S0-ELI-966

# CONCORDANCE

# OF

# A COURSE IN MIRACLES®

# CONCORDANCE OF A COURSE IN MIRACLES®

## A Complete Index

Kenneth Wapnick, Ph.D.
*Editor*

Rosemarie LoSasso, Ph.D.
*Associate Editor*

Veronica Whitson
*Associate Editor*

Foundation for Inner Peace

Viking

VIKING
Published by the Penguin Group
Penguin Books USA Inc., 375 Hudson Street, New York, New York 10014, U.S.A.
Penguin Books Ltd, 27 Wrights Lane, London W8 5TZ, England
Penguin Books Australia Ltd, Ringwood, Victoria, Australia
Penguin Books Canada Ltd, 10 Alcorn Avenue, Toronto, Ontario, Canada M4V 3B2
Penguin Books (N.Z.) Ltd, 182–190 Wairau Road, Auckland 10, New Zealand

Penguin Books Ltd, Registered Offices:
Harmondsworth, Middlesex, England

First published in 1997 by Viking Penguin,
a division of Penguin Books USA Inc.

1 3 5 7 9 10 8 6 4 2



ISBN 0-670-86995-3
CIP data is available from the Library of Congress.

This book is printed on acid-free paper.
∞



Printed in the United States of America
Set in Stone Print
Designed by Veronica Whitson

# Introduction

Simply stated, the purpose of this Concordance is to provide students with a handy, single-volume reference work that will enable them to locate quickly and easily a statement in *A Course in Miracles* by looking up any key word of that passage. The Concordance is keyed to the Viking-Penguin edition, fifth printing, of *A Course in Miracles,* and the fourth printing of the two scribed pamphlets, *Psychotherapy: Purpose, Process and Practice* and *The Song of Prayer*, published by Viking-Penguin under the title *Supplements to A Course in Miracles*.

If we may borrow a phrase from the preface to the world-famous *Strong's Exhaustive Concordance of the Bible,* we would say that our goal was to produce a complete index that would contain three essential qualities: *completeness, simplicity, and accuracy*. To this end, the Concordance lists every word found in *A Course in Miracles* as well as in the two supplements. The following pages, "Guide to the Use of the Concordance," provide the reader with simple and specific instructions regarding the structure and use of this reference work. Part of the long delay in publishing the Concordance was our insistence that it be as accurate as possible, which meant checking and rechecking the listings many times over. Throughout, we have tried to provide a reference work that would meet the needs and interests of all students—present and future—of *A Course in Miracles*.

A work of this magnitude would have been impossible without the tireless dedication of many, many people. Dr. Rosemarie LoSasso, Director of Publications of the Foundation for *A Course in Miracles* served as Associate Editor, and without her painstaking and loving conscientiousness, and unstinting devotion to the successful fulfillment of this task, the Concordance would never have been completed. Ronnie Whitson of CenterLink provided all of the computer work, and was as indefatigable as she was patient throughout the long process of arranging, rearranging, editing, and re-editing. Her work was far more than merely technical, however, as she was an integral part of all editorial decisions from beginning to end. Without her dedicated efforts, too, the Concordance would have remained an impossible dream. We owe a special debt of gratitude to Dale Vaughn, who made an invaluable contribution by developing computer programs that added to the accuracy of the work. Finally, there were Loral Reeves, Dr. Jeffrey Seibert and many other staff members of the Foundation for *A Course in Miracles*, as well as students in residence at the Foundation—all of whom so ably and selflessly assisted in the massive checking and proofreading required to bring this project to completion. To all of them, we at the Foundation for Inner Peace express our deep appreciation and gratitude.

I would also like to express my personal appreciation to Judith Skutch Whitson and Robert Skutch, President and Vice-President respectively of the Foundation for Inner Peace, for their constant support and encouragement for this project throughout these many years.

Kenneth Wapnick, Ph.D.
Foundation for Inner Peace
Foundation for *A Course in Miracles*

# Guide to the Use of the Concordance

To find a particular sentence or passage of interest, the student should seek under any key word within that sentence or passage. That word would appear in the reference under the initial letter, in bold face, followed by a period. These references are listed sequentially by book, as they appear in *A Course in Miracles* and *Supplements to A Course in Miracles: Psychotherapy: Purpose, Process and Practice; The Song of Prayer*. Key phrases or combinations of words can be found under each of the individual words. In addition, the most important terms and phrases of *A Course in Miracles* are indexed separately in Appendix C.

There are some words, called *noise words*, that are cited only by a word count. These words by and large include conjunctions, prepositions, lowercase pronouns, and auxiliary verbs. A separate list of these noise words can be found in Appendix B.

A complete list of *every* word in *A Course in Miracles* and the two supplements is provided in Appendix A. A word count for each book within the Course and the supplements is provided at the end of Appendix A. Hyphenated words are listed and cross referenced—indicated by *See* or *See also*—by both the prefix and suffix, as long as these are whole words.

Since certain characters present problems on a computer, the normal alphabetical order is modified when apostrophes and hyphens are encountered. For example, *day's* appears before *daylight*, *guilt's* appears before *guiltily*, *anti-religious* appears before *anticipate*, *clear-cut* appears before *cleared*.

Because of the centrality of the Holy Spirit in *A Course in Miracles*, the term *Holy Spirit* is treated as one word.

## SPLIT WORDS

Some words, called *split words*, have been listed according to their different meanings (or parts of speech) in the Course. While there are many words that have more than one meaning, only those that are distinctive within *A Course in Miracles* itself were selected for these "split" listings. One of the most important of these is *Will/will*, which is found as a noun (the *Will* of God or the *will* of the Son), a verb (I *will* there be light), or as an auxiliary verb (I *will* forgive), which is treated as a noise word. Each of these usages is listed separately, and is cross-referenced under the others. Another example is *rest*, which refers either to *peace/repose*, or to *remainder*.

A second category of split words consists of those pronouns that are found in both upper and lowercase, referring respectively to the Members of the Trinity (God, Christ, the Holy Spirit) and the Son of God in his separated state. References are listed for uppercase pronouns, while those in lowercase are treated as noise words and are listed as such with a word count only. Exceptions are those lowercase pronouns that relate to Jesus, where references are listed for these pronouns, which also include the collective pronouns *we*, *our*, and *us*. Many of these collective pronouns are the editorial *we* and *our*, while many others relate to Jesus and the student.

Finally, listings for many other words are also separated into uppercase followed by lowercase, where the uppercase refers to God, Christ, or the Holy Spirit. Examples are *Father/father*, *Self/self*, and *Voice/voice*.

A complete list of all the split words can be found in Appendix B.

### *Examples*

Each of the split words contains at least one subheading, and examples of these are as follows. Please note that capitalizations refer only to the *meaning* of the word, not to its placement at the beginning of a sentence. Capitalized words that begin a sentence are always treated as lowercase for the purpose of the Concordance, unless of course the meaning of the word calls for a capital:

**Love**
*love*

The split here is between the upper and lowercase, uppercase relating to God, Christ, or the Holy Spirit.

**he**
• Jesus
*noise word*
*He*

The bullet (black circle) before *Jesus* means that the list that follows includes all the references in which *he* refers to Jesus. The term *noise word* means that all the words *he* that do not relate to Jesus are regarded as *noise words*, and therefore only a word count is shown. The capitalized *He* refers to the listing of all references to God, Christ, or the Holy Spirit.

**arms**
• body
*weapon*
*Arms*

The bullet before *body* means that the list that follows includes all the references in which *arms* refers to the body part. The word *weapon* is a cross-reference to the listing of *arms* when the word means weapon. The word *Arms* is a cross-reference to the listing of *Arms* as it relates to God, as in *Everlasting Arms*.

**still**
• quiet, peaceful
*other*

The bullet before *quiet, peaceful* means that the list that follows includes all the references to *still* that mean quiet or peaceful. The word *other* refers to the list of all other usages of *still*.

## CROSS-REFERENCES

As mentioned above, cross-references are given for all hyphenated words. They are also given for the terms and phrases in Appendix C. An example follows for cross-references to pronouns:

**Holy Spirit**
*See also* He, Him, Himself, His, I, Me, My, Who, Whom, Whose, You, Your

*See also* indicates that there is a separate listing for each of the pronouns that relates to the Holy Spirit.

## CAPITALIZATION

The capitalization in *A Course in Miracles* has been a source of quizzical wonderment for many students. At times it can seem to have been done on a whim, and its seeming inconsistencies more of a hindrance than a help as students struggled to decipher the meaning of sentences. Yet, to paraphrase the famous phrase from *Hamlet*, there yet has been a method to its apparent madness. Since awareness of the capitalization of the Course will inevitably become part of any student's use of this Concordance, a complete explanation of the capitalization principles used in *A Course in Miracles* is presented here now, appearing for the first time in print.

We begin with a discussion of the capitalization philosophy of Helen Schucman, scribe of the Course, as described in the book on Helen and her scribing of *A Course in Miracles: Absence from Felicity: The Story of Helen Schucman and Her Scribing of "A Course in Miracles"** It should be noted at the outset that with the very few exceptions discussed below, the capitalization was not dictated by Jesus. It was thus left to Helen to determine how words should be capitalized.

> One can see an "evolution" in Helen's style as one traces the Course from its original dictation in the notebooks, through Bill's [William Thetford, Helen's close friend and colleague] first typing and Helen's subsequent retypings. The process culminated in Helen's feeling that every word even remotely (a slight, but only slight, exaggeration on my [Kenneth Wapnick] part) associated with God should be capitalized, including pronouns and relative pronouns. I should mention that while here again Jesus left Helen with the

* Kenneth Wapnick (Roscoe, NY: Foundation for *A Course in Miracles*, 1991.)

freedom to do as she wished, he did make some exceptions. Under his specific instructions, all pronouns referring to him were to be lowercase (in the earlier manuscript Helen always capitalized them), to reflect his unity with us. Jesus instructed Helen always to capitalize the term "Son of God," to emphasize the inclusion of all of us as part of God's one Son, in contradistinction to traditional Christianity's exclusion of all but Jesus from God's special Sonship. Pronouns referring to the Son, however, were to be lowercase, to emphasize our separated state. The exception, of course, would be when "Son of God" refers to our true Identity as Christ, where the pronouns would be capitalized. Also, Jesus asked Helen to capitalize all pronouns referring to the Trinity—God, Christ, and the Holy Spirit—otherwise the reader might not always know for whom (or Whom) the referent was meant.

In the manuscript from which Helen and I were editing, Helen's capitalization was quite inconsistent. While I did originally try to talk her out of what I believed to be the excessive stylistic emphasis on God's divinity, I soon abandoned this fruitless enterprise and ended by saying to Helen that I would capitalize the Course words any way she chose to have them be, but that the capitalization should be consistent. This clearly appealed to her sense of logic, and so we set out in writing the rules of capitalization we would follow, and kept to these as best we could (pp. 364-66).

## RULES OF CAPITALIZATION

### *Trinity*

Nouns for the three Members of the Trinity—God, Christ, and the Holy Spirit—are always capitalized, along with their pronouns.

### *God*

Nouns relating to God—Mind, Heart, Will, Everlasting Arms, Holiness, Presence, etc.—are capitalized, but the pronouns for these nouns are not capitalized, unless these nouns are used as synonyms for God (in the Concordance, these lowercase pronouns are considered noise words). Some words are capitalized when used as synonyms for God, but not capitalized when used more generally, even though they clearly relate to God. Examples of this principle would be *Truth, Life, Light*, and *Innocence.*

### *Christ*

Words used as synonyms for Christ are capitalized. For example: *Effect, Identity*, and *Self*. However, words associated with Christ are not capitalized, as, for example, *face, eyes, hands*, and *vision.*

### *Holy Spirit*

Words used as synonyms for the Holy Spirit are capitalized—for example: *Teacher, Guide, Answer, Voice for God*—as are their pronouns.

### *Jesus*

The first person (i.e., "I") used throughout *A Course in Miracles* is Jesus. Words associated with him are not capitalized; for example: all pronouns, *brother, man.*

### *Exceptions*

When a capital letter is needed for clarity and emphasis, exceptions to these principles are made. For example:

> *What*: Although demonstrative pronouns are not capitalized, this is allowed when it specifically refers to Christ, as in T-31.V.17:9.
>
> *Itself*: Pronouns for *Will* are not capitalized. However, one *itself* referring to *Will* is capitalized for clarity, so that readers would be able to distinguish this from other *itself*s in the same sentence (W-pII.253.2:2).

### *Pronouns*

Compound pronouns such as *both, either, they*, or *those* are capitalized when one or both subjects are part of the Trinity. An exception to this rule is when one of the two subjects refers to the ego, as in T-24.II.5:2.

## CONTENTS OF THE APPENDICES

Appendix A alphabetically lists all the words that appear in *A Course in Miracles* and *Supplements to A Course in Miracles: Psychotherapy: Purpose, Process and Practice; The Song of Prayer*.

Appendix B includes lists of split words and noise words.

Appendix C contains the index of selected terms and phrases.

## ABBREVIATIONS

T – text

- in – introduction (also found in workbook for students, manual for teachers, clarification of terms, *Psychotherapy: Purpose, Process and Practice* and *The Song of Prayer*)

W – workbook for students

- p – part (referring to parts I and II in the workbook for students)
- r – review lessons (I-VI)
- fl – final lessons
- ep – epilogue (also found in clarification of terms)

M – manual for teachers

C – clarification of terms

P – *Psychotherapy: Purpose, Process and Practice*

S – *The Song of Prayer*

# CONCORDANCE

# OF

# A COURSE IN MIRACLES®

**a** 4997

**abandon** 21

T-1........III.4:7 to a. them by following my guidance."
T-9..... VIII.1:3 dimly, you a. the ego automatically,
T-12......IV.3:3 you would have to a. the ego's guidance,
T-12... VIII.4:5 and did not a. you in your distress. You
T-14.....XI.4:2 Yet God did not a. you. And so you have
T-14....XI.6:11 in your awareness the instant you a. it,
T-14....XI.14:1 you want peace you must a. the teacher of
T-14....XI.14:2 The Teacher of peace will never a. you.
T-14....XI.14:5 lies His Holiness which He cannot a., for
T-16......IV.9:5 of God, be wholly willing to a. all illusions
T-17....... V.6:4 Do not a. faith, now that the rewards of
T-17..... V.7:13 A. Him not now, nor your brother. This
T-18......IX.3:7 Him not to a. you and leave you there. For
T-18......IX.3:9 severely tempted to a. Him at the outside
T19... IV.D.7:1 utterly a. you if you but raise your eyes.
T-29.........I.9:3 of God, what could induce you to a. Him?
T-31....IV.11:4 is merciful, and did not let His Son a. Him
W-pI.....64.1:3 It is the temptation to a. God and His Son
W-pI...131.5:1 in hell, for no one can a. his Creator, nor
W-pI...169.7:2 to a. all but this is now at hand. We do
S-3......IV.10:6 Do not a. Love. Remember this; whatever

**abandoned** 18

T-1........IV.4:8 that they have a. the belief in deprivation
T-6...........I.7:6 with them because I knew I could not *be* a.
T-6...........I.9:2 as God knows them, I was betrayed, a.,
T-6......V.A.6:5 perception you have not yet a., or the
T-14....XI.13:3 because you have a. the Teacher of peace.
T-15...VII.11:3 that by communicating you will be a..
T-20.......VI.6:3 For here is love made fearful and hope a..
T-26....... X.6:3 yourself deprived of light, a. to the dark,
T-28......III.3:3 you a. him to his own dream by sharing it
W-pI...123.3:1 Give thanks that He has not a. you, and
W-pI.153.13:1 you are lost to hope, a. by your Father,
W-pI...193.5:3 with which temptation ends, and guilt, a.,
W-pII..279.1:1 because God's Son is not a. by His Love.
W-pII..301.1:2 *pain, or feel I am a. or unneeded in the world.*
W-pII..327.1:5 that He has not a. me and loves me still,
M-4....... X.2:3 They have in truth a. the world, and let it
M-16........10:8 as true must be a. through his recognition
S-3........IV.5:8 on earth, which He a. to the devil's care,

**abandoning** 4

T-14....XI.13:4 to do so by a. the ego on behalf of Him.
W-pI...152.9:1 a. the false pretense by which the ego
W-pI...165.3:2 a. all else as worthless in comparison with
P-1.............1:2 Its aim is to aid the patient in a. his fixed

**abandonment** 5

T-5........VI.2:2 They induce fears of retaliation or a., and
T-6......V.B.1:1 have a basic fear of retaliation and a..
T-9...........I.8:5 no one really wants either a. or retaliation
W-pI.....41.1:1 and a. all the separated ones experience.
W-pI...190.2:5 It is a nightmare of a. by an Eternal Love,

**abasement**
*See* self-abasement

**abate** 2

W-pI...100.6:3 Son, and wills no sorrow rises to a. his joy
W-pI...196.7:1 as will permit fear of retaliation to a., and

**abated** 1

M-17.........5:9 him safe from fury that can never be a.,

**abide** 65

T-4.........in.1:8 are enlightened and cannot a. in darkness
T-5...........I.4:4 another Comforter and he will a. with you
T-6....... II.13:3 allow no darkness to a. in your own mind.
T-8......IV.2:12 and you cannot a. in darkness any more
T-8......IV.2:12 than darkness can a. wherever you go.
T-8........IV.3:9 to hear His Voice and a. in His Will. As
T-9.......VII.2:4 And you a. in peace when you so decide.
T-9.......VII.2:5 cannot a. in peace unless you accept the
T-11....... II.4:5 you invite as your guest will a. with you.
T-11...... III.4:4 go with you and a. with you on the way.
T-11...... III.6:1 children of light cannot a. in darkness, for
T-13.... III.12:6 that would a. with you in your insanity.
T-13....... V.5:2 For love cannot a. in a world apart, where
T-13...VII.17:4 God's most holy Son, where it cannot a..
T-14....... V.8:7 A. with me within it, as a teacher of
T-14...... IX.4:5 For God is life, and they a. in life. Life is as
T-14....XI.10:7 that no dark lesson of guilt can a. in what
T-15.... III.10:1 with me, who has decided to a. with you. I
T-15......IV.3:5 would have His host a. in perfect freedom
T-15......XI.2:7 to His Oneness can a. with Him there.
T-15......XI.9:1 lets Him enter and a. where He would be.
T-16......VI.9:3 because you invited it, it will a. with you.
T-18.........I.9:4 only the truth in your brother can a..
T19... IV.A.1:5 how can it a. within the Son of God? If it
T19... IV.A.7:3 Before the Holy Spirit entered to a. with
T-21....... V.5:5 a place in which the Holy Spirit can a.,
T-25.......in.2:7 does the Son of God a. exactly where he is
T-25...VII.10:2 And where does sanity a. except in Him?
T-26...VII.19:1 A. in peace, where God would have you
T-27...... III.4:3 and where He is there must the truth a..
T-28.......I.12:5 and lets Them enter where They would a..
T-29.........I.7:2 love, for in love's presence fear cannot a..
T-29....... V.1:4 Where Both a. are They remembered,
T-29....... V.3:3 the changeless and eternal that a. in him,
T-29.....VII.9:5 unto God, and where He is no idols can a.
T-31...... III.4:5 but the willing mind that would a. in it. It
T-31...... III.5:3 and sin cannot a. the joyous and the free,
T-31....IV.10:3 In unity with Him do they a., and in Their
W-pI.....53.4:6 decision, and recognize where I really a..
W-pI........93.h Light and joy and peace a. in me.
W-pI.....93.4:1 and that light and joy and peace a. in you
W-pI.....93.6:7 God, and light and joy and peace a. in you
W-pI.....93.7:7 Light and joy and peace a. in you because
W-pI.....93.8:2 *Light and joy and peace a. in me. My*
W-pI.....93.9:8 joy and peace a. in you because this is so.
W-pI...93.10:4 hour: *Light and joy and peace a. in me. My*
W-pI...93.11:3 *Light and joy and peace a. in you. Your*
W-pI...112.1:1 (93) Light and joy and peace a. in me. *I*
W-pI...112.3:2 Light and joy and peace a. in me. On the
W-pI...124.8:6 A. with Him this half an hour. He will do
W-pI...127.9:5 In loving gentleness He will a. with you,
W-pI...140.5:7 not, and nowhere sin and sickness can a..
W-pI...152.2:5 a mind where love and perfect holiness a.
W-pI...163.9:6 *And we a. where You have placed us, in the*
W-pI...165.3:1 he but recognized where they a.? Would
W-pI...165.7:5 Sureness must a. within you who are host
W-pI...167.6:3 cannot make a body, nor a. within a body
W-pI.167.10:5 we let imagined opposites to life a. even
W-pI...205.1:3 *my life, while I a. where I am not at home.* I
W-pII......6.2:1 of despair, for hope forever will a. in Him.
W-pII..326.1:4 *Where You established me I still a.. And all*
W-pII .326.1:5 *And all Your attributes a. in me, because it is*
W-pII .346.1:6 *I would a. in You, and know no laws except*
C-2.............2:4 as He created him a. in form or in a world
P-3........ III.8:3 an invitation to enter and a. with you. He

**abides** 57

T-6....... II.13:3 No darkness a. anywhere in the Kingdom,
T-8.......VII.9:7 Voice a. in it by directing the use to which
T-9.......VII.2:3 This, then, is where peace a.. And you
T-11.........II.7:8 a. with you merely by recognizing what is
T-11...... III.7:7 He Himself dwells there and a. in peace.
T-13.........I.6:6 of love he was created, and in love he a..
T-14... III.12:4 true. Peace a. in every mind that quietly
T-15...... III.9:6 where holiness a. in perfect peace. My
T-18.....VII.7:8 place the Holy Spirit comes, and there a..
T-23.......I.10:6 him. Illusions have no place where love a.,
T-23.......I.12:5 Peace is the state where love a., and seeks
T-23.......I.12:7 Where one a. the other cannot be; where
T-24...... VI.3:5 has no meaning in eternity where He a.,
T-25.........I.5:4 and Christ a. within your understanding,
T-25...... IV.3:1 comfort in another world where peace a..
T-28.....VII.3:6 to help you reach the home where God a..
T-29...... III.3:6 of light where God a. within the darkness,
T-29....... V.2:2 For your Identity a. in Them, and where
T-29....... V.4:1 which still a. in him as it abides in you. Be
T-29....... V.4:1 which still abides in him as it a. in you. Be
T-29...VII.1:10 glad that you are told where happiness a.,
T-29....VIII.4:3 for its source a. within your mind where
T-29...... IX.8:5 that a. forever deep within the Son of God
W-pI.....47.7:6 place in you where the strength of God a..
W-pI.....49.1:2 The part of your mind in which truth a. is
W-pI.....57.4:3 understand that peace, not war, a. in it.
W-pI.....57.4:4 I will perceive that peace also a. in the
W-pI.....59.1:3 of myself when perfect certainty a. in Him
W-pI.....66.7:4 home of the Holy Spirit, where truth a..
W-pI.....97.4:1 the spirit in whose mind a. the miracle in
W-pI.....97.4:4 with Him you are the spirit that a. in Him
W-pI...121.2:3 It suffers and a. in misery, peering about
W-pI...125.1:3 from deep within your mind where He a..
W-pI...125.4:3 place within the mind where He a. forever
W-pI...131.9:4 believes that he a. in what does not exist,
W-pI...140.5:3 God a. in holy temples. He is barred
W-pI.153.14:2 where truth a. and games are meaningless
W-pI.153.19:3 as we remember that His strength a. in us
W-pI...165.2:7 God has left you not, and still a. with you.
W-pI.170.13:2 *No cruelty a. in us, for there is none in You.*
W-pI...182.6:4 does He know that in you still a. His sure
W-pI...207.1:2 *upon me from within my heart, where He a..*
W-pII .253.1:6 Heaven where my holy Self a. with them
W-pII ....266.h My holy Self a. in you, God's Son.
W-pII ..... 6.1:3 still a. within the Mind that is His Source.
W-pII ..... 6.1:5 a. unchanged forever in the Mind of God.
W-pII ....283.h My true Identity a. in You.
W-pII ....299.h Eternal holiness a. in me.
W-pII .320.1:6 in whom the power of my Father's Will a..
W-pII .322.1:3 memory a. in every gift that I receive of
W-pII .322.1:4 the Holy One Who still a. in Him forever,
W-pII .322.1:4 abides in Him forever, as He still a. in me.
W-pII ... 12.3:2 and the death of God, when he a. in Him?
W-pII ... 14.1:6 *Itself, for in my purity a. His Own.*
W-pII .359.1:4 *You created sinless so a. forever and forever.*
C-1.............3:1 Who a. in this part but sees the other part
C-6.............4:1 The Holy Spirit a. in the part of your

**abideth** 3

T-12........II.9:3 and a. in you in the peace out of which He
T-12.... III.10:3 The altar of God where Christ a. is there.

| | |
|---|---|
| T-29....VIII.4:3 | within your mind where God **a.** not. |

**abiding** 6

| | |
|---|---|
| T-27....... V.3:1 | The holy instant is the miracle's **a.** place. |
| W-pI.....92.8:2 | eyes, and strength and light **a.** in his heart |
| W-pI...122.1:6 | that never can be hurt, a deep, **a.** comfort, |
| W-pII .327.2:4 | *and surety of Your* **a.** *Love is gained at last.* |
| W-pII .336.2:2 | *my mind, Your Love is still* **a.** *in my heart.* |
| W-pII .341.1:3 | *safe, how holy, then, are we,* **a.** *in Your Smile* |

**abilities** 23

| | |
|---|---|
| T-2........ IV.3:9 | world. Its **a.** can be and frequently are |
| T-3........ IV.1:1 | The **a.** you now possess are only shadows |
| T-3......... V.1:1 | I have said that the **a.** you possess are |
| T-6......... II.4:2 | because its **a.** are directed by the mind, |
| T-6........ IV.8:1 | The introduction of **a.** into being was the |
| T-6........ IV.8:1 | of uncertainty, because **a.** are potentials, |
| T-6........ IV.8:2 | Your **a.** are useless in the presence of |
| T-6........ IV.8:4 | When they are perfect, **a.** are meaningless |
| T-6........ IV.9:1 | **A.** must be developed before you can use |
| T-6........ IV.9:3 | develop your **a.** to the point where they |
| T-7........ IV.3:6 | If different **a.** are applied long enough to |
| T-7........ IV.3:6 | goal, the **a.** themselves become unified. |
| T-7........ IV.4:1 | All **a.** should therefore be given over to |
| T-7......... V.1:1 | more than a framework for developing **a.**, |
| T-9........ IV.3:2 | reminds you of the natural use of your **a.**. |
| T-9........ IV.3:4 | on your **a.** through the eyes of the ego, or |
| M-25 ......... 1:3 | each individual has many **a.** of which he is |
| M-25 ......... 1:4 | he may well develop **a.** that seem quite |
| M-25 ......... 3:1 | seemingly new **a.** that may be gathered on |
| M-25 ......... 4:2 | deception, and He can use only genuine **a.** |
| M-25 ......... 4:5 | unusual **a.** that can be curiously tempting |
| M-25 ......... 6:4 | Salvation has need of all **a.**, for what the |
| M-25 ......... 6:5 | "Psychic" **a.** have been used to call upon |

**ability** 68

| | |
|---|---|
| T-1.........I.38:3 | from the false by His **a.** to perceive totally |
| T-1......... III.1:9 | Doing them will bring conviction in the **a.** |
| T-1...... III.1:10 | The **a.** is the potential, the achievement is |
| T-2...........I.1:6 | this **a.** because it is inherent in what he is, |
| T-2...........I.4:1 | you have the **a.** to usurp the power of God |
| T-2........ II.1:11 | the **a.** of anything not of God to affect you |
| T-2......... II.5:4 | The **a.** to learn has no value when change |
| T-2........ III.3:3 | Who set the limits on your **a.** to miscreate |
| T-2........ IV.2:8 | that there is a creative **a.** in matter which |
| T-2........ V.1:11 | of creative **a.** that is truly meaningful. |
| T-2......... V.9:1 | an **a.** that developed after the separation, |
| T-2......VIII.1:4 | Since creative **a.** rests in the mind, |
| T-2......VIII.3:7 | the **a.** to choose can be directed rationally |
| T-3........ IV.6:1 | **a.** to perceive made the body possible, |
| T-3........ VI.5:7 | curious that an **a.** so debilitating would be |
| T-3........ VI.9:5 | does not depend on your **a.** to identify it, |
| T-3....... VII.4:1 | for usurping the **a.** for self-creating. This |
| T-4..... VII.3:12 | cannot totally lose the **a.** to communicate, |
| T-5........ III.7:2 | His **a.** to deal with symbols enables Him |
| T-5........ III.7:3 | **a.** to look beyond symbols into eternity |
| T-5........ IV.1:4 | Truth is beyond your **a.** to destroy, but |
| T-5........ IV.1:4 | but entirely within your **a.** to accept. It |
| T-5........ VI.8:3 | the thoughts from the **a.** to produce fear. |
| T-6.........I.17:1 | develop your weakened **a.** to be grateful, |
| T-6......... II.4:2 | Every **a.** of the ego has a better use, |
| T-6........ IV.7:6 | mind has become only the **a.** for certainty |
| T-7........ IV.3:4 | **a.** that was applied to the learning. All |
| T-7......... V.3:1 | Healing is the one **a.** everyone can |
| T-7........ VI.2:6 | **a.** to direct your thinking as you choose is |
| T-7......... X.2:4 | **a.** to see a logical outcome depends on the |
| T-8..... VII.14:6 | that is interfering with his **a.** to accept its |
| T-8........ IX.1:4 | establish your **a.** to evaluate its questions. |
| T-9...........I.6:4 | This loses the **a.** to communicate simply |
| T-9........ III.8:7 | Spirit's use of an **a.** that you do not need, |
| T-9........ IV.3:3 | By reinterpreting the **a.** to attack into the |
| T-9........ IV.3:3 | the ability to attack into the **a.** to share, |
| T-10....... II.3:3 | The **a.** to accept truth in this world is the |
| T-10....... IV.2:4 | and because of your **a.** to evaluate it truly, |
| T-11.......I.5:10 | nor have your closed eyes lost the **a.** to see |
| T-11.........I.7:5 | Your **a.** to accept Him depends on your |
| T-12 ........I.2:2 | own **a.** to understand what you perceive. |
| T-12 ...... V.6:4 | of the **a.** to generalize is a crucial learning |
| T-15 ..... VI.1:4 | one, for its **a.** to satisfy you completely, |
| T-15 ..... VI.8:7 | Through your **a.** to do this you will learn |
| T-15 .. VII.12:1 | the body and its **a.** to overcome loneliness |
| T-16 . IV.11:13 | to forget and your **a.** to remember. In |
| T-18 .......II.4:5 | For the dream of your **a.** to control reality |
| T-21 .....II.11:4 | feel, and place your faith in its **a.** to do so, |
| T-22 ........I.7:1 | So in each holy relationship is the **a.** to |
| T-22 ..... VI.2:1 | used as means whose value lies in its **a.** to |
| T-26 ..... III.7:3 | this is so lies the **a.** to give up all attempts |
| T-29 ........I.5:4 | and limits your **a.** to make communion |
| T-30 ... VII.6:5 | your **a.** to see relationships among events. |
| T-31 ........I.5:1 | is an **a.** you made and gave yourself. It |
| W-in.......... 7:1 | to increase your **a.** to extend the ideas you |
| W-pI..... 47.1:4 | What would give you the **a.** to be aware of |
| W-pI..... 98.3:4 | not doubt their own **a.** because they know |
| W-pI... 134.8:3 | By its **a.** to overlook what is not there, it |
| W-pI... 154.3:1 | His **a.** to hear one Voice which is His Own |
| W-pI... 181.1:1 | in your **a.** to transcend doubt and lack of |
| W-pI... 199.6:4 | in the **a.** to serve an undivided goal. In |
| W-pII . 299.1:1 | beyond my own **a.** to understand or know |
| M-4 .........I.1:1 | which their **a.** to fulfill their function rests |
| M-4 ..... I.A.4:3 | before will merely hinder his **a.** to transfer |
| M-25 ......... 5:6 | the "power" is no longer a genuine **a.**, and |
| M-25 ......... 6:1 | Any **a.** that anyone develops has the |
| P-1............ 4:1 | the **a.** to make his own decisions. He must |
| S-1..........II.4:3 | have also limited your **a.** to receive and to |

**abject** 1

| | |
|---|---|
| W-pI... 170.8:2 | be the time of your release from **a.** slavery |

**able** 36

| | |
|---|---|
| T-2 ..........I.4:2 | neither can nor have been **a.** to do this. |
| T-2 ...... VII.2:1 | or you will not be **a.** to help me. Miracle |
| T-3 .........II.1:8 | one, therefore, is **a.** to deny truth totally, |
| T-3 ........ V.6:5 | be **a.** to recognize what you already have. |
| T-4 ..........I.6:6 | I would not be **a.** to devote myself to |
| T-4 ..........I.9:7 | awaken you will not be **a.** to understand |
| T-6 .........I.10:5 | being **a.** to hear the Holy Spirit in others |
| T-7 .... VII.1:13 | never be **a.** to exclude yourself from your |
| T-9 ..........II.5:9 | his words and making you **a.** to hear them |
| T-10 ...... III.9:4 | him you made yourself **a.** to hear him. Yet |
| T-10 ...... IV.3:4 | and you will not be **a.** to limit the split, |
| T-13 ..... VI.2:3 | will be **a.** to learn from what you see *now.* |
| T-15 ..... IV.9:6 | for it. You will not be **a.** to accept perfect |
| T-15 .........X.7:5 | in part, but **a.** to be neither completely. |
| T-16 .........II.2:2 | you might be better **a.** to understand. For |
| T-18 . VIII.12:3 | not be **a.** to give love welcome separately. |
| T-28 ...... V.4:7 | It is as little **a.** to perceive as it can judge |
| W-pI....... 9.1:2 | you may be **a.** to accept it intellectually, it |
| W-pI..... 15.5:1 | Although you will obviously not be **a.** to |
| W-pI..... 26.6:4 | will not be **a.** to use very many for any one |
| W-pI..... 45.8:7 | you should be **a.** to remind yourself that |
| W-pI... 93.10:1 | You may not be willing or even **a.** to use |
| W-pI..... 97.6:3 | nor will you be **a.** to forget the way again. |
| W-pI..... 98.5:1 | your time each hour to be **a.** to accept the |
| W-pI... 126.2:2 | and **a.** to behave in ways which have no |
| W-pI... 154.6:3 | that they become **a.** to bring them further |
| W-pI... 159.5:3 | never **a.** to obscure the light that shines |
| W-pII . 268.1:4 | *For thus will I be* **a.**, *too, to recognize my Self* |
| M-8 ........... 2:8 | and **a.** to gratify its needs at the expense |
| P-in ........... 1:6 | Sometimes he is **a.** to start to open his |
| P-2.........in.2:3 | aim is to be **a.** to retain their self-concept |
| P-2....... VII.5:6 | self of one alone against the universe **a.** to |
| P-3..........I.4:9 | only thus will he be **a.** to hear the call and |
| P-3..........II.1:8 | be far more **a.** teachers outside of them. |
| P-3..........II.5:6 | be **a.** to accept help from them if they did. |
| S-2.........I.10:3 | you will not be **a.** to attain your freedom. |

**abode** 5

| | |
|---|---|
| T-14 ... III.15:8 | his **a.** was fixed in perfect peace forever. |
| T-16 ..... IV.9:2 | Fear not to cross to the **a.** of peace and |
| T-18 ..... VI.7:2 | holy Son can enter an **a.** that harbors hate |
| T-31 .VIII.12:2 | in the **a.** You set for Him before time was, |
| W-pI..... 92.8:2 | none who enters its **a.** can leave without a |

**abolish** 4

| | |
|---|---|
| T-1 ........I.24:1 | death yourself, and can therefore **a.** both. |
| T-1 .........V.1:6 | But you cannot **a.** it. You can destroy your |
| T-2 .........II.6:6 | but like the miracle it serves, does not **a.** it |
| T-4 ...... VII.2:2 | establish separateness rather than to **a.** it. |

**abolished** 6

| | |
|---|---|
| T-1 ........I.28:2 | a state in which fear has already been **a.**. |
| T-2 ....... VI.8:8 | accept the remedy, you have **a.** the fear. |
| T-2 ...... VII.5:4 | light enters darkness, the darkness is **a.**. |
| T-2 .... VII.5:12 | It only seems to be **a.** by degrees, because |
| T-5 ..... VI.12:4 | device to be **a.** when it is no longer useful. |
| W-pI .. 154.4:2 | with guilt **a.** in the mind that God created |

**abolishes** 3

| | |
|---|---|
| T-2 ... V.A.11:1 | The miracle **a.** the need for lower-order |
| T-3 ..........I.7:7 | form of evil, as light **a.** forms of darkness. |
| T-3 ....... IV.6:6 | light **a.** darkness merely by showing you it |

**abolishing** 2

| | |
|---|---|
| T-1 .........II.6:5 | thus has the unique property of **a.** time to |
| T-2 ..... VIII.2:6 | the device for shortening but not **a.** time. |

**about** 403

**above** 68

| | |
|---|---|
| T-4 ....... IV.6:3 | can focus and rise **a.** fatigue and heal. Yet |
| T-5 ....... IV.5:1 | is done in many ways, **a.** all by example. |
| T-11 ..... VI.1:7 | does rise **a.** the ego and all its works, and |
| T-15 ... III.12:6 | rises **a.** the stars and reaches even to |
| T-16 ..... IV.3:2 | It makes no attempt to rise **a.** the storm, |
| T-18 ........I.6:9 | in reality. And **a.** all, *be not afraid of it.* |
| T-18 ..... IV.1:4 | of recognizing that you want it **a.** all else. |
| T-18 ... VI.13:6 | experience of peace and joy, and, **a.** all, |
| T-18 ... VIII.7:7 | Arched high **a.** it and surrounding it with |
| T-18 ..... IX.6:3 | softly to the mountain tops that rise **a.** it, |
| T-18 ..... IX.6:3 | willing to climb **a.** it and see the sun. It is |
| T-18 ... IX.13:2 | lifted high **a.** the darkness and gently |
| T-20 .... VII.2:7 | be sincere and say, "I want this **a.** all else, |
| T-22 ..... III.9:1 | newly born, must value holiness **a.** all else |
| T-23 ...... in.5:4 | help him rise **a.** it and perceive the light of |
| T-23 .....II.20:2 | quite possible to value some **a.** the others. |
| T-23 ..... III.6:6 | on it in safety from **a.** and not be touched. |
| T-23 ........ IV.h | **A.** the Battleground |
| T-23 ..... IV.4:5 | relationship is raised **a.** the battleground, |
| T-23 ..... IV.5:6 | Yet from **a.**, the choice is miracles instead |
| T-23 ..... IV.6:1 | remember you *can* see the battle from **a.**. |
| T-23 ..... IV.6:3 | a stab of pain, a twinge of guilt, and **a.** all, |
| T-23 ..... IV.7:7 | From **a.**, the limits it exerts on those in |
| T-23 ..... IV.9:5 | from the quiet sphere **a.** the battleground. |
| T-24 ........I.4:2 | of being like what he condemns, "**a.**" it, |
| T-25 ........I.2:4 | your sinfulness, your evil and, **a.** all, your |
| T-25 ... VIII.7:2 | were a messenger from hell, sent from **a.**, |
| T-26 ..... IV.3:4 | altar to rise and tower far **a.** the world, |
| T-27 ..... III.2:1 | love," a "weakened power," and **a.** all, a |
| T-27 ... VIII.1:8 | **A.** all, it tries to teach itself its pains and |
| T-28 ...... III.3:6 | for it is His coming that you want **a.** all |
| T-31 ........I.6:1 | so small and still It cannot rise **a.** the |
| T-31 ........V.5:2 | that smiles **a.** it must forever look away, |
| T-31 ... VIII.9:3 | to lift us high **a.** the thorny roads we |
| W-pI ....... 27.h | **A.** all else I want to see. |
| W-pI .... 27.2:1 | when you say you want to see **a.** all else. If |
| W-pI ....... 28.h | **A.** all else I want to see things differently. |
| W-pI .... 28.2:1 | for example, "**A.** all else I want to see this |
| W-pI .... 28.3:1 | you say, "**A.** all else I want to see this table |
| W-pI .... 28.4:3 | saying, "**A.** all else I want to see this table |
| W-pI .... 28.8:2 | ***A.*** *all else I want to see this_differently.* |
| W-pI .... 35.9:1 | idea in the form stated **a.** to each of them. |
| W-pI .. 44.11:3 | **A.** all, be determined not to forget today. |
| W-pI .... 50.3:2 | raise you high **a.** all the perceived dangers |
| W-pI .... 56.2:1 | (27) **A.** all else I want to see. Recognizing |
| W-pI .... 56.3:1 | (28) **A.** all else I want to see differently. |
| W-pI .... 73.7:5 | you. **A.** all else, you want the freedom to |
| W-pI .... 80.5:5 | peace. **A.** all, remember that you have one |

W-pI...121.2:1 peace and soar a. the turmoil of the world
W-pI...123.4:1 in gratitude we lift our hearts a. despair,
W-pI...123.8:2 His Son, that he might rise a. the world,
W-pI...125.9:2 today lift you a. the thinking of the world,
W-pI...128.6:1 and see how far you rise a. the world,
W-pI.136.15:5 prayer, to help us rise a. defensiveness,
W-pI...157.3:2 to alter time sufficiently to rise a. its laws,
W-pI...164.8:5 sought a. the world's unsatisfying goals?
W-pI.170.10:6 And He is terrible a. all else, cruel beyond
W-pI...182.4:6 to earth the pure reflection of the light a.,
W-pI.185.10:4 intent with what they seek a. all things,
W-pI...186.9:6 off. Or like mirages seen a. a desert, rising
W-pI...191.5:1 and you have risen far a. the world, and
W-pI...192.9:4 realize you hold a sword a. your head.
W-pII..303.2:5 *He is the Son You love a. all things. He is my*
M-4........ X.2:6 And a. all are all things welcoming, for
C-1.............7:3 receiving messages from a. or below;
P-2......... V.2:6 the lesson of defenselessness a. all else, to
S-2.........in.1:2 vain to try to rise a. prayer's bottom step,
S-2........ I.10:5 to ascend a. the world of chaos into peace

## Abraham 1

T-3........III.6:5 and the end," and "Before A. was I am."

## abrupt 1

W-pI.....33.1:4 but without an a. sense of shifting.

## abruptly 3

T-9.......VII.4:7 shift a. from suspiciousness to viciousness
T-16......VI.8:1 will be a. lifted up and hurled into reality.
T-17....... V.2:6 the goal of the relationship is a. shifted to

## absence 11

T-4........VI.5:4 him to associate his misery with its a.,
T-9........ I.13:4 unreal because the a. of reality is fearful,
T-14......XI.5:4 a. of perfect peace means but one thing:
T-17......VI.3:7 The a. of a criterion for outcome, set in
T-19.........I.5:8 Truth is the a. of illusion; illusion the
T-19.........I.5:8 absence of illusion; illusion the a. of truth.
T-21.....III.11:9 on the a. of the other does each depend.
T-21....... V.8:6 for it depends entirely on reason's a.. The
W-pI.....91.1:5 its a. is not the result of your failure to see
W-pII.......3.2:3 And what is fear except love's a.? Thus
M-4.......IV.1:7 demonstrates the a. of God's curriculum,

## absent 25

T-1......... V.4:2 him, even though he may be a. in spirit.
T-7......... II.1:3 are seeing him as if he were a. from the
T-7........III.1:8 I am not a. to anyone in any situation.
T-7........III.2:4 meaning perceive yourself as a. from it?
T-11.........I.5:3 If you believe you are a. from God, you
T-11.........I.5:3 you will believe that He is a. from you.
T-11.....VII.4:5 Truth is not a. here, but it is obscure. You
T-14..... X.12:9 will the power of all His Love be a. from
T-14....XI.12:6 so where one is a. the other cannot be.
T-17....... V.9:6 from which your true intent was never a..
T-18.....VII.8:5 It is this center, from which the body is a.,
T19. IV.A.11:6 is wholly a. from love's gentle perception.
T-23....III.6:12 safety? Can guilt be a. from a battlefield?
T-24......VI.3:3 within His Mind is a. from your own. It is
T-27......III.3:7 you see is wholly a. and has never been.
T-28.........I.8:5 Yet was It never a. from your mind, for it
T-29.........I.1:1 time, no place, no state where God is a..
T-29......IV.2:5 But never is it a. from the dream, for fear
T-30......III.6:4 Thoughts were a. or could suffer change.
W-pI...107.8:4 and how could He be a. where you are?
W-pI...140.4:3 Sickness where guilt is a. cannot come,
W-pI...165.7:4 And the Thought of Him is never a..
M-11........4:12 "Is it not impossible that peace be a. here
M-16..........1:7 Not one is a. whom he needs; not one is
P-2........III.1:4 this One be wholly a. if the goal is healing.

## absolute 1

W-pI.....59.1:4 anything when He rests in me in a. peace?

## absolutely 2

T-3.......VII.2:8 of no real worth. This makes a. no sense.
T-14....... II.1:5 learning goal depends means a. nothing.

## absolution 1

T-19....... II.1:5 unless a mind not part of it can give it a..

## absolve 1

T-4...........I.6:3 my goal will always be to a. you finally

## absolved 6

T-15.........I.9:6 and it is here that you are completely a.,
T-15... VIII.1:7 nothing to forgive, you are a. completely.
W-pI.....97.1:5 for your mind has been a. from madness,
W-pI.....98.2:5 For we have been a. from errors. All our
W-pI.184.15:5 *may be a. from all effects our errors seemed*
M-29 .........3:3 guidance is to let yourself be a. of guilt. It

## absolving 1

W-pI.188.10:2 a. all the world from what we thought it

## abstract 8

T-3......... V.2:8 of the a. creativity of God's creations.
T-4......... II.1:4 A. thought applies to knowledge because
T-4.......VII.1:2 specific, although the mind is naturally a..
T-4.......VII.2:6 generalization which is really not a. at all.
T-4.......VII.3:9 This communication is perfectly a., since
W-pI.....35.7:1 not think of these terms in an a. way.
M-21 .........2:2 Even when they seem most a., the picture
M-29 .........1:7 to start at the more a. level of the text.

## Abstraction 1

*abstraction*

T-4.......VII.5:4 you. Divine A. takes joy in sharing. That is

## abstraction 3

*Abstraction*

W-pI...161.2:1 Complete a. is the natural condition of
W-pI...161.4:7 a. in the sense that it is all-encompassing.
P-2........III.4:4 the egoless psychotherapist is an a. that

## absurd 1

T-27.....VII.2:5 the problem is a. when clearly seen. No

## absurdity 1

W-pI...156.6:4 is sin gone, because its quaint a. is seen. It

## abundance 15

T-1........IV.4:8 the a. they have learned belongs to them.
T-1......... V.4:6 which is a state of completion and a..
T-1......... V.6:2 The a. of Christ is the natural result of
T-4......... II.6:1 lasting sense of a. can be truly charitable.
T-4......... II.7:3 The ego never gives out of a., because it
T-7.......VII.7:7 Give, therefore, of your a., and teach your
T-7.....VII.10:5 See His a. in everyone, and you will know
T-7..... VIII.1:9 produces a. or scarcity, depending on
T-9..... VIII.5:1 bless, because your grandeur is your a..
T-12....... III.5:5 they dwell in a. and that salvation is come
T-26...VII.13:3 idea the mind conceives but adds to its a.,
T-28...... III.9:6 no gap in which a. falters and grows thin.
W-pI.....54.5:4 to replace tears, and a. to replace loss. I
W-pI...165.6:6 A. dwells in him, and deprivation cannot
W-pII..249.1:5 The world becomes a place of joy, a.,

## abundant 2

T-1........ IV.3:4 Truth is always a.. Those who perceive
M-17 .........8:4 but it requires patience and a. willingness

## abuse 3

T-28........II.8:5 which they a. because the motives he has
T-31....... V.3:4 irritation, and at last to open insult and a.
W-pI... 135.7:3 a. it by assigning it to roles it cannot fill,

## accept 499

*See also* Appendix C

T-1.........I.21:2 miracles you a. God's forgiveness by
T-1........ III.1:6 to a. error in yourself and others, you
T-2........ IV.4:1 All material means that you a. as
T-2......... V.2:4 unable to a. the real Source of the healing.
T-2......... V.4:4 of refusal to a. the Atonement for yourself
T-2......... V.4:5 If you do a. it, you are in a position to
T-2......... V.5:1 *worker is to a. the Atonement for himself.*
T-2......... V.5:3 Once you a. this, your mind can only heal
T-2......... V.8:1 a. unequivocally that healing is necessary.
T-2........ V.10:3 help, and a recognition that he will a. it.
T-2........ VI.8:8 However, as soon as you a. the remedy,
T-3...........I.2:2 It is unwise to a. any concept if you have
T-3.........I.7:10 If you can a. this one generalization now,
T-3..........II.6:3 willing to a. what is true in everything you
T-3..........II.6:6 their truth so they can a. it for themselves
T-3........ III.6:7 becomes "Know God and a. His certainty.
T-3........ III.7:8 what you know, and therefore a. as yours.
T-3........ VI.4:1 you have perceived but have refused to a..
T-3........ VI.4:2 that, because you have refused to a. it,
T-3........ VI.4:4 to a. can be brought into awareness. It is
T-3....... VI.10:2 is free to refuse to a. his inheritance, but
T-3....... VI.11:8 what I am and I a. my own inheritance."
T-4.........in.3:3 can a. it as your own last useless journey,
T-4...........I.6:7 I do not a. either perception for myself.
T-4...........I.8:4 a fearful attempt, but to a. it as it is. You
T-4.........I.10:7 do not a. such a picture of them yourself.
T-4........ IV.8:4 refuse to a. anything but this as your goal.
T-4......... V.2:3 either distorts them or refuses to a. them.
T-4......... V.4:4 a. it as good enough to be its home. Here
T-4.......VII.6:3 has no ego with which to a. such praise,
T-5.........I.1:14 If you can a. the concept that the world is
T-5........ III.9:2 you a. are the foundations of your beliefs.
T-5........ IV.1:4 but entirely within your ability to a.. It
T-5......... V.4:1 you a. into your mind has reality for you.
T-5......... V.6:7 the alternatives the mind can a. and obey.
T-5......... V.7:8 worker is to a. the Atonement for himself,
T-5........ V.7:12 you a. the remedy for disordered thought,
T-5........ VI.2:9 Your ego cannot a. this freedom, and will
T-5.......VII.1:7 but you can choose to a. His care and use
T-6.........in.2:3 the moment you a. any premise at all, and
T-6...........I.6:7 to a. them as false justifications for anger.
T-6...........I.8:6 a. me as a model are literally my disciples.
T-6........ II.6:11 is impossible to a. one without the other.
T-6........ II.11:1 The ego can a. the idea that return is
T-6........ III.3:2 Once it can a. this fully, it sees no need to
T-6......V.A.6:7 this point they may try to a. the conflict,
T-6...... V.B.5:2 if you a. two thought systems which are in
T-6...... V.B.5:3 you will surely do as long as you a. both,
T-7......... V.3:3 a. the ego's confusion of mind and body.
T-7....... V.11:5 He will a. it and give it to the Sonship,
T-7........ VI.7:2 only reason you may find this hard to a. is
T-7...... VI.10:2 belief you a. apart from this will obscure
T-7.......VII.6:5 and a. His gift for yourself and as yourself
T-7.....VII.10:2 Do not a. anything else as your will, or
T-7......VIII.5:4 are willing to a. sole responsibility for the
T-7........ X.1:11 that will determine what you a. into your
T-7......... X.2:1 that you can both a. into your mind what
T-7......... X.8:3 you are God's Will and do not a. His Will,
T-7........ XI.5:4 your brother is to a. your own inheritance
T-8........ III.6:5 at it you *will* a. the Atonement for yourself.
T-8........ IV.3:8 If you will a. the fact that I am with you,
T-8........ IV.4:6 You must a. guidance from within. The
T-8........ VI.5:9 you a. anything else or give anything else,
T-8........ VI.6:7 No one who does not a. his function can
T-8........ VI.6:7 and no one can a. his function unless he
T-8.......VII.1:3 attack physically to a. this interpretation.

T-8 VII.6:3 Will for you when you **a.** it for yourself.
T-8 VII.14:4 Are you willing to **a.** this, when your
T-8 VII.14:6 his ability to **a.** its purpose as his own.
T-8 VIII.8:5 choose not to **a.** anything except truth.
T-8 IX.1:5 for this would merely be to **a.** the ego's
T-8 IX.2:10 **A.**, then, your little part, and let the whole
T-8 IX.8:7 is split, and does not **a.** a unified purpose.
T-9 II.9:2 To believe is to **a.**, and to side with. To
T-9 II.9:3 to be credulous, but to **a.** and appreciate.
T-9 II.11:5 But to receive is to **a.**, not to get. It is
T-9 III.5:2 If you perceive his errors and **a.** them, you
T-9 III.6:4 your brother, but merely to **a.** him as he is
T-9 III.7:2 of you. **A.** his errors as real, and you have
T-9 III.8:3 **A.** only the function of healing in time,
T-9 IV.1:4 **A.** as true only what your brother is, if
T-9 IV.4:7 insisting that you must **a.** the meaningless
T-9 IV.6:4 and unless you **a.** this you cannot learn
T-9 VI.2:6 decision to receive is the decision to **a.**.
T-9 VI.3:1 brothers are part of you, will you **a.** them?
T-9 VI.4:9 brother's, and will **a.** it as you accept his.
T-9 VI.4:9 brother's, and will accept it as you **a.** his.
T-9 VI.7:5 Could you but **a.** one of them you would
T-9 VI.7:8 **A.** your brother in this world and accept
T-9 VI.7:8 brother in this world and **a.** nothing else,
T-9 VII.2:5 in peace unless you **a.** the Atonement,
T-9 VII.8:5 and **a.** nothing that you would not offer to
T-9 VIII.3:5 you **a.** its offer of grandiosity it will attack
T-9 VIII.10:8 To **a.** yourself as God created you cannot
T-9 VIII.10:9 To **a.** your littleness *is* arrogant, because it
T-10 in.3:10 me?" Then **a.** His decision, for it is indeed
T-10 II.3:2 you merely **a.** again what is already there,
T-10 II.3:3 The ability to **a.** truth in this world is the
T-10 III.8:1 that you always receive as much as you **a.**.
T-10 III.8:2 You could **a.** peace now for everyone, and
T-10 III.9:6 your willingness to **a.** only the eternal.
T-10 III.10:3 **a.** other gods before Him is to place other
T-10 III.11:6 And if you **a.** him you will bow down and
T-10 V.4:3 joy, because he would not **a.** the fact that,
T-10 V.6:6 And if you **a.** denial, you can accept its
T-10 V.6:6 you accept denial, you can **a.** its undoing.
T-10 V.9:5 If you will **a.** yourself as God created you,
T-10 V.11:2 to **a.** what had been created for him, and
T-10 V.12:4 may take, are refusals to **a.** creation as it is
T-10 V.13:7 Only if you **a.** the Fatherhood of God will
T-10 V.14:9 If you will **a.** only what is timeless as real,
T-11 I.5:8 unwillingness to **a.** His Fatherhood has
T-11 I.7:5 Your ability to **a.** Him depends on your
T-11 II.2:5 Every healing thought that you **a.**, either
T-11 II.7:2 You will **a.** only whom you invite. You are
T-11 III.6:3 Him, and **a.** His Will for you in peace. For
T-11 III.6:4 in peace. For you cannot **a.** it otherwise.
T-11 III.8:1 mind you can **a.** the whole Sonship and
T-11 V.10:3 will not **a.** the cost of fear if you recognize
T-11 V.12:8 him but recognize it and he will not **a.** it.
T-11 V.17:2 **A.** His Son and you will remember Him.
T-11 V.17:5 be. **A.** what God does not deny, and it will
T-11 V.18:5 You cannot **a.** false witness of him unless
T-11 VI.3:3 what it means and therefore do not **a.** it.
T-11 VI.6:4 And you can **a.** it by His grace, for God is
T-11 VI.9:4 or you will not **a.** what I can do *for* you. Yet
T-11 VII.3:3 entirely, for that you could not **a.**. But it
T-11 VIII.3:6 Recognize this but do not **a.** it, for
T-11 VIII.9:3 **A.** him as his Father accepts him and heal
T-11 VIII.10:3 willing to **a.** this Help by asking for It, you
T-11 VIII.11:1 **a.** your brother's variable perception of
T-11 VIII.11:1 you will not **a.** your healing without his.
T-11 VIII.12:5 **A.** His healing power and use it for all He
T-11 VIII.15:4 you will **a.** the real world in place of the
T-12 I.4:3 for your unwillingness to **a.** reality as it is,
T-12 I.8:7 then. Having taught you to **a.** only loving
T-12 II.4:2 If they ask for enlightenment and **a.** it,
T-12 III.3:5 if you **a.** their poverty as yours. If you had
T-12 III.4:8 is valuable and wants to **a.** nothing else.
T-12 III.9:2 to **a.** even death to deny your Father. Yet
T-12 V.2:2 For if you **a.** your invulnerability, you are
T-12 VI.4:4 see with love if you **a.** His vision as yours.
T-12 VII.7:5 and you will **a.** it from the world because
T-13 in.4:3 you **a.** the eternal fact that God's Son is
T-13 I.1:4 coexist, and to **a.** one is to deny the other.
T-13 II.8:2 may reject it and do not **a.** it for yourself.
T-13 III.5:1 You can **a.** insanity because you made it,
T-13 III.5:1 you cannot **a.** love because you did not.
T-13 III.9:1 you may **a.** the magnitude of your Father
T-13 IV.8:4 of salvation that you must learn to **a.**, if
T-13 IV.9:2 If you **a.** your function in the world of
T-13 V.8:7 what denial does, for by it you **a.** insanity,
T-13 VI.7:3 refusing to **a.** the light that is offered you.
T-13 VI.12:3 Those who **a.** love of you become your
T-13 VIII.9:5 no healing, nor do you, when you **a.** them
T-13 IX.3:3 You *will* **a.** your treasure, and if you place
T-13 IX.6:3 it, **a.** His offer of Atonement for all your
T-13 X.8:6 look upon the Atonement and **a.** it wholly
T-14 II.7:8 **A.** this key to freedom from the hands of
T-14 III.3:8 *I would **a.** my guiltlessness by making it*
T-14 III.8:6 and **a.** the Cause of God as yours. The
T-14 III.10:1 who **a.** the Atonement *are* invulnerable.
T-14 III.11:6 Instead, **a.** His answer, for He knows that
T-14 IV.1:1 When you **a.** a brother's guiltlessness you
T-14 IV.7:3 **a.** the necessary conditions for knowing
T-14 V.1:7 **A.**, then, the immutable. Leave the world
T-14 V.11:5 of you. Refuse to **a.** anyone as without the
T-14 VII.7:7 not to **a.** what God would have you have.
T-14 X.1:2 The reflections you **a.** into the mirror of
T-14 XI.4:7 Who teaches light He will **a.** from you,
T-14 XI.5:6 will replace the dark ones you do not **a.**,
T-14 XI.8:6 so limiting the guidance that you would **a.**
T-14 XI.10:2 have you **a.** His accomplishments as yours
T-15 III.1:4 this in place of magnitude, and you **a.** it.
T-15 III.2:4 you. It is essential that you **a.** the fact, and
T-15 III.2:4 that you accept the fact, and **a.** it gladly,
T-15 III.6:6 Neither give littleness, nor **a.** it. All honor
T-15 III.8:3 it is sacrifice to **a.** anything less than glory
T-15 III.10:4 **A.** no less, remembering that everything I
T-15 III.10:5 and I can no more **a.** it as what it is not,
T-15 III.10:7 When you have learned to **a.** what you are
T-15 III.10:7 and unable to **a.** anything for yourself.
T-15 IV.5:2 to which you learn to **a.** me is the measure
T-15 IV.6:8 nothing, but merely to **a.** everything.
T-15 IV.9:6 for it. You will not be able to **a.** perfect
T-15 VI.1:6 be guilt as long as you **a.** the possibility,
T-15 VI.2:1 to **a.** the fact that perfect love is in you.
T-15 VI.4:5 you find difficult to **a.** is the fact that, like
T-15 VII.7:6 he demands that the other **a.** the guilt and
T-15 VII.9:2 united at its altar **a.** suffering and sacrifice
T-15 VIII.3:6 **A.** your sense of failure as nothing more
T-15 VIII.6:2 It is His holy function to **a.** them both,
T-15 IX.3:2 to **a.** the fact that the ego has no purpose
T-15 X.1:8 gift I can **a.** of you is the gift I gave to you.
T-15 X.3:2 are willing to **a.** our relationship as real,
T-15 X.3:3 in our union you will **a.** all of our brothers
T-15 X.5:6 **a.** the fact that sacrifice gets nothing.
T-15 X.5:10 If you would **a.** but this one idea, your
T-15 X.8:2 so fearful that you cannot **a.** it where it is.
T-15 XI.2:2 and **a.** it as the sign the time of Christ has
T-15 XI.10:10 **A.** the holy instant as this year is born,
T-16 I.4:4 that to recognize and **a.** the fact that you
T-16 I.4:4 and **a.** the fact that He *does* know. You are
T-16 II.8:5 let us resolve together to **a.** the joyful
T-16 II.8:7 no greater love than to **a.** this and be glad.
T-16 III.1:2 how to **a.** the comfort of your teaching. If
T-16 III.4:8 **a.** into your mind does not really change
T-16 IV.9:6 you are wholly willing to **a.** completion,
T-16 IV.10:2 Every illusion you **a.** into your mind by
T-16 V.5:2 both the ego and the Holy Spirit **a.** it.
T-16 VII.11:4 with Him is to **a.** relationships as real,
T-16 VII.12:1 *help us to **a.** our true relationship with You,*
T-16 VII.12:6 ***a.** but this into the minds which You created*
T-17 IV.10:3 are truth **a.** an idea so dangerous to truth,
T-17 IV.11:3 **a.** this gift you will not see the frame at all
T-17 IV.13:1 **a.** this and be glad: These pictures are
T-17 V.6:5 Spirit was there to **a.** the relationship,
T-17 V.8:1 **A.** with gladness what you do not
T-17 V.15:1 As you begin to recognize and **a.** the gifts
T-17 V.15:1 will also **a.** the effects of the holy instant
T-17 VII.5:9 **A.** not the illusion of peace it offers, but
T-18 I.1:1 substitute is to **a.** instead. If you would
T-18 I.10:4 never **a.** something else instead of you. He
T-18 I.10:9 **a.** His gift as our most holy and perfect
T-18 I.13:4 **A.** it here, and you will give as you have
T-18 II.4:6 fearful, but this you are not willing to **a.**.
T-18 IV.7:3 find it difficult to **a.** the idea that you need
T-18 VII.4:1 impossible to **a.** the holy instant without
T-18 VIII.7:1 Do not **a.** this little, fenced-off aspect as
T-19 III.5:7 must **a.** as true what it is told through it.
T-19 IV.3:9 And the Father will **a.** them in His Name.
T19 IV.B.9:2 And to **a.** the peace He gives instead,
T19 IV.B.10:2 It will **a.** you wholly, and give you peace.
T19 IV.D.9:7 and that you will **a.** it for my love and His.
T19 IV.D.13:2 his sins against him, or **a.** his gift to you?
T-20 II.2:2 For bodies can neither offer nor **a.**; hold
T-20 II.5:3 Those who **a.** the Holy Spirit's purpose as
T-20 IV.8:4 Once you **a.** His plan as the one function
T-20 VI.3:2 Idols **a.**, but never make return. They can
T-20 VI.11:8 it. Here he can **a.** the holy instant, offered
T-20 VII.2:4 Are you not also willing to **a.** the means?
T-20 VIII.8:5 Once you **a.** this simple fact and take unto
T-20 VIII.11:1 need persuade you to **a.** the gift of vision?
T-21 in.2:7 yourself to see in you, and to **a.** as yours.
T-21 I.9:4 **A.** the vision that can show you this, and
T-21 II.4:9 You must **a.** its strength, and not its
T-21 II.4:10 and can **a.** correction if it is willing to see
T-21 III.2:1 If you **a.** this change, you have accepted
T-21 V.7:7 Here is the part you can **a.**. What reason
T-21 VI.1:4 Yet if you will not **a.** the help you call for,
T-21 VI.7:2 neither can **a.** a miracle instead without
T-22 VI.4:7 is, and here will you **a.** Atonement. And
T-22 VI.8:7 **A.** this one and serve it willingly, for what
T-23 I.4:3 you not now **a.** the peace offered you here
T-23 II.6:6 He must **a.** His Son's belief in what he is,
T-23 III.3:2 is to **a.** but part of what you want; to take
T-23 III.5:3 **a.** forgiveness side by side with the belief
T-23 III.5:4 Would they be willing to **a.** the fact their
T-24 II.14:1 to you when you were ready to **a.** His plan
T-25 II.7:1 **A.** God's frame instead of yours, and you
T-25 VII.10:5 **A.** the function that has been assigned to
T-25 VIII.9:5 as well that you cannot **a.** it for yourself. It
T-25 VIII.9:7 that you **a.** brings joy to Him as well as
T-25 VIII.9:8 Heaven is richer made by each one you **a.**.
T-25 IX.2:1 the gift, because you are reluctant to **a.** it.
T-26 I.3:7 And to **a.** the limits of a body is to impose
T-27 I.4:4 This sick and sorry picture *you* **a.**, if only it
T-27 II.16:7 he may **a.** his other half as part of him.
T-27 V.1:3 **A.** the miracle of healing, and it will go
T-27 V.4:4 **a.** the blessing that the holy instant brings
T-27 V.11:2 you when you **a.** the healing for yourself.
T-27 VII.14:1 **A.** the dream He gave instead of yours. It
T-28 II.5:2 dream, and can **a.** another dream as well.
T-28 II.10:5 you can **a.** the role of maker of their hate,
T-28 III.1:6 When you **a.** a miracle, you do not add
T-28 III.2:3 If you withhold agreement and **a.** the part
T-28 V.2:7 You have the one that you **a.**, because it is
T-28 VII.2:8 You **a.** it wholly or accept it not. What is
T-28 VII.2:8 You accept it wholly or **a.** it not. What is
T-29 II.4:7 They will be healed when you **a.** your gifts
T-29 V.3:3 him. Nothing is asked of you but to **a.** the
T-30 I.7:6 by simple methods that you can **a.**.
T-31 V.15:3 matters it which concept you **a.** while you
T-31 VIII.10:4 They will **a.** the gift I offer them, because
W-in 9:1 believe the ideas, you need not **a.** them,
W-pI 9.1:2 you may be able to **a.** it intellectually, it is
W-pI 12.5:3 If you could **a.** the world as meaningless
W-pI 13.3:1 the meaningless, and **a.** it without fear. If
W-pI 58.1:4 I can **a.** the innocence that is the truth
W-pI 61.3:1 True humility requires that you **a.** today's
W-pI 63.2:4 you. **A.** no trivial purpose or meaningless
W-pI 63.2:6 to **a.** salvation that it may be yours to give
W-pI 65.3:1 try to understand and **a.** what the idea for
W-pI 65.8:5 when you **a.** today's idea completely.
W-pI 66.5:5 even if you do not yet **a.** the conclusion. It
W-pI 66.6:6 believing if you do not **a.** the first premise
W-pI 71.1:3 you also believe that to **a.** God's plan in
W-pI 72.6:4 Let us **a.** this and be glad. As a body, do
W-pI 72.9:5 plan for salvation, and to **a.** it instead.
W-pI 72.13:4 *Let me **a.** it instead. What is salvation,*
W-pI 73.7:2 to **a.** God's plan because you share in it.
W-pI 75.3:3 Today we will **a.** the new world as what
W-pI 78.4:5 or untrue to the ideal he should **a.** as his,

W-pI.....79.6:2 **a.** the answer because you would see its
W-pI.....80.1:8 **A.** that fact, and you are ready to take
W-pI.....80.3:6 **A.** the peace this simple statement brings.
W-pI.....86.3:6 I would **a.** God's plan for salvation, and
W-pI.....89.1:4 And I would **a.** the miracles in place of the
W-pI.....89.1:5 Now I would **a.** only what the laws of God
W-pI.....89.3:3 By this idea do I **a.** my release from hell.
W-pI.....90.4:3 *this problem is already given me, if I will **a.** it.*
W-pI.....95.1:5 You do not **a.** this, and you fail to realize
W-pI...96.12:2 who asks for it, and will **a.** the gift. Think,
W-pI.....97.5:2 that will **a.** the healing gifts they bring,
W-pI.....97.7:3 will **a.** this gift that you received of Him,
W-pI........98.h will **a.** my part in God's plan for salvation.
W-pI.....98.1:8 In gladness we **a.** it as it is, and take the
W-pI.....98.5:1 **a.** the happiness that God has given you?
W-pI.....98.7:6 *I will **a.** my part in God's plan for salvation.*
W-pI.....98.8:1 He will **a.** your words and give them back
W-pI...98.11:2 Tell Him once more that you **a.** the part
W-pI...100.4:4 all who will **a.** their Father's gifts as theirs.
W-pI...101.4:3 would he try to listen and **a.** Its offering?
W-pI...101.5:3 **A.** Atonement with an open mind, which
W-pI...102.4:2 *for me, and I **a.** it as my function now.* Then
W-pI...105.1:2 Today we will **a.** them, knowing they
W-pI...105.3:3 **A.** God's peace and joy, and you will learn
W-pI...105.4:1 when you **a.** them as God's gift to you, so
W-pI...105.4:1 when you **a.** His joy and peace as yours.
W-pI...105.5:1 Today **a.** God's peace and joy as yours.
W-pI...105.7:4 Now are you ready to **a.** the gift of peace
W-pI...106.1:1 you will not **a.** its petty gifts that give you
W-pI...109.5:6 Let it be still and thankfully **a.** its healing.
WpI . rIII.in4:6 And so **a.** their offering and be at peace.
W-pI...114.2:1 will **a.** my part in God's plan for salvation.
W-pI...114.2:2 *can my function be but to **a.** the Word of God*
W-pI...114.3:4 will **a.** my part in God's plan for salvation.
W-pI...117.2:4 *gave to me. I would **a.** all that is mine in truth.*
W-pI...118.1:2 *Today I will **a.** God's peace and joy, in glad*
W-pI...119.2:2 *that I may learn how to **a.** the truth in me,*
W-pI...122.7:3 **A.** salvation now. It is the gift of God, and
W-pI...124.9:2 You may not be ready to **a.** the gain today
W-pI...128.1:3 No one but must **a.** this thought as true, if
W-pI...130.8:6 *Let me **a.** the strength God offers me and see*
W-pI.130.11:1 **A.** a little part of hell as real, and you
W-pI...132.6:4 Not everyone is ready to **a.** it, and each
W-pI...132.7:1 is no world, and can **a.** the lesson now.
W-pI.132.13:4 Deny illusions, but **a.** the truth. Deny you
W-pI...134.2:1 can **a.** the fact that pardon is not asked for
W-pI.135.18:1 What could you not **a.**, if you but knew
W-pI.136.15:7 *I will **a.** the truth of what I am, and let my*
W-pI...137.3:4 and to **a.** his Self with all Its parts intact
W-pI...137.4:4 healed is merely to **a.** what always was the
W-pI......139.h I will **a.** Atonement for myself.
W-pI...139.1:2 decision to **a.** ourselves as God created us.
W-pI...139.2:2 Only refusal to **a.** yourself could make the
W-pI...139.9:5 What we **a.** as what we are proclaims
W-pI.139.10:2 he is. Today **a.** Atonement, not to change
W-pI.139.10:2 but merely to **a.** the truth about yourself,
W-pI.139.11:3 *I will **a.** Atonement for myself, For I remain*
W-pI.139.12:4 *I will **a.** Atonement for myself, For I remain*
W-pI...150.1:1 (139) I will **a.** Atonement for myself.
W-pI...151.9:2 you. **A.** His Word for what you are, for He
W-pI...152.2:7 **A.** no opposites and no exceptions, for to
W-pI...152.3:2 before, but may not yet **a.** both parts of it.
W-pI...152.8:1 and **a.** what we have made as what it is.
W-pI...152.8:3 Decide but to **a.** your rightful place as co-
W-pI.152.10:2 And we **a.** of Him that which we are, and
W-pI.152.11:4 *This day I will **a.** myself as what my Father's*
W-pI...154.5:3 It is enough that he **a.** it, give it to the
W-pI...154.6:3 is only as they can **a.** them for themselves
W-pI.154.14:4 prove that we **a.** no will we do not share,
W-pI...155.8:2 It asks that you **a.** the truth, and let it go
W-pI...156.5:5 **A.** their reverence, for it is due to Holiness
W-pI...159.2:2 **a.** forgiveness as accomplished in yourself
W-pI.160.10:5 and thus refusing to **a.** the gift of sight by
W-pI.161.10:4 you will not be willing to **a.** the witnesses
W-pI...162.5:2 is the right to perfect holiness you now **a.**.
W-pI...163.6:5 position, which we must **a.** if we be sane;
W-pI...163.9:7 *We **a.** Your Thoughts as ours, and our will is*
W-pI...164.3:4 to you who will today **a.** the gifts He gives.
W-pI...165.5:6 **a.** the Thought of God as your inheritance
W-pI...166.3:2 He must believe that to **a.** God's gifts,
W-pI.166.12:7 becomes your will when you **a.** these gifts,
W-pI.166.15:4 becomes which chooses to **a.** His gifts,
W-pI...169.3:6 and thus is ready to **a.** a state completely
W-pI.169.14:1 and **a.** the gifts that grace provided you.
WpI...rV.in3:6 *And we **a.** the Word You offer us to unify our*
Wi181-200 3:3 be there, but you cannot **a.** its presence.
W-pI.182.12:7 and you **a.** it in exchange for all the toys of
W-pI...183.9:4 **a.** today the part you play in its salvation,
W-pI...184.6:7 to **a.** its presence is the proof of sanity.
W-pI.184.11:2 Yet **a.** them not as your reality. The Holy
W-pI.184.12:6 our purpose is to let our minds **a.** what
W-pI.184.13:3 first you must **a.** the Name for all reality,
W-pI.184.15:6 *And we **a.** the truth You give, in place of*
W-pI...186.2:5 to do is to **a.** our part in genuine humility,
W-pI...186.5:2 **A.** the plan you did not make instead.
W-pI...186.8:2 We will **a.** the function God has given us,
W-pI.186.10:1 when you **a.** the function given you. The
W-pI...187.3:2 world, you first **a.** salvation for yourself.
W-pI...187.7:2 **A.** not suffering, and you remove the
W-pI...188.8:2 urge you gently to **a.** His Word for what
W-pI...190.5:7 them, they will **a.** your holy will as theirs.
W-pI...191.5:3 who can **a.** his true Identity is truly saved.
W-pI.191.11:5 They die till you **a.** your own eternal life.
W-pI.192.10:3 asks that you **a.** the way to freedom now.
W-pI.192.10:6 that you may **a.** him back as your Identity
W-pI...194.2:1 **A.** today's idea, and you have passed all
W-pI...194.2:2 **A.** today's idea, and you have released the
W-pI...194.9:4 If we **a.** an unforgiving thought, it will be
W-pI...196.6:1 you **a.** the fearful thought you can attack
W-pI...198.5:2 salvation, and **a.** His gift with gratitude?
W-pI.198.10:1 **A.** the one illusion which proclaims there
W-pI...199.3:1 in this course that you **a.** today's idea, and
W-pI...199.7:5 **A.** salvation now, and give your mind to
W-pI...200.1:3 **A.** this fact, and save yourself the agony of
W-pI.200.11:3 is ours, and only this will we **a.** and want.
W-pI...207.1:3 *away, as I **a.** His boundless Love for me.* I am
W-pI...212.1:4 *this I seek, and only this will I **a.** as mine.*
W-pI...214.1:5 *I **a.** but what He gives as what belongs to me.* I
W-pII.....in.6:5 **A.** these little gifts of thanks from us, as
W-pII...in.10:6 We will **a.** the way God's plan will end, as
W-pII..221.2:4 **A.** my confidence, for it is yours. Our
W-pII..228.1:3 I **a.** as true what He proclaims as false? Or
W-pII..234.1:5 the Son. This we **a.** as wholly true today.
W-pII..236.2:3 *it to You. **A.** my gift, for it is Yours to me.*
W-pII..237.1:1 Today I will **a.** the truth about myself. I
W-pII..246.2:1 *will **a.** the way You choose for me to come to*
W-pII..247.1:4 Let me **a.** what His sight shows me as the
W-pII..248.1:8 I ready to **a.** him back as God created him
W-pII..253.1:5 This must I **a.**. For thus am I led past this
W-pII..272.1:6 *I will **a.** no less than You have given me. I am*
W-pII..276.1:5 Let us **a.** His Fatherhood, and all is given
W-pII..278.1:1 If I **a.** that I am prisoner within a body, in
W-pII..279.2:1 *I will **a.** Your promises today, and give my*
W-pII.......7.5:1 **A.** your Father's gift. It is a Call from
W-pII..282.1:2 insane, and to **a.** myself as God Himself,
W-pII..285.1:3 joyous things the instant I **a.** my holiness.
W-pII..285.1:4 me today, and I **a.** my holiness instead?
W-pII..291.1:3 And I **a.** this vision in its name, both for
W-pII..291.2:2 *And I **a.** what comes from You, instead of*
W-pII..297.1:4 will be saved as I **a.** Atonement for myself.
W-pII..298.1:5 I **a.** instead what God establishes as mine,
W-pII..305.2:2 *Help us today but to **a.** Your gift, and judge it*
W-pII..307.1:5 *only You can give, I must **a.** Your Will for me,*
W-pII.....10.3:1 **a.** this holy truth: God's Judgment is the
W-pII..316.2:1 *Father, I would **a.** Your gifts today. I do not*
W-pII..318.2:1 *Your request that I **a.** Atonement for myself.*
W-pII..329.2:1 Today we will **a.** our union with each
W-pII..330.1:1 day **a.** forgiveness as our only function.
W-pII..330.1:4 mind that is made willing to **a.** God's gifts
W-pII..334.1:3 me not **a.** such meager gifts again today.
W-pII..337.1:4 I must **a.** Atonement for myself, and
W-pII..337.1:6 of myself, for I need but **a.** my Self, my
W-pII..337.2:2 *I sinned, but I **a.** Atonement for myself.*
W-pII..349.1:5 *Each one that I **a.** gives me a miracle to give.*
W-pII.....14.3:2 We **a.** our part as saviors of the world,
W-pII......355.h that I will give, When I **a.** God's Word.
M-2 ...........3:5 Because your will is free you can **a.** what
M-2 ...........3:8 it. And as you **a.** it, it is already learned.
M-5 ..... II.3:12 Yet to **a.** this release, the insignificance of
M-7 ...........3:2 worker is to **a.** the Atonement for himself.
M-7 ...........3:4 Yet he must first **a.** them. He need do no
M-13 .........2:1 to realize and to **a.** the fact that the world
M-16 .......6:14 only then will you **a.** your real protection.
M-16 .......10:3 he may **a.** as real can but deceive him. But
M-16 .......10:8 each temptation to **a.** magic as true must
M-17 .........6:6 **A.** it as a fact, and then forget it. Do not
M-17 .........6:9 **A.** your separation, but do not remember
M-18 .........4:5 teacher is to **a.** the Atonement for himself
M-22 .........1:5 **A.** Atonement and you are healed.
M-22 .........1:7 **A.** His Word and what remains to make
M-22 .........1:8 **A.** His Word and every miracle has been
M-22 .........4:3 Perhaps he can **a.** the idea in theory, but
M-22 .........5:4 refused to **a.** the Atonement for himself,
M-24 .........5:9 He need merely **a.** the idea that what he
M-24 .........6:1 and it is at this moment that you can **a.** it.
M-26 .........4:6 the answer, and then **a.** it when it comes.
M-26 .........4:8 All the help you can **a.** will be provided,
M-27 .........7:1 **A.** no compromise in which death plays a
M-28 .........5:7 And we **a.** His Holiness as ours; as it is. As
M-29 .........5:2 to **a.** the power given him by God is but to
M-29 .........5:2 acknowledge his Creator and **a.** His gifts.
M-29 .........5:4 you is simply to **a.** your true inheritance.
C-6.............1:3 possible to **a.** Him and to hear His Voice.
P-1.............2:6 helps the patient to recognize and **a.** it.
P-1.............5:2 illusions as false and to **a.** the truth as true
P-2.........in.4:4 and therapists alike **a.** unrealistic goals
P-2..........II.8:6 **a.** Atonement and learn to give it as it was
P-2.......VII.6:1 insane not to **a.** a function God has given
P-3..........II.5:6 be able to **a.** help from them if they did.
P-3..........II.6:7 no patient can **a.** more than he is ready to
P-3..........II.6:8 as much good as each can **a.** and use.
S-1...........I.1:7 already given; to **a.** what is already there.
S-1...........I.2:5 You cannot be asked to **a.** answers which
S-1..........II.4:3 and to **a.** to the same narrow margins.
S-2..........II.5:4 must **a.** the guilt and heavy-laid reproach
S-3........IV.3:4 nor **a.** an idol for rememberance of Him

## acceptable 24

T-6......V.B.4:2 which would be much less **a.** to it, would
T-7.......V.11:5 it is **a.** to Him and therefore to His Sons.
T-8........IV.7:9 He gives equally whatever is **a.** to Him.
T-8......IV.7:10 it is **a.** to Him it is the gift of freedom,
T-10....... V.9:4 His Son anything that is not **a.** to Him? If
T-14....VIII.2:4 by gifts wholly **a.** to Father and to Son.
T-14........X.8:2 ego, if the form is **a.** the content must be.
T-16......IV.3:5 special love partner is **a.** only as long as he
T-16....... V.3:3 usually judged to be **a.** and even natural.
T-17...... VI.3:6 is whether or not the ego likes it; is it **a.**,
T-19.......I.12:3 and wholly **a.** to his Father as to Him.
T-25.....VII.7:5 form of sanity which makes it most **a.** to
W-pI.....26.8:3 occur to you toward the end, less **a.** to you
W-pI.....71.3:2 is **a.** provided that it will not work. This
WpIrIII.in11:6 of God's Son, **a.** to God and to your Self.
W-pI...166.3:1 The gifts of God are not **a.** to anyone who
W-pI...185.8:6 now. Let not some dreams be more **a.**,
W-pI...187.2:7 Nor can the form it takes be less **a.**. It
M-4 ...... III.1:8 judgment are all things equally **a.**, for
M-5 ..... II.3:12 insignificance of the body must be an **a.**
M-24 .........3:4 with any concept that is not **a.** to anyone,
M-27 .........4:8 Not one can be **a.** to God's teachers,
M-27 .........4:8 because not one could be **a.** to God. He
P-2........ VI.3:4 and translating them into **a.** and pleasant

## acceptance 88

T-1.........I.44:1 of Christ and the **a.** of His Atonement.
T-1........ VI.4:4 Belief produces the **a.** of existence. That is
T-2...........I.4:4 about by your **a.** of the Atonement, which
T-2.........I.5:12 and capable, through your **a.** of miracles,
T-2........ III.3:1 **a.** of the Atonement by everyone is only a
T-3..........II.6:6 you offer them your **a.** of their truth so
T-5......... V.4:2 It is your **a.** of it that makes it real. If you
T-7........ IX.4:5 Kingdom because of its **a.** of wholeness.
T-8....... V.2:10 of God shine upon you by your **a.** of me.
T-9................h THE **A.** OF THE ATONEMENT
T-9.............I.h The **A.** of Reality

T-9.........I.11:5 not require belief, but it does require **a.**. It
T-9.........I.14:2 be. This is the simple **a.** of reality, because
T-9...........VI.h The A. of Your Brother
T-9........VI.6:3 are a way of giving **a.** and receiving it. In
T-10........II.2:3 of yourself for you, waiting for your **a.**.
T-10........II.4:3 denial of reality precludes the **a.** of God's
T-10.......III.3:4 **a.** of God in him acknowledges the Love
T-10.......III.7:2 it. The **a.** of peace is the denial of illusion,
T-10.......IV.2:2 **a.** depends on your willingness to have it.
T-11.......IV.7:3 Christ waits for your **a.** of Him as yourself
T-11......V.13:2 of wholeness comes only through **a.**, for
T-12.....VII.1:5 Atonement will radiate from your **a.** of it
T-12.....VII.7:7 for it represents the **a.** of two goals, each
T-13.......in.2:1 The **a.** of guilt into the mind of God's Son
T-13.......in.2:1 as the **a.** of the Atonement is its end. The
T-14......III.3:7 *I choose to testify to my* **a.** *of the Atonement,*
T-14.....VII.4:4 their joint **a.** becomes impossible. But if
T-14.....VII.4:6 **a.** must be withdrawn from one of them.
T-15......IV.1:8 in shimmering readiness for your **a.**. Yet
T-15......IV.8:6 willingness, being the **a.** of the single Will
T-15.......X.2:7 you have limited **a.** of the gift I offer you.
T-15.......X.3:7 by your **a.** of it, you offer it to everyone.
T-16......III.2:5 And this **a.** means that you are willing to
T-16......IV.8:6 A. of your creations is the acceptance of
T-16......IV.8:6 your creations is the **a.** of the Oneness of
T-17....IV.10:2 defense against your **a.** of the gift of death
T-17......VI.6:2 faith. Faith is implicit in the **a.** of the Holy
T-18.........I.3:7 comparison of **a.** or rejection for acting
T-18......IV.2:9 willingness for this lies also your **a.** of
T-19........II.4:2 and the **a.** of the self as sinful is perceived
T19....IV.C.6:1 have been given through your **a.**, the
T-20.........I.1:1 of victory and the **a.** of the truth. Let us
T-20.........I.2:2 the **a.** of the truth and its expression. This
T-20.......II.1:5 own interpretation of its value by his **a.**.
T-20.......II.1:6 as his **a.** and delight acknowledges the
T-21......IV.5:3 freedom; the **a.** of release to come to you.
T-21......VI.9:7 still. Spend but an instant in the glad **a.** of
T-22......IV.5:6 God's offer still is open, yet it waits **a.**.
T-24.....II.10:2 in need of your **a.** of himself as part of you
T-24.....II.14:5 to the **a.** of yourself as God created you.
T-26....VIII.6:2 Yet the **a.** of the working out can seem to
T-27.....II.16:5 **a.** of this function lies the means whereby
T-31......IV.6:1 of **a.** that there is a real alternative instead
W-pI.....65.1:5 full **a.** of salvation as your only function
W-pI.....65.7:1 the relief its **a.** will bring you by resolving
W-pI.....66.4:1 as its purpose your **a.** of the fact that not
W-pI...72.10:2 this goal, we must replace attack with **a.**.
W-pI.....80.5:1 the peace that your **a.** brings be given you
W-pI.....81.3:4 My **a.** does not depend on my recognizing
W-pI.....93.7:1 requires the **a.** of but one thought;–you
W-pI...102.4:1 today with this **a.** of God's Will for you: *I*
W-pI.122.11:1 and what your **a.** of the answer brings.
W-pI...138.5:3 recognition its **a.** lies, and as it is accepted
W-pI...139.8:1 Only **a.** can be asked of you, for what you
W-pI...154.7:2 their **a.** of His messages as for themselves,
W-pI...154.8:7 giving is his own **a.** of what he received.
W-pI...159.7:6 except the gift of his **a.** of his welcoming.
W-pI...162.5:3 this **a.** is salvation brought to everyone,
W-pI...164.9:1 you receiving your consent and your **a.**.
W-pI...164.9:3 not see the value your **a.** gives the world.
W-pI...165.4:8 to receive what only your **a.** can bestow.
W-pI...168.5:2 Our faith lies in the Giver, not our own **a.**.
W-pI...169.1:3 until the mind prepares itself for true **a.**.
W-pI...169.2:1 Grace is **a.** of the Love of God within a
W-pI...185.6:4 will meet with **a.** and be truly learned.
W-pI...186.1:3 It offers your **a.** of a part assigned to you,
W-pI...199.5:5 be exempt from the **a.** of the gifts you give
W-pII .284.1:8 and arrive at full **a.** of the truth in them.
W-pII ...10.4:6 And the world awaits your glad **a.**, which
M-4 ......IX.2:8 It implies **a.** of the Word of God and His
M-5 .......II.2:1 **a.** of sickness as a decision of the mind,
M-22 .........2:3 has learned all that his **a.** holds out to him
M-24 .........3:6 be an advantage in his premature **a.** of the
M-28 .........1:3 **a.** of the Holy Spirit's interpretation of the
M-28 .........1:3 the **a.** of the Atonement for oneself. It is
P-3.......II.10:9 between the offering and the **a.** of healing.
S-1..........I.6:2 their asking is not yet based upon **a.**. Help

**accepted** 163

T-2 .......III.1:1 Atonement can only be **a.** within you by
T-2 ......VII.5:9 the Atonement can be **a.** without delay. It
T-3 ........V.6:4 Once forgiveness has been **a.**, prayer in
T-3 ......V.10:2 those who perceive have not totally **a.** the
T-4 .......III.9:6 which implies a lack, has already been **a.**.
T-4 .......VI.3:7 that you have already **a.** this difference,
T-6 ........in.1:2 be **a.** as one's own responsibility, rather
T-6 ..........I.7:4 in it, and therefore **a.** it as true for me.
T-6 .....V.B.8:7 difficulty in miracles has not yet been **a.**,
T-7 .......III.3:6 you have **a.** the impossible as true. Is that
T-7 ........V.9:4 it part of you, you have **a.** it with love.
T-7 ......VII.3:6 picture in anyone, or you have **a.** it *as* you.
T-7 .....VIII.5:5 But having **a.** the errors as yours, do not
T-8 ....VII.14:6 poor learner. He has **a.** a learning goal in
T-8 .....VIII.2:5 of every end that the ego has **a.** as its own.
T-8 .....VIII.7:3 how you feel because you have **a.** the ego's
T-9 ......VII.3:4 in your mind, because you have **a.** it there
T-10 .......II.1:6 When what you have dissociated is **a.**, it
T-10 .......II.4:3 you have **a.** something else in its place. If
T-10 .....III.2:2 not matter where in the Sonship He is **a.**.
T-10 .....III.2:3 He is always **a.** for all, and when your
T-10 ...III.11:5 of sickness anywhere, you have **a.** him.
T-10 .....IV.2:2 mind. It is always there to be **a.**, but its
T-11 .....III.7:9 until you have **a.** them *you* cannot enter.
T-11 ...VIII.3:4 not misguided; you have **a.** no guide at all
T-12 ..VII.7:11 you have **a.** only one and want but one.
T-12 ....VII.8:3 upon your mind and **a.** opposition there,
T-12 ..VII.11:1 When you have **a.** your mission to extend
T-13 ........I.2:3 rose in the black cloud of guilt that you **a.**,
T-13 ........I.6:1 you have **a.** the Atonement for yourself,
T-13 .....VI.7:4 received, and can be **a.** only without limit.
T-13 .....IX.4:1 **a.** into your mind without distinction.
T-13 .......X.5:5 you. For you will have **a.** the Atonement,
T-13 ...XI.10:7 it, the Will of God must be **a.** as your will.
T-14 ........I.1:5 And you must also have **a.** it as yours, for
T-14 .....III.7:4 which you have **a.** for yourself, is also his.
T-14 ...VIII.5:5 worthy of the Father will be **a.** by the Son,
T-14 .....XI.9:5 to light, having **a.** them instead of you,
T-15 .....IV.4:5 have **a.** for finding magnitude in littleness
T-15 .....VI.5:2 For gain and loss are both **a.**, and so no
T-15 .....VI.6:6 because He offered it to me and I **a.** it.
T-15 .....IX.1:5 have **a.** it as the only perception you want,
T-15 .....IX.4:7 be **a.** and the loneliness in Heaven is gone
T-15 .....XI.3:3 have **a.** it with me you will give it with me.
T-16 .....III.2:4 are immediately **a.** as your choice. And
T-16 ......V.3:8 the illusion of love is **a.** in love's place,
T-17 .....IV.5:1 **a.** is very anxious to preserve its reason, as
T-17 ...IV.11:3 all, because the gift can only be **a.** through
T-17 ...IV.12:2 is complete, and cannot be partially **a.**.
T-17 ......V.3:1 This invitation is **a.** immediately, and the
T-17 ......V.3:5 to the purpose that has been **a.** for it. In
T-17 ......V.3:9 relationship has **a.** the goal of holiness, it
T-17 ......V.4:6 and **a.** as the only way out of the conflict,
T-17 ....V.12:5 thus enable its results to be **a.** and shared.
T-17 ....V.14:4 that has been **a.** and the means as they
T-17 ...VIII.1:5 Faith has **a.** every aspect of the situation,
T-17 ...VIII.5:4 **a.** the Cause of his awakening as yours.
T-17 ...VIII.6:1 **a.** truth as the goal for your relationship,
T-17 ...VIII.6:2 cannot be **a.** apart from its conditions,
T-17 ...VIII.6:3 change, for you **a.** what can never change.
T-18 ......I.13:4 it here, and you will give as you have **a.**.
T-18 ......I.13:6 him together must extend, as you **a.** it.
T-18 .....III.2:3 The goal you **a.** is the goal of knowledge,
T-18 .....III.4:9 You have **a.** God. The holiness of your
T-18 ...III.4:11 You do not understand what you **a.**, but
T-18 ......V.3:7 to Him. You have **a.** one; the other will be
T-18 ......V.4:5 even realize you have **a.** the Holy Spirit's
T-18 . VI.11:11 You have **a.** this instead of the body, and
T-18 ....VII.4:6 a very long road to the goal you have **a.**. It
T-19 ........I.9:2 you have **a.** the Atonement for yourself,
T19..IV.A.6:10 truth which you **a.** must all illusions end.
T19..IV.B.17:2 is offered them but they have not **a.** it,
T19....IV.C.1:2 For it was offered you, and you **a.**. Yet you
T19..IV.C.2:13 When you **a.** the Holy Spirit's purpose in
T19....IV.C.5:7 mind which heard His Answer and **a.** It.
T19...IV.D.9:1 of God unterrified, unless he has **a.** the
T19. IV.D.16:5 you laid upon him and he **a.** as his own,
T-20 .....III.7:3 light the Holy Spirit offered, and you **a.**.
T-20 .....IV.4:7 for those with little wings have not **a.** for
T-20 ...VIII.7:6 have faith in what you see, if you **a.** this?
T-21 .....III.1:5 from the **a.** purpose of the relationship.
T-21 .....III.2:1 have **a.** the idea of making room for truth.
T-21 .....III.4:6 have **a.** them completely instead of yours,
T-21 .....IV.4:5 Holy Spirit's purpose was **a.** by the part of
T-21 .......V.5:2 It must have been **a.** by the Son of God,
T-21 .......V.9:2 Spirit's purpose **a.** and accomplished,
T-21 .....VI.2:1 Correction cannot be **a.** or refused by you
T-22 .......II.3:2 The form in which they are **a.** is irrelevant
T-22 .....IV.5:7 From you who have **a.** it is it received.
T-22 .....VI.5:3 then the same Atonement you **a.** in your
T-22 ...VI.14:5 For when you have **a.** it with gladness,
T-23 .......II.9:2 law of chaos, which, if the others are **a.**,
T-23 .....III.3:6 is denied where compromise has been **a.**,
T-27 .....V.1:12 because you have **a.** what He says.
T-28 .........I.7:7 instead, the new effects of cause **a.** *now,*
T-29 .......II.2:1 You have **a.** healing's cause, and so it
T-30 .......V.7:7 Yet is the Love of Christ **a.** first. And then
T-31 .....II.11:1 remembered and **a.** by you both. Alone it
T-31 ....VII.4:5 unto him, has been **a.** now for both of you
W-pI ....26.2:4 and invulnerability cannot be **a.** together.
W-pI ....58.4:4 Once I have **a.** my holiness, nothing can
W-pI ....60.1:3 **a.** their innocence see nothing to forgive.
W-pI ....70.2:4 This is not a role that can be partially **a.**.
W-pI ....72.9:6 instead. And wherever His plan is **a.**, it is
W-pI ....77.6:4 The fact that you **a.** must be so. There is
W-pI ....79.2:2 solution that solves them all is to be **a.**.
W-pI ....80.2:5 **a.** salvation for yourself by bringing the
W-pI ....80.4:5 You are answered, and have **a.** the answer
W-pI ....93.6:2 over this must be repeated, until it is **a.**. It
W-pI ....96.2:1 must be **a.** if you would be saved. Until
W-pI ....96.2:2 Until you have **a.** this, you will attempt an
W-pI ....96.7:3 Voice **a.** it for you and answered in your
W-pI ..102.5:3 that you have now **a.** happiness as your
W-pI ..110.2:3 It is enough to let the present be **a.** as it is.
W-pI 122.14:4 *Today I have* **a.** *this as true. Today I have*
W-pI ..124.7:3 We have **a.**, and we now would give. For
W-pI 135.12:3 But when it has **a.** this as true, then is it
W-pI ..138.5:3 acceptance lies, and as it is **a.** it is known.
W-pI ..138.5:6 you have **a.** as the truth of what you are,
W-pI ..138.6:5 only choice in which is truth **a.** or denied.
W-pI ..139.4:4 He has **a.** it because he lives; has judged
W-pI ..139.7:3 come again until the time Atonement is **a.**
W-pI ..139.9:3 Let us not forget the goal that we **a.**. It is
W-pI 152.10:5 from hell, are joyously **a.** as our own.
W-pI ..192.6:4 for, met with thanks and joyously **a.**? We
W-pI ..197.4:5 In your gratitude are they **a.** universally,
W-pI ..197.4:6 back, when He has gratefully **a.** them?
W-pI ..198.7:3 You may think They have **a.**. But if you
W-pI ..200.5:5 as you free the one, the other is **a.** as he is.
WpI.rVI.in.2:2 curriculum if understood, practiced, **a.**,
W-pII ....in.4:4 We will offer it, and it will be **a.**. So our
W-pII . 284.1:5 times; and next to be **a.** as but partly true,
W-pII . 284.1:6 more and more, and finally **a.** as the truth
W-pII . 298.1:1 permits my love to be **a.** without fear.
W-pII ... 10.1:3 At first you see a world that has **a.** this as
W-ep ......... 2:4 follow Him Whom you **a.** as your voice, to
M-5 ...... III.2:3 to question what the patient has **a.** as true
M-6 ........... 1:5 Having **a.** the Atonement for himself, he
M-6 ........... 1:5 for himself, he has also **a.** it for the patient
M-6 ........... 2:8 to him to judge when his gift should be **a.**.
M-6 ........... 2:9 received, and trust that it will be **a.** when
M-7 ........... 2:3 the Holy Spirit so **a.** it and so used it. Now
M-11 ......... 1:8 at differently, if His promises are to be **a.**.
M-12 ....... 1:10 him. He has **a.** Christ, and he is saved.
M-15 ......... 3:9 and His alone, will be **a.** in the end. It is
M-16 ......... 7:1 teacher of God who has **a.** His protection!
M-16 ......... 7:6 was before illusions were **a.** into his mind,
M-20 ......... 4:3 War is again **a.** as the one reality. Now
M-22 ......... 2:3 teacher of God may have **a.** the function
M-22 ....... 6:12 Having been received, it must be **a.**. It is
M-23 ......... 2:1 who has perfectly **a.** the Atonement for
M-23 ......... 2:5 has overcome death because he has **a.** life.
M-27 ......... 1:5 but to be **a.** as the "natural" law of life.
C-in ........... 2:4 belief and can therefore be **a.** or rejected.
P-1............ 4:4 Until this is at least in part **a.**, the patient
P-2........ III.1:6 little light that can be then **a.** is all there is
P-2........ IV.6:5 word, error is **a.** as real and dealt with by

P-2........VI.7:5 seen in the patient and **a.** in the therapist,
P-3.........II.3:9 it. He has **a.** the Atonement for himself.
P-3.........II.7:5 **a.** the gift entirely in order to stay and let
P-3........III.1:7 last illusion be **a.** by everyone everywhere.
S-1........III.2:7 forgiven, and who **a.** their forgiveness,
S-3........III.3:4 assumed and then **a.** as the truth, and

## accepting 64

T-1........I.50:1 **a.** what is in accord with it as true, and
T-2........VI.6:9 can be corrected only by **a.** a unified goal.
T-2........VI.7:3 of **a.** the Atonement as the remedy. These
T-3.........V.7:7 is a continual process of **a.** and rejecting,
T-4.........II.6:8 the ego has deluded itself into **a.** its reality
T-5.........V.7:7 recognizing that, by **a.** this responsibility,
T-5.........V.7:9 except by **a.** the solution of undoing. You
T-6...........I.4:5 are **a.** false premises and teaching them to
T-6......V.B.4:6 he is receiving conflicting messages and **a.**
T-6......V.C.5:5 Therefore, you are **a.** it as it is. Since it is
T-7...........I.2:9 **a.** this power as yours you have learned to
T-7........III.4:2 not true, you are **a.** conflict as your choice
T-7.........V.5:4 By **a.** exceptions and acknowledging that
T-7.........V.5:4 the healer is obviously **a.** inconsistency.
T-7.....VIII.7:3 By **a.** the Atonement for yourself, you are
T-8........IV.3:5 problem in **a.** it is the problem of this
T-8........IV.3:8 you are denying the world and **a.** God.
T-8.......VII.1:4 **a.** it simply by the belief that attack can
T-9........III.5:2 errors and accept them, you are **a.** yours.
T-9.........V.7:8 extending it and **a.** its acknowledgment.
T-9........VI.4:8 your magnitude by **a.** His limitlessness as
T-10.......III.2:4 your brothers simply by **a.** God for them.
T-10.......IV.5:3 them with chaos, and **a.** it of them. All
T-11.......V.8:5 continue if you realize that, by **a.** it, you
T-11.......VI.6:4 Son, **a.** him without question as His Own.
T-11.....VII.2:8 you are **a.** both the false and the true and
T-13.........I.7:6 your mind, and by **a.** his purity as yours,
T-13.........I.9:1 **A.** the Atonement teaches you what
T-13.........I.9:1 for by **a.** your guiltlessness you learn that
T-13.........I.9:3 **A.** the guiltlessness of the Son of God as
T-14.........I.1:7 go, **a.** the Atonement for yourself and
T-14.......IV.7:5 **A.** His Son as guilty is denial of the Father
T-14.....VII.7:8 Behold your will, **a.** it as His, with all His
T-15.......IX.7:4 **A.** it as undivided you join Him wholly, in
T-15........X.8:3 real price of not **a.** this has been so great
T-16........II.5:2 would be in joyously **a.** truth for what it is
T-18........V.5:6 gave to your relationship by **a.** it for you,
T-18..VI.11:10 no questions of reality, but merely **a.** it.
T-20.......IV.3:1 you by **a.** their results as your just due.
T-21.......VI.3:8 it simply by **a.** reason where madness was
T-21.....VII.6:7 hope of finding sin, and not **a.** power.
T-22........in.3:3 **A.** his completion, he would extend it by
T-28.......IV.1:1 **A.** the Atonement for yourself means not
T-28.......IV.2:3 yourself by not **a.** them as causing you,
W-pI.....61.2:3 of **a.** your role in salvation and in taking
W-pI.....61.3:2 step in **a.** your real function on earth. It is
W-pI.....65.5:6 *is preventing me from* **a.** *my only function.*
W-pI.....70.2:1 The seeming cost of **a.** today's idea is this
W-pI.....70.2:5 surely begin to see that **a.** it is salvation.
W-pI.....70.5:3 Therefore, in **a.** the idea for today, we are
W-pI.....81.3:2 It is through **a.** my function that I will see
W-pI.....98.3:5 and thus increase it by **a.** it ourselves.
W-pI...122.9:2 **a.** Heaven's answer to the hell we made,
W-pI...164.2:5 glad consent; **a.** your deliverance for you.
W-pII..255.1:6 what my Father wills for me, **a.** it as mine,
W-pII..284.2:2 *in You today,* **a.** *but the joyous as Your gifts;*
W-pII..284.2:2 *as Your gifts;* **a.** *but the joyous as the truth.*
W-pII..339.2:2 *me,* **a.** *only Thoughts You share with me.*
M-7............3:6 By **a.** healing he can give it. If he doubts
M-22........1:10 heal. The teacher of God has taken **a.** the
M-22..........7:8 Son of God, **a.** him as God created him.
C-5............2:5 he saw the false without **a.** it as true. And
C-5............6:6 from them without **a.** him into your life.
S-2.........II.4:4 Is it not kind to be **a.** of another's spite,

## accepts 40

T-1.........V.2:3 therefore, **a.** the time-control factor gladly
T-3........VI.7:5 it **a.** the one inconceivable thought as its
T-4........VI.6:4 and **a.** my Atonement decisions because
T-5.........I.1:13 if the one to whom you give it **a.** it as his,
T-5........III.6:4 is the ego's domain, **a.** it without question
T-5.........V.8:6 at any minute if it **a.** the Atonement first.
T-6......V.C.1:4 partly in accord with it He **a.** and purifies.
T-6......V.C.1:7 that what the Holy Spirit rejects the ego **a.**
T-7.........V.3:2 in this world, and the only one He **a.**. He
T-7........VI.2:1 The mind that **a.** attack cannot love. That
T-9........VI.5:5 the Sonship comes together and **a.** its
T-11.....V.13:1 The ego analyzes; the Holy Spirit **a.**. The
T-11......VI.5:3 for he will obey only the god he **a.**. The
T-11...VIII.9:3 as his Father **a.** him and heal him unto
T-14...III.12:4 that quietly **a.** the plan God set for its
T-14.......X.2:2 the only perception the Son of God **a.**.
T-15....VI.5:10 God **a.** the laws of God as what he gladly
T-15...VII.10:3 basis the ego **a.** for special relationships.
T-17...VIII.6:2 no one **a.** what he does not believe is real.
T-18.......II.6:1 **a.** your dreams and uses them as means
T-18.....VII.1:4 No one **a.** Atonement for himself who still
T-18.....VII.1:4 for himself who still **a.** sin as his goal. You
T-21......III.2:4 and protected as is a goal the mind **a.**.
T-24.......II.6:4 as his mind **a.** the truth about himself, as
T-28.........I.12:5 Son **a.** gives welcome to eternity and Him,
T-28......IV.7:3 sick if someone else **a.** his union with him.
T-28....VI.1:10 It **a.** no role, but does what it is told,
W-pI.....97.1:2 It **a.** no split identity, nor tries to weave
W-pI.....97.5:3 time someone **a.** them as his thoughts,
W-pI...125.1:5 **a.** the message that the world must hear
W-pI.137.11:3 **a.** it not within his mind becomes a haven
W-pI...140.1:1 to any remedy the world **a.** as beneficial.
W-pI.151.17:2 with us and happily **a.** our holy thoughts,
W-pI...154.2:2 He chooses and **a.** your part for you. He
W-pI.166.14:5 **a.** God's gifts can never suffer anything.
W-pI...184.6:2 learns to think that it is so **a.** the signs and
W-pI...184.8:7 you, and he **a.** this separate name as his.
M-14.........3:4 any one of them **a.** Atonement for himself
M-19.........5:6 It **a.** all evidence that is brought before it,
M-21.........4:7 God **a.** the words which are offered him,

## access 1

T-21.......V.8:8 The partially insane have **a.** to it, and only

## accessibility 1

W-pI...107.6:3 It stands in open light, in obvious **a.**. It is

## accessible 3

T-14.....X.11:2 Him is perfectly open and freely **a.** to all,
W-pI...168.1:6 He remains entirely **a.**. He loves His Son.
W-pII......1.2:3 and more obscure; less easily **a.** to doubt,

## accident 5

T-21.......II.3:3 he seems to find himself by chance or **a.**.
T-21.......II.3:4 No **a.** nor chance is possible within the
W-pI...136.2:1 Sickness is not an **a.**. Like all defenses, it
M-9...........1:3 that no one is where he is by **a.**, and
P-3........III.6:2 pay. No one is sent by **a.** to anyone.

## accidental 1

M-3...........4:4 the first level, these meetings are not **a.**,

## accidents 1

M-3...........1:6 There are no **a.** in salvation. Those who

## acclaim 1

T-29.......II.1:2 Why would you not **a.** the truth instead of

## accommodate 1

T-29.........I.6:1 The body will **a.** to this, if you would

## accompanied 1

M-17.........4:5 of intense rage, **a.** by thoughts of violence,

## accomplish 38

T-2.......VII.7:4 there is usually some degree of desire to **a.**
T-5.......II.12:5 What we can **a.** together has no limits,
T-6......V.A.4:4 We have too much to **a.** on behalf of the
T-7......VI.13:7 Sonship can only **a.** perfectly, extending
T-8.......VII.6:3 with which you can perfectly **a.** His holy
T-8........IX.7:1 separate and to **a.** all things in my name.
T-9........IV.3:4 **a.** this through Him you cannot look on
T-11........II.2:4 Every miracle that you **a.** speaks to you of
T-11........II.4:4 not **a.** with the Fatherhood of God in him
T-11.....V.12:3 ego believes that to **a.** its goal is happiness
T-12........II.6:2 and you must **a.** it because it is His Will.
T-12........II.8:5 and we will easily **a.** the goal of perfection
T-12........II.8:7 **a.** together will be believed when you see
T-14......XI.4:6 But to **a.** this, all your dark lessons must
T-15......XI.5:5 Yet how could you **a.** this yourself, when
T-15....XI.10:2 faith in you to do all that you would **a.**.
T-16........II.2:7 to **a.** what you do not understand. And so
T-16......IV.7:3 love relationship would **a.** the impossible.
T-16.......V.7:3 it thinks it can **a.** this it gives itself away,
T-17.........I.6:4 He will **a.** it; not you. But forget not this:
T-17.....VII.6:6 goal's reality will call forth and **a.** every
T-18.........I.1:2 Spirit has given you, and would **a.** for you
T-18.....VII.6:8 will **a.** more than is given to a century of
T-21......III.9:8 The faith you give your brother can **a.** this
T-25....IX.10:4 can **a.** when it is offered to everyone alike.
T-27....VI.6:10 The purpose of a miracle is to **a.** this. And
W-in..........1:3 An untrained mind can **a.** nothing. It is
W-pI.....25.5:2 "good" or "bad," is the only way to **a.** this
W-pI...102.2:1 a cause and with no power to **a.** anything.
W-pI...134.4:5 It is delusional in what it thinks it can **a.**.
W-pI...135.7:3 and to exalted aims which it cannot **a.**.
W-pII.......1.3:3 the means by which it would **a.** it as well.
W-pII.225.2:5 as we **a.** these few final steps which end a
M-16.........4:5 an hour with closed eyes and **a.** nothing.
M-28.........5:4 What remains that vision could **a.**? We
S-2.......in.1:10 go. **A.** this and you have been redeemed.
S-2.......in.1:11 **A.** this and you have been transformed.
S-2.......in.1:12 **A.** this and you will save the world.

## accomplished 101

T-2.......VII.7:6 develop fully until mastery has been **a.**.
T-3.........V.1:3 which was **a.** by the union of my will with
T-4.........in.3:2 Do not dwell upon it, but dismiss it as **a.**.
T-6......V.A.1:2 Perhaps you think this is **a.** through death
T-6......V.A.1:2 death, but nothing is **a.** through death,
T-6......V.A.1:3 Everything is **a.** through life, and life is of
T-7.........X.7:1 guards so jealously, is not **a.** by your wish.
T-7.........X.7:2 It was **a.** for you by the Will of God, Who
T-8........III.2:2 When this is **a.**, then, there is no other
T-8........IV.3:2 this was done, it was perfectly **a.** by all.
T-8........IV.3:3 all. How else could it be perfectly **a.**? My
T-8.....VII.12:7 **a.** only if the mind extends to other minds
T-10.........I.3:5 What is possible has not yet been **a.**. Yet
T-11........II.2:3 willingness to join them is your healing **a.**
T-11.....V.11:1 be **a.** God's purpose could be defeated,
T-11.....V.11:3 goal can be **a.** and God's purpose can *not.*
T-11.....V.11:4 teaching, *only* God's purpose can be **a.**,
T-11.....V.11:4 can be accomplished, and it is **a.** already.
T-11......VI.4:6 in the resurrection because it has been **a.**,
T-11......VI.4:6 accomplished, and it has been **a.** in you.
T-11......VI.4:8 will not perceive what has been **a.** for you.
T-12........II.6:4 What has been **a.** for you must be yours.
T-12........II.8:7 will be believed when you see it as **a.**.
T-12......VI.6:7 When this has been **a.**, perception and
T-13......IV.9:3 Healing cannot be **a.** in the past. It must
T-13......IV.9:4 be **a.** in the present to release the future.
T-13....VIII.3:2 the future, was **a.** by God in your creation
T-13......XI.5:3 God would have **a.** from accomplishment.
T-13....XI.11:5 *of* everyone, will not be perfectly **a.**. You
T-14........II.1:1 in whom His mission can be happily **a.**.
T-14......IV.3:4 to be forgiven, for this has already been **a.**
T-14...VII.5:10 easy that it was **a.** the instant it was given
T-14...VII.5:15 see how easily all that He asks can be **a.**.
T-14...VIII.4:8 is **a.** by the Creator and by His creations.
T-14......XI.3:2 has been **a.** before its effects are manifest.
T-15........II.5:6 instant, complete, **a.** and given wholly.
T-15...VII.14:1 instant that what seems impossible is **a.**,

T-15...... IX.1:2 shift to vision that is **a.** in the holy instant
T-15...... IX.3:4 This will never be **a.**. Yet you have surely
T-16.........I.1:7 that healing pain is not **a.** by delusional
T-16....... II.4:5 reality of what has clearly been **a.** through
T-16....... II.7:3 been **a.** in a mind firmly convinced that
T-16....... V.5:3 on what completion is, and how it is **a.**.
T-17.........I.2:1 wish you think you have **a.** what you wish
T-17.........I.6:3 except your willingness to have this be **a.**.
T-17....... V.2:4 as it begins, develops and becomes **a.**, it
T-17....... V.3:3 This is **a.** very rapidly, but it makes the
T-17....... V.5:3 As this change develops and is finally **a.**,
T-18.........I.6:8 guilt, for guilt implies it was **a.** in reality.
T-18....... II.9:8 this Will would have **a.** has never *not* been
T-18....... V.1:3 and all the means by which salvation is **a.**,
T-19....... II.7:7 which in its madness it believes it has **a.**.
T-19...... IV.3:6 the Holy Spirit's function here will be **a.**.
T19... IV.A.5:5 How can this fail to be **a.**, wherever it is
T19..IV.B.16:2 places in it all its faith that this can be **a.**.
T19....IV.C.6:2 that seems to be the hardest can be **a.** first
T19. IV.D.10:6 is over unless you realize its purpose is **a.**?
T19. IV.D.16:1 return until redemption is **a.** and received
T-20....... V.5:6 take so many holy instants to let this be **a.**
T-21...... III.9:1 this is how they think *their* purpose is **a.**.
T-21....... V.5:3 the Will of God wait upon time to be **a.**.
T-21....... V.9:2 the Holy Spirit's purpose accepted and **a.**,
T-22....... II.6:2 to let the Holy Spirit's purpose be **a.**, they
T-24...... VI.4:3 Son as all you wish to be **a.** by the world,
T-26......VII.1:2 before the purpose of the course can be **a.**
T-27....... III.5:8 When its aim has been **a.** it is functionless
T-29...... IX.4:2 you from what you believe you have **a.**,
T-31.........I.2:8 But you **a.** it because you wanted to, and
W-pI.....44.3:5 this training must be **a.** if you are to see.
W-pI.....47.1:5 and the guarantee that it will be **a.**?
W-pI.....72.9:6 His plan is accepted, it is **a.** already.
W-pI...72.10:1 for salvation has already been **a.** in us. To
W-pI.....77.5:3 you be given the means by which this is **a.**
W-pI.....80.1:6 Salvation is **a.**. Freedom from conflict has
W-pI.....91.5:2 This is **a.** very simply, as you instruct
W-pI.....94.1:4 idea. Here is salvation **a.**. Here is sanity
W-pI. 134.14:4 That this may be **a.**, let us give a quarter
W-pI...137.3:6 But healing is **a.** as he sees the body has
W-pI...137.5:2 overlooks all sins that never were **a.**,
W-pI...138.3:5 There is no sense of gain, for nothing is **a.**;
W-pI. 153.11:4 come to you, and your escape has been **a.**.
W-pI...154.9:4 part of your appointed task is yet to be **a.**.
W-pI...158.6:5 goal, for it transcends what needs to be **a.**.
W-pI...159.2:2 accept forgiveness as **a.** in yourself when
W-pI...169.8:1 was already in His Mind, **a.** and complete.
W-pI...183.9:5 own as well. And both can be **a.** perfectly.
W-pI...186.2:4 given us by which it will be perfectly **a.**.
W-pI...196.7:3 Until this shift has been **a.**, you can not
W-pII ..... 7.2:3 And when this is entirely **a.**, learning has
W-pII .297.2:1 *salvation set already, and* **a.** *by Your grace.*
W-pII ... 10.1:4 its goal **a.** and its mission done.
M-5 ..............h HOW IS HEALING A.?
M-5 .........I.1:1 Healing is **a.** the instant the sufferer no
M-18 ......... 4:7 When this has been **a.**, the teacher of God
M-22 ......... 1:8 His Word and every miracle has been **a.**.
M-24 ......... 4:2 When this is finally **a.**, issues such as the
M-28 ......... 3:9 The whole reversal is **a.**. Nothing is left to
P-2.........in.2:6 In illusions the impossible is easily **a.**, but
P-2...... IV.11:2 guilt it carries so wearily, and healing is **a.**
P-3.........I.3:10 of the Holy Spirit. It cannot fail to be **a.**.
P-3........ III.3:5 offer the only gift whereby all healing is **a.**

## accomplishment 34

T-1........ III.1:9 because conviction comes through **a.**. The
T-2........VII.7:2 Readiness is only the prerequisite for **a.**.
T-4........ IV.8:5 carefully for any beliefs that hinder its **a.**,
T-5........ II.12:4 is beyond belief, but not beyond **a.**. What
T-6........ II.11:4 experience perfection as a difficult **a.**,
T-6...... V.C.7:4 His perfect **a.** is not apparent to you. This
T-7...... VI.13:7 Being a perfect **a.**, the Sonship can only
T-8........ III.2:3 wish for other experience will block its **a.**,
T-12....... IV.4:6 His is the journey to **a.**, and the goal He
T-13....... XI.5:3 God would have accomplished from **a.**.
T-15....... IX.3:3 which it tries to turn its purpose into **a.**.
T-17....... II.3:1 still the greatest **a.** of all in God's plan of
T-17 ...... V.2:3 relationship is a phenomenal teaching **a.**.
T-17 .... V.14:3 will gladly arrange the means for its **a.**? It
T-17 ..... VI.4:2 interferes with the **a.** of your objective,
T-17 ..... VI.6:5 involved in it will play his part in its **a.**.
T-18 ..... III.5:2 And in your desire lies its **a.**. Your desire
T-18 ...... V.4:5 merely bring unholy means to its **a.**. The
T19.... IV.B.4:5 you place between your will and its **a.**?
T19..IV.B.10:8 only the mind can see the means for its **a.**,
T-20 ...VIII.6:9 holy purpose bereft of means for its **a.**.
T-21 .... V.10:6 that it serves, and all the means for its **a.**.
T-24 ..... VI.9:2 a purpose and without **a.** of any kind, is
T-24 ... VI.12:5 the means, and guarantee the goal's **a.**.
T-24 ... VI.13:7 comes the means for effortless **a.** and rest.
T-26 ...... V.9:5 on a mission whose **a.** can only be unreal.
T-27 ...VIII.6:3 and possible of both **a.** and real effects.
T-31 ........I.4:4 world arises from the first **a.** of learning;
W-pI.... 44.8:2 Salvation is your happiest **a.**. It is also the
W-pI. 135.11:5 its progress to **a.** of any goal that serves
W-pI. 135.21:2 we need is given us for our **a.** of this today
W-pI... 199.7:6 joy, and hope that finds its full **a.** in God.
W-pII .... in.5:3 remains for time to separate from its **a.**.
W-pII . 296.2:2 and possible of easy reach and quick **a.**.

## accomplishments 9

T-2 ...... V.10:1 gone far beyond his actual **a.** in time.
T-6 ....... IV.8:1 because abilities are potentials, not **a.**.
T-6 ....... IV.8:2 are useless in the presence of God's **a.**,
T-6 ....... IV.8:3 A. are results that have been achieved.
T-7 ..........I.2:5 God's **a.** are not yours, but yours are like
T-7 ..............I.7:1 take steps, because His **a.** are not gradual.
T-14 ... XI.10:2 would but have you accept His **a.** as yours
W-in.......... 5:3 true perception makes its **a.** anywhere
M-25 ......... 2:8 special, and there is no magic in his **a.**.

## accord 45

T-1 ........I.50:1 accepting what is in **a.** with it as true, and
T-1 ........I.50:1 and rejecting what is out of **a.** as false.
T-2 .........II.5:7 into closer and closer **a.** with the Sonship;
T-2 ....... VI.4:9 ask me if your choice is in **a.** with mine. If
T-2 ....... VI.5:6 the mind and the behavior are out of **a.**,
T-3 .........II.4:6 Father are One, their perfect **a.** is Heaven.
T-3 ........ IV.3:6 in conflict because it is out of **a.** with itself
T-4 ....... VI.6:4 because my will is never out of **a.** with His
T-5 ...... VII.4:3 made that is not in **a.** with His holy Will. I
T-6 ........I.11:5 is that no perception that is out of **a.** with
T-6 ..... V.C.1:3 there. Whatever is in **a.** with this light He
T-6 ..... V.C.1:4 partly in **a.** with it He accepts and purifies
T-6 ..... V.C.1:5 of **a.** entirely He rejects by judging against
T-7 ....... IV.5:6 perception is therefore in **a.** with the laws
T-7 ....... IV.5:6 in a state of mind that is out of **a.** with His
T-7 ....... IV.5:7 that it brings the mind into **a.** with His,
T-7 ........ V.6:9 by His Voice, and is in **a.** with His laws.
T-7 ...... V.6:13 meaning cannot be out of **a.** with His,
T-7 ...... V.6:14 God cannot be out of **a.** with Himself, and
T-7 ...... V.6:14 and you cannot be out of **a.** with Him.
T-7 ..... VI.13:3 If your mind could be out of **a.** with God's
T-7 .........X.8:1 Miracles are in **a.** with the Will of God,
T-7 ....... XI.1:5 nature, being out of **a.** with God's laws.
T-8 .........II.3:6 cannot be out of **a.** because they are one.
T-8 ....... V.6:4 us. Never **a.** the ego the power to interfere
T-9 ...... VII.4:6 clearly out of **a.** with its perception of you.
T-10 ........I.3:1 that reality is in **a.** with neither? You do
T-11 ...... V.5:2 being out of **a.** with your true nature. I
T-12 ...... V.9:3 the means and the end are in complete **a.**.
T-14 ...... V.7:5 From everyone whom you **a.** release from
T-18 ..... III.5:3 Your desire is now in complete **a.** with all
T-25 ..... III.1:3 in **a.** with perception's fundamental law:
T-25 ..... VI.1:8 And being in **a.** with what God wills, he
T-25 .VIII.14:6 what justice must **a.** the Son of God. Let
T-27 ...... V.9:4 in **a.** with laws that have been properly
T-30 .... VII.1:5 can affect its aim, but must be in **a.** with it
T-30 .... VII.3:2 But it must **a.** *one* meaning to them all. If
W-pI.... 43.6:1 are clearly out of **a.** with today's idea, or if
W-pI.... 67.2:7 Any attribute which is in **a.** with God as
W-pI.... 69.7:3 You are in **a.** with His Will. You cannot
W-pI.... 71.4:2 is in strict **a.** with the ego's basic doctrine,
W-pI.... 73.6:9 it with your blessing and your glad **a.**.
W-pI .... 73.9:1 and only His, is wholly in **a.** with your will
W-pI .... 73.9:3 you and your Father are in perfect **a.**. You
W-pI .. 191.9:4 Yet when you **a.** it mercy, will its mercy

## accordance 7

T-7 ....... IV.6:9 by thinking in **a.** with the laws of God,
T-7 .........V.2:4 can act in **a.** with what you do not believe.
T-8 .........II.3:5 His Voice teaches only in **a.** with His Will,
T-8 ..... VIII.9:3 Everything used in **a.** with its function as
T-16 .......V.9:4 strict **a.** with the ego's goals, is to destroy
W-pI .... 73.4:1 reach the world that is in **a.** with your will
W-pI .... 87.4:2 *me perceive this in* **a.** *with the Will of God. It*

## accorded 8

T-2 ..........I.4:7 dream, which is then no longer **a.** reality.
T-2 .......V.10:3 charity. The charity that is **a.** him is both
T-25 ..... IX.3:7 Thus is justice not **a.** to the Son of God.
T-31 . VIII.12:5 Not one illusion is **a.** faith, and not one
W-pI .... 28.7:2 but each one should be **a.** equal sincerity
W-pI .. 130.1:5 can see a world his mind has not **a.** value.
W-pII . 333.1:3 and with the purpose that the mind **a.** it.
M-4 ..... I.A.4:6 should be **a.** them in this world of illusion

## according 47

T-1 ....... VI.1:9 You act **a.** to the particular order of needs
T-1 ...... VII.3:4 attempt to control reality **a.** to false needs
T-4 .........V.1:5 **a.** to the thought system which gave rise
T-5 ..........I.1:6 mind thinks **a.** to the laws spirit obeys,
T-5 ........ III.8:7 because, **a.** to its interpretation of reality,
T-5 .........V.6:1 it can interpret them **a.** to what it wants,
T-7 ....... IV.1:2 and certainty is of God **a.** to His laws.
T-8 ..... III.5:10 imprisoned or released **a.** to your decision
T-8 ...... VII.4:3 or harmful, **a.** to the use to which it is put.
T-8 ....... IX.4:5 have you utilized sleep **a.** to His purpose.
T-11 .....V.11:3 A. to the ego's teaching, *its* goal can be
T-11 .....V.11:4 A. to the Holy Spirit's teaching, *only* God's
T-13 ..... VI.4:5 have it be **a.** to your use for it *is* delusional.
T-14 .... VII.5:7 His perception of them, **a.** to His purpose,
T-15 ........I.7:7 For time, **a.** to its teaching, is nothing but
T-16 ..... III.2:3 certain that you judge yourself **a.** to your
T-17 .........V.5:1 reinterpret each slow step **a.** to its liking.
T-17 ..... VI.5:9 it, and is experienced **a.** to the goal.
T-19 ......I.16:5 **a.** to which it chooses as its purpose for
T19 . IV.C.11:4 **a.** to the truth or falsity of the idea which
T19 IV.D.13:4 you will receive of him **a.** to your choice.
T-20 ..... III.8:4 and adjusted it **a.** to its insane answer.
T-20 ..... IV.4:3 sharing their power **a.** to the Will of God.
T-20 ...VIII.6:1 **a.** to the laws brought to it by His calm
T-24 .... VII.6:3 to it, **a.** to the purpose that you serve.
T-27 .... VII.8:7 leaping up and down **a.** to a senseless plot
T-30 ..... IV.4:4 little while, **a.** to the rules you set for them
T-30 .... VII.2:3 are made **a.** to the roles the script assigns.
W-pI .... 43.7:1 the form may vary **a.** to the circumstances
W-pI .... 51.2:6 me, and I do not want to see **a.** to them.
W-pI .... 71.3:2 A. to this insane plan, any perceived
W-pI .... 78.4:5 accept as his, **a.** to the role you set for him
W-pI .... 89.3:4 truth, **a.** to God's plan for my salvation. I
W-pI .... 93.3:2 These thoughts are not **a.** to God's Will.
W-pI .. 100.7:1 arise in us **a.** to our Father's Will and ours
W-pI .. 100.7:7 You but receive **a.** to God's plan, and
W-pI 133.10:3 no mistakes, **a.** to the dictates of his guide
W-pI 135.20:2 for your happiness **a.** to the ancient plan,
W-pI .. 165.8:5 dreams and in our minds, **a.** to His Will.
W-pI .. 199.4:5 goal that it must reach, **a.** to God's plan.
W-pII . 292.1:7 will seek and we will find **a.** to His Will,
M-8 ........... 4:3 bring to it **a.** to its preconceived values,
C-ep .......... 2:3 stone away, and it is done **a.** to His Will.
P-2........ IV.8:2 of threat differs **a.** to the form it takes.
P-2..........V.4:6 He directs, because it is **a.** to His Will. We
S-3...........I.1:2 and to be just, **a.** to the usage of the world
S-3..........II.5:1 This is not death **a.** to the world, for

## accordingly 23

T-1 ....... VI.2:4 one, and your needs become one **a.**.
T-4 .......II.10:3 without judgment, and is laid aside **a.**.

T-4........IV.2:5 what you have done and left undone **a.**,
T-6......V.B.3:2 **A.**, the Holy Spirit's first lesson was "To
T-7.........V.3:7 insane premise, and so it proceeds **a.**.
T-8........IV.5:8 or join, and experience pain or joy **a.**. My
T-13......VI.4:7 of your past experience, and plan for it **a.**.
T-14.......X.6:5 recognizes what it is, and answers **a.**. It
T-15.......III.5:3 answer this, and invites sorrow or joy **a.**.
T-16.......III.2:5 that you are willing to judge yourself **a.**.
T-18.........I.1:5 thus fragmented, and its purpose split **a.**.
T-19.........I.3:6 the instrument of illusion, acting **a.**;
T-24........IV.2:9 be changed, and body states must shift **a.**.
T-28.....VII.4:9 is its opposite. And you are sick or well, **a.**
T-30.....VII.1:8 element, and every meaning shifts **a.**.
T-30.....VII.3:9 wrote a fearful script, and are afraid **a.**.
T-31......VI.4:8 will be done." And it is done to you **a.**.
W-pI.....91.5:3 you want, and you instruct your mind **a.**.
W-pI...124.7:2 and healed; that we can save and heal **a.**.
W-pI...132.5:2 to see, and all the world must change **a.**.
W-pI...155.4:3 of loss, and have not been released **a.**.
W-pI...181.2:3 focus, and what you behold will change **a.**
M-29..........6:7 And He responds with help **a.**. God would

## accords 2

T-7.......VII.6:2 the appreciation God **a.** them always,
T-31.......V.3:2 at the injustices the world **a.** to those who

## account 5

T-1........III.9:3 selectivity takes no **a.** of the magnitude of
T-4.........II.9:2 generally include some **a.** of "the creation,
T-9........IV.8:2 regardless of how you may **a.** for the
T-9.........V.5:2 evident inconsistencies **a.** for why no one
W-pI...101.2:5 form that evens the **a.** they owe to God.

## accounts 1

T-9...........I.8:3 former **a.** for the atheist and the latter for

## accurate 6

T-1........III.6:3 that the perception of both must be **a.**.
T-3........IV.4:3 state of mind that induces **a.** perception.
T-4.......II.11:2 while **a.** perception is a steppingstone
W-pI.......5.1:2 feeling in whatever term seems **a.** to you.
W-pI.....67.1:1 and **a.** statement of what you are. This is
W-pI.158.11:2 so **a.** its image shares its unseen holiness;

## accurately 4

T-22.........I.2:2 this strange idea which it does **a.** describe,
W-pI.....22.1:1 Today's idea **a.** describes the way anyone
W-pI.....95.1:1 idea **a.** describes you as God created you.
W-pI...138.9:2 alternatives are **a.** seen and understood.

## accusation 3

T-27.........I.9:4 from it all signs of **a.** and of blamefulness.
T-27.......II.1:3 yes. For **a.** is a bar to love, and damaged
T-27.......V.7:6 world of **a.** is replaced by one in which all

## accuse 9

T-14.......V.3:6 To **a.** is *not to understand.* The happy
T19IV.B.14:12 Who would **a.**, make guilty and condemn
T-27.........I.3:1 **a.** your brother of attack upon God's Son.
T-27.....II.10:4 is but to forgive, and never to **a.**. Alone,
T-27.......V.6:4 And suffering eyes no longer will **a.**, but
W-pI...134.9:2 that you are tempted to **a.** someone of sin
W-pI...134.9:3 instead, "Would I **a.** myself of doing this?
W-pI.134.17:4 *Would I* **a.** *myself of doing this? I will not lay*
W-pI...152.6:5 You but **a.** Him of insanity, to think He

## accused 1

*See also* self-accused

T-31.....V.13:6 stand **a.** of guilt for what your brother is.

## accuser 2

T-27.....II.14:3 can never be returned to its **a.**, who had
T-31.....V.16:5 role of the **a.** will appear in many places

## accusers 2

T-27.......II.1:3 a bar to love, and damaged bodies are **a.**.
T-27.......II.3:4 The sick remain **a.**. They cannot forgive

## accusing 2

*See also* self-accusing

T-31.......V.6:4 he does, for your **a.** finger points to him,
T-31.....V.16:6 And each will seem to be **a.** you. Yet have

## accustomed 12

T-13.......X.1:1 **a.** to the notion that the mind can see the
T-14......III.2:1 Perhaps you are **a.** to using guiltlessness
T-21.........I.4:1 blind become **a.** to their world by their
T-25......VI.2:1 **a.** to the dim effects perceived at twilight.
T-28.........I.4:3 You are so long **a.** to believe that memory
W-pI.....24.3:1 more honesty than you are **a.** to using. A
W-pI.....30.5:3 you to become more **a.** to this idea as well
W-pI.....91.9:5 You will be **a.** to keeping faith with the
W-pI...126.8:2 alien to the thoughts to which you are **a.**.
W-pI...137.4:5 Yet eyes **a.** to illusions must be shown
W-pI.161.11:2 can, in that same form to which you are **a.**
W-pII..303.1:3 and the sights to which I am **a.** disappear.

## achieve 30

T-1.........II.1:3 Physical closeness cannot **a.** it. Miracles,
T-1.......VII.2:4 your perception so you can **a.** real vision,
T-2........III.5:2 Until they **a.** this, they waste themselves
T-2.....VIII.5:8 to "give you time" to **a.** this judgment. It
T-4.........V.6:2 but has systematically failed to **a.**. The
T-8........III.6:2 To **a.** the goal of the curriculum, then,
T-9.........I.11:2 believing that to **a.** it is to succeed? The
T-11. VIII.11:3 perceive part of you as sick and **a.** your
T-12.......V.8:2 that the way to **a.** a goal is not to attain it?
T-18......IV.2:7 must **a.** the state its coming brings with it.
T-20.....VII.8:3 a holy relationship **a.** its purpose through
T-21.......II.2:4 *and I decide upon the goal I would* **a.**. *And*
T-22......VI.2:1 to contrive ways to **a.** the body's freedom.
T-26.........I.1:2 and all conflicts **a.** a seeming balance. It is
T-26.......V.2:3 to reach a goal as high as learning can **a.**?
T-29......IV.4:8 *should* represent, and *should* **a.** for you. If it
T-30......III.3:4 you will **a.** completion in a form you like.
T-31......IV.7:3 let me repeat that to **a.** a goal you must
W-pI.....11.3:4 from worry that we are trying to **a.**. On
W-pI.....42.1:2 in your efforts to **a.** the goal of the course.
W-pI...72.10:2 us. To **a.** this goal, we must replace attack
W-pI...127.7:1 If you **a.** the faintest glimmering of what
W-pI...131.2:5 they **a.** that offers any hope of being real?
WpI. rIV.in1:4 the readiness that we would now **a.**.
W-pI...158.8:1 and must be taught by all who would **a.** it.
W-pI...183.9:1 Today you can **a.** a state in which you will
W-pII..257.1:4 and **a.** only what God would have us do
W-pII..340.1:6 *I was born into this world but to* **a.** *this day,*
M-4 ....IV.1:11 realize that harm can actually **a.** nothing.
S-2...........I.9:1 But to **a.** this end you first must learn,

## achieved 30

T-4.......II.10:1 be **a.** before One-mindedness is restored.
T-6.........IV.8:3 are results that have been **a.**. When they
T-8.....VIII.2:6 When you have **a.** it, *it has not satisfied you*
T-9.........II.2:3 certain specific forms of healing are not **a.**
T-18.....VII.4:4 have indeed **a.** their instants of success.
T-18.....VII.5:7 or when the goal is finally **a.** by anyone, it
T19. IV.A.17:3 and so atonement is **a.** through murder.
T-20......IV.7:5 this has been **a.** that you will rest without
T-27.........I.11:1 simple way to let this be **a.** is merely this;
T-27......VI.1:7 because their purpose cannot be **a.**. Thus
T-29... VIII.1:9 or wanted, or a right demanded or **a.**, it is
T-30.......I.13:3 When this has been **a.**, the sorry dream of
T-30......VI.3:3 The real world is **a.** when you perceive the
W-in..........5:2 has been **a.** in connection with any person
W-pI...131.1:1 while you seek for goals that cannot be **a.**.
W-pI...132.2:1 Yet is salvation easily **a.**, for anyone is
W-pI.135.12:1 which is best, the means by which it is **a.**,
W-pI...184.2:1 by which the world's perception is **a.**. You
W-pI...184.5:3 goal by which communication is **a.**, and
W-pII .273.1:2 satisfied to learn how such a day can be **a.**
W-pII .....7.2:3 has **a.** the only goal it has in truth. For
M-4 ........II.1:2 Once that has been **a.**, the others cannot
M-4 ....... X.2:8 Now is the goal **a.**. Forgiveness is the final
M-28 .........3:5 The goal of the curriculum has been **a.**.
P-2.........in.1:4 for reality, it has **a.** its ultimate success.
P-2...........I.1:1 the ideal outcome is rarely **a.**. Therapy
P-2..........II.1:3 for one who had **a.** that point could teach
P-2........IV.7:2 emphasized, correction cannot be **a.** by
P-2........VI.5:5 That is **a.** by only one recognition; that
S-2...........I.9:6 God established for returning be **a.** at last

## achievement 3

T-1......III.1:10 is the potential, the **a.** is its expression,
Wi181-200 3:2 remains beyond **a.** while it is denied. It
M-4 .....I.A.8:1 And finally, there is "a period of **a.**." It is

## achievements 1

M-25 .........3:6 lie in proving anything; **a.** from the past,

## achieving 4

W-pI.....66.1:1 fulfilling your function and **a.** happiness.
W-pI.....66.3:3 and determining the means for **a.** it. We
M-4 ......IX.1:9 each degree, however small, is worth **a.**.
M-9 ...........2:5 training is directed toward **a.** a goal in

## aching 2

T-13.....VII.3:6 This **a.** world has not the power to touch
W-pI.....97.5:1 carry them around this **a.** world where

## acknowledge 34

T-1........IV.3:5 Those who perceive and **a.** that they have
T-5.....III.2:10 Call for God in him, and thus **a.** Its being.
T-5........III.3:5 **a.** in your brother you are acknowledging
T-7........IV.7:8 of you, because it is a refusal to **a.** fear.
T-8..........II.8:3 you **a.** this you bring the acknowledgment
T-8........IV.1:1 this you must be refusing to **a.** His Will.
T-8........IV.6:2 power, which I can only **a.** in honor of His
T-10.......V.8:2 When you **a.** Him you will know that He
T-10.......V.8:2 know that He has never ceased to **a.** you,
T-10.......V.9:6 do this you must **a.** Him as your Creator.
T-14......XI.8:3 you are willing to **a.** that it *is* impossible. It
T-15....IV.9:10 you ready to **a.** that you are host to God,
T-16........II.6:6 that to **a.** Him is to deny all that you think
T-21........II.2:7 **A.** but that you have been mistaken, and
T-22......IV.2:5 nothing you will not be told, if you **a.** this.
T-28......IV.4:4 Let him **a.** who he is, by not supporting
W-pI........7.4:3 at. **A.** this by applying the idea for today
W-pI.....28.7:2 attempt to **a.** the equal value of them all
W-pI.....83.1:5 All doubt must disappear as I **a.** that my
W-pI.131.11:1 **a.** as we start upon our practice periods.
W-pI.135.26:5 special day for learning, and **a.** it with this
W-pI...164.9:2 We can change the world, if you **a.** them.
W-pI...167.2:6 discomfort or the merest frown, **a.** death.
W-pI...168.5:3 We **a.** our mistakes, but Him to Whom all
W-pI.170.10:6 striking down all who **a.** Him to be their
W-pI...183.8:1 and you **a.** Him as sole Creator of reality.
W-pI...183.8:2 you **a.** also that His Son is part of Him,
W-pI.188.10:1 **a.** that the peace of God still shines in us,
W-pII .223.2:7 *is Yours, and we* **a.** *that we are Your Son.*
W-pII .276.1:7 need but to **a.** Him Who gave His Word
W-pII .....9.4:3 the Sons of God **a.** that they all are one.
M-8 ...........6:2 let itself be healed will no longer **a.** them.
M-12 .......6:11 God's teachers **a.** as behind the dream,
M-29 .........5:2 but to **a.** his Creator and accept His gifts.

## acknowledged 11

T-7........XI.5:6 have **a.** what He has given you. Nothing is

|  |  |
|---|---|
| T-8 II.8:3 | to everyone, because you *have* **a.** everyone. |
| T-10 IV.8:5 | returning the little light must be **a.** first, |
| T-10 V.13:5 | real Fatherhood must be **a.** if the real Son |
| T-14 IV.1:5 | you will see the truth of what you have **a.**. |
| T-17 VIII.4:1 | who have **a.** the Call of your Redeemer, |
| T19..IV.B.4:11 | to join your brother, you **a.** this is so. This |
| W-pI 168.3:1 | within our hearts, waiting to be **a.**. This |
| W-pI 188.5:6 | In quietness is it **a.** universally. For what |
| W-pI 192.2:7 | merely waits for your return to be **a.**, not |
| W-pI 197.4:5 | thankfully **a.** by the Heart of God Himself |

## acknowledges 17

|  |  |
|---|---|
| T-1 I.40:1 | miracle **a.** everyone as your brother and |
| T-1 IV.2:4 | to spirit, and the miracle **a.** only truth. It |
| T-10 III.3:4 | him **a.** the Love of God he has forgotten. |
| T-14 V.5:3 | The miracle **a.** the guiltlessness that must |
| T-14 XI.7:7 | miracle **a.** His changelessness by seeing |
| T-15 VII.6:4 | Yet the ego **a.** "reality" as it sees it, and |
| T-17 I.2:2 | strange position, in a sense, **a.** your power |
| T-20 II.1:6 | acceptance and delight **a.** the lack of value |
| T-28 II.12:5 | the mind **a.** "this is not done to me, but *I* |
| W-pI.135.20:1 | which Heaven gratefully **a.** to be its own. |
| W-pI 185.7:6 | mean these words **a.** illusions are in vain, |
| W-pI 186.1:5 | It but **a.** the Will of God is done on earth |
| W-pII .270.1:4 | *forgiven signifies Your Son* **a.** *his Father, lets* |
| W-pII .299.1:2 | Who created it, **a.** my holiness as His. Our |
| W-pII 10.4:3 | of pain the Son whom God **a.** as His. Be |
| M-17 5:3 | mere presence, **a.** a separation from God. |
| S-1 II.5:6 | for it **a.** the Son of God as he was created. |

## acknowledging 12

|  |  |
|---|---|
| T-2 II.1:4 | anything, you are **a.** its power to hurt you. |
| T-5 III.3:5 | in your brother you are **a.** in yourself, and |
| T-6 V.C.5:4 | you are **a.** your mind as God created it. |
| T-7 V.5:4 | By accepting exceptions and **a.** that he |
| T-7 XI.6:5 | you are **a.** his power to create and yours. |
| T-9 V.6:3 | by **a.** darkness in yourself and looking for |
| W-pI 53.3:8 | fear, because I am **a.** that it does not exist. |
| W-pI 63.3:2 | We will begin the day by **a.** it, and close |
| W-pI.138.12:4 | with this, **a.** we chose but what we want: |
| W-pI 152.9:3 | But truth is humble in **a.** its mightiness, |
| W-pI 158.8:4 | he is, **a.** that he is one with you in holiness |
| W-pII .266.2:1 | and on our own, **a.** our Self in each of us; |

## acknowledgment 34

|  |  |
|---|---|
| T-2 V.10:3 | him is both an **a.** that he needs help, and |
| T-4 II.8:5 | to gain the spirit's **a.** and thus establish its |
| T-6 II.5:7 | it is the **a.** that you are not in this world, |
| T-8 II.8:2 | is, and for its own **a.** of what it is. When |
| T-8 II.8:3 | bring the **a.** automatically to everyone, |
| T-8 IV.8:1 | being an **a.** of what they are and what He |
| T-9 V.7:6 | And by his **a.** the healer knows it is there. |
| T-9 V.7:8 | extending it and accepting its **a.**. Its |
| T-10 V.8:1 | God of love, for healing is the **a.** of Him. |
| T-10 V.8:2 | and that in His **a.** of you lies your being. |
| T-10 V.9:8 | It is merely because your **a.** of your Father |
| T-10 V.9:8 | your Father is the **a.** of yourself as you are. |
| T-14 V.5:4 | Do not withhold this glad **a.**, for hope of |
| T-14 V.8:2 | For peace is the **a.** of perfect purity, from |
| T-18 IX.12:6 | Whose **a.** of you and yours of Him so far |
| T-19 I.10:2 | Faith is the **a.** of union. It is the gracious |
| T-19 I.10:3 | It is the gracious **a.** of everyone as a Son of |
| T-19 III.10:2 | in glad **a.** of the grace that has been given |
| T19 IV.A.6:1 | of gladness in **a.** of the journey's end. For |
| T-24 VI.1:9 | your **a.** that He created you as part of Him |
| T-24 VII.2:3 | your changelessness is recognized in its **a.** |
| T-30 I.12:1 | is but **a.** of lack of opposition to be helped |
| T-30 VI.9:5 | the glad **a.** that guilt has not succeeded by |
| T-31 V.12:3 | and some **a.** that interaction must have |
| W-pI 50.4:8 | It is your **a.** of the truth about yourself. |
| W-pI 61.3:4 | and an **a.** of the power that is given you to |
| W-pI 61.6:2 | with an **a.** of the truth about yourself, |
| W-pI 76.12:3 | It is our **a.** that God is our Father, and |
| W-pI 95.15:1 | Your own **a.** you are one Self, united with |
| W-pI 110.9:4 | Christ in you is waiting your **a.** as you. |
| W-pI 135.2:2 | of threat is an **a.** of an inherent weakness; |
| W-pI.152.11:1 | do we join in glad **a.** that lies are false, |
| W-pI 168.2:5 | grace is yours by your **a.**. And memory of |
| W-pI.184.10:2 | all things share; the one **a.** of what is true. |

## acquired 7

|  |  |
|---|---|
| T-1 VI.1:2 | No learning is **a.** by anyone unless he |
| T-14 I.1:2 | but its conditions must be **a.** for it is they |
| T-15 V.2:1 | define your own needs and **a.** methods for |
| T-21 I.3:2 | And gentle lessons are **a.** joyously, and |
| T-30 V.2:1 | that understanding is **a.** by attack. There, |
| W-pI 121.6:1 | Forgiveness is **a.**. It is not inherent in the |
| M-4 1:3 | yet **a.** the deeper characteristics that will |

## acquires 1

|  |  |
|---|---|
| M-4 X.1:1 | last of the attributes the teacher of God **a.** |

## acquisition 1

|  |  |
|---|---|
| W-in 3:1 | the second with the **a.** of true perception. |

## across 58

|  |  |
|---|---|
| T-4 VI.2:5 | easily flow **a.** it and obliterate it forever. |
| T-5 I.4:9 | that God Himself can flow **a.** the little gap |
| T-12 I.9:11 | that you have drawn **a.** the face of love |
| T-13 VI.11:8 | and spreads **a.** this world in quiet joy. All |
| T-13 VII.16:10 | it like a veil of light **a.** the world's sad face, |
| T-14 X.5:2 | unceasingly **a.** the mirror of your mind, |
| T-14 X.5:3 | darkness sweep constantly **a.** your mind. |
| T-15 VI.6:2 | veil that has been drawn **a.** reality is lifted |
| T-16 III.8:3 | which carries him **a.** the gap as soon as he |
| T-16 III.9:2 | wait for you will not draw you safely **a.**. |
| T-16 IV.9:1 | A. the bridge is your completion, for you |
| T-16 IV.13:4 | you **a.** lifts you from time into eternity. |
| T-16 IV.13:7 | But as you step lightly **a.** it, upheld *by* |
| T-16 VI.6:1 | A. the bridge it is so different! For a time |
| T-16 VI.11:2 | it seems to be outside and **a.** the bridge. |
| T-17 II.6:2 | reaching quietly and gently **a.** chaos, |
| T-18 VIII.10:3 | So will it grow and stretch **a.** the desert, |
| T-19 IV.2:2 | flow **a.** the obstacles you placed before it. |
| T19 IV.A.1:1 | must flow **a.** is your desire to get rid of it. |
| T19 IV.A.1:6 | If it would spread **a.** the whole creation, it |
| T19 IV.A.4:6 | Peace will flow **a.** it, and join you without |
| T19 IV.B.1:3 | second obstacle that peace must flow **a.**, |
| T19 IV.B.4:2 | It flows **a.** all else. The second obstacle is |
| T19 IV.C.1:3 | the third obstacle that peace must flow **a.**. |
| T19 IV.C.1:9 | its dark shadow falls **a.** all living things, |
| T19 IV.C.7:5 | peace must flow **a.** seems to be very great. |
| T19 IV.D.5:1 | Every obstacle that peace must flow **a.** is |
| T-22 III.3:2 | and without a key, **a.** the road to peace. |
| T-25 II.7:3 | and casts a veil of light **a.** the picture's |
| T-26 V.6:6 | shore, and dream himself **a.** an ocean, to |
| T-28 I.15:3 | to allow the memory of God to flow **a.** it, |
| T-28 I.15:7 | it is He Who will transport His Son **a.** it. |
| T-29 I.3:2 | that peace must flow **a.** has not yet gone. |
| T-29 VIII.4:1 | world of idols *is* a veil **a.** the face of Christ, |
| T-30 V.8:1 | light and easy is the step **a.** the narrow |
| T-31 VI.3:8 | veil of ignorance is drawn **a.** the evil and |
| T-31 VII.9:1 | The veil **a.** the face of Christ, the fear of |
| W-pI 56.4:3 | every veil I have drawn **a.** the face of love, |
| W-pI 75.5:2 | we see Heaven's reflection lie **a.** the world. |
| W-pI 109.8:3 | and let them come from far **a.** the world, |
| W-pI 122.3:2 | can arise **a.** the threshold of your mind. |
| W-pI 125.4:2 | Word, to spread **a.** the world the tidings |
| W-pI 128.3:3 | add another bar **a.** the door that leads to |
| W-pI. 132.16:1 | comes to many brothers far **a.** the world, |
| W-pI. 134.11:1 | A. this bridge, as powerful as love which |
| W-pI. 134.16:3 | up, a lightening of weight **a.** your chest, a |
| W-pI. 136.16:1 | Healing will flash **a.** your open mind, as |
| W-pI. 184.15:3 | *we have tried to cast* **a.** *Your Own reality.* |
| W-pI 186.9:5 | blow **a.** his mind like wind-swept leaves |
| W-pI. 198.11:3 | is there tranquil light **a.** the face of earth, |
| W-pII in.9:5 | God is shimmering **a.** the wide horizons |
| W-pII 7.1:3 | A. the bridge that He provides are dreams |
| M-15 1:10 | and silence lies **a.** the world that everyone |
| M-26 1:3 | this memory can arise **a.** the threshold of |
| M-28 2:5 | of God shines unimpeded **a.** the world. |
| M-28 3:8 | The last illusion spreads **a.** the world, |
| P-3 II.10:10 | This is the veil **a.** the face of Christ. Yet it |
| S-3 IV.9:1 | Creation leans **a.** the bars of time to lift |

## act 36

|  |  |
|---|---|
| T-1 III.1:6 | learn to undo error and **a.** to correct it. |
| T-1 VI.1:9 | You **a.** according to the particular order |
| T-2 II.4:3 | love and the Atonement was an ***a.*** of love. |
| T-2 IV.2:5 | The body can **a.** wrongly only when it is |
| T-4 VI.2:3 | you **a.** egotistically towards another, you |
| T-5 IV.2:11 | be understood as a pure **a.** of sharing. |
| T-5 V.4:10 | lack of love, but as a positive **a.** of assault. |
| T-7 V.2:3 | you that the body can **a.** like the mind, |
| T-7 V.2:4 | since you can **a.** in accordance with what |
| T-10 IV.7:1 | The miracle is the **a.** of a Son of God who |
| T-10 IV.7:2 | an **a.** of faith, because it is the recognition |
| T-12 VII.2:6 | in their existence as they enable you to **a.**. |
| T-16 V.9:3 | of the giving of specialness as an **a.** of love |
| T-16 VII.3:4 | its chosen relationships in which to **a.** out |
| T-16 VII.4:3 | Would you **a.** out the dream, or let it go? |
| T-17 V.6:3 | That was an **a.** of faith. Do not abandon |
| T-18 II.5:6 | that you are making them **a.** out for you, |
| T-18 VI.3:5 | and direct the body to **a.** them out. Yet it |
| T-18 VI.6:2 | It is impossible to **a.** out fantasies. For it is |
| T-18 IX.5:1 | will **a.** as it directs as long as you believe |
| T19 .IV.A.14:4 | be as careful to let no little **a.** of charity, |
| T-21 VII.3:6 | dream of power and to **a.** out their dream. |
| T-21 VII.3:7 | How would an army **a.** in dreams? Any |
| T-23 II.18:1 | these senseless laws, nor **a.** upon them. |
| T-25 VI.5:2 | **a.** of special faithfulness to one perceived |
| T-26 V.5:5 | Yet in each unforgiving **a.** or thought, in |
| T-27 I.6:5 | No worldly thought or **a.** or feeling has a |
| T-27 II.1:8 | To forgive may be an **a.** of charity, but not |
| T-29 II.9:3 | be perceived and thought to feel and **a.**, |
| T-31 III.3:4 | actions. Bodies **a.**, and minds do not. And |
| T-31 III.3:9 | mind. The body must **a.** on its own, and |
| W-pI 54.4:4 | of God cannot think or speak or **a.** in vain |
| W-pI .. 187.4:1 | you value by the **a.** of giving them away, |
| M-in 1:4 | the **a.** of teaching is regarded as a special |
| M-4 II.1:6 | any other thought; no **a.** belies your word; |
| M-4 IV.1:4 | the dishonest **a.** that follows a dishonest |

## acted 6

|  |  |
|---|---|
| T-16 V.10:5 | it is this theme that is **a.** out in the special |
| T-31 V.2:6 | the face of innocence, the aspect **a.** on. It |
| W-pI 71.2:2 | if someone else spoke or **a.** differently, if |
| W-pI .. 132.4:3 | **a.** out so you can look on them and think |
| M-17 4:5 | of violence, fantasied or apparently **a.** out |
| P-1 3:6 | This self he sees as being **a.** on, reacting to |

## acting 11

|  |  |
|---|---|
| T-1 III.4:4 | will be **a.** under direct communication. |
| T-3 III.5:7 | say you are **a.** on the basis of knowledge, |
| T-4 VI.1:3 | as if it were a separate thing, **a.** on its own |
| T-12 III.3:5 | **a.** destructively if you accept their poverty |
| T-16 VII.5:1 | to be an **a.** out of vengeance that you seek. |
| T-16 VII.5:3 | is the **a.** out of vengeance on yourself. Yet |
| T-18 I.3:4 | a different form of **a.** out for satisfaction. |
| T-18 I.3:7 | rejection for **a.** out a special form of fear. |
| T-18 VI.3:7 | the body is actually **a.** out its fantasies, it |
| T-19 I.3:6 | the instrument of illusion, **a.** accordingly; |
| T-19 III.1:3 | so acute that the sin is denied the **a.** out. |

## action 10

|  |  |
|---|---|
| T-1 II.1:8 | Consciousness is the state that induces **a.**, |
| T-1 II.2:4 | Miracles, on the other hand, induce **a.**. |
| T-1 III.8:4 | but the **a.** aspect of the miracle should be |
| T-1 VI.2:5 | Unified needs lead to unified **a.**, because |
| T-3 III.5:6 | Certainty does not require **a.**. When you |
| W-pI 24.1:2 | you have no guide to appropriate **a.**, and |
| W-pII 1.3:2 | In frantic **a.** it pursues its goal, twisting |
| W-pII. 267.1:2 | breath; in every **a.** and in every thought. |
| M-9 2:2 | and it is this he follows as his guide for **a.**. |
| M-10 1:6 | the same person classifies the same **a.** as |

**actions** 16

T-1 VII.3:3 A. that stem from distortions are literally
T-2 II.3:6 and to bring them into all your a., you
T-3 III.2:9 what you do, and a. must occur in time.
T-12 VII.2:7 act. And the results of your a. you *can* see.
T-14 II.2:4 and feelings and a. and reactions that you
T-18 IX.7:3 stand out and move about, a. seem real,
T-27 VIII.7:7 control its a. nor its purpose nor its fate.
T-31 III.3:3 They are not seen as purposes, but a..
T-31 VII.3:2 a. of the body are perceived as coming
T-31 VIII.2:5 by never using weakness to direct your a.,
W-pI 60.4:3 thoughts, guide my a. and lead my feet. I
W-pII 222.1:3 and move; the Spirit which directs my a.,
W-pII 254.2:h let no ego thoughts direct our words or a..
W-pII 257.1:1 of what I am, and thus conflicted in my a..
W-pII 257.1:4 unify our thoughts and a. meaningfully,
M-1 3:6 It can be taught by a. or thoughts; in

**activate** 1

W-pI 135.1:4 you attempt to plan the future, a. the past

**activating** 1

C-1 1:1 term *mind* is used to represent the a. agent

**active** 11

T-3 IV.5:2 The mind is very a.. When it chooses to
T-3 IV.6:8 be an a. process of correction because, as
T-3 VII.2:4 be extremely powerful and extremely a..
T-3 VII.5:2 It is powerful, a., destructive and clearly
T-14 V.3:5 is to devote yourself, with a. willingness,
T-28 II.12:3 deny the a. role in making up the dream.
T-31 V.12:3 and at least makes way for a. choice, and
W-pI 9.2:2 with a. resistance in any number of forms
W-pI 20.1:2 and not even a. cooperation and interest
W-pI 42.6:1 that a. searching for relevant thoughts is
W-pI 72.1:1 that it is an a. attack on His plan, and a

**actively** 10

T-4 IV.7:1 if you a. refuse to let your mind slip away.
T-5 VII.6:3 to recognize that you a. decided wrongly,
T-5 VII.6:3 wrongly, but can as a. decide otherwise.
T-10 II.5:6 you are a. choosing not to remember Him
T-12 IV.1:3 encouraging the search for love very a.,
W-in 9:2 Some of them you may a. resist. None of
W-pI 16.4:1 and a. seek not to overlook any "little"
W-pI 72.4:4 a. trying to hold him to it by confusing it
W-pI 121.10:1 you should meet him; one you a. despise,
W-pI 182.1:6 times hardly remembered, a. dismissed,

**activities** 5

T-6 IV.2:9 most inventive a. of the ego have never
T-18 VII.7:9 body's a. return to occupy your conscious
W-pI 49.1:1 interrupting your regular a. in any way.
M-8 4:1 out and categorizing a. of the mind that
P-3 II.1:8 kinds of needs in their professional a.,

**activity** 6

T-7 VIII.3:12 constant a. in order not to recognize this.
T-18 VII.7:7 make a place within you where the a. of
T-18 VII.8:2 center of the storm than all its raging a..
T-18 VIII.4:1 of all this strange and meaningless a..
M-in 1:4 act of teaching is regarded as a special a.,
P-2 IV.1:2 Son of God, and judgment is a mental a..

**acts** 12

T-1 I.37:2 It a. as a catalyst, breaking up erroneous
T-2 II.4:4 of love. A. were not necessary before the
T-2 VI.1:2 constructive a. should be involuntary. My
T-7 VII.2:1 When a brother a. insanely, he is offering
T-24 VII.10:5 it. You brand it sinful and you hate its a.,
T-27 VIII.1:2 exist without the dream in which it a. as if
T-28 VI.3:5 And you despise its a., but not your own.
T-28 VI.3:6 It sees and a. for *you*. It hears your voice.
T-31 III.3:7 are sin you *are* a body, for the mind a. not.
T-31 III.3:10 to its prison house, which a. instead of it.
W-pII 233.1:4 *I give You all my a. as well, that I may do*
W-pII 12.4:1 the ego and its thoughts, its works, its a.,

**actual** 8

T-2 IV.3:5 no power in itself to introduce a. learning
T-2 V.10:1 beyond his a. accomplishments in time.
T-4 VII.7:4 cannot be done with the a. revelation; its
T-14 IX.8:5 but rather the a. condition of what was
T-16 VI.7:4 a sense of a. disorientation may occur.
T-16 VI.8:5 which precedes the a. transition, is far
T-18 VI.11:3 It is a sense of a. escape from limitations.
S-1 II.4:2 The contradiction lies not in the a. words,

**actually** 41

T-1 III.5:2 it. Only the error is a. vulnerable. You are
T-2 I.2:1 of what a. occurred in the separation, or
T-2 I.2:2 the separation, nor does it a. exist now.
T-2 II.6:3 is a. incomprehensible in temporal terms,
T-2 VI.9:10 because you are a. afraid of them. This
T-2 VII.3:11 A., "Cause" is a term properly belonging
T-2 VIII.3:2 A. it will be undertaken by my brothers
T-4 V.4:5 Here is where the mind becomes a. dazed.
T-6 I.2:7 and how it a. led to the resurrection was
T-8 VI.7:1 in terms that a. means nothing. When
T-8 IX.6:2 the ego a. believes that it is protecting it.
T-9 I.8:6 as these, and a. expect to receive them?
T-11 VII.2:6 The real world can a. be perceived. All
T-12 I.1:7 you will respond as if he had a. done so,
T-13 II.2:2 of it, but you are a. merely concealing it.
T-15 VII.6:2 is a. the root of its bitter resentment. For
T-18 VI.3:7 the body is a. acting out its fantasies, it
W-pI 8.2:3 Very few have realized what is a. entailed
W-pI 8.2:4 The mind is a. blank when it does this,
W-pI 8.4:2 is because you a. cannot see anything,
W-pI 13.1:2 A., a meaningless world is impossible.
W-pI 30.4:2 range as well as those you can a. see, as
W-pI 32.2:1 and outer worlds, which are a. the same.
W-pI 44.10:1 approaching, if not a. entering into light.
W-pI 49.3:2 will try a. to hear God's Voice reminding
W-pI 66.4:1 happiness, but that they are a. identical.
W-pI 72.1:2 which are a. associated with the ego,
W-pI 133.11:3 dangerous to be the nothingness it a. is.
M-in 1:1 is a. reversed in the thinking of the world.
M-3 5:3 the teaching-learning balance is a. perfect
M-4 I.A.5:7 only as he a. does give up the valueless.
M-4 II.1:5 The term a. means consistency. There is
M-4 IV.1:11 realize that harm can a. achieve nothing.
M-5 II.1:9 A., such terms merely state or describe
M-5 II.2:11 They are not a. needed at all. The patient
M-10 1:2 world. It is a. confused with wisdom, and
M-10 2:4 He has a. merely become more honest.
M-22 4:2 anyone a. believe he wants to be sick.
P-2 VII.3:1 in this relationship is a. one in which the
P-3 I.3:2 gifts to you limited to the few you a. see.
P-3 II.3:2 selfish, unconcerned, and a. dishonest.

**acute** 5

T-2 III.3:9 as conflict, which can become very a.. But
T-5 V.3:11 the guilt is so a. that it must be projected.
T-6 V.A.6:6 a long time, experiencing very a. conflict.
T-19 III.1:3 so a. that the sin is denied the acting out.
W-pI 96.1:2 feelings of a. and constant conflict, and

**Adam** 4

T-2 I.3:2 A. listened to the "lies of the serpent," all
T-2 I.3:6 Bible says that a deep sleep fell upon A.,
T-2 I.4:5 upon A. could he experience nightmares.
T-3 I.3:9 the belief that God rejected A. and forced

**Adam's** 1

T-13 in.3:6 A. "sin" could have touched no one, had

**adapt** 2

T-7 XI.2:4 He therefore cannot a. to it, nor can he
T-7 XI.2:4 cannot adapt to it, nor can he a. it to him.

**adapted** 6

T-7 II.2:7 Laws must be a. to circumstances if they
T-7 II.2:9 been a. to the circumstances of this world
T-7 II.3:1 law that prevails inside is a. to "What you
T-7 II.3:7 That form of the law is not a. at all, being
T-25 III.1:6 This is perception's form, a. to this world,
T-25 III.4:1 but in some form a. to the need the Son of

**adapts** 2

T-20 VII.5:6 Seeing a. to wish, for sight is always
C-3 3:5 The form a. itself to need; the content is

**add** 44

T-7 I.2:7 You have the power to a. to the Kingdom,
T-7 I.2:7 not to a. to the Creator of the Kingdom.
T-8 VI.1:3 their weakness and a. their strength to us.
T-8 VI.2:1 world can a. nothing to the power and the
T-8 VI.6:1 is to a. to God's treasure by creating yours
T-10 in.2:4 Your creations a. to Him as you do, but
T-14 II.1:8 Yet you will a. another burden to your
T-18 IV.1:6 will a. the ego to Him and confuse the two
T-18 IV.5:12 *I need a. nothing to His plan. But to receive it*
T-18 IV.6:2 A. more, and you will merely take away
T-18 IV.6:4 And it is only fear that you will a., if you
T-20 V.6:4 from it, and the future will a. no more.
T-21 VII.11:5 you a. sincerity to the decisions you have
T-24 VII.7:3 nothing to a. and nothing taken from; not
T-25 VIII.1:7 This much is necessary to a. to the idea no
T-26 I.5:4 a. a limitless supply to every meager scrap
T-26 X.5:3 you seek to a. unto the purpose given it.
T-26 X.5:6 To a. or take away from this one goal is
T-27 II.1:10 a. to all the guilt that he has really earned.
T-27 IV.5:5 they a. nothing new and nothing has been
T-28 I.1:4 It does not a., but merely takes away. And
T-28 III.1:6 do not a. your dream of fear to one that is
T-29 VIII.2:4 and a. the value that you do not have. No
T-30 III.3:3 to a. to you to make yourself complete,
T-30 VII.1:7 a. an element into the script you write for
W-pI 10.4:2 Then a.: *This idea will help to release me*
W-pI 10.5:4 applying it specifically, and also to a.: *This*
W-pI 12.4:3 At the end of the practice period, a.: *But I*
W-pI 27.2:2 about the lack of reservation involved, a.:
W-pI 27.2:4 If fear of loss still persists, a. further: *It can*
W-pI 35.7:4 After you have named each one, a.: *But my*
W-pI 38.5:1 a. some relevant thoughts of your own.
W-pI 40.3:2 and then a. several of the attributes you
W-pI 43.5:2 a. to the idea in your own personal way.
W-pI 62.5:6 attention wander, repeat the idea and a.: *I*
W-pI 123.2:1 day devoted now to gratitude will a. the
W-pI 124.12:1 A. further jewels to the golden frame that
W-pI 128.3:3 and a. another bar across the door that
WpI rIV.in9:1 We a. no other thoughts, but let these be
W-pI 157.2:2 We a. a new dimension now; a fresh
WpI rVI.in.6:5 we will a. but a few formal expressions or
W-pII 301.2:2 who look on it can only a. their joy to it,
W-pII 11.2:2 For He would a. to love by its extension.
M-24 3:5 it is not the part of wisdom to a. sectarian

**added** 11

T-10 in.2:4 but nothing is a. that is different because
T-16 III.5:4 God's Answer to the separation a. more
T-25 IX.3:3 has a. to it and made it greater, harder to
T-25 IX.4:7 can bring another problem a. to the first,
T-26 X.5:5 And to this purpose nothing can be a., for
W-pI 45.6:3 mind. After you have a. some four or five
W-pI 151.14:2 to be deceived by what was falsely a.. All
W-pI 159.9:4 to which they go again with a. fragrance.

W-pI... 199.5:3 none which will not gain in **a.** gifts to you
W-pII .316.1:4 not one gift is lost, and only more are **a.**.
S-1 ...........I.3:5 All the rest is merely **a.**. You have sought

**adding** 11

W-pI..... 35.9:1 **a.** the idea in the form stated above to
W-pI... 39.10:4 idea in its original form once more, and **a.**
W-pI..... 44.1:1 for yesterday, **a.** another dimension to it.
W-pI..... 46.5:4 practice period to **a.** related ideas such as:
W-pI..... 67.2:2 a few minutes **a.** some relevant thoughts,
W-pI..... 67.4:2 and that you need to continue **a.** other
W-pI..... 70.7:1 **a.** a statement signifying your recognition
W-pI..... 74.3:4 minutes in **a.** some related thoughts, such
W-pI... 105.4:4 already, not in simple terms of **a.** more,
W-pI... 188.4:4 **a.** to the gifts you have to offer to the
W-pI... 197.5:3 out, extending love and **a.** to your never-

**addition** 6

W-pI..... 10.5:2 at any time. In **a.**, five practice periods are
W-pI..... 21.1:2 in **a.** to applying the idea to particular
W-pI... 29.5:10 In **a.** to the assigned practice periods,
W-pI..... 31.4:1 In **a.**, repeat the idea for today as often as
W-pI..... 68.7:4 *Self.* In **a.**, repeat the idea several times an
W-pI..... 95.5:2 In **a.** to recognizing your difficulties with

**additional** 5

T-2....... VII.7:1 but some **a.** points might be helpful here.
T-4........ VI.3:3 chaos and disaster needs **a.** convincing.
W-pI..... 34.2:2 an **a.** one to be undertaken at any time in
W-pI..... 95.9:3 to continue is to make **a.** mistakes, based
P-1 ............. 5:6 and to prepare **a.** teachers for His work.

**addressed** 1

S-1 ......... II.3:2 asking may be **a.** to God in honest belief,

**adds** 14

T-2........ III.4:6 realizing that it only **a.** unnecessary pain.
T-4....... VII.8:6 Every mind that is changed **a.** to this joy
T-9........ VI.4:5 of creation. Each part you remember **a.** to
T-11..... VII.3:4 always **a.** something that is not real to the
T-18...... IV.1:8 is He Who **a.** the greatness and the might.
T-21... VII.11:4 last question **a.** the wish for constancy in
T-25...... IX.2:6 Each gift but **a.** to the supply. For God is
T-26...... IV.5:3 a voice that **a.** its power to the song, and
T-26... VII.13:3 mind conceives but **a.** to its abundance,
W-pI... 105.4:4 It **a.** to all that is complete already, not in
W-pI... 105.4:5 It **a.** by letting what cannot contain itself
W-pI... 135.1:3 It **a.** illusions to illusions, thus making
W-pI. 135.10:4 all, but merely **a.** to your distress of mind.
W-pI. 153.16:1 Each hour **a.** to our increasing peace, as

**adequacy** 3

T-8....... VII.8:2 learn. His sense of **a.** suffers, and he must
W-pI. 135.11:4 its **a.** to fulfill the plans assigned to it. It is
W-pI... 186.4:2 doubt our **a.** for the function He will offer

**adhere** 3

W-pI..... 27.3:4 and attempt to **a.** to it throughout the day
W-pI..... 40.1:3 schedule and to **a.** to it whenever possible
W-pI..... 65.4:2 and then **a.** to it as closely as possible. The

**adheres** 1

T-4....... II.10:5 by the thought system to which it **a.**.

**adhering** 1

W-pI..... 70.6:3 then **a.** to your own decisions as closely as

**adjectives** 1

W-pI..... 12.3:6 these "nice" **a.** belong in these exercises

**adjust** 14

T-1 ........I.30:1 miracles **a.** the levels of perception and
T-2 ... V.A.11:3 arrange both time and space to **a.** to it.
T-20 ..... III.1:7 Who need **a.** to truth, which calls on only
T-20 ..... III.3:3 without attempting to **a.** themselves to it,
T-20 ..... III.3:6 You make the world and then **a.** to it, and
T-20 ..... III.4:6 those who would **a.** themselves to a world
T-20 ..... III.5:7 And to this world must you **a.** as long as
T-20 ..... III.7:1 to make the Son of God **a.** to his insanity.
T-20 ..... III.7:7 and it is to his answer that you would **a.**.
T-20 ..... III.8:2 answer, and **a.** to it as if it were the truth?
T-20 ..... III.8:3 given it power to **a.** the world to make its
T-20 ... III.8:11 Give it no power to **a.** the means and end.
T-20 ... VIII.6:6 Its eyes **a.** to sin, unable to overlook it in
T-21 ........I.5:4 And they **a.** to loneliness, believing that

**adjusted** 4

T-20 ..... III.8:4 and **a.** it according to its insane answer.
T-21 ..... III.1:2 toward which the seeming union is **a.**.
T-21 ...... V.8:2 in madness, nor can it be **a.** to fit its end.
T-31 ...... V.1:1 concept of the self **a.** to the world's reality

**adjusting** 1

T-21 ........I.5:1 they live, **a.** to it as they think they must,

**adjustment** 5

*See also* level-adjustment

T-12 ..... III.6:6 outside himself, for this is crucial to his **a.**
T-20 ........ III.h Sin as an **A.**
T-20 ..... III.1:1 belief in sin is an **a.**. And an adjustment is
T-20 ..... III.1:2 an **a.** is a change; a shift in perception, or
T-20 ..... III.1:3 Every **a.** is therefore a distortion, and calls

**adjustments** 10

T-20 ..... III.1:4 Knowledge requires no **a.** and, in fact, is
T-20 ..... III.1:6 this impaired condition *are* **a.** necessary,
T-20 ..... III.2:1 **A.** of any kind are of the ego. For it is the
T-20 ..... III.2:2 that all relationships depend upon **a.**, to
T-20 ..... III.2:4 making whatever **a.** it deems necessary
T-20 ..... III.4:6 to a world made fearful by their **a.**. And
T-20 ..... III.6:4 they did not make **a.** to fit their orders.
T-21 ........I.4:1 accustomed to their world by their **a.** to it
T-21 .......II.9:3 Faith in the unreal leads to **a.** of reality to
T-21 .......II.9:6 the **a.** you have introduced to make it so.

**adjusts** 1

T-20 ... VIII.9:6 **a.** to sin and seems to witness to its reality

**admit** 3

T-20 .... VII.2:5 are not, let us **a.** that *you* are inconsistent.
T-21 ..... IV.1:4 This you would not be fearful to **a.**. Fear
T-21 .... VII.5:4 he **a.** that no one made him powerless?

**admitted** 1

T-13 .......II.5:2 not **a.** to this "terrible" secret because you

**adopted** 2

T-28 .......II.8:5 he has given it have they **a.** as their own.
T-30 ........I.1:5 set, **a.** consciously each time you wake,

**adopting** 1

T-5 ....... III.4:6 you because, by **a.** the ego's viewpoint,

**adored** 1

W-pI .... 92.4:7 and **a.** that strength may be dispelled,

**adorn** 1

T-20 .......II.2:5 It will **a.** its chosen home most carefully,

**adornment** 1

T-27 ........I.6:9 **A.** of the body seeks to show how lovely

**adult** 3

M-3 ........... 2:2 he is going running into an **a.** "by chance,
M-3 ........... 2:5 perhaps the **a.** will not scold the child for
M-13 ......... 4:3 **a.** resent the giving up of children's toys?

**advance** 27

T-17 ..... VI.3:7 of a criterion for outcome, set in **a.**, makes
T-17 ..... VI.4:1 The value of deciding in **a.** what you want
T-17 .... VII.6:2 in any situation dedicated in **a.** to truth,
T-18 ..... III.2:2 But you will **a.**, because your goal is the
T-18 ..... III.2:2 your goal is the **a.** from fear to truth. The
T-18 ..... III.5:6 you and walk with you in your **a.** to truth.
T-18 ..... III.8:3 is joined with you in your **a.** to Heaven.
T-18 .......V.1:5 cannot distinguish between **a.** and retreat
T19 ... IV.A.9:2 eagle's flight, or hinder the **a.** of summer?
T-26 ... III.1:11 a necessary step in the **a.** toward oneness.
T-26 ... VIII.6:8 in disaster's form is difficult to credit in **a.**
T-30 .... VII.2:2 thus you judge disaster and success, **a.**,
T-31 .......II.6:7 with us, and we fall back if he does not **a.**.
T-31 ..... IV.7:4 way will not **a.** the purpose to be found. If
W-pI .... 64.5:3 Prepare yourself in **a.** for all the decisions
W-pI .... 65.4:2 Try, also, to determine this time in **a.**, and
W-pI .... 70.6:3 to decide in **a.** when would be a good time
W-pI .... 95.4:5 this, for it is indeed a hindrance to your **a.**
W-pI 110.10:4 make a great **a.** to truth by letting idols go
W-pI .. 127.6:5 in your **a.** towards its established goal.
W-pI .. 162.1:3 It will mean far more to you as you **a.**.
W-pI 196.11:6 Step back from fear, and make **a.** to love.
M-10 ......... 3:4 One would have to recognize in **a.** all the
M-12 ......... 4:2 body. As they **a.** in their profession, they
M-24 ......... 5:5 is detrimental to his pupil's **a.** or his own.
P-2...........I.1:5 again and **a.** in the same relationship,
P-2..........V.6:5 just the smallest willingness, the least **a.**,

**advanced** 18

T-6 ..... V.B.8:2 It is, however, more **a.** than the first step,
T-6 ..... V.C.3:3 It has **a.** far from the first lesson, which is
W-pI .. 127.7:1 you have **a.** in distance without measure
M-4 ........... 1:6 of God who have **a.** in their own learning.
M-4 ........... 2:2 in time it can be said that the **a.** teachers
M-4 ........II.2:1 The peace of mind which the **a.** teachers
M-4 ...... VI.1:6 No one can become an **a.** teacher of God
M-5 ...... III.3:1 once do the **a.** teachers of God consider
M-16 ......... 1:1 To the **a.** teacher of God this question is
M-16 ......... 1:8 day. For the **a.** teacher of God, then, this
M-16 ......... 9:5 of God has reached the most **a.** state. All
M-23 ......... 1:2 most **a.** of God's teachers will give way to
P-2............I.4:4 and the more **a.** he is the more he teaches
P-2........ III.4:4 too **a.** to believe in sickness and too near
P-2....... VII.3:6 needs the help of a very **a.** therapist,
P-2....... VII.6:2 The **a.** therapist in no way can ever doubt
P-3...........I.4:1 A holy therapist, an **a.** teacher of God,
P-3........ III.1:3 **a.** therapist has some earthly needs while

**advancement** 2

M-4 ...... IX.1:1 is the measure of his **a.** in the curriculum.
M-4 ...... IX.1:3 If so, his **a.** is limited, and his trust not yet

**advances** 5

T-18 .......V.1:6 Some of your greatest **a.** you have judged
W-pI .... 61.7:4 to build a firm foundation for these **a.**.
W-pI 108.10:3 for today as quick **a.** in your learning,

WpIrIII.in12:3 these ideas will bring such large **a.** that we
M-9............2:1 As the teacher of God **a.** in his training,

## advancing 4

T-2.........II.6:5 your steps without **a.** to your return. In
T-18......III.3:7 it. You are **a.** to love's meaning, and away
T-31.......II.9:4 same, **a.** only when he would step back,
WpI rVI.in.7:4 by day, **a.** toward the goal He set for us;

## advantage 9

T-4.........V.6:1 The ego thinks it is an **a.** not to commit
T-9.........V.3:1 **a.** to bringing nightmares into awareness,
T-31.....V.13:5 The main **a.** of the shifting to the second
M-24..........3:6 Nor would there be an **a.** in his premature
M-29..........3:1 is another **a.**, –and a very important one,
P-3.........II.9:1 The professional therapist has one **a.** that
S-1........III.3:7 value or **a.** to himself in setting others free
S-1........III.3:9 indeed to be a real **a.** in having enemies,
S-1........III.4:4 Yet what **a.** has an illusion of escape ever

## advantageous 1

W-pI.....95.6:3 **a.**, however, for those whose motivation

## advantages 5

T-17......VI.5:1 The goal of truth has further practical **a.**.
T-31.......II.3:3 each seeming to possess **a.** you would not
W-pI.....95.4:1 for the day has special **a.** at the stage of
W-pI.....95.5:1 periods have other **a.** for you at this time.
M-16..........2:8 are obvious **a.** in terms of saving time.

## advent 3

W-pI...169.4:3 and speed its **a.** into every mind that
W-pII......9.2:1 and hold you safe within its gentle **a.**,
S-3........IV.9:2 Lift up your hearts to greet its **a.**. See the

## adventures 1

T-27... VIII.3:1 The body's serial **a.**, from the time of

## adverse 2

W-pI.....34.6:1 the form of more generalized **a.** emotions,
W-pI.....37.6:3 seems to cause an **a.** reaction in you. Offer

## adversely 1

T-2........IV.2:2 is amiss on one level can **a.** affect another.

## advertise 1

T-15.........I.6:4 The ego does not **a.** its final threat, for it

## advice 5

T-12.........I.5:1 It is surely good **a.** to tell you not to judge
T-13...VII.11:5 and your **a.** to yourself will hurt you. For
T-13......XI.1:1 even death become the ego's best **a.** for
T-30...... I.15:3 ask **a.** before you can decide on anything.
S-1...........I.4:6 for a bit of trifling **a.** about a problem of

## advised 3

W-pI.....34.2:2 the morning and one in the evening are **a.**
M-24..........5:3 the belief unless his internal Teacher so **a.**
M-24..........5:5 might be **a.** that he is misusing the belief

## adviser 3

T-30...... I.16:2 For you and your **a.** must agree on what
T-30...... I.16:6 They are made by you and your **a.**, for
T-30...... I.16:7 reinforce the rule of your **a.** in the world.

## advocate 2

T-9......... V.3:4 condemnation and **a.** a fearful solution.
T19....IV.B.7:9 death, when its great **a.** is heard no more?

## advocated 1

W-pI.....44.8:1 approach is **a.** for this form of exercise,

## advocates 2

T-11... VIII.5:2 you have not done what it specifically **a.**.
M-24.........3:6 because it **a.** a long-held belief of his own.

## advocating 1

W-pI...181.4:2 is **a.** are from those you held before. And

## aesthetic 1

W-pI.......7.3:3 Are not your **a.** reactions to the cup, too,

## affect 15

T-2....... II.1:11 ability of anything not of God to **a.** you.
T-2........IV.2:2 on one level can adversely **a.** another. We
T-5......... V.8:3 decision of the mind will **a.** both behavior
T-7........ VI.1:5 and they will **a.** his total perception. That
T-10......IV.6:6 yourself and your reality **a.** truth at all.
T-21..... V.3:10 that miracles do not **a.** another's mind,
T-26....... V.5:2 What disappeared too quickly to **a.** the
T-26.....VII.4:4 the laws of time do not **a.** its workings. It
T-30.....VII.1:5 And no situation can **a.** its aim, but must
T-31.....VII.2:6 his, because you let them all **a.** you not.
W-pI.....19.1:1 why your seeing does not **a.** you alone.
W-pI...131.5:1 abandon his Creator, nor **a.** His perfect,
W-pII..227.1:4 *not* **a.** *my own reality at all by my illusions.*
W-pII......9.4:1 event in time which time itself can not **a.**.
M-8 ...........5:5 **a.** their credibility in his perception? His

## affected 3

W-pI.....52.1:7 Nothing in God's creation is **a.** in any way
W-pI.....91.1:6 only your awareness of miracles that is **a.**.
W-pII.....338.h I am **a.** only by my thoughts.

## affecting 2

T-28.....VII.5:2 and think without **a.** those apart from you
W-pI...126.2:4 sin without **a.** your perception of yourself,

## affects 2

T-27. VIII.11:5 The form **a.** His answer not at all, for He
W-pI...190.5:4 No one but yourself **a.** you. There is

## affirm 3

T-1.........I.29:3 deny body-identification and **a.** spirit-
T-13......IX.6:1 you will **a.** the truth of guiltlessness unto
W-pI...95.10:4 Today we will **a.** this truth again, and try

## affirmation 4

T-2....V.A.14:1 a denial of this error and an **a.** of the truth
T-3.....III.1:10 the **a.** of truth and beyond all perceptions
T-6......V.B.8:3 step is a positive **a.** of what you want. This
T-12.........I.9:7 as a positive **a.** of the underlying belief it

## affirmations 2

T-1.........I.13:2 They are always **a.** of rebirth, which seem
T-1......... V.4:6 Miracles are **a.** of Sonship, which is a

## affirming 5

T-1.........I.29:2 His creations, **a.** their perfection. They
T-2......... V.5:6 By **a.** this you release the mind from
T-3......IV.5:10 in miscreation the mind is **a.** its Source,
T-4.........in.2:4 are disclaiming knowledge instead of **a.** it,
T-7......VIII.7:3 the idea of separation and **a.** your true

## affliction 2

T-26........II.7:5 without a remedy, or an **a.** without a cure,
T-29....VIII.8:8 wealth, or even more **a.** and more pain.

## afford 4

T-7........ VI.4:1 The ego cannot **a.** to know anything.
W-pI...41.10:1 can indeed **a.** to laugh at fear thoughts,
M-4 ........II.1:3 Only the trusting can **a.** honesty, for only
M-4 ....VIII.1:1 are certain of the outcome can **a.** to wait,

## affront 2

T-6......IV.10:5 creations are perfect, does not **a.** them.
W-pI...186.5:5 to experience which might **a.** their stance.

## affronted 1

T-6......IV.10:6 as the ego's notion that it has **a.** Him.

## afraid 187

T-2...........I.4:6 itself as part of his dream and be **a.** of it.
T-2..........II.1:4 fear. When you are **a.** of anything, you are
T-2..........II.1:7 If you are **a.**, you are valuing wrongly.
T-2.........III.5:9 Whenever you are **a.** you *are* deceived, and
T-2......... V.2:2 but if you are **a.** to use the mind to heal,
T-2......... V.2:3 The very fact that you are **a.** makes your
T-2......... V.7:2 because you are **a.** of what your spiritual
T-2........ VI.1:1 Being **a.** seems to be involuntary;
T-2...... VI.2:10 Whenever you are **a.**, it is a sure sign that
T-2........ VI.8:3 It is obvious, then, that when you are **a.**,
T-2...... VI.9:10 because you are actually **a.** of them. This
T-2...... VI.9:12 is ineffectual you may cease to be **a.** of it,
T-2........VII.3:5 You are **a.** of God, of me and of yourself.
T-2........VII.3:7 if you were not **a.** of your own thoughts.
T-3...........I.1:6 led many people to be bitterly **a.** of God.
T-3..........II.4:1 **a.** of God's Will because you have used
T-3........ III.7:5 him a stranger that you are **a.** of him.
T-3........ IV.3:8 reason to feel **a.** as you perceive yourself.
T-4...........I.6:2 as merely "a larger ego" you will be **a.**,
T-4...........I.8:6 When you are **a.**, be still and know that
T-4...........I.9:6 has chosen to be **a.** instead of meeting it.
T-4.........I.10:1 The ego is **a.** of the spirit's joy, because
T-4........ III.9:3 not exist, and this makes it profoundly **a.**.
T-5........ VI.4:7 Being **a.**, you do not appeal to the Higher
T-6.........I.17:4 **a.** of what you are you do not appreciate it
T-6........ IV.2:9 have the answer and *the ego is* **a.** *of you.*
T-6........ IV.4:8 If you side with this alliance you will be **a.**,
T-6...... IV.11:9 created for you, what could you be but **a.**?
T-6......... V.2:4 understand they need not be **a.** of dreams
T-6......... V.3:3 and be safe, and then you will not be **a.**."
T-7....VIII.3:10 **a.** that their projections will return and
T-7......VIII.5:1 *Do not be* **a.** *of the ego.* It depends on your
T-8..........II.4:2 making you **a.** of your will *because* it is free
T-9...........I.1:2 it possible for it to be **a.** of what it really is
T-9...........I.1:4 demonstrates that you *are* **a.** of what you
T-9...........I.1:5 then, the Will of God of which you are **a.**,
T-9...........I.6:7 Yet as long as you are **a.** of your will, that
T-9...........I.7:3 is because you are **a.** you might receive it,
T-9..........II.2:1 you really want, but you are still **a.** of it.
T-9.......VII.2:7 ego is **a.** of the obvious, since obviousness
T-9.....VIII.4:8 and are **a.** of it because it is a form of
T-9....VIII.11:6 tell you, but do not be **a.** of His answer,
T-10........II.1:5 because you are **a.** of your dissociation,
T-10........II.6:6 vigilance that makes you **a.** to remember
T-10.... III.1:11 you. Do not be **a.** of it, because it is your
T-10... III.4:10 to save? Are you really **a.** of losing this?
T-10...... III.9:1 you may believe you are **a.** of nothingness
T-10...... III.9:1 but you are really **a.** of nothing. And in
T-10...... IV.1:7 **a.** of him because he cannot be reconciled
T-10....... V.1:4 Many are **a.** of blasphemy, but they do
T-11......in.3:10 everything of which you have been **a.** was
T-11.......I.10:3 You are **a.** to know God's Will, because
T-11....... V.2:3 Be not **a.**, therefore, for what you will be

| | |
|---|---|
| T-11....... V.2:8 | Do not be a., then, to look upon fear, for |
| T-11....... V.8:1 | wishes you to realize is that you are a. of it |
| T-11....... V.9:1 | and even desperate, but not really a.. |
| T-11..... V.10:7 | then, you have become a. of yourself. And |
| T-11.... VIII.5:7 | You may be a. of His specificity, for fear |
| T-11.... VIII.7:4 | You are a. of the world as you see it, but |
| T-11.. VIII.13:3 | "dragon" into a dream he is no longer a., |
| T-11.. VIII.14:1 | are a. of your brothers and of your Father |
| T-11.. VIII.14:5 | they learn to perceive truly they are not a. |
| T-12....... II.5:2 | the covers and look at what you are a. of. |
| T-12...... III.6:3 | for self-hate, making him a. of himself. He |
| T-12...... III.9:7 | from your mind because you are a. of it. |
| T-12...... IV.2:3 | for love it is seeking what it is a. to find. |
| T-12... VII.10:1 | a. of me because you looked within and |
| T-12... VII.10:1 | looked within and are a. of what you saw. |
| T-12... VII.10:4 | *upon it.* If you are a., it is because you saw |
| T-13....... II.3:5 | and it will try to destroy it because it is a.. |
| T-13....... II.5:3 | very fearful, and so you are a. to find him. |
| T-13....... II.7:2 | Yet you are a. of it. You have been told |
| T-13....... II.8:4 | you are a. of redemption and you believe |
| T-13...... III.1:5 | state of mind you are not a. of fear. You |
| T-13...... III.1:8 | because you are more a. of what it covers. |
| T-13.... III.1:10 | You are not really a. of crucifixion. Your |
| T-13...... III.2:1 | God, and it is of this that you are really a.. |
| T-13...... III.4:2 | You are a. it would sweep you away from |
| T-13...... III.5:4 | You are more a. of God than of the ego, |
| T-13...... IV.1:1 | are a. of this course should be apparent. |
| T-13...... VI.2:4 | the present, *unless you are a. of light.* And |
| T-13...... IX.7:4 | You are a. of what you would see there, |
| T-13...... IX.8:1 | Do not be a. to look within. The ego tells |
| T-13...... IX.8:5 | are too a. to look upon the light within. |
| T-14...... III.6:5 | he became a. of darkness and of light. The |
| T-14...... VI.2:5 | illusion out of nothing are now a. of them |
| T-15......... I.7:3 | the present, because you are a. of it. The |
| T-15....... V.1:6 | You are a. of this because you believe that |
| T-15....... V.5:7 | then, be a. to let go your imagined needs, |
| T-15... VII.10:6 | and will be a. to hear the Holy Spirit, |
| T-16...... IV.1:1 | Be not a. to look upon the special hate |
| T-16...... IV.6:5 | perceive hatred within, and are a. of it. |
| T-16..... V.10:8 | and unworthy, because you are a. of it. |
| T-18......... I.6:9 | in reality. And above all, *be not a. of it.* |
| T-18...... III.2:4 | when you are a. you have stepped back. |
| T-18...... III.3:5 | and terribly a. of its judgment upon you. |
| T-18...... III.3:6 | do not realize that you are not a. of love, |
| T19. IV.A.10:7 | wholly without attack, it could not be a.. |
| T19. IV.A.14:6 | you. Be not a. of them. They offer you |
| T19... IV.D.4:4 | are no more a. of death than of the ego. |
| T19. IV.D.11:5 | a. of God *because* you fear your brother. |
| T-20....... II.7:4 | Who is a. to look upon illusions, knowing |
| T-20...... III.3:2 | They are not a. of it, for it is within the |
| T-20....... V.1:7 | single purpose, unified and sure, can be a. |
| T-20...... VI.7:1 | Idolaters will always be a. of love, for |
| T-21......... I.5:1 | must, a. to lose the little that they have. |
| T-21......... I.7:3 | could remember, yet you are a., believing |
| T-21...... III.9:4 | Him, you will hate Him because you are a. |
| T-21...... IV.1:3 | You are indeed a. to look within and see |
| T-21...... IV.4:7 | now identify, is not a. to look upon itself. |
| T-21...... IV.6:3 | and not been made a. because you did not |
| T-21...... IV.7:1 | And now the ego *is* a.. Yet what it hears in |
| T-21....... V.2:3 | will see yourself as tiny, vulnerable and a.. |
| T-21..... VII.2:4 | and by their envy make themselves a. of it |
| T-21..... VII.2:5 | are the dark ones, silent and a., alone and |
| T-25....... V.2:2 | you not be a. with "enemies" like these? |
| T-25.... VIII.6:5 | that Heaven is hell, and *are* a. of love. And |
| T-26. VII.11:11 | And he could only be a. of it. Is fear a |
| T-26.... VIII.3:2 | you so perceive it, you will be a. of it, |
| T-27....... V.2:7 | But if you are a. of healing, then it cannot |
| T-27....... V.4:5 | Be not a. of blessing, for the One Who |
| T-27....... V.5:1 | back because he was a. of being healed? |
| T-28....... I.12:6 | do nothing that would make himself a.. |
| T-28....... II.7:3 | No one is a. of them when he perceives he |
| T-28...... III.8:1 | Be not a., my child, but let your world be |
| T-29......... I.2:3 | No one who hates but is a. of love, and |
| T-29......... I.2:3 | love, and therefore must he be a. of God. |
| T-29......... I.9:5 | not a. to find a loss of self in finding God? |
| T-29...... IV.2:7 | a. because you did not recognize the fear. |
| T-29...... IX.6:7 | is a. of all the chaos in a world he thinks is |
| T-30...... IV.2:4 | And he is a., because he thought the rules |
| T-30...... VI.7:6 | and will remain a. to look within and find |
| T-30 .... VII.3:9 | a fearful script, and are a. accordingly. |
| T-30 ... VIII.6:3 | made guilty and a. when you are tempted |
| T-31 ....... II.9:3 | be. He is a. to walk with you, and thinks |
| T-31 .... V.17:6 | that the world is more a. to hear than this |
| W-pI....... 4.2:2 | a. to use "good" thoughts as well as "bad. |
| W-pI....... 5.2:4 | *I think. I am not a. of _for the reason I think.* |
| W-pI..... 13.5:2 | remind yourself that you are really a. of |
| W-pI..... 14.5:1 | anything you are a. might happen to you, |
| W-pI..... 15.3:3 | Do not be a. of them. They are signs that |
| W-pI..... 26.7:4 | specifically, saying: *I am a. _will happen.* |
| W-pI..... 26.9:1 | named each outcome of which you are a., |
| W-pI..... 58.4:4 | my holiness, nothing can make me a.. |
| W-pI..... 87.1:3 | fearful of shadows and a. of things unseen |
| W-pI..... 87.3:3 | can become a. only when I believe there is |
| W-pI..... 87.3:4 | I try to attack only when I am a., and only |
| W-pI..... 92.3:3 | dying, those in need, the helpless and a., |
| W-pI..... 93.2:3 | deceiving and a. of foolish fantasies and |
| W-pI... 103.2:5 | *To fear Him is to be a. of joy.* Begin your |
| W-pI... 106.3:1 | Be not a. today to circumvent the voices |
| W-pI... 121.3:1 | about itself and all it sees; a. and angry, |
| W-pI... 121.3:1 | weak and blustering, a. to go ahead, |
| W-pI... 121.3:1 | blustering, afraid to go ahead, a. to stay, |
| W-pI... 121.3:1 | afraid to stay, a. to waken or to go to sleep |
| W-pI... 121.3:1 | waken or to go to sleep, a. of every sound, |
| W-pI... 121.3:1 | of every sound, yet more a. of stillness; |
| W-pI... 124.5:2 | sad and the distressed, the lonely and a., |
| W-pI... 130.2:3 | can choose to see a world of which he is a. |
| W-pI... 151.4:5 | how weak you are; how helpless and a., |
| W-pI... 152.6:4 | sinful and the guilty, the a., the suffering |
| W-pI... 152.9:4 | says that we are sinners, guilty and a., |
| W-pI. 153.20:2 | Be not a. nor timid. There can be no |
| W-pI... 163.8:1 | Death's worshippers may be a.. And yet, |
| W-pI... 166.4:3 | he made is he an outcast; homeless and a. |
| W-pI... 166.4:4 | not realize that it is here he is a. indeed, |
| W-pI. 166.11:4 | you perceive yourself as lonely and a.. |
| W-pI... 186.5:5 | a. to go beyond them to experience which |
| W-pI... 187.9:4 | Be not a. to look. The blessedness you will |
| W-pI... 191.1:4 | God. What could it be but vicious and a., |
| W-pI... 195.5:2 | you; the sick, the weak, the needy and a., |
| W-pI... 199.2:4 | And who can be a. who lives in Innocence |
| W-pI... 199.7:3 | themselves as bound and helpless and a.. |
| W-pII . 244.2:4 | make a. what will forever be a part of Him |
| W-pII . 245.1:4 | *I bring it to the desolate and lonely and a.. I* |
| W-pII . 259.2:2 | *I would not be a. of love, nor seek for refuge* |
| W-pII .... 282.h | I will not be a. of love today. |
| W-pII . 282.2:5 | *a mistake. Let me not be a. of truth today.* |
| W-pII ... 10.4:2 | Be not a. of love. For it alone can heal all |
| W-pII ... 10.4:4 | Be not a. of this. Salvation asks you give it |
| W-pII . 348.1:6 | *Can I be a., when Your eternal promise goes* |
| M-16 ......... 6:9 | this. How foolish to be so a. of nothing! |
| M-19 ......... 4:9 | You are a. of Him, and do not see you |
| C-ep........... 3:1 | Be not a.. We only start again an ancient |
| P-2......... V.2:1 | who come to us for help are bitterly a.. |
| P-2........ VII.7:1 | are not a. to offer weakness to God's Son. |
| S-2.......... II.8:5 | You do not want to be a. of God. You |

## after 51

| | |
|---|---|
| T-2 .......... I.4:5 | Only a. the deep sleep fell upon Adam |
| T-2 ......... II.3:2 | The means are easier to understand a. the |
| T-2 ......... II.4:5 | only a. the separation that the Atonement |
| T-2 ........ V.9:1 | an ability that developed a. the separation |
| T-2 ..... VIII.2:4 | brought into being only a. the separation, |
| T-2 ..... VIII.3:7 | is not. A. this, the ability to choose can be |
| T-3 ....... IV.2:1 | into the mind a. the separation, making |
| T-3 ........ V.1:1 | was introduced only a. the separation. No |
| T-3 ....... VI.1:2 | A. the Last Judgment there will be no |
| T-4 .......... II.9:5 | will continue to exist a. a temporary lapse |
| T-18 ..... III.8:5 | a. a long and meaningless journey that |
| T-18 ...... V.2:1 | Never approach the holy instant a. you |
| T-19 ... III.11:4 | is the rest that waits for all, a. the journey. |
| T19... IV.D.1:5 | obstacle, a. which is salvation completed, |
| T-20 . VIII.11:2 | And a. vision, who is there who could |
| T-20 . VIII.11:2 | who could refuse what must come a.? |
| T-22 ..... IV.3:6 | Think what will happen a.. The Love of |
| T-22 ..... IV.4:3 | a. such a long and lonely journey where |
| T-25 ..... IV.5:6 | Nothing before and nothing a. it. No |
| W-pI..... 24.7:1 | A. covering the list of as many hoped-for |
| W-pI..... 26.9:1 | A. you have named each outcome of |
| W-pI .... 35.7:4 | A. you have named each one, add: *But my* |
| W-pI .... 42.3:1 | today, one as soon as possible a. you wake |
| W-pI .... 42.4:3 | A. this, try to think of nothing except |
| W-pI .... 45.6:3 | A. you have added some four or five |
| W-pI .... 46.5:2 | A. you have applied the idea to all those |
| WpI... rI.in.1:3 | a few short comments a. each of the ideas, |
| WpI... rI.in.2:3 | related comments a. reading them over. |
| WpI... rI.in.3:3 | A. you have read the idea and the related |
| W-pI .... 64.8:3 | your eyes open a. reviewing the thoughts, |
| W-pI .... 65.6:1 | A. a while, interfering thoughts will |
| W-pI .... 67.3:1 | A. you have gone over several such |
| W-pI .... 69.6:1 | A. you have thought about the |
| W-pI .... 71.1:5 | a. we have considered just what the ego's |
| W-pI .. 73.10:1 | A. reminding yourself of this, and |
| W-pI .... 74.5:1 | A. you have cleared your mind in this |
| W-pI .... 77.5:1 | A. this brief introductory phase, wait |
| W-pI .. 92.11:2 | A. the morning meeting, we will use the |
| W-pI .... 93.1:3 | living on a. seeing this being impossible. |
| W-pI .. 124.3:1 | is our eternal gift to those who follow a., |
| W-pI .. 133.1:1 | particularly a. you have gone through |
| WpI..rIV.in7:1 | A. your preparation, merely read each of |
| W-pII ... 11.1:5 | unchanged through time and a. time is |
| W-pII . 336.1:2 | is restored a. perception first is changed, |
| W-ep ......... 2:1 | sun laid down before it rises, a. it has set, |
| M-13 ......... 2:9 | seeking a. such things the mind associates |
| M-16 ......... 3:8 | A. completion of the more structured |
| M-16 ......... 4:7 | as possible a. waking take your quiet time |
| M-16 ......... 4:7 | or two a. you begin to find it difficult. You |
| M-26 ......... 3:3 | be won a. much devotion and dedication, |
| C-6 ............ 1:1 | the earth a. he ascended into Heaven, or |

## afterwards 11

| | |
|---|---|
| T-3 ....... IV.5:5 | A. it can only choose ambiguously, and |
| T-18 .... VII.2:4 | A. you will see the body again, but never |
| T-20 ....... V.5:8 | all the same; nothing before it, nothing a.. |
| T-28 ...... I.11:5 | place will not be wholly unremembered a. |
| T-31 .. .... II.2:4 | But a., the truth is given you. You would |
| W-pI .... 27.3:4 | the idea when you wake or shortly a., and |
| W-pI .. 128.7:2 | And when your eyes are opened a., you |
| W-pI .. 136.4:3 | But a., your plan requires that you must |
| W-pII .. in.11:2 | deep experience which should come a.. |
| W-pII . 294.1:7 | And a., without a purpose, it is laid aside. |
| C-in ........... 5:2 | A. and soon, it drops away to make way |

## again 301

| | |
|---|---|
| T-2 ......... V.6:1 | It should be emphasized a. that the body |
| T-3 ....... III.2:2 | or God. To recognize means to "know a.," |
| T-4 .......... I.7:6 | A., –nothing you do or think or wish or |
| T-4 ....... III.3:7 | of this can ever fully believe in the ego a.. |
| T-4 ....... III.5:1 | you will never want to cover or hide it a.. |
| T-5 ......... II.3:8 | to where you were before and will be a.. It |
| T-5 ......... II.4:5 | You knew as you will know a., but as you |
| T-5 ......... V.1:5 | But a., remember that both are in you. |
| T-6 .......... I.1:1 | let us consider the crucifixion a.. I did not |
| T-6 ......... I.18:6 | as He thinks if you are to know Him a.. |
| T-6 ..... V.A.2:5 | A. as always, He reinterprets what the ego |
| T-10 ......... I.3:4 | that you will know it can be so a.. What is |
| T-10 ....... II.2:5 | Him and know your own reality a.. Let |
| T-10 ....... II.3:2 | you merely accept a. what is already there |
| T-11 ...... in.4:3 | from our Father to offer you everything a. |
| T-11 ......... I.1:3 | a. the thought system you share with Him |
| T-11 ..... VII.1:5 | To perceive anew is merely to perceive a., |
| T-11 . VIII.14:6 | ask for truth a. when they are frightened. |
| T-13 ....... II.7:3 | told a. and again that it will set you free, |
| T-13 ....... II.7:3 | told again and a. that it will set you free, |
| T-13 ....... V.3:6 | it. A. and again have you attacked your |
| T-13 ....... V.3:6 | and a. have you attacked your brother, |
| T-13 ..... VI.3:5 | To be born a. is to let the past go, and |
| T-13 ..... VI.4:8 | between them, to free you to be born a.. |
| T-13 ..... VI.5:1 | his past, and so perceive him as born a.. |
| T-13 .. VII.11:2 | the ego urges you a. and again to get, it |
| T-13 .. VII.11:2 | the ego urges you again and a. to get, it |
| T-13 ....... X.5:2 | but with each one each day be born a.. A |
| T-15 ....... I.4:12 | A. the ego tries, and all too frequently |
| T-15 ......... I.9:7 | holy instant wherein holiness was born a. |
| T-15 ....... II.6:7 | one instant, and you will never deny it a.. |
| T-16 ..... II.6:12 | Never a. will you be wholly willing not to |

T-17......III.6:8 be unwilling ever to lose the sight of it **a.**.
T-17....IV.16:1 you will experience **a.** the meaning of
T-17.......V.3:9 of holiness, it can never **a.** be what it was.
T-17.......V.9:3 that you and your brother have started **a.**,
T-17......VI.5:8 **a.** you see the opposite of the ego's way of
T-18.........I.4:3 splintered and subdivided and divided **a.**,
T-18.....VII.2:4 Afterwards you will see the body **a.**, but
T-19......I.14:3 as it was made **a.** through faith. And there
T-19....III.11:1 and let not sin arise **a.** to blind your eyes.
T19...IV.D.7:6 mad desire, no trivial impulse to forget **a.**,
T19.IV.D.10:8 on, only to return and make the choice **a.**.
T19.IV.D.16:1 place of resurrection, to which we come **a.**
T19.IV.D.18:5 rise **a.** to glad remembrance of his Father,
T-20....VI.11:6 he makes his choice **a.** between idolatry
T-20... VIII.2:3 be free of misery, and learn **a.** of joy?
T-20. VIII.8:10 same. **A.** there is no order; only a seeming
T-21.........I.5:3 reach each other, and they fail, and fail **a.**.
T-21.......II.7:8 simply to recognize **a.** the presence of
T-21......IV.5:2 but to join with him and to be free **a.**, as
T-21...VII.10:4 be made, and then unmade and made **a.**.
T-21...VII.11:6 the option to change your mind **a.**. When
T-22.......II.9:5 And here we see **a.** another form of the
T-22......VI.5:6 you fill **a.** with the eternal light you bring,
T-23.......in.2:3 think that you succeeded, and attack **a.**. It
T-23.......II.5:2 it appears that They can never be One **a.**.
T-24...VII.6:10 not till you make **a.** a holy home for your
T-25......IV.1:8 And then the means are chosen once **a.**,
T-25......IV.5:3 Each bird that ever sang will sing **a.** in you
T-25.......V.6:5 hell. Look once **a.** upon your brother, not
T-26.........I.7:1 can you be reborn, and given life **a.**. His
T-26.........I.7:7 Born **a.** each instant, untouched by time,
T-26.......II.1:7 will recur and then recur **a.** and yet again,
T-26.......II.1:7 will recur and then recur again and yet **a.**,
T-26.......II.1:7 for all time and will not rise **a.** in any form
T-26.......II.6:5 Consider once **a.** your special function.
T-26......IV.1:8 which his forgiveness offers him **a.**.
T-26......IV.3:8 and all their radiance made whole **a.**.
T-26.......V.5:5 back, as if it could be made **a.** in time.
T-26.......V.8:2 be made real **a.** and seen as here and now,
T-26.....V.13:2 And so you die each day to live **a.**, until
T-26.....V.13:3 from birth to death and on to life **a.**, a
T-26.....V.14:4 repeat **a.** a journey that was over long ago.
T-26...VII.16:5 God reborn until he chooses not to die **a.**.
T-26......IX.3:1 hatred fades to let the grass grow green **a.**,
T-26......IX.3:4 Presence which has lifted holiness **a.** to
T-26......IX.4:5 The incomplete is made complete **a.**, and
T-26......IX.8:1 as host **a.** to Him by Whom it was created
T-27.........I.9:9 mind made free **a.** to choose what it is for.
T-27.......II.1:6 He has attacked and will attack **a.**. Protect
T-27......VI.2:1 from pain to pleasure, and **a.** to pain. For
T-27... VIII.3:4 This single lesson does it try to teach **a.**,
T-27... VIII.3:4 does it try to teach again, and still **a.**, and
T-28.........I.5:8 that they be brought to you, and lived **a.**.
T-28......IV.8:1 of God and put the pieces into place **a.**.
T-28......VI.4:4 apart. This is the secret oath you take **a.**,
T-29.........I.3:6 and him, lest he turn **a.** into an enemy.
T-29.........I.4:3 separate till you and he elect to meet **a.**.
T-29.........I.4:7 in which to build **a.** your separate self,
T-29......IX.8:6 And when he hears this song **a.**, he knows
T-30.........I.1:9 Then try **a.** to have the day you want.
T-30.........I.4:1 tell yourself **a.** the kind of day you want;
T-30.........I.5:5 need a quick restorative before you ask **a.**.
T-30.........I.6:1 (3) Remember once **a.** the day you want,
T-30......I.13:5 then, consider once **a.** the very first of the
T-30.......II.3:1 Look once **a.** upon your enemy, the one
T-30......III.7:3 An unremembered thought is born **a.** to
T-30......IV.4:5 But then they fall and cannot rise **a.**. They
T-30.......V.6:3 Yet God need not create His Son **a.**, that
T-30.......V.6:5 of God knew in creation he must know **a.**.
T-30.....VII.7:8 to us all, and thus we can communicate **a.**
T-30... VIII.1:4 it real before, and now you think it real **a.**.
T-31......I.13:4 Now is he born **a.** to you, and you are
T-31......I.13:4 again to you, and you are born **a.** to him,
T-31.......II.2:1 Let us review **a.** what seems to stand
T-31......IV.8:2 choose the better to deceive yourself **a.**.
T-31......VIII.h Choose Once **A.**
T-31... VIII.1:5 *Choose once **a.** if you would take your place*
T-31... VIII.3:1 that you failed to learn presented once **a.**,
T-31... VIII.3:2 and gently says, "My brother, choose **a.**."
T-31... VIII.4:2 see it as it is; another chance to choose **a.**,
T-31... VIII.6:5 Choose once **a.** what you would have him
T-31... VIII.9:1 gift can once **a.** be recognized as ours!
T-31... VIII.9:6 For you *will* hear, and you *will* choose **a.**.
W-pI.......5.3:1 But **a.**, this should not be substituted for
W-pI.......6.1:2 **A.**, it is necessary to name both the form
W-pI.......6.3:1 **A.**, if you resist applying the idea to some
W-pI.......9.5:1 It is emphasized **a.** that while complete
W-pI.....10.1:3 this distinction before, and will do so **a.**.
W-pI.....19.2:1 Today we are **a.** emphasizing the fact that
W-pI.....31.1:2 **A.**, the idea should be applied to both the
W-pI.....32.2:2 practice periods for today will **a.** include
W-pI.....32.3:1 **A.** we will begin the practice periods for
W-pI.....36.4:1 idea; look about you as you repeat it **a.**;
W-pI.....37.5:1 you may open your eyes **a.** and apply the
W-pI.....40.1:4 try **a.**. If there are long interruptions, try
W-pI.....40.1:5 If there are long interruptions, try **a.**.
W-pI.....40.1:6 try again. Whenever you remember, try **a.**
W-pI.....42.4:2 close your eyes and repeat the idea **a.**,
W-pI.....43.5:2 close your eyes, repeat today's idea **a.**,
W-pI.....43.6:1 and then attempt the second phase **a.**. Do
W-pI.....45.6:3 idea, repeat it **a.** and tell yourself gently:
W-pI.....52.4:6 Now I would choose **a.**, that I may see.
W-pI.....64.5:2 of it in the morning and **a.** at night, and
W-pI.....65.5:2 eyes, repeat the idea to yourself once **a.**,
W-pI.....68.4:5 never be a problem in motivation ever **a.**.
W-pI.....70.6:3 **a.** be well to decide in advance when
W-pI.....70.8:1 we will try **a.** to reach the light in you,
W-pI...73.11:1 **a.** make a declaration of what you really
W-pI.....74.6:3 repeat the idea for today and try **a.**. Do
W-pI.....76.2:3 tells you once **a.** how simple is salvation.
W-pI.....77.1:4 **A.**, how simple is salvation! It is merely a
W-pI.....79.5:5 only to be hidden **a.** but still unsolved.
W-pI.....92.7:6 to darkness till the morning comes **a.**.
W-pI.....92.9:3 His Son, is waiting now to meet Itself **a.**,
W-pI...92.11:2 time at night when we will meet **a.** in trust
W-pI...93.11:1 of fear by repeating these thoughts **a.**.
W-pI.....94.3:1 Today we will **a.** devote the first five
W-pI.....95.3:2 We will **a.** direct our exercises towards
W-pI.....95.3:3 In patience and in hope we try **a.** today.
W-pI.....95.7:3 not to return to it **a.** as soon as you can.
W-pI.....95.7:5 corrected, and an unwillingness to try **a.**.
W-pI...95.10:4 Today we will affirm this truth **a.**, and try
W-pI...95.11:3 Then close your eyes and tell yourself **a.**,
W-pI...96.10:3 it will **a.** flow out from spirit to the spirit
W-pI.....97.2:1 We state **a.** the truth about your Self, the
W-pI.....97.6:3 nor will you be able to forget the way **a.**.
W-pI.....98.4:3 they have come to make their choice **a.**.
W-pI...98.10:1 five minutes you will spend **a.** with Him.
W-pI...98.10:2 wait for the glad time to come to you **a.**.
W-pI...98.11:1 and spend a happy time **a.** with Him. Tell
W-pI...101.6:8 and then attempt **a.** to find the joy these
W-pI...103.2:3 error we will try **a.** to bring to truth today,
W-pI...106.9:3 will **a.** release a thousand more who pause
W-pI...107.4:2 nor come and go and go and come **a.**. It
W-pI.107.10:1 you will be glad to look **a.** upon this world
W-pI...109.2:6 in which the Son of God is born **a.**, to
W-pI...109.6:1 sing, a stream long dry begins to flow **a.**.
W-pI...109.6:2 The world is born **a.** each time you rest,
W-pI...109.7:3 to sing and see the stream begin to flow **a.**
WpIrIII.in11:1 If you are shaken, think of it **a.**. These
W-pI...122.2:4 when you wake **a.**, it offers you another
W-pI...122.7:2 Do not turn away in aimless wandering **a.**
W-pI.122.13:3 you return **a.** to meet a world of shifting
W-pI...124.1:1 will **a.** give thanks for our Identity in God.
W-pI...129.5:2 back to see **a.** the world you do not want.
W-pI...132.6:5 step back a while and then return **a.**.
W-pI...132.9:1 repeated once must now be stressed **a.**,
W-pI...134.5:5 and once **a.** by those who pardon them.
W-pI.135.25:4 And you rise **a.** from what was seeming
W-pI...136.6:3 in effect, and never to be seen as whole **a.**.
W-pI.136.19:2 to come, you have **a.** misplaced yourself,
W-pI...137.3:4 healing is his own decision to be one **a.**,
W-pI...138.9:3 raised to understanding, to be judged **a.**,
W-pI.138.12:3 passed, we have declared our choice **a.**, in
W-pI...139.7:3 will come **a.** until the time Atonement is
W-pI.140.11:1 end the day by listening **a.** five minutes
WpI. rIV.in1:1 Now we review **a.**, this time aware we are
WpIrIV.in10:2 to the ideas for the day **a.** before you sleep
WpIrIV.in10:2 and are learning now to claim **a.** as your
W-pI. 151.13:4 and give them back **a.** as clean ideas that
W-pI. 152.11:6 never left will come **a.** to our awareness,
W-pI...153.1:1 the "gifts" it merely lends to take away **a.**;
W-pI...153.1:4 It attacks, and then attacks **a.**. No peace
W-pI...153.3:2 iron overlaid, returning but to start **a.**.
W-pI...154.4:3 mind becomes aware **a.** of Who created it,
W-pI...155.8:7 As they step back, he finds himself **a.**.
W-pI...157.9:4 knew that instant, and will surely know **a.**
W-pI...158.4:5 back on it, imagining we make it once **a.**;
W-pI...159.7:2 For here it is repaired, made new **a.**, but
W-pI...159.9:4 to which they go **a.** with added fragrance.
W-pI...160.9:5 And He leads them gently home **a.**, where
W-pI...161.8:2 attack, and howling to unite with him **a.**.
W-pI...163.5:4 And this it writes **a.** and still again, while
W-pI...163.5:4 And this it writes again and still **a.**, while
W-pI...163.6:5 For here **a.** we see an obvious position,
W-pI. 170.13:5 *We choose **a.**, and make our choice for all*
WpI...rV.in1:1 We now review **a.**. This time we are ready
WpI...rV.in1:4 that we may go on **a.** more certain, more
WpI...rV.in4:2 Self we share and now prepare to know **a.**
WpI...rV.in7:1 My resurrection comes **a.** each time I
WpI...rV.in8:1 Release me as you practice once **a.** the
WpI.rV.in11:3 once **a.** with these same words upon our
WpI.rV.in12:4 try **a.** to go beyond them to their meaning
W-pI...181.4:3 you will inevitably lose your way **a.**.
W-pI...182.1:6 dismissed, but surely to return to mind **a.**
W-pI...182.4:1 childhood home that you would find **a.**.
W-pI...182.5:4 **a.** the holy air that fills His Father's house.
W-pI...182.7:5 not return **a.** where He does not belong,
W-pI...183.6:1 God's Name slowly **a.** and still again.
W-pI...183.6:1 God's Name slowly again and still **a.**.
W-pI...186.9:5 an instant, break apart to group **a.**, and
W-pI. 190.11:1 And so **a.** we make the only choice that
W-pI...191.8:4 God's Son has come **a.** at last to set it free
W-pI. 191.10:1 eyes, return **a.** to bless the world he made.
W-pI...192.5:7 the Son to look **a.** upon his holiness.
W-pI...192.8:1 can be born **a.** in Christ but him who has
W-pI...193.9:5 each one, and that His Son be free **a.**.
W-pI...194.7:8 to choose **a.** when he has been deceived;
W-pI...194.8:2 you call the memory of Him to come **a.**,
W-pI...195.7:4 An ancient door is swinging free **a.**; a long
W-pI...195.7:4 clarity as we are willing once **a.** to hear.
W-pI...197.1:3 Yet you turn them to attack **a.**, unless you
W-pI...197.5:3 joy while you forgive but to attack **a.**.
W-pI...197.6:2 before He snatches them away **a.** in death.
W-pI...198.7:4 you will look **a.** upon the place where you
W-pI...200.3:6 than to seek and seek and seek **a.** for hell,
W-pI...200.9:1 Let us not lose our way **a.** today. We go to
WpI rVI.in.1:4 and invite the memory of God to come **a.**.
W-pII .....in.9:6 A moment more, and it will rise **a.**. A
W-pII .227.2:3 The Son of God this day comes home **a.**,
W-pII ..... 2.4:5 Earth is being born **a.** in new perspective.
W-pII .....234.h Father, today I am Your Son **a.**.
W-pII .238.2:1 And so, **a.** today, we pause to think how
W-pII .241.2:1 *now, and so we come at last to You **a.**. Father,*
W-pII .248.2:1 *returns, and lets me love Your Son **a.** as well.*
W-pII .249.2:3 *Now would we rest **a.** in You, as You created*
W-pII .260.1:6 *my sinlessness arise **a.** before Christ's vision*
W-pII .303.1:6 here, for He is born **a.** in me today.
W-pII .304.2:3 *Son, that he may find **a.** the memory of You,*
W-pII .323.2:4 And we are at peace **a.**, for fear has gone
W-pII .....330.h I will not hurt myself **a.** today.
W-pII .332.2:1 *We would not bind the world **a.** today. Fear*
W-pII .334.1:3 me not accept such meager gifts **a.** today.
W-pII .342.1:6 *Let me not wait **a.** today. Let me forgive all*
W-pII .352.1:4 *have given me a way to find Your peace **a.**. I*
Wfl........in.1:5 For we would not return **a.** to the belief in
M-2 ........... 1:4 **A.**, it is only a matter of time. Once he has
M-2 ........... 4:2 that is relived **a.** and again and still again,
M-2 ........... 4:2 that is relived again and **a.** and still again,
M-2 ........... 4:2 that is relived again and again and still **a.**,
M-3 ........... 4:5 **A.**, each has learned the most he can at
M-3 ........... 4:6 Yet all who meet will someday meet **a.**,
M-4 .........I.2:1 to trust one's own petty strength **a.**. Who
M-5 ........II.3:4 will never **a.** appear to rule the mind. For
M-11 ......... 2:1 **A.** we come to the question of judgment.
M-11 ....... 4:10 it leans down in answer, to raise it up **a.**.
M-16 ......... 2:7 It is always possible to begin **a.**, should

M-16 ..... 11:11 light can shine **a.** on an untroubled mind.
M-17 ......... 6:4 Magic **a.** must help. Forget the battle.
M-19 ......... 5:9 rests, the mind is still, and light returns **a.**
M-20 ......... 4:2 form, will drop the heavy curtain once **a.**,
M-20 ......... 4:3 War is **a.** accepted as the one reality. Now
M-20 ......... 4:4 must you once **a.** lay down your sword,
M-20 ......... 4:4 recognize that you have picked it up **a.**.
M-20 ......... 4:5 you must have taken it **a.** as your defense.
M-23 ....... 5:11 Why would you choose to start **a.**, when
M-29 ......... 4:1 Here **a.** is the paradox often referred to in
C-ep........... 1:2 way will come and go and go to come **a.**.
C-ep........... 3:2 We only start **a.** an ancient journey long
C-ep........... 3:3 begun **a.** upon a road we travelled on
C-ep........... 3:4 And now we try **a.**. Our new beginning
C-ep........... 4:5 we know that we will never lose the way **a.**
C-ep........... 4:6 song begins **a.** which had been stopped
P-2........... I.1:5 Perhaps they will come together **a.** and
P-2........ IV.1:3 Judgment is a decision, made **a.** and again
P-2........ IV.1:3 Judgment is a decision, made again and **a.**
P-2........ IV.3:6 and we have said already and will say **a.**,
P-2....... VII.3:5 Nor will it return **a.**, once its cause has
P-3....... II.9:10 is One Who says, "My brother, choose **a.**.
P-3........ III.3:7 if it does, it merely crucifies God's Son **a.**.
P-3........ III.6:9 A. will both be blessed. Only in terms of
S-1......... II.7:7 can **a.** become what it was meant to be.
S-1......... V.1:2 And here **a.** it rises slowly up, and grows
S-2........ III.6:7 and death become **a.** the holy gift of God.
S-3......... II.1:3 to fear, so sickness will be free to strike **a.**.
S-3......... II.2:4 light that we have learned to look upon **a.**.
S-3......... II.6:1 ready to strike **a.** until it brings a cruel
S-3........ III.6:4 cause, it cannot come **a.** in different form.
S-3........ IV.6:1 Come unto Me, My children, once **a.**,

**against** 311

T-2......... II.7:6 can be turned **a.** you very unexpectedly.
T-2........ III.1:2 entirely to defend ***a.*** the Atonement, and
T-2........ III.2:4 the one effective defense **a.** all separation
T-3........... I.3:6 He does not hold your "evil" deeds **a.** you.
T-3........... I.3:7 Is it likely that He would hold them **a.** me
T-3......... II.5:1 Nothing can prevail **a.** a Son of God who
T-3......... II.5:8 instead of defending themselves **a.** it.
T-3........ VI.2:7 that what you judged **a.** has no effect.
T-3........ VI.2:8 that what you judged **a.** does not exist.
T-3........ VI.2:9 this, or you would not have judged **a.** it.
T-3........ VI.5:9 that it will someday be used **a.** you. This
T-4........... I.5:3 this, because it goes **a.** all of its own laws.
T-4...... III.1:12 *protected, and the ego will not prevail* ***a.*** *it.*
T-4........ III.2:6 A. our united strength the ego cannot
T-4........ III.3:6 A. this sense of temporary existence spirit
T-4........ III.3:8 to you prevail **a.** the glorious gift of God?
T-4........ IV.2:6 it is much easier than trying to think **a.** it.
T-4........ IV.4:2 as vigilant **a.** the ego's dictates as for them
T-4........ IV.6:4 Yet you are not sufficiently vigilant **a.** the
T-4........ IV.7:3 with me consistently **a.** this deception,
T-4......... V.1:6 would inevitably judge **a.** the ego, and
T-4....... VII.2:2 The ego is thus **a.** communication, except
T-5...... IV.1:10 The ego cannot prevail **a.** the Kingdom
T-5........ IV.4:5 cannot hurt you and hold nothing **a.** him,
T-5........ IV.4:5 against him, or you hold it **a.** yourself.
T-5........ VI.4:7 believe its judgment would also be **a.** you.
T-5...... VI.10:2 you. It will merely dismiss the case **a.** you.
T-5...... VI.10:3 There can be no case **a.** a child of God,
T-5...... VI.10:5 It will dismiss the case **a.** you, however
T-6......... II.2:3 you have also judged **a.** what you project,
T-6....... II.10:8 The ego cannot prevail **a.** this because it is
T-6........ IV.4:1 that part of the mind that made it is **a.** it.
T-6........ IV.5:1 uses the body to conspire **a.** your mind,
T-6...... V.A.2:5 for separation into a demonstration **a.** it.
T-6...... V.C.1:5 of accord entirely He rejects by judging **a.**.
T-6...... V.C.3:2 there is something you must be vigilant ***a.***.
T-6...... V.C.4:1 this step calls for consistent vigilance **a.** it.
T-6...... V.C.4:2 you can be as vigilant **a.** the ego as for it.
T-6...... V.C.4:8 long as you must be vigilant **a.** anything,
T-6...... V.C.7:6 ego speaks **a.** His creation, and therefore
T-6...... V.C.8:9 for truth, but it is necessary **a.** illusions.
T-6...... V.C.9:6 vigilance **a.** this sickness is the way to heal
T-6.... V.C.10:6 you must now turn your effort **a.** it. Only
T-7........ III.3:5 underestimate your need to be vigilant ***a.***
T-7 ....... VI.7:6 It is necessary **a.** beliefs that are not true,
T-7 ...... VI.12:3 and you must be vigilant **a.** this divided
T-7 ..... VIII.7:3 are deciding **a.** the belief that you can be
T-7 ....... IX.1:6 and it responds as if it were being sided **a.**
T-7 ....... IX.2:3 prevail **a.** a totality that includes God, and
T-7 ....... XI.1:5 The world goes **a.** your nature, being out
T-8 ......... II.2:8 When you are taught **a.** your nature,
T-8 ......... II.2:9 your nature, and therefore cannot go **a.** it.
T-8 ..... IV.4:11 you would have decided **a.** healing, and
T-8 ..... IV.5:12 mine, and God Himself would not go **a.** it.
T-8 ........ V.4:6 all. Nothing can prevail **a.** our united wills
T-8 ........ V.4:6 wills because nothing can prevail **a.** God's
T-8 .... VII.10:7 to attack, because it has turned **a.** itself.
T-8 ..... VIII.3:5 recognized this and also decided **a.** attack
T-9 .......... I.2:1 the ego's, and that is why the ego is **a.** you
T-9 ........ I.12:2 Willing **a.** reality, though impossible, can
T-9 ......... II.9:1 To disbelieve is to side **a.**, or to attack. To
T-9 ........ V.3:7 there have been revolts **a.** this concept,
T-9 ........ V.3:7 but to revolt **a.** it is still to believe in it.
T-9 ...... VII.4:5 and you are going **a.** its judgment. The
T-9 ...... VII.7:6 The Holy Spirit judges **a.** the reality of the
T-9 ..... VIII.4:5 and mobilize its energies **a.** your release.
T-10 ..... in.3:11 God will never decide **a.** you, or He would
T-10 ..... in.3:11 you, or He would be deciding **a.** Himself.
T-10 ......... I.1:1 **a.** them as long as your mind is split, and
T-10 ........ II.6:5 at it. By deciding **a.** your reality, you have
T-10 ........ II.6:5 yourself vigilant ***a.*** God and His Kingdom.
T-10 ...... IV.1:7 He is the symbol of deciding **a.** God, and
T-10 ....... V.4:1 to enter the mind of God's Son **a.** His Will
T-10 ....... V.6:2 knowing that you could not sin **a.** Him.
T-11 ........ II.5:6 you have allied yourself **a.** Him. Whatever
T-11 ...... IV.2:4 without the intervention of God **a.** it, and
T-11 ..... V.18:5 you have evoked false witnesses **a.** him. If
T-11 ...... VI.3:2 it is because you are interpreting **a.** it, and
T-11 .... VIII.4:3 make, and do not defend yourself **a.** truth
T-11 . VIII.12:4 of God's Son **a.** himself and perceive no
T-12 ......... I.2:5 pitting one level within it **a.** another.
T-12 ....... I.10:1 than to recognize, in every defense **a.** it,
T-12 ....... II.9:6 them, for to lay aside means to judge **a.**. If
T-12 ...... III.9:4 You still cannot will **a.** Him, and that is
T-12 ....... V.7:4 the learning this strange curriculum is **a.**.
T-12 ....... V.7:7 the curriculum you have chosen is **a.** love,
T-12 ..... V.7:10 Yet your mind speaks **a.** your learning as
T-12 ..... V.7:10 as your learning speaks **a.** your mind, and
T-12 ..... V.7:10 so you fight **a.** all learning and succeed,
T-12 .. VII.12:8 You will judge **a.** yourself, but He will
T-13 ........ II.4:5 for the ego cannot protect you **a.** truth,
T-13 ...... VI.7:2 Would you, then, hold the past **a.** them?
T-13 .. VII.11:6 serve to tighten up your world **a.** the light,
T-13 ...... X.12:1 illusion that you have ever held **a.** him has
T-13 ...... XI.7:3 not prevail **a.** the peace God wills for you.
T-14 ...... III.3:3 to it, you are deciding **a.** your happiness,
T-14 ...... III.5:5 it and cherishes it by holding it **a.** you.
T-14 .... III.12:3 Do not decide **a.** it, for being of Him it
T-14 .... III.13:5 and **a.** this strange distortion of the purity
T-14 .... III.14:4 and will decide **a.** your peace as surely as
T-14 .... III.15:1 is to evaluate his Father and judge **a.** Him.
T-14 ...... IV.5:1 have decided **a.** your function in Heaven,
T-14 ...... IV.5:2 only to decide **a.** deciding what you want,
T-14 ..... VII.5:2 Truth does not struggle **a.** ignorance, and
T-14 ..... VII.5:6 of truth only because you made them **a.** it
T-14 .... XI.11:4 and do not raise your voice **a.** Him. For
T-14 .... XI.15:5 that nothing will prevail **a.** your peace.
T-15 ...... III.4:4 your striving must be directed **a.** littleness
T-15 ...... III.6:2 side **a.** Him in what He wills for you.
T-15 ...... IV.9:8 then, try only to be vigilant **a.** deception,
T-15 ....... V.6:4 them, but you have also judged **a.** both.
T-15 ....... V.6:5 Yet you had judged **a.** yourself first, or
T-16 ........ II.8:1 Do not interpret **a.** God's Love, for you
T-16 ...... IV.2:1 The symbols of hate **a.** the symbols of
T-16 ...... IV.3:3 by attempting to build barricades **a.** it,
T-16 .... IV.4:10 When the barricades **a.** it are broken, fear
T-16 ...... IV.6:1 within yourself that you have built **a.** it. It
T-16 ....... V.2:1 to make guilty is always directed **a.** God.
T-16 ..... VII.3:5 For the ego holds the past **a.** you, and in
T-16 ..... VII.6:1 A. the ego's insane notion of salvation
T-16 ..... VII.9:1 There is nothing you can hold **a.** reality.
T-16 ..... VII.9:2 illusions you have held **a.** your brothers.
T-16 ..... VII.9:4 God holds nothing **a.** anyone, for He is
T-17 ...... III.8:1 alliance with the ego **a.** the present. For
T-17 ..... IV.10:2 do need defense **a.** your acceptance of the
T-17 ...... VI.5:6 truly, for deception cannot prevail **a.** you.
T-17 .. VII.3:10 used ***a.*** truth will always destroy faith. If
T-17 ..... VII.6:3 and used your faithlessness **a.** him. No
T-17 ..... VII.8:1 think you hold **a.** your brother what he
T-17 ..... VII.8:3 is not his past but yours you hold **a.** him.
T-17 .. VII.10:6 Use not your faithlessness **a.** it, for it calls
T-17 .... VIII.2:7 But rise you not **a.** it, for against your
T-17 .... VIII.2:7 it, for **a.** your opposition it cannot come.
T-17 .... VIII.5:3 you let yourself use faithlessness **a.** him.
T-18 ...... II.5:15 They are your protest **a.** reality, and your
T-18 ...... VI.6:8 place of God's Son, and turning it **a.** him.
T-18 ..... VII.4:7 to reach Atonement by fighting **a.** sin.
T-18 ..... VII.5:7 and fight **a.** the giving in to sin; when the
T-18 ..... VII.6:8 or of struggle **a.** temptation.
T-18 .... VIII.3:2 of dust it bids you fight **a.** the universe.
T-18 .... VIII.3:5 holding itself apart **a.** the universe. The
T-18 . VIII.12:2 all the barriers you hold **a.** your brother.
T-18 ...... IX.8:2 yourself **a.** them in traveling through. Let
T-19 ......... I.3:5 becomes its weapon, used **a.** this Purpose,
T-19 ........ II.3:1 turn the power of his mind **a.** himself. But
T-19 ...... III.7:5 God created holy could not prevail **a.** it,
T-19 .... III.10:3 not prevail **a.** a union Heaven has smiled
T19 .IV.A.2:10 remnant of attack you cherish still **a.** your
T19 .... IV.A.5:6 Guilt can raise no real barriers **a.** it. And
T19 .... IV.C.3:2 to madness and set **a.** the peace of Heaven
T19 .... IV.C.8:1 He created **a.** the ego's savage wish to kill.
T19 .. IV.D.7:4 thoughts that come to you **a.** your will. It
T19 .. IV.D.7:6 of seeming death can stand **a.** your will.
T19 IV.D.13:2 Would you hold his sins **a.** him, or accept
T19 IV.D.16:6 Press it not like thorns **a.** his brow, nor
T-20 ........ II.4:3 who offers thorns to anyone is **a.** me still,
T-20 ...... III.1:3 calls upon defenses to uphold it **a.** reality.
T-20 .... IV.8:10 God's guarantee will hold **a.** all obstacles,
T-20 ...... VI.8:9 this mad idea **a.** reality but for an instant?
T-20 . VIII.10:3 you saw at all or merely judged **a.**. Vision
T-21 ........ II.1:5 choose **a.** it now it will not be because it is
T-21 ........ II.6:5 will, a mad revolt **a.** what must forever be.
T-21 ........ V.9:5 can serve to open doors you closed **a.** it.
T-21 ...... VI.4:5 you would defend the body **a.** your reason
T-21 ..... VII.1:8 And you are for him or **a.** him; either you
T-21 ..... VII.2:5 and raising up their helplessness **a.** him.
T-21 ..... VII.4:6 And as it runs it turns **a.** itself, thinking it
T-21 .. VII.12:5 No one decides **a.** his happiness, but he
T-21 .. VII.12:6 attached to nothing, he does decide **a.** it.
T-22 ........ II.4:4 One illusion cherished and defended **a.**
T-22 ...... III.9:4 other what impels him to sin **a.** his will.
T-22 ........ V.1:4 reality. They go **a.** what must be true. The
T-22 ........ V.2:2 Always to justify what goes **a.** the truth,
T-22 ........ V.2:7 offers must be defended **a.** and sacrificed.
T-22 ........ V.3:6 your Father Whom you would defend **a.**.
T-23 ............. h THE WAR A. YOURSELF
T-23 ....... in.2:1 indeed becomes this war **a.** yourself!
T-23 ....... in.2:3 And you will fight **a.** it, and try to weaken
T-23 ......... I.1:2 for a mind at war **a.** itself remembers not
T-23 ......... I.2:1 a war **a.** yourself would be a war on God?
T-23 ......... I.4:1 the war **a.** yourself is almost over. The
T-23 ......... I.5:1 The war **a.** yourself was undertaken to
T-23 ......... I.6:1 The war **a.** yourself is but the battle of
T-23 ......... I.7:3 Truth does not fight **a.** illusions, nor do
T-23 ......... I.7:3 do illusions fight **a.** the truth. Illusions
T-23 ...... III.5:4 savage purpose is directed **a.** themselves?
T-23 ...... III.6:9 of protection stands **a.** the faith in murder
T-23 ...... IV.1:7 not asked to fight **a.** your wish to murder.
T-24 ......... I.4:7 On its behalf they fight **a.** the universe,
T-24 ......... I.8:2 demand your brother bow to it **a.** his will.
T-24 ......... I.9:1 special must defend illusions **a.** the truth.
T-24 ......... I.9:3 while it is this you would defend **a.** him.
T-24 ......... I.9:5 ground of battle which you wage **a.** him.
T-24 ........ II.1:6 A. the littleness you see in him you stand
T-24 ........ II.4:2 defend your specialness **a.** the truth of
T-24 ........ II.6:4 the sins he held in its defense **a.** himself,
T-24 ...... III.2:2 all your puny might **a.** the Will of God.
T-24 ...... III.2:3 And thus it stands **a.** yourself; *your* enemy,
T-24 .... VI.10:8 Would you decide **a.** the holiness He sees?
T-24 .... VI.11:3 itself, with every entry shut **a.** intrusion,
T-24 .... VI.11:3 and every window barred **a.** the light.
T-24 .... VI.13:2 judging **a.** the Christ and setting forth for

T-25.......V.4:8 If you decide **a.** his proper function, the
T-25.......V.6:1 **A.** the hatred that the Son of God may
T-25......VI.7:5 employ on his behalf, and not **a.** himself.
T-25.....VII.2:7 What wish can rise **a.** His Will, and be
T-25.....VII.6:1 that you believe **a.** this one requirement,
T-25... VIII.1:3 He wrested it from you **a.** your will. And
T-25... VIII.2:5 still **a.** himself would find impossible.
T-25. VIII.10:6 come to plead for him, and not **a.** his life?
T-25......IX.2:8 He does not fight **a.** His Son's reluctance
T-26...VII.6:11 wish that seems to go **a.** His Will has no
T-27......II.3:11 would hold **a.** himself or any living thing.
T-27......VI.4:1 Witness sees no witnesses **a.** the body.
T-27.....VII.1:3 of what brought on the attack **a.** himself,
T-28.........I.6:7 so it is a way to hold the past **a.** the now.
T-28......I.10:3 for what was causeless and **a.** His Will.
T-28.......II.8:3 But what he made has turned **a.** him,
T-28....VII.7:3 blow upon it and the rain will beat **a.** it,
T-29....VII.9:8 you must protect **a.** the light of truth. And
T-29... VIII.2:3 massed **a.** your confidence and peace of
T-29. VIII.8:13 more. And it is this that is **a.** God's Will.
T-29......IX.5:2 toys have turned **a.** the child who thought
T-29......IX.5:7 can turn **a.** him for his treachery to them.
T-30.........I.9:3 This works **a.** the sense of opposition, and
T-30......I.12:6 Nor will you fight **a.** it, for you see that it
T-30.....II.2:10 Him is to make a choice **a.** yourself, and
T-30....IV.5:12 God's Son needs no defense **a.** his dreams
T-31.......II.1:2 nor fought **a.** to lose to truth's appeal.
T-31.......II.1:4 an ancient battle being waged **a.** the truth
T-31......IV.6:2 fight **a.** this step is to defeat your purpose
T-31......VI.5:1 will stand **a.** the truth of what you are.
T-31...VII.13:7 and dear **a.** the vision of the Christ in you.
T-31...VII.14:1 **a.** temptation, then, remembering that it
T-31...VII.14:5 Can this be difficult to choose ***a.?*** Consider
T-31... VIII.4:1 images you make cannot prevail **a.** what
W-pI.......7.3:2 a cup, feeling the rim of a cup **a.** your lips,
W-pI.....26.1:6 own best interests, rather than **a.** them.
W-pI.....52.2:4 I hold the past **a.** everyone and everything
W-pI.....52.3:5 that I am trying to use time **a.** God. Let
W-pI.....53.5:6 images I have made cannot prevail **a.** Him
W-pI.....68.5:1 those **a.** whom you hold what you regard
W-pI.....68.5:3 **a.** those you like and even think you love.
W-pI.....68.5:4 that there is no one **a.** whom you do not
W-pI.....68.7:1 any thought of grievance arises **a.** anyone,
W-pI.....69.9:8 are tempted to hold anything **a.** anyone
W-pI.....72.7:4 your grievances **a.** Him and His creation,
W-pI.....73.7:7 will is free, and nothing can prevail **a.** it.
W-pI.....78.5:3 the grievances that you have held **a.** him,
W-pI.....89.2:3 *Let me not hold a grievance* ***a.*** *you, [name],*
W-pI.....95.6:3 who remain heavily defended **a.** learning.
W-pI.....95.9:4 you would defend illusions **a.** the truth.
W-pI.....96.5:3 attacked by armies massed **a.** itself and
W-pI.....97.8:4 Use them **a.** temptation, and escape its
W-pI...100.2:2 Why should you choose to go **a.** His Will?
W-pI...135.3:5 what you defend, and how, and **a.** what?
W-pI.135.17:1 plans you undertake to make **a.** the truth.
W-pI.135.26:8 *Son of God needs no defense* ***a.*** *the truth of*
W-pI......136.h Sickness is a defense **a.** the truth.
W-pI.136.13:4 defense you made **a.** the truth. Yet what
W-pI.136.15:6 *Sickness is a defense* ***a.*** *the truth. I will accept*
W-pI.136.19:2 or make plans **a.** uncertainties to come,
W-pI.136.20:4 *Sickness is a defense* ***a.*** *the truth. But I am*
W-pI...137.8:2 that dreams will not prevail **a.** the truth.
W-pI...138.8:2 to be safe, and magically armored **a.** truth
W-pI...139.4:4 lives; has judged **a.** it and denied its worth
W-pI...148.2:1 (136) Sickness is a defense **a.** the truth.
W-pI.153.14:4 defense **a.** a vengeance he can not escape,
W-pI...160.1:6 he is what he is not, and judge **a.** himself?
W-pI...161.1:1 differently, and take a stand **a.** our anger,
W-pI...166.3:2 is to be pressed to treachery **a.** himself.
W-pI...166.7:2 the self you savagely defend **a.** all reason,
W-pI...169.3:5 It is not shut tight **a.** God's Voice. It has
W-pI...170.2:6 *You make what you defend* ***a.****, and by your*
W-pI...170.2:6 *own defense* ***a.*** *it is it real and inescapable.*
W-pI...170.3:3 your defense **a.** the threat of what you
W-pI...181.5:3 concerns are but defenses **a.** present
W-pI.182.11:1 you raised **a.** an enemy without existence.
W-pI...184.4:1 vision, purposefully set **a.** the given truth.
W-pI...190.9:4 of judgment that you hold **a.** your throat,
W-pI...191.3:2 tiny particle of dust **a.** the legions of your
W-pI...192.7:4 thoughts, our eyes shut tight **a.** the light;
W-pI...195.7:1 heads **a.** our shoulders as they rest a while
W-pI...197.1:1 belief in outside force pitted **a.** your own.
W-pI...198.1:4 for yourself can be now used **a.** you, till
W-pII..268.1:1 *be Your critic, Lord, today, and judge* ***a.*** *You.*
W-pII......8.3:3 and what is there that it would judge **a.**?
W-pII..311.1:1 made to be a weapon used **a.** the truth. It
W-pII..311.1:2 It separates what it is being used **a.**, and
W-pII..311.1:6 the judgments we have made **a.** ourselves,
W-pII.....347.h is The weapon I would use **a.** myself, To
W-pII..347.1:1 *Father, I want what goes* ***a.*** *my will, and do*
M-4 ......VI.1:2 no dreams that need defense **a.** the truth.
M-4 .......X.1:3 shuts the mind **a.** God's Teacher, so open-
M-5 .......II.2:4 If he decides **a.** recovery, he will not be
M-8 ...........2:6 the mind revolts **a.** truth and gives itself
M-13 .........8:3 Decide **a.** Him, and you choose nothing,
M-14 .......3:11 It goes **a.** all the thinking of the world, but
M-17 .........6:7 not remember the impossible odds **a.** you
M-17 .........8:5 an intense white light **a.** a black horizon,
C-in ...........2:3 recognizing that it is a defense **a.** truth in
P-1.............4:5 will fight **a.** his freedom because he thinks
P-2...........I.3:3 Holy Spirit fight **a.** the intrusions of the
P-2.........II.3:5 all its forces **a.** this one awareness, for in it
P-2........IV.1:3 and again, **a.** creation and its Creator. It is
P-2........IV.6:8 circle closed **a.** the "inroads" of salvation.
P-2.......VII.5:6 tiny self of one alone **a.** the universe able
P-3.........II.5:2 **a.** the day when they can recognize that
P-3......III.5:11 Where God's Son turns **a.** himself, he can
S-1.........V.1:3 that thought it was alone and stood **a.** the
S-3........IV.6:5 a heavy heart made hard **a.** the love that is

## age 2
*See also* age-old

T-31......III.5:1 evil, sickness and attack; of pain and **a.**, of
W-pI.....56.1:3 loss, **a.** and death seem to threaten me.

## age-old 1
M-18 .........1:7 **a.** impossible dream in but another form.

## ageless 1
T19..IV.C.10:6 The miracle of life is **a.**, born in time but

## agent 1
C-1............1:1 to represent the activating **a.** of spirit,

## agents 3
T-2........IV.4:3 attempt to heal it through non-creative **a.**.
T-2........IV.4:4 of such **a.** for corrective purposes is evil.
M-5 .......II.2:8 Special **a.** seem to be ministering to him,

## aggrandizement
*See* self-aggrandizement

## aging 2
M-27 .........1:2 madness to think of life as being born, **a.**,
S-3...........I.2:2 pain and **a.** and the mark of death upon it

## ago 14
T19. IV.A.16:4 as long **a.** I promised and promise still.
T-21.........I.7:5 you knew so long **a.** and held more dear
T-26.......V.4:3 upon you saw but for an instant, long **a.**,
T-26.......V.4:5 so long **a.** that it is hard indeed to hold it
T-26.......V.5:4 So very long **a.**, for such a tiny interval of
T-26.......V.9:1 has been so long **a.** corrected and undone.
T-26......V.13:3 gone by long **a.** that cannot be relived.
T-26.....V.14:4 again a journey that was over long **a.**.
T-28.........I.1:6 This world was over long **a.**. The thoughts
M-2 ...........2:7 In time this happened very long **a.**. In
M-2 ...........3:2 happened long **a.** seems to be happening
M-2 ...........3:4 and understood and long **a.** passed by is
C-ep...........2:5 Long **a.** the end was written in the stars
C-ep...........3:2 journey long **a.** begun that but seems new

## agony 7
T-6...........I.7:6 during the so-called "**a.** in the garden,"
T19. IV.D.18:4 in the garden of seeming **a.** and death. So
T-31....VIII.5:6 as natural as fear and **a.** appeared to be
W-pI...191.6:5 with the world twisting in **a.** because your
W-pI...200.1:3 the **a.** of yet more bitter disappointments,
W-pII .311.1:6 for it. He will relieve us of the **a.** of all the
S-3........III.3:4 the mind that suffers from the **a.** of doubt

## agree 10
T-19........II.8:3 Perhaps you would be tempted to **a.** with
T-24.......V.9:4 doubts, if you **a.** that He is One with you,
T-28.......VI.5:3 Unless you both **a.** that is your wish, it
T-29.........I.4:6 you and he **a.** to meet from time to time,
T-30.......I.16:2 adviser must **a.** on what you want before
W-pI...159.1:3 Here the laws of Heaven and the world **a.**.
W-pI...163.5:4 while all the while its worshippers **a.**, and
W-pI...185.2:9 should any two **a.** these words express the
M-8 ...........5:3 Will he **a.** more quickly to the unreality of
M-21 .........1:5 are contradictory; sometimes they **a.**. It

## agreeable 1
P-2........VI.3:3 task is to make **a.** whatever is called on,

## agreed 8
T-4..........II.5:5 you have **a.** to cooperate in the effort to
T-17.......V.5:8 serves the purpose they have **a.** to meet.
T-18......III.4:2 the darkness that you **a.** to leave with me?
T-18......III.5:5 as surely as you **a.** to take your brother's.
T19..IV.B.4:11 When you **a.** to join your brother, you
T19... IV.D.4:6 you have **a.** never to let the fear of God be
T-29.........I.3:9 was a point you both **a.** to keep intact.
T-30...VII.6:11 No one has **a.** with you on what it means.

## agreeing 2
T-9.......VII.4:9 that you are **a.** with the ego's evaluation
T-12......III.3:2 If he attacks, you are **a.** with this belief;

## agreement 11
T-6......V.C.9:9 must be in **a.** about what they believe.
T-25.....VII.4:3 **a.** of their thought that makes the Son a
T-28.........III.h The **A.** to Join
T-28.......III.2:3 If you withhold **a.** and accept the part you
T-28......VI.5:2 **a.** with another's secret wish to be apart
T-28......VI.6:1 Let this be your **a.** with each one; that
T-30.......I.16:3 this **a.** that permits all things to happen.
T-30.....VII.5:6 **a.** makes interpretation stabilize and last.
W-pI.....70.5:3 for today, we are really in **a.** with God. He
M-1 ...........1:6 entered an **a.** with God even if he does not
M-4 ........II.1:6 word; and no word lacks **a.** with another.

## agrees 2
T-28......III.2:1 another mind **a.** that they are separate.
M-4 ......VI.1:8 teacher of God finally **a.** to look past them

## ahead 23
T-2..........II.6:4 free yourself from the past as you go **a.**. It
T-22......IV.1:1 road is quite apparent, you cannot go **a.**.
T-22......IV.1:3 For now if you go straight **a.**, the way you
T-30.........I.1:5 each time you wake, will put you well **a.**.
T-30.........I.9:4 to let you go **a.** with just a few more steps
T-30.......V.9:3 lies **a.** is all you ever wanted in your heart.
T-31........II.9:3 bit **a.** would be a safer place for him to be.
T-31........II.9:4 and falling back when he would go **a.**? For
W-pI.....69.7:1 a sense of being lifted up and carried **a.**.
W-pI...121.3:1 weak and blustering, afraid to go **a.**,
W-pI.134.12:5 his foot to stride **a.** a star is left behind, to
W-pI...155.2:5 To let illusions walk **a.** of truth is madness
W-pI...155.6:4 Nor can the truth, which walks **a.** of you,

| | |
|---|---|
| W-pI...155.9:2 | you are tempted still to walk **a.** of truth, |
| W-pI...166.5:4 | lot but dwindles, as he goes **a.** to nowhere |
| W-pI...181.9:4 | We look neither **a.** nor backwards. We |
| W-pI...196.8:2 | From there we go **a.** quite rapidly. For |
| W-pII ....in.6:4 | We look **a.**, and fix our eyes upon the |
| W-pII .225.1:2 | *beloved, with fear behind and only peace* **a.**. |
| W-pII .325.1:6 | and help his brothers walk **a.** with him, |
| P-2........ III.1:1 | that he walks slightly **a.** of the patient, |
| P-2........ III.1:2 | for One should walk **a.** of him to give him |
| P-3......... II.8:4 | is reached another can be dimly seen **a.**. |

## Aid 1

*aid*

| | |
|---|---|
| T-31.....VII.3:5 | see without the **A.** that God has given you |

## aid 19

*Aid*

| | |
|---|---|
| T-6.........I.11:6 | serve as a good teaching **a.** to those whose |
| T-12....... V.7:4 | Every legitimate teaching **a.**, every real |
| T-15.........I.9:4 | as a teaching **a.** to happiness and peace. |
| T-16...... VI.3:2 | The holy instant is His most helpful **a.** in |
| T-27...... III.5:7 | No learning **a.** has use that can extend |
| T-27...... III.6:9 | place of every learning **a.** will merely *be.* |
| T-28...... III.2:3 | without your **a.** in letting it perceive itself |
| T-28..... VII.3:6 | but merely as an **a.** to help you reach the |
| W-pI.....30.5:3 | To **a.** in helping you to become more |
| W-pI.131.14:2 | and through His **a.** slip effortlessly past it, |
| W-pI...192.4:3 | as what it is; a simple teaching **a.**, to be |
| WpI rVI.in.6:5 | or specific thoughts to **a.** in practicing. |
| M-5 ..... II.2:12 | merely rise up without their **a.** and say, "I |
| M-17 .........2:7 | of God gives to those who need his **a.**? |
| P-1.............1:2 | Its aim is to **a.** the patient in abandoning |
| P-2......... II.9:6 | an **a.** in helping him to see that this is so? |
| P-2......... V.5:1 | A brother seeking **a.** can bring us gifts |
| S-3.........in.1:2 | Forgiveness' witness and an **a.** to prayer, a |
| S-3........ IV.2:1 | As witness to forgiveness, **a.** to prayer, |

## aids 11

| | |
|---|---|
| T-1......... V.1:1 | that both are learning **a.** for facilitating a |
| T-12....... V.6:5 | failed to learn what learning **a.** are for? |
| T-12....... V.6:7 | If they could interpret the **a.** correctly, |
| T-13...... XI.6:3 | and differences are necessary teaching **a.**, |
| T-27...... III.5:6 | until the time when **a.** are meaningless |
| T-27...... III.6:8 | you need no pictures and no learning **a.**. |
| WpI.rV.in12:1 | Yet are the words but **a.**, and to be used, |
| M-1 ...........3:3 | So do the particular teaching **a.** involved. |
| M-25 .........3:2 | direction, they are valuable teaching **a.**. |
| P-2.......... II.5:1 | Different teaching **a.** appeal to different |
| S-3.........in.1:1 | Prayer has both **a.** and witnesses which |

## aim 74

| | |
|---|---|
| T-in ...........1:6 | *does not* **a.** *at teaching the meaning of love,* |
| T-in ...........1:7 | *It does* **a.**, *however, at removing the blocks* |
| T-2........ IV.5:6 | The whole **a.** of the miracle is to raise the |
| T-2......VIII.3:4 | **a.** of the Last Judgment is to restore right- |
| T-4.........I.13:7 | who share my **a.** of healing the mind. |
| T-8.....VIII.5:4 | Its sole **a.** is to lose sight of the function of |
| T-8........ IX.1:5 | that the body is the proper **a.** of healing. |
| T-12....... V.7:5 | the **a.** of your teaching is to defeat itself, |
| T-12....... V.7:8 | split that makes its primary **a.** believable. |
| T-13.........I.1:1 | whose ultimate **a.** is to make themselves |
| T-14....... V.6:3 | which has one **a.** however it is taught. |
| T-14..... V.10:6 | Crucifixion is always the ego's **a.**. It sees |
| T-17....... IV.3:3 | **a.** of occupying your mind so completely |
| T-18..... VII.4:5 | in time, but it does **a.** at saving time. You |
| T-24..... VII.7:5 | uncertain, or one wish with a divided **a.**. |
| T-25.........I.6:1 | **a.** of specialness can be corrected where |
| T-25...... IV.1:6 | It is not the **a.**, as such, that varies. Yet it |
| T-25...... IV.1:7 | way in which the **a.** is seen that makes the |
| T-25...... IV.1:7 | hope of change unless the **a.** is changed. |
| T-25...... IV.5:5 | What **a.** can supersede the Will of God |
| T-25....... V.1:3 | the cause and **a.** and justifier of the other. |
| T-25...... VI.3:6 | no **a.** which only they can perfectly fulfill. |
| T-26...... III.5:5 | set. It will not go beyond this **a.**. Its only |
| T-27...... III.5:8 | When its **a.** has been accomplished it is |
| T-28 ........I.3:7 | use. They have no dedication and no **a.**. |
| T-29 ..... VI.4:5 | Forgiveness does not **a.** at keeping time, |
| T-30 ...... V.1:2 | for the escape from guilt becomes its **a.**. |
| T-30 .... VII.1:5 | And no situation can affect its **a.**, but |
| T-30 .... VII.1:6 | For only if its **a.** could change with every |
| T-31 .... IV.10:6 | that there could be a road with such an **a.**! |
| T-31 ...... V.6:4 | to him, unwavering and deadly in its **a.**. It |
| T-31 ...... V.8:2 | **a.** of teaching you this concept of yourself, |
| W-in.......... 7:1 | overall **a.** of the exercises is to increase |
| W-pI....... 4.3:2 | The **a.** here is to train you in the first steps |
| W-pI....... 9.1:7 | indeed be circular to **a.** at understanding, |
| W-pI... 105.4:5 | its **a.** of giving everything it has away, |
| WpI..rIII.in2:4 | Rituals are not our **a.**, and would defeat |
| W-pI. 126.11:1 | **a.** which makes this day of special value to |
| W-pI. 135.17:2 | Their **a.** is to select what you approve, and |
| W-pI... 136.2:4 | The **a.** of all defenses is to keep the truth |
| W-pI... 136.5:6 | They **a.** at doing this, and it is this they do |
| W-pI. 136.15:1 | This is our **a.** today. And we will give a |
| W-pI... 138.3:2 | the **a.** of effort and expenditure of time. |
| W-pI. 139.12:1 | that would distract us from our holy **a.**. |
| WpI. rIV.in1:3 | Such is our **a.** for this review, and for the |
| W-pI. 193.10:6 | what time you can to serve its proper **a.**, |
| W-pI... 205.1:3 | *is my one goal; the* **a.** *of all my living here, the* |
| W-pII ..... 1.2:4 | the **a.** that it has chosen as its wanted goal |
| W-pII ..... 3.3:3 | Their **a.** is to fulfill the purpose which the |
| W-pII ..... 4.2:4 | the body serves a different **a.** for striving. |
| W-pII ..... 4.2:5 | for now is chosen by the **a.** the mind has |
| W-pII ..... 4.2:6 | Truth can be its **a.** as well as lies. The |
| W-pII . 258.1:5 | We have no **a.** but to remember Him. |
| W-pII . 308.1:1 | of time in such a way that I defeat my **a.**. |
| W-pII . 318.1:2 | the parts have but one purpose and one **a.** |
| W-pII . 319.2:3 | *What* **a.** *but the salvation of the world could* |
| W-pII ... 14.5:2 | changed about the **a.** for which we came, |
| WfI ........in.3:2 | us the **a.** is given to forgive the world. It is |
| M-4 ......X.2:12 | Forgiveness is its single **a.**, at which all |
| M-10 ......... 3:1 | The **a.** of our curriculum, unlike the goal |
| M-13 ......... 6:2 | and it is the course's **a.** to set him free. But |
| M-17 ......... 3:5 | single **a.** of the teacher turns the divided |
| P-1............. 1:2 | Its **a.** is to aid the patient in abandoning |
| P-1............. 2:3 | transcendent **a.** can there be than to recall |
| P-2.........in.2:3 | **a.** is to be able to retain their self-concept |
| P-2..........II.7:3 | he can best reach the **a.** it sets for him. |
| P-2......... III.2:2 | The **a.** of the process, therefore, is to |
| P-2....... VII.2:2 | prayer, and healing is its **a.** and its result. |
| P-2....... VII.5:1 | passing of guilt is the true **a.** of therapy |
| P-2....... VII.5:1 | therapy and the obvious **a.** of forgiveness. |
| P-3..........II.2:4 | the **a.** of making the therapist a judge. |
| S-1........ IV.3:5 | The **a.** of prayer is to release the present |
| S-2..........II.4:3 | Here must the **a.** be clearly seen, for this |
| S-3........ III.3:1 | **a.** of healing as the world conceives of it. |

## aimed 5

| | |
|---|---|
| T-12 .....II.10:1 | and carefully planned program **a.** at |
| T-16 .... V.12:2 | **a.** at raising the form to take the place of |
| T-18 .... VII.4:9 | **a.** at detachment from the body necessary |
| T-31 ...... V.8:4 | be unlearned except by lessons **a.** to teach |
| W-pI. 135.24:1 | All your defenses have been **a.** at not |

## aiming 1

| | |
|---|---|
| T-17 ..... IV.2:6 | rather than **a.** to make a substitute for it. |

## aimless 2

| | |
|---|---|
| T19....IV.A.7:4 | Now it is **a.**, wandering pointlessly, |
| W-pI... 122.7:2 | Do not turn away in **a.** wandering again. |

## aimlessly 3

| | |
|---|---|
| T19....IV.A.7:2 | this little wish, uprooted and floating **a.**, |
| T-28 .... VI.2:5 | follow **a.** the path on which it has been set |
| T-29 .... VII.2:5 | And thus he wanders **a.** about, in search |

## aimlessness 1

| | |
|---|---|
| T-17 ...... V.8:3 | A sense of **a.** will come to haunt you, and |

## aims 17

| | |
|---|---|
| T-1 ....... III.9:4 | miracle **a.** at restoring the awareness of |
| T-1 ....... III.9:4 | laws that govern the error it **a.** to correct. |
| T-6 ..... IV.12:4 | Teaching **a.** at change, but God created |
| T-8 ..........I.4:3 | If learning **a.** at change, and that is always |
| T-15 ........I.4:5 | ego **a.** at death and dissolution as an end, |
| T-15 ......I.4:12 | its contradictory **a.** together so that they |
| T-25 .. VII.13:1 | because your **a.** can not be reconciled. |
| T-27 .......V.8:8 | All learning **a.** at transfer, which becomes |
| T-31 ... IV.11:1 | all senseless journeys and all goal-less **a.**. |
| W-pI .. 135.7:3 | to exalted **a.** which it cannot accomplish. |
| W-pI .. 155.7:2 | defeat, and **a.** that will remain impossible. |
| W-pII . 258.1:1 | minds to overlook all little senseless **a.**, |
| W-pII . 319.1:4 | it must seek for **a.** which are curtailed and |
| M-10 ......... 1:3 | and his education **a.** at strengthening the |
| M-24 ......... 4:1 | that this course **a.** at a complete reversal |
| C-in ........... 1:6 | of overlooking at which the course **a.**. |
| P-2...........I.3:2 | psychotherapy because it restricts its **a.**. |

## air 5

| | |
|---|---|
| W-pI .. 156.3:3 | to grow with roots suspended in the **a.**. |
| W-pI .. 161.8:4 | claws the **a.** in frantic hope it can reach to |
| W-pI .. 182.5:4 | the holy **a.** that fills His Father's house. |
| W-pII . 222.1:2 | of life, the life within, the **a.** I breathe, the |
| S-3..........II.3:4 | go in peace to freer **a.** and gentler climate, |

## airplane 1

| | |
|---|---|
| W-pI .... 14.4:6 | *God did not create that* **a.** *crash, and so it is* |

## alarm 1

| | |
|---|---|
| W-pI .. 167.2:5 | It is the **a.** to which you give response of |

## alcove 1

| | |
|---|---|
| T-29 ... VIII.7:4 | a dismal **a.** separated off from what is |

## alert 5

| | |
|---|---|
| T-1 .........II.5:1 | and **a.** to the revelation-readiness of my |
| T-17 ..... IV.5:1 | The ego is always **a.** to threat, and the |
| W-pI .. 71.10:2 | Be **a.** to all temptation to hold grievances |
| W-pI 132.15:4 | Then merely rest, **a.** but with no strain, |
| P-2........ VI.1:3 | its loving protection and **a.** defense, -- all |

## alertness 2

| | |
|---|---|
| T-9 ........ III.1:1 | **a.** of the ego to the errors of other egos is |
| W-pI .... 74.5:4 | a deep sense of joy and an increased **a.**, |

## alien 60

*See also* ego-alien

| | |
|---|---|
| T-3 .........V.9:5 | entirely **a.** to the world's thinking. The |
| T-5 ..........I.1:9 | this kind of thinking is totally **a.** to having |
| T-6 ....... IV.4:5 | something **a.** to itself in your mind, the |
| T-8 ..........I.3:8 | a condition so **a.** to the Kingdom that you |
| T-9 ..........I.3:7 | attempting to force an **a.** will upon you. |
| T-9 ...........I.6:1 | impossible to communicate in **a.** tongues. |
| T-11 .......II.5:2 | but His Voice grows faint in **a.** company. |
| T-13 ... III.10:3 | not give it for the request was **a.** to Him, |
| T-14 .......II.2:5 | Nothing is so **a.** to you as the simple truth |
| T-14 ..... VI.7:2 | perceives the meaning in your **a.** language |
| T-15 ..... XI.2:7 | no thought **a.** to His Oneness can abide |
| T-16 ..... III.1:3 | how **a.** it is to what you thought you knew |
| T-20 .........I.4:5 | **a.** to you and yet your ancient Friend, lies |
| T-20 ..... IV.2:1 | where its results are **a.** and can no more |
| T-21 .......V.5:9 | Your reason's **a.** nature to the ego is proof |
| T-21 .......V.9:3 | Reason is **a.** to insanity, and those who |
| T-21 ... VIII.2:1 | condition quite **a.** to your understanding. |
| T-22 ........I.5:6 | What needs interpretation must be **a.**. |
| T-22 ........I.8:3 | For his will be no **a.** tongue. He will need |
| T-24 .......II.2:9 | To value specialness is to esteem an **a.** will |
| T-24 ..... III.5:2 | would have no separation, like an **a.** will, |
| T-24 .. VII.11:8 | son of man perceives an **a.** will and wishes |
| T-25 .......V.2:5 | something **a.** to yourself and "something |

T-25... VIII.5:5 Vengeance is a. to God's Mind *because* He
T-28....... II.4:1 dream in which you were an a. to yourself
T-28...... III.6:2 not destroy the a. will that He created not
T-28....... V.3:6 and walk upon an a. ground which your
T-31.........I.4:5 forgotten, and His Son an a. to himself, in
T-31.....VII.1:2 as yet too a. to your thinking to be helpful
W-pI.....29.4:2 with today's idea because of its wholly a.
W-pI.....29.4:3 order you impose is equally a. to reality.
W-pI.....73.9:2 will. It is not the purpose of an a. power,
W-pI.....81.4:4 *my will. I will not use this for an a. purpose.*
W-pI.....84.3:2 Grievances are completely a. to love.
W-pI.....84.3:5 Self. My Self thus becomes a. to me. I am
W-pI.....96.4:5 peace, and happiness is a. to its thoughts.
W-pI...126.1:1 completely a. to the ego and the thinking
W-pI...126.8:2 it is so a. to the thoughts to which you are
W-pI...131.8:5 an a. will upon God's single purpose. He
W-pI.134.13:3 is as a. to the world as is your own reality.
W-pI...160.1:4 your Self remains an a. to the part of you
W-pI...160.2:2 to him, while he is a. now who is at home.
W-pI...160.6:7 in, and took no a. thought to be Itself.
W-pI.166.10:4 not know about a plan so a. to His Will.
W-pI...167.6:4 What is a. to the mind does not exist,
W-pI...167.9:2 to assume an a. power which it does not
W-pI...170.3:2 within; an a. thought at war with you,
W-pI...170.3:3 an "enemy," an opposite; and fear, the a.,
W-pI...182.1:4 you of. Yet still you feel an a. here, from
W-pI...182.4:3 house, and knows that He is a. here. This
W-pI...182.7:5 lives an outcast in a world of a. thoughts.
W-pI.182.10:4 today. You are as much an a. here as He.
W-pI...184.5:2 to teach the mind a thousand a. names,
W-pI...188.1:5 bear the light in you are a. here as well.
W-pI...198.8:2 of any kind are strange and a. to the truth
W-pI...200.4:2 in a. forms that have no meaning to you,
W-pII..292.1:3 let an a. will appear to be opposing His.
M-4......VII.1:6 it is perhaps more a. to the thinking of the
P-2........IV.8:4 is a mockery so a. to God that it must be
P-2.......VII.7:7 a. to the truth and poor in wisdom,

### aligning 2

T-1........ I.36:1 a. your perceptions with truth as God
T-13......VI.4:8 Yet by doing so you are a. past and future,

### alignment 6

T-1........ I.30:1 of perception and show them in proper a.
T-2......... V.6:6 easily brought into a. with a mind that
T-6......... II.9:8 mind is not in perfect a. with the idea,
T-6....... II.13:4 This a. with light is unlimited, because it
T-6....... II.13:4 it is in a. with the light of the world. Each
T-18....... V.4:4 otherwise." The a. of means and purpose

### alike 25

T-1......... V.3:3 all His gifts are freely given to everyone a..
T-4.........I.1:2 and pupil are a. in the learning process.
T-8.........IV.6:3 me I will help you, knowing that we are a.
T-14....III.17:1 Whose equal Love is given equally to all a.
T-17....IV.16:8 holy instant shines a. on all relationships,
T-20..... II.10:3 chill of fear and withering blight of sin a..
T-24.........I.8:6 it teaches you you and your brother are a.
T-24.... II.10:3 You are a. to God as God is to Himself.
T-25.... II.10:6 He offers unto the Father and the Son a..
T-25......VI.7:7 and will remain in time and in eternity a..
T-25....IX.10:4 when it is offered to everyone a.. It is
T-27.........I.8:1 end a. within the termination of the grave
T-27......VI.2:6 for this, the witnesses of sin are all a.. Call
T-27......VI.4:9 Its pains and pleasures does He heal a.,
T-27...VII.12:2 of your brother and the world a.. Here is
W-pI.....26.8:4 to treat them all a. to whatever extent you
W-pI.....45.2:4 To share is to make a., or to make one.
W-pII..260.2:3 Sons are like each other, and a. to Him.
M-4............1:1 traits of God's teachers are not at all a..
M-4............1:2 They do not look a. to the body's eyes,
M-4............1:7 learning. In this respect they are all a..
M-17..........2:5 always come to teacher and to pupil a..
C-4............7:2 Gone is perception, false and true a..
P-2.........in.4:4 and therapists a. accept unrealistic goals
P-3........III.4:3 a right the therapist and patient share a..

### alive 26

T-2..... VIII.5:4 No one who lives in fear is really a.. Your
T-5.........in.2:2 to be wholly fearful and remain a., the
T-5......... II.1:6 it. God Himself keeps your will a. by
T-10......IV.8:2 Yet God has kept the spark a. so that the
T-11.......in.1:6 them. Nothing a. is Fatherless, for life is
T-14.....VII.4:5 them both a. and equal in their reality.
T-17....... II.5:4 His reason touches grows a. with beauty,
T-17.......III.5:7 yet there to come a. as the relationship is
T19....IV.C.4:2 to sin to feed upon and keep itself a.; a
T-20...... VI.5:3 and seeks for crumbs to keep itself a..
T-24...... VI.2:4 Nothing a. that is not part of Him, and
T-24...... VI.2:4 of Him, and nothing is but is a. in Him.
T-28.........I.5:8 associations made to keep the past a., the
T-29....... II.6:2 What you have given "life" is not a., and
T-29....... II.6:2 but your wish to be a. apart from life,
T-29....... II.6:2 wish to be alive apart from life, a. in death
T-29....... IX.3:3 an idol keep the dream a. and terrible, for
T-29....... IX.5:7 Yet do they keep his thoughts a. and real,
T-30...... VI.4:1 world employs to keep the sense of sin a..
W-pI.....17.3:2 anything that is really a. or really joyous.
W-pI...139.3:2 To be a. and not to know yourself is to
W-pI...139.3:3 and what but you can be a. instead? Who
W-pI...139.4:2 could never be a. at all unless he knew the
W-pI...163.7:2 God was once a. and somehow perished;
W-pI...189.1:7 anew, shining in innocence, a. with hope,
P-2......... V.1:5 are forces to be overcome to be a. at all.

### All 3

*all*
*See also* All-Loving

T-7.........IV.7:4 God is A. in all in a very literal sense. All
T-8.........IV.1:4 Yet He is A. in all. His peace is complete,
W-pII.... 12.2:2 beyond the Everywhere, apart from A., in

### all 3027

*All*
*See also* all-embracing, all-encompassed, all-encompassing, all-inclusive, all-inclusiveness

T-1...........I.1:3 They are a. the same. All expressions of
T-1...........I.1:4 same. A. expressions of love are maximal.
T-1...........I.4:1 A. miracles mean life, and God is the
T-1...........I.4:3 You will be told a. you need to know.
T-1...........I.9:2 Like a. expressions of love, which are
T-1.........I.19:2 Sonship is the sum of a. that God created.
T-1.........I.23:1 and place a. levels in true perspective.
T-1.........I.25:2 Atonement works a. the time and in all
T-1.........I.25:2 the time and in a. the dimensions of time.
T-1.........I.27:1 from God through me to a. my brothers.
T-1.........I.32:1 I inspire a. miracles, which are really
T-1.........I.48:2 it, having nothing to do with time at a..
T-1........ III.1:4 is the cancelling out of a. errors that you
T-1........ III.3:4 for the salvation or release of a. of God's
T-1........ III.5:7 undoes a. errors in this respect, and thus
T-1........ III.7:3 uniting a. creations with their Creator. As
T-1......... V.1:4 shell, but you cannot express nothing at a.
T-1......... V.3:1 a. talents will be shared by all the Sons of
T-1......... V.3:1 will be shared by a. the Sons of God. God
T-1......... V.3:3 A. His children have His total Love, and
T-1......... V.3:3 a. His gifts are freely given to everyone
T-1......... V.3:6 A. my brothers are special. If they believe
T-1......... V.6:3 Him. A. shallow roots must be uprooted,
T-1........ VI.1:7 There were no needs at a.. Needs arise
T-1........ VI.3:1 of perceiving levels at a. can be corrected.
T-1........ VI.5:1 A. aspects of fear are untrue because they
T-1........ VI.5:1 level, and therefore do not exist at a.. To
T-1.......VII.1:4 A. real pleasure comes from doing God's
T-1.......VII.4:2 A. learning involves attention and study
T-2...........I.2:8 because a. loving creation is freely given
T-2...........I.2:8 in which a. aspects are of the same order.
T-2...........I.3:2 of the serpent," a. he heard was untruth.
T-2...........I.3:4 so. A. that can literally disappear in the
T-2...........I.4:1 A. fear is ultimately reducible to the basic
T-2...........I.5:6 by a. expressions of lack of love. These
T-2......... II.1:8 and by endowing a. thoughts with equal
T-2....... II.1:14 It brings a. error into the light, and since
T-2......... II.3:6 and to bring them into a. your actions,
T-2..........II.7:2 a mistake a. the separated Sons of God
T-2......... III.1:7 that a temple is not a structure at a.. Its
T-2...... III.1:11 structure at a. because it is perfect vision.
T-2......... III.2:4 you the one effective defense against a.
T-2......... III.4:2 Atonement. A. solutions the physical eye
T-2......... III.4:4 the right defense it passes over a. others,
T-2......... III.5:3 not involve any effort at a. on their part.
T-2......... IV.1:7 A. healing is essentially the release from
T-2......... IV.2:1 plan is to undo error at a. levels. Sickness
T-2......... IV.2:3 a. mistakes must be corrected at the level
T-2......... IV.2:6 error, produces a. physical symptoms.
T-2......... IV.4:1 A. material means that you accept as
T-2......... V.4:4 A. forms of not-right-mindedness are the
T-2......... V.9:2 Like a. aspects of the belief in space and
T-2....V.A.12:2 essential. A. forms of healing rest on this
T-2....V.A.16:2 It has no element of judgment at a.. The
T-2......... VI.9:3 one remains fully aware of it a. the time.
T-2....... VI.9:14 A. thinking produces form at some level.
T-2..... VII.1:10 way. A. miracle workers need that kind of
T-2..... VII.3:14 A. fear is implicit in the second, and all
T-2..... VII.3:14 in the second, and a. love in the first. The
T-2..... VII.5:11 which a. compromise in this respect can
T-2....... VII.6:2 If a. His creations are His Sons, every one
T-2....... VII.6:5 a. the parts of the Sonship have returned.
T-3...........I.2:9 It is so essential that a. such thinking be
T-3...........I.7:9 that a. the other lessons I taught are true.
T-3.........I.7:11 released from a. errors if you believe this.
T-3..........II.1:4 They are a. true or all false. It is essential
T-3..........II.1:4 They are all true or a. false. It is essential
T-3..........II.3:7 This, then, is a. the innocent can see. They
T-3..........II.5:3 A. sense of separation disappears. The
T-3..........II.6:4 Truth overcomes a. error, and those who
T-3........ III.1:8 certainty because a. perception varies.
T-3...... III.1:10 is the affirmation of truth and beyond a.
T-3........ III.2:1 A. your difficulties stem from the fact
T-3........ III.3:4 fear inhibits the tendency to question at a.
T-3........ III.4:5 that perception is involved at a. removes
T-3........ IV.1:2 A. of your present functions are divided
T-3........ IV.1:6 a. conflict arises from the concept of levels
T-3........ IV.2:4 are, because that is a. you can be sure of.
T-3........ IV.7:7 but I can erase a. misperceptions from
T-3...... IV.7:12 be, "A. are called but few choose to listen.
T-3......... V.4:1 properly be directed to yourself at a.. You
T-3......... V.8:4 A. of it is equally true, and knowing any
T-3......... V.8:4 knowing any part of it is to know a. of it.
T-3......... V.8:7 It is a. one and has no separate parts. You
T-3....... V.10:3 anyone who perceives at a. needs healing.
T-3........ VI.3:4 A. uncertainty comes from the belief that
T-3........ VI.3:6 knowledge a. judgment is automatically
T-3........ VI.5:4 A. this makes you feel tired because it is
T-3........ VI.7:2 for a. of them: the authority problem.
T-3........ VI.7:3 This *is* "the root of a. evil." Every symptom
T-3........ VI.8:4 This is the fundamental error of a. those
T-3...... VI.8:10 even doubt whether you really exist at a..
T-3........ VI.9:1 Only those who give over a. desire to
T-3...... VI.10:4 A. fear comes ultimately, and sometimes
T-3....... VII.3:3 A. beliefs are real to the believer. The fruit
T-3....... VII.4:9 and a. your defenses are used to attack
T-3..... VII.6:11 truth can be known by a. those for whom
T-4...........I.5:3 because it goes against a. of its own laws.
T-4...........I.6:1 any situation, but spirit cannot clash at a..
T-4...........I.8:1 The ego tries to exploit a. situations into
T-4.........I.10:1 will withdraw a. protection from the ego,
T-4..........II.5:6 because a. attitudes are ego-based. This
T-4..........II.8:7 it; it merely cannot conceive of it at a..
T-4....... II.11:3 that *a.* perception is unnecessary. This
T-4..... II.11:10 will be, because it implies no change at a..
T-4........ III.3:4 A. it can offer is a sense of temporary
T-4......... V.1:1 A. things work together for good. There
T-4......... V.3:4 identifies so closely, makes no sense at a..
T-4......... V.6:3 just as it does with a. issues touching on
T-4......... V.6:7 In a. these diversionary tactics, however,
T-4........ VI.4:3 this, it denies a. truly natural impulses,
T-4........ VI.7:6 Love does not conquer a. things, but it
T-4........ VI.7:6 all things, but it does set a. things right.
T-4....... VII.2:6 which is really not abstract at a.. It merely
T-4....... VII.3:1 does not respond at a. to anything else.
T-4....... VII.4:5 total only by recognizing a. reality in the
T-4....... VII.5:1 God, Who encompasses a. being, created

T-4 VII.8:7 we are a. united in the joy of the Kingdom
T-5 I.1:7 getting is meaningless and giving is a..
T-5 I.1:12 A. of it is still yours although all of it has
T-5 I.1:12 still yours although a. of it has been given
T-5 I.4:6 and foremost that this Inspiration is for a.
T-5 I.7:1 the shared Inspiration of a. the Sonship,
T-5 II.9:2 only my decision that gave me a. power in
T-5 III.2:4 of yourself, as well as of a. His creations.
T-5 IV.5:1 done in many ways, above a. by example.
T-5 IV.6:1 Holy Spirit atones in a. of us by undoing,
T-5 IV.8:2 A. your past except its beauty is gone, and
T-5 IV.8:3 I have saved a. your kindnesses and every
T-5 V.2:12 the belief from which a. guilt really stems.
T-5 V.5:9 It tries to usurp a. the functions of God as
T-5 V.6:7 a decision. Together they constitute a. the
T-5 V.6:12 like God, you are not really thinking at a..
T-5 V.7:10 for the effects of a. your wrong thinking if
T-5 VI.1:2 A. the Sons of God are waiting for your
T-5 VII.1:6 you always that a. hope is yours because
T-5 VII.1:7 of His care for a. those He created by it.
T-5 VII.6:10 *Holy Spirit will undo a. the consequences of*
T-6 in.2:2 Everyone teaches, and teaches a. the time.
T-6 in.2:3 the moment you accept any premise at a.,
T-6 I.8:7 chosen to save them pain in a. respects,
T-6 I.10:6 led to demonstrate His way for a..
T-6 I.16:6 for a. behavior teaches the beliefs that
T-6 I.18:1 of the Sons of God is present a. the time,
T-6 I.18:3 that a. forms of rejection are meaningless.
T-6 II.8:2 A. His Thoughts are thus perfectly united
T-6 II.11:5 bringing a. of your perceptions into the
T-6 II.11:7 means that a. perception is guided by the
T-6 II.12:4 the Holy Spirit perceives is a. the same.
T-6 II.13:1 impartially can you recognize Him at a..
T-6 IV.3:4 answers truly He answers for a. time,
T-6 IV.5:2 is perhaps the strangest perception of a.,
T-6 IV.6:1 the one answer of the Holy Spirit to a. the
T-6 IV.6:8 the Kingdom and a. that you have created
T-6 V.A.h To Have, Give A. to All
T-6 V.A.h To Have, Give All to A.
T-6 V.A.1:6 to resolve conflict by not deciding at a..
T-6 V.A.5:10 only what each one can give to a.. He
T-6 V.A.5:13 with the lesson: *To have, give a. to all.*
T-6 V.A.5:13 with the lesson: *To have, give all to a..*
T-6 V.B.1:1 A. who believe in separation have a basic
T-6 V.B.2:1 A. good teachers realize that only
T-6 V.B.2:4 in the learner is a. that a teacher need do
T-6 V.B.3:2 first lesson was "To have, give a. to all." I
T-6 V.B.3:2 first lesson was "To have, give all to a.." I
T-6 V.C.4:9 teach you that you need not choose at a..
T-7 I.2:4 way can a. creative power extend outward
T-7 II.3:7 That form of the law is not adapted at a.,
T-7 II.5:2 original meaning in a. respects and in all
T-7 II.5:2 original meaning in all respects and in a.
T-7 II.5:7 inheritance and requires no learning at a.,
T-7 III.1:1 applies it to a. individuals in all situations
T-7 III.1:1 applies it to all individuals in a. situations
T-7 III.1:2 He maximizes a. efforts and all results. By
T-7 III.1:2 He maximizes all efforts and a. results. By
T-7 III.1:3 He teaches you that a. power is yours. Its
T-7 III.1:6 enable you to use it always and in a. ways.
T-7 III.3:2 recognize a. whom you see as brothers,
T-7 III.3:5 because a. your conflicts come from it. It
T-7 IV.2:9 else, as a. incorrect perception does.
T-7 IV.2:10 of conflict, as a. proper perception can.
T-7 IV.3:1 want to teach everyone a. it has learned,
T-7 IV.3:2 Therefore it does not really learn at a..
T-7 IV.3:5 A. you need do is make the effort to learn,
T-7 IV.3:8 then, they a. contribute to one result, and
T-7 IV.4:1 A. abilities should therefore be given over
T-7 IV.5:7 it serves His Voice, which is in a. of you.
T-7 IV.6:5 It is nothing at a.. God has given you a gift
T-7 IV.6:11 since a. meaning is contained by them
T-7 IV.7:4 God is All in a. in a very literal sense. All
T-7 IV.7:5 A. being is in Him Who is all Being. You
T-7 IV.7:5 All being is in Him Who is a. Being. You
T-7 IV.7:10 It comes freely to a. the Sonship, being
T-7 V.5:6 of God not be for a. and for always? Love
T-7 V.10:11 because it encompasses a. things within
T-7 V.11:2 we share is shared by a. our brothers, and
T-7 V.11:8 and therefore governs a. thought.
T-7 VI.1:2 of it that you will not attribute to a. of it.
T-7 VI.1:4 entirely it is not relinquished at a.. Fear
T-7 VI.1:8 appreciate a. of Them if he regards Them
T-7 VI.5:1 ego therefore opposes a. appreciation, all
T-7 VI.5:1 opposes all appreciation, a. recognition,
T-7 VI.5:1 a. sane perception and all knowledge. It
T-7 VI.5:1 all sane perception and a. knowledge. It
T-7 VI.5:2 that a. commitments the mind makes are
T-7 VI.6:1 because He cannot perceive them at a..
T-7 VI.8:9 the idea of conflict entirely and for a. time
T-7 VI.9:3 and is not influenced by it at a.. Perceived
T-7 VI.11:4 That is a. the world of the ego is. Nothing.
T-7 VI.13:6 that opposes this means anything at a..
T-7 VII.1:8 you have lost the awareness of a. of it. Yet
T-7 VII.1:11 part of reality, and thus appreciate a. of it.
T-7 VII.3:7 A. illusions about the Sonship are dispelled
T-7 VII.4:4 is to withdraw a. investment from them,
T-7 VII.5:5 A. confusion comes from not extending
T-7 VII.6:6 honored a. those who were created like
T-7 VII.7:2 another. One Teacher is in a. minds and
T-7 VII.7:2 and He teaches the same lesson to a.. He
T-7 VII.8:5 ultimate basis for a. the ego's projection.
T-7 VII.11:1 and you have correctly evaluated a. of it.
T-7 VII.11:6 A. power and glory are yours because the
T-7 VIII.5:4 will have laid aside a. anger and all attack,
T-7 VIII.5:4 will have laid aside all anger and a. attack,
T-7 VIII.5:6 a. their effects will vanish from your mind
T-7 IX.2:1 of a. its brothers is included in its own, as
T-7 IX.2:4 He created is given a. His power, because
T-7 X.5:13 and refuses to follow any guidance at a.. If
T-7 XI.1:8 difficulty at a. *because* it is a state of grace.
T-7 XI.5:2 Its own radiance shines a. around it, and
T-7 XI.7:8 But you must also know a. He created, to
T-7 XI.7:10 Kingdom of God includes a. His Sons and
T-7 XI.7:11 of God, and you will know a. creation.
T-8 I.5:10 curriculum teaches them that *a.* directions
T-8 II.7:1 "A. power and glory are yours because the
T-8 II.7:1 limit, and a. power and glory lie within it.
T-8 II.7:3 encompasses a. things because it created
T-8 II.7:3 all things because it created a. things. By
T-8 II.7:4 By creating a. things, it made them part of
T-8 II.7:7 are part of Him Who is a. power and glory
T-8 II.8:1 To what else except a. power and glory
T-8 III.7:4 Holy Spirit teaches that a. strength is in
T-8 III.7:8 power and glory a. your wrong decisions
T-8 IV.1:4 Yet He is All in a.. His peace is complete,
T-8 IV.3:2 done, it was perfectly accomplished by a..
T-8 IV.5:11 A. things are possible through our joint
T-8 IV.6:7 and the perfect equality of a. God's Sons
T-8 IV.6:8 in will, a. being the Will of their Father.
T-8 IV.7:9 which He will share with a. His creations,
T-8 IV.7:10 freedom, which is His Will for a. His Sons
T-8 V.3:3 His power in you, but in that lies a. truth.
T-8 V.3:6 A. glory lies in Them *because* They are
T-8 V.4:4 this confidence for both of us and a. of us.
T-8 V.4:5 of us. I bring God's peace back to a. His
T-8 V.4:5 because I received it of Him for us a..
T-8 V.6:2 Holy Spirit has one direction for a. minds,
T-8 V.6:3 for which God's Voice speaks in a. of us.
T-8 V.6:6 true. Leave a. illusions behind, and reach
T-8 V.6:6 beyond a. attempts of the ego to hold you
T-8 VI.1:1 of the Sonship, whose Wholeness is for a..
T-8 VI.1:3 Every gain in our strength is offered for a.,
T-8 VI.1:4 God's welcome waits for us a., and He will
T-8 VI.8:4 from each other we cannot function at a..
T-8 VI.8:5 whole power of God's Son lies in a. of us,
T-8 VI.9:4 God has joined a. His Sons with Himself.
T-8 VI.10:5 of a. those who are as blessed as you are.
T-8 VII.5:1 Yet a. loss comes only from your own
T-8 VII.10:3 A. mind is whole, and the belief that part
T-8 VII.12:8 arrest is the cause of a. illness, because
T-8 VII.13:6 the mind the body has no purpose at a..
T-8 VII.15:8 Yet if a. condemnation is unreal, and it
T-8 VIII.6:5 does not bother to analyze it at a.. If data
T-8 VIII.6:9 it is not necessary to examine a. possible
T-8 VIII.9:9 Health is the result of relinquishing a.
T-8 IX.3:2 A. forms of sickness, even unto death, are
T-8 IX.5:2 since a. healing involves replacing fear
T-8 IX.7:1 enjoins you to be perfect, to heal a. errors,
T-8 IX.7:1 and to accomplish a. things in my name.
T-8 IX.8:7 A. forms of sickness are signs that the
T-8 IX.9:8 Will must stand forever and in a. things.
T-9 I.3:3 truth is. A. this could mean is that you are
T-9 II.2:7 request is, therefore, not for healing at a..
T-9 II.3:1 emphasizes that a. prayer is answered,
T-9 II.6:11 except as He answers a. of God's Sons?
T-9 II.7:6 The answer to a. prayers lies in them. You
T-9 II.12:4 His answer is a. you can ask for and want.
T-9 III.1:4 To the Holy Spirit it makes no sense at a..
T-9 III.4:1 When you react at a. to errors, you are
T-9 III.5:4 the one way in which you handle a. errors,
T-9 III.5:4 understand how a. errors are undone.
T-9 III.6:6 can have no effect at a. on the truth in you
T-9 III.7:4 Holy Spirit in you forgives a. things in you
T-9 III.8:6 For that a. learning was made. This is the
T-9 III.8:11 to you, and a. your errors will be forgiven.
T-9 IV.1:1 Atonement is for a., because it is the way
T-9 IV.2:6 sense of limitation is where a. errors arise.
T-9 IV.3:5 does. A. their harmfulness lies in the ego's
T-9 IV.3:6 A. their helpfulness lies in the judgment
T-9 IV.5:6 consistently cancelling out a. its effects,
T-9 IV.5:6 its effects, everywhere and in a. respects,
T-9 IV.7:2 ego believes that a. functions belong to it,
T-9 IV.7:4 anyone and anything for no reason at a..
T-9 IV.12:2 God, and is perfectly satisfying to a. of Us.
T-9 V.3:3 A. unhealed healers follow the ego's plan
T-9 V.8:16 good *can* work. Nothing else works at a..
T-9 V.9:5 you will learn the simplest of a. lessons: *By*
T-9 VI.1:3 How, then, can you perceive Him at a.? If
T-9 VI.3:5 has but one Son, knowing them a. as One.
T-9 VII.2:1 that in this joint will you are a. united,
T-9 VII.3:1 Spirit looks with love on a. He perceives,
T-9 VII.7:3 therefore is to deny a. knowledge, and
T-9 VII.8:7 will give you a. of Himself in exchange for
T-9 VIII.4:2 will give up a. investment in it. Grandeur
T-9 VIII.9:5 to the Will of God does not exist at a..
T-10 I.2:4 happen in the dream did not happen at a..
T-10 I.2:5 though a. the laws of what you awaken to
T-10 II.5:1 A. attack is Self attack. It cannot be
T-10 III.2:3 He is always accepted for a., and when
T-10 III.2:6 with a. His children joins them together,
T-10 III.4:3 A. forms of idolatry are caricatures of
T-10 III.4:5 you are part of God, Who is a. power. A
T-10 III.8:2 and offer them perfect freedom from a.
T-10 IV.1:1 A. magic is an attempt at reconciling the
T-10 IV.1:2 A. religion is the recognition that the
T-10 IV.3:1 it that way is not to perceive it at a.. If the
T-10 IV.3:2 the Sonship is One, it is One in a. respects
T-10 IV.5:4 A. this has never been. Nothing but the
T-10 IV.5:8 it is. You will see nothing at a.. And your
T-10 IV.5:9 it, to what is in you and a. around you.
T-10 IV.6:6 yourself and your reality affect truth at a..
T-10 IV.7:1 of God who has laid aside a. false gods,
T-10 IV.7:5 because a. the lamps of God were lit by
T-10 IV.8:7 Put a. your faith in it, and God Himself
T-10 V.1:6 as a. forms of denial replace what is with
T-10 V.12:4 A. of these illusions, and the many other
T-11 in.1:4 are diametrically opposed in a. respects so
T-11 I.4:3 so you believe that a. creation is limited.
T-11 III.1:7 Conflict is the root of a. evil, for being
T-11 III.2:3 and amid a. his brothers he is friendless.
T-11 III.5:5 companions, the dark way, are a. illusions
T-11 III.5:6 it can sweep you out of a. darkness forever
T-11 III.7:9 A. your brothers must enter with you, for
T-11 IV.1:6 of your Self a. your understanding is lost,
T-11 IV.5:4 yourself, for only the ego blames at a.. Self-
T-11 V.2:1 of a. that stands in the way of knowledge?
T-11 V.3:6 *A. power is of God. What is not of Him has*
T-11 V.6:8 ego sees a. dependency as threatening,
T-11 V.8:4 this belief you would not listen to it at a..
T-11 VI.1:7 does rise above the ego and a. its works,
T-11 VI.2:4 These questions are a. the same, and are
T-11 VI.3:7 perceive with Him involves no strain at a..
T-11 VI.6:6 The Father has given you a. that is His,
T-11 VI.9:5 unless you give a. that you have received
T-11 VI.10:5 a. of God's Sons are of equal value, and
T-11 VI.10:8 To God a. things are possible. And to

|  |  |
|---|---|
| T-11.....VII.1:5 | between, you were not perceiving at **a.**. |
| T-11.....VII.2:7 | A. that is necessary is a willingness to |
| T-11.....VII.4:9 | The real world is **a.** that the Holy Spirit |
| T-11... VIII.1:9 | the transfer of **a.** perception to knowledge |
| T-11... VIII.3:4 | have accepted no guide at **a.**. Instruction |
| T-11. VIII.12:4 | Let the Holy Spirit remove **a.** offenses of |
| T-11. VIII.12:4 | He would save you from **a.** condemnation |
| T-11. VIII.12:5 | power and use it for **a.** He sends you, for |
| T-12.........I.3:2 | it requires no effort at **a.** on your part. |
| T-12.........I.4:1 | you from recognizing **a.** calls for help as |
| T-12.........I.6:3 | And **a.** your sense of strain comes from |
| T-12.........I.6:5 | reality, for reality evokes no conflict at **a.**. |
| T-12.........I.9:8 | not work at **a.** are automatically discarded |
| T-12....... II.2:4 | remembering that **a.** power is of God. You |
| T-12....... II.2:5 | You can remember this for **a.** the Sonship. |
| T-12...... III.1:1 | I once asked you to sell **a.** you have and |
| T-12.... III.10:1 | If you will recognize that **a.** the attack you |
| T-12......IV.2:4 | split off, or it could not be believed at **a.**. |
| T-12......IV.3:2 | presence, for it could not respond at **a.**. |
| T-12......IV.6:8 | for God is whole and **a.** His extensions are |
| T-12......IV.7:6 | will not see life though it is **a.** around you. |
| T-12....... V.3:3 | place you can cancel out **a.** reinforcement |
| T-12....... V.7:4 | be misinterpreted, since they are **a.** for |
| T-12....... V.7:9 | for **a.** your learning will be on its behalf. |
| T-12..... V.7:10 | you fight against **a.** learning and succeed, |
| T-12......VI.4:1 | Correction is for **a.** who cannot see. To |
| T-12......VI.6:5 | more common elements in **a.** situations, |
| T-12......VII.1:3 | when you apply them to **a.** situations. |
| T-12......VII.1:4 | them to **a.** situations you will gain the real |
| T-12......VII.3:3 | you to do is clearly beyond **a.** of them. |
| T-12...VII.10:5 | looked upon me and **a.** your brothers, in |
| T-12...VII.11:9 | And **a.** that you see but witnesses to your |
| T-12...VII.12:7 | reserving no judgment at **a.** for yourself. |
| T-12... VIII.2:5 | For a split mind and **a.** its works were not |
| T-12... VIII.7:4 | in His sight, and encompasses **a.** of it. He |
| T-12. VIII.7:11 | the function of love to unite **a.** things unto |
| T-12. VIII.7:11 | to hold **a.** things together by extending its |
| T-13.......in.1:5 | A. this is but the delusional attempt of the |
| T-13.......in.2:4 | and **a.** the laws that seem to govern it are |
| T-13.......in.2:9 | love, perhaps the most insane belief of **a.**. |
| T-13.........I.1:1 | Spirit shares the goal of **a.** good teachers, |
| T-13.........I.1:1 | by teaching their pupils **a.** they know. The |
| T-13.........I.1:2 | He seeks to remove **a.** guilt from his mind |
| T-13....... II.1:3 | issue, then, the deepest split of **a.** occurs, |
| T-13....... II.4:4 | withstand your raising **a.** else to question, |
| T-13......III.6:6 | Not **a.** the tricks and games you offer it |
| T-13......III.7:4 | Lay before His eternal sanity **a.** your hurt, |
| T-13......III.8:1 | Beneath **a.** the grandiosity you hold so |
| T-13.....III.11:4 | remain in peace, he could not remain at **a.** |
| T-13......IV.1:4 | and you have no function at **a.** in Heaven. |
| T-13......IV.3:3 | and needs this to prove that it was at **a.**. |
| T-13....... V.1:5 | one thing in common; they are **a.** insane. |
| T-13....... V.1:8 | maker, and so they have no meaning at **a.**. |
| T-13....... V.5:7 | it, and **a.** the love your brothers offer you, |
| T-13....... V.6:4 | as if you were alone in **a.** the universe. In |
| T-13....... V.7:8 | You will see **a.** that you denied in your |
| T-13..... V.7:11 | The Father welcomes **a.** of us in gladness, |
| T-13....... V.8:5 | go and **a.** you made you will no longer see, |
| T-13....... V.9:2 | vision of Christ, Who looks on **a.** in light. |
| T-13..... V.11:2 | **a.** who would behold Him can see Him, |
| T-13..... V.11:5 | And **a.** this will they understand, because |
| T-13..... V.11:7 | vision of the truth in them came **a.** the |
| T-13......VI.1:1 | perceive truly is to be aware of **a.** reality |
| T-13......VI.2:3 | with no reference at **a.** to the past, either |
| T-13......VI.5:2 | His errors are **a.** past, and by perceiving |
| T-13......VI.6:3 | true. **A.** healing lies within it because its |
| T-13......VI.6:4 | extends to **a.** aspects of the Sonship at the |
| T-13......VI.6:6 | In it are **a.** things that are eternal, and |
| T-13......VI.8:2 | Reach out to **a.** your brothers, and touch |
| T-13......VI.8:6 | Call **a.** your brothers to witness to his |
| T-13....VI.11:9 | A. those you brought with you will shine |
| T-13....VI.13:2 | them through **a.** your nightmares, and |
| T-13.....VII.3:6 | the power to touch the living world at **a.**. |
| T-13.....VII.4:4 | A. that you need to give this world away |
| T-13.....VII.5:3 | A. seeing starts with the perceiver, who |
| T-13.....VII.7:5 | love, for it is **a.** about him and within him. |
| T-13.....VII.8:5 | For **a.** else you have lent yourself in time, |
| T-13.....VII.9:3 | world of dreams, where **a.** perception is. |
| T-13.VII.10:13 | altar it demands you lay **a.** of the things it |
| T-13...VII.12:2 | For He will give you **a.** things that do not |
| T-13...VII.12:4 | gives you **a.** the things that you need have, |
| T-13...VII.12:6 | but last until you step aside from **a.** your |
| T-13...VII.12:6 | realize that **a.** of them have been fulfilled. |
| T-13...VII.13:2 | them with no emphasis at **a.** upon them. |
| T-13...VII.15:1 | lead you safely through **a.** dangers to your |
| T-13...VII.16:9 | Take it of me in glad exchange for **a.** the |
| T-13... VIII.1:1 | A. healing is release from the past. That is |
| T-13... VIII.1:5 | eternity, and utilizes no perception at **a.**. |
| T-13... VIII.2:4 | A. knowledge must be yours, for in you is |
| T-13... VIII.2:4 | must be yours, for in you is **a.** knowledge. |
| T-13... VIII.3:5 | formulation of reality, with no effect at **a.**. |
| T-13... VIII.5:6 | gift of light to **a.** who think they wander in |
| T-13... VIII.6:1 | They are **a.** the same; all beautiful and |
| T-13... VIII.6:1 | **a.** beautiful and equal in their holiness. |
| T-13... VIII.6:4 | every miracle you do contains them **a.**, as |
| T-13... VIII.7:5 | part of it and **a.** of it need only realize that |
| T-13... VIII.8:3 | we will **a.** unite in the eternity of God the |
| T-13....... IX.6:3 | offer of Atonement for **a.** your brothers. |
| T-13....... IX.8:2 | tells you **a.** is black with guilt within you, |
| T-13....... X.1:4 | willing to look upon **a.** kinds of "sources," |
| T-13....... X.1:4 | which they bear no real relationship at **a.**. |
| T-13....... X.2:3 | For **a.** relationships that guilt has touched |
| T-13....... X.2:5 | are holy, and cannot be used by you at **a.**. |
| T-13....... X.4:4 | whom you find no real relationships at **a.**. |
| T-13....... X.5:5 | you **a.** the while you dreamed of guilt, and |
| T-13... X.10:10 | A. else He would have you see. And in |
| T-13..... X.11:1 | Sons unless you love them **a.** and equally. |
| T-13..... X.11:3 | imposing guilt on **a.** your relationships |
| T-13..... X.13:3 | I love **a.** that He created, and all my faith |
| T-13..... X.13:3 | **a.** my faith and my belief I offer unto it. |
| T-13..... X.13:4 | is as strong as **a.** the love I give my Father. |
| T-13..... X.14:2 | Alone we are **a.** lowly, but together we |
| T-13...... XI.3:1 | When we are **a.** united in Heaven, you |
| T-13...... XI.3:2 | wholly, and so you do not value it at **a.**. |
| T-13...... XI.5:1 | gave Him the mission to remove **a.** doubt |
| T-13...... XI.7:2 | blackest nightmares **a.** mean nothing. |
| T-14.........I.2:5 | everything, and **a.** this has been denied, |
| T-14.........I.3:3 | have **a.** the power that he gives to them. |
| T-14.........I.4:7 | not believe **a.** that *is* possible to learn to do |
| T-14........ II.2:4 | Consider **a.** the distortions you have made |
| T-14........ II.2:4 | **a.** the strange forms and feelings and |
| T-14........ II.3:1 | A. this the Holy Spirit sees, and teaches, |
| T-14........ II.3:1 | and teaches, simply, that **a.** this is not true |
| T-14........ II.4:5 | nothing and from **a.** the works of nothing. |
| T-14........ II.6:4 | up before you in **a.** its gracious simplicity. |
| T-14........ II.7:2 | A. this lies in the Holy Spirit's plan to free |
| T-14........ II.8:4 | Where everything is clear, it is **a.** holy. |
| T-14...... III.1:4 | and serves no useful function at **a.**. |
| T-14...... III.4:3 | The power of decision is **a.** that is yours. |
| T-14...... III.8:7 | in place of **a.** the happy teaching the Holy |
| T-14.... III.10:5 | A. this arises because they do not believe |
| T-14.... III.10:6 | and will bring to them **a.** that they need, |
| T-14.... III.11:3 | is **a.** that you alone can offer yourself, |
| T-14.... III.12:6 | leave **a.** decisions to His gentle counsel. |
| T-14.... III.13:4 | that **a.** salvation is escape from guilt. You |
| T-14.... III.16:3 | to anticipate **a.** you cannot know, when |
| T-14.... III.16:3 | **a.** knowledge lies behind every decision |
| T-14.... III.17:1 | gracious it is to decide **a.** things through |
| T-14.... III.17:1 | equal Love is given equally to **a.** alike! He |
| T-14.... III.18:3 | and learn of **a.** the happy communication |
| T-14.... III.19:4 | *communicate to me **a.** that He knows for me.* |
| T-14...... IV.3:1 | let **a.** that obscured the truth in your most |
| T-14...... IV.3:2 | Giving Himself is **a.** He knows, and so it is |
| T-14...... IV.3:2 | is all He knows, and so it is **a.** knowledge. |
| T-14...... IV.3:7 | must learn that it is **a.** you want to learn. |
| T-14...... IV.3:9 | function in God's Mind with **a.** of yours. |
| T-14...... IV.5:4 | Leave **a.** decisions to the One Who speaks |
| T-14...... IV.6:1 | **a.** decisions become as easy and as right |
| T-14...... IV.7:3 | Him, though He is **a.** around you. He |
| T-14.... IV.10:7 | with God is life. Nothing without it is at **a.** |
| T-14....... V.1:2 | Would you have **a.** of it transformed into |
| T-14....... V.1:2 | with **a.** the lonely ones who have denied |
| T-14....... V.2:7 | **a.** the love you share with God He holds in |
| T-14....... V.3:5 | to the denial of guilt in **a.** its forms. To |
| T-14....... V.3:7 | that is the right of **a.** that God created. |
| T-14....... V.5:1 | We are **a.** joined in the Atonement here, |
| T-14....... V.8:6 | and attract **a.** tortured minds to join with |
| T-14..... V.11:7 | in peace on **a.** who think they are outside. |
| T-14..... V.11:9 | holy place of peace which is for **a.** of us, |
| T-14...... VI.3:4 | They do nothing at **a.**, being nothing at all |
| T-14...... VI.3:4 | They do nothing at all, being nothing at **a.** |
| T-14...... VI.4:4 | A. you have done by keeping them apart |
| T-14...... VI.5:3 | A. things you made have use to Him, for |
| T-14...... VI.5:5 | are. **A.** this and nothing else would He |
| T-14...... VI.7:4 | He will separate out **a.** that has meaning, |
| T-14...... VI.8:4 | which nothing at **a.** is carefully concealed. |
| T-14...... VI.8:5 | must open **a.** doors and let the light come |
| T-14..... VII.3:6 | It is therefore not a point of view at **a.**, but |
| T-14... VII.5:15 | easily **a.** that He asks can be accomplished |
| T-14..... VII.6:8 | **a.** your dark and secret thoughts to Him, |
| T-14..... VII.7:5 | with Him will show you that **a.** meaning, |
| T-14..... VII.7:7 | you could not wish, for **a.** the world, not |
| T-14..... VII.7:8 | it as His, with **a.** His Love as yours. All |
| T-14..... VII.7:9 | yours. **A.** honor to you through Him, and |
| T-14.... VIII.1:2 | A. this lies hidden in every darkened place |
| T-14.... VIII.1:5 | but let **a.** that would hide your glory be |
| T-14.. VIII.2:10 | A. this is safe within you, where the Holy |
| T-14.. VIII.2:14 | A. interference in the communication |
| T-14.... VIII.3:4 | before which **a.** separation vanishes. |
| T-14.. VIII.4:10 | is one link that joins Them **a.** together, |
| T-14.... VIII.5:2 | Heaven itself is union with **a.** of creation, |
| T-14...... IX.3:2 | **a.** its power will rush to your assistance |
| T-14...... IX.4:3 | and cover **a.** their sense of pain and loss |
| T-14...... IX.5:1 | shines forth from you to **a.** around you. |
| T-14...... IX.5:5 | the mirror clean and clear of **a.** the images |
| T-14...... IX.7:1 | shining in you, can bring to **a.** the world, |
| T-14...... IX.7:4 | A. bring their different problems to its |
| T-14...... IX.7:4 | **a.** their problems find but healing there. |
| T-14........X.1:3 | But eternity itself is beyond **a.** time. Reach |
| T-14........X.1:5 | holiness calls everyone to lay **a.** guilt aside |
| T-14........X.1:7 | they enter into it they leave **a.** reflections |
| T-14........X.3:3 | you conceive of them as possible at **a.**. |
| T-14........X.5:6 | For the ego *is* chaos, and if it were **a.** of you |
| T-14........X.5:6 | all of you, no order at **a.** would be possible |
| T-14........X.6:1 | no basis at **a.** for ordering your thoughts. |
| T-14..... X.6:11 | gives equal blessing to **a.** who share in it, |
| T-14........X.7:4 | you consider content is not content at **a.**. |
| T-14..... X.11:2 | is perfectly open and freely accessible to **a.** |
| T-14..... X.11:2 | and freely accessible to all, being for **a.**. |
| T-14..... X.12:8 | His Son with **a.** the Love He holds for him |
| T-14..... X.12:9 | will the power of **a.** His Love be absent |
| T-14...... XI.1:2 | is power, and **a.** power is of God. You who |
| T-14...... XI.1:9 | **a.** that stands between you and the power |
| T-14...... XI.2:1 | Be willing, then, for **a.** of it to be undone, |
| T-14...... XI.2:4 | And can His Son, given **a.** power by Him, |
| T-14...... XI.3:4 | gives the present no meaning at **a.**. |
| T-14...... XI.3:7 | *Let it **a.** go.* Do not attempt to understand |
| T-14...... XI.3:9 | Put no confidence at **a.** in darkness to |
| T-14...... XI.4:1 | You who have not yet brought **a.** of the |
| T-14...... XI.4:6 | this, **a.** your dark lessons must be brought |
| T-14...... XI.5:2 | and if **a.** those who meet or even think of |
| T-14...... XI.5:3 | own. Unless **a.** this is true, there are dark |
| T-14...... XI.8:6 | miracles to answer **a.** your problems for |
| T-14...... XI.9:5 | He has brought **a.** of them to light, having |
| T-14...... XI.9:8 | They do not exist in His Mind at **a.**. For |
| T-14.... XI.10:9 | And **a.** His works are yours. He offers you |
| T-14.... XI.11:8 | This is the Will of God for **a.** creation, and |
| T-14.... XI.11:8 | and **a.** creation joins in willing this. |
| T-14.... XI.13:1 | are with them, can really learn at **a.**. For |
| T-15.........I.1:1 | to be perfectly calm and quiet **a.** the time? |
| T-15.........I.1:3 | until it constitutes **a.** your learning. He |
| T-15.........I.2:6 | And **a.** the waste that time seems to bring |
| T-15.........I.4:2 | and their fears are **a.** associated with it. |
| T-15.........I.4:3 | this is what **a.** its teaching is directed to. |
| T-15.........I.4:12 | ego tries, and **a.** too frequently succeeds, |
| T-15.........I.8:1 | Holy Spirit would undo **a.** of this *now.* Fear |
| T-15.........I.9:3 | it takes no time at **a.** to be what you are. |
| T-15.........I.9:5 | now, and think of it as **a.** there is of time. |
| T-15.......I.13:3 | of freedom to **a.** who are enslaved by time |
| T-15.......I.14:5 | to transcend **a.** of the ego's making, and |
| T-15.......I.15:8 | not. And so it is no longer time at **a.**. For |
| T-15........II.1:7 | blessed instant you will let go **a.** your past |
| T-15........II.1:8 | when **a.** the obstacles to learning it have |
| T-15........II.1:9 | beyond time that **a.** of it happens at once. |
| T-15.......II.1:10 | so its oneness depends not on time at **a.**. |
| T-15........II.2:1 | instant of holiness that will remove **a.** fear |
| T-15........II.3:3 | A. that you have, you have forever. The |

| | |
|---|---|
| T-15....... II.3:6 | instant you will unchain **a.** your brothers, |
| T-15....... II.5:6 | And here it is, **a.** in this instant, complete, |
| T-15...... III.2:5 | but **a.** you will be doing is to delay your |
| T-15...... III.3:1 | you must learn to remember **a.** the time. |
| T-15...... III.4:4 | A. your striving must be directed against |
| T-15...... III.5:6 | A. your attempts to deny His magnitude, |
| T-15...... III.6:1 | hold your magnitude, clean of **a.** littleness |
| T-15...... III.6:5 | that lie in you from God are for **a.** who, |
| T-15...... III.6:7 | it. A. honor is due the host of God. Your |
| T-15...... III.7:3 | beyond **a.** your littleness to give the gift of |
| T-15...... III.7:7 | Yet He brings **a.** His extensions to you, as |
| T-15...... III.8:7 | appreciation of yourself and **a.** the little |
| T-15... III.11:3 | may release **a.** those who would be bound |
| T-15...... IV.2:1 | your willingness to let **a.** littleness go. The |
| T-15...... IV.6:7 | that **a.** minds are in communication. It |
| T-15...... IV.7:5 | God Who surrounds **a.** of you together. |
| T-15...... IV.8:6 | of the single Will that governs **a.** thought. |
| T-15...... IV.9:9 | bring **a.** your awareness to the readiness |
| T-15....... V.1:6 | that without the ego, **a.** would be chaos. |
| T-15....... V.1:7 | you that without the ego, **a.** would be love |
| T-15....... V.4:1 | **a.** special relationships have elements of |
| T-15....... V.5:5 | A. the guilt in it arises from your use of it. |
| T-15....... V.5:6 | it. A. the love from His. Do not, then, be |
| T-15....... V.8:3 | see them **a.** the same and like yourself. |
| T-15....... V.9:3 | by bringing **a.** perception out of the past, |
| T-15..... V.10:1 | A. your relationships are blessed in the |
| T-15..... V.10:6 | He needs them **a.** equally, and so do you. |
| T-15..... V.10:8 | God, and **a.** your brothers join in Christ. |
| T-15...... VI.1:3 | the Holy Spirit's teaching **a.** relationships |
| T-15...... VI.2:3 | faith in you, in place of **a.** your doubts. |
| T-15...... VI.2:4 | as perfect in **a.** your brothers as it is in you |
| T-15...... VI.3:1 | A. separation vanishes as holiness is |
| T-15...... VI.5:5 | to hold **a.** of your brothers in your mind, |
| T-15...... VI.5:9 | this world cease to hold any meaning at **a.** |
| T-15...... VI.7:7 | full communication with **a.** that ever was. |
| T-15...... VI.8:1 | language of communication with **a.** your |
| T-15...... VI.8:5 | your Source, and that of **a.** your brothers, |
| T-15..... VII.2:6 | so weak that it would have no hold at **a.**, |
| T-15..... VII.2:7 | and has no attraction at **a.** to anyone who |
| T-15..... VII.7:4 | He is not in love with the other at **a.**. He |
| T-15..... VII.7:8 | that holds **a.** its relationships together. |
| T-15..... VII.9:1 | which the ego would "bless" **a.** unions. |
| T-15... VII.10:2 | will learn that love brings no guilt at **a.**, |
| T-15... VII.10:3 | A. anger is nothing more than an attempt |
| T-15... VII.14:7 | **a.** are invited and made welcome. And |
| T-15.... VIII.2:1 | have need of no special relationships at **a.**. |
| T-15.... VIII.2:3 | aside, but still desire with **a.** your heart. |
| T-15.... VIII.2:4 | in making the holy instant **a.** that there is, |
| T-15.... VIII.2:4 | is, by desiring that it *be* **a.** that there is. |
| T-15.... VIII.4:5 | sum of **a.** the separate bodies you perceive |
| T-15.... VIII.4:6 | For **a.** its parts are joined in God through |
| T-15...... IX.2:1 | of looking straight at **a.** the interference |
| T-15...... IX.3:5 | will strive for them with **a.** its might, and |
| T-15...... IX.6:1 | idea of **a.** the loveliness that you could see. |
| T-15...... IX.7:2 | will learn you have no need of a body at **a.** |
| T-15...... IX.7:6 | that you could ever want. A. truth *is* here. |
| T-15....... X.3:3 | union you will accept **a.** of our brothers. |
| T-15....... X.4:2 | It is possible to do this **a.** at once because |
| T-15....... X.4:3 | It seems like many, but it is **a.** the same. |
| T-15....... X.5:1 | not necessary to follow fear through **a.** the |
| T-15....... X.5:2 | the principle that governs **a.** of them. |
| T-15....... X.6:1 | give **a.** your guilt away whenever you want |
| T-15....... X.6:7 | for the one idea that hides behind them **a.** |
| T-15...... XI.2:5 | whole idea of sacrifice loses **a.** meaning. |
| T-15...... XI.3:4 | A. pain and sacrifice and littleness will |
| T-15...... XI.6:1 | So is it that, in **a.** your seeking for love, |
| T-15...... XI.6:5 | while **a.** that you would keep away holds |
| T-15...... XI.6:5 | away holds **a.** the meaning of the universe |
| T-15...... XI.7:5 | and still would teach to **a.** my brothers, is |
| T-15.... XI.10:2 | in you to do **a.** that you would accomplish |
| T-15.. XI.10:11 | year different by making it **a.** the same. |
| T-15.. XI.10:12 | let **a.** your relationships be made holy for |
| T-16......... I.3:4 | is. A. you have learned of empathy is from |
| T-16......... I.7:4 | **a.** to Him Whose function is to meet them |
| T-16....... II.1:6 | how the miracle extends to **a.** the Sonship |
| T-16....... II.1:8 | If miracles *are* at **a.**, their attributes would |
| T-16....... II.5:6 | turn away from **a.** the witnesses that He |
| T-16....... II.6:6 | Him is to deny **a.** that you think you know |
| T-16....... III.1:1 | everyone teaches, and teaches **a.** the time. |

| | |
|---|---|
| T-16 ..... III.2:6 | **a.** your learning has been directed toward |
| T-16 ..... III.6:3 | are the universe, **a.** else must be outside, |
| T-16 ..... III.7:8 | A. this is *you*, and nothing outside of this *is* |
| T-16 ..... III.8:1 | holy Self **a.** praise is due for what you are, |
| T-16 ..... III.8:4 | united will of **a.** who make Heaven what it |
| T-16 ..... IV.5:2 | at **a.** concerned with the "triumph of love. |
| T-16 ..... IV.6:1 | merely to seek and find **a.** of the barriers |
| T-16 ..... IV.8:5 | to look on **a.** your brothers with gratitude, |
| T-16 ..... IV.9:5 | be wholly willing to abandon **a.** illusions. |
| T-16 ... IV.10:4 | needful to value truth beyond **a.** fantasy, |
| T-16 . IV.11:14 | willingness to love and **a.** the Love of God, |
| T-16 ... IV.12:5 | with me firmly away from **a.** illusions now |
| T-16 ...... V.1:2 | despair, guilt and attack **a.** enter into it, |
| T-16 ...... V.1:3 | A. these must be understood for what |
| T-16 ...... V.3:5 | that it is not natural at **a.** seem to be the |
| T-16 ...... V.7:1 | Most curious of **a.** is the concept of the |
| T-16 ...... V.8:5 | Yet if **a.** illusions are of fear, and they can |
| T-16 .. V.12:11 | of God have any influence at **a.** upon it. |
| T-16 .... V.15:5 | complete escape from **a.** its consequences. |
| T-16 .... V.16:2 | illusion and not confused with it at **a.**. |
| T-16 .... V.17:2 | on the other side, and nothing at **a.** is here |
| T-16 ..... VI.1:3 | meaning, for it perceives **a.** love as special. |
| T-16 ..... VI.1:4 | and **a.** relationships that are unlike this |
| T-16 ..... VI.6:4 | you will see no need at **a.** to magnify it. |
| T-16 ... VI.11:4 | that for **a.** this you gave up *nothing!* The |
| T-16 .... VII.1:3 | and deprivations **a.** enter into the special |
| T-16 .... VII.2:5 | now, it cannot have any real meaning at **a.** |
| T-16 .... VII.7:1 | of the complete difference, in **a.** respects, |
| T-16 .... VII.9:2 | A. that must be forgiven are the illusions |
| T-16 .. VII.10:2 | power of God and **a.** His Love, without |
| T-16 .. VII.10:4 | to place **a.** your investment in salvation in |
| T-16 .. VII.11:1 | instant, where **a.** illusions are forgiven. |
| T-16 .. VII.11:2 | bless everyone and to resolve **a.** problems, |
| T-16 .. VII.11:4 | their reality to give over **a.** illusions for the |
| T-17 ......... I.1:1 | **a.** his "sins" are but his own imagining. |
| T-17 ......... I.1:7 | that they had no effect upon reality at **a.**, |
| T-17 ......... I.3:1 | **a.** you mean is that there are some things |
| T-17 ......... I.3:3 | in the power that heals **a.** pain arises from |
| T-17 ......... I.4:5 | which it cannot really be compared at **a.**. |
| T-17 ......... I.6:1 | to give **a.** you have held outside the truth |
| T-17 ......... I.6:1 | truth, and in Whom **a.** is brought to truth |
| T-17 ......... I.6:2 | would be complete, or will not be at **a.**. Be |
| T-17 ........ II.1:9 | And **a.** His teaching leads to seeing it and |
| T-17 ........ II.2:5 | thing that touches on this world at **a.**. |
| T-17 ........ II.2:6 | beyond **a.** ugliness into beauty that will |
| T-17 ........ II.3:1 | of **a.** in God's plan of Atonement. All else |
| T-17 ........ II.3:2 | A. else is learned, but this is given, |
| T-17 ........ II.3:5 | Fantasies are **a.** undone, and no one and |
| T-17 ........ II.5:3 | show you that there is no reason here at **a.** |
| T-17 ........ II.6:1 | A. this beauty will rise to bless your sight |
| T-17 ........ II.6:2 | removing **a.** illusions that had twisted |
| T-17 ...... III.1:2 | A. the rest must be forgotten. Forgiveness |
| T-17 ...... III.2:2 | and **a.** relationships into which they enter |
| T-17 ...... III.2:6 | finally, why **a.** such relationships become |
| T-17 ...... III.2:7 | to **a.** unholy relationships is evident. Your |
| T-17 ...... III.2:9 | may not realize are **a.** the reasons that go |
| T-17 ...... III.4:5 | does not enter at **a.** to "spoil" the dream. |
| T-17 ...... III.5:3 | do so. If **a.** but loving thoughts have been |
| T-17 ...... III.6:5 | He is not at **a.** confused by any "reasons" |
| T-17 ...... III.6:6 | A. He perceives in separation is that it |
| T-17 ...... III.7:1 | A. this you will do gladly, if you but let |
| T-17 ...... III.8:4 | alliance are retained, and **a.** the rest let go. |
| T-17 ...... III.8:5 | And what is thus let go is **a.** the truth the |
| T-17 ...... III.9:4 | freedom or slavery–it is **a.** the same. For |
| T-17 ...... III.9:6 | and **a.** their attributes come simply from |
| T-17 ...... III.9:8 | And **a.** that follows from them comes |
| T-17 ... III.10:1 | I would enter into **a.** your relationships, |
| T-17 ...... IV.2:4 | And **a.** that is meant by that is that He will |
| T-17 ...... IV.4:7 | **a.** your holy relationships been carefully |
| T-17 ...... IV.5:5 | And **a.** their defenses are as insane as |
| T-17 ...... IV.7:1 | **a.** defenses *do* what they would defend |
| T-17 ...... IV.7:5 | frame is very elaborate, **a.** set with jewels, |
| T-17 ...... IV.8:1 | frame of **a.** the defenses the ego uses. Its |
| T-17 ...... IV.8:3 | structure. Into the frame are woven **a.** |
| T-17 ... IV.11:3 | this gift you will not see the frame at **a.**, |
| T-17 ... IV.11:3 | to focus **a.** your attention on the picture. |
| T-17 ... IV.12:3 | Each is a picture of **a.** that you can have, |
| T-17 . IV.12:10 | tiny picture, hard to see at **a.** beneath the |
| T-17 ... IV.16:8 | instant shines alike on **a.** relationships, |

| | |
|---|---|
| T-17 ....... V.2:4 | In **a.** its aspects, as it begins, develops and |
| T-17 ....... V.3:6 | goal was **a.** that seemed to give it meaning |
| T-17 ....... V.8:3 | and to remind you of **a.** the ways you once |
| T-17 ..... V.10:5 | For **a.** it needs now is your blessing, that |
| T-17 ..... V.10:7 | which **a.** the Sonship is together blessed. |
| T-17 ..... V.11:4 | appreciation for **a.** you have done for Him |
| T-17 ..... V.11:5 | Nor does He see the mistakes at **a.**. Have |
| T-17 ..... V.15:1 | and use them to correct **a.** your mistakes |
| T-17 ..... V.15:2 | also learned how to release **a.** the Sonship, |
| T-17 ..... VI.2:9 | but only that. It has no positive goal at **a.**. |
| T-17 .... VII.2:4 | that **a.** your problems have been solved, |
| T-17 .... VII.3:7 | error, but be not at **a.** concerned with that |
| T-17 .... VII.7:3 | Yet for **a.** its might, so great it reaches |
| T-17 ... VIII.2:1 | courtesy is **a.** the Holy Spirit asks of you. |
| T-17 ... VIII.3:4 | power instantly transforms **a.** situations |
| T-17 ... VIII.3:8 | truth with faith entails no strain at **a.**. |
| T-18 ........ I.4:4 | and life to death, was **a.** you ever made. |
| T-18 ........ I.6:6 | and take no part in **a.** the mad projection |
| T-18 ........ I.6:9 | in reality. And above **a.**, *be not afraid of it.* |
| T-18 ........ I.7:7 | patterns that need not be judged at **a.**. To |
| T-18 ........ I.7:9 | in form are no real differences at **a.**. None |
| T-18 ...... I.7:12 | else is necessary to make them **a.** the same |
| T-18 ........ I.8:1 | Let them **a.** go, dancing in the wind, |
| T-18 ........ I.8:4 | He brings **a.** your insane projections and |
| T-18 ...... I.11:1 | is restored to **a.** the Sonship through your |
| T-18 ...... I.11:2 | **a.** illusions have been gently brought unto |
| T-18 ..... II.5:12 | A. your time is spent in dreaming. Your |
| T-18 ..... II.5:13 | have different forms, and that is **a.**. Their |
| T-18 ....... II.7:2 | share with **a.** who come within your sight. |
| T-18 ....... II.8:6 | choice between the truth and ***a.*** illusions. |
| T-18 ...... III.3:7 | and away from **a.** illusions in which you |
| T-18 .... III.4:12 | A. that was necessary was merely the *wish* |
| T-18 ...... III.5:3 | with **a.** the power of the Holy Spirit's Will. |
| T-18 ...... III.7:5 | for **a.** the fear that you and your brother |
| T-18 ..... IV.1:4 | recognizing that you want it above **a.** else. |
| T-18 ..... IV.6:1 | And that is **a.**. Add more, and you will |
| T-18 ....... V.1:3 | and **a.** the means by which salvation is |
| T-18 ....... V.1:4 | For they are **a.** but aspects of the plan to |
| T-18 ....... V.2:1 | **a.** fear and hatred from your mind. That |
| T-18 ....... V.2:5 | to let Him remove **a.** fear and hatred, and |
| T-18 ....... V.4:6 | needed to change the purpose is **a.** that is |
| T-18 ....... V.5:3 | A. that remains of dreams within it is that |
| T-18 ..... VI.4:4 | **a.** it does when it believes it has attacked |
| T-18 ..... VI.5:4 | destroy can have no real effect at **a.**. What |
| T-18 ..... VI.5:7 | your will conflicts with His, but that is **a.**. |
| T-18 ... VI.12:5 | suspending **a.** the "laws" your body obeys |
| T-18 ... VI.13:1 | There is no violence at **a.** in this escape. |
| T-18 ... VI.13:6 | experience of peace and joy, and, above **a.** |
| T-18 ... VI.13:6 | the questioning whether or not **a.** this is |
| T-18 .... VII.3:1 | no single instant does the body exist at **a.**. |
| T-18 .. VII.4:10 | A. such attempts will ultimately succeed |
| T-18 .. VII.4:11 | **a.** of them look to the future for release |
| T-18 .... VII.7:4 | in which sin loses **a.** attraction *right now.* |
| T-18 .... VII.8:2 | of the storm than **a.** its raging activity. |
| T-18 ... VIII.4:1 | of **a.** this strange and meaningless activity |
| T-18 ... VIII.7:5 | king, a bitter ruler of **a.** that he surveys, |
| T-18 ... VIII.7:7 | offers **a.** its happiness and deep content to |
| T-18 . VIII.10:4 | **a.** the Love of its Creator shining upon it. |
| T-18 . VIII.12:2 | because you have not yet let go of **a.** the |
| T-18 ..... IX.4:2 | Here are **a.** the illusions, all the twisted |
| T-18 ..... IX.4:2 | all the illusions, **a.** the twisted thoughts, |
| T-18 ..... IX.4:2 | the twisted thoughts, **a.** the insane attacks |
| T-18 ..... IX.6:3 | has no power at **a.** to hold back anyone |
| T-18 ..... IX.7:2 | a lake, a city, **a.** rise in your imagination, |
| T-18 ... IX.12:3 | when you have recognized **a.** it is *not.* That |
| T-18 ... IX.12:6 | yours of Him so far transcend **a.** learning |
| T-18 ... IX.13:3 | to remind you of **a.** that lies beyond it. Yet |
| T-19 ........ I.2:7 | joined the Mind in which **a.** healing rests. |
| T-19 ........ I.5:3 | remove **a.** limitations and make whole. |
| T-19 ........ I.5:5 | faith would remove **a.** obstacles that seem |
| T-19 ........ I.6:7 | together, **a.** attempts to keep both truth |
| T-19 ........ I.9:5 | past **a.** barriers between yourself and him, |
| T-19 ...... I.11:3 | free of **a.** the guilt he laid upon himself. |
| T-19 ...... I.14:5 | of healing with equal ease to **a.** of them. |
| T-19 ...... I.16:3 | Son is slave to nothing, being lord of **a.**, |
| T-19 ....... II.2:6 | underlying **a.** the ego's grandiosity. For by |
| T-19 ....... II.3:5 | Yet for **a.** the wild insanity inherent in the |
| T-19 ....... II.5:4 | "best" defense, which **a.** the others serve. |
| T-19 ....... II.7:1 | no stone in **a.** the ego's embattled citadel |

T-19....... II.8:1 **a.** this be nothing more than a mistake,
T-19....... II.8:2 For that is **a.** it is. Perhaps you would be
T-19...... III.4:2 them **a.** as God entrusted Him to do. But
T-19...... III.9:5 You will be healed of sin and **a.** its ravages
T-19.... III.11:3 a place where **a.** the weary ones can come
T-19.... III.11:4 Here is the rest that waits for **a.**, after the
T-19.... III.11:5 brought nearer to **a.** by your relationship.
T-19...... IV.1:1 to embrace **a.** the Sonship and give it rest,
T-19...... IV.2:1 **A.** this will you do. Yet the peace that
T-19...... IV.3:5 them will show you **a.** that you need to see
T-19...... IV.3:8 the Holy Spirit will gather **a.** the thanks
T19. IV.A.4:12 its messengers from you to **a.** the world,
T19... IV.A.5:3 in miracles, for they are **a.** the same. Each
T19... IV.A.5:7 And **a.** that seems to stand between you
T19. IV.A.6:10 which you accepted must **a.** illusions end.
T19... IV.A.8:1 is **a.** that remains of what once seemed to
T19. IV.A.10:1 for love would never look on guilt at **a.**. It
T19. IV.A.14:5 with **a.** the happy things they found, to
T19. IV.A.15:2 of **a.** guilt and softly brushed with beauty.
T19....IV.B.4:2 It flows across **a.** else. The second obstacle
T19....IV.B.5:4 We will surmount **a.** obstacles together,
T19....IV.B.6:2 Forgive me **a.** the sins you think the Son
T19....IV.B.7:6 Send forth to **a.** the world the joyous
T19....IV.B.7:6 end of guilt, and **a.** the world will answer.
T19....IV.B.8:5 perception that will bring light to **a.** the
T19..IV.B.11:3 But **a.** that lies in it will come with it, and
T19..IV.B.12:3 It is not really punitive at **a.**. It is but the
T19..IV.B.12:7 It will share the pain of **a.** illusions, and
T19..IV.B.13:5 It is this idea that underlies **a.** of the ego's
T19..IV.B.14:7 for them. **A.** of the feeling with which they
T19..IV.B.15:3 urges you to send out **a.** your messages of
T19..IV.B.16:2 it **a.** its faith that this can be accomplished
T19... IV.C.1:7 Yet it could have no hold at **a.** except on
T19... IV.C.1:9 dark shadow falls across **a.** living things,
T19... IV.C.4:5 **a.** are part of your unrecognized
T19... IV.C.7:6 For in it lie hidden **a.** the ego's secrets, all
T19... IV.C.7:6 **a.** its strange devices for deception, all its
T19... IV.C.7:6 **a.** its sick ideas and weird imaginings.
T19...IV.D.6:3 **a.** rise and bid you not to raise your eyes.
T19...IV.D.6:5 **A.** of your "friends," your "protectors"
T19...IV.D.7:2 Yet **a.** that will occur is you will leave the
T19...IV.D.8:6 ready to look on terror with no fear at **a.**.
T19. IV.D.12:6 **a.** the pity and forgiveness that would
T19. IV.D.12:8 your eyes in faith together, or not at **a.**.
T19 IV.D15:10 and **a.** the guilt you think you see in him.
T19. IV.D.16:4 remove **a.** trace of guilt from his disturbed
T-20....... II.1:1 Look upon **a.** the trinkets made to hang
T-20....... II.1:2 See **a.** the useless things made for its eyes
T-20....... II.1:3 remember **a.** these were made to make
T-20....... II.7:1 the vision now to look past **a.** illusions. It
T-20....... II.8:4 Yet **a.** you need you have. Your home has
T-20....... II.8:8 from **a.** the terror that kept it hidden.
T-20..... II.10:2 his communion with **a.** that is within him.
T-20...... III.2:2 the ego's fixed belief that **a.** relationships
T-20...... III.2:4 mediator of **a.** relationships, making
T-20...... III.4:6 **A.** these are but the fearful thoughts of
T-20...... III.5:3 It is not there at **a.**. Yet judgment lays a
T-20...... III.6:6 watches over **a.** perception answered.
T-20...... III.7:6 in **a.** the universe that does not know. Yet
T-20.... III.7:10 in **a.** the seeing universe of truth you ask,
T-20...... III.8:6 give him thanks for **a.** the happiness that
T-20.... III.10:5 **a.** thoughts of any separation between us
T-20...... IV.1:3 lose. It is not up to you to give power at **a.**.
T-20...... IV.1:8 already given and received **a.** that is true.
T-20...... IV.2:7 It lies in him to overlook **a.** your mistakes,
T-20...... IV.4:5 upheld through **a.** temptation to imprison
T-20...... IV.5:4 separately, though they are **a.** the same.
T-20...... IV.5:5 they are **a.** the same need not salvation.
T-20...... IV.6:4 For in your part lies **a.** of it, without which
T-20...... IV.7:4 forgetting **a.** the rest and yearning only to
T-20...... IV.7:4 fulfilled in them and **a.** their brothers.
T-20.... IV.8:10 guarantee will hold against **a.** obstacles,
T-20....... V.3:2 but **a.** it means is that it wants the other
T-20....... V.3:6 worth when **a.** you want for him is peace.
T-20....... V.5:8 through time like golden light is **a.** the
T-20....... V.6:3 **A.** that it ever held or will ever hold is
T-20...... VI.4:6 **a.** that it could offer is seen as valueless.
T-20...... VI.5:7 in **a.** the universe where it can not be seen
T-20...... VI.8:6 possible, **a.** your relationships were made
T-20..... VII.2:7 sincere and say, "I want this above **a.** else,
T-20..... VII.6:2 see him as sinful; he does not see him at **a.**
T-20... VIII.2:4 Your holy relationship offers **a.** this to you
T-20... VIII.2:8 **A.** this is given you who would but see
T-20... VIII.2:9 **A.** this is given, waiting on your desire but
T-20... VIII.3:2 For peace will come to **a.** who ask for it
T-20... VIII.5:8 **A.** is redeemed when looked upon with
T-20... VIII.6:8 **A.** that could save you, you will never see.
T-20... VIII.7:2 But vision sets **a.** things right, bringing
T-20... VIII.8:4 **a.** you need to do is recognize that *you* did
T-20... VIII.8:9 Yet they are **a.** the same. Again there is no
T-20... VIII.9:8 Yet upon nothing are **a.** projections made.
T-20... VIII.9:9 the "nothing" **a.** the meaning that it holds
T-20. VIII.10:3 out. **A.** meaning that you give the world
T-20. VIII.10:3 if you saw at **a.** or merely judged against.
T-20. VIII.10:4 that show you **a.** the fearful outcomes of
T-20. VIII.10:6 substitutes for **a.** the terrifying sights and
T-21....... in.2:2 and **a.** you see is what you did to hurt the
T-21......... I.5:2 And so it is with **a.** who see the body as all
T-21......... I.5:2 as **a.** they have and all their brothers have.
T-21......... I.5:2 as all they have and **a.** their brothers have.
T-21......... I.8:2 And **a.** the circle fills with light before
T-21......... I.8:3 what is in it is no longer contained at **a.**.
T-21......... I.9:3 you are; a part of this, with **a.** of it within,
T-21......... I.9:3 joined to **a.** as surely as all is joined in you.
T-21......... I.9:3 joined to all as surely as **a.** is joined in you.
T-21....... I.10:6 not? The light in one awakens it in **a.**. And
T-21....... II.2:1 escape from sin, **a.** to be given you. Say
T-21....... II.2:7 **a.** effects of your mistakes will disappear.
T-21....... II.6:4 **A.** that the ego is, is an idea that it is
T-21....... II.7:6 **A.** that is asked of you is to make room for
T-21....... II.7:8 **A.** you are asked to do is *let it in;* only to
T-21....... II.9:6 you will uphold it by not realizing **a.** the
T-21..... II.13:4 **A.** its effects are gone, because its source
T-21....... III.1:1 **A.** special relationships have sin as their
T-21....... III.4:2 from **a.** illusions where your faith was laid
T-21....... III.4:5 and His belief and vision are **a.** for you.
T-21....... III.6:1 The Holy Spirit has a use for **a.** the means
T-21....... III.6:6 of a holy relationship is **a.** you *want* to see.
T-21....... III.7:1 as **a.** the means that once served sin are
T-21....... III.8:2 choosing to let **a.** limitations be removed.
T-21....... III.8:6 For **a.** who choose to look away from sin
T-21....... IV.6:6 you have realized that **a.** the gifts it would
T-21....... V.1:6 for God is not drowned out by **a.** the ego's
T-21....... V.4:5 **A.** sorts of questions may arise in it, but if
T-21....... V.4:6 Like **a.** that stems from reason, the basic
T-21....... V.7:5 threatens dissociation as much as **a.** of it.
T-21....... V.7:6 And **a.** of it will come with any part. Here
T-21....... V.8:2 But reason has no place at **a.** in madness,
T-21....... V.8:4 But reason enters not at **a.** in this. For the
T-21..... V.10:6 and **a.** the means for its accomplishment.
T-21...... VI.2:9 alone have no effect at **a.** on what *is* yours?
T-21...... VI.8:5 Heaven is what you want, and **a.** you want
T-21..... VII.1:1 Do you not see that **a.** your misery comes
T-21..... VII.3:8 Any way at **a.**. It could be seen attacking
T-21..... VII.6:3 would assure you they are **a.** the same.
T-21..... VII.8:3 **a.** you need do is simply ask yourself: *Is*
T-21... VII.11:1 In content **a.** the questions are the same.
T-21... VII.11:5 you have already made to **a.** the rest. For
T-21... VIII.3:7 has already given **a.** that he really wants.
T-22....... in.2:4 And **a.** this would be real if sin were so.
T-22....... in.4:8 and finally removes **a.** sense of differences
T-22....... in.4:8 lies beneath them **a.** becomes apparent.
T-22......... I.3:2 no messages at **a.** you understand. For
T-22......... I.3:3 to what can never communicate at **a.**.
T-22......... I.6:1 Of **a.** the messages you have received and
T-22....... II.2:6 **A.** that is possible in the dark world of
T-22....... II.4:4 the truth makes **a.** truth meaningless, and
T-22....... II.4:4 all truth meaningless, and **a.** illusions real
T-22....... II.7:4 course will be believed entirely or not at **a.**
T-22....... II.7:6 escape from misery entirely or not at **a.**.
T-22....... II.9:6 that the self he made, and **a.** it made,
T-22..... II.10:5 And **a.** the misery you made has been
T-22..... II.13:1 **A.** you need do to dwell in quiet here with
T-22..... II.13:3 be released entirely from **a.** effects of sin.
T-22...... III.4:6 preserve **a.** errors and make them sins.
T-22...... III.9:1 born, must value holiness above **a.** else.
T-22...... IV.6:1 **a.** who share the Love of God the grace is
T-22...... IV.6:3 **A.** barriers disappear before their coming,
T-22....... V.2:7 cost. **A.** that the Holy Spirit offers must be
T-22..... V.3:12 **a.** uncertainty is doubt about yourself.
T-22....... V.6:3 This is the cost of **a.** illusions. Not one but
T-22...... VI.3:1 Be not disturbed at **a.** to think how He
T-22...... VI.4:2 Be thankful that it serves yours not at **a.**.
T-22...... VI.4:4 relationship has the power to heal **a.** pain,
T-22...... VI.4:5 you nor your brother alone can serve at **a.**
T-22...... VI.5:2 with love, looks quietly on **a.** confusion,
T-22...... VI.6:6 now His means must love **a.** that He loves.
T-22...... VI.9:8 to it **a.** the power that God has given Him,
T-22.... VI.12:4 and **a.** were separate from your Creator.
T-22.... VI.15:2 And in Him is **a.** creation joined. Would
T-22.... VI.15:3 is there, which makes **a.** fear impossible?
T-23....... in.4:5 you, for **a.** these meaningless distractions,
T-23....... in.6:3 So will you come to understand **a.** that is
T-23......... I.4:5 was God Himself, to Whom **a.** conflict,
T-23......... I.4:5 and attack of any kind are **a.** unknown.
T-23......... I.8:9 Let **a.** this madness be undone for you,
T-23....... I.10:3 and let forgiveness sweep away **a.** trace of
T-23........ II.2:2 everyone. Like **a.** these principles, this one
T-23........ II.3:3 they are **a.** the same and equally untrue, it
T-23........ II.3:3 that miracles apply to **a.** of them. Errors
T-23........ II.8:3 From where **a.** this begins, there is no
T-23........ II.9:5 Yet **a.** the other laws must lead to this. For
T-23...... II.10:1 **A.** of the mechanisms of madness are
T-23...... II.12:5 is the magic that will cure **a.** of your pain;
T-23... II.12:12 **a.** your relationships have but the purpose
T-23...... II.16:7 takes seem to have meaning, and that is **a.**
T-23...... II.19:7 impossible and beyond **a.** reason, and yet
T-23...... II.20:1 The laws of chaos govern **a.** illusions.
T-23...... II.22:5 it is possible to have **a.** this undone. How
T-23...... IV.1:6 and what is **a.** the same cannot conflict.
T-23...... IV.2:9 creations **a.** that it is and never suffer loss
T-23...... IV.4:2 so it cannot be extended to **a.** creation.
T-23...... IV.4:3 you have the power to extend to **a.**. Yet
T-23...... IV.6:3 of pain, a twinge of guilt, and above **a.**, a
T-23...... IV.6:6 God Himself and **a.** the lights of Heaven
T-24..... in.2:10 your beliefs as certainly as **a.** creation rose
T-24......... I.1:6 has given it **a.** the reality it seems to have.
T-24......... I.2:3 power to direct **a.** subsequent decisions.
T-24......... I.2:8 **A.** that can be denied is their reality, but
T-24......... I.3:1 **A.** that is ever cherished as a hidden
T-24......... I.5:9 can he live, with **a.** your sins upon him?
T-24........ II.1:3 clear in sight, **a.** lacks it can perceive. This
T-24........ II.3:3 an evil flower with no roots at **a.**. Here is
T-24........ II.4:4 praise of what you are, is **a.** you listen to.
T-24........ II.5:5 which does not see his specialness at **a.**.
T-24........ II.6:4 And **a.** the world he made, and all his
T-24........ II.6:4 the world he made, and **a.** his specialness,
T-24........ II.6:4 **a.** the sins he held in its defense against
T-24........ II.7:1 the power to forgive you **a.** the sins you
T-24........ II.8:5 it. Let him forgive you **a.** your specialness,
T-24........ II.9:6 Leave **a.** illusions of yourself outside this
T-24...... II.12:6 the great defender of **a.** illusions from the
T-24...... II.13:3 apart and separate from **a.** your brothers;
T-24...... II.13:3 from **a.** intrusions of sanity upon illusions
T-24...... II.14:2 save through the sight of **a.** your misery,
T-24...... III.1:3 Forgiveness is release from **a.** illusions,
T-24...... III.2:2 strongly defended with **a.** your puny
T-24...... III.4:4 or creeps or crawls, or even lives at **a.**.
T-24...... III.5:6 one Mind They wait for **a.** illusions to be
T-24...... III.7:1 special ones are **a.** asleep, surrounded by
T-24...... IV.2:8 What they are, and **a.** their attributes,
T-24.... IV.3:10 but only in the sense that **a.** illusions are
T-24...... IV.4:6 **A.** that is real proclaims his sinlessness.
T-24...... IV.4:7 **A.** that is false proclaims his sins as real. If
T-24....... V.6:2 in gentleness and blessing **a.** the way. His
T-24....... V.6:3 His Love for God replaces **a.** the fear you
T-24....... V.7:2 hand holds **a.** His brothers in Himself. He
T-24....... V.7:4 that everyone may bless **a.** living things,
T-24....... V.7:6 you may save **a.** living things from death,
T-24....... V.7:7 The sight of Christ is **a.** there is to see. The
T-24....... V.7:8 The song of Christ is **a.** there is to hear.
T-24....... V.7:9 The hand of Christ is **a.** there is to hold.
T-24....... V.9:4 exchange His certainty for **a.** your doubts,
T-24...... VI.1:7 offered you that **a.** your doubts about
T-24...... VI.3:1 Nothing is lost to you in **a.** the universe.
T-24...... VI.4:1 healing of God's Son is **a.** the world is for.
T-24...... VI.4:3 the healing of the Son as **a.** you wish to be

| | |
|---|---|
| T-24...... VI.4:3 | by the world, by time and **a.** appearances, |
| T-24...... VI.4:5 | you to be beyond its laws in **a.** respects, in |
| T-24...... VI.4:5 | in **a.** temptation to perceive what is not |
| T-24...... VI.4:5 | and **a.** belief God's Son can suffer pain |
| T-24...... VI.5:5 | one judgment made for **a.** it looks upon. |
| T-24...... VI.9:2 | kind, is **a.** the other choice can offer you. |
| T-24...... VI.9:5 | to laws that have no power over him at **a.**. |
| T-24.... VI.10:3 | part of God holds not for **a.** the rest. You |
| T-24.... VI.11:3 | with **a.** the power to hold itself complete |
| T-24.... VI.11:5 | **a.** this grim determination was for this; |
| T-24.... VI.12:5 | and **a.** the power of Heaven and the might |
| T-24.... VI.13:5 | Him this judgment makes no sense at **a.**. |
| T-24..... VII.2:2 | your brother still contains **a.** of creation, |
| T-24..... VII.2:6 | to you. **A.** of the tribute you have given |
| T-24..... VII.2:7 | to you. **A.** of the love and care, the strong |
| T-24..... VII.7:4 | one, nor does this one have any end at **a.**. |
| T-24..... VII.7:5 | **A.** this is true, and yet it has no meaning |
| T-24..... VII.8:5 | it be kept in mind that **a.** perception still |
| T-24... VII.11:6 | and separates each from **a.** aspects with a |
| T-25......... I.2:4 | your sinfulness, your evil and, above **a.**, |
| T-25......... I.4:3 | release **a.** that it looks upon unto itself. Its |
| T-25......... I.4:4 | brushes **a.** its darkness into light merely |
| T-25......... I.5:3 | as **a.** your brothers join as one in truth. |
| T-25......... I.7:1 | **A.** this takes note of time and place as if |
| T-25......... I.7:2 | which unites **a.** things within Itself. And |
| T-25......... I.7:3 | mind, and does unite **a.** things together, |
| T-25......... I.7:5 | It must use **a.** learning to transfer illusions |
| T-25......... I.7:5 | truth, taking **a.** false ideas of what you are |
| T-25......... I.7:6 | **A.** this can very simply be reduced to this: |
| T-25....... II.2:4 | hopes, and no suggestions of success at **a.**. |
| T-25....... II.5:3 | set within this frame is **a.** there is to see. |
| T-25....... II.5:8 | of this? And see the picture not at **a.**? |
| T-25....... II.6:8 | God creates is safe from **a.** corruption, |
| T-25....... II.9:8 | And **a.** His thanks and gladness shine on |
| T-25..... II.10:4 | that **a.** His praise is given not to you. For |
| T-25..... II.11:5 | apart from **a.** God's Love as given equally. |
| T-25...... III.2:3 | world where this reflection is, is real at **a.**. |
| T-25...... III.6:8 | And he will reinterpret **a.** temptation as |
| T-25...... III.7:2 | sin? Let **a.** your brother's errors be to you |
| T-25...... III.9:8 | when **a.** time becomes a means to reach a |
| T-25...... IV.3:2 | world you bring with you to **a.** the weary |
| T-25...... IV.3:5 | there is a vision that extends to **a.** of them, |
| T-25...... IV.3:7 | **a.** their "evil" thoughts and "sinful" hopes |
| T-25...... IV.5:1 | In you is **a.** of Heaven. Every leaf that falls |
| T-25.... IV.5:11 | This can you bring to **a.** the world, and all |
| T-25.... IV.5:11 | and **a.** the thoughts that entered it and |
| T-25....... V.4:8 | depriving him of **a.** the joy he would have |
| T-25...... VI.1:6 | with **a.** the tenderness it offers others. For |
| T-25...... VI.1:8 | power to heal and bless **a.** those he looks |
| T-25...... VI.5:5 | Forgiveness is for **a.**. But when it rests on |
| T-25...... VI.5:6 | But when it rests on **a.** it is complete, and |
| T-25...... VI.5:9 | for on his part does **a.** the plan depend. |
| T-25...... VI.6:3 | you think you see in it is really there at **a.**. |
| T-25...... VI.7:4 | you. **A.** that you made can serve salvation |
| T-25...... VI.7:7 | plan to save the Son of God from **a.** attack |
| T-25..... VII.1:2 | thing in **a.** the world that cannot change. |
| T-25..... VII.3:3 | makes any sense at **a.** within this world. |
| T-25..... VII.3:4 | as true has any meaning in His Mind at **a.**. |
| T-25..... VII.3:8 | **a.** beliefs the world gives any meaning to |
| T-25..... VII.3:8 | to are false, and make no sense at **a.**. This |
| T-25..... VII.7:3 | and **a.** that you believe must limit you. |
| T-25..... VII.9:1 | nor fail completely to perceive at **a.**. To |
| T-25..... VII.9:3 | and **a.** the sin he sees within the world, |
| T-25... VII.10:6 | And that in Heaven *They* are **a.** the same, |
| T-25... VII.11:6 | be the total cost of any gain at **a.**. You who |
| T-25... VII.12:5 | for **a.** insane beliefs can be corrected here. |
| T-25... VII.13:1 | Remember **a.** temptation is but this; a |
| T-25.... VIII.1:1 | Holy Spirit can use **a.** that you give to Him |
| T-25.... VIII.2:2 | attack from **a.** beliefs opposed to it. You |
| T-25.... VIII.4:2 | Justice looks on **a.** in the same way. It is |
| T-25.... VIII.4:7 | to "atone" for **a.** that you would keep, and |
| T-25.... VIII.5:8 | mind that can conceive of specialness at **a.** |
| T-25.... VIII.8:2 | and give them **a.** the honor they deserve |
| T-25.... VIII.9:1 | ask of you who think that **a.** of this is true |
| T-25.... VIII.9:5 | justice does He recognize **a.** you deserve, |
| T-25.. VIII.10:2 | indeed to **a.** the holiness that is in him, |
| T-25.. VIII.10:4 | death, and could not see his worth at **a.**. |
| T-25.. VIII.10:8 | from **a.** unfairness you might seek to offer |
| T-25.. VIII.12:3 | but shadows of **a.** that is really happening |
| T-25 . VIII.14:1 | You have the right to **a.** the universe; to |
| T-25 . VIII.14:1 | complete deliverance from **a.** effects of sin |
| T-25 . VIII.14:2 | and **a.** the Holy Spirit brings to earth. |
| T-25 . VIII.14:4 | you are safe from vengeance in **a.** forms. |
| T-25 ..... IX.1:3 | willing to be released from **a.** effects of sin |
| T-25 ..... IX.1:4 | you see **a.** that the answer must entail. For |
| T-25 ..... IX.1:5 | it means you will forego **a.** values of this |
| T-25 ..... IX.1:8 | has greater value now than **a.** illusions. |
| T-25 ..... IX.2:4 | where **a.** of the treasures given to God's |
| T-25 ..... IX.8:1 | Unless you think that **a.** your brothers |
| T-25 ... IX.10:2 | rests; that justice must be done to **a.**, if |
| T-26 ........ I.1:2 | It is the pivot upon which **a.** compromise, |
| T-26 ........ I.1:2 | **a.** desperate attempts to strike a bargain, |
| T-26 ........ I.1:2 | and **a.** conflicts achieve a seeming balance |
| T-26 ........ I.1:8 | itself. **A.** seeming entities can come a little |
| T-26 ........ I.3:1 | preserved through sacrifice of **a.** the rest. |
| T-26 ........ I.3:2 | And **a.** the rest must lose this little part, |
| T-26 ........ I.4:9 | song of union and of love be heard at **a.**. |
| T-26 ........ I.8:1 | keeps him safe from **a.** injustice the world |
| T-26 ....... II.1:1 | Holy Spirit to solve **a.** problems for you. |
| T-26 ....... II.1:7 | until it has been answered for **a.** time and |
| T-26 ....... II.4:1 | miracle of justice can correct **a.** errors. |
| T-26 ....... II.7:1 | to receive correction for **a.** your problems. |
| T-26 ....... II.7:4 | For **a.** of them *are* little in His sight, and |
| T-26 ....... II.7:7 | shine away **a.** memory of sacrifice and loss |
| T-26 ....... II.8:5 | And **a.** you need to do is but to wish that |
| T-26 ..... III.1:2 | How could it be, when **a.** He knows is One |
| T-26 ..... III.2:3 | conflicting values meet and **a.** illusions |
| T-26 ..... III.4:7 | to make a choice at **a.** is this distinction. |
| T-26 ..... III.7:2 | **A.** illusions are but one. And in the |
| T-26 ..... III.7:3 | up **a.** attempts to choose between them, |
| T-26 ..... III.7:7 | **a.** reality has been withdrawn from what |
| T-26 ..... IV.3:4 | universe to touch the Heart of **a.** creation? |
| T-26 ..... IV.3:8 | and **a.** their radiance made whole again. |
| T-26 ...... V.1:1 | understand that miracles are **a.** the same. |
| T-26 ...... V.1:3 | for only that is **a.** there is to learn. And |
| T-26 ...... V.1:5 | **A.** learning is a help or hindrance to the |
| T-26 ...... V.2:4 | the way to Heaven's gate is difficult at **a.**. |
| T-26 ...... V.3:4 | And so is **a.** time past, and everything |
| T-26 ...... V.3:5 | and **a.** of them within that one mistake, |
| T-26 ...... V.3:5 | and **a.** of them that came within the first. |
| T-26 ...... V.3:6 | time was gone, for that was **a.** it ever was. |
| T-26 ...... V.5:5 | in every judgment and in **a.** belief in sin, is |
| T-26 .... V.12:4 | for **a.** time and every circumstance. And |
| T-26 .... V.13:2 | past and present, which is not a gap at **a.**. |
| T-26 .... V.13:4 | And **a.** of time is but the mad belief that |
| T-26 ..... VI.1:5 | perceived reality has entered **a.** the world |
| T-26 ..... VI.1:6 | **A.** belief in sin, in power of attack, in hurt |
| T-26 ..... VI.2:3 | Whom **a.** power in earth and Heaven rests |
| T-26 .... VII.1:3 | that summarizes **a.** that must occur for |
| T-26 .... VII.2:1 | **A.** sickness comes from separation. |
| T-26 .... VII.4:2 | of sickness, which applies to **a.** its forms. |
| T-26 .... VII.4:6 | is real, and dwells where **a.** reality must be |
| T-26 .... VII.4:9 | external to the mind, is not outside at **a.**, |
| T-26 .... VII.6:4 | although this clearly makes no sense at **a.**. |
| T-26 .... VII.6:5 | **A.** that a hierarchy of illusions can show is |
| T-26 .... VII.6:9 | and **a.** must yield with equal ease to what |
| T-26 .... VII.6:9 | to what God gave as answer to them **a.**. |
| T-26 .... VII.7:4 | and **a.** creation be subjected to the laws of |
| T-26 .... VII.8:6 | and **a.** beliefs that rise from mists of guilt. |
| T-26 .. VII.10:4 | a unity which holds **a.** things within itself? |
| T-26 .. VII.15:3 | God gave to **a.** illusions that were made |
| T-26 .. VII.15:4 | In every miracle **a.** healing lies, for God |
| T-26 .. VII.15:4 | for God gave answer to them **a.** as one. |
| T-26 .. VII.17:4 | from hell and death, **a.** glory be forever. |
| T-26 .. VII.17:6 | And in your hands does **a.** salvation lie, to |
| T-26 .. VII.18:2 | make use of what He gave to answer **a.** His |
| T-26 .. VII.19:4 | can save each one of us can save us **a.**. |
| T-26 .. VII.19:6 | that specialness denies will save them **a.**, |
| T-26 .. VII.19:9 | To get from one is to deprive them **a.**. |
| T-26 VII.19:10 | but one gives blessing to them **a.** as one. |
| T-26 .. VII.20:3 | has already answered **a.** who call on Him? |
| T-26 .. VII.20:4 | A miracle can make no change at **a.**. But it |
| T-26 .. VII.20:5 | **a.** creation freed to call upon the Name of |
| T-26 ... VIII.5:1 | The plans you make for safety **a.** are laid |
| T-26 ... VIII.5:9 | but which is **a.** there is to time. |
| T-26 ... VIII.6:1 | working out of **a.** correction takes no time |
| T-26 ... VIII.6:1 | out of all correction takes no time at **a.**. |
| T-26 ... VIII.6:3 | has in it **a.** effects that you will see. They |
| T-26 ... VIII.7:3 | Its cause is here, if it appears at **a.**. Why |
| T-26 . VIII.7:10 | asks for what He gave without a cost at **a.**. |
| T-26 ..... IX.2:1 | you, that you may be forgiven **a.** your sins |
| T-26 ..... IX.3:1 | let the flowers be **a.** white and sparkling |
| T-26 ..... IX.3:8 | **a.** the blight and withering have passed |
| T-26 ..... IX.6:1 | holiest of **a.** the spots on earth is where an |
| T-26 ..... IX.6:6 | And **a.** the lights in Heaven brighter grow, |
| T-26 ..... IX.7:1 | to keep away **a.** darkened thoughts of sin, |
| T-26 ....... X.1:6 | If it occurs at **a.** it will be total. And its |
| T-26 ....... X.1:8 | They are known with clarity or not at **a.**. |
| T-26 ....... X.2:6 | this denies the fact that ***a.*** are senseless, |
| T-26 ....... X.5:6 | is but to take away **a.** purpose from the |
| T-26 ....... X.6:2 | not a trace of **a.** the happy sparkle that |
| T-26 ....... X.6:4 | and there has **a.** unfairness been resolved |
| T-27 ........ I.1:9 | If it could occur at **a.** it would entail the |
| T-27 ........ I.3:4 | you show yourself, and give it **a.** your faith |
| T-27 ........ I.3:5 | there is no pain and no reproach at **a.**. |
| T-27 ........ I.5:3 | and therefore never suffered pain at **a.**. It |
| T-27 ...... I.6:11 | vanity of real concern with anything at **a.**. |
| T-27 ........ I.7:1 | that bolsters **a.** the rest and helps them |
| T-27 ........ I.7:6 | death will pay the price for **a.** of them, if |
| T-27 ........ I.9:4 | not. It only takes away from it **a.** signs of |
| T-27 ........ I.9:6 | that it may be judged in any way at **a.**. It |
| T-27 ........ I.9:8 | stands apart from **a.** experience of love or |
| T-27 ..... II.1:10 | to **a.** the guilt that he has really earned. |
| T-27 ....... II.6:4 | Thus does the miracle undo **a.** things the |
| T-27 ....... II.7:4 | that healing sees no specialness at **a.**. It |
| T-27 ....... II.7:6 | prove **a.** suffering is but a vain imagining, |
| T-27 ....... II.8:4 | his, and cannot be apart from his at **a.**. As |
| T-27 ..... II.13:3 | half the error, which you think is **a.** of it. |
| T-27 ..... II.14:5 | his presence is perceived as **a.** of you. To |
| T-27 ......... III.h | Beyond **A.** Symbols |
| T-27 ..... III.2:1 | love," a "weakened power," and above **a.**, |
| T-27 ..... III.3:4 | And thus the picture has no cause at **a.**. |
| T-27 ..... III.7:7 | no other kind can be at **a.**. Give welcome |
| T-27 ..... IV.1:1 | In quietness are **a.** things answered, and |
| T-27 ..... IV.1:6 | be clear you cannot answer anything at **a.**, |
| T-27 ..... IV.2:5 | It is here that **a.** your problems should be |
| T-27 ..... IV.4:1 | **A.** questions asked within this world are |
| T-27 ..... IV.4:7 | bring escape from **a.** the pain of which |
| T-27 ... IV.4:13 | get that you would want the most of **a.**? It |
| T-27 ..... IV.5:3 | Thus is **a.** questioning within the world a |
| T-27 ..... IV.6:7 | asking not if sacrifice is meaningful at **a.**. |
| T-27 ....... V.3:4 | **a.** the hurt that war has sought to bring, |
| T-27 ....... V.4:2 | attack is necessary that **a.** this occur. In |
| T-27 ....... V.4:3 | in that single instant is **a.** healing done. |
| T-27 ....... V.4:5 | One Who blesses you loves **a.** the world, |
| T-27 ....... V.5:2 | The eyes of **a.** the dying bring reproach, |
| T-27 ....... V.6:5 | give them sight to see beyond **a.** suffering |
| T-27 ....... V.7:6 | in which **a.** eyes look lovingly upon the |
| T-27 ....... V.8:6 | and generalizes to include them **a.**. This is |
| T-27 ....... V.8:8 | forms. **A.** learning aims at transfer, which |
| T-27 ..... V.8:11 | made in spite of **a.** the differences you see, |
| T-27 ....... V.9:4 | **A.** healing must proceed in lawful manner |
| T-27 ..... V.10:3 | by **a.** the many different witnesses it finds. |
| T-27 ..... V.11:7 | Yet **a.** the witnesses that you behold will |
| T-27 ..... V.11:7 | will be far less than **a.** there really are. |
| T-27 ..... VI.1:6 | unites **a.** those who share in it within itself |
| T-27 ..... VI.2:6 | for this, the witnesses of sin are **a.** alike. |
| T-27 ..... VI.3:1 | itself, holds **a.** your memories and all your |
| T-27 ..... VI.3:1 | all your memories and **a.** your hopes. You |
| T-27 ..... VI.4:9 | alike, for **a.** sin's witnesses do His replace. |
| T-27 ..... VI.5:6 | the miracle perceives them **a.** as one, and |
| T-27 ..... VI.8:2 | holy instant will replace **a.** sin if you but |
| T-27 .... VII.1:1 | Suffering is an emphasis upon **a.** that the |
| T-27 .... VII.2:2 | **A.** that is needed is you look upon the |
| T-27 .... VII.2:4 | will emerge in **a.** its primitive simplicity. |
| T-27 .... VII.7:1 | to sin **a.** stand within one little space. And |
| T-27 .... VII.7:4 | Of **a.** the many causes you perceived as |
| T-27 .... VII.7:6 | This is how **a.** illusions came about. The |
| T-27 .. VII.10:6 | Awaken and forget **a.** thoughts of death, |
| T-27 .. VII.12:4 | hate, the instant of disaster, **a.** are here. |
| T-27 .. VII.15:5 | to him for **a.** the helpfulness he gave. And |
| T-27 .. VII.16:3 | Let **a.** your brother's gifts be seen in light |
| T-27 ... VIII.1:8 | Above **a.**, it tries to teach itself its pains |
| T-27 ... VIII.4:3 | That this is **a.** the body does is true, for it |
| T-27 ... VIII.5:1 | of **a.** the dreams the world has ever had? |
| T-27 ... VIII.6:2 | Into eternity, where **a.** is one, there crept a |
| T-27 ... VIII.7:1 | a mind within a body **a.** are forms of |

T-27... VIII.7:6 which it punishes because of a. the sinful
T-27... VIII.8:4 to perceive the jest when a. around you do
T-27. VIII.10:5 For you would not react at a. to figures in
T-27. VIII.11:5 The form affects His answer not at a., for
T-27. VIII.11:5 you but the single cause of a. of them, no
T-27. VIII.12:1 a. forms of suffering to Him Who knows
T-27. VIII.12:3 None has a different cause from a. the rest
T-27. VIII.12:3 and a. of them are easily undone by but a
T-27. VIII.12:6 Yet to its witnesses you pay no heed at a..
T-28.........I.1:2 A. it does is to undo. And thus it cancels
T-28.........I.2:1 A. the effects of guilt are here no more.
T-28.........I.2:8 And like a. the things you made, it can be
T-28.........I.3:1 represents an effort to do anything at a..
T-28.........I.3:4 A. things the Holy Spirit can employ for
T-28.........I.5:7 of a. the body's past is hidden there. All of
T-28.........I.5:8 A. of the strange associations made to
T-28.........I.6:2 It works hand in hand with a. the other
T-28...... I.11:3 the Mind which caused a. minds to be.
T-28...... I.11:4 delay in hastening to a. unquiet minds,
T-28...... I.12:2 to offer a. its treasures to the Son of God,
T-28...... I.14:2 made is causeless, having no effects at a..
T-28....... II.1:8 in itself it holds the universe of a. creation
T-28....... II.2:8 Yet must a. healing come about because
T-28....... II.2:8 apart from it, and where a. healing is.
T-28....... II.4:1 Nothing at a. has happened but that you
T-28....... II.5:1 holds a. your shreds of memories and
T-28.... II.12:7 until a. the steps have been retraced, the
T-28.... II.12:7 and a. the dreaming of the world undone.
T-28...... III.3:6 coming that you want above a. things that
T-28...... III.4:5 of the gap is a. the cause that sickness has.
T-28...... III.6:4 The miracle will brush them a. aside, and
T-28...... III.7:1 as a. the treasures you would keep within
T-28...... III.8:7 a. those may come who would no longer
T-28...... III.9:2 the more is left for a. the rest to share. The
T-28...... IV.8:5 clean of a. the seeds of sickness and of sin.
T-28...... IV.9:3 joined because what is in one is in them a.
T-28.... IV.10:8 go is a. the Healer of God's Son requires.
T-28....... V.4:1 to be the place where a. your safety lies,
T-28....... V.6:1 it shares the function a. creation shares. It
T-28....... V.6:2 perhaps, a. put together to attest its truth.
T-28...... VI.4:1 own and a. the rest of what is really yours.
T-28..... VII.2:1 you have with a. your brothers is a part of
T-28..... VII.2:5 it. For healing will be one or not at a., its
T-28..... VII.4:6 A. miracles are based upon this choice,
T-28..... VII.5:5 Yet a. it means is that you tried to keep a
T-29.........I.1:6 A. this do you believe, when you perceive
T-29.........I.9:1 Yet a. that happens when the gap is gone
T-29....... II.3:6 loss, and a. effects of hatred and attack.
T-29....... II.4:6 help in giving them to a. who walk apart,
T-29....... II.5:4 and a. the happiness His Presence brings,
T-29....... II.8:4 it asks that God be less than a. He really is
T-29...... III.2:7 the world has built to keep apart a. living
T-29...... IV.2:5 of dreams, from which they a. are made.
T-29...... IV.6:5 can utilize a. dreams as means to serve the
T-29....... V.5:1 you but that you see in a. creation but the
T-29....... V.5:2 to whom is a. creation given as his own.
T-29....... V.7:2 forgiven him for a. his dreams of death; a
T-29....... V.8:6 And leading finally beyond a. dreams,
T-29...... VI.2:6 thing in a. the universe that must be one.
T-29...... VI.2:7 What *seems* eternal a. will have an end.
T-29...... VI.2:9 A. things that come and go, the tides, the
T-29...... VI.2:9 men; a. things that change with time and
T-29...... VI.4:1 gave to a. that you would make eternal, to
T-29...... VI.4:4 A. other goals are set in time and change
T-29..... VII.1:7 a. your pain comes simply from a futile
T-29..... VII.2:3 off and found where a. the rest of it is not.
T-29..... VII.3:2 And each will fail him, a. excepting one;
T-29..... VII.6:1 A. idols of this world were made to keep
T-29..... VII.7:2 dreams, in which a. idols fail you, one by
T-29..... VII.8:1 To change a. this, and open up a road of
T-29..... VII.9:9 a. the world becomes the means by which
T-29... VIII.2:6 apart from a. the misery the world reflects
T-29... VIII.3:5 A. forms of anti-Christ oppose the Christ.
T-29... VIII.6:5 of God, forever given to a. living things,
T-29... VIII.7:4 A place of darkness set where a. is light, a
T-29... VIII.7:5 where God has set a. things forever, and
T-29... VIII.9:7 God gave you a. there is. And to be sure
T-29...... IX.3:1 A. figures in the dream are idols, made to
T-29...... IX.6:3 Put them a. away, for you have need of
T-29...... IX.6:7 and he is afraid of a. the chaos in a world
T-29...... IX.7:5 for childish things have a. been put away.
T-29...... IX.7:6 has changed into a dream where a. is joy,
T-29...... IX.8:4 has not heard it since before a. time began
T-29...... IX.9:2 conceal completely a. your sense of doom.
T-29.... IX.10:6 And a. the while he is remembering what
T-30.......I.13:1 prevent unhappiness from entering at a..
T-30.......I.14:5 That is really a.. The first rule, then, is not
T-30.......I.16:3 that permits a. things to happen. Nothing
T-30.......I.17:1 this day to promise it to a. the world. It
T-30.......I.17:3 and gives it a. effects that it will ever have.
T-30....... II.1:4 And a. He knows is but your knowledge,
T-30....... II.3:5 with God Himself in a. creation's birth.
T-30......... III.h Beyond A. Idols
T-30...... III.1:5 and that, by limiting, is a. attained. It is as
T-30...... III.2:3 form can take the place of a. the love in
T-30.... III.2:11 because what shares in a. creation cannot
T-30...... III.5:2 He has no need to seek for it at a.. Beyond
T-30...... III.5:3 Beyond a. idols stands his holy will to be
T-30...... III.7:2 a. this means is that you are sometimes
T-30...... III.8:1 Thoughts of God are far beyond a. change
T-30...... III.8:6 and lovely will it shine through a. eternity
T-30.... III.10:1 Beyond a. idols is the Thought God holds
T-30.... III.10:4 completely unaware of a. the world that
T-30...... IV.1:8 A. idols are the false ideas you made to fill
T-30...... IV.4:3 safety. A. illusions that you believe about
T-30.... IV.4:10 See one in them and you will see them a..
T-30...... IV.5:7 a power that can have no real effects at a.?
T-30.... IV.5:13 His idols do not threaten him at a.. His
T-30...... IV.7:3 you forgive a. things that no one ever did;
T-30...... IV.7:5 of a. the dreams of what you never were,
T-30....... V.1:5 a wish to understand a. things created as
T-30....... V.1:6 it is recognized that a. things must be first
T-30....... V.2:8 of the world is one which a. must share, if
T-30....... V.3:7 step in which is a. forgiveness left behind.
T-30....... V.6:2 And a. that stood between your image of
T-30....... V.9:2 And with it goes a. hatred and all fear.
T-30....... V.9:2 And with it goes all hatred and a. fear.
T-30....... V.9:3 ahead is a. you ever wanted in your heart.
T-30...... VI.3:6 And this is a. the world can ever give. It
T-30...... VI.6:2 are not prepared, as yet, to let a. idols go.
T-30...... VI.6:3 are real and not appearances at a.. Be not
T-30...... VI.7:1 must be true the miracle can heal a. forms
T-30...... VI.7:4 And you could not escape a. guilt, but
T-30...... VI.9:2 guilt in a. its consequences and its forms.
T-30..... VII.1:7 a. that happens now means something
T-30..... VII.2:3 These judgments a. are made according to
T-30..... VII.3:2 But it must accord *one* meaning to them a.
T-30..... VII.3:4 And this is a. the meaning that they have.
T-30..... VII.4:1 given to the world and a. experiences here
T-30..... VII.4:5 And so you offer it to a. events, and let
T-30..... VII.5:1 lies in this; a. things have but one purpose
T-30..... VII.5:1 which you share with a. the world. And
T-30..... VII.5:3 purpose is the end of a. ideas of sacrifice,
T-30..... VII.6:5 A. sacrifice entails the loss of your ability
T-30..... VII.7:7 so that they mean the same to a. of us.
T-30..... VII.7:8 language lets us speak to a. our brothers,
T-30..... VII.7:8 them forgiveness has been given to us a.,
T-30... VIII.1:3 It does not deceive at a., and if you fail to
T-30... VIII.1:7 and keeps it separate from a. appearances
T-30... VIII.1:8 It must transcend a. form to be itself. It
T-30... VIII.2:1 to demonstrate that a. appearances can
T-30... VIII.2:5 his perfect freedom from a. forms of lack,
T-30... VIII.2:5 lack, and safety from disaster of a. kinds.
T-30... VIII.4:2 is unreal, and does not interfere at a.. The
T-30... VIII.4:4 be withheld from power to heal a. dreams
T-30... VIII.4:7 Who gives a. miracles has not been given
T-30... VIII.5:1 already there to heal a. things that change
T-31.........I.1:2 A. it says is what was never true is not
T-31.........I.1:4 And that is a.. Can this be hard to learn by
T-31.........I.2:4 from one to another, with no strain at a..
T-31.........I.5:5 skill the Holy Spirit sees in a. the world.
T-31.........I.6:5 and far beyond a. doubt and question?
T-31.........I.9:3 you remembers God with a. the certainty
T-31.......I.11:6 a. the world will give you joy and peace.
T-31.......I.12:1 and forget a. things we ever learned, all
T-31.......I.12:1 we ever learned, a. thoughts we had, and
T-31....... II.3:2 Thus is it really not a choice at a.. The
T-31....... II.7:1 you will be saved from a. appearances and
T-31........II.7:5 Christ calls to a. with equal tenderness,
T-31........II.7:5 and hearing but one answer to them a..
T-31........II.8:2 Come without a. thought of what you ever
T-31........II.8:2 before, and put aside a. images you made.
T-31........II.9:1 Forgive your brother a. appearances, that
T-31........II.9:2 for mercy and release from a. the fearful
T-31...... III.1:3 your first response to a. temptation, and
T-31...... III.2:7 occur to you to give attack to anyone at a..
T-31...... III.3:6 and doing nothing of itself at a.. If you are
T-31...... III.4:8 Learning is a. that causes change. And so
T-31.... III.4:10 can learn, and there is a. change made.
T-31...... IV.2:3 A. its roads but lead to disappointment,
T-31...... IV.2:7 not deceived by a. the different names its
T-31...... IV.2:9 end, for it is here that a. its roads will lead
T-31.... IV.2:11 A. of them will lead to death. On some
T-31...... IV.3:2 Perhaps you would prefer to try them a.,
T-31...... IV.3:7 A. must reach this point, and go beyond it
T-31...... IV.3:8 true indeed there is no choice at a. within
T-31...... IV.4:2 to the search that a. must undertake who
T-31...... IV.5:1 away from a. the roadways of the world,
T-31...... IV.8:4 A. choices in the world depend on this;
T-31...... IV.8:5 when a. the lesson's purpose is to teach
T-31...... IV.9:4 What road in a. the world will lead within
T-31...... IV.9:5 A. roads that lead away from what you are
T-31.... IV.11:1 forget a. senseless journeys and all goal-
T-31.... IV.11:1 all senseless journeys and a. goal-less aims
T-31....... V.2:2 It bears no likeness to yourself at a.. It is
T-31....... V.6:6 shrouded vaults are a. his sins and yours
T-31....... V.7:9 For a. of them are made within the world,
T-31....... V.8:2 is a. learning that the world directs begun
T-31..... V.10:5 And who is deceived by a. your goodness,
T-31..... V.11:2 see, if a. its underpinnings were removed?
T-31..... V.15:7 of the self embraces a. you look upon, and
T-31..... V.17:2 come a time when images have a. gone by,
T-31...... VI.1:5 What you decide in this determines a. you
T-31...... VI.1:6 this one choice does a. your world depend
T-31...... VI.1:8 and a. Heaven bends to touch your eyes
T-31...... VI.2:2 and happenings that make no sense at a..
T-31...... VI.2:6 dust? Salvation is undoing of a. this. For
T-31.... VI.3:10 It is not done at a.. What could there be
T-31...... VI.6:6 So is a. the world perceived as treacherous
T-31..... VII.2:6 his, because you let them a. affect you not.
T-31..... VII.5:3 a. this shift requires is that you be willing
T-31..... VII.7:2 A. things you see are images, because you
T-31..... VII.7:7 A. that is given you is for release; the sight
T-31..... VII.7:7 the vision and the inner Guide a. lead you
T-31..... VII.8:2 a. salvation from the misery of hell. And
T-31..... VII.9:1 a. are different names for just one error;
T-31... VII.10:4 rest. To everyone has God entrusted a.,
T-31... VII.10:5 are; a. those you saw an instant and forgot
T-31... VII.11:5 he see his innocence in a. he looks upon,
T-31... VII.13:2 It sees no past in anyone at a.. And thus it
T-31.... VIII.1:1 one lesson it would teach, in a. its forms,
T-31.... VIII.1:4 if Christ appeared to you in a. His glory,
T-31.... VIII.3:1 thus escape a. pain that what you chose
T-31.... VIII.3:2 In every difficulty, a. distress, and each
T-31.... VIII.3:4 remove a. misery from you whom God
T-31.... VIII.4:5 joined in a. the power of the Will of God.
T-31.... VIII.5:1 happy habit of response to a. temptation
T-31.... VIII.5:5 prevail, replacing a. your weakness with
T-31.... VIII.6:3 Yield not to this, and you will see a. pain,
T-31.... VIII.9:2 And thus will a. the vestiges of hell, the
T-31.... VIII.9:3 a. the loveliness which they concealed
T-31.. VIII.12:6 perfectly, and a. creation recognizes You,
T-31.. VIII.12:8 we have reached where a. of us are one,
W-in.......... 8:4 do. You are not asked to judge them at a..
W-pI.......... 2.h place] a. the meaning that it has for me.
W-pI....... 3.2:1 clear your mind of a. past associations, to
W-pI....... 5.1:3 a. of which will be perceived as different.
W-pI....... 5.1:6 in ultimately recognizing they are a. the
W-pI....... 5.4:4 *a. equally disturbing to my peace of mind.*
W-pI....... 5.6:4 *then, I will regard them a. as the same.*
W-pI....... 6.3:3 *a. equally disturbing to my peace of mind.*
W-pI....... 6.3:6 *then, I will regard them a. as the same.*
W-pI....... 7.1:2 the rationale for a. of the preceding ones.
W-pI....... 7.1:4 you see a. the meaning that it has for you.
W-pI....... 8.2:2 To think about it at a. is therefore to think
W-pI....... 8.3:1 when it is not really thinking at a.. While
W-pI..... 10.1:1 to a. the thoughts of which you are aware,

| | |
|---|---|
| W-pI.....10.1:2 | The reason the idea is applicable to **a.** of |
| W-pI.....10.4:3 | *help to release me from* **a.** *that I now believe.* |
| W-pI.....10.4:4 | searching your mind for **a.** the thoughts |
| W-pI.....10.5:5 | *help to release me from* **a.** *that I now believe.* |
| W-pI.....12.1:3 | **A.** these attributes are given it by you. The |
| W-pI.....12.2:7 | in learning to give them **a.** equal value. |
| W-pI.....12.3:7 | one. **A.** terms which cross your mind are |
| W-pI.....13.2:1 | intense anxiety in **a.** the separated ones. It |
| W-pI.....14.4:1 | think of **a.** the horrors in the world that |
| W-pI.....16.3:3 | recognize them **a.** as equally destructive, |
| W-pI.....19.2:4 | it must be true if salvation is possible at **a.** |
| W-pI.....19.4:2 | of subjects for **a.** practice periods remains |
| W-pI.....20.3:1 | decision to see is **a.** that vision requires. |
| W-pI.....20.3:7 | His will is done because **a.** power is given |
| W-pI.....21.4:1 | As you search your mind for **a.** the forms |
| W-pI.....22.2:5 | and kill. **A.** that you fear does not exist. |
| W-pI.....24.5:4 | situation, or even to be inherent in it at **a.**. |
| W-pI.....25.3:1 | are **a.** concerned with "personal" interests |
| W-pI.....25.3:3 | them, therefore, you have no goals at **a.**. |
| W-pI.....26.8:4 | them **a.** alike to whatever extent you can. |
| W-pI........27.h | Above **a.** else I want to see. |
| W-pI.....27.2:1 | you say you want to see above **a.** else. If |
| W-pI........28.h | **a.** else I want to see things differently. |
| W-pI.....28.2:1 | "Above **a.** else I want to see this table |
| W-pI.....28.2:2 | In itself it is not important at **a.**. Yet what |
| W-pI.....28.2:5 | really means you are not seeing at **a.**. You |
| W-pI.....28.2:7 | you will see **a.** things differently. The light |
| W-pI.....28.2:8 | is the same light you will see in them **a.**. |
| W-pI.....28.3:1 | say, "Above **a.** else I want to see this table |
| W-pI.....28.4:3 | "Above **a.** else I want to see this table |
| W-pI.....28.5:1 | would withdraw **a.** your own ideas from it |
| W-pI.....28.5:3 | Hidden under **a.** your ideas about it is its |
| W-pI.....28.5:3 | the purpose it shares with **a.** the universe. |
| W-pI.....28.7:2 | **a.** in their contribution to your seeing. |
| W-pI.....28.8:2 | *Above* **a.** *else I want to see this_differently.* |
| W-pI.....29.1:1 | why you can see **a.** purpose in everything. |
| W-pI.....29.1:4 | thus far, and **a.** subsequent ones as well. |
| W-pI.....29.3:1 | to learn how to look on **a.** things with love |
| W-pI.....30.5:1 | it does not depend on the body's eyes at **a.** |
| W-pI.....34.2:3 | **A.** applications should be done with your |
| W-pI.....34.3:3 | Note them **a.** casually, repeating the idea |
| W-pI.....35.4:2 | Include **a.** the ego-based attributes which |
| W-pI.....35.4:3 | **A.** of them are equally unreal, because |
| W-pI.....36.4:2 | **A.** applications should, of course, be |
| W-pI.....37.3:2 | are **a.** things blessed along with you. |
| W-pI.....38.1:1 | holiness reverses **a.** the laws of the world. |
| W-pI.....38.2:4 | Your holiness, then, can remove **a.** pain, |
| W-pI.....38.2:4 | can remove all pain, can end **a.** sorrow, |
| W-pI.....38.2:4 | end all sorrow, and can solve **a.** problems. |
| W-pI.....38.3:2 | holy because **a.** things He created are holy |
| W-pI.....38.3:3 | And **a.** things He created are holy because |
| W-pI.....38.3:4 | the power of your holiness to **a.** problems, |
| W-pI.....38.5:5 | over **a.** things because of what you are. |
| W-pI.....39.2:5 | and you would not need a workbook at **a.**. |
| W-pI.....41.1:1 | and abandonment **a.** the separated ones |
| W-pI.....41.2:4 | idea for today has the power to end **a.** this |
| W-pI.....41.3:2 | will cure **a.** sorrow and pain and fear and |
| W-pI.....41.4:2 | of **a.** joy goes with you wherever you go. |
| W-pI.....41.4:3 | of **a.** life goes with you wherever you go. |
| W-pI.....41.5:1 | understand that you do not believe **a.** this |
| W-pI.....41.5:2 | and obscuring, yet representing **a.** you see |
| W-pI.....41.6:5 | past **a.** the idle thoughts of the world. Try |
| W-pI.....41.7:2 | most of **a.**, try to sink down and inward, |
| W-pI.....41.7:2 | and **a.** the foolish thoughts of the world. |
| W-pI.....41.7:3 | are trying to reach past **a.** these things. |
| W-pI.....42.5:4 | no thoughts at **a.** seem to come to mind. If |
| W-pI.....43.7:6 | not to make distinctions of this kind at **a.**. |
| W-pI.....44.5:4 | **a.** the thoughts that you have made up. |
| W-pI.....44.8:3 | only one that has any real use to you at **a.**. |
| W-pI...44.11:3 | Above **a.**, be determined not to forget |
| W-pI.....45.6:6 | Then try to go past **a.** the unreal thoughts |
| W-pI.....45.7:1 | Under **a.** the senseless thoughts and mad |
| W-pI.....45.9:3 | from **a.** thoughts that are unworthy of |
| W-pI.....46.3:5 | have forgiven them entirely or not at **a.**. |
| W-pI.....46.5:2 | idea to **a.** those who have come to mind, |
| W-pI.....47.1:4 | to be aware of **a.** the facets of any problem |
| W-pI.....47.3:2 | His Voice speaks for Him in **a.** situations |
| W-pI.....47.3:2 | and in every aspect of **a.** situations, telling |
| W-pI.....47.5:1 | Now try to slip past **a.** concerns related to |
| W-pI.....47.5:4 | of God in you is successful in **a.** things. |
| W-pI.....47.6:2 | in every respect and in **a.** circumstances. |
| W-pI.....47.7:3 | Let go **a.** the trivial things that churn and |
| W-pI........49.h | God's Voice speaks to me **a.** through the |
| W-pI.....49.1:1 | to listen to God's Voice **a.** through the day |
| W-pI.....49.4:3 | Go past **a.** the raucous shrieks and sick |
| W-pI.....50.2:1 | **A.** these things are your replacements for |
| W-pI.....50.2:2 | **A.** these things are cherished to ensure a |
| W-pI.....50.3:1 | God will protect you in **a.** circumstances. |
| W-pI.....50.3:2 | and raise you high above **a.** the perceived |
| W-pI.....50.4:3 | Put **a.** your faith in the Love of God within |
| W-pI.....50.4:5 | can resolve **a.** seeming difficulties without |
| WpI...rI.in.2:6 | be sure to review **a.** of them once more. |
| W-pI.....51.2:1 | what I see **a.** the meaning it has for me. I |
| W-pI.....51.4:8 | but **a.** creation lies in the thoughts I think |
| W-pI.....51.5:4 | I make **a.** things my enemies, so that my |
| W-pI.....52.2:7 | with love on **a.** that I failed to see before. |
| W-pI.....52.5:7 | than to obscure **a.** that is really mine with |
| W-pI.....53.2:6 | not see it at **a.** unless I choose to value it. |
| W-pI.....53.3:8 | escape **a.** the effects of the world of fear, |
| W-pI.....53.4:3 | it? He is the Source of **a.** meaning, and |
| W-pI.....54.1:2 | because **a.** thoughts have power. They will |
| W-pI.....54.4:3 | I think or say or do teaches **a.** the universe |
| W-pI.....56.1:4 | **A.** my hopes and wishes and plans appear |
| W-pI.....56.2:1 | (27) Above **a.** else I want to see. |
| W-pI.....56.3:1 | (28) Above **a.** else I want to see differently |
| W-pI.....56.4:4 | Beyond **a.** my insane wishes is my will, |
| W-pI.....56.4:6 | of Him will yet look past **a.** appearances, |
| W-pI.....56.4:6 | and recognize the truth beyond them **a.**. |
| W-pI.....56.5:2 | mind, behind **a.** my insane thoughts of |
| W-pI.....56.5:2 | is the knowledge that **a.** is one forever. I |
| W-pI.....57.2:3 | **A.** I need do is recognize this and I am |
| W-pI.....57.4:4 | hearts of **a.** who share this place with me. |
| W-pI.....57.5:6 | understand the holiness of **a.** living things |
| W-pI.....58.1:5 | eyes, the holiness of the world is **a.** I see, |
| W-pI.....58.3:4 | **a.** illusions except false ideas about myself |
| W-pI.....58.3:5 | My holiness undoes them **a.** by asserting |
| W-pI.....58.3:6 | I share with God Himself, **a.** idols vanish. |
| W-pI.....58.4:2 | Since my holiness saves me from **a.** guilt, |
| W-pI.....58.5:2 | lies my claim to **a.** good and only good. I |
| W-pI.....58.5:4 | **A.** good things are mine, because God |
| W-pI.....58.5:6 | protects me, and directs me in **a.** things. |
| W-pI.....60.2:5 | earth. I forgive **a.** things because I feel the |
| W-pI.....60.4:1 | (49) God's Voice speaks to me **a.** through |
| W-pI.....61.4:2 | It is the perfect answer to **a.** illusions, and |
| W-pI.....61.4:2 | illusions, and therefore to **a.** temptation. |
| W-pI.....61.4:3 | brings **a.** the images you have made about |
| W-pI.....62.2:2 | is why **a.** forgiveness is a gift to yourself. |
| W-pI.....62.3:3 | It will remove **a.** sense of weakness, strain |
| W-pI.....62.3:4 | It will take away **a.** fear and guilt and pain |
| W-pI.....64.2:2 | use for **a.** the illusions you have made, |
| W-pI.....64.3:3 | the Son of God escape from **a.** illusions, |
| W-pI.....64.3:3 | all illusions, and thus from **a.** temptation. |
| W-pI.....64.5:2 | at night, and **a.** through the day as well. |
| W-pI.....64.5:3 | Prepare yourself in advance for **a.** the |
| W-pI.....64.5:3 | they are **a.** really very simple. Each one |
| W-pI.....65.1:5 | relinquishment of **a.** the other goals you |
| W-pI.....65.3:2 | escape from **a.** your perceived difficulties. |
| W-pI.....65.3:4 | It gives you the answer to **a.** the searching |
| W-pI.....65.4:3 | as well as for **a.** the trivial purposes and |
| W-pI.....65.7:1 | by resolving your conflicts once and for **a.** |
| W-pI...66.10:6 | On one side stand **a.** illusions. All truth |
| W-pI...66.10:7 | **A.** truth stands on the other. Let us try |
| W-pI.....67.3:1 | try to let **a.** thoughts drop away for a brief |
| W-pI.....67.3:1 | and then try to reach past **a.** your images |
| W-pI.....68.2:2 | Can **a.** this arise from holding grievances? |
| W-pI.....68.4:1 | grievances if you believed **a.** this were so? |
| W-pI.....68.5:5 | This has left you alone in **a.** the universe |
| W-pI.....68.6:1 | now to see **a.** these people as friends. Say |
| W-pI.....68.6:2 | Say to them **a.**, thinking of each one in |
| W-pI.....68.6:9 | *When I let* **a.** *my grievances go I will know I* |
| W-pI.....68.7:6 | *I would wake to my Self by laying* **a.** *my* |
| W-pI.....69.3:1 | to reach what is dearer to us than **a.** else. |
| W-pI.....69.4:1 | closed, try to let go of **a.** the content that |
| W-pI.....69.5:3 | reality. They seem to be **a.** there is to see. |
| W-pI.....70.1:1 | **A.** temptation is nothing more than some |
| W-pI.....70.1:5 | that **a.** guilt is solely an invention of your |
| W-pI.....70.9:1 | Since **a.** illusions of salvation have failed |
| W-pI...70.10:2 | You are free from **a.** external interference. |
| W-pI ....71.4:3 | to channelize **a.** your efforts in searching |
| W-pI ....71.5:3 | that are diametrically opposed in **a.** ways. |
| W-pI ....71.6:1 | How can you escape **a.** this? Very simply. |
| W-pI ....71.7:3 | **A.** things are possible to God. Salvation |
| W-pI ....71.8:4 | your full release from **a.** your own insane |
| W-pI ..71.10:2 | to **a.** temptation to hold grievances today, |
| W-pI ....73.1:3 | with God has **a.** the power of creation in it |
| W-pI ....73.1:4 | and therefore have no power at **a.**. Its |
| W-pI ....73.6:1 | seek to prove **a.** this is really Heaven. You |
| W-pI ....73.7:5 | Above **a.** else, you want the freedom to |
| W-pI ....73.9:4 | of God from hell and from **a.** idle wishes. |
| W-pI ....74.1:1 | toward which **a.** our exercises are directed |
| W-pI ....75.6:2 | washed of **a.** past ideas and clean of every |
| W-pI ....76.3:1 | you are not bound by **a.** the strange and |
| W-pI ....76.9:2 | Dismiss **a.** foolish magical beliefs today, |
| W-pI ..76.12:2 | of freedom from **a.** danger and all tyranny |
| W-pI ..76.12:2 | of freedom from all danger and **a.** tyranny |
| W-pI .......78.h | Let miracles replace **a.** grievances. |
| W-pI ....78.1:4 | Yet **a.** the while it waits for you in light, |
| W-pI ....78.6:3 | **a.** the little and the larger hurts he gave. |
| W-pI ....78.9:2 | you are saved, and **a.** the world with you. |
| W-pI ..78.10:4 | you both, and **a.** the sightless ones as well, |
| W-pI ..78.10:5 | we pray: *Let miracles replace* **a.** *grievances.* |
| W-pI ....79.2:2 | Yet they are **a.** the same, and must be |
| W-pI ....79.2:2 | that solves them **a.** is to be accepted. Who |
| W-pI ....79.5:1 | No one could solve **a.** the problems the |
| W-pI ....79.6:1 | **A.** this complexity is but a desperate |
| W-pI ....79.6:3 | Perceiving the underlying constancy in **a.** |
| W-pI ....79.6:3 | that you have the means to solve them **a.**. |
| W-pI ....79.7:3 | will try to free our minds of **a.** the many |
| W-pI ....79.8:2 | in letting **a.** your preconceived notions go, |
| W-pI ....79.8:3 | **A.** that is necessary is to entertain some |
| W-pI ....79.9:4 | this recognition are **a.** problems resolved. |
| W-pI ..79.10:4 | to suspend **a.** judgment about what the |
| W-pI ....80.3:3 | not forget that **a.** problems are the same. |
| W-pI ....80.5:5 | Above **a.**, remember that you have one |
| WpI..rII.in.4:4 | has power over **a.** fantasies and dreams. |
| WpI..rII.in.4:5 | through, and carry you beyond them **a.**. |
| W-pI ....81.1:4 | its calm light let **a.** my conflicts disappear. |
| W-pI ....83.1:3 | recognition releases me from **a.** conflict, |
| W-pI ....83.1:5 | to think. **A.** doubt must disappear as I |
| W-pI ....83.3:2 | **A.** things that come from God are one. |
| W-pI ....85.2:3 | *The light of the world will shine* **a.** *this away.* |
| W-pI ....87.3:5 | recognize that **a.** this has not occurred. I |
| W-pI ....88.2:3 | *The light in you is* **a.** *that I would see, [name].* |
| W-pI ....88.3:6 | They have no real effect on me at **a.**. I am |
| W-pI ....88.3:7 | I am perfectly free of the effects of **a.** laws |
| W-pI ....89.1:3 | His laws release me from **a.** grievances, |
| W-pI ....89.3:1 | (78) Let miracles replace **a.** grievances. By |
| W-pI ....89.3:4 | to have **a.** my illusions be replaced with |
| W-pI ....89.3:6 | I want **a.** of Heaven and only Heaven, as |
| W-pI ....89.4:4 | *by which* **a.** *my grievances are replaced.* |
| W-pI ....91.4:4 | makes **a.** miracles within your easy reach, |
| W-pI ....91.5:4 | has **a.** the strength to do what it desires. |
| W-pI ....91.8:5 | *I am not helpless, but* **a.** *powerful. I am not* |
| W-pI ....91.9:3 | Remember that **a.** sense of weakness is |
| W-pI ..91.10:1 | the strength of God and **a.** His Thoughts. |
| W-pI ....92.2:3 | lights the sun and gives it **a.** its warmth; |
| W-pI ....92.5:5 | that lack in anyone would be a lack in **a.**. |
| W-pI ....92.5:6 | its light that **a.** may see and benefit as one |
| W-pI ....92.5:7 | may bring to **a.** the miracle in which they |
| W-pI ....92.6:2 | It sees **a.** others different from itself, and |
| W-pI ....93.2:3 | – **a.** this is true by what you now believe. |
| W-pI ....93.4:1 | not be overjoyed to be assured that **a.** the |
| W-pI ....93.4:1 | never done, that **a.** your sins are nothing, |
| W-pI ....93.5:2 | Therefore, this self does not exist at **a.**. |
| W-pI ....94.1:1 | makes **a.** forms of temptation powerless; |
| W-pI ....94.1:3 | and **a.** the thoughts that this world ever |
| W-pI ....94.4:1 | except to lay **a.** idols and self-images aside |
| W-pI ....94.4:2 | that it will be revealed to **a.** who ask for it. |
| W-pI ....95.1:3 | Yours is the unity of **a.** creation. Your |
| W-pI ..95.10:1 | Let **a.** these errors go by recognizing |
| W-pI ..95.11:1 | your mind with **a.** the certainty that you |
| W-pI ..95.12:2 | awareness of this oneness to **a.** minds, |
| W-pI ..95.13:1 | Self, in perfect harmony with **a.** there is, |
| W-pI ..95.13:1 | with all there is, and **a.** that there will be. |
| W-pI ..95.13:3 | let It shine away **a.** your illusions and your |
| W-pI ..95.13:5 | and to cast **a.** your illusions out of the one |
| W-pI ..95.14:2 | part in bringing happiness to **a.** the world |

| | |
|---|---|
| W-pI...95.15:1 | a call to **a.** the world to be at one with you. |
| W-pI...96.10:3 | in **a.** things created by the Spirit as Itself. |
| W-pI...96.10:4 | Your mind will bless **a.** things. Confusion |
| W-pI...96.12:2 | **a.** of it is given everyone who asks for it, |
| W-pI.....97.2:2 | endowed with **a.** your Father's Love and |
| W-pI.....97.4:1 | the miracle in which **a.** time stands still; |
| W-pI.....97.4:3 | He will offer **a.** His strength to every little |
| W-pI.....97.7:2 | *Spirit am I, a holy Son of God, free of* ***a.*** *limits* |
| W-pI.....98.2:2 | **A.** our doubts we lay aside today, and take |
| W-pI.....98.2:6 | **A.** our sins are washed away by realizing |
| W-pI.....98.4:1 | **a.** who took the stand we take today will |
| W-pI.....98.4:1 | we take today will gladly offer us **a.** that |
| W-pI.....98.7:4 | will bring the light to **a.** the words you say |
| W-pI.....98.8:1 | to you **a.** bright with faith and confidence |
| W-pI.....98.9:4 | He will respond with **a.** His faith and joy |
| W-pI...98.11:1 | be thankful and lay down **a.** earthly tasks, |
| W-pI...98.11:1 | tasks, **a.** little thoughts and limited ideas, |
| W-pI.....99.3:1 | meeting place at **a.** where earth and |
| W-pI.....99.7:4 | you. **A.** the world of pain is not His Will. |
| W-pI.....99.7:6 | which He has replaced **a.** your mistakes |
| W-pI.....99.9:1 | seek out and lighten up **a.** darkened spots, |
| W-pI.....99.9:8 | what you need to learn to lay **a.** fear aside, |
| W-pI...99.10:1 | Forgive **a.** thoughts which would oppose |
| W-pI...99.11:1 | which has the power to remove **a.** forms |
| W-pI...99.12:5 | mind and let **a.** fear be gently laid aside, |
| W-pI...100.1:3 | one of them is equally essential to them **a.** |
| W-pI...100.3:4 | no one laughs because **a.** laughter can but |
| W-pI...100.4:2 | joy on earth calls to **a.** minds to let their |
| W-pI...100.4:4 | for **a.** who will accept their Father's gifts |
| W-pI...100.6:2 | and **a.** the world is thus deprived of joy, |
| W-pI...100.6:5 | bring His happiness to **a.** you look upon; |
| W-pI...100.8:1 | to us and **a.** the world God's Will for us. It |
| W-pI...100.8:5 | undismayed by **a.** the little thoughts and |
| W-pI...101.5:2 | and **a.** that you believe must come from |
| W-pI...101.6:4 | you free from **a.** the consequences sin has |
| W-pI...102.2:2 | It cannot purchase anything at **a.**. It offers |
| W-pI...103.3:2 | Then welcome **a.** the happiness it brings |
| W-pI...103.3:4 | and quiet **a.** your fears with this assurance |
| W-pI...104.2:1 | Today we would remove **a.** meaningless |
| W-pI...104.4:1 | **A.** this we lay aside, and seek instead that |
| W-pI...104.5:5 | *God's gifts of joy and peace are* ***a.*** *I want.* |
| W-pI...105.2:3 | pervades **a.** levels of the world you see. It |
| W-pI...105.2:4 | It strips **a.** meaning from the gifts you give |
| W-pI...105.4:4 | It adds to **a.** that is complete already, not |
| W-pI...105.7:3 | of **a.** that would prevent success today. |
| W-pI...105.8:2 | let **a.** bars to peace and joy be lifted up, |
| W-pI...106.3:5 | Go past **a.** things which do not speak of |
| W-pI...106.4:9 | to you and **a.** your brothers to be kept. |
| W-pI...106.5:1 | wakes **a.** those who sleep and cannot see. |
| W-pI...106.5:4 | to speak to **a.** the multitude who wait to |
| W-pI...106.6:5 | The bringer of **a.** miracles has need that |
| W-pI......107.h | Truth will correct **a.** errors in my mind. |
| W-pI...107.3:3 | When truth has come **a.** pain is over, for |
| W-pI...107.3:4 | you from **a.** beliefs in the ephemeral. They |
| W-pI...107.4:3 | and trusted with a perfect trust in **a.** the |
| W-pI...107.6:9 | dreams be gone. Let truth correct them **a.**. |
| W-pI...107.7:6 | into **a.** the exercises that we do this day. |
| W-pI...107.9:1 | Truth will correct **a.** errors in your mind |
| W-pI...107.9:5 | *Truth will correct* ***a.*** *errors in my mind, And* |
| W-pI.107.11:2 | "Truth will correct **a.** errors in my mind," |
| W-pI.107.11:2 | you speak for **a.** the world and Him Who |
| W-pI...108.1:2 | in it, for it reconciles **a.** seeming opposites |
| W-pI...108.1:3 | of **a.** your conflicts and mistaken thoughts |
| W-pI...108.2:2 | that darkness cannot be perceived at **a.**. |
| W-pI...108.4:3 | base on which **a.** opposites are reconciled, |
| W-pI...108.5:1 | unified, will serve to unify **a.** thought. |
| W-pI...108.5:2 | correction will suffice for **a.** correction, or |
| W-pI...108.5:2 | is enough to bring salvation to **a.** minds. |
| W-pI...108.6:3 | the one Thought which underlies them **a.**. |
| W-pI...108.9:5 | the others, and through him you give to **a.** |
| W-pI...109.1:2 | of **a.** the turmoil born of clashing dreams. |
| W-pI...109.2:5 | is the end of suffering for **a.** the world, |
| W-pI...109.4:5 | You call to **a.** to join you in your rest, and |
| W-pI...109.5:2 | rest can never change in any way at **a.**. |
| W-pI...109.5:5 | your mind that **a.** its frantic fantasies were |
| W-pI...109.7:2 | is comes closer to **a.** worn and tired minds |
| W-pI...109.8:3 | bid them **a.** enter here and rest with you. |
| W-pI...110.2:1 | Today's idea is therefore **a.** you need to |
| W-pI...110.2:1 | give you perfect vision that will heal **a.** the |
| W-pI...110.2:4 | for **a.** the world to learn escape from time, |
| W-pI...110.3:2 | **A.** this has not occurred, if you remain as |
| W-pI...110.4:1 | In this one thought is **a.** the past undone; |
| W-pI...110.5:2 | It is the birthplace of **a.** miracles, the great |
| W-pI...110.5:6 | This is the Word in which **a.** sorrow ends. |
| W-pI.110.10:2 | your Savior from **a.** idols you have made. |
| W-pI.110.11:1 | thoughts for **a.** who meet with us today. |
| WpI. rIII.in5:3 | seeming problems and **a.** your concerns. |
| WpIrIII.in11:5 | And it is meant to serve you in **a.** ways, all |
| WpIrIII.in11:5 | serve you in all ways, **a.** times and places, |
| W-pI...113.1:2 | *whole, at one with* ***a.*** *creation and with God.* |
| W-pI...115.1:2 | *the world for* ***a.*** *the errors I have made. For* |
| W-pI...115.1:3 | *am I released from them with* ***a.*** *the world.* |
| W-pI...116.2:3 | *What He has given me is* ***a.*** *I want. What He* |
| W-pI...116.2:4 | *I want. What He has given me is* ***a.*** *there is.* |
| W-pI...117.2:4 | *to me. I would accept* ***a.*** *that is mine in truth.* |
| W-pI...118.1:2 | *in glad exchange for* ***a.*** *the substitutes that I* |
| W-pI...119.1:1 | Truth will correct **a.** errors in my mind. *I* |
| W-pI...119.2:2 | *I will forgive* ***a.*** *things today, that I may learn* |
| W-pI...119.3:2 | Truth will correct **a.** errors in my mind. |
| W-pI...120.2:3 | *Today I lay aside* ***a.*** *sick illusions of myself,* |
| W-pI...121.1:3 | and bring uncertainty to **a.** your hopes of |
| W-pI...121.1:4 | Here are **a.** questions answered; here the |
| W-pI...121.1:4 | the end of **a.** uncertainty ensured at last. |
| W-pI...121.3:1 | doubt, confused about itself and **a.** it sees; |
| W-pI...121.3:3 | behold except the proof that **a.** its sins are |
| W-pI...121.7:7 | **a.** your teaching and your learning will be |
| W-pI...122.2:1 | **A.** this forgiveness offers you, and more. |
| W-pI...122.2:5 | **A.** this forgiveness offers you, and more. |
| W-pI...122.3:2 | clears your memory of **a.** dead thoughts |
| W-pI...122.6:2 | stand outside while **a.** of Heaven waits for |
| W-pI...122.6:7 | **A.** the complexities the world has spun of |
| W-pI.122.13:2 | Today **a.** things you want are given you. |
| W-pI...123.2:1 | of **a.** the gains which you have made; the |
| W-pI...124.1:2 | is safe, protection guaranteed in **a.** we do, |
| W-pI...124.1:2 | available to us in **a.** our undertakings. We |
| W-pI...124.4:5 | behold His loveliness in **a.** we look upon. |
| W-pI...124.5:4 | life. **A.** this we see because we saw it first |
| W-pI...124.6:2 | to heal **a.** forms of suffering in anyone, in |
| W-pI.124.12:2 | *God, at one with* ***a.*** *my brothers and my Self,* |
| W-pI...125.3:1 | without **a.** judgment of His holy Word. |
| W-pI...125.3:3 | stand apart from **a.** the judgments which |
| W-pI......126.h | **A.** that I give is given to myself. |
| W-pI.126.11:1 | value to yourself and **a.** your brothers. Do |
| W-pI.126.11:3 | *A. that I give is given to myself. The Help I* |
| W-pI...127.3:2 | As it is one itself, it looks on **a.** as one. Its |
| W-pI...127.3:5 | is no love but God's, and **a.** of love is His. |
| W-pI...127.6:4 | of **a.** the laws you think you must obey; of |
| W-pI...127.6:4 | obey; of **a.** the limits under which you live |
| W-pI...127.6:4 | and **a.** the changes that you think are part |
| W-pI...127.8:4 | Withdraw **a.** value you have placed upon |
| W-pI...127.8:4 | and let the gift of God replace them **a.**. |
| W-pI.127.11:2 | to shed its blessing upon **a.** who come to |
| W-pI.127.11:3 | Now are they **a.** made free, along with us. |
| W-pI.127.11:4 | us. Now are they **a.** our brothers in God's |
| W-pI...128.1:1 | anything at **a.** that serves to give you joy. |
| W-pI...128.3:3 | **A.** things you seek to make your value |
| W-pI...128.5:1 | Today we practice letting go **a.** thought of |
| W-pI...128.5:3 | and loosen it from **a.** we wish it were. |
| W-pI...128.5:4 | go beyond **a.** little values and diminished |
| W-pI...129.2:2 | loss in letting go **a.** thought of value here. |
| W-pI...129.2:4 | and takes away **a.** things that you have |
| W-pI...129.2:6 | is the world of time, where **a.** things end. |
| W-pI...129.3:2 | Is it loss to find **a.** things you really want, |
| W-pI...129.4:1 | as day, remains unlimited for **a.** eternity. |
| W-pI...129.6:5 | the place of **a.** the things you seek but do |
| W-pI...129.7:5 | loses **a.** meaning as they blend in one. |
| W-pI...130.4:2 | **A.** separation, all distinctions, and the |
| W-pI...130.4:2 | All separation, **a.** distinctions, and the |
| W-pI...130.5:5 | unreal are **a.** there are to choose between, |
| W-pI...130.6:5 | It is **a.** a piece because it stems from one |
| W-pI...130.7:1 | that ends **a.** compromise and doubt, and |
| W-pI...130.7:1 | and doubt, and go beyond them **a.** as one. |
| W-pI...130.8:3 | of **a.** the petty treasures of this world. You |
| W-pI.130.11:3 | to you. **A.** you need say to any part of hell, |
| W-pI...131.1:1 | Failure is **a.** about you while you seek for |
| W-pI...131.7:1 | strange world you made and **a.** its ways; |
| W-pI.131.13:2 | light the way, so that **a.** darkness vanishes |
| W-pI.131.13:2 | that you can understand **a.** things you see. |
| W-pI.131.14:5 | will find the goal of **a.** your searching here |
| W-pI.131.14:5 | here, and **a.** the seeking of the world, |
| W-pI.131.15:5 | this: *Today I seek and find* ***a.*** *that I want. My* |
| W-pI......132.h | I loose the world from **a.** I thought it was. |
| W-pI...132.2:1 | mind, and **a.** his thoughts change with it. |
| W-pI...132.2:2 | changed the source of **a.** ideas you think |
| W-pI...132.2:4 | free the future from **a.** ancient thoughts of |
| W-pI...132.3:4 | have enslaved the world with **a.** your fears |
| W-pI...132.3:4 | and tears, and **a.** your sorrows press on it, |
| W-pI...132.5:2 | and **a.** the world must change accordingly |
| W-pI...132.8:3 | loose it from **a.** things you ever thought it |
| W-pI...132.8:3 | it was by merely changing **a.** the thoughts |
| W-pI...132.8:4 | as you let go **a.** thoughts of sickness, and |
| W-pI...132.8:4 | replace **a.** thoughts you ever held of death |
| W-pI.132.11:4 | it does, it is not real, and cannot be at **a.**. |
| W-pI.132.14:1 | **a.** the idle thoughts we ever held about it, |
| W-pI.132.14:1 | and about **a.** living things we see upon it. |
| W-pI.132.15:2 | *loose the world from* ***a.*** *I thought it was. For I* |
| W-pI.132.17:1 | sent through your ideas to **a.** the world, |
| W-pI.132.17:2 | *I loose the world from* ***a.*** *I thought it was, and* |
| W-pI...133.3:1 | which to test **a.** things you think you want |
| W-pI...133.3:2 | they are not worth desiring at **a.**, for they |
| W-pI...133.4:3 | you had considered **a.** of them in time; |
| W-pI...133.6:2 | A temporary value is without **a.** value. |
| W-pI...133.8:5 | Here it is easiest of **a.** to be deceived. For |
| W-pI.133.12:1 | **A.** things are valuable or valueless, |
| W-pI.133.12:1 | worthy or not of being sought at **a.**, |
| W-pI...134.2:5 | **A.** truth belongs to Him, reflects His laws |
| W-pI...134.4:3 | forgiveness really but a sin, like **a.** the rest. |
| W-pI.134.11:1 | **a.** dreams of evil and of hatred and attack |
| W-pI.134.11:4 | now he cannot feel that **a.** escape has been |
| W-pI.134.13:2 | is no thought in **a.** the world that leads to |
| W-pI.134.14:3 | lighting up the way for **a.** our brothers, |
| W-pI.134.15:2 | but to save the world from **a.** ideas of sin. |
| W-pI.134.15:3 | consider **a.** the evil things you thought of |
| W-pI.134.16:1 | from **a.** the thoughts you had of sin in him |
| W-pI.134.16:4 | the escape from **a.** the heavy chains you |
| W-pI...135.2:4 | And **a.** its structures, all its thoughts and |
| W-pI...135.2:4 | its structures, **a.** its thoughts and doubts, |
| W-pI...135.2:4 | **a.** serve but to preserve its sense of threat. |
| W-pI...135.5:3 | medicine, no care and no concern at **a.**. |
| W-pI...135.6:4 | the body **a.** the functions that you see in it |
| W-pI...135.9:4 | And you will impose upon the body **a.** the |
| W-pI.135.10:4 | a kind from which it gains no benefit at **a.**, |
| W-pI.135.14:1 | purpose **a.** of them were made to realize. |
| W-pI.135.16:5 | Anticipation plays no part at **a.**, for |
| W-pI.135.18:1 | that everything that happens, **a.** events, |
| W-pI.135.21:3 | our defenselessness is **a.** that is required |
| W-pI.135.24:1 | **A.** your defenses have been aimed at not |
| W-pI.135.26:2 | conceive of **a.** the happiness that comes to |
| W-pI.135.26:4 | And **a.** the world will take this giant stride |
| W-pI...136.1:3 | intent of any kind, it cannot be at **a.**. |
| W-pI...136.1:5 | approach that carries **a.** of them to truth, |
| W-pI...136.2:2 | Like **a.** defenses, it is an insane device for |
| W-pI...136.2:3 | And like **a.** the rest, its purpose is to hide |
| W-pI...136.2:4 | The aim of **a.** defenses is to keep the truth |
| W-pI...136.4:2 | **A.** this cannot be done unconsciously. But |
| W-pI...136.6:1 | regard to **a.** their true relationships, and |
| W-pI...136.7:3 | and **a.** your world appears to totter and |
| W-pI.136.10:2 | **a.** the universe made slave to laws which |
| W-pI.136.11:5 | What is created is apart from **a.** of this. |
| W-pI.136.16:4 | will be healed of **a.** the sickly wishes that it |
| W-pI.136.17:2 | well by this: The body should not feel at **a.** |
| W-pI.136.17:4 | at **a.** is in the mind to what the body does. |
| W-pI.136.18:2 | enough to serve **a.** truly useful purposes. |
| W-pI...137.1:2 | healing is the opposite of **a.** the world's |
| W-pI...137.2:2 | to keep one self apart from **a.** the rest, to |
| W-pI...137.3:4 | Self with **a.** Its parts intact and unassailed. |
| W-pI...137.5:2 | Just as forgiveness overlooks **a.** sins that |
| W-pI...137.5:3 | take the place of what has never been at **a.** |
| W-pI...137.7:1 | Just as forgiveness shines away **a.** sin and |
| W-pI...137.7:2 | **a.** the laws that hold it cannot but be real, |
| W-pI...137.9:1 | and the glad exchange of **a.** the world of |
| W-pI.137.10:1 | be healed, you see **a.** those around you, or |
| W-pI.137.10:2 | Perhaps you will not recognize them **a.**, |
| W-pI.137.10:2 | how great your offering to **a.** the world, |
| W-pI.137.11:2 | and **a.** the grace of healing it is given them |
| W-pI.137.11:4 | and here are **a.** illusions brought to truth. |
| W-pI.137.15:2 | to take the place of **a.** the foolish thoughts |

W-pI.137.15:3 together to make well a. that was sick, and
W-pI...138.1:2 We think that a. things have an opposite,
W-pI...138.4:3 confuse yourself with a. the doubts that
W-pI...138.4:5 you will perceive it was no choice at a..
W-pI...138.6:2 Of a. the choices you have tried to make
W-pI...138.6:2 definitive and prototype of a. the rest, the
W-pI...138.6:2 the rest, the one which settles a. decisions.
W-pI...138.6:4 a. decisions but conceal this one by taking
W-pI...138.9:3 understood. A. that is veiled in shadows
W-pI...138.9:4 And a. mistakes in judgment that the
W-pI...139.4:2 be alive at a. unless he knew the answer. If
W-pI...139.8:3 It is so far beyond a. doubt and question
W-pI...139.8:3 what it must be is a. the proof you need to
W-pI.139.11:5 for in creation are a. minds as one. And in
W-pI.139.11:6 how our Father's Love contains them a..
W-pI.139.12:1 In thanks for a. creation, in the Name of
W-pI.139.12:1 His Oneness with a. aspects of creation,
W-pI.139.12:1 lay aside a. thoughts that would distract
W-pI.139.12:2 mind be cleared of a. the foolish cobwebs
W-pI...140.3:5 gone. And thus they cure for a. eternity.
W-pI...140.4:1 heals with certainty, and cures a. sickness.
W-pI...140.8:1 sickness, for we seek a cure for a. illusions,
W-pI...140.9:5 A. of them are false, and can be cured
W-pI.140.10:2 of healing, which will cure a. ills as one,
W-pI.140.10:4 to us of truth, where a. illusions end, and
W-pI.140.11:2 not separately, but a. of them as one.
WpI. rIV.in5:2 clear it of a. thoughts that would deceive,
WpI. rIV.in5:4 of a. the thoughts you will receive that day
WpI. rIV.in6:1 alone, for they will a. be shared with Him.
WpI. rIV.in9:2 and a. our Father wills that we receive as
W-pI...143.2:1 (126) A. that I give is given to myself.
W-pI...146.2:1 I loose the world from a. I thought it was.
W-pI......151.h A. things are echoes of the Voice for God.
W-pI...151.1:6 because of a. the doubting underneath.
W-pI...151.4:4 the ego's judgments, a. of which are false.
W-pI...151.7:4 holy light of what He sees do a. the ego's
W-pI.151.10:1 will remove a. faith that you have placed
W-pI.151.10:2 the gentle face of Christ in a. of them. You
W-pI.151.10:3 of God, for He will judge a. happenings,
W-pI.151.10:3 teach the single lesson that they a. contain
W-pI.151.11:2 And He will reinterpret a. you see, and all
W-pI.151.11:2 reinterpret all you see, and a. occurrences,
W-pI.151.14:3 A. the threads of fantasy are gone. And
W-pI.151.15:2 begins as a. your thoughts are purified. So
W-pI...152.1:6 Here is your world, complete in a. details.
W-pI...152.2:6 must be all-inclusive, if it be the truth at a.
W-pI...152.5:2 false. And that includes a. shifts in feeling,
W-pI...152.5:2 mind; in a. awareness and in all response.
W-pI...152.5:2 mind; in all awareness and in a. response.
W-pI...152.7:1 to triumph over life; a. this is arrogance.
W-pI...152.8:3 and a. you think you made will disappear.
W-pI...152.8:4 awareness then will be a. that there ever
W-pI.152.10:3 that a. self-concepts have been laid aside,
W-pI.152.11:5 in silence, giving up a. self-deceptions, as
W-pI.152.12:3 peace of God for a. your frantic thoughts,
W-pI...153.1:1 its brief relationships and a. the "gifts" it
W-pI...153.1:3 a. its "gifts" of seeming safety are illusory
W-pI...153.4:1 of a. the prices which the ego would exact.
W-pI...153.4:3 idea of a. the devastation it has wrought.
W-pI...153.7:3 you see at work in a. the evils of the world
W-pI...153.9:1 without a. thought or wish or dream in
W-pI...153.9:2 for we have left a. fearful thoughts behind
W-pI.153.11:2 God has elected a., but few have come to
W-pI.153.11:5 light, until you offer it to a. your brothers.
W-pI.153.14:4 of terrifying destiny, defeat of a. his hopes
W-pI.153.17:2 while thanking Him for a. the gifts He
W-pI.153.20:4 them to a. their brothers come from Him.
W-pI.153.20:6 Defenselessness is a. you need to give Him
W-pI...154.4:2 which promises salvation from a. sin,
W-pI...154.7:1 his role by giving a. his messages away.
W-pI...155.7:1 A. roads will lead to this one in the end.
W-pI...155.7:3 A. this steps back as truth comes forth in
W-pI.155.10:2 And a. illusions walking in the way you
W-pI.155.11:1 time has closed the door on a. the things
W-pI...156.4:2 A. things that live bring gifts to you, and
W-pI...156.5:2 A. living things are still before you, for
W-pI...156.5:5 transforming in Its gentle light a. things
W-pI...156.7:2 The past is gone, with a. its fantasies.
W-pI...156.8:6 *I light my mind and a. the minds which God*
W-pI...157.2:2 a light on a. that we have learned already,
W-pI...157.7:1 experience increases and a. goals but this
W-pI...157.9:2 be an instant which transcends a. vision,
W-pI...158.2:1 You have received a. this. No one who
W-pI...158.2:4 A. this cannot be learned. What, then, are
W-pI...158.6:3 Here are a. contradictions reconciled, for
W-pI...158.7:5 a. happenings and all events, without the
W-pI...158.7:5 all happenings and a. events, without the
W-pI...158.8:1 must be taught by a. who would achieve it
W-pI...158.9:1 vision that has power to overlook them a..
W-pI...158.9:6 And a. effects they seemed to have are
W-pI...159.2:4 you cannot give, for a. are given you.
W-pI...159.4:1 the miracle in which a. miracles are born.
W-pI...159.6:1 for a. the things that can contribute to
W-pI...159.6:2 A. are laid here already. All can be
W-pI...159.6:3 A. can be received but for the asking.
W-pI...160.4:8 if fear is real, then you do not exist at a..
W-pI...160.5:3 and give him a. I thought belonged to me.
W-pI...160.5:4 who he is, uncertain of a. things but this;
W-pI.160.10:4 Him until you look on a. as He does. Who
W-pI...161.2:5 The purpose of a. seeing is to show you
W-pI...161.2:6 A. hearing but brings to your mind the
W-pI...161.4:1 One brother is a. brothers. Every mind
W-pI...161.4:2 Every mind contains a. minds, for every
W-pI.161.11:5 of one who can forgive you a. your sins;
W-pI...162.1:5 and a. things seen within its misty clouds
W-pI...162.4:3 God places a. His gifts and all His Love, to
W-pI...162.4:3 God places all His gifts and a. His Love, to
W-pI...162.4:3 His Love, to be distributed to a. the world
W-pI...162.5:4 to a. as remedy for grief and misery, all
W-pI...162.5:4 for grief and misery, a. sense of loss, and
W-pI...163.1:2 a. forms in which the wish to be as you are
W-pI...163.1:3 A. such thoughts are but reflections of the
W-pI...163.2:1 and the lord of a. illusions and deceptions
W-pI...163.2:2 to hold a. living things within its withered
W-pI...163.2:2 a. hopes and wishes in its blighting grasp;
W-pI...163.2:2 a. goals perceived but in its sightless eyes.
W-pI...163.3:1 A. things but death are seen to be unsure,
W-pI...163.3:4 never fail to take a. life as hostage to itself.
W-pI...163.4:3 of God proclaimed as lord of a. creation,
W-pI...163.5:4 while a. the while its worshippers agree,
W-pI...163.6:3 Either a. things die, or else they live and
W-pI...163.9:6 *we share with You and with a. living things,*
W-pI...164.1:6 them a. He hears the song of Heaven, and
W-pI...164.3:3 How easily are a. your seeming sins forgot
W-pI...164.3:3 and a. your sorrows unremembered. On
W-pI...164.4:4 touched. A. this today you will remember.
W-pI...164.4:5 different from a. things you sought before
W-pI...164.5:2 while a. the shadows which appeared to
W-pI...164.6:2 you from far beyond a. things within the
W-pI...164.7:4 A. that we see will but increase our joy,
W-pI...164.7:5 with a. the world forgiven in our own. We
W-pI...164.8:1 letting go a. things you think you want.
W-pI...164.9:4 exchange a. suffering for joy this very day.
W-pI...165.3:2 found, abandoning a. else as worthless in
W-pI...165.6:1 Now is a. doubting past, the journey's
W-pI...165.7:6 This course removes a. doubts which you
W-pI...165.8:5 is still beyond a. dreams and in our minds
W-pI...166.1:1 A. things are given you. God's trust in
W-pI...166.5:1 gifts go with him, a. unknown to him. He
W-pI...166.7:2 self you savagely defend against a. reason,
W-pI...166.7:2 a. the witnesses with proof to show this is
W-pI...166.8:5 And what becomes of a. the tragedy you
W-pI.166.10:6 That is a.. And you who have this Answer
W-pI.166.11:3 a. your fears with this one merciful reply,
W-pI.166.11:4 points to a. the gifts you have each time
W-pI.166.12:6 you of a. the gifts that God has given you.
W-pI.166.13:1 give to a. who chose the lonely road you
W-pI.166.15:3 God has entrusted a. His gifts to you. Be
W-pI.166.15:6 of His gifts to a. who have received them.
W-pI...167.1:3 is the one condition in which a. that God
W-pI...167.1:4 Like a. His Thoughts, it has no opposite.
W-pI...167.2:4 one idea which underlies a. feelings that
W-pI...167.2:6 A. sorrow, loss, anxiety and suffering and
W-pI...167.5:3 can extend a. that their source contains.
W-pI...167.6:1 The mind can think it sleeps, but that is a.
W-pI...167.6:5 For mind creates a. things that are, and
W-pI...167.9:3 substanceless, and a. events are nowhere.
W-pI.167.11:3 that we share with Him, with a. creation,
W-pI .. 168.2:3 His grace His answer is to a. despair, for
W-pI .. 168.3:3 A. steps but this we learn, instructed by
W-pI .. 168.3:6 It restores a. memories the sleeping mind
W-pI .. 168.3:6 a. certainty of what Love's meaning is.
W-pI .. 168.4:3 see a light that covers a. the world in love,
W-pI .. 168.5:3 but He to Whom a. error is unknown is
W-pI .. 169.3:2 The final step must go beyond a. learning.
W-pI .. 169.5:2 in His Being, He encompasses a. things.
W-pI .. 169.6:1 speak nor write nor even think of this at a.
W-pI .. 169.6:4 beyond salvation; past a. thought of time,
W-pI .. 169.6:6 The world has never been at a.. Eternity
W-pI .. 169.7:2 to abandon a. but this is now at hand. We
W-pI .. 169.8:1 A. learning was already in His Mind,
W-pI .. 169.8:2 He recognized a. that time holds, and
W-pI .. 169.8:2 gave it to a. minds that each one might
W-pI 169.11:4 part is still what a. the rest depends on.
W-pI 169.12:1 a. its parts in meaningful relationships,
W-pI 169.13:2 to a. who see the light that lingers in your
W-pI .. 170.5:4 you lay down a. defense as merely foolish.
W-pI 170.10:6 And He is terrible above a. else, cruel
W-pI 170.10:6 down a. who acknowledge Him to be their
W-pI 170.13:5 *and make our choice for a. our brothers,*
WpI...rV.in6:2 which a. fears and doubts are overcome.
WpI.rV.in10:7 it is free of a. illusions every time we say:
W-pI .. 171.1:1 (151) A. things are echoes of the Voice
Wi181-200 1:2 for total dedication a. the time as yet. But
Wi181-200 3:4 past a. defenses for a little while each day.
W-pI .. 181.3:1 we first let a. such little focuses give way
W-pI .. 181.8:4 When seeing this is a. we want to see,
W-pI .. 181.8:4 when this is a. we seek for in the name of
W-pI .. 182.1:4 alien here, from somewhere a. unknown.
W-pI .. 182.2:3 sad, and do not recognize their tears at a..
W-pI .. 182.3:7 for Heaven. A. he ever made was hell.
W-pI .. 182.8:3 silent and at peace, beyond a. words,
W-pI 182.12:7 it in exchange for a. the toys of battle you
W-pI .. 183.3:1 and a. the world responds by laying down
W-pI .. 183.4:3 forget the names of a. the gods you valued
W-pI .. 183.5:2 Name, and a. the tiny, nameless things on
W-pI .. 183.6:4 Let a. your thoughts become anchored on
W-pI .. 183.8:4 Let a. thoughts be still except this one.
W-pI .. 183.8:5 to a. other thoughts respond with this,
W-pI .. 183.8:5 that there is one Name for a. there is, and
W-pI .. 183.8:5 for all there is, and a. that there will be.
W-pI .. 183.9:2 You can escape a. bondage of the world,
W-pI 183.10:2 is necessary, for it holds them a. within it.
W-pI 183.10:3 and a. requests unneeded when God's
W-pI 183.10:5 He makes his claim to a. his Father gave,
W-pI 183.10:6 He calls on Him to let a. things he thought
W-pI 183.11:1 A. little things are silent. Little sounds are
W-pI 183.11:6 communication far transcends a. words,
W-pI .. 184.1:6 space you lay between a. things to which
W-pI .. 184.1:6 a. happenings in terms of place and time;
W-pI .. 184.1:6 a. bodies which are greeted by a name.
W-pI .. 184.2:1 This space you see as setting off a. things
W-pI .. 184.2:2 there is unity; a space between a. things,
W-pI .. 184.2:2 all things, between a. things and you.
W-pI .. 184.7:5 a. the arbitrary names the world bestows
W-pI .. 184.9:1 to go beyond a. symbols of the world,
W-pI .. 184.9:4 They do not stand for anything at a., and
W-pI 184.10:2 the one Identity which a. things share; the
W-pI 184.11:1 Use a. the little names and symbols
W-pI 184.11:3 The Holy Spirit uses a. of them, but He
W-pI 184.11:3 and a single Source which unifies a. things
W-pI 184.11:4 Use a. the names the world bestows on
W-pI 184.12:2 the final lesson that a. things are one, and
W-pI 184.12:2 and at this lesson does a. learning end. All
W-pI 184.12:3 A. names are unified; all space is filled
W-pI 184.12:3 a. space is filled with truth's reflection.
W-pI 184.13:3 you must accept the Name for a. reality,
W-pI 184.13:3 but have not interfered with truth at a..
W-pI 184.14:3 a. foolish separations disappear which
W-pI 184.15:2 *In It we are united with a. living things, and*
W-pI 184.15:5 *A. our mistakes we give to You, that we may*
W-pI 184.15:5 *may be absolved from a. effects our errors*
W-pI .. 185.1:4 the resurrection of a. creation fully
W-pI .. 185.2:5 For that is a. he wants, and that is all he
W-pI .. 185.2:5 all he wants, and that is a. he will receive.
W-pI .. 185.5:1 the peace of God is to renounce a. dreams
W-pI .. 185.5:4 offer nothing more than a. the others.

W-pI...185.6:1 The mind which means that a. it wants is
W-pI...185.7:5 can succeed where a. the rest have failed.
W-pI...185.8:8 question should be asked of a. of them,
W-pI.185.10:2 And so do a. who seem to seek for dreams
W-pI.185.10:4 intent with what they seek above a. things
W-pI.185.13:5 you share one Will with a. your brothers,
W-pI...186.1:1 take a. arrogance away from every mind.
W-pI...186.1:6 It unites a. wills on earth in Heaven's plan
W-pI...186.2:5 A. that we are asked to do is to accept our
W-pI...186.3:2 meaning. A. it says is that your Father still
W-pI...186.4:1 A. false humility we lay aside today, that
W-pI...186.6:2 and the holiness to go beyond a. images.
W-pI...186.7:1 A. this the Voice for God relates to you.
W-pI...186.7:6 Why need he be concerned with it at a.?
W-pI...186.8:2 for a. illusions rest upon the weird belief
W-pI...186.9:4 A. the images His Son appears to make
W-pI.186.11:5 A. of them point to one goal, and one you
W-pI.186.12:4 that speaks for the Creator of a. things,
W-pI.186.12:4 Who knows a. things exactly as they are,
W-pI...187.4:1 Protect a. things you value by the act of
W-pI...187.6:5 the one idea that stands behind them a.,
W-pI...187.7:3 you choose to see a. suffering as what it is.
W-pI...187.7:4 The thought of sacrifice gives rise to a. the
W-pI...187.9:5 behold will take away a. thought of form,
W-pI.187.10:3 Whose innocence has joined us a. as one,
W-pI...188.1:4 is but a recognition, not a change at a..
W-pI...188.2:5 to look within, for there a. vision starts.
W-pI...188.3:4 removes a. thoughts of the ephemeral and
W-pI...188.3:5 It brings renewal to a. tired hearts, and
W-pI...188.3:5 hearts, and lights a. vision as it passes by.
W-pI...188.3:6 by. A. of its gifts are given everyone, and
W-pI...188.4:2 radiates with gifts beyond a. measure,
W-pI...188.5:5 shining in you now, and in a. living things
W-pI...188.8:3 you are the co-creator of a. things that live
W-pI...188.9:2 with a. the thoughts we share with God.
W-pI.188.10:1 us to a. living things that share our life.
W-pI.188.10:2 We will forgive them a., absolving all the
W-pI.188.10:2 all, absolving a. the world from what we
W-pI.188.10:7 *Let a. things shine upon me in that peace,*
W-pI...189.3:3 Only one can be perceived at a.. The other
W-pI...189.7:1 and lay aside a. thoughts of what you are
W-pI...189.7:1 is; a. concepts you have learned about the
W-pI...189.7:1 world; a. images you hold about yourself.
W-pI...189.7:2 and a. the ideas of which it is ashamed.
W-pI...189.8:3 Your part is simply to allow a. obstacles
W-pI...190.1:3 It is not a fact at a.. There is no form it
W-pI...190.5:6 power to dominate a. things you see by
W-pI...190.6:2 It has no effects at a.. It merely represents
W-pI...190.8:5 pain that waits to end a. joy in misery.
W-pI...190.9:1 Heaven's peace holds a. things still at last.
W-pI...190.9:2 down a. thoughts of danger and of fear.
W-pI.190.10:3 that contains a. of salvation's power. It is
W-pI...191.1:2 And here as well is a. the world released.
W-pI...191.1:4 punitive and wild, lacking a. reason, blind
W-pI...191.4:3 A. else but this one thing is folly to believe
W-pI...191.4:5 In this one truth are a. illusions gone. In
W-pI...191.5:1 and a. the worldly thoughts that hold it
W-pI...191.7:4 *loss, nor fail to do a. that salvation asks.* And
W-pI...191.8:1 has lighted up a. dark and ancient caverns
W-pI...191.9:1 A. power is given unto you in earth and
W-pI.191.11:7 Remember this, and a. the world is free.
W-pI...192.3:4 being Heaven-born, it has no form at a..
W-pI...192.4:1 looks upon a. things unknown in Heaven,
W-pI...192.4:3 but hardly changing him who learns at a..
W-pI...192.5:4 those who have lost the source of a. attack
W-pI......193.h A. things are lessons God would have me
W-pI...193.2:4 God does not perceive at a.. Yet it is He
W-pI...193.3:2 His Will reflects them a., and they reflect
W-pI...193.3:3 a central thought, the same in a. of them.
W-pI...193.4:1 Certain it is that a. distress does not
W-pI...193.4:4 yet is recognized as easily in a. of them, if
W-pI...193.5:2 Holy Spirit speaks in a. your tribulations,
W-pI...193.5:2 in all your tribulations, a. your pain, all
W-pI...193.5:2 pain, a. suffering regardless of its form.
W-pI...193.5:5 by which salvation comes to a. the world.
W-pI...193.6:2 power to release a. minds from bondage?
W-pI...193.6:3 give you power over a. events that seem to
W-pI...193.8:4 and a. the gifts His Love brings with it.
W-pI...193.8:6 that a. pain may disappear and God may
W-pI...193.9:1 A. things are lessons God would have you
W-pI...193.9:4 He would have a. tears be wiped away,
W-pI.193.11:1 Give a. you can, and give a little more.
W-pI.193.11:4 let us think about a. things we saved to
W-pI.193.11:5 Let us give them a. to Him Who knows
W-pI.193.13:2 To a. that speaks of terror, answer thus: *I*
W-pI...194.2:1 idea, and you have passed a. anxiety, all
W-pI...194.2:1 you have passed all anxiety, a. pits of hell,
W-pI...194.2:1 all pits of hell, a. blackness of depression,
W-pI...194.2:2 world from a. imprisonment by loosening
W-pI...194.5:4 and a. his glory shines upon a world made
W-pI...194.6:3 as you learn to see salvation in a. things,
W-pI...194.7:6 For he who has escaped a. fear of future
W-pI...194.8:2 replacing a. your thoughts of sin and evil
W-pI...195.1:7 Who made a. cause of sorrow disappear
W-pI...195.2:2 certain means whereby a. pain is healed,
W-pI...195.3:2 Now is vengeance a. there is to wish for.
W-pI...195.4:4 that in us a. things will find their freedom.
W-pI...195.5:2 room for a. who will escape with you; the
W-pI...195.5:3 A. these go with you. Let us not compare
W-pI.195.10:3 the Love which is the Source of a. creation
W-pI...196.2:1 limitless and with a. things held in its sure
W-pI...196.3:4 past a. thoughts of crucifixion and of
W-pI...196.7:1 To question it at a., its form must first be
W-pI.196.10:2 When you realize, once and for a., that it
W-pI...197.3:3 Your gratitude is a. your gifts require,
W-pI...197.7:5 to a. They have created has no end, for
W-pI...197.8:2 you contain a. things within your Self.
W-pI...197.8:7 A. gratitude belongs to you, because of
W-pI...197.9:2 you free of a. ingratitude to anyone who
W-pI...197.9:4 Give thanks for a. the countless channels
W-pI...197.9:5 A. that you do is given unto Him. All that
W-pI...197.9:6 Him. A. that you think can only be His
W-pI...198.2:6 and its effects have not occurred at a.. Yet
W-pI...198.3:1 Forgiveness sweeps a. other dreams away
W-pI...198.3:2 A. illusions save this one must multiply a
W-pI...198.4:1 that leads out of disaster, past a. suffering
W-pI...198.6:3 His words contain a. hope, all blessing
W-pI...198.6:3 a. blessing and all joy that ever can be
W-pI...198.6:3 all blessing and a. joy that ever can be
W-pI...198.6:6 the words in which a. merge as one at last.
W-pI...198.7:2 Yet a. are one; a place where death is
W-pI.198.10:1 a. its weird beliefs forgotten with it, as the
W-pI.198.11:1 Now is there silence a. around the world.
W-pI...199.2:1 Holy Spirit is unlimited forever, in a. ways
W-pI...200.2:1 to lay aside a. hope of finding happiness
W-pI...200.5:3 till a. the world is seen by you as blessed,
W-pI...200.9:7 And that is a. there is to what appears to
WpI rVI.in.2:2 and applied to a. the seeming happenings
WpI rVI.in.2:5 to use them a. and let them blend as one,
WpI rVI.in.4:1 We will attempt to get beyond a. words
WpI rVI.in.4:3 and then forget a. that we thought we
WpI rVI.in.4:4 For thus is freedom given us from a. we
W-pI...205.1:3 *is my one goal; the aim of a. my living here,*
W-pI...212.1:2 *me free from a. the vain illusions of the world*
W-pI...213.1:1 (193) A. things are lessons God would
W-pI...216.1:2 *A. that I do I do unto myself. If I attack, I*
W-pII.....in.3:1 a central thought for a. the days to come,
W-pII.....in.4:2 He has not left His Son in a. his madness,
W-pII.....in.5:2 are a. ancient promises upheld and fully
W-pII.....in.7:7 Son, Whose holy Will created a. that is,
W-pII.....in.9:4 Now we are glad that this is a. undone,
W-pII...in.10:2 call to God, and a. temptations disappear.
W-pII...in.10:5 but be still and let a. things be healed. We
W-pII......1.1:4 And in that view are a. your sins forgiven.
W-pII.....221.h to my mind. Let a. my thoughts be still.
W-pII..222.1:3 and guarantees my safety from a. pain. He
W-pII..225.1:1 *same, and You have given a. Your Love to me*
W-pII..227.1:4 *not affect my own reality at a. by my illusions*
W-pII..229.2:1 *the midst of a. the thoughts of sin my foolish*
W-pII..230.2:2 *time, and still remains beyond a. change.*
W-pII......2.1:3 and a. the thoughts that have been born
W-pII......2.4:3 a hint of a. the glory given us by God. The
W-pII......2.5:2 to a. the world that freedom is returned,
W-pII......2.5:2 world, and only Heaven now exists at a..
W-pII..232.1:4 *let a. my thoughts be still of You and of Your*
W-pII..232.2:4 Trust a. things to Him. Let Him reveal all
W-pII..232.2:5 Let Him reveal a. things to you, and be
W-pII..233.1:1 *Father, I give You a. my thoughts today. I*
W-pII .233.1:4 *I give You a. my acts as well, that I may do*
W-pII .233.2:2 give this day to Him with no reserve at a..
W-pII .234.2:2 *for a. the gifts You have bestowed on us, for*
W-pII .234.2:2 *on us, for a. the loving help we have received,*
W-pII .235.1:1 look upon a. things that seem to hurt me,
W-pII .236.1:2 times, it does not seem I am its king at a..
W-pII ....238.h On my decision a. salvation rests.
W-pII .239.2:3 *You, at peace with a. creation and ourselves.*
W-pII .....3.1:4 where a. the world must disappear and all
W-pII .....3.1:4 must disappear and a. its errors vanish.
W-pII .....3.4:2 a. perception can be given a new purpose
W-pII .....3.4:4 His Voice alone in a. that speaks to you.
W-pII .241.1:7 will be united now, as you forgive them a..
W-pII .241.2:3 *to us, and to remember that we a. are one.*
W-pII .242.1:3 is One Who knows a. that is best for me.
W-pII .242.2:5 *You know a. our desires and our wants. And*
W-pII .243.1:3 my perception, which are a. that I can see.
W-pII .243.2:2 *I honor a. its parts, in which I am included.*
W-pII .243.2:3 *and truth must shine in a. of us as one.*
W-pII .245.2:2 To a. the world we give the message that
W-pII .246.1:3 my mind conceive of a. the love my Father
W-pII .246.1:3 me, and a. the love which I return to Him.
W-pII .247.2:3 *them, and gave them a. to me as part of You,*
W-pII ....249.h Forgiveness ends a. suffering and loss.
W-pII .....4.1:7 What would they sense at a.? To sense is
W-pII .....4.3:1 Sin is the home of a. illusions, which but
W-pII .....4.4:4 But a. the while his Father shines on him,
W-pII .....4.4:4 which his pretenses cannot change at a..
W-pII .251.1:2 I seek but one, for in that one is a. I need,
W-pII .251.1:3 A. that I sought before I needed not, and
W-pII .251.1:6 In that a. needs are satisfied, all cravings
W-pII .251.1:6 that all needs are satisfied, a. cravings end
W-pII .251.1:6 a. hopes are finally fulfilled and dreams
W-pII .252.1:1 My Self is holy beyond a. the thoughts of
W-pII .252.1:3 an intensity that holds a. things within it,
W-pII .255.1:6 mine, and giving it to a. my Father's Sons,
W-pII .256.1:8 him in whom a. sin remains impossible,
W-pII .258.1:1 A. that is needful is to train our minds to
W-pII .258.1:1 minds to overlook a. little senseless aims,
W-pII ....263.h My holy vision sees a. things as pure.
W-pII .263.1:1 *Father, Your Mind created a. that is, Your*
W-pII .263.1:4 *instead of a. the loveliness with which You*
W-pII .263.1:4 *which You blessed creation; a. its purity, its*
W-pII .263.2:1 let us look on a. we see through holy
W-pII .263.2:2 Let a. appearances seem pure to us, that
W-pII .264.1:2 *I go. You are in a. the things I look upon, the*
W-pII .264.1:5 *the Love which holds a. things within Itself.*
W-pII ....265.h Creation's gentleness is a. I see.
W-pII .266.1:1 *Father, You gave me a. Your Sons, to be my*
W-pII .267.1:1 is a. the life that God created in His Love.
W-pII .267.1:4 and a. I need to save the world is given me
W-pII ....268.h Let a. things be exactly as they are.
W-pII .268.1:6 *when I let a. things be exactly as they are?*
W-pII .269.1:4 *illusion which transcends a. those I made.*
W-pII .270.1:1 *has power to translate a. that the body's eyes*
W-pII .....6.2:3 lies; where a. decisions are already made,
W-pII .....6.4:1 from the Christ in you to a. your dreams,
W-pII .271.1:3 come together a. perception disappears.
W-pII .272.2:2 hell, and love will happily replace a. fear.
W-pII .274.1:1 *I would let a. things be as You created them,*
W-pII .274.1:3 *illusions were, light will replace a. darkness,*
W-pII ....275.h healing Voice protects a. things today.
W-pII .275.1:5 It is in this that a. things are protected.
W-pII .275.2:1 *Your healing Voice protects a. things today,*
W-pII .275.2:1 *things today, and so I leave a. things to You. I*
W-pII .275.2:5 *Your Voice protects a. things through me.*
W-pII .276.1:5 accept His Fatherhood, and a. is given us.
W-pII .276.2:2 *it is this that I would speak to a. my brothers,*
W-pII .278.1:1 world in which a. things that seem to live
W-pII .278.1:4 And I am lost to a. reality. For truth is free
W-pII .279.1:2 and awaits a future freedom, if it be at a..
W-pII .280.1:4 No Thought of God is limited at a.. No
W-pII .....7.1:3 are dreams a. carried to the truth, to be
W-pII .....7.4:3 And the memory of a. your Father's Love
W-pII .....7.5:4 when a. He wills is that you be complete?
W-pII .281.2:2 For I am far beyond a. pain. My Father
W-pII .282.1:1 would be reached for a. the world. This
W-pII .283.2:2 us. And so we offer blessing to a. things,
W-pII .283.2:2 things, uniting lovingly with a. the world,

W-pII ....284.h I can elect to change a. thoughts that hurt
W-pII .284.1:3 There is no grief with any cause at a.. And
W-pII .284.1:7 I can elect to change a. thoughts that hurt.
W-pII .284.1:8 words today, and past a. reservations, and
W-pII .286.1:2 *How quietly do a. things fall in place! This is*
W-pII .289.2:5 *be the end of a. his dreams and all his pain?*
W-pII .289.2:5 *to be the end of all his dreams and a. his pain*
W-pII ....290.h My present happiness is a. I see.
W-pII .290.1:1 not there, my present happiness is a. I see.
W-pII .291.1:2 shows me a. things forgiven and at peace,
W-pII ....292.h A happy outcome to a. things is sure.
W-pII .292.1:4 as the outcome of a. problems we perceive
W-pII .292.1:4 all problems we perceive, a. trials we see,
W-pII ....293.h A. fear is past and only love is here.
W-pII .293.1:1 A. fear is past, because its source is gone,
W-pII .293.1:1 is gone, and a. its thoughts gone with it.
W-pII .293.1:3 with a. my past mistakes oppressing it,
W-pII .293.1:5 A. the world shines in reflection of its
W-pII .293.2:2 *Nor let my ears be deaf to a. the hymns of*
W-pII .293.2:3 *the present holds safe from a. past mistakes.*
W-pII .294.2:3 *that we awaken from a. dreams we made.*
W-pII .295.1:2 to me, and take away a. terror and all pain
W-pII .295.1:2 to me, and take away all terror and a. pain
W-pII .295.1:6 For a. of us must be redeemed together.
W-pII .295.2:2 *to bless a. things which I may look upon, that*
W-pII .296.1:1 *that a. the world may listen to Your Voice,*
W-pII .298.1:3 at last. A. that intruded on my holy sight
W-pII .299.2:6 *In it are a. things healed, for they remain as*
W-pII .300.1:1 are the certain lot of a. who come here, for
W-pII .....9.1:3 to let forgiveness rest upon a. things
W-pII .....9.2:1 encompasses a. living things with you.
W-pII .....9.3:2 Second Coming is the time in which a.
W-pII .....9.4:3 of God acknowledge that they a. are one.
W-pII .....9.5:4 And most of a. it needs your willingness.
W-pII ....301.h And God Himself shall wipe away a. tears
W-pII .301.1:4 *forgiveness has released from a. distortion.*
W-pII .301.1:6 *And a. the tears I shed will be forgotten, for*
W-pII .303.1:2 Let a. God's holy Thoughts surround me,
W-pII .303.2:5 *He is the Son You love above a. things. He is*
W-pII .304.1:6 that a. my sins have been forgiven me.
W-pII .305.1:3 And a. the world departs in silence as this
W-pII ....306.h The gift of Christ is a. I seek today.
W-pII .306.1:3 I made. Today I can go past a. fear, and be
W-pII .310.1:1 *as You have chosen a. my days should be.*
W-pII .310.1:2 *And what I will experience is not of time at a.*
W-pII .310.2:2 And a. the world joins with us in our song
W-pII ...10.2:5 And a. the figures in the dream in which
W-pII ...10.3:1 Correction He bestowed on a. your errors,
W-pII ...10.3:1 and a. effects they ever seemed to have.
W-pII ...10.4:3 For it alone can heal a. sorrow, wipe away
W-pII ...10.4:3 can heal all sorrow, wipe away a. tears,
W-pII ....311.h I judge a. things as I would have them be.
W-pII .311.1:6 it. He will relieve us of the agony of a. the
W-pII ....312.h I see a. things as I would have them be.
W-pII .312.2:1 *set free from a. the judgments I have made.*
W-pII .313.1:1 *is a vision which beholds a. things as sinless,*
W-pII .313.1:5 *In His sight are a. its sins forgiven, for He sees*
W-pII .314.1:4 a. the needed means are happily provided
W-pII ....315.h A. gifts my brothers give belong to me.
W-pII .315.1:2 beyond a. things of which I can conceive.
W-pII .315.2:2 *brothers are unlimited in a. their gifts to me.*
W-pII ....316.h A. gifts I give my brothers are my own.
W-pII .316.1:3 a brother has received throughout a. time,
W-pII .316.1:3 all time, and past a. time as well. My
W-pII .317.1:4 given a. my brothers and already mine as
W-pII .317.2:5 *And a. my sorrows end in Your embrace,*
W-pII .318.1:1 are reconciled a. parts of Heaven's plan to
W-pII .318.1:2 a. the parts have but one purpose and one
W-pII .319.1:1 which a. arrogance has been removed,
W-pII .319.1:6 I learn that what one gains is given unto a.
W-pII ....320.h My Father gives a. power unto me.
W-pII .320.1:4 and lays before it a. the strength and love
W-pII .320.1:5 I am he to whom a. this is given. I am he
W-pII .320.2:1 *Your Will can do a. things in me, and then*
W-pII .320.2:1 *extend to a. the world as well through me.*
W-pII .320.2:3 *And so a. power has been given to Your Son.*
W-pII ...11.1:1 Creation is the sum of a. God's Thoughts,
W-pII ...11.1:1 infinite, and everywhere without a. limit.
W-pII ...11.1:3 time when a. that it created was not there.
W-pII ...11.2:1 God's Thoughts are given a. the power
W-pII ...11.3:1 Creation is the opposite of a. illusions, for
W-pII ...11.3:3 holy Will, beyond a. possibility of harm,
W-pII ...11.4:3 Yet back of a. our doubts, past all our
W-pII ...11.4:3 back of all our doubts, past a. our fears,
W-pII ...11.4:4 For love remains with a. its Thoughts, its
W-pII .321.2:3 And how sure is a. the world's salvation,
W-pII .322.2:1 *a. sacrifice remains forever inconceivable.*
W-pII .323.1:1 *Son; You ask him to give up a. suffering, all*
W-pII .323.1:1 *up all suffering, a. sense of loss and sadness,*
W-pII .323.1:1 *of loss and sadness, a. anxiety and doubt,*
W-pII .324.1:6 *brothers a. can follow in the way I lead them.*
W-pII ....325.h A. things I think I see reflect ideas.
W-pII .326.1:5 *And a. Your attributes abide in me, because*
W-pII .326.1:8 *and a. separate thoughts unite in glory as the*
W-pII .327.1:5 give me a. the help I need to come to Him.
W-pII .328.1:1 for a. things we perceive are upside down
W-pII .328.1:3 Yet a. we find is sickness, suffering and
W-pII .329.1:6 *That choice was made for a. eternity. It*
W-pII .329.2:2 a. of us are one because His Will is shared
W-pII .329.2:2 one because His Will is shared by a. of us.
W-pII .330.1:6 and thus escape forever from a. things the
W-pII .330.2:3 *to be made free forever from a. our mistakes,*
W-pII ...12.3:4 a. there is surrounding him is everlasting
W-pII .333.2:1 *chose to shine away a. conflict and all doubt,*
W-pII .333.2:1 *chose to shine away all conflict and a. doubt,*
W-pII .334.1:2 Illusions are a. vain, and dreams are gone
W-pII .334.1:4 to a. who hear and choose to follow Him.
W-pII .336.1:3 the memory that lies beyond them a..
W-pII ....337.h My sinlessness protects me from a. harm.
W-pII .337.1:1 freedom forever from a. thought of loss;
W-pII .337.1:3 What must I do to know a. this is mine? I
W-pII .337.1:5 already done a. things that need be done.
W-pII .338.1:1 this to let salvation come to a. the world.
W-pII .338.1:4 and he is safe from a. external things. His
W-pII .338.2:2 *Yours. A. other plans will fail. And I will have*
W-pII .340.1:4 *and be free forever from a. suffering. Thanks*
W-pII ...13.1:2 It does not create, nor really change at a..
W-pII ...13.3:2 to a. they look upon in mercy and in love.
W-pII ...13.3:4 Each lily of forgiveness offers a. the world
W-pII .341.1:3 *Smile, with a. Your Love bestowed upon us,*
W-pII ....342.h I let forgiveness rest upon a. things, For
W-pII .342.1:7 *Let me forgive a. things, and let creation be*
W-pII .343.1:7 *And so a. things are given unto me forever*
W-pII .345.2:1 Peace to a. seeking hearts today. The
W-pII ....346.h me, And I forget a. things except His Love
W-pII .346.1:1 *correcting my perception of a. things. And*
W-pII .346.1:4 *today transcends a. laws of time and things*
W-pII .346.1:5 *I would forget a. things except Your Love. I*
W-pII .346.1:7 *Son, forgetting a. the foolish toys I made as I*
W-pII .346.2:2 we forget a. things except God's Love.
W-pII .347.1:5 *I give a. judgment to the One You gave to me*
W-pII ....349.h upon A. things for me and judge them not
W-pII .349.1:1 *So would I liberate a. things I see, and give to*
W-pII .349.2:2 He gives us grace to meet them a.. And so
W-pII .350.1:2 *Son of God incorporates a. things within*
W-pII ...14.3:4 perceive a. things as kindly and as good.
W-pII ...14.4:4 we have attained we call to a. our brothers
W-pII ....352.h one Come a. the sorrows of the world. But
W-pII .353.1:1 *Father, I give a. that is mine today to Christ,*
W-pII ....355.h There is no end to a. the peace and joy,
W-pII ....355.h joy, And a. the miracles that I will give,
W-pII .358.1:4 *as well, and a. I want is what You offer me, in*
W-pII .358.1:5 *Let me remember a. I do not know, and let*
W-pII .358.1:7 *not forget myself is nothing, but my Self is a..*
W-pII ....359.h A. pain Is healed; all misery replaced with
W-pII ....359.h pain Is healed; a. misery replaced with joy
W-pII ....359.h A. prison doors are opened. And all sin Is
W-pII ....359.h a. sin Is understood as merely a mistake.
W-pII .359.1:2 *We have misunderstood a. things. But we*
W-pII ....360.h me. Let a. the world be blessed with peace
W-pII .360.1:4 *Peace be to me, and peace to a. the world. In*
Wfl........in.1:5 and destroying, dangerous in a. its ways,
Wfl........in.3:1 directing a. our thoughts to serve the
Wfl........in.3:5 For a. that we forgive we will not fail to
Wfl........in.5:3 from a. the wrath we thought belonged to
Wfl........in.6:3 say, "This is My Son, and a. I have is his"?
Wfl........in.6:5 ever have, for in these words is a. there is,
Wfl........in.6:5 a. that there will be throughout all time
Wfl........in.6:5 will be throughout a. time and in eternity.
W-ep......... 1:6 He will not withhold a. answers that you
W-ep......... 1:7 He knows the way to solve a. problems,
W-ep......... 1:7 solve all problems, and resolve a. doubts.
W-ep......... 4:1 and a. pain that you may think is real.
W-ep......... 6:2 in His way, and trust a. things to Him. In
W-ep......... 6:7 God's angels hover near and a. about. His
M-in.......... 2:2 believe one or the other is true a. the time.
M-1........... 2:1 They come from a. over the world. They
M-1........... 2:2 They come from a. religions and from no
M-1........... 2:5 It goes on a. the time everywhere. It calls
M-1........... 2:8 Yet it is a. a matter of time. Everyone will
M-1........... 4:2 of other forms, a. with the same outcome.
M-1........... 4:7 wears out the world and a. things in it.
M-2........... 2:5 So is a. reality, being of Him. The instant
M-2........... 2:8 long ago. In reality it never happened at a.
M-2........... 4:1 so ancient that it is beyond a. memory,
M-2........... 5:6 a. the differences they thought separated
M-3........... 4:6 Yet a. who meet will someday meet again,
M-3........... 4:6 destiny of a. relationships to become holy
M-4........... 1:1 traits of God's teachers are not at a. alike.
M-4........... 1:6 become characteristic of a. teachers of
M-4........... 1:7 learning. In this respect they are a. alike.
M-4........... 2:1 A. differences among the Sons of God are
M-4.........I.1:6 It is this power that keeps a. things safe. It
M-4..... I.A.4:2 he must now decide a. things on the basis
M-4..... I.A.4:5 learning to understand that a. things,
M-4..... I.A.7:3 A. that he really learned so far was that he
M-4..... I.A.7:8 He must learn to lay a. judgment aside,
M-4..... I.A.8:3 on in a. "emergencies" as well as tranquil
M-4........II.1:1 A. other traits of God's teachers rest on
M-4........II.2:8 In this, as in a. things, they are honest.
M-4......II.2:10 They choose for a. mankind; for all the
M-4......II.2:10 for a. the world and all things in it; for the
M-4......II.2:10 for all the world and a. things in it; for the
M-4...... III.1:7 Let this be lost, and a. his learning goes.
M-4...... III.1:8 judgment are a. things equally acceptable,
M-4...... III.1:9 Without judgment are a. men brothers,
M-4.... IV.1:11 Nor can God's Teacher be heard at a.,
M-4......V.1:11 God's Voice directs them in a. things. Joy
M-4...... VII.1:3 carefully. Like a. the other attributes of
M-4... VII.2:10 want to keep for himself a. things that are
M-4.... VIII.1:3 A. he sees is certain outcome, at a time
M-4.... VIII.1:8 willing to reconsider a. his past decisions,
M-4..VIII.1:10 interpretation of a. things in time, no
M-4...... IX.1:4 in the Word of God to set a. things right;
M-4...... IX.1:4 to set all things right; not some, but a..
M-4...... IX.1:6 To give up a. problems to one Answer is
M-4.... IX.2:12 that alone to which a. faithfulness is due.
M-4........X.2:2 have let go a. things that would prevent
M-4........X.2:6 And above a. are all things welcoming, for
M-4........X.2:6 And above all are a. things welcoming, for
M-4......X.2:10 way for what goes far beyond a. learning.
M-4......X.2:12 at which a. learning ultimately converges.
M-5.........I.1:8 eager to keep a. power for Himself. Only
M-5.........I.2:4 It stands for a. that he would hide from
M-5........II.1:2 gain at a. to me in this" and he is healed.
M-5........II.2:2 And this is so for healing in a. forms. A
M-5......II.2:11 They are not actually needed at a.. The
M-5........II.4:2 idea goes also a. confusion about creation.
M-5........II.4:7 pain, disaster and a. suffering mean now?
M-5........II.4:9 also go a. the effects they seemed to cause.
M-5...... III.3:2 is to forget that a. of them have the same
M-6........... 4:1 It is the relinquishing of a. concern about
M-7........... 4:5 It has a. the appearances of love. Yet love
M-8........... 3:1 Where do a. these differences come from
M-8........... 3:5 does not exist in the world outside at a..
M-8........... 4:7 this the judgment of a. differences rests,
M-8........... 5:1 merely because a. sickness is illusion. Is it
M-8........... 5:6 His mind has categorized them a. as real,
M-8........... 5:6 all as real, and so they are a. real to him.
M-8........... 5:7 they are a. illusions they will disappear.
M-8........... 6:4 mind will put them a. in one category;
M-8........... 6:9 The one answer to a. illusions is truth.
M-9........... 1:8 and a. dark cornerstones of unforgiveness
M-10......... 3:4 to recognize in advance a. the effects of
M-10......... 4:1 a. the "facts" you needed for judgment,
M-10......... 4:8 He does know a. the facts; past, present
M-10......... 4:9 know a. the effects of His judgment on

M-10 5:3 And it was **a.** illusion. Nothing more.
M-10 6:4 A. of the ugliness he sees about him is its
M-10 6:5 A. of the pain he looks upon is its result.
M-10 6:6 A. of the loneliness and sense of loss; of
M-10 6:6 and fear of death; **a.** these have come of it.
M-11 3:1 the Answer to **a.** problems you have made
M-12 3:3 Only very few can hear God's Voice at **a.**,
M-12 5:6 is done it is laid by, and that is **a.**. The
M-12 5:7 it makes **a.** decisions that are responsible
M-12 6:4 that **a.** choices are made consciously, with
M-12 6:11 beyond **a.** seeming and yet surely theirs.
M-13 1:2 Like **a.** things in the world, its meaning is
M-13 1:4 Like **a.** lessons it is an illusion, for in
M-13 2:6 "hero" to whom **a.** these things belong?
M-13 3:1 to understand that **a.** the "pleasures" of
M-13 3:2 –and it is sacrifice indeed!– **a.** this entails
M-13 3:7 is. He can doubt **a.** things, but never this.
M-13 4:5 who has escaped the world and **a.** its ills
M-13 4:6 Yet he must rejoice that he is free of **a.** the
M-13 4:7 him. To them he sacrifices **a.** his peace. To
M-13 4:8 To them he sacrifices **a.** his freedom. And
M-13 6:1 requires sacrifice of **a.** you really hold dear
M-13 6:9 is no other hope in **a.** the world that they
M-13 6:10 voice in **a.** the world that echoes God's. If
M-13 8:2 everything is given you at no cost at **a.**.
M-14 1:4 in gentleness, will cover it, hiding **a.** evil,
M-14 1:4 concealing **a.** sin and ending guilt forever.
M-14 1:9 How but in this way are **a.** illusions ended
M-14 2:8 The world will end when **a.** things in it
M-14 3:5 forgive one sin than to forgive **a.** of them.
M-14 3:11 It goes against **a.** the thinking of the world
M-14 5:7 only complete forgiveness brings **a.** this to
M-14 5:10 that **a.** God would have you do you can do
M-15 1:9 the Judgment in which **a.** things are freed
M-15 2:13 Judgment comes to **a.** who stand aside in
M-15 3:11 and offer it to **a.** the world to keep it safe.
M-16 1:5 He will be told **a.** that his role should be,
M-16 6:2 because **a.** things are freed within it. You
M-16 6:4 **a.** the fearful things you see in dreams. It
M-16 6:10 Nothing at **a.**! Your defenses will not
M-16 7:2 A. that he did before in the name of safety
M-16 7:5 for He to Whom he turns with **a.** of them
M-16 7:7 places, because they are **a.** one to God.
M-16 9:2 For **a.** temptation is nothing more than
M-16 9:5 **a.** magic is recognized as merely nothing,
M-16 9:6 A. intermediate lessons will but lead to
M-16 9:7 For magic of any kind, in **a.** its forms,
M-16 10:4 is safe from **a.** deception if he so decides.
M-16 10:7 other words, or only one, or none at **a.**.
M-16 10:9 merely chooses to give up **a.** that he never
M-16 11:8 A. belief in magic is maintained by just
M-16 11:9 A. through their training, every day and
M-17 4:7 A. of these reactions are the same. They
M-17 7:1 now be your reaction to **a.** magic thoughts
M-17 9:13 Love is Cause of everything beyond **a.** fear
M-18 2:4 condition of **a.** that God created. Now He
M-18 2:6 is He free to teach **a.** minds the truth of
M-18 3:6 Correction has one answer to **a.** this, and
M-18 4:1 to let **a.** his own mistakes be corrected. If
M-19 1:2 the basis for **a.** the judgments of the world
M-19 1:5 justice, since **a.** attack can only be unjust.
M-19 1:7 and laying **a.** injustices aside. If God's Son
M-19 2:6 along. Nor could **a.** the magnificence, the
M-19 2:7 fall short indeed of **a.** that wait when the
M-19 3:1 A. concepts of your brothers and yourself
M-19 3:1 **a.** fears of future states and all concerns
M-19 3:1 all fears of future states and **a.** concerns
M-19 3:4 **a.** thought of wholeness must be lost.
M-19 5:6 accepts **a.** evidence that is brought before
M-19 5:6 as separate and apart from **a.** the rest.
M-19 5:8 **a.** attack and condemnation becomes
M-19 5:12 peace of God descends on **a.** the world,
M-20 2:2 it is totally unlike **a.** previous experiences.
M-20 2:6 yes, between this thing and **a.** the past.
M-20 6:9 The Will of God is One and **a.** there is.
M-20 6:11 **a.** the thoughts of which you can conceive,
M-21 1:1 words play no part at **a.** in healing. The
M-21 3:4 in his heart, **a.** this becomes his own. The
M-21 3:10 that which has no human symbols at **a.**.
M-21 5:4 A. these are judgments that have no value
M-22 2:2 lesson of the Atonement to **a.** situations,
M-22 2:3 **a.** that his acceptance holds out to him. It
M-22 4:3 applied to **a.** specific forms of sickness,
M-22 4:3 of himself and of **a.** others as well. Nor is
M-22 4:5 correcting **a.** mistakes and healing all
M-22 4:5 all mistakes and healing **a.** perception.
M-22 4:8 It is true of **a.** things that God created. In
M-22 4:9 God created. In it are **a.** illusions healed.
M-22 5:5 be unable to recognize his brother at **a.**,
M-22 6:2 to **a.** individuals in all circumstances. And
M-22 6:2 to all individuals in **a.** circumstances. And
M-22 6:3 heal **a.** individuals of all forms of sickness.
M-22 6:3 heal all individuals of **a.** forms of sickness.
M-22 6:14 lies. A. else must follow from this single
M-23 2:6 recognized **a.** living things as part of him.
M-23 4:3 names of **a.** the gods to which you pray. It
M-23 4:5 for **a.** the gifts that God has given you.
M-23 6:8 Then turn to one who laid **a.** limits by,
M-24 4:4 wise to step away from **a.** such questions,
M-24 5:7 A. that must be recognized, however, is
M-24 5:9 is not necessarily **a.** there is to learn. His
M-24 6:9 A. beliefs will point to this if properly
M-24 6:11 A. beliefs that lead to progress should be
M-25 1:6 is. Let **a.** his learning and all his efforts be
M-25 1:6 is. Let all his learning and **a.** his efforts be
M-25 2:6 that surround **a.** the separate places of the
M-25 6:4 Salvation has need of **a.** abilities, for what
M-26 1:3 **a.** barriers to truth have been removed. In
M-26 2:7 A. needs are known to them, and all
M-26 2:7 them, and **a.** mistakes are recognized and
M-26 2:9 they give **a.** their gifts to the teachers of
M-26 2:9 asking **a.** things in their name and in no
M-26 3:7 A. worldly states must be illusory. If God
M-26 4:8 delayed. A. the help you can accept will be
M-26 4:11 could you desire, when this is **a.** you need
M-27 1:1 dream from which **a.** illusions stem. Is it
M-27 1:4 that **a.** things in it are born only to die.
M-27 1:6 path,– **a.** this is taken as the Will of God.
M-27 2:2 who has decreed that **a.** things pass away,
M-27 3:6 And so do **a.** things live because of death.
M-27 6:4 A. dreams will end with this one. This is
M-27 6:5 final goal; the end of **a.** illusions. And in
M-27 6:6 And in death are **a.** illusions born. What
M-27 6:10 in Him **a.** created things must be eternal.
M-28 1:9 is the relinquishment of **a.** other purposes
M-28 1:9 of all other purposes, **a.** other interests, all
M-28 1:9 **a.** other wishes and all other concerns. It
M-28 1:9 all other wishes and **a.** other concerns. It
M-28 2:2 of life. Thus is **a.** the thinking of the world
M-28 3:3 wholly corrected and **a.** mistakes undone.
M-28 3:7 A. longings are satisfied, for what remains
M-28 3:8 forgiving **a.** things and replacing all attack
M-28 3:8 forgiving all things and replacing **a.** attack
M-28 4:1 A. living hearts are tranquil with a stir of
M-28 4:6 A. things are seen in light, and in the light
M-28 5:5 His sinlessness, His Love behind **a.** forms,
M-28 5:5 behind all forms, beyond **a.** purposes.
M-28 6:1 These things await us **a.**, but we are not
M-28 6:9 And **a.** he sought before to crucify are
M-29 1:1 to answer **a.** questions that both teacher
M-29 2:6 and **a.** aspects are under the Holy Spirit's
M-29 4:2 I can do nothing" is to gain **a.** power. And
M-29 4:4 As God created you, you *have* **a.** power.
M-29 4:8 image assumes it knows **a.** things because
M-29 4:11 it. His decisions bring benefit to **a.**, being
M-29 7:6 it so. Ask **a.** things of His Teacher, and all
M-29 7:6 His Teacher, and **a.** things are given you.
M-29 8:1 *And now in* ***a.*** *your doings be you blessed.*
M-29 8:3 *And* ***a.*** *the world stands silent in the grace*
M-29 8:4 *around the world, To close* ***a.*** *things of time;*
M-29 8:4 *of time; to end the sight Of* ***a.*** *things visible;*
M-29 8:4 *visible; and to undo* ***A.*** *things that change.*
M-29 8:7 *And for* ***a.*** *those who walk to God with me.*
C-in 2:1 A. terms are potentially controversial,
C-in 3:2 with what is beyond **a.** error because it is
C-2 1:7 It is a thing of madness, not reality at **a.**. A
C-2 1:8 all. A name for namelessness is **a.** it is. A
C-2 1:11 this except a dream which, like **a.** dreams,
C-2 4:3 from this that we deduce **a.** that the ego is
C-2 5:2 we find **a.** that is not the ego in this world.
C-2 5:3 for here we see **a.** that it seemed to do,
C-2 7:3 But look at **a.** the aspects of *this* dream and
C-2 7:5 at the helpers **a.** along the way you travel,
C-2 8:1 This was the ego– **a.** the cruel hate, the
C-2 8:1 self that seemed alone in **a.** the universe.
C-2 8:4 Would it not answer **a.** you thought to ask
C-3 1:4 Unlike **a.** other illusions it leads away
C-3 3:3 He is not at **a.** concerned with form, but
C-3 6:1 God's Will is **a.** there is. We can but go
C-3 8:4 behind **a.** joining but beyond them all.
C-3 8:4 behind all joining but beyond them **a.**.
C-4 1:5 when **a.** things visible will have an end.
C-4 3:6 Atonement, true perception, **a.** are one.
C-4 5:6 as surely as forgiveness takes **a.** guilt away
C-4 5:7 once **a.** guilt is gone what more remains to
C-4 6:3 Here are **a.** illusions brought to truth and
C-4 8:3 out of **a.** fear and given back to love.
C-5 1:8 But He creates **a.** Helpers of His Son while
C-5 2:1 in **a.** his brothers and remembered God.
C-5 2:3 to hold his self from Self, as **a.** illusions do
C-5 3:1 –Jesus became what **a.** of you must be. He
C-5 4:1 **a.** your sins have been forgiven because
C-5 4:1 because they carried no effects at **a.**. And
C-5 5:3 mighty lesson that he learned for **a.** of you
C-5 6:8 most of **a.** that he would have you learn,
C-5 6:12 *bring with you* ***a.*** *those whom He has sent to*
C-6 2:3 A. power in Heaven and earth is therefore
C-ep 1:9 farther on the road where **a.** illusions end?
C-ep 2:5 eternity and through **a.** time as well. And
C-ep 4:4 God is here, and with Him **a.** our brothers
C-ep 4:7 **a.** that the dream of sin had made of it.
C-ep 5:3 and the end of **a.** we thought we made.
P-1 5:8 **a.** psychotherapy leads to God in the end.
P-1 5:10 We are **a.** His psychotherapists, for He
P-1 5:10 for He would have us **a.** be healed in Him.
P-2 I.3:7 Only then is **a.** conflict over, for only then
P-2 II.1:4 learned **a.** things does not need a teacher,
P-2 II.2:2 without perceiving the contradiction at **a.**.
P-2 II.3:2 then, is **a.** that need be taught, because it
P-2 II.3:2 because it is **a.** that need be learned. All
P-2 II.3:3 A. blocks to the remembrance of God are
P-2 II.3:5 world has marshalled **a.** its forces against
P-2 II.3:5 ending of the world and **a.** it stands for.
P-2 II.4:6 and it is to this that **a.** unforgiveness leads
P-2 II.5:6 are **a.** insane or they would not be here.
P-2 II.8:4 doing, lose **a.** sense of separate interests.
P-2 III.1:6 is **a.** there is to light the way to truth.
P-2 III.2:3 for transcending **a.** limitations has been
P-2 IV.1:1 As **a.** therapy is psychotherapy, so all
P-2 IV.1:1 **a.** illness is mental illness. It is a judgment
P-2 IV.2:3 received. And **a.** who ask for illness have
P-2 IV.2:4 for **a.** external things are only shadows of
P-2 IV.3:3 Yet **a.** these things, however real they
P-2 IV.3:6 will say again, **a.** therapy is psychotherapy
P-2 IV.6:4 overcome **a.** limits perceived in the self, at
P-2 IV.7:8 form, being the source of **a.** illusions.
P-2 IV.8:1 Sickness is insanity because **a.** sickness is
P-2 IV.8:3 Herein lies the basis of **a.** errors, for all of
P-2 IV.8:3 errors, for **a.** of them are but attempts to
P-2 IV.11:1 single doctrine is the goal of **a.** therapy.
P-2 IV.11:7 Given this single shift, **a.** else will follow.
P-2 IV.11:10 The truth is simple, being one for **a.**.
P-2 V.1:5 are forces to be overcome to be alive at **a.**.
P-2 V.2:6 the lesson of defenselessness above **a.** else,
P-2 V.3:6 less than **a.** he has to give is worthy of the
P-2 V.6:7 can serve His Son in **a.** his present needs.
P-2 V.7:1 **a.** gifts of God must be received. In time
P-2 V.7:6 him to forgive himself for **a.** the trespasses
P-2 V.8:2 which we come to where **a.** dreams began.
P-2 V.8:10 that **a.** his sins have been forgiven him.
P-2 VI.1:3 **a.** this is but the grim refusal to forgive.
P-2 VI.2:6 **a.** these and more are heard instead of
P-2 VI.4:4 Here is **a.** sickness cherished, but without
P-2 VI.6:3 therapist sees in the patient **a.** that he has
P-2 VI.7:2 joyous song salvation sings to **a.** who hear
P-2 VI.7:3 by **a.** who see themselves as therapists.
P-2 VII.3:1 that **a.** his sins have been forgiven him,

| Reference | Context |
|---|---|
| P-2 ....... VII.3:6 | a. sense of separation finally is overcome. |
| P-2 ....... VII.4:2 | God. A. "unhealed healers" make this |
| P-2 ....... VII.5:4 | of a. the effects that may occur in them. |
| P-2 ....... VII.6:4 | He understands a. power in earth and |
| P-2 ....... VII.8:2 | And then forget the world and a. its little |
| P-2 ....... VII.8:4 | that brushes lightly past a. sickly dreams. |
| P-3 ......... II.4:1 | on a. He created and pronounced it good. |
| P-3 ....... II.4:10 | for a. your sins have been forgiven you. |
| P-3 ......... II.6:6 | of fear, which is the content of a. dreams. |
| P-3 ......... II.6:8 | is a place for a. relationships in this world, |
| P-3 ......... II.7:4 | mind, offering it to a. who come to him. |
| P-3 ......... II.8:7 | Yet a. the laws of healing can be theirs in |
| P-3 ........ III.3:5 | gift whereby a. healing is accomplished. |
| P-3 ........ III.5:7 | A. that they need will thus be given them. |
| P-3 ........ III.5:8 | that a. they have comes only from God. If |
| P-3 ........ III.8:5 | is in every circumstance and at a. times. |
| S-1 ......... in.1:7 | what a. prayer will be throughout eternity |
| S-1 ........... I.3:5 | A. the rest is merely added. You have |
| S-1 ........... I.3:6 | and a. else has indeed been given you. |
| S-1 ........... I.4:8 | still a. little answers are contained in this. |
| S-1 ......... II.7:3 | of earth are left behind, a. unremembered |
| S-1 ......... II.7:5 | beyond a. change and incorruptible. The |
| S-1 ......... II.7:8 | desires, unneedful now of anything at a.. |
| S-1 ......... II.8:6 | a. things will be transformed together, |
| S-1 ........ III.1:2 | then, should you pray for others at a.? |
| S-1 ...... III.6:10 | well. A. other goals are at the cost of God. |
| S-1 ........ IV.3:1 | pray together do not ask, before a. else, |
| S-1 ........ IV.3:2 | come in which are a. specifics satisfied; all |
| S-1 ........ IV.3:2 | satisfied; a. separate wishes unified in one |
| S-1 ........ IV.3:4 | – a. these are but illusions from the past. |
| S-1 ........ IV.3:6 | prayer can offer now so far exceeds a. that |
| S-1 ........ IV.4:2 | to free yourself from a. of them at once? |
| S-1 ......... V.1:4 | judge a. things as you would have them be |
| S-1 ......... V.1:5 | be. A. little gods it gladly lays aside, not in |
| S-2 ......... in.1:2 | step, or even to attempt to climb at a.. |
| S-2 ........... I.2:4 | It carefully picks out a. evil things, and |
| S-2 ........... I.2:5 | this it sees in a. it looks upon and hates. |
| S-2 ........... I.4:5 | it is the only happy dream in a. the world; |
| S-2 ........... I.6:3 | Yet God Himself has given a. His Sons a |
| S-2 ........... I.6:3 | for a. illusions that they think they see. |
| S-2 ........... I.6:5 | still remains unchanged behind them a.. |
| S-2 ........... I.8:6 | beyond a. limits into timelessness, with |
| S-2 ........... I.8:6 | song that a. creation sings unto its God. |
| S-2 ........... I.9:5 | must be unveiled in a. its treachery, and |
| S-2 ......... II.1:2 | Not a. of them are obvious, and some are |
| S-2 ......... II.1:3 | Yet a. the forms that it may seem to take |
| S-2 ......... II.6:9 | A. else is mockery. For who would try to |
| S-2 ......... II.7:7 | Christ is for a. because He is in all. It is |
| S-2 ......... II.7:7 | Christ is for all because He is in a.. It is |
| S-2 ......... II.8:1 | A. forms forgiveness takes that do not |
| S-2 ........ III.2:4 | Give up a. else, for there *is* nothing else. |
| S-2 ........ III.2:6 | A. that you need do is to step back and |
| S-2 ........ III.4:9 | and purpose. Here a. dreams are done. |
| S-3 ........... I.3:3 | a. shadows on the holy face of Christ, |
| S-3 ......... II.2:2 | then, for a. the service it has given us. But |
| S-3 ......... II.6:3 | overcome until a. faith in it has been laid |
| S-3 ........ III.5:1 | understand that a. their Source creates is |
| S-3 ........ III.5:3 | It will remain to bless for a. eternity. It |
| S-3 ........ III.6:2 | and to bless a. those who serve with Him |
| S-3 ........ IV.1:9 | and given up a. separate dreams of special |
| S-3 ........ IV.2:3 | and a. the living things upon the earth. |
| S-3 ........ IV.2:4 | for love has come in a. its holy oneness. |
| S-3 ........ IV.2:6 | This instant is the goal of a. true healers, |
| S-3 ........ IV.6:4 | arise and lay a. dreaming down forever. |
| S-3 ........ IV.6:6 | Give a. your dreams to Christ and let Him |
| S-3 ........ IV.7:3 | joyful thanks in unison with a. creation, |

### all-embracing 3

| Reference | Context |
|---|---|
| W-pI ... 130.6:2 | already made a choice as a. as its opposite |
| W-pI ... 189.6:1 | is true in us, and feel its a. tenderness, its |
| M-14 ......... 2:2 | grows and becomes stronger and more a.. |

### all-encompassed 1

| Reference | Context |
|---|---|
| T-24 ..... VII.7:3 | A perfect being, all-encompassing and a., |

### all-encompassing 8

| Reference | Context |
|---|---|
| T-in ........... 1:8 | *is fear, but what is* a. *can have no opposite.* |
| T-15 ........ I.7:7 | for compounding guilt until it becomes a. |
| T-24 .... VII.7:3 | A perfect being, a. and all-encompassed, |
| T-29 ... VIII.6:4 | deathless come to die, the a. to suffer loss, |
| W-pI ... 152.9:3 | its eternal wholeness, a., God's perfect |
| W-pI ... 161.4:7 | grasp abstraction in the sense that it is a.. |
| W-pI ... 183.8:3 | and let His Name become the a. idea that |
| M-4 ...... IV.2:7 | a. and limitless strength of gentleness? |

### all-inclusive 4

| Reference | Context |
|---|---|
| T-17 ..... VI.6:2 | Holy Spirit's purpose, and this faith is a.. |
| W-pI ... 152.2:6 | Truth must be a., if it be the truth at all. |
| W-pI ... 199.4:5 | extended to the a. goal that it must reach, |
| W-pII ..... 9.2:1 | a. nature of Christ's Second Coming that |

### all-inclusiveness 1

| Reference | Context |
|---|---|
| W-pI ... 152.5:3 | This is the a. which sets the truth apart |

### All-Loving 1

| Reference | Context |
|---|---|
| T-26 ...... V.9:6 | your A. Father has ensured must come to |

### allay 2

| Reference | Context |
|---|---|
| T-2 ..... VI.9:11 | This may a. awareness of the guilt, but at |
| T19 .. IV.A.13:4 | seem to a. their savage pangs of hunger. |

### allays 1

| Reference | Context |
|---|---|
| T-14 ..... III.3:1 | escape the pain that only guiltlessness a.. |

### allegiance 31

| Reference | Context |
|---|---|
| T-4 ....... III.4:3 | the Father, the ego has no a. to its maker. |
| T-4 ....... IV.8:9 | Without your own a., protection and love |
| T-4 ..... IV.8:10 | be judged truly and you must withdraw a. |
| T-4 ....... VI.1:2 | your a. to it gives the ego any power over |
| T-5 ........ V.5:9 | it recognizes that only total a. can be |
| T-6 ........ in.2:5 | capacity for a. to a thought system may be |
| T-6 ..... V.A.5:9 | Egos do join together in temporary a., but |
| T-7 ..... III.2:12 | mind cannot be unified in a. to the ego, |
| T-7 ....... VI.4:6 | This is its a., and this allegiance makes it |
| T-7 ....... VI.4:6 | and this a. makes it treacherous to love |
| T-7 ....... VI.8:4 | of its weakness the ego wants your a., but |
| T-7 ....... VI.9:1 | is dividing its a. between two kingdoms, |
| T-7 ..... VI.12:2 | your thought system and divide your a.. |
| T-7 ...... VII.9:1 | for itself, and being without a. to God, the |
| T-8 ....... I.1:10 | it away when the ego asks for your a.. |
| T-8 ..... VIII.2:2 | of shifting its a. from one to the other, |
| T-10 ...... V.1:2 | for depression is the sign of a. to him. |
| T-10 ...... V.3:1 | A. to the denial of God is the ego's |
| T-11 ...... in.1:4 | all respects so that partial a. is impossible |
| T-11 ...... V.8:3 | to your a. is that it can give power to you. |
| T-11 ...... VI.6:1 | Resurrection must compel your a. gladly, |
| T-15 ...... I.4:10 | to keep fear from you to hold your a.. Yet |
| T-15 ...... IV.3:6 | Every a. to a plan of salvation apart from |
| T-18 .... VII.6:7 | "I need do nothing" is a statement of a., a |
| T-25 ... VIII.2:3 | to it. You have no fixed a.. But remember |
| T-27 .... VII.6:7 | They support its claim on your a.. What |
| T-28 .... VII.3:2 | and no a. to be split between the two. A |
| T-28 .... VII.3:3 | A split a. is but faithlessness to both, and |
| T-29 ........ I.7:5 | not see how limited and weak is your a., |
| T-29 .... VII.6:1 | and to maintain a. to the dream that you |
| W-pI ..... 41.3:2 | real, and suffered out of its a. to them. |

### allegorical 1

| Reference | Context |
|---|---|
| T-18 ... VIII.1:4 | Think not that this is merely a., for it was |

### alliance 8

| Reference | Context |
|---|---|
| T-6 ....... IV.4:7 | It is an a. frankly based on separation. If |
| T-6 ....... IV.4:8 | If you side with this a. you will be afraid, |
| T-6 ....... IV.4:8 | because you are siding with an a. of fear. |
| T-16 .... VII.3:6 | without your a. in your own destruction, |
| T-17 ..... III.8:1 | unholy a. with the ego against the present |
| T-17 ..... III.8:3 | the relationships the unholy a. dictates |
| T-17 ..... III.8:4 | the purpose of the unholy a. are retained, |
| T19 .. IV.D.4:6 | secret a. with them you have agreed never |

### alliances 3

| Reference | Context |
|---|---|
| T-15 .... VII.9:3 | angry a., born of the fear of loneliness |
| T-17 ... III.1:12 | into unholy a. to support the ego's goals, |
| T-23 ........ I.3:2 | and make your strange a. on grounds that |

### allied 1

| Reference | Context |
|---|---|
| T-11 ....... II.5:6 | but you have a. yourself against Him. |

### allies 2

| Reference | Context |
|---|---|
| T-6 ....... IV.4:4 | it, and the ego feels badly in need of a., |
| T-7 ....... III.3:1 | itself at war and therefore in need of a.. |

### allness 1

| Reference | Context |
|---|---|
| W-pI .. 95.12:2 | may extend the a. and the unity of God. |

### allot 1

| Reference | Context |
|---|---|
| T-26 ........ I.5:4 | crumb of happiness that you a. yourself. |

### allots 2

| Reference | Context |
|---|---|
| T-25 . VIII.11:5 | Each special function He a. is but for this; |
| P-3 ........ III.2:7 | money where God's plan a. it has no cost. |

### allotted 4

| Reference | Context |
|---|---|
| T-25 ..... VI.5:9 | And each must do what is a. him, for on |
| T-25 . VIII.14:7 | yourself of what God's justice has a. you. |
| T-27 ... VIII.1:4 | In the brief time a. it to live, it seeks for |
| T-29 ..... IV.4:1 | has failed to fill the function you a. him? |

### allow 70

| Reference | Context |
|---|---|
| T-4 .......... I.2:4 | You believe that if you a. no change to |
| T-5 ...... VII.5:5 | If you a. yourself to feel guilty, you will |
| T-5 ...... VII.5:5 | rather than a. it to be undone for you. |
| T-6 ........ I.16:2 | I do not want you to a. any fear to enter |
| T-6 ....... II.13:3 | part is only to a. no darkness to abide in |
| T-6 ..... V.B.6:5 | you remind yourself to a. the Holy Spirit |
| T-6 ..... V.C.1:2 | to judge every thought you a. to enter it in |
| T-6 ..... V.C.5:4 | you a. yourself to have in your mind only |
| T-7 ....... XI.3:4 | fear, and a. him to give always, without |
| T-8 ...... VII.5:6 | not a. him to belittle himself in your mind |
| T-8 .... VII.16:1 | a. yourself to suffer from imagined results |
| T-8 .... VIII.9:5 | a. the body to be a mirror of a split mind. |
| T-9 ..... VIII.4:4 | unless you do not a. the ego to attack it. |
| T-10 ....... V.9:3 | God. Would He a. Himself to suffer? And |
| T-10 ..... V.14:6 | If you a. yourself to become preoccupied |
| T-11 ....... V.9:1 | can and does a. you to regard yourself as |
| T-12 ....... II.2:6 | Do not a. your brother not to remember, |
| T-12 ...... III.5:4 | of this, and never a. yourself to believe, |
| T-13 ... III.11:6 | God did not a. this to happen. Yet you |
| T-14 ...... III.7:4 | and by refusing to a. him to think he can, |
| T-14 ....... V.4:5 | Never a. purity to remain hidden, but |
| T-16 ...... VI.9:4 | for it will not a. you to betray yourself, |
| T-17 ..... V.12:1 | forgotten if you a. time to close over it. It |
| T-19 ....... II.8:4 | before you a. yourself to make this choice. |
| T19 .. IV.D.3:4 | to a. union to call you out of separation; |
| T-21 ..... VI.1:7 | If it can correct, and you a. it not to do so, |
| T-25 ....... V.5:6 | that you a. him freedom to complete the |
| T-25 . VIII.10:4 | He would not a. His Son be judged by |
| T-26 ..... V.10:1 | Would God a. His Son to lose his way |
| T-26 ..... VI.3:2 | Would you a. one shadow to usurp the |
| T-27 ..... II.12:4 | Him, and you a. Him only half your mind |
| T-27 .. VII.14:3 | and a. His gentle dreams to take the place |
| T-28 ..... I.15:3 | to a. the memory of God to flow across it, |
| T-28 ....... II.3:1 | and not a. himself to be his Father's Son. |
| T-28 ..... III.1:2 | For you have barely started to a. your first |
| T-28 ..... III.3:3 | Do not a. your brother to be sick, for if he |
| T-29 ........ I.6:2 | It will a. but limited indulgences in "love, |

| | |
|---|---|
| T-29.........I.9:5 | you a. the body to say "no" to Heaven's |
| T-30... VIII.6:2 | a dream a. uncertainty to enter here. Be |
| W-in..........9:4 | But do not a. yourself to make exceptions |
| W-pI.....12.2:4 | Do not a. the time of the shift to become |
| W-pI.....43.6:2 | Do not a. any protracted period to occur |
| W-pI.....43.9:2 | Try today not to a. any long periods of |
| W-pI.....50.5:2 | a. peace to flow over you like a blanket of |
| W-pI.....71.8:3 | Do not a. yourself to become depressed |
| W-pI.....74.6:5 | in refusing to a. retreat into withdrawal, |
| W-pI...78.10:2 | when we a. each one we meet to save us, |
| W-pI...78.10:3 | the past, a. the role of savior to be given, |
| WpI. rII.in.4:1 | Do not a. your intent to waver in the face |
| W-pI.....88.4:4 | *Let me a. God's laws to work in this, and not* |
| W-pI.....95.4:2 | this point not to a. your mind to wander, |
| W-pI.....95.9:3 | To a. a mistake to continue is to make |
| W-pI...95.11:3 | and thoughtfully, attempting to a. the |
| W-pI...103.3:1 | A. this one correction to be placed within |
| W-pI...106.4:9 | Today a. your Father's ancient pledge to |
| WpI. rIII.in4:3 | given them, a. your practice periods to be |
| WpIrIII.in10:5 | a. your mind to rest a little time in silence |
| W-pI...126.5:4 | Think you the Lord of Heaven would a. |
| W-pI...127.9:5 | a. His Voice to teach love's meaning to |
| W-pI...134.9:2 | do not a. your mind to dwell on what you |
| W-pI.134.17:2 | a. your mind to see through this illusion |
| W-pI.135.16:1 | that plans is thus refusing to a. for change |
| W-pI...139.8:5 | Let us not a. our holy minds to occupy |
| W-pI...189.8:3 | Your part is simply to a. all obstacles that |
| W-pII..237.1:2 | a. the light in me to shine upon the world |
| W-pII..240.2:2 | *Would You a. Your Son to suffer? Give us* |
| W-pII..258.1:3 | to a. God's grace to shine in unawareness, |
| W-pII..290.1:5 | I would not a. my mind to be deceived by |
| W-pII..295.2:2 | *and thus a. the Holy Spirit's Love to bless all* |
| W-pII..296.2:3 | we a. His teaching to persuade the world, |

## allowance 2

| | |
|---|---|
| T-30.....VII.3:7 | make a. for stability of meaning anywhere |
| W-pI.......1.3:1 | make no a. for differences in the kinds of |

## allowed 18

| | |
|---|---|
| T-2......VI.2:10 | a sure sign that you have a. your mind to |
| T-2......VI.2:10 | miscreate and have not a. me to guide it. |
| T-6......V.C.2:2 | would hardly be consistent if He a. you to |
| T-8.....VII.10:7 | that has been blocked has a. itself to be |
| T-16......VI.9:3 | You have a. the Thought of your reality to |
| T-21.......in.2:7 | joy you have a. yourself to see in you, and |
| T-21....... V.4:3 | And nothing you have a. to stay in your |
| T-26...VII.20:5 | be itself, the Son of God a. to be himself, |
| T-26....... X.1:2 | you think it is unfair and not to be a.. |
| T-27...VII.13:4 | and a. his calmer mind to welcome, not to |
| T-28...... I.12:2 | For in that instant is God's memory a. to |
| T-29...... I.3:10 | to be a breach of treaty not to be a.. |
| T-29......IV.2:7 | indeed if it a. you still to be afraid because |
| T-31.....VII.8:3 | And to each one has He a. the grace to be |
| W-pI.....78.8:8 | a. the Holy Spirit to express through him |
| W-pI.133.11:2 | a. the ego's goals to come between the |
| W-pI.136.14:1 | remain where truth has been a. to enter. |
| S-2........III.6:8 | as true forgiveness is a. to come from His |

## allowing 17

| | |
|---|---|
| T-5......... V.4:3 | your a. it to enter makes it your reality. |
| T-5.....VII.6:11 | *let Him, by a. Him to decide for God for me.* |
| T-6......V.C.7:1 | a. you to identify only with the center, |
| T-7......VI.12:1 | A. insanity to enter your mind means |
| T-12....III.10:9 | a. the Holy Spirit to extend the real world |
| T-13......VI.4:8 | past and future, and not a. the miracle, |
| T-13......XI.4:4 | a. Him to demonstrate which must be |
| T-15......XI.9:5 | And by a. Him to enter, the remembrance |
| T-16.....VII.3:7 | In the special relationship you are a. your |
| T-28...... I.10:9 | lesson in a. Cause to have Its Own Effects, |
| W-pI.....21.1:3 | are urged, a. a full minute for each. |
| W-pI.....53.5:4 | and am not a. my real thoughts to cast |
| W-pI.....78.2:2 | see by not a. sight to stop before it sees. |
| W-pI.....91.8:2 | to a. your mistaken thoughts about your |
| W-pI.136.20:1 | a. your defensiveness to hurt you longer. |
| WpI rVI.in.7:4 | He set for us; a. Him to teach us how to go |
| M-22..........5:3 | In a. this to happen, he has identified |

## allows 8

| | |
|---|---|
| T-5...........I.4:8 | He calls it forth; or better, a. it to come. I |
| T-15.........I.5:4 | The only time the ego a. anyone to look |
| T-15.........I.6:6 | The only way in which the ego a. the fear |
| T-16.....VII.5:3 | Yet the one thing the ego never a. to reach |
| T19. IV.A.12:5 | who a. them to feast only upon what they |
| T-21...... III.2:4 | No one a. a purpose to be replaced while |
| W-pI.....55.3:4 | As forgiveness a. love to return to my |
| W-pII..316.1:2 | me. Each one a. a past mistake to go, and |

## ally 8

| | |
|---|---|
| T-6........ IV.4:5 | mind, the ego turns to the body as its a., |
| T-8..... VIII.4:9 | it has already made the witness an a.. |
| T-15.........I.3:1 | The ego is an a. of time, but not a friend. |
| T-16.....VII.3:9 | while you pursue the ego's goal as its a.. |
| T-16...VII.10:3 | Be an a. of God and not the ego in seeking |
| T-24.... VI.13:3 | apply to what you do with it as your a.. |
| T-25...... IX.7:2 | less deserving, then is He a. to specialness |
| S-2.........in.1:3 | all. Forgiveness is prayer's a.; sister in the |

## almost 32

| | |
|---|---|
| T-1......... II.6:2 | the Sonship appears to involve a. endless |
| T-1......... V.1:5 | or reduce your creativity a. to nothing. |
| T-2........ III.1:2 | defenses have been used a. entirely to |
| T-2.......IV.3:10 | it is a. impossible to deny its existence in |
| T-3.........I.3:11 | use words that are a. impossible to distort |
| T-3........ IV.6:5 | This makes spirit a. inaccessible to the |
| T-3........ VI.7:1 | at that level there is a. endless variation. |
| T-5...........I.6:2 | so high they could reach a. back to Him. |
| T-5.......... V.3:5 | simultaneously; or a. simultaneously, for |
| T-16.... IV.12:3 | that seemed endless is a. complete, for |
| T-16.... IV.12:4 | You have a. recognized it. Turn with me |
| T-17...... III.4:3 | to fade and to be questioned a. at once. |
| T-17...... IV.8:2 | is a. obliterated by its imposing structure. |
| T-18.........I.4:3 | now a. impossible to perceive it once was |
| T-18... VIII.3:4 | this a. imperceptible ripple hails itself as |
| T19. IV.D.17:4 | It is a. Easter, the time of resurrection. Let |
| T-20.....VII.1:7 | This course requires a. nothing of you. It |
| T-20.....VII.2:1 | from sin to holiness may now be a. over. |
| T-22...... IV.3:5 | Yet it is a. over in your awareness, and |
| T-23..........I.4:1 | the war against yourself is a. over. The |
| T-29...... IX.7:7 | dreams can enter here, for time is a. over. |
| T-31..... V.13:6 | But this gain is paid in a. equal loss, for |
| W-pI...182.6:3 | call for help a. unheard amid the grating |
| W-pII...in.10:1 | Now is the need for practice a. done. For |
| W-pII.......2.5:2 | freedom is returned, that time is a. over, |
| W-pII....14.2:1 | Our use for words is a. over now. Yet in |
| W-pII..353.1:3 | *has learning come a. to its appointed end. A* |
| M-9 ...........1:6 | change their life situation a. immediately, |
| M-25 ...........5:7 | is a. inevitable that, unless the individual |
| M-26 .........3:2 | world, it is a. impossible that this endure. |
| P-2........ III.2:6 | it can reach a. to Heaven or go no further |
| S-1......... V.3:6 | You have come a. to Heaven. There is |

## alone 362

| | |
|---|---|
| T-2..... VIII.1:5 | that whatever you a. make is real in your |
| T-5........ III.4:6 | a. your thoughts will frighten you because |
| T-5........ III.8:1 | You cannot understand yourself a.. This |
| T-5........ IV.2:9 | You cannot cancel out your past errors a.. |
| T-5........ IV.4:1 | that I could not atone for myself a.. |
| T-6....... II.6:10 | perfect inclusion in Him Who a. is perfect |
| T-6........ IV.7:4 | *been. Being* a. lives in the Kingdom, where |
| T-6......V.A.6:9 | chosen what they cannot complete a., |
| T-6......V.A.6:9 | complete alone, they are no longer a.. |
| T-6.... V.C.1:11 | and so He a. can keep you wholly joyous. |
| T-7..... VIII.7:2 | cannot make this judgment a.. By |
| T-7..... VIII.7:3 | against the belief that you can be a., thus |
| T-8...........I.2:4 | not asked to dispel your hallucinations a.. |
| T-8...........I.4:2 | basis a. its value should be questioned. If |
| T-8......... II.2:5 | this a. disqualify it as your future teacher? |
| T-8......... II.2:6 | more harm to your learning than this a.. |
| T-8........ III.5:6 | The ego tries to find them in yourself a., |
| T-8........ III.6:1 | The Kingdom cannot be found a., and |
| T-8........ III.6:1 | are the Kingdom cannot find yourself a.. |
| T-8........ III.7:3 | ego teaches that your strength is in you a.. |
| T-8........ III.8:1 | Power and glory belong to God a.. So do |
| T-8........ IV.2:7 | the illusion of loneliness if you are not a.. |
| T-8...... IV.5:11 | decision, but mine a. cannot help you. |
| T-8......... V.1:6 | A. we can do nothing, but together our |
| T-8........ VI.8:5 | Son lies in all of us, but not in any of us a.. |
| T-8........ VI.8:6 | be a. because *He* does not will to be alone. |
| T-8........ VI.8:6 | be alone because *He* does not will to be a.. |
| T-8........ IX.1:6 | body, for perception a. can be distorted. |
| T-8........ IX.7:2 | is not my name a., for ours is a shared |
| T-8........ IX.7:6 | Yet you cannot withdraw from me a.. You |
| T-9...........I.8:4 | panic, because the atheist believes he is a., |
| T-9..........II.6:1 | no more pray for yourself a. than you can |
| T-9..........II.6:1 | alone than you can find joy for yourself a.. |
| T-9..........II.6:5 | hear the Voice for God in yourself a., |
| T-9..........II.6:5 | in yourself alone, because you are not a.. |
| T-9........ II.6:10 | God have created a Voice for you a.? |
| T-9........ IV.1:1 | undo the belief that anything is for you a.. |
| T-9....VIII.10:7 | God's Mind, and therefore not in yours a. |
| T-10....... V.4:4 | without the Father, Who a. is his Help. |
| T-11.......in.4:6 | You will not take this journey a.. I will |
| T-11.........I.1:6 | for God Himself did not will to be a.. |
| T-11.........I.2:1 | To be a. is to be separated from infinity, |
| T-11.........I.5:7 | He did not will to be a., He created a Son |
| T-11.........I.6:3 | Could you be a. there, when it was given |
| T-11.........I.6:3 | you because God did not will to be a.? |
| T-11.......I.11:2 | never forget that God did not will to be a.. |
| T-11...... III.2:4 | real, when He did not will to be a. Himself |
| T-11...... III.7:8 | beside you, but you also cannot enter a.. |
| T-11...... III.8:2 | Him, because it is your will not to be a.. |
| T-11....VIII.1:5 | but an instant to realize that this a. is true |
| T-12........II.2:7 | is his, for God cannot be remembered a.. |
| T-12........II.7:5 | Trust in my help, for I did not walk a., |
| T-12... VII.15:3 | I have overcome death for myself a.? And |
| T-13.... III.12:1 | To "single out" is to "make a.," and thus |
| T-13....... V.1:9 | all. In this world their maker moves a., for |
| T-13....... V.3:4 | and he a. believes they answered him. |
| T-13....... V.6:4 | isolated from reality as if you were a. in all |
| T-13....... V.6:7 | your sight, for you look upon yourself a.. |
| T-13..... V.11:3 | Nor will they see Him a., for He is no |
| T-13..... V.11:3 | alone, for He is no more a. than they are. |
| T-13.... VI.12:4 | In sleep you are a., and your awareness is |
| T-13.... VI.13:2 | faithful in your giving, for you were not a. |
| T-13..... VII.1:2 | streets where people walk a. and separate. |
| T-13... VII.17:1 | We cannot sing redemption's hymn a.. |
| T-13....VIII.8:2 | leave no one untouched and no one left a. |
| T-13........X.8:3 | a. in a dark world where pain is pressing |
| T-13..... X.14:2 | A. we are all lowly, but together we shine |
| T-13..... X.14:2 | that none of us a. can even think of it. |
| T-14.......in.1:7 | for there a. their seeming clearness seems |
| T-14...... III.2:3 | You do not want either a., for without |
| T-14...... III.9:3 | decisions by yourself or for yourself a.. |
| T-14.... III.10:8 | of deciding what they want and need a.. |
| T-14.... III.11:3 | which is all that you a. can offer yourself, |
| T-14.... III.13:3 | it. Every decision you undertake a. but |
| T-14.... III.14:4 | His guidance you will think you know a., |
| T-14.... III.14:4 | as you decided that salvation lay in you a.. |
| T-14....... V.3:8 | for you will not withhold it from them a.. |
| T-14....... V.8:4 | with no one left outside to suffer guilt a.. |
| T-14.... VII.6:7 | The vision of Christ is not for Him a., but |
| T-14..... VII.7:2 | You cannot see a.. Sharing perception |
| T-14..... VII.7:4 | that nothing you see means anything a.. |
| T-14........X.9:5 | For no one a. can judge the ego truly. Yet |
| T-14..... X.10:1 | to remember God in secret and a.. For |
| T-14..... X.10:2 | remembering Him means you are not a., |
| T-14...... XI.8:4 | or deal with certain aspects of your life a., |
| T-14... XI.12:4 | go together and never can be found a.. |
| T-14... XI.15:2 | think you know Him not, only because, a. |
| T-15.......I.12:2 | holiness is shared, and cannot be yours a. |
| T-15...... III.4:7 | Nor is it asked of you a.. The power of |
| T-15...... III.9:2 | that you learn not for yourself a., no more |
| T-15...... IV.4:7 | that you a. cannot know where it is, and |
| T-15...... IV.7:3 | lies in keeping thoughts to yourself a.. For |
| T-15...... IV.7:4 | a way to keep what you would have a., |
| T-15....... V.2:5 | to it for salvation is to believe you are a.. |
| T-15....... V.2:6 | To be a. *is* to be guilty. For to experience |
| T-15....... V.2:7 | For to experience yourself as a. is to deny |
| T-15....... V.4:3 | They are not based on changeless love a.. |
| T-15...... VI.5:7 | this a. is natural under the laws of God. In |
| T-15... VII.11:2 | to communicate is to make yourself a.? It |
| T-15....VIII.2:7 | You are not a. in this. The will of your |

T-15....VIII.6:1 In the Holy Spirit **a.** lies the awareness of
T-16.......I.3:10 *I am not* ***a.****, and I would not intrude the past*
T-16....... II.4:1 apparent that you have not done them **a.**.
T-16....... II.9:10 it. Can you be **a.** with witnesses like these?
T-16....... III.6:7 **A.**, you stand outside your teaching and
T-16....... V.2:2 ego would have you see Him, and Him **a.**,
T-17....VII.10:2 no longer wholly insane, nor no longer **a.**.
T-18....... II.6:8 It will not be for you **a.**, for therein lay its
T-18....... III.4:1 you joined each other you were not **a.**. Do
T-18...... IV.4:1 not come from your little willingness **a.**. It
T-18...... IV.5:7 Purification is of God **a.**, and therefore for
T-18....... V.2:8 Nor will you use it to ascend to Heaven **a.**.
T-18....... V.6:4 you or your brother to experience fear **a.**,
T-18....... V.6:4 fear alone, or to attempt to deal with it **a.**.
T-18...... VI.3:3 to be fragmented and private and **a.**. Its
T-18....VIII.3:5 Think how **a.** and frightened is this little
T-18....VIII.5:2 thought, living **a.** and in no way joined to
T-18....VIII.9:6 they will not depart as they had come, **a.**.
T-18....VIII.9:8 but has grown too weary to go on **a.**.
T-18..VIII.12:4 You could no more know God **a.** than He
T19... IV.A.2:6 are not asked to let it go for yourself **a.**.
T19... IV.D.9:2 No one can stand before this obstacle **a.**,
T19. IV.D.13:6 Neither can give it to himself **a.**. And yet
T-20...... III.4:2 constant dangers, **a.** and frightened,
T-20...... IV.3:6 God has given follows His laws, and His **a.**
T-20...... IV.7:2 of your brother serves but you two **a.**. For
T-21...... IV.2:1 Remember that the ego is not **a.**. Its rule
T-21....... V.7:4 yes, you know this, and more than this **a.**.
T-21.... VI.1:10 not make way for correction in you **a.**.
T-21...... VI.2:9 **a.** have no effect at all on what *is* yours? If
T-21...... VI.7:1 brother nor yourself can be attacked **a.**.
T-21.... VI.10:4 And here **a.** does reason tell you that you
T-21..... VII.2:5 and afraid, **a.** and not communicating,
T-22.......in.2:2 sin? Only the lonely and **a.**, who see their
T-22.........I.6:1 course **a.** is open to your understanding
T-22.........I.8:6 Where Christ has entered no one is **a.**, for
T-22........ II.7:2 the same will not decide **a.** nor differently
T-22...... IV.3:4 your brother **a.** will see it as a solid block,
T-22...... IV.4:3 and lonely journey where you walked **a.**.
T-22...... IV.7:3 it, he learned it was not given him **a.**.
T-22....... V.3:8 in this quiet state **a.** is strength and power
T-22....... V.6:2 feel that you are weak because you are **a.**.
T-22...... VI.4:5 Neither you nor your brother **a.** can serve
T-22.... VI.15:3 Would you regret you cannot fear **a.**,
T-23.......in.5:4 not frightened and **a.** in his temptation,
T-23... II.22:12 If not, you walk **a.**. Ask, then, your Friend
T-24.........I.6:5 it depends on goals that you **a.** can reach.
T-24..... II.10:4 not given to His Son but kept for Him **a.**.
T-24..... II.13:3 is sacred here but unto you, and you **a.**,
T-24..... III.2:7 to it, leaving him **a.** and unforgiven, and
T-24..... IV.1:2 Faith is invested in yourself **a.**. Everything
T-24.... VI.11:2 It stands for you **a.**, as self-created, self-
T-24.... VII.2:1 The memory of God shines not **a.**. What
T-25..... II.9:12 It is not His Will to be **a.**. And neither is it
T-25..... III.6:1 darkness, yet no one has entered it **a.**. Nor
T-25....... V.1:4 Each is meaningless **a.**, but seems to draw
T-25....... V.4:2 **A.** does neither have it. So must it remain
T-25....... V.4:9 But think not Heaven is lost to him **a.**.
T-25....... V.5:3 toward Heaven or toward hell, but not **a.**.
T-25..... VI.4:2 special function in salvation he **a.** can fill;
T-25... VII.13:5 Not for you **a.**, but for the Self that is the
T-25... VIII.1:6 take it than that you keep it for yourself **a.**
T-26.........I.3:4 and something still remains for you **a.**.
T-26....... V.2:6 indeed to wander off, **a.** and miserable,
T-26....... V.5:7 in memories **a.** is unaware of where he is.
T-26...... VI.1:8 find the safety that the truth **a.** can give?
T-26...... VI.3:1 Who dwells with shadows is **a.** indeed,
T-26...... X.4:2 innocence that is not Theirs but yours **a.**,
T-27.........I.1:5 You cannot crucify yourself **a.**. And if you
T-27.........I.1:7 see. You cannot sacrifice yourself **a.**. For
T-27..... II.10:5 **A.**, you cannot see they are the same, and
T-27..... II.15:1 function given both, but neither one **a.**.
T-28..... III.1:3 The miracle **a.** is your concern at present.
T-28..... VII.5:1 But never you **a.**. This world is but the
T-28..... VII.5:2 world is but the dream that you can be **a.**,
T-28..... VII.5:3 To be **a.** must mean you are apart, and if
T-28..... VII.7:4 for its strength lies not within itself **a.**. It
T-29.........I.7:5 away, and leave you quietly **a.** in "peace."
T-29....... II.4:6 apart, believing they are separate and **a.**.
T-29 ..... III.5:3 He is himself, but not himself **a.**. And as
T-29 ...VIII.3:6 to shut you off from Him, **a.** in darkness.
T-30 ......in.1:3 be reached depends on this one thing **a.**;
T-30 ......I.17:2 to understand that they cannot decide **a.**,
T-30 .......II.1:7 He did not set His Kingdom up **a.**. And
T-30 ..... III.3:7 sin is the idea you are **a.** and separated off
T-30 .... V.10:4 *at cost of pain, nor was it ever paid by you* ***a.***.
T-31 .......II.9:6 Thus it is a way you go together, not **a.**.
T-31 .....II.11:2 **A.** it is denied to both of you. Is it not
T-31 .....II.11:3 or on following, you think you walk **a.**,
T-31 .....II.11:4 light cannot be given while you walk **a.**,
T-31 .....II.11:5 back and forward in the darkness and **a.**.
T-31 ..... IV.1:5 a little time is given you to use for you **a.**;
T-31 .... VII.3:4 the sight your eyes **a.** can offer you to see.
T-31 .... VII.4:3 because it was not made for you **a.**. Born
T-31 ...VIII.3:5 leave you comfortless, **a.** in dreams of hell
W-pI..... 13.2:4 and unreality. And on this **a.** it is correct.
W-pI........ 18.h not **a.** in experiencing the effects of my
W-pI..... 18.3:2 *I am not* ***a.*** *in experiencing the effects of how*
W-pI..... 18.3:4 *I am not* ***a.*** *in experiencing the effects of my*
W-pI........ 19.h I am not **a.** in experiencing the effects of
W-pI..... 19.1:1 why your seeing does not affect you **a.**.
W-pI..... 19.3:4 *I am not* ***a.*** *in experiencing the effects of this*
W-pI..... 23.4:6 hate. For you will not be making them **a.**.
W-pI..... 41.4:3 You can never be **a.** because the Source of
WpI... rI.in.3:3 eyes closed and when you are **a.** in a quiet
W-pI..... 54.3:1 not **a.** in experiencing the effects of my
W-pI..... 54.4:1 (19) I am not **a.** in experiencing the
W-pI..... 54.4:2 I am **a.** in nothing. Everything I think or
W-pI..... 54.4:5 in vain. He cannot be **a.** in anything. It is
W-pI..... 58.2:2 of my holiness does not bless me **a.**.
W-pI..... 59.1:2 can I be **a.** when God always goes with me
W-pI..... 68.5:5 This has left you **a.** in all the universe in
W-pI..... 69.9:2 also that you are not searching for it **a.**,
W-pI..... 72.2:3 with a body, keeping it separate and **a.**,
W-pI..... 76.3:4 you are **a.** unless another body is with you
W-pI..... 91.3:7 it is impossible, but you are not **a.** in this.
W-pI..... 96.5:3 now, it thinks it is **a.** and separate,
W-pI... 109.7:2 minds, too weary now to go their way **a.**.
W-pI... 123.2:2 yourself, nor let you wander in the dark **a.**
W-pI... 123.5:1 We do not go **a.**. And we give thanks that
W-pI... 130.9:4 kind of seeing that your eyes **a.** have ever
W-pI. 131.11:4 *made. The world I seek I did not make* ***a.****, the*
W-pI. 132.16:2 as yet that you could never be released **a.**.
W-pI. 134.17:7 *No one is crucified* ***a.****, and yet no one can*
W-pI...... 137.h When I am healed I am not healed **a.**.
W-pI... 137.1:4 separate self, and keeps it isolated and **a.**.
W-pI... 137.3:2 It is impossible that anyone be healed **a.**.
W-pI. 137.10:3 But you are never healed **a.**. And legions
W-pI. 137.14:3 *When I am healed I am not healed* ***a.***. *And I*
W-pI. 137.15:5 *When I am healed I am not healed* ***a.***. *And I*
W-pI... 138.7:3 In death **a.** are opposites resolved, for
W-pI... 139.9:4 more than just our happiness **a.** we came
WpI. rIV.in5:2 and let this thought **a.** engage it fully, and
WpI. rIV.in6:1 They will not come from you **a.**, for they
W-pI... 149.1:1 When I am healed I am not healed **a.**.
W-pI... 151.5:4 It is itself **a.** that it condemns. It is within
W-pI... 151.7:1 and let the Voice for God **a.** be Judge of
W-pI. 152.11:2 true. We think of truth **a.** as we arise, and
W-pI. 153.13:1 left **a.** in terror in a fearful world made
W-pI. 154.10:3 He **a.** can speak to us and for us, joining
W-pI... 156.1:5 world **a.** and separate from your Source?
W-pI... 163.2:3 before its image, thinking it **a.** is real,
W-pI... 163.2:4 of their trust. For it **a.** will surely come.
W-pI... 163.9:3 *We live and move in You* ***a.***. *We are not*
W-pI... 166.2:4 in two creators; or in one, himself **a.**. But
W-pI... 166.5:5 and poverty, **a.** though God is with him,
W-pI... 166.9:2 shoulder, and you feel that you are not **a.**.
W-pI. 166.12:3 The gifts you have are not for you **a.**.
W-pI... 169.2:2 By grace **a.** the hate and fear are gone, for
W-pI... 170.5:3 is shorn of what belongs to it and it **a.**,
W-pI. 170.13:4 *with what we have received from You* ***a.***. *We*
WpI...rV.in4:4 This Self **a.** knows Love. This Self alone is
WpI...rV.in4:5 This Self **a.** is perfectly consistent in Its
WpI...rV.in9:2 For this **a.** I need; that you will hear the
WpI...rV.in9:6 hand, for this is not a way we walk **a.**. In
Wi181-200 2:3 Words **a.** can not convey the sense of
W-pI... 182.9:4 is far away, and He will not return to it **a.**.
W-pI... 185.4:1 Yet compromise **a.** a dream can bring.
W-pI 185.12:3 could your request be limited to you **a.**?
W-pI .. 188.6:3 It **a.** has power to give the gift of sight to
W-pI .. 190.5:1 It is your thoughts **a.** that cause you pain.
W-pI 190.10:6 Pain is deception; joy **a.** is truth.
W-pI .. 191.3:2 Identity, and you assail the universe **a.**,
W-pI .. 193.3:4 The form **a.** is changed, with different
W-pI .. 195.1:7 gratitude is due to Him **a.** Who made all
W-pI .. 195.6:1 We thank our Father for one thing **a.**;
W-pI 198.11:4 now the Word of God **a.** remains upon it.
W-pI .. 200.9:4 God **a.** is sure, and He will guide our
WpI.rVI.in.1:3 ideas **a.** would be sufficient for salvation,
W-pII .... in.1:3 now we seek direct experience of truth **a.**.
W-pII . 221.1:1 *today to seek the peace that You* ***a.*** *can give. I*
W-pII . 228.2:6 *to receive Your Word* ***a.*** *for what I really am.*
W-pII .... 236.h I rule my mind, which I **a.** must rule.
W-pII . 236.1:7 I thus direct my mind, which I **a.** can rule.
W-pII ..... 3.4:4 Hear His Voice **a.** in all that speaks to you
W-pII . 242.1:1 I will not lead my life **a.** today. I do not
W-pII . 242.1:2 to lead my life **a.** must be but foolishness.
W-pII . 265.1:3 was in the world, instead of in my mind **a.**
W-pII ..... 6.3:1 of the Holy Spirit, and at home in God **a.**,
W-pII . 275.1:4 tells us of things we cannot understand **a.**.
W-pII . 280.2:1 *to Your Son, for thus* ***a.*** *I find the way to You.*
W-pII . 281.1:7 *The Thoughts I think with You* ***a.*** *are true.*
W-pII . 296.2:1 today what we would learn, and that **a.**.
W-pII . 298.1:5 as mine, sure that in that **a.** I will be saved
W-pII . 307.1:4 *Your Will* ***a.*** *can bring me happiness, and*
W-pII ... 10.4:3 For it **a.** can heal all sorrow, wipe away all
W-pII . 317.1:1 have a special place to fill; a role for me **a.**.
W-pII . 318.1:3 could there be a single part that stands **a.**,
W-pII .... 321.h Father, my freedom is in You **a.**.
W-pII . 321.1:8 *Father, my freedom is in You* ***a.***. *Father, it is*
W-pII . 321.2:3 learn our freedom can be found in God **a.**.
W-pII . 325.2:2 *for Yours and Yours* ***a.*** *establish truth.*
W-pII ... 12.1:3 death, and what opposes God **a.** is true.
W-pII . 333.2:4 *For this* ***a.*** *will never fail in anything, being*
W-pII . 335.1:4 It is to this **a.** that I respond, however
W-pII . 338.1:5 but since these thoughts belong to him **a.**,
W-pII . 338.2:4 *Mine* ***a.*** *will fail, and lead me nowhere. But*
W-pII . 344.1:2 *thought to save what I desired for myself* ***a.***.
W-pII . 344.1:7 *with Heaven's treasures, which* ***a.*** *are real.*
W-pII . 345.1:7 *Then let me give this gift* ***a.*** *today, which,*
W-pII . 348.1:1 *me remember You are here, and I am not* ***a.***.
W-pII . 351.1:2 *of God;* ***a.*** *and friendless in a fearful world.*
W-pII . 351.1:7 *For He* ***a.*** *gives judgment in Your Name.*
W-pII . 352.1:1 *Forgiveness looks on sinlessness* ***a.****, and*
W-pII . 353.1:2 *Nothing is mine* ***a.****, for He and I have joined*
W-pII . 358.1:1 *I really am* ***a.*** *remember what I really want.*
W-ep......... 1:3 You are not **a.**. No one who calls on Him
W-ep......... 6:6 You do not walk **a.**. God's angels hover
M-in.......... 2:9 is not done by words **a.**. Any situation
M-1........... 4:4 Yet it is time **a.** that winds on wearily, and
M-4 ... I.A.6:13 going on. He will not go on from here **a.**.
M-4 ........II.2:9 because they never do their will **a.**. They
M-4 ...... IX.1:7 And that **a.** is faithfulness. Nothing but
M-4 .... IX.2:12 rests in quiet certainty on that **a.** to which
M-4 ........X.1:6 be at peace, for they **a.** see reason for it.
M-8 ......... 3:11 It **a.** decides whether what is seen is real
M-12 ......... 5:8 of God does not make this decision **a.**. To
M-12 ....... 6:10 Unity **a.** is not a thing of dreams. And it is
M-15 ......... 3:9 guaranteed His Judgment, and His **a.**, will
M-16 ......... 8:5 attempts to place reliance on himself **a.**.
M-17 ......... 5:9 And he must stand **a.** in his protection,
M-17 ....... 7:11 or be killed, for here **a.** is choice. Beyond
M-18 ......... 1:9 the form **a.** in which the difference lies.
M-18 ......... 3:3 eyes now "see"; its ears **a.** can "hear." Its
M-18 ....... 3:10 *laws* ***a.*** *prevail upon you and upon the world*
M-19 ......... 5:7 one standpoint does it judge, and this **a.**.
M-21 ....... 3:11 The Holy Spirit **a.** understands what this
M-23 ......... 6:9 take you with him, for he did not go **a.**.
M-25 ......... 6:9 offer them to Him and Him **a.** go with
M-26 ......... 1:9 **A.** they are nothing. But in their joining is
M-27 ......... 3:8 of life." God is insane, and fear **a.** is real.
M-29 ......... 2:2 Who would profit more from prayers **a.**?
M-29 ......... 2:4 attempt to answer these questions **a.**.
M-29 ......... 2:8 is His, and He **a.** is fit to assume it. To do
M-29 ......... 8:6 *holiness, for you are not* ***A.*** *and friendless. I*
C-in........... 2:7 **a.** consistency becomes possible because
C-in........... 2:7 possible because here **a.** uncertainty ends.

| | |
|---|---|
| C-2 1:2 | is sure and this a. is certain in their world. |
| C-2 2:3 | ego cannot be denied for it a. seems real. |
| C-2 5:3 | the ego's opposite and here a. we look on |
| C-2 8:1 | the self that seemed a. in all the universe. |
| C-3 5:1 | symbol of His Will a. it cannot be divided |
| C-5 1:2 | God a. established in reality. Helpers are |
| C-6 1:5 | which God a. knows along with Christ, |
| C-6 3:5 | in which the face of Christ a. is seen. He |
| C-6 5:3 | A. he cannot be the Helper of God's Son |
| C-6 5:3 | of God's Son for he a. is functionless. But |
| C-ep 4:3 | Now we are sure we do not walk a.. For |
| P-2 II.5:7 | pathway out, for no one will find sanity a. |
| P-2 II.9:1 | Communion is impossible a.. No one |
| P-2 III.2:3 | Neither can do this a., but when they join, |
| P-2 III.3:6 | goals a. can interfere with perfect healing. |
| P-2 V.2:2 | what they believe will harm a. can help. |
| P-2 V.8:2 | There is one way a. by which we come to |
| P-2 VI.7:1 | No one is healed a.. This is the joyous |
| P-2 VII.5:6 | the tiny self of one a. against the universe |
| S-1 IV.2:8 | For no one can receive effects a., asking a |
| S-1 V.1:3 | it was a. and stood against the world. |
| S-1 V.3:12 | he never left, and you, who seemed a., are |
| S-2 I.9:2 | the key was made, and where a. it fits? |
| S-3 I.4:2 | But not a.. For he has thrown away the |
| S-3 III.6:1 | God's Voice a. can tell you how to heal. |

## along 117

| | |
|---|---|
| T-1 II.6:4 | both emerge farther a. in time than they |
| T-1 V.5:4 | creates a. the line of its own creation. If it |
| T-1 VI.5:3 | true, the miracle proceeds a. these lines: |
| T-8 II.2:7 | is joyful if it leads you a. your natural path |
| T-8 II.4:4 | leads you steadily a. the path of freedom, |
| T-8 V.5:5 | intrudes anywhere a. the road to peace, it |
| T-12 III.9:8 | of its maker, a. with his real salvation. Do |
| T-13 I.3:5 | long carpet spread a. the past behind you, |
| T-13 I.3:6 | God is guilty you will walk a. this carpet, |
| T-14 V.11:8 | out, for here is what he seeks a. with you. |
| T-15 II.6:2 | very specific instructions as you go a.. To |
| T-15 VI.8:7 | is, and what His creation is a. with Him. |
| T-17 V.9:4 | walk together a. a road far more familiar |
| T-18 I.11:8 | on what is joined in it, a. with its Creator. |
| T-19 I.16:3 | being lord of all, a. with his Creator. You |
| T19 IV.B.17:5 | returns to Him, seeking itself a. the way, |
| T19 IV.C.2:5 | watch the chains fall away, a. with yours. |
| T-20 I.2:10 | forgiveness rests on Christ, a. with mine. |
| T-20 I.4:7 | and celebrate his holiness a. with me. For |
| T-20 I.4:8 | is the time of your salvation, a. with mine. |
| T-20 VI.3:6 | keep their secrets hidden a. with them. |
| T-20 VIII.3:1 | vision and to rejoice in a. with Him. For |
| T-22 I.5:1 | given you, a. with everything that you can |
| T-22 IV.2:1 | few steps a. the right way that seem hard, |
| T-23 in.2:5 | travels sinlessly a. the way love shows him |
| T-24 II.9:1 | You have come far a. the way of truth; |
| T-24 VI.6:4 | your brother lives, and you a. with him. |
| T-24 VI.9:4 | to save from condemnation, a. with you. |
| T-24 VII.6:4 | Here you are but means, a. with it. God is |
| T-25 II.9:8 | who would complete His joy, a. with Him. |
| T-25 II.9:10 | complete, and theirs a. with His. The |
| T-25 IV.2:7 | might be increased, and God's a. with his. |
| T-25 V.2:1 | Christ your enemy, and God a. with Him. |
| T-25 V.4:4 | the other, and save himself a. with him. |
| T-25 V.5:7 | that what he does you do, a. with him. |
| T-26 V.1:8 | you will go a. the way your chosen teacher |
| T-26 V.10:1 | God allow His Son to lose his way a. a |
| T-26 X.2:7 | belongs to every living thing a. with you. |
| T-27 II.6:3 | was never lost, and healed a. with you. |
| T-30 II.4:4 | you co-creator of the universe a. with Him |
| T-31 II.6:9 | And we go separately a. the way unless |
| T-31 IV.1:8 | you whatever road you choose to walk a.. |
| T-31 V.1:6 | without a self, and make one as you go a.. |
| T-31 V.13:8 | now must you be condemned a. with him |
| T-31 V.16:1 | concepts of the self as learning goes a.. |
| W-in 1:4 | to think a. the lines the text sets forth. |
| W-pI 12.3:5 | occur to you, use them a. with the rest. |
| W-pI 15.3:1 | As we go a., you may have many "light |
| W-pI 37.3:2 | holiness are all things blessed a. with you. |
| W-pI 41.8:6 | about this kind of practice as we go a.. |
| W-pI 54.4:6 | power to change every mind a. with mine, |
| W-pI 82.1:5 | world, that it may be healed a. with me. |
| W-pI 91.9:5 | with the more worthy in you as we go a.. |
| W-pI 99.6:5 | you entrusted with this plan, a. with Him. |
| W-pI 100.6:2 | world is thus deprived of joy, a. with you. |
| W-pI 106.9:3 | ask that truth be given them, a. with you. |
| W-pI 109.6:2 | that it might take its rest a. with you. |
| W-pI 109.7:3 | to walk with lightened steps a. the road |
| W-pI 109.8:1 | to draw them to their rest, a. with you. |
| W-pI 124.7:7 | from our Father, it is healed a. with us. |
| W-pI.127.11:3 | Now are they all made free, a. with us. |
| W-pI 132.6:4 | can let himself be led a. the road to truth. |
| W-pI.132.14:4 | home our Father set for us, a. with them. |
| W-pI.132.15:4 | so that the world is freed, a. with you. |
| W-pI.137.10:1 | no contact with you, healed a. with you. |
| W-pI 139.9:5 | what everyone must be, a. with us. Fail |
| WpI. rIV.in5:4 | the day a. the lines which God appointed, |
| W-pI.155.11:3 | progress a. the way that truth points out |
| W-pI.155.14:3 | *the way, For I would walk a. the road to Him.* |
| W-pI 157.3:2 | Yet you have come far enough a. the way |
| W-pI 158.3:3 | no step a. the road that anyone takes but |
| WpI rV.in2:5 | *a little child a. a way he does not understand.* |
| WpI rV.in6:6 | is crucified until you walk a. the road with |
| W-pI 182.6:6 | He will go home, and you a. with Him. |
| W-pI 182.7:7 | you to let Him go in peace, a. with you, to |
| W-pI 183.5:4 | Name a. with him within your quiet mind |
| W-pI.184.11:4 | they share the Name of God a. with you. |
| W-pI 192.8:5 | world in which his jailer lives, a. with him |
| W-pI 194.8:5 | the sick illusions of the world a. with his, |
| W-pI.195.10:4 | and the Source of love, a. with Him. Your |
| W-pI 196.7:2 | at least consider if you want to go a. this |
| W-pI 199.8:5 | you in it; the world is blessed a. with you, |
| WpI rVI.in.4:2 | reach a quickened pace a. a shorter path |
| W-pI 208.1:2 | *be still, and let the earth be still a. with me.* |
| W-pII in.2:5 | We have come far a. the road, and now |
| W-pII 225.1:3 | *still the way Your loving Son is led a. to You!* |
| W-pII 255.1:6 | it to all my Father's Sons, a. with me. |
| W-pII 5.4:3 | and to help him walk a. the road with him |
| W-pII 264.2:3 | join in what will save the world, a. with us |
| W-pII 286.2:1 | travelled far a. it to a wholly certain goal. |
| W-pII 288.1:5 | *His sins are in the past a. with mine, and I* |
| W-pII 291.2:5 | *Your Son a. the quiet path that leads to You.* |
| W-pII 10.3:1 | condemn the world to hell a. with you, |
| W-pII 321.2:1 | the world, which will be freed a. with us. |
| W-pII 340.1:6 | *made, which is released a. with him today.* |
| W-pII 355.1:7 | *is You I choose, and my Identity a. with You.* |
| M-10 5:8 | He has given it away, a. with judgment. |
| M-16 8:1 | will be temptations a. the way the teacher |
| M-19 2:5 | becomes quite different as one goes a.. |
| M-20 1:5 | for each reflects a different step a. the way |
| M-22 2:5 | Anywhere a. the way, the necessary |
| C-2 7:5 | at the helpers all a. the way you travel, |
| C-4 5:8 | For place has gone as well, a. with time. |
| C-5 5:2 | O yes, a. with you. His little life on earth |
| C-6 1:5 | which God alone knows a. with Christ, |
| C-6 5:2 | calls to you to be His Voice a. with him. |
| C-ep 1:2 | Doubt a. the way will come and go and go |
| C-ep 3:6 | where He has set your Name a. with His. |
| C-ep 4:2 | us arise and go in faith a. the way to Him. |
| P-2 III.1:1 | the pitfalls a. the road by seeing them first |
| P-2 VII.3:1 | have been forgiven him, a. with his own. |
| P-3 II.8:3 | Many holy instants can be his a. the way. |
| S-1 I.3:3 | the gift. A. with it come the overtones, the |
| S-1 III.5:7 | He is a Son of God, a. with you. He is no |
| S-2 II.8:7 | From here is prayer released, a. with you. |
| S-3 II.2:1 | the Son of God a. the way he goes to God. |
| S-3 IV.8:2 | love extends a. with Mine beyond infinity |

## Alpha 1

| | |
|---|---|
| T-3 III.6:5 | is the real meaning of "A. and Omega, the |

## already 207

| | |
|---|---|
| T-1 I.28:2 | a state in which fear has a. been abolished |
| T-1 III.5:9 | you reinforce errors they have a. made. |
| T-1 V.5:2 | unalterable because it is a. perfect, but |
| T-1 VI.2:3 | you had a. fragmented yourself into levels |
| T-1 VII.5:1 | fear and awe to which I have a. referred, |
| T-2 III.5:3 | But the real means are a. provided, and |
| T-2 IV.3:1 | create because spirit has a. been created, |
| T-2 IV.4:8 | They are a. in a fear-weakened state. If |
| T-2 V.1:2 | a belief that is a. very prevalent. This |
| T-2 V.1:8 | spirit is a. perfect and therefore does not |
| T-2 V.3:1 | have a. said that miracles are expressions |
| T-2 V.6:4 | Spirit is a. illuminated and the body in |
| T-2 V.10:1 | of looking at another as if he had a. gone |
| T-2 VI.1:2 | Yet I have said a. that only constructive |
| T-2 VII.1:2 | I have a. indicated that you cannot ask me |
| T-2 VII.4:1 | It has a. been said that you believe you |
| T-2 VII.7:1 | I have a. briefly spoken about readiness, |
| T-2 VII.7:7 | a. attempted to correct the fundamental |
| T-3 IV.6:8 | as I have a. emphasized, knowledge does |
| T-3 V.3:1 | Knowing, as we have a. observed, does |
| T-3 V.6:5 | may be able to recognize what you a. have |
| T-3 VI.1:1 | We have a. discussed the Last Judgment, |
| T-3 VII.1:2 | creating, a difference we have a. discussed |
| T-4 III.6:4 | it asks only for what He has a. willed. |
| T-4 III.9:6 | which implies a lack, has a. been accepted |
| T-4 VI.3:7 | that you have a. accepted this difference, |
| T-5 I.3:2 | I have said a. that I can reach up and |
| T-5 III.1:2 | I have a. said that the Holy Spirit is the |
| T-5 III.10:2 | uses only what your mind a. understands |
| T-5 IV.2:5 | that continues has a. been born. It will |
| T-5 VII.6:2 | realize that you must a. have decided not |
| T-6 I.2:5 | I have a. told you that you can always call |
| T-6 I.7:2 | dawning on your mind of what is a. in it. |
| T-6 III.1:1 | As we have a. emphasized, every idea |
| T-6 V.1:2 | Him. You had a. taught yourself wrongly, |
| T-6 V.C.4:2 | it. I have a. told you that you can be as |
| T-6 V.C.10:8 | since it is a. true and needs no protection. |
| T-7 I.1:5 | I have a. told you that only in this respect |
| T-7 V.3:5 | body has a. been confused with the mind. |
| T-7 VI.6:6 | As I have a. said, understanding brings |
| T-7 XI.6:4 | I have a. said that only the whole Sonship |
| T-8 III.1:2 | be given you, because it has a. *been* given. |
| T-8 VI.8:3 | Him, and learned of what He had a. given |
| T-8 VII.4:7 | because you have a. done so *by* misusing it |
| T-8 VIII.4:9 | witness, it has a. made the witness an ally. |
| T-9 I.1:2 | unless the mind were a. profoundly split, |
| T-9 I.14:1 | then, that God's Will is a. possible, and |
| T-9 II.3:6 | have a. received but have not yet heard. I |
| T-10 II.3:1 | to restore to your mind *what is a. there.* |
| T-10 II.3:2 | you merely accept again what is a. there, |
| T-11 II.7:8 | merely by recognizing what is there a., |
| T-11 V.11:4 | accomplished, and it is accomplished a.. |
| T-11 VI.9:5 | Yet it is done a., and unless you give all |
| T-11 VII.4:3 | you do you will not know it is yours a.. |
| T-11 VIII.4:7 | for you will see it as it is, and it is yours a.. |
| T-12 I.8:11 | We have a. learned that fear and attack |
| T-12 II.8:2 | perfect to you what is a. perfect in you. |
| T-13 I.4:5 | He has a. undone everything unworthy of |
| T-13 VII.16:1 | In me you have a. overcome every |
| T-14 II.1:8 | add another burden to your a. burdened |
| T-14 III.19:5 | your guiltlessness, which is a. there. |
| T-14 IV.3:4 | for this has a. been accomplished. Ask, |
| T-14 X.12:5 | have a. learned that this Identity is shared |
| T-14 XI.4:3 | a. learned for every child of light by Him |
| T-14 XI.9:6 | no dark lessons He has not a. lightened |
| T-14 XI.9:7 | would teach yourself He has corrected a.. |
| T-14 XI.12:3 | for learning by thinking they a. know. |
| T-15 IX.4:7 | Yet your minds are a. continuous, and |
| T-15 XI.2:7 | need but invite Him in Who is there a., by |
| T-16 II.9:6 | a. proved their power sufficiently for you |
| T-16 III.1:1 | We have a. learned that everyone teaches |
| T-16 III.5:1 | Your teaching has a. done this, for the |
| T-16 VII.2:10 | cannot really *not* let go what has a. gone. It |
| T-17 III.3:2 | a. a severely limited perception of him, is |
| T-17 IV.16:9 | is only healing, a. complete and perfect. |
| T-17 VI.3:1 | makes no sense until it has a. happened. |
| T-18 I.12:5 | apart what is a. broken and hopeless? Is it |
| T-18 IV.8:4 | is not only possible, but has a. happened. |
| T-18 V.1:2 | you a. understood the difference between |
| T-19 I.11:3 | of faith, the Son of God is seen a. forgiven |
| T-19 I.15:2 | what has a. been prepared for loveliness. |
| T-19 IV.2:2 | peace that a. lies deeply within must first |
| T19 IV.B.5:3 | for in your holy relationship I am there a.. |
| T19 IV.B.8:4 | to keep away One Who is there a.. And in |
| T19 IV.B.8:5 | our communion, where we are joined a., |

T19..IV.B.10:3 unite only with what **a.** is at peace in you,
T-20.........I.3:2 promise of the resurrection, **a.** given him.
T-20...... IV.1:8 has **a.** given and received all that is true.
T-20....... V.6:6 means and end in perfect harmony **a.**.
T-20....... V.6:7 day offer to your brother **a.** offered you;
T-20....... V.6:7 forgiveness you will give him **a.** given, the
T-20....... V.6:7 of Christ you yet will look upon **a.** seen.
T-21....... II.9:1 We have **a.** said that wishful thinking is
T-21....... III.9:7 your awareness to what has been **a.** joined
T-21....... IV.3:6 And your belief in sin has been **a.** shaken,
T-21....... IV.5:6 perfectly from what you have **a.** learned.
T-21.... VI.11:3 freedom lie but in himself, if he be free **a.**?
T-21.... VII.6:1 You may **a.** have answered the first three
T-21... VII.11:5 decisions you have **a.** made to all the rest.
T-21.... VIII.3:7 God has **a.** given all that he really wants.
T-21.... VIII.4:2 it possible to help you be **a.** partly sane.
T-21.... VIII.5:5 For here the final question is **a.** answered,
T-24.......in.1:5 Where He can enter, there He is **a.**. And
T-24....... V.4:8 with flesh **a.** loosened from the bone and
T-26....... III.3:6 place, and every choice has been **a.** made.
T-26... VII.20:3 when He has **a.** answered all who call on
T-26.... VIII.5:6 if its effects **a.** have been judged as fearful.
T-26.... VIII.5:9 It stands **a.** here, in present grace, within
T-26.... VIII.6:5 fear they may not come, although **a.** there
T-26.... VIII.8:1 though untrue, must be **a.** in your mind.
T-27...... IV.1:7 for what He wills **a.** has been done.
T-27...... IV.2:3 of mind in which the answer is **a.** there.
T-28...... III.1:6 of fear to one that is **a.** being dreamed.
T-30.........I.5:1 will still be times when you have judged **a.**
T-30.........I.7:2 For you have **a.** gotten angry. And your
T-30.... III.4:10 to give the Son of God what he **a.** has?
T-30....... V.7:1 they stand **a.** at the edge of the real world.
T-30.... VIII.5:1 *Because* reality is changeless is a miracle **a.**
W-pI....... 4.1:4 If you are **a.** aware of unhappy thoughts,
W-pI....... 9.1:6 need to practice what you **a.** understand.
W-pI....... 9.1:7 and assume that you have it **a.**.
W-pI..... 23.4:4 is gone? Vision **a.** holds a replacement for
W-pI..... 23.5:5 Your images have **a.** been replaced. By
W-pI..... 28.4:1 not question what you have **a.** defined.
W-pI..... 39.2:6 one needs practice to gain what is **a.** his.
W-pI..... 39.3:1 We have **a.** said that your holiness is the
W-pI..... 45.8:7 little understanding you have **a.** gained,
W-pI..... 46.6:4 *I have* **a.** *been forgiven. No fear is possible in*
WpI... rI.in.1:2 will cover five of the ideas **a.** presented,
WpI... rI.in.4:3 in those that **a.** seem to be calm and quiet
W-pI..... 72.9:6 His plan is accepted, it is accomplished **a.**.
W-pI... 72.10:1 salvation has **a.** been accomplished in us.
W-pI..... 78.5:1 his name has crossed your mind **a.**. He
W-pI..... 79.1:2 solved **a.** you will still have the problem,
W-pI..... 79.1:4 the only problem, has **a.** been solved. Yet
W-pI..... 79.7:2 We will not assume that we **a.** know. We
W-pI..... 88.1:2 choose to recognize what is **a.** there.
W-pI..... 88.1:3 Salvation is a decision made **a.**. Attack
W-pI..... 90.3:7 a problem which has not been solved **a.**.
W-pI..... 90.4:3 *The answer to this problem is* **a.** *given me, if I*
W-pI..... 95.1:5 believe that you have changed yourself **a.**.
W-pI..... 95.7:4 you have **a.** failed to do what is required.
W-pI... 104.5:1 recognizing that His Will is done **a.**, and
W-pI... 105.4:4 It adds to all that is complete **a.**, not in
W-pI... 109.9:3 what we give today we have received **a.**.
W-pI. 121.10:3 You probably have chosen him **a.**. He will
W-pI... 130.6:2 world you see is proof you have **a.** made a
W-pI... 132.4:4 but came unwillingly to what was made **a.**
W-pI... 133.1:1 far from what the student has **a.** learned,
W-pI... 133.4:1 We have **a.** stressed there are but two,
W-pI. 154.12:3 has left no gift beyond what you **a.** have;
W-pI... 157.2:2 sheds a light on all that we have learned **a.**
W-pI... 158.3:1 The time is set **a.**. It appears to be quite
W-pI... 158.3:4 It has **a.** been taken by him, although he
W-pI... 159.6:2 All are laid here **a.**. All can be received but
W-pI... 159.6:5 There is no sickness not **a.** healed, no lack
W-pI... 165.1:4 keep from you what you **a.** have except
W-pI... 169.4:1 Father and the Son as One has been **a.** set.
W-pI... 169.8:1 All learning was **a.** in His Mind,
W-pI. 169.10:3 which explain what is to come is past **a.**.
W-pI. 185.11:3 unsatisfied who asks for what he has **a.**?
W-pI. 186.13:3 He knows that you have everything **a.**. He
W-pI... 188.2:2 in the future, or believe it has been lost **a.**,
W-pI... 192.3:6 that the light of day **a.** shines in them,
W-pI... 192.3:6 eyes **a.** opening behold the joyful sights
W-pI... 194.3:4 in passing, with the next one given Him **a.**
W-pI... 200.3:3 To ask for what you have **a.** must succeed.
W-pI. 200.10:6 Peace is **a.** recognized at last, and you can
W-pII ..... 1.5:2 He has forgiven you **a.**, for such is His
W-pII . 243.1:2 I will not think that I **a.** know what must
W-pII ..... 6.2:3 lies; where all decisions are **a.** made, and
W-pII . 279.1:4 And now is freedom his **a.**. Should I wait
W-pII . 286.1:4 *In You is every choice* **a.** *made. In You has*
W-pII . 286.1:6 *You is everything I hope to find* **a.** *given me.*
W-pII . 290.2:3 *What I ask have You* **a.** *given me. And I am*
W-pII . 297.2:1 *faithfully is every step in my salvation set* **a.**,
W-pII . 317.1:4 then will I recognize salvation is **a.** here,
W-pII . 317.1:4 **a.** given all my brothers and already mine
W-pII . 317.1:4 given all my brothers and **a.** mine as well.
W-pII .... 329.h I have **a.** chosen what You will.
W-pII . 330.1:3 Love, and bids them take what is **a.** theirs
W-pII . 337.1:5 has **a.** done all things that need be done.
W-pII . 337.1:6 sinlessness, created for me, now **a.** mine,
Wfl........in.2:4 yet, in truth, it is **a.** here; already serving
Wfl........in.2:4 **a.** serving us as gracious guidance in the
M-2 ........... 3:5 has **a.** happened at any time you choose,
M-2 ........... 3:8 it. And as you accept it, it is **a.** learned.
M-3 ........... 3:4 it. We have covered the illusion of time **a.**,
M-4 ..... I.A.8:8 anywhere, if peace of mind is **a.** complete
M-4 .. VIII.1:10 outcome **a.** seen or yet to come can cause
M-5 ...... III.1:4 For those **a.** willing to change their minds
M-5 ...... III.2:7 of the remedy God has **a.** given them. It is
M-7 ........... 1:4 healing is certain, as we have **a.** said it is,
M-7 ........... 2:3 That was **a.** maximal, because the Holy
M-13 ......... 4:4 one whose vision has **a.** glimpsed the face
M-16 ......... 1:7 one is sent without a learning goal **a.** set,
M-17 ......... 7:6 thought has guilt **a.** raised madness to the
M-23 ......... 2:2 Indeed, he has **a.** done so. Temptation
P-2.........in.2:7 The patient has **a.** paid this price. Now he
P-2...........I.1:2 have come together who **a.** believe this. It
P-2......... IV.2:4 are only shadows of a decision **a.** made.
P-2......... IV.3:6 and we have said **a.** and will say again, all
P-2......... IV.7:2 And as we have **a.** emphasized, correction
P-2......... V.1:1 still be taught to those who have **a.** lost
P-2......... V.7:4 We are deceived **a.**, if we think there is a
S-1...........I.1:7 Ask, rather, to receive what is **a.** given; to
S-1...........I.1:7 is already given; to accept what is **a.** there.

## also 262

## altar 99

T-1 .........I.20:1 the spirit, not the body, is the **a.** of truth.
T-2 ........... III.h The **A.** of God
T-2 ........ III.1:8 the inner **a.** around which the structure is
T-2 ........ III.1:9 and an unwillingness to reach the **a.** itself.
T-2 ...... III.1:12 however, see the **a.** with perfect clarity.
T-2 ........ III.2:1 belongs at the center of the inner **a.**,
T-2 ........ III.2:3 of the **a.** to receive the Atonement. This
T-2 ........ III.4:3 that the **a.** has been defiled and needs to
T-2 ........ III.5:4 is worthy of being offered at the **a.** of God
T-2 ........ III.5:4 of God, because of the value of the **a.** itself
T-2 ......... V.7:5 to look upon the defilement of the **a.**, He
T-2 ......... V.8:4 cannot endure to see your own defiled **a.**.
T-2 ......... V.8:5 But since the **a.** has been defiled, your
T-3 ...........I.8:3 is the only appropriate gift for God's **a.**,
T-3 ...... III.5:12 Knowledge comes from the **a.** within and
T-5 ..........II.8:9 must choose at which **a.** you want to serve
T-6 ...........I.8:4 church is where an **a.** is, and the presence
T-6 ...........I.8:4 of the **a.** is what makes the church holy. A
T-6 ...........I.8:5 that does not inspire love has a hidden **a.**
T-6 ...... V.C.7:1 where God placed the **a.** to Himself.
T-7 ........ III.4:8 The **a.** there is the only reality. The altar is
T-7 ........ III.4:9 **a.** is perfectly clear in thought, because it
T-7 ....... V.11:6 Spirit, Who sees the **a.** of God in everyone
T-10 ... III.11:1 Only at the **a.** of God will you find peace.
T-10 ... III.11:2 this **a.** is in you because God put it there.
T-11 ...... IV.1:7 are denying Him His place in His Own **a.**.
T-11 ...... IV.3:3 Every **a.** to God is part of you, because the
T-11 ...... IV.6:1 Christ is at God's **a.**, waiting to welcome
T-11 ...... IV.7:1 God's **a.** Christ waits for the restoration of
T-11 ...... VI.5:2 For he places himself at the **a.** of his god,
T-12 .... III.10:3 **a.** of God where Christ abideth is there.
T-12 .... III.10:4 You have defiled the **a.**, but not the world.
T-12 .... III.10:5 placed the Atonement on the **a.** for you.
T-12 .... III.10:6 your perceptions of the world to this **a.**,
T-12 .... III.10:6 world to this altar, for it is the **a.** to truth.
T-12 .... III.10:9 the real world to you from the **a.** of God.
T-12 ...... VI.5:8 peace He waits for you at His Father's **a.**,
T-12 ...... VI.6:3 led you to Christ at the **a.** to His Father,
T-12 ...... VI.7:2 At the **a.** of God, the holy perception of
T-13 VII.10:13 And at its **a.** it demands you lay all of the
T-13 ...... IX.7:6 and in peace upon the **a.** to your Father.
T-13 ........X.9:7 The **a.** to your Father is as pure as He
T-14 ... V.10:10 The temple you restore becomes your **a.**,
T-14 ... VIII.2:2 upon the **a.** to your Father and His Son.
T-14 ... VIII.2:3 No **a.** stands to God without His Son.
T-14 ... VIII.5:7 Your little gifts will vanish on the **a.**,
T-14 ...... IX.3:8 you. God has not left His **a.**, though His
T-15 ........II.2:7 Through Him you stand before God's **a.**,
T-15 ...... III.9:6 into a manger, but into the **a.** to holiness,
T-15 .... III.12:6 Lay not littleness before His holy **a.**,
T-15 ...... IV.4:1 and immaculate is the holy **a.** on which
T-15 ..... VII.9:2 And those who are united at its **a.** accept
T-15 ..... VII.9:6 ego's **a.** far exceeds your awareness of it.
T-16 ...... V.11:5 An **a.** is erected in between two separate
T-19 ....... I.13:3 There is the **a.** where the grace was given,
T-19 ....... I.13:4 stand at the same **a.** where grace was laid
T-19 ....... I.14:1 before the **a.** God has raised unto Himself
T-19 ....... I.14:6 the **a.** from which they were sent forth.
T-20 ........II.3:2 sees his chosen home as an **a.** to himself.
T-20 ........II.3:4 And each has set a light upon his **a.**, that
T-20 ........II.4:5 you first upon the **a.** in your chosen home
T-20 ........II.4:8 will see your **a.** is no longer what it was.
T-20 ........II.5:4 from every **a.** now is yours as well as His.
T-20 ........II.9:2 and shining from the holy **a.** within him
T-20 ......II.11:5 And come before his holy **a.** where the
T-20 ... VIII.4:4 brother, you will see an **a.** to your Father,
T-21 ........II.7:2 left open and unoccupied the **a.** where the
T-23 ....... I.11:3 The **a.** disappears, the light grows dim,
T-25 ...... III.6:7 gave attack is but another **a.** where he can
T-26 ...... IV.3:4 **a.** to rise and tower far above the world,
T-26 ...... IV.5:1 a world that will become an **a.** to the truth
T-26 ...... IV.5:4 joins the singing at the **a.** that was raised
T-29 ..... VII.9:5 there. Your holy mind is **a.** unto God, and
T-29 ...... IX.8:5 the **a.** that abides forever deep within the
T-31 ... VIII.3:4 from you whom God created **a.** unto joy.
W-pI ..... 45.8:4 approach it as you would an **a.** dedicated
W-pI .. 104.2:1 upon the holy **a.** where God's gifts belong
W-pI .. 104.4:2 holy place within our minds before His **a.**,
W-pI .. 152.8:5 to usurp the **a.** to the Father and the Son.
W-pI .. 169.1:4 received; an **a.** clean and holy for the gift.
W-pI .. 183.5:4 you have established there an **a.** which
W-pI .. 187.9:1 brother offers you are laid upon your **a.**,
W-pI 187.10:2 And here, before the **a.** to one God, one
W-pI 187.11:6 us in form of lilies we can lay upon our **a.**,
W-pII ..... 2.3:4 an **a.** to the holy Name of God whereon
W-pII . 309.2:2 *Your* **a.** *stands serene and undefiled. It is the*
W-pII . 309.2:3 *It is the holy* **a.** *to my Self, and there I find my*
W-pII . 313.1:6 *undefiled upon the* **a.** *to Your holy Son, the*
W-pII ... 12.4:2 blood must flow before the **a.** where its
W-pII ... 12.5:1 **a.** to illusions to the shrine of Life Itself.
W-pII . 336.1:4 and opens the hidden **a.** to the truth. Its
W-pII ... 13.3:5 God, upon the universal **a.** to Creator and
C-4 ............ 6:2 For there the **a.** to the Son is set, and
C-4 ............ 6:3 brought to truth and laid upon the **a.**.
C-4 ............ 6:7 lie together, side by side, upon one **a.**.
C-4 ............ 7:4 light upon the **a.** to the Son of God. God
C-4 ............ 8:1 but rush to meet Him where His **a.** is.
C-5 ............ 1:3 forms, although upon the **a.** they are one.
S-1............I.5:7 That nothingness becomes the **a.** of God.

## altars 11

T-3 ...........I.8:5 That is why their **a.** are truly radiant.
T-3 ....... III.6:1 God can communicate directly to His **a.**,
T-5 ..........II.8:6 for God comes from your own **a.** to Him.
T-5 ..........II.8:7 to Him. These **a.** are not things; they are
T-6 ..... V.C.7:2 **A.** are beliefs, but God and His creations
T-13 .. VII.15:2 Kneel not before the **a.** to sacrifice, and
T-14 ... VIII.5:4 Lay no gifts other than this upon your **a.**,

T19 IV.C.8:3 There is no funeral, no dark **a.**, no grim
T-21 II.6:7 idea you have enshrined upon your **a.**,
T-21 II.8:1 leave your **a.** free of what you placed upon
T-26 IV.3:6 of **a.** is set where once sin was believed to

## alter 10

T-1 I.13:1 and so they **a.** the temporal order. They
T-7 II.4:3 he must **a.** the form of what he translates,
T-9 VI.4:2 did, and your dissociation will not **a.** this.
T-29 II.7:7 health, and with events that seem to **a.** it.
T-30 VIII.2:8 in Heaven or on earth could ever **a.**. But
W-pI 12.4:1 sure that you do not **a.** the time intervals
W-pI 107.4:2 It does not shift and **a.** in its form, nor
W-pI 136.12:3 attempts to plan defenses that would **a.** it.
W-pI 157.3:2 way to **a.** time sufficiently to rise above its
W-pII 285.2:5 *part of You. And what can* **a.** *Holiness Itself?*

## alterable 1

T-5 VI.1:5 Yet your election is both free and **a.**. You

## alteration 3

T-4 II.2:4 is important to realize that this **a.** can and
T-4 VII.3:9 to any judgment, any exception or any **a.**.
T-5 II.1:3 This **a.** of the time sequence should be

## alterations 1

W-pI 152.5:2 **a.** in conditions of the body and the mind

## Alternate 2

*alternate*

T-28 V.h The **A.** to Dreams of Fear
T-28 V.1:6 God is the **A.** to dreams of fear. Who

## alternate 1

• adjective
*verb*
*Alternate*

T-5 VI.3:6 **A.** interpretations were unnecessary until

## alternate 5

• verb
*adjective*
*Alternate*

T-9 VIII.6:4 coexist, nor is it possible for them to **a.**.
T-9 VIII.6:5 and grandiosity can and must **a.**, since
W-pI 33.1:4 **A.** between surveying your outer and
W-pI 37.5:1 you may **a.** between applying the idea to
W-pI 167.4:2 emotions **a.** because of causes you cannot

## alternating 3

T-2 III.3:9 The **a.** investment in the two levels of
T-14 X.5:3 **a.** patterns of light and darkness sweep
W-pI 42.6:3 spend the practice period **a.** between slow

## Alternative 1

*alternative*

M-5 III.2:6 They stand for the **A.**. With God's Word

## alternative 25

*Alternative*

T-6 II.h The **A.** to Projection
T-6 II.4:1 however, that there *is* an **a.** to projection.
T-6 V.B.4:2 this is its only **a.** since the other possibility
T-9 VIII.1:6 of the ego is its **a.** to the grandeur of God.
T-10 V.4:3 This was his **a.** to joy, because he would
T-13 II.8:3 not yet look upon the **a.** with gladness. In
T-18 VI.9:8 changeless forever, and forever without **a.**
T-24 in.2:8 What God creates has no **a.**. The truth
T-24 I.1:5 come with the one **a.** that you can choose
T-24 VI.13:5 possible, and there is no **a.** for Him to see.
T-25 VII.8:4 This One but points to an **a.**, another way
T-25 VII.9:1 of the **a.** is one which he cannot deny, nor
T-25 VII.9:2 as it proves to him that it is an **a.** he really
T-25 VII.10:3 this, in the **a.** He chose especially for you.
T-27 VII.9:1 can see; the one **a.** that you can choose,
T-28 II.12:3 They are the dream's **a.**, the choice to be
T-31 II.2:9 them to the one **a.** that *is* a different choice
T-31 IV.h The Real **A.**
T-31 IV.6:1 of acceptance that there is a real **a.** instead
W-pI 66.9:8 ego is the only **a.** to the Holy Spirit's Voice
W-pI 71.6:5 no possible **a.** to God's plan that will save
W-pI 88.1:7 I can but choose the light, for it has no **a.**.
W-pI 131.7:1 Heaven remains your one **a.** to this
W-pI 133.11:3 the **a.** you think you chose seems fearful,
S-2 I.1:6 remedy appears to be a terrible **a.** to life.

## alternatives 26

T-5 V.6:5 that the **a.** themselves are unalterable.
T-5 V.6:7 all the **a.** the mind can accept and obey.
T-6 V.B.8:4 conflict, since it means that **a.** have been
T-14 III.4:4 there are no **a.** except truth and illusion.
T-15 X.5:6 You see no other **a.**, for you cannot accept
T-15 X.9:3 bondage, for there are no **a.** but these.
T-22 II.1:2 do they appear to be the only **a.**, and
T-22 VI.13:9 Of the **a.**, this seems more natural and
T-26 III.6:3 but in the perception of **a.** for choice.
T-28 V.2:4 must come, because there are but these **a.**
T-31 IV.2:4 is no choice in its **a.**. Seek not escape from
T-31 IV.8:1 to make when you have seen the real **a.**.
T-31 V.12:1 are **a.** about the thing that you must be.
T-31 V.12:7 be, **a.** were there to choose among, and
T-31 VII.6:5 **A.** are in your mind to use, and you can
T-31 VII.14:6 is, and see the real **a.** you choose between.
T-31 VIII.5:7 false distinctions gone, illusory **a.** laid by,
W-pI 133.3:3 more than you can make **a.** from which to
W-pI 133.3:5 choose, and what **a.** you choose between.
W-pI 133.4:3 ungenerous to you to let **a.** be limitless,
W-pI 133.11:2 ego's goals to come between the real **a.**.
W-pI 134.10:1 Thus will you see **a.** for choice in terms
W-pI 138.1:1 we believe there are **a.** to choose between.
W-pI 138.9:2 The choice cannot be made until **a.** are
W-pI 138.10:3 to make a choice between **a.** when only
S-2 I.10:3 Yet you must learn **a.** for choice, or you

## alters 4

T-2 III.1:5 this distortion, because it **a.** only part of it
T-4 II.2:3 Their interaction is a process that **a.** both,
W-pI 127.1:6 never **a.** with a person or a circumstance.
M-12 2:3 mind. Nothing external **a.**, but everything

## although 103

T-1 VII.3:7 But **a.** you can perceive false associations,
T-2 II.4:6 not be misused, **a.** it could be refused.
T-3 I.2:6 **a.** the error itself is no harder to correct
T-4 II.5:2 **a.** they may well harm themselves if you
T-4 II.8:10 myths, **a.** creative effort can be turned to
T-4 VII.1:2 specific, **a.** the mind is naturally abstract.
T-5 I.1:12 it. All of it is still yours **a.** all of it has been
T-5 I.4:11 can obstruct it, **a.** you can never lose it.
T-5 I.7:4 that **a.** it does not engender knowledge, it
T-5 II.1:5 and **a.** you can keep it asleep you cannot
T-5 III.10:4 the ego, **a.** the ego does not recognize it.
T-5 V.6:13 real thoughts, **a.** you can believe in them.
T-6 I.10:1 learners, **a.** we do not need to have equal
T-6 I.15:1 **a.** its gospel is really only the message of
T-6 II.9:6 **A.** perception of any kind is unreal, you
T-6 IV.2:8 since, **a.** it has raised a great many. The
T-6 V.B.7:1 insane decisions, **a.** you can think you are.
T-6 V.B.8:6 **a.** this step is essential for the ultimate
T-6 V.B.9:1 **a.** it is a giant step toward the unified
T-6 V.C.4:5 **a.** it does not deny that the temptation to
T-7 II.4:3 translator, **a.** he must alter the form of
T-7 VI.1:1 **A.** you can love the Sonship only as one,
T-8 IV.1:7 from His laws, **a.** you can disobey them.
T-8 VI.4:1 of any value, **a.** he had not understood its
T-8 IX.1:3 question is, **a.** it asks an endless number.
T-9 I.11:6 **a.** it is impossible for you to change them.
T-9 V.5:8 is real, **a.** he does not know it himself.
T-10 III.1:7 **a.** those who make idols do worship them
T-10 III.6:8 you. It is for you **a.** you may not ask for it.
T-10 III.11:8 **A.** it is clear this has nothing to do with
T-10 V.3:8 but **a.** he may seem to be many different
T-10 V.4:3 accept the fact that, **a.** he was a creator, he
T-11 II.7:5 there, **a.** He cannot help you without your
T-12 I.6:8 **A.** your interpretations of reality are
T-12 I.8:2 from it, **a.** the recognition is necessary to
T-12 V.2:3 **A.** you have attacked yourself, you will be
T-12 V.8:1 for **a.** the curriculum you set yourself is
T-13 I.4:3 **a.** he believes in it the Holy Spirit knows it
T-13 IV.5:3 from the past, and **a.** the past is over, the
T-13 V.8:3 you see in dreams **a.** your eyes are closed.
T-13 VI.3:7 it has not gone from you, **a.** it is not there.
T-13 VI.13:8 **A.** he slept, Christ's vision did not leave
T-13 VII.3:7 that, and so **a.** you turn in sadness from it
T-13 VII.5:7 Christ is still there, **a.** you know Him not.
T-13 VII.11:2 For **a.** the ego urges you again and again
T-15 I.4:5 **a.** the ego aims at death and dissolution
T-15 V.8:1 and **a.** this is not so in Heaven, the Holy
T-15 VII.6:5 *is* direct attack, **a.** it does not seem to be.
T-17 II.8:3 would not wait, **a.** He waits in patience.
T-17 IV.4:2 For **a.** the ego did not understand what
T-17 V.11:3 **A.** you may have made many mistakes
T-21 VIII.2:2 would desire it **a.** you understand it not.
T-22 IV.1:7 make the wrong decision, **a.** he can delay.
T-22 IV.2:1 **a.** you still may think you can go back and
T-24 V.1:4 takes joy in what it sees, **a.** it is not true.
T-26 VII.6:4 **a.** this clearly makes no sense at all. All
T-26 VII.9:5 **A.** it falls far short of giving you your full
T-26 VIII.6:5 fear they may not come, **a.** already there?
T-27 VII.11:7 which you do not perceive **a.** it caused the
T-27 VII.14:6 from your sight, **a.** your eyes are closed. A
T-28 VI.2:1 sounds you do not like, **a.** it cannot hear.
T-29 II.6:4 **a.** it seems to be in constant change. Yet
T-31 V.13:1 **A.** this step has gains, it does not yet
W-pI 15.5:1 **A.** you will obviously not be able to apply
W-pI 19.4:1 day, **a.** it will occasionally be included as a
W-pI 26.5:2 **a.** the time may be reduced to a minute if
W-pI 35.8:3 you. **A.** nothing that does occur should be
W-pI 39.5:2 are recommended, **a.** both are suggested.
W-pI 40.2:1 **a.** you will probably find it more helpful if
W-pI 43.5:1 **A.** this part of the exercise period should
W-pI 46.2:1 Yet **a.** God does not forgive, His Love is
W-pI 61.5:1 **a.** each one need not exceed a minute or
W-pI 71.3:3 that, **a.** this hope has always failed, there
W-pI 72.3:1 **A.** the attempt to keep the limitations
W-pI 96.1:1 **A.** you are one Self, you experience
W-pI 109.1:3 **a.** we seem to look on danger and on
W-pI 127.2:4 remain itself **a.** it is withheld from others.
W-pI 131.11:5 your mind and see, **a.** your eyes are closed
W-pI 132.16:2 **a.** you may not fully understand as yet
W-pI 135.12:1 **a.** it cannot know the outcome which is
W-pI 155.1:1 world that is not here, **a.** it seems to be.
W-pI 155.5:3 be distinct from them, **a.** you are indeed.
W-pI 158.3:4 by him, **a.** he has not yet embarked on it.
WpI rV.in6:4 and pain, **a.** I know they have no meaning
W-pI 182.1:3 return, **a.** you do not recognize the voice,
W-pI 183.4:5 **a.** before you let the Name of God replace
W-pI 186.13:2 comfort you, **a.** He knows no sorrow. He
W-pI 186.13:3 **a.** He knows that you have everything
W-pI 186.13:4 His Son perceives, **a.** He sees them not.
W-pI 186.14:4 here, **a.** what love will mean to you when
W-pII 1.2:1 it will not raise to doubt, **a.** it is not true.
W-pII 260.1:1 *myself,* **a.** *in my insanity I thought I did. Yet,*
M-in 5:7 more, **a.** their thoughts remain a source of
M-3 1:2 **a.** the ultimate goal is always the same; to
M-13 1:1 **A.** in truth the term sacrifice is altogether
M-16 2:4 **a.** each one must use them as best he can
M-16 3:3 **a.** it remains important throughout the
M-20 4:4 **a.** you do not recognize that you have
M-25 5:4 here, **a.** they are not particularly subtle.
M-26 2:2 because, **a.** they are no longer visible,
C-5 1:3 forms, **a.** upon the altar they are one.
P-3 II.1:8 **a.** they may be far more able teachers

P-3......... II.6:2 a. both patient and therapist may change

## altogether 5

T-2........ III.3:4 in the extreme, becomes a. intolerable.
T-9....VIII.10:1 are a. irreplaceable in the Mind of God.
T-15...... IX.3:5 the ego, whose goals are a. unattainable,
T-21.........I.6:1 dim, perhaps, and yet not a. unfamiliar,
M-13 ......... 1:1 truth the term sacrifice is a. meaningless,

## always 438

T-1...........I.9:2 which are a. miraculous in the true sense,
T-1.........I.13:2 They are a. affirmations of rebirth, which
T-1.........I.35:1 they may not a. have observable effects.
T-1........ III.5:1 threaten truth, which can a. withstand it.
T-1........ III.5:8 is a. because you are defending misplaced
T-1........ III.8:2 The miracle will a. bless *you*. Miracles you
T-1........ IV.3:4 Truth is a. abundant. Those who perceive
T-1....... VII.3:2 they a. involve twisting perception into
T-2........ IV.2:2 because it a. entails the belief that what is
T-2......... V.4:3 a. because fear has intruded on your right-
T-2......... V.7:1 learning a. begins with the awakening of
T-2....V.A.14:1 (4) The miracle is a. a denial of this error
T-2........ VI.4:4 conditions a. entail a willingness to be
T-2........ VI.4:8 The correction is a. the same. Before you
T-2........ VI.5:1 Fear is a. a sign of strain, arising
T-2........ VI.8:1 is a. a sign of respect *from* the worthy *to* the
T-3...........I.2:1 The best defense, as a., is not to attack
T-3.........I.3:11 a. possible to twist symbols around if you
T-3......... II.2:5 you never misperceive and a. see truly.
T-3......... II.2:6 what does not exist, and a. see what does.
T-3........ III.5:2 Certainty is a. of God. When you love
T-3........ III.7:3 Attack is a. made upon a stranger. You
T-3........ IV.3:7 condition, in which attack is a. possible.
T-3........ IV.5:1 Perception a. involves some misuse of
T-3........ IV.6:7 Truth will a. overcome error in this way.
T-3...... IV.6:10 that knowledge can a. be remembered,
T-3......... V.3:3 Knowledge is a. stable, and it is quite
T-3......... V.4:6 The word "image" is a. perception-related
T-3......... V.5:2 is a. open to error because it refers to the
T-3......... V.5:5 a. happens when method and content are
T-3........ VI.2:4 Judgment a. involves rejection. It never
T-3........ VI.8:2 a. because you believe you are the author
T-3...... VI.11:4 freedom. Judgment a. imprisons because
T-4...........I.2:2 Change is a. fearful to the separated,
T-4...........I.2:3 a. perceive it as a move toward further
T-4...........I.6:3 my goal will a. be to absolve you finally
T-4......... II.1:5 Perception, however, is a. specific, and
T-4......... II.6:5 a. evaluates itself in relation to other egos.
T-4......... II.6:9 "self-esteem" is a. vulnerable to stress, a
T-4....... II.10:5 Its direction is a. automatic, because it
T-4....... III.1:10 but your spirit and your Creator will a. be
T-4........ III.6:5 Those who call truly are a. answered.
T-4........ VI.1:7 and a. will be totally unaffected by your
T-4........ VI.6:1 the moment, but it will not a. be that way.
T-4....... VII.5:8 of being the mind gives everything a..
T-5.........I.4:10 Knowledge is a. ready to flow everywhere,
T-5......... II.3:3 that the ego a. dissolves at Its sound. That
T-5......... II.7:7 The Voice for God is a. quiet, because It
T-5......... II.8:2 mind that a. speaks for the right choice,
T-5......... II.9:1 My mind will a. be like yours, because we
T-5....... II.12:2 the Holy Spirit, Whose Will is for God a..
T-5...... III.11:8 He is in communion with God a., and He
T-5........ IV.8:9 Hold it and share it, that it may a. be ours
T-5......... V.2:6 whole. Guilt is *a.* disruptive. Anything that
T-5......... V.4:9 thinking will a. be attended with guilt,
T-5....... V.6:12 you made can a. be changed because,
T-5......... V.7:3 Guilt feelings are a. a sign that you do not
T-5........ VI.3:1 Remember the Kingdom a., and
T-5........ VI.3:3 Holy Spirit remind you a. of His fairness,
T-5........ VI.3:5 simultaneously, for the ego a. speaks first.
T-5........ VI.4:2 The ego's decisions are a. wrong, because
T-5...... VI.10:8 verdict will a. be "thine is the Kingdom,"
T-5....... VII.1:6 His Voice reminds you a. that all hope is
T-6.........in.1:1 of anger to fear is not a. so apparent.
T-6.........in.1:2 Anger a. involves projection of separation
T-6...........I.2:5 you can a. call on me to share my decision
T-6...........I.3:2 who a. refuse to consider what they have
T-6 .........I.6:10 Remember a. that what you believe you
T-6 .........II.3:1 projection will a. hurt you. It reinforces
T-6 .........II.3:5 is a. a means of justifying attack. Anger
T-6 .......II.12:5 is united He offers the whole Kingdom a..
T-6 ....... IV.1:2 The ego a. speaks first. It is capricious
T-6 ....... IV.3:2 does not speak first, *but He a. answers.*
T-6 ........ V.4:2 Yet He a. answers their call, and His
T-6 ........ V.4:6 away. His light is a. the Call to awaken,
T-6 .....V.A.2:4 The Holy Spirit, as a., takes what you
T-6 .....V.A.2:5 Again as a., He reinterprets what the ego
T-6 .....V.A.3:2 He a. tells you that only the mind is real,
T-6 .....V.A.5:8 and attack a. breaks communication,
T-6 .....V.A.5:9 a. for what each one can get *separately*.
T-6 ..... V.B.4:1 Upside down as a., the ego perceives the
T-6 ..... V.B.4:3 judgment, here as a., is predetermined by
T-7 ..........I.3:7 God's creations have a. been, because He
T-7 ..........I.3:7 have always been, because He has a. been.
T-7 ..........I.3:8 Your creations have a. been, because you
T-7 ..........I.4:1 other hand, a. demands reciprocal rights,
T-7 ..........I.4:2 It is a. willing to strike a bargain, but it
T-7 ..........I.7:3 last, because He created first and for a.. It
T-7 ..........I.7:9 What is timeless is a. there, because its
T-7 .........II.5:3 emphasizing a. that *these differences do*
T-7 .........II.5:4 meaning of His message is a. the same;
T-7 ....... III.1:5 It is a. maximal. Your vigilance does not
T-7 ....... III.1:6 does enable you to use it a. and in all ways
T-7 ....... III.1:7 When I said "I am with you a.," I meant it
T-7 ....... III.1:9 Because I am a. with you, *you* are the way,
T-7 ....... III.2:9 teach. Yet you are a. teaching. You must,
T-7 ..... III.2:11 ego, then, is a. being undone, and does
T-7 ....... IV.5:2 The ego a. seeks to divide and separate.
T-7 ....... IV.5:3 The Holy Spirit a. seeks to unify and heal.
T-7 ........ V.3:6 that magic a. involves the belief that
T-7 ........ V.4:2 Magic a. tries to weaken. Healing
T-7 ........ V.4:4 Magic a. sees something "special" in the
T-7 ........ V.5:1 and healing that is of Him *a.* works
T-7 ........ V.5:2 the healer a. heals by Him the results will
T-7 ........ V.5:6 anything of God not be for all and for a.?
T-7 ........ V.6:3 Fear a. makes exceptions. Healing never
T-7 ........ V.6:6 Healing a. produces harmony, because it
T-7 ....... VI.4:4 Mind a. reproduces as it was produced.
T-7 ...... VII.6:2 the appreciation God accords them a.,
T-7 ...... VII.7:3 He a. teaches you the inestimable worth
T-7 ...... VII.9:4 Projection a. sees your wishes in others. If
T-7 .... VII.11:4 to the ego are a. experienced as sacrifices,
T-7 .... VII.11:5 They will a. be treasured by God because
T-7 .....VIII.1:2 mind, and therefore one that a. operates.
T-7 .....VIII.2:2 The ego a. tries to preserve conflict. It is
T-7 .....VIII.4:4 that it can, an error the ego a. makes,
T-7 ....... IX.1:5 between them a. in favor of the spirit. To
T-7 .........X.5:1 Spirit a. sides with you and with your
T-7 .........X.5:5 asks for sacrifice, but the ego a. does.
T-7 .........X.5:9 this case, it a. means that the follower is.
T-7 .........X.6:3 will a. remain beyond question, however
T-7 ....... XI.1:1 The Holy Spirit will a. guide you truly,
T-7 ....... XI.3:4 by fear, and allow him to give a., without
T-8 ..........I.4:3 aims at change, and that is a. its purpose,
T-8 ....... III.4:8 it yourself. For I am a. there with you, in
T-8 ....... IV.2:4 I said that I am with you a., even unto the
T-8 ....... IV.7:5 I will a. remember you, and in my
T-8 ....... VI.9:6 of the knowledge of where you are a., and
T-8 ...... VII.1:1 Attack is a. physical. When attack in any
T-8 ...... VII.1:6 a body you will a. experience depression.
T-8 .....VIII.1:2 and are a. based on what it believes the
T-8 .....VIII.2:3 between means and end as it a. does.
T-8 ....... IX.6:1 ego, which a. wants to weaken the mind,
T-9 .......II.11:3 laws are a. fair and perfectly consistent.
T-9 ..... III.2:10 His ego is a. wrong, no matter what it
T-9 ....... IV.1:6 Remember a. that your Identity is shared,
T-9 ....... IV.4:3 situation, to which the ego a. leads you.
T-9 ........ V.5:5 His ego will a. seek to get something from
T-9 ........ V.7:1 situation" to which the ego a. leads. It
T-9 ....... VI.2:3 inconsistent you will not a. give rise to joy
T-9 ....... VI.2:3 you will not a. recognize His consistency.
T-9 ....... VI.7:1 is one time, its only dimension being "a.."
T-9 ....... VI.7:3 Like Him, *you* are "a."; in His Mind and
T-9 ...... VII.7:2 is. Lack of knowledge of any kind is a.
T-9 .....VIII.2:1 Grandiosity is a. a cover for despair. It is
T-9 .....VIII.2:5 it a. involves attack. It is a delusional
T-9 .....VIII.5:3 of God. Remember a. that you cannot be
T-9 .....VIII.7:2 Truth does not vacillate; it is a. true.
T-9 .....VIII.7:6 deceive you, but your illusions a. will.
T-10 ......in.2:4 different because everything has a. been.
T-10 .......II.4:4 that this is a. an attack on truth, and truth
T-10 .......II.4:4 is God, you will realize why it is a. fearful.
T-10 .......II.4:5 why it is that you a. attack yourself first.
T-10 ..... III.2:3 He is a. accepted for all, and when your
T-10 ..... III.8:1 that you a. receive as much as you accept.
T-10 ..... IV.2:2 mind. It is a. there to be accepted, but its
T-10 .....V.14:7 As a., your choice is determined by what
T-11 ......in.1:7 decision is a. an answer to the question,
T-11 .......I.11:4 A. remember that what He gives He keeps
T-11 ..... III.1:8 Yet it a. attacks the Son of God, and the
T-11 ..... III.3:2 He wills has happened, for it was a. true.
T-11 ..... III.4:7 Great Light a. surrounds you and shines
T-11 .......V.5:1 purpose is a. the natural outcome of what
T-11 .......V.7:1 The ego a. attacks on behalf of separation
T-11 .....V.13:6 ego will a. substitute chaos for meaning,
T-11 .... VII.3:4 But it a. adds something that is not real to
T-12 ..... III.2:5 in is a. related to your notion of salvation.
T-12 ..... III.2:6 The question is a. twofold; first, *what* is to
T-12 ..... III.6:5 a. tries to handle it by making some sort
T-12 ..... III.6:6 a. perceives this world as outside himself,
T-12 ..... IV.1:1 and this is a. its central teaching. It never
T-12 ..... IV.4:5 For His promise is a., "Seek and you *will*
T-12 .......V.3:4 you are a. the first point of your attack,
T-12 ..... VI.2:4 Remembering you a., He cannot let you
T-12 ..... VI.7:5 where everything eternal in it has a. been.
T-12 .... VII.6:3 Remember a. that you see what you seek,
T-12 .... VII.6:8 The mind a. strives for integration, and if
T-12 .. VII.13:3 is what it a. reserves for you in the end.
T-12 ... VIII.4:8 no more past than future, being forever a.
T-12 ... VIII.8:4 it you will remember that it was a. so.
T-13 ........I.3:4 A. has no direction. Time seems to go in
T-13 ........I.4:6 by God. And what God gives has a. been.
T-13 ........I.5:2 He has a. sought his guiltlessness, and he
T-13 ........I.5:7 God's Son will a. be as he was created.
T-13 ........I.6:7 and mercy have a. followed him, for he
T-13 ........I.6:7 he has a. extended the Love of his Father.
T-13 ........I.7:5 And so it has a. been. Let the holiness of
T-13 ........I.8:4 this can understand what "a." means, and
T-13 ........I.8:5 you are eternal, and "a." must be now.
T-13 ........I.9:2 in time, is a. associated with expiation,
T-13 .......II.1:1 ultimate purpose of projection is a. to get
T-13 .......II.8:1 Atonement has a. been interpreted as the
T-13 ..... IV.6:9 Spirit teaches that you a. meet yourself,
T-13 ... IV.6:10 teaches that you a. encounter your past,
T-13 .......V.9:5 looking a. on the real world, and calling
T-13 ... VI.10:4 Love a. leads to love. The sick, who ask
T-13 .... VII.4:3 Love a. answers, being unable to deny a
T-13 .... VII.6:7 Christ will a. offer you the Will of God, in
T-13 .... VII.8:6 But this one thing is a. yours, being the
T-13 .... VII.9:7 world is but your welcome of what a. was.
T-13 ..... IX.1:2 The guilty a. condemn, and having done
T-13 ..... IX.2:6 For faith is a. given what is treasured, and
T-13 ..... IX.6:5 you. Remember a. that it is impossible to
T-13 ..... IX.6:7 Guilt is a. in your mind, which has
T-13 .......X.1:3 Displacement a. is maintained by the
T-13 .......X.6:1 where you would a. find Atonement. The
T-13 .......X.6:3 must learn that guilt is a. totally insane,
T-13 .......X.7:4 would have Him do, and has a. done so.
T-13 .....X.10:2 as God Himself has a. loved His Son. *And*
T-13 .....X.10:5 have a. loved your Father can have no fear
T-13 ..... XI.8:7 Heaven, and will a. will you nothing else.
T-13 ... XI.11:7 true, or not remember what has a. been?
T-14 ........I.3:1 Seeing is a. outward. Were your thoughts
T-14 ..... III.8:5 Remember a. that mind is one, and cause
T-14 ..... IV.3:1 will give Himself to you as He has a. done.
T-14 ..... IV.3:5 to restore what a. was to your unforgiving
T-14 .......V.2:1 message given to each one is a. the same;
T-14 .....V.10:6 Crucifixion is a. the ego's aim. It sees
T-14 ..... VI.1:8 but value a. lies in joint appreciation.
T-14 ..... VI.2:2 will a. yield to love if it is brought to love,
T-14 ..... IX.1:9 interposed between what a. was and now.
T-14 ... IX.1:10 represents only the denial of what a. was.
T-14 ..... IX.8:1 to any form of error is a. the same. There
T-14 .....X.6:13 limitless. And being a. maximal, it offers
T-14 ..... XI.7:7 by seeing His Son as he a. was, and not as

| | |
|---|---|
| T-14....XI.10:6 | He a. gives His gifts in place of yours. He |
| T-14....XI.11:1 | God's Son will a. be indivisible. As we are |
| T-14....XI.11:6 | that you have a. created like your Father. |
| T-14....XI.12:1 | who remember a. that they know nothing |
| T-15.........I.6:5 | must lead to the belief in hell, and a. does. |
| T-15.........I.6:6 | hell here, but a. as a foretaste of the future |
| T-15.......II.4:7 | Holy Spirit in a brother is a. recognized. |
| T-15......III.1:8 | will a. choose one at the expense of the |
| T-15.......V.1:3 | Judgment a. rests on the past, for past |
| T-15.......V.9:2 | having a. known you exactly as He knows |
| T-15......VI.3:4 | must a. lose if you perceive yourself as |
| T-15......VI.6:1 | nothing happens that has not a. been. |
| T-15.....VII.1:1 | love relationship, and a. obscured by it, is |
| T-15.....VII.2:7 | the ego a. seems to attract through love, |
| T-15.....VII.8:3 | It is a. this that the ego demands, and it |
| T-15.....VII.9:5 | seems a. to be attacking and wounding |
| T-15...VII.12:4 | will a. teach that loneliness is solved by |
| T-15......IX.4:2 | Love would *a.* give increase. Limits are |
| T-15.......X.4:4 | takes many forms, it is a. the same idea. |
| T-15.......X.4:5 | What is not love is a. fear, and nothing |
| T-15.......X.8:7 | but a. to make the sacrifice complete. |
| T-16.........I.1:2 | is a. used to form a special relationship in |
| T-16.........I.2:5 | the ego a. empathizes to weaken, and to |
| T-16.........I.2:5 | to weaken, and to weaken is a. to attack. |
| T-16.........I.6:6 | since they a. contain some element of |
| T-16......IV.5:3 | a. at the price of making both illusions. |
| T-16.......V.1:4 | they are a. an attack on the self to make |
| T-16.......V.2:1 | to make guilty is a. directed against God. |
| T-16.......V.8:1 | the ego seeks is a. one that is more special |
| T-16.....VII.8:7 | Son will a. be exactly as he was created. |
| T-16...VII.10:1 | you a. choose between truth and illusion; |
| T-17.......II.7:2 | knows that he has a. rested there in peace. |
| T-17......III.2:2 | shadow figures a. speak for vengeance, |
| T-17......IV.5:1 | The ego is a. alert to threat, and the part |
| T-17......IV.7:4 | the gift is a. a miniature of the thought |
| T-17.......V.1:4 | The experience of it is a. felt. Yet without |
| T-17...VII.3:10 | used *against* truth will a. destroy faith. If |
| T-18.......II.1:6 | with the ego, which a. looks upon itself, |
| T-18......IV.4:2 | It is a. the result of your small willingness |
| T-18.....VII.1:3 | this a. means you still find sin attractive. |
| T-18.....VII.3:2 | It is a. remembered or anticipated, but |
| T-18.....VII.5:7 | a. comes with just one happy realization; |
| T-18.....VII.8:1 | Yet there will a. be this place of rest to |
| T-18...VIII.2:4 | on love will a. seem to shut Him out, and |
| T-19.........I.5:3 | Faithlessness would a. limit and attack; |
| T-19.........I.7:3 | But illusions are a. connected, as is truth. |
| T-19.........I.9:7 | for faithlessness, but faith is a. justified. |
| T-19.......II.5:1 | sin as error is a. indefensible to the ego. |
| T-19.......II.7:3 | from which escape will a. be impossible. |
| T-19......III.1:7 | the ego thinks you are, you will a. want it. |
| T-19......III.2:1 | is really called upon by sin, *and a. answers.* |
| T-19......III.2:4 | Punishment is a. the great preserver of sin |
| T19..IV.B.10:1 | Faith in the eternal is a. justified, for the |
| T19..IV.B.15:1 | ego's messages are a. sent away from you, |
| T19. IV.C.11:1 | over it, remember it is a. for *one* reason; |
| T-20......III.2:3 | no interferences, are a. seen as dangerous. |
| T-20......VI.7:1 | Idolaters will a. be afraid of love, for |
| T-20.....VII.4:3 | be lifted, so what was a. true is recognized |
| T-20.....VII.5:6 | to wish, for sight is a. secondary to desire. |
| T-20.....VII.6:6 | brought to truth, and a. hidden from it. |
| T-20...VIII.6:2 | for everything He looks upon is a. sure. |
| T-20...VIII.8:7 | never is whether you want them, but a., |
| T-20. VIII.10:2 | And meaning a. looks within to find itself |
| T-21.........I.2:5 | Judgment will a. give you false directions, |
| T-21......III.2:5 | but a. with faith and with the persistence |
| T-21......III.2:7 | But it is a. recognized if it is placed in love |
| T-21.....V.3:11 | They a. change *your* mind. There *is* no |
| T-21....VI.10:1 | The Son of God is a. blessed as one. And |
| T-21.....VII.4:6 | who a. eludes its murderous attack by |
| T-21...VIII.3:2 | you need ask for it but once to have it a.. |
| T-21...VIII.3:3 | And if you do not have it a., being what it |
| T-21...VIII.5:2 | the awareness of what is a. there to see, |
| T-21...VIII.5:2 | see, the happiness that could be a. yours. |
| T-22.........I.4:9 | a. leads to sight of differences and loss of |
| T-22.......I.10:3 | For what is time to what was a. so? Think |
| T-22.......I.11:2 | For He is a. drawn unto Himself. What is |
| T-22.......I.11:6 | for faith in another is a. faith in Him. You |
| T-22.......V.2:2 | A. to justify what goes against the truth, |
| T-23.........I.2:6 | The ego a. marches to defeat, because it |
| T-23.......II.5:3 | For One must a. be condemned, and by |
| T-23......III.1:2 | you do not a. recognize the source of pain |
| T-23......IV.8:5 | their present and their future; a. the same |
| T-24.........I.3:2 | but a. clashes with the reality of God's |
| T-24.........I.7:9 | Is it not a. your belief your specialness is |
| T-24.......II.1:2 | Specialness a. makes comparisons. It is |
| T-24.......II.1:5 | And a. whom it thus diminishes would be |
| T-24.......II.2:1 | Pursuit of specialness is a. at the cost of |
| T-24....VI.11:4 | A. attacked and always furious, with |
| T-24....VI.11:4 | Always attacked and a. furious, with |
| T-24....VI.11:4 | furious, with anger a. fully justified, you |
| T-25.........I.3:4 | And a. is it faithful to your purpose, from |
| T-25.......II.1:5 | hopes and fancies, a. does despair result. |
| T-25.......II.3:3 | to uphold pursuit of what has a. failed, on |
| T-25......VI.6:5 | He has the means for either, as he a. did. |
| T-25......VI.7:7 | that he is safe, as he has a. been, and will |
| T-25......IX.3:1 | solves will a. be one in which no one loses |
| T-26.........I.1:4 | for it is a. an attempt to limit loss. The |
| T-26......IV.1:7 | Forgiveness a. rests upon the one who |
| T-26...VII.13:2 | God wills you learn what a. has been true: |
| T-26...VII.20:5 | But it can make what a. has been true be |
| T-28.......II.3:1 | A. in sickness does the Son of God |
| T-28......IV.7:2 | not, for what is joined in Him is a. one. |
| T-29.........I.4:5 | But a. is it possible for you and him to go |
| T-30.........I.1:2 | not a. know when you are making them. |
| T-30.......I.15:3 | You a. ask advice before you can decide |
| T-30......III.7:5 | It was a. there, but you were unaware of it |
| T-30......III.7:7 | will a. be exactly as it was before the time |
| T-30....III.10:2 | holds of you remains exactly as it a. was. |
| T-30......IV.1:2 | it up. You a. fight illusions. For the truth |
| T-30......VI.2:1 | Pardon is *a.* justified. It has a sure |
| T-30......VI.6:5 | It a. means you think forgiveness must be |
| T-31.........I.8:4 | everything within the world has a. made, |
| T-31.........I.8:7 | had lost a friend who a. wanted to be part |
| T-31.....V.14:1 | The concept of the self has a. been the |
| T-31...VII.12:1 | a. but reflects a wish to be a self that you |
| T-31...VIII.2:3 | a. choose between your weakness and the |
| W-pI.....17.1:3 | is a. the thought that comes first, despite |
| W-pI.....26.3:1 | thought that you a. attack yourself first. If |
| W-pI.....41.8:5 | and sooner or later it is a. successful. We |
| W-pI.....44.2:4 | It is with you a., making vision possible in |
| W-pI.....45.7:3 | They will a. be in your mind, exactly as |
| W-pI.....45.7:3 | be in your mind, exactly as they a. were. |
| W-pI.....49.2:1 | God is calm, a. at rest and wholly certain. |
| W-pI.....52.1:5 | it is a. because I have replaced reality with |
| W-pI.....52.1:8 | of mine. I am a. upset by nothing. |
| W-pI.....59.1:2 | can I be alone when God a. goes with me? |
| W-pI.....61.2:5 | be for you, and arrogance is a. of the ego. |
| W-pI.....66.7:5 | but the fear that the ego a. engenders, |
| W-pI.....66.7:5 | that the Holy Spirit a. offers to replace it. |
| W-pI.....71.3:3 | that, although this hope has a. failed, |
| W-pI.....72.3:3 | a. associated with something a body does |
| W-pI.....78.3:2 | see the Son of God where he has a. been. |
| W-pI.....83.1:4 | purpose only, I am a. certain what to do, |
| W-pI.....88.1:5 | That is why I a. choose between truth and |
| W-pI.....90.1:2 | today that the problem is a. some form of |
| W-pI.....90.1:3 | also understand that the solution is a. a |
| W-pI.....91.1:4 | The miracle is a. there. Its presence is not |
| W-pI.....97.2:4 | He is with you a., as you are with Him. |
| W-pI...107.4:3 | again. It stays exactly as it a. was, to be |
| W-pI...108.6:2 | this special case has proved it a. works, in |
| W-pI...122.1:5 | and the warmth of sure protection a.? Do |
| W-pI.136.15:5 | and let truth be as it has a. been: *Sickness* |
| W-pI.136.18:2 | strength the body has will a. be enough to |
| W-pI...137.4:4 | healed is merely to accept what a. was the |
| W-pI...137.4:4 | and a. will remain exactly as it has forever |
| W-pI...153.6:3 | the text maintains that choice is a. made |
| W-pI.155.12:6 | and leads us to where He has a. been. |
| W-pI...162.3:2 | and wakens with the truth before him a.. |
| W-pI...165.5:3 | you have the treasure you have a. sought. |
| W-pI...167.9:4 | mind awakes, it but continues as it a. was. |
| W-pI.167.12:1 | remaining a. in the holy minds which He |
| W-pI...169.9:2 | be a constant state, forever as it a. was; |
| W-pI...170.6:4 | insane, while they are a. merciful and just. |
| W-pI...187.5:8 | What he seems to lose is a. something he |
| W-pII.....in.1:5 | end toward which our practicing was a. |
| W-pII..232.1:3 | *and a. will be there to hear my call to You and* |
| W-pII..283.1:2 | *Yet is creation as it a. was, for Your creation* |
| W-pII..324.1:5 | *Your loving Voice will a. call me back, and* |
| W-pII .358.1:6 | *promise to Your Son in my awareness a.. Let* |
| M-1...........3:5 | Its central theme is a., "God's Son is |
| M-2...........3:5 | then will you realize that it was a. there. |
| M-3...........1:2 | although the ultimate goal is a. the same; |
| M-3...........3:6 | Salvation is a. ready and always there. |
| M-3...........3:6 | Salvation is always ready and a. there. |
| M-3...........3:7 | levels, but the result is a. the same. |
| M-4.....I.A.3:7 | These changes are a. helpful. When the |
| M-4.....I.A.4:2 | This is a. somewhat difficult because, |
| M-4.....I.A.4:2 | that the changes in his life are a. helpful, |
| M-4....IV.2:10 | And so their will, which a. was His Own, |
| M-4.......V.1:3 | The open hands of gentleness are a. filled. |
| M-4......IX.2:9 | faithfulness in the true sense is a. directed |
| M-6...........1:1 | Healing is a. certain. It is impossible to |
| M-6...........2:1 | Healing will a. stand aside when it would |
| M-7...........5:1 | Teacher for resolution is a. self-doubt. |
| M-7...........6:1 | The mistake is a. some form of concern |
| M-8...........2:1 | Illusions are a. illusions of differences. |
| M-9...........1:5 | since training is a. highly individualized. |
| M-10.........2:5 | that judgment was a. impossible for him, |
| M-12.........1:4 | was a. wholly spirit now no longer sees |
| M-12.........5:1 | The central lesson is a. this; that what |
| M-13.........6:4 | a. means the giving up of what you want. |
| M-16.........2:7 | It is a. possible to begin again, should the |
| M-16.........4:1 | This course is a. practical. It may be that |
| M-17.........2:2 | it. Nor is this a. obvious. It can, in fact, be |
| M-17.........2:5 | will a. come to teacher and to pupil alike. |
| M-17.........4:2 | It is a. an interpretation that gives rise to |
| M-17.......9:13 | all fear, and thus forever real and a. true. |
| M-21.........2:5 | It a. requests some kind of experience, the |
| M-23.........7:8 | with him, for he is with you; he is a. here. |
| M-24.........2:7 | There is a. some risk in seeing the present |
| M-24.........2:8 | There is a. some good in any thought |
| M-24.........6:1 | of this course a. remains the same;–it is |
| M-25.........2:5 | Whose Presence is a. there and Whose |
| M-29.......2:13 | His answers are a. right. Would you say |
| C-1.............4:4 | This Will is a. unified and therefore has |
| C-1.............7:1 | a. between two choices or two voices. Will |
| C-3.............7:5 | And what He gives is a. like Himself. This |
| P-in............1:6 | but even then it is a. some change in his |
| P-2...........I.3:5 | His goal is wholly undivided a.. Whatever |
| P-2.......VII.2:5 | cure, when another is a. there to choose? |
| P-3.....II.10:11 | the Will of God has a. been exactly as it is. |
| P-3.......III.6:1 | One rule should a. be observed: No one |
| P-3.......III.6:3 | anyone. Relationships are a. purposeful. |
| P-3.......III.6:4 | them, they are a. His potential temple; |
| S-1...........I.2:9 | is a. a song of thanksgiving and of Love. |
| S-1..........II.2:1 | asking-out-of-need, a. involve feelings of |
| S-1..........II.6:1 | that prayer at any level is a. for yourself. If |
| S-1........III.1:1 | We said that prayer is a. for yourself, and |
| S-1........III.6:1 | a. made to set up jailers and to hide from |
| S-1........IV.3:3 | Prayer for specifics a. asks to have the |
| S-2...........I.4:1 | prayer is a. for yourself, so is forgiveness |
| S-2...........I.4:1 | for yourself, so is forgiveness a. given you. |
| S-2...........I.5:2 | It a. seems to be another who is evil, and |

**am** 589

**amazing** 1

| | |
|---|---|
| T-18....VIII.3:4 | In its a. arrogance, this tiny sunbeam has |

**ambiguity** 3

| | |
|---|---|
| T-3........IV.5:5 | the only way out of a. is clear perception. |
| W-pI.....39.2:3 | is not due to the a. of the question. But do |
| W-pI.200.11:5 | simple, happy way to leave the world of a. |

**ambiguous** 4

| | |
|---|---|
| T-4.......II.8:12 | a. in form and characteristically good-and- |
| T-21........II.1:4 | Rejected yes, but not a.. And if you |
| T-22......III.1:8 | it is plain, and what is obvious is not a.. It |
| W-pI.186.10:2 | impermanent and vague, uncertain and a. |

**ambiguously** 1

| | |
|---|---|
| T-3........IV.5:5 | Afterwards it can only choose a., and the |

**ambivalence** 3

T-4........ III.4:6 it. No love in this world is without this **a.**,
T-4........ III.4:6 no ego has experienced love without **a.**
T-4........ III.4:8 This means that it wants it without **a.**,

**Amen** 17

T-4...... III.1:13 *and the ego will not prevail against it.* **A.**.
T-15.. XI.10:14 be made holy for you. This is our will. **A.**.
T-16... VII.12:7 *which You created and which You love.* **A.**.
T-31..VIII.12:1 And now we say "**A.**." For Christ has
W-pI... 163.9:8 *and our will is one with Yours eternally.* **A.**.
WpI 170.13:11 *has set us free. And we give thanks.* **A.**.
W-pI. 184.15:9 *which is our inheritance and peace.* **A.**.
WpI 189.10:10 *that it become a part of Heaven now.* **A.**.
W-pII . 229.2:3 *thanks to You for saving me from them.* **A.**.
W-pII . 237.2:3 *is Your Son, and my true Self as well.* **A.**.
W-pII . 246.2:5 *that. And so I choose to love Your Son.* **A.**.
W-pII . 331.2:3 that we may find the peace of God. **A.**.
W-pII . 337.2:4 *myself. Father, my dream is ended now.* **A.**.
W-pII . 360.1:7 *And with this thought we gladly say "***A.***."*
W-ep ......... 5:2 well. To this we say "**A.**." You will be told
W-ep ......... 6:1 We trust our ways to Him and say "**A.**."
M-29 ......... 8:8 *for all those who walk to God with me.* **A.**

**amenable** 1

T-26..... VII.6:1 illusion be less **a.** to truth than are the rest

**amid** 3

T-11...... III.2:3 and **a.** all his brothers he is friendless.
T-17.... IV.13:4 as you search it out **a.** its wrappings. As
W-pI... 182.6:3 call for help almost unheard **a.** the grating

**amiss** 9

T-2........ IV.2:2 always entails the belief that what is **a.** on
T-6.......... I.7:5 that it is true for you, or you will teach **a.**.
T-11.... VIII.3:8 learned **a.** should not be your own teacher
W-pI..... 51.3:2 what I see when I have judged it **a.**? What
W-pI..... 99.1:2 something **a.** that needs corrective change
W-pI... 193.6:4 you see or any brother looks upon **a.**.
W-pI... 195.1:1 for those who look upon the world **a.**. The
S-3........... I.5:3 ask **a.** and seeming charity forgive to kill,
S-3........ IV.5:3 Do not choose **a.**, or you will think that it

**amnesia** 1

T19... IV.D.3:4 the great **a.** in which the memory of God

**among** 51

T-1......... I.49:1 distinction **a.** degrees of misperception. It
T-1......... II.3:4 is therefore a sign of love **a.** equals. Equals
T-2........... I.5:2 makes no distinctions **a.** misperceptions.
T-6......... V.4:4 Spirit makes no distinction **a.** dreams. He
T-7....... VII.5:8 God, and count yourself **a.** them gladly.
T-8........ IX.5:3 cannot distinguish **a.** degrees of error, for
T-11....... II.2:3 But be sure to count yourself **a.** them, for
T-12...... III.1:4 you to help them, since you are **a.** them.
T-12...... III.5:5 you will surely place yourself **a.** the poor,
T-14....... X.4:1 of lack of competition **a.** your thoughts,
T-14... X.12:10 there be any order of difficulty **a.** them?
T-18......... II.8:6 used to choosing **a.** dreams you do not see
T-21...... III.6:5 that you might choose **a.** your brothers,
T-22....... IV.4:7 will they be to see you come **a.** them,
T-23....... II.3:2 establishes degrees of truth **a.** illusions,
T-24......... I.9:7 Never can there be peace **a.** the different.
T-26... VII.19:5 There is no difference **a.** the Sons of God.
T-27..... V.10:4 Your brother first **a.** them will be seen,
T-27..... VI.3:5 You cannot choose **a.** them which are real
T-27..... VII.6:6 look **a.** the mighty legions of its witnesses
T-27..... VII.7:4 to you, your guilt was not **a.** them. Nor
T-30..... VII.6:5 your ability to see relationships **a.** events.
T-31....... IV.1:3 a place where choice **a.** illusions seems to
T-31.... IV.2:10 is certain, for there is no choice **a.** them.
T-31..... V.12:7 be, alternatives were there to choose **a.**,
T-31.... VIII.1:5 *take your place* ***a.*** *the saviors of the world, or*
W-pI..... 27.1:2 It gives vision priority **a.** your desires.
W-pI..... 31.3:2 to establish any kind of hierarchy **a.** them
WpI... rI.in.6:4 now emphasizing the relationships **a.** the
W-pI..... 56.5:5 And I, who am **a.** them, am one with
W-pI..... 65.2:1 rightful place **a.** the saviors of the world.
W-pI..... 92.1:5 This is **a.** the many magical beliefs that
W-pI..... 96.7:4 Thus is salvation kept **a.** the Thoughts
W-pI..... 96.9:7 have. Salvation is **a.** them; find it there.
W-pI... 100.7:4 to take his place **a.** God's messengers.
W-pI. 121.13:4 unforgiving mind, with yours **a.** them.
W-pI... 140.6:2 does not make distinctions **a.** unrealities.
W-pI... 140.8:1 for all illusions, not another shift **a.** them.
W-pI. 153.10:6 ones who are **a.** the chosen ones of God,
W-pI...... 154.h I am **a.** the ministers of God.
W-pI. 154.13:2 thus: *I am* ***a.*** *the ministers of God, and I am*
W-pI... 165.6:3 now you are **a.** the saviors of the world.
W-pI... 172.2:1 (154) I am **a.** the ministers of God. God is
W-pI... 191.5:1 But let today's idea find a place **a.** your
W-pII . 239.1:4 And can it be that we are not **a.** them,
W-pII . 316.1:5 home, **a.** the gifts that God has given me.
M-4 ........... 2:1 All differences **a.** the Sons of God are
M-16 ......... 7:5 distinctions **a.** the problems he perceives,
C-ep........... 3:6 Look up and see His Word **a.** the stars,
P-2........ IV.4:1 word "cure" has come into disrepute **a.**
S-3........... I.3:3 **a.** which sickness should be seen as one.

**amount** 8

T-2 ...... VII.7:9 this implies that an enormous **a.** of time is
T-13 .... VII.2:4 to you as the **a.** to which you hold it dear.
T-16 ...... V.1:1 to realize that it involves a great **a.** of pain
T-22 ....... II.1:4 Both bring the same **a.** of misery, though
T-25 .. VII.11:5 and pay exact **a.** in blood and suffering.
T-29 ........ I.3:8 in scope and carefully restricted in **a.**,
W-pI..... 42.5:2 be astonished at the **a.** of course-related
W-pI... 108.9:2 come to you in the **a.** in which you gave it.

**amounts** 1

T-12 ...... V.7:7 **a.** to a course in how to attack yourself. A

**amplified** 1

T-1 ...... VII.4:6 of the implications that will be **a.** later on.

**amplify** 1

T-2 ........ V.1:8 level. To **a.** an earlier statement, spirit is

**amulets** 1

W-pI. 140.10:1 So do we lay aside our **a.**, our charms and

**an** 980

**analyses** 1

P-2...... IV.11:9 There is no need for long **a.** and wearying

**analysis** 1

T-12 ........ I.2:1 **a.** of ego motivation is very complicated,

**analyze** 3

T-8 ..... VIII.6:5 situation, does not bother to **a.** it at all. If
T-11 .... V.13:2 **a.** means to break down or to separate out
T-14 ........ X.8:7 undertakings of students who would "**a.**"

**analyzes** 1

T-11 .... V.13:1 The ego **a.**; the Holy Spirit accepts. The

**analyzing** 4

T-8 ..... VIII.6:6 meaningless there is no point in **a.** them.
T-9 ........ V.6:3 Can you find light by **a.** darkness, as the
T-11 .... V.15:2 **A.** to attack meaning, the ego succeeds in
T-12 ........ I.1:6 why **a.** the motives of others is hazardous

**anchor** 2

T-22 ..... III.4:7 its heavy **a.** in the shifting world it made;
T-22 ... VI.10:7 lies buried the heavy **a.** that seems to keep

**anchored** 2

T-30 ..... III.9:1 holds it safe, forever lifted up and **a.** sure.
W-pI .. 183.6:4 Let all your thoughts become **a.** on this.

**anchors** 1

T-28 .... VII.6:2 further locks and chains and heavy **a.**,

**ancient** 70

T-18 . VIII.13:1 have reached the end of an **a.** journey, not
T-20 ........ I.4:5 alien to you and yet your **a.** Friend, lies
T-21 ........ I.6:1 perhaps you catch a hint of an **a.** state not
T-21 ........ I.7:5 and see if you remember an **a.** song you
T-21 ........ I.9:5 You know the **a.** song, and know it well.
T-21 ........ I.9:6 to you as is this **a.** hymn of love the Son of
T-22 ........ I.7:2 yet more **a.** than the old illusion it has
T-22 ........ I.8:7 Yet must He be reborn into His **a.** home,
T-26 ....... V.5:3 Only in the past,–an **a.** past, too short to
T-26 ....... V.5:6 You keep an **a.** memory before your eyes.
T-26 .. VII.16:1 miracle but calls your **a.** Name, which you
T-26 .. VII.20:1 Your **a.** Name belongs to everyone, as
T-26 ..... IX.2:3 And would you trade Them for an **a.** hate
T-26 ..... IX.3:4 to take its **a.** place upon an ancient throne
T-26 ..... IX.3:4 to take its ancient place upon an **a.** throne
T-26 ..... IX.3:8 The shadow of an **a.** hate has gone, and
T-26 ..... IX.6:1 an **a.** hatred has become a present love.
T-26 ..... IX.8:4 and **a.** scars are healed within His sight.
T-26 ..... IX.8:5 An **a.** miracle has come to bless and to
T-26 ..... IX.8:5 to replace an **a.** enmity that came to kill.
T-27 ....... II.6:5 disappear before the **a.** clarion call of life.
T-27 ....... II.6:7 The **a.** calling of the Father to His Son,
T-27 .. VII.12:1 separated from yourself, an **a.** enemy, a
T-27 .. VII.12:4 of fear, the time of terror and of **a.** hate,
T-27 ... VIII.8:1 The world but demonstrates an **a.** truth;
T-28 ........ I.5:6 And if it seems to serve to cherish **a.** hate,
T-28 ........ I.7:3 one? When **a.** memories of hate appear,
T-28 ........ I.7:9 **a.** new ideas they bring will be the happy
T-28 ........ I.7:9 happy consequences of a Cause so **a.** that
T-29 ....... V.7:6 sword, to keep his **a.** promises to die.
T-30 ....... V.9:1 An **a.** hate is passing from the world. And
T-31 ........ I.5:4 Now does your **a.** overlearning stand
T-31 ........ I.9:2 have heard its calling as the **a.** call to life,
T-31 ...... I.13:5 free, because an **a.** learning passed away,
T-31 ....... II.1:1 **a.** lesson is not overcome by the opposing
T-31 ....... II.1:4 an **a.** battle being waged against the truth,
T-31 ....... II.7:3 Think not **a.** thoughts. Forget the dismal
T-31 ....... II.9:1 **a.** lessons you have taught yourself about
T-31 ..... III.7:3 and there will be no **a.** penalty exacted
T-31 .. VII.13:7 veil of old ideas and **a.** concepts held so
W-pI .... 69.3:5 Let us end the **a.** search today by finding
W-pI .. 106.4:9 Today allow your Father's **a.** pledge to
W-pI .. 122.8:3 heart with deep tranquility as **a.** truths,
W-pI 131.14:4 God keeps His **a.** promise to His holy Son,
W-pI .. 132.2:4 You free the future from all **a.** thoughts of
W-pI .. 132.3:3 and release the future from your **a.** fears,
W-pI 135.20:2 your happiness according to the **a.** plan,
W-pI .. 156.7:5 the senseless, **a.** dream that now is past.
W-pI 161.10:5 will see will sing to you of **a.** melodies you
W-pI .. 164.2:3 an **a.** call to which He gives an ancient
W-pI .. 164.2:3 call to which He gives an **a.** answer. You
W-pI .. 164.4:2 **a.** peace you carry in your heart and have
W-pI .. 166.9:1 Your **a.** fear has come upon you now, and
WpI... rV.in8:8 whole we go together to our **a.** home,
WpI. rV.in10:6 practice but an **a.** truth we knew before
W-pI .. 191.8:1 has lighted up all dark and **a.** caverns,
W-pI .. 195.7:4 An **a.** door is swinging free again; a long
W-pII .... in.5:2 are all **a.** promises upheld and fully kept.
W-pII .... in.7:5 We ask but that Your **a.** promises be kept
W-pII . 248.2:1 *Father, my* ***a.*** *love for You returns, and lets*
W-pII . 275.1:1 Voice for God, which speaks an **a.** lesson,

W-pII..306.1:1 Heaven that an **a.** memory returns to me?
W-pII..322.1:2 readiness to give God's **a.** messages to me.
M-2............4:1 goes backward to an instant so **a.** that it is
M-2............4:5 in that **a.** instant which he now relives. So
M-2............4:6 an inevitable choice out of an **a.** past.
C-2...........1:10 that it is nothing but an **a.** thought that
C-ep.........1:11 up an **a.** door that leads beyond the world
C-ep...........3:2 We only start again an **a.** journey long
S-1........IV.4:2 you stifle and imprison it in **a.** prisons,

## and 15958

## anew 6

T-11.....VII.1:5 To perceive **a.** is merely to perceive again,
T-17.......V.2:2 relationship, transformed and seen **a.**.
T-18......IX.9:2 Here the world outside is seen **a.**, without
T-31...... I.13:3 free to learn of him, and learn of him **a.**.
W-pI...189.1:7 of God within you is to see the world **a.**,
W-pII..306.1:4 born **a.** into a world of mercy and of care;

## angel's 2

T-25... VIII.7:3 dressed to deceive within an **a.** cloak. And
P-2........VI.2:6 of the universe," "the herald **a.** song," all

## angels 9

T19... IV.C.9:4 Your newborn purpose is nursed by **a.**,
T-26......IX.7:1 Around you **a.** hover lovingly, to keep
W-pI.131.13:2 it. **A.** light the way, so that all darkness
W-pI...161.9:1 the **a.** love and God created perfect. This
W-pI...183.2:2 invite the **a.** to surround the ground on
W-pII..303.1:1 Watch with me, **a.**, watch with me today.
W-pII..316.1:4 **a.** watch its open doors that not one gift is
W-ep .........6:7 God's **a.** hover near and all about. His
S-2........III.7:5 fail to send His **a.** down to answer you in

## anger 89

T-6.........in.1:1 The relationship of **a.** to attack is obvious
T-6.........in.1:1 relationship of **a.** to fear is not always so
T-6.........in.1:2 apparent. **A.** always involves projection of
T-6.........in.1:3 **A.** cannot occur unless you believe that
T-6...........I.3:3 Projection means **a.**, anger fosters assault,
T-6...........I.3:3 Projection means anger, **a.** fosters assault,
T-6...........I.4:4 destruction, therefore, does not justify **a.**.
T-6...........I.4:7 respond with **a.**, you must be equating
T-6...........I.6:7 to accept them as false justifications for **a.**
T-6........ I.11:6 to **a.** and assault would not be so extreme.
T-6........ I.14:4 of the crucifixion entirely without **a.**,
T-6......... II.3:6 **A.** without projection is impossible. The
T-6......... II.5:3 Instead of **a.** this arouses love for both,
T-7..... VIII.1:1 that without projection there can be no **a.**
T-7..... VIII.2:1 projection and **a.** can be finally undone.
T-7..... VIII.5:4 will have laid aside all **a.** and all attack,
T-12.........I.3:5 with **a.** to a brother's plea for help? No
T-12......III.6:3 he experiences then is depression or **a.**,
T-13......III.6:4 mind that thought it made them in **a.**.
T-13......VI.5:7 Your past was made in **a.**, and if you use it
T-15.....VII.2:3 to enter into any relationship without **a.**,
T-15.....VII.2:3 for the ego believes that **a.** makes friends.
T-15.....VII.4:5 it will enable you to direct its **a.** outward,
T-15.....VII.4:6 out of **a.** and dedicated to but one insane
T-15.....VII.4:6 the more **a.** you invest outside yourself,
T-15...VII.10:1 the ego has "blessed," for **a.** *is* its blessing.
T-15...VII.10:2 **A.** takes many forms, but it cannot long
T-15...VII.10:2 brings guilt cannot be love and *must* be **a.**.
T-15...VII.10:3 All **a.** is nothing more than an attempt to
T-18....... II.4:4 **A.** and fear pervade it, and in an instant
T-22....... V.1:2 Surely not by force or **a.**, nor by opposing
T-23..........I.4:7 as nature roaring at the wind in **a.**,
T-24....VI.11:4 furious, with **a.** always fully justified, you
T-25......III.6:5 before was means to justify his **a.** turned
T-26....... X.1:3 you think that a response of **a.** now is just.
T-28......VI.5:1 Sickness is **a.** taken out upon the body, so
T-30....... II.4:1 What cause have you for **a.** in a world
T-30......VI.1:1 **A.** is *never* justified. Attack has *no*
T-31....... II.6:8 Take not his hand in **a.** but in love, for in
W-pI.......5.1:3 to be fear, worry, depression, anxiety, **a.**,
W-pI.......6.1:2 to name both the form of upset (**a.**, fear,
W-pI.....21.2:2 or anticipated that arouse **a.** in you. The
W-pI.....21.2:3 The **a.** may take the form of any reaction
W-pI.....21.3:1 let the "little" thoughts of **a.** escape you in
W-pI.....21.3:2 really recognize what arouses **a.** in you,
W-pI.....21.5:2 focus your **a.** on a particular attribute of a
W-pI.....21.5:2 that the **a.** is limited to this aspect. If your
W-pI.....22.1:2 Having projected his **a.** onto the world, he
W-pI.....26.6:2 take the form of depression, worry, **a.**, a
W-pI.....39.6:2 they appear; uneasiness, depression, **a.**,
W-pI.....47.2:2 fear, anxiety, depression, **a.** and sorrow.
W-pI.....51.5:4 so that my **a.** is justified and my attacks
W-pI.....71.8:5 They have led to depression and **a.**; but
W-pI.121.10:2 not matter what the form your **a.** takes.
W-pI...153.2:2 For threat brings **a.**, anger makes attack
W-pI...153.2:2 anger, **a.** makes attack seem reasonable,
W-pI...153.7:2 the Christ and come to fear His Father's **a.**
W-pI...161.1:1 and take a stand against our **a.**, that our
W-pI...161.1:3 where fear and **a.** had prevailed before.
W-pI.161.12:4 is your safe escape from **a.** and from fear.
W-pI...163.1:2 as sadness, fear, anxiety or doubt; as **a.**,
W-pI...181.6:1 this goal if **a.** blocks our way in any form.
W-pI...192.5:3 **A.** becomes impossible, and where is
W-pI...192.6:1 With **a.** gone, you will indeed perceive
W-pI...192.9:4 Every time you feel a stab of **a.**, realize
W-pI...195.9:1 learn to think of gratitude in place of **a.**,
W-pII..249.1:1 impossible and **a.** makes no sense. Attack
W-pII.....347.h **A.** must come from judgment. Judgment
W-pII.....348.h I have no cause for **a.** or for fear, For You
W-pII..348.1:4 *with You. What need have I for* **a.** *or for fear?*
Wfl........in.5:4 in which we understand that **a.** is insane,
M-17 ......... 1:6 If a magic thought arouses **a.** in any form,
M-17 .........4:3 of the intensity of the **a.** that is aroused. It
M-17 .........5:1 **A.** in response to perceived magic
M-17 .........8:6 **a.** comes from an interpretation and not a
M-17 .........9:5 Can nothing give rise to **a.**? Hardly so.
M-17 .........9:7 **a.** recognizes a reality that is not there; yet
M-17 .........9:7 **a.** certain witness that you do believe in it
M-18 .........2:1 react to magic thoughts wholly without **a.**
M-18 .........3:1 **A.** but screeches, "Guilt is real!" Reality is
M-20 .........3:3 God's peace can never come where **a.** is,
M-20 .........3:3 is, for **a.** must deny that peace exists.
M-20 .........3:4 Who sees **a.** as justified in any way or any
M-20 .........4:2 Returning **a.**, in whatever form, will drop
C-1.............6:1 illusions; perceiving sin and justifying **a.**,
P-2.........in.1:5 the belief that **a.** brings him something he
S-2......... II.4:5 the **a.** and the hurt another gives, and do
S-2......... II.8:1 takes that do not lead away from **a.**,
S-3......... II.1:9 thoughts and raging **a.** at the universe. It

## angered 2

T-8......... V.5:6 do so. Sensing defeat and **a.** by it, the ego
W-pI.....78.4:5 someone you think you love who **a.** you;

## angry 24

T-6...........I.7:6 but I could not be **a.** with them because I
T-6.........I.14:4 their sense of guilt had made them **a.**.
T-12........ III.3:1 Whenever you become **a.** with a brother,
T-15.....VII.9:3 In their **a.** alliances, born of the fear of
T-15...VII.10:1 Whenever you are **a.**, you can be sure
T-16..... V.12:7 God is not **a.**. He merely could not let this
T-25... VIII.6:4 "fires" of Heaven by God's Own **a.** Hand.
T-29......IV.4:1 you are **a.**, is it not because someone has
T-30.........I.3:5 therefore **a.**. There are rules by which this
T-30.........I.7:2 For you have already gotten **a.**. And your
T-31....... V.3:1 This aspect can grow **a.**, for the world is
W-pI........5.2:3 *I am not* **a.** *at_for the reason I think. I am not*
W-pI........6.1:4 *I am* **a.** *at_because I see something that is not*
W-pI.....71.8:3 become depressed or **a.** at the second part
W-pI.....72.6:1 where **a.** animals seek for prey and mercy
W-pI....93.11:2 be tempted to become **a.** with someone,
W-pI....121.3:1 about itself and all it sees; afraid and **a.**,
W-pI...153.7:3 you now from your delusion of an **a.** god,
W-pI...192.9:6 you to be **a.** represent your savior from
Wfl........in.5:7 a father **a.** at his son because he failed to
M-4 ......IV.1:9 him confused, fearful, **a.** and suspicious.
M-15 .........3:1 who are sometimes sad and sometimes **a.**;
M-17 .........4:1 remember that no one can be **a.** at a fact.
M-17 .......7:10 An **a.** father pursues his guilty son. Kill or

## anguish 1

W-pI...192.5:4 attack, the core of **a.** and the seat of fear?

## animals 2

T-4..........II.4:1 Think of the love of **a.** for their offspring,
W-pI.....72.6:1 angry **a.** seek for prey and mercy cannot

## animate 1

W-pI.....17.3:1 what you believe to be **a.** or inanimate;

## annoyance 1

W-pI.....21.2:5 a slight twinge of **a.** is nothing but a veil

## anonymous 3

T-3........ VI.8:7 but you prefer to be **a.** when you choose
T-3........ VI.8:8 you believe that your creation was **a.**. This
W-pI...183.4:5 They become **a.** and valueless to you,

## Another 1

*another*

T-27......II.10:7 your function with the function of **A.**, you

## another 375

*Another*

T-1...........I.1:2 One is not "harder" or "bigger" than **a.**.
T-1.........I.18:2 the maximal service you can render to **a.**.
T-1..........II.3:5 of one **a.** because awe implies inequality.
T-1........VII.2:3 still be expressed through one body to **a.**,
T-2..........II.7:2 Sons of God make in one way or **a.**. It is
T-2........ IV.2:2 amiss on one level can adversely affect **a.**.
T-2....... V.9:4 way of perceiving the perfection of **a.** even
T-2....... V.10:1 Charity is a way of looking at **a.** as if he
T-2....... V.10:7 that whenever you offer a miracle to **a.**,
T-3...........I.5:4 God" is **a.** way of saying the same thing. A
T-3........ III.7:1 If you attack error in **a.**, you will hurt
T-4.......in.3:11 We have **a.** journey to undertake, and if
T-4...........I.1:4 he teaches, but he must meet **a.** condition;
T-4..........II.2:5 Thinking about **a.** ego is as effective in
T-4....... II.4:10 Belief that there is **a.** way of perceiving is
T-4..........II.8:1 which is merely **a.** way of describing how
T-4...... IV.10:1 Christ is merely **a.** name for the creation,
T-4........ VI.2:3 Whenever you act egotistically towards **a.**,
T-4........ VI.3:3 and joy while **a.** brings chaos and disaster
T-5...........I.4:4 I go I will send you **a.** Comforter and he
T-5..........II.5:7 broken because you had made **a.** voice.
T-5........ III.6:1 of the mind is not understandable to **a.**.
T-5........ III.9:3 is merely **a.** term for a split mind. The ego
T-6...........I.3:4 of some of the Sons of God upon **a.**. This,
T-6...........I.4:2 is little doubt that one body can assault **a.**,
T-6........ IV.3:3 one time or **a.** and in one way or another,
T-6........ IV.3:3 one time or another and in one way or **a.**,
T-6......V.C.9:4 it. By making **a.** kingdom that you valued,
T-7...........I.4:2 understand that to be like **a.** means that
T-7...... III.1:11 belonging to anyone at the expense of **a.**.
T-7.......VII.2:6 denied it in **a.** and are therefore not aware
T-7.......VII.7:1 teacher sufficiently worthy to teach **a.**.
T-7.......VII.9:3 Whenever a brother attacks **a.**, that *is*
T-7......VIII.3:3 of **a.** part does not really mean anything.
T-7......VIII.4:1 perpetuate an illusion about **a.** without
T-8........ III.4:6 meet, they are given **a.** chance at salvation
T-8........ III.5:4 you have **a.** opportunity to find them.
T-8........ IV.6:7 the dominion of one mind over **a.**. God's
T-8......... V.6:3 only illusions of **a.** direction can obscure
T-8.......VII.4:4 And in the body of **a.** you will see the use
T-8.......VII.7:2 translation of one order of reality into **a.**.
T-8.....VII.14:3 you see **a.** as limited to or by the body,
T-8......VIII.2:7 to shift ceaselessly from one goal to **a.**, so

| | |
|---|---|
| T-8.....VIII.7:4 | feel. Sickness is merely **a.** example of your |
| T-8........IX.5:3 | form of sickness is more serious than **a.**, |
| T-8........IX.5:3 | that one error can be more real than **a.**. |
| T-9.........III.2:8 | He needs correction at **a.** level, because |
| T-9.........III.2:8 | level, because his error is at **a.** level. He is |
| T-9.........III.6:2 | Is it possible, then, for you to correct **a.**? |
| T-9.........V.3:3 | plan for forgiveness in one form or **a.**. If |
| T-10.........I.2:6 | you merely shifted from one dream to **a.**, |
| T-10.........IV.7:5 | The power of one mind can shine into **a.**, |
| T-11.....VII.1:3 | there must be **a.** world that you do not see |
| T-12.........I.2:5 | mind, pitting one level within it against **a.** |
| T-12........II.1:7 | the light in **a.** mind must shine into theirs |
| T-12........II.3:1 | Perceive in sickness but **a.** call for love, |
| T-12........III.5:4 | even for an instant, that there is **a.** answer |
| T-12........IV.4:4 | The Holy Spirit offers you **a.** promise, and |
| T-13.......in.1:2 | judgment of one mind by **a.** as unworthy |
| T-13.......in.1:4 | judged, believing that by punishing **a.**, it |
| T-13.........I.6:3 | a belief in condemnation of one by **a.**, |
| T-13.....VI.11:5 | you will lay aside the world and find **a.**. |
| T-13.....VII.3:7 | road that leads away from it into **a.** world. |
| T-14........II.1:8 | Yet you will add **a.** burden to your already |
| T-14........III.6:2 | him to heal is **a.** opportunity to replace |
| T-14.....IV.10:1 | totally incapable of understanding one **a.**. |
| T-14........X.2:6 | brings the laws of **a.** world to this one. |
| T-14........XI.4:3 | And so you have **a.** lesson sent from Him, |
| T-14........XI.5:5 | dark lesson teaches this, in one form or **a.**. |
| T-15........V.6:1 | you would substitute for **a.** has not been |
| T-15........V.6:3 | to substitute one aspect of love for **a.**, you |
| T-15........V.7:1 | while it prefers different parts of **a.** aspect. |
| T-15........VI.1:1 | at the expense of **a.** and not to suffer guilt. |
| T-15........VI.1:3 | they do not conflict with one **a.** in any way |
| T-15........VI.3:3 | must believe that strength comes from **a.**, |
| T-15........VI.3:5 | is **a.** interpretation of relationships that |
| T-15........VI.4:1 | believe that when **a.** calls on God for love, |
| T-15.....VII.6:1 | In one way or **a.**, every relationship the |
| T-15.....VII.7:7 | believes that to forgive **a.** is to lose him. It |
| T-15.....VII.8:6 | they bring the body of **a.** closer or farther. |
| T-15.....VII.8:8 | makes **a.** guilty and holds him through |
| T-15........X.7:4 | is who is to be destroyed, you or **a.**? You |
| T-16.........I.1:6 | does not relate through your ego to **a.** ego. |
| T-16.........I.7:2 | the needs of one you do not jeopardize **a.**, |
| T-16........II.2:3 | For this is but **a.** way in which you would |
| T-16........II.4:2 | have reached **a.** mind and joined with it. |
| T-16.......IV.6:4 | escape from one illusion into **a.** must fail. |
| T-16........V.7:3 | and tries to "trade" itself for the self of **a.**. |
| T-16......V.10:6 | your self you think you can attack **a.** self, |
| T-16......V.11:5 | body raise **a.** self to take its power from |
| T-17.........I.4:2 | some of it to one teacher, and some to **a.**. |
| T-17.........I.4:3 | in one way, and in **a.** way the other part. |
| T-17.........I.6:5 | mind because **a.** is attempting to solve his |
| T-17.....III.1:10 | think guiltily of **a.** and not harm yourself. |
| T-17.....IV.16:7 | with Him lies in our relationship to one **a.** |
| T-17........V.3:8 | old goal re-established in **a.** relationship. |
| T-17........V.7:1 | substitute for this **a.** relationship to which |
| T-18.........I.2:2 | one person as a replacement for **a.**, the |
| T-18.........I.12:4 | brother out of this world and through **a.**, |
| T-18......II.5:10 | to make **a.** world that is not real remains |
| T-18......II.5:11 | you seem to waken to is but **a.** form of this |
| T-18....VIII.5:3 | self-contained, needing **a.** for some things |
| T-19........III.2:3 | Yet punishment is but **a.** form of guilt's |
| T-19........III.8:2 | capable of making **a.** will that could attack |
| T19IV.A.17:15 | it. Communion is **a.** kind of completion, |
| T19..IV.B.15:4 | the body search for pain in attack upon **a.**, |
| T19....IV.C.5:1 | You have **a.** dedication that would keep |
| T-20........II.5:2 | you have asked for and received **a.** sight. |
| T-20.....III.10:1 | for each of you for one **a.** and for himself. |
| T-20........IV.6:5 | the beginning of **a.** world goes with them. |
| T-21........III.8:4 | should **a.** point of view be given them. |
| T-21.....III.10:2 | must be exacted of a body, and by **a.** body |
| T-21........IV.2:8 | to look within because of sin is yet **a.** fear, |
| T-21........IV.7:4 | which sings the praises of **a.** world, brings |
| T-21........V.3:1 | **a.** vision and another Voice in which your |
| T-21........V.3:1 | another vision and **a.** Voice in which your |
| T-21........V.3:2 | in Them, you will perceive **a.** self in you. |
| T-21.....VII.4:5 | it attacks, so that it runs at once to find **a.**, |
| T-22.......in.3:3 | he would extend it by joining with **a.**, |
| T-22.........I.1:1 | Let reason take **a.** step. If you attack |
| T-22.........I.4:3 | secrets be except **a.** "will" that is your own |
| T-22.......I.11:6 | for faith in **a.** is always faith in Him. You |
| T-22........II.2:3 | of misery and seek **a.** is hardly an escape. |
| T-22........II.5:4 | Yet reason looks on this **a.** way, for reason |
| T-22........II.9:5 | And here we see again **a.** form of the same |
| T-22......VI.8:5 | not to change it, nor to substitute **a.** goal. |
| T-22....VI.11:7 | seems safer to attack **a.** or yourself than to |
| T-22....VI.12:5 | Father; and to attack **a.** without yourself, |
| T-23.........I.7:8 | illusion about yourself can battle with **a.**, |
| T-23........II.2:4 | it true by his attack on what **a.** values. |
| T-23........II.3:6 | be more resistant to the truth than can **a.**. |
| T-23........II.9:6 | For enemies do not give willingly to one **a.** |
| T-23......II.21:5 | Think not one step is smaller than **a.**, nor |
| T-23......III.1:2 | much as in **a.** form that you *do* recognize, |
| T-23......IV.2:3 | same, and indistinguishable from one **a.**. |
| T-24........II.1:3 | It is established by a lack seen in **a.**, and |
| T-24....VI.12:1 | you pursue **a.** goal with far less vigilance; |
| T-24..VII.1:12 | has found **a.** son whom he prefers to them |
| T-24.....VII.4:6 | Save it for show, as bait to catch **a.** fish, to |
| T-24.....VII.5:9 | it immortality, setting **a.** light in Heaven, |
| T-24 VII.11:10 | Yet can perception serve **a.** goal. It is not |
| T-25......III.4:1 | is **a.** Maker of the world, the simultaneous |
| T-25......III.5:1 | is **a.** purpose in the world that error made |
| T-25......III.5:1 | **a.** Maker Who can reconcile its goal with |
| T-25......III.6:7 | he gave attack is but **a.** altar where he can, |
| T-25......III.6:8 | temptation as just **a.** chance to bring him |
| T-25......IV.1:8 | defined **a.** way and sought for differently. |
| T-25......IV.3:1 | comfort in **a.** world where peace abides. |
| T-25......VI.1:4 | himself for his mistakes than damn **a.**. He |
| T-25.....VII.5:1 | can be based, **a.** world perceived. And one |
| T-25.....VII.8:4 | **a.** way of looking at what he has seen |
| T-25..VII.11:2 | it seems that one must gain *because* **a.** lost. |
| T-25....VIII.4:3 | just that one should lack for what **a.** has. |
| T-25....VIII.4:7 | The rest is taken from **a.**, to be laid beside |
| T-25 .VIII.13:5 | give **a.** must be an injustice to them both, |
| T-25......IX.4:4 | The world solves problems in **a.** way. It |
| T-25......IX.4:7 | can bring **a.** problem added to the first, in |
| T-25......IX.8:4 | be received because **a.** could receive it not. |
| T-25......IX.9:5 | have no mercy to bestow upon **a.**. That is |
| T-26.........I.1:6 | To see a brother in **a.** body, separate from |
| T-26........II.2:4 | for Him to bring to truth than is **a.**. For |
| T-26.....V.1:10 | never will **a.** road be made except the way |
| T-26.......V.6:9 | imagine he is elsewhere, and in **a.** time. In |
| T-26......VI.2:6 | Seek not **a.** friend to take His place. There |
| T-26.....VII.8:8 | a little space to you, **a.** little space to him. |
| T-26..VII.15:3 | to all illusions that were made **a.** purpose |
| T-26........X.3:3 | The belief you are is but **a.** form of the |
| T-27........I.11:3 | in which a different view, **a.** purpose, can |
| T-27......III.4:8 | your picture is **a.** picture of another kind. |
| T-27......III.4:8 | your picture is another picture of **a.** kind. |
| T-27......IV.1:4 | point of view is not an answer in **a.** light. |
| T-27......IV.2:3 | a way of reaching to **a.** state of mind in |
| T-27......IV.7:4 | the answers merely raise **a.** question, |
| T-27.......V.1:6 | No one can ask **a.** to be healed. But he can |
| T-27.......V.1:8 | can bestow upon **a.** what he does not have |
| T-27......VI.2:9 | to name, as one steps forward and **a.** back |
| T-27.....VII.2:3 | be **a.** way to solve a problem that is very |
| T-27.....VII.6:6 | to. Seek not **a.** cause, nor look among the |
| T-27..VII.12:2 | Yet underneath this dream is yet **a.**, in |
| T-28.........I.2:8 | made, it can be used to serve **a.** purpose, |
| T-28.........I.6:1 | time is but **a.** phase of what does nothing. |
| T-28.......I.15:5 | glimpse **a.** shore that he can never reach. |
| T-28........II.5:2 | dream, and can accept **a.** dream as well. |
| T-28........II.5:8 | It does not ask you make **a.**; only that you |
| T-28......II.12:6 | the mind is free to make **a.** choice instead. |
| T-28......III.2:1 | until **a.** mind agrees that they are separate |
| T-28......VI.2:6 | path is changed, it walks as easily **a.** way. |
| T-28......VI.4:7 | Yet it is a promise to **a.** to be hurt by him, |
| T-29......VI.3:6 | your mind, and see **a.** purpose there. |
| T-29 .VIII.8:10 | And when one fails **a.** takes its place, with |
| T-29....IX.10:2 | **a.** try to worship idols and to keep attack. |
| T-30.........I.2:6 | And then **a.** answer cannot but produce |
| T-30.......I.11:4 | *I want **a.** way to look at this.* Now you have |
| T-30.......I.12:3 | *Perhaps there is **a.** way to look at this. What* |
| T-30.....VII.1:8 | else. You take away **a.** element, and every |
| T-30.....VII.2:5 | you see **a.** meaning in what went before. |
| T-31.........I.2:4 | steps that lead you gently from one to **a.**, |
| T-31.......I.7:11 | God's Son is innocent, and see **a.** world. |
| T-31.......I.11:2 | **a.** outcome seen to be preferred. You are |
| T-31......IV.3:3 | begins to see how like they are to one **a.**. |
| T-31......IV.4:1 | Why would you seek to try **a.** road, |
| T-31......IV.4:1 | another road, **a.** person or another place, |
| T-31......IV.4:1 | another road, another person or **a.** place, |
| T-31......IV.4:2 | still believe there is **a.** answer to be found. |
| T-31......IV.4:5 | this. Seek not **a.** signpost in the world that |
| T-31......IV.4:5 | world that seems to point to still **a.** road. |
| T-31......IV.5:2 | begin with this, to seek **a.** way instead? |
| T-31......VI.3:4 | see **a.** world your eyes could never find. Be |
| T-31.....VII.2:3 | yourself and blacken it with still **a.** "crime |
| T-31.....VII.3:6 | you. And in His sight there *is* **a.** world. |
| T-31.....VII.6:5 | to use, and you can see yourself **a.** way. |
| T-31.....VII.9:3 | holds the mirror to **a.** view of what he is, |
| T-31....VIII.4:2 | but see it as it is; **a.** chance to choose again |
| T-31....VIII.9:1 | so many chances to perceive **a.** situation |
| W-pI.......1.3:7 | excluded. One thing is like **a.** as far as the |
| W-pI.......3.2:3 | this purpose one thing is like **a.**; equally |
| W-pI.....10.3:3 | is merely **a.** way of repeating our earlier |
| W-pI.....11.3:1 | move from one thing to **a.** fairly rapidly, |
| W-pI.....12.2:3 | **a.** involves a fairly constant time interval. |
| W-pI.....13.1:1 | idea is really **a.** form of the preceding one, |
| W-pI.....13.5:1 | to avoid resistance, in one form or **a.**, to |
| W-pI.....14.3:1 | The idea for today is **a.** step in learning to |
| W-pI.....17.1:1 | This idea is **a.** step in the direction of |
| W-pI.....18.1:1 | The idea for today is **a.** step in learning |
| W-pI.....22.3:2 | eyes move slowly from one object to **a.**, |
| W-pI.....22.3:2 | one object to another, from one body to **a.** |
| W-pI.....25.3:1 | A. way of describing the goals you now |
| W-pI........33.h | There is **a.** way of looking at the world. |
| W-pI.....33.3:4 | say: *There is **a.** way of looking at this.* |
| W-pI.....37.5:2 | of the idea with your eyes closed, and **a.**, |
| W-pI.....40.3:6 | A. might take this form: *I am blessed as a* |
| W-pI.....42.3:1 | and **a.** as close as possible to the time you |
| W-pI.....44.1:1 | for yesterday, adding **a.** dimension to it. |
| W-pI.....57.3:1 | There is **a.** way of looking at the world. |
| W-pI.....57.3:2 | to it, there must be **a.** way of looking at it. |
| W-pI.....64.1:1 | Today's idea is merely **a.** way of saying |
| W-pI.....64.2:2 | learned that the Holy Spirit has **a.** use for |
| W-pI.....64.2:2 | and therefore He sees **a.** purpose in them. |
| W-pI...66.10:5 | us. Today's idea is **a.** giant stride in the |
| W-pI.....69.2:1 | let us make **a.** real attempt to reach the |
| W-pI.....71.3:4 | A. person will yet serve better; another |
| W-pI.....71.3:4 | better; **a.** situation will yet offer success. |
| W-pI.....76.3:4 | really think you are alone unless **a.** body is |
| W-pI.....77.4:3 | are never taken from one and given to **a.**, |
| WpI..rII.in.1:1 | We are now ready for **a.** review. We will |
| W-pI.....87.3:3 | afraid only when I believe there is **a.** will. I |
| W-pI.....95.9:4 | it is but **a.** way in which you would defend |
| W-pI...96.11:5 | offer Him **a.** treasure to be kept for you. |
| W-pI...96.12:1 | you lay **a.** treasure in your growing store. |
| W-pI...99.10:3 | You do not want to be **a.** self. You have no |
| W-pI...100.5:3 | is the sign that you would play **a.** part, |
| W-pI...105.1:7 | that one can gain because **a.** loses. This |
| W-pI...105.9:4 | him, see it as but **a.** chance to let yourself |
| W-pI...107.2:5 | and then be multiplied **a.** hundred more. |
| W-pI...109.4:6 | will not hear **a.** voice than yours because |
| WpI..rIII.in9:4 | to you. Here is **a.** chance to use it well. |
| W-pI...116.1:3 | *from the belief there is **a.** will apart from His.* |
| W-pI...121.8:3 | in the morning, and at night **a.** ten, to |
| W-pI...122.2:4 | it offers you **a.** day of happiness and peace |
| W-pI...122.4:5 | no more. You will not find **a.** one instead. |
| W-pI 122.12:1 | and you will see **a.** world arise you have |
| W-pI...127.1:2 | loving one, **a.** way of loving still another. |
| W-pI...127.1:2 | loving one, another way of loving still **a.**. |
| W-pI...128.3:3 | and add **a.** bar across the door that leads |
| W-pI...129.7:5 | until where one begins **a.** ends loses all |
| W-pI 132.10:1 | What is the lesson for today except **a.** way |
| W-pI...133.5:1 | A. kindly and related law is that there is |
| W-pI...134.5:2 | to be concealed, denied or called **a.** name, |
| W-pI 135.23:4 | they are answers to **a.** kind of question, |
| W-pI 136.13:4 | For time is but **a.** meaningless defense you |
| W-pI...140.1:5 | One belief in sickness takes **a.** form, and |
| W-pI...140.3:2 | perceive do not induce **a.** form of sleep, so |
| W-pI...140.3:2 | so that the dreamer dreams **a.** dream. His |
| W-pI...140.4:3 | cannot come, for it is but **a.** form of guilt. |
| W-pI...140.7:6 | how can one illusion differ from **a.** but in |
| W-pI...140.8:1 | for all illusions, not **a.** shift among them. |
| W-pI 151.15:1 | give **a.** fifteen more before you go to sleep. |
| W-pI...153.3:1 | wherein **a.** circle bound it and another |
| W-pI...153.3:1 | another circle bound it and **a.** one in that, |
| W-pI...154.9:4 | Yet **a.** part of your appointed task is yet to |

W-pI...155.5:1 Between these paths there is a. road that
W-pI...157.2:1 a. crucial turning point in the curriculum.
W-pI.158.10:5 you meet today provides a. chance to let
W-pI...160.3:3 were a. home more suited to his tastes.
W-pI...162.1:2 repeat it, as we reach a. stage in learning.
W-pI...166.1:6 make you think there is a. will than His?
W-pI...166.2:3 it real must still believe there is a. will,
W-pI.166.13:4 of Christ there is a. way for them to walk.
W-pI...167.7:1 opposite of life can only be a. form of life.
W-pI...170.1:4 you believe to hurt a. brings you freedom.
W-pI...170.8:5 Or will you make a. idol to replace it? For
W-pI...170.8:7 takes many forms. A. can be found.
W-pI.170.11:3 cruel god remain with you in still a. form.
WpI .. rV.in1:3 preparing for a. phase of understanding.
WpI .. rV.in7:5 was begun, to make a. choice with me.
WpI rV.in11:3 same words upon our lips, to greet a. day.
W-pI...183.7:5 or that His Son receive a. name than His.
W-pI...184.2:1 you see as setting off all things from one a.
W-pI...184.7:5 from which a. kind of learning can begin,
W-pI...185.3:5 gain takes on a different aspect or a. form.
W-pI...185.5:4 recognizing that a. dream would offer
W-pI...185.7:4 words do not request a. dream be given us
W-pI...185.7:5 nor try to make a. bargain in the hope
W-pI...186.1:3 to you, without insisting on a. role. It does
W-pI...186.8:2 belief that we can make a. for ourselves.
W-pI...187.5:6 giver who retains; a. who will give as well.
W-pI.193.10:3 Do not try to hold it off a. day, another
W-pI.193.10:3 another day, a. minute or another instant.
W-pI.193.10:3 another day, another minute or a. instant.
W-pI.193.13:1 that lets it be to you a. step to Him, and to
W-pI...194.1:1 idea takes a. step toward quick salvation,
W-pI...195.1:3 because a. seems to suffer more than they.
W-pI...195.1:6 suffer less because he sees a. suffer more?
W-pI...196.1:2 that to attack a. is but to attack yourself.
W-pI...196.6:1 you can attack a. and be free yourself.
W-pI...197.4:1 not matter if a. thinks your gifts unworthy
W-pI...198.4:2 How could there be a. way, when this one
W-pI...200.7:6 Yet can he learn to look on it a. way, and
W-pII..227.1:2 *I thought to make a. will. Yet nothing that I*
W-pII......3.1:4 will the world be seen in quite a. light;
W-pII..241.2:1 *We have forgiven one a. now, and so we*
W-pII......6.1:2 is the Self we share, uniting us with one a.,
W-pII..282.2:3 *truth be changed by merely giving it a. name*
W-pII..294.1:2 And can I be a. thing as well? Did God
W-pII..307.1:3 *to have. Let me not try to make a. will, for it is*
W-pII..309.1:5 I think I made a. will that is not true, and
W-pII..315.1:3 A brother smiles upon a., and my heart is
W-pII..333.1:2 seen somewhere else, called by a. name,
W-pII..334.1:1 I will not wait a. day to find the treasures
W-pII..344.2:1 How near we are to one a., as we go to
W-pII.....356.h Sickness is but a. name for sin. Healing is
W-pII.....356.h sin. Healing is but a. name for God. The
M-2............5:6 they thought separated them from one a.,
M-2............5:9 in a. person the same interests as his own.
M-3............2:5 in the elevator will smile to one a.,
M-4........ II.1:6 and no word lacks agreement with a..
M-5....... III.2:1 to represent a. choice which they had
M-5....... III.3:8 So are they dispelled, not by the will of a.,
M-8............1:4 from a. with less intensity of appeal. And
M-10...........1:5 judgment to one is "bad" judgment to a..
M-10...........1:6 at one time and "bad" judgment at a. time
M-12...........5:9 to give the body a. purpose from the one
M-13...........1:5 device; a. illusion that replaces the first,
M-13...........1:6 before a. thought system can take hold, is
M-16...........9:2 the attempt to substitute a. will for God's.
M-18...........1:7 age-old impossible dream in but a. form.
M-28...........5:9 Illusions of a. will are lost, for unity of
M-29...........3:1 is a. advantage,–and a very important
C-in............3:5 The course merely gives a. answer, once a
C-4.............3:1 for false perception since, being a. level,
P-2...........I.1:6 of them will enter into a. commitment. Be
P-2......... III.3:4 a. hears and tries to answer in the form of
P-2........ IV.5:4 temporary, or a. illness rise instead, for
P-2........ IV.7:8 It will escape and take a. form, being the
P-2........ VI.6:3 and is thus given a. chance to look at it,
P-2....... VII.2:5 cure, when a. is always there to choose?
P-2....... VII.4:2 fundamental confusion in one form or a.,
P-3......... II.1:4 of one sort or a. as their chief function.
P-3......... II.7:3 a brother from one dream than from a..
P-3......... II.8:4 goal is reached a. can be dimly seen ahead
S-1...........I.6:3 that a. mediates between you and God.
S-1...........I.6:4 But it does mean that a. stands beside you
S-1...........I.7:9 if you are genuinely attuned to one a.. It
S-1......... II.6:5 You do not choose for a.. You can but
S-1......... III.2:5 Hell cannot be asked for a., and then
S-1......... III.4:6 be recognized as long as he hides it in a.,
S-2...........I.4:2 It is impossible to forgive a., for it is only
S-2...........I.4:4 That is why forgiveness of a. is an illusion.
S-2...........I.5:2 It always seems to be a. who is evil, and in
S-2......... II.2:4 And who can tell a. he is steeped in sin,
S-2......... II.3:1 A. form, still very like the first if it is
S-2......... II.4:5 saintliness the anger and the hurt a. gives,
S-2........ III.3:4 be to you a. step to Heaven and to peace.
S-3......... III.1:6 false, there is some power that a. has, not
S-3........ III.3:2 And to this wiser one a. goes to profit by

## another's 14

T-3...........I.2:1 as always, is not to attack a. position, but
T-21..... V.3:10 that miracles do not affect a. mind, only
T-23....... II.9:4 By this, a. loss becomes your gain, and
T-25. VIII.13:8 He is no judge of what must be a. due,
T-25VIII.13:10 and cannot fairly see a. rights because his
T-27..... VII.4:8 And he must see it in a. hand, if he would
T-28....... II.7:7 fear his own attack, but sees it at a. hands.
T-28...... VI.5:2 with a. secret wish to be apart from you,
W-pI...185.4:8 each to his gain and to a. loss.
M-22 .........5:2 is. A. sickness thus becomes his own. In
M-22 .........5:3 to happen, he has identified with a. ego,
S-1......... IV.3:4 to be; what was a. and he seemed to love,
S-2......... II.4:2 who seek the role of martyr at a. hand.
S-2......... II.4:4 Is it not kind to be accepting of a. spite,

## Answer 42

*answer*

T-5......... II.2:5 Holy Spirit is God's A. to the separation;
T-5........ III.5:3 that the Holy Spirit is God's A. to the ego.
T-6...........IV.h The Only A.
T-6........ IV.1:1 Remember that the Holy Spirit is the A.,
T-6.... IV.12:10 He merely gave the A.. His Answer is your
T-6.... IV.12:11 gave the Answer. His A. is your Teacher.
T-7........ III.5:3 The A. merely undoes the question by
T-8........ IX.1:1 I said before that the Holy Spirit is the A..
T-8........ IX.1:2 He is the A. to everything, because He
T-9......... II.4:3 you would know God and His A., believe
T-9......... II.8:7 Hear only God's A. in His Sons, and you
T-9... VIII.11:9 with His Own exalted A. to what you are,
T-11... VIII.4:2 Yet God will not refuse you the A. He gave
T-11. VIII.10:5 not disappear in the Presence of God's A.?
T-12.........I.5:7 you will not recognize God's A. to you.
T-12.........I.7:3 recognize God's A. as you want It to be,
T-12..... II.2:10 and God's A. to your forgetting is but the
T-12... VIII.4:4 what you have not heard is the only A..
T-13....... V.7:5 sane A. tells you what you have offered
T-13...... VI.9:3 return your thanks in His clear A. to your
T-16...... III.5:4 God's A. to the separation added more to
T-17...... IV.4:1 Who was God's A. to the separation. For
T19....IV.C.5:7 with His Own; an A. which left Him not,
T19....IV.C.5:7 mind which heard His A. and accepted It.
T19....IV.C.7:2 the light of truth, the answer to the A., the
T19....IV.C.7:4 Only God's A. is its end. The obstacle of
T-26..... V.12:4 it took for God to give His A. to illusion
T-30....... II.2:6 your will when He gave you His perfect A.
W-pI.135.23:4 of answering until the A. comes to you at
W-pI.166.10:5 not understand, to which He gave an A..
W-pI.166.10:7 And you who have this A. given you have
W-pII..267.2:1 *Let me attend Your A., not my own. Father,*
W-pII......6.2:3 He is the part in which God's A. lies;
M-2 ...........2:6 in that same instant was God's A. given.
M-4 ...... IX.1:6 To give up all problems to one A. is to
M-11 .........3:1 is the A. to all problems you have made.
M-16 .........1:9 he keeps in constant contact with the A..
M-23 .........7:7 In him you find God's A.. Do you, then,
P-1.............2:2 to learn to call upon God and hear His A.?
P-2......... V.6:7 He will send His A. through the therapist
P-2....... VII.7:8 in him, for what you see will be your A..
S-2........ III.5:9 own. He is the A.. You the one who hears.

## answer 364

*Answer*

T-3........ III.2:5 It is the right a. to a question, but you do
T-3........ III.2:7 The miracle, or the right a., corrects them
T-3......... V.4:3 that the a. is not only one you know, but
T-4..........II.1:3 no point in giving an a. in terms of the
T-4.......... III.6:4 He has never failed to a. this request,
T-4..... IV.11:10 I have called and you will a.. I understand
T-4..... IV.11:12 My calling you is as natural as your a.,
T-4.......... V.4:9 has no real a. to this because there is none
T-5....... II.8:10 call you a. now is an evaluation because it
T-5....... II.10:8 Everyone will a. the Call of the Holy Spirit
T-5....... II.12:6 away as you a. the Holy Spirit within you.
T-6........ IV.2:6 was ever asked, but one it can never a..
T-6........ IV.2:9 you have the a. and *the ego is afraid of you.*
T-6........ IV.3:4 means that everyone has the a. *now.*
T-6........ IV.6:1 the one a. of the Holy Spirit to all the
T-8..........II.2:4 never given you a sensible a. to anything.
T-8..........II.8:5 the Kingdom, in a. to the Call for God.
T-8...... VIII.7:4 of a teacher who does not know the a..
T-8....... IX.1:2 He knows what the a. to everything is.
T-9...........I.7:1 insist that the Holy Spirit does not a. you,
T-9.........I.10:1 cannot a. because nothing can hurt you,
T-9........... II.h The A. to Prayer
T-9..........II.3:4 It is possible that His a. will not be heard.
T-9........ II.5:10 His words are the Holy Spirit's a. to you.
T-9..........II.6:6 And His a. is only for what you are. You
T-9........ II.6:11 you hear His a. except as He answers all of
T-9..........II.7:6 The a. to all prayers lies in them. You will
T-9..........II.7:7 answered as you hear the a. in everyone.
T-9..........II.8:3 will a. you if you learn to ask only truth of
T-9....... II.12:4 is the way, and the only way to have His a.
T-9....... II.12:4 His a. is all you can ask for and want. Say,
T-9......... V.2:3 not have the a. to the problem of healing.
T-9......... V.7:5 his mind will therefore a. the questioner,
T-9...... VIII.6:3 ego. Your grandeur is God's a. to the ego,
T-9.... VIII.11:6 will tell you, but do not be afraid of His a.,
T-9.... VIII.11:7 It is an exalted a. because of its Source,
T-9.... VIII.11:7 but the Source is true and so is Its a..
T-10...... IV.8:7 faith in it, and God Himself will a. you.
T-11.......in.1:7 decision is always an a. to the question,
T-11.......in.4:8 Will you not a. the call of love with joy?
T-11.......VIII.h The Problem and the A.
T-11.... VIII.4:6 *Do I want the problem or do I want the a.?*
T-11.... VIII.4:7 Decide for the a. and you will have it, for
T-11.... VIII.5:5 Holy Spirit will a. every specific problem
T-11.... VIII.5:6 His a. is both many and one, as long as
T-11.... VIII.6:4 the question you must ask to learn His a.?
T-11.... VIII.6:5 heard the a., but you have misunderstood
T-11.... VIII.7:7 learn that His a. is the release from fear.
T-11.... VIII.8:7 Not one of us but has the a. in him, to give
T-11.... VIII.9:1 of God's Son and his Father will a. you,
T-11..VIII.14:3 the Teacher of reality, and hearing His a.,
T-12.........I.7:4 Every appeal you a. in the Name of Christ
T-12.........I.7:5 for help as what it is, so God can a. *you.*
T-12........II.3:5 A. his call for love, and yours is answered.
T-12...... III.5:3 "how" of salvation, and this is the only a..
T-12...... III.5:4 for an instant, that there is another a.. For
T-12... VII.11:3 will not look upon me nor hear the a. that
T-12... VIII.4:3 it. A Voice will a. every question you ask,
T-13...... III.2:6 you to a. His Call and leap into Heaven.
T-13... III.12:6 He could but a. your insane request with a
T-13... III.12:6 your insane request with a sane a. that
T-13... III.12:8 who hears His a. but will give up insanity.
T-13... III.12:9 a. is the reference point beyond illusions,
T-13....... V.3:3 are not there, and it is they who a. them.
T-13....... V.3:4 no one hears their a. save him who called
T-13... VII.10:7 Without the Holy Spirit the a. would be
T-13... VII.10:8 Yet because of Him the a. is a joyous *yes!*
T-13....... XI.6:4 you will find the a. that makes the need
T-14.... III.11:2 bereft of help, and Help that knows the a..
T-14.... III.11:6 Instead, accept His a., for He knows that
T-14.... III.16:4 teach His a. to everyone who struggles in
T-14.... III.17:5 Trust Him to a. quickly, surely, and with
T-14.... IV.10:4 only the Holy Spirit can a. God for you,
T-14....... V.4:4 to light, in a. to the call of the Atonement.
T-14........X.6:8 The a. is very simple. The power of God,
T-14...... X.10:4 only the a. with which He answers you.
T-14...... XI.8:6 miracles to a. all your problems for you.

| | |
|---|---|
| T-15...... III.5:3 | For every decision you make does **a.** this, |
| T-15.... III.12:4 | that his call is yours, and **a.** him with me. |
| T-15...... IV.8:4 | **a.** is no, then the Holy Spirit's readiness to |
| T-15...... VI.4:2 | him, your hope of **a.** is diminished. On |
| T-15....... X.7:5 | seek to **a.** this question in your special |
| T-15....... X.9:8 | In you are both the question and the **a.**; |
| T-16.... IV.11:7 | He not **a.** you whose completion is His? |
| T-16.... IV.12:6 | in joyous **a.** to His Call for His completion |
| T-16.... IV.13:5 | and **a.** fearlessly the Call of Him Who gave |
| T-17...... IV.3:2 | it does constantly, you **a.** with a substitute |
| T-17...... IV.4:1 | special relationship was the ego's **a.** to the |
| T-17....... V.7:8 | Has He not been very explicit in His **a.**? |
| T-17.... VIII.1:3 | that faith might **a.** to the call of truth. The |
| T-17.... VIII.3:8 | **a.** truth with faith entails no strain at all. |
| T-18...... IV.1:2 | It is the **a.**. The desire and the willingness |
| T-18...... IV.5:2 | The **a.** is given. Seek not to answer, but |
| T-18...... IV.5:3 | Seek not to **a.**, but merely to receive the |
| T-18...... IV.5:3 | but merely to receive the **a.** as it is given. |
| T-18.... VI.14:7 | you, in **a.** to its gentle call to be at peace. |
| T-18.. VIII.11:2 | Love's **a.** is inevitable. It will come |
| T-19...... IV.1:8 | for you will call to him and he will **a.** you, |
| T19.... IV.B.7:6 | of the end of guilt, and all the world will **a.** |
| T19.... IV.C.7:2 | the light of truth, the **a.** to the Answer, the |
| T-20...... III.4:1 | question yet remains, and needs an **a.**. Do |
| T-20...... III.6:7 | of the world as **a.** to the question, "What |
| T-20...... III.7:7 | and it is to his **a.** that you would adjust. |
| T-20...... III.8:2 | And if you have, would you believe the **a.**, |
| T-20...... III.8:3 | world you look on is the **a.** that it gave you |
| T-20...... III.8:3 | to adjust the world to make its **a.** true. |
| T-20...... III.8:4 | and adjusted it according to its insane **a.**. |
| T-21....... V.4:7 | But think not reason could not **a.** it. |
| T-21....... V.5:9 | ego is proof you will not find the **a.** there. |
| T-21....... V.6:5 | for this must have an **a.** if the plan of God |
| T-21....... V.7:1 | Where would the **a.** be but in the Source? |
| T-21....... V.7:2 | are you but there, where this same **a.** is? |
| T-21....... V.7:3 | true Effect of this same Source as is the **a.**, |
| T-21..... VII.8:1 | Consider carefully your **a.** to the last |
| T-21... VII.12:3 | been made, the **a.** is both "yes" and "no." |
| T-21.... VIII.3:6 | whom God Himself will never fail to **a.**. |
| T-21.... VIII.4:1 | how you would **a.** the final question. Your |
| T-21.... VIII.4:2 | Your **a.** to the others has made it possible |
| T-24....... II.4:3 | **a.** that the Holy Spirit gives can reach you, |
| T-24....... II.4:4 | Its tiny **a.**, soundless in the melody that |
| T-24...... IV.4:3 | To specialness the **a.** must be "no." A |
| T-24..... VII.6:2 | The **a.** makes it what it is for you. It has no |
| T-25....... V.3:5 | **a.** by returning unto God what is His Own |
| T-25.... VIII.4:1 | not of justice still can ask, and learn the **a.** |
| T-25...... IX.1:4 | You cannot **a.** this until you see all that |
| T-25...... IX.1:4 | until you see all that the **a.** must entail. |
| T-25...... IX.1:5 | For if you **a.** "yes" it means you will forego |
| T-25...... IX.3:1 | certain any **a.** to a problem the Holy Spirit |
| T-25...... IX.3:3 | An **a.** which demands the slightest loss to |
| T-26....... V.3:7 | God gave **a.** to is answered and is gone. |
| T-26....... V.5:3 | too short to make a world in **a.** to creation |
| T-26..... VII.4:2 | has God given **a.** to the world of sickness, |
| T-26..... VII.4:3 | God's **a.** is eternal, though it works in |
| T-26..... VII.5:1 | God's **a.** lies where the belief in sin must |
| T-26..... VII.6:9 | ease to what God gave as **a.** to them all. |
| T-26... VII.10:2 | In joyous **a.** will creation rise within you, |
| T-26... VII.15:4 | lies, for God gave **a.** to them all as one. |
| T-26... VII.17:2 | Forgiveness is the **a.** to attack of any kind. |
| T-26... VII.18:2 | to make use of what He gave to **a.** all His |
| T-26... VII.18:5 | There is no circumstance it cannot **a.**, and |
| T-26... VII.20:2 | on your brother's name and God will **a.**, |
| T-26... VII.20:3 | Could He refuse to **a.** when He has already |
| T-27......... IV.h | The Quiet A. |
| T-27...... IV.1:2 | there can be no **a.** and no resolution, for |
| T-27...... IV.1:2 | possible, and to ensure no **a.** will be plain. |
| T-27...... IV.1:3 | A problem set in conflict has no **a.**, for it |
| T-27...... IV.1:4 | And what would be an **a.** from one point |
| T-27...... IV.1:4 | point of view is not an **a.** in another light. |
| T-27...... IV.1:6 | be clear you cannot **a.** anything at all, for |
| T-27...... IV.1:7 | Yet if God gave an **a.** there must be a way |
| T-27...... IV.2:3 | of mind in which the **a.** is already there. |
| T-27...... IV.2:6 | Here they belong, for here their **a.** is. And |
| T-27...... IV.2:7 | is. And where its **a.** is, a problem must be |
| T-27...... IV.2:8 | to solve a problem where the **a.** cannot be. |
| T-27...... IV.2:9 | resolved, if it is brought to where the **a.** is. |
| T-27...... IV.3:3 | for there is no **a.** there that could be found |
| T-27 ..... IV.4:2 | be answered, because it is an **a.** in itself. A |
| T-27 ..... IV.5:1 | A pseudo-question has no **a.**. It dictates |
| T-27 ..... IV.5:2 | It dictates the **a.** even as it asks. Thus is all |
| T-27 ..... IV.5:8 | *want* an honest **a.** where the conflict ends. |
| T-27 ..... IV.6:2 | does the meaningfulness of the **a.** come. |
| T-27 ..... IV.6:3 | to separate your wishes from the **a.**, so it |
| T-27 ..... IV.6:4 | The **a.** is provided everywhere. Yet it is |
| T-27 ..... IV.6:6 | An honest **a.** asks no sacrifice because it |
| T-27 ..... IV.6:8 | And so, unless the **a.** tells "of whom," it |
| T-27 ..... IV.6:8 | intact because it gave the **a.** to itself. The |
| T-27 ..... IV.6:9 | to hear an **a.** that is not entailed within |
| T-27 ..... IV.7:1 | a world from which the **a.** has been barred |
| T-27 ..... IV.7:2 | place that holds the **a.** lovingly for you. |
| T-27 ..... IV.7:5 | you can bring the question to the **a.**, and |
| T-27 ..... IV.7:5 | and receive the **a.** that was made for you. |
| T-27 .... V.10:7 | And their common **a.** shows the questions |
| T-27 ..... VI.2:5 | and so it seems to **a.** to a different sound. |
| T-27 .VIII.11:3 | will make **a.** with this very simple truth. |
| T-27 .VIII.11:4 | one **a.** takes away the cause of every form |
| T-27 .VIII.11:5 | The form affects His **a.** not at all, for He |
| T-29 .... VII.1:4 | when God calls will never **a.** in His place. |
| T-29 .... VII.1:5 | There is no other **a.** you can substitute, |
| T-29 .... VII.1:5 | and find the happiness His **a.** brings. Seek |
| T-30 ........ I.2:6 | And then another **a.** cannot but produce |
| T-30 ........ I.5:2 | Now the **a.** will provoke attack, unless you |
| T-30 ........ I.5:2 | your mind to want an **a.** that will work. Be |
| T-30 ........ I.5:3 | to sit by and ask to have the **a.** given you. |
| T-30 ........ I.6:2 | and must have set an **a.** in your terms. |
| T-30 ........ I.6:6 | lets the **a.** show you what the question |
| T-30 ........ I.7:3 | in which you get *your* **a.** to *your* question. |
| T-30 ....... I.12:5 | and so the **a.** will make sense as well. Nor |
| T-30 ..... III.4:6 | **a.** you in terms that have no meaning. |
| T-30 ..... VI.1:9 | the **a.** to attack that has been made. And |
| T-30 ... VIII.3:5 | And Heaven gives no **a.** to the prayer, nor |
| T-31 ........ I.9:2 | Without your **a.** is it left to die, as it is |
| T-31 ....... I.10:5 | give Him **a.** in the language that He calls. |
| T-31 ....... I.11:7 | For as you hear, you **a.**. And behold! Your |
| T-31 ....... I.11:9 | Your **a.** is the proof of what you learned. |
| T-31 ..... II.5:10 | with him and in your **a.** is salvation found |
| T-31 ....... II.6:1 | Before you **a.**, pause to think of this: *The* |
| T-31 ....... II.6:2 | ***a.*** *that I give my brother is what I am asking* |
| T-31 ....... II.7:1 | and **a.** to the Christ Who calls to you. Be |
| T-31 ....... II.7:5 | hearing but one **a.** to them all. Because He |
| T-31 ....... II.7:6 | He cannot hear a different **a.** from the one |
| T-31 .... II.10:4 | in him, but it is not the form you **a.** to. He |
| T-31 ..... III.2:5 | You **a.** "yes" whenever you attack, for by |
| T-31 ..... IV.4:2 | Its purpose is the **a.** to the search that all |
| T-31 ..... IV.4:2 | still believe there is another **a.** to be found |
| T-31 ..... IV.4:3 | despair, there is no hope of **a.** in the world |
| T-31 ..... V.14:2 | he must find the **a.** to the riddle of himself |
| T-31 ..... V.14:7 | the self appear to **a.** what it does not know |
| T-31 .. VII.13:6 | Then is the **a.** given. And the door held |
| W-pI..... 22.3:9 | *I really want to see?* The **a.** is surely obvious. |
| W-pI..... 27.4:3 | A. one of these questions, and you have |
| W-pI..... 39.4:1 | is the **a.** to every question that was ever |
| W-pI..... 47.8:2 | often. Use it as your **a.** to any disturbance. |
| W-pI..... 50.1:1 | **a.** to every problem that will confront you |
| W-pI..... 50.4:4 | is the **a.** to whatever confronts you today. |
| W-pI..... 61.4:2 | It is the perfect **a.** to all illusions, and |
| W-pI..... 65.3:4 | It gives you the **a.** to all the searching you |
| W-pI..... 69.8:2 | You may not recognize His **a.** yet, but you |
| W-pI..... 71.6:3 | The idea for today is the **a.**. Only God's |
| W-pI..... 71.7:2 | And let us rejoice that there is an **a.** to |
| W-pI..... 71.9:7 | will **a.** in proportion to your willingness |
| W-pI... 71.9:10 | enough to establish your claim to God's **a.** |
| W-pI... 72.10:9 | Then we will wait in quiet for His **a.**. We |
| W-pI... 72.11:7 | **a.** will be true because of Whom you ask. |
| W-pI... 72.12:5 | He will **a.**. Be determined to hear. |
| W-pI... 72.13:6 | with your eyes closed, and listen for His **a.** |
| W-pI..... 77.6:7 | **a.** is a simple statement of a simple fact. |
| W-pI..... 77.8:1 | to be satisfied with less than the perfect **a.** |
| W-pI..... 79.2:4 | Even if he is given the **a.**, he cannot see its |
| W-pI..... 79.3:2 | You have the **a.**, but you are still uncertain |
| W-pI..... 79.4:2 | of problems, each requiring a different **a.**. |
| W-pI..... 79.6:2 | the **a.** because you would see its relevance. |
| W-pI..... 79.7:1 | the problem is, and what is the **a.** to it. |
| W-pI..... 79.7:5 | We will ask what it is, and wait for the **a.**. |
| W-pI..... 79.8:4 | given the **a.** by recognizing the problem, |
| W-pI..... 79.8:4 | so that the problem and the **a.** can be |
| W-pI .... 79.9:2 | problems today, each one calling for an **a.** |
| W-pI .... 79.9:3 | that there is only one problem and one **a.**. |
| W-pI .... 80.2:3 | for the Holy Spirit to give you God's **a.**. |
| W-pI .... 80.2:5 | yourself by bringing the problem to the **a.** |
| W-pI .... 80.2:6 | And you can recognize the **a.**, because the |
| W-pI .... 80.4:1 | and the **a.** have been brought together. |
| W-pI .... 80.4:2 | be gone, because God's **a.** cannot fail. |
| W-pI .... 80.4:5 | are answered, and have accepted the **a.**. |
| W-pI .... 90.2:4 | *The* ***a.*** *to this problem is the miracle that it* |
| W-pI .... 90.3:4 | the **a.** as simultaneous in their occurrence. |
| W-pI .... 90.3:5 | placed the **a.** together with the problem, |
| W-pI .... 90.4:3 | *The* ***a.*** *to this problem is already given me, if I* |
| W-pI .... 98.4:3 | and **a.** it when they have come to make |
| W-pI .... 98.9:3 | trust will be His gifts; His **a.** to your words |
| W-pI .... 99.6:6 | He has one **a.** to appearances; regardless |
| W-pI 100.10:7 | And it is Him you **a.**, every time you tell |
| W-pI .. 106.8:1 | Ask and expect an **a.**. Your request is one |
| W-pI .. 106.8:2 | request is one whose **a.** has been waiting |
| W-pI .. 109.1:4 | will **a.** our asking with what we request. |
| W-pI .. 121.1:1 | Here is the **a.** to your search for peace. |
| W-pI .. 122.4:1 | Why would you seek an **a.** other than the |
| W-pI .. 122.4:1 | than the **a.** that will answer everything? |
| W-pI .. 122.4:1 | than the answer that will **a.** everything? |
| W-pI .. 122.4:2 | Here is the perfect **a.**, given to imperfect |
| W-pI .. 122.4:3 | Here is the **a.**! Seek for it no more. You |
| W-pI .. 122.6:1 | Here is the **a.**! Would you stand outside |
| W-pI .. 122.6:6 | that this is so, for here we have an **a.**, clear |
| W-pI .. 122.7:1 | is the **a.**! Do not turn away in aimless |
| W-pI .. 122.9:2 | accepting Heaven's **a.** to the hell we made, |
| W-pI 122.11:1 | and what your acceptance of the **a.** brings. |
| W-pI .. 127.9:1 | your Father, certain that His Voice will **a.**. |
| W-pI 133.14:2 | be quick to **a.** with this simple thought: *I* |
| W-pI .. 139.3:7 | Whom does he question? Who can **a.** him |
| W-pI .. 139.4:2 | never be alive at all unless he knew the **a.**. |
| W-pI 139.5:10 | For it asks of one who knows the **a.**. Were |
| W-pI 140.12:6 | to hear the **a.** to our prayer be given us as |
| W-pI 152.12:2 | God's Voice will **a.**, for He speaks for you |
| W-pI .. 161.1:3 | Here is the **a.** to temptation which can |
| W-pI .. 161.1:5 | Here is the **a.** of the Voice for God. |
| W-pI 161.12:1 | And He will **a.** Whom you called upon. |
| W-pI 161.12:2 | Voice for God in you, and **a.** in your own. |
| W-pI .. 162.1:4 | God gave in **a.** to the world you made. By |
| W-pI .. 162.2:5 | The dead awake in **a.** to its call. And those |
| W-pI .. 164.2:3 | call to which He gives an ancient **a.**. You |
| W-pI .. 164.2:4 | are but your **a.** to your Father's Call to you |
| W-pI .. 168.2:3 | His grace His **a.** is to all despair, for in it |
| W-pI .. 168.3:5 | His gift of grace is more than just an **a.**. It |
| WpI...rV.in8:1 | and knows the **a.** God has given Him. |
| W-pI .. 183.7:2 | And God will come, and **a.** it Himself. |
| W-pI 183.11:5 | Voice gives **a.** in his Father's holy Name. |
| W-pI 184.12:6 | what God has given as the **a.** to the pitiful |
| W-pI 185.11:4 | who requests an **a.** which is his to give? |
| W-pI 186.13:4 | has Thoughts which **a.** every need His Son |
| W-pI 193.13:2 | To all that speaks of terror, **a.** thus: *I will* |
| W-pI 198.2:10 | Forgiveness is illusion that is **a.** to the rest. |
| W-pI .. 198.5:1 | hold the **a.** to your problems in your hand |
| W-pI .. 200.8:3 | Peace is the **a.** to conflicting goals, to |
| W-pII . 221.1:5 | *love, sure You will hear my call and* ***a.*** *me.* |
| W-pII . 221.2:6 | intent; to hear our Father's **a.** to our call, |
| W-pII . 232.1:3 | *will be there to hear my call to You and* ***a.*** *me* |
| W-pII . 321.2:1 | Today we **a.** for the world, which will be |
| W-pII .... 327.h | I need but call and You will **a.** me. |
| W-pII . 327.1:2 | He will hear my call, and **a.** me Himself. |
| W-pII . 356.1:1 | *to* ***a.*** *any call Your Son might make to You. It* |
| W-pII . 356.1:3 | *He is Your Son, and You will* ***a.*** *him. The* |
| W-pII . 356.1:6 | *Your Name gives* ***a.*** *to Your Son, because to* |
| W-pII .... 358.h | can be sure; His **a.** is the one I really want. |
| W-pII .... 359.h | God's **a.** is some form of peace. All pain Is |
| Wfl........ in.6:3 | Son? Or would He rush to **a.** him, and say, |
| Wfl........ in.6:4 | Be certain He will **a.** thus, for these are His |
| WpII361-5.1:5 | And He will hear and **a.** me, because He |
| W-ep......... 1:5 | troubles you, be certain that He has the **a.**, |
| M-in........ 5:12 | manual attempts to **a.** these questions. |
| M-1........... 2:7 | Many hear It, but few will **a.**. Yet it is all a |
| M-1........... 2:9 | Everyone will **a.** in the end, but the end |
| M-4.... VIII.1:4 | The time will be as right as is the **a.**. And |
| M-5...... II.1:10 | or describe the problem. They do not **a.** it. |
| M-8........... 6:8 | one **a.** to sickness of any kind is healing. |
| M-8........... 6:9 | healing. The one **a.** to all illusions is truth. |

M-9............2:2 decisions; he asks his Teacher for His **a.**,
M-11..........3:4 –God has sent His Judgment to **a.** yours.
M-11..........4:7 And peace descends on it in joyous **a.**.
M-11........4:10 gracious Presence, and it leans down in **a.**,
M-12..........1:1 **a.** to this question is–one. One wholly
M-14..........2:7 It is His Call God's teachers **a.**, turning to
M-17..........3:6 is easily responded to with just one **a.**, and
M-17..........3:6 **a.** will enter the teacher's mind unfailingly
M-18..........3:6 Correction has one **a.** to all this, and to
M-23..........7:6 Jesus has come to **a.** yours. In him you
M-24..........5:2 The **a.** is, certainly not! If he does believe
M-25..........1:1 The **a.** to this question is much like the
M-26..........4:6 Behold the problem, ask for the **a.**, and
M-29..........1:1 manual is not intended to **a.** all questions
M-29..........2:4 one should attempt to **a.** these questions
M-29..........2:7 Ask and He will **a.**. The responsibility is
C-in............3:5 The course merely gives another **a.**, once a
C-in............3:6 However, this **a.** does not attempt to
C-in............4:2 of a question to which an **a.** is impossible.
C-in............4:4 Yet there is no **a.**; only an experience.
C-2.............3:5 And yet there is an **a.** even here.
C-2.............4:4 you can see the only **a.** that is meaningful.
C-2.............8:4 Would it not **a.** all you thought to ask,
C-2.............9:1 Your questions have no **a.**, being made to
C-2...........10:4 is? Problem and **a.** lie together here, and
C-6.............2:1 as giving us the **a.** to the separation and
P-2........III.3:4 hears and tries to **a.** in the form of help.
P-2.........V.4:5 that He will hear and **a.** them in truth.
P-2.........V.6:8 Perhaps the **a.** does not seem to be a gift
P-2.........V.8:4 Hear a brother call for help and **a.** him. It
P-2.........V.8:5 It will be God to Whom you **a.**, for you
P-2........VI.3:4 may be. They **a.** the decisions of the mind,
P-2.......VII.7:7 What **a.** can he give to one who seems to
P-2.......VII.9:6 in him an **a.** that you have refused to give?
P-3...........I.2:4 And that is the **a.**; listen. Do not demand,
P-3...........I.4:9 Yet would he not rejoice that he can **a.**,
P-3.........II.1:1 Strictly speaking the **a.** is no. How could a
S-1...........I.2:1 told to ask the Holy Spirit for the **a.** to any
S-1...........I.2:1 you will receive a specific **a.** if such is your
S-1...........I.2:2 that there is only one problem and one **a.**.
S-1...........I.2:7 The form of the **a.**, if given by God, will
S-1...........I.4:5 His **a.** be but your remembrance of Him?
S-1........III.2:4 god, and it is he who seems to **a.** them.
S-1........III.3:1 to recognize that prayer will bring an **a.**
S-1........IV.3:2 Cause only can the **a.** come in which are
S-2........III.2:5 in any form, He is the One to **a.** for you.
S-2........III.5:6 knows the need; the question and the **a.**.
S-2......III.6:11 His **a.** will be clear as morning, nor is His
S-2........III.7:5 angels down to **a.** you in His Own Name.
S-3........III.4:2 In arrogance the **a.** must be "no." But in

### answered 76

T-4........III.6:5 Those who call truly are always **a.**. Thou
T-4........V.4:11 it cannot be **a.** because it cannot be asked.
T-5.........V.6:2 "What do you want?" must be **a.**. You are
T-6........IV.2:8 The ego has never **a.** any questions since,
T-6........IV.3:3 in one way or another, and has been **a.**.
T-6........IV.7:3 Having finally been wholly **a.**, *it has never*
T-7........III.5:2 and when you question it you are **a.**. The
T-9...........I.9:9 Ask for this and you will be **a.**, because
T-9.........II.3:1 The Bible emphasizes that all prayer is **a.**,
T-9.........II.4:1 If you would know your prayers are **a.**,
T-9.........II.7:7 be **a.** as you hear the answer in everyone.
T-9.........II.8:7 God's Answer in His Sons, and you are **a.**.
T-10.......V.7:3 When you think He has not **a.** your call,
T-10.......V.7:3 answered your call, you have not **a.** His.
T-10.......V.7:5 If you hear His message He has **a.** you,
T-11......VI.2:4 are all the same, and are **a.** together.
T-11... VIII.4:4 You made the problem God has **a.**. Ask
T-12.......II.3:5 Answer his call for love, and yours is **a.**.
T-12...VII.11:3 I have heard your call and I have **a.** it, but
T-13.......V.3:4 them, and he alone believes they **a.** him.
T-13......VI.9:6 Him. And in Him you are **a.** by His peace.
T-17.......V.7:6 Have faith in Him Who **a.** you. He heard.
T-17... VIII.6:7 you separate from Him Whose Call you **a.**
T-18......III.6:7 when you joined your brother, you **a.** me.
T-19......IV.2:5 He **a.** you, and entered your relationship.
T19... IV.A.5:7 fall away because of the appeal you **a.**.
T19... IV.A.5:8 From you who **a.**, He Who answered you
T19... IV.A.5:8 who answered, He Who **a.** you would call.
T19....IV.C.5:7 God has **a.** this insane idea with His Own;
T19... IV.D.5:9 them, you **a.** and they disappeared.
T-20......III.6:6 He Who watches over all perception **a.**.
T-21.....VII.6:1 already have **a.** the first three questions,
T-21.....VII.8:2 let your reason tell you that it must be **a.**,
T-21.....VII.8:2 be answered, and is **a.** in the other three.
T-21...VII.11:7 you do not want, the rest are wholly **a.**.
T-21...VII.12:1 you are unsure the others have been **a.**?
T-21...VII.12:4 For you have **a.** "yes" without perceiving
T-21... VIII.5:5 For here the final question is already **a.**,
T-22......VI.8:4 is your function here, and have been **a.**.
T-22....VI.13:7 only question to be **a.** in order to decide
T-26.......II.1:7 until it has been **a.** for all time and will
T-26.......V.3:7 God gave answer to is **a.** and is gone.
T-26...VII.17:3 effects, and hate is **a.** in the name of love.
T-26...VII.20:3 He has already **a.** all who call on Him? A
T-27......IV.1:1 In quietness are all things **a.**, and is every
T-27......IV.2:1 and every problem can be **a.** *now.* Yet it
T-27......IV.3:2 there the problem *will* be **a.** and resolved.
T-27......IV.3:8 do. It does not ask a question to be **a.**, but
T-27......IV.4:2 A question asked in hate cannot be **a.**,
T-27....IV.6:11 How could it be **a.** if it but repeats itself?
T-27......IV.7:3 apart from them, and see what can be **a.**;
T-30.........I.7:3 And your fear of being **a.** in a different
T-31.......I.10:6 He will appear when you have **a.** Him,
W-pI.....27.4:3 these questions, and you have **a.** the other
W-pI.....69.8:1 certain that He has heard you and **a.** you.
W-pI...72.11:3 Ask and you will be **a.**. Seek and you will
W-pI...79.10:6 it is. You will be heard and you will be **a.**.
W-pI.....80.1:2 Your one central problem has been **a.**,
W-pI.....80.4:5 You are **a.**, and have accepted the answer.
W-pI.....96.7:3 you and **a.** in your name that it was done.
W-pI...121.1:4 Here are all questions **a.**; here the end of
W-pI.122.11:1 the sure rewards of questions **a.** and what
W-pI...137.7:2 but be real, then questions have been **a.**.
W-pI...160.8:3 has **a.** you who ask, "Who is the stranger?
W-pI.166.11:2 The wish for death is **a.**, and the sight that
W-pI.170.12:5 The Call for God is heard and **a.**. Now has
W-pI.189.10:2 *But we have called, and You have* **a.** *us. We*
W-pII..267.1:7 Name, and every one is **a.** by His Voice,
W-pII..285.1:2 and realize my invitation will be **a.** by the
M-1...........2:3 They are the ones who have **a.**. The Call is
M-2...........1:1 look for him as soon as he has **a.** the Call.
M-13.........6:6 have been called by God, and you have **a.**.
M-16.........1:9 It has been asked and **a.**, and he keeps in
P-2.........V.5:5 distress can be but **a.** by his Father. Yet
S-1...........I.7:7 one who knows that this is true is to be **a.**.
S-3.........II.1:7 wish is death a certainty, for prayer *is* **a.**.

### answering 9

T-5.........V.6:3 are **a.** it every minute and every second,
T-12.........I.5:6 for only by **a.** his appeal *can* you be helped.
T-12.......I.10:2 than by **a.** the appeal for it by giving it?
T-14......IV.6:4 delay in **a.** your every question what to do
T-21...VII.11:5 By **a.** the final question "yes," you add
W-pI.....39.2:3 hesitation you may feel in **a.** is not due to
W-pI.135.23:4 of **a.** until the Answer comes to you at last
W-pI...156.8:4 you in **a.** your question with these words:
M-1...........3:8 He has become a savior by his **a.**. He has

### answers 49

T-3........III.3:1 in time, and therefore looks for future **a.**.
T-3........IV.3:2 but not of perceiving meaningful **a.**,
T-5.......II.10:2 it hears only one Voice and **a.** in only one
T-6........IV.3:2 not speak first, *but He always* **a.**. Everyone
T-6........IV.3:4 Since the Holy Spirit **a.** truly He answers
T-6........IV.3:4 the Holy Spirit answers truly He **a.** for all
T-6.........V.4:2 always **a.** their call, and His dependability
T-9.........II.3:6 are many **a.** you have already received but
T-9.........II.6:4 from your mind to his, and **a.** *you.* You
T-9.......II.6:11 you hear His answer except as He **a.** all of
T-13.....VII.4:3 Love always **a.**, being unable to deny a
T-14.......X.6:5 recognizes what it is, and **a.** accordingly.
T-14.....X.10:4 give only the answer with which He **a.** you
T-15......VI.4:2 Nor do you think that when God **a.** him,
T-19......III.2:1 is really called upon by sin, *and always* **a.**.
T-20......III.3:5 and it is what they see that **a.** them. You
T-24.......II.4:3 to which you listen, and which asks and **a.**
T-26......IX.1:1 awake in him the Voice that **a.** to your call
T-27......IV.3:6 One with many **a.** can have no answers.
T-27......IV.3:6 One with many answers can have no **a.**.
T-27......IV.4:3 itself. A double question asks and **a.**, both
T-27......IV.4:9 is real, and **a.** in the form of preference.
T-27......IV.5:4 so are the **a.** to the questions of the world
T-27......IV.5:5 Where **a.** represent the questions, they
T-27......IV.6:6 because it **a.** questions truly asked. The
T-27......IV.7:3 **a.** that will solve your problems because
T-27......IV.7:4 *is.* Within the world the **a.** merely raise
T-29....VIII.8:3 This is the only question that has many **a.**
W-pI.....28.4:2 is to ask questions and receive the **a.**. In
W-pI.135.23:3 nor indeed the **a.** to the problems which
W-pI.135.23:4 they are **a.** to another kind of question,
W-pI...164.2:5 Christ **a.** for you, echoing your Self, using
W-pI...164.3:1 and **a.** in your name the Call He hears!
W-pI.166.11:3 be. One walks with you Who gently **a.** all
W-pI...168.5:3 the One Who **a.** our mistakes by giving us
W-pI...193.2:6 Who **a.** what His Son would contradict,
W-pII .356.1:4 *miracle reflects Your Love, and thus it* **a.** *him*
W-pII ....357.h Truth **a.** every call we make to God,
W-ep .........1:6 He will not withhold all **a.** that you need
W-ep .........6:3 In confidence we wait His **a.**, as we ask
M-7 ...........1:1 This question really **a.** itself. Healing
M-29 .......2:13 His **a.** are always right. Would you say
M-29 .........6:2 the requests of your heart, and **a.** them.
C-in ...........4:1 ego will demand many **a.** that this course
S-1...........I.2:5 You cannot be asked to accept **a.** which
S-1...........I.4:7 God **a.** only for eternity. But still all little
S-1...........I.4:8 But still all little **a.** are contained in this.
S-2........III.5:4 his release, and it is this that **a.** to his call.
S-3........IV.4:2 up and called to God, Who hears and **a.**.

### antagonistic 2

T-12......III.7:7 it, because you think it is **a.** to you. This is
T-12......III.7:9 outward what is **a.** to what is inward, and

### antecedents 1

T-7........VI.4:3 does not love you it *is* faithful to its own **a.**,

### anti-Christ 6

T-29.......VIII.h The **A.**
T-29....VIII.3:1 or a false belief; some form of **a.**, that
T-29....VIII.3:5 All forms of **a.** oppose the Christ. And fall
T-29....VIII.6:2 This is the **a.**; the strange idea there is a
T-30.......I.14:9 And you ask help of **a.** or Christ, and
W-pI...137.6:2 **a.** becomes more powerful than Christ to

### anti-religious 1

T-3...........I.1:7 **a.** concepts enter into many religions. Yet

### anticipate 6

T-13......VI.4:7 You would **a.** the future on the basis of
T-14.....III.16:3 so frantically to **a.** all you cannot know,
T-24......III.3:1 that you did not **a.** upsets your world, and
W-pI.135.21:1 We will **a.** that time today with present
W-pII .234.1:1 Today we will **a.** the time when dreams of
W-pII .322.2:5 *What loss can I* **a.** *except the loss of fear, and*

### anticipated 7

T-18....VI.12:2 occur with something past, present or **a.**.
T-18.....VII.3:2 It is always remembered or **a.**, but never
W-pI.....21.2:2 present or **a.** that arouse anger in you.
W-pI.....26.8:3 the list of **a.** outcomes for each situation
W-pI.....32.4:3 select a time when few distractions are **a.**,
W-pI...184.6:5 It can be seen, as is **a.**. What denies that it
M-4 .....I.A.5:8 this, he learns that where he **a.** grief, he

## anticipating 1

| | |
|---|---|
| W-pI.......8.2:3 | in picturing the past or in a. the future. |

## anticipation 4

| | |
|---|---|
| T-12....... II.5:3 | of. Only the a. will frighten you, for the |
| W-pI.135.16:5 | beliefs. A. plays no part at all, for present |
| W-pI...157.4:3 | and let it rest in still a. and in quiet joy, |
| M-28 .........4:1 | hearts are tranquil with a stir of deep a., |

## antithetical 1

| | |
|---|---|
| T-13.........I.1:3 | Peace and guilt are a., and the Father can |

## anxieties 2

| | |
|---|---|
| T-15.........I.1:1 | means to have no cares, no worries, no a., |
| W-pI...124.4:2 | No meaningless a. can come between our |

## anxiety 20

*See also* anxiety-provoking

| | |
|---|---|
| T-4...........I.6:2 | would be to increase a. about separation. |
| T-4........ IV.4:1 | anxious, realize that a. comes from the |
| T-6........ III.3:6 | Without a. the mind is wholly kind, and |
| T-7........ VI.3:2 | it, which must result in extreme a.. That |
| T-9.........I.14:4 | do distort reality you will experience a., |
| T-12...... III.6:5 | is fully aware of a. he does not perceive its |
| T-16....... V.1:2 | A., despair, guilt and attack all enter into |
| W-pI.......5.1:3 | may seem to be fear, worry, depression, a. |
| W-pI.....13.2:1 | intense a. in all the separated ones. It |
| W-pI.....34.6:1 | emotions, such as depression, a. or worry, |
| W-pI.....34.6:4 | *a. or worry [or my thoughts about this* |
| W-pI.....41.1:3 | are a., worry, a deep sense of helplessness |
| W-pI.....47.2:2 | is unwarranted, and to justify fear, a., |
| W-pI...109.5:1 | cares and no concerns, no burdens, no a., |
| W-pI...138.8:1 | grip the mind with terror and a. so strong |
| W-pI...163.1:2 | It may appear as sadness, fear, a. or doubt |
| W-pI...167.2:6 | All sorrow, loss, a. and suffering and pain |
| W-pI...194.2:1 | today's idea, and you have passed all a., |
| W-pII .323.1:1 | *all sense of loss and sadness, all a. and doubt,* |
| M-4 ....VIII.1:1 | can afford to wait, and wait without a.. |

## anxiety-provoking 1

| | |
|---|---|
| W-pI.....34.3:2 | your mind for fear thoughts, a. situations, |

## anxious 4

| | |
|---|---|
| T-4........IV.4:1 | When you are a., realize that anxiety |
| T-17.......IV.5:1 | accepted is very a. to preserve its reason, |
| W-pI.....47.1:1 | reason to be apprehensive, a. and fearful. |
| W-pII .275.2:2 | *I need be a. over nothing. For Your Voice will* |

## any 596

| | |
|---|---|
| T-1......... II.2:2 | is why a. attempt to describe it in words is |
| T-1......... II.4:1 | but by me" does not mean that I am in a. |
| T-1........ III.1:2 | you offer a miracle to a. of my brothers, |
| T-1........ IV.3:5 | have everything have no needs of a. kind. |
| T-1......... V.1:2 | body nor the miracle serves a. purpose. |
| T-1......... V.2:1 | to wait on time a. longer than is necessary |
| T-1......... V.4:4 | God *would* be mocked if a. of His creations |
| T-1.......VII.3:2 | Fantasies of a. kind are distortions, |
| T-1.......VII.3:5 | needs. Twist reality in a. way and you are |
| T-2...........I.3:7 | has not yet experienced a. comprehensive |
| T-2...........I.5:1 | which can heal a. of them with equal ease. |
| T-2....... II.1:10 | of being shaken by errors of a. kind. It |
| T-2......... II.2:2 | deny a. belief that error can hurt you. |
| T-2........ III.5:3 | do not involve a. effort at all on their part. |
| T-2........ IV.1:5 | a remedy and a. type of healing is a result. |
| T-2......... V.1:6 | device than a. form of level confusion, |
| T-2......... V.2:4 | to misunderstand a. healing that might |
| T-2......... V.5:4 | heal. By denying your mind a. destructive |
| T-2......... V.6:1 | does not learn a. more than it creates. As |
| T-2......... V.8:2 | error be corrected by a. device that can be |
| T-2......... V.9:6 | that is far beyond a. form of charity you |
| T-2....V.A.13:2 | to a. form of error with anything except a |
| T-2 ...V.A.14:2 | can correct in a way that has a. real effect. |
| T-2 ......VII.4:2 | a. attempt to resolve the error through |
| T-2 ......VII.6:4 | as long as a. of its parts is missing. That is |
| T-2 ......VII.6:7 | A. part of the Sonship can believe in error |
| T-2 .....VIII.5:6 | at a. time to everything you have made, |
| T-3 ..........I.1:1 | before a. residual fear still associated with |
| T-3 ..........I.2:2 | unwise to accept a. concept if you have to |
| T-3 ..........I.2:6 | itself is no harder to correct than a. other, |
| T-3 ........I.2:11 | with this kind of distortion in a. form. |
| T-3 ..........I.4:3 | Sacrificing in a. way is a violation of my |
| T-3 ..........I.7:7 | Good can withstand a. form of evil, as |
| T-3 .........II.3:6 | with the same Will has a. real existence. |
| T-3 ........ III.2:9 | at a. given time determines what you do, |
| T-3 ........ V.8:4 | knowing a. part of it is to know all of it. |
| T-3 ..... VI.2:12 | cannot be avoided in a. type of judgment, |
| T-3 ........ VI.3:2 | them in a. way is without meaning. In fact |
| T-3 ....... VII.2:3 | it, a. more than you can weaken God. The |
| T-3 ....... VII.3:9 | but you may be sure that a. interpretation |
| T-4 ..........I.6:1 | Egos can clash in a. situation, but spirit |
| T-4 ..........I.7:3 | particularly a. situation that lends itself to |
| T-4 ........I.7:10 | A. confusion on this point is delusional, |
| T-4 ..........I.9:9 | A. attempt to increase its believableness |
| T-4 ........I.9:11 | avoid Him a. more than He can avoid you |
| T-4 .........II.6:9 | term which refers to a. perceived threat to |
| T-4 ........ III.4:7 | into a. mind that truly wants it, but it |
| T-4 ........ III.7:8 | never forsake you a. more than God will, |
| T-4 ........ III.9:6 | everything. A. distinction in this respect |
| T-4 ........ IV.8:5 | Watch your mind carefully for a. beliefs |
| T-4 ........ IV.8:7 | Judgment, like a. other defense, can be |
| T-4 ........ V.3:1 | A. thought system that confuses God and |
| T-4 ........ V.6:3 | touching on the real question in a. way. |
| T-4 ........ VI.1:2 | to it gives the ego a. power over you. I |
| T-4 ....... VII.1:1 | It is clear that while the content of a. |
| T-4 ....... VII.3:2 | make a. attempt to establish what is true. |
| T-4 ....... VII.3:9 | and not subject to a. judgment, any |
| T-4 ....... VII.3:9 | judgment, a. exception or any alteration. |
| T-4 ....... VII.3:9 | judgment, any exception or a. alteration. |
| T-4 ....... VII.8:1 | God is praised whenever a. mind learns |
| T-5 ........in.3:1 | thought of a. of your brothers anywhere. |
| T-5 ..........I.7:4 | it does not obstruct it in a. way. Finally, it |
| T-5 .......II.10:9 | for a. part of the Kingdom than to restore |
| T-5 ........ IV.3:1 | Every loving thought held in a. part of |
| T-5 ........ IV.6:6 | and God if you forsake a. of your brothers |
| T-5 ........ IV.7:3 | as a. of God's ideas is withheld from the |
| T-5 ........ V.6:1 | the laws of God a. more than you can, but |
| T-5 ........ V.8:3 | A. decision of the mind will affect both |
| T-5 ........ V.8:6 | it will turn it back to full creation at a. |
| T-6 ........in.2:3 | the moment you accept a. premise at all, |
| T-6 ........in.2:4 | developed a thought system of a. kind, |
| T-6 ..........I.2:2 | value, like the value of a. teaching device, |
| T-6 ..........I.4:6 | perceive a. form of assault in persecution, |
| T-6 ........I.14:1 | interpret the crucifixion in a. other way, |
| T-6 ........I.16:2 | I do not want you to allow a. fear to enter |
| T-6 ........I.16:5 | A. concept of punishment involves the |
| T-6 ........I.19:3 | in them, and do not respond to a. other, |
| T-6 .........II.1:1 | A. split in mind must involve a rejection |
| T-6 .........II.9:6 | Although perception of a. kind is unreal, |
| T-6 ........ III.3:9 | attack in a. form and you have learned it, |
| T-6 ........ IV.1:4 | his support from it at a. moment. If it |
| T-6 ........ IV.2:8 | ego has never answered a. questions since |
| T-6 ........ IV.9:6 | and never detract from it in a. way. You |
| T-6 ........ V.1:1 | Like a. good teacher, the Holy Spirit |
| T-6 ......V.A.1:7 | Like a. other impossible solution the ego |
| T-6 ......V.C.7:4 | is assailed by a. doubts in your mind, His |
| T-7 ..........I.4:6 | God does not limit His gifts in a. way. |
| T-7 ........ III.1:8 | I am not absent to anyone in a. situation. |
| T-7 ..... III.1:10 | not make this power, a. more than I did. |
| T-7 ........ III.3:4 | Yet if they perceive a. of their brothers as |
| T-7 ........ IV.5:1 | be reconciled in a. way or to any extent. |
| T-7 ........ IV.5:1 | be reconciled in any way or to a. extent. |
| T-7 ........ V.5:7 | Love is incapable of a. exceptions. Only if |
| T-7 ........ VI.1:7 | He will not appreciate a. of Them if he |
| T-7 ...... VI.4:12 | And if it recognized a. part of the Sonship |
| T-7 ........ VI.9:4 | at a. level are not problems of fact. They |
| T-7 ...... VI.10:2 | A. belief you accept apart from this will |
| T-7 ....... VII.1:8 | why denying a. part of it means you have |
| T-7 .... VII.11:1 | Perceive a. part of the ego's thought |
| T-7 .... VII.11:2 | perceive a. part of creation as wholly real, |
| T-7 ..... VIII.3:3 | A. attempt to keep part of it and get rid of |
| T-7 ..... VIII.6:2 | ego can be completely forgotten at a. time |
| T-7 ........ IX.1:7 | cannot conceive of a. part from which it is |
| T-7 ........ IX.2:3 | God, and a. totality *must* include God. |
| T-7 ........ IX.3:2 | contained, a. more than can the fullness |
| T-7 ........ IX.4:3 | Exclude a. part of the Kingdom from |
| T-7 ........ IX.7:5 | including a. part of totality in the lesson, |
| T-7 ..........X.1:4 | you could possibly want a. part of it is |
| T-7 ..........X.5:2 | long as you avoid His guidance in a. way, |
| T-7 ........X.5:13 | and refuses to follow a. guidance at all. If |
| T-7 ........ XI.3:4 | to give always, without a. sense of loss? |
| T-7 ........ XI.3:7 | it, a. more than you can make yourself. It |
| T-7 ........ XI.7:4 | a. more than you can establish God's. But |
| T-8 .........II.2:1 | Is there a. possible reason for choosing a |
| T-8 .........II.4:3 | Holy Spirit opposes a. imprisoning of the |
| T-8 ........ III.7:8 | thought a. part of the Sonship holds. |
| T-8 ..... IV.2:12 | and you cannot abide in darkness a. more |
| T-8 ........ IV.3:1 | done completely by a. part of the Sonship |
| T-8 ........ IV.6:7 | cannot be learned by tyranny of a. kind, |
| T-8 ........ VI.4:1 | squandered everything for nothing of a. |
| T-8 ........ VI.5:4 | you a. more than you left your Creator, |
| T-8 ........ VI.8:5 | lies in all of us, but not in a. of us alone. |
| T-8 ...... VII.1:2 | When attack in a. form enters your mind |
| T-8 ...... VII.5:2 | Loss of a. kind is impossible. But when |
| T-8 .... VII.15:6 | No more are a. of its seeming results. |
| T-8 ..... VIII.5:5 | A sick body does not make a. sense. It |
| T-8 ..... VIII.6:8 | *A.* way you handle error results in nothing. |
| T-9 ........I.10:2 | A. wish that stems from the ego is a wish |
| T-9 ........I.12:1 | A. attempt to deny what *is* must be fearful |
| T-9 ........ III.7:1 | not of him, a. more than yours are of you. |
| T-9 ........ III.7:8 | A. attempt you make to correct a brother |
| T-9 ........ IV.5:4 | let a. belief in its realness enter your mind |
| T-9 .........V.7:4 | longer believes in nightmares of a. kind. |
| T-9 .........V.8:5 | He makes healing clear in a. situation in |
| T-9 ...... VII.7:2 | is. Lack of knowledge of a. kind is always |
| T-10 .........I.1:5 | A. part of your mind that does not know |
| T-10 .......V.5:5 | a. more than He could have created a Son |
| T-10 .......V.9:9 | and wholly without suffering of a. kind. If |
| T-10 .....V.11:4 | anywhere else, or in a. other condition. |
| T-11 .........I.7:1 | Could a. part of God be without His Love |
| T-11 .........I.7:1 | could a. part of His Love be contained? |
| T-11 ........II.1:6 | Yet when you attack a. part of God and |
| T-11 ...... III.1:4 | yourself you could never suffer in a. way, |
| T-11 ...... IV.2:4 | and a. limitation on your power is not the |
| T-11 .......V.4:2 | have a. effects if its source is not real. Fear |
| T-11 .......V.4:3 | which is so clearly senseless that a. effort |
| T-11 .......V.4:5 | independent of a. power except its own. |
| T-11 ...VIII.8:6 | Ask for truth of a. Son of God, and you |
| T-12 .........I.3:1 | of motivation that makes a. sense. And |
| T-12 ........II.9:5 | not by denying its full import in a. way– |
| T-12 ...... III.5:3 | A. response other than love arises from a |
| T-12 ...... III.9:6 | "laws," and without meaning of a. kind. |
| T-12 .......V.2:5 | you will no longer see a. sense in attack, |
| T-12 ...... VI.6:4 | transfers to love without a. interference, |
| T-13 .......II.6:4 | You do not yet understand that a. fear |
| T-13 ...... III.7:5 | leave a. spot of pain hidden from His light |
| T-13 ...... III.7:5 | your mind carefully for a. thoughts you |
| T-13 ...... VI.1:2 | for reality leaves no room for a. error. |
| T-13 .. VII.12:5 | from you as long as you have a. need of it. |
| T-13 ...... IX.5:4 | In a. form, in anyone, *believe this not.* For |
| T-13 .......X.2:9 | No one who would unite in a. way with |
| T-13 .......X.3:1 | a. union with a brother in which you seek |
| T-13 .......X.6:1 | you believe that guilt is justified in a. way, |
| T-13 .....X.10:5 | your Father can have no fear, for a. reason |
| T-13 .....X.11:1 | enter into real relationships with a. of |
| T-13 .....X.12:1 | him has touched his innocence in a. way. |
| T-13 ...... XI.6:4 | the need for a. differences disappear. |
| T-13 ...... XI.6:6 | over you without a difference of a. kind. |
| T-14 .........I.4:1 | A. direction that would lead you where |
| T-14 ...... III.2:6 | To wish for guilt in a. way, in any form, |
| T-14 ...... III.2:6 | To wish for guilt in any way, in a. form, |
| T-14 ...... III.8:4 | it, and do not foster belief in it in a. mind. |
| T-14 ... III.16:2 | light, error of a. kind becomes impossible |
| T-14 ... III.17:5 | will be touched in a. way by the decision. |
| T-14 ...... IV.5:1 | Before you make a. decisions for yourself, |
| T-14 ...... VI.4:6 | other is wholly without sense of a. kind. |
| T-14 .. VII.3:10 | does not retain a. conviction of reality. |
| T-14 ...... IX.8:1 | response of holiness to a. form of error is |
| T-14 .......X.5:5 | and bring a. order into chaos shows you |
| T-14 .......X.8:9 | lack a. consistent sense when they are put |

T-14..... X.12:9 from **a.** miracle you offer to His Son. How
T-14... X.12:10 there be **a.** order of difficulty among them
T-14...... XI.1:8 and truth is beyond semblance of **a.** kind.
T-14...... XI.3:8 Do not attempt to understand **a.** event or
T-14...... XI.4:9 you. Never believe that **a.** lesson you have
T-14...... XI.5:2 If you are wholly free of fear of **a.** kind,
T-14...... XI.6:6 peace is threatened or disturbed in **a.** way
T-15....... II.5:3 gift of God is recognized in **a.** other way.
T-15...... IV.3:3 by your decision to join in **a.** plan but His.
T-15...... IV.4:4 instant **a.** time and anywhere you want it.
T-15....... V.5:4 You can place **a.** relationship under His
T-15....... V.6:1 A. relationship you would substitute for
T-15....... V.8:4 see **a.** separation between yourself and
T-15..... V.10:4 Give to it **a.** meaning apart from His, and
T-15...... VI.1:3 do not conflict with one another in **a.** way
T-15...... VI.5:9 this world cease to hold **a.** meaning at all.
T-15.... VI.5:10 that he be bound, or limited in **a.** way. In
T-15..... VII.1:6 for **a.** relationship in which the ego enters
T-15..... VII.2:3 to enter into **a.** relationship without anger
T-15...... IX.5:3 sure and loving relationships that **a.** limit
T-15....... X.2:6 me. Learn now that sacrifice of **a.** kind is
T-15....... X.6:6 you will not be deceived by **a.** form the
T-15...... XI.2:4 No sacrifice of **a.** kind, of anyone, is asked
T-16......... I.3:8 tempted you may be to judge **a.** situation,
T-16......... I.6:1 in **a.** relationship that looks to weakness,
T-16....... II.9:1 never given **a.** problem to the Holy Spirit
T-16...... IV.4:5 ones as partners in **a.** aspect of living, and
T-16...... IV.4:5 use them for **a.** purpose which they would
T-16...... IV.9:6 In **a.** relationship in which you are wholly
T-16.... IV.13:1 of **a.** kind would hinder God's completion
T-16.... IV.13:1 completion, can they have **a.** value to you
T-16..... V.12:1 Whenever **a.** form of special relationship
T-16..... V.12:1 love is content, and not form of **a.** kind.
T-16... V.12:11 of God have **a.** influence at all upon it.
T-16...... VI.8:7 of love in **a.** special relationship here. For
T-16..... VII.2:5 now, it cannot have **a.** real meaning at all.
T-16..... VII.9:4 for He is incapable of illusions of **a.** kind.
T-17...... III.6:5 confused by **a.** "reasons" for separation.
T-17...... VI.1:6 guidelines He provides for **a.** situation,
T-17...... VI.2:1 In **a.** situation in which you are uncertain
T-17...... VI.7:1 Confronted with **a.** aspect of the
T-17..... VII.2:1 no problem in **a.** situation that faith will
T-17..... VII.2:2 is no shift in **a.** aspect of the problem but
T-17..... VII.4:1 not given can be lacking in **a.** situation.
T-17..... VII.6:2 part in **a.** situation dedicated in advance
T-17..... VII.8:8 Cause has entered **a.** situation that shares
T-17... VIII.1:5 has not forced **a.** exclusion on it. It is a
T-17... VIII.6:7 **a.** situation that could hold you back, and
T-18..... VII.3:5 In **a.** single instant the attraction of guilt
T-18... VIII.5:3 needing the whole to give it **a.** meaning,
T-18... VIII.5:4 Nor has it **a.** life apart and by itself.
T-18.... IX.11:2 Nor is there **a.** need for us to try to speak
T-19......... I.6:7 with truth, in **a.** respect or in any way.
T-19......... I.6:7 with truth, in any respect or in **a.** way.
T-19...... I.16:4 **a.** way except by the mind that thought it.
T-19....... II.3:3 would really change his reality in **a.** way,
T-19....... II.5:1 A. attempt to reinterpret sin as error is
T-19....... II.6:7 A. mistake can be corrected, if truth be
T19. IV.A.12:7 sin they pounce on **a.** living thing they see
T19.. IV.B.14:5 Like **a.** communication medium the body
T19... IV.C.2:5 Touch **a.** one of them with the gentle
T19. IV.C.11:1 when **a.** situation strikes you with terror
T19. IV.D.18:2 upon him with condemnation of **a.** kind.
T-20...... III.1:4 is lost if **a.** shift or change is undertaken.
T-20...... III.2:1 Adjustments of **a.** kind are of the ego. For
T-20...... III.3:7 **a.** difference between yourself and it in
T-20.... III.10:5 all thoughts of **a.** separation between us
T-20...... IV.3:7 to suffer the results of **a.** other source.
T-20....... V.7:2 Would you exchange this gift for **a.** other?
T-20...... VI.2:4 A. relationship in which the body enters
T-20...... VI.3:4 and **a.** relationship in which they enter
T-20... VIII.6:6 it in **a.** form and seeing it everywhere, in
T-21......... I.7:5 and held more dear than **a.** melody you
T-21..... II.11:3 by your Creator has **a.** influence over you.
T-21...... III.1:3 **a.** brother with whom you have a limited
T-21.... III.11:4 and cannot meaningfully join in **a.** way. It
T-21....... V.7:5 alone. Yet **a.** part of knowledge threatens
T-21....... V.7:6 And all of it will come with **a.** part. Here
T-21....... V.9:4 is far beyond attainment of **a.** kind. But
T-21...... VI.1:6 For uncorrected error of **a.** kind deceives
T-21...... VI.7:7 And **a.** instant serves to bring complete
T-21..... VII.3:8 A. way at all. It could be seen attacking
T-21..... VII.8:3 as you look on the effects of sin in **a.** form,
T-21... VIII.2:3 has no exceptions; no change of **a.** kind. It
T-22......... I.1:7 a plan of **a.** kind except to wander off, for
T-22....... II.3:5 be sure indeed that **a.** seeming happiness
T-22..... II.10:2 Nothing you made has **a.** power over you
T-22....... V.1:2 or anger, nor by opposing them in **a.** way.
T-22...... VI.9:7 no blessing from it, nor limit it in **a.** way.
T-22.... VI.12:2 believe attack of **a.** kind means anything.
T-22.... VI.12:3 It is unjustified in **a.** form, because it has
T-23....... in.1:3 cannot fear, for sin of **a.** kind is weakness.
T-23....... in.4:7 is at variance with littleness of **a.** kind.
T-23......... I.4:5 and attack of **a.** kind are all unknown. He
T-23......... I.6:8 truth, nor can they threaten it in **a.** way.
T-23....... II.3:4 Errors of **a.** kind can be corrected *because*
T-23..... II.17:2 Can an attack in **a.** form be love? What
T-23..... II.18:5 Can **a.** form of this be tenable? Yet you
T-23..... II.19:3 **a.** state apart from Heaven life is illusion.
T-23..... II.20:7 lack of faith in love, in **a.** form, attests to
T-23..... II.22:4 Attack in **a.** form has placed your foot
T-23..... II.22:5 Yet **a.** instant it is possible to have all this
T-23...... III.1:2 If it is true attack in **a.** form will hurt you,
T-23...... III.1:3 Attack in **a.** form is equally destructive.
T-23...... III.2:1 Is death in **a.** form, however lovely and
T-23...... III.3:1 Salvation is no compromise of **a.** kind.
T-23...... III.4:7 assault upon your peace in **a.** form, if only
T-23...... IV.1:4 and no illusion in **a.** form stalks Heaven.
T-23...... IV.4:6 realize that murder in **a.** form is not your
T-23...... IV.8:3 Sorrow of **a.** kind is inconceivable. Only
T-23...... IV.8:6 happiness could ever suffer change of **a.**
T-24......... I.3:6 of **a.** kind imposes orders of reality, and a
T-24......... I.7:7 of **a.** kind between you and him? Look
T-24....... II.7:2 **a.** more than you can change the truth in
T-24..... II.14:2 fail to bring you peace and joy of **a.** kind?
T-24...... IV.5:2 and when you suffer pain of **a.** kind, you
T-24...... VI.9:2 and without accomplishment of **a.** kind,
T-24..... VII.6:9 **a.** way to learn what this condition means
T-24..... VII.7:3 held to limits or uncertainties of **a.** kind.
T-24..... VII.7:4 as one, nor does this one have **a.** end at all
T-25......... I.1:7 **a.** differences perceived to stand between
T-25....... II.2:2 respect, at **a.** time or place, has anything
T-25....... II.5:4 for a while, without obscuring it in **a.** way.
T-25....... II.6:7 you not the picture is destroyed in **a.** way.
T-25....... II.9:5 when **a.** part of Him joins in His praise, to
T-25...... III.6:3 him out of darkness into light at **a.** time.
T-25...... III.6:4 The time he chooses can be **a.** time, for
T-25.... IV.5:10 In **a.** form. This can you bring to all the
T-25..... VII.3:3 His makes **a.** sense at all within this world
T-25..... VII.3:4 as true has **a.** meaning in His Mind at all.
T-25..... VII.3:8 all beliefs the world gives **a.** meaning to
T-25..... VII.4:7 Who thinks the world is sane in **a.** way, is
T-25..... VII.4:7 or is maintained by **a.** form of reason,
T-25... VII.11:6 be the total cost of **a.** gain at all. You who
T-25... VII.13:2 life, but life is not maintained at **a.** cost.
T-25... VIII.4:5 for **a.** sacrifice is made that sin may be
T-25...... IX.3:1 certain **a.** answer to a problem the Holy
T-25...... IX.4:3 attack, and loss of **a.** kind He cannot see.
T-25...... IX.6:3 he does not merit an attack of **a.** kind.
T-26......... I.4:6 be denied if **a.** sacrifice is asked of anyone.
T-26......... I.7:7 far beyond the reach of **a.** sacrifice of life
T-26....... II.1:7 all time and will not rise again in **a.** form.
T-26....... II.3:1 This one mistake, in **a.** form, has one
T-26....... II.3:4 or **a.** attribute which you perceive that
T-26....... II.3:5 on what you see can limit God in **a.** way.
T-26....... II.7:2 one, for pain in **a.** form you will not want.
T-26...... IV.4:3 and none is cherished more than **a.** other.
T-26....... V.7:2 Is **a.** echo from the past that he may hear
T-26..... V.14:4 **a.** need that you repeat again a journey
T-26..... VII.6:3 help. No illusion has **a.** truth in it. Yet it
T-26..... VII.6:9 Not one is true in **a.** way, and all must
T-26... VII.6:11 And **a.** wish that seems to go against His
T-26... VII.14:5 is his, unlimited by loss of **a.** kind. A tiny
T-26... VII.14:7 If loss in **a.** form is possible, then is God's
T-26... VII.17:2 is the answer to attack of **a.** kind. So is
T-26....... X.2:6 and cannot have effects of **a.** kind. Their
T-26....... X.2:7 Their Presence is obscured by **a.** veil that
T-27......... I.5:7 ever done, or ever had effects of **a.** kind.
T-27......... I.9:6 that it may be judged in **a.** way at all. It
T-27..... II.3:11 hold against himself or **a.** living thing.
T-27...... III.6:1 vacant will not need defense of **a.** kind.
T-27....... V.9:2 solved as **a.** one of them has been escaped
T-27...... VI.3:5 real, for **a.** one you choose is like the rest.
T-27...... VI.7:2 There is no need to suffer **a.** more. But
T-27..... VII.7:5 you in **a.** way request them for yourself.
T-27..... VII.8:6 as it will in **a.** role that satisfies its dream.
T-27.. VIII.10:4 the cause of **a.** pain and suffering you feel,
T-28....... V.6:5 left no room for them in **a.** place or time.
T-28..... VII.2:7 no middle ground in **a.** aspect of salvation
T-28..... VII.3:3 grasp uncertainly at **a.** straw that seems
T-29........ II.1:4 a simple way, without a sacrifice or **a.** loss
T-29....... V.3:2 and not for **a.** purpose you may see in him
T-29....... V.6:1 you would not keep hold on **a.** thought,
T-29...... IX.9:1 Whenever you feel fear in **a.** form,–and
T-30......... I.4:1 at **a.** time you think of it and have a quiet
T-30..... III.5:5 reduced to **a.** form and limited to what is
T-30.... III.5:11 Not in **a.** form that would content you not
T-30...... IV.5:2 Dwell not on them in **a.** form. They but
T-30....... V.2:4 as the sole cause of pain in **a.** form. No
T-30... VII.6:10 In **a.** thought of loss there is no meaning.
T-30.... VIII.2:6 not bound by loss or suffering in **a.** form,
T-31....... I.13:1 unaware of **a.** thoughts of evil or of good
T-31...... IV.9:3 Him, nor **a.** worldly goal be one with His.
T-31....... V.8:3 if **a.** peace of mind is to be given you. Nor
T-31... V.15:10 your suffering of **a.** kind you see your own
T-31... VII.13:1 is free of **a.** judgment made upon yourself
T-31... VIII.3:3 nor **a.** image left to veil the truth. He
W-in.......... 5:2 achieved in connection with **a.** person,
W-pI....... 1.3:1 statements are not arranged in **a.** order,
W-pI....... 3.1:1 without making distinctions of **a.** kind.
W-pI....... 5.1:1 preceding one, can be used with **a.** person
W-pI....... 5.1:3 hatred, jealousy or **a.** number of forms, all
W-pI....... 5.2:1 perceived cause of an upset in **a.** form, use
W-pI....... 6.1:2 specifically for **a.** application of the idea.
W-pI....... 7.5:1 not linger over **a.** one thing in particular,
W-pI....... 8.6:3 or **a.** emotion that the idea for today may
W-pI....... 9.2:2 active resistance in **a.** number of forms.
W-pI....... 9.2:4 is required for these or **a.** other exercises.
W-pI..... 10.4:5 Try to avoid classification of **a.** kind. In
W-pI..... 10.4:6 has little if **a.** personal meaning to you. As
W-pI..... 10.5:1 **a.** thought that distresses you at any time.
W-pI..... 10.5:1 any thought that distresses you at **a.** time.
W-pI..... 13.5:4 **a.** signs of overt or covert fear which it
W-pI..... 16.4:1 and actively seek not to overlook **a.** "little
W-pI..... 17.3:3 as yet of **a.** thought that is really true, and
W-pI..... 20.5:3 should be applied to **a.** situation, person
W-pI..... 21.2:3 anger may take the form of **a.** reaction
W-pI..... 24.1:5 only goal in **a.** situation which is correctly
W-pI..... 25.4:1 Before you can make **a.** sense out of the
W-pI..... 26.6:3 A. problem as yet unsettled that tends to
W-pI..... 26.6:4 use very many for **a.** one practice period,
W-pI..... 28.2:8 The light you will see in **a.** one of them is
W-pI..... 29.4:3 Remember that **a.** order you impose is
W-pI..... 31.3:2 to establish **a.** kind of hierarchy among
W-pI..... 31.3:4 Do not dwell on **a.** one in particular, but
W-pI..... 31.3:4 without **a.** special investment on your
W-pI..... 31.5:1 to **a.** form of temptation that may arise. It
W-pI..... 32.6:1 to **a.** situation that may distress you.
W-pI..... 33.3:2 when **a.** situation arises which tempts you
W-pI..... 34.2:2 to be undertaken at **a.** time in between
W-pI..... 34.4:2 not to make **a.** specific exclusions.
W-pI..... 34.5:1 peace of mind is threatened in **a.** way. The
W-pI..... 34.6:2 change your mind in **a.** specific context,
W-pI..... 35.7:3 up **a.** specific situation that occurs to you,
W-pI..... 37.2:2 A. other way of seeing will inevitably
W-pI..... 37.2:4 Nor will he have **a.** idea why he is losing.
W-pI..... 37.4:5 the idea to **a.** person who occurs to you,
W-pI..... 37.5:1 you may use **a.** combination of these two
W-pI..... 38.1:2 time, space, distance and limits of **a.** kind.
W-pI..... 38.3:4 difficulties or suffering in **a.** form that you
W-pI..... 38.4:1 and then search your mind for **a.** sense of
W-pI..... 38.4:1 or unhappiness of **a.** kind as you see it.
W-pI..... 39.7:1 unloving thoughts of **a.** kind are suitable
W-pI..... 39.8:1 undue emphasis on **a.** one in particular,
W-pI..... 40.2:4 practice quite well under **a.** circumstances
W-pI..... 41.6:6 keeping it clear of **a.** thoughts that might
W-pI..... 42.2:2 you can receive it **a.** time and anywhere,

W-pI.....42.5:1 A. thought that is clearly related to the
W-pI.....43.5:8 A. thought related more or less directly to
W-pI.....43.5:9 bear a. obvious relationship to the idea,
W-pI.....43.6:2 not allow a. protracted period to occur in
W-pI.....43.8:1 those which seem to distress you in a. way
W-pI.....43.9:2 Try today not to allow a. long periods of
W-pI.....44.8:3 It is also the only one that has a. meaning,
W-pI.....44.8:3 only one that has a. real use to you at all.
W-pI.....44.9:1 If resistance rises in a. form, pause long
W-pI.....45.1:2 think you see is related to vision in a. way.
W-pI.....45.1:4 resemble your real thoughts in a. respect.
W-pI.....45.1:5 you think you see bears a. resemblance to
W-pI.....46.7:3 They will be needed at a. time during the
W-pI.....46.7:3 of a. kind of negative reaction to anyone,
W-pI.....47.1:4 to be aware of all the facets of a. problem,
W-pI.....47.5:2 It is obvious that a. situation that causes
W-pI.....47.8:2 Use it as your answer to a. disturbance.
W-pI.....48.2:3 eyes open at a. time and in any situation.
W-pI.....48.2:3 eyes open at any time and in a. situation.
W-pI.....49.1:1 your regular activities in a. way. The part
W-pI.....49.2:3 distraught, but without reality of a. kind.
WpI...rI.in.2:2 follow a. particular order in considering
WpI...rI.in.2:5 If a. one of the five ideas appeals to you
WpI...rI.in.5:1 to embrace a. situation in which you are.
W-pI.....52.1:7 in a. way by this confusion of mine. I am
W-pI.....58.5:5 I cannot suffer a. loss or deprivation or
W-pI.....61.1:5 not refer to a. of the characteristics with
W-pI.....64.5:8 is impossible that a. decision on earth can
W-pI.....67.2:7 A. attribute which is in accord with God
W-pI.....68.6:6 that nothing can harm you in a. way. At
W-pI.....68.7:1 whenever a. thought of grievance arises
W-pI.....70.2:2 disturb your peace or upset you in a. way.
W-pI.....70.7:7 *My salvation cannot come from a. of these*
W-pI.....71.3:2 plan, a. perceived source of salvation is
W-pI...73.11:6 are tempted to hold a grievance of a. kind
W-pI...74.3:10 be sure to deal quickly with a. conflict
W-pI...76.12:1 as well as in response to a. temptation to
W-pI.....77.2:2 It does not depend on a. magical powers
W-pI.....77.2:2 nor on a. of the rituals you have devised.
W-pI...79.10:2 Whenever a. difficulty seems to rise, tell
W-pI.....80.6:3 to a. specific problem that may arise. Say
W-pI.....82.4:4 *but cannot change my function in a. way.*
W-pI.....99.6:6 depth or a. attribute they seem to have:
W-pI...109.5:2 your rest can never change in a. way at all.
W-pI...110.2:1 a. mind has made at any time or place. It
W-pI...110.2:1 any mind has made at a. time or place. It
WpIrIII.in11:5 and whenever you need help of a. kind.
W-pI...119.1:2 *mistaken when I think I can be hurt in a. way.*
W-pI...122.7:5 The world can give no gifts of a. value to a
W-pI...126.2:3 help are not in a. way related to your own
W-pI...128.1:1 you; nothing that you can use in a. way,
W-pI...130.5:1 worlds which have no overlap of a. kind.
W-pI.130.11:3 to you. All you need say to a. part of hell,
W-pI...131.2:5 achieve that offers a. hope of being real?
W-pI.131.12:4 Nothing but this has a. meaning now; no
W-pI.133.11:2 If you feel a. guilt about your choice, you
W-pI...134.9:2 to accuse someone of sin in a. form, do
W-pI.134.13:2 to a. understanding of the laws it follows,
W-pI.134.15:2 Be certain not to dwell on a. one of them,
W-pI.135.11:5 accomplishment of a. goal that serves the
W-pI.135.16:4 a continuity of a. old ideas and sick beliefs
W-pI...136.1:3 without a meaningful intent of a. kind, it
W-pI.136.11:4 sickness or distort the truth in a. way.
W-pI.136.14:2 to a. mind that would lay down its arms,
W-pI.136.14:3 It is found at a. time; today, if you will
W-pI.136.18:3 drink, or a. laws you made it serve before.
W-pI...139.2:3 known by a. living thing is what it is.
W-pI...140.1:1 a. remedy the world accepts as beneficial.
W-pI.151.11:2 in a. way from His one frame of reference,
W-pI...153.9:1 or dream in which attack has a. meaning.
W-pI.155.12:3 Could a. way be holier, or more deserving
W-pI...163.6:1 is impossible to worship death in a. form,
W-pI...167.2:5 response of a. kind that is not perfect joy.
W-pI...167.8:4 unopposed by opposites of a. kind, the
W-pI.167.10:4 We will not ask for death in a. form today
W-pI...168.2:2 satisfied; despair of a. kind unthinkable.
W-pI...181.6:1 goal if anger blocks our way in a. form.
W-pI...183.6:6 we have, the only sound with a. meaning,
W-pI...185.1:3 further sorrow possible for you in a. form
W-pI...185.1:3 for you in any form; in a. place or time.
W-pI...185.2:9 should a. two agree these words express
W-pI.185.13:1 and everyone must gain whenever a. gift
W-pI...186.3:3 be different in a. way from what you are.
W-pI...187.8:2 no place for sacrifice in what has a. value.
W-pI...190.1:2 When it is experienced in a. form, it is a
W-pI...190.1:6 cruel. How could it be real in a. form? It
W-pI...190.5:2 mind can hurt or injure you in a. way.
W-pI...193.6:4 you see or a. brother looks upon amiss.
W-pI...193.9:2 or nail to hurt His holy Son in a. way. He
W-pI...198.8:1 unaware of a. condemnation which could
W-pI...198.8:2 Dreams of a. kind are strange and alien to
W-pI...199.2:1 and space, unbound by a. preconceptions
W-pII.239.1:3 shares His glory a. trace of sin and guilt?
W-pII.....240.h Fear is not justified in a. form.
W-pII.252.1:2 is a. light that I have ever looked upon. Its
W-pII.275.1:1 no more true today than a. other day. Yet
W-pII.277.1:3 *He is not subject to a. laws I made by which I*
W-pII.277.1:5 *He is not slave to a. laws of time. He is as You*
W-pII.277.2:1 nor believe in a. law idolatry would make
W-pII.278.1:3 If I am bound in a. way, I do not know my
W-pII.281.1:2 *When I think that I am hurt in a. way, it is*
W-pII.284.1:3 There is no grief with a. cause at all. And
W-pII.284.1:4 of a. kind is nothing but a dream. This is
W-pII.298.2:1 *because I would not follow a. way but Yours.*
W-pII.320.1:2 joy, nor a. attributes his Father gave in his
W-pII...11.1:4 anything that it created suffers a. loss.
W-pII...11.3:3 imperfection and of a. spot upon its
W-pII.328.1:4 for us, nor is there a. second to His Will.
W-pII.333.1:2 name, or hidden by deceit of a. kind, if it
W-pII.345.1:6 *to Your gifts than a. other gift that I can give.*
W-pII.353.1:1 *use in a. way that best will serve the purpose*
W-pII.356.1:1 *answer a. call Your Son might make to You.*
M-in........2:10 A. situation must be to you a chance to
M-in..........3:3 use the content of a. situation on behalf of
M-1...........3:6 in a. language or in no language; in any
M-1...........3:6 language; in a. place or time or manner. It
M-2...........3:5 already happened at a. time you choose,
M-2...........5:3 God's Teacher speaks to a. two who join
M-2...........5:4 to send His Spirit into a. holy relationship
M-3...........3:5 simply to say that a. level of the teaching-
M-4.....I.A.4:6 to which they are helpful that a. degree of
M-4........II.1:6 do; no thought opposes a. other thought;
M-5.........I.1:1 the sufferer no longer sees a. value in pain
M-7...........5:1 about the outcome of a. problem that has
M-8...........6:8 answer to sickness of a. kind is healing.
M-10.........1:7 can a. consistent criteria for determining
M-10.........1:8 At a. time the student may disagree with
M-10.........3:4 and everything involved in them in a. way
M-10.........4:9 and everything involved in a. way. And
M-13.........7:9 if you attack a. brother for anything. For
M-14.........3:4 remain the instant a. one of them accepts
M-16.........8:4 of him, but will be given him at a. time, in
M-16.........8:4 in a. place and circumstance he calls for it
M-16.........9:7 For magic of a. kind, in all its forms,
M-17.........1:6 a magic thought arouses anger in a. form,
M-20.........3:4 Who sees anger as justified in a. way or
M-20.........3:4 as justified in any way or a. circumstance
M-21.......3:10 Only the Word of God has a. meaning,
M-23.........1:6 an invocation call forth a. special power.
M-24.........1:3 cannot, then, be true in a. real sense. Our
M-24.........1:7 Is a. other question about it really useful
M-24.........2:1 would not, under a. circumstances, be the
M-24.........2:8 There is always some good in a. thought
M-24.........3:1 to take a. definite stand on reincarnation.
M-24.........3:4 course is not concerned with a. concept
M-24.........4:6 to a. concept or belief that will be helpful,
M-25.........2:7 transcends these limits in a. way is merely
M-25.........3:7 and no one has a. powers that are not
M-25.........6:1 A. ability that anyone develops has the
M-27.........4:1 God nor re-establish a. grounds for trust.
M-27.........7:5 deceived by the "reality" of a. changing
M-28.........2:3 and misery of a. kind perceived as hell.
M-28.........6:2 long as a. mind remains possessed of evil
C-1............7:2 is not involved in perception at a. level,
C-2............7:3 and you will never question a. more. Look
C-5............3:5 life in a. way be changed by sin and evil,
P-1.............2:1 better purpose could a. relationship have
P-2.........in.3:3 his self-concept to a. significant extent.
P-2.........II.1:1 to believe in God to a. recognizable extent
P-2.........II.6:5 If a. two are joined, He must be there. It
P-2........IV.6:1 Illness of a. kind may be defined as the
P-2..........V.5:1 beyond the heights perceived in a. dream.
P-2........VI.5:5 possibly give rise to sickness of a. kind.
P-3..........II.1:3 could a. limits be laid on an interaction in
P-3........II.4:11 only message that a. two should ever give
P-3........II.10:1 forget that a. form of specialness must be
P-3........II.10:7 does not limit the Holy Spirit in a. way.
S-1...........I.2:1 for the answer to a. specific problem, and
S-1...........I.5:2 be confused with supplication of a. kind,
S-1..........II.3:4 that inevitably underlie a. prayer of need.
S-1..........II.6:1 prayer at a. level is always for yourself. If
S-1..........II.7:7 Now, without needs of a. kind, and clad
S-1........III.6:1 human love, for external "gifts" of a. kind
S-1........III.6:5 lost in the quest for lesser goals of a. kind,
S-2........III.1:2 for proof of innocence, nor pay of a. kind.
S-2........III.2:5 When someone calls for help in a. form,
S-3........III.2:2 said of a. form of healing that is based on
S-3........III.2:2 that is based on inequality of a. kind.
S-3........III.6:5 Nor will death a. more be feared because

## anyone 143

T-1.......IV.4:6 you that I will witness for a. who lets me,
T-1.......VI.1:2 No learning is acquired by a. unless he
T-3........V.9:6 world believes that if a. has everything,
T-3.......V.10:3 that a. who perceives at all needs healing.
T-5.........V.5:3 conceive of attacking a. or anything. I said
T-6..........I.2:6 release from fear to a. who understands it
T-6..........I.9:3 I had not harmed a. and had healed many
T-6.........I.10:6 One, and a. who listens is inevitably led to
T-6.........I.14:2 the same reason that a. misunderstands it
T-7.......III.1:8 I am not absent to a. in any situation.
T-7.....III.1:11 belonging to a. at the expense of another.
T-7......VII.3:6 Do not see this picture in a., or you have
T-7.....VIII.5:3 for your belief in it onto a. else, or you
T-7.......XI.5:6 If you recognize His gift in a., you have
T-8.......III.4:1 When you meet a., remember it is a holy
T-8.......III.4:7 Do not leave a. without giving salvation
T-8.......III.5:4 lost. Whenever you are with a., you have
T-8.......III.7:6 not will a. to suffer for a wrong decision,
T-8.......IV.4:5 Healing does not come from a. else. You
T-8.......IV.8:4 Therefore, when you seek to imprison a.,
T-8.....VIII.8:5 a. doubt your willingness to listen until
T-9.......III.6:7 To perceive errors in a., and to react to
T-9.......IV.7:4 attack a. and anything for no reason at all
T-9.......IV.8:4 A. who elects a totally insane guide must
T-9.........V.8:8 to do to help a. He sends to you for help,
T-11........I.3:4 Mind cannot be filled by a. except you,
T-11...VIII.8:7 in him, to give to a. who asks it of him.
T-12........I.3:5 a. be justified in responding with anger to
T-12.......V.5:5 either for themselves or for a. else. You
T-12.....VII.9:4 give anything but love to a. or anything,
T-13.......IX.5:4 In any form, in a., *believe this not.* For sin
T-13.......X.2:9 who would unite in any way with a. for
T-13.......X.6:1 that guilt is justified in any way, in a.,
T-14.......II.5:1 When you teach a. that truth is true, you
T-14.....IV.4:9 therefore, be a. without His Holiness, nor
T-14.....IV.4:9 nor a. unworthy of His perfect Love. Fail
T-14.......V.11:5 Refuse to accept a. as without the blessing
T-14......X.6:13 it offers everything to every call from a..
T-14.......XI.3:8 any event or anything or a. in its "light,"
T-15.........I.5:4 The only time the ego allows a. to look
T-15....VII.2:7 has no attraction at all to a. who perceives
T-15..VII.14:6 desire to exclude a. from your completion
T-15.....XI.2:4 No sacrifice of any kind, of a., is asked by
T-15.....XI.8:2 peace by demanding no sacrifice of a., for
T-16........I.5:7 His, for this will never bring peace to a..
T-16....VII.9:4 God holds nothing against a., for He is
T-17.....IV.4:6 separate from a. since the separation.
T-17....VII.6:2 truth. If you lack faith in a. to fulfill, and
T-18........II.7:4 He has forgotten a. in the purpose He has
T-18.......V.3:9 the means to a. who shares His purpose.
T-18....VII.5:7 or when the goal is finally achieved by a.,
T-18.....IX.6:3 no power at all to hold back a. willing to
T19 .IV.A.17:8 No one can die for a., and death does not
T-20.......II.4:3 who offers thorns to a. is against me still,
T-21....VII.3:9 could be seen attacking a. with anything.

T-22.........I.8:5 He could not come to a. but you, never to
T-22........II.5:2 it is impossible for you to see no guilt in a.
T-22......II.13:2 is His vision given a. who is but willing to
T-22.......VI.2:3 so impossible that a. who chooses this has
T-22.....VI.8:10 overlook the tiniest mistake be lost to a..
T-23......II.14:1 nor does a. cling to his madness if he sees
T-24.......IV.1:1 is a lack of trust in a. except yourself.
T-24......VII.7:5 has no meaning to a. who still retains one
T-25...VII.12:1 of the idea no one can lose for a. to gain.
T-25...VII.12:2 everyone *must* gain, if a. would be a gainer
T-25.......IX.2:4 Nothing you give is lost to you or a., but
T-25.......IX.2:4 and offered a. who but holds out his hand
T-25.......IX.3:2 be true, because He asks no sacrifice of a..
T-25.......IX.3:3 loss to a. has not resolved the problem,
T-25.......IX.3:8 When a. is seen as losing, he has been
T-25.....IX.10:2 must be done to all, if a. is to be healed.
T-26.........I.4:6 be denied if any sacrifice is asked of a..
T-26........II.2:5 is possible, and could result in gain for a..
T-26........II.8:2 He cannot be unjust to a. or anything,
T-27......II.11:2 a. perceive a function unified which has
T-28........II.6:1 is every dream that a. has dreamed within
T-28.......III.9:2 For here, the more that a. receives, the
T-28.......IV.1:9 You could be a. or anything, depending
T-30........V.1:4 no demands are made of a. or anything to
T-31.........I.1:5 hard to learn by a. who wants it to be true
T-31.......I.13:1 of good that ever crossed your mind of a..
T-31.......III.2:7 occur to you to give attack to a. at all.
T-31......VII.1:7 "bad." Nor does he trust the "good" in a.,
T-31...VII.13:2 It sees no past in a. at all. And thus it
T-31. VIII.12:5 remains to hide the face of Christ from a..
W-pI.....14.5:1 or to a. about whom you are concerned.
W-pI.....22.1:1 the way a. who holds attack thoughts in
W-pI.....27.2:3 *Vision has no cost to a..* If fear of loss still
W-pI.....35.1:3 It is difficult for a. who thinks he is in this
W-pI.....37.1:4 one loses; nothing is taken away from a.;
W-pI.....37.6:2 helpful to apply it silently to a. you meet,
W-pI.....37.6:3 It is essential to use the idea if a. seems to
W-pI.....38.2:5 connection with yourself and with a. else.
W-pI.....38.2:6 It is equal in its power to help a. because
W-pI.....38.2:6 because it is equal in its power to save a..
W-pI.....46.4:2 that a. you do not like is a suitable subject
W-pI.....46.7:3 of any kind of negative reaction to a.,
W-pI.....68.7:1 any thought of grievance arises against a.,
W-pI.....69.9:8 tempted to hold anything against a. today
W-pI...75.10:4 say to a. who seems to pull you back into
W-pI.....92.5:5 It sees that lack in a. would be a lack in all
W-pI.....93.1:2 You think if a. could see the truth about
W-pI.....94.5:5 sure to respond to a. who seems to irritate
W-pI...100.7:4 Only this is asked of you or a. who wants
W-pI...107.6:4 It is impossible that a. could seek it truly,
W-pI...124.6:2 power to heal all forms of suffering in a.,
W-pI...127.2:1 to a. who thinks that love can change. He
W-pI...127.8:3 escaped by a. who does not hold it dear.
W-pI...132.2:1 achieved, for a. is free to change his mind,
W-pI...133.9:2 obvious to a. who cares to look for them.
W-pI...137.3:2 It is impossible that a. be healed alone. In
W-pI...158.3:3 along the road that a. takes but by chance
W-pI...158.5:4 He has a vision He can give to a. who asks
W-pI...159.4:4 Christ beholds no sin in a.. And in His
W-pI...166.3:1 to a. who holds such strange beliefs. He
W-pI.185.13:1 has been requested and received by a..
W-pI...192.8:2 could be set free while he imprisons a.? A
W-pI...196.6:4 real to a. who thinks this thought is true.
W-pI...197.9:2 you free of all ingratitude to a. who makes
W-pI...200.4:5 seems to be a prison house or jail for a..
W-pII..312.1:5 holy sight of a. who takes the Holy Spirit's
M-1............1:1 of God is a. who chooses to be one. His
M-4........II.1:9 them to be in conflict with a. or anything.
M-4.....VIII.1:8 decisions, if they are causing pain to a..
M-10..........4:2 there a. who has not had this experience?
M-14..........3:9 No; it is meaningless to a. here. Yet it is
M-17........7:13 and a. who bears this stain on him must
M-18..........4:2 irritation in himself as he responds to a.,
M-18..........4:9 How can he then condemn a.? And who is
M-22..........4:2 a. actually believe he wants to be sick.
M-23..........7:4 God leave a. without a very present help
M-24..........3:4 any concept that is not acceptable to a.,
M-25..........6:1 that a. develops has the potentiality for
M-26..........2:6 Nor is there a. of whom they are unaware.
C-2.............9:3 No miracle is now withheld from a.. The
P-1.............2:2 higher goal could there be for a. than to
P-3.........III.6:2 pay. No one is sent by accident to a..
S-1...........I.7:1 Praying to Christ in a. is true prayer
S-1.........II.6:2 If you unite with a. in prayer, you make
S-1........III.3:7 this step cannot be reached by a. who sees
S-2...........I.4:8 think you can see sin in a. except yourself.
S-2.........II.6:3 Say this to a. and you are slave. And you
S-2........III.6:6 be heard by a. who calls upon His Name,

## anything 344

T-1.........V.3:7 If they believe they are deprived of a.,
T-1.........V.6:7 a. that holds it upside down be conducive
T-1.......VII.1:7 God or to your brothers with a. external.
T-2.........II.1:1 You can do a. I ask. I have asked you to
T-2.........II.1:4 or fear. When you are afraid of a., you are
T-2.......II.1:11 denies the ability of a. not of God to affect
T-2.......II.1:13 It is not used to hide a., but to correct
T-2....V.A.13:2 any form of error with a. except a desire
T-2........VI.3:7 Change does not mean a. at the symptom
T-2........VI.4:9 Before you choose to do a., ask me if your
T-3...........I.6:1 Innocence is incapable of sacrificing a.,
T-3...........I.7:3 if it arose from a. but perfect innocence.
T-3.........II.3:5 seeing cannot see a. but perfection. I have
T-3........III.1:2 straightened out before you can know a..
T-3........IV.6:8 emphasized, knowledge does not do a.. It
T-3.........V.1:2 No one has been sure of a. since. I have
T-3.........V.2:3 A. made for a specific purpose has no true
T-3.........V.3:2 literally impossible for you to know a..
T-4.........II.5:1 as painful, even though this is a. but true.
T-4.........II.6:3 to give a. implies that you will have to do
T-4........III.1:2 is inside, and this does not mean a.. The
T-4........III.5:1 kind of experience so different from a. the
T-4........IV.8:4 do. Do not settle for a. less than this, and
T-4........IV.8:4 refuse to accept a. but this as your goal.
T-4.........V.6:1 not to commit itself to a. that is eternal,
T-4.......VII.3:1 true, and does not respond at all to a. else
T-5...........I.7:2 instant that sharing it involves a. but gain
T-5........IV.4:4 want to show your brother a. except your
T-5.........V.2:7 A. that engenders fear is divisive because
T-5.........V.5:3 cannot conceive of attacking anyone or a..
T-5.........V.6:3 is a judgment that is a. but ineffectual. Its
T-6...........I.4:3 a. that is destructible cannot be real. Its
T-6.........II.6:9 A. that God created is as true as He is. Its
T-6........IV.3:1 the basic fact that the ego cannot know a..
T-6........IV.9:2 This is not true of a. that God created, but
T-6....V.A.5:11 He never takes a. back, because He wants
T-6......V.C.4:8 As long as you must be vigilant against a.,
T-7........III.3:4 as a. other than their perfect equals, the
T-7.........V.5:6 Can a. of God not be for all and for always
T-7........VI.4:1 ego cannot afford to know a.. Knowledge
T-7........VI.5:3 you, it is willing to attach itself to a. else.
T-7........VI.7:1 vigilant for a. *but* God and His Kingdom.
T-7......VI.13:6 nothing that opposes this means a. at all.
T-7.......VII.8:2 cannot lose a. unless you do not value it,
T-7.....VII.10:2 Do not accept a. else as your will, or you
T-7.....VIII.3:3 of another part does not really mean a..
T-7.........X.4:9 The ego's wishes do not mean a., because
T-7.........X.6:8 decide that you do not have to decide a..
T-7........XI.2:8 his own worth is beyond a. he can make.
T-8.........II.1:7 does not understand a. else. As a teacher,
T-8.........II.2:2 of a. it teaches make anything but sense?
T-8.........II.2:2 of anything it teaches make a. but sense?
T-8.........II.2:4 never given you a sensible answer to a..
T-8.........II.3:1 ego cannot teach you a. as long as your
T-8........III.6:3 know this, because it does not know a..
T-8........VI.1:5 Kingdom of God for a. the world has to
T-8........VI.3:2 God can find joy in a. except the eternal;
T-8........VI.3:2 not because he is deprived of a. else, but
T-8........VI.5:9 you accept a. else or give anything else,
T-8........VI.5:9 you accept anything else or give a. else,
T-8........VI.7:1 An "unwilling will" does not mean a.,
T-8......VI.8:11 this belief, you cannot understand a..
T-8.......VII.3:6 because He knows the only reality of a. is
T-8.......VII.4:5 will not see a. physical except as what it is
T-8.......VII.4:8 it. Interpret a. apart from the Holy Spirit
T-8.....VII.11:5 loses its usefulness if it is used for a. else.
T-8.....VII.13:3 To see a body as a. except a means of
T-8......VIII.1:2 The ego's definitions of a. are childish,
T-8......VIII.4:8 judge gives a. but an impartial judgment.
T-8......VIII.7:6 When I said that the ego does not know a.
T-8......VIII.8:5 you choose not to accept a. except truth.
T-8......VIII.9:8 Spirit, Who perceives no attack on a..
T-8........IX.9:2 is the only level at which healing means a.
T-9...........I.1:3 cannot "threaten" a. except illusions,
T-9...........I.2:3 to learn a. consistently in a state of panic.
T-9...........I.5:1 will never call upon you to sacrifice a.. But
T-9...........I.6:4 communication does not mean a.. A
T-9.........I.10:5 The ego cannot ask the Holy Spirit for a.,
T-9..........II.3:2 been asked for a. will ensure a response.
T-9..........II.7:8 listen to a. else or you will not hear truly.
T-9........III.3:3 to understand a. that arises from it. Since
T-9........III.3:4 that nothing the ego makes means a..
T-9........IV.1:1 to undo the belief that a. is for you alone.
T-9........IV.7:4 attack anyone and a. for no reason at all.
T-9.........V.3:1 and that a. they contain is meaningless.
T-9........VI.7:2 mean a. to you until you remember God's
T-9........VI.7:5 would not want a. the world has to offer.
T-9.......VII.2:2 There may be disagreement on a. else,
T-9.......VII.4:3 He is not deceived by a. you do, because
T-9.......VII.7:7 nothing that arises from it means a.. He
T-9.......VII.8:6 You do not want a. else. Return your part
T-10.......in.1:3 long as you believe that a. happening to
T-10.......in.3:5 holy. Can a. exceed the Love of God? Can
T-10.......in.3:6 Can a., then, exceed your will? Nothing
T-10.......in.3:9 When a. threatens your peace of mind,
T-10........II.5:2 It cannot be a. else. Arising from your
T-10.......V.9:4 His Son a. that is not acceptable to Him?
T-10.....V.13:1 Do not perceive a. God did not create or
T-10.....V.13:7 the Fatherhood of God will you have a.,
T-11.........I.1:2 Would you bring a. else to the Sonship,
T-11......IV.1:4 is. You are not saved *from* a., but you are
T-11......IV.4:1 *Only you can deprive yourself of a..* Do not
T-11.......V.3:1 that the term itself does not mean a.. It
T-11.......V.3:3 belief that the ego *has* the power to do a..
T-11.......V.3:7 *What is not of Him has no power to do a..*
T-11.....V.16:5 without meaning cannot demonstrate a.,
T-11....VIII.3:1 not know the meaning of a. you perceive.
T-11....VIII.5:8 that nothing of God demands a. of you.
T-11....VIII.9:1 Ask a. of God's Son and his Father will
T-12.........I.1:3 to believe in truth *you do not have to do a..*
T-12.........I.1:4 that you do not respond to a. directly, but
T-12.........I.3:7 Offer him a. else, and you are assuming
T-12.......III.1:2 you have no investment in a. in this world
T-12.......V.2:4 by attacking you have not done a.. Once
T-12.....VII.9:4 cannot really give a. but love to anyone or
T-12.....VII.9:4 give anything but love to anyone or a.,
T-12.....VII.9:4 you really receive a. but love from them.
T-12.....VII.9:5 If you think you have received a. else, it is
T-13....VIII.1:6 concept "where" does not mean a. to it. It
T-13.....XI.11:6 and you will not remember a. you made
T-14.........I.4:2 A. you deny that He knows to be true you
T-14.......III.9:5 a constellation larger than a. you ever
T-14.....III.10:7 to provide that offers them a. of value.
T-14.......IV.4:4 will not fail, nor ever has in a.. Decide
T-14.......IV.7:8 not, and a. you understand is not of Him.
T-14.......VI.4:5 you do not realize that only one means a..
T-14.......VI.6:3 how can this tongue mean a.? Yet even
T-14.....VII.7:4 that nothing you see means a. alone.
T-14....VIII.3:6 You cannot join with a. except reality.
T-14........X.2:3 no longer be satisfied with a. but his own
T-14........X.2:5 true that a. without order of difficulty can
T-14......XI.3:8 any event or a. or anyone in its "light," for
T-14......XI.4:9 have learned apart from Him means a..
T-14......XI.6:7 *I do not know what a., including this, means*
T-14....XI.12:4 Think not you understand a. until you
T-14....XI.13:5 Call not upon the ego for a.; it is only this
T-15......III.1:6 When you strive for a. in this world in the
T-15......III.8:3 it is sacrifice to accept a. less than glory.
T-15....III.10:7 and unable to accept a. for yourself. But
T-15....III.10:9 The host of God needs not seek to find a..
T-15.......V.1:4 for without it you do not understand a..
T-15.......V.1:5 you do not understand what a. means.
T-15......IX.7:1 no value on it as a means of getting a.,
T-15........X.1:3 time nor season means a. in eternity. But
T-16.........I.3:1 you do not want a. you value to come of a
T-16........II.9:2 to solve a. yourself and been successful. Is

T-17 I.6:3 concerned with a. except your willingness
T-17 II.1:2 no fantasy have you ever seen a. so lovely.
T-17 IV.1:2 The purpose God ascribed to a. is its only
T-17 VI.2:5 of the outcome, which can be a.. The
T-17 VI.6:7 No one will fail in a.. This seems to ask for
T-17 VII.3:5 of faithlessness, for bodies cannot solve a.
T-18 V.6:1 of your relationship is threatened by a.,
T-18 VI.12:3 The "something" can be a. and anywhere;
T-18 VII.7:1 To do a. involves the body. And if you
T-19 I.9:4 not use a. your brother has done before to
T19 IV.A.7:2 can land and settle briefly upon a., for it
T19 IV.B.14:1 Why should the body be a. to you?
T19 IV.C.11:1 a. seems to you to be a source of fear,
T19 IV.D.20:7 given a. in hell or Heaven to interfere with
T-20 IV.6:1 nor need you be concerned with a. except
T-20 V.1:4 Only in time can a. be lost, and never lost
T-21 in.1:11 Nothing perceived without it means a..
T-21 I.6:2 not to a person or a place or a. particular.
T-21 I.8:6 to imagine that a. could be outside, for
T-21 II.6:8 And a. that threatens this seems to attack
T-21 III.9:5 than a. that stands this side of Heaven.
T-21 VII.3:9 It could be seen attacking anyone with a..
T-22 I.7:5 nor was received by a. except yourself.
T-22 I.9:3 it possible that a. not part of Him *can* join.
T-22 II.12:5 will, nor the desire that a. be separate. Its
T-22 V.1:12 for a. that needs defense will weaken you.
T-22 V.6:1 feel the need arise to be defensive about a.
T-22 VI.6:8 No trace of a. in time can long remain in a
T-22 VI.12:2 you believe attack of any kind means a.. It
T-23 I.8:5 whenever you look on a. that God created
T-23 I.8:5 that God created with a. but love. Conflict
T-23 IV.8:8 it be a. that offers you a perfect calmness,
T-24 II.11:6 God and you as one seem a. but Heaven,
T-24 III.3:5 *It* can be thrown off balance by a.. What
T-24 VI.11:2 and unjoined with a. beyond the body. In
T-24 VII.1:6 hint of threat, or a. but deepest reverence.
T-25 I.3:4 nor gives the slightest witness unto a. the
T-25 II.2:2 has a. but fear and guilt been your reward
T-25 III.4:1 belief that a. could be established and
T-25 VII.4:7 sane in any way, is justified in a. it thinks,
T-25 VII.7:4 by time nor place nor a. God did not will.
T-25 VIII.10:1 how can it be that a. be kept from him?
T-26 I.1:7 see nothing attached to a. beyond itself.
T-26 II.8:2 He cannot be unjust to anyone or a.,
T-26 III.1:14 on a. that cannot be immediately grasped
T-26 V.5:1 too soon for a. to notice it had come.
T-26 VI.1:1 A. in this world that you believe is good
T-26 VII.4:1 true of knowledge is not true of a. that is
T-26 VII.11:4 It is impossible that a. be lost, if what you
T-27 I.3:1 deprived, unfairly treated or in need of a.,
T-27 I.6:11 and vanity of real concern with a. at all.
T-27 IV.1:6 must be clear you cannot answer a. at all,
T-27 VIII.5:6 ridiculous for a. but to be laughed away.
T-28 I.3:1 healing represents an effort to do a. at all.
T-28 I.14:4 he never had a need for doing a., and
T-28 IV.1:9 You could be anyone or a., depending on
T-29 V.6:2 the cost of holding a. God did not give in
T-29 VIII.7:5 left no room for a. to be except His Will.
T-29 IX.5:9 And so he makes of a. a toy, to make his
T-30 I.15:3 ask advice before you can decide on a..
T-30 V.1:4 or a. to twist and fit into the dream of fear
T-30 V.3:3 He has no wish for a. but this. And fear
T-30 V.10:3 *idol brought you a. except the "gift" of guilt.*
T-30 VIII.2:8 no effects that a. in Heaven or on earth
T-31 II.2:6 time you think you must decide on a..
T-31 V.15:8 If you can be hurt by a., you see a picture
W-pI 1.h from this window, in this place] means a..
W-pI 1.1:2 *This table does not mean a.. This chair does*
W-pI 1.1:3 *This chair does not mean a.. This hand does*
W-pI 1.1:4 *This hand does not mean a.. This foot does*
W-pI 1.1:5 *This foot does not mean a.. This pen does*
W-pI 1.1:6 *mean anything. This pen does not mean a..*
W-pI 1.2:2 *That door does not mean a.. That body does*
W-pI 1.2:3 *That body does not mean a.. That lamp does*
W-pI 1.2:4 *That lamp does not mean a.. That sign does*
W-pI 1.2:5 *That sign does not mean a.. That shadow*
W-pI 1.2:6 *anything. That shadow does not mean a..*
W-pI 1.3:3 should merely be applied to a. you see. As
W-pI 2.1:6 do not concentrate on a. in particular,
W-pI 2.2:4 sole criterion for applying the idea to a. is
W-pI 2.2:5 Make no attempt to include a. particular,
W-pI 3.h I do not understand a. I see in this room
W-pI 3.1:3 suitability of a. for application of the idea.
W-pI 3.1:5 A. is suitable if you see it. Some of the
W-pI 3.1:7 these things exactly as you would a. else.
W-pI 4.h These thoughts do not mean a.. They are
W-pI 4.1:7 or "bad." This is why they do not mean a.
W-pI 4.4:2 *This thought about_does not mean a.. It is*
W-pI 6.2:1 application to a. that seems to upset you,
W-pI 7.1:3 reason why nothing that you see means a.
W-pI 7.1:5 why you do not understand a. you see. It
W-pI 7.1:6 reason why your thoughts do not mean a.
W-pI 8.1:2 No one really sees a.. He sees only his
W-pI 8.1:6 time, and cannot, in fact, understand a..
W-pI 8.2:4 because it is not really thinking about a..
W-pI 8.4:2 This is because you actually cannot see a.,
W-pI 8.4:2 picture a thought, you are not seeing a..
W-pI 9.1:2 unlikely that it will mean a. to you as yet.
W-pI 10.h My thoughts do not mean a..
W-pI 10.1:5 were your thoughts did not mean a..
W-pI 10.4:8 *My thought about_does not mean a.. My*
W-pI 10.4:9 *My thought about_does not mean a..*
W-pI 11.3:1 they should not linger on a. in particular.
W-pI 14.5:1 a. you are afraid might happen to you, or
W-pI 14.7:1 applied to a. that disturbs you during the
W-pI 17.3:2 see a. that is really alive or really joyous.
W-pI 21.3:2 you believe in this connection means a..
W-pI 25.h I do not know what a. is for.
W-pI 25.1:2 explains why nothing you see means a..
W-pI 25.2:3 incapable of understanding what a. is for.
W-pI 25.3:4 And thus you do not know what a. is for.
W-pI 27.3:6 sentence to yourself without disturbing a.
W-pI 28.4:5 to the table just as much as to a. else,
W-pI 29.1:3 it explains why nothing you see means a..
W-pI 34.3:2 or a. else about which you are harboring
W-pI 34.4:1 without applying it to a. in particular. Be
W-pI 37.3:2 not by preaching to it, not by telling it a.,
W-pI 39.9:2 relax and do not seem to be thinking of a.
W-pI 41.6:4 Then make no effort to think of a.. Try,
W-pI 43.6:1 or if you seem to be unable to think of a.,
W-pI 48.2:5 should a. disturb your peace of mind.
W-pI 51.1:1 (1) Nothing I see means a.. The reason
W-pI 51.3:1 (3) I do not understand a. I see. How
W-pI 51.4:1 (4) These thoughts do not mean a.. The
W-pI 51.4:2 which I am aware do not mean a. because
W-pI 51.4:6 that my thoughts do not mean a., and to
W-pI 52.5:1 (10) My thoughts do not mean a.. I have
W-pI 53.1:2 of which I am aware do not mean a., the
W-pI 54.4:5 He cannot be alone in a.. It is therefore in
W-pI 55.2:4 It is a. but a reflection of the Love of God
W-pI 55.5:1 (25) I do not know what a. is for. To me,
W-pI 59.1:4 I be disturbed by a. when He rests in me
W-pI 59.3:4 I cannot see a. else. Beyond His Will lie
W-pI 60.3:3 not look a. like what I imagine I see now.
W-pI 64.2:1 to see can be a. but a form of temptation,
W-pI 66.9:7 happiness from a. the ego ever proposed.
W-pI 69.9:8 tempted to hold a. against anyone today.
W-pI 70.8:6 that you have never found a. in the cloud
W-pI 77.6:1 In doing this, you do not really ask for a..
W-pI 93.5:3 a. it seems to do and think means nothing
W-pI 102.2:1 cause and with no power to accomplish a.
W-pI 102.2:2 cannot purchase a. at all. It offers nothing
W-pI 121.5:1 which can offer a. but more despair. Yet it
W-pI 128.1:1 nor a. at all that serves to give you joy.
W-pI 128.4:1 world holds a. you want to hold you back.
W-pI 128.7:2 will not value a. you see as much as when
W-pI 131.2:3 and hope through them to gain in a.?
W-pI 135.11:4 not depend upon itself for a. except its
W-pI 140.6:6 or a. that is related to the form it takes. It
W-pI 140.7:3 provides that can effect a change in a..
W-pI 151.12:1 for your life is not a part of a. you see. It
W-pI 158.8:2 the world can not give a. that faintly can
W-pI 159.7:6 No one asks for a. of him except the gift of
W-pI 166.10:7 you have need no more of a. but this.
W-pI 166.14:5 accepts God's gifts can never suffer a..
W-pI 167.7:5 It is not its opposite in a. created, nor in
W-pI 169.5:3 No mind holds a. but Him. We say "God
W-pI 181.9:2 conceive of a. without Its sinlessness. We
W-pI 184.9:4 They do not stand for a. at all, and in your
W-pI 187.11:4 have it be withheld from a. we look upon.
W-pI 189.7:4 one belief you ever learned before from a.
W-pI 190.2:2 Can they be a. but wholly false? Pain is
W-pI 190.4:4 could conceive of them as cause of a.?
W-pII 1.3:4 without concern for a. that would appear
W-pII 242.2:3 *do not ask for a. that we may think we want.*
W-pII 253.1:1 that a. should come to me unbidden by
W-pII 6.2:4 untouched by a. the body's eyes perceive.
W-pII 6.5:3 or of time, or a. except the holy Self, the
W-pII 273.2:2 *What need have I to fear that a. can rob me of*
W-pII 286.1:3 *the lesson that there is no need that I do a..*
W-pII 8.3:5 No danger lurks in a. it sees, for it is kind,
W-pII 313.1:5 *for He sees no sin in a. He looks upon. Now*
W-pII 11.1:4 when a. that it created suffers any loss.
W-pII 333.2:4 *For this alone will never fail in a., being Your*
W-pII 340.2:3 is no room for a. but joy and thanks today
W-pII 344.1:6 *give me gifts beyond the worth of a. on earth.*
W-pII 348.1:3 *I have no cause for a. except the perfect peace*
W-ep 1:6 you need for a. that seems to trouble you.
M-4 II.1:9 them to be in conflict with anyone or a..
M-4 VII.2:3 God does not want a. he cannot give away
M-5 II.3:10 Nor does he do a. to the world, because
M-8 4:8 "reasoning" be depended on for a.?
M-10 1:9 in these terms, does not mean a.. No
M-10 3:3 In order to judge a. rightly, one would
M-13 2:7 Could they mean a. except to a body? Yet
M-13 7:9 It is denied if you attack any brother for a.
M-17 3:4 been the case if the result is a. but joy.
M-17 9:2 In truth it has no power to make a.. Like
M-25 3:6 Nor does their value lie in proving a.;
M-27 4:2 trust. If death is real for a., there is no life.
M-29 5:5 you cannot say a. without consulting Him
C-3 1:2 to think of a. He created that could need
P-1 2:5 Could a. be holier? For psychotherapy,
P-2 VI.1:1 forgiveness, for no healing can be a. else.
P-3 I.2:10 Could a. be holier? Or a greater gift to you
P-3 III.5:9 If they believe they need a. from a brother
S-1 II.7:8 or vain desires, unneedful now of a. at all.
S-3 IV.3:2 Can a. be holier than this? God thanks

## anywhere 32

T-5 in.3:1 thought of any of your brothers a.. You
T-6 II.6:2 You cannot be a. God did not put you,
T-6 II.11:7 There is no conflict a. in this perception,
T-6 II.13:3 No darkness abides a. in the Kingdom,
T-8 V.5:5 fear intrudes a. along the road to peace, it
T-9 VIII.5:3 cannot be a. except in the Mind of God.
T-10 III.7:3 power to deny illusions a. in the Kingdom
T-10 III.11:5 For if you see the god of sickness a., you
T-10 V.11:4 Son. You are not at home a. else, or in any
T-10 V.12:2 it is blasphemous to perceive suffering a..
T-13 II.3:5 Yet let it perceive guiltlessness a., and it
T-13 VI.8:5 There is no darkness in him a., for he is
T-15 IV.4:4 claim the holy instant any time and a. you
T-18 VI.8:11 you. There is nothing else, a. or ever.
T-18 VI.12:3 The "something" can be anything and a.;
T-21 I.8:4 shining and with no break or limit a..
T-22 VI.7:1 what mistake can there be a. you cannot
T-22 VI.14:9 There is no difference a. in it, for every
T-23 II.19:6 what is not in Heaven is not a.. Outside of
T-26 X.6:5 If you perceive injustice a., you need but
T-27 III.7:3 There is no choice of function a.. The
T-30 VII.3:7 allowance for stability of meaning a.. Fear
W-in 5:3 makes its accomplishments a. impossible.
W-pI 11.2:3 about, near and far, up and down,– a..
W-pI 42.2:2 that you can receive it any time and a.,
W-pI 53.2:3 a world in which there is no order a..
W-pI 70.1:2 seems to come from a. except from you.
W-pI 70.7:4 *It cannot come from a. else.* Then devote a
W-pI 132.13:3 Can it be a.? Deny illusions, but accept
W-pII 247.1:2 attack. Behold it a., and I will suffer. For
M-4 I.A.8:8 Who would "go" a., if peace of mind is
M-22 2:5 is certain. A. along the way, the necessary

## apart 289

T-1 I.49:2 effective quite a. from either the degree or

T-5 I.4:3 **a.** from the Father and from the Son. I
T-5 III.8:2 meaning **a.** from your rightful place in the
T-5 V.6:16 Thought, you *cannot* think **a.** from Him.
T-5 V.7:4 you believe you can think **a.** from God,
T-7 V.1:1 is quite **a.** from what they are used for.
T-7 VI.10:2 belief you accept **a.** from this will obscure
T-7 VII.5:6 You can do nothing **a.** from Him, and you
T-7 VII.5:6 Him, and you *do* do nothing **a.** from Him.
T-7 VII.6:3 You cannot be **a.** from them because you
T-7 VII.6:3 them because you are not **a.** from Him.
T-7 X.3:5 function is to teach you to tell them **a.**.
T-8 II.5:4 to be the same, how can you tell them **a.**?
T-8 VI.8:4 **a.** from each other we cannot function at
T-8 VII.4:8 Interpret anything **a.** from the Holy Spirit
T-8 VII.13:6 because **a.** from the mind the body has no
T-11 I.9:6 Even in time you cannot live **a.** from Him.
T-11 V.6:6 that autonomy is meaningful **a.** from Him
T-11 V.10:1 of the form it takes and quite **a.** from how
T-11 V.12:4 cannot be found **a.** from Your joint Will.
T-13 III.12:3 Could He set you **a.**, knowing that your
T-13 IV.3:1 even **a.** from the fact that you were wrong
T-13 V.5:2 For love cannot abide in a world **a.**, where
T-13 VI.13:6 his Father, he has no past **a.** from Him. So
T-13 VIII.4:1 **A.** from the Father and the Son, the Holy
T-13 IX.3:1 it has no meaning **a.** from what you found
T-13 X.11:5 Him, for there is no love **a.** from His.
T-14 IV.8:5 nothing you have ever felt **a.** from Him
T-14 V.6:2 is no unity of learning goals **a.** from this.
T-14 VI.1:8 The hidden is kept **a.**, but value always
T-14 VI.2:4 What is kept **a.** from love cannot share its
T-14 VI.4:3 Keep not guilt and guiltlessness **a.**, for
T-14 VI.4:4 All you have done by keeping them **a.** is
T-14 VII.1:3 must be brought together, not kept **a.**.
T-14 VII.4:8 **A.**, this fact is lost from sight, for each in a
T-14 VIII.2:7 For They are not **a.**, and gifts to One are
T-14 IX.1:6 is safe, but where is your safety **a.** from it?
T-14 X.4:4 the mind of those who think they live **a.**.
T-14 XI.4:9 learned **a.** from Him means anything.
T-15 IV.3:6 of salvation **a.** from Him diminishes the
T-15 V.10:4 Give to it any meaning **a.** from His, and it
T-15 VII.11:6 way in which they would keep minds **a.**.
T-15 X.1:10 for it has no meaning if we are **a.**.
T-15 X.5:7 **a.** from sacrifice means nothing to you.
T-15 XI.1:5 try longer to keep **a.** your thoughts and
T-15 XI.6:4 and it has no meaning **a.** from you. It is
T-15 XI.6:6 joined in you it would be **a.** from God,
T-15 XI.8:1 time of Christ is meaningless **a.** from joy.
T-16 III.6:7 stand outside your teaching and **a.** from it
T-16 IV.3:4 from which hatred is split off and kept **a.**.
T-16 V.12:5 even **a.** from its evident impossibility? If it
T-16 VI.9:4 for you would not want to be **a.** from it.
T-16 VII.8:2 God's gifts have no reality **a.** from your
T-17 IV.1:6 nothing God created is **a.** from happiness,
T-17 VI.5:3 this is quite **a.** from what the outcome *is.* If
T-17 VII.10:4 the Holy Spirit's goal are set **a.** from
T-17 VIII.6:2 cannot be accepted **a.** from its conditions,
T-18 I.12:5 still further weaken and break **a.** what is
T-18 II.6:9 As its unholiness kept it a thing **a.**, its
T-18 III.8:5 journey that you undertook **a.**, and that
T-18 VI.1:4 not his Father and dwells not **a.** from Him
T-18 VI.9:1 others and keeping you **a.** from them, and
T-18 VIII.2:4 shut Him out, and keep you **a.** from Him.
T-18 VIII.3:5 holding itself **a.** against the universe. The
T-18 VIII.4:3 for it could not survive **a.** from them. And
T-18 VIII.5:4 Nor has it any life **a.** and by itself.
T-18 VIII.6:4 the rest, and keeping it **a.** from its Creator
T-18 VIII.7:8 that you think you set **a.** is no exception.
T-18 IX.1:5 sole ruler of the kingdom it set **a.** to
T-18 IX.4:4 kept **a.** from what was made to keep it
T-19 I.4:4 and kept you both **a.** from being healed.
T-19 I.6:6 For God gave healing not **a.** from sickness
T-19 I.12:6 faithlessness has driven you and him **a.**,
T-19 III.7:4 seem to be split **a.** and overthrown. For
T-19 III.8:2 it; and give His Son a will **a.** from His, and
T-19 IV.3:3 looking where He *is,* and not **a.** from Him.
T19 IV.A.4:9 You cannot choose **a.** from this. You have
T19 IV.A.4:10 have no purpose **a.** from your brother,
T19 IV.A.4:10 **a.** from the one you asked the Holy Spirit
T19 IV.A.17:6 I teach that bodies cannot keep us **a.**?

T19 IV.B.7:5 And keep you not **a.** from what is offered
T19 IV.B.11:3 you think you are can never be **a.** from it.
T-20 VI.2:6 nothing that it would keep **a.** and hide. It
T-20 VI.6:4 and kept **a.** from those who worship them
T-20 VI.12:11 keep remembrance of His Love **a.** from
T-20 VII.7:5 as a separate thing **a.** from the intention.
T-21 II.12:4 **A.** from this he has no power to create,
T-21 IV.8:2 What it would keep **a.** has met and joined
T-21 V.5:3 For God wills not **a.** from him, nor does
T-21 VI.2:5 world and look upon himself **a.** from it?
T-21 VI.10:2 it cannot be you stand **a.** from blessing.
T-22 in.1:2 and need no longer look on sin **a.**. No two
T-22 in.2:8 in the same room and yet a world **a.**.
T-22 I.4:3 "will" that is your own, **a.** from His?
T-22 II.4:7 and holds it out, **a.** from its forgiveness.
T-22 II.10:2 you still would be **a.** from your Creator,
T-23 I.4:9 shall be part of you and what is kept **a.**.
T-23 I.7:10 And truth stands radiant, **a.** from conflict
T-23 I.10:2 Both of You, Who dwell as One and not **a.**
T-23 II.19:3 In any state **a.** from Heaven life is illusion.
T-24 I.4:4 For specialness not only sets **a.**, but serves
T-24 I.7:8 let you think that you are better off **a.**. Is
T-24 II.5:5 convince them they are different and **a.**;
T-24 II.13:3 **a.** and separate from all your brothers;
T-24 II.13:4 your special kingdom, **a.** from God, away
T-24 VII.10:4 And you cannot conceive of you **a.** from it
T-25 in.1:5 certain that you cannot be **a.** from what is
T-25 I.3:6 what seems to have a life **a.** has none.
T-25 I.4:1 not separate, nor with a life **a.** from His.
T-25 I.4:6 that seems to keep you separate and **a.**
T-25 II.3:1 you have found some hope **a.** from this;
T-25 II.6:4 serves His purpose, not yours **a.** from His.
T-25 II.11:5 **a.** from all God's Love as given equally.
T-25 IV.2:3 or beneficent **a.** from what you wish. It is
T-25 VII.4:4 lie **a.** from both the Father and the Son.
T-25 VIII.8:6 by being separate and **a.** from love. And
T-25 IX.6:7 condemned, and thus **a.** from healing.
T-25 IX.7:2 and kept **a.** from others as less deserving,
T-26 I.4:2 body, **a.** from you and separate in his cell,
T-26 I.8:6 be a task **a.** and separate from His Own?
T-26 III.2:2 and when you reach it is **a.** from time.
T-26 IV.2:4 between to keep them separate and **a.**.
T-26 IV.2:6 of them has not been kept **a.** and separate
T-26 VII.3:9 Kept **a.** from truth, it seems to have a
T-26 VII.4:1 is not true of anything that is **a.** from it.
T-26 VII.4:7 their effects but seem to be **a.** from them.
T-26 VII.7:4 becomes impatient, splits the world **a.**,
T-26 VII.8:9 which is clearly separate and a thing **a.**.
T-26 VII.8:10 is but your wish to *be* **a.** and separate.
T-26 VII.9:2 that you be joined with him, and not **a.**.
T-26 VII.11:6 It is not understood **a.** from Him, and
T-26 VII.12:8 What is thus kept **a.** can never join.
T-26 VIII.2:1 you would keep **a.** from your brother, and
T-26 IX.5:3 what was held **a.** from light is given up,
T-27 I.9:8 It stands **a.** from all experience of love or
T-27 II.8:4 unto his, and cannot be **a.** from his at all.
T-27 II.16:4 **a.** from that its Giver keeps *because* it has
T-27 IV.7:3 because they stand **a.** from them, and see
T-27 V.4:4 done. What stands **a.** from you, when you
T-27 VII.3:2 wrath, and you exist and think **a.** from me
T-27 VII.5:4 be changed by seeing it **a.** from its effects.
T-27 VII.7:8 they have is something quite **a.** from him,
T-27 VIII.1:8 and joys are different and can be told **a.**.
T-28 I.5:1 use of memory is quite **a.** from time. He
T-28 II.2:8 body, and its innocence is quite **a.** from it,
T-28 III.2:3 perceive itself as separate and **a.** from you
T-28 III.4:3 it is a wish to keep **a.** and not to join. And
T-28 III.7:4 a little gap perceived to tear eternity **a.**,
T-28 III.9:8 seemed to keep your Guests **a.** from you.
T-28 IV.2:4 You stand **a.** from them, but not apart
T-28 IV.2:4 but not **a.** from him who dreams them.
T-28 IV.2:10 you do not know and cannot tell **a.**.
T-28 VI.4:3 with every brother who would walk **a.**.
T-28 VI.5:2 another's secret wish to be **a.** from you, as
T-28 VI.5:2 from you, as you would be **a.** from him.
T-28 VI.6:1 one; that you be one with him and not **a.**.
T-28 VI.6:5 Myself, for you can never be **a.** from Me."
T-28 VII.2:4 Nor are you **a.** from it. For healing will be
T-28 VII.5:2 think without affecting those **a.** from you.

T-28 VII.5:3 To be alone must mean you are **a.**, and if
T-28 VII.5:4 This seems to prove that you must be **a.**.
T-28 VII.5:9 cannot be judged **a.** from its foundation.
T-29 I.2:2 fear, since fear and hate can never be **a.**.
T-29 I.4:6 and keep **a.** in intervals of separation,
T-29 II.4:6 help in giving them to all who walk **a.**,
T-29 II.6:2 but your wish to be alive **a.** from life, alive
T-29 III.2:7 to keep **a.** all living things who know not
T-29 III.3:10 gap so long perceived as keeping you **a.**.
T-29 V.8:1 that has been kept **a.** from use by Him
T-29 VIII.2:6 and stand **a.** from all the misery the world
T-29 VIII.2:7 you from the world, and lets you stand **a.**,
T-29 VIII.3:4 is its form **a.** from the idea it represents.
T-29 VIII.4:4 has been excluded and been kept **a.**?
T-30 II.4:9 be free **a.** from Him Whose holy Will you
T-30 III.6:6 nor have they a separate life **a.** from his.
T-30 III.11:2 Is your reality a thing **a.** from you, and in
T-30 VI.6:7 and everyone who seems **a.** from you?
T-30 VI.7:3 appearance must remain **a.** from healing,
T-30 VII.5:4 no thought of sacrifice **a.** from this idea.
T-31 I.5:2 a will **a.** from it was yet more real than it.
T-31 V.7:3 **A.** from learning they do not exist. They
T-31 VI.3:3 how to behold a world **a.** from it. It is
T-31 VII.9:1 kept **a.** by an illusion of yourself that
T-31 VII.11:2 holiness while you see him **a.** from yours?
T-31 VII.12:6 you see, or keep yourself **a.** and separate.
T-31 VIII.4:4 of their own weakness, seen **a.** from Him.
W-in 5:3 hand, one exception held **a.** from true
W-pI 14.6:5 can only be in your own mind **a.** from His
W-pI 19.5:1 **A.** from the "as needed" application of
W-pI 20.2:7 You are now learning how to tell them **a.**.
W-pI 30.2:4 we see, rather than keeping it **a.** from us.
W-pI 43.h is my Source. I cannot see **a.** from Him.
W-pI 43.3:1 You cannot see **a.** from God because you
W-pI 43.3:1 God because you cannot be **a.** from God.
W-pI 43.3:3 purpose, then you cannot see **a.** from God
W-pI 43.4:8 *I cannot see this desk* ***a.*** *from Him. God is my*
W-pI 43.4:10 *I cannot see that picture* ***a.*** *from Him.*
W-pI 43.7:4 *I cannot see you* ***a.*** *from Him.* This form is
W-pI 43.8:4 *is my Source. I cannot see this* ***a.*** *from Him.*
W-pI 51.2:4 have been made quite **a.** from reality. I
W-pI 58.2:4 There is nothing that is **a.** from this joy,
W-pI 59.3:2 I cannot see **a.** from Him. I can see what
W-pI 59.3:6 choose when I think I can see **a.** from Him
W-pI 59.5:3 I have no thoughts **a.** from Him, because I
W-pI 59.5:3 Him, because I have no mind **a.** from His.
W-pI 65.4:3 so that you have set **a.** the time for God,
W-pI 69.4:3 outside the circle and quite **a.** from it.
W-pI 83.4:4 *illusion of happiness* ***a.*** *from my function.*
W-pI 89.4:2 *not hold this grievance* ***a.*** *from my salvation.*
W-pI 96.5:1 Yet mind **a.** from spirit cannot think. It
W-pI 99.1:2 something **a.** or different from the Will of
W-pI 99.5:2 **a.** from time in that its Source is timeless.
W-pI 103.1:2 love. It cannot be **a.** from it. Nor can it be
W-pI 107.9:1 which tell you you could be **a.** from Him.
W-pI 116.1:3 *the belief there is another will* ***a.*** *from His.*
W-pI 124.6:3 and **a.** from distance as apart from time.
W-pI 124.6:3 and apart from distance as **a.** from time.
W-pI 125.3:3 We stand **a.** from all the judgments which
W-pI 125.7:1 minutes set **a.** from listening to the world,
W-pI 126.2:2 to you that other people are **a.** from you,
W-pI 126.2:4 yet remain **a.** from condemnation and at
W-pI 126.4:4 Someone **a.** from you committed it. And
W-pI 132.5:1 There is no world **a.** from what you wish,
W-pI 132.6:1 quite **a.** from what you chance to think it
W-pI 132.10:3 no world **a.** from your ideas because ideas
W-pI 132.11:1 you, you cannot think **a.** from Him, nor
W-pI 132.12:4 What He creates is not **a.** from Him, and
W-pI 132.13:1 world because it is a thought **a.** from God,
W-pI 135.8:2 merely be perceived as quite **a.** from you,
W-pI 135.9:4 **a.** from other minds and separate from its
W-pI 135.17:4 attack, obscure, and take **a.** and crucify.
W-pI 136.11:5 way. What is created is **a.** from all of this.
W-pI 136.13:3 Thoughts of God are quite **a.** from time.
W-pI 136.15:3 will come, for it has never been **a.** from us
W-pI 137.2:2 seems to keep one self **a.** from all the rest,
W-pI 137.2:3 split **a.** and held in pieces by a solid wall
W-pI 137.3:1 serves, but healing operates **a.** from them.
W-pI 137.3:3 In sickness must he be **a.** and separate.

W-pI...138.8:3 **a.** from question and from reason and
W-pI.139.12:3 of yourself **a.** from your awareness, as you
W-pI...152.5:3 which sets the truth **a.** from falsehood,
W-pI...153.6:3 your own weakness, seen **a.** from Him.
W-pI...154.4:1 Son, that sets **a.** salvation from the world.
W-pI.154.10:2 minds **a.** from Him Who speaks for us,
W-pI.155.10:2 keep the truth **a.** from God's completion,
W-pI...156.1:4 this be true, how can you be **a.** from God?
W-pI...156.2:4 You cannot walk the world **a.** from God,
W-pI...156.2:9 Nothing can be **a.** from Him and live.
W-pI...156.3:3 be of ice; the sea elect to be **a.** from water,
W-pI...157.1:3 is a time Heaven has set **a.** to shine upon,
W-pI...165.2:2 have you ever been **a.** from it an instant.
W-pI...167.4:3 **a.** from it in kind as well as distance, time
W-pI...184.3:1 of bodies kept **a.** and holding bits of mind
W-pI.185.12:5 attribute that sets the gifts of God **a.** from
W-pI...186.9:5 an instant, break **a.** to group again, and
W-pI.189.10:7 *We have no thoughts we think **a.** from You,*
W-pI.193.11:4 by ourselves, and kept **a.** from healing.
W-pI...200.9:7 what appears to be a world **a.** from God,
W-pI...210.1:3 *one I thought **a.** from Him and from His Will*
W-pII .223.1:1 when I thought I lived **a.** from God, a
W-pII .223.1:2 home, and I do not exist **a.** from Him. He
W-pII .227.1:3 *Yet nothing that I thought **a.** from You exists*
W-pII .230.2:2 *here now, for my creation was **a.** from time,*
W-pII .....3.2:4 and where His Son could be **a.** from Him.
W-pII .....3.3:4 where truth exists, upheld **a.** from lies.
W-pII .....3.3:5 is but illusion which is kept **a.** from truth.
W-pII .275.1:4 we cannot understand alone, nor learn **a.**.
W-pII .296.1:2 *have no thoughts which are **a.** from Yours,*
W-pII .311.1:2 and sets it off as if it were a thing **a.**. And
W-pII .325.2:1 *and mine **a.** from Yours but make up dreams*
W-pII .329.2:2 We have no will **a.** from His, and all of us
W-pII ...12.2:2 beyond the Everywhere, **a.** from All, in
M-1 ...........1:2 see his interests as **a.** from someone else's.
M-2 ...........2:4 the Will of God is entirely **a.** from time.
M-4 ......III.1:9 brothers, for who is there who stands **a.**?
M-4 ......IX.1:2 to his learning, while keeping others **a.**? If
M-8 ...........6:7 **a.** from size and shape and time and place
M-19 .........5:6 as separate and **a.** from all the rest. From
M-20 .........6:8 your tiny frail imaginings **a.** from Him?
M-22 .........7:9 No longer does he stand **a.** from God,
M-24 .........4:4 has much to teach and learn **a.** from them
M-26 .........1:7 This is what sets them **a.** from the world.
M-27 .........4:1 that may go on **a.** from what will die, does
M-28 .........2:6 darkness, **a.** from the light of forgiveness.
C-2.............1:6 thought you are **a.** from your Creator and
P-2 ........ II.9:2 who stands **a.** can receive Christ's vision.
S-1 ......... V.2:1 have goals so far **a.** they cannot coexist,
S-3...........I.1:1 nor think that sickness is **a.** and separate
S-3 ........ III.4:8 no point in giving remedy **a.** from where

### Apocalypse 1

T-2......VIII.4:2 and reflects the true meaning of the **A.**.

### Apostles 3

T-6.........I.14:2 The **A.** often misunderstood it, and for
T-6.........I.15:2 If the **A.** had not felt guilty, they never
T-6.........I.16:1 read the teachings of the **A.**, remember

### appalled 1

T-17....... V.5:6 of this new purpose, they are inevitably **a.**

### apparent 70

T-1........ VI.1:3 God, it is very **a.** in what you have made.
T-1.....VII.3:11 becomes **a.** to both giver and receiver.
T-2....... V.10:4 making it **a.** that charity still lies within
T-2.......VIII.5:3 quite **a.** that it is really the doorway to life
T-3...........I.6:4 meaning of the Atonement is perfectly **a.**.
T-3...... VI.11:2 in this position would be quite **a.**. Free
T-4......... II.3:3 This is so **a.** that one need only recognize
T-4.........III.3:1 It is surely **a.** by now why the ego regards
T-5......... V.8:8 ordering of thought becomes quite **a.**.
T-6.........in.1:1 of anger to fear is not always so **a.**. Anger
T-6...........I.3:4 the crucifixion lies in the ***a.*** intensity of the
T-6 ..... V.B.1:4 it is quite **a.** that you can teach wrongly,
T-6 ..... V.B.1:5 them, even though it was **a.** I was not. An
T-6 ..... V.C.7:4 perfect accomplishment is not **a.** to you.
T-7 .........II.7:2 **a.** that confusion interferes with meaning,
T-7 ........ V.1:3 are so **a.** that they need no elaboration,
T-7 ....... VI.6:3 He resolves the **a.** conflict they engender
T-7 ..... VI.8:11 share truth, your need for vigilance is **a.**.
T-7 .....VIII.6:5 perception based on the unbelievable is **a.**
T-9 .....VIII.1:3 of the ego becomes perfectly **a.**. When
T-12 .........I.3:8 of this to your own mind is not yet fully **a.**
T-12 ...... IV.3:3 be quite **a.** that it had not taught you the
T-13 ...... III.6:5 And the pain in this mind is so **a.**, when it
T-13 ..... IV.1:1 you are afraid of this course should be **a.**.
T-13 ...VIII.2:1 and knowledge becomes quite **a.** if you
T-14 .......II.2:6 what is true and what is not is perfectly **a.**,
T-14 .......II.2:7 simple and the obvious are not **a.** to those
T-14 ....VII.4:9 complete incompatibility is instantly **a.**.
T-15 ...... V.1:5 it would be quite **a.** to you that you do not
T-16 .......II.4:1 it is quite **a.** that you have not done them
T-16 ..... III.4:3 and effect relationship that is perfectly **a.**.
T-16 ..... VI.3:4 the more **a.** it becomes that it must foster
T-17 .........I.1:7 then does it become perfectly **a.** that they
T-17 ...... V.4:3 is so **a.** that they cannot coexist. Yet now
T-17 ..... VI.1:3 and for this it is **a.** that it must be clear.
T-18 .......II.2:3 outrageously violated in them becomes **a.**
T-18 ..... IX.5:3 are not **a.** until you see the light behind it.
T-19 .........I.5:2 difference in how they operate is less **a.**,
T-22 ......in.4:8 that lies beneath them all becomes **a.**.
T-22 ..... IV.1:1 where the branch in the road is quite **a.**,
T-23 .......II.6:1 could not be more **a.** than emerges here.
T-23 ...II.13:11 That is **a.**. The means of madness must be
T-23 ..... III.6:4 that haunts the place of death is not **a.**.
T-23 ..... IV.9:5 of conquest is quite **a.** from the quiet
T-25 .........I.7:2 It is **a.** that a mind so split could never be
T-26 .........I.1:4 Its focus on the body is **a.**, for it is always
T-26 ....VII.3:8 to truth, its senselessness is quite **a.**. Kept
T-26 ...VIII.4:1 and your brother is **a.** only in the present,
T-26 ...VIII.7:4 Why are not its effects **a.**, then? Why in
T-27 ...... V.8:6 But healing is **a.** in specific instances, and
T-27 ...... V.9:2 it will also be **a.** that your many different
T-27 .....VII.1:6 Yet is his own attack upon himself **a.** still,
T-31 .........I.2:4 merely goes from one **a.** lesson to the next
W-pI..... 68.5:4 will quickly become **a.** that there is no one
W-pI..... 72.3:1 perhaps not so **a.** why holding grievances
W-pI..... 72.5:4 The body's **a.** reality makes this view of
W-pI...121.1:3 way to safety in **a.** dangers that appear to
W-pI...127.6:3 is perfectly **a.** to the eyes that see and ears
W-pI...181.3:1 need to let our sinlessness become **a.**. We
W-pI...189.6:4 the world's **a.** reasoning but serve to hide.
W-pI...193.3:4 and different themes, **a.** but not real.
W-pI...195.5:2 who mourn a seeming loss or feel **a.** pain,
W-pII .293.1:4 present love is obvious, and its effects **a.**.
M-3 ...........2:2 meeting of two **a.** strangers in an elevator,
M-17 .........3:1 let error be corrected where it is most **a.**,
M-17 .........4:9 Either truth is **a.**, or it is not. It cannot be
M-17 .........5:2 in the world's thought system becomes **a.**.
M-20 .......3:10 the initial contrast stands out clear and **a.**
P-2..........II.3:4 This is never **a.** to the patient, and only
S-1........ III.3:7 It is **a.** that this step cannot be reached by

### apparently 3

T-24 ....VII.2:2 as yet, still in the future or **a.** gone by.
W-pI...163.7:2 alive and somehow perished; killed, **a.**, by
M-17 .........4:5 of violence, fantasied or **a.** acted out. It

### appeal 65

T-2 ...V.A.16:4 do. It is an **a.** to God to heal their minds.
T-2 ...V.A.17:2 **a.** for cooperation from miracle workers.
T-5 ..... III.8:10 The idea itself is an **a.** to the ego. The
T-5 ...... VI.4:7 you do not **a.** to the Higher Court because
T-5 ..... VI.10:4 **A.** everything you believe gladly to God's
T-8 .........II.8:1 Holy Spirit **a.** to restore God's Kingdom?
T-8 .........II.8:2 **a.**, then, is merely to what the Kingdom is
T-8 ......VII.1:5 idea of attack would have no **a.** for you.
T-9 .......IV.4:7 where the ego is forced to **a.** to "mysteries
T-11 .....V.16:1 Do not underestimate the **a.** of the ego's
T-12 .........I.3:4 Everything else is an **a.** for healing and
T-12 .........I.3:9 believe that an **a.** for help is something
T-12 .........I.5:3 to perceive an **a.** for help as what it is, it is
T-12 .........I.5:6 you refuse to recognize a brother's **a.**, for
T-12 .........I.5:6 only by answering his **a.** *can* you be helped
T-12 .........I.7:4 Every **a.** you answer in the Name of Christ
T-12 .........I.8:7 to regard everything else as an **a.** for help,
T-12 .........I.8:7 taught you that fear itself is an **a.** for help.
T-12 .......I.10:1 defense against it, the underlying **a.** *for* it?
T-12 .......I.10:2 than by answering the **a.** for it by giving it
T-12 .......II.3:3 for to perceive in sickness the **a.** for health
T-15 ... III.12:3 Hear not his **a.** to hell and littleness, but
T-15 .......V.2:5 and to **a.** to it for salvation is to believe
T-16 .......V.3:1 and one which has the most **a.** to those
T-16 .......V.9:1 **a.** of hell lies only in the terrible attraction
T-16 ..... VI.3:3 You do not recognize that this is its real **a.**
T-18 ... VI.14:2 is the irresistible **a.** the holy instant holds.
T-19 ..... III.1:5 making itself a willing captive to its sick **a.**
T-19 ..... III.3:3 results, but without the loss of its **a.**. And
T19 ...IV.A.5:4 from the **a.** of guilt to the appeal of love.
T19 ...IV.A.5:4 from the appeal of guilt to the **a.** of love.
T19 ...IV.A.5:7 fall away because of the **a.** you answered.
T19 ...IV.A.7:4 more than tiny interruptions in love's **a.**.
T19 ...IV.C.9:1 as its **a.** is yielded to love's real attraction.
T19 .. IV.D.5:5 And the **a.** of death is lost forever as love's
T19 .. IV.D.6:3 "loveliness" of sin, the delicate **a.** of guilt,
T-21 .... VII.1:5 Enormity has no **a.** save to the little. And
T-21 ...VIII.5:1 What is the holy instant but God's **a.** to
T-21 ...VIII.5:2 you? Here is the great **a.** to reason; the
T-23 .......II.7:3 Who caused it, to Whom **a.** is useless.
T-27 ..... III.4:2 that would enhance the invitation's real **a.**
T-30 .......V.2:5 form. No one is tempted by its vain **a.**, for
T-30 ...VIII.3:3 of idols have a powerful **a.** that makes
T-31 .........I.8:2 but calls to you in soft **a.** to be your friend
T-31 .......II.1:2 nor fought against to lose to truth's **a.**.
W-pI .... 38.5:4 *it.* Introduce whatever variations **a.** to you,
W-pI .... 98.3:2 do not **a.** to magic, nor invent escapes
W-pI 136.12:2 It does not make **a.** to might nor triumph.
W-pI .. 140.6:5 It is merely an **a.** to truth, which cannot
W-pI .. 159.6:1 to which you can **a.** with perfect certainty
W-pI .. 184.8:4 brother, it is to his body that you make **a.**.
W-pI .. 194.9:5 we will **a.** to Him Who guards our rest to
W-pII ..... 7.3:1 you would not let His Voice **a.** in vain, nor
M-8 ........... 1:4 from another with less intensity of **a.**.
M-17 ......... 3:5 with the call for help becoming his one **a.**.
M-23 ......... 1:5 Is this merely an **a.** to magic? A name
M-23 ......... 1:9 Why is the **a.** to him part of healing?
M-23 ......... 6:3 It is to them that wisdom should **a.**. There
M-23 ......... 7:2 tongues and **a.** to different symbols?
M-25 ......... 1:2 and it is obviously merely an **a.** to magic
M-25 ......... 4:5 particular **a.** in unusual abilities that can
C-4 ........... 7:7 and the grim **a.** of guilt and death is there
P-2..........II.5:1 teaching aids **a.** to different people. Some
P-3..........II.6:6 temporary **a.** and turn to dreams of fear,
S-1..........II.1:4 not, and often does not, make **a.** to God,

### appealed 1

W-pI .. 194.8:4 he has himself **a.** for comfort and security.

### appealing 2

T-8 .....VIII.3:4 **a.** argument from the ego's point of view,
W-pI 151.13:3 **a.** silently to Him Who sees the elements

### appeals 6

T-12 ........I.6:2 his loving thoughts and his **a.** for help, for
T-31 ......I.11:5 deeper call beyond it that **a.** for peace and
W-pI .. 39.10:1 periods in whatever form **a.** to you. Do
WpI... rI.in.2:5 five ideas **a.** to you more than the others,
W-pI .... 70.9:2 the clouds by whatever means **a.** to you. If
W-pI .. 126.2:3 and their **a.** for help are not in any way

### appear 99

T-1 .........II.4:7 This may **a.** to contradict the statement "I
T-2 ....... III.3:2 This may **a.** to contradict free will because
T-3 ..........I.1:5 it does **a.** as if God permitted and even
T-3 .......II.5:10 **a.** (or be perceived) we shall be like him,

| | |
|---|---|
| T-4....... II.11:5 | as long as you **a.** to be living in this world. |
| T-6......V.A.5:7 | Yet this is not so real as it may **a.**. Those |
| T-6......V.A.6:4 | step may **a.** to exacerbate conflict rather |
| T-7...... VI.7:8 | makes it **a.** as if you are attacking Him. |
| T-8.......VII.7:3 | orders of reality merely **a.** to exist, just as |
| T-9......... V.3:5 | onto God, they make Him **a.** retaliative, |
| T-10.......IV.1:9 | him in whatever form he may **a.** to you, |
| T-10..... V.14:2 | As long as both **a.** to you to be desirable |
| T-11.........I.9:1 | it **a.** as if God's Will is outside yourself, |
| T-13.......in.2:9 | They **a.** to lose what they love, perhaps |
| T-13...... III.6:2 | In concealment they **a.** to do so, and thus |
| T-16....... V.2:4 | It does not **a.** to be a weapon, but if you |
| T-18......IX.7:3 | and forms **a.** and shift from loveliness to |
| T19... IV.A.8:3 | makes its results **a.** to be more erratic and |
| T19IV.A.17:10 | The body does **a.** to be the symbol of sin |
| T19... IV.D.2:3 | His face with glory **a.** as streams of blood, |
| T19.IV.D.20:1 | look on him so will the gift itself **a.** to be. |
| T-21..... II.10:2 | the effect, and make effect **a.** to be a cause |
| T-21.....VII.4:7 | How treacherous does this enemy **a.**, who |
| T-22....... II.1:2 | do they **a.** to be the only alternatives, and |
| T-23....... II.1:3 | **a.** to be an obstacle to reason and to truth |
| T-23..... II.14:7 | by which the laws of God **a.** to be reversed |
| T-23..... II.14:8 | do the laws of sin **a.** to hold love captive, |
| T-23..... II.15:1 | the great reversal they **a.** to be the laws of |
| T-23..... II.15:7 | lovely do the laws of fear make death **a.**. |
| T-24...VII.11:1 | and both **a.** to walk this earth without a |
| T-25......VI.7:6 | does your specialness **a.** to be attack. In |
| T-26....... II.1:5 | A problem can **a.** in many forms, and it |
| T-26....... V.5:3 | to creation,–did this world **a.** to rise. So |
| T-26... VIII.7:1 | Why should the good **a.** in evil's form? |
| T-27..... II.12:7 | two halves **a.** to represent a split within a |
| T-27... VIII.5:2 | wish to let no dream **a.** to be the cause of |
| T-27... VIII.5:7 | How serious they now **a.** to be! And no |
| T-28.........I.5:9 | do their effects **a.** to be increased by time, |
| T-28.........I.7:3 | one? When ancient memories of hate **a.**, |
| T-29....... II.7:7 | The body can **a.** to change with time, with |
| T-29......IV.5:4 | The coverings may not **a.** to change, but |
| T-29....... V.6:1 | light the touch of evil on it may **a.** to be. |
| T-29......IX.4:7 | Yet everything their toys **a.** to do is in the |
| T-30......IV.3:4 | It must **a.** to break your rules for safety, |
| T-30......IV.5:8 | an illusion, making things **a.** like to itself? |
| T-31...... I.10:6 | He will **a.** when you have answered Him, |
| T-31......III.1:6 | Whatever form his sins **a.** to take, it but |
| T-31..... V.14:7 | self **a.** to answer what it does not know. |
| T-31..... V.16:5 | will **a.** in many places and in many forms. |
| T-31... VIII.9:3 | all the loveliness which they concealed **a.** |
| W-pI.......3.2:1 | to see things exactly as they **a.** to you now, |
| W-pI.....15.1:1 | thoughts you think you think **a.** as images |
| W-pI.....24.5:4 | if some of them do not **a.** to be directly |
| W-pI.....39.6:2 | thoughts in whatever form they **a.**; |
| WpI...rI.in.4:3 | most in situations that **a.** to be upsetting, |
| W-pI.....56.1:4 | All my hopes and wishes and plans **a.** to |
| W-pI.....78.3:1 | lay them down he will **a.** in shining light |
| W-pI.....97.5:1 | world where pain and misery **a.** to rule. |
| W-pI...108.1:4 | behind it will **a.** instead to take its place. |
| W-pI...121.1:3 | that **a.** to threaten you at every turn, and |
| W-pI...133.4:1 | are but two, however many there **a.** to be. |
| W-pI.133.10:2 | His ineffectual mistakes **a.** as sins to him, |
| W-pI...134.1:2 | this course **a.** to rest salvation on a whim. |
| W-pI...134.7:2 | the thousand forms in which they may **a.**. |
| W-pI.135.26:5 | the day, as foolish little things **a.** to raise |
| W-pI...137.3:5 | does his Self **a.** to be dismembered, and |
| W-pI...152.4:3 | that do not **a.** to be entirely your own. |
| W-pI...155.4:1 | **a.** to them as if it asked the sacrifice of |
| W-pI...157.7:3 | in the same form in which you now **a.**, for |
| W-pI...163.1:2 | It may **a.** as sadness, fear, anxiety or |
| W-pI...167.7:3 | may change; it may **a.** to be what it is not. |
| W-pI...187.2:5 | thought seems to **a.** is changed in giving. |
| W-pI...189.8:6 | road to God by which He should **a.** to you |
| W-pI...190.8:4 | In pain does fear **a.** to triumph over love, |
| W-pI...193.4:1 | does not **a.** to be but unforgiveness. Yet |
| W-pI...196.2:2 | **a.** to be a sign that punishment can never |
| W-pI...196.2:4 | and deny the meaning they **a.** to have. |
| W-pI...199.4:4 | the body will **a.** as useful form for what |
| W-pII......1.3:4 | that would **a.** to pose a contradiction to |
| W-pII..240.1:4 | matter what the form in which it may **a.**. |
| W-pII..278.1:1 | which all things that seem to live **a.** to die, |
| W-pII..292.1:3 | we let an alien will **a.** to be opposing His. |
| M-2............3:3 | Choices made long since **a.** to be open; yet |
| M-3 ...........4:3 | situation and then **a.** to separate. As with |
| M-4 ....... X.3:2 | and eternal truth do not **a.** in this context. |
| M-5 ....... II.3:4 | world will never again **a.** to rule the mind. |
| M-6 ...........2:7 | and it does not **a.** to have been received. It |
| M-7 ...........4:4 | It does **a.** unreasonable at first to be told |
| M-12 .........2:5 | God's teachers **a.** to be many, for that is |
| M-12 .........2:7 | it matter if they then **a.** in many forms? |
| M-12 .........4:6 | God **a.** to share the illusion of separation, |
| M-22 .........4:1 | sickness does not **a.** to be a decision. Nor |
| M-26 .........2:3 | And they will **a.** when and where it is |
| C-1.............2:1 | is split, the Sons of God **a.** to be separate. |
| C-3.............2:3 | makes God **a.** to be an enemy instead of |
| C-5.............2:6 | his form that He might **a.** to men and save |
| P-in............1:4 | This does not **a.** to be the case, for the |
| S-2 ......... II.3:1 | not **a.** in quite such blatant arrogance. |
| S-2 ......... II.3:4 | This can **a.** to be a humble thought, and |

## appearance 19

| | |
|---|---|
| T-18...... IX.6:2 | Its impenetrable **a.** is wholly an illusion. It |
| T-30...... VI.5:4 | can be no **a.** that can not be overlooked. |
| T-30...... VI.7:3 | If one **a.** must remain apart from healing, |
| T-30... VIII.2:3 | in him beyond **a.** and deception, both. It |
| T-30... VIII.2:5 | the form of the **a.** of his perfect health, his |
| T-30... VIII.6:1 | you decide there is not one **a.** you would |
| T-30... VIII.6:5 | There is no false **a.** but will fade, if you |
| T-30... VIII.6:9 | free of guilt, for his **a.** is your own to you. |
| W-pI.....64.1:3 | and His Son by taking on a physical **a.**. It |
| W-pI.....64.2:4 | the physical **a.** of temptation becomes the |
| W-pI.....66.4:4 | to go beyond these differences in **a.**, and |
| W-pI.....81.2:3 | *the light of the world shine through this* ***a.***. |
| W-pI...107.6:1 | change, in this **a.** now and then in that, |
| W-pI...109.3:5 | And no **a.** but will turn to truth before the |
| W-pI.138.11:2 | what has nothing but an **a.** of the truth. |
| W-pI...155.1:2 | You do not change **a.**, though you smile |
| W-pI...170.9:3 | a seeming obstacle with the **a.** of a solid |
| W-pII..265.1:6 | it. Let no **a.** of my sins obscure the light of |
| M-7 ...........4:1 | a healing because of the **a.** of continuing |

## appearances 49

| | |
|---|---|
| T-24...... VI.4:3 | by the world, by time and all **a.**, you will |
| T-24...VII.11:9 | serve his wish by giving it **a.** of truth. Yet |
| T-30...... IV.5:1 | A. deceive *because* they are appearances |
| T-30...... IV.5:1 | deceive *because* they are **a.** and not reality. |
| T-30...... IV.6:1 | A. can but deceive the mind that wants |
| T-30...... VI.5:8 | some **a.** that could withstand the miracle, |
| T-30...... VI.6:3 | thus you think that some **a.** are real and |
| T-30...... VI.6:3 | appearances are real and not **a.** at all. Be |
| T-30...... VI.6:4 | **a.** are harder to look past than others are. |
| T-30...... VI.7:2 | forms are real, and which **a.** are true. If |
| T-30...... VI.7:8 | be **a.** that have replaced the truth about |
| T-30... VIII.1:1 | A. deceive, but can be changed. Reality is |
| T-30... VIII.1:3 | if you fail to see beyond **a.** you *are* deceived |
| T-30... VIII.1:7 | it real, and keeps it separate from all **a.**. It |
| T-30... VIII.2:1 | to demonstrate that all **a.** can change |
| T-30... VIII.2:1 | can change because they *are* **a.**, and cannot |
| T-30... VIII.2:2 | from **a.** by showing they can change. Your |
| T-30... VIII.2:9 | But **a.** are shown to be unreal *because* they |
| T-30... VIII.3:5 | miracle be given you to heal **a.** you do not |
| T-30... VIII.4:3 | the belief there must be some **a.** beyond |
| T-31....... II.7:1 | will be saved from all **a.** and answer to the |
| T-31....... II.9:1 | Forgive your brother all **a.**, that are but |
| T-31..... II.11:6 | Yet these are but **a.** of what the journey is, |
| T-31...... III.4:9 | mind preferred the body change in its **a.**, |
| W-pI.....41.7:4 | are trying to leave **a.** and approach reality |
| W-pI.....56.4:6 | are part of Him will yet look past all **a.**, |
| W-pI.....92.4:1 | overlooks these things by seeing past **a.**. It |
| W-pI.....99.6:1 | and sees them as **a.** behind which is the |
| W-pI.....99.6:6 | He has one answer to **a.**; regardless of |
| W-pI...99.11:2 | remember that **a.** can not withstand the |
| W-pI...107.4:3 | that the **a.** the world presents engender. |
| W-pI...109.1:1 | and quietness unshaken by the world's **a.**. |
| W-pI...109.2:4 | whose vision sees beyond **a.** to that same |
| W-pI...109.4:4 | A. cannot intrude on you. You call to all |
| W-pI...110.3:1 | created you, **a.** cannot replace the truth, |
| W-pI.122.13:3 | a world of shifting change and bleak **a.**. |
| W-pI.122.13:4 | of change; the light of truth behind **a.**. |
| W-pI...124.5:1 | We see it in **a.** of pain, and pain gives way |
| W-pI...132.8:3 | all the thoughts that gave it these **a.**. The |
| W-pI...140.9:2 | beyond **a.** today and reach the source of |
| W-pI.151.10:2 | which can look beyond these grim **a.**, and |
| W-pI...158.4:2 | is a plan behind **a.** that does not change. |
| W-pII ..... 1.4:2 | of reality, nor seeks to twist it to **a.** it likes. |
| W-pII .263.2:2 | Let all **a.** seem pure to us, that we may |
| M-4 ..... II.2:10 | unchanging and unchangeable beyond **a.**; |
| M-7 ...........4:5 | It has all the **a.** of love. Yet love without |
| M-8 ...........6:3 | eyes will report their changed **a.** as before. |
| M-12 .........4:6 | do not believe in the illusion despite **a.**. |
| M-26 .........2:4 | to whom such **a.** would be frightening, |

## appeared 10

| | |
|---|---|
| T-27..... VII.7:3 | of everything the world **a.** to thrust upon |
| T-29..... VII.8:1 | what **a.** to be an endless circle of despair, |
| T-30....VIII.5:9 | And when He has **a.** to you, you will be |
| T-31....VIII.1:4 | be this, if Christ **a.** to you in all His glory, |
| T-31....VIII.5:6 | and agony **a.** to be before the choice for |
| T-31....VIII.9:3 | roads we travelled on before the Christ **a.**. |
| W-pI... 158.9:4 | took, nor how enormous they **a.** to be, |
| W-pI... 164.5:2 | which **a.** to hide it merely sink away. Now |
| W-pI... 169.4:1 | We have perhaps **a.** to contradict our |
| C-5............. 2:3 | a body that **a.** to hold his self from Self, as |

## appearing 1

| | |
|---|---|
| T-28........II.9:2 | of what has gone before, **a.** as a cause. The |

## appears 75

| | |
|---|---|
| T-1..........II.6:2 | Sonship **a.** to involve almost endless time. |
| T-2........ VI.9:9 | It **a.** at first glance that to believe such |
| T-6...... V.B.3:5 | it is, *having* **a.** to be the opposite of *giving*. |
| T-8....... VII.9:2 | other, so that it **a.** to be ruled by chaos. |
| T-8......VIII.4:2 | **a.** to be innocent and trustworthy because |
| T-9..........II.1:1 | has experienced what **a.** to be failure. This |
| T-10........II.1:3 | has been forgotten then **a.** to be fearful, |
| T-11.........I.8:9 | the Holy Spirit tells you **a.** to be coercive, |
| T-13....... V.4:3 | and where what is within **a.** to be without. |
| T-18.........I.3:5 | While this **a.** to introduce quite variable |
| T-19.......I.10:5 | Each one **a.** just as he is perceived in the |
| T-23........II.5:2 | Son. Now it **a.** that They can never be One |
| T-23........II.5:7 | God and of each other now **a.** as sensible, |
| T-23......II.13:4 | the laws on which your "sanity" **a.** to rest. |
| T-23......II.16:3 | how it **a.** to function many times before. |
| T-25......VII.7:1 | **a.** most sensible and meaningful to you. |
| T-26......VII.6:4 | Yet it **a.** some are more true than others, |
| T-26.....VIII.7:3 | Its cause is here, if it **a.** at all. Why are not |
| T-26.....VIII.8:3 | to be the form in which the "good" **a.**, is |
| T-26........X.5:7 | each unfairness that the world **a.** to lay |
| T-27...... III.7:5 | Yet only this **a.** to interfere with power |
| T-28..........I.1:5 | in memory **a.** to have immediate effects. |
| T-28..........I.4:7 | a part of time where guilt **a.** to linger still. |
| T-28........II.8:7 | the body which **a.** to prove the dreamer |
| T-28...... IV.6:2 | because what is the same **a.** to be unlike. |
| T-28....... V.2:5 | Where one **a.**, the other disappears. And |
| T-29...... VI.3:3 | is not fixed, however changeless it **a.** to be |
| T-29..... VII.3:3 | Its form **a.** to be outside himself. Yet does |
| T-29... VII.9:10 | Salvation thus **a.** to threaten life and offer |
| T-31........II.3:4 | So in their fusion there **a.** to be the hope |
| T-31....... V.2:4 | teach is not the thing that it **a.** to be. For it |
| T-31...... VI.2:3 | This one **a.** and disappears in death; that |
| T-31...VII.14:8 | not deceived by what **a.** as many choices. |
| T-31...VIII.4:3 | For what **a.** to hide the face of Christ is |
| W-pI.....29.3:4 | Nothing is as it **a.** to you. Its holy purpose |
| W-pI.....66.4:3 | be happiness, even if it **a.** to be different. |
| W-pI.....68.2:1 | weaves illusions in its sleep **a.** to be awake |
| W-pI.....72.1:2 | the ego **a.** to take on the attributes of God |
| W-pI.....79.5:1 | solve all the problems the world **a.** to hold |
| W-pI.....92.4:5 | It brings the light in which your Self **a.**. In |
| W-pI...108.4:1 | as first, nor which **a.** to be in second place |
| W-pI...110.2:4 | change that time **a.** to bring in passing by. |
| W-pI...136.3:2 | when truth **a.** to threaten what you would |
| W-pI...136.7:3 | your world **a.** to totter and prepare to fall. |
| W-pI...138.3:1 | obvious escape from what **a.** as opposites. |
| W-pI...138.6:1 | Heaven **a.** to take the form of choice, |
| W-pI...140.9:1 | will not be misled today by what **a.** to us |
| W-pI...152.4:4 | thus the truth **a.** to have some aspects |

W-pI...155.6:1 Illusion still a. to cling to you, that you
W-pI...158.3:2 It a. to be quite arbitrary. Yet there is no
W-pI...167.2:1 there a. to be a state that is life's opposite.
W-pI...170.9:5 love a. to be invested now with cruelty.
W-pI.170.10:5 The blood a. to be upon His Lips; the fire
W-pI...186.9:4 All the images His Son a. to make have no
W-pI...187.7:4 to all the forms that suffering a. to take.
W-pI...193.4:4 very obvious that it a. in countless forms,
W-pI.196.10:1 so wholly that escape a. quite hopeless.
W-pI...198.7:1 has no meaning, and attack a. as justified.
W-pI.198.10:1 the face of Christ a. unveiled at last in this
W-pI...200.6:6 while there a. to be a choice to make
W-pI...200.9:7 is to what a. to be a world apart from God
W-pII.....4.4:1 frightening, and sin a. indeed to terrify.
W-pII .279.1:2 is there a time when he a. to be in prison,
W-pII .295.1:7 Fear a. in many different forms, but love
W-pII .330.1:6 all things the dream of fear a. to offer us.
M-3...........2:1 level of teaching a. to be quite superficial.
M-3...........4:4 a. to be the end of the relationship a real
M-8...........6:5 from what a. to be the outside world. And
M-14.........3:2 not one thought of sin remains" a. to be a
M-17.........4:2 seeming justification by what *a.* as facts.
M-21.........5:3 that a. to be very embarrassing to him.
C-4............4:5 was perceived the face of Christ a., and in
S-2...........I.1:6 remedy a. to be a terrible alternative to
S-2...........I.6:2 this illusion of a world a. to be your home
S-3........III.2:8 be healed a. to be to find a wiser one who,

## appease 1

T-15.......X.8:7 you. No partial sacrifice will a. this savage

## appeased 1

W-pI...101.3:3 more than bones before salvation is a.. Its

## appetites 3

T-4.........II.7:5 system. A. are "getting" mechanisms,
T-4.........II.7:6 This is as true of body a. as it is of the so-
T-4.........II.7:7 Body a. are not physical in origin. The ego

## apple 1

W-pI.......2.2:3 a button, a fly or a floor, an arm or an a..

## applicability 2

T-12......VI.6:6 and everything, for its a. is universal.
M-22.........2:2 and complete awareness of the perfect a.

## applicable 8

T-1.........II.3:1 to which it is perfectly and correctly a.. It
T-3........IV.4:1 because it is a. only to right perception.
T-12.........I.8:1 that His criteria are equally a. to you. For
W-in..........4:2 a. to everyone and everything you see.
W-pI.....10.1:2 The reason the idea is a. to all of them is
W-pI.....35.7:3 are a. to your reactions to that situation,
W-pI.....43.7:5 This form is equally a. to strangers as it is
M-22.........6:2 It is equally a. to all individuals in all

## application 38

T-1........III.4:5 because it enables me to direct its a., and
T-2........IV.3:6 of the Atonement to two-edged a.. This is
T-2........V.1:11 its miscreations is the only a. of creative
T-3.........II.2:4 with universal a. that it becomes wisdom.
T-4.......VII.3:9 in a. and not subject to any judgment, any
T-5.........II.6:5 as freedom to create, but its a. is different.
T-7.........III.1:4 yours. Its a. does not matter. It is always
T-11....VIII.5:3 the play of ideas, but in their practical a..
T-16.......II.9:4 for the a. of the ideas that have been given
T-17......VI.1:1 practical a. of the Holy Spirit's purpose is
T-17......VI.1:5 you to make it specific, for a. *is* specific.
T-17......VI.1:6 you do not yet realize their universal a..
T-28.........I.3:5 They are but skills without an a.. They
W-pI.......1.3:7 as far as the a. of the idea is concerned.
W-pI.......2.1:6 as possible in selecting subjects for its a.,
W-pI.......3.1:3 suitability of anything for a. of the idea.
W-pI.......4.2:1 the subjects for the a. of today's idea, the
W-pI.......4.4:1 your thoughts for a. of the idea for today,
W-pI.......6.1:2 very specifically for any a. of the idea. For
W-pI.......6.2:1 for a. to anything that seems to upset you,
W-pI.......6.2:2 and the a. of the idea to each upsetting
W-pI.......9.3:1 the need for its indiscriminate a., and the
W-pI.....14.5:1 Suitable subjects for the a. of today's idea
W-pI.....15.4:4 specific subjects for the a. of today's idea.
W-pI.....15.5:3 Do not have more than three a. periods
W-pI.....18.3:1 selecting subjects for the a. of the idea for
W-pI.....19.5:1 from the "as needed" a. of today's idea, at
W-pI.....24.5:2 of each a. should be roughly as follows: *In*
W-pI.....28.1:1 giving specific a. to the idea for yesterday.
W-pI.....28.8:3 Each a. should be made quite slowly, and
W-pI.....33.4:3 eyes will probably help in this form of a..
W-pI.....34.6:2 If you find you need more than one a. of
W-pI.....35.3:3 kind of a. for today's idea because the
W-pI.....37.5:1 of these two phases of a. that you prefer.
W-pI.....46.6:1 The form of the a. may vary considerably
W-pI...66.11:1 an hour, this form of the a. is suggested:
W-pI.....68.7:1 a quick a. of today's idea in this form,
W-pI.193.12:2 it a. to the happenings the hour brought,

## applications 34

T-3..........I.2:3 procedure is painful in its minor a. and
W-pI.....27.4:4 You will probably miss several a., and
W-pI.....28.8:1 a. should include the name of the subject
W-pI.....31.1:4 frequent a. of the idea throughout the day
W-pI.....32.5:2 shorter a. consist of repeating the idea
W-pI.....33.1:2 be devoted to the morning and evening a.
W-pI.....33.1:3 though unhurried a. are essential.
W-pI.....33.3:2 Specific a. of today's idea should also be
W-pI.....33.3:3 For these a., say: *There is another way of*
W-pI.....34.2:3 All a. should be done with your eyes
W-pI.....34.2:4 inner world to which the a. of today's idea
W-pI.....34.5:1 The shorter a. are to be frequent, and
W-pI.....36.2:2 and make the shorter a. frequently, to
W-pI.....36.4:2 All a. should, of course, be made quite
W-pI.....38.6:1 In the frequent shorter a., apply the idea
W-pI...39.11:1 In the shorter a., which should be made
W-pI.....46.7:2 make more specific a. if they are needed.
W-pI.....64.7:1 frequent a. of today's idea throughout the
WpI..rII.in.6:1 the original form of the idea for general a.
W-pI.....83.2:1 specific a. of this idea might take these
W-pI.....83.4:1 useful forms for specific a. of this idea are:
W-pI.....85.2:1 Specific a. for this idea might be made in
W-pI.....85.4:1 the idea are suitable for more specific a.:
W-pI.....86.4:1 Specific a. for this idea might be in these
W-pI.....87.2:1 of this idea would be helpful for specific a.
W-pI.....87.4:1 useful forms of this idea for specific a.: *Let*
W-pI.....88.2:1 useful forms for specific a. of this idea:
W-pI.....89.2:1 use these suggestions for specific a. of this
W-pI.....90.2:1 Specific a. of this idea might be in these
W-pI.....90.4:1 of the idea will be useful for specific a.: *I*
W-pI.....95.5:3 the short a. of the idea for the day, and
W-pI...196.2:4 But you can learn to see these foolish a.,
WpI rVI.in.6:5 Beyond such special a. of each day's idea,
P-3..........II.1:9 to use special a. of the general principles

## applied 32

T-2.......IV.1:6 to which Atonement is a. is irrelevant. All
T-7..........I.7:4 "first" as a. to Him is not a time concept.
T-7.......IV.3:4 ability that was a. to the learning. All you
T-7.......IV.3:6 If different abilities are a. long enough to
T-16........I.2:1 in the fact that it is a. only to certain types
T-21......V.8:5 would fall away at once, if reason were a..
T-21......V.9:3 gained a means which cannot be a. to sin.
T-27.....VI.8:5 suffer not the laws of sin to be a. to you.
T-31.....IV.5:5 decision has power if it be a. in situations
W-in..........3:3 by which the idea for the day is to be a..
W-pI.......1.3:1 in the kinds of things to which they are a..
W-pI.......1.3:3 should merely be a. to anything you see.
W-pI.......3.2:2 to which the idea for the day is to be a..
W-pI.....14.7:1 be a. to anything that disturbs you during
W-pI.....15.5:4 can be a. as needed throughout the day.
W-pI.....20.5:3 repetitions should be a. to any situation,
W-pI....26.6:5 one. Today's idea should be a. as follows:
W-pI....28.7:1 and then a. to whatever you see about you
W-pI....28.7:2 equal sincerity as today's idea is a. to it, in
W-pI....30.3:1 Today's idea should be a. as often as
W-pI....31.1:2 the idea should be a. to both the world
W-pI....32.6:1 for today should also be a. immediately to
W-pI....43.8:1 idea should also be a. throughout the day
W-pI....46.5:2 After you have a. the idea to all those who
WpIrIII.in12:1 the one to be a. on each half hour as well.
W-pI..140.1:1 "Cure" is a word that cannot be a. to any
W-pI..140.7:2 but where it is, and then a. to what is sick,
WpI..rIV.in1:1 part of learning how the truth can be a..
W-pI..154.2:2 equally aware of where they can be best a.
W-pI..167.3:4 It can be then a. as mind directs it. But its
WpI.rVI.in.2:2 and a. to all the seeming happenings
M-22.........4:3 rarely if ever consistently a. to all specific

## applies 13

T-3..........I.4:4 to realize that this a. to themselves. Good
T-3.......IV.4:3 and a. to the state of mind that induces
T-4.........II.1:4 Abstract thought a. to knowledge because
T-7..........I.7:7 time a. neither to Him nor to what He
T-7.......III.1:1 and a. it to all individuals in all situations.
T-14.....IV.2:7 Learning a. only to the condition in which
T-26....VII.4:2 world of sickness, which a. to all its forms
W-pI....10.1:1 This idea a. to all the thoughts of which
W-pI....28.4:5 It is a commitment that a. to the table just
W-pI....30.3:2 the idea a. to everything you do see now,
W-pI....30.5:4 without. Today's idea a. equally to both.
W-pI....32.2:1 ones, a. to your inner and outer worlds,
W-pI....76.6:2 until you realize it a. to everything that

## apply 50

T-2...V.A.11:2 of time and space do not a.. When you
T-2.....VIII.5:6 a. it meaningfully and at any time to
T-4.........II.9:7 However, salvation does not a. to spirit,
T-7.....VIII.1:9 depending on how you choose to a. it.
T-12.....VI.6:6 learn to a. it to everyone and everything,
T-12....VII.1:3 when you a. them to all situations. There
T-12....VII.1:4 is no situation to which miracles do not a.
T-14.....VI.5:7 to a. it to the holy cause of restoration.
T-23.......II.3:3 understand that miracles a. to all of them.
T-24...VI.13:3 must a. to what you do with it as your ally
T-27.....V.10:2 to a. what He has taught you to yourself,
W-in..........8:3 are merely asked to a. the ideas as you are
W-pI......1.2:1 area, and a. the idea to a wider range:
W-pI......1.3:5 not attempt to a. it to everything you see,
W-pI......2.1:2 and a. the idea to whatever your glance
W-pI......2.1:5 and a. the idea to what was behind you.
W-pI......2.2:3 Try to a. the exercise with equal ease to a
W-pI......3.1:1 A. this idea in the same way as the
W-pI......4.1:3 a. the idea to them. If you are already
W-pI......5.1:2 A. it specifically to whatever you believe is
W-pI......5.6:1 also find yourself less willing to a. today's
W-pI......5.7:2 A. the idea for today to each of them,
W-pI....15.4:1 then a. it to whatever you see around you,
W-pI....15.5:1 will obviously not be able to a. the idea to
W-pI....25.6:8 next subject, and a. today's idea as before.
W-pI....29.4:1 a. it to randomly chosen subjects about
W-pI....30.4:2 you can actually see, as you a. today's idea
W-pI....31.1:4 you a. the idea on a more sustained basis,
W-pI....31.2:4 and a. the same idea to your inner world.
W-pI....32.6:2 you. A. the idea by telling yourself: *I have*
W-pI....33.4:1 Remember to a. today's idea the instant
W-pI....35.9:1 the time and a. the idea for today to them
W-pI....37.4:1 you as you a. the idea to whatever you see:
W-pI....37.4:5 Then close your eyes and a. the idea to
W-pI....37.5:1 you may open your eyes again and a. the
W-pI....37.6:2 helpful to a. it silently to anyone you meet
W-pI....38.3:4 we will a. the power of your holiness to all
W-pI....38.6:1 a. the idea in its original form unless a
W-pI....39.3:6 salvation? Today's exercises will a. to you,
W-pI....39.3:7 As you a. the exercises to your world, the
W-pI....39.8:2 A. the idea for today to each of them in
W-pI....43.8:2 For this purpose, a. the idea in this form:
WpI...rI.in.4:2 in which to a. what you have learned. You
WpI...rI.in.6:3 nor to a. the ideas as was suggested then.

W-pI...73.11:6 **a.** today's idea in this form immediately
W-pI.....80.6:3 And be particularly sure to **a.** the idea for
W-pI...193.6:4 forget these words **a.** to everything you
M-4......I.A.4:7 The word "value" can **a.** to nothing else.
M-4........ II.1:4 Honesty does not **a.** only to what you say.
M-16..........2:4 There are some general rules which do **a.**,

## applying 46

T-12.........I.8:1 By **a.** the Holy Spirit's interpretation of
T-12.....VII.1:4 and by **a.** them to all situations you will
W-in ..........9:4 in **a.** the ideas the workbook contains,
W-pI........1.1:1 and practice **a.** this idea very specifically
W-pI........2.2:4 sole criterion for **a.** the idea to anything is
W-pI........3.1:2 becomes a proper subject for **a.** the idea.
W-pI........5.1:6 the day. **A.** the same idea to each of them
W-pI........6.3:1 if you resist **a.** the idea to some upsetting
W-pI........7.4:3 Acknowledge this by **a.** the idea for today
W-pI........9.2:3 Yet that does not preclude **a.** it. No more
W-pI........9.3:1 involve looking about you and **a.** the idea
W-pI.....10.5:4 the idea slowly before **a.** it specifically,
W-pI.....12.4:1 the time intervals between **a.** today's idea
W-pI.....14.7:2 Be very specific in **a.** it. Say: *God did not*
W-pI.....16.4:1 In **a.** the idea for today, search your mind
W-pI.....16.4:4 it, is a suitable subject for **a.** today's idea.
W-pI.....17.2:1 In **a.** today's idea, say to yourself, with
W-pI.....21.1:2 in addition to **a.** the idea to particular
W-pI.....23.6:1 periods are required in **a.** today's idea. As
W-pI.....24.5:1 **a.** the idea for today, name each situation
W-pI.....26.5:1 periods are required in **a.** today's idea. A
W-pI.....28.6:1 table as a subject for **a.** the idea for today,
W-pI.....30.5:3 to **a.** today's idea with your eyes closed,
W-pI.....31.1:3 **a.** the idea, we will use a form of practice
W-pI.....34.4:1 without **a.** it to anything in particular. Be
W-pI.....35.6:1 suitable unselected list for **a.** the idea for
W-pI.....35.7:3 situation, and use them in **a.** today's idea.
W-pI.....36.3:2 **a.** the idea specifically to whatever you
W-pI.....37.5:1 you may alternate between **a.** the idea to
W-pI.....38.4:4 Use this form in **a.** the idea for today: *In*
W-pI.....38.6:2 the more specific form in **a.** the idea to it.
W-pI...39.10:2 idea itself as you vary the method of **a.** it.
W-pI.....40.3:2 being a Son of God, **a.** them to yourself.
W-pI.....43.4:4 **a.** the idea specifically to what you see.
W-pI.....43.7:1 In **a.** today's idea in the shorter practice
W-pI.....45.4:1 form that we used in **a.** yesterday's idea.
W-pI.....65.8:1 an hour, use this form in **a.** today's idea:
W-pI.....81.2:1 Some specific forms for **a.** this idea when
W-pI.....82.2:1 for specific forms for **a.** this idea are: *Let*
W-pI.....84.2:1 these specific forms helpful in **a.** the idea:
W-pI.....84.4:1 forms for **a.** this idea would be helpful:
W-pI.....86.2:1 are some suggested forms for **a.** this idea
W-pI.....88.4:1 For specific forms in **a.** this idea, these
W-pI.....89.4:1 specific forms for **a.** this idea would be: *I*
WpI. rIII.in9:2 without **a.** what you learned to them. As a
WpIrIII.in11:2 the habit of **a.** what you learn each day to

## appoint 2

T-25......VI.6:6 God **a.** to be the means for his salvation,
T-28.........I.5:4 not write the message, nor **a.** what it is for

## appointed 57

*See also* self-appointed
T-14... VIII.3:2 together only by the Guide **a.** for you. He
T-15.......II.2:3 He has **a.** to translate time into eternity.
T-15.......III.7:2 to the host whom God **a.** for Himself. It is
T-15....... X.3:6 Christ is the time **a.** for the gift of freedom
T-20......IV.5:4 world of separation each is **a.** separately,
T-24......IV.5:4 you saved what you **a.** to be your savior,
T-25.........I.1:1 to do the task that Christ **a.** you to do,
T-25....... V.5:8 let him be what God **a.** that he be to you.
T-25.....VII.8:2 Because He is not mad has God **a.** One as
T-25. VIII.14:1 in every way, as God **a.** for His holy Son.
T-26.........VI.h The **A.** Friend
T-26......VI.2:8 What God **a.** has no substitute, for what
T-26......VI.3:2 the throne that God **a.** for your Friend, if
T-29....VI.2:12 and as he is, for time **a.** not his destiny,
T-31....... II.7:6 He gave when God **a.** Him His only Son.
W-pI.....63.3:5 *the means God has* **a.** *for the salvation of the*
W-pI.....67.1:3 is why God **a.** you as the world's savior.
W-pI.....73.9:4 the time **a.** for the release of the Son of
W-pI.....78.7:3 **a.** *as the one for me to ask to lead me to the*
W-pI.....92.4:7 and darkness rule where God **a.** that there
W-pI...100.3:4 the light that God Himself **a.** as the means
W-pI...106.2:1 Father speak to you through His **a.** Voice,
WpI. rIII.in2:2 because it is impossible at the **a.** time.
WpI. rIII.in9:2 been inclined to practice only at **a.** times,
W-pI.122.10:4 close indeed to the **a.** ending of the dream
W-pI...123.4:3 footsteps as we go to do what is **a.** us to
W-pI...131.4:6 wanders off, he is led back to his **a.** task.
W-pI.131.14:5 come to the **a.** time and place where you
W-pI.135.20:2 And it will lead you on in ways **a.** for your
WpI. rIV.in5:4 set the day along the lines which God **a.**,
W-pI...154.2:1 Whatever your **a.** role may be, it was
W-pI...154.8:3 You are **a.** now. And yet you wait to give
W-pI...154.9:2 For that is part of your **a.** role. God has
W-pI...154.9:4 of your **a.** task is yet to be accomplished.
W-pI...155.5:2 This is the way **a.** for you now. You walk
W-pI...158.5:2 It revealed itself to him at its **a.** time. But
W-pI.159.10:2 the gift, when God **a.** it be given you?
W-pI...166.7:4 not. You go on your **a.** way, with eyes cast
W-pI...193.9:4 and none but waiting their **a.** time to fall.
W-pI...196.4:2 us, taking every step in its **a.** sequence, as
W-pII......3.4:2 One Whom God **a.** Savior to the world.
W-pII..256.2:1 *Father, would we come to You in Your* **a.** *way*
W-pII......6.4:2 dream which God **a.** as the end of dreams
W-pII..292.1:4 we will not find the end He has **a.** as the
W-pII..308.2:3 *is the time You have* **a.** *for Your Son's release*
W-pII.... 10.4:1 every step in His **a.** plan to bless His Son,
W-pII.....317.h I follow in the way **a.** me.
W-pII..317.1:4 go the way my Father's plan **a.** me to go,
W-pII..324.1:2 *the role to take, and every step in my* **a.** *path.*
W-pII..336.1:1 is the means **a.** for perception's ending.
W-pII..353.1:3 *Thus has learning come almost to its* **a.** *end.*
W-pII..357.1:4 *way to You, as You* **a.** *that the way shall be:*
Wfl ........in.2:2 because it is this ending God Himself **a.**.
M-1 ...........4:8 the teachers of God are **a.** to bring about.
M-24 .........4:5 time, draining it away from its **a.** purpose.
C-ep...........1:4 one can fail to do what God **a.** him to do.
S-1 ......... V.4:3 the place **a.** for the time when you should

## appoints 3

W-pI...154.3:2 And that one Voice **a.** your function, and
W-pI...154.6:1 sets them off from those the world **a.**. The
W-pI.154.11:3 and carry them to those whom He **a.**. He

## appraisal 2

*See also* self-appraisal
T-12....... V.8:5 merely the result of an honest **a.** of what
T-14.... III.12:1 place your pitiful **a.** of yourself in place of

## appraise 1

T-14.... III.15:1 Seek not to **a.** the worth of God's Son

## appraised 1

T-27..... V.11:3 Its total value need not be **a.** by you to let

## appreciate 19

T-2........ VI.9:3 Few **a.** the real power of the mind, and no
T-6.........I.17:1 to be grateful, or you cannot **a.** God. He
T-6.........I.17:3 You cannot love what you do not **a.**, for
T-6.........I.17:4 are afraid of what you are you do not **a.** it,
T-7......... V.9:6 makes, does not **a.** it and does not love it.
T-7....... V.11:7 You can **a.** the Sonship only as one. This
T-7......... VI.1:7 He will not **a.** any of Them if he regards
T-7......... VI.1:8 He will **a.** all of Them if he regards Them
T-7.....VII.1:11 part of reality, and thus **a.** all of it. Mind
T-7....... XI.5:3 for you to recognize and **a.** and know.
T-9......... II.9:3 not to be credulous, but to accept and **a.**.
T-9......... II.9:4 What you do not believe you do not **a.**,
T-9......... II.10:6 you will not **a.** it and you will not want it.
T-17..... V.12:5 To give thanks to your brother is to **a.** the
T-18....VIII.3:3 part of it that, could you but **a.** the whole,
T-19..... IV.2:7 forever impossible to **a.** your brother.
T-25.........II.9:1 not be glad if you **a.** His masterpiece?
W-pI.....45.9:2 the day, to **a.** your mind's holiness. Stand
W-pI.....93.9:4 Try to **a.** Its Holiness and the love from

## appreciated 5

T-6..........II.1:2 cannot be **a.** except by a whole mind that
T-7...... VI.11:8 is therefore capable of being **a.** and loved.
T-7....... VII.1:7 *Reality* cannot be partly **a.**. That is why
T-13...... XI.3:5 It can merely be **a.** or not. To value it
T-17..... V.11:7 Have you consistently **a.** the good efforts,

## appreciating 1

T-7..........II.7:2 therefore prevents the learner from **a.** it.

## appreciation 31

T-6.........I.17:2 He does not need your **a.**, but *you* do. You
T-6.........I.17:3 appreciate, for fear makes **a.** impossible.
T-6......V.A.4:7 the equal Sons of God, and that is full **a.**.
T-7......... V.9:4 it. Understanding is **a.**, because what you
T-7......... V.9:5 you; in understanding, in **a.** and in love.
T-7....... V.11:6 in everyone, and by bringing it to your **a.**,
T-7........ VI.5:1 therefore opposes all **a.**, all recognition,
T-7......... VI.6:6 understanding brings **a.** and appreciation
T-7......... VI.6:6 brings appreciation and **a.** brings love.
T-7....... VII.6:2 them the **a.** God accords them always,
T-7........ IX.4:6 full **a.** of the mind's Self-fullness makes
T-9........ VI.5:3 their gratitude and their **a.** of what you
T-10....... III.6:1 is great **a.** for everything that God created
T-11....... IV.7:2 is approached through the **a.** of His Son.
T-11..... V.13:2 The **a.** of wholeness comes only through
T-12.........I.6:1 Only **a.** is an appropriate response to
T-13..........I.8:4 guilt must deprive you of the **a.** of eternity
T-13...... IV.7:6 that the beginning of the **a.** of eternity lies
T-13...... X.12:5 and gladness and **a.** for what you see will
T-14....... III.2:6 lose **a.** of the value of your guiltlessness,
T-14.... IV.4:12 For this small gift of **a.** for His Love, God
T-14....... VI.1:8 kept apart, but value always lies in joint **a.**
T-15........II.6:8 the universe bows to, in **a.** and gladness?
T-15...... III.8:7 your poor **a.** of yourself and all the little
T-15...... VI.2:5 in our **a.** of his worth we cannot doubt his
T-17..........I.3:4 what this must do to your **a.** of the whole!
T-17..... V.11:4 lacking in **a.** for all you have done for Him
T-17..... V.11:8 Or has your **a.** flickered and grown dim in
T-27... VII.16:4 your dream of deep **a.** for his gifts to you.
W-pI.....29.3:1 things with love, **a.** and open-mindedness
M-15 .........3:1 meet with lack of **a.** and even contempt;

## apprehension 1

W-pI.193.13:4 To every **a.**, every care and every form of

## apprehensive 2

W-pI.....47.1:1 strength, you have every reason to be **a.**,
W-pI...151.4:5 and afraid, how **a.** of just punishment,

## approach 34

T-1....... VII.5:7 involve a more direct **a.** to God Himself. It
T-2......... IV.4:6 utilize a compromise **a.** to mind and body
T-3..... VII.5:10 As you **a.** the Beginning, you feel the fear
T-4......... VI.8:1 you **a.** me, and as you withdraw from him
T-6.......... V.3:1 A wise teacher teaches through **a.**, not
T-9......... V.4:4 This would be a healing **a.** if the dreamer
T-9......... V.7:1 Both forms of the ego's **a.**, then, must
T-11..........in.3:4 The more you **a.** the center of His thought
T-11..... V.13:3 contradictory **a.** of the ego to everything.
T-17....... VI.2:6 reason for this disorganized **a.** is evident.
T-17....... VI.4:3 is quite noticeable that this **a.** has brought
T-18........ V.2:1 Never **a.** the holy instant after you have
T-19..........II.8:5 **A.** it not lightly, for it is the choice of hell
T19... IV.D.3:2 to the ego never to lift this veil, not to **a.** it
T-20........ VI.7:1 so severely threatens them as love's **a.**. Let
T-26..........II.1:3 the same respect and through the same **a.**

T-31..... V.13:1 gains, it does not yet a. a basic question.
W-pI.....20.1:3 This a. has been intentional, and very
W-pI.....41.7:4 trying to leave appearances and a. reality.
W-pI.....44.8:1 While no particular a. is advocated for
W-pI.....45.8:4 a. it as you would an altar dedicated in
W-pI.....49.3:3 We will a. this happiest and holiest of
W-pI...107.7:4 footsteps of illusion are not our a. today.
W-pI...121.3:1 yet more terrified at the a. of light. What
W-pI.131.14:2 you, that you might a. this door some day
W-pI...136.1:5 same a. that carries all of them to truth,
W-pI...156.6:5 but who would waste an instant in a. to
W-pI...156.7:4 The a. to God is near. And in the little
WpI...rV.in1:6 we hasten on, for we a. a greater certainty
WpI.rV.in12:5 as we a. the Source of meaning. It is Here
M-2 ........... 3:4 a new thought, a fresh idea, a different a..
M-5 ....... II.1:5 sickness is but a faulty problem-solving a.
M-14 ......... 4:5 He need merely learn how to a. it; to be
P-2......... II.7:2 no good teacher uses one a. to every pupil

## approached 3
T-11...... IV.7:2 is a. through the appreciation of His Son.
T-13....... II.4:4 a. the darkest and deepest cornerstone in
T-29.........I.3:7 to you, and you jumped back; as you a.,

## approaches 3
T-4........ VI.5:3 learn how his misery lessens as he a. it.
T-14.........I.5:6 to be deceived will merely attack direct a.,
Wi181-200 2:1 and direct a. to the special blocks that

## approaching 4
T-7........ IV.6:9 is a way of a. knowledge by thinking in
W-pI...44.10:1 and even a feeling that you are a., if not
WpI...rV.in5:3 as we practice it is this to which we are a..
W-pI...194.1:5 How close are we a. to our goal! How

## appropriate 16
T-1......... II.3:2 It is not a. for miracles because a state of
T-1........ III.6:4 Golden Rule is the rule for a. behavior.
T-1........VII.5:6 awe is not an a. reaction to me because of
T-3...........I.8:3 sacrifice, is the only a. gift for God's altar,
T-5......... V.2:2 The word "create" is a. here because, once
T-12.........I.3:6 for help? No response can be a. except the
T-12.........I.6:1 appreciation is an a. response to your
T-17....... V.7:1 to which your former goal was quite a..
T-20..... VII.7:3 one a. to the end for which it is employed.
T-21...... IV.1:5 with sin the ego deems quite a., and
W-pI.....23.3:4 hallucination a more a. term for the result
W-pI.....24.1:2 Therefore, you have no guide to a. action,
W-pI.....42.6:1 thoughts is not a. for today's exercises.
W-pI.....67.2:7 God as He defines Himself is a. for use.
W-pI...135.2:2 power to call on you to make a. defense.
M-6 ........... 3:7 to be sure it is used as the giver deems a.?

## appropriately 3
T-1........ III.6:5 behave a. unless you perceive correctly.
T-9........ IV.8:1 happening, how a. can you expect to react
T-30...... VI.2:5 it merely asks that you respond a. to what

## approval 1
T-31....... V.5:4 of the self the world smiles with a., for it

## approve 1
W-pI.135.17:2 Their aim is to select what you a., and

## approves 1
T-14....... X.8:7 and thoroughly a. the undertakings of

## approving 1
T-14....... X.8:7 would "analyze" it, thus a. its importance

## approvingly 1
T-21 ..... IV.1:5 deems quite appropriate, and smiles a.. It

## approximately 1
W-pI..... 65.4:1 periods at a. the same time each day. Try,

## approximation 1
T-13 ..... IV.7:5 closest a. of eternity that this world offers.

## apt 12
T-2 ....... VI.6:5 but particularly a. to be overlooked. I will
T-2 .....VIII.1:2 You are a. to forget this when you become
T-3 .........II.2:3 innocent are a. to be quite foolish at times
T-6 ..........I.2:4 only because the fearful are a. to perceive
T-6 ..... V.B.3:3 this is a. to increase conflict temporarily,
T-7 .........X.3:4 and are, in fact, very a. to confuse the two
W-pI..... 72.3:2 of things you are a. to hold grievances for.
W-pI... 134.1:1 is a. to be distorted and to be perceived as
W-pI... 163.3:1 a. to fail the hopes they once engendered,
M-4 ..... I.A.5:5 period of overlap is a. to be one in which
M-9 ........... 2:4 a. to be perceived as personally insulting.
M-21 ......... 2:2 picture that comes to mind is a. to be very

## arbiter 2
T-18 ..... IV.8:2 have become the a. of what is possible,
T-25 ..... VI.1:5 is not an a. of vengeance, nor a punisher

## arbitrarily 2
T-9 ..........I.3:3 you are a. associating something beyond
M-19 ......... 3:3 Selectively and a. is every concept of the

## arbitrary 4
T-12 ..... III.9:6 governed by a. and senseless "laws," and
W-pI... 158.3:2 It appears to be quite a.. Yet there is no
W-pI... 184.7:5 all the a. names the world bestows can be
M-10 ......... 4:4 such an a. basis for decision making?

## arc 1
T-21 ........I.8:1 an a. of golden light that stretches as you

## arched 1
T-18 ...VIII.7:7 A. high above it and surrounding it with

## are 4422

## area 5
T-14 ........I.2:7 There is no a. of your perception that it
T-26 .... III.6:3 real world is the a. of choice made real,
W-pI....... 1.2:1 look farther away from your immediate a.
W-pI....... 2.1:6 to include everything you see in a given a.
W-pI..... 74.4:1 is one conflict a. that seems particularly

## areas 7
T-3 ....... IV.5:1 it brings the mind into a. of uncertainty.
T-12 ...... V.5:2 There are a. in your learning skills that
T-17 ...... V.7:4 you must exclude major a. of fantasy from
T-20 .... VII.1:4 are merely indications of a. where means
W-pI... 108.6:2 to other a. of doubt and double vision.
M-22 ......... 1:4 just as special a. of hell in Heaven are
M-22 ......... 2:1 a time excludes some problem a. from it.

## arena 1
W-pI..... 72.6:1 this carefully prepared a., where angry

## argue 3
T-9 ..... VIII.4:6 and a. that grandeur cannot be a real part
W-pI .... 98.1:6 be. We will not a. it is something else. We
S-2........ III.1:3 It does not a., nor evaluate the errors that

## argued 1
T-13 ..... IV.3:2 be a. that death suggests there *was* life, no

## argues 3
T-8 ....... IX.8:3 I ask, and everything a. *for* your doing it. I
W-pI .. 132.6:1 But it is pride that a. you have come into
M-18 ......... 1:2 a. with his pupil about a magic thought,

## argument 5
T-4 .........V.4:2 its own best a. that you cannot be of God.
T-6 ..... V.A.2:5 what the ego uses as an a. for separation
T-8 ..... VIII.3:4 appealing a. from the ego's point of view,
T-8 ..... VIII.6:3 as its best a. for your need for *its* guidance.
T-27 .......II.9:7 reason with an a. for sickness such as this

## arguments 3
W-pI .... 66.3:2 not engage in senseless a. about what it is.
W-pI .... 73.6:1 Forget the ego's a. which seek to prove all
W-pI .. 188.2:3 easily be looked upon that a. which prove

## aright 4
T-10 .......V.7:5 and you will learn of Him if you hear a..
T-12 .......V.9:6 you. For you really want to learn a., and
W-pI .. 190.1:4 it takes that will not disappear if seen a..
W-pII . 324.1:5 *will always call me back, and guide my feet a.*

## arise 57
T-1 ........I.14:2 because they a. from conviction. Without
T-1 ........I.43:1 Miracles a. from a miraculous state of
T-1 ....... III.7:1 Miracles a. from a mind that is ready for
T-1 ....... VI.1:8 Needs a. only when you deprive yourself.
T-2 ....... III.1:4 which minds engage a. from the distorted
T-8 ..... VIII.1:9 are part of being since they a. from it, but
T-9 ....... IV.2:6 sense of limitation is where all errors a..
T-13 .....V.10:2 worlds a. from their different sights. See
T-14 ... XI.15:1 power of God, from which they both a., is
T-18 .......II.1:1 a world that seems quite real a. in dreams
T-19 ... III.11:1 and let not sin a. again to blind your eyes.
T-19 ..... IV.1:3 Others will seem to a. from elsewhere;
T-21 .......V.4:5 All sorts of questions may a. in it, but if
T-22 ........I.1:6 fear of lack of meaning in yourself a.? It is
T-22 .......V.6:1 you feel the need a. to be defensive about
T-24 .......V.3:1 could your peace a. *but* from forgiveness?
T-26 .. VII.12:4 error does the world of sin and sacrifice a.
T-27 ..... VI.5:9 The dying live, the dead a., and pain has
T-29 ..... IV.4:5 that they exist from which the fears a..
T-30 ........I.4:3 for opposition will not first a. and then
T-30 .......V.3:6 heart made ready to a. and go with him.
T-30 ..... VI.3:2 Fear cannot a. unless attack is justified,
T-31 .......II.4:3 you want to let the follower in you a., and
T-31 .......V.8:5 of self, and greater terror would a. in you.
W-pI .... 21.1:2 to particular situations as they may a..
W-pI .... 31.5:1 to any form of temptation that may a.. It
W-pI .... 34.3:3 slowly as you watch them a. in your mind,
W-pI .. 39.11:2 If temptations a., a particularly helpful
W-pI .... 68.2:2 Can all this a. from holding grievances?
W-pI .... 73.1:2 out of which darkness and nothingness a.
W-pI .... 79.3:3 one is settled the next one and the next a..
W-pI .... 80.6:3 today to any specific problem that may a..
W-pI .... 81.2:1 special difficulties seem to a. might be: *Let*
W-pI .. 100.7:1 by feeling happiness a. in us according to
W-pI .. 122.3:2 can a. across the threshold of your mind.
W-pI .. 122.8:3 forever newly born, a. in your awareness.
W-pI 122.12:1 see another world a. you have no words
W-pI .. 132.8:4 and the dead a. when you let thoughts of
W-pI 136.16:1 peace and truth a. to take the place of war
W-pI .. 137.5:3 Just as the real world will a. to take the
W-pI 152.11:2 We think of truth alone as we a., and

| | |
|---|---|
| W-pI.153.15:5 | ceases to **a.** to turn us from our purpose, |
| W-pI...181.6:3 | should such blocks **a.** we will transcend |
| W-pI...183.3:3 | The sick **a.**, healed of their sickly thoughts |
| W-pI.193.11:2 | now we would **a.** in haste and go unto our |
| W-pII..237.1:2 | I will **a.** in glory, and allow the light in me |
| W-pII..260.1:6 | *sinlessness* **a.** *again before Christ's vision,* |
| M-4......I.A.4:3 | he has learned to new situations as they **a.** |
| M-25..........3:3 | the question of how they **a.** is irrelevant. |
| M-26..........1:3 | awareness and this memory can **a.** across |
| C-5............4:3 | **A.** with him who showed you this because |
| C-ep...........4:2 | us **a.** and go in faith along the way to Him |
| P-2........VI.2:4 | of the song of condemnation must **a.**. The |
| S-2........III.3:2 | **a.** in haste to go at last unto your Father's |
| S-2........III.7:4 | Let it **a.** to Christ, Who welcomes it as gift |
| S-3........IV.6:4 | **a.** and lay all dreaming down forever. You |
| S-3........IV.9:8 | **A.** and let My thanks be given you. And |

## arisen 4

| | |
|---|---|
| T-1........VI.2:2 | sense of separation would never have **a.** if |
| T-2........VI.7:2 | not to love, or the fear could not have **a.**. |
| W-pI...187.8:3 | error has **a.** and correction must be made. |
| S-3........III.1:8 | and idols have **a.** to obscure the unity that |

## arises 41

| | |
|---|---|
| T-2.........V.1:3 | This misperception **a.** in turn from the |
| T-2.........V.8:1 | The fear of healing **a.** in the end from an |
| T-2........VI.5:2 | This situation **a.** in two ways: First, you |
| T-2........VI.7:6 | Fear **a.** from lack of love. The only remedy |
| T-3...........I.3:8 | is, and how entirely it **a.** from projection. |
| T-3...........I.4:2 | God. It **a.** solely from fear, and frightened |
| T-3........IV.1:6 | all conflict **a.** from the concept of levels. |
| T-9........III.3:3 | to understand anything that **a.** from it. |
| T-9.......VII.7:7 | nothing that **a.** from it means anything. |
| T-11...... I.10:5 | symptom of sickness and fear **a.** here, |
| T-12.......III.5:3 | it. Any response other than love **a.** from a |
| T-14....III.10:5 | All this **a.** because they do not believe that |
| T-14.......IV.3:9 | your guilt **a.** from your failure to fulfill |
| T-14....... X.9:2 | the system of thought that **a.** from joining |
| T-15....... V.5:5 | All the guilt in it **a.** from your use of it. All |
| T-15.......VI.1:4 | **a.** only from perfect faith in yourself. And |
| T-16.....V.11:8 | complete, for life **a.** not from death, nor |
| T-17..........I.3:3 | the power that heals all pain **a.** from your |
| T-18........IV.3:3 | with the holy instant **a.** from your fixed |
| T-19...... I.12:2 | faith **a.** from the Holy Spirit's perception, |
| T-24.......in.2:9 | The truth **a.** from what He knows. And |
| T-24.........I.8:4 | or stab of hate or wish to separate **a.** here. |
| T-25......III.5:3 | Nothing **a.** but is met with instant and |
| T-28...... I.13:1 | How instantly the memory of God **a.** in |
| T-31.........I.4:4 | that makes up the world **a.** from the first |
| T-31......VI.2:7 | constancy **a.** in the sight of those whose |
| W-pI.....23.6:1 | using it throughout the day as the need **a.**, |
| W-pI.....24.1:1 | In no situation that **a.** do you realize the |
| W-pI.....33.3:2 | situation **a.** which tempts you to become |
| W-pI.....34.1:4 | that a peaceful perception of the world **a.**. |
| W-pI.....34.5:3 | form of temptation **a.** in your awareness, |
| W-pI.....38.6:1 | concerning you or someone else **a.**, or |
| W-pI.....54.1:5 | the world I see **a.** from my thinking errors |
| W-pI.....65.5:4 | each thought that **a.** to interfere with it. |
| W-pI.....68.7:1 | thought of grievance **a.** against anyone, |
| W-pI.....77.7:4 | a situation **a.** in which they are called for. |
| W-pI....93.11:1 | a situation **a.** that seems to be disturbing, |
| W-pI.130.10:1 | temptation easily today whenever it **a.**, |
| W-pI...136.7:3 | truth **a.** in your own deluded mind, and |
| W-pII......8.3:4 | sees **a.** from a mind at peace within itself. |
| W-pII..344.1:9 | *And thus Your Son* **a.** *and returns to You.* |

## arising 6

| | |
|---|---|
| T-2........VI.5:1 | **a.** whenever what you want conflicts with |
| T-10....... II.5:3 | **A.** from your own decision not to be what |
| T-16...VII.10:2 | the plan of Atonement **a.** from His Love. |
| T-26.......IV.3:2 | you see the face of Christ, **a.** in its place. |
| W-pI.131.10:3 | with true ideas **a.** in the place of thoughts |
| W-pI...162.3:1 | words his own; **a.** with them in his mind, |

## ark 4

| | |
|---|---|
| T-20.........IV.h | Entering the **A.** |
| T-20......IV.6:5 | The **a.** of peace is entered two by two, yet |
| T-28........VII.h | The **A.** of Safety |
| T-28.....VII.7:5 | an **a.** of safety, resting on God's promise |

## arm 3

| | |
|---|---|
| T-20..... II.10:4 | his strong **a.** is free to guide you safely |
| W-pI.......2.2:3 | a button, a fly or a floor, an **a.** or an apple. |
| W-pI.......9.3:5 | *as it is now. I do not see this* **a.** *as it is now.* |

## armaments 1

| | |
|---|---|
| W-pI...135.2:4 | and doubts, its penalties and heavy **a.**, its |

## armature 1

| | |
|---|---|
| W-pI...135.2:5 | For no one walks the world in **a.** but must |

## armies 1

| | |
|---|---|
| W-pI.....96.5:3 | attacked by **a.** massed against itself and |

## armor 3

| | |
|---|---|
| T-19....... II.5:5 | serve. Here is its **a.**, its protection, and the |
| W-pI.134.12:4 | and useless **a.** made to chain his mind to |
| W-pI...135.3:5 | your **a.** thicker and your locks more tight, |

## armored 1

| | |
|---|---|
| W-pI...138.8:2 | to be safe, and magically **a.** against truth. |

## Arms 12

*arms*

| | |
|---|---|
| T-9........VI.7:2 | to you until you remember God's open **A.**, |
| T-20.....VI.10:5 | behind and resting in the Everlasting **A.**. |
| T-20.....VI.10:6 | Love's **A.** are open to receive you, and give |
| W-pI...168.3:4 | and takes us in His **A.** and sweeps away |
| W-pII..226.2:2 | *Your* **A.** *are open and I hear Your Voice.* |
| W-pII..235.1:3 | that I am saved and safe forever in His **A.**. |
| W-pII..267.1:6 | quiet and at peace within His loving **A.**. |
| W-pII..303.2:8 | *Safe in Your* **A.** *let me receive Your Son.* |
| W-pII..317.2:5 | *from the sure protection of Your loving* **A.**. |
| S-3........IV.6:2 | still surrounds you with the **A.** of peace. |
| S-3........IV.7:3 | My **A.** are open to the Son I love, who |
| S-3........IV.9:6 | I hold you in My Heart and in My **A.**. |

## arms 4

• body
*weapons*
*Arms*

| | |
|---|---|
| T-13.....VII.7:6 | he perceives the **a.** of love around him. |
| T-24...... III.6:6 | Will it is you rest forever in the **a.** of peace |
| W-pI...156.4:4 | extend their **a.** to shield you from the heat |
| M-27 .........3:4 | he is "laid to rest" in devastation's **a.**, |

## arms 4

• weapons
*body*
*Arms*

| | |
|---|---|
| W-pI.136.14:2 | to any mind that would lay down its **a.**, |
| W-pI...170.2:7 | *Lay down your* **a.**, *and only then do you* |
| W-pI...170.5:5 | your **a.** indeed would crumble into dust. |
| W-pI...190.9:1 | Lay down your **a.**, and come without |

## army 6

| | |
|---|---|
| T-21.....VII.2:6 | They join the **a.** of the powerless, to wage |
| T-21.....VII.2:8 | They are indeed a sorry **a.**, each one as |
| T-21.....VII.3:5 | **a.** of the powerless must be disbanded in |
| T-21.....VII.3:7 | How would an **a.** act in dreams? Any way |
| T-21...VII.3:13 | This is no **a.**, but a madhouse. What |
| T-21.....VII.4:1 | The **a.** of the powerless is weak indeed. It |

## arose 18

| | |
|---|---|
| T-1....... VI.2:3 | The idea of order of needs **a.** because, |
| T-3...........I.1:6 | interpretation, which **a.** out of projection, |
| T-3...........I.7:3 | it **a.** from anything but perfect innocence. |
| T-4...........I.3:5 | to teach you how its thought system **a.**. |
| T-4..........II.7:4 | of "getting" **a.** in the ego's thought system |
| T-4........ III.3:2 | The ego **a.** from the separation, and its |
| T-5........ IV.5:3 | learned, which **a.** in me *because* I learned it |
| T-6...... IV.12:6 | of communication **a.** as the ego's voice. It |
| T-18.........I.6:2 | The world **a.** to hide it, and became the |
| T-18.........I.6:4 | down **a.** from this projection of error? It |
| T-18...... IX.4:5 | for the body **a.** from this for its protection |
| T-21....... V.5:6 | have been there since the need for Him **a.**, |
| T-24........II.3:3 | For sin **a.** from it, out of nothingness; an |
| T-26...VII.12:2 | outside the mind where the belief **a.**. Here |
| T-30......IV.1:8 | think **a.** between yourself and what is true |
| T-31...... VI.3:6 | how what you see **a.** to meet your sight. |
| C-2............2:5 | how it **a.** can be but he who thinks it real, |
| C-6............5:5 | as him for you **a.** with him when he began |

## around 62

| | |
|---|---|
| T-2........ III.1:8 | inner altar **a.** which the structure is built. |
| T-3.........I.3:11 | possible to twist symbols **a.** if you wish. |
| T-4........ III.7:4 | can see through a wall, but I can step **a.** it. |
| T-6........IV.6:7 | you will see the truth **a.** you and in you, |
| T-7........ XI.5:2 | light. Its own radiance shines all **a.** it, and |
| T-10.......IV.5:9 | beyond it, to what is in you and all **a.** you. |
| T-12......IV.7:6 | you will not see life though it is all **a.** you. |
| T-13.....VII.7:6 | he perceives the arms of love **a.** him. And |
| T-14......IV.7:3 | not recognize Him, though He is all **a.** you |
| T-14...... IX.5:1 | Creator shines forth from you to all **a.** you |
| T-14...... XI.5:3 | hurt and hinder you, and everyone **a.** you. |
| T-15.......IV.7:5 | in full communication with those **a.** you, |
| T-15.....VII.5:2 | belongs not **a.** the chosen host of God, |
| T-16....... V.3:2 | that center **a.** it are often quite overt. Here |
| T-16...... VI.7:6 | frame of reference is built **a.** the special |
| T-18........II.1:4 | solely **a.** what you would have preferred. |
| T-18.... VI.9:10 | it is. You cannot put a barrier **a.** yourself, |
| T-18....VIII.2:5 | The body is a tiny fence **a.** a little part of a |
| T-18....VIII.2:6 | small, **a.** a very little segment of Heaven, |
| T-20.... VI.11:2 | seems to be a wall of flesh **a.** the mind, |
| T-22.........I.6:6 | he will communicate with those **a.** him, |
| T-23.......in.6:1 | Nothing **a.** you but is part of you. Look |
| T-23.......II.14:6 | Such a reversal, completely turned **a.**, |
| T-24......VII.4:6 | or weave a frame of loveliness **a.** your hate |
| T-24......VII.4:8 | rather, then, a frame of holiness **a.** him, |
| T-25........II.6:1 | the frame God set **a.** the part of Him that |
| T-26.........I.2:3 | **A.** each entity is built a wall so seeming |
| T-26...... IX.7:1 | **A.** you angels hover lovingly, to keep |
| T-27....VIII.8:4 | easy to perceive the jest when all **a.** you do |
| T-29.........I.8:7 | of seeming fear **a.** the happy message, |
| W-in..........3:2 | exercises are planned **a.** one central idea, |
| W-pI.......1.1:1 | Now look slowly **a.** you, and practice |
| W-pI.......2.1:5 | turn **a.** and apply the idea to what was |
| W-pI.......2.2:1 | glance easily and fairly quickly **a.** you, |
| W-pI.....10.2:3 | link is made overtly with the things **a.** you |
| W-pI.....12.2:2 | Look **a.** you, this time quite slowly. Try to |
| W-pI.....15.2:2 | edges of light **a.** the same familiar objects |
| W-pI.....15.4:1 | then apply it to whatever you see **a.** you, |
| W-pI.....17.1:3 | to believe that it is the other way **a.**. This |
| W-pI.....32.3:1 | **a.** at the world you see as outside yourself. |
| W-pI.....32.3:2 | your eyes and look **a.** your inner world. |
| W-pI.....33.2:1 | Merely glance casually **a.** the world you |
| W-pI.....37.5:1 | what you see **a.** you and to those who are |
| W-pI.....43.4:4 | open. Then glance **a.** you for a short time, |
| W-pI.....62.4:3 | be. And it will help those **a.** you, as well as |
| W-pI.....64.8:3 | then look slowly and unselectively **a.** you, |
| W-pI.....71.2:1 | for salvation centers **a.** holding grievances |
| W-pI.....74.5:2 | you. Sink into it and feel it closing **a.** you. |
| W-pI.....97.5:1 | carry them **a.** this aching world where |
| W-pI.121.12:2 | to see **a.** your former "enemy" to him. |
| W-pI...124.9:4 | like a diamond set **a.** the mirror that this |
| W-pI...125.1:5 | until His Word is heard **a.** the world; until |
| W-pI.137.10:1 | yourself be healed, you see all those **a.** you |
| W-pI.139.12:2 | world would weave **a.** the holy Son of God |
| W-pI...162.2:4 | of awakening that sounds **a.** the world. |
| W-pI...185.2:8 | see **a.** you to be sure how very few they are |
| W-pI...188.3:1 | and from your heart extends **a.** the world. |

W-pI.198.11:1 Now is there silence all a. the world. Now
M-15 .........1:6 proclaimed a. and around the world,
M-15 .........1:6 proclaimed around and a. the world,
M-28 .........4:8 The song of Heaven sounds a. the world,
M-29 .........8:4 *which His Voice is heard a. the world, To*

**arouse** 4
T-9........ VI.2:1 you do not consistently a. joy in others.
W-pI.....13.5:4 of overt or covert fear which it may a..
W-pI.....14.5:4 attacks, or whatever may a. fear in you.
W-pI.....21.2:2 present or anticipated that a. anger in you

**aroused** 4
T-2......... V.7:8 Discomfort is a. only to bring the need for
T-29.........I.8:6 is a wariness that is a. by learning that the
W-pI.....13.1:1 it is more specific as to the emotion a..
M-17 .........4:3 too, of the intensity of the anger that is a..

**arouses** 7
T-2........ VI.5:7 do. This a. a sense of coercion that usually
T-6......... II.5:3 Instead of anger this a. love for both,
T-26....VIII.5:5 Belief in sin a. fear, and like its cause, is
W-pI.....13.2:1 of meaninglessness a. intense anxiety in
W-pI.....16.5:4 of a particular thought that a. uneasiness.
W-pI.....21.3:2 not really recognize what a. anger in you,
M-17 .........1:6 If a magic thought a. anger in any form,

**arousing** 1
M-29 .......4:12 And therefore incapable of a. guilt.

**arrange** 8
T-2....V.A.11:3 I will a. both time and space to adjust to it
T-14....... X.5:8 order is to judge, and to a. by judgment.
T-17..... V.14:3 Think you not the goal itself will gladly a.
T-18....... II.3:4 gone. In dreams *you* a. everything. People
T-18....... V.3:1 blessed in every holy instant you do not a.
T-20...... IV.8:4 will not a. for you without your effort. He
T-26..... VII.1:3 and a. them in a way that summarizes all
W-pI.....65.4:3 The purpose of this is to a. your day so

**arranged** 2
T-31....... V.9:1 Holy Spirit's lesson plans a. in easy steps,
W-pI.......1.3:1 these statements are not a. in any order,

**arrangement** 2
T-12...... III.6:5 some sort of insane "a." with the world.
T-13....... II.2:1 how strange a solution the ego's a. is. You

**array** 1
W-pI...152.4:3 It is concealed behind a vast a. of choices

**arrest** 4
T-8.....VII.12:7 and does not a. itself in its extension. This
T-8.....VII.12:8 This a. is the cause of all illness, because
T-8.....VII.16:8 Do not a. your thought in this world, and
T-11.........I.3:7 Your denial of its reality may a. it in time,

**arrival** 2
W-pI...163.3:3 when the time has come for its a.. It will
W-ep .........4:6 of the goal, and of your safe a. in the end.

**arrive** 6
T-7......... II.2:8 can a. at diametrically opposed results.
T-9......... V.7:1 approach, then, must a. at an impasse;
T-17...... III.2:5 by which you a. at the connection may be.
W-pI.....66.3:1 and a. at the truth about your function.
W-pI...108.6:3 and finally a. at the one Thought which

W-pII .284.1:8 a. at full acceptance of the truth in them.

**arriving** 1
W-ep .........2:1 certain of a. home as is the pathway of the

**arrogance** 40
T-5 .........II.7:1 command, because It is incapable of a.. It
T-9 ....... III.7:8 and this can only be the a. of the ego.
T-9 ....... III.7:9 is of God, Who does not know of a..
T-9 ...VIII.10:8 yourself as God created you cannot be a.,
T-9 ...VIII.10:8 be arrogance, because it is the denial of a..
T-10 .... V.14:1 A. is the denial of love, because love
T-10 .... V.14:1 love, because love shares and a. withholds
T-11 ...... V.6:4 ascribe the ego's a. to Him Who wills not
T-18 ..... IV.2:7 Come to it not in a., assuming that you
T-18 ...VIII.3:4 In its amazing a., this tiny sunbeam has
T-19 .......II.2:1 entails an a. which the idea of error lacks.
T-19 .......II.4:2 Purity is seen as a., and the acceptance of
T19...IV.C.2:8 This is no a.. It is the Will of God. What is
T19...IV.C.4:5 a. of sin, the pride of guilt, the sepulchre
T-20 ..... III.7:8 This one wild thought, fierce in its a., and
T-22 ... VI.10:2 only a. that would deny the power of your
T-23 .......II.6:1 a. on which the laws of chaos stand could
T-25 ..... IX.1:1 but a. to think your little errors cannot be
T-31 ..... VI.4:1 Only in a. could you conceive that you
W-pI.....61.1:3 the opposite of a statement of pride, of a.,
W-pI.....61.2:5 It is only a. that would assert this function
W-pI.....61.2:5 be for you, and a. is always of the ego.
W-pI.....64.3:2 It is only the a. of the ego that leads you to
W-pI...152.6:1 to think you made the world you see is a.?
W-pI...152.7:1 death to triumph over life; all this is a..
W-pI...152.9:4 aside the a. which says that we are sinners
W-pI.152.10:4 false. Their a. has been perceived. And in
W-pI...154.1:7 we believe to be our strength is often a..
W-pI...186.1:1 one day take all a. away from every mind.
W-pI...186.2:5 with self-deceiving a. that we are worthy.
W-pI...186.3:5 And what could a. deny but this? Today
W-pI...186.4:5 we are. It is but a. that judges otherwise.
W-pI...186.6:1 A. makes an image of yourself that is not
W-pII .319.1:1 from which all a. has been removed, and
W-pII .319.1:2 For a. opposes truth. But when there is no
W-pII .319.1:3 is no a. the truth will come immediately,
S-1......... V.3:2 as God's Son, and recognize the a. of sin.
S-2..........II.2:2 from love that a. could never be dislodged
S-2..........II.3:1 does not appear in quite such blatant a..
S-3........ III.4:2 In a. the answer must be "no." But in

**arrogant** 15
T-2 ....... VI.9:9 to believe such power about yourself is a.,
T-5 ........ V.5:7 Yet even in this it is a.. It attributes to
T-9 .....VIII.9:1 be a. when God Himself witnesses to it?
T-9 ...VIII.10:9 To accept your littleness *is* a., because it
T-18 ..... IV.4:4 to make a. preparations for holiness, and
T19...IV.C.4:3 condemned the Son of God to this *are* a..
T-26 .. VII.18:2 It is not a. to be as He created you, nor to
T-26 .. VII.18:3 it is a. to lay aside the power that He gave,
W-pI...152.7:5 be. And what could be more a. than this?
W-pI...152.9:1 by which the ego seeks to prove it a.. Only
W-pI...152.9:2 Only the ego can be a.. But truth is
W-pI...154.1:1 us today be neither a. nor falsely humble.
W-pI...186.5:5 The a. must cling to words, afraid to go
M-14 .......5:11 Do not be a. and say you cannot learn His
P-3..........II.3:2 The unhealed healer may be a., selfish,

**arsenals** 1
S-1........ IV.1:6 Their separate wishes are their a.; their

**artificial** 5
T-9 ..........I.3:2 fear, which would be highly a. at most, is
T-13 .... VII.1:4 It is not lit with a. light, and night comes
T-18 ..... IX.6:1 barrier, this a. floor that looks like rock, is
W-pI..... 16.4:3 hard for you not to make a. distinctions.
W-pII .298.1:4 journeys, mad careers and a. values. I

**arts** 1
S-3........ III.2:8 a wiser one who, by his a. and learning,

**as** 4589

**ascend** 8
T-11 ..... VI.2:3 your prison and a. to the Father? These
T-11 ..... VI.4:9 For we a. unto the Father together, as it
T-15 ......I.14:5 the ego's making, and a. unto your Father
T-17 ... IV.16:2 Let us a. in peace together to the Father,
T-18 .......V.2:8 Nor will you use it to a. to Heaven alone.
W-pI .. 100.8:5 pass as you a. to meet the Christ in you.
S-1.........in.3:3 as you a. the shining stairway to the lawns
S-2.........I.10:5 waits its freedom to a. above the world of

**ascendance** 3
T-17 ... IV.16:2 the Father, by giving Him a. in our minds.
T-17 ... IV.16:4 They are in us, through His a.. What He
P-2..........II.5:4 therapist restores the place of God to a.,

**ascended** 1
C-6 ............ 1:1 upon the earth after he a. into Heaven, or

**ascending** 1
S-1........ III.1:6 prayer, of rising power and with a. goals,

**ascends** 2
T-11 ..... VI.1:7 and a. to the Father and His Kingdom.
T-17 ... IV.16:1 God a. into His rightful place and you to

**ascent** 3
S-1........ III.3:4 The next a. begins with this: *What I have*
S-1........ IV.2:2 This step begins the quicker a., but there
S-3.........in.1:1 the steep a. more gentle and more sure,

**ascribe** 6
T-11 .......V.6:4 a. the ego's arrogance to Him Who wills
T-29 ..... IV.4:3 the needs which you a. to you are met. It
T-29 ..... IV.6:3 Do not a. a role to him that you imagine
T-29 .... VII.8:5 do, and have the power you a. to them.
W-pI ...... 5.2:1 the upset, and the cause which you a. to it
W-pI .... 35.4:2 the ego-based attributes which you a. to

**ascribed** 5
T-15 .......X.8:5 Him. To Him you a. the ego's treachery,
T-17 ..... IV.1:2 The purpose God a. to anything is its only
W-pI .... 57.3:2 of the world is not the one I a. to it, there
W-pI .... 77.2:2 magical powers you have a. to yourself,
W-pI .... 94.4:1 good and bad, you have a. to yourself;

**ascribes** 2
T-4 .........II.9:1 magic to the powers the ego a. to itself.
T-8 ..... VIII.1:3 what it sees with the function it a. to it. It

**ascribing** 1
W-pI .... 35.9:1 or attributes you are a. to yourself at the

**ashamed** 4
T-8 ....... VI.4:2 He was a. to return to his father, because
T-21 ..... IV.1:6 It has no fear to let you feel a.. It doubts
W-pI .. 152.9:4 guilty and afraid, a. of what we are; and
W-pI .. 189.7:2 worthy, and all the ideas of which it is a..

**ashen** 1
T-23 .....II.15:6 And fear, with a. lips and sightless eyes,

## ashes 2

| | |
|---|---|
| W-pI...128.1:2 | hopes that turn to bitter **a.** of despair. No |
| W-pI...163.3:1 | leave the taste of dust and **a.** in their wake |

## aside 87

| | |
|---|---|
| T-4....... II.10:3 | judgment, and is laid **a.** accordingly. The |
| T-7..... VIII.5:4 | will have laid **a.** all anger and all attack, |
| T-8........ VI.1:3 | so they too can lay **a.** their weakness and |
| T-8..... VIII.8:6 | When you lay the ego **a.**, it will be gone. |
| T-10....... IV.7:1 | a Son of God who has laid **a.** all false gods |
| T-12....... II.9:6 | lay **a.** the obstacles to real vision without |
| T-12....... II.9:6 | them, for to lay **a.** means to judge against. |
| T-13... VI.11:5 | you will lay **a.** the world and find another. |
| T-13... VII.12:6 | and will but last until you step **a.** from all |
| T-14....... X.1:5 | of holiness calls everyone to lay all guilt **a.** |
| T-15...... VI.6:4 | swiftly as the veil of time is pushed **a.**. No |
| T-15... VIII.2:3 | learn the value of what you have cast **a.**, |
| T-15...... XI.5:3 | thrust Heaven and its Creator **a.** without |
| T-16......... I.3:7 | Step gently **a.**, and let healing be done for |
| T-17......... I.5:6 | Reserve not one idea **a.** from truth, or you |
| T-17... VIII.3:2 | given wherever faithlessness is laid **a.**, |
| T-18...... VI.8:2 | place you set **a.** to house your hate is not a |
| T-18... VI.12:5 | body obeys and gently setting them **a.**. |
| T-19....... I.14:2 | of you. Lay faithlessness **a.**, and come to it |
| T19... IV.C.2:6 | See him throw **a.** the black robe he was |
| T19... IV.D.2:2 | the veil **a.** and run to meet Him, and to |
| T-20....... II.6:5 | to be tossed about a while and laid **a.**. |
| T-20...... VI.9:5 | lay **a.** the body and quietly transcend it, |
| T-21....... V.5:5 | You must have set **a.** a place in which the |
| T-23........ in.4:5 | meaningless distractions, lay Heaven **a.**? |
| T-25......... I.4:6 | to let Him draw **a.** the veil that seems to |
| T-25. VIII.5:10 | the idea of punishment that they lay it **a.**, |
| T-26... VII.18:3 | arrogant to lay **a.** the power that He gave, |
| T-27... VII.15:6 | brush **a.** his many gifts because he is not |
| T-28...... III.6:4 | The miracle will brush them all **a.**, and |
| T-29...... III.5:2 | and steps **a.** from heavy shadows that |
| T-29....... V.8:5 | are means to step **a.** from dreaming of a |
| T-31....... II.8:2 | before, and put **a.** all images you made. |
| W-pI....... 3.1:7 | Try to lay such feelings **a.**, and merely use |
| W-pI..... 14.7:1 | the day, **a.** from the practice periods. Be |
| W-pI..... 44.6:1 | can stand **a.** from the ego by ever so little, |
| W-pI..... 45.9:3 | Stand **a.**, however briefly, from all |
| W-pI..... 65.3:1 | set **a.** ten to fifteen minutes for a more |
| W-pI..... 68.7:6 | *all my grievances* **a.** *and wakening in Him.* |
| W-pI..... 69.6:4 | Brush them **a.** with your hand; feel them |
| W-pI..... 70.6:3 | be a good time to lay **a.** for each of them, |
| W-pI... 72.10:5 | we are going to try to lay judgment **a.**, |
| W-pI..... 78.4:4 | and lay the grievances **a.** and look at him. |
| W-pI..... 78.9:1 | today in which you laid your images **a.**, |
| W-pI..... 80.2:4 | You have laid deception **a.**, and seen the |
| W-pI..... 85.1:6 | To see, I must lay grievances **a.**. I want to |
| W-pI..... 91.5:1 | set **a.** about ten minutes for a quiet time |
| W-pI..... 94.4:1 | except to lay all idols and self-images **a.**; |
| W-pI..... 95.9:4 | It is this process that must be laid **a.**, for it |
| W-pI..... 98.2:2 | All our doubts we lay **a.** today, and take |
| W-pI..... 99.9:8 | what you need to learn to lay all fear **a.**, |
| W-pI... 99.12:5 | your mind and let all fear be gently laid **a.** |
| W-pI... 104.3:4 | Then lay **a.** the conflicts of the world that |
| W-pI... 104.4:1 | All this we lay **a.**, and seek instead that |
| W-pI... 106.1:1 | If you will lay **a.** the ego's voice, however |
| W-pI... 120.2:3 | *Today I lay* **a.** *all sick illusions of myself, and* |
| W-pI.127.11:2 | all who come to learn to cast **a.** the world |
| W-pI.133.13:2 | state today, with self-deception laid **a.**, |
| W-pI.135.20:4 | lay **a.** their cumbersome defenses, which |
| W-pI.136.18:2 | As these are laid **a.**, the strength the body |
| W-pI.139.12:1 | lay **a.** all thoughts that would distract us |
| W-pI.140.10:1 | So do we lay **a.** our amulets, our charms |
| W-pI.140.11:2 | is to let our interfering thoughts be laid **a.** |
| W-pI.152.9:4 | We lay **a.** the arrogance which says that |
| W-pI.152.10:3 | that all self-concepts have been laid **a.**, |
| W-pI.153.12:5 | The game of fear is gladly laid **a.**, when |
| W-pI.153.20:7 | You lay **a.** but what was never real, to |
| W-pI... 165.5:6 | your mind has come to lay **a.** denial, and |
| W-pI.182.11:1 | to lay **a.** your shield which profits nothing |
| W-pI... 186.4:1 | All false humility we lay **a.** today, that we |
| W-pI... 189.7:1 | and lay **a.** all thoughts of what you are |
| W-pI... 190.9:4 | put **a.** the withering assaults with which |
| W-pI... 194.8:5 | lays **a.** the sick illusions of the world along |
| W-pI... 195.8:2 | is forgotten when we lay comparisons **a.**. |
| W-pI... 200.2:1 | lay **a.** all hope of finding happiness where |
| W-pII..272.2:2 | dream, we turn **a.** and ask ourselves if we, |
| W-pII...... 7.1:4 | are sights and sounds forever laid **a.**. And |
| W-pII..294.1:7 | afterwards, without a purpose, it is laid **a.** |
| W-pII..333.1:2 | be evaded, set **a.**, denied, disguised, seen |
| W-pII..346.1:2 | *share eternity, for time has stepped* **a.** *today.* |
| M-4 ..... I.A.7:8 | He must learn to lay all judgment **a.**, and |
| M-6 ........... 2:1 | will always stand **a.** when it would be seen |
| M-15 ....... 2:10 | Have you yet learned to stand **a.** and hear |
| M-15 ....... 2:13 | to all who stand **a.** in quiet listening, and |
| M-19 ......... 1:7 | interpretations and laying all injustices **a.**. |
| S-1 ........... I.5:1 | Prayer is a stepping **a.**; a letting go, a |
| S-1 ......... V.1:5 | be. All little gods it gladly lays **a.**, not in |

## ask 338

| | |
|---|---|
| T-1........ III.4:3 | **A.** me which miracles you should perform |
| T-2......... II.1:1 | You can do anything I **a.**. I have asked |
| T-2......... II.3:7 | The means are available whenever you **a.**. |
| T-2........ VI.4:2 | When you **a.** for release from fear, you are |
| T-2........ VI.4:3 | You should **a.**, instead, for help in the |
| T-2........ VI.4:9 | **a.** me if your choice is in accord with mine |
| T-2........ VI.6:2 | cannot **a.** more than you are willing to do. |
| T-2....... VII.1:2 | you cannot **a.** me to release you from fear. |
| T-3........... I.1:8 | Yet the real Christian should pause and **a.** |
| T-3...... III.2:11 | when you have ceased to **a.** questions. |
| T-3........ III.5:5 | While you **a.** questions about him you are |
| T-3......... V.4:1 | continually **a.** yourself cannot properly be |
| T-4......... II.1:1 | It is reasonable to **a.** how the mind could |
| T-4......... II.1:2 | In fact, it is the best question you could **a.** |
| T-4....... II.11:5 | You may **a.** how this is possible as long as |
| T-4........ III.5:3 | are for you, but for which you must **a.**. |
| T-4........ III.6:3 | Let us **a.** the Father in my name to keep |
| T-4........ III.7:5 | or you will be unable to **a.** me to do so. I |
| T-4........ III.7:9 | in impatience, you will surely **a.** me truly. |
| T-4......... V.6:8 | learn to **a.** in connection with everything. |
| T-7......... XI.6:1 | your natural environment you may well **a.** |
| T-8......... II.5:5 | **a.** the part of your mind that taught you |
| T-8........ III.1:2 | **A.** and it shall be given you, because it has |
| T-8........ III.1:3 | **A.** for light and learn that you *are* light. If |
| T-8......... V.5:2 | **A.** it of me who know it for you and you |
| T-8........ VI.8:1 | but one you should ever **a.** of yourself;– |
| T-8..... VIII.8:1 | might well **a.** how the voice of something |
| T-8........ IX.1:5 | do not **a.** the Holy Spirit to heal the body, |
| T-8........ IX.1:6 | **A.**, rather, that the Holy Spirit teach you |
| T-8........ IX.8:2 | says. I would not **a.** you to do things you |
| T-8........ IX.8:3 | prevent you from doing exactly what I **a.**, |
| T-9........... I.5:2 | if you **a.** the sacrifice of reality of yourself, |
| T-9........... I.6:6 | be, when you **a.** for what you do not want |
| T-9........... I.7:2 | are. You do not **a.** only for what you want. |
| T-9........... I.8:6 | **a.** the Holy Spirit for "gifts" such as these, |
| T-9........... I.8:8 | When you **a.** the Universal Giver for what |
| T-9........... I.9:9 | will. **A.** for this and you will be answered, |
| T-9......... I.10:1 | **a.** the Holy Spirit for what would hurt you |
| T-9......... I.10:2 | nothing, and to **a.** for it is not a request. It |
| T-9......... I.10:5 | ego cannot **a.** the Holy Spirit for anything |
| T-9......... I.10:6 | *you* can **a.** for everything of the Holy Spirit |
| T-9......... II.1:1 | tried to use prayer to **a.** for something has |
| T-9......... II.2:1 | that what you **a.** of the Holy Spirit is what |
| T-9......... II.2:4 | An individual may **a.** for physical healing |
| T-9......... II.4:4 | Can you **a.** of the Holy Spirit truly, and |
| T-9......... II.8:3 | you if you learn to **a.** only truth of them. |
| T-9......... II.8:4 | not **a.** for blessings without blessing them |
| T-9........ II.12:1 | You can **a.** of the Holy Spirit, then, only |
| T-9........ II.12:4 | His answer is all you can **a.** for and want. |
| T-9........ IV.8:2 | You might **a.** yourself, regardless of how |
| T-9....... VII.6:7 | taken for granted there and you do not **a.**, |
| T-9... VIII.11:6 | *is.* **A.** the Holy Spirit what it is and He will |
| T-10....... in.3:9 | threatens your peace of mind, **a.** yourself, |
| T-10...... III.6:8 | It is for you although you may not **a.** for it |
| T-11......... I.8:5 | must **a.** what God's Will is in everything, |
| T-11......... I.8:7 | **A.** Him, therefore, what God's Will is for |
| T-11....... II.5:5 | Whenever you **a.** the ego to enter, you |
| T-11... VIII.2:2 | perceive, and so they **a.** what it means. Do |
| T-11... VIII.2:5 | you will see no need to **a.** it of Him. |
| T-11... VIII.4:3 | **A.**, then, for what is yours, but which you |
| T-11... VIII.4:5 | **A.** yourself, therefore, but one simple |
| T-11... VIII.5:4 | to be told that if you **a.** you will receive. |
| T-11..VIII.5:10 | When you refuse to **a.**, it is because you |
| T-11.... VIII.6:4 | question you must **a.** to learn His answer? |
| T-11.... VIII.6:6 | You believe that to **a.** for guidance of the |
| T-11.... VIII.6:6 | of the Holy Spirit is to **a.** for deprivation. |
| T-11.... VIII.7:7 | willing to **a.** the truth of God without fear, |
| T-11.... VIII.8:6 | **A.** for truth of any Son of God, and you |
| T-11.... VIII.9:1 | **A.** anything of God's Son and his Father |
| T-11..VIII.10:6 | **A.**, then, to learn of the reality of your |
| T-11..VIII.13:2 | Yet if they **a.** someone they trust for the |
| T-11..VIII.14:3 | **A.** what they are of the Teacher of reality, |
| T-11..VIII.14:6 | And because of this they will **a.** for truth |
| T-11..VIII.14:9 | **A.** what their reality is from the One Who |
| T-12........ II.4:2 | If they **a.** for enlightenment and accept it, |
| T-12....... III.4:1 | and if your brothers **a.** you for something |
| T-12....... V.6:5 | you **a.** those who have failed to learn what |
| T-12.... VIII.4:3 | A Voice will answer every question you **a.**, |
| T-12.... VIII.5:1 | You have but to **a.** for this memory, and |
| T-13.... III.10:3 | and you could not **a.** this of a Father Who |
| T-13...... VI.1:6 | **a.** yourself if it is really sane to perceive |
| T-13.... VI.10:5 | The sick, who **a.** for love, are grateful for |
| T-13... VII.11:5 | **a.** not of yourself what you need, for you |
| T-14.... III.11:4 | will never **a.** what you have done to make |
| T-14.... III.11:5 | **A.** it not therefore of yourself. Instead, |
| T-14.... III.12:6 | it lies, but **a.** the Holy Spirit everything, |
| T-14...... IV.3:4 | **A.** not to be forgiven, for this has already |
| T-14...... IV.3:5 | **A.**, rather, to learn how to forgive, and to |
| T-14....... V.4:2 | you will **a.** for guilt and will experience it. |
| T-14...... XI.6:5 | **A.** to be taught, and do not use your |
| T-15....... I.11:1 | your mind so completely, **a.** yourself, |
| T-15...... IV.8:3 | **A.** yourself honestly, "Would I want to |
| T-15........ X.2:5 | sacrifice you **a.** of yourself you ask of me. |
| T-15........ X.2:5 | sacrifice you ask of yourself you **a.** of me. |
| T-16......... I.7:9 | He will fulfill it if you but **a.** Him to enter |
| T-17......... I.2:4 | to two masters who **a.** conflicting things |
| T-17...... VI.6:8 | This seems to **a.** for faith beyond you, and |
| T-17... VII.3:11 | **a.** that it be restored where it was lost, |
| T-18...... IV.1:6 | give the Holy Spirit what He does not **a.**, |
| T-18...... IV.3:1 | will never **a.** that you remain content with |
| T-18...... IV.5:1 | You merely **a.** the question. The answer |
| T-18....... V.2:3 | guilt before you **a.** the Holy Spirit's help. |
| T-18..VIII.11:4 | you **a.** of love only what it offers everyone, |
| T19. IV.A.15:4 | none you cannot **a.** love's messengers to |
| T19.... IV.B.2:4 | too great to make, too much to **a.** of you. |
| T19.... IV.B.6:4 | I **a.** for your forgiveness, for if you are |
| T19.. IV.B.11:5 | but only if you **a.** of it what it cannot give. |
| T19.... IV.C.8:4 | **A.** not release of *it.* But free it from the |
| T-20...... III.7:5 | **A.** not this transient stranger, "What am I |
| T-20...... III.7:7 | Yet it is he you **a.**, and it is to his answer |
| T-20...... III.7:9 | you turn to **a.** the meaning of the universe |
| T-20.... III.7:10 | in all the seeing universe of truth you **a.**, |
| T-20...... III.8:1 | Does one **a.** judgment of what is totally |
| T-20.... III.8:10 | **A.** not the means of its attainment of the |
| T-20...... IV.4:6 | that you should **a.** what freedom is. Ask |
| T-20...... IV.4:7 | is. **A.** not the sparrow how the eagle soars, |
| T-20...... IV.8:3 | **a.** yourself if it is possible that God would |
| T-20..... VII.9:2 | **A.** only, "Do I really wish to see him |
| T-20..... VII.9:3 | sinless?" And as you **a.**, forget not that his |
| T-20.. VIII.2:10 | is freely given to those who **a.** to see. |
| T-20.... VIII.3:2 | For peace will come to all who **a.** for it |
| T-21........ II.2:5 | *that seems to happen to me I* **a.** *for, and* |
| T-21.... III.10:3 | could neither **a.** it nor receive it of itself. |
| T-21...... IV.3:3 | **a.** it now are threatening the ego's whole |
| T-21....... V.4:5 | stems from reason, it will not **a.** it. Like all |
| T-21....... V.6:4 | not meaningful to **a.** if what must be is so. |
| T-21....... V.6:5 | to **a.** why you are unaware of what is so, |
| T-21..... V.10:2 | asked the question the ego will never **a.**. |
| T-21... VII.5:10 | let him only **a.** himself these questions, |
| T-21..... VII.8:3 | form, all you need do is simply **a.** yourself |
| T-21.... VIII.3:1 | Reason will tell you that you cannot **a.** for |
| T-21.... VIII.3:2 | need **a.** for it but once to have it always. |
| T-21.... VIII.3:3 | being what it is, you did not **a.** for it. For |
| T-21.... VIII.3:4 | it. For no one fails to **a.** for his desire of |
| T-21.... VIII.3:6 | Yet he will **a.** because desire is a request, |
| T-21.... VIII.5:5 | answered, and what you **a.** for given. Here |
| T-23.... II.22:13 | **A.**, then, your Friend to join with you, |
| T-24...... III.6:4 | **A.** not He enter this. The way is barred to |
| T-24...... III.8:9 | They **a.** of you but that your will be done. |
| T-24..... VII.4:1 | **A.** yourself this: Can *you* protect the mind |
| T-25.... VIII.4:1 | You who know not of justice still can **a.**, |

T-25....VIII.8:1 punish those who a. for punishment, but
T-25....VIII.9:1 Love a. of you who think that all of this is
T-25..VIII.11:4 the Holy Spirit a. if he will be that one, so
T-26.........I.5:1 to illusion merely a. that they might see a
T-26....... II.1:1 why you do not a. the Holy Spirit to solve
T-26....... II.5:4 But a. not God to punish him because *you*
T-26....... II.6:7 you will a. no sacrifice of him because you
T-26...VII.11:7 Here does the Son of God a. not too much
T-26...... IX.2:1 it too much to a. a little trust for him who
T-26....... X.3:5 Yet it is you who a. this of yourself, in
T-27...... IV.3:5 The world can only a. a double question.
T-27...... IV.3:8 It does not a. a question to be answered,
T-27...... IV.5:8 in a conflict state is free to a. this question
T-27...... IV.6:7 questions of the world but a. of whom is
T-27....... V.1:6 No one can a. another to be healed. But
T-28....... II.5:8 It does not a. you make another; only that
T-28.....VII.1:1 His Son, like Him, need a. for nothing.
T-29...... IX.1:4 and a. yourself if it be not the truth that
T-30.........I.3:2 and *then* decide to a. what you should do.
T-30.........I.5:3 sit by and a. to have the answer given you.
T-30.........I.5:5 a quick restorative before you a. again.
T-30.......I.11:7 in conflict when you a. for what you want,
T-30.......I.11:7 and see that it is this for which you a..
T-30.......I.12:5 now can a. a question that makes sense,
T-30.......I.14:9 And you a. help of anti-Christ or Christ,
T-30.......I.15:3 always a. advice before you can decide on
T-30....... II.5:1 God turns to you to a. the world be saved
T-30...... III.1:9 yours. Decide for idols and you a. for loss.
T-30...... III.4:2 want indeed and have the right to a. for.
T-30....VIII.3:7 What you a. *is* given you, but not of God
T-31..... II.5:12 What does he a. you for? And listen well!
T-31...... VI.3:1 Salvation does not a. that you behold the
T-31....VIII.7:1 Deny me not the little gift I a., when in
T-31....VIII.8:2 I a. for nothing but your own release.
W-pI.....22.3:7 end of each practice period, a. yourself: *Is*
W-pI.....23.3:3 One can well a. if this can be called seeing
W-pI.....28.4:2 is to a. questions and receive the answers.
W-pI...39.11:1 you may a. yourself this question, repeat
W-pI.....71.9:2 A. Him very specifically: *What would You*
W-pI...72.10:5 aside, and a. what God's plan for us is:
W-pI...72.11:3 A. and you will be answered. Seek and
W-pI...72.11:7 will be true because of Whom you a..
W-pI.....77.3:4 We a. no more than what belongs to us in
W-pI.....77.6:1 this, you do not really a. for anything.
W-pI.....77.7:4 A. for them whenever a situation arises in
W-pI.....77.7:6 fully entitled to receive it whenever you a.
W-pI.....78.5:2 whom we a. God's Son be shown to you.
W-pI.....78.7:1 Then let us a. of Him Who knows this
W-pI.....78.7:2 We a. Him in the holy Name of God and
W-pI.....78.7:3 *one for me to a. to lead me to the holy light in*
W-pI.....79.7:1 today we will a. what the problem is, and
W-pI.....79.7:5 We will a. what it is, and wait for the
W-pI.....79.7:7 Then we will a. for the solution to it. And
W-pI...79.10:5 your eyes for a moment and a. what it is.
W-pI.....91.8:2 you? A. this in honesty, and then devote
W-pI.....92.8:2 No one can a. in vain to share its sight,
W-pI.....94.4:2 that it will be revealed to all who a. for it.
W-pI...101.2:4 death and pain, and it is this they a. for.
W-pI...104.4:1 we a. to recognize what God has given us.
W-pI...106.8:1 A. and expect an answer. Your request is
W-pI...106.9:3 who pause to a. that truth be given them,
W-pI...107.7:1 We do not a. for what we do not have.
W-pI...107.7:2 We merely a. for what belongs to us, that
W-pI...107.8:4 It is your Self you a. to go with you, and
W-pI...109.1:1 a. for rest today, and quietness unshaken
W-pI...109.1:2 We a. for peace and stillness, in the midst
W-pI...109.1:3 a. for safety and for happiness, although
W-pI...121.5:4 It does not a., because it thinks it knows.
W-pI...126.7:2 He a. you for a gift unless it was for you?
W-pI...126.8:4 and a. Him that He share your practicing
W-pI.126.10:2 a. for help in understanding what it really
W-pI...131.2:6 while you seek for life you a. for death.
W-pI.131.10:3 and we will a. to see the rising of the real
W-pI.131.11:3 this: *I a. to see a different world, and think a*
W-pI...133.2:1 You do not a. too much of life, but far too
W-pI...133.2:2 as valued by the world, you a. for sorrow,
W-pI...134.9:3 A. instead, "Would I accuse myself of
W-pI.134.14:5 teach it. Let us a. of Him: *Let me perceive*
W-pI.134.15:3 thought of him, and each time a. yourself,
W-pI...135.3:5 Is it not strange you do not pause to a., as
W-pI.136.15:2 will give a quarter of an hour twice to a.
W-pI.137.12:4 A. the inevitable to occur, and you will
W-pI.137.12:5 other choice is but to a. what cannot be to
W-pI.137.12:6 Today we a. that only truth will occupy
W-pI...139.2:1 Yet who could a. this question except one
W-pI...139.5:8 not a. what part of you can really doubt
W-pI...139.8:3 and question that to a. what it must be is
W-pI...151.2:3 Nor do you a. why you believe it, even
W-pI.152.11:5 humbly a. our Self that He reveal Himself
W-pI...154.5:2 nor a. why he has chosen those who will
W-pI...157.4:1 for what you a. for now is what He wills.
W-pI...160.8:3 He has answered you who a., "Who is the
W-pI...161.9:6 A. him but for this, and he will give it to
W-pI...161.9:7 A. him not to symbolize your fear. Would
W-pI.161.11:1 symbol of the rest, and a. salvation of him
W-pI.161.11:6 A. this of him, that he may set you free:
W-pI...165.4:4 to you. A. to receive, and it is given you.
W-pI...165.5:1 A. with desire. You need not be sure that
W-pI.167.10:4 We will not a. for death in any form today
W-pI...168.3:1 Today we a. of God the gift He has most
W-pI...168.6:8 *And You will come to me who a.. I am the*
W-pI.169.12:2 And now we a. for grace, the final gift
W-pI.169.14:5 We a. for grace, and for experience that
W-pI.169.14:7 We do not a. for the unaskable. We do
W-pI.169.15:2 what could be more than what we a. this
W-pI.169.15:2 this day of Him Who gives the grace we a.
W-pI...170.5:4 For love would a. you lay down all defense
W-pI...170.6:3 those who a. if the demands are sensible
W-pI...181.8:1 Nor do we a. for fantasies. For what we
W-pI...181.9:6 our trust to the experience we a. for now.
W-pI...182.5:4 not a. for more than just a few instants of
W-pI.182.11:3 to a. your help in letting Him go home
W-pI...185.7:5 They do not a. for compromise, nor try to
W-pI...185.8:2 What do you a. for in your heart? Forget
W-pI.185.10:3 a. but this when you make this request
W-pI.185.12:2 when you but a. for what He wills for you
W-pI...186.3:3 It does not a. that you be different in any
W-pI...189.8:5 A. and receive. But do not make demands
W-pI.189.10:9 *And we a. but that Your Will, which is our*
W-pI...200.3:1 you can a. as easily for love, for happiness
W-pI...200.3:2 A. for this, and you can only win. To ask
W-pI...200.3:3 a. for what you have already must succeed
W-pI...200.3:4 a. that what is false be true can only fail.
W-pII ....in.7:5 We a. but that Your ancient promises be
W-pII .222.2:1 *now, and a. to rest with You in peace a while.*
W-pII .230.1:5 Now I a. but to be what I am. And can
W-pII .242.2:3 *a. for anything that we may think we want.*
W-pII .254.1:3 *but this: I come to You to a. You for the truth.*
W-pII .269.1:1 *I a. Your blessing on my sight today. It is the*
W-pII .269.1:4 *I a. for the illusion which transcends all*
W-pII .272.2:2 we turn aside and a. ourselves if we, the
W-pII .278.2:1 *Father, I a. for nothing but the truth. I have*
W-pII .285.1:2 me. I a. but them to come, and realize my
W-pII .285.1:3 I will a. for only joyous things the instant
W-pII .290.2:1 *and a. Your strength to hold me up today,*
W-pII .290.2:3 *What I a. have You already given me. And I*
W-pII .323.1:1 *only "sacrifice" You a. of Your beloved Son;*
W-pII .323.1:1 *Son; You a. him to give up all suffering, all*
W-pII .323.1:2 *Such is the "sacrifice" You a. of me, and one I*
W-pII .339.1:9 resolve today to a. for what we really want
W-pII ... 13.4:1 because to a. for it implies the mind has
Wfl........in.6:1 and a. Him to help us to learn His lessons,
W-ep......... 1:5 if you simply turn to Him and a. it of Him
W-ep......... 1:9 You need but a. it of Him, and it will be
W-ep......... 6:3 as we a. His Will in everything we do. He
M-4 ..... I.A.7:8 and a. only what he really wants in every
M-5 ...... III.2:3 thoughts a. for the right to question what
M-5 ...... III.2:5 They a. the patient for forgiveness for
M-6 ........... 1:8 nothing to live for, he may a. for death.
M-11 ......... 1:1 is a question everyone must a.. Certainly
M-11 ......... 2:2 time a. yourself whether your judgment
M-21 ......... 1:3 What you a. for you receive. But this
M-21 ......... 2:4 prayer of the heart does not really a. for
M-23 ......... 1:4 Bible says, "A. in the name of Jesus Christ
M-23 ......... 3:7 a. yourself honestly whether it is likely
M-26 ......... 4:6 Behold the problem, a. for the answer,
M-29 ......... 2:7 A. and He will answer. The responsibility
M-29 ......... 5:4 To a. the Holy Spirit to decide for you is
M-29 ......... 5:8 to a. for help when and where you can,
M-29 ......... 5:9 a. the Holy Spirit's help when it is feasible
M-29 ....... 6:10 He may a. for injury, but his father will
M-29 ......... 7:6 A. all things of His Teacher, and all things
C-in ........... 4:3 The ego may a., "How did the impossible
C-in ........... 4:3 happen?", and may a. this in many forms.
C-2 .......... 6:16 Who has need to a.? Where is the ego?
C-2 ............ 8:4 Would it not answer all you thought to a.,
C-2 ............ 9:2 A. this instead of what the ego is, and you
C-ep .......... 2:3 A. but my help to roll the stone away, and
P-2........ IV.2:3 received. And all who a. for illness have
P-2..........V.6:6 To a. for help, whatever form it takes, is
P-2....... VII.2:9 with which the patient came to a. for help
P-3.........I.1:10 a. of Perfection that He be imperfect?
P-3..........II.3:6 the therapist will silently a. him for help.
P-3........ III.2:4 will be those from whom He does not a..
S-1...........I.1:7 A., rather, to receive what is already given
S-1...........I.2:1 told to a. the Holy Spirit for the answer to
S-1...........I.3:1 You cannot, then, a. for the echo. It is the
S-1...........I.4:2 To a. for the specific is much the same as
S-1...........I.5:6 to a. because there is nothing left to want.
S-1...........I.7:2 To a. that Christ be but Himself is not an
S-1..........II.2:6 A. and you have received, for you have
S-1..........II.3:4 at this level to continue to a. for things of
S-1..........II.3:4 to a. for gifts such as honesty or goodness
S-1........ III.2:6 Only those who are in hell can a. for hell.
S-1........ III.6:4 One need not a. explicitly. The goal of
S-1........ IV.1:2 each one must a. for different things. But
S-1........ IV.2:5 Even together you may a. for things, and
S-1........ IV.2:6 You may a. together for specifics, and not
S-1........ IV.3:1 if those who pray together do not a.,
S-2...........I.7:1 A., then, His help, and ask Him how to
S-2...........I.7:1 and a. Him how to learn forgiveness as
S-2..........II.6:7 God gives and does not a. for recompense
S-2........ III.1:2 It does not a. for proof of innocence, nor
S-2........ III.5:1 be the only thing you ever a. when help is
S-3...........I.5:3 As prayer within the world can a. amiss
S-3........ IV.3:4 Do not a. partial healing, nor accept an
S-3...... IV.10:5 I a. but this; that you be comforted and

**asked** 166

T-1 ....... III.8:3 not a. to perform have not lost their value
T-2 ..........II.1:2 I have a. you to perform miracles, and
T-4 .......V.4:11 be answered because it cannot be a..
T-4 .........V.5:1 *must* be a.: "Where can I go for protection
T-4 .........V.6:7 one question that is never a. by those who
T-4 ....... VI.6:3 You are a. to live so as to demonstrate
T-5 ...... VII.2:6 merely a. to return to God the mind as He
T-5 ...... VII.4:2 You have not been a. to work out the plan
T-6 ........in.2:1 a. to take me as your model for learning,
T-6 ..........I.6:6 You are not a. to be crucified, which was
T-6 ..........I.6:7 You are merely a. to follow my example in
T-6 ........I.11:2 a. to repeat my experiences because the
T-6 ....... IV.2:6 raised the first question that was ever a.,
T-6 ....... IV.7:2 because the first question was never a..
T-6 ..... V.B.7:1 You are not a. to make insane decisions,
T-8 ..........I.2:4 not a. to dispel your hallucinations alone.
T-8 ..........I.2:5 are merely a. to evaluate them in terms of
T-8 ....... VI.8:3 revealed it to me because I a. it of Him,
T-9 .........II.3:2 very fact that the Holy Spirit has been a.
T-11 ......I.11:1 a. to trust the Holy Spirit only because He
T-11 ... VIII.8:6 any Son of God, and you have a. it of me.
T-12 ..... III.1:1 I once a. you to sell all you have and give
T-13 ... III.10:2 were at peace until you a. for special favor
T-13 ... III.11:1 he needed nothing and a. for nothing. In
T-13 .....V.11:2 can see Him, for they have a. for light.
T-14 ..... III.6:1 No penalty is ever a. of God's Son except
T-14 .. VII.5:13 You are not a. to do mighty tasks yourself
T-14 .. VII.5:14 merely a. to do the little He suggests you
T-14 .......X.6:7 still bound to judgment can be a. to do
T-15 ..... III.4:6 is a. of you, in tribute to your magnitude
T-15 ..... III.4:7 Nor is it a. of you alone. The power of
T-15 ..... III.5:1 I a. you earlier, "Would you be hostage to
T-15 ..... III.5:2 Let this question be a. you by the Holy
T-15 .... VII.6:6 and having a. for it they are attracted to it
T-15 ..... XI.2:4 of any kind, of anyone, is a. by Him. In
T-16 .......V.8:4 one will recognize that he has a. for hell,
T-17 ... VIII.2:5 Not even faith is a. of you, for truth asks

T-18......IV.6:2 will merely take away the little that is a..
T-18.....VII.2:3 You are not a. to let this happen for more
T19... IV.A.2:6 are not a. to let it go for yourself alone.
T19. IV.A.4:10 you a. the Holy Spirit to share with you.
T19IV.A.10:10 language in which their going forth was a.
T19....IV.B.5:2 and sacrifice cannot be a. of you? There is
T-20....... II.5:2 you have a. for and received another sight
T-20....... II.7:8 a. for and been given the strength to look
T-20..... III.8:4 a. this puff of madness for the meaning of
T-21....... II.1:1 how little is a. of you to learn this course.
T-21....... II.2:5 *me I ask for, and receive as I have a..* Deceive
T-21....... II.7:6 that is a. of you is to make room for truth.
T-21....... II.7:7 You are not a. to make or do what lies
T-21....... II.7:8 All you are a. to do is *let it in;* only to stop
T-21..... V.10:2 have a. the question the ego will never ask
T-21... VII.12:2 Could it be necessary they be a. so often,
T-21... VIII.5:7 have a. that nothing stand between the
T-22...... VI.8:4 For you have a. what is your function here
T-23....... II.6:3 seen as even necessary that He be a. about
T-23..... IV.1:7 a. to fight against your wish to murder.
T-23..... IV.1:8 But you are a. to realize the form it takes
T-24.........I.1:4 you a. a substitute to take its place. And
T-24.... VI.12:1 Now you are merely a. that you pursue
T-24.... VI.12:5 as God established it no sacrifice is a., no
T-25... VIII.2:7 thankful that only little faith is a. of you.
T-25... VIII.9:3 You are not a. to trust Him far. No more
T-26.........I.4:6 be denied if any sacrifice is a. of anyone.
T-26....... X.3:7 a. to sacrifice his Father's Love and yours
T-27...... IV.3:4 outside a single, simple question is ever a.
T-27...... IV.4:1 All questions a. within this world are but
T-27...... IV.4:1 are but a way of looking, not a question a.
T-27...... IV.4:2 A question a. in hate cannot be answered,
T-27...... IV.5:4 contained within the questions that are a.
T-27...... IV.6:1 can an honest question honestly be a..
T-27...... IV.6:6 because it answers questions truly a.. The
T-27...... IV.6:9 that is not entailed within the question a..
T-27....... V.5:4 It is a. of you on your behalf. A dying
T-28.........I.5:6 is what you a. its message be and that it is
T-28....... II.5:6 no one a. to be the victim and the sufferer
T-28...... III.8:8 Guests the miracle has a. to come to you.
T-29....... II.4:2 You a. Him, and He came. You did not
T-29....... II.8:5 for it is you of whom the sacrifice is a.?
T-29....... II.9:1 body that is a. to be a god will be attacked
T-29..... II.10:1 "something" is the body a. to be God's
T-29....... V.3:3 him. Nothing is a. of you but to accept the
T-29... VIII.8:3 the one of whom the question has been a..
T-30.........I.6:2 that you have a. a question by yourself,
T-30...... I.16:7 world, for it will be what you have a. for,
T-30...... I.17:2 the joy they a. for will be wholly shared.
T-30...... III.5:9 But what is really a. for cannot be denied.
T-30...... IV.7:4 You are but a. to let your will be done,
T-30...... IV.7:5 And you are a. to let yourself be free of all
T-30...... IV.8:3 No more than this is a.. Be glad indeed
T-30...... VI.1:6 not a. to offer pardon where attack is due,
T-30...... VI.2:4 Salvation does not lie in being a. to make
T-30...... VI.2:6 a. to sacrifice your rights when you return
T-30...... VI.2:7 But you are merely a. to see forgiveness as
T-30... VIII.4:4 For you have a. it be withheld from power
T-31....... II.8:7 No more than this will you be a. to learn.
T-31...... III.7:4 has said there *is* no sacrifice that can be a.;
T-31....... V.8:5 be a. to make exchange of what you now
T-31..... VII.5:4 No more than this is a.. On its behalf,
W-in..........8:3 are merely a. to apply the ideas as you are
W-in..........8:4 You are not a. to judge them at all. You
W-in..........8:5 You are a. only to use them. It is their use
W-pI.....20.1:2 cooperation and interest have been a..
W-pI.....20.3:3 Do not mistake the little effort that is a. of
W-pI.....23.7:3 and you are a. at this time only to treat
W-pI.....27.2:1 of sacrifice is being a. of you when you say
W-pI.....39.4:1 answer to every question that was ever a.,
W-pI.....39.4:1 that was ever asked, is being a. now, or
W-pI.....39.4:1 asked now, or will be a. in the future.
W-pI.....63.2:5 is no idle request that is being a. of you.
W-pI.....63.2:6 You are being a. to accept salvation that it
W-pI.....77.5:2 You have a. for the salvation of the world,
W-pI.....78.8:1 What you have a. for cannot be denied.
W-pI.....98.6:3 you are being a. for nothing in return for
W-pI...100.7:4 be happy. Only this is a. of you or anyone
W-pI...100.7:6 wrong in your belief that sacrifice is a..
W-pI...108.9:3 have exact return, for that is what you a..
WpI. rIII.in3:1 devote the time to it that you are a. to give
W-pI...134.2:1 fact that pardon is not a. for what is true.
W-pI...139.8:1 Only acceptance can be a. of you, for
W-pI.139.10:3 It is but this that we are a. to do. It is but
W-pI...155.4:1 it a. the sacrifice of something that is real.
W-pI...156.8:2 should be a. a thousand times a day, till
W-pI...160.3:2 had a. this stranger in to take your place,
W-pI...160.6:7 It a. no stranger in, and took no alien
Wi181-200 1:2 a. for total dedication all the time as yet.
Wi181-200 1:3 But you are a. to practice now in order to
Wi181-200 3:5 No more than this is a., because no more
W-pI...184.9:1 indeed be strange if you were a. to go
W-pI...184.9:1 yet were a. to take a teaching function.
W-pI...185.8:8 one question should be a. of all of them,
W-pI...185.9:4 God's peace, or you have a. for dreams.
W-pI...186.2:5 All that we are a. to do is to accept our
W-pI...192.6:1 and the gift of sight, no sacrifice was a.,
W-pI...194.4:4 And so you are not a. to understand the
W-pI...194.4:5 You are but a. to let the future go, and
W-pI...199.2:1 strength and power to do whatever it is a.
W-pII..295.2:1 *My Father, Christ has a. a gift of me, and one*
W-pII..313.1:2 *in. And love will come wherever it is a..* This
W-pII..327.1:1 I am not a. to take salvation on the basis
W-pII..339.1:8 He has a. for what will frighten him, and
W-pII.....343.h I am not a. to make a sacrifice To find the
M-4 ..... I.A.5:8 he thought something was a. of him, he
M-8 ...........4:5 it has itself a. to be given what will fit into
M-16 .........1:9 It has been a. and answered, and he keeps
M-17 .........1:7 sure as well that he has a. for depression,
M-21 .........2:5 specific things a. for being the bringers of
M-21 .........2:6 then, are symbols for the things a. for,
M-22 .........2:8 What more was a. of him? And having
M-23 .........5:3 He has a. for love, but only that he might
M-27 .........1:3 We have a. this question before, but now
M-28 .......3:13 will it come as it is a. to enter and envelop
C-in ...........5:3 Since you have a. for clarification,
P-2........ IV.2:2 It has been a. for and will be received.
P-2......... V.3:6 No more than that is a. of psychotherapy;
P-2......... V.5:3 What he asks is a. by God through him.
P-2......... V.6:5 For He has never a. for more than just the
P-2......... V.7:3 our perfection that is a. in our attempts to
P-3......... II.3:8 a. the Holy Spirit to enter the relationship
P-3...... III.8:12 *darkness of the world until you a. for light.*
S-1 ...........I.2:5 You cannot be a. to accept answers which
S-1 ...........I.2:6 the question that matters, nor how it is a..
S-1 ........ III.2:5 Hell cannot be a. for another, and then
S-1 ........ III.3:5 *have a. for for my brother is not what I would*
S-1 ........ IV.2:4 is likely at first that what is a. for even by
S-1 ........ IV.3:6 so far exceeds all that you a. before that it

## asker 1

M-21 .........2:5 desired experience in the opinion of the a.

## asking 79

*See also* asking-out-of-need

T-3........ IV.3:2 It is capable of a. questions but not of
T-3......... V.4:2 at all. You keep a. what it is you are. This
T-3......... V.6:1 Prayer is a way of a. for something. It is
T-4........ III.8:1 and see what it is you are really a. for. Be
T-5.... III.11:10 a. only that you increase it in His Name
T-8...... VIII.7:4 example of your insistence on a. guidance
T-9...........I.6:7 will, that is precisely what you are a. for.
T-9...........I.7:4 That is why you persist in a. the teacher
T-9...........I.8:8 a. for what cannot be given because it was
T-9...........I.9:9 will be a. only for what belongs to you.
T-9.........I.10:1 hurt you, and so you are a. for nothing.
T-9......... II.2:6 he is not really a. for release from fear,
T-9....... II.12:2 consider how much you will be a. of Him,
T-9........ IV.4:1 of forgiveness because you are a. for one,
T-10....... II.3:7 He will give you everything but for the a..
T-10...... III.7:1 is sick it is because he is not a. for peace,
T-11... VIII.5:8 Yet only by a. will you learn that nothing
T-11. VIII.5:10 you believe that a. is taking rather than
T-11... VIII.7:4 but the real world is still yours for the a..
T-11... VIII.8:1 you are a. only for what I promised you.
T-11. VIII.10:3 willing to accept this Help by a. for It, you
T-11..VIII.15:1 truth, if the exchange is yours for the a.?
T-12.........I.3:6 for this and only this is what he is a. for.
T-12.........I.7:2 By giving help you are a. for it, and if you
T-12........II.1:3 are a. for the love that would heal them,
T-12..... III.4:6 He is a. for salvation, as you are. Poverty
T-17....... V.3:1 the practical results of a. Him to enter. At
T-18.. VI.11:10 fear to peace, a. no questions of reality,
T-18.. VIII.11:5 A. for everything, you will receive it. And
T19. IV.A.11:3 each a. for messages of different things in
T-20.... VIII.2:7 Rejoice in what is yours but for the a., and
T-21.... VIII.3:6 ask because desire is a request, an a. for,
T-22.........I.3:8 a. it to explain to you the world it sees,
T-23... II.13:10 There is no point in a. what they mean.
T-27...... IV.6:7 a. not if sacrifice is meaningful at all. And
T-30.......I.11:7 for a. brought to your awareness, for you
T-30.......I.12:4 *What can I lose by a.?* Thus you now can
T-31.....II.5:14 well! For he is a. what will come to you,
T-31........II.6:2 *that I give my brother is what I am a. for. And*
T-31.......II.10:1 is and what he should be a. for, will be
T-31.... VIII.1:4 to you in all His glory, a. you but this:
T-31.... VIII.1:6 *there.* For He *has* come, and He *is* a. this.
W-pI.....28.3:3 You are a. what it is, rather than telling it
W-pI.....28.6:1 really a. to see the purpose of the universe
W-pI.....37.2:6 holiness blesses him by a. nothing of him.
W-pI.....71.9:1 periods to a. God to reveal His plan to us.
W-pI...72.11:5 no longer a. the ego what salvation is and
W-pI...72.11:6 We are a. it of truth. Be certain, then, that
W-pI...72.12:1 are a. of the infinite Creator of infinity,
W-pI.....77.4:2 you are a. only for what is rightfully yours
W-pI.....77.4:3 to another, and that in a. for your rights,
W-pI.....77.5:5 are but a. that the Will of God be done.
W-pI.....77.6:6 We are a. a real question at last. The
W-pI...92.10:4 closing the body's eyes and a. truth to
W-pI.....94.4:3 You are a. now. You cannot fail because
W-pI...107.8:1 Begin by a. Him Who goes with you
W-pI...109.1:4 thought that will answer our a. with what
W-pI...110.8:1 lightly, a. for the Word that tells him he is
W-pI...130.8:1 by a. for a strength beyond your own, and
W-pI...157.4:2 day, what you are a. must be given you.
W-pI...159.6:3 All can be received but for the a.. Here the
W-pI...165.4:2 It is yours today, but for the a.. Nor need
W-pI...185.6:3 he can not mistake it, if his a. is sincere.
W-pI...200.2:3 to live. You cannot but be a. for defeat.
W-pII ....in.7:6 We will with You in a. this. The Father
W-pII .306.2:2 *open hearts and minds, a. but what You give*
W-pII ... 14.4:4 brothers, a. them to share our peace and
W-ep .........3:3 a. for His sure direction and His certain
M-13 .........5:6 He does not see what he is a. for. And so
M-21 .........1:2 The motivating factor is prayer, or a..
M-26 .........2:9 a. all things in their name and in no other
S-1 ...........I.1:6 must avoid the pitfall of a. to entreat. Ask
S-1 ...........I.6:2 their a. is not yet based upon acceptance.
S-1 ..........II.1:4 In its a. form it need not, and often does
S-1 ..........II.3:2 the a. may be addressed to God in honest
S-1 ..........II.7:4 is no a., for there is no lack. Identity in
S-1 ........ IV.2:6 realize that you are a. for effects without
S-1 ........ IV.2:8 a. a cause from which they do not come to
S-1 ........ IV.4:3 Do not restrict your a.. Prayer can bring

## asking-out-of-need 2

S-1 ..........II.2:1 forms of prayer, or a., always involve
S-1 ..........II.3:1 also possible to reach a higher form of a.,

## asks 138

T-1........ III.6:2 The Golden Rule a. you to do unto others
T-4.........in.1:1 go with a brother twice as far as he a.. It
T-4........ III.6:4 it a. only for what He has already willed.
T-4......... V.4:7 Therefore, the mind a., "Where can I go
T-5...........I.3:6 It a. that you may think as I thought,
T-5..........II.3:6 by God, Who a. you only to listen to it.
T-5....... VII.2:7 He a. you only for what He gave, knowing
T-5....... VII.3:2 and a. that you commend yours to Him.
T-7......... X.5:5 The Holy Spirit never a. for sacrifice, but
T-8.........I.1:10 ready to throw it away when the ego a. for
T-8........ IX.1:3 is, although it a. an endless number. Yet
T-11.... VIII.8:7 in him, to give to anyone who a. it of him.
T-12...... III.3:4 Their poverty a. for gifts, not for further

| | |
|---|---|
| T-12....VIII.2:2 | and needing nothing, he a. for nothing. |
| T-14...VII.5:14 | small extent of believing that, if He a. it, |
| T-14...VII.5:15 | easily all that He a. can be accomplished. |
| T-14.....VII.6:1 | The Holy Spirit a. of you but this; bring |
| T-15.......I.11:3 | He a. no more, for He has no need of |
| T-15.....VII.1:4 | Being complete, it a. nothing. Being |
| T-15....VIII.5:3 | Holy Spirit a. you to respond as God does |
| T-16.........I.6:4 | a brother a. a foolish thing of you to do it. |
| T-16....... II.8:8 | For love a. only that you be happy, and |
| T-16...... VI.3:1 | way in which the Holy Spirit a. your help, |
| T-16.... VI.12:1 | The Holy Spirit a. only this little help of |
| T-17..... V.7:11 | Now He a. for faith a little longer, even in |
| T-17....VIII.2:1 | courtesy is all the Holy Spirit a. of you. |
| T-17....VIII.2:5 | faith is asked of you, for truth a. nothing. |
| T-18...... IV.1:7 | two. He a. but little. It is He Who adds the |
| T-18...... IV.6:8 | Give Him but what He a., that you may |
| T-18...... IV.7:7 | it a. nothing you cannot give right now. |
| T-19...... IV.2:4 | Holy Spirit a. that you offer Him a resting |
| T-19...... IV.3:1 | to Him He a. but that you receive for Him |
| T19... IV.A.2:7 | Christ a. it of you for Himself. He would |
| T19....IV.B.3:7 | is the only "sacrifice" the Holy Spirit a., |
| T-20...... III.3:5 | Their looking merely a. a question, and it |
| T-20..... VII.1:8 | impossible to imagine one that a. so little, |
| T-20..... VII.3:1 | the goal the Holy Spirit indeed a. little. |
| T-20..... VII.3:2 | He a. no more to give the means as well. |
| T-21...... III.9:1 | must think the Holy Spirit a. for sacrifice, |
| T-21...... IV.3:2 | "fearful" question is one the ego never a.. |
| T-21...VII.11:2 | each one a. if you are willing to exchange |
| T-21...VIII.3:5 | it. He may be wrong in what he a., where, |
| T-21...VIII.4:3 | final one that really a. if you are willing to |
| T-24...... II.4:3 | you listen, and which a. and answers? Its |
| T-24...... III.5:1 | God a. for your forgiveness. He would |
| T-24...... III.8:7 | God a. your mercy on His Son and on |
| T-24.... IV.3:12 | keep the gift your Father a. from Him, |
| T-25....... V.4:1 | The Son of God a. only this of you; that |
| T-25..VIII.11:3 | Simple justice a. no more. Of each one |
| T-25...... IX.3:2 | true, because He a. no sacrifice of anyone. |
| T-26.....VII.3:1 | Guilt a. for punishment, and its request |
| T-26...VII.10:1 | a. but a little wish that what is true be |
| T-26..VIII.7:10 | cost the Holy Spirit a. for what He gave |
| T-27...... IV.4:3 | A double question a. and answers, both |
| T-27...... IV.4:4 | The world a. but one question. It is this: |
| T-27...... IV.4:9 | same. It a. but to establish sin is real, and |
| T-27...... IV.5:2 | It dictates the answer even as it a.. Thus is |
| T-27...... IV.5:6 | honest question is a learning tool that a. |
| T-27...... IV.5:7 | merely a. what the response should be. |
| T-27...... IV.6:6 | An honest answer a. no sacrifice because |
| T-27....... V.5:5 | A dying world a. only that you rest an |
| T-28....VII.1:1 | God a. for nothing, and His Son, like |
| T-29.........I.7:1 | It is not love that a. a sacrifice. But fear |
| T-29....... II.4:5 | a. you now that you will look on them |
| T-29....... II.8:4 | it a. that God be less than all He really is. |
| T-29...... IV.6:5 | He a. for help in every dream he has, and |
| T-29....... V.5:1 | is no gift the Father a. of you but that you |
| T-29...... VI.1:5 | This is the "sacrifice" salvation a., and |
| T-30.........I.7:3 | of the question a. will gain momentum, |
| T-30....... II.1:5 | God *a.* you do your will. He joins with *you.* |
| T-30..... II.1:12 | He a. no more than that He hear you call |
| T-30..... IV.7:3 | a. you but that you forgive all things that |
| T-30..... IV.8:4 | Be glad indeed salvation a. so little, not so |
| T-30..... IV.8:5 | It a. for nothing in reality. And even in |
| T-30..... IV.8:6 | it but a. forgiveness be the substitute for |
| T-30...... VI.2:5 | merely a. that you respond appropriately |
| T-31.........I.2:2 | in the simple things salvation a. you learn |
| T-31..... II.10:3 | He a. for what you want, and needs the |
| T-31..... II.10:5 | He a. and you receive, for you have come |
| T-31..... V.11:6 | merely a. if just a little question might be |
| T-31...... VI.3:2 | merely a. that this should be your choice. |
| T-31...VII.13:5 | And recognizing this, it merely a., "What |
| T-31...VII.13:7 | of Christ to shine upon the one who a., in |
| T-31...VII.15:5 | learn that it is you for whom He a. release |
| W-pI.....92.5:4 | It gives its strength to everyone who a., in |
| W-pI...96.12:2 | And all of it is given everyone who a. for it |
| W-pI.....97.4:4 | thing; offers His sight to everyone who a.; |
| W-pI...100.6:3 | God a. you to be happy, so the world can |
| W-pI...101.1:3 | still believe it a. for suffering as penance |
| W-pI...126.7:1 | having given Him the gift He a. of you, |
| W-pI. 135.24:3 | Heaven a. nothing. It is hell that makes |
| W-pI...136.9:1 | stronger than the truth, which a. you live, |
| W-pI...137.9:3 | extend the little help He a. in freeing you |
| W-pI...139.4:3 | If he a. as if he does not know, it merely |
| W-pI...139.5:9 | really be a part of you that a. this question |
| W-pI. 139.5:10 | For it a. of one who knows the answer. |
| W-pI...155.8:2 | It a. that you accept the truth, and let it |
| W-pI. 155.14:1 | And now He a. but that you think of Him |
| W-pI...158.5:4 | has a vision He can give to anyone who a.. |
| W-pI...159.7:6 | No one a. for anything of him except the |
| W-pI...168.2:6 | in the mind that a. the means of Him |
| W-pI...182.9:4 | He a. that they protect Him, for His home |
| W-pI. 182.11:5 | a. unceasingly that you return with Him, |
| W-pI...185.6:4 | But if he a. without sincerity, there is no |
| W-pI. 185.11:2 | For he merely a. that he deceive himself |
| W-pI. 185.11:3 | unsatisfied who a. for what he has already |
| W-pI. 186.12:2 | a. a thing of you which seems impossible, |
| W-pI. 186.12:2 | impossible, remember Who it is that a., |
| W-pI...191.7:4 | *suffer loss, nor fail to do all that salvation a..* |
| W-pI. 192.10:3 | It is he who a. that you accept the way to |
| W-pI. 193.13:7 | deny the little steps He a. you take to Him |
| W-pII . 295.1:1 | Christ a. that He may use my eyes today, |
| W-pII . 295.1:2 | He a. this gift that He may offer peace of |
| W-pII ... 10.4:5 | Salvation a. you give it welcome. And the |
| M-9 ........... 2:2 | he a. his Teacher for His answer, and it is |
| M-13 ......... 5:4 | and no one a. for pain if he recognizes it. |
| M-21 ......... 3:2 | If the prayer of the heart a. for this, this |
| M-21 ......... 3:3 | in the perception of the one who a.. If he |
| M-21 ......... 3:4 | If he a. for the impossible, if he wants |
| M-27 ......... 1:7 | one a. if a benign Creator could will this. |
| C-2 ............ 2:5 | Who a. you to define the ego and explain |
| C-2 ............ 9:1 | which a. of everyone one question only: |
| C-3 ............ 3:2 | knows what His Son needs before he a.. |
| P-2..........II.8:3 | requirement salvation a. of everyone. |
| P-2......... III.3:4 | One a. for help; another hears and tries to |
| P-2......... V.4:2 | is holier than helping one who a. for help. |
| P-2......... V.5:3 | What he a. is asked by God through him. |
| P-3...........I.2:2 | do not yet recognize who he is who a.. |
| P-3.......... III.1:1 | healing is of God and He a. for nothing. It |
| P-3.......... III.2:3 | Spirit a. some payment for His purpose. |
| P-3.......... III.7:8 | look. Whoever a. your help can show you |
| S-1...........I.1:3 | until you realize that it a. for nothing. |
| S-1...........I.7:5 | It a. nothing and receives everything. This |
| S-1......... III.2:5 | and then escaped by him who a. for it. |
| S-1......... IV.3:3 | Prayer for specifics always a. to have the |
| S-2......... III.1:4 | nor promise freedom while it a. for death. |
| S-2......... III.1:6 | a. for trust and willingness to learn how |
| S-2......... III.1:7 | He gives His Teacher to whoever a., and |

## asleep 20

| | |
|---|---|
| T-4 ..... III.10:2 | odds, whether you are a. or awake. |
| T-4 ..... IV.11:2 | Holy Spirit, whether you are a. or awake, |
| T-5 ..........II.1:5 | you can keep it a. you cannot obliterate it. |
| T-6 ........ IV.6:6 | was only because you were a. and did not |
| T-10 .........I.2:3 | dreams you think is real while you are a.. |
| T-11 ..... VI.8:5 | the Son of God as crucified, you are a.. |
| T-14 ........II.8:2 | them, and they will not leave you a.. The |
| T-18 ........II.6:2 | You would have used them to remain a.. I |
| T-24 ..... III.7:1 | The special ones are all a., surrounded by |
| T-24 ..... VI.9:3 | will haunt you while your brother lies a., |
| T-27 .. VII.11:8 | How could you doubt it while you lie a., |
| T-27 ...VIII.5:4 | No one a. and dreaming in the world |
| T-28 ........II.4:3 | is a choice of dreams while you are still a., |
| T-29 .... VII.9:1 | Yet where are dreams but in a mind a.? |
| W-pI...167.6:7 | seems to die is but the sign of mind a.. |
| W-pI. 168.1:10 | When his mind remains a., He loves him |
| W-pII . 256.1:6 | And who would yet remain a., in heavy |
| W-pII . 282.1:3 | determination not to be a. in dreams of |
| M-26 ....... 3:10 | who are still in bondage and still a., so |
| M-28 ......... 6:3 | the goal of wakening the minds of those a. |

## aspect 59

| | |
|---|---|
| T-1 ....... III.8:4 | but the action a. of the miracle should be |
| T-2 ..........I.1:1 | extend is a fundamental a. of God which |
| T-2 ..... IV.3:13 | this unfortunate a. of the mind's power, |
| T-3 ....... IV.3:1 | questioning a. of the post-separation self, |
| T-4 ...... VII.3:4 | communication with every a. of creation, |
| T-5 ....... III.6:5 | The only a. of time that is eternal is *now.* |
| T-6 ..... V.C.3:2 | Yet it still has an a. of thought reversal, |
| T-13 ..... IV.4:2 | is the only a. of time that is meaningful. |
| T-13 ..... IV.7:5 | is therefore on the only a. of time that can |
| T-13 ..... IV.9:2 | the a. of time in which healing can occur. |
| T-13 ... VIII.2:2 | Every a. is whole, and therefore no aspect |
| T-13 ... VIII.2:2 | is whole, and therefore no a. is separate. |
| T-13 ... VIII.2:3 | You are an a. of knowledge, being in the |
| T-13 ... VIII.5:2 | the true perception of one a. of the whole. |
| T-13 ... VIII.5:3 | Though every a. *is* the whole, you cannot |
| T-13 ... VIII.5:3 | this until you see that every a. is the same, |
| T-13 ... VIII.6:4 | every a. of reality you see blends quietly |
| T-15 .......V.6:3 | to substitute one a. of love for another, |
| T-15 .......V.7:1 | one part of one a. suits its purposes, while |
| T-15 .......V.7:1 | it prefers different parts of another a.. |
| T-16 ...... IV.4:5 | certain ones as partners in any a. of living |
| T-17 ..... IV.9:8 | enclose the whole, complete in every a.. |
| T-17 ..... VI.7:1 | Confronted with any a. of the situation |
| T-17 ..... VI.7:1 | ego will attempt to take this a. elsewhere, |
| T-17 .... VII.2:2 | There is no shift in any a. of the problem |
| T-17 .. VII.8:11 | in every a. and complete in every part. |
| T-17 ... VIII.1:5 | has accepted every a. of the situation, and |
| T-18 ........I.1:3 | one a. of the Sonship in favor of the other. |
| T-18 ... VIII.6:5 | little a. is no different from the whole, |
| T-18 ... VIII.7:1 | accept this little, fenced-off a. as yourself. |
| T-18 ... VIII.7:8 | The little a. that you think you set apart is |
| T-18 . VIII.11:6 | lift the tiny a. that you tried to hide from |
| T-19 ..... IV.1:6 | will quietly extend to every a. of your life, |
| T-23 .......II.7:4 | every a. seems to be at war with Him, and |
| T-25 ........I.4:3 | Each a. of Himself is framed in holiness |
| T-26 .... VII.8:5 | this world denies to every a. of God's Son |
| T-26 ... VIII.8:3 | one a. of the little space that lies between |
| T-28 ..... IV.9:7 | And every a. of the Son of God is just the |
| T-28 ... VII.2:7 | is no middle ground in any a. of salvation. |
| T-31 .......V.2:6 | the face of innocence, the a. acted on. It is |
| T-31 .......V.3:1 | This a. can grow angry, for the world is |
| T-31 .......V.3:3 | This a. never makes the first attack. But |
| W-pI .... 10.3:1 | This a. of the correction process began |
| W-pI .... 18.2:2 | emphasize this a. of your perception. The |
| W-pI .... 21.5:2 | that the anger is limited to this a.. If your |
| W-pI .... 44.1:3 | life, and is therefore an a. of creation. |
| W-pI .... 47.3:2 | situations and in every a. of all situations, |
| W-pI .. 95.10:2 | Creator, at one with every a. of creation, |
| W-pI .. 95.11:2 | *my Creator, at one with every a. of creation,* |
| W-pI .. 128.8:2 | value in an a. or an image of the world, |
| W-pI .. 169.1:1 | Grace is an a. of the Love of God which is |
| WpI...rV.in4:2 | one but clarifies some a. of this thought, |
| W-pI 184.14:1 | for each awareness of an a. of God's Son, |
| W-pI .. 185.3:5 | takes on a different a. or another form. |
| W-pI 195.10:3 | gratitude is but an a. of the Love which is |
| W-pII ..... 1.4:2 | It offends no a. of reality, nor seeks to |
| W-pII ... 11.3:2 | creation is His Will complete in every a., |
| M-21 ......... 5:1 | major hindrance in this a. of his learning |
| M-29 ......... 3:2 | Perhaps you have not thought of this a., |

## aspects 47

| | |
|---|---|
| T-1 ....... VI.5:1 | All a. of fear are untrue because they do |
| T-2 ..........I.2:8 | line, in which all a. are of the same order. |
| T-2 .........V.9:2 | Like all a. of the belief in space and time, |
| T-3 ....... IV.1:5 | introduced degrees, a. and intervals. |
| T-3 ....... IV.3:7 | This makes its a. strangers to each other, |
| T-3 ....... VI.2:5 | emphasizes only the positive a. of what is |
| T-13 ..... VI.6:4 | to all a. of the Sonship at the same time, |
| T-13 ... VIII.3:7 | A. of reality can still be seen, and they will |
| T-13 ... VIII.3:7 | seen, and they will replace a. of unreality. |
| T-13 ... VIII.3:8 | A. of reality can be seen in everything and |
| T-13 ... VIII.4:6 | The golden a. of reality that spring to |
| T-14 ..... XI.8:4 | or deal with certain a. of your life alone, |
| T-15 .......V.2:3 | you seek to separate out certain a. of the |
| T-15 .......V.3:5 | How can you decide that special a. of the |
| T-16 ..... IV.3:6 | is welcome in some a. of the relationship, |
| T-16 .......V.1:5 | some a. of what is really being attempted |
| T-17 ........I.3:3 | to retain some a. of reality for fantasy. If |
| T-17 ..... IV.6:4 | than we have at many other a. of the ego's |
| T-17 ..... IV.9:8 | most superficial a. of this thought system, |
| T-17 ..... IV.9:8 | system, for these a. enclose the whole, |
| T-17 .......V.2:4 | In all its a., as it begins, develops and |
| T-17 .... VII.1:1 | The substitutes for a. of the situation are |
| T-18 ........I.5:5 | it? Its fragmented a. are fearful enough, as |
| T-18 .......V.1:4 | are all but a. of the plan to change your |

T-19......IV.1:3 and from various a. of the world outside.
T-22.......II.2:6 of misery is to select some a. out of it, see
T-23.......II.5:5 just as the separate a. of the Son meet
T-24...VII.11:6 each from all a. with a different purpose.
T-25.........I.1:7 to stand between the a. of His Holiness,
T-26.......II.1:4 The a. that need solving do not change,
T-30.....VII.2:4 made on different a. of experience. And
W-pI.....31.1:4 speaking, the form includes two a., one in
W-pI.....33.1:1 of the world in both its outer and inner a..
W-pI.....35.5:1 negative a. of your perception of yourself.
W-pI.....44.1:4 together, being but different a. of creation
W-pI.....96.1:2 the contradictory a. of this self-perception
W-pI...108.4:1 seen as different a. of one Thought whose
W-pI...128.5:2 gave its a. and its phases and its dreams.
W-pI.139.12:1 and His Oneness with all a. of creation,
W-pI.151.11:1 those a. which reflect but idle dreams.
W-pI...152.4:4 to have some a. that belie consistency,
W-pI.184.13:3 gave its a. have distorted what you see,
M-4.......IX.1:2 he still select some a. of his life to bring to
M-16........10:9 two a. of one error and no more, he
M-24..........4:6 If there are a. to any concept or belief that
M-29..........2:6 and all a. are under the Holy Spirit's
C-2............7:3 But look at all the a. of *this* dream and you

### aspiration 1

W-pI...169.1:2 It is the world's most lofty a., for it leads

### aspirations 1

W-pI...163.3:1 in their wake, in place of a. and of dreams

### aspire 1

T-12... VIII.5:4 should hardly a. to control the universe.

### aspires 1

W-pI...169.3:3 is not the goal this course a. to attain. Yet

### assail 5

T-7.......II.7:11 That is its reality, and nothing can a. it.
T-8........V.1:3 delusional believe that truth will a. them,
T19. IV.C.10:1 What danger can a. the wholly innocent?
W-pI...191.3:2 Identity, and you a. the universe alone,
W-pI...192.5:4 fears could still a. those who have lost the

### assailable 1

T-6...........I.6:5 it yourself, or you are believing that it is a.

### assailed 4

T-6...........I.6:4 in you, and realize that it cannot *be* a.. Do
T-6......V.C.7:4 is a. by any doubts in your mind, His
T-6......V.C.8:4 needs protection, since being cannot be a.
T-31.......II.1:7 in truth. And can he be a. by dreams?

### assault 15

T-5.......V.4:10 as a lack of love, but as a positive act of a..
T-6...........I.3:3 Projection means anger, anger fosters a.,
T-6...........I.3:3 fosters assault, and a. promotes fear. The
T-6...........I.3:4 *apparent* intensity of the a. of some of the
T-6...........I.4:1 A. can ultimately be made only on the
T-6...........I.4:2 little doubt that one body can a. another,
T-6...........I.4:6 to perceive any form of a. in persecution,
T-6...........I.9:1 demonstrate that the most outrageous a.,
T-6........I.11:6 to anger and a. would not be so extreme. I
T-6........I.14:1 you are using it as a weapon for a. rather
T-13.....VII.3:3 has withstood the crumbling a. of time.
T-23.....III.4:7 recognize a. upon your peace in any form,
T-23....IV.1:12 Every illusion is an a. on truth, and every
T-29......IV.3:3 or a. must be the theme of every dream,
T-31.......II.8:5 will be no a. upon your wish to hear a call

### assaulted 1

W-pI...135.4:2 something that is very weak and easily a..

### assaults 2

T-31.......V.3:4 things make small a. upon its innocence,
W-pI...190.9:4 and put aside the withering a. with which

### assemble 1

T-15.......V.7:2 aspect. Thus does it a. reality to its own

### assembles 1

W-pI...136.6:1 a. them without regard to all their true

### assent 1

W-pII..253.2:2 *my own, which can but offer glad a. to Yours,*

### assert 6

T-3.........II.4:4 limited, and the will is not free to a. itself.
T-31......III.2:5 for by attack do you a. that you are guilty,
W-pI.....40.1:1 Today we will begin to a. some of the
W-pI.....61.2:5 only arrogance that would a. this function
W-pI...73.10:4 Then let your will a. itself, joined with the
W-pI...184.6:2 signs and symbols that a. the world is real

### asserting 1

W-pI.....58.3:5 undoes them all by a. the truth about me.

### assertion 4

T-30... VIII.3:3 it is an a. that some forms of idols have a
W-pI.....61.3:4 It is a positive a. of your right to be saved,
W-pI.....71.2:4 and an a. in which you believe, that says,
M-28.........2:1 is the denial of death, being the a. of life.

### asserts 3

T-2.......VII.4:3 In fact, it a. the power of fear by the very
W-pI.....72.5:9 And it a. that his salvation must be death,
W-pI...187.1:7 the world a. that you have lost what you

### assessing 1

M-19.........5:6 it, omitting nothing and a. nothing as

### asset 1

T-18......VI.6:4 make it a liability where it could be an a..

### assign 4

T-11......VI.8:3 and you cannot a. to death whom God
T19..IV.B.10:7 for reaching the goal that you a. to it.
W-pI.....16.4:4 regardless of the qualities that you a. to it,
W-pI...135.5:2 has no needs but those which you a. to it.

### assigned 27

T-24......VI.9:3 till what has been a. to you is done and he
T-25......VI.4:3 function, and fulfills the part a. to him, to
T-25...VII.10:5 Accept the function that has been a. to
T-29......IV.4:8 represents some function that you have a.
T-29......IV.6:4 he fails to take the part that you a. to him,
T-29.....VII.3:5 idol has, for this the role that is a. to it,
T-30.....VII.2:7 But you a. a meaning in the light of goals
W-pI.....25.2:5 the goals you have a. to the world, instead
W-pI...29.5:10 In addition to the a. practice periods,
W-pI.....61.2:4 world if that is the function God a. to you.
W-pI.....64.3:2 of the task a. to you by God Himself. The
W-pI.....71.3:1 The role a. to your own mind in this plan
W-pI.....72.1:2 God is a. the attributes which are actually
W-pI.....78.5:4 the holy role the Holy Spirit has a. to him.
W-pI...78.10:1 the role a. to us as part of God's salvation
W-pI...93.11:6 part in salvation that God has a. to you.
W-pI.....98.1:8 it as it is, and take the part a. to us by God
W-pI...100.5:3 instead of what has been a. to you by God
WpI. rIII.in5:1 it, to considering the thoughts that are a..
W-pI.135.11:4 its adequacy to fulfill the plans a. to it. It
WpI. rIV.in7:1 ideas a. to you to be reviewed that day.
W-pI...169.9:3 We merely take the part a. long since, and
W-pI.169.11:5 As you take the role a. to you, salvation
W-pI...186.1:3 offers your acceptance of a part a. to you,
W-pI...186.2:7 part a. to us by One Who knows us well.
W-ep.........3:1 No more specific lessons are a., for there
M-2...........1:1 have been a. to each of God's teachers,

### assigning 3

T-18......VI.3:2 Only by a. to the mind the properties of
W-pI.....51.5:5 everything I see by a. this role to it. I have
W-pI...135.7:3 not abuse it by a. it to roles it cannot fill,

### assignment 4

T-15....VIII.1:2 For a teaching a. such as His, He must use
W-pI.139.11:1 to dedicate our minds to our a. for today.
W-pI...186.3:6 Today we will not shrink from our a. on
M-27.........7:1 your one a. could be stated thus: Accept

### assignments 2

WpI..rII.in.2:1 the comments that are included in the a..
WpIrIII.in12:1 Each day's review a. will conclude with a

### assigns 3

T-3...........I.3:1 which one a. his own "evil" past to God.
T-30.....VII.2:3 made according to the roles the script a..
W-pII.....5.2:3 work, and do the task his mind a. to them

### assistance 3

T-14......IX.3:2 its power will rush to your a. and support.
WpI. rIII.in6:5 wisdom of your mind will come to your a.
M-16.........8:6 and magic is a sorry substitute for true a..

### associate 11

T-4..........II.6:4 it. When you a. giving with sacrifice, you
T-4..........II.9:2 a. this with its particular form of magic.
T-4........VI.1:1 and if you a. yourself with the ego, you do
T-4........VI.5:4 him to a. his misery with its absence, and
T-4........VI.5:6 I am teaching you to a. misery with the
T-6...........I.1:2 fearful connotations you may a. with it.
T-13........II.2:4 you a. it with a weird assortment of "ego
T-13......III.3:2 You a. love with weakness and hatred
T-22......III.8:4 attack except what you a. with his body,
W-pI.....39.7:1 you a. with unloving thoughts of any kind
W-pI.....40.3:2 attributes you a. with being a Son of God,

### associated 20

T-1.........I.22:1 Miracles are a. with fear only because of
T-2..........II.7:2 You may still think this is a. with loss, a
T-3...........I.1:1 fear still a. with miracles can disappear.
T-4..........II.9:1 Myths and magic are closely a., since
T-4..........II.9:4 beginning is usually a. with physical birth
T-5.........in.1:5 Radiance is not a. with sorrow. Joy calls
T-5...........I.2:5 *idea. How, then, can giving and losing be a.?*
T-9....... II.10:3 If paying is a. with giving it cannot be
T-9.......VII.7:2 is always a. with unwillingness to know,
T-12.......I.8:11 that fear and attack are inevitably a.. If
T-13.........I.9:2 future, in time, is always a. with expiation
T-15.........I.4:2 and their fears are all a. with it. The ego
T-17......III.3:3 be most readily a. with those on whom
W-pI.....47.5:2 concern is a. with feelings of inadequacy,
W-pI.....72.1:2 which are actually a. with the ego, while
W-pI.....72.3:3 not always a. with something a body does
W-pI.....91.9:3 is a. with the belief you are a body, a
W-pI...103.2:1 Fear is a. then with love, and its results
M-7...........5:5 and shame a. with a sense of inadequacy.
M-15.........1:4 not come until it is no longer a. with fear.

**associates** 3

T-3 I.5:6 because it **a.** innocence with strength, not
T-7 X.5:13 without fear, he **a.** fear with guidance,
M-13 2:9 things the mind **a.** itself with the body,

**associating** 1

T-9 I.3:3 you are arbitrarily **a.** something beyond

**association** 6

T-2 VIII.5:1 also because of the **a.** of "last" with death.
T-5 I.1:14 whole belief in the false **a.** the ego makes
T-7 VIII.2:1 the inevitable **a.** between projection and
T-9 I.3:2 The **a.** of truth and fear, which would be
T-21 IV.1:5 Fear in **a.** with sin the ego deems quite
W-pI 103.2:6 periods of practicing today with this **a.**,

**associations** 7

T-1 VII.3:6 of making false **a.** and attempting to
T-1 VII.3:7 But although you can perceive false **a.**,
T-13 X.4:3 weird **a.** to it have no meaning in the
T-17 III.2:5 no matter how distorted the **a.** by which
T-28 I.5:8 the strange **a.** made to keep the past alive,
W-pI 3.2:1 to help you clear your mind of all past **a.**,
M-20 2:4 It brings with it no past **a.**. It is a new

**assorted** 1

W-pI 10.4:6 watching an oddly **a.** procession going by,

**assortment** 1

T-13 II.2:4 associate it with a weird **a.** of "ego ideals,"

**assume** 17

T-2 II.7:8 you become more and more secure you **a.**
T-6 in.2:3 you inevitably **a.** the moment you accept
T-6 IV.11:2 To command is to **a.** inequality, which
T-18 IV.6:7 Do not **a.** His function for Him. Give Him
T-23 IV.4:2 yet **a.** the holy function God gave His Son,
T-27 II.10:3 If you **a.** correction's role, you lose the
T-30 VI.1:9 For it would **a.** that, by responding in a
T-30 VII.5:3 which must **a.** a different purpose for the
W-pI 9.1:7 and **a.** that you have it already.
W-pI 79.7:2 We will not **a.** that we already know. We
W-pI 167.9:2 **a.** an alien power which it does not have,
M-4 III.1:2 judge is to **a.** a position you do not have.
M-29 2:8 is His, and He alone is fit to **a.** it. To do so
P-2 VII.5:6 **a.** he has such wisdom except in madness.
P-3 I.1:5 **a.** that you know what to offer everyone
P-3 I.1:7 a tendency to **a.** that you are being called
P-3 II.9:3 he escapes the temptation to **a.** a function

**assumed** 5

T-8 VII.13:6 can only be an **a.** purpose of the body,
T-17 VIII.5:5 You have **a.** your part in his redemption,
T-19 I.1:2 of the dedication can be safely **a.**. Yet we
C-6 3:2 the Holy Spirit has **a.** a dual function. He
S-3 III.3:4 **a.** and then accepted as the truth, and

**assumes** 3

T-19 II.2:4 It **a.** the Son of God is guilty, and has thus
M-29 4:8 this image **a.** it knows all things because
M-29 5:1 Who **a.** a power that he does not possess

**assuming** 3

T-12 I.3:7 you are **a.** the right to attack his reality by
T-18 IV.2:7 **a.** that you must achieve the state its
T-31 II.4:3 and you hate as well his not **a.** it at times

**assumption** 2

T-2 VII.4:3 by the very **a.** that it need be mastered.
T-3 I.3:8 recognize how utterly impossible this **a.** is

**assumptions** 1

T-31 V.17:5 made on no **a.** that would stand the light,

**assurance** 10

T-14 IX.4:3 the immortal **a.** of their Father's Love.
T-23 III.4:4 uphold a quiet, calm **a.** it has come.
T-24 VI.1:4 In him is your **a.** God is here, and with
T-29 IX.9:1 of help, a calm **a.** Heaven goes with you,–
W-pI 77.5:1 wait quietly for the **a.** that your request is
W-pI 77.6:8 fact. You will receive the **a.** that you seek.
W-pI 95.11:1 the practice periods today with this **a.**,
W-pI 97.8:3 Listen for His **a.** every time you speak the
W-pI 103.3:4 day, and quiet all your fears with this **a.**,
S-3 in.1:2 prayer, a giver of **a.** of success in ultimate

**assure** 21

T-1 IV.4:6 I **a.** you that I will witness for anyone who
T-3 VII.3:6 His children, and I **a.** you that He does,
T-4 IV.10:6 I **a.** you this is a mistake of your ego. Do
T-4 IV.10:9 and I **a.** you that it *is* knowledge, means
T-5 V.7:8 for himself, and I **a.** you that it is, then the
T-7 II.2:8 and I **a.** you that you must obey them,
T-9 II.3:7 I **a.** you that they are waiting for you.
T-9 IV.10:4 And I **a.** you that God *is* right. Be glad,
T-9 V.7:9 Its effects **a.** him it is there.
T-14 X.8:4 me **a.** you that you understand nothing of
T-15 V.1:7 I **a.** you that without the ego, all would be
T-21 VII.6:3 reason would **a.** you they are all the same.
T-22 II.5:2 ego will **a.** you now that it is impossible
W-pI 70.9:4 And I **a.** you this will be no idle fantasy.
W-pI 77.6:3 but **a.** you that your request is granted.
W-pI 80.6:1 **A.** yourself often today that your
W-pI 105.8:3 let His Voice **a.** you that the words you
W-pI 118.2:2 *Itself* ***a.*** *me that I am God's perfect Son.*
W-pI 160.8:4 Hear His Voice **a.** you, quietly and sure,
WpI rVI.in.5:3 deny its hold and hasten to **a.** your mind
W-pII 235.1:1 me, and with perfect certainty **a.** myself,

**assured** 8

T-5 II.10:1 I have **a.** you that the Mind that decided
T-27 II.15:5 And you can rest **a.** that He will not fulfill
W-pI 40.3:8 *I am calm, quiet,* ***a.*** *and confident.* If only a
W-pI 77.3:3 **a.** that the Kingdom of God is within you,
W-pI 77.5:4 You cannot fail to be **a.** in this. You are
W-pI 93.4:1 to be **a.** that all the evil that you think you
W-pI 135.13:3 while. In this capacity is health **a.**. For
P-2 I.1:7 Be **a.** of this; each will progress.

**assures** 7

T-15 I.3:6 but **a.** you that Heaven is not for you.
T-21 VI.8:5 Reason **a.** you Heaven is what you want,
W-pI 186.5:4 If God's Voice **a.** you that salvation needs
W-pI 186.6:2 for God **a.** you that you have the strength,
W-pII 255.1:2 my God **a.** me that His Son is like Himself
M-11 1:6 His Word **a.** us that He loves the world.
M-11 2:6 Word **a.** you that He loves the world; your

**assuring** 4

T-6 III.3:3 it, **a.** it that it is perfectly safe forever. The
T-18 IX.7:2 return to you, **a.** you that it is there.
W-pII 267.1:7 by His Voice, **a.** me I am at home in Him.
W-pII 347.2:2 and hear the gentle Voice for God **a.** you

**astonished** 1

W-pI 42.5:2 fact, be **a.** at the amount of course-related

**astonishing** 1

P-2 II.2:2 **a.** tendency to join contradictory words

**astonishment** 1

T-16 VI.11:4 And you will think, in glad **a.**, that for all

**astray** 1

T-14 VIII.3:2 brother may choose to lead yourselves **a.**,

**asunder** 1

T-17 III.7:3 has joined as one, the ego cannot put **a.**.

**at** 1150

**atheist** 2

T-9 I.8:3 former accounts for the **a.** and the latter
T-9 I.8:4 panic, because the **a.** believes he is alone,

**atone** 8

T-1 I.33:3 They thus **a.** for your errors by freeing
T-1 I.41:2 They thus correct, or **a.** for, the faulty
T-5 IV.4:1 I understood that I could not **a.** for myself
T-16 VI.12:4 It is His task to **a.** for your unwillingness
T-16 VII.1:5 cling, and for which must someone else **a.**
T-18 IV.5:6 to those who think that they must first **a.**,
T19 .IV.A.17:8 for anyone, and death does not **a.** for sin.
T-25 VIII.4:7 to "**a.**" for all that you would keep, and

**atoned** 1

T-5 V.7:8 responsibility for *what* is **a.** for cannot be

**Atonement** 248

*atonement*
*See also* Appendix C

T-1 I.25:1 when completed, is the **A.**. Atonement
T-1 I.25:2 Atonement. **A.** works all the time and in
T-1 I.26:3 essential part of the **A.** value of miracles.
T-1 I.37:3 This places you under the **A.** principle,
T-1 I.44:1 of Christ and the acceptance of His **A.**.
T-1 III.h **A.** and Miracles
T-1 III.1:1 I am in charge of the process of **A.**, which
T-1 III.1:3 that I do not need miracles for my own **A.**,
T-1 III.1:4 My part in the **A.** is the cancelling out of
T-1 III.1:5 naturally become part of the **A.** yourself.
T-1 III.1:10 achievement is its expression, and the **A.**,
T-1 III.3:1 The forgiven are the means of the **A.**.
T-1 III.3:3 their brothers, for this is the plan of the **A.**
T-1 III.4:1 indiscriminately, because I am the **A.**.
T-1 III.4:2 a role in the **A.** which I will dictate to you.
T-1 III.5:7 **A.** undoes all errors in this respect, and
T-1 III.7:3 of miracles is because the **A.** itself is one,
T-1 III.9:2 to others, a strong chain of **A.** is welded.
T-1 IV.2:6 The miracle joins in the **A.** by placing the
T-1 IV.2:10 the **A.** restores spirit to its proper place.
T-1 IV.3:6 of the **A.** is to restore everything to you; or
T-1 V.3:1 When the **A.** has been completed, all
T-1 VII.5:4 **A.** without either over- or understating it.
T-2 h THE SEPARATION AND THE **A.**
T-2 I.4:4 about by your acceptance of the **A.**, which
T-2 II.h The **A.** as Defense
T-2 II.4:1 The **A.** is the only defense that cannot be
T-2 II.4:2 The **A.** *principle* was in effect long before
T-2 II.4:2 was in effect long before the **A.** began.
T-2 II.4:3 was love and the **A.** was an *act* of love. Acts
T-2 II.4:5 that the **A.** and the conditions necessary
T-2 II.4:8 **A.** thus becomes the only defense that is
T-2 II.5:1 **A.** was built into the space-time belief to
T-2 II.5:2 The **A.** is the final lesson. Learning itself,
T-2 II.6:4 The **A.** is the device by which you can free
T-2 II.6:6 In this sense the **A.** saves time, but like the

| | |
|---|---|
| T-2 II.6:7 | it. As long as there is need for A., there is |
| T-2 II.6:8 | the A. as a completed plan has a unique |
| T-2 II.6:9 | time. Until the A. is complete, its various |
| T-2 II.6:9 | but the whole A. stands at time's end. At |
| T-2 II.7:1 | The A. is a total commitment. You may |
| T-2 II.7:8 | the defense of A. to your real protection, |
| T-2 III.1:1 | The A. can only be accepted within you |
| T-2 III.1:2 | almost entirely to defend *against* the A., |
| T-2 III.1:6 | *does* recognize that A. in physical terms is |
| T-2 III.1:9 | structures is a sign of the fear of A., and |
| T-2 III.2:1 | perfect effectiveness the A. belongs at the |
| T-2 III.2:3 | the opening of the altar to receive the A.. |
| T-2 III.3:1 | the A. by everyone is only a matter of time |
| T-2 III.4:1 | cannot see error, and merely looks for A.. |
| T-2 III.5:4 | A. is the only gift that is worthy of being |
| T-2 III.5:13 | The A. is the guarantee that they will |
| T-2 IV.1:2 | is the means, the A. is the principle, and |
| T-2 IV.1:5 | The A., or the final miracle, is a remedy |
| T-2 IV.1:6 | of error to which A. is applied is irrelevant |
| T-2 IV.2:1 | in the A. plan is to undo error at all levels. |
| T-2 IV.3:6 | shares the invulnerability of the A. to two- |
| T-2 IV.4:5 | person temporarily inaccessible to the A.. |
| T-2 IV.5:1 | value of the A. does not lie in the manner |
| T-2 V.4:4 | of refusal to accept the A. for yourself. If |
| T-2 V.5:1 | *miracle worker is to accept the A. for himself* |
| T-2 V.5:2 | and that its errors are healed by the A.. |
| T-2 V.7:3 | of looking beyond it to the defense of A.. |
| T-2 V.7:5 | He also looks immediately toward the A.. |
| T-2 V.10:2 | is faulty he cannot see the A. for himself, |
| T-2 VI.7:3 | process of accepting the A. as the remedy. |
| T-2 VI.7:8 | love is perfect love. Perfect love is the A.. |
| T-2 VI.8:1 | that the miracle, or the expression of A., |
| T-2 VI.8:2 | of this worth is re-established by the A.. It |
| T-2 VI.8:3 | yourself in a position where you need A.. |
| T-2 VI.8:5 | the situation for which the A. was offered. |
| T-2 VII.5:9 | the A. can be accepted without delay. It |
| T-2 VII.6:9 | The correction of this error is the A.. |
| T-2 VIII.5:11 | with you. This is your part in the A.. |
| T-3 I.h | A. without Sacrifice |
| T-3 I.1:2 | The crucifixion did not establish the A.; |
| T-3 I.2:11 | The wholly benign lesson the A. teaches is |
| T-3 I.6:4 | in which the meaning of the A. is perfectly |
| T-3 I.6:5 | The A. is entirely unambiguous. It is |
| T-3 I.7:1 | The A. itself radiates nothing but truth. It |
| T-3 I.7:8 | The A. is therefore the perfect lesson. It is |
| T-3 I.8:3 | His Son as he is, you realize that the A., |
| T-3 II.5:9 | the A. they are without the wish to attack, |
| T-3 V.10:2 | the A. and given themselves over to truth. |
| T-4 III.1:6 | This is the whole message of the A.; a |
| T-4 IV.5:3 | to me. That is what A. is for. But until you |
| T-4 IV.5:4 | ego has hurt, the A. cannot release you. |
| T-4 VI.6:4 | accepts my A. decisions because my will is |
| T-4 VI.6:5 | said before that I am in charge of the A.. |
| T-5 I.5:2 | inspiring the A. principle at the same time |
| T-5 I.5:4 | Voice of the Holy Spirit is the Call to A., |
| T-5 I.5:5 | When the A. is complete and the whole |
| T-5 I.6:3 | The Holy Spirit is the Mind of the A.. He |
| T-5 II.2:5 | the means by which the A. heals until the |
| T-5 II.3:1 | principle of A. and the separation began |
| T-5 IV.1:2 | Joining the A. is the way out of fear. The |
| T-5 IV.1:9 | The A. is the guarantee of the safety of the |
| T-5 IV.2:10 | disappear from your mind without the A., |
| T-5 IV.2:11 | The A. must be understood as a pure act |
| T-5 IV.6:3 | My part in the A. is not complete until |
| T-5 IV.7:1 | A. gives you the power of a healed mind, |
| T-5 V.2:1 | the Kingdom is attained through the A., |
| T-5 V.7:8 | worker is to accept the A. for himself, and |
| T-5 V.7:11 | The purpose of the A. is to save the past in |
| T-5 V.8:6 | at any minute if it accepts the A. first. It |
| T-5 VI.9:1 | shall perish" becomes a statement of A., if |
| T-5 VII.3:4 | Excluding yourself from the A. is the ego's |
| T-5 VII.6:5 | made, and give it over to the A. in peace. |
| T-6 II.5:5 | This invites A. automatically, because |
| T-6 II.5:5 | because A. is the one need in this world |
| T-6 II.10:7 | The full awareness of the A., then, is the |
| T-7 VIII.7:3 | By accepting the A. for yourself, you are |
| T-8 I.5:1 | curriculum of the A. is the opposite of the |
| T-8 III.6:5 | at it you *will* accept the A. for yourself. |
| T-9 h | THE ACCEPTANCE OF THE A. |
| T-9 III.7:6 | yours. A. is no more separate than love. |
| T-9 III.7:7 | A. cannot be separate because it comes |
| T-9 IV.1:1 | A. is for all, because it is the way to undo |
| T-9 IV.2:1 | You have a part to play in the A., but the |
| T-9 IV.2:1 | but the plan of the A. is beyond you. You |
| T-9 IV.3:1 | The A. is a lesson in sharing, which is |
| T-9 VII.2:5 | abide in peace unless you accept the A., |
| T-9 VII.2:5 | because the A. *is* the way to peace. The |
| T-12 III.10:5 | Christ has placed the A. on the altar for |
| T-12 IV.7:1 | The A. is not the price of your wholeness, |
| T-12 VII.1:5 | A. will radiate from your acceptance of it |
| T-12 VIII.8:8 | A. is but the way back to what was never |
| T-13 in.2:1 | as the acceptance of the A. is its end. The |
| T-13 in.4:6 | The A. is the final lesson he need learn, |
| T-13 I.6:1 | you have accepted the A. for yourself, you |
| T-13 I.9:1 | the A. teaches you what immortality is, |
| T-13 II.8:1 | The A. has always been interpreted as the |
| T-13 III.1:3 | interposed between yourself and the A.. |
| T-13 IX.1:8 | A. stands between them, like a lamp |
| T-13 IX.4:1 | A. brings a re-evaluation of everything |
| T-13 IX.6:3 | accept His offer of A. for all your brothers. |
| T-13 IX.7:6 | look within you would see only the A., |
| T-13 X.5:3 | and give your mind in peace over to the A. |
| T-13 X.5:5 | For you will have accepted the A., which |
| T-13 X.6:1 | within, where you would always find A.. |
| T-13 X.6:5 | If guilt were real, A. would not be. The |
| T-13 X.6:6 | The purpose of A. is to dispel illusions, |
| T-13 X.8:6 | to look upon the A. and accept it wholly. |
| T-14 I.1:7 | accepting the A. for yourself and learning |
| T-14 III.3:7 | *I choose to testify to my acceptance of the A.*, |
| T-14 III.7:4 | to think he can, you teach him that the A., |
| T-14 III.10:1 | Those who accept the A. *are* invulnerable. |
| T-14 III.12:4 | quietly accepts the plan God set for its A., |
| T-14 IV.h | Your Function in the A. |
| T-14 IV.1:1 | guiltlessness you will see the A. in him. |
| T-14 IV.1:4 | His guiltlessness is *your* A.. Grant it to him |
| T-14 IV.3:6 | A. becomes real and visible to those who |
| T-14 IV.9:2 | The A. was established as the means of |
| T-14 IV.9:3 | A. teaches you the true condition of the |
| T-14 V.h | The Circle of A. |
| T-14 V.2:1 | has a special part to play in the A., but the |
| T-14 V.3:7 | The happy learners of the A. become the |
| T-14 V.4:4 | to light, in answer to the call of the A.. |
| T-14 V.5:1 | are all joined in the A. here, and nothing |
| T-14 V.6:1 | part in the unified curriculum of the A.. |
| T-14 V.7:6 | The circle of A. has no end. And you will |
| T-14 V.8:7 | Abide with me within it, as a teacher of A. |
| T-14 V.10:1 | The crucifixion had no part in the A.. |
| T-14 V.11:1 | the holy circle of A. or leave outside, |
| T-14 V.11:5 | anyone as without the blessing of A., and |
| T-14 IX.1:1 | The A. does not make holy. You were |
| T-14 IX.3:2 | A. is so gentle you need but whisper to it, |
| T-14 IX.3:5 | The A. offers you God. The gift that you |
| T-14 XI.3:1 | A. teaches you how to escape forever |
| T-15 II.1:1 | The A. is *in* time, but not *for* time. Being in |
| T-15 IV.9:5 | A. would not be if there were no need for |
| T-15 V.3:4 | is the complete equality of the A. in which |
| T-15 IX.1:5 | the part that God Himself plays in the A., |
| T-15 IX.6:6 | Seek not A. in further separation. And |
| T-16 VII.5:7 | vengeance becomes your substitute for A. |
| T-16 VII.10:1 | between the real A. that would heal and |
| T-16 VII.10:2 | in the plan of A. arising from His Love. Be |
| T-16 VII.10:3 | the ego in seeking how A. can come to you |
| T-17 II.3:1 | accomplishment of all in God's plan of A.. |
| T-17 III.5:8 | That is why A. centers on the past, which |
| T-17 III.10:6 | let not the holy purpose of A. be lost to |
| T-18 IV.5:6 | A. cannot come to those who think that |
| T-18 IV.6:3 | from guilt has been to bring A. to it, and |
| T-18 V.1:2 | illusion, the A. would have no meaning. |
| T-18 V.2:6 | He will build your part in the A. and make |
| T-18 VII.1:4 | No one accepts A. for himself who still |
| T-18 VII.1:6 | A. is not welcomed by those who prefer |
| T-18 VII.2:3 | this instant that the miracle of A. happens |
| T-18 VII.4:7 | difficult to reach A. by fighting against sin |
| T-19 I.9:2 | that you have accepted the A. for yourself, |
| T19 IV.B.2:8 | focus of the perception of A. as murder. |
| T19 IV.D.9:1 | unless he has accepted the A. and learned |
| T19 IV.D.13:1 | you is one who offers you the chalice of A. |
| T-22 VI.4:7 | healing is, and here will you accept A.. |
| T-22 VI.5:3 | same A. you accepted in your relationship |
| T-23 II.8:2 | A. thus becomes a myth, and vengeance, |
| T-28 IV.1:1 | Accepting the A. for yourself means not |
| W-pI 101.5:3 | Accept A. with an open mind, which |
| W-pI 139.h | I will accept A. for myself. |
| W-pI 139.5:2 | It is for this denial that you need A.. Your |
| W-pI 139.6:1 | A. remedies the strange idea that it is |
| W-pI 139.7:3 | come again until the time A. is accepted, |
| W-pI 139.10:1 | This does A. teach, and demonstrates the |
| W-pI 139.10:2 | is. Today accept A., not to change reality, |
| W-pI 139.11:3 | is: *I will accept A. for myself, For I remain as* |
| W-pI 139.12:4 | *I will accept A. for myself, For I remain as* |
| W-pI 140.4:1 | A. heals with certainty, and cures all |
| W-pI 140.4:4 | A. does not heal the sick, for that is not a |
| W-pI 150.1:1 | (139) I will accept A. for myself. |
| W-pI 161.1:4 | Here is A. made complete, the world |
| W-pII 6.5:1 | the goal of the A. has been reached at last |
| W-pII 297.1:4 | that will be saved as I accept A. for myself. |
| W-pII 318.2:1 | *me in Your request that I accept A. for myself* |
| W-pII 337.1:4 | I must accept A. for myself, and nothing |
| W-pII 337.2:2 | *I thought I sinned, but I accept A. for myself.* |
| M-2 2:2 | A. corrects illusions, not truth. Therefore, |
| M-3 3:5 | situation is part of God's plan for A., and |
| M-4 1:4 | they have a special role in His plan for A.. |
| M-6 1:5 | Having accepted the A. for himself, he has |
| M-7 3:2 | worker is to accept the A. for himself. The |
| M-13 8:7 | A. is for you. Your learning claims it and |
| M-14 3:4 | any one of them accepts A. for himself. It |
| M-18 4:5 | teacher is to accept the A. for himself. |
| M-18 4:6 | A. means correction, or the undoing of |
| M-22 h | HOW ARE HEALING AND A. RELATED |
| M-22 1:1 | Healing and A. are not related; they are |
| M-22 1:2 | because there are no degrees of A.. It is |
| M-22 1:4 | Partial A. is a meaningless idea, just as |
| M-22 1:5 | Accept A. and you are healed. Atonement |
| M-22 1:6 | A. is the Word of God. Accept His Word |
| M-22 1:10 | the A. for himself as his only function. |
| M-22 2:2 | of the lesson of the A. to all situations, but |
| M-22 3:4 | could be sick A. would be impossible. A |
| M-22 5:4 | he has refused to accept the A. for himself |
| M-22 6:1 | The offer of A. is universal. It is equally |
| M-22 6:11 | A. is received and offered. Having been |
| M-22 7:8 | mistake. Herein does he receive A., for he |
| M-23 2:1 | the A. for himself can heal the world. |
| M-24 6:3 | A. might be equated with total escape |
| M-28 1:3 | the acceptance of the A. for oneself. It is |
| M-29 3:4 | It is the essence of the A.. It is the core of |
| C-in 1:2 | concerned only with A., or the correction |
| C-in 1:3 | The means of the A. is forgiveness. The |
| C-4 3:6 | Forgiveness, salvation, A., true perception |
| C-6 2:1 | and bringing the plan of the A. to us, |
| C-6 2:4 | A. principle was given to the Holy Spirit |
| P-2 II.8:6 | I, accept A. and learn to give it as it was |
| P-3 II.3:9 | heal it. He has accepted the A. for himself. |

## atonement 4

*Atonement*

| | |
|---|---|
| T-2 III.1:4 | can be used as a means for attaining "a.." |
| T-13 I.10:3 | it. The ego believes in a. through attack, |
| T-16 VII.10:1 | heal and the ego's "a." that would destroy |
| T19 IV.A.17:3 | and so a. is achieved through murder. |

## Atonement's 1

| | |
|---|---|
| M-22 2:1 | he recognizes the A. inclusiveness, or for |

## atones 1

| | |
|---|---|
| T-5 IV.6:1 | The Holy Spirit a. in all of us by undoing, |

## atoning 3

| | |
|---|---|
| T-1 I.26:2 | "A." means "undoing." The undoing of |
| T-1 I.34:2 | to its fullness. By a. for lack they establish |
| T-13 I.10:1 | guilt by making it real, and then a. for it. |

### attach 1

T-7 VI.5:3 it is willing to **a.** itself to anything else.

### attached 5

T-21 I.6:2 **a.** not to a person or a place or anything
T-21 III.7:1 Faith and belief become **a.** to vision, as all
T-21 VII.12:6 and now an elusive shadow **a.** to nothing,
T-26 I.1:7 see nothing **a.** to anything beyond itself.
W-pI 199.2:2 enter in a mind that has **a.** itself to love. It

### attaches 1

W-pI 161.5:5 true. But fear **a.** to specifics, being false.

### attack 606

*See also* attack-defense, counter-attack

T-2 II.4:7 not, however, turn it into a weapon of **a.**,
T-2 II.7:3 defense that cannot **a.** is the best defense.
T-3 I.2:1 as always, is not to **a.** another's position,
T-3 I.4:6 To terrorize is to **a.**, and this results in
T-3 II.5:9 they are without the wish to **a.**, and
T-3 III.7:1 If you **a.** error in another, you will hurt
T-3 III.7:2 know your brother when you **a.** him.
T-3 III.7:3 A. is always made upon a stranger. You
T-3 IV.3:7 condition, in which **a.** is always possible.
T-3 IV.6:9 perceived as an attacker, but it cannot **a.**.
T-3 IV.6:10 What you perceive as its **a.** is your own
T-3 VII.4:9 all your defenses are used to **a.** ideas that
T-4 I.3:5 I will never **a.** your ego, but I am trying to
T-4 II.8:2 or **a.** them in an equally feeble show of
T-4 II.8:7 It does not **a.** it; it merely cannot conceive
T-4 II.10:2 right perception is uniformly without **a.**,
T-4 IV.8:7 other defense, can be used to **a.** or protect
T-4 IV.11:1 I do not **a.** your ego. I do work with your
T-5 I.7:3 incapable of **a.** and is therefore truly open
T-5 II.7:3 does not overcome, because It does not **a.**
T-5 V.2:10 It is the symbol of **a.** on God. This is a
T-5 V.3:10 that you believe it is possible to **a.** God,
T-5 VII.5:2 become defensive because you expect **a.**.
T-6 in.1:1 The relationship of anger to **a.** is obvious,
T-6 in.1:3 attacked, that your **a.** is justified in return
T-6 in.1:4 of **a.** rather than of love must follow.
T-6 in.1:7 cannot *be* attacked, **a.** *has* no justification,
T-6 I.5:5 offered a different interpretation of **a.**,
T-6 II.2:3 you continue to **a.** it because you continue
T-6 II.3:5 Projection and **a.** are inevitably related,
T-6 II.3:5 is always a means of justifying **a.**. Anger
T-6 III.h The Relinquishment of A.
T-6 III.3:7 is the complete relinquishment of **a.**. No
T-6 III.3:9 in this. Teach **a.** in any form and you have
T-6 IV.2:2 why **a.** within the Kingdom is impossible.
T-6 IV.4:3 It believes that the best defense is **a.**, and
T-6 IV.5:1 part of you, they join in the **a.** together.
T-6 IV.12:8 because to eradicate it would be to **a.** it.
T-6 V.A.5:3 The ego uses the body for **a.**, for pleasure
T-6 V.A.5:8 who communicate fear are promoting **a.**,
T-6 V.A.5:8 and **a.** always breaks communication,
T-6 V.B.1:2 They believe in **a.** and rejection, so that is
T-6 V.B.1:8 it therefore perceive this as an **a.** on them.
T-7 VI.1:3 That is why **a.** is never discrete, and why
T-7 VI.2:1 The mind that accepts **a.** cannot love.
T-7 VI.8:1 that the ego does believe it can **a.** God,
T-7 VI.8:2 If the mind cannot **a.**, the ego proceeds
T-7 VI.11:1 who see themselves as weakened do **a.**.
T-7 VI.11:2 The **a.** must be blind, however, because
T-7 VI.11:2 however, because there is nothing to **a.**.
T-7 VI.11:3 and **a.** them for their unworthiness. That
T-7 VI.12:2 it will **a.** your thought system and divide
T-7 VII.1:10 destructive, because it will be used for **a.**.
T-7 VII.7:4 Every **a.** is a call for His patience, since
T-7 VII.7:4 His patience can translate **a.** into blessing.
T-7 VII.7:5 who **a.** do not know they are blessed.
T-7 VII.7:6 **a.** because they believe they are deprived.
T-7 VII.8:1 A. could never promote attack unless you
T-7 VII.8:1 Attack could never promote **a.** unless you
T-7 VII.10:3 Deny this and you will **a.**, believing you
T-7 VIII.4:3 pieces, and mind cannot **a.** or be attacked
T-7 VIII.5:4 you will have laid aside all anger and all **a.**
T-8 IV.2:9 I do not **a.** it, but my light must dispel it
T-8 IV.2:10 is. Light does not **a.** darkness, but it does
T-8 VII.1:1 A. is always physical. When attack in any
T-8 VII.1:2 When **a.** in any form enters your mind
T-8 VII.1:3 **a.** physically to accept this interpretation.
T-8 VII.1:4 that **a.** can get you something you want. If
T-8 VII.1:5 idea of **a.** would have no appeal for you.
T-8 VII.3:1 If you use the body for **a.**, it is harmful to
T-8 VII.3:3 and only for this, you cannot use it for **a.**.
T-8 VII.4:2 A. promotes it. The body is beautiful or
T-8 VII.4:9 will lead you to hatred and **a.** and loss of
T-8 VII.10:7 has allowed itself to be vulnerable to **a.**,
T-8 VII.11:6 of **a.** is an obvious confusion in purpose.
T-8 VII.12:1 is to join and to **a.** is to separate. How can
T-8 VII.13:6 A. can only be an assumed purpose of the
T-8 VII.14:5 of the body as a means of **a.** and to believe
T-8 VII.15:8 it must be unreal since it is a form of **a.**,
T-8 VII.16:6 them. There is no **a.**, but there *is* unlimited
T-8 VIII.1:1 toward the body are attitudes toward **a.**.
T-8 VIII.1:5 To the ego the body is to **a.** *with.* Equating
T-8 VIII.1:6 the body, it teaches that *you* are to **a.** with.
T-8 VIII.3:1 with the belief in **a.** as an end. The ego has
T-8 VIII.3:4 the obvious **a.** that underlies the sickness.
T-8 VIII.3:5 this and also decided against **a.**, you could
T-8 VIII.5:7 body rests are true; that the body is for **a.**,
T-8 VIII.9:7 Do not let it reflect your decision to **a.**.
T-8 VIII.9:8 Spirit, Who perceives no **a.** on anything.
T-8 IX.6:8 Believing in the power of **a.**, the ego wants
T-8 IX.6:8 in the power of attack, the ego wants **a.**.
T-9 II.9:1 To disbelieve is to side against, or to **a.**.
T-9 IV.3:3 By reinterpreting the ability to **a.** into the
T-9 IV.7:4 that makes the ego likely to **a.** anyone and
T-9 V.1:6 **a.** is real for both himself and the patient,
T-9 VII.4:5 likely to **a.** you when you react lovingly,
T-9 VII.4:6 The ego will **a.** your motives as soon as
T-9 VII.4:8 Yet it is surely pointless to **a.** in return.
T-9 VIII.2:5 it always involves **a.**. It is a delusional
T-9 VIII.2:10 offers you the illusion of **a.** as a "solution.
T-9 VIII.3:3 of judgment except in terms of **a.**. When
T-9 VIII.3:4 to **a.** now or to withdraw to attack later. If
T-9 VIII.3:4 to attack now or to withdraw to **a.** later. If
T-9 VIII.3:5 offer of grandiosity it will **a.** immediately.
T-9 VIII.4:4 unless you do not allow the ego to **a.** it.
T-9 VIII.4:8 are afraid of it because it is a form of **a.**,
T-9 VIII.5:4 forget this, you *will* despair and you *will* **a.**.
T-9 VIII.11:3 Nothing can **a.** it nor prevail over it. It
T-10 I.1:1 to **a.** what you have created is impossible.
T-10 II.1:3 because the dissociation is an **a.** on truth.
T-10 II.4:1 When you **a.**, you are denying yourself.
T-10 II.4:4 that this is always an **a.** on truth, and
T-10 II.4:5 why it is that you always **a.** yourself first.
T-10 II.5:1 All **a.** is Self attack. It cannot be anything
T-10 II.5:1 All attack is Self **a.**. It cannot be anything
T-10 II.5:3 you are, it is an **a.** on your identification.
T-10 II.5:4 identification. A. is thus the way in which
T-10 II.5:4 identification is lost, because when you **a.**
T-10 II.5:5 you **a.** you are not remembering Him.
T-10 III.3:2 Love cannot suffer, because it cannot **a.**.
T-10 III.5:2 willing to **a.** the Divinity of your brothers,
T-10 IV.1:8 If you **a.** him, you will make him real to
T-10 V.4:2 The "**a.** on God" made His Son think he
T-10 V.10:3 interfere with you would be to **a.** Himself,
T-11 II.1:2 Every **a.** is a step away from this, and
T-11 II.1:6 Yet when you **a.** any part of God and His
T-11 III.1:5 knows no **a.** and His peace surrounds you
T-11 IV.5:6 *enter God's Presence if you* **a.** *His Son.* When
T-11 V.10:6 truth, you are believing that **a.** has power.
T-11 V.12:9 could believe that love can be gained by **a.**
T-11 V.12:10 realize that only **a.** could produce fear,
T-11 V.13:4 and to establish this belief it must **a.**.
T-11 V.15:2 Analyzing to **a.** meaning, the ego
T-11 VI.1:6 the ego, not by **a.** but by transcendence.
T-12 I.1:7 to **a.** you or desert you or enslave you, you
T-12 I.2:5 split or an **a.** on the integrity of your mind
T-12 I.3:7 and you are assuming the right to **a.** his
T-12 I.4:1 are except your own imagined need to **a.**.
T-12 I.8:10 in learning to perceive **a.** as a call for love.
T-12 I.8:11 that fear and **a.** are inevitably associated.
T-12 I.8:12 If only **a.** produces fear, and if you see
T-12 I.8:12 if you see **a.** as the call for help that it is,
T-12 III.3:1 ego is to be saved, and to be saved by **a.**. If
T-12 III.3:2 are agreeing with this belief; and if you **a.**,
T-12 III.3:3 *Remember that those who* **a.** *are poor.* Their
T-12 III.6:1 the ego is to **a.** yourself and make yourself
T-12 III.10:1 will recognize that all the **a.** you perceive
T-12 V.1:2 strong do not **a.** because they see no need
T-12 V.1:3 Before the idea of **a.** can enter your mind,
T-12 V.1:4 and believed that the **a.** was effective, you
T-12 V.1:6 You use **a.** to do so because you believe
T-12 V.1:6 that **a.** was successful in weakening you.
T-12 V.2:2 you are recognizing that **a.** has no effect.
T-12 V.2:5 this you will no longer see any sense in **a.**,
T-12 V.3:1 of **a.** except by recognizing that your
T-12 V.3:1 that your **a.** on yourself has no effects. For
T-12 V.3:2 For others do react to **a.** if they perceive it,
T-12 V.3:2 are trying to **a.** them you will be unable to
T-12 V.3:4 you are always the first point of your **a.**,
T-12 V.4:2 cannot trust your own love when you **a.** it
T-12 V.7:7 amounts to a course in how to **a.** yourself.
T-12 VIII.1:3 You **a.** the real world every day and every
T-12 VIII.1:4 If you seek love in order to **a.** it, you will
T-12 VIII.1:7 But offer **a.** and love will remain hidden,
T-12 VIII.2:3 chose to **a.** him and he disappeared from
T-13 in.1:1 If you did not feel guilty you could not **a.**,
T-13 in.1:1 attack, for condemnation is the root of **a.**.
T-13 in.3:4 If it did, **a.** would be salvation, and this is
T-13 I.10:3 The ego believes in atonement through **a.**,
T-13 I.10:3 to the insane notion that **a.** is salvation.
T-13 I.11:1 ego teaches you to **a.** yourself because you
T-13 I.11:1 the guilt, for guilt is the result of **a.**. In the
T-13 I.11:3 For **a.** makes guilt real, and if it is real
T-13 I.11:6 being true for you, you cannot **a.** yourself,
T-13 I.11:6 yourself, for without guilt **a.** is impossible
T-13 II.4:3 who do not **a.** are its "enemies" because,
T-13 III.1:6 your desire to **a.** that really frightens you.
T-13 III.2:3 Your fear of **a.** is nothing compared to
T-13 III.2:7 You believe that **a.** is salvation because it
T-13 III.4:2 lies in defiance, and that **a.** is grandeur.
T-13 IV.2:5 For you believe that **a.** is your reality, and
T-13 IV.6:3 mind, directing you to **a.** in the present in
T-13 V.3:7 And thus it is you must **a.** yourself first,
T-13 V.3:7 first, for what you **a.** is not in others. Its
T-13 VI.5:7 in anger, and if you use it to **a.** the present
T-13 IX.1:1 the Father, for guilt is the **a.** upon His Son
T-13 IX.5:3 of God can **a.** himself and make himself
T-14 I.5:6 deceived will merely **a.** direct approaches,
T-14 III.5:5 Everyone you **a.** keeps it and cherishes it
T-14 V.5:7 have failed to learn need teaching, not **a.**.
T-14 V.5:8 To **a.** those who have need of teaching is
T-14 VI.2:2 A. will always yield to love if it is brought
T-14 VI.3:3 They do not protect; neither do they **a.**.
T-14 VI.8:3 His sight, for He will not **a.** your sentinels.
T-14 VII.5:2 ignorance, and love does not **a.** fear.
T-14 X.8:3 be. Otherwise it will **a.** the form. If you
T-14 XI.14:1 peace you must abandon the teacher of **a.**.
T-15 I.12:3 when you are tempted to **a.** a brother,
T-15 I.15:6 forever beyond **a.** and without variability.
T-15 V.2:7 Father and His Son, and thus to **a.** reality.
T-15 VII.6:3 For it would prefer to **a.** directly, and
T-15 VII.6:4 no one could interpret direct **a.** as love.
T-15 VII.6:5 Yet to make guilty *is* direct **a.**, although it
T-15 VII.6:6 For the guilty expect **a.**, and having asked
T-15 VII.7:8 is only by **a.** without forgiveness that the
T-15 IX.7:2 separation and **a.** which the ego sees in it,
T-15 X.5:9 that you must look upon; sacrifice is **a.**,
T-15 X.6:7 is therefore inseparable from **a.** and fear.
T-15 XI.5:6 Deprivation breeds **a.**, being the belief
T-15 XI.5:6 attack, being the belief that **a.** is justified.
T-15 XI.5:7 the deprivation, **a.** becomes salvation and
T-16 I.2:5 to weaken, and to weaken is always to **a.**.
T-16 II.7:2 the weakness of **a.** are both being brought
T-16 II.7:3 that holiness is weakness and **a.** is power.
T-16 V.1:2 despair, guilt and **a.** all enter into it,
T-16 V.1:4 an **a.** on the self to make the other guilty. I
T-16 V.2:2 open to **a.** and unprotected from it. The
T-16 V.10:6 your self you think you can **a.** another self
T-17 IV.10:5 to defend you from your own **a.**. For you

T-17....IV.10:6 For you **a.** Them, being part of Them, and
T-17.....V.12:6 **a.** your brother is not to lose the instant,
T-17.....V.13:4 this every time you **a.** your brother, for
T-17.....V.13:4 for the **a.** must blind you to yourself. And
T-17.....VII.3:4 must have entered, for minds cannot **a.**
T-17... VIII.2:3 not intrude upon it, do not **a.** it, do not
T-18....... II.1:5 to make over whatever seemed to **a.** you,
T-18....... II.1:5 your ego, which was outraged by the "**a.**."
T-18....... II.1:6 as under **a.** and highly vulnerable to it.
T-18......VI.3:5 Mind cannot **a.**, but it can make fantasies
T-18......VI.3:7 fantasies, it will **a.** the body by increasing
T-18......VI.4:2 It cannot **a.**, but it maintains it can, and
T-18......VI.4:3 The mind cannot **a.**, but it can deceive
T-18......VI.6:1 directing its **a.** and blaming it for what
T-18......IX.1:9 guarded by **a.** and reinforced by hate.
T-18......IX.9:5 Here there is no **a.** upon the Son of God,
T-19.........I.5:3 Faithlessness would always limit and **a.**;
T-19........ I.5:10 a means for seeking out reality through **a.**
T-19.........I.7:8 identification safe from the "**a.**" of truth.
T-19.........I.8:2 for faithlessness is an **a.** that seems to be
T-19...... I.10:1 fear, as much a part of love as fear is of **a.**.
T-19....... II.1:4 conviction that minds, not bodies, can **a.**.
T-19....... II.2:3 the proclamation that **a.** is real and guilt
T-19......III.8:2 that could **a.** His Will and overcome it;
T19.IV.A.2:10 this little remnant of **a.** you cherish still
T19.IV.A.10:7 Being wholly without **a.**, it could not be
T19..IV.B.11:6 retaliative **a.** on what you think has failed
T19IV.B.14:11 send messages of hatred and **a.** if he but
T19..IV.B.15:1 belief that for your message of **a.** and guilt
T19..IV.B.15:4 body search for pain in **a.** upon another,
T19..IV.B.15:4 and offering it to you as freedom *from* **a.**.
T19... IV.C.9:3 from every thought that would **a.** it, and
T19.IV.C.10:2 What can **a.** the guiltless? What fear can
T19.IV.D.12:3 And you **a.** him still, to keep what seems
T19.IV.D.14:6 of sin, know not Whom they **a.**.
T-20......III.4:2 have made?–a world of murder and **a.**,
T-20... VIII.7:5 **a.** and murder and destroy themselves,
T-21....... II.6:8 that threatens this seems to **a.** your faith,
T-21......VI.4:1 an **a.** on reason that drives it out of mind,
T-21......VI.4:2 Reason does not **a.**, but takes the place of
T-21.....VII.1:8 against him; either you love him or **a.** him
T-21.....VII.1:8 or see him shattered and slain by your **a.**.
T-21.....VII.2:8 each one as likely to **a.** his brother or turn
T-21...VII.3:14 What seems to be a planned **a.** is bedlam.
T-21.....VII.4:6 **a.** by turning into something else. How
T-21.....VII.7:1 is the choice of whether to **a.** or heal. For
T-21.....VII.7:2 comes of power, and **a.** of helplessness.
T-21.....VII.7:3 Whom you **a.** you *cannot* want to heal.
T-21.....VII.7:4 the one you chose to be protected from **a.**.
T-22.........I.1:2 If you **a.** whom God would heal and hate
T-22...... I.11:5 His gentle innocence protected from **a.**.
T-22......III.8:4 is there in him that you would **a.** except
T-22....... V.3:9 for here is no **a.** and therefore no illusions
T-22....... V.4:3 mouse that would **a.** the universe. How
T-22....VI.11:1 can **a.** the Son of God and not attack his
T-22....VI.11:1 the Son of God and not **a.** his Father?
T-22....VI.11:3 and justify *is* an **a.** upon your Father. And
T-22....VI.11:7 For it seems safer to **a.** another or yourself
T-22....VI.11:7 to **a.** the great Creator of the universe,
T-22....VI.12:2 you believe **a.** of any kind means anything
T-22....VI.12:5 only then would it be possible to **a.** a part
T-22....VI.12:5 Father; and to **a.** another without yourself
T-22....VI.12:7 value, except in the desire to **a.** in safety?
T-22....VI.12:8 **A.** is neither safe nor dangerous. It is
T-22..VI.12:11 You would not choose **a.** on its reality if it
T-22..VI.12:11 to **a.** to see it separated from its maker.
T-22..VI.12:12 And thus it seems as if love could **a.** and
T-22....VI.13:1 Only the different can **a.**. So you
T-22....VI.13:2 So you conclude *because* you can **a.**, you
T-22....VI.13:4 brother are not different, you cannot **a.**.
T-22....VI.13:8 you seem to be, and therefore can **a.**. Of
T-23.......in.1:4 show of strength **a.** would use to cover
T-23.......in.1:5 and no one can **a.** unless he thinks he has.
T-23.......in.2:3 think that you succeeded, and **a.** again. It
T-23.......in.2:4 It is as certain you will fear what you **a.** as
T-23.......in.2:7 he will see only the sinless, who can not **a.**
T-23.........I.4:5 and **a.** of any kind are all unknown. He
T-23.........I.8:3 you could **a.** that is not part of you. And
T-23....... II.1:5 to make meaningless, and to **a.** the truth.
T-23....... II.2:4 it true by his **a.** on what another values.
T-23....... II.4:1 sin, and therefore deserves **a.** and death.
T-23....... II.7:4 be at war with Him, and justified in its **a.**.
T-23..... II.10:1 justified position and **a.** for what has been
T-23..... II.10:3 Were they not forced into this foul **a.** by
T-23..... II.11:9 may live. And you **a.** only in self-defense.
T-23..... II.12:2 sure your murderous **a.** is justified unless
T-23..... II.12:6 This is the reason why you must **a.**. Here
T-23..... II.13:2 cease his **a.** on you for what you stole. Nor
T-23..... II.14:6 sanity, illusions true, **a.** a kindness,
T-23..... II.17:2 Can an **a.** in any form be love? What form
T-23..... II.17:5 not the form of the **a.** on him deceive you.
T-23..... II.17:7 find safety from **a.** by turning on himself?
T-23..... II.20:5 seeming gentler forms of the **a.** are no less
T-23..... II.22:4 **A.** in any form has placed your foot upon
T-23......III.1:1 recognize some of the forms **a.** can take?
T-23......III.1:2 If it is true **a.** in any form will hurt you,
T-23......III.1:3 **A.** in any form is equally destructive. Its
T-23......III.2:5 from your brother and you **a.** him. You
T-23......III.3:7 It would maintain you can **a.** a little, love
T-23......III.4:3 They do not see that, if it is, salvation is **a.**
T-23......III.4:6 Nor is it possible to **a.** for this and love for
T-23......III.5:1 that **a.** is justified on its behalf, cannot
T-23......IV.1:1 in conflict, for there *is* no war without **a.**.
T-23......IV.1:4 In Him is no **a.**, and no illusion in any
T-23....IV.1:11 What is not loving must be an **a.**. Every
T-23......IV.4:3 Each form of murder and **a.** that still
T-23......IV.6:1 When the temptation to **a.** rises to make
T-23......IV.6:7 and no illusion can **a.** the peace of God
T-23......IV.7:3 For only bodies could **a.** and murder, and
T-24.........I.2:1 Beliefs will never openly **a.** each other
T-24.........I.2:6 least decision to choose **a.** instead of love,
T-24.........I.3:3 What else could justify **a.**? For who could
T-24.........I.4:4 serves as grounds from which **a.** on those
T-24.........I.5:5 Illusions can **a.** it, and they do. For what
T-24.........I.6:2 **a.** him if you realized you journey with
T-24.........I.7:7 Could you **a.** your brother if you chose to
T-24.........I.9:2 but an **a.** upon the Will of God? You love
T-24....... II.2:2 Who can **a.** his savior and cut him down,
T-24....... II.8:3 Not one **a.** you thought you made on him
T-24......III.3:1 vulnerable and open to **a.** that just a word
T-24......III.4:5 Nothing is safe from its **a.**, and it is safe
T-24......III.5:5 are powerless to make **a.** upon illusions.
T-24......IV.3:4 Yet to those who wish to heal and not **a.**,
T-24......IV.3:5 The purpose of **a.** is in the mind, and its
T-24.....VII.1:6 from the least slight, the tiniest **a.**, the
T-25......III.1:1 perceive a world in which **a.** is justified.
T-25......III.1:2 that extent you will perceive **a.** cannot *be*
T-25......III.6:7 gave **a.** is but another altar where he can,
T-25......IV.1:2 For they cannot **a.**, and they rejoice that
T-25....... V.1:1 merely this: The whole desire to **a.** is gone
T-25....... V.1:3 **A.** and sin are bound as one illusion, each
T-25....... V.2:1 **A.** makes Christ your enemy, and God
T-25....... V.2:6 would **a.** whatever he perceives as wholly
T-25....... V.2:7 And who, *because* he wishes to **a.**, can fail
T-25....... V.6:4 you; through your **a.** believe He hates you
T-25......VI.7:6 does your specialness appear to be **a.**. In
T-25......VI.7:7 the plan to save the Son of God from all **a.**
T-25.....VII.8:3 one which will not **a.** the world he sees,
T-25... VIII.2:2 without **a.** from all beliefs opposed to it.
T-25VIII.11:10 can be to warrant an **a.** upon the innocent
T-25......IX.4:2 perception leaves no ground for an **a.**.
T-25......IX.4:3 Only a loss could justify **a.**, and loss of any
T-25......IX.6:3 he does not merit an **a.** of any kind. What
T-25......IX.7:6 and lasting in its power of injustice and **a.**
T-26.........I.1:1 the "dynamics" of **a.** is sacrifice a key idea
T-26....... II.2:6 possible, **a.** be justified and vengeance fair
T-26....... II.8:3 loves but must be sinless and beyond **a.**.
T-26......III.3:4 knowledge makes no **a.** upon perception.
T-26......VI.1:6 All belief in sin, in power of **a.**, in hurt
T-26.....VII.7:4 apart, and relegates **a.** unto Himself. Thus
T-26...VII.12:2 Sin is belief **a.** can be projected outside
T-26...VII.12:5 prove your innocence, while cherishing **a.**
T-26...VII.17:2 Forgiveness is the answer to **a.** of any kind
T-26...VII.17:3 So is **a.** deprived of its effects, and hate is
T-26......IX.1:4 you as well while you **a.** His chosen home,
T-26....... X.1:2 a differential view of when **a.** is justified,
T-26....... X.2:1 mean if you perceive **a.** in certain forms to
T-26....... X.3:1 Unfairness and **a.** are one mistake, so
T-26........X.4:4 that your **a.** on him attempts to get? Is it
T-26........X.4:5 retribution for your own **a.** upon the Son
T-27.........I.1:1 that would combine **a.** and innocence.
T-27.........I.2:2 do you see as proof that he is guilty of **a.**.
T-27.........I.3:1 accuse your brother of **a.** upon God's Son.
T-27.........I.3:3 are beyond **a.** and prove his innocence.
T-27.........I.5:3 one has not been used for purpose of **a.**,
T-27.........I.5:8 and no **a.** can ever touch him with the
T-27........II.1:6 He has attacked and will **a.** again. Protect
T-27...... III.3:2 There is nothing to **a.** or to deny; to love
T-27....... V.2:12 if only for an instant, you love without **a.**.
T-27....... V.4:2 without **a.** is necessary that all this occur.
T-27....... V.5:5 you rest an instant from **a.** upon yourself,
T-27....... V.11:4 in without **a.** will stay with you forever.
T-27.....VII.1:3 of what brought on the **a.** against himself,
T-27.....VII.1:6 is his own **a.** upon himself apparent still,
T-27.....VII.3:3 me. While you **a.** I must be innocent. And
T-27.....VII.3:4 And what I suffer from is your **a.**." No one
T-27.....VII.4:8 would be a victim of **a.** he did not choose.
T-27.....VII.6:4 was the first **a.** upon yourself begun. And
T-27....VIII.5:4 the world remembers his **a.** upon himself.
T-27....VIII.7:1 made real; a part of God that can **a.** itself;
T-27..VIII.10:2 No matter what the form of the **a.**, this
T-28........II.5:5 In dreams of murder and **a.** are you the
T-28........II.7:7 Thus does he fear his own **a.**, but sees it at
T-28........II.7:9 He authored not his own **a.**, and he is
T-28....... V.3:7 be your enemy; and will **a.** your brother,
T-28.... VI.1:10 role, but does what it is told, without **a.**.
T-28...... VI.4:5 not see himself attacked, and losing by **a.**.
T-28...... VI.4:7 to be hurt by him, and to **a.** him in return.
T-29.........I.1:5 hate, His gentleness turn sometimes to **a.**,
T-29........II.3:3 as are hate and fear, **a.** and guilt but one.
T-29........II.3:6 and loss, and all effects of hatred and **a.**.
T-29...... IV.3:1 it can be said **a.** is a response to function
T-29...... IV.4:2 become the "reason" your **a.** is justified?
T-29....... V.6:4 would you **a.** him with the hands of hate?
T-29....... V.8:2 they lose the function of **a.** and separation
T-29...... IX.3:7 of judgment you **a.** and are condemned;
T-29...... IX.5:3 Yet can a dream **a.**? Or can a toy grow
T-29.... IX.10:2 try to worship idols and to keep **a.**.
T-30.........I.5:2 Now the answer will provoke **a.**, unless
T-30...... IV.1:1 You will **a.** what does not satisfy, and
T-30...... IV.1:7 You **a.** but false ideas, and never truthful
T-30...... IV.1:9 And you **a.** them for the things you think
T-30...... IV.5:4 Do not **a.** what you have made to let you
T-30...... IV.5:5 **A.** has power to make illusions real. Yet
T-30.... IV.5:11 Yet this is equally forgotten in **a.**. God's
T-30....... V.2:1 that understanding is acquired by **a.**.
T-30....... V.2:2 it is clear that by **a.** is understanding lost.
T-30...... VI.1:2 **A.** has *no* foundation. It is here escape
T-30...... VI.1:6 not asked to offer pardon where **a.** is due,
T-30...... VI.1:9 the answer to **a.** that has been made. And
T-30...... VI.2:3 a real **a.** that calls for punishment.
T-30...... VI.2:6 rights when you return forgiveness for **a.**.
T-30...... VI.3:2 Fear cannot arise unless **a.** is justified, and
T-30...... VI.3:5 Unjustified forgiveness is **a.**. And this is
T-31........I.10:3 that sings behind each murderous **a.** and
T-31........II.8:4 will be no **a.** upon the things you thought
T-31...... III.1:6 yours, and therefore meriting a "just" **a.**.
T-31...... III.2:3 why do you **a.** them everywhere except
T-31...... III.2:5 You answer "yes" whenever you **a.**, for by
T-31...... III.2:5 for by **a.** do you assert that you are guilty,
T-31...... III.2:7 If you did not believe that you deserved **a.**
T-31...... III.2:7 would occur to you to give **a.** to anyone at
T-31...... III.5:1 dogs of hate and evil, sickness and **a.**; of
T-31....... V.3:3 This aspect never makes the first **a.**. But
T-31....... V.4:1 wears can tolerate **a.** in self-defense, for is
T-31.....VII.2:1 thoughts as long as you see value in **a.**.
W-pI.....21.3:5 forms of **a.** are more justified than others.
W-pI.....21.4:1 in which **a.** thoughts present themselves,
W-pI.....22.1:1 the way anyone who holds **a.** thoughts in
W-pI.....22.1:3 own **a.** is thus perceived as self defense.
W-pI.....22.1:5 thoughts of **a.** and counter-attack will
W-pI.....22.2:4 that you hate and would **a.** and kill. All
W-pI.........23.h the world I see by giving up **a.** thoughts.
W-pI.....23.2:1 cause of the world you see is **a.** thoughts,
W-pI.....23.3:2 representation of your own **a.** thoughts.
W-pI.....23.6:2 for as many **a.** thoughts as occur to you.
W-pI.....23.6:4 *world I see by giving up* ***a.*** *thoughts about–.*

W-pI.....23.6:5 Hold each a. thought in mind as you say
W-pI.....23.7:5 that thoughts of a. and of being attacked
W-pI........26.h My a. thoughts are attacking my
W-pI.....26.1:2 You see a. as a real threat. That is because
W-pI.....26.1:3 because you believe that you can really a..
W-pI.....26.2:1 your a. thoughts will be projected, you
W-pI.....26.2:1 thoughts will be projected, you will fear a.
W-pI.....26.2:2 And if you fear a., you must believe that
W-pI.....26.2:3 invulnerable. A. thoughts therefore make
W-pI.....26.2:3 mind, which is where the a. thoughts are.
W-pI.....26.2:4 A. thoughts and invulnerability cannot be
W-pI.....26.3:1 thought that you always a. yourself first.
W-pI.....26.3:2 a. thoughts must entail the belief that you
W-pI.....26.4:2 Nothing except your thoughts can a. you.
W-pI.....26.9:2 *That thought is an a. upon myself.* Conclude
W-pI.....39.6:2 depression, anger, fear, worry, a.,
W-pI.....46.6:6 *is no need to a. because love has forgiven me.*
W-pI.....55.2:3 picture of a. on everything by everything.
W-pI.....55.2:5 my own a. thoughts that give rise to this
W-pI.....55.3:1 from this world by giving up a. thoughts.
W-pI.....55.3:3 else. Without a. thoughts I could not see a
W-pI.....55.3:3 thoughts I could not see a world of a.. As
W-pI.....56.1:1 (26) My a. thoughts are attacking my
W-pI.....56.1:2 am when I see myself as under constant a.
W-pI.....56.5:2 my insane thoughts of separation and a.,
W-pI.....62.2:5 this a. must be replaced by forgiveness, so
W-pI.....62.3:1 every a. you call upon your own weakness
W-pI........72.h Holding grievances is an a. on God's plan
W-pI.....72.1:1 that it is an active a. on His plan, and a
W-pI.....72.1:2 it. In the a., God is assigned the attributes
W-pI.....72.3:1 is an a. on God's plan for salvation. But
W-pI.....72.5:9 be death, projecting this a. onto God, and
W-pI.....72.9:5 to end the a. on God's plan for salvation,
W-pI...72.10:2 goal, we must replace a. with acceptance.
W-pI...72.10:3 As long as we a. it, we cannot understand
W-pI...72.13:3 *Holding grievances is an a. on God's plan for*
W-pI.....73.2:2 it with figures that seem to a. you and call
W-pI.....84.3:3 love. Grievances a. love and keep its light
W-pI.....84.3:6 I am determined not to a. my Self today,
W-pI.....84.4:3 *I will not use this to a. love. Let this not tempt*
W-pI.....84.4:4 *love. Let this not tempt me to a. myself.*
W-pI.....86.3:1 (72) Holding grievances is an a. on God's
W-pI.....86.4:4 *my salvation. This calls for salvation, not a..*
W-pI.....87.3:4 I try to a. only when I am afraid, and only
W-pI.....87.3:4 and only when I try to a. can I believe that
W-pI.....88.1:2 In choosing salvation rather than a., I
W-pI.....88.1:4 A. and grievances are not there to choose.
W-pI.....93.5:7 It does not hurt him, nor a. his peace. It
W-pI.....99.4:2 without a. and with no touch of pain?
W-pI...107.3:2 there could be no fear, no doubt and no a.
W-pI...107.5:2 no defense, and therefore no a. is possible
W-pI...121.4:2 rising to a. its miserable parody of life. It
W-pI...122.2:3 no dreams of fear and evil, malice and a.
W-pI...126.6:2 you see it, it is but a check upon overt a.,
W-pI.134.11:1 of hatred and a. brought silently to truth.
W-pI.134.17:1 you forget its meaning and a. yourself.
W-pI...135.1:1 he were attacked, that the a. were real,
W-pI.135.17:4 the "threat" which your defenses would a.
W-pI...136.2:3 the rest, its purpose is to hide reality, a. it,
W-pI...136.6:3 symbols standing for a. upon the whole;
W-pI.136.19:2 If you let your mind harbor a. thoughts,
W-pI.136.19:2 a bodily identity which will a. the body,
W-pI.136.20:6 *And my mind cannot a.. So I can not be sick.*
W-pI...137.3:6 to a. the universal Oneness of God's Son.
W-pI.137.15:3 sick, and offer blessing where there was a.
W-pI...153.1:3 It is rooted in a., and all its "gifts" of
W-pI...153.2:2 anger, anger makes a. seem reasonable,
W-pI...153.3:2 A., defense; defense, attack, become the
W-pI...153.3:2 Attack, defense; defense, a., become the
W-pI...153.5:5 of God as but a victim to a. by fantasies,
W-pI...153.6:4 it recognizes strength so great a. is folly,
W-pI...153.9:1 or dream in which a. has any meaning.
W-pI...161.6:1 Bodies a., but minds do not. This
W-pI...161.6:5 The body is the target for a., for no one
W-pI...161.6:6 Yet what but mind directs the body to a.?
W-pI...161.8:2 And he will a., because what he beholds is
W-pI...161.8:2 own fear external to himself, poised to a.,
W-pI...161.9:5 A. on him is enemy to you, for you will
W-pI.161.12:5 be tempted to a. a brother and perceive in
W-pI...170.1:3 you think that you a. in self-defense, you
W-pI...170.1:5 mean that to a. is to exchange the state in
W-pI...170.2:1 is the idea that to defend from fear is to a.
W-pI...170.3:1 to be the enemy without that you a.. Yet
W-pI...170.4:2 their source, for it is you who make a.,
W-pI...170.4:3 Yet you a. outside yourself, and separate
W-pI...181.1:2 When you a. a brother, you proclaim that
W-pI.185.14:1 beyond despair, the love a. would hide,
W-pI...186.7:2 and seeks to a. the threat it does not know
W-pI...189.3:5 who see a world of hatred rising from a.,
W-pI...190.2:4 for a. on what is wholly unassailable. It is
W-pI...190.9:3 Let no a. enter with you. Lay down the
W-pI...192.1:2 within a world of envy, hatred and a.?
W-pI...192.5:2 it will die, nor be the prey of merciless a..
W-pI...192.5:4 those who have lost the source of all a.,
W-pI...192.7:2 reason but to justify our rage and our a..
W-pI...194.9:5 if we are tempted to a., we will appeal to
W-pI...196.1:2 You will not a. yourself, and you will
W-pI...196.1:2 that to a. another is but to attack yourself.
W-pI...196.1:2 that to attack another is but to a. yourself.
W-pI...196.1:3 belief that to a. a brother saves yourself.
W-pI...196.6:1 you can a. another and be free yourself.
W-pI.196.10:3 you believed a. could be directed outward
W-pI...197.1:3 Yet you turn them to a. again, unless you
W-pI...197.5:3 joy while you forgive but to a. again.
W-pI...198.7:1 no meaning, and a. appears as justified.
W-pI...198.7:6 How foolish to believe you can a.! How
W-pI...199.2:2 A. thoughts cannot enter such a mind,
W-pI...216.1:3 *If I a., I suffer. But if I forgive, salvation will*
W-pII.....3.2:1 The world was made as an a. on God. It
W-pII.247.1:1 Sin is the symbol of a.. Behold it
W-pII.249.1:2 A. is gone, and madness has an end.
W-pII.250.1:2 him with which I would a. his sovereignty
W-pII.259.1:5 giving love the attributes of fear and of a.?
W-pII.....5.2:4 who could a. and who could be attacked?
W-pII.261.1:3 attempt to find my peace in murderous a.
W-pII.281.2:4 And I would not a. the Son He loves, for
W-pII.288.1:8 *Let me not a. the savior You have given me.*
W-pII.....8.3:1 for thoughts of death, a. and murder?
W-pII.299.2:3 *It is not mine to suffer from a.. Illusions can*
W-pII.330.1:2 Why should we a. our minds, and give
W-pII...12.3:4 of sin and guilt, of hatred and a., when all
W-pII.332.1:3 Truth never makes a.. It merely is. And by
W-pII.....341.h I can a. but my own sinlessness, And it is
W-pII.341.2:1 Let us not, then, a. our sinlessness, for it
Wfl........in.5:4 understand that anger is insane, a. is mad
M-4.......V.1:8 gentleness as surely as grief attends a..
M-7...........4:2 As such it is an a.. Usually it seems to be
M-7...........4:4 to be told that continued concern is a.. It
M-12.........5:2 Use it for sin or for a., which is the same
M-13.........7:9 denied if you a. any brother for anything.
M-17.........1:5 first responsibility in this is not to a. it. If
M-17.........3:3 A. can enter only if perception of separate
M-19.........1:5 on justice, since all a. can only be unjust.
M-19.........5:8 Here all a. and condemnation becomes
M-20.........3:8 For what except a. will lead to war? And
M-22.........3:3 mind, and keeps the idea of a. inviolate. If
M-27.........7:2 nor let a. conceal the truth from you.
M-28.........3:4 A. is meaningless and peace has come.
M-28.........3:8 forgiving all things and replacing all a..
M-29.......4:11 benefit to all, being wholly devoid of a..
M-29.........6:3 that, while a. remains attractive to you,
M-29.........6:6 He understands that an a. is a call for help
P-1.............3:3 which can a. and be attacked as well, is a
P-2.........in.1:5 by justifying a. he is protecting himself.
P-2........IV.9:2 will a. the one who tries to save him from
P-2.......IV.10:2 He must meet a. without attack, and
P-2.......IV.10:2 He must meet attack without a., and
P-2.........V.2:6 who will a. because they feel endangered,
P-2........VI.4:1 to justify a. and thus keep unforgiveness
S-3........IV.4:6 heart, and no desire to a. the Son of God.

## attack-defense 1

P-2........IV.9:3 This curious circle of a. is one of the most

## attacked 65

T-6........in.1:3 unless you believe that you have been a.,
T-6........in.1:7 cannot *be* a., attack *has* no justification
T-6.........II.2:4 fact that you a. yourself out of awareness,
T-7....VII.10:3 you will attack, believing you have been a.
T-7.....VIII.4:3 pieces, and mind cannot attack or be a..
T-8......VII.5:4 You have a. him, but you must have
T-8......VII.5:4 him, but you must have a. yourself first.
T-9.......III.7:2 his errors as real, and you have a. yourself
T-10.....III.1:1 You have not a. God and you do love
T-10.....III.1:5 And this, and only this, can be a. by you.
T-11.....V.10:6 that you have successfully a. truth, you
T-12.......V.1:4 Because you a. yourself and believed that
T-12.......V.2:3 Although you have a. yourself, you will be
T-13...III.10:6 having a. his own glorious equality with
T-13.......V.3:6 Again and again have you a. your brother,
T-14.....VII.5:7 into a call for what you have a. with them.
T-14.....IX.2:4 What disappears in light is not a.. It
T-16.....V.11:1 power to what you think you have a.? So
T-18.....VI.3:4 suffers and dies because it is a. to hold the
T-18.....VI.4:4 it does when it believes it has a. the body.
T-18...VI.13:2 The body is not a., but simply properly
T-21.....VI.7:1 your brother nor yourself can be a. alone.
T-23........I.2:8 the Will of God can be a. and overthrown
T-24........I.4:1 What God created cannot be a., for there
T-24........I.5:7 He who is "worse" than you must be a., so
T-24.....III.4:4 that is a. by everything that walks and
T-24.....IV.1:3 else becomes your enemy; feared and a.,
T-24...VI.11:4 Always a. and always furious, with anger
T-24....VII.5:4 What is immortal cannot be a.; what is
T-25...III.8:12 Sin is a. by punishment, and so preserved
T-27........II.1:6 He has a. and will attack again. Protect
T-27....VII.1:3 himself a. unjustly and by something not
T-28.....VI.4:4 again, whenever you perceive yourself a..
T-28.....VI.4:5 one can suffer if he does not see himself a.
T-29........II.9:1 body that is asked to be a god will be a.,
T-29.....IV.3:2 where it is perceived it will be there it is a.
T-29...IX.10:1 you live in safety and have not a. yourself.
T-30........I.3:4 what you perceive and so you feel a.. And
T-30.....IV.1:4 The truth could never be a.. And this you
T-30...IV.1:10 What lies beyond them cannot be a..
T-30.....IV.4:9 They must be neither cherished nor a.,
T-31...V.10:11 And what but is a. could need defense?
W-pI....23.7:1 your thoughts of attacking and of being a.
W-pI....23.7:5 of attack and of being a. are not different,
W-pI....26.1:1 is surely obvious that if you can be a. you
W-pI....26.3:3 eyes. Thus they have a. your perception of
W-pI....72.4:5 Herein is God a., for if His Son is only a
W-pI 72.10:10 have a. God's plan for salvation without
W-pI....96.5:3 a. by armies massed against itself and
W-pI.....135.h If I defend myself I am a..
W-pI..135.1:1 himself unless he thought he were a., that
W-pI..135.9:1 the body and you have a. your mind. For
W-pI 135.22:4 as we say: *If I defend myself I am a.. But in*
W-pI 136.11:6 are plans to defeat what cannot be a..
W-pI..148.1:1 (135) If I defend myself I am a..
W-pI..153.6:4 Defenselessness can never be a., because
W-pI..161.7:2 There must be a thing to be a.. An enemy
W-pI..170.4:3 your mind from him who is to be a., with
W-pII.....5.2:4 who could attack and who could be a.?
W-pII.261.1:2 citadel where I am safe and cannot be a..
M-14.......2:11 not be destroyed nor a. nor even touched.
M-17.........1:2 has hurt himself and has also a. his pupil.
C-3............8:6 His Son is not a. but recognized.
P-1.............3:3 "self," which can attack and be a. as well,
P-2........IV.9:6 source of danger, to be a. and even killed.

## attacker 3

T-3.......IV.6:9 It can be perceived as an a., but it cannot
T-22.....VI.8:1 place of the a. who he thought was there.
T-27.VIII.10:3 Whoever takes the role of enemy and of a.

## attackers 1

T-22...VI.10:6 mercy of countless a. more powerful than

## attacking 32

T-5........V.3:2 detach itself without believing it is a. Him
T-5........V.3:8 idea of a. God may be to the sane mind,

T-5 V.5:3 cannot conceive of **a.** anyone or anything.
T-6 III.1:4 By **a.** nothing, He presents no barrier to
T-6 IV.4:2 this as a justification for **a.** its maker. It
T-6 V.B.1:5 Many thought I was **a.** them, even though
T-7 VI.6:1 Spirit undoes illusions without **a.** them,
T-7 VI.7:8 this makes it appear as if you are **a.** Him.
T-7 VII.8:4 you believe that your brother is **a.** you to
T-8 I.3:4 peace, which you are giving up by **a.** them
T-10 III.1:4 When you think you are **a.** yourself, it is a
T-12 V.2:4 by **a.** you have not done anything. Once
T-13 III.3:4 Spirit, then, seems to be **a.** your fortress,
T-13 V.3:8 and by **a.** others you are literally attacking
T-13 V.3:8 others you are literally **a.** what is not there
T-15 VII.9:5 seems always to be **a.** and wounding him,
T-18 II.3:8 You do not realize you are **a.** it, trying to
T-21 VII.3:9 It could be seen **a.** anyone with anything.
T-23 I.8:4 *by* **a.** it you make two illusions of yourself,
W-pI 23.7:1 your thoughts of **a.** and of being attacked.
W-pI 26.h attack thoughts are **a.** my invulnerability.
W-pI 56.1:1 attack thoughts are **a.** my invulnerability.
W-pI 62.2:3 having denied your Identity by **a.** creation
W-pI 72.7:4 you are **a.** God's plan for salvation, and
W-pI 72.10:4 are therefore **a.** what we do not recognize.
W-pI 84.3:4 If I hold grievances I am **a.** love, and
W-pI 84.3:4 attacking love, and therefore **a.** my Self.
W-pII 12.2:5 it before it can ensure its safety by **a.** them
Wfl in.1:5 seem ugly and unsafe, **a.** and destroying,
P-1 3:1 of the form of his distress, is **a.** himself,
P-2 IV.9:2 from them, believing that he is **a.** him.
P-2 IV.9:5 The therapist is seen as one who is **a.** the

## attacks 34

T-4 IV.10:4 cannot be wrong because it never **a.**.
T-7 VI.3:2 means that the ego **a.** what is preserving it
T-7 VII.9:3 Whenever a brother **a.** another, that *is*
T-11 III.1:7 for being blind it does not see whom it **a.**.
T-11 III.1:8 Yet it always **a.** the Son of God, and the
T-11 V.7:1 The ego always **a.** on behalf of separation
T-11 V.13:5 ego **a.** everything it perceives by breaking
T-12 III.3:2 If he **a.**, you are agreeing with this belief;
T-12 V.2:7 **a.** on yourself have failed to weaken you,
T-15 I.5:2 Even when it **a.** so savagely that it tries to
T-18 IX.4:2 all the twisted thoughts, all the insane **a.**,
T-21 VII.4:5 an enemy, but this will shift even as it **a.**,
T-23 III.1:6 justify his savagery with smiles as he **a.**.
T-24 I.9:4 This is what he **a.**, and you protect. Here
T-27 III.1:7 that contradicts the concept that it **a.**.
T-29 IV.5:6 shadow figure who **a.** becomes a brother
T-31 V.10:5 deceived by all your goodness, and **a.** it so
W-pI 14.5:4 "God did not create cancer," or heart **a.**,
W-pI 51.5:4 anger is justified and my **a.** are warranted.
W-pI 66.2:4 The ego **a.** and the Holy Spirit does not
W-pI 66.3:4 the ego by listening to its **a.** on truth. We
W-pI 72.8:1 to stop these senseless **a.** on salvation. We
W-pI 76.5:5 enemy; that it **a.** itself and wants to die. It
W-pI 92.7:1 It fears and it **a.** and hates itself, and
W-pI 131.7:3 denies its own existence and **a.** itself is not
W-pI 135.7:4 for the many mad **a.** you make upon it.
W-pI 136.10:2 Heaven quails before such mad **a.** as these
W-pI 153.1:4 It **a.**, and then attacks again. No peace of
W-pI 153.1:4 It attacks, and then **a.** again. No peace of
W-pI 170.1:1 No one **a.** without intent to hurt. This
W-pI 196.5:1 hopeless thought that you can make **a.** on
W-pII 259.1:3 What else but sin engenders our **a.**? What
M-17 9:3 its servant, it neither **a.** nor protects. To
M-18 1:2 with his pupil about a magic thought, **a.** it

## attain 20

T-1 II.3:10 is nothing about me that you cannot **a.**. I
T-2 IV.5:3 means that a miracle, to **a.** its full efficacy,
T-12 V.8:2 the way to achieve a goal is not to **a.** it?
T-14 IV.2:3 This state, and only this, must you **a.**,
T-19 I.5:10 is to set up a goal forever impossible to **a.**,
T-24 VI.13:2 forth for you the purpose that you can **a.**,
T-25 II.1:3 Perhaps you fancy to **a.** some peace and
T-29 II.7:3 To change is to **a.** a state unlike the one in
W-pI 157.2:3 past the highest reaches it can possibly **a.**.
W-pI 158.6:7 is with Christ's vision. This we can **a.**.
W-pI 169.3:3 is not the goal this course aspires to **a.**.
W-pI 169.13:4 How could you finally **a.** to it forever,
Wi181-200 1:3 asked to practice now in order to **a.** the
W-pI 186.11:5 point to one goal, and one you can **a.**.
W-pII 7.3:2 you would **a.** what is forever unattainable.
W-pII 339.1:6 the things he wants; the state he would **a.**.
M-4 I.A.7:7 now he must **a.** a state that may remain
M-20 6:13 **A.** His peace, and you remember Him.
S-1 I.6:1 level of prayer that everyone can **a.** as yet.
S-2 I.10:3 or you will not be able to **a.** your freedom.

## attainable 2

T-16 IV.10:2 **a.** removes your own sense of completion,
P-2 V.3:4 the insane within the bounds of the **a.**.

## attained 24

T-2 V.9:7 limited sense in which it can now be **a.**.
T-5 V.2:1 the Kingdom is **a.** through the Atonement
T-12 III.5:1 is for the mind, and it is **a.** through peace.
T-17 II.5:1 real world is **a.** simply by the complete
T-18 IX.11:5 is not for us to dwell on what cannot be **a.**
T-18 IX.11:7 readiness for knowledge still must be **a.**.
T-19 I.1:3 that peace without faith will never be **a.**,
T19 IV.B.10:9 are both conditions of the mind, to be **a.**.
T-20 VII.2:6 A purpose is **a.** by means, and if you want
T-20 VII.5:4 It cannot be **a.** but in illusion, and so the
T-21 VII.13:2 **a.** by giving up the wish for the *inconstant*
T-22 II.5:3 by which escape from guilt can be **a.**, then
T-24 in.1:2 in which God is remembered is **a.**. It is
T-24 IV.4:1 not the means by which salvation is **a.**,
T-27 V.8:9 Yet this can only be **a.** by One Who does
T-30 I.10:3 But this much reason have you now **a.**;
T-30 III.1:5 happiness, and that, by limiting, is all **a.**.
W-pI 126.7:5 forgiveness, as the means by which it is **a.**,
W-pI 131.2:1 Goals that are meaningless are not **a.**.
W-pI 138.5:5 be **a.** through learning how to reach them
W-pI 157.9:3 teach, for you **a.** it not through learning.
W-pII 14.4:4 that we have **a.** we call to all our brothers,
M-26 1:6 not **a.** the necessary understanding as yet,
S-3 IV.4:6 be **a.** until there is no hatred in your heart

## attaining 2

T-2 III.1:4 can be used as a means for **a.** "atonement.
T-30 in.1:2 now you need specific methods for **a.** it.

## attainment 12

T-9 II.2:2 **a.** of it would no longer *be* what you want
T-13 VII.h **A.** of the Real World
T-19 h THE **A.** OF PEACE
T-19 I.1:2 **a.** is the criterion by which the wholeness
T-20 III.8:10 Ask not the means of its **a.** of the one
T-20 VII.8:10 its **a.** will be evaluated as worth the seeing
T-21 V.9:4 Knowledge is far beyond **a.** of any kind.
T-22 II.5:6 means for its **a.** are more than possible.
T-24 in.1:1 **a.** and the keeping of the state of peace.
T-24 I.6:3 if his **a.** of it were perceived as yours? You
S-1 II.8:8 The stages necessary to its **a.**, however,
S-3 in.1:2 of success in ultimate **a.** of the goal, is

## attains 2

T-5 I.7:2 and no one who **a.** it could believe for one
T-18 IX.11:3 remember only that whoever **a.** the real

## attempt 201

T-1 II.2:2 is why any **a.** to describe it in words is
T-1 VII.3:4 they do. Fantasy is an **a.** to control reality
T-2 IV.4:3 is a second misstep to **a.** to heal it through
T-2 V.2:2 mind to heal, you should not **a.** to do so.
T-2 V.2:6 you should not **a.** to perform miracles.
T-2 VII.4:2 **a.** to resolve the error through attempting
T-3 I.2:4 Persecution frequently results in an **a.** to
T-3 III.3:3 state that is usually an **a.** to counteract an
T-3 IV.2:3 The ego is a wrong-minded **a.** to perceive
T-3 IV.6:3 the body as yourself in an **a.** to escape
T-3 IV.7:4 not **a.** to counteract error with knowledge
T-3 V.5:5 a futile **a.** to escape from an inescapable
T-3 VI.6:3 an **a.** to teach you the meaning of mercy.
T-4 I.8:4 change reality, which is indeed a fearful **a.**
T-4 I.9:9 **a.** to increase its believableness is merely
T-4 II.6:7 is only an **a.** to convince itself that *it* is real.
T-4 II.8:2 with them in a feeble **a.** at identification,
T-4 VII.3:2 it make any **a.** to establish what is true. It
T-5 in.1:7 **a.** to heal without being wholly joyous
T-5 V.4:11 automatically **a.** to remedy the situation.
T-5 VI.8:2 an **a.** to guarantee the ego's own survival.
T-6 V.A.1:6 Death is an **a.** to resolve conflict by not
T-7 VI.11:11 meaningful. This can only be an insane **a.**.
T-7 VIII.2:6 in an **a.** to persuade you that you have
T-7 VIII.3:1 are two major errors involved in this **a.**.
T-7 VIII.3:3 **a.** to keep part of it and get rid of another
T-7 VIII.5:4 because they come from an **a.** to project
T-8 II.4:2 and the **a.** to learn it is a violation of your
T-8 V.5:9 Do not **a.** to hold on to both, or you will
T-8 IX.6:1 it from the body in an **a.** to destroy it. Yet
T-9 I.12:1 Any **a.** to deny what *is* must be fearful,
T-9 I.12:1 and if the **a.** is strong it will induce panic.
T-9 III.3:3 the Holy Spirit does not **a.** to understand
T-9 III.7:8 **a.** you make to correct a brother means
T-9 VIII.2:3 It is an **a.** to counteract your littleness,
T-9 VIII.2:6 It is a delusional **a.** to outdo, but not to
T-10 IV.1:1 is an **a.** at reconciling the irreconcilable.
T-10 IV.6:6 No false gods you **a.** to interpose between
T-11 V.13:3 The **a.** to understand totality by breaking
T-11 V.15:1 The ego makes no **a.** to understand this,
T-11 V.15:1 ego does make every **a.** to demonstrate it,
T-12 I.2:2 whole process represents a clear-cut **a.** to
T-12 I.6:10 Do not **a.** to "help" a brother in your way,
T-12 III.7:5 **a.** to maintain your ego identification, for
T-12 V.1:5 **a.** to "equalize" the situation you made.
T-12 V.6:2 Do not **a.** to teach yourself what you do
T-12 V.7:7 This **a.** at "learning" has so weakened
T-13 in.1:5 the delusional **a.** of the mind to deny itself
T-13 in.1:6 It is not an **a.** to relinquish denial, but to
T-13 II.6:2 of God's Son it did **a.** to kill him, and the
T-13 X.3:4 those who suffer guilt will **a.** to displace it,
T-14 IV.5:6 Give up this frantic and insane **a.** that
T-14 VI.7:3 not **a.** to communicate the meaningless.
T-14 XI.3:8 **a.** to understand any event or anything or
T-14 XI.6:10 refusal to **a.** to teach yourself what you do
T-15 II.3:5 **a.** to support it and uphold its weakness,
T-15 III.11:1 unwilling to **a.** to grasp for peace yourself,
T-15 IV.6:2 nothing more than the ego's **a.** to obscure
T-15 V.1:5 You would make no **a.** to judge, because it
T-15 V.6:3 If you would **a.** to substitute one aspect of
T-15 VI.7:8 **a.** to be nothing else and something else
T-15 VII.10:3 than an **a.** to make someone feel guilty,
T-15 VII.10:3 this **a.** is the only basis the ego accepts for
T-15 VII.12:2 you will be compelled to **a.** to keep your
T-15 VIII.5:1 The Holy Spirit is God's **a.** to free you of
T-15 VIII.5:2 And because of the Source of the **a.**, it will
T-15 X.9:4 have tried many compromises in the **a.** to
T-16 I.5:5 **A.** to teach Him not. You are the learner;
T-16 I.7:1 *You* will **a.** to do this only in secrecy. And
T-16 IV.1:7 it into sight, and to make no **a.** to hide it.
T-16 IV.1:8 **a.** to balance hate with love that makes
T-16 IV.3:1 The special love relationship is an **a.** to
T-16 IV.3:2 It makes no **a.** to rise above the storm,
T-16 IV.6:4 And the **a.** to escape from one illusion
T-16 IV.7:1 is an **a.** to bring love into separation. And,
T-16 IV.7:2 it is nothing more than an **a.** to bring love
T-16 V.2:1 the **a.** to make guilty is always directed
T-16 V.4:2 the **a.** to secure for the self the specialness
T-16 V.6:2 And the **a.** to find the imagined "best" of
T-16 V.6:4 basis for the **a.** at union rests on exclusion
T-16 V.13:1 **a.** to raise other gods before Him, and by
T-16 VII.1:2 special relationship is an **a.** to re-enact the
T-16 VII.7:1 you may **a.** to bring illusions into the holy
T-16 VII.7:2 Yet you will not **a.** this long. In the holy
T-17 I.6:5 to forgive yourself for just this same **a.**.
T-17 III.4:7 **a.** at union becomes a way of excluding
T-17 VI.7:1 ego will **a.** to take this aspect elsewhere,

T-17...... VI.7:2 except that this a. conflicts with unity,
T-18...... IV.1:6 Do not a. to give the Holy Spirit what He
T-18...... IV.5:4 not a. to make yourself holy to be ready to
T-18....... V.2:3 Never a. to overlook your guilt before you
T-18....... V.6:4 fear alone, or to a. to deal with it alone.
T-18..... VII.4:5 course does not a. to teach more than
T-18..... VII.4:8 Enormous effort is expended in the a. to
T-18...... IX.6:6 disappears; a. to grasp it and your hands
T-19....... II.4:5 an a. to wrest creation away from truth,
T-19....... II.5:1 a. to reinterpret sin as error is always
T19. IV.A.5:10 Do not a. to stand between Him and His
T-20....... V.3:4 fear that rises from the meaningless a. to
T-20..... VII.8:8 A. to see him not in darkness, for your
T-21.........I.2:1 to a. to judge what could be seen instead.
T-21...... III.1:4 may a. to keep the bargain in the name of
T-21...... III.1:5 Thus in the "fairness" you a. to ease the
T-22...... III.3:4 thick it would be madness to a. to pass it.
T-22.... VI.11:5 You do not see that this is your a. because
T-22.... VI.15:4 a. to keep a little of the ego with this gift.
T-24..... VII.8:1 course makes no a. to teach what cannot
T-25... VII.3:10 Do not a. to see it differently, nor twist it
T-26.........I.1:4 for it is always an a. to limit loss. The
T-26....... II.1:6 purpose to a. to solve it in a special form.
T-26... VII.12:5 world is an a. to prove your innocence,
T-27.........I.1:1 is a compromise a. that would combine
T-27...... IV.2:8 must be pointless to a. to solve a problem
T-27...... IV.3:1 A. to solve no problems but within the
T-27...... IV.7:1 a. to solve no problems in a world from
T-28..... II.2:11 sickness is a meaningless a. to give effects
T-28....... II.3:1 Son of God a. to make himself his cause,
T-29....... II.3:1 It has been hopeless to a. to find the hope
T-29..... VII.4:1 Whenever you a. to reach a goal in which
W-pI....... 1.3:5 Do not a. to apply it to everything you see
W-pI....... 2.1:6 a. to include everything you see in a given
W-pI....... 2.2:5 Make no a. to include anything particular
W-pI....... 4.3:3 It is a first a. in the long-range purpose of
W-pI..... 13.6:1 our first a. at stating an explicit cause and
W-pI..... 19.5:2 if necessary. Do not a. more than four.
W-pI..... 20.1:2 no a. to direct the time for undertaking
W-pI..... 20.2:1 This is our first a. to introduce structure.
W-pI..... 27.3:4 and a. to adhere to it throughout the day.
W-pI..... 28.7:2 in an a. to acknowledge the equal value of
W-pI..... 33.1:1 Today's idea is an a. to recognize that
W-pI..... 40.1:3 and you are urged to a. this schedule and
W-pI..... 41.5:3 our first real a. to get past this dark and
W-pI..... 43.6:1 and then a. the second phase again. Do
W-pI..... 44.3:1 we are going to a. to reach that light. For
W-pI..... 45.3:2 Today we will a. to reach them. We will
W-pI..... 45.4:2 will a. to leave the unreal and seek for the
W-pI..... 45.8:7 holiness and an a. to reach the Kingdom
W-pI..... 55.5:3 that I a. to use everyone and everything. It
W-pI..... 65.5:3 first, make no a. to concentrate only on
W-pI..... 66.4:4 Today's exercises are an a. to go beyond
W-pI..... 69.2:1 another real a. to reach the light in you.
W-pI..... 69.5:4 not a. to go through them and past them,
W-pI..... 69.5:5 of substance. We will make this a. today.
W-pI..... 69.8:3 a. to go through the clouds to the light, to
W-pI..... 70.4:1 to do just the opposite, making every a.,
W-pI..... 71.5:3 your purpose is divided and you will a. to
W-pI..... 72.1:1 His plan, and a deliberate a. to destroy it.
W-pI..... 72.3:1 the a. to keep the limitations that a body
W-pI..... 78.4:1 Today we will a. to see God's Son. We
W-pI..... 78.6:2 You will a. to hold him in your mind, first
W-pI..... 79.6:1 desperate a. not to recognize the problem
W-pI..... 86.3:2 Holding grievances is an a. to prove that
W-pI..... 91.4:3 to the a. to let you feel this strength.
W-pI..... 94.3:1 hour to the a. to feel the truth in you.
W-pI..... 95.3:1 We will a. today to be aware only of what
W-pI... 95.11:5 then a. to feel the meaning that the words
W-pI..... 96.2:2 will a. an endless list of goals you cannot
W-pI..... 96.3:5 Make no a. to reconcile the two, for one
W-pI..... 96.8:1 We will a. today to find this thought,
W-pI... 100.6:1 will a. to understand joy is our function
W-pI... 101.4:2 a. in every way he can to drown the Voice
W-pI... 101.6:8 a. again to find the joy these thoughts will
W-pI... 108.7:4 we will a. to offer peace to everyone, and
WpIrIII.in10:2 A. to give your daily two ideas a brief but
W-pI... 124.8:4 first a. at an extended period for which we
W-pI... 126.9:1 today to the a. to understand today's idea
W-pI... 130.6:1 we will a. no compromise where none is
W-pI... 130.7:2 a. to bring with us a little part of unreality
W-pI... 133.2:3 course does not a. to take from you the
W-pI. 133.13:2 We will a. to reach this state today, with
W-pI... 134.3:2 as a vain a. to look past what is there; to
W-pI... 135.1:4 this you do when you a. to plan the future
W-pI... 136.3:4 recognize exactly what you would a. to do
W-pI... 168.1:4 He makes no a. to hide from us. We try to
Wi181-200 3:4 So we now a. to go past all defenses for a
W-pI. 185.10:5 for it, and where to turn for help in the a..
W-pI. 193.10:1 We will a. today to overcome a thousand
W-pI... 196.1:1 you will not a. to harm yourself, nor make
W-pI... 200.2:2 A. no more to win through losing, nor to
W-pI... 200.9:3 Only if we a. to wander can there be delay
WpI rVI.in.4:1 will a. to get beyond all words and special
WpI rVI.in.4:2 For we a., this time, to reach a quickened
W-pII..... in.2:1 Now we a. to let the exercise be merely a
W-pII..... 3.5:3 And let us not a. to change our function.
W-pII . 261.1:3 a. to find my peace in murderous attack. I
W-pII . 268.1:2 *Let me not a. to interfere with Your creation,*
W-pII . 327.2:2 *Let me a. therefore to try them, and to judge*
W-pII ... 13.1:4 but does not a. to go beyond perception,
M-4 .........I.2:2 Who would a. to fly with the tiny wings of
M-8 ........... 2:3 an illusion is an a. to make something real
M-15 ....... 2:11 do you still a. to take His role from Him?
M-16 ......... 9:2 the a. to substitute another will for God's.
M-27 ......... 4:7 and will a. a thousand more. Not one can
M-29 ......... 2:4 should a. to answer these questions alone.
C-in ........... 3:6 does not a. to resort to inventiveness or
P-2..........II.2:3 a. to formalize religion is so obviously an
P-2..........II.2:3 is so obviously an ego a. to reconcile the
P-2......... V.4:3 And two come very close to God in this a.
P-3....... III.7:6 and to a. to do what is impossible. Then
S-2.........in.1:2 bottom step, or even to a. to climb at all.
S-2........ III.7:3 in this; do not a. to judge forgiveness, nor

## attempted 12

T-2 ...... VII.7:7 already a. to correct the fundamental
T-8 ........ V.5:5 ego has a. to join the journey with us and
T-10 ..... III.8:7 replacements you have a. are nothing.
T-15 ..... IX.6:5 a. to separate the Father from the Son,
T-16 ...... V.1:5 being a. that have not been touched upon
T-17 ..... III.3:1 body of the other with which union is a.,
T-30 ...... in.1:4 one will help a little, every time it is a..
W-pI....... 1.4:2 they be a. for more than a minute or so,
W-pI....... 9.5:1 while complete inclusion should not be a.
W-pI..... 26.5:2 two minutes should be a. for each of them
W-pI..... 41.8:5 startling results even the first time it is a.,
W-pI. 161.10:1 we practice in a form we have a. earlier.

## attempting 20

T-1 ...... VII.3:6 and a. to obtain pleasure from them. But
T-2 ...... VII.4:2 through a. the mastery of fear is useless.
T-9 ..........I.3:7 He is not a. to force an alien will upon you
T-9 ........I.11:2 you say of someone who persists in a. the
T-15 ...... V.2:3 you are a. to use separation to save you.
T-15 ..... XI.1:2 seek not safety by a. to protect yourself
T-15 ..... XI.5:4 and loss without a. to restore himself?
T-16 ..... IV.3:3 haven by a. to build barricades against it,
T-17 ........I.6:5 a. to solve his problems through fantasy,
T-18 .... VII.4:6 may be a. to follow a very long road to the
T-20 ..... III.3:3 without a. to adjust themselves to it, or it
W-pI..... 20.5:1 an hour today, a. to do so every half hour.
W-pI..... 25.2:5 the world, instead of a. to reinforce them.
W-pI..... 30.2:2 We are not a. to get rid of what we do not
W-pI..... 44.6:4 in which you see. You are a. to reach Him.
W-pI..... 44.8:1 awareness that you are a. something very
W-pI..... 65.6:2 a. to catch a few of the idle thoughts that
W-pI..... 69.2:3 We are literally a. to get in touch with the
W-pI... 95.11:3 a. to allow the meaning of the words to
Wi181-200 2:2 goal. We are a. now to lift these blocks,

## attempts 60

T-2 ....... III.5:2 their true creative powers on useless a. to
T-2 ........ V.8:3 your a. at correction will be misdirected.
T-3 ..........I.6:7 Only the a. to shroud it in darkness have
T-3 .........V.5:3 incongruities are the result of a. to regard
T-4 ........ in.3:5 the futile a. of the ego at reparation, and
T-4 .........II.8:5 The ego's ceaseless a. to gain the spirit's
T-4 .........V.2:7 the ego a. to save itself from being swept
T-4 ....... VI.1:7 unaffected by your a. to dissociate it.
T-5 ..... III.10:4 Despite the ego's a. to conceal this part, it
T-6 ....... IV.5:3 which is not real, a. to persuade the mind,
T-6 ..... V.A.1:7 any other impossible solution the ego a.,
T-8 .........V.6:6 beyond all a. of the ego to hold you back.
T-8 ..... VIII.9:9 all a. to use the body lovelessly. Health is
T-8 ....... IX.3:3 They are a. to reinforce sleeping out of
T-9 .........V.4:3 a. to dispel its effects by depreciating the
T-9 ..... VIII.1:4 a. to offer gifts to induce you to return to
T-12 ........I.6:3 comes from your a. not to do just this.
T-13 .......II.1:2 ego a. to get rid of guilt from its viewpoint
T-13 ... XI.11:3 surely as the ego will not effect what it a..
T-14 ..... XI.1:9 the false, and of your a. to undo the true.
T-15 ..... III.5:6 All your a. to deny His magnitude, and
T-15 .... VII.4:1 the ego a. to maintain and increase guilt,
T-15 ..... IX.2:4 more than a. to limit communication,
T-15 ..... XI.5:5 when the basis of your a. is the belief in
T-16 ........I.1:7 accomplished by delusional a. to enter
T-17 ..... III.2:6 become a. at union through the body, for
T-18 .......II.4:6 Your a. to blot out reality are very fearful,
T-18 .. VII.4:10 body necessary. All such a. will ultimately
T-19 ........I.6:7 all a. to keep both truth and illusion in
T-25 ..... III.5:4 the pitiful a. of specialness to put it out of
T-26 ........I.1:2 all desperate a. to strike a bargain, and all
T-26 ..... III.7:3 to give up all a. to choose between them,
T-26 .......X.4:4 that your attack on him a. to get? Is it not
T-29 ... VIII.8:5 and still a. to seek for one that yet might
T-31 ..... IV.8:3 This course a. to teach no more than that
W-pI .... 71.8:4 a. and mad proposals to free yourself.
W-pI .... 74.5:3 to mistake these a. for withdrawal, but
W-pI .... 95.6:1 of your goal and regular a. to reach it.
W-pI .. 95.10:2 a. to keep you unaware you are one Self,
W-pI .... 96.1:2 and leads to frantic a. to reconcile the
W-pI 122.14:1 your mind by your a. to think of them at
W-pI .. 132.6:3 the central thought the course a. to teach.
W-pI .. 135.1:2 reality, and then a. to handle them as real
W-pI .. 135.7:4 Such a., ridiculous yet deeply cherished,
W-pI 136.12:3 a. to plan defenses that would alter it.
W-pI .. 154.1:4 These are but a. to hold decision off, and
W-pI .. 167.3:7 our a. to change your mind about yourself
W-pI .. 197.1:2 You make a. at kindness and forgiveness.
W-pII ..... 1.3:4 It sets about its furious a. to smash reality
M-in........ 5:12 This manual a. to answer these questions.
M-5 ........II.1:8 "reflexes" and the like represent a. to
M-8 ........... 2:5 creation; a. to bring truth to lies. Finding
M-10 ......... 2:5 impossible for him, he no longer a. it.
M-16 ......... 8:5 a. to place reliance on himself alone.
M-16 ......... 9:3 These a. may indeed seem frightening,
M-27 ......... 4:7 The world a. a thousand compromises,
M-27 ......... 6:9 the world fosters in its vain a. to cling to
P-2....... IV.8:3 for all of them are but a. to compromise
P-2..........V.7:3 perfection that is asked in our a. to heal.
P-3..........II.9:7 The a. of therapists to compromise in this

## attend 9

T-7 ....... III.4:2 you believe you can a. to what is not true,
T-9 ....... III.4:2 if you a. to them you are not hearing Him.
W-pI .. 106.2:4 belief. A. them not, but listen to the truth.
W-pI 140.12:6 be given us as we a. in silence and in joy.
W-pI .. 153.1:1 to take away again; a. this lesson well. The
W-pI 154.10:2 it is but our voice we hear as we a. Him.
W-pII . 267.2:1 *Let me a. Your Answer, not my own. Father,*
W-pII . 268.2:1 today, nor let our ears a. to lying tongues.
W-pII . 275.1:1 Let us today a. the Voice for God, which

## attended 3

T-5 .........V.4:9 thinking will always be a. with guilt,
T-5 .........V.7:5 thought is a. by guilt at its inception, and
T-13 ...... in.2:6 Their growth is a. by suffering, and they

## attends 3

W-ep......... 5:6 Joy a. our way. For we go homeward to an

M-4........ V.1:8 with gentleness as surely as grief a. attack.
M-4..... IX.2:11 Defenselessness a. it naturally, and joy is

**attention** 15

T-1....... VII.4:2 involves a. and study at some level. Some
T-7........ III.4:1 is merely to focus your full a. on it. As
T-12....... V.9:4 accord. You need offer only undivided a..
T-13....... X.1:3 source of guilt, from which a. is diverted,
T-17...... IV.7:6 to divert your a. from what it encloses.
T-17.... IV.11:3 to focus all your a. on the picture. The
T-18..... VII.7:7 activity of the body ceases to demand a..
T-27...... VI.1:3 Pain compels a., drawing it away from
W-pI..... 12.2:6 glance rests on equal a. and equal time.
W-pI..... 41.6:6 of any thoughts that might divert your a..
W-pI..... 62.5:6 Should your a. wander, repeat the idea
W-pI..... 65.6:2 idle thoughts that escaped your a. before,
W-pI..... 95.5:2 your difficulties with sustained a., you
W-pI.153.15:2 will begin each day by giving our a. to the
M-8............ 1:4 brighter thing draws the a. from another

**attentively** 1

WpI. rII.in.3:1 part of the time listening quietly but a..

**attest** 14

T-9..... VIII.8:4 They a. to your grandeur, but they cannot
T-9..... VIII.8:4 a. to pride because pride is not shared.
T-11..... V.16:8 Its witnesses do a. to its denial, but hardly
T-12..... VII.8:4 they a. only to your decision about reality
T-14...... III.8:4 Do not a. to it, and do not foster belief in
T-15...... I.12:5 They a. to your willingness to *be* released,
T-27......... I.6:1 A. his innocence and not his guilt. Your
T-27....... II.4:2 You must a. his sins have no effect on you
T-27...... VI.6:5 And they a. to different sufferings. Yet to
T-27..... VII.5:3 The means a. the purpose, but are not
T-27. VIII.12:7 they a. the thing you do not want to know
T-28...... IV.6:5 to his, and his a. the truth of yours. Yet if
T-28....... V.6:2 perhaps, all put together to a. its truth.
M-in .......... 2:7 call to witnesses to a. to what you believe.

**attested** 1

W-pI...190.2:1 Can such projections be a. to? Can they

**attesting** 3

T-3......... II.3:1 you are a. to your belief that he is not in
T-14...... III.5:3 a. to your happiness that comes from
T-27...... IV.4:3 both a. the same thing in different form.

**attests** 15

T-1......... II.1:9 and what you do a. to what you believe.
T-12...... I.10:6 a. to your eternal knowledge that union is
T-21.... VI.11:2 It but a. to it. Where could his freedom lie
T-21..... VII.6:6 And this imagined difference a. to your
T-23..... II.20:7 in love, in any form, a. to chaos as reality.
T-25....... V.1:6 truth, for each a. the other must be true.
T-25..... VII.5:3 joy. Nothing a. to death and cruelty; to
T-27....... II.6:4 things the world a. can never be undone.
T-27...... VI.6:7 It is their sameness that the miracle a.. It
T-30... VIII.2:2 miracle a. salvation from appearances by
W-pI..... 56.2:3 The world I see a. to the fearful nature of
W-pI... 153.2:4 For it a. to weakness, and sets up a system
W-pI... 181.9:2 love for everyone we look upon a. to our
W-pII..229.1:5 upon a. the truth of the Identity I sought
W-pII..240.1:2 It a. that you have seen yourself as you

**attitude** 2

T-1........ VI.4:3 In a., then, though not in content, you
S-2......... II.2:2 Forgiveness here rests on an a. of gracious

**attitudes** 8

T-4......... II.5:6 Your a. even toward this are necessarily
T-4......... II.5:6 conflicted, because all a. are ego-based.
T-4........ IV.1:2 of your ego is demonstrated by your a.,
T-4....... VII.7:5 the a. the knowledge from the revelation
T-8..... VIII.1:1 A. toward the body are attitudes toward
T-8..... VIII.1:1 toward the body are a. toward attack. The
W-pI...126.2:3 Therefore, your a. have no effect on them,
M-9 ........... 1:4 is most unlikely that changes in a. would

**attract** 10

T-5....... II.11:2 increase its power to a. the whole Sonship
T-13.... VI.11:4 will a. you as nothing in this world can do
T-14...... III.3:3 Whenever the pain of guilt seems to a.
T-14....... V.8:6 and a. all tortured minds to join with you
T-15..... VII.2:7 the ego always seems to a. through love,
T-15...... IX.7:1 When the body ceases to a. you, and
T-17...... III.6:8 Its loveliness will so a. you that you will
T-20....... II.1:4 brother to you, and to a. his body's eyes?
T-20....... II.2:5 its chosen home, or those it would a. to it.
T-20...... VI.9:7 For no illusions can a. the mind that has

**attracted** 5

T-15..... VII.6:6 and having asked for it they are a. to it.
T19. IV.A.10:5 Love is a. only to love. Overlooking guilt
T19. IV.A.10:8 Fear is a. to what love sees not, and each
T19....IV.C.1:7 on those who are a. to it and seek it out.
T-22...... III.9:5 and is a. to him to perpetuate his sins.

**attraction** 60

T-12...... VIII.h The A. of Love for Love
T-12. VIII.7:10 the a. of love for love remains irresistible.
T-13.... VI.12:2 The a. of light must draw you willingly,
T-13..... VII.2:5 because their real a. to you is unequal.
T-15..... VII.1:1 the poor a. of the special love relationship
T-15..... VII.1:1 the powerful a. of the Father for His Son.
T-15..... VII.2:6 This is its one a.; an attraction so weak
T-15..... VII.2:6 an a. so weak that it would have no hold
T-15..... VII.2:7 no a. at all to anyone who perceives that it
T-15..... VII.3:1 The sick a. of guilt must be recognized
T-15..... VII.3:4 Yet the a. of guilt has value to you only
T-15..... VII.7:1 the a. of what you do not want seems to
T-15..... VII.7:1 stronger than the a. of what you do want.
T-15... VII.14:2 In the holy instant guilt holds no a., since
T-15......... IX.h The Holy Instant and the A. of God
T-15...... IX.5:1 you would experience the a. of the eternal
T-15...... IX.6:2 a. of guilt opposes the attraction of God.
T-15...... IX.6:2 attraction of guilt opposes the a. of God.
T-15...... IX.6:3 His a. for you remains unlimited, but
T-15...... IX.7:3 and you experience only the a. of God.
T-15....... X.1:2 the a. of guilt does stand between them.
T-15....... X.3:2 as real, guilt will hold no a. for you. For in
T-16....... II.6:9 now, and you *will* yield to its compelling a.
T-16...... III.9:2 no fear that the a. of those who stand on
T-16....... V.3:2 for counting on the a. of this offering, the
T-16....... V.9:1 of hell lies only in the terrible a. of guilt,
T-16...... VI.3:2 aid in protecting you from the a. of guilt,
T-17...... III.4:3 The a. of the unholy relationship begins
T-17....... V.4:2 its former goal completely without a., and
T-18..... VII.3:5 In any single instant the a. of guilt would
T-18..... VII.3:6 It has no a. *now.* Its whole attraction is
T-18..... VII.3:7 Its whole a. is imaginary, and therefore
T-18..... VII.7:4 the way in which sin loses all a. *right now.*
T-19...... III.1:1 The a. of guilt is found in sin, not error.
T-19...... III.1:2 Sin will be repeated because of this a..
T19.... IV.A.i.h The A. of Guilt
T19. IV.A.10:1 The a. of guilt produces fear of love, for
T19. IV.A.11:6 fierce a. that guilt holds for fear is wholly
T19....IV.B.1:2 Where the a. of guilt holds sway, peace is
T19....IV.B.1:4 the a. of guilt made manifest in the body,
T19.....IV.B.i.h The A. of Pain
T19..IV.B.12:6 The a. of guilt *must* enter with it, and
T19..IV.B.13:2 guilt, serving its master whose a. to guilt
T19..IV.B.13:3 This, then, is the a. of pain. Ruled by this
T19..IV.B.16:4 to the a. of guilt is the escape from pain.
T19...... IV.C.h The Third Obstacle: The A. of Death
T19....IV.C.1:5 seems to be the fear of death is really its a.
T19....IV.C.9:1 go as its appeal is yielded to love's real a..
T19... IV.D.1:2 feel and think if death held no a. for you?
T19... IV.D.3:1 the belief in death and protected by its a..
T19... IV.D.4:3 a. of death that makes life seem to be ugly
T19... IV.D.5:5 forever as love's a. stirs and calls to you.
T19... IV.D.5:7 by the power of the a. of what lies beyond
T-20...... VI.9:4 false a. your preference to the holy instant
T-21..... VII.1:6 that they are little could see a. there.
T-22......... I.4:6 correction, for the a. of guilt is only fear.
T-23....... in.4:2 There can be no a. of guilt in innocence.
T-23....... in.4:4 sin, nor for a tiny stirring of guilt's a..
T-24...... IV.1:6 first. And such is guilt's a.. Here is death
W-pI... 192.4:2 it holds no fierce a. now and guilt is gone.

**attractive** 7

T-15... VII.10:4 identify with it, guilt will remain a. to you
T-16....... V.8:5 is nothing more than an "a." form of fear,
T-18..... VII.1:3 and this always means you still find sin a..
T-19...... III.1:4 the guilt remains a. the mind will suffer,
T-19...... III.3:1 An error, on the other hand, is not a..
T-19...... III.7:2 you will find guilt a. and believe that sin is
M-29 ......... 6:3 mean that, while attack remains a. to you,

**attracts** 11

T-3....... VII.2:7 Yet he a. men rather than repels them,
T-13....... V.5:6 it. Yet fear a. you, and believing it is love,
T-15..... VII.2:7 who perceives that it a. through guilt.
T-15... VII.14:5 to communicate a. communication to it,
T-16...... VI.12:1 to a special relationship which still a. you,
T-17...... III.2:5 you of your past grievances a. you, and
T19... IV.D.7:7 For what a. you from beyond the veil is
T-21... VII.10:7 same desire as a little glint of sin a. you.
T-22...... III.4:1 Only the form of error a. the ego.
T-23...... IV.4:3 of murder and attack that still a. you and
W-pI... 133.8:3 What a. your mind to it? What purpose

**attributable** 1

T-13........ II.4:1 is directly a. to its definition of guilt. To

**attribute** 22

T-2........... I.5:8 Peace is an a. *in* you. You cannot find it
T-2...... VIII.2:3 it. Judgment is not an a. of God. It was
T-3.......... II.2:1 Innocence is not a partial a.. It is not real
T-3........ III.1:7 As an a. of the belief in space and time, it
T-4...... IV.11:7 that life is an eternal a. of everything that
T-7........ VI.1:2 in part of it that you will not a. to all of it.
T-10....... V.2:4 Do not a. your denial of joy to them, or
T-14....... V.8:4 Son. Joy is its unifying a., with no one left
T-16........ II.1:7 One a. is no more difficult to understand
T-17...... IV.5:6 no "reason," and no a. that is not insane.
T-26........ II.3:4 or any a. which you perceive that makes
W-pI..... 21.5:2 on a particular a. of a particular person,
W-pI..... 21.5:4 *the a.] in_[name of person] differently.*
W-pI..... 35.9:1 pick up a specific a. or attributes you are
W-pI..... 43.1:1 Perception is not an a. of God. His is the
W-pI..... 67.2:7 Any a. which is in accord with God as He
W-pI..... 99.6:6 their depth or any a. they seem to have:
W-pI... 103.1:1 Happiness is an a. of love. It cannot be
W-pI. 127.10:4 a future dawns unlike the past in every a..
W-pI... 137.8:4 And by this a. it proves that laws unlike
W-pI... 156.3:2 as life. No a. of His remains unshared by
W-pI. 185.12:5 It is this a. that sets the gifts of God apart

**attributed** 1

T-17.... VIII.4:3 was there, but you a. it to something else,

**attributes** 41

T-4.......... II.5:5 and helpful, a. that must go together.
T-5......... V.5:8 It a. to God a punishing intent, and then
T-14...... IV.7:7 not endow Him with a. you understand.
T-15...... XI.4:8 Heaven out and giving it the a. of hell,
T-16........ II.1:8 all, their a. would have to be miraculous,
T-16........ II.3:5 their a. could hardly cause you perplexity.
T-16....... V.10:3 only a. of the whole religion of separation
T-17...... III.9:6 their a. come simply from what they are.

T-20.....VII.4:6 be invested with a. of Christ or of the ego.
T-20.....VII.4:7 would place the a. where they cannot be.
T-24......IV.2:8 they are, and all their a., they cannot
T-25...VII.1:11 not should share the a. of His creation,
T-25.....VII.2:6 And what can share its a. except itself?
T-28.........I.6:2 the other a. with which you seek to keep
T-30......III.6:6 die. They share the a. of their creator, nor
W-pI.....12.1:3 All these a. are given it by you. The world
W-pI.....13.3:2 the world with a. that it does not possess,
W-pI.....35.4:2 ego-based a. which you ascribe to yourself
W-pI.....35.9:1 pick up a specific attribute or a. you are
W-pI.....40.3:2 add several of the a. you associate with
W-pI.....72.1:2 God is assigned the a. which are actually
W-pI.....72.1:2 the ego appears to take on the a. of God.
W-pI.....91.8:2 thoughts about your a. to be corrected,
W-pI.....94.4:1 and self-images aside; go past the list of a.
W-pI...140.7:6 another but in a. that have no substance,
W-pI...167.6:5 that are, and cannot give them a. it lacks,
W-pI...170.5:1 the a. of love bestowed upon its "enemy."
W-pI...170.5:3 it alone, love is endowed with a. of fear.
W-pI.170.10:2 has not confused its a. with those of fear.
W-pI.170.12:4 chosen Him in place of idols, and your a.,
W-pI...184.1:5 By this you designate its special a., and
W-pI...186.9:3 changeless shares His a. with His creation
W-pII .259.1:5 giving love the a. of fear and of attack?
W-pII .320.1:2 nor any a. his Father gave in his creation.
W-pII .326.1:5 *And all Your a. abide in me, because it is*
M-4 .....VII.1:3 Like all the other a. of God's teachers this
M-4 ......IX.2:7 in itself the other a. of God's teachers. It
M-4 ....... X.1:1 last of the a. the teacher of God acquires,
M-4 ....... X.3:1 You may have noticed that the list of a. of
C-in ...........3:7 are a. of the ego. *The course is simple.* It has
S-3........IV.1:9 of special a. through which they can

### attune 1

T-13....VIII.7:2 through the Holy Spirit, a. you to reality.

### attuned 1

S-1...........I.7:9 if you are genuinely a. to one another. It

### attunement 1

M-25 .........3:6 the past, unusual a. with the "unseen," or

### Author 2
*author*

T-3........VI.8:7 choose to separate yourself from your A..
W-pI.....72.5:3 Himself as the A. of life and not of death,

### author 4
*Author*

T-3........VI.5:8 Yet if you wish to be the a. of reality, you
T-3........VI.8:2 you believe you are the a. of yourself and
T-4...........I.9:1 God is not the a. of fear. You are. You
T-28....... II.7:4 he did not see that he was a. of the dream,

### authored 1

T-28....... II.7:9 cause. He a. not his own attack, and he is

### Authoritative 1

T-1......... V.5:5 under tyrannous rather than A. control.

### Authority 1
*authority*

T-1......... V.5:7 means to place it at the disposal of *true* A..

### authority 12
*Authority*

T-3...........VI.h Judgment and the A. Problem
T-3........VI.5:10 as a weapon of defense for your own a..
T-3........VI.7:2 one cause for all of them: the a. problem.
T-3 ....... VI.7:5 position is the result of the a. problem
T-3 ....... VI.8:1 of a. is really a question of authorship.
T-3 ....... VI.8:2 When you have an a. problem, it is always
T-3 ..... VI.10:7 This strange perception *is* the a. problem.
T-3 ..... VII.2:1 resolve the a. problem by depreciating the
T-3 .... VII.6:10 is the idea of an a. problem meaningful.
T-5 ......... V.3:3 spoke before of the a. problem as based
T-11 ......in.2:3 The a. problem is still the only source of
W-pI... 154.7:3 no roles that are not given them by His a..

### authorize 1

W-pI. 136.16:4 wishes that it tried to a. the body to obey.

### Authorship 4
*authorship*

T-3 ....... VI.8:7 God's creations are given their true A.,
T-3 ....... VI.8:8 Being uncertain of your true A., you
T-3 ..... VI.10:4 very devious routes, from the denial of A..
T-3 ..... VI.10:6 deny His A. is to deny yourself the reason

### authorship 4
*Authorship*

T-3 ....... VI.8:1 issue of authority is really a question of a..
T-3 ....... VI.8:3 others are literally fighting you for your a.
T-3 ..... VI.8:10 dispute over a. has left such uncertainty
T-3 ..... VI.10:3 decide is the fundamental question of a..

### automatic 3

T-4 .......II.10:5 move. Its direction is always a., because it
W-pI..... 95.5:3 the idea as an a. response to temptation.
W-pI... 136.1:4 When this is seen, healing is a.. It dispels

### automatically 15

T-1 .........I.39:2 perceiving light, darkness a. disappears.
T-2 .......II.1:14 darkness are the same, it corrects error a..
T-2 .........II.3:4 defends his treasure, and will do so a..
T-2 ....... VI.2:9 This is controlled by me a. as soon as you
T-3 ....... VI.3:6 knowledge all judgment is a. suspended,
T-4 .......II.10:2 leads to the next step a., because right
T-4 ...... V.6:10 Whatever it is, it will direct your efforts a.
T-5 ...... V.4:11 will a. attempt to remedy the situation.
T-5 ........ V.6:4 will follow a. until the decision is changed
T-6 .........II.5:5 needs. This invites Atonement a., because
T-8 .........II.8:3 bring the acknowledgment a. to everyone
T-9 .....VIII.1:3 it, however dimly, you abandon the ego a.
T-10 ..... IV.5:9 And your vision will a. look beyond it, to
T-12 ........I.9:8 that do not work at all are a. discarded. If
W-pI..... 23.2:7 the cause. The effect will change a..

### autonomous 1

T-27 ...VIII.2:1 in many ways to prove it is a. and real. It

### Autonomy 2
*autonomy*

T-11 ...... V.6:5 He has included you in His A.. Can you
T-11 .... V.12:1 Him, because His A. encompasses yours,

### autonomy 16
*Autonomy*

T-2 ....... VI.2:8 from the truth by "giving" a. to behavior.
T-4 ........... II.h The Ego and False A.
T-11 ...... V.4:4 The ego's goal is quite explicitly ego a..
T-11 ...... V.6:1 is the independence of creation, not of a..
T-11 ...... V.6:6 that a. is meaningful apart from Him?
T-11 ...... V.6:7 The belief in ego a. is costing you the
T-11 ...... V.7:2 else, because its goal of a. *is* nothing else.
T-11 .... V.10:2 Its dream of a. is shaken to its foundation
T-11 .... V.11:1 the ego's goal of a. could be accomplished
T-11 .... V.12:2 establish your a. by identifying with Him,
T-11 .... VII.3:7 To establish your personal a. you tried to
T-15 .. VII.12:1 illusion of the a. of the body and its ability
T-15 .. VII.12:1 of the ego's plan to establish its own a.. As
W-pII . 328.1:2 gain a. but by our striving to be separate,
W-pII ... 12.2:4 And in its terrible a. it "sees" the Will of
M-22 ......... 3:3 This thought gives the body a., separates

### avail 3

T-25 ..... III.6:5 chooses to a. himself of what is given him,
W-pI 185.10:7 you not a. yourself of it by sharing it?
W-pII . 285.1:4 and loss a. me if insanity departs from me

### available 11

T-2 .........II.3:7 The means are a. whenever you ask. You
W-pI .... 10.4:4 for all the thoughts that are a. to you,
W-pI .... 26.8:1 possibilities a. for each situation you use,
W-pI .... 38.2:2 your holiness the power of God is made a.
W-pI .... 40.3:9 If only a brief period is a., merely telling
W-pI .. 124.1:2 strength a. to us in all our undertakings.
W-pI .. 162.5:4 a. to all as remedy for grief and misery, all
WpI.rVI.in.7:3 He will not fail to be a. to you, each time
M-23 ......... 3:5 Is he still a. for help? What did he say
M-25 ......... 2:5 and Whose Voice is a. but for the hearing.
M-25 ......... 3:7 has any powers that are not a. to everyone

### availed 1

W-pI 135.20:4 a. them nothing and could only terrify.

### avenge 2

W-pI .. 129.2:3 you, quick to a. and pitiless with hate. It
W-pI .. 189.3:5 of hatred rising from attack, poised to a.,

### avenger 2

T-19 ..... III.1:8 And only an a., with a mind unlike your
M-27 ......... 5:8 He is not Creator, but a.. Terrible His

### avenger's 1

T-27 .... VII.4:7 Otherwise is the a. knife in his own hand,

### avert 1

T19 .IV.A.13:5 and would a. the punishment of him who

### averted 1

W-pI .. 192.9:5 And it will fall or be a. as you choose to be

### avoid 32

T-2 ...... VII.2:2 of thought in order to a. miscreation.
T-3 ....... VI.1:4 you will be unable to a. judging your own.
T-4 .........I.9:11 a. Him any more than He can avoid you.
T-4 .........I.9:11 avoid Him any more than He can a. you.
T-6 .........V.3:2 not emphasize what you must a. to escape
T-6 ..... V.C.2:2 to strengthen what you must learn to a..
T-7 .........X.3:1 Spirit will direct you only so as to a. pain.
T-7 .........X.5:2 As long as you a. His guidance in any way,
T-12 ........V.3:2 to a. interpreting this as reinforcement.
T-13 ........X.2:3 are used but to a. the person *and* the guilt.
T-13 ..... XI.6:3 you learn what to a. and what to seek.
T-15 .... VII.6:3 and a. delaying what it really wants. Yet
T-15 ........X.9:4 in the attempt to a. recognizing the one
T-16 ..... III.4:3 have been very careful to a. the obvious,
T-22 ........II.6:8 no point in trying to a. this one decision.
T-25 ... VIII.6:2 a. the vengeance that their own belief in
T-27 ... VIII.1:7 and a. the things that would be hurtful.
T-30 ..... VI.4:4 himself as guilty can a. the fear of God.
W-pI ...... 2.2:1 around you, trying to a. selection by size,
W-pI ...... 4.5:4 You are too inexperienced as yet to a. a
W-pI ...... 5.4:1 a. giving greater weight to some subjects
W-pI .... 10.4:5 Try to a. classification of any kind. In fact,
W-pI .... 13.5:1 You may find it difficult to a. resistance,
W-pI .... 29.4:2 specifically. Try to a. the tendency toward
W-pI .. 105.3:2 and so you would a. the only means by
W-pI .. 155.2:2 can be illusions, and a. their own reality.

| | |
|---|---|
| W-pI...163.6:1 | you would not cherish and would yet **a.**, |
| W-pII..339.1:3 | No one would **a.** his happiness. But he |
| M-21..........4:1 | then, to **a.** the use of words in his teaching |
| P-2........ III.1:1 | helps him to **a.** a few of the pitfalls along |
| S-1 ...........I.1:6 | True prayer must **a.** the pitfall of asking |
| S-1 ......... II.2:3 | of his Identity can **a.** praying in this way. |

## avoidance 3

| | |
|---|---|
| T-6......... V.3:1 | teacher teaches through approach, not **a.**. |
| M-16..........9:1 | **a.** of magic is the avoidance of temptation |
| M-16..........9:1 | avoidance of magic is the **a.** of temptation |

## avoided 5

| | |
|---|---|
| T-3...... VI.2:12 | This cannot be **a.** in any type of judgment |
| T-5......... II.5:2 | one to be chosen and the other to be **a.**. |
| T-18..... VII.3:5 | as pain and nothing else, and would be **a.**. |
| W-pI ........9.5:1 | attempted, specific exclusion must be **a.**. |
| M-8...............h | OF ORDER OF DIFFICULTIES BE **A.**? |

## avoiding 5

| | |
|---|---|
| T-8..... VIII.6:4 | for **a.** catastrophic outcomes. The Holy |
| T-13...... IV.4:3 | like the past, and thus **a.** the present. By |
| T-16....... II.2:2 | And this is but a way of **a.**, or looking |
| T-16...... III.2:8 | and in **a.** those which spoke for the cause |
| WpI ...rI.in.4:5 | This is not done by **a.** them and seeking a |

## avoids 1

| | |
|---|---|
| W-pI...189.6:4 | For its simplicity **a.** the snares the foolish |

## await 9

| | |
|---|---|
| T-2......... V.3:3 | miracle need not **a.** the right-mindedness |
| T-12...VII.13:4 | for you, it lets you live but to **a.** death. It |
| T-14... VIII.3:3 | God and His Son **a.** your recognition. |
| T-28.........I.3:6 | **a.** their use. They have no dedication and |
| T-30...... III.8:2 | They **a.** not birth. They wait for welcome |
| W-pI...125.6:3 | **A.** His Word in quiet. There is peace |
| W-pI.191.11:1 | They must **a.** your own release. They stay |
| W-pI...194.1:3 | you **a.** with certainty the final step of God. |
| M-28..........6:1 | These things **a.** us all, but we are not |

## awaiting 5

| | |
|---|---|
| T-21....... V.3:1 | your freedom lies, **a.** but your choice. And |
| T-25...... III.6:4 | time, for help is there, **a.** but his choice. |
| W-pI...102.4:3 | mind, for it is there, **a.** but your choice. |
| W-pII..322.1:2 | tried to hide, **a.** me in shining welcome, |
| W-pII..327.1:5 | still, **a.** but my call to give me all the help I |

## awaits 18

| | |
|---|---|
| T-11..... VII.1:6 | that **a.** your perception when you see it? |
| T-12...... IV.7:5 | Your inheritance **a.** only the recognition |
| T-16...... III.9:3 | you would be, and where your Self **a.** you. |
| T-16...... IV.2:6 | its reality, which **a.** you on the other side, |
| T-16.... VI.10:7 | and learn how much **a.** you for the simple |
| T-18.... IX.14:5 | *now.* And it is there that peace **a.** you. |
| T-27...... VI.8:1 | world **a.** your healing and your happiness |
| T-30....... II.4:6 | This world **a.** the freedom you will give |
| W-pI.....64.3:3 | The world's salvation **a.** your forgiveness, |
| W-pI...121.7:2 | Each one **a.** release from hell through you, |
| W-pI...125.6:2 | His Voice **a.** your silence, for His Word |
| W-pII.....226.h | My home **a.** me. I will hasten there. |
| W-pII..226.2:1 | *Father, my home **a.** my glad return. Your* |
| W-pII..279.1:2 | to be in prison, and **a.** a future freedom, if |
| W-pII..302.1:2 | *Your holy world **a.** us, as our sight is finally* |
| W-pII..302.2:1 | Our Love **a.** us as we go to Him, and |
| W-pII....10.4:6 | And the world **a.** your glad acceptance, |
| W-pII..317.2:4 | *The memory of You **a.** me there. And all my* |

## awake 29

| | |
|---|---|
| T-4...... III.10:2 | odds, whether you are asleep or **a.**. |
| T-4...... IV.11:2 | Holy Spirit, whether you are asleep or **a.**, |
| T-6........ IV.6:3 | sleep is not real and God calls you to **a.**. |
| T-8........ IX.4:9 | can rest in peace only because you are **a.**. |
| T-9....... VI.4:8 | When you **a.** in Him you will know your |
| T-9........ VI.5:1 | You are not yet **a.**, but you can learn how |
| T-10.........I.3:2 | You do not remember being **a.**. When |
| T-11...... VI.6:7 | for otherwise you will not **a.** in God, |
| T-11...... VI.9:1 | own call, for the Call to **a.** is within you. If |
| T-11...... VI.9:2 | If I live in you, you are **a.**. Yet you must |
| T-12....... II.6:3 | **A.** and remember your purpose, for it is |
| T-13.... VI.13:3 | the real world for you when you **a.**. In |
| T-13... VII.14:3 | *I go? What need have I but to **a.** in Him?* |
| T-16....... II.8:3 | **A.** and share it, for that is the only reason |
| T-17....... II.7:5 | Who, **a.** in Heaven, could dream that |
| T-26...... IX.1:1 | may **a.** in him the Voice that answers to |
| T-28....... II.6:7 | do. The dreamer of a dream is not **a.**, but |
| T-29...... IV.1:7 | some, for you are either sleeping or **a.**. |
| T-29...... IV.2:8 | You would not then be willing to **a.**, for |
| W-pI.....68.2:1 | illusions in its sleep appears to be **a.**. Can |
| W-pI...122.2:2 | It sparkles on your eyes as you **a.**, and |
| W-pI...140.3:1 | where one can merely dream he is **a.**. The |
| W-pI.151.15:1 | Spend fifteen minutes thus when you **a.**, |
| W-pI...162.2:5 | The dead **a.** in answer to its call. And |
| W-pI...167.7:4 | Yet mind is mind, **a.** or sleeping. It is not |
| W-pI...167.8:1 | God creates only mind **a.**. He does not |
| W-pII..340.2:6 | Himself, **a.** in Heaven in the Heart of Love |
| P-3......... II.4:8 | must enter, for only that is the call to **a.**. |
| P-3....... II.4:10 | **A.** and be glad, for all your sins have been |

## awaken 30

| | |
|---|---|
| T-4...........I.9:7 | **a.** you will not be able to understand this, |
| T-5....... II.10:5 | Holy Spirit is the Call to **a.** and be glad. |
| T-6........ IV.6:4 | when you hear Him, because you will **a.**. |
| T-6......... V.4:6 | His light is always the Call to **a.**, whatever |
| T-8......... II.8:4 | By your recognition you **a.** theirs, and |
| T-8........ IX.4:5 | Spirit. Only when you **a.** joyously have |
| T-9........ V.8:12 | As you **a.** other minds to the Holy Spirit |
| T-9........ VI.5:1 | not yet awake, but you can learn how to **a.** |
| T-9........ VI.5:2 | the Holy Spirit teaches you to **a.** others. |
| T-10.........I.2:5 | laws of what you **a.** to were violated while |
| T-11...... VI.9:1 | You will **a.** to your own call, for the Call |
| T-12....... II.7:2 | will **a.** you as surely as I awakened myself, |
| T-12...... VI.4:3 | **a.** them from the sleep of forgetting to the |
| T-12...... VI.5:3 | Only then will you decide to **a.**. And then |
| T-13..... VII.9:1 | will first dream of peace, and then **a.** to it. |
| T-13... VII.16:5 | teach you to **a.** unto us and to yourself. |
| T-15....... II.1:6 | in that instant you will **a.** gently in Him. |
| T-24...... III.7:5 | They hate the call that would **a.** them, |
| T-27... VII.10:6 | **A.** and forget all thoughts of death, and |
| T-27... VII.15:2 | of Heaven will Himself **a.** His beloved Son |
| T-28....... II.4:2 | The miracle does not **a.** you, but merely |
| T-29...... IV.1:5 | want to live in dreams or to **a.** from them. |
| T-29...... IX.2:3 | How can God's Son **a.** from the dream? It |
| W-pI.....54.3:6 | real thoughts **a.** the real thoughts in them |
| W-pI.....61.6:2 | Thus you will **a.** with an acknowledgment |
| W-pI.121.13:7 | *I will **a.** from the dream that I am mortal,* |
| W-pI...140.2:4 | seen the light that would **a.** him and end |
| W-pI.191.10:1 | Then let the Son of God **a.** from his sleep, |
| W-pII..294.2:3 | *plan that we **a.** from all dreams we made.* |
| W-pII.... 10.5:2 | Therefore **a.** and return to Me. I am your |

## awakened 7

| | |
|---|---|
| T-6......... V.1:8 | "My children sleep and must be **a.**." |
| T-11...... VI.9:5 | liveth, and that you have **a.** with him. |
| T-12....... II.7:2 | I will awaken you as surely as I **a.** myself, |
| T-17.........I.1:3 | He need not be forgiven but **a.**. In his |
| T-20..... II.10:1 | from the past, and has **a.** to the present. |
| T-20...... VI.9:6 | you not back on what you have **a.** from. |
| W-pI...140.2:3 | Yet he has not **a.** from the dream, and so |

## Awakening 1

*awakening*

| | |
|---|---|
| T-15.. XI.10:10 | so long left unfulfilled, in the Great **A.**. |

## awakening 24

*Awakening*

| | |
|---|---|
| T-2......... V.7:1 | learning always begins with the **a.** of spirit |
| T-7...... IV.7:11 | By your **a.** to it, you are merely forgetting |
| T-8..........II.8:5 | **A.** runs easily and gladly through the |
| T-8......... IX.3:2 | are physical expressions of the fear of **a.**. |
| T-10.........I.2:1 | exile but perfectly capable of **a.** to reality. |
| T-11...... VI.8:8 | the **a.** of others to share your redemption. |
| T-12...... VI.4:9 | **a.** of His Son begins with his investment |
| T-13.........I.7:1 | that there is no journey, but only an **a.**. |
| T-13...... IV.6:6 | from **a.** and understanding they are past. |
| T-13...... VII.9:8 | response is your **a.** to what you have not |
| T-13...... IX.1:3 | fidelity to darkness and forbids **a.**. The |
| T-15...... III.9:5 | My birth in you is your **a.** to grandeur. |
| T-15....... XI.1:6 | them is nothing more than a gentle **a.**, |
| T-17.... VIII.5:4 | have accepted the Cause of his **a.** as yours. |
| T-18........II.3:3 | Yet on **a.**, you do not expect it to be gone. |
| T-28.......I.13:3 | in the way of glad **a.** to present peace. The |
| T-29.............h | THE **A.** |
| T-31...... III.6:4 | your sleep, nor interfere with your **a.**. |
| W-pI... 162.2:4 | of **a.** that sounds around the world. The |
| W-pI... 165.3:1 | peace of mind, his quiet rest, his calm **a.**, |
| W-pI. 190.10:5 | is but sleep; joy is **a.**. Pain is deception; joy |
| W-pII . 331.1:8 | *Conflict is sleep, and peace **a.**. Death is* |
| W-pII ... 13.1:6 | for the return of timelessness and love's **a.** |
| M-26 ....... 3:10 | that by their **a.** can God's Voice be heard. |

## awakens 8

| | |
|---|---|
| T-2...........I.4:7 | However, when he **a.**, the light is correctly |
| T-3..........II.5:2 | mind **a.** from its sleep and remembers its |
| T-6........ III.4:7 | It **a.** in your mind through the conviction |
| T-10...... III.2:3 | of Him **a.** throughout the Sonship. Heal |
| T-21.......I.10:6 | The light in one **a.** it in all. And when you |
| W-pI. 159.10:7 | His dream **a.** us to truth. His vision gives |
| W-pI... 168.2:6 | And memory of Him **a.** in the mind that |
| W-pI... 198.3:7 | Son of God **a.** to his Self and to his Father, |

## awakes 3

| | |
|---|---|
| W-pI... 167.9:4 | When the mind **a.**, it but continues as it |
| W-pI. 168.1:11 | And when his mind **a.**, He loves him with |
| M-16 ......... 4:2 | that fosters quiet thought as he **a.**. If this |

## awaking 10

| | |
|---|---|
| T-13.... VI.12:1 | **A.** unto Christ is following the laws of |
| T-13...... XI.9:6 | him. He will learn the lesson of **a.**. God |
| T-14....... V.2:5 | for your **a.** is as perfect as yours is fallible. |
| T-18........II.2:3 | take them seriously on **a.** because the fact |
| T-18........II.3:1 | what you see in sleep and on **a.** disturbing |
| T-18........II.9:4 | from which **a.** is so easy and so natural. |
| T-24.......II.14:4 | your death, but your **a.** into life eternal. |
| T-27... VII.13:4 | unless a gentler dream preceded his **a.**, |
| T-29...... IV.1:3 | depends, not on the dream, but only on **a.** |
| W-pII . 332.1:5 | recalled from fantasies, **a.** to the real. |

## aware 82

| | |
|---|---|
| T-1.........I.45:2 | in situations of which you are not even **a.**. |
| T-2........ III.4:4 | Perfectly **a.** of the right defense it passes |
| T-2........ VI.9:3 | no one remains fully **a.** of it all the time. |
| T-3...........I.7:5 | perfectly **a.** of everything that is true. The |
| T-5...........I.5:1 | which is **a.** of the knowledge that lies |
| T-5........ III.2:8 | Your brother does not have to be **a.** of the |
| T-5....... III.2:10 | you become **a.** of the Call for God in him, |
| T-5....... VII.6:4 | yourself fully **a.** that the undoing process, |
| T-6....... II.12:8 | it must shine outward to make you **a.** of it |
| T-6.... V.B.3:10 | Still strongly **a.** of the ego in yourself, and |
| T-7....... V.11:3 | to them make them **a.** of the light in them |
| T-7........ VI.8:4 | be. **A.** of its weakness the ego wants your |
| T-7....... VII.2:6 | and are therefore not **a.** of it in yourself. |
| T-8......... IV.3:4 | by being **a.** of the Father's Will myself. |
| T-8...... VI.9:10 | can make you **a.** of the conditions of truth |
| T-8...... VIII.6:5 | Spirit, perfectly **a.** of the same situation, |
| T-9...........I.10:4 | with form, being **a.** only of meaning. The |
| T-9....... VI.1:1 | become increasingly **a.** of the Holy Spirit |
| T-9...... VIII.1:3 | Whenever you become **a.** of it, however |
| T-9...... VIII.3:2 | that the ego is **a.** of threat to its existence, |
| T-10...... III.2:7 | To be **a.** of this is to heal them because it |
| T-11...... VI.2:6 | you cannot be **a.** without interpretation, |
| T-11...... VI.8:7 | beginning to wake are still **a.** of dreams, |

T-12...... III.6:5 Even if he is fully **a.** of anxiety he does not
T-12...... VI.2:2 perfectly **a.** that you do not know yourself
T-12...... VI.2:2 and perfectly **a.** of how to teach you to
T-12..... VII.4:5 For you can be **a.** of what you cannot see,
T-13...... VI.1:1 To perceive truly is to be **a.** of all reality
T-14....... X.4:1 Perhaps you have been **a.** of lack of
T-15...... VI.5:2 so no one is **a.** that perfect love is in him.
T-17...... IV.4:2 what had been created, it was **a.** of threat.
T-17...... VI.2:8 It is **a.** of what it does not want, but only
T-18..... VII.8:2 will be more **a.** of this quiet center of the
T-18.... VIII.4:1 Yet neither sun nor ocean is even **a.** of all
T-21.......... I.1:5 fail to be **a.** you can go through the doors
T-21....... V.3:9 This other self is perfectly **a.** of this. And
T-25......... I.6:3 by mind perceived as one, **a.** that it is one,
T-25..VIII.13:7 or less is not **a.** that he has everything. He
T-28........ I.14:1 is the Son of God at last **a.** of present
T-30...... III.7:2 is that you are sometimes **a.** of them, and
T-30.... III.11:6 Nor can you be **a.** of more than one. An
T-30...... IV.1:3 **a.** of it you would forget defensiveness
T-30...... VI.3:7 but remains **a.** that they have sinned. And
W-pI....... 4.1:4 If you are already **a.** of unhappy thoughts,
W-pI..... 10.1:1 to all the thoughts of which you are **a.**, or
W-pI..... 10.1:1 or become **a.** in the practice periods. The
W-pI..... 10.3:1 of which you are **a.** are meaningless,
W-pI..... 16.5:4 use today's idea whenever you are **a.** of a
W-pI..... 21.2:5 You will become increasingly **a.** that a
W-pI..... 33.4:1 idea the instant you are **a.** of distress. It
W-pI..... 43.6:1 if you begin to be **a.** of thoughts which are
W-pI..... 44.9:1 your eyes closed unless you are **a.** of fear.
W-pI..... 46.7:3 the day when you become **a.** of any kind
W-pI..... 47.1:4 to be **a.** of all the facets of any problem,
W-pI..... 49.1:2 with God, whether you are **a.** of it or not.
W-pI..... 51.4:2 thoughts of which I am **a.** do not mean
W-pI..... 51.4:5 I am not **a.** of them because I have made
W-pI..... 52.5:3 it is only private thoughts of which I am **a.**
W-pI..... 53.1:2 of which I am **a.** do not mean anything,
W-pI..... 68.2:1 remains **a.** of Its likeness to Its Creator,
W-pI... 72.10:1 to become **a.** that God's plan for salvation
W-pI..... 82.1:3 I become **a.** of the light of the world in me
W-pI..... 91.7:2 You need to be **a.** of what the Holy Spirit
W-pI..... 95.3:1 to be **a.** only of what can hear and see,
W-pI..... 95.4:5 It is necessary that you be **a.** of this, for it
W-pI... 104.4:3 **a.** that what belongs to us in truth is what
W-pI... 122.9:2 **a.** we hold the key within our hands,
W-pI.124.10:3 thankfully **a.** no time was ever better
W-pI.137.12:6 healed, **a.** that they will both occur as one.
W-pI... 139.7:3 yourself, and not to be **a.** of what you are.
WpI. rIV.in1:1 time **a.** we are preparing for the second
W-pI... 154.2:2 and equally **a.** of where they can be best
W-pI... 154.3:1 become **a.** at last there is one Voice in you
W-pI... 154.4:3 mind becomes **a.** again of Who created it,
W-pI... 166.5:4 on, **a.** of the futility he sees about him
W-pI... 169.3:6 become **a.** that there are things it does not
W-pI... 169.5:5 that it is now **a.** of something not itself. It
W-pII .232.1:5 *of Your care, and happily* ***a.*** *I am Your Son.*
W-pII .237.1:4 see, **a.** it ends the bitter dream of death;
W-pII .237.1:4 of death; **a.** it is my Father's Call to me.
M-10 ......... 3:3 rightly, one would have to be fully **a.** of an
C-1............ 7:5 its highest it becomes **a.** of the real world,

## awareness 219

T-in ........... 1:7 *the blocks to the* ***a.*** *of love's presence, which*
T-1......... I.20:1 Miracles reawaken the **a.** that the spirit,
T-1......... I.44:1 expression of an inner **a.** of Christ and the
T-1........ III.7:2 the **a.** of the miracle worker himself. The
T-1........ III.8:4 of my complete **a.** of the whole plan. The
T-1........ III.9:4 miracle aims at restoring the **a.** of reality,
T-1........ IV.3:6 to you; or rather, to restore it to your **a.**.
T-1....... VII.1:1 it hard for them to reach your own **a.**. The
T-2......... V.7:7 Everything that results from spiritual **a.** is
T-2......... V.7:8 to bring the need for correction into **a.**.
T-2.... V.A.17:4 Only the latter involves an **a.** of time,
T-2...... VI.9:11 This may allay **a.** of the guilt, but at the
T-3......... V.8:5 of it. Only perception involves partial **a.**.
T-3........ VI.4:4 refused to accept can be brought into **a.**.
T-4......... V.1:3 vigilance about what it permits into **a.**,
T-4......... V.1:4 keeps its primary motivation from your **a.**
T-4....... V.4:10 the question from the mind's **a.**. Once out
T-4 ...... V.4:11 Once out of **a.** the question can and does
T-6 ......... II.2:4 fact that you attacked yourself out of **a.**,
T-6 ....... II.10:7 The full **a.** of the Atonement, then, is the
T-6 ..... IV.10:3 themselves to the **a.** of their perfection,
T-6 ..... V.B.9:4 **a.** that the Holy Spirit will lead you on.
T-6 ..... V.C.8:2 you will lose **a.** of its wholeness and will
T-6 ..... V.C.8:3 but your **a.** of its wholeness does. It is
T-6 ..... V.C.8:4 It is only your **a.** that needs protection,
T-7 ....... VI.2:4 This loses the **a.** of being, induces feelings
T-7 ...... VII.1:8 of it means you have lost the **a.** of all of it.
T-7 ...... IX.2:1 Spirit knows that the **a.** of all its brothers
T-7 ...... IX.5:1 into your **a.** whenever you will let Him.
T-7 ...... IX.7:3 and of your **a.** that your identification is
T-8 ....... IV.3:5 This is the **a.** I came to give you, and your
T-8 ....... V.2:12 signifying your **a.** that the Will of God is
T-8 ....... IX.2:3 also the condition of your **a.** of its reality.
T-9 .......... I.3:3 your **a.** with something you do not want.
T-9 .......... I.3:8 to re-establish your own will in your **a.**.
T-9 .......... I.4:1 imprisoned your will beyond your own **a.**,
T-9 ... IV.11:10 The Second Coming is the **a.** of reality,
T-9 ..... IV.12:3 of Us. Only this **a.** heals, because it is the
T-9 ..... IV.12:3 heals, because it is the **a.** of truth.
T-9 ........ V.3:1 advantage to bringing nightmares into **a.**,
T-10 ....... II.1:5 have replaced your knowledge by an **a.** of
T-10 ..... III.2:7 because it is the **a.** that no one is separate,
T-10 ..... III.9:2 And in that **a.** you are healed. You will
T-11 .... V.10:2 is shaken to its foundation by this **a.**. For
T-11 ..... VI.2:5 the word is used both for **a.** and for the
T-11 ..... VI.2:5 awareness and for the interpretation of **a.**.
T-11 ..... VI.3:8 His perceptions are your natural **a.**, and it
T-11 ..... VI.8:8 forgetting of dreams and the **a.** of Christ
T-11 ... VI.10:2 Bring only this **a.** to the Sonship, and you
T-11 .... VII.4:3 this **a.** you have not met its conditions,
T-12 ........ I.6:2 into your **a.** if you perceive them truly.
T-12 ........ I.7:4 of your Father closer to your **a.**. For the
T-12 ........ I.8:1 will gain an increasing **a.** that His criteria
T-12 ...... I.10:3 it, for the **a.** of truth cannot be denied.
T-12 ....... II.9:4 exchange this **a.** for the awareness of fear?
T-12 ....... II.9:4 exchange this awareness for the **a.** of fear?
T-12 ..... IV.7:1 it *is* the price of your **a.** of your wholeness.
T-12 ..... VI.1:6 sell your soul, but you can sell your **a.** of it
T-12 ... VIII.7:1 to interpose between your **a.** and truth.
T-13 ....... II.3:1 holds your belief in guilt from your **a.**. For
T-13 ..... III.1:2 the need for you to raise it to **a.** yourself.
T-13 ..... VI.1:1 of all reality through the **a.** of your own.
T-13 ... VI.10:3 in light brings your light closer to your **a.**.
T-13 ... VI.12:4 alone, and your **a.** is narrowed to yourself
T-13 ....... X.1:2 your **a.** the full perception that it is insane
T-14 ...... V.2:3 will suffer the pain of dim **a.** that his true
T-14 ..... XI.1:4 it and your **a.** of it that you cannot use it.
T-14 ... XI.6:11 in your **a.** the instant you abandon it, and
T-15 ..... III.4:5 To hold your magnitude in perfect **a.** in a
T-15 ..... III.5:7 brings you the **a.** of what you decided for.
T-15 ..... III.7:2 It is our task together to restore the **a.** of
T-15 ..... III.9:4 with the glad **a.** of the glory that is in him.
T-15 ..... IV.1:9 it into glad **a.** while you do not want it, for
T-15 ..... IV.9:9 all your **a.** to the readiness for purity He
T-15 ..... VI.6:4 Yet the **a.** of changelessness comes swiftly
T-15 ..... VI.8:5 all your brothers, to replace it in your **a.**.
T-15 ... VII.9:6 at the ego's altar far exceeds your **a.** of it.
T-15 .. VII.14:9 your completion makes you His in your **a.**
T-15 ... VIII.3:3 Refuse not the **a.** of your completion, and
T-15 ... VIII.6:1 alone lies the **a.** of what God cannot know
T-15 ..... IX.3:1 the Great Rays replace the body in **a.**, the
T-15 ..... XI.4:3 as peace is the condition for the **a.** of your
T-16 ....... II.4:3 first link in the **a.** of the Sonship as One
T-16 ....... II.7:2 attack are both being brought into your **a.**
T-16 .... VII.5:3 the ego never allows to reach **a.** is that the
T-16 .... VII.7:1 your full **a.** of the complete difference, in
T-17 .... V.12:2 shining and gracious in your **a.** of time,
T-18 ... IV.5:11 *to restore to me my own* ***a.*** *of my readiness,*
T-18 ..... VI.1:6 It is merely an **a.** of perfect Oneness, and
T-18 ..... VI.2:3 you the **a.** of Heaven and of your Identity.
T-18 ... VI.11:7 have given up the illusion of a limited **a.**,
T-18 ... VI.13:6 and, above all, the lack of **a.** of the body,
T-18 ... VI.14:2 sudden expansion of **a.** that takes place
T-18 .... VII.2:5 every instant that you spend without **a.** of
T-18 .... VII.8:5 absent, that will keep it so in your **a.** of it.
T-18 ... VIII.1:1 is only the **a.** of the body that makes love
T-18 ... VIII.2:2 while you limit your **a.** to its tiny senses,
T-18 ..... IX.2:5 it to limit your **a.** are little and limited,
T-19 ..... IV.1:6 and the calm **a.** of complete protection.
T19 ... IV.B.9:2 back, and so would limit your **a.** of it. For
T19 ... IV.C.5:7 the Creator to the **a.** of every mind which
T-20 ..... II.10:1 in which we join in glad **a.** that the Son of
T-20 ..... II.11:5 receive the bright **a.** that leads you home.
T-20 . VI.12:11 of His Love apart from their **a.**?
T-20 . VIII.10:6 ego's purpose brought to your horrified **a.**
T-21 ..... III.9:7 your **a.** to what has been already joined.
T-21 ..... V.1:11 in which **a.** of reality is possible, or those
T-21 ....... V.2:2 But your **a.** of it needs your help, because
T-21 ....... V.4:2 other self you have cut off from your **a.**.
T-21 ....... V.4:3 to stay in your **a.** is capable of reason.
T-21 ... VIII.5:2 the **a.** of what is always there to see, the
T-21 ... VIII.5:7 relationship and your ***a.*** of its holiness.
T-22 ...... I.10:2 make it through **a.** older than perception,
T-22 ..... III.1:2 is it possible for them to coexist in your **a.**
T-22 ..... III.8:3 Let your **a.** of your brother not be blocked
T-22 ..... III.9:2 values will produce confusion, and in **a.**.
T-22 ..... IV.3:5 Yet it is almost over in your **a.**, and peace
T-22 ....... V.5:1 your **a.** of your union with your brother!
T-23 ...... in.3:3 **a.** of the truth releases everything from
T-23 ...... in.5:5 so is yours protected and kept in your **a.**.
T-23 ..... II.22:9 Is peace in your **a.**? Are you certain which
T-23 ..... III.1:7 meet his horrified **a.** and pursue him still.
T-23 ..... III.3:5 **a.** of salvation's purpose is lost because it
T-23 ..... IV.8:4 Only the light they love is in **a.**, and only
T-23 ..... IV.9:1 the strength of God in their **a.** could never
T-24 ..... II.14:2 and the **a.** that your plan has failed, and
T-25 ... IX.10:6 **a.** that giving and receiving are the same.
T-26 .... VII.2:4 in a relationship kept hidden from **a.** that
T-26 ....... X.2:7 **a.** that it is your own and equally belongs
T-27 ..... II.15:8 him, preserves yourself from the **a.** of a
T-27 ..... III.2:8 What can interfere with the **a.** of reality is
T-27 ..... VI.1:2 says, and keep His words from your **a.**.
T-29 ..... VI.4:7 God established for His Son in full **a.**.
T-30 ...... I.11:7 readiness for asking brought to your **a.**,
T-30 ..... III.7:3 again to you when it returns to your **a.**.
T-30 ....... V.6:1 world's purpose gently brought into **a.**, to
T-30 ..... V.11:4 the Will of God must reach to their **a.**.
T-30 ... VIII.4:2 between reality and your **a.** is unreal, and
W-pI .... 16.5:1 mind hold it in **a.** while you tell yourself:
W-pI .... 31.3:1 cross your mind come into your **a.**, each
W-pI .... 32.3:4 your imagination presents to your **a.**.
W-pI .... 34.5:3 form of temptation arises in your **a.**, the
W-pI .... 37.2:5 wholeness restored to his **a.** through your
W-pI .... 37.6:4 you may learn to keep it in your own **a.**.
W-pI .... 43.2:4 for the restoration of his holiness to his **a.**
W-pI .... 43.9:1 presents itself to your **a.** at the time,
W-pI .... 44.8:1 **a.** that you are attempting something very
W-pI .... 46.2:3 returning the mind to the **a.** of God. For
W-pI .... 47.6:2 You must also gain an **a.** that confidence
W-pI .... 48.3:2 The **a.** that there is nothing to fear shows
W-pI .... 55.3:4 forgiveness allows love to return to my **a.**,
W-pI .... 56.3:3 as I see it now, truth cannot enter my **a.**. I
W-pI .... 62.3:5 and power God gave His Son to your **a.**.
W-pI .... 62.5:5 and in your mind is the **a.** they are true.
W-pI .... 63.3:2 the day with the thought of it in our **a.**.
W-pI .... 67.4:3 interval of thoughtlessness to the **a.** of a
W-pI .... 67.4:4 will do much today to bring that **a.** nearer
W-pI .... 69.9:1 hiding the light of the world from your **a.**.
W-pI .... 72.8:4 from your **a.** by the body's limitations.
W-pI .... 73.2:4 between your **a.** and your brothers' reality
W-pI .... 73.9:5 His will is now restored to his **a.**. He is
W-pI .. 75.11:2 be. Keep it in your **a.** of yourself and see it
W-pI .... 85.4:3 *this interfere with my* ***a.*** *of the Source of my*
W-pI .... 86.3:4 my only hope of salvation from my **a.**. I
W-pI .... 91.1:6 is only your **a.** of miracles that is affected.
W-pI .... 91.4:5 leap into **a.** as you feel the strength in you.
W-pI .. 91.6:10 to your **a.** what the mistake conceals.
W-pI .. 95.12:2 to bring **a.** of this oneness to all minds,
W-pI .. 96.11:4 for you, and it will yet be yours in full **a.**.
W-pI .... 97.3:2 **a.** is brought a little nearer at least;
W-pI .. 107.8:1 that He be in your **a.** as you go with Him.
W-pI .. 110.5:2 restorer of the truth to the **a.** of the world.
W-pI .. 122.8:3 forever newly born, arise in your **a.**. What
W-pI 122.13:4 Retain your gifts in clear **a.** as you see the
W-pI 122.14:2 hold your gifts in your **a.** through the day:

W-pI...124.4:2 our faith and our **a.** of His Presence. We
W-pI...124.7:1 this **a.** as we say that we are one with God.
W-pI...124.8:2 Secure your peace by practicing **a.** you are
W-pI...126.6:5 to restore your unity with him to your **a.**.
W-pI...128.3:3 the door that leads to true **a.** of your Self.
W-pI...136.3:1 nor are they made without **a.**. They are
W-pI.139.12:3 knowledge of yourself apart from your **a.**,
WpI.rIV.in2:7 blocks this thought from his **a.**. Yet it is
W-pI...151.3:7 This is **a.** that you understand, and think
W-pI...152.5:2 and the mind; in all **a.** and in all response.
W-pI...152.8:4 to **a.** then will be all that there ever was,
W-pI.152.11:6 Who never left will come again to our **a.**,
W-pI...157.1:4 a different kind of feeling and **a.**. You
W-pI...181.1:4 becoming blocks to your **a.** of the Self
W-pI.184.14:1 for each **a.** of an aspect of God's Son, we
W-pI...185.1:4 would be completely given back to full **a.**,
W-pI...193.6:4 when you hold these words in full **a.**, and
W-pI...195.5:4 our **a.** of the unity we share with them, as
W-pI...196.1:1 is firmly understood and kept in full **a.**,
W-pII..225.1:2 *I must return it, for I want it mine in full* **a.**,
W-pII..246.1:3 believe that my **a.** can contain my Father,
W-pII..323.1:1 *let Your Love come streaming in to his* **a.**,
W-pII..323.2:3 Love has now returned to our **a.**. And we
W-pII..347.1:8 *miracles my dreams would hide from my* **a.**.
W-pII..358.1:6 *Your promise to Your Son in my* **a.** *always.*
M-4.......IV.1:8 obliterates his function from his **a.**. It will
M-12..........6:4 with full **a.** of their consequences. The
M-12..........6:6 are? **A.** of dreaming is the real function of
M-13..........8:3 at the expense of the **a.** of everything.
M-16......10:10 "sacrifice" is Heaven restored to his **a.**.
M-19..........4:2 It restores to your **a.** the wholeness of the
M-22..........2:2 is a sudden and complete **a.** of the perfect
M-25..........1:4 As his **a.** increases, he may well develop
M-26..........1:2 His **a.** is in everyone's memory, and His
M-26..........1:3 **a.** and this memory can arise across the
M-26..........3:8 God were reached directly in sustained **a.**,
M-27..........3:2 it from **a.** like a shield held up to obscure
M-28..........1:4 the glad **a.** of the Holy Spirit's final dream
C-1............7:4 levels and **a.** can shift quite dramatically,
P-1............4:1 must restore to his **a.** the ability to make
P-2.........II.2:7 to remove the seeming obstacles to true **a.**
P-2.........II.3:5 all its forces against this one **a.**, for in it
P-2.........II.4:1 Yet it is not the **a.** of God that constitutes
P-2.......VII.4:3 This confusion is rarely if ever in **a.**, or the

## awarenesses 2

W-pI...184.3:1 and holding bits of mind as separate **a.**?
P-2........VI.2:2 These fleeting **a.** represent the many

## away 327

T-1........I.17:2 into invisibility, **a.** from the bodily level.
T-1........III.2:1 "Heaven and earth shall pass **a.**" means
T-1........III.2:2 life, shall not pass **a.** because life is eternal
T-2.........V.7:1 turning **a.** from the belief in physical sight
T-3...........I.5:1 of God who taketh **a.** the sins of the world
T-3...........I.6:4 The lamb "taketh **a.** the sins of the world"
T-3.......VII.6:1 no fruit will be cut off and will wither **a.**.
T-4.........II.3:2 knowledge **a.** it is as if you never had it.
T-4.........II.5:2 Babies scream in rage if you take **a.** a knife
T-4........IV.7:1 you actively refuse to let your mind slip **a.**
T-4........IV.8:3 and mine can unite in shining your ego **a.**,
T-4........IV.8:5 accomplishment, and step **a.** from them.
T-4.........V.2:7 attempts to save itself from being swept **a.**
T-4........VI.2:3 you are throwing **a.** the graciousness of
T-4........VI.5:1 something he has deliberately thrown **a.**?
T-4........VI.5:2 must have thrown it **a.** because he did not
T-5........I.1:12 yours although all of it has been given **a.**.
T-5...........I.2:2 *Thoughts increase by being given* **a.**. *The*
T-5.........II.4:3 the glory before which dissociation falls **a.**
T-5.......II.12:6 to hear and give **a.** as you answer the Holy
T-5........III.2:6 It is strengthened by being given **a.**. It
T-5......IV.1:11 be as one, the ego fades **a.** and is undone.
T-5......IV.3:11 purified He lets you give them **a.**. The
T-5........IV.6:3 complete until you join it and give it **a.**.
T-5.......V.3:10 that a part of Him has been torn **a.** by you
T-6........III.4:5 win back the knowledge that you threw **a.**
T-6.........V.4:5 He merely shines them **a.**. His light is
T-6......V.A.4:4 Kingdom to let this crucial concept slip **a.**
T-6......V.C.9:3 When you threw truth **a.** you saw yourself
T-7.........V.9:7 it. It incorporates to take **a.**. It literally
T-7......VIII.3:6 something you do not want by giving it **a.**
T-8.........I.1:10 it **a.** when the ego asks for your allegiance.
T-8......IV.2:10 not attack darkness, but it does shine it **a.**
T-8......IV.2:11 you everywhere, you shine it **a.** with me.
T-9......VIII.7:3 When grandeur slips **a.** from you, you
T-10.........I.4:1 you will have willed **a.** the separation,
T-11.......II.1:2 Every attack is a step **a.** from this, and
T-11.......VI.5:6 nothing, for He does not will to take **a.**.
T-11....VIII.2:4 restore to you what you have thrown **a.**.
T-12.........I.8:4 would have taken a step **a.** from reality,
T-12.......II.9:8 He cannot shine **a.** what you keep hidden,
T-12....VIII.1:2 him far **a.** from your destructive thoughts
T-13.........I.7:6 Let the holiness of God's Son shine **a.** the
T-13.........I.8:9 is the opposite of time, for time passes **a.**,
T-13......III.4:2 it would sweep you **a.** from yourself and
T-13......III.4:3 you do, you would throw this world **a.**,
T-13.......V.5:5 react with fear to love, and draw **a.** from it
T-13.....VII.3:7 that leads **a.** from it into another world.
T-13.....VII.4:4 All that you need to give this world **a.** in
T-13.....VII.5:5 judgment enters reality has slipped **a.**.
T-13...VII.14:1 journey that would lead **a.** from light,
T-13...VII.16:9 for all the world has offered but to take **a.**.
T-13.......X.14:3 radiance of the Kingdom guilt melts **a.**,
T-14.......in.1:8 Let us now turn **a.** from them, and follow
T-14.........I.1:2 for it is they that have been thrown **a.**.
T-14.........I.1:5 as yours, for how else could you give it **a.**?
T-14.......II.7:7 The key is only the light that shines **a.** the
T-14......III.6:4 throws **a.** the joyous opportunity to learn
T-14....III.18:3 you have thrown **a.** but could not lose.
T-14......IV.7:5 knowledge is swept **a.** from recognition in
T-14......IV.8:3 throw yourself **a.** and valued God so little,
T-14.......V.4:3 would steal it **a.** and keep it from his sight
T-14.......V.4:5 but shine **a.** the heavy veils of guilt within
T-14.......V.5:2 So will the world of separation slip **a.**, and
T-14......VI.1:3 and shrink **a.** from it to further darkness.
T-14......VI.4:2 of guiltlessness shines guilt **a.** because,
T-14.....VII.1:6 so ignorance fades **a.** when knowledge
T-14.....VII.6:1 every secret you have locked **a.** from Him.
T-14.....VII.6:2 Him enter the darkness and lighten it **a.**.
T-14....VIII.3:1 darkened corridors, **a.** from light's center.
T-15......IV.2:2 you is but as far **a.** as your desire for it. As
T-15......IV.9:9 Let the Holy Spirit's purity shine them **a.**,
T-15....VIII.2:2 but seek in them what you have thrown **a.**
T-15......IX.6:3 as great as His, you can turn **a.** from love.
T-15.......X.6:1 give all your guilt **a.** whenever you want,
T-15.......X.8:3 have given God **a.** rather than look at it.
T-15.......X.8:4 to project Him outward and **a.** from you,
T-15......XI.6:5 while all that you would keep **a.** holds all
T-16.......II.2:2 of avoiding, or looking **a.** from the whole,
T-16.......II.5:6 and do not turn **a.** from all the witnesses
T-16......III.5:4 more to you than you tried to take **a.**. He
T-16.....IV.12:5 with me firmly **a.** from all illusions now,
T-16.....IV.12:6 last useless journey **a.** from truth together
T-16.......V.7:3 it can accomplish this it gives itself **a.**, and
T-16.......V.7:7 that he would give **a.** to get a "better" one
T-16.....V.15:4 to lead **a.** from truth and into fantasy. Yet
T-17.........I.3:5 take **a.** from Him Who would release you.
T-17.........I.6:6 of you **a.** from truth and from salvation.
T-18.......II.6:5 not destroy it, nor snatch it **a.** from you.
T-18......III.3:7 and **a.** from all illusions in which you
T-18......III.3:9 travel surely and very swiftly **a.** from fear?
T-18......III.4:5 tempted not to snatch **a.** the gift of faith
T-18......III.8:7 to shine **a.** the past and so make room for
T-18......IV.6:2 will merely take **a.** the little that is asked.
T-18....VI.12:5 rush to meet it, letting your limits melt **a.**,
T-18. VIII.10:3 lonely little kingdoms locked **a.** from love,
T-18. VIII.13:7 and with happy laughter, and it will fall **a.**
T-19.......II.4:5 an attempt to wrest creation **a.** from truth
T19...IV.A.4:1 salvation **a.** from the giver of salvation?
T19. IV.A.4:11 will fall **a.** so quietly beneath the wings of
T19. IV.A.4:12 barriers will fall **a.** before their coming as
T19...IV.A.5:7 fall **a.** because of the appeal you answered
T19...IV.A.9:4 this little wisp is lifted up and carried **a.**,
T19. IV.A.12:5 steal guiltily **a.** in hungry search of guilt,
T19....IV.B.8:4 to keep **a.** One Who is there already. And
T19..IV.B.15:1 messages are always sent **a.** from you, in
T19....IV.C.2:4 chorus, plodding so heavily **a.** from life,
T19....IV.C.2:5 of forgiveness, and watch the chains fall **a.**
T19. IV.D.16:5 and with happy laughter **a.** from him.
T-20.........I.2:7 Join now with me and throw **a.** the thorns
T-20......IV.8:7 but will melt **a.** before you reach it. You
T-20......VI.4:6 The rest it merely throws **a.**, for all that it
T-20..VIII.10:7 They step **a.** from sin, reminding you that
T-20..VIII.11:1 in dancing brooks that never waste **a.**;
T-21........II.4:3 it. Give it **a.**, and everything you see goes
T-21........II.7:8 presence of what you thought you gave **a.**.
T-21......III.3:6 you give to sin you take **a.** from holiness.
T-21......III.4:2 and **a.** from all illusions where your faith
T-21......III.6:2 But as He uses them they lead **a.** from sin,
T-21......III.8:6 choose to look **a.** from sin are given vision
T-21.......V.8:5 For the perception would fall **a.** at once, if
T-21......VI.5:6 enters part be kept **a.** from other parts?
T-21....VI.7:10 steadily **a.** from madness toward the goal
T-22....VI.9:10 look **a.** from it and toward your brother.
T-23.......I.10:3 and let forgiveness sweep **a.** all trace of
T-23........II.9:4 you can never take **a.** save from yourself.
T-23.......II.21:4 still deeper into terror and **a.** from truth.
T-24........II.9:2 of the fear of God will melt **a.** in love.
T-24......II.13:4 God, **a.** from truth and from salvation.
T-24......II.14:1 key you threw **a.** God gave your brother,
T-24......III.2:6 seems to give you power has taken it **a.**.
T-25.......in.1:9 Then will their bodies melt **a.**, that they
T-25......IV.3:6 that they thought was there is pushed **a.**,
T-25......IV.3:6 until it is but distant shadows, far **a.**, not
T-25......IV.4:4 increasingly remote and far **a.** from you.
T-25......IV.4:5 they may be pushed **a.** before the light.
T-25......IV.4:6 in twisted forms too far **a.** for recognition,
T-25......IV.4:8 can never fall **a.** and leave you homeless.
T-25......VI.2:2 And they turn **a.** from sunlight and the
T-25..VIII.13:9 and try to take **a.** from whom he judges.
T-26.........I.2:3 join with what is locked **a.** within the wall.
T-26........II.4:7 And so He takes the thorns and nails **a.**.
T-26........II.7:7 shine **a.** all memory of sacrifice and loss.
T-26........II.8:5 locked will merely fall **a.** and disappear.
T-26.....V.1:11 to go toward Heaven, or **a.** to nowhere.
T-26.......V.5:1 passed **a.** in Heaven too soon for anything
T-26.....VII.9:1 Forgiveness takes **a.** what stands between
T-26...VII.13:3 but adds to its abundance, never takes **a.**.
T-26.......IX.7:1 to keep **a.** all darkened thoughts of sin,
T-26........X.5:6 To add or take **a.** from this one goal is but
T-26........X.5:6 but to take **a.** all purpose from the world
T-26........X.6:7 *injustice, which Their Presence shines* **a.**.
T-27.........I.5:5 tear is wiped **a.** in laughter and in love.
T-27.........I.9:4 it is not. It only takes **a.** from it all signs of
T-27.......II.10:9 for you must lose what you would take **a.**.
T-27.......VI.1:3 it **a.** from Him and focusing upon itself.
T-27...VII.11:6 but a part of your own dream you gave **a.**,
T-27....VIII.2:3 and tosses them **a.** for senseless things it
T-27....VIII.5:6 for anything but to be laughed **a.**. How
T-27....VIII.6:1 Let us return the dream he gave **a.** unto
T-27....VIII.6:4 Together, we can laugh them both **a.**, and
T-27..VIII.11:4 this one answer takes **a.** the cause of every
T-28.........I.1:4 It does not add, but merely takes **a.**. And
T-28.........I.1:5 And what it takes **a.** is long since gone,
T-28.........I.5:9 by time, which took **a.** their cause.
T-28.........I.6:3 Time neither takes **a.** nor can restore.
T-28........I.13:1 that has no fear to keep the memory **a.**!
T-28.......III.1:7 the dream will fade **a.** without effects. For
T-28......IV.6:4 your own **a.** would he be free of them, and
T-28.....VII.7:4 will wash **a.** and yet this house will stand
T-29.........I.4:7 for it gets **a.** from total sacrifice and gives
T-29.........I.7:5 you have demanded that love go **a.**, and
T-29......VI.4:1 that only Heaven would not pass **a.**. You
T-29......IX.6:3 Put them all **a.**, for you have need of them
T-29......IX.7:5 for childish things have all been put **a.**.
T-29......IX.8:7 dreams of judgment have been put **a.**?
T-29....IX.10:2 So do your childish terrors melt **a.**, and
T-30.......III.5:7 For can he give a part of him **a.**? What is
T-30.......V.3:4 And fear has dropped **a.**, because he is
T-30.......V.6:2 you are, forgiveness washes joyfully **a.**.
T-30.......V.7:3 surely set **a.** from idols toward reality. For
T-30.......V.8:2 perfect confidence **a.** from fear forever,
T-30.....VII.1:8 You take **a.** another element, and every
T-31.......I.12:4 be loosened from our minds and swept **a.**.
T-31.......I.13:5 because an ancient learning passed **a.**,

T-31....... II.4:3 arise, and give a. the role of leadership.
T-31....... II.6:6 as near or far a. from what we want as we
T-31....... II.8:3 The old will fall a. before the new without
T-31....... II.8:8 but come a. without the thoughts you did
T-31...... IV.1:5 a. from difficulties that concern you not.
T-31...... IV.5:1 be willing to be turned a. from all the
T-31...... IV.7:1 ever found by following a road a. from it.
T-31...... IV.7:3 proceed in its direction, not a. from it.
T-31...... IV.9:5 All roads that lead a. from what you are
T-31.... IV.10:4 There is no road that leads a. from Him.
T-31...... V.5:2 that smiles above it must forever look a.,
T-31..... VII.9:1 him off from you, and you a. from him.
W-pI....... 1.2:1 look farther a. from your immediate area,
W-pI....... 9.2:5 step will clear a little of the darkness a.,
W-pI..... 37.1:4 loses; nothing is taken a. from anyone;
W-pI..... 41.7:2 a. from the world and all the foolish
W-pI..... 52.3:6 Let me learn to give the past a., realizing
W-pI..... 56.1:6 to give my inheritance a. in exchange for
W-pI..... 61.5:7 mind wanders a. from the central thought
W-pI..... 62.3:4 It will take a. all fear and guilt and pain. It
W-pI..... 62.4:3 who seem to be far a. in space and time,
W-pI..... 67.3:1 try to let all thoughts drop a. for a brief
W-pI..... 72.8:4 you, locked a. from your awareness by the
W-pI..... 78.4:3 as we look out toward truth, a. from fear.
W-pI... 78.10:2 Temptation falls a. when we allow each
W-pI..... 85.2:3 *The light of the world will shine all this a.. I*
W-pI..... 85.4:2 *me to look a. from me for my salvation. I will*
W-pI..... 92.8:1 sure as love, forever glad to give itself a.,
W-pI... 92.11:3 led a. from darkness to the light where
W-pI..... 93.8:4 Then put a. your foolish self-images, and
W-pI..... 94.1:3 held are wiped a. forever by this one idea.
W-pI... 95.13:3 shine a. all your illusions and your doubts
W-pI..... 98.2:6 All our sins are washed a. by realizing
W-pI... 101.3:3 taking everything a. before it grants the
W-pI... 105.3:4 will never lessen when they are given a..
W-pI... 105.4:5 fulfill its aim of giving everything it has a.,
W-pI... 106.7:1 is yours and everything is given a., it will
W-pI. 106.10:1 is kept through your receiving it to give a.
W-pI... 107.4:4 They will merely blow a., when truth
W-pI... 109.5:5 but the dreams of fever that has passed a..
W-pI... 109.5:8 to slip a. from dreams and into peace.
W-pI... 122.7:2 Do not turn a. in aimless wandering again
W-pI... 129.2:4 takes a. all things that you have cherished
W-pI... 129.4:5 far a. from this are you who stay bound to
W-pI... 129.5:1 an instant's space a. from timelessness.
W-pI... 131.5:3 Everything you seek but this will fall a..
W-pI... 131.9:2 God make time to take a. the Will of God
W-pI. 131.13:3 quite forget in wandering a. in dreams.
W-pI. 132.13:1 and break a. a part of God Himself and
W-pI... 133.6:3 Time can never take a. a value that is real.
W-pI... 133.7:1 to take a thing a. from someone else, you
W-pI... 133.7:4 Who seeks to take a. has been deceived by
W-pI. 135.10:5 but merely take a. the hope of healing, for
W-pI... 136.7:4 that truth may go a. and threaten your
W-pI. 136.12:5 it sighs a little when you throw a. its gifts,
W-pI... 137.7:1 Just as forgiveness shines a. all sin and
W-pI... 140.4:5 takes a. the guilt that makes the sickness
W-pI... 153.1:1 the "gifts" it merely lends to take a. again;
W-pI. 153.13:3 come, in which we put a. the toys of guilt,
W-pI. 153.18:3 keep your mind a. from Him a moment,
W-pI... 154.7:1 his role by giving all his messages a.. The
W-pI... 154.7:2 the messages by giving them a.. They
W-pI... 154.7:4 gain by every message that they give a..
W-pI... 155.5:1 road that leads a. from loss of every kind,
W-pI... 159.2:5 where they are laid, and giving them a..
W-pI... 159.7:4 one will be turned a. from this new home,
W-pI. 161.11:5 hands can take a. the nails which pierce
W-pI... 162.2:3 that will not fade a. before their might.
W-pI... 164.2:1 The world fades easily a. before His sight.
W-pI... 164.5:2 which appeared to hide it merely sink a..
W-pI... 164.8:2 Your trifling treasures put a., and leave a
W-pI... 165.5:5 induce you now to let it fade a. from your
W-pI... 166.4:4 wandering so far from home, so long a.,
W-pI... 168.3:4 and sweeps a. the cobwebs of our sleep.
W-pI... 182.9:4 they protect Him, for His home is far a.,
W-pI. 185.13:3 To take a. is meaningless to Him. And
W-pI... 186.1:1 day take all arrogance a. from every mind
W-pI... 187.2:2 it is sure that if you give a finite thing a.,
W-pI... 187.2:4 lack for proof that when you give ideas a.,
W-pI... 187.4:1 you value by the act of giving them a., and
W-pI... 187.9:5 will behold will take a. all thought of form
W-pI... 187.9:5 to increase, forever yours, forever given a.
W-pI... 193.9:4 And He would have all tears be wiped a.,
W-pI... 195.8:5 some other things still locked a. as "sins."
W-pI... 197.6:2 But learn to let forgiveness take a. the sins
W-pI... 197.6:2 before He snatches them a. again in death
W-pI... 198.3:1 Forgiveness sweeps all other dreams a.,
W-pI... 198.4:1 all suffering, and finally a. from death.
W-pI... 198.6:7 And as this one will fade a., the Word of
W-pI... 207.1:3 *but turn to Him, and every sorrow melts a.,*
W-pII . 229.1:4 I will turn a. no longer from the holy face
W-pII ..... 2.5:2 are done, eternity has shined a. the world,
W-pII ..... 3.4:1 As sight was made to lead a. from truth,
W-pII ..... 3.4:5 and certainty, which you have thrown a.,
W-pII . 241.1:4 when sorrows pass a. and pain is gone.
W-pII ..... 4.5:2 put a. these sharp-edged children's toys?
W-pII ..... 7.3:1 nor turn a. from His replacement for the
W-pII . 295.1:2 to me, and take a. all terror and all pain.
W-pII . 298.1:3 on my holy sight forgiveness takes a.. And
W-pII .... 301.h And God Himself shall wipe a. all tears.
W-pII . 306.2:1 *to You, remembering we never went a.;*
W-pII ... 10.2:3 sight, it merely slips a. to nothingness.
W-pII ... 10.2:6 now are useless, and will therefore fade a.,
W-pII ... 10.4:3 alone can heal all sorrow, wipe a. all tears,
W-pII . 332.1:2 undoes its evil dreams by shining them a..
W-pII . 333.2:1 *chose to shine a. all conflict and all doubt,*
W-pII . 336.1:4 all. Forgiveness sweeps a. distortions, and
W-pII . 336.2:1 *quiet may forgiveness wipe a. my dreams of*
W-pII ... 13.1:6 fear must slip a. under the gentle remedy
W-pII . 343.1:4 *You never take a.. And You created me to be*
W-pII .... 347.h myself, To keep the miracle a. from me.
W-ep ......... 4:2 will He give you pleasures that will pass a.
M-4 ..... I.A.3:3 It seems as if things are being taken a.,
M-4 ..... VII.1:4 "giving a." in the sense of "giving up." To
M-4 ..... VII.1:5 of God, it means giving a. in order to keep
M-4 ..... VII.2:3 does not want anything he cannot give a.,
M-4 ... VII.2:12 These he can give a. in true generosity,
M-5 .... III.2:11 brothers to turn a. from death: "Behold,
M-10 ......... 5:8 He has given it a., along with judgment.
M-14 ......... 3:1 this seems to be a long, long while a..
M-16 ......... 4:8 the difficulty will diminish and drop a.. If
M-16 ......... 5:7 of rest, and orients you a. from fear. If it is
M-20 ......... 2:8 The past just slips a., and in its place is
M-24 ......... 4:4 wise to step a. from all such questions, for
M-24 ......... 4:5 draining it a. from its appointed purpose.
M-27 ......... 2:2 who has decreed that all things pass a.,
M-28 ......... 3:6 Thoughts turn to Heaven and a. from hell
C-in ........... 5:2 it drops a. to make way for the central
C-3 ............ 1:4 it leads a. from error and not towards it.
C-4 ............ 5:6 as surely as forgiveness takes all guilt a..
C-4 ............ 7:6 of Christ has shone a. time's final instant,
C-ep ........ 1:11 before a lifeless image when a step a. the
C-ep .......... 2:3 Ask but my help to roll the stone a., and it
P-2.......... V.8:3 them down, to come a. in peace forever.
P-2....... VII.6:6 he has the gifts of God Himself to give a..
P-3........ III.6:1 be turned a. because he cannot pay. No
P-3........ III.7:4 How much is lost by throwing God a.?
S-2.......... II.5:7 to keep the witnesses of guilt a. from love
S-2.......... II.8:1 takes that do not lead a. from anger,
S-3........... I.4:3 For he has thrown a. the prison's key; his
S-3........ IV.2:5 earth an instant, as the world is shined a..
S-3........ IV.9:3 See the shadows fade a. in gentleness; the

**awe** 14

T-1 ........ I.31:1 Miracles should inspire gratitude, not a..
T-1 ......... II.3:1 A. should be reserved for revelation, to
T-1 ......... II.3:2 for miracles because a state of a. is
T-1 ......... II.3:3 experience a. only in the Presence of the
T-1 ......... II.3:5 Equals should not be in a. of one another
T-1 ......... II.3:5 one another because a. implies inequality.
T-1 ...... VII.5:1 and a. to which I have already referred,
T-1 ...... VII.5:2 I have said that a. is inappropriate in
T-1 ...... VII.5:2 not experience a. in the presence of your
T-1 ...... VII.5:3 it was also emphasized that a. is proper in
T-1 ...... VII.5:6 yours. I have stressed that a. is not an
T-1 ...... VII.5:8 or a. will be confused with fear, and the
T-19 ....... II.5:2 except with reverence and a.. It is the
T-20 ..... VI.6:6 of separation perceived in a. and held in

**awesome** 1

T-28 ....... V.7:5 are no a. secrets and no darkened tombs

**awful** 1

T-14 ..... IV.5:5 will He teach you to remove the a. burden

**awhile** 3

T-30 ...... in.1:7 So now we need to practice them a., until
W-pI .. 155.3:2 mad illusion will remain a. in evidence,
W-pI .. 190.6:1 of this a.: The world you see does nothing

**awoke** 2

T-12 ....... II.7:2 as I awakened myself, for I a. for you. In
W-pI 138.12:2 day to the decision with which we a.. As

**axis** 1

T-1 ......... II.4:2 of a vertical rather than a horizontal a..

# B

## babe 1
T19. IV.C.10:8 Here is the **b.** of Bethlehem reborn. And

## babies 1
T-4......... II.5:2 **B.** scream in rage if you take away a knife

## baby 3
T-4......... II.5:3 In this sense you are still a **b.**. You have
T-22.........I.6:4 The sounds a **b.** makes and what he hears
T-22.........I.7:2 has replaced, is like a **b.** now in its rebirth

## baby's 1
T-22.........I.6:3 your whole communication is like a **b.**.

## back 162
T-1........ I.13:2 which seem to go **b.** but really go forward.
T-3......... II.4:3 not free because it is possessed, or held **b.**
T-3.......VII.5:9 You have not yet gone **b.** far enough, and
T-4.........in.1:2 suggest that you set him **b.** on his journey
T-4.........in.1:3 to a brother cannot set you **b.** either. It
T-4...........I.4:7 it very gently and lead you **b.** to God.
T-4........IV.7:3 permit this shabby belief to pull you **b.**.
T-4........VI.7:7 Kingdom of God I can lead you **b.** to your
T-5...........I.6:2 so high they could reach almost **b.** to Him
T-5.......... II.3:8 His is the Voice that calls you **b.** to where
T-5........ II.11:2 to bring it **b.** into the oneness in which it
T-5.......III.11:7 looks **b.** to God in remembrance of me.
T-5........IV.6:2 you are led **b.** to God where you belong,
T-5......... V.8:6 and it will turn it **b.** to full creation at any
T-6........III.4:5 Only thus can you win **b.** the knowledge
T-6... V.A.5:11 He never takes anything **b.**, because He
T-7....... V.11:4 will shine **b.** upon you and on the whole
T-7... VIII.3:11 their projections are trying to creep **b.** in.
T-8................h THE JOURNEY **B.**
T-8......... II.4:4 beyond everything that would hold you **b.**
T-8......... V.4:5 I bring God's peace **b.** to all His children
T-8......... V.5:4 the journey **b.** to God Who is our home.
T-8......... V.6:6 all attempts of the ego to hold you **b.**. I go
T-8........VI.1:2 all. We begin the journey **b.** by setting out
T-9.......VII.6:3 it, look **b.** from a point where sanity exists
T-11....... II.6:4 Invite this knowledge **b.** into your mind,
T-11.......IV.3:6 As you bring him **b.**, so will you return.
T-12......IV.7:2 for you, since you could not "buy" it **b.**.
T-12... VIII.8:8 is but the way **b.** to what was never lost.
T-13....III.12:9 look **b.** on them and see them as insane.
T-13...VII.16:1 every temptation that would hold you **b.**.
T-14........ II.6:5 truth before you, you will not look **b.**.
T-15......XI.4:5 peace you invite them **b.**, realizing that
T-16....VI.10:1 look not **b.** with longing on the travesty it
T-17.........I.3:6 Unless you give it **b.**, it is inevitable that
T-17......VI.3:2 Then you look **b.** at it, and try to piece
T-17... VIII.6:7 any situation that could hold you **b.**, and
T-18.........I.8:3 gently **b.** to the truth and safety within.
T-18......III.2:4 when you are afraid you have stepped **b.**.
T-18......III.4:8 You cannot take it **b.**. You have accepted
T-18......III.7:3 Carry it **b.** to darkness, from the holy
T-18......III.8:7 light will the Great Rays extend **b.** into
T-18......IX.1:7 Give it **b.** to Heaven. Heaven has not lost
T-18......IX.3:3 these messengers to bring this **b.** to you.
T-18......IX.6:3 and has no power at all to hold **b.** anyone
T-18......IX.7:4 And **b.** and forth they go, as long as you
T19... IV.A.3:7 hold **b.** the universe and its Creator. This
T19....IV.B.9:2 the limits that would hold its extension **b.**
T-20.........I.3:5 Hold him not **b.** with thorns and nails
T-20......III.5:9 if mercilessness seems to look **b.** at you, it
T-20...... VI.9:6 temple, look you not **b.** on what you have
T-20.. VI.12:10 held **b.** from looking on the face of Christ
T-21....... II.5:3 in its testimony, and as it gave it **b.** to you
T-21.... III.12:7 now be given **b.** to what produced them,
T-21......IV.8:4 not held **b.** by fear's insane insistence that
T-22.........I.2:4 seeing such as this send **b.** its messages?
T-22...... III.5:9 It is held **b.** by form, having been made to
T-22......IV.2:1 you can go **b.** and make the other choice.
T-24.......in.1:8 believe a shadow can hold **b.** the Will that
T-24.........I.1:4 Hold **b.** but one belief, one offering, and
T-24...... III.7:7 on him, and give him **b.** his birthright. It
T-25.....VII.3:1 Let us go **b.** to what we said before, and
T-26.........I.8:4 and give you **b.** the gift of freedom by
T-26......IV.6:1 **b.** the happy opening of Heaven's gate.
T-26....... V.5:5 in sin, is that one instant still called **b.**, as
T-26....... V.9:4 You can *not* go **b.**. And everything that
T-26..... V.11:4 there? Now you are shifting **b.** and forth
T-26... VIII.5:5 its cause, is looking forward, looking **b.**,
T-27....... V.5:1 stepped **b.** because he was afraid of being
T-27...... VI.2:9 as one steps forward and another **b.**. Yet
T-28.......I.11:3 its radiant extension **b.** into the Mind
T-28....... II.9:3 is the first step in giving **b.** to cause the
T-28..... II.12:4 glad effects of taking **b.** the consequence
T-29.........I.3:7 come close to you, and you jumped **b.**; as
T-29.........I.9:4 to hold you **b.** an instant from His Love?
T-29......IV.2:1 you **b.** as much as those in which the fear
T-30....... V.6:3 again, that what is his be given **b.** to him.
T-30....... V.7:2 Perhaps they still look **b.**, and think they
T-30....... V.9:3 Look **b.** no longer, for what lies ahead is
T-30..... V.10:1 Do not look **b.** except in honesty. And
T-30..... V.10:7 For he will be delayed when you look **b.**,
T-30.....VII.2:5 And then, in looking **b.**, you think you see
T-31....... II.6:7 us, and we fall **b.** if he does not advance.
T-31....... II.9:4 advancing only when he would step **b.**,
T-31....... II.9:4 and falling **b.** when he would go ahead?
T-31..... II.11:5 **b.** and forward in the darkness and alone.
W-pI.....42.6:2 Try merely to step **b.** and let the thoughts
W-pI.....45.4:4 let the thoughts of the world hold us **b.**.
W-pI.....57.5:4 and shines forgiveness **b.** at me. In this
W-pI...70.10:7 *me. Nothing outside of me can hold me* **b.**.
W-pI.....73.3:1 in which guilt is traded **b.** and forth, and
W-pI...75.10:4 who seems to pull you **b.** into darkness:
W-pI.....92.7:6 and **b.** to darkness till the morning comes
W-pI.....95.8:2 held **b.** only by your unwillingness to let
W-pI.....97.7:3 increase its power and give it **b.** to you.
W-pI.....98.8:1 your words and give them **b.** to you all
W-pI...100.9:4 little thought has power to hold you **b.**?
WpI. rIII.in6:6 at the outset; then lean **b.** in quiet faith,
W-pI...123.1:3 There is no thought of turning **b.**, and no
W-pI...123.6:3 gives them **b.** a thousand and a hundred
W-pI...128.4:1 holds anything you want to hold you **b.**.
W-pI...129.5:2 never **b.** to see again the world you do not
W-pI...131.4:6 off, he is led **b.** to his appointed task.
W-pI...132.6:5 or perhaps step **b.** a while and then return
W-pI...133.1:1 to bring him **b.** to practical concerns.
W-pI.151.13:4 and give them **b.** again as clean ideas that
W-pI.151.14:1 He will give them **b.** as miracles which
W-pI.......155.h I will step **b.** and let Him lead the way.
W-pI...155.2:3 then they step **b.** and let it lead the way.
W-pI...155.6:2 Yet it has stepped **b.**. And it is not illusion
W-pI...155.7:3 this steps **b.** as truth comes forth in you,
W-pI...155.8:7 As they step **b.**, he finds himself again.
W-pI.155.10:3 Step **b.** in faith and let truth lead the way.
W-pI.155.14:3 *I will step* **b.** *and let Him lead the way, For I*
W-pI...156.6:2 As you step **b.**, the light in you steps
W-pI...158.4:5 point at which it ended, looking **b.** on it,
W-pI...159.8:3 can be brought from here **b.** to the world,
W-pI...159.9:2 when they are carried **b.** into the world.
W-pI...164.6:2 the world, looks **b.** on them in a new light
W-pI...166.1:4 holding nothing **b.** that can contribute to
W-pI.169.13:3 he felt an instant **b.** to bless the world?
W-pI.169.14:2 you. You carry them **b.** to yourself. And
WpI...rV.in3:4 *off, but You will not forget to call us* **b.**.
WpI...rV.in7:5 you **b.** to where the journey was begun, to
W-pI...173.1:1 I will step **b.** and let Him lead the way.
W-pI...182.7:5 For He would bring you **b.** with Him, that
W-pI.184.10:3 And then step **b.** to darkness, not because
W-pI...185.1:4 be completely given **b.** to full awareness,
W-pI...188.1:8 and leads you **b.** to where it came from
W-pI...188.7:5 They lead you **b.** to peace, from where
W-pI...188.9:2 gently bring them **b.** to where they fall in
W-pI...188.9:6 But now we call them **b.**, and wash them
W-pI.192.10:6 you may accept him **b.** as your Identity.
W-pI...193.2:3 lead him **b.** to where perception ceases.
W-pI...196.8:5 be welcomed **b.** within the holy mind He
W-pI.196.11:6 Step **b.** from fear, and make advance to
W-pI...197.3:4 you would undo by taking **b.** your gifts,
W-pI...197.4:6 And would you take them **b.**, when He
W-pII .233.1:6 *I will step* **b.** *and merely follow You. Be You*
W-pII .248.1:8 to accept him **b.** as God created him, and
W-pII .....4.5:7 Would you still hold return to Heaven **b.**?
W-pII .254.2:2 occur, we quietly step **b.** and look at them
W-pII .265.1:1 sins on it and saw them looking **b.** at me.
W-pII .266.1:2 *does Christ look* **b.** *upon me from my Self.*
W-pII ... 11.4:3 Yet **b.** of all our doubts, past all our fears,
W-pII .324.1:5 *Your loving Voice will always call me* **b.**, *and*
W-pII .341.1:2 *deep and still the universe smiles* **b.** *on You,*
W-pII .345.1:4 *miracles I give are given* **b.** *in just the form I*
Wfl........in.3:6 thus His memory is given **b.**, completely
M-13.........4:4 look **b.** with longing on a slaughter house
M-13.........4:5 its ills looks **b.** on it with condemnation.
M-19.........3:2 of the distorted world **b.** to the mind that
M-21.........4:6 "I will step **b.** and let Him lead the way."
M-22.........5:7 Step **b.** now, teacher of God. You have
M-25.........5:3 temptation to win **b.** strength by guile.
C-4.............8:3 out of all fear and given **b.** to love.
C-5.............3:3 He leads you **b.** to God because he saw
P-2......VII.6:8 Christ's shining face as it looks **b.** at them.
S-2...........I.8:6 with nothing of the past to hold it **b.** from
S-2........ III.2:6 need do is to step **b.** and not to interfere.
S-3...........I.1:5 healing but delays its turning **b.** to dust,
S-3...........I.2:4 hands, which cannot hold them **b.**. And

## background 1
M-8...........1:2 on uneven **b.** and shifting foreground, on

## backgrounds 1
M-4...........1:2 eyes, they come from vastly different **b.**,

## backward 2
W-pII ....in.6:3 We look not **b.** now. We look ahead, and
M-2...........4:1 goes **b.** to an instant so ancient that it is

## backwards 2
T-18.........I.6:4 that a world in which everything is **b.** and
W-pI...181.9:4 We look neither ahead nor **b.**. We look

## bad 29
T-3.........I.2:10 I was not "punished" because *you* were **b.**.
T-6........IV.6:3 a sleep in which you have had **b.** dreams,
T-6......... V.2:5 And so when **b.** dreams come, they will
T-11....VIII.1:6 will be forgotten; the good and the **b.**, the
T-15.....VII.8:7 terms that it evaluates ideas as good or **b.**.

T-15.....VII.8:9 What releases him from guilt is "**b.**,"
T-27.........I.9:5 as neither sick nor well, nor **b.** nor good.
T-29......IX.6:7 And **b.** things seem to happen, and he is
T-31.....VII.1:5 In this world's concepts are the guilty "**b.**
T-31.....VII.1:6 counts the "good" to pardon him the "**b.**.
T-31.....VII.1:7 believing that the "**b.**" must lurk behind.
T-31.....VII.1:9 change while you perceive the "**b.**" in you.
W-pI.......4.1:5 select only the thoughts you think are "**b.**.
W-pI.......4.1:6 none of them can be called "good" or "**b.**.
W-pI.......4.2:2 to use "good" thoughts as well as "**b.**."
W-pI.......4.2:5 The "**b.**" ones are blocks to sight, and
W-pI.....12.3:6 that a "good world" implies a "**b.**" one,
W-pI.....12.5:1 is meaningless is neither good nor **b.**.
W-pI.....25.5:2 meaningless, rather than "good" or "**b.**,"
W-pI.....93.5:4 It is neither **b.** nor good. It is unreal, and
W-pI.....94.4:1 the list of attributes, both good and **b.**,
W-pI...189.7:2 thinks is either true or false, or good or **b.**,
W-pII .294.2:2 *be sinful nor sinless; neither good nor* ***b.**. Let*
M-10 .........1:3 is capable of "good" and "**b.**" judgment,
M-10 .........1:5 "good" judgment to one is "**b.**" judgment
M-10 .........1:6 time and "**b.**" judgment at another time.
M-10 .......1:10 not mean anything. No more does "**b.**."
M-10 .........2:8 this judgment is neither "good" nor "**b.**."
M-16 .........9:4 can have no effects; neither good nor **b.**,

### badgered 1
W-pI...195.9:3 pursuit, where we are **b.** ceaselessly, and

### badly 3
T-6........IV.4:4 it, and the ego feels **b.** in need of allies,
T-6......... V.2:2 that frightened them so **b.** are not real,
T-28.........I.7:1 taught yourself, for you were **b.** taught.

### bait 1
T-24.....VII.4:6 it for show, as **b.** to catch another fish, to

### balance 8
T-4......... V.1:4 The ego is thrown further off **b.** because it
T-16......IV.1:8 attempt to **b.** hate with love that makes
T-24......III.3:5 *It* can be thrown off **b.** by anything. What
T-26.........I.1:2 and all conflicts achieve a seeming **b.**. It is
T-27........ II.9:6 to prevent a shift of **b.** in the sacrifice.
W-pI...164.5:3 Now is the **b.** righted, and the scale of
M-3 ...........5:3 the teaching-learning **b.** is actually perfect
M-8 ...........1:5 completely upsets the mental **b.**. What

### balanced 1
*See also* off-balanced
T-4......... V.1:3 is not the way a **b.** mind holds together.

### band 1
T-31......IV.1:5 within the narrow **b.** from birth to death,

### bands 1
W-pI...153.3:2 in heavy **b.** of steel with iron overlaid,

### banish 8
T-5......... II.4:2 that you must let **b.** the idea of darkness.
T-12....... II.9:1 have tried to **b.** love have not succeeded,
T-12....... II.9:1 you who choose to **b.** fear must succeed.
T-13...VII.17:4 The sound of it will **b.** sorrow from the
T-13..... X.12:5 for what you see will **b.** guilt forever. I
T-14.....VIII.1:5 **B.** not power from your mind, but let all
T-29.....VIII.3:9 a veil can **b.** what it seems to separate, nor
W-pI...196.8:5 And God, Whom you had thought to **b.**,

### banished 3
T-4........ III.10:1 is ruthlessly **b.** from the part of the mind
T-10.........I.1:5 know this has **b.** itself from knowledge,
W-pI.137.14:4 *may be* ***b.*** *from the mind of God's one Son,*

### banishment 1
T-10 ........I.1:7 the realization that your **b.** is not of God,

### bank 3
T-18 ..... IX.6:1 is like a **b.** of low dark clouds that seem to
T-18 ..... IX.7:1 cloud **b.** it is easy to see a whole world
T19....IV.A.2:9 Would you let a little **b.** of sand, a wall of

### bankrupt 1
T-24 ... IV.3:15 given specialness has left you **b.** and your

### banner 1
T-13 ...VIII.8:2 with me under the holy **b.** of His teaching,

### bar 8
T-11 ..... IV.6:5 cannot **b.** the door that Christ holds open
T19....IV.B.8:3 raise to freedom, and **b.** my way to you.
T-20 ..... IV.8:5 trip on, and no obstacles to **b.** your way.
T-27 .......II.1:3 yes. For accusation is a **b.** to love, and
T-28 .. VII.5:10 there is no need to **b.** the door and lock
W-pI... 126.9:3 from every **b.** to what forgiveness means,
W-pI... 128.3:3 and add another **b.** across the door that
W-pI... 128.5:4 Thus do we lift the chains that **b.** the door

### barely 3
T-17 .......II.4:4 you will **b.** have time to thank God for it.
T-28 ..... III.1:2 For you have **b.** started to allow your first,
T-30 ...... V.3:5 he can **b.** stay and wait a little longer,

### bargain 17
T-7 ..........I.4:2 It is always willing to strike a **b.**, but it
T-7 ..........I.4:3 To gain you must give, not **b.**. To bargain
T-7 ..........I.4:4 To **b.** is to limit giving, and this is not
T-8 ..........I.1:5 This is not a **b.** made by God, Who makes
T-9 .......II.11:2 is to believe that you can **b.** with God.
T-15 ..... XI.1:4 you would **b.** with them for a few special
T19.... IV.D.3:3 This is the secret **b.** made with the ego to
T-21 ..... III.1:3 Forget not this; to **b.** is to set a limit, and
T-21 ..... III.1:4 may attempt to keep the **b.** in the name of
T-26 ........I.1:2 all desperate attempts to strike a **b.**, and
T-29 ..... VI.2:2 You make a **b.** that you cannot keep. The
W-pI..... 98.6:4 Here is a **b.** that you cannot lose. And
W-pI... 185.4:5 They merely **b.**. And what bargain can
W-pI... 185.4:6 what **b.** can give them the peace of God?
W-pI... 185.7:5 nor try to make another **b.** in the hope
W-pI... 195.4:6 For who can **b.** in the name of love?
S-2........II.6:10 try to strike a **b.** with the Son of God, and

### bargaining 1
S-2..........II.6:1 also take the form of **b.** and compromise.

### bargains 10
T-7 ..........I.4:2 like another means that no **b.** are possible
T-8 ..........I.1:5 bargain made by God, Who makes no **b.**.
T-15 .......X.9:1 keeps no **b.** and would leave you nothing.
T-21 ..... III.1:2 For they are **b.** with reality, toward which
T-21 ..... III.9:3 He makes no **b.**. And if you seek to limit
T-24 .....II.12:5 but seeks for **b.** and for compromise that
W-pI..... 98.5:4 made a thousand losing **b.** at the least.
W-pI... 105.1:5 Such are not gifts, but **b.** made with guilt.
S-2..........II.6:4 guilt in further **b.** which can give no hope,
S-2..........II.6:6 Have mercy on yourself who **b.** thus. God

### barred 7
T-11 ..... IV.6:2 that the door is **b.** and you cannot enter.
T-11 ..... IV.6:3 The door is not **b.**, and it is impossible
T-24 ..... III.6:5 The way is **b.** to love and to salvation. Yet
T-24 ... VI.11:3 and every window **b.** against the light.
T-26 .......II.8:5 hold the door securely **b.** and locked will

T-27 ..... IV.7:1 world from which the answer has been **b.**.
W-pI .. 140.5:4 He is **b.** where sin has entered. Yet there

### barren 5
T-18 ... VIII.9:1 inside and shine upon the **b.** ground. See
T-18 ..... IX.2:4 is. The **b.** sands, the darkness and the
T-19 ...... I.15:1 keep your little kingdoms **b.** and separate,
T-24 ... IV.3:15 and your treasure house **b.** and empty,
T-26 ..... IX.3:5 as grass and flowers on the **b.** ground that

### barricade 1
T-31 .... VII.7:1 like a shield, a silent **b.** before the truth,

### barricades 3
T-16 ..... IV.3:3 haven by attempting to build **b.** against it,
T-16 ... IV.4:10 When the **b.** against it are broken, fear
T-18 ... IX.1:10 its **b.** is still a tiny segment of the Son of

### barrier 17
T-6 ....... III.1:4 presents no **b.** to the communication of
T-18 ..... VI.9:3 There is no **b.** between God and His Son,
T-18 ... VI.9:10 it is. You cannot put a **b.** around yourself,
T-18 ... VIII.9:1 waiting at the **b.** you built to come inside
T-18 ..... IX.6:1 This heavy-seeming **b.**, this artificial floor
T-19 ........I.8:3 beyond the **b.** to what is joined with you.
T19 ...IV.A.2:4 The little **b.** of sand still stands between
T19 ...IV.A.2:9 of sand, a wall of dust, a tiny seeming **b.**,
T19 ...IV.A.3:7 still contain behind your little **b.** and keep
T19 ...IV.A.5:2 of your holy relationship, without this **b.**,
T19 ...IV.A.8:2 It is no longer an unrelenting **b.** to peace.
T-21 ..... VI.5:3 see the body as a **b.** between what reason
T-23 ....II.19:7 yet perceived as an eternal **b.** to Heaven.
T-26 .......II.8:5 and every bolt and **b.** that seems to hold
T-28 .......II.2:4 uncontained, without a **b.** or limitation.
T-31 .... VII.7:2 as through a **b.** that dims your sight and
W-pI .... 73.5:5 that the **b.** of grievances is easily passed,

### barriers 16
T-4 ....... III.2:5 so truth can break through the **b.** the ego
T-14 ..... IV.4:2 God breaks no **b.**; neither did He make
T-16 ..... IV.6:1 merely to seek and find all of the **b.** within
T-18 ... VI.13:6 the lifting of the **b.** of time and space, the
T-18 . VIII.11:3 no **b.** to interfere with its glad coming. In
T-18 . VIII.12:2 of all the **b.** you hold against your brother
T-18 ... IX.13:1 safely brought through the **b.** of guilt,
T-19 ........I.9:5 past all **b.** between yourself and him, and
T-19 ... III.10:6 The **b.** to Heaven will disappear before
T19 .IV.A.4:12 and **b.** will fall away before their coming
T19 ...IV.A.5:6 Guilt can raise no real **b.** against it. And
T19 ... IV.B.4:5 peace and its going forth but **b.** you place
T19 ... IV.B.5:6 be difficult for us to walk past **b.** together,
T-22 ..... IV.6:3 All **b.** disappear before their coming, as
M-25 ......... 2:5 **b.** to direct experience of the Holy Spirit,
M-26 ......... 1:3 where all **b.** to truth have been removed.

### bars 4
W-pI .. 105.8:2 have let all **b.** to peace and joy be lifted up
W-pI .. 192.8:5 The **b.** that limit him become the world in
W-pI .. 197.2:3 as bound, and **b.** become your home. Nor
S-3........ IV.9:1 Creation leans across the **b.** of time to lift

### bartering 1
W-pI .... 73.3:1 Your will is lost to you in this strange **b.**,

### base 5
T-24 .......II.3:2 even to imagine without this **b.**. For sin
T-25 .......II.2:4 gives no support to **b.** your future hopes,
W-pI .. 108.4:3 this understanding is the **b.** on which all
W-pII ..... 3.3:4 illusions but a solid **b.** where truth exists,
W-pII . 359.1:7 *fact forgiveness rests upon a certain* ***b.*** *more*

### based 38
*See also* ego-based, miracle-based
T-3.......V.10:3 Perception is **b.** on a separated state, so
T-3.......VII.1:6 that a thought system **b.** on lies is weak.
T-4.......VII.2:3 of the ego is **b.** on its own thought system,
T-5.........V.3:3 of the authority problem as **b.** on the
T-5........VI.4:2 **b.** on the error they were made to uphold.
T-6........IV.4:7 It is an alliance frankly **b.** on separation.
T-7.....VIII.6:5 of perception **b.** on the unbelievable is
T-8.....VIII.1:2 always **b.** on what it believes the thing is
T-9.......VII.3:2 evaluation of you is **b.** on His knowledge
T-9.....VIII.2:3 **b.** on the belief that the littleness is real.
T-11....in.3:10 you have been afraid was **b.** on nothing.
T-14.......X.2:7 order, being **b.** not on differences but on
T-15.......V.4:3 They are not **b.** on changeless love alone.
T-15......VII.6:1 is **b.** on the idea that by sacrificing itself,
T-17......III.1:3 remembering, **b.** not on your selection.
T-18.......IX.2:3 being **b.** on what this little kingdom really
T-18.......IX.4:1 foundation on which the world is **b.**. Here
T-19........II.1:4 belief in sin is necessarily **b.** on the firm
T-20......VI.2:2 The first is **b.** on love, and rests on it
T-20......VI.2:4 in which the body enters is **b.** not on love,
T-22.......in.2:5 an unholy relationship is **b.** on differences
T-24.......in.2:5 a decision is a conclusion **b.** on everything
T-25......VII.5:1 on which a sane perception can be **b.**,
T-26.........I.2:1 you see is **b.** on "sacrifice" of oneness. It is
T-28......VII.4:6 All miracles are **b.** upon this choice, and
T-29.......II.6:3 for on confusion has this world been **b.**,
W-pI.......7.3:3 to the cup, too, **b.** on past experiences?
W-pI.....76.8:5 Many "religions" have been **b.** on this.
W-pI.....93.2:1 help you see that they are **b.** on nothing.
W-pI.....95.9:3 mistakes, **b.** on the first and reinforcing it
W-pI...108.3:3 **b.** upon one frame of reference, from
W-pI...135.2:3 The world is **b.** on this insane belief. And
W-pI...151.1:3 an opinion **b.** on ignorance and doubt. Its
M-4.......IX.2:4 Being **b.** on fearlessness, it is gentle. Being
M-12..........1:7 of himself is **b.** upon God's Judgment, not
M-19..........4:7 an evaluation **b.** entirely on love,–you
S-1...........I.6:2 their asking is not yet **b.** upon acceptance.
S-3........III.2:2 that is **b.** on inequality of any kind. These

### baser 2
T-31.....VII.3:2 as coming from the "**b.**" part of you, and
S-2.........II.2:1 to save a "**b.**" one from what he truly is.

### basic 25
T-1.........V.2:1 The **b.** decision of the miracle-minded is
T-2...........I.4:1 to the **b.** misperception that you have the
T-2.......VII.1:4 with a **b.** law of cause and effect; the most
T-2.....VIII.1:6 This **b.** distinction leads directly into the
T-3.........II.1:1 I have stated that the **b.** concepts referred
T-6.........II.9:4 cannot escape the **b.** laws of mind. You
T-6.......IV.3:1 **b.** fact that the ego cannot know anything
T-6.......V.B.1:1 who believe in separation have a **b.** fear of
T-8.....VIII.5:7 only if the two **b.** premises on which the
T-11.....V.10:1 it, is therefore the **b.** ego threat. Its dream
T-12.........I.9:2 the loss, the **b.** cause of fear is removed.
T-13.VII.10:12 a **b.** cornerstone in the churches it builds
T-21.......V.4:5 but if the **b.** question stems from reason,
T-21.......V.4:6 from reason, the **b.** question is obvious,
T-25......III.1:6 to this world, of God's more **b.** law; that
T-25......IV.2:1 Perception's **b.** law could thus be said,
T-25...VII.11:4 belief except a form of the more **b.** tenet,
T-30......I.17:3 the **b.** law that makes decision powerful,
T-31.....V.13:1 it does not yet approach a **b.** question.
W-pI.....70.1:1 than some form of the **b.** temptation not
W-pI.....71.4:2 in strict accord with the ego's **b.** doctrine,
W-pI...103.2:3 This **b.** error we will try again to bring to
W-pI...156.1:3 It follows surely from the **b.** thought so
W-pI...170.9:4 Here is the **b.** premise which enthrones
M-17..........5:1 perceived magic thoughts is a **b.** cause of

### basically 2
T-15.....VII.8:6 Ideas are **b.** of no concern, except as they
W-pI...126.4:1 Thus is forgiveness **b.** unsound; a

### basis 48
T-2...........I.4:3 is the real **b.** for your escape from fear.
T-3......III.1:10 True perception is the **b.** for knowledge,
T-3........III.5:7 say you are acting on the **b.** of knowledge,
T-5.......II.8:12 It is made on the **b.** of which call is worth
T-7.......VII.8:5 the ultimate **b.** for all the ego's projection.
T-8...........I.2:6 not want them on the **b.** of loss of peace,
T-8...........I.4:2 **b.** alone its value should be questioned. If
T-11......VI.1:2 are built up on the **b.** of experience, and
T-13......VI.4:7 future on the **b.** of your past experience,
T-14.......X.6:1 no **b.** at all for ordering your thoughts.
T-15.......V.1:3 experience is the **b.** on which you judge.
T-15......VI.8:3 and with it goes the whole **b.** for exclusion
T-15......VII.1:6 This is not the **b.** for any relationship in
T-15...VII.10:3 attempt is the only **b.** the ego accepts for
T-15.......XI.5:5 when the **b.** of your attempts is the belief
T-16......III.1:5 the **b.** of a very different thought system,
T-16.......V.6:4 and the **b.** for the attempt at union rests
T-16......VII.1:4 What **b.** would you have for choosing a
T-17......IV.7:2 The underlying **b.** for their effectiveness is
T-17....IV.12:7 And only on this **b.** are you really free to
T-18..........II.h The **B.** of the Dream
T-25......VII.2:2 **b.** of a world He did not make be firm and
T-25......VII.5:1 you see to something else; a **b.** not insane,
T-25......VII.6:4 Love is the **b.** for a world perceived as
T-26......III.6:1 is no **b.** for a choice in this complex and
T-29.......II.6:4 Its **b.** does not change, although it seems
T-29......IV.1:3 equal lack of truth becomes the **b.** for the
T-30......VI.3:3 when you perceive the **b.** of forgiveness is
W-pI.....10.1:4 You have no **b.** for comparison as yet.
W-pI.....29.1:5 Today's idea is the whole **b.** for vision.
W-pI.....31.1:4 you apply the idea on a more sustained **b.**
W-pI.....46.2:1 Love is nevertheless the **b.** of forgiveness.
W-pI.....54.3:3 it could form the **b.** of the world I see. Yet
W-pI...101.5:5 today, because it is the **b.** for today's idea.
W-pI.135.16:2 before becomes the **b.** for its future goals.
W-pI...186.7:2 it does not know, sensing its **b.** crumble.
W-pII..327.1:1 on the **b.** of an unsupported faith. For
M-in..........2:5 teach on the **b.** of what you want to learn.
M-4.....I.A.4:2 he must now decide all things on the **b.** of
M-5.......II.2:1 it would use the body, is the **b.** of healing.
M-7...........5:1 The real **b.** for doubt about the outcome
M-8...........1:1 is the **b.** for the world's perception. It
M-8...........4:4 best. What **b.** could be faultier than this?
M-9...........1:9 old thought system still has a **b.** for return
M-10.........4:4 such an arbitrary **b.** for decision making?
M-19.........1:2 is the **b.** for all the judgments of the world
M-29.........3:6 of functions not your own is the **b.** of fear.
P-2........IV.8:3 Herein lies the **b.** of all errors, for all of

### basket 1
W-pI.....29.5:9 *God is in that waste **b.***. In addition to the

### battle 27
T-4.........II.9:3 The so-called "**b.** for survival" is only the
T-23.........I.6:1 yourself is but the **b.** of two illusions,
T-23.........I.7:4 Illusions **b.** only with themselves. Being
T-23.........I.7:8 about yourself can **b.** with another, yet
T-23.........I.8:7 of nothing cannot win reality through **b.**.
T-23........I.11:6 do **b.** only to establish which form is true.
T-23......IV.5:7 this choice shows you the **b.** is not real,
T-23......IV.5:8 Bodies may **b.**, but the clash of forms is
T-23....IV.5:10 How can a **b.** be perceived as nothingness
T-23......IV.6:1 remember you *can* see the **b.** from above.
T-23......IV.7:7 limits it exerts on those in **b.** still are gone
T-23......IV.9:1 in their awareness could never think of **b.**.
T-24.........I.9:5 ground of **b.** which you wage against him.
T-24.......V.7:3 hear no more the sound of **b.** and of death
T-26......IX.1:4 His chosen home, and **b.** with His host.
T-30....III.10:3 no sound of **b.** comes remotely near, it
T-31.......II.1:3 There is no **b.** that must be prepared; no
T-31.......II.1:4 ancient **b.** being waged against the truth,
W-pI.....66.2:1 ego does constant **b.** with the Holy Spirit
W-pI.....66.2:2 do constant **b.** with the Holy Spirit about
W-pI.....66.2:3 It is not a two-way **b.**. The ego attacks and
W-pI.....66.3:1 to go past this wholly meaningless **b.** and
W-pI.....93.5:6 It does not **b.** with the Son of God. It does
W-pI.182.12:7 for all the toys of **b.** you have made. And
W-pII.....8.2:1 sounds of **b.** which your world contains.
M-17.........6:1 How can this unfair **b.** be resolved? Its
M-17.........6:5 Forget the **b.**. Accept it as a fact, and then

### battlefield 1
T-23....III.6:12 offer safety? Can guilt be absent from a **b.**

### battleground 14
T-23.......I.12:8 in minds that have become illusions' **b.**.
T-23......III.6:3 The door is open; you have left the **b.**.
T-23......III.6:5 There *is* no safety in a **b.**. You can look
T-23.........IV.h Above the **B.**
T-23......IV.4:5 your relationship is raised above the **b.**, in
T-23......IV.4:7 overlooking of the **b.** is now your purpose
T-23......IV.7:1 See no one from the **b.**, for there you look
T-23......IV.8:7 you think the **b.** can offer something you
T-23......IV.9:3 everything fought for on the **b.** is of the
T-23......IV.9:5 from the quiet sphere above the **b.**. What
T-25......III.3:5 to set it off; the perfect **b.** to wage its wars,
T-27.......V.3:3 from the place of peace into the **b.**, and
T-29........II.3:1 to find the hope of peace upon a **b.**. It has
M-27.........2:7 life's symbol. His world is now a **b.**, where

### battles 2
T-12.........I.4:2 to engage in endless "**b.**" with reality, in
T-13......XI.1:5 torn in endless **b.** if he himself perceives

### battling 1
T-3.......VII.2:5 **b.** Him for possession of His creations.

### bay 3
T-31......III.5:1 it chose and guards and holds itself at **b.**,
P-2.........V.1:6 if these forces can be held at **b.** only by an
S-3..........II.6:2 It can be held at **b.** a little while, and there

### be 5913

### bear 19
T-1.........I.14:1 Miracles **b.** witness to truth. They are
T-8.........V.3:7 The miracles we do **b.** witness to the Will
T-13......VI.9:2 whom you heal **b.** witness to your healing
T-13........X.1:4 to which they **b.** no real relationship at all
T-18......IX.3:2 these messages **b.** witness to this world,
T-26.........I.7:3 and make your eyes and ears **b.** witness to
T-27.....VII.5:5 effects, which then **b.** witness to the cause
T-28.......V.5:3 a dream; your ears **b.** witness to illusion.
T-30......IV.2:2 soft and silent woolly **b.** begins to squeak
W-pI.....43.5:9 The thoughts need not **b.** any obvious
W-pI...103.2:2 in truth, **b.** witness to the fear of God,
W-pI...151.7:3 merely **b.** false witness to God's Son. He
W-pI...154.6:4 they did not write the messages they **b.**,
W-pI...169.4:3 urge you to **b.** witness to the Word of God
W-pI...169.7:2 the experiences which **b.** witness that the
W-pI...188.1:5 **b.** the light in you are alien here as well.
W-pII.255.1:4 let the peace I choose be mine today **b.**
W-pII.262.1:6 *For Your Son must **b.** Your Name, for You*
S-2..........II.4:5 how good are you who **b.** with patience

### bearer 2
C-5............6:4 Jesus is for you the **b.** of Christ's single
S-3........III.4:5 not make yourself the **b.** of the special gift

### bearers 1
W-pII.266.1:1 *in sight; the **b.** of Your holy Voice to me. In*

### bearing 3
T-5......VI.10:3 is **b.** false witness to God Himself. Appeal
W-pI...126.2:2 ways which have no **b.** on your thoughts,

P-3 I.4:5 They come **b.** God. Would he refuse this

**bears** 13

T-3 VII.6:1 The branch that **b.** no fruit will be cut off
T-24 II.12:3 No gift that **b.** its seal but offers treachery
T-25 IX.7:3 He cannot perceive He **b.** no witness to.
T-27 VII.1:6 still, for it is he who **b.** the suffering. And
T-27 VII.6:5 And it is this the world **b.** witness to. Seek
T-30 IV.2:3 made for boxes and for **b.** have failed him
T-30 IV.2:5 the boxes and the **b.** did not deceive him,
T-31 V.2:2 It **b.** no likeness to yourself at all. It is an
W-pI 45.1:5 Nothing that you think you see **b.** any
W-pI 121.5:3 what it sees **b.** witness that its judgment is
W-pI 151.9:2 He **b.** witness to your beautiful creation,
W-pII 288.1:9 *But let me honor him who **b.** Your Name,*
M-17 7:13 who **b.** this stain on him must meet with

**beat** 4

T-20 V.2:3 hearts of everyone, to let them **b.** as one.
T-25 IV.3:2 that look on sin and **b.** its sad refrain.
T-28 VII.7:3 blow upon it and the rain will **b.** against it
W-pI 169.11:5 that does not **b.** as yet in tune with God.

**beaten** 1

T-6 I.9:2 them, I was betrayed, abandoned, **b.**, torn

**beatific** 1

T-1 VII.5:8 experience will be more traumatic than **b.**

**beating** 3

T-3 I.2:7 you," and feels exonerated in **b.** a child.
W-pII 267.h My heart is **b.** in the peace of God.
W-pII 267.2:2 *is **b.** in the peace the Heart of Love created. It*

**beats** 1

T-30 V.10:8 **b.** in hope and does not pound in fear.

**beautiful** 35

T-1 VII.2:1 to create the good, the **b.** and the holy. Do
T-2 III.1:9 The emphasis on **b.** structures is a sign of
T-3 V.10:6 How **b.** indeed are the Thoughts of God
T-5 in.3:5 children are worthy channels of His **b.** joy
T-5 in.3:5 they are **b.** enough to hold it by sharing it.
T-6 IV.6:8 for you, because they are **b.** and true.
T-8 VII.3:4 service of uniting it becomes a **b.** lesson in
T-8 VII.4:3 The body is **b.** or ugly, peaceful or savage,
T-11 VIII.8:1 **B.** child of God, you are asking only for
T-13 VIII.6:1 the same; all **b.** and equal in their holiness
T-15 I.8:6 is so **b.** and so clean and free of guilt that
T-17 II.1:1 how **b.** those you forgive will look to you?
T-18 I.11:1 for in it lies the Sonship, whole and **b.**,
T19 IV.A.13:4 To them such things are **b.**, because they
T19 IV.A.14:3 they will see only the blameless and the **b.**
T19 IV.D.14:2 How holy and how **b.** He is! You thought
T-20 III.6:3 is **b.** because they see their innocence in it
T-21 III.9:9 that makes the sight of it as **b.** as Heaven.
T-22 IV.4:2 think how **b.** will you and your brother
T-22 IV.4:6 How **b.** the sight you saw beyond the veil,
T-23 in.6:5 How **b.** it is to walk, clean and redeemed
T-23 III.2:3 empty box, however **b.** and gently given,
T-24 V.3:7 How **b.** His hand that holds His brother's,
T-25 V.5:4 How **b.** his sinlessness will be when you
T-28 VII.2:1 The **b.** relationship you have with all
W-pI 28.5:2 something **b.** and clean and of infinite
W-pI 121.11:4 him, and makes the picture **b.** and good.
W-pI 135.5:4 gifts to make it **b.** or walls to make it safe,
W-pI 151.9:2 for He bears witness to your **b.** creation,
W-pI 161.9:3 so holy and so **b.** that you could scarce
W-pI 193.2:5 and **b.** enough to let the light of Heaven
W-pII 313.2:2 How **b.** we are! How holy and how loving!
M-12 6:9 real than to regard it as healthy and **b.**.
M-23 5:7 and no stain to mar your **b.** perfection. In

P-2 VI.2:5 make this ugly sound seem truly **b.**. "The

**beauty** 27

T-2 III.1:10 The real **b.** of the temple cannot be seen
T-4 I.12:5 **b.** and dignity are far beyond doubt,
T-5 IV.8:2 All your past except its **b.** is gone, and
T-11 III.3:3 such **b.** that you will know it is not of you.
T-11 III.3:4 of your joy you will create **b.** in His Name,
T-11 VIII.10:6 and you will see your **b.** reflected in his.
T-13 V.11:7 all the **b.** of the world to shine upon them.
T-13 VI.10:9 them. And seeing it, its **b.** calls you home.
T-16 VI.10:2 the illusion of the **b.** and holiness of guilt.
T-16 VI.10:5 See no illusion of truth and **b.** there. And
T-16 VI.10:6 *is* a place where truth and **b.** wait for you.
T-17 II.1:7 will behold the **b.** the Holy Spirit loves to
T-17 II.2:6 all ugliness into **b.** that will enchant you,
T-17 II.4:1 that opened up the world to **b.** will vanish
T-17 II.5:4 His reason touches grows alive with **b.**,
T-17 II.5:5 spark of **b.** that gentleness could release.
T-17 II.6:1 All this **b.** will rise to bless your sight as
T-17 II.8:5 into the real world of **b.** and forgiveness.
T-17 III.5:7 is the spark of **b.** hidden in the ugliness of
T-17 III.5:7 is given to Him Who gives it life and **b.**.
T-17 III.6:7 hidden spark of **b.** in your relationships,
T-17 III.6:11 conditions in which this **b.** can be seen.
T-17 III.9:3 choose you will endow with **b.** and reality,
T-17 III.9:4 The spark of **b.** or the veil of ugliness, the
T19 IV.A.15:2 of all guilt and softly brushed with **b.**. The
T-29 VIII.8:8 not really matter more of what; more **b.**,
W-pI 122.1:4 of worth and **b.** that transcends the world

**became** 26

T-2 VIII.2:4 **b.** one of the many learning devices to be
T-7 II.5:7 disinherited yourself you **b.** a learner of
T-11 II.6:3 for His function **b.** yours with His gift.
T-11 V.6:3 **b.** as dependent on you as you are on Him
T-12 VIII.3:1 is not true, what *is* true **b.** invisible to you.
T-14 III.6:5 he **b.** afraid of darkness and of light. The
T-14 V.10:2 Only the resurrection **b.** my part in it.
T-17 IV.1:3 relationships **b.** forever "to make happy."
T-17 V.1:6 in which the relationship **b.** what it is.
T-17 VIII.6:1 **b.** a giver of peace as surely as your Father
T-18 I.6:2 **b.** the screen on which it was projected
T-18 I.12:3 And what **b.** of peace in those who heard?
T19 IV.A.17:2 For I **b.** the symbol of your sin, and so I
T-25 VI.6:8 grace. His special hate **b.** his special love.
T-26 VII.11:5 is the miracle by which creation **b.** your
T-29 I.3:8 **b.** the treaty that you had made with him.
W-pI 162.2:1 the Word by which the Son **b.** his Father's
W-pI 196.10:5 thus a god outside yourself **b.** your mortal
W-pII 2.2:4 the split **b.** a part of every fragment of the
W-pII 329.1:5 *where my will **b.** forever one with Yours.*
C-5 2:2 So he **b.** identified with *Christ*, a man no
C-5 3:1 Him–Jesus **b.** what all of you must be.
C-6 1:1 or **b.** completely identified with the Christ
P-2 VII.4:5 patient's errors thus **b.** his own failures,
P-2 VII.4:5 his own failures, and guilt **b.** the cover,
P-3 II.2:2 because the curriculum by which he **b.** a

**because** 2180

**become** 280

T-1 III.1:5 you naturally **b.** part of the Atonement
T-1 IV.1:5 When you have **b.** willing to hide nothing
T-1 V.1:1 a state in which they **b.** unnecessary.
T-1 V.3:4 "Except ye **b.** as little children" means
T-1 V.5:4 mind can **b.** the medium by which spirit
T-1 VI.2:4 As you integrate you **b.** one, and your
T-1 VI.2:4 one, and your needs **b.** one accordingly.
T-1 VII.3:11 Fantasies **b.** totally unnecessary as the
T-1 VII.4:5 you may **b.** much too fearful of what is to
T-2 II.5:6 and can **b.** a better and better learner.
T-2 II.7:8 and as you **b.** more and more secure you
T-2 III.3:9 as conflict, which can **b.** very acute. But
T-2 VIII.1:2 apt to forget this when you **b.** egocentric,
T-2 VIII.2:7 number **b.** truly miracle-minded, this
T-3 V.2:1 "create" and "make" have **b.** confused.
T-3 V.3:2 that it has **b.** literally impossible for you
T-3 V.5:5 Your mind may have **b.** very ingenious,
T-3 VII.5:9 enough, and that is why you **b.** so fearful.
T-4 I.10:1 and **b.** totally without investment in fear.
T-4 II.5:5 the effort to **b.** both harmless and helpful,
T-4 II.7:9 which has **b.** completely confused about
T-4 VI.8:1 withdraw from him I **b.** distant to you.
T-5 I.1:1 minds perceive their oneness and **b.** glad.
T-5 I.2:3 *who believe in them the stronger they **b.**.*
T-5 III.2:10 as you **b.** aware of the Call for God in him,
T-5 V.1:1 some of our concepts will **b.** clearer and
T-5 VII.5:2 Perceiving this as "sin" you **b.** defensive
T-6 I.6:11 with me, and we will **b.** equal as teachers.
T-6 IV.7:6 once certain in your mind has **b.** only the
T-6 V.A.4:2 by now, but it has not yet **b.** believable.
T-7 I.2:8 claim this power when you **b.** vigilant
T-7 IV.3:6 goal, the abilities themselves **b.** unified.
T-7 VI.7:4 and vigilance has therefore **b.** essential.
T-7 XI.4:4 Everyone who learns this lesson has **b.** the
T-8 VII.8:2 suffers, and he must **b.** depressed. Being
T-8 VII.9:7 sense the body does **b.** a temple to God;
T-8 VIII.6:9 The more complicated the results **b.** the
T-9 VI.1:1 How can you **b.** increasingly aware of the
T-9 VI.5:4 They will **b.** the witnesses to your reality,
T-9 VII.4:6 your motives as soon as they **b.** clearly out
T-9 VIII.1:3 Whenever you **b.** aware of it, however
T-10 III.6:5 you do not value yourself you **b.** sick, but
T-10 IV.3:6 and then the mind does **b.** unreasonable.
T-10 V.14:6 to **b.** preoccupied with the temporal, you
T-11 II.2:1 it the better teacher and learner you **b.**. If
T-11 V.10:7 then, you have **b.** afraid of yourself. And
T-11 VI.3:6 you will **b.** less and less willing to deny.
T-11 VIII.1:7 For as Heaven and earth **b.** one, even the
T-11 VIII.2:1 The Bible tells you to **b.** as little children.
T-11 VIII.10:3 **b.** willing to accept this Help by asking for
T-12 I.5:2 truth to him has **b.** what he wants it to be.
T-12 III.3:1 Whenever you **b.** angry with a brother,
T-12 III.7:7 You have **b.** at odds with the world as you
T-12 V.8:6 you will **b.** an excellent learner and an
T-12 VI.6:3 because perception has **b.** so holy that its
T-12 VI.6:7 perception and knowledge have **b.** so
T-12 VII.4:5 **b.** compellingly real to you as its presence
T-12 VII.11:5 Yet as I **b.** more real to you, you will learn
T-12 VIII.8:5 Nothingness will **b.** invisible, for you will
T-13 II.6:4 **b.** increasingly convinced that this is so.
T-13 VI.12:3 Those who accept love of you **b.** your
T-13 VII.13:3 He will ensure it never can **b.** a dark spot,
T-13 VII.13:6 However holy his perception may **b.**, no
T-13 IX.4:2 guilt has **b.** as true for you as innocence.
T-13 IX.6:6 as guilty **b.** the witnesses to guilt in you,
T-13 XI.1:1 and sleep and even death **b.** the ego's best
T-14 I.5:2 which has **b.** so twisted and so complex
T-14 II.4:9 they will **b.** your teachers in release and
T-14 IV.6:1 all decisions **b.** as easy and as right as
T-14 V.3:7 learners of the Atonement **b.** the teachers
T-14 IX.5:1 In this world you can **b.** a spotless mirror
T-14 XI.12:1 who have **b.** willing to learn everything,
T-15 I.1:4 until you have **b.** such a consistent learner
T-15 VII.4:6 invest outside yourself, the safer you **b.**.
T-15 VII.5:5 know, but you will **b.** willing to find out,
T-15 VIII.4:6 Christ, where they **b.** like to their Father.
T-15 IX.1:3 you will **b.** willing to make it permanent.
T-15 X.7:1 How fearful, then, has God **b.** to you, and
T-15 XI.1:3 your Father have **b.** very fearful to you.
T-16 V.11:2 fearful has the truth **b.** to you that unless
T-16 V.16:3 How simple does this choice **b.** when it is
T-16 VI.5:2 in separate unions and to **b.** one by losing
T-16 VI.5:3 When two individuals seek to **b.** one, they
T-16 VI.11:3 it will join with you and **b.** one with you.
T-17 I.1:7 for only then does it **b.** perfectly apparent
T-17 I.6:5 **b.** disturbed and lose your peace of mind
T-17 II.7:3 Even salvation will **b.** a dream, and vanish
T-17 III.2:6 such relationships **b.** attempts at union
T-17 III.6:10 and **b.** increasingly unwilling to let it be
T-17 V.5:7 may even **b.** quite disorganized. And yet,
T-18 I.4:3 It has **b.** so splintered and subdivided and
T-18 II.3:5 People **b.** what you would have them be,

T-18 II.6:9 its holiness will **b.** an offering to everyone
T-18 II.8:4 your brother has now **b.** one in which the
T-18 IV.8:2 you have **b.** the arbiter of what is possible,
T-18 V.5:5 It will **b.** the happy dream through which
T-18 VI.11:6 And both **b.** whole, as neither is perceived
T-19 I.8:1 your own identification has **b.** because of
T-19 III.1:3 Fear can **b.** so acute that the sin is denied
T19 IV.A.4:2 For such have you **b.**. Peace could no
T19 IV.B.12:5 invites fear to enter and **b.** your purpose.
T-20 II.7:5 your vision has **b.** the greatest power for
T-20 III.10:5 any separation between us **b.** impossible.
T-21 I.4:1 The blind **b.** accustomed to their world
T-21 III.7:1 Faith and belief **b.** attached to vision, as
T-22 I.6:7 about him will **b.** to him his comforters,
T-22 III.9:6 must **b.** impossible for each to see himself
T-22 IV.3:9 You will **b.** His messenger, returning Him
T-22 IV.5:8 have **b.** its willing guardian and protector.
T-22 VI.6:9 of a relationship that has **b.** the means of
T-22 VI.12:12 seems as if love could attack and **b.** fearful
T-23 in.2:2 for sin can hurt you and **b.** your enemy.
T-23 I.12:8 minds that have **b.** illusions' battleground
T-23 II.7:3 He has **b.** the "enemy" Who caused it, to
T-23 II.7:6 because the Savior has **b.** the enemy.
T-23 III.4:7 it **b.** impossible that you lose sight of it? It
T-24 I.2:3 to **b.** beliefs now given power to direct all
T-24 I.4:3 thus does specialness **b.** a means and end
T-24 I.5:6 brother must **b.** to keep your specialness
T-24 VII.10:7 Thus does the "son" **b.** the means to serve
T-25 VI.2:1 Eyes **b.** used to darkness, and the light of
T-25 VI.5:11 thus **b.** a means to save instead of lose.
T-25 IX.9:1 that you keep and hide **b.** your secret sins,
T-26 I.5:3 **b.** a treasure house as rich and limitless as
T-26 IV.5:1 a world that will **b.** an altar to the truth,
T-26 VIII.3:4 you still, and let you instantly **b.** as one.
T-26 IX.3:2 now **b.** a living temple in a world of light.
T-26 IX.6:1 an ancient hatred has **b.** a present love.
T-27 I.10:3 The body can **b.** a sign of life, a promise of
T-27 II.11:4 And thus does he **b.** your victim, not your
T-27 II.13:4 sins **b.** the central target for correction,
T-27 III.4:1 **b.** a silent invitation to the truth to enter,
T-27 VII.12:2 yet another, in which you **b.** the murderer
T-27 VIII.6:3 his forgetting did the thought **b.** a serious
T-28 IV.1:7 And you **b.** a figure in his dream of pain,
T-28 IV.1:8 do you and your brother both **b.** illusions,
T-28 IV.5:3 when you **b.** a passive figure in his dreams
T-29 II.6:6 and shift and change **b.** the law on which
T-29 IV.4:2 this **b.** the "reason" your attack is justified
T-29 IV.5:1 How happy would your dreams **b.** if you
T-29 IX.10:2 and dreams **b.** a sign that you have made
T-30 I.1:4 wise to let yourself **b.** preoccupied with
T-30 I.4:3 first arise and then **b.** a problem in itself.
T-30 VI.1:9 your pardon will **b.** the answer to attack
T-30 VI.10:4 For he has **b.** to you a graven image and a
T-30 VII.5:6 In one united goal does this **b.** impossible
T-31 I.1:9 and just what to do if you **b.** confused.
T-31 III.1:3 It must **b.** a habit of response so typical of
T-31 III.4:6 of the mind that would **b.** its prisoner.
T-31 V.6:2 For what you are has now **b.** his sin. For
W-pI 1.3:5 for these exercises should not **b.** ritualistic
W-pI 4.5:4 a tendency to **b.** pointlessly preoccupied.
W-pI 10.1:1 aware, or **b.** aware in the practice periods.
W-pI 12.2:4 the shift to **b.** markedly longer or shorter,
W-pI 21.2:5 You will **b.** increasingly aware that a
W-pI 25.1:7 recognizing this that your goals **b.** unified
W-pI 27.2:2 **b.** uneasy about the lack of reservation
W-pI 30.5:3 to **b.** more accustomed to this idea as well
W-pI 33.3:2 arises which tempts you to **b.** disturbed.
W-pI 39.9:4 will **b.** much easier as your mind becomes
W-pI 43.1:5 God, perception will **b.** so changed and
W-pI 43.2:4 it must **b.** the means for the restoration of
W-pI 43.6:2 **b.** preoccupied with irrelevant thoughts.
W-pI 46.7:3 when you **b.** aware of any kind of negative
W-pI 65.6:1 interfering thoughts will **b.** harder to find
W-pI 66.3:3 will not **b.** hopelessly involved in defining
W-pI 68.1:7 that He is like what you think you have **b.**,
W-pI 68.2:4 has **b.** fearful to him in his dream of hate.
W-pI 68.5:4 It will quickly **b.** apparent that there is no
W-pI 71.8:3 allow yourself to **b.** depressed or angry at
W-pI 72.10:1 to **b.** aware that God's plan for salvation
W-pI 73.2:3 figures **b.** the middlemen the ego employs
W-pI 82.1:3 the means by which I **b.** aware of the light
W-pI 87.3:3 I can **b.** afraid only when I believe there is
W-pI 91.3:2 It is very difficult to **b.** convinced that it is
W-pI 93.11:2 you be tempted to **b.** angry with someone
W-pI 101.4:5 is real, salvation has **b.** your bitter enemy,
W-pI 103.2:1 results **b.** the heritage of minds that think
W-pI 105.3:2 For giving has **b.** a source of fear, and so
W-pI 106.6:5 and thus **b.** the joyous giver of what you
W-pI 108.2:2 It is a state of mind that has **b.** so unified
W-pI 121.7:3 It has no hope, but you **b.** its hope. And
W-pI 121.7:4 And as its hope, do you **b.** your own. The
W-pI 123.6:1 for you **b.** the messenger who brings His
W-pI 135.20:1 you **b.** a light which Heaven gratefully
W-pI 136.6:3 they **b.** symbols standing for attack upon
W-pI 136.18:4 it well, for sickness has **b.** impossible.
W-pI 137.11:1 are healed **b.** the instruments of healing.
W-pI 138.3:2 of conflicting goals **b.** the aim of effort
W-pI 153.3:2 **b.** the circles of the hours and the days
W-pI 154.3:1 **b.** aware at last there is one Voice in you.
W-pI 154.6:3 that they **b.** able to bring them further,
W-pI 154.6:4 **b.** their first receivers in the truest sense,
W-pI 154.8:2 For thus do you **b.** His messenger. You
W-pI 157.7:1 and all goals but this **b.** of little worth, the
W-pI 159.8:6 And they **b.** His messengers, who give as
W-pI 161.6:3 the reason bodies easily **b.** fear's symbols.
W-pI 163.5:1 he has **b.** what death would have him be.
W-pI 166.3:2 God's gifts, however evident they may **b.**,
W-pI 166.15:2 **B.** the living proof of what Christ's touch
W-pI 169.3:6 **b.** aware that there are things it does not
W-pI 170.6:1 love as enemy, must cruelty **b.** a god. And
WpI rV.in10:1 Let this review **b.** a time in which we
Wi181-200 2:5 that words **b.** of little consequence. You
W-pI 181.3:1 need to let our sinlessness **b.** apparent.
W-pI 181.8:6 This will **b.** the only thing we see reflected
W-pI 182.9:2 For He was willing to **b.** a little Child that
W-pI 183.4:5 They **b.** anonymous and valueless to you,
W-pI 183.6:2 **B.** oblivious to every name but His. Hear
W-pI 183.6:4 Let all your thoughts **b.** anchored on this.
W-pI 183.8:3 and let His Name **b.** the all-encompassing
W-pI 183.10:4 His Father's Thoughts **b.** his own. He
W-pI 184.4:4 **b.** the threats which it must overcome,
W-pI 184.9:5 They **b.** but means by which you can
W-pI 185.3:1 Two minds with one intent **b.** so strong
W-pI 188.2:3 which prove it is not there **b.** ridiculous.
W-pI 188.6:6 **b.** the holy messengers of God Himself.
W-pI 189.10:9 *in the world, that it* ***b.*** *a part of Heaven now.*
W-pI 192.8:5 that limit him **b.** the world in which his
W-pI 197.2:2 and weakness must **b.** salvation to you.
W-pI 197.2:3 yourself as bound, and bars **b.** your home
WpI rVI.in.7:4 **b.** a loving gift of freedom to the world.
W-pII 3.2:7 Now mistakes **b.** quite possible, for
W-pII 3.4:2 Sounds **b.** the call for God, and all
W-pII 4.4:3 The Son of God may play he has **b.** a body
W-pII 269.1:2 *which You have chosen to* ***b.*** *the way to show*
W-pII 276.1:3 did God **b.** the Father of the Son He loves,
W-pII 318.2:2 *reconciled in me* ***b.*** *as surely reconciled to*
W-pII 12.2:3 thinks it has **b.** a victor over God Himself.
W-pII 356.1:2 *his problem, nor what he believes he has* ***b.***.
M-in 5:6 Yet it is their mission to **b.** perfect here,
M-1 1:7 He has **b.** a bringer of salvation. He has
M-1 1:8 of salvation. He has **b.** a teacher of God.
M-1 3:8 He has **b.** a savior by his answering. He
M-3 2:5 him; perhaps the students will **b.** friends.
M-3 4:6 the destiny of all relationships to **b.** holy.
M-3 5:7 they **b.** the saviors of the teachers who
M-4 1:6 **b.** characteristic of all teachers of God
M-4 I.A.8:3 as merely shadows before **b.** solid gains,
M-4 VI.1:6 No one can **b.** an advanced teacher of
M-5 III.1:4 for they have **b.** teachers of God with him.
M-7 2:6 His position has thus **b.** untenable, for he
M-7 6:3 and you have **b.** deceived about yourself.
M-10 2:4 He has actually merely **b.** more honest.
M-12 2:1 does the son of man **b.** the Son of God. It
M-12 4:2 **b.** more and more certain that the body's
M-12 5:1 what you use the body for it will **b.** to you.
M-16 2:5 they easily **b.** gods in their own right,
M-18 3:4 little space and tiny breath **b.** the measure
M-22 3:7 The body has **b.** lord of the mind. How
M-23 2:4 He has **b.** the risen Son of God. He has
M-23 2:8 So has his name **b.** the Name of God, for
M-23 5:6 **b.** the symbol of his Father here on earth.
M-23 6:6 No one who has **b.** a true and dedicated
M-24 4:2 validity of reincarnation **b.** meaningless.
M-27 2:6 Death has **b.** life's symbol. His world is
C-3 7:2 Even the wished-for can **b.** unwelcome.
C-3 8:1 How lovely does the world **b.** in just that
P-1 4:2 He must **b.** willing to reverse his thinking,
P-2 I.3:6 **b.** completely reconciled as one until they
P-2 II.2:5 At the highest levels they **b.** one. Neither
P-2 IV.9:6 And since this picture has **b.** the patient's
P-2 VI.1:8 To question it must then **b.** his choice.
P-2 VII.4:3 healer would instantly **b.** a teacher of God
P-3 II.5:4 the therapeutic relationship must **b.** like
S-1 in.1:2 It was then what it is to **b.**; the single
S-1 I.4:4 There they **b.** your gifts to Him, for they
S-1 II.5:5 It has **b.** a statement of the unity of Christ
S-1 II.5:6 sinlessness. And now it has **b.** holy, for it
S-1 II.6:4 Christ. Before it can **b.** holy, then, prayer
S-1 II.7:7 can again **b.** what it was meant to be. For
S-1 V.4:6 Prayer has **b.** what it was meant to be, for
S-2 I.1:2 It has, in fact, **b.** a scourge; a curse where
S-2 I.2:6 God's mercy has **b.** a twisted knife that
S-2 II.6:5 How fearful has forgiveness now **b.**, and
S-2 III.2:3 the eyes of Christ **b.** the sight you choose.
S-2 III.6:7 sin and death **b.** again the holy gift of God
S-3 I.4:5 him the body may **b.** his chosen home,
S-3 III.1:2 Its separate goals **b.** quite clear in this, for
S-3 IV.5:8 loss **b.** the lot of everyone on earth, which

## becomes 298

T-1 III.7:6 bring in the stranger, he **b.** your brother.
T-1 V.3:7 of anything, their perception **b.** distorted.
T-1 VII.3:11 **b.** apparent to both giver and receiver.
T-2 II.4:8 The Atonement thus **b.** the only defense
T-2 III.3:4 in the extreme, **b.** altogether intolerable.
T-2 III.3:7 recognition **b.** more firmly established, it
T-2 III.3:7 firmly established, it **b.** a turning point.
T-2 III.4:7 the mind **b.** increasingly sensitive to what
T-2 V.6:2 it **b.** a serious obstruction to the very
T-2 V.8:5 your state **b.** doubly dangerous unless it *is*
T-2 VI.5:9 and your behavior inevitably **b.** erratic.
T-2 VI.7:3 of correction **b.** nothing more than a
T-2 VII.3:10 effect principle now **b.** a real expediter,
T-3 II.2:4 until their innocence **b.** a viewpoint with
T-3 II.2:4 universal application that it **b.** wisdom.
T-3 III.6:7 **b.** "Know God and accept His certainty."
T-3 V.6:4 in the usual sense **b.** utterly meaningless.
T-3 V.8:2 Perception **b.** impossible. Truth can only
T-4 II.7:2 its grasp, and charity **b.** impossible. The
T-4 V.4:5 Here is where the mind **b.** actually dazed.
T-4 VI.5:5 It gradually **b.** desirable as he changes his
T-4 VII.1:3 Part of the mind **b.** concrete, however,
T-4 VII.4:5 **b.** total only by recognizing all reality in
T-5 III.8:8 The ego **b.** strong in strife. If you believe
T-5 V.8:8 ordering of thought **b.** quite apparent.
T-5 VI.8:2 It **b.** merely an attempt to guarantee the
T-5 VI.9:1 shall perish" **b.** a statement of Atonement
T-6 II.1:5 it occurs projection **b.** its main defense, or
T-6 V.A.5:5 is sharing it **b.** communion. Perhaps you
T-7 X.5:7 given this confusion, trust **b.** impossible.
T-7 XI.2:3 Everything he does **b.** a strain, because he
T-8 I.6:1 a real change in direction **b.** possible. You
T-8 IV.2:12 The light **b.** ours, and you cannot abide in
T-8 V.5:6 regards itself as rejected and **b.** retaliative.
T-8 VII.3:4 service of uniting it **b.** a beautiful lesson
T-8 VII.4:5 the body **b.** a means you give to the Holy
T-8 VII.9:5 **b.** a means by which the part of the mind
T-8 VII.9:6 The ego's temple thus **b.** the temple of the
T-8 VII.13:5 it **b.** whole because the mind's purpose is
T-9 III.5:4 Unless this **b.** the one way in which you
T-9 VI.3:4 as you call upon it in them it **b.** real to you
T-9 VIII.1:3 of the ego **b.** perfectly apparent. When
T-10 IV.6:1 God, the making of idols **b.** inconceivable
T-11 in.3:4 thought system, the clearer the light **b.**.
T-11 in.3:5 the darker and more obscure **b.** the way.
T-11 II.2:1 thus **b.** a lesson in understanding, and the

T-11....... II.5:4 and the little spark **b.** a blazing light that
T-11....... II.5:4 your mind so that He **b.** your only Guest.
T-11....... V.4:3 Fear **b.** more obviously inappropriate if
T-11..... V.12:5 and it **b.** difficult to maintain that fear is
T-11..... V.15:3 This, then, **b.** the universe it perceives.
T-11..... V.15:4 **b.** its demonstration of its own reality.
T-11..... V.18:1 meet **b.** a witness for Christ or for the ego,
T-12.........I.1:5 thus **b.** the justification for the response.
T-12.........I.9:9 predominance, fear **b.** meaningless. You
T-12....... II.1:5 task of the miracle worker thus **b.** *to deny*
T-12....... V.5:3 He **b.** your Resource because of yourself
T-12...... VI.6:5 guidance increases and **b.** generalized.
T-12...... VI.7:2 the holy perception of God's Son **b.** so
T-12...... VI.7:2 the Mind of the Father and **b.** one with it.
T-12..... VII.4:4 cannot see **b.** real to you only through the
T-12..... VII.4:5 as its presence **b.** manifest through you.
T-13...... IV.1:7 When it **b.** overtly savage, it offers you
T-13...... IV.4:4 the past **b.** the determiner of the future,
T-13.... VIII.2:1 and knowledge **b.** quite apparent if you
T-14... III.16:2 this light, error of any kind **b.** impossible.
T-14..... IV.3:6 Atonement **b.** real and visible to those
T-14....... V.8:1 unto everyone who **b.** a teacher of peace.
T-14... V.10:10 The temple you restore **b.** your altar, for it
T-14..... VII.1:8 deceit, for otherwise it **b.** the messenger
T-14..... VII.2:6 it **b.** unreal to you *because* you hid it and
T-14..... VII.2:8 see it, and the clearer what it conceals **b.**.
T-14..... VII.4:4 their joint acceptance **b.** impossible. But
T-14..... VII.4:6 Their joining thus **b.** the source of fear,
T-14....... X.2:2 its truth **b.** the only perception the Son of
T-14...... X.12:6 The miracle **b.** the means of sharing It. By
T-14.... XI.3:10 a condition in which seeing **b.** impossible.
T-15.........I.7:7 for compounding guilt until it **b.** all-
T-15....... V.1:4 Judgment **b.** impossible without the past,
T-15....... V.4:6 every relationship **b.** a lesson in love.
T-15..... V.10:2 united in your blessing it **b.** one to you.
T-15...... VI.5:5 The holy instant thus **b.** a lesson in how
T-15..... VII.6:1 idea that by sacrificing itself, it **b.** bigger.
T-15..... VII.7:7 Forgiveness **b.** impossible, for the ego
T-15... VII.11:6 union of bodies thus **b.** the way in which
T-15...... IX.7:5 The reality of this relationship **b.** the only
T-15...... XI.5:7 attack **b.** salvation and sacrifice becomes
T-15...... XI.5:7 becomes salvation and sacrifice **b.** love.
T-16...... IV.3:7 relationship is broken or **b.** unsatisfying
T-16...... VI.3:4 the more apparent it **b.** that it must foster
T-16..... VII.1:3 **b.** a way in which you seek to restore your
T-16..... VII.5:6 the relationship **b.** your substitute for it.
T-16..... VII.5:7 it. And vengeance **b.** your substitute for
T-16..... VII.5:7 the escape from vengeance **b.** your loss.
T-17....... II.6:3 The smallest leaf **b.** a thing of wonder,
T-17...... III.4:5 of the unholy relationship thus **b.** one in
T-17...... III.4:6 to the relationship, the "better" it **b.**.
T-17...... III.4:7 attempt at union **b.** a way of excluding
T-17...... III.8:1 past **b.** the justification for entering into a
T-17.... IV.13:5 is exposed to light, it **b.** dull and lifeless,
T-17....... V.2:4 it begins, develops and **b.** accomplished,
T-17....... V.4:1 The temptation of the ego **b.** extremely
T-17...... VI.2:5 The situation **b.** the determiner of the
T-17...... VI.4:4 true **b.** what can be used to meet the goal.
T-17...... VI.4:5 false **b.** the useless from this point of view
T-17..... VII.3:6 **b.** the justification for your lack of faith.
T-17.... VIII.3:6 Now it **b.** a fact, from which faith can no
T-18....... II.2:3 violated in them **b.** apparent. Yet they are
T-18.... VI.11:5 It **b.** part of you, as you unite with it. And
T-18.... VIII.3:6 sun **b.** the sunbeam's "enemy" that would
T-18.... VIII.9:3 The desert **b.** a garden, green and deep
T-19.........I.2:1 **b.** an opportunity to heal the Son of God.
T-19.........I.3:5 When this occurs the body **b.** its weapon,
T-19.........I.3:6 body thus **b.** the instrument of illusion,
T-19.........I.4:3 in which uniting with him **b.** impossible.
T-19...... III.9:3 it seems to be seen, and it **b.** invisible.
T19..IV.B.13:4 perception the body **b.** the servant of pain
T-20.........I.1:5 a risen Christ **b.** the symbol of the Son of
T-20...... III.7:8 the universe of truth, **b.** your guide. To it
T-20.... VIII.6:4 it. Destructiveness **b.** benign, and sin is
T-21..... II.10:1 confusion of cause and effect **b.** inevitable
T-21..... II.10:2 purpose now **b.** to keep obscure the cause
T-21... VII.3:11 a child **b.** a giant and a mouse roars like a
T-21... VII.11:4 so the desire **b.** the only one you have. By
T-22.......in.4:8 that lies beneath them all **b.** apparent.
T-22 ........I.3:5 have made to be yourself **b.** your sight.
T-23 ......in.2:1 indeed **b.** this war against yourself! You
T-23 ......I.11:3 temple of the Holy One **b.** a house of sin.
T-23 .......II.4:5 which his own destruction **b.** inevitable.
T-23 .......II.5:6 join. One **b.** weak, the other strong by his
T-23 .......II.7:2 Now it **b.** impossible to turn to Him for
T-23 .......II.8:2 escape. Atonement thus **b.** a myth, and
T-23 .......II.9:4 By this, another's loss **b.** your gain, and
T-24 ........I.8:5 share **b.** obscured from both of you. You
T-24 ..... IV.1:3 Everything else **b.** your enemy; feared and
T-24 ...... V.9:6 His quietness **b.** your certainty. And
T-25 .......II.8:5 His gentleness **b.** your strength, and both
T-25 ..... III.9:8 when all time **b.** a means to reach a goal.
T-25 ..... IX.3:9 punishment **b.** his due instead of justice.
T-25 ... IX.10:2 Each one **b.** an illustration of the law on
T-26 ........I.3:1 little that the body fences off **b.** the self,
T-26 ........I.3:4 bodies **b.** the sign that sacrifice is limited,
T-26 ..... IV.1:6 Forgiveness thus **b.** the means by which
T-26 .... VII.7:4 opposing powers, until God **b.** impatient,
T-26 ..... IX.6:5 What hatred has released to love **b.** the
T-27 ........I.3:6 to his guilt **b.** the perfect witness to his
T-27 ........I.8:4 For it **b.** the symbol of reproach, the sign
T-27 ...... V.8:8 **b.** complete within two situations that are
T-27 .... VII.8:2 He **b.** a part of someone else's dream. He
T-28 .......II.8:8 and then reversed, so that effect **b.** a cause
T-28 ...... V.2:6 which you share **b.** the only one you have.
T-29 .......II.8:5 then, **b.** of you, for it is you of whom the
T-29 .......II.8:8 And what is gone from Him **b.** your god,
T-29 ..... III.3:5 he **b.** your savior from your dreams. And
T-29 ..... IV.1:3 lack of truth **b.** the basis for the miracle,
T-29 ..... IV.5:6 A shadow figure who attacks **b.** a brother
T-29 ..... IV.5:6 help, if this **b.** the function of the dream.
T-29 ..... IV.6:6 dream, each dream **b.** an offering of love.
T-29 .... VII.9:9 And all the world **b.** the means by which
T-29 ..... IX.5:6 And their reality **b.** his own, because they
T-29 ..... IX.6:4 game, in which the child **b.** the father,
T-30 ......in.1:1 now **b.** the focus of the curriculum. The
T-30 ...... V.1:2 goal, for the escape from guilt **b.** its aim.
T-30 ...... V.2:7 The world **b.** a place of hope, because its
T-30 ...VIII.4:9 And he **b.** the willing slave of what he
T-31 .......I.11:2 state of mind unwanted that **b.** the means
T-31 .......II.3:6 And every friend or enemy **b.** a means to
T-31 ..... III.1:3 it **b.** your first response to all temptation,
T-31 .... VII.1:8 treachery, and trust **b.** impossible. Nor
W-pI....... 3.1:2 Whatever you see **b.** a proper subject for
W-pI....... 5.1:5 each form **b.** a proper subject for the
W-pI..... 22.1:4 This **b.** an increasingly vicious circle until
W-pI..... 39.9:4 as your mind **b.** more disciplined and less
W-pI..... 43.2:7 Healed perception **b.** the means by which
W-pI..... 64.2:4 of temptation **b.** the spiritual recognition
W-pI..... 64.4:2 means by which happiness **b.** inevitable.
W-pI..... 84.3:5 my Self. My Self thus **b.** alien to me. I am
W-pI... 91.10:6 Their strength **b.** your eyes, that you may
W-pI..... 97.4:1 these ideas **b.** a time that has no limit and
W-pI..... 99.2:2 The impossible **b.** the thing you need
W-pI..... 99.2:3 Salvation now **b.** the borderland between
W-pI... 103.3:2 joy **b.** what you expect to take the place of
W-pI... 106.8:4 the world **b.** ready to understand and to
W-pI. 122.10:2 point at which the road **b.** far easier. And
W-pI... 134.8:2 that it **b.** the undeceiver in the face of lies;
W-pI. 134.14:3 practicing **b.** the footsteps lighting up the
W-pI... 135.8:2 quite apart from you, and it **b.** a healthy,
W-pI. 135.15:3 Time **b.** a future emphasis, to be
W-pI. 135.16:2 before **b.** the basis for its future goals. Its
W-pI. 135.19:1 increases, as this life **b.** a holy instant, set
W-pI. 135.19:2 and this life **b.** a meaningful encounter
W-pI... 137.1:4 It **b.** a door that closes on a separate self,
W-pI... 137.6:2 anti-Christ **b.** more powerful than Christ
W-pI... 137.6:4 And love **b.** a dream, while fear remains
W-pI... 137.9:3 His life **b.** your own, as you extend the
W-pI. 137.11:3 his mind **b.** a haven where the weary can
W-pI... 139.4:1 **b.** a questioner of what that something is.
W-pI... 139.5:1 Thus he **b.** uncertain of his life, for what
W-pI... 153.6:4 **b.** too sleepy to remember what he wants.
W-pI. 153.15:3 Five minutes now **b.** the least we give to
W-pI... 154.3:3 Son **b.** His messenger of unity with Him.
W-pI... 154.4:3 mind **b.** aware again of Who created it,
W-pI... 157.5:3 your mind that it **b.** the touchstone for
W-pI... 157.7:1 return **b.** a little closer to the end of time;
W-pI .. 159.7:3 home of sin **b.** the center of redemption
W-pI .. 164.6:3 you see **b.** the healing and salvation of the
W-pI .. 164.7:3 world. Our practicing today **b.** our gift of
W-pI .. 166.8:5 And what **b.** of all the tragedy you sought
W-pI 166.12:7 speaks as well of what **b.** your will when
W-pI 166.14:5 Your hand **b.** the giver of Christ's touch;
W-pI 166.14:5 your change of mind **b.** the proof that
W-pI 166.15:4 mind **b.** which chooses to accept His gifts,
W-pI 167.12:5 It **b.** the thing reflected, and the light
W-pI .. 169.1:4 Grace **b.** inevitable instantly in those who
W-pI .. 170.5:2 fear **b.** your safety and protector of your
W-pI 170.10:4 And what **b.** more fearful than the Heart
W-pI .. 181.8:5 the Love He feels for us **b.** our own as well
W-pI .. 181.9:1 our sins **b.** the proof that we are sinless.
W-pI .. 183.4:2 No temptation but **b.** a nameless and
W-pI .. 183.6:6 then God's Name **b.** our only thought,
W-pI 183.10:6 the holy Name of God **b.** his judgment of
W-pI .. 184.1:3 Each one **b.** a separate entity, identified
W-pI .. 184.3:1 the world **b.** a series of discrete events, of
W-pI 184.10:1 learning of the world **b.** a transitory phase
W-pI 184.12:2 Name **b.** the final lesson that all things
W-pI .. 185.3:1 that what they will **b.** the Will of God. For
W-pI .. 190.5:8 now **b.** a source of innocence and holiness
W-pI .. 190.8:5 And the world **b.** a cruel and a bitter place
W-pI .. 192.5:3 Anger **b.** impossible, and where is terror
W-pI .. 193.6:1 and death **b.** our choice instead of life?
W-pI .. 194.2:3 your salvation thus **b.** the gift you give the
W-pI .. 194.5:2 **b.** the instant in which time escapes the
W-pI .. 194.6:2 As it **b.** a thought that rules your mind, a
W-pI .. 195.9:4 future. Gratitude **b.** the single thought we
W-pI .. 199.4:5 thus **b.** a vehicle which helps forgiveness
W-pI .. 199.6:4 And it **b.** perfect in the ability to serve an
W-pI .. 213.1:3 *What I learn of Him* ***b.*** *the way I am set free.*
W-pII . 249.1:1 loss **b.** impossible and anger makes no
W-pII . 249.1:5 The world **b.** a place of joy, abundance,
W-pII . 264.1:3 *and place* ***b.*** *a meaningless belief. For what*
W-pII ..... 7.2:4 for it, **b.** the means to go beyond itself, to
W-pII . 296.2:2 our learning goal **b.** an unconflicted one,
W-pII . 313.2:6 in our vision it **b.** as holy as the light in us.
W-pII . 315.1:5 who finds the way to God **b.** my savior,
W-pII . 343.1:5 *sacrifice* ***b.*** *impossible for me as well as You.*
W-pII . 350.1:1 *we forgive* ***b.*** *a part of us, as we perceive*
M-in .......... 4:8 hope, their learning finally **b.** complete.
M-2 ........... 5:8 who was the learner **b.** a teacher of God
M-4 ...... IV.2:2 this that the function of salvation **b.** easy.
M-6 ......... 4:11 of God have about what **b.** of his gifts?
M-7 ........... 6:9 what you want, and doubt **b.** impossible.
M-9 ........... 2:3 This **b.** easier and easier, as the teacher of
M-12 ......... 1:3 **b.** the Self Who is the Son of God. He who
M-12 ......... 3:4 which communication **b.** possible to
M-12 ......... 5:4 who have it not, and the body **b.** holy.
M-13 ......... 3:1 **b.** impossible for the mind to understand
M-14 ......... 2:2 **b.** the home in which forgiveness is born,
M-14 ......... 2:2 and **b.** stronger and more all-embracing.
M-16 ......... 3:3 process, **b.** less and less emphasized. At
M-16 ......... 3:8 individual need **b.** the chief consideration
M-17 ......... 1:4 deal with magic thus **b.** a major lesson for
M-17 ......... 5:2 in the world's thought system **b.** apparent
M-17 ......... 9:3 Like the magic which **b.** its servant, it
M-18 ......... 3:5 And truth **b.** diminutive and meaningless
M-18 ......... 4:1 it thus **b.** essential for the teacher of God
M-18 ......... 4:7 of God **b.** a miracle worker by definition.
M-19 ......... 2:3 This **b.** possible because, while it is not
M-19 ......... 2:5 path **b.** quite different as one goes along.
M-19 ......... 5:8 attack and condemnation **b.** meaningless
M-21 ......... 3:4 illusions in his heart, all this **b.** his own.
M-22 ......... 5:2 is. Another's sickness thus **b.** his own. In
M-23 ......... 4:4 It **b.** the shining symbol for the Word of
M-23 ......... 4:6 gratitude to God **b.** the way in which He
M-27 ......... 5:4 world of illusions **b.** more sharply evident
M-27 ......... 7:4 Now it **b.** your task to let the illusion be
C-in ........... 2:7 alone consistency **b.** possible because
C-1 ............ 7:5 At its highest it **b.** aware of the real world,
C-3 ............ 5:2 so the unity that it reflects **b.** His Will. It
P-1............. 1:5 earthly patient-therapist relationship **b.**
P-2........ III.2:6 Progress **b.** a matter of decision; it can
P-2........ III.4:6 psychotherapist **b.** his patient, working
P-2........ IV.2:1 Son is seen as guilty, illness **b.** inevitable.
P-2........ IV.6:6 reality now **b.** a threat and is perceived as

P-2........IV.6:7 evil. Love **b.** feared because reality is love.
P-2........V.2:3 Progress **b.** impossible until the patient is
P-2........V.5:4 we do for him **b.** the gift we give to God.
P-2........VII.1:10 him. He thus **b.** his patient. God does not
P-2........VII.8:4 The room **b.** a temple, and the street a
S-1........I.5:7 That nothingness **b.** the altar of God. It
S-1........II.5:3 thus **b.** a prayer for your own freedom.
S-1........II.6:4 can become holy, then, prayer **b.** a choice.
S-1........III.1:4 **b.** a means for lifting your projections of
S-1........III.6:5 kind, and prayer **b.** requests for enemies.
S-1........IV.1:3 an instant, it **b.** possible to join in prayer.
S-2........in.1:8 it **b.** unneeded when the rising up is done.
S-2........I.1:6 Guilt **b.** salvation, and the remedy
S-2........I.7:5 His sight the world **b.** as holy as Himself.
S-3........IV.5:5 He Who is Love **b.** the source of fear, for

## becoming 7

T-4........V.6:4 By **b.** involved with tangential issues, it
W-pI...167.4:3 **b.** different from their own origin, apart
W-pI...181.1:4 **b.** blocks to your awareness of the Self
M-3........2:4 of them has the potential for **b.** a teaching-
M-17........3:5 with the call for help **b.** his one appeal.
M-25........2:7 in any way is merely **b.** more natural. He
P-1........5:2 and **b.** increasingly willing to see illusions

## bedlam 1

T-21...VII.3:14 What seems to be a planned attack is **b.**.

## bedrock 1

M-4........III.1:6 and trust remains the **b.** of the teacher of

## been 728

## before 445

T-1........II.3:2 one of a lesser order stands **b.** his Creator.
T-1........III.1:3 The reason you come **b.** me is that I do
T-1........VI.3:1 requires correction at its own level **b.** the
T-2........I.2:2 None of this existed **b.** the separation, nor
T-2........II.4:2 was in effect long **b.** the Atonement began
T-2........II.4:4 Acts were not necessary **b.** the separation,
T-2........III.2:2 the mind. **B.** the separation the mind was
T-2........V.1:1 **B.** miracle workers are ready to
T-2........V.7:3 I said **b.** that the Holy Spirit cannot see
T-2........V.9:1 separation, **b.** which it was unnecessary.
T-2........V.10:5 I said **b.** that only revelation transcends
T-2........VI.4:9 **B.** you choose to do anything, ask me if
T-3........I.1:1 A further point must be perfectly clear **b.**
T-3........III.1:2 out **b.** you can know anything. To know is
T-3........III.2:2 "know again," implying that you knew **b.**.
T-3........III.6:1 Right perception is necessary **b.** God can
T-3........III.6:5 and the end," and "**B.** Abraham was I am.
T-3........VI.2:3 I have discussed this **b.** in terms of the
T-3........VII.3:1 have discussed the fall or separation **b.**,
T-3........VII.4:8 as I said **b.**, when you finally perceive
T-4........II.9:4 that the ego existed **b.** that point in time.
T-4........II.9:5 may believe that the soul existed **b.**, and
T-4........II.10:1 achieved **b.** One-mindedness is restored.
T-4........III.6:6 other gods **b.** Him because there *are* none.
T-4........VI.6:5 I have said **b.** that I am in charge of the
T-5........I.4:9 I have spoken **b.** of the higher or "true"
T-5........I.5:3 **B.** that there was no need for healing, for
T-5........II.1:2 of God were **b.** healing was needed, and
T-5........II.2:4 because **b.** that it had only being, and
T-5........II.3:8 to where you were **b.** and will be again. It
T-5........II.4:3 the glory **b.** which dissociation falls away,
T-5........II.4:4 own. **B.** the separation you did not need
T-5........III.4:3 be increased in strength **b.** you can hear It
T-5........III.5:3 I have said **b.** that the Holy Spirit is God's
T-5........V.3:3 We spoke **b.** of the authority problem as
T-5........V.4:5 I said **b.** that you must learn to think with
T-5........V.5:4 I said **b.** that illness is a form of magic. It
T-5........V.8:2 feelings. We have said this **b.**, but did not
T-5........VII.4:2 salvation yourself because, as I told you **b.**
T-6........I.1:2 I did not dwell on it **b.** because of the
T-6........I.2:7 I emphasized only the resurrection **b.**, the
T-6........I.6:1 As I have said **b.**, "As you teach so shall
T-6........II.1:5 We have said **b.** that the separation was
T-6........III.2:4 said **b.** that the message of the crucifixion
T-6........IV.9:1 must be developed **b.** you can use them.
T-6........V.B.6:5 is why I suggested **b.** that you remind
T-6........V.C.1:1 said **b.** that the Holy Spirit is evaluative,
T-7........II.6:4 I said **b.** that He teaches remembering
T-7........III.3:1 said **b.** that the ego's friend is not part of
T-7........IV.2:7 I said **b.** that forgetting is merely a way of
T-7........VI.6:4 meaningless. I have said **b.** that the Holy
T-7........VIII.2:1 of projection must be fully understood **b.**
T-7........X.6:4 I said **b.** that you are the Will of God. His
T-8........I.6:1 curriculum must be fully recognized **b.** a
T-8........V.6:7 I go **b.** you because I am beyond the ego.
T-8........IX.1:1 said **b.** that the Holy Spirit is the Answer.
T-9........VIII.2:7 We said **b.** that the ego vacillates between
T-10........III.8:3 no other gods **b.** Him or you will not hear.
T-10........III.10:3 accept other gods **b.** Him is to place other
T-10........III.10:3 Him is to place other images **b.** yourself.
T-10........III.11:3 when you place no other gods **b.** Him.
T-10........IV.1:5 sick, you have placed other gods **b.** Him.
T-10........V.5:1 **b.** that of yourself you can do nothing,
T-11........III.6:3 there *are* no other gods to place **b.** Him,
T-11........V.5:3 I said **b.** that to will contrary to God is
T-11........VII.1:5 merely to perceive again, implying that **b.**
T-12........III.7:10 and not outside it **b.** you can get rid of it;
T-12........III.7:10 and why you must get rid of it **b.** you can
T-12........III.8:1 I said **b.** that God so loved the world that
T-12........IV.4:6 the goal He sets **b.** you He will give you.
T-12........V.1:3 **B.** the idea of attack can enter your mind,
T-12........VII.7:1 I said **b.** that what you project or extend
T-12........VII.7:1 and you must look in **b.** you look out. As
T-13........III.7:4 Lay **b.** His eternal sanity all your hurt,
T-13........VI.6:5 The present is **b.** time was, and will be
T-13........VII.15:1 peace of mind this world may set **b.** you.
T-13........VII.15:2 Kneel not **b.** the altars to sacrifice, and
T-13........X.14:3 **B.** the glorious radiance of the Kingdom
T-13........X.14:6 United in this praise we stand **b.** the gates
T-14........II.5:7 I said **b.**, "Be not content with nothing,"
T-14........II.6:4 up **b.** you in all its gracious simplicity.
T-14........II.6:5 With truth **b.** you, you will not look back.
T-14........IV.3:1 therefore stand in grace **b.** your Father,
T-14........IV.4:1 do what must be done **b.** that knowledge
T-14........IV.5:1 **B.** you make any decisions for yourself,
T-14........VIII.3:4 oneness, **b.** which all separation vanishes.
T-14........XI.3:2 accomplished **b.** its effects are manifest.
T-14........XI.11:5 and **b.** His lesson division disappears.
T-15........I.4:9 paradox in the ego's thought system **b.**,
T-15........II.2:7 Through Him you stand **b.** God's altar,
T-15........II.6:9 **B.** the recognition of the universe that
T-15........III.8:7 **B.** the greatness that lives in you, your
T-15........III.12:6 Lay not littleness **b.** His holy altar, which
T-15........IV.3:1 Be humble **b.** Him, and yet great *in* Him.
T-15........IV.3:2 no plan of the ego **b.** the plan of God. For
T-15........VII.4:1 said **b.** that the ego attempts to maintain
T-16........III.1:6 with what you taught **b.** He came. And
T-16........IV.1:4 salvation will rise clearly **b.** your open
T-16........V.1:5 I have spoken of this **b.**, but there are
T-16........V.13:1 attempt to raise other gods **b.** Him, and
T-16........V.13:3 raise to place **b.** Him stands before *you*, in
T-16........V.13:3 raise to place before Him stands **b.** *you*, in
T-16........VI.12:6 Delay will hurt you now more than **b.**,
T-16........VII.6:2 We said **b.** that the Holy Spirit must teach
T-17........III.7:1 if you but let Him hold the spark **b.** you,
T-17........VIII.4:1 to His Call seems to be greater than **b.**.
T-17........VIII.4:3 is not so. **B.**, the strain was there, but you
T-17........VIII.5:3 Think carefully **b.** you let yourself use
T-18........II.1:3 clearly not the world you saw **b.** you slept.
T-18........II.6:3 I said **b.** that the first change, before
T-18........II.6:3 that the first change, **b.** dreams disappear
T-18........III.4:4 And fear must disappear **b.** you now. Be
T-18........V.2:3 your guilt **b.** you ask the Holy Spirit's help
T-18........IX.5:4 then you see it as a fragile veil **b.** the light.
T-18........IX.6:1 that seem to be a solid wall **b.** the sun. Its
T-18........IX.11:4 for learning ends **b.** Him Who is complete
T-18........IX.13:2 and gently placed **b.** the gates of Heaven.
T-19........I.1:1 We said **b.** that when a situation has
T-19........I.9:4 brother has done **b.** to condemn him now
T-19........I.14:1 brother stand **b.** the altar God has raised
T-19........I.14:6 brother who stand together **b.** the altar
T-19........II.8:4 think you carefully **b.** you allow yourself
T-19........III.7:5 it, nor remain itself **b.** the power of sin.
T-19........III.7:6 God, **b.** which God Himself must bow,
T-19........III.8:7 cherished but a little while **b.** it vanishes.
T-19........III.10:6 barriers to Heaven will disappear **b.** your
T-19........IV.2:2 flow across the obstacles you placed **b.** it.
T-19........IV.3:8 and lay them gently **b.** His Creator in the
T19. IV.A.4:12 and barriers will fall away **b.** their coming
T19........IV.A.7:3 **B.** the Holy Spirit entered to abide with
T19........IV.A.8:3 be more erratic and unpredictable than **b.**
T19........IV.A.9:1 little feather be **b.** the great wings of truth
T19. IV.A.11:2 them respectfully **b.** their lord and master
T19. IV.A.15:2 world will be transformed **b.** your sight,
T19. IV.A.16:1 Love, too, would set a feast **b.** you, on a
T19. IV.A.16:3 in gentleness **b.** the table of communion.
T19........IV.B.5:3 obstacle that you can place **b.** our union,
T19........IV.C.8:1 Himself is powerless **b.** the ego's might,
T19........IV.D.2:1 hangs like a heavy veil **b.** the face of Christ
T19........IV.D.6:1 And now you stand in terror **b.** what you
T19........IV.D.9:2 No one can stand **b.** this obstacle alone,
T19. IV.D.10:7 Here, with the journey's end **b.** you, you
T19. IV.D.11:4 **B.** complete forgiveness you still stand
T19. IV.D.16:2 brother is, **b.** you would condemn him.
T-20........II.11:5 come **b.** his holy altar where the strength
T-20........III.1:2 what was so **b.** has been made different.
T-20........III.4:2 **b.** it overtakes you and you disappear.
T-20........III.7:3 he will not remain **b.** the shining light the
T-20........IV.8:1 must be done **b.** the way to peace is open.
T-20........IV.8:5 will go **b.** you making straight your path,
T-20........IV.8:7 but will melt away **b.** you reach it. You
T-20........V.5:8 golden light is all the same; nothing **b.** it,
T-20........VI.11:8 him to replace the unholy one he chose **b.**.
T-20........VII.1:1 brought in line **b.** your holy relationship
T-20........VII.3:8 with it. **B.** we look at them a little closer,
T-20........VII.6:7 the cause of sin an instant **b.** he dies.
T-20........VIII.3:3 may rise **b.** your vision and give you joy.
T-20........VIII.6:7 everything will stand condemned **b.** you.
T-21........I.1:5 but which stand open **b.** unseeing eyes,
T-21........I.2:3 be seen **b.** you recognize it for what it is.
T-21........I.8:2 all the circle fills with light **b.** your eyes.
T-21........III.4:7 only **b.** the state of certainty is reached. In
T-22........II.9:5 illusion we have seen many times **b.**. Only
T-22........IV.1:3 way you went **b.** you reached the branch,
T-22........IV.3:1 **b.** the veil of sin that hangs between you
T-22........IV.3:5 has reached you even here, **b.** the veil.
T-22........IV.6:3 All barriers disappear **b.** their coming, as
T-22........IV.6:3 that seemed to rise and block their way **b.**
T-22........IV.7:5 Standing **b.** the veil, it still seems difficult.
T-22........V.4:2 How insignificant **b.** the quiet strength of
T-22........VI.3:5 from hate to gratitude **b.** forgiving eyes.
T-22........VI.5:1 **B.** a holy relationship there is no sin. The
T-23........I.4:4 peace is here transformed, **b.** your sight,
T-23........II.14:5 must its opposite, which was the truth **b.**,
T-23........II.16:3 how it appears to function many times **b.**.
T-23........III.4:8 of it? It can be kept shining **b.** your vision,
T-24........II.4:5 silent and unheard **b.** its "mightiness."
T-24........III.2:7 misery, **b.** the idol that can save you not.
T-24........IV.3:11 truth. They will not stand **b.** it. Yet what
T-24........V.4:6 first, nor hated him **b.** it hated you. The
T-24........V.9:1 must be doubt **b.** there can be conflict.
T-24........V.9:5 you, yet He walks beside you and **b.**,
T-24........VI.1:1 **B.** your brother's holiness the world is
T-24........VI.1:7 yourself may disappear **b.** his holiness.
T-24........VI.3:2 has He failed to lay **b.** you lovingly, as
T-24........VI.3:4 as He conceived of you **b.** the world began
T-24........VI.10:6 will disappear **b.** the Will of God, Who
T-25........I.4:6 You and your brother stand **b.** Him now,
T-25........II.3:3 and bring what it has never brought **b.**?
T-25........II.5:1 empty frame upon a wall and stands **b.** it,
T-25........III.6:5 that he thought **b.** was means to justify
T-25........III.6:6 to war he heard **b.** are really calls to peace
T-25........IV.3:7 die, will disappear **b.** the sun you bring.
T-25........IV.4:5 that they may be pushed away **b.** the light
T-25........IV.5:6 Nothing **b.** and nothing after it. No other
T-25........V.2:9 Christ stands **b.** you, each time you look
T-25........VII.3:1 Let us go back to what we said **b.**, and
T-25........VII.8:4 way of looking at what he has seen **b.**, and

T-25.....VII.8:4 he lives, and thought he understood **b.**.
T-26.......I.4:10 him to make the world recede **b.** his song,
T-26....... II.7:3 resolved **b.** the Holy Spirit's gentle sight.
T-26....... II.7:4 than just a tiny sigh **b.** they disappear, to
T-26......IV.4:1 little miracles to lay **b.** the gate of Heaven.
T-26....... V.3:4 was **b.** the way to nothingness was made.
T-26....... V.4:3 long ago, **b.** its unreality gave way to truth
T-26....... V.4:5 it to your heart, as if it were **b.** you still.
T-26....... V.5:6 You keep an ancient memory **b.** your eyes
T-26.....VII.1:2 laws of healing must be understood **b.** the
T-26.....VII.9:7 they were known **b.** they were denied.
T-27.........I.3:2 a picture of your crucifixion **b.** his eyes,
T-27.........I.3:2 in your blood and death, and go **b.** him,
T-27....... II.3:7 not the proof of sin **b.** his brother's eyes.
T-27....... II.6:5 disappear **b.** the ancient clarion call of life
T-28.......I.13:6 Son of God remembers from **b.** his own
T-28....... II.9:2 final step is an effect of what has gone **b.**,
T-28...... III.8:7 enjoy the feast of plenty set **b.** them there.
T-28...... III.9:5 Here is a feast the Father lays **b.** His Son,
T-28...... VI.6:8 vows are powerless **b.** the Will of God,
T-29....... II.7:3 the one in which you found yourself **b.**.
T-29...... III.1:3 first, **b.** he can remember what he is. And
T-29...... III.3:7 **B.** this light the body disappears, as heavy
T-29....VIII.3:6 fall **b.** His face like a dark veil that seems
T-29....VIII.5:3 be believed **b.** it seems to come to life, and
T-29...... IX.8:4 he has not heard it since **b.** all time began.
T-30.........I.5:5 need a quick restorative **b.** you ask again.
T-30.......I.15:3 ask advice **b.** you can decide on anything.
T-30.......I.16:2 agree on what you want **b.** it can occur. It
T-30.......I.17:5 two are joined **b.** there can be a decision.
T-30...... III.7:7 as it was **b.** the time when you forgot, and
T-30....... V.7:5 face of Christ is looked upon **b.** the Father
T-30.....VII.2:5 you see another meaning in what went **b.**.
T-30....VIII.1:4 will change, and yet you thought it real **b.**,
T-31.........I.4:4 seems small and still **b.** its magnitude.
T-31.........I.5:4 stand implacable **b.** the Voice of truth,
T-31....... II.2:9 **b.** you can look past them to the one
T-31....... II.6:1 **B.** you answer, pause to think of this: *The*
T-31....... II.8:2 all thought of what you ever learned **b.**,
T-31....... II.8:3 The old will fall away **b.** the new without
T-31..... II.11:7 to you is One Who holds the light **b.** you,
T-31.... IV.2:12 gaily for a while, **b.** the bleakness enters.
T-31...... IV.3:2 all, **b.** you really learn they are but one.
T-31....... V.9:6 he see your future and ordain, **b.** it comes,
T-31..... V.13:2 have gone **b.** these concepts of the self.
T-31..... V.13:8 While only he was treacherous **b.**, now
T-31...... VI.5:4 fit the picture as it was perceived **b.** will
T-31.....VII.7:1 a shield, a silent barricade **b.** the truth,
T-31.....VII.8:7 For there is light where darkness was **b.**,
T-31....VIII.3:1 choice **b.** you now can make a better one,
T-31....VIII.3:1 that what you chose **b.** has brought to you
T-31....VIII.4:2 place you raised an image of yourself **b.**.
T-31....VIII.4:3 face of Christ is powerless **b.** His majesty,
T-31....VIII.4:3 majesty, and disappears **b.** His holy sight.
T-31....VIII.5:6 to be **b.** the choice for holiness was made.
T-31....VIII.6:3 occurs, but disappear as mists **b.** the sun.
T-31....VIII.7:1 in exchange I lay **b.** your feet the peace of
T-31....VIII.8:4 the pain and sorrow that you saw **b.**. Yet
T-31....VIII.9:3 we travelled on **b.** the Christ appeared.
T-31..VIII.12:2 in the abode You set for Him **b.** time was,
W-pI.......6.2:2 by a minute or so of mind searching, as **b.**
W-pI.....10.1:3 We have made this distinction **b.**, and
W-pI.....10.4:4 The exercises consist, as **b.**, in searching
W-pI.....10.5:4 the idea slowly **b.** applying it specifically,
W-pI.....16.3:4 in many forms **b.** you really understand it
W-pI.....25.4:1 **B.** you can make any sense out of the
W-pI.....25.6:8 next subject, and apply today's idea as **b.**.
W-pI.....30.1:2 this idea will the world open up **b.** you,
W-pI.....30.1:2 and see in it what you have never seen **b.**.
W-pI.....30.1:3 you saw **b.** be even faintly visible to you.
W-pI...36.3:11 Then open your eyes, and continue as **b.**.
W-pI.....42.4:2 repeat the idea again, even slower than **b.**.
W-pI.....44.3:2 of exercise which has been suggested **b.**,
W-pI.....46.1:2 condemnation **b.** forgiveness is necessary.
W-pI.....51.3:8 this a better choice than the one I made **b.**
W-pI.....52.2:7 look with love on all that I failed to see **b.**.
W-pI.....53.5:7 His, and I will place no other gods **b.** Him
W-pI.....54.1:5 will the real world rise **b.** my eyes as I let
W-pI.....54.3:3 to be shared **b.** it could form the basis of
W-pI.....65.6:2 thoughts that escaped your attention **b.**,
W-pI.....69.2:2 in you. **B.** we undertake this in our more
W-pI.....70.8:5 the clouds **b.** you can reach the light. But
W-pI.....73.7:6 the ego that stands powerless **b.** your will.
W-pI.....75.4:4 the real world rises **b.** us in gladness, to
W-pI.....75.6:4 look upon it now as if you never saw it **b.**.
W-pI.....76.1:1 We have observed **b.** how many senseless
W-pI.....78.1:2 of hate **b.** the miracle it would conceal.
W-pI.....78.1:3 And as you raise it up **b.** your eyes, you
W-pI.....78.2:2 see by not allowing sight to stop **b.** it sees.
W-pI.....78.2:3 We will not wait **b.** the shield of hate, but
W-pI.....78.3:1 in shining light where each one stood **b.**.
W-pI.....81.1:3 Let me be still **b.** my holiness. In its calm
W-pI.....81.2:4 *This shadow will vanish* ***b.*** *the light.*
W-pI.....81.3:3 and perfectly unambiguous **b.** my sight.
W-pI.....90.3:3 time must elapse **b.** it can be worked out.
W-pI.....92.1:4 by putting little bits of glass **b.** your eyes.
W-pI.....92.8:2 can leave without a miracle **b.** his eyes,
W-pI.....96.2:2 and doubt, each one as futile as the one **b.**
W-pI...101.3:3 taking everything away **b.** it grants the
W-pI...101.3:3 more than bones **b.** salvation is appeased.
W-pI...104.2:3 are the gifts that we inherited **b.** time was,
W-pI...104.4:2 a holy place within our minds **b.** His altar,
W-pI...105.4:4 more, for that implies that it was less **b.**.
W-pI...109.3:5 to truth **b.** the eyes of you who rest in God
WpI..rIII.in8:2 other in the hour just **b.** you go to sleep.
W-pI...122.5:3 Changelessly it stands **b.** you like an open
W-pI...122.6:7 of fragile cobwebs disappear **b.** the power
W-pI. 122.12:1 **B.** the light you will receive today the
W-pI...124.3:1 who went **b.** or stayed with us a while.
W-pI. 127.10:1 **b.** the timelessness of what you learn. Let
W-pI...128.7:2 see as much as when you looked at it **b.**.
W-pI...130.9:4 that your eyes alone have ever seen **b.**.
W-pI. 131.12:2 But **b.** you try to open it, remind yourself
W-pI. 131.12:4 nothing **b.** this door you really want, and
W-pI. 131.13:3 will make you pause **b.** you realize the
W-pI. 131.13:3 you realize the world you see **b.** you in the
W-pI...132.2:3 free the past from what you thought **b.**.
W-pI. 135.16:2 learned **b.** becomes the basis for its future
W-pI. 136.10:2 quails **b.** such mad attacks as these, with
W-pI. 136.18:3 drink, or any laws you made it serve **b.**.
W-pI...137.7:1 which you hold **b.** the simple truth. When
W-pI...138.9:4 mind had made **b.** are open to correction,
W-pI. 138.12:1 **B.** we close our eyes in sleep tonight, we
W-pI...140.2:3 so his mind remains exactly as it was **b.**.
W-pI. 140.11:1 again five minutes more **b.** we go to sleep.
WpIrIV.in10:2 to the ideas for the day again **b.** you sleep,
W-pI...151.7:4 you are vanish **b.** the splendor He beholds
W-pI...151.8:1 great that doubt is meaningless **b.** Its face
W-pI...151.8:4 witnesses **b.** the rapture of Christ's holy
W-pI. 151.15:1 gladly give another fifteen more **b.** you go
W-pI...152.3:2 This you have heard **b.**, but may not yet
W-pI...155.1:5 that you are like them, as you were **b.**.
W-pI...155.8:2 you accept the truth, and let it go **b.** you,
W-pI...155.9:4 It goes **b.** you now, that they may see
W-pI. 155.11:6 For as truth goes **b.** us, so it goes before
W-pI. 155.11:6 it goes **b.** our brothers who will follow us.
W-pI. 155.12:6 that walks **b.** us now is one with Him, and
W-pI...156.4:4 you. The waves bow down **b.** you, and the
W-pI...156.4:4 and lay their leaves **b.** you on the ground
W-pI...156.5:2 All living things are still **b.** you, for they
W-pI...161.1:3 where fear and anger had prevailed **b.**.
W-pI...162.2:3 that will not fade away **b.** their might.
W-pI...162.3:2 and wakens with the truth **b.** him always.
W-pI...163.2:3 the helpless and the sick bow down **b.** its
W-pI...164.2:1 The world fades easily away **b.** His sight.
W-pI...164.4:5 different from all things you sought **b.**,
W-pI...164.5:4 unfold in perfect innocence **b.** your eyes.
W-pI...165.4:3 your mind will be **b.** it comes to you. Ask
W-pI...166.5:5 contains is valueless **b.** its magnitude.
W-pI...169.8:3 We have repeated several times **b.** that
W-pI...170.8:3 You make a choice, standing **b.** this idol,
W-pI...170.8:4 it and lay **b.** this mindless piece of stone?
W-pI. 170.11:3 You have reached this place **b.**, but you
WpI...rV.in8:8 for us **b.** time was and kept unchanged by
WpI.rV.in10:6 but an ancient truth we knew **b.** illusion
WpI.rV.in11:4 the thoughts to hold it up **b.** our minds,
W-pI...181.2:4 which has replaced the one you held **b.**.
W-pI...181.4:2 is advocating are from those you held **b.**.
W-pI .. 183.4:2 and unwanted thing **b.** God's Name.
W-pI .. 183.4:5 **b.** you let the Name of God replace their
W-pI .. 183.4:5 names, you stood **b.** them worshipfully,
W-pI .. 187.1:3 We have made this point **b.**. What seems
W-pI .. 187.3:1 must first belong to you, **b.** you give them
W-pI .. 187.8:6 and suffering can long endure **b.** the face
W-pI .. 187.9:3 **b.** the purity that you will look on here.
W-pI 187.10:2 And here, **b.** the altar to one God, one
W-pI .. 189.7:4 belief you ever learned **b.** from anything.
W-pI .. 190.8:5 sorrow rules and little joys give way **b.** the
W-pI .. 192.4:1 the senseless symbols written there **b.**.
W-pI .. 193.8:6 lessons Heaven's Teacher sets **b.** you, that
W-pI 193.12:2 so that the next one is free of the one **b.**.
W-pI .. 195.2:3 and follow in the way He sets **b.** them, to
W-pI .. 197.6:2 **b.** He snatches them away again in death.
W-pI 198.11:2 Now is there stillness where **b.** there was a
W-pI .. 200.3:6 open eyes to find that Heaven lies **b.** you,
W-pI 200.10:3 the trees of hopelessness you sought **b.**.
W-pII . 227.1:5 *up, and lay them down* ***b.*** *the feet of truth, to*
W-pII ..... 2.2:2 There was no need for such a Thought **b.**,
W-pII ..... 2.3:4 with the gifts of your forgiveness laid **b.** it,
W-pII . 251.1:3 All that I sought **b.** I needed not, and did
W-pII . 260.1:6 *my sinlessness arise again* ***b.*** *Christ's vision,*
W-pII . 264.1:1 *Father, You stand* ***b.*** *me and behind, beside*
W-pII ..... 6.3:4 fade **b.** His glory and reveal your holy Self
W-pII ..... 7.1:3 to be dispelled **b.** the light of knowledge.
W-pII ..... 7.1:5 aside. And where they were perceived **b.**,
W-pII . 287.1:3 gift could I prefer **b.** the peace of God?
W-pII . 293.2:4 *I would see only this world* ***b.*** *my eyes today.*
W-pII . 300.1:1 their joys are gone **b.** they are possessed,
W-pII . 305.1:2 Comparisons are still **b.** this peace. And
W-pII . 320.1:4 and lays **b.** it all the strength and love in
W-pII ... 11.2:4 remaining as it was **b.** the thought of time
W-pII . 325.1:6 he can rest a while **b.** he journeys on, and
W-pII ... 12.2:5 who seek to murder it **b.** it can ensure its
W-pII ... 12.4:2 and blood must flow **b.** the altar where its
W-pII ... 13.2:3 perception which was upside down **b.**,
W-pII ... 13.3:5 love. And each is laid **b.** the Word of God,
W-pII ... 13.4:3 a world more real than what you saw **b.**; a
W-pII . 342.1:5 *I stand* ***b.*** *the gate of Heaven, wondering if I*
W-pII ... 14.5:5 sees the gate of Heaven stand open **b.** him
W-ep ......... 2:1 pathway of the sun laid down **b.** it rises,
M-1 ........... 3:7 who the teacher was **b.** he heard the Call.
M-2 ........... 4:3 each other as if they had not met **b.**. The
M-3 ........... 5:6 lesson is **b.** them and can be learned. And
M-4 .........I.2:3 ego when the gifts of God are laid **b.** him?
M-4 ..... I.A.4:3 if not most of the things he valued **b.** will
M-4 ... I.A.6:12 a while, and gathers them **b.** going on. He
M-4 ..... I.A.8:3 as merely shadows **b.** become solid gains,
M-4 ......V.1:10 they are sure His Teacher goes **b.** them,
M-4 ........X.2:5 now which seemed so dull and lifeless **b.**.
M-6 ........... 2:4 And what is time **b.** the gifts of God? We
M-8 ........... 6:3 report their changed appearances as **b.**.
M-11 ....... 4:10 earth bows down **b.** its gracious Presence,
M-13 ......... 1:6 must be displaced **b.** another thought
M-16 ....... 1:10 walks stretch surely and smoothly **b.** him.
M-16 ......... 5:2 for you to take it just **b.** going to sleep. It
M-16 ......... 5:6 just **b.** going to sleep is a desirable time to
M-16 ......... 7:2 All that he did **b.** in the name of safety no
M-16 ......... 7:6 safe in the present as he was **b.** illusions
M-19 ......... 3:2 is the lens which, held **b.** the body's eyes,
M-19 ......... 5:6 It accepts all evidence that is brought **b.** it
M-20 ......... 2:3 It calls to mind nothing that went **b.**. It
M-22 ......... 2:3 the function God has given him long **b.** he
M-27 ......... 1:3 We have asked this question **b.**, but now
M-28 ......... 6:9 sought **b.** to crucify are resurrected with
C-2 ............ 7:4 extend **b.** you as you walk in gentleness.
C-3 ............ 3:2 God knows what His Son needs **b.** he asks
C-3 ............ 4:1 be seen **b.** the memory of God can return.
C-4 ............ 4:1 world stands like a block **b.** Christ's face.
C-5 ............ 3:3 to God because he saw the road **b.** him,
C-6 ............ 2:4 Holy Spirit long **b.** Jesus set it in motion.
C-ep ........ 1:11 Who stands **b.** a lifeless image when a
C-ep ........... 3:3 on **b.** and lost our way a little while. And
P-2..........V.8:1 Let us stand silently **b.** God's Will, and
P-2....... VII.4:4 **B.** he reached this point, he thought he
P-3..........II.8:2 Yet well **b.** he reaches this in time he can
P-3.......... III.6:4 have been **b.** the Holy Spirit entered them
S-1.........in.1:8 For such it was **b.** time seemed to be.

S-1 I.4:4 Him that you would have no gods **b.** Him;
S-1 II.6:4 **B.** it can become holy, then, prayer
S-1 III.1:5 be relinquished **b.** *you* can be saved from
S-1 IV.3:1 who pray together do not ask, **b.** all else,
S-1 IV.3:4 What was enjoyed **b.**, or seemed to be;
S-1 IV.3:6 **b.** that it is pitiful to be content with less.
S-1 V.3:7 more to learn **b.** the journey is complete.
S-1 V.4:2 Now you stand **b.** the gate of Heaven, and
S-2 I.9:1 **b.** you reach where learning cannot go.
S-3 II.6:4 prepared **b.** time was and still but waits

## began 28

T-2 II.4:2 in effect long before the Atonement **b.**.
T-5 II.3:1 and the separation **b.** at the same time.
T-6 II.7:5 Your perception will end where it **b.**.
T-13 VII.3:1 for it has disappointed you since time **b.**.
T-20 II.8:5 Your home has called to you since time **b.**
T-21 IV.5:1 recognized him perfectly since time **b.**.
T-24 VI.3:4 He conceived of you before the world **b.**,
T-29 IX.8:4 he has not heard it since before all time **b.**
T-31 I.4:5 The world **b.** with one strange lesson,
T-31 I.6:6 since time **b.** and learning had been made
T-31 VIII.12:3 closes, ending at the place where it **b.**. No
W-pI 10.3:1 of the correction process **b.** with the idea
W-pI 65.3:4 the searching you have done since time **b.**
W-pI 75.8:5 that has been promised you since time **b.**,
W-pI 122.12:2 been held in store for us since time **b.**,
WpI rIV.in8:1 mind the thought with which the day **b.**,
WpI rIV.in9:3 practicing, as we review, we close as we **b.**
W-pI 152.12:1 Him with the words with which the day **b.**
W-pI 191.8:1 the rites of death echoed since time **b.**.
W-pI 191.10:2 made. In error it **b.**, but it will end in the
W-pII in.8:5 has called to us unceasingly since time **b.**.
W-pII 249.1:7 the journey which the Son of God **b.** has
W-pII 10.2:5 the dream in which the world **b.** go with it
W-pII 11.2:4 as it was before the thought of time **b.**.
M-14 1:2 The world will end in an illusion, as it **b.**.
M-14 5:8 it departs, for it will not end as it **b.**. To
C-6 5:5 with him when he **b.** to save the world.
P-2 V.8:2 by which we come to where all dreams **b.**.

## begets 1

T-7 VI.1:5 ego or the Holy Spirit **b.** or inspires them,

## begetting 1

T-7 VI.4:3 its own antecedents, **b.** as it was begotten.

## begin 140

T-1 III.1:1 of Atonement, which I undertook to **b.**.
T-1 VII.4:6 you will **b.** to see some of the implications
T-2 VIII.4:4 the mind can **b.** to look with love on its
T-6 II.9:1 Thoughts **b.** in the mind of the thinker,
T-6 V.B.2:1 will last, but they do not **b.** at that level.
T-6 V.B.6:4 As you **b.** to realize the quiet power of the
T-8 VI.1:2 all. We **b.** the journey back by setting out
T-9 V.1:5 for example, he may **b.** with the premise,
T-10 V.14:9 will **b.** to understand eternity and make it
T-11 II.6:8 you will **b.** to remember creation.
T-11 V.3:1 Let us **b.** this lesson in "ego dynamics" by
T-13 IV.4:1 that your questioning might well **b.**. The
T-14 I.5:1 must **b.** His teaching by showing you
T-14 II.6:2 And then **b.** to learn the joyous lessons
T-15 I.9:4 **B.** to practice the Holy Spirit's use of time
T-15 II.6:3 **b.** to experience yourself as not separate.
T-15 VI.8:7 will **b.** to understand what your Creator is
T-15 XI.10:8 So will the year **b.** in joy and freedom.
T-16 III.7:1 This year you will **b.** to learn, and make
T-17 V.15:1 **b.** to recognize and accept the gifts you
T-18 I.5:5 fearful enough, as you **b.** to look at them.
T-19 I.15:3 the process of making lovely that they **b.**.
T19 IV.A.1:6 the whole creation, it must **b.** with you,
T-20 VI.7:2 of their temple **b.** to shake and loosen.
T-27 V.1:2 help, but you are needed that it can **b.**.
T-28 III.1:4 Here is where we must **b.**. And having
T-30 I.8:1 you can **b.** to change your mind with this:
T-30 I.14:1 We said you can **b.** a happy day with the
T-31 IV.5:2 it not needful that he should **b.** with this,
T-31 IV.5:4 The great release of power must **b.** with
W-pI 2.1:2 **B.** with the things that are near you, and
W-pI 4.1:1 exercises do not **b.** with the idea for the
W-pI 4.1:2 periods, **b.** with noting the thoughts that
W-pI 8.3:1 of the exercises for today is to **b.** to train
W-pI 9.4:1 **B.** with things that are nearest you, and
W-pI 11.2:2 **B.** with your eyes closed, and repeat the
W-pI 15.2:2 You will **b.** to understand it when you
W-pI 15.5:2 practice periods, if you **b.** to feel uneasy.
W-pI 21.2:1 **b.** by repeating the idea to yourself. Then
W-pI 24.2:3 your mind so that learning can **b.**.
W-pI 24.4:1 practice periods should **b.** with repeating
W-pI 25.6:2 Each practice period should **b.** with a
W-pI 26.6:1 practice period should **b.** with repeating
W-pI 29.3:1 **b.** to learn how to look on all things with
W-pI 29.4:1 **B.** with repeating the idea to yourself, and
W-pI 30.4:2 To help you **b.** to get used to this idea, try
W-pI 32.3:1 Again we will **b.** the practice periods for
W-pI 34.1:3 It must **b.** with your own thoughts, and
W-pI 34.4:1 **b.** to experience difficulty in thinking of
W-pI 35.4:1 **b.** by repeating today's idea to yourself,
W-pI 37.4:1 **b.** with the repetition of the idea for today
W-pI 38.5:5 The purpose of today's exercises is to **b.** to
W-pI 39.6:1 **B.** the practice periods as usual, by
W-pI 40.1:1 Today we will **b.** to assert some of the
W-pI 42.4:1 **B.** these practice periods by repeating the
W-pI 43.6:1 you **b.** to be aware of thoughts which are
W-pI 44.7:1 **B.** the practice period by repeating
W-pI 45.6:1 **B.** the exercises for today by repeating
W-pI 46.3:2 possible. **B.** the longer practice periods by
W-pI 47.4:3 urged. Close your eyes and **b.**, as usual, by
WpI rI.in.2:1 **B.** the day by reading the five ideas, with
W-pI 57.5:3 I **b.** to understand that this peace comes
W-pI 57.5:5 In this light I **b.** to see what my illusions
W-pI 57.5:6 I **b.** to understand the holiness of all
W-pI 60.2:4 As I **b.** to see, I recognize His reflection on
W-pI 60.2:6 And I **b.** to remember the Love I chose to
W-pI 61.5:2 They should **b.** with telling yourself: *I am*
W-pI 61.6:1 both to **b.** and end the day with a practice
W-pI 61.7:4 Try today to **b.** to build a firm foundation
W-pI 62.3:2 **b.** to understand what forgiveness will do
W-pI 62.4:1 Let us be glad to **b.** and end this day by
W-pI 63.3:2 We will **b.** the day by acknowledging it,
W-pI 65.5:1 **b.** by reviewing the idea for the day. Then
W-pI 66.5:1 **B.** the ten-to-fifteen-minute practice
W-pI 67.2:2 will **b.** by repeating this truth about you,
W-pI 68.5:1 **B.** today's extended practice period by
W-pI 69.3:1 Let us **b.** our longer practice period today
W-pI 69.7:1 you will **b.** to feel a sense of being lifted
W-pI 70.2:5 must surely **b.** to see that accepting it is
W-pI 70.7:1 **B.** these practice periods by repeating the
W-pI 71.8:1 **B.** the two longer practice periods for
W-pI 72.13:2 usual. These exercises should **b.** with this:
W-pI 73.9:1 We will **b.** our longer practice periods
W-pI 74.3:1 **B.** the longer practice periods by
W-pI 75.5:3 **B.** the longer practice periods by telling
W-pI 76.8:1 will **b.** the longer practice periods today
W-pI 77.4:1 **B.** the longer practice periods by telling
WpI rII.in.1:2 We will **b.** where our last review left off,
WpI rII.in.2:1 **b.** by thinking about the ideas for the day,
W-pI 91.6:1 **B.** the longer practice periods with this
W-pI 93.8:1 hour, **b.** by stating the truth about your
W-pI 94.3:2 **B.** these times of searching with these
W-pI 95.11:1 **B.** the practice periods today with this
W-pI 96.9:1 **B.** with saying this: *Salvation comes from*
W-pI 97.7:1 **B.** these happy exercises with the words
W-pI 100.7:2 **B.** the exercises with the thought today's
W-pI 102.4:1 **B.** your practice periods today with this
W-pI 103.2:6 **B.** your periods of practicing today with
W-pI 104.3:2 for your salvation, should **b.** with this: *I*
W-pI 105.6:2 **B.** today by thinking of those brothers
W-pI 106.7:4 Each hour's exercises should **b.** with this
W-pI 106.8:3 It will **b.** the ministry for which you came,
W-pI 107.8:1 **B.** by asking Him Who goes with you
W-pI 108.8:1 So we **b.** the practice periods with the
W-pI 109.7:3 And they will hear the bird **b.** to sing and
W-pI 109.7:3 to sing and see the stream **b.** to flow again
W-pI 110.6:1 **b.** with this quotation from the text: *I am*
WpI rIII.in5:3 And then **b.** to think about them, while
W-pI 121.10:1 **B.** the longer practice periods by thinking
W-pI 122.10:2 **B.** in hopefulness, for we have reached the
W-pI 122.11:1 happiness as you **b.** these practice periods
W-pI 129.7:2 **B.** with this: *Beyond this world there is a*
W-pI 130.8:1 **B.** your searching for the other world by
W-pI 131.11:2 **B.** with this: *I ask to see a different world,*
W-pI 132.12:4 Son **b.** as something separate from Him.
W-pI 132.15:1 **B.** the fifteen-minute periods in which we
W-pI 133.13:3 of fifteen minutes each **b.** with this: *I will*
W-pI 133.14:2 Should you **b.** to let yourself collect some
W-pI 134.16:3 honesty, you will **b.** to sense a lifting up, a
W-pI 137.14:2 And so we will **b.** the day with this, and
W-pI 138.7:1 **b.** today considering the choice that time
WpI rIV.in1:2 applied. Today we will **b.** to concentrate
WpI rIV.in3:1 Let us **b.** our preparation with some
WpI rIV.in5:1 **B.** each day with time devoted to the
W-pI 153.15:2 will **b.** each day by giving our attention to
W-pI 153.20:1 will now **b.** to take the earnestness of love,
W-pI 184.7:5 which another kind of learning can **b.**, a
WpI rVI.in.7:4 us offer Him the whole review we now **b.**,
W-pII in.1:5 we **b.** to reach the goal this course has set,
W-pII 290.1:2 see. Eyes that **b.** to open see at last. And I
M-2 1:1 and they will **b.** to look for him as soon as
M-3 3:3 the teacher of God seems to **b.** to change
M-16 2:7 It is always possible to **b.** again, should
M-16 2:7 begin again, should the day **b.** with error.
M-16 4:7 or two after you **b.** to find it difficult. You
M-29 1:6 might do better to **b.** with the workbook.
P-in 1:5 individual can **b.** to question their reality.
P-1 1:2 and to **b.** to reconsider the spurious cause
P-1 5:2 he must **b.** to separate truth from illusion,
S-2 I.1:3 to **b.** the steps of prayer cannot but use it

## beginner 2

M-21 1:8 can be helpful, particularly for the **b.**, in
M-24 5:8 even this much is not required of the **b.**.

## Beginning 2

*beginning*

T-3 VII.5:6 is truth, and you must return to your **B.**.
T-3 VII.5:10 As you approach the **B.**, you feel the fear

## beginning 78

*Beginning*

T-2 VII.7:8 Readiness is only the **b.** of confidence.
T-3 III.6:5 of "Alpha and Omega, the **b.** and the end,
T-4 II.9:3 itself, and its interpretation of its own **b.**.
T-4 II.9:4 **b.** is usually associated with physical birth
T-4 III.3:4 its own **b.** and ends with its own ending.
T-5 IV.2:4 Physical birth is not a **b.**; it is a continuing
T-6 IV.2:7 "What are you?" was the **b.** of doubt. The
T-6 IV.8:1 into being was the **b.** of uncertainty,
T-6 V.A.6:4 because it is the **b.** step in reversing your
T-6 V.B.8:2 is really only the **b.** of the thought reversal
T-6 V.C.3:3 is merely the **b.** of the thought reversal,
T-7 I.7:8 God will take was therefore true in the **b.**,
T-8 VIII.4:5 of witnesses should be suspect from the **b.**
T-8 VIII.9:10 Health is the **b.** of the proper perspective
T-9 IV.5:3 in looking beyond error from the **b.**, and
T-11 I.1:3 this lies the **b.** of the return to knowledge;
T-11 I.11:9 is why healing is the **b.** of the recognition
T-11 IV.4:2 for it is truly the **b.** of the dawn of light.
T-11 IV.4:5 The **b.** phases of this reversal are often
T-11 V.2:3 and you are **b.** to learn that fear is not real
T-11 V.4:5 From the **b.**, then, its purpose is to be
T-11 V.16:4 reasoning ends at its **b.**, and no thought
T-11 VI.4:9 the Father together, as it was in the **b.**, is
T-11 VI.8:7 are **b.** to wake are still aware of dreams,
T-11 VIII.3:3 The recognition of this is your firm **b.**.
T-13 in.2:1 of God's Son was the **b.** of the separation,
T-13 IV.7:6 the **b.** of the appreciation of eternity lies.
T-15 IV.6:3 instant, **b.** now and reaching to eternity,
T-17 V.2:5 in this; the only difficult phase is the **b.**.
T-17 V.5:4 But at the **b.**, the situation is experienced

|  |  |
|---|---|
| T-17 VI.2:3 | clarification of the goal belongs at the **b.**, |
| T19. IV.D.19:5 | seek, the reason for the journey from its **b.** |
| T-20 IV.6:5 | the **b.** of another world goes with them. |
| T-22 III.1:1 | thought system is the **b.** of its undoing, |
| T-22 III.1:5 | here is the **b.** of a vision that has meaning. |
| T-27 VIII.5:3 | let us merely look upon the dream's **b.**, |
| T-27 VIII.7:1 | of circularity whose ending starts at its **b.**, |
| T-28 II.1:8 | creation, without **b.** and without an end. |
| T-28 II.12:7 | **B.** here, salvation will proceed to change |
| T-29 IX.10:2 | a sign that you have made a new **b.**, not |
| T-30 h | THE NEW **B.** |
| T-30 in.1:1 | The new **b.** now becomes the focus of the |
| T-31 IV.6:1 | is the **b.** of acceptance that there is a real |
| W-pI 4.3:4 | It is also the **b.** of training your mind to |
| W-pI 12.2:7 | a **b.** step in learning to give them all equal |
| W-pI 15.2:3 | That is the **b.** of real vision. You can be |
| W-pI 16.1:1 | idea for today is a **b.** step in dispelling the |
| W-pI 28.1:5 | to keeping them. And we are still at the **b.** |
| W-pI 41.6:3 | At the **b.** of the practice period, repeat |
| W-pI 42.7:2 | is a **b.** step in bringing thoughts together, |
| W-pI 43.4:3 | At the **b.** of these practice periods, repeat |
| W-pI 45.7:1 | that you thought with God in the **b.**. They |
| WpI...rI.in.1:1 | **B.** with today we will have a series of |
| W-pI 61.3:2 | **b.** step in accepting your real function on |
| W-pI 75.3:1 | passing of the old and the **b.** of the new. |
| W-pI 75.9:5 | that on this day there is a new **b.**. Without |
| W-pI 75.11:2 | as we celebrate the **b.** of your vision and |
| W-pI. 151.13:1 | except at the **b.** of the time we spend with |
| WpI.rV.in12:1 | at the **b.** and the end of practice periods, |
| W-pI 183.6:5 | No other word we use except at the **b.**, |
| W-pII in.2:1 | attempt to let the exercise be merely a **b.**. |
| Wfl in.1:2 | use them but at the **b.** of our practicing, |
| W-ep 1:1 | course is a **b.**, not an end. Your Friend |
| M-3 1:2 | involves a different relationship at the **b.**, |
| M-4 1:3 | **b.** stages of their functioning as teachers |
| M-14 1:1 | Can what has no **b.** really end? The world |
| M-16 3:1 | At the **b.**, it is wise to think in terms of |
| M-19 2:9 | one must start. Justice is the **b.**. |
| M-24 5:7 | however, is that birth was not the **b.**, and |
| C-4 3:7 | They are the one **b.**, with the end to lead |
| C-ep 3:5 | Our new **b.** has the certainty the journey |
| P-2 in.3:1 | At the **b.**, then, the patient's goal and the |
| P-2 in.4:4 | At the **b.**, it is inevitable that patients and |
| P-2 III.2:5 | may come from either one at the **b.**, and |
| P-3 II.8:4 | marks the end of a journey, not the **b.**, |
| P-3 II.8:5 | start of the **b.** stage of the first journey. |
| S-1 II.1:1 | Prayer has no **b.** and no end. It is a part of |
| S-1 II.8:2 | Nor has it a **b.**, because the goal has never |

## beginnings 3

|  |  |
|---|---|
| T-1 I.13:1 | Miracles are both **b.** and endings, and so |
| T-11 I.2:3 | There are no **b.** and no endings in God, |
| T-11 I.4:2 | that neither **b.** nor endings were created |

## begins 52

|  |  |
|---|---|
| T-2 III.3:6 | limit. Eventually everyone **b.** to recognize, |
| T-2 V.7:1 | always **b.** with the awakening of spirit, |
| T-3 VII.1:2 | It **b.** with either a making or a creating, a |
| T-4 III.3:4 | which **b.** with its own beginning and ends |
| T-6 II.3:8 | The process **b.** by excluding something |
| T-6 II.5:1 | Holy Spirit **b.** by perceiving you as perfect |
| T-6 III.1:1 | every idea **b.** in the mind of the thinker. |
| T-6 V.A.5:12 | Therefore, His teaching **b.** with the lesson |
| T-9 V.7:8 | The miracle worker **b.** by perceiving light, |
| T-12 III.10:1 | its source, and where it **b.** it must end. |
| T-12 VI.4:9 | The awakening of His Son **b.** with his |
| T-14 II.2:1 | elsewhere, **b.** His lesson in simplicity with |
| T-17 III.4:3 | attraction of the unholy relationship **b.** to |
| T-17 V.2:4 | In all its aspects, as it **b.**, develops and |
| T-18 I.5:6 | But nothing you have seen **b.** to show you |
| T-18 IX.11:4 | Where learning ends there God **b.**, for |
| T-18 IX.11:4 | before Him Who is complete where He **b.**, |
| T-20 I.2:1 | week **b.** with palms and ends with lilies, |
| T-20 V.1:2 | **b.** to find the certainty his Father has in |
| T-23 II.8:3 | From where all this **b.**, there is no sight of |
| T-28 II.9:1 | which proceeds to go the other way, **b.**. |
| T-30 I.1:3 | set **b.** to form which sees you through the |
| T-30 IV.2:2 | and silent woolly bear **b.** to squeak as he |
| T-30 IV.8:2 | For here the gap that is not there **b.** to be |
| T-30 VI.1:3 | It is here escape from fear **b.**, and will be |
| T-31 IV.3:3 | time must come when everyone **b.** to see |
| W-pI 34.1:1 | The idea for today **b.** to describe the |
| W-pI 75.2:4 | the time of light **b.** for you and everyone. |
| W-pI 109.6:1 | glad, a bird with broken wings **b.** to sing, |
| W-pI 109.6:1 | to sing, a stream long dry **b.** to flow again. |
| WpI..rIII.in1:1 | Our next review **b.** today. We will review |
| W-pI 129.7:5 | until where one **b.** another ends loses all |
| W-pI. 140.11:1 | Him speak to us five minutes as the day **b.** |
| W-pI. 151.13:2 | of the thought with which the day **b.**. And |
| W-pI. 151.15:2 | Your ministry **b.** as all your thoughts are |
| W-pI 200.8:2 | peace **b.** within the world perceived as |
| WpI rVI.in.3:6 | *me.* The day **b.** and ends with this. And we |
| W-pII. 346.1:2 | *so b. the day I share with You as I will share* |
| M-1 2:12 | Each one **b.** as a single light, but with the |
| M-2 5:1 | together, a teaching-learning situation **b.**. |
| M-4 I.A.6:4 | Now he **b.** to see the transfer value of |
| M-4 IX.1:5 | his faithfulness **b.** by resting on just some |
| C-ep 4:6 | song **b.** again which had been stopped |
| P-1 5:7 | end to the help that He **b.** and He directs. |
| P-2 I.1:2 | achieved. Therapy **b.** with the realization |
| P-2 VI.1:5 | Healing occurs as a patient **b.** to hear the |
| P-2 VI.3:5 | the mind grows fearful and **b.** to doubt its |
| P-3 II.5:8 | understanding **b.** with recognizing this, |
| S-1 III.3:4 | The next ascent **b.** with this: *What I have* |
| S-1 IV.1:1 | Until the second level at least **b.**, one |
| S-1 IV.2:2 | This step **b.** the quicker ascent, but there |
| S-1 V.1:3 | leave the ground where it **b.** to rise to God |

## begot 2

|  |  |
|---|---|
| T-31 VII.12:4 | self whose image has the wish **b.** of you. |
| W-pI 170.2:2 | For here is fear **b.** and fed with blood, to |

## begotten 4

|  |  |
|---|---|
| T-2 VII.5:14 | the world that he gave his only **b.** Son, |
| T-2 VII.5:14 | this context; "He gave it *to* His only **b.** Son. |
| T-7 VI.4:3 | its own antecedents, begetting as it was **b.** |
| T-12 III.8:1 | world that He gave it to His only **b.** Son. |

## begrudge 1

|  |  |
|---|---|
| T-21 II.4:1 | **B.** not then this little offering. Withhold |

## begun 19

|  |  |
|---|---|
| T-8 IX.8:1 | You have surely **b.** to realize that this is a |
| T-18 VI.10:2 | have **b.** to reach beyond the body, but not |
| T-23 IV.5:9 | it is over when you realize it never was **b.**. |
| T-24 VI.8:3 | both may end a journey that has never **b.**, |
| T-27 VII.6:4 | was the first attack upon yourself **b.**. And |
| T-31 IV.4:4 | judge the lesson that is but **b.** with this. |
| T-31 V.8:2 | that the world directs **b.** and ended with |
| W-pI. 135.20:2 | the ancient plan, **b.** when time was born. |
| W-pI. 151.17:3 | Now has our ministry **b.** at last, to carry |
| WpI...rV.in7:5 | lead you back to where the journey was **b.** |
| W-pII. 225.2:5 | steps which end a journey that was not **b.**. |
| M-24 5:10 | all there is to learn. His journey has **b.**. |
| C-ep 1:1 | Forget not once this journey is **b.** the end |
| C-ep 2:4 | We *have* **b.** the journey. Long ago the end |
| C-ep 3:2 | journey long ago **b.** that but seems new. |
| C-ep 3:3 | have **b.** again upon a road we travelled on |
| C-ep 4:7 | **b.** will grow in life and strength and hope, |
| P-2 V.6:3 | count as nothing, for the healing has **b.**. |
| P-3 II.8:6 | **b.** to understand what they must do may |

## behalf 54

|  |  |
|---|---|
| T-2 V.A.18:1 | much on **b.** of your own healing and that |
| T-3 I.2:4 | His Own Son on **b.** of salvation. The very |
| T-4 VII.3:12 | it may refuse to utilize it on **b.** of being. |
| T-5 III.7:7 | Spirit to reinterpret you on **b.** of God. |
| T-6 V.A.4:4 | We have too much to accomplish on **b.** of |
| T-6 V.C.7:5 | is why you must be vigilant on God's **b.**. |
| T-8 I.1:6 | on **b.** of an imaginary will that is not His. |
| T-8 V.1:5 | them your unified mind on their **b.**, as I |
| T-8 V.1:5 | as I am offering you mine on **b.** of yours. |
| T-8 VII.3:6 | God on **b.** of the function He gives it. |
| T-8 VII.4:5 | Spirit to use on **b.** of union of the Sonship |
| T-8 VIII.4:3 | a strong witness on **b.** of the ego's views. |
| T-8 IX.3:8 | dreams on **b.** of waking if you will let Him |
| T-8 IX.4:6 | if you have misused it on **b.** of sickness. |
| T-10 III.10:4 | gods, and how vigilant you are on their **b.** |
| T-11 III.8:5 | from God if you use it on **b.** of the eternal. |
| T-11 V.4:3 | its **b.** is necessarily expended on nothing. |
| T-11 V.7:1 | ego always attacks on **b.** of separation. |
| T-11 V.15:2 | perceptions which it unifies on **b.** of itself. |
| T-12 V.7:9 | for all your learning will be on its **b.**. Yet |
| T-13 VII.12:7 | not use them on **b.** of lingering in time. |
| T-14 V.6:4 | Each effort made on its **b.** is offered for |
| T-14 VI.5:6 | He would teach you how to use on your **b.** |
| T-14 VII.5:6 | Holy Spirit uses defenses on **b.** of truth |
| T-14 XI.13:4 | do so by abandoning the ego on **b.** of Him |
| T-15 I.12:1 | the Holy Spirit on **b.** of your release while |
| T-15 I.12:1 | to give it to your brothers on **b.** of theirs. |
| T-15 II.1:6 | Holy Spirit is offered to God on your **b.**, |
| T-15 III.4:8 | effort you make on **b.** of His dear Son. |
| T-15 VIII.1:4 | whatever you offer Him on **b.** of this. His |
| T-16 II.4:4 | you to use His understanding on your **b.**. |
| T-16 III.8:3 | some little effort on **b.** of bridging it. His |
| T-16 VI.8:2 | is kind, and if you use it on **b.** of reality, it |
| T-18 II.2:5 | willingness to change reality on its **b.**. |
| T-20 VII.7:4 | is a *choice* of purpose, employed on its **b.**. |
| T-21 V.7:8 | because the witnesses on its **b.** are clear. |
| T-22 I.1:5 | in this and see much evidence on its **b.**. |
| T-23 III.5:1 | that attack is justified on its **b.**, cannot |
| T-24 I.4:7 | On its **b.** they fight against the universe, |
| T-25 VI.7:5 | the Holy Spirit cannot employ on his **b.**, |
| T-25 VIII.10:5 | could they call forth to speak on his **b.**? |
| T-26 I.6:3 | the rest his witness offers on **b.** of peace. |
| T-27 V.5:4 | It is asked of you on your **b.**. A dying |
| T-31 V.9:1 | of what seems to be the evidence on its **b.**. |
| T-31 VII.5:5 | On its **b.**, remember what the concept of |
| T-31 VIII.10:4 | them, because You gave it me on their **b.**. |
| W-pI 89.1:5 | it on **b.** of the function He has given me. |
| W-pI 121.8:2 | to happiness, and use it on your own **b.**. |
| M-in 3:3 | situation on **b.** of what you really teach, |
| M-4 I.A.5:5 | his own best interests on **b.** of truth. He |
| M-4 X.1:4 | be judged by the Voice for God on His **b.**. |
| M-29 8:7 | *for you, And join your efforts on* **b.** *of God,* |
| M-29 8:7 | *of God, Knowing they are on my* **b.** *as well,* |
| P-1 3:4 | willing to "sacrifice" his "life" on its **b.**. |

## behave 8

|  |  |
|---|---|
| T-1 III.6:1 | and as you perceive so shall you **b.**. The |
| T-1 III.6:5 | You cannot **b.** appropriately unless you |
| T-1 VI.3:2 | corrected. You cannot **b.** effectively while |
| T-2 VI.5:4 | you can **b.** as you think you should, but |
| T-5 II.12:1 | I have enjoined you to **b.** as I behaved, |
| T-5 II.12:3 | your thought, and to **b.** like me as a result |
| T-31 V.9:3 | learned by now that you **b.** as if it were. |
| W-pI 126.2:2 | able to **b.** in ways which have no bearing |

## behaved 1

|  |  |
|---|---|
| T-5 II.12:1 | I have enjoined you to behave as I **b.**, but |

## behaves 2

|  |  |
|---|---|
| T-9 III.5:1 | When a brother **b.** insanely, you can heal |
| T-28 VI.2:3 | It **b.** in ways you want, but never makes |

## behaving 1

|  |  |
|---|---|
| T-19 I.3:6 | what truth has never said and **b.** insanely, |

## behavior 19

|  |  |
|---|---|
| T-1 III.6:4 | Golden Rule is the rule for appropriate **b.**. |
| T-2 VI.2:2 | You would not excuse insane **b.** on your |
| T-2 VI.2:8 | the truth by "giving" autonomy to **b.**. |
| T-2 VI.3:4 | You must change your mind, not your **b.**, |
| T-2 VI.5:3 | This produces conflicted **b.**, which is |
| T-2 VI.5:5 | This produces consistent **b.**, but entails |

T-2........VI.5:6 the mind and the **b.** are out of accord,
T-2........VI.5:9 and your **b.** inevitably becomes erratic.
T-3.........V.3:5 In this sense, when your **b.** is unstable,
T-4........IV.1:2 your attitudes, your feelings and your **b.**.
T-4........IV.2:1 change your mind by changing your **b.**,
T-5.........V.8:3 mind will affect both **b.** and experience.
T-6........I.16:6 all **b.** teaches the beliefs that motivate it.
T-7.........V.2:4 Yet we have learned that **b.** is not the level
T-13........II.4:1 Much of the ego's strange **b.** is directly
T-18.........I.3:5 this appears to introduce quite variable **b.**
T-18.........I.3:5 perception from which the **b.** stems. No
T-23.....II.10:3 by the unscrupulous **b.** of the enemy, they
W-pI.....72.3:6 He "betrays" his hostile thoughts in his **b.**

## behavioral 1

T-2......VI.5:10 Correcting at the **b.** level can shift the

## behaviorally 1

T-12.........I.2:4 You may then control your reactions **b.**,

## beheld 7

T-11.....V.17:7 is the sign that they have **b.** God's Son,
T-12...VII.12:4 is a judgment of what you **b.** within. If it
T-24......IV.5:2 you have **b.** some sin within your brother,
T-27.....VII.6:3 And this is where your guilt was first **b.**.
W-pI.170.11:6 by its weight; **b.** not in its sightless eyes,
W-pI...198.7:4 upon the place where you **b.** Their blood,
W-pI...200.5:1 where you **b.** but chains and iron doors.

## behind 100

T-4........I.10:3 Leave it **b.**! Do not listen to it and do not
T-7......VII.3:4 escape from this image by leaving it **b.**.
T-8.........V.6:6 Leave all illusions **b.**, and reach beyond
T-11.........I.4:2 You who made delay can leave time **b.**
T-11......VI.6:3 The freedom to leave **b.** everything that
T-13.........I.3:5 a long carpet spread along the past **b.** you
T-13......VI.6:1 Judgment and condemnation are **b.** you,
T-13.....VII.5:9 and waits for you to leave the past **b.** and
T-14.......II.7:6 this door of nothing, and **b.** it *is* nothing.
T-14....III.16:3 when all knowledge lies **b.** every decision
T-14.......V.1:8 Leave the world of death **b.**, and return
T-14......VI.8:4 serve to guard the dark doors **b.** which
T-14... VIII.1:3 **B.** the dark doors you have closed lies
T-14.......X.1:7 enter into it they leave all reflections **b.**.
T-14.......X.8:9 this fact **b.** impressive sounding words,
T-15......III.8:1 Is it a sacrifice to leave littleness **b.**, and
T-15......VI.6:5 drawn irresistibly into the light **b.** it, can
T-15.......X.6:7 for the one idea that hides **b.** them all;
T-15......XI.3:3 Leave nothing **b.**, for release is total, and
T-16.....IV.10:3 are the veil **b.** which truth is hidden. To
T-18......IX.5:3 not apparent until you see the light **b.** it.
T19....IV.A.3:7 What you would still contain **b.** your little
T19....IV.B.8:3 me **b.** the obstacles you raise to freedom,
T-20.........I.4:2 glimpses of the face of Christ **b.** the veil,
T-20......VI.9:1 and leave no trace **b.** their going. The
T-20......VI.9:7 transcended them, and left them far **b.**.
T-20.....VI.10:5 the body thankfully **b.** and resting in the
T-21......VI.8:7 would direct you how to leave insanity **b.**.
T-21......VI.8:8 not **b.** insanity in order to escape from
T-24......III.5:6 be brought to Them, and left **b.**. Salvation
T-26......IV.1:2 the gate **b.** which total lack of limits lies.
T-27.......V.6:1 is left **b.** on your returning to the world.
T-27.....V.10:4 will be seen, but thousands stand **b.** him,
T-27......VI.2:8 pain **b.** the pleasure will be felt no more.
T-28......III.7:3 They have nothing left **b.** the open door.
T-29.........I.8:4 there is no gap **b.** which you can hide?
T-30......III.3:1 **B.** the search for every idol lies the
T-30.........IV.h The Truth **b.** Illusions
T-30......IV.1:3 For the truth **b.** them is so lovely and so
T-30.......V.3:7 the step in which is all forgiveness left **b.**.
T-31......I.10:3 that sings **b.** each murderous attack and
T-31.......II.9:3 walk with you, and thinks perhaps a bit **b.**
T-31......IV.1:7 you escape from them by leaving them **b.**
T-31.....VII.1:7 believing that the "bad" must lurk **b.**.
W-pI.......2.1:5 and apply the idea to what was **b.** you.
W-pI.....44.5:4 leave **b.** everything that you now believe,
W-pI.....56.3:4 the door **b.** this world be opened for me,
W-pI.....56.4:2 see. **B.** every image I have made, the truth
W-pI.....56.4:3 **B.** every veil I have drawn across the face
W-pI.....56.5:2 **b.** all my insane thoughts of separation
W-pI.....78.3:1 He waits for you **b.** your grievances, and
W-pI.....78.5:3 Through seeing him **b.** the grievances
W-pI...78.10:2 refuse to hide his light **b.** our grievances.
W-pI.....89.2:2 *B. this is a miracle to which I am entitled. Let*
W-pI.....90.2:3 *miracle **b.** this grievance will resolve it for*
W-pI.....91.5:1 in which you try to leave your weakness **b.**
W-pI.....93.9:5 by hiding Its majesty **b.** the tiny idols of
W-pI.....99.6:1 as appearances **b.** which is the changeless
W-pI...108.1:4 Thought **b.** it will appear instead to take
W-pI...108.6:2 thought **b.** it can be generalized to other
WpI. rIII.in3:3 **b.** a cloak of situations you cannot control
W-pI.122.13:4 change; the light of truth **b.** appearances.
W-pI...124.2:5 the way because the light we carry stays **b.**
W-pI.127.10:3 Today we leave the past **b.** us, nevermore
W-pI...128.1:3 if he would leave the world **b.** and soar
W-pI.131.10:1 Leave foolish thoughts like these **b.** today
W-pI.134.12:5 lifts his foot to stride ahead a star is left **b.**
W-pI...152.4:3 is concealed **b.** a vast array of choices that
W-pI...153.9:2 for we have left all fearful thoughts **b.**.
W-pI...155.2:6 But to let illusion sink **b.** the truth and let
W-pI...155.5:1 and deprivation both are quickly left **b.**.
W-pI...157.4:3 wherein you quickly leave the world **b.**.
W-pI...158.4:2 plan **b.** appearances that does not change.
W-pI.169.14:3 revelation stands not far **b.**. Its coming is
W-pI...187.4:6 It is the thought **b.** the form of things that
W-pI...187.6:5 the one idea that stands **b.** them all, and
W-pI...194.1:2 with the goal in sight and obstacles **b.**.
W-pI...194.9:5 choice for us that leaves temptation far **b.**.
W-pI...196.9:3 the deadly fear of God projection hides **b.**
W-pI...200.8:1 everyone will cross, to leave this world **b.**.
W-pII..225.1:2 *beloved, with fear **b.** and only peace ahead.*
W-pII......2.3:4 it, and the memory of God not far **b.**.
W-pII..264.1:1 *Father, You stand before me and **b.**, beside*
W-pII..314.2:2 *in Your Hands, leaving **b.** our past mistakes,*
M-12 .......6:11 teachers acknowledge as **b.** the dream,
M-14 .........3:6 of God must learn to pass by and leave **b.**.
M-21 .........5:5 self-perception which he would leave **b.**.
M-21 .........5:8 have God's Word **b.** their symbols. And
M-23 .........4:6 far **b.** a grateful heart and thankful mind.
M-25 .........6:9 their hearts, and His holy sight not far **b.**.
M-26 .........3:9 to those remaining **b.** are few indeed. And
M-28 .........5:5 His sinlessness, His Love **b.** all forms,
C-2............2:5 **b.** the words that seem to make it so.
C-2............7:6 you left **b.** at last and finally passed by.
C-3............8:4 stands **b.** all joining but beyond them all.
C-ep...........1:8 **B.** each one there is reality and there is
P-2........VI.3:5 the thought **b.** the form breaks through,
S-1.........II.7:3 of you. The things of earth are left **b.**, all
S-2...........I.6:5 which still remains unchanged **b.** them all
S-2.........II.5:1 Forgiveness-to-destroy will often hide **b.**

## behold 138

T-8........VI.2:1 blind the Sons to the Father if they **b.** it.
T-8........VI.2:2 You cannot **b.** the world and know God.
T-9.......IV.12:1 **B.**, my child, reality is here. It belongs to
T-9..... VIII.8:5 to **b.** what He created because it is His joy.
T-10........II.3:6 your will to remember Him, and **b.**! He
T-11.....V.17:6 stand in His light and **b.** what He created.
T-12....III.10:8 look out in peace and **b.** the world truly.
T-12......IV.6:1 **B.** the Guide your Father gave you, that
T-12.......V.1:4 was effective, you **b.** yourself as weakened
T-12.....VII.7:3 then you look out and **b.** his witnesses.
T-12...VII.12:4 Everything you **b.** without is a judgment
T-12... VIII.6:6 it. Yet what He does see is yours to **b.**, and
T-13.....V.11:2 And all who would **b.** Him can see Him,
T-13...X.11:10 *B. the Son of God, and look upon his purity*
T-14.......II.8:1 **B.** your brothers in their freedom, and
T-14.....VII.7:8 **B.** your will, accepting it as His, with all
T-15... VIII.2:6 **B.** the only need that God and His Son
T-17.......II.1:7 will **b.** the beauty the Holy Spirit loves to
T-19....III.11:1 and **b.** what He would show you in your
T19..IV.C.10:7 **B.** this infant, to whom you gave a resting
T19.IV.D.14:1 **B.** your Friend, the Christ Who stands
T19.IV.D.17:6 **B.** the gift of freedom that I gave the Holy
T-20.........I.4:2 will **b.** your brother's face and recognize it
T-20......II.11:3 singing as you **b.** the open door of Heaven
T-20..VIII.11:3 you can **b.** the holiness God gave His Son.
T-21.......in.2:3 If you **b.** disaster and catastrophe, you
T-22......II.10:1 **B.** the great projection, but look on it
T-22......III.3:4 it. The body's eyes **b.** it as solid granite, so
T-23......II.12:8 **B.**, unveiled, the ego's secret gift, torn
T-24.......V.4:7 The sin its eyes **b.** in him and love to look
T-24......VI.5:1 and **b.** in him the whole reversal of the
T-25.........I.2:3 **B.** the body, and you will believe that you
T-25.........I.3:5 is a part of what it is your purpose to **b.**,
T-25........II.8:7 your only function to **b.** in him what he
T-25.....IV.1:4 it is their purpose to **b.** it and rejoice.
T-25......VI.3:2 Would you **b.** your brother? God is glad
T-26......IV.3:3 Who could **b.** the face of Christ and not
T-26.....V.14:5 and **b.** the world in which perception of
T-26......IX.1:6 that you may **b.** his glory and rejoice that
T-27.........I.4:6 an easy price, if they can say, "**B.** me,
T-27.......I.10:7 to your brother let its message be, "**B.** me,
T-27.....V.11:6 you go, will you **b.** its multiplied effects.
T-27.....V.11:7 Yet all the witnesses that you **b.** will be far
T-27....VIII.8:4 do your eyes **b.** its heavy consequences,
T-27....VIII.9:7 holy Son of God, **b.** your idle dream, in
T-28.......V.5:3 Let not your eyes **b.** a dream; your ears
T-28.......V.7:6 you **b.** the innocence and emptiness of sin
T-29........II.2:8 and you will not **b.** a reason for regret,
T-29......II.10:2 when you **b.** the body as a thing you love,
T-29.......V.3:1 and would **b.** him waken and be glad. He
T-29.......V.5:2 **B.** His Son, His perfect gift, in whom his
T-29.......V.5:3 and where it lies in him **b.** your peace.
T-30....VIII.6:8 You but **b.** yourself in what you see. As he
T-31.......I.11:8 And **b.**! Your answer is the proof of what
T-31.....V.15:6 world, and you **b.** it as you see yourself.
T-31......VI.2:2 see the body, you **b.** a world of separation
T-31......VI.3:1 Salvation does not ask that you **b.** the
T-31......VI.3:3 how to **b.** a world apart from it. It is your
T-31.....VII.7:2 vision, so that you **b.** nothing with clarity.
T-31.....VII.8:1 **B.** your role within the universe! To every
T-31...VII.12:4 you will **b.** your brother in the likeness of
T-31...VII.13:5 asks, "What is the meaning of what I **b.**?"
T-31....VIII.6:2 What you **b.** as sickness and as pain, as
T-31....VIII.8:5 you see, for otherwise you will **b.** it not.
W-pI.....54.5:4 I would **b.** the proof that what has been
W-pI...73.10:3 *Let me **b.** the light that reflects God's Will*
W-pI.....78.1:4 light, but you **b.** your grievances instead.
W-pI.....78.2:3 our eyes in silence to **b.** the Son of God.
W-pI.....78.7:3 *Let me **b.** my savior in this one You have*
W-pI.....92.3:3 in darkness to **b.** the likeness of itself; the
W-pI...108.2:1 possible is not the light the body's eyes **b.**.
W-pI...121.3:3 **b.** except the proof that all its sins are real
W-pI...124.4:5 eyes **b.** His loveliness in all we look upon.
W-pI...129.8:2 Here is light your eyes can not **b.**. And yet
W-pI.130.11:1 sight, and what you will **b.** is hell indeed.
W-pI...132.4:3 And what you **b.** upon it are your wishes,
W-pI...132.7:4 because what they **b.** must be the truth,
W-pI...151.7:2 be judged by what your eyes **b.** in him,
W-pI.151.10:2 **b.** the gentle face of Christ in all of them.
W-pI...153.5:5 For you **b.** the Son of God as but a victim
W-pI...156.5:1 in you is what the universe longs to **b.**. All
W-pI.159.10:1 **B.** the store of miracles set out for you to
W-pI...161.7:5 consuming everything its eyes **b.**, seeing
W-pI...161.9:1 eyes **b.** in one whom Heaven cherishes,
W-pI.161.11:8 *I would **b.** you with the eyes of Christ, and see*
W-pI.161.12:3 own. **B.** him now, whom you have seen as
W-pI...164.7:6 as we **b.** it in the light in which our Savior
W-pI...181.2:3 and what you **b.** will change accordingly.
W-pI...181.8:3 mistakes, we will **b.** a wholly sinless world
W-pI...187.9:5 will **b.** will take away all thought of form,
W-pI.187.11:3 We would **b.** it shining with the grace of
W-pI...192.3:6 eyes already opening **b.** the joyful sights
W-pI.198.12:5 that to **b.** the Son is to perceive no more,
W-pI...211.1:2 *b. it in the Son whom He created as my Self.* I
W-pI...218.1:3 *Yet today I can **b.** this glory and be glad.* I am
W-pII .....in.6:5 Christ's vision we **b.** a world beyond the
W-pII .226.1:4 But if I see no value in the world as I **b.** it,
W-pII .237.1:4 And I **b.** the world that Christ would have
W-pII .....3.5:5 it must **b.** it through the eyes of Christ,
W-pII .247.1:2 **B.** it anywhere, and I will suffer. For

W-pII .250.1:1 Let me b. the Son of God today, and
W-pII .250.2:2 *today I would b. his gentleness instead of my*
W-pII .....4.1:4 eyes, for what is there the sinless would b.
W-pII .261.1:2 b. myself where I perceive my strength,
W-pII .270.1:1 *eyes b. into the sight of a forgiven world.*
W-pII .....6.5:3 As we b. His glory, will we know we have
W-pII .288.2:2 know you have forgiven me if you b. your
W-pII .290.1:4 I made is frightening and painful to b..
W-pII .....9.5:6 B., the Son of God is one in us, and we
W-pII .301.1:4 *Let me today b. it uncondemned, through*
W-pII .304.1:2 can I b. the holy sights Christ looks upon,
W-pII .312.1:4 and fail to see what we have chosen to b..
W-pII .313.2:1 today b. each other in the sight of Christ.
W-pII .316.2:3 *provide the means by which I can b. them,*
W-pII .325.2:2 *Let me b. what only Yours reflect, for Yours*
W-pII .326.2:1 Let us today b. earth disappear, at first
W-pII .334.2:4 *Today I would b. my brother sinless. This*
W-pII .334.2:5 *Will for me, for so will I b. my sinlessness.*
W-pII .335.1:7 having chosen to b. my brother in its holy
W-pII .346.1:7 *toys I made as I b. Your glory and my own.*
W-pII .347.1:6 *He sees what I b., and yet He knows the truth*
W-pII ....351.h pain. And which I choose to see I will b..
W-pII .357.1:5 *be: "B. his sinlessness, and be you healed."*
W-ep .........6:5 teaches us how to b. him through His eyes
M-5 .... III.2:11 brothers to turn away from death: "B.,
M-8 ...........1:6 What the body's eyes b. is only conflict.
M-8 ...........3:3 the mind that judges what the eyes b.. It
M-12 .........6:9 They recognize that to b. a dream figure
M-26 .........4:6 B. the problem, ask for the answer, and
C-3............8:2 you are sinless and b. your sinlessness.
C-5............5:8 b. how dear a brother he would be to you.
P-2......... V.7:8 of God, we will b. in him the face of Christ
P-2....... VII.6:8 b. Christ's shining face as it looks back at
P-2....... VII.7:8 B. your God in him, for what you see will
S-2.........in.1:5 B. the greatest help that God ordained to
S-2......... II.4:5 B., how good are you who bear with
S-2........ III.7:8 B. your brother there beyond the door;
S-3......... II.2:4 Now we can b. Him without blinders, in

## beholden 1

T-20.... VI.11:2 tiny spot of space and time, b. unto death

## beholder 1

T-25...... VI.1:1 they look on speaks of Him to the b.. He

## beholders 1

T-25.........I.4:5 hides the face of Christ from its b.. You

## beholding 4

T-12....VIII.8:3 else invisible, for b. it is total perception.
T-19...... IV.3:2 upon your brother, you are b. Him. For
T-31... VII.15:3 unknown, b. them with eyes unopened.
W-pI.....73.2:5 B. them, you do not know your brothers

## beholds 21

T-13..... V.10:3 for through Christ's vision He b. Himself.
T-13....VIII.2:7 the vision of Christ b. everything in light.
T-18........I.11:5 it! Heaven b. it, and rejoices that you have
T-22...... VI.8:1 each one is released as he b. his savior in
T-24....... V.6:8 in each living thing that He b. and loves.
T-24...... VI.8:7 The Christ in you b. his holiness. Your
T-24...... VI.8:8 specialness looks on his body and b. him
T-27.........I.5:6 it to the innocence that he b. in you. Here
T-31..... VII.8:5 what he looks upon, to judge what he b..
T-31..... VII.8:6 he looks on everyone as he b. this one.
W-pI... 121.4:2 shrieks as it b. its own projections rising
W-pI... 151.7:4 you are vanish before the splendor He b..
W-pI... 158.5:6 sees because the Mind of Christ b. it too.
W-pI... 158.7:3 It b. a light beyond the body; an idea
W-pI... 159.4:4 Christ b. no sin in anyone. And in His
W-pI... 160.9:2 b. His Own and joyously unites with them
W-pI... 161.8:2 he b. is his own fear external to himself,
W-pI... 188.2:4 deny the presence of what he b. in him? It
W-pII .....3.4:3 His light, and see the world as He b. it.

W-pII .271.2:2 *b. invites Your memory to be restored to me.*
W-pII .313.1:1 *there is a vision which b. all things as sinless,*

## Being 14

*being*

T-4 ...... VII.6:6 knows it in His Own B. and its experience
T-7 ....... IV.7:5 All being is in Him Who is all B.. You are
T-7 ...... V.6:15 created you by sharing His B. with you.
T-7 ....... IX.2:4 is part of Him and shares His B. with Him
T-7 ...... IX.2:10 to contain God, but wills to extend His B..
T-7 ....... IX.3:1 The extension of God's B. is spirit's only
T-7 ....... XI.7:7 Because God shared His B. with you, you
T-11 ...VIII.7:6 and whose freedom is protected by His B..
T-12 ...VIII.7:9 share God's B. with Him could never be
T-13 .... VII.5:8 not. His B. does not depend upon your
T-13 ...VIII.6:7 to you. His B. is His Father's gift to Him.
T-24 ..... VI.5:6 in everything that lives and shares His B..
W-pI... 169.5:2 And in His B., He encompasses all things.
W-pI... 197.7:4 His B. in His Father is secure, because

## being 63

• existence

*verb, adverb*

*Being*

*See also* pseudo-being

T-2 .....VIII.2:4 brought into b. only after the separation,
T-4 ....... III.3:6 of permanence and unshakable b.. No
T-4 ..... III.10:1 The calm b. of God's Kingdom, which in
T-4 ....... IV.9:4 creation and brought your mind into b..
T-4 ...... VII.2:1 without the relationships that imply b..
T-4 .... VII.3:12 it may refuse to utilize it on behalf of b..
T-4 ...... VII.4:1 as well as b. rest on communication.
T-4 ...... VII.4:3 undertaking. B. is completely without
T-4 ...... VII.5:1 God, Who encompasses all b., created
T-4 ...... VII.5:7 is no difference between *having* and *b., as*
T-4 ...... VII.5:8 of b. the mind gives everything always.
T-5 ..........I.1:5 no difference between *having* and *b.*. The
T-5 ..........I.5:2 into b. with the separation as a protection
T-5 .........II.2:4 because before that it had only b., and
T-5 ..... III.2:10 God in him, and thus acknowledge Its b..
T-5 ..... IV.8:13 Whose Heart and Hands we have our b..
T-6 ....... III.1:5 Therefore, b. is never threatened. Your
T-6 ....... IV.7:4 *been. B.* alone lives in the Kingdom, where
T-6 ....... IV.8:1 into b. was the beginning of uncertainty,
T-6 .....V.A.5:1 to God, translates communication into b.,
T-6 .....V.B.3:4 of *having* and b. is not yet perceived. Until
T-6 .....V.B.8:1 since *having* and *b.* are still not equated. It
T-6 .....V.C.5:2 You create by your true b., but what you
T-6 .....V.C.5:8 the translation of *having* into *b.* by the very
T-6 .....V.C.7:3 is the preparation for *b.* without question.
T-6 .....V.C.8:4 protection, since b. cannot be assailed.
T-6 .....V.C.8:5 real sense of b. cannot be yours while you
T-6 .....V.C.8:7 about b. must not enter your mind, or
T-6 ...V.C.10:7 upon the b. which you both *have* and *are*.
T-7 ..........I.7:9 because its b. is eternally changeless. It
T-7 .........II.3:6 God and His Sons, in the surety of b.,
T-7 ....... III.4:7 *having* and *b.* are ultimately reconciled
T-7 ....... IV.7:5 All b. is in Him Who is all Being. You are
T-7 ....... IV.7:6 are therefore in Him since your b. is His.
T-7 ....... VI.2:4 This loses the awareness of b., induces
T-7 ....... VI.3:9 *you*, and perceiving your b. as nonexistent.
T-7 ..... VI.10:1 because your b. *is* the knowledge of God.
T-7 ...... VII.5:4 and *are*, and so you do not know your b..
T-7 .....VIII.7:5 wholeness has no limits because b. is
T-7 ....... IX.2:6 B. *must* be extended. That is how it retains
T-7 ....... IX.2:8 Spirit yearns to share its b. as its Creator
T-7 ....... IX.3:7 of your spirit can interfere with its b..
T-7 ....... IX.5:2 They are there as part of your own b.,
T-7 ....... XI.7:6 B. is known by sharing. Because God
T-8 ....... III.2:7 this is the natural outcome of their b..
T-8 ....... VI.9:5 be separated from your life and your b.?
T-8 .....VIII.1:9 are part of b. since they arise from it, but
T-8 .....VIII.7:7 only knowledge has b. and the ego has no
T-8 .....VIII.7:7 has no knowledge, then the ego has no b..
T-9 ........I.11:8 your cooperation is the law of its b.. You
T-10 ...... V.8:2 in His acknowledgment of you lies your b.
T-11 .......II.1:4 *having* and *b.* is to unite your will with His,

T-12 ..... VI.6:1 for his b. is in Christ as Christ's is in God.
T-12 .... VII.2:4 what it does, you recognize its b.. And by
T-13 ........I.6:5 You have denied the condition of his b.,
T-18 ...VIII.4:4 its total dependence on them for its b.. Its
T-18 ...VIII.6:6 *is* the oneness in which its b. was created.
T-22 ... VI.14:8 extends its b. and creates more of itself.
T-24 .... VII.7:3 A perfect b., all-encompassing and all-
W-pI .. 130.4:5 have no cause, no b. and no consequence.
W-pI .. 186.8:5 very b. seems to change as we experience
W-pII . 307.1:5 *Your Son is one with You in b. and in will,*
C-5 ............ 2:3 illusion, for he seemed to be a separate b.,

## being 311

• verb, adverb

*existence*

*Being*

T-1 ....... III.3:2 B. filled with spirit, they forgive in return.
T-1 ....... III.7:2 b. united this mind goes out to everyone,
T-1 .... VII.5:10 means are b. carefully explained to you.
T-2 .......II.1:10 of b. shaken by errors of any kind. It
T-2 ....... III.5:4 is worthy of b. offered at the altar of God,
T-2 ... V.A.14:5 B. without substantial content, it lends
T-2 ....... VI.1:1 B. afraid seems to be involuntary;
T-3 ....... III.2:4 The miracle, b. a way of perceiving, is not
T-3 ....... VI.5:1 have judged yourself as capable of b. tired
T-3 ....... VI.5:3 idea of b. more unworthy than they are.
T-3 ....... VI.5:5 You are not really capable of b. tired, but
T-3 ....... VI.8:8 B. uncertain of your true Authorship, you
T-4 ..........I.6:7 I am constantly b. perceived as a teacher
T-4 .........II.1:3 errors were not b. repeated in the present.
T-4 .........II.8:8 perceive itself as b. rejected by something
T-4 .....II.11:11 nor is it understood by b. compared to an
T-4 ....... III.4:3 B. made out of the denial of the Father,
T-4 ....... III.9:7 *having* the Kingdom of God and *b.* the
T-4 ....... IV.3:2 of b. deprived of something you want and
T-4 .........V.2:6 to it. B. concerned primarily with its own
T-4 .........V.2:7 attempts to save itself from b. swept away
T-4 .........V.4:6 B. told by the ego that it is really part of
T-4 ...... VII.8:2 is impossible without b. wholly harmless,
T-5 ........in.1:7 attempt to heal without b. wholly joyous
T-5 ........in.3:1 b. blessed by every beneficent thought of
T-5 ..........I.2:2 *Thoughts increase by b. given away. The*
T-5 ....... III.2:2 B. thought, the idea gains as it is shared.
T-5 ....... III.2:3 B. the Call *for* God, it is also the idea *of* God
T-5 ....... III.2:6 It is strengthened by b. given away. It
T-5 ..... IV.3:10 making them, too, worthy of b. shared.
T-5 .........V.5:2 B. sane, the mind heals the body because
T-5 ....... VI.4:7 B. afraid, you do not appeal to the Higher
T-5 ....... VI.7:1 that ideas increase only by b. shared. The
T-5 ...... VII.2:5 of b. healed *because* God created it whole.
T-6 ........in.1:2 rather than b. blamed on others. Anger
T-6 ..........I.3:1 for years as if you were b. crucified. This is
T-6 ........I.10:5 by b. able to hear the Holy Spirit in others
T-6 ..... IV.12:9 it. B. questioned, He did not question. He
T-6 ..... V.B.3:6 since it is b. learned by a conflicted mind.
T-6 ... V.B.3:10 b. taught to react to both as if what you
T-6 ..... V.C.1:8 b. in fundamental disagreement about
T-7 ..........I.3:5 B. limitless it does not stop. It creates
T-7 .........II.3:7 is not adapted at all, b. the law of creation
T-7 ....... III.1:2 B. conflict-free, He maximizes all efforts
T-7 ..... III.2:11 ego, then, is always b. undone, and does
T-7 ....... IV.5:5 b. the only way of perceiving the Sonship
T-7 ..... IV.7:10 to all the Sonship, b. what the Sonship is.
T-7 ....... VI.9:6 this totally, b. fully committed to it. It is
T-7 ..... VI.11:8 capable of b. appreciated and loved. That
T-7 ..... VI.13:7 B. a perfect accomplishment, the Sonship
T-7 ...... VII.1:9 of b. used positively as well as negatively.
T-7 ...... VII.9:1 B. the part of your mind that does not
T-7 ...... VII.9:1 for itself, and b. without allegiance to God
T-7 .....VIII.6:5 may not be recognized as b. beyond belief
T-7 ....... IX.1:6 it responds as if it were b. sided against.
T-7 ....... IX.5:3 b. created for the Sonship as a whole.
T-7 .........X.8:5 B. a lesson in sharing it is a lesson in love,
T-7 ....... XI.1:5 nature, b. out of accord with God's laws.
T-8 ....... III.2:3 you, b. an experience of total willingness.
T-8 ....... IV.1:2 does not vacillate, b. changeless forever.
T-8 ....... IV.3:4 by b. aware of the Father's Will myself.
T-8 ....... IV.6:8 equal in will, all b. the Will of their Father

T-8 IV.8:1 **b.** an acknowledgment of what they are
T-8 V.1:7 By not **b.** separate, the Mind of God is
T-8 V.2:1 creator, **b.** wholly in the likeness of God,
T-8 VI.7:1 **b.** a contradiction in terms that actually
T-8 VI.9:2 **b.** born of my knowledge of myself and
T-8 VII.2:2 **B.** the Communication Link between God
T-8 VII.8:3 **B.** faced with an impossible learning
T-8 VIII.9:10 what life is, **b.** the Voice for Life Itself.
T-9 I.10:4 with form, **b.** aware only of meaning. The
T-9 I.10:6 to Him are real, **b.** of your right mind.
T-9 II.11:8 **b.** the exact measure of the value you put
T-9 III.6:8 not because you are **b.** punished for it, but
T-9 V.8:3 **b.** *for* him, it must also be for his patient.
T-9 VI.7:1 is one time, its only dimension **b.** "always.
T-9 VIII.6:6 **B.** the level of shift, it is experienced as
T-10 in.3:7 you from beyond it because, **b.** in God,
T-10 I.3:2 You do not remember **b.** awake. When
T-10 I.4:3 want only truth, and **b.** at last your will, it
T-11 I.7:9 And **b.** an extension of His Will, yours
T-11 II.3:3 And **b.** without meaning to you, you will
T-11 III.1:7 **b.** blind it does not see whom it attacks.
T-11 V.5:2 **b.** out of accord with your true nature. I
T-11 VII.2:5 And **b.** loving they are like the Father, and
T-11 VII.3:7 you made is capable of **b.** unlike Him. Yet
T-11 VIII.9:6 **b.** deceived in yourself you are deceived in
T-12 IV.3:2 **B.** unable to love, the ego would be totally
T-12 VI.7:7 and **b.** in God it must also be in you.
T-12 VIII.4:8 more past than future, **b.** forever always.
T-12 VIII.8:7 **B.** corrected it gives place to knowledge,
T-13 in.1:4 itself as separate from the mind **b.** judged,
T-13 I.5:4 **B.** in him, he has found it. *When* he finds it
T-13 I.7:4 **b.** forever unwilling to be without him.
T-13 I.9:4 His Son, and **b.** guiltless he is eternal.
T-13 I.10:3 **b.** fully committed to the insane notion
T-13 I.11:6 And **b.** true for you, you cannot attack
T-13 I.11:8 And **b.** wholly pure, you are invulnerable.
T-13 V.1:2 **b.** offered by the eternal to the eternal. In
T-13 V.2:4 **b.** perceived in one separate mind only.
T-13 VII.4:3 answers, **b.** unable to deny a call for help,
T-13 VII.8:6 yours, **b.** the gift of God unto His Son.
T-13 VIII.2:3 of knowledge, **b.** in the Mind of God,
T-13 VIII.4:2 from Either, **b.** in the Mind of Both, and
T-13 IX.3:1 it, for **b.** nothing but your own projection,
T-13 XI.4:2 you what is capable of **b.** wholly shared. It
T-14 III.3:2 is living here, as creating is **b.** in Heaven.
T-14 III.7:7 without cause, and **b.** without cause,
T-14 III.12:3 against it, for **b.** of Him it must be true.
T-14 IV.6:2 you will be led as gently as if you were **b.**
T-14 VI.3:4 They do nothing at all, **b.** nothing at all.
T-14 VII.2:4 It is there, wherever you are, **b.** within you
T-14 IX.3:1 Merely by **b.** what it is, does truth release
T-14 X.2:7 order, **b.** based not on differences but on
T-14 X.6:13 limitless. And **b.** always maximal, it offers
T-14 X.11:2 open and freely accessible to all, **b.** for all.
T-14 XI.7:6 And **b.** yours He cannot change Himself,
T-15 II.1:2 *for* time. **B.** in you, it is eternal. What holds
T-15 II.2:3 It will come, **b.** the lesson God gives you,
T-15 IV.8:6 **b.** the acceptance of the single Will that
T-15 VII.1:4 **B.** complete, it asks nothing. Being wholly
T-15 VII.1:5 **B.** wholly pure, everyone joined in it has
T-15 VIII.4:5 this universe, **b.** of God, is far beyond the
T-15 IX.6:3 but because your power, **b.** His, is as great
T-15 X.9:1 succeed in **b.** partial hostage to the ego,
T-15 X.9:6 is simple, **b.** of God, and therefore very
T-15 XI.5:6 attack, **b.** the belief that attack is justified.
T-15 XI.9:4 Him, **b.** host to Him Who created them.
T-16 II.1:8 have to be miraculous, **b.** part of them.
T-16 II.7:2 are both **b.** brought into your awareness.
T-16 III.8:4 make Heaven what it is, **b.** joined within it
T-16 V.1:5 aspects of what is really **b.** attempted that
T-16 V.3:6 of Heaven, **b.** made to be its opposite, and
T-16 V.4:4 **b.** the one condition in which Heaven
T-16 VII.7:5 not prevent the timeless from **b.** what it is
T-17 III.3:3 separated off as **b.** the only parts of value.
T-17 IV.10:6 For you attack Them, **b.** part of Them,
T-17 V.6:4 that the rewards of faith are **b.** introduced
T-17 VI.7:4 been denied, **b.** withheld from where it
T-17 VII.3:1 a relationship, **b.** the joining of thoughts.
T-18 I.2:4 **B.** united, they are one because they are
T-18 II.7:10 in one purpose, **b.** of one mind with Him.
T-18 VI.5:5 only what He would have it be, **b.** His Will
T-18 VI.7:5 incapable of reaching out as **b.** reached.
T-18 VI.11:1 a sense of **b.** transported beyond himself.
T-18 VIII.6:5 **b.** continuous with it and at one with it. It
T-18 IX.2:3 **b.** based on what this little kingdom really
T-19 I.3:6 insanely, **b.** imprisoned *by* insanity.
T-19 I.4:4 and kept you both apart from **b.** healed.
T-19 I.16:3 His Son is slave to nothing, **b.** lord of all,
T-19 I.16:4 incapable of **b.** kept in prison or limited
T19. IV.A.10:7 **B.** wholly without attack, it could not be
T-20 IV.1:8 **B.** without illusion of what you are, the
T-20 VII.1:3 **B.** so simple and direct, this course has
T-21 II.1:3 And **b.** true, it is so simple that it cannot
T-21 V.5:4 of God must be in you now, **b.** eternal.
T-21 VI.7:2 instead without the other **b.** blessed by it,
T-21 VI.9:5 Love plans is like Itself in this: **B.** united,
T-21 VI.9:6 And **b.** one with It, it must be given you to
T-21 VII.1:2 **B.** helpless is the cost of sin. Helplessness
T-21 VIII.3:3 if you do not have it always, **b.** what it is,
T-22 I.1:6 uneasiness, your sense of **b.** disconnected,
T-22 I.9:2 what is part of Him is worthy of **b.** joined.
T-22 II.6:4 to do what holds no hope of ever **b.** done.
T-23 in.1:7 **B.** opposed to it, it is God's "enemy." And
T-23 I.3:9 The ego joins with nothing, **b.** nothing.
T-23 I.7:5 **B.** fragmented, they fragment. But truth is
T-23 I.10:1 no illusion, **b.** as true and holy as Himself.
T-23 II.4:5 **b.** the belief the Son of God can make
T-24 I.4:2 incapable of **b.** like what he condemns,
T-25 II.9:7 thank His perfect Son for **b.** what he is.
T-25 III.8:5 damned forever, **b.** forever unforgivable.
T-25 VI.1:8 And **b.** in accord with what God wills, he
T-25 VII.9:4 him and whatever hope he has of **b.** sane.
T-25. VIII.4:10 And justice, **b.** blind, is satisfied by being
T-25. VIII.4:10 justice, being blind, is satisfied by **b.** paid,
T-25 VIII.8:6 by **b.** separate and apart from love. And
T-27 I.9:9 to nothing yet, its purpose **b.** open, and
T-27 II.13:1 that is its purpose, **b.** what it really is.
T-27 V.5:1 back because he was afraid of **b.** healed?
T-27 V.6:2 And **b.** blessed you will bring blessing.
T-27 VII.2:1 Now you are **b.** shown you *can* escape. All
T-27 VIII.7:3 think that what you did is **b.** done to you.
T-27 VIII.7:4 you thought is **b.** placed outside yourself,
T-28 I.1:5 but **b.** kept in memory appears to have
T-28 I.2:5 as selective as perception, **b.** its past tense
T-28 III.1:6 of fear to one that is already **b.** dreamed.
T-28 IV.9:4 is recognized as **b.** part of the completed
T-28 VII.2:5 at all, its oneness **b.** where the healing is.
T-29 I.9:6 God? Yet can your self be lost by **b.** found
T-29 II.2:2 And **b.** healed, the power to heal must
T-29 II.8:8 god, protecting you from **b.** part of Him.
T-29 V.5:7 And **b.** empty they receive, instead, a
T-29 VII.6:1 the truth within from **b.** known to you,
T-29 VIII.5:6 truth shine unencumbered, **b.** what it is.
T-29. VIII.9:11 But you will never be content with **b.** less.
T-29 IX.8:3 the dream is **b.** dreamed by someone else.
T-30 I.7:3 your fear of **b.** answered in a different way
T-30 I.9:3 and reminds you that help is not **b.** thrust
T-30 I.10:2 your happiness depends on **b.** right. But
T-30 I.11:6 the goal of **b.** right when you are wrong.
T-30 III.1:2 But your will is universal, **b.** limitless.
T-30 III.4:4 God's Will, and this is given you by **b.** His
T-30 VI.1:10 by **b.** granted where it is not due.
T-30 VI.2:4 Salvation does not lie in **b.** asked to make
T-30 VI.2:9 It *keeps* your rights from **b.** sacrificed.
T-30 VI.8:5 and **b.** glad there cannot be some forms of
T-31 I.6:6 the simple lessons **b.** taught to you in
T-31 II.1:4 ancient battle **b.** waged against the truth,
T-31 IV.6:5 this would *keep* the truth from **b.** reached.
W-pI 4.2:3 which are **b.** covered up by them. The
W-pI 7.3:2 experiences of picking up a cup, **b.** thirsty,
W-pI 11.2:4 to yourself, **b.** sure to do so without haste,
W-pI 20.1:6 not see if you regard yourself as **b.** coerced
W-pI 23.7:1 thoughts of attacking and of **b.** attacked.
W-pI 23.7:5 attack and of **b.** attacked are not different,
W-pI 27.2:1 some sort of sacrifice is **b.** asked of you
W-pI 39.4:1 that was ever asked, is **b.** asked now, or
W-pI 40.1:1 to which you are entitled, **b.** what you are.
W-pI 40.3:2 attributes you associate with **b.** a Son of
W-pI 44.1:4 **b.** but different aspects of creation.
W-pI 45.3:5 Mind of God is eternal, **b.** part of creation
W-pI 50.1:3 clothing, influence, prestige, **b.** liked,
W-pI 51.3:7 now for this merely by **b.** willing to do so.
W-pI 63.2:5 is no idle request that is **b.** asked of you.
W-pI 63.2:6 You are **b.** asked to accept salvation that it
W-pI 65.6:5 but try to get the sense of **b.** willing to
W-pI 66.8:4 **b.** itself an illusion and offering only the
W-pI 69.7:1 to feel a sense of **b.** lifted up and carried
W-pI 91.6:9 a body calls for correction, **b.** a mistake.
W-pI 92.11:3 that we are **b.** introduced to sight, and led
W-pI 93.1:3 living on after seeing this **b.** impossible.
W-pI 96.1:2 sense of **b.** split into opposites induces
W-pI 98.6:3 you are **b.** asked for nothing in return for
W-pI 103.h God, **b.** Love, is also happiness.
W-pI 103.1:4 Love has no limits, **b.** everywhere. And
W-pI 103.2:2 to the fear of God, forgetting **b.** Love, He
W-pI 103.2:4 *God,* ***b.*** *Love, is also happiness. To fear Him*
W-pI 103.3:3 God, **b.** Love, it will be given you. Bolster
W-pI 103.3:5 *God,* ***b.*** *Love, is also happiness. And it is*
W-pI 104.3:1 wills, and recognize the same as **b.** one.
W-pI 108.3:1 shows no opposites, and vision, **b.** healed,
WpI. rIII.in6:2 **b.** helped in its decisions by the One Who
W-pI 117.1:1 (103) God, **b.** Love, is also happiness. *Let*
W-pI 117.3:2 God, **b.** Love, is also happiness. On the
W-pI 131.2:5 they achieve that offers any hope of **b.** real
W-pI.133.12:1 valueless, worthy or not of **b.** sought at all
W-pI 136.1:3 **B.** causeless and without a meaningful
W-pI 136.2:4 is to keep the truth from **b.** whole. The
W-pI 138.2:2 But here is opposition part of **b.** "real." It
W-pI 138.6:1 of choice, rather than merely **b.** what it is.
W-pI 139.4:1 himself, and therefore, **b.** something else,
WpI. rIV.in3:2 thoughts from **b.** seen and recognized.
W-pI 156.1:2 for guilt, and **b.** causeless it does not exist.
W-pI 157.6:1 only purpose **b.** now to bring the vision of
W-pI 161.5:4 Love needs no symbols, **b.** true. But fear
W-pI 161.5:5 true. But fear attaches to specifics, **b.** false
W-pI 185.8:8 And **b.** one, one question should be asked
W-pI 191.9:3 You play the game of death, of **b.** helpless,
W-pI 192.3:4 For **b.** Heaven-born, it has no form at all.
W-pI 195.8:6 has earned the right to love by **b.** loving,
W-pI.195.10:4 to you, His Son, for **b.** what you are; His
W-pI 199.3:4 sheltered it from **b.** found illusory itself.
W-pI 200.2:1 is none; of **b.** saved by what can only hurt;
W-pII 2.4:5 Earth is **b.** born again in new perspective.
W-pII 4.1:3 And **b.** mad, it sees illusions where the
W-pII .311.1:2 It separates what it is **b.** used against, and
W-pII .314.1:3 its idols and its images, and **b.** formless, it
W-pII 11.4:4 with all its Thoughts, its sureness **b.** theirs
W-pII .333.2:4 *anything,* ***b.*** *Your gift to Your beloved Son.*
M-2 2:5 So is all reality, **b.** of Him. The instant the
M-3 3:5 have no levels, **b.** a reflection of His Will.
M-4 I.A.3:3 It seems as if things are **b.** taken away,
M-4 I.A.3:3 their lack of value is merely **b.** recognized.
M-4 IX.2:2 **B.** consistent, it is wholly honest. Being
M-4 IX.2:3 **B.** unswerving, it is full of trust. Being
M-4 IX.2:4 **B.** based on fearlessness, it is gentle. Being
M-4 IX.2:5 gentle. **B.** certain, it is joyous. And being
M-4 IX.2:6 is joyous. And **b.** confident, it is tolerant.
M-5 II.1:7 on the body **b.** the decision maker. Terms
M-8 2:3 but is recognized as **b.** untrue. The mind
M-11 4:9 hell to Heaven merely by **b.** what it is?
M-12 1:6 And **b.** limitless, his thoughts are joined
M-12 2:6 Yet **b.** joined in one purpose, and one
M-12 5:3 Because it is sinful it is weak, and **b.** weak,
M-19 4:5 forever like its Creator, **b.** one with Him.
M-20 1:4 And **b.** found, how can it be retained? Let
M-21 2:5 specific things asked for **b.** the bringers of
M-21 4:3 words, **b.** as yet unable to hear in silence.
M-27 1:2 Is it not madness to think of life as **b.** born
M-28 2:1 the denial of death, **b.** the assertion of life.
M-29 2:3 but a smile, **b.** as yet unready for more?
M-29 4:11 benefit to all, **b.** wholly devoid of attack.
C-1 3:3 with the understanding that, **b.** of God, it
C-2 9:1 no answer, **b.** made to still God's Voice,
C-4 3:1 for false perception since, **b.** another level
C-4 5:9 for **b.** separate it could not remain where
C-5 1:5 for time needs symbols, **b.** itself unreal.
C-6 1:2 Spirit, **b.** a creation of the one Creator,

| | |
|---|---|
| C-6.............4:3 | God and also for you, **b.** joined with Both. |
| P-1.............3:6 | This self he sees as **b.** acted on, reacting to |
| P-2........ III.3:7 | world without a word, merely by **b.** there. |
| P-2........ IV.6:6 | Truth **b.** brought to illusions, reality now |
| P-2........ IV.7:8 | another form, **b.** the source of all illusions |
| P-2...... IV.10:7 | function to teach that guilt, **b.** unreal, |
| P-2.... IV.11:10 | The truth is simple, **b.** one for all. |
| P-3...........I.1:7 | tendency to assume that you are **b.** called |
| S-1...........I.5:3 | **b.** fully entitled to everything Love has to |
| S-1......... II.8:7 | **B.** beyond learning, this state cannot be |
| S-2...........I.5:6 | And **b.** evil, he can only give of what he is. |
| S-2......... II.1:1 | forms, **b.** a weapon of the world of form. |

## beings 2

| | |
|---|---|
| T-4....... VII.3:8 | Since only **b.** of a like order can truly |
| T-4....... VII.5:1 | all being, created **b.** who have everything |

## belie 1

| | |
|---|---|
| W-pI... 152.4:4 | to have some aspects that **b.** consistency, |

## belief 406

| | |
|---|---|
| T-1.........I.10:1 | use of miracles as spectacles to induce **b.** |
| T-1.........I.22:1 | because of the **b.** that darkness can hide. |
| T-1........ IV.3:3 | It is an example of the "scarcity" **b.**, from |
| T-1........ IV.4:7 | it. Your witnessing demonstrates your **b.**, |
| T-1........ IV.4:8 | abandoned the **b.** in deprivation in favor |
| T-1........ VI.4:4 | **B.** produces the acceptance of existence. |
| T-1....... VII.3:9 | will be equally strong in your **b.** in them. |
| T-1..... VII.3:10 | then sustain the **b.** of the miracle receiver. |
| T-2......... II.2:2 | deny any **b.** that error can hurt you. This |
| T-2......... II.4:4 | because **b.** in space and time did not exist |
| T-2......... II.5:1 | into the space-time **b.** to set a limit on the |
| T-2......... II.5:1 | to set a limit on the need for the **b.** itself, |
| T-2......... II.5:8 | a **b.** in differences is learning meaningful. |
| T-2........ III.1:4 | the distorted **b.** that the body can be used |
| T-2........ IV.2:2 | because it always entails the **b.** that what |
| T-2........ IV.2:6 | body cannot create, and the **b.** that it can, |
| T-2........ IV.2:7 | Physical illness represents a **b.** in magic. |
| T-2........ IV.2:8 | that made magic rests on the **b.** that there |
| T-2........ IV.4:6 | outside is temporarily given healing **b.**. |
| T-2...... IV.4:10 | has induced the **b.** that miracles are |
| T-2......... V.1:2 | foster the **b.** that release is imprisonment, |
| T-2......... V.1:2 | a **b.** that is already very prevalent. This |
| T-2......... V.1:3 | the **b.** that harm can be limited to the |
| T-2......... V.7:1 | turning away from the **b.** in physical sight |
| T-2......... V.9:2 | Like all aspects of the **b.** in space and time |
| T-2........ VI.9:8 | to recognize that thought and **b.** combine |
| T-2....... VII.4:1 | and your **b.** in it seems to render it out of |
| T-2...... VIII.1:2 | where a **b.** in magic is virtually inevitable. |
| T-2...... VIII.4:5 | disown its miscreations which, without **b.** |
| T-3...........I.1:4 | No one who is free of the **b.** in scarcity |
| T-3...........I.3:9 | including the **b.** that God rejected Adam |
| T-3......... II.3:1 | to your **b.** that he is not in his right mind. |
| T-3........ III.1:7 | As an attribute of the **b.** in space and time |
| T-3......... V.7:5 | is impossible without a **b.** in "more" and |
| T-3........ VI.2:7 | is the **b.** that what you judged against has |
| T-3...... VI.2:11 | way you are placing your **b.** in the unreal. |
| T-3...... VI.2:12 | implies the **b.** that reality is yours to select |
| T-3........ VI.3:4 | All uncertainty comes from the **b.** that |
| T-3...... VI.5:10 | This **b.** can exist only to the extent that |
| T-3........ VI.8:5 | This **b.** is very frightening to them, but |
| T-3....... VII.1:5 | for systems of **b.** by which one lives. It is a |
| T-3....... VII.4:3 | The **b.** that they are is implicit in the "self- |
| T-3....... VII.4:9 | **b.** that you can is the foundation stone in |
| T-3....... VII.5:1 | mind can make the **b.** in separation very |
| T-3....... VII.5:1 | and very fearful, and this **b.** *is* the "devil." |
| T-3..... VII.5:11 | There is no death, but there *is* a **b.** in death |
| T-4...........I.7:3 | to the **b.** in superiority and inferiority. |
| T-4......... II.4:8 | **B.** is an ego function, and as long as your |
| T-4......... II.4:8 | as long as your origin is open to **b.** you are |
| T-4....... II.4:10 | **B.** that there is another way of perceiving |
| T-4......... II.6:6 | with the **b.** in scarcity that gave rise to it. |
| T-4......... II.8:4 | mind's **b.** that it is completely on its own. |
| T-4........ III.3:2 | on your continuing **b.** in the separation. |
| T-4........ III.3:3 | sort of reward for maintaining this **b.**. All |
| T-4........ III.5:2 | It is necessary to repeat that your **b.** in |
| T-4 ..... III.10:4 | then protect this **b.** at the cost of truth? |
| T-4 ...... IV.7:2 | of concentration; it is the **b.** that no one, |
| T-4 ....... IV.7:3 | not permit this shabby **b.** to pull you back |
| T-4 ........ V.4:3 | is the **b.** that the ego sponsors eagerly. Yet |
| T-4 ....... VI.1:6 | more than a part of your **b.** about yourself |
| T-4 ....... VI.4:4 | The ego is a device for maintaining this **b.** |
| T-5 ........I.1:14 | the whole **b.** in the false association the |
| T-5 .........II.4:1 | let the **b.** in darkness enter your mind and |
| T-5 .......II.12:4 | of our joint motivation is beyond **b.**, but |
| T-5 ....... III.6:4 | Time is a **b.** of the ego, so the lower mind, |
| T-5 ...... V.2:11 | the power of the ego's **b.** in it. This is the |
| T-5 ...... V.2:12 | is the **b.** from which all guilt really stems. |
| T-5 ........ V.4:9 | with guilt, because it is the **b.** in sin. The |
| T-6 .........II.1:1 | of part of it, and this *is* the **b.** in separation |
| T-6 .........II.3:2 | reinforces your **b.** in your own split mind, |
| T-6 .........II.6:8 | It is not a **b.**, but a Fact. Anything that |
| T-6 ..... IV.10:3 | and thus side with the **b.** that those who |
| T-6 ..... V.A.4:6 | it, because it is a **b.** in perfect equality. |
| T-6 ..... V.C.6:4 | excluded yourself from it in your **b.**. It is |
| T-6 ..... V.C.6:5 | and that the **b.** that you are not is the only |
| T-6 ..... V.C.7:2 | but God and His creations are beyond **b.** |
| T-6 ..... V.C.7:3 | God speaks only for **b.** beyond question, |
| T-6 ..... V.C.7:4 | As long as **b.** in God and His Kingdom is |
| T-6 ..... V.C.7:7 | go beyond **b.** until you believe fully. |
| T-7 .........II.3:4 | or learning, because there is no **b.**. There |
| T-7 ....... III.3:6 | it. It *is* the **b.** that conflicting interests are |
| T-7 ....... IV.5:5 | is the way to undo the **b.** in differences, |
| T-7 ........ V.3:6 | involves the **b.** that healing is harmful. |
| T-7 ........ V.3:7 | This **b.** is its totally insane premise, and |
| T-7 ....... VI.2:7 | and thus rendered it powerless in your **b.**. |
| T-7 ....... VI.7:3 | **B.** does not require vigilance unless it is |
| T-7 ....... VI.8:2 | logically to the **b.** that you must be a body |
| T-7 ....... VI.9:5 | since their presence implies a **b.** that what |
| T-7 ..... VI.10:2 | **b.** you accept apart from this will obscure |
| T-7 ...... VII.9:2 | Projecting its insane **b.** that you have |
| T-7 ........VIII.h | The Unbelievable **B.** |
| T-7 .....VIII.3:8 | The **b.** that by seeing it outside you have |
| T-7 .....VIII.4:4 | The **b.** that it can, an error the ego always |
| T-7 .....VIII.4:6 | on your mind, because the ego is your **b.**. |
| T-7 .....VIII.5:2 | can dispel it by withdrawing **b.** from it. |
| T-7 .....VIII.5:3 | project the responsibility for your **b.** in it |
| T-7 .....VIII.5:3 | anyone else, or you will preserve the **b.**. |
| T-7 .....VIII.6:1 | will teach you to perceive beyond your **b.**, |
| T-7 .....VIII.6:1 | is beyond **b.** and His perception is true. |
| T-7 .....VIII.6:2 | time, because it is a totally incredible **b.**, |
| T-7 .....VIII.6:2 | keep a **b.** he has judged to be unbelievable |
| T-7 .....VIII.6:5 | may not be recognized as being beyond **b.** |
| T-7 .....VIII.6:5 | beyond belief, because it is made *by* **b.**. |
| T-7 .....VIII.7:3 | against the **b.** that you can be alone, thus |
| T-7 .....VIII.7:4 | is as beyond doubt as it is beyond **b.**. |
| T-7 .......X.5:10 | this, too, is merely a matter of his own **b.**. |
| T-8 ....... IV.3:7 | the world *is* the **b.** that love is impossible. |
| T-8 ........ V.2:3 | the **b.** that your will is separate from mine |
| T-8 ...... VI.8:11 | Given this **b.**, you cannot understand |
| T-8 ...... VII.1:4 | You are accepting it simply by the **b.** that |
| T-8 ...... VII.5:6 | give him freedom from his **b.** in littleness, |
| T-8 ...... VII.7:4 | cannot be made into flesh except by **b.**, |
| T-8 .... VII.10:3 | whole, and the **b.** that part of it is physical |
| T-8 .... VII.16:2 | mind from the **b.** that this is possible. In |
| T-8 .....VIII.3:1 | to overcome the ego's **b.** in the body as an |
| T-8 .....VIII.3:1 | is synonymous with the **b.** in attack as an |
| T-8 .....VIII.3:3 | ego's firm **b.** that you are not invulnerable |
| T-8 ....... IX.1:5 | merely be to accept the ego's **b.** that the |
| T-9 ..........I.7:9 | is nothing more than the **b.** that it is |
| T-9 .........I.11:3 | The **b.** that you must have the impossible |
| T-9 .........I.11:5 | fact that God is Love does not require **b.**, |
| T-9 .........II.8:1 | you will learn that my **b.** in you is justified |
| T-9 ....... IV.1:1 | the way to undo the **b.** that anything is for |
| T-9 ....... IV.5:4 | let any **b.** in its realness enter your mind, |
| T-9 ........ V.1:6 | the equally incredible **b.** that attack is real |
| T-9 ...... VII.6:1 | evaluate an insane **b.** system from within |
| T-9 ...... VII.7:8 | He judges every **b.** you hold in terms of |
| T-9 .....VIII.2:3 | based on the **b.** that the littleness is real. |
| T-9 .....VIII.2:4 | this **b.** grandiosity is meaningless, and |
| T-9 .....VIII.7:4 | Perhaps it is the **b.** in littleness; perhaps it |
| T-9 .....VIII.7:4 | perhaps it is the **b.** in grandiosity. Yet it |
| T-9 ...VIII.11:9 | He would have you replace the ego's **b.** in |
| T-10 ..... III.4:4 | the **b.** that power can be taken from you. |
| T-10 ... III.11:7 | **b.** that you can choose which god is real. |
| T-10 ..... IV.7:4 | brother by weakening his **b.** in sickness, |
| T-11 ......I.10:4 | **b.** is your whole sickness and your whole |
| T-11 ......I.10:5 | is the **b.** that makes you *want* not to know. |
| T-11 .......V.3:3 | whole separation fallacy lies in the **b.** that |
| T-11 .......V.5:2 | ego is the natural outcome of its central **b.** |
| T-11 .......V.6:7 | The **b.** in ego autonomy is costing you the |
| T-11 .......V.8:4 | Without this **b.** you would not listen to it |
| T-11 .....V.13:4 | and to establish this **b.** it must attack. |
| T-11 .....V.13:5 | that the **b.** cannot be established, and |
| T-11 ..... VI.3:3 | And since **b.** determines perception, you |
| T-12 ........I.9:6 | and denial depends on the **b.** in what is |
| T-12 ........I.9:7 | affirmation of the underlying **b.** it masks, |
| T-12 ..... III.3:2 | If he attacks, you are agreeing with this **b.** |
| T-12 .. VII.4:10 | For this **b.** is the destruction of peace, a |
| T-13 ...... in.2:9 | love, perhaps the most insane **b.** of all. |
| T-13 ...... in.3:7 | **b.** the knowledge of the Father was lost, |
| T-13 ........I.6:3 | of guilt brings a **b.** in condemnation of |
| T-13 .......II.3:1 | your **b.** in guilt from your awareness. For |
| T-13 ..... III.4:1 | built your whole insane **b.** system because |
| T-13 ..... IX.2:4 | of the **b.** in which the faith was placed. |
| T-13 ..... IX.2:5 | Faith makes the power of **b.**, and where it |
| T-13 ..... IX.5:5 | and the **b.** in one is faith in the other, |
| T-13 .....X.13:1 | and my **b.** are centered on what I treasure |
| T-13 .....X.13:3 | and all my faith and my **b.** I offer unto it. |
| T-13 ..... XI.8:2 | and this **b.** does interfere with the deep |
| T-14 ........I.3:4 | he shares with God are beyond his **b.**, but |
| T-14 ..... III.7:3 | your perfect freedom from the **b.** that you |
| T-14 ..... III.8:4 | to it, and do not foster **b.** in it in any mind |
| T-14 ..... VI.4:3 | for your **b.** that you can have them both is |
| T-14 .... VII.2:7 | you have erected your insane system of **b.** |
| T-14 .... VII.3:6 | a **b.** in something that does not exist. It is |
| T-14 .... VII.3:7 | It is only this **b.** that the unknowing have, |
| T-14 .... VII.4:3 | of thinking whereby two systems of **b.** |
| T-14 .... VII.4:8 | place can be endowed with firm **b.**. Bring |
| T-15 ........I.2:1 | may suffer is your **b.** that this takes time, |
| T-15 ........I.2:6 | uses time to support its **b.** in destruction. |
| T-15 ........I.4:1 | The **b.** in hell is inescapable to those who |
| T-15 ........I.6:5 | **b.** in guilt must lead to the belief in hell, |
| T-15 ........I.6:5 | belief in guilt must lead to the **b.** in hell, |
| T-15 ........I.7:3 | The **b.** in hell is what prevents you from |
| T-15 ..... III.1:5 | strange **b.** that littleness can content you. |
| T-15 ..... III.1:6 | world in the **b.** that it will bring you peace |
| T-15 ..... III.6:4 | **b.** that you can be content with littleness, |
| T-15 .......V.3:3 | is the **b.** that separation is salvation. For it |
| T-15 .... VII.4:4 | Yet its survival depends on your **b.** that |
| T-15 .... VII.4:6 | anger and dedicated to but one insane **b.**; |
| T-15 ..... IX.6:8 | For his **b.** in limits *has* imprisoned him. |
| T-15 ..... XI.5:5 | is the **b.** in the reality of the deprivation? |
| T-15 ..... XI.5:6 | attack, being the **b.** that attack is justified. |
| T-16 .... VII.6:3 | opposite of the ego's fixed **b.** in salvation |
| T-17 ........I.5:4 | keep them by justifying your **b.** in them. |
| T-18 ..... IV.8:3 | whole **b.** in orders of difficulty in miracles |
| T-18 ..... VI.2:3 | **b.** that you could give and get something |
| T-18 ... VIII.1:3 | The **b.** in limited love was its origin, and |
| T-19 ........I.6:1 | inevitable compromise is the **b.** that the |
| T-19 .......II.1:4 | The **b.** in sin is necessarily based on the |
| T-19 .......II.1:6 | and the **b.** that punishment *is* correction is |
| T-19 ..... III.5:7 | But sin is the **b.** that your perception is |
| T-19 ..... III.7:3 | For the **b.** that bodies limit mind leads to |
| T-19 ..... III.8:5 | and the **b.** in sin has been uprooted in its |
| T-19 ..... III.9:6 | joyously releasing him from the **b.** in sin. |
| T19 ...IV.A.8:1 | this microscopic remnant of the **b.** in sin, |
| T19 ......IV.B.h | **B.** the Body is Valuable for What It Offers |
| T19 ...IV.B.1:3 | is the **b.** that the body is valuable for what |
| T19 ...IV.B.2:6 | your strange **b.** that in it lies salvation? |
| T19 ...IV.B.2:7 | Do you not see that this is the **b.** in death? |
| T19 ...IV.B.7:8 | can guilt be, when the **b.** in sin is gone? |
| T19 .IV.B.15:1 | the **b.** that for your message of attack and |
| T19 .. IV.D.3:1 | upheld by the **b.** in death and protected |
| T19 .. IV.D.4:1 | the **b.** in death would seem to "save" you. |
| T-20 ..... III.1:1 | The **b.** in sin is an adjustment. And an |
| T-20 ..... III.1:2 | **b.** that what was so before has been made |
| T-20 ..... III.2:2 | it is the ego's fixed **b.** that all relationships |
| T-20 ..... III.6:8 | but the **b.** that made it as you see it is not |
| T-20 ... VI.11:1 | **b.** in sin made flesh and then projected |
| T-21 ........II.6:9 | your **b.** and trust in this is strong indeed. |
| T-21 ........ III.h | Faith, **B.** and Vision |
| T-21 ..... III.4:1 | Faith and **b.** and vision are the means by |
| T-21 ..... III.4:5 | faith and His **b.** and vision are all for you. |

T-21......III.4:7 For faith and vision and **b.** are meaningful
T-21......III.5:5 For faith, perception and **b.** you made, as
T-21......III.7:1 Faith and **b.** become attached to vision,
T-21......III.7:4 so the body has your faith and your **b.**.
T-21......III.8:3 of their **b.** and faith sees far beyond the
T-21....III.10:6 an inescapable **b.** of those who value sin.
T-21....III.12:5 and the **b.** you gave it belongs beyond.
T-21....III.12:6 and **b.** and faith from mind to body. Let
T-21......IV.1:7 It doubts not your **b.** and faith in sin. Its
T-21......IV.3:4 their **b.** that their identity lies in the ego.
T-21......IV.3:6 your **b.** in sin has been already shaken,
T-21.......V.1:9 entirely your whole **b.** in what you are.
T-21.......V.8:1 and perception and **b.** can be misplaced,
T-21.......V.8:3 end. Faith and **b.** are strong in madness,
T-21.....V.10:2 Faith and **b.** have shifted, and you have
T-21.....V.10:4 Faith and **b.**, upheld by reason, cannot
T-21......VI.1:5 will not give it, thus maintaining the **b.**.
T-21......VI.1:8 he shares this same **b.** you both will think
T-21.....VII.1:1 the strange **b.** that you are powerless?
T-21.....VII.6:6 imagined difference attests to your **b.** that
T-22.......in.4:2 Here is **b.** in differences undone. Here is
T-22.......II.4:5 real. Such is the power of **b.**. It cannot
T-22.......II.4:7 **b.** excludes one living thing and holds it
T-22.......II.5:3 then the **b.** in sin must be eternal. Yet
T-22.....II.6:10 Faith and **b.** can fall to either side, but
T-22.......II.9:2 is the same **b.** that caused the separation.
T-22......III.2:1 on its **b.** you cannot learn this course.
T-22......III.2:2 Share this **b.**, and reason will be unable to
T-22......III.2:6 its fixed **b.** in sin and disregard of errors.
T-22.......V.2:6 fear? **B.** in sin needs great defense, and at
T-22.......V.6:4 but rests on the **b.** that you are separate.
T-22....VI.10:5 You do not see what this **b.** has done. You
T-22....VI.12:6 And this **b.** you want. Yet wherein lies its
T-23.......in.1:6 **B.** in enemies is therefore the belief in
T-23.......in.1:6 in enemies is therefore the **b.** in weakness,
T-23.........I.1:4 unless **b.** in victory is cherished. Conflict
T-23.........I.1:9 Yet just as certain is its fixed **b.** it has an
T-23.........I.2:8 only the mad **b.** the Will of God can be
T-23.........I.2:9 You may identify with this **b.**, but never
T-23.........I.6:1 the **b.** the one that conquers will be true.
T-23......I.10:3 the **b.** in sin that keeps God homeless and
T-23.......II.2:3 principle evolves from the **b.** there is a
T-23.......II.4:5 being the **b.** the Son of God can make
T-23.......II.6:3 of what has been established for His **b.**.
T-23.......II.6:5 leads directly to the *third* preposterous **b.**
T-23.......II.6:6 He must accept His Son's **b.** in what he is,
T-23.......II.9:3 is the **b.** you have what you have taken. By
T-23.....II.14:2 protects madness is the **b.** that it is true. It
T-23.....II.16:5 No law of chaos could compel **b.** but for
T-23.....II.20:3 Yet each one rests as surely on the **b.** the
T-23.....II.21:1 From the **b.** in sin, the faith in chaos
T-23......III.3:6 is the **b.** salvation is impossible. It would
T-23......III.4:4 certain the **b.** that salvation is impossible
T-23......III.5:3 the **b.** that murder takes some forms by
T-24.......in.2:3 No **b.** is neutral. Every one has the power
T-24.......in.2:6 It is the outcome of **b.**, and follows it as
T-24.........I.1:4 Hold back but one **b.**, one offering, and
T-24.........I.2:2 an unrecognized **b.** is a decision to war in
T-24.........I.3:1 All that is ever cherished as a hidden **b.**,
T-24.........I.7:9 Is it not always your **b.** your specialness is
T-24.........I.8:1 from each unrecognized **b.** in specialness.
T-24......VI.4:5 all **b.** God's Son can suffer pain because
T-25.......II.3:3 Can it make sense to hold the fixed **b.** that
T-25......III.2:4 His Son's **b.** He could not let Himself be
T-25......III.4:1 Corrector of the mad **b.** that anything
T-25......III.7:7 from the **b.** there are two ways to see.
T-25......III.8:4 is the fixed **b.** perception cannot change.
T-25.......V.6:3 see the picture of your own **b.** in what the
T-25.....VII.3:7 If one **b.** so deeply valued here were true,
T-25.....VII.4:6 Think not that this **b.** depends upon the
T-25...VII.11:1 whole **b.** that someone loses but reflects
T-25...VII.11:4 **b.** except a form of the more basic tenet,
T-25...VII.13:1 a mad **b.** that God's insanity would make
T-25... VIII.6:2 the vengeance that their own **b.** in justice
T-26.........I.6:5 his holiness a sacrifice to your **b.** in sin.
T-26.......V.5:5 in every judgment and in all **b.** in sin, is
T-26.....V.6:10 mere imagining into **b.** and into madness,
T-26.....V.13:4 all of time is but the mad **b.** that what is
T-26......VI.1:6 All **b.** in sin, in power of attack, in hurt
T-26.....VII.5:1 answer lies where the **b.** in sin must be,
T-26.....VII.7:2 the **b.** that it is real has made some errors
T-26...VII.12:2 Sin is **b.** attack can be projected outside
T-26...VII.12:2 outside the mind where the **b.** arose. Here
T-26... VIII.5:5 **B.** in sin arouses fear, and like its cause, is
T-26.......X.3:3 The **b.** you are is but another form of the
T-27.........I.4:1 power of witness is beyond **b.** because it
T-27.........I.8:1 witnesses unto the strange **b.** that sin and
T-27.......II.5:4 The power of witness comes from your **b.**.
T-27......III.2:8 is the **b.** that there is something there.
T-27.......V.2:3 must provide a witness that compels **b.**.
T-28......III.3:5 cherished, and upheld by firm **b.**, lest
T-28....IV.10:6 from the **b.** that there is joy in separation,
T-29.......II.7:8 in its **b.** of what the purpose of the body is
T-29... VIII.3:1 An idol is a false impression, or a false **b.**;
T-29... VIII.5:7 It does not need **b.** to be itself, for it has
T-29... VIII.6:1 An idol is established by **b.**, and when it
T-30.......I.11:6 by the insane **b.** you want it for the goal of
T-30......III.1:5 They are the **b.** that there are forms that
T-30......III.3:5 source of the **b.** that you are incomplete.
T-30.......V.2:8 world has been united in **b.** the purpose
T-30......VI.6:1 than a **b.** there are some forms of sickness
T-30......VI.6:4 about the meaning of a fixed **b.** that some
T-30... VIII.4:3 all. The cost of the **b.** there must be some
T-31......VI.1:6 you are, as flesh or spirit in your own **b.**.
W-pI.....16.1:1 the **b.** that your thoughts have no effect.
W-pI.....21.3:5 is merely an example of the **b.** that some
W-pI.....26.3:2 must entail the **b.** that you are vulnerable,
W-pI.....50.4:7 declaration of release from the **b.** in idols.
W-pI.....53.3:6 reality, and have suffered from my **b.** in it.
W-pI.....53.3:7 it. Now I choose to withdraw this **b.**, and
W-pI.....57.2:5 I was bitterly mistaken in this **b.**, which I
W-pI.....72.5:8 It reinforces your **b.** that he is a body, and
W-pI.....72.7:1 is the universal **b.** of the world you see.
W-pI.....73.1:5 in which your **b.** can be very strong. But
W-pI.....73.8:3 and end forever the insane **b.** that it is hell
W-pI.....74.1:4 The **b.** that conflict is possible has gone.
W-pI...76.10:6 creation; denied to Him by his **b.** in hell.
W-pI.....88.3:5 I suffer only because of my **b.** in them.
W-pI.....91.6:7 you think you are is a **b.** to be undone.
W-pI.....91.6:9 The **b.** you are a body calls for correction,
W-pI.....91.9:3 is associated with the **b.** you are a body, a
W-pI.....91.9:3 a **b.** that is mistaken and deserves no faith
W-pI.....97.8:4 yield to the **b.** that you are something else
W-pI.....99.5:3 time, because of your **b.** that time is real.
W-pI...100.1:2 Salvation must reverse the mad **b.** in
W-pI...100.7:6 have indeed been wrong in your **b.** that
W-pI...101.5:3 which cherishes no lingering **b.** that you
W-pI...101.7:1 yourself with the insane **b.** that sin is real.
W-pI...102.1:3 Yet this **b.** is surely shaken now, at least
W-pI...103.1:7 This strange **b.** would limit happiness by
W-pI...103.2:6 which corrects the false **b.** that God is fear
W-pI...106.2:3 of life and offer it to you for your **b.**.
W-pI...107.1:5 They are gone because, without **b.**, they
W-pI...116.1:3 *but from the* **b.** *there is another will apart*
W-pI...127.9:3 your mind wherever you give up a false **b.**
W-pI...132.1:3 **B.** is powerful indeed. The thoughts you
W-pI...135.2:1 operate from the **b.** you must protect
W-pI...135.2:2 a **b.** that there is danger which has power
W-pI...135.2:3 The world is based on this insane **b.**. And
W-pI...135.6:3 right to serve you thus except your own **b.**
W-pI.135.12:1 mind is relieved of the **b.** that it must plan
W-pI...139.6:5 sad **b.** that what is universal here is true?
W-pI.139.10:1 by his **b.** he knows not what he is. Today
W-pI...140.1:5 One **b.** in sickness takes another form,
W-pI...151.7:1 be Judge of what is worthy of your own **b.**.
W-pI.154.12:2 a hundred times, and yet **b.** is lacking still
W-pI.154.12:3 But this is sure; until **b.** is given it, you
W-pI...167.4:2 It is the **b.** conditions change, emotions
W-pI...167.4:3 is the fixed **b.** ideas can leave their source,
W-pI.170.10:1 insane **b.** in gods of vengeance come from
W-pI...186.8:2 all illusions rest upon the weird **b.** that we
W-pI...189.7:4 nor one **b.** you ever learned before from
W-pI...196.1:3 will be free of the insane **b.** that to attack
W-pI...196.5:3 merely stood for the **b.** the fear of God is
W-pI...197.1:1 to free your mind from the **b.** in outside
W-pI...197.7:1 with the end of this **b.** is fear forever over.
W-pII..264.1:3 *and place becomes a meaningless* **b.**. *For*
W-pII..290.1:5 to be deceived by the **b.** the dream I made
W-pII ... 12.4:1 its salvation, and the cost **b.** in it entails.
Wfl........in.1:5 For we would not return again to the **b.** in
M-8 ........... 1:1 The **b.** in order of difficulties is the basis
M-8 ........... 5:2 it harder to dispel the **b.** of the insane in a
M-14 ......... 1:6 illusions is the **b.** that they have a purpose
M-15 ......... 2:6 One instant of complete **b.** in this, and
M-15 ......... 2:6 and you will go beyond **b.** to Certainty.
M-16 ....... 11:8 All **b.** in magic is maintained by just one
M-17 ......... 1:6 own **b.** in sin and has condemned himself
M-18 ......... 3:2 Reality is blotted out as this insane **b.** is
M-20 ......... 4:2 and the **b.** that peace cannot exist will
M-24 ......... 3:6 it advocates a long-held **b.** of his own.
M-24 ......... 4:6 to any concept or **b.** that will be helpful,
M-24 ......... 5:3 him to renounce the **b.** unless his internal
M-24 ......... 5:5 he is misusing the **b.** in some way that is
M-27 ......... 1:4 unchangeable **b.** of the world that all
M-27 ......... 4:1 The curious **b.** that there is part of dying
M-27 ......... 5:1 rooted in the **b.** that God's Son is a body.
M-29 ......... 4:8 things because you have given that **b.** to it
C-in ........... 2:4 since they depend on **b.** and can therefore
C-4............. 7:7 at last there is no journey, no **b.** in sin, no
P-2.........in.1:5 the **b.** that anger brings him something
P-2.........in.2:4 rests on the insane **b.** that this is possible.
P-2..........II.4:3 unfair indeed if **b.** in God were necessary
P-2..........II.4:4 is **b.** in God a really meaningful concept,
P-2..........II.4:5 **B.** implies that unbelief is possible, but
P-2..........II.4:7 without knowledge one can have only **b.**.
P-2........IV.5:2 error lies in the **b.** that it can cure itself.
P-2........IV.8:2 real is the **b.** that illness varies in intensity
P-2......IV.10:6 the **b.** that guilt is real and fully justified.
P-2......... V.1:3 In its wake comes the inevitable **b.** that,
P-2......... V.1:4 strange **b.** relies on certain steps which
P-2......... V.1:5 ushered in by the **b.** that there are forces
S-1..........II.1:4 appeal to God, or even involve **b.** in Him.
S-1..........II.3:2 may be addressed to God in honest **b.**,

## beliefs 61

T-1........ VI.3:6 meaningless as time. Both are merely **b.**.
T-1........ VI.5:2 are willing to submit your **b.** to this test,
T-3........VII.3:3 All **b.** are real to the believer. The fruit of
T-4........ IV.8:5 for any **b.** that hinder its accomplishment
T-4.......VII.8:2 harmless, because the two **b.** must coexist
T-5........ III.7:2 work with the ego's **b.** in its own language
T-5........ III.9:2 you accept are the foundations of your **b.**.
T-6.........I.16:6 all behavior teaches the **b.** that motivate it
T-6......V.C.1:9 The ego's **b.** on this crucial issue vary, and
T-6......V.C.7:2 Altars are **b.**, but God and His creations
T-7........ VI.7:6 It is necessary against **b.** that are not true,
T-7........ X.1:11 Whatever these **b.** may be, they are the
T-9...........I.1:1 **b.** the human mind has ever made. It
T-9.......... V.2:1 said that **b.** of the ego cannot be shared,
T-9......VIII.3:1 impulses and ego-alien **b.** of its own. I
T-11...... VI.1:2 of experience, and experience leads to **b.**.
T-11...... VI.1:3 It is not until **b.** are fixed that perceptions
T-11...... VI.3:4 different experiences lead to different **b.**,
T-11...... VI.3:5 For perceptions are learned *with* **b.**, and
T-11...... VI.3:9 little **b.** that are unworthy of God's Son.
T-11.....VII.4:4 these **b.** are the world as you perceive it.
T-14.........I.3:4 his belief, but those he made *are* his **b.**.
T-16...... III.4:9 it. Illusions are but **b.** in what is not there.
T-23............I.h The Irreconcilable **B.**
T-23..........I.3:3 For your **b.** converge upon the body, the
T-23......II.20:6 fear because of the **b.** that they imply, not
T-24.....in.2:10 And your decisions come from your **b.** as
T-24.........I.2:1 **B.** will never openly attack each other
T-24.........I.2:3 to become **b.** now given power to direct
T-25.....VII.3:8 then all **b.** the world gives any meaning to
T-25...VII.12:5 for all insane **b.** can be corrected here.
T-25....VIII.2:2 without attack from all **b.** opposed to it.
T-26.....VII.8:6 and all **b.** that rise from mists of guilt.
T-26.....VII.8:7 Sins are **b.** that you impose between your
T-27....IV.4:17 for it. It leaves no room to question its **b.**,
W-pI.....45.4:5 We will not let the **b.** of the world tell us
W-pI......76.9:2 Dismiss all foolish magical **b.** today, and
W-pI......92.1:5 This is among the many magical **b.** that
W-pI......93.2:1 **b.** so firmly fixed that it is difficult to help
W-pI......93.3:3 weird **b.** He does not share with you. This
W-pI...107.3:4 you from all **b.** in the ephemeral. They

W-pI.126.10:1 thoughts are changed and false **b.** laid by.
W-pI...132.1:1 keeps the world in chains but your **b.**?
W-pI...132.3:4 and keep the world a prisoner to your **b.**.
W-pI.135.15:3 from past events and previous **b.**. It
W-pI.135.16:4 a continuity of any old ideas and sick **b.**.
W-pI.135.17:2 incompatible with your **b.** of your reality.
W-pI.135.25:6 plans or magical **b.** can still have value,
W-pI...138.8:1 These mad **b.** can gain unconscious hold
W-pI...140.9:4 and no **b.** that what does not exist is truer
W-pI...166.3:1 to anyone who holds such strange **b.**. He
W-pI...181.5:6 We do not look to past **b.**, and what we
W-pI.189.10:7 *from You, and cherish no* ***b.*** *of what we are,*
W-pI.198.10:1 forgotten, all its weird **b.** forgotten with it
W-pII .277.2:2 He is not bound except by his **b.**. Yet
W-pII ...12.4:1 its works, its acts, its laws and its **b.**, its
M-24 .........1:8 way? Like many other **b.**, it can be bitterly
M-24 .........3:4 to anyone, regardless of his formal **b.**. His
M-24 .........6:9 **b.** will point to this if properly interpreted
M-24 .......6:11 All **b.** that lead to progress should be
C-5.............1:2 circumscribed by false **b.** of your Identity,

### belies 2

W-pI...189.3:2 of malice and of fear, that one **b.** the other
M-4 ....... II.1:6 any other thought; no act **b.** your word;

### believable 2

T-6......V.A.4:2 you by now, but it has not yet become **b.**.
T-12....... V.7:8 the split that makes its primary aim **b.**.

### believableness 1

T-4...........I.9:9 its **b.** is merely to postpone the inevitable.

### believe 617

*See also* make-believe

T-1.........I.22:2 **b.** that what your physical eyes cannot see
T-1......... II.1:9 it. You are free to **b.** what you choose, and
T-1......... II.1:9 and what you do attests to what you **b.**.
T-1......... V.1:3 While you **b.** you are in a body, however,
T-1......... V.3:7 If they **b.** they are deprived of anything,
T-1........ VI.4:2 made fear, and you **b.** in what you made.
T-1........ VI.4:5 you can **b.** what no one else thinks is true.
T-1........ VI.5:9 **B.** this and you will be free. Only God can
T-1.......VII.3:8 You **b.** in what you make. If you offer
T-2...........I.1:7 occurs when you **b.** that some emptiness
T-2...........I.1:9 **b.** that what God created can be changed
T-2.........I.1:10 **b.** that what is perfect can be rendered
T-2.........I.1:11 you **b.** that you can distort the creations
T-2.........I.1:12 you **b.** that you can create yourself, and
T-2...........I.3:3 You do not have to continue to **b.** what is
T-2...........I.5:1 may **b.** are of no concern to the miracle,
T-2......... II.1:6 You **b.** in what you value. If you are afraid
T-2......... II.7:3 hard to **b.** a defense that cannot attack is
T-2......... V.8:3 as you **b.** in what your physical sight tells
T-2........ VI.2:5 You may **b.** that you are responsible for
T-2........ VI.3:1 It is pointless to **b.** that controlling the
T-2........ VI.9:9 It appears at first glance that to **b.** such
T-2........ VI.9:9 that is not the real reason you do not **b.** it.
T-2...... VI.9:10 prefer to **b.** that your thoughts cannot
T-2...... VI.9:12 If you **b.** that what you think is ineffectual
T-2.......VII.3:6 Us, and **b.** in what you have made. You
T-2.......VII.4:1 It has already been said that you **b.** you
T-2.......VII.4:5 you **b.** in the power of what does not exist
T-2.......VII.5:2 To **b.** in one is to deny the other. Fear is
T-2.......VII.5:5 What you **b.** is true for you. In this sense
T-2.......VII.6:7 Any part of the Sonship can **b.** in error or
T-3...........I.2:8 you **b.** our Father really thinks this way?
T-3...........I.3:4 God does not **b.** in retribution. His Mind
T-3.........I.3:10 is also why you may **b.** from time to time
T-3.........I.7:11 are released from all errors if you **b.** this.
T-3......... V.2:4 tacitly implying that you **b.** in separation.
T-3........ VI.2:8 be true unless you also **b.** that what you
T-3........ VI.2:9 exist. You evidently do not **b.** this, or you
T-3........ VI.4:2 You **b.** that, because you have refused to
T-3...... VI.5:10 to the extent that you **b.** in the efficacy of
T-3........ VI.8:2 always because you **b.** you are the author
T-3 ....... VI.8:4 of all those who **b.** they have usurped the
T-3 ....... VI.8:8 you **b.** that your creation was anonymous
T-3 ....... VI.8:9 meaningful to **b.** that you created yourself
T-3 ...... VII.1:6 It is a mistake to **b.** that a thought system
T-3 ...... VII.4:6 but you cannot do more than **b.** it. You
T-3 ....VII.4:10 You still **b.** you are an image of your own
T-3 ....VII.4:11 and there is no resolution while you **b.** the
T-3 ...... VII.6:7 **b.** that they can be reconciled is to believe
T-3 ...... VII.6:7 is to **b.** that God and His Son can *not.* Only
T-4 ..........I.1:4 teacher must **b.** in the ideas he teaches,
T-4 ..........I.1:4 must **b.** in the students to whom he offers
T-4 ..........I.2:4 You **b.** that if you allow no change to
T-4 ..........I.4:4 ego and **b.** in a world that rests upon it.
T-4 ..........I.5:5 to want to obey its laws unless *you* **b.** them
T-4 ..........I.6:6 be a devoted teacher as long as you **b.** it. I
T-4 ..........I.8:2 doubtful as long as you **b.** in its existence.
T-4 ..........I.9:8 *Do not* ***b.*** *the incredible now.* Any attempt
T-4 ........I.13:5 once been tempted to **b.** in them myself.
T-4 .........II.4:7 to the ego, but what you **b.** you are. Belief
T-4 .........II.6:4 you give only because you **b.** that you are
T-4 .........II.9:5 may **b.** that the soul existed before, and
T-4 .........II.9:6 ego life. Some even **b.** that the soul will be
T-4 ....... III.3:7 of this can ever fully **b.** in the ego again.
T-4 ....... III.4:1 with your ego cannot **b.** God loves you.
T-4 ..... III.10:4 insane would undertake to **b.** what is not
T-4 ..... IV.10:5 you **b.** I was mistaken in choosing you. I
T-4 ..... IV.11:8 Why do you **b.** it is harder for me to
T-4 ..... IV.11:9 the unstable? I do not **b.** that there is an
T-4 ........ V.5:6 You learn best when you **b.** what you are
T-4 ....... VI.1:5 here, or as long as you **b.** that you are here
T-4 ....... VI.3:7 may **b.** that you have already accepted
T-4 ....... VI.3:8 The fact that you **b.** you must escape from
T-4 ....... VI.4:3 but because you want to **b.** that *you* are.
T-5 ..........I.2:3 *who* ***b.*** *in them the stronger they become.*
T-5 ..........I.7:2 and no one who attains it could **b.** for one
T-5 ....... III.8:9 **b.** there is strife you will react viciously,
T-5 ...... V.3:10 that you **b.** it is possible to attack God,
T-5 ...... V.6:13 thoughts, although you can **b.** in them.
T-5 ........ V.7:4 that you **b.** you can think apart from God,
T-5 ........ V.7:6 who **b.** they order their own thoughts,
T-5 ....... VI.1:4 eternity, and therefore **b.** you *are* in time.
T-5 ....... VI.4:7 appeal to the Higher Court because you **b.**
T-5 ..... VI.10:4 you **b.** gladly to God's Own Higher Court,
T-5 ...... VII.1:1 Do you really **b.** you can make a voice
T-5 ...... VII.1:2 Do you really **b.** you can devise a thought
T-5 ...... VII.1:3 really **b.** you can plan for your safety and
T-5 ...... VII.2:4 **b.** that there is no order of difficulty in
T-5 ...... VII.4:5 His children who **b.** they are lost to Him.
T-6 ........in.1:3 unless you **b.** that you have been attacked
T-6 ........in.1:7 and you *are* responsible for what you **b.**.
T-6 ..........I.4:5 To the extent to which you **b.** that it does,
T-6 ..........I.5:6 If you will **b.** it, you will help me teach it.
T-6 ..........I.6:9 Do not **b.** there is, and do not teach that
T-6 ........I.6:10 always that what you **b.** you will teach.
T-6 ........I.6:11 **B.** with me, and we will become equal as
T-6 ..........I.7:5 of God, but first **b.** that it is true for you,
T-6 ........I.18:5 As long as you teach this you will **b.** it.
T-6 .........II.2:1 disown, and therefore do not **b.** is yours.
T-6 .........II.7:4 ego would prefer to **b.** that this memory is
T-6 .......II.10:1 Holy Spirit uses time, but does not **b.** in it
T-6 .......II.10:2 but He does not **b.** in what is not true.
T-6 .......II.10:3 your mind can also **b.** only what is true.
T-6 ....... III.1:8 have taught yourself to **b.** that you are not
T-6 ....... III.2:9 And what you project or extend you **b.**.
T-6 ....... IV.2:4 *is* love, you **b.** that you are without it. This
T-6 ....... IV.4:1 but it does **b.** that part of the mind that
T-6 ....... IV.4:3 defense is attack, and wants *you* to **b.** it.
T-6 ....... IV.4:4 you do **b.** it you will not side with it, and
T-6 ....... IV.5:4 in his right mind could possibly **b.** this,
T-6 ....... IV.5:4 and no one in his right mind does **b.** it.
T-6 ....... IV.6:7 will no longer **b.** in dreams because they
T-6 ....... IV.8:7 you **b.** that the impossible *is* possible.
T-6 ........ V.1:3 You did not **b.** in your own perfection.
T-6 ........ V.2:2 are not real, because children **b.** in magic.
T-6 ..... V.B.1:1 All who **b.** in separation have a basic fear
T-6 ..... V.B.1:2 They **b.** in attack and rejection, so that is
T-6 ..... V.B.1:8 Those who **b.** in it therefore perceive this
T-6 ..... V.B.1:9 system centers on what you **b.** you are. If
T-6 ... V.B.3:10 to both as if what you do **b.** is not true.
T-6 ..... V.B.7:2 insane to **b.** that it is up to you to decide
T-6 ..... V.C.4:8 and still **b.** that you can choose either one
T-6 ..... V.C.5:6 you are teaching peace *because* you **b.** in it.
T-6 ..... V.C.7:7 cannot go beyond belief until you **b.** fully.
T-6 ..... V.C.9:9 must be in agreement about what they **b.**.
T-6 ... V.C.10:1 is a statement of what you want to **b.**, and
T-7 ..........I.5:2 you **b.** you are determines your gifts, and
T-7 .........II.3:1 is adapted to "What you project you **b.**."
T-7 .........II.3:3 onto others, and therefore **b.** they are. In
T-7 ......... III.4:2 you **b.** you can attend to what is not true,
T-7 .........V.2:4 act in accordance with what you do not **b.**
T-7 .........V.2:5 emphasized, you teach what you *do* **b.**. An
T-7 .........V.4:5 may **b.** that the gift comes from God to
T-7 ....... VI.2:7 If you do not **b.** you can do this you have
T-7 ....... VI.4:2 is total, and the ego does not **b.** in totality
T-7 ....... VI.5:5 and if it does so it will **b.** in them, because
T-7 ....... VI.7:7 When you **b.** something, you have made
T-7 ....... VI.7:8 When you **b.** what God does not know,
T-7 ....... VI.8:1 that the ego does **b.** it can attack God,
T-7 ..... VI.8:11 what is true. While you **b.** that two totally
T-7 ..... VI.10:6 because you do not **b.** you are part of it.
T-7 ...... VII.7:6 attack because they **b.** they are deprived.
T-7 ...... VII.8:3 then **b.** that others are taking it from you.
T-7 ...... VII.8:4 must be fearful if you **b.** that your brother
T-7 ...... VII.9:1 that does not **b.** it is responsible for itself,
T-7 ...VIII.3:11 they also **b.** their projections are trying to
T-7 .......X.1:10 depend on what you **b.** about your mind.
T-7 .........X.4:3 You **b.** that doing the opposite of God's
T-7 .........X.4:4 also **b.** that it is possible to *do* the opposite
T-7 .........X.4:5 you **b.** that an impossible choice is open
T-8 .........II.5:5 that taught you to **b.** they are the same, to
T-8 ........ IV.1:3 be because you do not **b.** you are in Him.
T-8 .........V.1:3 delusional **b.** that truth will assail them,
T-8 ...... VII.1:5 If you did not **b.** this, the idea of attack
T-8 ...... VII.3:2 the minds of those who **b.** they are bodies
T-8 ...... VII.6:4 **b.** you have withdrawn them from Him.
T-8 .... VII.14:5 and to **b.** that joy could possibly result, is
T-8 .... VII.15:3 **B.** you can interfere with His purpose,
T-8 ....VIII.7:3 **b.** that a learning device *can* tell you how
T-9 ..........I.2:4 and if you **b.** that what you are is fearful,
T-9 ..........I.8:1 can **b.** that its will is stronger than God's.
T-9 ........I.13:5 As long as you **b.** that fear is possible, you
T-9 .........II.4:3 **b.** in me whose faith in you cannot be
T-9 .........II.4:5 **B.** his words are true because of the truth
T-9 .........II.6:8 or **b.** that it is for you unless you hear it in
T-9 .........II.8:1 **B.** in your brothers because I believe in
T-9 .........II.8:1 in your brothers because I **b.** in you, and
T-9 .........II.8:2 **B.** in me *by* believing in them, for the sake
T-9 .........II.9:2 To **b.** is to accept, and to side with. To
T-9 .........II.9:3 To **b.** is not to be credulous, but to accept
T-9 .........II.9:4 What you do not **b.** you do not appreciate
T-9 .......II.11:2 **b.** that it is possible to get much for little
T-9 .......II.11:2 is to **b.** that you can bargain with God.
T-9 ....... III.7:8 that you **b.** correction by you is possible,
T-9 ....... IV.1:3 for you will **b.** what your perception holds
T-9 ....... IV.2:3 to **b.** either that you do not make them, or
T-9 ....... IV.5:4 will also **b.** that you must undo what you
T-9 ..... IV.11:7 Children may **b.** them, and so, for a while,
T-9 .........V.3:2 cannot do this because he does not **b.** it.
T-9 .........V.3:7 but to revolt against it is still to **b.** in it.
T-9 ...VIII.10:9 it means that you **b.** your evaluation of
T-10 ......in.1:3 You cannot do this as long as you **b.** that
T-10 ......in.3:8 **B.** this, and you will realize how much is
T-10 .......II.6:2 still **b.** it can get you something you want.
T-10 ..... III.3:1 To **b.** that a Son of God can be sick is to
T-10 ..... III.3:1 be sick is to **b.** that part of God can suffer.
T-10 ..... III.4:1 To **b.** a Son of God is sick is to worship
T-10 ..... III.8:5 them, because you **b.** that they made you.
T-10 ..... III.9:1 you may **b.** you are afraid of nothingness,
T-10 ..... IV.1:5 If you **b.** you can be sick, you have placed
T-10 .......V.1:7 can and **b.** you have is beyond dispute.
T-10 .......V.2:1 will **b.** that others and not yourself have
T-10 .......V.2:3 You may **b.** that you judge your brothers
T-10 .....V.13:6 You **b.** that the sick things you have made
T-10 .....V.13:6 because you **b.** that the sick images you
T-11 ........I.2:6 Do you really **b.** that part of God can be
T-11 ........I.4:3 and so you **b.** that all creation is limited.
T-11 ........I.5:3 If you **b.** you are absent from God, you
T-11 ........I.5:3 you will **b.** that He is absent from you.

T-11......I.10:3 God's Will, because you **b.** it is not yours.
T-11......IV.6:2 for otherwise you will **b.** that the door is
T-11......V.3:4 ego is fearful to you because you **b.** this.
T-11......V.6:6 Can you **b.** that autonomy is meaningful
T-11.....V.12:6 this is what the ego would have you **b.**.
T-11.....V.12:7 God's Son is not insane, and cannot **b.** it.
T-11.....V.12:9 could **b.** that love can be gained by attack.
T-11......VI.1:1 It is impossible not to **b.** what you see,
T-11......VI.1:1 impossible to see what you do not **b.**.
T-11......VI.1:4 In effect, then, what you **b.** you *do* see.
T-11......VI.1:5 are ye who have not seen and still **b.**," for
T-11......VI.1:5 those who **b.** in the resurrection will see it
T-11......VI.3:2 against it, and therefore do not **b.** it. And
T-11......VI.4:6 **B.** in the resurrection because it has been
T-11......VI.8:6 as long as you **b.** that you can crucify him,
T-11......VI.9:4 set limits on what you **b.** I can do through
T-11....VI.10:4 me. If you **b.** that yours is limited, you are
T-11.....VII.3:6 If you **b.** in truth and illusion, you cannot
T-11.....VII.4:7 To **b.** that you can perceive the real world
T-11.....VII.4:7 world is to **b.** that you can know yourself.
T-11... VIII.1:3 But do you **b.** it? When you perceive the
T-11... VIII.1:4 you will recognize that you did not **b.** it.
T-11... VIII.5:5 long as you **b.** that problems are specific.
T-11... VIII.5:6 as long as you **b.** that the one is many.
T-11. VIII.5:10 it is because you **b.** that asking is taking
T-11... VIII.6:6 You **b.** that to ask for guidance of the
T-11... VIII.7:2 You **b.** in a world that takes, because you
T-11... VIII.7:2 because you **b.** that you can get by taking.
T-11... VIII.8:2 you. Do you **b.** I would deceive you? The
T-11... VIII.8:4 **B.** that the truth is in me, for I know that
T-12.........I.1:2 If you want to **b.** in error, you would have
T-12.........I.1:3 **b.** in truth *you do not have to do anything.*
T-12.........I.3:9 **b.** that an appeal for help is something
T-12.......II.4:5 Yet you **b.** that you do understand yours.
T-12......III.5:4 of this, and never allow yourself to **b.**,
T-12......III.9:9 Do not **b.** it is outside of yourself, for only
T-12......IV.5:3 **b.** it is outside you the search will be futile
T-12......IV.5:4 for you do not **b.** your home is there. Yet
T-12......IV.6:5 you will **b.** that you have purchased it,
T-12.......V.1:6 because you **b.** that attack was successful
T-12.....VII.4:9 long as you **b.** you have other functions,
T-12.....VII.5:5 For you will **b.** in what you manifest, and
T-12.....VII.6:8 it will still **b.** it has one goal by making it
T-12.....VII.7:9 enables it to **b.** that it is pursuing one goal
T-12.....VII.8:4 But do not then **b.** that the witnesses for
T-12...VII.14:2 a traitor to you who **b.** that you have been
T-12...VII.14:5 with the ego, you **b.** that you want death.
T-12... VIII.1:1 really **b.** that you can kill the Son of God?
T-13.......in.3:7 who do not understand Him could **b.** it.
T-13.........I.3:6 As long as you **b.** the Son of God is guilty
T-13...... I.10:4 And you who cherish guilt must also **b.** it,
T-13.......II.5:1 that you **b.** you have crucified God's Son.
T-13.......II.5:6 you identify with it you must **b.** its goal is
T-13.......II.7:5 must **b.** that by not learning the course
T-13.......II.8:4 afraid of redemption and you **b.** it will kill
T-13.......II.8:6 For you **b.** that, in the presence of truth,
T-13......III.1:9 cornerstone without fear if you did not **b.**
T-13......III.2:4 you did not **b.** that it saves you from love.
T-13......III.2:7 You **b.** that attack is salvation because it
T-13......III.4:2 you **b.** that magnitude lies in defiance,
T-13....III.11:5 where it can **b.** it is where it is not. God
T-13......IV.2:4 reality is questioned, you **b.** that yours is.
T-13......IV.2:5 For you **b.** that attack is your reality, and
T-13......VI.4:4 deceived, and then **b.** that this is how it is.
T-13......VI.4:5 For to **b.** reality is what you would have it
T-13......IX.1:6 who follow them **b.** that they are guilty,
T-13......IX.4:3 You do not **b.** the Son of God is guiltless
T-13......IX.5:4 In any form, in anyone, ***b.** this not.* For sin
T-13......IX.8:6 Within you is not what you **b.** is there,
T-13.......X.3:4 to displace it, because they do **b.** in it. Yet
T-13.......X.6:1 as you **b.** that guilt is justified in any way,
T-13.......X.6:2 as long as you **b.** there is a reason for it.
T-13......XI.8:2 You may **b.** you want It broken, and this
T-14.........I.4:7 will not **b.** all that *is* possible to learn to do
T-14.......II.1:3 for you **b.** that misery *is* happiness. This
T-14.......II.1:9 You will **b.** that nothing is of value, and
T-14.......II.7:5 the dark door that you **b.** is locked forever
T-14......III.2:2 **b.** that guilt and guiltlessness are both of
T-14....III.10:2 **b.** they are guilty will respond to guilt,
T-14....III.10:3 **b.** that increasing guilt is self-protection.
T-14....III.10:5 do not **b.** that what they want is good. Yet
T-14......IV.1:3 within him while you still **b.** it is not there
T-14.......V.9:7 **B.** not that you cannot teach His perfect
T-14.....VII.2:8 you see no reason to **b.** that the more you
T-14.......X.7:2 or to **b.** that everything else is nothing but
T-14.......X.8:4 you **b.** you understand something of the
T-14......XI.4:9 Never **b.** that any lesson you have learned
T-15.........I.4:5 and dissolution as an end, it does not **b.** it
T-15.........I.6:4 still **b.** that it can offer them escape. But
T-15.........I.6:7 can **b.** that punishment will end in peace.
T-15......III.3:4 **B.** the little can content you, and by
T-15......III.6:5 and **b.** that littleness can be blown up into
T-15......IV.1:1 unless you **b.** that what God wills takes
T-15......IV.7:3 **b.** you can harbor thoughts you would
T-15.......V.1:6 afraid of this because you **b.** that without
T-15.......V.2:5 to appeal to it for salvation is to **b.** you are
T-15.......V.3:3 it? To **b.** that *special* relationships, with
T-15......VI.3:3 must **b.** that strength comes from another
T-15......VI.4:1 find it difficult to **b.** that when another
T-15.....VII.8:9 no longer **b.** that bodies communicate,
T-15...VII.11:2 while you **b.** that to communicate is to
T-15...VII.11:3 alone? It is clearly insane to **b.** that by
T-15...VII.11:4 And yet many do **b.** it. For they think
T-15...VII.12:2 As long as you **b.** that to be with a body is
T-15...VII.13:2 who **b.** communication to be damnation
T-15... VIII.5:7 only you who **b.** that it is understandable.
T-15.......X.5:4 You **b.** it is possible to be host to the ego
T-15.......X.5:5 the decision you **b.** that you must make.
T-15.......X.6:1 **b.** that you can give all your guilt away
T-15.......X.7:1 a sacrifice do you **b.** His Love demands!
T-15......XI.4:1 You who **b.** that sacrifice is love must
T-16.......II.4:5 while you **b.** that you must understand it
T-16......III.2:7 have so diligently taught yourself to **b.**?
T-16......III.3:4 taught freedom unless you did **b.** in it.
T-16.......V.3:4 who **b.** that hate is sin merely feel guilty,
T-16.......V.4:3 ego that you **b.** this specialness is not hell,
T-17.........I.3:2 You **b.** truth cannot deal with them only
T-17.......II.2:4 not **b.** it is the meeting place of worlds so
T-17......IV.9:3 you take it you will **b.** that you *are* damned
T-17.......V.6:5 why would you now not still **b.** that He is
T-17.......V.9:4 a road far more familiar than you now **b.**.
T-17.....VII.1:2 They demonstrate that you did not **b.** the
T-17... VIII.6:2 no one accepts what he does not **b.** is real.
T-18.........I.4:1 You who **b.** that God is fear made but
T-18.........I.7:5 You but **b.** it is the other way; that truth is
T-18......III.4:2 **b.** that I would leave you in the darkness
T-18......IV.3:6 **b.** He cannot enter where He wills to be,
T-18......IV.4:4 and not **b.** that it is up to you to establish
T-18......IV.8:2 you **b.** the holy instant is difficult for you,
T-18.......V.5:5 on thousands who **b.** that love is fear, not
T-18.......V.6:5 Never **b.** that this is necessary, or even
T-18.....VII.6:8 **B.** it for just one instant, and you will
T-18......IX.5:1 it directs as long as you **b.** that guilt is real
T-19......III.5:5 see beyond it, but not while you **b.** in sin.
T-19......III.6:1 you are tempted to **b.** that sin is real,
T-19......III.6:6 easier to **b.** that you have been mistaken
T-19......III.6:6 you have been mistaken than to **b.** in this
T-19......III.7:1 While you **b.** that your reality or your
T-19......III.7:1 is bounded by a body, you will **b.** in sin.
T-19......III.7:2 While you **b.** that bodies can unite, you
T-19......III.7:2 guilt attractive and **b.** that sin is precious.
T19IV.A.17:10 you **b.** that it can get you what you want.
T19IV.A.17:11 While you **b.** that it can give you pleasure,
T19IV.A.17:11 you will also **b.** that it can bring you pain.
T19....IV.B.2:2 is what you **b.** that it would dispossess,
T19..IV.B.16:1 and **b.** not the impossible is true. Forget
T19..IV.B.16:4 Not one but must **b.** that yielding to the
T19....IV.C.4:3 You who **b.** you have condemned the Son
T19... IV.D.7:4 and you will nevermore **b.** that you are at
T-20......III.5:7 as long as you **b.** this picture is outside,
T-20......III.8:2 And if you have, would you **b.** the answer,
T-20... VIII.8:3 **B.** them not and they are gone. And all
T-21.........I.4:6 This they do not **b.**. And so they keep the
T-21......III.5:3 the Son of God **b.** that he is powerless.
T-21......III.9:1 Those who **b.** in sin must think the Holy
T-21......IV.2:4 This you **b.**, and so you do not look. Yet
T-21.......V.2:5 will **b.** that you are helpless prey to forces
T-21.......V.2:8 never **b.** because it is your faith it makes
T-21......VI.1:4 for, you will not **b.** that it is yours to give.
T-21......VI.4:3 their will, for they **b.** they see the body,
T-21.....VII.1:4 Only the helpless could **b.** in it. Enormity
T-21.....VII.1:6 And only those who first **b.** that they are
T-21.....VII.2:2 must **b.** that they are not the Son of God.
T-21.....VII.5:3 in sin would dare **b.** he has no enemy?
T-22.........I.1:3 must then **b.** is that you are not yourself.
T-22.........I.1:4 You can indeed **b.** this, and you do. And
T-22.........I.4:2 Yet you **b.** that you have secrets. What
T-22........II.4:3 To **b.** that one exception can exist is to
T-22......II.10:3 For only if you would **b.** His Son could be
T-22......III.8:4 with his body, which you **b.** can sin?
T-22.... VI.1:10 He will **b.** it possible of mind or body, and
T-22.... VI.12:2 you **b.** attack of any kind means anything.
T-23.......in.2:2 You will **b.** that everything you use for sin
T-23.........I.1:5 **b.** the ego has the power to be victorious.
T-23.........I.3:3 ego's chosen home, which you **b.** is yours.
T-23.........I.5:3 a body, you will **b.** you have forgotten it.
T-23........II.6:2 what He must think and what He must **b.**;
T-23......II.13:4 You who **b.** you walk in sanity with feet
T-23......II.18:1 that you do not **b.** these senseless laws,
T-23......II.18:3 Brother, you *do* **b.** them. For how else
T-23......II.18:6 Yet you **b.** them *for* the form they take,
T-23...... III.4:2 it seems difficult to those who still **b.** that
T-23...... III.5:1 Those who **b.** that peace can be defended
T-23...... IV.3:3 to **b.** the function of the Son is murder,
T-24.......in.1:8 Can you **b.** a shadow can hold back the
T-24.......in.2:5 based on everything that you **b.**. It is the
T-24....... V.4:8 and madness, and **b.** this crumbling thing
T-24.... VI.13:1 You who **b.** it easier to see your brother's
T-25.........I.2:3 body, and you will **b.** that you are there.
T-25.........I.5:1 Since you **b.** that you are separate,
T-25......II.10:4 **b.** that all His praise is given not to you.
T-25...... III.1:3 law: You see what you **b.** is there, and you
T-25...... III.1:3 you **b.** it there because you want it there.
T-25....... V.1:6 no one could **b.** in one unless the other
T-25....... V.2:5 And now you must **b.** you are not you,
T-25....... V.6:4 you; through your attack **b.** He hates you,
T-25..... VII.2:9 For it is this that you do not **b.**. Yet there
T-25... VII.2:10 Yet there is nothing else you could **b.**, if
T-25..... VII.4:4 he chooses to **b.** one thought opposed to
T-25..... VII.4:5 This you **b.**. Think not that this belief
T-25..... VII.6:1 that you **b.** against this one requirement,
T-25..... VII.6:4 sinners, who **b.** theirs is the way to sanity.
T-25..... VII.7:3 time, and all that you **b.** must limit you.
T-25... VII.11:7 at all. You who **b.** that God is mad, look
T-25....VIII.1:3 **b.** He wrested it from you against your
T-25....VIII.2:8 faith remains to those who still **b.** in sin?
T-25....VIII.6:1 who still **b.** sin meaningful to understand
T-25....VIII.6:2 must **b.** He shares their own confusion,
T-25....VIII.6:5 They *do* **b.** that Heaven is hell, and *are*
T-25....VIII.9:2 **b.** in your confusion you have much to
T-25...... IX.9:3 Not one right do you **b.** you have. And
T-26........II.5:1 **b.** it safe to give but some mistakes to be
T-26........II.6:2 **b.** that some injustices are fair and good,
T-26....... V.2:3 Yet since you do **b.** in it, why should you
T-26....... V.4:1 still **b.** you live in time and know not it is
T-26...... VI.1:1 Anything in this world that you **b.** is
T-26...... VI.1:9 Who can **b.** illusions are the same, and
T-26... VII.13:5 And to **b.** ideas can leave their source is to
T-26... VII.15:6 If you **b.** what is the same is different you
T-26....VIII.2:1 you still **b.** you are external to him. This
T-26....VIII.2:3 And you cannot **b.** that trust would settle
T-26........X.4:6 safer to **b.** that you are innocent of this,
T-27.........I.7:5 Are not the frail entitled to **b.** that every
T-27........II.5:3 What you would prove to him you will **b.**.
T-27...... VI.4:4 could contain what you **b.** it holds within.
T-27....VIII.8:1 you will **b.** that others do to you exactly
T-28.........I.4:3 long accustomed to **b.** that memory holds
T-28........II.3:2 he does not **b.** that he is Love's Effect, and
T-28...... IV.5:2 must **b.** that it is your reality as well as his
T-28....... V.3:4 you will **b.** you are the dream you share.
T-28....... V.7:1 You who **b.** there is a little gap between
T-29.........I.1:6 All this do you **b.**, when you perceive a
T-29.........I.4:7 which you truly **b.** diminishes as you and
T-29........II.5:7 you will **b.** His Presence must be there.
T-29...... IV.1:1 **b.** that truth can be but some illusions?
T-29....... V.6:7 death. **B.** him not. But learn, instead, how
T-29..... VII.4:2 For you **b.** that you can suffer lack, and

T-29....VIII.2:3 you **b.** they will complete your little self,
T-29......IX.1:4 the truth that you **b.** that it is not a dream
T-29......IX.4:2 from what you **b.** you have accomplished,
T-29......IX.5:5 This does the child **b.**, because he fears
T-29......IX.9:1 made an idol, and **b.** it will betray you.
T-30.........I.7:3 until you **b.** the day you want is one in
T-30.......I.10:2 will **b.** your happiness depends on being
T-30......III.3:3 mean that you **b.** some form is missing.
T-30......IV.4:3 that you **b.** about yourself obey no laws.
T-30......IV.6:4 do not want whatever you **b.** an idol gives
T-30.....VII.7:2 you will **b.** the world is an uncertain place
T-31.........I.2:6 For somehow you **b.** that what is totally
T-31........I.11:3 deceived if you **b.** you want disaster and
T-31......III.1:6 the fact that you **b.** them to be yours, and
T-31......III.2:1 not **b.** they could not be forgiven in you?
T-31......III.2:2 if you did not **b.** that they are your reality
T-31......III.2:7 If you did not **b.** that you deserved attack,
T-31......III.6:1 us be glad that you will see what you **b.**,
T-31......III.6:1 has been given you to change what you **b.**.
T-31......IV.4:2 **b.** there is another answer to be found.
T-31....... V.8:5 of what you now **b.** for total loss of self,
T-31......VI.4:5 It matters not where you **b.** you are, nor
T-31......VI.5:1 You who **b.** that you can choose to see
T-31....VIII.6:5 own identity as you will see it and **b.** it is.
W-in..........8:1 presents you will find hard to **b.**, and
W-in..........9:1 only this; you need not **b.** the ideas, you
W-pI.......5.1:2 whatever you **b.** is the cause of your upset
W-pI.......5.3:1 for "sources" of upset in which you **b.**,
W-pI.......7.1:1 idea is particularly difficult to **b.** at first.
W-pI.......7.2:1 everything you **b.** is rooted in time, and
W-pI.......9.2:1 for the untrained mind to **b.** that what it
W-pI.....10.4:3 *will help to release me from all that I now **b.**.*
W-pI.....10.5:5 *will help to release me from all that I now **b.**.*
W-pI.....13.5:3 expected to **b.** the statement at this point,
W-pI.....17.1:3 to **b.** that it is the other way around. This
W-pI.....17.3:1 what you **b.** to be animate or inanimate;
W-pI.....17.3:2 Regardless of what you may **b.**, you do
W-pI.....21.3:2 you **b.** in this connection means anything.
W-pI.....25.2:5 you **b.** this, you will try to withdraw the
W-pI.....26.1:3 because you **b.** that you can really attack.
W-pI.....26.2:2 you must **b.** that you are not invulnerable
W-pI.....26.3:4 And because you **b.** in them, you can no
W-pI.....26.3:4 in them, you can no longer **b.** in yourself.
W-pI.....27.2:1 may be a great temptation to **b.** that some
W-pI.....35.1:3 he is in this world to **b.** this of himself.
W-pI.....35.1:4 is in this world because he does not **b.** it
W-pI.....35.2:1 You will **b.** that you are part of where you
W-pI.....35.2:5 What you see while you **b.** you are in it is
W-pI.....39.2:4 But do you **b.** that guilt is hell? If you did,
W-pI.....41.2:1 what they **b.** to be "the ills of the world."
W-pI.....41.5:1 We understand that you do not **b.** all this
W-pI.....41.8:4 way will open, if you **b.** that it is possible.
W-pI.....44.5:4 leave behind everything that you now **b.**,
W-pI.....44.6:2 whatever you may **b.** to the contrary. God
W-pI.....47.2:2 **b.** that you can is to put your trust where
W-pI.....47.5:2 for otherwise you would **b.** that you could
W-pI.....48.1:2 It is not a fact to those who **b.** in illusions,
W-pI.....50.1:2 you **b.** you are sustained by everything
W-pI.....55.5:4 It is for this that I **b.** the world is for.
W-pI.....68.1:7 It makes you **b.** that He is like what you
W-pI.....68.6:6 Try to **b.**, however briefly, that nothing
W-pI.....69.5:1 see no reason to **b.** there is a brilliant light
W-pI.....70.1:1 temptation not to **b.** the idea for today.
W-pI.....71.1:2 It is this plan in which you **b.**. Since it is
W-pI.....71.1:3 you also **b.** that to accept God's plan in
W-pI.....71.1:5 preposterous it may be, you do **b.** in it.
W-pI.....71.2:4 and an assertion in which you **b.**, that
W-pI.....72.2:5 Yet the ego would have you **b.** that it is.
W-pI.....75.7:3 **B.** He will not fail you now. You have
W-pI.....76.8:3 further; you **b.** in the "laws" of friendship,
W-pI.....87.3:3 afraid only when I **b.** there is another will.
W-pI.....87.3:4 only when I try to attack can I **b.** that my
W-pI.....88.4:2 *of this shows me I **b.** in laws that do not exist.*
W-pI.....90.3:3 I **b.** that the problem comes first, and
W-pI.....92.1:4 Thus you **b.** that you can change what
W-pI.....92.2:1 You also **b.** the body's brain can think. If
W-pI.....92.2:4 foolish than to **b.** the body's eyes can see;
W-pI.....93.2:3 dust,–all this is true by what you now **b.**.
W-pI.....95.1:5 be so, only because you **b.** that you have
W-pI...99.11:2 mind. If you are tempted to **b.** them true,
W-pI....101.1:3 You still **b.** it asks for suffering as penance
W-pI....101.1:5 think it so while you **b.** that sin is real,
W-pI....101.5:2 that you **b.** must come from sin will never
W-pI....102.1:2 still **b.** a little that it buys you what you
W-pI....121.9:1 unforgiving mind does not **b.** that giving
W-pI....124.9:1 not be less if you **b.** that nothing happens.
W-pI....126.2:1 Let us consider what you do **b.**, in place
W-pI. 126.11:7 And what you hear of Him you will **b.**, for
W-pI....127.2:5 others. To **b.** these things of love is not to
W-pI....127.8:1 from every law in which you now **b.**.
W-pI....128.1:2 **B.** this thought, and you are saved from
W-pI....128.4:1 permit temptation to **b.** the world holds
W-pI....130.4:2 of differences you **b.** make up the world.
W-pI....133.9:4 will **b.** that he has served the ego's hidden
W-pI. 133.10:4 it is error to **b.** that sins are but mistakes,
W-pI. 133.11:1 for choice that is the hardest to **b.**,
W-pI. 133.14:2 **b.** you see some difficult decisions facing
W-pI....134.3:1 that you still **b.** you must forgive the truth
W-pI....134.4:2 of sin as true and not **b.** forgiveness is a lie
W-pI. 135.26:1 this day as you **b.** would benefit you most.
W-pI....136.3:2 appears to threaten what you would **b.**.
W-pI. 136.10:2 And you **b.** that Heaven quails before
W-pI....138.1:1 here we **b.** there are alternatives to choose
W-pI....139.3:2 yourself is to **b.** that you are really dead.
W-pI....139.8:3 to show that you **b.** the contradiction that
W-pI....151.2:3 eyes. Nor do you ask why you **b.** it, even
W-pI....151.2:4 That you **b.** them to the last detail which
W-pI....151.4:4 You merely can **b.** the ego's judgments,
W-pI....151.5:2 **b.** that this is so with stubborn certainty.
W-pI....151.5:3 reality with such conviction it does not **b.**.
W-pI....151.6:4 **b.** to doubt his vassals is to doubt yourself
W-pI....152.2:1 You may **b.** that this position is extreme,
W-pI....152.6:1 strange that you **b.** to think you made the
W-pI....152.7:4 To think you can is merely to **b.** you can
W-pI....153.7:3 fearful image you **b.** you see at work in all
W-pI....154.1:7 **b.** to be our strength is often arrogance.
W-pI....155.1:5 you also, and **b.** that you are like them, as
W-pI....160.1:6 a madman could **b.** he is what he is not,
W-pI....163.8:3 they saw that it is only this which they **b.**,
W-pI....166.2:3 it real must still **b.** there is another will,
W-pI....166.3:2 He must **b.** that to accept God's gifts,
W-pI....169.2:2 of grace can not **b.** the world of fear is real
W-pI....170.1:4 mean that you **b.** to hurt another brings
W-pI....170.9:3 The final one, the hardest to **b.** is nothing,
W-pI....181.5:6 we will **b.** will not intrude upon us now.
W-pI....184.5:3 Yet you **b.** this is what learning means; its
W-pI....184.8:5 from you by what you **b.** he really is. His
W-pI....185.8:4 but what you **b.** will comfort you, and
W-pI....187.3:3 But you will not **b.** that this is done until
W-pI....187.8:1 Never **b.** that you can sacrifice. There is
W-pI....188.2:2 in the future, or **b.** it has been lost already
W-pI....191.4:3 All else but this one thing is folly to **b.**. In
W-pI....193.6:1 we are tempted to **b.** that pain is real, and
W-pI....196.3:3 will not **b.** you are a body to be crucified.
W-pI....196.5:5 could **b.** his Father is his deadly enemy,
W-pI....196.6:1 Such is the form of madness you **b.**, if
W-pI....196.8:4 cannot then **b.** that fear is caused without
W-pI....198.7:5 How foolish to **b.** that They could die!
W-pI....198.7:6 How foolish to **b.** you can attack! How
W-pI....199.7:2 still **b.** they are enslaved within a body. Be
W-pII . 226.1:3 If I **b.** it has a value as I see it now, so will
W-pII . 228.1:2 and **b.** in what His knowledge makes
W-pII . 246.1:3 and still **b.** that my awareness can contain
W-pII ..... 5.5:2 may be, you will **b.** that it is one with you.
W-pII . 277.2:1 nor **b.** in any law idolatry would make to
W-pII . 278.1:2 And this do I **b.**, when I maintain the laws
W-pII . 331.1:1 *to **b.** Your Son could cause himself to suffer!*
M-in..........2:2 you **b.** one or the other is true all the time.
M-in..........2:7 a call to witnesses to attest to what you **b.**.
M-in..........3:1 you **b.** the relationship of others is to you.
M-in..........3:7 but reinforces what you **b.** about yourself.
M-1...........1:6 God even if he does not yet **b.** in Him. He
M-5.......III.1:7 they **b.** that sickness has chosen them.
M-5......III.3:3 himself as to **b.** God's Son can suffer. And
M-11.........3:2 is meaningless to those who **b.** in them.
M-12.........4:6 not **b.** in the illusion despite appearances.
M-13.........6:1 You may **b.** this course requires sacrifice
M-13.......7:13 Yet a split in which you surely will **b.**,
M-15.........2:2 Do you **b.** that this is wholly true? No; not
M-17.........6:3 How, then, can one **b.** in one's defenses?
M-17.......6:10 **B.** that you have won it, but do not retain
M-17.........9:7 certain witness that you do **b.** in it as fact.
M-20.........3:4 and must **b.** that it cannot exist. In this
M-22.........4:2 anyone actually **b.** he wants to be sick.
M-22.........6:4 Not to **b.** this is to be unfair to God, and
M-24.........2:5 who **b.** in reincarnation and by those who
M-24.........3:2 those who **b.** in it as to those who do not.
M-24.........5:1 should not **b.** in reincarnation himself, or
M-24.........5:3 If he does **b.** in reincarnation, it would be
M-27.........7:2 Do not **b.** in cruelty, nor let attack conceal
P-2...........I.1:2 have come together who already **b.** this. It
P-2..........II.1:1 to **b.** in God to any recognizable extent. It
P-2..........II.7:6 where many who **b.** they have found God
P-2.........III.4:4 advanced to **b.** in sickness and too near to
P-2........ IV.8:5 the insane **b.** it because they are insane.
P-2...... IV.10:5 emphasized that the insane **b.** that sanity
P-2..........V.2:2 What they **b.** will help can only harm;
P-2..........V.2:2 what they **b.** will harm alone can help.
P-2........ VI.7:4 that still **b.** that sin is there to look upon.
P-3........ III.5:9 they **b.** they need anything from a brother
S-1..........II.4:3 While you **b.** you have enemies, you have

## believed 54

T-2 ....... IV.2:9 it can be **b.** that the mind can miscreate in
T-4 ..........I.6:6 to devote myself to teaching if I **b.** this
T-6 ..........I.7:4 I **b.** in it, and therefore accepted it as true
T-6 ........I.15:5 of man with a kiss?" unless I **b.** in betrayal
T-6 .........V.1:2 wrongly, having **b.** what was not true.
T-6 ..... V.C.6:4 have **b.** that you are without the Kingdom
T-7 ..........I.5:1 Kingdom because I **b.** that was what I was
T-7 ....... VI.7:6 Holy Spirit if you had not **b.** the untrue.
T-7 .....VIII.6:3 the more you realize that it cannot be **b.**.
T-7 .......X.3:11 If you **b.** this, there would be no conflict.
T-8 ....... III.6:7 you will understand why you once **b.** that,
T-11 ......in.2:1 you say to someone who **b.** this question
T-12 .......II.8:7 will be **b.** when you see it as accomplished
T-12 ..... IV.2:4 wholly split off, or it could not be **b.** at all.
T-12 .......V.1:4 and **b.** that the attack was effective, you
T-13 ......in.3:6 one, had he not **b.** it was the Father Who
T-13 ... III.11:7 it happen, and therefore **b.** that it was so.
T-13 .......X.1:3 guilt onto what you **b.** to be less fearful.
T-13 .....X.10:6 You cannot be as you **b.** you were. Your
T-14 ....II.1:11 you have **b.** that nothing can be precious,
T-14 .......II.5:7 have **b.** that nothing could content you. *It*
T-17 .......V.6:5 **b.** the Holy Spirit was there to accept the
T-21 ........I.3:6 If you **b.** it would, the learning of it would
T-21 ........I.4:3 stern necessity of limits they **b.** they could
T-21 .... VII.1:3 one requirement that it demands to be **b.**.
T-22 ......in.1:4 other yet **b.** by each to be within himself.
T-22 ......in.1:7 the effects of what you both **b.** and saw.
T-22 ........I.9:9 him; such he **b.** *because* it was the truth.
T-22 .......II.7:4 This course will be **b.** entirely or not at all.
T-22 .......II.7:5 false, and cannot be but partially **b.**. And
T-23 ....II.14:4 It must be seen as truth to be **b.**. And if it
T-23 ....II.15:4 laws. To be **b.**, its seeming laws must be
T-23 ....II.16:1 can it be that laws like these can be **b.**?
T-23 ....II.18:2 look at what they say, they cannot be **b.**.
T-25 .......V.6:1 is God **b.** to be without the power to save
T-26 .... IV.1:5 No one forgives unless he has **b.** in sin,
T-26 .... IV.3:6 of altars is set where once sin was **b.** to be.
T-27 .......I.4:2 witness is **b.** because he points beyond
T-27 ......I.4:11 that it has shown to him have you **b.**,
T-27 ........I.6:6 the witnesses that are called forth to be **b.**
T-27 ... VIII.1:2 as if it were a person to be seen and be **b.**.
T-29 ... VIII.5:3 must be **b.** before it seems to come to life,
W-pI .... 10.1:5 that what you once **b.** were your thoughts
W-pI .... 68.4:1 your grievances if you **b.** all this were so?
W-pI .... 76.8:1 kinds of "laws" we have **b.** we must obey.
W-pI .. 110.1:2 you and the world, if you **b.** that it is true.
W-pI 110.10:3 false the images which you **b.** were you.
W-pI .. 126.1:2 If you **b.** this statement, there would be
W-pI .. 139.9:2 reinforce the madness that we once **b.** in.
W-pI 196.10:3 you **b.** attack could be directed outward,
W-pI .. 198.1:4 For you have **b.** that you can injure, and
W-pII .... in.9:3 **b.** that our insane desires were the truth.
W-pII ... 10.3:1 who **b.** that God's Last Judgment would

M-17..........5:6 that it can be **b.** as fact is equally obvious.

### believer 2

T-3.......VII.3:3 All beliefs are real to the **b.**. The fruit of
T-24.....II.12:5 Not one **b.** in its potency but seeks for

### believer's 1

T-29... VIII.5:4 Its life and power are its **b.** gift, and this is

### believers 1

T-22.......II.3:1 suffering, sickness and death, to their **b.**.

### believes 120

T-1........VI.1:2 it and **b.** in some way that he needs it.
T-3.........II.4:2 can miscreate only when it **b.** it is not free
T-3........III.3:2 closed mind **b.** the future and the present
T-3.........V.9:6 world **b.** that if anyone has everything,
T-3......VI.11:7 Yet no one in his right mind **b.** that what
T-4...........I.5:4 of the system in which the lawmaker **b.**. It
T-4.........II.8:1 The ego **b.** it is completely on its own,
T-4.......VII.1:4 The concrete part **b.** in the ego, because
T-4.......VII.1:5 ego is the part of the mind that **b.** your
T-5.........V.3:1 is the part of the mind that **b.** in division.
T-5.........V.3:4 ego **b.** that this is what you did because it
T-5.........V.3:4 is what you did because it **b.** that it *is* you.
T-5.........V.5:6 The ego **b.** that by punishing itself it will
T-6........III.4:1 exact opposite of everything the ego **b.**.
T-6........IV.1:4 It **b.**, and correctly, that its maker may
T-6........IV.2:5 part of your mind that **b.** *you* are separate
T-6........IV.4:3 It **b.** that the best defense is attack, and
T-7........IV.6:2 The ego **b.** that it can, and that it can offer
T-7.........V.4:4 **b.** he can offer as a gift to someone who
T-7.........V.9:8 It literally **b.** that every time it deprives
T-7........VI.2:2 That is because it **b.** it can destroy love,
T-7........VI.9:6 decide. The ego **b.** this totally, being fully
T-7.......VII.9:2 to your Creator, it **b.** that your brothers,
T-7.......VII.9:3 brother attacks another, that *is* what he **b.**.
T-7........X.5:11 he **b.** that everything can betray him. Yet
T-8.....VII.11:3 mind **b.** the body is its goal it will distort
T-8..... VIII.1:2 always based on what it **b.** the thing is *for.*
T-8........IX.6:2 the ego actually **b.** that it is protecting it.
T-8........IX.6:3 because the ego **b.** that mind is dangerous
T-9...........I.8:2 a mind **b.** that its will is different from His
T-9...........I.8:3 who **b.** that God demands sacrifices.
T-9...........I.8:4 panic, because the atheist **b.** he is alone,
T-9...........I.8:4 the martyr **b.** that God is crucifying him.
T-9........IV.7:2 The ego **b.** that all functions belong to it,
T-9.........V.5:8 **b.** that it is up to him to teach the patient
T-9.........V.7:4 no longer **b.** in nightmares of any kind.
T-9..... VIII.1:4 it, the ego **b.** that its "enemy" has struck,
T-9..... VIII.4:6 you because of the littleness in which it **b.**
T-10......III.3:4 presence of a Son of God even if he **b.** in it
T-11.....V.10:8 no one wants to find what he **b.** would
T-11.....V.12:3 The ego **b.** that to accomplish its goal is
T-11.....V.13:4 The ego **b.** that power, understanding
T-11.....VII.2:3 because he still **b.** that he is separate. Yet
T-12.......II.3:1 your brother what he **b.** he cannot offer
T-12......III.2:2 should tell you that he **b.** salvation lies in
T-12......III.7:5 everyone **b.** that identification is salvation
T-12......IV.1:2 everyone who **b.** that the ego is salvation
T-12......IV.2:5 mind that **b.** in it and gives existence to it.
T-12...VII.13:2 goal, for it fully **b.** that you are a criminal,
T-13.........I.4:3 **b.** in it the Holy Spirit knows it is not true
T-13.........I.8:4 No one who **b.** this can understand what
T-13...... I.10:3 The ego **b.** in atonement through attack,
T-13......IV.4:2 and in the end **b.** that the past is the only
T-13.......V.3:4 them, and he alone **b.** they answered him.
T-13.......X.8:3 The Son of God **b.** that he is lost in guilt,
T-13......XI.1:2 **b.** that both opponents in the war are real
T-14.....VII.5:1 darkness when a mind **b.** in darkness,
T-15.....VII.2:3 for the ego **b.** that anger makes friends.
T-15.....VII.2:5 For the ego really **b.** that it can get and
T-15.....VII.3:3 choose to let go what he **b.** has value. Yet
T-15.....VII.7:5 He merely **b.** he is in love with sacrifice.
T-15.....VII.7:7 the ego **b.** that to forgive another is to lose
T-15.....VII.9:4 each **b.** that this decreases guilt in him.
T-16.....VII.3:5 of the vengeance it **b.** you so justly merit.
T-17......VI.5:8 ego **b.** the situation brings the experience.
T-17......VI.6:9 the ego **b.** in "solving" conflict through
T-18......VI.3:7 Unless the mind **b.** the body is actually
T-18......VI.4:4 it does when it **b.** it has attacked the body
T-18......VI.9:4 This is not his reality, though he **b.** it is.
T-19.......II.7:7 in its madness it **b.** it has accomplished.
T19. IV.A.10:8 each **b.** that what the other looks upon
T19. IV.D.21:2 to do what he **b.** is meaningless. What
T-20......III.6:8 I?" The world **b.** in sin, but the belief that
T-21.......II.8:6 in hand, for everyone **b.** in what he wants.
T-21......III.3:3 in chains as long as he **b.** he is in chains.
T-21......III.3:4 be simply because he no longer **b.** in them
T-21...III.10:5 the means for sin in which the mind **b.**.
T-21......VI.5:2 and **b.** it also has the means to make its
T-21.....VII.2:1 No one **b.** the Son of God is powerless.
T-21.....VII.5:3 that **b.** in sin would dare believe he has no
T-21... VIII.3:4 for his desire of something he **b.** holds out
T-22.......II.6:5 possible, but what you made **b.** it is not so
T-22.......VI.1:9 will seek for it where he **b.** it is and can be
T-24.......V.2:2 maker of the dream **b.** that what he made
T-25.......in.2:3 And as long as he **b.** he is in a body, where
T-25......III.2:4 Only because His Son **b.** it is, and from
T-25......III.4:1 to the need the Son of God **b.** he has.
T-25.....VII.3:4 And nothing that the world **b.** as true has
T-25.....VII.4:7 by any form of reason, **b.** this to be true.
T-26......III.4:1 the Son of God **b.** can be destroyed. But
T-26......IV.1:5 still **b.** that he has much to be forgiven.
T-27.......II.2:4 no one can forgive a sin that he **b.** is real.
T-27... VIII.5:5 No one **b.** there really was a time when he
T-29... VIII.2:5 No one **b.** in idols who has not enslaved
T-29... VIII.8:4 The world **b.** in idols. No one comes
T-31.......V.2:9 It **b.** that it is good within an evil world.
T-31.....V.14:2 everyone **b.** that he must find the answer
W-pI...127.5:2 world **b.** was made to hide love's meaning
W-pI...130.1:6 can fail to look upon what he **b.** he wants.
W-pI...131.9:4 **b.** that he abides in what does not exist,
W-pI.134.11:2 the foolish dreamer who **b.** in them. He
W-pI.136.10:3 **b.** illusions but the one who made them
W-pI...139.7:1 Nothing the world **b.** is true. It is a place
W-pI...159.1:5 The world **b.** that to possess a thing, it
W-pI...166.2:4 trustworthy and true **b.** in two creators;
W-pI...166.4:2 is the only safety he **b.** that he can find.
W-pI...167.7:5 what it seems to make when it **b.** it sleeps.
W-pI...193.2:2 Yet His Son **b.** he sees them. Thus he has
W-pI...200.6:5 dreams that he imagines, yet **b.** are true, a
W-pII..356.1:2 *his problem, nor what he **b.** he has become.*
M-5 ......III.3:1 of sickness in which their brother **b.**. To
M-10 .........1:8 may well be inconsistent in what he **b.**.
M-11 .........3:3 And everyone **b.** in what he made, for it
M-13 .........3:6 and no one doubts what he **b.** he is. He
M-17 .........5:4 that the mind which **b.** it has a separate
M-17 .........5:4 the Will of God, also **b.** it can succeed.
M-22 .........6:8 what he **b.** about himself is not the truth.
C-5............1:8 His Son while he **b.** his fantasies are true.
P-2.........in.4:1 self-concept in some way that he **b.** is real.
P-3.........II.6:7 therapist can offer more than he **b.** he has

### believeth 1

T-2.....VII.5:14 whosoever **b.** in him should not perish

### believing 75

T-1.......VII.1:7 not deceive yourself into **b.** that you can
T-2........IV.4:2 the first step in **b.** that the body makes its
T-2.......VII.6:8 so, he is **b.** in the existence of nothingness
T-3........VI.5:9 **b.** that it will someday be used against
T-5.........V.3:2 detach itself without **b.** it is attacking Him
T-5........VI.2:4 by **b.** that you cannot escape from it. But
T-6...........I.6:5 yourself, or you are **b.** that it is assailable.
T-6.......V.A.4:6 cannot perform miracles without **b.** it,
T-7.......VI.11:8 you are **b.** that it can be understood and
T-7.....VII.10:3 you will attack, **b.** you have been attacked
T-7... VIII.3:11 **B.** they have blotted their projections
T-7..... VIII.5:2 your mind, and as you made it by **b.** in it,
T-7..... VIII.7:2 who made the ego by **b.** the unbelievable
T-7.......X.5:11 **B.** that he can betray, he believes that
T-8...........I.5:5 each **b.** in diametrically opposed ideas, it
T-8..........II.5:4 **B.** them to be the same, how can you tell
T-8........IV.4:9 must collaborate by **b.** that I know what
T-8.....VII.16:5 from illusions lies only in not **b.** them.
T-8........IX.6:8 **B.** in the power of attack, the ego wants
T-9.........I.11:2 **b.** that to achieve it is to succeed? The
T-9..........II.8:2 Believe in me *by* **b.** in them, for the sake of
T-11.......I.10:6 **B.** this you hide in darkness, denying that
T-11......III.2:1 what he does, **b.** his will is not his own.
T-11......IV.2:2 without **b.** that the Father has denied him
T-11.......V.7:2 separation. **B.** it has the power to do this
T-11.....V.10:6 By **b.** that you have successfully attacked
T-11.....V.10:6 truth, you are **b.** that attack has power.
T-11......VI.5:5 **b.** that the power of the Son of God is
T-11.....VII.3:7 **b.** that what you made is capable of being
T-11....VIII.2:3 Do not make the mistake of **b.** that you
T-12......III.2:3 **b.** that your salvation lies in *not* doing it.
T-12......III.3:1 you are **b.** that the ego is to be saved, and
T-13.......in.1:4 judged, **b.** that by punishing another, it
T-13.........I.3:6 along this carpet, **b.** that it leads to death.
T-13.........II.2:6 **B.** you are no longer you, you do not
T-13.......V.5:6 Yet fear attracts you, and **b.** it is love, you
T-13.......V.8:7 **b.** you can make a private world and rule
T-13......XI.1:3 **B.** this he must escape, for such a war
T-14.........II.1:4 **b.** that unless you learn it you will not be
T-14.........II.2:7 **b.** they are kings with golden crowns
T-14.........II.3:2 themselves into **b.** that it is not nothing,
T-14...VII.5:14 Him only to the small extent of **b.** that, if
T-17....VIII.4:3 **b.** that the "something else" produced it.
T-18......IV.4:8 the lesson by **b.** that you must make the
T-20.....VII.3:5 the error of **b.** the means are difficult. Yet
T-21.........I.4:4 And still **b.** this, they hold those lessons
T-21.........I.4:7 **b.** that their choice is that or nothing.
T-21.........I.5:4 **b.** that to keep the body is to save the
T-21.........I.7:3 **b.** you would lose the world you learned
T-21......II.11:4 and **b.** that you made yourself. For if you
T-21......III.6:7 desiring and **b.** in it because of your
T-22......III.4:7 bodies, **b.** the body's freedom is their own
T-23........II.6:2 believe; and how He must respond, **b.** it.
T-25......IV.2:5 **b.** them to be the bringers of rejoicing
T-25..VIII.10:8 to offer, **b.** vengeance is his proper due.
T-26....VIII.3:2 **b.** that the risk of loss is great between the
T-29........II.4:6 walk apart, **b.** they are separate and alone
T-29.....VII.2:5 he cannot find, **b.** that he is what he is not
T-31.....VII.1:7 **b.** that the "bad" must lurk behind. This
W-pI.......8.3:3 than **b.** that it is filled with real ideas, is
W-pI.....21.5:2 **b.** that the anger is limited to this aspect.
W-pI.....57.2:4 I have deluded myself into **b.** it is possible
W-pI.....66.6:6 definition of Him you are **b.** if you do not
W-pI...103.1:6 so, **b.** there are gaps in love where sin can
W-pI...130.1:4 want to see, **b.** what you see is really there
W-pI....155.4:2 the world while still **b.** its reality. And
W-pI...163.6:1 would yet avoid, while still **b.** in the rest.
W-pI...163.7:1 that even the insane have difficulty in **b.** it
W-pII .332.1:7 is the mind in chains, **b.** in its own futility
M-6 ........... 1:6 a way of life, **b.** healing is the way to death
M-11 .........3:3 what he made, for it was made by his **b.** it.
M-13 .........5:2 It is the cost of **b.** in illusions. It is the
M-13 .........5:7 a thousand places, each time **b.** it is there,
P-2........IV.9:2 from them, **b.** that he is attacking him.
P-2........VI.1:2 are sick, **b.** they are unforgiven. The

### belittle 1

T-8.......VII.5:6 not allow him to **b.** himself in your mind,

### belittled 1

T-8.......VII.1:7 and seeing his brothers as similarly **b.**.

### belittling 3

T-8.......VII.1:7 of himself in this way he is **b.** himself, and
T-11.......V.8:5 you are **b.** yourself and depriving yourself
T-15......III.1:6 **b.** yourself and blinding yourself to glory.

### belong 56

T-5........IV.6:2 you are led back to God where you **b.**, and

|  |  |
|---|---|
| T-5........IV.6:7 | and understand they **b.** to God as you do. |
| T-5........VI.1:6 | You do not **b.** in time. Your place is only |
| T-5........VI.7:3 | in you because it does not **b.** in your mind |
| T-7...........I.3:1 | Your creations **b.** in you, as you belong in |
| T-7...........I.3:1 | creations belong in you, as you **b.** in God. |
| T-7.......III.2:12 | ego, because the mind does not **b.** to it. |
| T-7.....VII.11:5 | God because they **b.** to His beloved Sons, |
| T-7.....VII.11:5 | to His beloved Sons, who **b.** to Him. All |
| T-7.........X.1:9 | you. They are exactly where they **b.**. They |
| T-7.......X.1:10 | They **b.** in your mind as part of your |
| T-8.........III.3:5 | You who **b.** in God have the holy function |
| T-8.........III.8:1 | Power and glory **b.** to God alone. So do |
| T-9........IV.7:2 | The ego believes that all functions **b.** to it, |
| T-11......III.7:5 | Thought and therefore does not **b.** to Him |
| T-13......XI.2:5 | Gladness and joy **b.** to God for your |
| T-13......XI.6:6 | you have learned that you **b.** to truth, it |
| T-14......IV.2:1 | You who **b.** to the First Cause, created by |
| T-14....VIII.3:7 | glory and His Son's **b.** to you in truth. |
| T-18.......V.3:6 | The means and purpose both **b.** to Him. |
| T-21.......II.7:2 | unoccupied the altar where the gifts **b.**. |
| T-21.......V.10:3 | that you do not know, but must **b.** to you |
| T-24.......V.2:4 | For the parts do not **b.** together, and the |
| T-24.....VII.2:7 | powerful conviction this is you, **b.** to him. |
| T-26.........I.3:5 | this little to **b.** to you are limits placed on |
| T-27......IV.2:6 | Here they **b.**, for here their answer is. And |
| T-31.........I.3:6 | your own, your thoughts do not **b.** to you, |
| T-31..VIII.11:2 | Give me my own, for they **b.** to You. And |
| W-pI.....12.3:6 | why these "nice" adjectives **b.** in these |
| W-pI.....70.2:3 | where you **b.** because of what you are. |
| W-pI.....77.3:1 | which are your right, since they **b.** to you. |
| W-pI...104.1:5 | received the gifts it made where His **b.**, as |
| W-pI...104.2:1 | upon the holy altar where God's gifts **b.**. |
| W-pI...104.2:6 | wait to have them. They **b.** to us today. |
| W-pI...104.5:1 | joy and peace **b.** to us as His eternal gifts. |
| W-pI...105.1:2 | will accept them, knowing they **b.** to us. |
| W-pI...122.5:3 | and make yourself at home, where you **b.**. |
| W-pI...128.7:5 | And you **b.** where it would be, and where |
| W-pI...160.2:4 | Here I **b.**, and will not leave because a |
| W-pI...160.9:5 | them gently home again, where they **b.**. |
| W-pI.170.12:1 | Now do your eyes **b.** to Christ, and He |
| W-pI...182.7:5 | not return again where He does not **b.**, |
| W-pI...187.3:1 | Ideas must first **b.** to you, before you give |
| W-pI.189.10:4 | *ways are not our own, for they* ***b.*** *to You. And* |
| W-pI.190.10:2 | Here does the joy of God **b.** to you. This is |
| W-pI...197.3:2 | Yet your thanks **b.** to you as well, for its |
| W-pI...200.4:3 | This world is not where you **b.**. You are a |
| W-pI...202.1:2 | *to stay an instant more where I do not* ***b.***, |
| W-pII .281.1:4 | *ideas in place of where Your Thoughts* ***b.***, |
| W-pII ....315.h | All gifts my brothers give **b.** to me. |
| W-pII .338.1:5 | but since these thoughts **b.** to him alone, |
| W-pII .349.1:6 | *I learn Your healing miracles* ***b.*** *to me.* |
| M-4 ...VII.2:11 | These are the things that **b.** to him. These |
| M-13 .........2:6 | is the "hero" to whom all these things **b.**? |
| M-20 .......6:11 | of which you can conceive, **b.** to you. |
| C-ep...........2:2 | But you **b.** to Him Who loves you as He |

## belonged 3

|  |  |
|---|---|
| T-17......VI.7:4 | being withheld from where it rightfully **b.** |
| W-pI...160.5:3 | and give him all I thought **b.** to me." Now |
| Wfl........in.5:3 | from all the wrath we thought **b.** to God, |

## belonging 3

|  |  |
|---|---|
| T-2.....VII.3:11 | "Cause" is a term properly **b.** to God, and |
| T-7.......III.1:11 | meaningfully perceived as **b.** to anyone at |
| T-11......IV.1:2 | creation It is yours, and **b.** to you It is His. |

## belongs 100

|  |  |
|---|---|
| T-1........III.1:7 | it. The power to work miracles **b.** to you. I |
| T-1........IV.2:3 | miracle sets reality where it **b.**. Reality |
| T-1........IV.2:4 | Reality **b.** only to spirit, and the miracle |
| T-1........IV.4:8 | abundance they have learned **b.** to them. |
| T-2........III.2:1 | perfect effectiveness the Atonement **b.** at |
| T-2.........V.1:7 | and that correction **b.** at the thought level |
| T-2....V.A.17:5 | my direction, but timelessness **b.** to God. |
| T-2........VI.3:6 | level. Correction **b.** only at the level where |
| T-3...........I.8:3 | altar, where nothing except perfection **b.**. |
| T-3 .....IV.5:11 | because the mind **b.** to spirit which God |
| T-5 ........in.1:4 | The light that **b.** to you is the light of joy. |
| T-5 .......IV.1:5 | It **b.** to you because, as an extension of |
| T-5 .......IV.3:1 | in any part of the Sonship **b.** to every part |
| T-5 .......VI.9:5 | the Kingdom, where your whole mind **b.**. |
| T-7 .......II.7:10 | It **b.** to Him and is therefore like Him. |
| T-7 .......III.2:3 | rests in the Kingdom because it **b.** there, |
| T-7 .......IX.5:3 | yours, since every creation **b.** to everyone, |
| T-7 .......XI.2:7 | strain, because that is where he **b.**. It is |
| T-8 .......III.8:3 | God gives whatever **b.** to Him because He |
| T-8 .......III.8:3 | of Himself, and everything **b.** to Him. |
| T-9 ..........I.9:9 | you will be asking only for what **b.** to you. |
| T-9 .....IV.12:2 | here. It **b.** to you and me and God, and is |
| T-9 .......VI.3:8 | of you, everything we do **b.** to you as well. |
| T-9 .....VI.3:10 | His glory **b.** to Him, but it is equally yours |
| T-9 ......VII.8:7 | **b.** to Him and renders Him complete. |
| T-10 .....IV.6:2 | are of one mind and that mind **b.** to Him. |
| T-10 .....IV.6:3 | It is yours *because* it **b.** to Him, for to Him |
| T-11 .....III.7:6 | as His, if you would know what **b.** to you. |
| T-11 .....IV.8:3 | Father the Son must share what **b.** to Him |
| T-12 .......II.5:7 | and it **b.** to you despite your dreams. |
| T-12 .....VI.3:6 | gift of the Holy Spirit, and so it **b.** to you. |
| T-13 ...VIII.1:3 | a fact which **b.** to the sphere of knowledge |
| T-14 .......II.3:7 | *place it gently in the holy place where it* ***b.***. |
| T-15 ....VII.3:6 | ugliness such as this **b.** not in your holy |
| T-15 ....VII.5:2 | the chain of savagery **b.** not around the |
| T-17 .....VI.2:3 | of the goal **b.** at the beginning, for it is |
| T-18 .....IV.6:5 | preparation for the holy instant **b.** to Him |
| T-21 ...III.12:5 | faith and the belief you gave it **b.** beyond. |
| T-23 .....II.11:6 | guilt, the hiding place for what **b.** to you. |
| T-23 .....II.11:7 | that you may have that which **b.** to you. |
| T-23 .....II.12:8 | in hatred for the one to whom the gift **b.**. |
| T-24 ....VII.2:4 | The holiness in you **b.** to him. And by |
| T-24 ....VII.2:6 | you have given specialness **b.** to him, and |
| T-25 . IX.10:10 | *What is God's* ***b.*** *to everyone, and* ***is*** *his due.* |
| T-26 .......II.8:2 | knows that everything that is **b.** to Him, |
| T-26 ..VII.19:7 | And everything **b.** to each of them. No |
| T-26 ..VII.20:1 | Your ancient Name **b.** to everyone, as |
| T-26 .......X.2:7 | **b.** to every living thing along with you. |
| T-27 .........I.2:5 | vengeance that you suffer now **b.** to him, |
| T-27 .....II.10:2 | It **b.** to One Who knows of fairness, not of |
| T-29 .......II.8:6 | told that part of Him **b.** to Him no longer. |
| T-30 ....VII.5:2 | be opposed to it, for it **b.** to everything, as |
| T-30 ....VII.5:2 | for it belongs to everything, as it **b.** to you |
| W-pI.....39.4:4 | your holiness **b.** be excluded from it? God |
| W-pI.....63.2:3 | It is yours to give him, for it **b.** to you. |
| W-pI.....77.3:4 | ask no more than what **b.** to us in truth. |
| W-pI.....77.8:4 | *I want only what* ***b.*** *to me. God has* |
| WpI..rII.in.3:4 | Remember that it **b.** to you, and that you |
| W-pI.....89.2:3 | *offer you the miracle that* ***b.*** *to you instead.* |
| W-pI.....99.8:1 | This part **b.** to God, as does the rest. It |
| W-pI...103.2:7 | It also emphasizes happiness **b.** to you, |
| W-pI........104.h | I seek but what **b.** to me in truth. |
| W-pI...104.3:3 | *I seek but what* ***b.*** *to me in truth, And joy and* |
| W-pI...104.4:3 | aware that what **b.** to us in truth is what |
| W-pI...104.4:4 | else, for nothing else **b.** to us in truth. |
| W-pI...104.5:4 | *I seek but what* ***b.*** *to me in truth. God's gifts* |
| W-pI...107.6:5 | Today **b.** to truth. Give truth its due, and |
| W-pI...107.7:2 | We merely ask for what **b.** to us, that we |
| W-pI...117.2:1 | (104) I seek but what **b.** to me in truth. |
| W-pI...117.3:4 | hour: I seek but what **b.** to me in truth. |
| W-pI.124.11:1 | the sinless light you see **b.** to you; the |
| W-pI...128.6:3 | It knows where it **b.**. But free its wings, |
| W-pI...128.7:4 | The world is not where it **b.**. And you |
| W-pI.133.14:3 | *is valueless, for what is valuable* ***b.*** *to me.* |
| W-pI...134.2:5 | All truth **b.** to Him, reflects His laws and |
| W-pI.151.17:3 | peace of God, through us, **b.** to everyone. |
| W-pI...160.2:2 | and yet maintains his home **b.** to him, |
| W-pI...160.7:6 | He is sure of what **b.** to Him. No stranger |
| W-pI...160.8:2 | Son **b.** where He has set His Son forever. |
| W-pI...160.9:1 | to search the world for what **b.** to Him. |
| W-pI...165.2:3 | **b.** to you. By it you live. It is your Source |
| W-pI...170.5:3 | love is shorn of what **b.** to it and it alone, |
| W-pI.170.12:2 | Now your voice **b.** to God and echoes His. |
| W-pI.192.10:5 | His Father's Love for him **b.** to you. Your |
| W-pI...197.5:2 | And what **b.** to God must be His Own. |
| W-pI...197.8:7 | All gratitude **b.** to you, because of what |
| W-pI...214.1:5 | *I accept but what He gives as what* ***b.*** *to me.* I |
| W-pII .244.1:3 | *experience unhappiness, when he* ***b.*** *to You,* |
| W-pII . 269.1:5 | *teaches me that what I look upon* ***b.*** *to me;* |
| W-pII . 272.1:1 | *Father, the truth* ***b.*** *to me. My home is set in* |
| W-pII ....274.h | Today **b.** to love. Let me not fear. |
| W-pII . 280.2:3 | *is Yours, and what is Yours* ***b.*** *to me as well.* |
| W-pII . 316.1:1 | give is mine, so every gift I give **b.** to me. |
| M-4 ........X.3:5 | the focus properly **b.** on the curriculum. |
| M-5 ........II.3:5 | is responsibility placed where it **b.**; not |
| M-11 .........4:8 | Peace now **b.** here, because a Thought of |
| M-19 .........4:8 | Now it **b.** to Him and not to you. You are |
| M-29 .........3:8 | to Whom it **b.** is thus the escape from fear |
| P-2.......VII.6:4 | Heaven **b.** to him because of who he is. |
| P-3.........III.2:8 | withhold it from where it rightfully **b.** has |

## beloved 33

|  |  |
|---|---|
| T-4 ..........I.8:6 | are His **b.** Son in whom He is well pleased |
| T-7 ......VII.6:2 | His **b.** Sons in whom He is well pleased. |
| T-7 ....VII.11:5 | God because they belong to His **b.** Sons, |
| T-8 .....VI.10:4 | You who are **b.** of God are wholly blessed. |
| T-11 .VIII.11:6 | Love him who is **b.** of his Father, and you |
| T-13 .VIII.10:7 | For never would He leave His Own **b.** Son |
| T-20 ...VIII.5:9 | brings with it the laws **b.** of Him Whose |
| T-22 .....II.12:1 | your holy relationship, **b.** of God Himself. |
| T-23 ......I.10:1 | You who are **b.** of Him are no illusion, |
| T-24 ....VII.1:7 | son, **b.** of you as you are to your Father. |
| T-24 ..VII.10:6 | whispers, "Here is my own **b.** son, in |
| T-24 ..VII.11:2 | perceive outside yourself, your own **b.** son |
| T-25 ....VII.4:2 | and His **b.** Son do not think differently. |
| T-27 ........I.1:9 | the Father with the sacrifice of His **b.** Son. |
| T-27 ..VII.15:2 | of Heaven will Himself awaken His **b.** Son |
| T-28 .....VI.6:4 | "You are **b.** of Me and I of you forever. Be |
| W-pI .....46.6:5 | *No fear is possible in a mind* ***b.*** *of God. There* |
| W-pI ....55.1:3 | be what God created for His **b.** Son. The |
| W-pI 151.10:3 | good can come to you who are **b.** of God, |
| W-pI .. 152.9:3 | God's perfect gift to His **b.** Son. We lay |
| W-pI .. 200.6:5 | of God's **b.** Son from evil dreams that he |
| W-pI .. 210.1:4 | *His Will is joy, and only joy for His* ***b.*** *Son.* |
| W-pII . 225.1:2 | *it within its kindly light, inviolate,* ***b.***, *with* |
| W-pII . 238.1:4 | *I must be* ***b.*** *of You indeed. And I must be* |
| W-pII . 244.1:3 | *when he belongs to You,* ***b.*** *and loving, in the* |
| W-pII ..... 7.5:3 | of Heaven is restored to God's **b.** Son. |
| W-pII . 283.1:6 | *Is not what is* ***b.*** *of You secure? Is not the light* |
| W-pII . 294.1:4 | use has God's **b.** Son for what must die? |
| W-pII . 323.1:1 | *is the only "sacrifice" You ask of Your* ***b.*** *Son* |
| W-pII . 333.2:4 | *in anything, being Your gift to Your* ***b.*** *Son.* |
| W-pII . 338.1:7 | planned that His **b.** Son will be redeemed. |
| M-4 ........V.1:7 | They are sure they are **b.** and must be safe |
| M-22 .......7:10 | can he say with God, "This is my **b.** Son, |

## below 9

|  |  |
|---|---|
| T-1 .........II.4:3 | You stand **b.** me and I stand below God. |
| T-1 .........II.4:3 | You stand below me and I stand **b.** God. |
| T-18 ..... IX.4:1 | of fear lies just **b.** the level the body sees, |
| T-18 ..... IX.7:5 | it, you do not confuse it with the world **b.**, |
| T-23 ..... IV.7:6 | From **b.**, it cannot be surmounted. From |
| T-31 .......V.6:5 | in the mists **b.** the face of innocence. And |
| W-pI .... 47.7:3 | reach down and **b.** them to the Kingdom |
| W-pI 131.11:7 | and sink **b.** them to the holy place where |
| C-1 ............ 7:3 | receiving messages from above or **b.**; |

## bend 1

|  |  |
|---|---|
| W-pI .. 129.8:1 | Today the lights of Heaven **b.** to you, to |

## bends 1

|  |  |
|---|---|
| T-31 ..... VI.1:8 | and all Heaven **b.** to touch your eyes and |

## beneath 22

|  |  |
|---|---|
| T-13 ..... III.6:4 | For **b.** them, and concealed as long as |
| T-13 ..... III.8:1 | **B.** all the grandiosity you hold so dear is |
| T-17 . IV.12:10 | hard to see at all **b.** the heavy shadows of |
| T-18 ..... IX.8:3 | for **b.** them is a world of light whereon |
| T19 .IV.A.4:11 | fall away so quietly **b.** the wings of peace. |
| T-21 ..... IV.2:8 | **B.** your fear to look within because of sin |
| T-22 ......in.4:8 | that lies **b.** them all becomes apparent. |
| T-23 .....II.13:5 | make the ground **b.** your feet seem solid. |

T-24.........I.4:4 "b." the special one is "natural" and "just.
T-25.......V.3:5 And yet, b. the ego's senseless shrieks,
T-28.....VII.6:4 what will collapse b. a feather's weight?
T-29......IX.9:2 For b. your hope that it will save you lie
T-30.......V.4:3 has a purpose still b. creation and eternity
T-31.......V.5:1 B. the face of innocence there is a lesson
W-pI.....12.5:7 B. your words is written the Word of God
W-pI...126.3:3 lowered him b. a true equality with you.
W-pI.131.11:8 There is a door b. them in your mind,
W-pI...163.4:4 and laid to rest b. the headstone death
M-10..........5:2 could merely stagger and fall down b. it.
M-17..........2:3 fact, be easily concealed b. a wish to help.
S-2.........II.1:2 and some are carefully concealed b. what
S-3........III.2:5 one who stands b. him in his patronage.

## benediction 4

T-23.....II.14:6 a kindness, hatred love, and murder b., is
T-24......VI.8:1 holiness is sacrament and b. unto you.
M-5.......III.2:7 Word in their minds they come in b., not
M-14..........2:9 The world will end with the b. of holiness

## beneficence 8

T-6........III.3:6 and because it extends b. it is beneficent.
T-14......VI.2:3 unless it is concealed from love's b.. What
T-18...VIII.9:8 under its b. your little garden will expand,
T-20......VI.9:3 of the holy instant and its unlimited b.? Is
T-29......IV.1:6 some dreams to leave untouched by its b..
W-pI.134.13:1 nor provide a guide to teach you its b..
W-pI...140.5:6 no home in which to hide from His b..
W-pI...159.9:4 their source, but carry its b. with them,

## beneficent 7

T-5.........in.3:1 being blessed by every b. thought of any
T-6........III.3:6 and because it extends beneficence it is b.
T-17.......V.5:3 it grows increasingly b. and joyous. But at
T-25......IV.2:3 is harmful or b. apart from what you wish
W-pI.....53.5:4 to cast their b. light on what I see. Yet
W-pII..224.1:1 and great, wholly b. and free from guilt,
P-2.........in.1:2 this "new" self is a more b. self-concept,

## beneficial 4

W-pI.....42.7:1 practice periods that would be b. today.
W-pI.....67.5:3 it would be most b. to remind yourself
W-pI.....95.6:2 the most b. form of practice in salvation.
W-pI...140.1:1 to any remedy the world accepts as b..

## beneficiary 1

T-29.....VII.4:1 the body's betterment is cast as major b.,

## benefit 18

T-17.....V.13:3 have denied yourself its b.. You reinforce
T-25....IX.10:3 No one can lose, and everyone must b..
T-31....III.2:11 And how could murder bring you b.?
W-pI.....11.3:1 To do these exercises for maximum b.,
W-pI.....17.4:1 than three are required for maximum b.,
W-pI.....27.3:1 needs many repetitions for maximum b..
W-pI.....39.3:7 your world, the whole world stands to b..
W-pI.....92.5:6 its light that all may see and b. as one. Its
W-pI...123.2:1 the b. of some insight into the real extent
W-pI...124.9:1 Your b. will not be less if you believe that
W-pI...133.1:1 Sometimes in teaching there is b.,
W-pI.135.10:4 of a kind from which it gains no b. at all,
W-pI.135.26:1 this day as you believe would b. you most.
M-4....VIII.1:6 nothing that did not serve to b. the world,
M-7..........1:10 so he has not received the b. of his gift.
M-10..........5:6 on. Yet it is not only this that is his b.. His
M-29........4:11 His decisions bring b. to all, being wholly
C-5............6:6 is possible to read his words and b. from

## benefited 1

T-27.....V.11:3 you understand that you have b. from it.

## benefits 8

T-5.........in.2:7 Every part b., and benefits equally.
T-5.........in.2:7 Every part benefits, and b. equally.
T-26...VIII.1:1 receive the b. of trusting in your brother.
T-27.........I.7:6 for all of them, if they enjoy their b. or not
T-28....IV.10:3 want to have the "b." of sickness when he
WpI.rIII.in8:1 We emphasize the b. to you if you devote
W-pI...133.1:3 ideas, but dwell instead on b. to you.
W-pI.153.12:5 children come to see the b. salvation

## benevolence 1

W-pI...189.2:6 and its snow, in thankfulness for your b..

## benevolent 2

T-4.......II.8:12 the most b. of them is not without fearful
W-pI...126.4:1 a charitable whim, b. yet undeserved, a

## benign 7

T-3.........I.2:11 wholly b. lesson the Atonement teaches is
T-6...........I.1:5 and therefore wholly b. in what it teaches,
T-6........III.3:4 The perfectly safe are wholly b.. They
T-20...VIII.6:4 it. Destructiveness becomes b., and sin is
T-28.......I.14:1 aware of present Cause and Its b. Effects.
W-pI...134.2:7 you forgive the sinless and eternally b.?
M-27.........1:7 no one asks if a b. Creator could will this.

## bent 2

T-13......IV.2:3 are b. on demonstrating their reality to
T-16.......II.5:1 while you are b. on making it unreal? And

## bequest 1

W-pI...194.5:2 freed from its b. of grief and misery, of

## bereft 10

T-5........VI.1:1 but His Kingdom is b. while *you* wait. All
T-8......IV.8:12 of It, the Holy Trinity is as b. as you are.
T-14....III.11:2 You are not b. of help, and Help that
T-20......III.8:1 of what is totally b. of judgment? And if
T-20....VI.11:3 b. of water and set uncertainly upon
T-20...VIII.6:9 its most holy purpose b. of means for its
T-24......IV.5:1 in which God is b. of what He loves, and
T-25...VIII.8:7 helpless hands, b. of justice and vitality,
T-27.......V.5:1 a world so bitterly b. be looked on as a
W-pII..245.1:5 *or think they are b. of hope and happiness.*

## beseech 1

W-pI.182.11:4 must b. his father for protection and for

## beset 3

W-pI.....95.2:1 and sinful, miserable and b. with pain.
W-pI...194.7:1 What worry can b. the one who gives his
S-3........IV.8:1 of retribution and a little life b. with fear,

## besets 1

W-pI...100.6:3 his joy; no fear b. him to disturb his peace

## besetting 1

P-2........VI.6:5 must think of evil as b. him here and now.

## beside 55

T-9........III.7:3 keep it, see only truth b. you for you walk
T-10.......in.2:1 God created nothing b. you and nothing
T-10.......in.2:1 beside you and nothing b. you exists, for
T-10......IV.4:4 good, and there are no other laws b. His.
T-11.......II.4:3 b. your small willingness to make whole
T-11.......III.7:8 with the dark companions b. you, but you
T-14.......II.3:4 *else is real, and everything b. it is not there.*
T-14......IV.2:3 this, must you attain, with God b. you.
T-14......IX.3:3 You are not frail with God b. you. Yet
T-15......IV.2:8 For peace is of God, and no one b. Him.
T-16....IV.10:1 for it was built with God b. you, and will
T-18......III.3:2 knew Who walks b. you on the way that
T-18....VIII.7:2 and ocean are as nothing b. what you are.
T19...IV.A.3:6 has no opposition, for there is none b. it.
T19...IV.D.9:2 this far unless his brother walked b. him.
T19.IV.D.11:7 And no one reaches love with fear b. him.
T19.IV.D.12:1 stands b. you still seems to be a stranger.
T19.IV.D.13:1 B. you is one who offers you the chalice of
T19.IV.D.13:7 And yet your savior stands b. each one.
T19.IV.D.14:1 Friend, the Christ Who stands b. you.
T-20.........I.2:6 You stand b. your brother, thorns in one
T-20........II.7:4 knowing his savior stands b. him? With
T-20......III.9:5 He seemed to be crucified b. you. And yet
T-20......III.9:6 and perfect, and with him b. you, you
T-20..VIII.11:1 life-giving water running happily b. them
T-23.......in.4:3 a happy world you walk, with truth b. you
T-24........II.5:1 never will you hear the Voice for God b. it
T-24......III.2:7 and unforgiven, and yourself in sin b. him
T-24......III.7:2 there, b. the bier on which they sleep, and
T-24.......V.3:7 how lovingly He walks b. him, showing
T-24.......V.9:5 you, yet He walks b. you and before,
T-24......VI.8:5 it is not a part of him who stands b. you.
T-25....VIII.4:7 another, to be laid b. your little payment,
T-26......III.2:3 and all illusions are laid down b. the truth
T-28.......I.14:6 never was a cause b. It that could generate
T-29......III.4:4 saw the light that he would keep b. him,
T-31........II.6:5 us, but walks b. us on the selfsame road.
T-31.....VII.7:7 you out of hell with those you love b. you,
W-pI.....69.1:2 stands in darkness, and you b. him. But
W-pI.....69.1:4 who stood b. you when you were in hell.
W-pI.....97.4:2 promised to lay timelessness b. them. He
W-pI...100.4:2 and take their place b. you in God's plan.
W-pI...124.6:2 as in the ones who walk b. them now.
W-pI.153.19:4 that He remains b. us through the day,
W-pI.185.14:2 it. With Help like this b. us, can we fail
W-pI...187.9:1 altar, with the ones you offer him b. them
W-pI...197.2:4 perceived as joined, with strength b. them
W-pII.264.1:1 *You stand before me and behind, b. me, in*
W-pII.298.2:2 *You are b. me. Certain is Your way. And I am*
W-pII.302.2:1 Him, and walks b. us showing us the way.
W-pII.351.1:5 *my everlasting Comforter and Friend b. me,*
M-4...I.A.6:11 he goes with mighty companions b. him.
S-1...........I.6:4 does mean that another stands b. you and
S-1.........V.4:2 and your brother stands b. you there. The
S-2........III.7:6 stands b. the door to which forgiveness is

## besides 5

T-25.....VII.2:5 What is immutable b. His Will? And
W-pI.....16.3:1 B. your recognizing that thoughts are
W-pI.....23.6:1 B. using it throughout the day as the
W-pI...102.5:3 B. these hourly five-minute rests, pause
WpI rVI.in.1:2 B. the time you give morning and evening

## best 51

T-1.......VII.2:4 use your body b. to help you enlarge your
T-2..........II.7:3 that cannot attack is the b. defense. This
T-3...........I.2:1 The b. defense, as always, is not to attack
T-4..........II.1:2 In fact, it is the b. question you could ask.
T-4.........V.4:2 its own b. argument that you cannot be of
T-4.........V.5:6 You learn b. when you believe what you
T-6.........IV.4:3 It believes that the b. defense is attack,
T-8......VIII.6:3 ego uses this as its b. argument for your
T-9.......VII.3:7 at b. and viciousness at worst. That is its
T-13......XI.1:1 even death become the ego's b. advice for
T-16.......V.6:2 find the imagined "b." of both worlds has
T-18........II.2:2 They are the b. example you could have of
T-19........II.5:4 For here lies its "b." defense, which all the
T-23......II.19:4 At b. it seems like life; at worst, like death
T-25......IX.4:7 at b. can bring another problem added to
T-26......VI.1:9 and still maintain that even one is b.?
W-pI........24.h I do not perceive my own b. interests.
W-pI.....24.1:4 you will not serve your own b. interests.
W-pI.....24.2:1 you do not perceive your own b. interests,
W-pI.....24.7:2 *my own b. interests in this situation,* and go

| | |
|---|---|
| W-pI.....25.1:5 | Everything is for your own **b.** interests. |
| W-pI.....25.2:2 | nothing to do with your own **b.** interests, |
| W-pI.....26.1:6 | it can be used for your own **b.** interests, |
| W-pI.....55.4:1 | I do not perceive my own **b.** interests. |
| W-pI.....55.4:2 | I recognize my own **b.** interests when I do |
| W-pI.....55.4:3 | What I think are my **b.** interests would |
| W-pI.....55.4:4 | to find out what my own **b.** interests are, |
| W-pI.....72.2:4 | the **b.** means to expand communication. |
| W-pI.....86.3:5 | my own **b.** interests in this insane way. I |
| W-pI...124.8:3 | Sometime today, whenever it seems **b.**, |
| W-pI...134.5:2 | sin is unforgivable, at **b.** to be concealed, |
| W-pI.135.12:1 | it cannot know the outcome which is **b.**, |
| W-pI...154.1:5 | nor can we know what role is **b.** for us; |
| W-pI...154.2:2 | aware of where they can be **b.** applied, for |
| W-pI...197.1:5 | so you think God's gifts are loans at **b.**; at |
| WpI rVI.in.7:4 | for the way each practice period can **b.** |
| W-pII .242.1:3 | is One Who knows all that is **b.** for me. |
| W-pII .336.1:3 | For sights and sounds, at **b.**, can serve but |
| W-pII .353.1:1 | *use in any way that* **b.** *will serve the purpose* |
| M-2 ........... 1:2 | that he will teach is **b.** for them in view of |
| M-3 ........... 3:5 | Perhaps the **b.** way to demonstrate that |
| M-4 ..... I.A.5:5 | his own **b.** interests on behalf of truth. He |
| M-8 ........... 4:3 | judging where each sense datum fits **b.**. |
| M-15 ......... 3:1 | **b.** efforts meet with lack of appreciation |
| M-16 ......... 2:4 | each one must use them as **b.** he can in |
| P-1............. 5:5 | The Holy Spirit uses time as He thinks **b.**, |
| P-2.........in.1:2 | **b.** this "new" self is a more beneficent self- |
| P-2......... II.7:3 | he can **b.** reach the aim it sets for him. |
| P-2.........IV.5:1 | **b.**, and the word is perhaps questionable |
| P-2......... V.6:7 | the therapist who **b.** can serve His Son in |
| S-1.........in.2:1 | takes the form that **b.** will suit your need. |

## bestow 14

| | |
|---|---|
| T-13....VIII.7:1 | with healing, for Christ's gift you can **b.**, |
| T-14....VIII.3:8 | and nothing else can you **b.** upon yourself |
| T-22...... VI.8:8 | He will **b.** them where they are received |
| T-25...... III.6:7 | and far more happiness, **b.** forgiveness. |
| T-25...... IX.9:5 | have no mercy to **b.** upon another. That is |
| T-27....... II.7:2 | For they **b.** an equal gift of full deliverance |
| T-27....... V.1:8 | **b.** upon another what he does not have? |
| T-30...... III.2:8 | one. It will not **b.** on you the gift you seek. |
| T-30....VIII.4:7 | freedom to **b.** His gifts upon God's Son. |
| W-pI...126.3:3 | which you **b.** on one unworthy of the gift, |
| W-pI...165.4:8 | receive what only your acceptance can **b.**. |
| W-pI.169.12:2 | for grace, the final gift salvation can **b.**. |
| Wi181-200 1:3 | of peace such unified commitment will **b.**, |
| S-3........IV.1:9 | **b.** unequal gifts on those less fortunate. |

## bestowed 14

| | |
|---|---|
| T-1........ III.8:5 | a position to know where they can be **b.**. |
| T-14....VIII.1:1 | the power He **b.** upon His guiltless Son. |
| T-29....VIII.9:6 | God **b.** upon your brother and on you, as |
| W-pI...126.4:1 | yet undeserved, a gift **b.** at times, at other |
| W-pI...127.2:4 | He also thinks that love can be **b.** on one, |
| W-pI.137.11:4 | rest. For here is truth **b.**, and here are all |
| W-pI...170.5:1 | the attributes of love **b.** upon its "enemy." |
| WpI rVI.in.2:1 | has **b.** on us in our last twenty lessons. |
| W-pII .234.2:2 | *give thanks for all the gifts You have* **b.** *on us,* |
| W-pII .294.1:5 | there, nor is a mockery of love **b.** upon it. |
| W-pII ...10.3:1 | of the Correction He **b.** on all your errors, |
| W-pII .341.1:3 | *in Your Smile, with all Your Love* **b.** *upon us,* |
| M-4 ..... I.A.5:8 | was asked of him, he finds a gift **b.** on him |
| S-3........ III.1:6 | another has, not equally **b.** on both as one |

## bestows 8

| | |
|---|---|
| T-23.......in.6:5 | that your innocence **b.** upon it! What can |
| T-29.....VII.2:4 | This is the purpose he **b.** upon the body; |
| W-pI...184.6:1 | is the sum of the inheritance the world **b.**. |
| W-pI...184.7:5 | the world **b.** can be withdrawn as they are |
| W-pI.184.11:4 | the world **b.** on them but for convenience |
| W-pI...189.6:1 | its sight which is the gift its Love **b.** on us. |
| W-pI...198.9:2 | The truth **b.** these words upon your mind |
| W-pII ....305.h | There is a peace that Christ **b.** on us. |

## Bethlehem 1

| | |
|---|---|
| T19..IV.C.10:8 | God. Here is the babe of **B.** reborn. And |

## betray 11

| | |
|---|---|
| T-6 ..........I.8:2 | I know they cannot really **b.** themselves |
| T-7 .......X.5:11 | Believing that he can **b.**, he believes that |
| T-7 .......X.5:11 | he believes that everything can **b.** him. |
| T-16 ..... VI.9:4 | love for it will not allow you to **b.** yourself |
| T-22 ...... V.4:9 | can a mouse **b.** whom God has joined? |
| T-29 ..... IX.7:3 | They are not seen as idols which **b.**. It is a |
| T-29 ..... IX.9:1 | made an idol, and believe it will **b.** you. |
| W-pI..... 68.7:3 | *Let me not* **b.** *my Self.* In addition, repeat |
| W-pI. 166.14:1 | Your sighs will now **b.** the hopes of those |
| W-pI. 166.15:1 | **B.** it not. Become the living proof of what |
| P-3...........I.4:7 | Let him not **b.** the Son of God. Who calls |

## betrayal 4

*See also* self-betrayal

| | |
|---|---|
| T-6 ........I.15:5 | man with a kiss?" unless I believed in **b.**. |
| T-17 ........I.1:1 | **b.** of the Son of God lies only in illusions, |
| T-18 ..... IX.4:2 | the vengeance and **b.** that were made to |
| T-29 ..... IV.5:2 | idea of him, and there is no **b.** but of this. |

## betrayed 6

| | |
|---|---|
| T-6 ..........I.9:2 | but not as God knows them, I was **b.**, |
| T-13 ........II.3:2 | the realization that you have **b.** God's Son |
| T-17 ........I.1:4 | his dreams he has **b.** himself, his brothers |
| W-pI... 188.9:5 | We have **b.** them, ordering that they |
| W-pII ....in.4:2 | in all his madness, nor **b.** his trust in Him. |
| W-pII . 249.2:2 | *You. We have* **b.** *them, held them in a vise of* |

## betrayer 1

| | |
|---|---|
| T19..IV.B.11:4 | The body is the great seeming **b.** of faith. |

## betrayest 1

| | |
|---|---|
| T-6 ........I.15:5 | "**B.** thou the Son of man with a kiss?" |

## betrays 1

| | |
|---|---|
| W-pI..... 72.3:6 | "**b.**" his hostile thoughts in his behavior. |

## better 92

| | |
|---|---|
| T-1 ....... VI.1:5 | Lack implies that you would be **b.** off in a |
| T-2 .........II.5:6 | and can become a **b.** and better learner. |
| T-2 .........II.5:6 | and can become a better and **b.** learner. |
| T-2 ....... III.3:6 | however dimly, that there *must* be a **b.** way |
| T-2 ........ V.1:6 | recognition is a far **b.** protective device |
| T-4 .........II.2:6 | There could be no **b.** example that the ego |
| T-4 .........II.6:4 | you are somehow getting something **b.**, |
| T-5 ..........I.4:8 | to knowledge that He calls it forth; or **b.**, |
| T-5 .......II.10:9 | What **b.** vocation could there be for any |
| T-5 ....... IV.6:8 | How could you treat your brother **b.** than |
| T-5 ........ V.5:5 | It might be **b.** to say that it is a form of |
| T-5 ......VII.1:3 | for your safety and joy **b.** than He can? |
| T-6 .........II.3:4 | that it makes you seem "**b.**" than they are, |
| T-6 .........II.4:2 | Every ability of the ego has a **b.** use, |
| T-6 .........II.4:2 | by the mind, which has a **b.** Voice. The |
| T-6 ........ V.3:4 | It is surely **b.** to use only three words: "Do |
| T-7 .........II.6:5 | You forget in order to remember **b.**. You |
| T-7 ....... IV.2:7 | is merely a way of remembering **b.**. It is |
| T-7 .........X.4:3 | opposite of God's Will can be **b.** for you. |
| T-10 ........I.3:3 | you may feel **b.** because loving then seems |
| T-11 .......II.2:1 | it the **b.** teacher and learner you become. |
| T-11 .......II.2:2 | what **b.** witnesses to its reality could you |
| T-12 ......I.10:1 | how could you do **b.** than to recognize, in |
| T-12 ......I.10:2 | And how could you **b.** learn of its reality |
| T-14 .......X.4:3 | thoughts as more important, larger or **b.**, |
| T-14 .......X.6:2 | is wrong, but that a **b.** way is offered you. |
| T-16 .......II.2:2 | think you might be **b.** able to understand. |
| T-16 .......II.2:4 | A **b.** and far more helpful way to think of |
| T-16 .......II.7:7 | God wills you **b.**. Could you not look with |
| T-16 ...... V.6:5 | What **b.** example could there be of the |
| T-16 .......V.7:7 | that he would give away to get a "**b.**" one? |
| T-16 .......V.8:1 | "**b.**" self the ego seeks is always one that is |
| T-17 ..... III.4:6 | to the relationship, the "**b.**" it becomes. |
| T-17 ... IV.13:1 | to fit the **b.** picture into the wrong frame |
| T-18 ........II.2:4 | world, and changing it to suit the ego **b.**. |
| T-19 .......II.8:3 | that it is far **b.** to be sinful than mistaken. |
| T19 .IV.A.17:7 | yours; no **b.** means for communication of |
| T19 ... IV.C.6:2 | **b.** way to teach the first and fundamental |
| T-20 ..... VI.2:1 | Nothing can show the contrast **b.** than |
| T-20 ... VIII.4:6 | Why do you think the body is a **b.** home, |
| T-20 . VIII.10:3 | thus reflect the sight you saw within; or **b.** |
| T-21 .......II.9:2 | is no **b.** demonstration of the power of |
| T-24 ........I.4:2 | and this must come from someone "**b.**," |
| T-24 ........I.7:8 | let you think that you are **b.** off apart. Is it |
| T-24 .... VII.4:6 | fish, to house your specialness in **b.** style, |
| T-25 .......II.2:3 | change that might result in **b.** outcome? |
| T-25 ... IV.5:12 | **b.** could your own mistakes be brought to |
| T-25 ..... VI.2:3 | Dimness seems **b.**; easier to see, and |
| T-25 ..... VI.2:3 | better; easier to see, and **b.** recognized. |
| T-26 ..... VI.2:3 | Yet God has given him a **b.** Friend, in |
| T-27 .......II.2:8 | and yet, because I am the **b.** of the two, I |
| T-27 ..... VI.8:4 | **b.** function could you serve than this? Be |
| T-28 ........I.7:2 | he can learn and can preserve a **b.** one? |
| T-28 ......I.15:3 | **b.** way to close the little gap between |
| T-30 ......I.10:3 | you would be **b.** off if you were wrong. |
| T-31 ..... IV.8:2 | choose the **b.** to deceive yourself again. |
| T-31 ... VIII.3:1 | choice before you now can make a **b.** one, |
| W-pI .... 20.4:3 | to change your present state for a **b.** one, |
| W-pI .... 23.3:4 | Is not fantasy a **b.** word for such a process |
| W-pI .... 42.3:2 | It is **b.**, however, to wait until you can sit |
| W-pI .... 42.6:3 | this difficult, it is **b.** to spend the practice |
| W-pI .. 44.11:1 | eyes open or closed as seems **b.** to you at |
| W-pI .... 51.3:8 | a **b.** choice than the one I made before? |
| W-pI .... 71.3:4 | Another person will yet serve **b.**; another |
| W-pI .. 71.10:6 | There could be no **b.** way to spend a half |
| W-pI .... 78.6:4 | body with its flaws and **b.** points as well, |
| W-pI 108.10:2 | and cause will be far **b.** understood from |
| W-pI 124.10:3 | thankfully aware no time was ever **b.** |
| W-pI .. 126.3:2 | merely to point out that you are **b.**, on a |
| W-pI .. 126.7:4 | Salvation is a **b.** gift than this. And true |
| W-pI .. 127.7:2 | and understand there is no **b.** use for time |
| W-pI .. 133.5:4 | from nothing, you will make the **b.** choice |
| W-pI .. 140.1:2 | is but what will make the body "**b.**." |
| W-pI 153.15:4 | Ten would be **b.**; fifteen better still. And |
| W-pI 153.15:4 | Ten would be better; fifteen **b.** still. And |
| W-pI .. 170.1:5 | state in which you are for something **b.**, |
| W-pI .. 195.1:2 | do is see themselves as **b.** off than others. |
| M-10 ......... 2:3 | He gives up an illusion; or **b.**, he has an |
| M-16 ......... 5:4 | It is **b.** to sit up, in whatever position you |
| M-17 ......... 2:7 | And where could this be **b.** shown than in |
| M-20 ......... 4:6 | you want, or is God's peace the **b.** choice? |
| M-29 ......... 1:6 | first. Others might do **b.** to begin with the |
| P-1............ 2:1 | What **b.** purpose could any relationship |
| P-2......... in.2:8 | this price. Now he wants a "**b.**" illusion. |
| P-2......... in.3:6 | is his god, and he seeks only to serve it **b.**. |
| P-3......... III.1:4 | but to help him **b.** serve the plan. Money |
| S-2...........I.2:1 | of the world far **b.** than its true objective, |
| S-2..........II.2:1 | there are the forms in which a "**b.**" person |
| S-2..........II.3:2 | the other does not claim to be the **b.**. Now |
| S-3......... III.2:4 | this. Someone knows **b.**, has been better |
| S-3......... III.2:4 | knows better, has been **b.** trained, or is |
| S-3........ III.3:1 | Someone knows **b.**; this the magic phrase |

## betterment 2

| | |
|---|---|
| T-29 .......V.8:3 | without the hope of change and **b.**, for |
| T-29 .... VII.4:1 | the body's **b.** is cast as major beneficiary, |

## between 380

| | |
|---|---|
| T-1 .........II.1:2 | communication **b.** God and His creations |
| T-1 .......II.3:12 | difference **b.** us now is that I have nothing |
| T-1 .........II.4:4 | the distance **b.** God and man would be |
| T-1 .........II.6:6 | no relationship **b.** the time a miracle takes |
| T-1 .........V.1:3 | can choose **b.** loveless and miraculous |
| T-1 ....... VI.1:4 | is, in fact, the essential difference **b.** them. |
| T-1 ...... VII.5:1 | necessary because of the confusion **b.** fear |
| T-2 ..........I.5:3 | is to distinguish **b.** truth on the one hand, |
| T-2 ... V.A.12:1 | (2) A clear distinction **b.** what is created |

T-2 VII.1:4 If I intervened **b.** your thoughts and their
T-2 VII.3:13 then, is **b.** creation and miscreation. All
T-2 VII.3:15 conflict is therefore one **b.** love and fear.
T-2 VII.5:10 is possible **b.** everything and nothing.
T-2 VII.7:9 is necessary **b.** readiness and mastery, but
T-2 VIII.3:8 the vacillations **b.** free and imprisoned
T-3 V.3:2 The confusion **b.** your real creation and
T-3 VI.7:4 is split **b.** the ego and the Holy Spirit, so
T-4 III.4:4 of the real relationship that exists **b.** God
T-4 III.9:7 why we make no distinction **b.** *having* the
T-4 V.2:1 **b.** the body and the Thoughts of God.
T-4 VII.5:7 there is no difference **b.** *having* and *being*,
T-5 in.2:3 There is no difference **b.** love and joy.
T-5 I.1:5 knows no difference **b.** *having* and *being*.
T-5 I.1:14 the ego makes **b.** giving and losing is gone
T-5 II.1:7 of this union of Will **b.** Father and Son.
T-5 III.1:3 the separation **b.** the two ways of thinking
T-5 III.7:1 The Holy Spirit is the Mediator **b.** the
T-6 I.16:7 perfect symbol of the "conflict" **b.** the ego
T-6 I.19:1 **b.** God the Father and His separated Sons
T-6 II.7:2 the Bridge **b.** perception and knowledge.
T-6 II.12:1 The difference **b.** the ego's projection and
T-6 V.2:4 the difference **b.** sleeping and waking, so
T-6 V.B.5:1 The way out of conflict **b.** two opposing
T-6 V.B.6:1 can be no conflict **b.** sanity and insanity.
T-6 V.C.3:4 the dichotomy **b.** the desirable and the
T-7 VI.9:1 is dividing its allegiance **b.** two kingdoms,
T-7 VIII.2:1 the inevitable association **b.** projection
T-7 IX.1:5 the mind that lies **b.** the ego and the spirit
T-7 IX.1:5 mediating **b.** them always in favor of the
T-7 X.7:3 you how to distinguish **b.** pain and joy,
T-7 X.8:6 are learning the difference **b.** pain and joy
T-8 II.h Difference **b.** Imprisonment and Freedom
T-8 II.5:1 teaches you the difference **b.** pain and joy.
T-8 II.5:2 difference **b.** imprisonment and freedom.
T-8 V.2:9 is no separation **b.** your will and mine.
T-8 VII.2:2 Link **b.** God and His separated Sons, the
T-8 VIII.1:11 difference **b.** knowledge and perception.
T-8 VIII.1:15 is no difference **b.** the part and whole.
T-8 VIII.2:3 confusion **b.** means and end as it always
T-8 IX.5:4 function is to distinguish only **b.** the false
T-9 I.5:3 is no difference **b.** your will and God's. If
T-9 I.10:5 complete communication failure **b.** them.
T-9 III.3:2 since there is no communication **b.** the
T-9 VIII.2:7 that the ego vacillates **b.** suspiciousness
T-9 VIII.3:1 difference **b.** grandeur and grandiosity,
T-9 VIII.3:1 because it sees no difference **b.** miracle
T-9 VIII.3:2 no distinctions **b.** these two very different
T-10 IV.6:6 you attempt to interpose **b.** yourself and
T-11 in.1:5 be reconciled by vacillations **b.** them.
T-11 IV.4:6 is no distinction **b.** within and without.
T-11 V.5:5 is **b.** the ego's idle wishes and the Will of
T-11 VII.1:5 implying that before, or in the interval **b.**,
T-11 VII.2:8 true and making no distinction **b.** them.
T-11 VII.4:4 have placed **b.** yourself and your Creator,
T-11 VII.4:6 not know the difference **b.** what you have
T-11 VII.4:6 the difference **b.** what you have made and
T-12 VIII.7:1 to interpose **b.** your awareness and truth.
T-13 II.9:3 no dark cloud will remain **b.** you and the
T-13 III.1:3 interposed **b.** yourself and the Atonement
T-13 VI.4:8 miracle, which could intervene **b.** them,
T-13 VII.10:9 As Mediator **b.** the two worlds, He knows
T-13 VIII.2:1 The very real difference **b.** perception
T-13 IX.1:7 **B.** the future and the past the laws of God
T-13 IX.1:8 Atonement stands **b.** them, like a lamp
T-13 X.4:4 let them stand **b.** you and your brothers,
T-13 XI.1:4 the war is **b.** real and unreal powers, he
T-14 II.2:6 contrast **b.** what is true and what is not is
T-14 III.4:1 are deciding **b.** the crucifixion and the
T-14 III.4:1 **b.** the ego and the Holy Spirit. The ego is
T-14 III.4:4 What you can decide **b.** is fixed, because
T-14 III.4:5 And there is no overlap **b.** them, because
T-14 IV.9:5 that stand **b.** you and what you know. His
T-14 V.5:2 full communication be restored **b.** the
T-14 VIII.2:12 Him. Communication **b.** what cannot be
T-14 VIII.2:15 constantly **b.** the Father and the Son, as
T-14 IX.1:9 interposed **b.** what always was and now.
T-14 X.1:1 no perception stands **b.** God and His
T-14 X.1:1 or **b.** His children and their own, the
T-14 XI.1:4 but you have interposed so much **b.** it and
T-14 XI.1:9 Yet all that stands **b.** you and the power
T-15 V.8:4 see any separation **b.** yourself and them.
T-15 IX.4:1 divide your strength **b.** Heaven and hell,
T-15 X.1:2 the attraction of guilt does stand **b.** them.
T-15 X.9:3 must choose **b.** total freedom and total
T-15 XI.1:6 the choice **b.** them is nothing more than a
T-16 III.2:6 establishing the relationship **b.** them.
T-16 III.4:10 seeming conflict **b.** truth and illusion can
T-16 III.8:2 the gap he imagines exists **b.** his selves.
T-16 IV.5:6 conflict in the choice **b.** truth and illusion.
T-16 IV.5:8 the choice seems to be one **b.** illusions,
T-16 IV.7:6 and only this stands **b.** you and the bridge
T-16 V.11:5 altar is erected in **b.** two separate people,
T-16 V.14:3 failing to make the simple choice **b.** truth
T-16 V.16:1 it is but the choice **b.** truth and illusion.
T-16 VII.7:1 **b.** your experience of truth and illusion.
T-16 VII.10:1 you always choose **b.** truth and illusion;
T-16 VII.10:1 **b.** the real Atonement that would heal
T-17 II.2:4 The bridge **b.** that world and this is so
T-17 III.9:5 never choose except **b.** God and the ego.
T-17 III.10:1 and step **b.** you and your fantasies. Let
T-17 III.10:5 truth that I would interpose **b.** you and
T-17 V.4:3 The conflict **b.** the goal and the structure
T-17 V.14:4 just this same discrepancy **b.** the purpose
T-18 I.1:3 To substitute is to choose **b.**, renouncing
T-18 I.2:3 He does not judge **b.** them, knowing they
T-18 I.2:7 separate. Nothing can come **b.** what God
T-18 I.2:8 one. But everything *seems* to come **b.** the
T-18 I.6:2 projected and drawn **b.** you and the truth.
T-18 II.3:1 not find the differences **b.** what you see in
T-18 II.8:6 the choice **b.** the truth and *all* illusions.
T-18 V.1:2 the difference **b.** truth and illusion, the
T-18 V.1:5 cannot distinguish **b.** advance and retreat
T-18 VI.7:3 your guilt stands **b.** you and other minds.
T-18 VI.9:3 There is no barrier **b.** God and His Son,
T-18 VI.9:10 God placed none **b.** Himself and you.
T-18 VI.12:1 that seems to be **b.** you and what you join
T-18. VIII.13:6 dust still stands **b.** you and your brother.
T-19 I.4:5 centered on the body, to stand **b.** you.
T-19 I.5:5 Faithlessness would interpose illusions **b.**
T-19 I.5:5 all obstacles that seem to rise **b.** them.
T-19 I.9:5 past all barriers **b.** yourself and him, and
T-19 III.5:3 of the difference **b.** time and eternity.
T-19 III.6:4 must be split, and torn **b.** good and evil;
T19 IV.A.2:4 sand still stands **b.** you and your brother.
T19 IV.A.2:9 stand **b.** your brothers and salvation?
T19 IV.A.5:7 all that seems to stand **b.** you and your
T19. IV.A.5:10 to stand **b.** Him and His holy purpose, for
T19 IV.A.6:3 stand **b.** you and your brother now. Look
T19 IV.B.4:5 that you would interpose **b.** peace and its
T19 IV.B.4:5 place **b.** your will and its accomplishment
T-20 I.2:2 intervene **b.** the journey and its purpose;
T-20 I.2:2 **b.** the acceptance of the truth and its
T-20 I.4:2 looking **b.** the snow-white petals of the
T-20 III.2:4 them **b.** those who would meet, to keep
T-20 III.3:7 any difference **b.** yourself and it in your
T-20 III.10:5 any separation **b.** us become impossible.
T-20 VI.1:4 unholy relationship **b.** him and his Father
T-20 VI.11:6 his choice again **b.** idolatry and love. Here
T-20 VII.7:1 indeed a difference **b.** this vain imagining
T-20 VIII.9:3 Nothing is in **b.**, and which you choose
T-21 in.2:5 no choice that lies **b.** these two decisions.
T-21 II.13:3 seems to stand **b.** you and your brother,
T-21 VI.5:3 see the body as a barrier **b.** what reason
T-21 VI.5:5 there be that stands **b.** what is continuous
T-21 VI.5:6 And if there is nothing in **b.**, how can
T-21 VIII.5:7 that nothing stand **b.** the holiness of your
T-22 in.3:4 He sees no difference **b.** these selves, for
T-22 II.6:6 you choose **b.** yourself and an illusion of
T-22 II.7:7 to choose **b.** the joy of Heaven and the
T-22 II.12:1 you interposed **b.** you and your brother,
T-22 III.2:4 can see the difference **b.** sin and mistakes,
T-22 III.5:7 the wall that stands **b.** you and the truth,
T-22 IV.3:1 that hangs **b.** you and the face of Christ.
T-22 IV.3:3 it is but a veil that stands **b.** you. Either
T-22 IV.5:3 everything that seems to rise **b.** you both.
T-22 IV.7:8 illusion stands **b.** you and your brother,
T-22 V.2:8 your peace, and laid **b.** you and its return.
T-22 V.3:4 brother stand together, with nothing in **b.**
T-22 V.5:1 little stands **b.** you and your awareness of
T-22 V.6:5 and immovable, **b.** you and your brother.
T-22 V.6:8 what seems to stand **b.** you and your
T-23 I.6:2 There *is* no conflict **b.** them and the truth.
T-23 I.8:1 Conflict must be **b.** two forces. It cannot
T-23 I.8:2 exist **b.** one power and nothingness.
T-23 I.9:2 as it is seen as war **b.** conflicting truths;
T-23 I.9:3 Thus, conflict is the choice **b.** illusions,
T-23 II.5:1 the relationship **b.** the Father and the Son
T-23 III.6:10 torn **b.** the natural desire to communicate
T-23 IV.7:8 body stands **b.** the Father and the Heaven
T-24 in.1:12 illusion that idly seems to drift **b.** Them
T-24 I.7:7 no specialness of any kind **b.** you and him
T-24 II.7:1 the sins you think you placed **b.** him and
T-24 II.7:7 the dream of specialness remain **b.** you.
T-24 III.4:7 like a flaming sword of death **b.** them,
T-24 III.5:2 rise **b.** what He wills for you and what you
T-25 I.1:7 any differences perceived to stand **b.** the
T-25 III.8:1 seems to stand **b.** you and His gentleness.
T-25 VII.9:4 and stands **b.** him and whatever hope he
T-26 III.1:10 for there is nothing to decide ***b.***. And only
T-26 III.2:1 that stands **b.** this world and Heaven. It is
T-26 III.4:8 herein lies the difference **b.** the worlds. In
T-26 III.5:3 Yet who can make a choice **b.** the wish for
T-26 III.7:3 to give up all attempts to choose **b.** them,
T-26 III.7:4 the choice **b.** two things so clearly unalike
T-26 IV.2:4 stands **b.** to keep them separate and apart
T-26 IV.2:5 for nothing stands **b.** to push the other off
T-26 IV.4:8 be to make the space **b.** you disappear?
T-26 IV.6:1 This tiny spot of sin that stands **b.** you
T-26 V.1:6 Nothing in **b.** is possible. There are two
T-26 V.11:4 back and forth **b.** the past and present.
T-26 V.11:8 This is the borderland **b.** the worlds, the
T-26 V.11:8 worlds, the bridge **b.** the past and present
T-26 V.13:2 you cross the gap **b.** the past and present,
T-26 V.14:2 on the ground that lies **b.** the worlds. You
T-26 VII.8:7 you impose **b.** your brother and yourself.
T-26 VII.9:1 what stands **b.** your brother and yourself.
T-26 VII.9:5 have placed **b.** the Heaven where you are,
T-26 VII.19:8 No wishes lie **b.** a brother and his own.
T-26 VIII.1:1 an interval **b.** the time when you forgive,
T-26 VIII.1:2 you would keep **b.** you and your brother,
T-26 VIII.2:6 The interval you think lies in **b.** the giving
T-26 VIII.3:2 risk of loss is great **b.** the time its purpose
T-26 VIII.3:4 wipe out the space you see **b.** you still,
T-26 VIII.3:8 a little space **b.** you and your brother still,
T-26 VIII.3:9 And this but makes the interval **b.** the
T-26 VIII.4:1 space **b.** you and your brother is apparent
T-26 VIII.8:3 aspect of the little space that lies **b.** you,
T-26 VIII.9:7 to time, but to the little space **b.** you still,
T-26 IX.2:2 Forget not that a shadow held **b.** your
T-26 IX.5:3 **b.** the light of Heaven and the world.
T-26 X.2:7 that stands **b.** Their shining innocence,
T-27 II.13:2 necessary view of function split **b.** the two
T-27 VII.9:4 The choice is yours to make **b.** a sleeping
T-27 VII.10:1 could you choose **b.** but life or death,
T-27 VII.10:7 **b.** exactly as they are and where they are.
T-27 VII.11:1 What choices can be made **b.** two states,
T-27 VII.11:2 Who could be free to choose **b.** effects,
T-27 VII.11:3 split **b.** a tiny you and an enormous world
T-27 VII.11:4 The gap **b.** reality and dreams lies not
T-27 VII.11:4 and dreams lies not **b.** the dreaming of
T-27 VII.12:3 the space **b.** your little dreams and your
T-28 I.13:6 came in **b.** the present and the past, to
T-28 I.15:3 way to close the little gap **b.** illusions and
T-28 III.3:4 and you have overlooked the gap **b.** you,
T-28 III.5:2 as unsubstantial as the empty place **b.** the
T-28 III.5:4 gap **b.** the waves when they have joined,
T-28 III.5:5 have joined to close the little gap **b.** them,
T-28 III.8:2 was seen to stand **b.** you and your brother
T-28 IV.4:1 And yet, **b.** your minds there is no gap.
T-28 IV.5:2 not to him to meet you in the gap **b.** you,
T-28 IV.7:2 The gap **b.** your bodies matters not, for
T-28 IV.7:6 dream, has left the space **b.** them vacant.
T-28 IV.9:1 lies **b.** the broken pieces of Your holy Son.
T-28 V.1:3 that is perceived **b.** you and your brother,
T-28 V.3:10 What can be **b.** illusion and the truth? A
T-28 V.4:1 conceived a little gap **b.** illusions and the

T-28....... V.7:1 is a little gap **b.** you and your brother, do
T-28...... VI.4:1 The body represents the gap **b.** the little
T-28...... VI.5:4 "There is no gap **b.** my mind and yours"
T-28..... VII.1:5 a gap **b.** the Father and the Son is not the
T-28..... VII.1:7 promise that there is no gap **b.** Himself
T-28..... VII.1:8 What will can come **b.** what must be One,
T-28..... VII.3:1 there is a gap **b.** you and your brother, or
T-28..... VII.3:2 There is no in **b.**, no other choice, and no
T-28..... VII.3:2 and no allegiance to be split **b.** the two. A
T-28..... VII.7:6 gap can interpose itself **b.** the safety of
T-29......... I.1:6 a gap **b.** your brother and yourself. How
T-29......... I.1:9 close, and leave a gap **b.** you and His Love
T-29......... I.3:6 without a gap perceived **b.** you and him,
T-29......... I.4:1 gap **b.** you and your brother is not one of
T-29......... I.4:1 is not one of space **b.** two separate bodies.
T-29......... I.5:1 and of distance seen **b.** you and him.
T-29......... I.6:2 in "love," with intervals of hatred in **b.**.
T-29......... I.8:3 nothing stands **b.** you and your brother?
T-29...... IV.1:5 The choice is not **b.** which dreams to keep
T-29.... VII.8:3 by splitting what you are **b.** the two. You
T-29.... VIII.3:1 a gap **b.** the Christ and what you see. An
T-29.... VIII.5:5 truth, the light the veil **b.** has not put out.
T-29...... IX.3:7 which are interposed **b.** your judgment
T-29...... IX.7:4 nor interposed **b.** the thoughts the mind
T-30...... IV.1:8 think arose **b.** yourself and what is true.
T-30....... V.6:2 all that stood **b.** your image of yourself
T-30....... V.6:4 The gap **b.** your brother and yourself was
T-30.... VIII.4:2 **b.** reality and your awareness is unreal,
T-31....... II.2:1 stand **b.** you and the truth of what you are
T-31....... II.3:1 What you would choose **b.** is not a choice
T-31....... II.3:5 both these roles, forever split **b.** the two.
T-31....... II.5:6 **B.** these two *is* choice, because from them
T-31...... IV.8:4 you choose **b.** your brother and yourself,
T-31...... VI.1:2 There is no compromise **b.** the two. If one
T-31..... VII.8:5 nothing stands **b.** his sight and what he
T-31..... VII.9:1 there is a space **b.** you and your brother,
T-31... VII.11:6 holds no concept of himself **b.** his calm
T-31... VII.14:6 and see the real alternatives you choose **b.**
T-31.... VIII.2:3 You always choose **b.** your weakness and
W-pI..... 12.4:1 the time intervals **b.** applying today's idea
W-pI..... 12.4:2 exercises, there is no difference **b.** them.
W-pI..... 17.3:1 to make no distinctions **b.** what you
W-pI..... 20.2:6 you cannot distinguish **b.** joy and sorrow,
W-pI..... 30.2:5 difference **b.** vision and the way you see.
W-pI..... 33.1:4 Alternate **b.** surveying your outer and
W-pI..... 34.2:2 to be undertaken at any time in **b.** that
W-pI..... 37.5:1 you may alternate **b.** applying the idea to
W-pI..... 38.4:2 **b.** a situation that is difficult for you, and
W-pI..... 39.8:1 that stands **b.** you and your salvation.
W-pI..... 42.6:3 the practice period alternating **b.** slow
W-pI..... 43.1:3 Mediator **b.** perception and knowledge.
W-pI..... 45.1:3 relationship **b.** what is real and what you
W-pI..... 66.1:1 the connection **b.** fulfilling your function
W-pI..... 66.1:3 is more than just a connection **b.** them;
W-pI..... 66.4:1 only is there a very real connection **b.** the
W-pI..... 66.7:5 are no other guides but these to choose **b.**
W-pI..... 73.2:4 They stand **b.** your awareness and your
W-pI..... 73.5:5 cannot stand **b.** you and your salvation.
W-pI..... 78.1:1 make is one **b.** a grievance and a miracle.
W-pI..... 86.4:2 forms: *I am choosing* ***b.*** *misperception and*
W-pI..... 88.1:5 why I always choose **b.** truth and illusion;
W-pI..... 88.1:5 illusion; **b.** what is there and what is not.
W-pI..... 96.8:3 Who is the Bridge **b.** your mind and It.
W-pI..... 98.1:4 We will not vacillate **b.** the two, but take a
W-pI..... 99.1:3 seen **b.** what is and what could never be.
W-pI..... 99.2:3 borderland **b.** the truth and the illusion.
W-pI... 99.12:2 Remind yourself of this **b.** the times you
W-pI. 100.10:5 for today **b.** your hourly practice periods.
W-pI... 104.5:2 of them **b.** the times we come to seek for
W-pI... 110.4:2 no split **b.** your mind and other minds,
WpIrIII.in10:1 lie idly by **b.** your longer practice periods.
W-pI... 124.4:2 No meaningless anxieties can come **b.** our
W-pI... 125.9:4 with no illusions interposed **b.** the wholly
W-pI... 127.2:6 to judge **b.** the righteous and the sinner,
W-pI... 127.3:8 the link **b.** the Father and the Son which
W-pI... 129.7:1 and at night, and once more in **b.**. Begin
W-pI... 130.5:5 the unreal are all there are to choose **b.**,
W-pI... 133.3:5 and what alternatives you choose **b.**.
W-pI... 133.5:2 give you just a little, for there is no in **b.**.
W-pI. 133.11:2 ego's goals to come **b.** the real alternatives
W-pI. 134.10:4 stands **b.** illusions and the truth; between
W-pI. 134.10:4 **b.** the world you see and that which lies
W-pI. 134.10:4 **b.** the hell of guilt and Heaven's gate.
W-pI. 137.11:2 time elapse **b.** the instant they are healed,
W-pI... 138.1:1 believe there are alternatives to choose **b.**.
W-pI. 138.10:2 can decide **b.** the clearly seen and the
W-pI. 138.10:3 fail to make a choice **b.** alternatives when
W-pI. 138.11:2 we make a conscious choice **b.** what has
W-pI. 138.12:1 choice that we have made each hour in **b.**.
W-pI... 140.2:7 sleeps or wakens. There is nothing in **b.**.
W-pI... 140.9:3 **b.** what is untrue and equally untrue.
W-pI... 151.9:7 bridge the gap **b.** illusions and the truth.
W-pI... 153.6:3 that choice is always made **b.** Christ's
W-pI... 155.5:1 **B.** these paths there is another road that
W-pI. 155.10:1 be no gap, no distance **b.** truth and you.
W-pI... 159.5:1 Christ's vision is the bridge **b.** the worlds.
W-pI... 160.7:7 No stranger can be interposed **b.** His
W-pI... 165.7:6 interposed **b.** Him and your certainty of
W-pI... 184.1:6 This space you lay **b.** all things to which
W-pI... 184.2:2 where there is unity; a space **b.** all things,
W-pI... 184.2:2 between all things, **b.** all things and you.
W-pI... 189.8:3 that you have interposed **b.** the Son and
W-pI. 190.11:1 we choose **b.** illusions and the truth, or
W-pI. 196.12:2 remain **b.** you and the holy peace of God.
W-pI. 198.12:6 so brief that not an instant stands **b.** this
W-pI. 198.13:1 would stand **b.** this vision and our sight.
W-pI... 200.6:6 be a choice to make **b.** success and failure;
WpI rVI.in.1:2 use the idea as often as you can **b.** them.
WpI rVI.in.3:7 the hour strikes, or we remember, in **b.**,
W-pII .... in.2:9 we forget our hourly remembrance in **b.**,
W-pII ..... 1.2:4 What can come **b.** a fixed projection and
W-pII . 234.1:2 has elapsed **b.** eternity and timelessness.
W-pII ..... 7.1:1 Spirit mediates **b.** illusions and the truth.
W-pII ..... 7.1:2 must bridge the gap **b.** reality and dreams
W-ep ......... 2:1 it has set, and in the half-lit hours in **b.**.
M-2 ........... 5:6 demarcations they have drawn **b.** their
M-19 ......... 2:4 is no inherent conflict **b.** justice and truth
M-20 ......... 2:6 contrast, yes, **b.** this thing and all the past
M-20 ......... 6:4 The contrast **b.** His Will and yours but
M-23 ......... 4:4 for that the little space **b.** the two is lost,
M-24 ....... 1:11 In **b.**, many kinds of folly are possible.
M-26 ......... 1:1 there is no distance **b.** Him and His Son.
M-27 ......... 5:4 at which the contrast **b.** the perception of
C-1 ............ 7:1 always **b.** two choices or two voices. Will
C-3 ............ 2:1 the gap **b.** their perception and the truth.
C-5 ............ 3:4 still obscure to you, **b.** the false and true.
C-6 ............ 3:1 Link **b.** God and His separated Sons. In
P-2.......... II.5:4 union of purpose **b.** patient and therapist
P-2........ VII.3:2 the difference **b.** healing and forgiveness?
P-3........ II.10:9 In time there can be a great lag **b.** the
P-3........ III.2:6 There is a difference **b.** payment and cost.
S-1........... I.6:3 that another mediates **b.** you and God.
S-2......... I.10:2 must choose **b.** them every instant while
S-3........... I.5:1 Distinctions therefore must be made **b.**

### beware 1

T-26 ....... X.4:1 **B.** of the temptation to perceive yourself

### bewildered 3

W-pI. 153.14:5 confused, **b.** memory of this distorted tale
W-pI. 186.12:4 a distorted image of yourself, confused, **b.**
W-pII . 334.2:3 *offering to his* ***b.*** *mind and frightened heart,*

### bewilderment 1

T-17 .... V.7:11 He asks for faith a little longer, even in **b.**.

### beyond 465

T-in ........... 1:6 *of love, for that is* ***b.*** *what can be taught. It*
T-1 .......... I.2:2 is their Source, which is far **b.** evaluation.
T-1 ......... I.32:3 placing you **b.** the physical laws they raise
T-2 ..... IV.2:10 level of creation, cannot create **b.** itself,
T-2 ........ V.6:6 has learned to look **b.** it toward the light.
T-2 ........ V.7:3 looking **b.** it to the defense of Atonement.
T-2 ........ V.9:6 that is far **b.** any form of charity you can
T-2 ....... V.10:1 far **b.** his actual accomplishments in time.
T-2 ....... VI.1:1 something **b.** your own control. Yet I
T-3 ..... III.1:10 affirmation of truth and **b.** all perceptions
T-3 ..... IV.3:10 and your creation is **b.** your own error.
T-3 ............ V.h **B.** Perception
T-3 ....... V.10:7 Your worth is **b.** perception because it is
T-3 ....... V.10:7 beyond perception because it is **b.** doubt.
T-3 ....... VI.1:3 more. Judgment is symbolic because **b.**
T-3 ..... VII.6:9 it was given you from **b.** this world. Only
T-4 .......... I.8:5 which stands unchanged **b.** the reach of
T-4 .......... I.8:7 know what is as far **b.** its reach as you are.
T-4 ........ I.12:3 Spirit is **b.** humility, because it recognizes
T-4 ........ I.12:5 whose beauty and dignity are far **b.** doubt
T-4 ........ I.12:5 are far beyond doubt, **b.** perception, and
T-4 ........ I.13:8 far **b.** the need of your protection or mine
T-4 ......... II.7:2 Equality is **b.** its grasp, and charity
T-4 ....... III.4:6 the concept is **b.** its understanding. Love
T-5 .......... I.5:1 of the knowledge that lies **b.** perception.
T-5 .......... I.7:5 the way **b.** the healing that it brings, and
T-5 .......... I.7:5 and leads the mind **b.** its own integration
T-5 ......... II.1:2 Spirit promotes healing by looking **b.** it to
T-5 ....... II.12:4 power of our joint motivation is **b.** belief,
T-5 ....... II.12:4 beyond belief, but not **b.** accomplishment
T-5 ....... III.7:3 ability to look **b.** symbols into eternity
T-5 ....... IV.1:4 Truth is **b.** your ability to destroy, but
T-5 ....... IV.8:5 They are **b.** destruction and beyond guilt.
T-5 ....... IV.8:5 They are beyond destruction and **b.** guilt.
T-5 ....... V.7:12 a remedy whose efficacy is **b.** doubt, how
T-6 ..... V.C.5:3 and goes **b.** them towards real integration
T-6 ..... V.C.7:2 but God and His creations are **b.** belief
T-6 ..... V.C.7:2 belief because they are **b.** question. The
T-6 ..... V.C.7:3 for God speaks only for belief **b.** question,
T-6 ..... V.C.7:7 cannot go **b.** belief until you believe fully.
T-7 .......... I.5:4 outward **b.** limits and beyond time, and
T-7 .......... I.5:4 outward beyond limits and **b.** time, and
T-7 .......... I.5:4 extend His Kingdom forever and **b.** limit.
T-7 ....... III.5:2 This is totally **b.** question, and when you
T-7 ....... VI.9:2 is totally **b.** question except by you, when
T-7 ..... VIII.6:1 will teach you to perceive **b.** your belief,
T-7 ..... VIII.6:1 is **b.** belief and His perception is true. The
T-7 ..... VIII.6:5 it may not be recognized as being **b.** belief
T-7 ..... VIII.7:4 is as **b.** doubt as it is beyond belief. Your
T-7 ..... VIII.7:4 is as beyond doubt as it is **b.** belief. Your
T-7 ......... X.6:2 your trustworthiness is **b.** question. It will
T-7 ......... X.6:3 will always remain **b.** question, however
T-7 ....... XI.2:8 his own worth is **b.** anything he can make
T-8 ......... II.4:4 or look **b.** everything that would hold you
T-8 ......... V.1:6 is far **b.** the power of its separate parts. By
T-8 ......... V.4:3 The truth in both of us is **b.** the ego. Our
T-8 ......... V.6:6 reach **b.** all attempts of the ego to hold
T-8 ......... V.6:7 I go before you because I am **b.** the ego.
T-8 ....... VII.5:9 is to reach **b.** the Kingdom to its Creator,
T-8 ....... VII.9:5 reach **b.** its distortions and return *to* spirit.
T-8 .... VII.10:4 physical if it uses the body to go **b.** itself.
T-8 .... VII.11:3 and by blocking its own extension **b.** it,
T-8 .... VII.12:6 Learning must lead **b.** the body to the re-
T-8 .... VII.14:2 if it goes **b.** it and does not interpret it as
T-9 .......... I.3:3 associating something **b.** your awareness
T-9 .......... I.4:1 your will **b.** your own awareness, where it
T-9 ........ I.14:5 do not try to look **b.** yourself for truth, for
T-9 ......... II.8:6 not going **b.** yourself but toward yourself.
T-9 ....... IV.1:3 **b.** error and do not let your perception
T-9 ....... IV.2:1 but the plan of the Atonement is **b.** you.
T-9 ....... IV.5:3 in looking **b.** error from the beginning,
T-9 ....... VI.2:4 cannot go **b.** your offering in His giving.
T-9 .... VII.3:10 can never go **b.** it because it can never *be*
T-9 ...... VII.6:3 You can only go **b.** it, look back from a
T-9 ...... VII.7:5 And this must be questioned from **b.** it,
T-10 ...... in.1:1 Nothing **b.** yourself can make you fearful
T-10 ...... in.1:1 fearful or loving, because nothing *is* **b.** you
T-10 ...... in.2:3 Nothing **b.** Him can happen, because
T-10 ...... in.3:7 Nothing can reach you from **b.** it because,
T-10 ....... II.3:5 Nothing is **b.** His Will for you. But signify
T-10 ..... IV.5:9 your vision will automatically look **b.** it,
T-10 ....... V.1:7 you can and believe you have is **b.** dispute
T-11 ........ I.2:2 No one can be **b.** the limitless, because
T-11 ....... II.4:3 go far **b.** the healing you would undertake
T-11 ....... V.1:5 for we must look first at this to see **b.** it,
T-11 ....... V.1:6 together, and then look **b.** it to truth.

T-11. VIII.10:4 It. Nothing will be **b.** your healing power,
T-12....... V.5:7 If they understood what is **b.** them, they
T-12..... VII.3:3 enables you to do is clearly **b.** all of them.
T-13.... III.12:9 answer is the reference point **b.** illusions,
T-13....... V.3:5 perception, and you cannot see **b.** it.
T-13....... V.7:6 can learn what insanity is, and look **b.** it.
T-13....... V.9:2 **B.** this darkness, and yet still within you,
T-13..... V.10:5 **B.** your darkest dreams He sees God's
T-13..... V.11:5 and saw **b.** the darkness the Christ in
T-13... VIII.4:6 glimpses of the Heaven that lies **b.** them.
T-13... VIII.7:4 is far **b.** your individual concern. You who
T-13. VIII.10:7 beloved Son outside them, and **b.** Himself
T-13....... X.3:7 outside themselves, **b.** their own control.
T-13..... X.13:2 you **b.** the value that you set on yourself,
T-14.........I.3:4 he shares with God are **b.** his belief, but
T-14...... IV.1:8 **B.** the First there is no other, for there is
T-14....... V.7:3 will not see yourself **b.** the power of God
T-14....... X.1:3 But eternity itself is **b.** all time. Reach out
T-14...... XI.1:8 and truth is **b.** semblance of any kind. Yet
T-15.........I.3:4 that it can pursue you **b.** the grave. And
T-15...... I.15:6 His changeless state is **b.** time, for his
T-15...... I.15:6 forever **b.** attack and without variability.
T-15....... II.1:9 so far **b.** time that all of it happens at once
T-15...... III.7:3 **b.** all your littleness to give the gift of God
T-15...... III.7:3 to give the gift of God, but not **b.** you. For
T-15...... III.7:5 and **b.** everyone to His Son's creations,
T-15...... III.7:6 Far **b.** your little world but still in you, He
T-15...... III.9:9 who must remain forever **b.** littleness.
T-15...... IV.1:1 This course is not **b.** immediate learning,
T-15...... IV.1:8 For **b.** the past and future, where you will
T-15..... V.11:2 God has created It **b.** judgment, out of
T-15..... VII.1:1 **B.** the poor attraction of the special love
T-15... VIII.1:1 the holy instant has extended far **b.** time.
T-15... VIII.3:7 For the holy host of God is **b.** failure, and
T-15... VIII.4:5 is far **b.** the petty sum of all the separate
T-16...... II.1:5 extension, far **b.** the limits you perceive,
T-16...... III.1:3 your Teacher came from **b.** your thought
T-16...... III.6:2 What is **b.** God? If you who hold Him and
T-16...... III.6:4 far off in the universe, yet not **b.** yourself,
T-16.... IV.10:4 is only needful to value truth **b.** all fantasy
T-17....... II.2:6 eternity, **b.** all ugliness into beauty that
T-17.... IV.14:8 For **b.** this picture you will see nothing.
T-17.... IV.15:1 transformed into what lies **b.** the picture.
T-17...... VI.1:7 you can more safely look **b.** each situation
T-17...... VI.6:8 This seems to ask for faith **b.** you, and
T-17...... VI.6:8 beyond you, and **b.** what you can give.
T-17..... VII.7:1 is so far **b.** your little conception of the
T-17..... VII.7:3 stars and to the universe that lies **b.** them,
T-17... VIII.6:7 demonstrate that you have risen far **b.**
T-18......... VI.h **B.** the Body
T-18.... VI.10:2 brother's have begun to reach **b.** the body
T-18.... VI.11:1 a sense of being transported **b.** himself.
T-18.. VI.11:11 let yourself be one with something **b.** it,
T-18...... IX.3:9 would lead you safely through and far **b.**.
T-18...... IX.8:4 Their shadows lie upon the world **b.** them
T-18.... IX.10:5 A step **b.** this holy place of forgiveness, a
T-18.... IX.11:1 itself is still **b.** the scope of our curriculum
T-18.... IX.11:2 to speak of what must forever lie **b.** words
T-18.... IX.11:3 real world, **b.** which learning cannot go,
T-18.... IX.11:3 which learning cannot go, will go **b.** it,
T-18.... IX.13:3 sent from **b.** forgiveness to remind you of
T-18.... IX.13:3 to remind you of all that lies **b.** it. Yet it is
T-19.........I.8:3 look **b.** the barrier to what is joined with
T-19...... I.13:2 that receives it looks instantly **b.** the body
T-19...... III.5:5 to look on time differently and see **b.** it,
T-19...... III.8:1 it must forever be **b.** the hope of healing.
T-19...... III.8:2 For there would be a power **b.** God's,
T19IV.A.17:15 kind of completion, which goes **b.** guilt,
T19IV.A.17:15 beyond guilt, because it goes **b.** the body.
T19.... IV.B.3:1 Spirit's messengers are sent far **b.** the
T19... IV.D.1:4 even **b.** them would you remember. And
T19... IV.D.2:2 Yet as His face rises **b.** it, shining with joy
T19... IV.D.2:3 light **b.** it when the fear of death is gone.
T19... IV.D.3:3 with the ego to keep what lies **b.** the veil
T19... IV.D.5:1 the fear that raised it yields to the love **b.**,
T19... IV.D.5:6 you. From **b.** each of the obstacles to love,
T19... IV.D.5:7 the power of the attraction of what lies **b.**.
T19... IV.D.5:9 when you heard the Voice of Love **b.** them
T19... IV.D.7:4 that you are at the mercy of things **b.** you,
T19... IV.D.7:7 attracts you from **b.** the veil is also deep
T19... IV.D.8:4 and bid you look on them and go **b.** them.
T19. IV.D.19:1 disappear into the Presence **b.** the veil,
T19. IV.D.21:3 strong that it would lift you far **b.** the veil,
T19. IV.D.21:5 **B.** this, they are meaningless. You and
T-20.........I.3:4 Help him to go in peace **b.** it, with the
T-20....... II.8:1 home is on the other side, **b.** the veil. It
T-20....... II.9:4 joy. We go **b.** the veil of fear, lighting each
T-20..... II.10:4 to guide you safely through them and **b.**.
T-20....... V.2:2 Each speaks in time of what is far **b.** it.
T-20....... V.3:4 **b.** your judgment you cannot even see it?
T-20.... VI.12:9 given one true relationship **b.** the body?
T-21.........I.8:1 **B.** the body, beyond the sun and stars,
T-21.........I.8:1 Beyond the body, **b.** the sun and stars,
T-21....... II.7:7 or do what lies **b.** your understanding. All
T-21...... III.8:3 their belief and faith sees far **b.** the body,
T-21.... III.12:5 faith and the belief you gave it belongs **b.**.
T-21....... V.2:5 prey to forces far **b.** your own control,
T-21..... V.7:12 For reason is **b.** the ego's range of means.
T-21....... V.9:4 sin. Knowledge is far **b.** attainment of any
T-21..... V.10:6 vision. Vision extends **b.** itself, as does the
T-22....... in.4:7 It must reach out **b.** itself, as you reached
T-22....... in.4:7 itself, as you reached out **b.** the body, to
T-22...... II.8:6 *How* He will do it is **b.** your understanding
T-22..... II.12:1 **B.** the body that you interposed between
T-22..... II.12:2 still it rests, in time and yet **b.**, immortal
T-22..... II.13:3 And no one can remain **b.** this willingness
T-22...... III.5:4 cannot see **b.** what they were made to see.
T-22...... III.5:6 unable to look **b.** the granite block of sin,
T-22...... III.6:5 eyes rest on externals and cannot go **b.**.
T-22...... III.6:6 unable to go **b.** the form to meaning.
T-22...... III.7:6 see **b.** what is not there must be distorted
T-22...... III.8:5 sin? **B.** his errors is his holiness and your
T-22...... IV.4:6 beautiful the sight you saw **b.** the veil,
T-22....... V.5:7 is quietly passed through and gone **b.**?
T-23....... in.4:6 Your destiny and purpose are far **b.** them,
T-23....... in.5:2 His glory is **b.** it, measureless and timeless
T-23.........I.7:6 is indivisible, and far **b.** their little reach.
T-23.......I.12:9 Yet far **b.** this senseless war it shines,
T-23....... II.1:4 them calmly, that we may look **b.** them,
T-23....... II.1:7 broken; merely looked upon and gone **b.**.
T-23....... II.4:3 him **b.** correction and beyond forgiveness
T-23....... II.4:3 him beyond correction and **b.** forgiveness
T-23....... II.7:5 made inevitable, **b.** the help of God. For
T-23..... II.19:7 senseless, impossible and **b.** all reason,
T-24...... IV.5:1 He loves, and you remain **b.** salvation.
T-24...... VI.4:5 is given you to be **b.** its laws in all respects
T-24.... VI.11:2 and unjoined with anything **b.** the body.
T-24... VII.10:1 no provisions made for evidence **b.** itself,
T-25.........I.7:5 you **b.** them to the truth that *is* beyond
T-25.........I.7:5 beyond them to the truth that *is* **b.** them.
T-25...... III.5:4 **b.** the pitiful attempts of specialness to
T-25...... III.8:8 He sees as far **b.** the chance of change. But
T-25...... IV.1:7 and **b.** the hope of change unless the aim
T-25...... IV.5:8 Nothing **b.** nor nearer. Nothing else. In
T-25.... IV.5:12 walk **b.** the world of darkness into light?
T-25..... VII.6:5 gentle eyes would look **b.** the madness
T-26.........I.1:7 see nothing attached to anything **b.** itself.
T-26.........I.7:7 and far **b.** the reach of any sacrifice of life
T-26....... II.8:3 He loves but must be sinless and **b.** attack
T-26....... II.8:4 the door **b.** which is the memory of His
T-26.... III.1:13 magnitude **b.** the scope of this curriculum
T-26...... III.2:4 borderland is just **b.** the gate of Heaven.
T-26...... III.5:5 It will not go **b.** this aim. Its only purpose
T-26...... IV.1:2 where justice can be reflected from **b.** the
T-26...... IV.3:4 reach **b.** the universe to touch the Heart
T-26..... VII.7:1 for it goes **b.** correction to impossibility.
T-26..... VII.9:3 yet reached **b.** the world of choice entirely
T-26... VII.12:7 seem to be **b.** you to control or to prevent.
T-26... VIII.1:4 projected **b.** your mind you think of it as
T-27.........I.3:3 you are **b.** attack and prove his innocence.
T-27.........I.4:1 The power of witness is **b.** belief because
T-27.........I.4:2 he points **b.** himself to what he represents
T-27.........I.5:4 points **b.** itself to both your innocence
T-27.........I.5:6 and with healed eyes will look **b.** it to the
T-27....... II.4:5 Sins are **b.** forgiveness just because they
T-27....... II.6:6 This call has power far **b.** the weak and
T-27......... III.h **B.** All Symbols
T-27...... III.4:6 Nothing points **b.** the truth, for what can
T-27...... III.5:7 use that can extend **b.** the goal of learning
T-27...... III.7:8 Give welcome to the power **b.** forgiveness
T-27...... III.7:8 **b.** the world of symbols and of limitations
T-27....... V.6:5 and give them sight to see **b.** all suffering
T-27..... V.10:4 **b.** each one of them there are a thousand
T-27..... VII.3:7 to go **b.** the obvious in terms of cause.
T-27..... VII.5:6 Look, then, **b.** effects. It is not here the
T-28.......I.14:7 Its Effects are changelessly eternal, **b.** fear
T-28.......I.15:3 a bridge an instant will suffice to reach **b.**
T-28...... III.1:1 certainty **b.** salvation is not our concern.
T-29...... III.1:2 For **b.** his dreams is his reality. But he
T-29....... V.6:1 the glorious goal that lies **b.** forgiveness,
T-29....... V.8:6 And leading finally **b.** all dreams, unto
T-29..... VII.3:1 and to seek **b.** them for a thousand more.
T-29.... VIII.2:6 And thus must seek **b.** his little self for
T-29.... VIII.6:2 past omnipotence, a place **b.** the infinite,
T-29.... VIII.7:5 is **b.** where God has set all things forever,
T-30......... III.h **B.** All Idols
T-30...... III.3:5 of an idol; that you will not look **b.** it, to
T-30...... III.3:8 **b.** the boundaries of limits on yourself.
T-30...... III.5:3 **B.** all idols stands his holy will to be but
T-30...... III.8:1 The Thoughts of God are far **b.** all change
T-30.... III.10:1 **B.** all idols is the Thought God holds of
T-30.... IV.1:10 What lies **b.** them cannot be attacked.
T-30...... IV.6:2 will forever place you far **b.** deception.
T-30....... V.3:2 is certain he will go **b.** forgiveness, and he
T-30....... V.7:6 reached **b.** forgiveness to the Love of God.
T-30...... VI.5:5 be some sin that stands **b.** forgiveness.
T-30...... VI.5:6 eternal, and **b.** correction or escape.
T-30.... VIII.1:3 fail to see **b.** appearances you *are* deceived.
T-30.... VIII.2:3 in him **b.** appearance and deception, both
T-30.... VIII.4:3 some appearances **b.** the hope of change
T-31.........I.6:5 as God, and far **b.** all doubt and question?
T-31.......I.10:4 understand Who calls to you **b.** each form
T-31.......I.11:5 deeper call **b.** it that appeals for peace and
T-31...... IV.3:7 All must reach this point, and go **b.** it. It
T-31...... IV.4:7 unless you go **b.** what you have learned to
T-31....... V.8:2 never seek to go **b.** its roads nor realize
T-31..... VII.3:4 when you have reached the world **b.** the
T-31..... VII.7:4 you glimpse a shadow of what lies **b.**. At
T-31... VII.13:7 to see **b.** the veil of old ideas and ancient
T-31.. VIII.11:1 light that shines **b.** in perfect constancy.
W-pI....... 4.2:4 ones are but shadows of what lies **b.**, and
W-pI..... 14.3:5 You will go far **b.** it. Our direction is
W-pI..... 29.3:5 holy purpose stands **b.** your little range.
W-pI..... 30.4:2 idea, try to think of things **b.** your present
W-pI..... 38.1:2 It is **b.** every restriction of time, space,
W-pI..... 41.5:3 cloud, and to go through it to the light **b.**.
W-pI..... 49.4:4 the peace that waits for you **b.** the frantic,
W-pI..... 56.4:4 **B.** all my insane wishes is my will, united
W-pI..... 56.4:6 and recognize the truth **b.** them all.
W-pI..... 59.3:5 **B.** His Will lie only illusions. It is these I
W-pI..... 61.7:1 Today's idea goes far **b.** the ego's petty
W-pI..... 66.4:4 to go **b.** these differences in appearance,
W-pI..... 70.8:4 It is past the clouds and in the light **b.**.
W-pI..... 73.6:4 is a point **b.** which illusions cannot go.
W-pI..... 78.1:3 your eyes, you will not see the miracle **b.**.
W-pI..... 78.2:1 Today we go **b.** the grievances, to look
W-pI..... 78.7:4 shown the light in him **b.** your grievances.
WpI..rII.in.4:5 you through, and carry you **b.** them all.
W-pI..... 85.3:7 But from within me it will reach **b.**, and
W-pI..... 89.1:4 are but illusions that hide the miracles **b.**.
W-pI..... 89.4:4 *[name]. B. this is the miracle by which all my*
W-pI..... 92.4:2 gaze upon the light that lies **b.** them. It
W-pI..... 98.7:4 will go **b.** their sound to what they really
W-pI... 107.5:1 falter in the face of pain, but looks **b.** it,
W-pI... 107.5:4 But the truth stands far **b.** illusions, and
W-pI... 109.2:4 whose vision sees **b.** appearances to that
W-pI... 122.5:3 and welcome calling from **b.** the doorway,
W-pI... 122.6:6 clear and plain, **b.** deceit in its simplicity.
W-pI... 127.7:1 time **b.** the count of years to your release.
W-pI... 128.1:3 and soar **b.** its petty scope and little ways.
W-pI... 128.5:4 go **b.** all little values and diminished goals
W-pI...... 129.h **B.** this world there is a world I want.
W-pI... 129.7:3 *B. this world there is a world I want. I choose*
W-pI... 129.8:1 as you rest **b.** the world of darkness. Here
W-pI... 129.9:5 *I want. B. this world there is a world I want.*
W-pI... 130.5:4 the range of choice **b.**which your decision
W-pI... 130.7:1 and doubt, and go **b.** them all as one. We

W-pI...130.8:1 by asking for a strength **b.** your own, and
W-pI...131.3:4 still are free to choose a goal that lies **b.**
W-pI...131.8:6 wills is present now, **b.** the reach of time.
W-pI.131.11:8 not completely lock to hide what lies **b.**.
W-pI.131.13:1 open with your one intent to go **b.** it.
W-pI.131.14:5 end together as you pass **b.** the door.
W-pI.134.10:4 the world you see and that which lies **b.**;
W-pI...135.6:4 value far **b.** a little pile of dust and water.
W-pI...135.7:3 roles it cannot fill, to purposes **b.** its scope
W-pI...136.4:3 intent; a happening **b.** your state of mind,
W-pI...136.5:1 defenses seem to be **b.** your own control.
W-pI...136.8:4 you might be something **b.** this little pile
W-pI.136.14:1 Truth has a power far **b.** defense, for no
W-pI...138.5:4 knowledge is **b.** the goals we seek to teach
W-pI...139.8:3 It is so far **b.** all doubt and question that
W-pI...140.9:2 We go **b.** appearances today and reach
W-pI...145.1:1 (129) **B.** this world there is a world I want
W-pI.151.10:2 which can look **b.** these grim appearances
W-pI.151.11:3 And you will see the love **b.** the hate, the
W-pI.151.12:2 It stands **b.** the body and the world, past
W-pI...153.4:2 but to be an idle dream, **b.** the possible.
W-pI...153.4:3 so far **b.** the frenzy and intensity of which
W-pI...154.1:2 We have gone **b.** such foolishness. We
W-pI.154.12:3 has left no gift **b.** what you already have;
W-pI...155.3:4 can look **b.** illusion to the simple truth in
W-pI...157.2:4 leaves us here an instant, and we go **b.** it,
W-pI...158.6:5 This is **b.** our goal, for it transcends what
W-pI...158.7:3 It beholds a light **b.** the body; an idea
W-pI...158.7:3 the body; an idea **b.** what can be touched,
W-pI...158.9:3 that lies **b.** them comes to take their place
W-pI...159.3:2 It comes from far **b.** itself, for it reflects
W-pI...159.5:3 to obscure the light that shines **b.** them.
W-pI...161.6:4 times been urged to look **b.** the body, for
W-pI...162.4:2 and they need no thoughts **b.** themselves
W-pI...163.8:9 us to look past death, and see the life **b.**.
W-pI...164.1:6 **b.** them all He hears the song of Heaven,
W-pI...164.2:3 melody from far **b.** the world increasingly
W-pI...164.3:2 you give to spend with Him, **b.** the world.
W-pI...164.5:1 like a curtain, to reveal what lies **b.** them.
W-pI...164.6:2 you from far **b.** all things within the world
W-pI...164.7:2 us from judgment made **b.** the world. Our
W-pI...165.1:1 your own denial of the truth that lies **b.**?
W-pI...165.8:3 His sureness lies **b.** our every doubt. His
W-pI...165.8:4 His Love remains **b.** our every fear. The
W-pI...165.8:5 Thought of Him is still **b.** all dreams and
W-pI...167.5:4 In that, they can go far **b.** themselves. But
W-pI...169.1:2 for it leads **b.** the world entirely. It is past
W-pI...169.3:2 The final step must go **b.** all learning.
W-pI...169.6:4 It lies **b.** salvation; past all thought of time
W-pI...169.7:1 This is **b.** experience we try to hasten. Yet
W-pI.169.10:3 for those in time can speak of things **b.**,
W-pI.169.14:8 We do not look **b.** what grace can give.
W-pI...170.9:3 impenetrable, fearful and **b.** surmounting
W-pI.170.10:6 terrible above all else, cruel **b.** conception
WpI.rV.in12:4 try again to go **b.** them to their meaning,
WpI.rV.in12:4 their meaning, which is far **b.** their sound.
Wi181-200 3:1 And so we start our journey **b.** words by
Wi181-200 3:2 Experience of what exists **b.** defensiveness
Wi181-200 3:2 remains **b.** achievement while it is denied.
W-pI...181.1:3 You do not look **b.** his errors. Rather,
W-pI...181.1:4 of the Self that lies **b.** your own mistakes,
W-pI...181.2:8 sight and see the sinlessness that lies **b.**.
W-pI...181.8:3 And as our focus goes **b.** mistakes, we will
W-pI...182.8:3 stillness, silent and at peace, **b.** all words,
W-pI...184.8:3 in earth and Heaven is **b.** your naming.
W-pI...184.9:1 asked to go **b.** all symbols of the world,
W-pI.184.14:4 And we are given strength to see **b.** them.
W-pI...185.5:4 Now he seeks to go **b.** them, recognizing
W-pI.185.14:1 every mind, the hope that lies **b.** despair,
W-pI...186.5:5 afraid to go **b.** them to experience which
W-pI...186.6:2 and the holiness to go **b.** all images. You
W-pI...188.4:2 salvation radiates with gifts **b.** all measure
W-pI...190.5:3 no cause **b.** yourself that can reach down
W-pI...192.2:2 understand a language far **b.** his simple
W-pI.196.12:1 reach that instant, and to go **b.** it quickly,
W-pI...199.2:1 in all ways, **b.** the laws of time and space,
W-pI...200.8:2 to the gate of Heaven and the way **b.**.
WpI rVI.in.3:8 see. **B.** this, and a repetition of the special
WpI rVI.in.4:1 We will attempt to get **b.** all words and
WpI rVI.in.6:5 **B.** such special applications of each day's
W-pII ....in.6:5 Christ's vision we behold a world **b.** the
W-pII .230.2:2 *from time, and still remains* ***b.*** *all change.*
W-pII .243.1:2 what must remain **b.** my present grasp. I
W-pII .252.1:1 My Self is holy **b.** all the thoughts of
W-pII .252.1:5 How far **b.** this world my Self must be,
W-pII .264.1:5 *its holiness; that stands* ***b.*** *Your one creation*
W-pII .269.1:2 *to show me my mistakes, and look* ***b.*** *them.*
W-pII .277.2:3 is, is far **b.** his faith in slavery or freedom.
W-pII .....7.2:4 for it, becomes the means to go **b.** itself,
W-pII .281.2:2 For I am far **b.** all pain. My Father placed
W-pII .284.1:8 And I would go **b.** these words today, and
W-pII .299.1:1 is far **b.** my own ability to understand or
W-pII .300.2:5 *We would go* ***b.*** *that tiny instant to eternity.*
W-pII .....9.3:1 one last summary that will extend **b.** itself
W-pII .315.1:2 far **b.** all things of which I can conceive. A
W-pII ... 11.3:3 His holy Will, **b.** all possibility of harm, of
W-pII ... 12.2:2 In fear it stands **b.** the Everywhere, apart
W-pII .335.1:2 as he is, for that is far **b.** perception. What
W-pII .336.1:3 to recall the memory that lies **b.** them all.
W-pII ... 13.1:4 but does not attempt to go **b.** perception,
W-pII .342.1:4 *I have reached the door* ***b.*** *which lies the end*
W-pII .344.1:6 *me gifts* ***b.*** *the worth of anything on earth.*
W-pII .354.1:1 *me as Your Son,* ***b.*** *the reach of time, and*
Wfl........in.1:2 to remind us that we seek to go **b.** them.
Wfl........in.1:5 and treacherous **b.** the hope of trust and
M-2 ........... 4:1 instant so ancient that it is **b.** all memory,
M-4 .......II.2:10 and unchangeable **b.** appearances; and
M-4 .......X.2:10 the way for what goes far **b.** all learning.
M-4 ........X.3:4 God has given is so far **b.** our curriculum
M-12 ........ 6:11 **b.** all seeming and yet surely theirs.
M-13 ........ 7:6 is this that makes it holy and **b.** the world.
M-14 ......... 4:3 to leave the world and go **b.** its tiny reach.
M-15 ......... 2:6 this, and you will go **b.** belief to Certainty.
M-17 ....... 7:12 **B.** this there is none, for what was done
M-17 ....... 9:13 His Love is Cause of everything **b.** all fear,
M-20 ....... 6:11 The universe **b.** the sun and stars, and all
M-22 ......... 7:2 must remain **b.** God's power to forgive?
M-23 ......... 6:8 and went **b.** the farthest reach of learning.
M-28 ......... 5:5 His Love behind all forms, **b.** all purposes
C-in ........... 3:2 is not concerned with what is **b.** all error
C-in ........... 3:3 and cannot express what lies **b.** symbols.
C-3 ............ 8:4 stands behind all joining but **b.** them all.
C-4 ............ 3:7 end to lead to oneness far **b.** themselves.
C-4 ............ 6:4 is seen outside must lie **b.** forgiveness, for
C-5 ............ 1:2 But there is need for help **b.** yourself as
C-5 ............ 1:4 **B.** each one there is a Thought of God,
C-5 ............ 1:6 go **b.** the names the course itself employs.
C-ep......... 1:11 up an ancient door that leads **b.** the world
P-2...........I.1:3 for no one learns **b.** his own readiness.
P-2......... V.4:8 lean upon a strength **b.** our little scope for
P-2......... V.5:1 can bring us gifts **b.** the heights perceived
P-3...........I.4:8 calls on him is far **b.** his understanding.
S-1...........I.2:5 asked to accept answers which are **b.** the
S-1..........II.7:5 forever, **b.** all change and incorruptible.
S-1.........II.8:7 Being **b.** learning, this state cannot be
S-2.........in.1:9 it has a purpose **b.** which you cannot go,
S-2...........I.8:6 **b.** all limits into timelessness, with
S-2........ III.1:8 God. His readiness to give lies far **b.** your
S-2........ III.2:3 seek to understand what is **b.** you yet, but
S-2........ III.7:8 Behold your brother there **b.** the door;
S-3........ IV.6:6 in prayer **b.** the sorry reaches of the world
S-3........ IV.8:2 love extends along with Mine **b.** infinity,

## Bible 17

T-1 ........ IV.4:2 what the **B.** means by "There is no death,
T-2 ..........I.3:6 **B.** says that a deep sleep fell upon Adam,
T-2 .........II.1:9 That is why the **B.** speaks of "the peace of
T-3 .......II.5:10 This is what the **B.** means when it says,
T-3 ....... III.5:1 The **B.** tells you to know yourself, or to be
T-3 ....... VI.1:4 **B.** says "Judge not that ye be not judged,"
T-4 ........in.1:1 **B.** says that you should go with a brother
T-4 ....... III.5:3 enter. The **B.** gives many references to the
T-4 ...... VII.6:1 The **B.** repeatedly states that you should
T-5 ...........I.3:4 The **B.** says, "May the mind be in you that
T-5 ....... VI.4:5 **B.** is a fearful thing in the ego's judgment.
T-8 ...... VII.7:1 The **B.** says, "The Word (or thought) was
T-8 ....... IX.7:1 The **B.** enjoins you to be perfect, to heal
T-9 .........II.3:1 **B.** emphasizes that all prayer is answered,
T-11 .... VII.1:4 The **B.** speaks of a new Heaven and a new
T-11 .... VIII.2:1 **B.** tells you to become as little children.
M-23 ......... 1:4 The **B.** says, "Ask in the name of Jesus

## biblical 1

C-1 ............ 3:2 term "soul" is not used except in direct **b.**

## bid 11

T-14 .... VII.6:2 **b.** Him enter the darkness and lighten it
T-16 .......II.6:5 **B.** Him welcome, and honor the witnesses
T19 ...IV.C.7:1 to it, and **b.** it come to save them from
T19 .. IV.D.6:3 all rise and **b.** you not to raise your eyes.
T19 .. IV.D.8:4 **b.** you look on them and go beyond them.
T-21 .... VII.5:5 Reason would surely **b.** him seek no
T-27 ........I.5:7 nothing which his madness **b.** him do was
W-pI .. 105.2:2 are but a **b.** for a more valuable return; a
W-pI .. 109.8:3 **b.** them all enter here and rest with you.
C-ep .......... 5:3 us. Let us go and **b.** Him welcome Who
P-3........ III.8:7 Let the Christ in you **b.** him welcome, for

## bidding 2

T-31 ..... III.4:6 It sickens at the **b.** of the mind that would
W-pI .. 122.5:3 **b.** you to enter in and make yourself at

## bids 12

T-13 VII.10:13 you lay all of the things it **b.** you get,
T-13 ..... IX.8:2 guilt within you, and **b.** you not to look.
T-13 ..... IX.8:3 Instead, it **b.** you look upon your brothers
T-15 ........I.5:3 and **b.** him leap from hell into oblivion.
T-15 ..... XI.4:5 they are where your invitation **b.** them be.
T-16 .......II.4:4 this joining as the Holy Spirit **b.** you, and
T-18 ... VIII.3:2 of dust it **b.** you fight against the universe.
T19 . IV.B.15:4 **b.** the body search for pain in attack upon
T-27 ... VIII.9:3 **b.** you bring each terrible effect to Him
W-pII ..... 6.4:1 your dreams, and **b.** them come to Him,
W-pII . 330.1:3 and **b.** them take what is already theirs?
W-pII . 332.1:6 Forgiveness **b.** this presence enter in, and

## bier 1

T-24 ..... III.7:2 there, beside the **b.** on which they sleep,

## big 1

W-pI .... 16.1:4 Thoughts are not **b.** or little; powerful or

## bigger 2

T-1 ..........I.1:2 One is not "harder" or "**b.**" than another.
T-15 .... VII.6:1 that by sacrificing itself, it becomes **b.**.

## bind 12

T-14 .......II.4:6 The heavy chains that seem to **b.** them to
T-21 ... VI.11:4 And who could **b.** him but himself, if he
T-24 ..... VI.5:3 law of death you **b.** him to will you escape
T-29 ..... VI.5:1 world will **b.** your feet and tie your hands
T-30 .......II.4:4 Think not He wills to **b.** you, Who has
W-pI .... 55.4:3 **b.** me closer to the world of illusions. I am
W-pI .... 76.1:5 you **b.** yourself to laws that make no sense
W-pI .. 153.3:2 the hours and the days that **b.** the mind in
W-pI .. 192.9:2 Release instead of **b.**, for thus are you
W-pII .... 277.h Let me not **b.** Your Son with laws I made.
W-pII . 332.2:1 *We would not* ***b.*** *the world again today.*
W-pII . 352.1:3 *Judgment will* ***b.*** *my eyes and make me blind*

## binding 2

W-pI .... 28.3:4 **b.** its meaning to your tiny experience of
W-pI .... 46.1:4 forgiveness are **b.** themselves to them. As

### binds 9
T-13......IX.4:6 mind the cloud of guilt that **b.** him to it.
T-14......III.6:3 If he refuses it he **b.** himself to darkness,
T-14......XI.9:9 all. For the past **b.** Him not, and therefore
T-14......XI.9:9 binds Him not, and therefore **b.** not you.
T-15......III.9:4 the shabby littleness that **b.** the host of
T-15.....VII.5:1 this chain that **b.** the Son of God to guilt,
T-16.....VII.4:1 in the special relationship that **b.** you to it
W-pI...128.2:1 is but a chain that **b.** you to the world,
W-pII.....332.h Fear **b.** the world. Forgiveness sets it free.

### bird 4
T-25......IV.5:3 Each **b.** that ever sang will sing again in
T-26......IV.2:2 and every **b.** sings of the joy of Heaven.
W-pI...109.6:1 a **b.** with broken wings begins to sing, a
W-pI...109.7:3 will hear the **b.** begin to sing and see the

### birds 1
W-pII......2.4:4 **b.** have come to live within their branches

### birth 27
T-4.........II.9:4 is usually associated with physical **b.**,
T-5........IV.2:4 born. Physical **b.** is not a beginning; it is a
T-7...........I.1:7 Parents give **b.** to children, but children
T-7...........I.1:7 but children do not give **b.** to parents.
T-7...........I.1:8 do, however, give **b.** to their children, and
T-7...........I.1:8 and thus give **b.** as their parents do.
T-15.........I.8:4 Each instant is a clean, untarnished **b.**, in
T-15......I.10:4 **b.** into the holy present is salvation from
T-15......III.7:1 the **b.** of holiness into this world, join
T-15......III.9:5 in him. My **b.** in you is your awakening to
T-15........X.1:5 you would celebrate my **b.** into the world.
T-15........X.1:7 and let me celebrate *your* **b.** through Him.
T-21......IV.5:3 It has been waiting for the **b.** of freedom;
T-23.........I.8:6 Conflict is fearful, for it is the **b.** of fear.
T-26.....V.13:3 seeming interval from **b.** to death and on
T-27... VIII.3:1 from the time of **b.** to dying are the theme
T-29....VI.2:12 the hour of his **b.** and death. Forgiveness
T-30.......II.3:5 with God Himself in all creation's **b.**.
T-30......III.8:2 They await not **b.**. They wait for welcome
T-30....III.10:2 the dreams of **b.** and death that here are
T-31......IV.1:5 within the narrow band from **b.** to death,
W-pI...167.5:5 not give **b.** to what was never given them.
W-pI...167.5:7 they were born, so will they then give **b.**.
W-pII......3.1:3 the thought that gave it **b.** is cherished.
W-pII..308.1:6 The **b.** of Christ is now, without a past or
M-24..........1:2 the idea of **b.** into a body has no meaning
M-24..........5:7 however, is that **b.** was not the beginning,

### birthplace 3
T-27...VII.12:4 not even see, the **b.** of illusions and of fear
W-pI...110.5:2 is the **b.** of all miracles, the great restorer
M-17..........5:7 herein lies the **b.** of guilt. Who usurps the

### birthright 3
T-24......III.2:7 For you have given your brother's **b.** to it,
T-24......III.7:7 look on him, and give him back his **b.**. It
W-pI.....37.1:6 everything because it is his **b.** as a Son of

### bit 10
T-28......III.7:5 within a separate and uncertain **b.** of clay
T-28......IV.8:3 broken **b.** that he insisted was himself.
T-28......VI.4:1 the little **b.** of mind you call your own and
T-31.......II.9:3 with you, and thinks perhaps a **b.** behind,
T-31.......II.9:3 a **b.** ahead would be a safer place for him
W-pI...123.1:4 A **b.** of wavering remains, some small
W-pI.170.11:2 upon this **b.** of carven stone you made,
M-13..........7:4 cannot be a little **b.** in hell. The Word of
P-2........IV.8:3 by seeing just a little **b.** of hell. This is a
S-1...........I.4:6 traded for a **b.** of trifling advice about a

### bits 7
T-18.........I.5:6 meaningless **b.** of disunited perceptions,
T-28.......V.6:2 It is not made of little **b.** of glass, a piece
W-pI.....92.1:4 putting little **b.** of glass before your eyes.
W-pI.140.10:1 chants and **b.** of magic in whatever form
W-pI....184.3:1 bodies kept apart and holding **b.** of mind
W-pII..243.1:3 the whole from **b.** of my perception,
M-14.........4:2 **b.** and pieces of its thinking will still seem

### bitter 21
T-13......XI.2:2 a **b.** war from which you *have* escaped. The
T-15.....VII.6:2 is actually the root of its **b.** resentment.
T-18... VIII.7:5 sorry king, a **b.** ruler of all that he surveys,
T-23.......in.6:5 a world in **b.** need of the redemption that
T-26......IX.7:3 him from **b.** winter and the freezing cold.
T-27.......I.4:10 The bleak and **b.** picture you have sent
T-29......IX.9:2 so deep and **b.** that the dream cannot
T-30.....V.9:12 free from **b.** cost and joyless consequence.
T-31.....VII.6:2 a **b.** sense of deep depression and futility.
W-pI...101.4:5 real, salvation has become your **b.** enemy,
W-pI...128.1:2 hopes that turn to **b.** ashes of despair. No
W-pI...132.3:5 **b.** thoughts of death within your mind.
W-pI...153.1:1 world, its twists of fortune and its **b.** jests,
WpI...rV.in8:1 to you from Him Who sees your **b.** need,
W-pI...190.8:5 the world becomes a cruel and a **b.** place,
W-pI...195.3:1 but a black despair so **b.** and relentless
W-pI...200.1:3 the agony of yet more **b.** disappointments
W-pII..237.1:4 see, aware it ends the **b.** dream of death;
C-5.............5:7 is. Some **b.** idols have been made of him
S-2.........II.4:5 and do not show the **b.** pain you feel.
S-3........IV.7:5 sounds of harsh and **b.** striving and defeat

### bitterly 8
T-3...........I.1:6 led many people to be **b.** afraid of God.
T-20......VI.9:4 powerful and so **b.** misunderstood and so
T-21.........I.4:9 that they are incomplete and **b.** deprived.
T-24.....VII.1:1 **b.** does everyone tied to this world defend
T-27.......V.5:1 Would not a world so **b.** bereft be looked
W-pI.....57.2:5 I was **b.** mistaken in this belief, which I no
M-24.........1:8 many other beliefs, it can be **b.** misused.
P-2.........V.2:1 ones who come to us for help are **b.** afraid

### bitterness 5
T-21.....VII.2:6 war of vengeance, **b.** and spite on him, to
T-25......IX.9:4 And **b.**, with vengeance justified and
T-28.......V.2:1 dreams of hate and malice, **b.** and death,
W-pI...195.9:3 it, we are not entitled therefore to our **b.**,
W-pII..249.2:2 *have betrayed them, held them in a vise of* **b.**,

### bizarre 1
T-16.......V.3:4 considers it **b.** to love and hate together,

### black 7
*See also* black-draped
T-13.........I.2:3 in the **b.** cloud of guilt that you accepted,
T-13.......IX.8:2 ego tells you all is **b.** with guilt within you,
T19....IV.C.2:6 the **b.** robe he was wearing to his funeral,
T-31...VII.14:3 death; a thing of treachery and **b.** despair,
W-pI...151.4:5 of just punishment, how **b.** with sin, how
W-pI...195.3:1 and leaves you nothing but a **b.** despair so
M-17.........8:5 an intense white light against a **b.** horizon

### black-draped 2
T19....IV.C.2:4 dedication is not to live; the **b.** "sinners,"
T19....IV.C.4:1 And what is the **b.** body they would bury

### blacken 1
T-31.....VII.2:3 yourself and **b.** it with still another "crime

### blackest 1
T-13...... XI.7:2 your **b.** nightmares all mean nothing.

### blackness 3
T-13...... III.4:4 you go into the **b.** of the ego's foundation,
T-18...... III.1:5 And you sought a **b.** so complete that you
W-pI... 194.2:1 anxiety, all pits of hell, all **b.** of depression

### blade 3
T-17........II.6:3 a **b.** of grass a sign of God's perfection.
T-29....VIII.4:2 the power to change one **b.** of grass from
S-3........IV.2:3 its merciful reprieve upon each **b.** of grass

### blame 13
*See also* self-blame
T-6.........I.16:5 punishment involves the projection of **b.**,
T-6.........I.16:5 and reinforces the idea that **b.** is justified.
T-6.........I.16:6 justified. The result is a lesson in **b.**, for all
T-11...... IV.4:5 for as **b.** is withdrawn from without, there
T-11...... IV.5:1 you and you **b.** them for your deprivation
T-11...... IV.5:2 cannot **b.** yourself without blaming them.
T-11...... IV.5:3 That is why **b.** must be undone, not seen
T-16.....VII.2:9 not seek to lay the **b.** for deprivation on it,
T-17....... V.8:2 to **b.** your brother for the "failure" of your
T-17..... V.11:9 campaign to **b.** him for the discomfort of
T-17.....VII.8:2 really **b.** him for is what *you* did to *him.* It is
T-28...... VI.2:1 and **b.** it for the sounds you do not like,
W-pI..... 60.1:3 The blameless cannot **b.**, and those who

### blamed 4
T-6.........in.1:2 rather than being **b.** on others. Anger
T-28.....VII.4:3 Nor is it idly **b.** for what it did not do. It
T-31....... V.6:7 You can be neither **b.** for what you are,
S-3........IV.5:4 He is **b.** for your deception and your guilt.

### blamefulness 1
T-27.........I.9:4 from it all signs of accusation and of **b.**.

### blameless 5
T-11...... IV.7:2 knows His Son as wholly **b.** as Himself,
T-14.... IV.4:11 instead offer to God and you His **b.** Son.
T19. IV.A.14:3 they will see only the **b.** and the beautiful,
W-pI..... 60.1:3 The **b.** cannot blame, and those who have
W-pI... 134.4:4 corrupt as if they were as **b.** as the grass;

### blamelessness 3
T-13.........I.1:5 for it is the denial of the **b.** of God's Son.
T-13.........I.2:4 **b.** of Christ is the proof that the ego never
T-13.........I.6:5 of his being, which is his perfect **b.**. Out of

### blames 1
T-11...... IV.5:4 know yourself, for only the ego **b.** at all.

### blaming 5
T-11...... IV.5:1 for your deprivation, you are **b.** yourself.
T-11...... IV.5:2 cannot blame yourself without **b.** them.
T-11...... IV.5:5 and as much an ego defense as **b.** others.
T-18...... VI.6:1 and **b.** it for what you wished it to do. It is
T-27....VIII.8:2 But once deluded into **b.** them you will

### blank 3
W-pI........ 8.2:4 The mind is actually **b.** when it does this,
W-pI........ 8.3:3 that your mind has been merely **b.**, rather
W-pI..... 10.3:3 statement that your mind is really a **b.**. To

### blanket 1
W-pI..... 50.5:2 over you like a **b.** of protection and surety

**blankets** 1

T-12....... II.4:6 the heavy **b.** you have laid upon yourself.

**blasphemous** 5

T-10..... V.12:1 sinless, it is **b.** to perceive them as guilty.
T-10..... V.12:2 it is **b.** to perceive suffering anywhere. If
T-10..... V.12:3 be wholly joyous, it is **b.** to feel depressed.
T-13....... II.6:2 it gave was that guiltlessness is **b.** to God.
W-pII .268.2:1 Let not our sight be **b.** today, nor let our

**blasphemy** 4

T-10....... V.1:4 Many are afraid of **b.**, but they do not
T-10....... V.3:5 them. **B.**, then, is *self-destructive,* not God-
T-10....... V.8:5 Remember, though, that to do this is **b.**,
T-10..... V.12:4 the many other forms that **b.** may take,

**blatant** 1

S-2......... II.3:1 not appear in quite such **b.** arrogance.

**blaze** 1

W-pI... 189.9:4 His Love will **b.** its pathway of itself.

**blazing** 7

T-11....... II.5:4 and the little spark becomes a **b.** light that
T19... IV.D.2:3 fades in the **b.** light beyond it when the
T-22...... VI.4:1 and **b.** with a light far brighter than the
W-pI..... 67.4:3 to the awareness of a **b.** light in which you
W-pII .225.1:2 ***b.*** *in my mind and keeping it within its*
W-pII .342.1:8 *at last, forget illusions in the* ***b.*** *light of truth,*
C-4............ 7:4 gone are bodies in the **b.** light upon the

**bleak** 9

T-11...... III.3:5 His. The **b.** little world will vanish into
T-15.........I.6:1 **b.** and despairing is the ego's use of time!
T-16....... IV.9:4 Seek not for this in the **b.** world of illusion
T-18..VIII.11:1 to enter into your **b.** and joyless kingdom,
T-18...... IX.2:5 Its **b.** sight is distorted, and the messages
T-27.......I.4:10 The **b.** and bitter picture you have sent
T-29.........I.3:3 seem dark and fearful, perilous and **b.**.
W-pI. 122.13:3 of shifting change and **b.** appearances.
W-pI... 200.1:3 more bitter disappointments, **b.** despair,

**bleakness** 1

T-31.... IV.2:12 gaily for a while, before the **b.** enters. And

**bleed** 2

W-pI... 166.6:1 feet that **b.** a little from the rocky road he
S-3........ IV.6:5 in a savage world with feet that **b.**, and

**bleeding** 2

W-pI. 161.11:5 which you have placed upon your **b.** head
S-3........ IV.9:3 the thorns fall softly from the **b.** brow of

**blend** 3

W-pI... 129.7:5 ends loses all meaning as they **b.** in one.
Wi181-200 1:1 your scattered goals **b.** into one intent.
WpI rVI.in.2:5 to use them all and let them **b.** as one, as

**blends** 2

T-12...... VI.7:4 The world has no purpose as it **b.** into the
T-13.... VIII.6:4 aspect of reality you see **b.** quietly into the

**bless** 77

T-1...... III.5:11 The miracle worker can only **b.** them, and
T-1........ III.8:2 The miracle will always **b.** *you.* Miracles
T-5........in.3:2 You should want to **b.** them in return, out
T-5 ..........I.5:7 to **b.** their creations and keep them in the
T-5 .... VI.12:6 and remain to **b.** your creations there. He
T-6 ....... III.3:5 They **b.** because they know that they are
T-7 ...... VII.2:1 is offering you an opportunity to **b.** him.
T-9 ..... VIII.5:1 From your grandeur you can only **b.**,
T-11 ..... III.8:1 and **b.** it with the light your Father gave it
T-11 ..... III.8:4 If you will **b.** him in time, you will be in
T-14 ........ I.1:3 You can learn to **b.**, and cannot give what
T-14 .....X.12:8 will **b.** each recognition of His Son with
T-15 .... VII.9:1 with which the ego would "**b.**" all unions.
T-16 ........ I.7:9 your relationships, and **b.** them for you.
T-16 .. VII.11:2 to **b.** everyone and to resolve all problems
T-17 ........II.6:1 All this beauty will rise to **b.** your sight as
T19.... IV.B.5:5 to let peace through to **b.** the tired world!
T-20 ..... III.8:6 your brother with joy to **b.** the Son of God
T-20 ..... III.8:8 you and your brother, to **b.** the other?
T-20 ... VIII.3:6 **b.** the Son of God in your relationship,
T-22 ....... II.8:4 And vision cannot damn, but only **b.**.
T-22 ... VI.9:11 and confidence with which you **b.** your
T-24 ...... V.7:4 that everyone may **b.** all living things, and
T-25 ..... VI.1:7 For he would only heal and only **b.**. And
T-25 ..... VI.1:8 he has the power to heal and **b.** all those
T-26 VII.19:10 to **b.** but one gives blessing to them all as
T-26 ..... IX.8:5 An ancient miracle has come to **b.** and to
T-27 ..... VI.6:6 Who sends forth miracles to **b.** the world,
T-29 ...... V.6:2 in minds that can direct the hand to **b.**,
T-31 ..... VI.1:8 to touch your eyes and **b.** your holy sight,
T-31 ..... VI.1:8 more except to heal and comfort and to **b.**
W-pI..... 27.2:5 still persists, add further: *It can only* ***b.***.
W-pI..... 52.2:5 am, I will **b.** everyone and everything I see
W-pI..... 58.2:2 of my holiness does not **b.** me alone.
W-pI..... 60.3:4 I see will lean toward me to **b.** me. I will
W-pI..... 92.3:4 eyes that cannot see and cannot **b.**.
W-pI... 96.10:4 Your mind will **b.** all things. Confusion
W-pI... 105.9:5 Then **b.** your brother thankfully, and say:
W-pI... 123.6:4 He will **b.** your gifts by sharing them with
W-pI... 127.9:6 And He will **b.** the lesson with His Love.
W-pI. 127.12:4 Self: *I* ***b.*** *you, brother, with the Love of God,*
W-pI. 132.16:1 send out these thoughts to **b.** the world.
W-pI. 137.15:6 *And I would* ***b.*** *my brothers, for I would be*
W-pI... 162.6:5 The light is come today to **b.** the world.
W-pI... 163.9:1 *Our Father,* ***b.*** *our eyes today. We are Your*
W-pI... 164.7:6 We **b.** the world, as we behold it in the
W-pI. 169.13:3 he felt an instant back to **b.** the world?
W-pI. 170.13:4 *we* ***b.*** *the world with what we have received*
W-pI... 183.3:5 as happy laughter comes to **b.** the world.
W-pI...... 187.h I **b.** the world because I bless myself.
W-pI...... 187.h I bless the world because I **b.** myself.
W-pI. 187.11:1 are we blessed, and now we **b.** the world.
W-pI. 188.10:7 *And let me* ***b.*** *them with the light in me.*
W-pI. 191.10:1 eyes, return again to **b.** the world he made
W-pI... 194.5:3 in God's Son is freed to **b.** the world. Now
W-pI... 207.1:1 I **b.** the world because I bless myself.
W-pI... 207.1:1 I bless the world because I **b.** myself.
W-pII . 270.2:1 The quiet of today will **b.** our hearts, and
W-pII . 281.1:6 *The Thoughts I think with You can only* ***b.***.
W-pII . 295.2:2 *Love to* ***b.*** *all things which I may look upon,*
W-pII . 301.2:2 and **b.** it as a cause of further joy in them.
W-pII . 304.1:5 I would **b.** the world by looking on it
W-pII ... 10.4:1 step in His appointed plan to **b.** His Son,
W-pII ... 13.3:3 what was meant to curse has come to **b.**.
W-pII . 345.2:2 light has come to offer miracles to **b.** the
W-pII . 349.2:3 in Him to send us miracles to **b.** the world
W-pII ... 14.4:3 that join together as we **b.** the world. And
W-pII ..... 353.h given Christ To use to **b.** the world with
M-10 ........ 5:12 where he came to judge, he comes to **b.**.
M-14 ......... 5:7 forgiveness brings all this to **b.** the world.
P-2........... I.4:1 which brothers meet to **b.** each other and
S-1......... in.3:2 and **b.** you as you lift your heart to Him in
S-1......... III.5:4 This enemy has come to **b.** you. Take his
S-2........... I.1:2 scourge; a curse where it was meant to **b.**,
S-3.......... II.4:2 to **b.** the mind with loving pardon for the
S-3......... III.5:3 It will remain to **b.** for all eternity. It heals
S-3......... III.6:2 and to **b.** all those who serve with Him in

**blessed** 84

T-1 ........I.16:1 for demonstrating it is as **b.** to give as to
T-3 ..........I.5:4 "**B.** are the pure in heart for they shall see
T-5 ........ in.3:1 being **b.** by every beneficent thought of
T-5 .......... I.6:2 But He also **b.** His children with a way of
T-5 .......... II.2:2 God **b.** the minds of His separated Sons.
T-5 ..... IV.8:14 His quiet children are His **b.** Sons. The
T-5 ......... V.2:2 the **b.** residue is restored and therefore
T-5 ......... V.2:3 truly **b.** is incapable of giving rise to guilt,
T-5 ..... VI.12:7 you can truly give, because He is truly **b.**.
T-6 ....... III.3:5 bless because they know that they are **b.**.
T-7 ..... V.10:12 **B.** are you who perceive only this, because
T-7 ...... VII.7:5 Those who attack do not know they are **b.**
T-8 ..... VI.10:4 You who are beloved of God are wholly **b.**
T-8 ..... VI.10:5 will of all those who are as **b.** as you are.
T-9 ......... II.8:4 in this way can you learn how **b.** you are.
T-11 ......... I.1:4 you place upon it but will be **b.** by Him,
T-11 ....... I.11:6 **B.** are you who learn that to hear the Will
T-11 ..... III.8:3 God **b.** His Son forever. If you will bless
T-11 ..... IV.8:1 **B.** is the Son of God whose radiance is of
T-11 ..... VI.1:5 "**B.** are ye who have not seen and still
T-11 ... VIII.7:7 **B.** are you who are willing to ask the truth
T-14 ...... in.1:1 Yes, you are **b.** indeed. Yet in this world
T-14 ........ I.1:1 If you are **b.** and do not know it, you
T-14 ........ I.1:6 offer *you* the testimony that you are **b.**. If
T-14 ..... V.1:12 God is **b.** in His Son as the Son is blessed
T-14 ..... V.1:12 blessed in His Son as the Son is **b.** in Him.
T-14 ....... V.3:1 **B.** Son of a wholly blessing Father, joy
T-14 ....... V.3:2 Who can condemn whom God has **b.**?
T-14 ....... V.9:1 **B.** are you who teach with me. Our power
T-15 ...... I.13:3 Practice giving this **b.** instant of freedom
T-15 ...... I.13:4 gives their **b.** instant to you through your
T-15 ....... II.1:7 the **b.** instant you will let go all your past
T-15 ....... II.2:4 **B.** is God's Teacher, Whose joy it is to
T-15 ....... II.3:4 **b.** instant reaches out to encompass time,
T-15 ..... V.10:1 relationships are **b.** in the holy instant,
T-15 .. VII.10:1 special relationship which the ego has "**b.**
T-17 ...... IV.4:3 response to the gift with which God **b.** it,
T-17 ..... V.10:3 God Himself has **b.** your holy relationship
T-17 ..... V.10:7 in which all the Sonship is together **b.**.
T-18 ....... II.7:1 **b.** through your holy relationship. It will
T-18 ....... V.3:1 reborn and **b.** in every holy instant you do
T-21 ..... VI.7:2 instead without the other being **b.** by it,
T-21 ..... VI.9:8 To give is no more **b.** than to receive. But
T-21 ... VI.10:1 The Son of God is always **b.** as one. And
T-21 ... VI.10:2 his gratitude goes out to you who **b.** him,
T-22 ..... VI.5:4 How **b.** are you who let this gift be given!
T-26 ..... IX.2:4 have **b.** it with Their innocence and peace
T-27 ....... V.6:2 And being **b.** you will bring blessing. Life
T-29 ....... V.6:8 how **b.** are you who can release him, just
T-29 ..... IX.6:5 him is destroyed; what helps him, **b.**.
W-pI .... 37.1:3 Thus are you and the world **b.** together.
W-pI .... 37.3:2 holiness are all things **b.** along with you.
W-pI ....... 40.h I am **b.** as a Son of God.
W-pI .... 40.3:4 *am* ***b.*** *as a Son of God. I am happy, peaceful,*
W-pI .... 40.3:7 *I am* ***b.*** *as a Son of God. I am calm, quiet,*
W-pI .... 40.3:9 that you are **b.** as a Son of God will do.
W-pI .... 43.5:5 *I see the world as* ***b.***. *The world can show me*
W-pI .... 46.5:6 *love myself. God is the Love in which I am* ***b.***.
W-pI .... 58.5:1 (40) I am **b.** as a Son of God. Herein lies
W-pI .... 58.5:3 I am **b.** as a Son of God. All good things
W-pI .... 58.5:8 me forever. I am eternally **b.** as His Son.
W-pI .... 63.1:2 **b.** are you who can learn to recognize the
W-pI .. 159.9:5 Now are they twice **b.**. The messages they
W-pI .. 162.5:3 when holiness like this has **b.** the world?
W-pI 184.14:5 Now our sight is **b.** with blessings we can
W-pI .. 187.8:6 one who has forgiven and has **b.** himself.
W-pI 187.11:1 Now are we **b.**, and now we bless the
W-pI .. 189.1:7 hope, and **b.** with perfect charity and love
W-pI .. 199.8:5 you in it; the world is **b.** along with you,
W-pI .. 200.5:3 till all the world is seen by you as **b.**, and
W-pI .. 201.1:3 *I am* ***b.*** *with oneness with the universe and*
W-pII .. in.11:4 one of the holy and **b.** instants in the day.
W-pII . 263.1:4 *all the loveliness with which You* ***b.*** *creation;*
W-pII . 269.2:1 Today our sight is **b.** indeed. We share
W-pII . 276.2:2 *own, as I am loved and* ***b.*** *and saved by You.*
W-pII . 315.1:2 I am **b.** with gifts throughout the day, in
W-pII .... 360.h all the world be **b.** with peace through us.
M-4 ........ X.3:9 world. **B.** indeed are they, for they are the
M-29 ......... 8:1 *And now in all your doings be you* ***b.***. *God*
P-2.......... II.6:7 impossible to share a goal not **b.** by Christ
P-3.......... II.5:3 **b.** by the Holy Spirit as a gift from their

P-3 III.6:7 Both will be **b.** thereby. Perhaps he was
P-3 III.6:9 Again will both be **b.**. Only in terms of
S-1 in.1:1 with which God **b.** His Son at his creation

## blessedness 2

W-pI 187.9:5 The **b.** you will behold will take away all
W-pI 187.10:3 has joined us all as one, we stand in **b.**,

## blesses 16

T-1 V.4:2 to return because it **b.** and honors him,
T-12 VI.4:10 the Holy Spirit **b.** the real world in Their
T-16 I.6:2 that hovers over it and **b.** it silently by
T-27 V.4:5 the One Who **b.** you loves all the world,
W-pI 37.h My holiness **b.** the world.
W-pI 37.2:6 holiness **b.** him by asking nothing of him.
W-pI 37.4:2 see: *My holiness **b.** this chair. My holiness*
W-pI 37.4:3 *My holiness **b.** that window. My holiness*
W-pI 37.4:4 *My holiness **b.** this body.* Then close your
W-pI 37.4:6 and saying: *My holiness **b.** you, [name].*
W-pI 58.2:1 (37) My holiness **b.** the world. The
W-pI 124.1:4 on a shining light that **b.** and that heals.
W-pI 157.5:1 you touch, and **b.** those you look upon. A
W-pI 189.2:4 It **b.** you throughout the day, and watches
W-pI 197.5:1 God **b.** every gift you give to Him, and
W-pII 8.1:4 except through eyes forgiveness **b.**, so

## blessing 106

T-1 I.27:1 A miracle is a universal **b.** from God
T-3 I.7:2 harmlessness and sheds only **b.**. It could
T-5 I.3:4 also in Christ Jesus," and uses this as a **b.**.
T-5 I.3:5 It is the **b.** of miracle-mindedness. It asks
T-5 IV.8:2 beauty is gone, and nothing is left but a **b.**
T-5 IV.8:8 You go with my **b.** and for my blessing.
T-5 IV.8:8 You go with my blessing and for my **b.**.
T-5 VI.12:7 there. He is the only **b.** you can truly give,
T-6 I.19:2 many need your **b.** to help them hear this
T-7 VII.1:1 Whenever you deny a **b.** to a brother *you*
T-7 VII.2:3 You need the **b.** you can offer him. There
T-7 VII.3:1 God's **b.** because that you have forever,
T-7 VII.7:4 His patience can translate attack into **b.**.
T-7 IX.2:5 of loss, as **b.** is the opposite of sacrifice.
T-8 IX.3:5 "Rest in peace" is a **b.** for the living, not
T-9 II.8:4 Do not ask for blessings without **b.** them,
T-9 VIII.5:2 By **b.** you hold it in your mind, protecting
T-12 VI.5:8 in the quiet light of the Holy Spirit's **b.**.
T-12 VII.1:5 the Holy Spirit sends you for your **b.**. In
T-12 VII.1:6 In every child of God His **b.** lies, and in
T-12 VII.1:6 **b.** of the children of God is His blessing to
T-12 VII.1:6 of the children of God is His **b.** to you.
T-14 I.1:4 If, then, you offer **b.**, it must have come
T-14 IV.8:6 cannot even give a **b.** in perfect gentleness
T-14 IV.9:1 live in the light of the **b.** of their Father,
T-14 V.3:1 Blessed Son of a wholly **b.** Father, joy was
T-14 V.11:5 anyone as without the **b.** of Atonement,
T-14 V.11:5 and bring him into it by **b.** him. Holiness
T-14 X.6:11 gives equal **b.** to all who share in it, and
T-15 V.10:1 holy instant, because the **b.** is not limited.
T-15 V.10:2 united in your **b.** it becomes one to you.
T-15 VII.10:1 the ego has "blessed," for anger *is* its **b.**.
T-17 II.3:6 with the **b.** of your forgiveness on it. And
T-17 II.3:7 this final **b.** of God's Son upon himself,
T-17 IV.4:3 it, and by His **b.** enabled it to be healed.
T-17 IV.4:4 This **b.** holds within itself the truth about
T-17 V.10:4 Join in His **b.**, and withhold not yours
T-17 V.10:5 it. For all it needs now is your **b.**, that you
T-18 I.11:2 upon you, **b.** your relationship with truth.
T-18 II.7:3 the **b.** the Holy Spirit has laid upon it will
T-18 V.6:4 The power of joining its **b.** lies in the fact
T-18 V.7:6 *Holy Spirit, that His **b.** may descend on us,*
T-18 VIII.10:2 quiet garden, and receive their **b.** there.
T-19 I.13:4 then, offer grace and **b.** to your brother,
T-19 III.9:1 your lips, and Heaven's **b.** on your sight.
T-20 VI.9:3 substitute you want for the eternal **b.** of
T-20 VI.10:3 smile and tender **b.** it offers to its own.
T-20 VIII.6:4 sin is turned to **b.** under His gentle gaze.
T-21 VI.10:2 that it cannot be you stand apart from **b.**.
T-22 VI.9:1 What can it be but universal **b.** to look on
T-22 VI.9:7 He will withhold no **b.** from it, nor limit it
T-23 II.17:3 What form of condemnation is a **b.**? Who
T-23 III.2:1 a **b.** and a sign the Voice for God speaks
T-24 II.9:5 receive you and your brother in silent **b.**,
T-24 V.6:2 you there in gentleness and **b.** all the way.
T-24 VI.1:1 it in gentleness and **b.** so complete that
T-24 VI.8:2 cannot withhold God's **b.** from himself,
T-25 VII.1:1 that you laid upon yourself into a **b.**, then
T-26 II.7:5 has been transformed into a universal **b.**.
T-26 VII.19:3 us unite in bringing **b.** to the world of sin
T-26 VII.19:10 to bless but one gives **b.** to them all as one
T-27 V.4:4 accept the **b.** that the holy instant brings?
T-27 V.4:5 Be not afraid of **b.**, for the One Who
T-27 V.4:6 But if you shrink from **b.**, will the world
T-27 V.6:2 And being blessed you will bring **b.**. Life
T-27 V.6:4 but shine in thanks to you who **b.** gave.
T-29 VI.3:3 the only thing that can be made a **b.** here,
T-29 VI.6:2 how filled with **b.** and with happiness!
T-30 II.1:10 ever had but waited for your **b.** to be born
T-30 II.4:1 world that merely waits your **b.** to be free
T-30 V.8:5 His **b.** lies on you as surely as His Father's
W-pI 37.6:4 him the **b.** of your holiness immediately,
W-pI 39.7:3 **b.** on them that will save you and give you
W-pI 73.6:9 undertake it with your **b.** and your glad
W-pI 121.13:1 friend unite in **b.** you with what you gave.
W-pI 127.11:2 to shed its **b.** upon all who come to learn
W-pI 134.6:1 who offer it; a quiet **b.** where it is received
W-pI 134.11:1 as powerful as love which laid its **b.** on it,
W-pI 135.18:3 loving **b.** shine in every step you ever took
W-pI 137.13:1 to the world, exchanging curse for **b.**,
W-pI 137.15:3 sick, and offer **b.** where there was attack.
WpI rIV.in9:3 special time of **b.** and of happiness for us;
W-pI 151.11:3 in sin, and only Heaven's **b.** on the world.
W-pI 153.9:3 ministry extends its holy **b.** through the
W-pI 161.h Give me your **b.**, holy Son of God.
W-pI 161.11:7 *Give me your **b.**, holy Son of God. I would*
W-pI 176.1:1 (161) Give me your **b.**, holy Son of God.
W-pI 187.7:3 Your **b.** lies on everyone who suffers,
W-pI 187.8:4 Your **b.** will correct it. Given first to you,
W-pI 188.3:2 leaves a **b.** with it that remains forever
W-pI 188.4:4 His **b.** does the light in you shine brighter,
W-pI 188.10:5 And we lay our saving **b.** on it, as we say:
W-pI 198.6:3 all **b.** and all joy that ever can be found
W-pI 207.1:2 *God's **b.** shines upon me from within my*
W-pII 269.1:1 *I ask Your **b.** on my sight today. It is the*
W-pII 274.2:1 A special **b.** comes to us today, from Him
W-pII 283.2:2 And so we offer **b.** to all things, uniting
W-pII 308.1:7 come to give His present **b.** to the world,
W-pII 10.1:4 gives a silent **b.** and then disappears, its
M-6 2:9 it is recognized as a **b.** and not a curse.
M-14 5:8 In **b.** it departs, for it will not end as it
M-28 6:4 The thought of murder is replaced with **b.**
P-3 III.6:11 everyone must gain a **b.** without cost.
S-1 III.5:5 Take his **b.**, and feel how your heart is
S-3 II.5:2 sin. How could it be a **b.**, then? And how
S-3 IV.2:1 effect of mercy truly taught, healing is **b.**.

## blessings 3

T-9 II.8:4 Do not ask for **b.** without blessing them,
W-pI 154.12:3 nor has denied the tiniest of **b.** to His Son.
W-pI 184.14:5 blessed with **b.** we can give as we receive.

## blight 2

T-20 II.10:3 chill of fear and withering **b.** of sin alike.
T-26 IX.3:8 and all the **b.** and withering have passed

## blighting 1

W-pI 163.2:2 hand; all hopes and wishes in its **b.** grasp;

## blind 34

T-7 VI.11:2 The attack must be **b.**, however, because
T-8 VI.2:1 **b.** the Sons to the Father if they behold it.
T-11 III.1:7 being **b.** it does not see whom it attacks.
T-12 VI.4:2 eyes of the **b.** is the Holy Spirit's mission,
T-13 II.3:4 who the Son of God is because it is **b.**. Yet
T-13 IX.7:1 Guilt makes you **b.**, for while you see one
T-13 IX.8:4 this you cannot do without remaining **b.**.
T-15 II.5:5 literally **b.** you to this world by its own
T-16 II.8:1 speak of it so clearly that only the **b.** and
T-17 V.13:4 for the attack must **b.** you to yourself.
T-19 III.11:1 and let not sin arise again to **b.** your eyes.
T-20 III.7:10 And of the one **b.** thing in all the seeing
T-21 I.4:1 **b.** become accustomed to their world by
T-21 I.4:5 not understand the lessons *keep* them **b.**.
T-21 I.10:1 And now the **b.** can see, for that same
T-21 III.12:3 to serve as means to help the **b.** to see. But
T-21 IV.2:3 light on sin, and God will strike you **b.**.
T-22 I.4:10 Here is the one emotion that keeps you **b.**
T-25 VIII.4:10 And justice, being **b.**, is satisfied by being
T-28 V.4:8 Its eyes are **b.**; its ears are deaf. It can not
W-pI 78.4:2 We will not let ourselves be **b.** to him; we
W-pI 95.2:4 does not see the oneness in you, for it is **b.**
W-pI 130.2:4 Fear must make **b.**, for this its weapon is:
W-pI 130.3:4 can be real in **b.** imaginings of panic born
W-pI 136.10:2 these, with God made **b.** by your illusions
W-pI 151.6:3 faith in them is **b.** because you would not
W-pI 159.5:4 been restored to vision, and the **b.** can see
W-pI 183.3:4 The **b.** can see; the deaf can hear. The
W-pI 184.14:3 separations disappear which kept us **b.**.
W-pI 191.1:4 punitive and wild, lacking all reason, **b.**,
W-pII 247.h Without forgiveness I will still be **b.**.
W-pII 259.1:2 What else could **b.** us to the obvious, and
W-pII 352.1:3 *Judgment will bind my eyes and make me **b.**.*
M-13 5:5 It is the idea of sacrifice that makes him **b.**

## blinded 3

T-23 II.15:6 eyes, **b.** and terrible to look upon, is lifted
T-24 VI.6:5 him. Let not your eyes be **b.** by the veil of
W-pI 189.1:2 see this light, for you are **b.** by the world.

## blinders 1

S-3 II.2:4 Now we can behold Him without **b.**, in

## blindfold 1

T-31 II.11:8 A **b.** can indeed obscure your sight, but

## blinding 2

T-15 III.1:6 belittling yourself and **b.** yourself to glory
T-22 III.6:7 Nothing so **b.** as perception of form. For

## blindly 3

T-4 V.5:2 that you should seek **b.** and desperately
T-13 II.5:5 projected guilt **b.** and indiscriminately,
P-2 III.1:3 will merely stumble **b.** on to nowhere. It

## blindness 3

T-21 I.10:2 The **b.** that they made will not withstand
W-pI 164.7:3 for our release from **b.** and from misery.
W-pI 165.5:6 your **b.** for the seeing eyes of Christ; your

## bliss 2

T-17 III.4:8 join with fantasies in uninterrupted "**b.**."
W-pI 186.8:3 mourner to ecstatic **b.** of love and loving.

## block 22

T-4 II.11:2 misperception is a **b.** to knowledge, while
T-4 II.11:4 This removes the **b.** entirely. You may ask
T-4 III.7:3 through the walls you make to **b.** it, and it
T-8 III.2:3 experience will **b.** its accomplishment,
T-8 V.1:4 their illusions which **b.** knowledge. Help
T-13 VII.12:2 all things that do not **b.** the way to light.
T-22 III.3:2 Sin is a **b.**, set like a heavy gate, locked
T-22 III.5:6 to look beyond the granite **b.** of sin, and
T-22 IV.3:4 your brother alone will see it as a solid **b.**,
T-22 IV.6:3 seemed to rise and **b.** their way before.

T-22......IV.7:6 and touch this heavy-seeming **b.**, and you
T-22....... V.2:8 sin is carved into a **b.** out of your peace,
T-22......VI.7:2 form of suffering could **b.** your sight,
T-25......IX.7:8 then must problems rise to **b.** your way,
T-26....... X.1:9 Confused perception will **b.** knowledge. It
T-29.........I.3:3 but this one still remains to **b.** your path,
T-29....VIII.4:5 hand could be held up to **b.** God's way?
W-pI.....78.3:2 For every grievance is a **b.** to sight, and as
W-pI.....85.2:2 *Let me not use this as a* **b.** *to sight. The light*
W-pI...170.9:3 obstacle with the appearance of a solid **b.**,
W-pI...181.7:3 each obstruction seems to **b.** the vision of
C-4............4:1 world stands like a **b.** before Christ's face.

## blocked 9

T-4.......VII.6:7 Love is **b.** when His channels are closed,
T-6......... V.1:7 His completeness, is **b.** when the Sonship
T-8.....VII.10:6 body, for if it does it is **b.** in its purpose. A
T-8.....VII.10:7 A mind that has been **b.** has allowed itself
T-11.........I.3:5 Extension cannot be **b.**, and it has no
T-14.........I.4:5 which has been **b.** by the capricious and
T-22...... III.8:3 your brother not be **b.** by your perception
W-pI.......8.3:2 ideas preoccupy your mind, the truth is **b.**
W-pI...134.8:3 which has been **b.** by dreams of guilt.

## blocking 2

T-7...... VI.12:4 mind is **b.** the extension of the Kingdom,
T-8.....VII.11:3 and by **b.** its own extension beyond it,

## blocks 17

T-in ...........1:7 *at removing the* **b.** *to the awareness of love's*
T-7........ IX.3:4 ego's whole thought system **b.** extension,
T-7........ IX.3:4 extension, and thus **b.** your only function.
T-7........ IX.3:5 therefore **b.** your joy, so that you perceive
T-8.....VII.11:1 The removal of **b.**, then, is the only way
T-8.....VII.12:5 confusion that **b.** the understanding of
T-14...... IV.9:5 how to remove the **b.** that stand between
W-pI.......4.2:5 The "bad" ones are **b.** to sight, and make
W-pI. 135.22:1 that **b.** the truth from entering our minds.
WpI. rIV.in2:7 Lack of forgiveness **b.** this thought from
Wi181-200 2:1 special **b.** that keep your vision narrow,
Wi181-200 2:2 We are attempting now to lift these **b.**,
W-pI...181.1:4 becoming **b.** to your awareness of the Self
W-pI...181.6:1 this goal if anger **b.** our way in any form.
W-pI...181.6:3 such **b.** arise we will transcend them with
P-1............1:1 is to remove the **b.** to truth. Its aim is to
P-2......... II.3:3 All **b.** to the remembrance of God are

## blood 15

*See also* blood-red, blood-stained
T-17...... IV.8:4 The glitter of **b.** shines like rubies, and the
T19... IV.D.2:3 face with glory appear as streams of **b.**,
T19... IV.D.6:3 of the ego you swore in **b.** not to desert,
T-25...VII.11:5 and pay exact amount in **b.** and suffering.
T-26...... IX.3:1 The **b.** of hatred fades to let the grass
T-27.........I.3:2 are writ in Heaven in your **b.** and death,
T-27..... II.6:10 He thinks your **b.** is on his hands, and so
T-27....... II.7:7 your brother with no **b.** upon his hands,
W-pI...107.8:2 are not made of flesh and **b.** and bone,
W-pI...170.2:2 For here is fear begot and fed with **b.**, to
W-pI...170.7:2 that though his lips are smeared with **b.**,
W-pI. 170.10:5 The **b.** appears to be upon His Lips; the
W-pI...198.7:4 upon the place where you beheld Their **b.**
W-pII ...12.4:2 and **b.** must flow before the altar where
M-17 .......7:13 The stain of **b.** can never be removed, and

## blood-red 1

T-20....... II.4:6 whose points gleam sharply in a **b.** light,

## blood-stained 1

T-3...........I.5:1 but those who represent the lamb as **b.** do

## bloodied 1

T-26 ..... IX.4:6 it. The **b.** earth is cleansed, and the insane

## bloody 1

T-29 ...... V.6:5 Who would lay **b.** hands on Heaven itself,

## bloom 1

T-29 ..... VI.2:9 with time and **b.** and fade will not return.

## bloomed 1

T-25 ..... IV.5:4 And every flower that ever **b.** has saved its

## blot 3

T-6 ..... IV.12:8 God did not **b.** it out, because to eradicate
T-18 .......II.4:6 attempts to **b.** out reality are very fearful,
W-pI... 196.5:5 and waiting to destroy his life and **b.** him

## blots 1

T-14 .......X.5:2 and grow dim, as darkness **b.** them out.

## blotted 6

T-7 ... VIII.3:11 Believing they have **b.** their projections
T-18 .......II.3:2 you see on waking is **b.** out in dreams. Yet
T19... IV.D.3:3 the veil forever **b.** out and unremembered
T-26 ........I.7:2 in you be **b.** out because he sees it not.
M-18 ......... 3:2 Reality is **b.** out as this insane belief is
M-27 ......... 3:2 His Love is **b.** out in the idea, which holds

## blow 5

T-18 .VIII.13:7 **B.** on it lightly and with happy laughter,
T-24 ......I.8:10 does not change with every seeming **b.**,
T-28 .... VII.7:3 The winds will **b.** upon it and the rain will
W-pI... 107.4:4 They will merely **b.** away, when truth
W-pI... 186.9:5 They **b.** across his mind like wind-swept

## blown 1

*See also* blown-up
T-15 ..... III.6:5 believe that littleness can be **b.** up into a

## blown-up 1

T-30 ..... IV.2:1 gods you made are **b.** children's toys. A

## blurred 1

S-1..........II.3:3 to be **b.** by a deep-rooted sense of sin. It is

## bluster 1

W-pI. 134.11:2 They are not kept to swell and **b.**, and to

## blustering 1

W-pI... 121.3:1 all it sees; afraid and angry, weak and **b.**,

## boasted 1

T-16 ...... V.3:1 love relationship is the ego's most **b.** gift,

## bodies 90

T-7 ........ V.3:5 in the service of the ego can hurt other **b.**,
T-8 ...... VII.2:5 because you do not regard **b.** solely as a
T-8 ...... VII.3:2 the minds of those who believe they are **b.**
T-13 ........in.2:7 its powers to decline if their **b.** are hurt.
T-13 .....in.2:10 And their **b.** wither and gasp and are laid
T-15 .... VII.8:2 to the ego, mean only that **b.** are together.
T-15 .... VII.8:9 no longer believe that **b.** communicate,
T-15 .. VII.11:5 **b.** are together their minds remain their
T-15 .. VII.11:6 The union of **b.** thus becomes the way in
T-15 .. VII.11:7 For **b.** cannot forgive. They can only do as
T-15 ... VIII.4:5 sum of all the separate **b.** you perceive.
T-15 ..... IX.7:3 all. In the holy instant there are no **b.**, and
T-16 ..... VI.5:2 bridge you see the world of separate **b.**,
T-17 ..... III.2:6 body, for only **b.** can be seen as means for
T-17 ..... III.2:7 **b.** are central to all unholy relationships is
T-17 ..... III.3:1 but the **b.** of those who are not there. For
T-17 .... VII.3:4 Some idea of **b.** must have entered, for
T-17 .... VII.3:5 thought of **b.** is the sign of faithlessness,
T-17 .... VII.3:5 faithlessness, for **b.** cannot solve anything
T-18 ..... VI.3:1 Minds are joined; **b.** are not. Only by
T-18 ... VIII.5:1 in a world inhabited by **b.** seem to be.
T-18 ... VIII.8:1 Love knows no **b.**, and reaches to
T-18 ..... IX.3:1 From the world of **b.**, made by insanity,
T-19 ...... I.11:5 eyes, nor looks to **b.** for its justification. It
T-19 .......II.1:4 on the firm conviction that minds, not **b.**,
T-19 .......II.6:5 ego wants; a world it rules, made up of **b.**,
T-19 ..... III.7:2 While you believe that **b.** can unite, you
T-19 ..... III.7:3 For the belief that **b.** limit mind leads to a
T19 .IV.A.17:6 would I teach that **b.** cannot keep us apart
T-20 .......II.2:1 Gifts are not made through **b.**, if they be
T-20 .......II.2:2 For **b.** can neither offer nor accept; hold
T-20 ..... VI.4:7 ego seeks as many **b.** as it can collect to
T-20 ..... VI.8:7 **b.** made to house the mad idea and give it
T-20 .... VII.5:2 The unholy instant *is* the time of **b.**. But
T-20 .... VII.6:7 in unholy relationships with other **b.**,
T-21 ..... VI.3:2 Only were Both in **b.** could this be. Nor
T-21 ..... VI.3:4 For only **b.** can be separate, and therefore
T-21 ... VIII.1:2 To **b.**, yes! The thoughts that seem to kill
T-22 ...... in.2:8 themselves, living with their **b.** perhaps
T-22 ........I.9:4 join, for this they could not do through **b.**
T-22 ..... III.4:7 where its worshippers are bound to **b.**,
T-23 ..... IV.5:8 **B.** may battle, but the clash of forms is
T-23 ..... IV.7:3 For only **b.** could attack and murder, and
T-24 ..... III.5:6 They are not **b.**; as one Mind They wait
T-24 ..... IV.2:5 Yet **b.** have no goal. Purpose is of the
T-25 ...... in.1:8 see Him where they thought their **b.** were.
T-25 ...... in.1:9 Then will their **b.** melt away, that they
T-25 ...... in.2:2 *Except* in **b.**. And as long as he believes he
T-26 ........I.3:4 sight of **b.** becomes the sign that sacrifice
T-26 ........I.4:7 Son is seen within a world of separate **b.**,
T-27 .......II.1:3 bar to love, and damaged **b.** are accusers.
T-27 .......V.3:4 the broken **b.** and the shattered limbs,
T-27 ... VIII.1:3 the story of how it was made by other **b.**,
T-27 ... VIII.1:3 in the dust with other **b.** dying like itself.
T-27 ... VIII.1:4 for other **b.** as its friends and enemies. Its
T-27 ... VIII.2:4 It hires other **b.**, that they may protect it
T-27 ... VIII.2:5 It looks about for special **b.** that can share
T-27 ... VIII.2:6 it is a conqueror of **b.** weaker than itself.
T-27 ... VIII.2:7 slave of **b.** that would hurt and torture it.
T-28 .......II.3:6 within a body and a world of other **b.**,
T-28 .....II.10:6 and the **b.** that still seem to move about
T-28 ..... III.3:2 and separate minds are seen as **b.**, which
T-28 ..... IV.7:2 The gap between your **b.** matters not, for
T-29 ........I.4:1 not one of space between two separate **b.**.
T-29 ........I.4:4 And then your **b.** seem to get in touch,
T-29 ..... III.3:1 Within the dream of **b.** and of death is
T-31 ..... III.3:1 Sins are in **b.**. They are not perceived in
T-31 ..... III.3:4 **B.** act, and minds do not. And therefore
W-pI .... 17.2:7 *my thoughts about* **b.** *are not neutral.*
W-pI .. 100.1:2 in separate thoughts and separate **b.**,
W-pI .. 161.5:2 Yet **b.** are but symbols for a concrete form
W-pI .. 161.6:1 **B.** attack, but minds do not. This thought
W-pI .. 161.6:3 reason **b.** easily become fear's symbols.
W-pI .. 163.1:2 and lack of trust; concern for **b.**, envy,
W-pI .. 183.5:3 for grace, nor **b.** for the holy Son of God.
W-pI .. 184.1:6 time; all **b.** which are greeted by a name.
W-pI .. 184.3:1 of **b.** kept apart and holding bits of mind
W-pI .. 200.9:7 apart from God, where **b.** have reality.
W-pII ... 10.2:6 **B.** now are useless, and will therefore fade
M-2 ........... 5:6 between their roles, their minds, their **b.**,
M-22 ......... 5:5 at all, for his Father did not create **b.**, and
M-27 ......... 5:2 body. And if God created **b.**, death would
C-4 ............ 5:2 It was the home of **b.**. But forgiveness
C-4 ............ 5:3 But forgiveness looks past **b.**. This is its
C-4 ............ 5:5 The world of **b.** is the world of sin, for
C-4 ............ 7:4 And gone are **b.** in the blazing light upon
C-4 ............ 7:7 journey, no belief in sin, no walls, no **b.**,
P-3..........II.9:8 to collect **b.** to worship at their shrine,

S-1 ......... V.3:1 is lifted from the world of things, of **b.**,
S-3 ........... I.2:5 And they feel fear as **b.** change and sicken

## bodily 7

T-1 ........ I.12:2 the lower or **b.** level of experience, or the
T-1 ........ I.17:2 into invisibility, away from the **b.** level.
T-2 ........ IV.4:1 that you accept as remedies for **b.** ills are
T-9 ......... II.2:4 healing because he is fearful of **b.** harm.
W-pI ... 133.2:2 let your mind be drawn to **b.** concerns, to
W-pI ... 135.9:3 the mind as separate from **b.** conditions.
W-pI.136.19:2 a **b.** identity which will attack the body,

## body 763

*See also* body-identification, ego-body

T-1 ........ I.17:1 Miracles transcend the **b.**. They are
T-1 ........ I.20:1 the awareness that the spirit, not the **b.**, is
T-1 ......... V.1:1 The miracle is much like the **b.** in that
T-1 ......... V.1:2 the **b.** nor the miracle serves any purpose.
T-1 ......... V.1:3 While you believe you are in a **b.**,
T-1 ....... VII.2:3 be expressed through one **b.** to another,
T-1 ....... VII.2:4 use your **b.** best to help you enlarge your
T-2 ........ III.1:3 generally seen as a need to protect the **b.**.
T-2 ........ III.1:4 many **b.** fantasies in which minds engage
T-2 ........ III.1:4 the distorted belief that the **b.** can be used
T-2 ........ III.1:5 Perceiving the **b.** as a temple is only the
T-2 ........ IV.2:5 The **b.** can act wrongly only when it is
T-2 ........ IV.2:6 The **b.** cannot create, and the belief that it
T-2 ........ IV.2:9 that the mind can miscreate in the **b.**, or
T-2 ........ IV.2:9 or that the **b.** can miscreate in the mind.
T-2 ........ IV.3:1 the **b.** is a learning device for the mind.
T-2 ........ IV.3:6 The **b.**, if properly understood, shares the
T-2 ........ IV.3:7 This is not because the **b.** is a miracle, but
T-2 ........ IV.3:8 **b.** is merely part of your experience in the
T-2 ........ IV.4:2 first step in believing that the **b.** makes its
T-2 ........ IV.4:6 a compromise approach to mind and **b.**,
T-2 ......... V.1:3 belief that harm can be limited to the **b.**.
T-2 ......... V.1:9 The **b.** does not exist except as a learning
T-2 ......... V.6:1 be emphasized again that the **b.** does not
T-2 ......... V.6:4 and the **b.** in itself is too dense. The mind,
T-2 ......... V.6:5 can bring its illumination to the **b.** by
T-2 ......... V.6:6 The **b.** is, however, easily brought into
T-2 ........ VI.1:6 raised **b.** thoughts to the level of the mind
T-3 ...... III.5:11 form perception involves the **b.**.
T-3 ........ IV.6:1 ability to perceive made the **b.** possible,
T-3 ........ IV.6:3 permits you to interpret the **b.** as yourself
T-3 ........ IV.6:5 mind and entirely inaccessible to the **b.**.
T-3 ........ IV.7:5 of the **b.** and the power of the mind. By
T-4 ........ in.3:5 and finally the crucifixion of the **b.**, or
T-4 ........ I.13:3 can protect the child's **b.** and his ego, but
T-4 ........ I.13:4 I can be entrusted with your **b.** and your
T-4 ........ II.7:6 This is as true of **b.** appetites as it is of the
T-4 ........ II.7:7 **B.** appetites are not physical in origin.
T-4 ........ II.7:8 The ego regards the **b.** as its home, and
T-4 ........ II.7:8 and tries to satisfy itself through the **b.**.
T-4 ......... V.2:1 between the **b.** and the Thoughts of God.
T-4 ......... V.2:5 not only "unacceptable" **b.** impulses, but
T-4 ......... V.3:1 confuses God and the **b.** must be insane.
T-4 ......... V.3:4 ego. But fear of the **b.**, with which the ego
T-4 ......... V.4:1 **b.** is the ego's home by its own election. It
T-4 ......... V.4:4 Yet the ego hates the **b.**, because it cannot
T-4 ......... V.4:6 of the **b.** and that the body is its protector
T-4 ......... V.4:6 of the body and that the **b.** is its protector
T-4 ......... V.4:6 is also told that the **b.** cannot protect it.
T-4 ......... V.4:8 insisted that it is identified with the **b.**, so
T-5 ......... V.5:2 the mind heals the **b.** because *it* has been
T-6 ........... I.4:1 can ultimately be made only on the **b.**.
T-6 ........... I.4:2 doubt that one **b.** can assault another,
T-6 ........ IV.4:5 mind, the ego turns to the **b.** as its ally,
T-6 ........ IV.4:5 as its ally, because the **b.** is *not* part of you.
T-6 ........ IV.4:6 This makes the **b.** the ego's friend. It is an
T-6 ........ IV.5:1 uses the **b.** to conspire against your mind,
T-6 ........ IV.5:3 that the **b.** is more real than the mind is.
T-6 ...... V.A.1:1 your **b.** and your ego and your dreams are
T-6 ...... V.A.1:4 The **b.** neither lives nor dies, because it
T-6 ...... V.A.2:1 God did not make the **b.**, because it is
T-6 ...... V.A.2:2 **b.** is the symbol of what you think you are
T-6 ...... V.A.2:6 If the mind can heal the **b.**, but the body
T-6 ...... V.A.2:6 the body, but the **b.** cannot heal the mind
T-6 ...... V.A.2:6 the mind must be stronger than the **b.**.
T-6 ...... V.A.3:3 The **b.** is separate, and therefore cannot
T-6 ...... V.A.3:4 but to be one **b.** is meaningless. By the
T-6 ...... V.A.3:5 laws of mind, then, the **b.** is meaningless.
T-6 ...... V.A.5:3 ego uses the **b.** for attack, for pleasure and
T-6 ...... V.A.5:5 the **b.** only as a means of communication,
T-7 ......... V.1:1 The **b.** is nothing more than a framework
T-7 ......... V.1:3 to use the **b.** only for communication has
T-7 ......... V.2:2 the **b.** can both communicate and create,
T-7 ......... V.2:3 teach you that the **b.** can act like the mind
T-7 ......... V.3:3 accept the ego's confusion of mind and **b.**
T-7 ......... V.3:5 The **b.** in the service of the ego can hurt
T-7 ......... V.3:5 but this cannot occur unless the **b.** has
T-7 ....... V.10:7 yours. I do not want to share my **b.** in
T-7 ........ VI.8:2 to the belief that you must be a **b.**. By not
T-8 .......... VII.h The **B.** as a Means of Communication
T-8 ....... VII.1:2 mind you are equating yourself with a **b.**,
T-8 ....... VII.1:2 this is the ego's interpretation of the **b.**.
T-8 ....... VII.1:6 equate yourself with a **b.** you will always
T-8 ....... VII.2:1 the **b.** only as a means of communication.
T-8 ....... VII.2:3 is. The ego separates through the **b.**. The
T-8 ....... VII.2:6 This interpretation of the **b.** will change
T-8 ....... VII.3:1 If you use the **b.** for attack, it is harmful
T-8 ....... VII.3:2 them *through* the **b.** that this is not so, you
T-8 ....... VII.3:3 If you use the **b.** for this and only for this,
T-8 ....... VII.3:6 Holy Spirit does not see the **b.** as you do,
T-8 ....... VII.4:3 it. The **b.** is beautiful or ugly, peaceful or
T-8 ....... VII.4:4 **b.** of another you will see the use to which
T-8 ....... VII.4:5 If the **b.** becomes a means you give to the
T-8 ....... VII.7:5 for which the **b.** can be used. This is the
T-8 ....... VII.7:7 To use the **b.** unnaturally is to lose sight
T-8 ....... VII.9:1 not even the **b.** is perceived as whole. Its
T-8 ....... VII.9:7 sense the **b.** does become a temple to God
T-8 ..... VII.10:1 of using the **b.** solely for communication.
T-8 ..... VII.10:4 if it uses the **b.** to go beyond itself. By
T-8 ..... VII.10:6 It does not stop at the **b.**, for if it does it is
T-8 ..... VII.11:2 of a mind that is working through the **b.**,
T-8 ..... VII.11:3 If the mind believes the **b.** is its goal it will
T-8 ..... VII.11:3 goal it will distort its perception of the **b.**,
T-8 ..... VII.11:4 Perceiving the **b.** as a separate entity
T-8 ..... VII.12:3 the **b.** can be unified only by one purpose.
T-8 ..... VII.12:4 temptation to see the **b.** in many lights,
T-8 ..... VII.12:6 Learning must lead beyond the **b.** to the
T-8 ..... VII.13:3 To see a **b.** as anything except a means of
T-8 ..... VII.13:5 the **b.** is brought under the purpose of the
T-8 ..... VII.13:6 can only be an assumed purpose of the **b.**,
T-8 ..... VII.13:6 from the mind the **b.** has no purpose at
T-8 ..... VII.14:1 are not limited by the **b.**, and thought
T-8 ..... VII.14:2 mind can be manifested through the **b.** if
T-8 ..... VII.14:3 you see another as limited to or by the **b.**,
T-8 ..... VII.14:5 To conceive of the **b.** as a means of attack
T-8 ..... VII.15:7 When you see a brother as a **b.**, you are
T-8 ......... VIII.h The **B.** as Means or End
T-8 ...... VIII.1:1 toward the **b.** are attitudes toward attack.
T-8 ...... VIII.1:5 it *is*. To the ego the **b.** is to attack *with*.
T-8 ...... VIII.1:6 Equating you with the **b.**, it teaches that
T-8 ...... VIII.1:7 The **b.**, then, is not the source of its own
T-8 ...... VIII.2:1 **b.** exists in a world that seems to contain
T-8 ...... VIII.2:2 In this perceived constellation the **b.** is
T-8 ...... VIII.2:4 Regarding the **b.** as an end, the ego has
T-8 ...... VIII.3:1 overcome the ego's belief in the **b.** as an
T-8 ...... VIII.5:1 true that the **b.** has no function of itself,
T-8 ...... VIII.5:5 A sick **b.** does not make any sense. It
T-8 ...... VIII.5:6 because sickness is not what the **b.** is for.
T-8 ...... VIII.5:7 ego's interpretation of the **b.** rests are true
T-8 ...... VIII.5:7 rests are true; that the **b.** is for attack, and
T-8 ...... VIII.5:7 body is for attack, and that you are a **b.**.
T-8 ...... VIII.9:1 to use your **b.** only to reach your brothers
T-8 ...... VIII.9:5 allow the **b.** to be a mirror of a split mind.
T-8 ...... VIII.9:9 of relinquishing all attempts to use the **b.**
T-8 ........ IX.1:5 do not ask the Holy Spirit to heal the **b.**,
T-8 ........ IX.1:5 that the **b.** is the proper aim of healing.
T-8 ........ IX.1:6 teach you the right *perception* of the **b.**, for
T-8 ........ IX.6:1 mind, tries to separate it from the **b.** in an
T-8 ........ IX.7:1 take no thought of the **b.** as separate and
T-8 ........ IX.8:6 Yet sickness is not of the **b.**, but of the
T-14 ...... II.1:10 speck of dust, a **b.** or a war are one to you.
T-15 ..... VII.8:4 as the **b.** is there to receive its sacrifice, it
T-15 ..... VII.8:5 is private, and only the **b.** can be shared.
T-15 ..... VII.8:6 bring the **b.** of another closer or farther.
T-15 ... VII.10:5 this; to be with a **b.** is not communication
T-15 ... VII.12:1 illusion of the autonomy of the **b.** and its
T-15 ... VII.12:2 that to be with a **b.** is companionship,
T-15 ... VII.12:2 to attempt to keep your brother in his **b.**,
T-15 ...... IX.1:1 your perception of your brothers to the **b.**
T-15 ...... IX.2:3 The **b.** is the symbol of the ego, as the ego
T-15 ...... IX.3:1 Great Rays replace the **b.** in awareness,
T-15 ...... IX.3:2 to give up every use the ego has for the **b.**,
T-15 ...... IX.3:3 the ego would limit everyone to a **b.** for its
T-15 ...... IX.4:4 Limit your sight of a brother to his **b.**,
T-15 ...... IX.4:5 you. His **b.** cannot give it. And seek it not
T-15 ...... IX.5:5 For the **b.** *is* little and limited, and only
T-15 ...... IX.7:1 When the **b.** ceases to attract you, and
T-15 ...... IX.7:2 **b.** only for purposes of communication,
T-15 ...... IX.7:2 will learn you have no need of a **b.** at all.
T-15 ...... XI.5:1 long as you perceive the **b.** as your reality,
T-15 ...... XI.7:2 unbroken even if the **b.** is destroyed,
T-15 ...... XI.7:2 provided that you see not the **b.** as the
T-15 ...... XI.7:3 to sacrifice the **b.** is to sacrifice nothing,
T-16 ..... V.11:5 and on his **b.** raise another self to take its
T-16 ...... VI.4:1 is totally meaningless without a **b.**. If you
T-16 ...... VI.4:2 If you value it, you must also value the **b.**.
T-16 ...... VI.4:4 is a device for limiting your self to a **b.**,
T-16 ...... VI.4:6 For in seeing them the **b.** would disappear
T-16 ...... VI.6:2 For a time the **b.** is still seen, but not
T-16 ...... VI.6:4 the value of the **b.** is so diminished in
T-16 ...... VI.6:5 will realize that the only value the **b.** has
T-17 ...... III.2:6 become attempts at union through the **b.**,
T-17 ...... III.3:1 it is not the **b.** of the other with which
T-17 ...... III.3:2 For even the **b.** of the other, already a
T-17 ...... III.5:1 His interpretation of the **b.** as a means of
T-18 ......... I.3:7 **b.** is emphasized, with special emphasis
T-18 ......... VI.h Beyond the **B.**
T-18 ...... VI.2:5 your guilt to your **b.** from your mind. Yet
T-18 ...... VI.2:6 Yet a **b.** cannot be guilty, for it can do
T-18 ...... VI.2:7 think you hate your **b.** deceive yourself.
T-18 ...... VI.3:2 the **b.** does separation seem to be possible
T-18 ...... VI.3:4 keeps it separate, is projected to the **b.**,
T-18 ...... VI.3:5 fantasies and direct the **b.** to act them out
T-18 ...... VI.3:6 it is never what the **b.** does that seems to
T-18 ...... VI.3:7 the **b.** is actually acting out its fantasies, it
T-18 ...... VI.3:7 it will attack the **b.** by increasing the
T-18 ...... VI.4:2 what it does to hurt the **b.** to prove it can.
T-18 ...... VI.4:4 when it believes it has attacked the **b.**. It
T-18 ...... VI.4:6 can misperceive the function of the **b.**, it
T-18 ...... VI.4:7 be. The **b.** was not made by love. Yet love
T-18 ...... VI.5:3 perception of the **b.** can clearly be sick,
T-18 ...... VI.5:3 be sick, but project not this upon the **b.**.
T-18 ...... VI.6:1 is insane to use the **b.** as the scapegoat for
T-18 ...... VI.6:3 have nothing to do with what the **b.** does.
T-18 ...... VI.6:5 fantasies have made your **b.** your "enemy
T-18 ...... VI.8:3 The **b.** is a limit imposed on the universal
T-18 ...... VI.9:1 The **b.** is outside you, and but seems to
T-18 .... VI.10:2 have begun to reach beyond the **b.**, but
T-18 .... VI.10:5 Is *He* a **b.**, and did He create you as He is
T-18 .... VI.11:4 that it is a sudden unawareness of the **b.**,
T-18.. VI.11:11 You have accepted this instead of the **b.**,
T-18 .... VI.12:5 all the "laws" your **b.** obeys and gently
T-18 .... VI.13:2 escape. The **b.** is not attacked, but simply
T-18 .... VI.13:6 above all, the lack of awareness of the **b.**,
T-18 ..... VII.1:1 faith in the **b.** as a source of strength.
T-18 ..... VII.1:3 This makes the **b.** an end and not a means
T-18 ..... VII.2:1 you have not utterly forgotten the **b.**. It
T-18 ..... VII.2:4 Afterwards you will see the **b.** again, but
T-18 ..... VII.3:1 At no single instant does the **b.** exist at all
T-18 ..... VII.4:9 at detachment from the **b.** necessary. All
T-18 ..... VII.7:1 To do anything involves the **b.**. And if
T-18 ..... VII.7:7 of the **b.** ceases to demand attention. Into
T-18 ..... VII.8:4 you be directed how to use the **b.** sinlessly
T-18 ..... VII.8:5 is this center, from which the **b.** is absent,
T-18 .... VIII.1:1 is only the awareness of the **b.** that makes
T-18 .... VIII.1:2 For the **b.** *is* a limit on love. The belief in
T-18 .... VIII.1:5 see yourself within a **b.** know yourself as
T-18 .... VIII.1:7 cannot even think of God without a **b.**, or
T-18 .... VIII.2:1 The **b.** cannot know. And while you limit
T-18 .... VIII.2:3 God cannot come into a **b.**, nor can you
T-18 .... VIII.2:5 The **b.** is a tiny fence around a little part

T-18....VIII.5:2 Each **b.** seems to house a separate mind, a
T-18..VIII.11:3 come because you came without the **b.**,
T-18...... IX.3:5 for it is not the **b.** that could speak of this.
T-18...... IX.4:1 of fear lies just below the level the **b.** sees,
T-18...... IX.4:5 The **b.** cannot see this, for the body arose
T-18...... IX.4:5 the **b.** arose from this for its protection,
T-18...... IX.5:1 The **b.** will remain guilt's messenger, and
T-19.........I.2:7 **b.** is healed because you came without it,
T-19.........I.3:1 The **b.** cannot heal, because it cannot
T-19.........I.3:5 this occurs the **b.** becomes its weapon,
T-19.........I.3:6 The **b.** thus becomes the instrument of
T-19.........I.4:2 is the perception of a brother as a **b.**, and
T-19.........I.4:2 **b.** cannot be used for purposes of union.
T-19.........I.4:3 If, then, you see your brother as a **b.**, you
T-19.........I.4:5 and brought illusions, centered on the **b.**,
T-19.........I.4:6 And the **b.** will seem to be sick, for you
T-19.......I.5:10 for part of it is sought through the **b.**,
T-19.......I.5:11 calls upon the mind and not the **b.**.
T-19.........I.6:1 is the belief that the **b.** must be healed,
T-19.........I.6:2 the mind is limited to the **b.** and divided
T-19.........I.6:3 This will not harm the **b.**, but it *will* keep
T-19.........I.7:7 produced the **b.** and remains connected
T-19.........I.7:8 think you are protecting the **b.** by hiding
T-19.......I.13:1 Grace is not given to a **b.**, but to a mind.
T-19.......I.13:2 receives it looks instantly beyond the **b.**,
T-19.......I.16:4 You can enslave a **b.**, but an idea is free,
T-19....... III.5:9 held to the **b.** by the fear of changed
T-19....... III.7:1 or your brother's is bounded by a **b.**, you
T19. IV.A.17:5 Yet would I offer you my **b.**, you whom I
T19IV.A.17:10 The **b.** does appear to be the symbol of
T19IV.A.17:15 guilt, because it goes beyond the **b.**.
T19.......IV.B.h Belief the **B.** is Valuable for What It Offers
T19....IV.B.1:3 that the **b.** is valuable for what it offers.
T19....IV.B.1:4 attraction of guilt made manifest in the **b.**
T19....IV.B.2:6 the **b.** really given you that justifies your
T19....IV.B.3:1 messengers are sent far beyond the **b.**,
T19....IV.B.3:3 only the messengers of fear that see the **b.**
T19..IV.B.10:4 The **b.** can bring you neither peace nor
T19..IV.B.10:7 **b.** will seem to be whatever is the means
T19..IV.B.11:4 **b.** is the great seeming betrayer of faith.
T19..IV.B.12:1 pleasure through the **b.** and not find pain.
T19..IV.B.12:4 result of equating yourself with the **b.**,
T19..IV.B.12:6 directs the **b.** to do is therefore painful. It
T19..IV.B.13:2 Under fear's orders the **b.** will pursue
T19..IV.B.13:4 perception the **b.** becomes the servant of
T19..IV.B.13:5 all of the ego's heavy investment in the **b.**.
T19..IV.B.14:1 Why should the **b.** be anything to you?
T19..IV.B.14:5 the **b.** receives and sends the messages
T19..IV.B.15:4 bids the **b.** search for pain in attack upon
T19..IV.B.16:2 ego has dedicated the **b.** to the goal of sin,
T19..IV.B.16:5 Not one but must regard the **b.** as himself
T19.... IV.C.i.h The Incorruptible **B.**
T19....IV.C.4:1 is the black-draped **b.** they would bury? A
T19....IV.C.4:2 A **b.** which they dedicated to death, a
T19....IV.C.4:6 of guilt you laid upon the **b.** would kill it.
T19....IV.C.5:1 the **b.** incorruptible and perfect as long as
T19....IV.C.5:2 The **b.** no more dies than it can feel. It
T19....IV.C.6:3 The **b.** can but serve your purpose. As you
T19....IV.C.8:3 condemnation to which the **b.** leads you.
T19..IV.C.11:1 and makes your **b.** tremble and the cold
T19... IV.D.5:4 of the **b.** is given up in favor of the spirit,
T19... IV.D.5:4 you love as you could never love the **b.**.
T-20....... II.1:1 all the trinkets made to hang upon the **b.**,
T-20....... II.4:6 light, the **b.** is your chosen home and it is
T-20....... V.5:1 brother's **b.** is as little use to you as it is to
T-20....... V.5:3 minds need not the **b.** to communicate.
T-20....... V.5:4 sight that sees the **b.** has no use which
T-20....... V.7:5 This is no gift your brother's **b.** offers you.
T-20...... VI.2:3 The **b.** does not intrude upon it. Any
T-20...... VI.2:4 in which the **b.** enters is based not on love
T-20...... VI.4:3 **b.** is the ego's chosen weapon for seeking
T-20...... VI.5:1 The Holy Spirit's temple is not a **b.**, but a
T-20...... VI.5:2 The **b.** is an isolated speck of darkness; a
T-20...... VI.6:1 make the **b.** the Holy Spirit's temple, and
T-20...... VI.7:2 love draw near them and overlook the **b.**,
T-20...... VI.7:8 safe in your relationship, and not your **b.**.
T-20...... VI.7:9 You have escaped the **b.**. Where you are
T-20..... VI.7:10 Where you are the **b.** cannot enter, for the
T-20...... VI.9:5 lay aside the **b.** and quietly transcend it,
T-20 .... VI.10:5 leaving the **b.** thankfully behind and
T-20 .... VI.11:1 The **b.** is the ego's idol; the belief in sin
T-20 .... VI.11:7 spend this instant paying tribute to the **b.**
T-20 .... VI.12:9 given one true relationship beyond the **b.**
T-20 .... VII.4:1 as sinless and yet to look upon him as a **b.**
T-20 .... VII.4:4 see a sinless **b.** is impossible, for holiness
T-20 .... VII.4:4 is positive and the **b.** is merely neutral. It
T-20 .... VII.4:6 **b.** cannot meaningfully be invested with
T-20 .... VII.5:1 The **b.** *is* the means by which the ego tries
T-20 .... VII.5:4 and so the illusion of a brother as a **b.** is
T-20 .... VII.5:7 And if you see the **b.**, you have chosen
T-20 .... VII.6:1 a brother's **b.** has laid a judgment on him,
T-20 .... VII.6:7 is your brother's reality imagined as a **b.**,
T-20 .... VII.8:1 **b.** cannot be looked upon except through
T-20 .... VII.8:2 see the **b.** is the sign that you lack vision,
T-20 .... VII.8:5 vision cannot see the **b.** because it cannot
T-20 .... VII.9:1 "How can I see my brother without the **b.**
T-20 ... VIII.3:4 And place no value on your brother's **b.**,
T-20 ... VIII.4:3 vision that enables you to see the **b.** not.
T-20 ... VIII.4:6 Why do you think the **b.** is a better home,
T-20 ... VIII.5:1 **b.** is the sign of weakness, vulnerability
T-21 ........I.5:2 And so it is with all who see the **b.** as all
T-21 ........I.5:4 that to keep the **b.** is to save the little that
T-21 ........I.8:1 Beyond the **b.**, beyond the sun and stars,
T-21 ........I.9:4 that can show you this, and not the **b.**.
T-21 ..... III.7:2 limit to the **b.** you hate because you fear.
T-21 ..... III.7:3 would condemn him to the **b.** because the
T-21 ..... III.7:4 so the **b.** has your faith and your belief.
T-21 ..... III.8:1 free their brothers from the **b.** can have
T-21 ..... III.8:3 belief and faith sees far beyond the **b.**,
T-21 ... III.10:2 For sacrifice must be exacted of a **b.**, and
T-21 ... III.10:2 be exacted of a body, and by another **b.**.
T-21 ... III.10:4 And no more could the **b.**. The intention
T-21 ... III.10:5 which tries to use the **b.** to carry out the
T-21 ... III.10:6 Thus is the joining of mind and **b.** an
T-21 ... III.12:1 The **b.** was made to be a sacrifice to sin,
T-21 ... III.12:6 and belief and faith from mind to **b.**. Let
T-21 ...... V.3:4 and as natural to it as breathing to the **b.**.
T-21 ..... VI.3:3 only for itself unless the **b.** *were* the mind.
T-21 ..... VI.4:3 their will, for they believe they see the **b.**,
T-21 ..... VI.4:5 would defend the **b.** against your reason,
T-21 ..... VI.4:5 you will not understand the **b.** or yourself
T-21 ..... VI.5:1 The **b.** does not separate you from your
T-21 ..... VI.5:3 To see the **b.** as a barrier between what
T-22 ...... in.3:4 selves, for differences are only of the **b.**.
T-22 ...... in.4:7 itself, as you reached out beyond the **b.**,
T-22 ........I.2:9 The brain interprets to the **b.**, of which it
T-22 ........I.4:8 secrecy, of private thoughts and of the **b.**.
T-22 ........I.9:6 each other through a vision not of the **b.**,
T-22 ........I.9:6 in a language the **b.** does not speak. Nor
T-22 .....II.12:1 Beyond the **b.** that you interposed
T-22 ..... III.8:3 your perception of his sins and of his **b.**.
T-22 ..... III.8:4 except what you associate with his **b.**,
T-22 ...... V.5:3 eyes it looks like an enormous solid **b.**,
T-22 ...... V.5:5 This **b.** only seems to be immovable; this
T-22 ..... VI.1:1 you want freedom of the **b.** or of the mind
T-22 ... VI.1:10 He will believe it possible of mind or **b.**,
T-22 ..... VI.2:1 Where freedom of the **b.** has been chosen
T-22 ..... VI.2:2 Yet freedom of the **b.** has no meaning,
T-22 ..... VI.3:4 serve this end the **b.** must be perceived as
T-22 ..... VI.3:6 using your **b.** only to serve the sinless.
T-23 ........I.3:3 For your beliefs converge upon the **b.**, the
T-23 ........I.5:3 body's life, and if you think you are a **b.**,
T-23 .....II.11:6 He hid it in his **b.**, making it the cover for
T-23 .....II.11:7 to you. Now must his **b.** be destroyed and
T-23 .....II.12:8 secret gift, torn from your brother's **b.**,
T-23 ... III.6:10 Here stands the **b.**, torn between the
T-23 ..... IV.2:4 they be to those who see God's Son a **b.**.
T-23 ..... IV.2:5 is not the **b.** that is like the Son's Creator.
T-23 ..... IV.2:7 can a **b.** be extended to hold the universe?
T-23 ..... IV.3:1 God does not share His function with a **b.**
T-23 ..... IV.7:5 The **b.** has no purpose of itself, and must
T-23 ..... IV.7:8 The **b.** stands between the Father and the
T-23 ..... IV.9:3 fought for on the battleground is of the **b.**
T-24 ........I.5:3 make the **b.** dear and worth preserving.
T-24 .....II.13:1 the **b.** as the prison house that keeps His
T-24 ..... IV.2:1 the purpose of the **b.** be but specialness?
T-24 ..... IV.2:9 and **b.** states must shift accordingly. Of
T-24 ... IV.2:10 Of itself the **b.** can do nothing. See it as
T-24 ..... VI.6:7 Your brother's **b.** shows not Christ to you
T-24 ..... VI.7:1 **b.** or his holiness as what you want to see,
T-24 ..... VI.7:4 where is your salvation, if he is but a **b.**?
T-24 ..... VI.8:8 specialness looks on his **b.** and beholds
T-24 ... VI.11:2 unjoined with anything beyond the **b.**. In
T-24 ... VI.13:1 to see your brother's **b.** than his holiness,
T-24 .... VII.4:2 The **b.**, yes, a little; not from time, but
T-24 .... VII.9:1 Look at yourself, and you will see a **b.**.
T-24 .... VII.9:2 at this **b.** in a different light and it looks
T-24 .. VII.10:1 Thus is the **b.** made a theory of yourself,
T-24 VII.10:10 does the **b.** testify to the idea that made it,
T-25 ...... in.1:1 The Christ in you inhabits not a **b.**. Yet
T-25 ...... in.1:3 it must be that you are not within a **b.**.
T-25 ...... in.2:3 And as long as he believes he is in a **b.**,
T-25 ...... in.2:7 as is his specialness set forth within his **b.**.
T-25 ...... in.3:1 The **b.** needs no healing. But the mind
T-25 ...... in.3:2 mind that thinks it is a **b.** is sick indeed!
T-25 ...... in.3:4 His purpose folds the **b.** in His light, and
T-25 ...... in.3:5 that the **b.** says or does but makes Him
T-25 ........I.1:2 it will you learn the **b.** merely seems to be
T-25 ........I.1:5 the **b.** through the mind at one with Him.
T-25 ........I.2:3 Behold the **b.**, and you will believe that
T-25 ........I.2:4 And every **b.** that you look upon reminds
T-25 ........I.2:8 in his **b.** you will see your sinfulness,
T-25 ........I.4:4 shines through each **b.** that it looks upon,
T-25 .......II.5:2 Yet if you see your brother as a **b.**, it is but
T-25 .......II.5:4 to see. The **b.** holds it for a while, without
T-25 ..... III.5:4 it must be, and light the **b.** up instead of it
T-26 ........I.1:4 *lose.* Its focus on the **b.** is apparent, for it is
T-26 ........I.1:5 The **b.** is itself a sacrifice; a giving up of
T-26 ........I.1:6 To see a brother in another **b.**, separate
T-26 ........I.3:1 that the **b.** fences off becomes the self,
T-26 ........I.3:7 accept the limits of a **b.** is to impose these
T-26 ........I.4:1 **b.** *is* a loss, and *can* be made to sacrifice.
T-26 ........I.4:2 And while you see your brother as a **b.**,
T-26 ........I.7:4 God's Son is not imprisoned in a **b.**, nor is
T-26 .... VII.8:9 a **b.** which is clearly separate and a thing
T-26 ... VIII.3:7 Time is as neutral as the **b.** is, except in
T-27 ........I.5:2 It is a picture of a **b.** still, for what you
T-27 ........I.6:9 Adornment of the **b.** seeks to show how
T-27 ......I.6:10 Concerns about the **b.** demonstrate how
T-27 ........I.8:3 Yet in this picture is the **b.** not perceived
T-27 ........I.9:3 not the **b.** into something it is not. It only
T-27 ......I.10:3 death. The **b.** can become a sign of life, a
T-27 ......I.11:1 let the **b.** have no purpose from the past,
T-27 .......II.1:7 because your damaged **b.** shows that *you*
T-27 .......II.5:1 A broken **b.** shows the mind has not been
T-27 .......II.5:6 Your **b.** can be means to teach that it has
T-27 ... IV.4:13 **b.** get that you would want the most of all
T-27 ..... VI.1:1 Pain demonstrates the **b.** must be real. It
T-27 ..... VI.1:4 they both are means to make the **b.** real.
T-27 ..... VI.2:2 one message: "You are here, within this **b.**
T-27 ..... VI.3:1 This **b.**, purposeless within itself, holds
T-27 ..... VI.4:1 Witness sees no witnesses against the **b.**.
T-27 ..... VI.4:8 He brings is witness that the **b.** is not real.
T-27 .. VII.10:2 world equates the **b.** with the Self which
T-27 ... VIII.1:1 **b.** is the central figure in the dreaming of
T-27 ... VIII.1:3 bodies, born into the world outside the **b.**
T-27 ... VIII.2:1 the **b.** seeks in many ways to prove it is
T-27 ... VIII.4:3 That this is all the **b.** does is true, for it is
T-27 ... VIII.5:5 was a time when he knew nothing of a **b.**,
T-27 ... VIII.7:1 enemy; a mind within a **b.** all are forms of
T-27 ... VIII.7:6 keeps you narrowly confined within a **b.**,
T-27 ... VIII.7:6 sinful things the **b.** does within its dream.
T-27 ... VIII.7:7 You have no power to make the **b.** stop its
T-28 ........I.5:5 for. Like to the **b.**, it is purposeless within
T-28 .......II.2:5 Thus is purity not of the **b.**. Nor can it be
T-28 .......II.2:7 The **b.** can be healed by its effects, which
T-28 .......II.2:8 mind is recognized as not within the **b.**,
T-28 .......II.3:6 within a **b.** and a world of other bodies,
T-28 .......II.5:5 are you the victim in a dying **b.** slain. But
T-28 .......II.8:5 His **b.** is their slave, which they abuse
T-28 .......II.8:7 It is their vengeance on the **b.** which
T-28 .....II.11:4 Thus is the **b.** healed by miracles because
T-28 .....II.11:4 and employed the **b.** to be victim, or
T-28 .....II.11:6 if you learn but that the **b.** can be healed,
T-28 .....II.11:7 was sick that thought the **b.** could be sick;
T-28 .....II.12:5 cause. The **b.** is released because the mind
T-28 ..... III.2:4 Thus is the **b.** not perceived as sick by

| | |
|---|---|
| T-28......III.4:6 | **b.** which you see as if it were the cause of |
| T-28......III.5:1 | The cause of pain is separation, not the **b.** |
| T-28......IV.3:4 | made by what he dreams, nor is his **b.**, |
| T-28......IV.3:7 | His **b.** and his dreams but seem to make a |
| T-28....... V.4:4 | sights and sounds the **b.** can perceive are |
| T-28......VI.1:1 | Who punishes the **b.** is insane. For here |
| T-28......VI.3:1 | loathe and want, the **b.** does not know. |
| T-28......VI.4:1 | The **b.** represents the gap between the |
| T-28......VI.5:1 | Sickness is anger taken out upon the **b.**, |
| T-28.....VII.3:5 | The **b.** can be made a home like this, |
| T-28.....VII.4:1 | With *this* as purpose is the **b.** healed. It is |
| T-28.....VII.7:7 | From here the **b.** can be seen as what it is, |
| T-29.........I.4:7 | The **b.** saves you, for it gets away from |
| T-29.........I.5:1 | The **b.** could not separate your mind |
| T-29.........I.6:1 | The **b.** will accommodate to this, if you |
| T-29.........I.8:1 | The **b.**, innocent of goals, is your excuse |
| T-29.........I.8:1 | you hold, and force the **b.** to maintain. |
| T-29.........I.8:6 | aroused by learning that the **b.** is not real. |
| T-29.........I.9:5 | you allow the **b.** to say "no" to Heaven's |
| T-29....... II.7:1 | The **b.** does not change. It represents the |
| T-29....... II.7:7 | The **b.** can appear to change with time, |
| T-29....... II.7:8 | its belief of what the purpose of the **b.** is. |
| T-29....... II.8:1 | is a demand the **b.** be a thing that it is not. |
| T-29....... II.9:1 | The **b.** that is asked to be a god will be |
| T-29..... II.10:1 | "something" is the **b.** asked to be God's |
| T-29..... II.10:2 | you behold the **b.** as a thing you love, or |
| T-29......III.1:1 | savior not because he thinks he is a **b.**. For |
| T-29......III.2:7 | He must see someone else as not a **b.**, one |
| T-29......III.3:6 | will see that God Himself is where his **b.** is |
| T-29......III.3:7 | is. Before this light the **b.** disappears, as |
| T-29......IV.4:8 | assigned; some goal which an event, or **b.**, |
| T-29......VI.5:1 | tie your hands and kill your **b.** only if you |
| T-29.....VII.2:4 | is the purpose he bestows upon the **b.**; |
| T-29... VIII.1:9 | Be it a **b.** or a thing, a place, a situation or |
| T-31......III.3:5 | must the **b.** be at fault for what it does. It |
| T-31......III.3:7 | all. If you are sin you *are* a **b.**, for the mind |
| T-31......III.3:8 | And purpose must be in the **b.**, not the |
| T-31......III.3:9 | The **b.** must act on its own, and motivate |
| T-31.....III.3:10 | are sin you lock the mind within the **b.**, |
| T-31......III.4:1 | Yet is the ***b.*** prisoner, and not the mind. |
| T-31......III.4:2 | The **b.** thinks no thoughts. It has no |
| T-31......III.4:9 | And so the **b.**, where no learning can |
| T-31......III.4:9 | preferred the **b.** change in its appearances |
| T-31......III.5:1 | purpose; that the **b.** be the source of sin, |
| T-31......III.6:2 | The **b.** will but follow. It can never lead |
| T-31......III.6:5 | Release your **b.** from imprisonment, and |
| T-31......VI.1:7 | will escape the **b.** as your own reality, for |
| T-31......VI.2:2 | If you choose to see the **b.**, you behold a |
| T-31......VI.3:1 | behold the spirit and perceive the **b.** not. |
| T-31......VI.3:3 | For you can see the **b.** without help, but |
| T-31......VI.6:5 | Are you a **b.**? So is all the world perceived |
| T-31.....VII.3:1 | it is thus you see him more than just a **b.**, |
| T-31.....VII.3:1 | the good is never what the **b.** seems to be. |
| T-31.....VII.3:2 | actions of the **b.** are perceived as coming |
| T-31.....VII.3:3 | the **b.** grows decreasingly persistent in |
| T-31.....VII.9:3 | you must perceive the **b.** as yourself, for |
| T-31... VIII.1:2 | persuade the holy Son of God he is a **b.**, |
| W-pI........1.2:3 | *That* ***b.*** *does not mean anything. That lamp* |
| W-pI........2.2:3 | with equal ease to a **b.** or a button, a fly or |
| W-pI........7.4:8 | *I see only the past in that* ***b.***. *I see only the* |
| W-pI......17.2:7 | *neutral. I do not see a neutral* ***b.***, *because my* |
| W-pI......22.3:2 | object to another, from one **b.** to another, |
| W-pI......29.5:7 | *God is in that* ***b.***. *God is in that door. God is* |
| W-pI......36.1:8 | to your ego, and therefore not to your **b.**. |
| W-pI......36.3:8 | *My holiness envelops that* ***b.***. *My holiness* |
| W-pI......37.4:4 | *My holiness blesses this* ***b.***. Then close your |
| W-pI......50.2:2 | are cherished to ensure a **b.** identification |
| W-pI......64.2:1 | since this was the purpose of the **b.** itself. |
| W-pI......68.1:3 | hold a grievance is to see yourself as a **b.**. |
| W-pI......68.1:4 | mind and to condemn the **b.** to death. |
| W-pI......72.2:3 | seems to surround the mind with a **b.**, |
| W-pI......72.2:3 | the **b.** that was made to imprison it. The |
| W-pI......72.3:1 | that a **b.** would impose is obvious here, it |
| W-pI......72.3:3 | associated with something a **b.** does? A |
| W-pI......72.4:2 | concerned with what he does in a **b.**. You |
| W-pI......72.4:5 | is God attacked, for if His Son is only a **b.**, |
| W-pI......72.5:1 | If God is a **b.**, what must His plan for |
| W-pI......72.5:5 | In fact, if the **b.** were real, it would be |
| W-pI......72.5:6 | that you hold insists that the **b.** is real. It |
| W-pI......72.5:8 | is. It reinforces your belief that he is a **b.**, |
| W-pI......72.6:2 | you. God made you a **b.**. Very well. Let us |
| W-pI......72.6:5 | As a **b.**, do not let yourself be deprived of |
| W-pI......72.6:5 | yourself be deprived of what the **b.** offers. |
| W-pI......72.6:8 | The **b.** is your only savior. It is the death |
| W-pI......72.7:2 | see. Some hate the **b.**, and try to hurt and |
| W-pI......72.7:3 | Others love the **b.**, and try to glorify and |
| W-pI......72.7:4 | while the **b.** stands at the center of your |
| W-pI......72.8:4 | yourself in a **b.** and the truth outside you, |
| W-pI......72.9:2 | It is the **b.** that is outside us, and is not |
| W-pI......72.9:3 | without a **b.** is to be in our natural state. |
| W-pI......72.9:5 | To see our Self as separate from the **b.** is |
| W-pI......76.3:4 | are alone unless another **b.** is with you. |
| W-pI......76.4:4 | Protect the **b.**, and you will be saved. |
| W-pI......76.5:2 | The **b.** is endangered by the mind that |
| W-pI......76.5:3 | The **b.** suffers just in order that the mind |
| W-pI......76.5:6 | is from this your "laws" would save the **b.** |
| W-pI......76.5:7 | body. It is for this you think you are a **b.**. |
| W-pI......78.6:4 | will regard his **b.** with its flaws and better |
| W-pI......84.1:4 | die. I am not a **b.**. I would recognize my |
| W-pI......91.5:2 | you instruct yourself that you are not a **b.**. |
| W-pI......91.5:5 | You can escape the **b.** if you choose. You |
| W-pI......91.6:4 | *But I am not a* ***b.***. *What am I?* The question |
| W-pI......91.6:9 | The belief you are a **b.** calls for correction, |
| W-pI......91.7:1 | If you are not a **b.**, what are you? You |
| W-pI......91.7:2 | to replace the image of a **b.** in your mind. |
| W-pI......91.7:3 | put your faith in, as you lift it from the **b.**. |
| W-pI......91.8:1 | If you are not a **b.**, what are you? Ask this |
| W-pI......91.9:3 | is associated with the belief you are a **b.**, a |
| W-pI......92.1:3 | tied up with the **b.** and its eyes and brain. |
| W-pI......92.1:5 | come from the conviction you are a **b.**, |
| W-pI......96.1:1 | and evil, loving and hating, mind and **b.**. |
| W-pI......96.3:4 | A mind and **b.** cannot both exist. Make |
| W-pI......96.3:7 | the **b.** must be meaningless to your reality |
| W-pI......96.4:4 | perceive itself within a **b.** it confuses with |
| W-pI....114.1:3 | *No* ***b.*** *can contain my spirit, nor impose on* |
| W-pI....128.4:1 | Let nothing that relates to **b.** thoughts |
| W-pI....135.4:4 | **b.** has such frailty that constant care and |
| W-pI....135.4:5 | **b.** falters and must fail to serve the Son of |
| W-pI....135.5:1 | Yet it is not the **b.** that can fear, nor be a |
| W-pI....135.6:3 | Yet what endowed the **b.** with the right to |
| W-pI....135.6:4 | the **b.** all the functions that you see in it, |
| W-pI....135.7:1 | The **b.** is in need of no defense. This |
| W-pI....135.8:2 | The **b.**, valueless and hardly worth the |
| W-pI....135.9:1 | the **b.** and you have attacked your mind. |
| W-pI....135.9:2 | which you think the **b.** must be saved. |
| W-pI....135.9:4 | And you will impose upon the **b.** all the |
| W-pI.135.10:1 | and the **b.** will respond with health when |
| W-pI.135.12:2 | the **b.** in its plans until it recognizes this is |
| W-pI.135.12:3 | as true, then is it healed, and lets the **b.** go |
| W-pI.135.13:1 | Enslavement of the **b.** to the plans the |
| W-pI.135.13:1 | sets up to save itself must make the **b.** sick |
| W-pI....136.8:2 | it proves the **b.** is not separate from you, |
| W-pI....136.8:3 | You suffer pain because the **b.** does, and |
| W-pI....136.9:1 | Thus is the **b.** stronger than the truth, |
| W-pI....136.9:2 | **b.** is more powerful than everlasting life, |
| W-pI.136.16:4 | that it tried to authorize the **b.** to obey. |
| W-pI.136.17:1 | Now is the **b.** healed, because the source |
| W-pI.136.17:2 | well by this: The **b.** should not feel at all. |
| W-pI.136.17:4 | at all is in the mind to what the **b.** does. |
| W-pI.136.18:1 | upon the **b.** by the purposes you gave to it |
| W-pI.136.18:2 | strength the **b.** has will always be enough |
| W-pI.136.19:2 | a bodily identity which will attack the **b.**, |
| W-pI.136.20:3 | *I really am, for I mistook my* ***b.*** *for myself.* |
| W-pI.136.20:5 | *truth. But I am not a* ***b.***. *And my mind cannot* |
| W-pI....137.2:3 | the **b.** final power to make the separation |
| W-pI....137.3:6 | he sees the **b.** has no power to attack the |
| W-pI....137.6:3 | **b.** seems to be more solid and more stable |
| W-pI....137.8:6 | within a **b.** free to join with other minds, |
| W-pI....140.1:2 | is but what will make the **b.** "better." |
| W-pI....140.1:3 | mind, it sees no separation from the **b.**, |
| W-pI....151.9:3 | **b.** mean to Him Who knows the glory of |
| W-pI.151.12:2 | It stands beyond the **b.** and the world, |
| W-pI....152.5:2 | alterations in conditions of the **b.** and the |
| W-pI....152.6:4 | mind that lives within a **b.** that must die? |
| W-pI....157.6:1 | Your **b.** will be sanctified today, its only |
| W-pI....158.7:2 | It does not look upon a **b.**, and mistake it |
| W-pI....158.7:3 | It beholds a light beyond the **b.**; an idea |
| W-pI....158.8:3 | this you give today: See no one as a **b.**. |
| W-pI....161.5:1 | be the **b.** that we feel limits our freedom, |
| W-pI....161.6:4 | times been urged to look beyond the **b.**, |
| W-pI....161.6:5 | The **b.** is the target for attack, for no one |
| W-pI....161.6:6 | Yet what but mind directs the **b.** to attack |
| W-pI....161.8:1 | a brother as a **b.** sees him as fear's symbol |
| W-pI....162.3:2 | secure, his safety certain and his **b.** healed |
| W-pI....163.4:4 | placed upon the **b.** of the holy Son of God |
| W-pI....167.3:1 | You think that death is of the **b.**. Yet it is |
| W-pI....167.6:3 | It cannot make a **b.**, nor abide within a |
| W-pI....167.6:3 | make a body, nor abide within a **b.**. What |
| W-pI....182.4:2 | The childhood of your **b.**, and its place of |
| W-pI....184.8:4 | it is to his **b.** that you make appeal. His |
| W-pI....184.8:6 | **b.** makes response to what you call him, |
| W-pI....190.3:7 | The **b.** is the Son of God, corruptible in |
| W-pI....192.4:3 | lets the **b.** be perceived as what it is; a |
| W-pI....192.5:1 | without the **b.** cannot make mistakes. It |
| W-pI....192.5:5 | mind of thinking that the **b.** is its home. |
| W-pI....196.1:1 | nor make your **b.** slave to vengeance. You |
| W-pI....196.3:3 | will not believe you are a **b.** to be crucified |
| W-pI.......199.h | I am not a **b.**. I am free. |
| W-pI....199.1:1 | as long as you perceive a **b.** as yourself. |
| W-pI....199.1:2 | The **b.** is a limit. Who would seek for |
| W-pI....199.1:3 | for freedom in a **b.** looks for it where it |
| W-pI....199.1:4 | free when it no longer sees itself as in a **b.**, |
| W-pI....199.3:3 | holds the **b.** dear because it dwells in it, |
| W-pI....199.4:3 | The **b.** disappears, because you have no |
| W-pI....199.4:4 | the **b.** will appear as useful form for what |
| W-pI....199.6:5 | of freedom as its goal, the **b.** serves, and |
| W-pI....199.7:2 | still believe they are enslaved within a **b.**. |
| W-pI....199.8:7 | *I am not a* ***b.***. *I am free. I hear the Voice that* |
| WpI rVI.in.3:3 | *I am not a* ***b.***. *I am free. For I am still as God* |
| W-pI.......201.h | I am not a **b.**. I am free. For I am still as |
| W-pI....201.1:4 | I am not a **b.**. I am free. For I am still as |
| W-pI.......202.h | I am not a **b.**. I am free. For I am still as |
| W-pI....202.1:3 | I am not a **b.**. I am free. For I am still as |
| W-pI.......203.h | I am not a **b.**. I am free. For I am still as |
| W-pI....203.1:3 | I am not a **b.**. I am free. For I am still as |
| W-pI.......204.h | I am not a **b.**. I am free. For I am still as |
| W-pI....204.1:3 | I am not a **b.**. I am free. For I am still as |
| W-pI.......205.h | I am not a **b.**. I am free. For I am still as |
| W-pI....205.1:4 | I am not a **b.**. I am free. For I am still as |
| W-pI.......206.h | I am not a **b.**. I am free. For I am still as |
| W-pI....206.1:4 | I am not a **b.**. I am free. For I am still as |
| W-pI.......207.h | I am not a **b.**. I am free. For I am still as |
| W-pI....207.1:4 | I am not a **b.**. I am free. For I am still as |
| W-pI.......208.h | I am not a **b.**. I am free. For I am still as |
| W-pI....208.1:5 | I am not a **b.**. I am free. For I am still as |
| W-pI.......209.h | I am not a **b.**. I am free. For I am still as |
| W-pI....209.1:6 | I am not a **b.**. I am free. For I am still as |
| W-pI.......210.h | I am not a **b.**. I am free. For I am still as |
| W-pI....210.1:6 | I am not a **b.**. I am free. For I am still as |
| W-pI.......211.h | I am not a **b.**. I am free. For I am still as |
| W-pI....211.1:3 | I am not a **b.**. I am free. For I am still as |
| W-pI.......212.h | I am not a **b.**. I am free. For I am still as |
| W-pI....212.1:5 | I am not a **b.**. I am free. For I am still as |
| W-pI.......213.h | I am not a **b.**. I am free. For I am still as |
| W-pI....213.1:5 | I am not a **b.**. I am free. For I am still as |
| W-pI.......214.h | I am not a **b.**. I am free. For I am still as |
| W-pI....214.1:6 | I am not a **b.**. I am free. For I am still as |
| W-pI.......215.h | I am not a **b.**. I am free. For I am still as |
| W-pI....215.1:5 | I am not a **b.**. I am free. For I am still as |
| W-pI.......216.h | I am not a **b.**. I am free. For I am still as |
| W-pI....216.1:5 | I am not a **b.**. I am free. For I am still as |
| W-pI.......217.h | I am not a **b.**. I am free. For I am still as |
| W-pI....217.1:4 | I am not a **b.**. I am free. For I am still as |
| W-pI.......218.h | I am not a **b.**. I am free. For I am still as |
| W-pI....218.1:4 | I am not a **b.**. I am free. For I am still as |
| W-pI.......219.h | I am not a **b.**. I am free. For I am still as |
| W-pI....219.1:1 | (199) I am not a **b.**. I am free. *I am God's* |
| W-pI....219.1:6 | I am not a **b.**. I am free. For I am still as |
| W-pI.......220.h | I am not a **b.**. I am free. For I am still as |
| W-pI....220.1:4 | I am not a **b.**. I am free. For I am still as |
| W-pII .223.1:1 | unattached, and housed within a **b.**. Now |
| W-pII .228.2:2 | *not left that Source to enter in a* ***b.*** *and to die.* |
| W-pII ..... 4.1:4 | Sin gave the **b.** eyes, for what is there the |
| W-pII ..... 4.2:1 | The **b.** is the instrument the mind made |
| W-pII ..... 4.2:4 | the **b.** serves a different aim for striving. |
| W-pII ..... 4.4:3 | Son of God may play he has become a **b.**, |
| W-pII .........5.h | What Is the **B.**? |

W-pII .....5.1:1 The **b.** is a fence the Son of God imagines
W-pII .....5.1:5 he be certain he remains within the **b.**,
W-pII .....5.2:1 The **b.** will not stay. Yet this he sees as
W-pII .....5.3:1 The **b.** is a dream. Like other dreams it
W-pII .....5.3:4 must the **b.** serve the purpose given it.
W-pII .....5.3:5 that the **b.** will obey by changing what we
W-pII .....5.4:1 The **b.** is the means by which God's Son
W-pII .....5.4:4 Now is the **b.** holy. Now it serves to heal
W-pII .267.1:3 my **b.** with the purpose of forgiveness.
W-pII .277.1:2 *him with the laws I made to rule the* **b.**. *He is*
W-pII .277.1:3 *by which I try to make the* **b.** *more secure. He*
W-pII .278.1:1 If I accept that I am prisoner within a **b.**,
W-pII ....294.h My **b.** is a wholly neutral thing.
W-pII .294.2:1 *My* **b.**, *Father, cannot be Your Son. And*
W-pII ...12.1:1 of limited and separated self, born in a **b.**,
M-5 ....... II.1:4 decisions are of the mind, not of the **b.**. If
M-5 ....... II.1:6 it is the mind and not the **b.** that makes it.
M-5 ....... II.1:7 it depends on the **b.** being the decision
M-5 ....... II.1:8 endow the **b.** with non-mental motivators
M-5 ....... II.2:1 a purpose for which it would use the **b.**, is
M-5 ....... II.3:2 mind, and has nothing to do with the **b.**.
M-5 ..... II.3:12 the insignificance of the **b.** must be an
M-5 ...... III.1:9 **b.** tells them what to do and they obey.
M-12 ......... 1:4 spirit now no longer sees himself as a **b.**,
M-12 ......... 1:4 sees himself as a body, or even as in a **b.**.
M-12 ......... 3:5 are spirit. A **b.** they can see. A voice they
M-12 ......... 3:8 So do God's teachers need a **b.**, for their
M-12 ......... 4:1 of the proper purpose of the **b.**. As they
M-12 ......... 4:6 but because of what they use the **b.** for,
M-12 ......... 5:1 you use the **b.** for it will become to you.
M-12 ......... 5:4 who have it not, and the **b.** becomes holy.
M-12 ......... 5:9 To do that would be to give the **b.** another
M-13 ......... 2:4 world's terms that does not involve the **b.**
M-13 ......... 2:7 Could they mean anything except to a **b.**?
M-13 ......... 2:8 Yet a **b.** cannot evaluate. By seeking after
M-13 ......... 2:9 the mind associates itself with the **b.**,
M-22 ......... 3:2 The idea that a **b.** can be sick is a central
M-22 ......... 3:3 This thought gives the **b.** autonomy,
M-22 ......... 3:4 If the **b.** could be sick Atonement would
M-22 ......... 3:5 A **b.** that can order a mind to do as it sees
M-22 ......... 3:7 The **b.** has become lord of the mind. How
M-22 ......... 3:8 to the Holy Spirit unless the **b.** is killed?
M-22 ......... 4:5 He overlooks the mind *and* **b.**, seeing only
M-22 ......... 5:3 ego, and has thus confused him with a **b.**.
M-23 ....... 3:10 the **b.** has transcended limitation. Would
M-24 ......... 1:2 the idea of birth into a **b.** has no meaning
M-24 ......... 2:8 idea that life and the **b.** are not the same.
M-26 ......... 3:8 the **b.** would not be long maintained.
M-26 ......... 3:9 Those who have laid the **b.** down merely
M-27 ......... 5:1 rooted in the belief that God's Son is a **b.**.
M-28 ......... 1:6 dream in which the **b.** functions perfectly,
C-4............. 5:5 for only if there were a **b.** is sin possible.
C-4............. 5:9 Only the **b.** makes the world seem real,
C-5............. 2:3 within a **b.** that appeared to hold his self
P-2........ IV.4:3 but make the **b.** real in their own minds,
P-2...... IV.11:3 **b.** is not cured. It is merely recognized as
S-3........... I.1:4 Healing the **b.** is impossible, and this is
S-3........... I.1:5 The **b.** yet must die, and so its healing but
S-3........... I.3:1 The **b.** can be healed as an effect of true
S-3........... I.3:5 For he has damned his **b.** as his prison,
S-3........... I.4:5 him the **b.** may become his chosen home,
S-3....... II.1:10 has come for usefulness of **b.** functioning.
S-3......... II.2:1 **b.** has been kindly used to help the Son of
S-3......... II.2:2 We thank the **b.**, then, for all the service it
S-3........ III.1:1 False healing heals the **b.** in a part, but
S-3........ III.2:3 These forms may heal the **b.**, and indeed
S-3........ III.2:6 of the **b.** can be done by this because, in
S-3........ III.3:1 magic phrase by which the **b.** seems to be

## body's 96

T-1...... VII.2:5 to do this is the **b.** only true usefulness.
T-4......... V.4:2 since the **b.** vulnerability is its own best
T-8...... VIII.1:8 health. The **b.** condition lies solely in your
T-15...... XI.7:1 are joined without the **b.** interference,
T-18..... VII.7:2 withdrawn the **b.** value from your mind.
T-18..... VII.7:9 and the **b.** activities return to occupy your
T-18...... IX.2:4 are seen only through the **b.** eyes. Its
T-18...... IX.4:6 The **b.** eyes will never look on it. Yet they
T-19 ...... I.11:5 It sees not through the **b.** eyes, nor looks
T-19 ...... I.12:7 holiness you see, not through the **b.** eyes,
T19.... IV.B.3:5 you sacrifice the hope of the **b.** pleasure; it
T19.. IV.B.13:7 it teaches that the **b.** pleasure is happiness
T19.. IV.B.16:3 disciples chant the **b.** praise continually,
T-20 ....... II.1:4 brother to you, and to attract his **b.** eyes?
T-20 ....... II.5:1 You look still with the **b.** eyes, and they
T-20 ....... II.8:3 You will not see it with the **b.** eyes. Yet all
T-20 ..... VI.3:6 the sunlight and happy in the **b.** darkness
T-20 ... VIII.6:5 What can the **b.** eyes perceive, with power
T-21 .... VII.7:5 whether to see him through the **b.** eyes, or
T-21 .. VII.10:8 the **b.** eyes and change what you desire.
T-22 ..... III.1:7 literally. If it is not the **b.** sight, it *must* be
T-22 ..... III.3:4 The **b.** eyes behold it as solid granite, so
T-22 ..... III.4:3 Everything the **b.** eyes can see is a mistake
T-22 ..... III.4:7 believing the **b.** freedom is their own.
T-22 ..... III.5:3 The **b.** eyes see only form. They cannot
T-22 ..... III.6:4 For this the **b.** eyes are perfect means, but
T-22 ..... III.6:5 See how the **b.** eyes rest on externals and
T-22 ..... III.8:2 kept from you by what the **b.** eyes can see.
T-22 ...... V.5:3 the **b.** eyes it looks like an enormous solid
T-22 ..... VI.2:1 to contrive ways to achieve the **b.** freedom
T-23 ........ I.5:3 It *is* forgotten in the **b.** life, and if you
T-23 ..... IV.9:4 nor could he value the **b.** offerings. The
T-25 ....... II.1:1 that what the **b.** eyes perceive fills you
T-26 ........ I.3:3 perception of yourself the **b.** loss would
T-26 ...... I.4:10 song, and sight of him replace the **b.** eyes.
T-27 ..... IV.5:4 Just as the **b.** witnesses are but the senses
T-27 ..... VI.4:7 And for each witness to the **b.** death He
T-27 ... VIII.3:1 The **b.** serial adventures, from the time of
T-28 ........ I.5:7 history of all the **b.** past is hidden there.
T-28 ...... V.4:2 and this the world the **b.** eyes perceive.
T-28 ...... V.5:8 Let not the **b.** ears and eyes perceive these
T-29 ..... II.10:6 His **b.** nothingness releases yours from
T-29 .... VII.4:1 **b.** betterment is cast as major beneficiary,
W-pI..... 15.1:4 the function you have given your **b.** eyes.
W-pI..... 30.5:1 it does not depend on the **b.** eyes at all.
W-pI..... 59.3:7 when I try to see through the **b.** eyes. Yet
W-pI..... 64.1:4 It is this the **b.** eyes look upon.
W-pI..... 64.2:1 Nothing the **b.** eyes seem to see can be
W-pI..... 72.4:3 in freeing him from the **b.** limitations.
W-pI..... 72.5:4 The **b.** apparent reality makes this view of
W-pI..... 72.8:4 from your awareness by the **b.** limitations
W-pI..... 76.5:4 The **b.** suffering is a mask the mind holds
W-pI..... 76.8:2 of the **b.** protection in innumerable ways.
W-pI..... 78.7:4 The **b.** eyes are closed, and as you think of
W-pI..... 91.3:3 You do not doubt that the **b.** eyes can see.
W-pI..... 91.6:3 *The* **b.** *eyes do not perceive the light. But I am*
W-pI..... 92.1:5 you are a body, and the **b.** eyes can see.
W-pI..... 92.2:1 You also believe the **b.** brain can think. If
W-pI..... 92.2:4 foolish than to believe the **b.** eyes can see;
W-pI..... 92.3:3 weakness that sees through the **b.** eyes,
W-pI..... 92.9:1 that the **b.** eyes provide for self-deception.
W-pI... 92.10:4 closing the **b.** eyes and asking truth to
W-pI..... 96.5:3 itself and hiding in the **b.** frail support.
W-pI... 108.2:1 possible is not the light the **b.** eyes behold
W-pI. 124.11:2 a sight too holy for the **b.** eyes to see. And
W-pI... 125.9:2 and free your vision from the **b.** eyes.
W-pI. 135.10:2 This is the **b.** only real defense. Yet is this
W-pI. 136.18:3 The **b.** health is fully guaranteed, because
W-pI... 151.2:2 what is shown you through the **b.** eyes.
W-pI... 151.7:2 nor what his **b.** mouth says to your ears,
W-pI... 151.8:4 unheeding of the **b.** witnesses before the
W-pI... 161.9:1 This do the **b.** eyes behold in one whom
W-pI. 161.10:4 the witnesses your **b.** eyes call forth.
W-pI... 187.2:2 your **b.** eyes will not perceive it yours. Yet
W-pI... 199.6:3 The **b.** purpose now is unambiguous. And
W-pI. 200.10:5 with the **b.** eyes but serving for an instant
W-pII ....270.h I will not use the **b.** eyes today.
W-pII . 270.1:1 *power to translate all that the* **b.** *eyes behold*
W-pII ..... 6.2:4 by anything the **b.** eyes perceive. For
M-4 ........... 1:2 They do not look alike to the **b.** eyes, they
M-8 ........... 1:6 What the **b.** eyes behold is only conflict.
M-8 ........... 3:7 outward, and it sends the **b.** eyes to find it
M-8 ........... 3:8 The **b.** eyes will never see except through
M-8 ........... 4:3 The mind classifies what the **b.** eyes bring
M-8 ........... 6:1 **b.** eyes will continue to see differences.
M-8 ........... 6:3 and the **b.** eyes will report their changed
M-12 ......... 4:2 and more certain that the **b.** function is
M-12 ......... 4:4 of God, of what the **b.** purpose really is;
M-12 ......... 5:7 that are responsible for the **b.** condition.
M-18 ......... 3:3 The **b.** eyes now "see"; its ears alone can
M-19 ......... 3:2 is the lens which, held before the **b.** eyes,
C-4 ............ 2:1 The **b.** eyes are therefore not the means
P-3........... I.3:3 for seeing is not limited to the **b.** eyes.
S-3........... I.2:1 The **b.** cause is unforgiveness of the Son
S-3.......... II.6:1 False healing rests upon the **b.** cure,
S-3........ III.6:3 The **b.** healing will occur because its cause

## body-identification 1

T-1 ........ I.29:3 deny **b.** and affirm spirit-identification.

## bolster 2

W-pI .. 103.3:4 **B.** this expectation frequently throughout
M-25 ......... 5:7 he will **b.** his "power's" uncertainties with

## bolsters 1

T-27 ........ I.7:1 that **b.** all the rest and helps them paint

## bolt 1

T-26 ....... II.8:5 and every **b.** and barrier that seems to

## bolts 2

T-25 ... VIII.6:4 to strike them dead with lightning **b.** torn
T-28 .. VII.5:10 lock the windows and make fast the **b.**.

## bond 2

W-pI .. 159.4:3 It is the **b.** by which the giver and receiver
W-pI .. 183.1:4 thus are they united in a **b.** to which they

## bondage 15

T-10 ..... IV.4:2 of freedom, but yours are the laws of **b.**.
T-10 ..... IV.4:3 Since freedom and **b.** are irreconcilable,
T-15 ....... X.9:3 between total freedom and total **b.**, for
T-16 ..... VI.2:2 in **b.** is to separate yourself from it. For
T-16 ..... VI.2:3 union in separation, nor for freedom in **b.**
T-28 ..... IV.4:5 and you are kept in **b.** to his dreams. And
W-pI .... 31.5:2 will not yield to it, and put yourself in **b.**.
W-pI .. 183.9:2 You can escape all **b.** of the world, and
W-pI .. 191.1:1 declaration of release from **b.** of the world
W-pI .. 193.6:2 their power to release all minds from **b.**?
W-pI .. 194.5:2 the **b.** of illusions where it runs its pitiless
W-pI .. 196.4:1 us from **b.** to the state of perfect freedom.
W-pI .. 199.7:3 can make use of your escape from **b.**, to
WpI.rVI.in.1:4 and to the world from every form of **b.**,
M-26 ....... 3:10 helpers who are still in **b.** and still asleep,

## bone 3

T-24 ....... V.4:8 from the **b.** and sightless holes for eyes, is
W-pI .. 107.8:2 are not made of flesh and blood and **b.**,
W-pI 161.12:3 you have seen as merely flesh and **b.**, and

## bones 4

T19 .IV.A.13:2 bring you word of **b.** and skin and flesh.
T-25 ....... II.7:2 Mind that thought it, not in flesh and **b.**,
T-28 ....... V.7:5 where terror rises from the **b.** of death.
W-pI .. 101.3:3 more than **b.** before salvation is appeased

## bony 1

W-pI .. 189.5:4 in death's sharp-pointed, **b.** fingers. If you

## boon 1

W-pI .. 101.3:3 before it grants the welcome **b.** of death

## borderland 6

| | |
|---|---|
| T-26 III.h | The **B.** |
| T-26 III.2:1 | is a **b.** of thought that stands between this |
| T-26 III.2:4 | This **b.** is just beyond the gate of Heaven. |
| T-26 III.3:6 | Salvation is a **b.** where place and time and |
| T-26 V.11:8 | This is the **b.** between the worlds, the |
| W-pI 99.2:3 | the **b.** between the truth and the illusion. |

## born 106

*See also* heaven-born

| | |
|---|---|
| T-5 IV.2:3 | It does not die; it was merely never **b.**. |
| T-5 IV.2:5 | that continues has already been **b.**. It will |
| T-7 VII.7:3 | teaching it with infinite patience **b.** of the |
| T-7 IX.6:9 | only the whole can be **b.** of Its Wholeness. |
| T-8 VI.9:2 | being **b.** of my knowledge of myself and |
| T-9 VI.7:4 | in perfect communication **b.** of perfect |
| T-11 VI.5:5 | the Son of God is **b.** of sacrifice and pain. |
| T-13 in.2:5 | Children are **b.** into it through pain and |
| T-13 VI.3:5 | To be **b.** again is to let the past go, and |
| T-13 VI.4:8 | between them, to free you to be **b.** again. |
| T-13 VI.5:1 | his past, and so perceive him as **b.** again. |
| T-13 X.5:2 | but with each one each day be **b.** again. A |
| T-14 III.3:4 | conviction **b.** of the Love of God and of |
| T-15 I.9:7 | this holy instant wherein holiness was **b.** |
| T-15 III.8:4 | **b.** in you in honor of Him Whose host |
| T-15 VII.9:3 | alliances, **b.** of the fear of loneliness and |
| T-15 X.3:4 | union is the only gift that I was **b.** to give. |
| T-15 XI.7:2 | The Prince of Peace was **b.** to re-establish |
| T-15 XI.7:5 | The lesson I was **b.** to teach, and still |
| T-15 XI.10:1 | will soon be **b.** from the time of Christ. I |
| T-15 XI.10:10 | Accept the holy instant as this year is **b.**, |
| T-16 V.4:1 | **b.** of the hidden wish for special love from |
| T-17 II.3:7 | **b.** of the new perspective he has learned, |
| T19 IV.C.10:6 | **b.** in time but nourished in eternity. |
| T19 IV.D.8:7 | **b.** of complete forgiveness of his illusions, |
| T-20 VI.8:7 | In that unholy instant time was **b.**, and |
| T-21 III.8:5 | follow this decision are also **b.** of faith. |
| T-21 IV.4:1 | limited and incomplete, yet **b.** within you. |
| T-22 in.4:10 | **b.** into a holy relationship can never end. |
| T-22 III.9:1 | A holy relationship, however newly **b.**, |
| T-23 I.8:7 | **b.** of nothing cannot win reality through |
| T-23 I.12:4 | War is the condition in which fear is **b.**, |
| T-23 II.12:10 | for love, **b.** of your enmity to your brother |
| T-24 VII.2:2 | and creating, **b.** and unborn as yet, still in |
| T-24 VII.7:3 | from; not **b.** of size nor place nor time, |
| T-26 I.7:7 | **B.** again each instant, untouched by time, |
| T-27 V.1:4 | nature to extend itself the instant it is **b.**. |
| T-27 V.1:5 | is **b.** the instant it is offered and received. |
| T-27 V.3:2 | each one is **b.** into this world as witness to |
| T-27 VIII.1:3 | bodies, **b.** into the world outside the body |
| T-28 I.11:4 | **B.** out of sharing, there can be no pause in |
| T-28 VI.2:4 | It is not **b.** and does not die. It can but |
| T-28 VI.6:6 | "I will," though in that promise he was **b.**. |
| T-29 VI.4:2 | away. You were not **b.** to die. You cannot |
| T-30 II.1:10 | had but waited for your blessing to be **b.**. |
| T-30 II.3:2 | For thus was hatred **b.** into the world, |
| T-30 II.3:7 | thanks, for it is by your will that it was **b.**. |
| T-30 III.6:5 | Thoughts are not **b.** and cannot die. They |
| T-30 III.7:3 | An unremembered thought is **b.** again to |
| T-31 I.13:4 | Now is he **b.** again to you, and you are |
| T-31 I.13:4 | again to you, and you are **b.** again to him, |
| T-31 V.7:5 | hot with hatred and distortions **b.** of fear. |
| T-31 V.7:9 | made within the world, **b.** in its shadow, |
| T-31 V.17:8 | Yet in this learning is salvation **b.**. And |
| T-31 VII.4:4 | **B.** as a gift for someone not perceived to |
| T-31 VII.7:5 | guilty thoughts and concepts **b.** of fear. |
| T-31 VII.10:5 | the unremembered and the not yet **b.**. For |
| T-31 VIII.1:2 | of God he is a body, **b.** in what must die, |
| W-pI 75.2:5 | It is a new era, in which a new world is **b.**. |
| W-pI 101.4:4 | the vicious wishes in which sin is **b.**. If sin |
| W-pI 107.7:3 | note of certainty that has been **b.** of truth. |
| W-pI 108.1:3 | is light except the resolution, **b.** of peace, |
| W-pI 109.1:2 | of all the turmoil **b.** of clashing dreams. |
| W-pI 109.2:6 | in which the Son of God is **b.** again, to |
| W-pI 109.6:2 | The world is **b.** again each time you rest, |
| W-pI 109.9:5 | Thoughts were **b.** and where they rest. |
| W-pI 122.8:3 | as ancient truths, forever newly **b.**, arise |
| W-pI 127.11:1 | The world in infancy is newly **b.**. And we |
| W-pI 130.3:4 | can be real in blind imaginings of panic **b.** |
| W-pI 135.20:2 | the ancient plan, begun when time was **b.** |
| W-pI 159.4:1 | is the miracle in which all miracles are **b.**. |
| W-pI 167.5:7 | be. As they were **b.**, so will they then give |
| W-pI 188.7:4 | as well, for they were **b.** within your mind |
| W-pI 188.7:4 | your mind, as yours was **b.** in God's. They |
| W-pI 191.9:1 | and devastated dreams, **b.** but to die, to |
| W-pI 192.7:3 | understand is but confusion **b.** of error. |
| W-pI 192.8:1 | can be **b.** again in Christ but him who has |
| W-pI 198.6:4 | His words are **b.** in God, and come to you |
| W-pII 230.2:3 | *The peace in which Your Son was **b.** into* |
| W-pII 2.1:3 | that have been **b.** in time will end as well. |
| W-pII 2.4:5 | Earth is being **b.** again in new perspective. |
| W-pII 3.1:2 | It is **b.** of error, and it has not left its |
| W-pII 3.2:5 | Here was perception **b.**, for knowledge |
| W-pII 3.3:1 | of illusion have been **b.** instead. And now |
| W-pII 5.3:2 | revert to fear, where every dream is **b.**. |
| W-pII 276.1:4 | with Him, because in this His Son was **b.**. |
| W-pII 303.h | The holy Christ is **b.** in me today. |
| W-pII 303.1:2 | be still with me while Heaven's Son is **b.**. |
| W-pII 303.1:6 | here, for He is **b.** again in me today. |
| W-pII 306.1:4 | **b.** anew into a world of mercy and of care; |
| W-pII 10.2:4 | There it was **b.**, and there it ends as well. |
| W-pII 12.1:1 | of limited and separated self, **b.** in a body, |
| W-pII 340.1:6 | *was **b.** into this world but to achieve this day,* |
| W-pII 13.5:4 | up, to show that what is **b.** can never die, |
| W-pII 345.1:7 | *alone today, which, **b.** of true forgiveness,* |
| M-4 1:6 | **b.** in the holy relationship toward which |
| M-14 2:2 | the home in which forgiveness is **b.**, and |
| M-14 2:4 | **b.** where sin was made and guilt seemed |
| M-27 1:2 | it not madness to think of life as being **b.**, |
| M-27 1:4 | world that all things in it are **b.** only to die |
| M-27 6:6 | And in death are all illusions **b.**. What |
| M-27 6:7 | What can be **b.** of death and still have life |
| M-27 6:8 | But what is **b.** of God and still can die? |
| C-1 3:3 | of God, it is eternal and was never **b.**. |
| C-5 5:6 | whom you knew since you were **b.**, for |
| S-3 I.1:5 | to dust, where it was **b.** and will return. |

## borne 2

| | |
|---|---|
| T-24 VI.12:4 | wearisome and tedious, too heavy to be **b.** |
| W-pI 132.5:4 | text, and must be **b.** in mind if you would |

## borrowed 3

| | |
|---|---|
| T-9 IV.9:1 | The ego literally lives on **b.** time, and its |
| T-9 IV.9:2 | the ego's time is "**b.**" from your eternity. |
| T-17 IV.11:8 | **b.** from eternity and set in time for you. |

## borrowing 1

| | |
|---|---|
| W-pI 98.4:2 | too, will join with us, and, **b.** our certainty |

## Both 12

*both*

| | |
|---|---|
| T-13 VIII.4:2 | from Either, being in the Mind of **B.**, and |
| T-14 VIII.2:4 | there that is not equally worthy of **B.**, but |
| T-14 VIII.2:15 | Father and the Son, as **B.** would have it be |
| T-21 VI.3:2 | Only were **B.** in bodies could this be. Nor |
| T-22 I.11:9 | as **B.** are drawn to every holy relationship, |
| T-23 I.10:2 | Him and of yourself is home to **B.** of You, |
| T-29 V.1:4 | Where **B.** abide are They remembered, |
| T-29 V.1:4 | Both abide are They remembered, **B.**. And |
| T-31 IV.10:3 | in Their Oneness **B.** are kept complete. |
| W-pI 73.3:4 | Creation is the Will of **B.** together. Would |
| W-pI 198.10:4 | Be kind to **B.**, as you forgive the trespasses |
| C-6 4:3 | God and also for you, being joined with **B.** |

## both 356

*Both*

| | |
|---|---|
| T-1 I.9:3 | more love **b.** to the giver *and* the receiver. |
| T-1 I.13:1 | Miracles are **b.** beginnings and endings, |
| T-1 I.24:1 | yourself, and can therefore abolish **b.**. *You* |
| T-1 I.38:2 | He recognizes **b.** God's creations and your |
| T-1 II.1:7 | **b.** are experienced there. Consciousness is |
| T-1 II.6:4 | the giver and receiver **b.** emerge farther |
| T-1 III.6:3 | that the perception of **b.** must be accurate |
| T-1 III.6:6 | as you perceive **b.** so you will do to both. |
| T-1 III.6:6 | as you perceive both so you will do to **b.**. |
| T-1 V.1:1 | that **b.** are learning aids for facilitating a |
| T-1 VI.3:6 | meaningless as time. **B.** are merely beliefs. |
| T-1 VII.3:11 | becomes apparent to **b.** giver and receiver |
| T-2 I.2:7 | includes **b.** the creation of the Son by God |
| T-2 II.7:8 | knowing yourself as **b.** a brother and a |
| T-2 III.2:3 | exist. **B.** the separation and the fear are |
| T-2 V.10:3 | The charity that is accorded him is **b.** an |
| T-2 V.10:4 | **B.** of these perceptions clearly imply their |
| T-2 V.10:7 | are shortening the suffering of **b.** of you. |
| T-2 V.A.11:3 | I will arrange **b.** time and space to adjust |
| T-2 VI.5:6 | In **b.** cases, the mind and the behavior are |
| T-2 VII.3:1 | **B.** miracles and fear come from thoughts. |
| T-3 III.6:4 | preceded **b.** perception and time, and will |
| T-3 IV.7:5 | I demonstrated **b.** the powerlessness of |
| T-3 VII.1:5 | **B.** are cornerstones for systems of belief |
| T-4 I.12:1 | can do everything for the salvation of **b.**. |
| T-4 II.2:3 | Their interaction is a process that alters **b.** |
| T-4 II.5:5 | effort to become **b.** harmless and helpful, |
| T-4 III.9:5 | you **b.** *have* everything and *are* everything. |
| T-4 IV.2:9 | and see in **b.** the glorious creations of a |
| T-4 V.2:5 | of God, because **b.** are threatening to it. |
| T-5 II.6:1 | Holy Spirit calls you **b.** to remember and |
| T-5 II.8:5 | **B.** Heaven and earth are in you, because |
| T-5 II.8:5 | you, because the call of **b.** is in your mind. |
| T-5 III.2:10 | This dissociation is healed in **b.** of you as |
| T-5 III.3:2 | They must **b.** be in your mind, because |
| T-5 III.5:2 | **B.** time and delay are meaningless in |
| T-5 V.1:5 | But again, remember that **b.** are in you. |
| T-5 V.8:3 | will affect **b.** behavior and experience. |
| T-5 VI.1:5 | Yet your election is **b.** free and alterable. |
| T-5 VII.3:5 | It reflects **b.** the ego's need to separate, |
| T-6 II.3:7 | of **b.** yourself and your brothers. The |
| T-6 II.5:2 | it in others, thus strengthening it in **b.**. |
| T-6 II.5:3 | Instead of anger this arouses love for **b.**, |
| T-6 II.6:3 | That is **b.** where you are and what you are |
| T-6 II.11:3 | idea of return **b.** necessary and difficult. |
| T-6 IV.5:1 | that its "enemy" can end them **b.** merely |
| T-6 IV.9:5 | with **b.** a Guide to find it and a means to |
| T-6 V.B.3:10 | to **b.** as if what you do believe is not true. |
| T-6 V.B.4:6 | conflicting messages and accepting **b.**. |
| T-6 V.B.5:3 | If you teach **b.**, which you will surely do as |
| T-6 V.B.5:3 | you will surely do as long as you accept **b.**, |
| T-6 V.C.10:7 | upon the being which you **b.** *have* and *are.* |
| T-7 II.1:3 | the Kingdom itself obscure to **b.** of you. |
| T-7 II.2:2 | This places you **b.** within the Kingdom, |
| T-7 IV.1:3 | **B.**, therefore, come from the same Source, |
| T-7 IV.6:6 | God has given you a gift that you **b.** *have* |
| T-7 IV.7:8 | strengthens the Holy Spirit in **b.** of you, |
| T-7 V.2:2 | the body can **b.** communicate and create, |
| T-7 V.2:7 | If you teach **b.** sickness *and* healing, you |
| T-7 V.2:7 | are **b.** a poor teacher and a poor learner. |
| T-7 VI.13:7 | itself with **b.** its Creator and its creations, |
| T-7 VII.5:4 | not extending the gift you **b.** *have* and *are,* |
| T-7 IX.7:3 | reflections of **b.** your proper identification |
| T-7 X.2:1 | is surely clear that you can **b.** accept into |
| T-7 X.4:5 | and one which is **b.** fearful and desirable. |
| T-7 XI.7:5 | But you can *know* **b.**. Being is known by |
| T-8 I.6:4 | that **b.** are teaching you about yourself. |
| T-8 I.6:5 | Your reality is unaffected by **b.**, but if you |
| T-8 I.6:5 | unaffected by both, but if you listen to **b.**, |
| T-8 V.4:3 | The truth in **b.** of us is beyond the ego. |
| T-8 V.4:4 | I share this confidence for **b.** of us and all |
| T-8 V.5:9 | Do not attempt to hold on to **b.**, or you |
| T-8 VI.5:12 | only the decision to be unworthy of **b.**. |
| T-8 VII.12:2 | do **b.** simultaneously with the same thing |
| T-8 VII.12:5 | that blocks the understanding of **b.**. |
| T-8 VIII.2:2 | of **b.** health and sickness meaningful. The |
| T-9 I.8:5 | even though many may seek **b.**. Can you |
| T-9 V.1:6 | is real for **b.** himself and the patient, but |
| T-9 V.7:1 | **B.** forms of the ego's approach, then, |
| T-9 VII.4:1 | in your mind, and they cannot **b.** be true. |
| T-9 VIII.6:5 | since **b.** are untrue and are therefore on |
| T-10 in.1:2 | Time and eternity are **b.** in your mind, |
| T-10 I.3:1 | dismiss **b.** together if you discovered that |
| T-10 V.14:2 | As long as **b.** appear to you to be desirable |
| T-10 V.14:8 | Time and eternity cannot **b.** be real, |

T-11 in.1:2 examine the evidence on **b.** sides fairly,
T-11 II.1:3 The Son of God *has* **b.** Father and Son,
T-11 II.1:3 and Son, because he *is* **b.** Father and Son.
T-11 VI.2:5 because the word is used **b.** for awareness
T-11 VII.2:8 For if you perceive **b.** good and evil, you
T-11 VII.2:8 you are accepting **b.** the false and the true
T-11 VIII.5:6 His answer is **b.** many and one, as long as
T-12 I.6:2 Gratitude is due him for **b.** his loving
T-12 I.6:2 **b.** are capable of bringing love into your
T-12 III.2:4 and are making his error real to **b.** of you.
T-12 III.4:5 so is to deny yourself and impoverish **b.**.
T-12 VII.6:7 are the same because you want **b.** of them.
T-12 VII.12:2 manifest it you will see it **b.** without and
T-13 III.7:2 Here is **b.** his pain and his healing, for the
T-13 VII.2:2 *You cannot see **b.** worlds,* for each of them
T-13 VII.2:4 **B.** are not true, yet either one will seem as
T-13 XI.1:2 that **b.** opponents in the war are real.
T-14 III.2:2 that guilt and guiltlessness are **b.** of value,
T-14 III.2:3 for without **b.** you do not see yourself as
T-14 III.4:5 be reconciled and cannot **b.** be true. You
T-14 IV.1:7 is God the Father, Who is **b.** First and One
T-14 IV.10:2 making **b.** unable to communicate,
T-14 VI.4:3 that you can have them **b.** is meaningless.
T-14 VII.1:2 ignorance are yours, but not **b.**. Opposites
T-14 VII.4:3 which cannot coexist are **b.** maintained. If
T-14 VII.4:5 them **b.** alive and equal in their reality.
T-14 VII.4:7 You cannot have them **b.**, for each denies
T-14 VII.6:10 when **b.** of You together look on them.
T-14 X.11:5 teach you **b.** his love and his call for love.
T-14 XI.15:1 power of God, from which they **b.** arise, is
T-15 I.4:12 all too frequently succeeds, in doing **b.**, by
T-15 IV.6:6 your mind is open, **b.** to receive and give.
T-15 V.6:4 them, but you have also judged against **b.**.
T-15 VI.5:2 For gain and loss are **b.** accepted, and so
T-15 VIII.6:2 It is His holy function to accept them **b.**,
T-15 IX.2:4 And **b.** are nothing more than attempts to
T-15 X.1:4 is the Holy Spirit's function to use them **b.**
T-15 X.7:5 to be **b.** destroyer and destroyed in part,
T-15 X.9:8 In you are **b.** the question and the answer;
T-16 I.6:8 you how to meet **b.** without losing either.
T-16 II.7:2 are **b.** being brought into your awareness.
T-16 III.5:3 He is **b.** God and you, as you are God and
T-16 III.5:5 He protected **b.** your creations and you
T-16 IV.5:3 always at the price of making **b.** illusions.
T-16 IV.11:13 In His link with you lie **b.** His inability to
T-16 V.5:2 **b.** the ego and the Holy Spirit accept it.
T-16 V.6:2 imagined "best" of **b.** worlds has merely
T-16 V.6:2 worlds has merely led to fantasies of **b.**,
T-16 V.8:3 Where **b.** partners see this special self in
T-17 I.6:6 And you are holding **b.** of you away from
T-17 I.6:7 to truth what was denied by **b.** of you.
T-17 III.2:4 This is why you see in **b.** what is not there,
T-17 III.2:4 and make of **b.** the slaves of vengeance.
T-17 IV.12:9 **B.** of them. One is a tiny picture, hard to
T-17 IV.14:4 of **b.** pictures can at last occur. And each
T-17 IV.14:5 when **b.** are seen in relation to each other.
T-18 I.3:3 Fear is **b.** a fragmented and fragmenting
T-18 I.10:5 He loves you **b.**, equally and as one. And
T-18 II.2:5 **b.** of the ego's inability to tolerate reality,
T-18 V.3:6 The means and purpose **b.** belong to Him.
T-18 V.6:7 it will come to **b.** at the request of either.
T-18 V.7:1 pay his debt by bringing happiness to **b.**.
T-18 V.7:6 *may descend on us, and keep us **b.** in peace.*
T-18 VI.11:6 it. And **b.** become whole, as neither is
T-18 VII.5:3 brother restores the universe to **b.** of you.
T-18 VIII.13:8 the garden love has prepared for **b.** of you
T-19 I.4:4 and kept you **b.** apart from being healed.
T-19 I.5:9 **B.** cannot be together, nor perceived in
T-19 I.5:10 To dedicate yourself to **b.** is to set up a
T-19 I.6:2 divided goal has given **b.** an equal reality,
T-19 I.6:7 to keep **b.** truth and illusion in the mind,
T-19 I.6:7 illusion in the mind, where **b.** must be,
T-19 I.13:4 altar where grace was laid for **b.** of you.
T-19 I.14:1 God has raised unto Himself and **b.** of you
T-19 III.6:1 this: If sin is real, **b.** God and you are not.
T-19 III.10:1 shining on **b.** you and your brother. And
T19 IV.B.10:9 and guilt are **b.** conditions of the mind, to
T19 IV.B.14:8 ego and the Holy Spirit **b.** recognize this,
T19 IV.B.14:8 and **b.** also recognize that here the sender

T19 IV.B.17:4 Spirit is **b.** the sender and the receiver.
T19 IV.D.15:4 truly, for it will be **b.** offered and received.
T-20 II.3:6 Here is your gift to **b.**; your judgment on
T-20 III.3:7 it in your perception, which made them **b.**
T-20 III.8:8 that shone in **b.** you and your brother, to
T-20 V.4:7 is your choice, but never **b.** of these.
T-20 V.7:9 brother will offer and receive it for you **b.**.
T-20 VI.2:1 of **b.** a holy and an unholy relationship.
T-20 VII.4:7 for **b.** would place the attributes where
T-20 VII.4:8 **b.** must be undone for purposes of truth.
T-20 VII.7:3 **B.** are but means, each one appropriate to
T-21 I.3:7 you have learned that **b.** you cannot have.
T-21 II.10:8 is merely to fail to understand them **b.**.
T-21 II.13:1 brother were **b.** created by a loving Father
T-21 IV.8:1 ego's weakness is revealed in **b.** your sight
T-21 V.9:2 accepted and accomplished, **b.** at once.
T-21 VI.1:8 this same belief you **b.** will think that you
T-21 VI.9:7 with him what has been given **b.** of you.
T-21 VII.12:3 been made, the answer is **b.** "yes" and "no
T-22 in.1:7 effects of what you **b.** believed and saw.
T-22 II.1:4 **B.** bring the same amount of misery,
T-22 II.5:1 **B.** reason and the ego will tell you this,
T-22 II.6:7 Not **b.**, but one. There is no point in
T-22 III.9:7 where **b.** give errors gladly to correction,
T-22 III.9:7 that **b.** may happily be healed as one.
T-22 IV.5:3 that seems to rise between you **b.**. So shall
T-22 VI.1:2 For **b.** you cannot have. Which do you
T-22 VI.13:6 Either could be maintained, but never **b.**.
T-23 I.6:4 **B.** are not true. And so it matters not what
T-23 II.5:7 has done **b.** to himself and his Creator.
T-23 II.13:3 Nor will God end His vengeance upon **b.**,
T-23 II.13:3 this substitute for love, and kill you **b.**.
T-23 II.19:5 Yet **b.** are judgments on what is not life,
T-23 IV.2:3 Yet if they **b.** are true, then must they be
T-24 I.8:5 share becomes obscured from **b.** of you.
T-24 II.7:3 certain that the truth is just the same in **b.**
T-24 II.7:5 you and your brother **b.** can understand,
T-24 II.7:5 and one that brings release to **b.** of you.
T-24 II.10:7 that **b.** might share the universe with Him
T-24 III.2:7 yourself in sin beside him, **b.** in misery,
T-24 III.8:5 to join His Will to save you **b.** from hell.
T-24 V.4:2 And **b.** will walk in danger, each intent, in
T-24 V1.5:4 sin you see in him but keeps you **b.** in hell.
T-24 VI.5:5 will his perfect sinlessness release you **b.**,
T-24 VI.8:3 that **b.** may end a journey that has never
T-24 VI.8:6 the judgment you have laid on **b.** of you.
T-24 VI.9:5 And **b.** shall see God's glory in His Son,
T-24 VII.4:5 in that choice lie **b.** its health and harm.
T-24 VII.11:1 and **b.** appear to walk this earth without a
T-25 I.6:2 still is one with **b.** the Father and the Son,
T-25 II.8:5 strength, and **b.** will gladly look within,
T-25 III.11:2 since He gave the same to **b.** of you. His
T-25 V.4:3 So must it remain useless to **b.**. Together,
T-25 VII.4:4 lie apart from **b.** the Father and the Son.
T-25 VII.11:7 God or this must be insane, but hardly **b.**.
T-25 VIII.11:6 And **b.** are strengthened by their union
T-25 VIII.13:5 another must be an injustice to them **b.**,
T-25 VIII.13:6 Father gave the same inheritance to **b.**.
T-26 VII.14:9 and made Them **b.** his enemies in hate.
T-26 VII.17:6 lie, to be **b.** offered and received as one.
T-27 I.5:4 beyond itself to **b.** your innocence and his
T-27 I.6:8 And yet to **b.** the message is the same.
T-27 I.11:7 and your function **b.** be reconciled at last
T-27 II.11:5 yours, and gives you **b.** a different role.
T-27 II.15:1 Correction is the function given **b.**, but
T-27 III.2:4 it cancelled out, and so they **b.** are gone.
T-27 IV.4:3 **b.** attesting the same thing in different
T-27 V.6:7 the other, for they cannot **b.** be there.
T-27 VI.1:4 they **b.** are means to make the body real.
T-27 VII.11:6 saw as if it were its start and ending, **b.**.
T-27 VII.15:7 you see as offering **b.** life and death to you
T-27 VIII.6:3 of **b.** accomplishment and real effects.
T-27 VIII.6:4 Together, we can laugh them **b.** away, and
T-27 VIII.13:6 learn that **b.** of you are innocent or guilty.
T-27 VIII.13:7 be unlike each other; that they **b.** be true.
T-28 III.2:4 the body not perceived as sick by **b.** your
T-28 IV.1:8 you and your brother **b.** become illusions,
T-28 IV.7:1 The Holy Spirit is in **b.** your minds, and
T-28 IV.7:5 **b.** are gone if someone wills to be united

T-28 V.3:2 a part of yours, from which you **b.** are free
T-28 VI.5:3 Unless you **b.** agree that is your wish, it
T-28 VII.3:3 A split allegiance is but faithlessness to **b.**,
T-29 I.3:9 was a point you **b.** agreed to keep intact.
T-29 IV.2:3 The fear is seen within, without, or **b.**. Or
T-29 VIII.1:5 and they are feared and worshipped, **b.**,
T-30 VII.6:4 In symbols that you **b.** can understand
T-30 VII.6:18 shared. They mean the same to **b.** of you.
T-30 VIII.2:3 him beyond appearance and deception, **b.**
T-31 II.2:9 Yet must we see them **b.**, before you can
T-31 II.3:5 see yourself divided into **b.** these roles,
T-31 II.9:7 for Christ has been reborn to **b.** of you.
T-31 II.11:1 remembered and accepted by you **b.**.
T-31 II.11:2 Alone it is denied to **b.** of you. Is it not
T-31 V.11:4 And **b.** would go, if either one were ever
T-31 V.12:4 that you chose for **b.** of you, and what he
T-31 VI.3:8 and must be passed that **b.** may disappear
T-31 VII.4:2 For **b.** are concepts of yourself, which can
T-31 VII.4:5 him, has been accepted now for **b.** of you.
W-pI 5.2:1 use **b.** the name of the form in which you
W-pI 5.7:2 using the name of **b.** the source of the
W-pI 6.1:2 to name **b.** the form of upset (anger, fear,
W-pI 23.7:1 be sure to include **b.** your thoughts of
W-pI 30.5:4 without. Today's idea applies equally to **b.**
W-pI 31.1:2 the idea should be applied to **b.** the world
W-pI 31.2:5 You will escape from **b.** together, for the
W-pI 32.2:3 that **b.** are in your own imagination.
W-pI 32.3:3 Try to treat them **b.** as equally as possible.
W-pI 33.1:1 the world in **b.** its outer and inner aspects.
W-pI 33.2:2 Try to remain equally uninvolved in **b.**,
W-pI 39.5:2 recommended, although **b.** are suggested.
W-pI 39.11:1 repeat today's idea, and preferably **b.**. If
W-pI 42.1:1 thoughts, **b.** of major importance. It also
W-pI 61.6:1 Be sure **b.** to begin and end the day with a
W-pI 65.1:3 **B.** these thoughts are obviously necessary
W-pI 66.11:2 *are one, because God has given me **b.**.* It will
W-pI 69.1:5 in the light of the world that saves you **b.**.
W-pI 78.8:5 what you see through Him will free you **b.**
W-pI 78.10:4 For you **b.**, and all the sightless ones as
W-pI 83.3:4 because **b.** come from the same Source.
W-pI 94.4:1 past the list of attributes, **b.** good and bad
W-pI 95.15:4 *and What He is, Who loves us **b.** as One.*
W-pI 96.1:1 yourself as two; as **b.** good and evil, loving
W-pI 96.3:4 A mind and body cannot **b.** exist. Make
W-pI 99.1:2 **b.** imply that something has gone wrong;
W-pI 99.1:3 of God. Thus do **b.** terms imply a thing
W-pI 99.2:1 Truth and illusions **b.** are equal now, for
W-pI 99.2:1 both are equal now, for **b.** have happened.
W-pI 99.3:1 within a mind where **b.** of them exist? The
W-pI 101.2:3 be illusion, for they cannot **b.** be true. The
W-pI 107.8:3 Father knows that You are **b.** the same. It
W-pI 108.4:1 Here are **b.** giving and receiving seen as
W-pI 108.4:2 it is understood that **b.** occur together,
W-pI 121.9:3 And as you learn to see them **b.** as one, we
W-pI 127.3:8 which holds Them **b.** forever as the same.
W-pI 137.12:6 aware that they will **b.** occur as one.
W-pI 152.3:2 but may not yet accept **b.** parts of it.
W-pI 155.5:1 and deprivation **b.** are quickly left behind.
W-pI 164.2:4 You will recognize them **b.**, for they are
W-pI 164.6:4 valuable and valueless are **b.** perceived
W-pI 183.9:5 And **b.** can be accomplished perfectly.
W-pI 185.3:4 the outcome wanted not the same for **b.**.
W-pI 187.5:7 And **b.** must gain in this exchange, for
W-pI 192.8:6 the way to liberty depends for **b.** of them.
W-pI 194.8:5 along with his, and offers peace to **b.**.
W-pI 196.9:7 You have sought to be **b.** weak and bound
W-pI 198.10:3 be celebrated **b.** on earth and in your holy
W-pI 214.1:3 *Now am I freed from **b.**. For what God gives*
W-pII 291.1:3 **b.** for myself and for the world as well.
W-pII 352.1:7 *I have within me **b.** the memory of You, and*
M-3 1:2 **b.** can look upon the Son of God as sinless
M-5 II.3:11 is the release from guilt and sickness **b.**,
M-13 1:5 the first, so **b.** can finally disappear. The
M-13 2:1 It takes great learning **b.** to realize and to
M-17 1:1 a crucial question **b.** for teacher and pupil
M-17 1:3 the magic seem quite real to **b.** of them.
M-18 1:3 has "proved," **b.** to his pupil and himself,
M-22 4:3 sickness, **b.** in the individual's perception
M-22 7:6 **B.** are equally meaningless. Yet this will

M-24..........4:5 **b.** learn and teach that theoretical issues
M-27........4:10 fear. **B.** are equally meaningless to Him.
M-29..........1:1 that **b.** teacher and pupil may raise. In
C-1............6:2 real. **B.** this world and the real world are
C-5............6:7 and leave them **b.** to find the peace of God
P-1.............1:5 which He offers His greater gifts to **b.**.
P-2.........in.4:3 **b.** will learn to give up their original goals,
P-2.........in.4:5 are finally given up in the minds of **b.**.
P-2...........I.4:7 give for now. Yet **b.** will find sanity at last.
P-2......... II.2:6 is truth itself, but **b.** can lead to truth.
P-2......... II.7:2 But **b.** have many forms, because no good
P-2........ III.1:3 One, **b.** will merely stumble blindly on to
P-2......IV.4:10 cure? Are not these **b.** one question?
P-2......... V.6:3 The limits laid on **b.** the patient and the
P-2........VI.7:5 offer the mind of **b.** a covenant in which
P-2.......VII.1:2 In the end, everyone is **b.**. He who needs
P-3...........I.3:6 way can be most helpful to **b.** of you. It
P-3......... II.1:3 which everyone is **b.** patient and therapist
P-3......... II.4:5 **B.** must have denied their perfection, for
P-3......... II.5:2 And that good is saved for **b.**, against the
P-3......... II.6:2 **b.** patient and therapist may change their
P-3......... II.6:3 will not be the same dream for **b.** of them,
P-3......... II.6:3 forgiveness in which **b.** will someday wake
P-3........ III.4:5 made holy, for herein **b.** are healed. The
P-3........ III.4:8 But thanks are due to **b.**, for the release
P-3........ III.6:7 **B.** will be blessed thereby. Perhaps he was
P-3........ III.6:9 Again will **b.** be blessed. Only in terms of
S-1.........in.3:2 until **b.** high and low have disappeared.
S-1...........I.7:9 which. Perhaps it will reach **b.**, if you are
S-1........ I.7:10 have realized that Christ is in **b.** of you.
S-2.........in.1:4 **B.** must come to hold you up and keep
S-2......... II.3:3 since **b.** have been unworthy and deserve
S-3.........in.1:1 Prayer has **b.** aids and witnesses which
S-3........ III.1:6 has, not equally bestowed on **b.** as one.

## bother 3

T-8..... VIII.6:5 situation, does not **b.** to analyze it at all. If
T-10.........I.3:1 you **b.** to reconcile what happened in
T-21......IV.3:3 for it to **b.** to pretend it is your friend.

## bothering 1

W-pI.....16.3:3 trivial and not worth **b.** about that it is

## bottom 4

T-1........VI.3:3 be introduced vertically from the **b.** up.
T-3........IV.7:4 but to correct error from the **b.** up. I
S-1........III.2:1 forms of prayer, at the **b.** of the ladder,
S-2.........in.1:2 vain to try to rise above prayer's **b.** step,

## bought 6

T-12......IV.6:7 inheritance can neither be **b.** nor sold.
T-27.... VIII.2:2 It puts things on itself that it has **b.** with
T-30....... V.9:8 moment of content has not been **b.** at
T-30.... V.10:4 *Not one was **b.** except at cost of pain, nor was*
P-3........III.3:5 A "**b.**" relationship cannot offer the only
P-3......III.4:10 could possibly imagine that it could be **b.**

## bound 56

*See also* time-bound

T-1........III.9:4 it would not be useful if it were **b.** by laws
T-5........III.4:7 ego as guide. This is **b.** to produce fear.
T-12......IV.2:1 undertakes is therefore **b.** to be defeated.
T-13......IX.1:8 in which you **b.** yourself will disappear.
T-14......III.4:6 are guilty or guiltless, **b.** or free, unhappy
T-14....... V.2:4 but God would not have you **b.** by it. His
T-14....... X.6:7 who are still **b.** to judgment can be asked
T-14....... X.7:3 You are too **b.** to form, and not to content
T-14......XI.2:1 be glad that you are not **b.** to it forever.
T-14......XI.8:1 so firmly **b.** to guilt and committed so to
T-15.........I.2:3 time in His Own way, and is not **b.** by it.
T-15....... II.1:3 of God cannot be **b.** by time. No more are
T-15....... II.1:5 For unless God is **b.**, you cannot be. An
T-15.....III.11:3 we may release all those who would be **b.**,
T-15....VI.5:10 gladly wills, it is impossible that he be **b.**,
T-15....VI.5:12 For the instant he refuses to be **b.**, he is
T-15....VI.5:12 he refuses to be bound, he is not **b.**.
T-15.....VII.2:2 keep the giver **b.** to itself through guilt. It
T-17....... II.3:5 one and nothing remain still **b.** by them,
T19....IV.C.3:3 death, wills not that you be **b.** by them.
T-20...... III.9:1 Prisoners **b.** with heavy chains for years,
T-22...... III.4:7 where its worshippers are **b.** to bodies,
T-24....... II.9:3 and **b.** in hate to kill each other and deny
T-24...... IV.5:5 So are you **b.** with him, for you are one.
T-24...... VI.9:5 **b.** to laws that have no power over him at
T-24.VII.11:11 is not **b.** to specialness but by your choice.
T-25....... V.1:3 Attack and sin are **b.** as one illusion, each
T-25......VII.7:4 The Son of God cannot be **b.** by time nor
T-25... VIII.8:2 In justice He is **b.** to set them free, and
T-27....... II.9:5 that they are free *because* they hold him **b.**.
T-27...... VI.6:3 is **b.** by laws that it came solely to undo!
T-29...... IV.3:5 and not the wrappings in which it is **b.**.
T-30..... II.2:10 yourself, and choose that you be **b.**.
T-30....... II.3:4 boundless; it is not your will that it be **b.**.
T-30.... VIII.2:6 he is not **b.** by loss or suffering in any
T-31.....VII.9:3 for you are **b.** to separation from the sight
T-31.... VIII.1:2 and **b.** by what it orders him to feel. It sets
W-pI.....25.2:4 As a result, you are **b.** to misuse it. When
W-pI.....76.1:3 as itself. You are not **b.** by them. Yet to
W-pI.....76.3:1 that you are not **b.** by all the strange and
W-pI.....92.2:3 your hand, securely **b.** until you let it go.
W-pI...129.4:5 away from this are you who stay **b.** to this
W-pI...153.3:1 circle **b.** it and another one in that, until
W-pI...156.7:3 keep you **b.** no longer. The approach to
W-pI...192.8:3 free, for he is **b.** together with his prisoner
W-pI...195.4:5 some are loosed while others still are **b.**.
W-pI...196.9:7 You have sought to be both weak and **b.**,
W-pI...197.2:3 See yourself as **b.**, and bars become your
W-pI...199.7:3 themselves as **b.** and helpless and afraid.
W-pI...200.5:3 You will be **b.** till all the world is seen by
W-pII..277.1:2 *Let me not imagine I have **b.** him with the*
W-pII..277.2:2 He is not **b.** except by his beliefs. Yet what
W-pII..277.2:5 he cannot be **b.** unless God's truth can lie,
W-pII.....278.h If I am **b.**, my Father is not free.
W-pII..278.1:3 If I am **b.** in any way, I do not know my
W-pII..278.1:5 is free, and what is **b.** is not a part of truth

## boundaries 4

T-8......... II.7:3 no **b.** because its extension is unlimited,
T-30...... III.3:8 made beyond the **b.** of limits on yourself.
T-30....... V.8:1 the step across the narrow **b.** of the world
P-2......... II.8:5 **b.** the ego would impose upon the self.

## bounded 1

T-19...... III.7:1 reality or your brother's is **b.** by a body,

## boundless 9

T-7........ IX.6:7 Your Self-fullness is as **b.** as God's. Like
T-8......... II.7:2 is **b.** in strength and in love and in peace.
T-11.........I.6:8 Your love is as **b.** as His because it *is* His.
T-26...... IV.1:3 Nothing in **b.** love could need forgiveness
T-30....... II.3:4 Your will is **b.**; it is not your will that it be
W-pI...101.3:4 Its wrath is **b.**, merciless, but wholly just.
W-pI...109.8:2 everyone into the **b.** circle of your peace,
W-pI...207.1:3 *melts away, as I accept His **b.** Love for me.* I
W-pII..252.1:4 but from the **b.** Love of God Himself.

## bounds 1

P-2......... V.3:4 the insane within the **b.** of the attainable.

## bow 7

T-10.... III.11:6 accept him you will **b.** down and worship
T-19...... III.7:6 God, before which God Himself must **b.**,
T-24.........I.8:2 your brother **b.** to it against his will. And
T-29...... IX.1:2 to let himself **b.** down in worship to what
W-pI...156.4:4 The waves **b.** down before you, and the
W-pI...163.2:3 and the sick **b.** down before its image,
W-pI...163.4:1 Would you **b.** down to idols such as this?

## bowed 2

W-pI.....93.2:3 and have **b.** down to idols made of dust,–
W-pI. 136.11:3 And Heaven has not **b.** to hell, nor life to

## bows 2

T-15........II.6:8 the Presence of what the universe **b.** to, in
M-11 ....... 4:10 is? The earth **b.** down before its gracious

## box 2

T-23...... III.2:3 give. An empty **b.**, however beautiful and
T-30...... IV.2:2 up as a closed **b.** is opened suddenly, or

## boxes 2

T-30...... IV.2:3 made for **b.** and for bears have failed him,
T-30...... IV.2:5 the **b.** and the bears did not deceive him,

## brain 6

T-13.......in.2:7 minds seem to be trapped in their **b.**, and
T-22.........I.2:7 **b.** cannot interpret what your vision sees.
T-22.........I.2:9 The **b.** interprets to the body, of which it
W-pI.....92.1:3 tied up with the body and its eyes and **b.**.
W-pI.....92.2:1 You also believe the body's **b.** can think.
W-pI.....92.2:4 the body's eyes can see; the **b.** can think.

## branch 4

T-3.......VII.6:1 The **b.** that bears no fruit will be cut off
T-22...... IV.1:1 where the **b.** in the road is quite apparent,
T-22...... IV.1:3 way you went before you reached the **b.**,
T-22...... IV.1:4 was to decide which **b.** you will take now.

## branches 2

T-22...... IV.1:8 futile than standing where the road **b.**,
W-pII ..... 2.4:4 birds have come to live within their **b.**.

## branching 1

T-22.........IV.h The **B.** of the Road

## brand 1

T-24...VII.10:5 it. You **b.** it sinful and you hate its acts,

## bravely 1

T-11.......in.3:7 and **b.** hold it up to the foundation of the

## breach 1

T-29.......I.3:10 to be a **b.** of treaty not to be allowed.

## breaches 1

T-13...... IX.1:4 are strict, and **b.** are severely punished.

## bread 1

T-2.... III.5:10 starves you by denying you your daily **b.**.

## break 17

T-4........ III.2:5 so truth can **b.** through the barriers the
T-7......VIII.4:3 To fragment is to **b.** into pieces, and mind
T-10.... IV.5:10 cannot **b.** through the obstructions you
T-11..... V.13:2 means to **b.** down or to separate out. The
T-16.....VII.5:2 and the savagery **b.** briefly through, the
T-18.......I.12:5 still further weaken and **b.** apart what is
T-21.........I.8:4 shining and with no **b.** or limit anywhere.
T-28...... III.7:4 and **b.** it into days and months and years?
T-30...... IV.3:2 one seems to **b.** the rules you set for it. It
T-30...... IV.3:4 It must appear to **b.** your rules for safety,
T-30...... IV.3:8 that they can seem to **b.** and frighten him.
W-pI.......7.3:4 not this kind of cup will **b.** if you drop it?

W-pI.132.13:1 and **b.** away a part of God Himself and
W-pI...153.3:3 There seems to be no **b.** nor ending in the
W-pI...186.9:5 an instant, **b.** apart to group again, and
W-pII .234.1:3 **b.** in thoughts which are forever unified
M-27 .........2:3 ready to **b.** it off without regret or care,

**breakfast** 1
W-pI.......7.3:2 cup against your lips, having **b.** and so on

**breaking** 8
T-1.........I.37:2 catalyst, **b.** up erroneous perception and
T-11..... V.13:3 to understand totality by **b.** it down is
T-11..... V.13:5 everything it perceives by **b.** it into small,
T-13...... VI.4:6 destroy time's continuity by **b.** it into past
T-14...... VI.5:1 regarded the separation as a means for **b.**
T-15...... IV.8:2 **b.** communication holds value to you.
T-17...... III.3:4 maintaining and the **b.** off of the unholy
T-18.... VI.14:6 through destruction, not through a **b.** out

**breaks** 5
T-5......... II.4:3 of Heaven **b.** through into its own. Before
T-6......V.A.5:8 and attack always **b.** communication,
T-13...... XI.7:6 it **b.** communication with you with whom
T-14...... IV.4:2 God **b.** no barriers; neither did He make
P-2........ VI.3:5 the thought behind the form **b.** through,

**breath** 8
T19. IV.A.14:4 no little **b.** of love escape their notice.
T-20....... V.5:8 The little **b.** of eternity that runs through
T-27.......I.10:3 a **b.** of immortality to those grown sick of
W-pI...191.2:6 no **b.** you draw that does not seem to
W-pII .267.1:2 to me in every heartbeat and in every **b.**;
W-pII .267.1:5 peace; each **b.** infuses me with strength. I
M-18 ......... 3:4 and tiny **b.** become the measure of reality.
S-3...........I.2:3 and linked to its unstable, tiny **b.**. Death

**breathe** 4
T-17....... V.8:4 and do not **b.** life into your failing ego.
W-pI...107.7:5 sure we live and hope and **b.** and think.
W-pI...182.5:4 He can return to **b.** again the holy air that
W-pII .222.1:2 Source of life, the life within, the air I **b.**,

**breathes** 1
T-24...... III.4:4 attacked by everything that walks and **b.**,

**breathing** 3
T-14...... IV.6:1 become as easy and as right as **b.**. There is
T-21....... V.3:4 and as natural to it as **b.** to the body.
T-27.......I.10:3 grown sick of **b.** in the fetid scent of death

**bred** 1
T-28...... III.3:4 you, where the sickness has been **b.**. Thus

**breeds** 2
T-15...... XI.5:6 Deprivation **b.** attack, being the belief
W-pI...198.3:1 though it is itself a dream, it **b.** no others.

**breeze** 1
T-24...... III.3:7 and turn and whirl about with every **b.**.

**Bridge** 4
*bridge*
T-5........ III.1:2 the Holy Spirit is the **B.** for the transfer of
T-6......... II.7:2 the **B.** between perception and knowledge
T-16....IV.12:2 it. The Holy Spirit is the **B.** to Him, made
W-pI.....96.8:3 Who is the **B.** between your mind and It.

**bridge** 39
*Bridge*
T-1 .........II.4:5 I **b.** the distance as an elder brother to you
T-2 .......II.6:10 that point the **b.** of return has been built.
T-4 ....... VI.7:1 my perception He can **b.** the little gap.
T-16 ..... III.8:2 Sooner or later must everyone **b.** the gap
T-16 ..... III.8:3 Each one builds this **b.**, which carries him
T-16 ..... III.9:1 **b.** is builded stronger than you think, and
T-16 ..... IV.2:5 and you will cross the **b.** in perfect safety,
T-16 ..... IV.7:6 you and the **b.** that leads you into it.
T-16 ..... IV.9:1 Across the **b.** is your completion, for you
T-16 ... IV.10:1 **b.** that leads to union in yourself *must* lead
T-16 ... IV.13:4 The **b.** that He would carry you across lifts
T-16 ... IV.13:6 On this side of the **b.** to timelessness you
T-16 .... V.17:2 You will cross the **b.** into reality simply
T-16 ........ VI.h The **B.** to the Real World
T-16 ..... VI.5:2 side of the **b.** you see the world of separate
T-16 ..... VI.6:1 Across the **b.** it is so different! For a time
T-16 ..... VI.6:4 Once you have crossed the **b.**, the value of
T-16 ..... VI.6:5 to bring your brothers to the **b.** with you,
T-16 ..... VI.7:1 **b.** itself is nothing more than a transition
T-16 ... VI.11:2 it seems to be outside and across the **b.**.
T-17 .......II.2:4 The **b.** between that world and this is so
T-17 .......II.2:5 Yet this little **b.** is the strongest thing that
T-26 .... V.11:8 the **b.** between the past and present. Here
T-28 .......I.15:3 a **b.** an instant will suffice to reach beyond
T-28 .......I.15:7 He has built the **b.**, and it is He Who will
T-28 ..... III.3:5 come to **b.** the little gap that leads to Him.
T-28 ..... III.6:1 God builds the **b.**, but only in the space
T-28 ..... III.6:2 and the shame of guilt He cannot **b.**, for
T-28 ..... III.6:4 and **b.** His Son's returning to Himself.
W-pI. 134.11:1 Across this **b.**, as powerful as love which
W-pI... 151.9:7 His lessons will enable you to **b.** the gap
W-pI... 159.5:1 vision is the **b.** between the worlds. And
W-pI... 198.8:3 which builds a **b.** to it that brings illusions
W-pI... 200.8:1 Peace is the **b.** that everyone will cross, to
W-pI... 200.8:4 easy, sloping gently toward the **b.** where
W-pII ..... 7.1:2 Since He must **b.** the gap between reality
W-pII ..... 7.1:3 Across the **b.** that He provides are dreams
C-3 ........... 2:1 a way in which the unknowing can **b.** the
C-3 ........... 5:3 world in part, and yet the **b.** to Heaven.

**bridging** 1
T-16 ..... III.8:3 expend some little effort on behalf of **b.** it.

**brief** 16
T-13 ..... IV.4:5 only as a **b.** transition to the future, in
T-27 ... VIII.1:4 In the **b.** time allotted it to live, it seeks
W-pI..... 40.3:9 If only a **b.** period is available, merely
W-pI..... 67.3:1 drop away for a **b.** preparatory interval,
W-pI..... 77.5:1 After this **b.** introductory phase, wait
WpIrIII.in10:2 ideas a **b.** but serious review each hour.
W-pI. 138.12:3 in a **b.** quiet time devoted to maintaining
W-pI... 153.1:1 its **b.** relationships and all the "gifts" it
W-pI. 198.12:6 **b.** that not an instant stands between this
W-pII . 234.1:3 So **b.** the interval there was no lapse in
M-16 ......... 5:8 be sure that you do not forget a **b.** period,
M-26 ......... 3:1 a **b.** experience of direct union with God.
M-29 ......... 1:2 in terms of a **b.** summary of some of the
C-in ........... 5:1 on structural issues in the course is **b.** and
S-3...........I.1:4 is shown by the **b.** nature of the " cure."
S-3..........II.6:2 **b.** respite as it waits to take its vengeance

**briefly** 16
T-2 ........ V.3:5 worker be in his right mind, however **b.**,
T-2 ...... VII.7:1 I have already **b.** spoken about readiness,
T-16 .... VII.5:2 hatred and the savagery break **b.** through,
T19....IV.A.7:2 can land and settle **b.** upon anything, for
T-20 ... VI.11:4 Here does the Son of God stop **b.** by, to
W-pI....... 7.5:2 Glance **b.** at each subject, and then move
W-pI..... 44.9:2 it more reassuring to open your eyes **b.**.
W-pI..... 45.9:3 Stand aside, however **b.**, from all
W-pI..... 47.7:2 you feel a sense of deep peace, however **b.**
W-pI..... 68.6:6 Try to believe, however **b.**, that nothing
W-pI..... 74.4:2 Think about it **b.** but very specifically,
W-pI... 129.9:3 you have, and dwelling **b.** only upon this:

W-pI 132.13:5 are a shadow **b.** laid upon a dying world.
W-pI 134.15:3 **B.** consider all the evil things you thought
Wi181-200 2:2 now to lift these blocks, however **b.**.
P-2........ VI.3:5 the form breaks through, but only very **b.**,

**bright** 19
T-13 ... VI.11:6 This other world is **b.** with love which you
T-13 .....X.12:2 guilt and wholly loving, is **b.** within you.
T-13 ..... XI.3:9 Everything is clear and **b.**, and calls forth
T-14 ..... XI.4:8 for the **b.** lesson He has learned for you.
T-14 ..... XI.5:6 And each **b.** lesson with which the Holy
T-14 ... XI.10:7 establish His **b.** teaching so firmly in your
T-15 ......I.10:7 which you see yourself as **b.** with freedom
T-17 .......II.2:2 It is the real world, **b.** and clean and new,
T-18 ..... IX.9:4 is **b.** and shining with innocence, washed
T-18 ... IX.14:3 the **b.** world of new and clean perception.
T19 .. IV.D.2:3 and the **b.** Rays of His Father's Love that
T-20 .....II.11:5 and receive the **b.** awareness that leads
T-22 .....II.12:1 golden light that reaches it from the **b.**,
T-29 ..... III.5:5 light in you must be as **b.** as shines in him
W-pI .... 98.8:1 and give them back to you all **b.** with faith
W-pI .... 99.8:4 and see how **b.** this light still shines in you
W-pI 131.13:2 standing in a light so **b.** and clear that you
W-pII .... 285.h My holiness shines **b.** and clear today.
W-pII . 293.1:3 seem **b.** and clear and safe and welcoming

**brightens** 1
T-13 .... VII.1:5 it. There is no day that **b.** and grows dim.

**brighter** 6
T-22 ..... VI.4:1 blazing with a light far **b.** than the sun
T-26 ..... IX.4:4 the lights grow ever **b.** as each one comes
T-26 ..... IX.6:6 And all the lights in Heaven **b.** grow, in
T-29 ..... III.5:4 the light in him is **b.** still because you gave
W-pI .. 188.4:4 His blessing does the light in you shine **b.**,
M-8 ........... 1:4 **b.** thing draws the attention from another

**brightest** 1
T-26 ..... IX.6:5 becomes the **b.** light in Heaven's radiance

**brightly** 3
T-12 .......II.2:1 light in them shines as **b.** regardless of the
T-13 ..... IX.1:8 like a lamp shining so **b.** that the chain of
T-20 .......V.4:4 will shine so **b.** in your grateful vision that

**brightness** 9
T-13 ........I.5:6 and the **b.** of his purity shines untouched
T-13 .....X.14:2 but together we shine with **b.** so intense
T-14 .... VII.7:7 and **b.** so intense you could not wish, for
T-18 ..... IX.9:1 of light, this circle of **b.** is the real world,
T-21 .......V.1:3 laws of size and shape and **b.** would hold,
W-pI ...... 2.2:1 you, trying to avoid selection by size, **b.**,
W-pI 121.11:3 Try to find some little spark of **b.** shining
C-2 ........... 9:2 will see a sudden **b.** cover up the world
C-4 ........... 6:8 its single remedy joined in one healing **b.**.

**brilliance** 2
T-15 .......II.5:5 so. Yet its shining and glittering **b.**, which
W-pI .... 97.6:3 The steady **b.** of this light remains and

**brilliant** 3
T-25 ..... VI.2:1 and the light of **b.** day seems painful to
W-pI .... 69.5:1 there is a **b.** light hidden by the clouds.
W-pII . 252.1:2 and perfect purity is far more **b.** than is

**bring** 295
T-1 ..........I.9:3 They **b.** more love both to the giver *and*
T-1 .........II.5:2 I can thus **b.** down to them more than
T-1 ....... III.1:9 them will **b.** conviction in the ability,
T-1 ........ III.7:6 When you **b.** in the stranger, he becomes

T-2......... II.3:6 and to **b.** them into all your actions, you
T-2......... II.5:7 will **b.** you into closer and closer accord
T-2......... V.6:5 can **b.** its illumination to the body by
T-2......... V.7:8 Discomfort is aroused only to **b.** the need
T-2........ VI.6:1 to reach a state in which you **b.** your mind
T-2..... VIII.2:8 if you are to **b.** peace to other minds.
T-3........ III.6:2 knowledge will **b.** peace without question
T-3........ IV.7:7 mind if you will **b.** it under my guidance.
T-3....... VII.4:9 to attack ideas that might **b.** it to light.
T-4........ VI.5:3 slowly **b.** it nearer so he can learn how his
T-4........ VI.7:3 I will **b.** it to God for you, knowing that to
T-5........... I.3:2 up and **b.** the Holy Spirit down to you,
T-5........... I.3:2 but I can **b.** Him to you only at your own
T-5....... II.11:2 **b.** it back into the oneness in which it was
T-6......... I.15:2 "I come not to **b.** peace but a sword." This
T-6...... IV.10:3 to **b.** themselves to the awareness of their
T-7......... IX.5:1 knows of them and can **b.** them into your
T-8......... II.8:3 is. When you acknowledge this you **b.** the
T-8......... V.4:5 I **b.** God's peace back to all His children
T-8....... VII.5:5 own salvation, which must **b.** him his. Do
T-8........ IX.2:9 little part is so powerful that it will **b.** the
T-9......... V.8:2 darkness but he cannot **b.** light of himself
T-9..... VIII.8:3 you lies in the joy you **b.** to its witnesses,
T-10...... III.8:1 I do not **b.** God's message with deception
T-10...... IV.5:3 gods do not **b.** chaos; you are endowing
T-10....... V.2:4 the spark in them that would **b.** joy to you
T-10..... V.9:10 If you deny Him you **b.** sin, pain and
T-11....... in.3:7 it. **B.** this light fearlessly with you, and
T-11....... in.3:9 which it rests, and **b.** it out into the light.
T-11......... I.1:2 you **b.** anything else to the Sonship,
T-11......... I.6:7 because only this can **b.** you the joy that is
T-11...... IV.3:6 As you **b.** him back, so will you return.
T-11.... VI.10:2 **B.** only this awareness to the Sonship,
T-12.... III.10:6 **B.** your perceptions of the world to this
T-12... VII.10:3 only **b.** you peace *if you really looked upon*
T-13....... II.9:2 and if you will but **b.** it to the light, the
T-13...... III.7:3 from His sight, but **b.** it gladly to Him.
T-13...... IV.6:2 no hold over you unless you **b.** them with
T-13...... VI.2:5 would you choose to **b.** darkness with you
T-13...... VI.6:1 you, and unless you **b.** them with you,
T-13...... IX.2:2 you **b.** its condemnation on yourself, and
T-14....... II.4:6 as nothing, until you **b.** the light to them.
T-14...... III.3:9 *Let me* ***b.*** *peace to God's Son from his Father*
T-14.... III.10:6 and will **b.** to them all that they need,
T-14.... III.17:7 for deciding what can **b.** only good to
T-14...... IV.6:8 For you can **b.** your guilt into sleeping,
T-14....... V.4:4 **B.** innocence to light, in answer to the call
T-14....... V.7:7 **b.** within its safety and its perfect peace.
T-14...... V.11:2 If you **b.** him into the circle of purity, you
T-14...... V.11:5 **b.** him into it by blessing him. Holiness
T-14...... VI.8:4 But **b.** them to Him and let His gentleness
T-14..... VII.4:9 **B.** them together, and the fact of their
T-14..... VII.6:1 **b.** to Him every secret you have locked
T-14..... VII.6:8 you. **B.**, therefore, all your dark and secret
T-14..... VII.7:7 you will **b.** this oneness to your mind with
T-14...... IX.2:1 the ego to God is but to **b.** error to truth,
T-14...... IX.7:1 shining in you, can **b.** to all the world, you
T-14...... IX.7:4 same. All **b.** their different problems to its
T-14....... X.1:2 in time but **b.** eternity nearer or farther.
T-14....... X.1:6 Heaven here, and **b.** this world to Heaven.
T-14....... X.5:5 and **b.** any order into chaos shows you
T-14...... X.10:6 you **b.** with you a light so powerful that
T-14...... XI.4:7 Every dark lesson that you **b.** to Him Who
T-14...... XI.7:8 the effects that only guiltlessness can **b.**,
T-15......... I.2:6 all the waste that time seems to **b.** with it
T-15......... I.6:6 of hell to be experienced is to **b.** hell here,
T-15...... III.1:6 world in the belief that it will **b.** you peace
T-15...... IV.1:9 **b.** it into glad awareness while you do not
T-15...... IV.2:4 much as you want it will you **b.** it nearer.
T-15...... IV.2:7 you, and nothing else can **b.** you peace.
T-15...... IV.9:9 and **b.** all your awareness to the readiness
T-15....... V.2:2 is to **b.** guilt into your relationships, and
T-15....... V.8:1 how to **b.** a touch of Heaven to them here.
T-15..... V.10:7 Spirit **b.** to you those who are seeking you
T-15..... VII.3:5 As we **b.** it to light, your only question
T-15..... VII.8:6 as they **b.** the body of another closer or
T-16......... I.5:3 the form of empathy which would **b.** this
T-16......... I.5:7 His, for this will never **b.** peace to anyone.
T-16....... II.6:5 who **b.** you the glad tidings He has come.
T-16...... III.1:7 results have been to **b.** peace where there
T-16...... IV.1:7 It is essential to **b.** it into sight, and to
T-16...... IV.7:1 is an attempt to **b.** love into separation.
T-16...... IV.7:2 more than an attempt to **b.** love into fear,
T-16... V.12:10 delights you can **b.** death to the eternal.
T-16...... VI.6:5 to **b.** your brothers to the bridge with you
T-16...... VII.7:1 you may attempt to **b.** illusions into the
T-16...... VII.7:4 The illusions you **b.** with you will weaken
T-16...... VII.9:7 to **b.** you the true condition of Heaven.
T-17......... I.5:1 you that you can **b.** truth to fantasy, and
T-17......... I.5:4 When you try to **b.** truth to illusions, you
T-17...... II.1:5 part of the happiness this sight will **b.** you
T-17...... III.1:6 you **b.** with you to demonstrate he did
T-17...... III.1:7 Because you **b.** them, you will hear them.
T-17.... III.1:10 You **b.** them with you only that you may
T-17...... III.5:1 Holy Spirit **b.** His interpretation of the
T-17.... III.10:2 and let me **b.** reality to your perception of
T-17.... III.10:8 in the Name of God and **b.** you peace,
T-17...... IV.7:3 and as they operate they **b.** it to you.
T-17..... V.7:12 faith emerge, to **b.** you shining conviction
T-17...... VI.3:5 was set with which to **b.** the means in line
T-17...... VI.7:5 of the situation the goal of truth would **b.**.
T-17...... VI.7:6 solutions **b.** but the illusion of experience,
T-17... VIII.2:4 every situation and **b.** you peace. Not
T-18......... I.9:8 Let Him **b.** it here, where *you* would have
T-18...... III.1:3 and every fantasy that seemed to **b.** a light
T-18...... III.6:2 been willing to **b.** the darkness to light,
T-18...... IV.6:3 from guilt has been to **b.** Atonement to it,
T-18....... V.4:5 you would merely **b.** unholy means to its
T-18... VIII.8:7 love would **b.** to it from where it comes,
T-18... VIII.9:5 will **b.** love with him from Heaven for you
T-18. VIII.10:1 find them, for they **b.** your Self with them
T-18...... IX.1:1 been told to **b.** the darkness to the light,
T-18...... IX.3:3 you sent forth these messengers to **b.** this
T-18...... IX.3:7 God can **b.** you there, if you are willing to
T-18...... IX.4:3 and to **b.** despair and loneliness to it and
T-18...... IX.7:5 of how much imagination you **b.** to it, you
T-19...... III.5:9 its Teacher, Who is one with it, would **b.**.
T-19...... IV.1:5 to others, to **b.** them gently in, is the way
T-19...... IV.1:5 in which He will **b.** means and goal in line
T19... IV.A.1:6 who calls, and **b.** him rest by joining you.
T19... IV.A.2:8 He would **b.** peace to everyone, and how
T19. IV.A.13:2 will **b.** you word of bones and skin and
T19IV.A.17:11 will also believe that it can **b.** you pain. To
T19.... IV.B.3:6 But neither can it **b.** you fear of pain. Pain
T19.... IV.B.8:5 new perception that will **b.** light to all the
T19.. IV.B.10:4 can **b.** you neither peace nor turmoil;
T-20..... VII.1:1 your holy relationship can **b.** you only joy
T-21......... I.3:5 learned will **b.** to you the joy it promises.
T-21...... VI.7:7 instant serves to **b.** complete correction of
T-22....... II.1:4 same. Both **b.** the same amount of misery,
T-22...... IV.4:6 which you will **b.** to light the tired eyes of
T-22...... VI.5:5 part of Heaven that you **b.** is given you.
T-22...... VI.5:6 you fill again with the eternal light you **b.**,
T-22...... VI.6:2 The light you **b.** you do not recognize,
T-22...... VI.6:7 And what you **b.** is your remembrance of
T-23..... II.20:6 Certain it is illusions will **b.** fear because
T-24....... II.2:6 Its pursuit will **b.** you joy. But the pursuit
T-24....... II.2:7 pursuit of specialness must **b.** you pain.
T-24..... II.14:2 will forever fail to **b.** you peace and joy of
T-25....... II.3:3 and **b.** what it has never brought before?
T-25...... III.6:8 as just another chance to **b.** him joy.
T-25......... IV.h The Light You **B.**
T-25...... IV.1:5 for what will **b.** him joy as he defines it. It
T-25...... IV.1:8 will **b.** rejoicing is defined another way
T-25...... IV.2:2 think that suffering and sin will **b.** you joy
T-25...... IV.2:7 The Son of God creates to **b.** him joy,
T-25...... IV.3:2 world you **b.** with you to all the weary
T-25...... IV.3:7 die, will disappear before the sun you **b.**.
T-25.... IV.5:11 This can you **b.** to all the world, and all
T-25.... IV.5:12 to **b.** the light of Heaven with you, as you
T-25...... IX.4:7 can **b.** another problem added to the first,
T-26....... II.2:4 for Him to **b.** to truth than is another. For
T-26...... III.1:9 and **b.** complexity where oneness is? The
T-26..... VII.8:5 and serves to **b.** the joy this world denies
T-27...... IV.4:7 And which can **b.** escape from all the pain
T-27...... IV.7:2 But **b.** the problem to the only place that
T-27...... IV.7:5 you can **b.** the question to the answer,
T-27....... V.3:4 For all the hurt that war has sought to **b.**,
T-27....... V.5:2 The eyes of all the dying **b.** reproach, and
T-27....... V.6:2 And being blessed you will **b.** blessing.
T-27....... V.9:3 to their opposites and **b.** the same results.
T-27.... VIII.9:3 He bids you **b.** each terrible effect to Him
T-27.. VIII.11:3 Whatever hurt you **b.** to Him He will
T-27.. VIII.12:1 **B.**, then, all forms of suffering to Him
T-28......... I.7:9 The ancient new ideas they **b.** will be the
T-28...... III.8:5 guilt to **b.** you witness to what never was.
T-29......... I.2:6 little gap must **b.** to those who cherish it,
T-29...... IV.6:3 you imagine would **b.** happiness to you.
T-29..... VII.2:1 that will **b.** happiness and peace to him. If
T-29..... VII.4:1 you try to **b.** about your death. For you
T-29.... IX.10:4 **b.** the dreamer full release from dreams of
T-30...... III.1:5 that there are forms that will **b.** happiness
T-30...... IV.5:3 they **b.** fear *because* they hide the truth.
T-30....... V.9:7 you sought here that did not **b.** you pain?
T-31.... III.2:11 And how could murder **b.** you benefit?
T-31..... VII.6:4 the function given you to **b.** you peace,
T-31.... VIII.7:1 and power to **b.** this peace to everyone
T-31.... VIII.8:4 tired eyes I **b.** a vision of a different world,
W-pI..... 27.1:5 of today's exercises is to **b.** the time when
W-pI..... 41.8:5 This exercise can **b.** very startling results
WpI... rI.in.4:4 is to enable you to **b.** the quiet with you,
W-pI..... 60.1:6 will **b.** me near enough to Heaven that the
W-pI..... 62.1:1 will **b.** the world of darkness to the light.
W-pI..... 62.5:4 the happiness and release it will **b.** you.
W-pI..... 63.1:1 have the power to **b.** peace to every mind!
W-pI..... 63.1:3 purpose could you have that would **b.** you
W-pI..... 65.7:1 the relief its acceptance will **b.** you by
W-pI..... 66.9:5 Did they **b.** you peace? We need great
W-pI..... 67.4:4 much today to **b.** that awareness nearer,
W-pI..... 71.5:4 The result can only **b.** confusion, misery
W-pI..... 75.1:5 you **b.** peace with you wherever you go.
W-pI... 91.6:10 calls on the strength in you to **b.** to your
W-pI..... 92.5:7 that it may **b.** to all the miracle in which
W-pI... 93.11:6 You can do much today to **b.** you closer to
W-pI... 93.11:7 much today to **b.** the conviction to your
W-pI... 95.12:2 **b.** awareness of this oneness to all minds,
W-pI..... 96.6:8 the release of His dear Son **b.** pain to him,
W-pI..... 97.1:4 for it will **b.** your mind from conflict to
W-pI..... 97.3:1 try to **b.** reality still closer to your mind.
W-pI..... 97.5:2 that will accept the healing gifts they **b.**,
W-pI..... 98.7:4 will **b.** the light to all the words you say,
W-pI..... 99.4:2 yet recognize the need illusions **b.**, and
W-pI... 100.6:5 You **b.** His happiness to all you look upon
W-pI... 103.2:3 error we will try again to **b.** to truth today
W-pI... 104.5:3 will we **b.** to mind as often as we can: *I*
W-pI. 107.10:2 For you will **b.** with you the promise of
W-pI... 108.5:2 is enough to **b.** salvation to all minds. For
W-pI... 109.2:2 thought will **b.** to you the rest and quiet,
W-pI... 109.6:2 to **b.** the peace of God into the world, that
W-pI... 110.2:4 change that time appears to **b.** in passing
WpIrIII.in12:3 with each of these ideas will **b.** such large
W-pI... 121.1:3 and **b.** uncertainty to all your hopes of
W-pI... 126.1:1 reversal that this course will **b.** about. If
W-pI... 130.7:2 to **b.** with us a little part of unreality, as
W-pI... 132.7:2 Their readiness will **b.** the lesson to them
W-pI... 132.9:3 no time that can **b.** change to your eternal
W-pI... 133.1:1 to **b.** him back to practical concerns. This
W-pI... 133.5:1 compromise in what your choice must **b.**.
WpI. rIV.in6:2 one will **b.** the message of His Love to you
WpI. rIV.in8:1 **b.** to your mind the thought with which
W-pI. 153.14:4 day **b.** the last chapter closer to the world,
W-pI... 154.6:3 that they become able to **b.** them further,
W-pI. 154.11:4 He needs our feet to **b.** us where He wills,
W-pI... 155.6:3 nor illusion that you **b.** their eyes to look
W-pI... 156.4:2 All things that live **b.** gifts to you, and
W-pI... 157.6:1 only purpose being now to **b.** the vision of
W-pI... 157.7:2 And you who **b.** it light will come to see
W-pI... 161.4:5 words **b.** perfect clarity with them to you?
W-pI... 164.4:5 practicing today will **b.** rewards so great
W-pI. 170.13:6 ***b.*** *them Your salvation as we have received it*
WpI... rV.in3:1 *So do we* ***b.*** *our practicing to You. And if we*
W-pI... 181.7:3 from the misery the focus upon sin will **b.**
W-pI... 182.7:5 For He would **b.** you back with Him, that
W-pI. 184.13:4 One Name we **b.** into our practicing. One
W-pI... 185.4:1 Yet compromise alone a dream can **b.**.
W-pI... 185.5:2 seeks the means which **b.** illusions. He
W-pI... 185.5:6 one will **b.** the same despair and misery as

W-pI...185.8:4 will comfort you, and b. you happiness.
W-pI...188.1:7 the only thing you b. with you from Him
W-pI...188.9:2 and gently b. them back to where they fall
W-pI...189.7:4 Do not b. with you one thought the past
W-pI...190.5:3 that can reach down and b. oppression.
W-pI...190.7:6 Your strange desires b. it evil dreams.
W-pI...191.2:6 that does not seem to b. you nearer death;
W-pI.191.10:8 willing to b. your weary brothers rest?
W-pI...194.7:3 him pain, or b. experience of loss to him?
W-pI...195.3:3 to b. him down to lie in death with you, as
W-pI...196.7:3 it is but your thoughts that b. you fear,
W-pII .237.1:3 day. I b. the world the tidings of salvation
W-pII .245.1:4 *I b. it to the desolate and lonely and afraid. I*
W-pII .245.1:7 *Let me b. Your peace with me. For I would*
W-pII .254.2:3 not want what they would b. with them.
W-pII .272.1:4 *Can illusions b. me happiness? What but*
W-pII .275.2:4 *The safety that I b. is given me. Father, Your*
W-pII .281.1:3 *Your Thoughts can only b. me happiness. If*
W-pII .307.1:4 *Your Will alone can b. me happiness, and*
W-pII .334.2:3 *heart, to give him certainty and b. him peace*
W-pII .339.1:8 will frighten him, and b. him suffering.
W-pII .340.1:1 *and for the freedom I am certain it will b..*
W-pII ...13.4:2 Yet faith will b. its witnesses to show that
W-pII ...14.5:3 We b. glad tidings to the Son of God, who
M-1 ...........4:8 teachers of God are appointed to b. about
M-4 ...... IX.1:2 aspects of his life to b. to his learning,
M-4 ....... X.3:6 teachers to b. true learning to the world.
M-4 ....... X.3:7 speaking it is unlearning that they b., for
M-4 ....... X.3:8 It is given to the teachers of God to b. the
M-5 ....... II.2:9 chooses them in order to b. tangible form
M-8 ...........2:5 of creation; attempts to b. truth to lies.
M-8 ...........3:9 the messages they b. on which perception
M-8 ...........4:3 mind classifies what the body's eyes b. to
M-10 .......6:10 of God, this step will b. you peace. Can it
M-12 .........1:8 b. His Thoughts to still deluded minds.
M-12 .........5:4 Use it to b. the Word of God to those who
M-15 .........2:7 One instant out of time can b. time's end.
M-16 .........9:6 this, and b. this goal nearer to recognition
M-17 .........8:2 b. the light of hope from God Himself.
M-18 .........2:5 ears, and b. Christ's vision to eyes that see
M-21 .........3:1 world will b. experiences of this world. If
M-29 .......4:11 it. His decisions b. benefit to all, being
M-29 .........8:3 *stands silent in the grace You b. from Him.*
C-5...........6:12 *And b. with you all those whom He has sent*
P-2......... II.8:2 must the therapist do to b. healing about?
P-2........ IV.3:7 heal the sick is but to b. this realization to
P-2......... V.5:1 brother seeking aid can b. us gifts beyond
P-2........ VI.4:1 which the senses b. have but one purpose;
P-3......... II.6:8 and they will b. as much good as each can
S-1........ III.3:1 to recognize that prayer will b. an answer
S-1........ III.4:3 recognized they b. their fear with them.
S-1........ IV.4:4 Prayer can b. the peace of God. What
S-2......... II.8:8 prayer will lift you up and b. you home
S-3........ III.6:2 will never fail to b. His kindly remedy to

## bringer 6

T-18...... III.7:1 You who are now the b. of salvation have
W-pI....61.7:2 is. As a b. of salvation, this is obviously
W-pI...106.6:5 b. of all miracles has need that you receive
W-pI...154.5:4 perform his proper part as b. of the Word
M-1 ...........1:7 He has become a b. of salvation. He has
C-6.............3:4 principle; the b. of true perception, the

## bringers 6

T-25...... IV.2:5 them to be the b. of rejoicing and of joy.
W-pII ...14.3:1 We are the b. of salvation. We accept our
M-4 ....... X.3:9 are they, for they are the b. of salvation.
M-21 .........2:5 for being the b. of the desired experience
P-2....... VI.7:4 can but be seen as the b. of forgiveness,
S-3........ IV.1:3 love. B. of peace,–the Holy Spirit's voice,

## bringing 31

T-5...... III.11:1 as a teaching device for b. you home. The
T-6........ II.11:5 b. all of your perceptions into the one line
T-7........ V.11:6 and by b. it to your appreciation, He calls
T-9......... V.3:1 to b. nightmares into awareness, but only
T-12 ........I.6:2 for both are capable of b. love into your
T-13 ... VIII.5:4 end of time by b. healed and healing sight
T-14 ....... II.7:8 may join Him in the holy task of b. light.
T-14 ..... VII.4:1 on b. what is undesirable to the desirable;
T-14 ..... IX.1:4 B. illusion to truth, or the ego to God, is
T-14 ..... IX.2:1 B. the ego to God is but to bring error to
T-15 ...... V.9:3 by b. all perception out of the past, thus
T-17 ...........I.h B. Fantasy to Truth
T-17 ... VIII.5:8 and it will be a means for b. only this.
T-18 ..... III.1:1 have spent your life in b. truth to illusion,
T-18 ..... III.6:1 with me in b. Heaven to the Son of God,
T-18 ..... III.7:1 have the function of b. light to darkness.
T-18 ...... V.7:1 can pay his debt by b. happiness to both.
T-20 ... VIII.7:2 b. them gently within the kindly sway of
T-22 ..... VI.8:3 This is your part in b. peace. For you have
T-26 .. VII.19:3 Let us unite in b. blessing to the world of
T-27 .... VII.7:4 perceived as b. pain and suffering to you,
T-28 ...... I.11:4 minds, and b. them an instant's stillness,
T-31 ....... II.1:3 plans that need be laid for b. in the new.
W-pI..... 42.7:2 a beginning step in b. thoughts together,
W-pI..... 80.2:5 yourself by b. the problem to the answer.
W-pI... 95.14:2 little part in b. happiness to all the world.
W-pI... 103.1:6 where sin can enter, b. pain instead of joy
W-pI... 109.8:2 b. everyone into the boundless circle of
W-pI. 121.13:4 in b. happiness to every unforgiving mind
W-pI... 162.3:1 night b. them with him as he goes to sleep
C-6 ........... 2:1 and b. the plan of the Atonement to us,

## brings 153

T-1 ....... IV.1:4 This step b. escape from fear. When you
T-1 ........ V.2:4 collapse of time b. everyone closer to the
T-1 ...... VII.1:6 correction of the error b. release from it.
T-2 ...... II.1:14 It b. all error into the light, and since
T-2 ....... III.4:5 of its vision, it b. the mind into its service.
T-3 ....... III.1:8 neither b. certainty because all perception
T-3 ....... III.4:3 which b. it into the proper domain of the
T-3 ....... IV.5:1 it b. the mind into areas of uncertainty.
T-4 ....... VI.3:3 that one choice b. peace and joy while
T-4 ....... VI.3:3 peace and joy while another b. chaos and
T-4 ..... VII.7:5 the knowledge from the revelation b..
T-5 ......... I.7:5 the way beyond the healing that it b., and
T-5 ......... II.7:6 you of. It b. to your mind the other way,
T-5 ..... III.11:9 and to come, and b. them to the present.
T-6 ..... V.C.5:3 which b. together the lessons implied in
T-7 ...... IV.5:7 that it b. the mind into accord with His,
T-7 ...... VI.6:6 said, understanding b. appreciation and
T-7 ....... VI.6:6 appreciation and appreciation b. love.
T-9 ......... I.4:4 perception of your mind b. its reality to
T-10 ....... II.2:1 of reality b. more than merely lack of fear.
T-10 ..... III.3:3 of love therefore b. invulnerability with it.
T-10 ...... V.2:5 the denial of the spark that b. depression,
T-11 ....... II.1:2 this, and every healing thought b. it closer
T-12 ........ I.7:4 the Name of Christ b. the remembrance
T-13 ........ I.6:3 idea of guilt b. a belief in condemnation
T-13 ..... IV.4:5 it b. the past to the future by interpreting
T-13 ... VI.10:3 it. Each one you see in light b. your light
T-13 ... VIII.5:4 the past thus b. you nearer to the end of
T-13 ..... IX.4:1 Atonement b. a re-evaluation of
T-14 ....... II.4:3 He b. the light of truth into the darkness,
T-14 ....... II.4:5 learners of the lesson this light b. to them,
T-14 .... VII.6:4 He b. the light to darkness if you make
T-14 ..... IX.1:3 It merely b. unholiness to holiness; or
T-14 ....... X.2:6 Who b. the laws of another world to this
T-14 ..... XI.7:8 himself. The miracle b. the effects that
T-14 ... XI.12:5 Each b. the other with it, for it is the law
T-15 ..... III.5:7 b. you the awareness of what you decided
T-15 ..... III.7:7 Yet He b. all His extensions to you, as
T-15 .. VII.10:2 who will learn that love b. no guilt at all,
T-15 .. VII.10:2 b. guilt cannot be love and *must* be anger.
T-15 ..... XI.4:2 sacrifice b. guilt as surely as love brings
T-15 ..... XI.4:2 brings guilt as surely as love b. peace.
T-16 .... VII.3:4 fantasies it b. to its chosen relationships
T-17 ....... II.5:3 In the light of the real reason that He b.,
T-17 ..... III.4:6 less the other really b. to the relationship,
T-17 ..... VI.5:8 believes the situation b. the experience.
T-18 ........ I.8:4 He b. all your insane projections and the
T-18 .... IV.2:7 achieve the state its coming b. with it. The
T-19 ...... I.14:5 which b. the miracle of healing with equal
T-19 ...... I.15:2 For faith b. peace, and so it calls on truth
T-19 ..... III.2:2 For the ego b. sin to fear, demanding
T19 ... IV.C.5:7 b. the Creator to the awareness of every
T-20 ....... II.9:3 that looks upon the lilies and b. you joy.
T-20 ... VIII.5:9 b. with it the laws beloved of Him Whose
T-21 ..... III.2:5 the persistence that faith inevitably b..
T-21 ..... III.9:2 Spirit knows that sacrifice b. nothing. He
T-21 ..... IV.7:4 of another world, b. to it hope of peace.
T-21 ..... VI.8:6 and b. your reason into line with His. Be
T-22 ....... II.1:4 be the way to lose the misery the other b..
T-22 ..... III.3:1 but it makes way for peace and b. you to a
T-22 ..... VI.6:3 himself the vision that he b. to others?
T-22 ... VI.14:7 And every thought in one b. gladness to
T-24 ....... II.7:5 and one that b. release to both of you.
T-25 ..... III.7:7 For it is seeing them as one that b. release
T-25 ..... VI.2:2 the clarity it b. to what they look upon.
T-25 ..... VI.3:1 and b. the gift of light that makes sight
T-25 ... VIII.1:6 that what b. loss to no one you would not
T-25 ... VIII.9:7 that you accept b. joy to Him as well as
T-25 . VIII.14:2 knows, and all the Holy Spirit b. to earth.
T-26 ..... IV.4:1 Forgiveness b. no little miracles to lay
T-26 ..... IV.4:2 each gift that b. him nearer to his home.
T-26 ..... VI.3:5 He b. you gifts that are not of this world,
T-26 ... VIII.6:6 everything b. good that comes from God.
T-26 ....... X.6:2 all the happy sparkle that salvation b. can
T-27 ........ I.4:1 belief because it b. conviction in its wake.
T-27 ....... II.4:1 is not real unless it b. a healing to your
T-27 ....... V.4:4 the blessing that the holy instant b.? Be
T-27 ..... VI.4:8 He b. is witness that the body is not real.
T-27 ..... VI.5:6 Who b. the miracle perceives them all as
T-27 ..... VI.5:8 can deny, for it is the effects of life it b..
T-27 .. VII.14:4 He b. forgiving dreams, in which the
T-27 .. VII.14:5 the dreams He b. there is no murder and
T-27 ... VIII.7:5 It b. its vengeance, not your own. It keeps
T-27 . VIII.11:2 of the form of suffering that b. you pain.
T-28 ..... VI.3:9 hatred for the limitations that it b. to you.
T-29 ....... II.5:4 joy, and all the happiness His Presence b.,
T-29 ....... V.3:5 thought of love you offer him but b. you
T-29 .... VII.1:5 and find the happiness His answer b..
T-29 ..... IX.3:7 your judgment and the penalty it b..
T-29 ..... IX.8:5 complete, b. timelessness so close the
T-31 ........ I.8:8 the world this second lesson b..
T-31 .... VII.5:7 changed to one that b. the peace of God.
T-31 .. VII.11:7 He b. the light to what he looks upon,
W-pI .... 16.3:1 thought you have b. either peace or war;
W-pI .... 52.1:4 Reality b. only perfect peace. When I am
W-pI .... 58.2:3 see in its light shares in the joy it b. to me.
W-pI .... 61.4:3 It b. all the images you have made about
W-pI ....... 63.h The light of the world b. peace to every
W-pI .... 63.3:4 *The light of the world b. peace to every mind*
W-pI .... 74.2:5 experience the peace this recognition b..
W-pI .... 80.3:6 Accept the peace this simple statement b..
W-pI .... 80.5:1 that your acceptance b. be given you.
W-pI .... 82.1:1 light of the world b. peace to every mind
W-pI .... 92.4:5 It b. the light in which your Self appears.
W-pI .... 94.1:1 the one idea which b. complete salvation;
W-pI .... 99.6:1 the Thought that b. illusions to the truth,
W-pI .. 101.7:3 now today's idea b. wings to speed you on
W-pI .. 103.3:2 the happiness it b. as truth replaces fear,
W-pI .. 108.3:2 that b. your peace of mind to other minds
W-pI .. 108.3:3 that heals because it b. single perception,
W-pI .. 117.1:2 *love is happiness, and nothing else b. joy.*
W-pI .. 122.3:5 hold more hope than what forgiveness b.?
W-pI 122.11:1 what your acceptance of the answer b..
W-pI .. 123.6:1 the messenger who b. His Voice with you,
W-pI .. 133.5:3 you make b. everything to you or nothing
W-pI .. 136.7:2 makes you weak and b. you suffering. It is
W-pI .. 140.3:1 The happy dreams the Holy Spirit b. are
W-pI .. 140.7:4 mind that b. illusions to the truth is really
W-pI .. 153.2:2 For threat b. anger, anger makes attack
W-pI 153.12:5 come to see the benefits salvation b..
W-pI .. 154.5:2 who will receive the message that he b.. It
W-pI .. 157.2:3 It b. us to the door where learning ceases,
W-pI .. 157.3:3 b. you more swiftly to this holy place and
W-pI .. 161.2:6 to see. All hearing but b. to your mind the
W-pI .. 169.7:2 b. with it the experiences which bear
W-pI .. 170.1:4 believe to hurt another b. you freedom.
WpI...rV.in5:2 Every step we take b. us a little nearer.
Wi181-200 2:3 sense of liberation which their lifting b..

W-pI...182.4:6 and that **b.** to earth the pure reflection of
W-pI...187.3:3 miracles it **b.** to everyone you look upon.
W-pI...188.3:5 It **b.** renewal to all tired hearts, and lights
W-pI...193.8:4 Love, and all the gifts His Love **b.** with it.
W-pI.193.13:5 and **b.** the Love of God the Father down
W-pI...198.8:3 to it that **b.** illusions to the other side?
W-pI...199.8:5 increase of joy your practice **b.** even to it.
W-pII..267.1:5 Each heartbeat **b.** me peace; each breath
W-pII..288.1:1 *leads the way to You, and* **b.** *me to my goal. I*
W-pII......8.1:3 **b.** the witnesses of terror to your mind.
W-pII......9.2:2 end to the release the Second Coming **b.**,
W-pII....13.1:6 slip away under the gentle remedy it **b.**.
W-ep .........5:4 each choice you make **b.** Heaven nearer to
M-14..........2:6 He **b.** the ending of the world with Him.
M-14..........4:3 lesson, which **b.** the ending of the world,
M-14..........5:7 forgiveness **b.** all this to bless the world.
M-19..........3:2 distorts perception and **b.** witness of the
M-20..........2:4 It **b.** with it no past associations. It is a
C-4.............6:1 shift that true perception **b.**: What was
C-6.............3:9 And He **b.** the Love of your Father to you
P-2.........in.1:5 the belief that anger **b.** him something he
S-1.........V.1:4 Humility **b.** peace because it does not
S-3.........II.6:1 until it **b.** a cruel death in seeming victory
S-3........III.4:5 of the special gift that **b.** the healing. You
S-3........III.5:2 the remedy that **b.** relief which cannot fail

### broader 1

T-17......VI.1:7 in an understanding far **b.** than you now

### broadly 1

M-16..........2:6 **B.** speaking, then, it can be said that it is

### broke 2

T-30......IV.2:5 the bears did not deceive him, **b.** no rules,
W-pII..329.1:1 *from Your Will, defied it,* **b.** *its laws, and*

### broken 26

T-5.........II.5:7 Direct communication was **b.** because
T-13......XI.8:1 joining your mind with His, cannot be **b.**.
T-13......XI.8:2 You may believe you want It **b.**, and this
T-14......VI.5:2 means of re-establishing what was not **b.**,
T-16......IV.3:7 relationship is **b.** or becomes unsatisfying
T-16....IV.4:10 When the barricades against it are **b.**, fear
T-16.......V.1:2 **b.** into by periods in which they seem to
T-17......IV.4:6 relationship with Him has never been **b.**,
T-17.......V.3:8 Many relationships have been **b.** off at
T-18......I.12:5 apart what is already **b.** and hopeless? Is
T-18......I.12:7 you not prefer to heal what has been **b.**,
T-18......I.13:2 and reaches out to every **b.** fragment of
T-20.....VI.1:6 **b.** into fragments and full of fear. The one
T-23.......II.1:7 they govern nothing, and need not be **b.**;
T-26...VII.10:4 What can remain unhealed and **b.** from a
T-27.......II.5:1 A **b.** body shows the mind has not been
T-27.......V.3:4 the **b.** bodies and the shattered limbs, the
T-28......III.7:5 a picture of the Son of God in **b.** pieces,
T-28......IV.8:1 is to take the **b.** picture of the Son of God
T-28......IV.8:3 a little, **b.** bit that he insisted was himself.
T-28......IV.9:1 between the **b.** pieces of Your holy Son.
T-28......IV.9:5 the **b.** pieces seem to take mean nothing.
T-30......IV.2:3 **b.** his "control" of what surrounds him.
W-pI...109.6:1 glad, a bird with **b.** wings begins to sing, a
W-pI...159.3:4 can show but twisted images in **b.** parts.
M-19..........4:2 you perceive as **b.** off and separate. And it

### brooding 1

T-20.........I.1:2 week **b.** on the crucifixion of God's Son,

### brooks 1

T-20. VIII.11:1 them in dancing **b.** that never waste away;

### Brother 1

*brother*

W-pI...107.8:3 well. He is your **B.**, and so like to you your

### brother 606

*Brother*

T-1.........I.40:1 everyone as your **b.** and mine. It is a way
T-1.........II.1:6 Miracles unite you directly with your **b.**.
T-1.........II.3:7 An elder **b.** is entitled to respect for his
T-1.........II.3.8 is also entitled to love because he is a **b.**,
T-1.........II.4:5 as an elder **b.** to you on the one hand, and
T-1........III.7:6 bring in the stranger, he becomes your **b.**.
T-2.........II.7:8 knowing yourself as both a **b.** and a Son.
T-3........III.2:1 do not recognize yourself, your **b.** or God.
T-3........III.7:2 cannot know your **b.** when you attack him
T-3.........V.9:2 Correct perception of your **b.** is necessary,
T-4.........in.1:1 should go with a **b.** twice as far as he asks.
T-4.........in.1:3 to a **b.** cannot set you back either. It can
T-4.........I.13:2 **b.** who has shown himself responsible,
T-4.........I.13:3 **b.** can protect the child's body and his ego
T-4........IV.2:3 wrongly about some **b.** God created, and
T-4........IV.2:9 loving **b.** I am deeply concerned with your
T-4........IV.2:9 as you look at yourself and at your **b.**, and
T-4......IV.11:6 your **b.** will yet come together in my name
T-4........VI.2:1 to your **b.** is something you must never
T-4........VI.7:2 gratitude to your **b.** is the only gift I want.
T-4........VI.7:3 that to know your **b.** *is* to know God. If you
T-4........VI.7:4 God. If you are grateful to your **b.**, you are
T-4........VI.7:5 your gratitude you come to know your **b.**,
T-4........VI.7:5 **b.** because each of them is of your Father.
T-4........VI.8:1 you come closer to a **b.** you approach me,
T-5.........in.3:8 is: *Let me know this* **b.** *as I know myself.*
T-5........III.1:1 way to recognize your **b.** is by recognizing
T-5........III.2:7 It increases in you as you give it to your **b.**
T-5........III.2:8 Your **b.** does not have to be aware of the
T-5........III.3:1 opposed ways of seeing your **b.**. They
T-5........III.3:5 your **b.** you are acknowledging in yourself
T-5........IV.4:4 not want to show your **b.** anything except
T-5........IV.6:2 the way except by taking your **b.** with you
T-5........IV.6:8 you treat your **b.** better than by rendering
T-5......VI.11:4 with your **b.** is your patience with yourself
T-6.........in.1:4 that a **b.** is worthy of attack rather than of
T-6.........I.15:8 Judas was my **b.** and a Son of God, as
T-6......V.A.4:9 be no range in what you offer to your **b.**.
T-7.........II.1:2 When a **b.** perceives himself as sick, he is
T-7.........II.2:1 correct perception in your **b.** and yourself
T-7........IV.7:7 by not recognizing its existence in your **b.**.
T-7.........V.8:2 your **b.** by realizing that he could not have
T-7.......VII.1:1 Whenever you deny a blessing to a **b.** *you*
T-7.......VII.2:1 When a **b.** acts insanely, he is offering
T-7.......VII.3:9 Your **b.** is the mirror in which you see the
T-7.......VII.8:4 if you believe that your **b.** is attacking you
T-7.......VII.9:3 Whenever a **b.** attacks another, that *is*
T-7........XI.5:4 your **b.** is to accept your own inheritance.
T-7........XI.6:5 Whenever you heal a **b.** by recognizing his
T-8........III.5:8 are. Whenever you are with a **b.**, you are
T-8........III.7:8 releasing you and your **b.** from every
T-8.......VII.5:3 you look upon a **b.** as a physical entity, his
T-8.....VII.15:7 When you see a **b.** as a body, you are
T-9.........II.4:4 of the Holy Spirit truly, and doubt your **b.**
T-9.........II.5:1 message your **b.** gives you is up to you.
T-9.........II.5:6 What can so holy a **b.** tell you except truth
T-9.........II.5:8 it? Your **b.** may not know who he is, but
T-9.........II.6:3 Salvation is of your **b.**. The Holy Spirit
T-9.........II.6:9 It must be for your **b.** *because* it is for you.
T-9.........II.6:12 Hear of your **b.** what you would have me
T-9.........II.12:6 *myself, I see you as God's Son and my* **b.**.
T-9........III.2:4 When you correct a **b.**, you are telling him
T-9........III.4:3 sense as the **b.** whose errors you perceive.
T-9........III.5:1 When a **b.** behaves insanely, you can heal
T-9........III.5:6 Your **b.** is as right as you are, and if you
T-9........III.6:4 It is not up to you to change your **b.**, but
T-9........III.7:4 forgives all things in you and in your **b.**.
T-9........III.7:8 attempt you make to correct a **b.** means
T-9........IV.1:4 Accept as true only what your **b.** is, if you
T-9.........VI.h The Acceptance of Your **B.**
T-9........VI.2:4 you offer to your **b.** you offer to Him,
T-9........VI.3:8 If what you do to my **b.** you do to me, and
T-9........VI.7:8 your **b.** in this world and accept nothing
T-9........VI.7:9 learn that your **b.** is co-creator with you.
T-10......III.7:1 a **b.** is sick it is because he is not asking for
T-10......IV.7:2 it is the recognition that his **b.** can do it. It
T-10......IV.7:4 sick **b.** by weakening his belief in sickness,
T-11.......in.4:1 My **b.**, you are part of God and part of
T-11.........I.1:6 dwell in the Mind of God with your **b.**, for
T-11........II.2:5 either from your **b.** or in your own mind,
T-11......IV.3:4 you cut off a **b.** from the light that is yours
T-11.....V.18:1 Every **b.** you meet becomes a witness for
T-11.....V.18:4 Every **b.** has the power to release you, if
T-11......VI.4:4 perceive unworthiness in a **b.** and not
T-11....VIII.9:2 Do not, then, be deceived in your **b.**, and
T-11..VIII.10:6 Ask, then, to learn of the reality of your **b.**
T-11..VIII.11:4 **B.**, we heal together as we live together
T-11..VIII.12:1 in a **b.** pluck the offense from your mind,
T-12.........I.6:1 is an appropriate response to your **b.**.
T-12........I.6:10 Do not attempt to "help" a **b.** in your way,
T-12........II.2:6 Do not allow your **b.** not to remember, for
T-12........II.2:9 To perceive the healing of your **b.** as the
T-12........II.3:1 offer your **b.** what he believes he cannot
T-12........II.3:4 And to give a **b.** what he really wants is to
T-12........II.3:4 wills you to know your **b.** as yourself.
T-12......III.2:1 Suppose a **b.** insists on having you do
T-12......III.3:1 Whenever you become angry with a **b.**,
T-12......III.4:3 and every request of a **b.** is for you. Why
T-13......IV.5:5 to your **b.** as though he were someone else
T-13......IV.5:7 of release that every **b.** offers you *now.*
T-13.......V.3:6 and again have you attacked your **b.**,
T-13.......V.5:3 If you see your own hatred as your **b.**, you
T-13......VI.1:3 you perceive a **b.** only as you see him *now.*
T-13......VI.1:7 the past as you look upon your **b.**, you will
T-13......VI.5:1 miracle enables you to see your **b.** without
T-13....VIII.9:3 is as His. Deny a **b.** here, and you deny the
T-13......IX.4:4 When you condemn a **b.** you are saying,
T-13.........X.3:1 In any union with a **b.** in which you seek
T-13.....X.11:7 is like. No one who condemns a **b.** can see
T-14......III.6:3 to free his **b.** and enter light with him. By
T-14....VIII.3:2 **b.** may choose to lead yourselves astray,
T-14.........X.7:6 not respond to what a **b.** really offers you,
T-14.....X.11:4 you would lay upon a **b.** is senseless. Let
T-14.....X.12:2 **b.** must give it to you because of what it is.
T-15.......I.12:3 then, when you are tempted to attack a **b.**,
T-15.......I.13:2 It is as short for your **b.** as it is for you.
T-15........II.4:7 Holy Spirit in a **b.** is always recognized.
T-15....III.12:2 For where you would have your **b.** be,
T-15.....V.10:5 it. God loves every **b.** as He loves you;
T-15......VI.1:6 that you can make a **b.** into what he is not
T-15...VII.12:2 to attempt to keep your **b.** in his body,
T-15......IX.4:4 Limit your sight of a **b.** to his body, which
T-15....XI.10:4 Say, then, to your **b.**: *I give you to the Holy*
T-16.........I.5:1 is not what you would offer to a **b.**. And
T-16.........I.6:4 if a **b.** asks a foolish thing of you to do it.
T-17....III.10:1 My holy **b.**, I would enter into all your
T-17.......V.6:6 in your **b.** in what but seems to be a trying
T-17.......V.7:2 your distress only by getting rid of your **b.**
T-17.......V.7:4 major areas of fantasy from your **b.**, to
T-17.....V.7:13 Abandon Him not now, nor your **b.**. This
T-17.......V.8:2 **b.** for the "failure" of your relationship,
T-17.......V.9:3 that you and your **b.** have started again,
T-17.....V.10:7 come to join you and your **b.** together in a
T-17.....V.11:6 you been similarly grateful to your **b.**?
T-17.....V.12:5 to your **b.** is to appreciate the holy instant
T-17.....V.12:6 To attack your **b.** is not to lose the instant,
T-17.....V.13:4 this every time you attack your **b.**, for the
T-17.....V.14:1 **b.** stand together in the holy presence of
T-17.....V.15:1 gifts you have so freely given to your **b.**,
T-17.....VII.4:3 faith in your **b.** was so limited and little.
T-17.....VII.4:6 faith, and remain faithful to your **b.**?
T-17.....VII.6:3 And so you have been faithless to your **b.**,
T-17.....VII.8:1 against your **b.** what he has done to you.
T-17.....VII.9:1 situation with the faith you give your **b.**,
T-18.........I.9:1 In your relationship with your **b.**, where
T-18.........I.9:3 you love your **b.** with a perfect love. Here
T-18.........I.9:4 where only the truth in your **b.** can abide.
T-18.........I.9:9 Give Him but a little faith in your **b.**, to
T-18.......I.10:1 no substitute can keep you from your **b.**.
T-18.......I.10:8 God is with you, my **b.**. Let us join in Him
T-18.......I.11:7 stands with you, together with your **b.**.

T-18.......I.12:4 walking together with your **b.** out of this
T-18.......I.13:1 have been called, together with your **b.**, to
T-18.......I.13:5 purpose in which you join with your **b.**.
T-18....... II.8:4 relationship with your **b.** has now become
T-18...... III.4:5 the gift of faith you offered to your **b.**. You
T-18...... III.6:7 to me? For when you joined your **b.**, you
T-18...... III.7:5 you and your **b.** experience is really past.
T-18...... III.8:5 and your **b.** are coming home together,
T-18...... III.8:6 You have found your **b.**, and you will light
T-18....... V.5:1 It is no dream to love your **b.** as yourself.
T-18....... V.6:4 for you or your **b.** to experience fear alone
T-18....... V.7:3 *for myself, that I may share it with my* **b.**,
T-18..... VII.5:3 your **b.** restores the universe to both of
T-18..... VII.6:3 you because you and your **b.** are together.
T-18..VIII.12:2 of all the barriers you hold against your **b.**
T-18..VIII.12:4 alone than He knows you without your **b.**.
T-18..VIII.13:6 dust still stands between you and your **b.**.
T-18.... IX.13:1 Your relationship with your **b.** has been
T-18.... IX.13:3 which you and your **b.** were united is but
T-19.........I.4:2 is the perception of a **b.** as a body, and the
T-19.........I.4:3 If, then, you see your **b.** as a body, you
T-19.........I.9:4 your **b.** has done before to condemn him
T-19.......I.10:4 It is His Love that joins you and your **b.**,
T-19.......I.12:5 offers you faith to give unto your **b.**. Your
T-19.......I.13:4 then, offer grace and blessing to your **b.**,
T-19.......I.14:1 **b.** stand before the altar God has raised
T-19.......I.14:6 and your **b.** who stand together before the
T-19...... III.9:5 that you give it no power over your **b.**.
T-19.... III.10:1 Heaven shining on both you and your **b.**.
T-19.... III.11:1 what He would show you in your **b.**, and
T-19.... III.11:2 have you look upon your **b.** as yourself.
T-19...... IV.1:6 peace He lay, deep within you and your **b.**
T-19...... IV.1:6 life, surrounding you and your **b.** with
T-19...... IV.2:7 forever impossible to appreciate your **b.**.
T-19...... IV.3:2 with gentle graciousness upon your **b.**,
T19... IV.A.2:4 sand still stands between you and your **b.**.
T19. IV.A.2:10 you cherish still against your **b.** *is* the first
T19... IV.A.3:7 your **b.** seems mightier than the universe,
T19. IV.A.4:10 You have no purpose apart from your **b.**,
T19... IV.A.5:7 you and your **b.** must fall away because of
T19... IV.A.6:3 stand between you and your **b.** now. Look
T19. IV.A.15:5 **b.** and return to you with what love sees.
T19..IV.B.4:11 When you agreed to join your **b.**, you
T19....IV.B.5:8 you stop now to look for guilt in your **b.**?
T19....IV.B.6:1 upon your **b.** as you would look on me.
T19....IV.B.8:2 I taught by teaching freedom to your **b.**,
T19....IV.C.1:1 To you and your **b.**, in whose special
T19....IV.C.8:2 My **b.**, child of our Father, this is a *dream*
T19....IV.C.9:2 protected by your union with your **b.**, and
T19..IV.C.10:7 place by your forgiveness of your **b.**, and
T19... IV.D.8:1 came this far together, you and your **b.**.
T19... IV.D.8:7 lift up your eyes and look on your **b.** in
T19... IV.D.9:2 this far unless his **b.** walked beside him.
T19... IV.D.9:3 complete forgiveness of his **b.** in his heart.
T19. IV.D.10:3 Once he has found his **b.** he *is* ready. Yet
T19. IV.D.11:3 it until you look upon your **b.** with perfect
T19. IV.D.11:5 are afraid of God *because* you fear your **b.**.
T19. IV.D.12:1 This **b.** who stands beside you still seems
T19. IV.D.12:7 **B.**, you need forgiveness of your brother,
T19. IV.D.12:7 Brother, you need forgiveness of your **b.**,
T19. IV.D.15:1 is your **b.**, crucified by sin and waiting for
T19. IV.D.15:5 of Heaven that you cannot offer to your **b.**
T19. IV.D.15:8 has been given you to give your **b.**, and
T19 IV.D15:10 the sins your **b.** thinks he has committed,
T19. IV.D.16:2 Think who your **b.** is, before you would
T19. IV.D.17:1 Give faith to your **b.**, for faith and hope
T19. IV.D.17:3 Look on your **b.**, and see in him the gift of
T19. IV.D.17:7 And be you and your **b.** free together, as
T19. IV.D.18:1 Free your **b.** here, as I freed you. Give him
T19. IV.D.18:4 your **b.** freedom and complete release
T19. IV.D.19:6 Heaven is the gift you owe your **b.**, the
T19. IV.D.21:6 You and your **b.** stand together, still
T-20.........I.2:5 sins. Offer your **b.** the gift of lilies, not the
T-20.........I.2:6 You stand beside your **b.**, thorns in one
T-20....... II.1:4 this hated thing to draw your **b.** to you,
T-20....... II.3:5 that you lay upon your **b.** and on yourself.
T-20....... II.6:1 look with different eyes upon your **b.**. You
T-20....... II.9:1 you not have your holy **b.** lead you there?
T-20..... II.11:3 gladly will you and your **b.** walk the way
T-20 .....II.11:4 Give joyously to your **b.** the freedom and
T-20 .....II.11:6 The lamp is lit in you for your **b.**. And by
T-20 ..... III.8:6 your **b.** with joy to bless the Son of God,
T-20 ..... III.8:7 you recognize your **b.** as the eternal gift of
T-20 ..... III.8:8 that shone in both you and your **b.**, to
T-20 ... III.10:1 Such is my will for you and your **b.**, and
T-20 ... III.10:7 with you, my friend, my **b.** and my Self.
T-20 ... III.11:1 Your gift unto your **b.** has given me the
T-20 ... III.11:7 You and your **b.** now will lead the other to
T-20 ... III.11:8 **b.** is the light of God's eternal promise of
T-20 ..... IV.2:2 lies your need to see your **b.** sinless. In
T-20 ..... IV.5:2 the power of sinlessness within your **b.**,
T-20 ..... IV.7:2 of your **b.** serves but you two alone. For
T-20 ...... V.2:6 You give to your **b.** for everyone, and in
T-20 ...... V.5:5 And while you look upon your **b.** thus, the
T-20 ...... V.6:7 day offer to your **b.** already offered you;
T-20 ...... V.7:9 **b.** will offer and receive it for you both.
T-20 ..... VI.6:8 not realize is what you fear within your **b.**,
T-20 ..... VI.7:3 **B.**, you tremble with them. Yet what you
T-20 ... VI.10:5 which you and your **b.** walk together,
T-20 ... VI.12:8 Perhaps you fear your **b.** a little yet;
T-20 ... VII.4:1 *is* impossible to see your **b.** as sinless and
T-20 ... VII.5:4 so the illusion of a **b.** as a body is quite in
T-20 ... VII.8:7 holy **b.**, sight of whom is your release, is
T-20 ... VII.9:1 "How can I see my **b.** without the body?"
T-20 ...VIII.1:1 what is given you who see your **b.** sinless.
T-20 ...VIII.2:8 you who would but see your **b.** sinless. All
T-20 ...VIII.3:3 willing, then, to see your **b.** sinless, that
T-20 ...VIII.4:4 And as you look upon your **b.**, you will see
T-21 ......I.10:7 all. And when you see it in your **b.**, you *are*
T-21 .......II.5:7 This was your gift to you and to your **b.**.
T-21 .....II.12:6 **b.** thinks he made the world with you.
T-21 .....II.13:1 truth is you and your **b.** were both created
T-21 .....II.13:3 seems to stand between you and your **b.**,
T-21 ..... III.1:3 and any **b.** with whom you have a limited
T-21 ..... III.7:5 belief. But holiness would set your **b.** free,
T-21 ..... III.9:2 **B.**, the Holy Spirit knows that sacrifice
T-21 ..... III.9:8 faith you give your **b.** can accomplish this.
T-21 ..... IV.5:1 part has seen your **b.**, and recognized him
T-21 ..... IV.8:1 Look gently on your **b.**, and remember
T-21 ..... VI.1:7 so, you deny it to yourself and to your **b.**.
T-21 ..... VI.2:1 or refused by you without your **b.**. Sin
T-21 ..... VI.2:3 that you cannot see your **b.** or yourself as
T-21 ..... VI.2:6 Sin would maintain you and your **b.** must
T-21 ..... VI.2:8 If you and your **b.** are joined, how could it
T-21 ..... VI.5:1 body does not separate you from your **b.**,
T-21 ..... VI.7:1 your **b.** nor yourself can be attacked alone
T-21 ..... VI.8:1 and your **b.** are joined is your salvation;
T-21 ..... VI.9:7 of what is given you to give your **b.**, and
T-21 ... VI.10:5 Your Father is as close to you as is your **b.**.
T-21 .... VII.2:8 each one as likely to attack his **b.** or turn
T-22 ......in.1:6 **B.**, it is the same, made by the same, and
T-22 ......in.1:7 your relationship forgives you and your **b.**
T-22 ......in.4:5 Reason now can lead you and your **b.** to
T-22 ......in.4:7 the body, to let you and your **b.** be joined.
T-22 ........I.8:1 Think what is given you, my holy **b.**. This
T-22 ......I.11:4 and your **b.** together draws Him to you.
T-22 ......I.11:7 in looking on your **b.** as His chosen home,
T-22 .......II.7:1 Forsake not now your **b.**. For you who are
T-22 .....II.12:1 you interposed between you and your **b.**,
T-22 .....II.13:2 who is but willing to see his **b.** sinless.
T-22 .....II.13:7 Look on your holy **b.**, sinless as yourself,
T-22 ..... III.8:3 see. Let your awareness of your **b.** not be
T-22 ..... IV.3:1 And so you and your **b.** stand, here in
T-22 ..... IV.3:3 Raise it together with your **b.**, for it is but
T-22 ..... IV.3:4 or your **b.** alone will see it as a solid block,
T-22 ..... IV.4:2 will you and your **b.** look to the other!
T-22 ..... IV.5:1 Every mistake you and your **b.** make, the
T-22 ..... IV.6:4 veil you and your **b.** lift together opens
T-22 ..... IV.7:8 illusion stands between you and your **b.**,
T-22 ...... V.3:4 In truth you and your **b.** stand together,
T-22 ...... V.4:8 **b.** are not joined together by this mouse,
T-22 ...... V.5:1 awareness of your union with your **b.**! Be
T-22 ...... V.6:5 and immovable, between you and your **b.**.
T-22 ...... V.6:7 If you forgive your **b.**, this *must* happen.
T-22 ...... V.6:8 your **b.** that makes it look impenetrable,
T-22 ..... VI.3:6 You will be sanctified by your **b.**, using
T-22 ..... VI.4:5 Neither you nor your **b.** alone can serve at
T-22 ..... VI.7:1 upon your **b.** with complete forgiveness,
T-22 ..... VI.8:7 Spirit does with gifts you give your **b.**, to
T-22 ..... VI.9:9 Each little gift you offer to your **b.** lights
T-22 ... VI.9:10 look away from it and toward your **b.**.
T-22 ... VI.9:11 confidence with which you bless your **b.**.
T-22 ... VI.12:4 and your **b.** were separate from the other,
T-22 ... VI.13:2 attack, you and your **b.** must be different.
T-22 ... VI.13:4 *Because* you and your **b.** are not different,
T-22 ... VI.13:7 is whether you and your **b.** are different.
T-22 ... VI.15:1 your **b.** shines throughout the universe,
T-22 ... VI.15:7 if you and your **b.** be different or the same
T-23 ........I.4:1 **B.**, the war against yourself is almost over
T-23 ......I.10:5 Welcome your **b.** to the home where God
T-23 ...II.12:10 for love, born of your enmity to your **b.**,
T-23 .....II.13:2 And never will your **b.** cease his attack on
T-23 .....II.18:3 **B.**, you *do* believe them. For how else could
T-23 .....II.22:1 **B.**, take not one step in the descent to hell
T-23 ..... III.2:1 for God speaks through you to your **b.**?
T-23 ..... III.2:5 Withhold forgiveness from your **b.** and
T-23 ..... IV.4:2 of your **b.** is not complete as yet, and so it
T-24 ........I.5:2 of what you are and what your **b.** is. And
T-24 ........I.5:6 **b.** must become to keep your specialness
T-24 ........I.6:1 it be possible for you to hate your **b.** if you
T-24 ........I.7:1 Your **b.** is your friend because his Father
T-24 ........I.7:3 to your **b.** that love might be extended,
T-24 ........I.7:5 God gave you and your **b.** Himself, and to
T-24 ........I.7:7 Could you attack your **b.** if you chose to
T-24 ........I.7:8 you give your **b.** only partial welcome, or
T-24 ......I.7:10 you and your **b.** illusions to each other?
T-24 ........I.8:1 The fear of God and of your **b.** comes
T-24 ........I.8:2 demand your **b.** bow to it against his will.
T-24 ........I.8:5 and your **b.** share becomes obscured from
T-24 ........I.8:6 it teaches you you and your **b.** are alike.
T-24 ........I.9:3 love your **b.** not while it is this you would
T-24 .......II.7:5 one you and your **b.** both can understand,
T-24 .......II.7:6 stands your **b.** with the key to Heaven in
T-24 .......II.9:5 receive you and your **b.** in silent blessing,
T-24 .....II.10:5 Son to be like Him, and your **b.** *is* like you.
T-24 .....II.10:7 Himself to you and your **b.** in equal love,
T-24 .....II.14:1 The key you threw away God gave your **b.**
T-24 ..... III.6:6 release your **b.** from the depths of hell,
T-24 ..... IV.4:2 wish that you might see your **b.** sinless.
T-24 ..... IV.4:4 A sinless **b.** *is* its enemy, while sin, if it
T-24 ..... IV.5:2 you have beheld some sin within your **b.**,
T-24 .......V.4:6 think not that it looked upon your **b.** first,
T-24 .......V.8:4 And would He give a **b.** unto you except
T-24 ..... VI.1:7 And the sign that this is so lies in your **b.**,
T-24 ..... VI.3:6 Your **b.** *is* as He created him. And it is this
T-24 ..... VI.5:1 Look on your **b.**, and behold in him the
T-24 ..... VI.6:4 memory of Him in Whom your **b.** lives,
T-24 ..... VI.9:3 will haunt you while your **b.** lies asleep,
T-24 ... VI.10:7 The Christ in you can see your **b.** truly.
T-24 .... VII.2:2 within your **b.** still contains all of creation
T-24 .. VII.11:3 Father's Son, within your **b.** as he is in you
T-25 ......in.3:7 is the mission that your **b.** has for you.
T-25 ........I.1:6 And you are manifest unto your holy **b.**,
T-25 ........I.2:7 one. And you must see your **b.** as yourself.
T-25 ........I.4:6 You and your **b.** stand before Him now,
T-25 .......II.5:2 Yet if you see your **b.** as a body, it is but
T-25 .......II.8:1 your **b.** as his Father's Mind shows him to
T-25 .......II.9:6 This **b.** is His perfect gift to you. And He is
T-25 .....II.10:1 Forgive your **b.**, and you cannot separate
T-25 .....II.10:8 and your **b.** with you and at one with you.
T-25 .....II.11:1 **b.** are the same, as God Himself is One
T-25 .....II.11:3 by offering completion to your **b.**. See not
T-25 .....II.11:5 and your **b.** is given the power of salvation
T-25 .......V.2:9 you, each time you look upon your **b.**. He
T-25 .......V.6:3 In your **b.** you see the picture of your own
T-25 .......V.6:5 be hell. Look once again upon your **b.**, not
T-25 ..... VI.3:2 Would you behold your **b.**? God is glad to
T-25 ... VI.5:11 in form, to let it serve his **b.** and himself,
T-25 ..... VI.7:8 This is the function given you for your **b.**.
T-26 ........I.1:6 To see a **b.** in another body, separate from
T-26 ........I.3:7 these limits on each **b.** whom you see. For
T-26 ........I.4:2 And while you see your **b.** as a body, apart
T-26 ........I.6:3 Hear, then, the song your **b.** sings to you,
T-26 ..... IV.6:1 and your **b.** still is holding back the happy
T-26 .....V.14:5 Look gently on your **b.**, and behold the
T-26 .... VII.8:7 you impose between your **b.** and yourself.
T-26 .... VII.9:1 what stands between your **b.** and yourself.

T-26...VII.16:2 this Name your **b.** calls for his release and
T-26...VII.19:2 And be the means whereby your **b.** finds
T-26...VII.19:8 No wishes lie between a **b.** and his own.
T-26... VIII.1:1 receive the benefits of trusting in your **b.**.
T-26... VIII.1:2 you would keep between you and your **b.**,
T-26... VIII.2:1 you would keep apart from your **b.**, and
T-26... VIII.3:8 a little space between you and your **b.** still
T-26... VIII.4:1 your **b.** is apparent only in the present,
T-26......IX.1:1 Voice for God calls lovingly unto your **b.**,
T-26......IX.2:2 your **b.** and yourself obscures the face of
T-26........X.5:1 You think your **b.** is unfair to you because
T-27.........I.1:4 which your **b.** and yourself will not escape
T-27.........I.3:1 accuse your **b.** of attack upon God's Son.
T-27.........I.4:6 easy price, if they can say, "Behold me, **b.**,
T-27...... I.4:10 sent your **b.** *you* have looked upon in grief.
T-27.........I.5:5 Show this unto your **b.**, who will see that
T-27.........I.6:7 your **b.** and yourself in different tongues.
T-27.........I.9:1 is to show your **b.** sin can have no cause.
T-27...... I.10:7 And to your **b.** let its message be, "Behold
T-27...... I.10:7 brother let its message be, "Behold me, **b.**,
T-27....... II.1:5 Who has been injured by his **b.**, and could
T-27....... II.2:8 Who can say and mean, "My **b.**, you have
T-27....... II.3:3 grant your **b.** mercy but retain the proof
T-27....... II.4:1 it brings a healing to your **b.** and yourself.
T-27....... II.4:7 offering salvation to your **b.** and yourself.
T-27....... II.6:8 **B.**, there is no death. And this you learn
T-27....... II.6:9 show your **b.** that you had no hurt of him.
T-27....... II.7:2 from guilt upon your **b.** and yourself.
T-27....... II.7:7 see your **b.** with no blood upon his hands,
T-27..... II.11:4 does he become your victim, not your **b.**,
T-27..... II.14:4 fear. This is your **b.**, focus of your hate,
T-27...... III.2:1 that your **b.** is a symbol for a "hateful love
T-27...... III.3:1 The picture of your **b.** that you see means
T-27...... III.3:7 picture of your **b.** that you see is wholly
T-27...... III.6:1 picture of your **b.** given you to occupy the
T-27....... V.7:7 And happily your **b.** will perceive the
T-27...... V.10:4 Your **b.** first among them will be seen, but
T-27..... VII.6:4 In separation from your **b.** was the first
T-27...VII.12:1 A **b.** separated from yourself, an ancient
T-27...VII.12:2 destroyer of your **b.** and the world alike.
T-27...VII.13:4 healed and where his **b.** was his friend.
T-27...VII.15:1 Dream softly of your sinless **b.**, who
T-27...VII.16:1 **B.**, He gives but life. Yet what you see as
T-27...VII.16:2 Yet what you see as gifts your **b.** offers
T-27... VIII.7:1 can attack itself; a separate **b.** as an enemy
T-27... VIII.9:7 But hear Him say, "My **b.**, holy Son of
T-27. VIII.13:5 world, and kept your **b.** separate from you
T-28....... II.7:5 that he dreams he gave his **b.**. And it is
T-28...... III.3:3 Do not allow your **b.** to be sick, for if he is,
T-28...... III.8:2 seen to stand between you and your **b.**,
T-28...... IV.1:8 do you and your **b.** both become illusions,
T-28...... IV.3:1 Like you, your **b.** thinks he is a dream.
T-28...... IV.3:3 persist, but as a mind which **b.** is to you.
T-28...... IV.3:4 He is not **b.** made by what he dreams, nor
T-28...... IV.3:4 is his body, "hero" of the dream, your **b.**.
T-28...... IV.3:5 It is his reality that is your **b.**, as is yours
T-28...... IV.7:6 that he was separated from his **b.** who, by
T-28....... V.1:3 that is perceived between you and your **b.**,
T-28....... V.3:7 to be your enemy; and will attack your **b.**,
T-28....... V.7:1 is a little gap between you and your **b.**, do
T-28...... VI.4:3 made with every **b.** who would walk apart
T-28...... VI.5:5 death. And by his healing is his **b.** healed.
T-28..... VII.3:1 there is a gap between you and your **b.**, or
T-29.........I.1:6 a gap between your **b.** and yourself. How
T-29.........I.3:4 had decided that your **b.** is your enemy.
T-29.........I.3:9 and your **b.** but shared a qualified entente
T-29.........I.4:1 gap between you and your **b.** is not one of
T-29.........I.4:7 diminishes as you and your **b.** meet.
T-29.........I.5:4 it determines when your **b.** and you meet,
T-29.........I.8:3 nothing stands between you and your **b.**?
T-29.... III.3:10 In glory will you see your **b.** then, and
T-29...... III.4:2 On earth this means forgive your **b.**, that
T-29...... IV.5:6 becomes a **b.** giving you a chance to help,
T-29...... IV.6:1 What is your **b.** for? You do not know,
T-29....... V.6:6 Your **b.** thinks he holds the hand of death.
T-29...... VI.1:1 How willing are you to forgive your **b.**?
T-29..... VII.9:3 Save time, my **b.**; learn what time is for.
T-29... VIII.1:6 idol is an image of your **b.** that you would
T-29... VIII.4:1 is to separate your **b.** from yourself. A
T-29... VIII.9:6 God bestowed upon your **b.** and on you,
T-30...... II.5:4 you chose to look upon your **b.** as a friend
T-30....... V.6:4 The gap between your **b.** and yourself was
T-30..... V.10:5 Be merciful unto your **b.**, then. And do
T-30..... VI.4:7 If you can see your **b.** merits pardon, you
T-30..... VI.4:8 judgment that your **b.** does not merit. For
T-30..... VI.8:1 Look on your **b.** with the willingness to
T-30.... VI.10:1 Look on your **b.** with this hope in you,
T-30..... VII.6:2 meaningful to you and to your **b.**. Thus
T-30..... VII.7:5 Do not continue thus, my **b.**. We have one
T-30... VIII.2:3 **b.** has a changelessness in him beyond
T-30... VIII.5:2 be given you to look upon your **b.** thus.
T-30... VIII.5:9 He is the changeless in your **b.** and in you.
T-30... VIII.6:1 hold in place of what your **b.** really is. Let
T-31....... II.4:4 And this is what you made your **b.** for,
T-31....... II.6:2 *that I give my* **b.** *is what I am asking for. And*
T-31....... II.6:5 This **b.** neither leads nor follows us, but
T-31....... II.9:1 Forgive your **b.** all appearances, that are
T-31..... II.10:5 you love your **b.** with a brother's love.
T-31..... II.10:6 And as a **b.**, must his Father be the same
T-31...... III.1:5 You never hate your **b.** for his sins, but
T-31...... III.7:3 penalty exacted from your **b.** or yourself.
T-31...... IV.8:4 you choose between your **b.** and yourself,
T-31...... IV.8:5 teach that what your **b.** loses *you* have lost,
T-31....... V.6:1 ensures your **b.** is condemned eternally.
T-31....... V.6:8 Your **b.** then is symbol of your sins to you
T-31....... V.6:8 still your **b.** for the hated thing you are.
T-31....... V.9:2 is that you are what your **b.** made of you.
T-31..... V.10:1 your **b.** made of you seems most unlikely.
T-31..... V.10:7 If one were generated by your **b.**, who was
T-31..... V.12:2 be the thing you chose to have your **b.** be.
T-31..... V.12:7 first? If you are what you chose your **b.** be,
T-31..... V.13:6 stand accused of guilt for what your **b.** is.
T-31..... VII.2:5 But should *one* **b.** dawn upon your sight as
T-31..... VII.8:4 upon one **b.** as he looks upon himself, and
T-31..... VII.9:1 there is a space between you and your **b.**,
T-31..... VII.9:2 that holds your **b.** off unoccupied by love.
T-31...VII.10:3 to see his **b.** not as this has saved himself,
T-31...VII.12:4 you will behold your **b.** in the likeness of
T-31...VII.13:1 as innocent of what your **b.** is as it is free
T-31... VIII.3:2 Christ calls to you and gently says, "My **b.**
T-31. VIII.11:1 to every **b.** who would join with me in
W-pI..... 43.2:7 by which the Son of God forgives his **b.**,
W-pI..... 69.1:5 He is your **b.** in the light of the world that
W-pI..... 72.5:7 It overlooks entirely what your **b.** is. It
W-pI... 105.7:2 *My* **b.**, *peace and joy I offer you, That I may*
W-pI... 105.9:4 a **b.** seems to tempt you to deny God's gift
W-pI... 105.9:5 Then bless your **b.** thankfully, and say: *My*
W-pI... 105.9:6 *My* **b.**, *peace and joy I offer you, That I may*
W-pI... 108.5:2 or that to forgive one **b.** wholly is enough
W-pI... 109.9:2 Each **b.** comes to take his rest, and offer it
W-pI... 110.8:1 in you, the Son of God and **b.** to the world
W-pI... 110.8:1 the Word that tells him he is **b.** unto Him.
W-pI. 127.12:4 *I bless you,* **b.**, *with the Love of God, which I*
W-pI... 134.7:5 eyes, and merely says to them, "My **b.**,
W-pI... 134.8:5 For if one **b.** has received this gift of you,
W-pI. 134.15:1 Then choose one **b.** as He will direct, and
W-pI. 134.16:4 chains you sought to lay upon your **b.**, but
W-pI... 151.7:2 He will not tell you that your **b.** should be
W-pI. 158.10:3 remember in your **b.** you but see yourself.
W-pI. 158.10:5 Each **b.** whom you meet today provides
W-pI... 159.2:3 You recognize your **b.** as yourself, and
W-pI. 160.10:5 Who denies his **b.** is denying Him, and
W-pI... 161.4:1 One **b.** is all brothers. Every mind
W-pI... 161.8:1 Who sees a **b.** as a body sees him as fear's
W-pI. 161.11:1 Select one **b.**, symbol of the rest, and ask
W-pI. 161.12:5 should you be tempted to attack a **b.** and
W-pI... 162.6:1 And who would not be **b.** to you now;
W-pI... 164.6:1 **B.**, this day is sacred to the world. Your
WpI...rV.in7:1 again each time I lead a **b.** safely to the
WpI...rV.in7:2 I am renewed each time a **b.** learns there
W-pI... 181.1:2 When you attack a **b.**, you proclaim that
W-pI. 182.11:2 Christ has called you friend and **b.**. He has
W-pI... 183.5:4 you join a **b.** as you sit with him in silence,
W-pI... 184.8:4 When you call upon a **b.**, it is to his body
W-pI... 187.9:1 your **b.** offers you are laid upon your altar
W-pI. 187.10:3 not distant from one **b.** who is part of our
W-pI... 190.6:1 My holy **b.**, think of this awhile: The
W-pI... 193.6:4 to everything you see or any **b.** looks upon
W-pI... 195.3:1 **b.** is your "enemy" because you see in him
W-pI... 195.4:1 because your **b.** is more slave than you,
W-pI... 196.1:3 belief that to attack a **b.** saves yourself.
W-pI... 201.1:2 me. *No one but is my* **b.**. *I am blessed with*
W-pII ..... 1.1:1 your **b.** did to you has not occurred. It
W-pII . 225.2:1 **B.**, we find that stillness now. The way is
W-pII . 231.2:1 This is your will, my **b.**. And you share
W-pII . 247.1:5 **B.**, come and let me look on you. Your
W-pII ..... 5.4:3 of God extends his hand to reach his **b.**,
W-pII . 274.1:1 *the love of* **b.** *to his brother and his Friend.*
W-pII . 274.1:1 *the love of brother to his* **b.** *and his Friend.*
W-pII . 288.1:2 *I cannot come to You without my* **b.**. *And to*
W-pII . 288.1:7 *My* **b.** *is my savior. Let me not attack the*
W-pII . 288.2:2 you behold your **b.** in the light of holiness.
W-pII . 313.2:4 **B.**, come and join with me today. We save
W-pII . 315.1:3 A **b.** smiles upon another, and my heart is
W-pII . 316.1:3 gift a **b.** has received throughout all time,
W-pII . 334.2:4 *Today I would behold my* **b.** *sinless. This*
W-pII . 335.1:2 I never see my **b.** as he is, for that is far
W-pII . 335.1:7 having chosen to behold my **b.** in its holy
W-pII . 342.2:1 **B.**, forgive me now. I come to you to take
W-pII .... 344.h that what I give my **b.** is my gift to me.
W-pII ... 14.3:4 We look on everyone as **b.**, and perceive
W-pII .... 351.h My sinless **b.** is my guide to peace. My
W-pII .... 351.h My sinful **b.** is my guide to pain. And
W-pII . 351.1:1 *Who is my* **b.** *but Your holy Son? And if I see*
W-pII . 351.1:4 *I can also see my* **b.** *sinless, as Your holy Son.*
W-pII . 357.1:2 *holy Son is pointed out to me, first in my* **b.**;
W-pII .... 360.h Peace to my **b.**, who is one with me. Let all
Wfl........in.4:3 And shall we not forgive our **b.**, who can
W-ep ......... 4:4 of your Father and your **b.** and your Self.
M-4 ...... IV.1:5 a verdict of guilt upon a **b.**, and therefore
M-5 ...... III.3:1 of sickness in which their **b.** believes. To
M-5 ...... III.3:3 They seek for God's Voice in this **b.** who
M-13 ......... 7:9 is denied if you attack any **b.** for anything.
M-22 ......... 5:4 hardly offer it to his **b.** in Christ's Name.
M-22 ......... 5:5 in fact, be unable to recognize his **b.** at all,
M-22 ......... 5:5 so he is seeing in his **b.** only the unreal.
C-5............. 5:6 a **b.** whom you knew since you were born,
C-5............. 5:7 of him who would be only **b.** to the world.
C-5............. 5:8 behold how dear a **b.** he would be to you.
C-6............. 5:2 Your **b.** calls to you to be His Voice along
P-2......... V.3:7 out his **b.** as his savior from the world.
P-2......... V.5:1 A **b.** seeking aid can bring us gifts beyond
P-2......... V.8:4 Hear a **b.** call for help and answer him. It
P-2....... VII.5:3 for his **b.** in the role of guide for him?
P-2....... VII.9:3 Son. Who is your **b.** now? What saint can
P-3........... I.2:1 Who, then, decides what each **b.** needs?
P-3.......... II.7:3 that it is no harder to wake a **b.** from one
P-3....... II.9:10 meeting there is One Who says, "My **b.**,
P-3........ III.5:9 they believe they need anything from a **b.**,
P-3........ III.5:9 they will recognize him as a **b.** no longer.
P-3........ III.6:6 sent to give his **b.** the money he needed.
S-1 ........ III.1:4 your projections of guilt from your **b.**,
S-1 ........ III.3:5 *asked for for my* **b.** *is not what I would have.*
S-1 ......... V.4:2 and your **b.** stands beside you there. The
S-2.......... II.7:1 What would you show your **b.**? Would
S-2........ III.7:8 Behold your **b.** there beyond the door; the
S-3........... I.3:4 of judgment made by **b.** upon brother,
S-3........... I.3:4 of judgment made by brother upon **b.**,

## brother's 81

T-9........ III.3:1 point out the errors of your **b.** ego you
T-9........ III.7:1 Your **b.** errors are not of him, any more
T-9........ VI.4:9 you will judge it as you judge your **b.**, and
T-11..VIII.11:1 not accept your **b.** variable perception of
T-12......... I.3:5 in responding with anger to a **b.** plea for
T-12......... I.5:6 when you refuse to recognize a **b.** appeal,
T-12......... I.7:1 of your **b.** needs are your interpretation of
T-14...... IV.1:1 When you accept a **b.** guiltlessness you
T-14...... IV.1:3 not see the symbol of your **b.** guiltlessness
T-18...... III.4:1 who hold your **b.** hand also hold mine,
T-18...... III.5:5 as surely as you agreed to take your **b.**.
T-18...... VI.2:8 it would remain separate from your **b.**,
T-18.... VI.10:2 hand is joined with your **b.** have begun to
T-19...... III.7:1 reality or your **b.** is bounded by a body,
T-20......... I.4:2 will behold your **b.** face and recognize it. I
T-20...... III.9:3 feebly in the dust and found your **b.** hand

| | |
|---|---|
| T-20 V.3:1 | impossible to overestimate your **b.** value. |
| T-20 V.3:6 | It will be given you to see your **b.** worth |
| T-20 V.5:1 | **b.** body is as little use to you as it is to him |
| T-20 V.7:5 | This is no gift your **b.** body offers you. |
| T-20 VII.6:1 | sees a **b.** body has laid a judgment on him |
| T-20 VII.6:7 | is your **b.** reality imagined as a body, in |
| T-20 VIII.3:1 | **b.** sinlessness is given you in shining light |
| T-20 VIII.3:4 | joy. And place no value on your **b.** body, |
| T-21 VI.9:1 | *are* your **b.** savior. He is yours. Reason |
| T-22 II.h | Your **B.** Sinlessness |
| T-22 IV.5:3 | And you will be your **b.** strong protector |
| T-22 IV.5:8 | Into your hand, joined with your **b.**, is it |
| T-22 IV.7:6 | hold out your hand, joined with your **b.**, |
| T-22 VI.4:8 | *because* your will and your **b.** are joined. |
| T-22 VI.8:1 | will see your value through your **b.** eyes, |
| T-22 VI.14:3 | except your mind and your **b.** are one? |
| T-23 II.12:8 | ego's secret gift, torn from your **b.** body, |
| T-24 II.9:3 | Your **b.** specialness and yours *are* enemies, |
| T-24 II.11:1 | *are* your **b.**; part of love was not denied to |
| T-24 III.2:7 | For you have given your **b.** birthright to it |
| T-24 IV.4:5 | Your **b.** sin would justify itself, and give it |
| T-24 V.3:7 | How beautiful His hand that holds His **b.**, |
| T-24 V.7:1 | same hand that holds your **b.** in your own |
| T-24 VI.1:1 | Before your **b.** holiness the world is still, |
| T-24 VI.2:5 | Your **b.** holiness shows you that God is |
| T-24 VI.6:4 | Within your **b.** holiness, the perfect frame |
| T-24 VI.6:7 | Your **b.** body shows not Christ to you. He |
| T-24 VI.7:6 | of Him He set forever in your **b.** holiness, |
| T-24 VI.8:1 | **b.** holiness is sacrament and benediction |
| T-24 VI.13:1 | believe it easier to see your **b.** body than |
| T-24 VII.4:7 | And if you see this purpose in your **b.**, |
| T-25 III.7:2 | Let all your **b.** errors be to you nothing |
| T-25 VI.7:9 | Take it gently, then, from your **b.** hand, |
| T-26 I.5:4 | in which your **b.** holiness cannot be seen, |
| T-26 V.2:5 | holding your **b.** hand and keeping step to |
| T-26 VII.20:2 | Call on your **b.** name and God will answer |
| T-27 I.4:3 | suffering you but represents your **b.** guilt; |
| T-27 II.3:7 | not the proof of sin before his **b.** eyes. |
| T-27 II.9:2 | Only those to whom their **b.** sacrifice and |
| T-27 II.13:4 | Your **b.** sins become the central target for |
| T-27 V.11:5 | will be one of its effects, as will your **b.**. |
| T-27 VII.15:3 | Dream of your **b.** kindnesses instead of |
| T-27 VII.16:3 | you. Let all your **b.** gifts be seen in light of |
| T-27 VIII.9:8 | your laughter and your **b.** joined with His. |
| T-28 III.2:5 | Uniting with a **b.** mind prevents the cause |
| T-28 IV.4:6 | you have supported in your **b.** mind. |
| T-28 IV.8:5 | If you share not your **b.** evil dream, this is |
| T-28 IV.10:1 | not your **b.** dreams but join with him, |
| T-28 VII.7:1 | Your home is built upon your **b.** health, |
| T-29 I.5:1 | your **b.** unless you wanted it to be a cause |
| T-29 I.5:4 | to make communion with your **b.** mind. |
| T-29 III.3:4 | You can overlook your **b.** dreams. So |
| T-29 V.5:7 | a **b.** hand in which completion lies. |
| T-31 II.10:5 | learn you love your brother with a **b.** love. |
| WpI rV.in7:3 | I am reborn each time a **b.** mind turns to |
| WpI rV.in9:6 | Take your **b.** hand, for this is not a way |
| W-pI 181.2:5 | Remove your focus on your **b.** sins, and |
| W-pI 181.6:2 | And if a **b.** sins occur to us, our narrowed |
| W-pII 288.h | Let me forget my **b.** past today. |
| W-pII 288.1:4 | *My **b.** is the hand that leads me on the way to* |
| W-pII 335.h | I choose to see my **b.** sinlessness. |
| W-pII 335.1:6 | My **b.** sinlessness shows me that I would |
| W-pII 335.2:1 | *to me, except to see my **b.** sinlessness? His* |
| P-2 II.9:4 | still and recognize his **b.** need is his own. |
| P-2 II.9:5 | And let him then meet his **b.** need as his |

## brotherhood 4

| | |
|---|---|
| T-28 IV.3:6 | Your mind and his are joined in **b.**. His |
| T-28 IV.4:3 | release him, merely by your claim on **b.**, |
| W-pI 185.14:1 | hide, the **b.** that hate has sought to sever, |
| W-pII 341.1:3 | *with You, in **b.** and Fatherhood complete; in* |

## brotherless 2

| | |
|---|---|
| T-24 V.8:3 | His Son could never will that you be **b.**. |
| C-2 8:1 | **b.** illusion and the self that seemed alone |

## brothers 206

| | |
|---|---|
| T-1 I.27:1 | from God through me to all my **b.**. It is |
| T-1 II.4:6 | to my **b.** has placed me in charge of the |
| T-1 II.5:1 | alert to the revelation-readiness of my **b.**. |
| T-1 III.1:2 | When you offer a miracle to any of my **b.**, |
| T-1 III.3:3 | are released must join in releasing their **b.** |
| T-1 III.8:1 | miracle may have effects on your **b.** that |
| T-1 V.3:6 | All my **b.** are special. If they believe they |
| T-1 VII.1:7 | God or to your **b.** with anything external. |
| T-2 VIII.3:2 | will be undertaken by my **b.** with my help |
| T-3 VI.3:1 | and your **b.** totally without judgment. |
| T-3 VI.3:2 | what you are and what your **b.** are, you |
| T-4 VI.8:4 | you only as you will give Him to your **b.**. |
| T-5 in.3:1 | thought of any of your **b.** anywhere. You |
| T-5 II.10:10 | your **b.** to listen as I am teaching you. |
| T-5 IV.6:6 | and God if you forsake any of your **b.**. |
| T-5 VI.3:3 | me teach you how to share it with your **b.**. |
| T-5 VII.2:8 | and the sanity of your **b.** is yours. |
| T-6 I.7:5 | our **b.** in the name of the Kingdom of God |
| T-6 I.7:6 | My **b.** slept during the so-called "agony in |
| T-6 I.8:1 | I am sorry when my **b.** do not share my |
| T-6 I.11:4 | My **b.** and yours are constantly engaged |
| T-6 II.3:3 | from your **b.** and separated from them. |
| T-6 II.3:7 | perception of both yourself and your **b.**. |
| T-6 II.3:8 | directly to excluding you from your **b.**. |
| T-6 IV.4:4 | badly in need of allies, though not of **b.**. |
| T-7 III.3:2 | for **b.** and recognize all whom you see as |
| T-7 III.3:2 | and recognize all whom you see as **b.**, |
| T-7 III.3:4 | perceive any of their **b.** as anything other |
| T-7 III.4:10 | Your right mind sees only **b.**, because it |
| T-7 V.7:1 | healer wants gratitude from his **b.**, but he |
| T-7 V.10:3 | you. Our **b.** are forgetful. That is why they |
| T-7 V.11:2 | The mind we share is shared by all our **b.**, |
| T-7 VII.7:7 | your abundance, and teach your **b.** theirs. |
| T-7 VII.9:2 | to your Creator, it believes that your **b.**, |
| T-7 IX.2:1 | of all its **b.** is included in its own, as it is |
| T-7 IX.7:3 | your proper identification with your **b.**, |
| T-7 XI.6:3 | because you do not know your **b.**, who |
| T-8 VI.1:2 | gather in our **b.** as we continue together. |
| T-8 VII.1:7 | and seeing his **b.** as similarly belittled. |
| T-8 VII.2:5 | perceive your **b.** as the Holy Spirit does, |
| T-8 VIII.9:1 | to use your body only to reach your **b.**, so |
| T-9 II.7:5 | hear my **b.** in whom God's Voice speaks. |
| T-9 II.8:1 | Believe in your **b.** because I believe in you |
| T-9 VI.3:1 | If your **b.** are part of you, will you accept |
| T-9 VII.1:4 | Your **b.** are everywhere. You do not have |
| T-9 VII.1:10 | that this is not also the will of your **b.**? |
| T-10 III.2:4 | your **b.** simply by accepting God for them |
| T-10 III.5:2 | willing to attack the Divinity of your **b.**, |
| T-10 III.11:4 | can give up the god of sickness for your **b.** |
| T-10 IV.7:1 | gods, and calls on his **b.** to do likewise. It |
| T-10 V.2:3 | your **b.** by the messages they give you, but |
| T-10 V.2:5 | for whenever you see your **b.** without it, |
| T-10 V.7:7 | Look with peace upon your **b.**, and God |
| T-11 III.2:3 | lonely, and amid all his **b.** he is friendless. |
| T-11 III.7:9 | All your **b.** must enter with you, for until |
| T-11 IV.2:5 | is His, and join with your **b.** in His peace. |
| T-11 IV.5:1 | **b.** are part of you and you blame them for |
| T-11 VI.2:2 | Would you condemn your **b.** or free them |
| T-11 VIII.14:1 | your **b.** and of your Father and of yourself |
| T-11 VIII.14:7 | not the reality of your **b.** or your Father or |
| T-12 II.2:10 | For you forgot your **b.** with Him, and |
| T-12 III.4:1 | **b.** ask you for something "outrageous," |
| T-12 IV.5:7 | your **b.** home you are but following Him. |
| T-12 V.1:5 | perceiving yourself and your **b.** as equal, |
| T-12 VII.10:5 | have looked upon me and all your **b.**, in |
| T-13 III.8:4 | this place of truth as you see it in your **b.**, |
| T-13 V.2:2 | are made up only of his reactions to his **b.** |
| T-13 V.4:4 | reality of their **b.** they cannot recognize. |
| T-13 V.5:7 | into it, and all the love your **b.** offer you, |
| T-13 V.7:8 | your **b.** because you denied it in yourself. |
| T-13 VI.2:5 | as a dark cloud that shrouds your **b.** and |
| T-13 VI.7:1 | The present offers you your **b.** in the light |
| T-13 VI.8:2 | Reach out to all your **b.**, and touch them |
| T-13 VI.8:6 | all your **b.** to witness to his wholeness, as |
| T-13 VI.9:1 | your **b.** in remembrance of your Creator, |
| T-13 VI.12:7 | closed. You do not see your **b.**, and in the |
| T-13 VII.16:3 | for what except your **b.** can you need? We |
| T-13 VII.16:10 | in which we hide our **b.** from the world, |
| T-13 VIII.8:1 | When you have seen your **b.** as yourself |
| T-13 VIII.8:4 | in every miracle you offered to your **b.**, |
| T-13 VIII.9:1 | miracles in this world join you to your **b.**, |
| T-13 IX.6:3 | His offer of Atonement for all your **b.**. For |
| T-13 IX.8:3 | Instead, it bids you look upon your **b.**, |
| T-13 IX.8:5 | For those who see their **b.** in the dark, |
| T-13 X.4:4 | let them stand between you and your **b.**, |
| T-13 X.4:5 | use your **b.** as a means to "solve" the past, |
| T-13 X.4:6 | **b.** to resolve problems that are not there. |
| T-13 X.9:2 | And looking without mercy upon your **b.**, |
| T-14 II.4:4 | on you. And as it shines your **b.** see it, and |
| T-14 II.7:9 | For, like your **b.**, you do not realize the |
| T-14 II.8:1 | Behold your **b.** in their freedom, and |
| T-15 I.12:1 | to give it to your **b.** on behalf of theirs. |
| T-15 II.3:5 | even years in chaining your **b.** to your ego |
| T-15 II.3:6 | holy instant you will unchain all your **b.**, |
| T-15 II.4:1 | you have misused your **b.** by seeing them |
| T-15 V.6:5 | that you needed your **b.** as they were not. |
| T-15 V.8:2 | on no one to make your **b.** seem different. |
| T-15 V.9:3 | you have built by which to judge your **b.**. |
| T-15 V.10:8 | with God, and all your **b.** join in Christ. |
| T-15 VI.2:4 | be as perfect in all your **b.** as it is in you, |
| T-15 VI.5:5 | in how to hold all of your **b.** in your mind, |
| T-15 VI.8:1 | with all your **b.** is remembered with Him. |
| T-15 VI.8:5 | your Source, and that of all your **b.**, to |
| T-15 IX.1:1 | your perception of your **b.** to the body, so |
| T-15 X.3:3 | in our union you will accept all of our **b.**. |
| T-15 XI.1:3 | Your **b.** and your Father have become |
| T-15 XI.4:4 | your Father and your **b.** from yourself. |
| T-15 XI.7:5 | to teach, and still would teach to all my **b.** |
| T-16 IV.8:5 | you to look on all your **b.** with gratitude, |
| T-16 VI.6:5 | to bring your **b.** to the bridge with you, |
| T-16 VII.9:2 | the illusions you have held against your **b.** |
| T-16 VII.9:5 | Release your **b.** from the slavery of their |
| T-17 I.1:4 | has betrayed himself, his **b.** and his God. |
| T-17 III.10:2 | bring reality to your perception of your **b.** |
| T-19 IV.1:3 | to arise from elsewhere; from your **b.**, and |
| T-19 IV.3:4 | Holy Spirit, but you can see your **b.** truly. |
| T19 IV.A.2:9 | stand between your **b.** and salvation? |
| T-20 IV.7:4 | perfectly fulfilled in them and all their **b.**. |
| T-20 VI.5:4 | Here it would drag its **b.**, holding them |
| T-21 I.5:2 | body as all they have and all their **b.** have. |
| T-21 III.6:5 | that you might choose among your **b.**, |
| T-21 III.8:1 | their **b.** from the body can have no fear. |
| T-21 III.8:3 | desire to look upon their **b.** in holiness, |
| T-21 IV.3:4 | joined their **b.** have detached themselves |
| T-22 in.2:2 | see their **b.** different from themselves. It |
| T-22 I.7:6 | no two **b.** can unite except through Christ |
| T-24 II.13:3 | alone, apart and separate from all your **b.**; |
| T-24 V.7:2 | Christ's hand holds all His **b.** in Himself. |
| T-25 I.5:3 | as One, as all your **b.** join as one in truth. |
| T-25 IX.8:1 | Unless you think that all your **b.** have an |
| T-27 II.3:5 | forgive their **b.** and themselves as well. |
| T-28 III.7:2 | not to thieves, but to your starving **b.**, |
| T-28 VII.2:1 | your **b.** is a part of you because it is a part |
| T-29 IX.7:8 | in the dream are now perceived as **b.**, not |
| T-30 V.7:1 | **b.** join in purpose in the world of fear, |
| T-30 VII.7:8 | language lets us speak to all our **b.**, and to |
| T-31 VIII.1:5 | *would remain in hell, and hold your **b.** there.* |
| T-31 VIII.8:1 | My **b.** in salvation, do not fail to hear my |
| T-31 VIII.9:4 | Hear me, my **b.**, hear and join with me. |
| T-31 VIII.10:1 | ones who are my **b.** as they are Your Sons. |
| T-31 VIII.11:4 | I give You thanks for what my **b.** are. And |
| W-pI 57.5:3 | I share the peace of the world with my **b.**, |
| W-pI 73.2:5 | you do not know your **b.** or your Self. |
| W-pI 95.13:2 | of God, united with your **b.** in that Self; |
| W-pI 97.8:2 | with Him and God, your **b.** and your Self. |
| W-pI 105.6:2 | Begin today by thinking of those **b.** who |
| W-pI 106.4:9 | pledge to you and all your **b.** to be kept. |
| W-pI 109.8:1 | and call upon your **b.** from your rest to |
| W-pI 109.8:3 | your distant **b.** and your closest friends; |
| W-pI 124.12:2 | *with God, at one with all my **b.** and my Self,* |
| W-pI 126.11:1 | of special value to yourself and all your **b.**. |
| W-pI 127.11:4 | us. Now are they all our **b.** in God's Love. |
| W-pI 132.16:1 | comes to many **b.** far across the world, as |
| W-pI 134.14:3 | footsteps lighting up the way for all our **b.** |
| W-pI 135.20:4 | joy. And gladly will our **b.** lay aside their |
| W-pI 137.15:6 | *And I would bless my **b.**, for I would be* |
| W-pI 139.9:6 | Fail not your **b.**, or you fail yourself. Look |

W-pI.139.11:6 memory is the recall how dear our **b.** are
W-pI.153.11:1 to help their **b.** choose as they have done.
W-pI.153.11:5 the light, until you offer it to all your **b.**.
W-pI.153.20:4 from them to all their **b.** come from Him.
W-pI...155.7:3 to lead your **b.** from the ways of death,
W-pI...155.9:3 Your holy **b.** have been given you, to
W-pI.155.11:6 so it goes before our **b.** who will follow us.
W-pI.155.13:4 given you your **b.** in His trust that you are
W-pI.155.13:7 You will not fail your **b.** nor your Self.
W-pI...161.4:1 One brother is all **b.**. Every mind
W-pI.170.13:5 *again, and make our choice for all our* ***b.***,
WpI.. rV.in8:4 And together we will teach them to our **b.**
W-pI......181.h I trust my **b.**, who are one with me.
W-pI...181.1:1 your **b.** is essential to establishing and
W-pI...181.6:5 *upon. I trust my* ***b.***, *who are one with me.*
W-pI...183.1:4 His **b.** share his name, and thus are they
W-pI.185.13:5 know you share one Will with all your **b.**,
W-pI.191.10:8 heart willing to bring your weary **b.** rest?
W-pI...195.7:1 let our **b.** lean their tired heads against
W-pI...199.8:5 Your **b.** stand released with you in it; the
W-pI...201.1:1 (181) I trust my **b.**, who are one with me.
W-pII..247.2:2 *My* ***b.*** *are Your Sons. Your Fatherhood*
W-pII..260.1:6 *I would look upon my* ***b.*** *and myself today.*
W-pII..263.2:2 house as **b.** and the holy Sons of God.
W-pII..264.2:1 My **b.**, join with me in this today. This is
W-pII..276.2:2 *And it is this that I would speak to all my* ***b.***,
W-pII.....315.h All gifts my **b.** give belong to me.
W-pII..315.2:2 *My* ***b.*** *are unlimited in all their gifts to me.*
W-pII.....316.h All gifts I give my **b.** are my own.
W-pII..316.1:1 As every gift my **b.** give is mine, so every
W-pII..317.1:4 given all my **b.** and already mine as well.
W-pII..324.1:6 *My* ***b.*** *all can follow in the way I lead them.*
W-pII..325.1:6 on, and help his **b.** walk ahead with him,
W-pII..344.1:7 *on earth. Let my forgiven* ***b.*** *fill my store with*
W-pII....14.4:4 that we have attained we call to all our **b.**,
Wfl ........in.2:6 our many **b.** who are seeking for the way,
M-4.......III.1:4 that you have been deceived in your **b.**.
M-4.......III.1:9 Without judgment are all men **b.**, for who
M-5.....III.2:11 their **b.** to turn away from death: "Behold
M-5.......III.3:6 out to the truth in the minds of their **b.**,
M-19..........3:1 All concepts of your **b.** and yourself; all
M-23..........6:6 dedicated teacher of God forgets his **b.**.
C-4............8:1 O my **b.**, if you only knew the peace that
C-5............2:1 Christ in all his **b.** and remembered God.
C-ep...........4:4 For God is here, and with Him all our **b.**.
P-2...........I.4:1 series of holy encounters in which **b.** meet
P-2.........V.4:7 Word to guide us, as we try to help our **b.**.
P-2.......VII.8:1 what the joining of two **b.** really means.
S-3........IV.1:2 their **b.** share their healing and their love.

## brothers' 1

W-pI.....73.2:4 between your awareness and your **b.**

## brought 144

T-1........IV.4:5 their minds who **b.** the "hell-fire" concept
T-2..........I.4:4 The escape is **b.** about by your acceptance
T-2.......... V.6:6 easily **b.** into alignment with a mind that
T-2........VI.4:3 the conditions that have **b.** the fear about.
T-2..... VIII.2:4 **b.** into being only after the separation,
T-3........VI.4:4 refused to accept can be **b.** into awareness
T-4........IV.8:8 ego *should* be **b.** to judgment and found
T-4........IV.9:4 creation and **b.** your mind into being. His
T-4.......VII.7:3 but He does want it **b.** to others. This
T-6........IV.1:5 when He has **b.** you home and you no
T-8...........I.4:3 with the changes your learning has **b.** you
T-8.....VII.13:5 body is **b.** under the purpose of the mind,
T-11.......V.12:5 so diligently, has merely **b.** you fear, and
T-13....VI.11:9 those you **b.** with you will shine on you,
T-13....VI.11:9 in gratitude because they **b.** you here.
T-13....XI.3:13 ever **b.** even a dim imagining of what it is.
T-14......VI.2:2 will always yield to love if it is **b.** to love,
T-14......VI.4:2 away because, when they are **b.** together,
T-14.....VII.1:3 Opposites must be **b.** together, not kept
T-14.....VII.1:7 by which ignorance is **b.** to knowledge.
T-14...VII.3:10 certainty. Uncertainty **b.** to certainty does
T-14.....VII.4:4 are **b.** together, their joint acceptance
T-14... VIII.1:5 be **b.** to the judgment of the Holy Spirit,
T-14... VIII.2:4 And nothing **b.** there that is not equally
T-14... VIII.3:2 **b.** together only by the Guide appointed
T-14... VIII.4:2 you as you are **b.** into the place where you
T-14... VIII.5:5 little offerings are **b.** together with the gift
T-14......IX.8:3 healing, without regard for what is **b.** to it
T-14......XI.4:1 yet **b.** all of the darkness you have taught
T-14......XI.4:6 dark lessons must be **b.** willingly to truth,
T-14......XI.9:5 He has **b.** all of them to light, having
T-15......XI.1:6 **b.** together and perceived where they are,
T-15......XI.3:5 be **b.** to us and disappear in our presence,
T-16.........II.7:2 are both being **b.** into your awareness.
T-16.........II.7:5 interpretation the results have **b.** you joy.
T-16.........II.9:3 time you **b.** these facts together and made
T-17.........I.6:1 the truth, and in Whom all is **b.** to truth.
T-17.........II.1:5 your heart sing with joy has ever **b.** you
T-17.........III.6:4 and more undone, and union **b.** closer.
T-17....IV.14:6 dark picture, **b.** to light, is not perceived
T-17....IV.14:6 that it is just a picture is **b.** home at last.
T-17......VI.4:3 that this approach has **b.** you closer to the
T-17.....VII.3:9 matter. Faithlessness **b.** to faith will never
T-18.........I.4:4 That one error, which **b.** truth to illusion,
T-18.........I.6:6 truth **b.** to this could only remain within
T-18........I.11:2 have been gently **b.** unto the truth in you,
T-18........I.13:6 that **b.** you and him together must extend
T-18......III.7:2 The darkness in you has been **b.** to light.
T-18......III.7:3 from the holy instant to which you **b.** it.
T-18... VIII.9:7 love they **b.** with them will stay with them
T-18......IX.2:1 Who does surround it has **b.** union to you
T-18....IX.13:1 safely **b.** through the barriers of guilt,
T-19.........I.1:3 truth as its only goal is **b.** to truth *by* faith.
T-19.........I.4:5 the Holy Spirit's purpose, and **b.** illusions
T-19.........I.6:7 to illusion; and given up when **b.** to truth,
T-19....... II.6:8 the status of truth, to what can it be **b.**?
T-19..... II.6:10 and everything is **b.** to *it* for judgment. As
T-19..... II.6:11 As a mistake, *it* must be **b.** to truth. It is
T-19.... III.11:5 it is **b.** nearer to all by your relationship.
T19....IV.B.5:1 nothing you have paid for **b.** you peace.
T19...IV.D.8:6 Guide Who **b.** you here remains with you,
T19...IV.D.9:7 And let us join in faith that He Who **b.** us
T-20....... V.1:5 each joining is the end of time **b.** nearer.
T-20....... V.5:5 means and end have not been **b.** in line.
T-20.....VII.1:1 and how these must be **b.** in line before
T-20.....VII.6:6 Here are illusions never **b.** to truth, and
T-20... VIII.6:1 laws **b.** to it by His calm and certain sight.
T-20. VIII.10:6 purpose **b.** to your horrified awareness.
T-21....... II.4:6 world you do not want **b.** to the one you
T-22.......I.10:4 always so? Think what that instant **b.**; the
T-22..... II.12:7 true. Every illusion **b.** to its forgiveness is
T-23.........I.9:1 illusions disappears when it is **b.** to truth!
T-23....... II.1:1 The "laws" of chaos can be **b.** to light,
T-23....... II.3:5 When **b.** to truth instead of to each other,
T-24.........I.2:2 are kept unknown and never **b.** to reason,
T-24......III.5:6 wait for all illusions to be **b.** to Them, and
T-25....... II.3:3 and bring what it has never **b.** before?
T-25....... II.8:3 who **b.** him forth for you to look upon.
T-25..... II.11:3 His Will is **b.** together as you join in will,
T-25....IV.5:12 better could your own mistakes be **b.** to
T-26......III.2:3 place where thoughts are **b.** together;
T-26......III.3:5 are **b.** together, and only one continues
T-26......III.4:2 But what is truth to him must be **b.** to the
T-26....... V.4:5 Uncertainty was **b.** to certainty so long
T-26.....VII.2:3 soon as the idea that **b.** it has been healed,
T-26.....VII.3:8 **B.** to truth, its senselessness is quite
T-26.....VII.7:5 **b.** His Love at last to vengeance's heels.
T-26...VII.14:1 cause and consequence are **b.** together,
T-26... VIII.1:5 The nearer it is **b.** to where it is, the more
T-26... VIII.6:3 the Holy Spirit **b.** to your relationship has
T-26....... X.6:4 Spirit has **b.** injustice to the light within,
T-27......IV.2:5 all your problems should be **b.** and left.
T-27......IV.2:9 resolved, if it is **b.** to where the answer is.
T-27....... V.7:5 of Christ to you who **b.** the sight to them,
T-27....... V.7:6 upon the Friend who **b.** them their release
T-27....... V.9:1 will be **b.** to problems that you thought
T-27.....VII.1:3 dreamer is unconscious of what **b.** on the
T-28.........I.5:8 your command that they be **b.** to you,
T-28......III.9:3 have **b.** unlimited supply with Them. And
T-29....... II.5:5 are where He is Who **b.** them with Him,
T-29....... II.5:6 your Guest, but you can see the gifts He **b.**
T-30.......I.11:7 readiness for asking **b.** to your awareness,
T-30...... IV.4:7 them. Their dancing never **b.** you joy. But
T-30...... IV.6:4 changes have been quickly **b.** about, when
T-30....... V.6:1 world's purpose gently **b.** into awareness,
T-30..... V.10:3 *idol* ***b.*** *you anything except the "gift" of guilt*
T-31.....VII.5:5 that now you hold has **b.** you in its wake,
T-31....VIII.2:7 For you have **b.** your weakness unto Him,
T-31....VIII.3:1 that what you chose before has **b.** to you.
W-pI.....79.8:4 be **b.** together and you can be at peace.
W-pI.....80.4:1 and the answer have been **b.** together.
W-pI.....85.3:6 It is not found outside and then **b.** in. But
W-pI...92.10:2 Let yourself be **b.** unto your Self. Its
W-pI.....97.3:2 awareness is **b.** a little nearer at least;
W-pI...107.5:3 Illusions can be **b.** to truth to be corrected
W-pI...107.5:4 not be **b.** to them to turn them into truth.
W-pI...133.4:3 and not been **b.** so clearly to the place
W-pI.134.11:1 of hatred and attack **b.** silently to truth.
W-pI.137.11:4 and here are all illusions **b.** to truth.
W-pI...138.2:7 be the error truth can be **b.** to illusions.
W-pI.138.10:1 shield of unawareness, and is **b.** to light.
W-pI.138.11:3 Its pseudo-being, **b.** to what is real, is
W-pI...159.8:3 can be **b.** from here back to the world, but
W-pI...159.9:6 they **b.** from Christ have been delivered,
W-pI...162.5:3 this acceptance is salvation **b.** to everyone
W-pI.169.13:3 **b.** a clear reflection of the unity he felt an
WpI...rV.in8:1 again the thoughts I **b.** to you from Him
W-pI...186.5:1 to prove the false is true has **b.** to you.
W-pI.193.12:2 application to the happenings the hour **b.**
W-pI...194.2:1 of sin, and devastation **b.** about by guilt.
W-pI.198.13:2 recognize that He Who **b.** us here will not
W-pII ..in.10:8 complete. This year has **b.** us to eternity.
W-pII .270.1:4 *his Father, lets his dreams be* ***b.*** *to truth, and*
W-pII .278.2:2 *and have* ***b.*** *a dream of fear into my mind.*
M-5 .........I.1:2 unless he thought it **b.** him something,
M-5 ...... III.3:7 They are thus **b.** to truth; truth is not
M-5 ...... III.3:7 brought to truth; truth is not **b.** to them.
M-6 ........... 1:2 is impossible to let illusions be **b.** to truth
M-14 ....... 1:10 They have been **b.** to truth, and truth saw
M-19 ......... 5:6 It accepts all evidence that is **b.** before it,
M-28 ......... 4:8 the world, as it is lifted up and **b.** to truth.
C-4............. 6:3 all illusions **b.** to truth and laid upon the
P-2........ IV.6:6 Truth being **b.** to illusions, reality now
S-1 ........ III.4:4 has an illusion of escape ever **b.** a prisoner

## brow 2

T19. IV.D.16:6 Press it not like thorns against his **b.**, nor
S-3........ IV.9:3 the bleeding **b.** of him who is the holy Son

## bruise 1

T-18...... IX.8:2 You will not **b.** yourself against them in

## brush 4

T19... IV.D.2:2 peace will lightly **b.** the veil aside and run
T-27...VII.15:6 **b.** aside his many gifts because he is not
T-28...... III.6:4 The miracle will **b.** them all aside, and
W-pI.....69.6:4 **B.** them aside with your hand; feel them

## brushed 1

T19. IV.A.15:2 of all guilt and softly **b.** with beauty. The

## brushes 3

T-25.........I.4:4 and **b.** all its darkness into light merely by
T-31..... V.7:10 of idols, painted with the **b.** of the world,
P-2....... VII.8:4 stars that **b.** lightly past all sickly dreams.

## bubble 1

W-pI.....47.7:3 churn and **b.** on the surface of your mind,

## budding 1

W-pII .....2.4:4 through the soil, the trees are **b.** now, and

**build** 12

T-4.........I.11:1 for you, because it cannot **b.** otherwise.
T-6...........I.8:2 it is still on them that I must **b.** my church
T-9......... V.5:1 of the mind, how can this **b.** ego strength?
T-11.........I.1:3 which God will help **b.** again the thought
T-16...... IV.3:3 by attempting to **b.** barricades against it,
T-18....... V.2:6 He will **b.** your part in the Atonement and
T-18....... V.2:7 you will **b.** a ladder planted in the solid
T-20...... VI.5:6 Holy Spirit does not **b.** His temples where
T-28..... VII.3:4 Yet who can **b.** his home upon a straw,
T-28..... VII.6:4 Would you **b.** your home upon what will
T-29.........I.4:7 in which to **b.** again your separate self,
W-pI..... 61.7:4 to begin to **b.** a firm foundation for these

**builded** 2

T-14....... II.6:3 For what is **b.** there *is* true, and built on
T-16...... III.9:1 Your bridge is **b.** stronger than you think

**building** 2

T-8......VIII.8:4 one can doubt the ego's skill in **b.** up false
T-31....... V.1:5 The **b.** of a concept of the self is what the

**buildings** 1

T-13..... VII.1:2 It has no **b.** and there are no streets where

**builds** 6

T-3....... VII.2:6 and **b.** kingdoms in which everything is in
T-13. VII.10:12 cornerstone in the churches it **b.** to itself.
T-16...... III.8:3 Each one **b.** this bridge, which carries him
T-28...... III.6:1 God **b.** the bridge, but only in the space
W-pI... 182.3:4 He does not understand he **b.** in vain. The
W-pI... 198.8:3 truth could have a Thought which **b.** a

**built** 29

T-2......... II.5:1 The Atonement was **b.** into the space-
T-2....... II.6:10 point the bridge of return has been **b.**.
T-2........ III.1:8 altar around which the structure is **b.**.
T-2......VIII.2:4 devices to be **b.** into the overall plan. Just
T-4.........I.11:1 The ego has **b.** a shabby and unsheltering
T-5...... VI.10:5 you, however carefully you have **b.** it up.
T-8....VIII.1:12 perception the whole is **b.** up of parts that
T-11...... VI.1:2 are **b.** up on the basis of experience, and
T-13...... III.4:1 have **b.** your whole insane belief system
T-13..... VII.3:2 homes you **b.** have never sheltered you.
T-13..... VII.3:3 and no city that you **b.** has withstood the
T-14....... II.6:3 is builded there *is* true, and **b.** on truth.
T-15....... V.9:3 have **b.** by which to judge your brothers.
T-16...... IV.6:1 within yourself that you have **b.** against it.
T-16.... IV.10:1 for it was **b.** with God beside you, and will
T-16...... VI.7:6 frame of reference is **b.** around the special
T-18 ... VIII.9:1 waiting at the barrier you **b.** to come
T-22 ..... III.4:7 it made; the rock on which its church is **b.**
T-26 ........I.2:3 Around each entity is **b.** a wall so seeming
T-26 .... VII.3:2 world of shadows and illusions **b.** on sin.
T-28 ......I.15:7 He has **b.** the bridge, and it is He Who
T-28 .... VII.7:1 home is **b.** upon your brother's health,
T-29 .....II.10:4 dwell in what was **b.** as temple unto death
T-29 ..... III.2:7 the wall the world has **b.** to keep apart all
T-31 ........I.4:3 until a world was **b.** that suited you. And
T-31 ...... V.1:1 learning of the world is **b.** upon a concept
W-pI..... 61.7:6 God has **b.** His plan for the salvation of
W-pII ..... 5.1:1 a fence the Son of God imagines he has **b.**,
M-19 ......... 3:3 concept of the world **b.** up in just this way

**bumping** 1

M-3 .......... 2:5 will not scold the child for **b.** into him;

**burden** 20

T-5 .......II.11:3 "join together," and "**b.**" means "message
T-5 .......II.11:4 yoke is easy and my **b.** light" in this way;
T-5 ....... IV.2:8 You have carried the **b.** of unshared ideas
T-5 ....... IV.6:1 lifts the **b.** you have placed in your mind.
T-14 ........I.5:4 escape the heavy **b.** of its dullness that lies
T-14 .......II.1:8 add another **b.** to your already burdened
T-14 ... III.10:8 or the impossible **b.** of deciding what they
T-14 ..... IV.5:5 to remove the awful **b.** you have laid upon
T-14 ...... V.2:4 The **b.** of guilt is heavy, but God would
T19. IV.D.16:5 Help him to lift the heavy **b.** of sin you
T-21 ... VI.7:11 you will lay down the **b.** of denying truth.
T-21 ... VI.7:12 *This* is the **b.** that is terrible, and not the
T-21 ..... VI.8:2 Does Heaven seem to be a **b.** to you? In
T-22 ... VI.14:4 think not that it lays a heavy **b.** on you.
T-24 ... VI.12:4 you, you find a **b.** wearisome and tedious,
T-28 .... VII.6:2 Why **b.** it with further locks and chains
M-8 ........... 2:7 Finding health a **b.**, it retreats into
M-10 ......... 5:2 Now are you free of a **b.** so great that you
P-2...... IV.11:2 the insane **b.** of guilt it carries so wearily,
S-3........ IV.9:1 of time to lift the heavy **b.** from the world.

**burdened** 1

T-14 .......II.1:8 another burden to your already **b.** mind.

**burdens** 4

W-pI... 109.5:1 you have no cares and no concerns, no **b.**,
W-pI. 133.14:2 to let yourself collect some needless **b.**, or
W-pI... 196.4:2 as the mind relinquishes its **b.** one by one.
M-24 ......... 3:5 to add sectarian controversies to his **b.**.

**buried** 2

T-16 ...... V.8:5 is **b.** deep and rises in the form of "love."
T-22 ... VI.10:7 for here lies **b.** the heavy anchor that

**burning** 2

T-13 ..... III.2:8 ever be, is your intense and **b.** love of God
W-pII . 252.1:4 from **b.** impulses which move the world,

**burrows** 1

T-15 .......X.5:1 it **b.** underground and hides in darkness,

**bury** 2

T-13 ..... IV.1:5 thus destroy you here and **b.** you here,
T19 ... IV.C.4:1 is the black-draped body they would **b.**?

**business** 2

WpIrIII.in11:6 you in the **b.** of the day and make it holy,
W-pI 153.16:4 times the **b.** of the world will close on us,

**busy** 2

T-18 .... VII.8:3 of every **b.** doing on which you are sent.
W-pI .. 164.1:5 sounds the senseless, **b.** world engenders,

**busyness** 1

T-4 .........V.6:5 ego's characteristic **b.** with nonessentials

**but** 3322

**button** 1

W-pI ...... 2.2:3 exercise with equal ease to a body or a **b.**,

**button's** 1

T-18 ..... IX.6:4 It is not strong enough to stop a **b.** fall,

**buy** 3

T-12 ..... IV.7:2 for you, since you could not "**b.**" it back.
T-13 .... VII.1:3 There are no stores where people **b.** an
W-pI .. 133.2:2 to bodily concerns, to things you **b.**, to

**buys** 2

W-pI .. 102.1:2 You may think it **b.** you something, and
W-pI .. 102.1:2 may still believe a little that it **b.** you what

**by** 1961

**byways** 1

W-pI .. 200.9:3 and needless wasted time on thorny **b.**.

# C

## calculate 1

| | |
|---|---|
| T-26 X.6:1 | who see as you have judged, you cannot **c.** |

## calendar 1

| | |
|---|---|
| W-pI 157.1:2 | special time of promise in your **c.** of days. |

## Call 50

*call*

| | |
|---|---|
| T-5 I.5:4 | of the Holy Spirit is the **C.** to Atonement, |
| T-5 I.5:5 | is healed there will be no **C.** to return. But |
| T-5 II.2:2 | **C.** to return with which God blessed the |
| T-5 II.2:4 | have understood the **C.** to right thinking. |
| T-5 II.3:2 | God placed in the mind the **C.** to joy. This |
| T-5 II.3:3 | This **C.** is so strong that the ego always |
| T-5 II.10:5 | Spirit is the **C.** to awaken and be glad. The |
| T-5 II.10:7 | joyous one of waking it to the **C.** for God. |
| T-5 II.10:8 | will answer the **C.** of the Holy Spirit, or |
| T-5 II.12:5 | the **C.** for God is the Call to the unlimited. |
| T-5 II.12:5 | the Call for God is the **C.** to the unlimited. |
| T-5 III.2:3 | Being the **C.** *for* God, it is also the idea *of* |
| T-5 III.2:9 | He may have dissociated the **C.** for God, |
| T-5 III.2:10 | become aware of the **C.** for God in him, |
| T-5 IV.1:11 | who hear the Holy Spirit's **C.** to be as one, |
| T-6 V.4:6 | away. His light is always the **C.** to awaken, |
| T-8 II.8:5 | the Kingdom, in answer to the **C.** for God. |
| T-11 VI.9:1 | own call, for the **C.** to awake is within you. |
| T-13 III.2:6 | to answer His **C.** and leap into Heaven. |
| T-13 VI.9:5 | His **C.** to you is but your call to Him. And |
| T-13 XI.10:1 | him the glad **C.** to waken and be glad? He |
| T-13 XI.10:3 | sleep will not withstand the **C.** to wake. |
| T-16 IV.12:6 | to God, in joyous answer to His **C.** for His |
| T-16 IV.13:5 | and answer fearlessly the **C.** of Him Who |
| T-16 VI.12:6 | Call upon Him, for Heaven is at His **C.**. |
| T-17 VIII.4:1 | acknowledged the **C.** of your Redeemer, |
| T-17 VIII.4:1 | to His **C.** seems to be greater than before. |
| T-17 VIII.6:7 | you separate from Him Whose **C.** you |
| T-19 IV.1:8 | recognizing in your call the **C.** for God. |
| T-24 II.4:6 | the **C.** of God Himself is soundless to you. |
| T-25 V.3:5 | that you might hear in him His **C.** to you, |
| T-28 VII.2:2 | help, the **C.** to healing and the Call to heal |
| T-28 VII.2:2 | help, the Call to healing and the **C.** to heal |
| W-pI 164.2:4 | but your answer to your Father's **C.** to you |
| W-pI 164.3:1 | and answers in your name the **C.** He hears |
| W-pI 169.3:4 | an open mind can hear the **C.** to waken. It |
| W-pI 170.12:5 | The **C.** for God is heard and answered. |
| W-pI 186.3:7 | that would deny the **C.** for God Himself. |
| W-pII 237.1:4 | of death; aware it is my Father's **C.** to me. |
| W-pII 7.5:2 | It is a **C.** from Love to Love, that It be but |
| M-1 2:4 | The **C.** is universal. It goes on all the time |
| M-1 2:12 | **C.** at its center it is a light that cannot be |
| M-1 2:14 | it. To the **C.** Itself time has no meaning. |
| M-1 3:7 | the teacher was before he heard the **C.**. He |
| M-2 1:1 | for him as soon as he has answered the **C.**. |
| M-13 6:7 | Would you now sacrifice that **C.**? Few |
| M-14 2:7 | It is His **C.** God's teachers answer, turning |
| M-21 5:9 | meaningless symbols to the **C.** of Heaven |
| C-ep 4:1 | called to us and helped us hear His **C.**. |
| S-3 IV.8:7 | Do not refuse to hear the **C.** for Love. Do |

## call 267

*Call*

| | |
|---|---|
| T-4 III.6:5 | Those who **c.** truly are always answered. |
| T-4 III.7:10 | in response to a single unequivocal **c.**. |
| T-5 in.1:7 | without being wholly joyous themselves **c.** |
| T-5 II.8:5 | you, because the **c.** of both is in your mind |
| T-5 II.8:10 | The **c.** you answer now is an evaluation |
| T-5 II.8:12 | the basis of which **c.** is worth more to you. |
| T-5 II.11:1 | **c.** on me to remind you how to heal by |
| T-5 III.8:11 | is as vigilant as the ego to the **c.** of danger, |
| T-5 IV.5:4 | it. I **c.** upon you to teach what you have |
| T-6 I.2:5 | can always **c.** on me to share my decision, |
| T-6 I.14:1 | the **c.** for peace for which it was intended. |
| T-6 I.16:3 | I do not **c.** for martyrs but for teachers. |
| T-6 V.2:5 | themselves **c.** on the light to dispel them. |
| T-6 V.4:2 | Yet He always answers their **c.**, and His |
| T-6 V.C.10:7 | **c.** upon the being which you both *have* and |
| T-7 VII.7:4 | Every attack is a **c.** for His patience, since |
| T-7 XI.4:1 | I **c.** upon you to remember that I have |
| T-8 I.3:1 | Every response to the ego is a **c.** to war, |
| T-8 VIII.4:6 | The ego does not **c.** upon witnesses who |
| T-9 I.5:1 | never **c.** upon you to sacrifice anything. |
| T-9 VI.3:3 | **c.** upon in them you call upon in yourself. |
| T-9 VI.3:3 | call upon in them you **c.** upon in yourself. |
| T-9 VI.3:4 | **c.** upon it in them it becomes real to you. |
| T-10 IV.7:3 | It is a **c.** to the Holy Spirit in his mind, a |
| T-10 IV.7:3 | mind, a **c.** that is strengthened by joining. |
| T-10 IV.8:6 | because it is the remaining **c.** of creation. |
| T-10 V.7:2 | retaliate, but He does **c.** to you to return. |
| T-10 V.7:3 | you think He has not answered your **c.**, |
| T-11 in.4:8 | Will you not answer the **c.** of love with joy |
| T-11 VI.9:1 | You will awaken to your own **c.**, for the |
| T-12 I.5:4 | to recognize a **c.** for help is to refuse help. |
| T-12 I.6:11 | But hear his **c.** for the Help of God, and |
| T-12 I.7:5 | then, hear every **c.** for help as what it is, so |
| T-12 I.8:10 | learning to perceive attack as a **c.** for love. |
| T-12 I.8:12 | if you see attack as the **c.** for help that it is, |
| T-12 I.8:13 | you. For fear *is* a **c.** for love, in unconscious |
| T-12 II.3:1 | in sickness but another **c.** for love, and |
| T-12 II.3:3 | is to recognize in hatred the **c.** for love. |
| T-12 II.3:5 | Answer his **c.** for love, and yours is |
| T-12 VII.11:3 | have heard your **c.** and I have answered it, |
| T-13 III.3:3 | response to the **c.** of love if you heard it, |
| T-13 III.8:1 | you hold so dear is your real **c.** for help. |
| T-13 III.8:2 | For you **c.** for love to your Father as your |
| T-13 V.5:6 | believing it is love, you **c.** it to yourself. |
| T-13 VI.7:5 | you look at Christ and **c.** His witnesses to |
| T-13 VI.8:6 | **C.** all your brothers to witness to his |
| T-13 VI.9:1 | you **c.** forth the witnesses to His creation. |
| T-13 VI.9:3 | your thanks in His clear Answer to your **c.** |
| T-13 VI.9:5 | His Call to you is but your **c.** to Him. And |
| T-13 VI.11:3 | to **c.** you from the world and follow it. For |
| T-13 VI.13:9 | And so it is that he can **c.** unto himself the |
| T-13 VII.4:2 | what you **c.** with love will come to you. |
| T-13 VII.4:3 | being unable to deny a **c.** for help, or not |
| T-13 VII.9:8 | Therefore the **c.** of joy is in it, and your |
| T-13 IX.5:6 | **c.** for punishment upon yourself must be |
| T-14 V.4:4 | light, in answer to the **c.** of the Atonement |
| T-14 VII.5:7 | a **c.** for what you have attacked with them. |
| T-14 X.6:3 | the same response to every **c.** for help. It |
| T-14 X.6:4 | for help. It does not judge the **c.**. It merely |
| T-14 X.6:6 | consider which **c.** is louder or greater or |
| T-14 X.6:13 | offers everything to every **c.** from anyone. |
| T-14 X.6:15 | difficulty here. A **c.** for help is given help. |
| T-14 X.7:1 | one of love, and the other the **c.** for love. |
| T-14 X.7:2 | everything else is nothing but a **c.** for love. |
| T-14 X.11:5 | teach you both his love and his **c.** for love. |
| T-14 X.12:3 | But where there is a **c.** for love, you must |
| T-14 XI.10:5 | Him, but you cannot **c.** on Him in vain. |
| T-14 XI.13:5 | **C.** not upon the ego for anything; it is |
| T-15 III.12:1 | **C.** forth in everyone only the |
| T-15 III.12:3 | but only his **c.** for Heaven and greatness. |
| T-15 III.12:4 | Forget not that his **c.** is yours, and answer |
| T-15 IV.3:4 | I **c.** you to fulfill your holy part in the plan |
| T-15 IV.5:3 | I **c.** to you to make the holy instant yours |
| T-15 VI.4:1 | on God for love, your **c.** remains as strong |
| T-16 IV.11:4 | stay. Hear not the **c.** of hate, and see no |
| T-16 IV.11:6 | See in the **c.** of hate, and in every fantasy |
| T-16 IV.11:6 | **c.** for help that rises ceaselessly from you |
| T-16 VI.12:6 | **C.** upon Him, for Heaven is at His Call. |
| T-16 VI.12:7 | Call. And let Him **c.** on Heaven for you. |
| T-17 IV.3:3 | that you will not hear the **c.** of truth. |
| T-17 VI.3:6 | is it acceptable, or does it **c.** for vengeance |
| T-17 VII.h | The **C.** for Faith |
| T-17 VII.4:5 | The goal's reality will **c.** this forth, for you |
| T-17 VII.6:6 | goal's reality will **c.** forth and accomplish |
| T-17 VII.9:2 | will **c.** the others to share your purpose, as |
| T-17 VII.10:1 | **c.** for faith because of Him Who walks |
| T-17 VII.10:5 | Its **c.** for faith is strong. Use not your |
| T-17 VIII.1:3 | that faith might answer to the **c.** of truth. |
| T-17 VIII.2:6 | and it will **c.** forth and secure for you the |
| T-18 I.6:7 | **C.** it not sin but madness, for such it was |
| T-18 I.12:2 | **c.** is but an echo of the original error that |
| T-18 VI.11:1 | he would **c.** a sense of being transported |
| T-18 VI.14:7 | in answer to its gentle **c.** to be at peace. |
| T-18 VIII.8:5 | be there that you would **c.** on love to enter |
| T-19 III.4:5 | *for* correction, and they **c.** for nothing else. |
| T-19 III.4:6 | calls for punishment must **c.** for nothing. |
| T-19 III.4:7 | Every mistake *must* be a **c.** for love. What, |
| T-19 III.4:9 | a **c.** for help that you would keep unheard |
| T-19 IV.1:8 | you will **c.** to him and he will answer you, |
| T-19 IV.1:8 | recognizing in your **c.** the Call for God. |
| T19 IV.A.1:3 | it radiates outward, to **c.** the others in. |
| T19 IV.A.5:8 | He Who answered you would **c.**. His |
| T19 IV.C.2:15 | is the result of the thought we **c.** the ego, |
| T19 IV.C.7:1 | not how often and how loudly they **c.** to it |
| T19 IV.D.3:4 | to allow union to **c.** you out of separation; |
| T-20 V.2:3 | together **c.** to the hearts of everyone, to let |
| T-20 VIII.5:4 | pitifully little the perfect choice to **c.** upon |
| T-21 VI.1:3 | when you think you sin, you **c.** for help. |
| T-21 VI.1:4 | if you will not accept the help you **c.** for, |
| T-23 II.4:2 | the demand that errors **c.** for punishment |
| T-24 I.4:6 | they protect its enmity and **c.** it "friend." |
| T-24 III.7:2 | and **c.** them to come forth and waken |
| T-24 III.7:5 | They hate the **c.** that would awaken them, |
| T-25 in.1:8 | that He may **c.** to them to come to Him |
| T-25 V.3:4 | to see. Nor do you hear his plaintive **c.**, |
| T-25 V.3:4 | in content in whatever form the **c.** is made |
| T-25 V.3:5 | such is the **c.** that God has given him, that |
| T-25 VIII.10:5 | could they **c.** forth to speak on his behalf? |
| T-25 VIII.12:5 | Your special function is a **c.** to Him, that |
| T-26 II.6:8 | The miracle of justice you **c.** forth will rest |
| T-26 VII.9:3 | We **c.** it "wish" because it still conceives |
| T-26 VII.20:2 | **C.** on your brother's name and God will |
| T-26 VII.20:2 | and God will answer, for on Him you **c.**. |
| T-26 VII.20:3 | has already answered all who **c.** on Him? |
| T-26 VII.20:5 | freed to **c.** upon the Name of God as One. |
| T-26 IX.1:1 | in him the Voice that answers to your **c.**! |
| T-27 II.6:5 | before the ancient clarion **c.** of life. This |
| T-27 II.6:6 | This **c.** has power far beyond the weak |
| T-27 V.7:5 | will **c.** forth its witnesses to show the face |
| T-27 VI.2:7 | **C.** pleasure pain, and it will hurt. Call |
| T-27 VI.2:8 | **C.** pain a pleasure, and the pain behind |
| T-27 VI.2:11 | Sin's witnesses hear but the **c.** of death. |
| T-27 VI.3:4 | you **c.** forth the witnesses to its reality. |
| T-27 VI.3:9 | **c.** him by the holy Name of God Himself. |
| T-27 VI.6:6 | are but a single sound; a **c.** for healing, |
| T-27 VI.6:9 | laws that **c.** them different are dissolved, |
| T-27 VIII.2:4 | senseless things that it can **c.** its own. It |
| T-28 II.9:5 | Nor will the **c.** to wakening be heard, |
| T-28 II.9:5 | heard, because it seems to be the **c.** to fear |
| T-28 IV.5:2 | **C.** not to him to meet you in the gap |
| T-28 VI.4:1 | of mind you **c.** your own and all the rest of |
| T-30 II.1:12 | than that He hear you **c.** Him "Friend." |
| T-31 I.5:6 | **c.** from God and from your Self to you. |

T-31 I.8:3 you. And never does a **c.** remain unheard,
T-31 I.8:3 selfsame tongue in which the **c.** was made.
T-31 I.8:4 it was this **c.** that everyone and everything
T-31 I.8:6 deceived by forms the **c.** was hidden in.
T-31 I.9:1 and that you do not leave its **c.** unheard.
T-31 I.9:2 heard its calling as the ancient **c.** to life,
T-31 I.10:3 are you who fail to hear the **c.** that echoes
T-31 I.10:3 that echoes past each seeming **c.** to death,
T-31 I.10:4 beyond each form of hate; each **c.** to war.
T-31 I.11:4 Hear not the **c.** for this within yourself.
T-31 I.11:5 deeper **c.** beyond it that appeals for peace
T-31 II.4:1 Perhaps you **c.** it love. Perhaps you think
T-31 II.8:5 wish to hear a **c.** that never has been made
T-31 II.9:2 Hear but his **c.** for mercy and release from
T-31 VII.11:4 they **c.** it forth in everyone they look upon
T-31 VIII.9:5 God has ordained I cannot **c.** in vain, and
W-pI 15.2:1 of image making that you **c.** seeing will
W-pI 47.3:2 telling you exactly what to do to **c.** upon
W-pI 49.2:6 Try to hear God's Voice **c.** to you lovingly,
W-pI 51.4:3 What I **c.** "my" thoughts are not my real
W-pI 52.2:3 I **c.** this seeing. I hold the past against
W-pI 54.3:5 I can also **c.** upon my real thoughts, which
W-pI 54.3:6 As my thoughts of separation **c.** to the
W-pI 59.2:6 Let me **c.** upon this gift today, so that this
W-pI 60.4:2 ceases to **c.** on my forgiveness to save me.
W-pI 62.3:1 that in every attack you **c.** upon your own
W-pI 62.3:1 you **c.** upon the strength of Christ in you.
W-pI 69.7:2 little effort and small determination **c.** on
W-pI 73.2:2 you and **c.** for "righteous" judgment.
W-pI 76.4:2 You **c.** them laws, and put them under
W-pI 78.4:5 who angered you; someone you **c.** a friend
W-pI 95.15:1 a **c.** to all the world to be at one with you.
W-pI 98.4:3 as yet unborn will hear the **c.** we heard,
W-pI 105.9:2 **c.** to Him to give you what He wills to give
W-pI 106.1:1 voice, however loudly it may seem to **c.**, if
W-pI 109.4:5 You **c.** to all to join you in your rest, and
W-pI 109.8:1 and **c.** upon your brothers from your rest
W-pI 121.12:1 and turn your mind to one you **c.** a friend.
W-pI 127.9:1 **C.** to your Father, certain that His Voice
W-pI 135.2:2 to **c.** on you to make appropriate defense.
W-pI 153.19:5 We **c.** upon His strength each time we feel
W-pI 155.6:4 now, while on the way you **c.** to them,
W-pI 155.8:1 Such is salvation's **c.**, and nothing more.
W-pI 160.6:8 will **c.** Its Own unto Itself in recognition of
W-pI 161.10:4 the witnesses your body's eyes **c.** forth.
W-pI 162.2:5 The dead awake in answer to its **c.**. And
W-pI 164.2:3 an ancient **c.** to which He gives an ancient
W-pI 167.2:2 You **c.** it death. Yet we have learned that
W-pI 170.7:6 no strength to **c.** upon in danger, and no
W-pI 170.11:2 stone you made, and **c.** it god no longer.
WpI rV.in3:4 *off, but You will not forget to c. us back.*
WpI rV.in9:4 Self from which I **c.** to you is but your own
W-pI 181.6:2 which we will magnify and **c.** our "sins."
W-pI 182.6:3 His **c.** for help almost unheard amid the
W-pI 182.12:4 and this the **c.** which cannot be denied.
W-pI 183.h I **c.** upon God's Name and on my own.
W-pI 183.1:2 **c.** upon His Name is but to call upon your
W-pI 183.1:2 call upon His Name is but to **c.** upon your
W-pI 183.5:1 the Name of God, and **c.** upon your Self,
W-pI 183.5:3 Those who **c.** upon the Name of God can
W-pI 183.6:6 of everything that we **c.** our own.
W-pI 183.7:3 little prayers of those who **c.** on Him with
W-pI 184.8:4 When you **c.** upon a brother, it is to his
W-pI 184.8:6 body makes response to what you **c.** him,
W-pI 184.15:3 *made and c. by many different names is but a*
W-pI 185.14:1 need of every heart, the **c.** of every mind,
W-pI 186.9:2 He create such instability and **c.** it Son?
W-pI 188.9:6 But now we **c.** them back, and wash them
W-pI 194.8:2 you **c.** the memory of Him to come again,
W-pI 196.11:4 And you can **c.** on Him to save you from
W-pI 199.5:4 sound the **c.** of freedom round the world
WpI rVI.in.7:3 you, each time you **c.** to Him to help you.
W-pI 202.1:2 *has given me His Voice to c. me home?* I am
W-pI 203.1:1 I **c.** upon God's Name and on my own.
W-pII in.10:2 to understand that we need only **c.** to God
W-pII in.10:4 of prayers, we need but **c.** His Name.
W-pII 221.1:5 *sure You will hear my c. and answer me.*
W-pII 221.2:6 to hear our Father's answer to our **c.**, to
W-pII 230.2:5 *need but c. on You to find the peace You gave*
W-pII 2.5:2 The song of our rejoicing is the **c.** to all
W-pII 232.1:3 *be there to hear my c. to You and answer me.*
W-pII 3.4:2 Sounds become the **c.** for God, and all
W-pII 244.1:2 *He need but c. upon Your Name, and he will*
W-pII 272.2:2 temptation **c.** to us to stay and linger in a
W-pII 283.1:1 *of myself, and it is this I c. the Son of God. Yet*
W-pII 10.4:1 and **c.** him to return to the eternal peace
W-pII 324.1:5 *Your loving Voice will always c. me back,*
W-pII 327.h I need but **c.** and You will answer me.
W-pII 327.1:2 For God has promised He will hear my **c.**,
W-pII 327.1:5 awaiting but my **c.** to give me all the help I
W-pII 336.1:5 mind, and **c.** it to return and look within,
W-pII347.1:11 *for me, and c. Your miracles to come to me.*
W-pII 14.4:4 we have attained we **c.** to all our brothers,
W-pII 356.h for God. The miracle is thus a **c.** to Him.
W-pII 356.1:1 *answer any c. Your Son might make to You.*
W-pII 356.1:6 *to c. Your Name is but to call his own.*
W-pII 356.1:6 *to call Your Name is but to c. his own.*
W-pII 357.h Truth answers every **c.** we make to God,
W-pII 358.h No **c.** to God can be unheard nor left
W-ep 1:4 No one who calls on Him can **c.** in vain.
M-in 2:7 Teaching is but a **c.** to witnesses to attest
M-4 I.A.3:6 the plan will sometimes **c.** for changes in
M-5 III.2:11 Very gently they **c.** to their brothers to
M-17 3:5 the **c.** for help becoming his one appeal.
M-23 1:6 an invocation **c.** forth any special power.
M-23 1:7 What does it mean to **c.** on Jesus Christ?
M-25 6:5 have been used to **c.** upon the devil, which
M-26 2:5 No one can **c.** on them in vain. Nor is
M-29 6:6 understands that an attack is a **c.** for help.
C-2 5:1 effect and consequence–we **c.** a miracle.
P-1 2:2 learn to **c.** upon God and hear His Answer
P-2 II.6:4 for they have found the way to **c.** to Him.
P-2 V.6:6 whatever form it takes, is but to **c.** on Him
P-2 V.8:4 Hear a brother **c.** for help and answer him
P-2 VII.6:7 who **c.** upon his sanctity to make it theirs.
P-3 I.4:9 to hear the **c.** and understand that it is his
P-3 II.4:8 must enter, for only that is the **c.** to awake
S-1 III.2:2 They **c.** for vengeance, not for love. Nor
S-1 III.2:4 They **c.** upon a vengeful god, and it is he
S-2 I.8:1 Forgiveness is the **c.** to sanity, for who
S-2 III.3:2 the way to make of every **c.** a help to you,
S-2 III.5:4 release, and it is this that answers to his **c.**
S-3 II.3:1 We **c.** it death, but it is liberty. It does not
S-3 IV.10:7 your Father needs you and will **c.** to you

## called 83

*See also* so-called

T-2 VIII.3:5 might be **c.** a process of right evaluation.
T-3 IV.7:12 are **c.** but few are chosen" should be, "All
T-3 IV.7:12 be, "All are **c.** but few choose to listen."
T-4 IV.10:3 have **c.** you to join with me in the Second.
T-4 IV.11:10 you do. I have **c.** and you will answer. I
T-6 I.10:4 one Voice you are never **c.** on to sacrifice.
T-6 I.15:7 "punishment" I was said to have **c.** forth
T-6 IV.3:3 Everyone has **c.** upon Him for help at one
T-6 V.B.5:4 **c.** upon the Voice for peace to help you.
T-6 V.C.4:6 your consistency is **c.** on despite chaos.
T-7 VI.7:6 and would never have been **c.** upon by the
T-12 VII.11:2 surround you because you **c.** upon them,
T-13 V.3:4 their answer save him who **c.** upon them,
T-13 VI.7:5 to shine on you *because you c. them forth.*
T-13 VI.9:4 that His Son **c.** upon Him and remained
T-14 VI.8:8 can fail to come where God has **c.** him, if
T-16 II.6:4 The One you **c.** upon *is* with you. Bid Him
T-16 II.6:11 The Host of God has **c.** to you, and you
T-16 II.8:3 for that is the only reason He has **c.** to you
T-17 VII.9:2 the same purpose **c.** forth the faith in you.
T-17 VIII.3:5 has been demonstrated has **c.** for faith,
T-18 I.12:1 God has **c.** should hear no substitutes.
T-18 I.13:1 You have been **c.**, together with your
T-18 III.3:1 rushed to meet you since you **c.** upon it. If
T-19 III.2:1 that love, not fear, is really **c.** upon by sin,
T19 IV.A.12:2 depends on which emotion was **c.** on to
T19 IV.D.5:6 of the obstacles to love, Love Itself has **c.**.
T-20 II.8:5 Your home has **c.** to you since time began
T-20 III.11:3 and recognize the home that **c.** to you.
T-22 I.3:8 and you have **c.** upon this thing to lead
T-24 VI.12:5 it no sacrifice is asked, no strain **c.** forth,
T-25 VIII.2:5 not **c.** upon to do what one divided still
T-26 V.5:5 in sin, is that one instant still **c.** back, as if
T-26 VI.3:3 of Him Whom God has **c.** your Friend.
T-27 I.6:6 witnesses that are **c.** forth to be believed,
T-27 VI.3:7 true because you **c.** him by truth's name.
T-27 VI.5:1 the names by which sin's witnesses are **c.**.
T-27 VI.5:4 the name by which you **c.** your suffering.
T-27 VI.5:6 them all as one, and **c.** by name of fear. As
T-30 I.2:4 you will be **c.** upon to make response. For
T-30 II.2:3 that ever should be **c.** by freedom's name.
T-30 III.4:10 What idol can be **c.** upon to give the Son
W-pI 4.1:6 none of them can be **c.** "good" or "bad."
W-pI 14.3:2 exchange, which can truly be **c.** salvation,
W-pI 16.2:2 of a whole world can hardly be **c.** idle.
W-pI 23.3:3 One can well ask if this can be **c.** seeing. Is
W-pI 46.2:4 forgiveness can truly be **c.** salvation. It is
W-pI 77.7:4 a situation arises in which they are **c.** for.
W-pI 125.6:4 is peace within you to be **c.** upon today, to
W-pI 130.9:2 For you have **c.** upon the great unfailing
W-pI 134.5:2 be concealed, denied or **c.** another name,
W-pI 137.5:1 might thus be **c.** a counter-dream, which
W-pI 161.12:1 And He will answer Whom you **c.** upon.
W-pI 166.3:2 he may be **c.** to claim them as his own, is
W-pI 182.1:3 if there were a place that **c.** you to return,
W-pI 182.11:2 Christ has **c.** you friend and brother. He
W-pI 189.10:2 *But we have c., and You have answered us.*
W-pII in.3:4 We have **c.** on Him, and He has promised
W-pII in.8:5 has **c.** to us unceasingly since time began.
W-pII 231.1:2 *else; a something I have c. by many names.*
W-pII 333.1:2 seen somewhere else, **c.** by another name,
W-ep 2:3 course of those whom God has **c.** to Him.
M-4 I.A.3:1 what might be **c.** "a period of undoing."
M-4 I.A.5:1 go can be **c.** "a period of relinquishment."
M-4 I.A.5:5 which the teacher of God feels **c.** upon to
M-9 1:6 are **c.** upon to change their life situation
M-13 6:6 You have been **c.** by God, and you have
M-23 4:4 the moment that the name is **c.** to mind.
M-26 2:2 be **c.** the Teachers of teachers because,
M-26 2:2 visible, their image can yet be **c.** upon.
M-29 1:4 While it is **c.** a manual for teachers, it
C-3 2:1 might be **c.** a kind of happy fiction; a way
C-6 1:1 Whom he **c.** down upon the earth after he
C-6 1:3 was "**c.** down upon the earth" in the sense
C-ep 4:1 Who **c.** to us and helped us hear His Call.
P-2 I.2:8 nothingness cannot be **c.** new or different
P-2 V.8:5 to Whom you answer, for you **c.** on Him.
P-2 VI.3:3 is to make agreeable whatever is **c.** on,
P-3 I.1:7 you are being **c.** on constantly to make
P-3 II.1:9 may be **c.** upon to use special applications
P-3 II.7:6 could hardly be **c.** professional therapists.
S-2 I.4:6 for you have **c.** him guilty of your sins,
S-3 IV.4:2 Your prayer has risen up and **c.** to God,

## calling 26

T-2 V.A.18:1 that of others if, in a situation **c.** for help,
T-4 IV.11:12 My **c.** you is as natural as your answer,
T-5 II.2:4 The mind had no **c.** until the separation,
T-13 V.9:5 **c.** forth its witnesses and drawing them to
T-13 VI.8:6 wholeness, as I am **c.** you to join with me.
T-13 IX.5:5 other, **c.** for punishment instead of love.
T-14 V.3:5 Your only **c.** here is to devote yourself,
T-14 V.9:4 I stand within the circle, **c.** you to peace.
T19 IV.B.3:1 **c.** the mind to join in holy communion
T19 IV.B.15:4 **c.** it pleasure and offering it to you as
T-27 II.6:7 The ancient **c.** of the Father to His Son,
T-29 I.9:5 allow the body to say "no" to Heaven's **c.**,
T-31 I.8:8 The soft eternal **c.** of each part of God's
T-31 I.9:2 have heard its **c.** as the ancient call to life,
W-pI 79.9:2 today, each one **c.** for an answer. Our
W-pI 100.2:6 hear God **c.** to them in your happy laugh.
W-pI 106.5:3 except his Father, **c.** through your Self?
W-pI 122.5:3 and welcome **c.** from beyond the doorway
W-pI 182.7:7 within you, **c.** you to let Him go in peace,
W-pI 186.13:1 is **c.** from the known to the unknowing.
W-pI 196.11:4 Love, **c.** Him Father and yourself His Son.
W-pII in.2:9 **c.** to God when we have need of Him as
W-pII 266.2:1 **c.** upon God's Name and on our own,

W-pII..310.1:4 *You, Your gracious c. to Your holy Son, the*
M-23..........1:8 What does c. on his name confer? Why is
P-2.........V.5:5 sacred c. of God's holy Son for help in his

## callous 1

T-11.......V.9:1 distant, emotionally shallow, c.,

## calls 128

T-1.........V.4:2 miracle c. him to return because it blesses
T-5.........in.1:6 Joy c. forth an integrated willingness to
T-5...........I.1:2 gladness c. to every part of the Sonship to
T-5...........I.4:8 is so close to knowledge that He c. it forth
T-5.........II.3:8 His is the Voice that c. you back to where
T-5.........II.6:1 Holy Spirit c. you both to remember and
T-5.......VI.12:3 Infinite patience c. upon infinite love, and
T-5.......VII.3:1 insane c. you think are made upon you,
T-6.......IV.6:3 sleep is not real and God c. you to awake.
T-6......V.C.4:1 step c. for consistent vigilance against it. I
T-7.......V.11:6 c. upon you to love God and His creation.
T-8.....VIII.4:9 the ego c. on a witness, it has already
T-9......IV.11:6 fearful, but no one c. them true. Children
T-10....III.11:3 His Voice still c. you to return, and He
T-10.......IV.7:1 gods, and c. on his brothers to do likewise
T-10.......V.7:4 c. to you from every part of the Sonship,
T-12..........I.4:1 to prevent you from recognizing all c. for
T-12.......IV.3:4 and teach you that love really c. forth the
T-12......VI.4:8 Him your Father c. His Son to remember.
T-13.....III.8:2 Father as your Father c. you to Himself. In
T-13.......V.6:6 God c. you and you do not hear, for you
T-13....VI.10:9 And seeing it, its beauty c. you home.
T-13.....XI.3:9 and bright, and c. forth one response.
T-14.......V.9:9 only purpose to which my teaching c. you
T-14......IX.8:2 no contradiction in what holiness c. forth
T-14.......X.1:5 holiness c. everyone to lay all guilt aside.
T-15......VI.4:1 that when another c. on God for love,
T-15... VIII.2:8 The will of your creations c. to you, to
T-15... VIII.3:8 it c. to everyone to escape from loneliness
T-16....IV.11:3 be. Love c., but hate would have you stay.
T-17......IV.3:2 predominance that, when truth c. to you,
T-17......VII.8:9 to whom the situation's purpose c.. It
T-17...VII.8:10 It c. to everyone. There is no situation
T-17......VII.9:4 Truth c. for faith, and faith makes room
T-17...VII.10:6 it, for it c. you to salvation and to peace.
T-17... VIII.1:3 It c. forth just the same suspension of
T-18........II.7:6 uses everyone who c. on Him as means
T-18....VI.14:3 It c. to you to be yourself, within its safe
T-18. VIII.11:7 No part of love c. on the whole in vain.
T-18.....IX.13:2 it c. to you to follow the course it took,
T-19...... I.5:11 c. upon the mind and not the body.
T-19...... I.15:2 c. on truth to enter and make lovely what
T-19.......II.1:6 c. for punishment as error for correction,
T-19......III.1:5 For guilt still c. to it, and the mind hears
T-19......III.3:7 for it is sin that c. for punishment, not
T-19......III.4:6 c. for punishment must call for nothing.
T19....IV.A.1:6 and from you reach to everyone who c.,
T-19 . IV.A.12:3 their master c. on them to serve him. For
T19IV.A.17:12 that you would have c. upon pain to fill
T19IV.B.10:10 home of the emotion that c. them forth,
T19....IV.D.5:5 as love's attraction stirs and c. to you.
T-20......III.1:3 and c. upon defenses to uphold it against
T-20......III.1:7 to truth, which c. on only what he is, to
T-21.......V.3:5 are the obvious response to c. for help,
T-22...... I.10:6 It is denial of illusions that c. on truth, for
T-24.........I.4:2 But what is different c. for judgment, and
T-24......III.1:5 And so he c. it "unforgivable," and makes
T-24......III.8:5 God c. to you from him to join His Will to
T-24.....VII.1:5 while it c. to him he hears no other Voice.
T-25......III.6:6 He will hear plainly that the c. to war he
T-25......III.6:6 war he heard before are really c. to peace.
T-25......VI.3:1 to see c. down the grace of God upon your
T-26.......V.8:1 unforgiven is a voice that c. from out a
T-26...VII.15:7 What God c. One will be forever One, not
T-26...VII.16:1 The miracle but c. your ancient Name,
T-26...VII.16:2 your brother c. for his release and yours.
T-26......IX.1:1 for God c. lovingly unto your brother,
T-27...VII.13:4 the Voice that c. with love to waken him;
T-29.......V.7:5 form it takes in some way c. for death.
T-29.....VII.1:4 God c. will never answer in His place.
T-30......VI.2:3 a real attack that c. for punishment.
T-30......VI.2:7 that rests on error, and thus c. for help.
T-31..........I.8:2 Nothing but c. to you in soft appeal to be
T-31.......I.10:4 Who c. to you beyond each form of hate;
T-31.......I.10:5 Him answer in the language that He c..
T-31....... II.5:5 Two c. you make to him, as he to you.
T-31....... II.5:8 But if he c. for death or calls for life, for
T-31....... II.5:8 But if he calls for death or c. for life, for
T-31....... II.7:1 and answer to the Christ Who c. to you.
T-31....... II.7:4 about this Son of God who c. to you.
T-31....... II.7:5 you. Christ c. to all with equal tenderness,
T-31... VIII.3:2 perplexity Christ c. to you and gently says
W-pI.....86.4:4 *salvation. This c. for salvation, not attack.*
W-pI.....91.6:9 The belief you are a body c. for correction
W-pI...91.6:10 truth of what you are c. on the strength in
W-pI.....95.9:2 This c. for correction, and for nothing
W-pI.....97.4:4 c. through His Voice to every living thing;
W-pI...100.4:2 earth c. to all minds to let their sorrows
W-pI...100.9:5 when He Who c. to you is God Himself?
W-pI.100.10:6 It is your Self Who c. to you today. And it
W-pI...106.5:2 God c. to them through you. He needs
W-pI...125.1:3 He c. to you from deep within your mind
W-pI...160.7:2 Is he not the one your Self c. not? You are
W-pI...161.5:3 Fear without symbols c. for no response,
W-pI...161.7:4 it c. for death as surely as God's Voice
W-pI...182.8:2 So poignantly He c. to you that you will
W-pI...182.9:3 of Heaven in His hand and c. them friend,
W-pI...183.2:1 echo in the mind that c. you to remember
W-pI.183.10:3 when God's Son c. on his Father's Name.
W-pI.183.10:6 He c. on Him to let all things he thought
W-pI.183.11:4 the Son of God, who c. upon his Father.
W-pI...195.9:5 God has cared for us, and c. us Son. Can
W-pI...199.7:5 your mind to Him Who c. to you to make
W-pI...200.9:6 The Father c.; the Son will hear. And that
W-pII.....in.3:4 remain unanswered when he c. His Name
W-pII.....in.7:8 which will not fail the Son who c. to You.
W-pII..260.1:3 *Your Son, my Father, c. on You today. Let*
W-pII..267.1:2 It c. to me in every heartbeat and in every
W-pII..267.1:7 Each heartbeat c. His Name, and every
W-pII......7.4:1 placed by God, the Holy Spirit c. to you,
W-pII......8.5:4 Who c. to us and comes to take us home,
W-pII....11.5:1 Our Father c. to us. We hear His Voice,
W-ep.........1:4 No one who c. on Him can call in vain.
M-1...........2:6 c. for teachers to speak for It and redeem
M-13.........2:5 a while about what the world c. sacrifice.
M-16.........8:4 in any place and circumstance he c. for it.
M-20.........2:3 It c. to mind nothing that went before. It
M-22.........4:4 of God c. forth the miracle of healing. He
C-6............5:2 brother c. to you to be His Voice along
P-2.....VII.1:14 God comes to him who c., and in Him he
P-2.....VII.7:6 He does not see the Christ in him who c..
P-3...........I.4:8 c. on him is far beyond his understanding
S-1........III.2:3 understands that they are c. for death,
S-2...........I.8:3 God c. on you to save His Son from death
S-2........III.2:5 When someone c. for help in any form,
S-2........III.6:6 heard by anyone who c. upon His Name,
S-3........III.4:6 your oneness with the one who c. for help
S-3........IV.8:6 Listen, My child, your Father c. to you.

## calm 29

T-4......III.10:1 The c. being of God's Kingdom, which in
T-5.......III.8:6 vision frightens the ego because it is so c..
T-7........III.5:6 The certain are perfectly c., because they
T-10......III.6:1 c. knowledge that each one is part of Him.
T-11.......V.1:4 Let us be very c. in doing this, for we are
T-13.......I.11:4 the c. recognition that it has never been.
T-13....... II.5:1 In the c. light of truth, let us recognize
T-14....III.12:1 of His c. and unswerving value of His Son
T-15.........I.1:1 to be perfectly c. and quiet all the time?
T-18.........I.8:2 you. And turn you to the stately c. within,
T-19.......I.14:5 No error interferes with its c. sight, which
T-19......IV.1:6 the c. awareness of complete protection.
T-20......VI.2:7 It walks in sunlight, open-eyed and c., in
T-20... VIII.6:1 brought to it by His c. and certain sight.
T-20. VIII.10:4 of imagined sin into the c. and reassuring
T-23......III.4:4 uphold a quiet, c. assurance it has come.
T-29... VIII.2:7 quiet c. that liberates you from the world,
T-29......IX.9:1 help, a c. assurance Heaven goes with you
T-31...VII.11:6 his c. and open eyes and what he sees. He
T-31..VIII.12:2 set for Him before time was, in c. eternity.
W-pI.....40.3:8 *I am c., quiet, assured and confident.* If only
W-pI.....49.2:1 that is listening to the Voice for God is c.,
W-pI.....50.3:3 upon the eternal c. of the Son of God.
WpI...rI.in.4:3 those that already seem to be c. and quiet.
W-pI.....81.1:4 In its c. light let all my conflicts disappear
W-pI...165.3:1 of mind, his quiet rest, his c. awakening,
W-pII ....in.3:1 times of rest, and c. our minds at need.
W-pII .252.1:3 within it, in the c. of quiet certainty. Its
S-3........III.3:4 to c. the mind that suffers from the agony

## calmer 1

T-27...VII.13:4 and allowed his c. mind to welcome, not

## calmly 5

T-10......III.5:1 Look c. at the logical conclusion of the
T-17.....VII.5:4 Let it enter and look upon it c., but do not
T-23........II.1:4 Let us, then, look upon them c., that we
T-30......IV.5:9 Look c. at its toys, and understand that
W-pI.....31.3:4 to let the stream move on evenly and c.,

## calmness 1

T-23......IV.8:8 it be anything that offers you a perfect c.,

## came 68

T-1.........IV.4:3 I c. to fulfill the law by reinterpreting it.
T-5...........I.4:6 c. from the Holy Spirit or the Universal
T-5...........I.5:2 He c. into being with the separation as a
T-5........IV.8:6 They c. from the Holy Spirit within you,
T-5......VI.11:1 meant that I c. to share the light with you.
T-8........IV.3:5 This is the awareness I c. to give you, and
T-8........IV.6:9 This is the only lesson I c. to teach.
T-8........VI.4:3 c. home the father welcomed him with joy
T-13.......V.11:7 this vision of the truth in them c. all the
T-13......XI.2:8 one into the unreality from which they c..
T-16.......III.1:3 c. from beyond your thought system.
T-16.......III.1:6 with what you taught before He c.. And
T-16.......III.3:5 be that what you taught c. from yourself.
T-17......III.1:8 understand how they c. into your mind,
T-17......III.9:8 as is the holy Source from which they c..
T-18......IV.2:5 it. That is why you c.. If you could come
T-18..VIII.11:3 come because you c. without the body,
T-19.........I.2:7 body is healed because you c. without it,
T19....IV.C.3:1 From the ego c. sin and guilt and death,
T19... IV.D.8:1 Forget not that you c. this far together,
T19. IV.D.21:1 You c. this far because the journey was
T-20......III.7:3 He c. without a purpose, but he will not
T-21......IV.7:2 hear since first the ego c. into your mind.
T-22.......I.10:5 And truth c. instantly, to show you where
T-22......IV.1:5 The way you c. no longer matters. It can
T-22.....VI.10:7 us look straight at how this error c. about,
T-26.......V.3:5 and all of them that c. within the first.
T-26......IX.8:5 to replace an ancient enmity that c. to kill
T-27......VI.6:3 is bound by laws that it c. solely to undo!
T-27.....VII.7:6 This is how all illusions c. about. The one
T-28.........I.9:2 c. from causelessness which you confused
T-28.......I.13:6 c. in between the present and the past, to
T-29........II.4:2 You asked Him, and He c.. You did not
T-29........II.4:4 And yet His gifts c. with Him. He has laid
T-29.....VII.5:2 You c. to die, and what would you expect
T-29......IX.2:1 dream of judgment c. into the mind that
W-pI...100.8:3 For this you c.. Let this one be the day
W-pI...106.8:3 It will begin the ministry for which you c.,
W-pI...107.1:6 to nothingness, returning whence they c..
W-pI...107.2:3 when nothing c. to interrupt your peace
W-pI...109.2:5 everyone who ever c. and yet will come to
W-pI...109.6:2 and hourly remember that you c. to bring
W-pI.127.12:2 and who c. to learn what you must learn.
W-pI...131.3:2 For this you c., and you will surely do the
W-pI...131.3:2 and you will surely do the thing you c. for.
W-pI...132.4:4 c. unwillingly to what was made already,
W-pI...132.4:5 exactly what you looked for when you c..
W-pI...139.9:4 just our happiness alone we c. to gain.

W-pI... 159.9:4 into a garden like the one they **c.** from,
W-pI... 166.4:4 realize he has forgotten where he **c.** from,
W-pI. 167.11:3 leave the Source of life from where it **c.**.
W-pI... 182.7:3 He **c.** because He knew you would not fail
W-pI... 188.1:6 light **c.** with you from your native home,
W-pI... 188.1:8 to where it **c.** from and you are at home.
W-pI... 188.7:5 **c.** but to remind you how you must return
W-pI... 189.2:2 It welcomes you, rejoices that you **c.**, and
W-pII . 228.2:1 *I failed to realize the Source from which I* **c.**.
W-pII . 249.1:7 has ended in the light from which he **c.**.
W-pII ..... 9.4:2 For every one who ever **c.** to die, or yet
W-pII .... 319.h I **c.** for the salvation of the world.
W-pII ... 14.5:2 changed about the aim for which we **c.**,
M-4 ...... IV.2:8 understood their evil thoughts **c.** neither
M-10 ....... 5:12 And where he **c.** to judge, he comes to
M-13 ......... 1:2 it **c.** when there is no more use for it. Now
M-17 ......... 6:9 but do not remember how it **c.** about.
C-4............. 4:5 spins into nothingness from where it **c.**.
P-2....... VII.2:9 with which the patient **c.** to ask for help.
P-3........ III.1:8 part in this one purpose, for which he **c.**.

**camouflage** 2
WpI. rIII.in3:4 to uphold a **c.** for your unwillingness.
W-pI... 133.9:1 Yet is its **c.** a thin veneer, which could

**campaign** 1
T-17..... V.11:9 you are now entering upon a **c.** to blame

**camps** 1
W-pI... 170.3:2 two **c.** which seem wholly irreconcilable.

**can** 3283

**cancel** 3
T-5........ IV.2:9 You cannot **c.** out your past errors alone.
T-6.... V.C.10:7 it. Only this can **c.** out the need for effort,
T-12....... V.3:3 can **c.** out all reinforcement is in yourself.

**cancelled** 5
T-27...... III.2:3 where half is **c.** out by the remaining half.
T-27...... III.2:4 is quickly contradicted by the half it **c.** out
T-27...... III.3:3 weak. The picture has been wholly **c.** out,
T-27...... III.3:3 symbolized a contradiction that **c.** out the
T-27...... III.6:6 remains unknown, but is not **c.** out. And

**cancelling** 3
T-1........ III.1:4 My part in the Atonement is the **c.** out of
T-3......... II.6:5 solace. If you perceive truly you are **c.** out
T-9........ IV.5:6 By steadily and consistently **c.** out all its

**cancels** 4
T-28......... I.1:3 And thus it **c.** out the interference to what
T-30......... I.6:6 This **c.** out the terms that you have set,
W-pI... 137.5:1 which **c.** out the dream of sickness in the
M-19 ......... 1:3 which injustice gives rise, and **c.** them out

**cancer** 1
W-pI..... 14.5:4 create illness," but, "God did not create **c.**

**candle** 1
W-pI... 131.6:7 time as is a tiny **c.** from a distant star, or

**cannot** 1502

**capable** 46
T-1......... I.24:2 a miracle, **c.** of creating in the likeness of
T-2......... I.5:12 by lack of love from without and **c.**,
T-2 ....... III.3:3 can temporize and you are **c.** of enormous
T-2 ....... IV.2:4 Only the mind is **c.** of error. The body can
T-2 ....... IV.5:4 level of communication of which he is **c.**.
T-2 ....... IV.5:5 of communication of which he is **c.** *now.*
T-2 ........ V.6:3 Only the mind is **c.** of illumination. Spirit
T-2 ........ V.7:3 **c.** only of looking beyond it to the defense
T-2 ........ V.9:5 which you are **c.** now are time-dependent.
T-3 .......... I.1:9 Is it likely that God Himself would be **c.** of
T-3 ....... IV.1:7 the Levels of the Trinity are **c.** of unity.
T-3 ....... IV.3:2 It is **c.** of asking questions but not of
T-3 ....... VI.5:1 have judged yourself as **c.** of being tired.
T-3 ....... VI.5:5 You are not really **c.** of being tired, but
T-3 ....... VI.5:5 but you are very **c.** of wearying yourself.
T-3 ....... VI.6:4 It is judgmental only because you are **c.** of
T-3 ...... VII.3:9 or His creations as **c.** of destroying Their
T-4 ....... II.4:10 the loftiest idea of which ego thinking is **c.**
T-5 ........ V.4:4 is **c.** of creating reality or making illusions
T-7 ..... VI.11:8 **c.** of being appreciated and loved. That
T-7 ...... VII.1:9 and so it is as **c.** of being used positively
T-8 ..... VIII.2:2 as **c.** of shifting its allegiance from one to
T-9 ....... VI.1:4 something in you that is **c.** of producing it
T-9 ...... VII.3:7 The ego is therefore **c.** of suspiciousness
T-10 ........ I.2:1 but perfectly **c.** of awakening to reality. Is
T-10 .... V.9:11 Your mind is **c.** of creating worlds, but it
T-11 ........ I.9:4 Who wants only your will, be **c.** of this?
T-11 .... VII.3:7 what you made is **c.** of being unlike Him.
T-11 .... VII.3:9 it will make you **c.** of understanding it.
T-11 ... VIII.6:4 be **c.** of misinterpreting the question you
T-12 ........ I.6:2 for both are **c.** of bringing love into your
T-12 ........ I.9:5 are the only emotions of which you are **c.**.
T-12 ... VIII.8:6 for only perception is **c.** of error and
T-13 ..... XI.4:2 you what is **c.** of being wholly shared. It
T-14 ... III.13:2 is. Only His wisdom is **c.** of guiding you to
T-19 ....... II.6:5 and **c.** of complete corruption and decay.
T-19 ..... III.8:2 God's, **c.** of making another will that
T-21 ..... II.10:3 and **c.** of serving as a cause of the events
T-21 ...... V.4:3 to stay in your awareness is **c.** of reason.
T-30 ... VIII.1:5 is thus reduced to form, and **c.** of change.
W-pI... 129.1:3 with joy, and **c.** of offering you peace.
M-10 ......... 1:3 is **c.** of "good" and "bad" judgment, and
M-19 ......... 1:7 for no one in the world is **c.** of making
P-1............ 4:4 himself as really **c.** of making decisions.
P-2........... I.2:2 the ego fosters; that it is **c.** of true change,
P-2....... VII.3:6 **c.** of joining with the patient in a holy

**capacity** 4
T-6 ........ in.2:5 Your **c.** for allegiance to a thought system
T-16 ........ I.1:3 The **c.** to empathize is very useful to the
T-16 ........ I.4:2 of it if you let Him use your **c.** for strength
W-pI. 135.13:3 In this **c.** is health assured. For everything

**capitalized** 1
C-1 ........... 1:2 the term is **c.** it refers to God or Christ

**capricious** 4
T-6 ....... IV.1:3 It is **c.** and does not mean its maker well.
T-14 ........ I.4:5 blocked by the **c.** and unholy whim of
T-15 ...... V.7:2 does it assemble reality to its own **c.** liking
W-pI..... 95.2:2 held together by its erratic and **c.** maker,

**capriciousness** 1
T-4 ....... IV.4:1 that anxiety comes from the **c.** of the ego,

**captive** 2
T-19 ..... III.1:5 making itself a willing **c.** to its sick appeal.
T-23 ..... II.14:8 do the laws of sin appear to hold love **c.**,

**capture** 1
W-pI... 107.6:1 in that, evading **c.** and escaping grasp. It

**care** 38
T-5 ...... VII.1:5 You are His **c.** because He loves you. His
T-5 ...... VII.1:6 that all hope is yours because of His **c.**.
T-5 ...... VII.1:7 choose to escape His **c.** because that is not
T-5 ...... VII.1:7 but you can choose to accept His **c.** and
T-5 ...... VII.1:7 of His **c.** for all those He created by it.
T-11 ....... II.5:3 your **c.** is a sign that you want Him. Think
T-15 ....... V.5:4 place any relationship under His **c.** and be
T-15 ... VIII.1:5 His concern and **c.** for you are limitless.
T-16 ..... III.2:8 remember how much **c.** you have exerted
T-24 ... VI.10:6 each part of Him with equal love and **c.**.
T-24 .... VII.2:7 to you. All of the love and **c.**, the strong
T-31 ....... II.8:4 thought were precious and in need of **c.**.
T-31 .... VII.8:3 the holy ones especially entrusted to his **c.**
W-pI .... 31.3:5 idea to yourself as often as you **c.** to, but
W-pI .... 58.5:7 His **c.** for me is infinite, and is with me
W-pI .. 122.1:5 world? Do you want **c.** and safety, and the
W-pI .. 123.8:1 how deep and limitless His **c.** for you,
W-pI .. 124.4:1 us, nor question His protection and His **c.**
W-pI .. 126.5:5 Would not His **c.** for you be small indeed,
W-pI .. 135.4:4 such frailty that constant **c.** and watchful,
W-pI .. 135.5:3 medicine, no **c.** and no concern at all.
W-pI .. 159.8:4 and kindly **c.** Christ's charity provides.
W-pI 166.13:1 The gifts are yours, entrusted to your **c.**,
W-pI .. 181.3:3 We do not **c.** about our future goals. And
W-pI .. 193.9:3 untroubled and serene, without a **c.**, in an
W-pI 193.13:4 every **c.** and every form of suffering,
W-pI .. 194.7:6 of **c.** the world can never threaten. He is
W-pI .. 195.9:3 a thought or **c.** for us or for our future.
W-pII . 222.1:4 He covers me with kindness and with **c.**,
W-pII . 232.1:5 *me sleep sure of my safety, certain of Your* **c.**,
W-pII . 306.1:4 born anew into a world of mercy and of **c.**
W-pII . 358.1:6 *let me not forget Your Love and* **c.**, *keeping*
M-10 ......... 5:7 His sense of **c.** is gone, for he has none.
M-27 ......... 2:3 ready to break it off without regret or **c.**,
M-29 ......... 2:6 Holy Spirit's particular **c.** and guidance.
C-5 .......... 6:12 *all those whom He has sent to you to* **c.** *for as I*
C-5 .......... 6:12 *He has sent to you to care for as I* **c.** *for you.*
S-3........ IV.5:8 which He abandoned to the devil's **c.**,

**cared** 1
W-pI .. 195.9:5 God has **c.** for us, and calls us Son. Can

**careers** 1
W-pII . 298.1:4 journeys, mad **c.** and artificial values. I

**careful** 14
T-1 ...... VII.4:3 sections not to require their **c.** study. You
T-1 ...... VII.5:4 I have been **c.** to clarify my role in the
T-1 ...... VII.5:8 on these steps without **c.** preparation, or
T-4 ....... II.11:7 You must be **c.**, however, that you really
T-5 ...... VII.1:4 You need be neither **c.** nor careless; you
T-14 ....... X.8:9 though **c.** to conceal this fact behind
T-16 ..... III.4:3 have been very **c.** to avoid the obvious,
T-17 ....... II.5:2 with you the **c.** searching of the mind that
T19 .IV.A.14:4 will be as **c.** to let no little act of charity,
T-26 ... VIII.2:4 to remain a little **c.** and a little watchful of
W-pI 136.19:1 needs to be preserved by **c.** watching. If
W-pI .. 185.8:1 periods to **c.** searching of your mind, to
M-19 ......... 3:4 and justified by **c.** selectivity in which all
P-2........ VI.5:3 that a **c.** study of the form a sickness takes

**carefully** 58
T-1 .... VII.5:10 The means are being **c.** explained to you.
T-2 ...... VII.1:7 do not guard your thoughts **c.** enough.
T-4 ...... in.3:11 and if you will read these lessons **c.** they
T-4 ....... III.8:1 Watch **c.** and see what it is you are really
T-4 ....... IV.8:5 Watch your mind **c.** for any beliefs that
T-5 ..... VI.10:5 you, however **c.** you have built it up. The
T-9 ......... V.1:3 consider the unhealed healer more **c.** now
T-11 ...... in.2:7 is **c.** hidden in the dark cornerstone of its
T-11 ..... III.7:7 you. Guard **c.** His temple, for He Himself
T-11 ..... V.16:2 perception chooses its witnesses **c.**, and
T-12 ..... III.10:1 well-structured and **c.** planned program
T-13 ...... in.2:3 Look **c.** at this world, and you will realize
T-13 ..... III.7:5 and search your mind **c.** for any thoughts
T-14 ..... IV.5:1 and then consider **c.** whether you want to

| | |
|---|---|
| T-14......VI.2:5 | The sentinels of darkness watch over it **c.**, |
| T-14......VI.8:4 | which nothing at all is **c.** concealed. We |
| T-16.....V.15:4 | whole thought system is a **c.** contrived |
| T-17......IV.4:7 | your holy relationships been **c.** preserved, |
| T-17... VIII.5:3 | him. Think **c.** before you let yourself use |
| T-19.......II.8:4 | Yet think you **c.** before you allow yourself |
| T19... IV.C.9:3 | infancy of salvation is **c.** guarded by love, |
| T19. IV.D.20:1 | Think **c.** how you would look upon the |
| T-20.......II.2:5 | It will adorn its chosen home most **c.**, |
| T-20.......II.6:6 | Listen and hear this **c.**, nor think it but a |
| T-20.......II.8:2 | It has been **c.** prepared for you, and it is |
| T-20......III.5:6 | sickly picture of yourself is **c.** preserved |
| T-20......VI.5:2 | a meaningless enclosure **c.** protected, yet |
| T-21.....VII.8:1 | Consider **c.** your answer to the last |
| T-21... VIII.4:1 | think **c.** why you have not yet decided |
| T-24.......II.3:7 | instead of peace, and wrapped it **c.** in sin, |
| T-25.....VII.3:1 | we said before, and think of it more **c.**. It |
| T-25...VII.11:7 | believe that God is mad, look **c.** at this, |
| T-26.....VII.2:4 | it may be **c.** preserved from reason's light. |
| T-28......III.3:5 | sickness is kept **c.** protected, cherished, |
| T-28.......V.7:3 | The gap is **c.** concealed in fog, and misty |
| T-29.........I.3:8 | and limited in scope and **c.** restricted in |
| T-31.........I.3:1 | you have learned, how **c.** you learned it, |
| W-pI.....13.5:4 | Note **c.**, however, any signs of overt or |
| W-pI.....19.3:2 | and then the mind should be **c.** searched |
| W-pI.....20.1:3 | has been intentional, and very **c.** planned. |
| W-pI.....21.2:2 | search your mind **c.** for situations past, |
| W-pI.....24.3:2 | honestly and **c.** considered in each of the |
| W-pI.....24.5:1 | and then enumerate **c.** as many goals as |
| W-pI.....65.5:2 | and watch your mind **c.** to catch whatever |
| W-pI.....72.6:1 | To this **c.** prepared arena, where angry |
| WpI. rIII.in3:3 | Unwillingness can be most **c.** concealed |
| WpI. rIV.in3:1 | of true forgiveness may be **c.** concealed. |
| W-pI...151.4:5 | It guides your senses **c.**, to prove how |
| W-pI...155.9:1 | Walk safely now, yet **c.**, because this path |
| W-pI...168.3:1 | has most **c.** preserved within our hearts, |
| W-pI...170.4:1 | you consider **c.** the means by which your |
| WpI rVI.in.2:1 | **c.** review the thoughts the Holy Spirit has |
| M-4......VII.1:2 | that must be learned and learned very **c.**. |
| M-4.......IX.1:5 | problems, remaining **c.** limited for a time. |
| M-27..........1:3 | but now we need to consider it more **c.**. It |
| P-2.......VII.2:1 | Think **c.**, teacher and therapist, for |
| S-2...........I.2:4 | its sight. It **c.** picks out all evil things, and |
| S-2.........II.1:2 | and some are **c.** concealed beneath what |

## careless 5

| | |
|---|---|
| T-5.......VII.1:4 | You need be neither careful nor **c.**; you |
| T-20.......II.6:6 | it but a dream, a **c.** thought to play with, |
| T-20......IV.8:8 | **c.** of everything except the only purpose |
| T-25.....VII.9:6 | and pass him by in **c.** thoughtlessness. |
| T-27.....VII.8:5 | **C.** indeed of him this mind must be, as |

## carelessly 1

| | |
|---|---|
| T-20......III.7:2 | who wandered **c.** into the home of truth |

## cares 9

| | |
|---|---|
| T-5.......VII.1:4 | you need merely cast your **c.** upon Him |
| T-13......III.5:5 | it enters of its own volition and **c.** not for |
| T-15.........I.1:1 | you imagine what it means to have no **c.**, |
| T-25. VIII.11:1 | specialness **c.** not who pays the cost of sin |
| W-pI...109.5:1 | In Him you have no **c.** and no concerns, |
| W-pI...133.9:2 | to anyone who **c.** to look for them. Here is |
| W-pI...165.2:6 | Thought of God protects you, **c.** for you, |
| W-pI...193.9:3 | care, in an eternal home which **c.** for him. |
| W-pII..255.1:5 | says. God's Son can have no **c.**, and must |

## caress 1

| | |
|---|---|
| W-pI...188.3:2 | It pauses to **c.** each living thing, and |

## careth 1

| | |
|---|---|
| T-5.......VII.1:4 | cares upon Him because He **c.** for you. |

## caricatures 1

| | |
|---|---|
| T-10......III.4:3 | All forms of idolatry are **c.** of creation, |

## carpet 2

| | |
|---|---|
| T-13.........I.3:5 | a long **c.** spread along the past behind you |
| T-13.........I.3:6 | of God is guilty you will walk along this **c.** |

## carpeted 1

| | |
|---|---|
| W-pI.200.10:3 | come to where the road is **c.** with leaves of |

## carried 14

| | |
|---|---|
| T-5...........I.6:6 | literal meaning of transferred or "**c.** over, |
| T-5........IV.2:8 | You have **c.** the burden of unshared ideas |
| T-7.........X.1:2 | You may have **c.** the ego's reasoning to its |
| T-8...........I.5:6 | be integrated. If it is **c.** out by these two |
| T-14......IV.6:2 | being **c.** down a quiet path in summer. |
| T19... IV.A.9:4 | this little wisp is lifted up and **c.** away, |
| T-28.......I.15:6 | that he be lifted up and gently **c.** over. He |
| W-pI.....69.7:1 | feel a sense of being lifted up and **c.** ahead |
| W-pI...154.5:4 | purpose is, or where they should be **c.**, he |
| W-pI...159.9:2 | when they are **c.** back into the world. |
| W-pII......7.1:3 | He provides are dreams all **c.** to the truth, |
| M-27.........7:3 | but been misperceived and **c.** to illusion. |
| M-27.........7:4 | task to let the illusion be **c.** to the truth. |
| C-5............4:1 | forgiven because they **c.** no effects at all. |

## carries 15

| | |
|---|---|
| T-16......III.8:3 | which **c.** him across the gap as soon as he |
| T-22.......II.1:5 | Every illusion **c.** pain and suffering in the |
| T-25.......in.2:1 | No one who **c.** Christ in him can fail to |
| T-25.......in.2:4 | And so he **c.** Him unknowingly, and does |
| T-25.......in.3:6 | Him not it **c.** Him in gentleness and love, |
| T-26......IX.1:6 | eyes on him who **c.** Christ within him, |
| T-26......IX.2:1 | a little trust for him who **c.** Christ to you, |
| T-27.......V.3:3 | It **c.** comfort from the place of peace into |
| T-27......VI.2:2 | and **c.** but one message: "You are here, |
| W-pI.135.11:2 | It **c.** out the plans that it receives through |
| W-pI...136.1:5 | same approach that **c.** all of them to truth |
| W-pI...189.6:3 | It is as sure as Love itself, to which it **c.** us. |
| W-pII..305.1:3 | peace envelops it, and gently **c.** it to truth, |
| P-2........III.4:5 | for thus he **c.** out the plan established for |
| P-2......IV.11:2 | the insane burden of guilt it **c.** so wearily, |

## carry 30

| | |
|---|---|
| T-13......IV.6:3 | They **c.** the spots of pain in your mind, |
| T-16....IV.13:4 | The bridge that He would **c.** you across |
| T-17.....VII.5:6 | it, and it will **c.** you straight to illusions. |
| T-18......III.5:7 | And where we go we **c.** God with us. |
| T-18......III.7:3 | light. **C.** it back to darkness, from the holy |
| T-19......IV.1:7 | will **c.** its message of love and safety and |
| T19. IV.A.12:7 | see, and **c.** it screaming to their master, to |
| T-21.....III.10:5 | which tries to use the body to **c.** out the |
| T-22.......II.3:1 | Illusions **c.** only guilt and suffering, |
| T-22......VI.5:7 | fear because they **c.** only love with them. |
| T-27......VI.8:2 | all sin if you but **c.** its effects with you. |
| T-28...VII.5:11 | and rain will come and **c.** it into oblivion. |
| W-pI.....19.2:2 | since it seems to **c.** with it an enormous |
| WpI..rII.in.4:5 | you through, and **c.** you beyond them all. |
| W-pI......97.5:1 | **c.** them around this aching world where |
| W-pI.107.10:2 | that goes with you will **c.** to the world. |
| W-pI...109.3:2 | will **c.** you through storms and strife, past |
| W-pI...124.2:5 | way because the light we **c.** stays behind, |
| W-pI.137.13:1 | may **c.** healing to the world, exchanging |
| W-pI.151.17:3 | **c.** round the world the joyous news that |
| W-pI.153.18:4 | for you who chose to **c.** out His plan for |
| W-pI.154.11:3 | and **c.** them to those whom He appoints. |
| W-pI...156.5:3 | The light you **c.** is their own. And thus |
| W-pI...159.5:2 | you safely trust to **c.** you from this world |
| W-pI...159.9:4 | source, but **c.** its beneficence with them, |
| W-pI...164.4:2 | an ancient peace you **c.** in your heart and |
| W-pI.169.14:2 | you. You **c.** them back to yourself. And |
| W-pI...199.7:2 | And **c.** freedom as your gift to those who |
| M-12.........4:3 | these ears will **c.** to the mind of the hearer |
| C-5............5:9 | at last and **c.** it with you unto your God. |

## carrying 8

| | |
|---|---|
| T-18......III.6:4 | with me in **c.** their light into the darkness, |
| T-18.....IX.14:3 | the shadows from the world and **c.** it, safe |
| T-22......IV.6:5 | and **c.** His message of hope and freedom |
| W-pII ...14.5:1 | and **c.** His Word to everyone whom He |
| M-8...........5:5 | number of pitchforks the devils he sees **c.** |
| C-6.............2:2 | the leader in **c.** out His plan since he was |
| P-3........III.1:2 | the Holy Spirit to help in **c.** out the plan. |
| P-3........III.8:2 | will come to you **c.** the gift of healing, if |

## carve 1

| | |
|---|---|
| W-pI....184.1:4 | By this you **c.** it out of unity. By this you |

## carved 2

| | |
|---|---|
| T-17......IV.7:5 | with jewels, and deeply **c.** and polished. |
| T-22.......V.2:8 | For sin is **c.** into a block out of your peace, |

## carven 1

| | |
|---|---|
| W-pI.170.11:2 | time upon this bit of **c.** stone you made, |

## case 23

| | |
|---|---|
| T-1.......III.1:3 | stand at the end in **c.** you fail temporarily. |
| T-2........IV.4:6 | **c.** it may be wise to utilize a compromise |
| T-4........IV.2:3 | every **c.** you have thought wrongly about |
| T-5......VI.10:2 | It will merely dismiss the **c.** against you. |
| T-5......VI.10:3 | There can be no **c.** against a child of God, |
| T-5......VI.10:5 | It will dismiss the **c.** against you, however |
| T-5......VI.10:6 | The **c.** may be fool-proof, but it is not God- |
| T-6.........I.11:6 | to show this was true in an extreme **c.**, |
| T-7.........X.5:9 | this **c.**, it always means that the follower |
| T-8.......VIII.4:6 | witnesses who would disagree with its **c.**, |
| T-9..........II.2:2 | Should this be the **c.**, your attainment of |
| T-9..........II.2:6 | In this **c.** he is not really asking for release |
| T-11.....V.16:3 | The **c.** for insanity is strong to the insane. |
| T-17....VIII.1:1 | instant is nothing more than a special **c.**, |
| T-18....VI.12:4 | in every **c.**, you join it without reservation |
| W-pI.....14.5:2 | In each **c.**, name the "disaster" quite |
| W-pI.....44.9:2 | In that **c.**, you will probably find it more |
| W-pI...108.6:2 | this special **c.** has proved it always works, |
| W-pI...108.7:1 | with the special **c.** of giving and receiving. |
| M-17.........3:4 | been the **c.** if the result is anything but joy |
| M-21.........4:6 | process is merely a special **c.** of the lesson |
| M-26.........1:4 | In how many is this the **c.**? Here, then, is |
| P-in...........1:4 | This does not appear to be the **c.**, for the |

## cases 6

| | |
|---|---|
| T-2........VI.5:6 | In both **c.**, the mind and the behavior are |
| T-8.......VIII.8:4 | doubt the ego's skill in building up false **c.** |
| W-pI...108.5:3 | some special **c.** of one law which holds for |
| M-9...........1:6 | but these are generally special **c.**. By far |
| M-22.........2:2 | from it. In some **c.**, there is a sudden and |
| M-29.........1:5 | In some **c.**, it may be helpful for the pupil |

## cast 22

| | |
|---|---|
| T-5.......VII.1:4 | you need merely **c.** your cares upon Him |
| T-13......VI.2:4 | can **c.** no shadow to darken the present, |
| T-14.....V.11:8 | **C.** no one out, for here is what he seeks |
| T-15.....VIII.2:3 | learn the value of what you have **c.** aside, |
| T-15......XI.4:6 | you endow it with fear and try to **c.** it out, |
| T-15......XI.6:4 | lies in what you have **c.** outside yourself, |
| T-18.........I.5:6 | which seemed to **c.** you out of Heaven, to |
| T-18......IX.8:3 | of light whereon they **c.** no shadows. |
| T19. IV.D.14:3 | You thought He sinned because you **c.** the |
| T-20......III.9:1 | and with eyes so long **c.** down in darkness |
| T-29.....VII.4:1 | betterment is **c.** as major beneficiary, you |
| W-pI.....53.5:4 | to **c.** their beneficent light on what I see. |
| W-pI.....95.13:5 | to **c.** all your illusions out of the one Mind |
| W-pI.127.11:2 | all who come to learn to **c.** aside the world |
| W-pI...154.1:6 | Our part is **c.** in Heaven, not in hell. And |
| W-pI...157.1:3 | and **c.** a timeless light upon this day, |
| W-pI...166.7:4 | with eyes **c.** down lest you might catch a |
| W-pI...183.3:5 | The sorrowful **c.** off their mourning, and |
| W-pI.184.15:3 | *we have tried to **c.** across Your Own reality.* |

W-pI.193.12:4 hour c. its shadow on the one that follows
W-pII.294.1:9 It is but functionless, unneeded and c. off.
W-pII.314.1:3 Past mistakes can c. no shadows on it, so

### casting 1

T-15......XI.4:8 of Heaven and hell in him by c. Heaven

### casts 3

T-1........VI.5:4 *Perfect love c. out fear. If fear exists, Then*
T-25.......II.7:3 and c. a veil of light across the picture's
T-27.....VII.8:6 c. him as it will in any role that satisfies

### casual 4

W-pI.....20.1:1 quite c. about our practice periods thus
W-pI.....36.3:2 to whatever you note in your c. survey.
M-3 ...........2:2 of what seem to be very c. encounters; a
M-3 ...........2:6 Even at the level of the most c. encounter,

### casually 3

W-pI.....11.3:3 should be practiced as c. as possible. It
W-pI.....33.2:1 Merely glance c. around the world you
W-pI.....34.3:3 Note them all c., repeating the idea for

### casualness 1

W-pI.....33.2:1 survey your inner thoughts with equal c..

### catalogue 2

W-pI.....76.4:2 different names in a long c. of rituals that
W-pI.134.15:1 brother as He will direct, and c. his "sins,

### catalyst 1

T-1.........I.37:2 me. It acts as a c., breaking up erroneous

### catastrophe 1

T-21.......in.2:3 If you behold disaster and c., you tried to

### catastrophic 1

T-8......VIII.6:4 prescriptions for avoiding c. outcomes.

### catch 10

T-21.........I.6:1 perhaps you c. a hint of an ancient state
T-21.......IV.6:7 trinkets still seem to shine and c. your eye
T-24.....VII.4:6 Save it for show, as bait to c. another fish,
W-pI.....25.6:2 rest on whatever happens to c. your eye,
W-pI.....65.5:2 carefully to c. whatever thoughts cross it.
W-pI.....65.6:2 attempting to c. a few of the idle thoughts
WpI. rIII.in2:3 sure that you c. up in terms of numbers.
W-pI...126.8:5 And if you only c. a tiny glimpse of the
W-pI...157.2:3 and we c. a glimpse of what lies past the
W-pI...166.7:4 eyes cast down lest you might c. a glimpse

### catches 1

W-pI.......7.4:3 indiscriminately to whatever c. your eye.

### categories 6

T-14.......X.7:1 the Holy Spirit's one division into two c.;
M-8 ...........4:5 to be given what will fit into these c.. And
M-8 ...........4:6 so, it concludes that the c. must be true.
M-8 ...........6:5 the understanding that only two c. are
M-10 .........1:4 confusion about what these c. mean.
M-10 .........1:7 what these c. are be really taught. At any

### categorized 1

M-8 ...........5:6 His mind has c. them all as real, and so

### categorizing 1

M-8 ...........4:1 It is in the sorting out and c. activities of

### category 1

M-8 ...........6:4 healed mind will put them all in one c.;

### caught 3

T-15 .......I.15:9 For c. in the single instant of the eternal
T-21 ....VII.4:6 thinking it c. a glimpse of the great enemy
W-pI...166.9:1 now, and justice has c. up with you at last.

### causation 3

T-28 .......II.1:3 create their cause, but they establish its c..
T-28 .......II.9:3 in giving back to cause the function of c.,
T-28 .....II.11:2 the function of c. is to have effects. And

### Cause 27

*cause*

T-2 ....VII.3:11 "C." is a term properly belonging to God,
T-2 ....VII.3:12 entails a set of C. and Effect relationships
T-9 ..........I.9:6 without a cause, and God is the only C..
T-14 .....III.8:1 God is the only C., and guilt is not of Him
T-14 .....III.8:6 and accept the C. of God as yours. The
T-14 .....IV.2:1 You who belong to the First C., created
T-14 ....V.11:9 of us, united as one within the C. of peace.
T-17 ....VII.8:7 for faithlessness, but there *is* C. for faith.
T-17 ....VII.8:8 C. has entered any situation that shares
T-17 ...VIII.5:4 accepted the C. of his awakening as yours.
T-21 .....II.10:6 Son is the Effect, whose C. he would deny.
T-28 .........I.7:9 the happy consequences of a C. so ancient
T-28 .........I.8:1 the C. the Holy Spirit has remembered for
T-28 .........I.8:4 that you remembered not their C.. Yet
T-28 .........I.9:4 The miracle reminds you of a C. forever
T-28 .......I.10:9 in allowing C. to have Its Own Effects, and
T-28 .......I.13:5 but rather is the C. that fear was made to
T-28 .......I.14:1 aware of present C. and Its benign Effects.
T-28 .......I.14:5 did. His C. *is* Its Effects. There never was a
T-28 ........II.3:3 of healing is the only C. of everything. It
W-pII.326.1:2 *and You forever and forever are my C.. As*
W-pII.326.1:5 *it is Your Will to have a Son so like his C. that*
W-pII.326.1:5 *that C. and Its Effect are indistinguishable.*
M-17 .......9:13 Love is C. of everything beyond all fear,
S-1........IV.3:2 From this C. only can the answer come in
S-3........IV.3:3 for He knows the C. of healing is Himself,
S-3........IV.5:3 He is then no longer C. but only an effect.

### cause 237

*Cause*

T-2 .........VII.h C. and Effect
T-2 ......VII.1:4 tampering with a basic law of c. and effect
T-2 ......VII.2:4 respect for true c. and effect as a necessary
T-2 ....VII.3:10 The c. and effect principle now becomes a
T-3 .......VI.2:1 than to know is the c. of the loss of peace.
T-3 .......VI.7:2 only one c. for all of them: the authority
T-4 ........V.4:8 The mind, and not without c., reminds
T-7 .........X.3:7 is the c. of the whole idea of sacrifice.
T-8 ...VII.12:8 This arrest is the c. of all illness, because
T-9 ..........I.9:6 Fear cannot be real without a c., and God
T-12 .........I.9:2 the loss, the basic c. of fear is removed.
T-12 .....II.10:7 at the c. of fear and letting it go forever?
T-14 .....III.5:2 It is not a c., but an effect. It is the natural
T-14 .....III.7:7 His guilt is wholly without c., and being
T-14 .....III.7:7 without cause, and being without c.,
T-14 .....III.8:5 always that mind is one, and c. is one.
T-14 .....VI.5:7 to apply it to the holy c. of restoration.
T-14 ...XI.12:6 They are c. and effect, each to the other,
T-15 ..VII.12:4 that communication is the c. of loneliness
T-16 .......II.3:5 attributes could hardly c. you perplexity.
T-16 .....III.2:6 C. and effect are very clear in the ego's
T-16 .....III.2:8 spoke for the c. of truth and its effects.
T-16 .....III.4:3 see the real c. and effect relationship that
T-17 .......II.2:6 will never cease to c. you wonderment at
T-17 ....VII.8:1 learn the c. of faithlessness: You think you
T-17 ....VII.8:7 There is no c. for faithlessness, but there *is*
T-20 ....VII.6:7 serving the c. of sin an instant before he
T-21 ......in.1:8 Perception is a result and not a c.. And
T-21 .....II.10:1 of c. and effect becomes inevitable. The
T-21 .....II.10:2 to keep obscure the c. of the effect, and
T-21 .....II.10:2 effect, and make effect appear to be a c..
T-21 .....II.10:3 and capable of serving as a c. of the events
T-21 .....II.10:7 And so he seems to *be* the c., producing
T-21 .....II.10:8 Nothing can have effects without a c., and
T-21 ....VII.2:8 that they thought they had a common c..
T-21 ....VII.7:8 This is a course in c. and not effect.
T-24 .......V.2:2 In dreams effect and c. are interchanged,
T-24 .....VI.8:3 His mistakes can c. delay, which it is given
T-25 .......V.1:3 the c. and aim and justifier of the other.
T-25 .VIII.11:9 love is fair, and cannot chasten without c..
T-25VIII.11:10 What c. can be to warrant an attack upon
T-26 ....VII.2:4 and sin are seen as consequence and c., in
T-26 ....VII.5:1 effects be utterly undone and without c..
T-26 ..VII.13:1 C. and effect are one, not separate. God
T-26 ..VII.14:1 is possible when c. and consequence are
T-26 ..VII.14:2 healing of effect without the c. can merely
T-26 ...VIII.4:6 now? A future c. as yet has no effects. And
T-26 ...VIII.4:7 it be that if you fear, there is a present c..
T-26 ...VIII.5:2 yet, and what will happen has as yet no c..
T-26 ...VIII.5:3 Who can predict effects without a c.? And
T-26 ...VIII.5:5 Belief in sin arouses fear, and like its c., is
T-26 ...VIII.5:6 Yet only here and now its c. must be, if its
T-26 ...VIII.7:3 Its c. is here, if it appears at all. Why are
T-26 ...VIII.8:1 Yet this illusion has a c. which, though
T-26 ...VIII.9:3 For you have c. for freedom *now*. What
T-26 ...VIII.9:6 c. must be delayed until a future time, is
T-26 ...VIII.9:6 consequence and c. must come as one.
T-26 .......X.2:6 equally without a c. or consequence, and
T-26 .......X.3:4 Projection of the c. of sacrifice is at the
T-27 ........I.8:4 to see, so that the c. can never be denied.
T-27 ........I.9:1 is to show your brother sin can have no c..
T-27 .......II.8:6 is purposeless and wholly without c..
T-27 .....III.3:4 And thus the picture has no c. at all. Who
T-27 .....III.3:5 all. Who can perceive effect without a c.?
T-27 ....VII.3:1 is simply this: "*You* are the c. of what I do.
T-27 ....VII.3:7 to go beyond the obvious in terms of c..
T-27 ....VII.5:3 the purpose, but are not themselves a c..
T-27 ....VII.5:4 Nor will the c. be changed by seeing it
T-27 ....VII.5:5 The c. produces the effects, which then
T-27 ....VII.5:5 effects, which then bear witness to the c.,
T-27 ....VII.5:7 here the c. of suffering and sin must lie.
T-27 ....VII.5:8 sin, for they are but reflections of their c..
T-27 ....VII.6:6 Seek not another c., nor look among the
T-27 ....VII.7:2 you find the c. of your perspective on the
T-27 ....VII.7:3 Once you were unaware of what the c. of
T-27 ....VII.7:8 Whatever c. they have is something quite
T-27 ....VII.9:1 you can choose, the other possibility of c.,
T-27 ....VII.9:2 deny the c. of suffering is in your mind. Be
T-27 ..VII.11:8 and dream in secret that its c. is real?
T-27 ..VII.12:3 alike. Here is the c. of suffering, the space
T-27 ..VII.12:5 Here is the c. of unreality. And it is here
T-27 ..VII.13:2 No other c. it has, nor ever will. Nothing
T-27 ...VIII.3:4 yet once more; that it is c. and not effect.
T-27 ...VIII.3:5 And you are its effect, and cannot be its c.
T-27 ...VIII.5:2 appear to be the c. of what it is you do?
T-27 ...VIII.5:3 the second part, whose c. lies in the first.
T-27 ...VIII.5:9 this, if we but look directly at their c.. And
T-27 .VIII.5:10 the grounds for laughter, not a c. for fear.
T-27 ...VIII.7:1 starts at its beginning, ending at its c..
T-27 ...VIII.8:2 you will not see the c. of what they do,
T-27 ...VIII.8:4 consequences, but without their trifling c.
T-27 ...VIII.8:5 Without the c. do its effects seem serious
T-27 ...VIII.8:7 c. that follows nothing and is but a jest.
T-27 ...VIII.9:1 does the Holy Spirit perceive the c., and
T-27 ...VIII.9:2 error, who have overlooked the c. entirely
T-27 ...VIII.9:3 its foolish c. and laugh with Him a while.
T-27 ...VIII.9:4 judge effects, but *He* has judged their c..
T-27 .VIII.10:4 be the c. of any pain and suffering you feel
T-27 .VIII.11:4 the c. of every form of sorrow and of pain.
T-27 .VIII.11:5 teach you but the single c. of all of them,
T-27 .VIII.12:3 None has a different c. from all the rest,
T-28 ........I.1:9 has no effects. Remembering a c. can but
T-28 ........I.2:3 went its consequences, left without a c..
T-28 ........I.5:9 by time, which took away their c..
T-28 ........I.6:4 be made possible because its c. has gone.

T-28.........I.6:5 Yet change must have a **c.** that will endure
T-28.........I.6:6 can be made in the present if its **c.** is past.
T-28.........I.7:3 appear, remember that their **c.** is gone.
T-28.........I.7:5 Let not the **c.** that you would give them
T-28.........I.7:7 instead, the new effects of **c.** accepted *now*
T-28.........I.9:2 causelessness which you confused with **c.**.
T-28...... I.11:4 no pause in time to **c.** the miracle delay in
T-28...... I.14:6 There never was a **c.** beside It that could
T-28.......... II.h Reversing Effect and **C.**
T-28....... II.1:1 Without a **c.** there can be no effects, and
T-28....... II.1:1 and yet without effects there is no **c.**. The
T-28....... II.1:2 The **c.** a cause is *made* by its effects; the
T-28....... II.1:2 The cause a **c.** is *made* by its effects; the
T-28....... II.1:3 Effects do not create their **c.**, but they
T-28..... II.2:10 Only where its **c.** is given its effects. For
T-28..... II.2:11 to causelessness, and make it be a **c.**.
T-28....... II.3:1 Son of God attempt to make himself his **c.**
T-28....... II.3:2 and must be **c.** because of what he is. The
T-28....... II.3:3 he is. The **c.** of healing is the only Cause of
T-28....... II.5:4 and you would not be **c.** of this effect. In
T-28....... II.6:3 be expected from a thing that has no **c.**?
T-28....... II.6:4 Yet if it has no **c.**, it has no purpose. You
T-28....... II.6:5 You may **c.** a dream, but never will you
T-28....... II.6:6 For that would change its **c.**, and it is this
T-28....... II.6:8 without a stable **c.** with guaranteed effects
T-28....... II.7:8 suffering from its effects, but not their **c.**.
T-28..... II.7:11 fears is **c.** without the consequences that
T-28..... II.7:11 the consequences that would make it **c.**.
T-28....... II.8:8 Effect and **c.** are first split off, and then
T-28....... II.8:8 then reversed, so that effect becomes a **c.**;
T-28....... II.8:8 so that effect becomes a cause; the **c.**,
T-28....... II.9:2 of what has gone before, appearing as a **c.**.
T-28....... II.9:3 giving back to **c.** the function of causation
T-28..... II.11:1 returns the **c.** of fear to you who made it.
T-28..... II.11:2 shows that, having no effects, it is not **c.**,
T-28..... II.11:3 And where effects are gone, there is no **c.**.
T-28..... II.12:4 back the consequence of sickness to its **c.**.
T-28...... III.2:5 the **c.** of sickness and perceived effects.
T-28...... III.3:4 has not seen the **c.** of sickness where it is,
T-28...... III.4:4 thus it seems to give a **c.** to sickness which
T-28...... III.4:4 give a cause to sickness which is not its **c.**.
T-28...... III.4:5 of the gap is all the **c.** that sickness has.
T-28...... III.4:6 which you see as if it were the **c.** of pain.
T-28...... III.5:1 The **c.** of pain is separation, not the body,
T-28...... III.8:3 so sickness will now be seen without a **c.**.
T-28...... IV.5:5 because by sharing is a **c.** produced.
T-28...... IV.7:4 can not remain without a witness or a **c.**.
T-29.........I.5:1 you wanted it to be a **c.** of separation and
T-29....... II.1:8 Their **c.** has been effected, and they must
T-29....... II.1:8 be present where their **c.** has entered in.
T-29....... II.2:1 You have accepted healing's **c.**, and so it
T-29....... II.2:3 suddenly, as an effect without a **c.**. Nor is
T-29....... II.2:4 Nor is it, in itself, a **c.**. But where its cause
T-29....... II.2:5 But where its **c.** is must it be. Now is it
T-29....... II.2:8 **c.** indeed for glad rejoicing and for hope
T-30...... I.16:5 Decisions **c.** results *because* they are not
T-30....... II.4:1 What **c.** have you for anger in a world
T-30....... V.2:4 guilt is understood as the sole **c.** of pain in
W-pI.......5.1:2 you believe is the **c.** of your upset, using
W-pI.......5.2:1 perceived **c.** of an upset in any form, use
W-pI.......5.2:1 upset, and the **c.** which you ascribe to it.
W-pI.......8.1:4 is the **c.** of the misconception about time
W-pI.....13.6:1 first attempt at stating an explicit **c.** and
W-pI.....17.1:1 the direction of identifying **c.** and effect as
W-pI.....17.1:5 were not so, perception would have no **c.**,
W-pI.....17.1:5 cause, and would itself be the **c.** of reality.
W-pI.....19.1:4 for **c.** and effect are never separate.
W-pI.....20.5:6 of **c.** and effect as it operates in the world.
W-pI.....23.2:1 **c.** of the world you see is attack thoughts,
W-pI.....23.2:6 Here you are changing the **c.**. The effect
W-pI.....23.4:2 the world, but you can escape from its **c.**.
W-pI.....23.4:3 is the world you see when its **c.** is gone?
W-pI.....23.5:1 you see, because its **c.** can be changed.
W-pI.....23.5:2 that the **c.** be identified and then let go, so
W-pI.....23.7:4 of identifying the **c.** of the world you see.
W-pI.....23.7:5 different, you will be ready to let the **c.** go.
W-pI.....31.2:5 for the inner is the **c.** of the outer.
W-pI.....32.1:1 to develop the theme of **c.** and effect. You
W-pI.....37.6:3 seems to **c.** an adverse reaction in you.
W-pI.....42.1:2 also sets forth a **c.** and effect relationship
W-pI.....91.6:1 with this statement of true **c.** and effect
W-pI...101.5:2 from sin will never happen, for it has no **c.**
W-pI...102.2:1 is purposeless, without a **c.** and with no
W-pI.108.10:2 Effect and **c.** will be far better understood
W-pI.121.10:1 to **c.** regret in you if you should meet him;
W-pI...130.4:5 can have no enemy, and so they have no **c.**
W-pI.139.12:1 our dedication to our **c.** today each hour,
W-pI...156.1:2 It promises there is no **c.** for guilt, and
W-pI...167.3:9 It is the **c.** of healing. It is why you cannot
W-pI...184.3:4 be seen as meaningful; a **c.** of true effect,
W-pI...190.4:4 could conceive of them as **c.** of anything?
W-pI...190.5:1 It is your thoughts alone that **c.** you pain.
W-pI...190.5:3 There is no **c.** beyond yourself that can
W-pI...190.7:1 The world may seem to **c.** you pain. And
W-pI...190.7:2 the world, as causeless, has no power to **c.**
W-pI...194.7:3 What can **c.** him pain, or bring experience
W-pI...195.1:5 **c.** for thanks while others have less cause?
W-pI...195.1:5 cause for thanks while others have less **c.**?
W-pI...195.1:7 to Him alone Who made all **c.** of sorrow
W-pII......3.2:5 could not **c.** such insane thoughts. But
W-pII..284.1:3 There is no grief with any **c.** at all. And
W-pII..301.2:2 and bless it as a **c.** of further joy in them.
W-pII..307.1:3 *will, for it is senseless and will **c.** me pain.*
W-pII....10.2:3 Without a **c.**, and now without a function
W-pII..331.1:1 *to believe Your Son could **c.** himself to suffer*
W-pII.....348.h I have no **c.** for anger or for fear, For You
W-pII..348.1:3 *I have no **c.** for anything except the perfect*
M-4 .........I.1:3 because **c.** and effect are never separated.
M-4 . VIII.1:10 seen or yet to come can **c.** them fear.
M-5 ....... II.4:4 Place **c.** and effect in their true sequence
M-5 ....... II.4:9 also go all the effects they seemed to **c.**.
M-5 ..... II.4:10 **C.** and effect but replicate creation. Seen
M-10 .........6:9 For he has given up their **c.**, and they,
M-12 .........2:4 for the mind sees no **c.** for punishment.
M-17 .........5:1 perceived magic thoughts is a basic **c.** of
C-2...............5:3 do, and **c.** and its effects must still be one.
C-4...............7:6 world without a purpose and without a **c.**.
P-1...............1:2 the spurious **c.** and effect relationships on
P-2......... V.7:6 he would condemn himself without a **c.**.
P-2....... VII.3:5 return again, once its **c.** has been removed
S-1 ........ IV.2:6 you are asking for effects without the **c.**.
S-1 ........ IV.2:8 asking a **c.** from which they do not come
S-3 ...............I.h The **C.** of Sickness
S-3 ...........I.1:1 Do not mistake effect for **c.**, nor think
S-3 ...........I.1:1 and separate from what its **c.** must be. It
S-3 ...........I.2:1 body's **c.** is unforgiveness of the Son of
S-3 ......... II.1:5 the **c.** remains, and will not lack effects.
S-3 ......... II.1:6 The **c.** is still the wish to die and overcome
S-3 ......... II.6:1 leaving the **c.** of illness still unchanged,
S-3 ........ III.5:5 Now the **c.** of every malady has been
S-3 ........ III.6:3 healing will occur because its **c.** has gone.
S-3 ........ III.6:4 And now without a **c.**, it cannot come

## caused 21

T-10.......in.1:3 to you is **c.** by factors outside yourself.
T-13...... III.2:5 For this wish **c.** the separation, and you
T-18....... II.5:9 to recognize is that what **c.** the dream has
T-22....... II.9:2 is the same belief that **c.** the separation. It
T-23....... II.7:3 He has become the "enemy" Who **c.** it, to
T-26... VIII.5:4 effects unless he thought they had been **c.**
T-27... VII.11:7 although it **c.** the part you see and do not
T-27. VIII.12:2 and He will teach you how each one is **c.**.
T-28.........I.6:4 use of it, as if the past had **c.** the present,
T-28........I.11:3 into the Mind which **c.** all minds to be.
T-28....... II.5:2 much at least: that you have **c.** the dream,
T-28....... II.5:4 It is but an effect that *you* have **c.**, and you
T-28....... II.7:9 attack, and he is innocent of what he **c.**.
T-28..... II.11:7 be sick; projecting out its guilt **c.** nothing,
T-29....... II.2:6 Now is it **c.**, though not as yet perceived.
T-30........I.16:4 can be **c.** without some form of union, be
W-pI......26.7:3 connection and which has **c.** you concern,
W-pI......78.6:3 you have had with him, the pain he **c.** you
W-pI......91.1:5 Its presence is not **c.** by your vision; its
W-pI...137.9:3 you from everything that ever **c.** you pain.
W-pI...196.8:4 cannot then believe that fear is **c.** without.

## causeless 17

T-14...... III.8:3 *The **c.** cannot be.* Do not attest to it, and do
T-14...... III.8:6 only when you learn to deny the **c.**, and
T-17..... VII.8:6 What never was is **c.**, and is not there to
T-27...... III.3:6 What can the **c.** be but nothingness? The
T-28.........I.9:3 that were **c.** and could never be effects.
T-28.......I.10:3 for what was **c.** and against His Will.
T-28.......I.14:2 he understand what he has made is **c.**,
T-28.......I.15:1 What has been lost, to see the **c.** not?
T-28........II.6:1 This world is **c.**, as is every dream that
T-28......II.10:4 Their enmity is seen as **c.** now, because
T-29........II.3:4 Where they are **c.** their effects are gone,
W-pI...101.6:1 because there is no sin, and suffering is **c.**.
W-pI...136.1:3 Being **c.** and without a meaningful intent
W-pI...138.9:4 as the truth dismisses them as **c.**. Now are
W-pI...156.1:2 for guilt, and being **c.** it does not exist. It
W-pI...190.7:2 And yet the world, as **c.**, has no power to
M-17 ....... 9:12 exist. The fear of God is **c.**. But His Love is

## causelessness 3

T-28.........I.9:2 from **c.** which you confused with cause. It
T-28......II.2:11 a meaningless attempt to give effects to **c.**
T-28........II.3:5 **c.** is given no effects and none is seen. A

## causes 8

T-14........X.4:2 so used to this that it **c.** you little surprise.
T-21......III.10:3 events and feelings its maker thinks it **c.**.
T-27..... VII.7:4 all the many **c.** you perceived as bringing
T-27... VII.10:7 then you must see the **c.** of the things you
T-31...... III.4:8 Learning is all that **c.** change. And so the
W-pI.....47.5:2 It is obvious that any situation that **c.** you
W-pI...167.4:2 alternate because of **c.** you cannot control
P-1............ 1:3 everyone can reconsider its **c.** and learn to

## causing 7

T19....IV.A.7:4 **c.** no more than tiny interruptions in
T-22...... III.9:6 as **c.** sin by his desire to have sin real. Yet
T-27.... VIII.4:5 by **c.** them and making them seem real.
T-28...... IV.2:3 yourself by not accepting them as **c.** you,
W-pI.......5.1:1 situation or event you think is **c.** you pain.
W-pI.....26.6:1 whose outcomes are **c.** you concern. The
M-4 ....VIII.1:8 decisions, if they are **c.** pain to anyone.

## cautions 1

W-pI.......6.3:1 of the two **c.** stated in the previous lesson:

## cautious 1

T-29.........I.3:8 A **c.** friendship, and limited in scope and

## caverns 1

W-pI...191.8:1 has lighted up all dark and ancient **c.**,

## cease 22

T-1.........I.15:4 Time will **c.** when it is no longer useful in
T-2........ VI.9:12 is ineffectual you may **c.** to be afraid of it,
T-3....... IV.5:10 its Source, or it would merely **c.** to be.
T-4......... V.2:4 It cannot, however, make them **c.** to be. It
T-9....VIII.11:9 **c.** to question it and know it for what it is.
T-10..... V.10:6 God will never **c.** to love His Son, and His
T-10..... V.10:6 Son, and His Son will never **c.** to love Him
T-12....VIII.8:9 Your Father could not **c.** to love His Son.
T-13..... X.14:5 for He will never **c.** His praise of you.
T-14..VIII.2:12 what cannot be divided cannot **c.**. The
T-15...... VI.5:9 of this world **c.** to hold any meaning at all
T-17........II.2:6 will never **c.** to cause you wonderment at
T-23......II.13:2 never will your brother **c.** his attack on
T-24..... VI.11:4 and effort that you never thought to **c.**.
W-pI...136.8:5 commanding you to die and **c.** to be.
W-pI.136.14:2 down its arms, and **c.** to play with folly. It
W-pI.153.18:1 practice, you will never **c.** to think of Him,
W-pI...156.8:3 Today let doubting **c.**. God speaks for you

W-pI... 169.5:4 We say "God is," and then we c. to speak,
W-pI... 182.8:1 valueless ideas c. to have value in your
W-pI... 198.1:5 Then does illusion c. to have effects, and
M-14 ....... 2:12 touched. It will merely c. to seem to be.

### ceased 9

T-3...... III.2:11 know when you have c. to ask questions.
T-4........ III.1:8 c. to create because of the ego's illusions.
T-10....... V.8:2 that He has never c. to acknowledge you,
T-11......... I.3:8 your creations have not c. to be extended,
T-13.... VI.13:7 never c. to be his Father's witness and his
T-14.... XI.11:7 The miracle of creation has never c.,
W-pI... 197.9:8 that He has ever c. to offer thanks to you.
M-18 ......... 1:1 has c. to confuse interpretation with fact,
S-3 ........ IV.7:3 and that his prayers have never c. to sing

### ceaseless 3

T-4......... II.8:5 The ego's c. attempts to gain the spirit's
T-31....... V.6:8 are but silently, and yet with c. urgency,
S-2 .......... I.8:6 c. song that all creation sings unto its God

### ceaselessly 3

T-8...... VIII.2:7 forced to shift c. from one goal to another
T-16.... IV.11:6 help that rises c. from you to your Creator
W-pI... 195.9:3 pursuit, where we are badgered c., and

### ceases 12

T-10....... II.1:6 dissociated is accepted, it c. to be fearful.
T-12...... VI.2:5 Father never c. to remind Him of His Son,
T-12...... VI.2:5 never c. to remind His Son of the Father.
T-15...... IX.7:1 When the body c. to attract you, and
T-17.... IV.13:5 and c. to distract you from the picture.
T-18..... VII.7:7 of the body c. to demand attention. Into
W-pI..... 60.4:2 a moment in which God's Voice c. to call
W-pI. 153.15:5 distraction c. to arise to turn us from our
W-pI... 157.2:3 It brings us to the door where learning c.,
W-pI... 193.2:3 will lead him back to where perception c..
M-19 ......... 2:7 the pathway c. and time ends with it. But
P-3......... II.7:1 it is when judgment c. that healing occurs

### ceasing 2

M-21 ......... 4:5 by c. to decide for himself what he will say
S-1......... II.2:5 Everyone prays without c.. Ask and you

### celebrate 13

T-15....... X.1:5 you would c. my birth into the world. Yet
T-15....... X.1:7 you, and let me c. *your* birth through Him.
T-15..... X.1:10 The time of Christ we c. together, for it
T-15...... XI.3:2 let us c. our release together by releasing
T-15...... XI.9:3 but c. His Wholeness as we welcome Him
T-20......... I.2:3 This week we c. life, not death. And we
T-20......... I.4:7 Friend, and c. his holiness along with me.
T-29..... II.10:2 loss you c. when you behold the body as a
W-pI..... 75.2:1 Today we c. the happy ending to your
W-pI... 75.11:2 as we c. the beginning of your vision and
W-pI..... 77.1:6 Identity. It is this that we will c. today.
W-pI. 135.26:4 stride, and c. your Eastertime with you.
C-ep........... 5:3 Who returns to us to c. salvation and the

### celebrated 1

W-pI. 198.10:3 Let today be c. both on earth and in your

### celebrates 1

T-15...... III.7:1 season (Christmas) which c. the birth of

### celebrating 2

T-15...... XI.8:2 Let us join in c. peace by demanding no
W-pI... 157.1:5 spent long days and nights in c. death.

### celebration 7

T-15 ..... XI.8:5 He joins us in the c. of His Son's creation.
T19.. IV.B.16:3 continually, in solemn c. of the ego's rule.
T-20 ........ I.1:1 the c. of victory and the acceptance of the
T-20 ........ I.1:2 Son, but happily in the c. of his release.
T-20 ........ I.4:1 Easter is not the c. of the *cost* of sin, but of
W-pI..... 75.9:2 or so that today is a time for special c..
W-pII . 241.1:2 It is a time of special c.. For today holds

### celestial 3

T-1 ........ I.32:3 they raise you into the sphere of c. order.
T-25 ........ I.4:3 love c. and so complete it wishes only that
W-pII . 265.1:4 Today I see the world in the c. gentleness

### cell 1

T-26 ........ I.4:2 apart from you and separate in his c., you

### censoring 1

W-pI..... 42.5:3 Let them come without c. unless you find

### center 22

T-1 ........ I.30:2 This places spirit at the c., where it can
T-2 ....... III.2:1 belongs at the c. of the inner altar, where
T-6 ... V.B.1:10 are. If the c. of the thought system is true,
T-6 ... V.B.1:11 it. But if a lie is at its c., only deception
T-6 ..... V.B.9:2 you will be pushing toward the c. of your
T-6 ..... V.C.7:1 allowing you to identify only with the c.,
T-11 ...... in.3:4 more you approach the c. of His thought
T-14 ... VIII.3:1 darkened corridors, away from light's c..
T-16 ... IV.13:8 God. At its c., and only there, you are safe
T-16 ...... V.3:2 fantasies that c. around it are often quite
T-17 .... VII.8:9 of truth shines from the c. of the situation
T-18 .... VII.8:2 will be more aware of this quiet c. of the
T-18 .... VII.8:3 This quiet c., in which you do nothing,
T-18 .... VII.8:4 For from this c. will you be directed how
T-18 .... VII.8:5 It is this c., from which the body is absent
T19.... IV.A.1:3 are the c. from which it radiates outward,
T-22 ..... II.12:8 For at its c. Christ has been reborn, to
T-25 ...... in.1:5 from what is at the very c. of your life.
T-29 ..... IV.6:7 For at its c. is His Love for you, which
W-pI..... 72.7:4 the body stands at the c. of your concept
W-pI... 159.7:3 home of sin becomes the c. of redemption
M-1 ......... 2:12 at its c. it is a light that cannot be limited.

### centered 5

*See also* Self-centered, self-centered

T-13 ..... X.13:1 and my belief are c. on what I treasure.
T-17 ..... III.3:3 c. on and separated off as being the only
T-18 ..... IV.8:3 orders of difficulty in miracles is c. on this
T-19 ........ I.4:5 and brought illusions, c. on the body, to
WpI rVI.in.3:1 are c. round a central theme with which

### centers 3

T-6 ..... V.B.1:9 and every thought system c. on what you
T-17 ..... III.5:8 That is why Atonement c. on the past,
W-pI..... 71.2:1 for salvation c. around holding grievances

### central 38

T-6 ....... IV.9:7 the c. place in your imagined enslavement
T-11 ...... V.5:2 ego is the natural outcome of its c. belief,
T-12 ..... IV.1:1 and this is always its c. teaching. It never
T-16 .... V.10:4 The c. theme in its litany to sacrifice is
T-17 ..... III.2:7 bodies are c. to all unholy relationships is
T-17 ..... III.3:2 of him, is not the c. focus as it is, or in
T-26 ........ I.1:3 the symbol of the c. theme that *somebody*
T-27 .... II.13:4 sins become the c. target for correction,
T-27 ... VIII.1:1 the c. figure in the dreaming of the world.
T-27 ... VIII.1:3 It takes the c. place in every dream, which
T-31 ...... V.6:1 the c. lesson that ensures your brother is
W-in .......... 3:2 exercises are planned around one c. idea,
W-pI....... 4.4:1 identify each thought by the c. figure or
W-pI ...... 8.4:4 one by the c. figure or theme it contains,
W-pI ..... 19.3:3 name it in terms of the c. person or theme
W-pI ..... 46.6:1 but the c. idea should not be lost sight of.
WpI... rI.in.3:2 Try, rather, to emphasize the c. point,
W-pI .... 61.5:7 mind wanders away from the c. thought.
W-pI .... 74.1:1 as the c. thought toward which all our
W-pI .... 80.1:2 Your one c. problem has been answered,
W-pI .... 91.1:3 It is a c. idea in your new thought system,
W-pI .. 132.5:4 This c. theme is often stated in the text,
W-pI .. 132.6:3 c. thought the course attempts to teach.
W-pI .. 137.1:1 the c. thought on which salvation rests.
WpI..rIV.in1:4 the recent lessons and their c. thoughts in
WpI..rIV.in2:1 There is a c. theme that unifies each step
W-pI 169.12:1 is the c. theme that runs throughout
W-pI .. 191.4:6 c. core of its existence and its guarantee of
W-pI .. 193.3:3 Each lesson has a c. thought, the same in
WpI.rVI.in.3:1 are centered round a c. theme with which
W-pII .... in.3:1 with a c. thought for all the days to come,
M-1 ........... 3:5 c. theme is always, "God's Son is guiltless,
M-4 ..... I.A.7:5 sacrifice, so c. to his own thought system,
M-12 ......... 5:1 The c. lesson is always this; that what you
M-22 ......... 3:2 is a c. concept in the ego's thought system
M-27 ......... 1:1 the c. dream from which all illusions stem
C-in ........... 5:2 away to make way for the c. teaching.
P-2........ IV.9:4 deal. In fact, this is his c. task; the core of

### centrality 4

W-pI .. 167.3:7 that idea is due to its c. in our attempts to
M-4 ........ X.1:1 The c. of open-mindedness, perhaps the
M-17 ......... 5:2 c. in the world's thought system becomes
M-29 ......... 3:2 thought of this aspect, but its c. is obvious

### centuries 1

T-18 .... VII.7:3 through which you slip past c. of effort,

### century 1

T-18 .... VII.6:8 than is given to a c. of contemplation, or

### certain 169

T-1 ......... II.6:9 it, thus eliminating c. intervals within it.
T-2 ..... III.3:10 acute. But the outcome is as c. as God.
T-3 ......... II.1:2 degree. C. fundamental concepts cannot
T-3 ....... III.1:3 To know is to be c.. Uncertainty means
T-3 ....... III.1:5 Knowledge is power because it is c., and
T-3 ....... III.5:1 tells you to know yourself, or to be c..
T-3 ..... III.5:12 altar within and is timeless because it is c.
T-3 ....... IV.1:3 you are not c. how you will use them, and
T-3 ....... IV.7:9 way. Without them your choice is c.. Sane
T-4 ........ I.11:6 it. Of this you can be wholly c.. God is as
T-4 ......... II.5:8 and remember that the outcome is as c. as
T-4 ...... VII.2:7 It merely responds in c. specific ways to
T-6 ....... IV.7:1 you are and what you are is perfectly c..
T-6 ....... IV.7:6 c. as God because you are as true as He is,
T-6 ....... IV.7:6 once c. in your mind has become only the
T-6 ......... V.4:2 His dependability makes them more c..
T-7 ....... III.5:6 The c. are perfectly calm, because they are
T-9 ......... II.2:3 This is why c. specific forms of healing are
T-9 ......... II.3:3 Yet it is equally c. that no response given
T-9 ....... III.2:5 no sense at the time, and it is c. that, if he
T-9 ..... IV.10:2 c. that you will never find satisfaction in
T-9 .... VII.3:10 go beyond it because it can never *be* c..
T-11 ....... V.7:4 are, because it is perfectly c. of its purpose
T-12 ..... IV.1:1 The ego is c. that love is dangerous, and
T-13 .. VII.12:7 except to make c. that you will not use
T-14 ..... XI.8:4 or deal with c. aspects of your life alone,
T-14 ..... XI.8:5 for keeping c. dark lessons from Him.
T-15 ....... V.2:3 you seek to separate out c. aspects of the
T-15 .... VII.5:4 For it is c. that if you will look at them,
T-16 ........ I.2:1 c. types of problems and in certain people
T-16 ........ I.2:1 certain types of problems and in c. people
T-16 ........ I.6:5 But be c. that this does not mean to do a
T-16 ...... III.2:3 is c. that you judge yourself according to
T-16 ..... IV.4:5 It is sure that those who select c. ones as
T-16 ..... IV.6:5 can be c. that you perceive hatred within,
T-16 ..... IV.9:4 is c. and where everything fails to satisfy.

| | |
|---|---|
| T-17.......V.9:5 | Is it not **c.** that you will remember a goal |
| T-17......VI.1:6 | **c.** very specific guidelines He provides for |
| T-17... VIII.6:5 | it. Your release is **c.**. Give as you have |
| T-18.........I.3:7 | with special emphasis on **c.** parts, and |
| T-20....IV.8:12 | what can be more **c.** than a Son of God? |
| T-20... VIII.6:1 | laws brought to it by His calm and **c.** sight |
| T-21......IV.2:7 | proclamation, the ego is not **c.** it is so. |
| T-21......VI.3:9 | is **c.** that they look upon them differently. |
| T-22.........I.1:7 | to wander off, for only that seems **c.**. |
| T-22.........I.9:1 | Be **c.** God did not entrust His Son to the |
| T-22......VI.2:4 | as **c.** of the outcome as He is sure of His |
| T-23.......in.2:4 | It is as **c.** you will fear what you attack as |
| T-23.........I.1:8 | **C.** it is it has no enemy. Yet just as certain |
| T-23.........I.1:9 | just as **c.** is its fixed belief it has an enemy |
| T-23.........I.3:1 | **c.** that it is impossible God and the ego, |
| T-23... II.13:13 | as **c.** that you realize the goal is madness? |
| T-23..... II.20:4 | a **c.** witness that these laws are true. The |
| T-23..... II.20:5 | attack are no less **c.** in their witnessing, or |
| T-23..... II.20:6 | **C.** it is illusions will bring fear because of |
| T-23... II.22:10 | Are you **c.** which way you go? And are |
| T-23......III.4:4 | is **c.** the belief that salvation is impossible |
| T-24....... II.7:3 | **c.** that the truth is just the same in both. |
| T-24......IV.5:2 | Only this is **c.** in this shifting world that |
| T-25.......in.1:5 | And it is **c.** that you cannot be apart from |
| T-25......IX.3:1 | Be **c.** any answer to a problem the Holy |
| T-26....... V.2:5 | Nothing you undertake with **c.** purpose |
| T-26....... X.2:1 | if you perceive attack in **c.** forms to be |
| T-28......IV.5:1 | Be **c.**, if you do your part, he will do his, |
| T-29.........I.2:4 | **C.** it is he knows not what love means. He |
| T-30.........I.5:3 | **c.** this has happened if you feel yourself |
| T-30...... I.12:2 | is a statement of an open mind, not **c.** yet, |
| T-30....... V.3:2 | is **c.** he will go beyond forgiveness, and he |
| T-30... VIII.5:9 | to you, you will be **c.** you are like Him, for |
| T-31.........I.7:4 | **c.** outcome of the lesson that God's Son is |
| T-31....IV.2:10 | go. Their end is **c.**, for there is no choice |
| W-in..........5:2 | transfer to everyone and everything is **c.**. |
| W-pI.....13.3:2 | it is **c.** that you will endow the world with |
| W-pI.....15.2:4 | **c.** that real vision will come quickly when |
| W-pI.....49.2:1 | God is calm, always at rest and wholly **c.**. |
| W-pI.....61.4:3 | unburdened and **c.** of your purpose. |
| W-pI.....68.3:1 | it is **c.** that God created them like Himself |
| W-pI.....68.3:2 | is **c.** that those who forgive will find peace |
| W-pI.....68.3:3 | is **c.** that those who forgive will remember |
| W-pI.....69.8:1 | be **c.** that He has heard you and answered |
| W-pI.....71.6:6 | is the only plan that is **c.** in its outcome. |
| W-pI....72.11:7 | Be **c.**, then, that the answer will be true |
| W-pI.....73.8:1 | **c.** that we will find what it is your will to |
| W-pI.....80.3:3 | you. Only be **c.** you do not forget that all |
| W-pI.....83.1:4 | purpose only, I am always **c.** what to do, |
| W-pI.....91.8:7 | *I am not doubtful, but c.. I am not an illusion* |
| W-pI.....98.2:1 | How happy to be **c.**! All our doubts we |
| W-pI....106.1:1 | and completely **c.** in Its messages. |
| W-pI....107.2:3 | when you were **c.** you were loved and safe |
| W-pI....107.7:5 | We are as **c.** of success as we are sure we |
| W-pI....121.2:3 | not, yet **c.** of the danger lurking there. |
| W-pI....121.5:5 | knows. It does not question, **c.** it is right. |
| W-pI....124.8:5 | as He sees fit today, **c.** He will not fail. |
| W-pI....127.9:1 | your Father, **c.** that His Voice will answer. |
| W-pI....129.5:1 | Now is the last step **c.**; now you stand an |
| W-pI.134.15:2 | Be **c.** not to dwell on any one of them, but |
| W-pI.134.16:3 | your chest, a deep and **c.** feeling of relief. |
| W-pI....139.2:4 | it looks on other things as **c.** as itself. |
| W-pI....139.8:1 | can be asked of you, for what you are is **c.**. |
| W-pI....153.9:3 | stand secure, serenely **c.** of our safety now |
| W-pI.155.13:6 | trust has made your pathway **c.** and your |
| W-pI....160.7:4 | Self as **c.** of Its Own as God is of His Son. |
| W-pI....160.7:9 | not know of strangers. He is **c.** of His Son. |
| W-pI....162.3:2 | secure, his safety **c.** and his body healed, |
| W-pI....163.3:3 | will come with **c.** footsteps when the time |
| W-pI....165.6:1 | doubting past, the journey's end made **c.**, |
| W-pI....165.7:3 | doubts are meaningless, for God is **c.**. |
| W-pI....166.2:4 | looks upon the world and judges it as **c.**, |
| W-pI.170.11:1 | The choice you make today is **c.**. For you |
| WpI.. rV.in1:4 | that we may go on again more **c.**, more |
| W-pI....182.8:3 | doubt, sublimely **c.** that you are at home. |
| W-pI....186.4:3 | be **c.** only that He knows our strengths, |
| W-pI.186.11:1 | **c.** as the sun's return each morning to |
| W-pI.186.11:3 | error, and His Voice is **c.** of Its messages. |
| W-pI.186.12:6 | Hear instead a **c.** Voice, which tells you of |
| W-pI...193.4:1 | **C.** it is that all distress does not appear to |
| W-pI...195.2:2 | the **c.** means whereby all pain is healed, |
| W-pI...220.1:3 | *me home, and peace is c. as the Love of God.* I |
| W-pII.....in.7:1 | in silence, unafraid and **c.** of Your coming |
| W-pII.......1.5:1 | in hope, and **c.** of your ultimate success. |
| W-pII..232.1:5 | *let me sleep sure of my safety, c. of Your care,* |
| W-pII.......5.1:5 | could he be **c.** he remains within the body |
| W-pII..286.2:1 | travelled far along it to a wholly **c.** goal. |
| W-pII......8.4:2 | Love; the **c.** promise that he is redeemed. |
| W-pII..291.2:4 | *But You are wholly c.. Father, guide Your* |
| W-pII..292.1:5 | Yet is the ending **c.**. For God's Will is |
| W-pII..297.2:1 | *Father, how c. are Your ways; how sure their* |
| W-pII..298.2:3 | *C. is Your way. And I am grateful for Your* |
| W-pII..298.2:4 | *grateful for Your holy gifts of c. sanctuary,* |
| W-pII..300.1:1 | sorrow are the **c.** lot of all who come here, |
| W-pII..304.1:6 | And I will look upon the **c.** signs that all |
| W-pII..317.2:3 | *to do. Your way is c., and the end secure. The* |
| W-pII..321.2:2 | the **c.** way our Father has established. |
| W-pII..331.1:2 | *and be left without a c. way to his release?* |
| W-pII..340.1:1 | *and for the freedom I am c. it will bring. This* |
| W-pII..359.1:7 | *forgiveness rests upon a c. base more solid* |
| Wfl........in.6:4 | Be **c.** He will answer thus, for these are |
| WpII...361-5.h | **C.** that Your direction gives me peace. |
| W-ep .........1:5 | troubles you, be **c.** that He has the answer |
| W-ep .........2:1 | as **c.** of arriving home as is the pathway of |
| W-ep .........2:2 | Indeed, your pathway is more **c.** still. For |
| W-ep .........3:3 | for His sure direction and His **c.** Word. |
| W-ep .........4:6 | with Him, as **c.** as is He of where you go; |
| W-ep .........5:1 | The end is **c.**, and the means as well. To |
| M-2 ...........1:1 | **C.** pupils have been assigned to each of |
| M-2 ...........1:3 | been waiting for him, for his coming is **c.**. |
| M-4 ... VIII.1:1 | are **c.** of the outcome can afford to wait, |
| M-4 ... VIII.1:3 | of God. All he sees is **c.** outcome, at a time |
| M-4 ...... IX.2:5 | Being **c.**, it is joyous. And being confident |
| M-5 ....... II.1:3 | say this, one first must recognize **c.** facts. |
| M-6 ..............h | IS HEALING **C.**? |
| M-6 ...........1:1 | Healing is always **c.**. It is impossible to let |
| M-6 ...........2:9 | Let him be **c.** it has been received, and |
| M-7 ...........1:4 | And if the healing is **c.**, as we have already |
| M-7 ...........6:7 | If you are **c.** what the problem is, you |
| M-10 .........3:5 | And one would have to be **c.** there is no |
| M-12 .........4:2 | become more and more **c.** that the body's |
| M-17 .........9:7 | anger **c.** witness that you do believe in it |
| M-22 .........2:4 | It is only the end that is **c.**. Anywhere |
| M-24 .........2:5 | It is **c.**, however, that the way to salvation |
| M-27 .........1:6 | waning in a **c.** way upon a certain path,– |
| M-27 .........1:6 | waning in a certain way upon a **c.** path,– |
| M-27 .........2:4 | Or if he waits, yet is the ending **c.**. Who |
| C-2.............1:2 | is sure and this alone is **c.** in their world. |
| C-4.............7:1 | And now God's *knowledge*, changeless, **c.**, |
| C-ep...........1:1 | once this journey is begun the end is **c.**. |
| C-ep...........3:7 | His. Look up and find your **c.** destiny the |
| P-2......... V.1:4 | This strange belief relies on **c.** steps which |
| P-3......... II.1:8 | They are devoted to **c.** kinds of needs in |

## certainly 22

| | |
|---|---|
| T-3........VI.3:5 | you **c.** do not need it to organize yourself. |
| T-4.........in.1:2 | **c.** does not suggest that you set him back |
| T-16...... III.1:6 | For **c.** what He has taught, and what you |
| T19..IV.B.14:2 | **C.** what it is made of is not precious. And |
| T19..IV.B.14:3 | just as **c.** it has no feeling. It transmits to |
| T-24.....in.2:10 | decisions come from your beliefs as **c.** as |
| W-pI.....29.2:3 | **C.** God is not in a table, for example, as |
| W-pI....131.5:6 | as **c.** as God created you in sinlessness. |
| WpI...rV.in3:5 | *we may walk more c. and quickly unto You.* |
| W-pI....185.9:6 | Yet will God's peace come just as **c.**, and |
| W-pI....196.9:1 | Salvation's song can **c.** be heard in the |
| M-5 ...... III.1:3 | him? **C.** not. For those already willing to |
| M-8 ...........3:2 | **C.** they seem to be in the world outside. |
| M-11 .........1:2 | **C.** peace seems to be impossible here. Yet |
| M-14 .........3:1 | **C.** this seems to be a long, long while |
| M-20 .........4:2 | that peace cannot exist will **c.** return. War |
| M-22 .........4:1 | **C.** sickness does not appear to be a |
| M-23 .........7:3 | **C.** there are. Would God leave anyone |
| M-24 .........5:2 | The answer is, **c.** not! If he does believe in |
| M-25 .........2:1 | **C.** there are many "psychic" powers that |
| M-27 .........3:5 | as well are doomed to be destroyed as **c.**. |
| S-3......... II.3:5 | Voice, the Word of God, more **c.** our own. |

## Certainty 2

*certainty*

| | |
|---|---|
| W-pI...151.8:1 | because it rests on **C.** so great that doubt |
| M-15 .........2:6 | in this, and you will go beyond belief to **C.** |

## certainty 124

*Certainty*

| | |
|---|---|
| T-3........ III.1:5 | because it is certain, and **c.** is strength. |
| T-3........ III.1:8 | brings **c.** because all perception varies. |
| T-3........ III.2:10 | is timeless, because **c.** is not questionable. |
| T-3........ III.5:2 | **C.** is always of God. When you love |
| T-3........ III.5:6 | **C.** does not require action. When you say |
| T-3........ III.6:2 | There He can communicate His **c.**, and |
| T-3........ III.6:7 | becomes "Know God and accept His **c.**." |
| T-3........ III.7:9 | God knows His children with perfect **c.**. |
| T-6...... IV.7:6 | mind has become only the ability for **c.**. |
| T-6...... IV.11:6 | insanely? Can God lose His Own **c.**? I have |
| T-6...... V.C.8:7 | or you cannot know what you are with **c.**. |
| T-6...... V.C.8:8 | **C.** is of God for you. Vigilance is not |
| T-7...........I.6:1 | like God is to share His **c.** of what you are, |
| T-7..........II.3:5 | There is only **c.**. God and His Sons, in the |
| T-7........ III.5:5 | undo the questionable and thus lead to **c.**. |
| T-7........ IV.1:2 | and **c.** is of God according to His laws. |
| T-7........ IV.1:3 | God and **c.** comes from the laws of God. |
| T-12.........II.4:7 | in the darkness of your own false **c.**, and |
| T-13...... XI.9:4 | His **c.** suffices. Learn that even the darkest |
| T-14..... VII.3:9 | was not a point of view, but rather a **c.**. |
| T-14... VII.3:10 | Uncertainty brought to **c.** does not retain |
| T-15........II.5:2 | and you will recognize it with perfect **c.**. |
| T-20...... III.1:5 | in which **c.** is lost and doubt has entered. |
| T-20... III.11:1 | has given me the **c.** our union will be soon |
| T-20.... IV.8:10 | for it rests on **c.** and not contingency. It |
| T-20....... V.1:2 | begins to find the **c.** his Father has in him. |
| T-20....... V.8:2 | shares his Father's **c.** the universe rests in |
| T-20.... VI.10:2 | within it in the **c.** it will endure forever. Its |
| T-20....VIII.2:2 | not happily exchange your doubts for **c.**? |
| T-21...... III.4:7 | only before the state of **c.** is reached. In |
| T-21...... III.5:5 | as means for losing **c.** and finding sin. |
| T-21...... IV.8:3 | of sin, follow in gladness the way to **c.**. Be |
| T-22..... V.3:10 | Love rests in **c.**. Only uncertainty can be |
| T-23.......I.10:2 | stillness of your **c.** of Him and of yourself |
| T-23... II.22:13 | with you, and give you **c.** of where you go. |
| T-23...... IV.8:8 | no touch of doubt can ever mar your **c.**? |
| T-24....... V.9:3 | doubt, and from His **c.** His quiet comes. |
| T-24....... V.9:4 | He will exchange His **c.** for all your doubts |
| T-24....... V.9:6 | His quietness becomes your **c.**. And where |
| T-24....... V.9:7 | And where is doubt when **c.** has come? |
| T-26....... V.4:5 | Uncertainty was brought to **c.** so long ago |
| T-27.........I.4:9 | Yet it speaks with **c.** for what it represents |
| T-28...... III.1:1 | waits in perfect **c.** beyond salvation is not |
| T-28...... IV.2:1 | is a way of finding **c.** right here and now. |
| T-29....VIII.2:7 | penalty for looking not within for **c.** and |
| T-29...... IX.9:1 | you do not feel a deep content, a **c.** of help |
| T-30... III.10:3 | near, it rests in **c.** and perfect peace. Here |
| T-31..........I.9:3 | all the **c.** with which He knows His Love. |
| T-31......II.11:7 | step is made in **c.** and sureness of the road |
| T-31....VIII.9:5 | call in vain, and in His **c.** I rest content. |
| W-pI.....59.1:3 | of myself when perfect **c.** abides in Him? |
| W-pI.....71.7:1 | Let us practice recognizing this **c.** today. |
| W-pI....73.10:1 | yourself with gentle firmness and quiet **c.**: |
| W-pI.....75.8:2 | And tell yourself you wait in **c.** to look |
| W-pI....95.11:1 | your mind with all the **c.** that you can give |
| W-pI.....98.2:2 | and take our stand with **c.** of purpose, and |
| W-pI.....98.3:3 | They rest in quiet **c.** that they will do what |
| W-pI.....98.3:5 | may share their **c.** and thus increase it by |
| W-pI.....98.4:2 | will join with us, and, borrowing our **c.**, |
| W-pI.....98.6:2 | time for peace of mind and **c.** of purpose, |
| W-pI.....98.7:2 | the deep conviction and the **c.** you lack. |
| W-pI.....98.9:4 | and joy and **c.** that what you say is true. |
| W-pI....107.7:3 | note of **c.** that has been born of truth. The |
| W-pI....109.3:2 | and death, and onward to the **c.** of God. |
| W-pI....120.1:2 | *while I rest in Him in quiet and in perfect c..* |
| W-pI....122.1:4 | happiness, a quiet mind, a **c.** of purpose, |
| W-pI....124.9:3 | it when it dawns with **c.** upon your mind. |
| W-pI.124.11:2 | in **c.** that His return will be a sense of love |
| W-pI....126.1:2 | in complete forgiveness, **c.** of goal, and |
| W-pI....128.4:5 | nothing. **C.** of worth can not be found in |
| W-pI....128.8:2 | your mind, but tell yourself with quiet **c.**: |

| | |
|---|---|
| W-pI.135.11:5 | secure in **c.** that obstacles can not impede |
| W-pI.135.21:3 | the truth to dawn upon our minds with **c.**. |
| W-pI.136.12:5 | its gifts, and yet it knows, with perfect **c.**, |
| W-pI...139.2:4 | From this one point of **c.**, it looks on other |
| W-pI...139.4:4 | not know the only **c.** by which he lives. |
| W-pI.139.5:11 | it part of you, then **c.** would be impossible |
| W-pI...140.4:1 | Atonement heals with **c.**, and cures all |
| WpI. rIV.in9:2 | and rest, and endless quiet, perfect **c.**, and |
| W-pI...151.1:4 | doubt. Its seeming **c.** is but a cloak for the |
| W-pI...151.2:6 | which you would hide with show of **c.**? |
| W-pI...151.5:2 | you believe that this is so with stubborn **c.** |
| W-pI...151.6:2 | speak with **c.** of what they do not know. |
| W-pI...151.8:1 | for He has **c.** in which there is no doubt, |
| W-pI.153.19:5 | our defenses undermine our **c.** of purpose |
| W-pI...155.9:3 | as you walk with **c.** of purpose to the truth |
| W-pI...156.8:2 | till **c.** has ended doubting and established |
| W-pI...159.6:1 | you can appeal with perfect **c.** for all the |
| W-pI...160.8:1 | God's **c.** suffices. Who He knows to be |
| W-pI...165.7:6 | interposed between Him and your **c.** of |
| W-pI...165.8:1 | God, and not upon ourselves, to give us **c.** |
| W-pI...168.1:8 | There is no **c.** but this, yet this suffices. He |
| W-pI...168.3:6 | forgot; all **c.** of what Love's meaning is. |
| WpI...rV.in1:6 | we hasten on, for we approach a greater **c.** |
| W-pI...182.1:5 | you could say with **c.** you are an exile here |
| W-pI...194.1:3 | you await with **c.** the final step of God. |
| W-pI...194.7:6 | **c.** of care the world can never threaten. He |
| W-pI...198.3:6 | gives direction with the **c.** of God Himself. |
| W-pII ....in.7:8 | In this **c.**, we undertake these last few |
| W-pII .221.1:5 | *hear Your Voice in silence and in* **c.** *and love,* |
| W-pII .235.1:1 | hurt me, and with perfect **c.** assure myself |
| W-pII .238.1:5 | *me in* **c.** *that he is safe Who still is part of You,* |
| W-pII .....3.2:7 | become quite possible, for **c.** has gone. |
| W-pII .....3.4:5 | And let Him give you peace and **c.**, which |
| W-pII .252.1:3 | all things within it, in the calm of quiet **c.**. |
| W-pII .273.1:4 | We need but tell our minds, with **c.**, "The |
| W-pII .315.1:5 | and giving me his **c.** that what he learned |
| W-pII ...11.4:3 | doubts, past all our fears, there still is **c.**. |
| W-pII .334.2:3 | *heart, to give him* **c.** *and bring him peace?* |
| W-pII ....354.h | Christ and I, in peace And **c.** of purpose. |
| W-pII .360.1:3 | *I would reach to them in silence and in* **c.**, *for* |
| W-pII .360.1:3 | *in certainty, for nowhere else can* **c.** *be found* |
| W-ep .........1:8 | His **c.** is yours. You need but ask it of Him |
| M-4 .... IX.2:12 | it rests in quiet **c.** on that alone to which |
| M-7 ............4:9 | This is the **c.** that gives God's teachers the |
| M-16 .........2:1 | about those who have not reached his **c.**? |
| M-16 .........8:5 | There are times his **c.** will waver, and the |
| C-2.............7:5 | in the **c.** of Heaven and the surety of peace |
| C-4...........5:11 | just as its presence once had been your **c.**. |
| C-ep...........3:5 | Our new beginning has the **c.** the journey |
| P-2...........I.3:7 | conflict over, for only then can there be **c.**. |
| P-2.......VII.5:4 | that no one here can have; a **c.** of past, |
| S-2.........III.1:9 | way to Him, and in His willing there is **c.**. |
| S-3.........II.1:7 | And with this wish is death a **c.**, for prayer |

## chain 11

| | |
|---|---|
| T-1.........I.25:1 | of an interlocking **c.** of forgiveness which, |
| T-1........III.9:2 | **c.** of Atonement is welded. However, this |
| T-13......IX.1:8 | the **c.** of darkness in which you bound |
| T-15.....VII.4:6 | unrewarding **c.** of special relationships, |
| T-15.....VII.5:1 | this **c.** that binds the Son of God to guilt, |
| T-15.....VII.5:1 | **c.** the Holy Spirit would remove from his |
| T-15.....VII.5:2 | For the **c.** of savagery belongs not around |
| W-pI...128.2:1 | is but a **c.** that binds you to the world, |
| W-pI...128.8:2 | refuse to lay this **c.** upon your mind, but |
| W-pI.134.12:4 | made to **c.** his mind to fear and misery. |
| W-pI.134.17:5 | *this? I will not lay this* **c.** *upon myself.* In |

## chained 1

| | |
|---|---|
| T-24....... II.7:1 | have **c.** your savior to your specialness, |

## chaining 1

| | |
|---|---|
| T-15....... II.3:5 | hours and even years in **c.** your brothers |

## chains 29

| | |
|---|---|
| T-14....... II.4:6 | The heavy **c.** that seem to bind them to |
| T-14 .......II.4:7 | And then they see the **c.** have disappeared |
| T19....IV.C.2:4 | life, dragging their **c.** and marching in the |
| T19....IV.C.2:5 | of forgiveness, and watch the **c.** fall away, |
| T-20 ..... III.9:1 | Prisoners bound with heavy **c.** for years, |
| T-21 ..... III.3:3 | the Son of God in **c.** as long as he believes |
| T-21 ..... III.3:3 | in chains as long as he believes he is in **c.**. |
| T-21 . VI.11:10 | in **c.** his pardon on himself to set him free |
| T-26 .... V.10:8 | be kept in **c.** long since removed and gone |
| T-28 .... VII.6:2 | further locks and **c.** and heavy anchors, |
| T-30 ...... V.8:6 | enabled Him to rise from **c.** and go with |
| T-31 ..... III.6:6 | guilt your chosen enemies, nor keep in **c.**, |
| W-pI.....57.1:3 | My **c.** are loosened. I can drop them off |
| W-pI... 128.3:1 | Escape today the **c.** you place upon your |
| W-pI... 128.5:4 | Thus do we lift the **c.** that bar the door to |
| W-pI... 128.6:1 | when you release your mind from **c.** and |
| W-pI... 128.7:3 | every time you let your mind escape its **c.**. |
| W-pI... 132.1:1 | keeps the world in **c.** but your beliefs? |
| W-pI. 134.16:4 | **c.** you sought to lay upon your brother, |
| W-pI. 139.12:3 | And learn the fragile nature of the **c.** that |
| W-pI... 155.8:5 | but seem to hold in **c.** the holy Son of God |
| W-pI. 191.11:2 | They stay in **c.** till you are free. They |
| W-pI. 193.12:3 | The **c.** of time are easily unloosened in |
| W-pI... 194.2:2 | **c.** that locked the door to freedom on it. |
| W-pI... 200.5:1 | where you beheld but **c.** and iron doors. |
| W-pII ..... 1.2:3 | protects projection, tightening its **c.**, so |
| W-pII . 279.1:5 | in **c.** which have been severed for release, |
| W-pII . 332.1:7 | Without forgiveness is the mind in **c.**, |
| S-1........ IV.3:5 | the present from its **c.** of past illusions; to |

## chair 4

| | |
|---|---|
| W-pI....... 1.1:3 | *This* **c.** *does not mean anything. This hand* |
| W-pI..... 25.6:4 | *I do not know what this* **c.** *is for. I do not* |
| W-pI..... 36.3:7 | *My holiness envelops that* **c.**. *My holiness* |
| W-pI..... 37.4:2 | see: *My holiness blesses this* **c.**. *My holiness* |

## chalice 1

| | |
|---|---|
| T19. IV.D.13:1 | is one who offers you the **c.** of Atonement |

## challenge 4

| | |
|---|---|
| T-24 ........I.2:6 | love, unrecognized and swift to **c.** you to |
| W-pI.... 13.2:2 | which God and the ego "**c.**" each other as |
| M-4 ........II.2:5 | is no **c.** to a teacher of God. Challenge |
| M-4 ........II.2:6 | **C.** implies doubt, and the trust on which |

## challenges 1

| | |
|---|---|
| T-24 ..... III.5:7 | Salvation **c.** not even death. And God |

## chambers 1

| | |
|---|---|
| T-14 ..... VI.8:6 | There are no hidden **c.** in God's temple. |

## chance 33

| | |
|---|---|
| T-5 ....... VI.3:4 | the **c.** to claim it for yourself be given you |
| T-7 ........ V.5:1 | The Holy Spirit does not work by **c.**, and |
| T-8 ........ III.4:6 | they are given another **c.** at salvation. Do |
| T-9 ...... VII.1:6 | second gives you a **c.** to save yourself. Do |
| T-13 ...... XI.8:9 | is no **c.** that Heaven will not be yours, for |
| T-14 ...... III.6:2 | Every **c.** given him to heal is another |
| T-14 ...... IX.2:7 | It cannot change with time or mood or **c.**. |
| T-21 ........II.3:3 | he seems to find himself by **c.** or accident. |
| T-21 ........II.3:4 | No accident nor **c.** is possible within the |
| T-25 ........II.2:3 | long is needed for you to realize the **c.** of |
| T-25 ..... III.6:8 | temptation as just another **c.** to bring him |
| T-25 ..... III.7:2 | you nothing except a **c.** for you to see the |
| T-25 ..... III.8:8 | He sees as far beyond the **c.** of change. |
| T-29 ..... IV.5:6 | becomes a brother giving you a **c.** to help, |
| T-31 ...VIII.4:2 | see it as it is; another **c.** to choose again, |
| W-pI..... 63.4:3 | an opportunity. No **c.** should be lost for |
| W-pI..... 98.8:2 | one **c.** to be the glad receiver of His gifts, |
| W-pI... 105.9:4 | him, see it as but another **c.** to let yourself |
| WpI..rIII.in9:3 | your learning a fair **c.** to prove how great |
| WpI..rIII.in9:4 | to you. Here is another **c.** to use it well. |
| WpIrIII.in12:3 | This second **c.** with each of these ideas |
| W-pI... 132.6:1 | quite apart from what you **c.** to think it is. |
| W-pI .. 158.3:3 | along the road that anyone takes but by **c.** |
| W-pI 158.10:5 | **c.** to let Christ's vision shine on you, and |
| M-in........ 2:10 | be to you a **c.** to teach others what you are |
| M-3 ........... 2:2 | a "**c.**" meeting of two apparent strangers |
| M-3 ........... 2:2 | he is going running into an adult "by **c.**," |
| M-3 ........... 2:3 | These are not **c.** encounters. Each of them |
| M-9 ........... 1:3 | and **c.** plays no part in God's plan. It is |
| P-2........ VI.6:3 | and is thus given another **c.** to look at it, |
| P-2........ VII.1:7 | a therapist offers him a **c.** to heal himself. |
| S-1......... IV.4:1 | chosen a newborn **c.** each time you pray. |
| S-1......... IV.4:2 | the **c.** has come to free yourself from all of |

## chances 3

| | |
|---|---|
| T-9 ...... VII.1:7 | Do not lose these **c.**, not because they will |
| T-25 ..... III.7:8 | many **c.** to extend your own forgiveness. |
| T-31 ... VIII.9:1 | and find so many **c.** to perceive another |

## change 389

| | |
|---|---|
| T-1 .........V.5:1 | is eternal, and cannot **c.** or be changed. |
| T-1 .........V.5:7 | To **c.** your mind means to place it at the |
| T-2 .........II.5:4 | ability to learn has no value when **c.** is no |
| T-2 ....... VI.3:4 | for it. You must **c.** your mind, not your |
| T-2 ....... VI.3:6 | only at the level where **c.** is possible. |
| T-2 ....... VI.3:7 | is possible. **C.** does not mean anything at |
| T-2 ....... VII.7:5 | more than a potential for a **c.** of mind. |
| T-3 ......... III.2:8 | Since perceptions **c.**, their dependence on |
| T-4 ..........I.2:1 | they are, and learning means **c.**. Change is |
| T-4 ..........I.2:2 | **C.** is always fearful to the separated, |
| T-4 ..........I.2:3 | separation was their first experience of **c.**. |
| T-4 ..........I.2:4 | You believe that if you allow no **c.** to enter |
| T-4 ..........I.3:3 | This is the **c.** the ego must fear, because it |
| T-4 ..........I.4:1 | because they enable you to **c.** your mind |
| T-4 ..........I.4:1 | your mind and help others to **c.** theirs. |
| T-4 ..........I.4:2 | Refusing to **c.** your mind will not prove |
| T-4 ..........I.8:4 | only sane solution is not to try to **c.** reality |
| T-4 .....II.11:10 | ever will be, because it implies no **c.** at all. |
| T-4 ....... IV.2:1 | I have said that you cannot **c.** your mind |
| T-4 ....... IV.2:1 | and many times, that you *can* **c.** your mind |
| T-4 ....... IV.2:5 | then **c.** your mind to think with God's. |
| T-4 ....... IV.5:4 | until you **c.** your mind about those whom |
| T-4 .......V.6:11 | remain in effect unless you **c.** your mind. |
| T-5 ..........I.7:6 | point that sufficient quantitative **c.** occurs |
| T-5 .......II.10:1 | you can let it **c.** you just as it changed me. |
| T-5 ....... III.5:6 | would be unable to understand the **c.**. |
| T-6 .........II.6:6 | You cannot **c.** it now or ever. It is forever |
| T-6 ..... IV.12:4 | Teaching aims at **c.**, but God created only |
| T-6 .....V.A.6:5 | or the **c.** in direction would not have been |
| T-6 ..... V.B.2:1 | realize that only fundamental **c.** will last, |
| T-6 ..... V.B.2:2 | for **c.** is their first and foremost goal. It is |
| T-6 ..... V.B.2:4 | Increasing motivation for **c.** in the learner |
| T-6 ..... V.B.2:4 | all that a teacher need do to guarantee **c.**. |
| T-6 ..... V.B.2:5 | **C.** in motivation is a change of mind, and |
| T-6 ..... V.B.2:5 | Change in motivation is a **c.** of mind, and |
| T-6 ..... V.B.2:5 | produce fundamental **c.** because the |
| T-6 ..... V.B.4:4 | fundamental **c.** will still occur with the |
| T-6 ..... V.B.4:4 | occur with the **c.** of mind in the thinker. |
| T-6 ..... V.B.6:3 | by God, and your decision cannot **c.** it. As |
| T-6 ..... V.B.9:2 | where the fundamental **c.** will occur. At |
| T-6 ..... V.C.3:1 | is a major step toward fundamental **c.**. |
| T-7 ........I.7:10 | It does not **c.** by increase, because it was |
| T-7 .........II.4:4 | his whole purpose is to **c.** the form so that |
| T-7 .........II.4:6 | therefore **c.** the meaning to preserve the |
| T-7 .........V.7:5 | and so vital in its power for **c.** that a Son |
| T-7 .........V.7:5 | in one instant and **c.** the world in the next |
| T-7 .........V.7:6 | device that was ever given him for **c.**. This |
| T-7 .........V.7:8 | learn to **c.** your mind about your mind. |
| T-7 .........V.8:8 | help him undo the **c.** his ego thinks it has |
| T-7 .......V.10:5 | you can **c.** their minds about themselves, |
| T-7 .......V.10:5 | minds about themselves, as I can **c.** yours. |
| T-8 ..........I.4:3 | If learning aims at **c.**, and that is always |
| T-8 ..........I.5:2 | one, a **c.** in the curriculum is obviously |
| T-8 ..........I.5:3 | The first **c.** to be introduced is a change in |
| T-8 ..........I.5:3 | to be introduced is a **c.** in direction. A |
| T-8 ..........I.5:7 | This leads to fluctuation, but not to **c.**. |
| T-8 ..........I.6:1 | a real **c.** in direction becomes possible. |
| T-8 ....... IV.6:4 | I will wait until you **c.** your mind. I can |
| T-8 ...... VII.2:6 | will **c.** your mind entirely about its value. |

T-8... VIII.1:14 level of perception, where **c.** is possible.
T-9........ I.11:6 it is impossible for you to **c.** them. If you
T-9........ I.11:9 You cannot **c.** laws you did not make, and
T-9........ III.6:4 It is not up to you to **c.** your brother, but
T-9........ III.6:6 His errors cannot **c.** this, and can have no
T-9...... IV.10:2 only hope is to **c.** your mind about reality.
T-9......... V.6:5 Nothing will **c.** unless it is understood,
T-9......... V.7:2 unless he is also helped to **c.** his direction.
T-10........in.3:1 God does not **c.** His Mind about you, for
T-10.... in.3:10 and refuse to **c.** your mind about yourself.
T-10...... III.1:2 Can you **c.** your reality? No one can will
T-11...... I.10:1 you cannot **c.** this because it is immutable
T-12.........I.6:7 **c.** His Mind about reality because reality
T-12.........I.6:7 about reality because reality does not **c.**.
T-12... VIII.2:4 He did not **c.**, but you did. For a split
T-13...... VI.7:5 still dimension of time that does not **c.**,
T-13...... IX.8:12 deny His knowledge, but you cannot **c.** it.
T-13...... XI.5:5 you, because He does not **c.** His Mind. He
T-13...... XI.6:1 will not remember **c.** and shift in Heaven.
T-14... VIII.4:6 Nothing can **c.** the knowledge, given you
T-14...... IX.2:7 It cannot **c.** with time or mood or chance.
T-14...... IX.7:2 your mind is not obscure, and will not **c.**.
T-14...... XI.7:6 And being yours He cannot **c.** Himself,
T-15.........I.9:7 fear, and with no sense of **c.** with time.
T-15...... I.10:1 Time is inconceivable without **c.**, yet
T-15...... I.10:1 without change, yet holiness does not **c.**.
T-15...... I.10:4 And Heaven will not **c.**, for the birth into
T-15...... I.10:4 into the holy present is salvation from **c.**.
T-15...... I.10:5 **C.** is an illusion, taught by those who
T-15...... I.10:6 There is no **c.** in Heaven because there is
T-15...... I.10:6 in Heaven because there is no **c.** in God.
T-15...... I.11:1 would take to **c.** your mind so completely,
T-15...... IV.6:8 therefore seeks to **c.** nothing, but merely
T-15....... V.4:2 This is why they shift and **c.** so frequently.
T-16...... III.4:8 accept into your mind does not really **c.** it
T-16...... IV.4:4 illusion, and what can **c.** was never love. It
T-16..... V.12:9 You cannot **c.** His Mind. No rituals that
T-16..... VII.1:2 is an attempt to re-enact the past and **c.** it.
T-16..... VII.2:6 How can you **c.** the past except in fantasy
T-17.........I.1:7 effect upon reality at all, and did not **c.** it.
T-17.........I.1:8 Fantasies **c.** reality. That is their purpose.
T-17.........I.2:1 only your wish to **c.** reality that is fearful,
T-17....... II.4:3 Nothing will ever **c.**; no shifts nor
T-17...... III.7:8 Who can **c.** your mind about it for you.
T-17....... V.4:5 except to **c.** the relationship to fit the goal
T-17....... V.5:2 induce a complete **c.** of mind about what
T-17....... V.5:3 **c.** develops and is finally accomplished, it
T-17... VIII.6:3 purpose has not changed, and will not **c.**,
T-17... VIII.6:3 for you accepted what can never **c.**. And
T-18....... II.1:5 you, and **c.** it into a tribute to your ego,
T-18....... II.2:5 your willingness to **c.** reality on its behalf.
T-18...... II.5:15 fixed and insane idea that you can **c.** it. In
T-18....... II.6:3 I said before that the first **c.**, before
T-18....... V.1:4 to **c.** your dreams of fear to happy dreams
T-18....... V.3:5 it. Nor will He **c.** His Mind about it. The
T-18....... V.4:6 The little faith it needed to **c.** the purpose
T-18...... VI.4:6 **c.** its function from what the Holy Spirit
T-19....... II.3:3 that would really **c.** his reality in any way,
T-19....... II.7:5 his Father, and **c.** His Mind completely.
T-19...... III.3:4 you **c.** its status from a sin to a mistake.
T-19...... III.3:6 For then you will but **c.** the form of sin,
T-19...... III.3:7 This is not really a **c.** in your perception,
T-19...... III.5:9 could **c.** perception is thus kept impotent,
T-20...... III.1:2 an adjustment is a **c.**; a shift in perception
T-20...... III.1:4 fact, is lost if any shift or **c.** is undertaken.
T-20..... VII.2:1 discomfort that follows the sudden **c.** in a
T-20. VIII.11:1 seen it **c.** to sights of loveliness and peace;
T-20. VIII.11:1 watched them **c.** to quiet views of gardens
T-21........in.1:7 Therefore, seek not to **c.** the world, but
T-21........in.1:7 choose to **c.** your mind about the world.
T-21....... II.1:2 tiny **c.** of mind by which the crucifixion is
T-21....... II.5:9 And as you look upon the **c.** in him, it will
T-21...... III.1:6 And that is why the Holy Spirit must **c.** its
T-21...... III.2:1 If you accept this **c.**, you have accepted
T-21...... V.3:11 They always **c.** *your* mind. There *is* no
T-21...... V.10:5 in this **c.** is room made way for vision.
T-21...... VI.7:6 you it is given you to **c.** his whole mind,
T-21... VII.10:6 rule that rules you not, and **c.** your mind.
T-21... VII.10:8 use the body's eyes and **c.** what you desire
T-21... VII.11:6 the option to **c.** your mind again. When it
T-21... VIII.2:3 has no exceptions; no **c.** of any kind. It is
T-21... VIII.5:6 of your desire for what will never **c.**. For
T-22....... II.2:4 To **c.** illusions is to make no change. The
T-22....... II.2:4 To change illusions is to make no **c.**. The
T-22....... II.3:6 turn to sorrow, for the eternal cannot **c.**.
T-22....... II.3:8 but everything in time can **c.** with time.
T-22....... II.3:9 Yet if the **c.** be real and not imagined,
T-22...... III.7:2 You can **c.** form *because* it is not true. It
T-22...... VI.3:1 disturbed at all to think how He can **c.** the
T-22...... VI.8:5 Seek not to **c.** it, nor to substitute another
T-23...... III.1:4 Its purpose does not **c.**. Its sole intent is
T-23...... IV.8:6 happiness could ever suffer **c.** of any kind.
T-24.......I.8:10 that does not **c.** with every seeming blow,
T-24....... II.7:2 Nor will you **c.** his function, any more
T-24....... II.7:2 you can **c.** the truth in him and in yourself
T-24...... IV.2:7 And minds can **c.** as they desire. What
T-24...... IV.2:8 are, and all their attributes, they cannot **c.**
T-24...... IV.3:9 merely **c.** of purpose from hurt to healing.
T-25....... II.1:4 must be evident the outcome does not **c.**.
T-25....... II.2:3 chance of **c.** in this respect is hardly worth
T-25....... II.2:3 **c.** that might result in better outcome?
T-25...... III.8:4 Sin is the fixed belief perception cannot **c.**
T-25...... III.8:7 And thus is **c.** made possible. The Holy
T-25...... III.8:8 He sees as far beyond the chance of **c.**. But
T-25... III.8:13 it is to **c.** its state from error into truth.
T-25...... IV.1:7 the hope of **c.** unless the aim is changed.
T-25..... VII.1:2 only thing in all the world that cannot **c.**.
T-25... VII.1:10 Nor will it **c.**. Yet is it possible what God
T-25..... VII.5:1 Holy Spirit has the power to **c.** the whole
T-26....... II.1:4 The aspects that need solving do not **c.**,
T-26...... III.7:1 where the separation is undone by **c.** of
T-26...... IV.4:6 What but a miracle could **c.** his mind, so
T-26....... V.6:8 and does not **c.** whatever dreams he has.
T-26....... V.7:3 and place effect a **c.** in where he really is?
T-26...... V.12:1 do not **c.** the laws of time nor of eternity.
T-26... VII.20:4 A miracle can make no **c.** at all. But it can
T-26... VIII.6:3 The **c.** of purpose the Holy Spirit brought
T-26... VIII.7:9 Given a **c.** of purpose for the good, there
T-27... VII.14:2 It is not difficult to **c.** a dream when once
T-27... VIII.3:2 The "hero" of this dream will never **c.**,
T-28.........I.6:4 which no **c.** can be made possible because
T-28.........I.6:5 Yet **c.** must have a cause that will endure,
T-28.........I.6:6 No **c.** can be made in the present if its
T-28....... II.5:3 But for this **c.** in content of the dream, it
T-28....... II.6:6 For that would **c.** its cause, and it is this
T-28..... II.12:7 salvation will proceed to **c.** the course of
T-29....... II.6:4 Its basis does not **c.**, although it seems to
T-29....... II.6:4 although it seems to be in constant **c.**. Yet
T-29....... II.6:6 and shift and **c.** become the law on which
T-29....... II.7:1 The body does not **c.**. It represents the
T-29....... II.7:2 the larger dream that **c.** is possible. To
T-29....... II.7:3 To **c.** is to attain a state unlike the one in
T-29....... II.7:4 There is no **c.** in immortality, and Heaven
T-29....... II.7:7 The body can appear to **c.** with time, with
T-29...... IV.2:6 Their form can **c.**, but they cannot be
T-29...... IV.5:4 The coverings may not appear to **c.**, but
T-29....... V.2:1 not that you can **c.** Their dwelling place.
T-29....... V.8:3 without the hope of **c.** and betterment,
T-29...... VI.2:9 all things that **c.** with time and bloom and
T-29.... VI.2:11 can never **c.** by what men made of him.
T-29.... VI.2:13 Forgiveness will not **c.** him. Yet time
T-29...... VI.3:3 **C.** is the only thing that can be made a
T-29...... VI.3:6 can not remove the power to **c.** your mind
T-29...... VI.4:1 **C.** is the greatest gift God gave to all that
T-29...... VI.4:3 You cannot **c.**, because your function has
T-29...... VI.4:4 time and **c.** that time might be preserved,
T-29..... VII.8:1 To **c.** all this, and open up a road of hope
T-29... VIII.4:2 yet a thought without the power to **c.** one
T-29... VIII.6:5 Here does the changeless **c.**; the peace of
T-30.........I.8:1 you can begin to **c.** your mind with this:
T-30...... III.5:5 If there were **c.** in him, if he could be
T-30...... III.6:4 Thoughts were absent or could suffer **c.**.
T-30...... III.8:1 The Thoughts of God are far beyond all **c.**
T-30...... VI.3:1 This understanding is the only **c.** that lets
T-30.... VI.10:1 an error that could **c.** the truth in him. It
T-30..... VII.1:6 it. For only if its aim could **c.** with every
T-30..... VII.2:4 these labels **c.** with other judgments,
T-30..... VII.2:7 a meaning in the light of goals that **c.**,
T-30..... VII.2:7 with every meaning shifting as they **c.**.
T-30..... VII.4:4 It cannot **c.** *because* you would perceive it
T-30..... VII.5:5 makes perception shift and meaning **c.**. In
T-30.... VIII.1:4 For everything you see will **c.**, and yet you
T-30.... VIII.1:5 is thus reduced to form, and capable of **c.**.
T-30.... VIII.1:9 transcend all form to be itself. It cannot **c.**
T-30.... VIII.2:1 can **c.** because they *are* appearances, and
T-30.... VIII.2:2 from appearances by showing they can **c.**.
T-30.... VIII.2:9 are shown to be unreal *because* they **c.**.
T-30.... VIII.4:3 hope of **c.** is that the miracle cannot come
T-30.... VIII.5:1 already there to heal all things that **c.**, and
T-31...... III.4:8 Learning is all that causes **c.**. And so the
T-31...... III.4:9 could never **c.** unless the mind preferred
T-31...... III.4:9 preferred the body **c.** in its appearances,
T-31.... III.4:10 mind can learn, and there is all **c.** made.
T-31...... III.6:1 has been given you to **c.** what you believe.
T-31...... III.7:3 Open your mind to **c.**, and there will be
T-31....... V.6:7 nor can you **c.** the things it makes you do.
T-31...... VI.2:5 could have trust where so much **c.** is seen,
T-31...... VI.5:3 But concepts are not difficult to **c.**. One
T-31...... VI.5:4 will **c.** the world for eyes that learn to see,
T-31...... VI.7:3 your Father wills of you can never **c.**. The
T-31..... VII.1:1 Learning is **c.**. Salvation does not seek to
T-31..... VII.1:2 nor to make the kinds of **c.** you could not
T-31..... VII.1:4 which has no opposite and cannot **c.**. In
T-31..... VII.1:9 it **c.** while you perceive the "bad" in you.
T-31..... VII.5:1 your fearful concept of yourself may **c.**.
T-31..... VII.5:3 you be willing that this happy **c.** occur.
T-31..... VII.6:3 it past the hope of **c.** and keep it static and
W-pI........ 7.2:1 ideas about time are very difficult to **c.**,
W-pI..... 20.4:3 to **c.** your present state for a better one,
W-pI..... 22.1:4 circle until he is willing to **c.** how he sees.
W-pI..... 23.2:3 There is no point in trying to **c.** the world.
W-pI..... 23.2:4 It is incapable of **c.** because it is merely an
W-pI..... 23.2:7 the cause. The effect will **c.** automatically.
W-pI..... 23.5:2 This **c.** requires, first, that the cause be
W-pI..... 34.6:2 you **c.** your mind in any specific context,
W-pI... 39.10:2 **c.** the idea itself as you vary the method of
W-pI..... 45.7:4 you have thought since then will **c.**, but
W-pI..... 54.2:5 I know that my state of mind can **c.**. And
W-pI..... 54.2:6 I also know the world I see can **c.** as well.
W-pI..... 54.4:6 power to **c.** every mind along with mine,
W-pI..... 71.2:5 The **c.** of mind necessary for salvation is
W-pI..... 71.3:1 than itself, must **c.** if you are to be saved.
W-pI..... 82.4:4 *ego, but cannot **c.** my function in any way.*
W-pI..... 83.2:2 *perception of this does not **c.** my function.*
W-pI..... 92.1:4 Thus you believe that you can **c.** what you
W-pI..... 92.7:5 It does not **c.** and flicker and go out. It
W-pI..... 93.6:5 touch it, or **c.** what God created as eternal
W-pI..... 95.1:4 perfect unity makes **c.** in you impossible.
W-pI..... 99.1:2 something amiss that needs corrective **c.**;
W-pI... 107.4:1 while, to disappear or **c.** to something else
W-pI... 107.6:1 does not come and go nor shift nor **c.**, in
W-pI... 109.5:2 for your rest can never **c.** in any way at all.
W-pI... 110.2:4 and every **c.** that time appears to bring in
W-pI... 121.5:3 It thinks it cannot **c.**, for what it sees
W-pI... 122.5:1 God's plan for your salvation cannot **c.**,
W-pI. 122.13:3 of shifting **c.** and bleak appearances.
W-pI. 122.13:4 as you see the changeless in the heart of **c.**
W-pI... 123.3:1 remain shining on you, forever without **c.**
W-pI... 125.2:1 This world will **c.** through you. No other
W-pI... 127.2:1 to anyone who thinks that love can **c.**. He
W-pI... 129.7:1 this **c.** ten minutes in the morning and at
W-pI... 132.2:1 achieved, for anyone is free to **c.** his mind,
W-pI... 132.2:1 his mind, and all his thoughts **c.** with it.
W-pI... 132.2:2 **c.** your mind means you have changed the
W-pI... 132.5:2 **C.** but your mind on what you want to see
W-pI... 132.5:2 see, and all the world must **c.** accordingly.
W-pI... 132.5:5 and that it changes as you **c.** your mind.
W-pI... 132.9:3 time that can bring **c.** to your eternal state
W-pI. 132.10:2 pain is but to **c.** your mind about yourself.
W-pI. 132.17:1 deny the power of your simple **c.** of mind:
W-pI... 133.4:2 The range is set, and this we cannot **c.**. It
W-pI. 135.16:1 that plans is thus refusing to allow for **c.**.
W-pI... 136.2:3 its purpose is to hide reality, attack it, **c.** it
W-pI. 136.11:1 knows not of your plans to **c.** His Will.
W-pI. 136.11:7 What is unalterable cannot **c.**. And what
W-pI. 138.12:6 *I make it now, and will not **c.** my mind,*
W-pI... 139.5:3 Your denial made no **c.** in what you are.

W-pI.139.10:2 Today accept Atonement, not to **c.** reality
W-pI...140.7:3 provides that can effect a **c.** in anything.
W-pI...140.7:5 There is no **c.** but this. For how can one
W-pI...140.8:1 Today we seek to **c.** our minds about the
WpI.rIV.in4:3 **c.** the coming and the going of the tides,
W-pI.151.11:3 love beyond the hate, the constancy in **c.**,
W-pI...155.1:2 be. You do not **c.** appearance, though you
W-pI...158.4:2 plan behind appearances that does not **c.**.
W-pI...162.4:2 to **c.** the mind of him who uses them. So
W-pI...164.9:2 We can **c.** the world, if you acknowledge
W-pI.166.14:5 your **c.** of mind becomes the proof that
W-pI...167.3:5 is where it must be changed, if **c.** occurs.
W-pI...167.3:7 attempts to **c.** your mind about yourself.
W-pI...167.4:2 It is the belief conditions **c.**, emotions
W-pI...167.4:2 you did not make, and you can never **c.**. It
W-pI...167.6:2 all. It cannot **c.** what is its waking state. It
W-pI...167.6:5 attributes it lacks, nor **c.** its own eternal,
W-pI...167.7:3 Its form may **c.**; it may appear to be what
W-pI...181.2:3 **C.** but this focus, and what you behold
W-pI...181.2:3 and what you behold will **c.** accordingly.
W-pI...181.5:3 against present **c.** of focus in perception.
W-pI...181.6:3 instructions to our minds to **c.** their focus
W-pI...185.7:6 which seem to **c.** in what they offer, but
W-pI...185.9:7 forms which shift and **c.** with every step
W-pI...186.8:3 seem to **c.** from mourner to ecstatic bliss
W-pI...186.8:5 very being seems to **c.** as we experience a
W-pI.186.10:4 **c.** ten times an hour at their most secure.
W-pI.186.11:4 They will not **c.**, nor be in conflict. All of
W-pI...187.4:4 will **c.** and grow unrecognizable in time,
W-pI...188.1:4 is but a recognition, not a **c.** at all. Light is
W-pI...190.6:4 will **c.** entirely as you elect to change your
W-pI...190.6:4 entirely as you elect to **c.** your mind, and
W-pI...194.7:8 to **c.** his mind when he has made mistakes
W-pI...195.6:2 nor impair or **c.** our function to complete
W-pI...200.5:2 must **c.** your mind about the purpose of
W-pII....in.9:2 We wanted God to **c.** Himself, and be
W-pII.226.1:2 **c.** of mind about the purpose of the world
W-pII.230.1:3 It is not given me to **c.** my Self. How
W-pII.230.2:2 *from time, and still remains beyond all* **c.**.
W-pII.....3.5:3 And let us not attempt to **c.** our function.
W-pII.....4.2:3 Yet can the goal of striving **c.**. And now
W-pII.....4.4:4 Love which his pretenses cannot **c.** at all.
W-pII.....5.3:5 But we can **c.** the purpose that the body
W-pII....284.h I can elect to **c.** all thoughts that hurt.
W-pII.284.1:7 I can elect to **c.** all thoughts that hurt.
W-pII.308.1:2 must **c.** my perception of what time is for.
W-pII.309.1:2 as is His Own, can will no **c.** in this. For to
W-pII.329.1:3 *This am I, and this will never* **c.**. *As You are*
W-pII.329.1:7 *It cannot* **c.**, *and be in opposition to itself.*
W-pII...12.5:1 will one lily of forgiveness **c.** the darkness
W-pII.338.1:5 he has the power to **c.** them and exchange
W-pII...13.1:2 It does not create, nor really **c.** at all. It
W-ep.........2:3 For it can not be possible to **c.** the course
M-1...........4:6 outcome, for what can **c.** the Will of God?
M-1...........4:7 But time, with its illusions of **c.** and death
M-3...........3:3 to begin to **c.** his mind about the world
M-4.....I.A.8:9 And who would seek to **c.** tranquility for
M-4.......X.2:3 could never have conceived of such a **c.**.
M-5......III.1:1 must **c.** his mind in order to be healed,
M-5......III.1:2 do? Can he **c.** the patient's mind for him?
M-5......III.1:4 For those already willing to **c.** their minds
M-6...........4:3 Healing is the **c.** of mind that the Holy
M-7...........1:9 must be willing to **c.** his mind about it. He
M-9...........1:6 are called upon to **c.** their life situation
M-12.........2:2 It is not really a **c.**; it is a change of mind.
M-12.........2:2 It is not really a change; it is a **c.** of mind.
M-12.........6:7 dream figures come and go, shift and **c.**,
M-16.........1:2 is no program, for the lessons **c.** each day.
M-16.........1:3 of but one thing; they do not **c.** at random
M-23.........7:5 symbols must shift and **c.** to suit the need
M-28.........1:2 a **c.** of mind about the meaning of the
M-29.........8:4 *things visible; and to undo All things that* **c.**.
C-3............7:1 There are no wishes now for wishes **c.**.
C-5............1:4 is a Thought of God, and this will never **c.**
C-5...........6:10 *Nothing you can do can* **c.** *Eternal Love.*
P-in...........1:6 but even then it is always some **c.** in his
P-in...........1:8 the patient must be helped to **c.** his mind
P-2........in.4:1 must want to **c.** the patient's self-concept
P-2..........I.1:4 levels of readiness **c.**, and when therapist
P-2..........I.2:2 the ego fosters; that it is capable of true **c.**,
P-2........IV.2:4 be nothing that a **c.** of mind cannot effect,
P-2........IV.2:5 **C.** the decision, and how can its shadow
P-2......IV.11:8 is no need for complicated **c.**. There is no
P-2........VI.2:2 given us literally "to **c.** our tune." The
P-2........VI.3:6 its slaves to **c.** the forms they look upon;
P-3..........II.4:3 His creations do not **c.** and last forever, so
P-3..........II.6:2 may **c.** their dreams in the process. Yet it
S-1..........II.1:3 life. But it does **c.** in form, and grow with
S-1..........II.7:5 forever, beyond all **c.** and incorruptible.
S-1........IV.1:7 lies in this simple thought; this **c.** of mind
S-3.........in.1:3 of a **c.** of mind about the goal of prayer.
S-3...........I.2:5 And they feel fear as bodies **c.** and sicken.
S-3........III.2:7 and **c.** are what the dream is made of. To

## changeable 1

W-pII.277.1:4 *He is not changed by what is* **c.**. *He is not*

## changed 99

T-1.......IV.4:5 It is those who have not yet **c.** their minds
T-1........V.5:1 true is eternal, and cannot change or be **c.**
T-2..........I.1:9 God created can be **c.** by your own mind.
T-3.......IV.5:7 the service of spirit, where perception is **c.**
T-4......VII.8:6 Every mind that is **c.** adds to this joy with
T-5.......II.10:1 you can let it change you just as it **c.** me.
T-5........V.6:4 automatically until the decision is **c.**.
T-5......V.6:12 What you made can always be **c.** because,
T-7........V.7:6 **c.** the most powerful device that was ever
T-7........V.7:7 think that you have **c.** it as long as you
T-7........V.8:2 that he could not have **c.** his mind. That is
T-7........V.8:7 in him you have not really **c.** him. By
T-8.......VI.9:7 distance to a goal that has never **c.**. Truth
T-9........V.4:1 not matter and the content has not **c.**. In
T-9........V.7:4 of one whose direction has been **c.** *for* him,
T-10......in.3:9 yourself, "Has God **c.** His Mind about me
T-12...III.10:7 There you will see your vision **c.**, and
T-13........V.7:5 true, but His offering to you has never **c.**.
T-14.....IX.1:9 **c.** and interposed between what always
T-15.....VI.6:3 Nothing has **c.**. Yet the awareness of
T-17......V.4:2 yet been **c.** sufficiently to make its former
T-17......V.4:4 Yet now the goal will not be **c.**. Set firmly
T-17....VII.9:5 When the Holy Spirit **c.** the purpose of
T-17...VIII.6:3 real. Your purpose has not **c.**, and will not
T-18.......II.6:3 dreams of fear are **c.** to happy dreams.
T-18.......II.8:4 has been **c.** from one of dreams to one of
T-19.......II.2:7 For by it God Himself is **c.**, and rendered
T-19.......II.6:5 sin has **c.** creation from an idea of God to
T-19.....III.5:9 the fear of **c.** perception which its Teacher
T-20....VII.2:2 the means to Him Who **c.** the purpose.
T-21.......II.1:2 which the crucifixion is **c.** to resurrection.
T-21.....V.10:4 reason, cannot fail to lead to **c.** perception
T-22.....III.7:3 It could not be reality *because* it can be **c.**.
T-24.....IV.2:9 But what they hold as purpose can be **c.**,
T-25.....IV.1:7 the hope of change unless the aim is **c.**.
T-25....VI.5:11 His wish was not denied but **c.** in form, to
T-25....VII.2:4 that what He did not will cannot be **c.**?
T-26...VIII.9:8 its form is **c.** and what it is cannot be
T-27....VII.5:4 will the cause be **c.** by seeing it apart from
T-28........I.8:3 It has never **c.**, because there never was a
T-28........I.9:5 Never **c.** from what It is. And you are Its
T-28.....VI.2:6 set. And if that path is **c.**, it walks as easily
T-29.....IV.5:4 has **c.** because they cover something else.
T-29.....VI.2:5 What he is cannot be **c.**. He is the only
T-29.....VI.5:3 Let *this* be **c.**, and nothing in the world but
T-29.....VI.5:3 in the world but must be **c.** as well. For
T-29.....IX.2:2 And in that dream was Heaven **c.** to hell,
T-29.....IX.6:9 been **c.** because he does not understand.
T-29.....IX.7:2 Except the figures have been **c.**. They are
T-29.....IX.7:6 now has **c.** into a dream where all is joy,
T-30......I.11:5 Now you have **c.** your mind about the day
T-30...III.11:9 The star shines still; the sky has never **c.**.
T-30...VIII.1:1 Appearances deceive, but can be **c.**.
T-30...VIII.2:6 in any form, because it can so easily be **c.**.
T-31.......II.9:7 in this choice is learning's outcome **c.**, for
T-31.....V.16:2 as your perception of yourself is **c.**. There
T-31.....VI.5:4 see, because the concept of the self has **c.**.
T-31....VII.2:5 then your concept of yourself is wholly **c.**.
T-31....VII.5:7 be **c.** to one that brings the peace of God.
W-pI....23.1:5 if your perception of the world is to be **c.**.
W-pI....23.5:1 world you see, because its cause can be **c.**.
W-pI....43.1:5 perception will become so **c.** and purified
W-pI....54.5:3 me the thinking of the world has been **c.**.
W-pI....65.8:5 see now that will be totally **c.** when you
W-pI....71.2:2 external circumstance or event were **c.**,
W-pI....93.5:8 It has not **c.** creation, nor reduced eternal
W-pI....95.1:5 believe that you have **c.** yourself already.
W-pI..110.1:3 **c.** the universe so that what God created
WpI..rIII.in4:1 as you have **c.** your mind about your goal.
W-pI 121.12:1 Look at this **c.** perception for a while, and
W-pI 126.10:1 thoughts are **c.** and false beliefs laid by.
W-pI..132.2:2 change your mind means you have **c.** the
W-pI 132.15:4 quietness be **c.** so that the world is freed,
W-pI..140.7:4 brings illusions to the truth is really **c.**.
W-pI 154.14:3 they have **c.** our minds about ourselves,
W-pI..162.4:3 wholly is it **c.** that it is now the treasury in
W-pI..165.4:3 how **c.** your mind will be before it comes
W-pI..167.3:5 it. But its origin is where it must be **c.**, if
W-pI..185.2:9 The world would be completely **c.**, should
W-pI..187.2:5 the thought seems to appear is **c.** in giving
W-pI..191.5:4 that **c.** his whole perspective of the world.
W-pI..191.7:5 is everything you look on wholly **c.**.
W-pI..193.3:4 them. The form alone is **c.**, with different
W-pI..196.6:2 Until this form is **c.**, there is no hope.
W-pI..196.7:1 its form must first be **c.** at least as much
W-pII.....3.1:4 has been **c.** to one of true forgiveness, will
W-pII.....3.5:1 the world has joined our **c.** perception.
W-pII.277.1:4 *He is not* **c.** *by what is changeable. He is not*
W-pII.282.2:3 *truth be* **c.** *by merely giving it another name?*
W-pII...10.1:1 false is false, and what is true has never **c.**.
W-pII...11.2:4 not be **c.** throughout the course of time,
W-pII.336.1:2 is restored after perception first is **c.**, and
W-pII...14.5:2 are **c.** about the aim for which we came,
M-8...........6:3 will report their **c.** appearances as before.
M-17.........8:9 The interpretation can be **c.** at last. Magic
C-5............3:5 can his life in any way be **c.** by sin and evil
C-6............1:2 or spirit, is eternal and has never **c.**. He
S-1..........II.8:2 a beginning, because the goal has never **c.**
S-3........IV.3:4 Whose Love has never **c.** and never will.

## Changeless 1

*changeless*

W-pI..112.2:2 *as I was, created by the* **C.** *like Himself. And I*

## changeless 50

*Changeless*

T-6.....IV.12:4 at change, but God created only the **c.**.
T-7..........I.7:2 not teach, because His creations are **c.**. He
T-7..........I.7:9 there, because its being is eternally **c.**. It
T-7.........V.7:9 Only by this can you learn that it *is* **c.**.
T-7.........V.8:2 You are recognizing the **c.** mind in your
T-7.........V.8:7 the **c.** in him you have not really changed
T-8.......IV.1:2 Will does not vacillate, being **c.** forever.
T-10.....in.3:10 accept His decision, for it is indeed **c.**, and
T-13..........V.1:2 fear. One is **c.** but continually exchanged,
T-13.....VI.3:2 to you now has no past, for He is **c.**, and
T-14.......V.1:6 you. This is forever **c.**. Accept, then, the
T-14.....XI.7:6 change Himself, for your Identity is **c.**.
T-15......I.15:6 His **c.** state is beyond time, for his purity
T-15.......V.4:3 They are not based on **c.** love alone. And
T-17...VIII.6:4 forever **c.** can you now withhold from it.
T-18.....VI.9:8 love must be forever like itself, **c.** forever,
T-24....VII.2:3 gone by. What is in him is **c.**, and your
T-25....VII.2:8 realize nothing is **c.** but the Will of God,
T-25..VII.4:10 create the **c.** if it does not rest on truth?
T-25....VII.6:6 as each defines the **c.** and eternal truth of
T-26....VII.3:4 made to take the place of **c.** knowledge.
T-28........I.9:6 are Its Effect, as **c.** and as perfect as Itself.
T-29.........V.h The **C.** Dwelling Place
T-29.......V.3:3 accept the **c.** and eternal that abide in him
T-29.....VI.3:3 is not fixed, however **c.** it appears to be.
T-29.....VI.3:4 for you, and establish it as **c.** and eternal.
T-29...VIII.6:5 Here does the **c.** change; the peace of God,
T-30...III.11:3 is no eternal sky, no **c.** star and no reality.
T-30......VIII.h **C.** Reality

T-30... VIII.1:2 Reality is c.. It does not deceive at all, and
T-30... VIII.1:6 Reality is c.. It is this that makes it real,
T-30... VIII.2:8 For that is c., and has no effects that
T-30... VIII.4:1 Reality is c.. Miracles but show what you
T-30... VIII.5:1 *Because* reality is c. is a miracle already
T-30... VIII.5:9 for He is the c. in your brother and in you.
T-30... VIII.6:4 replace the c. in him in your sight of him.
W-pI.....45.7:4 Foundation on which it rests is wholly c..
W-pI.....50.4:3 you; eternal, c. and forever unfailing. This
W-pI.....99.6:1 behind which is the c. and the sure. This
W-pI.122.13:4 as you see the c. in the heart of change;
W-pI...123.3:2 Give thanks as well that you are c., for the
W-pI...123.3:2 for the Son He loves is c. as Himself. Be
W-pI...163.4:3 of love and Heaven's perfect, c. constancy.
W-pI...167.8:4 the Thoughts of God remain forever c.,
W-pI...186.9:3 c. shares His attributes with His creation.
W-pI...197.5:3 never realize His gifts are sure, eternal, c.,
W-pII..305.1:1 and quiet, undisturbable and wholly c.,
W-pII....10.5:1 completely c. and forever pure. Therefore
M-18..........1:5 Reality is c.. Magic thoughts are but
C-4............7:1 And now God's *knowledge*, c., certain,

### changelessly 5

T-28...... I.14:7 Its Effects are c. eternal, beyond fear, and
T-30...... III.6:2 And what He knows exists forever, c.. For
T-30.....VII.1:4 world as with one purpose, c. established.
W-pI...122.5:3 C. it stands before you like an open door,
W-pI...167.8:4 with the power to extend forever c., but

### changelessness 15

T-7............V.h Healing and the C. of Mind
T-7.........V.7:7 no way contradicts the c. of mind as God
T-13......VI.3:2 changeless, and in His c. lies your release.
T-14......IX.2:8 Its c. is what makes it real. This cannot be
T-14......XI.7:7 miracle acknowledges His c. by seeing His
T-15......VI.6:4 awareness of c. comes swiftly as the veil of
T-24.....VII.2:3 c. is recognized in its acknowledgment.
T-25.....VII.1:4 And on its c. the world depends. The
T-29....... V.2:3 The c. of Heaven is in you, so deep within
T-29....... V.8:3 for here is not where c. is found. Let us be
T-29......VI.4:8 can set no end to its fulfillment nor its c..
T-30....III.10:5 of its c. and of its rest in its eternal home,
T-30... VIII.2:1 and cannot have the c. reality entails. The
T-30... VIII.2:3 Your brother has a c. in him beyond
W-pI...152.9:3 its c. and its eternal wholeness, all-

### changes 44

T-1........ I.45:2 produce undreamed of c. in situations of
T-4........VI.5:5 as he c. his mind about its worth. I am
T-7......... II.4:3 what he translates, never c. the meaning.
T-7.........V.8:4 Holy Spirit in him that never c. His Mind.
T-8...........I.4:3 with the c. your learning has brought you
T-8... VIII.1:13 knowledge never c., so its constellation is
T-14......VII.5:7 merely c. them into a call for what you
T-15....... I.15:7 stands still in his holiness, and c. not.
T-18... VIII.4:4 And what it thinks it is in no way c. its
T-20....... V.6:2 It never c.. All that it ever held or will ever
T-21..... II.12:5 It c. nothing in creation, depends entirely
T-21.....VII.4:7 c. so it is impossible even to recognize
T-23..... II.18:7 It never c.. Can you paint rosy lips upon a
T-24......VI.3:5 God c. not His Mind about His Son with
T-26.....VII.3:4 Perception c., made to take the place of
T-27.........I.9:3 picture c. not the body into something it
T-30.....IV.6:4 that mighty c. have been quickly brought
T-30.....VII.1:3 it cannot be that meaning c. constantly,
T-31..... V.16:2 will show the c. in your own relationships
T-31.....VII.6:4 Who understands the c. that it needs to
W-pI.....31.1:3 used more and more, with c. as indicated.
W-pI.107.10:2 you the promise of the c. which the truth
W-pI...110.1:3 made no c. in yourself that have reality,
W-pI...127.6:4 all the c. that you think are part of human
W-pI...132.5:5 and that it c. as you change your mind.
W-pI...138.7:2 hell is real, hope c. to despair, and life
W-pI...167.9:3 the c. wrought are substanceless, and all
W-pI.167.10:3 Who c. life because he shuts his eyes, or
WpI.. rV.in4:5 never c. from Its constant state of union
W-pII..302.1:6 *Christ's vision c. darkness into light, for fear*
M-in..........4:4 here does follow it until he c. his mind,
M-1...........3:4 But the content of the course never c.. Its
M-4.....I.A.3:6 call for c. in what seem to be external
M-4.....I.A.3:7 These c. are always helpful. When the
M-4.....I.A.4:2 that the c. in his life are always helpful, he
M-9..............h C. REQUIRED IN THE LIFE SITUATION
M-9...........1:1 C. are required in the *minds* of God's
M-9...........1:2 may or may not involve c. in the external
M-9...........1:4 is most unlikely that c. in attitudes would
M-25.........5:7 individual c. his mind about its purpose,
P-2.........in.1:1 is a process that c. the view of the self. At
P-2.........in.3:3 patient hopes to learn how to get the c. he
P-2...........I.2:6 The c. the ego seeks to make are not really
P-2...........I.2:6 the ego seeks to make are not really c..

### changing 29

*See also* never-changing
T-3......... V.4:8 The idea of "c. your image" recognizes
T-3......... V.7:7 reorganizing, shifting and c.. Evaluation
T-4...........I.4:6 undo it by not c. your mind about it. If
T-4......... II.2:5 is as effective in c. relative perception as is
T-4.........IV.2:1 change your mind by c. your behavior,
T-7......... V.7:6 That is because, by c. his mind, he has
T-7......... V.8:8 By c. your mind about his *for* him, you
T-14....... X.5:1 c. pattern that never rests and is never
T-18....... II.2:4 the world, and c. it to suit the ego better.
T-21...VII.12:6 it. And if he sees his happiness as ever c.,
T-21...VII.13:1 in c. form that shifts with time and place,
T-27...... III.1:6 on it without c. it into something it is not.
T-28....... V.7:3 with vague uncertain forms and c. shapes,
T-30... VIII.2:4 It is obscured by c. views of him that you
T-31...... III.6:6 keep in chains, to the illusion of a c. love,
T-31.....VII.1:3 lasts, and c. concepts is salvation's task.
W-pI.....23.2:5 point in c. your thoughts about the world.
W-pI.....23.2:6 Here you are c. the cause. The effect will
W-pI...127.2:2 not see that c. love must be impossible.
W-pI...132.8:3 it was by merely c. all the thoughts that
W-pI...153.1:1 You who feel threatened by this c. world,
W-pI...181.3:4 of time wherein we practice c. our intent.
W-pI...185.3:5 gainer merely shift about in c. patterns, as
W-pI...192.4:3 but hardly c. him who learns at all.
W-pII......5.3:5 will obey by c. what we think that it is for.
M-27.........1:6 the c. and unsure; the undependable and
M-27.........7:5 deceived by the "reality" of any c. form.
P-2.........in.3:3 to get the changes he wants without c. his
P-2...........I.1:4 held out to them that meets the c. need.

### channel 8

T-1......... II.5:3 the direct c. from God to you open for
T-4.........VII.3:7 thus establishing it forever as a c. for the
T-10...... III.2:5 God has only one c. for healing because
T-15... VIII.5:5 And so He keeps this c. open to receive
W-pI...76.10:6 only Son, created as His c. for creation;
W-pI...184.5:1 direction for the mind to c. its perception.
M-7...........2:1 to be a c. for healing he has succeeded.
M-25.........6:6 also a great c. of hope and healing in the

### channelize 1

W-pI.....71.4:3 than to c. all your efforts in searching for

### channelized 2

T-2......... V.7:7 awareness is merely c. toward correction.
T-7.........IV.3:7 is because they are c. in one direction, or

### channels 10

T-1......... V.1:3 loveless and miraculous c. of expression.
T-4........ VI.6:3 ego, and I do not choose God's c. wrongly
T-4........ VI.6:7 My chosen c. cannot fail, because I will
T-4.........VII.6:7 His Love is blocked when His c. are closed
T-5.........in.3:5 children are worthy c. of His beautiful joy
T-6......... V.1:5 communication c. are not open to Him,
T-13....... XI.8:3 c. of reaching out cannot be wholly closed
W-pI...76.11:1 Let us today open God's c. to Him, and
W-pI...197.9:4 all the countless c. which extend this Self.
M-25.........2:2 the small range of c. the world recognizes.

### chant 1

T19..IV.B.16:3 disciples c. the body's praise continually,

### chants 2

T-29...VII.10:5 to drown His Voice in c. of deep despair
W-pI.140.10:1 our c. and bits of magic in whatever form

### chaos 39

T-4........ VI.3:3 while another brings c. and disaster needs
T-6...... V.C.4:6 your consistency is called on despite c..
T-6...... V.C.4:7 c. and consistency cannot coexist for long
T-8.......VII.9:2 other, so that it appears to be ruled by c..
T-10...... IV.4:8 exist. "Laws of c." is a meaningless term.
T-10...... IV.5:3 gods do not bring c.; you are endowing
T-10...... IV.5:3 chaos; you are endowing them with c.,
T-11..... V.13:6 ego will always substitute c. for meaning,
T-14........X.5:5 into c. shows you that you are not an ego,
T-14........X.5:6 For the ego *is* c., and if it were all of you,
T-15....... V.1:6 that without the ego, all would be c.. Yet I
T-17........II.6:2 reaching quietly and gently across c.,
T-21.....in.1:12 And where there is no meaning, there is c.
T-23.......... II.h The Laws of C.
T-23........II.1:1 The "laws" of c. can be brought to light,
T-23........II.4:1 The *second* law of c., dear indeed to every
T-23........II.6:1 arrogance on which the laws of c. stand
T-23........II.6:5 belief that seems to make c. eternal. For if
T-23........II.9:2 This leads to the *fourth* law of c., which, if
T-23......II.12:3 a *final* principle of c. comes to the "rescue.
T-23......II.14:6 is the goal the laws of c. serve. These are
T-23......II.15:1 These do not seem to be the goals of c.,
T-23......II.15:3 C. is lawlessness, and has no laws. To be
T-23......II.16:5 No law of c. could compel belief but for
T-23......II.20:1 The laws of c. govern all illusions. Their
T-23......II.20:3 of c. are the laws of order as do the others.
T-23......II.20:7 in love, in any form, attests to c. as reality.
T-23......II.21:1 the belief in sin, the faith in c. must follow
T-23......II.21:3 The steps to c. do follow neatly from their
T-24...... III.3:1 upsets your world, and hurls it into c..
T-29....VIII.6:5 given to all living things, give way to c..
T-29...... IX.6:7 is afraid of all the c. in a world he thinks is
W-pI.....53.2:4 Only c. rules a world that represents
W-pI.....53.2:4 chaotic thinking, and c. has no laws. I
W-pI... 136.9:3 and c. sits in triumph on His throne.
W-pI... 152.7:1 To think that God made c., contradicts
W-pI... 191.2:4 You look on c. and proclaim it is yourself.
W-pI... 200.2:1 what can only hurt; of making peace of c.,
S-2.........I.10:5 to ascend above the world of c. into peace

### chaotic 10

T-8........ IX.9:3 of meaning in a c. thought system *is* the
T-10...... IV.4:5 else is merely lawless and therefore c.. Yet
T-10...... IV.4:9 and the c. is without meaning because it
T-12...... III.9:6 The world you made is therefore totally c.
T-14........X.9:2 joining them is incoherent and utterly c..
T-18........II.2:1 Dreams are c. because they are governed
T-23........II.1:2 C. laws are hardly meaningful, and
T-23........II.2:1 The *first* c. law is that the truth is different
T-30...... IV.2:5 nor mean his world is made c. and unsafe.
W-pI.....53.2:4 rules a world that represents c. thinking,

### chapter 1

W-pI.153.14:4 day bring the last c. closer to the world,

### characteristic 11

T-2..........II.4:7 which is the inherent c. of other defenses.
T-4......... V.6:5 The ego's c. busyness with nonessentials
T-7..........II.2:8 The outstanding c. of the laws of mind as
T-8......VIII.2:5 c. of every end that the ego has accepted
T-9.......... V.7:1 the c. "impossible situation" to which the
T-9.......VII.2:7 obviousness is the essential c. of reality.

T-9......VIII.6:6 shifting and extremes are its essential **c.**.
T-14....... X.9:1 is **c.** of the ego's judgments. Separately,
M-in .......... 1:2 world. The reversal is **c.**. It seems as if the
M-4 .......... 1:6 become **c.** of all teachers of God who have
P-2..........I.3:1 be **c.** of a therapist as well as of a patient.

### characteristically 4
T-4....... II.8:12 and so ambiguous in form and **c.** good-
T-11..... V.13:3 **c.** contradictory approach of the ego to
T-11..... V.14:3 and with **c.** circular reasoning concludes
T-13....... II.1:2 Yet, **c.**, the ego attempts to get rid of guilt

### characteristics 5
T-12....... V.4:4 you wanted to retain the **c.** of creation,
W-pI..... 61.1:5 refer to any of the **c.** with which you have
M-4 .............h ARE THE **C.** OF GOD'S TEACHERS?
M-4 .......... 1:3 acquired the deeper **c.** that will establish
M-4 .......... 2:2 teachers of God have the following **c.**:

### characterizes 1
W-pI..... 74.6:1 Joy **c.** peace. By this experience will you

### characters 1
W-pI... 193.3:4 with different **c.** and different themes,

### charge 19
T-1......... II.4:6 has placed me in **c.** of the Sonship, which
T-1........ III.1:1 I am in **c.** of the process of Atonement,
T-4...... IV.10:4 I am in **c.** of the Second Coming, and my
T-4........ VI.6:5 before that I am in **c.** of the Atonement.
T-6........ IV.9:5 This leaves you in **c.** of the Kingdom, with
T-6...... V.A.6:3 you place yourself in **c.** of the journey,
T-18..........I.9:1 has taken **c.** of everything at your request,
T-18........ V.1:5 Put yourself not in **c.** of this, for you
T-31.... VIII.2:6 in you is given **c.** of everything you do.
W-pI..... 70.2:3 way. Today's idea places you in **c.** of the
W-pI... 70.10:3 You are in **c.** of your salvation. You are in
W-pI... 70.10:4 You are in **c.** of the salvation of the world.
W-pI..... 71.9:6 Give Him full **c.** of the rest of the practice
WpI. rIV.in5:4 to place His Mind in **c.** of all the thoughts
WpI rVI.in.7:2 I place you in His **c.**, and let Him teach
WpII...361-5.h You. Be You in **c.**. For I would follow You,
WpII361-5.1:4 He is in **c.** by my request. And He will
P-2....... VII.4:4 he thought he was in **c.** of the therapeutic
S-2......... III.3:4 Let Him take **c.** of how you would forgive,

### charged 1
W-pI....... 3.1:6 may have emotionally **c.** meaning for you.

### charitable 5
T-4......... II.6:1 lasting sense of abundance can be truly **c.**.
T-23...... III.2:1 however lovely and **c.** it may seem to be, a
W-pI..... 35.6:9 *out. I see myself as* **c.**. *I see myself as virtuous.*
W-pI... 126.3:3 He has not earned your **c.** tolerance,
W-pI... 126.4:1 forgiveness basically unsound; a **c.** whim,

### charity 28
T-2......... V.9:4 This is because healing rests on **c.**, and
T-2......... V.9:4 **c.** is a way of perceiving the perfection of
T-2......... V.9:6 **C.** is really a weaker reflection of a much
T-2......... V.9:6 any form of **c.** you can conceive of as yet.
T-2......... V.9:7 **C.** is essential to right-mindedness in the
T-2........ V.10:1 **C.** is a way of looking at another as if he
T-2........ V.10:2 himself, or he would have no need of **c.**.
T-2........ V.10:3 The **c.** that is accorded him is both an
T-2....... V.10:4 making it apparent that **c.** still lies within
T-2....... V.10:6 The miracle, as an expression of **c.**, can
T-4...........I.3:3 must fear, because it does not share my **c.**
T-4......... II.4:4 creations,–with love, protection and **c.**.
T-4......... II.7:2 its grasp, and **c.** becomes impossible. The
T-16....... II.7:8 with greater **c.** on whom God loves with
T19..IV.A.14:4 will be as careful to let no little act of **c.**,
T-20 ... III.11:4 Looking with **c.** within, what can it fear
T-22 ..... VI.9:1 to look on what your Father loves with **c.**?
T-26 ..... IV.1:4 And what is **c.** within the world gives way
T-27 .......II.1:8 To forgive may be an act of **c.**, but not his
T-27 .. VII.16:3 in light of **c.** and kindness offered you.
W-pI..... 56.2:6 the world and on myself with **c.** and love.
W-pI... 126.3:2 You give **c.** to one unworthy, merely to
W-pI... 159.8:4 and kindly care Christ's **c.** provides. They
W-pI... 189.1:7 hope, and blessed with perfect **c.** and love
W-pII . 249.1:5 of joy, abundance, **c.** and endless giving.
S-2..........II.1:2 concealed beneath what seems like **c.**. Yet
S-2..........II.4:3 may pass as meekness and as **c.** instead of
S-3...........I.5:3 ask amiss and seeming **c.** forgive to kill,

### charms 2
T-31 ...... V.2:7 that smiles and **c.** and even seems to love.
W-pI. 140.10:1 aside our amulets, our **c.** and medicines,

### chasten 1
T-25 . VIII.11:9 love is fair, and cannot **c.** without cause.

### cheat 1
W-pI... 197.1:5 which would **c.** you of defenses, to ensure

### cheats 1
T-14 ..... IV.5:6 this frantic and insane attempt that **c.** you

### check 1
W-pI... 126.6:2 you see it, it is but a **c.** upon overt attack,

### cheek 1
T-5 ....... IV.4:6 is the meaning of "turning the other **c.**."

### cheeks 1
W-pI..... 69.6:4 feel them resting on your **c.** and forehead

### cheer 1
T-4 ......I.13:11 *world. That is why you should be of good* **c.**.

### cherish 34
T-13 ......I.10:4 And you who **c.** guilt must also believe it,
T-13 ..... VI.1:5 him that you made and **c.** instead of him.
T-13 .... VII.2:2 of seeing, and depends on what you **c.**.
T-13 ..... IX.4:1 brings a re-evaluation of everything you **c.**
T-15 ..... IV.2:3 you desire it not and **c.** littleness instead,
T-15 ..... VI.1:6 as you accept the possibility, and **c.** it,
T19..IV.A.2:10 little remnant of attack you **c.** still against
T19..IV.A.11:2 and **c.** every scrap of evil and of sin that
T-21 ..........I.7:5 any melody you taught yourself to **c.** since
T-24 ..... III.2:1 Whatever form of specialness you **c.**, you
T-25 .......II.2:1 strange that you should **c.** still some hope
T-25 ...... V.6:1 the Son of God may **c.** toward himself, is
T-26 ..... IX.2:1 and left without a single one you **c.** still?
T-27 ........I.8:2 joys and **c.** little pleasures where you can.
T-27 ....III.12:5 a different purpose from the one you **c.**,
T-28 ........I.5:6 And if it seems to serve to **c.** ancient hate,
T-29 ........I.2:6 the little gap must bring to those who **c.** it
T-31 .. VII.12:4 But while you **c.** it, you will behold your
W-pI..... 59.1:6 Let me not **c.** illusions about myself. I am
W-pI..... 65.1:4 purpose you hold while you still **c.** others.
W-pI..... 68.5:4 you do not **c.** grievances of some sort.
W-pI..... 90.1:2 some form of grievance that I would **c.**.
W-pI... 125.5:3 not **c.** the illusions which you hold about
W-pI... 128.4:2 Nothing is here to **c.**. Nothing here is
W-pI... 162.5:3 **c.** sin when holiness like this has blessed
W-pI... 163.6:1 few you would not **c.** and would yet avoid,
W-pI... 185.8:1 your mind, to find the dreams you **c.** still.
W-pI. 189.10:7 *from You, and* **c.** *no beliefs of what we are, or*
W-pI... 199.5:1 **C.** today's idea, and practice it today and
W-pII . 276.2:2 *brothers, who are given me to* **c.** *as my own,*
W-pII . 288.1:6 *Let me not* **c.** *it within my heart, or I will lose*
W-pII . 316.2:3 *their worth, and* **c.** *only them as what I want.*
P-2......... in.3:2 as the patient may **c.** false self-concepts,
S-1........ III.2:3 made out of fear by those who **c.** guilt.

### cherished 25
T-3 ....... VI.5:7 so debilitating would be so deeply **c.**. Yet
T-17 ... III.10:7 such dreams are **c.** have excluded me. Let
T-19 ..... III.8:7 be **c.** but a little while before it vanishes.
T19 ...IV.C.9:4 **c.** by the Holy Spirit and protected by
T-20 .... VII.5:5 remain unquestioned while the end is **c.**.
T-21 ..... III.2:4 nothing is so **c.** and protected as is a goal
T-22 .......II.4:4 One illusion **c.** and defended against the
T-23 ........I.1:4 is impossible unless belief in victory is **c.**.
T-24 ........I.3:1 All that is ever **c.** as a hidden belief, to be
T-25 ..... IX.2:4 anyone, but **c.** and preserved in Heaven,
T-26 ..... IV.4:3 is lost, and none is **c.** more than any other
T-27 .... VII.8:4 a victim to a dream conceived and **c.** by a
T-28 ..... III.3:5 sickness is kept carefully protected, **c.**,
T-30 ..... IV.4:9 They must be neither **c.** nor attacked, but
W-pI .... 50.2:2 are **c.** to ensure a body identification.
W-pI .. 129.2:4 all things that you have **c.** for a while. No
W-pI .. 135.7:4 Such attempts, ridiculous yet deeply **c.**,
W-pI .. 137.7:3 the laws can be no longer **c.** nor obeyed.
W-pI .. 140.5:2 holiness can not be found where sin is **c.**.
W-pI .. 183.7:3 Him with names of idols **c.** by the world.
W-pII ..... 3.1:3 than the thought that gave it birth is **c.**.
W-pII . 256.1:3 If sin had not been **c.** by the mind, what
P-2........ IV.9:5 attacking the patient's most **c.** possession;
P-2........ VI.4:4 Here is all sickness **c.**, but without the
P-3..........II.6:4 The good is saved; indeed is **c.**. But only

### cherishes 8
T-14 ..... III.5:5 keeps it and **c.** it by holding it against you
T-23 .......II.8:7 which does not value what the ego **c.**.
T-25 .......II.6:5 the picture, and **c.** the frame instead of it.
T-25 .......II.9:4 God **c.** creation as the perfect Father that
W-pI .... 96.7:4 Thoughts your Self holds dear and **c.** for
W-pI .. 101.5:3 which **c.** no lingering belief that you have
W-pI .. 161.9:1 eyes behold in one whom Heaven **c.**, the
P-1............ 3:4 he **c.** it, defends it, and is sometimes even

### cherishing 3
T-26 .. VII.12:5 to prove your innocence, while **c.** attack.
W-pI .... 25.3:3 In **c.** them, therefore, you have no goals at
W-pI .. 73.11:7 go, instead of **c.** them and hiding them in

### chest 1
W-pI 134.16:3 up, a lightening of weight across your **c.**, a

### chief 6
T-15 .......V.2:1 The past is the ego's **c.** learning device,
T-16 .......V.2:3 special love relationship is the ego's **c.**
T-17 ..... IV.5:8 relationship, which is its **c.** defense, must
M-16 ......... 3:8 contains, individual need becomes the **c.**
M-25 ......... 2:5 the **c.** barriers to direct experience of the
P-3..........II.1:4 of one sort or another as their **c.** function.

### Child 10
*child*
W-pI .. 182.4:3 a **C.** in you Who seeks His Father's house,
W-pI .. 182.4:5 Where this **C.** shall go is holy ground. It is
W-pI .. 182.5:1 It is this **C.** in you your Father knows as
W-pI .. 182.5:2 It is this **C.** Who knows His Father. He
W-pI .. 182.6:1 This **C.** needs your protection. He is far
W-pI .. 182.7:1 This **C.** is your defenselessness; your
W-pI .. 182.9:2 to become a little **C.** that you might learn
W-pI 182.10:1 Christ is reborn as but a little **C.** each
W-pI 182.10:2 that what he would protect is but this **C.**,
W-pI 182.12:5 The holy **C.** remains with you. His home

## child 59

*Child*

T-1.......VII.2:1 C. of God, you were created to create the
T-2...........I.1:6 No c. of God can lose this ability because
T-3...........I.2:7 you," and feels exonerated in beating a c..
T-3.......VII.1:7 made by a c. of God is without power. It is
T-4........I.13:2 A father can safely leave a c. with an elder
T-5.........in.3:6 It is impossible for a c. of God to love his
T-5.......II.12:6 C. of God, my message is for you, to hear
T-5......VI.10:3 There can be no case against a c. of God,
T-5......VI.11:5 Is not a c. of God worth patience? I have
T-6........IV.6:1 ego raises: You are a c. of God, a priceless
T-6.........V.3:3 and confusion a c. would experience if he
T-7.......VII.7:1 One c. of God is the only teacher
T-7........XI.3:2 Is it worthy to be a home for a c. of God?
T-8.......VII.1:7 When a c. of God thinks of himself in this
T-9......IV.12:1 Behold, my c., reality is here. It belongs
T-11......III.3:1 O my c., if you knew what God wills for
T-11...VIII.7:1 Little c. of God, you do not understand
T-11...VIII.8:1 Beautiful c. of God, you are asking only
T-11.VIII.13:3 When a c. is helped to translate his "ghost
T-11.VIII.14:1 You, my c., are afraid of your brothers
T-12.......II.4:4 It is easy to help an uncertain c., for he
T-12.......II.4:6 Little c., you are hiding your head under
T-12.......II.6:1 can defeat a c. of God in his purpose. For
T-12.......VI.6:1 Every c. of God is one in Christ, for his
T-12.....VII.1:6 In every c. of God His blessing lies, and in
T-13.......II.9:1 Little c., this is not so. Your "guilty secret
T-13.......V.7:1 Little c., would you offer this to your
T-13....VI.10:1 C. of Light, you know not that the light is
T-13.......X.9:9 and He offers mercy to every c. of God, as
T-14......XI.4:3 already learned for every c. of light by
T-15......III.9:1 Holy c. of God, when will you learn that
T19...IV.C.8:2 brother, c. of our Father, this is a *dream* of
T-21......IV.8:3 Little c., innocent of sin, follow in
T-21...VII.3:11 c. becomes a giant and a mouse roars like
T-22.........I.8:2 This c. will teach you what you do not
T-22......VI.6:1 C. of peace, the light *has* come to you. The
T-24...VII.1:10 c. of earth on whom such love is lavished?
T-28......III.8:1 Be not afraid, my c., but let your world be
T-29......IX.4:3 you. Little c., the light is there. You do but
T-29......IX.5:2 the c. who thought he made them real.
T-29......IX.5:5 This does the c. believe, because he fears
T-29......IX.6:4 game, in which the c. becomes the father,
T-29......IX.6:4 but with the little wisdom of a c.. What
T-29......IX.6:6 Except he judges this as does a c., who
T-30......IV.2:2 A c. is frightened when a wooden head
T-30......IV.3:6 c. who learns they are no threat to him.
T-30......IV.4:6 They are but toys, my c., so do not grieve
T-31......VI.7:1 Your will be done, you holy c. of God. It
WpI.rIV.in4:3 No more than can a c. who throws a stick
W-pI...153.6:4 folly, or a silly game a tired c. might play,
WpI..rV.in2:5 *a little c. along a way he does not understand*
W-pI.182.11:4 He has come as does a little c., who must
M-3............2:2 a c. who is not looking where he is going
M-3............2:5 will not scold the c. for bumping into him
M-29...........6:9 father does not let his c. harm himself, or
C-2.............8:2 as a loving mother sings her c. to rest. Is
S-2........III.2:1 You c. of God, the gifts of God are yours,
S-3........IV.8:6 Listen, My c., your Father calls to you. Do
S-3........IV.9:4 How lovely are you, c. of Holiness! How

## child's 2

T-4........I.13:2 involves no confusion about the c. origin.
T-4........I.13:3 can protect the c. body and his ego, but

## childhood 4

T-29......IX.6:1 a time when c. should be passed and gone
W-pI...182.4:1 is your c. home that you would find again.
W-pI...182.4:2 c. of your body, and its place of shelter,
W-pI...182.4:4 This c. is eternal, with an innocence that

## childish 8

T-8.....VIII.1:2 The ego's definitions of anything are c.,
T-27...VIII.8:3 How c. is the petulant device to keep your
T-29......IX.5:1 Nightmares are c. dreams. The toys have
T-29......IX.7:5 is not, for c. things have all been put away
T-29....IX.10:2 So do your c. terrors melt away, and
W-pI...153.8:1 We will not play such c. games today. For
W-pI.153.13:3 and lock our quaint and c. thoughts of sin
W-pII......4.4:2 yet what sin perceives is but a c. game.

## childless 1

T-11.........I.5:6 God is not incomplete, and He is not c..

## children 58

T-1.........I.31:3 c. of God are holy and the miracle honors
T-1.......III.1:10 is the natural profession of the c. of God,
T-1.........V.3:3 All His c. have His total Love, and all His
T-1.........V.3:4 "Except ye become as little c." means that
T-2...........I.2:4 that the c. of the Father inherit from Him.
T-2........III.5:1 The c. of God are entitled to the perfect
T-3........III.7:9 God knows His c. with perfect certainty.
T-3........VI.8:6 eager to undo it, not to punish His c., but
T-3.......VII.3:6 If God knows His c., and I assure you that
T-5.........in.3:5 God's holy c. are worthy channels of His
T-5...........I.6:1 of His c. because they had made them.
T-5...........I.6:2 also blessed His c. with a way of thinking
T-5.........II.1:2 c. of God were before healing was needed,
T-5.........II.6:8 God did not leave His c. comfortless, even
T-5.......IV.8:14 His quiet c. are His blessed Sons. The
T-5.......VII.4:5 of His c. who believe they are lost to Him.
T-6.........V.1:5 and know that His c. are wholly joyous.
T-6.........V.1:8 "My c. sleep and must be awakened."
T-6.........V.2:1 How can you wake c. in a more kindly
T-6.........V.2:2 are not real, because c. believe in magic.
T-6.........V.4:1 errors because He does not frighten c.,
T-6.........V.4:1 and those who lack wisdom *are* c.. Yet He
T-6.........V.4:3 C. *do* confuse fantasy and reality, and they
T-7...........I.1:7 Parents give birth to c., but children do
T-7...........I.1:7 but c. do not give birth to parents. They
T-7...........I.1:8 They do, however, give birth to their c.,
T-7.......V.10:8 the most holy c. of a most holy Father?
T-7........XI.3:9 over His c. and denies them nothing. Yet
T-7......XI.7:10 of God includes all His Sons and their c.,
T-8.........V.4:5 to all His c. because I received it of Him
T-9.......IV.11:7 C. may believe them, and so, for a while,
T-10......III.2:1 Comforter can there be for the sick c. of
T-10......III.2:6 Link with all His c. joins them together,
T-10.....V.12:1 If God knows His c. as wholly sinless, it is
T-10.....V.12:2 God knows His c. as wholly without pain,
T-10.....V.12:3 If God knows His c. to be wholly joyous, it
T-11......III.6:1 The c. of light cannot abide in darkness,
T-11...VIII.2:1 The Bible tells you to become as little c..
T-11...VIII.2:2 children. Little c. recognize that they do
T-11.VIII.13:1 C. perceive frightening ghosts and
T-11.VIII.14:4 minds of c. who do not understand reality
T-12.........II.4:1 the frightening perceptions of little c.,
T-12.....VII.1:6 blessing of the c. of God is His blessing to
T-13.......in.2:5 C. are born into it through pain and in
T-13.......in.3:2 For no Father could subject His c. to this
T-14......IV.9:1 The c. of Heaven live in the light of the
T-14.......X.1:1 or between His c. and their own, the
T-29......IX.4:5 with. Who has need of toys but c.? They
T-29......IX.6:2 Seek not to retain the toys of c.. Put them
W-pI.153.12:1 thought of as a game that happy c. play. It
W-pI.153.12:2 It was designed by One Who loves His c.,
W-pI.153.12:5 when c. come to see the benefits salvation
W-pI.153.13:3 minds of Heaven's c. and the Son of God.
W-pI.167.10:1 Let us today be c. of the truth, and not
W-pII..253.1:6 this world to my creations, c. of my will,
M-28.........4:7 And we, God's c., rise up from the dust
S-3........IV.6:1 Come unto Me, My c., once again,
S-3........IV.8:1 Help Me to wake My c. from the dream

## children's 6

T-18......IX.7:4 would play the game of c. make-believe.
T-29......IX.6:4 The dream of judgment is a c. game, in
T-30......IV.2:1 gods you made are blown-up c. toys. A
T-30......IV.4:9 but merely looked upon as c. toys without
W-pII......4.5:2 we not put away these sharp-edged c. toys
M-13.........4:3 an adult resent the giving up of c. toys?

## chill 3

T-20......II.10:3 perfectly protected from the cold c. of
T-25....VIII.6:6 deep suspicion and the c. of fear comes
W-pI.....97.1:5 No c. of fear can enter, for your mind has

## choice 307

T-1........III.5:3 right c. is inevitable if you remember this:
T-1.........V.5:3 its c. is that it cannot serve two masters. If
T-2.........I.3:10 In reality this is your only c., because your
T-2........VI.2:6 is only at this level that you can exercise c.
T-2........VI.4:9 ask me if your c. is in accord with mine. If
T-3........IV.7:9 Without them your c. is certain. Sane
T-3.......IV.7:11 but I can help you make your own right c.
T-3........VI.2:1 The c. to judge rather than to know is the
T-4...........I.5:6 this c. because of the nature of its origin.
T-4........VI.3:2 this c. is the only sane one you can make.
T-4........VI.3:3 that one c. brings peace and joy while
T-5..........II.5:4 c. for the Holy Spirit is the choice for God
T-5..........II.5:4 choice for the Holy Spirit is the c. for God
T-5..........II.6:4 power is unlimited and c. is meaningless.
T-5..........II.8:2 mind that always speaks for the right c.,
T-5..........II.9:4 This decision is the c. to share it, because
T-5..........II.9:5 the one c. that resembles true creation. I
T-6...........I.8:3 There is no c. in this, because only you
T-6.....V.C.3:5 therefore makes the ultimate c. inevitable
T-6....V.C.4:10 will finally liberate your mind from c.,
T-7........III.4:2 true, you are accepting conflict as your c..
T-7........III.4:3 choice. Is it really a c.? It seems to be, but
T-7......VI.13:2 joy. This is not God's c. but yours. If your
T-7....VIII.1:10 This c. is up to you, but it is not up to you
T-7.........X.4:5 that an impossible c. is open to you, and
T-7.........X.6:6 His Will with me is not really open to c.,
T-8.........I.5:10 exist, and gives them no rationale for c..
T-8..........II.1:1 *is* a rationale for c.. Only one Teacher
T-8........III.6:6 What other c. could you make? Having
T-8........III.6:7 Having made this c. you will understand
T-8.......IV.4:11 Without this c. you could not be healed
T-8........VI.2:4 the c. of which is true is not yours to make
T-8........VI.7:7 c. does make the Son's function unknown
T-8......VIII.4:5 c. of witnesses should be suspect from the
T-8......VIII.8:8 without violating your freedom of c.,
T-9........IV.8:3 poor c. as a teacher of salvation. Anyone
T-9.........V.8:9 for helping, and the wrong c. will not help
T-9.......VII.6:6 dictated this c. the lament is inevitable.
T-10.....V.14:2 to you to be desirable the concept of c.,
T-10.....V.14:4 Time itself is your c.. If you would
T-10.....V.14:7 your c. is determined by what you value.
T-12.....V.7:11 can learn it because it *is* your c. to do so.
T-14......III.4:2 The ego is the c. for guilt; the Holy Spirit
T-14......III.4:2 the Holy Spirit the c. for guiltlessness.
T-14....III.15:6 Madness may be your c., but not your
T-15........II.4:5 your c. whether they support the ego or
T-15.......III.2:1 that your c. is your evaluation of yourself.
T-15........X.5:5 This is the c. you think you have, and the
T-15......XI.1:6 the c. between them is nothing more than
T-16......III.2:4 are immediately accepted as your c.. And
T-16......IV.4:6 This is the c. they see. And love, to them,
T-16......IV.5:5 And then the only c. remaining possible
T-16......IV.5:6 in the c. between truth and illusion. Seen
T-16......IV.5:8 the instant the c. seems to be one between
T-16......IV.5:8 illusions, but this c. does not matter.
T-16......IV.5:9 Where one c. is as dangerous as the other,
T-16..........V.h The C. for Completion
T-16.....V.14:3 are failing to make the simple c. between
T-16.....V.16:1 it is but the c. between truth and illusion.
T-16.....V.16:3 How simple does this c. become when it
T-16.....VII.1:5 the past? Every such c. is made because of
T-17......III.9:3 the c. depends on which you value more.
T-17.....V.10:1 freedom heard, in joyous echo of your c..
T-17.....V.10:3 not your c. will leave you comfortless, for
T-18........II.8:6 the c. between the truth and *all* illusions.
T-19........II.8:4 before you allow yourself to make this c..
T-19........II.8:5 not lightly, for it is the c. of hell or Heaven
T19..IV.B.11:2 Here is your c., and it *is* free. But all that
T19.IV.D.10:8 on, only to return and make the c. again.
T19.IV.D.13:4 will receive of him according to your c..
T19.IV.D.20:6 he will recognize his c. by what he gives,
T19.IV.D.21:1 this far because the journey was your c..

T-20....... V.4:7 Vision or judgment is your c., but never
T-20.... VI.11:6 is also here he makes his c. again between
T-20..... VII.7:4 of the other, for each one is a c. of purpose,
T-20.... VIII.5:4 the perfect c. to call upon for strength?
T-21.......in.2:5 There is no c. that lies between these two
T-21.......in.2:6 will see the witness to the c. you made,
T-21.........I.4:7 believing that their c. is that or nothing.
T-21........ II.3:2 that come to him were not his c.. His
T-21...... III.5:6 This mad direction was your c., and by
T-21....... V.1:7 It. Perception is a c. and not a fact. But on
T-21....... V.1:8 But on this c. depends far more than you
T-21....... V.2:2 of it needs your help, because it is your c..
T-21....... V.3:1 your freedom lies, awaiting but your c..
T-21...... VI.4:2 if it be the c. of the insane to listen to it.
T-21...... VI.6:2 tell him, by your c., that he is damned;
T-21...... VI.6:4 you choose he be is but your c. for you.
T-21..... VII.7:1 Forget not that the c. of sin or truth,
T-21..... VII.7:1 is the c. of whether to attack or heal. For
T-21..... VII.7:5 decision but the c. whether to see him
T-21..... VII.7:7 But what you want to see must be your c..
T-22....... II.8:6 understanding, but *when* must be your c..
T-22...... IV.2:1 you can go back and make the other c..
T-22...... IV.2:3 A c. made with the power of Heaven to
T-22.... VI.1:10 will make the other serve his c. as means
T-23.........I.9:3 Thus, conflict is the c. between illusions,
T-23....... II.6:4 and He has but the c. whether to take his
T-23...... IV.5:5 Here murder is your c.. Yet from above,
T-23...... IV.5:6 the c. is miracles instead of murder. And
T-23...... IV.5:7 this c. shows you the battle is not real,
T-23.... IV.5:11 be recognized if murder is your c.?
T-23...... IV.9:8 the c. of miracles or murder hard to make
T-24...... VI.9:2 any kind, is all the other c. can offer you.
T-24..... VII.4:5 For in that c. lie both its health and harm.
T-24. VII.11:11 is not bound to specialness but by your c..
T-24. VII.11:12 And it is given you to make a different c.,
T-25.........I.3:1 is a c. of what you want yourself to be; the
T-25....... II.2:6 Yet is this hopelessness your c., while you
T-25....... III.h Perception and C.
T-25...... III.6:4 time, for help is there, awaiting but his c..
T-25...... III.7:6 you see them as the same, your c. is made.
T-25...... III.9:7 he is to you will make this c. your future?
T-25...... III.9:9 Make, then, your c.. But recognize that in
T-25.... III.9:10 recognize that in this c. the purpose of the
T-25...... IV.1:7 seen that makes the c. of means inevitable
T-25...... VI.5:1 *one* perfect thing and make *one* perfect c..
T-25...... VI.6:6 from the very instant that the c. was made
T-25...... VI.7:5 Son of God can make no c. the Holy Spirit
T-25..... VII.3:9 This is the c. you make. Do not attempt to
T-25..... VII.7:5 to those who are insane requires special c.
T-25..... VII.7:6 Nor can this c. be made by the insane,
T-25..... VII.8:3 given the c. of form most suitable to him;
T-26...... III.1:7 For it is conflict that makes c. possible.
T-26...... III.3:6 place and time and c. have meaning still,
T-26...... III.3:6 place, and every c. has been already made
T-26...... III.4:7 thing to make a c. at all is this distinction.
T-26...... III.4:9 In this one, c. is made impossible. In the
T-26...... III.5:3 Yet who can make a c. between the wish
T-26...... III.5:6 leaving room to make the only c. that can
T-26...... III.6:1 There is no basis for a c. in this complex
T-26...... III.6:2 and seems to choose where no c. really is.
T-26...... III.6:3 The real world is the area of c. made real,
T-26...... III.6:3 but in the perception of alternatives for c.
T-26...... III.6:4 That there is c. is an illusion. Yet within
T-26...... III.7:4 is the c. between two things so clearly
T-26....... V.1:9 while time remains and c. is meaningful.
T-26..... VII.9:3 reached beyond the world of c. entirely.
T-27...... III.7:3 There is no c. of function anywhere. The
T-27...... III.7:4 The c. you fear to lose you never had. Yet
T-27..... VII.2:5 The c. will not be difficult, because the
T-27..... VII.9:4 c. is yours to make between a sleeping
T-27... VII.10:7 Yet if the c. is really given you, then you
T-27... VII.11:3 An honest c. could never be perceived as
T-27... VII.11:3 in which the c. is split between a tiny you
T-27.... VII.14:4 in which the c. is not who is the murderer
T-28....... II.4:3 is a c. of dreams while you are still asleep,
T-28..... II.12:3 alternative, the c. to be the dreamer,
T-28..... II.12:6 mind is free to make another c. instead.
T-28....... V.1:9 There is no other c.. Except you share it,
T-28...... VI.2:3 in ways you want, but never makes the c..
T-28 .... VII.3:2 There is no in between, no other c., and
T-28 .... VII.4:6 All miracles are based upon this c., and
T-28 .... VII.4:7 the c. cannot be made in terms of form.
T-28 .... VII.4:8 The c. of sickness seems to be of form, yet
T-29 .......II.1:6 see the many gains your c. has offered you
T-29 ..... IV.1:5 c. is not between which dreams to keep,
T-30 .....II.2:10 And to oppose Him is to make a c. against
T-30 ..... IV.6:2 And you can make a simple c. that will
T-31 ......I.11:2 the means whereby the c. is reassessed;
T-31 .......II.2:9 to the one alternative that *is* a different c..
T-31 .......II.3:1 not a c. and gives but the illusion it is free,
T-31 .......II.3:2 Thus is it really not a c. at all. The leader
T-31 .......II.5:6 you. Between these two *is* c., because from
T-31 .......II.9:7 in this c. is learning's outcome changed,
T-31 ..... III.1:2 you prepare to make a c. that will result in
T-31 ..... IV.1:3 a place where c. among illusions seems to
T-31 ..... IV.1:3 among illusions seems to be the only c..
T-31 ..... IV.2:1 Real c. is no illusion. But the world has
T-31 ..... IV.2:4 There is no c. in its alternatives. Seek not
T-31 ... IV.2:10 is certain, for there is no c. among them.
T-31 ... IV.2:14 The c. is not what will the ending be, but
T-31 ..... IV.3:1 There is no c. where every end is sure.
T-31 ..... IV.3:8 there is no c. at all within the world. But
T-31 ..... IV.5:3 For while he sees a c. where there is none,
T-31 ..... IV.5:5 if it be applied in situations without c.?
T-31 ..... IV.6:1 that the world can offer but one c., no
T-31 ..... IV.8:1 There *is* a c. that you have power to make
T-31 ..... IV.8:2 Until that point is reached you have no c.,
T-31 .... V.12:3 and at least makes way for active c., and
T-31 .... V.13:5 entered in the c. by your decision. But
T-31 .... V.14:5 And what can think has c., and can be
T-31 ..... VI.1:4 There is no c. in vision but this one. What
T-31 ..... VI.1:6 On this one c. does all your world depend
T-31 ..... VI.3:2 It merely asks that this should be your c..
T-31 .. VII.12:6 hate, depending only on the simple c. of
T-31 ... VIII.2:1 How do you make the c.? How easily is
T-31 ... VIII.3:1 made a faulty c. before you now can make
T-31 ... VIII.5:6 to be before the c. for holiness was made.
T-31 ... VIII.5:7 For in that c. are false distinctions gone,
T-31 ... VIII.6:5 be, remembering that every c. you make
T-31 ... VIII.9:7 And in this c. is everyone made free.
T-31 .VIII.10:7 the world with every c. they make. For we
W-pI..... 51.3:8 this a better c. than the one I made before
W-pI..... 52.4:4 The c. is not whether to see the past or
W-pI..... 52.4:4 the c. is merely whether to see or not.
W-pI..... 64.5:8 different from just this one simple c..
W-pI..... 64.5:9 That is the only c. the Holy Spirit sees.
W-pI... 64.5:10 sees. Therefore it is the only c. there is.
W-pI..... 66.7:5 a result of your c. but the fear that the ego
W-pI... 66.10:2 Try to make this c. as you think about the
W-pI..... 98.4:3 they have come to make their c. again.
W-pI... 98.11:2 He will make you sure you want this c.,
W-pI... 102.4:3 mind, for it is there, awaiting but your c..
W-pI... 102.4:4 fail to find it when you learn it is your c.,
W-pI. 106.10:2 Do not forget today to reinforce your c. to
W-pI... 129.6:1 Such is the c.. What loss can be for you in
W-pI... 129.9:2 and we are grateful that the c. is made.
W-pI... 129.9:3 and take a moment to confirm your c. by
W-pI... 130.1:3 thinking but reflects your c. of what you
W-pI... 130.5:4 of c. beyond which your decision cannot
W-pI... 130.6:2 made a c. as all-embracing as its opposite.
W-pI... 130.9:5 strength upheld you as you made this c..
W-pI. 130.10:1 by remembering the limits of your c.. The
W-pI. 130.10:3 Perception is consistent with your c., and
W-pI. 130.11:2 still remains within your range of c., to
W-pI... 133.3:3 The laws that govern c. you cannot make,
W-pI... 133.4:3 and thus delay your final c. until you had
W-pI... 133.4:3 there is but one c. that must be made.
W-pI... 133.5:1 compromise in what your c. must bring.
W-pI... 133.5:3 Each c. you make brings everything to
W-pI... 133.5:4 from nothing, you will make the better c..
W-pI... 133.8:2 Why is the c. you make of value to you?
W-pI. 133.11:1 to the criterion for c. that is the hardest to
W-pI. 133.11:2 If you feel any guilt about your c., you
W-pI. 134.10:1 Thus will you see alternatives for c. in
W-pI. 135.16:3 directs its c. of what will happen. And it
W-pI... 136.3:4 second, even less, in which the c. is made,
W-pI... 136.7:3 It is a c. you make, a plan you lay, when
W-pI... 136.9:1 live, but cannot overcome your c. to die.
W-pI 137.12:5 other c. is but to ask what cannot be to be
W-pI .. 138.1:1 In this world Heaven is a c., because here
W-pI .. 138.2:3 that makes the c. of Heaven seem to be
W-pI .. 138.3:1 C. is the obvious escape from what
W-pI .. 138.4:2 And even this but seems to be a c.. Do not
W-pI .. 138.4:5 made, you will perceive it was no c. at all.
W-pI .. 138.6:1 Heaven appears to take the form of c.,
W-pI .. 138.6:5 the final and the only c. in which is truth
W-pI .. 138.7:1 the c. that time was made to help us make
W-pI .. 138.9:2 The c. cannot be made until alternatives
W-pI 138.10:1 The conscious c. of Heaven is as sure as is
W-pI 138.10:3 can fail to make a c. between alternatives
W-pI 138.10:4 Who hesitates to make a c. like this? And
W-pI 138.11:1 We make the c. for Heaven as we wake,
W-pI 138.11:2 we make a conscious c. between what has
W-pI 138.12:1 we reaffirm the c. that we have made each
W-pI 138.12:3 passed, we have declared our c. again, in a
W-pI .. 139.1:1 Here is the end of c.. For here we come to
W-pI .. 139.1:3 is c. except uncertainty of what we are?
W-pI .. 152.1:2 pain except his c. elects this state for him.
W-pI .. 153.6:3 the text maintains that c. is always made
W-pI .. 155.2:4 What other c. is really theirs to make? To
W-pI .. 155.3:1 This is the simple c. we make today. The
W-pI .. 155.3:2 to find they were mistaken in their c..
W-pI .. 165.1:4 already have except your c. to see it not,
W-pI .. 170.8:3 You make a c., standing before this idol,
W-pI 170.11:1 The c. you make today is certain. For you
W-pI 170.11:6 in the vision that your c. restored to you.
W-pI 170.13:5 *again, and make our c. for all our brothers,*
WpI...rV.in7:5 was begun, to make another c. with me.
W-pI .. 185.9:1 This is the c. you make. Be not deceived
W-pI .. 189.5:2 The c. is given you. But learn and do not
W-pI .. 189.9:3 And with this c. we rest. And in our quiet
W-pI 190.11:1 we make the only c. that ever can be made
W-pI .. 193.6:1 and death becomes our c. instead of life?
W-pI .. 194.9:5 c. for us that leaves temptation far behind
W-pI .. 200.6:6 while there appears to be a c. to make
W-pII .... in.8:2 the c. to follow it as He would have us go.
W-pII . 263.1:4 *A madman's dream is hardly fit to be my c.,*
W-pII . 282.1:4 the c. to recognize the Self Whom God
W-pII . 286.1:4 *In You is every c. already made. In You has*
W-pII . 317.1:3 Until I make this c., I am the slave of time
W-pII . 329.1:6 *That c. was made for all eternity. It cannot*
W-pII . 334.1:5 This is my c. today. And so I go to find
W-pII . 335.1:1 Forgiveness is a c.. I never see my brother
W-pII . 351.1:3 *Yet this perception is a c. I make, and can*
W-pII . 351.1:5 *Son. And with this c. I see my sinlessness, my*
W-ep ......... 5:3 for you each time there is a c. to make.
W-ep ......... 5:4 and that each c. you make brings Heaven
M-in .......... 2:4 you will teach, for in that there is no c..
M-1 ............ 1:2 somewhere he has made a deliberate c. in
M-1 ......... 4:10 Such was their c., and it is given them.
M-2 ........... 1:6 Time waits on his c., but not on whom he
M-2 ........... 4:5 made the right c. in that ancient instant
M-2 ........... 4:6 an inevitable c. out of an ancient past.
M-4 ......II.2:12 honesty, sure of their c. as of themselves.
M-4 ...... IV.2:5 What c. but this has meaning to the sane?
M-5 .........I.1:5 It is the c. of weakness, in the mistaken
M-5 ........II.2:8 him, yet they but give form to his own c..
M-5 ...... III.2:1 another c. which they had forgotten. The
M-10 ......... 6:9 were but the effects of his mistaken c.,
M-12 ......... 6:3 It is a conscious c.. For they have learned
M-17 ....... 7:11 or be killed, for here alone is c.. Beyond
M-20 ......... 4:6 you want, or is God's peace the better c.?
C-1 ............ 7:1 remaining freedom is the freedom of c.;
C-1 ............ 7:2 at any level, and has nothing to do with c.
C-2 ............ 1:9 a c. for options that do not exist. We
C-2 .......... 10:4 here, and having met at last the c. is clear.
P-2........ VI.1:8 To question it must then become his c..
P-2....... VII.2:6 what c. is there except to have Him stay?
P-2....... VII.9:8 other c. of pathways that can ever lead to
S-1..........II.6:4 become holy, then, prayer becomes a c..
S-1........ IV.3:5 from every c. that stood for a mistake.
S-2...........I.8:2 This is the c. you make; the simplest one,
S-2.........I.10:3 Yet you must learn alternatives for c., or
S-3.........II.1:11 And so it is discarded as a c., as one lays
S-3..........II.2:1 This is what death should be; a quiet c.,

## choices 20

T-5......... II.6:3 As a result, there are c. you must make. In
T-5......... V.6:8 and the ego are the only c. open to you.
T-10..... V.14:3 time lasts in your mind there will be c..
T-12....... V.5:5 Poor learners are not good c. as teachers,
T-15...... III.1:7 Littleness and glory are the c. open to
T-25..... VII.7:6 whose problem is their c. are not free, and
T-26..... VII.9:3 because it still conceives of other c., and
T-27... VII.11:1 What c. can be made between two states,
T-31....... II.2:6 by your wish you set two c. to be made,
T-31...... IV.8:4 All c. in the world depend on this; you
T-31... VII.14:8 not deceived by what appears as many c..
W-pI.133.12:5 you make c. easily and without pain.
W-pI... 138.4:1 think a thousand c. are confronting you,
W-pI... 138.6:2 Of all the c. you have tried to make this is
W-pI... 152.4:3 concealed behind a vast array of c. that do
W-pI... 155.7:2 are paths that lead nowhere, c. for defeat,
W-pII.. 242.1:4 no c. for me but the ones that lead to God
M-2............3:3 C. made long since appear to be open; yet
M-12..........6:4 learned that all c. are made consciously,
C-1.............7:1 always between two c. or two voices. Will

## choose 321

T-1......... II.1:9 it. You are free to believe what you c., and
T-1........ III.4:7 and c. to abandon them by following my
T-1......... V.1:3 can c. between loveless and miraculous
T-2........... I.3:3 what is not true unless you c. to do so. All
T-2........ VI.1:3 direct everything that does, if you so c..
T-2........ VI.2:1 confusion, but you must c. to correct it.
T-2........ VI.4:9 Before you c. to do anything, ask me if
T-2........ VI.5:2 First, you can c. to do conflicting things,
T-2....... VII.3:2 If you are not free to c. one, you would
T-2....... VII.3:2 you would also not be free to c. the other.
T-2..... VIII.3:7 the ability to c. can be directed rationally.
T-2..... VIII.4:3 and c. to preserve only what is good, just
T-3........... I.6:7 inaccessible to those who do not c. to see.
T-3...... IV.3:11 must eventually c. to heal the separation.
T-3........ IV.5:5 Afterwards it can only c. ambiguously,
T-3...... IV.7:11 I cannot c. for you, but I can help you
T-3...... IV.7:12 be, "All are called but few c. to listen."
T-3...... IV.7:13 they do not c. right. The "chosen ones"
T-3...... IV.7:14 are merely those who c. right sooner.
T-3......... V.3:6 You can do this if you c., but you would
T-3........ VI.8:7 prefer to be anonymous when you c. to
T-4......... in.2:1 from the spirit or from the ego, as you c..
T-4......... in.3:9 free to crucify yourself as often as you c..
T-4........ I.11:5 is ready for you when you c. to enter it. Of
T-4........ III.7:8 wait as long as you c. to forsake yourself.
T-4........ IV.1:1 God, it is because you do not c. to listen.
T-4........ VI.5:8 You are still free to c., but can you really
T-4........ VI.6:3 and I do not c. God's channels wrongly.
T-5........... I.1:4 If you do not c. to be wholly joyous, your
T-5........... I.1:4 cannot have what it does not c. to be.
T-5......... II.3:4 why you must c. to hear one of two voices
T-5......... II.6:5 to c. is the same power as freedom to
T-5....... II.7:14 is therefore "lost" to you until you c. right
T-5......... II.8:9 must c. at which altar you want to serve.
T-5........ IV.5:6 that was in me rejoices as you c. to hear it.
T-5........ VI.2:7 When you c. to make this exchange, you
T-5....... VII.1:7 You cannot c. to escape His care because
T-5....... VII.1:7 but you can c. to accept His care and use
T-5..... VII.6:11 *I c. to let Him, by allowing Him to decide for*
T-6........... I.5:2 to perceive yourself as persecuted if you c.
T-6........... I.5:3 choose. When you do c. to react that way,
T-6...... V.B.5:1 clearly to c. one and relinquish the other.
T-6...... V.C.4:8 and still believe that you can c. either one.
T-6...... V.C.4:9 By teaching *what* to c., the Holy Spirit will
T-6...... V.C.4:9 teach you that you need not c. at all. This
T-6...... V.C.9:9 and those who c. to teach the same thing
T-7........ VI.2:6 your thinking as you c. is part of its power
T-7....... VII.9:5 If you c. to separate yourself from God,
T-7..... VIII.1:9 depending on how you c. to apply it. This
T-8........... I.5:9 They cannot c. one because they cannot
T-8........ III.5:1 regardless of the teacher you c., is "Know
T-8...... IV.4:10 Only then will your mind c. to follow me.
T-8........ IV.6:5 only you can c. to listen to my teaching.
T-8......... V.6:9 and if you c. to share it you will do so. I
T-8........ VI.7:6 the mind of God's Son, if they so c.. This
T-8..... VIII.8:5 you c. not to accept anything except truth
T-9......... V.8:9 that you c. the guide for helping, and the
T-9....... VII.5:1 c. to see yourself as unloving you will not
T-9....... VII.8:5 C., then, what you want in these terms,
T-9....... VIII.1:7 to the grandeur of God. Which will you c.
T-10.... III.11:7 the belief that you can c. which god is real
T-11........ in.1:8 you will be faithful to the father you c..
T-11....... II.5:7 Whatever journey you c. to take, He will
T-11..... V.12:9 the insane would c. fear in place of love,
T-11..... V.18:4 power to release you, if you c. to be free.
T-12....... II.9:1 you who c. to banish fear must succeed.
T-12..... VII.7:2 As you look in, you c. the guide for seeing.
T-13...... VI.2:5 if you are would you c. to bring darkness
T-13...... IX.4:4 saying, "I who was guilty c. to remain so."
T-13...... XI.5:4 may be, whatever voice you c. to listen to,
T-14.......... I.5:6 c. to be deceived will merely attack direct
T-14...... III.3:7 *to fear. I c. to testify to my acceptance of the*
T-14...... III.6:3 because he did not c. to free his brother
T-14...... III.8:7 and nothing else can His Son see or c. to
T-14...... III.9:1 Whenever you c. to make decisions for
T-14... VIII.3:2 brother may c. to lead yourselves astray,
T-15...... III.1:8 always c. one at the expense of the other.
T-15...... III.2:1 what you do not realize, each time you c.,
T-15...... III.2:2 C. littleness and you will not have peace,
T-15..... VII.3:3 No one would c. to let go what he believes
T-15...... IX.3:3 you will c. to utilize the means by which it
T-15....... X.1:9 Release me as I c. your own release. The
T-15....... X.2:3 offer me, when only this I c. to offer you?
T-15....... X.9:3 must c. between total freedom and total
T-15.... XI.10:7 *In the name of my freedom I c. your release,*
T-16.......... I.3:2 You c. neither to hurt it nor to heal it in
T-16... VII.10:1 you always c. between truth and illusion;
T-16... VII.11:7 and nowhere else. You c. this or nothing.
T-17...... III.9:1 you to c. to join with truth or with illusion
T-17...... III.9:2 that to c. one is to let the other go. Which
T-17...... III.9:3 you c. you will endow with beauty and
T-17...... III.9:5 never c. except between God and the ego.
T-17.... IV.12:7 only on this basis are you really free to c..
T-17....... V.7:3 not part entirely if you c. not to do so. But
T-18.......... I.1:3 To substitute is to c. between, renouncing
T-18....... V.7:6 *I c. this instant as the one to offer to the Holy*
T-19.......... I.9:5 now. You freely c. to overlook his errors,
T19... IV.A.4:9 You cannot c. apart from this. You have
T19. IV.D.10:8 c. whether to look upon it or wander on,
T19. IV.D.13:4 C. which he is, remembering that you will
T19. IV.D.20:5 he must c. what it will *be* that he receives.
T-20...... IV.4:1 c. freedom will experience only its results.
T-20...... VI.5:7 the face of Christ c. as His home the only
T-20.... VI.11:7 it is given him to c. to spend this instant
T-20.... VIII.9:3 and which you c. determines what you see
T-21........ in.1:7 c. to change your mind about the world.
T-21....... II.1:5 c. against it now it will not be because it is
T-21....... II.2:4 *see. I c. the feelings I experience, and I decide*
T-21...... III.5:1 but he can c. where he would have it be.
T-21...... III.6:5 perception that you might c. among your
T-21...... III.8:6 all who c. to look away from sin are given
T-21...... IV.6:3 afraid because you did not c. to share in it
T-21....... V.1:9 For on the voice you c. to hear, and on the
T-21....... V.1:9 to hear, and on the sights you c. to see,
T-21...... VI.6:1 If you c. sin instead of healing, you would
T-21...... VI.6:4 you c. he be is but your choice for you.
T-21...... VI.7:8 The instant that you c. to let yourself be
T-21..... VII.9:4 if you c. to see a world without an enemy,
T-21... VIII.2:8 to those who c. to heal and not to judge.
T-22....... II.6:6 Now must you c. between yourself and an
T-22....... II.7:7 waiting to c. between the joy of Heaven
T-22....... II.7:8 Until you c. Heaven, you *are* in hell and
T-22.. VI.12:11 You would not c. attack on its reality if it
T-23...... IV.6:5 but quickly c. a miracle instead of murder
T-24.......... I.1:5 the one alternative that you can c. for love
T-24.......... I.2:6 least decision to c. attack instead of love,
T-24...... VI.7:1 C., then, his body or his holiness as what
T-24...... VI.7:1 and which you c. is yours to look upon.
T-24...... VI.7:2 Yet will you c. in countless situations, and
T-25....... II.6:3 picture when you c. to see it in its place.
T-25...... III.5:5 for mind to c. to see them where it will. If
T-25....... V.4:7 of what you c. to have him be to you. If
T-25...... IX.9:1 did not c. to let them be removed for you.
T-26...... III.6:2 and seems to c. where no choice really is.
T-26...... III.7:3 to give up all attempts to c. between them
T-26...... III.7:7 hard to give it up, and c. what *must* be true
T-26..... V.1:11 You but c. whether to go toward Heaven,
T-26..... V.1:12 to nowhere. There is nothing else to c..
T-26....... V.5:2 be there, for you to c. to be your teacher.
T-26...... VI.1:8 can c. to keep the ones that he prefers,
T-26... VII.18:3 and c. a little senseless wish instead of
T-27.......... I.9:9 mind made free again to c. what it is for.
T-27.... IV.4:11 That is the one that you should c.. The
T-27...... VI.3:5 You cannot c. among them which are real
T-27...... VI.3:5 are real, for any one you c. is like the rest.
T-27...... VI.3:6 name or that, but nothing more, you c..
T-27..... VII.4:8 would be a victim of attack he did not c..
T-27..... VII.8:3 He cannot c. to waken from a dream he
T-27..... VII.9:1 see; the one alternative that you can c.,
T-27..... VII.9:2 c. if you deny the cause of suffering is in
T-27... VII.10:1 could you c. between but life or death,
T-27... VII.10:7 the things you c. between exactly as they
T-27... VII.11:2 Who could be free to c. between effects,
T-29...... III.3:8 The darkness cannot c. that it remain.
T-29..... VII.8:4 You c. your dreams, for they are what you
T-30........ I.14:4 really is with what you c. to make them.
T-30........ I.14:9 and which you c. will join with you and
T-30........ I.15:2 It is set by what you c. to live it with, and
T-30....... II.2:10 against yourself, and c. that you be bound
T-30..... V.10:6 then. And do not c. an idol thoughtlessly,
T-30.... VIII.4:7 it. C. what you would heal, and He Who
T-31........ II.3:1 c. between is not a choice and gives but
T-31........ II.5:4 for what you c. you choose as well for him
T-31........ II.5:4 for what you choose you c. as well for him
T-31...... IV.1:5 c. which road will lead you out of conflict,
T-31...... IV.1:8 you whatever road you c. to walk along.
T-31...... IV.8:2 but decide how you would c. the better to
T-31...... IV.8:4 you c. between your brother and yourself,
T-31....... V.8:2 that you will c. to follow this world's laws,
T-31..... V.12:7 be, alternatives were there to c. among,
T-31..... V.12:7 must have first decided on the one to c.,
T-31...... VI.1:7 If you c. flesh, you never will escape the
T-31...... VI.1:8 But c. the spirit, and all Heaven bends to
T-31...... VI.2:2 If you c. to see the body, you behold a
T-31...... VI.4:6 nor what you c. to feel or think or wish.
T-31...... VI.5:1 You who believe that you can c. to see the
T-31..... VII.2:7 No longer do you c. that you should be
T-31..... VII.6:3 unless you c. to hold it past the hope of
T-31... VII.14:5 Can this be difficult to c. *against?* Consider
T-31... VII.14:6 see the real alternatives you c. between.
T-31... VII.14:9 or Heaven, and of these you c. but one.
T-31....... VIII.h C. Once Again
T-31.... VIII.1:5 *C. once again if you would take your place*
T-31.... VIII.2:3 You always c. between your weakness and
T-31.... VIII.2:4 And what you c. is what you think is real.
T-31.... VIII.3:2 and gently says, "My brother, c. again."
T-31.... VIII.4:2 see it as it is; another chance to c. again,
T-31.... VIII.4:4 merely those who c. His strength instead
T-31.... VIII.6:5 C. once again what you would have him
T-31.... VIII.9:6 For you *will* hear, and you *will* c. again.
T-31.. VIII.10:5 but do Your holy Will, so will they c.. And
W-pI..... 32.5:3 world. It does not matter which you c..
W-pI..... 44.7:3 be stopped in this unless you c. to stop it.
W-pI..... 51.4:7 I c. to have them be replaced by what they
W-pI..... 52.4:6 Now I would c. again, that I may see.
W-pI..... 53.2:6 I need not see it at all unless I c. to value it
W-pI..... 53.2:7 I do not c. to value what is totally insane
W-pI..... 53.3:7 in it. Now I c. to withdraw this belief, and
W-pI..... 55.3:5 And it is this I c. to see, in place of what I
W-pI..... 57.1:2 that can be completely undone if I so c.?
W-pI..... 59.3:6 I c. when I think I can see apart from Him
W-pI..... 59.3:7 It is these I c. when I try to see through
W-pI..... 59.3:9 It is through this vision that I c. to see.
W-pI..... 64.4:4 time you c. whether or not to fulfill your
W-pI..... 66.7:5 no other guides but these to c. between,
W-pI..... 73.8:3 it is hell in place of Heaven that you c..
W-pI..... 78.5:1 You know the one to c.; his name has
W-pI..... 88.1:2 I merely c. to recognize what is already
W-pI..... 88.1:4 Attack and grievances are not there to c..
W-pI..... 88.1:5 why I always c. between truth and illusion
W-pI..... 88.1:7 come. I can but c. the light, for it has no
W-pI..... 91.5:5 You can escape the body if you c.. You
W-pI..... 98.4:4 We do not c. but for ourselves today.

W-pI...100.2:2 Why should you **c.** to go against His Will?
W-pI...104.3:1 Therefore, we **c.** to have them now, and
W-pI...117.1:3 *so I* **c.** *to entertain no substitutes for love.*
W-pI...125.7:1 **c.** instead a gentle listening to the Word
W-pI...126.5:2 you sometimes **c.** to give indulgently an
W-pI...129.6:3 but what you **c.** instead you want indeed!
W-pI...129.7:4 *I* **c.** *to see that world instead of this, for here is*
W-pI...130.2:3 can **c.** to see a world of which he is afraid?
W-pI...130.5:5 the unreal are all there are to **c.** between,
W-pI...131.3:4 still are free to **c.** a goal that lies beyond
W-pI...131.9:1 we will not **c.** a paradox in place of truth.
W-pI.132.17:2 *it was, and* **c.** *my own reality instead.*
W-pI...133.3:3 can make alternatives from which to **c.**.
W-pI...133.3:5 the laws you set in motion when you **c.**,
W-pI...133.3:5 and what alternatives you **c.** between.
W-pI...133.6:1 if you **c.** a thing that will not last forever,
W-pI...133.7:1 **c.** to take a thing away from someone else
W-pI.134.15:1 Then **c.** one brother as He will direct, and
W-pI...136.3:3 the rapidity with which you **c.** to use them
W-pI.136.11:4 You can but **c.** to think you die, or suffer
W-pI.136.14:3 will **c.** to practice giving welcome to the
W-pI...138.1:1 there are alternatives to **c.** between. We
W-pI...138.1:2 have an opposite, and what we want we **c.**
W-pI...138.4:7 There is no opposite to **c.** instead. There
W-pI.138.10:5 like this? And shall we hesitate to **c.** today
W-pI...152.1:5 wish, and nothing is omitted that you **c.**.
W-pI.153.11:1 to help their brothers **c.** as they have done
W-pI...154.7:3 They **c.** no roles that are not given them
W-pI...155.2:2 Those who **c.** to come to it are seeking for
W-pI.155.12:7 could be a path that you would **c.** instead?
W-pI...156.3:3 be sinful than the sun could **c.** to be of ice;
W-pI.170.13:5 *We* **c.** *again, and make our choice for all our*
W-pI...185.9:4 You **c.** God's peace, or you have asked for
W-pI...187.7:3 you **c.** to see all suffering as what it is. The
W-pI.188.10:4 Now we **c.** that it be innocent, devoid of
W-pI...189.9:1 today we do not **c.** the way in which we go
W-pI...189.9:2 But we do **c.** to let Him come. And with
W-pI......190.h I **c.** the joy of God instead of pain.
W-pI...190.6:4 **c.** the joy of God as what you really want.
W-pI.190.11:1 we **c.** between illusions and the truth, or
W-pI.190.11:2 as we are free to **c.** our joy instead of pain,
W-pI...192.9:5 averted as you **c.** to be condemned or free
W-pI...194.7:8 free to **c.** again when he has been deceived
W-pI...195.8:5 we cannot **c.** to overlook some things, and
WpI rVI.in.6:3 *I* **c.** *instead* _ And then repeat the idea for
W-pI...202.1:2 *Why would I* **c.** *to stay an instant more*
W-pI...210.1:1 (190) I **c.** the joy of God instead of pain.
W-pI...210.1:5 *And that I* **c.**, *instead of what I made.* I am
W-pI...213.1:4 *so I* **c.** *to learn His lessons and forget my own.*
W-pII .226.1:1 If I so **c.**, I can depart this world entirely.
W-pII .246.2:1 *accept the way You* **c.** *for me to come to You,*
W-pII .246.2:4 *that. And so I* **c.** *to love Your Son. Amen.*
W-pII .254.2:4 And so we do not **c.** to keep them. They
W-pII ....255.h This day I **c.** to spend in perfect peace.
W-pII .255.1:1 to me that I can **c.** to have but peace today
W-pII .255.1:4 And let the peace I **c.** be mine today bear
W-pII .255.2:3 *in his mind, and it is there I* **c.** *to spend today.*
W-pII .256.1:8 and it is this we **c.** to dream today. God is
W-pII .261.2:3 *I* **c.** *to be as You created me, and find the Son*
W-pII .269.1:5 *Today I* **c.** *to see a world forgiven, in which*
W-pII .271.1:2 me. Today I **c.** to look upon what Christ
W-pII .271.2:3 *And this I* **c.**, *to be what I would look upon*
W-pII .278.2:4 *I* **c.** *the way to You instead of madness and*
W-pII .....8.3:3 is there it would **c.** to be condemned, and
W-pII .314.2:1 *in the past, and* **c.** *to use the present to be free*
W-pII .317.1:2 until I take this part as what I **c.** to do.
W-pII .317.2:1 *Father, Your way is what I* **c.** *today. Where it*
W-pII .317.2:2 *Where it would lead me do I* **c.** *to go; what it*
W-pII .317.2:2 *to go; what it would have me do I* **c.** *to do.*
W-pII .324.1:4 *I can but* **c.** *to wander off a while, and then*
W-pII ....328.h I **c.** the second place to gain the first.
W-pII .330.1:6 Let us **c.** today that He be our Identity,
W-pII .334.1:4 God to all who hear and **c.** to follow Him.
W-pII ....335.h I **c.** to see my brother's sinlessness.
W-pII .335.1:5 I **c.** to see what I would look upon, and
W-pII .347.1:4 *freedom, and I* **c.** *to claim Your gift today.*
W-pII .348.2:2 only that we **c.** to be our will as well as His
W-pII ....351.h pain. And which I **c.** to see I will behold.
W-pII .351.1:6 *C., then, for me, my Father, through Your*
W-pII .355.1:7 *It is You I* **c.**, *and my Identity along with You.*
W-pII .358.1:4 *me, in just the form You* **c.** *that it be mine. Let*
M-2 ........... 3:5 has already happened at any time you **c.**,
M-2 ........... 3:6 you are not free to **c.** the curriculum, or
M-4 ......II.2:10 They **c.** for all mankind; for all the world
M-4 ......II.2:12 They **c.** in perfect honesty, sure of their
M-4 ...... IV.2:7 And who would **c.** the weakness that
M-5 .........I.1:2 Who would **c.** suffering unless he thought
M-5 .... III.2:12 Would you **c.** sickness in place of this?"
M-10 ......... 4:4 Why would you **c.** such an arbitrary basis
M-11 ....... 1:10 You cannot **c.** what this should be. But
M-11 ....... 1:11 be. But you can **c.** how you would see it.
M-11 ....... 1:12 you would see it. Indeed, you *must* **c.** this.
M-12 ......... 6:2 teachers **c.** to look on dreams a while. It is
M-13 ......... 8:3 Decide against Him, and you **c.** nothing,
M-20 ......... 4:9 Would you not rather live than **c.** to die?
M-23 ....... 5:11 Why would you **c.** to start again, when he
M-29 ......... 6:9 harm himself, or **c.** his own destruction.
P-2....... VII.2:5 cure, when another is always there to **c.**?
P-3...........I.1:2 **c.** the kind of treatment that is suitable.
P-3.........I.2:12 Would you rather **c.** who would be god,
P-3........II.9:10 is One Who says, "My brother, **c.** again."
S-1..........II.6:5 You do not **c.** for another. You can but
S-1..........II.6:6 You can but **c.** for yourself. Pray truly for
S-2..........I.10:2 must **c.** between them every instant while
S-2......... III.2:3 the eyes of Christ become the sight you **c.**.
S-2......... III.4:2 God did not **c.** this sorry path for you.
S-3......... IV.5:1 you **c.** to be to him so are you to yourself,
S-3......... IV.5:3 Do not **c.** amiss, or you will think that it is

## chooses 34

T-1 ........ V.5:2 but the mind can elect what it **c.** to serve.
T-2 ...... VII.6:7 in error or incompleteness if he so **c.**.
T-3 ....... IV.5:3 it **c.** to be separated it chooses to perceive.
T-3 ....... IV.5:3 it chooses to be separated it **c.** to perceive.
T-3 ....... IV.5:8 mind **c.** to divide itself when it chooses to
T-3 ....... IV.5:8 itself when it **c.** to make its own levels.
T-4 ....... IV.8:2 expression of his power as much as he **c.**.
T-11 ..... V.16:2 listen. Selective perception **c.** its witnesses
T-12 ... VIII.5:3 dawn only in a mind that **c.** to remember,
T-19 ....... I.16:5 according to which it **c.** as its purpose for
T19....IV.C.1:4 No one can die unless he **c.** death. What
T-21 ... VI.11:9 And where he **c.** to be merciful, there is he
T-21 . VI.11:10 free. But where he **c.** to condemn instead,
T-22 ..... VI.2:3 who **c.** this has no idea of what is valuable
T-25 ........I.3:2 It **c.** where you think your safety lies, at
T-25 ..... III.6:4 The time he **c.** can be any time, for help is
T-25 ..... III.6:5 he **c.** to avail himself of what is given him,
T-25 .... VII.4:4 **c.** to believe one thought opposed to truth
T-26 .. VII.16:5 of God reborn until he **c.** not to die again.
T-26 .. VII.16:6 In every wish to hurt he **c.** death instead
WpI..rIII.in6:1 your mind, and let it use them as it **c.**.
W-pI... 133.6:4 and makes no offering to him who **c.** it.
W-pI... 154.2:2 when, He **c.** and accepts your part for you
W-pI. 166.15:4 mind becomes which **c.** to accept His gifts
M-1 ........... 1:1 teacher of God is anyone who **c.** to be one
M-4 ...... IV.2:6 **c.** hell when he perceives a way to Heaven
M-5 .........I.2:7 But if he **c.** death himself, his weakness is
M-5 ........II.2:9 **c.** them in order to bring tangible form to
M-5 ........II.3:6 He looks on what he **c.** to see. No more
M-13 ....... 4:10 sane mind **c.** nothing as a substitute for
M-16 ......... 4:3 let him but remember that he **c.** to spend
M-16 ....... 10:9 merely **c.** to give up all that he never had.
C-2 .......... 10:5 Who **c.** hell when it is recognized? And
P-1............ 5:8 He directs. By whatever routes He **c.**, all

## choosing 44

T-1 ........ V.6:2 is the natural result of **c.** to follow Him.
T-2 ...... VII.3:3 By **c.** the miracle you *have* rejected fear, if
T-3 ..... IV.7:10 Sane perception induces sane **c.**. I cannot
T-3 ...... VII.6:5 You who fear salvation are **c.** death. Life
T-4 ..... IV.10:5 that you believe I was mistaken in **c.** you.
T-5 .........II.5:3 **c.** one you give up the other. The choice
T-5 .........II.6:6 **C.** depends on a split mind. The Holy
T-5 .........II.6:7 The Holy Spirit is one way of **c.**. God did
T-5 .........II.8:1 The Holy Spirit is your Guide in **c.**. He is
T-6 ..... V.C.5:1 **C.** through the Holy Spirit will lead you
T-8 .........II.2:1 reason for **c.** a teacher such as this? Does
T-10 .......II.5:6 you are actively **c.** not to remember Him.
T-13 ..... IV.6:5 you are **c.** a future of illusions and losing
T-13 ..... VI.7:3 you are **c.** to remain in the darkness that
T-14 ..... III.5:3 It is the natural result of **c.** right, attesting
T-14 ..... III.5:3 that comes from **c.** to be free of guilt.
T-16 ..... III.2:8 care you have exerted in **c.** its witnesses,
T-16 .....V.16:4 fantasies make confusion in **c.** possible,
T-16 .... VII.1:4 for **c.** a special partner without the past?
T-18 .......II.8:6 You are so used to **c.** among dreams you
T-21 ..... III.8:2 sin by **c.** to let all limitations be removed.
T-24 ........I.1:6 **c.** it has given it all the reality it seems to
T-25 ..... III.3:1 Perception rests on **c.**; knowledge does
T-25 ... VI.5:10 part in time for so he chose, and **c.** it, he
T-26 ... III.1:11 only if there were could **c.** be a necessary
T-26 ... III.4:10 In the real world is **c.** simplified.
T-30 ........I.2:3 that you are **c.** not to be the judge of what
T-31 ..... IV.1:4 you are in control of outcomes of your **c.**.
T-31 ..... IV.8:3 power of decision cannot lie in **c.** different
T-31 .....V.12:6 Yet who was it that did the **c.** first? If you
W-pI .... 53.3:8 In **c.** this, I will escape all the effects of the
W-pI .... 64.4:4 are really **c.** whether or not to be happy.
W-pI .... 86.4:2 forms: *I am* **c.** *between misperception and*
W-pI .... 88.1:2 In **c.** salvation rather than attack, I merely
W-pI .. 104.3:1 in **c.** them in place of what we made, we
W-pI .. 129.6:2 be for you in **c.** not to value nothingness?
W-pI .. 129.6:5 It waits but for your **c.** it, to take the place
W-pI .. 133.3:4 The **c.** you can do; indeed, you must. But
W-pI 133.12:2 **C.** is easy just because of this. Complexity
W-pI 134.10:1 choice in terms that render **c.** meaningful,
W-pI .. 138.5:1 **C.** depends on learning. And the truth
W-pII . 271.1:1 instant, I am **c.** what I want to look upon,
M-in.......... 2:5 means of **c.** what you want to teach on the
S-2...........I.3:5 the sin by **c.** in its place the face of Christ.

## chorus 4

T19 ... IV.C.2:4 "sinners," the ego's mournful **c.**, plodding
T-26 ..... IV.6:3 you join the mighty **c.** to the Love of God!
T-31 . VIII.11:5 **c.** from a world redeemed from hell, and
S-3......... IV.2:2 quickened **c.** through the voice of prayer.

## chose 54

T-5 .........II.5:6 When you **c.** to leave Him He gave you a
T-5 .........II.6:8 even though they **c.** to leave Him. The
T-12 ..... IV.7:2 you **c.** to "sell" had to be kept for you,
T-12 ..... VI.2:7 You **c.** to forget your Father but you do
T-12 ... VIII.2:3 **c.** to attack him and he disappeared from
T-14 ........I.5:5 you, because you **c.** to deceive yourself.
T19 . IV.C.2:10 to you who **c.** His Will as yours? What is
T-20 ... VI.11:8 him to replace the unholy one he **c.** before
T-21 ...... in.2:6 from this to recognize which one you **c.**.
T-21 ..... III.5:6 choice, and by your faith in what you **c.**,
T-21 ..... III.8:4 first they **c.** to recognize how much their
T-21 .... VII.7:4 the one you **c.** to be protected from attack
T-23 .....II.22:6 know whether you **c.** the stairs to Heaven
T-24 ........I.7:7 Could you attack your brother if you **c.** to
T-24 .......II.3:7 **c.** their specialness instead of Heaven and
T-24 .....II.10:7 Who **c.** that love could never be divided,
T-24 ..... III.6:2 Here is the hell you **c.** to be your home.
T-24 ..... III.6:3 He **c.** not this for you. Ask not He enter
T-25 ..... IV.2:5 **c.** it as a means to gain these same effects,
T-25 .... VI.5:10 He *has* a special part in time for so he **c.**,
T-25 ..... VI.6:6 The specialness he **c.** to hurt himself did
T-25 .... VII.8:2 everyone who **c.** insanity as his salvation.
T-25 .. VII.10:3 in the alternative He **c.** especially for you.
T-26 .....V.11:2 the instant that he **c.** to die instead of live.
T-27 ..... VI.8:6 who **c.** to let love's symbols take the place
T-27 . VIII.12:9 you need but learn you **c.** but not to listen
T-30 .......II.3:1 the one you **c.** to hate instead of love. For
T-30 .......II.5:4 **c.** to look upon your brother as a friend.
T-30 ... VIII.4:9 the willing slave of what he **c.** instead.
T-31 ..... III.5:1 it **c.** and guards and holds itself at bay, a
T-31 .....V.12:2 the thing you **c.** to have your brother be.
T-31 .....V.12:4 understanding that you **c.** for both of you,
T-31 .....V.12:7 If you are what you **c.** your brother be,
T-31 .....V.13:7 you **c.** it for him in the image of your own.
T-31 ..... VI.2:7 guilt, because they **c.** to let it go instead.

T-31... VIII.3:1 what you c. before has brought to you. In
W-pI.....60.2:6 begin to remember the Love I c. to forget,
W-pI...106.6:3 Who c. it in your Father's Name for you.
W-pI...131.6:7 or what you c. from what you really want.
W-pI...133.6:1 not last forever, what you c. is valueless. A
W-pI.133.11:3 alternative you think you c. seems fearful,
W-pI.138.12:4 acknowledging we c. but what we want:
W-pI.153.18:4 for you who c. to carry out His plan for
W-pI...155.3:2 for those to look upon who c. to come,
W-pI...166.6:3 you see that he is following the way he c.,
W-pI...166.9:6 and go the way you c. without your Self.
W-pI.166.13:1 who c. the lonely road you have escaped.
W-pI.184.12:5 to those who c. the teaching of the world
W-pII.....in.8:2 We have found the way He c. for us, and
W-pII..329.1:5 *And this I c. in my creation, where my will*
W-pII..333.2:1 *You c. to shine away all conflict and all doubt*
W-ep .........3:5 His is the Word you c. to be your own.
P-3.........II.3:4 may have been, when he c. to be a healer,
P-3.........II.4:7 the way God c. for the return of His Son.

## chosen 121

T-1.........V.6:1 has c. to be led by me in Christ's service.
T-2........VI.3:2 you are fearful, you have c. wrongly. That
T-2........VI.7:2 you must somehow have c. not to love, or
T-2........VI.8:4 loveless, having c. without love. This is
T-3......IV.7:12 are called but few are c." should be, "All
T-3......IV.7:14 "c. ones" are merely those who choose
T-3.........V.9:2 have c. to see themselves as separate.
T-4.........in.2:2 speak from spirit you have c. to "Be still
T-4...........I.9:3 are. You have c. to create unlike Him, and
T-4...........I.9:6 has c. to be afraid instead of meeting it.
T-4........I.11:4 who have c. to leave it empty by their own
T-4........IV.2:2 mood tells you that you have c. wrongly,
T-4.........V.5:8 may be c. *because* their value will not last.
T-4........VI.6:7 My c. channels cannot fail, because I will
T-5.........II.5:2 one to be c. and the other to be avoided.
T-5.........II.6:2 You have c. to be in a state of opposition
T-6...........I.8:7 the model they follow has c. to save them
T-6........IV.6:3 You have c. a sleep in which you have had
T-6......V.A.6:3 Having c. to go that way, you place
T-6......V.A.6:9 have c. what they cannot complete alone,
T-6......V.B.8:4 and one has been c. as more desirable.
T-7........XI.4:1 that I have c. you to teach the Kingdom *to*
T-8.........V.5:8 On this journey you have c. me as your
T-9........VI.5:3 and because you have c. to wake them,
T-9.......VII.6:5 c. to be little and to lament your littleness
T-10..III.10:11 have c. to fear love because of its perfect
T-11.......V.18:2 kingdom you have c. for your vigilance.
T-12.......V.7:7 the curriculum you have c. is against love,
T-12.....VII.5:6 will reflect the guidance you have c..
T-14.........I.3:5 truth, that he has c. to defend and love.
T-14.......III.5:1 teaches you that you have c. guiltlessness,
T-14.......X.9:4 therefore remains the ego's c. condition.
T-15.......II.4:6 which you have c. by *their* reactions. A Son
T-15.......V.4:5 which you have c. to support the ego, as
T-15.....VII.5:2 belongs not around the c. host of God,
T-16......III.7:2 c. this by your own willingness to teach.
T-16...V.12:11 c. substitute for the Wholeness of God
T-16.....VII.3:4 fantasies it brings to its c. relationships in
T-17.......V.9:6 For you have c. but the goal of God, from
T-18.......II.9:3 Its coming means that you have c. truth,
T-18......III.3:2 beside you on the way that you have c.,
T19...IV.D.4:5 ego. These are your c. friends. For in your
T-20.......II.2:5 It will adorn its c. home most carefully,
T-20.......II.2:5 to those who come unto its c. home,
T-20.......II.3:2 but sees his c. home as an altar to himself.
T-20.......II.4:5 you first upon the altar in your c. home,
T-20.......II.4:6 body is your c. home and it is separation
T-20.......II.8:1 c. home is on the other side, beyond the
T-20......VI.4:3 body is the ego's c. weapon for seeking
T-20.....VII.5:7 you have c. judgment and not vision. For
T-20... VIII.4:8 and c. to replace the holy home the Holy
T-22.......I.11:7 in looking on your brother as His c. home
T-22......IV.2:1 right way that seem hard, for you have c.,
T-22.......VI.2:1 Where freedom of the body has been c.,
T-22.......VI.4:1 c. of your Father as a means for His Own
T-23..........I.3:3 upon the body, the ego's c. home, which
T-23......IV.5:4 Here you have c. to be part of it. Here
T-23......IV.6:7 c. to remain where He would have you,
T-24.........II.1:5 had you not c. to make of him a tiny
T-25....III.9:10 the purpose of the world you see is c., and
T-25......IV.1:8 And then the means are c. once again, as
T-26.......V.1:8 will go along the way your c. teacher leads
T-26.......IX.1:4 you as well while you attack His c. home,
T-27.......III.5:4 Yet it sets no limits you have c. to impose.
T-28.....VII.4:5 own, and you have c. that it not be sick.
T-29.........II.1:5 regrets about the way that you have c..
T-30.........II.2:5 Son without what he has c. for himself?
T-31.......I.7:10 you may have overlearned your c. task,
T-31.......II.5:7 you it matters not, for you have c. death.
T-31.......III.6:6 not want to hold in guilt your c. enemies,
T-31.......VI.1:7 reality, for you have c. that you want it so.
W-pI.....28.7:2 only should the subjects be c. randomly,
W-pI.....29.4:1 apply it to randomly c. subjects about you
W-pI.....52.4:5 What I have c. to see has cost me vision.
W-pI.....72.7:5 Your c. savior takes His place instead. It is
WpI. rIII.in7:4 Holy Spirit's c. means for your salvation.
W-pI.121.10:3 You probably have c. him already. He will
W-pI...138.9:1 Heaven is c. consciously. The choice
W-pI...153.9:3 sure we will fulfill our c. purpose, as our
W-pI.153.10:2 have c. that the truth be with them. Who
W-pI.153.10:6 ones who are among the c. ones of God,
W-pI...154.5:2 ask why he has c. those who will receive
W-pI...155.4:2 Many have c. to renounce the world while
W-pI...155.4:4 Others have c. nothing but the world, and
W-pI...166.7:1 This is your c. self, the one you made as a
W-pI.170.11:3 but you have c. that this cruel god remain
W-pI.170.12:4 You have c. Him in place of idols, and
W-pI...194.9:6 enemy, for we have c. that we be its friend
W-pII......1.2:4 the aim that it has c. as its wanted goal?
W-pII......1.3:2 what it sees as interfering with its c. path.
W-pII......4.2:5 What it seeks for now is c. by the aim the
W-pII..254.2:6 our will, as we have c. to remember Him.
W-pII..257.2:1 *is Your c. means for our salvation. Let us not*
W-pII..269.1:2 *It is the means which You have c. to become*
W-pII..272.2:2 Heaven can be c. just as easily as hell, and
W-pII..275.1:2 Yet has this day been c. as the time when
W-pII..286.1:3 *This is the day that has been c. as the time in*
W-pII..310.1:1 *You, as You have c. all my days should be.*
W-pII..312.1:4 and fail to see what we have c. to behold.
W-pII.....329.h I have already c. what You will.
W-pII..335.1:7 having c. to behold my brother in its holy
W-pII..349.1:3 *because I have c. it as the gift I want to give.*
M-in ..........5:9 How are they c.? What do they do? How
M-2 ...........1:2 They were c. for him because the form of
M-2 ...........1:5 Once he has c. to fulfill his role, they are
M-3 ...........5:2 in which each person is given a c. learning
M-5 ......III.1:6 do not realize they have c. sickness. On
M-5 ......III.1:7 they believe that sickness has c. them.
M-10 .........5:9 Whose judgment he has c. now to trust,
M-17 .........2:9 he will give only what he has c. for himself
M-21 .........4:5 learns how to let his words be c. for him
P-2.........V.8:1 Will, and do what it has c. that we do.
P-3.........II.3:4 misguided the direction he may have c..
P-3.........II.7:9 remains, because they have c. that it be so
P-3.........II.9:2 He has c. a road in which there is great
S-1.........IV.3:5 to let it be a freely c. remedy from every
S-1........IV.4:1 c. a newborn chance each time you pray.
S-2...........I.1:3 Yet those who have not yet c. to begin the
S-2.........III.4:3 What you have c. still can be undone, for
S-3...........I.4:5 him the body may become his c. home,
S-3........IV.1:9 They have c. holiness, and given up all

## Christ 366

*See also* He, Him, Himself, His, I, My, One, We, Who, Whom, Whose, You, anti-Christ; Appendix C

T-1.........I.44:1 C. and the acceptance of His Atonement.
T-1.........V.6:2 The abundance of C. is the natural result
T-4.........IV.1:5 ego, and you do not seek the face of C..
T-4......IV.10:1 The First Coming of C. is merely another
T-4......IV.10:1 for the creation, for C. is the Son of God.
T-4......IV.10:2 The Second Coming of C. means nothing
T-4......IV.10:9 means that C. has come into your mind
T-5...........I.3:4 mind be in you that was also in C. Jesus,"
T-5...........I.3:6 I thought, joining with me in C. thinking.
T-5...........I.5:1 Holy Spirit is the C. Mind which is aware
T-9.........I.14:7 *C. is in me, and where He is God must be, for*
T-9.........I.14:7 *He is God must be, for C. is part of Him.*
T-11......IV.6:1 C. is at God's altar, waiting to welcome
T-11......IV.6:4 But love yourself with the Love of C., for
T-11......IV.6:5 cannot bar the door that C. holds open.
T-11......IV.7:1 At God's altar C. waits for the restoration
T-11......IV.7:3 C. waits for your acceptance of Him as
T-11......IV.7:4 For C. is the Son of God, Who lives in His
T-11......IV.7:5 C. is the extension of the Love and the
T-11.....V.17:7 of C. they need demonstrate nothing, for
T-11.....V.17:7 for C. speaks to them of Himself and of
T-11.....V.17:8 They are silent because C. speaks to them,
T-11.....V.18:1 becomes a witness for C. or for the ego,
T-11.....V.18:6 If he speaks not of C. to you, you spoke
T-11.....V.18:6 Christ to you, you spoke not of C. to him.
T-11.....V.18:7 own voice, and if C. speaks through you,
T-11......VI.1:6 is the complete triumph of C. over the ego
T-11......VI.1:7 For C. does rise above the ego and all its
T-11......VI.3:7 Learning of C. is easy, for to perceive with
T-11......VI.3:9 Let the C. in you interpret for you, and do
T-11....VI.3:10 For until C. comes into His Own, the Son
T-11......VI.8:4 awareness of C. come with the awakening
T-11.....VI.10:9 And to C. it is given to be like the Father.
T-11....VIII.9:1 for C. is not deceived in His Father and
T-11....VIII.9:3 Father accepts him and heal him unto C.,
T-11....VIII.9:3 Christ, for C. is his healing and yours.
T-11....VIII.9:4 C. is the Son of God Who is in no way
T-11..VIII.12:1 offended by C. and are deceived in Him.
T-11..VIII.12:2 Heal in C. and be not offended by Him,
T-12.........I.7:4 you answer in the Name of C. brings the
T-12........II.3:6 Love of C. for His Father and for Himself.
T-12........II.5:1 for they are not fitting offerings for C.,
T-12........II.6:5 withstand the Love of C. for His Father,
T-12.....III.10:3 The altar of God where C. abideth is there
T-12.....III.10:5 Yet C. has placed the Atonement on the
T-12.........VI.h The Vision of C.
T-12......VI.4:5 the vision of C. for every Son of God who
T-12......VI.5:4 spring to your sight, for C. has never slept
T-12......VI.5:9 to his Father, where C. waits as his Self.
T-12......VI.6:1 Every child of God is one in C., for his
T-12......VI.6:1 for his being is in C. as Christ's is in God.
T-12......VI.6:3 last led you to C. at the altar to His Father
T-12...VII.11:7 Through the eyes of C., only the real
T-12..VIII.6:11 And C. is invisible to you because of what
T-12.....VIII.8:2 Only take it from the hand of C. and look
T-13.........I.1:5 Guilt hides C. from your sight, for it is the
T-13.........I.2:4 of C. is the proof that the ego never was,
T-13.......V.6:7 And the vision of C. is not in your sight,
T-13.......V.9:2 and yet still within you, is the vision of C.,
T-13.....V.11:1 is the light in which C. stands revealed.
T-13.....V.11:5 saw beyond the darkness the C. in them,
T-13......VI.3:2 The C. as revealed to you now has no past
T-13......VI.7:5 look at C. and call His witnesses to shine
T-13......VI.8:2 and touch them with the touch of C.. In
T-13....VI.12:1 Awaking unto C. is following the laws of
T-13....VI.13:3 alone. Even in sleep has C. protected you,
T-13......VII.5:7 C. is still there, although you know Him
T-13......VII.6:7 C. will always offer you the Will of God,
T-13...VII.14:2 *The Holy Spirit leads me unto C., and where*
T-13....VIII.2:7 vision of C. beholds everything in light.
T-13........X.9:8 from you what C. would have you see. His
T-14........II.7:8 from the hands of C. Who gives it to you,
T-14........II.8:3 vision of C. is given the very instant that it
T-14......VII.6:7 The vision of C. is not for Him alone, but
T-15......III.6:9 then, with littleness in the Name of C.,
T-15.....V.10:8 with God, and all your brothers join in C..
T-15.....V.10:9 are joined in C. are in no way separate.
T-15....V.10:10 For C. is the Self the Sonship shares, as
T-15....V.10:10 shares, as God shares His Self with C..
T-15....VIII.4:6 all its parts are joined in God through C.,
T-15....VIII.4:7 Father. C. knows of no separation from
T-15......X.1:10 The time of C. we celebrate together, for
T-15........X.2:1 The holy instant is truly the time of C..
T-15........X.3:6 time of C. is the time appointed for the
T-15........X.4:1 your power to make the time of C. be now
T-15......XI.2:2 it as the sign the time of C. has come. He
T-15......XI.2:9 Host Who cradles God in the time of C.,
T-15......XI.8:1 time of C. is meaningless apart from joy.
T-15......XI.8:4 Such is the message of the time of C.,

T-15...... XI.8:5 the time of C. communication is restored,
T-15...... XI.10:1 year will soon be born from the time of C.
T-17.... IV.10:5 Heaven, the Love of God, the tears of C.,
T-19....... I.10:6 You see the C. in him, and he is healed
T19... IV.A.2:7 C. asks it of you for Himself. He would
T19... IV.D.2:1 like a heavy veil before the face of C.. Yet
T19... IV.D.2:3 the face of C. Himself like to a leper's, and
T19... IV.D.4:6 the face of C. and join Him in His Father.
T19. IV.D.14:1 Friend, the C. Who stands beside you.
T19. IV.D.14:6 The "enemies" of C., the worshippers of
T-20......... I.1:4 A slain C. has no meaning. But a risen
T-20......... I.1:5 But a risen C. becomes the symbol of the
T-20........ I.2:10 complete till your forgiveness rests on C.,
T-20........ I.4:2 glimpses of the face of C. behind the veil,
T-20...... IV.5:6 he is ready to look upon the face of C.,
T-20...... IV.7:4 the face of C. shines on them and they
T-20....... V.4:5 would see the face of C. and yet insist that
T-20....... V.6:7 of C. you yet will look upon already seen.
T-20...... VI.5:7 Would He Who sees the face of C. choose
T-20.. VI.12:10 held back from looking on the face of C.?
T-20..... VII.4:6 invested with attributes of C. or of the ego
T-20.... VIII.3:3 that C. may rise before your vision and
T-22......... I.7:6 two brothers can unite except through C.,
T-22......... I.8:6 Where C. has entered no one is alone, for
T-22........ I.11:1 C. comes to what is like Himself; the
T-22........ I.11:9 And who is drawn to C. is drawn to God
T-22...... II.12:8 For at its center C. has been reborn, to
T-22...... II.13:1 in quiet here with C. is share His vision.
T-22...... IV.3:1 that hangs between you and the face of C.
T-22...... IV.3:7 The Love of C. will light your face, and
T-22...... IV.4:5 looks upon the C. in you but will rejoice.
T-24.......... V.h The C. in You
T-24....... V.1:1 The C. in you is very still. He looks on
T-24....... V.3:2 The C. in you looks only on the truth, and
T-24....... V.5:2 Be glad that only C. can lend you His,
T-24....... V.6:1 C. in you is very still. He knows where you
T-24....... V.6:6 For what but C. is there to see and hear
T-24....... V.7:7 The sight of C. is all there is to see. The
T-24....... V.7:8 The song of C. is all there is to hear. The
T-24....... V.7:9 hear. The hand of C. is all there is to hold.
T-24....... V.9:3 C. has no doubt, and from His certainty
T-24...... VI.6:5 that hides the face of C. from him, and
T-24...... VI.6:7 Your brother's body shows not C. to you.
T-24...... VI.7:3 by still one more denial of C. in him. And
T-24...... VI.8:7 The C. in you beholds his holiness. Your
T-24.... VI.10:7 The C. in you can see your brother truly.
T-24.... VI.12:4 a nod to God, a greeting to the C. in you,
T-24.... VI.13:2 judging against the C. and setting forth
T-24.... VI.13:4 what you do through C. it does not know.
T-25....... in.1:1 The C. in you inhabits not a body. Yet He
T-25....... in.1:8 C. is within a frame of Holiness whose
T-25....... in.2:1 No one who carries C. in him can fail to
T-25....... in.2:6 is. The son of man is not the risen C.. Yet
T-25....... in.3:3 it is here that C. sets forth the remedy.
T-25......... I.1:1 to do the task that C. appointed you to do
T-25......... I.1:7 is the meeting of the holy C. unto Himself
T-25......... I.2:1 manifest the C. in you except to look on
T-25......... I.2:9 the C. in him proclaims Himself as you.
T-25......... I.4:5 and nothing hides the face of C. from its
T-25......... I.5:4 truth. C. and His Father never have been
T-25......... I.5:4 and C. abides within your understanding,
T-25......... I.5:5 separate, different and special–to the C.,
T-25...... II.8:8 that looks on C. instead of seeing death.
T-25....... V.2:1 Attack makes C. your enemy, and God
T-25....... V.2:9 C. stands before you, each time you look
T-25....... V.3:1 It is not C. you see by looking thus. It is
T-25....... V.3:2 It is the "enemy," confused with C., you
T-26...... IV.3:2 And here you see the face of C., arising in
T-26...... IV.3:3 behold the face of C. and not recall His
T-26...... IX.1:6 eyes on him who carries C. within him,
T-26...... IX.2:1 a little trust for him who carries C. to you,
T-26...... IX.2:2 the face of C. and memory of God. And
T-26...... IX.8:4 stood a cross stands now the risen C., and
T-27....... V.7:5 C. to you who brought the sight to them,
T-29.... VIII.3:1 a gap between the C. and what you see.
T-29.... VIII.3:5 All forms of anti-Christ oppose the C..
T-29.... VIII.4:1 world of idols *is* a veil across the face of C.,
T-30....... I.14:9 And you ask help of anti-Christ or C., and
T-30....... V.7:5 The face of C. is looked upon before the
T-30 ...... V.7:7 Yet is the Love of C. accepted first. And
T-30 ... VIII.5:5 The C. in him is perfect. Is it this that you
T-30 ... VIII.5:8 will see the C. in him because you let Him
T-30 ... VIII.6:7 Why should you fear to see the C. in him?
T-31 ........ I.9:3 The C. in you remembers God with all the
T-31 ......... II.h Walking with C.
T-31 ....... II.7:1 and answer to the C. Who calls to you. Be
T-31 ....... II.7:5 you. C. calls to all with equal tenderness,
T-31 ....... II.9:7 for C. has been reborn to both of you.
T-31 .... VII.8:6 this single vision does he see the face of C.
T-31 .... VII.9:1 The veil across the face of C., the fear of
T-31 .. VII.13:7 face of C. to shine upon the one who asks,
T-31 .. VII.13:7 dear against the vision of the C. in you.
T-31 ... VIII.1:4 this, if C. appeared to you in all His glory,
T-31 ... VIII.2:3 weakness and the strength of C. in you.
T-31 ... VIII.2:6 And the light of C. in you is given charge
T-31 ... VIII.3:2 perplexity C. calls to you and gently says,
T-31 ... VIII.4:3 face of C. is powerless before His majesty,
T-31 ... VIII.7:2 and through the C. in you unveil his eyes,
T-31 ... VIII.7:2 eyes, and let him look upon the C. in him.
T-31 ... VIII.9:3 we travelled on before the C. appeared.
T-31 . VIII.12:2 For C. has come to dwell in the abode You
T-31 . VIII.12:5 to hide the face of C. from anyone. Thy
W-pI..... 59.3:8 of C. has been given me to replace them.
W-pI..... 62.3:1 you call upon the strength of C. in you.
W-pI... 100.8:5 pass as you ascend to meet the C. in you.
W-pI... 110.8:1 Seek Him within you Who is C. in you,
W-pI... 110.9:4 Deep in your mind the holy C. in you is
W-pI. 110.11:3 His Son, our holy Self, the C. in each of us
W-pI... 122.3:1 that hides the face of C. from those who
W-pI... 137.6:2 C. to those who dream the world is real.
W-pI... 151.8:2 C. cannot doubt Himself. The Voice for
W-pI. 151.10:2 behold the gentle face of C. in all of them.
W-pI. 151.12:4 you see the holy face of C. in everything,
W-pI... 153.6:2 It testifies to recognition of the C. in you.
W-pI... 153.7:2 the C. and come to fear His Father's anger
W-pI. 153.19:3 day. We rise up strong in C., and let our
W-pI. 153.20:7 real, to look on C. and see His sinlessness.
W-pI... 158.5:6 sees because the Mind of C. beholds it too
W-pI... 158.9:1 C. has vision that has power to overlook
W-pI. 158.11:3 practice seeing with the eyes of C. today.
W-pI... 159.4:4 C. beholds no sin in anyone. And in His
W-pI... 159.6:5 unmet within this golden treasury of C..
W-pI... 159.9:6 they brought from C. have been delivered
W-pI. 159.10:4 C. has dreamed the dream of a forgiven
W-pI... 160.9:1 Today we offer thanks that C. has come
W-pI. 160.10:1 Not one does C. forget. Not one He fails
W-pI... 161.1:3 to welcome in the C. where fear and anger
W-pI. 161.11:8 *I would behold you with the eyes of C., and*
W-pI. 161.12:3 and recognize that C. has come to you.
W-pI. 161.12:6 enemy to savior; from the devil into C..
W-pI... 164.1:3 not in our sight, but in the eyes of C.. He
W-pI... 164.2:5 C. answers for you, echoing your Self,
W-pI... 164.3:1 as C. gives you His sight and hears for you
W-pI... 164.5:5 Now will you see it with the eyes of C..
W-pI... 164.7:5 We stand forgiven in the sight of C., with
W-pI... 164.8:2 within your mind where C. can come, and
W-pI... 165.5:6 your blindness for the seeing eyes of C.;
W-pI. 166.13:4 of C. there is another way for them to
W-pI. 166.13:5 comes to those who feel the touch of C.,
W-pI. 166.15:4 to accept His gifts, and feel the touch of C.
W-pI... 169.6:4 time, forgiveness and the holy face of C..
W-pI. 169.13:3 What is the face of C. but his who went a
W-pI. 170.12:1 Now do your eyes belong to C., and He
W-pI... 181.8:4 are the eyes of C. inevitably ours. And the
W-pI. 182.10:1 C. is reborn as but a little Child each time
W-pI. 182.11:2 C. has called you friend and brother. He
W-pI... 192.8:1 can be born again in C. but him who has
W-pI... 197.7:3 To everyone who lives will C. yet come,
W-pI. 198.10:1 as the face of C. appears unveiled at last in
W-pI. 198.10:4 shining upon you from the face of C..
W-pII . 223.2:1 *us see the face of C. instead of our mistakes.*
W-pII . 229.1:4 away no longer from the holy face of C..
W-pII . 237.1:4 I behold the world that C. would have me
W-pII . 237.2:1 *C. is my eyes today, and He the ears that*
W-pII ..... 3.5:5 it must behold it through the eyes of C.,
W-pII . 263.2:1 see through holy vision and the eyes of C..
W-pII . 266.1:2 *does C. look back upon me from my Self. Let*
W-pII . 269.1:5 *in which everyone shows me the face of C.,*
W-pII . 270.2:2 C. is our eyes today. And through His
W-pII ........ 6.h What Is the C.?
W-pII ..... 6.1:1 C. is God's Son as He created Him. He is
W-pII ..... 6.2:1 C. is the link that keeps you one with
W-pII ..... 6.3:1 C. remain at peace within the Heaven of
W-pII ..... 6.3:4 Yet will these dreams be given unto C., to
W-pII ..... 6.3:4 His glory and reveal your holy Self, the C.,
W-pII ..... 6.4:1 from the C. in you to all your dreams, and
W-pII ..... 6.5:3 Self, the C. Whom God created as His Son
W-pII . 271.1:2 to look upon what C. would have me see,
W-pII . 295.1:1 C. asks that He may use my eyes today,
W-pII . 295.2:1 *My Father, C. has asked a gift of me, and one*
W-pII . 295.2:2 *Help me to use the eyes of C. today, and thus*
W-pII ..... 9.3:2 all minds are given to the hands of C., to
W-pII ..... 9.4:3 this equality is C. restored as one Identity,
W-pII .... 303.h The holy C. is born in me today.
W-pII . 303.1:4 Let C. be welcomed where He is at home.
W-pII . 303.2:7 *It is not C. that can be crucified. Safe in Your*
W-pII .... 304.h Let not my world obscure the sight of C..
W-pII . 304.1:2 can I behold the holy sights C. looks upon
W-pII . 304.1:5 by looking on it through the eyes of C..
W-pII .... 305.h There is a peace that C. bestows on us.
W-pII . 305.2:1 *Father, the peace of C. is given us, because it*
W-pII .... 306.h The gift of C. is all I seek today.
W-pII . 306.2:4 *Son. But in Your Love the gift of C. is his.*
W-pII . 308.1:6 The birth of C. is now, without a past or
W-pII . 312.1:6 to look upon what C. would have him see,
W-pII . 313.1:4 *The eyes of C. look on a world forgiven. In*
W-pII . 313.2:1 today behold each other in the sight of C..
W-pII ... 13.3:2 The eyes of C. deliver them to all they
W-pII .... 353.h be given C. To use to bless the world with
W-pII . 353.1:1 *Father, I give all that is mine today to C., to*
W-pII . 353.1:5 *and recognize that C. is but my Self.*
W-pII .... 354.h We stand together, C. and I, in peace
W-pII . 354.1:1 *My oneness with the C. establishes me as*
W-pII . 354.1:2 *I have no self except the C. in me. I have no*
W-pII . 354.1:6 *is C. except Your Son as You created Him?*
W-pII . 354.1:7 *Him? And what am I except the C. in me?*
M-4 ...... V.1:13 C. looks down on them in thanks as well.
M-4 ........ X.2:7 No clouds remain to hide the face of C..
M-12 ....... 1:10 him. He has accepted C., and he is saved.
M-13 ......... 4:4 the face of C. look back with longing on a
M-22 ......... 4:5 only the face of C. shining in front of him,
M-23 ......... 1:4 Bible says, "Ask in the name of Jesus C.."
M-23 ......... 1:7 What does it mean to call on Jesus C.?
M-23 ......... 4:1 name of Jesus C. as such is but a symbol.
M-23 ......... 4:5 Remembering the name of Jesus C. is to
M-28 ......... 5:5 have seen the face of C., His sinlessness,
C-1 ........... 1:2 is capitalized it refers to God or C. (i.e., the
C-1 ........... 1:2 (i.e., the Mind of God or the Mind of C.).
C-1 ........... 1:4 The unified spirit is God's one Son, or C..
C-1 ........... 6:3 is not the *One-mindedness* of the C. Mind,
C-3 ............... h FORGIVENESS – THE FACE OF C.
C-3 ........... 4:1 *face of C.* has to be seen before the memory
C-3 ........... 4:3 Seeing the face of C. involves perception.
C-3 ........... 4:5 of C. is the great symbol of forgiveness. It
C-3 ........... 7:6 This is the purpose of the face of C.. It is
C-4 ........... 4:5 was perceived the face of C. appears, and
C-4 ........... 7:6 of C. has shone away time's final instant,
C-5 ............... h JESUS – C.
C-5 ........... 2:1 but saw the face of C. in all his brothers
C-5 ........... 2:2 So he became identified with C., a man no
C-5 ........... 2:6 C. needed his form that He might appear
C-5 ........... 3:1 In his complete identification with the C.
C-5 ........... 5:1 Is he the C.? O yes, along with you. His
C-5 ........... 5:5 be his vision, for the eyes of C. are shared.
C-5 ........... 6:3 C. takes many forms with different names
C-6 ........... 1:1 became completely identified with the C.,
C-6 ........... 1:5 which God alone knows along with C.,
C-6 ........... 3:4 the inherent power of the vision of C.. He
C-6 ........... 3:5 in which the face of C. alone is seen. He
C-6 ........... 4:1 of your mind that is part of the C. Mind.
C-ep .......... 5:1 knowing that C. has been reborn in it,
P-2.......... II.6:7 to share a goal not blessed by C., for what
P-2......... III.4:1 The ideal therapist is one with C.. But
P-2......... III.4:3 to receive the C. or he could not be sick.
P-2......... III.4:6 as he receives them from the Mind of C..
P-2.......... V.5:2 for he comes to us as C. and Savior. What
P-2.......... V.7:8 God, we will behold in him the face of C.,

P-2.......VII.2:3 in a relationship which C. can enter? This
P-2.......VII.2:6 But once C. enters in, what choice is there
P-2.......VII.3:3 Only C. forgives, knowing His sinlessness.
P-2.......VII.4:5 for what should be the Holiness of C..
P-2.......VII.7:6 He does not see the C. in him who calls.
P-3..... II.10:10 This is the veil across the face of C.. Yet it
P-3........III.6:4 the resting place of C. and home of God
P-3........III.8:7 Let the C. in you bid him welcome, for
P-3........III.8:7 for that same C. is in him as well. Deny
P-3........III.8:8 you have denied the C. in you. Remember
S-1...........I.7:1 Praying to C. in anyone is true prayer
S-1...........I.7:2 that C. be but Himself is not an entreaty.
S-1........ I.7:10 you have realized that C. is in both of you.
S-1......... II.4:6 that you may not seek to imprison C. and
S-1......... II.5:1 enemy is the symbol of an imprisoned C..
S-1......... II.5:5 of C. and a recognition of His sinlessness.
S-1......... II.6:3 The enemy is you, as is the C.. Before it
S-1......... II.7:5 in C. is fully recognized as set forever,
S-1........III.5:8 He is no jailer, but a messenger of C.. Be
S-1......... V.3:3 A dream has veiled the face of C. from you
S-1......... V.4:6 be, for you have recognized the C. in you.
S-2...........I.3:5 sin by choosing in its place the face of C..
S-2...........I.6:5 an instant only seem to hide the face of C.
S-2...........I.6:8 eyes that look past error to the C. in you.
S-2...........I.7:5 C. has forgiven you, and in His sight the
S-2...........I.8:1 when he could see the face of C. instead?
S-2......... II.7:7 C. is for all because He is in all. It is His
S-2........III.2:3 eyes of C. become the sight you choose.
S-2........III.5:4 The light of C. in him is his release, and it
S-2........III.5:5 Forgive him as the C. decides you should,
S-2........III.7:4 Let it arise to C., Who welcomes it as gift
S-2........III.7:7 silently open upon the shining face of C..
S-3...........I.3:3 all shadows on the holy face of C., among
S-3......... II.1:6 is still the wish to die and overcome the C.
S-3......... II.2:3 and to reach the C. in hidden forms and
S-3......... II.3:5 us. For C. is clearer now; His vision more
S-3........IV.2:6 C. has taught to see His likeness and to
S-3........IV.3:1 what it means to help the C. to heal! Can
S-3........IV.6:6 Give all your dreams to C. and let Him be
S-3........IV.8:8 Love. Do not deny to C. what is His Own.

## Christ's 90

*See also* His, My, Whose

T-1......... V.6:1 has chosen to be led by me in C. service.
T-12......VI.4:4 C. eyes are open, and He will look upon
T-12......VI.6:1 for his being is in Christ as C. is in God.
T-12......VI.6:2 C. Love for you is His Love for His Father,
T-13..... V.10:3 for through C. vision He beholds Himself.
T-13.....VI.13:8 he slept, C. vision did not leave him. And
T-13... VIII.4:4 is why C. vision looks on everything with
T-13... VIII.4:5 Yet even C. vision is not His reality. The
T-13... VIII.5:5 to make C. vision possible even here.
T-13... VIII.6:6 C. vision is His gift to you. His Being is
T-13... VIII.7:1 with healing, for C. gift you can bestow,
T-13... VIII.7:2 Offer C. gift to everyone and everywhere,
T-13... X.10:11 And in C. vision He would show you the
T-22.......IV.4:7 offering C. forgiveness to dispel their faith
T-24....... II.5:6 C. vision is their "enemy," for it sees not
T-24....... V.7:2 C. hand holds all His brothers in Himself.
T-25.........I.6:1 Spirit serves C. purpose in your mind, so
T-27....... V.6:5 to see beyond all suffering and see C. face
T-29... VIII.4:8 fear. C. enemy is nowhere. He can take no
T-30......... V.7:4 their hands it was C. hand they took, and
T-31... VIII.4:2 again, and let C. strength prevail in every
T-31... VIII.5:5 *Son.* Thus is C. strength invited to prevail,
W-pI.....59.2:5 C. vision is His gift, and He has given it to
W-pI...124.9:5 you. And you will see C. face upon it, in
W-pI...151.8:4 witnesses before the rapture of C. holy
W-pI...153.6:3 C. strength and your own weakness, seen
W-pI...157.9:1 Into C. Presence will we enter now,
W-pI...158.5:4 give directly, for C. knowledge is not lost,
W-pI...158.6:6 Our concern is with C. vision. This we can
W-pI...158.7:1 C. vision has one law. It does not look
W-pI.158.10:2 And thus C. vision looks on you as well.
W-pI.158.10:5 chance to let C. vision shine on you, and
W-pI.158.11:4 C. vision looks upon ourselves as well.
W-pI...159.3:1 C. vision is a miracle. It comes from far
W-pI...159.3:3 C. vision pictures Heaven, for it sees a
W-pI...159.4:1 C. vision is the miracle in which all
W-pI...159.5:1 C. vision is the bridge between the
W-pI...159.8:1 C. vision is the holy ground in which the
W-pI...159.8:4 and kindly care C. charity provides. They
W-pI...161.6:4 of love's "enemy" C. vision does not see.
W-pI...161.9:3 And in C. vision is his loveliness reflected
W-pI.161.10:2 and you will come today nearer C. vision.
W-pI...162.4:5 God. C. vision has restored your sight by
W-pI...164.8:5 Is not C. vision worthy to be sought above
W-pI...165.6:2 Now is C. power in your mind, to heal as
W-pI...166.8:1 should feel C. touch upon your shoulder,
W-pI...166.9:2 C. hand has touched your shoulder, and
W-pI.166.14:5 Your hand becomes the giver of C. touch;
W-pI.166.15:2 proof of what C. touch can offer everyone.
W-pI...192.6:1 that, for C. vision and the gift of sight, no
W-pII.....in.6:5 as through C. vision we behold a world
W-pII..247.1:3 means whereby C. vision comes to me.
W-pII..260.1:6 *my sinlessness arise again before C. vision,*
W-pII.....269.h My sight goes forth to look upon C. face.
W-pII..270.1:1 *Father, C. vision is Your gift to me, and it has*
W-pII......6.4:3 for what remains to see except C. face?
W-pII......6.5:2 to find C. face and look on nothing else.
W-pII.....271.h C. is the vision I will use today.
W-pII..271.1:3 In C. sight, the world and God's creation
W-pII..271.2:1 *Father, C. vision is the way to You. What He*
W-pII..290.1:3 have C. vision come to me this very day.
W-pII..291.1:1 C. vision looks through me today. His
W-pII......9.1:1 C. Second Coming, which is sure as God,
W-pII......9.2:1 It is the all-inclusive nature of C. Second
W-pII..302.1:6 *C. vision changes darkness into light, for*
W-pII..305.1:1 but C. vision finds a peace so deep and
W-pII..305.1:4 and healed the world by giving it C. peace
W-pII..306.1:1 What but C. vision would I use today,
W-pII....10.1:1 C. Second Coming gives the Son of God
W-pII....10.2:3 and now without a function in C. sight, it
W-pII..312.1:6 and share C. Love for what he looks upon.
W-pII..340.1:4 *him to find C. vision through forgiveness,*
W-pII.....349.h Today I let C. vision look upon All things
W-pII....14.4:1 eyes through which C. vision sees a world
M-4....... X.1:5 hell, so open-mindedness lets C. image be
M-18.........2:5 ears, and bring C. vision to eyes that see.
M-22.........5:4 hardly offer it to his brother in C. Name.
M-23.........5:8 eyes C. vision shines in perfect constancy.
M-25.........6:9 go with C. gratitude upon their hearts,
M-28.........2:6 C. face is seen in every living thing, and
M-28.........6:3 and seeing there the vision of C. face to
C-1............5:2 C. vision sees the real world in its place.
C-4............4:1 world stands like a block before C. face.
C-5............6:4 of C. single message of the Love of God.
P-2......... II.5:4 first through C. vision and then through
P-2......... II.9:2 who stands apart can receive C. vision. It
P-2.......VII.6:8 behold C. shining face as it looks back at
S-2...........I.6:4 C. vision does not use your eyes, but you
S-2...........I.8:3 from death by offering C. Love to him.
S-2........III.3:1 form should be that C. forgiveness takes.

## Christian 1

T-3...........I.1:8 Yet the real C. should pause and ask,

## Christians 2

T-3...........I.1:3 Many sincere C. have misunderstood this
T-3...........I.4:4 been hard for many C. to realize that this

## Christmas 5

T-15...... III.7:1 In this season (C.) which celebrates the
T-15.........XI.h C. as the End of Sacrifice
T-15....... XI.2:1 The sign of C. is a star, a light in darkness
T-15....... XI.3:1 This C. give the Holy Spirit everything
T-15....... XI.8:1 Let no despair darken the joy of C., for

## church 7

T-6...........I.8:2 it is still on them that I must build my c..
T-6...........I.8:3 you can be the foundation of God's c.. A
T-6...........I.8:4 A c. is where an altar is, and the presence
T-6...........I.8:4 of the altar is what makes the c. holy. A
T-6...........I.8:5 c. that does not inspire love has a hidden
T-6...........I.8:6 I must found His c. on you, because those
T-22...... III.4:7 it made; the rock on which its c. is built,

## churches 1

T-13. VII.10:12 cornerstone in the c. it builds to itself.

## churn 1

W-pI.....47.7:3 Let go all the trivial things that c. and

## circle 27

T-14......... V.h The C. of Atonement
T-14....... V.7:6 The c. of Atonement has no end. And you
T-14....... V.7:7 your safe inclusion in the c. with everyone
T-14....... V.8:3 Within its holy c. is everyone whom God
T-14....... V.8:6 Stand quietly within this c., and attract all
T-14....... V.9:4 I stand within the c., calling you to peace.
T-14..... V.11:1 the holy c. of Atonement or leave outside,
T-14..... V.11:2 If you bring him into the c. of purity, you
T-14..... V.11:7 Come gladly to the holy c., and look out
T-18....VIII.2:6 It draws a c., infinitely small, around a
T-18...... IX.4:1 The c. of fear lies just below the level the
T-18...... IX.9:1 light, this c. of brightness is the real world
T-21.........I.8:1 as you look into a great and shining c..
T-21.........I.8:2 all the c. fills with light before your eyes.
T-21.........I.8:3 The edges of the c. disappear, and what is
T-22.......in.4:9 golden c. where you recognize the Son of
T-22.......II.12:1 the bright, endless c. that extends forever,
T-28........II.1:6 The c. of creation has no end. Its starting
T-29..... VII.8:1 appeared to be an endless c. of despair,
W-pI....22.1:4 becomes an increasingly vicious c. until
W-pI.....69.4:2 Think of your mind as a vast c.,
W-pI.....69.4:3 outside the c. and quite apart from it.
W-pI...109.8:2 into the boundless c. of your peace, the
W-pI...153.3:1 It is as if a c. held it fast, wherein another
W-pI...153.3:1 wherein another c. bound it and another
P-2........IV.6:8 Thus is the c. closed against the "inroads"
P-2........IV.9:3 This curious c. of attack-defense is one of

## circles 1

W-pI...153.3:2 become the c. of the hours and the days

## circling 1

T-31..... VII.3:3 than just a shadow c. round the good.

## circuitous 1

T-15........X.5:1 to follow fear through all the c. routes by

## circular 6

T-2....... VII.2:3 a c. process that would not foster the time
T-3...... VI.11:2 or the c. reasoning in this position would
T-11..... V.14:3 and with characteristically c. reasoning
T-21........II.5:5 and you will also see how c. the reasoning
T-21....... V.6:1 simple; never c. and never self-defeating.
W-pI.......9.1:7 indeed be c. to aim at understanding, and

## circularity 1

T-27....VIII.7:1 of c. whose ending starts at its beginning,

## circumscribed 1

C-5............ 1:2 you are c. by false beliefs of your Identity,

## circumstance 24

T-24...... III.3:1 that you do not like, a c. that suits you not
T-24...... VI.3:5 His Mind about His Son with passing c.
T-24...... VI.4:5 in all respects, in every way and every c.,
T-25..VIII.12:2 You need not perceive, in every c., that
T-26..... V.12:4 to illusion for all time and every c.. And

T-26...VII.18:5 There is no **c.** it cannot answer, and no
T-29.........I.6:5 misuse each **c.** and everyone you meet,
T-29....VIII.1:9 body or a thing, a place, a situation or a **c.**
T-30.....VII.4:4 perceive it everywhere, unchanged by **c.**.
T-31....... V.9:6 it comes, what you should do in every **c.**?
T-31....VIII.4:2 let Christ's strength prevail in every **c.**
W-pI.....42.2:2 are, and in whatever **c.** you find yourself.
W-pI.....44.2:4 always, making vision possible in every **c.**.
W-pI.....47.3:1 God is your safety in every **c.**. His Voice
W-pI.....71.2:2 if some external **c.** or event were changed,
W-pI...108.6:2 always works, in every **c.** where it is tried,
W-pI...127.1:6 It never alters with a person or a **c.**. It is
W-pI.151.11:2 all you see, and all occurrences, each **c.**,
W-pI...158.7:5 And it looks on everyone, on every **c.**, all
W-pI...160.1:5 Who could be sane in such a **c.**? Who but
M-4 ..... I.A.7:8 ask only what he really wants in every **c.**.
M-16 .........8:4 any time, in any place and **c.** he calls for it
M-20 .........3:4 as justified in any way or any **c.** proclaims
P-3........ III.8:5 function is in every **c.** and at all times.

## circumstances 14

T-7......... II.2:7 adapted to **c.** if they are to maintain order
T-7......... II.2:9 have been adapted to the **c.** of this world,
T-13...... IV.3:1 Under the **c.**, would it not be more
T-21.........I.6:1 and the **c.** in which you heard completely
W-pI.....40.2:4 You can practice quite well under any **c.**,
W-pI.....43.4:2 suitable time that **c.** and readiness permit
W-pI.....43.7:1 the form may vary according to the **c.** and
W-pI.....47.6:2 fully justified in every respect and in all **c.**.
W-pI.....50.3:1 the Love of God will protect you in all **c.**.
W-pI...193.3:4 is changed, with different **c.** and events;
M-4 ..... I.A.3:6 for changes in what seem to be external **c.**
M-4 ..... I.A.4:5 events, encounters and **c.** are helpful. It is
M-22 .........6:2 applicable to all individuals in all **c.**. And
M-24 .........2:1 Reincarnation would not, under any **c.**,

## circumvent 2

T-27....VIII.6:5 to think that time can come to **c.** eternity,
W-pI...106.3:1 afraid today to **c.** the voices of the world.

## citadel 2

T-19....... II.7:1 no stone in all the ego's embattled **c.** that
W-pII .261.1:2 think I live within the **c.** where I am safe

## cite 2

T-5........ VI.4:4 does the ego **c.** Scripture for its purpose,
W-pI...196.2:2 is quick to **c.** the truth to save its lies. Yet

## city 2

T-13.....VII.3:3 and no **c.** that you built has withstood the
T-18...... IX.7:2 A solid mountain range, a lake, a **c.**, all

## clad 2

W-pII .227.2:3 again, released from sin and **c.** in holiness
S-1......... II.7:7 and **c.** forever in the pure sinlessness that

## claim 37

T-5........ VI.3:4 else can the chance to **c.** it for yourself be
T-7...........I.2:8 **c.** this power when you become vigilant
T-11....... V.8:3 one **c.** to your allegiance is that it can give
T-13...... IV.3:2 no one would **c.** that it proves there *is* life.
T-15...... IV.4:4 **c.** the holy instant any time and anywhere
T-25...... IX.8:1 you will not **c.** your right to them because
T-27..... VII.6:7 They support its **c.** on your allegiance.
T-28...... IV.4:3 him, merely by your **c.** on brotherhood,
W-pI.....58.5:2 lies my **c.** to all good and only good. I am
W-pI...71.9:10 is enough to establish your **c.** to God's
W-pI.....77.2:1 **c.** to miracles does not lie in your illusions
W-pI.....77.3:1 will **c.** the miracles which are your right,
W-pI.....80.4:1 will **c.** the peace that must be ours when
W-pI.....96.9:4 Its Thoughts, and **c.** them as your own.
W-pI...105.6:4 you must return to **c.** them as your own.
W-pI...126.3:4 He has no **c.** on your forgiveness. It holds
W-pI.133.13:1 to find everything and **c.** it as their own.
W-pI...139.7:2 to be a home where those who **c.** they do
WpIrIV.in10:2 and are learning now to **c.** again as your
W-pI...154.9:6 do you identify with Him and **c.** your own
W-pI...166.3:2 he may be called to **c.** them as his own, is
W-pI......168.h Your grace is given me. I **c.** it now.
W-pI...168.4:3 as hearts rise up and **c.** the light as theirs.
W-pI...168.6:6 *I c. it now. Father, I come to You. And You*
WpI.rV.in10:6 before illusion seemed to **c.** the world.
W-pI...179.2:2 I **c.** it now. God is but Love, and therefore
W-pI.183.10:5 He makes his **c.** to all his Father gave, is
W-pI...197.2:4 leave the prison house, or **c.** your strength
W-pII .314.1:4 Death will not **c.** the future now, for life is
W-pII ....334.h Today I **c.** the gifts forgiveness gives.
W-pII .347.1:4 *freedom, and I choose to c. Your gift today.*
W-ep .........5:4 thus making sure that hell will **c.** you not,
M-10 .........3:7 in grandiose fantasies would **c.** this for
M-16 .........3:7 **c.** that title until he has gone through the
C-4 ............6:9 God has come to **c.** His Own. Forgiveness
S-1......... V.1:4 not **c.** that you must rule the universe, nor
S-2..........II.3:2 the other does not **c.** to be the better.

## claimed 3

T-25 ... III.8:11 For what it **c.** could never be, has been.
T-26 ..... IX.4:4 What hatred **c.** is given up to love, and
W-pI...197.2:4 strength beside them, to be sought and **c.**,

## claims 4

T-13 .......II.2:4 ideals," which the ego **c.** you have failed.
T-21 ..... IV.2:6 Loudly indeed the ego **c.** it is; too loudly
T-24 .... VII.3:1 worth while specialness **c.** you instead?
M-13 ......... 8:8 learning **c.** it and your learning gives it.

## clamor 1

T-21 ..... IV.8:7 made meaningful by repetition and by **c.**.

## clarification 5

T-5 ....... III.1:5 This needs **c.**, not in statement but in
T-7 ........ V.1:3 with healing that it does need **c.**. The
T-17 ..... VI.2:3 **c.** of the goal belongs at the beginning, for
C-in ...........2:2 Yet those who seek **c.** will find it as well.
C-in ...........5:3 Since you have asked for **c.**, however,

## clarified 3

T-5 ........ V.1:1 meaningful if the ego's use of guilt is **c.**.
T-6 ..........I.2:7 led to the resurrection was not **c.** then.
W-pI...187.3:4 is the idea of giving **c.** and given meaning.

## clarifies 2

T-4 ..........I.1:1 A good teacher **c.** his own ideas and
WpI...rV.in4:2 one but **c.** some aspect of this thought, or

## clarify 4

T-1 ......VII.5:4 I have been careful to **c.** my role in the
T-3 ........ V.1:4 will **c.** some of our subsequent statements
T-6 ..... V.B.3:3 and we can **c.** this still further now. At
W-pI. 169.10:1 is no need to further **c.** what no one in the

## clarifying 1

T-2 .........II.3:6 will have little difficulty in **c.** the means.

## clarion 1

T-27 .......II.6:5 disappear before the ancient **c.** call of life.

## clarity 13

T-2 ..... III.1:12 can, however, see the altar with perfect **c.**.
T-6 ..... V.B.4:5 the increasing **c.** of the Holy Spirit's Voice
T-11 .......V.2:9 **C.** undoes confusion by definition, and to
T-12 ...VIII.3:2 for the Holy Spirit sees it with perfect **c.**.
T-14 ..... VI.6:7 He will interpret it to you with perfect **c.**,
T-14 .... VII.7:7 to your mind with **c.** and brightness so
T-17 ... IV.13:3 The other is framed for perfect **c.**. The
T-25 ..... VI.2:2 the **c.** it brings to what they look upon.
T-26 .......X.1:8 They are known with **c.** or not at all.
T-31 .... VII.7:2 vision, so that you behold nothing with **c.**
W-pI .. 161.4:5 words bring perfect **c.** with them to you?
W-pI .. 195.7:4 gathers **c.** as we are willing once again to
C-2 ............ 4:2 And this is shown to us with perfect **c.**. It

## clash 3

T-4 ..........I.6:1 Egos can **c.** in any situation, but spirit
T-4 ..........I.6:1 in any situation, but spirit cannot **c.** at all.
T-23 ..... IV.5:8 battle, but the **c.** of forms is meaningless.

## clashes 1

T-24 ........I.3:2 but always **c.** with the reality of God's

## clashing 1

W-pI .. 109.1:2 midst of all the turmoil born of **c.** dreams.

## classification 1

W-pI .... 10.4:5 Try to avoid **c.** of any kind. In fact, if you

## classifies 2

M-8 ........... 4:3 The mind **c.** what the body's eyes bring to
M-10 ......... 1:6 even the same person **c.** the same action

## classifying 1

T-14 .......X.4:3 Yet you are also used to **c.** some of your

## classrooms 1

T-2 .........II.5:3 itself, like the **c.** in which it occurs, is

## clause 1

T-29 ........I.3:9 in which a **c.** of separation was a point

## claws 1

W-pI .. 161.8:4 and **c.** the air in frantic hope it can reach

## clay 2

T19 ... IV.B.4:8 want your Father, not a little mound of **c.**,
T-28 ..... III.7:5 within a separate and uncertain bit of **c.**?

## clean 26

T-14 ..... IX.5:5 You need but leave the mirror **c.** and clear
T-14 ..... IX.6:5 **C.** but the mirror, and the message that
T-14 ..... IX.7:1 of your mind **c.** to receive the image of the
T-15 ........I.8:4 Each instant is a **c.**, untarnished birth, in
T-15 ........I.8:6 It is so beautiful and so **c.** and free of guilt
T-15 ..... III.6:1 hold your magnitude, **c.** of all littleness,
T-17 ..........II.2:2 It is the real world, bright and **c.** and new,
T-18 ... IX.14:3 the bright world of new and **c.** perception
T-23 ......in.4:6 the **c.** place where littleness does not exist
T-23 ......in.6:5 it is to walk, **c.** and redeemed and happy,
T-24 ........I.8:8 has been made **c.** of special goals. And
T-24 .......II.1:6 stand as tall and stately, **c.** and honest,
T-28 ..... III.6:1 the space left **c.** and vacant by the miracle
T-28 ..... IV.8:5 left **c.** of all the seeds of sickness and of
T-31 .....V.17:5 enter in its sanctuary, **c.** and free of guilt.
T-31 ...VIII.8:4 so new and **c.** and fresh you will forget the
W-pI .... 28.5:2 beautiful and **c.** and of infinite value, full
W-pI .... 65.6:4 *c. slate let my true function be written for me*
W-pI .... 75.6:2 and **c.** of every concept you have made.
W-pI .. 127.9:5 love's meaning to your **c.** and open mind.

W-pI.151.13:4 and give them back again as **c.** ideas that
W-pI...164.8:2 and leave a **c.** and open space within your
W-pI...169.1:4 received; an altar **c.** and holy for the gift.
W-pI...188.9:6 and wash them **c.** of strange desires and
W-pI...192.4:1 and leaves the world a **c.** and unmarked
C-4............4:4 there is an empty place made **c.** and ready

## cleanness 1

T-15...... I.13:7 In the crystal **c.** of the release you give is

## cleanse 1

T-13......III.7:6 kept to hurt you and **c.** it of its littleness,

## cleansed 5

T-18......IX.9:4 **c.** of every evil thought you laid upon it.
T-18....IX.14:2 every perception has been **c.** and purified,
T19.IV.A.15:2 **c.** of all guilt and softly brushed with
T-26......IX.4:6 it. The bloodied earth is **c.**, and the insane
S-2 ...........I.9:4 and **c.** from evil usages and hateful goals.

## cleanses 1

W-pII..222.1:2 the water which renews and **c.** me. He is

## clear 91

*See also* clear-cut

T-2......... II.1:2 have made it **c.** that miracles are natural,
T-2... V.A.12:1 **c.** distinction between what is created and
T-3...........I.1:1 further point must be perfectly **c.** before
T-3...........I.6:6 It is perfectly **c.** because it exists in light.
T-3........IV.5:5 only way out of ambiguity is **c.** perception
T-3......... V.1:3 I have also made it **c.** that the resurrection
T-3....... V.10:9 the miracle that is you is perfectly **c.**.
T-4.......VII.1:1 **c.** that while the content of any particular
T-5...........I.7:2 First, its universality is perfectly **c.**, and
T-6...........I.5:1 I have made it perfectly **c.** that I am like
T-6...........I.9:3 It was **c.** that this was only because of the
T-6........ I.13:1 message of the crucifixion is perfectly **c.**:
T-6....... II.11:4 is surely **c.** that the perfect need nothing,
T-6......... V.3:5 This simple statement is perfectly **c.**,
T-7........III.4:9 reality. The altar is perfectly **c.** in thought,
T-7......... X.2:1 is surely **c.** that you can both accept into
T-7........XI.5:8 that is immediate, **c.** and natural. You
T-9......... V.8:5 makes healing **c.** in any situation in which
T-10....... II.6:4 outcome of your decision is perfectly **c.**, if
T-10....III.11:8 it is **c.** this has nothing to do with reality,
T-10....III.11:8 it is equally **c.** that it has everything to do
T-11....III.4:10 for the light is here and the way is **c.**.
T-11......VI.3:1 This course is perfectly **c.**. If you do not
T-13......IV.7:2 The reason is equally **c.**, for they perceive
T-13......VI.9:3 your thanks in His **c.** Answer to your call.
T-13......XI.3:9 Everything is **c.** and bright, and calls forth
T-14....... II.8:4 Where everything is **c.**, it is all holy. The
T-14......VI.1:6 **c.** and you would be no longer in the dark
T-14......VI.4:2 make the falsity of its opposite perfectly **c.**
T-14......IX.5:5 need but leave the mirror clean and **c.** of
T-14......IX.5:7 Only the **c.** reflection of Himself can be
T-14......IX.6:4 It is **c.**. Clean but the mirror, and the
T-15.........I.8:3 stands **c.** and separated from the past,
T-15......IV.4:3 perfectly **c.** because you have been willing
T-15......IV.5:1 holy instant, as **c.** as you would have me.
T-16......III.2:6 Cause and effect are very **c.** in the ego's
T-17......III.7:1 to light your way and make it **c.** to you.
T-17....... V.3:4 distressing. The reason is quite **c.**. For the
T-17......VI.1:3 for this it is apparent that it must be **c.**.
T-17... VIII.1:4 the **c.** and unequivocal demonstration of
T-20. VIII.11:1 views of gardens under open skies, with **c.**
T-21....... V.7:8 because the witnesses on its behalf are **c.**.
T-21.....VII.8:3 And then it will be **c.** to you that, as you
T-23......III.4:8 vision, forever **c.** and never out of sight, if
T-24....... II.1:3 by searching for, and keeping **c.** in sight,
T-25.........I.5:5 make the oneness **c.** to what is really one.
T-25......VI.2:4 than what is wholly **c.** and unambiguous.
T-26... VIII.7:7 And then its meaning will be **c.**. This is
T-27......IV.1:6 be **c.** you cannot answer anything at all,
T-28..... II.10:1 Spirit requests you learn, the miracle is **c.**.
T-30.......in.1:2 The goal is **c.**, but now you need specific
T-30.......I.13:1 must be **c.** that it is easier to have a happy
T-30......... V.2:2 it is **c.** that by attack is understanding lost
T-31..... II.11:3 **c.** that while you still insist on leading or
T-31......IV.4:8 see the purpose of the lesson shining **c.**,
T-31. VIII.12:7 **C.** in Your likeness does the light shine
W-pI.......3.2:1 you **c.** your mind of all past associations,
W-pI.......9.2:5 step will **c.** a little of the darkness away,
W-pI.....39.1:2 simple, very **c.** and totally unambiguous.
W-pI.....41.6:6 keeping it **c.** of any thoughts that might
W-pI.....70.3:1 be **c.** to you why the recognition that guilt
W-pI.....78.1:1 Perhaps it is not yet quite **c.** to you that
W-pI.....81.3:3 And in this light will my function stand **c.**
W-pI...104.4:2 **c.** a holy place within our minds before
W-pI...104.5:1 do we **c.** the way for Him today by simply
W-pI...122.6:6 for here we have an answer, **c.** and plain,
W-pI.122.13:4 Retain your gifts in **c.** awareness as you
W-pI.131.13:2 standing in a light so bright and **c.** that
W-pI.133.10:1 tries to keep its halo **c.** within his vision,
WpI.rIV.in5:2 **c.** it of all thoughts that would deceive,
W-pI...151.7:1 will **c.** the way to recognize yourself, and
W-pI...161.4:4 thoughts make **c.** the meaning of creation
W-pI...164.1:6 of Heaven, and the Voice for God more **c.**,
W-pI...164.3:4 the world are **c.** to you who will today
W-pI...164.5:6 Now is its transformation **c.** to you.
W-pI.169.13:3 and brought a **c.** reflection of the unity he
WpI rV.in11:4 up before our minds, and keep it **c.** in our
W-pI.186.11:1 stands out **c.** and wholly unambiguous.
W-pII..259.1:2 strange and the distorted seem more **c.**?
W-pII.....285.h My holiness shines bright and **c.** today.
W-pII..293.1:3 the world seem bright and **c.** and safe and
W-pII..321.1:7 *the way to You is opening and **c.** to me at last.*
W-pII..351.1:5 *Friend beside me, and my way secure and **c.**.*
M-20 .......3:10 initial contrast stands out **c.** and apparent
C-2............3:3 **c.** because its nature seems to have a form
C-2...........10:4 and having met at last the choice is **c.**.
C-5............3:4 He made a **c.** distinction, still obscure to
S-2 .........I.10:4 freedom. Let it then be **c.** to you exactly
S-2 ......... II.1:4 The difference is **c.** in several forms where
S-2 ...... III.6:11 His answer will be **c.** as morning, nor is
S-3 ........ III.1:2 Its separate goals become quite **c.** in this,

## clear-cut 7

T-6......V.C.4:4 difficulty, but with **c.** priority for vigilance
T-8.....VII.14:5 result, is a **c.** indication of a poor learner.
T-12.........I.2:2 The whole process represents a **c.** attempt
T-12.........I.9:9 conceals to **c.** unequivocal predominance,
T-12....... V.5:2 progress only under constant, **c.** direction
T-17.....IV.15:1 of light, in **c.** and unmistakable contrast,
T-17......VI.3:1 Without a **c.**, positive goal, set at the

## cleared 3

W-pI.......9.2:5 has been **c.** of the debris that darkens it.
W-pI.....74.5:1 After you have **c.** your mind in this way,
W-pI.139.12:2 For several minutes let your mind be **c.** of

## clearer 4

T-5......... V.1:1 some of our concepts will become **c.** and
T-11.......in.3:4 thought system, the **c.** the light becomes.
T-14.....VII.2:8 see it, and the **c.** what it conceals becomes
S-3 ......... II.3:5 us. For Christ is **c.** now; His vision more

## clearest 4

T-16.........I.2:1 The **c.** proof that empathy as the ego uses
T-16....... V.3:2 The "dynamics" of the ego are **c.** here, for
M-4 .....VII.1:8 In the **c.** way possible, and at the simplest
M-17 .........5:4 It states, in the **c.** form possible, that the

## clearly 93

T-2...........I.4:9 free, but also shows you **c.** that you *are* free
T-2....... V.10:4 perceptions **c.** imply their dependence on
T-2........ VI.2:4 here that you would do well to look at **c.**.
T-3...........I.1:9 have **c.** stated is unworthy of His Son?
T-3........ III.5:5 are **c.** implying that you do not know God
T-3........ IV.4:2 **c.** demonstrating that knowledge is not
T-3.......VII.3:1 but its meaning must be **c.** understood.
T-3.......VII.5:2 destructive and **c.** in opposition to God,
T-4......... V.2:2 because they **c.** point to the nonexistence
T-4......... V.5:4 must be formulated **c.** and kept in mind.
T-4....... VII.7:3 to Him, which would **c.** be impossible,
T-6.........I.15:3 is **c.** the opposite of everything I taught.
T-6.........I.16:7 the result of **c.** opposed thought systems;
T-6......V.A.2:3 It is **c.** a separation device, and therefore
T-6...... V.B.1:3 ideas are **c.** the result of dissociation and
T-6...... V.B.5:1 **c.** to choose one and relinquish the other.
T-6...... V.B.8:6 ultimate decision, it is **c.** not the final one.
T-7........ III.2:7 That is so contradictory it is **c.** impossible
T-7........ VI.3:4 It is perfectly logical but **c.** insane. The
T-9........ IV.4:4 ego's plan is to have you see error **c.** first,
T-9........ IV.4:6 By seeing it **c.**, you have made it real and
T-9.......VII.4:6 **c.** out of accord with its perception of you
T-11....... V.4:3 which is so **c.** senseless that any effort on
T-11..... V.13:3 is **c.** the characteristically contradictory
T-11..... V.14:6 Holding error **c.** in mind, and protecting
T-11..... V.15:1 this, and it is **c.** not understandable, but
T-11...... VI.3:2 If you do not see it **c.**, it is because you are
T-12....... V.5:4 situation you **c.** require a special Teacher
T-12....... V.6:2 goals where yours have **c.** failed. Your
T-12.....VII.3:2 enables you to do is **c.** not of this world,
T-12.....VII.3:3 enables you to do is **c.** beyond all of them.
T-14.......in.1:3 means for learning it and seeing it quite **c.**
T-14.......in.1:5 pointing as **c.** to Heaven as the ego points
T-14.......in.1:7 seeming clearness seems to be **c.** seen. Let
T-14.....VII.3:4 These are **c.** opposite viewpoints on what
T-14....... IX.2:3 when its impossible nature is **c.** revealed?
T-15.........I.4:9 system before, but never so **c.** as here. For
T-15.......II.4:12 to Him will speak so **c.** of Him that you
T-15...... III.6:1 **c.** and in perfect safety in your mind,
T-15.....VII.3:2 real to you, it is essential to look at it **c.**,
T-15...VII.11:3 alone? It is **c.** insane to believe that by
T-15....VIII.1:6 perceives as **c.** as He knows forgiveness is
T-15........X.6:6 For when the recognition dawns **c.**, you
T-16........II.4:5 reality of what has **c.** been accomplished
T-16........II.8:1 many witnesses that speak of it so **c.** that
T-16........II.8:4 His Voice has spoken **c.**, and yet you have
T-16...... III.3:6 Yet this Self you **c.** do not know, and do
T-16...... IV.1:4 salvation will rise **c.** before your open eyes
T-17.... III.1:11 speak so **c.** for the separation that no one
T-17...... IV.2:5 have given them is **c.** not to make happy.
T-17....... V.3:5 and **c.** unsuited to the purpose that has
T-18.........I.2:5 Substitution is **c.** a process in which they
T-18........II.1:3 **c.** not the world you saw before you slept.
T-18........II.5:3 Yet here is a world, **c.** within your mind,
T-18...... VI.4:1 this, the mind is **c.** delusional. It cannot
T-18...... VI.4:6 though it **c.** can misperceive the function
T-18...... VI.5:3 Your perception of the body can **c.** be sick
T-19........II.1:6 that punishment *is* correction is **c.** insane.
T-19...... III.3:2 you see **c.** as a mistake you want corrected
T-19...... III.5:1 the Holy Spirit **c.** sees the Son of God can
T-20....... V.3:3 is inestimable **c.** cannot be evaluated. Do
T-21....... V.5:8 Yet such is **c.** not the ego's reasoning.
T-24... VI.13:2 Here is the voice of specialness heard **c.**,
T-26...... III.7:4 choice between two things so **c.** unalike.
T-26.....VII.6:4 although this **c.** makes no sense at all. All
T-26.....VII.8:9 which is **c.** separate and a thing apart. Yet
T-26....VIII.7:8 and **c.** hints at punishment until the time
T-27.....VII.1:2 demented version of salvation **c.** shown.
T-27.....VII.2:5 the problem is absurd when **c.** seen. No
T-27...VII.11:1 states, but one of which is **c.** recognized?
T-29........II.1:3 **c.** marked it is impossible to lose the way,
T-31...... VI.5:4 One vision, **c.** seen, that does not fit the
W-pI.....34.1:2 Peace of mind is **c.** an internal matter. It
W-pI.....42.5:1 that is **c.** related to the idea for today is
W-pI.....43.6:1 are **c.** out of accord with today's idea, or if
W-pI.....69.8:5 Try to keep the thought **c.** in mind that
W-pI...73.10:1 determining to keep your will **c.** in mind,
W-pI...132.7:4 truth, and yet it **c.** contradicts the world.
W-pI...133.4:3 and not been brought so **c.** to the place
W-pI.138.10:2 between the **c.** seen and the unrecognized
W-pI.160.10:5 of sight by which his Self is **c.** recognized,
W-pI.161.11:2 See him first as **c.** as you can, in that same
M-17 .........2:8 Here is his gift most **c.** given him. For he

M-17 ......... 4:4 perhaps too mild to be even **c.** recognized
M-17 ......... 7:3 Each one says **c.** to your frightened mind,
M-25 ......... 2:1 powers that are **c.** in line with this course.
P-2 ......... in.2:5 to the sane mind it is so **c.** impossible,
P-2 ......... VI.5:3 form a sickness takes will point quite **c.** to
P-2 ....... VII.5:2 In this their oneness can be **c.** seen. Yet
S-1 ........ III.6:6 of prayer can be quite **c.** recognized even
S-2 ......... II.4:3 Here must the aim be **c.** seen, for this may
S-3 ........... I.2:2 the mark of death upon it this is **c.** shown.
S-3 ......... II.2:3 forms and **c.** seen at most in lovely flashes

**clearness** 1

T-14 ....... in.1:7 their seeming **c.** seems to be clearly seen.

**clears** 1

W-pI ... 122.3:2 and **c.** your memory of all dead thoughts

**cleavage** 1

T19 ... IV.D.3:4 forgotten; the **c.** of your Self from you;–

**climate** 2

W-pI ..... 50.3:2 world into a **c.** of perfect peace and safety.
S-3 ......... II.3:4 we go in peace to freer air and gentler **c.**,

**climb** 2

T-18 ...... IX.6:3 willing to **c.** above it and see the sun. It is
S-2 ......... in.1:2 bottom step, or even to attempt to **c.** at all

**cling** 8

T-16 ..... VII.1:5 "evil" in the past to which you **c.**, and for
T-21 ......... I.4:4 and **c.** to them because they cannot see.
T-23 ..... II.14:1 nor does anyone **c.** to his madness if he
T-28 ......... I.2:4 Why would you **c.** to it in memory if you
W-pI. 140.12:1 With nothing in our hands to which we **c.**
W-pI ... 155.6:1 Illusion still appears to **c.** to you, that you
W-pI ... 186.5:5 The arrogant must **c.** to words, afraid to
M-27 ......... 6:9 its vain attempts to **c.** to death and yet to

**clinging** 2

T-4 ......... in.3:7 error of "**c.** to the old rugged cross." The
T-16 ....... II.6:8 What gain is there to you in **c.** to it, and

**clings** 2

T-24 ..... II.12:6 dear but **c.** to murder as safety's weapon,
T-24 ...... III.1:4 No one who **c.** to one illusion can see

**cloak** 4

T-25 .... VIII.7:3 dressed to deceive within an angel's **c.**.
WpI. rIII.in3:3 a **c.** of situations you cannot control.
W-pI ... 151.1:4 is but a **c.** for the uncertainty it would
S-2 ......... II.5:1 will often hide behind a **c.** like this. It

**close** 86

*See also* hugging-close

T-1 ......... II.5:1 by me because I am **c.** to the Holy Spirit,
T-4 ........ VI.2:4 as **c.** to knowledge as perception can. The
T-5 ........... I.4:8 is so **c.** to knowledge that He calls it forth;
T-5 ........... I.6:4 He represents a state of mind **c.** enough
T-14 ... III.18:2 remain in **c.** communication with Him,
T-14 ...... VI.8:8 **c.** not the door himself upon his Father's
T-16 ...... IV.7:6 You have come **c.** to truth, and only this
T-16 ... VII.11:4 To join in **c.** relationship with Him is to
T-17 ...... IV.4:5 Holy Spirit is in **c.** relationship with you,
T-17 ..... V.12:1 forgotten if you allow time to **c.** over it. It
T-18 ....... II.8:1 not the dream take hold to **c.** your eyes. It
T-21 ...... V.10:1 You have come very **c.** to this. Faith and
T-21 .... VI.10:5 Father is as **c.** to you as is your brother.
T-22 ....... in.3:7 but **c.** enough not to return to earth. For
T-28 ...... I.15:3 better way to **c.** the little gap between
T-28 ..... III.5:3 as fast, as water rushes in to **c.** the gap,
T-28 ..... III.5:5 joined to **c.** the little gap between them,
T-28 ..... IV.9:1 knowing You will come to **c.** each little
T-29 ........ I.1:9 Be wary, then; let Him not come too **c.**,
T-29 ........ I.3:7 Let him come **c.** to you, and you jumped
T-29 ..... IX.8:5 so **c.** the song of Heaven can be heard, not
T-31 ... VIII.6:4 **c.** the door upon his dreams of weakness,
W-pI ..... 10.4:1 **C.** your eyes for these exercises, and
W-pI ..... 11.3:5 **c.** your eyes and repeat the idea once
W-pI ..... 13.4:6 Then **c.** your eyes, and conclude with: *A*
W-pI ..... 21.2:2 Then **c.** your eyes and search your mind
W-pI ..... 23.6:2 and then **c.** your eyes and devote about a
W-pI ..... 31.2:4 Then **c.** your eyes, and apply the same
W-pI ..... 32.3:2 Then **c.** your eyes and look around your
W-pI ..... 33.2:1 then **c.** your eyes and survey your inner
W-pI ..... 35.4:1 **c.** your eyes and search your mind for the
W-pI ..... 36.3:1 **c.** your eyes and repeat the idea for today
W-pI ... 36.3:10 periods, **c.** your eyes and repeat the idea
W-pI ..... 36.4:1 periods, **c.** your eyes and repeat the idea;
W-pI ..... 37.4:5 Then **c.** your eyes and apply the idea to
W-pI ..... 38.4:1 repeat the idea for today, **c.** your eyes,
W-pI ..... 40.2:1 not **c.** your eyes for the exercise periods,
W-pI ..... 42.3:1 another as **c.** as possible to the time you
W-pI ..... 42.4:2 **c.** your eyes and repeat the idea again,
W-pI ..... 42.5:5 while looking slowly about; **c.** your eyes,
W-pI ..... 43.2:6 Spirit give it a meaning very **c.** to God's.
W-pI ..... 43.5:2 the second and longer phase, **c.** your eyes,
W-pI ..... 44.7:1 with your eyes open, and **c.** them slowly,
W-pI ..... 46.3:3 **C.** your eyes as you do so, and spend a
W-pI ..... 47.4:3 **C.** your eyes and begin, as usual, by
W-pI ..... 48.2:4 so whenever possible to **c.** your eyes and
W-pI ..... 63.3:2 **c.** the day with the thought of it in our
W-pI ..... 63.4:1 If you **c.** your eyes, you will probably find
W-pI ..... 65.5:2 day. Then **c.** your eyes, repeat the idea to
W-pI ..... 65.8:4 Sometimes **c.** your eyes as you practice
W-pI. 72.10:12 grievances to **c.** our eyes and stop our ears
W-pI ..... 74.5:1 way, **c.** your eyes and try to experience the
W-pI ... 79.10:5 **c.** your eyes for a moment and ask what it
W-pI ..... 80.5:2 **C.** your eyes, and receive your reward.
WpI .. rII.in.2:2 you wish, and then **c.** your eyes and listen
W-pI ... 91.11:5 *in light. Let me not c. my eyes because of this.*
W-pI ... 95.11:3 Then **c.** your eyes and tell yourself again,
W-pI ... 105.8:3 joy are mine," and **c.** your eyes a while,
W-pI ... 108.8:4 Then **c.** your eyes, and for five minutes
W-pI ... 109.5:4 And as you **c.** your eyes, sink into stillness
W-pI. 121.11:1 Now **c.** your eyes and see him in your
W-pI. 122.10:4 We are **c.** indeed to the appointed ending
W-pI. 126.10:1 **c.** your eyes upon the world that does not
W-pI ... 129.7:5 Then **c.** your eyes upon the world you see,
W-pI. 138.12:1 Before we **c.** our eyes in sleep tonight, we
W-pI. 138.12:4 we **c.** the day with this, acknowledging we
W-pI ... 140.8:4 own thoughts; so **c.** it is impossible to lose
WpI. rIV.in7:2 Then **c.** your eyes, and say them slowly to
WpI. rIV.in9:3 as we review, we **c.** as we began, repeating
W-pI ... 151.3:6 touch reality, and **c.** upon the truth. This
W-pI. 153.16:4 the business of the world will **c.** on us,
W-pI ... 188.6:1 Sit quietly and **c.** your eyes. The light
W-pI ... 192.3:6 but of a kind so **c.** to waking that the light
W-pI ... 194.1:5 How **c.** are we approaching to our goal!
W-pI. 200.11:8 We are **c.** to home, and draw still nearer
WpI rVI.in.4:3 We merely **c.** our eyes, and then forget all
W-pII .... in.6:1 I am so **c.** to you we cannot fail. Father,
W-pII . 252.1:5 be, and yet how near to me and **c.** to God!
W-pII . 344.2:3 us. How **c.** the ending of the dream of sin,
W-pII . 355.1:5 *It is very c.. I need not wait an instant more to*
M-16 ......... 5:8 which you **c.** your eyes and think of God.
M-23 ......... 4:4 **c.** to what it stands for that the little space
M-29 ......... 8:4 *around the world, To c. all things of time; to*
P-2 ......... V.4:3 two come very **c.** to God in this attempt,
P-3 ........... I.4:6 or would he **c.** the door on the savior of
P-3 .......... II.7:5 some in this world who have come very **c.**

**closed** 61

T-3 ....... III.3:2 The **c.** mind believes the future and the
T-4 ...... VII.6:7 Love is blocked when His channels are **c.**,
T-11 ....... I.5:10 nor have your **c.** eyes lost the ability to see
T-13 ...... V.8:3 see in dreams although your eyes are **c.**.
T-13 ... VI.12:6 of isolation because your eyes are **c.**. You
T-13 ..... XI.8:3 be wholly **c.** and separated from Him.
T-14 ........ I.2:5 your thought system is **c.** off and wholly
T-14 ... VIII.1:3 the dark doors you have **c.** lies nothing,
T-14 ..... XI.4:6 by hands open to receive, not **c.** to take.
T-18 ..... III.3:4 A little flicker of your eyelids, **c.** so long,
T-20 .... VII.8:9 You **c.** your eyes to shut him out. Such
T-20 ... VIII.1:3 you **c.** off by valuing the "something else,
T-21 ........ I.1:2 open doorways that they thought were **c.**.
T-21 ........ I.1:5 go through the doors you thought were **c.**
T-21 ....... V.9:5 can serve to open doors you **c.** against it.
T-22 ........ I.3:8 Yet if your eyes are **c.** and you have called
T-24 ..... II.13:4 are the gates of hell you **c.** upon yourself,
T-25 ..... V.2:10 He has not gone because your eyes are **c.**.
T-27 .. VII.14:6 from your sight, although your eyes are **c.**
T-28 ........ I.15:4 God has **c.** it with Himself. His memory
T-30 ..... IV.2:2 springs up as a **c.** box is opened suddenly,
W-pI ...... 8.4:1 for today should be done with eyes **c.**.
W-pI .... 11.2:2 Begin with your eyes **c.**, and repeat the
W-pI .... 13.4:2 ones. With eyes **c.**, repeat today's idea to
W-pI .... 14.2:1 to be practiced with eyes **c.** throughout.
W-pI .... 14.4:1 With eyes **c.**, think of all the horrors in
W-pI .... 16.4:1 your mind for a minute or so with eyes **c.**,
W-pI .... 19.3:1 require is to be undertaken with eyes **c.**.
W-pI .... 24.4:1 by searching the mind, with **c.** eyes, for
W-pI .... 30.5:3 to applying today's idea with your eyes **c.**,
W-pI .... 34.2:3 should be done with your eyes **c.**. It is
W-pI .... 35.9:2 repeat the idea to yourself, with **c.** eyes.
W-pI .... 36.4:1 one more repetition with your eyes **c.**. All
W-pI .... 37.5:1 the practice period with your eyes **c.**; you
W-pI .... 37.5:2 a repetition of the idea with your eyes **c.**,
W-pI .... 39.6:2 with **c.** eyes, search out your unloving
W-pI .... 41.6:2 three to five minutes, with your eyes **c.**. At
W-pI .... 41.9:1 it very slowly, preferably with eyes **c.**.
W-pI .... 42.6:3 the idea with eyes open, then with eyes **c.**,
W-pI .... 44.9:1 your eyes **c.** unless you are aware of fear.
W-pI .... 44.9:3 exercises with eyes **c.** as soon as possible.
W-pI .. 44.11:1 eyes open or **c.** as seems better to you at
W-pI .... 49.5:2 when necessary, but **c.** when possible.
WpI ... rI.in.3:3 your eyes **c.** and when you are alone in a
W-pI .... 61.5:6 with your eyes **c.** if the situation permits.
W-pI .... 64.6:5 today to reflecting on this with **c.** eyes.
W-pI .... 64.8:2 times, do the exercises with your eyes **c.**,
W-pI .... 65.3:3 of peace, which you have **c.** upon yourself,
W-pI .... 69.4:1 Very quietly now, with your eyes **c.**, try to
W-pI .... 70.7:5 devote a few minutes, with your eyes **c.**, to
W-pI .. 72.13:6 so in silence, preferably with your eyes **c.**,
W-pI .... 74.7:5 every half an hour, with eyes **c.** if possible,
W-pI .... 78.7:4 The body's eyes are **c.**, and as you think of
W-pI 131.11:5 mind and see, although your eyes are **c.**,
W-pI 155.11:1 time has **c.** the door on all the things that
W-pI 184.12:4 Every gap is **c.**, and separation healed.
W-pII ..... 1.2:2 The mind is **c.**, and will not be released.
W-pII . 236.2:1 *and c. today to every thought but Yours. I*
M-in .......... 4:7 this hopeless and **c.** learning situation,
M-16 ......... 4:5 hour with **c.** eyes and accomplish nothing
P-2 ........ IV.6:8 circle **c.** against the "inroads" of salvation

**closely** 14

T-3 ....... III.5:9 miracles and doing are **c.** related.
T-4 ......... II.9:1 Myths and magic are **c.** associated, since
T-4 ......... V.3:4 body, with which the ego identifies so **c.**,
T-5 ..... III.8:13 peace are as **c.** related as are time and war
T-11 ....... V.1:3 We are ready to look more **c.** at the ego's
T-15 .... VII.5:3 let us look more **c.** at the relationships the
T-16 ..... IV.7:5 is essential that we look very **c.** at exactly
T-17 .... VII.6:1 goal of illusion is as **c.** tied to faithlessness
T19 ... IV.B.1:3 flow across, and **c.** related to the first, is
T-23 ....... II.4:2 This principle, **c.** related to the first, is the
W-pI .... 65.4:2 and then adhere to it as **c.** as possible.
W-pI .... 70.6:3 to your own decisions as **c.** as possible.
WpI .. rIII.in1:3 are urged to follow just as **c.** as you can.
P-2 ........ VI.5:3 So **c.** is one translated into the other, that

**closeness** 2

T-1 ......... II.1:3 Physical **c.** cannot achieve it. Miracles,
T-1 ......... II.1:4 and result in true **c.** to others. Revelation

### closer 28

| | |
|---|---|
| T-1.........V.2:4 | **c.** to the ultimate release from time, in |
| T-2.........II.5:7 | into **c.** and closer accord with the Sonship |
| T-2.........II.5:7 | into closer and **c.** accord with the Sonship |
| T-4........VI.8:1 | come **c.** to a brother you approach me, |
| T-11.......in.3:5 | The **c.** you come to the foundation of the |
| T-11.......II.1:2 | and every healing thought brings it **c.**. |
| T-12.........I.7:4 | of your Father **c.** to your awareness. For |
| T-13......III.4:4 | the **c.** you come to the Love that is hidden |
| T-13....VI.10:3 | brings your light **c.** to your awareness. |
| T-15.....VII.8:6 | bring the body of another **c.** or farther. |
| T-16......VI.3:4 | the **c.** you look at the special relationship, |
| T-17......III.6:4 | and more undone, and union brought **c.**. |
| T-17......IV.6:4 | Yet we have looked at it far **c.** than we |
| T-17......VI.4:3 | you **c.** to the Holy Spirit's sorting out of |
| T-20.......II.4:8 | Look you still **c.** at them now, and you |
| T-20.....VII.3:8 | with it. Before we look at them a little **c.**, |
| T-21.......II.6:2 | Look **c.**, then, at what it is. And, very |
| T-22.......II.9:1 | Let us look **c.** at the whole illusion that |
| W-pI.....43.7:5 | as it is to those you think are **c.** to you. In |
| W-pI.....55.4:3 | bind me **c.** to the world of illusions. I am |
| W-pI...93.11:6 | You can do much today to bring you **c.** to |
| W-pI.....97.3:1 | we try to bring reality still **c.** to your mind |
| W-pI...109.7:2 | is comes **c.** to all worn and tired minds, |
| W-pI...125.7:3 | His Voice is **c.** than your hand. His Love is |
| W-pI.153.14:4 | day bring the last chapter **c.** to the world, |
| W-pI...157.7:1 | becomes a little **c.** to the end of time; a |
| W-pI.161.10:2 | Your readiness is **c.** now, and you will |
| W-pII..345.1:6 | *is* **c.** *to Your gifts than any other gift that I can* |

### closes 3

| | |
|---|---|
| T-13......IV.8:2 | and it **c.** over the present so that no gap in |
| T-31. VIII.12:3 | The journey **c.**, ending at the place where |
| W-pI...137.1:4 | becomes a door that **c.** on a separate self, |

### closest 4

| | |
|---|---|
| T-13......IV.7:5 | for *now* is the **c.** approximation of eternity |
| T-20.......V.1:1 | comes **c.** to himself in a holy relationship. |
| W-pI...109.8:3 | your distant brothers and your **c.** friends; |
| W-pI...192.3:3 | Forgiveness is the **c.** it can come to earth. |

### closing 15

| | |
|---|---|
| T-14... VIII.1:4 | It is the **c.** of the doors that interferes with |
| T-17.......II.7:4 | the **c.** of the dream will have no meaning. |
| T-27.........I.3:2 | **c.** off the gate and damning him to hell. |
| T-29...........I.h | The **C.** of the Gap |
| W-pI.....26.6:1 | **c.** your eyes and reviewing the unresolved |
| W-pI.....33.4:3 | **C.** your eyes will probably help in this |
| W-pI.....40.2:2 | when **c.** your eyes would not be feasible. |
| W-pI.....45.6:1 | idea to yourself, **c.** your eyes as you do so. |
| W-pI.....49.5:3 | you can, **c.** your eyes on the world, and |
| W-pI.....62.5:1 | often as you can, **c.** your eyes if possible, |
| W-pI.....74.5:2 | you. Sink into it and feel it **c.** around you. |
| W-pI.....77.4:2 | **C.** your eyes, remind yourself that you are |
| W-pI...92.10:4 | **c.** the body's eyes and asking truth to |
| W-pI...93.10:6 | to devote at least a minute or so to **c.** your |
| P-3.........II.7:5 | remain on earth until the **c.** of time. They |

### cloth 1

| | |
|---|---|
| T19.IV.A.16:1 | you, on a table covered with a spotless **c.**, |

### clothe 2

| | |
|---|---|
| T-18......IX.9:6 | waiting to **c.** you and protect you, and |
| W-pI.153.19:2 | We **c.** ourselves in it, as we prepare to |

### clothing 3

| | |
|---|---|
| W-pI.....50.1:3 | symbols; pills, money, "protective" **c.**, |
| W-pI.161.11:3 | See his face, his hands and feet, his **c.**. |
| W-pI...166.6:1 | figure; weary, worn, in threadbare **c.**, and |

### cloud 21

| | |
|---|---|
| T-13.........I.2:3 | in the black **c.** of guilt that you accepted, |
| T-13.........I.7:6 | the **c.** of guilt that darkens your mind, |
| T-13.......II.9:3 | And then no dark **c.** will remain between |
| T-13......III.2:6 | by removing the dark **c.** that obscures it, |
| T-13......VI.2:5 | mind, see it as a dark **c.** that shrouds your |
| T-13......VI.3:4 | No **c.** of guilt has risen to obscure Him, |
| T-13......VI.3:6 | The **c.** that obscures God's Son to you *is* |
| T-13......VI.5:4 | Let no dark **c.** out of your past obscure |
| T-13.........IX.h | The **C.** of Guilt |
| T-13......IX.4:6 | mind the **c.** of guilt that binds him to it. |
| T-13.......X.9:6 | the **c.** of guilt that dims your vision, and |
| T-18. VIII.13:2 | to **c.** your eyes and keep you sightless. Yet |
| T-18......IX.7:1 | Yet in this **c.** bank it is easy to see a whole |
| T-29... VIII.3:8 | A **c.** does not put out the sun. No more a |
| T-31.....VII.5:2 | thoughts because they do not **c.** your view |
| W-pI.....41.5:2 | under a heavy **c.** of insane thoughts, |
| W-pI.....41.5:3 | attempt to get past this dark and heavy **c.**, |
| W-pI.....70.8:6 | **c.** patterns you imagined that endured, or |
| W-pI.....79.5:5 | remain unsolved under a **c.** of denial, and |
| W-pII..300.1:2 | a passing **c.** upon a sky eternally serene. |
| P-2...........I.2:7 | shadows, or perhaps different **c.** patterns. |

### clouds 22

| | |
|---|---|
| T-18......IX.6:1 | is like a bank of low dark **c.** that seem to |
| T-18......IX.7:2 | the **c.** the messengers of your perception |
| T-18......IX.8:1 | So should it be with the dark **c.** of guilt, |
| T-19.......II.6:3 | strange illusion that makes the **c.** of guilt |
| T-27.....VII.2:3 | obscured by heavy **c.** of complication, |
| T-27.....VII.2:4 | Without the **c.** the problem will emerge in |
| W-pI.....39.1:4 | been overlooked in the **c.** of complexity in |
| W-pI.....69.4:2 | surrounded by a layer of heavy, dark **c.**. |
| W-pI.....69.4:3 | You can see only the **c.** because you seem |
| W-pI.....69.5:1 | there is a brilliant light hidden by the **c.**. |
| W-pI.....69.5:2 | The **c.** seem to be the only reality. They |
| W-pI.....69.6:2 | Determine to go past the **c.**. Reach out |
| W-pI.....69.6:5 | through them. Go on; **c.** cannot stop you. |
| W-pI.....69.8:3 | attempt to go through the **c.** to the light, |
| W-pI.....70.8:2 | find it in the **c.** that surround the light, |
| W-pI.....70.8:4 | It is past the **c.** and in the light beyond. |
| W-pI.....70.8:5 | the **c.** before you can reach the light. But |
| W-pI.....70.9:1 | surely you do not want to remain in the **c.** |
| W-pI.....70.9:2 | the **c.** by whatever means appeals to you. |
| W-pI...162.1:5 | and all things seen within its misty **c.** and |
| W-pII..256.1:6 | in heavy **c.** of doubt about the holiness of |
| M-4 .......X.2:7 | No **c.** remain to hide the face of Christ. |

### clutch 1

| | |
|---|---|
| T-28......III.6:3 | be gone and **c.** them not with eager hands |

### cluttered 1

| | |
|---|---|
| W-pI.....45.7:1 | and mad ideas with which you have **c.** up |

### clutters 1

| | |
|---|---|
| WpI rVI.in.3:8 | of everything that **c.** up the mind, and |

### co-creator 13

| | |
|---|---|
| T-7...........I.2:2 | and you would not be **c.** with God. As |
| T-7...........I.5:4 | and you who are **c.** with Him extend His |
| T-7......VI.13:1 | not fulfilling your function as **c.** with God |
| T-7........XI.6:4 | Sonship is worthy to be **c.** with God, |
| T-7........XI.6:7 | He is a **c.** with God with you. Deny his |
| T-9........VI.7:9 | You will never know that you are **c.** with |
| T-9........VI.7:9 | you learn that your brother is **c.** with you. |
| T-24.....VII.7:1 | A **c.** with the Father must have a Son. Yet |
| T-25.....VII.4:3 | their thought that makes the Son a **c.** with |
| T-30.......II.4:4 | you **c.** of the universe along with Him. He |
| WpI. rIV.in2:4 | establishing the Son as **c.** with Himself. It |
| W-pI...152.8:3 | your rightful place as **c.** of the universe, |
| W-pI...188.8:3 | They remind you that you are the **c.** of all |

### co-creators 3

| | |
|---|---|
| T-3.......VII.4:2 | in which God and His creations are not **c.**. |
| T-4...... III.1:10 | Your ego and your spirit will never be **c.**, |
| T-7...........I.7:6 | Prime Creator, because He created His **c.**. |

### co-makers 1

| | |
|---|---|
| W-pI.....73.2:1 | or **c.** in picturing the world you see. The |

### coat 2

| | |
|---|---|
| W-pI.......9.4:2 | *I do not see that* **c.** *rack as it is now. I do not* |
| W-pI.....29.5:3 | *God is in this* **c.** *hanger. God is in this* |

### cobwebs 3

| | |
|---|---|
| W-pI...122.6:7 | has spun of fragile **c.** disappear before the |
| W-pI.139.12:2 | of all the foolish **c.** which the world would |
| W-pI...168.3:4 | Arms and sweeps away the **c.** of our sleep. |

### codes 1

| | |
|---|---|
| W-pI...135.2:4 | armaments, its legal definitions and its **c.**, |

### coerced 2

| | |
|---|---|
| T-30.......I.11:2 | You are not **c.**, but merely hope to get a |
| W-pI.....20.1:6 | not see if you regard yourself as being **c.**, |

### coerces 1

| | |
|---|---|
| T-8..........II.3:4 | It is never God Who **c.** you, because He |

### coercion 4

| | |
|---|---|
| T-2........VI.5:7 | arouses a sense of **c.** that usually produces |
| T-3........VI.3:4 | that you are under the **c.** of judgment. |
| T-30.......I.14:6 | The first rule, then, is not **c.**, but a simple |
| T-30.......I.15:4 | and you can see there cannot be **c.** here, |

### coercive 1

| | |
|---|---|
| T-11.........I.8:9 | the Holy Spirit tells you appears to be **c.**, |

### coexist 20

| | |
|---|---|
| T-2....V.A.17:7 | other. In timelessness we **c.** with God. |
| T-2.......VII.5:1 | Nothing and everything cannot **c.**. To |
| T-4.......VII.8:2 | harmless, because the two beliefs must **c.**. |
| T-5.........in.2:2 | and love cannot **c.**, and if it is impossible |
| T-6......V.C.4:7 | chaos and consistency cannot **c.** for long, |
| T-7........VI.8:8 | **c.** in your mind without splitting it. If |
| T-7........VI.8:9 | If they cannot **c.** in peace, and if you want |
| T-9......VIII.6:4 | Littleness and grandeur cannot **c.**, nor is |
| T-13.........I.1:4 | Love and guilt cannot **c.**, and to accept |
| T-14.....VII.4:3 | which cannot **c.** are both maintained. If |
| T-14...VII.6:10 | **c.** when both of You together look on |
| T-14....VIII.5:4 | your altars, for nothing can **c.** with it. |
| T-17.......V.4:3 | is so apparent that they cannot **c.**. Yet |
| T-22......III.1:2 | possible for them to **c.** in your awareness. |
| W-pI.....44.1:4 | Creation and darkness cannot **c.**, but light |
| W-pI...160.4:6 | They cannot **c.**. If you are real, then fear |
| M-7 ...........4:6 | impossible, and doubt and trust cannot **c.** |
| M-12 .........6:1 | Oneness and sickness cannot **c.**. God's |
| M-27 .........3:3 | is enough to show it cannot **c.** with God. |
| S-1.........V.2:1 | have goals so far apart they cannot **c.**, nor |

### cohesive 1

| | |
|---|---|
| T-14........X.9:3 | of content makes a **c.** system impossible. |

### cohesiveness 1

| | |
|---|---|
| WpI...rI.in.6:4 | and the **c.** of the thought system to which |

### coincide 1

| | |
|---|---|
| M-in..........3:5 | It may **c.** with it, or it may not. It is the |

**coins** 1

T-30 V.9:8 bought at fearful price in **c.** of suffering?

**cold** 8

T-17 VIII.4:5 **c.** fantasies of fear and fiery dreams of hell
T19 IV.A.9:6 shiver in remembrance of the winter's **c.**?
T19. IV.A.12:5 are kept **c.** and starving and made very
T19 IV.C.11:1 and the **c.** sweat of fear comes over it,
T19 IV.D.7:6 no stab of fear nor the **c.** sweat of seeming
T-20 II.10:3 and perfectly protected from the **c.** chill
T-26 IX.7:3 him from bitter winter and the freezing **c.**
W-pI 195.5:2 apparent pain, who suffer **c.** or hunger, or

**collaborate** 1

T-8 IV.4:9 but you must **c.** by believing that I know

**collaborative** 2

T-4 VI.8:2 you. Salvation is a **c.** venture. It cannot be
T-8 IV.4:8 That is why healing is a **c.** venture. I can

**collapse** 3

T-1 V.2:4 He recognizes that every **c.** of time brings
T-2 VII.2:3 **c.** for which the miracle was intended.
T-28 VII.6:4 what will **c.** beneath a feather's weight?

**collapsing** 1

T-1 II.6:9 The miracle shortens time by **c.** it, thus

**collect** 6

T-8 VIII.6:7 function of truth is to **c.** information that
T-20 VI.4:7 bodies as it can **c.** to place its idols in, and
T-27 VIII.2:4 they may protect it and **c.** more senseless
W-pI 80.7:1 be determined not to **c.** grievances today.
W-pI 133.14:2 to let yourself **c.** some needless burdens,
P-3 II.9:8 to **c.** bodies to worship at their shrine,

**collects** 1

W-pI 134.6:2 countenance illusions, but **c.** them lightly,

**color** 1

W-pI 2.2:1 to avoid selection by size, brightness, **c.**,

**combat** 2

T-3 VII.2:5 He is perceived as a force in **c.** with God,
T-24 I.2:6 to challenge you to **c.** and to violence far

**combination** 2

T-9 IV.7:4 a particularly dangerous **c.** of grandiosity
W-pI 37.5:1 or you may use any **c.** of these two phases

**combine** 5

T-2 IV.1:3 to **c.** two orders of reality inappropriately.
T-2 VI.9:8 and belief **c.** into a power surge that can
T-17 IV.13:1 frame and so **c.** what cannot be combined
T-27 I.1:1 that would **c.** attack and innocence. Who
T-27 I.1:2 Who can **c.** the wholly incompatible, and

**combined** 2

T-17 IV.13:1 frame and so combine what cannot be **c.**,
T-18 IV.4:2 **c.** with the unlimited power of God's Will

**combines** 2

W-pI 42.1:1 for today **c.** two very powerful thoughts,
M-4 IX.2:7 **c.** in itself the other attributes of God's

**combining** 1

S-3 II.1:2 **c.** with forgiveness kindly meant but not

**come** 631

T-1 II.3:11 I have nothing that does not **c.** from God.
T-1 III.1:3 The reason you **c.** before me is that I do
T-1 VII.4:5 what is to **c.** to make constructive use of it
T-2 VII.3:1 Both miracles and fear **c.** from thoughts.
T-2 VIII.3:6 that everyone will finally **c.** to understand
T-4 III.7:10 will **c.** in response to a single unequivocal
T-4 III.8:4 for this together, for once He has **c.**, you
T-4 IV.10:9 Christ has **c.** into your mind and healed it
T-4 IV.11:6 brother will yet **c.** together in my name,
T-4 V.6:1 because the eternal must **c.** from God.
T-4 VI.2:4 **c.** as close to knowledge as perception can
T-4 VI.7:5 gratitude you **c.** to know your brother,
T-4 VI.8:1 **c.** closer to a brother you approach me,
T-4 VI.8:4 God will **c.** to you only as you will give
T-5 I.4:8 He calls it forth; or better, allows it to **c.**. I
T-5 II.10:4 Rest does not **c.** from sleeping but from
T-5 III.11:9 the remembrance of things past and to **c.**,
T-5 IV.2:7 I have **c.** to give you the foundation, so
T-5 VI.11:1 I said "I am **c.** as a light into the world," I
T-5 VII.6:4 process, which does not **c.** from you, is
T-6 I.15:2 "I **c.** not to bring peace but a sword." This
T-6 V.2:1 that the night is over and the light has **c.**?
T-6 V.2:5 And so when bad dreams **c.**, they will
T-7 III.3:5 idea, because all your conflicts **c.** from it.
T-7 IV.1:3 Both, therefore, **c.** from the same Source,
T-7 IV.1:4 Healing does not **c.** directly from God,
T-7 V.11:1 **C.** therefore unto me, and learn of the
T-7 VIII.5:4 attack, because they **c.** from an attempt to
T-8 IV.2:1 I am **c.** as a light into a world that does
T-8 IV.4:5 Healing does not **c.** from anyone else. You
T-8 VI.2:4 I am **c.** to tell you that the choice of which
T-9 III.6:5 do not **c.** from the truth that is in him,
T-9 IV.4:8 perfect sense because they **c.** from God.
T-9 VIII.9:3 What good can **c.** of it? And if no good
T-9 VIII.9:4 no good can **c.** of it the Holy Spirit cannot
T-10 V.7:7 and God will **c.** rushing into your heart in
T-11 in.3:5 The closer you **c.** to the foundation of the
T-11 in.4:3 I **c.** to you from our Father to offer you
T-11 II.4:5 And yet the invitation must **c.** from you,
T-11 IV.6:2 But **c.** wholly without condemnation, for
T-11 IV.6:6 **C.** unto me who hold it open for you, for
T-11 VI.8:8 awareness of Christ **c.** with the awakening
T-12 III.5:5 in abundance and that salvation is **c.**.
T-12 VI.3:5 of self-value **c.** from the extension of
T-12 VII.8:6 will **c.** to you because you invited them.
T-12 VII.11:2 called upon them, and they will **c.** to you.
T-12 VIII.1:6 Offer it and it will **c.** to you, because it is
T-13 III.4:4 the closer you **c.** to the Love that is hidden
T-13 IV.3:3 only have been futile if it must **c.** to this,
T-13 V.7:7 **c.** forth from your private world in peace.
T-13 V.8:9 disappear when light has **c.** and you can
T-13 VI.12:5 And that is why the nightmares **c.**. You
T-13 VII.4:2 And what you call with love will **c.** to you.
T-13 VIII.5:5 For light must **c.** into the darkened world
T-13 X.6:2 The end of guilt will never **c.** as long as
T-14 I.1:4 blessing, it must have **c.** first to yourself.
T-14 II.6:2 to learn the joyous lessons that **c.** quickly
T-14 II.7:9 realize the light has **c.** and freed you from
T-14 V.11:7 **C.** gladly to the holy circle, and look out
T-14 V.11:9 you. **C.**, let us join him in the holy place of
T-14 VI.8:5 and let the light **c.** streaming through.
T-14 VI.8:8 can fail to **c.** where God has called him, if
T-14 VII.4:2 that salvation must **c.** to you this way, if
T-14 X.3:4 as something that must **c.** from elsewhere
T-14 XI.14:7 peace, and it will **c.**. For understanding is
T-14 XI.14:8 is in you, and from it peace must **c.**.
T-15 II.2:3 It will **c.**, being the lesson God gives you,
T-15 IV.8:5 **c.** into a mind that has decided to oppose
T-15 VI.7:1 It is through *us* that peace will **c.**. Join me
T-15 XI.2:2 it as the sign the time of Christ has **c.**. He
T-16 I.3:1 anything you value to **c.** of a relationship.
T-16 II.6:5 who bring you the glad tidings He has **c.**.
T-16 II.6:9 **c.** too near to truth to renounce it now,
T-16 III.9:3 For you will **c.** where you would be, and
T-16 IV.4:8 in which it would gladly **c.** quietly to them
T-16 IV.6:6 will never **c.** from the illusion of love, but
T-16 IV.7:6 You have **c.** close to truth, and only this
T-16 VI.10:2 for you have **c.** too far to yield to the
T-16 VI.11:7 as it will surely do if you but let it **c.** to you
T-16 VII.10:3 in seeking how Atonement can **c.** to you.
T-17 III.5:7 **c.** alive as the relationship is given to Him
T-17 III.9:6 attributes **c.** simply from what they are.
T-17 V.8:3 A sense of aimlessness will **c.** to haunt you
T-17 V.10:6 salvation not, for it has **c.** to you. And
T-17 V.10:7 for it has **c.** to join you and your brother
T-17 VI.2:1 simply, is "What do I want to **c.** of this?
T-17 VI.2:7 know what it wants to **c.** of the situation.
T-17 VI.5:6 the truth has **c.** to you and you will see the
T-17 VI.7:4 has not **c.** because faith has been denied,
T-17 VII.4:5 that peace and faith will not **c.** separately.
T-17 VII.10:4 from loneliness because the truth has **c.**.
T-17 VIII.2:7 it, for against your opposition it cannot **c.**
T-18 I.2:7 Nothing can **c.** between what God has
T-18 I.2:8 But everything *seems* to **c.** between the
T-18 I.5:4 What else could **c.** of it? Its fragmented
T-18 I.11:5 and rejoices that you have let it **c.** to you.
T-18 II.5:4 the dream produces must **c.** from you. It
T-18 II.5:17 try to make your sleeping dreams **c.** true.
T-18 II.7:2 you will share with all who **c.** within your
T-18 II.9:3 has **c.** because you have been willing to let
T-18 IV.1:3 willingness to let it **c.** precede its coming.
T-18 IV.2:6 If you could **c.** without them you would
T-18 IV.2:7 **C.** to it not in arrogance, assuming that
T-18 IV.3:7 the strength of willingness to **c.** from you,
T-18 IV.4:1 not **c.** from your little willingness alone. It
T-18 IV.5:6 Atonement cannot **c.** to those who think
T-18 V.4:1 Happy dreams **c.** true, not because they
T-18 V.6:6 that the holy instant **c.** to either of you
T-18 V.6:7 it will **c.** to both at the request of either.
T-18 VI.14:5 **C.** to this place of refuge, where you can
T-18 VIII.2:3 God cannot **c.** into a body, nor can you
T-18 VIII.9:1 the barrier you built to **c.** inside and shine
T-18 VIII.9:6 but they will not depart as they had **c.**,
T-18 VIII.11:3 It will **c.** because you came without the
T-18 VIII.12:2 You do not recognize that love has **c.**,
T-18 VIII.13:3 He Whom you welcomed has **c.** to you,
T-18 IX.14:1 And when the memory of God has **c.** to
T-19 I.14:2 faithlessness aside, and **c.** to it together.
T-19 III.11:3 where all the weary ones can **c.** and rest.
T19 IV.B.7:4 O **c.** ye faithful to the holy union of the
T19 IV.B.11:3 But all that lies in it will **c.** with it, and
T19 IV.C.7:1 it **c.** to save them from communication.
T19 IV.D.7:4 thoughts that **c.** to you against your will.
T19 IV.D.10:2 which everyone must **c.** when he is ready.
T19 IV.D.16:1 place of resurrection, to which we **c.** again
T-20 II.2:5 to those who **c.** unto its chosen home, or
T-20 II.10:5 savior from illusions has **c.** to greet you,
T-20 II.11:5 **c.** before his holy altar where the strength
T-20 VII.1:2 to meet the Holy Spirit's goal will **c.** from
T-20 VIII.1:1 Vision will **c.** to you at first in glimpses,
T-20 VIII.3:2 For peace will **c.** to all who ask for it with
T-20 VIII.11:2 there who could refuse what must **c.** after
T-21 II.3:2 that **c.** to him were not his choice. His
T-21 II.13:3 and the instant of release has **c.** to you.
T-21 III.11:5 one because they **c.** with night and day,
T-21 IV.5:3 the acceptance of release to **c.** to you. And
T-21 IV.7:5 it sees that Heaven has **c.** to earth at last,
T-21 IV.7:6 Heaven has **c.** because it found a home in
T-21 V.7:6 And all of it will **c.** with any part. Here is
T-21 V.10:1 You have **c.** very close to this. Faith and
T-21 V.10:3 **c.** from something that you do not know,
T-21 VII.3:3 In hatred they have **c.** together, but have
T-21 VIII.2:8 peace must **c.** to those who choose to heal
T-22 in.1:2 Rejoice whom God hath joined have **c.**
T-22 in.2:6 not. They **c.** together, each to complete
T-22 I.8:5 He could not **c.** to anyone but you, never
T-22 IV.1:1 **c.** to the place where the branch in the
T-22 IV.4:7 will they be to see you **c.** among them,
T-22 V.5:6 then, must happen when they **c.** together
T-22 VI.6:1 Child of peace, the light *has* **c.** to you. The
T-23 in.6:3 you **c.** to understand all that is given you.
T-23 I.1:2 It cannot **c.** where there is conflict, for a
T-23 III.4:4 uphold a quiet, calm assurance it has **c.**.

T-24.... in.2:10 And your decisions **c.** from your beliefs as
T-24.........I.1:5 **c.** with the one alternative that you can
T-24.........I.4:2 and this must **c.** from someone "better,"
T-24........ II.9:1 You have **c.** far along the way of truth;
T-24........ II.9:6 to which you **c.** in hope and honesty.
T-24...... III.7:2 and call them to **c.** forth and waken from
T-24....... V.8:1 holy Lord of Heaven has Himself **c.** down
T-24....... V.9:7 And where is doubt when certainty has **c.**
T-24..... VII.8:2 is yours will **c.** to you when you are ready.
T-24..... VII.9:6 It is the means to make your wish **c.** true.
T-25.......in.1:8 that He may call to them to **c.** to Him and
T-25...... III.6:3 he has **c.** with Heaven's Help within him,
T-25...... IV.3:3 From you can **c.** their rest. From you can
T-25. VIII.10:6 And who would **c.** to plead for him, and
T-26.........I.1:8 All seeming entities can **c.** a little nearer,
T-26.........I.8:4 that he may **c.** forth to shine on you, and
T-26...... IV.3:7 And here does every light of Heaven **c.**, to
T-26...... IV.5:2 And as they **c.** to you to be complete, so
T-26....... V.5:1 too soon for anything to notice it had **c.**.
T-26....... V.9:6 Father has ensured must **c.** to you. And
T-26..... V.10:5 Resurrection has **c.** to take its place. And
T-26..... V.12:2 They **c.** from what is past and gone, and
T-26...... VI.1:6 harm, in sacrifice and death, has **c.** to you
T-26... VIII.3:2 is made yours and its effects will **c.** to you.
T-26... VIII.6:5 unfold in time and fear they may not **c.**,
T-26... VIII.9:6 consequence and cause must **c.** as one.
T-26.........IX.h For They Have **C.**
T-26...... IX.3:8 forever from the land where They have **c.**.
T-26...... IX.4:2 When They **c.**, time's purpose is fulfilled.
T-26...... IX.4:3 passes to nothingness when They have **c.**.
T-26...... IX.5:2 For They have **c.** to gather in Their Own.
T-26...... IX.6:2 And They **c.** quickly to the living temple,
T-26...... IX.6:4 have **c.** to dwell within the temple offered
T-26...... IX.8:5 An ancient miracle has **c.** to bless and to
T-26...... IX.8:8 For They have **c.**! For They have come at
T-26...... IX.8:9 They have come! For They have **c.** at last!
T-27.........I.2:4 been unfair will **c.** to him in righteousness
T-27.........I.7:7 The end of life must **c.**, whatever way that
T-27...... I.10:2 Here its peace can **c.**, and perfect healing
T-27....... II.7:5 all. It does not **c.** from pity but from love.
T-27...... III.7:2 A power wholly limitless has **c.**, not to
T-27...... IV.6:2 does the meaningfulness of the answer **c.**.
T-27....... V.2:7 of healing, then it cannot **c.** through you.
T-27....... V.4:1 no sadness where a miracle has **c.** to heal.
T-27....... V.6:1 **C.** to the holy instant and be healed, for
T-27...... VI.5:3 its own effects have **c.** to take their place.
T-27... VII.14:7 A smile has **c.** to lighten up your sleeping
T-27... VIII.6:5 that time can **c.** to circumvent eternity,
T-27... VIII.9:6 Perhaps you **c.** in tears. But hear Him say,
T-28...... I.11:5 and what has **c.** to take its place will not
T-28...... I.15:2 memory of God has **c.** to take the place of
T-28....... II.2:8 Yet must all healing **c.** about because the
T-28...... III.3:5 lest God should **c.** to bridge the little gap
T-28...... III.6:4 Him Who wills to **c.** and bridge His Son's
T-28...... III.8:7 those may **c.** who would no longer starve,
T-28...... III.8:8 Guests the miracle has asked to **c.** to you.
T-28...... IV.9:1 knowing You will **c.** to close each little
T-28.... IV.10:6 The seeds of sickness **c.** from the belief
T-28....... V.2:4 Where fear has gone there love must **c.**,
T-28..... VII.1:8 will can **c.** between what must be One,
T-28... VII.5:11 and rain will **c.** and carry it into oblivion.
T-29.........I.1:9 Be wary, then; let Him not **c.** too close,
T-29.........I.3:7 Let him **c.** close to you, and you jumped
T-29.........I.7:4 because it seems to **c.** and go uncertainly,
T-29....... II.3:4 and love must **c.** wherever they are not.
T-29....... II.4:1 Your Guest *has* **c.**. You asked Him, and He
T-29....... II.5:2 for you to **c.** where you invited Him to be.
T-29...... III.4:3 has **c.** to him through your forgiveness, he
T-29....... V.5:4 and from this quiet **c.** the happy dreams
T-29....... V.7:6 of death have **c.** to worship in a separated
T-29...... VI.2:9 All things that **c.** and go, the tides, the
T-29... VIII.5:3 be believed before it seems to **c.** to life,
T-29... VIII.6:4 deathless **c.** to die, the all-encompassing
T-29... VIII.6:6 as his Father, **c.** to hate a little while; to
T-29...... IX.3:4 terror, and the dream from which they **c.**.
T-30...... III.7:1 Thoughts seem to **c.** and go. Yet all this
T-30....... V.7:8 then will **c.** the knowledge They are One.
T-30....... V.8:4 Now that you have **c.**, would He delay in
T-30... VIII.4:3 cannot **c.** forth from you consistently. For
T-30... VIII.5:8 in him because you let Him **c.** to you. And
T-31..... II.5:14 well! For he is asking what will **c.** to you,
T-31....... II.8:2 **C.** without all thought of what you ever
T-31....... II.8:6 to which you **c.** to listen silently and learn
T-31....... II.8:8 you will understand you need but **c.** away
T-31..... II.10:5 for you have **c.** with but one purpose; that
T-31...... IV.3:3 time must **c.** when everyone begins to see
T-31.... IV.3:10 in this you **c.** to understand what it is for.
T-31...... IV.6:3 You did not **c.** to learn to find a road the
T-31....... V.1:6 is its purpose; that you **c.** without a self,
T-31....... V.7:5 and many **c.** from feverish imaginations,
T-31....... V.9:7 to have such prescience in the things to **c.**.
T-31..... V.17:2 will **c.** a time when images have all gone
T-31..... VII.2:3 so they **c.** in fearful form, with content
T-31..... VII.7:5 that **c.** from guilty thoughts and concepts
T-31... VIII.1:6 *there.* For He *has* **c.**, and He *is* asking this.
T-31... VIII.6:4 A miracle has **c.** to heal God's Son, and
T-31. VIII.10:3 I am as sure that they will **c.** to me as You
T-31. VIII.12:2 Christ has **c.** to dwell in the abode You set
W-pI....... 9.2:5 understanding will finally **c.** to lighten
W-pI..... 15.2:4 that real vision will **c.** quickly when this
W-pI..... 26.3:5 of yourself has **c.** to take the place of what
W-pI..... 30.5:3 closed, using whatever subjects **c.** to mind
W-pI..... 31.3:1 cross your mind **c.** into your awareness,
W-pI..... 31.3:3 Watch them **c.** and go as dispassionately
W-pI..... 42.5:3 Let them **c.** without censoring unless you
W-pI..... 42.5:4 no thoughts at all seem to **c.** to mind. If
W-pI..... 42.6:2 to step back and let the thoughts **c.**. If you
W-pI..... 46.5:2 the idea to all those who have **c.** to mind,
W-pI..... 47.1:4 in such a way that only good can **c.** of it?
W-pI..... 50.5:2 thoughts **c.** to help you recognize its truth
W-pI..... 58.1:2 does the perception of the real world **c.**.
W-pI..... 61.5:7 Let a few related thoughts **c.** to you, and
W-pI..... 62.5:5 Let related thoughts **c.** freely, for your
W-pI..... 63.4:1 to let the related thoughts **c.** to you in the
W-pI..... 64.6:6 Related thoughts will **c.** to help you, if
W-pI..... 68.6:3 *I may remember you are part of me and* **c.** *to*
W-pI..... 70.1:2 to **c.** from anywhere except from you. So,
W-pI..... 70.7:4 *me. It cannot* **c.** *from anywhere else.* Then
W-pI..... 70.7:7 *salvation cannot* **c.** *from any of these things.*
W-pI........ 75.h The light has **c.**.
W-pI..... 75.1:1 The light has **c.**. You are healed and you
W-pI..... 75.1:3 The light has **c.**. You are saved and you
W-pI..... 75.1:7 death have disappeared. The light has **c.**.
W-pI..... 75.2:3 The light has **c.**. Today the time of light
W-pI..... 75.2:7 a different world, because the light has **c.**.
W-pI..... 75.3:5 We will to see the light; the light has **c.**.
W-pI..... 75.4:5 Sight is given us, now that the light has **c.**.
W-pI..... 75.5:4 *The light has* **c.**. *I have forgiven the world.*
W-pI..... 75.6:8 *The light has* **c.**. *I have forgiven the world.*
W-pI... 75.7:10 The light has **c.**. You have forgiven the
W-pI..... 75.8:4 Today the light has **c.**. And you will see
W-pI... 75.10:2 *The light has* **c.**. *I have forgiven the world.*
W-pI... 75.10:5 *The light has* **c.**. *I have forgiven you.*
W-pI... 75.11:2 has **c.** to replace the unforgiven world you
W-pI..... 76.7:6 has **c.** because there are no laws but His.
W-pI..... 83.3:2 All things that **c.** from God are one. They
W-pI..... 83.3:3 one. They **c.** from Oneness, and must be
W-pI..... 83.3:4 because both **c.** from the same Source.
W-pI..... 88.1:1 The light has **c.**. In choosing salvation
W-pI..... 88.1:6 The light has **c.**. I can but choose the light
W-pI..... 88.2:2 *show me darkness, for the light has* **c.**. *The*
W-pI..... 90.1:6 I invite the solution to **c.** to me through
W-pI... 91.10:2 It is from Them that your strength will **c.**.
W-pI..... 92.1:5 that **c.** from the conviction you are a body
W-pI..... 93.9:6 Let It **c.** into Its Own. Here you are; This
W-pI... 95.12:3 and let the light in you **c.** through to teach
W-pI... 96.10:1 that **c.** to you will tell you you are saved,
W-pI..... 98.2:2 that doubt is gone and surety has **c.**. We
W-pI..... 98.4:3 answer it when they have **c.** to make their
W-pI... 98.10:2 wait for the glad time to **c.** to you again.
W-pI... 98.10:3 mind be readied for the happy time to **c.**.
W-pI... 101.5:2 must **c.** from sin will never happen, for it
W-pI... 104.1:3 They **c.** to you from God, Who cannot fail
W-pI... 104.4:2 **c.** to find what has been given us by Him.
W-pI... 104.4:3 We **c.** in confidence today, aware that
W-pI... 104.5:2 sight of them between the times we **c.** to
W-pI... 105.8:2 up, and what is yours can **c.** to you at last.
W-pI... 106.4:7 for they **c.** from God to His dear Son,
W-pI... 107.1:7 From dust to dust they **c.** and go, for only
W-pI... 107.3:1 mind will rest in when the truth has **c.**.
W-pI... 107.3:3 When truth has **c.** all pain is over, for
W-pI... 107.3:5 have no place because the truth has **c.**,
W-pI... 107.4:1 When truth has **c.** it does not stay a while
W-pI... 107.4:2 nor **c.** and go and go and come again. It
W-pI... 107.4:2 nor come and go and go and **c.** again. It
W-pI... 107.5:1 When truth has **c.** it harbors in its wings
W-pI... 107.6:1 does not **c.** and go nor shift nor change,
W-pI... 108.9:2 will **c.** to you in the amount in which you
W-pI... 109.2:5 came and yet will **c.** to linger for a while.
W-pI... 109.4:5 will hear and **c.** to you because you rest in
W-pI... 109.5:7 No more fearful dreams will **c.**, now that
W-pI... 109.8:3 and let them **c.** from far across the world,
W-pI... 110.3:3 to let redemption **c.** to light the world and
WpI. rIII.in6:5 The wisdom of your mind will **c.** to your
WpIrIII.in12:3 we **c.** from these reviews with learning
W-pI... 119.2:2 *in me, and* **c.** *to recognize my sinlessness.*
W-pI... 123.1:2 We have **c.** to gentler pathways and to
W-pI... 123.5:2 **c.** to speak the saving Word of God to us.
W-pI... 124.2:5 who **c.** to follow us will recognize the way
W-pI... 124.4:2 No meaningless anxieties can **c.** between
W-pI... 124.6:2 in times gone by and times as yet to **c.**, as
W-pI... 124.9:3 sometime, somewhere, it will **c.** to you,
W-pI. 127.11:2 shed its blessing upon all who **c.** to learn
W-pI... 130.8:3 **c.** to these five minutes emptying your
W-pI. 131.14:3 Today that day has **c.**. Today God keeps
W-pI. 131.14:5 for we **c.** to the appointed time and place
W-pI. 131.15:2 Salvation's time has **c.**. Today is set by
W-pI... 132.6:1 But it is pride that argues you have **c.** into
W-pI. 133.11:1 we **c.** to the criterion for choice that is the
W-pI. 133.11:2 allowed the ego's goals to **c.** between the
W-pI. 133.13:1 which **c.** with nothing to find everything
W-pI. 135.18:1 all events, past, present and to **c.**, are
W-pI. 135.25:5 in you, for now you **c.** without defense, to
W-pI. 136.15:2 to ask the truth to **c.** to us and set us free.
W-pI. 136.15:3 And truth will **c.**, for it has never been
W-pI. 136.19:2 or make plans against uncertainties to **c.**,
W-pI. 137.10:2 the world, when you let healing **c.** to you.
W-pI. 137.15:3 we **c.** together to make well all that was
W-pI... 138.2:6 Truth cannot **c.** where it could only be
W-pI... 138.2:8 the truth unwelcome, and it cannot **c.**.
W-pI... 139.1:2 **c.** to a decision to accept ourselves as God
W-pI... 139.7:2 can **c.** to question what it is they are. And
W-pI... 139.7:3 will **c.** again until the time Atonement is
W-pI... 139.9:2 We did not **c.** to reinforce the madness
W-pI... 140.4:3 Sickness where guilt is absent cannot **c.**,
W-pI... 140.5:2 cure must **c.** from holiness, and holiness
W-pI. 140.11:6 We hear Him now. We **c.** to Him today.
WpI. rIV.in6:1 They will not **c.** from you alone, for they
W-pI. 151.10:3 can **c.** to you who are beloved of God, for
W-pI. 152.11:6 never left will **c.** again to our awareness,
W-pI... 153.7:2 Christ and **c.** to fear His Father's anger.
W-pI. 153.11:2 have **c.** to realize His Will is but their own
W-pI. 153.11:4 Nor will you learn that light has **c.** to you,
W-pI. 153.12:5 children **c.** to see the benefits salvation
W-pI. 153.13:3 Now a quiet time has **c.**, in which we put
W-pI. 153.14:5 God's ministers have **c.** to waken him
W-pI. 153.17:2 would have us do the hour that is yet to **c.**
W-pI. 153.20:4 them to all their brothers **c.** from Him.
W-pI... 155.2:2 Those who choose to **c.** to it are seeking
W-pI... 155.3:2 for those to look upon who chose to **c.**,
W-pI... 157.3:2 Yet you have **c.** far enough along the way
W-pI... 157.6:3 may **c.** the sooner to the same experience
W-pI... 157.7:2 it light will **c.** to see the light more sure;
W-pI... 157.7:3 The time will **c.** when you will not return
W-pI... 158.2:8 Son are one will **c.** in time to every mind.
W-pI... 158.4:1 vast illusion in which figures **c.** and go as
W-pI... 158.4:4 will **c.** to end your doubting has been set.
W-pI... 160.6:5 The miracle will **c.**. For in his home his
W-pI... 160.9:1 that Christ has **c.** to search the world for
W-pI. 160.10:5 his home remembered and salvation **c.**.
W-pI. 161.10:2 you will **c.** today nearer Christ's vision. If
W-pI. 161.12:3 and recognize that Christ has **c.** to you.
W-pI... 162.1:6 words are spoken. For they **c.** from God.
W-pI... 162.6:5 The light is **c.** today to bless the world.
W-pI... 163.1:2 to be as you are not may **c.** to tempt you.
W-pI... 163.2:4 of their trust. For it alone will surely **c.**.
W-pI... 163.3:3 For it will **c.** with certain footsteps when

W-pI...163.3:3 when the time has c. for its arrival. It will
W-pI...164.1:3 we c. to look upon what is forever there;
W-pI...164.3:4 for sights and sounds that c. from nearer
W-pI...164.8:2 within your mind where Christ can c.,
W-pI...165.5:6 your mind has c. to lay aside denial, and
W-pI...166.9:1 Your ancient fear has c. upon you now,
W-pI.166.12:4 What He has c. to offer you, you now
W-pI...167.5:1 Death cannot c. from life. Ideas remain
W-pI...167.5:8 And where they c. from, there will they
W-pI...168.4:2 will disappear, and vision first will c.,
W-pI...168.6:1 He descends to meet us, as we c. to Him.
W-pI...168.6:7 *Father, I c. to You. And You will come to me*
W-pI...168.6:8 *And You will c. to me who ask. I am the Son*
W-pI...169.1:3 grace cannot c. until the mind prepares
W-pI.169.10:3 which explain what is to c. is past already.
W-pI.170.10:1 insane belief in gods of vengeance c. from
WpI...rV.in6:2 that you may c. to me who recognize the
Wi181-200 3:6 be enough to guarantee the rest will c..
W-pI.182.11:3 c. to ask your help in letting Him go home
W-pI.182.11:4 He has c. as does a little child, who must
W-pI...183.7:2 And God will c., and answer it Himself.
W-pI.184.13:2 must c. to supplement the Word. But first
W-pI...185.4:7 Illusions c. to take His place. And what
W-pI...185.9:5 And dreams will c. as you requested them
W-pI...185.9:6 Yet will God's peace c. just as certainly,
W-pI...186.6:5 misery can c. not near the holy home of
W-pI.186.14:1 because they c. from Formlessness Itself.
W-pI...188.9:4 within our minds direct them to c. home.
W-pI...189.7:5 and c. with wholly empty hands unto
W-pI...189.9:2 But we do choose to let Him c.. And with
W-pI...190.4:2 time has c. to laugh at such insane ideas.
W-pI...190.6:6 where living things must c. at last to die?
W-pI...190.9:1 and c. without defense into the quiet
W-pI...191.8:3 of God has c. in glory to redeem the lost,
W-pI...191.8:4 God's Son has c. again at last to set it free
W-pI...192.3:3 Forgiveness is the closest it can c. to earth
W-pI.193.10:2 Let mercy c. to you more quickly. Do not
W-pI.193.12:1 a little time today, and in the days to c., in
W-pI...194.8:2 you call the memory of Him to c. again,
W-pI...194.9:2 sure that only good can c. to us. If we
W-pI.196.12:6 your redemption, too, will c. from you.
W-pI...197.7:3 To everyone who lives will Christ yet c.,
W-pI...198.6:4 c. to you with Heaven's love upon them.
W-pI...198.6:7 the Word of God will c. to take its place,
W-pI...198.9:1 freedom c. to make its home with you.
W-pI.198.13:1 Today we c. still nearer to the end of
W-pI.198.13:2 And we are glad that we have c. this far,
W-pI.198.13:5 The time has c.. The time has come today.
W-pI.198.13:6 The time has come. The time has c. today.
W-pI...200.2:1 point to which each one must c. at last, to
W-pI...200.4:1 C. home. You have not found your
W-pI.200.10:3 You have c. to where the road is carpeted
WpI rVI.in.1:4 and invite the memory of God to c. again.
W-pII ....in.2:5 We have c. far along the road, and now
W-pII ....in.3:1 a central thought for all the days to c.,
W-pII ....in.4:1 Now do we c. to Him with but His Word
W-pII ....in.4:6 and then we wait for Him to c. to us.
W-pII ....in.5:6 He has willed to c. to you when you have
W-pII ....in.5:7 could have never c. this far unless you saw
W-pII ..in.10:2 will c. to understand that we need only
W-pII ..in.11:2 experience which should c. afterwards.
W-pII .....1.2:4 c. between a fixed projection and the aim
W-pII .221.1:1 *I c. to You today to seek the peace that You*
W-pII .221.1:2 *I c. in silence. In the quiet of my heart, the*
W-pII .221.1:5 *today. I c. to hear Your Voice in silence and*
W-pII .222.2:1 *as we c. quietly into Your Presence now, and*
W-pII .....2.4:1 Let us c. daily to this holy place, and
W-pII .....2.4:4 birds have c. to live within their branches.
W-pII .....2.4:6 gone, and we have c. together in the light.
W-pII .233.1:5 *Today I c. to You. I will step back and merely*
W-pII .235.1:2 to find that only happiness has c. to me.
W-pII .237.2:2 *I c. to You through Him Who is Your Son,*
W-pII ....241.h This holy instant is salvation c..
W-pII .241.1:4 The day has c. when sorrows pass away
W-pII .241.2:1 *another now, and so we c. at last to You again*
W-pII .242.2:2 *We c. with wholly open minds. We do not*
W-pII .244.2:2 No storms can c. into the hallowed haven
W-pII .244.2:4 For what can c. to threaten God Himself,
W-pII .245.1:8 *Your Will, that I may c. to recognize my Self.*
W-pII .245.2:3 And thus we c. to hear the Voice for God,
W-pII .246.2:1 *the way You choose for me to c. to You, my*
W-pII .247.1:5 Brother, c. and let me look on you. Your
W-pII .....4.5:3 How soon will you be ready to c. home?
W-pII .253.1:1 should c. to me unbidden by myself. Even
W-pII .254.1:2 *In deepest silence I would c. to You, to hear*
W-pII .254.1:3 *but this: I c. to You to ask You for the truth.*
W-pII .256.2:1 *would we c. to You in Your appointed way.*
W-pII .261.2:2 *I would c., my Father, home to You today. I*
W-pII .262.2:2 We would c. home, and rest in unity. For
W-pII .264.1:7 *We c. to You in Your Own Name today, to be*
W-pII .270.2:1 through them peace will c. to everyone.
W-pII .....6.4:1 all your dreams, and bids them c. to Him,
W-pII .....6.4:3 and peace has c. to every Son of God,
W-pII .271.1:3 they c. together all perception disappears.
W-pII .276.1:6 Father is, and for what purpose we have c.
W-pII .....7.4:3 return to signify the end of dreams has c..
W-pII .285.1:1 but the happy things of God to c. to me. I
W-pII .285.1:2 to me. I ask but them to c., and realize my
W-pII .286.1:3 *as the time in which I c. to understand the*
W-pII .288.1:2 *I cannot c. to You without my brother. And*
W-pII .290.1:3 have Christ's vision c. to me this very day.
W-pII .290.2:1 *With this resolve I c. to You, and ask Your*
W-pII .296.2:3 gladly does the Holy Spirit c. to rescue us
W-pII .298.2:1 *Father, I c. to You today, because I would*
W-pII .300.1:1 are the certain lot of all who c. here, for
W-pII .....9.4:2 to die, or yet will c. or who is present now
W-pII .302.1:6 *for fear must disappear when love has c.. Let*
W-pII .303.2:2 *He has c. to save me from the evil self I made.*
W-pII .305.1:4 For love has c., and healed the world by
W-pII .305.2:3 *has c. to us to save us from our judgment on*
W-pII .306.2:2 *us. In gratitude and thankfulness we c., with*
W-pII .307.2:1 into a state where conflict cannot c.,
W-pII .308.1:5 instant has forgiveness c. to set me free.
W-pII .308.1:7 He has c. to give His present blessing to
W-pII .310.1:4 *holy Son, the sign Your grace has c. to me,*
W-pII .312.1:5 must the real world c. to greet the holy
W-pII ....313.h Now let a new perception c. to me.
W-pII .313.1:2 *in. And love will c. wherever it is asked. This*
W-pII .313.1:6 *Now let His true perception c. to me, that I*
W-pII .313.2:4 Brother, c. and join with me today. We
W-pII .315.1:1 Each day a thousand treasures c. to me
W-pII .315.2:1 *many gifts that c. to me today and every day*
W-pII .316.1:5 Let me c. to where my treasures are, and
W-pII .319.1:3 arrogance the truth will c. immediately,
W-pII .323.1:1 *Your Love c. streaming in to his awareness,*
W-pII .327.1:3 and faith in Him must surely c. to me.
W-pII .327.1:5 to give me all the help I need to c. to Him.
W-pII .338.1:1 but this to let salvation c. to all the world.
W-pII ...13.3:3 what was meant to curse has c. to bless.
W-pII ...13.5:1 starved and thirsty creatures c. to die.
W-pII .342.2:2 I c. to you to take you home with me. And
W-pII .345.2:2 has c. to offer miracles to bless the tired
W-pII ....347.h Anger must c. from judgment. Judgment
W-pII347.1:11 *for me, and call Your miracles to c. to me.*
W-pII ....352.h From one C. all the sorrows of the world.
W-pII .352.1:2 *Through this I c. to You. Judgment will bind*
W-pII .353.1:3 *has learning c. almost to its appointed end.*
Wfl........in.6:1 We c. in honesty to God and say we did
W-ep.........3:3 mind, and when to c. to Him in silence,
M-1...........2:1 They c. from all over the world. They
M-1...........2:2 c. from all religions and from no religion.
M-2...........4:3 teacher seem to c. together in the present,
M-2...........5:1 When pupil and teacher c. together, a
M-3...........2:8 moment will be enough. Salvation has c..
M-4...........1:2 they c. from vastly different backgrounds,
M-4 ... I.A.6:10 He has not yet c. as far as he thinks. Yet
M-4 .... IV.1:12 achieve nothing. No gain can c. of it.
M-4 ...... IV.2:7 choose the weakness that must c. from
M-4 ....... V.1:2 and what could c. to interfere with joy?
M-4 ..... V.1:10 making sure no harm can c. to them.
M-4 ..VIII.1:10 no outcome already seen or yet to c. can
M-4 ........X.1:3 so open-mindedness invites Him to c. in.
M-5 ...... III.2:1 To them God's teachers c., to represent
M-5 ...... III.2:7 in their minds they c. in benediction, not
M-8...........3:1 Where do all these differences c. from?
M-10.........3:3 range of things; past, present and to c..
M-10.........4:8 know all the facts; past, present and to c..
M-10.......5:13 now he laughs, he used to c. to weep.
M-10.........6:6 and fear of death; all these have c. of it.
M-11.........2:1 Again we c. to the question of judgment.
M-12.........3:7 forget that truth can c. only where it is
M-12.........4:4 this understanding will c. the recognition,
M-12.........4:5 is enough to let the thought of unity c. in,
M-12.........6:7 They watch the dream figures c. and go,
M-14.........5:2 When joy has c., the purpose of the world
M-14.........5:4 When peace has c., what is the purpose of
M-15.........1:4 the Final Judgment will not c. until it is no
M-16.........5:5 must have c. to some conclusions in this
M-17.........1:7 pain, fear and disaster to c. to him. Let
M-17.........2:5 will always c. to teacher and to pupil alike
M-20.........3:3 God's peace can never c. where anger is,
M-21.........5:6 Judge not the words that c. to you, but
M-23.........7:1 course has c. from him because his words
M-23.........7:6 Jesus has c. to answer yours. In him you
M-25.........1:6 little ones that may c. to him on the way.
M-26.........2:8 The time will c. when this is understood.
M-28.........2:8 earth. The joy of Heaven has c. upon it.
M-28.........3:4 Attack is meaningless and peace has c..
M-28.......3:12 And now the truth can c. at last. How
M-28.......3:13 quickly will it c. as it is asked to enter and
M-29.........2:5 God has c. this far without realizing that.
C-2..........1:11 could c. of this except a dream which, like
C-2............6:8 Now the light has c.: Its opposite has
C-4............1:5 will c. when all things visible will have an
C-4............6:9 God has c. to claim His Own. Forgiveness
C-4............7:7 memory has c. at last there is no journey,
C-5..........6:11 *c. with me instead to share the resurrection*
C-ep..........1:2 the way will c. and go and go to come
C-ep..........1:2 way will come and go and go to c. again.
C-ep..........1:7 Illusions of despair may seem to c., but
P-2...........I.1:2 have c. together who already believe this.
P-2...........I.1:5 Perhaps they will c. together again and
P-2...........I.4:2 And this will one day c. to pass for every
P-2...........I.4:2 a patient could possibly have c. here? The
P-2..........II.4:2 will c. when psychotherapy is complete,
P-2..........II.4:2 where there is forgiveness truth must c..
P-2..........II.5:3 because He has been invited to c. in. In
P-2........ III.2:5 may c. from either one at the beginning,
P-2........ IV.4:1 word "cure" has c. into disrepute among
P-2..........V.2:1 who c. to us for help are bitterly afraid.
P-2..........V.4:3 two c. very close to God in this attempt,
P-2..........V.7:5 And the truth will c. to us only through
P-2..........V.7:8 as we see the sinlessness in him c. shining
P-2..........V.8:2 by which we c. to where all dreams began.
P-2..........V.8:3 them down, to c. away in peace forever.
P-2........ VI.7:4 for it is they who c. to demonstrate their
P-2....... VII.9:4 saint can c. to take you home with him?
P-2....... VII.9:9 patient in, for he has c. to you from God.
P-3...........I.1:7 sacrifices of yourself for those who c..
P-3...........I.3:7 It does not matter how they c.. They will
P-3...........I.4:5 They c. bearing God. Would he refuse
P-3..........II.5:1 Something good must c. from every
P-3..........II.7:4 his mind, offering it to all who c. to him.
P-3..........II.7:5 some in this world who have c. very close,
P-3........ III.8:2 will c. to you carrying the gift of healing,
S-1...........I.3:3 the gift. Along with it c. the overtones, the
S-1.........I.7:10 It will c. because you have realized that
S-1........ III.2:3 Nor do they c. from one who understands
S-1........ III.5:4 This enemy has c. to bless you. Take his
S-1........ IV.2:8 which they do not c. to offer them to him.
S-1........ IV.3:2 Cause only can the answer c. in which are
S-1........ IV.4:2 has c. to free yourself from all of them at
S-1..........V.1:3 and true humility will c. at last to grace
S-1..........V.2:2 Where one has c. the other disappears.
S-1..........V.3:2 last. Humility has c. to teach you how to
S-1..........V.3:6 You have c. almost to Heaven. There is
S-1..........V.4:3 you should c. has waited long for you.
S-2.........in.1:4 Both must c. to hold you up and keep
S-2.........in.1:6 Illusion's end will c. with this. Unlike the
S-2...........I.7:8 plan is made complete, and sanity has c..
S-2........ III.6:8 to c. from His eternal vigilance and Love.
S-3..........II.1:9 It does not c. because of hurtful thoughts
S-3........II.1:10 has c. for usefulness of body functioning.
S-3..........II.3:2 c. in forms that seem to be thrust down in
S-3..........II.4:2 Yet first true healing must have c. to bless
S-3........ III.3:4 True healing cannot c. from inequality
S-3........ III.6:4 cause, it cannot c. again in different form.

S-3 ........IV.2:4 here, for love has **c.** in all its holy oneness.
S-3 ........IV.6:1 **C.** unto Me, My children, once again,
S-3 ........IV.9:9 will **c.** the gift first of forgiveness, then
S-3 ......IV.10:7 to you until you **c.** to Him in peace at last.

## comes 221

T-1 ...........I.3:3 everything that **c.** from love is a miracle.
T-1 ........ I.23:2 This is healing because sickness **c.** from
T-1 ........III.1:9 conviction **c.** through accomplishment.
T-1 .......VII.1:4 All real pleasure **c.** from doing God's Will
T-2 ........III.5:1 perfect comfort that **c.** from perfect trust.
T-2 ........VI.2:7 What you do **c.** from what you think. You
T-2 ........VI.6:3 to do **c.** from your undivided decision.
T-3 ......III.5:12 Knowledge **c.** from the altar within and is
T-3 ........VI.3:1 that **c.** from meeting yourself and your
T-3 ........VI.3:4 All uncertainty **c.** from the belief that you
T-3 ......VI.10:4 All fear **c.** ultimately, and sometimes by
T-4 ........IV.3:2 *not be.* Depression **c.** from a sense of being
T-4 ........IV.4:1 anxious, realize that anxiety **c.** from the
T-5 ......... II.8:6 for God **c.** from your own altars to Him.
T-5 ........IV.1:7 be lost because it **c.** from the Holy Spirit,
T-5 ....... V.6:15 of thought **c.** from God and is in God. As
T-7 ......... II.7:4 This meaning **c.** from God and *is* God.
T-7 ........IV.1:3 since inspiration **c.** from the Voice for
T-7 ........IV.1:3 God and certainty **c.** from the laws of God
T-7 ......IV.7:10 It **c.** freely to all the Sonship, being what
T-7 ......... V.4:5 believe that the gift **c.** from God to him,
T-7 ....... V.6:13 only meaning **c.** from His and is like His.
T-7 .......VII.5:5 All confusion **c.** from not extending life,
T-8 .......VII.5:1 **c.** only from your own misunderstanding.
T-8 ........IX.3:5 not the dead, because rest **c.** from waking,
T-9 ........III.7:7 cannot be separate because it **c.** from love
T-9 ........VI.5:5 Yet when the Sonship **c.** together and
T-9 ........VI.6:4 In time the giving **c.** first, though they are
T-9 .......VII.7:8 you hold in terms of where it **c.** from. If it
T-9 .......VII.7:9 If it **c.** from God, He knows it to be true. If
T-9 ... VIII.11:6 of His answer, because it **c.** from God. It
T-10 ......III.6:7 Peace **c.** from God through me to you. It
T-11 ......III.3:3 true. When the light **c.** and you have said,
T-11 ..... V.13:2 of wholeness **c.** only through acceptance,
T-11 ....VI.3:10 For until Christ **c.** into His Own, the Son
T-12 .........I.6:3 And all your sense of strain **c.** from your
T-12 ......VI.3:5 As self-value **c.** from self-extension, so
T-12...VII.14:5 will think that death **c.** from God and not
T-13 ....... V.5:2 where when it **c.** it is not recognized. If
T-13 ....... V.9:3 Your "vision" **c.** from fear, as His from
T-13 .....VII.1:4 artificial light, and night **c.** not upon it.
T-13 .....VII.7:1 and nothing else **c.** nigh unto him. He is
T-13...VII.13:3 What **c.** to you of Him comes safely, for
T-13...VII.13:3 What comes to you of Him **c.** safely, for
T-13 ......XI.6:5 Truth **c.** of its own will unto its own.
T-14 ......III.5:3 that **c.** from choosing to be free of guilt.
T-14 ....... V.9:2 Our power **c.** not of us, but of our Father.
T-14 .....VII.7:5 including yours, **c.** not from double vision
T-15 ......VI.3:3 believe that strength **c.** from another, and
T-15 ......VI.6:4 awareness of changelessness **c.** swiftly as
T-15 ... VIII.3:5 you, for He **c.** from One Who cannot fail.
T-15 ......XI.2:3 He **c.** demanding nothing. No sacrifice of
T-15 ......XI.7:6 the peace it re-establishes, love **c.** of itself.
T-17 ....... II.1:3 or waking, **c.** near to such loveliness. And
T-17 ......III.9:8 follows from them **c.** from what they are,
T-17 ......VI.5:5 Truth **c.** of itself. If you experience peace,
T-18 ......III.2:1 light **c.** nearer you will rush to darkness,
T-18 ......IV.3:2 with less than greatness that **c.** not of you.
T-18 .....VII.5:7 peace **c.** at last to those who wrestle with
T-18 .....VII.5:7 the light **c.** at last into the mind given to
T-18 .....VII.5:7 always **c.** with just one happy realization;
T-18 .....VII.7:8 Into this place the Holy Spirit **c.**, and
T-18 ... VIII.8:7 love would bring to it from where it **c.**,
T19. IV.C.11:1 tremble and the cold sweat of fear **c.** over
T-20 ....... V.1:1 God's Son **c.** closest to himself in a holy
T-21 ....... II.8:3 recognition **c.** of vision and suspended
T-21 ......III.1:5 to ease the guilt that **c.** from the accepted
T-21 .....VII.1:1 your misery **c.** from the strange belief that
T-21 .....VII.4:5 another, and never **c.** to rest in victory.
T-21 .....VII.7:2 For healing **c.** of power, and attack of
T-21 ... VIII.2:8 It **c.** as surely unto those who see the final
T-22 ...... I.11:1 Christ **c.** to what is like Himself; the same
T-22 ....... V.1:5 The opposition **c.** from them, and not
T-23 .........I.1:1 The memory of God **c.** to the quiet mind.
T-23 ..... II.12:3 a *final* principle of chaos **c.** to the "rescue."
T-24 .........I.8:1 your brother **c.** from each unrecognized
T-24 ....... V.9:3 doubt, and from His certainty His quiet **c.**
T-24 ....VI.13:6 Out of His lack of conflict **c.** your peace.
T-24 ....VI.13:7 And from His purpose **c.** the means for
T-25 .....VII.9:4 he **c.** to understand it cost him his sanity,
T-25 ... VIII.6:6 the chill of fear **c.** over them when they
T-25. VIII.12:4 understanding that you need **c.** not of you
T-26 ......IV.4:2 Here the Son of God Himself **c.** to receive
T-26 .....VII.2:1 All sickness **c.** from separation. When
T-26 ... VIII.6:6 everything brings good that **c.** from God.
T-26 ......IX.4:4 grow ever brighter as each one **c.** home.
T-27 ....... II.5:4 The power of witness **c.** from your belief.
T-27 ..... II.13:2 there **c.** a necessary view of function split
T-28 .......I.11:1 The miracle **c.** quietly into the mind that
T-28 ......III.2:6 as sickness **c.** from minds that separate.
T-28 ......IV.7:7 Father **c.** to join His Son the Holy Spirit
T-29 .........I.8:5 There is a shock that **c.** to those who learn
T-29 ......III.5:2 See how eagerly he **c.**, and steps aside
T-29 ......VI.6:4 while till timelessness **c.** quietly to take
T-29 .....VII.1:7 all your pain **c.** simply from a futile search
T-29 .....VII.2:1 one who **c.** here but must still have hope,
T-29 ... VIII.8:5 No one **c.** unless he worshipped them,
T-30 ....III.10:3 no sound of battle **c.** remotely near, it
T-31 ....IV.2:14 what will the ending be, but when it **c.**.
T-31 ....... V.9:6 he see your future and ordain, before it **c.**,
T-31 ... VIII.5:5 that **c.** from God and that can never fail.
W-pI .....17.1:3 is always the thought that **c.** first, despite
W-pI .....38.6:1 you or someone else arises, or **c.** to mind.
W-pI .....57.5:3 that this peace **c.** from deep within myself
W-pI .....65.5:5 Note each one as it **c.** to you, with as little
W-pI ........70.h My salvation **c.** from me.
W-pI .....70.7:1 salvation **c.** from nothing outside of you.
W-pI .....70.7:3 *My salvation c. from me. It cannot come*
W-pI .....70.7:8 *My salvation c. from me and only from me.*
W-pI ...70.10:1 yourself that your salvation **c.** from you,
W-pI ...70.10:6 *My salvation c. from me. Nothing outside of*
W-pI .....72.6:1 mercy cannot enter, the ego **c.** to save you
W-pI .....85.3:1 (70) My salvation **c.** from me. Today I
W-pI .....90.3:3 I believe that the problem **c.** first, and
W-pI .....91.2:4 the premises from which the darkness **c.**.
W-pI .....92.5:1 Strength **c.** from truth, and shines with
W-pI .....92.7:6 back to darkness till the morning **c.** again.
W-pI ........96.h Salvation **c.** from my one Self.
W-pI .....96.4:3 Its power **c.** from spirit, and it is fulfilling
W-pI .....96.8:3 Salvation **c.** from this one Self through
W-pI .....96.9:2 *Salvation c. from my one Self. Its Thoughts*
W-pI ...96.12:1 mind salvation **c.** from your one Self, you
W-pI ...106.4:4 He **c.** with miracles a thousand times as
W-pI ...108.3:3 of reference, from which one meaning **c.**.
W-pI ...109.7:2 is **c.** closer to all worn and tired minds,
W-pI ...109.9:2 Each brother **c.** to take his rest, and offer
W-pI ...110.5:4 This is the truth that **c.** to set you free.
W-pI ...113.2:1 (96) Salvation **c.** from my one Self. *From*
W-pI ...113.3:4 half hour: Salvation **c.** from my one Self.
W-pI ...122.8:2 by which it **c.** to take the place of hell. In
W-pI ...126.1:3 the means by which salvation **c.** to you,
W-pI.127.12:3 learn. And as he **c.** to mind, give him this
W-pI ...129.5:3 Here is the world that **c.** to take its place,
W-pI.130.10:3 and hell or Heaven **c.** to you as one.
W-pI ...131.1:3 the place to which he **c.** to find stability?
W-pI ...131.3:4 thought, and one that **c.** to you from an
W-pI ...132.1:7 that the hope of freedom **c.** to him at last.
W-pI.132.13:2 a world which **c.** from this idea be real?
W-pI.132.16:1 need not realize that healing **c.** to many
W-pI.133.14:1 of Heaven, which swings open as he **c.**.
W-pI ...135.9:4 all the pain that **c.** from the conception of
W-pI.135.23:4 of answering until the Answer **c.** to you at
W-pI.135.26:2 that **c.** to you without your planning.
W-pI.136.14:2 it **c.** to any mind that would lay down its
W-pI.140.12:7 This is the day when healing **c.** to us. This
W-pI.151.13:4 evaluate each thought that **c.** to mind,
W-pI ...155.7:3 All this steps back as truth **c.** forth in you,
W-pI ...158.9:3 lies beyond them **c.** to take their place. It
W-pI.158.11:1 It matters not when revelation **c.**, for that
W-pI ...159.3:2 It **c.** from far beyond itself, for it reflects
W-pI ...160.2:1 **c.** from an idea so foreign to the truth he
W-pI ...160.2:2 yet, he does not recognize to whom he **c.**,
W-pI ...165.4:3 your mind will be before it **c.** to you. Ask
W-pI ...166.6:2 for everyone who **c.** here has pursued the
W-pI.166.13:5 **c.** to those who feel the touch of Christ,
W-pI.167.12:1 a Source from which perfection **c.** to us,
W-pI ...168.3:4 But finally He **c.** Himself, and takes us in
W-pI ...169.6:2 It **c.** to every mind when total recognition
W-pI.169.10:2 When revelation of your oneness **c.**, it will
W-pI.169.11:5 salvation **c.** a little nearer each uncertain
W-pI.169.14:5 and for experience that **c.** from grace. We
W-pI.170.10:5 to be upon His Lips; the fire **c.** from Him.
WpI...rV.in7:1 My resurrection **c.** again each time I lead
WpI.rV.in12:2 in the experience that **c.** from practice,
Wi181-200 2:4 and of peace that **c.** as you give up your
W-pI ...181.2:5 the peace that **c.** from faith in sinlessness.
W-pI ...182.9:2 how strong is he who **c.** without defenses,
W-pI.182.10:2 Who **c.** defenseless and Who is protected
W-pI ...183.3:5 as happy laughter **c.** to bless the world.
W-pI ...184.7:2 everyone who **c.** must go through. But the
W-pI.186.11:3 It **c.** from One Who knows no error, and
W-pI ...193.5:5 the words by which salvation **c.** to all the
W-pI.196.11:2 is the time as well in which salvation **c.**.
W-pII .227.2:3 The Son of God this day **c.** home again,
W-pII .232.1:4 *As evening c., let all my thoughts be still of*
W-pII .247.1:3 means whereby Christ's vision **c.** to me.
W-pII .252.1:4 Its strength **c.** not from burning impulses
W-pII .274.2:1 A special blessing **c.** to us today, from
W-pII .....8.5:4 He Who calls to us and **c.** to take us home
W-pII .291.2:2 *And I accept what c. from You, instead of*
W-pII .310.1:3 *The joy that c. to me is not of days nor hours,*
W-pII .310.1:3 *nor hours, for it c. from Heaven to Your Son.*
W-pII .314.1:1 new perception of the world there **c.** a
W-pII .325.1:4 From insane wishes **c.** an insane world.
W-pII .325.1:5 From judgment **c.** a world condemned.
W-pII .325.1:6 forgiving thoughts a gentle world **c.** forth,
W-pII .327.2:4 *You give the means whereby conviction c.,*
W-pII .346.2:1 And when the evening **c.** today, we will
W-pII ....352.h The other **c.** the peace of God Himself.
W-pII .358.1:3 *And what You give me c. from God Himself.*
M-2 ........... 4:4 pupil **c.** at the right time to the right place
M-4 ..... I.A.6:1 Now **c.** "a period of settling down." This
M-4 ...... VI.1:4 Their joy **c.** from their understanding
M-4 .... VI.1:11 that **c.** when defenses are laid down. It is
M-4 ....... X.1:2 **c.** with lack of judgment. As judgment
M-10 ....... 5:12 where he came to judge, he **c.** to bless.
M-15 ....... 1:10 him. Time pauses as eternity **c.** near, and
M-15 ....... 2:13 His Judgment **c.** to all who stand aside in
M-17 ......... 8:6 anger **c.** from an interpretation and not a
M-21 ......... 2:2 that **c.** to mind is apt to be very concrete.
M-26 ......... 4:6 the answer, and then accept it when it **c.**.
C-4............. 3:4 But for the time it lasts it **c.** to heal. For
C-4............. 5:6 From sin **c.** guilt as surely as forgiveness
P-2.........in.1:6 extent he **c.** to realize that this is an error,
P-2..........II.6:4 God **c.** to those who would restore His
P-2..........II.7:5 not understand that healing **c.** from God.
P-2......... V.1:3 In its wake **c.** the inevitable belief that, to
P-2......... V.5:2 for he **c.** to us as Christ and Savior. What
P-2........VII.1:7 Each patient who **c.** to a therapist offers
P-2.......VII.1:9 to heal from each patient who **c.** to him.
P-2.....VII.1:14 God **c.** to him who calls, and in Him he
P-3...........I.1:3 mean that no one **c.** to you by mistake.
P-3...........I.1:5 you know what to offer everyone who **c.**.
P-3........ III.5:8 that all they have **c.** only from God. If
P-3........ III.6:5 Whoever **c.** has been sent. Perhaps he was
S-1..........II.4:1 level also **c.** that curious contradiction in
S-1......... V.3:8 everyone who **c.** to join in prayer with you
S-2........ III.5:3 in which forgiveness **c.** to save God's Son.
S-3..........II.3:3 form in which death **c.** when it is time to
S-3..........II.4:4 Now its forgiveness **c.** to heal the world
S-3........ IV.7:1 He **c.** for Me and speaks My Word to you

## cometh 1

T-1..........II.4:1 "No man **c.** unto the Father but by me"

## comfort 23

T-2........ III.5:1 perfect **c.** that comes from perfect trust.
T-11...... III.2:1 God's Son is indeed in need of **c.**, for he

| | |
|---|---|
| T-11...... III.7:1 | Only God's Comforter can **c.** you. In the |
| T-16...... III.1:2 | how to accept the **c.** of your teaching. If |
| T-16...... VI.2:5 | Love will be unable to find you and **c.** you |
| T-16...... VI.8:7 | Find hope and **c.**, rather than despair, in |
| T-18....... I.13:2 | of the Sonship with healing and uniting **c.** |
| T-18..... VII.1:2 | that do not involve its **c.** or protection or |
| T-24.... IV.3:12 | it. Yet what **c.** has ever been in them, that |
| T-25...... IV.3:1 | rest and **c.** in another world where peace |
| T-27......... I.6:2 | healing is his **c.** and his health because it |
| T-27....... V.3:3 | carries **c.** from the place of peace into the |
| T-27....... V.4:6 | for you have withheld its peace and **c.**, |
| T-27.... VIII.1:6 | Its **c.** is its guiding rule. It tries to look for |
| T-31...... VI.1:8 | no more except to heal and **c.** and to bless |
| W-pI... 122.1:6 | that never can be hurt, a deep, abiding **c.**, |
| W-pI... 153.5:5 | by which illusions of his safety **c.** him. |
| W-pI... 185.8:4 | Consider but what you believe will **c.** you, |
| W-pI. 186.13:2 | He would **c.** you, although He knows no |
| W-pI... 194.8:4 | has himself appealed for **c.** and security. |
| W-pI. 200.10:6 | your heart and mind with **c.** and with love |
| M-24 ......... 2:4 | To some, there may be **c.** in the concept, |
| S-3......... in.1:1 | offering the **c.** and the promises of hope. |

## comfortable 5

| | |
|---|---|
| T-2........ III.5:2 | more **c.** by inappropriate means. But the |
| W-pI........ 1.4:3 | of hurry. A **c.** sense of leisure is essential. |
| W-pI..... 14.2:3 | with today's idea unless you find them **c.**. |
| W-pI..... 15.5:3 | idea unless you feel completely **c.** with it, |
| W-pI..... 33.1:3 | should be repeated as often as you find **c.**, |

## comforted 4

| | |
|---|---|
| T-17....... V.2:5 | Be **c.** in this; the only difficult phase is the |
| T-20....... V.8:1 | Be **c.**, and feel the Holy Spirit watching |
| T-27....... V.3:4 | the silent dead, are gently lifted up and **c.**. |
| S-3...... IV.10:5 | **c.** and live no more in terror and in pain. |

## Comforter 7

| | |
|---|---|
| T-5........... I.4:2 | to as the Healer, the **C.** and the Guide. He |
| T-5........... I.4:4 | you another **C.** and he will abide with you |
| T-10...... III.2:1 | **C.** can there be for the sick children of |
| T-11....... II.7:8 | comforters, for the **C.** of God is in you. |
| T-11...... III.1:2 | Your **C.** will rest you, but you cannot. You |
| T-11...... III.7:1 | Only God's **C.** can comfort you. In the |
| W-pII . 351.1:5 | *my everlasting **C.** and Friend beside me, and* |

## comforters 3

| | |
|---|---|
| T-11....... II.7:8 | and do not be satisfied with imaginary **c.**, |
| T-11...... III.6:2 | Do not be deceived by the dark **c.**, and |
| T-22......... I.6:7 | sees about him will become to him his **c.**, |

## comfortless 9

| | |
|---|---|
| T-5........... I.5:3 | was no need for healing, for no one was **c.** |
| T-5......... II.6:8 | God did not leave His children **c.**, even |
| T-7......... X.7:2 | the Will of God, Who has not left you **c.**. |
| T-17..... V.10:3 | Think not your choice will leave you **c.**, |
| T-31.... VIII.3:5 | joy. He would not leave you **c.**, alone in |
| W-pII . 352.1:6 | *You have not left me **c.**. I have within me* |
| W-ep ......... 6:8 | this be sure; that I will never leave you **c.**. |
| S-2........ III.7:5 | He will not leave you **c.**, nor fail to send |
| S-3......... II.6:3 | there is no veil of sin to keep it dark and **c.** |

## Coming 15

*coming*

| | |
|---|---|
| T-4...... IV.10:1 | First **C.** of Christ is merely another name |
| T-4...... IV.10:2 | The Second **C.** of Christ means nothing |
| T-4...... IV.10:4 | I am in charge of the Second **C.**, and my |
| T-9........ IV.9:3 | This is the Second **C.** that was made for |
| T-9........ IV.9:4 | Second **C.** is merely the return of sense. |
| T-9.... IV.11:10 | The Second **C.** is the awareness of reality, |
| W-pII ........ 9.h | What Is the Second **C.**? |
| W-pII ..... 9.1:1 | Christ's Second **C.**, which is sure as God, |
| W-pII ..... 9.2:1 | of Christ's Second **C.** that permits it to |
| W-pII ..... 9.2:2 | no end to the release the Second **C.** brings |
| W-pII ..... 9.3:1 | The Second **C.** ends the lessons that the |
| W-pII ..... 9.3:2 | Second **C.** is the time in which all minds |
| W-pII ..... 9.4:1 | Second **C.** is the one event in time which |
| W-pII ..... 9.5:1 | Pray that the Second **C.** will be soon, but |
| W-pII ... 10.1:1 | Christ's Second **C.** gives the Son of God |

## coming 32

*Coming*

| | |
|---|---|
| T-6 ....... II.10:2 | **C.** from God He uses everything for good, |
| T-12 .... VII.5:2 | your invitation, **c.** to you as you sent for it |
| T-12 .. VII.10:3 | **C.** only from God, its power and grandeur |
| T-14 ... III.10:6 | **c.** as naturally as peace that knows no |
| T-17 ... VIII.2:3 | it, do not attack it, do not interrupt its **c.**. |
| T-18 ....... II.9:3 | Its **c.** means that you have chosen truth, |
| T-18 ..... III.8:5 | and your brother are **c.** home together, |
| T-18 ..... IV.1:3 | the willingness to let it come precede its **c.** |
| T-18 ..... IV.2:7 | must achieve the state its **c.** brings with it. |
| T-18 . VIII.11:3 | no barriers to interfere with its glad **c.**. In |
| T-19 ...... I.11:6 | sent forth to gather witnesses unto its **c.**, |
| T19..IV.A.4:12 | before their **c.** as easily as those that you |
| T19IV.C.11:10 | *but let You use it for me, to facilitate its **c.**.* |
| T-20 ...... V.3:5 | never see it, but wait in patience for its **c.**. |
| T-22 ..... IV.1:4 | whole purpose of **c.** this far was to decide |
| T-22 ..... IV.6:3 | All barriers disappear before their **c.**, as |
| T-23 ..... IV.5:7 | perspective **c.** from this choice shows you |
| T-28 ..... III.3:6 | Fight not His **c.** with illusions, for it is His |
| T-28 ..... III.3:6 | His **c.** that you want above all things that |
| T-29 ......... II.h | The **C.** of the Guest |
| T-29 ..... III.3:9 | The **c.** of the light means it is gone. In |
| T-29 .... VII.2:3 | so. And therefore by his **c.**, he denies the |
| T-31 .... VII.3:2 | as **c.** from the "baser" part of you, and |
| WpI. rIV.in4:3 | change the **c.** and the going of the tides, |
| W-pI. 169.14:4 | Its **c.** is ensured. We ask for grace, and for |
| W-pI... 188.9:1 | practice **c.** nearer to the light in us today. |
| W-pII .... in.7:1 | in silence, unafraid and certain of Your **c.**. |
| W-pII . 229.1:4 | So still It waited for my **c.** home, that I |
| W-pII . 242.1:5 | to Him, for I would not delay my **c.** home, |
| M-2 ........... 1:3 | been waiting for him, for his **c.** is certain. |
| M-21 ......... 5:5 | **c.** from a shabby self-perception which he |
| M-26 ......... 4:7 | Nor will its **c.** be long delayed. All the help |

## Coming's 1

| | |
|---|---|
| W-pII ..... 9.2:3 | Forgiveness lights the Second **C.** way, |

## command 9

| | |
|---|---|
| T-4 ....... IV.5:5 | While you feel guilty your ego is in **c.**, |
| T-5 ......... II.7:1 | The Voice of the Holy Spirit does not **c.**, |
| T-6 ....... IV.9:6 | to follow who will strengthen your **c.**, and |
| T-6 ..... IV.11:2 | To **c.** is to assume inequality, which the |
| T-22 ....... II.8:7 | For time you made, and time you can **c.**. |
| T-28 ........ I.5:8 | it, waiting your **c.** that they be brought to |
| T-29 ........ I.6:3 | And it will take **c.** of when to "love," and |
| W-pI. 136.12:3 | It does not **c.** obedience, nor seek to prove |
| S-3........... I.2:3 | is tied to its **c.** and linked to its unstable, |

## commanded 1

| | |
|---|---|
| T19.... IV.C.8:6 | In its exaltation you **c.** it to die, for only |

## commander 1

| | |
|---|---|
| T-6 ....... IV.9:4 | them, but you have no **c.** except yourself. |

## commanding 1

| | |
|---|---|
| W-pI... 136.8:5 | your heart, **c.** you to die and cease to be. |

## commandments 3

| | |
|---|---|
| T-3 ....... III.6:7 | "Fear God and keep His **c.**" becomes |
| T-13 ..... IX.2:2 | by obeying the ego's harsh **c.** you bring its |
| T19.... IV.C.8:3 | altars, no grim **c.** nor twisted rituals of |

## commands 2

| | |
|---|---|
| T-6 ..... IV.11:1 | That is why the Holy Spirit never **c.**. To |
| T-31 ..... III.3:6 | seen to be a passive thing, obeying your **c.** |

## commend 1

| | |
|---|---|
| T-5 ...... VII.3:2 | to you, and asks that you **c.** yours to Him. |

## commended 1

| | |
|---|---|
| T-5 ...... VII.3:2 | God **c.** His Spirit to you, and asks that |

## commends 1

| | |
|---|---|
| T-3 ......... II.5:1 | **c.** his spirit into the Hands of his Father. |

## commensurate 1

| | |
|---|---|
| T-16 ..... III.7:1 | learn, and make learning **c.** with teaching. |

## comments 8

| | |
|---|---|
| WpI... rI.in.1:3 | be a few short **c.** after each of the ideas, |
| WpI... rI.in.2:1 | five ideas, with the **c.** included. Thereafter |
| WpI... rI.in.2:3 | and the related **c.** after reading them over. |
| WpI... rI.in.3:1 | necessary to cover the **c.** that follow each |
| WpI... rI.in.3:3 | you have read the idea and the related **c.**, |
| WpI.. rII.in.2:1 | **c.** that are included in the assignments. |
| WpI.. rII.in.6:2 | Some specific forms are included in the **c.** |
| WpI.. rIII.in5:2 | assigned. Read over the ideas and **c.** that |

## commit 2

| | |
|---|---|
| T-4 ......... V.6:1 | not to **c.** itself to anything that is eternal, |
| T-14 ... III.15:2 | in this world or Heaven could possibly **c.**. |

## commitment 15

| | |
|---|---|
| T-2 ......... II.7:1 | The Atonement is a total **c.**. You may still |
| T-3 ......... II.1:5 | until a firm **c.** to one or the other is made. |
| T-3 ......... II.1:6 | A firm **c.** to darkness or nothingness, |
| T-7 ....... VI.8:8 | **C.** to either must be total; they cannot |
| T-16 .... VII.2:2 | with the past and its total **c.** to it. No |
| W-pI .... 28.3:1 | you are making a **c.** to withdraw your |
| W-pI .... 28.4:4 | to seeing. It is not an exclusive **c.**. It is a |
| W-pI .... 28.4:5 | **c.** that applies to the table just as much as |
| W-pI .... 28.6:3 | And you are making a **c.** to each of them |
| W-pI .... 65.1:1 | for today reaffirms your **c.** to salvation. It |
| W-pI .... 65.1:3 | are obviously necessary for a total **c.**. |
| W-pI .. 154.1:4 | off, and to delay **c.** to our function. It is |
| Wi181-200 1:1 | willingness to make your weak **c.** strong; |
| Wi181-200 1:3 | sense of peace such unified **c.** will bestow, |
| P-2........... I.1:6 | each of them will enter into another **c.**. Be |

## commitments 3

| | |
|---|---|
| T-7 ....... VI.5:2 | senses that all **c.** the mind makes are total |
| T-15 ..... VI.1:3 | all relationships are seen as total **c.**, yet |
| W-pI .... 28.1:2 | you will be making a series of definite **c.**. |

## committed 12

| | |
|---|---|
| T-7 ....... VI.9:1 | and you are totally **c.** to neither. Your |
| T-7 ....... VI.9:6 | ego believes this totally, being fully **c.** to it |
| T-7 ....... VI.9:8 | The ego therefore is totally **c.** to untruth, |
| T-7 ...... VII.1:4 | cannot be totally **c.** sometimes. Denial |
| T-13 ...... I.10:3 | being fully **c.** to the insane notion that |
| T-14 ..... XI.8:1 | firmly bound to guilt and **c.** so to remain, |
| T-18 ........ I.9:7 | the Holy Spirit has **c.** your relationship. |
| T19 .... IV.B.6:2 | all the sins you think the Son of God **c.**. |
| T19 IV.D15:10 | the sins your brother thinks he has **c.**, and |
| T-28 ........ I.5:7 | it is. **C.** to its vaults, the history of all the |
| W-pI .. 126.4:4 | Someone apart from you **c.** it. And if you |
| W-pI .. 190.2:4 | retaliation for a crime that could not be **c.** |

## committing 1

| | |
|---|---|
| W-pI .... 28.4:3 | differently," you are **c.** yourself to seeing. |

## common 17

| | |
|---|---|
| T-12 ..... VI.6:5 | and more **c.** elements in all situations, the |
| T-13 ....... V.1:5 | Yet they have one thing in **c.**; they are all |

| | |
|---|---|
| T-13...VIII.3:1 | has many elements in **c.** with knowledge, |
| T-16...III.1:5 | and one with nothing in **c.** with yours. For |
| T-16...III.1:6 | nothing in **c.** with what you taught before |
| T-18...I.7:11 | *That* they have in **c.** and nothing else. Yet |
| T-18...I.9:2 | substituting have nothing in **c.** in reality. |
| T-21...VII.2:8 | that they thought they had a **c.** cause. |
| T-22...in.2:8 | under a **c.** roof that shelters neither; in |
| T-22...III.9:7 | as what it is; a **c.** state of mind, where |
| T-27...V.8:8 | seen as one, for only **c.** elements are there. |
| T-27...V.10:7 | And their **c.** answer shows the questions |
| T-27...VI.1:5 | What shares a **c.** purpose is the same. |
| T-27...VII.4:3 | Yet they do not recognize their **c.** need. |
| T-30...VII.4:1 | A **c.** purpose is the only means whereby |
| T-30...VII.7:8 | us. Our **c.** language lets us speak to all our |
| W-pI...66.4:4 | recognize a **c.** content where it exists in |

## communicate 47

| | |
|---|---|
| T-1...I.30:2 | spirit at the center, where it can **c.** directly |
| T-3...III.6:1 | before God can **c.** directly to His altars, |
| T-3...III.6:2 | There He can **c.** His certainty, and His |
| T-4...VII.3:8 | only beings of a like order can truly **c.**, His |
| T-4...VII.3:8 | naturally **c.** with Him and like Him. This |
| T-4...VII.3:12 | mind cannot totally lose the ability to **c.**, |
| T-4...VII.6:7 | minds He created do not **c.** fully with Him |
| T-6...V.1:7 | the Sonship does not **c.** with Him as one. |
| T-6...V.A.5:2 | You do not lose what you **c.**. The ego uses |
| T-6...V.A.5:8 | Those who **c.** fear are promoting attack, |
| T-7...I.1:2 | You **c.** fully with God, as He does with |
| T-7...V.2:1 | Only minds **c.**. Since the ego cannot |
| T-7...V.2:2 | **c.** because it is also the impulse to create, |
| T-7...V.2:2 | you that the body can both **c.** and create, |
| T-7...V.3:4 | Minds can **c.**, but they cannot hurt. The |
| T-8...VII.5:9 | To **c.** with part of God Himself is to reach |
| T-8...VII.12:1 | To **c.** is to join and to attack is to separate |
| T-9...I.6:1 | It is impossible to **c.** in alien tongues. |
| T-9...I.6:2 | and your Creator can **c.** through creation, |
| T-9...I.6:3 | Will. A divided mind cannot **c.**, because it |
| T-9...I.6:4 | This loses the ability to **c.** simply because |
| T-13...V.3:3 | do they **c.** with those who are not there, |
| T-13...V.6:4 | are. You **c.** with no one, and you are as |
| T-13...XI.7:6 | with you with whom He would **c.**. His |
| T-14...III.19:4 | *so I trust Him to c. to me all that He knows for* |
| T-14...IV.10:2 | as like himself, making both unable to **c.**, |
| T-14...IV.10:3 | God can **c.** only to the Holy Spirit in your |
| T-14...VI.6:4 | strange and twisted effort to **c.** through |
| T-14...VI.6:6 | Leave what you would **c.** to Him. He will |
| T-14...VI.7:3 | He will not attempt to **c.** the meaningless. |
| T-14...VI.7:4 | to those who would **c.** as truly with you. |
| T-15...VI.7:2 | the idea of peace, for in ideas minds can **c.** |
| T-15...VII.8:9 | he would no longer believe that bodies **c.**, |
| T-15...VII.10:6 | in His Voice your own need to **c.**. |
| T-15...VII.11:2 | And how can He **c.** with you, while you |
| T-15...VII.11:2 | believe that to **c.** is to make yourself alone |
| T-15...VII.14:5 | willingness to **c.** attracts communication |
| T-16...III.5:8 | They **c.** to you through the Holy Spirit, |
| T-20...V.5:3 | For minds need not the body to **c.**. The |
| T-22...I.3:3 | have listened to what can never **c.** at all. |
| T-22...I.6:6 | which he will **c.** with those around him, |
| T-22...I.7:1 | the ability to **c.** instead of separate reborn |
| T-23...III.6:10 | torn between the natural desire to **c.** and |
| T-30...VII.6:3 | Thus can you **c.** with him, and he with |
| T-30...VII.7:8 | given to us all, and thus we can **c.** again. |
| W-pI...184.9:5 | can **c.** in ways the world can understand, |
| M-12...3:3 | **c.** His messages directly through the |

## communicated 4

| | |
|---|---|
| T-6...V.A.5:6 | think that fear as well as love can be **c.**; |
| T-7...II.4:1 | Laws must be **c.** if they are to be helpful. |
| T-9...I.6:5 | cannot be **c.** unless it makes sense. How |
| T-22...I.9:6 | **c.** in a language the body does not speak. |

## communicates 2

| | |
|---|---|
| T-6...V.A.5:10 | Spirit **c.** only what each one can give to all |
| T-14...X.11:1 | As God **c.** to the Holy Spirit in you, so |

## communicating 6

| | |
|---|---|
| T-4...VII.3:7 | God created every mind by **c.** His Mind to |
| T-6...V.A.5:5 | **c.** is sharing it becomes communion. |
| T-14...III.18:1 | habit of not **c.** with your Creator. Yet you |
| T-14...VI.6:4 | to communicate through not **c.** holds |
| T-15...VII.11:3 | clearly insane to believe that by **c.** you will |
| T-21...VII.2:5 | ones, silent and afraid, alone and not **c.**, |

## Communication 5

*communication*

| | |
|---|---|
| T-6...I.19:1 | the Holy Spirit is the **C.** Link between God |
| T-8...VII.2:2 | Being the **C.** Link between God and His |
| T-10...III.2:6 | Son. God's remaining **C.** Link with all His |
| T-13...XI.8:1 | **C.** Link that God Himself placed within |
| C-6...3:1 | the remaining **C.** Link between God and |

## communication 139

*Communication*

| | |
|---|---|
| T-1...I.11:2 | It is a means of **c.** of the created with the |
| T-1...I.46:1 | The Holy Spirit is the highest **c.** medium. |
| T-1...I.46:2 | Miracles do not involve this type of **c.**, |
| T-1...I.46:2 | because they are *temporary* **c.** devices. |
| T-1...I.46:3 | form of **c.** with God by direct revelation, |
| T-1...II.1:2 | form of **c.** between God and His creations, |
| T-1...II.5:3 | Holy Spirit mediates higher to lower **c.**, |
| T-1...III.4:4 | because you will be acting under direct **c.**. |
| T-1...V.1:2 | spirit's original state of direct **c.** is reached |
| T-1...V.1:7 | You can destroy your medium of **c.**, but |
| T-2...IV.5:4 | highest level of **c.** of which he is capable. |
| T-2...IV.5:5 | level of **c.** of which he is capable *now.* The |
| T-2...IV.5:6 | aim of the miracle is to raise the level of **c.**, |
| T-4...I.2:12 | in **c.** and can never be in communication. |
| T-4...I.2:12 | in communication and can never be in **c.**. |
| T-4...VII.h | Creation and **C.** |
| T-4...VII.2:2 | The ego is thus against **c.**, except insofar |
| T-4...VII.2:3 | **c.** system of the ego is based on its own |
| T-4...VII.2:4 | **c.** is controlled by its need to protect itself |
| T-4...VII.2:4 | will disrupt **c.** when it experiences threat. |
| T-4...VII.3:4 | and direct **c.** with every aspect of creation, |
| T-4...VII.3:4 | in complete and direct **c.** with its Creator. |
| T-4...VII.3:5 | This **c.** is the Will of God. Creation and |
| T-4...VII.3:6 | Creation and **c.** are synonymous. God |
| T-4...VII.3:9 | Him. This **c.** is perfectly abstract, since its |
| T-4...VII.4:1 | Existence as well as being rest on **c.**. |
| T-4...VII.4:2 | **c.** is judged to be worth undertaking. |
| T-4...VII.4:4 | mind is in **c.** with everything that is real. |
| T-4...VII.7:2 | not enough, because it is only **c.** *from* God. |
| T-5...II.5:7 | Direct **c.** was broken because you had |
| T-5...II.8:3 | He is your remaining **c.** with God, which |
| T-6...II.11:6 | This line is the direct line of **c.** with God, |
| T-6...III.1:4 | He presents no barrier to the **c.** of God. |
| T-6...IV.12:5 | not a loss of perfection, but a failure in **c.**. |
| T-6...IV.12:6 | strident form of **c.** arose as the ego's voice. |
| T-6...V.1:5 | that His **c.** channels are not open to Him, |
| T-6...V.A.5:1 | Who leads to God, translates **c.** into being |
| T-6...V.A.5:5 | Spirit sees the body only as a means of **c.**, |
| T-6...V.A.5:8 | attack, and attack always breaks **c.**, |
| T-7...II.7:7 | **C.** is perfectly direct and perfectly united. |
| T-7...V.1:3 | use the body only for **c.** has such a direct |
| T-7...V.3:2 | is the Holy Spirit's form of **c.** in this world |
| T-8...VII.h | The Body as a Means of **C.** |
| T-8...VII.2:1 | interprets the body only as a means of **c.**. |
| T-8...VII.4:1 | **C.** ends separation. Attack promotes it. |
| T-8...VII.7:5 | Yet thought is **c.**, for which the body can |
| T-8...VII.10:1 | is the result of using the body solely for **c.**. |
| T-8...VII.11:5 | A medium of **c.** loses its usefulness if it is |
| T-8...VII.11:6 | use a medium of **c.** as a medium of attack |
| T-8...VII.13:3 | as anything except a means of **c.** is to limit |
| T-8...VII.16:6 | but there *is* unlimited **c.** and therefore |
| T-9...I.5:4 | that willing is salvation because it is **c.**. |
| T-9...I.6:4 | confused **c.** does not mean anything. A |
| T-9...I.10:5 | there is complete **c.** failure between them. |
| T-9...III.3:2 | no **c.** between the ego and the Holy Spirit. |
| T-9...VI.7:4 | perfect **c.** born of perfect understanding. |
| T-13...VI.6:7 | is timeless and their **c.** is unbroken, for |
| T-13...XI.7:6 | it breaks **c.** with you with whom He would |
| T-13...XI.8:2 | **c.** God would share with you is known. |
| T-14...III.8:6 | You will learn **c.** with this oneness only |
| T-14...III.18:2 | Yet you remain in close **c.** with Him, and |
| T-14...III.18:3 | and learn of all the happy **c.** that you have |
| T-14...IV.10:5 | in **c.** with the Mind of God has never been |
| T-14...IV.10:6 | **C.** with God is life. Nothing without it is |
| T-14...V.5:2 | and full **c.** be restored between the Father |
| T-14...VI.h | The Light of **C.** |
| T-14...VI.5:1 | for breaking your **c.** with your Father. The |
| T-14...VI.6:2 | It has no meaning, for its purpose is not **c.** |
| T-14...VI.6:2 | but rather the disruption of **c.**. If the |
| T-14...VI.6:3 | If the purpose of language is **c.**, how can |
| T-14...VI.6:7 | knows with Whom you are in perfect **c.**. |
| T-14...VI.7:4 | rest and offering your true **c.** to those who |
| T-14...VI.7:6 | only that one is possible for purposes of **c.** |
| T-14...VI.8:1 | The Holy Spirit's function is entirely **c.**. |
| T-14...VI.8:2 | interferes with **c.** in order to restore it. |
| T-14...VIII.2:12 | Him. **C.** between what cannot be divided |
| T-14...VIII.2:14 | All interference in the **c.** that God Himself |
| T-15...IV.6:5 | in which you receive and give perfect **c.**. |
| T-15...IV.6:7 | is the recognition that all minds are in **c.**. |
| T-15...IV.7:2 | **c.** that makes the holy instant what it is. |
| T-15...IV.7:5 | are not in full **c.** with those around you, |
| T-15...IV.8:1 | thought you would keep hidden shuts **c.** |
| T-15...IV.8:2 | is impossible to recognize perfect **c.** while |
| T-15...IV.8:2 | while breaking **c.** holds value to you. Ask |
| T-15...IV.8:3 | honestly, "Would I want to have perfect **c.** |
| T-15...IV.9:6 | You will not be able to accept perfect **c.** as |
| T-15...VI.7:7 | not be in full **c.** with all that ever was. Yet |
| T-15...VI.7:8 | you will not remember the language of **c.**, |
| T-15...VI.8:1 | the language of **c.** with all your brothers is |
| T-15...VI.8:2 | For **c.** is remembered together, as is truth. |
| T-15...VI.8:6 | you will experience the full **c.** of ideas with |
| T-15...VII.10:5 | remember this; to be with a body is not **c.**. |
| T-15...VII.10:6 | will feel guilty about **c.** and will be afraid |
| T-15...VII.12:3 | you will see safety in guilt and danger in **c.** |
| T-15...VII.12:4 | guilt, and that **c.** is the cause of loneliness. |
| T-15...VII.13:1 | in **c.** as surely as damnation lies in guilt. It |
| T-15...VII.13:2 | those who believe **c.** to be damnation that |
| T-15...VII.13:2 | to be damnation that **c.** is salvation. And |
| T-15...VII.14:2 | no attraction, since **c.** has been restored. |
| T-15...VII.14:3 | guilt, whose only purpose is to disrupt **c.**, |
| T-15...VII.14:5 | to communicate attracts **c.** to it, and |
| T-15...VIII.5:5 | this channel open to receive His **c.** to you, |
| T-15...VIII.5:6 | does not understand your problem in **c.**, |
| T-15...IX.2:4 | are nothing more than attempts to limit **c.** |
| T-15...IX.2:5 | For **c.** must be unlimited in order to have |
| T-15...IX.6:5 | the Father from the Son, and limit their **c.** |
| T-15...IX.7:1 | no interference in **c.** and your thoughts |
| T-15...IX.7:2 | to use the body only for purposes of **c.**, |
| T-15...XI.7:1 | and where there is **c.** there is peace. The |
| T-15...XI.7:2 | that **c.** remains unbroken even if the body |
| T-15...XI.7:2 | not the body as the necessary means of **c.**. |
| T-15...XI.7:3 | the body is to sacrifice nothing, and **c.**, |
| T-15...XI.7:6 | For **c.** embraces everything, and in the |
| T-15...XI.8:5 | For in the time of Christ **c.** is restored, and |
| T-17...III.5:1 | as a means of **c.** into relationships whose |
| T-18...VI.8:3 | the universal **c.** that is an eternal property |
| T-18...VI.8:4 | But the **c.** is internal. Mind reaches to |
| T19. IV.A.17:7 | yours; no better means for **c.** of salvation, |
| T19...IV.B.14:5 | Like any **c.** medium the body receives and |
| T19...IV.B.17:3 | For the Holy Spirit, too, is a **c.** medium, |
| T19...IV.C.6:5 | be the final and complete disruption of **c.**, |
| T19...IV.C.7:1 | to it, and bid it come to save them from **c.** |
| T19...IV.C.10:4 | its infancy, is in full **c.** with God and you. |
| T-22...I.6:3 | only because your whole **c.** is like a baby's. |
| T-22...I.9:4 | **C.** must have been restored to those who |
| T-30...VII.6:1 | How can **c.** really be established while the |
| T-30...VII.6:14 | This is not **c.**. Your dark dreams are but |
| W-pI...49.1:2 | truth abides is in constant **c.** with God, |
| W-pI...72.2:4 | The limit on **c.** cannot be the best means |
| W-pI...72.2:4 | cannot be the best means to expand **c.**. |
| W-pI...129.4:1 | **C.**, unambiguous and plain as day, |
| W-pI.183.11:6 | in which **c.** far transcends all words, and |
| W-pI...184.5:3 | one essential goal by which **c.** is achieved, |
| W-pI...184.9:5 | is not the unity where true **c.** can be found |
| M-12...3:4 | which **c.** becomes possible to those who |
| M-25...2:2 | **C.** is not limited to the small range of |
| M-25...2:5 | The limits the world places on **c.** are the |
| M-28...1:6 | perfectly, having no function except **c.**. It |

S-1 ........ II.1:3 state, and fuses into total **c.** with God. In

**communications** 2

T-14..... X.11:1 Holy Spirit translate His **c.** through you,
T-14..... X.11:2 God has no secret **c.**, for everything of

**communion** 20

T-1........ IV.1:5 not only be willing to enter into **c.** but will
T-1........ IV.2:5 and puts you in **c.** with yourself and God.
T-3....... V.10:4 C., not prayer, is the natural state of those
T-5....... III.11:8 me. He is in **c.** with God always, and He is
T-6......V.A.5:5 communicating is sharing it becomes **c.**.
T-7....... V.10:7 body in **c.** because this is to share nothing
T-7....... V.11:6 This is true **c.** with the Holy Spirit, Who
T-8....... VII.3:4 uniting it becomes a beautiful lesson in **c.**,
T-8....... VII.3:4 in communion, which has value until **c.** *is.*
T19. IV.A.16:3 join in gentleness before the table of **c.**.
T19IV.A.17:15 C. is another kind of completion, which
T19.... IV.B.3:1 the mind to join in holy **c.** and be at peace
T19.... IV.B.4:6 You want **c.**, not the feast of fear. You
T19..IV.B.4:10 Son. He has not lost **c.** with Him, nor with
T19.... IV.B.7:3 in the quiet **c.** in which the Father and the
T19.... IV.B.8:5 And in Him it *is* possible that our **c.**, where
T-20..... II.10:2 in his **c.** with all that is within him. Now
T-29......... I.5:4 to make **c.** with your brother's mind. And
WpI. rIV.in6:3 So will **c.** with the Lord of Hosts be yours,
P-2......... II.9:1 C. is impossible alone. No one who

**commute** 1

T-25..... VII.1:1 Yet if the Holy Spirit can **c.** each sentence

**Companion** 2
*companion*

W-pI... 124.2:4 our **C.** as we walk the world a little while.
W-pI... 156.7:5 you may perhaps lose sight of your **C.**,

**companion** 3
*Companion*

T-8......... V.5:8 chosen me as your **c.** *instead* of the ego. Do
T-20...... III.9:4 and raise your eyes unto your strong **c.**, in
T-31..... II.10:1 **c.** is and what he should be asking for, will

**companions** 8

T-11...... III.4:6 Walk in light and do not see the dark **c.**,
T-11...... III.4:6 for they are not fit **c.** for the Son of God,
T-11...... III.4:8 you see the dark **c.** in a light such as this?
T-11...... III.5:5 The dark **c.**, the dark way, are all illusions
T-11...... III.7:8 Presence with the dark **c.** beside you, but
T-13......... I.7:1 perceive the holy **c.** who travel with you,
T-31....... V.2:8 It searches for **c.** and it looks, at times
M-4 ... I.A.6:11 go on, he goes with mighty **c.** beside him.

**Companionship** 1
*companionship*

W-pI. 166.11:4 and speaks of His **C.** when you perceive

**companionship** 3
*Companionship*

T-15... VII.12:2 as you believe that to be with a body is **c.**,
W-pI..... 41.9:3 about you; on the unfailing **c.** that is yours
W-pI. 200.11:5 solitary dreams with single purpose and **c.**

**company** 2

T-11....... II.5:2 but His Voice grows faint in alien **c.**. He
T-13..... VII.6:4 you will rejoice that you have found His **c.**

**comparatively** 1

M-22 ......... 2:2 to all situations, but this is **c.** rare. The

**compare** 7

T-14 ..... IV.8:5 is nothing on earth with which it can **c.**,
T-17 ... IV.12:4 You cannot **c.** their value by comparing a
T-17 ... IV.12:5 It must be the pictures only that you **c.**, or
W-pI... 158.8:2 that faintly can **c.** with this in value; nor
W-pI... 195.5:4 Let us not **c.** ourselves with them, for thus
W-pII . 287.1:4 find and keep that can **c.** with my Identity
M-25 ......... 1:5 Yet nothing he can do can **c.** even in the

**compared** 3

T-4 ..... II.11:11 is it understood by being **c.** to an opposite
T-13 ..... III.2:3 of attack is nothing **c.** to your fear of love.
T-17 ........ I.4:5 reality to which it cannot really be **c.** at all

**compares** 1

T-1 ........ I.50:1 The miracle **c.** what you have made with

**comparing** 2

T-17 ... IV.12:4 their value by **c.** a picture to a frame. It
W-pI... 195.8:4 undone at last, and we forgive without **c.**.

**comparison** 12

T-17 ... IV.12:5 or the **c.** is wholly without meaning.
T-17 ... IV.14:4 And now, by real **c.**, a transformation of
T-18 ........ I.3:7 used as the standard for **c.** of acceptance
T-24 ........ I.4:2 condemns, "above" it, sinless by **c.** with it
T-24 ....... II.1:1 C. must be an ego device, for love makes
T-24 ....... II.1:6 and unsullied, by **c.** with what you see.
T-26 ..... III.4:2 to the last **c.** that he will ever make; the
W-pI..... 10.1:4 You have no basis for **c.** as yet. When you
W-pI... 165.3:2 all else as worthless in **c.** with them? And
M-17 ......... 6:8 and do not think about your frailty in **c.**.
P-3........ III.6:8 and how valueless is money in **c.**. Again
S-2.......... II.1:4 where the designed **c.** cannot be missed,

**comparisons** 8

T-4 ......... II.7:1 The ego literally lives by **c.**. Equality is
T-4 ..... II.11:12 Knowledge never involves **c.**. That is its
T-16 .... VII.6:2 that the Holy Spirit must teach through **c.**
T-24 ....... II.1:2 none. Specialness always makes **c.**. It is
W-pI... 195.4:2 Love makes no **c.**. And gratitude can only
W-pI... 195.8:2 hatred is forgotten when we lay **c.** aside.
W-pII . 305.1:2 C. are still before this peace. And all the
S-2.......... II.8:1 and **c.** of every kind are death. For that is

**compassion** 1

T19. IV.D.11:2 and raving madness with pity and **c.**, but

**compatible** 5

T-16 ... IV.10:1 your completion rests, wholly **c.** with His.
T19IV.B.10:10 them forth, and therefore is **c.** with them.
T19..IV.B.11:1 think you which it is that is **c.** with you.
W-pI..... 96.1:4 opposites you see in you will never be **c.**.
W-pI. 131.11:6 as well which are **c.** with such a world,

**compel** 3

T-11 ..... VI.6:1 must **c.** your allegiance gladly, because it
T-14 ..... XI.7:4 Yet He cannot **c.** His Son to turn to Him
T-23 ..... II.16:5 No law of chaos could **c.** belief but for the

**compelled** 3

T-15 .. VII.12:2 will be **c.** to attempt to keep your brother
T-16 ..... III.1:3 you will be **c.** to realize that your Teacher
W-pI... 161.7:5 **c.** to turn upon itself and to destroy.

**compelling** 8

T-5 ......... II.7:5 **c.** only because of what It reminds you *of.*
T-11 ..... VI.6:2 Its whole **c.** power lies in the fact that it
T-13 . VI.11:10 light will join with theirs in power so **c.**,
T-14 ....... II.8:5 The quietness of its simplicity is so **c.** that
T-15 ....... II.4:3 more **c.** witnesses for the Holy Spirit. And
T-16 ....... II.6:9 now, and you *will* yield to its **c.** attraction.
T-17 ..... V.12:1 of an instant, however **c.** it may be, is
T-17 .... VII.6:7 small or too enormous, too weak or too **c.**

**compellingly** 2

T-9 ..... VIII.4:3 and because it is real it is **c.** convincing.
T-12 .... VII.4:5 it can become **c.** real to you as its presence

**compels** 2

T-27 ....... V.2:3 and must provide a witness that **c.** belief.
T-27 ..... VI.1:3 Pain **c.** attention, drawing it away from

**compete** 1

T-7 ....... III.3:3 Sons have everything, they cannot **c.**. Yet

**competes** 1

M-8 ........... 1:2 which each thing seen **c.** with every other

**competing** 1

T-8 ..... IV.5:14 oppose your decision without **c.** with it

**competition** 4

T-7 ....... III.3:4 the idea of **c.** has entered their minds. Do
T-14 ....... X.3:1 Miracles are not in **c.**, and the number of
T-14 ....... X.4:1 aware of lack of **c.** among your thoughts,
W-pI .... 13.4:7 *fear because I think I am in c. with God.*

**competitive** 2

T-7 .......... I.4:1 rights, because it is **c.** rather than loving.
T-28 ..... VI.1:8 is. And so it has no need to be **c.**. It can be

**competitiveness** 1

T-9 ..... VIII.2:5 The essence of grandiosity is **c.**, because it

**complain** 2

T-2 ...... VII.1:1 still **c.** about fear, but you nevertheless
T-11 ... VIII.5:1 may **c.** that this course is not sufficiently

**complaint** 1

T-31 ........ I.4:3 every step, however difficult, without **c.**,

**complete** 229

T-1 ......... II.1:1 Revelation induces **c.** but temporary
T-1 ......... II.4:6 which I render **c.** because I share it. This
T-1 ....... III.8:4 of my **c.** awareness of the whole plan. The
T-1 ......... V.3:4 recognize your **c.** dependence on God,
T-1 ....... VI.1:1 peace can find it only by **c.** forgiveness.
T-1 .... VII.3:13 to walk the earth, your release is not **c.**.
T-1 .... VII.3:14 C. restoration of the Sonship is the only
T-2 ......... II.5:1 itself, and ultimately to make learning **c.**.
T-2 ......... II.6:9 Until the Atonement is **c.**, its various
T-3 ......... V.8:8 know yourself and your knowledge is **c.**.
T-4 ....... III.7:7 **c.** respect for what you have made, but I
T-4 ....... VI.6:6 a man, and can now **c.** it through others.
T-4 ...... VII.3:4 It is in **c.** and direct communication with
T-4 ...... VII.3:4 is in **c.** and direct communication with its
T-4 ...... VII.6:4 joy is not **c.** because yours is incomplete.
T-5 .......... I.5:5 When the Atonement is **c.** and the whole
T-5 ....... IV.6:3 is not **c.** until you join it and give it away.
T-5 ....... IV.7:4 because only the **c.** can think completely,
T-6 ....... III.3:7 Safety is the **c.** relinquishment of attack.
T-6 ..... V.A.6:2 necessary that you **c.** the step yourself,
T-6 ..... V.A.6:9 have chosen what they cannot **c.** alone,
T-6 ..... V.B.5:2 systems which are in **c.** disagreement,

T-7..........I.6:2 may be **c.** because the Kingdom of God is
T-7..... VIII.3:8 is a **c.** distortion of the power of extension
T-7......... IX.4:8 function, and only **c.** fulfillment is peace.
T-8........IV.1:1 If God's Will for you is **c.** peace and joy,
T-8........IV.1:5 His peace is **c.**, and you must be included
T-8.....VII.16:3 In its **c.** impossibility lies your only hope
T-8........IX.4:8 **C.** unconsciousness is impossible. You
T-9........ I.10:5 is **c.** communication failure between them
T-9.......VII.8:7 what belongs to Him and renders Him **c.**.
T-10....... II.6:1 If you realized the **c.** havoc this makes of
T-11....... II.4:3 His Own **c.** Will and make yours whole.
T-11......III.3:1 God wills for you, your joy would be **c.**!
T-11....... V.6:2 lies in your **c.** dependence on God, Whose
T-11......VI.1:6 is the **c.** triumph of Christ over the ego,
T-11......VI.5:3 is why his slavery is as **c.** as his freedom,
T-12....... II.8:5 in the name of the **c.** trust I have in you,
T-12....... V.9:3 the means and the end are in **c.** accord.
T-13.....III.9:4 Healing must be as **c.** as fear, for love
T-13... VIII.2:5 Perception, at its loftiest, is never **c.**. Even
T-14.........I.1:7 is **c.** forgiveness you must have let guilt go
T-14.....IV.7:5 Son as guilty is denial of the Father so **c.**,
T-14.....VII.4:9 fact of their **c.** incompatibility is instantly
T-15........ II.4:9 only because you have not given **c.** release
T-15....... II.5:6 it is, all in this instant, **c.**, accomplished
T-15....III.10:7 to yourself, for you will know you are **c.**,
T-15....... V.3:4 For it is the **c.** equality of the Atonement
T-15.....VII.1:4 Being **c.**, it asks nothing. Being wholly
T-15...VII.14:6 There is **c.** forgiveness here, for there is no
T-15...VII.14:8 Whose only need is to have you be **c.**. For
T-15... VIII.1:7 And that in **c.** forgiveness, in which you
T-15......IX.5:3 be in Heaven, where you are **c.** and quiet,
T-15....... X.8:7 but always to make the sacrifice **c.**.
T-15....XI.10:3 and you will make **c.** and not destroy. Say
T-16......IV.8:3 and it is they who render you **c.**. The
T-16......IV.8:6 without which you could never be **c.**. No
T-16....IV.12:3 journey that seemed endless is almost **c.**,
T-16....IV.13:8 are safe forever, because you are **c.** forever
T-16....... V.5:3 in **c.** disagreement on what completion is,
T-16....... V.7:2 seeks the relationship to make itself **c.**.
T-16.....V.11:8 The ritual of completion cannot **c.**, for life
T-16.....V.15:5 and **c.** escape from all its consequences.
T-16....VI.12:3 need not be **c.** because His is perfect. It is
T-16.....VII.7:1 your full awareness of the **c.** difference, in
T-17.........I.6:2 Salvation from separation would be **c.**, or
T-17....... II.3:2 but this is given, **c.** and wholly perfect. No
T-17....... II.3:3 Who planned salvation could **c.** it thus.
T-17....... II.5:1 simply by the **c.** forgiveness of the old, the
T-17......III.6:3 to make His resolutions **c.** and perfect,
T-17......IV.9:8 enclose the whole, **c.** in every aspect.
T-17....IV.12:2 you. Each is **c.**, and cannot be partially
T-17....IV.16:9 here is only healing, already **c.** and perfect
T-17..IV.16:10 where He is only the perfect and **c.** can be.
T-17....... V.5:2 shift in purpose could induce a **c.** change
T-17...VII.8:11 in every aspect and **c.** in every part. You
T-18.........I.3:6 No one is seen **c.**. The body is emphasized
T-18......III.1:5 sought a blackness so **c.** that you could
T-18......III.1:5 hide from truth forever, in **c.** insanity.
T-18......III.5:3 Your desire is now in **c.** accord with all
T-18... VIII.2:5 a little part of a glorious and **c.** idea. It
T-18... VIII.8:3 to preserve and keep **c.** what it would give
T-18....IX.1:10 segment of the Son of God, **c.** and holy,
T-18....IX.11:4 learning ends before Him Who is **c.** where
T-19.........I.7:4 Each is united, a **c.** thought system, but
T-19....... II.6:5 and capable of **c.** corruption and decay. If
T-19......IV.1:6 and the calm awareness of **c.** protection.
T19IV.A.17:12 your meager store and make your life **c.**.
T19... IV.C.6:5 final and **c.** disruption of communication,
T19...IV.D.8:7 born of **c.** forgiveness of his illusions, and
T19...IV.D.9:3 to look on it without **c.** forgiveness of his
T19.IV.D.11:4 **c.** forgiveness you still stand unforgiving.
T19.IV.D.18:4 Offer your brother freedom and **c.** release
T-20...... I.2:10 be **c.** till your forgiveness rests on Christ,
T-20......IV.6:4 lies all of it, without which is no part **c.**,
T-20......IV.6:9 Except you be there, he is not **c.**. And it is
T-21....... II.2:1 from pain and the **c.** escape from sin, all
T-21....... V.6:5 if the plan of God for your salvation is **c.**.
T-21....... V.6:6 And it must be **c.**, because its Source
T-21......VI.7:7 instant serves to bring **c.** correction of his
T-21......VI.7:8 his whole salvation seen as **c.** with yours.

T-21... VIII.4:1 who **c.** God's Will and are His happiness,
T-22.......in.2:6 each to **c.** himself and rob the other. They
T-22....... II.6:1 of you and the ego must be made **c.**. For if
T-22......VI.7:1 upon your brother with **c.** forgiveness,
T-23.......in.6:8 it must be **c.** if you would recognize it.
T-23..... II.13:1 Never is your possession made **c.**. And
T-23......III.3:4 It is **c.** for everyone. Let the idea of
T-23......IV.4:2 forgiveness of your brother is not **c.** as yet
T-23......IV.8:5 the same, eternally **c.** and wholly shared.
T-24..... II.11:2 it be that you have lost because he is **c.**?
T-24..... II.11:3 What has been given him makes you **c.**,
T-24....... V.6:7 first, but recognized that you were not **c.**.
T-24....... V.9:5 way that He must go to find Himself **c.**.
T-24......VI.1:1 it in gentleness and blessing so **c.** that not
T-24....VI.11:3 all the power to hold itself **c.** within itself,
T-25.........I.4:3 love celestial and so **c.** it wishes only that
T-25....... II.9:5 And so His joy is made **c.** when any part
T-25....... II.9:8 shine on you who would **c.** His joy, along
T-25..... II.9:10 will to make their Father's happiness **c.**,
T-25..... II.11:3 be made **c.** by offering completion to your
T-25......III.5:3 but is met with instant and **c.** forgiveness.
T-25....... V.5:6 allow him freedom to **c.** the task God gave
T-25......VI.4:3 plan **c.** until he finds his special function,
T-25......VI.4:3 to make himself **c.** within a world where
T-25......VI.5:6 But when it rests on all it is **c.**, and every
T-25. VIII.14:1 peace, **c.** deliverance from all effects of sin
T-25. VIII.14:1 the life eternal, joyous and **c.** in every way
T-26.........I.2:2 is a picture of **c.** disunity and total lack of
T-26.........I.2:4 sacrifice the other part, to keep itself **c.**.
T-26......IV.5:2 And as they come to you to be **c.**, so will
T-26...VII.10:1 Salvation, perfect and **c.**, asks but a little
T-26...VII.10:2 see with Heaven, wholly perfect and **c.**.
T-26......IX.4:5 The incomplete is made **c.** again, and
T-27......III.7:5 single thoughts, **c.** and happy, without
T-27....... V.8:8 becomes **c.** within two situations that are
T-28......IV.9:2 Your Holiness, **c.** and perfect, lies in every
T-29......III.2:4 are you the proof that He is perfect and **c.**
T-29....... V.4:3 the **c.** can be a part of God's completion,
T-29.....VII.2:4 and give him what would make himself **c.**.
T-29.....VII.6:1 is outside yourself to be **c.** and happy. It is
T-29.....VII.8:3 with power to make **c.** what is within by
T-29... VIII.2:3 way, you believe they will **c.** your little self
T-29......IX.8:5 Forgiveness, once **c.**, brings timelessness
T-30......III.3:3 a thing to add to you to make yourself **c.**,
T-30......III.4:4 Your will to be **c.** is but God's Will, and
T-30......III.4:9 thing the power to **c.** the Son of God.
T-30....III.10:3 Surrounded by a stillness so **c.** no sound
T-30......VI.1:3 from fear begins, and will be made **c.**.
T-31....IV.10:3 and in Their Oneness Both are kept **c.**.
T-31. VIII.12:6 Thy Will is done, **c.** and perfectly, and all
W-pI.......9.5:1 emphasized again that while **c.** inclusion
W-pI.....41.9:3 on the **c.** protection that surrounds you.
W-pI.....56.1:5 perfect security and **c.** fulfillment are my
W-pI.....67.1:1 is a **c.** and accurate statement of what you
W-pI.....75.6:7 several times, slowly and in **c.** patience:
W-pI.....94.1:1 the one idea which brings **c.** salvation; the
W-pI...95.12:3 You are one Self, **c.** and healed and whole,
W-pI.....98.6:2 of purpose, with the promise of **c.** success
W-pI...100.2:5 Your joy must be **c.** to let His plan be
W-pI...105.4:4 It adds to all that is **c.** already, not in
W-pI...105.5:2 Him **c.** Himself as He defines completion.
W-pI...105.5:3 completes Him must **c.** His Son as well.
W-pI...108.4:2 together, that the Thought remain **c.**.
W-pI...109.9:3 together here, for thus our rest is made **c.**,
W-pI...110.2:1 need to let **c.** correction heal your mind,
W-pI...126.1:2 would be no problem in **c.** forgiveness,
W-pI...134.1:1 undeserved, and a **c.** denial of the truth.
WpI. rIV.in6:4 with you who are **c.** as you unite with Him
W-pI...152.1:6 Here is your world, **c.** in all details. Here
W-pI.160.10:2 may be **c.** and perfect as it was established
W-pI...161.1:4 Here is Atonement made **c.**, the world
W-pI...161.2:1 **C.** abstraction is the natural condition of
W-pI...162.4:3 kept **c.** because its sharing is unlimited.
W-pI...162.5:4 loss, and for **c.** escape from sin and guilt?
W-pI...164.9:8 Hand holds out **c.** salvation to His Son?
W-pI...169.8:1 already in His Mind, accomplished and **c.**
W-pI.170.13:7 *we give thanks for them who render us* **c.**. *In*
WpI rV.in10:4 wholeness now **c.**, as God established it.
W-pI.186.13:3 would make a restitution, though He is **c.**;

W-pI...192.1:1 Father's holy Will that you **c.** Himself,
W-pI...192.2:7 return to be acknowledged, not to be **c.**.
W-pI...192.4:3 aid, to be laid by when learning is **c.**, but
W-pI...195.6:2 to **c.** the One Who is Himself completion.
W-pI...195.8:6 is **c.** you will have total gratitude, for you
W-pI...197.9:2 to anyone who makes your Self **c.**. And
W-pII ..in.10:7 Now it is **c.**. This year has brought us to
W-pII .238.2:2 to Him Whose Love is made **c.** in him.
W-pII ..... 3.5:2 until forgiveness has been made **c.**. And
W-pII ..... 4.3:4 loves, with but corruption to **c.** Himself,
W-pII ..... 7.5:4 God, when all He wills is that you be **c.**?
W-pII .291.2:6 *Let my forgiveness be* **c.**, *and let the memory*
W-pII ... 10.3:2 is but to fear **c.** release from suffering,
W-pII ... 11.3:2 in creation is His Will **c.** in every aspect,
W-pII .337.1:1 of loss; **c.** deliverance from suffering. And
W-pII .341.1:3 *You, in brotherhood and Fatherhood* **c.**; *in*
W-pII .343.1:9 *Son can make no sacrifice, for he must be* **c.**,
W-pII343.1:10 *I am* **c.** *because I am Your Son. I cannot lose,*
W-pII ... 14.1:1 *I am God's Son,* **c.** *and healed and whole,*
Wfl........in.3:6 memory is given back, completely and **c.**.
M-in.......... 4:8 hope, their learning finally becomes **c.**.
M-4 ..... I.A.8:8 anywhere, if peace of mind is already **c.**?
M-4 ....... X.3:8 glad tidings of **c.** forgiveness to the world.
M-12 ......... 1:2 perfect teacher, whose learning is **c.**,
M-12 ......... 2:8 Their minds are one; their joining is **c.**.
M-14 ......... 1:4 The illusion of forgiveness, **c.**, excluding
M-14 ......... 2:1 Until forgiveness is **c.**, the world does
M-14 ......... 3:7 one teacher of God can make salvation **c.**.
M-14 ......... 5:7 And only **c.** forgiveness brings all this to
M-15 ......... 2:6 One instant of **c.** belief in this, and you
M-22 ......... 1:3 the one **c.** concept possible in this world,
M-22 ......... 2:2 there is a sudden and **c.** awareness of the
M-23 ......... 5:5 But in his eyes your loveliness is so **c.** and
M-24 ......... 4:1 this course aims at a **c.** reversal of thought
M-24 ......... 6:1 moment that **c.** salvation is offered you,
M-29 ......... 4:8 Yet, despite its obvious and **c.** ignorance,
C-4........... 6:10 come to claim His Own. Forgiveness is **c.**.
C-5............. 3:1 In his **c.** identification with the Christ–
C-6............. 2:2 was the first to **c.** his own part perfectly.
C-6............. 5:4 part in its redemption you have made **c.**.
C-ep........... 5:5 We who **c.** Him offer thanks to Him, as
P-2...........II.1:3 Even in this, **c.** consistency is not required
P-2...........II.4:2 This will come when psychotherapy is **c.**,
P-2......... V.6:4 What they must start their Father will **c.**.
P-3...........I.4:2 recognize the whole when his part is **c.**.
S-1 ......... V.3:7 little more to learn before the journey is **c.**
S-2...........I.7:8 Salvation's plan is made **c.**, and sanity has
S-2...........I.9:6 be achieved at last, and learning be **c.**.
S-3 ....... II.5:10 true. If you are healed your healing is **c.**.

## completed 20

T-1.........I.25:1 chain of forgiveness which, when **c.**, is the
T-1......... V.3:1 When the Atonement has been **c.**, all
T-2..........II.6:8 a **c.** plan has a unique relationship to time
T-4........ VI.6:6 is only because I **c.** my part in it as a man,
T-13...VII.17:2 My task is not **c.** until I have lifted every
T-16...... IV.9:6 completion, and only this, there is God **c.**,
T-16..... V.11:7 it is never **c.**, nor ever will be completed.
T-16..... V.11:7 it is never completed, nor ever will be **c.**.
T-19...... III.5:4 And when correction is **c.**, time *is* eternity.
T19... IV.D.1:5 a final obstacle, after which is salvation **c.**.
T-20...... IV.6:4 nor is the whole **c.** without your part. The
T-25........II.9:9 Him. And thus is yours **c.**. Not one ray of
T-25...... VI.5:6 and every function of this world **c.** with it.
T-28...... IV.9:4 recognized as being part of the **c.** picture
W-pI.....25.6:7 until you have **c.** the statement about it.
W-pI...160.4:4 Is it fear that love completes, and is **c.** by?
W-pI.182.11:3 Him go home today, **c.** and completely.
M-2 ........... 2:4 was established and **c.** simultaneously,
M-23 ......... 3:4 **c.** learning guarantees your own success.
C-6............. 2:3 share it with you when you have **c.** yours.

## completely 122

T-2........ III.5:6 creations are **c.** dependent on Each Other.
T-2......... V.4:2 are **c.** unconcerned about your readiness,
T-3......... V.9:3 separate. Spirit knows God **c.**. That is its
T-3......... V.9:5 The fact that each one has this power **c.** is

T-4......... II.1:4 because knowledge is c. impersonal, and
T-4......... II.7:9 become c. confused about what is really
T-4......... II.8:1 The ego believes it is c. on its own, which
T-4......... II.8:4 is the mind's belief that it is c. on its own.
T-4........VII.4:3 Being is c. without these distinctions. It is
T-5........IV.7:4 because only the complete can think c.,
T-6......... II.6:4 It is c. unalterable. It is total inclusion.
T-7........ VI.3:8 the ego resolves this c. insane dilemma in
T-7........ VI.3:8 insane dilemma in a c. insane way. It does
T-7......VIII.5:6 quickly to the Holy Spirit to be undone c.,
T-7......VIII.6:2 The ego can be c. forgotten at any time,
T-8........ III.7:8 all your wrong decisions are undone c.,
T-8........IV.3:1 was done c. by any part of the Sonship.
T-9.......VII.4:2 realize how c. different these evaluations
T-10...... III.7:3 merely by denying them c. in himself.
T-10.....IV.5:10 will envelop you c. when you let them go.
T-10...... IV.8:2 so that the Rays can never be c. forgotten.
T-11... V.12:10 which the Love of God c. protects them.
T-12...... III.7:3 that it encompasses c. opposed thoughts
T-12...... IV.1:6 though severely impaired, is c. consistent.
T-13...... III.9:3 total love you will not be healed c..
T-13....... V.6:5 In your madness you overlook reality c.,
T-14...... XI.6:1 you can learn a lesson so c. different from
T-15.........I.9:3 It has taken time to misguide you so c.,
T-15.........I.9:6 and it is here that you are c. absolved,
T-15.........I.9:6 c. free and wholly without condemnation.
T-15.......I.11:1 it would take to change your mind so c.,
T-15..... II.4:10 given a single instant c. to the Holy Spirit.
T-15...... VI.1:4 in each one, for its ability to satisfy you c.,
T-15...... VI.3:5 transcends the concept of loss of power c.
T-15...... VI.4:6 And like Him, you can give yourself c.,
T-15.....VII.3:4 it is, and have judged it c. in the dark. As
T-15...VII.14:5 to it, and overcomes loneliness c.. There
T-15.....VIII.1:7 is nothing to forgive, you are absolved c..
T-15...... IX.2:5 of meaning, it will not satisfy you c.. Yet it
T-15....... X.7:5 destroyed in part, but able to be neither c.
T-15....... X.7:6 Whose total Love would c. destroy you.
T-15...... XI.3:2 Let yourself be healed c. that you may
T-16.........I.4:5 because you have never yet done yours c..
T-16...... VI.7:2 grossly distorted and c. out of perspective
T-16.... VI.12:2 to share His perspective to give it to you c.
T-16.....VII.3:2 It is c. savage and completely insane. For
T-16.....VII.3:2 It is completely savage and c. insane. For
T-17...... IV.3:3 aim of occupying your mind so c. that you
T-17....... V.4:2 make its former goal c. without attraction
T-18.........I.5:3 so vast and so c. incredible that from it a
T-18.....VII.2:2 sight, but it has not yet c. disappeared.
T-18....VIII.8:3 its meaning. It is c. impartial in its giving,
T-18... IX.10:5 transports you to something c. different.
T-19...... II.7:5 Father, and change His Mind c.. Mourn,
T-19...... IV.1:4 them, extending past c. unencumbered.
T19. IV.A.10:6 Overlooking guilt c., it sees no fear. Being
T19... IV.D.7:7 you, unseparated from it and c. one.
T-20...... VI.2:5 to be known, c. understood and shared. It
T-21.........I.6:1 in which you heard c. unremembered.
T-21....... II.1:3 that it cannot fail to be c. understood.
T-21...... III.4:6 have accepted them c. instead of yours,
T-22...... VI.7:3 through which you walk c. undismayed?
T-23.........I.4:6 He loves you perfectly, c. and eternally.
T-23..... II.14:6 Such a reversal, c. turned around, with
T-23..... II.20:4 Each one upholds these laws c., offering a
T-25.....VII.9:1 nor overlook, nor fail c. to perceive at all.
T-29...... IX.9:2 cannot conceal c. all your sense of doom.
T-30.... III.5:11 whole c. lovely Thought God holds of you
T-30.... III.10:2 you. C. unaffected by the turmoil and the
T-30.... III.10:4 c. unaware of all the world that worships
T-30....... V.5:1 and yet c. shared and perfectly fulfilled.
W-pI..... 15.5:3 idea unless you feel c. comfortable with it,
W-pI.....28.5:1 it, and look upon it with a c. open mind.
W-pI.....41.1:1 overcome c. the sense of loneliness and
W-pI.....41.8:7 along. But it will never fail c., and instant
W-pI.....45.7:2 are there in your mind now, c. unchanged
W-pI.....53.3:2 fear because it is c. undependable, and
W-pI.....57.1:2 world that can be c. undone if I so choose
W-pI.....65.8:5 changed when you accept today's idea c..
W-pI.....66.1:4 are different, but their content is c. one.
W-pI.....68.6:4 c. at peace with everyone and everything,
W-pI.....75.6:2 Keep a c. open mind, washed of all past
W-pI.....75.9:4 power of forgiveness to heal your sight c..
W-pI..... 79.3:5 you feel c. free of problems and at peace.
W-pI.....84.3:2 Grievances are c. alien to love. Grievances
W-pI.....98.3:4 be filled c. in the perfect time and place.
W-pI...106.1:1 in stillness, and c. certain in Its messages.
W-pI...107.3:4 Truth occupies your mind c., liberating
W-pI...108.5:1 One thought, c. unified, will serve to
W-pI...109.3:2 C. undismayed, this thought will carry
W-pI...109.4:2 of hate your rest remains c. undisturbed.
W-pI...113.1:2 *are mine, because I am one Self, c. whole, at*
W-pI...126.1:1 c. alien to the ego and the thinking of the
W-pI. 131.11:8 could not c. lock to hide what lies beyond.
W-pI...151.6:3 the doubts their lord can not c. vanquish.
W-pI...164.4:5 so great and so c. different from all things
W-pI...169.3:6 thus is ready to accept a state c. different
W-pI...169.6:2 has been c. given and received completely
W-pI...169.6:2 has been completely given and received c.
WpI...rV.in1:4 We would take this step c., that we may
W-pI. 182.11:3 Him go home today, completed and c..
W-pI...183.8:3 idea that holds your mind c.. Let all
W-pI...185.1:4 would be c. given back to full awareness,
W-pI...185.2:9 The world would be c. changed, should
W-pI. 198.11:6 you made c. vanished from the mind that
WpI rVI.in.7:4 trusting Him c. for the way each practice
W-pII .247.1:4 me as the simple truth, and I am healed c.
W-pII ... 10.5:1 c. changeless and forever pure. Therefore
W-pII .313.1:6 *kept c. undefiled upon the altar to Your holy*
W-pII ... 12.5:2 dwelling place, His joy, His love, c. His,
W-pII ... 12.5:2 His love, completely His, c. one with Him.
Wfl........in.3:6 memory is given back, c. and complete.
M-4 ...... IV.1:8 harmfulness c. obliterates his function
M-8 ........... 1:5 standards, c. upsets the mental balance.
M-14 ......... 4:1 its thought system has been c. reversed.
M-16 ......... 4:6 and in that instant join with Him c..
M-18 ......... 2:7 overlooked c. in His sight and in God's
C-6 ............ 1:1 or became c. identified with the Christ,
P-2.........in.4:4 goals not c. free of magical overtones.
P-2...........I.3:6 they cannot become c. reconciled as one
P-2..........II.1:3 that point could teach salvation c., within
S-3..........II.1:2 kindly meant but not c. understood as yet

## completeness 1

T-6 ........ V.1:7 extending outward, though not His c., is

## completes 6

T-16 .... VII.8:3 Your receiving c. His giving. You will
W-pI.....97.2:3 You are the spirit which c. Himself, and
W-pI...100.1:1 Just as God's Son c. his Father, so your
W-pI...100.1:1 so your part in it c. your Father's plan.
W-pI...105.5:3 will understand that what c. Him must
W-pI...160.4:4 Is it fear that love c., and is completed by?

## completing 7

T-16 ..... IV.9:1 like to Him, c. Him by your completion.
T-19 ......I.15:3 c. the process of making lovely that they
T-21 ... VI.10:3 thanks your Father gives you for c. Him.
WpI.rV.in10:5 are His Son, c. His extension in your own.
W-pII ..... 7.5:4 you refuse to take the function of c. God,
W-pII .341.1:3 *us as His Son, a universe of Thought c. Him.*
W-pII .343.1:9 *be complete, having the function of c. You.*

## completion 55

T-1 ........ V.4:6 which is a state of c. and abundance.
T-5 ....... VI.9:6 You can delay the c. of the Kingdom, but
T-15 ..... VI.5:5 in your mind, experiencing not loss but c.
T-15 .. VII.14:6 no desire to exclude anyone from your c.,
T-15 .. VII.14:8 And you understand that your c. is God's,
T-15 .. VII.14:9 your c. makes you His in your awareness.
T-15 ... VIII.3:3 Refuse not the awareness of your c., and
T-16 ..... IV.8:3 You seek but for your own c., and it is
T-16 ..... IV.9:1 Across the bridge is your c., for you will
T-16 ..... IV.9:1 like to Him, completing Him by your c..
T-16 ..... IV.9:3 Only there is the c. of God and of His Son
T-16 ..... IV.9:6 which you are wholly willing to accept c.,
T-16 ... IV.10:1 you straight to Him where your c. rests,
T-16 ... IV.10:2 attainable removes your own sense of c.,
T-16 ... IV.11:5 For your c. lies in truth, and nowhere else.
T-16 ... IV.11:7 Would He not answer you whose c. is His
T-16 . IV.11:12 c. lie the memory of His Wholeness and
T-16 . IV.11:12 and His gratitude to you for His c.. In His
T-16 ... IV.12:6 in joyous answer to His Call for His c..
T-16 ... IV.13:1 of any kind would hinder God's c., can
T-16 ... IV.13:3 does interference in God's c. seem to be
T-16 ..........V.h The Choice for C.
T-16 .......V.5:1 To everyone Heaven is c.. There can be
T-16 .......V.5:3 in complete disagreement on what c. is,
T-16 .......V.5:4 Spirit knows that c. lies first in union, and
T-16 .......V.5:5 To the ego c. lies in triumph, and in the
T-16 ......V.11:8 The ritual of c. cannot complete, for life
T-16 .....V.13:2 the name of your c. you do not want this.
T19 .IV.A.10:2 which it would unite in holy union and c..
T19IV.A.17:13 is c. as the ego sees it. For guilt creeps in
T19IV.A.17:15 Communion is another kind of c., which
T-20 ... IV.6:10 And it is his c. that he remembers there.
T-22 ...... in.3:3 Accepting his c., he would extend it by
T-24 .......V.6:8 sought for your c. in each living thing that
T-24 .......V.8:1 down to you, to offer you your own c..
T-24 .......V.8:2 His is yours because in your c. is His Own.
T-25 .....II.11:3 complete by offering c. to your brother.
T-29 .....II.10:3 not exist, and His c. is its nothingness.
T-29 .......V.4:3 the complete can be a part of God's c.,
T-29 .......V.5:7 instead, a brother's hand in which c. lies.
T-29 .... VII.6:3 dwells within, and your c. lies in Him. No
T-30 ..... III.3:1 for every idol lies the yearning for c..
T-30 ..... III.3:4 this, you will achieve c. in a form you like.
T-30 ..... III.5:1 C. is the *function* of God's Son. He has no
W-pI .. 99.10:1 which would oppose the truth of your c.,
W-pI .. 105.5:2 Him complete Himself as He defines c..
WpI..rIV.in6:4 And as His Own c. joins with Him, so will
W-pI 155.10:2 left to keep the truth apart from God's c.,
W-pI .. 162.2:1 Father's happiness, His Love and His c..
W-pI .. 195.6:2 to complete the One Who is Himself c..
W-pI 195.10:4 are; His Own c. and the Source of love,
Wfl........ in.4:1 as it is given us to be His Own c. in reality.
M-16 ......... 3:8 After c. of the more structured practice
M-29 ......... 7:1 Remember you are His c. and His Love.
S-3........ IV.3:3 restored as His c. and returned to share

## complex 3

T-14 ........I.5:2 so c. you cannot see that it means nothing
T-26 ..... III.6:1 in this c. and overcomplicated world. For
T-31 ........I.2:8 to judge it hard to learn or too c. to grasp.

## complexities 1

W-pI .. 122.6:7 All the c. the world has spun of fragile

## complexity 11

T-15 ..... IV.6:2 C. is of the ego, and is nothing more than
T-26 .......II.3:4 one by one, without regard to size, c., or
T-26 ..... III.1:1 C. is not of God. How could it be, when
T-26 ..... III.1:5 How, then, could there be c. in Him?
T-26 ..... III.1:9 presence, and bring c. where oneness is?
W-pI .... 39.1:4 clouds of c. in which you think you think.
W-pI .... 64.5:7 C. of form does not imply complexity of
W-pI .... 64.5:7 of form does not imply c. of content. It is
W-pI .... 79.6:1 All this c. is but a desperate attempt not
W-pI 133.12:3 this. C. is nothing but a screen of smoke,
P-2..........V.1:1 lost their way in endless mazes of c.. This

## complicated 5

T-8 .....VIII.6:9 more c. the results become the harder it
T-12 ........I.2:1 The analysis of ego motivation is very c.,
W-pI .. 135.5:3 it. It needs no c. structures of defense, no
W-pI .. 138.6:1 In this insanely c. world, Heaven appears
P-2...... IV.11:8 There is no need for c. change. There is

## complication 1

T-27 .... VII.2:3 has been obscured by heavy clouds of c.,

## comply 1
W-pI.....95.9:1 to c. with the requirements of this course,

## components 1
T-7........VI.7:4 conflicting c. within it that have led to a

## compounding 1
T-15.........I.7:7 nothing but a teaching device for c. guilt

## comprehend 3
W-pI.124.11:2 understand, a joy too deep for you to c., a
W-pI.124.11:3 you will understand and c. and see.
W-pII..233.1:7 *nor Love whose tenderness I cannot c., but*

## comprehensible 1
T-5...........I.1:9 the lower mind it is quite c. in connection

## comprehensive 1
T-2...........I.3:7 not yet experienced any c. reawakening or

## compromise 35
T-2........IV.4:6 to utilize a c. approach to mind and body,
T-2.....VII.5:10 that ultimately no c. is possible between
T-2.....VII.5:11 which all c. in this respect can be given up
T-6........III.3:8 No c. is possible in this. Teach attack in
T-14......III.3:1 is no c. that you can make with guilt, and
T-19.........I.6:1 The inevitable c. is the belief that the
T-22....... II.4:6 It cannot c.. And faith in innocence is
T-23.........III.h Salvation without C.
T-23......III.3:1 Salvation is no c. of any kind. To
T-23......III.3:2 c. is to accept but part of what you want;
T-23......III.3:5 Let the idea of c. but enter, and the
T-23......III.3:6 It is denied where c. has been accepted,
T-23......III.3:6 for c. is the belief salvation is impossible.
T-23......III.4:1 course is easy just because it makes no c..
T-23......III.4:2 those who still believe that c. is possible.
T-23......III.6:1 peace, nor c. for the escape from conflict.
T-24..... II.12:5 seeks for bargains and for c. that would
T-26.........I.1:2 idea. It is the pivot upon which all c., all
T-27.........I.1:1 wish to be unfairly treated is a c. attempt
T-28....... V.3:8 There is no c.. You are your Self or an
T-29.........I.1:4 His. The c. the least and littlest gap would
T-31......VI.1:2 There is no c. between the two. If one is
W-pI...130.6:1 will attempt no c. where none is possible.
W-pI...130.7:1 to the thought that ends all c. and doubt,
W-pI...133.5:1 is no c. in what your choice must bring. It
W-pI...163.6:4 No c. is possible. For here again we see an
W-pI...185.4:1 c. alone a dream can bring. Sometimes it
W-pI...185.4:8 is lost to sleeping minds intent on c., each
W-pI...185.7:5 us. They do not ask for c., nor try to make
W-pI...185.9:3 No c. is possible in this. You choose God's
M-27..........4:5 No c. in this is possible. There is either a
M-27..........7:1 Accept no c. in which death plays a part.
P-2.........IV.8:3 to c. by seeing just a little bit of hell. This
P-3......... II.9:7 to c. in this respect are strange indeed.
S-2......... II.6:1 also take the form of bargaining and c.. "I

## compromises 5
T-4......... V.6:3 The ego c. with the issue of the eternal,
T-15....... X.9:4 You have tried many c. in the attempt to
T-23......III.5:6 one c. with an enemy but hates him still,
M-27..........4:7 The world attempts a thousand c., and
M-27..........6:9 the c. and the rituals the world fosters in

## compromising 1
W-pI...185.4:3 the dream, for c. is the goal of dreaming.

## conceal 16
T-4......... V.2:5 tries to c. not only "unacceptable" body
T-5...... III.10:4 Despite the ego's attempts to c. this part,
T-12.......I.9:10 You have denied its power to c. love,
T-14....... X.8:9 is senseless, though careful to c. this fact
T-21...... VI.8:9 What madness would c., the Holy Spirit
T-22...... III.3:6 cannot c. its emptiness from reason's eyes
T-29...... IX.9:2 the dream cannot c. completely all your
W-pI.....69.1:1 can look upon what your grievances c..
W-pI.....78.1:2 of hate before the miracle it would c.. And
W-pI.135.19:2 the truth that only your defenses would c.
W-pI.136.16:2 will be no dark corners sickness can c.,
W-pI...138.6:4 but c. this one by taking different forms.
W-pI...151.1:4 but a cloak for the uncertainty it would c..
W-pII..322.1:4 only to c. the Self which is God's only Son
M-27 .........7:2 nor let attack c. the truth from you. What
C-2.............3:2 can there be a truth that lies c. effectively.

## concealed 25
T-13...... III.6:4 them, and c. as long as they are hidden, is
T-14...... VI.1:9 What is c. cannot be loved, and so it must
T-14...... VI.2:3 unless it is c. from love's beneficence.
T-14...... VI.8:4 behind which nothing at all is carefully c..
T-17..... V.12:2 awareness of time, but not c. within it.
T-28.........I.6:2 seek to keep c. the truth about yourself.
T-28...... III.7:5 each c. within a separate and uncertain
T-28....... V.7:3 The gap is carefully c. in fog, and misty
T-31... V.15:10 any kind you see your own c. desire to kill
T-31.....VII.2:3 come in fearful form, with content still c.,
T-31.....VII.6:3 and keep it static and c. within your mind
T-31... VIII.9:3 all the loveliness which they c. appear like
W-pI.....69.2:4 past the veil of darkness that keeps it c..
WpI. rIII.in3:3 Unwillingness can be most carefully c.
W-pI...134.5:2 that sin is unforgivable, at best to be c.,
W-pI...138.9:6 effects. They cannot be c., because their
WpI. rIV.in3:1 of true forgiveness may be carefully c..
W-pI...152.4:3 It is c. behind a vast array of choices that
W-pI...165.1:3 hide what cannot be c. except illusion?
W-pI...169.7:3 will offer was c. from Him Who teaches
W-pI.196.10:3 this had been c. while you believed attack
M-17 .........2:3 in fact, be easily c. beneath a wish to help.
C-2.............2:5 its illusive nature is c. behind the words
S-1 ....... III.4:1 Guilt must be given up, and not c.. Nor
S-2......... II.1:2 some are carefully c. beneath what seems

## concealing 2
T-13....... II.2:2 rid of it, but you are actually merely c. it.
M-14 .........1:4 all evil, c. all sin and ending guilt forever.

## concealment 5
T-2......... II.2:3 kind of denial is not a c. but a correction.
T-13...... III.6:2 In c. they appear to do so, and thus they
T-15...VII.14:4 here. Here there is no c., and no private
T-19.........I.7:8 c. seems to keep your identification safe
T-19.........I.8:1 understood how much this strange c. has

## conceals 10
T-12.........I.9:9 raise what fear c. to clear-cut unequivocal
T-13...... VI.2:5 brothers and c. their reality from your
T-14.....VII.2:8 see it, and the clearer what it c. becomes.
T-22...... III.5:2 If what the form c. is a mistake, the form
T-23.......in.1:4 attack would use to cover frailty c. it not,
T-23...... IV.1:8 are asked to realize the form it takes c. the
T-27.....VII.6:8 What c. the truth is not where you should
W-pI.....90.2:4 *to this problem is the miracle that it c..*
W-pI...91.6:10 to your awareness what the mistake c..
W-pI.161.11:5 What you are seeing now c. from you the

## concede 1
W-pI...129.2:2 Perhaps you will c. there is no loss in

## conceivable 4
T-11.........I.3:2 Is this c.? Can part of His Mind contain
T-18.........I.6:3 loss is meaningless and only increase is c..
T-23.........I.2:2 God? Is victory c.? And if it were, is this a
W-pII .249.1:3 What suffering is now c.? What loss can

## conceive 36
T-2........ V.9:6 any form of charity you can c. of as yet.
T-3.........II.1:3 It is impossible to c. of light and darkness
T-4...........I.2:2 because they cannot c. of it as a move
T-4..........II.8:7 not attack it; it merely cannot c. of it at all
T-4...... III.4:4 You cannot c. of the real relationship that
T-5......... V.5:3 sane mind cannot c. of illness because it
T-5......... V.5:3 cannot c. of attacking anyone or anything
T-7........ IX.1:7 its fullness and cannot c. of any part from
T-8..........II.6:3 Yet He cannot c. of God without you,
T-8.....VII.14:5 To c. of the body as a means of attack and
T-13.......in.3:5 this, for only the guilty could c. of it.
T-14........X.3:3 once you c. of them as possible at all.
T-15.......I.4:14 and because it cannot c. of its own death,
T-15....VIII.2:5 for this that you cannot c. of need so great
T-15........X.5:8 you cannot c. of love without sacrifice.
T-24....... V.1:5 you seek for is a source of joy as you c. it.
T-24...VII.10:4 And you cannot c. of you apart from it.
T-25....VIII.5:8 a mind that can c. of specialness at all. Yet
T-26....VIII.2:5 you cannot c. of gaining what forgiveness
T-31.........I.3:1 in every form you could c. of them, could
T-31...... VI.4:1 Only in arrogance could you c. that you
W-pI.....68.1:7 one can c. of his Creator as unlike himself
W-pI.....94.3:8 nor could c. of loss or suffering or death.
W-pI...121.4:5 can c. of none because it sees the sinful
W-pI...134.3:2 You c. of pardon as a vain attempt to look
W-pI.135.26:2 c. of all the happiness that comes to you
W-pI...153.4:3 frenzy and intensity of which you can c.,
W-pI...181.9:2 and never could c. of anything without Its
W-pI...190.4:4 could c. of them as cause of anything?
W-pII .246.1:3 mind c. of all the love my Father has for
W-pII .252.1:1 the thoughts of holiness of which I now c.
W-pII .315.1:2 far beyond all things of which I can c.. A
W-pII ... 13.4:1 to c. of what it cannot see and does not
M-4 ........II.2:3 at one with himself can even c. of conflict.
M-20 ....... 6:11 and all the thoughts of which you can c.,
S-3..........II.5:6 by the healing that the world cannot c..

## conceived 19
T-24...... IV.2:3 It was c. to make *you* frail and helpless.
T-24...... VI.3:4 as He c. of you before the world began,
T-27......II.16:4 is the function given it c. to be its Own,
T-27..... VII.8:4 to a dream c. and cherished by a separate
T-27..... VII.8:7 c. within the idle dreaming of the world.
T-27....VIII.5:5 and could never have c. this world as real.
T-28....... V.4:1 You have c. a little gap between illusions
T-29.........I.1:3 could be c. of in the Wholeness that is His
T-29...... VI.3:2 If it be c. to die, then die it must unless it
T-29.....VII.5:3 death, c. as real and given living form. Yet
W-pI...139.3:1 so vast, its magnitude can hardly be c.. To
W-pI...169.6:3 where the past and future cannot be c.. It
W-pI...170.4:2 make attack, and must have first c. of it.
W-pI...192.3:1 cannot even be c. of in the world. It has
W-pII .308.1:1 I have c. of time in such a way that I
M-4 ....... X.2:3 they could never have c. of such a change.
M-5 .........I.1:7 Sickness is a method, c. in madness, for
M-8 ........... 1:5 one c. of as more desirable by the world's
P-2......... V.3:3 is but a glimmer of a thought not yet c..

## conceives 8
T-26..... VII.9:3 it "wish" because it still c. of other choices
T-26... VII.13:3 that each idea the mind c. but adds to its
T-27......II.16:3 and c. a single function as its only one.
T-29...... IX.7:4 the thoughts the mind c. and what it sees.
W-pI...184.4:3 It c. of little things and looks upon them.
W-pI...187.5:5 receiver in the sense the world c. of them.
W-pII .341.1:3 *that the Lord of Sinlessness c. us as His Son, a*
S-3........ III.3:1 be the aim of healing as the world c. of it.

## concentrate 13
T-2....... VII.5:7 to c. on error is only a further error. The
T-17...... VI.4:2 c. on everything that helps you meet it. It
T-18...... IV.2:4 C. only on this, and be not disturbed that

T-18.....VII.5:6 far more profitable now merely to c. on
W-pI.......2.1:6 do not c. on anything in particular, and
W-pI......41.9:3 C. on the holiness that they imply about
WpI...rI.in.2:5 you more than the others, c. on that one.
W-pI.....64.7:3 my function" quite often to help you c..
W-pI.....64.8:2 trying to c. on the thoughts you are using.
W-pI.....65.5:3 make no attempt to c. only on thoughts
W-pI.....91.9:2 yourself. C. particularly on the experience
WpI. rIV.in1:2 Today we will begin to c. on readiness for
P-2........VI.4:9 c. your healing efforts here is but futility.

## concentrated 1

W-pI.186.10:3 or direct his energies and c. drive toward

## concentrating 1

Wi181-200 3:1 start our journey beyond words by c. first

## concentration 3

T-4........IV.7:2 The problem is not one of c.; it is the
W-pI.....39.9:3 Sustained c. is very difficult at first. It will
M-21.........1:8 in helping c. and facilitating the exclusion

## concept 90

*See also* self-concept

T-1........III.9:3 the c. of size exists on a plane that is itself
T-1.........IV.4:5 who brought the "hell-fire" c. into it.
T-2......VIII.3:4 a c. totally opposed to right-mindedness,
T-3...........I.2:2 It is unwise to accept any c. if you have to
T-3.........IV.1:6 and all conflict arises from the c. of levels.
T-3.......VII.2:4 The "devil" is a frightening c. because he
T-4.........II.7:4 That is why the c. of "getting" arose in the
T-4........III.4:6 the c. is beyond its understanding. Love
T-5.........I.1:14 accept the c. that the world is one of ideas
T-5........III.5:1 Delay is of the ego, because time is its c..
T-5.......V.2:11 a totally meaningless c. except to the ego,
T-5.........V.3:3 based on the c. of usurping God's power.
T-5........VI.9:6 you cannot introduce the c. of fear into it.
T-6.........I.16:5 c. of punishment involves the projection
T-6......V.A.4:4 Kingdom to let this crucial c. slip away. It
T-6.......V.B.3:1 process is the undoing of the getting c..
T-7...........I.7:4 "first" as applied to Him is not a time c..
T-7.......V.5:10 and is therefore a c. that only a conflicted
T-7........VI.1:6 includes his c. of God, of His creations
T-9.........V.3:7 that there have been revolts against this c.
T-10.....V.14:2 to you to be desirable the c. of choice,
T-13.VII.10:10 Ownership is a dangerous c. if it is left to
T-13....VIII.1:6 c. "where" does not mean anything to it.
T-14.......III.9:2 because of the c. of decision that led to it.
T-15......VI.3:5 that transcends the c. of loss of power
T-16.......V.7:1 Most curious of all is the c. of the self
T-19.......II.5:3 It is the most "holy" c. in the ego's system
T-25.........I.7:1 is separate, the c. of a Oneness joined as
T-27......III.1:7 that contradicts the c. that it attacks. And
T-27......III.1:9 Who can understand a double c., such as
T-31.......V.1:1 learning of the world is built upon a c. of
T-31.......V.1:5 The building of a c. of the self is what the
T-31.......V.2:1 A c. of the self is made by you. It bears no
T-31.......V.2:4 The c. of the self the world would teach is
T-31.......V.4:1 The face of innocence the c. of the self so
T-31.......V.5:1 that the c. of the self was made to teach. It
T-31.......V.7:6 c. but a thought to which its maker gives
T-31.......V.8:1 A c. of the self is meaningless, for no one
T-31.......V.8:2 aim of teaching you this c. of yourself,
T-31.......V.8:3 you see this c. of the self must be undone,
T-31.....V.11:1 this c. must be kept in darkness is that, in
T-31.....V.11:3 c. of the world depends upon this concept
T-31.....V.11:3 the world depends upon this c. of the self.
T-31.....V.12:3 shifts the c. of the self from what is wholly
T-31.....V.14:1 The c. of the self has always been the
T-31.....V.14:7 And vaguely does the c. of the self appear
T-31.....V.15:2 be no c. that can stand for what you are.
T-31.....V.15:3 What matters it which c. you accept while
T-31.....V.15:4 Your c. of yourself will still remain quite
T-31.....V.15:7 c. of the self embraces all you look upon,
T-31.....V.17:5 every c. has been raised to doubt and
T-31.....VI.5:1 forget not that no c. of yourself will stand
T-31.....VI.5:4 see, because the c. of the self has changed.
T-31....VII.1:6 And no one here but holds a c. of himself
T-31....VII.1:8 This c. emphasizes treachery, and trust
T-31....VII.2:3 to shake your sorry c. of yourself and
T-31....VII.2:5 then your c. of yourself is wholly changed.
T-31....VII.3:4 And this will be your c. of yourself, when
T-31....VII.4:3 think, for you will love this c. of yourself,
T-31....VII.5:1 that your fearful c. of yourself may change
T-31....VII.5:5 remember what the c. of yourself that
T-31....VII.5:7 And let the cruel c. of yourself be changed
T-31....VII.6:1 c. of yourself that now you hold would
T-31....VII.7:1 The c. of the self stands like a shield, a
T-31....VII.8:5 him. Thus is the c. of himself laid by, for
T-31..VII.10:6 Son to save from every c. that he ever held
T-31..VII.11:6 holds no c. of himself between his calm
T-31..VII.12:2 And from that wish a c. rises, teaching
T-31..VII.12:3 It will remain your c. of yourself until the
W-pI.....11.1:3 Today's idea introduces the c. that your
W-pI.....16.2:1 no more self-contradictory c. than that of
W-pI.....72.7:4 stands at the center of your c. of yourself,
W-pI.....75.6:2 ideas and clean of every c. you have made.
W-pI...108.1:3 thoughts into one c. which is wholly true?
W-pI...135.6:2 be at peace with such a c. of your home?
M-2...........2:1 necessary to grasp the c. of time that the
M-3...........3:1 is a c. as meaningless in reality as is time.
M-5....III.1:10 They have no idea how insane this c. is. If
M-19.........3:3 Selectively and arbitrarily is every c. of
M-22.........1:3 the one complete c. possible in this world,
M-22.........3:2 is a central c. in the ego's thought system.
M-24.........1:4 only question should be, "Is the c. helpful
M-24.........2:4 To some, there may be comfort in the c.,
M-24.........3:4 Our course is not concerned with any c.
M-24.........4:6 to any c. or belief that will be helpful, he
C-in...........1:4 is essentially irrelevant because it is a c.
C-1............2:3 the c. of an "individual mind" seems to be
P-1............3:3 and be attacked as well, is a c. he made up
P-2..........II.4:4 Nor is belief in God a really meaningful c.
P-2........IV.5:3 "degrees of error" is a meaningful c.. Yet

## concept's 1

T-31....V.10:6 it so? Let us forget the c. foolishness, and

## conception 6

T-14.......X.2:4 You on earth have no c. of limitlessness,
T-15....IX.6:1 You have no c. of the limits you have
T-17....VII.7:1 so far beyond your little c. of the infinite
T-31......V.5:4 On this c. of the self the world smiles with
W-pI...135.9:4 the c. of the mind as limited and fragile,
W-pI.170.10:6 is terrible above all else, cruel beyond c.,

## concepts 30

*See also* self-concepts

T-1.......VI.3:4 where c. such as "up" and "down" are
T-2........V.9:5 Most of the loftier c. of which you are
T-3..........I.1:7 anti-religious c. enter into many religions.
T-3.........II.1:1 I have stated that the basic c. referred to
T-3.........II.1:2 degree. Certain fundamental c. cannot be
T-5..........I.2:1 of reawakening with just a few simple c.:
T-5..........V.1:1 Perhaps some of our c. will become
T-8.....VIII.2:2 making the c. of both health and sickness
T-27.....III.6:4 It does not stand for double c.. Though it
T-31......V.7:1 C. are learned. They are not natural.
T-31......V.7:7 C. maintain the world. But they can not
T-31....V.13:2 must have gone before these c. of the self.
T-31....V.14:3 as nothing more than the escape from c..
T-31....V.16:1 many c. of the self as learning goes along.
T-31....V.17:4 Where c. of the self have been laid by is
T-31.....VI.5:3 But c. are not difficult to change. One
T-31....VII.1:3 C. are needed while perception lasts, and
T-31....VII.1:3 lasts, and changing c. is salvation's task.
T-31....VII.1:5 In this world's c. are the guilty "bad"; the
T-31....VII.3:1 In terms of c., it is thus you see him more
T-31....VII.4:2 For both are c. of yourself, which can be
T-31....VII.7:5 from guilty thoughts and c. born of fear.
T-31..VII.13:3 a wholly open mind, unclouded by old c.,
T-31..VII.13:7 the veil of old ideas and ancient c. held so
W-pI....30.4:1 is not limited to c. such as "near" and "far
W-pI..184.5:3 and c. can be meaningfully shared.
W-pI..189.7:1 is; all c. you have learned about the world;
M-19.........3:1 All c. of your brothers and yourself; all
M-29.........1:2 of the major c. in the text and workbook.
P-2.........in.2:2 the contrary, such c. mean little to them,

## concern 42

T-1.......III.8:1 that you may not recognize is not your c..
T-2..........I.5:1 you may believe are of no c. to the miracle
T-2..........I.5:3 Its sole c. is to distinguish between truth
T-6.....V.C.4:4 It does not c. itself with order of difficulty
T-13...VIII.7:4 is far beyond your individual c.. You who
T-13.......X.3:7 Their main c. is to perceive the source of
T-15....VII.8:6 Ideas are basically of no c., except as they
T-15...VIII.1:5 His c. and care for you are limitless. In the
T-16.......II.1:3 holy. C. yourself not with the extension of
T-18.......II.2:1 therefore they have no c. with what is true
T-22......VI.9:4 Let your c. be only that you give to Him
T-24...VII.2:7 the thought by day and night, the deep c.,
T-26.....V.10:3 perfectly corrected, is of no c. nor value.
T-27......I.6:11 and vanity of real c. with anything at all.
T-27...VIII.1:5 Its safety is its main c.. Its comfort is its
T-28.....III.1:1 certainty beyond salvation is not our c..
T-28.....III.1:3 The miracle alone is your c. at present.
T-30.....IV.6:3 not c. yourself with how this will be done,
T-31.....IV.1:5 and away from difficulties that c. you not.
T-31.....IV.1:6 Yet they *are* your c.. How, then, can you
T-31.....V.14:4 does not c. itself with content of the mind
W-pI....26.6:1 whose outcomes are causing you c.. The
W-pI....26.6:2 The c. may take the form of depression,
W-pI....26.7:3 connection and which has caused you c.,
W-pI....28.1:3 keep them in the future is not our c. here.
W-pI....47.5:2 causes you c. is associated with feelings of
W-pI....65.5:5 with as little involvement or c. as possible
W-pI....72.9:2 body that is outside us, and is not our c..
W-pI..135.4:4 deep c. are needful to protect its little life?
W-pI..135.5:3 medicine, no care and no c. at all. Defend
W-pI..158.6:6 Our c. is with Christ's vision. This we can
W-pI..163.1:2 and lack of trust; c. for bodies, envy, and
W-pI..181.3:4 saw an instant previous has no c. for us
W-pI..181.3:6 else. We seek for it with no c. but now.
W-pII.....1.3:4 without c. for anything that would appear
M-6...........4:1 of all c. about the gift that makes it truly
M-6.........4:11 What c., then, can a teacher of God have
M-7...........4:4 first to be told that continued c. is attack.
M-7...........6:1 mistake is always some form of c. with the
M-13.........8:6 learn. For it is here that your c. should be.
M-16.........4:4 so. Duration is not the major c.. One can
M-24.........6:8 not lead to this is of c. to God's teachers.

## concerned 40

T-4..........I.6:5 c. with the effect of his ego on other egos,
T-4........I.13:4 this enables you not to be c. with them,
T-4.......IV.2:9 a loving brother I am deeply c. with your
T-4.........V.2:6 to it. Being c. primarily with its own
T-7.......III.4:5 *are* the Kingdom are not c. with seeming.
T-9........I.10:4 The Holy Spirit is not c. with form, being
T-14.....XI.6:1 be c. about how you can learn a lesson so
T-15.......II.2:1 Do not be c. with time, and fear not the
T-16.......II.2:1 and then to be c. about the truth of just a
T-16.....IV.5:2 hate is at all c. with the "triumph of love."
T-17........I.6:3 c. with anything except your willingness
T-17....VII.3:7 this error, but be not at all c. with that.
T-20.....IV.6:1 nor need you be c. with anything except
T-21...III.11:1 Think you the Holy Spirit is c. with this?
T-22...VI.9:10 Be not c. with darkness; look away from it
T-31.....VI.3:5 Be not c. how this could ever be. You do
W-pI......1.3:7 as far as the application of the idea is c..
W-pI......9.1:5 These exercises are c. with practice, not
W-pI....14.5:1 you, or to anyone about whom you are c..
W-pI....24.4:1 about which you are currently c.. The
W-pI....25.3:1 they are all c. with "personal" interests.
W-pI....25.3:2 your goals are really c. with nothing. In
W-pI....26.7:2 *I am c. about–.* Then go over every
W-pI....38.4:3 and also the name of the person c.. Use

W-pI.....39.1:3 **c.** with intellectual feats nor logical toys.
W-pI.....42.3:2 than it is to be **c.** with the time as such.
W-pI.....72.4:2 exclusively **c.** with what he does in a body.
W-pI...136.5:3 in force, as far as your desires are **c.**.
W-pI...186.7:6 of God? Why need he be **c.** with it at all?
W-pI...199.3:2 Be not **c.** that to the ego it is quite insane.
W-pII....14.3:7 **c.** only with giving welcome to the truth.
M-6............3:4 can give if he is **c.** with the result of giving.
M-7............1:5 For a teacher of God to remain **c.** about
M-24..........3:4 Our course is not **c.** with any concept that
M-26..........4:9 **c.** with goals for which you are not ready.
M-29..........5:7 practical with which this course is most **c.**
C-in............1:1 nor is it **c.** with precise terminology. It is
C-in............1:2 **c.** only with Atonement, or the correction
C-in............3:2 **c.** with what is beyond all error because it
C-3.............3:3 He is not at all **c.** with form, but having

## concerning 1

W-pI.....38.6:1 problem **c.** you or someone else arises, or

## concerns 10

T-2... V.A.11:1 abolishes the need for lower-order **c.**.
T-27...... I.6:10 C. about the body demonstrate how frail
W-pI.....47.5:1 Now try to slip past all **c.** related to your
W-pI...109.5:1 In Him you have no cares and no **c.**, no
WpI . rIII.in5:3 your seeming problems and all your **c.**.
W-pI...133.1:1 learned, to bring him back to practical **c.**.
W-pI...133.2:2 you let your mind be drawn to bodily **c.**,
W-pI...181.5:3 These **c.** are but defenses against present
M-19..........3:1 of future states and all **c.** about the past,
M-28..........1:9 interests, all other wishes and all other **c.**.

## conclude 10

T-22....VI.13:2 So you **c.** *because* you can attack, you and
W-pI.....13.4:6 your eyes, and **c.** with: *A meaningless*
W-pI.....14.6:7 fact, **c.** the practice periods by repeating
W-pI.....18.3:3 C. each practice period by repeating the
W-pI.....26.9:3 C. each practice period by repeating
W-pI.....36.4:1 and **c.** with one more repetition with your
W-pI.....37.5:2 practice period should **c.** with a repetition
WpIrIII.in12:1 assignments will **c.** with a restatement of
W-pI.137.14:2 which we will **c.** today at night as well:
W-pII.....in.3:2 which **c.** the year that we have given God.

## concludes 3

T-11..... V.14:3 reasoning **c.** that because of the mistake
W-pI...76.11:5 with which the practice period **c.**: *I am*
M-8............4:6 so, it **c.** that the categories must be true.

## concluding 6

W-pI.......8.5:2 **c.** at the end of the mind-searching period
W-pI.....11.3:5 On **c.** the exercises, close your eyes and
W-pI.....13.5:1 one form or another, to this **c.** statement.
W-pI.....13.6:2 Do not dwell on the **c.** statement, and try
W-pI.152.12:1 **c.** it with this same invitation to your Self.
M-14..........4:4 of the teacher of God in this **c.** lesson? He

## conclusion 14

T-6.........in.1:4 the equally irrational **c.** that a brother is
T-6.........in.1:5 from insane premises except an insane **c.**?
T-6.........in.1:6 way to undo an insane **c.** is to consider
T-7......... X.1:2 carried the ego's reasoning to its logical **c.**
T-10...... III.5:1 Look calmly at the logical **c.** of the ego's
T-22.......in.4:5 brother to the logical **c.** of your union. It
T-22....VI.13:5 Either position is a logical **c.**. Either could
T-23..... II.21:2 it follows that it seems to be a logical **c.**; a
T-24.......in.2:5 a decision is a **c.** based on everything that
W-pI.....66.5:5 even if you do not yet accept the **c.**. It is
W-pI.....66.5:6 are wrong that the **c.** could be false. Let us
W-pI...66.10:2 about the premises on which our **c.** rests.
W-pI...66.10:3 We can share in this **c.**, but in no other.
W-pI.....72.5:5 would be difficult indeed to escape this **c.**.

## conclusions 4

T-14.......in.1:4 the ego, except that His **c.** are not insane.
T-14.......in.1:6 the ego's logic, and have seen its logical **c.**.
T-14.......in.1:8 teaches the simple **c.** that speak for truth,
M-16 .........5:5 must have come to some **c.** in this respect.

## concord 1

S-1 .........in.1:3 the joyous **c.** of the Love They give forever

## concrete 7

T-4......... II.1:5 is always specific, and therefore quite **c.**.
T-4.......VII.1:3 Part of the mind becomes **c.**, however,
T-4.......VII.1:4 The **c.** part believes in the ego, because
T-4.......VII.1:4 ego, because the ego depends on the **c.**.
W-pI...161.5:2 are but symbols for a **c.** form of fear. Fear
M-21 .........2:2 that comes to mind is apt to be very **c.**.
M-21 .........2:4 the heart does not really ask for **c.** things.

## condemn 41

T-5...... VI.10:1 need not fear the Higher Court will **c.** you.
T-6.........I.15:9 Was it likely that I would **c.** him when I
T-9......... V.3:4 they are likely to **c.** themselves, teach
T-9......... V.3:6 **c.** themselves because of this confusion. It
T-11...... VI.2:2 Would you **c.** your brothers or free them?
T-13.........I.6:4 You can **c.** only yourself, and by so doing
T-13...... IX.1:2 The guilty always **c.**, and having done so
T-13...... IX.1:2 having done so they will still **c.**, linking
T-13...... IX.1:6 that they are guilty, and so they must **c.**.
T-13...... IX.4:4 When you **c.** a brother you are saying, "I
T-13...... IX.6:5 is impossible to **c.** the Son of God in part.
T-14....... V.3:2 you. Who can **c.** whom God has blessed?
T-15...... VI.1:2 And it is equally impossible to **c.** part of a
T-17..... V.10:6 C. salvation not, for it has come to you.
T-18...... VI.4:8 love does not **c.** it and can use it lovingly,
T-19...........I.9:4 brother has done before to **c.** him now.
T19IV.B.14:12 would accuse, make guilty and **c.** himself?
T19. IV.D.16:2 your brother is, before you would **c.** him.
T-21...... III.7:3 you would **c.** him to the body because the
T-21...... VI.6:1 you would **c.** the Son of God to what can
T-21.. VI.11:10 But where he chooses to **c.** instead, there
T-22..... II.10:4 You would **c.** His joy to misery, and make
T-24...... III.8:3 God **c.** Himself to hell and to damnation?
T-24..... VII.4:6 hate, and you **c.** it to decay and death.
T-25...... VI.1:4 no more **c.** himself for his mistakes than
T-26.........I.8:3 him? C. him not by seeing him within the
T-29...... III.1:1 C. your savior not because he thinks he is
T-31...... III.1:1 Only the self-accused **c.**. As you prepare
W-pI.....46.1:5 As you **c.** only yourself, so do you forgive
W-pI.....52.2:2 As I look about, I **c.** the world I look upon
W-pI.....68.1:4 your mind and to **c.** the body to death.
W-pI. 134.10:2 It is but lies that would **c.**. In truth is
W-pI. 134.15:3 yourself, "Would I **c.** myself for doing this
W-pI...198.1:3 If you can **c.**, you can be injured. For you
W-pI...198.2:1 C. and you are made a prisoner. Forgive
W-pI...198.2:5 To **c.** is thus impossible in truth. What
W-pII....10.3:1 would **c.** the world to hell along with you,
M-11 .........2:4 salvation; your judgment would **c.** it. God
M-18 .........4:9 How can he then **c.** anyone? And who is
P-2......... V.7:6 which he would **c.** himself without a cause
S-2......... II.3:6 Son **c.** himself and still remember Him?

## condemnation 58

*See also* self-condemnation

T-6.........I.15:9 ready to demonstrate that **c.** is impossible
T-8.....VII.15:4 condemned yourself, but **c.** is not of God.
T-8.....VII.15:8 Yet if all **c.** is unreal, and it must be unreal
T-9...... III.8:10 teach you how to see yourself without **c.**,
T-9...... III.8:11 it. C. will then not be real to you, and all
T-9......... V.3:4 teach **c.** and advocate a fearful solution.
T-9......... V.3:5 Projecting **c.** onto God, they make Him
T-11....... IV.6:2 But come wholly without **c.**, for otherwise
T-11....... IV.8:2 There is no **c.** in the Son, for there is no
T-11....... IV.8:2 in the Son, for there is no **c.** in the Father.
T-11. VIII.12:4 for He would save you from all **c.**. Accept
T-13.......in.1:1 not attack, for **c.** is the root of attack. It is
T-13.........I.6:3 idea of guilt brings a belief in **c.** of one by
T-13....... V.4:2 not wish to die, yet they will not let **c.** go.
T-13...... VI.3:5 go, and look without **c.** upon the present.
T-13...... VI.6:1 Judgment and **c.** are behind you, and
T-13...... IX.2:2 you bring its **c.** on yourself, and you will
T-13...... IX.5:5 For sin and **c.** are the same, and the belief
T-13...... IX.6:2 In every **c.** that you offer the Son of God
T-14..... V.10:7 as guilty, and by its **c.** it would kill. The
T-15.........I.9:6 completely free and wholly without **c.**.
T19....IV.C.8:3 rituals of **c.** to which the body leads you.
T19. IV.D.18:2 nor look upon him with **c.** of any kind.
T-20...... VI.6:2 is the home of the idolater, and of love's **c.**
T-20..... VII.9:7 can judge, and what he sees is free of **c.**.
T-22.........II.7:3 or his judge, offering him sanctuary or **c.**.
T-22.........II.8:3 A savior cannot be a judge, nor mercy **c.**.
T-22.... VI.11:3 and every **c.** that you perceive and justify
T-23......II.17:3 What form of **c.** is a blessing? Who makes
T-24....... V.2:1 from pain, in which you suffer not your **c.**
T-24....... V.3:2 and sees no **c.** that could need forgiveness
T-24...... VI.9:4 you as well, is given you to save from **c.**,
T-24..... VII.4:7 brother's, such is your **c.** of your own.
T-25...... III.9:5 or not? Does he need help or **c.**? Is it your
T-27......II.3:11 retains no trace of **c.** that he still would
T-27....... V.5:1 as a **c.** by the one who could have saved it,
T-27..... VII.4:2 world's escape from **c.** is a need which
T-27..... VII.4:4 part, the **c.** of the world will rest on him.
T-27..... VII.6:1 the world from **c.** is your own escape.
W-pI.....46.1:2 must be **c.** before forgiveness is necessary.
W-pI... 126.2:4 and yet remain apart from **c.** and at peace
W-pI......198.h Only my **c.** injures me.
W-pI... 198.8:1 of any **c.** which could need forgiveness.
W-pI... 198.9:3 end: *Only my c. injures me. Only my own*
W-pI. 198.10:1 proclaims there is no **c.** in God's Son, and
W-pI. 198.12:1 There is no **c.** in him. He is perfect in his
W-pI...218.1:1 (198) Only my **c.** injures me. *My*
W-pI...218.1:2 *My c. keeps my vision dark, and through my*
W-pII ... 10.2:1 judgment on the world contains no **c.**. For
M-4 ....... X.1:4 in. As **c.** judges the Son of God as evil, so
M-13 ......... 4:5 and all its ills looks back on it with **c.**. Yet
M-17 ......... 8:10 Magic thoughts need not lead to **c.**, for
M-19 ......... 4:7 this,–a Judgment wholly lacking in **c.**; an
M-19 ......... 5:8 attack and **c.** becomes meaningless and
P-2..........II.1:2 to teach forgiveness rather than **c.**. Even
P-2........ VI.2:4 the "truth" of the song of **c.** must arise.
S-2..........II.8:1 **c.** and comparisons of every kind are
S-2........ III.4:5 know at last that **c.** is not real and makes

## condemned 44

T-8..... VII.15:4 You have **c.** yourself, but condemnation is
T-8..... VII.15:7 him because you have **c.** yourself. Yet if all
T-12... VII.13:1 yourself unworthy and have **c.** yourself to
T-12.... VIII.3:8 you would have **c.** yourself to oblivion.
T-13.......in.4:5 be **c.** because he has never condemned.
T-13.......in.4:5 be condemned because he has never **c.**.
T-13.........I.9:4 For God has never **c.** His Son, and being
T-13....... V.4:1 do not recognize they have **c.** themselves.
T-13...... IX.6:7 is always in your mind, which has **c.** itself.
T-13........X.8:5 loved him not, and looked upon him as **c.**
T19....IV.C.4:2 feed upon and keep itself alive; a thing **c.**,
T19....IV.C.4:3 have **c.** the Son of God to this *are* arrogant.
T-20.... VIII.6:7 and everything will stand **c.** before you.
T-23........II.5:3 For One must always be **c.**, and by the
T-24........II.8:7 It is not God Who has **c.** His Son, but you,
T-24...... VI.9:4 He who **c.** himself, and you as well, is
T-25.........I.2:8 see your sinfulness, wherein you stand **c.**.
T-25....... V.4:6 C. by you, he offers death to you. In
T-25...... IX.3:8 anyone is seen as losing, he has been **c.**.
T-25...... IX.6:7 from others as less worthy, more **c.**, and
T-26........II.5:3 If the Son of God is guilty then is he **c.**,
T-26...... IX.1:3 However much you wish he be **c.**, God is
T-27.........I.2:3 look on you to realize that he has been **c.**.
T-27.......I.9:10 Now is it not **c.**, but waiting for a purpose
T-27......II.6:10 blood is on his hands, and so he stands **c.**.
T-27......II.14:3 is **c.** can never be returned to its accuser,
T-28.......I.10:3 no time in which His Son could be **c.** for
T-29...... IX.2:8 Nor can he know the Self he has **c.**. Judge
T-29...... IX.3:7 dream of judgment you attack and are **c.**;
T-31....... V.5:3 on me, you stand **c.** because of what I am.

| | |
|---|---|
| T-31....... V.6:1 | that ensures your brother is c. eternally. |
| T-31...... V.13:8 | now must you be c. along with him. |
| W-pI..... 46.1:1 | does not forgive because He has never c.. |
| W-pI..... 60.1:2 | does not forgive because He has never c.. |
| W-pI... 121.5:2 | does not see it has c. itself to this despair. |
| W-pI... 134.5:5 | are real are pitifully mocked and twice c.; |
| W-pI... 192.9:5 | be averted as you choose to be c. or free. |
| W-pI... 198.7:7 | How mad to think that you could be c., |
| W-pII .... 228.h | God has c. me not. No more do I. |
| W-pII ..... 8.3:3 | What is there it would choose to be c., |
| W-pII . 325.1:5 | From judgment comes a world c.. And |
| M-13 ......... 3:3 | the mind c. itself to seek without finding; |
| M-17 ......... 1:6 | his own belief in sin and has c. himself. |
| P-2........ IV.2:3 | for illness have now c. themselves to seek |

## condemneth 1

| | |
|---|---|
| T-11..VIII.12:3 | condemning God's Son whom God c. not. |

## condemning 7

| | |
|---|---|
| T-8..... VII.15:7 | are c. him because you have condemned |
| T-9........ III.5:6 | you think he is wrong you are c. yourself. |
| T-9....... VII.5:2 | are c. yourself and must therefore regard |
| T-11..VIII.12:3 | offended in yourself and are c. God's Son |
| T-13....... II.3:2 | betrayed God's Son by c. him to death. |
| T-23.... II.17:9 | itself, c. what it says it wants to save. Be |
| T-31....... V.6:8 | c. still your brother for the hated thing |

## condemns 10

| | |
|---|---|
| T-11....... VI.7:2 | His Son whom the god of crucifixion c.. |
| T-13...... X.11:7 | No one who c. a brother can see himself |
| T-24......... I.4:2 | incapable of being like what he c., "above |
| T-25.... VIII.5:9 | He c. a sinner for the crimes he did not do |
| T-25...... IX.9:4 | lost, c. you as unworthy of forgiveness. |
| W-pI..... 46.2:2 | Fear c. and love forgives. Forgiveness thus |
| W-pI..... 72.5:8 | belief that he is a body, and c. him for it. |
| W-pI..... 92.6:3 | It judges and c., but does not love. In |
| W-pI... 151.5:4 | It is itself alone that it c.. It is within itself |
| M-18 ......... 4:8 | forgiven him, and he no longer c. himself. |

## condition 69

| | |
|---|---|
| T-2........... I.3:1 | Garden of Eden, or the pre-separation c., |
| T-2....... VII.2:4 | as a necessary c. for the miracle to occur. |
| T-3........ IV.3:7 | and this is the essence of the fear-prone c. |
| T-3......... V.9:5 | a c. entirely alien to the world's thinking. |
| T-4........... I.1:4 | he teaches, but he must meet another c.; |
| T-4....... II.8:11 | It can do so, however, only under one c.; |
| T-4........ III.5:4 | This is not a c. as the ego sets conditions. |
| T-4........ III.5:5 | It is the glorious c. of what you are. |
| T-6...... V.C.6:3 | is the c. for identifying with the Kingdom, |
| T-6...... V.C.6:3 | Kingdom, since it is the c. *of* the Kingdom. |
| T-8........... I.1:3 | and peace is the c. of knowledge because |
| T-8........... I.1:3 | of knowledge because it is the c. of the |
| T-8........... I.3:8 | is a c. so alien to the Kingdom that you |
| T-8........ IV.5:7 | by which you determine your own c., |
| T-8...... VIII.1:8 | body's c. lies solely in your interpretation |
| T-8........ IX.2:2 | total harmlessness is the c. of its reality. It |
| T-8........ IX.2:3 | also the c. of your awareness of its reality. |
| T-10..... V.10:7 | That was the c. of His Son's creation, |
| T-10..... V.11:4 | at home anywhere else, or in any other c.. |
| T-11........ VII.h | The C. of Reality |
| T-11.... VII.4:1 | a c. in which opposites do not exist. And |
| T-11.... VII.4:2 | And this *is* the c. of knowledge. Without |
| T-13......... I.6:5 | You have denied the c. of his being, which |
| T-14...... IV.2:2 | The state of guiltlessness is only the c. in |
| T-14...... IV.2:7 | only to the c. in which it happens of itself. |
| T-14...... IV.7:4 | guiltlessness is the c. for knowing Him. |
| T-14...... IV.9:3 | teaches you the true c. of the Son of God. |
| T-14...... IX.8:5 | the actual c. of what was but reflected to |
| T-14....... X.9:4 | therefore remains the ego's chosen c.. For |
| T-14.... XI.3:10 | is nothing more than a c. in which seeing |
| T-15...... IV.9:1 | The necessary c. for the holy instant does |
| T-15...... XI.4:3 | Guilt is the c. of sacrifice, as peace is the |
| T-15...... XI.4:3 | as peace is the c. for the awareness of your |
| T-15...... XI.7:1 | In the holy instant the c. of love is met, |
| T-15...... XI.7:2 | re-establish the c. of love by teaching that |
| T-16 ..... IV.7:3 | In fundamental violation of love's one c., |
| T-16 ...... V.3:5 | This is the "natural" c. of the separation, |
| T-16 ...... V.4:4 | the one c. in which Heaven could not be. |
| T-16 ...... V.5:8 | is a c. in which the ego cannot interfere, |
| T-16 .... VII.9:7 | in time, to bring you the true c. of Heaven |
| T-17 ...... V.3:6 | it. In its unholy c., *your* goal was all that |
| T-17 .... V.13:1 | established a c. in which you cannot use it |
| T-17 ..... VI.5:4 | *is*. If peace is the c. of truth and sanity, and |
| T-17 ..... VI.7:6 | the illusion of peace is not the c. in which |
| T-18 ..... VI.1:5 | Heaven is not a place nor a c.. It is merely |
| T-19 ........ I.4:3 | you have established a c. in which uniting |
| T-20 ..... III.1:6 | impaired c. *are* adjustments necessary, |
| T-21 ...... in.1:5 | mind, the outside picture of an inward c.. |
| T-21 .... VII.1:3 | cost of sin. Helplessness is sin's c.; the one |
| T-21 .... VII.9:1 | one decision; this the c. for what occurs. |
| T-21 ... VIII.2:1 | is a c. quite alien to your understanding. |
| T-23 ........ I.4:7 | his Creator is a c. as ridiculous as nature |
| T-23 ...... I.12:4 | War is the c. in which fear is born, and |
| T-24 ...... in.1:2 | and the c. in which God is remembered is |
| T-24 .... VII.6:9 | there any way to learn what this c. means. |
| T-25 ........ I.7:4 | in the c. in which it thinks it is. And It |
| W-pI... 161.2:1 | abstraction is the natural c. of the mind. |
| W-pI... 167.1:3 | one c. in which all that God created share. |
| W-pI... 167.9:2 | enter, or a false c. not within its Source, it |
| W-pII . 228.1:4 | the One Who knows the true c. of His Son |
| W-pII ..... 9.1:2 | a part of the c. that restores the never lost, |
| M-4 .... IX.2:11 | attends it naturally, and joy is its c.. And |
| M-9 ........... 2:7 | judgment as the necessary c. of salvation. |
| M-12 ......... 5:7 | that are responsible for the body's c.. Yet |
| M-18 ......... 2:4 | unchangeable c. of all that God created. |
| M-20 ......... 3:5 | exist. In this c., peace cannot be found. |
| M-20 ......... 3:6 | necessary c. for finding the peace of God. |
| M-20 ....... 6:12 | God's peace is the c. for His Will. Attain |
| C-1 ............ 5:3 | the c. in which God takes the final step |

## conditional 1

| | |
|---|---|
| T-29 ........ I.4:6 | C. upon the "right" to separate will you |

## conditions 40

| | |
|---|---|
| T-2 ........ I.5:12 | correcting the c. proceeding from lack of |
| T-2 ......... II.4:5 | the Atonement and the c. necessary for its |
| T-2 ........ V.2:5 | Under these c., it is safer for you to rely |
| T-2 ....... VI.4:3 | in the c. that have brought the fear about. |
| T-2 ....... VI.4:4 | These c. always entail a willingness to be |
| T-4 ....... III.5:4 | This is not a condition as the ego sets c.. It |
| T-8 .......... I.1:4 | can be restored only when you meet its c.. |
| T-8 ..... VI.9:10 | I can make you aware of the c. of truth, |
| T-8 ..... VI.9:11 | Together we can meet its c., but truth will |
| T-8 ....... IX.2:5 | you and find you when you meet its c.. Its |
| T-8 ....... IX.2:6 | Its c. are part of what it is. And this part |
| T-8 ....... IX.9:4 | task is only to meet the c. for meaning, |
| T-10 ........ I.1:5 | knowledge, because it has not met its c.. |
| T-11 .... VII.4:3 | this awareness you have not met its c., |
| T-12 ...... V.8:6 | Under the proper learning c., which you |
| T-14 ........... I.h | The C. of Learning |
| T-14 ......... I.1:2 | c. must be acquired for it is they that have |
| T-14 ........ II.7:1 | learner meets the c. of learning here, as he |
| T-14 ........ II.7:1 | meets the c. of knowledge in the Kingdom |
| T-14 ..... IV.7:3 | accept the necessary c. for knowing Him, |
| T-15 ..... IV.4:3 | you have been willing to meet its c.. You |
| T-15 ..... VI.7:6 | mind, and its c. are in the mind with it. If |
| T-17 ... III.6:11 | the c. in which this beauty can be seen. |
| T-17 ...... VIII.h | The C. of Peace |
| T-17 ... VIII.6:2 | peace cannot be accepted apart from its c. |
| T-18 ....... II.9:3 | to let your special relationship meet its c.. |
| T-18 ..... IV.4:4 | it is up to you to establish the c. for peace. |
| T19..IV.B.10:9 | Peace and guilt are both c. of the mind, to |
| T19 IV.B.10:10 | And these c. are the home of the emotion |
| T-21 .... V.1:11 | you the c. in which awareness of reality is |
| T-27 ..... IV.5:7 | It does not set c. for response, but merely |
| T-31 ..... III.4:4 | need serve, nor sets c. that it must obey. It |
| W-in.......... 7:3 | the c. necessary for this kind of transfer. |
| W-pI.... 34.1:1 | idea for today begins to describe the c. |
| W-pI.... 135.9:3 | see the mind as separate from bodily c.. |
| W-pI.... 152.5:2 | alterations in c. of the body and the mind; |
| W-pI.... 167.4:2 | is the belief c. change, emotions alternate |
| W-pI.... 167.8:2 | nor make c. which He does not share with |
| M-20 ......... 3:2 | can fail to find it who but seeks out its c.. |
| M-23 ......... 4:7 | these are the true c. for your homecoming |

## condone 1

| | |
|---|---|
| T-2 ....... VI.2:3 | it. Why should you c. insane thinking? |

## condoning 1

| | |
|---|---|
| T-2 ....... VI.4:6 | are passively c. your mind's miscreations. |

## conducive 2

| | |
|---|---|
| T-1 ......... V.6:7 | it upside down be c. to increased stability. |
| W-pI .... 34.2:2 | between that seems most c. to readiness. |

## confer 1

| | |
|---|---|
| M-23 ......... 1:8 | What does calling on his name c.? Why is |

## confidence 46

| | |
|---|---|
| T-2 ...... VII.7:6 | C. cannot develop fully until mastery has |
| T-2 ...... VII.7:8 | Readiness is only the beginning of c.. You |
| T-3 ......... II.3:1 | you lack c. in what someone will do, you |
| T-7 ....... IX.7:2 | Miracles are an expression of this c.. They |
| T-8 ......... V.4:4 | I share this c. for both of us and all of us. |
| T-12 .... VII.2:6 | but you gain c. in their existence as they |
| T-14 ....... V.7:7 | And you will find ever-increasing c. in |
| T-14 ..... XI.3:9 | Put no c. at all in darkness to illuminate |
| T-18 ..... III.3:4 | been sufficient to give you c. in yourself, |
| T-20 ....... V.8:1 | you in love and perfect c. in what He sees. |
| T-20 ....... V.8:3 | must learn, to share his Father's c. in him. |
| T-20 ....... V.8:6 | it is impossible the c. of God should be |
| T-22 ...... I.11:6 | And here can He return in c., for faith in |
| T-22 ... VI.9:11 | and c. with which you bless your brother. |
| T-25 .. VII.12:4 | saneness rest in perfect c. and perfect |
| T-26 ....... V.2:5 | purpose and high resolve and happy c., |
| T-29 ... VIII.2:3 | massed against your c. and peace of mind |
| T-30 ....... V.8:2 | with perfect c. away from fear forever, |
| T-30 ..... V.10:8 | in c. walk with a happy heart that beats in |
| T-31 ..... V.16:4 | and happy in the c. that it will go at last, |
| W-pI .... 47.5:3 | by trusting yourself that you will gain c.. |
| W-pI .... 47.6:1 | one in giving you the c. which you need, |
| W-pI .... 47.6:2 | also gain an awareness that c. in your real |
| W-pI .... 49.3:3 | happiest and holiest of thoughts with c., |
| W-pI .... 50.4:5 | difficulties without effort and in sure c.. |
| W-pI .... 69.8:1 | Have c. in your Father today, and be |
| W-pI .... 69.8:3 | to the light, to hold this c. in your mind. |
| W-pI .. 72.12:1 | Whenever you feel your c. wane and your |
| W-pI .... 73.8:1 | the exercises for today in happy c., certain |
| W-pI .. 95.14:3 | looks to you in c. that you will try today. |
| W-pI .... 98.7:4 | His c. in you will bring the light to all the |
| W-pI .... 98.8:1 | and c. so strong and steady they will light |
| W-pI .. 101.6:4 | But turn to it in c. that it will set you free |
| W-pI .. 104.4:3 | We come in c. today, aware that what |
| W-pI .. 107.9:4 | His c. is with you, as you say: *Truth will* |
| W-pI 107.11:2 | Each time you tell yourself with c., "Truth |
| WpI..rIII.in7:1 | in perfect c. that you would use them well |
| WpI..rIII.in7:2 | mind in that same trust and c. and faith. |
| W-pI 135.16:5 | part at all, for present c. directs the way. |
| W-pI 135.21:1 | anticipate that time today with present c., |
| W-pII .... in.7:8 | to You, and rest in c. upon Your Love, |
| W-pII . 221.2:4 | Accept my c., for it is yours. Our minds |
| W-ep ......... 6:3 | In c. we wait His answers, as we ask His |
| M-21 ......... 5:6 | that come to you, but offer them in c.. |
| M-29 ....... 5:10 | And your c. will be well founded indeed. |
| M-29 ....... 7:11 | In c. I place you in His Hands, and I give |

## confident 11

| | |
|---|---|
| T-4 ..... III.1:11 | Be c. that your creations are as safe as you |
| T-7 ....... IX.7:1 | c. that you have never lost your Identity |
| W-pI .... 40.3:8 | *I am calm, quiet, assured and c.*. If only a |
| W-pI .... 45.5:3 | every reason to feel c. that we will succeed |
| W-pI .... 67.4:4 | Be c. that you will do much today to bring |
| W-pI .... 75.9:5 | completely. Be c. that on this day there is |
| WpI.. rII.in.3:3 | Be c. that you will receive it. Remember |
| W-pI .. 91.10:1 | of the practice period, c. that your efforts, |

| | |
|---|---|
| W-ep .........4:6 | should proceed; as c. as He is of the goal, |
| M-4.......IX.2:6 | And being c., it is tolerant. Faithfulness, |
| M-29..........5:8 | be c. that wisdom will be given you when |

## confidently 1

| | |
|---|---|
| W-pI.....77.4:1 | quite c. that you are entitled to miracles. |

## confined 2

| | |
|---|---|
| T-27... VIII.7:6 | It keeps you narrowly c. within a body, |
| T-28....... II.2:3 | Purity is not c.. It is the nature of the |

## confirm 3

| | |
|---|---|
| T-4......... II.7:5 | representing the ego's need to c. itself. |
| T-14...... XI.6:5 | experiences to c. what you have learned. |
| W-pI...129.9:3 | take a moment to c. your choice by laying |

## conflict 183

*See also* conflict-free

| | |
|---|---|
| T-1........VI.2:5 | action, because this produces a lack of c.. |
| T-2........III.3:9 | of perception is usually experienced as c., |
| T-2...........VI.h | Fear and C. |
| T-2........VI.7:1 | first that the c. is an expression of fear. |
| T-2.....VII.3:13 | The fundamental c. in this world, then, is |
| T-2.....VII.3:15 | c. is therefore one between love and fear. |
| T-2.......VII.4:5 | however, the sense of c. is inevitable, |
| T-2.......VII.6:5 | That is why the c. cannot ultimately be |
| T-2..... VIII.2:8 | you must emerge from the c. if you are to |
| T-3...........I.5:3 | that strength and innocence are not in c., |
| T-3........IV.1:6 | and all c. arises from the concept of levels. |
| T-3........IV.1:8 | created by the separation cannot but c.. |
| T-3........IV.3:6 | in c. because it is out of accord with itself. |
| T-3........IV.6:3 | to escape from the c. you have induced. |
| T-3.......VII.5:8 | in peace, even though your mind is in c.. |
| T-3.......VII.6:8 | the oneness of knowledge is free of c.. |
| T-4...........I.2:7 | the ego nor reduce the c. within it. The |
| T-4...........III.h | Love without C. |
| T-5........IV.3:5 | them, nor can they c. with each other. |
| T-5........IV.3:6 | ideas of the ego can c. because they occur |
| T-6........ I.16:7 | the perfect symbol of the "c." between the |
| T-6........ I.16:8 | This c. seems just as real now, and its |
| T-6....... II.11:7 | There is no c. anywhere in this perception |
| T-6....... II.11:8 | God. Only the Holy Spirit can resolve c., |
| T-6........IV.3:1 | You cannot understand the c. until you |
| T-6......V.A.1:6 | attempt to resolve c. by not deciding at all |
| T-6......V.A.6:4 | step may appear to exacerbate c. rather |
| T-6......V.A.6:6 | for a long time, experiencing very acute c. |
| T-6......V.A.6:7 | At this point they may try to accept the c., |
| T-6......V.B.3:3 | that this is apt to increase c. temporarily, |
| T-6......V.B.3:8 | the mind of the learner projects its own c. |
| T-6......V.B.5:1 | The way out of c. between two opposing |
| T-6......V.B.5:3 | both, you are teaching c. and learning it. |
| T-6......V.B.5:5 | help you. Its lesson is not insane; the c. is. |
| T-6......V.B.6:1 | can be no c. between sanity and insanity. |
| T-6......V.B.7:3 | Holy Spirit perceives the c. exactly as it is. |
| T-6......V.B.8:4 | then, is a step in the direction out of c., |
| T-6......V.C.4:1 | the first step seems to increase c. and the |
| T-6......V.C.4:1 | second may still entail c. to some extent, |
| T-7........III.4:2 | true, you are accepting c. as your choice. |
| T-7........IV.2:9 | a perception of c. with something else, as |
| T-7.......IV.2:10 | perceived, it can be used as a way out of c. |
| T-7......... V.5:5 | is therefore in c., and is teaching conflict. |
| T-7......... V.5:5 | is therefore in conflict, and is teaching c.. |
| T-7........VI.6:3 | He resolves the apparent c. they engender |
| T-7........VI.6:3 | engender by perceiving c. as meaningless. |
| T-7........VI.6:4 | Holy Spirit perceives the c. exactly as it is, |
| T-7........VI.6:5 | Spirit does not want you to understand c. |
| T-7........VI.6:5 | to realize that, because c. is meaningless, |
| T-7........VI.8:9 | must give up the idea of c. entirely and for |
| T-7......VI.13:4 | is unchangeable, no c. of will is possible. |
| T-7..... VIII.2:2 | The ego always tries to preserve c.. It is |
| T-7..... VIII.2:3 | in devising ways that seem to diminish c., |
| T-7..... VIII.2:3 | because it does not want you to find c. so |
| T-7..... VIII.2:4 | to persuade you that *it* can free you of c., |
| T-7..... VIII.2:6 | It projects c. from your mind to other |
| T-7..... VIII.3:2 | c. cannot be projected because it cannot |
| T-7....... X.3:11 | If you believed this, there would be no c.. |
| T-8...........I.1:3 | those who are in c. are not peaceful, and |
| T-10.......in.1:2 | and will c. until you perceive time solely |
| T-11.......in.2:1 | believed this question really involves c.? If |
| T-11.......in.2:3 | problem is still the only source of c., |
| T-11.........I.9:2 | possible for God's Will and yours to c.. |
| T-11...... III.1:6 | God is very quiet, for there is no c. in Him |
| T-11...... III.1:7 | C. is the root of all evil, for being blind it |
| T-11....... V.5:5 | itself. The real c. you experience, then, is |
| T-11....... V.5:6 | which you share. Can this be a real c.? |
| T-11....... V.6:9 | deceived by its interpretation of your c.. |
| T-12.........I.6:5 | to reality, for reality evokes no c. at all. |
| T-12...... III.7:2 | an internal c. of this magnitude he cannot |
| T-13...... XI.1:2 | Yet no one sees himself in c. and ravaged |
| T-14...... III.2:5 | There is no c. here. To wish for guilt in |
| T-14....... V.6:3 | There is no c. in this curriculum, which |
| T-14...... VI.6:5 | You who made it are but expressing c., |
| T-14....... X.4:1 | thoughts, which even though they may c., |
| T-15..... V.11:4 | In the holy instant there is no c. of needs, |
| T-15...... VI.1:3 | do not c. with one another in any way. |
| T-15...... VI.4:7 | Herein lies peace, for here there *is* no c.. |
| T-15...... XI.4:8 | try to resolve the "c." of Heaven and hell |
| T-16.........I.6:6 | are foolish merely because they c., since |
| T-16.... III.4:10 | seeming c. between truth and illusion can |
| T-16...... III.6:1 | You are not two selves in c.. What is |
| T-16...... IV.2:1 | of love play out a c. that does not exist. |
| T-16...... IV.5:6 | *is* no c. in the choice between truth and |
| T-16...... IV.5:8 | But c. enters the instant the choice seems |
| T-17...... III.5:5 | No longer does the past c. with *now*. This |
| T-17...... IV.9:5 | value is the frame, for there you see no c.. |
| T-17...... IV.9:6 | is only the wrapping for the gift of c.. The |
| T-17....... V.4:3 | The c. between the goal and the structure |
| T-17....... V.4:6 | and accepted as the only way out of the c., |
| T-17...... VI.6:9 | in "solving" c. through fragmentation, |
| T-17..... VII.3:2 | the thoughts are judged to be in c.. But if |
| T19... IV.A.7:1 | in and push Him out *must* produce c.. As |
| T19....IV.C.7:3 | Yet the retreat to death is not the end of c. |
| T-22..... V.1:10 | *You* are the strong one in this seeming c.. |
| T-23.........I.1:2 | It cannot come where there is c., for a |
| T-23.........I.1:5 | C. within you must imply that you believe |
| T-23.........I.4:5 | God Himself, to Whom all c., triumph |
| T-23.........I.6:2 | There *is* no c. between them and the truth. |
| T-23.........I.7:7 | you have learned you cannot be in c.. One |
| T-23.......I.7:10 | And truth stands radiant, apart from c., |
| T-23.........I.8:1 | C. must be between two forces. It cannot |
| T-23.........I.8:4 | illusions of yourself, in c. with each other. |
| T-23.........I.8:6 | C. is fearful, for it is the birth of fear. Yet |
| T-23.........I.9:1 | See how the c. of illusions disappears |
| T-23.........I.9:3 | Thus, c. is the choice between illusions, |
| T-23.......I.11:5 | Illusions can c., because their forms are |
| T-23.......I.12:6 | C. and peace are opposites. Where one |
| T-23....... II.5:5 | of the Son meet only to c. but not to join. |
| T-23....... II.7:5 | And now is c. made inevitable, beyond |
| T-23..... II.19:7 | of Heaven, only the c. of illusion stands; |
| T-23..... II.20:2 | Their forms c., making it seem quite |
| T-23...... III.6:1 | nor compromise for the escape from c.. |
| T-23...... III.6:2 | be released from c. means that it is over. |
| T-23...... IV.1:1 | Do not remain in c., for there *is* no war |
| T-23...... IV.1:6 | enters, and what is all the same cannot c.. |
| T-23...... IV.9:6 | What can c. with everything? And what is |
| T-24.........I.2:2 | where the results of c. are kept unknown |
| T-24..... II.13:3 | safe from God and safe for c. everlasting. |
| T-24....... V.9:1 | must be doubt before there can be c.. And |
| T-24...... VI.1:1 | one trace of c. still remains to haunt you |
| T-24.... VI.13:6 | Out of His lack of c. comes your peace. |
| T-26...... III.1:7 | For it is c. that makes choice possible. The |
| T-26...... III.7:5 | unalike. There is no c. here. No sacrifice is |
| T-26....... V.3:1 | replace the one you made, not to c. with it |
| T-27...... IV.1:2 | resolved. In c. there can be no answer and |
| T-27...... IV.1:3 | A problem set in c. has no answer, for it is |
| T-27...... IV.1:5 | You *are* in c.. Thus it must be clear you |
| T-27...... IV.1:6 | at all, for c. has no limited effects. Yet if |
| T-27...... IV.5:8 | one in a c. state is free to ask this question |
| T-27...... IV.5:8 | *want* an honest answer where the c. ends. |
| T-27..... V.2:10 | This does not mean the c. must be gone |
| T-27....... V.3:2 | to a state of mind that has transcended c., |
| T-30.......I.11:7 | be in c. when you ask for what you want, |
| T-31...... IV.1:5 | choose which road will lead you out of c., |
| W-pI.....24.4:3 | goals are on different levels and often c.. |
| W-pI..... 71.6:5 | work. There can be no real c. about this, |
| W-pI..... 71.7:2 | to be a c. with no resolution possible. All |
| W-pI..... 74.1:4 | The belief that c. is possible has gone. |
| W-pI..... 74.2:4 | Without illusions c. is impossible. Let us |
| W-pI..... 74.3:3 | *God's. I cannot be in c..* Then spend several |
| W-pI... 74.3:10 | any c. thoughts that may cross your mind |
| W-pI... 74.3:13 | *God's. These c. thoughts are meaningless.* |
| W-pI..... 74.4:1 | there is one c. area that seems particularly |
| W-pI..... 80.1:7 | Freedom from c. has been given you. |
| W-pI..... 80.5:4 | Recognize that you are out of c.; free and |
| W-pI..... 83.1:3 | This recognition releases me from all c., |
| W-pI..... 96.1:2 | induces feelings of acute and constant c., |
| W-pI..... 96.3:2 | Two selves in c. could not be resolved, |
| W-pI..... 97.1:4 | will bring your mind from c. to the quiet |
| W-pI..... 99.1:3 | resulting in a state of c. seen between |
| W-pI... 131.8:1 | God does not suffer c.. Nor is His |
| W-pI... 138.7:4 | must be seen as death, for life is seen as c.. |
| W-pI... 138.7:5 | To resolve the c. is to end your life as well. |
| W-pI... 139.1:6 | is no c. that does not entail the single, |
| W-pI... 184.4:4 | which it must overcome, c. with and deny |
| W-pI. 186.11:4 | They will not change, nor be in c.. All of |
| W-pI. 190.11:2 | place of sin, the peace of God instead of c. |
| W-pII ..... 2.1:4 | thoughts of c. with the Thought of peace. |
| W-pII . 286.1:5 | *In You has every c. been resolved. In You is* |
| W-pII . 307.1:5 | *and enter into peace where c. is impossible,* |
| W-pII . 307.2:1 | silently into a state where c. cannot come, |
| W-pII . 318.1:2 | What could c., when all the parts have |
| W-pII .... 331.h | There is no c., for my will is Yours. |
| W-pII . 331.1:7 | *dream, and has no will that can c. with Yours* |
| W-pII . 331.1:8 | *C. is sleep, and peace awakening. Death is* |
| W-pII331.1:11 | *Your Will. There is no c., for my will is Yours.* |
| W-pII .... 333.h | Forgiveness ends the dream of c. here. |
| W-pII . 333.1:1 | C. must be resolved. It cannot be evaded, |
| W-pII . 333.2:1 | *You chose to shine away all c. and all doubt,* |
| M-4 ..... I.A.5:2 | desirable, it will engender enormous c.. |
| M-4 ........II.1:8 | At no level are they in c. with themselves. |
| M-4 ........II.1:9 | them to be in c. with anyone or anything. |
| M-4 ........II.2:3 | one with himself can even conceive of c.. |
| M-4 ........II.2:4 | C. is the inevitable result of self-deception |
| M-7 ........... 6:3 | C. about what you are has entered your |
| M-8 ........... 1:6 | What the body's eyes behold is only c.. |
| M-19 ......... 2:4 | no inherent c. between justice and truth; |
| M-20 ....... 3:12 | is c. now that is perceived as nonexistent |
| M-20 ......... 4:6 | now and think of this: Is c. what you want |
| M-20 ......... 6:5 | In truth there was no c., for His Will is |
| C-3............. 3:1 | a Thought of peace because they are in c.. |
| P-2...........I.3:7 | Only then is all c. over, for only then can |

## conflict's 1

| | |
|---|---|
| T-23.......I.2:11 | This is the c. purpose. And to those who |

## conflict-free 7

| | |
|---|---|
| T-6....... II.11:8 | conflict, because only the Holy Spirit is c.. |
| T-6........ III.2:2 | If you are to be c. yourself, you must learn |
| T-7........ III.1:2 | Being c., He maximizes all efforts and all |
| T-7......... V.5:3 | is consistent, since only consistency is c., |
| T-7......... V.5:3 | is conflict-free, and only the c. are whole. |
| W-pI... 199.6:5 | c. and unequivocal response to mind with |
| W-pII ... 12.3:4 | peace, forever c. and undisturbed, in |

## conflicted 12

| | |
|---|---|
| T-2........ VI.5:3 | produces c. behavior, which is intolerable |
| T-2........ VI.6:8 | does so whenever it is c. in what it wants, |
| T-4..........II.5:6 | even toward this are necessarily c., |
| T-4........ VI.1:5 | as necessarily c. as long as you are here, or |
| T-6...... IV.12:3 | God is not c.. Teaching aims at change, |
| T-6...... V.B.3:6 | since it is being learned by a c. mind. This |
| T-7..........II.4:6 | c. mind cannot be faithful to one meaning |
| T-7....... V.5:10 | only a c. mind could possibly perceive as |
| T-7........ VI.7:3 | does not require vigilance unless it is c.. If |
| T-7......VIII.3:4 | Remember that a c. teacher is a poor |
| T-8.........I.5:10 | Their c. curriculum teaches them that *all* |
| W-pII . 257.1:1 | of what I am, and thus c. in my actions. |

### conflicting 23

|  |  |
|---|---|
| T-2 VI.5:2 | ways: First, you can choose to do **c.** things |
| T-6 V.B.3:7 | This means **c.** motivation, and so the |
| T-6 V.B.4:6 | receiving **c.** messages and accepting both. |
| T-7 II.2:9 | because you can respond to two **c.** voices. |
| T-7 III.3:6 | It *is* the belief that **c.** interests are possible, |
| T-7 VI.7:4 | **c.** components within it that have led to a |
| T-9 VII.4:1 | have two **c.** evaluations of yourself in your |
| T-10 I.3:1 | to reconcile what happened in **c.** dreams, |
| T-10 III.7:6 | idolatrous, and does not know of **c.** laws. |
| T-12 VII.8:2 | merely the reflection of your **c.** invitations |
| T-17 I.2:4 | to two masters who ask **c.** things of you. |
| T-18 II.2:1 | they are governed by your **c.** wishes, and |
| T-23 I.9:2 | long as it is seen as war between **c.** truths; |
| T-24 I.2:1 | other because **c.** outcomes are impossible. |
| T-26 III.2:3 | where **c.** values meet and all illusions are |
| T-27 II.11:2 | which has **c.** purposes and different ends. |
| W-pI 74.1:5 | strange idea that you are torn by **c.** goals. |
| W-pI 83.1:3 | because it means I cannot have **c.** goals. |
| W-pI 138.3:2 | Decision lets one of **c.** goals become the |
| W-pI 186.10:2 | images you make give rise to but **c.** goals, |
| W-pI 200.8:3 | beyond. Peace is the answer to **c.** goals, to |
| W-pII 307.h | **C.** wishes cannot be my will. |
| M-7 6:8 | Doubt is the result of **c.** wishes. Be sure of |

### conflicts 17

|  |  |
|---|---|
| T-2 VI.5:1 | what you want **c.** with what you do. This |
| T-4 III.4:5 | and this **c.** with the love you feel for the |
| T-6 II.12:4 | Nothing **c.** in this perception, because |
| T-6 V.A.6:5 | This **c.** with the upside-down perception |
| T-7 III.3:5 | this idea, because all your **c.** come from it. |
| T-17 VI.7:2 | except that this attempt **c.** with unity, and |
| T-18 VI.5:7 | fantasies in which your will **c.** with His, |
| T-23 I.8:8 | you fill your world with **c.** with yourself? |
| T-26 I.1:2 | and all **c.** achieve a seeming balance. It is |
| T-26 III.1:4 | Son. Nothing **c.** with oneness. How, then, |
| T-31 IV.1:5 | alone; a time when everyone **c.** with you, |
| W-pI 65.7:1 | you by resolving your **c.** once and for all, |
| W-pI 74.4:5 | *it with Him. My* **c.** *about _ cannot be real.* |
| W-pI 81.1:4 | In its calm light let all my **c.** disappear. In |
| W-pI 96.6:2 | can resolve the senseless **c.** which a dream |
| W-pI 104.3:4 | Then lay aside the **c.** of the world that |
| W-pI 108.1:3 | of all your **c.** and mistaken thoughts into |

### confound 2

|  |  |
|---|---|
| T-9 II.4:2 | Do not question him and do not **c.** him, |
| T-21 VIII.2:7 | so. Nothing has power to **c.** its constancy, |

### confront 5

|  |  |
|---|---|
| W-pI 50.1:1 | answer to every problem that will **c.** you, |
| W-pI 79.3:3 | of different problems seems to **c.** you, and |
| W-pI 79.5:2 | they **c.** you with an impossible situation. |
| W-pI 79.6:3 | in all the problems that seem to **c.** you, |
| M-21 5:3 | in fact, **c.** the teacher with a situation that |

### confronted 6

|  |  |
|---|---|
| T-6 IV.11:9 | If He **c.** the self you made with the truth |
| T-13 II.6:2 | When it was **c.** with the real guiltlessness |
| T-16 V.17:1 | make the easiest decision that ever **c.** you, |
| T-17 VI.7:1 | **C.** with any aspect of the situation that |
| T19 IV.C.11:5 | **C.** with such seeming uncertainty of |
| W-pI 135.23:3 | to the problems which you thought **c.** you |

### confronting 1

|  |  |
|---|---|
| W-pI 138.4:1 | you think a thousand choices are **c.** you, |

### confronts 1

|  |  |
|---|---|
| W-pI 50.4:4 | is the answer to whatever **c.** you today. |

### confuse 20

|  |  |
|---|---|
| T-2 V.A.13:1 | Never **c.** right- and wrong-mindedness. |
| T-3 I.5:6 | It does not **c.** destruction with innocence |
| T-4 I.13:3 | but he does not **c.** himself with the father |
| T-6 V.4:3 | Children *do* **c.** fantasy and reality, and |
| T-7 X.3:4 | and are, in fact, very apt to **c.** the two. The |
| T-8 VII.7:7 | and thus to **c.** the goal of His curriculum. |
| T-8 VII.12:5 | To **c.** a learning device with a curriculum |
| T-10 V.8:4 | you can **c.** yourself with things that do. |
| T-16 I.5:7 | Do not **c.** your role with His, for this will |
| T-18 IV.1:6 | will add the ego to Him and **c.** the two. He |
| T-18 IV.5:5 | it. That is but to **c.** your role with God's. |
| T-18 IX.7:5 | to it, you do not **c.** it with the world below |
| T-21 II.10:8 | **c.** the two is merely to fail to understand |
| T-22 II.4:3 | **c.** what is the same with what is different. |
| T-27 II.10:7 | if you **c.** your function with the function |
| T-31 I.2:2 | But **c.** it not with difficulty in the simple |
| W-pI 138.4:3 | Do not **c.** yourself with all the doubts that |
| M-18 1:1 | has ceased to **c.** interpretation with fact, |
| M-19 5:1 | not **c.** His mercy with your own insanity. |
| S-2 III.5:8 | Do not **c.** His function with your own. He |

### confused 54

|  |  |
|---|---|
| T-1 VII.5:8 | preparation, or awe will be **c.** with fear, |
| T-2 VII.7:3 | The two should not be **c.**. As soon as a |
| T-3 IV.3:3 | The mind is therefore **c.**, because only |
| T-3 IV.3:4 | A separated or divided mind *must* be **c.**. It |
| T-3 IV.4:1 | Right-mindedness is not to be **c.** with the |
| T-3 V.2:1 | "create" and "make" have become **c.**. |
| T-4 II.7:9 | become completely **c.** about what is really |
| T-4 IV.11:3 | you are too **c.** to recognize your own hope |
| T-6 IV.6:5 | of the ego's symbols and they have **c.** you. |
| T-7 II.7:1 | of the Kingdom mean to those who are **c.**? |
| T-7 V.3:5 | body has already been **c.** with the mind. |
| T-7 VIII.3:5 | His lessons are **c.**, and their transfer value |
| T-7 X.3:6 | you are, you will be **c.** about joy and pain. |
| T-7 X.5:6 | are **c.** about this distinction in motivation |
| T-7 X.8:1 | because you are **c.** about what *you* will. |
| T-7 X.8:2 | means that you are **c.** about what you are. |
| T-8 II.1:8 | the ego is totally **c.** and totally confusing. |
| T-9 I.6:4 | because **c.** communication does not mean |
| T-11 V.7:3 | The ego is totally **c.** about reality, but it |
| T-11 V.7:5 | are **c.** because you do not recognize yours. |
| T-14 II.1:4 | **c.** you that you have undertaken to learn |
| T-14 X.7:2 | are much too **c.** either to recognize love, |
| T-16 V.16:2 | from illusion and not **c.** with it at all. How |
| T-17 III.6:5 | at all **c.** by any "reasons" for separation. |
| T-19 I.8:1 | and how **c.** your own identification has |
| T-19 II.1:1 | It is essential that error be not **c.** with sin, |
| T19 IV.C.11:2 | sign nor symbol should be **c.** with source, |
| T-22 II.3:3 | misery in reason's eyes can be **c.** with joy. |
| T-25 V.3:2 | It is the "enemy," **c.** with Christ, you look |
| T-26 X.1:9 | **C.** perception will block knowledge. It is |
| T-27 II.10:7 | be **c.** about yourself and who you are. |
| T-28 I.9:2 | causelessness which you **c.** with cause. It |
| T-28 IV.6:1 | You share confusion and you are **c.**, for in |
| T-29 II.6:6 | to those who are **c.** is meaningless, and |
| T-31 I.1:9 | and just what to do if you become **c.**. Why |
| T-31 I.2:5 | This cannot be confusing, yet you are **c.**. |
| T-31 I.2:6 | totally **c.** is easier to learn and understand |
| T-31 VII.2:4 | for you are too **c.** about yourself. But |
| W-pI 121.3:1 | with doubt, **c.** about itself and all it sees; |
| W-pI 136.20:2 | Do not be **c.** about what must be healed, |
| W-pI 153.2:6 | The mind is now **c.**, and knows not where |
| W-pI 153.14:5 | dreams this story has evoked in his **c.**, |
| W-pI 160.7:5 | He cannot be **c.** about creation. He is sure |
| W-pI 170.10:2 | has not **c.** its attributes with those of fear. |
| W-pI 186.12:4 | are, or a distorted image of yourself, **c.**, |
| W-pI 190.3:2 | demonstrates God is denied, **c.** with fear, |
| W-pI 197.2:1 | How easily are God and guilt **c.** by those |
| W-pII 257.1:1 | If I forget my goal I can be but **c.**, unsure |
| W-pII 339.1:6 | be **c.** indeed about the things he wants; |
| M-4 IV.1:9 | It will make him **c.**, fearful, angry and |
| M-8 4:8 | **c.** and senseless "reasoning" be depended |
| M-10 1:2 | world. It is actually **c.** with wisdom, and |
| M-22 5:3 | ego, and has thus **c.** him with a body. In |
| S-1 I.5:2 | not be **c.** with supplication of any kind, |

### confuses 3

|  |  |
|---|---|
| T-4 V.3:1 | that **c.** God and the body must be insane. |
| W-pI 96.4:4 | and perceive itself within a body it **c.** with |
| P-2 VII.4:1 | therapist in no way **c.** himself with God. |

### confusing 11

|  |  |
|---|---|
| T-1 I.23:2 | because sickness comes from **c.** the levels. |
| T-3 III.5:7 | are really **c.** knowledge with perception. |
| T-8 II.1:8 | the ego is totally confused and totally **c.**. |
| T-11 VII.3:4 | real to the real, thus **c.** illusion and reality |
| T-12 VII.14:5 | ego because, by **c.** yourself with the ego, |
| T-14 VI.4:4 | their meaning by **c.** them with each other. |
| T-21 II.11:5 | what it wills, you are **c.** Son and Father; |
| T-31 I.2:5 | This cannot be **c.**, yet you are confused. |
| W-pI 72.4:4 | trying to hold him to it by **c.** it with him, |
| W-pI 95.8:5 | and are **c.** strength with weakness. |
| W-pII 339.1:9 | in fearlessness, without **c.** pain with joy, |

### confusion 89

|  |  |
|---|---|
| T-1 VII.1:2 | The **c.** of miracle impulses with physical |
| T-1 VII.5:1 | is necessary because of the **c.** between fear |
| T-2 IV.2:2 | is the result of level **c.**, because it always |
| T-2 IV.2:3 | as the means of correcting level **c.**, for all |
| T-2 IV.2:10 | itself, neither type of **c.** need occur. |
| T-2 V.1:6 | protective device than any form of level **c.** |
| T-2 V.5:4 | in a position to undo the level **c.** of others. |
| T-2 V.A.13:2 | a desire to heal is an expression of this **c.**. |
| T-2 VI.1:8 | for them. This is an obvious **c.** of levels. |
| T-2 VI.2:1 | I do not foster level **c.**, but you must |
| T-2 VI.2:4 | There is a **c.** here that you would do well |
| T-2 VIII.1:1 | the magic-miracle **c.** is to remember that |
| T-3 II.5:5 | There is no **c.** within Its Levels, because |
| T-3 IV.3:3 | only One-mindedness can be without **c.**. |
| T-3 V.3:2 | The **c.** between your real creation and |
| T-3 V.5:4 | so fundamental a **c.** without increasing |
| T-3 V.5:4 | increasing your overall **c.** still further. |
| T-4 I.2:5 | This profound **c.** is possible only if you |
| T-4 I.7:10 | Any **c.** on this point is delusional, and no |
| T-4 I.13:2 | this involves no **c.** about the child's origin |
| T-4 V.3:2 | Yet this **c.** is essential to the ego, which |
| T-6 V.3:3 | joy. Consider the fear and **c.** a child would |
| T-7 II.7:2 | apparent that **c.** interferes with meaning, |
| T-7 II.7:3 | it. There is no **c.** in the Kingdom, because |
| T-7 V.3:3 | not accept the ego's **c.** of mind and body. |
| T-7 VI.2:4 | feelings of unreality and results in utter **c.** |
| T-7 VII.5:5 | All **c.** comes from not extending life, |
| T-7 VIII.3:5 | and their transfer value is limited by his **c.** |
| T-7 VIII.4:7 | The ego is a **c.** in identification. Never |
| T-7 X.h | The **C.** of Pain and Joy |
| T-7 X.1:2 | which is total **c.** about everything. If you |
| T-7 X.3:7 | This **c.** is the cause of the whole idea of |
| T-7 X.5:7 | Projection is a **c.** in motivation, and given |
| T-7 X.5:7 | confusion in motivation, and given this **c.** |
| T-7 X.5:14 | all. If the result of this decision is **c.**, this is |
| T-7 X.7:3 | will lead you out of the **c.** you have made. |
| T-7 X.7:4 | There is no **c.** in the mind of a Son of God |
| T-8 II.1:6 | you are. It is expert only in **c.**. It does not |
| T-8 VII.11:6 | of attack is an obvious **c.** in purpose. |
| T-8 VII.12:5 | **c.** that blocks the understanding of both. |
| T-8 VIII.2:3 | The ego makes a fundamental **c.** between |
| T-8 VIII.7:3 | because you have accepted the ego's **c.**, |
| T-9 IV.7:1 | The **c.** of functions is so typical of the ego |
| T-9 IV.7:3 | they are. This is more than mere **c.**. It is a |
| T-9 IV.7:4 | of grandiosity and **c.** that makes the ego |
| T-9 V.3:6 | condemn themselves because of this **c.**. It |
| T-9 V.4:6 | one which it usually notes even in its **c.**. |
| T-9 VII.4:4 | because at such times its **c.** increases. The |
| T-11 V.2:9 | Clarity undoes **c.** by definition, and to |
| T-11 VI.2:5 | much **c.** about what perception means, |
| T-12 III.5:3 | than love arises from a **c.** about the "what |
| T-12 V.7:5 | to defeat itself, what can you expect but **c.** |
| T-15 X.5:8 | **c.** of sacrifice and love is so profound that |
| T-16 V.6:3 | relationship is the triumph of this **c.**. It is |
| T-16 V.16:4 | is. For only fantasies make **c.** in choosing |
| T-16 VI.7:4 | In the transition there is a period of **c.**, in |
| T-20 VI.12:4 | Perhaps **c.**, but hardly discouragement. |
| T-21 II.10:1 | **c.** of cause and effect becomes inevitable. |

T-22......III.9:2 else. Unholy values will produce **c.**, and in
T-22......VI.2:4 Yet even in this **c.**, so profound it cannot
T-22......VI.5:2 joined with love, looks quietly on all **c.**,
T-25... VIII.6:2 They must believe He shares their own **c.**,
T-25... VIII.9:2 believe in your **c.** you have much to give?
T-26.......X.1:5 **C.** is not limited. If it occurs at all it will
T-26.....X.1:10 It is not a question of the size of the **c.**, or
T-28.......II.9:4 For this **c.** has produced the dream, and
T-28......IV.6:1 You share **c.** and you are confused, for in
T-29.......II.6:3 **C.** follows on confusion here, for on
T-29.......II.6:3 Confusion follows on **c.** here, for on
T-29.......II.6:3 here, for on **c.** has this world been based,
T-29.......II.6:5 is that except the state **c.** really means?
T-30.........I.2:6 but produce **c.** and uncertainty and fear.
T-30.....VII.3:6 **c.** be what meaning means? Perception
T-31.....II.11:5 go. And thus there is **c.**, and a sense of
T-31.....IV.9:5 you are will lead you to **c.** and despair.
T-31.....V.14:6 it thinks reflects the deep **c.** that it feels
T-31.....V.16:3 will be some **c.** every time there is a shift,
W-pI.....52.1:7 is affected in any way by this **c.** of mine.
W-pI.....71.5:4 The result can only bring **c.**, misery and a
W-pI...96.10:5 **C.** done, you are restored, for you have
W-pI.170.10:3 fear perceive their own **c.** in fear's "enemy
W-pI...192.7:3 we understand is but **c.** born of error. We
W-pI...219.1:5 *without* **c.** *as to what my Father loves forever*
M-5........II.4:2 this idea goes also all **c.** about creation.
M-7............6:2 Self, and thus represents a **c.** in identity.
M-10..........1:4 **c.** about what these categories mean.
M-13..........3:1 Once this **c.** has occurred, it becomes
P-2.......VII.4:2 fundamental **c.** in one form or another,
P-2.......VII.4:3 This **c.** is rarely if ever in awareness, or

## conjunction 1
M-21..........2:3 occur to the mind in **c.** with the word, the

## connect 1
T-19.........I.7:2 true, however much you seek to **c.** them.

## connected 2
T-19.........I.7:3 But illusions are always **c.**, as is truth.
T-19.........I.7:7 produced the body and remains **c.** to it,

## connection 25
T-1.......VII.5:2 inappropriate in **c.** with the Sons of God,
T-4.........V.6:8 *you* must learn to ask in **c.** with everything.
T-5...........I.1:9 it is quite comprehensible in **c.** with ideas.
T-7.........II.6:1 questions the **c.** of learning and memory.
T-7.........V.1:3 for communication has such a direct **c.**
T-9.........II.1:2 This is not only true in **c.** with specific
T-9.........II.1:2 also in **c.** with requests that are strictly in
T-13.......II.6:4 you may experience in **c.** with this course
T-17......III.2:5 by which you arrive at the **c.** may be. And
T-19.........I.6:2 of seeming wholeness, but without **c.**.
T-19.........I.7:1 Truth and illusion have no **c.**. This will
T-19.........I.7:8 are protecting the body by hiding this **c.**,
W-in..........5:2 has been achieved in **c.** with any person,
W-pI.......4.6:1 in **c.** with thoughts particularly difficult.
W-pI.....19.4:3 Lack of order in this **c.** will ultimately
W-pI.....21.3:2 that you believe in this **c.** means anything.
W-pI.....24.6:2 in **c.** with some of your goals, however the
W-pI.....26.7:3 that **c.** and which has caused you concern,
W-pI.....29.4:2 tempting in **c.** with today's idea because
W-pI.....38.2:5 so in **c.** with yourself and with anyone else
W-pI.....66.1:1 on the **c.** between fulfilling your function
W-pI.....66.1:2 This is because you do not really see the **c.**
W-pI.....66.1:3 there is more than just a **c.** between them;
W-pI.....66.4:1 not only is there a very real **c.** between the
P-2...........I.3:6 reach in **c.** with their own divergent goals,

## connotations 2
T-4.......II.8:12 of them is not without fearful **c.**.
T-6...........I.1:2 of the fearful **c.** you may associate with it.

## conquer 2
T-4........VI.7:6 Love does not **c.** all things, but it does set
T19....IV.C.8:6 it to die, for only death could **c.** life. And

## conquered 1
M-5.........I.1:9 Only by His death can He be **c.** by His Son

## conquering 1
W-pI.....92.6:4 itself, and dreams that it is strong and **c.**,

## conqueror 5
T-19......III.7:6 must bow, and offer His creation to its **c.**.
T-23.........I.9:2 conflicting truths; the **c.** to be the truer,
T-23.......II.15:6 is lifted to the throne of love, its dying **c.**,
T-24.......I.5:10 him? And who must be his **c.** but you?
T-27... VIII.2:6 it is a **c.** of bodies weaker than itself. But

## conquers 1
T-23.........I.6:1 in the belief the one that **c.** will be true.

## conquest 1
T-23......IV.9:5 The senselessness of **c.** is quite apparent

## conscious 8
T-1...........I.5:2 They should not be under **c.** control.
T-2........VI.6:1 mind under my guidance without **c.** effort
T-4......III.10:1 which in your sane mind is perfectly **c.**, is
T-18.....VII.7:9 activities return to occupy your **c.** mind.
W-pI.....39.8:1 without **c.** selection and without undue
W-pI.138.10:1 The **c.** choice of Heaven is as sure as is
W-pI.138.11:2 recognize we make a **c.** choice between
M-12.........6:3 It is a **c.** choice. For they have learned that

## consciously 7
T-1...........I.5:3 **C.** selected miracles can be misguided.
T-4.........V.5:3 Meaningful seeking is **c.** undertaken,
T-4.........V.5:3 **c.** organized and consciously directed.
T-4.........V.5:3 consciously organized and **c.** directed.
T-30.........I.1:5 proper set, adopted **c.** each time you wake
W-pI...138.9:1 Heaven is chosen **c.**. The choice cannot
M-12.........6:4 have learned that all choices are made **c.**,

## consciousness 11
T-1.........II.1:7 Neither emanates from **c.**, but both are
T-1.........II.1:8 **C.** is the state that induces action, though
T-3........IV.2:1 **C.**, the level of perception, was the first
T-3........IV.2:2 **C.** is correctly identified as the domain of
T-28......VI.4:6 unheard in **c.** is every pledge to sickness.
W-pI.....50.5:1 the idea for today sink deep into your **c.**.
W-pI.....69.4:1 content that generally occupies your **c.**.
C-in ...........1:4 structure of "individual **c.**" is essentially
C-1.............7:3 *C.* is the receptive mechanism, receiving
C-1.............7:4 **C.** has levels and awareness can shift quite
P-2.........V.1:4 on certain steps which never reach to **c.**.

## consent 9
T-21.......V.5:1 established without your will and your **c.**.
T-27.........I.3:1 Whenever you **c.** to suffer pain, to be
T-27.......II.8:7 healing, and he will **c.** no more to suffer.
T-30.......II.1:9 of life but was created with your glad **c.**,
W-pI...152.1:4 And no one dies without his own **c.**.
W-pI...154.2:3 He does not work without your own **c.**.
W-pI...164.2:5 Self, using your voice to give His glad **c.**;
W-pI...164.9:1 you receiving your **c.** and your acceptance
W-pI...165.6:5 God **c.** to let His Son remain forever

## consents 2
T-27.......II.8:5 all. As long as he **c.** to suffer, you will be
W-pI...184.8:6 for his mind **c.** to take the name you give

## consequence 19
T-12......III.7:8 is a necessary **c.** of what you have done.
T-26.....VII.2:4 Sickness and sin are seen as **c.** and cause,
T-26...VII.14:1 miracle is possible when cause and **c.** are
T-26....VIII.9:6 fact that **c.** and cause must come as one.
T-26........X.2:6 senseless, equally without a cause or **c.**,
T-28.........I.6:4 which is but a **c.** in which no change can
T-28......II.12:4 taking back the **c.** of sickness to its cause.
T-29.........I.2:6 This is the **c.** the little gap must bring to
T-30.....V.9:12 not free from bitter cost and joyless **c.**.
T-31.....V.14:5 that different thoughts have different **c.**.
W-pI.....41.1:2 is an inevitable **c.** of separation. So are
W-pI...101.6:7 *There is no sin; it has no* **c.**. So should you
W-pI...130.4:5 so they have no cause, no being and no **c.**.
Wi181-200 2:5 intensified that words become of little **c.**.
W-pI...184.3:4 of true effect, with **c.** inherent in itself.
W-pI...190.4:3 crimes, or secret sins with weighty **c.**.
M-25.........4:9 is given to fear, and will be fearful in **c.**.
C-2.............5:1 in every way,–in origin, effect and **c.**–
P-1.............3:1 and his peace of mind is suffering in **c.**.

## consequences 19
T-5.....VII.6:10 *all the* **c.** *of my wrong decision if I will let Him*
T-12......III.7:6 for thoughts do have **c.** to the thinker.
T-12.......V.3:4 and if this has never been, it has no **c.**.
T-16.....V.15:5 and complete escape from all its **c.**.
T-27.........I.8:4 sign of guilt whose **c.** still are there to see,
T-27........II.2:3 retain the **c.** of the guilt they overlook. Yet
T-27........II.2:5 And what has **c.** must be real, because
T-27....VIII.8:4 you do your eyes behold its heavy **c.**, but
T-28.........I.2:3 In its passing went its **c.**, left without a
T-28.........I.7:7 effects of cause accepted *now*, with **c.** *here.*
T-28.........I.7:9 they bring will be the happy **c.** of a Cause
T-28.........I.8:4 Its **c.** will indeed seem new, because you
T-28.........I.9:3 learn you have remembered **c.** that were
T-28........II.7:5 the **c.** that he dreams he gave his brother.
T-28......II.7:11 he fears is cause without the **c.** that would
T-30......VI.9:2 escape from guilt in all its **c.** and its forms
W-pI.....97.8:4 escape its sorry **c.** if you yield to the belief
W-pI...101.6:4 **c.** sin has wrought in feverish imagination
M-12.........6:4 consciously, with full awareness of their **c.**

## consequently 1
T-9.........V.5:6 know how to give, and **c.** cannot share.

## consider 75
T-2..........II.3:6 it? Once you have learned to **c.** these
T-4..........II.6:2 is obvious when you **c.** what is involved.
T-4......III.10:3 **C.** how much vigilance you have been
T-5........VI.6:1 you **c.** worth cultivating you will cultivate
T-6.........in.1:6 to **c.** the sanity of the premises on which
T-6...........I.1:1 purposes, let us **c.** the crucifixion again.
T-6...........I.2:8 own life, and if you will **c.** it without fear,
T-6...........I.3:2 always refuse to **c.** what they have done to
T-6........IV.5:2 of all, if you **c.** what it really involves. The
T-6.........V.3:3 **C.** the fear and confusion a child would
T-7........XI.3:1 **C.** the kingdom you have made and judge
T-8........IV.5:2 is obvious when you **c.** what healing is for
T-8......VIII.4:3 you would not **c.** sickness such a strong
T-9...........I.7:1 you, but it might be wiser to **c.** the kind of
T-9.........I.12:3 But **c.** the result of this strange decision.
T-9.......II.12:2 **c.** how much you will be asking of Him,
T-9.........V.1:3 us **c.** the unhealed healer more carefully
T-9.......VII.2:1 **C.**, then, that in this joint will you are all
T-10.......V.3:3 But **c.** what this means to you. Unless you
T-12.........I.8:6 of the ego. **C.** how well the Holy Spirit's
T-12......III.1:5 **C.** how perfectly your lesson would be
T-12......III.7:6 Yet **c.** what has happened, for thoughts
T-13.........I.3:2 Yet **c.** this: You are not guiltless in time,
T-13........II.2:1 Yet **c.** how strange a solution the ego's
T-13........II.6:4 but if you will **c.** your reactions to it you
T-13......VI.2:1 **c.** it "natural" to use your past experience
T-13....VIII.1:6 at all. It therefore does not **c.** where it is,

T-13....VIII.2:1 you c. this: There is nothing partial about
T-14....... II.2:4 C. all the distortions you have made of
T-14.....IV.5:1 and then c. carefully whether you want to
T-14.....VII.4:2 you this way, if you c. what dissociation is
T-14....... X.6:6 c. which call is louder or greater or more
T-14....... X.7:4 What you c. content is not content at all.
T-16...... III.1:3 If you will c. what you have taught, and
T-16........ V.2:4 but if you c. how you value it and why,
T-17...... VI.2:1 you are uncertain, the first thing to c.,
T-18.........I.1:2 you would but c. exactly what this entails,
T-18.... VI.11:4 If you will c. what this "transportation"
T-18.... VII.5:6 on this than to c. what you should do.
T-20....... V.8:3 Let us c. now what he must learn, to share
T-21.....VII.8:1 C. carefully your answer to the last
T-22....... V.2:1 C. what the ego wants defenses for.
T-23..... II.13:4 c. this: These *are* the laws on which your
T-24......IV.4:1 Earlier I said c. not the means by which
T-24......IV.4:2 But do c., and consider well, whether it is
T-24......IV.4:2 But do consider, and c. well, whether it is
T-24....... V.8:1 love, c. this: The holy Lord of Heaven has
T-26....... II.6:5 C. once again your special function. One
T-26...VII.12:1 Let us c. what the error is, so it can be
T-27..... II.13:1 C. how this self-perception must extend,
T-27....... V.5:3 C. well its question. It is asked of you on
T-30.......I.13:5 us, then, c. once again the very first of the
T-31........ V.9:2 Let us c., then, what proof there is that
T-31...VII.14:6 C. what temptation is, and see the real
W-pI.....19.3:3 As you c. each one, name it in terms of
W-pI.....35.5:1 you c. to be the more negative aspects of
WpI...rI.in.1:3 ideas, which you should c. in your review.
W-pI.....66.9:7 and c. also whether it was ever reasonable
W-pI.....72.3:2 let us c. the kinds of things you are apt to
W-pI.....78.6:2 him in your mind, first as you now c. him.
W-pI...121.9:2 enemy, and one whom you c. as a friend.
W-pI...126.2:1 Let us c. what you do believe, in place of
W-pI.134.15:3 Briefly c. all the evil things you thought of
W-pI...135.4:1 Let us c. first what you defend. It must be
W-pI.135.17:2 and disregard what you c. incompatible
W-pI...170.4:1 you c. carefully the means by which your
W-pI...185.8:4 C. but what you believe will comfort you,
W-pI.186.12:3 Then c. this; which is more likely to be
W-pI...196.7:2 From there you can at least c. if you want
W-pII ....in.2:7 will not c. time a matter of duration now.
M-5...... III.3:1 the advanced teachers of God c. the forms
M-17.........5:2 fear. C. what this reaction means, and its
M-20.........1:5 retained? Let us c. each of these questions
M-27.........1:3 but now we need to c. it more carefully. It
P-3......... II.9:9 too, c. this strange procedure as salvation

## considerable 1

M-10.........1:4 c. confusion about what these categories

## considerably 2

T-9......... II.2:5 to his thought system might be c. more
W-pI.....46.6:1 The form of the application may vary c.,

## consideration 4

W-pI.....74.4:1 to resolve, single it out for special c..
W-pI...133.8:1 next c. is the one on which the others rest.
M-16.........3:8 individual need becomes the chief c..
M-25.........3:4 only important c. is how they are used.

## considerations 2

T-2....V.A.11:2 the ordinary c. of time and space do not
C-in...........2:4 Theological c. as such are necessarily

## considered 11

T-4........IV.8:1 you really c. how many opportunities you
T-6......V.B.8:4 it means that alternatives have been c.,
T-10....... II.6:3 mind, but you have not c. what it must be
T-24.........I.2:2 brought to reason, to be c. sensible or not
W-pI.....24.3:2 honestly and carefully c. in each of the
W-pI.....31.3:1 awareness, each to be c. for a moment,
W-pI.....71.1:5 after we have c. just what the ego's plan is
W-pI...133.4:3 choice until you had c. all of them in time;
W-pI...182.2:4 not to be c. more than but a dream. Yet
W-pII .284.1:6 Then to be c. seriously more and more,
M-26.........3:4 so rare that it cannot be c. a realistic goal.

## considering 8

T-11...... V.4:1 we are not c. dynamics but delusions.
T-16........II.7:6 c. honestly what they have been? God
WpI...rI.in.2:2 to follow any particular order in c. them,
W-pI.....62.5:4 Then devote a minute or two to c. your
W-pI.....63.4:1 or two that you should devote to c. this.
W-pI.....73.1:1 Today we are c. the will you share with
WpI..rIII.in5:1 it, to c. the thoughts that are assigned.
W-pI...138.7:1 So we begin today c. the choice that time

## considers 3

T-4.........II.4:3 dismisses something he c. part of himself.
T-15.........I.6:7 For no one who c. himself as deserving of
T-16...... V.3:4 one c. it bizarre to love and hate together,

## consist 7

W-pI.....10.4:4 The exercises c., as before, in searching
W-pI.....20.4:1 The exercises for today c. in reminding
W-pI.....32.5:2 shorter applications c. of repeating the
W-pI.....37.6:1 exercises c. of repeating the idea as often
W-pI.....40.3:3 might, for example, c. of the following:
W-pI.....46.7:1 shorter practice periods may c. either of a
M-1...........1:2 be one. His qualifications c. solely in this;

## consistency 20

T-6..... V.B.3:8 thus does not perceive c. in the minds of
T-6..... V.B.6:4 the Holy Spirit's Voice, and Its perfect c.,
T-6..... V.C.4:6 then, your c. is called on despite chaos.
T-6..... V.C.4:7 Yet chaos and c. cannot coexist for long,
T-7.........II.6:8 This is the only way you can learn c., so
T-7.........II.7:1 What can the perfect c. of the Kingdom
T-7........ V.5:3 is consistent, since only c. is conflict-free,
T-7...... V.6:11 means c. because God means consistency.
T-7...... V.6:11 means consistency because God means c..
T-9....... VI.2:2 to you are your evaluations of His c..
T-9....... VI.2:3 so you will not always recognize His c..
T-14 ... XI.14:5 this c. lies His Holiness which He cannot
T-20.......VII.h The C. of Means and End
T-20 .... VII.5:5 Because of this c., the means remain
W-pI...152.4:4 appears to have some aspects that belie c.
W-pI...181.2:2 It is this that gives c. to what you see.
M-4..... I.A.8:4 learning, c. of thought and full transfer.
M-4.........II.1:5 say. The term actually means c.. There is
C-in...........2:7 Here alone c. becomes possible because
P-2..........II.1:3 Even in this, complete c. is not required,

## consistent 33

T-2........ V.4:2 readiness, but maintain a c. trust in mine.
T-2....... VI.5:5 so. This produces c. behavior, but entails
T-3....... III.2:3 and this means that it is not whole or c..
T-4....... IV.7:2 one, including yourself, is worth c. effort.
T-6..... V.C.1:6 the Kingdom perfectly c. and perfectly
T-6..... V.C.2:2 He would hardly be c. if He allowed you
T-6..... V.C.4:1 this step calls for c. vigilance against it.
T-7.........II.6:2 since it must be c. to be remembered.
T-7.........II.6:4 is only to make the remembering c.. You
T-7.........II.6:8 consistency, so that you can finally *be* c..
T-7........ V.5:3 will vary. Yet healing itself is c., since only
T-7...... V.6:10 if healing is c. it cannot be inconsistently
T-7..... VI.13:5 is the Holy Spirit's perfectly c. teaching.
T-7.....VIII.4:8 Never having had a c. model, it never
T-9.......II.11:3 God's laws are always fair and perfectly c.
T-11......in.1:4 system. Each is internally c., but they are
T-11 .... V.14:3 the mistake c. truth must be meaningless.
T-11 .... V.14:5 If c. truth is meaningless, inconsistency
T-11 .... V.16:2 carefully, and its witnesses are c.. The
T-12..... IV.1:6 though severely impaired, is completely c.
T-14.......X.8:9 which lack any c. sense when they are put
T-15........I.1:4 a c. learner that you learn only of Him.
T-20 .... VII.1:3 this course has nothing in it that is not c..
T-20 .... VII.4:2 not perfectly c. with the goal of holiness?
W-pI .. 130.1:1 Perception is c.. What you see reflects
W-pI .. 130.6:4 the one you see is quite c. from the point
W-pI 130.10:3 Perception is c. with your choice, and hell
WpI...rV.in4:5 Self alone is perfectly c. in Its Thoughts;
W-pI .. 194.6:1 to give as much c. effort as you can, to
M-4...... IX.2:2 Being c., it is wholly honest. Being
M-10.........1:7 any c. criteria for determining what these
C-in.........3:10 that does it remain wholly c. because only
C-in.........3:10 consistent because only that can *be* c..

## consistently 14

T-4....... IV.7:3 Side with me c. against this deception,
T-6..... V.B.3:7 so the lesson cannot be learned c. as yet.
T-7.....VIII.4:8 a consistent model, it never developed c..
T-9..........I.2:3 to learn anything c. in a state of panic. If
T-9....... IV.5:6 steadily and c. cancelling out all its effects
T-9....... VI.2:1 the Holy Spirit does not produce joy c. in
T-9....... VI.2:1 because you do not c. arouse joy in others
T-12........I.6:8 in your divided state, His remain c. true.
T-12........I.8:1 the reactions of others more and more c.,
T-17.....V.11:7 Have you c. appreciated the good efforts,
T-30 ... VIII.4:3 miracle cannot come forth from you c..
W-pI .... 65.4:4 it c. for the purpose He shares with you.
M-22.........4:3 if ever c. applied to all specific forms of
P-3..........II.7:4 hold this understanding c. in his mind,

## consisting 1

W-pI .... 31.1:4 and the other c. of frequent applications

## consists 3

W-pI .... 61.2:3 Humility c. of accepting your role in
W-pI 183.11:4 universe c. of nothing but the Son of God,
M-3...........2:2 superficial. It c. of what seem to be very

## consolation 1

T-31..... IV.1:1 to think the world can offer c. and escape

## consolidated 1

M-4..... I.A.8:2 It is here that learning is c.. Now what

## consolidates 1

M-4..... I.A.6:3 Now he c. his learning. Now he begins to

## conspire 1

T-6....... IV.5:1 ego uses the body to c. against your mind,

## constancy 15

T-21 .. VII.11:4 for c. in your desire to see the real world,
T-21 .. VII.13:4 can be given only those who wish for c..
T-21 ... VIII.1:5 he valued the inconstant more than c..
T-21 ... VIII.2:1 The c. of joy is a condition quite alien to
T-21 ... VIII.2:3 The c. of happiness has no exceptions; no
T-21 ... VIII.2:7 so. Nothing has power to confound its c.,
T-31..... VI.2:7 For c. arises in the sight of those whose
T-31 .VIII.11:1 the light that shines beyond in perfect c..
W-pI .... 79.6:3 Perceiving the underlying c. in all the
W-pI .. 107.5:1 it harbors in its wings the gift of perfect c.
W-pI 151.11:3 the love beyond the hate, the c. in change,
W-pI .. 163.4:3 love and Heaven's perfect, changeless c..
W-pII . 239.1:4 loves His Son forever and with perfect c.,
M-23.........5:8 his eyes Christ's vision shines in perfect c.
S-2...........I.6:6 His c. remains in tranquil silence and in

## constant 43

T-3....... VI.5:6 of c. judgment is virtually intolerable. It is
T-4.......II.11:9 is immortal, and immortality is a c. state.
T-4...... VII.6:7 c. going out of His Love is blocked when
T-7.........V.7:5 True learning is c., and so vital in its

T-7 ... VIII.3:12 in c. activity in order not to recognize this
T-11 ....... V.9:2 but not its undoing, is the ego's c. effort,
T-12 ....... V.5:2 that you can progress only under c., clear-
T-13 .........I.8:9 time passes away, while immortality is c..
T-13 ...... XI.8:2 in which the sweet and c. communication
T-15 .... III.10:2 wills, knowing His Will is c. and at peace
T-17 ....... V.1:6 The holy relationship is a c. reminder of
T-20 ...... III.4:2 thread your timid way through c. dangers
T-21 ...... IV.2:7 this c. shout and frantic proclamation,
T-21 ... VII.10:5 But truth is c., and implies a state where
T-21 ... VII.13:2 Happiness must be c., because it is
T-21 ... VII.13:3 be perceived except through c. vision.
T-21 ... VII.13:4 And c. vision can be given only those who
T-21 ... VIII.1:7 it was the truth, and therefore must be c..
T-21 ... VIII.3:2 you desire you receive, and happiness is c.
T-21 ... VIII.5:3 the c. peace you could experience forever.
T-27 ....... II.9:4 c. sting of guilt he suffers serves to prove
T-27 ....... II.9:5 The c. pain they suffer demonstrates that
T-29 ....... II.6:4 although it seems to be in c. change. Yet
T-30 ....... V.3:5 so sure and c. he can barely stay and wait
T-30 ..... VII.3:1 Only a c. purpose can endow events with
T-30 ..... VII.3:7 Perception cannot be in c. flux, and make
T-31 ... VIII.7:1 the world uncertain, lonely, and in c. fear.
W-pI ..... 12.2:3 another involves a fairly c. time interval.
W-pI ..... 49.1:2 abides is in c. communication with God,
W-pI ..... 56.1:2 I am when I see myself as under c. attack?
W-pI ..... 66.2:1 ego does c. battle with the Holy Spirit on
W-pI ..... 66.2:2 So does it do c. battle with the Holy Spirit
W-pI ..... 92.8:1 The light of strength is c., sure as love,
W-pI ..... 96.1:2 induces feelings of acute and c. conflict,
W-pI ... 135.4:4 has such frailty that c. care and watchful,
W-pI ... 169.6:7 been at all. Eternity remains a c. state.
W-pI ... 169.9:2 irrelevant to what must be a c. state,
WpI .. rV.in4:5 never changes from Its c. state of union
W-pI .186.10:3 Who could be c. in his efforts, or direct
M-in .......... 1:6 emphasizes that teaching is a c. process; it
M-16 .......... 1:9 he keeps in c. contact with the Answer.
C-3 ............ 7:4 But Will is c., as the gift of God. And what
P-2 ........ IV.6:1 and thus in need of c. defense. Yet if such

## constantly 14

T-4 ........... I.6:7 I am c. being perceived as a teacher either
T-6 ........ I.11:4 and yours are c. engaged in justifying the
T-11 ..... V.15:1 to demonstrate it, and this it does c..
T-14. VIII.2:15 flows c. between the Father and the Son,
T-14 ....... X.5:3 and darkness sweep c. across your mind.
T-17 ...... IV.3:2 that, when truth calls to you, as it does c.,
T-30 ..... VII.1:3 For it cannot be that meaning changes c.,
W-pI ..... 49.1:4 laws. It is this part that is c. distracted,
W-pI ..... 51.5:2 I am c. trying to justify my thoughts. I am
W-pI ..... 51.5:3 I am c. trying to make them true. I make
W-pI ..... 71.2:3 the source of salvation is c. perceived as
W-pI ..... 88.3:4 I am c. tempted to make up other laws
W-pI.135.19:1 of sorrow, and with joy that c. increases,
P-3 ........... I.1:7 to assume that you are being called on c.

## constellation 3

T-8 ... VIII.1:13 never changes, so its c. is permanent. The
T-8 ..... VIII.2:2 perceived c. the body is seen as capable of
T-14 ...... III.9:5 and influencing a c. larger than anything

## constellations 1

T-8 ... VIII.1:12 separate and reassemble in different c..

## constitute 1

T-5 ......... V.6:7 Together they c. all the alternatives the

## constitutes 3

T-15 ......... I.1:3 His teaching until it c. all your learning.
T-29 ... VIII.3:1 that c. a gap between the Christ and what
P-2 ......... II.4:1 the awareness of God that c. a reasonable

## constructive 5

T-1 ....... VII.4:5 of what is to come to make c. use of it.
T-2 ......... V.5:4 and reinstating its purely c. powers, you
T-2 ......... V.5:5 the truth that their minds are similarly c.,
T-2 ........ VI.1:2 I have said already that only c. acts should
T-2 ..... VIII.4:2 is a process of separation in the c. sense,

## constructively 2

T-1 ......... I.15:2 to enable you to learn how to use time c..
T-6 ......... I.11:3 To use my experiences c., however, you

## constructs 1

W-pI ... 136.6:1 and thus c. illusions of a whole that is not

## consulting 1

M-29 ......... 5:5 you cannot say anything without c. Him?

## consuming 2

T-18 ... VII.4:11 the means are tedious and very time c.,
W-pI ... 161.7:5 is insatiable, c. everything its eyes behold,

## consummate 1

W-pII .... 14.4:4 them to share our peace and c. our joy.

## consummated 1

M-28 ......... 1:7 ends, for it is c. and surpassed with this. It

## contact 4

W-pI ..... 25.4:6 makes your c. with him meaningful or
W-pI.137.10:1 or those who seem to have no c. with you,
M-16 ......... 1:9 he keeps in constant c. with the Answer.
C-1 ............. 3:1 in c. with God through the Holy Spirit,

## contacts 1

M-3 ........... 1:5 plan includes very specific c. to be made

## contagion 1

T-27 ......... I.4:5 to everyone, and in c. do they seek to kill.

## contain 30

T-6 ........ IV.6:5 Your dreams c. many of the ego's symbols
T-6 ...... V.A.1:4 dies, because it cannot c. you who are life.
T-6 ...... V.B.3:6 the first lesson seems to c. a contradiction
T-7 ...... IX.2:10 It does not wish to c. God, but wills to
T-8 ..... VIII.2:1 to c. two voices fighting for its possession.
T-9 ......... V.3:1 and that anything they c. is meaningless.
T-11 ......... I.3:3 Can part of His Mind c. nothing? If your
T-16 ......... I.6:6 always c. some element of specialness.
T-16 ..... VII.4:2 is no fantasy that does not c. the dream of
T-17 .... IV.14:1 lightly framed, for time cannot c. eternity.
T-18 .... VI.13:4 really "lifted out" of it; it cannot c. you.
T19 ... IV.A.3:7 What you would still c. behind your little
T19 ... IV.A.4:5 It cannot c. the Will of God. Peace will
T-27 ...... VI.4:4 could c. what you believe it holds within.
T-29 ... VIII.8:5 might offer him a gift reality does not c..
T-31 ...... IV.6:3 learn to find a road the world does not c..
W-pI ..... 42.5:2 understanding some of your thoughts c..
W-pI ..... 98.6:1 every kind, and joy the world does not c..
W-pI ... 99.11:2 withstand the truth these mighty words c.
W-pI ... 105.4:5 adds by letting what cannot c. itself fulfill
W-pI ... 114.1:3 *No body can c. my spirit, nor impose on me a*
W-pI ... 124.4:5 Our minds c. His Thoughts; our eyes
W-pI ... 135.2:1 because it must c. what threatens you. A
WpI. rIV.in8:2 enough to see the gifts that they c. for you
W-pI.151.10:3 and teach the single lesson that they all c..
W-pI ... 167.4:3 take on qualities the source does not c.,
W-pI ... 192.3:6 behold the joyful sights their offerings c..
W-pI ... 197.8:2 created, you c. all things within your Self.
W-pI ... 198.6:3 His words c. all hope, all blessing and all
W-pII .246.1:3 that my awareness can c. my Father, or

## contained 15

*See also* self-contained

T-7 ........... I.3:4 outward simply because it cannot be c..
T-7 ...... IV.6:11 all meaning is c. by them and in them.
T-7 ........ IX.3:2 Its fullness cannot be c., any more than
T-11 ......... I.7:1 Love, and could any part of His Love be c.
T-11 ...... III.3:4 for your joy could no more be c. than His.
T-15 ........ II.2:5 His joy is not c. in time. His teaching is
T-15 ...... XI.9:2 for what is c. in you who welcome Him is
T19 .... IV.A.5:2 without this barrier, is every miracle c..
T19. IV.A.5:11 relationship to everyone c. in it as it was
T19 .... IV.B.8:5 will bring light to all the world, c. in you.
T-21 ......... I.8:3 and what is in it is no longer c. at all. The
T-27 ...... IV.5:4 to the questions of the world c. within the
W-pI ... 188.5:1 The peace of God can never be c.. Who
W-pI ... 195.2:3 to escape a prison that they thought c. no
S-1 ........... I.4:8 But still all little answers are c. in this.

## container 1

W-pII ... 11.3:2 aspect, making every part c. of the whole.

## contains 42

T-4 ....... II.4:11 That is because it c. a hint of recognition
T-11 ....... V.3:2 It c. the very contradiction in terms that
T-13 .... VIII.6:4 And every miracle you do c. them all, as
T-18 ....... I.13:1 to the most holy function this world c.. It
T19. IV.A.10:4 For love c. the end of guilt, as surely as
T19. IV.A.15:3 world c. no fear that you laid not upon it.
T19 .... IV.C.1:3 for it c. the third obstacle that peace must
T-23 ...... III.2:3 beautiful and gently given, still c. nothing
T-24 ..... VII.2:2 within your brother still c. all of creation,
T-29 ...... IV.5:1 role to every figure which the dream c..
W-in .......... 9:4 in applying the ideas the workbook c.,
W-pI ........ 4.4:1 thought by the central figure or event it c.
W-pI ........ 8.4:4 one by the central figure or theme it c.,
W-pI ..... 11.3:4 c. the foundation for the peace, relaxation
W-pI ..... 12.1:1 lies in the fact that it c. a correction for a
W-pI ..... 19.3:2 searched for the thoughts it c. at that time
W-pI ..... 19.3:3 terms of the central person or theme it c.,
W-pI ..... 23.1:1 The idea for today c. the only way out of
W-pI ..... 37.1:1 This idea c. the first glimmerings of your
W-pI ..... 71.8:1 idea, and realizing that it c. two parts,
W-pI ... 100.7:2 exercises with the thought today's idea c..
W-pI ... 128.2:3 mind this world c. is that you pass it by,
W-pI ... 132.9:1 it c. the firm foundation for today's idea.
W-pI ... 133.2:4 ideas for satisfactions which the world c..
W-pI.139.11:6 us, and how our Father's Love c. them all.
W-pI ... 161.4:2 Every mind c. all minds, for every mind is
W-pI ... 162.2:3 and no illusion which the dream c. that
W-pI ... 166.5:5 world c. is valueless before its magnitude.
W-pI ... 167.5:3 They can extend all that their source c.. In
W-pI ... 169.2:2 so opposite to everything the world c.,
W-pI.190.10:3 the lesson that c. all of salvation's power.
WpI rVI.in.2:2 lessons. Each c. the whole curriculum if
W-pII .243.2:3 *are one because each part c. Your memory,*
W-pII ..... 8.2:1 and sounds of battle which your world c..
W-pII ..... 8.5:3 is our goal, for it c. the memory of God.
W-pII .305.1:1 world c. no counterpart. Comparisons are
W-pII ... 10.2:1 on the world c. no condemnation. For it
W-pII ... 13.2:1 A miracle c. the gift of grace, for it is
W-pII .341.2:1 for it c. the Word of God to us. And in its
Wfl ........ in.4:2 which c. the memory of God, and points
M-13 .......... 8:9 The world c. it not. But learn this course
M-16 ......... 3:8 practice periods, which the workbook c.,

## contemplate 1

T-17 ....... V.5:6 two c. their relationship from the point of

## contemplation 3

T-18 ..... VII.4:9 Nor is a lifetime of c. and long periods of
T-18 ..... VII.5:7 comes at last into the mind given to c.; or

T-18.....VII.6:8 more than is given to a century of **c.**, or of

## contempt 1

M-15 .........3:1 with lack of appreciation and even **c.**; give

## content 112

• happiness
*meaning*

T-2....V.A.18:5 *I am c. to be wherever He wishes, knowing*
T-12....VIII.6:1 Son of God, be not **c.** with nothing! What
T-12....VIII.7:9 Him could never be **c.** without reality.
T-13...... III.8:7 real, and he will be **c.** only with his reality.
T-13...VII.15:3 **C.** yourself with what you will as surely
T-13....VIII.7:1 Be you **c.** with healing, for Christ's gift
T-14....... II.5:7 I said before, "Be not **c.** with nothing," for
T-14....... II.5:7 have believed that nothing could **c.** you. *It*
T-14.... III.11:3 Would you be **c.** with little, which is all
T-15...... III.1:1 Be not **c.** with littleness. But be sure you
T-15...... III.1:2 is, and why you could never be **c.** with it.
T-15...... III.1:5 the strange belief that littleness can **c.** you
T-15...... III.2:4 is no form of littleness that can ever **c.** you
T-15...... III.2:6 For you will be **c.** only in magnitude,
T-15...... III.3:4 Believe the little can **c.** you, and by
T-15.... III.4:10 His Son be **c.** with less than everything.
T-15.... III.4:11 For He is not **c.** without His Son, and His
T-15.... III.4:11 Son cannot be **c.** with less than his Father
T-15...... III.6:4 the belief that you can be **c.** with littleness
T-15...... III.6:5 a sense of magnitude that can **c.** them.
T-15...... III.9:1 holiness can **c.** you and give you peace?
T-15.... III.10:3 You will be **c.** with nothing but His Will.
T-15...... IV.2:7 His will **c.** you, and nothing else can bring
T-15..... VII.8:4 body is there to receive its sacrifice, it is **c.**
T-18...... IV.3:1 ask that you remain **c.** with littleness. But
T-18...... IV.3:2 But it does require that you be not **c.** with
T-18....VIII.7:7 all its happiness and deep **c.** to every part.
T-23...... II.18:9 be **c.** with an illusion that you are living?
T-24......... V.8:1 You who would be **c.** with specialness,
T-25.........I.3:1 think your mind will be **c.** and satisfied. It
T-26....... II.6:9 Spirit be **c.** until it is received by everyone
T-26....... VI.2:2 nor one with which he could remain **c.**.
T-26...VII.14:4 God's Son could never be **c.** with less than
T-26....VIII.7:6 And you seek to be **c.** with sighing, and
T-26....VIII.9:1 Be not **c.** with future happiness. It has no
T-27.........I.8:2 be reason to remain **c.** to seek for passing
T-29..VIII.9:11 But you will never be **c.** with being less.
T-29...... IX.9:1 you *are* fearful if you do not feel a deep **c.**,
T-30...... III.1:3 is **c.** for its expression in the terms of form
T-30.... III.2:11 be **c.** with small ideas and little things.
T-30.... III.5:11 Not in any form that would **c.** you not,
T-30....... V.9:8 What moment of **c.** has not been bought
T-31....VIII.9:5 call in vain, and in His certainty I rest **c.**.
W-pI.....77.3:5 sure that we will not **c.** ourselves with less
W-pI...133.9:1 but those who are **c.** to be deceived. Its
W-pI.155.12:4 offer less and still **c.** the holy Son of God?
W-pI...195.1:3 they try to be **c.** because another seems to
W-pII ...in.3:2 Yet we will not **c.** ourselves with simple
W-pII ..... 3.5:1 Let us not rest **c.** until the world has
W-pII .272.1:3 *Can dreams c. me? Can illusions bring me*
W-pII .272.2:2 the Sons of God, could be **c.** with dreams,
W-pII .273.1:2 we are **c.** and even more than satisfied to
W-pII .334.2:2 *Son can be c. with nothing less than this.*
M-16 ......... 1:4 understanding that it is true, he rests **c.**.
M-22 ......... 2:6 If the way seems long, let him be **c.**. He
M-25 ......... 1:6 and he will not be **c.** to be delayed by the
S-1 ........ IV.3:6 before that it is pitiful to be **c.** with less.
S-1 ......... V.2:5 hide in shame because it is **c.** with what it

## content 112

• meaning
*happiness*

T-1.........I.41:1 is the perceptual **c.** of miracles. They thus
T-1........ VI.4:3 In attitude, then, though not in **c.**, you
T-2....V.A.14:5 Being without substantial **c.**, it lends itself
T-3......... V.5:5 when method and **c.** are separated, it is
T-4....... VII.1:1 is clear that while the **c.** of any particular
T-4....... VII.7:4 revelation; its **c.** cannot be expressed,
T-7 .........II.2:6 However, the **c.** is different in this world,
T-8 .........II.3:8 that must be unconflicted, but also the **c.**.
T-9 ......... V.4:1 not matter and the **c.** has not changed. In
T-12 ...... V.4:4 of creation, but with your own **c.**. Yet
T-13 ...... V.1:4 the **c.** of individual illusions differs greatly
T-14 .......X.7:3 You are too bound to form, and not to **c.**.
T-14 .......X.7:4 What you consider **c.** is not content at all.
T-14 .......X.7:4 What you consider content is not **c.** at all.
T-14 .......X.8:1 The ego is incapable of understanding **c.**,
T-14 .......X.8:2 if the form is acceptable the **c.** must be.
T-14 .......X.8:8 they but study form with meaningless **c.**.
T-14 .......X.9:3 of **c.** makes a cohesive system impossible.
T-14 .......X.9:6 the ego can no longer defend its lack of **c.**.
T-16 .... V.12:1 seek for love in ritual, remember love is **c.**
T-16 .... V.12:2 take the place of God at the expense of **c.**.
T-16 .... V.12:4 the sign that form has triumphed over **c.**,
T-18 ....II.5:14 Their **c.** is the same. They are your protest
T-21 .. VII.11:1 In **c.** all the questions are the same. For
T-23 ....II.16:5 the emphasis on form and disregard of **c.**.
T-23 ....II.18:4 the form they take, with **c.** such as this?
T-23 ....II.18:6 they take, and do not recognize the **c.**. It
T-23 ....II.19:9 are but forms. Their **c.** is never true.
T-25 .......II.4:3 Take not the form for **c.**, for the form is
T-25 .......II.4:3 content, for the form is but a means for **c.**
T-25 ....... V.3:4 unchanged in **c.** in whatever form the call
T-25 .... VII.7:2 The **c.** is the same. The form is suited to
T-28 ........I.3:4 without the **c.** and the purposes for which
T-28 ........II.5:3 But for this change in **c.** of the dream, it
T-28 ........II.7:1 dream a dream, and that its **c.** is not true.
T-31 .... V.14:4 does not concern itself with **c.** of the mind
T-31 .... VII.2:3 in fearful form, with **c.** still concealed, to
W-pI.... 64.5:7 of form does not imply complexity of **c.**. It
W-pI..... 64.5:8 that any decision on earth can have a **c.**
W-pI..... 66.1:4 different, but their **c.** is completely one.
W-pI..... 66.4:4 recognize a common **c.** where it exists in
W-pI..... 69.4:1 try to let go of all the **c.** that generally
W-pI..... 79.5:2 varying forms and with such varied **c.**,
W-pI... 140.2:5 difference does the **c.** of a dream make in
W-pI... 193.3:5 They are the same in fundamental **c.**. It is
W-pI... 193.4:2 Yet that is the **c.** underneath the form. It
M-in .......... 3:3 Yet it is impossible not to use the **c.** of any
M-in .......... 3:4 this the verbal **c.** of your teaching is quite
M-1 ........... 3:4 But the **c.** of the course never changes. Its
M-18 ......... 1:8 Yet the dream of salvation has new **c.**. It is
M-23 ......... 7:5 curriculum, not because of **c.** differences,
C-3 ............ 3:3 the **c.** it is His Will that it be understood.
C-3 ............ 3:5 adapts itself to need; the **c.** is unchanging,
P-3..........II.6:6 of fear, which is the **c.** of all dreams. Yet

## contented 1

W-pI..... 40.3:5 *I am happy, peaceful, loving and c.*. Another

## contents 1

W-pI... 182.3:3 he makes, yet none **c.** his restless mind.

## context 7

T-2 .... VII.5:14 correction to be meaningful in this **c.**; "He
T-4 ...... VII.1:1 correction is more helpful in a specific **c.**.
T-4 ...... VII.4:5 glorious **c.** of its real relationship to you.
T-5 ..........I.4:8 The word "know" is proper in this **c.**,
T-16 .... V.10:3 the total **c.** in which it is thought to occur.
W-pI..... 34.6:2 you change your mind in any specific **c.**,
M-4 ........X.3:2 and eternal truth do not appear in this **c.**.

## contingency 2

T-20 ... IV.8:10 for it rests on certainty and not **c.**. It rests
T-20 ..... VI.1:2 If it were elsewhere it would rest on **c.**,

## continual 2

T-3 ........ V.7:7 Perception is a **c.** process of accepting and
S-1..........II.2:4 And prayer is as **c.** as life. Everyone prays

## continually 5

T-3 ......... V.4:1 fundamental question you **c.** ask yourself
T-4 .........II.6:6 **c.** preoccupied with the belief in scarcity
T-9 .........V.7:8 perception into sureness by **c.** extending
T-13 .......V.1:2 One is changeless but **c.** exchanged, being
T19 . IV.B.16:3 Its sad disciples chant the body's praise **c.**

## continuance 5

T-5 .........V.7:5 and maintained by guilt in its **c.**. Guilt is
T-7 ..... VI.3:10 This ensures its **c.** if you side with it, by
T-15 .... VII.9:3 and yet dedicated to the **c.** of loneliness,
T-22 ..... III.2:1 The ego's whole **c.** depends on its belief
W-pI .... 56.3:2 self-image in place, and guarantees its **c.**.

## continuation 1

W-pI .... 21.1:1 for today is obviously a **c.** and extension

## continue 38

T-1 ....... III.2:1 they will not **c.** to exist as separate states.
T-2 ..........I.3:3 to **c.** to believe what is not true unless you
T-2 ..........I.3:8 as long as you **c.** to project or miscreate. It
T-2 .....VIII.3:8 free and imprisoned will cannot but **c.**.
T-4 .........II.9:5 and will **c.** to exist after a temporary lapse
T-6 .........II.2:3 you **c.** to attack it because you continue to
T-6 .........II.2:3 it because you **c.** to keep it separated. By
T-8 ....... VI.1:2 gather in our brothers as we **c.** together.
T-8 .....VIII.2:7 that you will **c.** to hope it can yet offer you
T-11 .........V.8:5 then, can its existence **c.** if you realize that
T-14 ..... VI.3:1 **c.** to give imagined power to these strange
T-14 .......X.1:1 the knowledge of creation must **c.** forever.
T-15 ..... IX.2:1 Our task is but to **c.**, as fast as possible,
T-18 ... VIII.4:2 They merely **c.**, unaware that they are
T-29 .......V.7:4 for hate, and will **c.** in death's services.
T-30 ........I.9:1 feel, what could be easier than to **c.** with:
T-30 .... VII.7:5 Do not **c.** thus, my brother. We have one
W-pI .... 15.4:5 **c.** to look at each subject while you repeat
W-pI .... 34.4:1 **c.** to repeat the idea to yourself in an
W-pI .. 36.3:11 Then open your eyes, and **c.** as before.
W-pI .... 37.5:1 You may **c.** the practice period with your
W-pI .... 42.5:5 and then **c.** to look for related thoughts in
W-pI .... 53.4:5 Why should I **c.** to suffer from the effects
W-pI .... 65.6:2 Try, however, to **c.** a minute or so longer,
W-pI .... 67.4:2 need to **c.** adding other thoughts related
W-pI .... 71.3:3 ensures that the fruitless search will **c.**, for
W-pI .... 94.1:1 Today we **c.** with the one idea which
W-pI .... 95.9:3 allow a mistake to **c.** is to make additional
W-pI .. 101.1:1 we will **c.** with the theme of happiness.
W-pI .. 102.3:1 For several days we will **c.** to devote our
WpIrIII.in12:3 so great we will **c.** on more solid ground,
W-pII .... in.2:6 We will **c.** spending time with Him each
W-pII .... in.3:1 We will **c.** with a central thought for all
W-pII . 258.1:3 Shall we **c.** to allow God's grace to shine
W-ep ......... 4:5 He will **c.**. Now you walk with Him, as
W-ep ......... 6:2 In peace we will **c.** in His way, and trust
M-8 ........... 6:1 The body's eyes will **c.** to see differences.
S-1..........II.3:4 possible at this level to **c.** to ask for things

## continued 6

T-4 ....... III.3:2 **c.** existence depends on your continuing
T-4 ....... VI.1:7 other life has **c.** without interruption, and
T-31 ........I.4:3 You have **c.**, taking every step, however
W-pI .... 32.5:1 exercises are also to be **c.** during the day,
W-pII .. in.11:3 of them to be **c.** till the next is given you.
M-7 ........... 4:4 at first to be told that **c.** concern is attack.

## continues 11

T-5 ....... IV.2:5 Everything that **c.** has already been born.
T-5 .........V.2:2 is restored and therefore **c.** in creation.
T-11 ........I.3:6 It **c.** forever, however much it is denied.
T-18 ... VIII.6:1 Like to the sun and ocean your Self **c.**,
T-26 ..... III.3:5 only one **c.** past the gate where oneness is.
W-pI .... 26.8:3 anticipated outcomes for each situation **c.**
W-pI .. 104.1:1 Today's idea **c.** with the thought that joy
W-pI .. 167.9:4 the mind awakes, it but **c.** as it always was

M-in ..........1:6 day, and **c.** into sleeping thoughts as well.
M-19..........2:6 that rise to meet one as the journey **c.**, be
C-1.............4:3 Creation **c.** unabated because that is the

## continuing 10

T-4........III.3:2 existence depends on your **c.** belief in the
T-5........IV.2:4 Physical birth is not a beginning; it is a **c.**.
T-5.........V.8:1 The **c.** decision to remain separated is the
T-5.........V.8:1 only possible reason for **c.** guilt feelings.
T-17......III.8:1 the justification for entering into a **c.**,
T-17.......V.1:7 unholy relationship is a **c.** hymn of hate in
W-pI.....32.1:1 Today we are **c.** to develop the theme of
W-pI.....44.1:1 Today we are **c.** the idea for yesterday,
M-7............4:1 appearance of **c.** symptoms is a mistake in
M-16..........4:7 **c.** a minute or two after you begin to find

## continuity 20

T-4...........I.5:4 up to protect the **c.** of the system in which
T-5........VI.2:3 This is the ego's **c.**. It gives the ego a false
T-5........VI.2:6 offers you the **c.** of eternity in exchange.
T-13.........I.8:6 future in your mind to ensure the ego's **c.**.
T-13.........I.8:7 be punished, the ego's **c.** is guaranteed.
T-13.........I.8:8 Yet the guarantee of your **c.** is God's, not
T-13......IV.4:3 its **c.** by making the future like the past,
T-13......IV.8:2 own. The **c.** of past and future, under its
T-13......IV.8:2 so that no gap in its own **c.** can occur. Its
T-13......IV.8:3 Its **c.**, then, would keep you in time, while
T-13......VI.4:2 continuous, unless you force **c.** on them.
T-13......VI.4:6 destroy time's **c.** by breaking it into past,
T-13......VI.6:3 healing lies within it because its **c.** is real.
T-13......VI.6:7 **c.** is timeless and their communication is
T-13......VI.8:3 In timeless union with them is your **c.**,
T-17......III.5:6 This **c.** extends the present by increasing
T-20......VI.1:5 is one of perfect union and unbroken **c.**.
T-21.........I.8:5 Within it everything is joined in perfect **c.**
W-pI.135.16:4 past, without a **c.** of any old ideas and sick
W-pII..234.1:3 brief the interval there was no lapse in **c.**,

## continuous 10

T-2...........I.2:8 creation is freely given in one **c.** line, in
T-13......IV.4:4 them **c.** without an intervening present.
T-13......VI.4:2 Past, present and future are not **c.**, unless
T-13......VI.4:3 You can perceive them as **c.**, and make
T-13.....VI.13:6 **C.** with his Father, he has no past apart
T-15......IX.4:7 Yet your minds are already **c.**, and their
T-17... VIII.3:4 and **c.** means for establishing His purpose
T-18... VIII.6:5 whole, being **c.** with it and at one with it.
T-21......VI.5:5 there be that stands between what is **c.**?
T-30.........I.1:1 Decisions are **c.**. You do not always know

## continuum 1

T-4..... II.11:11 It is not a **c.**, nor is it understood by being

## contradict 18

T-1......... II.4:7 may appear to **c.** the statement "I and my
T-2........III.3:2 This may appear to **c.** free will because of
T-7........VI.7:8 not know, your thought seems to **c.** His,
T-8........VI.7:5 God does not **c.** Himself, and His Sons,
T-8........VI.7:5 are like Him, cannot **c.** themselves or Him
T-10.....V.14:8 both be real, because they **c.** each other. If
T-11...... I.11:4 so that nothing He gives can **c.** Him. You
T-14......XI.3:9 for if you do you **c.** the light, and thereby
T-22.......V.1:3 letting reason tell you that they **c.** reality.
W-pI.....26.2:5 be accepted together. They **c.** each other.
W-pI.....93.5:9 possess, when it would **c.** the Will of God
W-pI.151.13:4 clean ideas that do not **c.** the Will of God.
W-pI...152.2:7 for to do so is to **c.** the truth entirely.
W-pI...156.2:3 be true. It cannot **c.** itself, nor be in parts
W-pI...166.3:3 He must deny their presence, **c.** the truth,
W-pI...169.4:1 perhaps appeared to **c.** our statement that
W-pI...193.2:6 is He Who answers what His Son would **c.**
M-28........3:10 Nothing is left to **c.** the Word of God.

## contradicted 3

T-8........VI.7:4 It cannot be **c.** *by* thought. God does not
T-25.....VII.5:2 And one in which nothing is **c.** that would
T-27......III.2:4 is quickly **c.** by the half it cancelled out,

## contradicting 1

W-pII..257.1:2 one can serve **c.** goals and serve them well

## contradiction 28

T-3........VI.7:4 the ego makes involves a **c.** in terms,
T-4...........I.2:8 The ego *is* a **c.**. Your self and God's Self *are*
T-6......V.B.3:6 the first lesson seems to contain a **c.**, since
T-7.......V.5:10 The "fearful healer" is a **c.** in terms, and is
T-7........VI.9:8 perceiving in total **c.** to the Holy Spirit
T-8........VI.7:1 a **c.** in terms that actually means nothing.
T-8.....VII.14:6 accepted a learning goal in obvious **c.** to
T-9.........V.4:6 This is a **c.** even in the ego's terms, and
T-11.........I.5:1 The laws of the universe do not permit **c.**.
T-11.......V.3:2 very **c.** in terms that makes it meaningless
T-14......IX.2:2 because the **c.** can no longer stand. How
T-14......IX.2:3 long can **c.** stand when its impossible
T-14......IX.8:2 There is no **c.** in what holiness calls forth.
T-16........II.3:4 for it involves a **c.** of what miracles mean.
T-22......VI.3:5 The lack of **c.** makes the soft transition
T-26......III.3:3 And yet there is a **c.** here, in that the
T-27......III.1:2 it, and weakened power is a **c.** in ideas.
T-27......III.3:3 because it symbolized a **c.** that cancelled
W-pI...131.1:3 could succeed where **c.** is the setting of his
W-pI...138.1:3 **c.** is the way we make what we perceive,
W-pI...138.4:8 choose instead. There is no **c.** to the truth.
W-pI...139.8:3 you believe the **c.** that you know not what
W-pII......1.3:4 appear to pose a **c.** to its point of view.
M-27 .........2:7 **c.** reigns and opposites make endless war.
P-2.........II.2:2 one term without perceiving the **c.** at all.
S-1.........II.4:1 At this level also comes that curious **c.** in
S-1.........II.4:2 The **c.** lies not in the actual words, but
S-1.........II.5:4 Now it is no longer a **c.** in terms. It has

## contradictions 4

W-pI...131.7:2 God made no **c.**. What denies its own
W-pI...152.4:4 not seem to be but **c.** introduced by you.
W-pI...158.6:3 Here are all **c.** reconciled, for here the
W-pI...193.2:1 God sees no **c.**. Yet His Son believes he

## contradictory 16

*See also* self-contradictory

T-3........VI.7:4 the ego makes is incomplete and **c.**. This
T-7........III.2:7 That is so **c.** it is clearly impossible. It is
T-7.........V.7:8 of needing to learn a lesson that seems **c.**;
T-7......VI.8:11 two totally **c.** thought systems share truth
T-11.....V.13:3 **c.** approach of the ego to everything. The
T-11....VI.10:6 nothing **c.** to His Will is either great or
T-12.....VII.8:2 **c.** nature of the witnesses you perceive is
T-15.......I.4:12 using dissociation for holding its **c.** aims
T-22......III.1:1 its undoing, for reason and the ego are **c.**.
T-22......VI.2:3 This is a situation so **c.** and so impossible
W-pI.....24.6:2 recognize that many of your goals are **c.**,
W-pI.....42.7:2 nothing is included that is **c.** or irrelevant.
W-pI.....96.1:2 the **c.** aspects of this self-perception. You
M-21 .........1:5 the words and the prayer are **c.**;
P-2.........II.2:2 to join **c.** words into one term without
S-1...........I.2:3 answer. In prayer this is not **c.**. There are

## contradicts 12

T-7.........V.7:7 This in no way **c.** the changelessness of
T-25... VIII.5:7 one **c.** the other and denies that it is real.
T-27......III.1:7 opposite that **c.** the concept that it attacks
T-30.........I.3:4 because it **c.** what you perceive and so you
W-pI...131.9:3 himself, and **c.** what has no opposite. He
W-pI...132.7:4 be the truth, and yet it clearly **c.** the world
W-pI...152.7:1 think that God made chaos, **c.** His Will,
W-pI...163.6:5 **c.** one thought entirely can not be true,
W-pII..307.1:5 *and nothing* **c.** *the holy truth that I remain as*
W-pII..328.2:2 *I imagine* **c.** *what You would have me be. It is*

M-4........II.1:6 nothing you say that **c.** what you think or
M-20 .........6:3 There is no thought that **c.** His Will, yet

## contrary 15

T-6.........I.10:5 On the **c.**, by being able to hear the Holy
T-7....... X.3:10 On the **c.**, you will be gaining everything.
T-11....... V.5:3 nature. I said before that to will **c.** to God
T-12...... IV.1:2 never puts it this way; on the **c.**, everyone
T-13........II.2:4 On the **c.**, you associate it with a weird
T-15...... VI.4:3 On the **c.**, you are more inclined to regard
T-16...... IV.3:3 On the **c.**, it emphasizes the guilt outside
W-pI..... 13.1:5 On the **c.**, you will be particularly likely to
W-pI..... 44.6:2 whatever you may believe to the **c.**. God is
W-pI..... 65.7:1 in spite of your own foolish ideas to the **c.**
W-pI..... 72.4:2 On the **c.**, you are exclusively concerned
M-5 ...... III.1:7 On the **c.**, they believe that sickness has
M-10 .........2:7 On the **c.**, he puts himself in a position
P-2.........in.2:2 On the **c.**, such concepts mean little to
P-2..........II.7:3 On the **c.**, he listens patiently to each one,

## contrast 22

T-4.......VII.3:1 In **c.**, spirit reacts in the same way to
T-9.......VII.6:3 a point where sanity exists and *see the* **c.**.
T-9.......VII.6:4 by this **c.** can insanity be judged as insane
T-13.... XI.3:10 There is no darkness and there is no **c.**.
T-13...... XI.4:4 The Holy Spirit points quietly to the **c.**,
T-13...... XI.6:2 You have need of **c.** only here. Contrast
T-13...... XI.6:3 **C.** and differences are necessary teaching
T-13...... XI.6:7 For you will need no **c.** to help you realize
T-14........II.1:3 Holy Spirit cannot teach without this **c.**,
T-14........II.2:6 **c.** between what is true and what is not is
T-17.... IV.15:1 of light, in clear-cut and unmistakable **c.**,
T-17....... V.5:1 more slowly, for the **c.** would be obscured
T-20...... VI.2:1 Nothing can show the **c.** better than the
T-31..... VII.4:3 The **c.** is far greater than you think, for
T-31..... VII.5:5 and welcome the glad **c.** offered you. Hold
W-pI. 186.11:1 In lovely **c.**, certain as the sun's return
M-20 .........2:6 There is a **c.**, yes, between this thing and
M-20 .........2:7 strangely, it is not a **c.** of true differences.
M-20 .......2:10 The **c.** first perceived has merely gone.
M-20 .......3:10 initial **c.** stands out clear and apparent.
M-20 .........6:4 **c.** between His Will and yours but seemed
M-27 .........5:4 There is no point at which the **c.** between

## contrasts 2

T-31..... VII.1:4 For it must deal in **c.**, not in truth, which
M-8 ........... 1:2 and thousands of **c.** in which each thing

## contribute 4

T-7........ IV.3:8 Ultimately, then, they all **c.** to one result,
T-10...... III.6:4 not my merit that I **c.** to you but my love,
W-pI... 159.6:1 the things that can **c.** to your happiness.
W-pI... 166.1:4 back that can **c.** to your happiness. And

## contributes 3

T-24....... V.2:4 whole **c.** nothing to the parts to give them
W-pI..... 16.2:3 thought you have **c.** to truth or to illusion;
WpI rVI.in.2:5 as one, as each **c.** to the whole we learn.

## contribution 9

T-1.........I.42:1 A major **c.** of miracles is their strength in
T-6...........I.2:8 has a definite **c.** to make to your own life,
T-6...........I.6:6 which was part of my own teaching **c.**.
T-9......... V.7:4 only meaningful **c.** the healer can make is
T-18...... IV.7:4 that your **c.** and the Holy Spirit's are so
T-18...... IV.7:5 is a powerful **c.** to the truth, and makes it
T-31..... V.10:3 Is this your **c.**? Who is, then, the "you"
W-pI..... 28.7:2 value of them all in their **c.** to your seeing.
W-pI..... 71.8:1 parts, each making equal **c.** to the whole.

## contributions 2

T-1......... V.2:6 individual **c.** to the Sonship will no longer
P-1............. 1:4 **c.** an earthly therapist can provide. Yet

**contrive** 1

T-22......VI.2:1 to **c.** ways to achieve the body's freedom.

**contrived** 1

T-16..... V.15:4 thought system is a carefully **c.** learning

**contrives** 2

T-15.....VII.5:3 closely at the relationships the ego **c.**, and
T-27....VIII.4:2 in and out of places and events that it **c.**.

**control** 45
*See also* time-control

T-1...........I.5:2 They should not be under conscious **c.**.
T-1......... III.4:6 A guide does not **c.** but he does direct,
T-1......... V.5:5 tyrannous rather than Authoritative **c.**.
T-1.........VI.4:2 can never **c.** the effects of fear yourself,
T-1.......VII.3:4 is an attempt to **c.** reality according to
T-2........IV.2:8 in matter which the mind cannot **c.**. This
T-2........VI.1:1 something beyond your own **c.**. Yet I have
T-2........VI.1:3 My **c.** can take over everything that does
T-2........VI.1:5 Fear prevents me from giving you my **c.**.
T-2........VI.1:7 removes them from my **c.**, and makes you
T-2.......VII.4:1 **c.** fear because you yourself made it, and
T-2.......VII.4:1 in it seems to render it out of your **c.**. Yet
T-2.......VII.7:9 you that time and space are under my **c.**.
T-3........VI.4:2 to accept it, you have lost **c.** over it. This is
T-4......... V.1:4 **c.** rather than sanity to predominance.
T-5.......... II.7:2 not demand, because It does not seek **c.**.
T-10......IV.3:5 This means it is out of **c.**. To be out of
T-10......IV.3:6 To be out of **c.** is to be out of reason, and
T-12.........I.2:4 may then **c.** your reactions behaviorally,
T-12...... III.9:4 you have no **c.** over the world you made.
T-12...... III.9:9 where it is will you gain **c.** over it. For you
T-12.... III.9:10 For you do have **c.** over your mind, since
T-12....VIII.5:3 relinquished the insane desire to **c.** reality
T-12....VIII.5:4 **c.** yourself should hardly aspire to control
T-12....VIII.5:4 should hardly aspire to **c.** the universe.
T-13...... III.3:3 For you could not **c.** your joyous response
T-13........ X.3:7 outside themselves, beyond their own **c.**.
T-18........ II.4:5 For the dream of your ability to **c.** reality
T19... IV.D.7:4 things beyond you, forces you cannot **c.**,
T-21........ V.2:5 prey to forces far beyond your own **c.**,
T-21.....VII.9:3 You *have* **c.** of this. And if you choose to
T-26...VII.12:7 seem to be beyond you to **c.** or to prevent.
T-27....VIII.7:7 **c.** its actions nor its purpose nor its fate.
T-30......IV.2:3 broken his "**c.**" of what surrounds him.
T-31......IV.1:4 are in **c.** of outcomes of your choosing.
W-pI.....47.1:2 What can you predict or **c.**? What is there
W-pI.....56.1:4 to be at the mercy of a world I cannot **c.**.
WpI. rIII.in3:3 behind a cloak of situations you cannot **c.**
W-pI. 135.15:1 in setting up **c.** of future happenings. It
W-pI...136.5:1 defenses seem to be beyond your own **c.**.
W-pI...167.4:2 alternate because of causes you cannot **c.**,
Wi181-200 2:4 tight **c.** of what you see speaks for itself.
M-21 ......... 1:8 facilitating the exclusion, or at least the **c.**,
M-21 ......... 4:8 does not **c.** the direction of his speaking.
P-2......... V.1:3 that, to be safe, one must **c.** the unknown.

**controlled** 6
*See also* self-controlled

T-1........ III.8:4 the miracle should be **c.** by me because of
T-2.......... II.7:7 possibility cannot be **c.** except by miracles
T-2.........VI.1:4 Fear cannot be **c.** by me, but it can be self-
T-2.........VI.2:9 This is **c.** by me automatically as soon as
T-4.......VII.2:4 is **c.** by its need to protect itself, and it will
W-pI. 135.15:3 be **c.** by learning and experience obtained

**controlling** 3

T-1.........I.48:1 at your immediate disposal for **c.** time.
T-2........VI.3:1 pointless to believe that **c.** the outcome of
T-4........VI.3:8 ego by humbling it or **c.** it or punishing it.

**controls** 1

T-18 .....VII.3:4 Time **c.** it entirely, for sin is never wholly

**controversial** 4

M-24 ......... 4:3 Until then, they are likely to be merely **c.**.
C-in ........... 2:1 All terms are potentially **c.**, and those
C-in ........... 2:4 considerations as such are necessarily **c.**,
C-1 ............ 3:2 quotations because of its highly **c.** nature.

**controversies** 1

M-24 ......... 3:5 wisdom to add sectarian **c.** to his burdens

**controversy** 2

C-in ........... 2:1 and those who seek **c.** will find it. Yet
C-in ........... 2:3 must, however, be willing to overlook **c.**,

**convenience** 1

W-pI. 184.11:4 the world bestows on them but for **c.**, yet

**convenient** 1

W-pI..... 43.4:2 at the most **c.** and suitable time that

**converge** 2

T-6 .......II.11:6 with God, and lets your mind **c.** with His.
T-23 ........I.3:3 For your beliefs **c.** upon the body, the

**convergence** 1

T-6 ..........II.9:8 This **c.** seems to be far in the future only

**converges** 1

M-4 ......X.2:12 aim, at which all learning ultimately **c.**. It

**conversation** 1

W-pI..... 27.3:5 to do this, even if you are engaged in **c.**, or

**conversion** 1

M-in .......... 2:8 It is a method of **c.**. This is not done by

**convey** 5

T-22 ........I.5:4 your vision can **c.** to you what you can see
W-pI... 95.11:5 to feel the meaning that the words **c.**.
W-pI. 169.10:4 meaning can the words **c.** to those who
Wi181-200 2:3 briefly. Words alone can not **c.** the sense
W-pI. 183.11:6 height whatever words could possibly **c.**,

**conviction** 43

T-1 .........I.14:2 are convincing because they arise from **c.**.
T-1 .........I.14:3 Without **c.** they deteriorate into magic,
T-1 ........ III.1:9 Doing them will bring **c.** in the ability,
T-1 ........ III.1:9 **c.** comes through accomplishment. The
T-1 .... VII.3:10 The strength of your **c.** will then sustain
T-4 ...........I.1:3 they share their lessons **c.** will be lacking.
T-6 ........ III.4:7 in your mind through the **c.** of teaching it.
T-9 .....VIII.4:4 Yet the **c.** of reality will not remain with
T-11 .... V.13:5 with the **c.** that separation is salvation,
T-13 ..... IX.6:2 Son of God lies the **c.** of your own guilt. If
T-14 ..... III.3:4 **c.** born of the Love of God and of His Son:
T-14 ... III.12:2 Nothing can shake God's **c.** of the perfect
T-14 .. VII.3:10 certainty does not retain any **c.** of reality.
T-15 .........I.3:4 **c.** that it can pursue you beyond the grave
T-16 ..... III.3:3 to teach successfully wholly without **c.**,
T-16 ..... III.3:3 impossible that **c.** be outside of you. You
T-16 ..... III.6:8 learned from the **c.** you shared with them.
T-16 ...... V.9:2 The **c.** of littleness lies in every special
T-17 .... V.7:12 your faith emerge, to bring you shining **c.**.
T-18 ..... IV.3:3 your fixed **c.** that you are not worthy of it.
T-19 ........II.1:4 based on the firm **c.** that minds, not
T19 IV.D.21:6 still without **c.** they have a purpose. Yet it
T-24 .... VII.2:7 deep concern, the powerful **c.** this is you,
T-26 .....V.11:7 but lacks **c.** in what he perceives. This is
T-26 .. VII.12:3 Here is the firm **c.** that ideas can leave
T-27 .........I.4:1 belief because it brings **c.** in its wake. The
T-27 .........I.6:6 and lend **c.** to the system they speak for
T-27 ........V.2:2 as it is unattested, it remains without **c.**.
W-pI .... 24.2:2 of your **c.** that you do know what they are,
W-pI .... 80.2:2 to yourself today, with gratitude and **c.**.
W-pI .... 80.6:2 solved. Repeat the idea with deep **c.**, as
W-pI .... 92.1:5 that come from the **c.** you are a body, and
W-pI .. 93.11:7 much today to bring the **c.** to your mind
W-pI .... 98.7:2 idea the deep **c.** and the certainty you lack
W-pI .... 98.9:5 will have **c.** then of Him Who knows the
W-pI .. 151.5:3 as reality with such **c.** it does not believe.
W-pI .. 165.4:5 C. lies within it. Till you welcome it as
WpI.rV.in12:3 and recognize that it is only here **c.** lies.
W-pI .. 181.1:1 doubt and lack of sure **c.** in yourself.
W-pII . 327.2:4 *You give the means whereby* **c.** *comes, and*
M-5 .........I.1:5 in the mistaken **c.** that it is strength.
M-5 .........I.2:1 And what, in this insane **c.**, does healing
M-16 ......... 8:3 depends on his **c.** that he will succeed. He

**convince** 16

T-4 ..........I.5:3 is impossible to **c.** the ego of this, because
T-4 .........II.6:7 is only an attempt to **c.** itself that *it* is real.
T-4 ..... IV.10:8 trying to **c.** you that it is real and I am not,
T-4 ....... VI.3:2 The results will **c.** you increasingly that
T-7 .........II.5:5 the use of truth to **c.** His Sons of truth.
T-7 ....... XI.1:8 in miracles, you will **c.** yourself that, in
T-9 .........V.9:4 They will **c.** you that the words are true.
T-14 .... VII.3:1 possible to **c.** the unknowing that they
T-15 ........I.2:7 uses time to **c.** you of the inevitability of
T-16 .......II.4:5 It is impossible to **c.** you of the reality of
T-16 .......II.6:1 No evidence will **c.** you of the truth of
T-17 ........I.1:6 is impossible to **c.** the dreamer that this is
T19 . IV.B.15:4 And to **c.** you this is possible, it bids the
T-24 .......II.5:5 hear **c.** them they are different and apart;
W-pI .. 151.9:5 What could **c.** Him that your sins are real
M-in.......... 4:4 teaches solely to **c.** himself that he is what

**convinced** 14

T-4 ....... VI.3:7 but you are by no means **c.** as yet. The
T-11 .....V.16:5 those who are **c.** by it must be deluded.
T-12 .... VII.5:4 Of whose presence would you be **c.**? For
T-13 .......II.6:4 will become increasingly **c.** that this is so.
T-14 ... XI.15:3 must be **c.** you did them through Him. It
T-16 .......II.7:3 accomplished in a mind firmly **c.** that
T-18 ..... IV.7:5 You are still **c.** that your understanding is
T-21 .......II.5:3 and **c.** yourself that what it saw was true.
T-22 .......V.6:6 lightly, and so easily that you must be **c.**,
T-26 .....V.6:10 quite **c.** that where he would prefer to be,
T-27 .......II.6:3 so is he **c.** his innocence was never lost,
W-pI .... 69.5:4 be really **c.** of their lack of substance. We
W-pI .... 91.2:3 Thus you are **c.** it is not there. This
W-pI .... 91.3:2 It is very difficult to become **c.** that it is

**convinces** 2

T-11 .....V.18:2 him. Everyone **c.** you of what you want to
T-27 .....V.8:11 you see, **c.** you that they could not be real.

**convincing** 8

T-1 .........I.14:2 are **c.** because they arise from conviction.
T-4 ....... VI.3:3 chaos and disaster needs additional **c.**.
T-9 .........V.9:3 Its results are more **c.** than its words.
T-9 .....VIII.4:3 and because it is real it is compellingly **c.**.
T-17 ... IV.13:4 **c.** as you search it out amid its wrappings.
T-17 ... IV.14:3 eternity grows more **c.** as you look at it.
W-pI .... 72.5:4 reality makes this view of God quite **c.**. In
W-pI .. 151.1:6 And its defense seems strong, **c.**, and

**convolutions** 1

W-pI .. 189.6:4 the snares the foolish **c.** of the world's

**cooperate** 2

T-4......... II.5:5 agreed to c. in the effort to become both
WpI . rIII.in4:2 are unwilling to c. in practicing salvation

**cooperation** 6

T-1........ I.19:2 They depend on c. because the Sonship is
T-2... V.A.17:2 is the appeal for c. from miracle workers.
T-9........ I.11:8 because your c. is the law of its being. You
T-21....... V.2:1 Reality needs no c. from you to be itself.
W-pI.....20.1:2 active c. and interest have been asked.
W-pI.....23.5:3 two steps in this process require your c..

**cope** 1

M-24..........3:5 His ego will be enough for him to c. with,

**core** 11

T-16..... V.15:1 c. of the separation illusion lies simply in
T-29...... IV.3:4 veils the heavy lump of fear that is their c.
T-29.....IV.4:11 whether it succeeds or fails is not its c.,
T-29...... IV.5:3 c. of dreams the Holy Spirit gives is never
T-29....... V.8:1 the c. of fear in every dream that has been
W-pI.133.10:1 its tarnished edges and its rusted c.. His
W-pI...140.7:6 that have no substance, no reality, no c.,
W-pI...191.4:6 everything, the central c. of its existence
W-pI...192.5:4 the c. of anguish and the seat of fear?
M-29..........3:5 is the c. of the curriculum. The imagined
P-2........IV.9:4 is his central task; the c. of psychotherapy

**corner** 2

W-pI.......9.2:5 to lighten every c. of the mind that has
W-pI...190.6:6 a little c. of your mind its own inheritance

**corners** 1

W-pI.136.16:2 will be no dark c. sickness can conceal,

**cornerstone** 8

T-11.......in.2:7 in the dark c. of its thought system. And
T-11.......in.3:2 The c. of God's creation is you, for His
T-11.......in.3:9 the dark c. of terror on which it rests, and
T-11.......in.4:4 refuse it in order to keep a dark c. hidden,
T-13....... II.4:4 and deepest c. in the ego's foundation,
T-13....... III.1:9 could look even upon the ego's darkest c.
T-13.VII.10:12 a basic c. in the churches it builds to itself
T-14.....VII.2:7 Under each c. of fear on which you have

**cornerstones** 3

T-3.......VII.1:5 are c. for systems of belief by which one
T-13....... II.3:1 The darkest of your hidden c. holds your
M-9............1:8 and all dark c. of unforgiveness removed.

**corollary** 2

T-8..... VIII.7:7 But there is a c.; if only knowledge has
P-2......IV.10:6 This is the c. of the "original sin"; the

**correct** 60

T-1........ I.41:2 thus c., or atone for, the faulty perception
T-1........III.1:4 all errors that you could not otherwise c..
T-1........III.1:6 you must join the great crusade to c. it;
T-1........III.1:6 voice, learn to undo error and act to c. it.
T-1........III.9:4 by laws that govern the error it aims to c..
T-1........VI.2:1 God is the only lack you really need c..
T-1........VI.4:1 of this world is to use it to c. your unbelief
T-2........ II.1:13 not used to hide anything, but to c. error.
T-2......... II.3:9 The c. focus will shorten it immeasurably.
T-2......... II.6:2 c. your previous missteps by stepping
T-2... V.A.14:2 Only right-mindedness can c. in a way
T-2........VI.2:1 confusion, but you must choose to c. it.
T-2.......VII.7:7 already attempted to c. the fundamental
T-2..... VIII.1:1 One of the ways in which you can c. the
T-3...........I.2:6 the error itself is no harder to c. than any
T-3......... II.6:1 The way to c. distortions is to withdraw
T-3........IV.7:4 but to c. error from the bottom up. I
T-3......... V.9:2 C. perception of your brother is necessary
T-4...........I.4:7 I will c. it very gently and lead you back to
T-5...... III.11:4 C. and learn, and be open to learning.
T-6........ III.1:3 The word "knows" is c. here, because the
T-7......... II.2:1 c. perception in your brother and yourself
T-9........ III.2:1 good to point out errors and "c." them.
T-9........ III.2:4 When you c. a brother, you are telling
T-9........ III.6:1 *You* cannot c. yourself. Is it possible, then,
T-9........ III.6:2 Is it possible, then, for you to c. another?
T-9........ III.7:8 attempt you make to c. a brother means
T-9........ IV.2:3 can c. them without a Guide to correction
T-9......... V.5:7 c. because he is not working correctively.
T-12.........I.2:3 to your interpretations as if they were c..
T-12... VIII.4:3 vision will c. the perception of everything
T-13....... II.8:1 from guilt, and this is c. if it is understood
T-16....... V.3:4 is sin merely feel guilty, but do not c. it.
T-17..... V.15:1 and use them to c. all your mistakes and
T-19...... III.4:2 c. them all as God entrusted Him to do.
T-20... VIII.6:5 the body's eyes perceive, with power to c.
T-21...... IV.1:2 Errors He will c., but this makes no one
T-21...... VI.1:7 If it can c., and you allow it not to do so,
T-22.......I.11:7 indeed c. in looking on your brother as
T-25...... III.5:6 must the Maker of the world c. your error
T-25VIII.11:11 In justice, then, does love c. mistakes, but
T-26....... II.4:1 The miracle of justice can c. all errors.
T-27..... II.13:3 what you would c. is only half the error,
T-27..... II.15:2 it must c. mistakes in you and him. It
T-27... VIII.9:2 How else could He c. your error, who
T-28..... VII.2:6 could c. for separation but its opposite?
W-pI..... 13.2:4 and unreality. And on this alone it is c..
W-pI......107.h Truth will c. all errors in my mind.
W-pI...107.1:1 What can c. illusions but the truth? And
W-pI...107.6:9 dreams be gone. Let truth c. them all.
W-pI...107.9:1 Truth will c. all errors in your mind
W-pI...107.9:5 *Truth will c. all errors in my mind, And I will*
W-pI.107.11:2 "Truth will c. all errors in my mind," you
W-pI...119.1:1 (107) Truth will c. all errors in my mind. *I*
W-pI...119.3:2 Truth will c. all errors in my mind. On the
W-pI...121.5:3 sees bears witness that its judgment is c..
W-pI...161.4:6 sounds; pretty, perhaps, c. in sentiment,
W-pI...187.8:4 Your blessing will c. it. Given first to you,
W-pI...193.2:3 a need for One Who can c. his erring sight
M-22 .........5:6 unreal. Mistakes do not c. mistakes, and

**correctable** 1

T-19....... II.8:1 nothing more than a mistake, entirely c.,

**corrected** 59

T-1........VI.3:1 error of perceiving levels at all can be c..
T-1........VI.5:2 test, to that extent are your perceptions c.
T-2........IV.2:3 all mistakes must be c. at the level on
T-2......... V.8:2 nor can error be c. by any device that can
T-2........VI.6:9 can be c. only by accepting a unified goal.
T-3.......VII.6:3 your own thought system will stand c.. It
T-8...........IX.h Healing as C. Perception
T-9........IV.2:4 this Guide, your errors will not be c.. The
T-10........ V.6:2 Yet this can be c. and God will help you,
T-12... VIII.8:7 been. Being c. it gives place to knowledge,
T-14...... IX.2:1 it stands c. because it is the opposite of
T-14...... XI.9:7 would teach yourself He has c. already.
T-17...... III.5:9 separation must be c. where it was made.
T-18...... IX.1:2 told that error must be c. at its source.
T-19....... II.1:2 For error can be c., and the wrong made
T-19....... II.6:7 Any mistake can be c., if truth be left to
T-19..... II.6:13 to have faith that a mistake can be c..
T-19...... III.1:6 Sin is an idea of evil that cannot be c., and
T-19...... III.3:2 you see clearly as a mistake you want c..
T-19...... III.4:3 He recognize mistakes that cannot be c..
T-19...... III.4:4 a mistake that cannot be c. is meaningless
T-19...... III.5:6 error, yes, for this can be c. by the mind.
T19....IV.C.5:6 mad idea of corruption that can be c.. For
T-20...... III.5:9 seems to look back at you, it can be c..
T-20. VIII.10:7 that the errors which you made can be c..
T-21...... VI.6:1 the Son of God to what can never be c..
T-22...... III.2:5 you thought was uncorrectable can be c.,
T-22...... III.2:7 It looks on nothing that can be c.. Thus
T-22...... III.4:4 regardless of their form, can be c.. Sin is
T-22...... IV.5:1 make, the other will gently have c. for you
T-23........II.3:4 any kind can be c. *because* they are untrue.
T-25.........I.6:1 the aim of specialness can be c. where the
T-25...... III.4:2 C. error is the error's end. And thus has
T-25...... III.8:9 encroach, for sin has been c. by His sight.
T-25... VII.12:5 for all insane beliefs can be c. here. And
T-25...... IX.3:5 is unfair must be c. *because* it is unfair.
T-26........II.2:3 error in perception that now has been c..
T-26........II.5:1 be c. while you keep the others to yourself
T-26....... V.9:1 that has been so long ago c. and undone.
T-26..... V.10:3 instant in a distant past, now perfectly c.,
T-26..... VII.5:4 be c. where the illusion of reversal lies.
T-26... VII.12:1 consider what the error is, so it can be c.,
W-pI..... 54.1:5 rise before my eyes as I let my errors be c..
W-pI..... 91.8:2 thoughts about your attributes to be c.,
W-pI..... 95.7:5 it is; a refusal to let your mistake be c.,
W-pI... 107.5:3 Illusions can be brought to truth to be c..
W-pI. 107.10:3 that surround the world will be c. as you
W-pI. 107.10:3 be corrected as you let them be c. in your
W-pI... 134.2:1 view of what forgiveness means is easily c.
W-pI. 135.10:1 they have been c. and replaced with truth.
W-pI. 151.17:2 which Heaven has c. and made pure. Now
W-pII ... 10.1:3 this as true, projected from a now c. mind
W-pII ... 13.3:3 Perception stands c. in His sight, and
M-7 ........... 3:8 Thus is his doubt c.. He thought the gifts
M-7 ......... 3:11 it for what it is, and let it be c. for him.
M-9 ........... 1:7 many previous mistakes as possible are c..
M-17 ......... 3:1 to let error be c. where it is most apparent
M-18 ......... 4:1 of God to let all his own mistakes be c.. If
M-28 ......... 3:3 is wholly c. and all mistakes undone.

**correcting** 7

T-2.........I.5:12 of c. the conditions proceeding from lack
T-2........ III.1:5 is only the first step in c. this distortion,
T-2........ IV.2:3 as the means of c. level confusion, for all
T-2...... VI.5:10 C. at the behavioral level can shift the
T-4....... II.11:1 that c. perception is merely a temporary
W-pII . 346.1:1 *I wake today with miracles c. my perception*
M-22 ......... 4:5 c. all mistakes and healing all perception.

**Correction** 4

*correction*

T-5....... VII.4:3 God Himself gave you the perfect C. for
T-26....... V.3:5 one mistake, held also the C. for that one,
W-pII . 290.1:4 What I perceive without God's Own C. for
W-pII ... 10.3:1 of the C. He bestowed on all your errors,

**correction** 125

*Correction*

T-1.........I.37:1 a c. introduced into false thinking by me.
T-1.........I.49:2 It is a device for perception c., effective
T-1........ VI.3:1 requires c. at its own level before the error
T-1........ VI.3:3 c. must be introduced vertically from the
T-1....... VII.1:6 while c. of the error brings release from it.
T-2..........II.2:3 of denial is not a concealment but a c..
T-2......... V.1:6 it introduces c. at the level of the error. It
T-2......... V.1:7 and that c. belongs at the thought level.
T-2......... V.1:8 perfect and therefore does not require c..
T-2......... V.3:3 However, as a c., the miracle need not
T-2......... V.7:7 is merely channelized toward c..
T-2......... V.7:8 to bring the need for c. into awareness.
T-2......... V.8:3 your attempts at c. will be misdirected.
T-2.... V.A.12:2 on this fundamental c. in level perception.
T-2.... V.A.15:3 is an empty gesture unless it entails c..
T-2.... V.A.16:1 (6) Miracle-minded forgiveness is *only* c..
T-2........ VI.3:6 C. belongs only at the level where change
T-2........ VI.4:1 The c. of fear *is* your responsibility. When
T-2........ VI.4:8 The c. is always the same. Before you
T-2........ VI.7:3 the whole process of c. becomes nothing
T-2....... VII.5:8 an indication that immediate c. is needed.
T-2....... VII.5:14 slight c. to be meaningful in this context;
T-2....... VII.6:9 The c. of this error is the Atonement.
T-3........ III.4:1 sight, but it is still a c. rather than a fact.

T-3........IV.4:3 used as the **c.** for "wrong-mindedness,"
T-3........IV.6:8 cannot be an active process of **c.** because,
T-4.......VII.1:1 its **c.** is more helpful in a specific context.
T-7.....VII.11:2 This **c.** enables you to perceive any part of
T-9...........III.h The **C.** of Error
T-9........III.2:2 unaware of what errors are and what **c.** is.
T-9........III.2:3 and **c.** of errors lies in the relinquishment
T-9........III.2:8 He needs **c.** at another level, because his
T-9........III.4:4 This cannot be **c.**. Yet it is more than
T-9........III.4:5 it is more than merely a lack of **c.** for him.
T-9........III.4:6 him. It is the giving up of **c.** in yourself.
T-9........III.7:8 that you believe **c.** by you is possible, and
T-9........III.7:9 ego. **C.** is of God, Who does not know of
T-9........IV.2:3 can correct them without a Guide to **c.**.
T-12.......VI.4:1 **C.** is for all who cannot see. To open the
T-12......VII.4:9 other functions, so long will you need **c.**.
T-13......VII.9:4 Knowledge needs no **c.**. Yet the dreams of
T-16.......V.15:5 God offers you **c.** and complete escape
T-19.......II.1:6 Sin calls for punishment as error for **c.**,
T-19.......II.1:6 the belief that punishment *is* **c.** is clearly
T-19.......II.8:1 easily escaped from that its whole **c.** is like
T-19......III.4:5 Him. Mistakes are *for* **c.**, and they call for
T-19......III.5:4 And when **c.** is completed, time *is* eternity.
T-19......III.9:4 quickly recognized and quickly given to **c.**
T19..IV.B.11:9 And the **c.** of your mistake will give you
T-21......II.4:10 accept **c.** if it is willing to see that it was
T-21.......VI.1:1 sin but can see errors, and leads to their **c.**
T-21.......VI.1:2 It does not value *them*, but their **c.**. Reason
T-21.......VI.1:6 about the power that is in you to make **c.**.
T-21......VI.1:10 would not make way for **c.** in you alone.
T-21.......VI.2:1 **C.** cannot be accepted or refused by you
T-21.......VI.7:7 instant serves to bring complete **c.** of his
T-22.........I.4:6 Let not your fear of sin protect it from **c.**,
T-22.......III.2:2 see your errors and make way for their **c.**.
T-22.......III.2:4 sin and mistakes, because it wants **c.**.
T-22.......III.2:6 The ego's opposition to **c.** leads to its
T-22.......III.5:2 is a mistake, the form cannot prevent **c.**.
T-22.......III.9:7 mind, where both give errors gladly to **c.**,
T-23.......II.4:2 that errors call for punishment and not **c.**.
T-23.......II.4:3 him beyond **c.** and beyond forgiveness.
T-26..........II.h Many Forms; One **C.**
T-26.......II.3:1 This one mistake, in any form, has one **c.**.
T-26.......II.7:1 willing to receive **c.** for all your problems.
T-26.....VII.7:1 for it goes beyond **c.** to impossibility. Yet
T-26....VIII.4:8 And it is *this* that needs **c.**, not a future
T-26....VIII.6:1 working out of all **c.** takes no time at all.
T-27......II.10:1 **C.** is not your function. It belongs to One
T-27......II.10:4 No one can forgive until he learns **c.** is but
T-27......II.10:5 the same, and therefore is **c.** not of you.
T-27......II.11:3 **C.**, to a mind so split, must be a way to
T-27......II.11:4 he is more guilty, thus in need of your **c.**,
T-27......II.12:1 **C.** *you* would do must separate, because
T-27......II.12:2 you perceive **c.** is the same as pardon,
T-27......II.13:4 sins become the central target for **c.**, lest
T-27......II.14:1 In this interpretation of **c.**, your own
T-27......II.14:2 of **c.** has been placed outside yourself, on
T-27......II.15:1 **C.** is the function given both, but neither
T-27......II.16:1 **C.** must be left to One Who knows
T-27......II.16:1 knows **c.** and forgiveness are the same.
T-27......II.16:3 Leave, then, **c.** to the Mind that is united,
T-30......VI.5:6 eternal, and beyond **c.** or escape. There
W-pI.....10.3:1 This aspect of the **c.** process began with
W-pI.....11.1:1 related to a major phase of the **c.** process;
W-pI.....12.1:1 in the fact that it contains a **c.** for a major
W-pI.....47.6:1 is a necessary step in the **c.** of your errors,
W-pI.....91.6:9 you. The belief you are a body calls for **c.**,
W-pI.....95.9:2 This calls for **c.**, and for nothing else. To
W-pI...103.3:1 Allow this one **c.** to be placed within your
W-pI...108.5:2 saying one **c.** will suffice for all correction,
W-pI...108.5:2 saying one correction will suffice for all **c.**,
W-pI...110.2:1 need to let complete **c.** heal your mind,
W-pI...126.6:2 attack, without requiring **c.** in your mind.
W-pI.126.11:6 opening your mind to His **c.** and His Love
W-pI...131.4:5 When he is wrong, he finds **c.**. When he
W-pI...135.1:3 illusions, thus making **c.** doubly difficult.
W-pI...138.9:4 the mind had made before are open to **c.**,
WpI. rIV.in3:3 hold **c.** off through self-deceptions made
W-pI...187.8:3 that error has arisen and **c.** must be made.
W-pI...193.9:2 leave an unforgiving thought without **c.**,
W-pI...194.7:7 may be faulty, but will never lack **c.**. He is
W-pII.....8.2:1 a sure **c.** for the sights of fear and sounds
W-pII.....9.1:1 is sure as God, is merely the **c.** of mistakes
W-pII...13.1:1 A miracle is a **c.**. It does not create, nor
M-2...........2:4 the plan for this **c.** was established and
M-6...........1:4 teacher of God has seen the **c.** of his errors
M-8...........4:2 And it is here **c.** must be made. The mind
M-18............h HOW IS **C.** MADE?
M-18.........1:1 **C.** of a lasting nature,–and only this is
M-18.........1:1 a lasting nature,–and only this is true **c.**,
M-18.........3:6 **C.** has one answer to all this, and to the
M-18.........4:6 Atonement means **c.**, or the undoing of
M-19.........1:1 Justice is the divine **c.** for injustice.
M-19.........1:4 for error is impossible and **c.** meaningless
C-in...........1:2 with Atonement, or the **c.** of perception.
C-in...........1:5 To study the error itself does not lead to **c.**
C-4............3:2 The one **c.** possible for false perception
C-6............3:4 He is the great **c.** principle; the bringer of
P-2........IV.3:6 Healing is therapy or **c.**, and we have said
P-2........IV.7:1 Illness is therefore a mistake and needs **c.**
P-2........IV.7:2 **c.** cannot be achieved by first establishing
P-3..........II.4:8 strange dream a strange **c.** must enter, for

## correction's 1

T-27.....II.10:3 of guilt. If you assume **c.** role, you lose the

## corrective 10

T-2.........II.1:2 made it clear that miracles are natural, **c.**,
T-2........IV.4:4 use of such agents for **c.** purposes is evil.
T-2.........V.7:1 **C.** learning always begins with the
T-2.........V.8:2 What the physical eye sees is not **c.**, nor
T-2........VI.7:1 The first **c.** step in undoing the error is to
T-2.......VII.5:8 The initial **c.** procedure is to recognize
T-2.....VII.5:13 made this necessary as a **c.** device. The
T-9.........V.4:5 mind's **c.** power through the Holy Spirit is
W-pI.....99.1:2 for; something amiss that needs **c.** change
M-13.........1:5 illusion must be replaced by a **c.** device;

## correctively 1

T-9.........V.5:7 correct because he is not working **c.**. He

## correctly 20

T-1.........II.3:1 to which it is perfectly and **c.** applicable.
T-1........III.6:5 appropriately unless you perceive **c.**.
T-2..........I.4:7 is **c.** perceived as the release from the
T-3..........I.5:1 I have been **c.** referred to as "the lamb of
T-3..........I.5:2 **C.** understood, it is a very simple symbol
T-3........III.7:6 Perceive him **c.** so that you can know him.
T-3........IV.2:2 is **c.** identified as the domain of the ego.
T-3.........V.4:4 Yet you cannot perceive yourself **c.**. You
T-3.......VII.4:8 perceive **c.** you can only be glad that you
T-5........VI.4:3 the ego perceives is interpreted **c.**. Not
T-6........IV.1:4 It believes, and **c.**, that its maker may
T-7.....VII.11:1 and you have **c.** evaluated all of it. This
T-10.......IV.2:4 nothingness is merely to judge it **c.**, and
T-12.........I.9:7 own existence. By interpreting fear **c.** as a
T-12........I.10:6 the denial of union, and **c.** interpreted,
T-12........V.6:7 If they could interpret the aids **c.**, they
W-pI.....24.1:5 goal in any situation which is **c.** perceived
W-pI...44.10:1 If you are doing the exercises **c.**, you
P-1.............1:3 its causes and learn to evaluate them **c.**.
P-1.............2:6 psychotherapy, **c.** understood, teaches

## Corrector 1

T-25.......III.4:1 the simultaneous **C.** of the mad belief that

## corrects 14

T-1........IV.2:7 function of the mind and **c.** its errors,
T-2.........II.1:14 are the same, it **c.** error automatically.
T-2.........V.10:8 **c.** retroactively as well as progressively.
T-3........III.2:7 The miracle, or the right answer, **c.** them.
T-13......VII.9:3 for the Holy Spirit **c.** the world of dreams,
T-14.....XI.9:11 miracle He offers you **c.** your use of time,
T-19......III.9:3 the new perception the mind **c.** it when it
T-22......VI.5:3 accepted in your relationship **c.** the error,
W-pI..103.2:6 which **c.** the false belief that God is fear. It
W-pI..107.4:4 when truth **c.** the errors in your mind.
M-2...........2:2 forth. Atonement **c.** illusions, not truth.
M-2...........2:3 Therefore, it **c.** what never was. Further,
M-19.........1:3 Justice **c.** the interpretations to which
C-2............8:2 the miracle **c.** as gently as a loving mother

## corridors 1

T-14...VIII.3:1 mind wander not through darkened **c.**,

## corrupt 2

T-19.......II.7:5 he has somehow managed to **c.** his Father
W-pI..134.4:4 and smiles on the **c.** as if they were as

## corruptible 5

T19.IV.A.13:3 They have been taught to seek for the **c.**,
T19...IV.C.5:4 Of itself it is neither **c.** nor incorruptible.
W-pI..135.5:4 to the thief of time, **c.** and crumbling, so
W-pI..190.3:7 The body is the Son of God, **c.** in death, as
W-pII.294.1:3 Did God create the mortal and **c.**? What

## corruption 7

T-19.......II.6:5 and capable of complete **c.** and decay. If
T19...IV.C.4:2 they dedicated to death, a symbol of **c.**, a
T19...IV.C.5:6 tiny, mad idea of **c.** that can be corrected.
T19...IV.C.6:1 acceptance, the power to release from **c.**.
T-25.......II.6:8 way. What God creates is safe from all **c.**,
T-31.....VI.6:7 of **c.** and the stain of sin upon you? So the
W-pII.....4.3:4 He loves, with but **c.** to complete Himself,

## cost 67

T-2.....VI.9:11 the **c.** of perceiving the mind as impotent.
T-4.....III.10:4 then protect this belief at the **c.** of truth?
T-11.....V.10:3 not accept the **c.** of fear if you recognize it
T-11.....V.10:4 it. Yet this is the **c.**, and the ego cannot
T-12.....VI.1:4 investment, but the **c.** to you is enormous
T-12.....VI.5:2 Yet you must learn the **c.** of sleeping, and
T-14.....III.5:8 The **c.** of giving *is* receiving. Either it is a
T-14.....IX.1:5 for hiding it has **c.** you knowledge of Him
T-18.....VI.2:3 has **c.** you the awareness of Heaven and of
T19...IV.A.2:3 to be the **c.** you are so unwilling to pay?
T19.IV.B.4:12 This has no **c.**, but it has release from cost
T19.IV.B.4:12 This has no cost, but it has release from **c.**
T-20........I.4:1 Easter is not the celebration of the *c.* of sin
T-21........II.1:5 but rather that this little **c.** seemed, in
T-21....VII.1:2 powerless? Being helpless is the **c.** of sin.
T-22.......V.2:6 needs great defense, and at enormous **c.**.
T-22.......V.6:3 This is the **c.** of all illusions. Not one but
T-24.......II.2:1 of specialness is always at the **c.** of peace.
T-24.......II.6:5 This is the only "**c.**" of truth: You will no
T-24...VI.12:3 nor do you deem this **c.** too heavy. But a
T-24....VII.1:6 No effort is too great, no **c.** too much, no
T-25....VII.1:6 Yet each one knows the **c.** of sin is death.
T-25....VII.9:4 comes to understand it **c.** him his sanity,
T-25..VII.11:6 be the total **c.** of any gain at all. You who
T-25..VII.13:2 life, but life is not maintained at any **c.**.
T-25...VIII.3:5 death must be the **c.** and must be paid.
T-25...VIII.4:6 It is a payment offered for the **c.** of sin,
T-25...VIII.4:6 for the cost of sin, but not the total **c.**. The
T-25...VIII.4:9 And in the total **c.**, the greater his the less
T-25.VIII.11:1 cares not who pays the **c.** of sin, so it be
T-26.VIII.7:10 **c.** the Holy Spirit asks for what He gave
T-26.VIII.7:10 asks for what He gave without a **c.** at all.
T-26.......X.4:2 alone, and at the **c.** of someone else's guilt
T-27.......II.8:1 The "**c.**" of your serenity is his. This is the
T-27.....VI.2:3 pleasure, too, but only at the **c.** of pain."
T-29.......V.6:2 understand how great the **c.** of holding
T-30.......V.9:9 Joy has no **c.**. It is your sacred right, and
T-30.....V.9:12 from bitter **c.** and joyless consequence.
T-30.....V.10:4 *Not one was bought except at c. of pain, nor*
T-30.....V.10:6 that he will pay the **c.** as well as you. For
T-30...VIII.4:3 The **c.** of the belief there must be some

T-31......VI.2:7 from looking at the **c.** of keeping guilt,
W-pI.....27.2:3 *Vision has no **c.** to anyone.* If fear of loss still
W-pI.....52.4:5 I have chosen to see has **c.** me vision. Now
W-pI.....70.2:1 seeming **c.** of accepting today's idea is this
W-pI...101.3:2 Pain is the **c.** of sin, and suffering can
W-pI.135.14:2 its own protection, at the **c.** of truth. This
W-pI...155.8:4 There is no **c.**, but only gain. Illusion can
W-pII..323.1:2 *"**c.**" of restoration of Your memory to me,*
W-pII....12.4:1 its salvation, and the **c.** belief in it entails.
W-pII..343.2:2 Salvation has no **c.**. It is a gift that must
M-5........II.3:3 What does this recognition "**c.**"? It costs
M-10..........6:3 happily the instant he recognizes its **c.**.
M-13..........5:2 It is the **c.** of believing in illusions. It is the
M-13..........8:1 you make must mean in terms of **c.**.
M-13..........8:2 and everything is given you at no **c.** at all.
P-2.........in.2:6 but only at the **c.** of making illusions true.
P-3........III.2:6 is a difference between payment and **c.**.
P-3........III.2:7 where God's plan allots it has no **c.**. To
P-3........III.2:8 it rightfully belongs has enormous **c.**. The
P-3........III.3:4 must demand payment, and the **c.** is great
P-3........III.3:6 Holy Spirit's only dream, must have no **c.**.
P-3........III.4:7 There is no **c.** to either. But thanks are
P-3......III.6:10 Only in terms of **c.** could one have more.
P-3......III.6:11 everyone must gain a blessing without **c.**.
S-1........III.6:9 Think of the **c.**, and understand it well.
S-1......III.6:10 it well. All other goals are at the **c.** of God.

**costing** 2

T-11.......V.6:7 The belief in ego autonomy is **c.** you the
T-13.....VII.2:1 for sight of it is **c.** you a different kind of

**costliest** 1

W-pI...153.4:1 Defenses are the **c.** of all the prices which

**costs** 2

T-12......VI.1:5 investment **c.** you the world's reality by
M-5........II.3:4 It **c.** the whole world you see, for the

**could** 799

**counsel** 2

T-14....III.12:6 and leave all decisions to His gentle **c.**.
T-30......I.15:2 friend whose **c.** you have sought perceives

**counselors** 1

W-pII..266.1:1 *Sons, to be my saviors and my **c.** in sight; the*

**counsels** 2

T-15.....VII.4:5 It **c.**, therefore, that if you are host to it, it
T-17.......V.7:1 Now the ego **c.** thus; substitute for this

**count** 13

T-7.......VII.5:8 God, and **c.** yourself among them gladly.
T-11.......II.2:3 But be sure to **c.** yourself among them, for
T-28.......III.7:1 **C.**, then, the silver miracles and golden
T-28.....VII.3:4 and **c.** on it as shelter from the wind? The
T-31.......II.6:8 for in his progress do you **c.** your own.
W-pI.....97.4:2 and **c.** on Him Who promised to lay
W-pI...107.7:6 and **c.** on it to enter into all the exercises
W-pI.124.11:2 **C.** this half hour as your gift to God, in
W-pI...127.7:1 time beyond the **c.** of years to your release
W-pI...165.8:1 We **c.** on God, and not upon ourselves, to
W-pI.169.10:4 convey to those who **c.** the hours still, and
WpI..rV.in3:3 *the way, we **c.** upon Your sure remembering*
P-2.........V.6:3 and the therapist will **c.** as nothing, for

**counted** 6

T-7.........V.6:7 It is predictable because it can be **c.** on.
T-7.........V.6:8 on. Everything that is of God can be **c.** on,
T-7.........V.6:9 can be **c.** on because it is inspired by His
W-pI.....47.1:3 What is there in you that can be **c.** on?
W-pI...163.3:2 But death is **c.** on. For it will come with
M-4.....I.A.8:3 to be **c.** on in all "emergencies" as well as

**countenance** 3

T-11.....V.10:3 you may **c.** a false idea of independence,
T-13......III.1:4 that no one will **c.** fear if he recognizes it.
W-pI...134.6:2 It does not **c.** illusions, but collects them

**counter** 2

*See also* counter-attack, counter-dream

T-5......III.10:3 learner without going **c.** to his mind,
T-24.......II.2:8 and thus run **c.** to the Will of God. To

**counter-attack** 1

W-pI.....22.1:5 thoughts of attack and **c.** will preoccupy

**counter-dream** 1

W-pI...137.5:1 Healing might thus be called a **c.**, which

**counteract** 4

T-3........III.3:3 state that is usually an attempt to **c.** an
T-3........IV.7:4 not attempt to **c.** error with knowledge,
T-9.........V.5:1 way to **c.** fear is to reduce the importance
T-9.....VIII.2:3 It is an attempt to **c.** your littleness, based

**counterpart** 8

T-6.........II.7:2 The ego's perception has no **c.** in God,
T-10.......II.3:3 perceptual **c.** of creating in the Kingdom.
T-10.......III.6:3 in this world is the **c.** of value in Heaven.
T-20....VI.12:2 now to you than its unholy seeming **c.**,
W-pII......8.2:1 real world holds a **c.** for each unhappy
W-pII..305.1:1 changeless, that the world contains no **c.**.
S-1........III.1:5 thought that he *is* your enemy, your evil **c.**,
S-3...........I.5:1 between true healing and its faulty **c.**. The

**counters** 1

T-5......III.8:12 Holy Spirit **c.** this welcome by welcoming

**counting** 3

T-16.......V.3:2 for **c.** on the attraction of this offering,
T-27.....V.11:8 by merely **c.** up its separate parts. God
T-27...VII.15:4 about instead of **c.** up the hurts he gave.

**countless** 9

T-22....VI.10:6 mercy of **c.** attackers more powerful than
T-24......VI.7:2 Yet will you choose in **c.** situations, and
T-28.......V.5:8 and eyes perceive these **c.** fragments seen
T-30......IV.3:1 is not there is filled with toys in **c.** forms.
W-pI...128.1:2 years of misery, from **c.** disappointments,
W-pI...193.4:4 so very obvious that it appears in **c.** forms
W-pI...197.9:4 all the **c.** channels which extend this Self.
W-pII..233.2:4 it is a day of **c.** gifts and mercies unto us.
W-pII..241.1:6 This is the time of hope for **c.** millions.

**country** 1

C-6.............4:6 He seems to be a Guide through a far **c.**,

**counts** 1

T-31.....VII.1:6 he **c.** the "good" to pardon him the "bad."

**course** 125

- *A Course in Miracles*
  *curriculum*
  *direction*
  *of course*
  *See also* course-related

T-in...........1:1 *This is a **c.** in miracles. It is a required course*
T-in...........1:2 *It is a required **c.**. Only the time you take it is*
T-in...........1:6 *The **c.** does not aim at teaching the meaning*
T-in...........2:1 This **c.** can therefore be summed up very
T-1.......VII.4:1 This is a **c.** in mind training. All learning
T-1.......VII.4:3 Some of the later parts of the **c.** rest too
T-1.......VII.5:7 Some of the later steps in this **c.**, however,
T-2...........I.5:5 But remember the first principle in this **c.**;
T-2.......VII.1:6 direct opposition to the purpose of this **c.**.
T-3..........II.1:1 to in this **c.** are not matters of degree.
T-7......VIII.7:1 The whole purpose of this **c.** is to teach
T-8...........I.1:1 is not the motivation for learning this **c.**.
T-8........IX.8:1 to realize that this is a very practical **c.**,
T-9...........I.2:4 purpose of this **c.** is to help you remember
T-9...........I.2:4 must follow that you will not learn this **c.**.
T-9...........I.2:5 reason for the **c.** is that you do not know
T-9..........II.1:2 that are strictly in line with this **c.**. The
T-9..........II.1:3 that the **c.** does not mean what it says.
T-9..........II.1:4 remember, however, that the **c.** states,
T-9............V.9:1 **c.** offers a very direct and a very simple
T-11......VI.3:1 This **c.** is perfectly clear. If you do not see
T-11....VIII.1:1 This is a very simple **c.**. Perhaps you do
T-11....VIII.1:2 you do not feel you need a **c.** which, in the
T-11....VIII.5:1 You may complain that this **c.** is not
T-11....VIII.5:3 This is not a **c.** in the play of ideas, but in
T-12.......V.7:7 amounts to a **c.** in how to attack yourself.
T-13........II.6:4 with this **c.** stems ultimately from this
T-13........II.7:1 **c.** has explicitly stated that its goal for you
T-13........II.7:5 learning the **c.** you are protecting yourself
T-13......IV.1:1 are afraid of this **c.** should be apparent.
T-13......IV.1:2 For this is a **c.** on love, because it is about
T-14.....X.12:4 Earlier I said this **c.** will teach you how to
T-14......XI.4:1 hardly judge the truth and value of this **c.**.
T-15......IV.1:1 This **c.** is not beyond immediate learning,
T-15......IV.6:1 The reason this **c.** is simple is that truth is
T-16......III.4:1 This is a **c.** in how to know yourself. You
T-16.....V.16:1 not to listen to this **c.** and follow it is but
T-18.....VII.4:5 This **c.** does not attempt to teach more
T-18.....VII.6:4 special means this **c.** is using to save you
T-18.....VII.6:5 making use of the **c.** if you insist on using
T-18....IX.11:1 **c.** will lead to knowledge, but knowledge
T19....IV.C.6:2 first and fundamental principle in a **c.** on
T-20.....VII.1:3 **c.** has nothing in it that is not consistent.
T-20.....VII.1:7 This **c.** requires almost nothing of you. It
T-21.........I.3:5 the means by which this **c.** is learned will
T-21........II.1:1 how little is asked of you to learn this **c.**. It
T-21.....VII.7:8 choice. This is a **c.** in cause and not effect.
T-22.........I.6:1 **c.** alone is open to your understanding
T-22........II.6:1 This is a crucial period in this **c.**, for here
T-22........II.7:4 **c.** will be believed entirely or not at all.
T-22......III.2:1 on its belief you cannot learn this **c.**.
T-23........II.8:7 That is the function of this **c.**, which does
T-23......III.4:1 This **c.** is easy just because it makes no
T-24.......in.1:1 this **c.** is the attainment and the keeping
T-24.......in.2:1 To learn this **c.** requires willingness to
T-24.........I.8:6 oppose this **c.** because it teaches you you
T-24.....VII.8:1 **c.** makes no attempt to teach what cannot
T-25.....VII.2:8 God, this **c.** would not be difficult for you.
T-25......IX.5:4 means no one can lose is crucial to this **c.**.
T-26......III.5:4 is the learning goal this **c.** has set. It will
T-26.......V.1:2 Yet teaching that is what this **c.** is for.
T-26.....V.10:2 This **c.** will teach you only what is now. A
T-26.....VII.1:1 This is a **c.** in miracles. As such, the laws
T-26.....VII.1:2 the purpose of the **c.** can be accomplished
T-31......IV.7:3 to find this **c.** to be too difficult to learn,
T-31......IV.7:5 then is this **c.** impossible to learn. But
T-31......IV.8:3 **c.** attempts to teach no more than that the
T-31...VII.15:6 what but this is what this **c.** would teach?
W-in..........1:2 that will make the goal of the **c.** possible.
W-pI.....42.1:2 in your efforts to achieve the goal of the **c.**
W-pI.....42.8:1 that the goal of the **c.** is important to you,
W-pI.....94.5:9 the thought system which this **c.** sets forth
W-pI.....95.9:1 to comply with the requirements of this **c.**
W-pI...105.3:1 A major learning goal this **c.** has set is to
W-pI...126.1:1 reversal that this **c.** will bring about. If
W-pI...127.4:1 No **c.** whose purpose is to teach you to
W-pI...127.6:5 the largest single step this **c.** requests in
W-pI...132.6:3 central thought the **c.** attempts to teach.
W-pI...132.8:1 And some will find it in this **c.**, and in the
W-pI...133.2:3 This **c.** does not attempt to take from you
W-pI...134.1:2 this **c.** appear to rest salvation on a whim.

W-pI...138.5:4 to teach within the framework of this **c.**.
W-pI...165.7:6 This **c.** removes all doubts which you have
W-pI...167.3:7 emphasis this **c.** has placed on that idea is
W-pI...169.3:3 is not the goal this **c.** aspires to attain. Yet
WpI...rV.in1:5 and slowly on the road this **c.** sets forth.
WpI...rV.in5:4 **c.** was sent to open up the path of light to
Wi181-200 1:4 to following the way the **c.** sets forth.
W-pI...181.4:2 the goals this **c.** is advocating are from
W-pI...189.7:5 Forget this world, forget this **c.**, and come
W-pI...199.3:1 in this **c.** that you accept today's idea, and
W-pII ....in.1:5 we begin to reach the goal this **c.** has set,
W-ep ......... 1:1 This **c.** is a beginning, not an end. Your
M-in .......... 1:5 The **c.**, on the other hand, emphasizes
M-in .......... 2:5 purpose of the **c.** might be said to provide
M-1 ........... 3:2 The form of the **c.** varies greatly. So do the
M-1 ........... 3:4 But the content of the **c.** never changes.
M-2 ........... 2:1 the concept of time that the **c.** sets forth.
M-2 ........... 3:6 As the **c.** emphasizes, you are not free to
M-13 ......... 6:1 You may believe this **c.** requires sacrifice
M-13 ....... 8:10 But learn this **c.** and it is yours. God holds
M-16 ......... 3:7 learning within the framework of our **c.**.
M-16 ......... 4:1 This **c.** is always practical. It may be that
M-20 ......... 5:8 In this one sentence is our **c.** explained. In
M-23 ......... 7:1 **c.** has come from him because his words
M-24 ......... 3:4 Our **c.** is not concerned with any concept
M-24 ......... 3:6 his premature acceptance of the **c.** merely
M-24 ......... 4:1 that this **c.** aims at a complete reversal of
M-24 ......... 6:1 of this **c.** always remains the same;–it is
M-24 ....... 6:12 This is the sole criterion this **c.** requires.
M-25 ......... 2:1 powers that are clearly in line with this **c.**.
M-29 ......... 4:1 is the paradox often referred to in the **c.**.
M-29 ......... 5:7 with which this **c.** is most concerned. If
C-in ........... 1:1 is not a **c.** in philosophical speculation,
C-in ........... 1:6 this process of overlooking at which the **c.**
C-in ........... 2:6 experience toward which the **c.** is directed
C-in ........... 3:1 This **c.** remains within the ego framework
C-in ........... 3:5 The **c.** merely gives another answer, once
C-in ........... 3:8 *The* **c.** *is simple.* It has one function and one
C-in ........... 4:1 many answers that this **c.** does not give. It
C-in ........... 5:1 structural issues in the **c.** is brief and early
C-1............. 2:4 described in the **c.** *as if* it has two parts;
C-5............. 1:6 go beyond the names the **c.** itself employs.
C-6............. 2:1 is described throughout the **c.** as giving us

**course** 4
• curriculum
*A Course in Miracles*
*direction*
*of course*

M-1 ........... 3:1 There is a **c.** for every teacher of God. The
M-1 ........... 4:1 of a special form of the universal **c.**. There
M-2 ........... 5:7 same **c.** share one interest and one goal.
M-3 ........... 3:1 that levels of teaching the universal **c.** is a

**course** 17
• direction
*A Course in Miracles*
*curriculum*
*of course*

T-17....... V.4:5 no **c.** except to change the relationship to
T-18.........I.7:6 and swirling lightly off on a mad **c.** like
T-18.........I.8:5 Thus He reverses the **c.** of insanity and
T-18.........I.9:1 set the **c.** inward to the truth you share. In
T-18.... IX.13:2 there it calls to you to follow the **c.** it took,
T-24...VII.10:2 Its **c.** is sure, when seen through its own
T-28..... II.12:7 salvation will proceed to change the **c.** of
W-pI.....44.7:4 it. It is merely taking its natural **c.**. Try to
W-pI. 135.15:4 enough to let the mind direct its future **c.**.
W-pI....157.8:1 we will embark upon a **c.** you have not
W-pI. 169.12:1 **c.** it runs directed and its outcome sure.
W-pI. 193.12:4 everything that happened in its **c.** go with
W-pI....194.5:2 where it runs its pitiless, inevitable **c.**.
W-pII ... 11.2:4 not be changed throughout the **c.** of time,
W-ep ......... 2:3 possible to change the **c.** of those whom
M-7 ........... 2:4 teacher of God has only one **c.** to follow.
P-2........IV.3:1 hell follows step by step in an inevitable **c.**

**course** 16
• of course
*A Course in Miracles*
*curriculum*
*direction*

T-2 ..........I.4:2 Of **c.**, you neither can nor have been able
T-6 ..........I.3:5 This, of **c.**, is impossible, and must be
T-9 ....... IV.4:2 The ego's plan, of **c.**, makes no sense and
T-22 .........I.3:7 Your vision would, of **c.**, render this quite
W-pI....... 8.1:1 This idea is, of **c.**, the reason why you see
W-pI..... 14.1:1 The idea for today is, of **c.**, the reason
W-pI..... 14.7:1 The idea for today can, of **c.**, be applied
W-pI..... 36.4:2 All applications should, of **c.**, be made
W-pI..... 66.6:2 This could be false, of **c.**, but in order to
W-pI..... 71.1:4 This sounds preposterous, of **c.**. Yet after
WpI..rIII.in2:1 We understand, of **c.**, that it may be
M-4 ........... 1:5 Their specialness is, of **c.**, only temporary;
M-24 ......... 1:5 And that depends, of **c.**, on what it is used
M-25 ......... 1:2 There are, of **c.**, no "unnatural" powers,
M-27 ......... 6:2 Of **c.**! Without the idea of death there is
P-3..........II.1:9 These people need no special rules, of **c.**,

**course's** 1
M-13 ......... 6:2 Son, and it is the **c.** aim to set him free.

**course-related** 1
W-pI..... 42.5:2 amount of **c.** understanding some of your

**Court** 3
*court*
T-5 ....... VI.4:7 not appeal to the Higher **C.** because you
T-5 ..... VI.10:1 not fear the Higher **C.** will condemn you.
T-5 ..... VI.10:4 believe gladly to God's Own Higher **C.**,

**court** 1
*Court*
T-5 ....... VI.4:1 much as a higher **c.** has the power to

**court's** 1
T-5 ....... VI.4:1 reverse a lower **c.** decisions in this world.

**courtesy** 1
T-17 ...VIII.2:1 simple **c.** is all the Holy Spirit asks of you.

**covenant** 1
P-2......... VI.7:5 offer the mind of both a **c.** in which they

**cover** 31
T-1 ...... VII.1:1 produce a dense **c.** over miracle impulses,
T-4 ....... III.5:1 you will never want to **c.** or hide it again.
T-9 .....VIII.2:1 Grandiosity is always a **c.** for despair. It is
T-12 .......II.4:6 you are hiding your head under the **c.** of
T-13 ...... III.4:4 you have used the world to **c.** your love,
T-14 ..... IX.4:3 and **c.** all their sense of pain and loss with
T-15 .......X.6:7 but a **c.** for the one idea that hides behind
T-18 ..... III.1:8 Darkness can **c.** it, but cannot put it out.
T-19 ..... IV.1:4 Yet peace will gently **c.** them, extending
T-20 .......II.1:1 upon the body, or to **c.** it or for its use.
T-23 ......in.1:4 would use to **c.** frailty conceals it not, for
T-23 .....II.11:6 it in his body, making it the **c.** for his guilt
T-23 ..... III.1:5 and what form of murder serves to **c.** the
T-25 ..... IX.9:2 until they **c.** everything that you perceive
T-28 ..... III.5:3 the gap, and as the waves in joining **c.** it.
T-28 ...... V.7:3 and misty pictures rise to **c.** it with vague
T-29 ..... IV.5:4 changed because they **c.** something else.
W-pI..... 24.5:4 so on. Try to **c.** as many different kinds of
W-pI..... 26.8:2 much more helpful to **c.** a few situations
W-pI..... 45.6:6 thoughts that **c.** the truth in your mind,
W-pI..... 49.4:3 that **c.** your real thoughts and obscure
WpI... rI.in.1:2 will **c.** five of the ideas already presented,
WpI... rI.in.3:1 necessary to **c.** the comments that follow
WpI..rII.in.1:2 review left off, and **c.** two ideas each day.
W-pI........85.h Today's review will **c.** these ideas:
W-pI ....... 87.h Our review today will **c.** these ideas:
W-pI 140.12:4 feel salvation **c.** us with soft protection,
M-14 ......... 1:4 no one, limitless in gentleness, will **c.** it,
M-20 ....... 2:11 gone. Quiet has reached to **c.** everything.
C-2 ........... 9:2 brightness **c.** up the world the ego made.
P-2....... VII.4:5 his own failures, and guilt became the **c.**,

**covered** 9
T19 ...IV.A.9:3 sun upon a garden **c.** by the snow? See
T19 .IV.A.16:1 you, on a table **c.** with a spotless cloth, set
T-22 .......II.1:6 garments are those who seek illusions **c.**,
T-26 .... VII.1:3 us review the principles that we have **c.**,
T-28 ..... III.5:3 And **c.** just as fast, as water rushes in to
T-28 ..... III.5:4 and **c.** up the space which seemed to keep
W-pI ...... 4.2:3 thoughts, which are being **c.** up by them.
WpI... rI.in.6:4 the first fifty of the ideas we have **c.**, and
M-3 ........... 3:4 it. We have **c.** the illusion of time already,

**covering** 3
T-29 ... IV.4:11 fails is not its core, but just the flimsy **c.**.
W-pI .... 24.7:1 After **c.** the list of as many hoped-for
W-pI .. 188.1:2 who seek the light are merely **c.** their eyes.

**coverings** 2
T-18 ..... IX.4:4 Yet its intensity is veiled by its heavy **c.**,
T-29 ..... IV.5:4 The **c.** may not appear to change, but

**covers** 13
T-1 .........II.6:6 the time a miracle takes and the time it **c.**.
T-12 .......II.5:2 the **c.** and look at what you are afraid of.
T-13 ...... III.1:8 because you are more afraid of what it **c.**.
T-21 ........I.8:4 all. The light expands and **c.** everything,
T-25 ..... IV.3:5 them, and **c.** them in gentleness and light.
W-pI ....... 51.h review for today **c.** the following ideas:
W-pI ....... 52.h Today's review **c.** these ideas:
W-pI ....... 56.h Our review for today **c.** the following:
W-pI .... 92.7:1 itself, and darkness **c.** everything it sees,
W-pI 121.11:4 try to let this light extend until it **c.** him,
W-pI .. 168.4:3 you see a light that **c.** all the world in love,
W-pII . 222.1:4 He **c.** me with kindness and with care,
M-29 ......... 1:2 it **c.** only a few of the more obvious ones,

**covert** 1
W-pI .... 13.5:4 any signs of overt or **c.** fear which it may

**cower** 1
W-pI .. 166.8:1 **c.** fearfully lest you should feel Christ's

**cowering** 1
T-23 ..... III.6:4 You have not lingered there in **c.** hope

**cradles** 1
T-15 ..... XI.2:9 the Host Who **c.** God in the time of Christ

**crash** 1
W-pI .... 14.4:6 *God did not create that airplane* **c.**, *and so it*

**craves** 1
T-15 ........I.4:6 goal of death, which it **c.** for you, leaves it

**cravings** 1
W-pII . 251.1:6 In that all needs are satisfied, all **c.** end,

**crawls** 1
T-24 ...... III.4:4 that walks and breathes, or creeps or **c.**,

**crazy** 1
W-pI .... 12.3:2 *a sad world, a wicked world, a* **c.** *world,* and

## create 123

| | |
|---|---|
| T-1.V.1:8 | your potential. You did not **c.** yourself. |
| T-1.VII.2:1 | of God, you were created to **c.** the good, |
| T-2.I.1:2 | them with the same loving Will to **c.**. You |
| T-2.I.1:12 | you believe that you can **c.** yourself, and |
| T-2.IV.2:6 | The body cannot **c.**, and the belief that it |
| T-2.IV.2:10 | level of creation, cannot **c.** beyond itself, |
| T-2.IV.3:1 | Only the mind can **c.** because spirit has |
| T-2.V.1:7 | to remember that only the mind can **c.**, |
| T-2.V.1:10 | to errors of its own, because it cannot **c.**. |
| T-2.VIII.1:1 | to remember that you did not **c.** yourself. |
| T-2.VIII.1:3 | will to **c.** was given you by your Creator, |
| T-2.VIII.1:4 | everything you **c.** is necessarily a matter |
| T-3.I.3:3 | did not **c.** it and He does not maintain it. |
| T-3.I.3:5 | His Mind does not **c.** that way. He does |
| T-3.II.3:6 | only what God creates or what you **c.** with |
| T-3.III.7:8 | **c.** as He created you can create only what |
| T-3.III.7:8 | He created you can **c.** only what you know |
| T-3.IV.3:9 | that you did not and could not **c.** yourself. |
| T-3.IV.5:9 | it derives its whole power to make or **c.**. |
| T-3.V.2:1 | the words "**c.**" and "make" have become |
| T-3.V.7:3 | God did **c.** spirit in His Own Thought and |
| T-3.VII.4:12 | why you cannot **c.** and are filled with fear |
| T-4.I.7:8 | is never at stake because God did not **c.** it. |
| T-4.I.9:3 | You have chosen to **c.** unlike Him, and |
| T-4.II.8:10 | The creations of God do not **c.** myths, |
| T-4.III.1:5 | What else *but* you did the Creator **c.**, and |
| T-4.III.1:8 | ceased to **c.** because of the ego's illusions. |
| T-4.VII.5:6 | everything, since it can **c.** only like itself. |
| T-5.II.6:5 | choose is the same power as freedom to **c.** |
| T-5.IV.7:1 | healed mind, but the power to **c.** is of God |
| T-5.IV.7:4 | the only creator that can **c.** like the Father |
| T-5.V.2:1 | the Atonement, which releases you to **c.**. |
| T-5.V.2:2 | The word "**c.**" is appropriate here because |
| T-6.II.8:4 | God created you to **c.**. You cannot extend |
| T-6.V.B.8:8 | To desire wholly is to **c.**, and creating |
| T-6.V.C.5:2 | You **c.** by your true being, but what you |
| T-7.I.1:3 | share it, you are inspired to **c.** like God. |
| T-7.I.1:4 | He created you but you did not **c.** Him. I |
| T-7.I.3:3 | To **c.** is to love. Love extends outward |
| T-7.I.3:8 | because you can **c.** only as God creates. |
| T-7.I.4:5 | To will with God is to **c.** like Him. God |
| T-7.I.6:1 | **c.** like Him is to share the perfect Love He |
| T-7.II.3:9 | And His Sons, who **c.** like Him, follow it |
| T-7.V.2:2 | because it is also the impulse to **c.**, it can |
| T-7.V.2:2 | the body can both communicate and **c.**, |
| T-7.VI.1:5 | Fear and love make or **c.**, depending on |
| T-7.VI.12:3 | You cannot **c.** in this divided state, and |
| T-7.VIII.1:3 | the law by which you **c.** and were created. |
| T-7.IX.2:9 | Created by sharing, its will is to **c.**. It does |
| T-7.IX.3:6 | Unless you **c.** you *are* unfulfilled, but God |
| T-7.IX.3:6 | unfulfillment and therefore you must **c.**. |
| T-7.XI.6:4 | only the whole Sonship can **c.** like Him. |
| T-7.XI.6:5 | acknowledging his power to **c.** and yours. |
| T-8.VI.3:3 | What God and His Sons **c.** is eternal, and |
| T-8.VI.6:9 | His Will created you to **c.**. Your will was |
| T-8.VI.8:7 | and gave him the power to **c.** with Him. |
| T-9.I.13:5 | believe that fear is possible, you will not **c.** |
| T-9.III.8:4 | gave you the function to **c.** in eternity. |
| T-9.VI.4:2 | Therefore you can **c.** as He did, and your |
| T-9.VI.4:4 | Because the Sonship must **c.** as one, you |
| T-10.in.3:3 | gave you the power to **c.** for yourself so |
| T-10.I.4:1 | it wholly, for if to desire wholly is to **c.**, |
| T-10.III.9:5 | Yet you did not **c.** him, because he is not |
| T-10.IV.8:4 | will heal, but knowing the light will **c.**. |
| T-10.V.5:4 | because your Father did not **c.** them. You |
| T-10.V.5:6 | is sharing, it cannot **c.** what is unlike itself |
| T-10.V.13:1 | God did not **c.** or you are denying Him. |
| T-11.I.4:2 | creation or upon those who **c.** like Him. |
| T-11.I.7:7 | God wills to **c.**, and your will is His. It |
| T-11.I.7:8 | It follows, then, that you will to **c.**, since |
| T-11.III.3:4 | of your joy you will **c.** beauty in His Name |
| T-11.VII.3:7 | autonomy you tried to **c.** unlike your |
| T-13.VIII.9:2 | you the power to **c.** the witnesses to yours |
| T-14.I.4:4 | You were created only to **c.**, neither to see |
| T-14.VIII.5:1 | the power to **c.** can never be dissolved. |
| T-17.III.10:4 | They were created to **c.** with you. This is |
| T-17.IV.2:1 | In this world it is impossible to **c.**. Yet it *is* |
| T-18.IV.3:5 | did not **c.** His dwelling place unworthy of |
| T-18.VI.9:6 | God would have had to **c.** differently, and |
| T-18.VI.9:7 | He would have had to **c.** different things, |
| T-18.VI.10:5 | *He* a body, and did He **c.** you as He is not, |
| T-18.IX.10:2 | does make lovely, but it does not **c.**. It is |
| T-21.II.10:4 | of your desire to **c.** your own creator, and |
| T-21.II.11:1 | you recognize that you did not **c.** yourself. |
| T-21.II.12:4 | Apart from this he has no power to **c.**, |
| T-23.IV.2:8 | Can it **c.**, and be what it creates? And can |
| T-23.IV.3:2 | to **c.** unto His Son because it is His Own. |
| T-24.V.1:8 | makes real, as surely as does will **c.**. The |
| T-25.VII.4:10 | Who could **c.** the changeless if it does not |
| T-28.II.1:3 | Son. Effects do not **c.** their cause, but they |
| T-28.V.1:11 | Will with you, that His creation might **c.**. |
| T-29.III.4:1 | Make way for love, which you did not **c.**, |
| T-30.V.4:1 | but God Who could **c.** a perfect Son and |
| T-30.V.6:3 | Yet God need not **c.** His Son again, that |
| T-31.VII.12:5 | a wish, because it has no power to **c.**. Yet |
| W-pI.14.h | God did not **c.** a meaningless world. |
| W-pI.14.1:2 | What God did not **c.** does not exist. And |
| W-pI.14.4:3 | God did not **c.** it, and so it is not real. Say, |
| W-pI.14.4:5 | *God did not* **c.** *that war, and so it is not real.* |
| W-pI.14.4:6 | *God did not* **c.** *that airplane crash, and so it is* |
| W-pI.14.4:7 | *God did not* **c.** *that disaster [specify], and so* |
| W-pI.14.5:4 | do not say, "God did not **c.** illness," but, |
| W-pI.14.5:4 | illness," but, "God did not **c.** cancer," or |
| W-pI.14.6:5 | What God did not **c.** can only be in your |
| W-pI.14.6:8 | idea: *God did not* **c.** *a meaningless world.* |
| W-pI.14.7:4 | *God did not* **c.** *a meaningless world. He did* |
| W-pI.14.7:5 | *He did not* **c.** *[specify the situation which is* |
| W-pI.16.1:6 | Those that are true **c.** their own likeness. |
| W-pI.53.4:1 | (14) God did not **c.** a meaningless world. |
| W-pI.53.4:2 | world exist if God did not **c.** it? He is the |
| W-pI.73.3:3 | Did God **c.** disaster for His Son? Creation |
| W-pI.73.3:5 | Would God **c.** a world that kills Himself? |
| W-pI.84.2:4 | *Creator. My Creator did not* **c.** *this as I see it.* |
| W-pI.132.11:3 | Does it **c.** like Him? Unless it does, it is |
| W-pI.186.9:2 | He **c.** such instability and call it Son? He |
| W-pII.276.1:4 | the Word His Son did not **c.** with Him, |
| W-pII.294.1:3 | Did God **c.** the mortal and corruptible? |
| W-pII.11.2:3 | and must therefore share in power to **c.**. |
| W-pII.326.1:6 | *of God, and so I have the power to* **c.** *like You.* |
| W-pII.13.1:2 | It does not **c.**, nor really change at all. It |
| M-20.5:7 | an end, and nothing He did not **c.** is real. |
| M-22.5:5 | at all, for his Father did not **c.** bodies, and |
| C-4.1:2 | God did not **c.** it, for what He creates |

## created 598

*See also* God-created, re-created, self-created; Appendix C

| | |
|---|---|
| T-1.I.11:2 | communication of the **c.** with the Creator. |
| T-1.I.19:2 | the Sonship is the sum of all that God **c.**. |
| T-1.I.36:1 | your perceptions with truth as God **c.** it. |
| T-1.IV.3:7 | were given everything when you were **c.**, |
| T-1.VI.4:3 | faith in His creations *because* He **c.** them. |
| T-1.VII.2:1 | of God, you were **c.** to create the good, the |
| T-2.I.1:3 | You have not only been fully **c.**, but have |
| T-2.I.1:3 | fully created, but have also been **c.** perfect |
| T-2.I.1:9 | God **c.** can be changed by your own mind |
| T-2.I.2:3 | Everything God **c.** is like Him. Extension, |
| T-2.III.5:5 | It was **c.** perfect and is entirely worthy of |
| T-2.III.5:7 | on them *because* He **c.** them perfect. He |
| T-2.IV.3:1 | create because spirit has already been **c.**, |
| T-2.V.A.12:1 | what is **c.** and what is made is essential. |
| T-2.VIII.4:3 | what He had **c.** and knew that it was good |
| T-3.II.4:1 | which He **c.** in the likeness of His Own, to |
| T-3.III.7:8 | He **c.** you can create only what you know, |
| T-3.III.7:10 | **c.** them by knowing them. He recognizes |
| T-3.IV.1:8 | The levels **c.** by the separation cannot but |
| T-3.IV.3:1 | self, which was made rather than **c.**. It is |
| T-3.IV.5:11 | God **c.** and which is therefore eternal. |
| T-3.V.3:4 | you are perfectly stable as God **c.** you. In |
| T-3.V.7:1 | statement "God **c.** man in his own image |
| T-3.VI.8:9 | meaningful to believe that you **c.** yourself. |
| T-3.VII.3:8 | Yet God **c.** knowledge and gave it freely to |
| T-3.VII.6:11 | by all those for whom the Kingdom was **c.** |
| T-4.I.10:5 | of deception as is the spirit He **c.**. Release |
| T-4.III.1:7 | too, have a Kingdom that your spirit **c.**. It |
| T-4.III.7:6 | I can help you only as our Father **c.** us. I |
| T-4.IV.2:3 | wrongly about some brother God **c.**, and |
| T-4.IV.10:3 | I was **c.** like you in the First, and I have |
| T-4.IV.11:7 | of everything that the living God **c.**. Why |
| T-4.VI.7:4 | you are grateful to God for what He **c.**. |
| T-4.VII.3:3 | that what is true is everything that God **c.**. |
| T-4.VII.3:7 | God **c.** every mind by communicating His |
| T-4.VII.3:10 | God **c.** you by this and for this. The mind |
| T-4.VII.5:1 | all being, **c.** beings who have everything |
| T-4.VII.5:3 | sharing. That is why God **c.** you. Divine |
| T-4.VII.6:7 | He **c.** do not communicate fully with Him |
| T-5.I.1:8 | giving it, and thus creates as the Father **c.**. |
| T-5.II.9:1 | be like yours, because we were **c.** as equals |
| T-5.II.11:2 | it back into the oneness in which it was **c.**. |
| T-5.IV.1:5 | as an extension of God, you **c.** it with Him |
| T-5.IV.1:6 | as you are part of God because He **c.** you. |
| T-5.IV.1:8 | Nothing that is not good was ever **c.**, and |
| T-5.IV.4:3 | drawn to every mind **c.** by God, because |
| T-5.IV.6:5 | be to forsake myself and God Who **c.** me. |
| T-5.V.6:9 | God **c.** one, and so you cannot eradicate it |
| T-5.V.7:2 | because your thought was **c.** by Him. |
| T-5.VII.1:7 | power of His care for all those He **c.** by it. |
| T-5.VII.2:5 | learned that every mind God **c.** is equally |
| T-5.VII.2:5 | of being healed *because* God **c.** it whole. |
| T-5.VII.2:6 | to return to God the mind as He **c.** it. He |
| T-6.I.18:1 | the time, because they were **c.** as creators. |
| T-6.II.6:2 | put you, and God **c.** you as part of Him. |
| T-6.II.6:9 | Anything that God **c.** is as true as He is. |
| T-6.II.7:6 | everything was **c.** by Him and in Him. |
| T-6.II.8:1 | **c.** His Sons by extending His Thought, |
| T-6.II.8:4 | God **c.** you to create. You cannot extend |
| T-6.IV.2:1 | God **c.** you He made you part of Him. |
| T-6.IV.6:1 | His Kingdom, which He **c.** as part of Him. |
| T-6.IV.6:8 | all that you have **c.** there will have great |
| T-6.IV.9:2 | This is not true of anything that God **c.**, |
| T-6.IV.11:3 | everything God **c.** is faithful to His laws. |
| T-6.IV.11:9 | self you made with the truth He **c.** for you |
| T-6.IV.12:4 | at change, but God **c.** only the changeless. |
| T-6.V.B.6:3 | teaches you that truth was **c.** by God, and |
| T-6.V.B.8:8 | difficult if God Himself **c.** you as a creator |
| T-6.V.C.5:4 | are acknowledging your mind as God **c.** it |
| T-7.I.1:4 | He **c.** you but you did not create Him. I |
| T-7.I.2:1 | If you **c.** God and He created you, the |
| T-7.I.2:1 | If you created God and He **c.** you, the |
| T-7.I.2:6 | He **c.** the Sonship and you increase it. You |
| T-7.I.3:9 | is yours, because He **c.** you eternal. |
| T-7.I.5:2 | if God **c.** you by extending Himself as you |
| T-7.I.7:3 | last, because He **c.** first and for always. It |
| T-7.I.7:6 | Creator, because He **c.** His co-creators. |
| T-7.I.7:7 | applies neither to Him nor to what He **c.**. |
| T-7.I.7:10 | because it was forever **c.** to increase. If |
| T-7.I.7:12 | it is. You also do not know Who **c.** it. God |
| T-7.II.3:8 | God Himself **c.** the law by creating *by* it. |
| T-7.III.1:11 | I did. It was **c.** to be shared, and therefore |
| T-7.V.6:15 | Who **c.** you by sharing His Being with you |
| T-7.V.7:7 | the changelessness of mind as God **c.** it, |
| T-7.V.9:5 | love. That is how God Himself **c.** you; in |
| T-7.V.9:9 | which can only be **c.** as you were. The |
| T-7.V.10:2 | is to forget yourself and Him Who **c.** you. |
| T-7.V.10:4 | of me and of Him Who **c.** me. Through |
| T-7.VI.12:5 | with your Creator and creating as He **c.**. |
| T-7.VI.13:7 | extending the joy in which it was **c.**, and |
| T-7.VII.6:1 | whom God Himself **c.** worthy of honor, |
| T-7.VII.6:5 | But love everything He **c.**, of which you |
| T-7.VII.6:6 | honored all those who were **c.** like you. |
| T-7.VIII.1:3 | is the law by which you create and were **c.** |
| T-7.IX.1:4 | is of spirit because that is how God **c.** it. |
| T-7.IX.2:4 | Everything He **c.** is given all His power, |
| T-7.IX.2:9 | **C.** by sharing, its will is to create. It does |
| T-7.IX.5:3 | being **c.** for the Sonship as a whole. |
| T-7.XI.2:3 | **c.** for the environment that he has made. |
| T-7.XI.3:8 | It has been **c.** for you, as you were created |
| T-7.XI.3:8 | been created for you, as you were **c.** for it. |
| T-7.XI.6:1 | by which and for which you were **c.**. You |
| T-7.XI.6:3 | your brothers, who **c.** them with you. I |
| T-7.XI.6:8 | are denying yours and that of God Who **c.** |
| T-7.XI.7:8 | But you must also know all He **c.**, to know |
| T-8.II.6:6 | His Kingdom, because He **c.** you for this. |
| T-8.II.7:3 | it encompasses all things because it **c.** all |
| T-8.II.7:5 | of God because that is how you were **c.**. |

T-8 III.1:6 His teaching because He was **c.** to teach.
T-8 III.3:3 This is perfect creation by the perfectly **c.**,
T-8 IV.6:1 Nothing God **c.** can oppose your decision
T-8 IV.6:1 as nothing God **c.** can oppose His Will.
T-8 IV.7:8 me in praise of Him and you whom He **c.**.
T-8 VI.2:6 His creations, having **c.** them for eternity.
T-8 VI.3:2 No one **c.** by God can find joy in anything
T-8 VI.5:3 Trinity, **c.** in gratitude for your creation.
T-8 VI.5:6 of God and those that are **c.** like His?
T-8 VI.6:9 His Will **c.** you to create. Your will was
T-8 VI.6:10 Your will was not **c.** separate from His,
T-8 VI.8:7 That is why He **c.** His Son, and gave him
T-8 IX.6:4 mean to make nothing out of what God **c.**
T-9 I.8:8 cannot be given because it was never **c.**. It
T-9 I.8:9 It was never **c.**, because it was never your
T-9 I.11:9 and the laws of happiness were **c.** for you,
T-9 I.12:6 If you do not want it, it was never **c.**. If it
T-9 I.12:7 If it were never **c.**, it is nothing. Can you
T-9 I.13:1 to you **c.** you devoted to everything, and
T-9 I.13:2 *to.* Otherwise you would not have been **c.**
T-9 I.13:4 of reality is fearful, and fear cannot be **c.**.
T-9 II.6:10 Would God have **c.** a Voice for you alone?
T-9 III.8:1 everything because God **c.** everything. Do
T-9 IV.3:3 what you have made into what God **c.**. If
T-9 IV.9:3 that was made for you as the First was **c.**.
T-9 VI.3:9 Everyone God **c.** is part of you and shares
T-9 VI.4:1 is more than you only because He **c.** you,
T-9 VI.5:4 reality, as you were **c.** witnesses to God's.
T-9 VI.7:8 creations because he **c.** them with you.
T-9 VIII.4:8 is of God, Who **c.** it out of His Love.
T-9 VIII.8:5 to behold what He **c.** because it is His joy.
T-9 VIII.9:7 Yet what God has **c.** cannot be replaced.
T-9 VIII.10:8 accept yourself as God **c.** you cannot be
T-10 in.2:1 God **c.** nothing beside you and nothing
T-10 in.2:5 God's only creation and He **c.** you eternal
T-10 in.3:3 He **c.** you for Himself, but He gave you
T-10 I.1:1 to attack what you have **c.** is impossible.
T-10 I.1:4 of you. Everything that was **c.** is therefore
T-10 III.4:2 God **c.** love, not idolatry. All forms of
T-10 III.6:1 appreciation for everything that God **c.**,
T-10 IV.1:4 If God **c.** you perfect, you *are* perfect. If
T-10 IV.4:6 protected everything He **c.** by His laws.
T-10 IV.5:6 were **c.** through His laws and by His Will,
T-10 IV.6:7 Peace is yours because God **c.** you. And
T-10 IV.6:8 God created you. And He **c.** nothing else.
T-10 V.4:3 although he was a creator, he had been **c.**.
T-10 V.5:5 could have **c.** a Son who was unlike Him.
T-10 V.5:8 isolation, and so it could not have been **c.**.
T-10 V.7:6 The Love of God is in everything He **c.**,
T-10 V.9:5 If you will accept yourself as God **c.** you,
T-10 V.9:9 Your Father **c.** you wholly without sin,
T-10 V.11:2 to accept what had been **c.** for him, and
T-10 V.11:2 what he had **c.** in the Name of his Father.
T-10 V.11:3 was **c.** as the dwelling place of God's Son.
T-10 V.11:5 the joy that was **c.** for you for the misery
T-10 V.12:5 If God **c.** His Son perfect, that is how you
T-11 I.4:2 nor endings were **c.** by the Eternal, Who
T-11 I.4:3 because you have tried to limit what He **c.**
T-11 I.5:7 will to be alone, He **c.** a Son like Himself.
T-11 I.5:9 Son, for yours were **c.** in honor of Him.
T-11 I.9:8 What He **c.** can sleep, but cannot die.
T-11 III.4:6 of God, who was **c.** *of* light and *in* light.
T-11 IV.1:6 on what God **c.** as yourself without love.
T-11 IV.1:7 And since what He **c.** is part of Him, you
T-11 IV.3:3 because the light He **c.** is one with Him.
T-11 V.17:6 stand in His light and behold what He **c.**.
T-11 VI.4:9 nature of God's Son as his Father **c.** him.
T-11 VI.5:2 the god he made or the God Who **c.** him.
T-11 VII.1:1 it cannot have been **c.** by the Father, for
T-11 VII.1:2 it. God **c.** only the eternal, and everything
T-11 VII.4:6 what you have made and what God **c.**,
T-11 VII.4:6 what you have made and what *you* have **c.**.
T-11 VIII.7:6 He **c.** free and whose freedom is protected
T-11 VIII.9:4 Thought of His Father by which He was **c.**
T-12 II.9:3 in you in the peace out of which He was **c.**
T-12 VII.10:5 the perfect safety of the Mind which **c.** us.
T-12 VIII.2:5 and all its works were not **c.** by the Father
T-12 VIII.3:7 He **c.** it, and He knows what it is. You
T-13 I.5:7 God's Son will always be as he was **c.**.
T-13 I.6:6 Out of love he was **c.**, and in love he
T-13 VI.3:3 For if He is as He was **c.**, there is no guilt
T-13 VII.8:7 you, and by it God **c.** you as one with Him
T-13 VIII.6:5 Son, **c.** in the one reality that is his Father.
T-13 VIII.9:4 The miracle that God **c.** is perfect, as are
T-13 X.9:4 is the perfect purity in which you were **c.**.
T-13 X.12:6 Son, whom You have **c.** guiltless forever.
T-13 X.13:3 I love all that He **c.**, and all my faith and
T-13 X.14:5 See only praise of Him in what He has **c.**,
T-13 XI.11:6 was not **c.** for you and by you in return.
T-14 I.4:4 You were **c.** only to create, neither to see
T-14 III.12:2 the perfect purity of everything that He **c.**,
T-14 III.15:1 the worth of God's Son whom He **c.** holy,
T-14 III.15:8 from the loving Mind wherein he was **c.**,
T-14 IV.2:1 **c.** by Him like unto Himself and part of
T-14 IV.4:6 He **c.** you out of Himself, but still within
T-14 V.3:1 wholly blessing Father, joy was **c.** for you.
T-14 V.3:7 that is the right of all that God **c.**. Deny
T-14 V.8:3 circle is everyone whom God **c.** as His Son
T-14 V.9:10 Restore to God His Son as He **c.** him, by
T-14 VII.3:8 defined themselves as they were not **c.**.
T-14 VIII.4:7 Everything God **c.** knows its Creator. For
T-14 IX.1:2 holy. You were **c.** holy. It merely brings
T-14 IX.4:6 as holy as the Holiness by which it was **c.**.
T-14 IX.4:7 in everything that lives, for Holiness **c.** life
T-14 IX.4:7 life, and leaves not what It **c.** holy as Itself.
T-14 XI.11:6 that you have always **c.** like your Father.
T-15 II.1:10 at once. For as it was **c.** one, so its oneness
T-15 V.11:2 God has **c.** It beyond judgment, out of His
T-15 VII.14:10 you experience yourself as you were **c.**,
T-15 VIII.4:3 Nothing that ever was **c.** but is yours.
T-15 VIII.6:6 For God **c.** the only relationship that has
T-15 XI.9:4 Him, being host to Him Who **c.** them.
T-16 III.5:2 **C.** by God, He left neither God nor His
T-16 III.8:1 and for what He is Who **c.** you as you are.
T-16 IV.8:5 your creations were **c.** in union with them
T-16 IV.12:2 Him and **c.** by His joy in union with you.
T-16 VI.1:5 For God **c.** love as He would have it be,
T-16 VII.8:7 His Son will always be exactly as he was **c.**
T-16 VII.12:6 *the minds which You c. and which You love.*
T-17 II.1:8 for. He was **c.** to see this for you, until you
T-17 III.10:3 **c.** to enable you to hurt yourself through
T-17 III.10:4 They were **c.** to create with you. This is
T-17 IV.1:6 nothing God **c.** is apart from happiness,
T-17 IV.1:6 and nothing God **c.** but would extend
T-17 IV.4:2 ego did not understand what had been **c.**,
T-18 I.11:6 glad that your relationship is as it was **c.**.
T-18 IV.5:10 *His dwelling place in me c. it as He would*
T-18 VI.1:3 you. For God **c.** only this, and He did not
T-18 VI.5:5 God **c.** is only what He would have it be,
T-18 VIII.5:2 joined to the Thought by which it was **c.**.
T-18 VIII.6:6 life *is* the oneness in which its being was **c.**.
T-18 VIII.8:1 and reaches to everything **c.** like itself. Its
T-19 I.16:3 God **c.** as His Son is slave to nothing,
T-19 II.2:4 and making himself what God **c.** not.
T-19 II.4:3 of the Son of God as his Father **c.** him,
T-19 III.6:5 must have **c.** what wills to destroy Him,
T-19 III.7:5 prove what God **c.** holy could not prevail
T19 IV.C.3:3 is sure; God, Who **c.** neither sin nor death
T19 IV.C.8:1 He **c.** against the ego's savage wish to kill.
T19. IV.D.15:3 as God **c.** every living thing and loves it.
T19. IV.D.19:6 he is, and what his Father **c.** him to be.
T-20 III.11:7 Father as surely as God **c.** His Son holy,
T-20 IV.2:10 them power to enforce what God **c.** not.
T-20 VI.1:7 The one **c.** by his Father is wholly Self-
T-21 II.3:4 is possible within the universe as God **c.** it
T-21 II.11:3 Nothing **c.** not by your Creator has any
T-21 II.13:1 brother were both **c.** by a loving Father,
T-21 II.13:1 Father, Who **c.** you together and as one.
T-21 II.13:6 of the Source by which you were **c.**, and
T-22 II.13:6 of perfect purity, and God **c.** it for you.
T-22 V.4:7 this tiny mouse or everything that God **c.**
T-23 I.7:2 you. For you must be as God **c.** you. Truth
T-23 I.8:5 anything that God **c.** with anything but
T-23 II.19:2 Where God **c.** life, there life must be. In
T-23 IV.7:8 **c.** for His Son *because* it has no purpose.
T-24 I.4:1 What God **c.** cannot be attacked, for
T-24 I.7:1 friend because his Father **c.** him like you.
T-24 II.3:6 Oneness which **c.** them as one with Him.
T-24 II.14:5 the acceptance of yourself as God **c.** you.
T-24 III.2:5 You would protect what God **c.** not. And
T-24 VI.1:9 acknowledgment that He **c.** you as part of
T-24 VI.3:2 that God **c.** has He failed to lay before you
T-24 VI.3:6 Your brother *is* as He **c.** him. And it is this
T-24 VI.3:7 that saves you from a world that He **c.** not
T-24 VII.2:2 all of creation, everything **c.** and creating,
T-24 VII.5:1 The Father keeps what He **c.** safe. You
T-24 VII.5:2 you made, because it was **c.** not by you.
T-24 VII.7:2 must this Son have been **c.** like Himself. A
T-25 II.5:5 Yet what God has **c.** needs no frame, for
T-25 II.5:5 **c.** He supports and frames within Himself
T-25 II.10:8 Will. It was for this you were **c.**, and your
T-25 III.2:1 for such a world could not have been **c.** by
T-25 III.4:1 law itself upholds the universe as God **c.** it
T-25 IV.5:5 him for whom it was **c.** as his only home?
T-25 V.6:1 to save what He **c.** from the pain of hell.
T-25 VII.1:11 possible what God **c.** not should share the
T-25 VII.4:3 with the Mind Whose Thought **c.** him. So
T-26 II.8:2 to Him, and will forever be as He **c.** it.
T-26 II.8:6 He gave, when He **c.** you in perfect love.
T-26 IV.3:5 everything **c.** to the Source of its creation?
T-26 V.11:1 God **c.** is as free as God created him. He
T-26 V.11:1 God created is as free as God **c.** him. He
T-26 VII.11:3 guaranteed when He **c.** him *as* everything.
T-26 VII.13:2 been true: that He **c.** you as part of Him,
T-26 VII.15:8 His Kingdom is united; thus it was **c.**, and
T-26 VII.18:2 It is not arrogant to be as He **c.** you, nor
T-26 IX.8:1 as host again to Him by Whom it was **c.**.
T-27 VII.10:2 the body with the Self which God **c.**. Yet a
T-28 II.1:5 be a father, who creates as God **c.** him.
T-28 III.6:2 not destroy the alien will that He **c.** not.
T-28 V.5:1 What is there God **c.** to be sick? And
T-28 V.5:2 And what that He **c.** not can be? Let not
T-29 III.2:1 the Father lost Himself when He **c.** you?
T-29 III.3:1 a tiny spark, a space of light **c.** in the dark,
T-29 V.4:1 which he was **c.** and which still abides in
T-29 V.4:3 is. He was **c.** that you might be whole, for
T-29 V.4:3 a part of God's completion, which **c.** you.
T-29 V.6:3 to him, **c.** by his Father as His home? If
T-29 VIII.5:7 need belief to be itself, for it has been **c.**;
T-29 IX.2:1 the mind that God **c.** perfect as Himself.
T-30 II.1:8 your will, where everything **c.** is for you.
T-30 II.1:9 of life but was **c.** with your glad consent,
T-30 II.3:6 Remember Him Who has **c.** you, and
T-30 II.3:6 you, and through your will **c.** everything.
T-30 II.3:7 Not one **c.** thing but gives you thanks, for
T-30 III.5:5 not in him, he would not be as God **c.** him
T-30 V.1:5 understand all things **c.** as they really are.
T-31 I.9:5 He **c.** innocent could be a slave to guilt.
T-31 VI.3:11 the universe that God **c.** that must still be
T-31 VIII.3:4 from you whom God **c.** altar unto joy. He
T-31 VIII.3:7 He is the Self that God **c.** as His only Son.
T-31 VIII.5:2 *I am as God c. me. His Son can suffer nothing*
T-31 VIII.6:1 You *are* as God **c.** you, and so is every
W-pI 14.1:3 everything that does exist exists as He **c.** it
W-pI 38.3:1 If you are holy, so is everything God **c.**.
W-pI 38.3:2 are holy because all things He **c.** are holy.
W-pI 38.3:3 all things He **c.** are holy because you are.
W-pI 43.1:3 He has **c.** the Holy Spirit as the Mediator
W-pI 53.4:4 in my mind too, because He **c.** it with me.
W-pI 55.1:3 be what God **c.** for His beloved Son. The
W-pI 57.2:7 He is as God **c.** him, and not what I would
W-pI 61.1:6 It refers to you as you were **c.** by God. It
W-pI 67.h Love **c.** me like itself.
W-pI 67.2:3 *Holiness c. me holy. Kindness created me*
W-pI 67.2:4 *Kindness c. me kind. Helpfulness created*
W-pI 67.2:5 *kind. Helpfulness c. me helpful. Perfection*
W-pI 67.2:6 *Perfection c. me perfect.* Any attribute
W-pI 67.3:2 If love **c.** you like itself, this Self must be
W-pI 67.4:3 you recognize yourself as love **c.** you. Be
W-pI 67.5:3 remind yourself that love **c.** you like itself.
W-pI 67.6:4 Son of God. You were **c.** by love like itself.
W-pI 68.1:1 who were **c.** by love like itself can hold no
W-pI 68.2:4 holds grievances denies he was **c.** by love,
W-pI 68.3:1 it is certain that God **c.** them like Himself,
W-pI 72.12:1 of infinity, Who **c.** you like Himself: *What*
W-pI 73.3:2 Can such a world have been **c.** by the Will
W-pI 76.10:6 only Son, **c.** as His channel for creation;

W-pI.....84.1:1 (67) Love **c.** me like itself. I am in the
W-pI.....84.1:8 of my Creator. Love **c.** me like itself.
W-pI.....93.4:1 you are as pure and holy as you were **c.**,
W-pI.....93.6:5 touch it, or change what God **c.** as eternal
W-pI.....93.7:1 but one thought;–you are as God **c.** you,
W-pI.....93.7:2 may think you did, you are as God **c.** you.
W-pI.....93.7:6 and will forever be exactly as you were **c.**.
W-pI.....93.9:1 You are what God **c.** or what you made.
W-pI.....93.9:4 and the love from which It was **c.**. Try not
W-pI.....93.9:5 with the Self which God **c.** as you, by
W-pI........94.h I am as God **c.** me.
W-pI.....94.1:2 You are as God **c.** you. The sounds of this
W-pI.....94.2:2 If you remain as God **c.** you, you must be
W-pI.....94.2:4 You are as God **c.** you. Darkness cannot
W-pI.....94.2:6 in the sinlessness in which you were **c.**,
W-pI.....94.3:3 *I am as God* **c.** *me. I am His Son eternally.*
W-pI.....94.5:2 *I am as God* **c.** *me. I am His Son eternally.*
W-pI.....94.5:4 today that you are as God **c.** you. And be
W-pI.....94.5:6 *are as God* **c.** *you. You are His Son eternally.*
W-pI.....95.1:1 accurately describes you as God **c.** you.
W-pI...96.10:3 spirit in all things **c.** by the Spirit as Itself.
W-pI.....99.6:2 what is not **c.** by the only Source it knows.
W-pI...102.5:2 Whose Love **c.** him as loving as Himself.
W-pI...107.8:2 **c.** by the selfsame Thought which gave
W-pI......110.h I am as God **c.** me.
W-pI...110.1:3 what God **c.** was replaced by fear and evil,
W-pI...110.1:4 remain as God **c.** you fear has no meaning
W-pI...110.3:1 If you remain as God **c.** you, appearances
W-pI...110.3:2 not occurred, if you remain as God **c.** you.
W-pI...110.4:2 If you are as God **c.** you, then there has
W-pI...110.6:2 *I am as God* **c.** *me. His Son can suffer nothing*
W-pI...110.9:1 You are as God **c.** you. Today honor your
W-pI.110.11:4 *I am as God* **c.** *me.* Let us declare this truth
W-pI...112.2:1 (94) I am as God **c.** me. *I will remain*
W-pI...112.2:2 *as I was,* **c.** *by the Changeless like Himself.*
W-pI...112.3:4 me. On the half hour: I am as God **c.** me.
W-pI...114.1:3 *nor impose on me a limitation God* **c.** *not.*
W-pI...114.2:2 *has* **c.** *me for what I am and will forever be?*
W-pI...120.2:1 (110) I am as God **c.** me. *I am God's Son.*
W-pI...120.3:4 God. On the half hour: I am as God **c.** me.
W-pI...124.3:2 us with the equal love in which we were **c.**
W-pI...124.5:2 and peace of mind in which they were **c.**.
W-pI...125.4:3 holiness that He **c.** and will never leave.
W-pI...131.5:6 as certainly as God **c.** you in sinlessness.
W-pI...132.9:2 You are as God **c.** you. There is no place
W-pI...132.9:4 place exist, if you remain as God **c.** you?
W-pI.132.11:1 Yet if you are as God **c.** you, you cannot
W-pI.132.11:6 it was His Thought by which you were **c.**,
W-pI.132.14:5 And we who are as He **c.** us would loose
W-pI.132.15:2 *I who remain as God* **c.** *me would loose the*
W-pI.136.11:5 way. What is **c.** is apart from all of this.
W-pI.136.13:5 wills is here, and you remain as He **c.** you.
W-pI...139.1:2 a decision to accept ourselves as God **c.** us
W-pI.139.11:3 *for myself, For I remain as God* **c.** *me.* We
W-pI.139.11:4 God gave to us when He **c.** us like Him.
W-pI.139.12:4 *for myself, For I remain as God* **c.** *me.*
W-pI...151.9:2 the Mind Whose Thought **c.** your reality.
W-pI...152.5:1 **c.** you, you must remain unchangeable,
W-pI...152.7:3 And can you see what God **c.** not? To
W-pI...152.9:4 instead to Him Who has **c.** us immaculate
W-pI.152.11:4 *myself as what my Father's Will* **c.** *me to be.*
W-pI...153.9:1 no defense because we are **c.** unassailable,
W-pI...154.4:2 abolished in the mind that God **c.** sinless.
W-pI...154.4:3 mind becomes aware again of Who **c.** it,
W-pI...156.8:6 *and all the minds which God* **c.** *one with me.*
W-pI...158.1:2 unafraid, because you were **c.** out of love.
W-pI...158.1:3 left your Source, remaining as you were **c.**
W-pI...158.7:2 and mistake it for the Son whom God **c.**.
W-pI...159.3:3 what God **c.** perfect can be mirrored there
W-pI...160.4:3 Is fear His Own, **c.** in His likeness? Is it
W-pI...161.9:1 the angels love and God **c.** perfect. This is
W-pI......162.h I am as God **c.** me.
W-pI...162.6:3 You are as God **c.** you. These words dispel
W-pI...165.2:1 The Thought of God **c.** you. It left you
W-pI...167.1:3 condition in which all that God **c.** share.
W-pI...167.1:5 death because what God **c.** shares His life.
W-pI...167.7:2 such, it can be reconciled with what **c.** it,
W-pI...167.7:5 It is not its opposite in anything **c.**, nor in
W-pI.167.11:3 whom He **c.** in a unity of life that cannot
W-pI.167.12:1 in the holy minds which He **c.** perfect. As
W-pI...176.2:1 (162) I am as God **c.** me. God is but Love,
W-pI.185.12:1 For you was peace **c.**, given you by its
W-pI.185.14:1 sever, but which still remains as God **c.** it.
W-pI.189.10:7 *no beliefs of what we are, or Who* **c.** *us. Yours*
W-pI...190.2:5 not leave the Son whom It **c.** out of love.
W-pI...191.4:2 You are as God **c.** you. All else but this
W-pI...192.1:1 as He, of love **c.** and in love preserved,
W-pI...192.3:5 all. Yet God **c.** One Who has the power to
W-pI.192.10:7 He is as God **c.** him. And you are what he
W-pI...197.7:5 gratitude to all They have **c.** has no end,
W-pI...197.8:2 For as you were **c.**, you contain all things
W-pI...197.8:3 And you are still as God **c.** you. Nor can
W-pI...200.7:3 have reality, because it never was **c.**. Is it
WpI rVI.in.3:5 *For I am still as God* **c.** *me.* The day begins
W-pI......201.h I am free. For I am still as God **c.** me.
W-pI...201.1:6 I am free. For I am still as God **c.** me.
W-pI......202.h I am free. For I am still as God **c.** me.
W-pI...202.1:5 I am free. For I am still as God **c.** me.
W-pI......203.h I am free. For I am still as God **c.** me.
W-pI...203.1:5 I am free. For I am still as God **c.** me.
W-pI......204.h I am free. For I am still as God **c.** me.
W-pI...204.1:5 I am free. For I am still as God **c.** me.
W-pI......205.h I am free. For I am still as God **c.** me.
W-pI...205.1:6 I am free. For I am still as God **c.** me.
W-pI......206.h I am free. For I am still as God **c.** me.
W-pI...206.1:6 I am free. For I am still as God **c.** me.
W-pI......207.h I am free. For I am still as God **c.** me.
W-pI...207.1:6 I am free. For I am still as God **c.** me.
W-pI......208.h I am free. For I am still as God **c.** me.
W-pI...208.1:7 I am free. For I am still as God **c.** me.
W-pI......209.h I am free. For I am still as God **c.** me.
W-pI...209.1:2 *The Love of God is what* **c.** *me. The Love of*
W-pI...209.1:8 I am free. For I am still as God **c.** me.
W-pI......210.h I am free. For I am still as God **c.** me.
W-pI...210.1:8 I am free. For I am still as God **c.** me.
W-pI......211.h I am free. For I am still as God **c.** me.
W-pI...211.1:2 *to behold it in the Son whom He* **c.** *as my Self.*
W-pI...211.1:5 I am free. For I am still as God **c.** me.
W-pI......212.h I am free. For I am still as God **c.** me.
W-pI...212.1:7 I am free. For I am still as God **c.** me.
W-pI......213.h I am free. For I am still as God **c.** me.
W-pI...213.1:7 I am free. For I am still as God **c.** me.
W-pI......214.h I am free. For I am still as God **c.** me.
W-pI...214.1:8 I am free. For I am still as God **c.** me.
W-pI......215.h I am free. For I am still as God **c.** me.
W-pI...215.1:7 I am free. For I am still as God **c.** me.
W-pI......216.h I am free. For I am still as God **c.** me.
W-pI...216.1:7 I am free. For I am still as God **c.** me.
W-pI......217.h I am free. For I am still as God **c.** me.
W-pI...217.1:6 I am free. For I am still as God **c.** me.
W-pI......218.h I am free. For I am still as God **c.** me.
W-pI...218.1:6 I am free. For I am still as God **c.** me.
W-pI......219.h I am free. For I am still as God **c.** me.
W-pI...219.1:8 I am free. For I am still as God **c.** me.
W-pI......220.h I am free. For I am still as God **c.** me.
W-pI...220.1:6 I am free. For I am still as God **c.** me.
W-pII.....in.7:7 and the Son, Whose holy Will **c.** all that is
W-pII.....in.9:1 to have the Son whom He **c.** for Himself.
W-pII.....229.h Love, which **c.** me, is what I am.
W-pII..229.1:1 find It in these words: "Love, which **c.** me,
W-pII..230.1:1 peace I was **c.**. And in peace do I remain.
W-pII..230.1:4 when He **c.** me He gave me peace forever.
W-pII..230.2:4 *I am as You* **c.** *me. I need but call on You to*
W-pII..235.2:2 *Your Love* **c.** *me, and made my sinlessness*
W-pII.....237.h Now would I be as God **c.** me.
W-pII..238.1:2 *You* **c.** *me, and know me as I am. And yet You*
W-pII..238.2:2 how dear His Son, **c.** by His Love, remains
W-pII..239.1:4 constancy, knowing he is as He **c.** him?
W-pII..243.1:6 I look upon, to be in peace as God **c.** us.
W-pII..247.2:3 *Your Fatherhood* **c.** *them, and gave them all*
W-pII..248.1:8 I ready to accept him back as God **c.** him,
W-pII..248.2:2 *Father, I am as You* **c.** *me. Now is Your Love*
W-pII..249.2:3 *would we rest again in You, as You* **c.** *us.*
W-pII..253.1:6 abides with them and Him Who has **c.** me
W-pII..253.2:1 *You are the Self Whom You* **c.** *Son, creating*
W-pII..256.1:6 the holiness of him whom God **c.** sinless?
W-pII.....260.h Let me remember God **c.** me.
W-pII..260.1:2 *left my Source, remaining part of Who* **c.** *me*
W-pII .260.1:4 *today. Let me remember You* **c.** *me. Let me*
W-pII .261.2:3 *I choose to be as You* **c.** *me, and find the Son*
W-pII .261.2:3 *me, and find the Son whom You* **c.** *as my Self.*
W-pII .262.1:6 *Son must bear Your Name, for You* **c.** *him.*
W-pII .263.1:1 *Father, Your Mind* **c.** *all that is, Your Spirit*
W-pII .263.1:2 *upon what You* **c.** *as if it could be made sinful*
W-pII .267.1:1 me is all the life that God **c.** in His Love. It
W-pII .267.2:2 *is beating in the peace the Heart of Love* **c.**. *It*
W-pII .268.1:3 *from its unity, and thus to let it be as You* **c.** *it*
W-pII .268.1:4 *able, too, to recognize my Self as You* **c.** *me.*
W-pII .268.1:5 *me. In love was I* **c.**, *and in love will I remain*
W-pII .270.2:3 Him, the holy Son whom God **c.** whole;
W-pII .270.2:3 whole; the holy Son whom God **c.** One.
W-pII ..... 6.1:1 Christ is God's Son as He **c.** Him. He is
W-pII ..... 6.1:4 nor lost the innocence in which He was **c.**.
W-pII ..... 6.5:3 Self, the Christ Whom God **c.** as His Son.
W-pII .272.1:8 *safe. God's Son must be as You* **c.** *him.*
W-pII .274.1:1 *today I would let all things be as You* **c.** *them,*
W-pII .274.1:3 *and Your Son will know he is as You* **c.** *him.*
W-pII .276.1:3 of the Son He loves, for thus was he **c.**.
W-pII .276.1:6 Deny we were **c.** in His Love and we deny
W-pII .277.1:6 *He is as You* **c.** *him, because he knows no law*
W-pII .279.2:2 *Father loves the Son Whom He* **c.** *as His Own*
W-pII .280.1:1 Whom God **c.** limitless is free. I can
W-pII .280.2:2 *on the Son You love and You* **c.** *limitless. The*
W-pII .281.1:2 *who I am, and that I am as You* **c.** *me. Your*
W-pII .282.1:2 Himself, my Father and my Source, **c.** me.
W-pII .282.1:4 the Self Whom God **c.** as the Son He loves
W-pII .283.1:8 *Identity, when You* **c.** *everything that is?*
W-pII .283.2:1 only Source, and everything **c.** part of us.
W-pII .285.2:3 *Your Son is still as You* **c.** *him. My holiness is*
W-pII .287.2:6 *Your Son would be as You* **c.** *him. What way*
W-pII .288.1:3 *must recognize what You* **c.** *one with me. My*
W-pII .294.2:2 *what is not* **c.** *cannot be sinful nor sinless;*
W-pII .299.1:2 God, my Father, Who **c.** it, acknowledges
W-pII .299.2:6 *healed, for they remain as You* **c.** *them. And I*
W-pII .299.2:8 *For Holiness Itself* **c.** *me, and I can know my*
W-pII .302.1:4 *But we had forgot the Son whom You* **c.**.
W-pII .303.2:6 *He is my Self as You* **c.** *me. It is not Christ that*
W-pII .304.2:3 *of You, and of Your Son as You* **c.** *him.*
W-pII .307.1:5 *the holy truth that I remain as You* **c.** *me.*
W-pII .309.1:4 within is but to find my will as God **c.** it,
W-pII .311.2:3 *what he whom You* **c.** *as Your Son must be.*
W-pII .318.1:5 I was **c.** as the thing I seek. I am the goal
W-pII ... 11.1:3 no time when all that it **c.** was not there.
W-pII ... 11.1:4 when anything that it **c.** suffers any loss.
W-pII ... 11.4:6 to sanity, and to be but as God **c.** us.
W-pII .322.2:3 *As You* **c.** *me, I can give up nothing You gave*
W-pII .326.1:1 *Father, I was* **c.** *in Your Mind, a holy*
W-pII .326.1:3 *As You* **c.** *me I have remained. Where You*
W-pII .330.1:5 The Self which God **c.** cannot sin, and
W-pII ... 12.5:2 the holy minds which God **c.** as His Son,
W-pII .335.2:2 *reminds me that he was* **c.** *one with me, and*
W-pII .337.1:6 accept my Self, my sinlessness, **c.** for me,
W-pII .337.2:1 **c.** *me in sinlessness are not mistaken about*
W-pII .343.1:5 *And You* **c.** *me to be like You, so sacrifice*
W-pII .343.1:8 *As I was* **c.** *I remain. Your Son can make no*
W-pII .346.1:7 *I would find the peace which You* **c.** *for Your*
W-pII .348.1:8 **c.** *me in holiness as perfect as Your Own?*
W-pII .350.1:2 *all things within himself as You* **c.** *him. Your*
W-pII .354.1:6 *who is Christ except Your Son as You* **c.** *Him*
W-pII .359.1:4 *You* **c.** *sinless so abides forever and forever.*
W-pII .360.1:2 *I am Your Son, forever just as You* **c.** *me, for*
W-pII .360.1:5 *In holiness were we* **c.**, *and in holiness do we*
M-4 ...... VI.1:4 from their understanding Who **c.** them.
M-4 ...... VI.1:5 And does what God **c.** need defense? No
M-5 ...... III.3:4 himself, and must remain as God **c.** him.
M-12 ......... 1:9 is forever one, because he is as God **c.** him
M-18 ......... 2:4 unchangeable condition of all that God **c.**
M-20 ......... 5:7 that God **c.** cannot have an end, and
M-22 ......... 4:8 It is true of all things that God **c.**. In it are
M-22 ......... 7:8 Son of God, accepting him as God **c.** him.
M-22 ....... 7:10 my beloved Son, **c.** perfect and forever so.
M-23 ......... 2:6 He has recognized himself as God **c.** him,
M-27 ......... 2:1 perception of the universe as God **c.** it, it
M-27 ......... 5:2 And if God **c.** bodies, death would indeed
M-27 ....... 6:10 and in Him all **c.** things must be eternal.
M-28 ......... 5:8 is. As God **c.** us so will we be forever and
M-29 ......... 4:4 As God **c.** you, you *have* all power. The

M-29 7:10 but His Son, and as he was c. so he is. In
C-1 1:3 Thought of God which He c. like Himself.
C-2 1:6 Creator and a wish to be what He c. not.
C-2 2:4 God's Son as He c. him abide in form or
C-3 1:2 to think of anything He c. that could need
C-4 2:4 While everything that God c. is forever
C-6 1:1 the Christ, the Son of God as He c. Him.
P-2 IV.1:4 the universe as you would have c. it. It is a
P-2 VII.9:2 in this, you have denied that God c. you,
P-3 II.4:1 on all He c. and pronounced it good. No,
S-1 in.2:3 God c. one must recognize its oneness,
S-1 in.3:1 Son of God, and rising up as God c. you,
S-1 II.5:6 acknowledges the Son of God as he was c.
S-2 I.3:8 you remember Him and hate what He c.?
S-2 II.1:3 to separate and make what God c. equal,
S-2 III.7:8 the door; the Son of God as He c. him.

## creates 36

T-1 I.12:3 the physical, and the other c. the spiritual
T-1 V.5:4 spirit c. along the line of its own creation.
T-2 V.6:1 body does not learn any more than it c..
T-3 II.3:6 I have said that only what God c. or what
T-3 II.5:6 This single purpose c. perfect integration
T-5 I.1:8 giving it, and thus c. as the Father created
T-5 I.5:6 But what God c. is eternal. The Holy
T-5 IV.8:6 you, and we know what God c. is eternal.
T-5 V.6:11 God c. is irreversible and unchangeable.
T-5 VI.3:2 *is* in you, for God c. with perfect fairness.
T-7 I.3:6 stop. It c. forever, but not in time. God's
T-7 I.3:8 because you can create only as God c..
T-7 IX.6:9 is so intense that It c. in perfect joy, and
T-8 II.7:6 Because your Creator c. only like Himself,
T-10 V.9:11 it can also deny what it c. because it is free
T-11 in.3:1 by projection, but God c. by extension.
T-11 I.6:5 He c. has the function of creating. Love
T-11 I.6:6 not limit, and what it c. is not limited. To
T-14 V.10:12 Thus He c., and thus must you restore.
T-15 XI.2:8 Holiness c. the holiness that surrounds it.
T-22 VI.14:8 love extends its being and c. more of itself
T-23 IV.2:8 Can it create, and be what it c.? And can
T-24 in.2:8 What God c. has no alternative. The truth
T-24 II.3:4 the "creator" who c. unlike the Father,
T-25 II.6:8 What God c. is safe from all corruption,
T-25 III.1:6 of God's more basic law; that love c. itself,
T-25 IV.2:7 Son of God c. to bring him joy, sharing
T-28 II.1:5 be a father, who c. as God created him.
W-pI 132.12:4 What He c. is not apart from Him, and
W-pI 167.6:5 For mind c. all things that are, and cannot
W-pI 167.8:1 God c. only mind awake. He does not
W-pII 5.3:3 For only love c. in truth, and truth can
W-pII 11.1:2 Only love c., and only like itself. There
C-4 1:2 for what He c. must be eternal as Himself.
C-5 1:8 But He c. all Helpers of His Son while he
S-3 III.5:1 that all their Source c. is one with them.

## creating 36

*See also* self-creating

T-1 I.24:2 of c. in the likeness of your Creator.
T-2 I.3:10 was given you for your joy in c. the perfect
T-2 VI.9:7 sleeps. Every instant it is c.. It is hard to
T-3 VII.h C. versus the Self-Image
T-3 VII.1:2 It begins with either a making or a c., a
T-4 I.11:7 God is as incapable of c. the perishable as
T-5 II.1:1 Healing is not c.; it is reparation. The
T-5 II.2:5 heals until the whole mind returns to c..
T-5 IV.3:3 Sharing is God's way of c., and also yours.
T-5 V.4:4 is capable of c. reality or making illusions.
T-6 V.B.8:8 and c. cannot be difficult if God Himself
T-7 II.3:8 God Himself created the law by c. *by* it.
T-7 VI.12:5 with your Creator and c. as He created.
T-7 IX.2:5 C. is the opposite of loss, as blessing is the
T-8 II.7:4 By c. all things, it made them part of itself
T-8 VI.6:1 is to add to God's treasure by c. yours.
T-8 VI.6:5 His joy lay in c. you, and He extends His
T-10 II.3:3 counterpart of c. in the Kingdom. God
T-10 V.9:11 Your mind is capable of c. worlds, but it
T-11 I.6:5 He creates has the function of c.. Love

T-13 IV.1:3 healing, and your function in Heaven is c.
T-14 III.3:2 is living here, as c. is being in Heaven.
T-17 IV.1:3 reason for c. His relationship with you,
T-18 IX.14:1 learning, for your only purpose will be c..
T-21 II.12:2 Yet in c. them the Son does not delude
T-21 II.12:3 His union with It is the source of his c..
T-23 IV.3:7 is. Life makes not death, c. like itself.
T-24 VII.2:2 all of creation, everything created and c.,
T-26 IV.1:8 is he returned to his real function of c.,
T-28 II.3:6 mind, c. with effects unlike yourself. And
W-pI 183.8:2 His Son is part of Him, c. in His Name. Sit
W-pI 192.1:1 preserved, extending love, c. in its name,
W-pII 253.2:1 *Son, c. like Yourself and One with You. My*
C-1 4:2 Spirit retains the potential for c., but its
C-6 1:2 c. with Him and in His likeness or spirit,
S-1 in.1:6 in the song of his c. in his Father's Name.

## creation 317

*See also* pseudo-creation

T-1 I.50:1 compares what you have made with c.,
T-1 II.1:2 sense of c. sometimes sought in physical
T-1 II.3:3 Creator. You are a perfect c., and should
T-1 V.4:5 holiness. The c. is whole, and the mark of
T-1 V.5:4 spirit creates along the line of its own c..
T-1 VI.1:3 While lack does not exist in the c. of God,
T-2 I.1:2 In the c., God extended Himself to His
T-2 I.1:12 the direction of your own c. is up to you.
T-2 I.2:7 sense the c. includes both the creation of
T-2 I.2:7 includes both the c. of the Son by God,
T-2 I.2:8 loving c. is freely given in one continuous
T-2 II.5:7 but the Sonship itself is a perfect c. and
T-2 IV.2:10 that the mind, the only level of c., cannot
T-2 VII.3:8 miscreate, because they misperceive c..
T-2 VII.3:13 then, is between c. and miscreation. All
T-2 VIII.1:3 was expressing the same Will in His c..
T-2 VIII.5:5 yourself, because you are not your own c..
T-3 III.7:7 There are no strangers in God's c.. To
T-3 IV.3:10 and your c. is beyond your own error.
T-3 IV.6:3 of perception, a distorted form of c., then
T-3 V.3:2 The confusion between your real c. and
T-3 V.3:5 are disagreeing with God's idea of your c..
T-3 V.6:8 God. C. is your Source and your only real
T-3 VI.8:8 you believe that your c. was anonymous.
T-3 VII.5:5 c. by God is the only Foundation that
T-4 I.3:6 When I remind you of your true c., your
T-4 I.12:6 worthy to be a gift for a c. of God Himself.
T-4 II.9:2 generally include some account of "the c.,
T-4 IV.9:4 your c. and brought your mind into being
T-4 IV.10:1 Christ is merely another name for the c.,
T-4 VII.h C. and Communication
T-4 VII.3:4 communication with every aspect of c.,
T-4 VII.3:6 C. and communication are synonymous.
T-4 VII.5:5 That is what c. means. "How," "what"
T-4 VII.5:6 irrelevant, because real c. gives everything
T-4 VII.6:4 it. But unless you take your part in the c.,
T-5 I.7:5 its own integration toward the paths of c..
T-5 II.9:5 the one choice that resembles true c.. I am
T-5 IV.1:7 from the Holy Spirit, the Voice for c..
T-5 IV.2:6 higher part, returning it undivided to c.. I
T-5 IV.7:3 The full power of c. cannot be expressed
T-5 V.2:2 is restored and therefore continues in c..
T-5 V.8:6 will turn it back to full c. at any minute if
T-5 V.8:7 return to full c. the instant it has done so.
T-6 II.1:2 that recognizes the Wholeness of God's c.
T-6 IV.7:5 has given way to c. and to its eternity.
T-6 V.C.4:10 direct it towards c. within the Kingdom.
T-6 V.C.7:6 behalf. The ego speaks against His c., and
T-6 V.C.10:10 inclusion is total and c. is without limit.
T-7 I.1:4 in c. you are not in a reciprocal relation to
T-7 I.2:2 C. would therefore be limited, and you
T-7 I.5:5 Eternity is the indelible stamp of c.. The
T-7 II.2:3 reflects c., because it unifies by increasing
T-7 II.3:7 is not adapted at all, being the law of c..
T-7 II.3:9 depends on it, just as their own c. did.
T-7 II.5:5 God's law of c. does not involve the use of
T-7 IV.2:3 because every part of c. is of one order.
T-7 V.11:6 He calls upon you to love God and His c..
T-7 V.11:8 This is part of the law of c., and therefore

T-7 VI.10:3 His c. truly you cannot know the Creator,
T-7 VI.10:3 since God and His c. are not separate. The
T-7 VI.10:4 the Creator and the c. is your wholeness,
T-7 VI.11:1 your part in it, God's c. is seen as weak,
T-7 VI.13:6 C., not separation, is your will *because* it is
T-7 VII.11:2 to perceive any part of c. as wholly real,
T-7 IX.5:3 yours, since every c. belongs to everyone,
T-7 XI.7:11 the Sons of God, and you will know all c..
T-8 III.3:3 This is perfect c. by the perfectly created,
T-8 IV.8:2 is. Freedom is c., because it is love. Whom
T-8 V.2:8 There is no separation of God and His c..
T-8 VI.5:3 Trinity, created in gratitude for your c..
T-8 VI.5:4 your c. as God extended Himself to you.
T-8 VI.5:7 as you love your Father for the gift of c..
T-8 VI.6:3 withhold c. from you because His joy is in
T-8 VI.6:8 C. is the Will of God. His Will created you
T-8 VII.16:8 and you will open your mind to c. in God.
T-9 I.6:2 your Creator can communicate through c.
T-9 I.11:3 totally at variance with the principle of c..
T-9 VI.4:4 you remember c. whenever you recognize
T-9 VI.4:4 whenever you recognize part of c.. Each
T-10 in.2:5 God's only c. and He created you eternal?
T-10 I.1:3 law of c. is that you love your creations as
T-10 II.2:2 lie joy and peace and the glory of c.. Offer
T-10 III.4:3 All forms of idolatry are caricatures of c.,
T-10 III.4:3 that c. shares power and never usurps it.
T-10 IV.4:9 C. is perfectly lawful, and the chaotic is
T-10 IV.5:6 of your c. established you a creator. What
T-10 IV.8:6 Light, because it is the remaining call of c.
T-10 V.5:6 If c. is sharing, it cannot create what is
T-10 V.8:5 looking without love on God and His c.,
T-10 V.10:7 That was the condition of His Son's c.,
T-10 V.10:10 God gave Himself to you in your c., and
T-10 V.12:4 may take, are refusals to accept c. as it is.
T-11 in.1:6 Nothing alive is Fatherless, for life is c..
T-11 in.3:2 The cornerstone of God's c. is you, for His
T-11 I.3:4 except you, and your filling it was your c.,
T-11 I.4:2 His c. or upon those who create like Him.
T-11 I.4:3 and so you believe that all c. is limited.
T-11 I.5:11 Look upon the glory of His c., and you
T-11 I.9:11 is like Him. C. is your will *because* it is His.
T-11 II.6:8 increase, you will begin to remember c..
T-11 IV.1:2 As God's c. It is yours, and belonging to
T-11 V.6:1 Yours is the independence of c., not of
T-12 V.4:4 wanted to retain the characteristics of c.,
T-12 V.4:5 Yet c. is not of you, and poor learners do
T-12 VII.4:7 As your function in Heaven is c., so your
T-13 III.12:4 for pain, for suffering is not of His c..
T-13 III.12:5 Having given you c., He could not take it
T-13 VI.9:1 as you call forth the witnesses to His c..
T-13 VIII.3:2 was accomplished by God in your c.. The
T-13 VIII.3:4 C. cannot be interrupted. The separation
T-13 VIII.5:1 is the miracle of c.; *that it is one forever.*
T-13 X.7:6 teaches healing, but He also knows of c..
T-13 XI.10:4 as surely as the c. will remain unchanged
T-14 IV.4:1 You need not understand c. to do what
T-14 V.3:4 C. is the natural extension of perfect
T-14 V.4:1 the right of God's Son, given him in his c..
T-14 V.6:4 to the eternal glory of God and His c..
T-14 V.7:4 but to restore what is the right of God's c.
T-14 VI.5:6 you made in place of the power of c., He
T-14 VII.3:9 c. was not a point of view, but rather a
T-14 VIII.4:8 For this is how c. is accomplished by the
T-14 VIII.4:10 in the oneness out of which c. happens.
T-14 VIII.5:2 Heaven itself is union with all of c., and
T-14 X.1:1 the knowledge of c. must continue forever
T-14 XI.11:7 The miracle of c. has never ceased, having
T-14 XI.11:8 it. This is the Will of God for all c., and all
T-14 XI.11:8 all creation, and all c. joins in willing this.
T-14 XI.14:4 Creator must encompass faith in His c..
T-15 I.15:9 instant of the eternal sanctity of God's c.,
T-15 III.5:4 When God gave Himself to you in your c.,
T-15 VI.8:7 is, and what His c. is along with Him.
T-15 VIII.4:1 Sonship to you, to ensure your perfect c..
T-15 VIII.4:2 not from you, He withheld not His c..
T-15 IX.4:1 and the ego, and release your power to c.,
T-15 XI.8:5 joins us in the celebration of His Son's c..
T-16 III.5:2 by God, He left neither God nor His c.. He
T-16 III.5:8 and gratitude to you for their c. they offer

T-16......IV.8:6 is the acceptance of the Oneness of c.,
T-16....IV.13:5 Him Who gave eternity to you in your c..
T-17......IV.4:1 ego's answer to the c. of the Holy Spirit,
T-17....IV.15:5 you the whole of c. in exchange for your
T-18...... I.10:2 Your reality was God's c., and has no
T-18...... I.11:3 and His whole c. have entered it together.
T-19....... II.2:5 not. Thus is c. seen as not eternal, and the
T-19....... II.4:5 an attempt to wrest c. away from truth,
T-19....... II.6:5 sin has changed c. from an idea of God to
T-19......III.6:2 If c. is extension, the Creator must have
T-19......III.7:4 God and His c. seem to be split apart and
T-19......III.7:6 bow, and offer His c. to its conqueror. Is
T-19......III.8:3 fragmented c. would have a different will,
T19... IV.A.1:6 If it would spread across the whole c., it
T19... IV.C.7:7 the triumph of the ego's making over c.,
T-21....... II.8:2 The holy instant is not an instant of c.,
T-21...... II.12:5 It changes nothing in c., depends entirely
T-21...... II.12:7 Thus he denies c.. With you, he thinks the
T-21... VIII.2:4 as is the Love of God for His c.. Sure in its
T-22....VI.12:5 attack a part of the c. without the whole,
T-22....VI.15:2 And in Him is all c. joined. Would you
T-23......IV.3:5 C. is the means for God's extension, and
T-23......IV.4:2 yet, and so it cannot be extended to all c..
T-24.... in.2:10 as all c. rose in His Mind *because* of what
T-24.........I.3:2 reality of God's c. and with the grandeur
T-24......VI.1:6 For He could never leave His Own c.. And
T-24......VI.1:8 See in him God's c.. For in him his Father
T-24...VII.1:11 of God's c. that takes the place of yours?
T-24.....VII.2:2 within your brother still contains all of c.,
T-24.....VII.6:7 Him. This is the state of true c., found not
T-24...VII.10:9 Such is the travesty on God's c.. For as
T-24.VII.10:10 Son's c. gave Him joy and witness to His
T-25....... II.9:4 cherishes c. as the perfect Father that He
T-25......IV.2:7 sharing his Father's purpose in his own c.,
T-25...VII.1:11 not should share the attributes of His c.,
T-26......III.1:3 He knows of one c., one reality, one truth
T-26......IV.3:4 the universe to touch the Heart of all c.?
T-26......IV.3:5 everything created to the Source of its c.?
T-26....... V.5:3 too short to make a world in answer to c.,
T-26.....VII.7:4 and all c. be subjected to the laws of two
T-26...VII.10:2 In joyous answer will c. rise within you, to
T-26...VII.11:5 miracle by which c. became your function
T-26...VII.20:5 and all c. freed to call upon the Name of
T-27.........I.1:9 at all it would entail the whole of God's c.,
T-27......III.4:4 power, with no opposite, is what c. is. For
T-28.........I.2:7 take the place of what God gave in your c.
T-28....... II.1:6 The circle of c. has no end. Its starting
T-28....... II.1:8 But in itself it holds the universe of all c.,
T-28....... II.2:1 Fatherhood *is* c.. Love must be extended.
T-28.....V.1:11 His Will with you, that His c. might create
T-28....... V.6:1 C. proves reality because it shares the
T-28....... V.6:1 because it shares the function all c. shares
T-28......VI.6:4 his. In his c. did his Father say, "You are
T-29......III.5:4 his Father lost not part of him in your c.,
T-29....... V.5:1 c. but the shining glory of His gift to you.
T-29....... V.5:2 and to whom is all c. given as his own.
T-30....III.2:11 because what shares in all c. cannot be
T-30......III.4:9 want. C. gives no separate person and no
T-30....III.11:4 of Son joined in c. which can have no end.
T-30....... V.4:3 has a purpose still beneath c. and eternity
T-30....... V.6:5 of God knew in c. he must know again.
T-30......VI.5:7 mistake that had the power to undo c.,
T-31.........I.8:8 of each part of God's c. to the whole is
T-31.........I.9:6 God's perfect Son remembers his c.. But
T-31.....VII.8:2 every part of true c. has the Lord of Love
T-31. VIII.12:6 and perfectly, and all c. recognizes You,
W-pI.....44.1:3 life, and is therefore an aspect of c..
W-pI.....44.1:4 C. and darkness cannot coexist, but light
W-pI.....44.1:4 together, being but different aspects of c..
W-pI.....45.3:5 Mind of God is eternal, being part of c..
W-pI.....51.4:8 all c. lies in the thoughts I think with God.
W-pI.....52.1:7 Nothing in God's c. is affected in any way
W-pI.....52.5:6 mind is part of c. and part of its Creator.
W-pI.....53.4:5 when the perfection of c. is my home? Let
W-pI.....62.2:3 Identity by attacking c. and its Creator.
W-pI.....72.4:6 wholly unlike his c. is inconceivable.
W-pI.....72.7:4 your grievances against Him and His c.,
W-pI.....73.1:3 share with God has all the power of c. in it
W-pI.....73.1:6 But they are idle indeed in terms of c..
W-pI.....73.3:4 C. is the Will of Both together. Would
W-pI...76.10:6 His only Son, created as His channel for c.
W-pI...76.11:2 Thus is c. endlessly increased. His Voice
W-pI.....77.2:5 It was ensured in your c., and guaranteed
W-pI.....93.5:8 It has not changed c., nor reduced eternal
W-pI.....93.7:4 C. is eternal and unalterable. Your
W-pI.....93.8:1 begin by stating the truth about your c.:
W-pI.....95.1:3 Yours is the unity of all c.. Your perfect
W-pI.....95.2:1 as a ridiculous parody on God's c.; weak,
W-pI...95.10:2 Creator, at one with every aspect of c.,
W-pI...95.11:2 *my Creator, at one with every aspect of c.,*
W-pI...95.12:2 that true c. may extend the allness and
W-pI...105.4:2 True giving is c.. It extends the limitless
W-pI...113.1:2 *whole, at one with all c. and with God.*
W-pI...123.2:3 made to take the place of Him and His c..
W-pI...131.8:2 Nor is His c. split in two. How could it be
W-pI.132.11:5 God's c. is unlike the world in every way.
W-pI...134.2:4 Truth is God's c., and to pardon that is
W-pI...138.2:1 C. knows no opposite. But here is
W-pI...138.2:5 Yet what is true in God's c. cannot enter
W-pI.139.11:5 for everyone, for in c. are all minds as one
W-pI.139.12:1 In thanks for all c., in the Name of its
W-pI.139.12:1 and His Oneness with all aspects of c., we
WpI. rIV.in2:4 by which the Father gave c. to the Son,
W-pI...151.9:2 for He bears witness to your beautiful c.,
W-pI...158.2:3 which you give, for that is what c. gave.
W-pI...160.7:5 He cannot be confused about c.. He is
W-pI...161.4:4 thoughts make clear the meaning of c.?
W-pI...162.2:2 Here c. is proclaimed, and honored as it is
W-pI...163.4:3 of God proclaimed as lord of all c.,
W-pI.167.11:3 and that we share with Him, with all c.,
W-pI.184.11:3 but He does not forget c. has one Name,
W-pI...185.1:4 the resurrection of all c. fully recognized.
W-pI...186.9:3 shares His attributes with His c.. All the
W-pI...191.3:1 that mocks c. and that laughs at God.
W-pI...192.2:4 It is not God's c., for it is the means by
W-pI...192.2:7 go. C. merely waits for your return to be
W-pI...192.3:1 C. cannot even be conceived of in the
W-pI...193.1:2 eternally expanding in the joy of full c.,
W-pI.195.10:3 of the Love which is the Source of all c..
W-pII..230.2:1 *I seek the peace You gave as mine in my c..*
W-pII..230.2:2 *be here now, for my c. was apart from time,*
W-pII..239.2:3 *with You, at peace with all c. and ourselves.*
W-pII..243.2:1 *Father, today I leave c. free to be itself. I*
W-pII......4.5:6 sin. C. is unchanged. Would you still hold
W-pII..259.1:5 be the source of fear, obscuring God's c.;
W-pII..262.1:3 *He is Your one c.. Why should I perceive a*
W-pII..263.1:4 *all the loveliness with which You blessed c.;*
W-pII..264.1:5 *its holiness; that stands beyond Your one c.,*
W-pII..265.1:4 celestial gentleness with which c. shines.
W-pII..268.1:2 *Let me not attempt to interfere with Your c.,*
W-pII..271.1:2 the witnesses to what is true in God's c..
W-pII..271.1:3 sight, the world and God's c. meet, and as
W-pII..271.1:4 Father and the Son; Creator and c. unified
W-pII..276.1:7 Him Who gave His Word to us in our c.,
W-pII..278.2:2 *foolish thoughts about myself and my c.,*
W-pII..283.1:2 *Yet is c. as it always was, for Your creation is*
W-pII..283.1:2 *as it always was, for Your c. is unchangeable.*
W-pII......9.2:2 brings, as God's c. must be limitless.
W-pII......9.3:2 in the name of true c. and the Will of God
W-pII......9.4:4 upon His Son, His one c. and His only joy.
W-pII..320.1:2 nor any attributes his Father gave in his c.
W-pII........11.h What Is C.?
W-pII....11.1:1 C. is the sum of all God's Thoughts, in
W-pII....11.2:3 Thus His Son shares in c., and must
W-pII....11.3:1 C. is the opposite of all illusions, for
W-pII....11.3:1 opposite of all illusions, for c. is the truth.
W-pII....11.3:2 C. is the holy Son of God, for in creation
W-pII....11.3:2 in c. is His Will complete in every aspect,
W-pII....11.4:1 We are c.; we the Sons of God. We seem
W-pII....11.5:2 we forgive c. in the Name of its Creator,
W-pII....11.5:2 Itself, Whose Holiness His Own c. shares;
W-pII..328.1:2 independence from the rest of God's c. is
W-pII..329.1:5 *You. And this I chose in my c., where my will*
W-pII....13.3:5 the universal altar to Creator and c. in the
W-pII..342.1:7 *let c. be as You would have it be and as it is.*
W-pII....14.1:2 *His c. sanctified and guaranteed eternal life.*
W-pII..359.1:1 *forgive Your world, and let c. be Your Own.*
M-5 ....... II.4:2 this idea goes also all confusion about c..
M-5 ..... II.4:10 Cause and effect but replicate c.. Seen in
M-7 ........... 6:4 you have denied the Source of your c.. If
M-8 ........... 2:5 Illusions are travesties of c.; attempts to
M-27 ......... 5:6 now His Own c. must stand in fear of Him
C-1............ 4:3 C. continues unabated because that is the
C-5............ 3:1 Son of God, His one c. and His happiness,
C-6............ 1:2 Holy Spirit, being a c. of the one Creator,
C-6............ 3:6 He never forgets the Creator or His c.. He
P-2......... IV.1:3 again and again, against c. and its Creator
S-1 .........in.1:1 with which God blessed His Son at his c..
S-1 .........in.1:2 the single voice Creator and c. share; the
S-1 .........in.1:4 And in this, c. is extended. God gives
S-1 .........in.1:6 His Son gives thanks for his c., in the song
S-1 ......... V.2:5 what it is, knowing c. is the Will of God.
S-2...........I.8:6 the ceaseless song that all c. sings unto its
S-2..........II.3:5 love for God's c. and the holiness that is
S-3........ IV.3:5 are as dear to Him as is the whole of His c.
S-3........ IV.5:2 will give the role to Him you see in His c..
S-3........ IV.7:3 sing his joyful thanks in unison with all c.,
S-3........ IV.8:4 Without you is c. unfulfilled. Return to
S-3........ IV.9:1 C. leans across the bars of time to lift the

## creation's 7

T-26...VII.13:3 Such is c. law; that each idea the mind
T-30.........II.3:5 has joined with God Himself in all c. birth
W-pII ....265.h C. gentleness is all I see.
W-pII265.1:10 And so I can perceive c. gentleness.
W-pII .265.2:2 *they are the same, and I will see c. gentleness.*
W-pII ....279.h C. freedom promises my own.
S-3........ IV.3:3 returned to share with Him c. holy joy.

## creations 118

T-1.........I.24:4 does not exist. Only the c. of light are real.
T-1.........I.29:2 you. They praise Him by honoring His c.,
T-1.........I.38:2 both God's c. and your illusions. He
T-1..........II.1:2 communication between God and His c.,
T-1......... III.3:4 the salvation or release of all of God's c..
T-1......... III.7:3 is one, uniting all c. with their Creator. As
T-1......... V.4:4 be mocked if any of His c. lacked holiness.
T-1........ VI.4:3 faith in His c. *because* He created them.
T-2.........I.1:2 to His c. and imbued them with the same
T-2.........I.1:11 believe that you can distort the c. of God,
T-2...........I.2:7 and the Son's c. when his mind is healed.
T-2........ III.5:6 God and His c. are completely dependent
T-2......... V.2:5 cannot misperceive them as your own c..
T-2........VII.6:2 If all His c. are His Sons, every one must
T-2.......VIII.4:3 his own c. and choose to preserve only
T-2.......VIII.4:4 on its own c. because of their worthiness.
T-2.......VIII.5:9 perfect judgment of your own perfect c..
T-3........ IV.7:1 God and His c. remain in surety, and
T-3......... V.2:8 of the abstract creativity of God's c..
T-3........ VI.8:7 God's c. are given their true Authorship,
T-3.......VII.2:5 God, battling Him for possession of His c.
T-3.......VII.3:8 knowledge and gave it freely to His c..
T-3.......VII.3:9 or His c. as capable of destroying Their
T-3.......VII.4:2 which God and His c. are not co-creators.
T-4.........I.11:4 make a home that is worthy of His c., who
T-4.........I.12:5 as the mark of the Love of God for His c.,
T-4..........II.4:4 to your ego much as God does to His c., –
T-4..........II.4:6 how you will one day react to your real c.,
T-4....... II.8:10 c. of God do not create myths, although
T-4....... III.1:9 c. are no more fatherless than you are.
T-4...... III.1:11 confident that your c. are as safe as you
T-4....... III.4:4 and His c. because of your hatred for the
T-4........ IV.2:9 in both the glorious c. of a glorious Father
T-4........ IV.7:1 habit of engaging with God and His c. is
T-4........ VI.7:7 of God I can lead you back to your own c..
T-4.......VII.3:8 His c. naturally communicate with Him
T-5...........I.4:6 As a man and also one of God's c., my
T-5...........I.5:7 their c. and keep them in the light of joy.
T-5....... III.2:4 the idea of yourself, as well as of all His c..
T-5...... VI.10:3 and every witness to guilt in God's c. is
T-5...... VI.12:6 eternity and remain to bless your c. there.
T-5.......VII.5:1 with a lack of love to one of God's c..
T-6....... II.11:5 way in which you must perceive God's c.,
T-6...... IV.10:5 God, Who knows that His c. are perfect,
T-6...... V.B.7:2 it is up to you to decide what God's c. are.

T-6......V.C.7:2 God and His **c.** are beyond belief because
T-7..........I.1:1 power of God and His **c.** is limitless, but
T-7..........I.2:3 thought proceed from you to your **c.**.
T-7..........I.3:1 Your **c.** belong in you, as you belong in
T-7..........I.3:7 God's **c.** have always been, because He
T-7..........I.3:8 Your **c.** have always been, because you
T-7..........I.7:2 not teach, because His **c.** are changeless.
T-7.......IV.1:4 Who knows His **c.** as perfectly whole. Yet
T-7.........V.9:9 of the increase of the Kingdom by your **c.**,
T-7.......VI.1:6 concept of God, of His **c.** and of his own.
T-7......VI.13:7 itself with both its Creator and its **c.**,
T-7.......IX.1:2 **c.** than He wills to deprive Himself of His.
T-7.......IX.2:2 rendering its **c.** equally whole and equal
T-7.......IX.3:7 You may not know your own **c.**, but this
T-7.......IX.5:1 Your **c.** are protected for you because the
T-7.......IX.5:3 The **c.** of every Son of God are yours,
T-7.........X.1:7 **c.** are the logical outcome of His premises
T-7.......XI.6:3 your **c.** because you do not know your
T-7.......XI.7:2 your **c.** because you do not know their
T-7.......XI.7:4 Your **c.** cannot establish your reality, any
T-8.........II.8:6 Voice for his **c.** and for his own extension.
T-8.......IV.7:9 to Him, which He will share with all His **c.**
T-8.......VI.2:6 God did not will the destruction of His **c.**,
T-8.......VI.5:2 You want your **c.** as He wants His. Your
T-8.......VI.5:3 Your **c.** are your gift to the Holy Trinity,
T-8.......VI.5:5 **c.** of God Himself take joy in what is not
T-8.......VI.5:6 And what is real except the **c.** of God and
T-8.......VI.5:7 **c.** love you as you love your Father for the
T-8.......VI.8:8 Our **c.** are as holy as we are, and we are
T-8.......VI.8:9 Through our **c.** we extend our love, and
T-9.......VI.5:5 its Oneness it will be known by its **c.**, who
T-9.......VI.7:4 In your open mind are your **c.**, in perfect
T-9.......VI.7:7 and you are incomplete without your **c.**.
T-9.......VI.7:8 your **c.** because he created them with you.
T-10.......in.2:4 is real. Your **c.** add to Him as you do, but
T-10.........I.1:1 You do not know your **c.** simply because
T-10.........I.1:3 law of creation is that you love your **c.** as
T-10.........I.4:1 to your Creator and your **c.**. Knowing
T-10.....V.13:3 your gifts to your **c.** are like His, because
T-10.....V.13:4 That is why your **c.** are as real as His. Yet
T-10.....V.13:6 sick things you have made are your real **c.**
T-11.........I.3:8 That is why your **c.** have not ceased to be
T-11.........I.4:4 then, could you know your **c.**, having
T-11.........I.5:9 See His **c.** as His Son, for yours were
T-12...VII.10:2 of your mind is the loveliest of God's **c.**.
T-13...VIII.8:5 is in you, your **c.** will be there with you, as
T-13...VIII.9:1 **c.** establish your fatherhood in Heaven.
T-14....VIII.4:8 by the Creator and by His **c.**. In the holy
T-14....VIII.4:9 place are joined the Father and His **c.**, and
T-14....VIII.4:9 and the **c.** of His Son with Them together.
T-14......IX.8:6 God is no image, and His **c.**, as part of
T-14........X.1:1 stands between God and His **c.**, or
T-15.......I.14:3 your immortal **c.** who share it with you.
T-15......III.7:5 and beyond everyone to His Son's **c.**, but
T-15....VIII.2:8 The will of your **c.** calls to you, to share
T-15......IX.5:1 need your **c.** have to be with you forever,
T-16......III.5:5 protected both your **c.** and you together,
T-16......IV.8:1 and your **c.** are holding out their hands to
T-16......IV.8:5 your **c.** were created in union with them.
T-16......IV.8:6 Acceptance of your **c.** is the acceptance of
T-17......IV.1:5 you relate to your **c.** as God to His. For
T-21...... II.12:1 The Son's **c.** are like his Father's. Yet in
T-23......IV.2:9 it offer its **c.** all that it is and never suffer
T-24....... II.6:3 memory, the Son remembers his own **c.**,
T-24.....VII.1:8 Yet it stands in place of your **c.**, who *are*
T-24.....VII.5:9 where your **c.** recognize a gift from you, a
T-24...VII.6:10 a holy home for your **c.** is it understood.
T-28....... II.3:6 each with separate minds, are your "**c.**,"
W-pI.132.12:2 Your real **c.** wait for this release to give
W-pI...167.8:2 and His **c.** cannot share what He gives not
W-pII .253.1:6 For thus am I led past this world to my **c.**,
M-27 .......5:10 His image. To look on His **c.** is to die.
P-3......... II.4:3 since His **c.** do not change and last forever

## creative 27

*See also* non-creative

T-1......... V.5:5 it retains its **c.** potential but places itself
T-1........VI.5:1 because they do not exist at the **c.** level,
T-2 ..........I.1:5 of your likeness to your Creator you are **c.**
T-2 .........II.5:5 The eternally **c.** have nothing to learn.
T-2 ....... III.5:2 waste themselves and their true **c.** powers
T-2 .......IV.2:8 on the belief that there is a **c.** ability in
T-2 ...... V.1:11 of **c.** ability that is truly meaningful.
T-2 ........ V.5:2 recognize that mind is the only **c.** level,
T-2 ....... VI.9:5 very powerful, and never loses its **c.** force.
T-2 .....VIII.1:4 creation. Since **c.** ability rests in the mind,
T-2 .....VIII.5:6 in your memory only what is **c.** and good.
T-3 ....... III.5:8 provides the strength for **c.** thinking, but
T-3 ........ V.2:6 None of them is **c.**. Inventiveness is
T-4 .......II.8:10 **c.** effort can be turned to mythology. It
T-4 .......II.8:11 what it makes is then no longer **c.**. Myths
T-5 .........II.6:4 that its **c.** power is unlimited and choice is
T-7 ..........I.1:1 The **c.** power of God and His creations is
T-7 ..........I.1:5 this respect your **c.** power differs from His
T-7 ..........I.2:1 not increase through its own **c.** thought.
T-7 ..........I.2:3 God's **c.** Thought proceeds from Him to
T-7 ..........I.2:3 must your **c.** thought proceed from you to
T-7 ..........I.2:4 this way can all **c.** power extend outward.
T-7 ....... IX.1:1 Only you can limit your **c.** power, but
T-7 ....... XI.6:8 Deny his **c.** power, and you are denying
T-11 ...... V.6:2 whole **c.** function lies in your complete
C-1 ........... 1:1 agent of spirit, supplying its **c.** energy.
P-2...........I.2:1 Psychotherapy itself cannot be **c.**. This is

## creativity 3

T-1 ........ V.1:5 or reduce your **c.** almost to nothing. But
T-3 ........ V.2:8 of the abstract **c.** of God's creations.
P-2...........I.2:2 of true change, and therefore of true **c.**.

## Creator 192

*creator*

T-1 ........I.11:2 communication of the created with the **C.**.
T-1 ........I.24:2 of creating in the likeness of your **C.**.
T-1 .........II.3:2 one of a lesser order stands before his **C.**.
T-1 .........II.3:3 in the Presence of the **C.** of perfection.
T-1 ....... III.7:3 is one, uniting all creations with their **C.**.
T-1 ....... VI.4:3 not in content, you resemble your **C.**,
T-1 ......VII.5:3 awe is proper in the Presence of your **C.**. I
T-2 ..........I.1:5 your likeness to your **C.** you are creative.
T-2 ....... III.3:3 you cannot depart entirely from your **C.**,
T-2 .....VIII.1:3 will to create was given you by your **C.**,
T-3 .........II.5:2 from its sleep and remembers its **C.**. All
T-3 ....... IV.7:6 By uniting my will with that of my **C.**, I
T-4 ....... III.1:5 What else *but* you did the **C.** create, and
T-4 ..... III.1:10 but your spirit and your **C.** will always be.
T-4 ......VII.3:4 and direct communication with its **C.**.
T-5 ..... VI.11:7 towards the Sonship in the Name of its **C.**.
T-6 .........II.1:3 this recognition it knows its **C.**. Exclusion
T-7 ..........I.2:7 not to add to the **C.** of the Kingdom. You
T-7 ..........I.7:6 He is the Prime **C.**, because He created
T-7 .........II.7:5 you share it and extend it as your **C.** did.
T-7 ...... V.6:15 cannot separate your Self from your **C.**,
T-7 ..... VI.10:3 His creation truly you cannot know the **C.**
T-7 ..... VI.10:4 the **C.** and the creation is your wholeness,
T-7 ..... VI.12:5 with your **C.** and creating as He created.
T-7 ..... VI.13:7 itself with both its **C.** and its creations,
T-7 ......VII.5:5 life, because that is not the Will of your **C.**
T-7 ......VII.9:2 that you have been treacherous to your **C.**
T-7 ....... IX.2:2 of its **C.** is therefore spirit's own fullness,
T-7 ....... IX.2:8 yearns to share its being as its **C.** did.
T-7 ....... IX.3:2 any more than can the fullness of its **C.**.
T-7 ....... XI.6:2 because you do not know your **C.**. You do
T-8 .........II.7:6 Because your **C.** creates only like Himself,
T-8 .........II.8:6 of every Son of God to the Voice for his **C.**
T-8 ....... III.3:3 created, in union with the perfect **C.**. The
T-8 ....... VI.5:4 leave you any more than you left your **C.**,
T-8 ....... VI.7:7 unknown to him, but never to his **C.**. And
T-8 ....... VI.7:8 And because it is not unknown to his **C.**,
T-8 ......VII.5:9 is to reach beyond the Kingdom to its **C.**,
T-9 ..........I.6:2 **C.** can communicate through creation,
T-10 .........I.4:1 to your **C.** and your creations. Knowing
T-10 ..... III.3:7 his wholeness and remember your **C.** with
T-10 ...... V.5:5 make creators who are unlike your **C.**, any
T-10 ...... V.9:6 you must acknowledge Him as your **C.**.
T-11 ..... III.5:7 For your Father *is* your **C.**, and you *are* like
T-11 ..... IV.1:5 you by your **C.** that you might extend it.
T-11 ..... IV.5:7 His Son lifts his voice in praise of his **C.**,
T-11 ..... IV.5:8 the **C.** cannot be praised without His Son,
T-11 ..... IV.7:4 lives in His **C.** and shines with His glory.
T-11 ..... IV.7:5 as perfect as His **C.** and at peace with Him
T-11 .... VII.4:4 have placed between yourself and your **C.**,
T-13 ..... VI.8:7 thanksgiving for the light to the **C.** of light
T-13 ..... VI.9:1 your brothers in remembrance of your **C.**,
T-13 ..... VI.9:3 of praise and gladness rise to your **C.**, He
T-14 ... III.18:1 habit of not communicating with your **C.**.
T-14 ...VIII.4:7 Everything God created knows its **C.**. For
T-14 ...VIII.4:8 by the **C.** and by His creations. In the holy
T-14 ...VIII.5:2 with all of creation, and with its one **C.**.
T-14 ..... IX.5:1 Holiness of your **C.** shines forth from you
T-14 ... XI.11:3 God's Teacher is as like to His **C.** as is His
T-14 ... XI.14:4 It is as firm as is His faith in His **C.**, and
T-14 ... XI.14:4 and He knows that faith in His **C.** must
T-15 ..... VI.8:7 will begin to understand what your **C.** is,
T-15 ..... XI.5:3 Heaven and its **C.** aside without a sense of
T-16 ... IV.11:6 that rises ceaselessly from you to your **C.**.
T-16 ..... VI.1:6 except as its **C.** defined it by His Will. It is
T-17 ..... III.7:5 For the **C.** of the one relationship has left
T-17 ..... IV.1:6 but would extend happiness as its **C.** did.
T-18 ..... I.11:8 on what is joined in it, along with its **C.**.
T-18 ... VIII.5:3 dependent on its one **C.** for everything;
T-18 ... VIII.6:4 the rest, and keeping it apart from its **C.**.
T-18 . VIII.10:4 with all the Love of its **C.** shining upon it.
T-18 ... IX.12:6 is useless in the Presence of your **C.**,
T-19 ........ I.5:5 between the Son of God and his **C.**; faith
T-19 ...... I.16:3 being lord of all, along with his **C.**. You
T-19 ..... III.6:2 the **C.** must have extended Himself, and it
T-19 ..... IV.3:8 His **C.** in the Name of His most holy Son.
T19 ...IV.A.3:7 it would hold back the universe and its **C.**.
T19 ... IV.C.3:5 procession march not in honor of their **C.**,
T19 ... IV.C.4:4 him are but honoring the Will of his **C.**.
T19 ... IV.C.5:7 brings the **C.** to the awareness of every
T19 .. IV.D.1:4 The **C.** of life, the Source of everything
T-20 ....... V.8:4 that the **C.** of the universe should offer it
T-20 ..... VI.1:1 lies solely in his relationship with his **C.**.
T-21 ...... I.10:1 of their **C.** gives praise to them as well.
T-21 ....... II.6:4 will; and thus without the Will of his **C.**,
T-21 ..... II.11:3 not by your **C.** has any influence over you.
T-21 ..... II.11:4 denying your **C.** and believing that you
T-21 ... VIII.2:5 in its vision as its **C.** is in what He knows,
T-22 ........ I.1:2 then you and your **C.** have a different will.
T-22 ....... II.6:5 *You* know what your **C.** wills is possible,
T-22 ..... II.10:2 you still would be apart from your **C.**, and
T-22 ....... V.4:5 out the hymn of praise to its **C.** that every
T-22 ..... VI.2:5 by one as dear to His **C.** as love is to itself.
T-22 ... VI.11:7 than to attack the great **C.** of the universe,
T-22 ... VI.12:4 other, and all were separate from your **C.**.
T-22 ... VI.14:5 of the union of the **C.** and His Son. From
T-22 ... VI.15:1 so it makes you and him one with your **C.**.
T-23 ........ I.4:7 The Son of God at war with his **C.** is a
T-23 ...... I.10:7 You dwell in peace as limitless as its **C.**,
T-23 ....... II.5:7 God has done both to himself and his **C.**.
T-23 ....... II.6:2 define what the **C.** of reality must be; what
T-23 ..... IV.2:5 it is not the body that is like the Son's **C.**.
T-24 ..... III.6:1 Forgive the great **C.** of the universe, the
T-25 ....... II.6:2 Yet its frame is joined to its **C.**, One with
T-25 ....... II.7:3 the light that shines from it to its **C.**.
T-25 ..... III.3:2 has but one law because it has but one **C.**.
T-28 ...... I.10:1 to lay a judgment on your own **C.** cannot
T-28 ...... I.12:4 And His **C.** shares His thanks, because He
T-28 ....... II.1:4 Thus, the Son gives Fatherhood to his **C.**,
T-28 ....... II.8:1 keep them since He was no longer their **C.**
T-28 ....... II.8:4 And as he hated his **C.**, so the figures in
T-28 ....... V.3:6 alien ground which your **C.** did not make,
T-29 ....... V.2:4 and quiet, tranquil in the might of its **C.**,
T-29 ..... VI.4:9 share the function their **C.** gave to them.
T-30 ... III.10:5 left the Mind of its **C.** Whom it knows, as
T-30 ... III.10:5 it knows, as its **C.** knows that it is there.
T-30 ..... VI.4:6 must think of its **C.** as it looks upon itself.
W-pI .... 29.2:5 of the universe shares the purpose of its **C.**
W-pI .... 38.1:3 Son of God, at one with the Mind of his **C.**
W-pI .... 49.2:6 that your **C.** has not forgotten His Son.
W-pI .... 52.5:6 mind is part of creation and part of its **C.**.
W-pI .... 62.2:3 Identity by attacking creation and its **C.**.
W-pI .... 68.1:7 for no one can conceive of his **C.** as unlike

W-pI.....68.2:1 remains aware of Its likeness to Its **C.**,
W-pI.....68.2:4 **C.** has become fearful to him in his dream
W-pI...72.12:1 you are asking of the infinite **C.** of infinity,
W-pI.....84.1:2 I am in the likeness of my **C.**. I cannot
W-pI.....84.1:7 I am in the likeness of my **C.**. Love created
W-pI.....84.2:3 *As I look on this, let me remember my* **C.**. *My*
W-pI.....84.2:4 *Creator. My* **C.** *did not create this as I see it.*
W-pI.........95.h I am one Self, united with my **C.**.
W-pI.....95.3:2 your one Self, which is united with Its **C.**.
W-pI...95.10:2 you are one Self, united with your **C.**, at
W-pI...95.11:2 *I am one Self, united with my* **C.**, *at one with*
W-pI...95.12:2 Son, one Self, with one **C.** and one goal; to
W-pI...95.13:4 the Son of God Himself, sinless as Its **C.**,
W-pI...95.15:3 *Self with me, united with our* **C.** *in this Self. I*
W-pI.....97.2:3 Himself, and shares His function as **C.**. He
W-pI...105.4:1 so does the joy of your **C.** grow when you
W-pI...113.1:1 (95) I am one Self, united with my **C.**.
W-pI...113.3:2 I am one Self, united with my **C.**. On the
W-pI...124.8:2 awareness you are one with your **C.**, as He
W-pI...125.6:4 mind to hear the Voice for its **C.** speak.
W-pI...128.6:5 Let it rest in its **C.**, there to be restored to
W-pI...131.5:1 in hell, for no one can abandon his **C.**, nor
W-pI.135.24:5 present yourself to your **C.** as you really
W-pI.139.12:1 Name of its **C.** and His Oneness with all
W-pI.151.12:3 you of nothing but your Self and your **C.**,
W-pI.154.14:2 the message sent to us today from our **C.**.
W-pI.154.14:4 our many gifts from our **C.** will spring to
W-pI...160.8:4 nor is your **C.** stranger made to you.
W-pI...167.4:1 that you are separate from your **C.**. It is
W-pI.170.12:4 and your attributes, given by your **C.**, are
WpI..rV.in4:5 consistent in Its Thoughts; knows Its **C.**,
W-pI...183.8:1 you acknowledge Him as sole **C.** of reality.
W-pI.184.15:2 *living things, and You Who are their one* **C.**.
W-pI.185.12:1 you was peace created, given you by its **C.**,
W-pI.186.12:4 Voice that speaks for the **C.** of all things,
W-pI.186.12:6 given you by your **C.** Who remembers you
W-pI.187.10:2 God, one Father, one **C.** and one Thought,
W-pI...201.1:3 *my Father, one* **C.** *of the whole that is my Self*
W-pII.....in.8:1 for truth and God, Who is its one **C.**. We
W-pII..228.1:4 His Word for what I am, since He is my **C.**
W-pII..271.1:4 and the Son; **C.** and creation unified.
W-pII....10.5:1 and forever loved, as limitless as your **C.**,
W-pII..315.2:3 *may lead me on to my* **C.** *and His memory.*
W-pII..320.1:3 with his **C.** and Redeemer must be done.
W-pII....11.2:1 given all the power that their own **C.** has.
W-pII....11.4:5 their oneness and their unity with their **C.**
W-pII....11.5:2 we forgive creation in the Name of its **C.**,
W-pII....13.3:5 of God, upon the universal altar to **C.** and
W-pII.....354.h And in Him Is His **C.**, as He is in me.
W-pII..355.1:8 *Himself, and know You as his Father and* **C.**,
M-4......II.2:10 and for the Son of God and his **C.**. How
M-4.......IV.2:8 came neither from God's Son nor his **C.**.
M-5..........I.2:8 thus entirely usurped the throne of his **C.**.
M-19..........4:5 It remains forever and forever like its **C.**,
M-23..........6:1 Heaven is, or what its one **C.** really means.
M-27..........1:7 no one asks if a benign **C.** could will this.
M-27..........5:8 He is not **C.**, but avenger. Terrible His
M-29..........5:2 to acknowledge his **C.** and accept His gifts
C-2.............1:6 you are apart from your **C.** and a wish to
C-3.............3:5 content is unchanging, as eternal as its **C.**.
C-3.............8:4 And now the mind returns to its **C.**; the
C-6.............1:2 Holy Spirit, being a creation of the one **C.**,
C-6.............3:6 He never forgets the **C.** or His creation.
C-6.............4:2 He represents your Self and your **C.**, Who
P-2........IV.1:3 and again, against creation and its **C.**. It is
P-2.......VII.6:5 is. And he is this because of his **C.**, Whose
P-3.........II.5:3 as a gift from their **C.** as a sign of His Love
S-1.........in.1:2 the single voice **C.** and creation share; the
S-1.........II.7:8 now it rises as a song of thanks to your **C.**,

## creator 14
*Creator*
*See also* co-creator

T-3........IV.2:1 the mind a perceiver rather than a **c.**.
T-5........IV.7:4 the only **c.** that can create like the Father,
T-6......V.B.8:8 difficult if God Himself created you as a **c.**
T-7........XI.7:2 because you do not know their **c.**. You do
T-8.........V.2:1 will of the Sonship is the perfect **c.**, being
T-10......IV.5:6 of your creation established you a **c.**.
T-10.......V.4:3 accept the fact that, although he was a **c.**,
T-16....III.5:10 nothing real has ever left the mind of its **c.**
T-21.....II.10:4 spoke of your desire to create your own **c.**,
T-24.......II.3:4 the "**c.**" who creates unlike the Father,
T-28.......II.8:3 against him, taking on the role of its **c.**, as
T-30......III.6:6 They share the attributes of their **c.**, nor
W-pI.....72.4:6 as well. A **c.** wholly unlike his creation is
S-3........IV.5:3 think that it is you who are **c.** in His place,

## Creator's 4

T-22......VI.2:4 the outcome as He is sure of His **C.** Love.
T-25......III.5:1 can reconcile its goal with His **C.** purpose.
W-pI...169.9:3 wrote salvation's script in His **C.** Name,
W-pI...169.9:3 Name, and in the Name of His **C.** Son.

## creators 3
*See also* co-creators

T-6.........I.18:1 the time, because they were created as **c.**.
T-10.......V.5:5 make **c.** who are unlike your Creator, any
W-pI...166.2:4 trustworthy and true believes in two **c.**; or

## creature 2

T-30.......II.3:3 a slave to death, a little **c.** with a little life.
W-pI...194.8:3 every living **c.** not respond with healed

## creatures 1

W-pII....13.5:1 where starved and thirsty **c.** come to die.

## credibility 1

M-8...........5:5 carrying affect their **c.** in his perception?

## credit 2

T-26... VIII.6:8 disaster's form is difficult to **c.** in advance
W-pI...187.1:4 seems to make it hard to **c.** is not this. No

## credulous 1

T-9.........II.9:3 To believe is not to be **c.**, but to accept

## creed 1

T-13.VII.10:12 its own sake is the ego's fundamental **c.**, a

## creep 1

T-7... VIII.3:11 their projections are trying to **c.** back in.

## creeps 2

T19IV.A.17:14 For guilt **c.** in where happiness has been
T-24......III.4:4 that walks and breathes, or **c.** or crawls,

## crept 1

T-27... VIII.6:2 eternity, where all is one, there **c.** a tiny,

## cries 4

T-13.....VII.4:3 or not to hear the **c.** of pain that rise to it
W-pI...182.5:3 voice **c.** unto you to let Him rest a while.
W-pII......8.2:4 There are no **c.** of pain and sorrow heard,
C-2.............8:1 the need for vengeance and the **c.** of pain,

## crime 4

T-14....III.15:2 And you *will* feel guilty for this imagined **c.**
T-31.....VII.2:3 and blacken it with still another "**c.**." You
W-pI...190.2:4 for a **c.** that could not be committed; for
S-2...........I.2:2 will overlook no sin, no **c.**, no guilt that it

## crimes 2

T-25....VIII.5:9 a sinner for the **c.** he did not do, but
W-pI...190.4:3 is no need to think of them as savage **c.**,

## criminal 1

T-12...VII.13:2 goal, for it fully believes that you are a **c.**,

## crippled 1

T-27.......I.11:2 For this insists your **c.** picture is a lasting

## criteria 3

T-12.........I.8:1 that His **c.** are equally applicable to you.
W-pI...133.3:1 Today we list the real **c.** by which to test
M-10.........1:7 Nor can any consistent **c.** for determining

## criterion 7

T-17......VI.3:7 The absence of a **c.** for outcome, set in
T-19.........I.1:2 is inevitable. Its attainment is the **c.** by
W-pI.......2.2:4 sole **c.** for applying the idea to anything is
W-pI.133.11:1 to the **c.** for choice that is the hardest to
M-9...........2:6 as the **c.** for maturity and strength. Our
M-16.........3:2 This is by no means the ultimate **c.**, but at
M-24.......6:12 This is the sole **c.** this course requires. No

## critic 1

W-pII.268.1:1 *Let me not be Your* **c.**, *Lord, today, and*

## critical 1

T-9........III.1:2 Egos are **c.** in terms of the kind of "sense"

## cross 8
• noun
*verb*

T-4.........in.3:1 the **c.** should be the last "useless journey."
T-4.........in.3:7 error of "clinging to the old rugged **c.**."
T-4.........in.3:8 is that you can overcome the **c.**. Until
T-11......VI.8:1 You have nailed yourself to a **c.**, and
T19..IV.C.10:9 him shelter will follow him, not to the **c.**,
T-26......IX.8:4 stood a **c.** stands now the risen Christ,
W-pI...196.5:1 escape yourself has nailed you to the **c.**.
S-3........IV.9:7 healed My Son and took him from the **c.**.

## cross 21
• verb
*noun*
*See also* cross-examined

T-5...........I.6:5 to knowledge, or **c.** over into it. It might
T-14........X.4:4 is true of the thoughts that **c.** the mind of
T-16......III.8:5 would **c.** over is literally transported there
T-16......IV.2:5 and you will **c.** the bridge in perfect safety
T-16......IV.8:1 hands to help you **c.** and welcome them.
T-16......IV.9:2 Fear not to **c.** to the abode of peace and
T-16.....V.17:2 You will **c.** the bridge into reality simply
T-16....VI.11:3 Yet as you **c.** to join it, it will join with you
T-17........II.2:4 world and this is so little and so easy to **c.**,
T-26.....V.13:2 until you **c.** the gap between the past and
W-pI.....12.3:7 All terms which **c.** your mind are suitable
W-pI.....14.4:1 the horrors in the world that **c.** your mind
W-pI.....31.3:1 merely let whatever thoughts **c.** your
W-pI.....35.5:2 descriptive terms may well **c.** your mind.
W-pI.....35.7:2 events in which you figure **c.** your mind.
W-pI.....65.5:2 carefully to catch whatever thoughts **c.** it.
W-pI...74.3:10 conflict thoughts that may **c.** your mind.
W-pI.134.15:1 "sins," as one by one they **c.** your mind.
W-pI.137.10:1 all those around you, or who **c.** your mind
W-pI...153.8:3 dream happened to **c.** our minds, and we
W-pI...200.8:1 Peace is the bridge that everyone will **c.**,

**cross-examined** 1
T-8......VIII.4:2 because you have not seriously **c.** him. If

**crossed** 3
T-16......VI.6:4 Once you have **c.** the bridge, the value of
T-31.......I.13:1 of good that ever **c.** your mind of anyone.
W-pI.....78.5:1 his name has **c.** your mind already. He

**crosses** 4
W-pI.....10.4:7 As each one **c.** your mind, say: *My thought*
W-pI.....16.5:1 and then as each one **c.** your mind hold it
W-pI.....23.6:3 As each one **c.** your mind say: *I can escape*
W-pI.....24.7:1 situation that **c.** your mind say to yourself

**crossing** 2
T-16....VI.11:1 you will gain from **c.** over will be the
W-pI.......4.1:2 that are **c.** your mind for about a minute.

**crowd** 1
W-pI.....13.3:2 and **c.** it with images that do not exist. To

**crown** 6
T-11......VI.8:1 placed a **c.** of thorns upon your own head.
T-20.........I.2:5 the gift of lilies, not the **c.** of thorns; the
T-20....... II.1:5 Learn you but offer him a **c.** of thorns, not
T-20....... II.7:8 the Son of God, and **c.** him king of death.
T-27.........I.1:4 will weave a **c.** of thorns from which your
W-pI.161.11:5 lift the **c.** of thorns which you have placed

**crowned** 1
T-23.........I.9:3 between illusions, one to be **c.** as real, the

**crowning** 1
T-13....VIII.3:9 by **c.** them as one with the final gift of

**crowns** 1
T-14....... II.2:7 are kings with golden **c.** because of them.

**crucial** 18
T-6......V.A.4:4 Kingdom to let this **c.** concept slip away.
T-6......V.C.1:9 The ego's beliefs on this **c.** issue vary, and
T-11......IV.4:4 This is a **c.** step in the reawakening. The
T-12.........I.8:5 as a **c.** step in the undoing of the ego.
T-12....... III.6:6 himself, for this is **c.** to his adjustment.
T-12....... V.6:4 ability to generalize is a **c.** learning failure
T-13....... III.1:1 You may wonder why it is so **c.** that you
T-22....... II.6:1 This is a **c.** period in this course, for here
T-25.......IX.5:4 means no one can lose is **c.** to this course.
T-28....... II.7:2 This is a **c.** step in dealing with illusions.
W-pI.....20.1:4 not lost sight of the **c.** importance of the
W-pI.....25.5:1 **c.** to your learning to be willing to give up
W-pI.....39.3:6 salvation is **c.** to the salvation of the world
W-pI.....64.6:6 you remember the **c.** importance of your
W-pI.....91.2:1 you, then, light is **c.**. While you remain in
W-pI...126.1:1 **c.** to the thought reversal that this course
W-pI...157.2:1 This is another **c.** turning point in the
M-17 .........1:1 is a **c.** question both for teacher and pupil

**crucified** 19
T-6...........I.3:1 reacted for years as if you were being **c.**.
T-6...........I.6:6 You are not asked to be **c.**, which was part
T-11......VI.8:5 While you perceive the Son of God as **c.**,
T-13.......in.4:2 you realize that God's Son cannot be **c.**,
T-13....... II.5:1 that you believe you have **c.** God's Son.
T-13...... III.7:1 And yet he is not **c.**. Here is both his pain
T19. IV.D.15:1 **c.** by sin and waiting for release from pain
T19. IV.D.20:3 The **c.** give pain because they are in pain.
T-20....... II.3:8 Offer him thorns and *you* are **c.**. Offer him
T-20 ......II.8:10 glad refrain the Son of God was never **c.**.
T-20 ..... III.9:5 He seemed to be **c.** beside you. And yet
T-24 ... III.8:13 Father it was not His Will that you be **c.**.
T-24 ..... IV.5:4 and **c.** the one whom God has given you
W-pI... 101.4:5 of God upon you who have **c.** His Son.
W-pI. 134.17:7 *No one is c. alone, and yet no one can enter*
WpI...rV.in6:6 God's Son is **c.** until you walk along the
W-pI... 196.3:3 will not believe you are a body to be **c.**.
W-pII . 303.2:7 *me. It is not Christ that can be c.. Safe in Your*
W-pII . 338.1:6 He **c.** himself. Yet God has planned that

**crucifies** 1
P-3........ III.3:7 For if it does, it merely **c.** God's Son again

**crucifixion** 52
T-3 ..........I.1:2 The **c.** did not establish the Atonement;
T-3 ..........I.1:5 **c.** is seen from an upside-down point of
T-4 .........in.3:5 reparation, and finally the **c.** of the body,
T-4 .........in.3:8 The only message of the **c.** is that you can
T-6 .............I.h The Message of the **C.**
T-6 ..........I.1:1 purposes, let us consider the **c.** again. I
T-6 ..........I.1:5 is a positive interpretation of the **c.** that is
T-6 ..........I.2:1 The **c.** is nothing more than an extreme
T-6 ..........I.2:6 I have also told you that the **c.** was the last
T-6 ..........I.2:7 the purpose of the **c.** and how it actually
T-6 ..........I.3:4 real meaning of the **c.** lies in the *apparent*
T-6 ..........I.4:6 The message the **c.** was intended to teach
T-6 ........I.12:1 The **c.** cannot be shared because it is the
T-6 ........I.13:1 The message of the **c.** is perfectly clear:
T-6 ........I.14:1 If you interpret the **c.** in any other way,
T-6 ........I.14:4 they speak of the **c.** entirely without anger
T-6 ........I.15:6 whole message of the **c.** was simply that I
T-6 ........I.16:7 it. The **c.** was the result of clearly opposed
T-6 ....... III.2:4 said before that the message of the **c.** was,
T-11 ..... VI.2:1 you join in the resurrection or the **c.**?
T-11 ..... VI.5:4 The god of **c.** demands that he crucify,
T-11 ..... VI.7:2 His Son whom the god of **c.** condemns.
T-11 ..... VI.7:5 undoing of the **c.** of God's Son is the work
T-11 ..... VI.8:3 Son has been redeemed from his own **c.**,
T-11 ..... VI.8:4 dream of **c.** still lies heavy on your eyes,
T-12 .......II.7:4 Our mission is to escape from **c.**, not from
T-13 ......in.4:1 world *is* a picture of the **c.** of God's Son.
T-13 .......II.3:3 **c.** of God's Son can ultimately satisfy it. It
T-13 .......II.6:1 I have said that the **c.** is the symbol of the
T-13 ... III.1:10 You are not really afraid of **c.**. Your real
T-13 .... III.5:2 of the **c.** than a Son of God in redemption
T-13 .... III.6:6 heal it, for here is the real **c.** of God's Son.
T-14 .... III.4:1 you are deciding between the **c.** and the
T-14 .... V.10:1 The **c.** had no part in the Atonement.
T-14 .... V.10:6 **C.** is always the ego's aim. It sees everyone
T-14 .... V.10:9 and therefore cannot crucify nor suffer **c.**.
T-14 .... V.11:1 judging him fit for **c.** or for redemption. If
T-17 ...VIII.5:1 Such was the **c.** of the Son of God. His
T-20 ........I.1:2 week brooding on the **c.** of God's Son, but
T-20 ........I.2:2 Let no dark sign of **c.** intervene between
T-20 ........I.2:9 We cannot be united in **c.** and in death.
T-20 ........I.3:3 him not wander into the temptation of **c.**,
T-20 ....II.11:1 released from **c.** through your vision, and
T-21 .......II.1:2 by which the **c.** is changed to resurrection
T-24 ..... IV.1:7 enthroned as savior; **c.** is now redemption
T-26 .. VII.17:1 In **c.** is redemption laid, for healing is not
T-26 .. VII.17:4 of God from **c.** and from hell and death,
T-27 ...........I.h The Picture of **C.**
T-27 ........I.3:2 hold a picture of your **c.** before his eyes,
W-pI... 196.3:4 past all thoughts of **c.** and of death, to
W-pII ... 12.4:2 is so immense that **c.** of the Son of God is
C-2 .......... 6:14 it. Where there was **c.** stands God's Son.

**crucify** 20
T-4 ........in.3:9 free to **c.** yourself as often as you choose.
T-11 ...... VI.5:4 The god of crucifixion demands that he **c.**
T-11 ...... VI.5:5 In his name they **c.** themselves, believing
T-11 ...... VI.8:2 Yet you cannot **c.** God's Son, for the Will
T-11 ...... VI.8:6 as long as you believe that you can **c.** him,
T-13 .......II.5:2 still wish to **c.** him if you could find him.
T-14 .... V.10:4 you perceive as guilty you would **c.**. Yet
T-14 .....V.10:9 therefore cannot **c.** nor suffer crucifixion.
T-14 ..... VI.5:7 You who made it to **c.** yourself must learn
T-20 .......II.7:8 no thorns nor nails to **c.** the Son of God,
T-21 ...... in.2:3 and catastrophe, you tried to **c.** him. If
T-27 ........I.1:5 You cannot **c.** yourself alone. And if you
T-29 ..... VI.5:1 think that it was made to **c.** God's Son.
W-pI 135.17:4 attack, obscure, and take apart and **c.**.
W-pI ..... 196.h It can be but myself I **c.**.
W-pI .. 196.9:2 If it can but be you you **c.**, you did not
W-pI 196.12:5 is indeed but you your mind can try to **c.**.
W-pI .. 216.1:1 (196) It can be but myself I **c.**. *All that I do*
M-13 ......... 6:2 you hold dear the things that **c.** God's Son
M-28 ......... 6:9 all he sought before to **c.** are resurrected

**crucifying** 1
T-9 .......... I.8:4 and the martyr believes that God is **c.** him

**cruel** 23
T-13 .... in.2:11 of them but has thought that God is **c.**.
T-13 ...... in.3:1 If this were the real world, God *would* be **c.**
T-13 ........ I.3:7 will seem long and **c.** and senseless, for so
T-13 ........ I.4:2 The Father is not **c.**, and His Son cannot
T-13 ..... XI.1:2 and ravaged by a **c.** war unless he believes
T-17 ..... III.4:2 For time *is* **c.** in the ego's hands, as it is
T-18 ..... III.3:3 into darkness has been long and **c.**, and
T19 .. IV.D.4:3 life seem to be ugly, **c.** and tyrannical.
T-31 .... VII.5:7 let the **c.** concept of yourself be changed
W-pI .. 101.4:4 meted out in **c.** form to match the vicious
W-pI .. 129.2:3 you see is merciless indeed, unstable, **c.**,
W-pI .. 170.1:3 you mean that to be **c.** is protection; you
W-pI .. 170.7:1 we look upon this **c.** god dispassionately.
W-pI 170.10:6 above all else, **c.** beyond conception,
W-pI 170.11:3 chosen that this **c.** god remain with you in
W-pI .. 190.1:5 For pain proclaims God **c.**. How could it
W-pI .. 190.8:5 the world becomes a **c.** and a bitter place,
W-pI .. 190.9:4 Lay down the **c.** sword of judgment that
M-29 ......... 6:8 be **c.** if He let your words replace His Own
C-2 ........... 8:1 This was the ego–all the **c.** hate, the
S-2...........I.1:2 was meant to bless, a **c.** mockery of grace,
S-3..........II.5:1 death is **c.** in its frightened eyes and takes
S-3..........II.6:1 it brings a **c.** death in seeming victory. It

**cruelly** 3
T-18 ...VIII.3:1 Within this kingdom the ego rules, and **c.**
W-pI .. 189.5:4 world, held **c.** in death's sharp-pointed,
W-pI .. 191.6:3 You have no need to use it **c.**, and then

**cruelty** 13
T-25 .... VII.5:3 joy. Nothing attests to death and **c.**; to
W-pI ..... 170.h There is no **c.** in God and none in me.
W-pI .. 170.1:3 is protection; you are safe because of **c.**.
W-pI .. 170.6:1 love as enemy, must **c.** become a god.
W-pI .. 170.8:6 it? For the god of **c.** takes many forms.
W-pI .. 170.9:5 love appears to be invested now with **c.**.
W-pI 170.10:3 fear's "enemy"; its **c.** as now a part of love
W-pI 170.12:6 way for love, as God Himself replaces **c.**.
W-pI 170.13:2 *No c. abides in us, for there is none in You.*
W-pI .. 180.2:1 There is no **c.** in God and none in me.
W-pII . 331.1:4 *desolate, to die within a world of pain and c..*
M-27 ......... 7:2 Do not believe in **c.**, nor let attack conceal
S-2..........II.4:3 as meekness and as charity instead of **c.**.

**crumb** 1
T-26 ........I.5:4 tiny **c.** of happiness that you allot yourself

**crumble** 3
T-29 .... VII.5:4 form. Yet each must fail and **c.** and decay,
W-pI .. 170.5:5 And your arms indeed would **c.** into dust.
W-pI .. 186.7:2 it does not know, sensing its basis **c.**. Let

**crumbled** 1
T-25 .......II.6:6 forever, when yours has **c.** into dust. But

**crumbles** 2
W-pII......5.1:2 thinks he lives, to die as it decays and **c.**.
S-1 ........IV.4:5 little space that lasts until it **c.** into dust?

**crumbling** 4
T-13.....VII.3:3 built has withstood the **c.** assault of time.
T-24......IV.4:8 that lasts an instant, **c.** into dust.
T-24....... V.4:8 and madness, and believe this **c.** thing,
W-pI ...135.5:4 to the thief of time, corruptible and **c.**, so

**crumbs** 1
T-20......VI.5:3 reality, and seeks for **c.** to keep itself alive.

**crusade** 1
T-1........III.1:6 you must join the great **c.** to correct it;

**crush** 1
T-13......III.4:1 think it would **c.** you into nothingness.

**cry** 2
T-27....... II.6:6 weak and miserable **c.** of death and guilt.
T-27......VI.6:6 a plaintive **c.** for help within a world of

**crystal** 1
T-15...... I.13:7 In the **c.** cleanness of the release you give

**cues** 1
T-21.........I.1:5 Your **c.** for inference are wrong, and so

**cultivate** 1
T-5........VI.6:1 worth cultivating you will **c.** in yourself.

**cultivating** 1
T-5........VI.6:1 worth **c.** you will cultivate in yourself.

**cumbersome** 1
W-pI.135.20:4 our brothers lay aside their **c.** defenses,

**cunning** 1
T-23..... II.11:2 from this most treacherous and **c.** enemy?

**cup** 9
W-pI .......7.3:1 Look at a **c.**, for example. Do you see a
W-pI .......7.3:2 you see a **c.**, or are you merely reviewing
W-pI .......7.3:2 your past experiences of picking up a **c.**,
W-pI .......7.3:2 up a cup, being thirsty, drinking from a **c.**
W-pI .......7.3:2 feeling the rim of a **c.** against your lips,
W-pI .......7.3:3 Are not your aesthetic reactions to the **c.**,
W-pI .......7.3:4 not this kind of **c.** will break if you drop it
W-pI .......7.3:5 this **c.** except what you learned in the past
W-pI .......7.3:6 You would have no idea what this **c.** is,

**cure** 25
T-23..... II.12:5 is the magic that will **c.** all of your pain;
T-26....... II.7:5 a remedy, or an affliction without a **c.**, has
W-pI.....41.3:2 It will **c.** all sorrow and pain and fear and
W-pI ......140.h Only salvation can be said to **c.**.
W-pI ...140.1:1 "**C.**" is a word that cannot be applied to
W-pI ...140.3:5 are gone. And thus they **c.** for all eternity.
W-pI ...140.4:4 does not heal the sick, for that is not a **c.**.
W-pI ...140.4:6 And that is **c.** indeed. For sickness now is
W-pI ...140.5:2 For **c.** must come from holiness, and
W-pI ...140.7:1 to seek to **c.** what cannot suffer sickness.
W-pI ...140.8:1 sickness, for we seek a **c.** for all illusions,
W-pI.140.10:2 of healing, which will **c.** all ills as one,
W-pI.140.10:3 No voice but this can **c.**. Today we hear a
W-pI.140.12:2 *Only salvation can be said to* **c.**. *Speak to us,*
W-pI...150.2:1 (140) Only salvation can be said to **c.**.
P-2........IV.4:1 word "**c.**" has come into disrepute among
P-2........IV.4:2 For not one of them can **c.**, and not one of
P-2........IV.4:4 it. How could such a process **c.**? It is
P-2........IV.4:9 And how could sickness **c.**? Are not these
P-2........IV.5:2 error lies in the belief that it can **c.** itself.
P-2......VI.4:10 **c.** what cannot be sick and make it well?
P-2........VI.5:4 Yet seeing this will not effect a **c.**. That is
P-2........VII.2:5 What is symptom **c.**, when another is
S-3 ...........I.1:4 is shown by the brief nature of the "**c.**."
S-3......... II.6:1 False healing rests upon the body's **c.**,

**cured** 6
W-pI.....41.2:3 be **c.** because the problem is not real. The
W-pI...140.5:1 Peace be to you who have been **c.** in God,
W-pI...140.7:2 applied to what is sick, so that it can be **c.**.
W-pI...140.9:5 and can be **c.** because they are not true.
M-5 ..... II.2:13 of sickness that would not be **c.** at once.
P-2......IV.11:3 The body is not **c.**. It is merely recognized

**cures** 4
W-pI.....41.2:1 separated ones have invented many "**c.**"
W-pI...140.4:1 heals with certainty, and **c.** all sickness.
W-pI...140.6:1 This is the thought that **c.**. It does not
P-2........IV.5:4 Yet must their **c.** remain temporary, or

**curious** 6
T-3........VI.5:7 **c.** that an ability so debilitating would be
T-6........IV.8:5 **c.** that the perfect must now be perfected.
T-16....... V.7:1 Most **c.** of all is the concept of the self
M-27 .........4:1 **c.** belief that there is part of dying things
P-2........IV.9:3 This **c.** circle of attack-defense is one of
S-1 ......... II.4:1 level also comes that **c.** contradiction in

**curiously** 1
M-25 .........4:5 unusual abilities that can be **c.** tempting.

**currently** 1
W-pI.....24.4:1 about which you are **c.** concerned. The

**curricular** 1
T-12....... V.7:2 Translated into **c.** terms this means, "Try

**curriculum** 70
T-in ...........1:4 *does not mean that you can establish the* **c.**.
T-8.............I.h The Direction of the **C.**
T-8...........I.5:1 **c.** of the Atonement is the opposite of the
T-8...........I.5:1 of the **c.** you have established for yourself,
T-8...........I.5:2 a change in the **c.** is obviously necessary.
T-8...........I.5:4 A meaningful **c.** cannot be inconsistent. If
T-8.........I.5:10 Their conflicted **c.** teaches them that *all*
T-8...........I.6:1 The total senselessness of such a **c.** must
T-8...........I.6:3 joint **c.** presents an impossible learning
T-8......... II.1:3 to that knowledge is the purpose of the **c.**,
T-8......... II.3:8 of the **c.** that must be unconflicted, but
T-8........ III.5:1 goal of the **c.**, regardless of the teacher
T-8........ III.6:2 To achieve the goal of the **c.**, then, you
T-8.......VII.7:7 and thus to confuse the goal of His **c.**.
T-8.......VII.8:1 to a learner as a **c.** he cannot learn. His
T-8.......VII.8:5 The Holy Spirit's **c.** is never depressing,
T-8.......VII.8:5 never depressing, because it is a **c.** of joy
T-8.......VII.8:6 true goal of the **c.** has been lost sight of.
T-8.....VII.12:5 To confuse a learning device with a **c.** goal
T-8.....VII.14:6 to the unified purpose of the **c.**, and one
T-12..............h THE HOLY SPIRIT'S **C.**
T-12.......... V.h The Sane **C.**
T-12....... V.5:4 require a special Teacher and a special **c.**.
T-12....... V.5:6 hardly turn to them to establish the **c.** by
T-12....... V.6:2 not try to set up **c.** goals where yours have
T-12....... V.7:3 The result of this **c.** goal is obvious. Every
T-12....... V.7:4 the learning this strange **c.** is against. If
T-12....... V.7:6 a **c.** does not make sense. This attempt at
T-12....... V.7:7 for the **c.** you have chosen is against love,
T-12....... V.7:8 A supplementary goal in this **c.** is learning
T-12....... V.7:9 you will not overcome the split in this **c.**,
T-12....... V.8:1 **c.** you set yourself is depressing indeed, it
T-12....... V.9:2 and understands His **c.** for learning it.
T-12....... V.9:3 it. The **c.** is totally unambiguous, because
T-14....... V.6:1 part in the unified **c.** of the Atonement.
T-14....... V.6:3 There is no conflict in this **c.**, which has
T-18.... IX.11:1 itself is still beyond the scope of our **c.**.
T-26.... III.1:13 magnitude beyond the scope of this **c.**.
T-30.......in.1:1 now becomes the focus of the **c.**. The goal
W-pI...156.2:1 in the thoughts that we present in our **c.**.
W-pI...157.2:1 is another crucial turning point in the **c.**.
WpI rVI.in.2:2 Each contains the whole **c.** if understood,
M-in ..........3:1 The **c.** you set up is therefore determined
M-in ..........4:4 Everyone who follows the world's **c.**, and
M-in ..........4:6 What else, then, would its **c.** be? Into this
M-1 ...........4:1 This is a manual for a special **c.**, intended
M-2 ...........1:2 form of the universal **c.** that he will teach
M-2 ...........3:6 you are not free to choose the **c.**, or even
M-4 ...... IV.1:7 It demonstrates the absence of God's **c.**,
M-4 .....VII.1:6 the world than many other ideas in our **c.**.
M-4 ...... IX.1:1 the measure of his advancement in the **c.**.
M-4 ....... X.2:9 Forgiveness is the final goal of the **c.**. It
M-4 ..... X.2:11 **c.** makes no effort to exceed its legitimate
M-4 ....... X.3:4 God has given is so far beyond our **c.** that
M-4 ....... X.3:5 the focus properly belongs on the **c.**. It is
M-9 ...........2:5 goal in direct opposition to that of our **c.**.
M-9 ...........2:7 Our **c.** trains for the relinquishment of
M-10 .........3:1 The aim of our **c.**, unlike the goal of the
M-14 .......5:11 and say you cannot learn His Own **c.**. His
M-20 .......5:10 Spirit's whole **c.** specified exactly as it is.
M-23 .........7:5 Yet do we need a many-faceted **c.**, not
M-24 .........2:6 be regarded as essential to the **c.**. There is
M-28 .........3:1 the **c.** ends. From here on, no directions
M-28 .........3:5 The goal of the **c.** has been achieved.
M-29 .........2:6 The **c.** is highly individualized, and all
M-29 .........3:5 the core of the **c.**. The imagined usurping
P-2..........II.7:3 one, and lets him formulate his own **c.**;
P-3...........I.4:1 thing; he did not make the **c.** of salvation,
P-3..........II.2:2 because the **c.** by which he became a
P-3..........II.2:4 world's teaching follows a **c.** in judgment,

**curriculum's** 1
P-2..........II.7:3 his own curriculum; not the **c.** goal, but

**curse** 10
T-24...... III.7:5 and they **c.** God because He did not make
T-24...... III.7:6 **C.** God and die, but not by Him Who
T-24...... IV.2:4 The goal of separation is its **c.**. Yet bodies
T-25....VIII.7:1 So do they think the loss of sin a **c.**. And
W-pI...101.4:5 **c.** of God upon you who have crucified
W-pI.137.13:1 to the world, exchanging **c.** for blessing,
W-pII ...13.3:3 what was meant to **c.** has come to bless.
M-6 ...........2:9 it is recognized as a blessing and not a **c.**.
S-2 ...........I.1:2 a scourge; a **c.** where it was meant to bless
S-3 ........ III.1:2 not removed the **c.** of sin that lies on it.

**cursed** 1
W-pI.130.11:1 have damned your eyes and **c.** your sight,

**cursory** 1
W-pI.....24.3:2 a more **c.** examination of a large number.

**curtailed** 2
T-4.......VII.4:5 this state to be **c.** you are limiting your
W-pII .319.1:4 seek for aims which are **c.** and limiting.

**curtain** 4
T-11..VIII.13:3 is helped to translate his "ghost" into a **c.**,
W-pI...164.5:1 day when vain imaginings part like a **c.**, to

W-pI....164.8:1 Open the **c.** in your practicing by merely
M-20.........4:2 form, will drop the heavy **c.** once again,

**curtains** 1
T-31.........I.3:4 **c.** to obscure the simple and the obvious.

**cut** 9
*See also* clear-cut
T-3......VII.6:1 no fruit will be **c.** off and will wither away.
T-8......VII.1:8 them, he has **c.** himself off from salvation.
T-11.....IV.3:4 **c.** off a brother from the light that is yours
T-16.....VI.7:3 strong and powerful **c.** down to littleness.
T-21......V.4:2 self you have **c.** off from your awareness.
T-24........I.7:3 might be extended, not **c.** off from him.
T-24.......II.2:2 can attack his savior and **c.** him down, yet
T-27........I.7:3 For who could live a life so soon **c.** short
W-pI..165.6:6 deprivation cannot **c.** him off from God's

**cutting** 1
T-17.....V.13:3 And by **c.** yourself off from its expression,

**cyclical** 1
M-27.........1:6 life. The **c.**, the changing and unsure; the

# D

**daily** 8
T-2......III.5:10 starves you by denying you your **d.** bread.
W-pI.....65.4:1 to undertake the **d.** extended practice
WpIrIII.in10:2 Attempt to give your **d.** two ideas a brief
W-pI.153.15:2 to the **d.** thought as long as possible. Five
W-pII..in.11:2 our **d.** lessons and the periods of wordless
W-pII.....2.4:1 Let us come **d.** to this holy place, and
W-pII...12.4:2 of God is offered **d.** at its darkened shrine,
W-ep.........4:4 earned your trust by speaking **d.** to you of

**damaged** 3
T-27.......II.1:3 is a bar to love, and **d.** bodies are accusers
T-27.......II.1:4 and that the **d.** have no grounds for peace
T-27.......II.1:7 because your **d.** body shows that *you* must

**damn** 4
T-22.......II.8:4 And vision cannot **d.**, but only bless.
T-22......III.2:8 Thus does the ego **d.**, and reason save.
T-25......VI.1:4 himself for his mistakes than **d.** another.
W-pI.....76.8:6 would not save but **d.** in Heaven's name.

**damnation** 7
T-15...VII.13:1 communication as surely as **d.** lies in guilt
T-15...VII.13:2 to be **d.** that communication is salvation.
T-17......IV.9:3 This gift is given you for your **d.**, and if
T-21.......in.2:1 **D.** is your judgment on yourself, and this
T-24......III.8:3 God condemn Himself to hell and to **d.**?
W-pI...121.3:2 the unforgiving mind perceive but its **d.**?
W-pII.331.1:2 *Could he make a plan for his* **d.**, *and be left*

**damned** 13
T-17......IV.9:3 you take it you will believe that you *are* **d.**.
T19....IV.C.4:2 **d.** by its maker and lamented by every
T-21.......in.2:2 See it as **d.**, and all you see is what you did
T-21......VI.1:8 belief you both will think that you are **d.**.
T-21......VI.6:2 You tell him, by your choice, that he is **d.**;
T-25......III.8:5 been **d.** is damned and damned forever,
T-25......III.8:5 been damned is **d.** and damned forever,
T-25......III.8:5 been damned is damned and **d.** forever,
T-25......III.9:6 Is it your purpose that he be saved or **d.**?
W-pI.....71.1:3 God's plan in place of the ego's is to be **d.**.
W-pI.130.11:1 have **d.** your eyes and cursed your sight,
W-pII.296.1:4 *For having* **d.** *it I would set it free, that I may*
S-3...........I.3:5 For he has **d.** his body as his prison, and

**damning** 1
T-27.........I.3:2 closing off the gate and **d.** him to hell. Yet

**damns** 1
C-2..........10:1 The miracle forgives; the ego **d.**. Neither

**dance** 4
T-16..V.12:10 in which the **d.** of death delights you can
T-30.....IV.4:4 They seem to **d.** a little while, according
T-30.....IV.5:9 they are idols which but **d.** to vain desires.
C-6............5:6 in which you **d.** to death's thin melody.

**dances** 1
T-18...VIII.7:3 the ripple **d.** as it rests upon the ocean.

**dancing** 5
T-18........I.7:6 like feathers **d.** insanely in the wind, have
T-18........I.8:1 Let them all go, **d.** in the wind, dipping
T-20.VIII.11:1 them in **d.** brooks that never waste away;
T-27....VII.8:7 is his worth that he is but a **d.** shadow,
T-30.....IV.4:7 them. Their **d.** never brought you joy. But

**danger** 31
T-4........II.9:7 not in **d.** and does not need to be salvaged
T-5.......III.8:9 the idea of **d.** has entered your mind. The
T-5.....III.8:11 is as vigilant as the ego to the call of **d.**,
T-7.......IV.7:7 the sense of **d.** the ego has induced in you,
T-12........I.3:8 Perhaps the **d.** of this to your own mind is
T-15..VII.12:3 safety in guilt and **d.** in communication.
T19..IV.C.10:1 What **d.** can assail the wholly innocent?
T-24.....IV.1:5 In **d.** of destruction it must kill, and you
T-24......V.4:2 And both will walk in **d.**, each intent, in
T-28....VII.6:1 safe in what was made for **d.** and for fear?
T-29.....VI.1:4 and the dream of **d.** and destruction, sin
T-30....VII.7:2 in which you walk in **d.** and uncertainty.
W-pI...76.12:2 of freedom from all **d.** and all tyranny. It
W-pI...109.1:3 we seem to look on **d.** and on sorrow.
W-pI...121.2:3 not, yet certain of the **d.** lurking there.
W-pI...131.1:2 there is none, for safety in the midst of **d.**;
W-pI...131.2:7 while in your heart you pray for **d.** and
W-pI...135.2:2 a belief that there is **d.** which has power
W-pI...153.1:5 mind is possible where **d.** threatens thus.
W-pI...170.7:6 guardian, no strength to call upon in **d.**,
W-pI...189.2:2 you safe from every form of **d.** and of pain
W-pI...190.9:2 Lay down all thoughts of **d.** and of fear.
W-pII....244.h I am in **d.** nowhere in the world.
W-pII.261.1:3 Let me today seek not security in **d.**, nor
W-pII.....8.3:5 No **d.** lurks in anything it sees, for it is
M-4....VI.1:11 It is not **d.** that comes when defenses are
M-5.........I.1:6 strength is seen as threat and health as **d.**.
M-16.......6:11 will not work, but you are not in **d.**. You
M-29.........7:9 your dreams of **d.** and selected "wrongs."
P-2........IV.9:6 cannot but be seen as a real source of **d.**,
S-2...........I.2:4 plague; a hateful thing of **d.** and of death.

**dangerous** 26
T-2.........V.8:5 becomes doubly **d.** unless it *is* perceived.
T-3.......VI.4:5 It is not **d.** in itself, but you have made it
T-3.......VI.4:5 itself, but you have made it seem **d.** to you
T-8.......IX.6:3 is because the ego believes that mind is **d.**,
T-9.......IV.7:4 It is a particularly **d.** combination of
T-11.......V.1:2 from illusions, for they cannot be **d.**. We
T-12.....IV.1:1 The ego is certain that love is **d.**, and this
T-13 VII.10:10 is a **d.** concept if it is left to you. The ego
T-16.....IV.5:9 Where one choice is as **d.** as the other, the
T-16...VI.10:4 has wrought is ugly, fearful and very **d.**.
T-17...IV.10:3 who are truth accept an idea so **d.** to truth
T-20.....III.2:3 are no interferences, are always seen as **d.**.
T-21...VIII.1:1 Are thoughts, then, **d.**? To bodies, yes!
T-22...VI.12:8 safety? Attack is neither safe nor **d.**. It is
T-24.....IV.1:3 feared and attacked, deadly and **d.**, hated
T-26...VIII.3:9 is withheld from you and given seem **d.**,
T-29...VIII.2:3 self, for safety in a world perceived as **d.**,
T-29.....IX.5:4 toy grow large and **d.** and fierce and wild?
W-pI....12.3:2 *I think I see a fearful world, a* **d.** *world, a*
W-pI 133.11:3 too **d.** to be the nothingness it actually is.
W-pI..170.1:5 secure from **d.** invasion and from fear.
W-pII.339.1:4 that joy is painful, threatening and **d.**.
Wfl........in.1:5 attacking and destroying, **d.** in all its ways
M-16.........2:5 way. Routines as such are **d.**, because they
M-16.......10:8 fearful, not that it is sinful, not that it is **d.**
S-1........III.3:8 it may seem to be **d.** instead of merciful.

**dangers** 5
T-10.....III.5:3 save you from the **d.** for which it stands,
T-13..VII.15:1 you safely through all **d.** to your peace of
T-20.....III.4:2 your timid way through constant **d.**,
W-pI....50.3:2 you high above all the perceived **d.** of this
W-pI..121.1:3 to safety in apparent **d.** that appear to

**dare** 3
T-16.....V.11:2 of value, you would not **d.** to look upon it.
T19..IV.D.9:3 no one would **d.** to look on it without
T-21....VII.5:3 in sin would **d.** believe he has no enemy?

**dark** 96
T-4.......IV.1:6 the ego seeks to see its face is **d.** indeed.
T-4.......IV.9:2 To the ego's **d.** glass you need but say, "I
T-5.....VI.11:2 my reference to the ego's **d.** glass, and
T-11......in.2:7 the **d.** cornerstone of its thought system.

T-11.......in.3:9 the **d.** cornerstone of terror on which it
T-11.......in.4:4 in order to keep a **d.** cornerstone hidden,
T-11......III.4:5 the **d.** journey is not the way of God's Son
T-11......III.4:6 in light and do not see the **d.** companions,
T-11......III.4:8 the **d.** companions in a light such as this?
T-11......III.5:5 The **d.** companions, the dark way, are all
T-11......III.5:5 The dark companions, the **d.** way, are all
T-11......III.6:2 Do not be deceived by the **d.** comforters,
T-11......III.7:8 with the **d.** companions beside you, but
T-13.......II.3:2 **d.** and secret place is the realization that
T-13.......II.9:3 no **d.** cloud will remain between you and
T-13......III.2:1 ego's **d.** foundation is the memory of God
T-13......III.2:6 by removing the **d.** cloud that obscures it,
T-13......III.9:2 you will be hiding a **d.** place in your mind
T-13......VI.2:5 see it as a **d.** cloud that shrouds your
T-13......VI.5:4 Let no **d.** cloud out of your past obscure
T-13...VII.13:3 will ensure it never can become a **d.** spot,
T-13......IX.7:2 And by projecting it the world seems **d.**,
T-13......IX.7:3 You throw a **d.** veil over it, and cannot see
T-13......IX.8:5 For those who see their brothers in the **d.**,
T-13......IX.8:5 guilty in the **d.** in which they shroud them
T-13......X.8:3 alone in a **d.** world where pain is pressing
T-14.........I.3:2 system you made would be forever **d.**.
T-14.......II.7:5 the key to the **d.** door that you believe is
T-14....III.16:4 to everyone who struggles in the **d.**. For
T-14......VI.1:1 together is the exchange of **d.** for light, of
T-14......VI.1:6 clear and you would be no longer in the **d.**
T-14......VI.6:1 speak in **d.** and devious symbols do not
T-14......VI.8:4 serve to guard the **d.** doors behind which
T-14.....VII.6:8 all your **d.** and secret thoughts to Him,
T-14... VIII.1:2 in guilt and in the **d.** denial of innocence.
T-14... VIII.1:3 the **d.** doors you have closed lies nothing,
T-14......XI.4:6 this, all your **d.** lessons must be brought
T-14......XI.4:7 Every **d.** lesson that you bring to Him
T-14......XI.5:3 are **d.** lessons in your mind that hurt and
T-14......XI.5:5 Every **d.** lesson teaches this, in one form
T-14......XI.5:6 will replace the **d.** ones you do not accept,
T-14......XI.8:5 for keeping certain **d.** lessons from Him.
T-14......XI.9:6 no **d.** lessons He has not already lightened
T-14....XI.10:7 no **d.** lesson of guilt can abide in what He
T-15.....VII.3:4 is, and have judged it completely in the **d.**
T-16....IV.10:4 To lift the veil that seems so **d.** and heavy,
T-17....IV.14:6 The **d.** picture, brought to light, is not
T-18......IX.6:1 is like a bank of low **d.** clouds that seem to
T-18......IX.8:1 So should it be with the **d.** clouds of guilt,
T-18......IX.9:7 the **d.** and heavy garments of guilt laid by,
T19... IV.C.1:9 its **d.** shadow falls across all living things,
T19... IV.C.7:2 the great **d.** savior from the light of truth,
T19... IV.C.8:3 There is no funeral, no **d.** altars, no grim
T19...IV.D.2:3 For this **d.** veil, which seems to make the
T-20.........I.2:2 Let no **d.** sign of crucifixion intervene
T-21.....VII.2:5 it? These are the **d.** ones, silent and afraid,
T-21.....VII.3:1 Frantic and loud and strong the **d.** ones
T-22.......II.1:5 and suffering in the **d.** folds of the heavy
T-22.......II.1:6 **d.** and heavy garments are those who seek
T-22.......II.2:6 All that is possible in the **d.** world of
T-22......VI.9:5 Save no **d.** secrets that He cannot use, but
T-24.......V.4:2 intent, in the **d.** forest of the sightless,
T-25..........II.h The Savior from the **D.**
T-25.......II.8:1 the darkness see the savior *from* the **d.**,
T-25.......II.8:2 on him, and you will see the **d.** no more.
T-26.......X.6:3 deprived of light, abandoned to the **d.**,
T-29.........I.3:3 make the way to light seem **d.** and fearful,
T-29......III.3:1 spark, a space of light created in the **d.**,
T-29......III.5:4 your light to him, to save him from the **d.**.
T-29... VIII.3:6 fall before His face like a **d.** veil that seems
T-29... VIII.4:2 A **d.** and fearful purpose, yet a thought
T-30...VII.6:15 Your **d.** dreams are but the senseless,
T-31......II.11:8 but cannot make the way itself grow **d.**.
T-31...VII.15:2 It needs the light, for it is **d.** indeed, and
W-pI.....41.5:3 to get past this **d.** and heavy cloud, and to
W-pI.....69.4:2 surrounded by a layer of heavy, **d.** clouds.
W-pI.....75.2:2 There are no **d.** dreams now. The light
W-pI.....78.1:2 Each grievance stands like a **d.** shield of
W-pI.....78.3:3 He stands in light, but you were in the **d.**.
W-pI.....78.8:7 No **d.** grievances obscure the sight of him.
W-pI.....91.1:7 the light; you will not see them in the **d.**.
W-pI...92.10:4 Leave, then, the **d.** a little while today,
W-pI...102.1:4 **d.** and hidden secret places of your mind.
W-pI...111.2:3 *me. My weakness is the* **d.** *His gift dispels, by*
W-pI...123.2:2 nor let you wander in the **d.** alone. Be
W-pI...127.5:2 meaning, and to keep it **d.** and secret.
W-pI...127.9:3 a **d.** illusion of your own reality and what
W-pI.136.16:2 will be no **d.** corners sickness can conceal,
W-pI.153.14:5 the **d.** dreams this story has evoked in his
W-pI...191.8:1 has lighted up all **d.** and ancient caverns,
W-pI...191.8:4 Who could see the world as **d.** and sinful,
W-pII...218.1:2 *My condemnation keeps my vision* **d.**, *and*
W-pII..263.1:3 *not perceive such* **d.** *and fearful images. A*
M-9 ...........1:8 and all **d.** cornerstones of unforgiveness
P-2.......VII.4:5 and guilt became the cover, **d.** and strong,
S-3.........II.6:3 no veil of sin to keep it **d.** and comfortless

## darken 8

T-11......IV.3:5 that you can **d.** only your own mind. As
T-13......VI.2:4 past can cast no shadow to **d.** the present,
T-15......XI.8:1 Let no despair **d.** the joy of Christmas, for
T-18.......I.10:7 that illusions cannot remain to **d.** the holy
T-25.......II.4:2 within your mind, to **d.** what is there.
T-29... VIII.3:9 nor **d.** by one whit the light itself.
W-pI.....73.5:3 Grievances **d.** your mind, and you look
W-pI.....75.3:2 remain to **d.** our sight and hide the world

## darkened 19

T-4........IV.2:3 images your ego makes in a **d.** glass.
T-13....III.11:5 For a **d.** mind cannot live in the light, and
T-13... VIII.5:5 light must come into the **d.** world to make
T-13.......XI.5:1 You whose mind is **d.** by doubt and guilt,
T-14... VIII.1:2 Son. All this lies hidden in every **d.** place,
T-14... VIII.3:1 mind wander not through **d.** corridors,
T-20......VI.4:1 Love has no **d.** temples where mysteries
T-22......IV.3:7 from it into a **d.** world that needs the light
T-23......IV.6:1 to make your mind **d.** and murderous,
T-25.......II.7:4 Think not this face was ever **d.** because
T-26......IX.7:1 to keep away all **d.** thoughts of sin, and
T-28.......V.7:5 are no awesome secrets and no **d.** tombs
W-pI.....73.5:3 mind, and you look out on a **d.** world.
W-pI.....99.7:6 your mistakes enter the **d.** places of your
W-pI.....99.9:1 light seek out and lighten up all **d.** spots,
W-pI...159.3:4 The **d.** glass the world presents can show
W-pI...189.3:2 see through **d.** eyes of malice and of fear,
W-pII..241.1:3 to the **d.** world where its release is set.
W-pII....12.4:2 Son of God is offered daily at its **d.** shrine,

## darkens 2

T-13.........I.7:6 away the cloud of guilt that **d.** your mind,
W-pI.......9.2:5 has been cleared of the debris that **d.** it.

## darker 1

T-11.......in.3:5 the **d.** and more obscure becomes the way

## darkest 6

T-13.......II.3:1 The **d.** of your hidden cornerstones holds
T-13.......II.4:4 They have approached the **d.** and deepest
T-13......III.1:9 look even upon the ego's **d.** cornerstone
T-13.....V.10:5 Beyond your **d.** dreams He sees God's
T-13......XI.9:5 Learn that even the **d.** nightmare that
T19...IV.D.3:1 This is the **d.** veil, upheld by the belief in

## darkness 254

T-1.........I.22:1 only because of the belief that **d.** can hide.
T-1.........I.39:2 light, **d.** automatically disappears.
T-1...........IV.h The Escape from **D.**
T-1.........IV.1:1 escape from **d.** involves two stages: First,
T-1.........IV.1:1 First, the recognition that **d.** cannot hide.
T-1.........IV.2:1 Holiness can never be really hidden in **d.**,
T-1.........IV.3:1 **D.** is lack of light as sin is lack of love. It
T-2.......II.1:14 light, and since error and **d.** are the same,
T-2.......VII.5:4 Whenever light enters **d.**, the darkness is
T-2.......VII.5:4 light enters darkness, the **d.** is abolished.
T-3...........I.6:7 Only the attempts to shroud it in **d.** have
T-3...........I.7:7 form of evil, as light abolishes forms of **d.**.
T-3..........II.1:3 conceive of light and **d.** or everything and
T-3..........II.1:6 A firm commitment to **d.** or nothingness,
T-3........IV.6:4 loss of power, because it is incapable of **d.**
T-3........IV.6:6 abolishes **d.** merely by showing you it is
T-3.......VII.6:6 Life and death, light and **d.**, knowledge
T-4.........in.1:8 are enlightened and cannot abide in **d.**.
T-4........III.5:2 to repeat that your belief in **d.** and hiding
T-5..........II.4:1 but you have let the belief in **d.** enter your
T-5..........II.4:2 that you must let banish the idea of **d.**.
T-6.......II.13:3 No **d.** abides anywhere in the Kingdom,
T-6.......II.13:3 part is only to allow no **d.** to abide in your
T-7........XI.5:2 extends out into the **d.** of other minds,
T-8......IV.2:10 Light does not attack **d.**, but it does shine
T-8......IV.2:12 and you cannot abide in **d.** any more than
T-8......IV.2:12 more than **d.** can abide wherever you go.
T-8........IV.3:1 You were in **d.** until God's Will was done
T-9.........V.6:3 Can you find light by analyzing **d.**, as the
T-9.........V.6:3 acknowledging **d.** in yourself and looking
T-9.........V.8:2 to **d.** but he cannot bring light of himself,
T-11.......I.10:6 Believing this you hide in **d.**, denying that
T-11.........III.h From **D.** to Light
T-11......III.5:6 that it can sweep you out of all **d.** forever.
T-11......III.6:1 The children of light cannot abide in **d.**,
T-11......III.6:1 abide in darkness, for **d.** is not in them.
T-11.......V.2:9 look upon **d.** through light must dispel it.
T-12........II.4:7 in the **d.** of your own false certainty, and
T-13....III.11:5 and it must seek a place of **d.** where it can
T-13.......V.8:2 You cannot see in **d.**. Yet in darkness, in
T-13.......V.8:3 Yet in **d.**, in the private world of sleep,
T-13.......V.8:5 But let the **d.** go and all you made you will
T-13.......V.9:1 way of seeing that you might see in **d.**,
T-13.......V.9:2 Beyond this **d.**, and yet still within you, is
T-13.....V.11:5 and saw beyond the **d.** the Christ in them,
T-13......VI.2:5 are would you choose to bring **d.** with you
T-13......VI.3:1 *This* **d.** *is in you.* The Christ as revealed to
T-13......VI.7:3 to remain in the **d.** that is not there, and
T-13......VI.8:5 There is no **d.** in him anywhere, for he is
T-13.. VI.11:10 will draw the others out of **d.** as you look
T-13....VI.12:7 the **d.** you cannot look upon the light you
T-13....VIII.5:4 healed and healing sight into the **d.**, and
T-13....VIII.5:6 to all who think they wander in the **d.**,
T-13.......IX.1:3 fidelity to **d.** and forbids awakening. The
T-13.......IX.1:8 that the chain of **d.** in which you bound
T-13.......IX.3:2 Be faithful unto **d.** and you will not see,
T-13........X.9:6 and look past **d.** to the holy place where
T-13....XI.3:10 There is no **d.** and there is no contrast.
T-14........in.1:5 as the ego points to **d.** and to death. We
T-14........II.4:3 He brings the light of truth into the **d.**,
T-14........II.7:9 come and freed you from the sleep of **d.**.
T-14........II.8:1 and learn of them how to be free of **d.**.
T-14......III.6:2 to replace **d.** with light and fear with love.
T-14......III.6:3 love. If he refuses it he binds himself to **d.**,
T-14......III.6:5 And by not dispelling **d.**, he became
T-14......III.6:5 he became afraid of **d.** and of light. The
T-14......III.6:6 The joy of learning that **d.** has no power
T-14....IV.4:10 a loveless place made out of **d.** and deceit,
T-14....IV.4:10 deceit, for thus are **d.** and deceit undone.
T-14......VI.1:3 It is only in **d.** and in ignorance that you
T-14......VI.1:3 and shrink away from it to further **d.**.
T-14......VI.2:3 no **d.** that the light of love will not dispel,
T-14......VI.2:4 it has been separated off and kept in **d.**.
T-14......VI.2:5 The sentinels of **d.** watch over it carefully,
T-14......VI.3:5 As guardians of **d.** and of ignorance look
T-14.....VII.1:2 Light or **d.**, knowledge or ignorance are
T-14.....VII.1:6 As **d.** disappears in light, so ignorance
T-14.....VII.4:5 But if one is kept in **d.** from the other,
T-14.....VII.5:1 enter **d.** when a mind believes in darkness
T-14.....VII.5:1 enter darkness when a mind believes in **d.**
T-14.....VII.6:2 bid Him enter the **d.** and lighten it away.
T-14.....VII.6:4 He brings the light to **d.** if you make the
T-14.....VII.6:4 darkness if you make the **d.** open to Him.
T-14.....VII.6:9 He holds the light, and you the **d.**. They
T-14....VIII.1:1 **d.** you have obscured the glory God gave
T-14......IX.5:5 of hidden **d.** you have drawn upon it. God
T-14......IX.6:2 In **d.** they are obscure, and their meaning
T-14........X.5:2 grow dim, as **d.** blots them out. Where
T-14........X.5:3 there was light, **d.** removes it in an instant
T-14........X.5:3 and **d.** sweep constantly across your mind
T-14......XI.3:8 for the **d.** in which you try to see can only

T-14...... XI.3:9 Put no confidence at all in **d.** to illuminate
T-14...... XI.3:9 the light, and thereby think you see the **d.**
T-14.... XI.3:10 Yet **d.** cannot be seen, for it is nothing
T-14...... XI.4:1 all of the **d.** you have taught yourself into
T-15.........I.8:7 No **d.** is remembered, and immortality
T-15....... X.5:1 it burrows underground and hides in **d.**,
T-15...... XI.2:1 sign of Christmas is a star, a light in **d.**.
T-17....... II.5:4 what seemed ugly in the **d.** of your lack of
T-17.... IV.13:4 The picture of **d.** and of death grows less
T-17.... IV.13:5 from the frame in **d.** is exposed to light, it
T-17....VIII.4:5 and pain, **d.** and dim imaginings of terror
T-18...... III.1:3 into the **d.** but made the darkness deeper.
T-18...... III.1:3 into the darkness but made the **d.** deeper.
T-18...... III.1:4 Your goal was **d.**, in which no ray of light
T-18...... III.1:8 you. **D.** can cover it, but cannot put it out.
T-18...... III.2:1 the light comes nearer you will rush to **d.**,
T-18...... III.2:4 Fear seems to live in **d.**, and when you are
T-18...... III.3:3 journey into **d.** has been long and cruel,
T-18...... III.4:2 in the **d.** that you agreed to leave with me
T-18...... III.6:1 Heaven to the Son of God, who hid in **d.**.
T-18...... III.6:2 have been willing to bring the **d.** to light,
T-18...... III.6:2 to everyone who would remain in **d.**.
T-18...... III.6:4 with me in carrying their light into the **d.**,
T-18...... III.6:4 when the **d.** in them is offered to the light,
T-18...... III.7:1 have the function of bringing light to **d.**.
T-18...... III.7:2 The **d.** in you has been brought to light.
T-18...... III.7:3 Carry it back to **d.**, from the holy instant
T-18...... III.8:4 of God Himself, can you remain in **d.**?
T-18...... III.8:7 back into **d.** and forward unto God, to
T-18...... IX.1:1 have been told to bring the **d.** to the light,
T-18...... IX.1:9 in which you set it off, surrounded by **d.**,
T-18...... IX.2:1 returning your little offering of **d.** to the
T-18...... IX.2:4 barren sands, the **d.** and the lifelessness,
T-18...... IX.4:3 its most external manifestations in **d.**,
T-18.... IX.13:2 lifted high above the **d.** and gently placed
T-20...... III.9:1 down in **d.** they remember not the light,
T-20...... VI.3:6 the sunlight and happy in the body's **d.**,
T-20...... VI.5:2 The body is an isolated speck of **d.**; a
T-20...... VI.7:5 This place of **d.** is not your home. Your
T-20..... VII.6:3 In the **d.** of sin he is invisible. He can but
T-20..... VII.6:4 He can but be imagined in the **d.**, and it is
T-20..... VII.6:7 And here, in **d.**, is your brother's reality
T-20..... VII.8:8 Attempt to see him not in **d.**, for your
T-21.........I.2:4 safety lies; and which way leads to **d.**,
T-21.... III.11:7 one with what depends on **d.** to be seen.
T-21.... III.12:1 to sin, and in the **d.** so it still is seen. Yet
T-22.... VI.9:10 Be not concerned with **d.**; look away from
T-22.... VI.9:11 let the **d.** be dispelled by Him Who knows
T-24...... VI.1:1 to haunt you in the **d.** of the night. He is
T-25.........I.4:4 and brushes all its **d.** into light merely by
T-25....... II.7:3 up the sinlessness the frame of **d.** hides,
T-25....... II.8:1 Within the **d.** see the savior *from* the dark,
T-25....... II.8:2 will step forth from **d.** as you look on him,
T-25....... II.8:3 The **d.** touched him not, nor you who
T-25....... II.8:7 in him and sees only a frame of **d.**, it is
T-25..... II.9:10 Not one ray of **d.** can be seen by those
T-25..... II.11:5 escape from **d.** into light be yours to share
T-25...... III.5:6 you remain in **d.** where the lamps are not.
T-25...... III.6:1 Everyone here has entered **d.**, yet no one
T-25...... III.6:3 to lead him out of **d.** into light at any time
T-25...... IV.3:6 light the **d.** that they thought was there is
T-25.... IV.5:12 you walk beyond the world of **d.** into light
T-25...... VI.2:1 Eyes become used to **d.**, and the light of
T-25...... VI.2:5 say that he prefers the **d.** and maintain he
T-25...... VI.7:6 Only in **d.** does your specialness appear to
T-29...... III.3:6 of light where God abides within the **d.**,
T-29...... III.3:8 The **d.** cannot choose that it remain. The
T-29...... III.4:2 that the **d.** may be lifted from your mind.
T-29...... III.4:4 walks through **d.** to the everlasting light.
T-29....VIII.3:6 to shut you off from Him, alone in **d.**. Yet
T-29....VIII.7:4 place of **d.** set where all is light, a dismal
T-31..... II.11:5 back and forward in the **d.** and alone. Yet
T-31....... V.6:6 sins and yours preserved and kept in **d.**,
T-31...... V.11:1 this concept must be kept in **d.** is that, in
T-31..... VII.7:5 least, you merely look on **d.**, and perceive
T-31..... VII.8:7 For there is light where **d.** was before, and
T-31..VIII.12:5 not one spot of **d.** still remains to hide the
W-pI....... 9.2:5 small step will clear a little of the **d.** away,
W-pI..... 44.1:2 it. You cannot see in **d.**, and you cannot
W-pI..... 44.1:3 can make **d.** and then think you see in it,
W-pI..... 44.1:4 Creation and **d.** cannot coexist, but light
W-pI..... 44.6:2 that to reach light is to escape from **d.**,
W-pI..... 59.4:2 I cannot see in **d.**. God is the only light.
W-pI..... 62.1:1 that will bring the world of **d.** to the light.
W-pI..... 69.1:2 of the world in you, everyone stands in **d.**,
W-pI..... 69.2:4 past the veil of **d.** that keeps it concealed.
W-pI..... 69.7:2 Himself will raise you from **d.** into light.
W-pI..... 73.1:2 out of which **d.** and nothingness arise.
W-pI..... 73.4:4 it. **D.** has vanished. The ego's idle wishes
W-pI..... 73.5:2 neither light nor **d.** can be found without.
W-pI..... 73.5:4 Forgiveness lifts the **d.**, reasserts your will
W-pI... 73.11:4 *D. is not my will.* This should be repeated
W-pI... 73.11:7 of cherishing them and hiding them in **d.**.
W-pI..... 75.1:6 you go. **D.** and turmoil and death have
W-pI..... 75.9:6 Without the **d.** of the past upon your eyes
W-pI... 75.10:4 who seems to pull you back into **d.**: *The*
W-pI..... 78.3:4 Each grievance made the **d.** deeper, and
W-pI..... 85.1:4 They keep me in **d.** and hide the light.
W-pI..... 87.1:3 It is not my will to grope about in **d.**,
W-pI..... 88.1:8 It has replaced the **d.**, and the darkness
W-pI..... 88.1:8 the darkness, and the **d.** has gone.
W-pI..... 88.2:2 *This cannot show me d., for the light has*
W-pI..... 91.2:2 While you remain in **d.**, the miracle
W-pI..... 91.2:4 the premises from which the **d.** comes.
W-pI..... 91.2:6 Failure to perceive light is to perceive **d.**.
W-pI..... 91.2:9 seeming reality of the **d.** makes the idea of
WpI..... 91.3:5 Your faith lies in the **d.**, not the light.
W-pI..... 91.8:9 *but a reality. I cannot see in d., but in light.*
W-pI..... 92.1:2 of strength, and **d.** in terms of weakness.
W-pI..... 92.3:3 about in **d.** to behold the likeness of itself;
W-pI..... 92.4:6 In **d.** you perceive a self that is not there.
W-pI..... 92.4:7 and **d.** rule where God appointed that
W-pI..... 92.5:1 it; weakness reflects the **d.** of its maker. It
W-pI..... 92.6:1 Weakness, which looks in **d.**, cannot see
W-pI..... 92.6:4 In **d.** it remains to hide itself, and dreams
W-pI..... 92.6:4 that but grow in **d.** to enormous size.
W-pI..... 92.7:1 itself, and **d.** covers everything it sees,
W-pI..... 92.7:6 back to **d.** till the morning comes again.
W-pI... 92.11:3 and led away from **d.** to the light where
W-pI..... 93.1:1 think you are the home of evil, **d.** and sin.
W-pI..... 94.2:5 **D.** cannot obscure the glory of God's Son.
W-pI... 95.12:3 power to lift the veil of **d.** from the world,
W-pI..... 97.6:3 this light remains and leads you out of **d.**,
W-pI... 108.2:2 unified that **d.** cannot be perceived at all.
W-pI... 111.1:2 *I cannot see in d.. Let the light of holiness*
W-pI... 121.2:3 and abides in misery, peering about in **d.**,
W-pI... 121.3:1 yet more afraid of stillness; terrified of **d.**,
W-pI... 127.6:2 Love is not found in **d.** and in death. Yet
W-pI... 129.7:5 and in the silent **d.** watch the lights that
W-pI... 129.8:1 eyelids as you rest beyond the world of **d.**.
W-pI... 130.2:5 hand, but fear obscures in **d.** what is there
W-pI... 130.3:2 What can be seen in **d.** that is real? Truth
W-pI... 131.1:2 within the **d.** of the dream of death. Who
W-pI. 131.13:2 light the way, so that all **d.** vanishes, and
WpI. rIV.in9:3 restored the world from **d.** to the light,
W-pI. 153.11:3 salvation waits and **d.** holds the world in
W-pI... 162.6:4 words dispel the night, and **d.** is no more.
W-pI... 182.3:2 search, seeking in **d.** what he cannot find;
W-pI. 184.10:1 you go into the sunlight and forget the **d.**.
W-pI. 184.10:3 And then step back to **d.**, not because you
W-pI. 184.10:3 have meaning in the world that **d.** rules.
W-pI. 184.11:1 symbols which delineate the world of **d.**.
W-pI. 190.11:2 the light of Heaven for the **d.** of the world.
W-pI... 192.7:2 Without its kindly light we grope in **d.**,
W-pI... 198.9:2 find the key to light and let the **d.** end:
W-pII ..... in.8:4 His Thoughts have lit the **d.** of our minds.
W-pII . 274.1:3 *where illusions were, light will replace all d.,*
W-pII ..... 302.h Where **d.** was I look upon the light.
W-pII . 302.1:5 *Now we see that d. is our own imagining,*
W-pII . 302.1:6 *Christ's vision changes d. into light, for fear*
W-pII . 304.2:1 *You lead me from the d. to the light; from*
W-pII ... 12.5:1 lily of forgiveness change the **d.** into light;
W-pII . 332.1:8 the light shine through the dream of **d.**,
M-1 ........... 1:4 A light has entered the **d.**. It may be a
M-8 ........... 1:2 sizes, on varying degrees of **d.** and light,
M-28 ......... 2:6 living thing, and nothing is held in **d.**,
C-2 ............ 6:1 Where there was **d.** now we see the light.
C-2 ............ 6:3 ego? What the **d.** was. Where is the ego?
C-2 ............ 6:5 Where the **d.** was. What is it now and
P-2.......... V.1:6 of self that holds in **d.** what is truly felt,
P-3...... III.5:11 against himself, he can look only upon **d.**.
P-3...... III.8:12 *in the d. of the world until you asked for light*
S-2........... I.9:3 prayer can be released from **d.** into light.

## dash 1

W-pI .. 186.8:5 or **d.** us to the ground in hopelessness.

## data 1

T-8 ..... VIII.6:6 If **d.** are meaningless there is no point in

## datum 1

M-8 ........... 4:3 judging where each sense **d.** fits best.

## dawn 13

T-6 ..... V.B.6:4 must **d.** on your mind that you are trying
T-7 ....... IX.4:4 of its wholeness to **d.** upon it and heal it.
T-8 ..... VI.9:11 but truth will **d.** upon you of itself.
T-10 ..... IV.2:1 can **d.** only on an unclouded mind. It is
T-10 ..... IV.2:5 go. Knowledge cannot **d.** on a mind full of
T-11 ..... IV.4:2 it is truly the beginning of the **d.** of light.
T-12 ...... I.8:12 it is, the unreality of fear must **d.** on you.
T-12 ... VIII.5:3 the memory of God can **d.** only in a mind
T-13 ..... VI.5:6 it where it is, and it will **d.** on eyes that see
T-31 .... VII.2:5 But should *one* brother **d.** upon your sight
W-pI .... 54.3:7 me will **d.** on their sight as well as mine.
W-pI 135.21:3 truth to **d.** upon our minds with certainty
W-pI .. 140.3:3 heralds of the **d.** of truth upon the mind.

## dawning 2

T-6 .......... I.7:2 but rebirth itself is merely the **d.** on your
W-pI .... 52.3:4 prevent the present from **d.** on my mind.

## dawns 9

T-6 ....... III.3:3 The protection of God then **d.** upon it,
T-9 ..... IV.11:8 Yet when reality **d.**, the fantasies are gone
T-14 .... VII.1:6 ignorance fades away when knowledge **d.**.
T-14 ....... X.2:3 remembrance of His Father **d.** on him,
T-15 ..... IV.2:2 The instant in which magnitude **d.** upon
T-15 ........ X.6:6 For when the recognition **d.** clearly, you
W-pI .. 124.9:3 when it **d.** with certainty upon your mind.
W-pI 127.10:4 future **d.** unlike the past in every attribute
W-pII . 241.1:5 of salvation **d.** today upon a world set free

## day 313

T-1 ........ I.15:1 Each **d.** should be devoted to miracles.
T-4 .......... I.5:1 that they will one **d.** no longer need him.
T-4 .......... II.4:6 you will one **d.** react to your real creations
T-12 ... VIII.1:3 every **d.** and every hour and every minute
T-13 .... VII.1:5 is no **d.** that brightens and grows dim.
T-13 ....... X.5:2 but with each one each **d.** be born again.
T-14 ..... III.4:1 Each **d.**, each hour and minute, even each
T-18 .... VII.6:1 everyone will one **d.** find in his own way,
T-20 ..... III.9:6 shall this **d.** enter with him to Paradise,
T-20 ....... V.6:7 perfect faith that you will one **d.** offer to
T-21 .. III.11:5 one because they come with night and **d.**,
T-24 .... VII.2:7 protection, the thought by **d.** and night,
T-25 ..... VI.2:1 and the light of brilliant **d.** seems painful
T-26 ..... V.13:1 Each **d.**, and every minute in each day,
T-26 ..... V.13:1 Each day, and every minute in each **d.**,
T-26 ..... V.13:2 And so you die each **d.** to live again, until
T-26 ... VIII.7:6 not understand it now, but will some **d.**.
T-26 ... VIII.7:9 "good" some **d.** but now in form of pain.
T-27 .... VII.8:5 as is the weather or the time of **d.**. It loves
T-29 ..... VI.2:8 and night and **d.** will be no more. All
T-30 ........ I.1:8 But think about the kind of **d.** you want,
T-30 ........ I.1:8 this very **d.** can happen just like that.
T-30 ........ I.1:9 Then try again to have the **d.** you want.
T-30 ........ I.4:1 (2) Throughout the **d.**, at any time you
T-30 ........ I.4:1 tell yourself again the kind of **d.** you want;
T-30 ........ I.4:2 *by myself, this is the d. that will be given me.*

T-30.........I.6:1 Remember once again the **d.** you want,
T-30.........I.7:3 until you believe the **d.** you want is one in
T-30.........I.7:4 destroy the **d.** by robbing you of what you
T-30.........I.7:5 the rules that promise you a happy **d.**. Yet
T-30...... I.11:5 you have changed your mind about the **d.**
T-30...... I.13:1 that it is easier to have a happy **d.** if you
T-30...... I.14:1 We said you can begin a happy **d.** with
T-30...... I.15:1 Your **d.** is not at random. It is set by what
T-30...... I.16:7 The **d.** you want you offer to the world,
T-30...... I.16:9 What kind of **d.** will you decide to have?
T-30...... I.17:1 this **d.** to promise it to all the world. It
T-30...... I.17:6 mind, and you will have the **d.** you want,
T-30...... I.17:7 the world by your decision for a happy **d.**.
T-30.....VII.1:7 script you write for every minute in the **d.**
T-30.....VII.2:1 your plans for what the **d.** *should* be? And
T-31.........I.6:6 taught to you in every moment of each **d.**,
T-31....... V.3:4 But every **d.** a hundred little things make
W-in..........2:6 to do more than one set of exercises a **d.**.
W-in..........3:3 which the idea for the **d.** is to be applied.
W-pI.......1.3:4 As you practice the idea for the **d.**, use it
W-pI.......1.4:1 not be done more than twice a **d.** each,
W-pI.......3.2:2 which the idea for the **d.** is to be applied.
W-pI.......4.1:1 do not begin with the idea for the **d.**. In
W-pI.......4.6:2 than three or four times during the **d.**.
W-pI.......5.1:5 proper subject for the exercises for the **d.**.
W-pI.......5.7:6 or four times during the **d.** is enough.
W-pI.......6.2:1 used throughout the **d.** for that purpose.
W-pI.......8.6:1 be done four or five times during the **d.**,
W-pI.......9.3:1 the idea for the **d.** to whatever you see,
W-pI.....14.7:1 anything that disturbs you during the **d.**,
W-pI.....15.5:4 be applied as needed throughout the **d.**.
W-pI.....19.4:1 and will no longer be repeated each **d.**,
W-pI.....20.4:1 throughout the **d.** that you want to see.
W-pI.....23.6:1 Besides using it throughout the **d.** as the
W-pI.....26.6:3 during the **d.** is a suitable subject. You
W-pI.....27.3:4 attempt to adhere to it throughout the **d.**.
W-pI.....27.4:6 only once during the **d.** you feel that you
W-pI.....28.7:1 in which the idea for the **d.** is stated first,
W-pI.....30.3:1 as often as possible throughout the **d.**.
W-pI.....31.1:4 applications of the idea throughout the **d.**
W-pI.....31.4:1 today as often as possible during the **d.**.
W-pI.....32.5:1 are also to be continued during the **d.**, as
W-pI.....33.2:2 as you repeat the idea throughout the **d.**.
W-pI.....34.5:2 from temptation throughout the **d.**. If a
W-pI.....35.9:1 As often as possible during the **d.**, pick
W-pI.....36.2:2 protect your protection throughout the **d.**
W-pI.....40.2:2 number of situations during the **d.** when
W-pI.....41.9:1 Throughout the **d.** use today's idea often,
W-pI.....42.4:3 to you in relation to the idea for the **d.**.
W-pI.....42.7:2 The idea for the **d.** is a beginning step in
W-pI.....42.8:1 often you repeat the idea during the **d.**,
W-pI.....43.4:1 early and one as late as possible in the **d.**.
W-pI.....43.7:1 in which you find yourself during the **d.**.
W-pI.....43.8:1 the **d.** to various situations and events
W-pI....44.11:1 Throughout the **d.** repeat the idea often,
W-pI.....45.9:2 as you repeat the idea throughout the **d.**,
W-pI.....46.7:3 the **d.** when you become aware of any
W-pI.....47.4:3 as usual, by repeating the idea for the **d.**.
W-pI.....47.8:1 During the **d.**, repeat the idea often. Use
W-pI........49.h Voice speaks to me all through the **d.**.
W-pI.....49.1:1 to God's Voice all through the **d.** without
WpI...rI.in.2:1 Begin the **d.** by reading the five ideas,
WpI...rI.in.2:4 Do this as often as possible during the **d.**.
WpI...rI.in.2:6 At the end of the **d.**, however, be sure to
W-pI.....59.2:6 **d.** may help me to understand eternity.
W-pI.....60.4:1 Voice speaks to me all through the **d.**.
W-pI.....61.6:1 sure both to begin and end the **d.** with a
W-pI.....61.6:2 yourself, reinforce it throughout the **d.**,
W-pI.....62.4:1 and end this **d.** by practicing today's idea,
W-pI.....62.4:1 frequently as possible throughout the **d.**.
W-pI.....62.4:2 will help to make the **d.** as happy for you
W-pI.....63.3:2 We will begin the **d.** by acknowledging it,
W-pI.....63.3:2 close the **d.** with the thought of it in our
W-pI.....63.3:3 the **d.** we will repeat this as often as we
W-pI.....64.5:2 at night, and all through the **d.** as well.
W-pI.....64.7:1 of today's idea throughout the **d.**, devote
W-pI.....65.3:1 what the idea for the **d.** really means.
W-pI.....65.4:1 at approximately the same time each **d.**.
W-pI.....65.4:3 your **d.** so that you have set apart the time
W-pI.....65.5:1 begin by reviewing the idea for the **d.**.
W-pI.....65.5:3 on thoughts related to the idea for the **d.**.
W-pI.....67.5:1 the idea for the **d.** as often as you can.
W-pI.....73.9:6 He is willing this very **d.** to look upon the
W-pI.....75.9:5 Be confident that on this **d.** there is a new
W-pI...75.11:1 dedicate this **d.** to the serenity in which
W-pI...76.12:1 as subject to other laws throughout the **d.**
W-pI...78.10:1 We will remember this throughout the **d.**
WpI..rII.in.1:2 left off, and cover two ideas each **d.**. The
WpI..rII.in.1:3 earlier part of each **d.** will be devoted to
WpI..rII.in.1:3 and the latter part of the **d.** to the other.
WpI..rII.in.2:1 by thinking about the ideas for the **d.**,
WpI..rII.in.5:4 Be determined each **d.** not to leave your
W-pI.....87.1:6 This **d.** I will experience the peace of true
W-pI.....92.7:6 out. It does not shift from night to **d.**, and
W-pI...92.11:2 will use the **d.** in preparation for the time
W-pI...93.11:7 that the idea for the **d.** is true indeed.
W-pI.....95.4:1 the idea for the **d.** has special advantages
W-pI.....95.5:3 short applications of the idea for the **d.**,
W-pI.....95.7:4 to regard the **d.** as lost because you have
W-pI...95.14:7 Throughout the **d.** do not forget your goal
W-pI...96.12:3 how much is given unto you to give this **d.**
W-pI.....98.1:1 Today is a **d.** of special dedication. We
W-pI...100.8:4 Let this one be the **d.** that you succeed!
W-pI...103.3:4 expectation frequently throughout the **d.**,
W-pI...107.7:6 into all the exercises that we do this **d.**.
W-pI...109.4:1 This is the **d.** of peace. You rest in God,
W-pI.110.11:1 the **d.** with thankful hearts and loving
WpI. rIII.in1:2 review two recent lessons every **d.** for ten
WpI. rIII.in2:1 optimal each **d.** and every hour of the day
WpI. rIII.in2:1 optimal each day and every hour of the **d.**
WpI. rIII.in5:1 is this: Devote five minutes twice a **d.**, or
WpI. rIII.in8:1 first five minutes of the **d.** to your reviews
WpI. rIII.in8:1 five minutes of your waking **d.** to them. If
WpI. rIII.in9:1 exercises to be done throughout the **d.** are
WpIrIII.in10:6 keep your peace throughout the **d.** as well
WpIrIII.in11:2 you learn each **d.** to everything you do.
WpIrIII.in11:6 in the business of the **d.** and make it holy,
W-pI.121.13:4 Do not forget, throughout the **d.**, the role
W-pI...122.2:2 gives you joy with which to meet the **d.**. It
W-pI...122.2:4 you another **d.** of happiness and peace.
W-pI...122.9:1 this will be the **d.** salvation will be ours.
W-pI.122.13:3 not your gifts recede throughout the **d.**, as
W-pI.122.14:2 gifts in your awareness through the **d.**:
W-pI...123.2:1 **d.** devoted now to gratitude will add the
W-pI...125.1:1 Let this **d.** be a day of stillness and of
W-pI...125.1:1 be a **d.** of stillness and of quiet listening.
W-pI...125.9:5 you have a special purpose for this **d.**; in
W-pI...126.8:5 today, this is a **d.** of glory for the world.
W-pI.126.11:1 aim which makes this **d.** of special value
W-pI.127.12:1 will remember them throughout the **d.**,
W-pI...128.8:1 your mind throughout the **d.** as well. And
W-pI...129.4:1 unambiguous and plain as **d.**, remains
W-pI...129.8:4 A **d.** of grace is given you today, and we
W-pI...129.8:5 This **d.** we realize that what you feared to
W-pI...130.4:8 this **d.** in seeking what can not be found.
W-pI.131.14:2 you might approach this door some **d.**,
W-pI.131.14:3 Today that **d.** has come. Today God keeps
W-pI.131.14:5 This is a **d.** of gladness, for we come to the
W-pI.132.14:5 this **d.** from every one of our illusions,
W-pI.132.17:1 Throughout the **d.**, increase the freedom
W-pI.134.17:1 should be practiced through the **d.**, for
W-pI.135.26:1 Try not to shape this **d.** as you believe
W-pI.135.26:5 Throughout the **d.**, as foolish little things
W-pI.135.26:5 yourself this is a special **d.** for learning,
W-pI.137.12:6 that thoughts of healing will this **d.** go
W-pI.137.14:2 And so we will begin the **d.** with this, and
W-pI.137.15:1 Let healing be through you this very **d.**.
W-pI.137.15:4 be forgot as every hour of the **d.** slips by,
W-pI.138.12:2 **d.** to the decision with which we awoke.
W-pI.138.12:4 And finally, we close the **d.** with this,
W-pI.140.11:1 speak to us five minutes as the **d.** begins,
W-pI.140.11:1 end the **d.** by listening again five minutes
W-pI.140.12:7 This is the **d.** when healing comes to us.
W-pI.140.12:8 This is the **d.** when separation ends, and
WpI. rIV.in5:1 Begin each **d.** with time devoted to the
WpI. rIV.in5:1 **d.** can offer you in freedom and in peace.
WpI. rIV.in5:4 **d.** along the lines which God appointed,
WpI. rIV.in5:4 of all the thoughts you will receive that **d.**.
WpI. rIV.in7:1 assigned to you to be reviewed that **d.**.
WpI. rIV.in7:5 that **d.** give you the gift that He has laid in
WpI. rIV.in8:1 Each hour of the **d.**, bring to your mind
WpI. rIV.in8:1 the thought with which the **d.** began, and
WpI. rIV.in8:2 ideas you practice for the **d.** unhurriedly,
WpI. rIV.in9:3 Each **d.** of practicing, as we review, we
WpI. rIV.in9:3 that made the **d.** a special time of blessing
WpIrIV.in10:2 the ideas for the **d.** again before you sleep,
W-pI.151.13:2 of the thought with which the **d.** begins.
W-pI.152.11:4 ***d.** I will accept myself as what my Father's*
W-pI.152.12:1 patience wait for Him throughout the **d.**,
W-pI.152.12:1 with the words with which the **d.** began,
W-pI.153.14:4 Let this **d.** bring the last chapter closer to
W-pI.153.15:2 will begin each **d.** by giving our attention
W-pI.153.15:3 to preparation for a **d.** in which salvation
W-pI.153.19:2 in it, as we prepare to meet the **d.**. We rise
W-pI.153.19:4 that He remains beside us through the **d.**,
W-pI.155.14:1 but that you think of Him a while each **d.**,
W-pI...156.8:2 should be asked a thousand times a **d.**, till
W-pI...157.1:1 This is a **d.** of silence and of trust. It is a
W-pI...157.1:3 and cast a timeless light upon this **d.**,
W-pI...157.1:4 This **d.** is holy, for it ushers in a new
W-pI...157.4:2 having joined your will with His this **d.**,
W-pI...157.5:1 From this **d.** forth, your ministry takes
W-pI...157.6:1 you experience this **d.** to light the world.
W-pI...157.8:2 this **d.** holds out to you to be your own.
W-pI...162.3:1 mind, recalling them throughout the **d.**,
W-pI...164.3:4 On this **d.** is grief laid by, for sights and
W-pI...164.5:1 This is the **d.** when vain imaginings part
W-pI...164.6:1 Brother, this **d.** is sacred to the world.
W-pI...164.9:4 exchange all suffering for joy this very **d.**.
W-pI...168.5:1 is a new and holy **d.** today, for we receive
W-pI.169.15:2 this **d.** of Him Who gives the grace we ask
WpI.rV.in11:1 With this we start each **d.** of our review.
WpI.rV.in11:3 words upon our lips, to greet another **d.**.
WpI.rV.in11:4 in our rememberance throughout the **d.**.
Wi181-200 3:4 past all defenses for a little while each **d.**.
W-pI...181.7:1 thought to keep us safe throughout the **d.**.
W-pI.184.10:1 you need are intervals each **d.** in which
W-pI...186.1:1 is the statement that will one **d.** take all
W-pI...186.8:4 greet the **d.** with welcome or with tears.
W-pI...189.2:4 It blesses you throughout the **d.**, and
W-pI.190.10:3 is the **d.** when it is given you to realize the
W-pI...192.3:6 that the light of **d.** already shines in them,
W-pI.193.10:1 seeming obstacles to peace in just one **d.**.
W-pI.193.10:3 not try to hold it off another **d.**, another
W-pI.193.12:1 in the form established for the **d.**. And try
W-pI...199.5:1 idea, and practice it today and every **d.**.
WpI rVI.in.1:1 this review we take but one idea each **d.**,
WpI rVI.in.1:2 you make throughout the **d.**, use the idea
WpI rVI.in.2:2 seeming happenings throughout the **d.**.
WpI rVI.in.3:6 The **d.** begins and ends with this. And we
WpI rVI.in.3:8 the special thought we practice for the **d.**,
WpI rVI.in.5:4 for the idea we practice for the **d.**.
WpI rVI.in.6:4 And then repeat the idea for the **d.**, and
WpI rVI.in.7:4 it has been given, as we practice **d.** by day,
WpI rVI.in.7:4 it has been given, as we practice day by **d.**,
W-pII ..in.11:3 thoughts should be reviewed each **d.**,
W-pII ..in.11:4 of the holy and blessed instants in the **d.**.
W-pII .227.2:2 Son of God this **d.** lays down his dreams.
W-pII .227.2:3 The Son of God this **d.** comes home again
W-pII ....232.h Be in my mind, my Father, through the **d.**
W-pII .232.1:1 *and shine on me throughout the **d.** today.*
W-pII .232.2:1 This is as every **d.** should be. Today,
W-pII .233.2:2 give this **d.** to Him with no reserve at all.
W-pII .233.2:3 at all. This is His **d.**. And so it is a day of
W-pII .233.2:4 a **d.** of countless gifts and mercies unto us
W-pII .237.1:2 shine upon the world throughout the **d.**. I
W-pII .241.1:4 The **d.** has come when sorrows pass away
W-pII ....242.h This **d.** is God's. It is my gift to Him.
W-pII .242.1:5 I give this **d.** to Him, for I would not delay
W-pII .247.2:4 *and thus I hope this **d.** to recognize my Self.*
W-pII .250.2:4 *that this **d.** I may at last identify with him.*
W-pII ....255.h This **d.** I choose to spend in perfect peace
W-pII .255.1:3 Let me this **d.** have faith in Him Who says
W-pII .255.2:1 *so, my Father, would I pass this **d.** with You.*
W-pII .257.1:4 only what God would have us do this **d.**.
W-pII .262.2:1 are one would recognize this **d.** the truth
W-pII .266.2:1 This **d.** we enter into Paradise, calling

W-pII .271.1:1 Each **d.**, each hour, every instant, I am
W-pII .273.1:1 ready for a **d.** of undisturbed tranquility.
W-pII .273.1:2 to learn how such a **d.** can be achieved. If
W-pII .274.2:2 Give this **d.** to Him, and there will be no
W-pII .274.2:2 today, because the **d.** is given unto love.
W-pII .275.1:1 no more true today than any other **d.**. Yet
W-pII .275.1:2 Yet has this **d.** been chosen as the time
W-pII .286.1:3 *This is the* **d.** *that has been chosen as the time*
W-pII .290.1:3 Christ's vision come to me this very **d.**.
W-pII .290.1:6 This the **d.** I seek my present happiness,
W-pII ....291.h This is a **d.** of stillness and of peace.
W-pII .291.2:1 *This* **d.** *my mind is quiet, to receive the*
W-pII .306.1:1 when it can offer me a **d.** in which I see a
W-pII .310.1:1 *This* **d.**, *my Father, would I spend with You,*
W-pII .310.1:4 **d.** *will be Your sweet reminder to remember*
W-pII .310.2:1 We spend this **d.** together, you and I.
W-pII .315.1:1 Each **d.** a thousand treasures come to me
W-pII .315.1:2 I am blessed with gifts throughout the **d.**,
W-pII .315.2:1 *me today and every* **d.** *from every Son of God*
W-pII .330.1:1 us this **d.** accept forgiveness as our only
W-pII .334.1:1 I will not wait another **d.** to find the
W-pII .339.1:9 that we may spend this **d.** in fearlessness,
W-pII .339.2:1 *Father, this is Your* **d.**. *It is a day in which I*
W-pII .339.2:2 *is a* **d.** *in which I would do nothing by myself,*
W-pII .340.1:2 *This* **d.** *is holy, for today Your Son will be*
W-pII .340.1:6 *born into this world but to achieve this* **d.**,
W-pII .340.2:4 Our Father has redeemed His Son this **d.**.
W-pII .346.1:2 *the* **d.** *I share with You as I will share eternity,*
M-in .......... 1:6 process; it goes on every moment of the **d.**
M-15 ......... 1:5 One **d.** each one will welcome it, and on
M-15 ......... 1:5 it, and on that very **d.** it will be given him.
M-16 ............h THE TEACHER OF GOD SPEND HIS **D.**?
M-16 ......... 1:2 program, for the lessons change each **d.**.
M-16 ......... 1:5 his role should be, this **d.** and every day.
M-16 ......... 1:5 his role should be, this day and every **d.**.
M-16 ......... 1:6 can learn the lessons for the **d.** together.
M-16 ......... 1:7 and one which can be learned that very **d.**
M-16 ......... 2:3 they do to learn to give the **d.** to God?
M-16 ......... 2:6 be said that it is well to start the **d.** right.
M-16 ......... 2:7 again, should the **d.** begin with error. Yet
M-16 ......... 3:4 starting the **d.** right does indeed save time
M-16 ......... 6:1 should be remembered throughout the **d.**
M-16 ......... 8:1 throughout the **d.** of his protection. How
M-16 ....... 10:2 fact that the teacher of God devotes his **d.**
M-16 ....... 11:5 the **d.** except to put your trust in magic,
M-16 ....... 11:9 their training, every **d.** and every hour,
M-29 ......... 5:9 God when you can throughout the **d.**, ask
C-ep........... 5:4 The morning star of this new **d.** looks on
P-2........... I.4:2 will one **d.** come to pass for every "patient
P-3......... II.5:2 against the **d.** when they can recognize

## day's 5

W-in .......... 3:2 each **d.** exercises are planned around one
W-pI..... 95.8:3 the instructions for practicing the **d.** idea.
WpI. rIII.in5:2 that are written down for each **d.** exercise.
WpIrIII.in12:1 Each **d.** review assignments will conclude
WpI rVI.in.6:5 such special applications of each **d.** idea,

## daylight 1

T-15...... XI.1:6 eyes to **d.** when you have no more need of

## days 14

T-9........ IV.9:1 borrowed time, and its **d.** are numbered.
T-15....... II.3:5 You who have spent **d.**, hours and even
T-28...... III.7:4 and break it into **d.** and months and years
W-pI..... 65.3:1 Today, and for a number of **d.** to follow,
W-pI... 102.3:1 For several **d.** we will continue to devote
WpI. rIII.in1:2 day for ten successive **d.** of practicing. We
W-pI... 153.3:2 the **d.** that bind the mind in heavy bands
W-pI... 157.1:2 time of promise in your calendar of **d.**. It
W-pI... 157.1:5 long **d.** and nights in celebrating death.
W-pI. 193.12:1 a little time today, and in the **d.** to come,
W-pII ....in.3:1 a central thought for all the **d.** to come,
W-pII .310.1:1 *You, as You have chosen all my* **d.** *should be.*
W-pII .310.1:3 *joy that comes to me is not of* **d.** *nor hours,*
W-pII ... 14.2:2 Yet in the final **d.** of this one year we gave

## dazed 1

T-4 ........ V.4:5 is where the mind becomes actually **d.**.

## dead 25

T-1 ........ I.24:1 heal the sick and raise the **d.** because you
T-4 ..... IV.11:7 I raised the **d.** by knowing that life is an
T-5 ...... VII.2:3 at times, but they have not raised the **d.**.
T-8 ....... IX.3:5 is a blessing for the living, not the **d.**,
T-15 ........ I.3:3 The ego wants *you* **d.**, but not itself. The
T-20 ... VI.11:5 And here he is more **d.** than living. Yet it
T-21 .... VII.2:5 of the Son of God will strike them **d.**, and
T-25 ...... V.2:8 Son of God as innocent and wish him **d.**?
T-25 ... VIII.6:4 they trust Him not to strike them **d.** with
T-26 .... V.10:4 the **d.** and gone be peacefully forgotten.
T-27 ........ I.9:7 It has no life, but neither is it **d.**. It stands
T-27 ...... V.3:4 the screaming dying and the silent **d.**, are
T-27 ..... VI.5:9 The dying live, the **d.** arise, and pain has
T-28 ........ I.5:8 made to keep the past alive, the present **d.**
T-29 ..... II.10:4 Your savior is not **d.**, nor does he dwell in
W-pI... 106.2:3 Be not deceived by voices of the **d.**, which
W-pI... 107.3:3 and **d.** ideas to linger in your mind. Truth
W-pI... 121.4:3 It wants to live, yet wishes it were **d.**. It
W-pI... 122.3:2 and clears your memory of all **d.** thoughts
W-pI... 124.5:3 we see it in the dying and the **d.** as well,
W-pI... 132.8:4 and the **d.** arise when you let thoughts of
W-pI... 139.3:2 yourself is to believe that you are really **d.**.
W-pI... 162.2:5 The **d.** awake in answer to its call. And
W-pI... 163.5:3 but this: "Here lies a witness God is **d.**."
W-pI... 190.3:6 and using pain to prove that God is **d.**,

## deadly 5

T-24 ..... IV.1:3 feared and attacked, **d.** and dangerous,
T-31 ...... V.6:4 to him, unwavering and **d.** in its aim. It
W-pI... 196.5:5 could believe his Father is his **d.** enemy,
W-pI... 196.9:3 the **d.** fear of God projection hides behind
M-17 ......... 5:8 takes it for himself now has a **d.** "enemy."

## deaf 7

T-16 ....... II.8:1 and **d.** could fail to see and hear them.
T-27 ..... VI.7:3 made it **d.** to its salvation and deliverance
T-28 ...... V.4:8 Its eyes are blind; its ears are **d.**. It can not
W-pI..... 95.2:3 It does not hear your prayers, for it is **d.**.
W-pI... 183.3:4 The blind can see; the **d.** can hear. The
WpI rVI.in.3:8 up the mind, and makes it **d.** to reason,
W-pII . 293.2:2 *let my ears be* **d.** *to all the hymns of gratitude*

## deal 18

T-3 ....... IV.7:2 Truth cannot **d.** with errors that you want
T-5 ....... III.7:2 ability to **d.** with symbols enables Him to
T-5 ..... III.10:3 Holy Spirit can **d.** with a reluctant learner
T-14 ..... XI.8:4 **d.** with certain aspects of your life alone,
T-17 ........ I.3:2 You believe truth cannot **d.** with them
T-17 ........ I.4:3 to **d.** with part of the truth in one way,
T-17 ... VI.6:10 the situation and **d.** with them separately,
T-18 ...... V.6:4 alone, or to attempt to **d.** with it alone.
T-24 .... VII.8:4 do we **d.** with them as if they were. It is
T-31 .... VII.1:4 For it must **d.** in contrasts, not in truth,
W-in.......... 2:2 They do not require a great **d.** of time,
W-pI..... 47.5:2 could **d.** with the situation successfully. It
W-pI... 74.3:10 be sure to **d.** quickly with any conflict
W-pI... 198.2:7 we **d.** with them a while as if they had.
M-17 ............h GOD'S TEACHERS **D.** WITH MAGIC
M-17 ......... 1:4 How to **d.** with magic thus becomes a
P-2......... in.1:5 the patient **d.** with one fundamental error
P-2........ IV.9:3 with which the psychotherapist must **d.**.

## dealing 5

T-13 ..... XI.1:1 advice for **d.** with the perceived and harsh
T-28 ....... II.7:2 This is a crucial step in **d.** with illusions.
W-in.......... 3:1 the first **d.** with the undoing of the way
W-pI..... 39.1:4 We are **d.** only in the very obvious, which
W-pI..... 72.4:1 are not **d.** here with what the person is.

## deals 2

T-21 ....... II.9:1 is how the ego **d.** with what it wants, to
T-31 ....... V.4:1 fact the world **d.** harshly with defenseless

## dealt 2

M-24 ......... 2:1 be the problem to be **d.** with *now*. If it
P-2........ IV.6:5 is accepted as real and **d.** with by illusions

## dear 51

T-13 ........ I.2:3 guilt that you accepted, and you hold it **d.**
T-13 ...... I.10:4 could you hold **d.** what you do not want?
T-13 ..... III.5:3 is given you is not so **d.** as what you made
T-13 ..... III.8:1 you hold so **d.** is your real call for help.
T-13 .... VII.2:4 you as the amount to which you hold it **d.**
T-13 .... VII.3:5 Hold it not **d.**, for it is old and tired and
T-13 .. VII.16:3 of God. Hold me **d.**, for what except your
T-13 ..... IX.3:4 Whatever you hold **d.** you think is yours.
T-13 ..... XI.5:1 guilt that His **d.** Son has laid upon himself
T-14 ..... III.5:9 happy purchase of a treasure to hold **d.**.
T-15 ..... III.4:8 effort you make on behalf of His **d.** Son.
T-17 ....... II.1:4 you value like unto this, nor hold so **d.**.
T19 .IV.A.13:5 forth by offering him what they hold **d.**.
T19 .IV.A.14:2 to you what they hold **d.** as are the others.
T-21 ........ I.4:4 believing this, they hold those lessons **d.**,
T-21 ........ I.7:2 if you remembered how **d.** it was to you.
T-21 ........ I.7:4 the world you learned is half so **d.** as this.
T-21 ........ I.7:5 so long ago and held more **d.** than any
T-21 ........ I.9:6 Nothing will ever be as **d.** to you as is this
T-21 ..... III.7:3 because the means for sin are **d.** to you.
T-21 ..... VI.6:7 with what you hold more **d.** than truth?
T-22 ..... VI.2:5 one as **d.** to His Creator as love is to itself.
T-23 ....... II.4:1 **d.** indeed to every worshipper of sin, is
T-24 ........ I.5:3 make the body **d.** and worth preserving.
T-24 ..... II.12:6 no relationship that holds its purpose **d.**
T-24 ... VII.1:6 no price too **d.** to save his specialness
T-25 ..... IX.1:7 will you hold **d.** that sin be kept in place.
T-27 ..... VI.4:6 is. Yet must He love whatever you hold **d.**.
T-30 ....... V.1:3 no longer, for their "gifts" are not held **d.**.
T-31 .. VII.12:3 wish that fathered it no longer is held **d.**.
T-31 .. VII.13:7 **d.** against the vision of the Christ in you.
W-pI .... 96.6:8 release of His **d.** Son bring pain to him,
W-pI .... 96.7:4 your Self holds **d.** and cherishes for you.
W-pI .. 106.4:7 for they come from God to His **d.** Son,
WpI..rIII.in4:2 if it interferes with goals you hold more **d.**
W-pI .. 127.8:3 by anyone who does not hold it **d.**.
W-pI 131.10:3 replace the foolish images that we hold **d.**,
W-pI 139.11:6 the recall how **d.** our brothers are to us in
W-pI .. 183.3:2 the world holds **d.** has suddenly gone by,
W-pI .. 197.8:6 He holds you **d.**, because you are Himself.
W-pI .. 199.3:1 accept today's idea, and hold it very **d.**. Be
W-pI .. 199.3:3 holds the body **d.** because it dwells in it,
W-pII . 238.2:2 And how **d.** His Son, created by His Love,
W-pII . 341.1:2 *smile in love and tenderness so* **d.** *and deep*
M-13 ......... 6:1 requires sacrifice of all you really hold **d.**.
M-13 ......... 6:2 hold **d.** the things that crucify God's Son,
M-19 ......... 3:2 that made the lens and holds it very **d.**.
C-5 ............ 5:8 how **d.** a brother he would be to you. For
S-2........... I.2:3 **D.** to its heart is error, and mistakes loom
S-3........ IV.3:5 **d.** to Him as is the whole of His creation,
S-3........ IV.9:7 **d.** is every gift to Me that you have made,

## dearer 2

T-24 ....... II.2:9 illusions of yourself are **d.** than the truth.
W-pI .... 69.3:1 to reach what is **d.** to us than all else.

## dearest 1

W-pI .... 60.3:5 I will recognize in everyone my **d.** Friend.

## dearly 2

T19 ... IV.B.5:1 You have paid very **d.** for your illusions,
T-20 ....... II.5:5 only **d.** loved and loving friends. He sees

**death** 492

T-1........ I.24:1 you made sickness and d. yourself, and
T-1........IV.4:2 is what the Bible means by "There is no d.
T-1........IV.4:2 I could demonstrate that d. does not exist
T-2..... VIII.5:1 of the association of "last" with d.. This is
T-3.....VII.5:10 system upon you as if it were the fear of d.
T-3.....VII.5:11 There is no d., but there *is* a belief in death
T-3.....VII.5:11 There is no death, but there *is* a belief in d.
T-3.......VII.6:5 You who fear salvation are choosing d..
T-3.......VII.6:6 death. Life and d., light and darkness,
T-3.....VII.6:11 The world is not left by d. but by truth,
T-4.........in.3:5 finally the crucifixion of the body, or d..
T-6......V.A.1:2 you think this is accomplished through d.
T-6......V.A.1:2 but nothing is accomplished through d.,
T-6......V.A.1:2 through death, because d. is nothing.
T-6......V.A.1:5 mind, you can overcome d. because I did.
T-6......V.A.1:6 D. is an attempt to resolve conflict by not
T-8........IX.3:2 All forms of sickness, even unto d., are
T-8........IX.4:7 Sleep is no more a form of d. than death
T-8........IX.4:7 than d. is a form of unconsciousness.
T-10....... V.1:5 and in this sense the wages of sin *is* d.. The
T-10....... V.4:1 Sickness and d. seemed to enter the mind
T-11..........I.9:7 Sleep is not d.. What He created can sleep
T-11...... I.9:10 God's Son cannot will d. for himself
T-11.......VI.8:3 assign to d. whom God has given eternal
T-12......III.8:2 its reality cannot see the world of d.. For
T-12......III.8:3 For d. is not of the real world, in which
T-12......III.8:4 split mind, and which is the symbol of d..
T-12......III.9:2 to accept even d. to deny your Father. Yet
T-12......IV.6:2 For d. is not your Father's Will nor yours,
T-12......IV.6:3 given you, but you do pay a price for d.,
T-12......IV.6:4 one. If d. is your treasure, you will sell
T-12......IV.7:6 must relinquish your investment in d., or
T-12...VII.13:1 and have condemned yourself to d.. The
T-12...VII.13:2 The d. penalty is the ego's ultimate goal,
T-12...VII.13:2 of d. as God knows you are deserving of
T-12...VII.13:3 d. penalty never leaves the ego's mind, for
T-12...VII.13:4 for you, it lets you live but to await d.. It
T-12...VII.14:4 to God and therefore deserve d.. You will
T-12...VII.14:5 You will think that d. comes from God
T-12...VII.14:5 with the ego, you believe that you want d.
T-12...VII.15:1 are tempted to yield to the desire for d.,
T-12...VII.15:3 I have overcome d. for myself alone? And
T-12...VII.15:5 make me manifest, you will never see d..
T-13.......in.2:4 that seem to govern it are the laws of d..
T-13.......in.2:6 learn of sorrow and separation and d..
T-13.........I.3:6 this carpet, believing that it leads to d..
T-13....... II.3:2 God's Son by condemning him to d.. You
T-13......III.5:3 Your individual d. seems more valuable
T-13......IV.3:2 be argued that d. suggests there *was* life,
T-13......IV.3:3 Even the past life that d. might indicate,
T-13......IV.3:6 might it not be more desirable than d.?
T-13.....VII.3:4 you made but has the mark of d. upon it.
T-13.....XI.1:1 and even d. become the ego's best advice
T-14......in.1:5 as the ego points to darkness and to d..
T-14.........I.4:5 the capricious and unholy whim of d. and
T-14....... V.1:8 Leave the world of d. behind, and return
T-14......VI.4:1 D. yields to life simply because
T-14......IX.4:4 fear of d. will be replaced with joy of life.
T-15.........I.2:8 To the ego the goal is d., which *is* its end.
T-15.........I.3:2 For it is as mistrustful of d. as it is of life,
T-15.........I.3:5 for you to find peace even in d., it offers
T-15.........I.4:5 ego aims at d. and dissolution as an end,
T-15.........I.4:6 it. The goal of d., which it craves for you,
T-15.........I.4:7 the ego's teaching is without the fear of d.
T-15.........I.4:8 Yet if d. were thought of merely as an end
T-15....... I.4:13 D. is the end as far as hope of Heaven
T-15....... I.4:14 because it cannot conceive of its own d., it
T-16......IV.4:7 love, to them, is only an escape from d..
T-16......IV.4:9 they find the fear of d. is still upon them,
T-16..... V.10:6 Through the d. of your self you think you
T-16..... V.11:5 another self to take its power from his d..
T-16..... V.11:8 complete, for life arises not from d., nor
T-16..... V.12:4 strength is extracted from the d. of God,
T-16... V.12:10 in which the dance of d. delights you can
T-16... V.12:10 delights you can bring d. to the eternal.
T-16.....VI.10:3 insane could look on d. and suffering,
T-17.....IV.9:9 D. lies in this glittering gift. Let not your
T-17....IV.9:11 picture, and realize that d. is offered you.
T-17....IV.10:2 against your acceptance of the gift of d..
T-17....IV.13:4 The picture of darkness and of d. grows
T-18.........I.4:4 to illusion, infinity to time, and life to d.,
T-18....... VI.7:2 the seeds of vengeance, violence and d..
T-19........ II.3:6 For the wages of sin *is* d., and how can the
T-19........ II.7:6 Mourn, then, the d. of God, Whom sin
T19. IV.A.11:2 find, losing none of them on pain of d.,
T19. IV.A.17:3 of you. To the ego sin means d., and so
T19. IV.A.17:8 for anyone, and d. does not atone for sin.
T19....IV.B.2:7 Do you not see that this is the belief in d.?
T19....IV.B.7:9 And where is d., when its great advocate
T19..IV.B.13:8 Yet to itself it whispers, "It is d.."
T19..IV.B.16:5 within which is his d. equally inevitable.
T19..IV.B.17:1 that they have dedicated themselves to d..
T19..IV.B.17:6 seeks. So does the ego find the d. *it* seeks,
T19...... IV.C.h The Third Obstacle: The Attraction of D.
T19....IV.C.1:1 and be released from the dedication to d..
T19....IV.C.1:4 No one can die unless he chooses d..
T19....IV.C.1:5 to be the fear of d. is really its attraction.
T19....IV.C.1:8 And so it is with d.. Made by the ego, its
T19....IV.C.2:4 that honors their grim master, lord of d.?
T19....IV.C.2:6 to his funeral, and hear him laugh at d..
T19..IV.C.2:11 What is d. to you? Your dedication is not
T19..IV.C.2:12 Your dedication is not to d., nor to its
T19..IV.C.2:13 in place of the ego's you renounced d.,
T19..IV.C.2:15 And d. is the result of the thought we call
T19....IV.C.3:1 From the ego came sin and guilt and d.,
T19....IV.C.3:3 sure; God, Who created neither sin nor d.
T19....IV.C.4:2 A body which they dedicated to d., a
T19....IV.C.4:5 of your unrecognized dedication to d..
T19....IV.C.6:5 be. D., were it true, would be the final and
T19....IV.C.7:1 Those who fear d. see not how often and
T19....IV.C.7:2 For d. is seen as safety, the great dark
T19....IV.C.7:3 the retreat to d. is not the end of conflict.
T19....IV.C.7:5 your seeming love for d. that peace must
T19....IV.C.8:2 child of our Father, this is a *dream* of d..
T19....IV.C.8:6 it to die, for only d. could conquer life.
T19....IV.C.9:1 fear of d. will go as its appeal is yielded to
T19....IV.C.9:6 deathless, and within it lies the end of d..
T19..IV.C.11:1 it as a symbol of fear, a sign of sin and d..
T19..IV.C.11:9 *Let me not see it as a sign of sin and d., nor*
T19... IV.D.1:1 What would you see without the fear of d.
T19... IV.D.1:2 and think if d. held no attraction for you?
T19... IV.D.2:3 light beyond it when the fear of d. is gone.
T19... IV.D.3:1 belief in d. and protected by its attraction
T19... IV.D.3:2 dedication to d. and to its sovereignty is
T19... IV.D.4:1 the belief in d. would seem to "save" you.
T19... IV.D.4:3 of d. that makes life seem to be ugly, cruel
T19... IV.D.4:4 are no more afraid of d. than of the ego.
T19... IV.D.5:5 And the appeal of d. is lost forever as
T19... IV.D.6:3 of guilt, the "holy" waxen image of d.,
T19... IV.D.7:6 of seeming d. can stand against your will.
T19. IV.D.17:5 as one in resurrection, not separate in d..
T19. IV.D.18:4 in the garden of seeming agony and d.. So
T19. IV.D.18:5 of his Father, Who knows no sin, no d.,
T-20.........I.2:3 This week we celebrate life, not d.. And
T-20.........I.2:9 cannot be united in crucifixion and in d..
T-20....... II.7:8 the Son of God, and crown him king of d..
T-20...... III.4:2 hoping at most that d. will wait a little
T-20...... III.4:5 *is* frightened, and those who kill fear d..
T-20...... IV.1:5 –sickness and d. and misery and pain.
T-20........ V.7:4 prisoner to pain and d. must be forgotten
T-20... VI.11:2 spot of space and time, beholden unto d.,
T-20... VIII.7:1 the idle game of d. in your imagination.
T-20. VIII.11:1 have looked on scenes of violence and d.,
T-21... VIII.1:5 He goes from life to d., the final proof he
T-22....... II.3:1 only guilt and suffering, sickness and d.,
T-22....... II.7:3 Either you give each other life or d.; either
T-23.........I.2:4 The d. of God, if it were possible, would
T-23.........I.2:4 God, if it were possible, would be your d..
T-23....... II.4:1 sin, and therefore deserves attack and d..
T-23..... II.11:8 His treachery demands his d., that you
T-23..... II.12:1 But what is it you want that needs his d.?
T-23..... II.15:7 lovely do the laws of fear make d. appear.
T-23..... II.15:8 who saved the Son of God for fear and d.!
T-23..... II.17:1 can some forms of murder not mean d.?
T-23..... II.19:4 At best it seems like life; at worst, like d..
T-23...... III.1:9 If the intent is d., what matter the form it
T-23...... III.2:1 Is d. in any form, however lovely and
T-23...... III.6:4 that haunts the place of d. is not apparent
T-23...... IV.1:2 fear of God is fear of life, and not of d..
T-23...... IV.3:7 is. Life makes not d., creating like itself.
T-24......II.12:4 from eyes it veils but looks on sight of d..
T-24......II.14:4 The d. of specialness is not your death,
T-24......II.14:4 The death of specialness is not your d.,
T-24....... III.4:7 like a flaming sword of d. between them,
T-24....... III.5:4 How could They will the d. of love itself?
T-24....... III.5:7 Salvation challenges not even d.. And
T-24....... III.5:8 Who knows that d. is not your will, must
T-24....... III.7:2 forth and waken from their dream of d..
T-24....... III.7:6 die, but not by Him Who made not d.;
T-24....... IV.1:7 Here is d. enthroned as savior; crucifixion
T-24....... V.4:4 What does it seek for but the sight of d.?
T-24....... V.7:3 no more the sound of battle and of d.. He
T-24....... V.7:6 that you may save all living things from d.
T-24....... VI.4:4 will not escape its laws of violence and d..
T-24....... VI.5:3 law of d. you bind him to will you escape.
T-24..... VII.4:6 hate, and you condemn it to decay and d..
T-25......in.1:6 gives you life cannot be housed in d.. No
T-25.........I.2:4 your evil and, above all, your d.. And
T-25.........I.2:5 who tells you this, and seek his d. instead
T-25........II.7:4 because you saw it in a frame of d.. God
T-25........II.8:8 that looks on Christ instead of seeing d..
T-25....... V.4:6 Condemned by you, he offers d. to you. In
T-25..... VII.1:6 Yet each one knows the cost of sin is d..
T-25..... VII.1:8 For sin is a request for d., a wish to make
T-25..... VII.2:1 "sinner's" wish for d. is just as strong as is
T-25..... VII.5:3 joy. Nothing attests to d. and cruelty; to
T-25... VII.13:2 reconciled. D. demands life, but life is not
T-25.... VIII.3:5 But d. must be the cost and must be paid.
T-25.... VIII.3:7 and d. is seen as victory and triumph over
T-25..VIII.10:4 Son be judged by those who seek his d.,
T-26.........I.6:6 time you see in him a sin deserving d..
T-26.........I.7:3 to the d. of God and of His holy Son,
T-26.........I.7:7 the reach of any sacrifice of life or d.. For
T-26..... V.10:6 you are a part of resurrection, not of d..
T-26..... V.10:7 the power to keep you in a place of d., a
T-26..... V.12:3 of the hallucination time and d. are real,
T-26..... V.13:3 a seeming interval from birth to d. and on
T-26..... VI.1:6 in hurt and harm, in sacrifice and d., has
T-26..... VII.8:6 see the role forgiveness plays in ending d.
T-26... VII.10:1 world that d. and desolation seem to rule.
T-26... VII.16:6 every wish to hurt he chooses d. instead
T-26... VII.17:4 from crucifixion and from hell and d., all
T-26... VII.19:3 blessing to the world of sin and d.. For
T-26.... VIII.9:5 should deliverance be disguised as d.?
T-26...... IX.3:2 What was a place of d. has now become a
T-27.........I.2:6 will not escape the d. you made for him.
T-27.........I.3:2 are writ in Heaven in your blood and d.,
T-27.........I.4:6 D. seems an easy price, if they can say,
T-27.........I.4:7 d. would prove his errors must be sins.
T-27.........I.4:8 sins. Sickness is but a "little" d.; a form of
T-27.........I.6:3 for d. that is the motivation for this world
T-27.......I.6:11 Depression speaks of d., and vanity of
T-27.........I.7:6 Their d. will pay the price for all of them,
T-27.........I.8:1 the strange belief that sin and d. are real,
T-27.......I.10:2 and perfect healing take the place of d..
T-27.......I.10:3 sick of breathing in the fetid scent of d..
T-27........II.6:5 And hopelessness and d. must disappear
T-27........II.6:6 the weak and miserable cry of d. and guilt
T-27........II.6:8 Brother, there is no d.. And this you learn
T-27...... III.2:1 power," and above all, a "living d.." And
T-27.... VI.2:11 Sin's witnesses hear but the call of d..
T-27...... VI.4:7 And for each witness to the body's d. He
T-27...... VI.4:7 to your life in Him Who knows no d..
T-27...... VI.5:7 of fear. As fear is witness unto d., so is the
T-27...... VI.6:6 throes of d. itself are but a single sound; a
T-27..... VII.9:4 yours to make between a sleeping d. and
T-27... VII.10:1 could you choose between but life or d.,
T-27... VII.10:2 There is a risk of thinking d. is peace,
T-27... VII.10:4 And d. is opposite to peace, because it is
T-27... VII.10:6 Awaken and forget all thoughts of d., and
T-27... VII.12:1 stalks you in the night and plots your d.,
T-27... VII.14:3 you dreamed in terror and in fear of d..
T-27... VII.14:5 there is no murder and there is no d.. The
T-27... VII.15:7 you see as offering both life and d. to you.
T-28........II.4:4 for dreams of healing, or for dreams of d.
T-28...... IV.1:1 to someone's dream of sickness and of d..

| | |
|---|---|
| T-28....... V.2:1 | of hate and malice, bitterness and **d.**, of |
| T-28....... V.7:5 | where terror rises from the bones of **d.**. |
| T-28...... VI.5:4 | his tiny oath to be forever faithful unto **d.**. |
| T-29....... II.6:2 | wish to be alive apart from life, alive in **d.**, |
| T-29....... II.6:2 | alive in death, with **d.** perceived as life, |
| T-29....... II.6:2 | with death perceived as life, and living, **d.**. |
| T-29..... II.10:4 | dwell in what was built as temple unto **d.**. |
| T-29..... II.10:6 | releases yours from sickness and from **d.**. |
| T-29...... III.3:1 | bodies and of **d.** is yet one theme of truth; |
| T-29....... V.6:6 | brother thinks he holds the hand of **d.**. |
| T-29....... V.7:2 | have forgiven him for all his dreams of **d.**; |
| T-29....... V.7:5 | Each form it takes in some way calls for **d.** |
| T-29....... V.7:6 | serve the lord of **d.** have come to worship |
| T-29...... VI.1:4 | of danger and destruction, sin and **d.**; of |
| T-29.... VI.2:12 | the hour of his birth and **d.**. Forgiveness |
| T-29...... VI.4:9 | There is no **d.** because the living share the |
| T-29...... VI.5:2 | For even though it was a dream of **d.**, you |
| T-29..... VII.3:2 | the idol that he seeks *is* but his **d.**. Its form |
| T-29..... VII.4:1 | beneficiary, you try to bring about your **d.** |
| T-29..... VII.4:2 | that you can suffer lack, and lack *is* **d.**. To |
| T-29..... VII.5:1 | no life, and what is lifeless is a sign of **d.**. |
| T-29..... VII.5:2 | but to perceive the signs of **d.** you seek? |
| T-29..... VII.5:3 | of life which, in its lifelessness, is really **d.**, |
| T-29..... VII.5:4 | decay, because a form of **d.** cannot be life, |
| T-29..... VII.7:2 | see **d.** and disappointment everywhere. |
| T-29... VII.9:10 | thus appears to threaten life and offer **d.**. |
| T-29... VII.10:2 | so. Salvation seeks to prove there is no **d.**, |
| T-29... VII.10:3 | The sacrifice of **d.** is nothing lost. An idol |
| T-29.... VIII.4:2 | grass from something living to a sign of **d.** |
| T-29...... IX.9:3 | to the frantic search for idols and for **d.**. |
| T-30....... II.3:3 | and be a prisoner to fear, a slave to **d.**, a |
| T-30....... II.5:2 | that he learn **d.** has no power over him, |
| T-30.... III.10:2 | of birth and **d.** that here are dreamed, the |
| T-30....... V.2:5 | for suffering and **d.** have been perceived |
| T-30.... VI.10:4 | to you a graven image and a sign of **d.**. Is |
| T-31.........I.9:2 | is saved from **d.** when you have heard its |
| T-31.......I.10:3 | that echoes past each seeming call to **d.**, |
| T-31....... II.4:6 | And thus he merits **d.**, because he has no |
| T-31....... II.5:4 | Herein is life as easily as **d.**, for what you |
| T-31....... II.5:7 | you it matters not, for you have chosen **d.** |
| T-31....... II.5:8 | But if he calls for **d.** or calls for life, for |
| T-31...... III.5:2 | ravages of fear except in murder and in **d.** |
| T-31...... III.5:4 | kill. In **d.** is sin preserved, and those who |
| T-31...... III.7:2 | their freedom from imprisonment and **d.**. |
| T-31...... IV.1:5 | within the narrow band from birth to **d.**, |
| T-31...... IV.2:3 | to disappointment, nothingness and **d.**. |
| T-31.... IV.2:11 | All of them will lead to **d.**. On some you |
| T-31.... IV.11:5 | is your escape from madness and from **d.**. |
| T-31...... VI.2:3 | This one appears and disappears in **d.**; |
| T-31..... VII.9:1 | of salvation, and the love of guilt and **d.**, |
| T-31... VII.14:3 | It is a thing of madness, pain and **d.**; a |
| T-31... VII.15:2 | vision is withheld and what they see is **d.**. |
| W-pI..... 53.5:4 | and loss and **d.** shows me that I am seeing |
| W-pI..... 55.1:2 | are but signs of disease, disaster and **d.**. |
| W-pI..... 56.1:3 | loss, age and **d.** seem to threaten me. All |
| W-pI..... 62.2:5 | of life may replace thoughts of **d.**. |
| W-pI..... 68.1:4 | your mind and to condemn the body to **d.** |
| W-pI..... 72.5:2 | be? What could it be but **d.**? In trying to |
| W-pI..... 72.5:3 | Himself as the Author of life and not of **d.** |
| W-pI..... 72.5:9 | it asserts that his salvation must be **d.**, |
| W-pI..... 72.6:9 | It is the **d.** of God and your salvation. |
| W-pI..... 75.1:6 | and turmoil and **d.** have disappeared. The |
| W-pI..... 76.3:3 | needle will ward off disease and **d.**. You |
| WpI..rII.in.5:2 | into detours, illusions and thoughts of **d.**. |
| W-pI..... 93.1:3 | you would rush to **d.** by your own hand, |
| W-pI..... 93.4:3 | You think that this is **d.**, but it is life. You |
| W-pI..... 94.3:8 | could conceive of loss or suffering or **d.**. |
| W-pI..... 99.5:4 | on what you see; on sin and pain and **d.**, |
| W-pI... 101.2:4 | The sinful warrant only **d.** and pain, and |
| W-pI... 101.3:3 | the welcome boon of **d.** to victims who |
| W-pI... 101.4:4 | If sin is real, its offering is **d.**, and meted |
| W-pI... 109.3:2 | past misery and pain, past loss and **d.**, |
| W-pI... 110.1:3 | replaced by fear and evil, misery and **d.**. If |
| W-pI... 110.1:4 | is not real, and misery and **d.** do not exist. |
| W-pI... 110.3:1 | sickness, nor can **d.** be substitute for life, |
| W-pI... 124.2:3 | and **d.** give place to everlasting life. Our |
| W-pI... 127.6:2 | Love is not found in darkness and in **d.**. |
| W-pI... 131.1:2 | within the darkness of the dream of **d.**. |
| W-pI... 131.2:6 | real? Pursuit of the imagined leads to **d.** |
| W-pI... 131.2:6 | and while you seek for life you ask for **d.**. |
| W-pI... 132.3:5 | **D.** strikes it everywhere because you hold |
| W-pI... 132.3:5 | bitter thoughts of **d.** within your mind. |
| W-pI... 132.7:3 | Some see it suddenly on point of **d.**, and |
| W-pI... 132.8:4 | replace all thoughts you ever held of **d.**. |
| W-pI. 135.18:4 | While you made plans for **d.**, He led you |
| W-pI. 135.25:4 | what was seeming **d.** and hopelessness. |
| W-pI. 136.11:3 | has not bowed to hell, nor life to **d.**. You |
| W-pI... 137.9:2 | you made to hold yourself a prisoner to **d.** |
| W-pI... 138.7:2 | itself must in the end be overcome by **d.**. |
| W-pI... 138.7:3 | In **d.** alone are opposites resolved, for |
| W-pI... 138.7:4 | And thus salvation must be seen as **d.**, for |
| W-pI. 151.16:2 | world, replacing witnesses to sin and **d.**. |
| W-pI... 152.7:1 | truth, and suffers **d.** to triumph over life; |
| W-pI... 155.7:3 | to lead your brothers from the ways of **d.**, |
| W-pI... 156.6:3 | not the end of sin in punishment and **d.**. |
| W-pI... 157.1:5 | long days and nights in celebrating **d.**. |
| W-pI. 159.10:5 | transition can be made from **d.** to life; |
| W-pI... 161.7:4 | it calls for **d.** as surely as God's Voice |
| W-pI... 161.7:4 | as God's Voice proclaims there is no **d.**. |
| W-pI... 162.2:6 | and hear this sound will never look on **d.**. |
| W-pI...... 163.h | There is no **d.**. The Son of God is free. |
| W-pI... 163.1:1 | **D.** is a thought that takes on many forms, |
| W-pI... 163.1:3 | of **d.** as savior and as giver of release. |
| W-pI... 163.2:1 | does the thought of **d.** seem mighty. For it |
| W-pI... 163.3:1 | All things but **d.** are seen to be unsure, |
| W-pI... 163.3:2 | But **d.** is counted on. For it will come with |
| W-pI... 163.4:4 | laid to rest beneath the headstone **d.** has |
| W-pI... 163.5:1 | has become what **d.** would have him be. |
| W-pI... 163.5:2 | His epitaph, which **d.** itself has written, |
| W-pI... 163.6:1 | It is impossible to worship **d.** in any form |
| W-pI... 163.6:2 | For **d.** is total. Either all things die, or else |
| W-pI... 163.7:1 | idea of the **d.** of God is so preposterous |
| W-pI... 163.7:3 | over His, and so eternal life gave way to **d.** |
| W-pI... 163.8:5 | There is no **d.**, and we renounce it now in |
| W-pI... 163.8:6 | God made not **d.**. Whatever form it takes |
| W-pI... 163.8:9 | And it is given us to look past **d.**, and see |
| W-pI... 163.9:5 | *life. There is no* **d.**, *for death is not Your Will.* |
| W-pI... 163.9:5 | *is no death, for* **d.** *is not Your Will. And we* |
| W-pI... 165.1:2 | and **d.** obscure the perfect happiness and |
| W-pI. 166.11:2 | The wish for **d.** is answered, and the sight |
| W-pI... 167.1:5 | There is no **d.** because what God created |
| W-pI... 167.1:6 | There is no **d.** because an opposite to God |
| W-pI... 167.1:7 | no **d.** because the Father and the Son are |
| W-pI... 167.2:2 | You call it **d.**. Yet we have learned that the |
| W-pI... 167.2:3 | that the idea of **d.** takes many forms. It is |
| W-pI... 167.2:6 | or the merest frown, acknowledge **d.**. And |
| W-pI... 167.3:1 | You think that **d.** is of the body. Yet it is |
| W-pI... 167.4:1 | **D.** is the thought that you are separate |
| W-pI... 167.5:1 | **D.** cannot come from life. Ideas remain |
| W-pI... 167.8:3 | of **d.** is not the opposite to thoughts of life |
| W-pI. 167.10:4 | We will not ask for **d.** in any form today. |
| W-pI. 167.11:3 | unity of life that cannot separate in **d.** and |
| W-pI... 177.1:1 | (163) There is no **d.**. The Son of God is |
| W-pI... 187.6:4 | at grief, at poverty, starvation and at **d.**. |
| W-pI... 190.1:7 | and His insane desire for revenge and **d.**. |
| W-pI... 190.3:6 | dead, has shown that **d.** is victor over life. |
| W-pI... 190.3:7 | body is the Son of God, corruptible in **d.**, |
| W-pI... 190.7:7 | Your thoughts of **d.** envelop it in fear, |
| W-pI... 191.2:6 | that does not seem to bring you nearer **d.**; |
| W-pI... 191.3:3 | own Identity, and look on evil, sin and **d.**, |
| W-pI... 191.6:5 | have laid the mark of **d.** upon its heart. |
| W-pI... 191.8:1 | the rites of **d.** echoed since time began. |
| W-pI... 191.9:3 | You play the game of **d.**, of being helpless, |
| W-pI. 191.10:3 | he will sleep no more and dream of **d.**. |
| W-pI... 192.4:2 | means by which the fear of **d.** is overcome |
| W-pI... 192.9:6 | your savior from the prison house of **d.**. |
| W-pI... 193.6:1 | and **d.** becomes our choice instead of life? |
| W-pI... 194.3:4 | from sadness, pain and even **d.** itself. |
| W-pI... 195.3:3 | try to bring him down to lie in **d.** with you |
| W-pI... 195.5:2 | walk the way of hatred and the path of **d.**. |
| W-pI... 196.3:4 | past all thoughts of crucifixion and of **d.**, |
| W-pI. 196.11:1 | perceived within you, eager for your **d.**, |
| W-pI... 197.6:2 | before He snatches them away again in **d.**. |
| W-pI... 197.6:3 | For **d.** will have no meaning for you then. |
| W-pI... 198.4:1 | past all suffering, and finally away from **d.** |
| W-pI... 198.7:2 | place where **d.** is offered to God's Son and |
| W-pII. 226.1:2 | It is not **d.** which makes this possible, but |
| W-pII. 237.1:4 | see, aware it ends the bitter dream of **d.**; |
| W-pII. 249.2:2 | *them with thoughts of violence and* **d.** *Now* |
| W-pII..... 4.3:4 | Himself, His Will forever overcome by **d.**, |
| W-pII..... 4.4:3 | guilt, with but a little life that ends in **d.**. |
| W-pII. 271.1:4 | kindly sight redeems the world from **d.**, |
| W-pII. 282.1:3 | not to be asleep in dreams of **d.**, while |
| W-pII..... 8.3:1 | need has such a mind for thoughts of **d.**, |
| W-pII. 294.1:5 | And yet a neutral thing does not see **d.**, |
| W-pII. 300.1:1 | to say that **d.** and sorrow are the certain |
| W-pII. 314.1:4 | **D.** will not claim the future now, for life is |
| W-pII. 328.1:3 | find is sickness, suffering and loss and **d.**. |
| W-pII... 12.1:1 | doomed to suffer and to end its life in **d.**. |
| W-pII... 12.1:3 | is weak and love is fearful, life is really **d.**, |
| W-pII... 12.3:2 | he know of madness and the **d.** of God, |
| W-pII. 331.1:9 | *D. is illusion; life, eternal truth. There is no* |
| M-in.......... 4:7 | which teaches nothing but despair and **d.**, |
| M-1........... 4:7 | time, with its illusions of change and **d.**, |
| M-5.........I.1:9 | by His **d.** can He be conquered by His Son |
| M-5.........I.2:7 | But if he chooses **d.** himself, his weakness |
| M-5.... III.2:11 | brothers to turn away from **d.**: "Behold, |
| M-6........... 1:6 | of life, believing healing is the way to **d.**? |
| M-6........... 1:8 | nothing to live for, he may ask for **d.**. |
| M-10......... 6:6 | of sickening despair and fear of **d.**; all |
| M-11......... 1:5 | It has also promised that there is no **d.**, |
| M-11......... 2:5 | it. God says there is no **d.**; your judgment |
| M-11......... 2:5 | judgment sees but **d.** as the inevitable end |
| M-17......... 6:2 | is inevitable, for its outcome must be **d.**. |
| M-17....... 7:13 | bears this stain on him must meet with **d.** |
| M-17....... 9:10 | There is no **d.**. This sword does not exist. |
| M-19......... 4:3 | And it is this that overcomes the fear of **d.** |
| M-20......... 5:1 | Living is joy, but **d.** can only weep. You |
| M-20......... 5:2 | You see in **d.** escape from what you made. |
| M-20......... 5:3 | But this you do not see; that you made **d.**, |
| M-20......... 5:4 | **D.** cannot be escape, because it is not life |
| M-20......... 5:6 | Life and **d.** seem to be opposites because |
| M-20......... 5:6 | because you have decided **d.** ends life. |
| M-23......... 2:5 | overcome **d.** because he has accepted life. |
| M-24......... 5:7 | not the beginning, and **d.** is not the end. |
| M-27............ h | WHAT IS **D.**? |
| M-27......... 1:1 | **D.** is the central dream from which all |
| M-27......... 2:6 | **D.** has become life's symbol. His world is |
| M-27......... 2:8 | Where there is **d.** is peace impossible. |
| M-27......... 3:1 | **D.** is the symbol of the fear of God. His |
| M-27......... 3:6 | And so do all things live because of **d.**. |
| M-27......... 4:2 | If **d.** is real for anything, there is no life. |
| M-27......... 4:3 | **D.** denies life. But if there is reality in life, |
| M-27......... 4:4 | But if there is reality in life, **d.** is denied. |
| M-27......... 4:9 | not make **d.** because He did not make fear |
| M-27......... 5:1 | "reality" of **d.** is firmly rooted in the belief |
| M-27......... 5:2 | created bodies, **d.** would indeed be real. |
| M-27......... 5:5 | **D.** is indeed the death of God, if He is |
| M-27......... 5:5 | Death is indeed the **d.** of God, if He is |
| M-27......... 6:1 | "And the last to be overcome will be **d.**." |
| M-27......... 6:3 | Without the idea of **d.** there is no world. |
| M-27......... 6:6 | And in **d.** are all illusions born. What can |
| M-27......... 6:7 | What can be born of **d.** and still have life? |
| M-27......... 6:9 | to cling to **d.** and yet to think love real are |
| M-27......... 7:1 | no compromise in which **d.** plays a part. |
| M-27......... 7:6 | nor sinks down to **d.** and dissolution. |
| M-27......... 7:7 | And what is the end of **d.**? Nothing but |
| M-28......... 1:1 | is the overcoming or surmounting of **d.**. It |
| M-28......... 2:1 | The resurrection is the denial of **d.**, being |
| M-28......... 4:2 | There is no **d.**. The Son of God is free. |
| C-1............ 6:1 | and seeing guilt, disease and **d.** as real. |
| C-2............ 1:2 | Their **d.** is sure and this alone is certain in |
| C-2.......... 1:11 | which, like all dreams, can only end in **d.**? |
| C-4............ 7:7 | of guilt and **d.** is there snuffed out forever. |
| C-5............ 3:5 | changed by sin and evil, malice, fear or **d.**. |
| C-5............ 6:9 | *is no* **d.** *because the Son of God is like his* |
| P-2........ IV.3:2 | Sickness and **d.** and misery now stalk the |
| P-2........ IV.5:4 | for **d.** has not been overcome until the |
| P-2........ VI.2:1 | to hear this song of **d.** only an instant, |
| P-2....... VII.8:2 | all its little triumphs and its dreams of **d.**. |
| S-1..........II.8:8 | with the illusion of **d.** and the fear of God. |
| S-1........ III.2:3 | who understands that they are calls for **d.**, |
| S-2...........I.2:4 | plague; a hateful thing of danger and of **d.**, |
| S-2...........I.2:5 | Forgiveness-to-destroy *is* **d.**, and this it |
| S-2...........I.4:5 | the only one that does not lead to **d.**. Only |
| S-2...........I.8:3 | from **d.** by offering Christ's Love to him. |
| S-2..........II.2:8 | grief. This is not really mercy. This is **d.**. |

| | |
|---|---|
| S-2 ......... II.7:6 | nothing else, or you have sought your **d.**, |
| S-2 ......... II.8:1 | and comparisons of every kind are **d.**. For |
| S-2 ......... III.1:4 | nor promise freedom while it asks for **d.**. |
| S-2 ......... III.6:3 | About the end of sin and guilt and **d.**. |
| S-2 ......... III.6:7 | and **d.** become again the holy gift of God. |
| S-3 ........... I.2:2 | and the mark of **d.** upon it this is clearly |
| S-3 ........... I.2:4 | **D.** stares at them as every moment goes |
| S-3 ........... I.2:6 | the heavy scent of **d.** upon their hearts. |
| S-3 ......... II.1:7 | And with this wish is **d.** a certainty, for |
| S-3 ......... II.1:8 | of seeming **d.** that has a different source. |
| S-3 ......... II.2:1 | This is what **d.** should be; a quiet choice, |
| S-3 ......... II.3:1 | We call it **d.**, but it is liberty. It does not |
| S-3 ......... II.3:3 | form in which **d.** comes when it is time to |
| S-3 ......... II.5:1 | This is not **d.** according to the world, for |
| S-3 ......... II.5:1 | **d.** is cruel in its frightened eyes and takes |
| S-3 ......... II.5:5 | **D.** is reward and not a punishment. But |
| S-3 ......... II.6:1 | it brings a cruel **d.** in seeming victory. It |
| S-3 ......... III.6:5 | Nor will **d.** any more be feared because it |
| S-3 ......... IV.5:7 | destroyer, **d.**. And sickness, suffering and |

## death's 5

| | |
|---|---|
| T-20.... VI.11:4 | his devotion to **d.** idols and then pass on. |
| T-29....... V.7:4 | for hate, and will continue in **d.** services. |
| W-pI ...163.8:1 | **D.** worshippers may be afraid. And yet, |
| W-pI ...189.5:4 | world, held cruelly in **d.** sharp-pointed, |
| C-6.............5:6 | in which you dance to **d.** thin melody. For |

## deathless 4

| | |
|---|---|
| T-12....VII.15:6 | will have looked upon the **d.** in yourself, |
| T19... IV.C.9:6 | For it is **d.**, and within it lies the end of |
| T-29.... VIII.6:4 | happened. Here the **d.** come to die, the all- |
| T-31...... VI.6:7 | you a spirit, **d.**, and without the promise |

## debased 1

| | |
|---|---|
| W-pI .....35.4:2 | desirable or undesirable, grandiose or **d.**. |

## debasement

*See* self-debasement

## debatable 1

| | |
|---|---|
| T-4...........I.7:7 | This point is not **d.** except in delusions. |

## debilitating 1

| | |
|---|---|
| T-3........VI.5:7 | is curious that an ability so **d.** would be so |

## debris 1

| | |
|---|---|
| W-pI .......9.2:5 | has been cleared of the **d.** that darkens it. |

## debt 7

| | |
|---|---|
| T-4........VI.2:1 | your **d.** to your brother is something you |
| T-4........VI.2:2 | It is the same **d.** that you owe to me. |
| T-18....... V.7:1 | be glad that he can pay his **d.** by bringing |
| T19 . IV.D.19:6 | the **d.** of gratitude you offer to the Son of |
| W-pI ...105.2:2 | meant to be a pledge of **d.** to be repaid |
| W-pII..323.2:1 | And as we pay the **d.** we owe to truth,–a |
| W-pII..323.2:1 | –a **d.** that merely is the letting go of self- |

## decay 7

| | |
|---|---|
| T-19....... II.6:5 | capable of complete corruption and **d.**. If |
| T19... IV.C.8:1 | orders, proof in his **d.** that God Himself is |
| T-24....... V.4:8 | Yet is it joy to look upon **d.** and madness, |
| T-24.....VII.4:6 | hate, and you condemn it to **d.** and death. |
| T-24.....VII.4:8 | shine on him, and give *you* safety from **d.**. |
| T-29.....VII.5:4 | Yet each must fail and crumble and **d.**, |
| M-19..........4:4 | For separate fragments must **d.** and die, |

## decayed 1

| | |
|---|---|
| T19 . IV.A.13:3 | gorges filled with things **d.** and rotted. To |

## decays 1

| | |
|---|---|
| W-pII......5.1:2 | he lives, to die as it **d.** and crumbles. For |

## deceit 9

| | |
|---|---|
| T-11... VIII.9:6 | in your Father, in Whom no **d.** is possible |
| T-11. VIII.15:3 | as part of God, **d.** in you is impossible. |
| T-11. VIII.15:4 | When you perceive yourself without **d.**, |
| T-14.... IV.4:10 | place made out of darkness and **d.**, for |
| T-14.... IV.4:10 | for thus are darkness and **d.** undone. Fail |
| T-14.... VII.1:8 | Yet the perception must be without **d.**, |
| W-pI ...122.6:6 | clear and plain, beyond **d.** in its simplicity |
| W-pII..333.1:2 | name, or hidden by **d.** of any kind, if it |
| M-15 .........3:6 | There is no **d.** in God. His promises are |

## deceits 1

| | |
|---|---|
| W-pII..248.1:7 | and **d.** and lies about the holy Son of God. |

## deceive 58

| | |
|---|---|
| T-1........ IV.2:1 | darkness, but you can **d.** yourself about it. |
| T-1....... VII.1:7 | Do not **d.** yourself into believing that you |
| T-3....... VII.2:2 | To do so is to **d.** yourself, and this will |
| T-3....... VII.4:5 | Knowledge cannot **d.**, but perception can. |
| T-6........ II.12:2 | projects to exclude, and therefore to **d.**. |
| T-9......... II.7:2 | Your deceptions may **d.** you, but they |
| T-9......... II.7:2 | may deceive you, but they cannot **d.** me. |
| T-9..... VIII.7:6 | Your grandeur will never **d.** you, but your |
| T-9... VIII.11:8 | what you hear, for God does not **d.**. He |
| T-11... VIII.8:2 | you. Do you believe I would **d.** you? The |
| T-12........ IV.4:7 | For He will never **d.** God's Son whom He |
| T-13........ III.8:4 | for though they may **d.** themselves, like |
| T-14...........I.5:5 | you, because you chose to **d.** yourself. |
| T-15....... IV.4:7 | know where it is, and can only **d.** yourself. |
| T-15... VII.10:2 | but it cannot long **d.** those who will learn |
| T-18....... VI.2:7 | who think you hate your body **d.** yourself. |
| T-18....... VI.4:3 | mind cannot attack, but it can **d.** itself. |
| T-19....... II.3:1 | of God can be mistaken; he can **d.** himself |
| T-19....... II.4:1 | truth, and it is innocence that would **d.**. |
| T-21....... II.2:6 | *asked*. **D.** yourself no longer that you are |
| T-22....... III.7:1 | have different forms, and so they can **d.**. |
| T-23..... II.17:5 | not the form of the attack on him **d.** you. |
| T-25..... VII.1:5 | sinners, and **d.** with glitter and with guile. |
| T-25.... VIII.7:3 | dressed to **d.** within an angel's cloak. And |
| T-26... VII.13:6 | be possible in trying to **d.** the Son of God. |
| T-26... VII.15:6 | is the same is different you but **d.** yourself |
| T-29.... VIII.2:1 | Let not their form **d.** you. Idols are but |
| T-30....... IV.2:5 | the boxes and the bears did not **d.** him, |
| T-30....... IV.5:1 | **d.** *because* they are appearances and not |
| T-30....... IV.6:1 | but **d.** the mind that wants to be deceived |
| T-30..... V.9:11 | not your experiences here **d.** in retrospect |
| T-30.... VIII.1:1 | Appearances **d.**, but can be changed. |
| T-30.... VIII.1:3 | It does not **d.** at all, and if you fail to see |
| T-31....... IV.8:2 | choose the better to **d.** yourself again. |
| W-pI .....64.5:6 | Let not the form of the decision **d.** you. |
| W-pI .....73.8:2 | us, nor **d.** us with an illusion of strength. |
| W-pI .....80.3:4 | will not **d.** you while you remember this. |
| W-pI .....80.7:4 | not **d.** yourself about what the problem is, |
| WpI . rIII.in3:2 | Do not **d.** yourself in this. Unwillingness |
| W-pI ...131.4:4 | **d.** himself and think that it is hell he seeks |
| W-pI ...133.9:1 | which could **d.** but those who are content |
| W-pI ...134.3:2 | unfounded effort to **d.** yourself by making |
| WpI . rIV.in5:2 | and clear it of all thoughts that would **d.**, |
| W-pI ...151.2:3 | a long while since your senses do **d.**. That |
| W-pI ...164.9:6 | Would God **d.** you? Can His promise fail? |
| W-pI. 185.11:2 | For he merely asks that he **d.** himself no |
| W-pI. 186.14:1 | These are the forms which never can **d.**, |
| W-pI ...196.3:2 | distort the truth will not **d.** you longer. |
| W-pI ...200.7:5 | as he looks on it, the world can but **d.**? |
| W-pII......3.2:6 | But eyes **d.**, and ears hear falsely. Now |
| W-pII......4.2:1 | the mind made in its efforts to **d.** itself. Its |
| W-pII..277.2:5 | lie, and God can will that He **d.** Himself. |
| M-in ..........5:2 | The self-deceiving must **d.**, for they must |
| M-4 ....... II.2:2 | It is only the wish to **d.** that makes for war |
| M-5 ...... III.3:3 | this brother who would so **d.** himself as to |
| M-16 .......10:3 | he may accept as real can but **d.** him. But |
| M-25 .........4:1 | Nothing that is genuine is used to **d.**. The |
| S-2 ........ III.1:5 | Would God **d.** you? He but asks for trust |

## deceived 78

| | |
|---|---|
| T-2........ III.5:8 | could not be shaken and could not be **d.**. |
| T-2........ III.5:9 | Whenever you are afraid you *are* **d.**, and |
| T-4........ IV.6:1 | of the ego, and do not be **d.** by it. It offers |
| T-9......... II.6:12 | you, for you would not want me to be **d.**. |
| T-9....... VII.4:3 | He is not **d.** by anything you do, because |
| T-9....... VII.4:4 | are. The ego is **d.** by everything you do, |
| T-11....... III.6:2 | Do not be **d.** by the dark comforters, and |
| T-11....... V.6:9 | be **d.** by its interpretation of your conflict. |
| T-11.... VIII.9:1 | for Christ is not **d.** in His Father and His |
| T-11.... VIII.9:1 | His Father and His Father is not **d.** in Him |
| T-11.... VIII.9:2 | Do not, then, be **d.** in your brother, and |
| T-11.... VIII.9:5 | Be not **d.** in God's Son, for thereby you |
| T-11.... VIII.9:5 | for thereby you must be **d.** in yourself. |
| T-11.... VIII.9:6 | And being **d.** in yourself you are deceived |
| T-11.... VIII.9:6 | in yourself you are **d.** in your Father, in |
| T-11.. VIII.11:5 | Be not **d.** in God's Son, for he is one with |
| T-11.. VIII.12:1 | are offended by Christ and are **d.** in Him. |
| T-11.. VIII.12:5 | heal the Son of God, in whom He is not **d.** |
| T-11.. VIII.14:2 | But you are merely **d.** in them. Ask what |
| T-11VIII.14:10 | are **d.** by what you see you need reality to |
| T-11.. VIII.15:2 | For if God is not **d.** in you, you can be |
| T-11.. VIII.15:2 | in you, you can be **d.** only in yourself. Yet |
| T-13....... V.9:1 | see in darkness, and in this you are **d.**. |
| T-13...... VI.4:4 | But do not be **d.**, and then believe that |
| T-14.........I.5:6 | be **d.** will merely attack direct approaches |
| T-15........ X.6:6 | will not be **d.** by any form the ego takes to |
| T-17...... IV.9:8 | Be not **d.** by the most superficial aspects |
| T-22....... V.5:2 | **d.** by the illusions it presents of size and |
| T-23... II.17:10 | Be not **d.** when madness takes a form you |
| T-23...... III.2:4 | the receiver nor the giver is long **d.**. |
| T-26..... VII.8:4 | Who looks on them is but **d.**. Forgiveness |
| T-26... VII.13:4 | willed, because the mind can wish to be **d.** |
| T-29.. VIII.8:11 | Be not **d.** by forms the "something" takes. |
| T-30...... IV.5:4 | what you have made to let you be **d.**, for |
| T-30...... IV.5:4 | for thus you prove that you have been **d.**. |
| T-30...... IV.6:1 | but deceive the mind that wants to be **d.**. |
| T-30...... VI.6:4 | **d.** about the meaning of a fixed belief that |
| T-30.... VI.10:7 | **d.** in him who has been given you to heal, |
| T-30.... VIII.1:3 | fail to see beyond appearances you *are* **d.**. |
| T-31.........I.8:6 | been **d.** by forms the call was hidden in. |
| T-31....... I.11:3 | You are **d.** if you believe you want disaster |
| T-31...... IV.2:7 | **d.** by all the different names its roads are |
| T-31..... V.10:5 | And who is **d.** by all your goodness, and |
| T-31... VII.14:8 | not **d.** by what appears as many choices. |
| W-pI ...79.10:1 | Be not **d.** by the form of problems today. |
| W-pI .....93.2:3 | salvation in strange ways; have been **d.**, |
| W-pI ...106.2:3 | Be not **d.** by voices of the dead, which tell |
| W-pI ...128.2:4 | Be you **d.** no more. The world you see |
| W-pI ...133.6:5 | **d.** by nothing in a form he thinks he likes. |
| W-pI ...133.7:4 | been **d.** by the illusion loss can offer gain. |
| W-pI ...133.8:5 | Here it is easiest of all to be **d.**. For what |
| W-pI ...133.9:1 | deceive but those who are content to be **d.** |
| W-pI ...133.9:3 | for the one who is **d.** will not perceive that |
| W-pI ...134.7:3 | It looks on lies, but it is not **d.**. It does not |
| W-pI ...140.4:2 | is not **d.** by forms the dream may take. |
| W-pI. 151.14:2 | failed to be **d.** by what was falsely added. |
| W-pI ...154.2:4 | But He is not **d.** in what you are, and |
| W-pI. 155.13:5 | He cannot be **d.**. His trust has made your |
| W-pI ...184.9:3 | But be you not **d.** by them as well. They |
| W-pI ...185.9:2 | make. Be not **d.** that it is otherwise. No |
| W-pI ...194.7:8 | free to choose again when he has been **d.**; |
| W-pII . 240.1:6 | Let us not be **d.** today. We are the Sons of |
| W-pII . 265.1:3 | **d.** was I to think that what I feared was in |
| W-pII . 290.1:5 | Yet I would not allow my mind to be **d.** by |
| W-pII . 323.2:2 | in joy. We are **d.** no longer. Love has now |
| M-4 ...... III.1:4 | that you have been **d.** in your brothers. |
| M-4 ...... III.1:5 | could you not have been **d.** in yourself? |
| M-7 ........... 6:3 | and you have become **d.** about yourself. |
| M-7 ........... 6:4 | And you are **d.** about yourself because |
| M-12 ......... 6:8 | Yet they are not **d.** by what they see. They |
| M-16 ....... 10:6 | I cannot be **d.**." Perhaps he prefers other |
| M-25 ......... 5:1 | world may still be **d.** by "psychic" powers. |
| M-25 ......... 5:5 | Yet, given a remaining wish to be **d.**, |
| M-27 ......... 7:5 | **d.** by the "reality" of any changing form. |
| C-6............ 4:8 | But He is not **d.** when you perceive your |
| C-ep........... 1:7 | come, but learn how not to be **d.** by them. |
| P-2......... V.7:4 | We are **d.** already, if we think there is a |
| S-2.......... II.8:3 | set. Be not **d.** by them, but lay them by as |

## deceiver 3

T19..IV.B.15:3 The great **d.** recognizes that this is not so,
W-pI.....72.5:3 life and not of death, He is a liar and a **d.**,
S-2...........I.5:1 the world, and you the great **d.** of yourself

## deceiver's 1

T-21....... V.8:1 serve the great **d.** needs as well as truth.

## deceives 7

T-3.......VII.2:6 The devil **d.** by lies, and builds kingdoms
T-14.........I.5:5 it. It **d.** you, because you chose to deceive
T-15...... III.6:8 of God. Your littleness **d.** you, but your
T-21.......IV.6:4 At times it still **d.** you. Yet in your saner
T-21...... VI.1:6 For uncorrected error of any kind **d.** you
T-25..VIII.14:5 The world **d.**, but it cannot replace God's
S-3........ III.1:3 Therefore it still **d.**. Nor is it made by one

## deceiving 3

*See also* self-deceiving

T-14....... II.3:6 *Your faith in nothing is* ***d.*** *you. Offer your*
W-pI.....93.2:3 **d.** and afraid of foolish fantasies and
M-29 .........5:1 that he does not possess is **d.** himself. Yet

## deception 28

*See also* self-deception

T-1........IV.2:2 **d.** makes you fearful because you realize
T-1........IV.2:2 because you realize in your heart it *is* a **d.**,
T-4.........I.10:5 incapable of **d.** as is the spirit He created.
T-4........IV.7:3 Side with me consistently against this **d.**,
T-6....V.B.1:11 lie is at its center, only **d.** proceeds from it
T-10...... III.8:1 I do not bring God's message with **d.**,
T-14.........I.5:6 seem to encroach upon **d.** and strike at it.
T-14....... II.3:8 *You will find no* ***d.*** *there, but only the simple*
T-15......IV.9:8 then, try only to be vigilant against **d.**,
T-17...... VI.5:6 truly, for **d.** cannot prevail against you.
T19....IV.C.7:6 ego's secrets, all its strange devices for **d.**,
T-24.......IV.1:4 Whatever gentleness it offers is but **d.**,
T-26....VIII.7:2 And is it not **d.** if it does? Its cause is here,
T-30...... IV.6:2 that will forever place you far beyond **d.**.
T-30....VIII.2:3 in him beyond appearance and **d.**, both.
W-pI.....80.2:4 You have laid **d.** aside, and seen the light
W-pI...133.9:3 Here is **d.** doubled, for the one who is
W-pI...134.4:1 sins are real, you look on pardon as **d.**.
W-pI...168.1:5 try to hide from Him, and suffer from **d.**.
W-pI.190.10:6 is awakening. Pain is **d.**; joy alone is truth.
W-pII .240.1:1 Fear is **d.**. It attests that you have seen
M-in ..........5:2 must deceive, for they must teach **d.**. And
M-16 .......10:4 But he is safe from all **d.** if he so decides.
M-25 .........4:2 The Holy Spirit is incapable of **d.**, and He
M-25 .........5:5 wish to be deceived, **d.** is made easy. Now
M-25 .........5:7 uncertainties with increasing **d.**.
S-2...........I.5:1 This is the great **d.** of the world, and you
S-3........IV.5:4 He is blamed for your **d.** and your guilt.

## deceptions 5

*See also* self-deceptions

T-9......... II.7:2 Your **d.** may deceive you, but they cannot
T-9......VIII.7:7 Illusions are **d.**. You cannot triumph, but
W-pI...153.1:3 its "gifts" of seeming safety are illusory **d.**.
W-pI...163.2:1 guilty and the lord of all illusions and **d.**,
W-pI...197.1:5 **d.** which would cheat you of defenses, to

## deceptive 2

T-17......IV.8:1 **d.** frame of all the defenses the ego uses.
T-29.........I.1:8 For He must be **d.** in His Love. Be wary,

## decide 95

T-3.....VI.10:3 is. The problem everyone must **d.** is the
T-4......... II.5:4 and are likely to **d.** that you need precisely
T-4........IV.3:3 own decisions, and then **d.** otherwise.
T-5.......VII.6:3 wrongly, but can as actively **d.** otherwise.
T-5 ......VII.6:8 *decision myself, but I can also* ***d.*** *otherwise. I*
T-5 ......VII.6:9 *I want to* ***d.*** *otherwise, because I want to be at*
T-5 .....VII.6:11 *Him, by allowing Him to* ***d.*** *for God for me.*
T-6 .....V.B.6:3 it is up to you to **d.** which voice is true,
T-6 .....V.B.6:5 allow the Holy Spirit to **d.** for God for you
T-6 .....V.B.7:2 is up to you to **d.** what God's creations are
T-7 ....... VI.9:5 belief that what you are is up to you to **d.**.
T-7 ...VIII.1:10 up to you to **d.** whether or not you will
T-7 .........X.6:8 The only way out of the error is to **d.** that
T-7 .........X.6:8 that you do not have to **d.** anything.
T-9 ..........I.8:2 it can only **d.** either that there is no God
T-9 ......... V.7:5 who must **d.** with God that there is light
T-9 ......VII.2:4 And you abide in peace when you so **d.**.
T-9 .....VIII.2:9 It shifts to viciousness when you **d.** not to
T-10 ....in.3:11 God will never **d.** against you, or He
T-10 .........I.1:1 you would **d.** against them as long as your
T-11 ...VIII.4:7 **D.** for the answer and you will have it, for
T-12 .........I.1:7 If you **d.** that someone is really trying to
T-12 ..... VI.2:7 do so, and therefore you can **d.** otherwise.
T-12 ..... VI.5:3 it. Only then will you **d.** to awaken. And
T-12 .....VII.9:2 You can **d.** to see it right. What you made
T-12 ..VII.11:8 As you **d.** so will you see. And all that you
T-12 ...VIII.3:4 to **d.** what is visible and what is invisible,
T-12 ...VIII.3:4 than it is up to you to **d.** what reality is.
T-14 .........I.2:4 If you **d.** to have and give and be nothing
T-14 ..... III.4:4 yours. What you can **d.** between is fixed,
T-14 .... III.11:9 not **d.** whether or not you are deserving of
T-14 ... III.12:3 Do not **d.** against it, for being of Him it
T-14 ... III.14:4 and will **d.** against your peace as surely as
T-14 ... III.16:1 Say to the Holy Spirit only, "**D.** for me,"
T-14 ... III.16:5 For you **d.** for them and for yourself.
T-14 ... III.17:1 How gracious it is to **d.** all things through
T-14 ..... IV.4:5 **D.** that God is right and you are wrong
T-14 ..... IV.5:2 only to **d.** against deciding what you want
T-14 ..... IV.5:3 then, can you **d.** what you should do?
T-14 ..... IV.6:1 you have learned how to **d.** with God, all
T-15 ..... III.6:3 **D.** for God through Him. For littleness,
T-15 ... III.10:1 **D.** with me, who has decided to abide
T-15 ..... IV.1:6 You must **d.** when it is. Delay it not. For
T-15 ...... V.3:5 How can you **d.** that special aspects of the
T-21 ........II.2:4 *and I* ***d.*** *upon the goal I would achieve. And*
T-21 ........II.3:6 to Him Who must **d.** for God for you.
T-21 ..VII.5:10 himself these questions, which he must **d.**
T-21 ....VII.6:5 which is indeed the last you need **d.**, still
T-21 ..VII.12:6 attached to nothing, he does **d.** against it.
T-22 ........II.7:2 the same will not **d.** alone nor differently.
T-22 ..... IV.1:4 was to **d.** which branch you will take now.
T-22 ... VI.13:7 to be answered in order to **d.** which must
T-22 ... VI.15:7 Let truth **d.** if you and your brother be
T-24 .........I.2:5 their mercy while you **d.** to leave it there.
T-24 ... VI.10:8 Would you **d.** against the holiness He sees
T-25 ...... V.4:8 If you **d.** against his proper function, the
T-25 .VIII.14:7 Let love **d.**, and never fear that you, in
T-25 ..... IX.7:6 help is to **d.** it should remain unsettled,
T-26 ..... III.1:6 What is there to **d.**? For it is conflict that
T-26 ... III.1:10 for there is nothing to **d.** *between.* And
T-29 ....VII.8:1 you need but to **d.** you do not know the
T-29 ....VII.8:2 not have, and thus do you **d.** what it is for
T-30 .........I.3:2 and *then* **d.** to ask what you should do.
T-30 .........I.6:5 *I forgot what to* ***d.***. This cancels out the
T-30 .........I.8:2 *At least I can* ***d.*** *I do not like what I feel now.*
T-30 .......I.14:7 decisions by yourself whatever you **d.**. For
T-30 .......I.15:3 ask advice before you can **d.** on anything.
T-30 .......I.16:9 What kind of day will you **d.** to have?
T-30 .......I.17:2 to understand that they cannot **d.** alone,
T-30 ..... III.1:9 **D.** for idols and you ask for loss. Decide
T-30 ... III.1:10 loss. **D.** for truth and everything is yours.
T-30 ..... III.2:9 you **d.** upon the form of what you want,
T-30 ..... IV.6:4 about, when you **d.** one very simple thing;
T-30 ...VIII.6:1 will you look upon when you **d.** there is
T-31 ........II.2:6 time you think you must **d.** on anything.
T-31 ........II.9:5 goal, which is but to **d.** to walk with him,
T-31 ..... IV.8:2 and you can but **d.** how you would choose
T-31 ..... VI.1:5 What you **d.** in this determines all you see
W-in..........6:3 sure that you do not **d.** for yourself that
W-pI.....70.6:2 still let you **d.** when to undertake them.
W-pI.....70.6:3 it would again be well to **d.** in advance
W-pI...138.6:3 If you could **d.** the rest, this one remains
W-pI. 138.10:2 Who can **d.** between the clearly seen and
W-pI .. 152.8:3 **D.** but to accept your rightful place as co-
W-pII . 311.2:3 *let Your Love* ***d.*** *what he whom You created*
M-2 ........... 3:7 however, to **d.** when you want to learn it.
M-3 ........... 5:6 Yet should they **d.** to learn it, the perfect
M-3 ........... 5:7 And if they **d.** to learn that lesson, they
M-4 ..... I.A.4:2 he must now **d.** all things on the basis of
M-13 ......... 8:2 **D.** for God, and everything is given you at
M-13 ......... 8:3 **D.** against Him, and you choose nothing,
M-21 ......... 4:5 ceasing to **d.** for himself what he will say.
M-29 ......... 5:4 ask the Holy Spirit to **d.** for you is simply
P-3...........I.1:6 This is not up to you to **d.**. There is a
P-3...........I.2:5 not demand, do not **d.**, do not sacrifice.

## decided 31

T-5 ........II.10:1 that the Mind that **d.** for me is also in you
T-5 ...... VII.6:2 realize that you must already have **d.** not
T-5 ...... VII.6:3 to recognize that you actively **d.** wrongly,
T-5 ...... VII.6:7 *I must have* ***d.*** *wrongly, because I am not at*
T-8 ..... IV.4:11 you would have **d.** against healing, and
T-8 .....VIII.3:5 recognized this and also **d.** against attack,
T-12 .. VII.12:1 be because you have **d.** to manifest truth.
T-14 ... III.14:4 as you **d.** that salvation lay in you alone.
T-14 ..... IV.5:1 have **d.** against your function in Heaven,
T-15 ..... III.5:7 you the awareness of what you **d.** for.
T-15 ..... III.7:1 join with me who **d.** for holiness for you.
T-15 ... III.10:1 with me, who has **d.** to abide with you. I
T-15 ..... IV.8:5 come into a mind that has **d.** to oppose it.
T-18 ... VIII.3:4 this tiny sunbeam has **d.** it is the sun; this
T-21 ........II.3:5 Suffer, and you **d.** sin was your goal. Be
T-21 ... VIII.4:1 not yet **d.** how you would answer the final
T-22 ..... IV.2:4 Your way is **d.**. There will be nothing you
T-25 .... VII.4:4 **d.** he is not his Father's Son because the
T-25 ..... IX.4:5 it is **d.** who shall win and who shall lose;
T-25 ..... IX.7:7 to you, unless you have **d.** first to *be* unjust
T-27 ..... III.2:1 You have **d.** that your brother is a symbol
T-29 .........I.3:4 had **d.** that your brother is your enemy.
T-30 .........I.5:4 This means you have **d.** by yourself, and
T-30 .........I.7:5 once you have **d.** by yourself the rules that
T-30 .........I.9:1 (5) Having **d.** that you do not like the way
T-30 .......I.10:1 you will gain if what you have **d.** is not so.
T-30 ........II.5:3 him, and because you have **d.** with him,
T-31 ......V.12:7 must have first **d.** on the one to choose,
W-pI .. 139.4:4 and has **d.** that he does not know the only
M-20 ......... 5:6 opposites because you have **d.** death ends
M-22 ......... 2:7 has **d.** on the direction he wants to take.

## decider 1

T-27 .... VII.9:3 are you the one **d.** of your destiny in time.

## decides 10

T-20 ........II.2:3 mind **d.** on what it would receive and give
T-21 .. VII.12:5 No one **d.** against his happiness, but he
W-pI .. 136.4:1 evaluates a threat, **d.** escape is necessary,
M-5 .........II.2:3 forms. A patient **d.** that this is so, and he
M-5 .........II.2:4 If he **d.** against recovery, he will not be
M-5 .........II.2:7 outcome is what he **d.** that it is. Special
M-8 ......... 3:11 It alone **d.** whether what is seen is real or
M-16 ....... 10:4 But he is safe from all deception if he so **d.**
P-3...........I.2:1 Who, then, **d.** what each brother needs?
S-2.......... III.5:5 Forgive him as the Christ **d.** you should,

## deciding 16

T-5 .........II.9:7 **d.** for God I showed you that this decision
T-6 ..... V.A.1:6 attempt to resolve conflict by not **d.** at all.
T-7 ..... VIII.7:3 **d.** against the belief that you can be alone,
T-10 .... in.3:11 you, or He would be **d.** against Himself.
T-10 ........II.6:5 By **d.** against your reality, you have made
T-10 ..... IV.1:7 He is the symbol of **d.** against God, and
T-14 ..... III.3:3 to it, you are **d.** against your happiness,
T-14 ..... III.4:1 you are **d.** between the crucifixion and the
T-14 ... III.10:8 impossible burden of **d.** what they want
T-14 ... III.17:7 **d.** what can bring only good to everyone?
T-14 ..... IV.5:2 is only to decide against **d.** what you want
T-14 ..... IV.6:3 your own volition seems to make **d.** hard.
T-17 ..... VI.4:1 The value of **d.** in advance what you want

T-20...... III.3:4 not **d.** first where they would have it be.
T-22...... IV.1:8 branches, and not **d.** on which way to go.
T-27...... III.6:3 in **d.** that it is the only one you want. It

## decision 211

*See also* decision-making

T-1......... V.2:1 The basic **d.** of the miracle-minded is not
T-2......... III.3:2 because of the inevitability of the final **d.**,
T-2......... VI.6:3 to do comes from your undivided **d.**.
T-4......... II.7:9 that this is possible is a **d.** of the mind,
T-4......... III.4:5 project onto the ego the **d.** to separate,
T-4....... V.6:11 When you make a **d.** of purpose, then,
T-4....... V.6:11 have made a **d.** about your future effort; a
T-4....... V.6:11 a **d.** that will remain in effect unless you
T-4........ VI.4:4 but it is still only your **d.** to use the device
T-5......... II.1:4 **d.** to heal the separation by letting it go.
T-5....... II.8:10 now is an evaluation because it is a **d.**.
T-5....... II.8:11 The **d.** is very simple. It is made on the
T-5......... II.9:2 It was only my **d.** that gave me all power
T-5......... II.9:3 gift to you is to help you make the same **d.**
T-5......... II.9:4 This **d.** is the choice to share it, because
T-5......... II.9:4 because the **d.** itself *is* the decision to share
T-5......... II.9:4 because the decision itself *is* the **d.** to share
T-5......... II.9:6 I am your model for **d.**. By deciding for
T-5......... II.9:7 I showed you that this **d.** can be made,
T-5....... II.11:1 by sharing my **d.** and making it stronger.
T-5...... IV.3:12 The **d.** to share them *is* their purification.
T-5........ IV.4:2 Listening to one Voice implies the **d.** to
T-5......... V.6:3 and each moment of **d.** is a judgment that
T-5......... V.6:4 automatically until the **d.** is changed.
T-5......... V.6:6 Holy Spirit, like the ego, is a **d.**. Together
T-5......... V.8:1 The continuing **d.** to remain separated is
T-5......... V.8:2 emphasize the destructive results of the **d.**
T-5......... V.8:3 **d.** of the mind will affect both behavior
T-5........ VI.4:1 and the Holy Spirit reverses its **d.**, much
T-5.........VII.h The **D.** for God
T-5.......VII.5:3 The **d.** to react in this way is yours, and
T-5.......VII.6:1 **D.** cannot be difficult. This is obvious, if
T-5.......VII.6:8 *I made the* **d.** *myself, but I can also decide*
T-5.....VII.6:10 *consequences of my wrong* **d.** *if I will let Him*
T-6...........I.2:5 you can always call on me to share my **d.**,
T-6...........I.5:1 be demonstrated only through joint **d.**.
T-6...........I.8:1 do not share my **d.** to hear only one Voice
T-6......V.B.6:3 by God, and your **d.** cannot change it. As
T-6......V.B.6:4 a **d.** that was irrevocably made for you.
T-6......V.B.8:6 this step is essential for the ultimate **d.**, it
T-7......... V.1:2 for. *That* is a **d.**. The effects of the ego's
T-7......... V.1:3 effects of the ego's **d.** in this matter are so
T-7......... V.1:3 but the Holy Spirit's **d.** to use the body
T-7......VI.4:11 only **d.** the ego could possibly encounter,
T-7......... X.5:4 **d.** mean except that you want to be fearful
T-7....... X.5:14 If the result of this **d.** is confusion, this is
T-7......... X.6:9 has been given you by God's **d.**. That is
T-8........ III.1:4 because your **d.** to learn it is the decision
T-8........ III.1:4 the **d.** to listen to the Teacher Who knows
T-8...... III.5:10 or released according to your **d.**, and so
T-8........ III.7:6 not will anyone to suffer for a wrong **d.**,
T-8........ IV.3:9 and your **d.** to hear me is the decision to
T-8........ IV.3:9 decision to hear me is the **d.** to hear His
T-8...... IV.4:11 my **d.** for you makes healing impossible.
T-8........ IV.5:6 The **d.** to unite must be unequivocal, or
T-8........ IV.5:7 because mind is the mechanism of **d.**. It is
T-8........ IV.5:9 My **d.** cannot overcome yours, because
T-8...... IV.5:11 things are possible through our joint **d.**,
T-8...... IV.5:14 but I cannot oppose your **d.** without
T-8........ IV.6:1 Nothing God created can oppose your **d.**,
T-8...... VI.5:12 made only the **d.** to be unworthy of both.
T-8..... VIII.9:7 Do not let it reflect your **d.** to attack.
T-8........ IX.5:1 and the substitution of the **d.** to wake.
T-8........ IX.5:2 The **d.** to wake is the reflection of the will
T-9......... I.12:3 But consider the result of this strange **d.**.
T-9......... II.5:4 **d.** about him determines the message you
T-9...... IV.10:3 Only if the **d.** that reality is fearful is
T-9........ VI.2:6 The **d.** to receive is the decision to accept.
T-9........ VI.2:6 The decision to receive is the **d.** to accept.
T-9..... VIII.3:4 its only **d.** is whether to attack now or to
T-10.... in.3:10 me?" Then accept His **d.**, for it is indeed
T-10.........I.2:2 Is it your **d.** to do so? You recognize from
T-10.......... II.h The **D.** to Forget
T-10....... II.1:2 is nothing more than a **d.** to forget. What
T-10....... II.2:2 In this **d.** lie joy and peace and the glory
T-10....... II.5:3 from your own **d.** not to be what you are,
T-10....... II.6:1 you could not make such an insane **d.**.
T-10....... II.6:4 the logical outcome of your **d.** is perfectly
T-11.......in.1:7 **d.** is always an answer to the question,
T-11....... II.1:1 the **d.** to heal and to be healed is the first
T-12.... III.9:10 since the mind is the mechanism of **d.**.
T-12........ V.9:6 nothing can oppose the **d.** of God's Son.
T-12...... VI.2:8 otherwise. As it was my **d.**, so is it yours.
T-12..... VII.8:4 they attest only to your **d.** about reality,
T-12..... VII.9:1 The power of **d.** is your one remaining
T-12..... VII.9:6 this **d.** that determined what you found,
T-12..... VII.9:6 for it was the **d.** for what you sought.
T-12... VII.11:9 all that you see but witnesses to your **d.**.
T-13..... IV.6:4 And this **d.** is one of future pain. Unless
T-14.........I.2:2 realize that to deny is the **d.** not to know.
T-14......... III.h The **D.** for Guiltlessness
T-14...... III.4:3 The power of **d.** is all that is yours. What
T-14...... III.9:1 destructively, and the **d.** will be wrong. It
T-14...... III.9:2 because of the concept of **d.** that led to it.
T-14...... III.9:5 Every **d.** is made for the whole Sonship,
T-14.... III.12:1 Would you deny the truth of God's **d.**,
T-14.... III.13:3 Every **d.** you undertake alone but signifies
T-14.... III.13:7 **d.** to undo everything that would obscure
T-14.... III.14:7 not and He will make every **d.** for you, for
T-14.... III.16:3 every **d.** the Holy Spirit makes for you?
T-14.... III.17:5 who will be touched in any way by the **d.**.
T-14...... VI.5:6 The power of **d.**, which you made in place
T-14...... IX.1:7 lay in the **d.** to be not as you are. Thus
T-15...... III.3:3 Every **d.** you make stems from what you
T-15...... III.5:2 the Holy Spirit every time you make a **d.**.
T-15...... III.5:3 For every **d.** you make does answer this,
T-15...... III.5:7 Every **d.** you make is for Heaven or for
T-15...... IV.3:3 me, by your **d.** to join in any plan but His.
T-15....... X.5:5 the **d.** you believe that you must make.
T-15....... X.9:4 recognizing the one **d.** you must make.
T-15....... X.9:5 And yet it is the recognition of the **d.**, *just*
T-15....... X.9:5 *just as it is,* that makes the **d.** so easy.
T-16...... IV.5:9 as the other, the **d.** must be one of despair
T-16..... V.14:4 in perceiving the **d.** as just what it is, and
T-16..... V.15:3 is only the **d.** *not* to know yourself. This
T-16..... V.16:1 **d.** whether or not to listen to this course
T-16..... V.17:1 the easiest **d.** that ever confronted you,
T-16..... V.17:3 to make the natural **d.** as this is realized.
T-18...... IV.8:1 Forget not that it has been your **d.** to
T19. IV.D.17:9 in this holy place, and make the same **d.**.
T19. IV.D.20:7 in hell or Heaven to interfere with his **d.**.
T-21....... II.3:3 His power of **d.** is the determiner of every
T-21....... II.3:6 and you gave the power of **d.** to Him Who
T-21....... III.8:5 that follow this **d.** are also born of faith.
T-21..... VII.7:5 this **d.** but the choice whether to see him
T-21..... VII.7:6 **d.** leads to its effects is not your problem.
T-21..... VII.9:1 This is your one **d.**; this the condition for
T-21... VII.12:3 had? Until the last **d.** has been made, the
T-22....... II.6:8 is no point in trying to avoid this one **d.**.
T-22..... II.10:1 on it with the **d.** that it must be healed,
T-22...... IV.1:7 reaches this far can make the wrong **d.**,
T-22...... VI.2:5 He knows this mad **d.** was made by one as
T-24.......in.2:4 has the power to dictate each **d.** you make
T-24.......in.2:5 a **d.** is a conclusion based on everything
T-24.........I.2:2 unrecognized belief is a **d.** to war in secret
T-24.........I.2:6 least **d.** to choose attack instead of love,
T-24.........I.6:8 And what **d.** can be made for this that will
T-24...... VI.7:2 to have no end, until the truth be your **d.**.
T-25.........I.3:2 you think your safety lies, at your **d.**. It
T-25... VII.3:11 For only this **d.** can you make. The rest is
T-26...... III.4:4 This is not your **d.**. It is but a simple
T-28...... III.2:2 And thus it is their joint **d.** to be sick. If
T-30............I.h Rules for **D.**
T-30.........I.7:6 Yet this **d.** still can be undone, by simple
T-30.......I.14:2 This seems to be a real **d.** in itself. And yet
T-30.......I.17:3 the basic law that makes **d.** powerful, and
T-30.......I.17:5 two are joined before there can be a **d.**.
T-30.......I.17:7 from the world by your **d.** for a happy day
T-30....... II.5:2 the earth but must depend on your **d.**,
T-31.......I.11:1 the wrong **d.** on what you would learn,
T-31....... II.2:3 first is a **d.** that you make. But afterwards,
T-31...... IV.5:3 there is none, what power of **d.** can he use
T-31...... IV.5:5 And what **d.** has power if it be applied in
T-31...... IV.8:3 than that the power of **d.** cannot lie in
T-31..... V.13:5 somehow entered in the choice by your **d.**
W-pI..... 20.3:1 Your **d.** to see is all that vision requires.
W-pI..... 53.4:6 Let me remember the power of my **d.**,
W-pI..... 64.5:5 such a simple **d.** really be difficult to make
W-pI..... 64.5:6 Let not the form of the **d.** deceive you.
W-pI..... 64.5:8 impossible that any **d.** on earth can have a
W-pI..... 78.1:1 yet quite clear to you that each **d.** that you
W-pI..... 88.1:3 Salvation is a **d.** made already. Attack and
W-pI... 129.9:3 Remember your **d.** hourly, and take a
W-pI... 130.5:4 of choice beyond which your **d.** cannot go
W-pI. 133.12:3 very simple fact that no **d.** can be difficult.
W-pI... 136.5:2 given willingness to reconsider the **d.**
W-pI... 136.5:3 the sign that this **d.** still remains in force,
W-pI... 136.6:4 but for your own **d.** of what should be real
W-pI... 136.7:1 Sickness is a **d.**. It is not a thing that
W-pI... 136.9:2 opposed by a **d.** stronger than His Will.
W-pI... 137.3:4 But healing is his own **d.** to be one again,
W-pI...... 138.h Heaven is the **d.** I must make.
W-pI... 138.3:2 **D.** lets one of conflicting goals become
W-pI... 138.3:3 Without **d.**, time is but a waste and effort
W-pI. 138.11:1 that we have made the one **d.** that is sane.
W-pI. 138.12:2 day to the **d.** with which we awoke. As
W-pI. 138.12:5 *Heaven is the* **d.** *I must make. I make it now,*
W-pI... 139.1:2 a **d.** to accept ourselves as God created us.
W-pI... 149.2:1 (138) Heaven is the **d.** I must make.
W-pI...... 152.h The power of **d.** is my own.
W-pI... 152.1:1 one can suffer loss unless it be his own **d.**.
W-pI... 152.8:2 The power of **d.** is our own. Decide but to
W-pI. 152.10:1 power of **d.** is our own. And we accept of
W-pI. 152.11:3 *The power of* **d.** *is my own. This day I will*
W-pI... 154.1:4 These are but attempts to hold **d.** off, and
W-pI... 171.2:1 (152) The power of **d.** is my own. God is
W-pII .... 238.h On my **d.** all salvation rests.
W-pII . 238.1:3 *in my hands, and let it rest on my* **d.**. *I must*
W-pII . 282.1:2 This the **d.** not to be insane, and to accept
M-2 ........... 5:8 the one **d.** that gave his teacher to him.
M-3 ........... 3:3 his mind about the world with a single **d.**,
M-5 .........I.1:4 For sickness is an election; a **d.**. It is the
M-5 ........II.1:5 faulty problem-solving approach, it is a **d.**
M-5 ........II.1:6 And if it is a **d.**, it is the mind and not the
M-5 ........II.1:7 depends on the body being the **d.** maker.
M-5 ........II.2:1 acceptance of sickness as a **d.** of the mind,
M-10 ......... 4:4 such an arbitrary basis for **d.** making?
M-12 ......... 5:7 The mind makes this **d.**, as it makes all
M-12 ......... 5:8 of God does not make this **d.** alone. To do
M-13 ......... 3:6 self-condemnation is a **d.** about identity,
M-13 ......... 8:1 remember what each **d.** you make must
M-21 ......... 3:5 The power of his **d.** offers it to him as he
M-22 ......... 4:1 sickness does not appear to be a **d.**. Nor
M-24 ......... 3:3 usefulness, as well as his own **d.** making.
P-2........ III.2:6 Progress becomes a matter of **d.**; it can
P-2........ IV.1:3 Judgment is a **d.**, made again and again,
P-2........ IV.1:4 a **d.** to perceive the universe as you would
P-2........ IV.1:5 It is a **d.** that truth can lie and must be lies
P-2........ IV.2:4 are only shadows of a **d.** already made.
P-2........ IV.2:5 Change the **d.**, and how can its shadow be
P-2........ IV.3:1 the **d.** that guilt is real has been made.

## decision-making 1

T-7......... X.7:1 of your false **d.** prerogative, which the ego

## decisions 59

T-4........ IV.3:3 of nothing except by your own **d.**, and
T-4........ VI.6:4 and accepts my Atonement **d.** because my
T-5........ VI.4:1 to reverse a lower court's **d.** in this world.
T-5........ VI.4:2 The ego's **d.** are always wrong, because
T-6...... V.B.7:1 You are not asked to make insane **d.**,
T-8........ III.7:8 His power and glory all your wrong **d.** are
T-8........ III.7:9 Wrong **d.** have no power, because they
T-9...........I.8:4 Either of these insane **d.** will induce panic
T-14...... III.9:1 Whenever you choose to make **d.** for
T-14...... III.9:3 make **d.** by yourself or for yourself alone.
T-14.... III.11:1 that you must make **d.** for yourself. You
T-14.... III.12:6 no **d.** about what it is or where it lies, but

T-14.... III.12:6 and leave all **d.** to His gentle counsel.
T-14.... III.16:2 His **d.** are reflections of what God knows
T-14...... IV.5:1 Before you make any **d.** for yourself,
T-14...... IV.5:1 whether you want to make **d.** here. Your
T-14...... IV.5:4 all **d.** to the One Who speaks for God, and
T-14...... IV.6:1 God, all **d.** become as easy and as right as
T-15...... III.6:4 littleness, are **d.** you make about yourself.
T-16...... III.2:4 because its **d.** are immediately accepted
T-21.......in.2:5 is no choice that lies between these two **d.**
T-21... VII.10:4 The others are **d.** that can be made, and
T-21... VII.11:5 add sincerity to the **d.** you have already
T-24.....in.2:10 **d.** come from your beliefs as certainly as
T-24.........I.2:3 meaningless **d.** have been made and kept
T-24.........I.2:3 given power to direct all subsequent **d.**.
T-24.........I.5:1 is the great dictator of the wrong **d.**. Here
T-26.... III.1:10 is? The truth makes no **d.**, for there is
T-30.........I.1:1 **D.** are continuous. You do not always
T-30.........I.2:2 this: *Today I will make no* **d.** *by myself.* This
T-30.........I.4:2 *If I make no* **d.** *by myself, this is the day that*
T-30.......I.13:5 very first of the **d.** which are offered here.
T-30.......I.14:1 determination not to make **d.** by yourself.
T-30.......I.14:3 And yet, you *cannot* make **d.** by yourself.
T-30.......I.14:7 make **d.** by yourself whatever you decide.
T-30.......I.16:5 **D.** cause results *because* they are not made
W-pI..... 64.5:3 advance for all the **d.** you will make today
W-pI..... 70.6:3 then adhering to your own **d.** as closely as
WpI. rIII.in6:2 being helped in its **d.** by the One Who
W-pI.133.14:2 you see some difficult **d.** facing you, be
W-pI... 138.4:3 the doubts that myriad **d.** would induce.
W-pI... 138.5:6 **D.** are the outcome of your learning, for
W-pI... 138.6:2 of all the rest, the one which settles all **d.**.
W-pI... 138.6:4 it, for all **d.** but conceal this one by taking
W-pI... 138.8:3 And these **d.** are made unaware, to keep
W-pII ..... 6.2:3 Answer lies; where all **d.** are already made
M-4 .... VIII.1:8 God is willing to reconsider all his past **d.**,
M-5 ....... II.1:4 First, it is obvious that **d.** are of the mind,
M-9 ........... 2:2 He does not make his own **d.**; he asks his
M-12 ......... 5:7 as it makes all **d.** that are responsible for
M-29 ....... 2:11 want to be responsible for **d.** about which
M-29 ......... 3:1 –in referring **d.** to the Holy Spirit with
M-29 ....... 4:11 it. His **d.** bring benefit to all, being wholly
P-1............ 4:1 awareness the ability to make his own **d.**.
P-1............ 4:4 see himself as really capable of making **d.**.
P-2....... VI.3:4 may be. They answer the **d.** of the mind,
P-2....... VII.4:6 use their judgment in making their **d.**.
P-3........ III.2:5 not be the therapist who makes these **d.**.
S-1...........I.2:4 There are **d.** to make here, and they must

## declaration 9

T-4........ III.2:2 It is a **d.** of independence. You will find it
T-4........ III.9:1 denied by the ego, is the **d.** of your release
W-pI..... 31.1:1 is the introduction to your **d.** of release.
W-pI..... 31.4:2 that you are making a **d.** of independence
W-pI..... 31.5:2 It is a **d.** that you will not yield to it, and
W-pI..... 50.4:7 It is a **d.** of release from the belief in idols.
W-pI..... 71.2:4 Each grievance you hold is a **d.**, and an
W-pI... 73.11:1 again make a **d.** of what you really want.
W-pI... 191.1:1 **d.** of release from bondage of the world.

## declare 2

W-pI.110.11:5 *me.* Let us **d.** this truth as often as we can.
W-pI... 199.4:2 **D.** your innocence and you are free. The

## declared 2

W-pI.138.12:3 hour passed, we have **d.** our choice again,
P-3......... II.4:2 No, He **d.** it perfect, and so it was. And

## declares 1

T-30...... IV.6:5 the Son of God **d.** that he is free of idols.

## decline 1

T-13.......in.2:7 its powers to **d.** if their bodies are hurt.

## decrease 2

T-16 ..... VI.5:3 one, they are trying to **d.** their magnitude.
W-in .......... 9:3 of this will matter, or **d.** their efficacy. But

## decreases 3

T-15 .... VII.9:4 For each believes that this **d.** guilt in him.
T-17 ..... III.3:5 whom they seem to be **d.** in importance.
T-22 ..... VI.1:7 end is reached the value of the means **d.**,

## decreasingly 1

T-31 .... VII.3:3 the body grows **d.** persistent in your sight

## decree 1

M-13 ......... 5:8 do not find" remains this world's stern **d.**,

## decreed 2

W-pI..... 93.8:4 in place of what you have **d.** for yourself.
M-27 ......... 2:2 For who has **d.** that all things pass away,

## dedicate 5

T-19 ...... I.5:10 To **d.** yourself to both is to set up a goal
W-pI... 75.11:1 We **d.** this day to the serenity in which
W-pI..... 98.1:5 We **d.** ourselves to truth today, and to
W-pI. 139.11:1 **d.** our minds to our assignment for today.
Wfl........ in.3:1 And to this purpose let us **d.** our minds,

## dedicated 18

T-14 ..... IX.1:8 past, and the present was **d.** to illusion.
T-15 .... VII.4:6 of anger and **d.** to but one insane belief;
T-15 .... VII.9:3 yet **d.** to the continuance of loneliness,
T-17 .... VII.6:2 his part in any situation **d.** in advance to
T-19 ........ I.1:1 a situation has been **d.** wholly to truth,
T-19 ........ I.1:3 is **d.** to truth as its only goal is brought to
T-19 ........ I.5:6 Faithlessness is wholly **d.** to illusions;
T19..IV.B.16:2 that the ego has **d.** the body to the goal of
T19..IV.B.17:1 that they have **d.** themselves to death.
T19....IV.C.3:2 **d.** to madness and set against the peace of
T19....IV.C.4:2 A body which they **d.** to death, a symbol
T19....IV.C.6:1 You who are **d.** to the incorruptible have
T-20 ..... VI.6:5 the temple **d.** to no relationships and no
T-21 ...... V.9:1 The part of mind where reason lies was **d.**
T-22 ..... VI.2:2 and so the mind is **d.** to serve illusions.
W-pI..... 45.8:4 approach it as you would an altar **d.** in
WpI..rII.in.5:3 You are **d.** to salvation. Be determined
M-23 ......... 6:6 and **d.** teacher of God forgets his brothers

## dedication 23

T-17 .... VII.6:2 in advance to truth, your **d.** is divided.
T-19 ........ I.1:2 wholeness of the **d.** can be safely assumed
T-19 ........ I.1:5 faith is limited and your **d.** incomplete.
T-19 ........ I.5:7 truth. Partial **d.** is impossible. Truth is the
T-19 ........ I.6:7 must be, are recognized as **d.** to illusion;
T-19 ...... I.16:1 Let, then, your **d.** be to the eternal, and
T19....IV.A.7:3 and unchangeable **d.** to sin and its results.
T19....IV.C.1:1 and be released from the **d.** to death. For
T19....IV.C.2:4 But what of those whose **d.** is not to live;
T19..IV.C.2:12 Your **d.** is not to death, nor to its master.
T19....IV.C.4:5 are part of your unrecognized **d.** to death.
T19....IV.C.5:1 You have another **d.** that would keep the
T19... IV.D.3:2 The **d.** to death and to its sovereignty is
T-24 ... VI.12:5 **d.** to the truth as God established it no
T-28 ........ I.3:7 their use. They have no **d.** and no aim.
T-30 ........ I.1:6 if you find resistance strong and **d.** weak,
W-pI... 76.11:5 as a **d.** with which the practice period
W-pI... 76.12:1 repeat this **d.** as often as possible today;
W-pI..... 98.1:1 Today is a day of special **d.**. We take a
W-pI..... 98.7:3 each repetition of today's idea a total **d.**,
W-pI. 139.12:1 our **d.** to our cause today each hour, as we
Wi181-200 1:2 not asked for total **d.** all the time as yet.
M-26 ......... 3:3 be won after much devotion and **d.**, and

## dedications 1

WpI..rII.in.5:1 these practice periods as **d.** to the way,

## deduce 1

C-2 ........... 4:3 It is from this that we **d.** all that the ego is.

## deeds 2

T-3 .......... I.3:6 does not hold your "evil" **d.** against you.
T-27 ... VIII.7:7 its evil **d.** because you did not make it,

## deem 1

T-24 ... VI.12:3 nor do you **d.** this cost too heavy. But a

## deems 4

T-20 ..... III.2:4 whatever adjustments it **d.** necessary and
T-21 ..... IV.1:5 with sin the ego **d.** quite appropriate, and
W-pI .. 186.4:4 And if He **d.** us worthy, so we are. It is but
M-6 ........... 3:7 sure it is used as the giver **d.** appropriate?

## deep 68

*See also* deep-rooted

T-1 ......... V.6:3 they are not **d.** enough to sustain you.
T-2 .......... I.3:6 Bible says that a **d.** sleep fell upon Adam,
T-2 .......... I.4:5 Only after the **d.** sleep fell upon Adam
T-3 ....... VI.3:1 the tremendous release and **d.** peace that
T-12 ........ I.9:1 is a symptom of your own **d.** sense of loss.
T-13 ... XI.3:13 sense of peace so **d.** that no dream in this
T-13 ..... XI.8:2 with the **d.** peace in which the sweet and
T-15 ..... III.3:1 is a **d.** responsibility you owe yourself,
T-16 ....... V.8:5 is buried **d.** and rises in the form of "love.
T-18 ..... III.3:3 and cruel, and you have gone **d.** into it. A
T-18 ....... V.7:1 how **d.** is his indebtedness to the other
T-18 ... VIII.7:7 its happiness and **d.** content to every part.
T-18 ... VIII.9:3 becomes a garden, green and **d.** and quiet
T-19 ..... IV.1:1 As peace extends from **d.** inside yourself
T-19 ..... IV.1:6 He lay, **d.** within you and your brother,
T19 ... IV.B.7:2 Salvation flows from **d.** within the home
T19 .. IV.D.7:7 from beyond the veil is also **d.** within you,
T-23 ..... IV.8:8 and a sense of love so **d.** and quiet that no
T-24 ... VII.2:7 thought by day and night, the **d.** concern,
T-25 ....... II.5:1 a wall and stands before it, **d.** in reverence
T-25 ... VIII.6:6 **d.** suspicion and the chill of fear comes
T-26 ....... X.3:5 yourself, in **d.** injustice to the Son of God.
T-27 .. VII.16:4 of **d.** appreciation for his gifts to you.
T-29 ....... V.2:3 so **d.** within that nothing in this world
T-29 .. VII.10:5 in chants of **d.** despair to idols of yourself.
T-29 ..... IX.8:5 abides forever **d.** within the Son of God.
T-29 ..... IX.9:1 *are* fearful if you do not feel a **d.** content, a
T-29 ..... IX.9:2 so **d.** and bitter that the dream cannot
T-31 ..... V.14:6 the **d.** confusion that it feels about how it
T-31 ... VII.6:2 a bitter sense of **d.** depression and futility.
W-pI .... 41.1:3 anxiety, worry, a **d.** sense of helplessness,
W-pI .... 41.3:1 **D.** within you is everything that is perfect
W-pI .... 41.5:2 you, when the truth is hidden **d.** within,
W-pI .... 47.7:2 reached it if you feel a sense of **d.** peace,
W-pI .... 49.4:1 Listen in **d.** silence. Be very still and open
W-pI .... 49.4:4 Sink **d.** into the peace that waits for you
W-pI .... 50.5:1 for today sink **d.** into your consciousness.
W-pI .... 57.5:3 this peace comes from **d.** within myself.
W-pI .... 71.5:4 and a **d.** sense of failure and despair.
W-pI .... 74.5:4 will feel a **d.** sense of joy and an increased
W-pI .... 80.6:2 Repeat the idea with **d.** conviction, as
W-pI .... 98.7:2 **d.** conviction and the certainty you lack.
W-pI .. 100.8:5 Look **d.** within you, undismayed by all the
W-pI .. 102.4:3 seek this function **d.** within your mind,
W-pI .. 107.9:6 and give you peace so **d.** and tranquil that
W-pI .. 110.9:4 **D.** in your mind the holy Christ in you is
W-pI .. 122.1:6 a gentleness that never can be hurt, a **d.**,
W-pI .. 122.8:3 heart with **d.** tranquility as ancient truths,
W-pI .. 123.8:1 how **d.** and limitless His care for you, how
W-pI 124.11:2 a joy too **d.** for you to comprehend, a
W-pI .. 125.1:3 He calls to you from **d.** within your mind
W-pI 133.10:2 a sign of **d.** unworthiness within himself.
W-pI .. 134.6:1 sane, a **d.** relief to those who offer it; a

W-pI.134.16:3 chest, a **d.** and certain feeling of relief.
W-pI...135.4:4 **d.** concern are needful to protect its little
W-pI.140.12:4 peace so **d.** that no illusion can disturb
W-pI...166.9:6 your plan to keep His Son in **d.** oblivion,
W-pI.185.10:3 you make this request with **d.** sincerity.
WpI rVI.in.3:8 except a **d.** relinquishment of everything
W-pII.. in.11:2 of wordless, **d.** experience which should
W-pII..221.1:3 *quiet of my heart, the* **d.** *recesses of my mind*
W-pII..257.1:3 without **d.** distress and great depression.
W-pII..305.1:1 but Christ's vision finds a peace so **d.** and
W-pII..341.1:2 *smile in love and tenderness so dear and* **d.**
M-6............1:7 a sense of loss so **d.** that the patient might
M-28..........4:1 are tranquil with a stir of **d.** anticipation,
S-1 ........ III.4:2 time be followed by a **d.** retreat into fear.
S-1 ......... V.4:3 The lawns are **d.** and still, for here the

## deep-rooted 1

S-1 ......... II.3:3 tends to be blurred by a **d.** sense of sin. It

## deepened 1

T-1......... V.6:4 The illusion that shallow roots can be **d.**,

## deeper 13

T-13...... III.2:8 For still **d.** than the ego's foundation, and
T-13...... III.4:4 and the **d.** you go into the blackness of
T-13....... X.1:4 provided they are not the **d.** source to
T-18...... III.1:2 sleeping, and on and on to a yet **d.** sleep.
T-18...... III.1:3 the darkness but made the darkness **d.**.
T-23..... II.21:4 leading still **d.** into terror and away from
T-31...... I.11:5 to the **d.** call beyond it that appeals for
T-31....... V.6:5 but this is kept still **d.** in the mists below
W-pI.....78.3:4 Each grievance made the darkness **d.**, and
W-pI...153.4:3 threat the world encourages is so much **d.**
W-pI...155.4:4 have suffered from a sense of loss still **d.**,
M-4............1:3 acquired the **d.** characteristics that will
P-2...........I.2:7 They are but **d.** shadows, or perhaps

## deepest 9

T-13....... II.1:3 this issue, then, the **d.** split of all occurs,
T-13....... II.4:4 darkest and **d.** cornerstone in the ego's
T-14...... XI.2:2 that only the insane, in **d.** sleep, could
T-18....... V.1:6 of your **d.** retreats you have evaluated as
T-24..... VII.1:6 of threat, or anything but **d.** reverence.
T-25... VII.10:4 emerge from **d.** mourning into perfect joy
W-pI.193.10:6 the time be less than meets your **d.** need.
W-pII..254.1:2 *In* **d.** *silence I would come to You, to hear*
W-pII....12.3:4 undisturbed, in **d.** silence and tranquility

## deeply 8

T-3........ VI.5:7 so debilitating would be so **d.** cherished.
T-4........ IV.2:9 a loving brother I am **d.** concerned with
T-17....... IV.7:5 with jewels, and **d.** carved and polished.
T-19....... IV.2:2 peace that already lies **d.** within must first
T-25..... VII.3:7 If one belief so **d.** valued here were true,
W-pI.....41.6:6 Try to enter very **d.** into your own mind,
W-pI...135.7:4 Such attempts, ridiculous yet **d.** cherished
W-pI...182.5:3 Father. He desires to go home so **d.**, so

## defeat 29

*See also* self-defeat

T-7........ IV.3:1 that would **d.** its purpose. Therefore it
T-7..... VIII.2:5 mind only to **d.** the mind's real purpose.
T-8........ III.6:2 ego, whose purpose is to **d.** its own goal.
T-8......... V.5:6 so. Sensing **d.** and angered by it, the ego
T-12....... II.6:1 can **d.** a child of God in his purpose. For
T-12...... IV.3:1 wants to find what would utterly **d.** him.
T-12....... V.7:5 and the aim of your teaching is to **d.** itself,
T-19....... II.2:5 the Will of God open to opposition and **d.**
T19... IV.C.8:7 insanity could look upon the **d.** of God,
T-23.........I.2:6 The ego always marches to **d.**, because it
T-23.........I.9:2 that was less real, made an illusion by **d.**.
T-23....... II.5:6 becomes weak, the other strong by his **d.**.
T-24.... in.1:12 has the power to **d.** what is Their Will?
T-24.........I.5:7 so that your specialness can live on his **d.**.
T-24.........I.5:8 and its victory is his **d.** and shame. How
T-24.........I.8:9 now **d.** the goal of holiness that Heaven
T-24....... II.2:8 Here is a goal that would **d.** salvation, and
T-31...... IV.6:2 this step is to **d.** your purpose here. You
W-pI..... 86.3:5 awareness. I would no longer **d.** my own
WpI. rIII.in2:4 are not our aim, and would **d.** our goal.
W-pI.136.11:6 are plans to **d.** what cannot be attacked.
W-pI.153.14:4 of terrifying destiny, **d.** of all his hopes,
W-pI...155.7:2 paths that lead nowhere, choices for **d.**,
W-pI...163.5:1 Unholy in **d.**, he has become what death
W-pI...166.6:2 felt **d.** and hopelessness as he is feeling
W-pI...200.2:3 to live. You cannot but be asking for **d.**.
W-pII..308.1:1 of time in such a way that I **d.** my aim. If I
M-5 .........I.2:2 It symbolizes the **d.** of God's Son and the
S-3 ........ IV.7:5 and bitter striving and **d.** there is a Voice

## defeated 4

T-11..... V.11:1 accomplished God's purpose could be **d.**,
T-12...... IV.2:1 undertakes is therefore bound to be **d.**.
T-12...... IV.4:5 and under His guidance you cannot be **d.**.
W-pI...163.4:4 is the Will of Father and of Son **d.** finally,

## defeating

*See* self-defeating

## defeats 1

T-23..... II.17:9 It is a judgment that **d.** itself, condemning

## defend 41

T-2......... II.3:1 You can **d.** truth as well as error. The
T-2........ III.1:2 entirely to **d.** *against* the Atonement, and
T-3......... II.5:8 the innocent **d.** true perception instead of
T-8.... VIII.4:4 who want the ego are predisposed to **d.** it.
T-11... VIII.4:3 and do not **d.** yourself against truth. You
T-14.........I.3:5 truth, that he has chosen to **d.** and love.
T-14..... VII.5:3 needs no protection does not **d.** itself.
T-14....... X.9:6 ego can no longer **d.** its lack of content.
T-17...... IV.7:1 that all defenses *do* what they would **d.**.
T-17...... IV.7:2 is that they offer what they **d.**. What they
T-17...... IV.7:3 they **d.** is placed in them for safe-keeping,
T-17.... IV.10:5 to **d.** you from your own attack. For you
T-18.... VIII.3:2 **d.** this little speck of dust it bids you fight
T-18.... VIII.7:5 on nothing yet who would still die to **d.** it
T-21...... VI.4:5 would **d.** the body against your reason,
T-22....... V.3:6 your Father Whom you would **d.** against.
T-23...... III.4:8 and never out of sight, if you **d.** it not.
T-24.........I.9:1 special must **d.** illusions against the truth.
T-24.........I.9:3 while it is this you would **d.** against him.
T-24....... II.4:2 and would **d.** your specialness against the
T-24....... II.5:1 You can **d.** your specialness, but never
T-24...... IV.5:1 Do not **d.** this senseless dream, in which
T-24..... VII.1:1 **d.** the specialness he wants to be the truth
T-25...... IX.4:5 take, and how much can the loser still **d.**.
W-pI.....51.5:6 this to **d.** a thought system that has hurt
W-pI.....95.9:4 you would **d.** illusions against the truth.
W-pI......135.h If I **d.** myself I am attacked.
W-pI...135.1:1 Who would **d.** himself unless he thought
W-pI...135.3:5 and your locks more tight, what you **d.**,
W-pI...135.4:1 Let us consider first what you **d.**. It must
W-pI...135.5:4 at all. **D.** its life, or give it gifts to make it
W-pI...135.9:1 **D.** the body and you have attacked your
W-pI.135.22:4 as we say: *If I* **d.** *myself I am attacked. But in*
W-pI.135.26:8 *I will not* **d.** *myself, because the Son of God*
W-pI...148.1:1 (135) If I **d.** myself I am attacked.
W-pI...151.5:1 This thing it speaks of, and would yet **d.**,
W-pI...153.7:4 What but illusions could **d.** you now,
W-pI...166.7:2 the self you savagely **d.** against all reason,
W-pI...170.2:1 is the idea that to **d.** from fear is to attack!
W-pI...170.2:6 *You make what you* **d.** *against, and by your*
P-2........ IV.9:1 madman will **d.** his own illusions because

## defended 12

T-19....... II.7:1 heavily **d.** than the idea that sin is real;
T-22........II.4:4 One illusion cherished and **d.** against the
T-22....... V.2:7 offers must be **d.** against and sacrificed.
T-22....... V.5:7 illusion of immovability be long **d.** from
T-23...... III.5:1 Those who believe that peace can be **d.**,
T-24.........I.3:1 belief, to be **d.** though unrecognized, is
T-24.........I.5:4 Specialness must be **d.**. Illusions can
T-24...... III.2:2 strongly **d.** with all your puny might
W-pI..... 95.6:3 who remain heavily **d.** against learning.
W-pI.135.24:2 thought that you must be **d.** from release.
W-pI.136.16:2 and keep **d.** from the light of truth. There
P-3........ II.10:1 that any form of specialness must be **d.**,

## defender 2

T-24......II.12:6 great **d.** of all illusions from the "threat"
T-24...... III.2:4 and make you separate from Him as its **d.**

## defending 2

T-1........ III.5:8 is always because you are **d.** misplaced or
T-3..........II.5:8 true perception instead of **d.** themselves

## defends 3

T-2..........II.3:4 Everyone **d.** his treasure, and will do so
T-22....... V.6:8 and **d.** the illusion of its immovability.
P-1............. 3:4 he cherishes it, **d.** it, and is sometimes

## defense 99

*See also* attack-defense, self-defense

T-2............ II.h The Atonement as **D.**
T-2..........II.2:5 Denial of error is a strong **d.** of truth, but
T-2..........II.4:1 The Atonement is the only **d.** that cannot
T-2..........II.4:6 Then a **d.** so splendid was needed that it
T-2..........II.4:8 Atonement thus becomes the only **d.** that
T-2..........II.7:3 to believe a **d.** that cannot attack is the
T-2..........II.7:3 a defense that cannot attack is the best **d.**.
T-2..........II.7:6 A two-way **d.** is inherently weak precisely
T-2..........II.7:8 miracle turns the **d.** of Atonement to your
T-2........ III.2:4 within you the one effective **d.** against all
T-2........ III.4:4 Perfectly aware of the right **d.** it passes
T-2......... V.7:3 looking beyond it to the **d.** of Atonement.
T-3...........I.2:1 The best **d.**, as always, is not to attack
T-3...........I.2:6 it up in view of its prominent value as a **d.**
T-3...... VI.5:10 as a weapon of **d.** for your own authority.
T-4........ IV.8:7 Judgment, like any other **d.**, can be used
T-5....... VII.3:4 the ego's last-ditch **d.** of its own existence.
T-6..........II.1:5 it occurs projection becomes its main **d.**,
T-6........ IV.4:3 It believes that the best **d.** is attack, and
T-7....... VII.1:9 Yet denial is a **d.**, and so it is as capable of
T-9.... VIII.11:2 establish your value and it needs no **d.**.
T-11...... IV.5:5 and as much an ego **d.** as blaming others.
T-12.......I.10:1 than to recognize, in every **d.** against it,
T-14..... VII.5:4 **D.** is of your making. God knows it not.
T-17...... IV.4:3 The whole **d.** system the ego evolved to
T-17...... IV.5:8 special relationship, which is its chief **d.**,
T-17...... IV.7:4 Every **d.** operates by giving gifts, and the
T-17...... IV.7:4 of the thought system the **d.** protects, set
T-17.... IV.10:1 instant is so important in the **d.** of truth.
T-17.... IV.10:2 The truth itself needs no **d.**, but you do
T-17.... IV.10:2 need **d.** against your acceptance of the gift
T-17.... IV.10:4 And your **d.** must now be undertaken, to
T-18.........I.1:6 the strongest **d.** the ego has for separation
T-19........II.5:3 protected with every **d.** at its disposal. For
T-19........II.5:4 For here lies its "best" **d.**, which all the
T-21..... VII.1:7 Treachery to the Son of God is the **d.** of
T-22....... V.1:7 What merely is needs no **d.**, and offers
T-22....... V.1:8 none. Only illusions need **d.** because of
T-22..... V.1:11 And you need no **d.**. Everything that
T-22..... V.1:12 Everything that needs **d.** you do not want,
T-22..... V.1:12 anything that needs **d.** will weaken you.
T-22....... V.2:6 fear? Belief in sin needs great **d.**, and at
T-24........II.6:4 the sins he held in its **d.** against himself,
T-24...... IV.2:2 makes it frail and helpless in its own **d.**. It
T-26..... VII.7:6 picture an insane **d.** can be expected, but
T-26..... VII.8:2 is. And truth needs no **d.** to make it true.
T-27....... III.6:1 and vacant will not need **d.** of any kind.
T-30.... IV.5:12 God's Son needs no **d.** against his dreams

T-31... V.10:11 And what but is attacked could need d.?
W-pI.....22.1:3 His own attack is thus perceived as self d..
W-pI...107.5:2 gift of healing, for the truth needs no d.,
W-pI...135.1:1 and that his own d. could save himself?
W-pI...135.1:2 And herein lies the folly of d.; it gives
W-pI...135.2:2 to call on you to make appropriate d.. The
W-pI...135.3:1 D. is frightening. It stems from fear,
W-pI...135.3:2 fear, increasing fear as each d. is made.
W-pI...135.4:3 to protect itself and needing your d..
W-pI...135.5:3 It needs no complicated structures of d.,
W-pI...135.6:5 make d. of something that he recognized
W-pI...135.7:1 The body is in need of no d.. This cannot
W-pI...135.8:2 valueless and hardly worth the least d.,
W-pI.135.10:2 This is the body's only real d.. Yet is this
W-pI.135.10:3 Yet is this where you look for its d.? You
W-pI.135.14:4 planning is not often recognized as a d..
W-pI.135.19:1 the d. that promises a future undisturbed,
W-pI.135.25:5 in you, for now you come without d., to
W-pI.135.26:8 *Son of God needs no d. against the truth of*
W-pI......136.h Sickness is a d. against the truth.
W-pI...136.6:1 Every d. takes fragments of the whole,
W-pI.136.10:1 Such is your planning for your own d..
W-pI.136.13:4 time is but another meaningless d. you
W-pI.136.14:1 Truth has a power far beyond d., for no
W-pI.136.15:6 *Sickness is a d. against the truth. I will accept*
W-pI.136.20:4 *Sickness is a d. against the truth. But I am not*
W-pI...148.2:1 (136) Sickness is a d. against the truth.
W-pI...151.1:5 needs irrational d. because it is irrational.
W-pI...151.1:6 And its d. seems strong, convincing, and
W-pI...153.2:4 sets up a system of d. that cannot work.
W-pI...153.3:2 Attack, d.; defense, attack, become the
W-pI...153.3:2 Attack, defense; d., attack, become the
W-pI...153.5:5 needful only of d. by still more fantasies,
W-pI...153.9:1 no d. because we are created unassailable,
W-pI.153.10:6 What d. could possibly be needed by the
W-pI.153.14:4 pitiful d. against a vengeance he can not
W-pI...170.2:6 *own d. against it is it real and inescapable.*
W-pI...170.3:2 Yet your d. sets up an enemy within; an
W-pI...170.3:3 now needs your d. against the threat of
W-pI...170.5:4 ask you lay down all d. as merely foolish.
W-pI...190.9:1 and come without d. into the quiet place
M-4 ...... VI.1:2 no dreams that need d. against the truth.
M-4 ...... VI.1:5 And does what God created need d.? No
M-20 ......... 4:5 you must have taken it again as your d..
C-in ........... 2:3 recognizing that it is a d. against truth in
P-2........... I.2:3 what we mean, but here is the ego's last d.
P-2........ IV.6:1 and thus in need of constant d.. Yet if
P-2........ IV.6:2 really the self, d. would be impossible.
P-2...... IV.10:2 without attack, and therefore without d..
P-2........ VI.1:3 its loving protection and alert d., – all this
S-1......... V.2:3 idols, and d. no longer serves a purpose.

## defenseless 4

T-31....... V.4:1 the world deals harshly with d. innocence
T-31.... VIII.6:2 to perceive yourself d. and in hell. Yield
W-pI.182.10:2 Who comes d. and Who is protected by
P-3....... II.10:2 The d. therapist has the strength of God

## defenselessness 17

W-pI.135.21:3 realize that our d. is all that is required
W-pI.135.22:5 *But in d. I will be strong, and I will learn what*
W-pI......153.h In my d. my safety lies.
W-pI...153.6:1 D. is strength. It testifies to recognition
W-pI...153.6:4 Him. D. can never be attacked, because it
W-pI...153.9:3 in d. we stand secure, serenely certain of
W-pI.153.18:1 quiet ways, where you will walk in true d..
W-pI.153.19:1 Today our theme is our d.. We clothe
W-pI.153.20:6 D. is all you need to give Him in return.
W-pI...172.1:1 (153) In my d. my safety lies. God is but
W-pI...182.7:1 This Child is your d.; your strength. He
W-pI.182.10:2 defenseless and Who is protected by d..
W-pI.182.12:7 yours. Today He gives you His d., and you
M-4 ......... VI.h Defenselessness
M-4 .... IX.2:11 finds. D. attends it naturally, and joy is its
P-2...... IV.10:3 are not necessary, and that d. is strength.
P-2......... V.2:6 who need the lesson of d. above all else, to

## defenses 48

T-2 .........II.4:7 is the inherent characteristic of other d..
T-2 ....... III.1:2 d. have been used almost entirely to
T-3 ...... VII.4:9 and all your d. are used to attack ideas
T-12 .........I.9:8 it useless. D. that do not work at all are
T-14 .... VII.5:6 The Holy Spirit uses d. on behalf of truth
T-14 .... VII.5:8 D., like everything you made, must be
T-17 ..... IV.5:5 And all their d. are as insane as what they
T-17 ..... IV.7:1 that all d. *do* what they would defend. The
T-17 ..... IV.7:8 D. operate to make you think you can.
T-17 ..... IV.8:1 deceptive frame of all the d. the ego uses.
T-20 ..... III.1:3 calls upon d. to uphold it against reality.
T-22 ...... V.2:1 Consider what the ego wants d. for.
W-pI.135.14:1 that self-initiated plans are but d., with
W-pI.135.17:1 D. are the plans you undertake to make
W-pI.135.17:4 is the "threat" which your d. would attack
W-pI.135.18:3 But your d. did not let you see His loving
W-pI.135.19:2 Let no d. but your present trust direct the
W-pI.135.19:2 the truth that only your d. would conceal.
W-pI.135.20:1 Without d., you become a light which
W-pI.135.20:4 brothers lay aside their cumbersome d.,
W-pI.135.22:5 *be strong, and I will learn what my d. hide.*
W-pI.135.24:1 All your d. have been aimed at not
W-pI...136.2:2 Like all d., it is an insane device for self-
W-pI...136.2:4 The aim of all d. is to keep the truth from
W-pI...136.3:1 D. are not unintentional, nor are they
W-pI...136.4:1 sets up a series of d. to reduce the threat
W-pI...136.5:1 d. seem to be beyond your own control.
W-pI...136.5:5 D. must make facts unrecognizable. They
W-pI.136.10:2 to laws which your d. would impose on it.
W-pI.136.11:6 D. are plans to defeat what cannot be
W-pI.136.12:3 attempts to plan d. that would alter it.
WpI. rIV.in3:2 d. that protect your unforgiving thoughts
W-pI...153.4:1 D. are the costliest of all the prices which
W-pI.153.19:5 d. undermine our certainty of purpose.
Wi181-200 3:4 to go past all d. for a little while each day.
W-pI...181.5:3 These concerns are but d. against present
W-pI...182.9:2 how strong is he who comes without d.,
W-pI...197.1:5 deceptions which would cheat you of d.,
W-pII .333.1:4 it. For only then are its d. lifted, and the
M-4 ...... VI.1:6 until he fully understands that d. are but
M-4 ...... VI.1:7 and more powerful its d. seem to be. Yet
M-4 .... VI.1:11 danger that comes when d. are laid down.
M-16 ....... 6:11 Your d. will not work, but you are not in
M-17 ......... 6:3 How, then, can one believe in one's d.?
M-25 ......... 5:4 have not seen through the ego's d. here,
P-2........ IV.6:3 the d. sought for must be magical. They
P-2...... IV.10:3 to demonstrate that d. are not necessary,
S-1........ III.4:3 For fear's d. are fearful in themselves, and

## defensive 5

T-5 ...... VII.5:2 you become d. because you expect attack.
T-21 ..... IV.3:3 the ego's whole d. system too seriously for
T-22 .... V.3:11 Only uncertainty can be d.. And all
T-22 ...... V.6:1 feel the need arise to be d. about anything
P-3........II.10:2 d. therapist has lost sight of the Source of

## defensiveness 11

T-22 ......... V.h Weakness and D.
T-30 ..... IV.1:3 aware of it you would forget d. entirely,
W-pI.135.26:5 as foolish little things appear to raise d. in
W-pI.136.15:5 a healing prayer, to help us rise above d.,
W-pI.136.20:1 by not allowing your d. to hurt you longer
W-pI...153.2:1 The world gives rise but to d.. For threat
W-pI...153.2:3 Yet is d. a double threat. For it attests to
W-pI...153.5:4 sabotage the holy peace of God by your d.
W-pI...153.7:1 D. is weakness. It proclaims you have
Wi181-200 3:2 still. Experience of what exists beyond d.
W-pI...182.2:5 honesty, without d. and self-deception,

## defiance 2

T-13 .... III.4:2 you believe that magnitude lies in d., and
M-5 .........I.2:3 represents the ultimate d. in a direct form

## defied 1

W-pII . 329.1:1 *I thought I wandered from Your Will, d. it,*

## defiled 5

T-2 ....... III.4:3 d. and needs to be repaired and protected
T-2 .........V.8:4 cannot endure to see your own d. altar.
T-2 .........V.8:5 But since the altar has been d., your state
T-6 ....... III.1:6 Your Godlike mind can never be d.. The
T-12 ... III.10:4 You have d. the altar, but not the world.

## defilement 1

T-2 .........V.7:5 permitted to look upon the d. of the altar,

## define 13

T-8 ... VIII.1:10 The whole does d. the part, but the part
T-8 ... VIII.1:10 part, but the part does not d. the whole.
T-14 ... III.13:3 that you would d. what salvation *is,* and
T-15 .......V.2:1 that you learned to d. your own needs
T-16 ..... VI.1:7 to d. it otherwise and understand it.
T-21 ........I.5:1 Thus they d. their life and where they live
T-22 .......II.2:6 as different, and d. the difference as joy.
T-23 .......II.6:2 a principle that would d. what the Creator
T-25 .......V.5:8 you d. the function he will have for you,
W-pI .... 59.4:5 I have tried to d. what seeing is, and I
W-pI .... 66.6:2 to d. God as something He is not. Love
C-2 ........... 2:5 Who asks you to d. the ego and explain
C-2 ........... 3:4 Who can d. the undefinable? And yet

## defined 12

T-4 ...... VII.1:5 believes your existence is d. by separation
T-14 .... VII.3:8 d. themselves as they were not created.
T-16 ..... VI.1:6 except as its Creator d. it by His Will. It is
T-25 ..... IV.1:8 rejoicing is d. another way and sought for
T-25 ...VIII.3:7 justice be d. without insanity where love
T-29 ..... VI.5:4 nothing here but is d. as what you see it
W-pI .... 28.4:1 not question what you have already d..
W-pI .... 68.3:1 like Himself, and d. them as part of Him.
C-2 .......... 10:2 Neither need be d. except by this. Yet
P-2........... I.3:1 as d. here can be characteristic of a
P-2........ IV.6:1 Illness of any kind may be d. as the result
P-2........ VI.1:1 then, can be d. simply as forgiveness, for

## defines 4

T-25 ..... IV.1:5 for what will bring him joy as he d. it. It is
T-25 .... VII.6:6 each d. the changeless and eternal truth
W-pI .... 67.2:7 as He d. Himself is appropriate for use.
W-pI .. 105.5:2 complete Himself as He d. completion.

## defining 4

T-10 ..... IV.3:7 By d. the mind wrongly, you perceive it as
W-pI .... 28.3:2 You are not d. it in past terms. You are
W-pI .... 66.3:3 involved in d. happiness and determining
W-pI .... 79.8:1 which you do not insist on d. the problem

## definite 7

T-6 ..........I.2:8 a d. contribution to make to your own life
W-pI .... 27.3:4 It is recommended that you set a d. time
W-pI .... 28.1:2 be making a series of d. commitments.
W-pI .... 74.6:5 is d. gain in refusing to allow retreat into
W-pI .. 182.1:5 Nothing so d. that you could say with
M-24 ......... 3:1 to take any d. stand on reincarnation. A
M-24 ......... 3:3 not. If a d. stand were required of him, it

## definition 21

T-9 .........V.1:4 By d., he is trying to give what he has not
T-11 .......V.2:9 Clarity undoes confusion by d., and to
T-12 ... VIII.3:6 The d. of reality is God's, not yours. He
T-13 .......II.4:1 is directly attributable to its d. of guilt. To
T-13 ..... IV.2:2 Your d. of Heaven *is* hell and oblivion, and
T-13 ..... IV.7:4 function, which is temporary by d.. His

| | |
|---|---|
| T-18.........I.3:2 | Fear involves substitution by **d.**, for it is |
| W-pI.....66.6:6 | And it is this **d.** of Him you are believing |
| W-pI.....67.2:8 | trying today to undo your **d.** of God and |
| W-pI.....67.2:9 | that you are part of His **d.** of Himself. |
| W-pI...152.5:1 | with transitory states by **d.** false. And that |
| M-4......VII.2:3 | realizes it would be valueless to him by **d.**. |
| M-4.......IX.2:8 | of the Word of God and His **d.** of His Son. |
| M-8............2:3 | By **d.**, an illusion is an attempt to make |
| M-18..........4:7 | of God becomes a miracle worker by **d.**. |
| M-29..........1:4 | so that the difference is temporary by **d.**. |
| C-2.............2:5 | and seeks by **d.** to ensure that its illusive |
| C-2.............3:1 | is no **d.** for a lie that serves to make it true |
| C-2.............4:1 | cannot really make a **d.** for what the ego is |
| C-2...........10:3 | Yet could a **d.** be more sure, or more in |
| P-2...........VI.h | The **D.** of Healing |

## definitions 3

| | |
|---|---|
| T-8..... VIII.1:2 | The ego's **d.** of anything are childish, and |
| T-10......IV.6:5 | for you. His **d.** *are* His laws, for by them He |
| W-pI...135.2:4 | armaments, its legal **d.** and its codes, its |

## definitive 1

| | |
|---|---|
| W-pI...138.6:2 | most **d.** and prototype of all the rest, the |

## deformed 1

| | |
|---|---|
| P-2........IV.2:7 | real, what could its shadow be except **d.**? |

## deformity 2

| | |
|---|---|
| P-2........IV.2:6 | grotesque and ugly since it mimics **d.**. If a |
| P-2........IV.2:7 | a **d.** is seen as real, what could its shadow |

## defy 1

| | |
|---|---|
| W-pI...170.7:4 | We need not **d.** his power. He has none. |

## degree 10

| | |
|---|---|
| T-1........ I.49:2 | either the **d.** or the direction of the error. |
| T-2......... II.5:7 | and perfection is not a matter of **d.**. Only |
| T-2......... II.6:1 | seem to proceed from one **d.** to the next. |
| T-2.......VII.7:4 | is usually some **d.** of desire to accomplish, |
| T-3......... II.1:1 | to in this course are not matters of **d.**. |
| W-pI.....21.2:4 | **d.** of the emotion you experience does not |
| M-4.......I.A.4:6 | that any **d.** of reality should be accorded |
| M-4.......IX.1:9 | Yet each **d.**, however small, is worth |
| M-17..........4:8 | truth, and this can never be a matter of **d.** |
| P-2........IV.8:2 | that the **d.** of threat differs according to |

## degrees 15

| | |
|---|---|
| T-1........ I.49:1 | no distinction among **d.** of misperception |
| T-2....VII.5:12 | up. It only seems to be abolished by **d.**, |
| T-3........IV.1:5 | exist until the separation introduced **d.**, |
| T-3........IV.4:2 | and even this is subject to **d.**, clearly |
| T-6......V.B.8:5 | still implies that the desirable has **d.**. |
| T-8........IX.5:3 | cannot distinguish among **d.** of error, for |
| T-23....... II.3:2 | establishes **d.** of truth among illusions, |
| W-pI...127.1:4 | one. It has no separate parts and no **d.**; no |
| W-pI...140.9:4 | Here there are no **d.**, and no beliefs that |
| W-pI...167.1:2 | It does not have **d.**. It is the one condition |
| M-8............1:2 | sizes, on varying **d.** of darkness and light, |
| M-22..........1:2 | because there are no **d.** of Atonement. It |
| C-1.............4:5 | in this world. It has no opposite and no **d.** |
| P-2........IV.5:3 | some merit in a world where "**d.** of error" |
| P-2........IV.8:1 | is mental illness, and in it there are no **d.**. |

## deigns 1

| | |
|---|---|
| S-2......... II.2:1 | the forms in which a "better" person **d.** to |

## deities 1

| | |
|---|---|
| T-29... VIII.8:6 | of idols harbors hope his special **d.** will |

## delay 50

| | |
|---|---|
| T-1......... V.1:5 | can wait, **d.**, paralyze yourself, or reduce |
| T-2......... III.4:6 | makes it increasingly unable to tolerate **d.** |
| T-2.......VII.5:9 | Atonement can be accepted without **d.**. It |
| T-5......... III.5:1 | **D.** is of the ego, because time is its |
| T-5......... III.5:2 | time and **d.** are meaningless in eternity. I |
| T-5......... VI.1:3 | **D.** does not matter in eternity, but it is |
| T-5......... VI.9:6 | can **d.** the completion of the Kingdom, |
| T-9.......VII.1:7 | return, but because **d.** of joy is needless. |
| T-10....... II.2:6 | this world **d.** your remembering of Him, |
| T-11.........I.4:2 | You who made **d.** can leave time behind |
| T-12....... II.5:4 | Let us not **d.** this, for your dream of |
| T-12....... II.5:6 | straight at every image that rises to **d.** you |
| T-13...VII.12:8 | He wills no **d.** to wait upon your joyous |
| T-14......IV.6:4 | The Holy Spirit will not **d.** in answering |
| T-14...VII.5:11 | **d.** in your return to peace by wondering |
| T-15...... III.2:5 | will be doing is to **d.** your homecoming. |
| T-15......IV.1:2 | means only that you would rather **d.** the |
| T-15......IV.1:7 | **D.** it not. For beyond the past and future, |
| T-15...... IX.1:6 | will be no **d.** when you are ready for it. |
| T-15....... X.1:1 | to **d.** the perfect union of the Father and |
| T-16..... II.6:10 | You can **d.** this now, but only a little |
| T-16....IV.11:6 | and in every fantasy that rises to **d.** you, |
| T-16...... VI.8:6 | **D.** will hurt you now more than before, |
| T-16...... VI.8:6 | before, only because you realize it *is* **d.**, |
| T-17....... II.8:4 | your impatience at **d.** in meeting Him. Go |
| T-20.........I.3:3 | of crucifixion, and **d.** him there. Help him |
| T-22......IV.1:7 | the wrong decision, although he can **d.**. |
| T-24...... VI.8:3 | His mistakes can cause **d.**, which it is |
| T-26... VIII.9:6 | **D.** is senseless, and the "reasoning" that |
| T-27...... III.6:3 | Nor **d.** an instant in deciding that it is the |
| T-28.......I.11:4 | to cause the miracle **d.** in hastening to all |
| T-30.........I.7:1 | Try to observe this rule without **d.**, |
| T-30....... V.8:4 | would He **d.** in showing you the way that |
| T-31...... III.1:4 | for it is here **d.** of happiness is shortened |
| W-pI.....95.8:4 | than give it power to **d.** our learning. If we |
| W-pI...128.4:1 | thoughts **d.** your progress to salvation, |
| W-pI...128.4:3 | here is worth one instant of **d.** and pain; |
| W-pI...128.8:3 | *This will not tempt me to* **d.** *myself. The* |
| W-pI...131.4:4 | not seek vainly, though he try to force **d.**, |
| W-pI...133.4:3 | and thus **d.** your final choice until you |
| W-pI.140.11:4 | and thus **d.** the time when we can hear |
| W-pI...154.1:4 | and to **d.** commitment to our function. It |
| W-pI...170.2:4 | which can save you more **d.** and needless |
| W-pI...200.9:3 | if we attempt to wander can there be **d.**, |
| W-pII..242.1:5 | Him, for I would not **d.** my coming home, |
| W-pII..292.2:2 | ***d.*** *the happy endings You have promised us* |
| M-2...........4:8 | What could **d.** the power of eternity? |
| M-15.........2:8 | yourself, and thus **d.** this Final Judgment. |
| M-25.........3:5 | matter how this is done, will **d.** progress. |
| C-in...........4:5 | only this, and do not let theology **d.** you. |

## delayed 11

| | |
|---|---|
| T-15....XI.10:9 | is much to do, and we have been long **d.**. |
| T-22...... VI.7:6 | remembrance of what they are be long **d.**? |
| T-26... VIII.9:6 | cause must be **d.** until a future time, is |
| T-27....... II.9:8 | And need your healing be **d.** because you |
| T-30..... V.10:7 | For he will be **d.** when you look back, and |
| W-pI.....95.8:1 | is not **d.** in His teaching by your mistakes. |
| W-pI.134.14:1 | that the time of joining be no more **d.**. For |
| W-pI...168.4:4 | now remains that Heaven be **d.** an instant |
| M-25.........1:6 | and he will not be content to be **d.** by the |
| M-26.........4:7 | Nor will its coming be long **d.**. All the |
| S-1........ III.3:8 | This may be long **d.**, because it may seem |

## delaying 4

| | |
|---|---|
| T-15.....VII.6:3 | directly, and avoid **d.** what it really wants. |
| T-25....... II.2:3 | this respect is hardly worth **d.** change that |
| W-pI...128.2:3 | without **d.** to perceive some hope where |
| C-in...........2:3 | against truth in the form of a **d.** maneuver |

## delays 1

| | |
|---|---|
| S-3...........I.1:5 | its healing but **d.** its turning back to dust, |

## deliberate 2

| | |
|---|---|
| W-pI.....72.1:1 | on His plan, and a **d.** attempt to destroy it |
| M-1...........1:2 | somewhere he has made a **d.** choice in |

## deliberately 1

| | |
|---|---|
| T-4........ VI.5:1 | value of something he has **d.** thrown away |

## delicate 1

| | |
|---|---|
| T19... IV.D.6:3 | "loveliness" of sin, the **d.** appeal of guilt, |

## delicately 1

| | |
|---|---|
| T-24....... V.2:1 | much it **d.** offers the hope of peace and |

## delight 2

| | |
|---|---|
| T-20........II.1:6 | acceptance and **d.** acknowledges the lack |
| T-24....... V.4:3 | For what can specialness **d.** in but to kill? |

## delights 1

| | |
|---|---|
| T-16... V.12:10 | **d.** you can bring death to the eternal. Nor |

## delineate 1

| | |
|---|---|
| W-pI.184.11:1 | symbols which **d.** the world of darkness. |

## deliver 4

| | |
|---|---|
| W-pI...154.6:2 | that they **d.** are intended first for them. |
| W-pII ... 13.3:2 | The eyes of Christ **d.** them to all they look |
| C-6.............4:9 | It is from these He would **d.** you. It is |
| S-3........ IV.5:8 | care, swearing He will **d.** it no more. |

## deliverance 20

| | |
|---|---|
| T-24...... VI.9:1 | what he is, that your **d.** may not be long. |
| T-25..VIII.14:1 | peace, complete **d.** from all effects of sin, |
| T-25...... IX.7:4 | to His gift of healing and **d.** and peace. To |
| T-26....VIII.9:5 | Why should **d.** be disguised as death? |
| T-27........II.7:2 | bestow an equal gift of full **d.** from guilt |
| T-27...... VI.7:3 | have made it deaf to its salvation and **d.**. |
| T-27..... VII.4:5 | this that he perceives to *be* his part in its **d.** |
| T-27..VIII.11:2 | lesson of **d.** until it has been learned, |
| T-30.... VI.10:7 | you to heal, for your salvation and **d.**? |
| W-pI...130.8:6 | *world, that I may find my freedom and* ***d.*** |
| W-pI.130.11:5 | *I seek my freedom and* ***d.****, and this is not a* |
| W-pI.151.17:1 | remember Him Who is salvation and **d.**. |
| W-pI...157.7:1 | Heaven in its ways; a little nearer its **d.**. |
| W-pI...164.2:5 | glad consent; accepting your **d.** for you. |
| W-pI...194.6:1 | the lesson for today as the **d.** it really is, |
| W-pI...195.2:3 | no door to the **d.** they now perceive. |
| W-pI...196.7:3 | you fear, and your **d.** depends on you. |
| W-pI.198.13:4 | Now is the time for your **d.**. The time has |
| W-pI...203.1:2 | *is my* ***d.*** *from every thought of evil and of sin,* |
| W-pII .337.1:1 | of loss; complete **d.** from suffering. And |

## delivered 4

| | |
|---|---|
| T-26....VIII.9:7 | space between you still, to be **d.** from. |
| T-30.... IV.8:12 | He is **d.** from illusions by his will, and but |
| W-pI.154.11:4 | those who wait in misery may be at last **d.** |
| W-pI...159.9:6 | they brought from Christ have been **d.**, |

## deliverer 1

| | |
|---|---|
| T-25....VIII.7:2 | on them in the guise of a **d.** and friend. |

## delivers 1

| | |
|---|---|
| W-pI...154.5:1 | not the one who writes the message he **d.**. |

## delivery 1

| | |
|---|---|
| W-pI...154.5:3 | it is intended, and fulfill his role in its **d.**. |

## delude 3

T-14....... II.3:2 and **d.** themselves into believing that it is
T-21..... II.12:2 the Son does not **d.** himself that he is
T-26..... V.6:10 extreme, he can **d.** himself that this is true

## deluded 8

T-4......... II.6:8 ego has **d.** itself into accepting its reality,
T-11..... V.16:5 those who are convinced by it must be **d.**.
T-27....VIII.8:2 But once **d.** into blaming them you will
W-pI.....57.2:4 free. I have **d.** myself into believing it is
W-pI...136.7:3 instant truth arises in your own **d.** mind,
W-pI.153.14:4 can not escape, is but his own **d.** fantasy.
M-12 .........1:8 and bring His Thoughts to still **d.** minds.
M-12 .........3:2 reality is not understandable to the **d.**.

## deludes 1

T-24..... V.1:10 itself. Except that one **d.**; the other heals.

## delusion 8

T-3........ VI.8:2 yourself and project your **d.** onto others.
T-4.........I.7:10 devotion is possible as long as this **d.** lasts
T-7........ IV.6:1 can oppose the Will of God is a real **d.**.
T-8......... V.1:2 Dissociation is not a solution; it is a **d.**.
T-8......... V.1:3 not recognize it because they prefer the **d.**
T-13..... IX.5:2 you, then, teach him he is right in his **d.**?
T-16.........I.1:7 into it, and lighten it by sharing the **d.**.
W-pI...153.7:3 you now from your **d.** of an angry god,

## delusional 27

T-4.........I.7:10 Any confusion on this point is **d.**, and no
T-4......... II.8:9 is why self-esteem in ego terms must be **d.**
T-5......... V.3:9 It represents a **d.** system, and speaks for it
T-5....... V.6:13 **D.** ideas are not real thoughts, although
T-5......... V.8:5 This is not **d.**. Your mind *does* make your
T-7........ VI.8:5 to engage your mind in its own **d.** system,
T-7.....VII.11:1 insane, wholly **d.** and wholly undesirable,
T-8......... V.1:3 The **d.** believe that truth will assail them,
T-9......VIII.2:6 It is a **d.** attempt to outdo, but not to
T-9......VIII.4:7 is not **d.** because you did not make it. You
T-9......VIII.9:6 all. Grandiosity is **d.**, because it is used to
T-11........in.2:4 is nothing more than a **d.** system in which
T-11....... V.4:2 can surely regard a **d.** system without fear
T-13........in.1:5 the **d.** attempt of the mind to deny itself,
T-13........in.2:2 the **d.** system of those made mad by guilt.
T-13....... V.4:1 The **d.** can be very destructive, for they
T-13...... VI.2:2 Yet this is *unnatural* because it is **d.**. When
T-13...... VI.4:5 have it be according to your use for it *is* **d.**.
T-13..... X.11:8 and in peace and sees it not, he is **d.**, and
T-16.........I.1:7 by **d.** attempts to enter into it, and lighten
T-18...... VI.4:1 In this, the mind is clearly **d.**. It cannot
T-18...... IX.1:5 wild and **d.** thought needs help because,
T-19.........I.6:3 keep the **d.** thought system in the mind.
T19... IV.A.8:4 than a tightly organized **d.** system? Its
W-pI...134.4:5 It is **d.** in what it thinks it can accomplish.
P-1............ 1:2 patient in abandoning his fixed **d.** system,
P-2...........I.2:5 be wrong of necessity, because they are **d.**

## delusions 4

T-4...........I.7:7 This point is not debatable except in **d.**.
T-11....... V.4:1 we are not considering dynamics but **d.**.
T-17...... IV.6:1 relationship protects is but a system of **d.**.
T-18...... IX.1:5 thought needs help because, in its **d.**, it

## demand 43

T-5......... II.7:2 It does not **d.**, because It does not seek
T-9....... II.10:1 will set the price low but **d.** a high return.
T-11...........I.9:3 to **d.** of you what you do not want to give,
T-11....VIII.5:7 for fear of what you think it will **d.** of you.
T-13........in.3:5 Only the world of guilt could **d.** this, for
T-13...VII.11:2 nothing, for what you get it will **d.** of you.
T-15..... VII.9:5 yet never without **d.** of sacrifice. The fury
T-15....... X.6:3 the ego does **d.** payment it never seems to
T-15....... X.7:2 For total love would **d.** total sacrifice. And
T-15 .......X.7:3 the ego seems to **d.** less of you than God,
T-15 .......X.8:1 you do not see that only you **d.** sacrifice,
T-15 .......X.8:2 Yet the **d.** of sacrifice is so savage and so
T-15 .......X.8:4 For if God would **d.** total sacrifice of you,
T-15 .......X.8:6 you, and does **d.** total sacrifice of you. No
T-15 .......X.9:8 the **d.** for sacrifice and the peace of God.
T-16 ...... V.9:3 The **d.** for specialness, and the perception
T-16 ..... V.10:7 think it offers the specialness that you **d.**.
T-18 .... VII.7:7 activity of the body ceases to **d.** attention.
T-19 ........I.2:2 every **d.** your ego would make of him.
T19.... IV.B.3:5 The Holy Spirit does not **d.** you sacrifice
T-23 ........II.4:2 **d.** that errors call for punishment and not
T-24 ........I.8:2 **d.** your brother bow to it against his will.
T-25 .... VII.6:1 meets this one **d.** is worthy of your faith.
T-25 ....VIII.3:3 The laws of sin **d.** a victim. Who it may be
T-26 .......II.2:2 is a **d.** that someone suffer loss and make
T-27 .VIII.13:3 Its innocence does not **d.** your guilt, nor
T-29 .......II.3:2 It has been futile to **d.** escape from sin
T-29 .......II.8:1 is a **d.** the body be a thing that it is not. Its
T-29 .......II.8:3 **d.** that it be more than this lies the idea of
T-29 ...VIII.4:6 Whose voice could make **d.** He enter not?
W-pI..... 37.2:2 Any other way of seeing will inevitably **d.**
W-pI... 170.6:2 And gods **d.** that those who worship them
W-pII . 289.2:5 *Shall I **d.** that You wait longer for Your Son*
M-4 ..... I.A.5:6 how wholly impossible such a **d.** would be
M-8 ........... 5:4 easily a whispered **d.** to kill than a shout?
M-13 ......... 4:6 all the sacrifice its values would **d.** of him.
M-13 ......... 5:4 pleasure of the world that does not **d.** this
C-in ........... 4:1 ego will **d.** many answers that this course
P-1............. 3:6 on, reacting to external forces as they **d.**,
P-3...........I.1:9 To **d.** sacrifice of yourself is to demand a
P-3...........I.1:9 of yourself is to **d.** a sacrifice of God, and
P-3...........I.2:5 Do not **d.**, do not decide, do not sacrifice.
P-3........ III.3:4 This, indeed, must **d.** payment, and the

## demanded 11

T-13 ... III.11:2 war he **d.** everything and found nothing.
T-13 ... III.11:7 Yet you **d.** that it happen, and therefore
T-15 ..... IX.4:3 Limits are **d.** by the ego, and represent its
T-25 .VIII.5:10 And where would justice be if He **d.** of the
T-26 .........I.4:3 What greater sacrifice could be **d.** than
T-27 ..... IV.6:7 the world but ask of whom is sacrifice **d.**,
T-29 ........I.7:5 frequently you have **d.** that love go away,
T-29 .......II.9:4 And it can fail to be what you **d.** that it be.
T-29 ...VIII.1:9 or wanted, or a right **d.** or achieved, it is
W-pI..... 71.2:5 for salvation is thus **d.** of everyone and
W-pI... 155.4:1 truth **d.** they give up the world, it would

## demanding 12

T-10 ...... V.1:1 the god of sickness are strange and very **d.**
T-13 ... III.10:4 **d.** of Him what only such a father could
T-15 ........I.7:7 all-encompassing, **d.** vengeance forever.
T-15 .......X.6:3 payment it never seems to be **d.** it of you.
T-15 ..... XI.2:3 He comes **d.** nothing. No sacrifice of any
T-15 ..... XI.8:2 peace by **d.** no sacrifice of anyone, for so
T-19 ..... III.2:2 the ego brings sin to fear, **d.** punishment.
T-21 ..... III.1:4 sometimes **d.** payment of yourself,
T-26 ........I.4:2 cell, you are **d.** sacrifice of him and you.
W-pI..... 78.4:5 as difficult at times or hard to please, **d.**,
W-pII . 259.1:4 of guilt, **d.** punishment and suffering?
M-16 ......... 9:4 bad, neither rewarding nor **d.** sacrifice,

## demands 39

T-4 ....... IV.6:4 the **d.** of the ego to disengage yourself.
T-7 ..........I.4:1 other hand, always **d.** reciprocal rights,
T-9 ..........I.8:3 who believes that God **d.** sacrifices. Either
T-10 ...... V.3:2 sickness obviously **d.** the denial of health,
T-10 ...... V.3:7 This is the offering your god **d.** because,
T-11 ...... VI.5:4 The god of crucifixion **d.** that he crucify,
T-11 ...... VI.5:6 The God of resurrection **d.** nothing, for
T-11 ...VIII.5:8 that nothing of God **d.** anything of you.
T-13 ... III.11:3 the gentleness of love respond to his **d.**,
T-13 VII.10:13 it **d.** you lay all of the things it bids you
T-13 ..... IX.1:3 for it **d.** fidelity to darkness and forbids
T-15 .... VII.7:6 for this sacrifice, which he **d.** of himself,
T-15 .... VII.7:6 he **d.** that the other accept the guilt and
T-15 .... VII.8:3 It is always this that the ego **d.**, and it
T-15 ..... IX.4:3 its **d.** to make little and ineffectual. Limit
T-15 .......X.6:7 behind them all; that love **d.** sacrifice, and
T-15 .......X.7:1 a sacrifice do you believe His Love **d.**! For
T-15 .......X.8:1 everyone outside yourself **d.** your sacrifice
T19 .IV.A.11:5 What fear **d.**, love cannot even see. The
T-21 ... III.11:8 Neither **d.** the sacrifice of the other. Yet
T-21 ... VII.1:3 one requirement that it **d.** to be believed.
T-23 ......II.11:8 His treachery **d.** his death, that you may
T-24 .....II.13:2 For it **d.** a special place God cannot enter,
T-24 ... VII.1:3 obeys. Nothing his specialness **d.** does he
T-25 .. VII.13:2 Death **d.** life, but life is not maintained at
T-25 ... VIII.4:5 Justice **d.** no sacrifice, for any sacrifice is
T-25 ..... IX.3:3 An answer which **d.** the slightest loss to
T-26 ........I.4:5 Yet every sacrifice **d.** that they be separate
T-26 .. VII.14:5 still **d.** that he must make some sacrifice,
T-29 ........I.7:2 But fear **d.** the sacrifice of love, for in
T-30 .......V.1:4 and no **d.** are made of anyone or anything
T-31 .......V.1:7 world on equal terms, at one with its **d.**.
W-pI .... 24.6:1 large number of **d.** of the situation which
W-pI .... 37.2:7 who see themselves as whole make no **d.**.
W-pI 135.24:4 that makes extravagant **d.** for sacrifice.
W-pI 138.11:4 **d.** obscurity for fear to be invested there.
W-pI .. 170.6:3 who ask if the **d.** are sensible or even sane.
W-pI .. 189.8:6 But do not make **d.**, nor point the road to
P-3........ III.3:2 They make **d.**, and so they cannot give.

## demarcations 1

M-2 ........... 5:6 **d.** they have drawn between their roles,

## demented 1

T-27 .... VII.1:2 the world's **d.** version of salvation clearly

## demonstrate 39

T-1 ....... IV.4:2 why I could **d.** that death does not exist. I
T-4 ....... VI.6:3 to live so as to **d.** that you are not an ego,
T-6 ..........I.9:1 to **d.** that the most outrageous assault, as
T-6 ........I.10:6 is inevitably led to **d.** His way for all.
T-6 ........I.15:9 to **d.** that condemnation is impossible?
T-6 ..... IV.10:3 **d.** that the perfect are inadequate to bring
T-7 ..........X.4:1 you need to **d.** the obvious to yourself. It
T-11 .....V.15:1 the ego does make every attempt to **d.** it,
T-11 .....V.16:5 without meaning cannot **d.** anything, and
T-11 .....V.17:3 Nothing can **d.** that His Son is unworthy,
T-11 .....V.17:5 God does not deny, and it will **d.** its truth.
T-11 .....V.17:7 Presence of Christ they need **d.** nothing,
T-12 ........I.2:2 to **d.** your own ability to understand what
T-12 ........I.8:2 is necessary to **d.** the need for escape. The
T-12 .... VII.1:1 Miracles **d.** that learning has occurred
T-13 .......X.7:1 you fearfully to **d.** what He has saved you
T-13 ..... XI.4:4 allowing Him to **d.** which must be true.
T-17 ..... III.1:6 with you to **d.** he did what he did not.
T-17 .... VII.1:2 **d.** that you did not believe the situation
T-17 .... VII.1:3 you **d.** when you remove it from its source
T-17 ...VIII.6:7 And **d.** that you have risen far beyond any
T-19 ........I.3:5 **d.** the "fact" that separation has occurred.
T-27 ......I.6:10 Concerns about the body **d.** how frail and
T-27 .......II.4:2 no effect on you to **d.** they are not real.
T-27 ..... VI.8:1 that you may **d.** the healing of the world.
T-30 ...VIII.2:1 The miracle is means to **d.** that all
T-31 ........I.5:3 it. And this has learning sought to **d.**, and
T-31 .......V.7:8 can not be used to **d.** the world is real. For
W-pI .... 13.2:3 to **d.** its own impotence and unreality.
W-pI .. 137.4:6 the truth, must **d.** that sickness is not real.
W-pI 154.14:3 Now we **d.** how they have changed our
W-pI .. 190.4:5 it shields, and tries to **d.** must still be true.
M-in.......... 2:1 To teach is to **d.**. There are only two
M-in.......... 2:2 **d.** that you believe one or the other is true
M-3 ........... 3:5 Perhaps the best way to **d.** that these
M-18 ......... 1:2 tries to establish its error or **d.** its falsity,
P-2...... IV.10:3 task to **d.** that defenses are not necessary,
P-2........ VI.7:4 come to **d.** their sinlessness to eyes that
P-3..........II.2:1 to **d.** that there is no order of difficulty in

## demonstrated 10

| | |
|---|---|
| T-3...........I.7:6 | resurrection **d.** that nothing can destroy |
| T-3........IV.7:5 | I **d.** both the powerlessness of the body |
| T-4........IV.1:2 | listen to the voice of your ego is **d.** by your |
| T-6...........I.5:1 | can be **d.** only through joint decision. You |
| T-12..........I.9:4 | yourself, and you have **d.** this by giving it. |
| T-12.....VII.1:2 | generalization is **d.** as you use it in more |
| T-17... VIII.3:5 | What has been **d.** has called for faith, and |
| T-27.......V.2:3 | Only when it has been **d.** is it proved, and |
| T-30.....VII.2:4 | they have no meaning in themselves is **d.** |
| M-25..........3:8 | by tricks of magic are special powers "**d.**." |

## demonstrates 21

| | |
|---|---|
| T-1........IV.4:7 | Your witnessing **d.** your belief, and thus |
| T-6........IV.9:7 | in itself **d.** that you are not enslaved. |
| T-6......IV.11:2 | which the Holy Spirit **d.** does not exist. |
| T-6......V.A.2:7 | than the body. Every miracle **d.** this. |
| T-6......V.C.8:1 | **d.** that you perceive its wholeness, and |
| T-9...........I.1:4 | **d.** that you *are* afraid of what you are. It is |
| T-16.......II.1:5 | you perceive, that **d.** you do not do them. |
| T-27.......II.9:5 | The constant pain they suffer **d.** that they |
| T-27.......V.3:3 | and **d.** that war has no effects. For all the |
| T-27.......VI.1:1 | Pain **d.** the body must be real. It is a loud, |
| T-27... VIII.8:1 | The world but **d.** an ancient truth; you |
| T-28.....II.10:2 | It **d.** what He would have you learn, and |
| T-30... VIII.2:7 | This **d.** that it was never real, and could |
| W-pI.136.13:1 | is this fact that **d.** that time is an illusion. |
| W-pI...137.4:2 | But healing **d.** that truth is true. The |
| W-pI...137.8:2 | **d.** that dreams will not prevail against the |
| W-pI.139.10:1 | **d.** the Oneness of God's Son is unassailed |
| W-pI...190.3:2 | It **d.** God is denied, confused with fear, |
| M-4.......IV.1:7 | It **d.** the absence of God's curriculum, and |
| M-6............1:3 | Truth **d.** illusions have no value. The |
| C-1.............7:6 | trained **d.** that it cannot reach knowledge. |

## demonstrating 9

| | |
|---|---|
| T-1........I.16:1 | for **d.** it is as blessed to give as to receive. |
| T-3........IV.4:2 | clearly **d.** that knowledge is not involved. |
| T-7........XI.1:8 | By **d.** to yourself there is no order of |
| T-8.....VIII.6:1 | is a way of **d.** that you can be hurt. It is a |
| T-11......VI.7:4 | Teach rather that I did not die by **d.** that I |
| T-12........V.2:3 | will be **d.** that nothing really happened. |
| T-13......IV.2:3 | bent on **d.** their reality to establish yours. |
| T-17... VIII.3:4 | His purpose, and **d.** its reality. What has |
| W-pI...138.7:2 | gave it; that it be a means for **d.** hell is real |

## demonstration 10

| | |
|---|---|
| T-3...........I.7:9 | It is the final **d.** that all the other lessons I |
| T-6......V.A.2:5 | for separation into a **d.** against it. If the |
| T-6......V.B.9:4 | Realizing that it *must* follow is a **d.** of a |
| T-11.....V.15:4 | in turn, becomes its **d.** of its own reality. |
| T-11.....V.17:4 | the ego is a **d.** that His Son does not exist, |
| T-17... VIII.1:4 | clear and unequivocal **d.** of the meaning |
| T-21.......II.9:2 | is no better **d.** of the power of wanting, |
| W-pI.....62.1:3 | is the **d.** that you are the light of the world |
| M-in ..........2:3 | From your **d.** others learn, and so do you. |
| C-5.............3:5 | offered you a final **d.** that it is impossible |

## demonstrations 1

| | |
|---|---|
| T-11.....V.16:1 | of the ego's **d.** to those who would listen. |

## denial 75

| | |
|---|---|
| T-1........I.22:3 | exist. This leads to a **d.** of spiritual sight. |
| T-1.......VII.1:5 | This is because *not* doing it is a **d.** of Self. |
| T-1.......VII.1:6 | of Self. **D.** of Self results in illusions, while |
| T-2.......II.1:12 | This is the proper use of **d.**. It is not used |
| T-2.........II.2:1 | True **d.** is a powerful protective device. |
| T-2.........II.2:3 | This kind of **d.** is not a concealment but a |
| T-2.........II.2:5 | it. **D.** of error is a strong defense of truth, |
| T-2.........II.2:5 | but **d.** of truth results in miscreation, the |
| T-2.........II.2:6 | right mind the **d.** of error frees the mind, |
| T-2.......IV.3:11 | in a particularly unworthy form of **d.**. The |
| T-2... V.A.14:1 | (4) The miracle is always a **d.** of this error |
| T-2.......VII.5:6 | deny it is merely to use **d.** inappropriately |
| T-3......VI.10:4 | devious routes, from the **d.** of Authorship |
| T-4........III.4:3 | Being made out of the **d.** of the Father, |
| T-7.......VII.1:1 | feel deprived, because **d.** is as total as love |
| T-7.......VII.1:5 | **D.** has no power in itself, but you can give |
| T-7.......VII.1:9 | Yet **d.** is a defense, and so it is as capable |
| T-8.........II.3:3 | That is why the ego is the **d.** of free will. It |
| T-9.........I.10:3 | It is merely a **d.** in the form of a request. |
| T-9... VIII.10:8 | it is the **d.** of arrogance. To accept your |
| T-10.......II.4:3 | **d.** of reality precludes the acceptance of |
| T-10......III.3:6 | strengthen his **d.** of God and thus lose |
| T-10......III.7:2 | acceptance of peace is the **d.** of illusion, |
| T-10..............V.h | The **D.** of God |
| T-10.......V.1:6 | very literal; **d.** of life perceives its opposite |
| T-10.......V.1:6 | of **d.** replace what is with what is not. No |
| T-10.......V.2:4 | Do not attribute your **d.** of joy to them, or |
| T-10.......V.2:5 | the **d.** of the spark that brings depression, |
| T-10.......V.3:1 | to the **d.** of God is the ego's religion. The |
| T-10.......V.3:2 | of sickness obviously demands the **d.** of |
| T-10.......V.3:8 | things he is but one idea;–the **d.** of God. |
| T-10.......V.6:4 | Your **d.** of Him therefore means that you |
| T-10.......V.6:6 | And if you accept **d.**, you can accept its |
| T-10.....V.14:1 | Arrogance is the **d.** of love, because love |
| T-11.........I.3:7 | Your **d.** of its reality may arrest it in time, |
| T-11.......II.2:6 | it, lies the **d.** of God's Fatherhood and of |
| T-11.......II.3:1 | And **d.** is as total as love. You cannot |
| T-11......IV.4:3 | Remember also that the **d.** of this simple |
| T-11.....V.16:8 | Its witnesses do attest to its **d.**, but hardly |
| T-11.....VII.4:1 | the **d.** of the opposite of goodness enables |
| T-12.........I.9:6 | One is false, for it was made out of **d.**; and |
| T-12.........I.9:6 | **d.** depends on the belief in what is denied |
| T-12........I.10:6 | For the separation is only the **d.** of union, |
| T-12.......II.1:1 | are merely the translation of **d.** into truth. |
| T-12.......II.1:5 | thus becomes *to deny the **d.** of truth.* The |
| T-12.......II.8:7 | deny the **d.** of perfection is not so difficult |
| T-12......VI.7:1 | **d.** of the separation is the reinstatement |
| T-13.......in.1:5 | to deny itself, and escape the penalty of **d.** |
| T-13.......in.1:6 | It is not an attempt to relinquish **d.**, but |
| T-13.........I.1:5 | the **d.** of the blamelessness of God's Son. |
| T-13.......V.8:7 | see. But this is what **d.** does, for by it you |
| T-14.........I.2:1 | a world made of **d.** and without direction. |
| T-14......IV.7:5 | as guilty is **d.** of the Father so complete, |
| T-14.......V.3:5 | to the **d.** of guilt in all its forms. To accuse |
| T-14... VIII.1:2 | in guilt and in the dark **d.** of innocence. |
| T-14....IX.1:10 | represents only the **d.** of what always was. |
| T-16.......II.9:6 | your faith in them, and not in their **d.**. |
| T-21...VII.11:3 | on sin are seeing the **d.** of the real world. |
| T-21... VIII.5:4 | Here is what **d.** has denied revealed to you |
| T-22........I.10:6 | It is **d.** of illusions that calls on truth, for |
| T-24......VI.7:3 | by still one more **d.** of Christ in him. And |
| T-26... VIII.9:6 | is merely a **d.** of the fact that consequence |
| W-pI.....79.5:5 | remain unsolved under a cloud of **d.**, and |
| W-pI.....91.2:5 | **D.** of light leads to failure to perceive it. |
| W-pI...134.1:1 | and a complete **d.** of the truth. In such a |
| W-pI.135.14:3 | where the **d.** of reality is very obvious. Yet |
| W-pI...139.5:2 | It is for this **d.** that you need Atonement. |
| W-pI...139.5:3 | Your **d.** made no change in what you are. |
| W-pI...165.1:1 | your own **d.** of the truth that lies beyond? |
| W-pI...165.5:6 | Christ; your mind has come to lay aside **d.** |
| W-pI...165.6:5 | his **d.** of the nourishment he needs to live |
| W-pI.186.12:2 | it is that asks, and who would make **d.**. |
| M-4 ......IV.1:6 | is the end of peace and the **d.** of learning. |
| M-13 .........5:3 | price that must be paid for the **d.** of truth. |
| M-28 .........2:1 | The resurrection is the **d.** of death, being |

## denials 1

| | |
|---|---|
| T-9..... VIII.7:1 | Truth and littleness are **d.** of each other |

## denied 131

| | |
|---|---|
| T-4........III.2:4 | because you have **d.** your own Guide and |
| T-4........III.9:1 | In your own mind, though **d.** by the ego, |
| T-7........VI.2:7 | you have **d.** the power of your thought, |
| T-7.......VII.2:6 | but because you have **d.** it in another and |
| T-9.........II.12:3 | nothing because you have **d.** Him nothing |
| T-9.........V.4:5 | power through the Holy Spirit is **d.**. This |
| T-10.......V.6:3 | Him. You **d.** Him because you loved Him, |
| T-10.......V.7:1 | Your Father has not **d.** you. He does not |
| T-10.....V.10:1 | realize how much you have **d.** yourself, |
| T-11.........I.3:6 | continues forever, however much it is **d.**. |
| T-11.........I.4:4 | know your creations, having **d.** infinity? |
| T-11.........I.5:8 | to accept His Fatherhood has **d.** you yours |
| T-11........II.2:2 | If you have **d.** truth, what better witnesses |
| T-11......IV.2:2 | believing that the Father has **d.** him? |
| T-11......IV.6:7 | and nothing is **d.** by God to His Son. |
| T-11.....V.10:5 | fear unreality *because* you have **d.** yourself. |
| T-11.....V.16:7 | truth? Can it perceive what it has **d.**? Its |
| T-11.....V.16:8 | to its denial, but hardly to what it has **d.**. |
| T-11.....V.16:9 | does not see Him, for it has **d.** His Son. |
| T-11..VIII.10:4 | nothing will be **d.** your simple request. |
| T-12........I.8:13 | recognition of what has been **d.**. |
| T-12.........I.9:6 | belief in what is **d.** for its own existence. |
| T-12.......I.9:10 | You have **d.** its power to conceal love, |
| T-12.......I.10:3 | it, for the awareness of truth cannot be **d.**. |
| T-12........II.8:6 | For perfection *is,* and cannot be **d.**. To |
| T-13.........I.5:3 | and the way to find release is not **d.** him. |
| T-13.........I.6:5 | You have **d.** the condition of his being, |
| T-13......III.6:5 | that its need of healing cannot be **d.**. Not |
| T-13....III.12:4 | He **d.** you only your request for pain, for |
| T-13.......V.7:8 | will see all that you **d.** in your brothers |
| T-13.......V.7:8 | your brothers because you **d.** it in yourself |
| T-13.....VII.2:1 | The world you see must be **d.**, for sight of |
| T-13.....VII.2:3 | is possible because you have **d.** the other. |
| T-13.....VII.5:6 | what is **d.** is there but is not recognized. |
| T-13......IX.4:5 | You have **d.** his freedom, and by so doing |
| T-13......IX.4:5 | doing you have **d.** the witness unto yours. |
| T-14.........I.2:5 | are everything, and all this has been **d.**, |
| T-14.........I.4:2 | He knows to be true you have **d.** yourself, |
| T-14......IV.7:3 | have **d.** Him and do not recognize Him, |
| T-14......IV.9:2 | guiltlessness to minds that have **d.** it, and |
| T-14......IV.9:2 | it, and thus **d.** Heaven to themselves. |
| T-14.......V.1:2 | with all the lonely ones who have **d.** Him? |
| T-14.......V.5:3 | been **d.** to produce the need of healing. |
| T-15........II.4:8 | He cannot be **d.**. If you remain uncertain, |
| T-15......VI.6:7 | it. Fear not the holy instant will be **d.** you, |
| T-15......VI.6:7 | instant will be denied you, for I **d.** it not. |
| T-15....VIII.3:7 | and nothing that he wills can be **d.**. You |
| T-15......IX.4:4 | from it, and you have **d.** his gift to you. |
| T-16.......V.4:2 | for the self the specialness that He **d.**. It is |
| T-16.....VII.5:6 | **d.** that it is there, and the relationship |
| T-17.........I.6:7 | to truth what was **d.** by both of you. And |
| T-17......V.13:3 | have **d.** yourself its benefit. You reinforce |
| T-17......VI.7:4 | has not come because faith has been **d.**, |
| T-18.....VII.7:5 | For here is time **d.**, and past and future |
| T-19......III.1:3 | so acute that the sin is **d.** the acting out. |
| T-20......IV.8:6 | Nothing you need will be **d.** you. Not one |
| T-20.....VII.8:2 | **d.** the means the Holy Spirit offers you to |
| T-21......II.10:1 | When vision is **d.**, confusion of cause and |
| T-21...VII.5:14 | *I want to see what I **d.** because it is the truth?* |
| T-21....VIII.5:4 | Here is what denial has **d.** revealed to you. |
| T-23......III.3:6 | **d.** where compromise has been accepted, |
| T-24.........I.2:8 | All that can be **d.** is their reality, but not |
| T-24......II.11:1 | brother's; part of love was not **d.** to him. |
| T-25.... VI.5:11 | His wish was not **d.** but changed in form, |
| T-25....VIII.8:2 | **d.** themselves because they are not fair, |
| T-25......IX.8:2 | Seek to deny and you will feel **d.**. Seek to |
| T-26.........I.4:6 | of God must be **d.** if any sacrifice is asked |
| T-26......III.2:6 | is sin **d.**, and everything that *is* received |
| T-26.....V.12:4 | terrible illusion was **d.** in but the time it |
| T-26......VI.1:2 | because you have **d.** it is but an illusion, |
| T-26.....VII.2:2 | When the separation is **d.**, it goes. For it is |
| T-26.....VII.9:7 | Yet facts can be **d.** and thus unknown, |
| T-26.....VII.9:7 | they were known before they were **d.**. |
| T-26........X.3:7 | of what he is, **d.** the right to be himself, |
| T-26........X.5:8 | simple justice has been thus **d.** to every |
| T-27.........I.8:4 | to see, so that the cause can never be **d.**. |
| T-27......II.14:4 | yourself; the other half, which is **d.**. And |
| T-27...VII.13:3 | he has lost his innocence, **d.** his Father, |
| T-28.......I.9:10 | It for your sins, It will no longer be **d.**. |
| T-28.......I.10:2 | His Effects, yet have They never been **d.**. |
| T-30......III.4:3 | Nor could it be possible it be **d.**. Your will |
| T-30......III.5:9 | But what is really asked for cannot be **d.**. |
| T-31.......II.11:2 | Alone it is **d.** to both of you. Is it not clear |
| W-pI.....62.2:3 | are, having **d.** your Identity by attacking |
| W-pI...76.10:6 | for creation; **d.** to Him by his belief in hell |
| W-pI.....77.6:2 | You state a fact that cannot be **d.**. The |
| W-pI.....78.8:1 | What you have asked for cannot be **d.**. |
| W-pI.....96.5:2 | It has **d.** its Source of strength, and sees |

W-pI.....96.9:5 are your own real thoughts you have d.,
W-pI...105.6:2 those brothers who have been d. by you
W-pI...105.6:3 Here you d. them to yourself. And here
W-pI...105.7:5 the joy and peace you have d. yourself.
W-pI...124.6:1 No miracle can ever be d. to those who
W-pI...133.7:2 right to everything, you have d. your own.
W-pI...134.5:2 be concealed, d. or called another name,
W-pI.134.11:4 feel that all escape has been d. to him.
W-pI...138.6:5 choice in which is truth accepted or d..
W-pI...139.4:4 has judged against it and d. its worth, and
W-pI...139.5:1 his life, for what it is has been d. by him.
W-pI...153.7:2 It proclaims you have d. the Christ and
W-pI.154.12:3 has d. the tiniest of blessings to His Son.
W-pI...155.3:3 the truth, because they have d. that it is so
W-pI...159.6:4 and no one is d. his least request or his
W-pI...160.5:2 Who fears has but d. himself and said, "I
W-pI...160.5:4 and that his home has been d. to him.
Wi181-200 3:2 remains beyond achievement while it is d.
W-pI.182.12:4 hear, and this the call which cannot be d..
W-pI...184.8:7 And thus his unity is twice d., for you
W-pI...189.9:5 What has not been d. is surely there, if it
W-pI...190.3:2 It demonstrates God is d., confused with
W-pI...190.8:3 free. In pain is God d. the Son He loves. In
W-pI...191.4:1 game you play in which Identity can be d.
W-pI.191.11:4 pain until you have d. its hold on you.
W-pI...197.9:7 you have d. yourself when you forgot the
WpI rVI.in.5:4 let the thought which you d. be given up,
W-pII .230.1:6 And can this be d. me, when it is forever
W-pII .251.2:2 *What we d. ourselves You have restored,*
W-pII .320.1:4 His holy will can never be d., because his
W-pII ...12.1:2 enemy, and takes a form in which it is d..
W-pII .333.1:2 cannot be evaded, set aside, d., disguised,
M-7 ...........6:4 you have d. the Source of your creation. If
M-13 .........7:9 d. if you attack any brother for anything.
M-23 .........1:3 fair if their pupils were d. healing because
M-27 .........2:5 of love, because he has d. that life is real.
M-27 .........4:4 But if there is reality in life, death is d.. No
C-2.............2:3 ego cannot be d. for it alone seems real.
C-2.............3:3 The ego's unreality is not d. by words nor
P-2.......VII.9:2 in this, you have d. that God created you,
P-3.........II.4:5 Both must have d. their perfection, for
P-3......III.5:12 He has himself d. the light, and cannot
P-3........III.8:8 you have d. the Christ in you. Remember

## denies 35

T-2....... II.1:11 It d. the ability of anything not of God to
T-2.......IV.3:13 If one d. this unfortunate aspect of the
T-3.......VII.5:2 because it literally d. His Fatherhood.
T-4........VI.4:3 done this, it d. all truly natural impulses,
T-7........VI.3:1 the very power of the mind the ego d..
T-7........XI.3:9 over His children and d. them nothing.
T-8.........V.5:3 deny you nothing, as God d. me nothing.
T-8........VI.3:1 Let us glorify Him Whom the world d.,
T-14......VII.4:7 have them both, for each d. the other.
T-16.....IV.10:2 and thus d. the Wholeness of your Father.
T-21..... II.12:7 Thus he d. creation. With you, he thinks
T-21..... II.12:9 made, made him. Thus he d. he made it.
T-21...VII.11:2 sees, since it is this the world of sin d..
T-22.......in.3:6 He d. not his own reality *because* it is the
T-22.... VI.15:6 you that you cannot separate d. the ego.
T-24......IV.4:5 and give it meaning that the truth d.. All
T-25....VIII.5:7 each one contradicts the other and d. that
T-26.....VII.8:5 this world d. to every aspect of God's Son
T-26...VII.14:5 sacrifice, and thus d. that everything is his
T-26...VII.19:6 unity that specialness d. will save them all
T-26.......X.2:6 And this d. the fact that *all* are senseless,
T-27..... II.2:10 One d. the other and must make it false.
T-27.......V.1:9 And who can share what he d. himself?
T-29.....VII.2:3 his coming, he d. the truth about himself,
T-30....VIII.4:8 When he is tempted, he d. reality. And he
T-31......VI.1:3 be false, for what is real d. its opposite.
W-pI.....68.2:4 holds grievances d. he was created by love
W-pI.....92.3:2 His strength d. your weakness. It is your
W-pI.....96.3:5 the two, for one d. the other can be real. If
W-pI...131.7:3 What d. its own existence and attacks
W-pI...131.9:3 He thus d. himself, and contradicts what
W-pI...139.8:4 or a statement which d. itself in statement
W-pI.160.10:5 Who d. his brother is denying Him, and
W-pI....184.6:6 What d. that it is true is but illusion, for it
M-27 .........4:3 Death d. life. But if there is reality in life,

## dense 3

T-1 ......VII.1:1 produce a d. cover over miracle impulses,
T-2 ........ V.6:4 illuminated and the body in itself is too d.
W-pI.....41.5:2 of insane thoughts, d. and obscuring, yet

## density 1

T-12 .......II.2:1 of the d. of the fog that obscures it. If you

## deny 184

T-1 ........I.29:3 heal because they d. body-identification
T-2 .........II.2:2 d. any belief that error can hurt you. This
T-2 .....IV.3:10 impossible to d. its existence in this world
T-2 ......VII.5:2 To believe in one is to d. the other. Fear is
T-2 ......VII.5:6 *has* occurred, and to d. it is merely to use
T-3 .........II.1:8 one, therefore, is able to d. truth totally,
T-3 .....VI.10:5 to God, but only to those who d. Him. To
T-3 .....VI.10:6 To d. His Authorship is to deny yourself
T-3 .....VI.10:6 is to d. yourself the reason for your peace,
T-4 ......III.8:5 How long will you d. Him His Kingdom?
T-6 .......II.6:11 To d. this is to deny yourself and Him,
T-6 .......II.6:11 To deny this is to d. yourself and Him,
T-6 ........III.2:3 You are only love, but when you d. this,
T-6 .....V.C.4:5 d. that the temptation to make exceptions
T-7 ....... VI.4:7 Love is your power, which the ego must d.
T-7 ....... VI.4:8 must also d. everything this power gives
T-7 ......VII.1:1 Whenever you d. a blessing to a brother
T-7 ......VII.1:2 impossible to d. part of the Sonship as it
T-7 ......VII.1:6 If you use it to d. reality, reality is gone for
T-7 ......VII.2:6 What you d. you lack, not because it is
T-7 ....VII.10:3 D. this and you will attack, believing you
T-7 .........X.2:1 mind what is not there, and d. what is.
T-7 .........X.2:2 gave your mind through His you may d.,
T-7 .........X.2:7 D. His Will as yours, and you are denying
T-7 .....XI.3:10 when they d. Him they do not know this,
T-7 .....XI.3:10 because they d. themselves everything.
T-7 .......XI.6:8 you. D. his creative power, and you are
T-7 .......XI.7:1 You cannot d. part of truth. You do not
T-8 .........II.6:6 D. yourself this and you are denying God
T-8 .......IV.2:1 into a world that does d. itself everything.
T-8 .......IV.7:4 by denying the Father you d. yourself. I
T-8 ........ V.5:3 it. I will d. you nothing, as God denies me
T-9 ...........I.9:5 To d. what is can only *seem* to be fearful.
T-9 .........I.10:7 Would the Holy Spirit d. the Will of God?
T-9 .........I.11:6 It is indeed possible for you to d. facts,
T-9 .........I.11:8 seeing. If you d. love, you will not know it
T-9 .........I.12:1 Any attempt to d. what *is* must be fearful,
T-9 .......II.12:3 He will d. you nothing because you have
T-9 ......VII.7:3 littleness therefore is to d. all knowledge,
T-10 ......III.7:3 to d. illusions anywhere in the Kingdom,
T-10 ......IV.5:1 free to give up freedom, but only to d. it.
T-10 ...... V.1:5 realize that to d. God is to deny their own
T-10 ...... V.1:5 realize that to deny God is to d. their own
T-10 ...... V.2:1 d. God will inevitably result in projection,
T-10 ...... V.6:3 your love for Him, you could not d. Him.
T-10 ...... V.6:5 what you d. you must have once known.
T-10 .... V.9:10 If you d. Him you bring sin, pain and
T-10 .... V.9:11 also d. what it creates because it is free.
T-10 .... V.10:4 When you d. Him *you* are insane. Would
T-10 .... V.10:9 To d. it is insanity. God gave Himself to
T-10 .. V.10:11 eternal. Would you d. yourself to Him?
T-10 .... V.11:5 not d. yourself the joy that was created for
T-10 .... V.13:8 That is why to d. Him is to deny yourself.
T-10 .... V.13:8 That is why to deny Him is to d. yourself.
T-11 .........I.5:8 Himself. Do not d. Him His Son, for your
T-11 .........I.8:2 strange when you realize that to d. is to
T-11 .........I.8:4 By denying this you d. your own will, and
T-11 .........II.3:2 You cannot d. part of yourself, because
T-11 .........II.3:4 it. To d. meaning is to fail to understand.
T-11 ... III.4:10 But d. them instead, for the light is here
T-11 ....... III.6:3 tempted to d. Him remember that there
T-11 ....... IV.2:2 Son d. the Father without believing that
T-11 ....... IV.2:4 experience when you d. your Father is still
T-11 .... V.17:5 Accept what God does not d., and it will
T-11 ..... VI.3:6 you will become less and less willing to d..
T-11 ....VIII.7:5 Do not d. it to yourself, for it can only free
T-12 ........I.4:2 in which you d. the reality of the need for
T-12 ........I.5:7 helped. D. him your help and you will not
T-12 .......II.1:5 thus becomes *to d. the denial of truth.* The
T-12 .......II.8:7 To d. the denial of perfection is not so
T-12 .......II.8:7 perfection is not so difficult as to d. truth,
T-12 ..... III.4:5 so is to d. yourself and impoverish both.
T-12 ..... III.9:2 to accept even death to d. your Father.
T-12 ..... IV.2:6 has the power to d. the ego's existence,
T-12 ....VIII.4:2 You can d. it, but you cannot lose it. A
T-13 ......in.1:5 delusional attempt of the mind to d. itself
T-13 ........I.1:4 and to accept one is to d. the other. Guilt
T-13 ........I.5:8 D. your world and judge him not, for his
T-13 ..... IV.5:7 thus d. yourself the message of release
T-13 .......V.7:7 It is given you to learn how to d. insanity,
T-13 ..... VI.7:6 *forth.* And they will not d. the truth in you,
T-13 .... VII.4:3 answers, being unable to d. a call for help,
T-13 .... VII.6:2 his own, he will d. the vision of the other,
T-13 .... VII.7:6 He must d. the world of pain the instant
T-13 ...VIII.9:3 His. D. a brother here, and you deny the
T-13 ...VIII.9:3 you d. the witnesses to your fatherhood in
T-13 ... IX.8:12 can d. His knowledge, but you cannot
T-14 ........I.2:2 that to d. is the decision not to know. The
T-14 ........I.4:2 Anything you d. that He knows to be true
T-14 ........I.4:2 He must therefore teach you not to d. it.
T-14 .......II.8:5 it is impossible to d. the simple truth. For
T-14 ..... III.8:6 only when you learn to d. the causeless,
T-14 ... III.12:1 Would you d. the truth of God's decision
T-14 .......V.1:4 Would you d. His yearning to be known?
T-14 .......V.3:8 D. them not what is their due, for you will
T-14 ... XI.10:5 You can d. Him, but you cannot call on
T-14 ... XI.15:4 It is impossible to d. the Source of effects
T-15 .......II.6:7 one instant, and you will never d. it again.
T-15 .......II.6:8 d. the Presence of what the universe bows
T-15 ..... III.4:9 the little, and you d. yourself His power.
T-15 ..... III.5:6 All your attempts to d. His magnitude,
T-15 ..... IV.7:2 way you could do that would be to d. the
T-15 .......V.2:7 as alone is to d. the Oneness of the Father
T-15 ..... XI.6:3 It is impossible to d. what love is and still
T-16 .......II.6:6 Him is to d. all that you think you know.
T-16 .......II.8:2 not to d. what has been given you by God.
T-16 ..... III.3:8 is only if you d. what It has done that you
T-16 ..... III.3:8 that you could possibly d. Its Presence.
T-16 ..... VI.5:4 Each would d. his power, for the separate
T-17 ........I.2:5 What you use in fantasy you d. to truth.
T-17 .....V.7:10 Can you d. that He has given you a most
T-17 .....V.13:5 And it is impossible to d. yourself, and to
T19 ... IV.B.2:3 for which you would d. a home to peace.
T-21 ........I.3:4 It is not this you would d.. Your question
T-21 .....II.10:6 is the Effect, whose Cause he would d..
T-21 .....II.13:2 otherwise, and you d. your whole reality.
T-21 ..... VI.1:7 you d. it to yourself and to your brother.
T-21 ... VI.11:4 bind him but himself, if he d. his freedom
T-22 ......I.10:6 for to d. illusions is to recognize that fear
T-22 ..... VI.6:3 can d. himself the vision that he brings to
T-22 ... VI.10:2 only arrogance that would d. the power of
T-23 ........I.6:9 reality that they d. is not a part of them.
T-23 ..... III.1:6 He may d. he is a murderer and justify his
T-24 ........I.2:7 d. their presence nor their terrible results.
T-24 .......II.9:3 to kill each other and d. they are the same
T-24 ..... III.8:8 D. Them not. They ask of you but that
T-24 ..... VII.1:4 It needs does he d. to what he loves. And
T-25 .... VII.4:1 is to d. your Father's sanity and yours. For
T-25 .... VII.9:1 the alternative is one which he cannot d.,
T-25 ..... IX.8:2 Seek to d. and you will feel denied. Seek
T-26 .......II.5:8 You d. the miracle of justice *can* be fair.
T-26 .. VII.16:4 D. him not, that you may be released.
T-26 .......X.6:6 *do I d. the Presence of the Father and the Son*
T-27 .....II.10:8 function from Him and d. that it is His?
T-27 ..... III.3:2 There is nothing to attack or to d.; to love
T-27 ..... VI.5:8 It is a witness no one can d., for it is the
T-27 .... VII.9:2 choose if you d. the cause of suffering is in
T-28 ........I.10:2 You would d. Him His Effects, yet have
T-28 .....II.12:3 than d. the active role in making up the
T-28 .......V.3:6 And you will d. your Self, and walk upon
T-28 .... VII.2:2 you d. yourself your wholeness and your
T-29 ..... III.2:5 D. Him not His witness in the dream His
T-31 ...VIII.7:1 D. me not the little gift I ask, when in

W-pI.....14.4:2 as it occurs to you, and then **d.** its reality.
W-pI.....45.4:3 We will **d.** the world in favor of truth. We
W-pI...103.1:6 as well. Yet can the mind **d.** that this is so,
W-pI...105.9:4 seems to tempt you to **d.** God's gift to him
W-pI...124.7:7 As we **d.** our separation from our Father,
W-pI.132.13:4 **D.** illusions, but accept the truth. Deny
W-pI.132.13:5 **D.** you are a shadow briefly laid upon a
W-pI.132.17:1 say whenever you are tempted to **d.** the
W-pI...133.7:2 when you **d.** his right to everything, you
W-pI......165.h Let not my mind **d.** the Thought of God.
W-pI...165.3:1 Who would **d.** his safety and his peace,
W-pI...165.4:1 **D.** not Heaven. It is yours today, but for
W-pI...166.3:3 He must **d.** their presence, contradict the
W-pI...167.2:7 acknowledge death. And thus **d.** you live.
W-pI.167.10:1 of the truth, and not **d.** our holy heritage.
W-pI...178.1:1 Let not my mind **d.** the Thought of God.
W-pI...182.2:3 Others will **d.** that they are sad, and do
W-pI...182.2:5 **d.** he understands the words we speak?
W-pI...184.4:4 it must overcome, conflict with and **d.**.
W-pI...186.2:5 and not **d.** with self-deceiving arrogance
W-pI...186.3:5 And what could arrogance **d.** but this?
W-pI...186.3:7 that would **d.** the Call for God Himself.
W-pI...188.2:4 **d.** the presence of what he beholds in him
W-pI...190.6:6 you **d.** a little corner of your mind its own
W-pI...191.2:3 **D.** your own Identity, and this is what
W-pI...191.3:1 **D.** your own Identity, and you will not
W-pI...191.3:2 **D.** your own Identity, and you assail the
W-pI...191.3:3 **D.** your own Identity, and look on evil,
W-pI.192.10:4 **D.** him not. His Father's Love for him
W-pI.193.13:7 **d.** the little steps He asks you take to Him.
W-pI...196.2:4 and **d.** the meaning they appear to have.
W-pI...197.2:2 do. **D.** your strength, and weakness must
WpI rVI.in.5:3 one, **d.** its hold and hasten to assure your
W-pII..228.1:2 Shall I **d.** His knowledge, and believe in
W-pII..276.1:6 us. **D.** we were created in His Love and we
W-pII..276.1:6 created in His Love and we **d.** our Self, to
W-pII..309.1:3 to **d.** my Father's Will is to deny my own.
W-pII..309.1:3 to deny my Father's Will is to **d.** my own.
M-20..........3:3 is, for anger must **d.** that peace exists.
P-3........III.8:8 **D.** him entrance, and you have denied the
S-3........IV.8:8 Do not **d.** to Christ what is His Own.

## denying 45

T-2......III.5:10 starves you by **d.** you your daily bread.
T-2......IV.3:12 to protect the mind by **d.** the unmindful.
T-2......IV.3:13 power, one is also **d.** the power itself.
T-2.........V.5:4 By **d.** your mind any destructive potential
T-3.........II.3:3 effect of **d.** the power of the miracle. The
T-4........IV.2:8 **D.** this and thinking otherwise has held
T-7.......VII.1:8 why **d.** any part of it means you have lost
T-7.....VII.10:2 as your will, or you are **d.** what you are.
T-7.........X.2:7 and you are **d.** His Kingdom *and* yours.
T-7.........X.8:3 and do not accept His Will, you are **d.** joy.
T-7......XI.3:11 are literally **d.** Heaven to yourself.
T-7........XI.6:8 are **d.** yours and that of God Who created
T-8.........II.6:6 Deny yourself this and you are **d.** God His
T-8........IV.1:8 because you are **d.** yourself everything.
T-8........IV.3:8 you are **d.** the world and accepting God.
T-8........IV.7:4 by **d.** the Father you deny yourself. I will
T-9........I.11:1 waste of energy you expend in **d.** truth.
T-10.......II.4:1 When you attack, you are **d.** yourself.
T-10......III.3:5 of the truth about himself, which he is **d.**.
T-10......III.7:3 merely by **d.** them completely in himself.
T-10.......V.2:5 your brothers without it, you are **d.** God.
T-10.....V.13:1 God did not create or you are **d.** Him. His
T-11.........I.8:4 By **d.** this you deny your own will, and
T-11.......I.10:6 hide in darkness, **d.** that the light is in you
T-11......III.4:9 it is only because you are **d.** the light. But
T-11......IV.1:7 you are **d.** Him His place in His Own altar
T-11.......V.2:4 can be dispelled merely by **d.** their reality.
T-11...VIII.9:2 for by **d.** that his mind is split you will
T-12.......II.1:3 them, but which they are **d.** to themselves
T-12.......II.9:5 it, and not by **d.** its full import in any way
T-12......III.4:4 Why would you insist in **d.** him? For to
T-12......VI.1:5 costs you the world's reality by **d.** yours,
T-13.......V.8:5 see, for sight of it depends upon **d.** vision.
T-13.......V.8:6 **d.** vision it does not follow you cannot see
T-16.......II.6:8 to it, and **d.** the evidence for truth? For
T-16.....V.14:3 And to the same extent you are **d.** truth,
T-21.....II.11:4 you are **d.** your Creator and believing that
T-21....VI.7:11 you will lay down the burden of **d.** truth.
T-22.........I.3:5 **D.** what you are, and firm in faith that
W-pI.....84.4:2 *This is no justification for* **d.** *my Self. I will*
W-pI...133.7:3 things you really have, **d.** they are there.
W-pI.160.10:5 Who denies his brother is **d.** Him, and
W-pI...165.1:4 your choice to see it not, **d.** it is there?
W-pI.185.11:2 longer by **d.** to himself what is God's Will.
W-pI...190.3:6 **d.** love and using pain to prove that God

## depart 15

T-2........III.3:3 you cannot **d.** entirely from your Creator,
T-4.........in.2:6 unwilling to **d.** from its Foundation.
T-5........IV.8:7 You can indeed **d.** in peace because I have
T-14....XI.13:3 think you know, peace will **d.** from you,
T-15.......II.6:6 that will **d.** from you in this practice, for it
T-18.........I.7:3 into the mad world and so **d.** from you.
T-18......VI.1:3 not **d.** from it nor leave it separate from
T-18...VIII.9:6 but they will not **d.** as they had come,
T19...IV.A.4:3 no more **d.** from you than from God. Fear
T-31....IV.10:2 He could no more **d.** from them than they
W-pI.....61.4:3 to the truth, and helps you **d.** in peace,
W-pI...188.9:5 them, ordering that they **d.** from us. But
W-pII..226.1:1 If I so choose, I can **d.** this world entirely.
W-pII..226.1:4 or search for as a goal, it will **d.** from me.
S-3.........II.4:4 the world and it is ready to **d.** in peace,

## departing 1

T-13....III.11:3 by **d.** in peace and returning to the Father

## departs 3

W-pII..285.1:4 loss avail me if insanity **d.** from me today,
W-pII..305.1:3 world **d.** in silence as this peace envelops
M-14.........5:8 In blessing it **d.**, for it will not end as it

## depend 33

T-1.........I.19:2 **d.** on cooperation because the Sonship is
T-2...........I.4:8 This release does not **d.** on illusions. The
T-3........VI.9:5 Its existence does not **d.** on your ability to
T-5........IV.5:4 because by so doing you can **d.** on it.
T-6.......V.C.8:3 Kingdom does not **d.** on your perception,
T-7.........X.1:10 it **d.** on what you believe about your mind
T-8........VIII.6:2 extreme need to **d.** on external guidance.
T-13.....VII.5:8 Being does not **d.** upon your recognition.
T-14......XI.7:2 means on which you can **d.** for miracles
T-14......XI.8:6 are unable to **d.** on miracles to answer all
T-20......III.2:2 that all relationships **d.** upon adjustments
T-21....III.11:9 on the absence of the other does each **d.**.
T-21.......V.8:9 of it. Knowledge does not **d.** on it, and
T-24.....VII.8:7 to which it must **d.** on what you see it for.
T-25......VI.5:9 him, for on his part does all the plan **d.**.
T-25......IX.5:5 For miracles **d.** on justice. Not as it is seen
T-27.....VII.7:7 them, and their reality does not **d.** on him
T-28.......V.6:3 Reality does not **d.** on this. There is no
T-30......II.5:2 the earth but must **d.** on your decision,
T-30......III.9:2 perfect purity does not **d.** on whether it is
T-31......IV.8:4 All choices in the world **d.** on this; you
T-31......VI.1:6 On this one choice does all your world **d.**,
W-pI.....30.5:1 but it does not **d.** on the body's eyes at all.
W-pI.....77.2:2 It does not **d.** on any magical powers you
W-pI.....81.3:4 sight. My acceptance does not **d.** on my
W-pI...108.4:1 truth does not **d.** on which is seen as first,
W-pI...126.5:4 allow the world's salvation to **d.** on this?
W-pI.135.11:4 not **d.** upon itself for anything except its
W-pII.....in.1:2 but as guides on which we do not now **d.**.
M-8...........4:7 it is on this that judgments of the world **d.**
M-16..........3:6 must **d.** on the teacher of God himself. He
M-29.........6:1 the Holy Spirit does not **d.** on your words.
C-in...........2:4 since they **d.** on belief and can therefore

## dependability 1

T-6.........V.4:2 call, and His **d.** makes them more certain.

## dependable 4

T-5........IV.5:5 Make it **d.** in my name because my name
T-25.....VII.1:8 foundation sure as love, **d.** as Heaven,
T-25...VII.10:1 What is **d.** except God's Love? And where
W-pI.....53.3:3 Nothing in madness is **d.**. It holds out no

## dependably 2

W-pI...126.5:1 no grounds on which to rest **d.** and sure.
M-25.........5:6 a genuine ability, and cannot be used **d.**.

## depended 4

T-9.........I.11:4 God could not will that happiness **d.** on
T-15.......V.4:4 cannot be **d.** on because it is not perfect.
W-pI...107.4:3 as it always was, to be **d.** on in every need,
M-8...........4:8 and senseless "reasoning" be **d.** on for

## dependence 6

T-1.........V.3:4 fully recognize your complete **d.** on God,
T-2.......V.10:4 perceptions clearly imply their **d.** on time,
T-3........III.2:8 change, their **d.** on time is obvious. How
T-11.......V.6:2 function lies in your complete **d.** on God,
T-11.......V.6:7 you the knowledge of your **d.** on God, in
T-18....VIII.4:4 changes its total **d.** on them for its being.

## dependency 1

T-11.......V.6:8 The ego sees all **d.** as threatening, and has

## dependent 7

*See also* time-dependent

T-2........III.5:6 creations are completely **d.** on Each Other
T-7.....VIII.4:6 are. Yet its existence is **d.** on your mind,
T-11.......V.6:3 became as **d.** on you as you are on Him.
T-11.....V.12:1 God is as **d.** on you as you are on Him,
T-18....VIII.5:3 no means totally **d.** on its one Creator for
T-22.......I.4:10 **d.** on the self you think you made to lead
T-22.........I.8:7 **d.** on the holiness of your relationship to

## depending 11

T-7........VI.1:5 **d.** on whether the ego or the Holy Spirit
T-7.....VIII.1:9 scarcity, **d.** on how you choose to apply it.
T-8........III.5:9 joy, **d.** on which teacher you are following
T-11.....V.18:1 the ego, **d.** on what you perceive in him.
T-13......VI.4:1 **d.** on whose interpretation of it you use.
T-28........II.4:3 **d.** on the purpose of your dreaming. Do
T-28......IV.1:9 **d.** on whose evil dream you share. You
T-29....VIII.8:3 each **d.** on the one of whom the question
T-31...VII.12:6 **d.** only on the simple choice of whether
M-22.........2:1 or rapid, **d.** on whether he recognizes the
C-1.............5:1 wrong, **d.** on the voice to which it listens.

## depends 70

T-1......VI.1:10 **d.** on your perception of what you are.
T-2..........II.2:4 Your right mind **d.** on it. Denial of error
T-2........III.5:7 He **d.** on them *because* He created them
T-4........III.3:2 and its continued existence **d.** on your
T-4.......VII.1:4 ego, because the ego **d.** on the concrete.
T-5..........II.6:6 Choosing **d.** on a split mind. The Holy
T-7..........II.3:9 that the increase of the Kingdom **d.** on it,
T-7......VIII.5:2 It **d.** on your mind, and as you made it by
T-7.........X.2:4 ability to see a logical outcome **d.** on the
T-9......VIII.6:1 The ego **d.** solely on your willingness to
T-10......IV.2:2 acceptance **d.** on your willingness to have
T-11.........I.7:5 Your ability to accept Him **d.** on your
T-11........II.7:4 freedom, for it still **d.** on how you see it.
T-11........II.7:7 Real freedom **d.** on welcoming reality,
T-11....VIII.3:8 Yet your willingness to learn of Him **d.** on
T-12.........I.9:6 denial **d.** on the belief in what is denied
T-13.........I.8:3 and thus **d.** on one-dimensional time,
T-13........II.4:4 for its existence **d.** on keeping this secret.
T-13.......V.8:1 Vision **d.** on light. You cannot see in
T-13.......V.8:5 see, for sight of it **d.** upon denying vision.

T-13.....VII.2:2 of seeing, and **d.** on what you cherish.
T-14....... II.1:5 learning goal **d.** means absolutely nothing
T-15....... II.1:10 one, so its oneness **d.** not on time at all.
T-15......IV.5:3 mind of the host of God **d.** on willingness,
T-15......VII.4:4 Yet its survival **d.** on your belief that you
T-17....... III.9:3 the choice **d.** on which you value more.
T-18....... IX.4:5 which **d.** on keeping it not seen. The
T-19.........I.3:3 or sickness **d.** entirely on how the mind
T19. IV.A.10:4 the end of guilt, as surely as fear **d.** on it.
T19. IV.A.12:2 And this **d.** on which emotion was called
T-20....... II.2:4 And every gift it offers **d.** on what it wants
T-21...... II.12:5 **d.** entirely upon the madness of its maker
T-21..... III.11:7 one with what **d.** on darkness to be seen.
T-21....... V.1:8 choice **d.** far more than you may realize as
T-21....... V.1:9 **d.** entirely your whole belief in what you
T-21....... V.8:6 for it **d.** entirely on reason's absence. The
T-22....... III.2:1 ego's whole continuance **d.** on its belief
T-22.... VI.10:1 your learning **d.** the welfare of the world.
T-24.........I.6:5 for it **d.** on goals that you alone can reach.
T-25....... V.1:5 Each **d.** upon the other for whatever sense
T-25..... VII.1:4 And on its changelessness the world **d.**.
T-25..... VII.4:6 that this belief **d.** upon the form it takes.
T-25.... VIII.6:7 Their world **d.** on sin's stability. And they
T-28...... IV.3:2 himself, for your Identity **d.** on his reality.
T-29...... III.1:5 On saving you **d.** his happiness. For who
T-29...... IV.1:3 dreams are dreams; and that escape **d.**,
T-30........in.1:3 can be reached **d.** on this one thing alone;
T-30........I.10:2 believe your happiness **d.** on being right.
T-31.........I.3:3 by it, and even now **d.** on nothing else.
T-31...... V.11:3 concept of the world **d.** upon this concept
W-pI........7.2:1 and **d.** on your not learning these new
W-pI......20.1:5 The salvation of the world **d.** on it. Yet
W-pI......80.1:4 thus **d.** on recognizing this one problem,
W-pI... 108.1:1 Vision **d.** upon today's idea. The light is
W-pI... 138.5:1 Choosing **d.** on learning. And the truth
W-pI. 169.11:4 For your part is still what all the rest **d.** on
W-pI...... 186.h Salvation of the world **d.** on me.
W-pI... 186.5:4 your part, and that the whole **d.** on you,
W-pI... 186.7:4 Salvation of the world **d.** on you, and not
W-pI. 186.14:5 Salvation of the world **d.** on you who can
W-pI... 192.8:6 that the way to liberty **d.** for both of them
W-pI... 196.7:3 you fear, and your deliverance **d.** on you.
W-pI... 206.1:1 (186) Salvation of the world **d.** on me. *I*
W-pII . 350.1:3 *Your memory* ***d.*** *on his forgiveness. What*
M-5 ....... II.1:7 as you perceive it **d.** on the body being the
M-16 ......... 8:3 success **d.** on his conviction that he will
M-19 ......... 1:5 world, however, forgiveness **d.** on justice,
M-24 ......... 1:5 And that **d.**, of course, on what it is used
P-2........ III.2:4 Now the extent of their success **d.** on how
S-2.........I.10:5 The level of your prayer **d.** on this, for

## depicts 1

T-27.... VIII.7:2 world you see **d.** exactly what you thought

## deprecating 1

W-pI... 195.1:4 How pitiful and **d.** are such thoughts! For

## depreciate 2

T-2......... V.3:2 The right-minded neither exalt nor **d.** the
T-7........ VI.3:6 power of this source, it is forced to **d.** it.

## depreciated 1

T-2....... VII.1:5 you if I **d.** the power of your own thinking

## depreciating 2

T-3....... VII.2:1 resolve the authority problem by **d.** the
T-9......... V.4:3 by **d.** the importance of the dreamer. This

## depressed 7

T-8....... VII.8:2 adequacy suffers, and he must become **d.**.
T-10...... V.12:3 wholly joyous, it is blasphemous to feel **d.**
T-28....... II.6:8 of himself as sick or well, **d.** or happy, but
W-pI....... 5.7:5 *I am not* ***d.*** *about for the reason I think.*
W-pI..... 35.6:3 *I see myself as* ***d.***. *I see myself as failing. I see*
W-pI..... 71.8:3 to become **d.** or angry at the second part;
W-pI... 129.1:2 else to hope for, you will only be **d.**. Our

## depressing 7

T-7 ..... VI.13:1 this **d.** state the Holy Spirit reminds you
T-8 ...... VII.8:3 situation is the most **d.** thing in the world
T-8 ...... VII.8:4 it is ultimately why the world itself is **d.**.
T-8 ...... VII.8:5 The Holy Spirit's curriculum is never **d.**,
T-12 ...... V.8:1 curriculum you set yourself is **d.** indeed, it
T-29 .... VII.7:2 like the past, and but a series of **d.** dreams
W-pI... 181.4:3 have also been dismayed by the **d.** and

## depression 37

T-4 ....... IV.3:2 **D.** comes from a sense of being deprived
T-8 ...... VII.1:6 with a body you will always experience **d.**.
T-8 ...... VII.8:6 Whenever the reaction to learning is **d.**, it
T-8 .... VII.13:1 The opposite of joy is **d.**. When your
T-8 .... VII.13:2 your learning promotes **d.** instead of joy,
T-9 ........I.14:4 anxiety, **d.** and ultimately panic, because
T-10 ...... V.1:2 for **d.** is the sign of allegiance to him.
T-10 ...... V.1:3 **D.** means that you have forsworn God.
T-10 ...... V.2:5 It is the denial of the spark that brings **d.**,
T-10 ...... V.4:2 of his **d.** he made the god of depression.
T-10 ...... V.4:2 of his depression he made the god of **d.**.
T-10 ...... V.5:8 is. **D.** is isolation, and so it could not have
T-12 ...... III.6:3 What he experiences then is **d.** or anger,
T-12 ...... IV.4:1 but lead to a sense of futility and **d.**? To
T-12 ...... V.8:4 This resignation will not lead to **d.**. It is
T-17 ... VIII.4:5 else" produced was sorrow and **d.**,
T19.. IV.B.11:6 grounds for **d.** and disillusionment, and
T-21 ...... V.2:4 afraid. You will experience **d.**, a sense of
T-27 ......I.6:11 **D.** speaks of death, and vanity of real
T-29 .... IV.3:3 **D.** or assault must be the theme of every
T-31 .... VII.6:2 you to a bitter sense of deep **d.** and futility
W-pI....... 5.1:3 The upset may seem to be fear, worry, **d.**,
W-pI....... 6.1:2 **d.** and so on) and the perceived source
W-pI..... 26.6:2 The concern may take the form of **d.**,
W-pI..... 34.6:1 generalized adverse emotions, such as **d.**,
W-pI..... 34.6:4 *I can replace my feelings of* ***d.***, *anxiety or*
W-pI..... 39.6:2 form they appear; uneasiness, **d.**, anger,
W-pI..... 41.1:2 **D.** is an inevitable consequence of
W-pI..... 47.2:2 and to justify fear, anxiety, **d.**, anger and
W-pI..... 71.8:5 They have led to **d.** and anger; but God's
W-pI..... 79.5:3 and **d.** are inevitable as you regard them.
W-pI... 194.2:1 anxiety, all pits of hell, all blackness of **d.**,
W-pI... 194.3:1 one instant is **d.** felt, or pain experienced
W-pII . 257.1:3 without deep distress and great **d.**. Let us
M-6 ........... 1:7 healing might precipitate intense **d.**, and
M-17 ......... 1:7 be sure as well that he has asked for **d.**,
M-18 ......... 1:3 **D.** is then inevitable, for he has "proved,"

## deprivation 14

T-1 ........I.42:1 your false sense of isolation, **d.** and lack.
T-1 ....... IV.4:8 the belief in **d.** in favor of the abundance
T-7 ..... VIII.1:8 To the ego it is the law of **d.**. It therefore
T-11 ..... IV.5:1 of you and you blame them for your **d.**,
T-11 ... VIII.6:6 guidance of the Holy Spirit is to ask for **d.**.
T-15 ..... XI.5:5 is the belief in the reality of the **d.**?
T-15 ..... XI.5:6 **D.** breeds attack, being the belief that
T-15 ..... XI.5:7 And as long as you would retain the **d.**,
T-16 .... VII.2:9 Do not seek to lay the blame for **d.** on it,
T-21 ... III.11:4 But "good" and "**d.**" are opposites, and
W-pI..... 58.5:5 or **d.** or pain because of Who I am. My
W-pI... 155.5:1 and **d.** both are quickly left behind. This
W-pI... 155.7:2 For sacrifice and **d.** are paths that lead
W-pI... 165.6:6 and **d.** cannot cut him off from God's

## deprivations 1

T-16 .... VII.1:3 injustices and **d.** all enter into the special

## deprive 16

T-1 ....... VI.1:8 all. Needs arise only when you **d.** yourself.
T-5 ........in.1:7 thus **d.** others of the joy of responding
T-7 ....... IX.1:2 no more wills you to **d.** yourself of your
T-7 ....... IX.1:2 than He wills to **d.** Himself of His. Do not
T-8 ..........I.3:1 a call to war, and war does **d.** you of peace
T-9 ..... VIII.8:2 will therefore **d.** you of the true witnesses
T-11 ........I.9:3 to give, and thus **d.** you of what you want.
T-11 ..... IV.4:1 *Only you can* ***d.*** *yourself of anything.* Do not
T-13 ........I.8:4 guilt must **d.** you of the appreciation of
T-17 ..... IV.2:3 not **d.** you of your special relationships,
T-21 ... III.11:3 You think He would **d.** you for your good.
T-23 .....II.12:9 He would **d.** you of the secret ingredient
T-25 . VIII.14:7 will **d.** yourself of what God's justice has
T-25 ..... IX.8:3 Seek to **d.**, and you have been deprived. A
T-26 .. VII.19:9 To get from one is to **d.** them all. And yet
T-28 ..... III.9:4 And no one is deprived or can **d.**. Here is

## deprived 33

T-1 .........V.3:7 If they believe they are **d.** of anything,
T-4 ....... IV.3:2 of being **d.** of something you want and do
T-4 ....... IV.3:3 Remember that you are **d.** of nothing
T-7 ...... VII.1:1 deny a blessing to a brother *you* will feel **d.**
T-7 ...... VII.3:2 The ego's picture of you is **d.**, unloving
T-7 ...... VII.7:6 attack because they believe they are **d.**.
T-7 ...... VII.8:3 it. This makes you feel **d.** of it, and by
T-8 ....... VI.3:2 not because he is **d.** of anything else, but
T-12 ..... III.6:2 who identifies with the ego feels **d.**. What
T-15 ..... IX.2:5 order to have meaning, and **d.** of meaning
T-15 ..... XI.5:1 will you perceive yourself as lonely and **d.**.
T-15 ..... XI.8:3 than to perceive we are **d.** of nothing?
T-16 .......V.9:2 for only the **d.** could value specialness.
T-16 .... VII.2:7 give you what you think the past **d.** you of
T-16 .... VII.3:5 escape from the past it sees itself **d.** of the
T-17 ... IV.15:5 without value and entirely **d.** of meaning.
T-17 .. VII.3:11 as if you had been unjustly **d.** of it.
T-20 ... VIII.6:9 of your salvation, will be **d.** of meaning,
T-21 ........I.4:9 that they are incomplete and bitterly **d.**.
T-25 . VIII.13:8 another's due, because he thinks he is **d.**.
T-25 ..... IX.4:6 loser; no one left unfairly treated and **d.**,
T-25 ..... IX.8:3 Seek to deprive, and you have been **d.**. A
T-26 .. VII.17:3 So is attack **d.** of its effects, and hate is
T-26 .......X.3:3 idea you are **d.** by someone not yourself.
T-26 .......X.3:7 more unjust than that he be **d.** of what he
T-26 .......X.6:3 way. And so you see yourself **d.** of light,
T-27 ........I.3:1 consent to suffer pain, to be **d.**, unfairly
T-28 ........I.12:4 because He would not be **d.** of His Effects.
T-28 ........II.8:1 the dream the Father was **d.** of His Effects,
T-28 ..... III.9:4 And no one is **d.** or can deprive. Here is a
W-pI ..... 41.4:1 can never be **d.** of your perfect holiness
W-pI ..... 72.6:5 let yourself be **d.** of what the body offers.
W-pI .. 100.6:2 and all the world is thus **d.** of joy, along

## deprives 2

T-7 .........V.9:8 every time it **d.** someone of something, it
T-16 ... IV.10:3 **d.** you of knowledge for fantasies are the

## depriving 5

T-7 ..... VI.13:1 God, and are therefore **d.** yourself of joy.
T-7 ...... VII.8:1 a means of **d.** you of something you want.
T-11 .......V.8:5 are belittling yourself and **d.** yourself of
T-25 .......V.4:8 you are **d.** him of all the joy he would have
W-pI .. 170.3:2 thought at war with you, **d.** you of peace,

## depth 4

T-13 .......II.8:5 Make no mistake about the **d.** of this fear.
W-pI ..... 99.6:6 their **d.** or any attribute they seem to have
W-pI .. 139.6:2 are. This is the **d.** of madness. Yet it is the
W-pI 183.11:6 and yet exceeds in **d.** and height whatever

## depths 1

T-24 ..... III.6:6 release your brother from the **d.** of hell,

## derive 1

T-26 .. VII.15:2 And from their purpose they **d.** whatever

**derives** 3

T-3........IV.5:9 spirit that it **d.** its whole power to make
T-5........III.9:1 **d.** meaning from relationships. Those you
T-17...VII.8:13 relationship, and **d.** its meaning from it.

**descend** 2

T-18.......V.7:6 *Holy Spirit, that His blessing may* **d.** *on us,*
T-25......III.7:9 to see peace and forgiveness **d.** on them,

**descends** 4

T-24......VI.1:1 peace **d.** on it in gentleness and blessing
W-pI...168.6:1 And He **d.** to meet us, as we come to Him
M-11..........4:7 And peace **d.** on it in joyous answer.
M-19........5:12 The peace of God **d.** on all the world, and

**descent** 6

T-10......IV.8:5 was a **d.** from magnitude to littleness. But
T-23.....II.21:6 whole **d.** from Heaven lies in each one.
T-23.....II.22:1 take not one step in the **d.** to hell. For
T-28.....II.12:7 of every step in the **d.** to separation, until
W-pI.....44.5:6 eyes, it is loss of identity and a **d.** into hell
P-2........IV.3:1 The **d.** into hell follows step by step in an

**describable** 1

T-24.....VII.6:8 To no one here is this **d.**. Nor is there any

**describe** 8

T-1.........II.2:2 attempt to **d.** it in words is impossible.
T-22.........I.2:2 strange idea which it does accurately **d.**,
W-pI.....34.1:1 idea for today begins to **d.** the conditions
W-pI.....35.1:1 does not **d.** the way you see yourself now.
W-pI.....35.1:2 however, **d.** what vision will show you. It
W-pI.....61.1:4 not **d.** the self-concept you have made. It
W-pII....14.2:4 we are is not for words to speak of nor **d.**.
M-5........II.1:9 such terms merely state or **d.** the problem

**described** 10

T-5...........I.4:3 He is also **d.** as something "separate,"
T-6........I.15:4 have **d.** my reactions to Judas as they did,
T-8........VI.9:9 It cannot be **d.** and it cannot be explained
T-22.......VI.2:4 confusion, so profound it cannot be **d.**,
W-pI...122.8:4 you will remember then can never be **d.**.
C-1.............2:4 **d.** in the course *as if* it has two parts; spirit
C-6.............2:1 Holy Spirit is **d.** throughout the course as
C-6.............3:1 The Holy Spirit is **d.** as the remaining
P-1.............3:2 are often **d.** as "self-destructive," and the
S-1.........II.8:7 beyond learning, this state cannot be **d.**.

**describes** 3

W-pI.....22.1:1 Today's idea accurately **d.** the way
W-pI.....35.3:2 it **d.** you as you must really be in truth.
W-pI.....95.1:1 idea accurately **d.** you as God created you.

**describing** 2

T-4.........II.8:1 way of **d.** how it thinks it originated. This
W-pI.....25.3:1 Another way of **d.** the goals you now

**description** 3

T-22.........I.2:1 we have heard a very similar **d.** earlier,
W-in..........3:3 followed by a **d.** of the specific procedures
W-pI.......5.1:2 using the **d.** of the feeling in whatever

**descriptive** 5

W-pI.....12.3:2 whatever **d.** terms happen to occur to you
W-pI.....35.4:1 of **d.** terms in which you see yourself.
W-pI.....35.5:2 self-inflating **d.** terms may well cross your
W-pI.....35.7:3 identify the **d.** term or terms you feel are
WpI..rV.in4:2 and more **d.** of the holy Self we share and

**desecrate** 1

T-4.......VII.4:7 Do not **d.** it or recoil from it. It is your

**desert** 12

T-12.........I.1:7 to attack you or **d.** you or enslave you,
T-13.......in.2:8 seem to love, yet they **d.** and are deserted.
T-14....XI.14:3 can **d.** Him but He will never reciprocate,
T-16.........I.4:3 He will not **d.** you, but be sure that you
T-16.........I.4:3 you, but be sure that you **d.** not Him.
T-18... VIII.8:6 Look at the **d.** –dry and unproductive,
T-18... VIII.9:3 The **d.** becomes a garden, green and deep
T-18... VIII.9:4 by love for them where once a **d.** was.
T-18. VIII.10:3 So will it grow and stretch across the **d.**,
T19...IV.D.6:3 of the ego you swore in blood not to **d.**, all
W-pI...186.9:6 off. Or like mirages seen above a **d.**, rising
W-pI...200.9:5 He will not **d.** His Son in need, nor let him

**desert's** 1

T-18. VIII.13:2 and the **d.** dust still seems to cloud your

**deserted** 2

T-12... VIII.6:4 the instant you thought you had **d.** Him.
T-13.......in.2:8 seem to love, yet they desert and are **d.**.

**deserts** 1

T-26.......X.3:4 perceived to be unfair and not your just **d.**

**deserve** 10

T-12...VII.14:4 to God and therefore **d.** death. You will
T-25... VIII.8:2 and give them all the honor they **d.** and
T-25... VIII.9:5 Own justice does He recognize all you **d.**,
T-25... VIII.9:6 hold out to you the gifts the innocent **d.**.
T-28.........I.9:3 It can **d.** but laughter, when you learn you
T-28......VI.3:9 thus **d.** your hatred for the limitations
T-31......III.2:5 you are guilty, and must give as you **d.**.
T-31......III.2:6 And what can you **d.** but what you are? If
W-pI...126.4:5 him by giving him what he does not **d.**,
S-2.........II.3:3 and **d.** the retribution of the wrath of God

**deserved** 2

T-2......VIII.3:3 you may think that punishment is **d.**.
T-31......III.2:7 If you did not believe that you **d.** attack, it

**deserves** 10

T-13.......in.4:4 He **d.** only love because he has given only
T-23.......II.4:1 sin, and therefore **d.** attack and death.
T-25.......IX.6:1 No one **d.** to lose. And what would be
T-25.......IX.6:4 someone **d.** to suffer more and others less
T-26.......II.5:3 he **d.** no mercy from the God of justice.
T-27.......II.3:2 what has been done to you **d.** no pardon.
T-31........V.3:1 provide the love and shelter innocence **d.**.
W-pI.....91.9:3 a belief that is mistaken and **d.** no faith.
W-pI.192.10:2 The Son of God **d.** your mercy. It is he
M-4......IX.1:8 Nothing but that really **d.** the name. Yet

**deserving** 9

T-12...VII.13:2 criminal, as **d.** of death as God knows you
T-12...VII.13:2 of death as God knows you are **d.** of life.
T-13.......in.1:2 as unworthy of love and **d.** of punishment
T-14....III.11:9 not decide whether or not you are **d.** of it.
T-15.........I.6:7 For no one who considers himself as **d.** of
T-19......III.2:3 for what is **d.** punishment must have been
T-25......IX.7:2 and kept apart from others as less **d.**, then
T-26.........I.6:6 die each time you see in him a sin **d.** death
W-pI.155.12:3 way be holier, or more **d.** of your effort, of

**design** 2

T-28.......II.6:2 and no **d.** exists that could be found and
W-pI...136.9:2 and God's **d.** for the salvation of His Son

**designate** 1

W-pI...184.1:5 By this you **d.** its special attributes, and

**designed** 4

T-16.....V.15:4 experience, **d.** to lead away from truth
T-25.....VII.9:2 function is **d.** to be perceived as possible,
W-pI.153.12:2 It was **d.** by One Who loves His children,
S-2..........II.1:4 the **d.** comparison cannot be missed, nor

**desirable** 27

T-4........VI.5:5 becomes **d.** as he changes his mind about
T-6......V.B.8:4 and one has been chosen as more **d.**.
T-6......V.B.8:5 the term "more **d.**" still implies that the
T-6......V.B.8:5 desirable" still implies that the **d.** has
T-6......V.C.3:3 the identification of what is more **d.**. This
T-6......V.C.3:4 between the **d.** and the undesirable. It
T-7.........V.7:2 receiving something equally **d.** in return.
T-7.......VI.12:1 you have not judged sanity as wholly **d.**. If
T-7......VII.11:2 wholly real, wholly perfect and wholly **d.**.
T-7.........X.4:5 you, and one which is both fearful and **d.**.
T-7........XI.1:7 the ego perceives nothing as wholly **d.**. By
T-8...........I.1:9 you do not yet regard this as wholly **d.**. If
T-10.....V.14:2 to you to be **d.** the concept of choice,
T-13......IV.3:1 it not be more **d.** to have been wrong,
T-13......IV.3:6 might it not be more **d.** than death? You
T-14.....VII.4:1 on bringing what is undesirable to the **d.**;
T-19......III.1:6 be corrected, and yet will be forever **d.**. As
W-pI.....35.4:2 positive or negative, **d.** or undesirable,
W-pI.....40.1:3 every ten minutes would be highly **d.**, and
W-pI.133.12:1 all, entirely **d.** or not worth the slightest
M-4.....I.A.5:2 If this is interpreted as giving up the **d.**, it
M-4.....I.A.8:9 change tranquility for something more **d.**
M-4...I.A.8:10 What could be more **d.** than this?
M-8...........1:5 of as more **d.** by the world's standards,
M-8.........3:11 is seen is real or illusory, **d.** or undesirable
M-16.........5:6 to sleep is a **d.** time to devote to God. It
M-25............h ARE "PSYCHIC" POWERS **D.**?

**desire** 106

T-2....V.A.13:2 of error with anything except a **d.** to heal
T-2.......VII.7:4 is usually some degree of **d.** to accomplish
T-3........VI.9:1 Only those who give over all **d.** to reject
T-3......VI.11:4 of reality by the unstable scales of **d.**.
T-4.........in.2:6 The ego may **d.** them, but spirit cannot
T-6......V.B.8:8 To **d.** wholly is to create, and creating
T-10.........I.4:1 everything the instant you **d.** it wholly,
T-10.........I.4:1 it wholly, for if to **d.** wholly is to create,
T-10.........I.4:2 but only the **d.** to waken and be glad.
T-12......III.9:5 it is governed by the **d.** to be unlike God,
T-12......III.9:5 to be unlike God, and this **d.** is not will.
T-12...VII.15:1 are tempted to yield to the **d.** for death,
T-12....VIII.5:3 the insane **d.** to control reality. You who
T-13......III.1:6 your **d.** to attack that really frightens you.
T-15......IV.2:2 you is but as far away as your **d.** for it. As
T-15......IV.2:3 you **d.** it not and cherish littleness instead
T-15...VII.14:6 for there is no **d.** to exclude anyone from
T-15....VIII.2:3 cast aside, but still **d.** with all your heart.
T-18....III.4:13 That wish was the **d.** to be holy. The Will
T-18....III.4:15 For you **d.** the only thing you ever had, or
T-18......III.5:1 and will strengthen your **d.** to reach it.
T-18......III.5:2 it. And in your **d.** lies its accomplishment.
T-18......III.5:3 Your **d.** is now in complete accord with
T-18......III.5:4 **d.** from His Will and from His strength. I
T-18......III.7:4 are made whole in our **d.** to make whole.
T-18......III.7:7 the **d.** for love without love's joining them
T-18......III.8:4 of your **d.** the power of God Himself, can
T-18......IV.1:3 The **d.** and the willingness to let it come
T-18.......V.7:3 *I d. this holy instant for myself, that I may*
T-18....VI.14:2 your **d.** for it is the irresistible appeal the
T-18.....VII.4:3 Release is given you the instant you **d.** it.
T19......IV.A.h First Obstacle: The **D.** to Get Rid of It
T19....IV.A.1:1 must flow across is your **d.** to get rid of it.
T19....IV.B.1:1 the obstacle of your **d.** to get rid of it.
T19...IV.D.5:3 The **d.** to get rid of peace and drive the
T19...IV.D.7:6 No mad **d.**, no trivial impulse to forget
T-20.....VII.5:6 to wish, for sight is always secondary to **d.**.

T-20....VIII.1:2 Truth is restored to you through your d.,
T-20....VIII.1:2 to you through your d. for something else
T-20....VIII.1:6 D. now its whole undoing, and it is done
T-20....VIII.2:9 given, waiting on your d. but to receive it.
T-20....VIII.3:2 for it with real d. and sincerity of purpose
T-20....VIII.3:5 is. It is his d. to see his sinlessness, as it is
T-21....... II.8:6 or not. Faith and d. go hand in hand, for
T-21....... II.9:5 you d., you will see. And if its reality is
T-21..... II.10:4 of your d. to create your own creator, and
T-21..... II.10:5 This is the same d.. The Son is the Effect,
T-21...... III.6:7 and believing in it because of your d..
T-21...... III.8:3 d. to look upon their brothers in holiness,
T-21...... IV.1:9 witnesses to your d. that it *be* there to see.
T-21.... VI.11:5 Son can be imprisoned save by his own d.
T-21.... VI.11:6 And it is by his own d. that he is freed.
T-21...VII.5:11 *I d. a world I rule instead of one that rules me*
T-21...VII.5:12 *Do I d. a world where I am powerful instead*
T-21...VII.5:13 *Do I d. a world in which I have no enemies*
T-21...VII.10:6 can d. a world you rule that rules you not,
T-21...VII.10:7 You can d. to exchange your helplessness
T-21...VII.10:7 and lose this same d. as a little glint of sin
T-21...VII.10:8 the body's eyes and change what you d..
T-21...VII.11:4 constancy in your d. to see the real world,
T-21...VII.11:4 so the d. becomes the only one you have.
T-21...VII.13:5 The power of the Son of God's d. remains
T-21...VII.13:6 D. what you want, and you will look on it
T-21....VIII.1:7 Yet he did not d. it *because* it was the truth
T-21....VIII.2:2 d. it although you understand it not. The
T-21....VIII.2:7 because its own d. cannot be shaken. It
T-21....VIII.3:2 if what you d. you receive, and happiness
T-21....VIII.3:4 no one fails to ask for his d. of something
T-21....VIII.3:6 Yet he will ask because d. is a request, an
T-21....VIII.3:9 does not d. it while he remains uncertain,
T-21....VIII.5:6 of your d. for what will never change. For
T-22...... II.12:5 will, nor the d. that anything be separate.
T-22...... III.9:6 as causing sin by his d. to have sin real.
T-22.... VI.12:7 value, except in the d. to attack in safety?
T-23.... III.6:10 the body, torn between the natural d. to
T-24...... IV.2:7 And minds can change as they d.. What
T-25.........I.5:5 part–the tiny, mad d. to be separate,
T-25....... V.1:1 merely this: The whole d. to attack is gone
T-27....... II.7:7 Your health is a result of your d. to see
T-28.........I.2:4 to it in memory if you did not d. its effects
T-28.........I.4:7 But only your d. made the link, and only
T-28....... II.3:2 For this impossible d., he does not believe
T-28...... IV.7:4 His d. to be a sick and separated mind
T-29...... VI.1:2 much do you d. peace instead of endless
T-30....VIII.4:5 you cannot have when you d. healing. But
T-31... V.15:10 kind you see your own concealed d. to kill
W-pI.....20.5:5 What you d. you will see. Such is the real
W-pI.....37.5:1 for today to your outer world if you so d.;
W-pI.....63.2:4 purpose or meaningless d. in its place, or
W-pI.....75.3:4 We will be given what we d.. We will to
W-pI...130.2:2 d. what he does not want to have reality?
W-pI.133.13:4 *value do I seek, for only that do I d. to find.*
W-pI...165.5:1 Ask with d.. You need not be sure that
W-pI.182.12:3 This is your heart's d.. This is the voice
W-pI...183.6:6 only Name of everything that we d. to see;
W-pI...190.1:7 and His insane d. for revenge and death.
W-pII ....in.2:8 as we will need for the result that we d..
W-pII .231.1:6 *else could I d. but the truth about myself?*
W-pII .253.1:3 What happens is what I d.. What does
W-pII .287.2:2 *What but You could I d. to have? What way*
W-pII .287.2:3 *but that which leads to You could I d. to walk*
M-8 ...........2:4 out of its intensity of d. to have it for itself
M-26 .......4:11 What more could you d., when this is all
M-28 .......1:10 It is the single d. of the Son for the Father.
S-1 ........ III.6:3 The d. for them *is* the prayer. One need
S-3........ IV.4:6 heart, and no d. to attack the Son of God.

### desired 9

T-6...... V.B.8:7 nothing is difficult that is *wholly* d.. To
T-21....... III.5:6 in what you chose, you made what you d..
T-21....... IV.5:2 d. nothing but to join with him and to be
T-25.....VII.9:2 as possible, and more and more d., as it
T-27....... II.9:6 sickness is d. to prevent a shift of balance
T-29...... IV.4:7 or less. They are d. or not. And each one
W-pI.....24.4:3 of goals in mind as part of the d. outcome
W-pII .344.1:2 *thought to save what I d. for myself alone.*
M-21 .........2:5 d. experience in the opinion of the asker.

### desires 23

T-21 ..... III.2:4 a purpose to be replaced while he d. it, for
T-21 ...VIII.2:6 for it d. everything be like itself, and sees
T-27 .........I.7:2 of their unnatural d. and strange needs.
T-30 ...... IV.5:9 they are idols which but dance to vain d..
W-pI.....27.1:2 It gives vision priority among your d..
W-pI.....91.5:4 will has all the strength to do what it d..
W-pI...125.3:1 petty thoughts, without our personal d.,
W-pI...125.6:2 and meaningless d. have been stilled.
W-pI...136.5:3 in force, as far as your d. are concerned.
W-pI...182.5:3 His Father. He d. to go home so deeply, so
W-pI. 185.14:1 our d. with the need of every heart, the
W-pI...188.9:6 clean of strange d. and disordered wishes.
W-pI...190.7:6 Your strange d. bring it evil dreams. Your
W-pI. 200.10:3 the road is carpeted with leaves of false d.,
W-pII ....in.9:3 believed that our insane d. were the truth.
W-pII .226.2:3 *in a place of vain d. and of shattered dreams,*
W-pII .242.2:5 *You know all our d. and our wants. And You*
W-pII .325.1:2 up an image of the thing the mind d.,
W-pII .339.1:1 No one d. pain. But he can think that
M-5 ........II.2:9 in order to bring tangible form to his d..
M-19 .........5:2 make whatever picture the mind d. to see.
P-2........ VI.3.4 reproducing its d. and translating them
S-1 ..........II.7:8 without words, or thoughts, or vain d.,

### desiring 5

T-15 ...VIII.2:4 that there is, by d. that it *be* all that there is
T-21 ..... III.6:7 d. and believing in it because of your
T-21 ..... III.8:4 d. to place its power elsewhere should
W-pI....57.1:4 I can drop them off merely by d. to do so.
W-pI...133.3:2 requirements, they are not worth d. at all,

### desk 1

W-pI.....43.4:8 *I cannot see this d. apart from Him. God is*

### desolate 3

T-26 ..... IX.3:5 that hate had scorched and rendered d..
W-pII .245.1:4 *I bring it to the d. and lonely and afraid. I give*
W-pII .331.1:4 *You could never leave me d., to die within a*

### desolation 3

T-26 ..VII.10:1 this world that death and d. seem to rule.
T-26 ...VIII.4:5 Who can feel d. except now? A future
T-29 ..... III.5:1 in the midst of dreams of d. and disaster.

### despair 55

T-9 .....VIII.2:1 Grandiosity is always a cover for d.. It is
T-9 .....VIII.2:8 suspicious as long as you d. of yourself. It
T-9 .....VIII.5:4 forget this, you *will* d. and you *will* attack.
T-9 .....VIII.6:2 to look upon your grandeur you cannot d.
T-12 ...VIII.7:6 You looked upon the unreal and found d..
T-12 ...VIII.7:8 The unreal world *is* a thing of d., for it can
T-14 .......II.4:6 them to d. they do not see as nothing,
T-15 ..... XI.8:1 Let no d. darken the joy of Christmas, for
T-16 ..... IV.5:9 the other, the decision must be one of d..
T-16 ...... V.1:2 Anxiety, d., guilt and attack all enter into
T-16 ..... VI.8:7 Find hope and comfort, rather than d., in
T-16 ... VI.10:3 on death and suffering, sickness and d.,
T-18 ..... IX.4:3 to bring d. and loneliness to it and keep it
T-20 ... VI.11:3 instant seems to be life; an instant of d., a
T-24 .....II.14:3 Through this d. you travel now, yet it is
T-24 .....II.14:3 you travel now, yet it is but illusion of d..
T-25 .......II.1:5 hopes and fancies, always does d. result.
T-29 .....II.10:1 what He is with littleness and limit and d.
T-29 .... VII.8:1 appeared to be an endless circle of d., you
T-29 ..VII.10:5 in chants of deep d. to idols of yourself.
T-29 ..VII.10:7 your hope. For hope of happiness is *not* d..
T-29 ..... IX.3:3 for one unless he were in terror and d.?
T-29 ..... IX.3:4 its worship is the worship of d. and terror
T-31 ........I.7:5 It is a world of terror and d.. Nor is there
T-31 ..... IV.4:3 Learn now, without d., there is no hope of
T-31 ..... IV.9:5 you are will lead you to confusion and d..
T-31 .. VII.14:3 death; a thing of treachery and black d.,
T-31 .. VII.15:2 and men d. because the savior's vision is
W-pI .... 71.5:4 misery and a deep sense of failure and d..
W-pI .. 100.4:3 joyous, and their joy heals sorrow and d..
W-pI .. 121.5:1 The unforgiving mind is in d., without
W-pI .. 121.5:1 which can offer anything but more d.. Yet
W-pI .. 121.5:2 not see it has condemned itself to this d..
W-pI .. 123.4:1 in gratitude we lift our hearts above d.,
W-pI .. 128.1:2 from hopes that turn to bitter ashes of d..
W-pI .. 138.7:2 hell is real, hope changes to d., and life
W-pI .. 151.5:6 sees the guilt. It is its own d. it sees in you.
W-pI .. 162.5:4 Who could d. when perfect joy is yours,
W-pI .. 168.2:1 Love, hope and d. would be impossible.
W-pI .. 168.2:2 satisfied; d. of any kind unthinkable. His
W-pI .. 168.2:3 His grace His answer is to all d., for in it
W-pI .. 185.5:6 the same d. and misery as do the rest.
W-pI 185.14:1 every mind, the hope that lies beyond d.,
W-pI .. 191.3:3 and watch d. snatch from your fingers
W-pI .. 195.3:1 leaves you nothing but a black d. so bitter
W-pI .. 200.1:3 yet more bitter disappointments, bleak d.
W-pII . 251.1:1 I sought for many things, and found d..
W-pII ..... 6.2:1 is no more than an illusion of d., for hope
M-in.......... 4:7 which teaches nothing but d. and death,
M-10 ......... 6:6 of sickening d. and fear of death; all these
M-26 ......... 4:1 Do not d., then, because of limitations. It
M-27 ......... 2:2 in dust and disappointment and d., can
C-ep .......... 1:6 Who could d. when hope like this is his?
C-ep .......... 1:7 his? Illusions of d. may seem to come, but
S-2........... I.5:4 your fate, your feelings, your d. or hope,

### despairing 1

T-15 ........ I.6:1 How bleak and d. is the ego's use of time!

### despairs 1

T-9 ..... IV.10:1 he d. of finding satisfaction in reality? Yet

### desperate 4

T-4 ..... III.10:2 The ego is d. because it opposes literally
T-11 .......V.9:1 shallow, callous, uninvolved and even d.,
T-26 ........I.1:2 all d. attempts to strike a bargain, and all
W-pI .... 79.6:1 this complexity is but a d. attempt not to

### desperately 2

T-4 .........V.5:2 d. for something you would not recognize
T-16 ..... IV.4:8 They seek it d., but not in the peace in

### despise 7

T-8 ....... IV.3:7 world must therefore d. and reject me,
T-16 .....V.10:6 the other to replace the self that you d..
T-16 .....V.10:7 And you d. it because you do not think it
T-25 ........I.2:5 you not d. the one who tells you this, and
T-28 ..... VI.3:5 And you d. its acts, but not your own. It
W-pI 121.10:1 you should meet him; one you actively d.,
S-2..........II.2:3 Who can forgive and yet d.? And who can

### despised 3

T-18 ..... III.3:4 give you confidence in yourself, so long d.
T-18 .... VII.4:8 to make holy what is hated and d.. Nor is
T-23 ........I.9:3 as real, the other vanquished and d.. Here

### despises 1

T-8 ....... IX.6:5 The ego d. weakness, even though it

### despite 14

T-5 ..... III.10:4 D. the ego's attempts to conceal this part,
T-6 ..... V.C.4:6 your consistency is called on d. chaos. Yet
T-12 .......II.5:7 and it belongs to you d. your dreams.
T-15 .. VII.12:5 And d. the evident insanity of this lesson,
T-25 .......II.1:5 D. your hopes and fancies, always does

T-26 X.4:6 of this, and victimized **d.** your innocence?
T-27 II.15:6 intact, **d.** Your separate views of what
T-27 V.8:7 are the same, **d.** their different forms. All
T-30 I.7:1 rule without delay, **d.** your opposition.
W-pI 17.1:3 **d.** the temptation to believe that it is the
W-pI 19.2:4 **D.** your initial resistance to this idea, you
W-pI 41.2:5 **d.** the serious and tragic forms it may take
M-12 4:6 not believe in the illusion **d.** appearances.
M-29 4:8 **d.** its obvious and complete ignorance,

## destiny 11

T-21 V.2:6 think the world you made directs your **d.**.
T-23 in.4:6 Your **d.** and purpose are far beyond them,
T-27 VII.9:3 are you the one decider of your **d.** in time.
T-29 VI.2:12 and as he is, for time appointed not his **d.**
W-pI 127.6:4 that you think are part of human **d.**.
W-pI 153.14:4 may learn the tale he reads of terrifying **d.**
W-pI 165.6:4 **d.** lies there and nowhere else. Would
W-pII 253.1:2 Even in this world, it is I who rule my **d.**.
W-pII 317.1:3 I am the slave of time and human **d.**. But
M-3 4:6 the **d.** of all relationships to become holy.
C-ep 3:7 His. Look up and find your certain **d.** the

## destroy 53

*See also* forgiveness-to-destroy

T-1 V.1:7 can **d.** your medium of communication,
T-2 II.1:8 with equal power will inevitably **d.** peace.
T-3 I.7:6 demonstrated that nothing can **d.** truth.
T-4 III.7:3 unwilling to **d.** what you have made. No
T-5 II.8:3 which you can interrupt but cannot **d.**.
T-5 IV.1:4 Truth is beyond your ability to **d.**, but
T-6 I.4:2 can assault another, and can even **d.** it.
T-6 II.3:7 The ego uses projection only to **d.** your
T-7 VI.2:2 That is because it believes it can **d.** love,
T-8 IX.6:1 it from the body in an attempt to **d.** it. Yet
T-9 IV.5:2 does it make real the unreal and then **d.** it
T-10 III.1:3 No one can will to **d.** himself. When you
T-11 V.10:8 to find what he believes would **d.** him.
T-13 II.3:5 and it will try to **d.** it because it is afraid.
T-13 II.8:6 might turn on yourself and **d.** yourself.
T-13 III.4:3 you have made a world God would **d.**;
T-13 IV.1:5 would thus **d.** you here and bury you here
T-13 VI.4:6 **d.** time's continuity by breaking it into
T-13 XI.1:3 end his peace of mind, and so **d.** him. Yet
T-15 V.5:2 which He would purify and not let you **d.**.
T-15 V.5:7 needs, which would **d.** the relationship.
T-15 X.7:6 total Love would completely **d.** you.
T-15 X.8:6 it is what you invited in that would **d.** you
T-15 XI.10:3 and you will make complete and not **d.**.
T-16 V.9:4 is to **d.** reality and substitute illusion. For
T-16 VII.10:1 and the ego's "atonement" that would **d.**.
T-17 I.4:4 fragment truth is to **d.** it by rendering it
T-17 VII.3:10 used *against* truth will always **d.** faith. If
T-18 I.2:8 relationships the ego sponsors to **d.**.
T-18 II.6:5 He does not **d.** it, nor snatch it away from
T-18 III.1:6 was simply that God cannot **d.** Himself.
T-18 VI.5:4 cannot **d.** can have no real effect at all.
T-18 VI.7:6 prison you have made, and would **d.** it.
T-19 I.5:4 Faithlessness would **d.** and separate; faith
T-19 III.6:5 must have created what wills to **d.** Him,
T-20 VIII.7:5 die, attack and murder and **d.** themselves,
T-24 IV.3:15 would disturb your peace to enter and **d.**.
T-25 IV.4:9 a home in Heaven the world cannot **d.**.
T-27 III.7:2 wholly limitless has come, not to **d.**, but
T-28 III.6:2 not **d.** the alien will that He created not.
T-30 I.7:4 for it would **d.** the day by robbing you of
T-30 VI.5:7 could replace it and **d.** the Will of God.
W-pI 22.2:4 You made what you would **d.**; everything
W-pI 41.4:4 go. Nothing can **d.** your peace of mind
W-pI 72.1:1 His plan, and a deliberate attempt to **d.** it.
W-pI 132.13:1 God Himself and thus **d.** His Wholeness.
W-pI 161.7:5 compelled to turn upon itself and to **d.**.
W-pI 161.9:8 Would you request that love **d.** itself? Or
W-pI 189.3:5 poised to avenge, to murder and **d.**.
W-pI 196.5:5 waiting to **d.** his life and blot him from
M-6 1:7 the patient might even try to **d.** himself.
M-25 6:4 the world would **d.** the Holy Spirit would
S-2 I.2:6 knife that would **d.** the holy Son He loves.

## destroyed 22

T-3 IV.6:10 be remembered, never having been **d.**.
T-5 VI.9:3 To the ego, to be undone means to be **d.**.
T-5 VI.9:4 ego will not be **d.** because it is part of your
T-8 VI.2:5 If it were, you would have **d.** yourself. Yet
T-14 XI.12:3 They have **d.** their motivation for learning
T-15 X.7:3 a little, perhaps, but the other to be **d.**.
T-15 X.7:4 and your only question is who is to be **d.**,
T-15 X.7:5 seem to be both destroyer and **d.** in part,
T-15 XI.7:2 remains unbroken even if the body is **d.**,
T-22 VI.10:6 yourself as vulnerable, frail and easily **d.**,
T-22 VI.11:2 and frail and easily **d.** unless his Father is?
T-23 II.11:7 Now must his body be **d.** and sacrificed,
T-25 II.6:7 think you not the picture is **d.** in any way.
T-26 III.4:1 Nothing the Son of God believes can be **d.**
T-27 I.6:10 is your life; how easily **d.** is what you love.
T-29 IX.6:5 What hurts him is **d.**; what helps him,
W-pI 93.4:4 You think you are **d.**, but you are saved.
W-pII 5.2:9 is there that God's eternal Son can be **d.**?
W-pII 299.2:2 *It is not mine to be* ***d.*** *by sin. It is not mine to*
W-pII 12.2:4 it "sees" the Will of God has been **d.**. It
M-14 2:11 not be **d.** nor attacked nor even touched.
M-27 3:5 as well are doomed to be **d.** as certainly.

## destroyer 4

T-15 X.7:5 seem to be both **d.** and destroyed in part,
T-27 VII.12:2 the **d.** of your brother and the world alike.
M-27 5:7 He is not Father, but **d.**. He is not Creator,
S-3 IV.5:7 is His. His great **d.**, death. And sickness,

## destroying 2

T-3 VII.3:9 as capable of **d.** Their Own purpose is in
Wfl in.1:5 seem ugly and unsafe, attacking and **d.**,

## destroys 1

M-4 III.1:10 Judgment **d.** honesty and shatters trust.

## destructible 3

T-6 I.4:3 anything that is **d.** cannot be real. Its
T-6 I.4:7 you must be equating yourself with the **d.**
T-6 V.A.2:1 did not make the body, because it is **d.**,

## destruction 41

*See also* self-destruction

T-3 I.5:6 not confuse **d.** with innocence because it
T-3 VII.3:6 position where their own **d.** was possible?
T-3 VII.5:10 you feel the fear of the **d.** of your thought
T-4 I.3:2 it leads to the relinquishment, not the **d.**,
T-5 III.7:4 makes, not by **d.** but by understanding.
T-5 IV.8:5 They are beyond **d.** and beyond guilt.
T-6 I.4:3 Yet if **d.** itself is impossible, anything that
T-6 I.4:4 Its **d.**, therefore, does not justify anger. To
T-8 VI.2:6 God did not will the **d.** of His creations,
T-10 III.1:7 Yet the **d.** is no more real than the image,
T-11 VIII.1:8 The end of the world is not its **d.**, but its
T-12 VII.4:10 For this belief is the **d.** of peace, a goal in
T-12 VII.13:6 **d.** is the one end toward which it works,
T-13 IV.1:4 teaches that your function on earth is **d.**,
T-13 IV.2:5 **d.** is the final proof that you were right.
T-13 IV.9:6 But if you interpret your function as **d.**,
T-14 VI.4:1 yields to life simply because **d.** is not true.
T-15 I.2:6 which uses time to support its belief in **d.**.
T-16 V.15:1 in the fantasy of **d.** of love's meaning. And
T-16 VII.3:4 to act out its hate are fantasies of your **d.**.
T-16 VII.3:6 Yet without your alliance in your own **d.**,
T-16 VII.3:7 you are allowing your **d.** to be. That this is
T-17 IV.10:3 to truth, you threaten truth with **d.**. And
T-18 VI.14:6 Not through **d.**, not through a breaking
T-18 VII.1:6 by those who prefer pain and **d.**.
T19 IV.C.11:9 *it as a sign of sin and death, nor use it for* ***d.***.
T-20 VIII.4:8 How can the engine of **d.** be preferred,
T-23 II.4:3 For the **d.** of the one who makes the error
T-23 II.4:5 for which his own **d.** becomes inevitable.
T-23 II.8:4 Only **d.** can be the outcome. And God
T-23 II.17:11 is intent on your **d.** is not your friend.
T-24 IV.1:3 dangerous, hated and worthy only of **d.**.
T-24 IV.1:5 In danger of **d.** it must kill, and you are
T-24 IV.1:7 salvation can only mean **d.** of the world,
T-24 V.4:5 Where does it lead but to **d.**? Yet think
T-25 VII.11:6 and **d.** be the total cost of any gain at all.
T-29 VI.1:4 and the dream of danger and **d.**, sin and
M-27 3:4 him and to last a little while by his **d.**. Yet
M-29 6:9 child harm himself, or choose his own **d.**.
C-4 4:5 Where **d.** was perceived the face of Christ
S-2 III.6:7 save it from **d.** and to make the means for

## destructive 20

*See also* God-destructive, self-destructive

T-1 I.14:3 magic, which is mindless and therefore **d.**
T-2 V.5:4 By denying your mind any **d.** potential
T-3 VII.5:2 active, **d.** and clearly in opposition to God
T-5 V.8:2 emphasize the **d.** results of the decision.
T-7 VII.1:10 Used negatively it will be **d.**, because it
T-10 III.1:6 image makes you do can be very **d.**. Yet
T-12 VIII.1:2 kept him far away from your **d.** thoughts,
T-13 II.3:3 the ego's **d.** urge is so intense that nothing
T-13 IV.9:6 hold on to the past to ensure a **d.** future.
T-13 V.4:1 The delusional can be very **d.**, for they do
T-13 XI.2:7 Nothing **d.** ever was or will be. The war,
T-15 X.7:4 For you see love as **d.**, and your only
T-16 I.2:1 the ego uses it is **d.** lies in the fact that it is
T-16 IV.3:1 is an attempt to limit the **d.** effects of hate
T-18 VI.5:4 wish to make **d.** what cannot destroy can
T-18 VI.5:6 You cannot make His Will **d.**. You can
T-23 III.1:3 pain. Attack in any form is equally **d.**. Its
T-25 VIII.6:8 as justice to be more **d.** to themselves and
W-pI 16.3:3 you recognize them all as equally **d.**, but
M-16 9:4 nor demanding sacrifice, healing nor **d.**,

## destructively 4

T-1 VII.3:5 in any way and you are perceiving **d.**.
T-2 II.4:1 **d.** because it is not a device you made.
T-12 III.3:5 **d.** if you accept their poverty as yours. If
T-14 III.9:1 decisions for yourself you are thinking **d.**,

## destructiveness 1

T-20 VIII.6:4 **D.** becomes benign, and sin is turned to

## detach 2

T-5 V.3:2 part of God **d.** itself without believing it is
T-7 VI.5:3 Forced, therefore, to **d.** itself from you, it

## detached 1

T-21 IV.3:4 joined their brothers have **d.** themselves

## detachment 2

T-18 VII.4:9 aimed at **d.** from the body necessary. All
W-pI 33.2:2 and to maintain this **d.** as you repeat the

## detail 3

T-3 VI.1:1 the Last Judgment, but in insufficient **d.**.
W-pI 41.8:6 We will go into more **d.** about this kind of
W-pI 151.2:4 to the last **d.** which they report is even

## details 1

W-pI 152.1:6 Here is your world, complete in all **d.**.

## detain 1

W-pI 73.8:2 No idle wishes can **d.** us, nor deceive us

**detected** 1
W-pI.....74.5:3 withdrawal, but the difference is easily **d.**.

**deteriorate** 1
T-1.........I.14:3 Without conviction they **d.** into magic,

**determination** 14
T-18...... II.5:19 The special relationship is your **d.** to keep
T-18...... IV.1:1 instant is the result of your **d.** to be holy.
T-18...... IV.3:4 the **d.** to be as you would make yourself?
T-24.... VI.11:5 And all this grim **d.** was for this; you
T-30........I.14:1 the **d.** not to make decisions by yourself.
T-31..VIII.11:1 and who looks with fixed **d.** toward the
W-pI.....20.3:8 earth. In your **d.** to see is vision given you.
W-pI.....27.1:1 something stronger than mere **d.**. It gives
W-pI.....69.3:1 and with real **d.** to reach what is dearer to
W-pI.....69.7:2 Your little effort and small **d.** call on the
W-pI.....74.3:1 firm **d.** to understand what they mean,
WpI..rII.in.4:3 Replace them with your **d.** to succeed. Do
WpI..rII.in.6:1 your **d.** in the shorter practice periods as
W-pII .282.1:3 the **d.** not to be asleep in dreams of death,

**determine** 15
T-7....... VII.2:8 then, must **d.** every response you make.
T-7....... X.1:11 premises that will **d.** what you accept into
T-8........ IV.5:7 mind is the means by which you **d.** your
T-11....... II.7:3 You are free to **d.** who shall be your guest,
T-13....... X.5:1 **D.**, then, to be not as you were. Use no
T-16.........I.3:8 and to **d.** your response *by* judging it.
T-16........ II.8:2 This year **d.** not to deny what has been
T-17...... VI.2:3 for it is this which will **d.** the outcome. In
W-pI.....11.1:3 that your thoughts **d.** the world you see.
W-pI.....65.4:2 Try, also, to **d.** this time in advance, and
W-pI.....68.6:1 **D.** now to see all these people as friends.
W-pI.....69.6:2 **D.** to go past the clouds. Reach out and
W-pI.....71.3:1 in this plan, then, is simply to **d.** what,
W-pI...105.9:3 **D.** not to interfere today with what He
W-pI...169.8:2 gave it to all minds that each one might **d.**

**determined** 27
T-7....... VII.2:7 you make is **d.** by what you think you are,
T-10..... V.14:7 your choice is **d.** by what you value. Time
T-12...... VII.9:6 only this decision that **d.** what you found,
T-29...... IV.5:5 Perceptions are **d.** by their purpose, in
W-pI........20.h I am **d.** to see.
W-pI.....20.4:3 you are stating that you are **d.** to change
W-pI........21.h I am **d.** to see things differently.
W-pI.....21.4:2 *I am **d.** to see_[name of person] differently. I*
W-pI.....21.4:3 ***d.** to see_[specify the situation] differently*
W-pI.....21.5:4 say: *I am **d.** to see_[specify the attribute] in_*
W-pI.....24.1:3 is **d.** by your perception of the situation,
W-pI...44.11:3 Above all, be **d.** not to forget today.
W-pI.....54.5:1 (20) I am **d.** to see. Recognizing the
W-pI.....54.5:2 nature of my thoughts, I am **d.** to see. I
W-pI.....55.1:1 (21) I am **d.** to see things differently.
W-pI.....55.1:7 I am **d.** to see the witnesses to the truth in
W-pI...72.12:6 *understand.* He will answer. Be **d.** to hear.
W-pI.....80.7:1 us be **d.** not to collect grievances today.
W-pI.....80.7:2 us be **d.** to be free of problems that do not
WpI..rII.in.5:4 Be **d.** each day not to leave your function
W-pI.....84.3:6 me. I am **d.** not to attack my Self today, so
W-pI.....95.8:3 Let us therefore be **d.**, particularly for the
W-pI...158.2:9 Yet is that time **d.** by the mind itself, not
W-pI...169.4:2 when that time will be, and has **d.** it. And
W-pI...169.7:2 **d.** to abandon all but this is now at hand.
W-pII .257.1:4 Let us therefore be **d.** to remember what
M-in.......... 3:1 therefore **d.** exclusively by what you think

**determiner** 3
T-13..... IV.4:4 the past becomes the **d.** of the future,
T-17...... VI.2:5 situation becomes the **d.** of the outcome,
T-21....... II.3:3 His power of decision is the **d.** of every

**determiners** 1
W-pI...130.1:4 Your values are **d.** of this, for what you

**determines** 14
T-3 ....... III.2:9 perceive at any given time **d.** what you do,
T-7 ..........I.5:2 What you believe you are **d.** your gifts,
T-9 .........II.5:4 about him **d.** the message you receive.
T-10 ......in.2:7 your mind **d.** your perception of it.
T-11 ..... VI.3:3 And since belief **d.** perception, you do not
T-13 ..... IX.2:5 and where it is invested **d.** its reward. For
T-14 ..... XI.3:3 but its influence **d.** the present by giving
T-17 ..... VI.5:9 knows that the situation is as the goal **d.** it
T-20 ...VIII.9:3 and which you choose **d.** what you see.
T-29 ........I.5:4 that it **d.** when your brother and you meet
T-31 ..... VI.1:5 What you decide in this **d.** all you see and
W-pI.....11.1:2 seems as if the world **d.** what you perceive
W-pI...154.5:4 If he **d.** what the messages should be, or
W-pI...169.4:2 said the mind **d.** when that time will be,

**determining** 4
W-pI.....66.3:3 and **d.** the means for achieving it. We will
W-pI...73.10:1 and **d.** to keep your will clearly in mind,
M-10 ......... 1:7 any consistent criteria for **d.** what these
M-22 ......... 7:9 **d.** where healing should be given and

**deterred** 1
T-27 .......II.9:7 could the Holy Spirit be **d.** an instant,

**detour** 1
T-2 ..........I.2:1 in the separation, or the "**d.** into fear."

**detours** 1
WpI..rII.in.5:2 Refuse to be sidetracked into **d.**, illusions

**detract** 2
T-6 ....... IV.9:6 and never **d.** from it in any way. You
T-24 .......II.2:3 Who can **d.** from his omnipotence, yet

**detrimental** 1
M-24 ......... 5:5 that is **d.** to his pupil's advance or his own

**devastated** 1
W-pI...191.9:1 and frail, with futile hopes and **d.** dreams,

**devastating** 2
T-31 ...... V.5:2 fear so **d.** that the face that smiles above it
W-pI...191.6:5 will not see a **d.** image of yourself walking

**devastation** 5
T-19 ........I.8:2 great the **d.** wrought by your faithlessness
T-29 .... VII.4:6 within and fear to look upon your **d.**, but
W-pI...153.4:3 have no idea of all the **d.** it has wrought.
W-pI...194.2:1 of sin, and **d.** brought about by guilt.
W-pII ...13.1:3 all. It merely looks on **d.**, and reminds the

**devastation's** 1
M-27 ......... 3:4 in which he is "laid to rest" in **d.** arms,

**develop** 9
T-2 ...... VII.7:6 Confidence cannot **d.** fully until mastery
T-4 ........ V.6:2 is the one function the ego has tried to **d.**,
T-6 ........I.17:1 to **d.** your weakened ability to be grateful,
T-6 ....... IV.9:3 **d.** your abilities to the point where they
T-6 ....... IV.9:4 You have a Guide to how to **d.** them, but
T-7 ........ V.3:1 the one ability everyone can **d.** and must
T-7 ........ V.3:1 develop and must **d.** if he is to be healed.
W-pI .... 32.1:1 to **d.** the theme of cause and effect. You
M-25 ......... 1:4 he may well **d.** abilities that seem quite

**developed** 6
T-2 .........V.9:1 is an ability that **d.** after the separation,
T-2 ....... VI.6:1 a willingness that you have not **d.** as yet.
T-6 ........in.2:4 you have **d.** a thought system of any kind,
T-6 ....... IV.9:1 must be **d.** before you can use them. This
T-7 ..... VIII.4:8 consistent model, it never **d.** consistently.
M-25 ......... 6:7 Those who have **d.** "psychic" powers have

**developing** 1
T-7 .........V.1:1 more than a framework for **d.** abilities,

**development** 2
T-8 .........II.2:7 and facilitates the **d.** of what you have.
M-4 ........ I.A.h **D.** of Trust

**develops** 3
T-17 .......V.2:4 it begins, **d.** and becomes accomplished,
T-17 .......V.5:3 this change **d.** and is finally accomplished
M-25 ......... 6:1 ability that anyone **d.** has the potentiality

**deviate** 1
M-4 ...... IX.2:1 True faithfulness, however, does not **d.**.

**device** 46
T-1 ........I.15:3 thus a teaching **d.** and a means to an end.
T-1 ........I.47:1 learning **d.** that lessens the need for time.
T-1 ........I.48:1 miracle is the only **d.** at your immediate
T-1 ........I.49:2 is a **d.** for perception correction, effective
T-2 .........II.2:1 True denial is a powerful protective **d.**.
T-2 .........II.4:1 destructively because it is not a **d.** you
T-2 .........II.6:4 Atonement is the **d.** by which you can free
T-2 ....... IV.3:1 and the body is a learning **d.** for the mind
T-2 ....... IV.3:4 worst a faulty use of a learning **d.** can do
T-2 .........V.1:6 better protective **d.** than any form of level
T-2 .........V.1:9 exist except as a learning **d.** for the mind.
T-2 .......V.1:10 learning **d.** is not subject to errors of its
T-2 .........V.5:6 from overevaluating its own learning **d.**,
T-2 .........V.6:2 a learning **d.** it merely follows the learner,
T-2 .........V.8:2 by any **d.** that can be seen physically. As
T-2 .... VII.5:11 nothing. Time is essentially a **d.** by which
T-2 .... VII.5:13 made this necessary as a corrective **d.**.
T-2 .....VIII.2:6 **d.** for shortening but not abolishing time.
T-3 ....... III.4:2 and therefore not a **d.** for knowing. It is,
T-4 ....... VI.4:4 The ego is a **d.** for maintaining this belief,
T-4 ....... VI.4:4 to use the **d.** that enables it to endure.
T-5 ..... III.11:1 as a teaching **d.** for bringing you home.
T-5 ..... VI.12:4 that time is a learning **d.** to be abolished
T-6 ........in.2:1 is a particularly helpful learning **d.**.
T-6 ..........I.2:2 Its value, like the value of any teaching **d.**,
T-6 .........II.1:5 main defense, or the **d.** that keeps it going
T-6 .........II.3:3 It is solely a **d.** of the ego to make you feel
T-6 ....... IV.5:3 real, that the mind is the ego's learning **d.**
T-6 .....V.A.2:3 It is clearly a separation **d.**, and therefore
T-6 .....V.A.2:4 made and translates it into a learning **d.**.
T-7 .........V.7:6 changed the most powerful **d.** that was
T-8 .... VII.12:5 confuse a learning **d.** with a curriculum
T-8 .....VIII.7:1 A learning **d.** is not a teacher. It cannot
T-8 .....VIII.7:3 that a learning **d.** *can* tell you how you feel.
T-15 ........I.7:7 teaching, is nothing but a teaching **d.** for
T-15 .......V.1:1 **d.** for teaching you love's meaning. For its
T-15 .......V.2:1 The past is the ego's chief learning **d.**, for
T-16 .......V.6:1 ego **d.** for joining hell and Heaven, and
T-16 ..... VI.4:4 is a **d.** for limiting your self to a body, and
T-17 .......V.1:2 salvation, the holy instant is a practical **d.**
T-19 .......II.6:9 sin is kept in place by just this strange **d.**.
T-23 .....II.16:2 is a strange **d.** that makes it possible. Nor
T-24 .......II.1:1 Comparison must be an ego **d.**, for love
T-27 ... VIII.8:3 How childish is the petulant **d.** to keep
W-pI .. 136.2:2 it is an insane **d.** for self-deception. And
M-13 ......... 1:5 must be replaced by a corrective **d.**;

**devices** 9

T-1........ I.16:1 are teaching **d.** for demonstrating it is as
T-1........ I.46:2 they are *temporary* communication **d.**.
T-2........IV.3:2 Learning **d.** are not lessons in themselves.
T-2......... V.2:5 to rely temporarily on physical healing **d.**,
T-2..... VIII.2:4 became one of the many learning **d.** to be
T-4......... V.6:6 ego **d.** for impeding learning progress. In
T19... IV.C.7:6 secrets, all its strange **d.** for deception, all
W-pI.....13.3:3 To the ego illusions are safety **d.**, as they
M-10..........1:1 Judgment, like other **d.** by which the

**devil** 9

T-3.......VII.2:4 The "**d.**" is a frightening concept because
T-3.......VII.2:6 **d.** deceives by lies, and builds kingdoms
T-3.......VII.5:1 and very fearful, and this belief *is* the "**d.**."
T-3.......VII.5:3 at your life and see what the **d.** has made.
T-25... VIII.7:3 What could He be to them except a **d.**,
W-pI...101.5:3 that you have made a **d.** of God's Son.
W-pI.161.12:6 enemy to savior; from the **d.** into Christ.
M-25..........6:5 have been used to call upon the **d.**, which
P-2........IV.4:7 God were the **d.** and must be found in evil

**devil's** 1

S-3........IV.5:8 earth, which He abandoned to the **d.** care,

**devils** 1

M-8............5:5 do the number of pitchforks the **d.** he sees

**devious** 2

T-3......VI.10:4 and sometimes by way of very **d.** routes,
T-14......VI.6:1 who speak in dark and **d.** symbols do not

**devise** 1

T-5.......VII.1:2 Do you really believe you can **d.** a thought

**devised** 1

W-pI.....77.2:2 nor on any of the rituals you have **d.**. It is

**devising** 1

T-7..... VIII.2:3 in **d.** ways that seem to diminish conflict,

**devoid** 6

T-6...........I.1:5 of the crucifixion that is wholly **d.** of fear,
T-21....... V.4:4 of the mind **d.** of reason understand what
T-30... VIII.5:1 to you to see in happy form, **d.** of fear. It
W-pI.188.10:4 innocent, **d.** of sin and open to salvation.
M-11..........3:4 one without meaning and **d.** of sense,
M-29........4:11 benefit to all, being wholly **d.** of attack.

**devote** 38

T-4...........I.6:6 to **d.** myself to teaching if I believed this,
T-5........IV.7:2 been forgiven must **d.** themselves first to
T-9.......... I.12:8 Can you really **d.** yourself to nothing?
T-14....... V.3:5 Your only calling here is to **d.** yourself,
W-pI.....23.6:2 and then close your eyes and **d.** about a
W-pI.....30.5:3 **d.** several practice periods to applying
W-pI.....34.6:2 try to take several minutes and **d.** them to
W-pI.....46.5:4 **d.** the remainder of the practice period to
WpI...rI.in.2:3 **D.** two minutes or more to each practice
W-pI.....62.5:4 Then **d.** a minute or two to considering
W-pI.....63.4:1 two that you should **d.** to considering this
W-pI.....64.6:5 least once **d.** ten or fifteen minutes today
W-pI.....64.7:1 day, **d.** several minutes to reviewing these
W-pI.....65.7:1 **d.** the rest of the practice period to trying
W-pI.....69.2:2 let us **d.** several minutes to thinking
W-pI.....70.7:5 *else.* Then **d.** a few minutes, with your eyes
W-pI.....71.9:1 let us **d.** the remainder of the extended
W-pI.....76.7:2 We will **d.** today to rejoicing that this is so
WpI. rII.in.2:2 **D.** some three or four minutes to reading
W-pI.....91.4:3 Today we will **d.** ourselves to the attempt
W-pI.....91.8:2 and then **d.** several minutes to allowing
W-pI...93.10:6 try to **d.** at least a minute or so to closing
W-pI.....94.3:1 Today we will again **d.** the first five
W-pI...102.3:1 days we will continue to **d.** our periods of
WpI. rIII.in3:1 **d.** the time to it that you are asked to give.
WpI. rIII.in5:1 reviews is this: **D.** five minutes twice a day
WpI. rIII.in8:1 if you **d.** the first five minutes of the day
W-pI...121.8:3 We will **d.** ten minutes in the morning,
W-pI...124.8:3 **d.** a half an hour to the thought that you
W-pI...130.7:2 **d.** our minds to finding only what is real.
W-pI.131.10:3 will **d.** ten minutes to this goal three times
W-pI.139.11:1 and at night we will **d.** to dedicate our
WpI...rV.in8:3 we **d.** our time and effort to them. And
W-pI...185.7:1 Let us today **d.** our practicing to
W-pI...185.8:1 Today **d.** your practice periods to careful
W-pI.193.10:6 **d.** what time you can to serve its proper
M-16.........5:6 to sleep is a desirable time to **d.** to God. It
P-3......... II.1:4 are those who **d.** themselves primarily to

**devoted** 17

T-1.........I.15:1 Each day should be **d.** to miracles. The
T-1......... II.3:8 he is a brother, and to devotion if he is **d.**.
T-4...........I.6:6 you will not be a **d.** teacher as long as you
T-4.........I.13:7 I need **d.** teachers who share my aim of
T-9.........I.13:1 to you created you **d.** to everything, and
T-9.........I.13:1 and gave you what you are **d.** *to.* Otherwise
T-14....... II.1:2 You who are steadfastly **d.** to misery must
T-27...... III.3:8 time **d.** to its seeing be perceived as idly
W-pI.....33.1:2 A full five minutes should be **d.** to the
W-pI.....75.4:1 Our longer practice periods will be **d.** to
W-pI.....77.7:1 also be **d.** to a reminder of a simple fact.
WpI..rII.in.1:3 earlier part of each day will be **d.** to one of
W-pI...123.2:1 A day **d.** now to gratitude will add the
W-pI.138.12:3 a brief quiet time **d.** to maintaining sanity
WpI. rIV.in5:1 Begin each day with time **d.** to the
M-16.........3:4 we can safely say that time **d.** to starting
P-3......... II.1:8 They are **d.** to certain kinds of needs in

**devotes** 1

M-16.......10:2 this fact that the teacher of God **d.** his day

**devoting** 3

T-9.........I.12:4 are **d.** your mind to what you do not want
T-17.........I.2:3 Yet by distorting it and **d.** it to "evil," it
P-2........VII.4:3 **d.** his life to the function of true healing.

**devotion** 19

T-1......... II.3:8 he is a brother, and to **d.** if he is devoted.
T-1......... II.3:9 It is only my **d.** that entitles me to yours.
T-1......... II.4:6 My **d.** to my brothers has placed me in
T-4.........in.1:3 **D.** to a brother cannot set you back either
T-4.........in.1:5 The result of genuine **d.** is inspiration, a
T-4.........I.7:10 of **d.** is possible as long as this delusion
T-5......... II.8:9 divided **d.** has given you the two voices,
T-8........ VI.9:2 My **d.** to you is of Him, being born of my
T-8........VII.9:6 **d.** to Him replaces devotion to the ego. In
T-8........VII.9:6 devotion to Him replaces **d.** to the ego. In
T-9.........I.12:5 How real can this **d.** be? If you do not
T-9.........I.13:1 God in His **d.** to you created you devoted
T-11...... VI.5:1 the power of the **d.** of God's Son, nor the
T19. IV.A.10:9 just the same **d.** that love looks on itself.
T19....IV.C.1:3 must learn still more about this strange **d.**
T-20....... II.3:3 upon it, making it worthy of their **d.**. And
T-20.... VI.11:4 his **d.** to death's idols and then pass on.
W-pI...157.5:1 forth, your ministry takes on a genuine **d.**
M-26.........3:3 be won after much **d.** and dedication, and

**devotions** 2

T-5......... II.8:7 These altars are not things; they are **d.**.
T-5......... II.8:8 Yet you have other **d.** now. Your divided

**devour** 2

T-18....VIII.3:6 the sunbeam's "enemy" that would **d.** it,
W-pI...161.8:4 hope it can reach to its maker and **d.** him.

**devoured** 1

T19. IV.A.12:7 carry it screaming to their master, to be **d.**

**devouring** 1

M-27.........3:7 **D.** is nature's "law of life." God is insane,

**diametrically** 7

T-5........ III.3:1 are two **d.** opposed ways of seeing your
T-7..........II.2:8 them, you can arrive at **d.** opposed results
T-7..........II.2:9 in which **d.** opposed outcomes seem
T-8...........I.5:5 each believing in **d.** opposed ideas, it
T-11.......in.1:4 but they are **d.** opposed in all respects so
T-13...... IV.7:2 perceive the goal of time as **d.** opposed.
W-pI.....71.5:3 salvation that are **d.** opposed in all ways.

**diamond** 1

W-pI...124.9:4 with every minute like a **d.** set around the

**diamonds** 1

T-17...... IV.8:4 and the tears are faceted like **d.** and gleam

**dichotomy** 1

T-6...... V.C.3:4 emphasizes the **d.** between the desirable

**dictate** 4

T-1........ III.4:2 in the Atonement which I will **d.** to you.
T-2......VIII.5:7 your right-mindedness cannot but **d.**. The
T-24.......in.2:4 the power to **d.** each decision you make.
W-pI...131.3:3 can not **d.** the goal for which you search,

**dictated** 2

T-4....... II.10:5 be **d.** by the thought system to which it
T-9......VII.6:6 that **d.** this choice the lament is inevitable

**dictates** 14

T-1......... V.5:6 because such are the **d.** of tyrants. To
T-4........ IV.4:2 as vigilant against the ego's **d.** as for them
T-4.......VII.2:3 thought system, as is everything else it **d.**.
T-5......... V.7:6 and must therefore obey their **d.**. This
T-8.......VIII.6:4 It **d.** endless prescriptions for avoiding
T-12...... IV.1:4 Its **d.**, then, can be summed up simply as:
T-13...... IV.5:4 **d.** your reactions to those you meet in the
T-13...... IV.5:5 if you follow the ego's **d.** you will react to
T-17...... III.8:3 the unholy alliance **d.** are not perceived
T-18...... IX.4:7 look on it. Yet they will see what it **d.**.
T-27...... IV.5:2 It **d.** the answer even as it asks. Thus is all
T-29...........I.5:6 do. It **d.** what its health can tolerate, and
W-pI.133.10:3 mistakes, according to the **d.** of his guide.
W-pI...170.6:2 those who worship them obey their **d.**,

**dictator** 1

T-24.........I.5:1 Specialness is the great **d.** of the wrong

**did** 291

**die** 102

T-5........ IV.2:3 It does not **d.**; it was merely never born.
T-10....... V.8:3 You are not sick and you cannot **d.**. But
T-10....... V.9:1 eternal can be loved, for love does not **d.**.
T-11.........I.9:8 What He created can sleep, but cannot **d.**.
T-11...... VI.7:4 not **d.** by demonstrating that I live in you.
T-11...... VI.8:2 God's Son, for the Will of God cannot **d.**.

T-11.....VII.2:5 like the Father, and therefore cannot **d.**
T-12......III.8:5 from the Mind of God you would **d.**.
T-12...VII.13:5 but its hatred is not satisfied until you **d.**.
T-12...VII.15:1 for death, *remember that I did not* ***d.*** You
T-12...VII.15:6 you look out upon a world that cannot **d.**.
T-13.......II.9:3 who did not **d.** because he is immortal.
T-13.......V.4:2 They do not wish to **d.**, yet they will not
T-16......IV.4:5 trying to live with guilt rather than **d.** of it
T-16......V.10:4 is that God must **d.** so you can live. And it
T-18....VIII.7:5 nothing yet who would still **d.** to defend it
T-19.......II.3:6 sin *is* death, and how can the immortal **d.?**
T19. IV.A.17:2 your sin, and so I had to **d.** instead of you.
T19. IV.A.17:8 No one can **d.** for anyone, and death does
T19..IV.B.16:5 as himself, without which he would **d.**,
T19....IV.C.1:4 No one can **d.** unless he chooses death.
T19....IV.C.8:6 In its exaltation you commanded it to **d.**,
T-20....VI.11:2 and grieve and **d.** in honor of its master.
T-20....VIII.7:5 seem to walk about in it, to sin and **d.**,
T-23....III.6:10 the unnatural intent to murder and to **d.**.
T-24......III.7:6 Curse God and **d.**, but not by Him Who
T-25......IV.3:7 and every wish to hurt and kill and **d.**,
T-26.........I.6:6 his, and **d.** each time you see in him a sin
T-26.........I.7:2 who cannot **d.** because his sinlessness is
T-26.......II.5:4 *you* find him guilty and would have him **d.**
T-26.....V.11:2 instant that he chose to **d.** instead of live.
T-26.....V.13:2 And so you **d.** each day to live again, until
T-26...VII.16:5 reborn until he chooses not to **d.** again. In
T-27.........I.4:6 "Behold me, brother, at your hand I **d.**."
T-27.......V.4:6 its peace and comfort, leaving it to **d.**.
T-28......VI.2:4 It is not born and does not **d.**. It can but
T-29.......V.7:6 sword, to keep his ancient promises to **d.**.
T-29......VI.2:1 Swear not to **d.**, you holy Son of God!
T-29......VI.3:2 If it be conceived to **d.**, then die it must
T-29......VI.3:2 then **d.** it must unless it does not take this
T-29......VI.4:2 You were not born to **d.**. You cannot
T-29....VI.4:10 Life's function cannot be to **d.**. It must be
T-29.....VII.3:2 fail him, all excepting one; for he will **d.**,
T-29.....VII.5:2 You came to **d.**, and what would you
T-29....VIII.6:4 Here the deathless come to **d.**, the all-
T-29....VIII.6:6 little while; to suffer pain and finally to **d.**.
T-30.....III.6:5 Thoughts are not born and cannot **d.**.
T-30.....III.7:4 Yet it did not **d.** when you forgot it. It was
T-31.........I.9:2 Without your answer is it left to **d.**, as it is
T-31.......I.13:4 without the past that sentenced him to **d.**,
T-31......III.5:4 sin must **d.** for what they think they are.
T-31......IV.9:6 Yet has He never left His Thoughts to **d.**,
T-31...VII.14:3 and no remaining hope except to **d.**, and
T-31....VIII.1:2 of God he is a body, born in what must **d.**,
W-pI.....73.5:8 you really want to weep and suffer and **d.**
W-pI.....76.5:5 that it attacks itself and wants to **d.**. It is
W-pI.....84.1:3 I cannot experience loss and I cannot **d.**. I
W-pI...100.7:7 plan, and never lose or sacrifice or **d.**.
W-pI...107.6:7 You were not meant to suffer and to **d.**.
W-pI...136.8:5 commanding you to **d.** and cease to be.
W-pI...136.9:1 but cannot overcome your choice to **d.**.
W-pI.136.11:4 You can but choose to think you **d.**, or
W-pI...138.7:3 resolved, for ending opposition is to **d.**.
W-pI...152.6:4 that lives within a body that must **d.?** You
W-pI...156.4:1 There is a light in you which cannot **d.**;
W-pI...163.6:3 Either all things **d.**, or else they live and
W-pI...163.6:3 things die, or else they live and cannot **d.**.
W-pI.166.11:1 Now do we live, for now we cannot **d.**.
W-pI.167.3:10 healing. It is why you cannot **d.**. Its truth
W-pI...167.6:7 seems to **d.** is but the sign of mind asleep.
W-pI...190.6:6 living things must come at last to **d.?**
W-pI...191.3:3 leaving you nothing but the wish to **d.**.
W-pI...191.9:1 and devastated dreams, born but to **d.**, to
W-pI.191.11:5 **d.** till you accept your own eternal life.
W-pI...192.5:2 It cannot think that it will **d.**, nor be the
W-pI...194.3:3 In no one instant can one even **d.**. And so
W-pI...198.7:5 How foolish to believe that They could **d.!**
W-pI...198.7:7 and that the holy Son of God can **d.!**
W-pI...200.2:2 to win through losing, nor to **d.** to live.
W-pII .228.2:2 *left that Source to enter in a body and to* ***d.***.
W-pII .....3.5:5 made to **d.** can be restored to everlasting
W-pII .....4.3:3 must have an end; eternal life must **d.**.
W-pII .....5.1:2 he lives, to **d.** as it decays and crumbles.
W-pII .....5.2:9 And if he did not **d.**, what "proof" is there
W-pII .278.1:1 all things that seem to live appear to **d.**,
W-pII .294.1:4 has God's beloved Son for what must **d.?**
W-pII .....9.4:2 For every one who ever came to **d.**, or yet
W-pII ...12.4:2 where its sickly followers prepare to **d.**.
W-pII .331.1:4 *to* ***d.*** *within a world of pain and cruelty. How*
W-pII ...13.5:1 starved and thirsty creatures come to **d.**.
W-pII ...13.5:4 up, to show that what is born can never **d.**
M-12.........5:5 it is holy it cannot be sick, nor can it **d.**.
M-12.........6:7 and go, shift and change, suffer and **d.**.
M-19.........4:4 For separate fragments must decay and **d.**
M-20.........4:9 you not rather live than choose to **d.?**
M-27.........1:4 that all things in it are born only to **d.**.
M-27.........4:1 that may go on apart from what will **d.**,
M-27.......5:10 image. To look on His creations is to **d.**.
M-27.........6:8 But what is born of God and still can **d.?**
M-27.........7:3 seems to **d.** has but been misperceived
S-3...........I.1:5 The body yet must **d.**, and so its healing
S-3..........II.1:6 cause is still the wish to **d.** and overcome

## died 3

T-11 .....VI.7:3 Teach not that I **d.** in vain. Teach rather
T-31 .....IV.3:4 Men have **d.** on seeing this, because they
W-pI...163.7:4 And with the Father **d.** the Son as well.

## dies 14

T-6 ......V.A.1:4 The body neither lives nor **d.**, because it
T-18 .....VI.3:4 which suffers and **d.** because it is attacked
T19....IV.C.5:2 The body no more **d.** than it can feel. It
T-20 ....VII.6:7 the cause of sin an instant before he **d.**.
T-21 ...VIII.1:4 so he "**d.**" because of what he learned. He
T-24 ..VII.10:3 It grows and withers, flourishes and **d.**.
T-27 ...VIII.1:3 outside the body, lives a little while and **d.**
T-29 ...VIII.6:1 and when it is withdrawn the idol "**d.**"
T-31 .....III.4:7 And it grows old and **d.**, because that
W-pI...133.6:4 What fades and **d.** was never there, and
W-pI...152.1:4 And no one **d.** without his own consent.
W-pI...159.3:2 and the rebirth of love which never **d.**,
W-pII .248.1:6 What **d.** was never living in reality, and
M-12.........5:3 weak, and being weak, it suffers and it **d.**.

## differ 6

T-13 ......V.2:1 is because of this that private worlds do **d.**
T-23 .......II.2:5 And this is justified because the values **d.**,
W-pI...140.7:6 For how can one illusion **d.** from another
W-pI...187.1:6 which the world and true perception **d.**.
C-5 ............1:5 But they have names which **d.** for a time,
P-2.........in.3:2 of "improvement" still must **d.**. The

## difference 74

T-1 .......II.3:12 **d.** between us now is that I have nothing
T-1 .......VI.1:4 It is, in fact, the essential **d.** between them
T-3 ......VII.1:2 a creating, a **d.** we have already discussed.
T-3 ......VII.1:4 Their **d.** lies in what rests upon them.
T-4 .....II.11:13 its main **d.** from everything else the mind
T-4 .......VI.3:7 that you have already accepted this **d.**,
T-4 ......VII.5:7 there is no **d.** between *having* and *being*, as
T-5 ........in.2:3 love. There is no **d.** between love and joy.
T-5 ........in.2:6 That is why it makes no **d.** to what part or
T-5 ..........I.1:5 knows no **d.** between *having* and *being*. The
T-6 .......II.12:1 The **d.** between the ego's projection and
T-6 ........V.2:4 the **d.** between sleeping and waking, so
T-6 ........V.4:3 because they do not recognize the **d.**. The
T-7 .........X.8:6 are learning the **d.** between pain and joy.
T-8 ...........II.h **D.** between Imprisonment and Freedom
T-8 .........II.5:1 teaches you the **d.** between pain and joy.
T-8 .........II.5:2 as saying He teaches you the **d.** between
T-8 ...VIII.1:11 **d.** between knowledge and perception. In
T-8 ...VIII.1:15 there is no **d.** between the part and whole.
T-9 ..........I.5:3 is no **d.** between your will and God's. If
T-9 .....VIII.3:1 the **d.** between grandeur and grandiosity,
T-9 .....VIII.3:1 sees no **d.** between miracle impulses and
T-11 ....VII.4:6 know the **d.** between what you have made
T-11 ....VII.4:6 know the **d.** between what you have made
T-13 ...VIII.2:1 The very real **d.** between perception and
T-13 ...IX.8:10 He knows there is no **d.**, for He knows not
T-13 .....X.13:2 The **d.** is that I love *only* what God loves
T-13 ..... XI.4:4 will finally let Him judge the **d.** for you,
T-13 ..... XI.6:6 lightly over you without a **d.** of any kind.
T-14 ..... III.5:6 he does this or does it not will make no **d.**
T-16 .... VII.7:1 your full awareness of the complete **d.**, in
T-18 .......V.1:2 already understood the **d.** between truth
T-19 ........I.5:2 the **d.** in how they operate is less apparent
T-19 ........I.5:2 from the fundamental **d.** in what they are.
T-19 ..... III.5:3 of the **d.** between time and eternity. And
T-20 ..... III.3:7 Nor is there any **d.** between yourself and
T-20 .... VII.7:1 is indeed a **d.** between this vain imagining
T-20 .... VII.7:2 **d.** lies not in them, but in their purpose.
T-21 .... VII.6:6 And this imagined **d.** attests to your belief
T-22 ......in.2:3 It is this **d.**, seen but not real, that makes
T-22 ......in.3:4 He sees no **d.** between these selves, for
T-22 .......II.2:6 them as different, and define the **d.** as joy.
T-22 .......II.2:7 Yet to perceive a **d.** where none exists will
T-22 .......II.2:7 none exists will surely fail to make a **d.**.
T-22 .....II.3:10 that are but equally unreal. This is no **d.**.
T-22 ..... III.2:4 can see the **d.** between sin and mistakes,
T-22 ... VI.14:9 There is no **d.** anywhere in it, for every
T-23 ..... III.3:7 a little, love a little, and know the **d.**. Thus
T-23 ..... IV.1:6 No **d.** enters, and what is all the same
T-24 ........I.3:6 **d.** of any kind imposes orders of reality,
T-24 ........I.7:2 There is no **d.**. You have been given to
T-24 .. VII.11:4 Their **d.** does not lie in how they look, nor
T-25 ... VIII.3:4 Who it may be makes little **d.**. But death
T-26 ..... III.4:8 And herein lies the **d.** between the worlds
T-26 ..... III.5:4 **d.** is the learning goal this course has set.
T-26 .. VII.19:5 all. There is no **d.** among the Sons of God.
T-27 ... VI.2:10 Yet which is foremost makes no **d.**. Sin's
T-31 ..... VI.4:6 It makes no **d.** what you look upon, nor
W-pI .... 12.4:2 exercises, there is no **d.** between them. At
W-pI .... 30.2:5 fundamental **d.** between vision and the
W-pI .... 74.5:3 withdrawal, but the **d.** is easily detected.
W-pI .. 127.4:1 **d.** in what you really are and what love is.
W-pI .. 140.2:5 **d.** does the content of a dream make in
W-pI .. 154.6:1 is one major **d.** in the role of Heaven's
W-pI .. 185.5:6 he has learned their only **d.** is one of form
M-4 ..... I.A.7:4 was meaningless in teaching him the **d.**.
M-16 ......... 7:7 is no **d.** in his state at different times and
M-18 ......... 1:9 is not the form alone in which the **d.** lies.
M-29 ......... 1:4 so that the **d.** is temporary by definition.
C-3 ........... 1:3 which is the Holy Spirit's, it has one **d.**.
P-2..........II.6:1 what **d.** does it make how the invitation is
P-2....... VII.3:2 be the **d.** between healing and forgiveness
P-3........ III.2:6 There is a **d.** between payment and cost.
S-2..........II.1:4 The **d.** is clear in several forms where the

## differences 49

T-2 .........II.5:8 is a belief in **d.** is learning meaningful.
T-7 .........II.5:3 the idea that **d.** in form are meaningful,
T-7 .........II.5:3 emphasizing always that *these* ***d.*** *do not*
T-7 ....... IV.3:8 their similarity rather than their **d.** is
T-7 ....... IV.5:5 Healing is the way to undo the belief in **d.**,
T-13 ... IX.8:10 is no difference, for He knows not of **d.**.
T-13 ..... XI.6:3 and **d.** are necessary teaching aids, for by
T-13 ..... XI.6:4 that makes the need for any **d.** disappear.
T-14 .......X.2:7 being based not on **d.** but on equality.
T-17 .......II.4:3 ever change; no shifts nor shadings, no **d.**,
T-18 ........I.7:9 tiny **d.** in form are no real differences at
T-18 ........I.7:9 differences in form are no real **d.** at all.
T-18 .......II.3:1 You do not find the **d.** between what you
T-18 ... VI.12:1 and of your **d.** in size and seeming quality
T-22 ......in.2:5 For an unholy relationship is based on **d.**,
T-22 ......in.3:4 these selves, for **d.** are only of the body.
T-22 ......in.4:2 Here is belief in **d.** undone. Here is the
T-22 ......in.4:3 Here is the faith in **d.** shifted to sameness.
T-22 ......in.4:4 here is sight of **d.** transformed to vision.
T-22 ......in.4:8 extends and finally removes all sense of **d.**
T-22 ........I.4:9 leads to sight of **d.** and loss of sameness.
T-24 ........I.4:5 ones feel weak and frail because of **d.**, for
T-25 ........I.1:7 nor any **d.** perceived to stand between the
T-25 .... VII.5:3 death and cruelty; to separation and to **d.**.
T-25 .. VII.10:6 without the **d.** which would have made a
T-25 ... IX.10:7 unlike, it sees no **d.** where none exists.
T-25 ... IX.10:8 for everyone, because it sees no **d.** in them
T-27 .......V.8:9 by One Who does not see the **d.** you see.
T-27 .....V.8:11 been made in spite of all the **d.** you see,

T-27.......V.9:3 be their **d.** which made this possible, for
T-27. VIII.12:2 He sees no **d.** where none exists, and He
T-31.........I.1:8 that you perceive no **d.** in false and true.
W-pI.......1.3:1 and make no allowance for **d.** in the kinds
W-pI.....66.4:4 to go beyond these **d.** in appearance, and
W-pI...130.4:2 of **d.** you believe make up the world. They
W-pII.....262.h Let me perceive no **d.** today.
M-2............5:6 and all the **d.** they thought separated
M-4............2:1 **d.** among the Sons of God are temporary.
M-8............1:2 It rests on **d.**; on uneven background and
M-8............2:1 Illusions are always illusions of **d.**. How
M-8............3:1 do all these **d.** come from? Certainly they
M-8............3:8 eyes will never see except through **d.**. Yet
M-8............4:7 true. On this the judgment of all **d.** rests,
M-8............6:1 The body's eyes will continue to see **d.**.
M-8............6:7 and place–for **d.** cannot exist within it–
M-20..........2:7 strangely, it is not a contrast of true **d.**.
M-23..........7:5 curriculum, not because of content **d.**,
M-28..........5:2 **D.** have disappeared and Love looks on
P-2.........in.4:2 of therapy is one of reconciling these **d.**.

### different 305

T-1.........II.4:1 separate or **d.** from you except in time,
T-1........VI.1:5 state somehow **d.** from the one you are in.
T-1........VI.2:3 yourself into levels with **d.** needs. As you
T-1........VI.3:2 effectively while you function on **d.** levels.
T-2.....VII.3:12 and Effect relationships totally **d.** from
T-3.......V.10:8 Do not perceive yourself in **d.** lights.
T-3........VI.7:1 I have spoken of **d.** symptoms, and at
T-4........III.5:1 There is a kind of experience so **d.** from
T-4........III.9:4 language, "to have" and "to be" are **d.**,
T-5..........in.1:7 **d.** kinds of responses at the same time,
T-5.........I.4:5 symbolism is open to **d.** interpretations.
T-5.........II.6:5 freedom to create, but its application is **d.**
T-5........IV.3:6 because they occur at **d.** levels and also
T-5........VI.3:5 two voices speak for **d.** interpretations of
T-6...........I.5:5 offered a **d.** interpretation of attack, and
T-6.........II.2:2 are **d.** from the one on whom you project.
T-6.........II.3:3 device of the ego to make you feel **d.** from
T-6......V.C.1:9 and that is why it promotes **d.** moods.
T-7.........II.2:6 However, the content is **d.** in this world,
T-7.........II.2:6 thoughts it governs are very **d.** from the
T-7.........II.4:2 must be translated for those who speak **d.**
T-7........III.3:7 **d.** from saying you perceive yourself as
T-7........IV.3:6 **d.** abilities are applied long enough to one
T-8...........I.5:2 you unhappy, and if you want a **d.** one, a
T-8...........I.6:4 you entirely **d.** things in entirely different
T-8...........I.6:4 different things in entirely **d.** ways, which
T-8.........II.5:5 are the same, to teach you how they are **d.**
T-8........IV.6:4 If you want to be **d.**, I will wait until you
T-8.........V.5:9 to go in **d.** directions and will lose the way
T-8.......VII.7:3 **D.** orders of reality merely appear to exist
T-8.......VII.7:3 to exist, just as **d.** orders of miracles do.
T-8... VIII.1:12 and reassemble in **d.** constellations. But
T-9...........I.6:3 it speaks for **d.** things to the same mind.
T-9...........I.7:9 nothing more than the belief that it is **d.**.
T-9...........I.8:2 a mind believes that its will is **d.** from His,
T-9........III.5:5 How is this **d.** from telling you that what
T-9.......VII.4:2 how completely **d.** these evaluations are,
T-9..... VIII.3:2 between these two very **d.** kinds of threat.
T-10.......in.2:4 is **d.** because everything has always been.
T-10.......V.3:8 to be many **d.** things he is but one idea;–
T-11.......in.1:5 their results are as **d.** as their foundations,
T-11......III.4:1 way is not hard, but it *is* very **d.**. Yours is
T-11......VI.3:4 Yet **d.** experiences lead to different beliefs
T-11......VI.3:4 Yet different experiences lead to **d.** beliefs
T-11......VI.3:4 beliefs, and with them **d.** perceptions. For
T-12.....VII.7:7 of two goals, each perceived in a **d.** place;
T-12.....VII.7:7 each other because you made them **d.**.
T-13.....V.10:2 **d.** worlds arise from their different sights.
T-13.....V.10:2 different worlds arise from their **d.** sights.
T-13.....VII.2:1 sight of it is costing you a **d.** kind of vision
T-13.....VII.2:2 each of them involves a **d.** kind of seeing,
T-13....XI.11:3 The Holy Spirit has a very **d.** kind of
T-14......IX.2:6 **D.** realities are meaningless, for reality
T-14......IX.7:4 bring their **d.** problems to its healing light
T-14......XI.6:1 so completely **d.** from everything that you
T-15.......V.7:1 while it prefers **d.** parts of another aspect.
T-15.......V.8:2 on no one to make your brothers seem **d.**.
T-15.......X.5:1 emerge in forms quite **d.** from what it is.
T-15.......X.5:3 but as **d.** manifestations of the same idea,
T-15..XI.10:11 this year **d.** by making it all the same. And
T-16.........I.1:4 in His way. His way is very **d.**. He does not
T-16........III.1:5 from the basis of a very **d.** thought system
T-16......VI.6:1 Across the bridge it is so **d.**! For a time
T-17.......I.1:10 in the mind that would have reality be **d.**.
T-17.......II.2:4 it is the meeting place of worlds so **d.**. Yet
T-17......IV.2:7 His because of the illusion that they are **d.**
T-17......IV.6:3 still seems to you somehow to be "**d.**." Yet
T-17......IV.6:6 For this one is not **d.**. Retain this one, and
T-18.........I.2:5 process in which they are perceived as **d.**.
T-18.........I.3:4 to require a **d.** form of acting out for
T-18.........I.5:1 how very **d.** is reality from what you see.
T-18.....II.5:13 and your waking dreams have **d.** forms,
T-18......IV.4:8 that you must make the learner **d.**. You
T-18......IV.4:9 the learner, nor can you make him **d.**.
T-18......VI.8:6 It is *not* made up of **d.** parts, which reach
T-18......VI.9:7 He would have had to create **d.** things,
T-18......VI.9:7 and to establish **d.** orders of reality, only
T-18.....VII.2:5 gives you a **d.** view of it when you return.
T-18.....VII.5:1 Your way will be **d.**, not in purpose but in
T-18... VIII.6:5 This little aspect is no **d.** from the whole,
T-18.....IX.10:5 you to something completely **d.**. Here is
T-18.....IX.11:3 go, will go beyond it, but in a **d.** way.
T-19......III.8:3 fragmented creation would have a **d.** will,
T19. IV.A.11:3 of **d.** things in different languages. What
T19. IV.A.11:3 of different things in **d.** languages. What
T-20.......II.6:1 look with **d.** eyes upon your brother. You
T-20.......III.1:2 that what was so before has been made **d.**
T-20.......V.6:1 look upon each holy instant as a **d.** point
T-20... VIII.8:8 each **d.** and with different values. Yet they
T-20... VIII.8:8 each different and with **d.** values. Yet they
T-22.......in.1:5 And each one seems to make a **d.** error,
T-22.......in.2:2 who see their brothers **d.** from themselves
T-22.......in.3:1 holy relationship starts from a **d.** premise.
T-22.........I.1:2 then you and your Creator have a **d.** will.
T-22.........I.6:4 meaning **d.** things to him at different
T-22.........I.6:4 meaning different things to him at **d.**
T-22........I.11:1 to what is like Himself; the same, not **d.**.
T-22.......II.1:2 only alternatives, and **d.** from each other.
T-22.......II.2:6 some aspects out of it, see them as **d.**, and
T-22.......II.4:2 they are **d.** from each other in every way,
T-22.......II.4:3 confuse what is the same with what is **d.**.
T-22.......II.9:3 mind, be **d.** from it and in opposition to it
T-22.......II.9:6 make himself **d.** and oppose His Will,
T-22.....II.10:4 His joy to misery, and make Him **d.**. And
T-22......III.7:1 Only mistakes have **d.** forms, and so they
T-22....VI.13:1 Only the **d.** can attack. So you conclude
T-22....VI.13:2 attack, you and your brother must be **d.**.
T-22....VI.13:4 *Because* you and your brother are not **d.**,
T-22....VI.13:7 is whether you and your brother are **d.**.
T-22....VI.15:7 if you and your brother be **d.** or the same,
T-23.........I.6:1 to make them **d.** from each other, in the
T-23.........I.6:3 Nor are they **d.** from each other. Both are
T-23........I.11:5 can conflict, because their forms are **d.**.
T-23.......II.2:1 law is that the truth is **d.** for everyone.
T-23.......II.2:2 and has a **d.** set of thoughts that set him
T-23.......II.5:4 Now are They **d.**, and enemies. And Their
T-23.....II.21:4 Each is a **d.** form in the progression of
T-23......III.3:8 teach a little of the same can still be **d.**,
T-23......IV.2:1 What can be equal to the truth, yet **d.**?
T-23......IV.3:4 What is the same can have no **d.** function.
T-23......IV.5:2 there will your perspective be quite **d.**.
T-24.........I.3:5 enemies, for they are **d.** and not the same.
T-24.........I.4:2 But what is **d.** calls for judgment, and this
T-24.........I.9:7 Never can there be peace among the **d.**.
T-24.......II.5:2 They speak a **d.** language and they fall on
T-24.......II.5:2 different language and they fall on **d.** ears.
T-24.......II.5:3 To every special one a **d.** message, and
T-24.......II.5:3 message, and one with **d.** meaning, is the
T-24.......II.5:4 Yet how can truth be **d.** to each one? The
T-24.......II.5:5 hear convince them they are **d.** and apart;
T-24.......II.7:4 both. It gives no **d.** messages, and has one
T-24.......V.5:4 And yet because they serve a **d.** purpose,
T-24.....VII.9:2 Look at this body in a **d.** light and it looks
T-24.....VII.9:2 body in a different light and it looks **d.**.
T-24...VII.11:5 do. They have a **d.** purpose. It is this that
T-24...VII.11:6 each from all aspects with a **d.** purpose.
T-24. VII.11:12 And it is given you to make a **d.** choice,
T-24. VII.11:12 and use perception for a **d.** purpose. And
T-25.........I.5:5 mad desire to be separate, **d.** and special
T-25.........I.7:7 *What is the same can not be* **d.**, *and what is*
T-25......III.3:4 To each it has a **d.** purpose, and to each it
T-25......VI.1:2 to fear, and no one who is **d.** from himself
T-25...VII.10:5 show His Son that hell and Heaven are **d.**,
T-25..VIII.9:10 For love and justice are not **d.**. *Because*
T-26........II.3:4 that makes each one seem **d.** from the rest
T-26......III.4:6 is the same and what is **d.** remain unclear.
T-26......III.5:6 is to teach what is the same and what is **d.**
T-26......III.7:3 between them, and to make them **d.**. How
T-26.......V.1:4 And you can learn it in many **d.** ways. All
T-26.......V.1:7 two teachers only, who point in **d.** ways.
T-26...VII.15:6 you believe what is the same is **d.** you but
T-26....VIII.1:3 are one illusion, which takes **d.** forms. If it
T-26........X.1:4 And thus you see what is the same as **d.**.
T-27.........I.5:1 the Holy Spirit lays a picture of a **d.** you.
T-27.........I.6:7 to your brother and yourself in **d.** tongues
T-27........I.11:3 This leaves no space in which a **d.** view,
T-27......II.11:2 has conflicting purposes and **d.** ends.
T-27......II.11:4 **d.** from you in that he is more guilty, thus
T-27......II.11:5 from yours, and gives you both a **d.** role.
T-27......II.12:5 seems to have a **d.** purpose from the one
T-27......II.14:7 you and him a function that is one, not **d.**.
T-27......IV.1:3 has no answer, for it is seen in **d.** ways.
T-27......IV.4:3 both attesting the same thing in **d.** form.
T-27....IV.6:10 something new and **d.** from the question.
T-27.......V.8:7 really are the same, despite their **d.** forms.
T-27.......V.9:2 your many **d.** problems will be solved as
T-27.....V.10:3 you by all the many **d.** witnesses it finds.
T-27.....V.10:5 to have a problem that is **d.** from the rest.
T-27......VI.2:5 more. Each one seems **d.** because it has a
T-27......VI.2:5 seems different because it has a **d.** name,
T-27......VI.2:5 and so it seems to answer to a **d.** sound.
T-27......VI.6:4 have **d.** witnesses with different strengths.
T-27......VI.6:4 have different witnesses with **d.** strengths.
T-27......VI.6:5 And they attest to **d.** sufferings. Yet to the
T-27......VI.6:9 The laws that call them **d.** are dissolved,
T-27...VII.11:3 with **d.** dreams about the truth in you.
T-27....VIII.1:8 and joys are **d.** and can be told apart.
T-27..VIII.12:3 None has a **d.** cause from all the rest, and
T-28.......I.14:6 It that could generate a **d.** past or future.
T-28......IV.6:2 What is the same seems **d.**, because what
T-29.......V.8:1 Him Who sees a **d.** function for a dream.
T-29......VI.1:3 These questions are the same, in **d.** form.
T-30.........I.7:3 of being answered in a **d.** way from what
T-30.....VII.1:6 which is **d.** every time you think of it. You
T-30.....VII.2:4 made on **d.** aspects of experience. And
T-30.....VII.3:3 If they are given **d.** meanings, it must be
T-30.....VII.3:3 must be that they reflect but **d.** purposes.
T-30.....VII.5:3 which must assume a **d.** purpose for the
T-30.....VII.5:5 And it is this idea of **d.** goals that makes
T-30.....VII.6:1 the symbols that are used mean **d.** things?
T-31.........I.7:2 Each has its outcome in a **d.** world. And
T-31........II.2:8 Nor are they **d.**. Yet must we see them
T-31........II.2:9 to the one alternative that *is* a **d.** choice.
T-31........II.5:6 because from them there is a **d.** outcome.
T-31........II.7:6 He cannot hear a **d.** answer from the one
T-31......II.10:4 It takes, perhaps, a **d.** form in him, but it
T-31.......III.1:2 a choice that will result in **d.** outcomes,
T-31......IV.2:7 deceived by all the **d.** names its roads are
T-31......IV.6:4 The search for **d.** pathways in the world is
T-31......IV.6:4 is but the search for **d.** forms of truth.
T-31......IV.8:3 of decision cannot lie in choosing **d.**
T-31.....V.14:5 be shown that **d.** thoughts have different
T-31.....V.14:5 different thoughts have **d.** consequence.
T-31.....VII.9:1 they all are **d.** names for just one error;
T-31....VIII.8:4 tired eyes I bring a vision of a **d.** world, so
W-in..........4:1 way to a **d.** perception of everyone and
W-pI.......4.3:1 from time to time in somewhat **d.** form.
W-pI.......4.3:4 recognize what is the same and what is **d.**.
W-pI.......5.1:3 forms, all of which will be perceived as **d.**.
W-pI.......5.7:1 try to identify a number of **d.** forms of
W-pI.....10.2:2 The form is only slightly **d.**. This time the
W-pI.....13.4:1 in a somewhat **d.** way from the preceding
W-pI.....15.3:2 They may take many **d.** forms, some of
W-pI.....23.7:5 of attack and of being attacked are not **d.**,

W-pI.....24.4:3 also that these goals are on **d.** levels and
W-pI.....24.5:4 so on. Try to cover as many **d.** kinds of
W-pI.....32.2:2 However, since you see them as **d.**, the
W-pI.....35.3:1 today presents a very **d.** view of yourself.
W-pI.....35.3:3 will use a somewhat **d.** kind of application
W-pI.....44.1:4 together, being but **d.** aspects of creation.
W-pI.....64.5:8 **d.** from just this one simple choice. That
W-pI.....66.1:4 Their forms are **d.**, but their content is
W-pI.....66.4:3 be happiness, even if it appears to be **d.**.
W-pI...66.10:5 same as the same, and the **d.** as different.
W-pI...66.10:5 same as the same, and the different as **d.**.
W-pI.....71.2:4 you believe, that says, "If this were **d.**, I
W-pI.....75.2:7 Today we see a **d.** world, because the light
W-pI.....76.4:2 and put them under **d.** names in a long
W-pI.....76.8:1 a short review of the **d.** kinds of "laws" we
W-pI.....78.7:1 truth, that we may look on him a **d.** way,
W-pI.....79.3:3 is. A long series of **d.** problems seems to
W-pI.....79.4:2 of problems, each requiring a **d.** answer.
W-pI.....79.7:3 **d.** kinds of problems we think we have.
W-pI.....87.2:4 *light, [name]. In the light this will look* **d.**.
W-pI.....92.6:2 love. It sees all others **d.** from itself, and
W-pI.....93.3:1 think, but from a very **d.** reference point,
W-pI.....99.1:2 apart or **d.** from the Will of God. Thus do
W-pI...105.3:3 you will learn a **d.** way of looking at a gift.
W-pI...108.4:1 and receiving seen as **d.** aspects of one
W-pI...127.1:1 think that **d.** kinds of love are possible.
W-pI.127.10:4 And we raise our eyes upon a **d.** present,
W-pI...128.2:2 given it, until you see a **d.** purpose there.
W-pI.131.11:3 *I ask to see a* **d.** *world, and think a different*
W-pI.131.11:3 *think a* **d.** *kind of thought from those I made.*
W-pI...138.6:4 but conceal this one by taking **d.** forms.
W-pI...140.3:1 are **d.** from the dreaming of the world,
W-pI...140.7:6 no core, and nothing that is truly **d.**?
W-pI.140.11:4 We have no need to make them **d.**, and
W-pI...157.1:4 a **d.** kind of feeling and awareness. You
W-pI...159.7:2 made new again, but in a **d.** light. What
W-pI...160.1:4 thinks that it is real, but **d.** from yourself.
W-pI...160.2:1 to the truth he speaks a **d.** language, looks
W-pI...161.3:3 which is **d.** from the one we gave to them.
W-pI...161.3:4 made, to teach us from a **d.** point of view,
W-pI...161.3:4 view, so we can see a **d.** use in everything.
W-pI...164.4:5 **d.** from all things you sought before, that
W-pI...167.1:1 There are not **d.** kinds of life, for life is
W-pI...167.4:3 becoming **d.** from their own origin, apart
W-pI...169.3:6 ready to accept a state completely **d.** from
W-pI...181.4:2 how extremely **d.** the goals this course is
W-pI...184.1:6 all things to which you give a **d.** name; all
W-pI.184.14:1 And though we use a **d.** name for each
W-pI.184.15:3 *What we made and call by many* **d.** *names is*
W-pI...185.3:4 To each, the hero of the dream is **d.**; the
W-pI...185.3:5 gain takes on a **d.** aspect or another form.
W-pI...186.3:3 you be **d.** in any way from what you are.
W-pI...189.3:2 It is so **d.** from the world you see through
W-pI...193.3:4 with **d.** circumstances and events; with
W-pI...193.3:4 with **d.** characters and different themes,
W-pI...193.3:4 with different characters and **d.** themes,
W-pI...200.8:2 begins within the world perceived as **d.**,
W-pII .....4.2:4 now the body serves a **d.** aim for striving.
W-pII .295.1:7 Fear appears in many **d.** forms, but love is
W-pII .311.1:5 a gift of it to Him Who has a **d.** use for it.
W-pII ....314.h I seek a future **d.** from the past.
W-pII .314.1:1 there comes a future very **d.** from the past
W-pII .345.1:5 *Father, in Heaven it is* **d.**, *for there, there are*
M-2 ...........3:4 a new thought, a fresh idea, a **d.** approach
M-3 ...........1:2 involves a **d.** relationship at the beginning
M-3 ...........3:4 of teaching seems to be something **d.**.
M-3 ...........3:7 God's teachers work at **d.** levels, but the
M-4 ...........1:2 they come from vastly **d.** backgrounds,
M-4 .....I.A.3:4 where he must see things in a **d.** light? He
M-5 ......III.3:2 purpose, and therefore are not really **d.**.
M-8 ...........2:8 the mind is separate, **d.** from other minds
M-8 ...........2:8 other minds, with **d.** interests of its own,
M-8 ...........5:9 seem to make them **d.** are really irrelevant
M-11 .........2:3 For they say **d.** things about the world,
M-11 .......4:11 Now is the question **d.**. It is no longer,
M-16 .........7:7 in his state at **d.** times and different places
M-16 .........7:7 in his state at different times and **d.** places
M-19 .........2:5 path becomes quite **d.** as one goes along.
M-20 .........1:5 for each reflects a **d.** step along the way.
M-23 .........7:2 way to those who speak in **d.** tongues and
M-23 .........7:2 in different tongues and appeal to **d.**
C-5 ............6:3 Christ takes many forms with **d.** names
C-ep...........5:4 of this new day looks on a **d.** world where
P-2...........I.2:7 shadows, or perhaps **d.** cloud patterns.
P-2...........I.2:8 of nothingness cannot be called new or **d.**
P-2..........II.5:1 **D.** teaching aids appeal to different
P-2..........II.5:1 teaching aids appeal to **d.** people. Some
S-1.......IV.1:2 point, each one must ask for **d.** things.
S-2..........II.1:3 and make what God created equal, **d.**.
S-3..........II.1:8 kind of seeming death that has a **d.** source
S-3........III.6:4 a cause, it cannot come again in **d.** form.

## differential 1

T-26 .......X.1:2 have a **d.** view of when attack is justified,

## differently 44

T-14 ...... V.2:2 Each one teaches the message **d.**, and
T-14 ...... V.2:2 the message differently, and learns it **d.**.
T-17 ... IV.12:3 of all that you can have, seen very **d.**. You
T-18 .......II.6:6 But He does use it **d.**, as a help to make
T-18 ..... VI.9:6 God would have had to create **d.**, and to
T-19 ..... III.5:5 how to look on time **d.** and see beyond it,
T-21 ... III.12:2 light of vision it is looked upon quite **d.**.
T-21 ..... VI.3:9 it is certain that they look upon them **d.**.
T-22 .......II.7:2 are the same will not decide alone nor **d.**.
T-22 ... VI.13:3 Yet does the Holy Spirit explain this **d.**.
T-25 ..... IV.1:8 is defined another way and sought for **d.**.
T-25 ...... V.5:8 until you see him **d.** and let him be what
T-25 .. VII.3:10 Do not attempt to see it **d.**, nor twist it
T-25 .... VII.4:2 God and His beloved Son do not think **d.**.
T-27 .......II.8:2 the Holy Spirit and the world interpret **d.**.
T-27 .VIII.13:1 How **d.** will you perceive the world when
T-31 ..... IV.2:9 will lead, however **d.** they seem to start;
T-31 ..... IV.2:9 seem to start; however **d.** they seem to go.
W-pI.....11.2:1 somewhat **d.** from the previous ones.
W-pI.....20.5:4 You can see them **d.**, and you will. What
W-pI........21.h I am determined to see things **d.**.
W-pI.....21.4:2 *I am determined to see_[name of person]* **d.**
W-pI.....21.4:3 *determined to see_[specify the situation]* **d.**
W-pI.....21.5:4 *the attribute] in_[name of person]* **d.**.
W-pI........28.h Above all else I want to see things **d.**.
W-pI.....28.2:1 "Above all else I want to see this table **d.**."
W-pI.....28.2:7 When you have seen one thing **d.**, you
W-pI.....28.2:7 thing differently, you will see all things **d.**.
W-pI.....28.3:1 "Above all else I want to see this table **d.**,"
W-pI.....28.4:3 "Above all else I want to see this table **d.**,"
W-pI.....28.8:2 *Above all else I want to see this_***d.**. Each
W-pI.....39.7:2 for your salvation that you see them **d.**.
W-pI.....55.1:1 (21) I am determined to see things **d.**.
W-pI.....56.3:1 (28) Above all else I want to see **d.**. The
W-pI.....71.2:2 that, if someone else spoke or acted **d.**, if
W-pI.....72.8:5 Now we are going to try to see this **d.**.
W-pI.....75.8:3 you. From this time forth you will see **d.**.
W-pI...105.6:1 our practice periods will start a little **d.**.
W-pI...161.1:1 Today we practice **d.**, and take a stand
W-pI...184.4:4 a sense of unity or vision that sees **d.**,
W-pI...193.3:7 It is this: *Forgive, and you will see this* **d.**.
W-pI...193.5:1 *Forgive, and you will see this* **d.**. These are
W-pII .....8.2:2 The real world shows a world seen **d.**,
M-11 .........1:8 is true that the world must be looked at **d.**

## differs 3

T-7 ..........I.1:5 respect your creative power **d.** from His.
T-13 ...... V.1:4 content of individual illusions **d.** greatly.
P-2........ IV.8:2 of threat **d.** according to the form it takes.

## difficult 103

T-3 ..........I.2:6 particularly **d.** to overcome this because,
T-5 ..........I.4:5 makes the Holy Spirit **d.** to understand,
T-5 ......VII.6:1 Decision cannot be **d.**. This is obvious, if
T-6 .......II.11:1 it can so easily make the idea seem **d.**. Yet
T-6 .......II.11:2 never happened cannot be **d.**. However,
T-6 .......II.11:3 the idea of return both necessary and **d.**.
T-6 .......II.11:4 you cannot experience perfection as a **d.**
T-6 ..... V.B.8:7 because nothing is **d.** that is *wholly* desired
T-6 ..... V.B.8:8 and creating cannot be **d.** if God Himself
T-7 ...... XI.5:9 it, and this has been very **d.** for you.
T-8 .....VIII.3:1 been particularly **d.** to overcome the ego's
T-11 ..... IV.4:6 It is **d.** at first to realize that this is exactly
T-11 .....V.12:5 and it becomes **d.** to maintain that fear is
T-12 .......II.8:7 of perfection is not so **d.** as to deny truth,
T-14 .......II.2:3 Simplicity is very **d.** for twisted minds.
T-14 .......X.3:3 This is not **d.** to understand, once you
T-14 .......X.3:4 is more **d.** to grasp is the lack of order of
T-14 .......X.6:1 will seem **d.** for you to learn that you have
T-15 ..... VI.4:1 You do not find it **d.** to believe that when
T-15 ..... VI.4:5 What you find **d.** to accept is the fact that,
T-16 .......II.1:7 One attribute is no more **d.** to understand
T-17 .......V.2:5 in this; the only **d.** phase is the beginning.
T-17 ..... VI.7:1 aspect of the situation that seems to be **d.**,
T-18 ..... IV.7:2 You make it **d.**, because you insist there
T-18 ..... IV.7:3 You find it **d.** to accept the idea that you
T-18 ..... IV.8:2 If you believe the holy instant is **d.** for you
T-18 ..... VII.4:7 It is extremely **d.** to reach Atonement by
T-19 ........I.5:1 It cannot be **d.** to realize that faith must
T19 ...IV.A.5:1 more **d.** than to surmount your little wall.
T19 ... IV.B.5:6 be **d.** for us to walk past barriers together,
T-20 ..... III.2:5 studied interference that makes it **d.** for
T-20 .... VII.1:4 or parts you find more **d.** than others, are
T-20 .... VII.3:5 the error of believing the means are **d.**.
T-20 .... VII.3:6 can they be **d.** if they are merely given you
T-22 ..... IV.7:2 has received it for himself could find it **d.**.
T-22 ..... IV.7:5 Standing before the veil, it still seems **d.**.
T-22 .......V.1:9 And how can it be **d.** to walk the way of
T-22 .......V.4:5 Can it be **d.** to disregard its feeble squeaks
T-23 ..... III.4:2 Yet it seems **d.** to those who still believe
T-24 ..... IV.3:2 been oft repeated, but is **d.** to grasp as yet
T-24 ... VI.12:2 of the two, it is this one you find more **d.**.
T-25 .... VII.2:8 God, this course would not be **d.** for you.
T-26 .......II.1:1 It is not **d.** to understand the reasons why
T-26 .......II.2:4 One mistake is not more **d.** for Him to
T-26 .......V.2:4 not the way to Heaven's gate is **d.** at all.
T-26 .......V.2:5 keeping step to Heaven's song, is **d.** to do.
T-26 ...VIII.6:8 disaster's form is **d.** to credit in advance.
T-27 .... VII.2:5 The choice will not be **d.**, because the
T-27 .. VII.14:2 is not **d.** to change a dream when once the
T-29 .......II.1:3 rough and far too **d.** for you to follow? Is
T-30 ... VI.10:2 It is not **d.** to overlook mistakes that have
T-31 ........I.1:6 learn it could make such an easy lesson **d.**
T-31 ........I.4:3 continued, taking every step, however **d.**,
T-31 ........I.5:4 not true; too hard to learn, too **d.** to see,
T-31 ..... IV.7:3 to find this course to be too **d.** to learn, let
T-31 ..... IV.7:5 If this be **d.** to understand, then is this
T-31 ..... VI.5:3 But concepts are not **d.** to change. One
T-31 .. VII.14:5 Can this be **d.** to choose *against?* Consider
W-pI ...... 4.2:4 lies beyond, and shadows make sight **d.**.
W-pI ...... 4.6:1 connection with thoughts particularly **d.**.
W-pI ...... 7.1:1 idea is particularly **d.** to believe at first.
W-pI ...... 7.2:1 ideas about time are very **d.** to change,
W-pI ...... 9.2:1 It is **d.** for the untrained mind to believe
W-pI .... 13.5:1 You may find it **d.** to avoid resistance, in
W-pI .... 14.3:2 can be quite **d.** and even quite painful.
W-pI .... 16.4:2 This is quite **d.** until you get used to it.
W-pI .... 27.3:5 It will not be **d.** to do this, even if you are
W-pI .... 29.2:1 find this idea very **d.** to grasp at this point
W-pI .... 29.3:7 how you could ever have found it **d.**.
W-pI .... 35.1:3 It is **d.** for anyone who thinks he is in this
W-pI .... 38.4:2 between a situation that is **d.** for you, and
W-pI .... 38.4:2 you, and one that is **d.** for someone else.
W-pI .... 39.2:2 This is not **d.**, surely. The hesitation you
W-pI .... 39.9:3 Sustained concentration is very **d.** at first.
W-pI .... 42.6:3 If you find this **d.**, it is better to spend the
W-pI .... 44.3:3 particularly **d.** form for the undisciplined
W-pI .... 44.4:3 unnatural and **d.** for the untrained mind.
W-pI .... 48.1:5 very **d.** to recognize it for those who want
W-pI .... 64.5:5 a simple decision really be **d.** to make? Let
W-pI .... 64.7:2 This will be **d.**, at first particularly, since
W-pI .... 72.5:5 be **d.** indeed to escape this conclusion.
W-pI .... 74.4:1 area that seems particularly **d.** to resolve,
W-pI .... 78.4:5 you see as **d.** at times or hard to please,
W-pI .... 91.3:2 It is very **d.** to become convinced that it is
W-pI .... 93.2:1 beliefs so firmly fixed that it is **d.** to help
W-pI .... 95.4:2 **d.** at this point not to allow your mind to

W-pI.133.12:3 very simple fact that no decision can be **d.**
W-pI.133.14:2 you see some **d.** decisions facing you, be
W-pI...135.1:3 thus making correction doubly **d.**. And it
W-pI.135.14:3 This is not **d.** to realize in some forms
W-pI...152.4:2 because it is a **d.** distinction to perceive. It
W-pI.158.10:3 well. This lesson is not **d.** to learn, if you
W-pI...188.2:5 It is not **d.** to look within, for there all
M-3............3:1 is **d.** to understand that levels of teaching
M-4.......I.A.4:2 out." This is always somewhat **d.** because,
M-7............4:1 One of the most **d.** temptations to
M-9............2:4 a fairly slow process, not because it is **d.**,
M-10..........6:1 It is not **d.** to relinquish judgment. But it
M-10..........6:2 But it is **d.** indeed to try to keep it. The
M-10........6:11 you peace. Can it be **d.** to want but this?
M-16..........4:7 minute or two after you begin to find it **d.**
P-2........IV.9:3 is one of the most **d.** problems with which
S-1........III.4:7 of escape makes it **d.** to welcome freedom

## difficulties 12

T-3........III.2:1 All your **d.** stem from the fact that you do
T-31......IV.1:5 and away from **d.** that concern you not.
W-pI.....38.3:4 problems, **d.** or suffering in any form that
W-pI.....50.4:5 all seeming **d.** without effort and in sure
W-pI.....65.3:2 you escape from all your perceived **d.**. It
W-pI.....78.6:3 his faults, the **d.** you have had with him,
W-pI.....81.2:1 when special **d.** seem to arise might be:
W-pI.....95.5:2 In addition to recognizing your **d.** with
W-pI...107.4:3 all the seeming **d.** and the doubts that the
M-8...............h CAN PERCEPTION OF ORDER OF **D.** BE
M-8............1:1 in order of **d.** is the basis for the world's
M-24..........2:2 it were responsible for some of the **d.** the

## difficulty 52

*See also* Appendix C

T-1...........I.1:1 There is no order of **d.** in miracles. One is
T-2...........I.5:5 course; there is no order of **d.** in miracles.
T-2......... II.3:6 will have little **d.** in clarifying the means.
T-4......IV.11:9 that there is an order of **d.** in miracles;
T-5.......VII.2:4 that there is no order of **d.** in miracles. He
T-6......V.A.4:1 Spirit, there is no order of **d.** in miracles.
T-6......V.A.4:9 a range, order of **d.** is meaningless, and
T-6......V.B.8:7 of order of **d.** in miracles has not yet been
T-6......V.C.4:4 It does not concern itself with order of **d.**,
T-7........IV.2:3 Spirit inspires can have no order of **d.**,
T-7........IV.5:4 Holy Spirit sees no order of **d.** in healing.
T-7........XI.1:6 world perceives orders of **d.** in everything
T-7........XI.1:8 yourself there is no order of **d.** in miracles
T-7........XI.1:8 is no **d.** at all *because* it is a state of grace.
T-11....VI.10:5 is no order of **d.** in miracles because all of
T-12.....VII.1:3 no order of **d.** in miracles when you apply
T-14....... X.2:5 anything without order of **d.** can occur.
T-14....... X.3:4 lack of order of **d.** that stamps the miracle
T-14..... X.6:14 There is no order of **d.** here. A call for
T-14... X.12:10 can there be any order of **d.** among them?
T-16....... II.3:4 order of **d.** in miracles is quite impossible,
T-16..... V.14:4 and you will have no **d.** in perceiving the
T-17.........I.3:1 there must be an order of **d.** in miracles,
T-17.........I.4:1 order of **d.** in miracles remain with you.
T-17......IV.6:1 little **d.** now in realizing that the thought
T-18......IV.3:3 Your **d.** with the holy instant arises from
T-18......IV.8:3 orders of **d.** in miracles is centered on this
T19... IV.A.5:3 There is no order of **d.** in miracles, for
T-20......IV.8:7 seeming **d.** but will melt away before you
T-21.......in.1:9 why order of **d.** in miracles is meaningless
T-22.........I.5:2 You will perceive no **d.** in understanding
T-26....... II.1:2 greater **d.** in resolving some than others.
T-27.....VII.2:6 No one has **d.** making up his mind to let a
T-31.........I.2:2 confuse it not with **d.** in the simple things
T-31.........I.6:6 and incredible in **d.** will withstand the
T-31... VIII.3:2 to you. In every **d.**, all distress, and each
W-pI.....34.4:1 you begin to experience **d.** in thinking of
W-pI.....44.6:1 you will have no **d.** in recognizing that its
W-pI.....46.4:1 exercises well you should have no **d.** in
W-pI...79.10:2 today. Whenever any **d.** seems to rise, tell
W-pI...134.3:1 The major **d.** that you find in genuine
W-pI...163.7:1 that even the insane have **d.** in believing it
W-ep .........4:1 Guide through every **d.** and all pain that
M-8 ...........5:1 no order of **d.** in healing merely because
M-14 .........3:6 The illusion of orders of **d.** is an obstacle
M-16 .........4:8 that the **d.** will diminish and drop away.
M-16 .........7:5 no order of **d.** in resolving them. He is as
M-22 .........1:2 is no order of **d.** in miracles because there
P-3......... II.2:1 that there is no order of **d.** in healing. For
P-3......... II.7:1 that there is no order of **d.** in healing.
P-3......... II.8:1 that order of **d.** in healing is meaningless.
P-3......... II.9:4 there is no order of **d.** in healing, he must

## dignity 1

T-4.........I.12:5 beauty and **d.** are far beyond doubt,

## dilemma 4

T-5......... V.7:9 **d.** cannot be resolved except by accepting
T-7........VI.3:8 ego resolves this completely insane **d.** in a
T-16......IV.7:5 solve the **d.** which seems very real to you,
T-30......VI.4:5 he is saved from this **d.** if he can forgive.

## diligence 3

T-31.........I.2:8 and did not pause in **d.** to judge it hard to
W-pI.....95.8:3 to forgive ourselves for our lapses in **d.**,
W-pI...122.4:2 and less than halfway **d.** and partial trust.

## diligently 2

T-11..... V.12:5 ego's goal, which you have pursued so **d.**,
T-16......III.2:7 you have so **d.** taught yourself to believe?

## dim 21

T-1.......VII.2:3 to another, because vision is still so **d.**.
T-13.....VII.1:5 is no day that brightens and grows **d.**.
T-13....XI.3:13 brought even a **d.** imagining of what it is.
T-14....... V.2:3 he will suffer the pain of **d.** awareness that
T-14......IX.5:3 images of other gods must **d.** the mirror
T-14....... X.5:2 of Heaven last but a moment and grow **d.**,
T-15......IX.6:5 your sight grows weak and **d.** and limited,
T-17......IV.8:4 the **d.** light in which the offering is made.
T-17..... V.11:8 appreciation flickered and grown **d.** in
T-17... VIII.4:5 darkness and **d.** imaginings of terror, cold
T-21.........I.6:1 of an ancient state not quite forgotten; **d.**,
T-23.......I.11:3 The altar disappears, the light grows **d.**,
T-25......VI.2:1 to the **d.** effects perceived at twilight. And
T-26....... X.6:2 The world grows **d.** and threatening, not
W-pI...100.3:4 to save the world is **d.** and lusterless, and
W-pI.136.16:3 will be no **d.** figures from your dreams,
W-pI...164.2:2 Its sounds grow **d.**. A melody from far
WpI rV.in12:5 The sound grows **d.** and disappears, as we
W-pI...197.8:4 can you **d.** the light of your perfection. In
W-pII..299.2:4 *can not put out its radiance, nor* **d.** *its light. It*
M-2 ...........5:6 another, fade and grow **d.** and disappear.

## dimension 4

T-9........VI.7:1 is one time, its only **d.** being "always."
T-13......VI.7:5 one, still **d.** of time that does not change,
W-pI.....44.1:1 idea for yesterday, adding another **d.** to it
W-pI...157.2:2 We add a new **d.** now, a fresh experience

## dimensional

*See* one-dimensional

## dimensions 1

T-1.........I.25:2 works all the time and in all the **d.** of time

## diminish 5

T-7..... VIII.2:3 in devising ways that seem to **d.** conflict,
T-11....... V.8:2 **d.** your independence and weaken your
T-24....... II.1:7 understand it is yourself that you **d.** thus.
M-in ..........3:8 fundamental purpose is to **d.** self-doubt.
M-16 .........4:8 that the difficulty will **d.** and drop away.

## diminished 4

T-15...... VI.4:2 answers him, your hope of answer is **d.**.
T-16...... VI.6:4 the value of the body is so **d.** in your sight
W-pI...128.5:4 go beyond all little values and **d.** goals.
W-pII .250.1:2 see his strength **d.** and reduced to frailty;

## diminishes 4

T-15...... IV.3:6 a plan of salvation apart from Him **d.** the
T-24........II.1:5 whom it thus **d.** would be your savior,
T-29.........I.4:7 believe **d.** as you and your brother meet.
W-pI...187.9:3 The great illusion of the fear of God **d.** to

## diminishing 1

T-22...... VI.1:6 increasing its importance by **d.** its own.

## diminutive 1

M-18 .........3:5 And truth becomes **d.** and meaningless.

## dimly 8

T-2........ III.3:6 everyone begins to recognize, however **d.**,
T-9......VIII.1:3 you become aware of it, however **d.**, you
T-15...... VI.4:4 That is because you recognize, however **d.**
T-25........II.3:1 inconstant, wavering, yet **d.** seen,–that
T-26..... V.11:9 but still a present light is **d.** recognized.
W-pII ....in.5:7 come this far unless you saw, however **d.**,
M-17 .........8:7 Once this is even **d.** grasped, the way is
P-3..........II.8:4 is reached another can be **d.** seen ahead.

## dimmed 1

T-9........ VI.4:3 nor yours is **d.** because you do not see.

## dimmer 1

T-30...... III.8:7 its light grew **d.** or less perfect ever was.

## dimness 1

T-25...... VI.2:3 **D.** seems better; easier to see, and better

## dims 2

T-13........X.9:6 the cloud of guilt that **d.** your vision, and
T-31..... VII.7:2 that **d.** your sight and warps your vision,

## dipping 1

T-18.........I.8:1 **d.** and turning till they disappear from

## direct 70

T-1...........I.4:2 life. His Voice will **d.** you very specifically.
T-1.........I.46:3 communication with God by **d.** revelation
T-1...........II.5:3 keeping the **d.** channel from God to you
T-1........ III.4:4 will be acting under **d.** communication.
T-1........ III.4:5 because it enables me to **d.** its application
T-1........ III.4:6 A guide does not control but he does **d.**,
T-1.......... V.1:2 spirit's original state of **d.** communication
T-1.......VII.5:7 a more **d.** approach to God Himself. It
T-2....V.A.18:4 *to do, because He Who sent me will* **d.** *me. I*
T-2........ VI.1:3 my guidance can **d.** everything that does,
T-2........VII.1:6 be in **d.** opposition to the purpose of this
T-3........VII.2:6 everything is in **d.** opposition to God. Yet
T-4....... V.6:10 it is, it will **d.** your efforts automatically.
T-4.......VII.3:4 It is in complete and **d.** communication
T-4.......VII.3:4 and **d.** communication with its Creator.
T-4.......VII.8:7 I **d.** until we are all united in the joy of the
T-4.......VII.8:8 I will **d.** you to wherever you can be truly
T-5..........II.5:7 **D.** communication was broken because
T-5........ III.5:4 is in **d.** opposition to the ego's notions,
T-6....... II.11:6 is the **d.** line of communication with God,
T-6.... V.C.4:10 and **d.** it towards creation within the
T-7..........II.7:7 is perfectly **d.** and perfectly united. It is
T-7......... V.1:3 only for communication has such a **d.**

T-7........VI.2:6 ability to **d.** your thinking as you choose
T-7........X.3:1 Spirit will **d.** you only so as to avoid pain.
T-9........V.9:1 offers a very **d.** and a very simple learning
T-10.......V.3:2 is in **d.** opposition to its own survival. But
T-12...VII.4:10 a goal in **d.** opposition to the Holy Spirit's
T-14.........I.2:4 you must **d.** your thoughts unto oblivion.
T-14.........I.5:6 deceived will merely attack **d.** approaches
T-15.....V.10:7 have been told to offer miracles as I **d.**,
T-15.....VII.4:5 it will enable you to **d.** its anger outward,
T-15.....VII.6:4 no one could interpret **d.** attack as love.
T-15.....VII.6:5 Yet to make guilty *is* **d.** attack, although it
T-18......VI.3:5 fantasies and **d.** the body to act them out.
T-20......III.2:3 be. **D.** relationships, in which there are no
T-20....III.10:3 what is Heaven but union, **d.** and perfect,
T-20....VII.1:3 Being so simple and **d.**, this course has
T-21......VI.8:7 **d.** you how to leave insanity behind. Hide
T-22.......I.10:1 the first **d.** perception that you can make.
T-24.........I.2:3 become beliefs now given power to **d.** all
T-24.......V.4:1 Yet let your specialness **d.** his way, and
T-29.......V.6:2 in minds that can **d.** the hand to bless,
T-31....VIII.2:5 never using weakness to **d.** your actions,
W-pI.....20.1:2 virtually no attempt to **d.** the time for
W-pI.....39.2:5 see at once how **d.** and simple the text is,
W-pI.....60.4:3 in which His Voice fails to **d.** my thoughts
W-pI.....95.3:2 We will again **d.** our exercises towards
W-pI...129.4:4 is **d.** and wholly shared and wholly one.
W-pI.134.15:1 Then choose one brother as He will **d.**,
W-pI.135.15:4 enough to let the mind **d.** its future course
W-pI.135.19:2 but your present trust **d.** the future, and
W-pI...157.4:1 He will **d.** your practicing today, for what
Wi181-200 2:1 and **d.** approaches to the special blocks
W-pI.186.10:3 or **d.** his energies and concentrated drive
W-pI.186.12:5 Let not its voice **d.** you. Hear instead a
W-pI...188.9:4 within our minds **d.** them to come home.
W-pI...195.7:3 **d.** them to the peace that we would find,
W-pII....in.1:3 now we seek **d.** experience of truth alone.
W-pII.236.1:7 I thus **d.** my mind, which I alone can rule.
W-pII.254.2:1 no ego thoughts **d.** our words or actions.
W-pII.324.1:7 *to You, as You* **d.** *me and would have me go.*
W-pII.350.1:5 *But what he looks upon is their* **d.** *result.*
W-ep.........3:3 He will **d.** your efforts, telling you exactly
W-ep.........3:3 exactly what to do, how to **d.** your mind,
M-5.........I.2:3 the ultimate defiance in a **d.** form which
M-9...........2:5 in **d.** opposition to that of our curriculum
M-25.........2:5 to **d.** experience of the Holy Spirit, Whose
M-26.........3:1 a brief experience of **d.** union with God.
C-1............3:2 "soul" is not used except in **d.** biblical

## directed 30

*See also* ego-directed, self-directed

T-1........III.9:1 in the sense that they are **d.** towards those
T-2......VIII.3:7 the ability to choose can be **d.** rationally.
T-2......VIII.5:5 judgment cannot be **d.** toward yourself,
T-3........V.4:1 cannot properly be **d.** to yourself at all.
T-4........V.5:3 consciously organized and consciously **d.**.
T-6........II.4:2 because its abilities are **d.** by the mind,
T-9........II.6:2 **d.** by the Holy Spirit under the laws of
T-14......III.9:5 made for the whole Sonship, **d.** in and out
T-15.........I.4:3 for this is what all its teaching is **d.** to.
T-15......III.4:4 your striving must be **d.** against littleness,
T-16......III.2:6 all your learning has been **d.** toward
T-16....IV.13:7 you are **d.** straight to the Heart of God. At
T-16.......V.2:1 to make guilty is always **d.** against God.
T-18.....VII.8:4 you be **d.** how to use the body sinlessly. It
T-23......III.5:4 savage purpose is **d.** against themselves?
T-28......III.1:2 uncertain steps to be **d.** up the ladder
T-30.........I.4:3 will serve to let you be **d.** without fear, for
W-in..........8:3 to apply the ideas as you are **d.** to do. You
W-pI.....45.8:1 which the exercises for today are **d.**. Here
W-pI.....74.1:1 toward which all our exercises are **d.**.
W-pI.....74.2:1 exercises for today are **d.** towards finding
W-pI.....79.9:3 Our efforts will be **d.** toward recognizing
W-pI...108.5:3 it be **d.** by the One Who knows the truth.
W-pI.169.12:1 the course it runs **d.** and its outcome sure.
W-pI.196.10:3 you believed attack could be **d.** outward,
W-pII.267.1:6 I am a messenger of God, **d.** by His Voice,
M-4......IX.2:9 faithfulness in the true sense is always **d.**.
M-9...........2:5 world's training is **d.** toward achieving a
M-25.........1:6 be **d.** toward this one great final surprise,
C-in...........2:6 experience toward which the course is **d.**.

## directing 7

T-8......VII.9:7 abides in it by **d.** the use to which it is put.
T-13.....IV.6:3 mind, **d.** you to attack in the present in
T-18.....VI.6:1 **d.** its attack and blaming it for what you
W-pI...166.8:1 gentle hand **d.** you to look upon your gifts
W-pII.321.1:2 *in vain until I heard Your Voice* **d.** *me. Now I*
W-pII.340.1:4 *will hear Your Voice* **d.** *him to find Christ's*
Wfl........in.3:1 **d.** all our thoughts to serve the function of

## direction 67

T-1.........I.49:2 either the degree or the **d.** of the error.
T-2.........I.1:12 the **d.** of your own creation is up to you.
T-2...V.A.17:5 Time is under my **d.**, but timelessness
T-4.........I.2:10 opposed in source, in **d.** and in outcome.
T-4.......II.10:4 then has only one **d.** in which it can move.
T-4.......II.10:5 Its **d.** is always automatic, because it
T-6.....V.A.6:2 but it is necessary that you turn in that **d.**.
T-6.....V.A.6:5 or the change in **d.** would not have been
T-6.....V.B.8:4 then, is a step in the **d.** out of conflict,
T-6.....V.B.9:2 As you take this step and hold this **d.**, you
T-7......IV.3:7 is because they are channelized in one **d.**,
T-8.............I.h The **D.** of the Curriculum
T-8..........I.5:3 change to be introduced is a change in **d.**.
T-8..........I.5:8 The volatile have no **d.**. They cannot
T-8..........I.6:1 a real change in **d.** becomes possible. You
T-8.........II.3:8 only the **d.** of the curriculum that must be
T-8.........II.6:1 takes only *one* **d.** and has only *one* goal. His
T-8.........II.6:2 His **d.** is freedom and His goal is God. Yet
T-8........V.6:2 The Holy Spirit has one **d.** for all minds,
T-8........V.6:3 not lose sight of His **d.** through illusions,
T-8........V.6:3 only illusions of another **d.** can obscure
T-9........V.7:2 unless he is also helped to change his **d.**.
T-9........V.7:4 of one whose **d.** has been changed *for* him,
T-12......V.5:2 progress only under constant, clear-cut **d.**
T-13.........I.3:4 Always has no **d.**. Time seems to go in
T-13.........I.3:5 Time seems to go in one **d.**, but when you
T-13.....IV.8:2 continuity of past and future, under its **d.**,
T-14........in.1:5 They take a **d.** exactly opposite, pointing
T-14.........I.2:1 in a world made of denial and without **d.**.
T-14.........I.4:1 Any **d.** that would lead you where the
T-16......V.3:6 takes a **d.** exactly opposite of what is true.
T-21......III.4:3 This is His **d.**; the only one He ever sees.
T-21......III.5:6 This mad **d.** was your choice, and by your
T-21......III.6:2 His purpose lies in the opposite **d.**. He
T-25..VII.12:7 and **d.** to the plan in which your special
T-26......V.9:5 everything that points the way in the **d.** of
T-31.....IV.7:3 achieve a goal you must proceed in its **d.**,
W-pI.....14.3:6 **d.** is toward perfect safety and perfect
W-pI.....17.1:1 This idea is another step in the **d.** of
W-pI.....25.5:3 this. The idea for today is a step in this **d.**.
W-pI.....35.5:3 mind. Try to recognize that the **d.** of your
W-pI.....35.5:4 Illusions have no **d.** in reality. They are
W-pI.....71.5:1 works simply because, by following His **d.**
WpI..rIII.in6:6 Give **d.** at the outset; then lean back in
W-pI...126.1:2 forgiveness, certainty of goal, and sure **d.**.
W-pI...157.2:4 beyond it, sure of our **d.** and our only goal
W-pI...158.3:5 it. For time but seems to go in one **d.**. We
W-pI...184.5:1 other vision still remain a natural **d.** for
W-pI...198.3:6 gives **d.** with the certainty of God Himself
WpII..361-5.h You, Certain that Your **d.** gives me peace.
W-ep.........3:3 for His sure **d.** and His certain Word. His
W-ep.........5:5 for guidance and for peace and sure **d.**.
M-1...........1:3 his road is established and his **d.** is sure.
M-3...........3:3 more about the new **d.** as he teaches it.
M-4.....I.A.7:9 each step in this **d.** so heavily reinforced,
M-14.........4:5 to approach it; to be willing to go in its **d.**.
M-17.........3:5 the divided goal of the pupil into one **d.**,
M-19.........2:4 the first small step in the **d.** of the other.
M-20.........5:9 sentence is our practicing given its one **d.**.
M-21.........4:8 He does not control the **d.** of his speaking
M-22.........2:7 He has decided on the **d.** he wants to take.
M-25.........3:2 to the Holy Spirit, and used under His **d.**,
C-in...........3:2 it is planned only to set the **d.** towards it.
P-1............5:6 Psychotherapy under His **d.** is one of the
P-2...........I.1:9 overall **d.** is one of progress toward the
P-2..........II.9:7 except a help in just this same **d.**? It is the
P-3..........II.3:4 misguided the **d.** he may have chosen.

## directions 6

T-8........I.5:10 curriculum teaches them that *all* **d.** exist,
T-8.........V.5:9 to go in different **d.** and will lose the way.
T-21........I.2:5 Judgment will always give you false **d.**,
T-21.....III.3:5 to place equal faith in opposite **d.**. What
T-26.......V.1:9 There are but two **d.** you can take, while
M-28.........3:2 From here on, no **d.** are needed. Vision is

## directly 37

T-1........I.30:2 the center, where it can communicate **d.**.
T-1.........II.1:5 Revelation unites you **d.** with God.
T-1.........II.1:6 Miracles unite you **d.** with your brother.
T-2.....VIII.1:6 This basic distinction leads **d.** into the
T-3.......III.6:1 God can communicate **d.** to His altars,
T-6........I.10:5 without experiencing them **d.** yourself.
T-6.........II.3:8 and leads **d.** to excluding you from your
T-7.......IV.1:4 Healing does not come **d.** from God, Who
T-11.......V.2:2 illusions except by looking at them **d.**,
T-12........I.1:4 that you do not respond to anything **d.**,
T-12....VII.7:7 want it. This leads **d.** to dissociation, for it
T-13.........II.4:1 is **d.** attributable to its definition of guilt.
T-15.....V.10:8 in the holy instant you unite **d.** with God,
T-15....VII.6:3 For it would prefer to attack **d.**, and avoid
T-19........I.5:2 apparent, though it follows **d.** from the
T-20.....III.3:3 They look on it **d.**, without attempting to
T-22........I.5:5 It reaches you **d.**, without a need to be
T-23.......II.6:5 This leads **d.** to the *third* preposterous
T-25.....III.2:1 not obtain **d.** to a world perception rules,
T-27....VIII.5:9 this, if we but look **d.** at their cause. And
W-pI....14.3:3 Some of them will lead you **d.** into fear.
W-pI....24.5:4 appear to be **d.** related to the situation, or
W-pI....43.5:8 thought related more or less **d.** to today's
W-pI 122.12:2 Now we walk **d.** into light, and we receive
W-pI..126.3:1 "forgive" a sin, there is no gain to you **d.**.
W-pI..155.3:3 They cannot learn **d.** from the truth,
W-pI..157.6:2 We cannot give experience like this **d.**.
W-pI..158.2:7 Experience cannot be shared **d.**, in the
W-pI..158.5:4 is his gift. This he can give **d.**, for Christ's
M-12.........3:3 His messages **d.** through the Spirit which
M-12.........3:8 for their unity could not be recognized **d.**.
M-23.........1:1 God's gifts can rarely be received **d.**. Even
M-26............h CAN GOD BE REACHED **D.**?
M-26.........1:1 God indeed can be reached **d.**, for there
M-26.........2:1 There are those who have reached God **d.**
M-26.........3:8 were reached **d.** in sustained awareness,
C-3...........2:2 They cannot go **d.** from perception to

## directs 22

T-15..VII.11:8 forgive. They can only do as the mind **d.**.
T-18.....IX.5:1 it **d.** as long as you believe that guilt is real
T19.IV.B.12:6 fear **d.** the body to do is therefore painful.
T-21.......V.1:2 It literally picks it out as the mind **d.**. The
T-21.......V.2:3 the ego says, and see what it **d.** you see,
T-21.......V.2:6 think the world you made **d.** your destiny.
T-25........I.1:5 Holiness **d.** the body through the mind at
T-31.......V.8:2 Yet is all learning that the world **d.** begun
W-pI....58.5:6 me, protects me, and **d.** me in all things.
W-pI 135.16:3 past experience **d.** its choice of what will
W-pI 135.16:5 at all, for present confidence **d.** the way.
W-pI..161.6:6 Yet what but mind **d.** the body to attack?
W-pI..165.8:2 Name we practice as His Word **d.** we do.
W-pI..167.3:4 It can be then applied as mind **d.** it. But
W-pI 186.12:1 Do as God's Voice **d.**. And if It asks a
W-pI..193.7:4 sees the pain through eyes the mind **d.**.
W-pI..195.2:3 sane refuse to take the steps which He **d.**,
W-pII.222.1:3 and move; the Spirit which **d.** my actions,
W-pII.321.1:7 *me. Your Voice* **d.** *me, and the way to You is*
M-4.....V.1:11 because God's Voice **d.** them in all things.
P-1............5:7 end to the help that He begins and He **d.**.
P-2..........V.4:6 can be sure that healing is a process He **d.**

**dirge** 2

T-14....... II.8:8 he sing the **d.** of sorrow when this is true?
P-2........ VI.1:5 as a patient begins to hear the **d.** he sings,

**dis-spirited** 3

T-4.........in.1:6 be fatigued is to be **d.**, but to be inspired
T-4.........in.1:7 To be egocentric is to be **d.**, but to be Self-
T-4......IV.11:8 inspire the **d.** or to stabilize the unstable?

**dis-spiriting** 2

T-4.........in.2:4 of affirming it, and are thus **d.** yourself.
T-4........IV.6:3 When you have given up this voluntary **d.**

**disagree** 2

T-8..... VIII.4:6 witnesses who would **d.** with its case, nor
M-10..........1:8 At any time the student may **d.** with what

**disagreeable** 1

P-2........VI.3:3 is called on, however **d.** it may be. They

**disagreeing** 1

T-3......... V.3:5 are **d.** with God's idea of your creation.

**disagreement** 8

T-6......V.B.5:2 thought systems which are in complete **d.**
T-6......V.C.1:8 are in fundamental **d.** about everything,
T-6......V.C.1:8 being in fundamental **d.** about what you
T-8...........I.6:2 who are in total **d.** about everything.
T-9.......VII.2:2 There may be **d.** on anything else, but not
T-15... VIII.6:2 and by removing every element of **d.**, to
T-16....... V.5:2 There can be no **d.** on this, because both
T-16....... V.5:3 in complete **d.** on what completion is,

**disagrees** 1

T-21......VI.6:7 How can a fact be fearful unless it **d.** with

**disappear** 91

T-2...........I.3:4 All that can literally **d.** in the twinkling of
T-3...........I.1:1 fear still associated with miracles can **d.**.
T-5......IV.2:10 They will not **d.** from your mind without
T-10......IV.1:9 will **d.** into the nothingness out of which
T-11. VIII.10:5 not **d.** in the Presence of God's Answer?
T-13.........I.3:5 along the past behind you, and will **d.**. As
T-13....... V.8:9 Dreams **d.** when light has come and you
T-13......IX.1:8 in which you bound yourself will **d.**.
T-13......XI.6:4 that makes the need for any differences **d.**
T-14......VI.3:8 can live in light. Everything else must **d.**.
T-14......VII.1:5 union, everything that is not real must **d.**,
T-15....... II.6:9 that witnesses to It, your doubts must **d.**.
T-15......XI.3:4 and littleness will **d.** in our relationship,
T-15......XI.3:5 be brought to us and **d.** in our presence,
T-16......VI.4:6 For in seeing them the body would **d.**,
T-17....... II.4:1 The stars will **d.** in light, and the sun that
T-18.........I.7:1 "God is not fear, but Love," and it will **d.**.
T-18.........I.8:1 dipping and turning till they **d.** from sight
T-18....... II.6:3 that the first change, before dreams **d.**, is
T-18......III.4:4 And fear must **d.** before you now. Be
T-19......III.10:6 The barriers to Heaven will **d.** before your
T19.IV.D.19:1 will **d.** into the Presence beyond the veil,
T-20......III.4:2 longer before it overtakes you and you **d.**.
T-20......VI.9:1 Idols must **d.**, and leave no trace behind
T-20... VIII.8:1 Hallucinations **d.** when they are
T-20... VIII.8:6 that purpose is no longer held they **d.**.
T-21.........I.8:3 The edges of the circle **d.**, and what is in it
T-21....... II.2:7 and all effects of your mistakes will **d.**.
T-22......IV.6:3 All barriers **d.** before their coming, as
T-23...... II.3:5 instead of to each other, they merely **d.**.
T-24......III.1:2 illusions can be forgiven, and then they **d.**
T-24......III.1:8 it so. And thus his secret guilt would **d.**,
T-24......VI.1:7 about yourself may **d.** before his holiness.
T-24....VI.10:6 specialness will **d.** before the Will of God,
T-25......IV.3:7 and die, will **d.** before the sun you bring.
T-26....... II.7:4 more than just a tiny sigh before they **d.**,
T-26....... II.8:5 and locked will merely fall away and **d.**.
T-26......IV.4:8 be to make the space between you **d.**?
T-26....... V.8:4 when Heaven seemed to **d.** and God was
T-27....... II.6:5 hopelessness and death must **d.** before
T-29......VI.2:8 The stars will **d.**, and night and day will
T-29....VI.2:14 of time may **d.** because they have no use.
T-30......IV.8:1 dream of separation start to fade and **d.**.
T-31......VI.3:8 and must be passed that both may **d.**, so
T-31... VIII.6:3 it occurs, but **d.** as mists before the sun. A
W-pI.....46.2:5 It is the means by which illusions **d.**.
W-pI.....69.2:5 the tears of God's Son **d.** in the sunlight.
W-pI.....81.1:4 In its calm light let all my conflicts **d.**. In
W-pI.....83.1:5 All doubt must **d.** as I acknowledge that
W-pI.....94.1:3 world are still, the sights of this world **d.**,
W-pI...107.1:3 Where truth has entered errors **d.**. They
W-pI...107.1:6 And so they **d.** to nothingness, returning
W-pI...107.4:1 a while, to **d.** or change to something else.
W-pI...108.1:4 true? Even that one will **d.**, because the
W-pI...121.6:4 the self you think you made, and let it **d.**.
W-pI...122.6:7 has spun of fragile cobwebs **d.** before the
W-pI...124.2:3 How easily do errors **d.**, and death give
W-pI...129.5:4 Value them not, and they will **d.**. Esteem
W-pI...134.6:3 feet of truth. And there they **d.** entirely.
W-pI...136.1:5 truth, and merely leaves them there to **d.**.
W-pI...137.7:2 sickness has been seen to **d.** in spite of all
W-pI...152.8:3 and all you think you made will **d.**. What
W-pI.153.19:3 strong in Christ, and let our weakness **d.**,
W-pI...158.8:2 merely **d.** when this has been perceived.
W-pI...158.9:3 Unseen by One they merely **d.**, because a
W-pI...161.1:1 our fears may **d.** and offer room to love.
W-pI...168.4:2 give the means by which this world will **d.**
W-pI...168.4:3 watch fear **d.** from every face as hearts
W-pI.184.14:3 foolish separations **d.** which kept us blind
W-pI...187.7:1 Illusion recognized must **d.**. Accept not
W-pI...190.1:4 form it takes that will not **d.** if seen aright.
W-pI...192.4:1 things unknown in Heaven, sees them **d.**,
W-pI...193.8:6 you, that all pain may **d.** and God may be
W-pI.193.11:5 way to look upon them so that they will **d.**
W-pI.193.13:3 *and this will* **d.**. To every apprehension,
W-pI...195.1:7 cause of sorrow **d.** throughout the world.
W-pI...196.8:3 own thoughts, the fear of God must **d.**.
W-pI.198.12:6 yourself, and then you **d.** forever into God
W-pII...in.10:2 only call to God, and all temptations **d.**.
W-pII..235.1:1 from this," and merely watch them **d.**. I
W-pII......3.1:4 the world must **d.** and all its errors vanish
W-pII..302.1:6 *light, for fear must* **d.** *when love has come.*
W-pII..303.1:3 the sights to which I am accustomed **d.**.
W-pII..326.2:1 Let us today behold earth **d.**, at first
W-pII....14.5:5 will enter in and **d.** into the Heart of God.
M-2 ...........5:6 one another, fade and grow dim and **d.**.
M-8 ...........5:7 realizes they are all illusions they will **d.**.
M-13 .........1:5 replaces the first, so both can finally **d.**.
M-16 .......6:13 Recognize this, and they will **d.**. And only
C-4............4:4 it is. And now it cannot fail to **d.**, for now
C-4............6:1 within, and there forgiveness lets it **d.**.

**disappeared** 18

T-12.......I.9:11 have drawn across the face of love has **d.**.
T-12... VIII.2:3 and he **d.** from your sight into his Father.
T-14....... II.4:7 And then they see the chains have **d.**, and
T-16....... III.1:7 and suffering has **d.** to be replaced by joy.
T-16.....VII.6:4 vengeance has been uprooted and has **d.**.
T-18.....VII.2:2 sight, but it has not yet completely **d.**.
T19...IV.D.5:9 beyond them, you answered and they **d.**.
T-21....III.11:6 is but the sign the other has **d.** from sight.
T-23.......in.3:6 And every error **d.** because they saw it not
T-26....... V.5:2 What **d.** too quickly to affect the simple
W-pI.....75.1:6 Darkness and turmoil and death have **d.**.
W-pI...169.6:5 Son of God has merely **d.** into his Father,
W-pI.183.11:3 The little things of earth have **d.**. The
W-pI.196.11:3 For fear of God has **d.**. And you can call
W-pII......8.5:2 God to take His final step, and time has **d.**
M-28 .........2:5 Idols have **d.**, and the remembrance of
M-28 .........5:2 have **d.** and Love looks on Itself. What
S-1.........in.3:2 still, until both high and low have **d.**.

**disappearing** 1

T19....IV.A.9:6 than fix your gaze upon a **d.** snowflake,

**disappears** 29

T-1.........I.39:2 light, darkness automatically **d.**.
T-3..........II.5:3 All sense of separation **d.**. The Son of God
T-14.... VII.1:6 As darkness **d.** in light, so ignorance fades
T-14..... IX.2:4 What **d.** in light is not attacked. It merely
T-14.... XI.11:5 oneness, and before His lesson division **d.**
T-18...... IX.6:6 Try but to touch it and it **d.**; attempt to
T-22......II.12:7 its forgiveness is gently overlooked and **d.**
T-23.........I.9:1 of illusions **d.** when it is brought to truth!
T-23.......I.11:3 The altar **d.**, the light grows dim, the
T-23.......I.12:7 cannot be; where either goes the other **d.**.
T-25...... IX.2:2 for you until reluctance to receive it **d.**,
T-28....... V.2:5 Where one appears, the other **d.**. And
T-29....... III.3:7 is. Before this light the body **d.**, as heavy
T-31...... VI.2:3 all. This one appears and **d.** in death; that
T-31....VIII.4:3 His majesty, and **d.** before His holy sight.
W-pI.122.12:1 today the world will fade until it **d.**, and
W-pI.127.10:1 years of waiting for salvation **d.** before the
W-pI...130.5:2 Seek for the one; the other **d.**. But one
W-pI...162.1:5 By them it **d.**, and all things seen within
WpI.rV.in12:5 sound grows dim and **d.**, as we approach
W-pI...199.4:3 The body **d.**, because you have no need of
W-pII.264.1:3 *my own. In You time* **d.**, *and place becomes a*
W-pII.271.1:3 as they come together all perception **d.**.
W-pII...10.1:4 gives a silent blessing and then **d.**, its goal
W-pII.333.1:4 and the truth can shine upon it as it **d.**.
M-4 ....... X.3:4 that learning but **d.** in its presence. Yet
P-2....... VII.3:4 vision heals perception and sickness **d.**.
S-1...........I.5:8 becomes the altar of God. It **d.** in Him.
S-1......... V.2:2 Where one has come the other **d.**. The

**disappointed** 3

T-13..... VII.3:1 you see, for it has **d.** you since time began.
M-6 ...........2:7 No teacher of God should feel **d.** if he has
M-13 .........5:7 it is there, and each time **d.** in the end.

**disappointment** 4

T-29..... VII.7:2 one, and you see death and **d.** everywhere
T-31...... IV.2:3 All its roads but lead to **d.**, nothingness
W-pI.....24.6:2 experience **d.** in connection with some of
M-27 .........2:2 away, ending in dust and **d.** and despair,

**disappointments** 3

T-16..... VII.1:3 slights, remembered pain, past **d.**,
W-pI....128.1:2 from years of misery, from countless **d.**,
W-pI...200.1:3 yourself the agony of yet more bitter **d.**,

**disaster** 20

T-4........ VI.3:3 chaos and **d.** needs additional convincing.
T-16........II.8:4 still greater faith in the **d.** you have made.
T-16........II.8:5 the joyful tidings that **d.** is not real and
T-16........II.8:5 is not real and that reality is not **d.**.
T-21.......in.2:3 If you behold **d.** and catastrophe, you
T-26......VIII.7:9 reason for an interval in which **d.** strikes,
T-27....VII.12:4 and of ancient hate, the instant of **d.**, all
T-29........ III.5:1 the midst of dreams of desolation and **d.**.
T-30......VII.2:2 be? And thus you judge **d.** and success,
T-30....VIII.2:5 of lack, and safety from **d.** of all kinds.
T-31.......I.11:3 believe you want **d.** and disunity and pain
W-pI.....14.4:7 *God did not create that* **d.** *[specify], and so it*
W-pI.....14.5:2 each case, name the "**d.**" quite specifically
W-pI.....55.1:2 now are but signs of disease, **d.** and death
W-pI.....73.3:3 Did God create **d.** for His Son? Creation is
W-pI.....75.2:1 happy ending to your long dream of **d.**.
W-pI.151.10:1 all faith that you have placed in pain, **d.**,
W-pI...198.4:1 is the only road that leads out of **d.**, past
M-5 ........II.4:7 pain, **d.** and all suffering mean now?
M-17 .........1:7 pain, fear and **d.** to come to him. Let him

**disaster's** 1
T-26....VIII.6:8 in **d.** form is difficult to credit in advance.

**disastrous** 2
T-3......... II.3:3 also has the **d.** effect of denying the power
T-26....VIII.5:4 they had been caused, and judged **d.** *now?*

**disbanded** 1
T-21.....VII.3:5 must be **d.** in the presence of strength.

**disbelief** 1
T-27....VIII.5:8 would have met with laughter and with **d.**

**disbelieve** 1
T-9......... II.9:1 To **d.** is to side against, or to attack. To

**discarded** 2
T-12.........I.9:8 do not work at all are automatically **d.**. If
S-3....... II.1:11 And so it is **d.** as a choice, as one lays by a

**disciples** 4
T-6...........I.8:6 accept me as a model are literally my **d.**.
T-6...........I.8:7 **D.** are followers, and if the model they
T19..IV.B.16:3 sad **d.** chant the body's praise continually
T19..IV.B.17:1 It is not given to the ego's **d.** to realize

**disciplinary** 1
W-pI.....65.4:4 is part of the long-range **d.** training your

**discipline** 2
W-pI.....64.7:2 proficient in the mind **d.** that it requires.
W-pI.....95.4:4 seen the extent of your lack of mental **d.**,

**disciplined** 1
W-pI.....39.9:4 becomes more **d.** and less distractible.

**disclaiming** 1
T-4.........in.2:4 you are **d.** knowledge instead of affirming

**discomfort** 11
T-2......... III.4:7 regarded as very minor intrusions of **d.**.
T-2......... V.7:4 is no doubt that this may produce **d.**, yet
T-2......... V.7:4 yet the **d.** is not the final outcome of the
T-2......... V.7:8 **D.** is aroused only to bring the need for
T-17..... V.11:9 to blame him for the **d.** of the situation in
T-20.....VII.1:5 And this produces great **d.**. This need not
T-20.....VII.2:1 The period of **d.** that follows the sudden
W-pI.....10.5:3 half a minute or less if you experience **d.**.
W-pI.....16.6:3 should also be reduced if there is **d.**.
W-pI.....26.5:2 reduced to a minute if the **d.** is too great.
W-pI...167.2:6 weariness, a slight **d.** or the merest frown,

**disconnected** 4
T-11..... V.13:5 breaking it into small, **d.** parts, without
T-18....VIII.5:2 to house a separate mind, a **d.** thought,
T-19.........I.7:4 system, but totally **d.** to each other. And
T-22.........I.1:6 strange uneasiness, your sense of being **d.**

**discontented** 1
M-13 .........3:3 finding; to be forever dissatisfied and **d.**;

**discordant** 3
T-2.........VI.6:8 strain because wanting and doing are **d.**.
T-7......... II.7:8 free, because nothing **d.** ever enters. That
P-2........ VI.2:6 more are heard instead of loud **d.** shrieks.

**discouragement** 2
T-15 ........I.2:1 One source of perceived **d.** from which
T-20 ... VI.12:4 Perhaps confusion, but hardly **d.**. You

**discover** 2
T-21 ...... V.1:5 look for you are far more likely to **d.** than
W-pI... 110.7:1 try to **d.** in your mind the Self Who is the

**discovered** 1
T-10 ........I.3:1 dismiss both together if you **d.** that reality

**discovery** 1
W-pI..... 22.2:3 not a happy **d.** to find that you can escape

**discrepancies** 1
T-20 .... VII.1:1 said much about **d.** of means and end,

**discrepancy** 1
T-17 .... V.14:4 It is just this same **d.** between the purpose

**discrepant** 1
T-20 .... VII.1:4 of areas where means and end are still **d.**.

**discrete** 4
T-7 ....... VI.1:3 That is why attack is never **d.**, and why it
T-25 ........I.7:1 note of time and place as if they were **d.**,
W-pI... 184.3:1 the world becomes a series of **d.** events, of
W-pII ... 11.4:2 We seem to be **d.**, and unaware of our

**discrimination** 2
T-4 ........ V.2:1 state is its lack of **d.** between the body and
W-pI..... 35.8:4 Neither force nor **d.** should be used.

**discs** 2
T-27 ... VIII.2:2 it has bought with little metal **d.** or paper
W-pI..... 76.3:2 of green paper strips and piles of metal **d.**.

**discuss** 1
M-24 ......... 5:1 himself, or **d.** it with others who do? The

**discussed** 4
T-3 ....... VI.1:1 We have already **d.** the Last Judgment,
T-3 ....... VI.2:3 rests. I have **d.** this before in terms of the
T-3 ...... VII.1:2 a creating, a difference we have already **d.**
T-3 ...... VII.3:1 We have **d.** the fall or separation before,

**discussion** 1
P-2...... IV.11:9 analyses and wearying **d.** and pursuits.

**disease** 5
T-18 ...... I.12:7 has been ravaged by separation and **d.**?
T-28 .... VII.4:2 witness to the dream of separation and **d.**.
W-pI..... 55.1:2 I see now are but signs of **d.**, disaster and
W-pI..... 76.3:3 needle will ward off **d.** and death. You
C-1 ........... 6:1 and seeing guilt, **d.** and death as real.

**disengage** 2
T-4 ...... IV.6:4 the demands of the ego to **d.** yourself.
T-4 ....... VI.8:3 who **d.** themselves from the Sonship,

**disengaging** 1
T-4 ....... VI.8:3 because they are **d.** themselves from me.

**disguise** 2
T-12 ........I.8:5 and face it without **d.** as a crucial step in
T-29 ..... IV.3:4 thin **d.** of pleasure and of joy in which

**disguised** 5
T-24 ....... V.2:1 however hidden or **d.** the form, however
T-26 ... VIII.9:5 Why should deliverance be **d.** as death?
T-26 ... VIII.9:8 And do not let it be **d.** as time, and so
T-29 ..... IV.2:4 Or it can be **d.** in pleasant form. But never
W-pII . 333.1:2 It cannot be evaded, set aside, denied, **d.**,

**disguises** 1
T-3 ....... VI.4:3 or in pleasant **d.** in what seem to be your

**disheartened** 2
T-4 ....... IV.7:4 **d.** are useless to themselves and to me,
T-4 ....... IV.7:4 and to me, but only the ego can *be* **d.**.

**disheartening** 1
T-3 ....... VI.5:4 you feel tired because it is essentially **d.**.

**dishonest** 4
M-4 ...... III.1:2 To judge is to be **d.**, for to judge is to
M-4 ...... IV.1:4 the **d.** act that follows a dishonest thought
M-4 ...... IV.1:4 the dishonest act that follows a **d.** thought
P-3..........II.3:2 selfish, unconcerned, and actually **d.**. He

**dishonesty** 1
M-4 ........II.2:4 of self-deception, and self-deception is **d.**.

**disillusionment** 5
T-16 ..... IV.3:7 unsatisfying on the grounds of **d.**.
T-16 ..... IV.4:3 Where **d.** is possible, there was not love
T19 . IV.B.11:5 In it lies **d.** and the seeds of faithlessness,
T19 . IV.B.11:6 reasonable grounds for depression and **d.**
T-22 ....... II.1:1 opposite of illusions is not **d.** but truth.

**disinherited** 2
T-7 .........II.5:7 but when you **d.** yourself you became a
T-12 ..... IV.6:8 There can be no **d.** parts of the Sonship,

**disjunctive** 1
T-17 ....... V.3:3 disturbed, **d.** and even quite distressing.

**dislodged** 1
S-2..........II.2:2 love that arrogance could never be **d.**.

**dislodging** 1
T-16 ..... VI.8:3 urgency is only in **d.** your mind from its

**dismal** 3
T-29 ... VIII.7:4 a **d.** alcove separated off from what is
T-31 ....... II.7:4 Forget the **d.** lessons that you learned
W-pI 131.15:1 refrain from **d.** thoughts and meaningless

**dismay** 1
W-pI .... 79.5:3 **D.** and depression are inevitable as you

**dismayed** 3
W-pI .. 96.11:3 while. Be not **d.** by this. The joy your Self

W-pI...181.4:3 have also been **d.** by the depressing and
W-pI...185.8:5 But be you not **d.** by lingering illusions,

**dismembered** 1
W-pI...137.3:5 In sickness does his Self appear to be **d.**,

**dismiss** 16
T-4.........in.3:2 dwell upon it, but **d.** it as accomplished. If
T-4........VI.1:4 persuade you that you cannot **d.** it lightly,
T-5......VI.10:2 you. It will merely **d.** the case against you.
T-5......VI.10:5 It will **d.** the case against you, however
T-10.........I.3:1 **d.** both together if you discovered that
T-13.......II.7:4 often **d.** it more readily than you dismiss
T-13.......II.7:4 than you **d.** the ego's thought system. To
W-pI.....13.5:3 and will probably **d.** it as preposterous.
W-pI.....16.3:3 to **d.** fear thoughts as unimportant, trivial
W-pI.....23.6:5 then **d.** that thought and go on to the next
W-pI.....76.9:2 **D.** all foolish magical beliefs today, and
W-pI.130.10:1 **D.** temptation easily today whenever it
W-pI...198.5:3 teach, instead of trying to **d.** His words,
W-pII..273.1:3 us learn how to **d.** it and return to peace.
M-8............5:4 one? Will he **d.** more easily a whispered
P-2........VI.2:1 an instant, and then **d.** it uncorrected.

**dismissed** 1
W-pI...182.1:6 times hardly remembered, actively **d.**, but

**dismisses** 4
T-4.........II.4:3 No one **d.** something he considers part of
T-14.........I.5:3 merely looks at its foundation and **d.** it.
W-pI...138.9:4 as the truth **d.** them as causeless. Now are
W-pI...187.7:5 is an idea so mad that sanity **d.** it at once.

**dismissing** 2
W-pI.....47.4:4 with fear, **d.** each one by telling yourself:
W-pI.....65.5:5 as possible, **d.** each one by telling yourself

**disobey** 1
T-8........IV.1:7 from His laws, although you can **d.** them.

**disobeying** 1
T-7........IX.6:5 so. **D.** God's Will is meaningful only to the

**disordered** 8
T-5.........V.7:1 Irrational thought is **d.** thought. God
T-5.........V.7:5 Every **d.** thought is attended by guilt at its
T-5.......V.7:12 If you accept the remedy for **d.** thought, a
T-5.........V.8:8 so. Having given up its **d.** thought, the
T-13.......III.1:5 **d.** state of mind you are not afraid of fear.
T-13.......V.4:3 private worlds, where everything is **d.**,
T-14.......IV.2:2 removed from the **d.** mind that thought it
W-pI...188.9:6 clean of strange desires and **d.** wishes. We

**disorganized** 3
T-17.......V.5:7 relationship may even become quite **d.**.
T-17.......VI.2:6 The reason for this **d.** approach is evident
W-pI.....49.1:4 distracted, **d.** and highly uncertain.

**disorientation** 2
T-16......VI.7:4 in which a sense of actual **d.** may occur.
T-16......VI.8:5 The period of **d.**, which precedes the

**disown** 3
T-2.....VIII.4:5 will inevitably **d.** its miscreations which,
T-6.........II.2:1 What you project you **d.**, and therefore
W-pII..248.1:7 Now I **d.** self-concepts and deceits and

**disowned** 1
W-pII..248.1:1 I have **d.** the truth. Now let me be as

**disowning** 1
W-pII..248.1:2 Now let me be as faithful in **d.** falsity.

**dispassionately** 2
W-pI.....31.3:3 them come and go as **d.** as possible. Do
W-pI...170.7:1 Today we look upon this cruel god **d.**.

**dispel** 26
T-1.........I.33:2 **d.** illusions about yourself and perceive
T-4.........V.3:3 since the idea of Him does **d.** the ego. But
T-6.........V.2:5 themselves call on the light to **d.** them.
T-7........VI.8:5 light of your understanding would **d.** it. It
T-7.......VII.4:4 only way to **d.** illusions is to withdraw all
T-7.....VIII.5:2 can **d.** it by withdrawing belief from it.
T-8...........I.2:4 not asked to **d.** your hallucinations alone.
T-8........IV.2:9 my light must **d.** it because of what it is.
T-9.........V.4:3 attempts to **d.** its effects by depreciating
T-11.......V.1:3 together we have the lamp that will **d.** it,
T-11.......V.2:2 And how else can one **d.** illusions except
T-11.......V.2:9 upon darkness through light must **d.** it.
T-11VIII.14:10 you see you need reality to **d.** your fears.
T-12.......I.10:3 Spirit's interpretation of fear does **d.** it,
T-13.......I.10:1 You cannot **d.** guilt by making it real,
T-13.......II.9:2 but bring it to the light, the light will **d.** it.
T-13......III.1:2 **d.** it without the need for you to raise it to
T-13.......X.6:4 The Holy Spirit seeks not to **d.** reality. If
T-13.......X.6:6 purpose of Atonement is to **d.** illusions,
T-14......VI.2:3 darkness that the light of love will not **d.**,
T-22......IV.4:7 Christ's forgiveness to **d.** their faith in sin.
W-pI...93.11:1 quickly **d.** the illusion of fear by repeating
W-pI...162.2:3 There is no dream these words will not **d.**;
W-pI...162.6:4 These words **d.** the night, and darkness is
W-pI.186.11:1 sun's return each morning to **d.** the night,
M-8...........5:2 Is it harder to **d.** the belief of the insane in

**dispelled** 13
T-3...........I.2:9 essential that all such thinking be **d.** that
T-7.......VII.3:7 the Sonship are **d.** together as they were
T-11.......V.2:4 can be **d.** merely by denying their reality.
T-13.......II.4:5 truth, and in its presence the ego is **d.**.
T-21......VI.8:4 what madness sees must be **d.** by reason.
T-22....VI.9:11 let the darkness be **d.** by Him Who knows
W-pI.....92.4:7 and adored that strength may be **d.**, and
W-pII......7.1:3 to be **d.** before the light of knowledge.
M-5.......III.3:8 So are they **d.**, not by the will of another,
C-4............4:2 so easily **d.** that it can last no longer than
C-5............4:3 shared your dreams that they might be **d.**
S-3.........II.4:3 Now are its dreams **d.** in quiet rest. Now
S-3........III.4:7 For in this oneness is his separate sense **d.**

**dispelling** 5
T-7.....VIII.7:3 alone, thus **d.** the idea of separation and
T-8........IV.3:6 **D.** it is salvation, and in this sense I *am* the
T-13.......I.10:2 ego's plan, which it offers instead of **d.** it.
T-14.......III.6:5 And by not **d.** darkness, he became afraid
W-pI.....16.1:1 idea for today is a beginning step in **d.** the

**dispels** 4
T-1........IV.2:5 It thus **d.** illusions about yourself, and
T-13.......I.11:4 The Holy Spirit **d.** it simply through the
W-pI...111.2:3 *My weakness is the dark His gift* **d.**, *by giving*
W-pI...136.1:5 It **d.** this meaningless illusion by the same

**dispense** 1
S-1.........in.3:1 you, **d.** with idols and remember Him.

**dispirited** 1
T-15.......I.11:1 tempted to be **d.** by thinking how long it

**dispiritedly** 1
T-8........IX.4:4 Whenever you wake **d.**, it was not given

**displace** 2
T-13........X.2:7 If you **d.** your guilt upon them, the Holy
T-13........X.3:4 those who suffer guilt will attempt to **d.** it,

**displaced** 3
T-13........X.1:3 or you would not have **d.** the guilt onto
T-18......VI.2:5 You have **d.** your guilt to your body from
M-13.........1:6 which must be **d.** before another thought

**displacement** 3
T-13........X.1:2 of such **d.** is to hide the real source of guilt
T-13........X.1:3 **D.** always is maintained by the illusion
T-31.......V.5:2 It is a lesson in a terrible **d.**, and a fear so

**displeases** 1
W-pI.....72.3:5 like. He does something that **d.** you. He

**disposal** 5
T-1.........I.48:1 at your immediate **d.** for controlling time.
T-1.........V.5:7 mind means to place it at the **d.** of *true*
T-5.........V.1:4 at its **d.** to side with Heaven or earth, as it
T-10.......in.1:4 must learn that time is solely at your **d.**,
T-19........II.5:3 protected with every defense at its **d.**. For

**dispossess** 2
T19....IV.A.2:2 think that it must **d.** to dwell with you?
T19....IV.B.2:2 This is what you believe that it would **d.**,

**dispossessed** 1
W-pI...160.3:3 one would let himself be **d.** so needlessly,

**dispossession** 1
T-4.........I.11:4 chosen to leave it empty by their own **d.**.

**disproportionate** 2
T-17..IV.12:10 shadows of its enormous and **d.** enclosure
T-18......IV.7:4 and the Holy Spirit's are so extremely **d.**.

**dispute** 4
T-3......VI.8:10 The **d.** over authorship has left such
T-4...........I.7:3 long as you **d.** this everything you do will
T-4...........I.8:7 Do not let your ego **d.** this, because the
T-10.......V.1:7 you can and believe you have is beyond **d.**

**disqualify** 1
T-8..........II.2:5 not this alone **d.** it as your future teacher?

**disregard** 9
T-8..........II.1:9 if you could **d.** the Holy Spirit entirely,
T-8..........II.2:2 Does the total **d.** of anything it teaches
T-8..........II.4:4 teaching you how to **d.** or look beyond
T-21.......V.7:9 Only the totally insane can **d.** them, and
T-22.......III.2:6 to its fixed belief in sin and **d.** of errors. It
T-22.......V.4:5 Can it be difficult to **d.** its feeble squeaks
T-23......II.16:5 the emphasis on form and **d.** of content.
W-pI.135.17:2 and **d.** what you consider incompatible
W-pI.151.11:1 and **d.** those aspects which reflect but idle

**disregarded** 1

T-9........ III.4:2 He has merely **d.** them, and if you attend

**disrepute** 1

P-2........ IV.4:1 The word "cure" has come into **d.** among

**disrupt** 3

T-4....... VII.2:4 and it will **d.** communication when it
T-15... VII.14:3 only purpose is to **d.** communication, has
T-24......... I.2:4 of these hidden warriors to **d.** your peace.

**disrupted** 1

T-17....... V.8:5 For your relationship has not been **d.**. It

**disruption** 4

T-4....... VII.2:5 This **d.** is a reaction to a specific person or
T-5......... V.2:5 It is invulnerable to **d.** because it is whole.
T-14...... VI.6:2 but rather the **d.** of communication. If the
T19.... IV.C.6:5 final and complete **d.** of communication,

**disruptive** 1

T-5......... V.2:6 is whole. Guilt is *always* **d.**. Anything that

**dissatisfaction** 1

T-8........... I.4:4 **D.** with learning outcomes is a sign of

**dissatisfied** 1

M-13......... 3:3 finding; to be forever **d.** and discontented

**dissatisfying** 1

T-30...... IV.2:1 **d.** gods you made are blown-up children's

**dissipated** 1

W-pI... 138.3:3 decision, time is but a waste and effort **d.**.

**dissociate** 4

T-4........ VI.1:7 unaffected by your attempts to **d.** it.
T-6........ III.4:4 because you cannot teach what you still **d.**
T-7...... VI.10:6 **d.** your mind from it you are perceiving
T-10....... II.1:1 you first know something you cannot **d.** it

**dissociated** 5

T-4........ VI.1:8 now, but what has been **d.** is still there.
T-5........ III.2:9 He may have **d.** the Call for God, just as
T-10....... II.1:5 your dissociation, not of what you have **d.**
T-10....... II.1:6 When what you have **d.** is accepted, it
W-pI..... 96.5:3 **D.** from its function now, it thinks it is

**dissociating** 3

T-4........ VI.4:2 maintain the separation except by **d.**.
T-8........ IV.2:2 this simply by **d.** itself from everything. It
T-9........ VI.1:5 joy in others, you must be **d.** it in yourself

**dissociation** 19

T-5......... II.4:3 His is the glory before which **d.** falls away,
T-5...... III.2:10 **d.** is healed in both of you as you become
T-6......... II.1:4 are synonymous, as are separation and **d.**.
T-6......... II.1:5 before that the separation was and is **d.**,
T-6...... V.B.1:3 are clearly the result of **d.** and projection.
T-7......... V.6:5 does. Fear produces **d.**, because it induces
T-8......... V.1:2 **D.** is not a solution; it is a delusion. The
T-9........ VI.4:2 as He did, and your **d.** will not alter this.
T-10....... II.1:2 it. Knowledge must precede **d.**, so that
T-10....... II.1:2 so that **d.** is nothing more than a decision
T-10....... II.1:3 only because the **d.** is an attack on truth.
T-10 ....... II.1:5 dreams because you are afraid of your **d.**,
T-10 ....... II.2:1 give up the **d.** of reality brings more than
T-12 .... VII.7:7 This leads directly to **d.**, for it represents
T-14 .... VII.4:2 to you this way, if you consider what **d.** is.
T-14 .... VII.4:3 is. **D.** is a distorted process of thinking
T-15 ...... I.4:12 by using **d.** for holding its contradictory
T19... IV.D.3:4 *–the fear of God,* the final step in your **d.**.
T-21 ...... V.7:5 threatens **d.** as much as all of it. And all of

**dissolution** 3

T-15 ........ I.4:5 the ego aims at death and **d.** as an end, it
W-pI... 191.9:3 pitifully tied to **d.** in a world which shows
M-27 ......... 7:6 wavers nor sinks down to death and **d.**.

**dissolve** 3

T-2 ....... III.4:2 All solutions the physical eye seeks **d.**.
T-3 ...... VII.5:4 making will surely **d.** in the light of truth,
W-pI... 191.2:6 no hope you hold but will **d.** in tears.

**dissolved** 2

T-14 ... VIII.5:1 gives the power to create can never be **d.**.
T-27 ..... VI.6:9 The laws that call them different are **d.**,

**dissolves** 2

T-1 ........ I.39:1 miracle **d.** error because the Holy Spirit
T-5 ......... II.3:3 strong that the ego always **d.** at Its sound.

**distance** 19

T-1 ......... II.4:4 because without me the **d.** between God
T-1 ......... II.4:5 I bridge the **d.** as an elder brother to you
T-8 ....... VI.9:7 It is a journey without **d.** to a goal that has
T-9 ........ V.6:3 to remove it, while emphasizing the **d.**?
T-12 ... VIII.7:1 not matter how much **d.** you have tried to
T-18 ... VI.12:1 occur regardless of the physical **d.** that
T-26 ... VIII.2:1 There is a **d.** you would keep apart from
T-26 ..... IX.5:3 space nor **d.** lingering between the light of
T-29 ........ I.5:1 and of **d.** seen between you and him.
T-30 ..... III.9:4 It is not the **d.** nor the time that keeps this
W-pI..... 30.5:1 is not only unlimited by space and **d.**, but
W-pI..... 38.1:2 of time, space, **d.** and limits of any kind.
W-pI... 124.6:3 and apart from **d.** as apart from time.
W-pI... 127.7:1 you have advanced in **d.** without measure
W-pI. 155.10:1 be no gap, no **d.** between truth and you.
W-pI... 167.4:3 origin, apart from it in kind as well as **d.**,
W-pI... 194.1:2 So great the **d.** is that it encompasses, it
M-26 ......... 1:1 there is no **d.** between Him and His Son.
S-3........ IV.8:2 where time and **d.** have no meaning.

**distant** 10

T-4 ....... VI.8:1 withdraw from him I become **d.** to you.
T-9 ........ V.6:3 and looking for a **d.** light to remove it,
T-11 ...... V.9:1 unbelieving, "lighthearted," **d.**,
T-25 ..... IV.3:6 is pushed away, until it is but **d.** shadows,
T-26 ...... V.6:6 And who can stand upon a **d.** shore, and
T-26 .... V.10:3 now. A dreadful instant in a **d.** past, now
W-pI... 109.8:3 your **d.** brothers and your closest friends;
W-pI... 131.6:7 from time as is a tiny candle from a **d.** star
W-pI... 168.1:3 He is not **d.**. He makes no attempt to hide
W-pI. 187.10:3 not **d.** from one brother who is part of

**distinct** 6

T-27 ..... II.15:8 inability to see His goal divided and **d.** for
W-pI... 155.5:3 walk, nor do you seem to be **d.** from them
W-pI... 157.7:2 see the light more sure; the vision more **d.**
W-pI... 164.2:3 world increasingly is more and more **d.**;
W-pI... 169.5:5 and no part of mind sufficiently **d.** to feel
M-4 .......... 1:2 superficial "personalities" are quite **d.**.

**distinction** 22

T-1 ........ I.49:1 no **d.** among degrees of misperception. It
T-2 ... V.A.12:1 clear **d.** between what is created and what
T-2 ..... VIII.1:6 This basic **d.** leads directly into the real
T-2 ..... VIII.3:8 Until this **d.** is made, however, the
T-3 ......... V.1:4 We can now establish a **d.** that will clarify
T-4 ....... III.9:6 Any **d.** in this respect is meaningful only
T-4 ....... III.9:7 is why we make no **d.** between *having* the
T-6 ......... V.4:4 Holy Spirit makes no **d.** among dreams.
T-7 ......... X.5:6 are confused about this **d.** in motivation,
T-8 ......... II.5:3 You cannot make this **d.** without Him
T-11 ..... IV.4:6 there is no **d.** between within and without
T-11 .... VII.2:8 the true and making no **d.** between them.
T-13 ..... IX.4:1 have accepted into your mind without **d.**.
T-14 ....... II.3:5 *the one* **d.** *for you that you cannot make, but*
T-19 ....... II.1:1 it is this **d.** that makes salvation possible.
T-26 ..... III.4:7 thing to make a choice at all is this **d.**.
W-pI ...... 9.5:2 are honest with yourself in making this **d.**
W-pI .... 10.1:3 We have made this **d.** before, and will do
W-pI .... 38.4:2 see it. Try to make as little **d.** as possible
W-pI .. 140.9:3 that there can never be a meaningful **d.**
W-pI .. 152.4:2 not because it is a difficult **d.** to perceive.
C-5 ............ 3:4 it. He made a clear **d.**, still obscure to you,

**distinctions** 23

T-2 .......... I.5:2 It makes no **d.** among misperceptions. Its
T-4 ...... VII.4:3 Being is completely without these **d.**. It is
T-9 ..... VIII.3:2 but makes no **d.** between these two very
T-27 ..... VI.5:1 The miracle makes no **d.** in the names by
T-31 ... VIII.5:7 made. For in that choice are false **d.** gone,
W-pI ....... 3.1:1 ones, without making **d.** of any kind.
W-pI .... 16.4:3 still hard for you not to make artificial **d.**.
W-pI .... 17.3:1 it is essential to make no **d.** between what
W-pI .... 38.3:5 no **d.** because there are no distinctions.
W-pI .... 38.3:5 no distinctions because there are no **d.**.
W-pI .... 43.7:6 fact, try not to make **d.** of this kind at all.
W-pI .. 127.1:4 nor levels, no divergencies and no **d.**. It is
W-pI .. 127.2:6 If it could make such **d.**, it would have to
W-pI .. 130.4:2 All separation, all **d.**, and the multitude of
W-pI .. 130.7:2 will not make a thousand meaningless **d.**,
W-pI 132.12:3 for He makes no **d.** in what is Himself and
W-pI .. 140.6:2 It does not make **d.** among unrealities.
W-pI .. 152.4:1 This is the simplest of **d.**, yet the most
M-8 ........... 6:7 within it–so too are illusions without **d.**.
M-16 ......... 7:5 no **d.** among the problems he perceives,
M-28 ......... 5:1 Now there are no **d.**. Differences have
S-2........... I.9:3 Therefore we make **d.**, so that prayer can
S-3........... I.5:1 **D.** therefore must be made between true

**distinguish** 10

T-2 .......... I.5:3 sole concern is to **d.** between truth on the
T-7 ......... X.7:3 teach you how to **d.** between pain and joy,
T-8 ....... IX.5:3 Spirit cannot **d.** among degrees of error,
T-8 ....... IX.5:4 to **d.** only between the false and the true,
T-9 ..... VIII.8:1 It is easy to **d.** grandeur from grandiosity,
T-11 ..... V.11:2 you finally learn to **d.** the possible from
T-18 ....... V.1:5 cannot **d.** between advance and retreat.
W-pI .... 20.2:6 you cannot **d.** between joy and sorrow,
WpI..rIII.in3:4 Learn to **d.** situations that are poorly
W-pI .. 133.5:4 you can **d.** everything from nothing, you

**distinguished** 1

T-16 ..... IV.7:1 if it is to be **d.** from illusion: The special

**distort** 12

T-2 ........ I.1:11 believe that you can **d.** the creations of
T-3 ........ I.3:11 words that are almost impossible to **d.**,
T-4 .... VII.3:11 this. The mind can **d.** its function, but it
T-8 .... VII.11:3 its goal it will **d.** its perception of the body
T-9 ........ I.14:3 You cannot **d.** reality and know what it is.
T-9 ........ I.14:4 do **d.** reality you will experience anxiety,
T-12 ..... IV.3:4 The ego will therefore **d.** love, and teach
W-pI .. 136.2:3 attack it, change it, render it inept, **d.** it,
W-pI 136.11:4 suffer sickness or **d.** the truth in any way.
W-pI .. 196.3:2 ways in which the ego would **d.** the truth
W-pII . 268.1:2 *Your creation, and* **d.** *it into sickly forms. Let*
S-1........ III.6:2 and therefore **d.** the purpose of prayer.

**distorted** 35

T-1......III.5:10 their own perception of themselves is **d.**.
T-1......... V.3:7 of anything, their perception becomes **d.**.
T-1........ VI.2:2 if you had not **d.** your perception of truth,
T-1....... VII.1:1 **d.** perceptions produce a dense cover over
T-1....... VII.3:1 Fantasy is a **d.** form of vision. Fantasies of
T-2........ III.1:4 the **d.** belief that the body can be used as
T-3......... II.3:8 They do not suffer from **d.** perception.
T-3........ IV.6:3 of perception, a **d.** form of creation, then
T-4...... IV.10:5 Yours may be so **d.** that you believe I was
T-7..... VIII.4:9 by **d.** minds that are misusing their power
T-8........ IX.1:6 the body, for perception alone can be **d.**.
T-8........ IX.3:7 the ego's **d.** notions about what joining is.
T-14..... VII.4:3 is. Dissociation is a **d.** process of thinking
T-16.........I.5:3 this about is so **d.** that it would imprison
T-16...... VI.7:2 you see is grossly **d.** and completely out of
T-16...... VI.7:5 go your hold on the **d.** frame of reference
T-17...... III.2:5 love, no matter how **d.** the associations by
T-18...... IX.2:5 Its bleak sight is **d.**, and the messages it
T19... IV.C.8:1 Under the dusty edge of its **d.** world the
T-22...... III.4:3 a **d.** fragment of the whole without the
T-22...... III.5:7 **d.** form of vision the outside of everything
T-22...... III.7:6 what is not there must be **d.** perception,
T-30... VII.6:12 It is a part of a **d.** script, which cannot be
W-pI..... 70.4:1 however **d.** and fantastic it might be, to
W-pI... 134.1:1 for it is apt to be **d.** and to be perceived as
W-pI. 153.14:5 bewildered memory of this **d.** tale. God's
W-pI... 182.4:2 are a memory now so **d.** that you merely
W-pI. 184.13:3 you gave its aspects have **d.** what you see,
W-pI. 186.12:4 as they are, or a **d.** image of yourself,
W-pII.. 259.1:2 the strange and the **d.** seem more clear?
W-pII.. 293.1:3 it, and showing me **d.** forms of fear? Yet
M-11.......... 4:6 Yet has God's Judgment on this **d.** world
M-19.......... 3:2 brings witness of the **d.** world back to the
M-22.......... 5:6 mistakes, and **d.** perception does not heal
S-2......... II.6:5 become, and how **d.** is the end it seeks.

**distorting** 2

T-8..... VIII.8:2 the **d.** power of something you want, even
T-17.........I.2:3 Yet by **d.** it and devoting it to "evil," it

**distortion** 16

T-1....... VII.1:2 physical impulses is a major perceptual **d.**
T-2........ III.1:5 is only the first step in correcting this **d.**,
T-2........ IV.2:8 The whole **d.** that made magic rests on
T-3......... I.2:11 is tainted with this kind of **d.** in any form.
T-7..... VIII.3:8 is a complete **d.** of the power of extension.
T-14.... III.13:5 and against this strange **d.** of the purity of
T-18....... II.1:4 Rather it is a **d.** of the world, planned
T-20...... III.1:3 Every adjustment is therefore a **d.**, and
W-pI...... 12.1:1 a correction for a major perceptual **d.**.
W-pI..... 21.5:3 is suffering from this form of **d.**, say: *I am*
W-pI... 105.2:3 strange **d.** of what giving means pervades
W-pII...... 1.3:3 **D.** is its purpose, and the means by which
W-pII.. 301.1:4 *eyes forgiveness has released from all* **d.**. *Let*
M-5...... II.4:11 perspective, without **d.** and without fear,
M-10.......... 3:5 be certain there is no **d.** in his perception,
M-10........ 4:10 for there is no **d.** in His perception.

**distortions** 16

T-1...... III.5:10 makes them vulnerable to the **d.** of others
T-1...... III.5:11 this undoes their **d.** and frees them from
T-1......... V.6:4 is one of the **d.** on which the reverse of the
T-1.......... VII.h **D.** of Miracle Impulses
T-1....... VII.3:2 Fantasies of any kind are **d.**, because they
T-1....... VII.3:3 Actions that stem from **d.** are literally the
T-2.......... I.2:1 These related **d.** represent a picture of
T-3......... II.6:1 The way to correct **d.** is to withdraw your
T-8....... VII.9:5 can reach beyond its **d.** and return *to* spirit
T-11...... VI.3:8 is only the **d.** you introduce that tire you.
T-14....... II.2:4 all the **d.** you have made of nothing; all
T-31....... V.7:5 hot with hatred and **d.** born of fear. What
W-pII...... 1.2:3 that **d.** are more veiled and more obscure;
W-pII.. 336.1:4 Forgiveness sweeps away **d.**, and opens
W-pII.... 13.2:3 it ends the strange **d.** that were manifest.
P-2........ VI.2:5 strange **d.** woven inextricably into the self-

**distorts** 3

T-4......... V.2:3 either **d.** them or refuses to accept them.
T-8..... VIII.8:3 of how what you want **d.** perception. No
M-19......... 3:2 **d.** perception and brings witness of the

**distract** 4

T-8.......... I.2:1 but the ego has no power to **d.** you unless
T-17..... IV.9:2 Do not let the frame **d.** you. This gift is
T-17.... IV.13:5 and ceases to **d.** you from the picture.
W-pI. 139.12:1 that would **d.** us from our holy aim. For

**distracted** 2

T-13..... VII.6:1 No one in this **d.** world but has seen
W-pI..... 49.1:4 laws. It is this part that is constantly **d.**,

**distractible** 1

W-pI..... 39.9:4 becomes more disciplined and less **d.**.

**distracting** 2

W-pI..... 67.4:1 from time to time to replace **d.** thoughts.
WpI..rII.in.4:1 intent to waver in the face of **d.** thoughts.

**distraction** 2

T-17.... IV.14:2 There is no **d.** here. The picture of Heaven
W-pI. 153.15:5 And as **d.** ceases to arise to turn us from

**distractions** 3

T-8.......... I.2:1 The **d.** of the ego may seem to interfere
T-23...... in.4:5 Would you, for all these meaningless **d.**,
W-pI..... 32.4:3 select a time when few **d.** are anticipated,

**distraught** 1

W-pI..... 49.2:3 other part is a wild illusion, frantic and **d.**

**distress** 16

T-12... VIII.4:5 and did not abandon you in your **d.**. You
T-17....... V.7:2 your **d.** only by getting rid of your brother
T-20... VIII.5:3 turn in your **d.** and need for help unto the
T-30...... VI.2:7 natural reaction to **d.** that rests on error,
T-31....... V.9:1 be some lack of ease at times and some **d.**,
T-31... VIII.3:2 every difficulty, all **d.**, and each perplexity
W-pI..... 32.6:1 to any situation that may **d.** you. Apply
W-pI..... 33.4:1 idea the instant you are aware of **d.**. It
W-pI..... 43.8:1 to those which seem to **d.** you in any way.
WpI... rI.in.4:4 quiet with you, and to heal **d.** and turmoil
W-pI. 135.10:4 at all, but merely adds to your **d.** of mind.
W-pI... 193.4:1 Certain it is that all **d.** does not appear to
W-pII.. 257.1:3 without deep **d.** and great depression. Let
M-4..... I.A.5:3 teachers of God escape this **d.** entirely.
P-1............ 3:1 help, regardless of the form of his **d.**, is
P-2......... V.5:5 **d.** can be but answered by his Father. Yet

**distressed** 2

W-pI..... 20.5:2 Do not be **d.** if you forget to do so, but
W-pI... 124.5:2 see it in the frantic, in the sad and the **d.**,

**distresses** 1

W-pI..... 10.5:1 for any thought that **d.** you at any time. In

**distressing** 4

T-17....... V.3:3 disturbed, disjunctive and even quite **d.**.
T-19..... III.3:3 over and over, with obviously **d.** results,
W-pI....... 5.5:1 examine your mind for whatever is **d.** you
W-pI..... 26.8:1 some five or six **d.** possibilities available

**distribute** 1

W-pI..... 36.2:2 Try to **d.** them fairly evenly, and make the

**distributed** 1

W-pI... 162.4:3 and all His Love, to be **d.** to all the world,

**disturb** 13

T19..IV.C.10:3 can enter and **d.** the peace of sinlessness?
T-22...... VI.6:9 And no illusion can **d.** the peace of a
T-24.... IV.3:15 would **d.** your peace to enter and destroy.
T-27... VII.16:4 And let no pain **d.** your dream of deep
T-28........ I.13:4 throughout the stillness, yet **d.** it not. And
W-pI..... 48.2:5 should anything **d.** your peace of mind.
W-pI..... 50.3:3 that nothing can threaten, nothing can **d.**,
W-pI..... 50.5:3 to **d.** the holy mind of the Son of God.
W-pI..... 70.2:2 or **d.** your peace or upset you in any way.
W-pI..... 74.3:6 *Nothing can* **d.** *me. My will is God's. My will*
W-pI... 100.6:3 his joy; no fear besets him to **d.** his peace.
W-pI. 140.12:4 so deep that no illusion can **d.** our minds,
W-pII. 234.1:4 one. Nothing has ever happened to **d.** the

**disturbance** 3

T-13..... VII.7:4 **D.** of his peace can never be. In perfect
W-pI..... 47.8:2 often. Use it as your answer to any **d.**.
W-pII. 273.1:3 If we give way to a **d.**, let us learn how to

**disturbed** 12

T-13...... III.1:7 You are not seriously **d.** by your hostility.
T-14...... XI.6:6 your peace is threatened or **d.** in any way,
T-17......... I.6:5 When you become **d.** and lose your peace
T-17....... V.3:3 but it makes the relationship seem **d.**,
T-18...... IV.2:4 and be not **d.** that shadows surround it.
T19. IV.D.16:4 remove all trace of guilt from his **d.** and
T-22...... VI.3:1 **d.** at all to think how He can change the
T-23....... I.10:8 sure that its peace can never be **d.**.
W-pI..... 27.4:5 Do not be **d.** by this, but do try to keep on
W-pI..... 33.3:2 arises which tempts you to become **d.**.
W-pI..... 59.1:4 I be **d.** by anything when He rests in me in
W-pI... 122.1:6 Do you want a quietness that cannot be **d.**

**disturbing** 8

T-18........ II.3:1 what you see in sleep and on awaking **d.**.
W-pI....... 5.4:4 *They are all equally* **d.** *to my peace of mind.*
W-pI....... 5.7:1 of different forms of upset that are **d.** you,
W-pI....... 6.3:3 *They are all equally* **d.** *to my peace of mind.*
W-pI....... 9.2:2 This idea can be quite **d.**, and may meet
W-pI..... 14.7:5 *create [specify the situation which is* **d.** *you],*
W-pI..... 27.3:6 sentence to yourself without **d.** anything.
W-pI.... 93.11:1 If a situation arises that seems to be **d.**,

**disturbs** 2

T-13...... XI.9:5 the darkest nightmare that **d.** the mind of
W-pI..... 14.7:1 applied to anything that **d.** you during the

**disunited** 1

T-18......... I.5:6 into meaningless bits of **d.** perceptions,

**disunity** 2

T-26......... I.2:2 of complete **d.** and total lack of joining.
T-31....... I.11:3 believe you want disaster and **d.** and pain.

**ditch**

*See* last-ditch

**divergencies** 1

W-pI... 127.1:4 kinds nor levels, no **d.** and no distinctions

**divergent** 1

| | |
|---|---|
| P-2 I.3:6 | in connection with their own **d.** goals, |

**diverse** 1

| | |
|---|---|
| M-8 1:2 | unequal heights and **d.** sizes, on varying |

**diversionary** 1

| | |
|---|---|
| T-4 V.6:7 | In all these **d.** tactics, however, the one |

**divert** 2

| | |
|---|---|
| T-17 IV.7:6 | to **d.** your attention from what it encloses. |
| W-pI 41.6:6 | any thoughts that might **d.** your attention |

**diverted** 1

| | |
|---|---|
| T-13 X.1:3 | source of guilt, from which attention is **d.**, |

**divide** 6

| | |
|---|---|
| T-3 IV.5:8 | mind chooses to **d.** itself when it chooses |
| T-5 I.1:10 | possession, you do **d.** its ownership. If |
| T-7 IV.5:2 | The ego always seeks to **d.** and separate. |
| T-7 VI.12:2 | thought system and **d.** your allegiance. |
| T-15 IX.4:1 | to **d.** your strength between Heaven and |
| WpI. rIII.in8:2 | least try to **d.** them so you undertake one |

**divided** 38

| | |
|---|---|
| T-3 IV.1:2 | are **d.** and open to question and doubt. |
| T-3 IV.3:4 | A separated or **d.** mind *must* be confused. |
| T-5 II.8:9 | **d.** devotion has given you the two voices, |
| T-7 VI.12:3 | You cannot create in this **d.** state, and you |
| T-7 VI.12:3 | this **d.** state because only peace can be |
| T-7 VI.12:4 | Your **d.** mind is blocking the extension of |
| T-8 IV.5:6 | or the mind itself is **d.** and not whole. |
| T-9 I.6:3 | A **d.** mind cannot communicate, because |
| T-10 III.4:3 | taught by sick minds too **d.** to know that |
| T-10 III.10:2 | reality with Him, because reality is not **d.**. |
| T-10 IV.3:3 | Oneness cannot be **d.**. If you perceive |
| T-12 I.6:8 | of reality are meaningless in your **d.** state, |
| T-12 V.4:1 | for yours is **d.** and therefore not real. You |
| T-12 V.9:3 | because the goal is not **d.** and the means |
| T-12 VII.7:8 | mind then sees a **d.** world outside itself, |
| T-14 VIII.2:12 | between what cannot be **d.** cannot cease. |
| T-17 V.14:7 | remain still separate and **d.** on the means. |
| T-17 VII.6:2 | in advance to truth, your dedication is **d.**. |
| T-18 I.4:3 | so splintered and subdivided and **d.** again |
| T-19 I.6:2 | **d.** goal has given both an equal reality, |
| T-19 I.6:2 | **d.** into little parts of seeming wholeness, |
| T-23 I.11:2 | when the house of God perceives itself **d.**. |
| T-24 II.10:7 | Who chose that love could never be **d.**, |
| T-24 VII.7:5 | still uncertain, or one wish with a **d.** aim. |
| T-25 II.11:1 | God Himself is One and not **d.** in His Will |
| T-25 VIII.2:5 | do what one **d.** still against himself would |
| T-27 II.11:1 | a split mind, identity must seem to be **d.**. |
| T-27 II.12:6 | Thus does your function seem **d.**, with a |
| T-27 II.15:4 | free. That is **d.** purpose, which can not be |
| T-27 II.15:7 | is. If He upheld **d.** function, you were lost |
| T-27 II.15:8 | inability to see His goal **d.** and distinct for |
| T-31 II.3:5 | You see yourself **d.** into both these roles, |
| W-in 3:1 | workbook is **d.** into two main sections, |
| W-pI 71.5:3 | your purpose is **d.** and you will attempt to |
| W-pI 95.2:2 | yourself; a self **d.** into many warring parts |
| M-17 3:5 | the **d.** goal of the pupil into one direction, |
| C-3 5:1 | symbol of His Will alone it cannot be **d.**. |
| P-2 III.3:6 | **D.** goals alone can interfere with perfect |

**divides** 1

| | |
|---|---|
| M-29 1:4 | be remembered that only time **d.** teacher |

**dividing** 2

| | |
|---|---|
| T-7 VI.9:1 | is **d.** its allegiance between two kingdoms, |
| T-29 I.4:2 | seems to be **d.** off your separate minds. It |

**Divine** 2
*divine*

| | |
|---|---|
| T-1 I.37:4 | knowledge of the **D.** Order is impossible. |
| T-4 VII.5:4 | **D.** Abstraction takes joy in sharing. That |

**divine** 1
*Divine*

| | |
|---|---|
| M-19 1:1 | Justice is the **d.** correction for injustice. |

**Divinity** 3

| | |
|---|---|
| T-10 III.5:2 | willing to attack the **D.** of your brothers, |
| T-30 II.1:3 | you. In His **D.** is but your own. And all He |
| T-30 III.2:3 | of all the love in the **D.** of God the Son? |

**division** 9

| | |
|---|---|
| T-5 II.7:9 | War is **d.**, not increase. No one gains |
| T-5 V.2:7 | is divisive because it obeys the law of **d.**. If |
| T-5 V.3:1 | is the part of the mind that believes in **d.**. |
| T-11 VIII.10:1 | for there is no separation and no **d.**. Only |
| T-14 VIII.2:11 | He shines not in **d.**, but in the meeting |
| T-14 X.7:1 | Holy Spirit's one **d.** into two categories; |
| T-14 X.7:2 | You cannot safely make this **d.**, for you |
| T-14 XI.11:5 | and before His lesson **d.** disappears. |
| W-pI 125.8:3 | nor **d.** in the single Mind of Father and of |

**divisive** 1

| | |
|---|---|
| T-5 V.2:7 | that engenders fear is **d.** because it obeys |

**divorced** 2

| | |
|---|---|
| T-3 V.5:6 | Ingenuity is totally **d.** from knowledge, |
| W-pI 96.4:4 | Yet mind can also see itself **d.** from spirit, |

**do** 1945

**doctrine** 4

| | |
|---|---|
| T-15 VII.4:2 | ego's fundamental **d.** that what you do to |
| T-19 II.4:3 | And it is this **d.** that replaces the reality of |
| W-pI 71.4:2 | it is in strict accord with the ego's basic **d.** |
| P-2 IV.11:1 | single **d.** is the goal of all therapy. Relieve |

**does** 1213

**dogs** 2

| | |
|---|---|
| T19 IV.A.15:6 | given to replace the hungry **d.** of fear you |
| T-31 III.5:1 | prisoner to the snarling **d.** of hate and evil |

**doing** 68

| | |
|---|---|
| T-1 III.1:9 | **D.** them will bring conviction in the |
| T-1 VII.1:4 | real pleasure comes from **d.** God's Will. |
| T-1 VII.1:5 | This is because *not* **d.** it is a denial of Self. |
| T-2 VI.5:6 | are **d.** what you do not wholly want to do. |
| T-2 VI.6:4 | There is no strain in **d.** God's Will as soon |
| T-2 VI.6:8 | because wanting and **d.** are discordant. |
| T-3 II.5:2 | **d.** this the mind awakens from its sleep |
| T-3 III.5:8 | for creative thinking, but not for right **d.**. |
| T-3 III.5:9 | miracles and **d.** are closely related. |
| T-3 V.3:1 | have already observed, does not lead to **d.** |
| T-5 IV.5:4 | because by so **d.** you can depend on it. |
| T-6 II.2:4 | By **d.** this unconsciously, you try to keep |
| T-7 IV.3:8 | all contribute to one result, and by so **d.**, |
| T-7 VI.3:3 | why the ego never recognizes what it is **d.**. |
| T-7 VII.9:5 | is what you will think others are **d.** to you. |
| T-7 X.4:3 | You believe that **d.** the opposite of God's |
| T-8 IX.8:3 | nothing can prevent you from **d.** exactly |
| T-8 IX.8:3 | I ask, and everything argues *for* your **d.** it. |
| T-11 V.1:4 | Let us be very calm in **d.** this, for we are |
| T-11 V.9:3 | to it if you recognized this is what it is **d.**? |
| T-12 III.2:3 | that your salvation lies in *not* **d.** it. You, |
| T-13 I.6:4 | so **d.** you cannot know that you are God's |
| T-13 VI.4:8 | by **d.** so you are aligning past and future, |
| T-13 IX.4:5 | **d.** you have denied the witness unto yours |
| T-14 I.4:3 | *is* indirect, as **d.** is. You were created only |
| T-15 I.4:12 | and all too frequently succeeds, in **d.** both |
| T-15 II.5:4 | instant, and will learn much from **d.** so. |
| T-15 III.2:5 | wish, but all you will be **d.** is to delay your |
| T-18 VII.6:6 | preparation, and practice **d.** nothing else. |
| T-18 VII.8:3 | of every busy **d.** on which you are sent. |
| T-25 I.1:2 | And in the **d.** of it will you learn the body |
| T-27 VIII.2:3 | It works to get them, **d.** senseless things, |
| T-27 VIII.10:1 | but this: that you are **d.** this unto yourself |
| T-28 I.10:9 | and **d.** nothing that would interfere. |
| T-28 I.11:3 | they will join in **d.** nothing to prevent its |
| T-28 I.14:4 | he never had a need for **d.** anything, and |
| T-28 II.12:5 | "this is not done to me, but *I* am **d.** this." |
| T-28 III.5:2 | space, enclosing nothing, **d.** nothing, and |
| T-31 III.3:6 | commands, and **d.** nothing of itself at all. |
| T-31 V.17:7 | *am, and therefore do not know what I am* **d.**, |
| W-in 1:2 | Yet it is **d.** the exercises that will make the |
| W-pI 5.5:1 | much or how little you think it is **d.** so. |
| W-pI 16.2:4 | but you will not extend it by **d.** so. |
| W-pI 26.8:1 | If you are **d.** the exercises properly, you |
| W-pI 44.8:1 | of the importance of what you are **d.**; its |
| W-pI 44.10:1 | If you are **d.** the exercises correctly, you |
| W-pI 45.5:2 | fail in **d.** what He would have us do. There |
| W-pI 46.4:1 | If you are **d.** the exercises well you should |
| W-pI 49.3:3 | knowing that in **d.** so we are joining our |
| W-pI 52.3:6 | that in so **d.** I am giving up nothing. |
| W-pI 65.6:2 | not strain or make undue effort in **d.** this. |
| W-pI 69.7:1 | If you are **d.** the exercises properly, you |
| W-pI 71.9:9 | The very fact that you are **d.** the exercises |
| W-pI 72.4:3 | **d.** more than failing to help in freeing him |
| W-pI 77.6:1 | **d.** this, you do not really ask for anything. |
| W-pI 102.5:4 | you are joining with God's Will in **d.** this. |
| W-pI 134.9:3 | instead, "Would I accuse myself of **d.** this |
| W-pI 134.15:3 | "Would I condemn myself for **d.** this?" |
| W-pI 134.17:4 | *Would I accuse myself of* **d.** *this? I will not lay* |
| W-pI 136.5:6 | They aim at **d.** this, and it is this they do. |
| M-22 5:4 | In so **d.**, he has refused to accept the |
| M-23 2:6 | so **d.** he has recognized all living things as |
| M-25 2:8 | He is **d.** nothing special, and there is no |
| P-2 II.8:4 | one goal with someone else, and in so **d.**, |
| P-2 II.8:5 | Only by **d.** this is it possible to transcend |
| P-2 II.8:6 | self. Only by **d.** this can teacher and pupil, |
| S-1 IV.1:3 | the reason for **d.** so has been recognized if |
| S-2 I.3:1 | Would you forgive yourself for **d.** this? |

**doings** 1

| | |
|---|---|
| M-29 8:1 | *And now in all your* **d.** *be you blessed. God* |

**domain** 3

| | |
|---|---|
| T-3 III.4:3 | brings it into the proper **d.** of the miracle. |
| T-3 IV.2:2 | is correctly identified as the **d.** of the ego. |
| T-5 III.6:4 | so the lower mind, which is the ego's **d.**, |

**dominate** 2

| | |
|---|---|
| T-23 I.12:4 | fear is born, and grows and seeks to **d.**. |
| W-pI 190.5:6 | But it is you who have the power to **d.** all |

**dominion** 2

| | |
|---|---|
| T-8 IV.6:7 | through the **d.** of one mind over another. |
| W-pI 38.5:5 | **d.** over all things because of what you are. |

**done** 214

**doom** 3

| | |
|---|---|
| T-5 V.4:13 | The ego regards this as **d.**, but you must |
| T-20 VI.11:9 | are his salvation, and not his **d.**. |
| T-29 IX.9:2 | conceal completely all your sense of **d.**. |

### doomed 3

T-31......VI.2:3 death; that one is d. to suffering and loss.
W-pII....12.1:1 d. to suffer and to end its life in death. It
M-27..........3:5 as well are d. to be destroyed as certainly.

### dooms 1

T-31.....VII.6:2 And thus it d. you to a bitter sense of

### door 61

T-11......IV.6:2 that the d. is barred and you cannot enter
T-11......IV.6:3 The d. is not barred, and it is impossible
T-11......IV.6:5 cannot bar the d. that Christ holds open.
T-14....... II.7:5 dark d. that you believe is locked forever.
T-14....... II.7:6 You made this d. of nothing, and behind
T-14......VI.8:8 the d. himself upon his Father's welcome.
T-14.....VII.6:2 Open every d. to Him, and bid Him enter
T-18.....VII.7:3 quick and open d. through which you slip
T-20..... II.8:12 only a pathway to the open d. of Heaven,
T-20..... II.11:3 singing as you behold the open d. of
T-23...... I.10:3 Open the d. of His most holy home, and
T-23......III.6:3 it is over. The d. is open; you have left the
T-24....IV.3:15 an open d. inviting everything that would
T-25... VIII.7:4 escape has He for them except a d. to hell
T-26.........I.8:4 function to ensure the d. be opened, that
T-26....... II.8:4 special function opens wide the d. beyond
T-26....... II.8:5 that seems to hold the d. securely barred
T-26..... X.1:11 Its simple presence shuts the d. to Theirs,
T-28....... II.5:1 An empty storehouse, with an open d.,
T-28......III.7:2 The d. is open, not to thieves, but to your
T-28......III.7:3 They have nothing left behind the open d.
T-28......III.8:7 The d. is open, that all those may come
T-28...VII.5:10 there is no need to bar the d. and lock the
T-31...VII.13:7 And the d. held open for the face of Christ
T-31... VIII.6:4 close the d. upon his dreams of weakness,
W-pI.......1.2:2 *That d. does not mean anything. That body*
W-pI.......9.4:3 *I do not see that d. as it is now. I do not see*
W-pI.....29.5:8 *God is in that d.. God is in that waste basket.*
W-pI.....56.3:4 the d. behind this world be opened for me
W-pI.....57.1:5 The prison d. is open. I can leave simply
W-pI.....65.3:3 It places the key to the d. of peace, which
W-pI...122.5:3 it stands before you like an open d., with
W-pI...128.3:3 and add another bar across the d. that
W-pI...128.5:4 that bar the d. to freedom from the world
W-pI.131.11:8 There is a d. beneath them in your mind,
W-pI.131.12:1 Seek for that d. and find it. But before
W-pI.131.12:4 nothing before this d. you really want,
W-pI.131.13:1 and see how easily the d. swings open
W-pI.131.14:2 that you might approach this d. some day
W-pI.131.14:5 end together as you pass beyond the d..
W-pI...134.8:5 this gift of you, the d. is open to yourself.
W-pI...134.9:1 way to find the d. to true forgiveness, and
W-pI...137.1:4 becomes a d. that closes on a separate self
W-pI.155.11:1 time has closed the d. on all the things
W-pI...157.2:3 brings us to the d. where learning ceases,
W-pI...159.6:4 Here the d. is never locked, and no one is
W-pI...189.9:8 Through every opened d. His Love shines
W-pI...194.2:2 chains that locked the d. to freedom on it.
W-pI...195.2:3 no d. to the deliverance they now perceive
W-pI...195.7:4 us. An ancient d. is swinging free again; a
W-pI...200.3:6 a d. that opens easily to welcome you?
W-pII..342.1:4 *the d. beyond which lies the end of dreams. I*
W-pII..342.1:8 *that I am Your Son, and opening the d. at last*
W-ep .........5:7 For we go homeward to an open d. which
C-ep.........1:11 an ancient d. that leads beyond the world
P-3 ...........I.4:6 or would he close the d. on the savior of
P-3 ........III.8:4 to open the d. to your salvation, for such
S-2 ...........I.9:2 has lost the d. for which the key was made
S-2 ........III.7:6 the d. to which forgiveness is the only key
S-2 ........III.7:7 and you will see the d. swing silently open
S-2 ........III.7:8 Behold your brother there beyond the d.;

### doors 12

T-14......VI.8:4 serve to guard the dark d. behind which
T-14......VI.8:5 must open all d. and let the light come
T-14... VIII.1:3 the dark d. you have closed lies nothing,
T-14... VIII.1:4 is the closing of the d. that interferes with
T-21.........I.1:5 through the d. you thought were closed,
T-21.........I.2:4 You can be shown which d. are open, and
T-21....... V.9:5 can serve to open d. you closed against it.
W-pI...109.8:3 Open the temple d. and let them come
W-pI.134.12:3 iron d. he thought would make him safe.
W-pI...200.5:1 where you beheld but chains and iron d..
W-pII..316.1:4 watch its open d. that not one gift is lost,
W-pII.....359.h All prison d. are opened. And all sin Is

### doorway 2

T-2..... VIII.5:3 apparent that it is really the d. to life. No
W-pI...122.5:3 and welcome calling from beyond the d.,

### doorways 1

T-21.........I.1:2 walk unharmed through open d. that they

### double 13

T-14.....VII.7:5 including yours, comes not from d. vision
T-27......III.1:9 Who can understand a d. concept, such
T-27......III.2:3 He represents a d. thought, where half is
T-27......III.6:4 It does not stand for d. concepts. Though
T-27......IV.3:5 The world can only ask a d. question. One
T-27......IV.4:3 A d. question asks and answers, both
T-27....... V.2:4 No one is healed through d. messages. If
T-29........ II.7:5 Yet here on earth it has a d. purpose, for
W-pI...108.6:2 to other areas of doubt and d. vision. And
W-pI.136.16:3 pursuits with d. purposes insanely sought
W-pI...153.2:3 Yet is defensiveness a d. threat. For it
W-pII......5.2:2 Yet this he sees as d. safety. For the Son of
M-17 .........2:4 d. wish that makes the help of little value,

### doubled 1

W-pI...133.9:3 Here is deception d., for the one who is

### doubly 3

T-2......... V.8:5 state becomes d. dangerous unless it *is*
W-pI...135.1:3 thus making correction d. difficult. And it
W-pI...136.5:2 decision which is d. shielded by oblivion.

### doubt 138

*See also* self-doubt

T-1......... II.1:1 but temporary suspension of d. and fear.
T-2......... II.1:3 be performed in the spirit of d. or fear.
T-2......... V.7:4 is no d. that this may produce discomfort,
T-3........IV.1:2 are divided and open to question and d..
T-3....... V.10:7 beyond perception because it is beyond d.
T-3......VI.8:10 may even d. whether you really exist at all
T-4.........I.12:5 beauty and dignity are far beyond d.,
T-5....... V.7:12 a remedy whose efficacy is beyond d.,
T-6...........I.4:2 little d. that one body can assault another
T-6........IV.2:7 "What are you?" was the beginning of d..
T-6........IV.7:2 There is no d., because the first question
T-6....IV.11:10 You would d. your right mind, which is
T-6......V.C.7:6 His creation, and therefore engenders d..
T-6......V.C.8:2 in your mind because, if you let d. enter,
T-7.........III.5:6 perfectly calm, because they are not in d..
T-7..... VIII.7:4 is as beyond d. as it is beyond belief. Your
T-7......... X.3:6 long as you are in d. about what you are,
T-8..... VIII.8:4 No one can d. the ego's skill in building
T-8..... VIII.8:5 anyone d. your willingness to listen until
T-9......... II.4:1 are answered, never d. a Son of God. Do
T-9......... II.4:4 the Holy Spirit truly, and d. your brother?
T-9......... II.7:3 Knowing what you are, I cannot d. you. I
T-13...... XI.4:6 you. To d. this would be to doubt that His
T-13...... XI.4:6 this would be to d. that His mission will
T-13...... XI.5:1 whose mind is darkened by d. and guilt,
T-13...... XI.5:1 the mission to remove all d. and every
T-14....III.19:1 you are in d. what you should do, think of
T-15.......... II.h The End of D.
T-15..... II.4:13 will d. until you hear one witness whom
T-15..... II.4:14 Spirit. And then you will d. no more.
T-15......III.4:1 There is no d. about what your function
T-15......III.4:2 There is no d. about its magnitude, for it
T-15...... VI.2:5 of his worth we cannot d. his holiness.
T-17...... III.4:4 it is formed, d. must enter in, because its
T-18........II.5:2 while you see it you do not d. that it is real
T-18...... III.3:8 is little d. that what you think it means *is*
T-20...... III.1:5 which certainty is lost and d. has entered.
T-21...... IV.8:4 insane insistence that sureness lies in d..
T-22..... V.3:12 And all uncertainty is d. about yourself.
T-23...... IV.8:8 no touch of d. can ever mar your certainty
T-24....... V.9:1 must be d. before there can be conflict.
T-24....... V.9:2 And every d. must be about yourself.
T-24....... V.9:3 Christ has no d., and from His certainty
T-24....... V.9:7 And where is d. when certainty has come?
T-24.... VI.10:6 And never d. but that your specialness
T-24..... VII.1:6 slight, the tiniest attack, the whispered d.,
T-25..VIII.12:4 holy that He could not d. His innocence.
T-25...... IX.1:7 And not one d. that this is possible will
T-27..... VII.7:9 He cannot d. his dreams' reality, because
T-27... VII.11:7 the part you see and do not d. is real.
T-27... VII.11:8 How could you d. it while you lie asleep,
T-31.........I.3:1 ever d. the power of your learning skill.
T-31.........I.6:5 God, and far beyond all d. and question?
T-31..... V.11:4 go, if either one were ever raised to d..
T-31..... V.17:5 has been raised to d. and question, and
W-pI.... 10.1:5 you will have no d. that what you once
W-pI..... 77.6:5 is no room for d. and uncertainty today.
W-pI..... 79.8:3 is to entertain some d. about the reality of
W-pI..... 83.1:5 All d. must disappear as I acknowledge
W-pI..... 91.3:3 You do not d. that the body's eyes can see
W-pI..... 91.3:4 d. the images they show you are reality.
W-pI..... 91.4:4 within your easy reach, you will not d..
W-pI.... 95.10:4 which there is no d. that only this is true.
W-pI..... 96.2:2 of time and effort, hopefulness and d.,
W-pI..... 98.2:2 with thanks that d. is gone and surety has
W-pI..... 98.3:4 They do not d. their own ability because
W-pI... 99.11:1 of d. and fear forever from your mind. If
W-pI... 107.3:2 could be no fear, no d. and no attack.
W-pI... 107.7:6 We do not d. we walk with truth today,
W-pI... 108.6:2 to other areas of d. and double vision.
W-pI... 121.3:1 The unforgiving mind is torn with d.,
W-pI... 124.4:1 Today we will not d. His Love for us, nor
W-pI... 128.4:3 pain; one moment of uncertainty and d..
W-pI... 130.7:1 thought that ends all compromise and d.,
W-pI... 130.9:4 You will not d. what you will look upon,
W-pI... 132.1:5 world he sees is real, and does not d. it.
W-pI... 138.8:3 question and from reason and from d..
W-pI... 139.1:4 are? There is no d. that is not rooted here.
W-pI... 139.5:6 There is no d. of this. And yet you doubt
W-pI... 139.5:7 And yet you d. it. But you do not ask what
W-pI... 139.5:8 ask what part of you can really d. yourself
W-pI... 139.6:1 idea that it is possible to d. yourself, and
W-pI... 139.7:3 they learn it is impossible to d. yourself,
W-pI... 139.8:3 It is so far beyond all d. and question that
W-pI... 151.1:3 an opinion based on ignorance and d.. Its
W-pI... 151.1:6 without a d. because of all the doubting
W-pI... 151.2:1 You do not seem to d. the world you see.
W-pI... 151.2:6 Why but because of underlying d., which
W-pI... 151.5:3 the hidden d. that what it shows you as
W-pI... 151.6:4 You believe to d. his vassals is to doubt
W-pI... 151.6:4 to doubt his vassals is to d. yourself.
W-pI... 151.7:1 Yet you must learn to d. their evidence
W-pI... 151.8:1 He has certainty in which there is no d.,
W-pI... 151.8:1 great that d. is meaningless before Its face
W-pI... 151.8:2 Christ cannot d. Himself. The Voice for
W-pI.151.10:3 You will no longer d. that only good can
W-pI.153.20:3 be no d. that you will reach your final goal
W-pI... 156.7:5 in the little interval of d. that still remains
W-pI... 158.6:1 joining of the world of d. and shadows
W-pI... 163.1:2 may appear as sadness, fear, anxiety or d.;
W-pI... 165.8:3 His sureness lies beyond our every d.. His
W-pI... 181.1:1 d. and lack of sure conviction in yourself.
W-pI... 182.8:3 all words, untouched by fear and d.,
W-pI... 184.6:4 leave no d. that what is named is there. It
W-pI... 184.7:5 can be withdrawn as they are raised to d..
W-pI... 186.4:2 d. our adequacy for the function He will
W-pI.186.11:2 There is no d. of its validity. It comes
W-pI... 187.1:5 No one can d. that you must first possess
W-pI... 200.1:3 and sense of icy hopelessness and d.. Seek
W-pII ..... 1.2:1 a judgment that it will not raise to d.,
W-pII ..... 1.2:3 more obscure; less easily accessible to d.,

W-pII .244.1:3 *he fear or d. or fail to know he cannot suffer,*
W-pII .256.1:6 in heavy clouds of d. about the holiness of
W-pII .286.2:2 Today we will not d. the end which God
W-pII .323.1:1 *sense of loss and sadness, all anxiety and d.,*
W-pII .333.2:1 *chose to shine away all conflict and all d.,*
M-4 ....... II.2:6 Challenge implies d., and the trust on
M-4 ....... II.2:6 teachers rest secure makes d. impossible.
M-4 ....VIII.1:3 unknown to him as yet, but not in d.. The
M-7 ...........2:2 he be tempted to d. this, he should not
M-7 ...........3:8 Thus is his d. corrected. He thought the
M-7 ...........4:1 to recognize is that to d. a healing because
M-7 ...........4:6 and d. and trust cannot coexist. And hate
M-7 ...........4:8 D. not the gift and it is impossible to
M-7 ...........4:8 the gift and it is impossible to d. its result.
M-7 ...........5:1 real basis for d. about the outcome of any
M-7 ...........6:5 are offering only healing, you cannot d.. If
M-7 ...........6:6 want the problem solved, you cannot d..
M-7 ...........6:7 the problem is, you cannot d.. Doubt is
M-7 ...........6:8 D. is the result of conflicting wishes. Be
M-7 ...........6:9 you want, and d. becomes impossible.
M-13 .........3:7 he is. He can d. all things, but never this.
C-ep...........1:2 D. along the way will come and go and go
P-2........VI.3:5 grows fearful and begins to d. its sanity.
P-2.......VII.6:2 way can ever d. the power that is in him.
P-2.......VII.6:3 Nor does he d. its Source. He understands
P-3........III.4:8 release from long imprisonment and d..
S-3........III.3:4 the mind that suffers from the agony of d.

## doubted 2

T-26..... V.11:6 from the past are heard and then are d..
M-7 ...........5:2 illusory self, for only such a self can be d..

## doubter 1

W-pI...139.3:4 Who is the d.? What is it he doubts?

## doubtful 7

T-4...........I.8:2 will remain d. as long as you believe in its
T-6......V.C.8:5 be yours while you are d. of what you are.
T-13....... X.1:2 The d. service of such displacement is to
T-17...... VI.3:7 makes understanding d. and evaluation
W-pI.....59.1:3 I be d. and unsure of myself when perfect
W-pI.....91.8:7 *I am not d., but certain. I am not an illusion,*
W-pI...184.7:3 are its premises, how d. its results, the

## doubting 6

T-31...... II.11:5 and a sense of endless d. as you stagger
W-pI...151.1:6 a doubt because of all the d. underneath.
W-pI...156.8:2 till certainty has ended d. and established
W-pI...156.8:3 Today let d. cease. God speaks for you in
W-pI...158.4:4 will come to end your d. has been set. For
W-pI...165.6:1 Now is all d. past, the journey's end

## doubts 32

T-4...........I.4:3 dreamer who d. the reality of his dream
T-4...........I.8:1 praise for itself in order to overcome its d.
T-6......V.C.7:4 is assailed by any d. in your mind, His
T-6......V.C.8:7 D. about being must not enter your mind,
T-15....... II.6:9 witnesses to It, your d. must disappear.
T-15...... VI.2:3 perfect faith in you, in place of all your d..
T-20....VIII.2:2 not happily exchange your d. for certainty
T-21...... IV.1:7 It d. not your belief and faith in sin. Its
T-24....... V.9:4 will exchange His certainty for all your d.,
T-24...... VI.1:7 offered you that all your d. about yourself
T-28...... VI.1:6 it has no will, no preferences and no d.. It
W-pI.....91.4:2 great this strength, your d. would vanish.
W-pI...95.13:3 shine away all your illusions and your d..
W-pI.....98.2:2 All our d. we lay aside today, and take our
W-pI...107.4:3 all the seeming difficulties and the d. that
W-pI...132.3:4 with all your fears, your d. and miseries,
W-pI...135.2:4 all its structures, all its thoughts and d.,
W-pI...138.4:3 the d. that myriad decisions would induce
W-pI...139.3:5 What is it he d.? Whom does he question
W-pI...151.6:3 d. their lord can not completely vanquish.
W-pI...165.7:3 d. are meaningless, for God is certain.
W-pI... 165.7:6 This course removes all d. which you have
W-pI... 170.5:2 turn for solace and escape from d. about
WpI...rV.in1:5 and d. have made us walk uncertainly and
WpI...rV.in2:2 *Let our d. be quiet and our holy minds be still*
WpI...rV.in6:2 For I share your d. and fears a little while,
WpI...rV.in6:2 by which all fears and d. are overcome.
W-pII ... 11.4:3 Yet back of all our d., past all our fears,
W-ep......... 1:7 to solve all problems, and resolve all d..
M-7 ........... 3:7 If he d. this, let him remember Who gave
M-13 ......... 3:6 and no one d. what he believes he is. He
C-in ........... 3:4 questions because it is only the ego that d.

## down 94

*See also* upside-down

T-1 .........II.5:2 I can thus bring d. to them more than
T-1 .........II.5:2 more than they can draw d. to themselves
T-1 ........ V.6:7 that holds it upside d. be conducive to
T-1 ....... VI.3:4 such as "up" and "d." are meaningful.
T-2 ........ V.4:3 and has turned it upside d.. All forms of
T-3 .........I.5:3 The lion and the lamb lying d. together
T-5 ..........I.3:2 up and bring the Holy Spirit d. to you,
T-6 ..... V.B.4:1 Upside d. as always, the ego perceives the
T-10 ... III.11:6 accept him you will bow d. and worship
T-11 .... V.13:2 means to break d. or to separate out. The
T-11 .... V.13:3 to understand totality by breaking it d. is
T-11 .VIII.15:5 Father will lean d. to you and take the last
T-14 .... IV.6:2 being carried d. a quiet path in summer.
T-14 .... XI.4:6 joyously laid d. by hands open to receive,
T-16 .... VI.7:3 is strong and powerful cut d. to littleness.
T-18 ........I.6:4 d. arose from this projection of error? It
T-19 .......II.6:2 a world could everything be upside d..
T19... IV.D.6:2 Your eyes look d., remembering your
T-20 ..... III.9:1 and with eyes so long cast d. in darkness
T-21 ........I.1:5 and fall d. upon the stones you did not
T-21 ... VI.7:11 will lay d. the burden of denying truth.
T-23 .... III.6:6 You can look d. on it in safety from above
T-23 .... IV.5:1 and from a higher place look d. upon it.
T-24 .......II.2:2 Who can attack his savior and cut him d.,
T-24 ...... V.8:1 of Heaven has Himself come d. to you, to
T-24 ... VII.8:5 d. until its purpose has been understood.
T-25 ..... VI.3:1 wish to see calls d. the grace of God upon
T-26 ..... III.2:3 all illusions are laid d. beside the truth,
T-26 ...... V.2:6 d. a road that leads to nothing and that
T-26 .... VII.5:3 be reversed; yet can be seen as upside d..
T-27 .... VII.8:7 leaping up and d. according to a senseless
T-28 .... III.1:2 up the ladder separation led you d.. The
T-29 .... IX.1:2 bow d. in worship to what has no life, and
W-pI.....11.2:3 and look about, near and far, up and d., –
W-pI.....41.7:2 But most of all, try to sink d. and inward,
W-pI.....47.7:1 try to reach d. into your mind to a place
W-pI.....47.7:3 reach d. and below them to the Kingdom
W-pI.....57.3:3 at it. I see everything upside d., and my
W-pI.....60.1:6 reach d. to me and raise me up to Him.
W-pI.....69.6:1 world, try to settle d. in perfect stillness,
W-pI.....78.2:3 lay it d. and gently lift our eyes in silence
W-pI.....78.3:1 lay them d. he will appear in shining light
W-pI.....93.2:3 and have bowed d. to idols made of dust,
W-pI...98.11:1 be thankful and lay d. all earthly tasks, all
WpI..rIII.in5:2 that are written d. for each day's exercise.
WpIrIII.in11:3 Do not repeat the thought and lay it d..
W-pI.136.14:2 to any mind that would lay d. its arms,
W-pI...156.4:4 The waves bow d. before you, and the
W-pI...163.2:3 the helpless and the sick bow d. before its
W-pI...163.4:1 Would you bow d. to idols such as this?
W-pI...163.5:4 kneeling d. with foreheads to the ground,
W-pI...166.7:4 eyes cast d. lest you might catch a glimpse
W-pI...168.5:3 by giving us the means to lay them d., and
W-pI...170.2:7 *Lay d. your arms, and only then do you*
W-pI...170.5:4 ask you lay d. all defense as merely foolish
W-pI.170.10:6 striking d. all who acknowledge Him to
W-pI.182.11:1 and lay d. the spear and sword you raised
W-pI...183.3:1 the world responds by laying d. illusions.
W-pI...190.5:3 that can reach d. and bring oppression.
W-pI...190.9:1 Lay d. your arms, and come without
W-pI...190.9:2 Lay d. all thoughts of danger and of fear.
W-pI...190.9:4 Lay d. the cruel sword of judgment that
W-pI.193.13:5 Love of God the Father d. to earth at last,
W-pI...194.1:2 it sets you d. just short of Heaven, with
W-pI .. 195.3:3 try to bring him d. to lie in death with you
W-pI .. 198.1:4 against you, till you lay it d. as valueless,
W-pII . 227.1:5 *up, and lay them d. before the feet of truth, to*
W-pII . 227.2:2 Son of God this day lays d. his dreams.
W-pII ..... 2.3:3 it merely lets them quietly go d. to dust.
W-pII . 328.1:1 all things we perceive are upside d. until
W-pII ... 13.2:3 perception which was upside d. before,
W-ep......... 2:1 pathway of the sun laid d. before it rises,
M-4 ..... I.A.6:1 Now comes "a period of settling d.." This
M-4 ......V.1:13 Christ looks d. on them in thanks as well.
M-4 ... VI.1:11 that comes when defenses are laid d.. It is
M-10 ......... 5:1 lay judgment d., not with regret but with
M-10 ......... 5:2 could merely stagger and fall d. beneath it
M-10 ......... 6:3 The teacher of God lays it d. happily the
M-11 ....... 4:10 earth bows d. before its gracious Presence
M-11 ....... 4:10 Presence, and it leans d. in answer, to
M-14 ....... 5:10 And now sit d. in true humility, and
M-16 ......... 5:3 It is not wise to lie d. for it. It is better to
M-20 ......... 4:4 must you once again lay d. your sword,
M-26 ......... 3:9 Those who have laid the body d. merely
M-27 ......... 7:6 nor sinks d. to death and dissolution.
C-4 ............ 8:3 Here He leans d. to lift you up to Him, out
C-6 ............ 1:1 called d. upon the earth after he ascended
C-6 ............ 1:3 He was "called d. upon the earth" in the
C-ep .......... 4:1 and kneel d. an instant in our gratitude to
P-2..........V.8:3 And it is there that we will lay them d., to
S-1.........in.3:1 Lay d. your dreams, you holy Son of God,
S-2........ III.7:5 angels d. to answer you in His Own Name
S-3..........II.3:2 be thrust d. in pain upon unwilling flesh,
S-3........ IV.6:4 Then arise and lay all dreaming d. forever

## downward 1

W-pI .. 123.4:1 eyes, no longer looking d. to the dust. We

## drag 1

T-20 ..... VI.5:4 Here it would d. its brothers, holding

## dragging 1

T19 ...IV.C.2:4 d. their chains and marching in the slow

## dragon 1

T-11 . VIII.13:3 "d." into a dream he is no longer afraid,

## dragons 3

T-11 . VIII.13:1 frightening ghosts and monsters and d.,
T-11 . VIII.14:8 them as ghosts and monsters and d.. Ask
W-pI 134.12:2 kill the d. which he thought pursued him.

## draining 1

M-24 ......... 4:5 d. it away from its appointed purpose. If

## dramatically 1

C-1 ............ 7:4 has levels and awareness can shift quite d.

## draped

*See* black-draped

## drapery 1

T-22 ..... IV.3:4 realize how thin the d. that separates you

## draw 19

T-1 .........II.5:2 than they can d. down to themselves. The
T-13 .......V.5:5 with fear to love, and d. away from it. Yet
T-13 .......V.7:9 unto them you will d. them to yourself,
T-13 .....V.7:10 we will d. them from their private worlds,
T-13 . VI.11:10 that it will d. the others out of darkness as
T-13 ... VI.12:2 attraction of light must d. you willingly,
T-16 .... III.9:2 wait for you will not d. you safely across.
T-19 ..... IV.1:9 And you will d. him in and give him rest,

| | |
|---|---|
| T-20.......II.1:4 | this hated thing to **d.** your brother to you, |
| T-20.......II.3:3 | to himself. No one but seeks to **d.** to it the |
| T-20......VI.7:2 | love **d.** near them and overlook the body, |
| T-25.........I.4:6 | to let Him **d.** aside the veil that seems to |
| T-25.......V.1:4 | but seems to **d.** a meaning from the other. |
| T-26...V.11:11 | It must **d.** you from the past into the |
| W-pI...109.8:1 | from your rest to **d.** them to their rest, |
| W-pI...191.2:6 | no breath you **d.** that does not seem to |
| W-pI.200.11:8 | and **d.** still nearer every time we say: |
| W-pII..298.1:4 | I **d.** near the end of senseless journeys, |
| S-2........III.2:3 | but let it be a way to **d.** you up to where |

## drawing 3

| | |
|---|---|
| T-13.......V.7:9 | and by **d.** nigh unto them you will draw |
| T-13.......V.9:5 | forth its witnesses and **d.** them to you. He |
| T-27......VI.1:3 | **d.** it away from Him and focusing upon |

## drawn 17

| | |
|---|---|
| T-5........IV.4:3 | Mind that was in me is still irresistibly **d.** |
| T-12........I.9:11 | The veil that you have **d.** across the face of |
| T-12...VIII.1:6 | it will come to you, because it is **d.** to itself |
| T-14......IX.5:5 | of hidden darkness you have **d.** upon it. |
| T-15......VI.6:2 | been. Only the veil that has been **d.** across |
| T-15......VI.6:5 | felt himself **d.** irresistibly into the light |
| T-18.........I.6:2 | and **d.** between you and the truth. For |
| T-22......I.11:2 | For He is always **d.** unto Himself. What is |
| T-22......I.11:9 | is **d.** to Christ is drawn to God as surely as |
| T-22......I.11:9 | is drawn to Christ is **d.** to God as surely as |
| T-22......I.11:9 | as Both are **d.** to every holy relationship, |
| T-24......IV.1:5 | must kill, and you are **d.** to it to kill it first |
| T-31......VI.3:8 | veil of ignorance is **d.** across the evil and |
| W-pI.....21.2:5 | is nothing but a veil **d.** over intense fury. |
| W-pI.....56.4:3 | every veil I have **d.** across the face of love, |
| W-pI...133.2:2 | let your mind be **d.** to bodily concerns, to |
| M-2............5:6 | demarcations they have **d.** between their |

## draws 9

| | |
|---|---|
| T-7........VI.3:5 | ego **d.** upon the one source that is totally |
| T-13.......V.5:4 | Everyone **d.** nigh unto what he loves, and |
| T-14.......V.8:5 | The power of God **d.** everyone to its safe |
| T-14.......X.1:7 | the reflection of truth **d.** everyone to truth |
| T-18...VIII.2:6 | It **d.** a circle, infinitely small, around a |
| T-19......IV.1:7 | to everyone who **d.** nigh unto your temple |
| T-22......I.11:4 | **d.** you and your brother together draws |
| T-22......I.11:4 | and your brother together **d.** Him to you. |
| M-8............1:4 | A brighter thing **d.** the attention from |

## dread 3

| | |
|---|---|
| T-26...VIII.4:4 | But present joining is your **d.**. Who can |
| W-pI...194.4:6 | and future **d.** will now be meaningless. |
| W-pI...196.9:4 | thing you **d.** the most is your salvation. |

## dreadful 1

| | |
|---|---|
| T-26.....V.10:3 | is now. A **d.** instant in a distant past, now |

## dream 357

*See also* counter-dream; Appendix C

| | |
|---|---|
| T-2...........I.4:6 | on while someone is dreaming a fearful **d.** |
| T-2...........I.4:6 | itself as part of his **d.** and be afraid of it. |
| T-2...........I.4:7 | perceived as the release from the **d.**, |
| T-4...........I.4:3 | doubts the reality of his **d.** while he is still |
| T-4...........I.4:4 | You **d.** of a separated ego and believe in a |
| T-6........IV.6:4 | be nothing left of your **d.** when you hear |
| T-6........IV.7:5 | in the **d.** has given way to creation and to |
| T-10.........I.2:4 | to happen in the **d.** did not happen at all. |
| T-10.........I.2:6 | you merely shifted from one **d.** to another |
| T-11.....V.10:2 | threat. Its **d.** of autonomy is shaken to its |
| T-11......VI.8:4 | **d.** of crucifixion still lies heavy on your |
| T-11. VIII.13:3 | "dragon" into a **d.** he is no longer afraid, |
| T-12......I.10:5 | **d.** of separation with the fact of unity. For |
| T-12........II.5:4 | for your **d.** of hatred will not leave you |
| T-13....VI.12:6 | You **d.** of isolation because your eyes are |
| T-13.....VII.9:1 | will first **d.** of peace, and then awaken to |
| T-13....XI.3:13 | a sense of peace so deep that no **d.** in this |
| T-14.........I.2:4 | have and give and be nothing except a **d.**, |
| T-14.........I.2:7 | not touched, and your **d.** *is* sacred to you. |
| T-14.........I.2:8 | Spirit in you, where you placed the **d.**. |
| T-14......XI.2:2 | in deepest sleep, could even **d.** of it. Can |
| T-16.....VII.4:2 | contain the **d.** of retribution for the past. |
| T-16.....VII.4:3 | Would you act out the **d.**, or let it go? |
| T-17.......II.7:3 | Even salvation will become a **d.**, and |
| T-17.......II.7:4 | the closing of the **d.** will have no meaning |
| T-17.......II.7:5 | could **d.** that there could ever be need of |
| T-17.......III.4:5 | does not enter at all to "spoil" the **d.**. And |
| T-17...VII.10:3 | For loneliness in God must be a **d.**. You |
| T-18.............h | THE PASSING OF THE **D.** |
| T-18..........II.h | The Basis of the **D.** |
| T-18.......II.4:3 | And yet the **d.** cannot escape its origin. |
| T-18.......II.4:5 | For the **d.** of your ability to control reality |
| T-18.......II.5:4 | the **d.** produces must come from you. It is |
| T-18.......II.5:5 | It is the figures in the **d.** and what they do |
| T-18.......II.5:5 | what they do that seem to make the **d.**. |
| T-18.......II.5:8 | You seem to waken, and the **d.** is gone. |
| T-18.......II.5:9 | what caused the **d.** has not gone with it. |
| T-18.......II.7:2 | It will be a happy **d.**, and one which you |
| T-18.......II.8:1 | Let not the **d.** take hold to close your eyes |
| T-18.......II.8:5 | you think it may be this that is the **d.**. You |
| T-18.......II.9:2 | This is no **d.**. Its coming means that you |
| T-18.......II.9:6 | The **d.** of waking is easily transferred to |
| T-18.......II.9:7 | For this **d.** reflects your will joined with |
| T-18.........III.h | Light in the **D.** |
| T-18......III.1:3 | Each **d.** has led to other dreams, and |
| T-18..........V.h | The Happy **D.** |
| T-18.......V.5:1 | It is no **d.** to love your brother as yourself |
| T-18.......V.5:2 | Nor is your holy relationship a **d.**. All that |
| T-18.......V.5:5 | will become the happy **d.** through which |
| T-18......VI.6:4 | It does not **d.** of them, and they but make |
| T-18.....VI.11:2 | feeling of liberation far exceeds the **d.** of |
| T19....IV.C.8:2 | child of our Father, this is a ***d.*** of death. |
| T-20.......II.6:6 | hear this carefully, nor think it but a **d.**, a |
| T-21.....VII.3:6 | have no need to **d.** of power and to act out |
| T-21.....VII.3:6 | to dream of power and to act out their **d.**. |
| T-21.....VII.4:5 | Yes, it can ***d.*** it found an enemy, but this |
| T-24.......II.7:7 | the **d.** of specialness remain between you. |
| T-24.......III.7:2 | forth and waken from their **d.** of death. |
| T-24.......III.7:5 | because He did not make their **d.** reality. |
| T-24.......III.7:6 | Who made not death; but only in the **d.**. |
| T-24......IV.4:8 | a **d.** of specialness that lasts an instant, |
| T-24......IV.5:1 | Do not defend this senseless **d.**, in which |
| T-24.......V.2:1 | There is no **d.** of specialness, however |
| T-24.......V.2:2 | for here the maker of the **d.** believes that |
| T-26.......V.6:6 | shore, and **d.** himself across an ocean, to a |
| T-26.......V.6:7 | real a hindrance can this **d.** be to where |
| T-27.............h | THE HEALING OF THE **D.** |
| T-27.....II.6:11 | his guilt is but the fabric of a senseless **d.**. |
| T-27........VII.h | The Dreamer of the **D.** |
| T-27.....VII.1:3 | Like to a **d.** of punishment, in which the |
| T-27.....VII.8:1 | No one can waken from a **d.** the world is |
| T-27.....VII.8:2 | He becomes a part of someone else's **d.**. |
| T-27.....VII.8:3 | to waken from a **d.** he did not make. |
| T-27.....VII.8:4 | a victim to a **d.** conceived and cherished |
| T-27.....VII.8:6 | as it will in any role that satisfies its **d.**. So |
| T-27...VII.11:4 | of the world and what you **d.** in secret. |
| T-27...VII.11:6 | is but a part of your own **d.** you gave away |
| T-27...VII.11:7 | Yet was it started by your secret **d.**, which |
| T-27...VII.11:8 | and **d.** in secret that its cause is real? |
| T-27...VII.12:1 | it be lingering and slow; of this you **d.**. |
| T-27...VII.12:2 | Yet underneath this **d.** is yet another, in |
| T-27...VII.13:3 | than an idle **d.** has terrified God's Son, |
| T-27...VII.13:4 | So fearful is the **d.**, so seeming real, he |
| T-27...VII.13:4 | unless a gentler **d.** preceded his awaking, |
| T-27...VII.13:4 | calls with love to waken him; a gentler **d.**, |
| T-27...VII.14:1 | Accept the **d.** He gave instead of yours. It |
| T-27...VII.14:2 | It is not difficult to change a **d.** when once |
| T-27...VII.14:6 | The **d.** of guilt is fading from your sight, |
| T-27...VII.15:1 | **D.** softly of your sinless brother, who |
| T-27...VII.15:2 | And from this **d.** the Lord of Heaven will |
| T-27...VII.15:3 | **D.** of your brother's kindnesses instead of |
| T-27...VII.15:4 | Select his thoughtfulness to **d.** about |
| T-27...VII.16:2 | the gifts you **d.** your Father gives to you. |
| T-27...VII.16:4 | And let no pain disturb your **d.** of deep |
| T-27......VIII.h | The "Hero" of the **D.** |
| T-27....VIII.1:2 | There is no **d.** without it, nor does it exist |
| T-27....VIII.1:2 | nor does it exist without the **d.** in which it |
| T-27....VIII.1:3 | It takes the central place in every **d.**, |
| T-27....VIII.2:5 | for special bodies that can share its **d.**. |
| T-27....VIII.2:7 | But in some phases of the **d.**, it is the slave |
| T-27....VIII.3:1 | theme of every **d.** the world has ever had. |
| T-27....VIII.3:2 | The "hero" of this **d.** will never change, |
| T-27....VIII.3:3 | Though the **d.** itself takes many forms, |
| T-27....VIII.3:3 | finds itself, the **d.** has but one purpose, |
| T-27....VIII.4:1 | Thus are you not the dreamer, but the **d.**. |
| T-27....VIII.4:3 | does is true, for it is but a figure in a **d.**. |
| T-27....VIII.4:4 | who reacts to figures in a **d.** unless he sees |
| T-27....VIII.5:2 | Is it your wish to let no **d.** appear to be the |
| T-27....VIII.6:1 | Let us return the **d.** he gave away unto |
| T-27....VIII.6:1 | perceives the **d.** as separate from himself |
| T-27....VIII.7:6 | sinful things the body does within its **d.**. |
| T-27....VIII.9:7 | holy Son of God, behold your idle **d.**, in |
| T-27..VIII.10:5 | to figures in a **d.** you knew that you were |
| T-27..VIII.10:6 | unless you failed to recognize it is your **d.**. |
| T-28........II.4:1 | a **d.** in which you were an alien to yourself |
| T-28........II.4:1 | and but a part of someone else's **d.**. The |
| T-28........II.4:5 | A **d.** is like a memory in that it pictures |
| T-28........II.5:2 | much at least: that you have caused the **d.** |
| T-28........II.5:2 | dream, and can accept another **d.** as well. |
| T-28........II.5:3 | But for this change in content of the **d.**, it |
| T-28........II.6:1 | every **d.** that anyone has dreamed within |
| T-28........II.6:5 | You may cause a **d.**, but never will you |
| T-28........II.6:7 | do. The dreamer of a **d.** is not awake, but |
| T-28........II.7:1 | The miracle establishes you **d.** a dream, |
| T-28........II.7:1 | The miracle establishes you dream a **d.**, |
| T-28........II.7:4 | he did not see that he was author of the **d.** |
| T-28........II.7:4 | of the dream, and not a figure in the **d.**. |
| T-28........II.7:6 | **d.** has put together and has offered him, |
| T-28........II.8:1 | separation started with the **d.** the Father |
| T-28........II.8:2 | In the **d.**, the dreamer made himself. But |
| T-28........II.8:4 | so the figures in the **d.** have hated him. |
| T-28........II.8:7 | dreamer could not be the maker of the **d.**. |
| T-28........II.9:4 | For this confusion has produced the **d.**, |
| T-28......II.10:6 | are you freed from this much of the **d.**; |
| T-28......II.12:2 | next to every **d.** of pain and suffering, of |
| T-28......II.12:3 | deny the active role in making up the **d.**. |
| T-28......III.1:5 | up to waking and the ending of the **d.**. |
| T-28......III.1:6 | you do not add your **d.** of fear to one that |
| T-28......III.1:7 | the **d.** will fade away without effects. For |
| T-28......III.3:3 | him to his own **d.** by sharing it with him. |
| T-28......III.3:6 | all things that seem to glisten in the **d.**. |
| T-28......III.8:4 | The **d.** of healing in forgiveness lies, and |
| T-28......IV.1:1 | to someone's **d.** of sickness and of death. |
| T-28......IV.1:7 | And you become a figure in his **d.** of pain, |
| T-28......IV.1:9 | depending on whose evil **d.** you share. |
| T-28......IV.2:5 | you separate the dreamer from the **d.**, |
| T-28......IV.2:6 | go. The **d.** is but illusion in the mind. And |
| T-28......IV.2:7 | you would unite, but never with the **d.**. It |
| T-28......IV.2:8 | It is the **d.** you fear, and not the mind. |
| T-28......IV.2:9 | because you think that *you* are but a **d.**. |
| T-28......IV.3:1 | Like you, your brother thinks he is a **d.**. |
| T-28......IV.3:4 | dreams, nor is his body, "hero" of the **d.**, |
| T-28......IV.5:4 | because the dreamer and the **d.** are one. |
| T-28......IV.5:5 | shares a **d.** must be the dream he shares, |
| T-28......IV.5:5 | shares a dream must be the **d.** he shares, |
| T-28......IV.6:6 | and he will understand what made the **d.**. |
| T-28......IV.7:6 | his brother who, by sharing not his **d.**, |
| T-28......IV.8:5 | If you share not your brother's evil **d.**, this |
| T-28.......V.3:1 | and perceive that he is not the **d.** he made |
| T-28.......V.3:3 | separates the dreamer from the evil **d.**, |
| T-28.......V.3:4 | Remember if you share an evil **d.**, you will |
| T-28.......V.3:4 | you will believe you are the **d.** you share. |
| T-28.....V.3:11 | you, must be a **d.** and cannot be the truth. |
| T-28.......V.5:3 | Let not your eyes behold a **d.**; your ears |
| T-28.....VII.4:2 | not used to witness to the **d.** of separation |
| T-28.....VII.5:2 | world is but the **d.** that you can be alone, |
| T-29........II.7:2 | the larger **d.** that change is possible. To |
| T-29......III.2:5 | in the **d.** His Son prefers to his reality. He |
| T-29......III.2:6 | He must be savior from the **d.** he made, |
| T-29......III.3:1 | Within the **d.** of bodies and of death is |
| T-29......III.5:6 | This is the spark that shines within the **d.**; |
| T-29.........IV.h | **D.** Roles |
| T-29......IV.1:3 | and that escape depends, not on the **d.**, |
| T-29......IV.1:7 | **d.** some dreams and wake from some, for |

T-29......IV.2:2 For every **d.** is but a dream of fear, no
T-29......IV.2:2 For every dream is but a **d.** of fear, no
T-29......IV.2:5 But never is it absent from the **d.**, for fear
T-29......IV.3:3 or assault must be the theme of every **d.**,
T-29......IV.4:9 If it succeeds you think you like the **d.**. If
T-29....IV.4:10 If it should fail you think the **d.** is sad. But
T-29......IV.5:1 role to every figure which the **d.** contains.
T-29......IV.5:6 help, if this becomes the function of the **d.**
T-29......IV.6:4 in what you **d.** your life was meant to be.
T-29......IV.6:5 He asks for help in every **d.** he has, and
T-29......IV.6:5 of the **d.** as He perceives its function,
T-29......IV.6:6 Because He loves the dreamer, not the **d.**,
T-29......IV.6:6 each **d.** becomes an offering of love. For at
T-29....... V.7:1 **d.** is given you in which he is your savior,
T-29....... V.7:2 **d.** is given you in which you have forgiven
T-29....... V.7:2 of death; a **d.** of hope you share with him,
T-29....... V.7:3 Why does it seem so hard to share this **d.**?
T-29....... V.7:4 the Holy Spirit gives the **d.** its function, it
T-29....... V.8:1 core of fear in every **d.** that has been kept
T-29....... V.8:1 Who sees a different function for a **d.**.
T-29....... V.8:2 it was for this that every **d.** was made. Yet
T-29...... VI.1:4 and the **d.** of danger and destruction, sin
T-29...... VI.5:2 For even though it was a **d.** of death, you
T-29..... VII.2:1 some **d.** that there is something outside of
T-29..... VII.6:1 and to maintain allegiance to the **d.** that
T-29..... VII.8:6 And you pursue them vainly in the **d.**,
T-29..... VII.9:2 And can a **d.** succeed in making real the
T-29......... IX.h The Forgiving **D.**
T-29...... IX.1:4 Hear, then, your story in the **d.** you made,
T-29...... IX.1:4 truth that you believe that it is not a **d.**.
T-29...... IX.2:1 **d.** of judgment came into the mind that
T-29...... IX.2:2 in that **d.** was Heaven changed to hell,
T-29...... IX.2:3 How can God's Son awaken from the **d.**?
T-29...... IX.2:4 It is a **d.** of judgment. So must he judge
T-29...... IX.2:6 **d.** will seem to last while he is part of it.
T-29...... IX.3:1 All figures in the **d.** are idols, made to
T-29...... IX.3:1 are idols, made to save you from the **d.**.
T-29...... IX.3:3 does an idol keep the **d.** alive and terrible,
T-29...... IX.3:4 terror, and the **d.** from which they come.
T-29...... IX.3:5 laid upon himself within the **d.** he made.
T-29...... IX.3:7 But in the **d.** of judgment you attack and
T-29...... IX.4:1 salvation in the **d.** as you are dreaming it.
T-29...... IX.4:4 You do but **d.**, and idols are the toys you
T-29...... IX.4:4 and idols are the toys you **d.** you play with
T-29...... IX.4:8 up the **d.** in which their toys are real, nor
T-29...... IX.5:3 Yet can a **d.** attack? Or can a toy grow
T-29...... IX.6:4 The **d.** of judgment is a children's game,
T-29...... IX.7:1 The real world still is but a **d.**. Except the
T-29...... IX.7:4 a **d.** in which no one is used to substitute
T-29...... IX.7:6 And what was once a **d.** of judgment now
T-29...... IX.7:6 now has changed into a **d.** where all is joy,
T-29...... IX.7:8 in the **d.** are now perceived as brothers,
T-29...... IX.8:3 the **d.** is being dreamed by someone else.
T-29...... IX.9:2 deep and bitter that the **d.** cannot conceal
T-29.... IX.10:3 are kind to everyone who figures in the **d.**.
T-30....... I.13:3 the sorry **d.** of judgment has forever been
T-30....... I.16:4 a **d.** of judgment or the Voice for God.
T-30...... IV.7:2 What could it be except a happy **d.**? It
T-30...... IV.8:1 does the **d.** of separation start to fade and
T-30....... V.1:4 anything to twist and fit into the **d.** of fear
T-30....... V.2:8 must share, if hope be more than just a **d.**.
T-30.... VIII.2:5 The happy **d.** about him takes the form of
T-30.... VIII.6:2 prefer a **d.** allow uncertainty to enter here
T-30.... VIII.6:3 you are tempted by a **d.** of what he is. But
T-31... VII.14:3 hope except to die, and end the **d.** of fear.
W-pI..... 68.2:4 has become fearful to him in his **d.** of hate
W-pI..... 68.2:5 Who can **d.** of hatred and not fear God?
W-pI..... 75.2:1 happy ending to your long **d.** of disaster.
W-pI..... 96.6:2 the senseless conflicts which a **d.** presents
W-pI... 106.4:7 They end the **d.** instead; and last forever,
W-pI... 108.1:5 are at peace forever, for the **d.** is over then
W-pI. 121.13:7 *I will awaken from the* **d.** *that I am mortal,*
W-pI. 122.10:4 indeed to the appointed ending of the **d.**.
W-pI... 130.3:6 What would you wish to keep in such a **d.**
W-pI... 131.1:2 within the darkness of the **d.** of death.
W-pI... 131.2:7 and protection for the little **d.** you made.
W-pI. 134.11:3 his **d.** by understanding what he thought
W-pI... 137.5:1 out the **d.** of sickness in the name of truth
W-pI... 137.6:2 Christ to those who **d.** the world is real.
W-pI... 137.6:4 And love becomes a **d.**, while fear remains
W-pI... 140.2:2 He merely had a **d.** that he was sick, and
W-pI... 140.2:2 and in the **d.** he found a magic formula to
W-pI... 140.2:3 Yet he has not awakened from the **d.**, and
W-pI... 140.2:4 that would awaken him and end the **d.**.
W-pI... 140.2:5 does the content of a **d.** make in reality?
W-pI... 140.3:1 where one can merely **d.** he is awake. The
W-pI... 140.3:2 so that the dreamer dreams another **d.**.
W-pI... 140.4:2 that sickness can be nothing but a **d.** is
W-pI... 140.4:2 is not deceived by forms the **d.** may take.
W-pI... 153.4:2 hope of sanity seems but to be an idle **d.**,
W-pI... 153.8:3 senseless **d.** happened to cross our minds,
W-pI... 153.9:1 or **d.** in which attack has any meaning.
W-pI... 156.6:5 foolish thought, a silly **d.**, not frightening,
W-pI... 156.7:5 the senseless, ancient **d.** that now is past.
W-pI. 159.10:4 has dreamed the **d.** of a forgiven world. It
W-pI. 159.10:6 Let us an instant **d.** with Him. His dream
W-pI. 159.10:7 His **d.** awakens us to truth. His vision
W-pI... 162.2:3 There is no **d.** these words will not dispel;
W-pI... 162.2:3 and no illusion which the **d.** contains that
W-pI... 182.2:4 not to be considered more than but a **d.**.
W-pI... 183.3:2 illusions. Every **d.** the world holds dear
W-pI... 185.2:2 with dreams, nor think he is himself a **d.**.
W-pI... 185.3:4 To each, the hero of the **d.** is different; the
W-pI... 185.4:1 Yet compromise alone a **d.** can bring.
W-pI... 185.4:3 The meaning must escape the **d.**, for
W-pI... 185.5:4 recognizing that another **d.** would offer
W-pI... 185.7:4 words do not request another **d.** be given
W-pI. 185.12:5 gifts of God apart from every **d.** that ever
W-pI... 188.6:6 the **d.** of worldly things outside yourself,
W-pI... 190.2:4 is a **d.** of fierce retaliation for a crime that
W-pI. 191.10:3 And he will sleep no more and **d.** of death
W-pI... 193.5:4 are the words which end the **d.** of sin, and
W-pI. 195.10:1 time by more than you could ever **d.** of.
W-pI... 198.3:1 dreams away, and though it is itself a **d.**,
W-pI... 198.3:4 end of dreams, because it is a **d.** of waking
W-pI... 198.3:7 It is a **d.** in which the Son of God awakens
W-pI. 198.10:1 appears unveiled at last in this one **d.**.
W-pI. 198.12:5 And who could **d.** of offering forgiveness
W-pII ..... 2.4:2 Here we share our final **d.**. It is a dream in
W-pII ..... 2.4:3 It is a **d.** in which there is no sorrow, for it
W-pII . 237.1:4 see, aware it ends the bitter **d.** of death;
W-pII . 256.1:7 Here we can but **d.**. But we can dream we
W-pII . 256.1:8 **d.** we have forgiven him in whom all sin
W-pII . 256.1:8 and it is this we choose to **d.** today. God is
W-pII ..... 5.3:1 The body is a **d.**. Like other dreams it
W-pII ..... 5.3:2 revert to fear, where every **d.** is born. For
W-pII . 263.1:4 *A madman's* **d.** *is hardly fit to be my choice,*
W-pII ..... 6.4:2 will exchange them for the final **d.** which
W-pII . 272.2:2 call to us to stay and linger in a **d.**, we
W-pII . 278.2:2 *and have brought a* **d.** *of fear into my mind.*
W-pII . 278.2:3 *Today, I would not* **d.**. *I choose the way to*
W-pII . 284.1:4 suffering of any kind is nothing but a **d.**.
W-pII . 290.1:5 the **d.** I made is real an instant longer.
W-pII ..... 8.4:1 symbol that the **d.** of sin and guilt is over,
W-pII . 294.2:3 *use this* **d.** *to help Your plan that we awaken*
W-pII ... 10.2:5 the **d.** in which the world began go with it
W-pII ... 10.4:3 and gently waken from his **d.** of pain the
W-pII . 313.1:6 *that I may waken from the* **d.** *of sin and look*
W-pII . 322.1:4 And every **d.** serves only to conceal the
W-pII . 330.1:6 all things the **d.** of fear appears to offer us.
W-pII . 331.1:7 *Fear is a* **d.**, *and has no will that can conflict*
W-pII . 332.1:8 the light shine through the **d.** of darkness,
W-pII ..... 333.h Forgiveness ends the **d.** of conflict here.
W-pII . 333.2:2 *No light but this can end our evil* **d.**. *No light*
W-pII . 337.2:3 *myself. Father, my* **d.** *is ended now. Amen.*
W-pII . 344.1:4 *will be. Who can share a* **d.**? *And what can*
W-pII . 344.2:3 How close the ending of the **d.** of sin, and
Wfl........ in.2:3 In the **d.** of time it seems to be far off.
Wfl........ in.3:4 It is His ending to the **d.** we seek, and not
Wfl........ in.5:3 belonged to God, and found it was a **d.**.
M-4 ...... VI.1:7 The more grotesque the **d.**, the fiercer
M-12 ......... 6:5 The **d.** says otherwise, but who would put
M-12 ......... 6:7 They watch the **d.** figures come and go,
M-12 ......... 6:9 They recognize that to behold a **d.** figure
M-12 ....... 6:11 teachers acknowledge as behind the **d.**,
M-18 ......... 1:7 age-old impossible **d.** in but another form
M-18 ......... 1:8 Yet the **d.** of salvation has new content. It
M-27 ......... 1:1 central **d.** from which all illusions stem. Is
M-28 ......... 1:4 glad awareness of the Holy Spirit's final **d.**
M-28 ......... 1:6 **d.** in which the body functions perfectly,
M-28 ......... 6:3 face to take the place of what they **d.**. The
C-2 ............ 1:5 But a **d.** of what you really are. A thought
C-2 .......... 1:11 what could come of this except a **d.** which
C-2 .......... 6:13 an evil **d.** that but seemed real while you
C-2 ............ 7:2 A **d.** as well. But look at all the aspects of
C-2 ............ 7:3 look at all the aspects of *this* **d.** and you
C-ep .......... 4:7 forgets all that the **d.** of sin had made of it
P-2.......... I.2:3 of "the saving illusion" or "the final **d.**,"
P-2.......... V.5:1 beyond the heights perceived in any **d.**.
P-2.......... V.7:5 one who seems to share our **d.** of sickness.
P-3.......... II.4:8 strange **d.** a strange correction must enter
P-3.......... II.6:3 it will not be the same **d.** for both of them
P-3.......... II.6:3 and so it is not the **d.** of forgiveness in
P-3.......... II.7:3 a brother from one **d.** than from another.
P-3........ III.3:6 Forgiveness, the Holy Spirit's only **d.**,
P-3........ III.3:9 Can this be how the **d.** of sin will end?
S-1.......... V.3:3 A **d.** has veiled the face of Christ from you
S-2.......... I.4:5 Yet it is the only happy **d.** in all the world;
S-3.......... II.1:1 one; a **d.** of sickness for a dream of health.
S-3.......... II.1:1 one; a dream of sickness for a **d.** of health.
S-3........ III.2:7 and change are what the **d.** is made of. To
S-3........ IV.6:3 **D.** now of healing. Then arise and lay all
S-3........ IV.8:1 the **d.** of retribution and a little life beset

## dream's 2

T-27 ... VIII.5:3 let us merely look upon the **d.** beginning,
T-28 ..... II.12:3 They are the **d.** alternative, the choice to

## dreamed 14

T-13 ....... X.5:5 within you all the while you **d.** of guilt,
T-14 ..... III.9:5 larger than anything you ever **d.** of.
T-27 .. VII.14:3 those you **d.** in terror and in fear of death.
T-28 ....... II.4:1 **d.** a dream in which you were an alien to
T-28 ....... II.5:3 who **d.** the dreaming that you do not like.
T-28 ....... II.6:1 is every dream that anyone has **d.** within
T-28 ..... III.1:6 of fear to one that is already being **d.**.
T-29 ..... IX.8:3 the dream is being **d.** by someone else.
T-30 ... III.10:2 dreams of birth and death that here are **d.**
W-pI .. 106.4:4 you ever **d.** or wished for in your dreams.
W-pI .. 157.8:1 embark upon a course you have not **d.** of.
W-pI .. 157.8:2 **d.** for you this journey which you make
W-pI 159.10:4 has **d.** the dream of a forgiven world. It is
S-3.......... II.4:2 sins it **d.** about and laid upon the world.

## dreamer 28

T-4 .......... I.4:3 **d.** who doubts the reality of his dream
T-9 ......... V.4:3 by depreciating the importance of the **d.**.
T-9 ......... V.4:4 if the **d.** were also identified as unreal. Yet
T-9 ......... V.4:5 Yet if the **d.** is equated with the mind, the
T-17 ......... I.1:6 impossible to convince the **d.** that this is
T-27 ....... VII.h The **D.** of the Dream
T-27 .... VII.1:3 **d.** is unconscious of what brought on the
T-27 .... VII.9:1 cause, if you be not the **d.** of your dreams.
T-27 .. VII.13:1 *You* are the **d.** of the world of dreams. No
T-27 .. VII.14:2 when once the **d.** has been recognized.
T-27 ... VIII.4:1 Thus are you not the **d.**, but the dreamer.
T-27 ... VIII.6:1 the dream he gave away unto the **d.**, who
T-28 ....... II.4:2 you, but merely shows you who the **d.** is.
T-28 ....... II.5:2 Yet if you are the **d.**, you perceive this
T-28 ....... II.6:7 The **d.** of a dream is not awake, but does
T-28 ....... II.8:2 In the dream, the **d.** made himself. But
T-28 ....... II.8:3 on the role of its creator, as the **d.** had.
T-28 ....... II.8:7 **d.** could not be the maker of the dream.
T-28 ..... II.12:3 alternative, the choice to be the **d.**, rather
T-28 ..... IV.2:5 Thus you separate the **d.** from the dream,
T-28 ..... IV.5:3 in his dreams, instead of **d.** of your own.
T-28 ..... IV.5:4 because the **d.** and the dream are one.
T-28 ....... V.3:1 share no evil dreams if you forgive the **d.**,
T-28 ....... V.3:3 separates the **d.** from the evil dream, and
T-29 ..... IV.6:6 Because He loves the **d.**, not the dream,
T-29 ... IX.10:4 the **d.** full release from dreams of fear. He
W-pI 134.11:2 terrify the foolish **d.** who believes in them
W-pI .. 140.3:2 so that the **d.** dreams another dream. His

## dreaming 29

T-2...........I.4:6 on while someone is **d.** a fearful dream, he
T-4...........I.4:3 still **d.** is not really healing his split mind.
T-6.........V.4:6 to awaken, whatever you have been **d.**.
T-10.........I.2:1 in God, **d.** of exile but perfectly capable of
T-18.....II.5:12 All your time is spent in **d.**. Your sleeping
T-27.....VII.8:1 from a dream the world is **d.** for him. He
T-27.....VII.8:7 conceived within the idle **d.** of the world.
T-27...VII.11:4 and dreams lies not between the **d.** of the
T-27...VII.11:6 The **d.** of the world is but a part of your
T-27... VIII.1:1 is the central figure in the **d.** of the world.
T-27... VIII.2:1 The **d.** of the world takes many forms,
T-27... VIII.5:4 first. No one asleep and **d.** in the world
T-27. VIII.10:5 in a dream you knew that you were **d.**. Let
T-28....... II.4:3 depending on the purpose of your **d.**. Do
T-28....... II.5:3 who dreamed the **d.** that you do not like.
T-28..... II.12:7 gone, and all the **d.** of the world undone.
T-28...... III.3:2 Yet in the **d.** has this been reversed, and
T-28...... III.4:1 The end of **d.** is the end of fear, and love
T-28...... III.9:1 to those the **d.** of the world has shown.
T-29..... IV.1:8 And **d.** goes with only one of these.
T-29....... V.7:2 instead of **d.** evil separate dreams of hate.
T-29....... V.8:5 aside from **d.** of a world outside yourself.
T-29...... IX.4:1 no salvation in the dream as you are **d.** it.
W-pI...106.4:6 They will not fade when **d.** ends. They
W-pI...140.3:1 are different from the **d.** of the world,
W-pI...185.4:3 dream, for compromising is the goal of **d.**
M-12..........6:6 of **d.** is the real function of God's teachers
C-2...........6:13 that but seemed real while you were **d.** it.
S-3 ........IV.6:4 Then arise and lay all **d.** down forever.

## dreamless 2

W-pI...170.5:2 your strength, and hope of rest in **d.** quiet
W-pI.198.11:3 the face of earth, made quiet in a **d.** sleep.

## dreams 337

T-2...........I.3:5 What is seen in **d.** seems to be very real.
T-3........VI.4:3 in what seem to be your happier **d.**.
T-6........IV.6:3 a sleep in which you have had bad **d.**, but
T-6........IV.6:5 **d.** contain many of the ego's symbols and
T-6........IV.6:7 will no longer believe in **d.** because they
T-6......... V.2:4 understand they need not be afraid of **d.**.
T-6......... V.2:5 when bad **d.** come, they will themselves
T-6......... V.4:4 Spirit makes no distinction among **d.**. He
T-6......... V.4:7 Nothing lasting lies in **d.**, and the Holy
T-6......V.A.1:1 body and your ego and your **d.** are gone,
T-8........IX.3:7 **D.** are illusions of joining, because they
T-8........IX.3:8 use **d.** on behalf of waking if you will let
T-10.........I.2:3 in **d.** you think is real while you are asleep
T-10.........I.3:1 reconcile what happened in conflicting **d.**
T-10.........I.4:3 **D.** will be impossible because you will
T-10....... II.1:5 your knowledge by an awareness of **d.**
T-11......VI.8:4 eyes, but what you see in **d.** is not reality.
T-11......VI.8:7 are beginning to wake are still aware of **d.**
T-11......VI.8:8 The forgetting of **d.** and the awareness of
T-12....... II.5:7 and it belongs to you despite your **d.**.
T-13....IV.6:10 past, and because your **d.** were not holy,
T-13....... V.8:3 see in **d.** although your eyes are closed.
T-13....... V.8:9 **D.** disappear when light has come and
T-13.....V.10:5 Beyond your darkest **d.** He sees God's
T-13.....V.10:5 radiance that is undimmed by your **d.**.
T-13.....VII.9:2 of nightmares for the happy **d.** of love. In
T-13.....VII.9:3 for the Holy Spirit corrects the world of **d.**
T-13.....VII.9:5 Yet the **d.** of love lead unto knowledge. In
T-13...VII.17:7 You travel but in **d.**, while safe at home.
T-13....XI.10:1 Can God's Son lose himself in **d.**, when
T-17.........I.1:4 In his **d.** he has betrayed himself, his
T-17.........I.1:5 is done in **d.** has not been really done. It is
T-17.........I.1:6 so, for **d.** are what they are *because* of their
T-17....... II.7:4 For salvation is the end of **d.**, and with the
T-17......III.8:6 is kept but witnesses to the reality of **d.**.
T-17....III.10:6 purpose of Atonement be lost to you in **d.**
T-17....III.10:7 such **d.** are cherished have excluded me.
T-17......IV.8:3 of love, set with **d.** of sacrifice and self-
T-17... VIII.4:5 cold fantasies of fear and fiery **d.** of hell.
T-18........ II.1:1 a world that seems quite real arise in **d.**?
T-18....... II.2:1 **D.** are chaotic because they are governed
T-18....... II.3:2 you see on waking is blotted out in **d.**. Yet
T-18....... II.3:4 gone. In **d.** *you* arrange everything. People
T-18....... II.4:1 **D.** are perceptual temper tantrums, in
T-18....... II.5:1 **D.** show you that you have the power to
T-18....... II.5:7 In **d.** these features are not obscure. You
T-18..... II.5:11 form of this same world you see in **d.**. All
T-18..... II.5:13 and your waking **d.** have different forms,
T-18..... II.5:16 In your waking **d.**, the special relationship
T-18..... II.5:17 try to make your sleeping **d.** come true.
T-18....... II.6:1 accepts your **d.** and uses them as means
T-18....... II.6:3 that the first change, before **d.** disappear,
T-18....... II.6:3 **d.** of fear are changed to happy dreams.
T-18....... II.6:3 dreams of fear are changed to happy **d.**.
T-18....... II.8:2 that **d.** can make a world that is unreal. It
T-18....... II.8:4 has been changed from one of **d.** to one of
T-18....... II.8:6 used to choosing among **d.** you do not see
T-18....... II.9:4 laid the real world; the world of happy **d.**,
T-18....... II.9:5 sleeping and your waking **d.** represent the
T-18...... III.1:1 to fantasy, have walked the way of **d.**. For
T-18...... III.1:3 Each dream has led to other **d.**, and every
T-18....... V.1:4 to change your **d.** of fear to happy dreams
T-18....... V.1:4 to change your dreams of fear to happy **d.**
T-18....... V.4:1 Happy **d.** come true, not because they are
T-18....... V.4:1 come true, not because they are **d.**, but
T-18....... V.5:3 All that remains of **d.** within it is that it is
T-20. VIII.10:4 translates your nightmares into happy **d.**;
T-21.....VII.3:7 How would an army act in **d.**? Any way at
T-21...VII.3:10 **D.** have no reason in them. A flower turns
T-22....... II.3:9 not to other **d.** that are but equally unreal
T-22....... V.3:3 and the material of evil **d.** are nothing. In
T-23..... II.16:4 In truth it does not function, yet in **d.**,
T-24...... III.7:4 They are lost in **d.** of specialness. They
T-24....... V.2:2 In **d.** effect and cause are interchanged,
T-24...... VI.1:2 He is your savior from the **d.** of fear. He is
T-25...... IV.3:7 their **d.** of guilt and merciless revenge,
T-26....... V.6:8 and does not change whatever **d.** he has.
T-27.....VII.9:1 if you be not the dreamer of your **d.**. And
T-27.....VII.9:4 to make between a sleeping death and **d.**
T-27...VII.10:1 peace or war, your **d.** or your reality?
T-27...VII.11:3 with different **d.** about the truth in you.
T-27...VII.11:4 The gap between reality and **d.** lies not
T-27...VII.12:3 the space between your little **d.** and your
T-27...VII.13:1 *You* are the dreamer of the world of **d.**. No
T-27...VII.14:3 and allow His gentle **d.** to take the place
T-27...VII.14:4 brings forgiving **d.**, in which the choice is
T-27...VII.14:5 **d.** He brings there is no murder and there
T-27...VII.14:8 is peaceful now, for these are happy **d.**.
T-27...VII.15:3 of dwelling in your **d.** on his mistakes.
T-27...VII.15:6 gifts because he is not perfect in your **d.**.
T-27... VIII.2:6 dream. Sometimes it **d.** it is a conqueror
T-27... VIII.5:1 effects of all the **d.** the world has ever had
T-27... VIII.7:4 and on a guilty world that **d.** your dreams
T-27... VIII.7:4 your **d.** and thinks your thoughts instead
T-28....... II.4:3 is a choice of **d.** while you are still asleep,
T-28....... II.4:4 you wish for **d.** of healing, or for dreams
T-28....... II.4:4 for dreams of healing, or for **d.** of death?
T-28....... II.5:1 holds all your shreds of memories and **d.**.
T-28....... II.5:5 In **d.** of murder and attack are you the
T-28....... II.5:6 But in forgiving **d.** is no one asked to be
T-28....... II.5:7 happy **d.** the miracle exchanges for your
T-28....... II.7:5 that he **d.** he gave his brother. And it is
T-28..... II.10:3 In His forgiving **d.** are the effects of yours
T-28...... III.4:1 fear, and love was never in the world of **d.**
T-28...... III.7:1 silver miracles and golden **d.** of happiness
T-28...... IV.1:5 free of **d.** of pain because you let him be.
T-28....IV.1:10 you are evil, for you share in **d.** of fear.
T-28...... IV.2:2 part of fearful **d.** whatever form they take,
T-28...... IV.2:4 but not apart from him who **d.** them.
T-28...... IV.3:4 He is not brother made by what he **d.**, nor
T-28...... IV.3:7 and his **d.** but seem to make a little gap,
T-28...... IV.4:2 To join his **d.** is thus to meet him not,
T-28...... IV.4:2 because his **d.** would separate from you.
T-28...... IV.4:3 on brotherhood, and not on **d.** of fear. Let
T-28...... IV.4:5 and you are kept in bondage to his **d.**.
T-28...... IV.4:6 And **d.** of fear will haunt the little gap,
T-28...... IV.5:3 you become a passive figure in his **d.**,
T-28...... IV.5:4 Identity in **d.** is meaningless because the
T-28...... IV.6:3 His **d.** are yours because you let them be.
T-28...... IV.6:5 Your **d.** are witnesses to his, and his attest
T-28...... IV.6:6 there is no truth in yours, his **d.** will go,
T-28...... IV.7:6 He has **d.** that he was separated from his
T-28.... IV.10:1 not your brother's **d.** but join with him,
T-28.......... V.h The Alternate to **D.** of Fear
T-28....... V.1:6 in. God is the Alternate to **d.** of fear. Who
T-28....... V.2:1 sharing of the evil **d.** of hate and malice,
T-28....... V.3:1 share no evil **d.** if you forgive the dreamer
T-28....... V.6:4 the truth from **d.** and from illusions.
T-29...... III.1:2 For beyond his **d.** is his reality. But he
T-29...... III.3:4 You can overlook your brother's **d.**. So
T-29...... III.3:5 he becomes your savior from your **d.**.
T-29...... III.5:1 the midst of **d.** of desolation and disaster.
T-29...... IV.1:2 They are **d.** *because* they are not true.
T-29...... IV.1:3 you have understood that **d.** are dreams;
T-29...... IV.1:3 you have understood that dreams are **d.**;
T-29...... IV.1:4 Could it be some **d.** are kept, and others
T-29...... IV.1:5 choice is not between which **d.** to keep,
T-29...... IV.1:5 want to live in **d.** or to awaken from them.
T-29...... IV.1:6 **d.** to leave untouched by its beneficence.
T-29...... IV.1:7 dream some **d.** and wake from some, for
T-29...... IV.2:1 The **d.** you think you like would hold you
T-29...... IV.2:5 the dream, for fear is the material of **d.**,
T-29...... IV.4:3 **d.** you think you like are those in which
T-29...... IV.4:6 **D.** are not wanted more or less. They are
T-29...... IV.5:1 How happy would your **d.** become if you
T-29...... IV.5:3 core of **d.** the Holy Spirit gives is never
T-29...... IV.5:7 And **d.** of sadness thus are turned to joy.
T-29...... IV.6:5 Who can utilize all **d.** as means to serve
T-29....... V.5:4 and from this quiet come the happy **d.** in
T-29....... V.5:5 are not hands that grasp in **d.** of pain.
T-29....... V.7:2 have forgiven him for all his **d.** of death; a
T-29....... V.7:2 of dreaming evil separate **d.** of hate. Why
T-29....... V.8:2 When **d.** are shared they lose the function
T-29....... V.8:3 Yet nothing in the world of **d.** remains
T-29....... V.8:5 Forgiving **d.** are means to step aside from
T-29....... V.8:6 And leading finally beyond all **d.**, unto
T-29..... VII.7:2 the past, and but a series of depressing **d.**,
T-29..... VII.8:4 You choose your **d.**, for they are what you
T-29..... VII.9:1 Yet where are **d.** but in a mind asleep?
T-29...... IX.2:9 you make yourself a part of evil **d.**, where
T-29...... IX.5:1 Nightmares are childish **d.**. The toys have
T-29...... IX.7:7 Only forgiving **d.** can enter here, for time
T-29...... IX.8:1 Forgiving **d.** have little need to last. They
T-29...... IX.8:4 these **d.** a melody is heard that everyone
T-29...... IX.8:7 when **d.** of judgment have been put away?
T-29.... IX.10:1 Forgiving **d.** remind you that you live in
T-29.... IX.10:2 and **d.** become a sign that you have made
T-29.... IX.10:3 Forgiving **d.** are kind to everyone who
T-29.... IX.10:4 the dreamer full release from **d.** of fear.
T-30.......in.1:5 these steps lead you from **d.** of judgment
T-30.......in.1:5 to forgiving **d.** and out of pain and fear.
T-30.... III.10:2 the **d.** of birth and death that here are
T-30.... IV.5:12 God's Son needs no defense against his **d.**
T-30...... IV.7:5 be free of all the **d.** of what you never were
T-30...... IV.8:7 Such is the only rule for happy **d.**. The
T-30...... IV.8:9 **D.** are for nothing. And the Son of God
T-30...... VI.1:4 world given in exchange for **d.** of terror.
T-30...... VI.3:1 world rise to take the place of **d.** of terror.
T-30...VII.6:15 dark **d.** are but the senseless, isolated
T-30...VII.6:16 Look not to separate **d.** for meaning. Only
T-30...VII.6:17 Only **d.** of pardon can be shared. They
T-30....VIII.3:4 a prayer the miracle touch not some **d.**,
T-30....VIII.4:4 it be withheld from power to heal all **d.**.
T-30....VIII.5:7 Then let there be no **d.** about him that
T-31........II.1:7 in truth. And can he be assailed by **d.**?
T-31......II.2:10 But not in **d.** you made, that this might be
T-31...VII.14:3 failing **d.** and no remaining hope except
T-31....VIII.3:5 leave you comfortless, alone in **d.** of hell,
T-31....VIII.6:4 close the door upon his **d.** of weakness,
W-pI.....75.2:2 There are no dark **d.** now. The light has
WpI..rII.in.4:4 will has power over all fantasies and **d.**.
W-pI.....92.6:4 and **d.** that it is strong and conquering, a
W-pI.....92.7:1 it sees, leaving its **d.** as fearful as itself. No
W-pI.....93.2:3 afraid of foolish fantasies and savage **d.**;
W-pI.....96.9:5 your mind go wandering in a world of **d.**,
W-pI... 104.1:1 that joy and peace are not but idle **d.**.
W-pI... 104.3:4 them, and sought for only in a world of **d.**
W-pI... 106.4:4 you ever dreamed or wished for in your **d.**
W-pI... 107.6:8 Your Father wills these **d.** be gone. Let

W-pI...109.1:2 of all the turmoil born of clashing **d.**. We
W-pI...109.5:5 but the **d.** of fever that has passed away.
W-pI...109.5:7 No more fearful **d.** will come, now that
W-pI...109.5:8 today to slip away from **d.** and into peace.
W-pI...122.2:3 eyelids so you see no **d.** of fear and evil,
W-pI...122.7:6 intricacies of your **d.** no longer hide their
W-pI...125.5:4 remain as part of Him regardless of his **d.**;
W-pI...128.5:2 gave its aspects and its phases and its **d.**.
W-pI.131.13:3 not quite forget in wandering away in **d.**.
W-pI...134.8:3 which has been blocked by **d.** of guilt.
W-pI.134.11:1 are all **d.** of evil and of hatred and attack
W-pI...135.7:5 your needs, your values and your **d.**.
W-pI.136.16:3 There will be no dim figures from your **d.**,
W-pI...137.5:3 **d.** embroider into pictures of the truth.
W-pI...137.8:2 that **d.** will not prevail against the truth.
W-pI...140.3:1 The happy **d.** the Holy Spirit brings are
W-pI...140.3:2 The **d.** forgiveness lets the mind perceive
W-pI...140.3:2 so that the dreamer **d.** another dream.
W-pI...140.3:3 happy **d.** are heralds of the dawn of truth
W-pI...140.3:4 sleep to gentle waking, so that **d.** are gone
W-pI...140.5:1 have been cured in God, and not in idle **d.**
W-pI...151.7:4 He sees do all the ego's **d.** of what you are
W-pI.151.11:1 those aspects which reflect but idle **d.**.
W-pI.151.13:4 comes to mind, remove the elements of **d.**
W-pI...153.5:5 but a victim to attack by fantasies, by **d.**,
W-pI...153.5:5 **d.** by which illusions of his safety comfort
W-pI...153.9:1 We look past **d.** today, and recognize
W-pI.153.14:5 **d.** this story has evoked in his confused,
W-pI.155.11:1 When **d.** are over, time has closed the
W-pI.155.13:3 **D.** are not a worthy guide for you who are
W-pI...157.8:2 Holy One, the Giver of the happy **d.** of life
W-pI...158.7:3 and fearful thoughts of guilt from **d.** of sin
W-pI...162.3:2 His **d.** are happy and his rest secure, his
W-pI...163.3:1 wake, in place of aspirations and of **d.**.
W-pI...165.8:5 Thought of Him is still beyond all **d.** and
W-pI...167.9:3 It **d.** of time; an interval in which what
W-pI.167.10:3 and sees in **d.** an opposite to what he is?
W-pI...185.2:2 He cannot play with **d.**, nor think he is
W-pI...185.3:3 In **d.**, no two can share the same intent.
W-pI...185.4:4 Minds cannot unite in **d.**. They merely
W-pI...185.5:1 the peace of God is to renounce all **d.**. For
W-pI...185.5:5 **D.** are one to him. And he has learned
W-pI...185.7:6 place of shifting **d.** which seem to change
W-pI...185.8:1 your mind, to find the **d.** you cherish still.
W-pI...185.8:6 now. Let not some **d.** be more acceptable,
W-pI...185.9:4 God's peace, or you have asked for **d.**.
W-pI...185.9:5 And **d.** will come as you requested them.
W-pI.185.10:2 And so do all who seem to seek for **d.**. For
W-pI...188.2:6 no sight, be it of **d.** or from a truer Source
W-pI...190.7:6 Your strange desires bring it evil **d.**. Your
W-pI...191.9:1 frail, with futile hopes and devastated **d.**,
W-pI...192.3:6 What He makes are **d.**, but of a kind so
W-pI...192.7:4 mists of shifting **d.** and fearful thoughts,
W-pI...198.3:1 Forgiveness sweeps all other **d.** away, and
W-pI...198.3:4 Forgiveness is the end of **d.**, because it is a
W-pI...198.8:2 **D.** of any kind are strange and alien to the
W-pI...200.6:5 beloved Son from evil **d.** that he imagines,
W-pI.200.11:5 and solitary **d.** with single purpose and
W-pII .226.2:3 *in a place of vain desires and of shattered* **d.**,
W-pII .227.2:2 The Son of God this day lays down his **d.**.
W-pII .228.2:4 *And my mistakes about myself are* **d.**. *I let*
W-pII .....2.3:1 to support the world of **d.** and malice.
W-pII .....2.5:2 his Father is remembered, **d.** are done,
W-pII .234.1:1 the time when **d.** of sin and guilt are gone,
W-pII .....4.4:1 A madman's **d.** are frightening, and sin
W-pII .251.1:6 hopes are finally fulfilled and **d.** are gone.
W-pII .....5.3:2 a dream. Like other **d.** it sometimes seems
W-pII .270.1:4 *his Father, lets his* **d.** *be brought to truth,*
W-pII .....6.2:3 are already made, and **d.** are over. He
W-pII .....6.3:3 The rest is **d.**. Yet will these dreams be
W-pII .....6.3:4 Yet will these **d.** be given unto Christ, to
W-pII .....6.4:1 from the Christ in you to all your **d.**, and
W-pII .....6.4:2 which God appointed as the end of **d.**. For
W-pII .272.1:3 *Can* **d.** *content me? Can illusions bring me*
W-pII .272.2:2 the Sons of God, could be content with **d.**
W-pII .279.1:1 The end of **d.** is promised me, because
W-pII .279.1:2 Only in **d.** is there a time when he appears
W-pII .279.1:3 Yet in reality his **d.** are gone, with truth
W-pII .....7.1:2 bridge the gap between reality and **d.**,
W-pII .....7.1:3 He provides are **d.** all carried to the truth,
W-pII .....7.2:1 Spirit's teaching sets is just this end of **d.**.
W-pII .....7.3:1 for the fearful images and **d.** you made.
W-pII .....7.4:1 you, to let forgiveness rest upon your **d.**,
W-pII .....7.4:2 will your **d.** remain to terrify you. And the
W-pII .....7.4:3 return to signify the end of **d.** has come.
W-pII .282.1:3 not to be asleep in **d.** of death, while truth
W-pII .287.2:4 *of* **d.** *and futile substitutions for the truth?*
W-pII .289.2:5 *to be the end of all his* **d.** *and all his pain?*
W-pII .294.2:3 *plan that we awaken from all* **d.** *we made.*
W-pII .295.1:3 the **d.** that seemed to settle on the world
W-pII .309.2:1 *Father, is my sure release from idle* **d.** *of sin.*
W-pII .322.2:2 *And so I cannot sacrifice except in* **d.**. *As You*
W-pII .325.2:1 *and mine apart from Yours but make up* **d.**.
W-pII ...12.2:5 It **d.** of punishment, and trembles at the
W-pII ...12.2:5 and trembles at the figures in its **d.**; its
W-pII ...12.4:1 its acts, its laws and its beliefs, its **d.**, its
W-pII .332.1:2 undoes its evil **d.** by shining them away.
W-pII .334.1:2 and **d.** are gone even while they are woven
W-pII .336.2:1 *In quiet may forgiveness wipe away my* **d.** *of*
W-pII .342.1:4 *the door beyond which lies the end of* **d.**. *I*
W-pII .347.1:8 *gives the miracles my* **d.** *would hide from my*
M-4 ...... VI.1:2 no **d.** that need defense against the truth.
M-8 ........... 2:7 a burden, it retreats into feverish **d.**. And
M-8 ........... 2:8 And in these **d.** the mind is separate,
M-12 ......... 6:2 teachers choose to look on **d.** a while. It is
M-12 ......... 6:5 but who would put his faith in **d.** once
M-12 ....... 6:10 Unity alone is not a thing of **d.**. And it is
M-16 ......... 6:4 from all the fearful things you see in **d.**. It
M-27 ......... 6:4 All **d.** will end with this one. This is
M-28 ......... 1:4 It is the end of **d.** of misery, and the glad
M-28 ......... 4:5 illusions, **d.** of fear and misperceptions of
M-28 ......... 6:2 as any mind remains possessed of evil **d.**,
M-29 ......... 7:9 your **d.** of danger and selected "wrongs."
C-2 .......... 1:11 of this except a dream which, like all **d.**,
C-2 .......... 6:18 seek for an illusion now that **d.** are gone?
C-5 ............ 4:2 And so they were but **d.**. Arise with him
C-5 ............ 4:3 your **d.** that they might be dispelled. And
C-5 .......... 6:11 *Forget your* **d.** *of sin and guilt, and come*
C-6 ............ 5:6 over and no trace remains of **d.** of spite in
P-2......... V.8:2 by which we come to where all **d.** began.
P-2....... VII.8:2 all its little triumphs and its **d.** of death.
P-2....... VII.8:4 stars that brushes lightly past all sickly **d.**.
P-3..........II.6:2 may change their **d.** in the process. Yet it
P-3..........II.6:6 new **d.** will lose their temporary appeal
P-3..........II.6:6 temporary appeal and turn to **d.** of fear,
P-3..........II.6:6 of fear, which is the content of all **d.**. Yet
P-3........II.7:10 of other images, and help with kindly **d.**.
P-3..........II.8:8 The journey is not long except in **d.**.
S-1..........in.3:1 Lay down your **d.**, you holy Son of God,
S-2........ III.4:6 matters not the form that **d.** may seem to
S-2........ III.4:9 in Will and purpose. Here all **d.** are done.
S-3..........II.4:3 Now are its **d.** dispelled in quiet rest. Now
S-3..........II.6:3 placed upon God's substitute for evil **d.**; a
S-3........ III.2:6 body can be done by this because, in **d.**,
S-3........ IV.1:9 and given up all separate **d.** of special
S-3........ IV.3:6 you for shifting **d.** within a sorry world?
S-3........ IV.6:6 Give all your **d.** to Christ and let Him be
S-3........ IV.7:2 Son to Me from **d.** of malice to the sweet

### dreams' 1
T-27 .... VII.7:9 He cannot doubt his **d.** reality, because he

### dreary 1
W-pI...196.5:1 The **d.**, hopeless thought that you can

### dress 1
T-23 .....II.18:8 lips upon a skeleton, **d.** it in loveliness,

### dressed 1
T-25 ...VIII.7:3 devil, **d.** to deceive within an angel's cloak

### drew 1
T-22 ........I.9:7 fearful sight or sound that **d.** them gently

### dried 1
W-pI .. 183.3:5 the tears of pain are **d.** as happy laughter

### drift 2
T-24 .... in.1:12 that idly seems to **d.** between Them has
W-pI 122.14:1 your gifts slip by and **d.** into forgetfulness

### drink 1
W-pI 136.18:3 by weather or fatigue, by food and **d.**, or

### drinking 1
W-pI ...... 7.3:2 up a cup, being thirsty, **d.** from a cup,

### drive 7
T-4 ....... III.4:8 is wholly without the ego's "**d.** to get."
T-16 ..... IV.1:6 merely **d.** it underground and out of sight
T-16 .... VII.3:1 of the ego's **d.** for vengeance on the past.
T-16 .... VII.6:4 and with its passing the **d.** for vengeance
T19 .. IV.D.5:3 The desire to get rid of peace and **d.** the
T-23 ........I.9:5 and **d.** Him out of what He loves forever.
W-pI 186.10:3 concentrated **d.** toward goals like these?

### driven 4
T-13 ...... in.1:7 you, and it is guilt that has **d.** you insane.
T-19 ......I.12:6 faithlessness has **d.** you and him apart,
T-21 .......II.3:1 be merely **d.** by events outside of him. It
W-pII ..... 4.1:2 is the means by which the mind is **d.** mad,

### drives 3
T-9 .....VIII.4:2 reality literally **d.** the ego from your mind
T-15 ........I.7:4 as steadily to Heaven as the ego **d.** to hell.
T-21 ..... VI.4:1 an attack on reason that **d.** it out of mind,

### drop 6
T-14 ... III.15:8 His Son **d.** from the loving Mind wherein
W-pI ...... 7.3:4 not this kind of cup will break if you **d.** it?
W-pI ..... 57.1:4 I can **d.** them off merely by desiring to do
W-pI .... 67.3:1 thoughts **d.** away for a brief preparatory
M-16 ......... 4:8 the difficulty will diminish and **d.** away. If
M-20 ......... 4:2 form, will **d.** the heavy curtain once again,

### dropped 1
T-30 .......V.3:4 And fear has **d.** away, because he is united

### dropping 1
T-14 ..... VI.7:4 **d.** off the rest and offering your true

### drops 2
W-pII ... 13.5:1 Miracles fall like **d.** of healing rain from
C-in ........... 5:2 it **d.** away to make way for the central

### drove 1
T-13 ...... in.3:6 the Father Who **d.** him out of Paradise.

### drown 4
T-5 ...... VII.1:1 can make a voice that can **d.** out God's?
T-22 .......V.4:5 and would **d.** out the hymn of praise to its
T-29 .. VII.10:5 and do not seek to **d.** His Voice in chants
W-pI .. 101.4:2 can to **d.** the Voice which offers it to him?

### drowned 1
T-21 .......V.1:6 small Voice for God is not **d.** out by all

## drowsiness 1

W-pI.....74.5:4 rather than a feeling of **d.** and enervation.

## drugged 1

T-8........IX.4:6 You can indeed be "**d.**" by sleep, if you

## dry 4

T-18... VIII.8:6 Look at the desert– **d.** and unproductive,
T-20.... VI.11:3 instant of despair, a tiny island of **d.** sand,
W-pI...109.6:1 sing, a stream long **d.** begins to flow again
W-pII....13.5:1 rain from Heaven on a **d.** and dusty world

## dual 1

C-6.............3:2 the Holy Spirit has assumed a **d.** function.

## due 36

T-7......... X.5:6 motivation, it can only be **d.** to projection
T-10.... III.10:6 Place honor where it is **d.**, and peace will
T-10.... III.10:9 Honor is not **d.** to illusions, for to honor
T-10..III.10:10 Yet fear is not **d.** them either, for nothing
T-12.........I.6:2 Gratitude is **d.** him for both his loving
T-14....... V.3:8 Deny them not what is their **d.**, for you
T-15.........I.2:6 **d.** but to your identification with the ego,
T-15..... III.6:7 it. All honor is **d.** the host of God. Your
T-16..... III.8:1 holy Self all praise is **d.** for what you are,
T-18....... V.7:1 other and how much gratitude is **d.** him,
T-20..... IV.3:1 by accepting their results as your just **d.**.
T-24..... VII.2:8 you gave to specialness but is his **d.**. And
T-24..... VII.2:9 And nothing **d.** him is not due to you.
T-24..... VII.2:9 And nothing due him is not **d.** to you.
T-25....... V.4:1 you; that you return to him what is his **d.**,
T-25... VIII.9:9 what loving justice knows to be his **d.**. For
T-25. VIII.10:8 offer, believing vengeance is his proper **d.**
T-25. VIII.13:8 is no judge of what must be another's **d.**,
T-25...... IX.3:9 punishment becomes his **d.** instead of
T-25..IX.10:10 *is God's belongs to everyone, and* ***is his d.***.
T-26....... X.3:7 his Father's Love and yours as not his **d.**?
T-27....... II.1:8 may be an act of charity, but not his **d.**.
T-30...... VI.1:6 asked to offer pardon where attack is **d.**,
T-30.... VI.1:10 by being granted where it is not **d.**.
W-pI.....37.1:5 because it offers everyone his full **d.**. And
W-pI.....39.2:3 is not **d.** to the ambiguity of the question.
W-pI...107.6:6 Give truth its **d.**, and it will give you yours
W-pI...156.5:5 reverence, for it is **d.** to Holiness Itself,
W-pI...167.3:7 this course has placed on that idea is **d.** to
W-pI...195.1:7 Your gratitude is **d.** to Him alone Who
W-pI...217.1:3 *I find the Self to Whom my thanks are* ***d.****?* I
W-pII..274.1:1 *give Your Son the honor* ***d.*** *his sinlessness;*
M-4........ II.2:1 is largely **d.** to their perfect honesty. It is
M-4..... IX.2:12 that alone to which all faithfulness is **d.**.
M-15..........3:1 feel your just **d.** is not given you, and your
P-3........ III.4:8 But thanks are **d.** to both, for the release

## dug 1

W-pI.....35.8:3 nothing should be "**d.** out" with effort.

## dull 2

T-17.... IV.13:5 exposed to light, it becomes **d.** and lifeless
M-4........ X.2:5 which seemed so **d.** and lifeless before.

## dullness 1

T-14.........I.5:4 burden of its **d.** that lies upon your mind,

## duration 4

W-pI.....25.6:1 practice periods, each of two-minutes **d.**,
W-pII.....in.2:7 will not consider time a matter of **d.** now.
M-16..........4:4 so. **D.** is not the major concern. One can
S-1...........I.4:6 advice about a problem of an instant's **d.**?

## during 26

T-6...........I.7:6 slept **d.** the so-called "agony in the garden
W-pI.......4.6:2 more than three or four times **d.** the day.
W-pI.......5.7:6 Three or four times **d.** the day is enough.
W-pI.......8.6:1 can be done four or five times **d.** the day,
W-pI.....11.2:4 **D.** the minute or so to be spent in using
W-pI.....13.6:2 think of it except **d.** the practice periods.
W-pI.....14.7:1 to anything that disturbs you **d.** the day,
W-pI.....15.5:1 to very many things **d.** the minute or so of
W-pI.....26.6:3 thoughts **d.** the day is a suitable subject.
W-pI.....27.4:6 If only once **d.** the day you feel that you
W-pI.....31.2:3 **D.** that time, look about you slowly while
W-pI.....31.4:1 for today as often as possible **d.** the day.
W-pI.....32.5:1 are also to be continued **d.** the day, as
W-pI.....35.8:1 **D.** the longer exercise periods, there will
W-pI.....35.9:1 As often as possible **d.** the day, pick up a
W-pI...36.3:10 Several times **d.** these practice periods,
W-pI.....39.9:1 short periods **d.** which you merely repeat
W-pI.....40.2:2 of situations **d.** the day when closing your
W-pI.....42.8:1 more often you repeat the idea **d.** the day,
W-pI.....43.7:1 in which you find yourself **d.** the day.
W-pI.....46.7:3 They will be needed at any time **d.** the day
W-pI.....47.8:1 **D.** the day, repeat the idea often. Use it as
WpI...rI.in.2:4 Do this as often as possible **d.** the day. If
W-pI.....66.9:1 this **d.** the longer practice period today.
W-pI...74.3:10 *Son.* **D.** this introductory phase, be sure to
M-16 .........8:2 particularly **d.** the time when his mind is

## dust 38

T-13...... IV.1:5 leaving you no inheritance except the **d.**
T-13..... VII.3:5 ready to return to **d.** even as you made it.
T-13... VII.11:3 it will be wrenched and hurled into the **d.**.
T-14..... II.1:10 A little piece of glass, a speck of **d.**, a body
T-18... VIII.3:2 of **d.** it bids you fight against the universe.
T-18... VIII.9:3 who lost their way and wander in the **d.**.
T-18. VIII.13:2 desert's **d.** still seems to cloud your eyes
T-18. VIII.13:6 Only a little wall of **d.** still stands between
T19... IV.A.2:9 you let a little bank of sand, a wall of **d.**, a
T-20...... III.9:3 in the **d.** and found your brother's hand,
T-24...... IV.4:8 that lasts an instant, crumbling into **d.**.
T-24...... VI.1:3 will scatter with the wind and turn to **d.**.
T-25...... II.6:6 forever, when yours has crumbled into **d.**.
T-25...... IX.9:2 And so they gather **d.** and grow, until
T-27... VIII.1:3 the **d.** with other bodies dying like itself.
T-28...... VI.1:4 joy and look for lasting pleasure in the **d.**.
T-31...... VI.2:5 is seen, for who is worthy if he be but **d.**?
W-pI.....93.2:3 and have bowed down to idols made of **d.**
W-pI...107.1:7 From **d.** to dust they come and go, for
W-pI...107.1:7 From dust to **d.** they come and go, for
W-pI...123.4:1 no longer looking downward to the **d.**.
W-pI...135.6:4 far beyond a little pile of **d.** and water.
W-pI...136.8:4 this little pile of **d.** silenced and stilled.
W-pI...136.8:5 For see, this **d.** can make you suffer, twist
W-pI...136.9:3 His Son is **d.**, the Father incomplete, and
W-pI...163.3:1 the taste of **d.** and ashes in their wake, in
W-pI...163.4:2 perceived within an idol made of **d.**. Here
W-pI...163.5:2 no name to him, for he has passed to **d.**. It
W-pI...170.5:5 your arms indeed would crumble into **d.**.
WpI...rV.in5:4 Let us raise our hearts from **d.** to life, as
W-pI...186.7:4 on you, and not upon this little pile of **d.**.
W-pI...186.9:6 seen above a desert, rising from the **d.**.
W-pI...191.3:2 of **d.** against the legions of your enemies.
W-pII......2.3:3 it merely lets them quietly go down to **d.**.
M-27 .........2:2 in **d.** and disappointment and despair,
M-28 .........4:7 up from the **d.** and look upon our perfect
S-1........ IV.4:5 space that lasts until it crumbles into **d.**?
S-3...........I.1:5 healing but delays its turning back to **d.**,

## dusty 2

T19....IV.C.8:1 Under the **d.** edge of its distorted world
W-pII.... 13.5:1 rain from Heaven on a dry and **d.** world,

## dutifully 1

T19..IV.B.13:4 seeking it **d.** and obeying the idea that

## dwell 34

T-4.........in.3:2 **d.** upon it, but dismiss it as accomplished
T-6...........I.1:2 I did not **d.** on it before because of the
T-11.........I.1:6 **d.** in the Mind of God with your brother,
T-11...... III.8:2 be worthy to **d.** in the temple with Him,
T-12...... III.5:5 not understand that they **d.** in abundance
T-12.... III.10:8 God and His Son **d.** in peace and where
T-13... VII.17:6 You **d.** not here, but in eternity. You
T-13...... XI.5:6 is invariable as the peace in which you **d.**,
T-15...... III.6:8 Who dwells in you, and in Whom you **d.**.
T-17.... IV.9:10 gift. Let not your gaze **d.** on the hypnotic
T-18.... IX.11:5 for us to **d.** on what cannot be attained.
T19....IV.A.2:2 that it must dispossess to **d.** with you?
T-20.... VIII.4:8 Spirit offers, where He will **d.** with you?
T-22......II.13:1 All you need do to **d.** in quiet here with
T-23.......I.10:2 of You, Who **d.** as One and not apart.
T-23.......I.10:7 You **d.** in peace as limitless as its Creator,
T-26.... III.1:14 Nor is it necessary we **d.** on anything that
T-26...... IX.6:4 to **d.** within the temple offered Them, to
T-27..... VII.5:8 And **d.** not on the suffering and sin, for
T-29......II.10:4 **d.** in what was built as temple unto death.
T-29...... VI.6:3 is to **d.** a little while in such a happy place!
T-30...... IV.5:2 **D.** not on them in any form. They but
T-31..VIII.12:2 For Christ has come to **d.** in the abode
W-pI..... 13.6:2 Do not **d.** on the concluding statement,
W-pI.....21.3:3 You will probably be tempted to **d.** more
W-pI.....31.3:4 Do not **d.** on any one in particular, but try
W-pI.....75.6:1 **D.** not upon the past today. Keep a
W-pI.....92.9:1 and guide your seeing so you do not **d.** on
W-pI... 133.1:3 ideas, but **d.** instead on benefits to you.
W-pI... 134.9:2 your mind to **d.** on what you think he did,
W-pI.134.15:2 Be certain not to **d.** on any one of them,
W-pI... 137.1:2 **d.** on sickness and on separate states.
WpI. rIV.in2:6 can **d.** but those his Father shares. Lack of
W-pII . 232.1:2 *every minute be a time in which I* ***d.*** *with You*

## dwelling 15

T-5...... III.10:5 it perfectly because it is His Own **d.** place;
T-10...... V.11:3 it was created as the **d.** place of God's Son
T-11.........I.1:4 be restoring the holy **d.** place of His Son,
T-18..... IV.3:5 God did not create His **d.** place unworthy
T-18.... IV.5:10 *established His* ***d.*** *place in me created it as*
T-18...... VI.1:4 Kingdom of Heaven is the **d.** place of the
T-18...... VI.6:8 proclaiming it to be the **d.** place of God's
T19....IV.A.1:4 its tranquil **d.** place from which it gently
T-27... VII.15:3 of **d.** in your dreams on his mistakes.
T-29.......... V.h The Changeless **D.** Place
T-29....... V.2:1 not that you can change Their **d.** place.
W-pI... 129.9:3 you have, and **d.** briefly only upon this:
W-pII ... 12.5:2 God created as His Son, His **d.** place, His
W-pII . 336.1:6 for this the **d.** place of God Himself.
S-1......... V.2:1 nor share a **d.** place where they can meet.

## dwells 21

T-11...... III.7:7 He Himself **d.** there and abides in peace.
T-13... VII.17:5 establish its eternal reign where sorrow **d.**
T-13.... VIII.1:5 unequivocally knows also it **d.** in eternity,
T-14...... VI.2:1 in which the Holy Spirit **d.** within you is
T-14...... IX.3:9 the Presence that **d.** within it *is* Holiness.
T-15...... III.6:8 your magnitude is of Him Who **d.** in you,
T-15...... III.8:6 Love is not little and love **d.** in you, for
T-15.... III.12:5 it protects only the peace in which He **d.**.
T-18.........I.8:2 stillness **d.** the living God you never left,
T-18...... VI.1:4 not his Father and **d.** not apart from Him.
T-23.......I.10:5 in serenity and peace, and **d.** with him.
T-23.......I.11:1 seek to overcome the One Who **d.** there?
T-26...... VI.3:1 Who **d.** with shadows is alone indeed,
T-26..... VII.4:6 it is real, and **d.** where all reality must be.
T-26...... IX.8:2 Where He **d.**, His Son dwells with Him,
T-26...... IX.8:2 Where He dwells, His Son **d.** with Him,
T-29....... V.5:4 The quiet that surrounds you **d.** in him,
T-29..... VII.6:3 God **d.** within, and your completion lies
W-pI... 165.6:6 Abundance **d.** in him, and deprivation
W-pI. 187.11:6 **d.** in us and offers us His Holiness as ours.
W-pI... 199.3:3 ego holds the body dear because it **d.** in it,

## dwindles 1

W-pI...166.5:4 perceiving how his little lot but **d.**, as he

## dying 16

T-23..... II.15:6 to the throne of love, its **d.** conqueror, its
T-27....... V.3:4 the screaming **d.** and the silent dead, are
T-27....... V.5:2 The eyes of all the **d.** bring reproach, and
T-27....... V.5:5 **d.** world asks only that you rest an instant
T-27....... V.6:3 Life is given you to give the **d.** world. And
T-27 ..... VI.5:9 The **d.** live, the dead arise, and pain has
T-27 ...VIII.1:3 in the dust with other bodies **d.** like itself.
T-27 ...VIII.3:1 from the time of birth to **d.** are the theme
T-28 .......II.5:5 are you the victim in a **d.** body slain. But
T-31 .......I.10:3 and pleads that love restore the **d.** world.
W-pI..... 92.3:3 the small, the weak, the sickly and the **d.**,
W-pI... 124.5:3 we see it in the **d.** and the dead as well,
W-pI. 132.13:5 are a shadow briefly laid upon a **d.** world.
M-27 ......... 1:2 aging, losing vitality, and **d.** in the end?
M-27 ......... 4:1 that there is part of **d.** things that may go
C-2 ............ 8:1 of pain, the fear of **d.** and the urge to kill,

## dynamics 8

T-11 ..........V.h The "**D.**" of the Ego
T-11 .......V.1:5 The "**d.**" of the ego will be our lesson for a
T-11 .......V.3:1 Let us begin this lesson in "ego **d.**" by
T-11 .......V.3:3 "**D.**" implies the power to do something,
T-11 .......V.4:1 we are not considering **d.** but delusions.
T-14 .......X.8:4 something of the "**d.**" of the ego, let me
T-16 .......V.3:2 The "**d.**" of the ego are clearest here, for
T-26 ........I.1:1 In the "**d.**" of attack is sacrifice a key idea.

---

# E

## Each 2

*each*

T-2........ III.5:6 are completely dependent on **E.** Other. He
S-1 .........in.1:3 of the Love They give forever to **E.** Other.

## each 591

*Each*

T-1.........I.15:1 **E.** day should be devoted to miracles. The
T-2....V.A.17:6 In time we exist for and with **e.** other. In
T-3........ III.6:3 and His Sons are not strangers to **e.** other.
T-3...... III.7:12 When they do not recognize **e.** other, they
T-3........ IV.1:9 because they are meaningless to **e.** other.
T-3........ IV.3:7 makes its aspects strangers to **e.** other,
T-3......... V.9:5 fact that **e.** one has this power completely
T-4........ III.8:2 for we must hide nothing from **e.** other. If
T-4........ VI.4:1 ego and the spirit do not know **e.** other.
T-4........ VI.7:5 because **e.** of them is of your Father. Love
T-5........ IV.3:5 them, nor can they conflict with **e.** other.
T-5......... V.6:3 and **e.** moment of decision is a judgment
T-6.........I.18:2 influence on **e.** other is without limit, and
T-6.........I.18:3 **E.** one must learn to teach that all forms
T-6......... II.8:2 within themselves and with **e.** other. The
T-6....... II.13:5 **E.** of us is the light of the world, and by
T-6......V.A.5:9 always for what **e.** one can get *separately.*
T-6....V.A.5:10 only what **e.** one can give to all. He never
T-8...........I.5:5 **e.** believing in diametrically opposed
T-8...........I.5:6 **e.** one merely interferes with the other.
T-8........ IV.7:6 of **e.** other lies our remembrance of God.
T-8........ VI.8:4 apart from **e.** other we cannot function at
T-8....... VII.9:2 with little or no relationship to **e.** other,
T-9........ VI.4:5 of creation. **E.** part you remember adds to
T-9........ VI.4:5 to your wholeness because **e.** part *is* whole.
T-9......VIII.7:1 of **e.** other because grandeur is truth.
T-10...... III.6:1 calm knowledge that **e.** one is part of Him
T-10..... V.14:8 be real, because they contradict **e.** other.
T-11.......in.1:4 **E.** is internally consistent, but they are
T-12...... VI.7:6 join in perfect love of God and of **e.** other.
T-12.....VII.7:7 two goals, **e.** perceived in a different place
T-12.....VII.7:7 separated from **e.** other because you made
T-13....... V.2:1 **E.** one peoples his world with figures
T-13....... V.5:1 to **e.** of them as though it were the other.
T-13...... V.10:2 **E.** is a way of seeing, and different worlds
T-13...... VI.6:4 and thus enables them to reach **e.** other.
T-13...... VI.8:7 with me. **E.** voice has a part in the song of
T-13.... VI.10:3 it. **E.** one you see in light brings your light
T-13.....VII.2:2 for **e.** of them involves a different kind of
T-13....... X.5:2 but with **e.** one each day be born again. A
T-13....... X.5:2 but with each one **e.** day be born again. A
T-14...... III.2:2 **e.** representing an escape from what the
T-14 ..... III.4:1 **E.** day, each hour and minute, even each
T-14 ..... III.4:1 Each day, **e.** hour and minute, even each
T-14 ..... III.4:1 each hour and minute, even **e.** second,
T-14 ... IV.10:2 **E.** perceives the other as like himself,
T-14 ... IV.10:2 because **e.** sees the other unlike the way
T-14 ...... V.2:1 message given to **e.** one is always the same
T-14 ...... V.2:2 **E.** one teaches the message differently,
T-14 ...... V.6:1 Teachers of innocence, **e.** in his own way,
T-14 ...... V.6:4 **E.** effort made on its behalf is offered for
T-14 .... V.11:1 **E.** one you see you place within the holy
T-14 ..... VI.4:4 meaning by confusing them with **e.** other.
T-14 .... VII.2:7 Under **e.** cornerstone of fear on which you
T-14 .... VII.4:7 have them both, for **e.** denies the other.
T-14 .... VII.4:8 for **e.** in a separate place can be endowed
T-14 .....X.12:8 will bless **e.** recognition of His Son with
T-14 ..... XI.4:8 And He will gladly exchange **e.** one for the
T-14 ..... XI.5:6 And **e.** bright lesson with which the Holy
T-14 ... XI.9:11 And **e.** miracle He offers you corrects your
T-14 ... XI.12:5 **E.** brings the other with it, for it is the law
T-14 ... XI.12:6 They are cause and effect, **e.** to the other,
T-15 ........I.8:3 in the present when **e.** instant stands clear
T-15 ........I.8:4 **E.** instant is a clean, untarnished birth, in
T-15 ..... III.2:1 you do not realize, **e.** time you choose, is
T-15 ...... V.8:5 see in **e.** relationship what it will be when
T-15 ..... VI.1:4 Perfect faith in **e.** one, for its ability to
T-15 .... VII.7:2 For **e.** one thinks that he has sacrificed
T-15 .... VII.9:3 **e.** seeks relief from guilt by increasing it in
T-15 .... VII.9:4 **e.** believes that this decreases guilt in him.
T-15 .......X.5:2 it *is* necessary to examine **e.** one as long as
T-15 .......X.6:7 **E.** form will be recognized as but a cover
T-16 ........I.7:2 them separate and secret from **e.** other.
T-16 ..... III.8:3 **E.** one builds this bridge, which carries
T-16 ...... V.7:5 **E.** partner tries to sacrifice the self he does
T-16 ...... V.8:3 partners see this special self in **e.** other,
T-16 ..... V.11:5 people, on which **e.** seeks to kill his self,
T-16 ..... VI.5:2 seeking to join **e.** other in separate unions
T-16 ..... VI.5:4 **E.** would deny his power, for the separate
T-16 ... VI.11:5 increased with **e.** light that returns to take
T-17 .......II.5:4 all. **E.** spot His reason touches grows alive
T-17 ..... III.6:4 **e.** step in His undoing is the separation
T-17 ... IV.12:2 **E.** is complete, and cannot be partially
T-17 ... IV.12:3 **E.** is a picture of all that you can have,
T-17 ... IV.13:1 These pictures are **e.** framed perfectly for
T-17 ... IV.13:5 As **e.** senseless stone that seems to shine
T-17 ... IV.14:5 **e.** is given its rightful place when both are
T-17 ... IV.14:5 when both are seen in relation to **e.** other.
T-17 ...... V.5:1 ego given time to reinterpret **e.** slow step
T-17 ..... VI.1:7 to use them in **e.** situation separately,
T-17 ..... VI.1:7 can more safely look beyond **e.** situation,
T-17 .... VII.9:1 Enter **e.** situation with the faith you give
T-18 ........I.3:4 **e.** one seems to require a different form of
T-18 ..... III.1:3 **E.** dream has led to other dreams, and
T-18 ..... III.4:1 you joined **e.** other you were not alone.
T-18 ..... III.5:1 **E.** instant that we spend together will
T-18 ..... III.8:6 brother, and you will light **e.** other's way.
T-18 ..... VI.8:6 up of different parts, which reach **e.** other.
T-18 ... VIII.5:2 **E.** body seems to house a separate mind, a
T-18 ... VIII.5:3 created. **E.** tiny fragment seems to be self-
T-19 ........I.7:4 **E.** is united, a complete thought system,
T-19 ........I.7:4 but totally disconnected to **e.** other. And
T-19 ......I.10:5 **E.** one appears just as he is perceived in
T-19 ..... III.8:3 And **e.** part of God's fragmented creation
T-19 ..... III.8:3 eternal opposition to Him and to **e.** other.
T19 ...IV.A.5:4 same. **E.** is a gentle winning over from the
T19 .IV.A.10:8 and **e.** believes that what the other looks
T19IV.A.10:10 **e.** has messengers which it sends forth,
T19 .IV.A.11:3 **e.** asking for messages of different things
T19 .. IV.D.5:6 From beyond **e.** of the obstacles to love,
T19 .. IV.D.5:7 **e.** has been surmounted by the power of
T19 IV.D.13:7 And yet your savior stands beside **e.** one.
T19 IV.D.17:5 give redemption to **e.** other and share in it
T-20 .......II.3:1 **E.** gift is an evaluation of the receiver and
T-20 .......II.3:4 And **e.** has set a light upon his altar, that
T-20 .......II.9:4 the veil of fear, lighting **e.** other's way.
T-20 ... III.10:1 **e.** of you for one another and for himself.
T-20 ... III.10:4 gentleness upon **e.** other and on ourselves
T-20 ..... IV.5:3 To **e.** who walks this earth in seeming
T-20 ..... IV.5:4 of separation **e.** is appointed separately,
T-20 ..... IV.5:6 **e.** one finds his savior when he is ready to
T-20 ..... IV.6:6 **E.** holy relationship must enter here, to
T-20 .......V.1:5 with **e.** joining is the end of time brought
T-20 .......V.1:6 **E.** miracle of joining is a mighty herald of
T-20 .......V.2:1 **E.** herald of eternity sings of the end of
T-20 .......V.2:2 **E.** speaks in time of what is far beyond it.
T-20 .......V.6:1 upon **e.** holy instant as a different point in
T-20 .. VI.12:6 God as equal things are like unto **e.** other.
T-20 .... VII.7:3 **e.** one appropriate to the end for which it
T-20 .... VII.7:4 the other, for **e.** one is a *choice* of purpose,
T-20 ....VIII.8:8 **e.** different and with different values. Yet
T-21 ........I.5:3 They try to reach **e.** other, and they fail,
T-21 .....II.13:3 you from **e.** other and separate from your
T-21 ... III.11:9 the absence of the other does **e.** depend.
T-21 .......V.3:6 how separate minds can influence **e.** other
T-21 .... VII.2:8 **e.** one as likely to attack his brother or
T-21 .... VII.3:3 together, but have not joined **e.** other. For
T-21 .. VII.11:2 **e.** one asks if you are willing to exchange
T-22 ......in.1:4 seen in the other yet believed by **e.** to be
T-22 ......in.1:5 **e.** one seems to make a different error,
T-22 ......in.2:5 where **e.** one thinks the other has what he
T-22 ......in.2:6 **e.** to complete himself and rob the other.
T-22 ......in.3:2 **E.** one has looked within and seen no lack.
T-22 ........I.7:1 So in **e.** holy relationship is the ability to

T-22.........I.9:6 **e.** other through a vision not of the body,
T-22.........I.9:8 in **e.** the other saw a perfect shelter where
T-22....... II.1:2 alternatives, and different from **e.** other.
T-22....... II.1:4 though **e.** one seems to be the way to lose
T-22....... II.4:2 are different from **e.** other in every way, in
T-22....... II.7:3 Either you give **e.** other life or death;
T-22....... II.7:3 either you are **e.** other's savior or his judge
T-22....... III.9:3 relationship, **e.** one is valued because he
T-22....... III.9:4 **E.** sees within the other what impels him
T-22....... III.9:6 for **e.** to see himself as causing sin by his
T-22...... VI.5:5 **E.** part of Heaven that you bring is given
T-22...... VI.8:1 **e.** one is released as he beholds his savior
T-22...... VI.9:6 He will take **e.** one and make of it a potent
T-22...... VI.9:8 to make **e.** little gift of love a source of
T-22...... VI.9:9 **E.** little gift you offer to your brother
T-22.... VI.9:11 and lays it gently in **e.** quiet smile of faith
T-22.... VI.14:8 because **e.** shining thought of love extends
T-23.........I.6:1 to make them different from **e.** other, in
T-23.........I.6:3 Nor are they different from **e.** other. Both
T-23.........I.8:4 of yourself, in conflict with **e.** other. And
T-23....... II.2:2 this one maintains that **e.** is separate and
T-23....... II.2:4 **E.** one establishes this for himself, and
T-23....... II.3:5 brought to truth instead of to **e.** other,
T-23....... II.4:1 worshipper of sin, is that **e.** one *must* sin,
T-23....... II.5:7 fear of God and of **e.** other now appears as
T-23..... II.20:3 Yet **e.** one rests as surely on the belief the
T-23..... II.20:4 **E.** one upholds these laws completely,
T-23..... II.21:4 **E.** is a different form in the progression of
T-23..... II.21:6 whole descent from Heaven lies in **e.** one.
T-23...... IV.4:3 **E.** form of murder and attack that still
T-24.......in.2:4 the power to dictate **e.** decision you make.
T-24.........I.2:1 Beliefs will never openly attack **e.** other
T-24...... I.7:10 you and your brother illusions to **e.** other?
T-24.........I.8:1 from **e.** unrecognized belief in specialness
T-24...... I.8:10 change with every seeming blow, **e.** slight,
T-24....... II.3:5 never one, **e.** one in exile from himself,
T-24....... II.5:4 Yet how can truth be different to **e.** one?
T-24....... II.5:5 **e.** in his special sins and "safe" from love,
T-24....... II.9:3 to kill **e.** other and deny they are the same
T-24....... V.4:2 And both will walk in danger, **e.** intent, in
T-24....... V.6:8 for your completion in **e.** living thing that
T-24....... V.6:9 that **e.** might offer you the Love of God.
T-24....... V.7:6 receiving from **e.** one the gift of life that
T-24.... VI.10:6 loves **e.** part of Him with equal love and
T-24... VII.11:6 and separates **e.** from all aspects with a
T-25.........I.4:3 **E.** aspect of Himself is framed in holiness
T-25.........I.4:4 shines through **e.** body that it looks upon,
T-25...... III.3:4 To **e.** it has a different purpose, and to
T-25...... III.3:4 and to **e.** it is a perfect means to serve the
T-25...... III.6:5 will he see **e.** situation that he thought
T-25...... IV.5:3 **E.** bird that ever sang will sing again in
T-25....... V.1:3 **e.** the cause and aim and justifier of the
T-25....... V.1:4 **E.** is meaningless alone, but seems to
T-25....... V.1:5 **E.** depends upon the other for whatever
T-25....... V.1:6 truth, for **e.** attests the other must be true.
T-25....... V.2:9 you, **e.** time you look upon your brother.
T-25....... V.4:4 will give to **e.** an equal strength to save the
T-25...... VI.4:2 **e.** He gives a special function in salvation
T-25...... VI.5:9 And **e.** must do what is allotted him, for
T-25...... VI.6:4 and understood as **e.** one takes his part in
T-25..... VII.1:1 Holy Spirit can commute **e.** sentence that
T-25..... VII.1:6 Yet **e.** one knows the cost of sin is death.
T-25..... VII.5:4 one, and no one loses that **e.** one may gain
T-25..... VII.6:6 **E.** sees a world immutable, as each defines
T-25..... VII.6:6 **e.** defines the changeless and eternal truth
T-25..... VII.6:7 And **e.** reflects a view of what the Father
T-25..... VII.9:2 To **e.** his special function is designed to be
T-25... VIII.5:7 for **e.** one contradicts the other and denies
T-25... VIII.9:8 is richer made by **e.** one you accept. And
T-25. VIII.11:4 Of **e.** one does the Holy Spirit ask if he will
T-25. VIII.11:5 **E.** special function He allots is but for this;
T-25. VIII.11:5 that **e.** one learn that love and justice are
T-25. VIII.11:6 strengthened by their union with **e.** other.
T-25...... IX.2:6 **E.** gift but adds to the supply. For God is
T-25.... IX.10:2 **E.** one becomes an illustration of the law
T-25.... IX.10:4 **E.** miracle is an example of what justice
T-26.........I.2:3 Around **e.** entity is built a wall so seeming
T-26.........I.2:4 **E.** part must sacrifice the other part, to
T-26.........I.2:5 joined **e.** one would lose its own identity,
T-26.........I.3:7 these limits on **e.** brother whom you see.
T-26.........I.6:6 die **e.** time you see in him a sin deserving
T-26.........I.7:7 Born again **e.** instant, untouched by time,
T-26....... II.1:3 because **e.** one is solved in just the same
T-26....... II.2:2 They are the same to Him because **e.** one,
T-26....... II.3:4 makes **e.** one seem different from the rest.
T-26....... II.5:7 **E.** time you keep a problem for yourself to
T-26....... II.7:3 will see **e.** little hurt resolved before the
T-26....... IV.2:2 **E.** flower shines in light, and every bird
T-26....... IV.4:2 Son of God Himself comes to receive **e.**
T-26...... IV.4:4 **E.** reminds him of his Father's Love as
T-26...... IV.4:5 **e.** one teaches him that what he feared he
T-26...... IV.5:4 And **e.** one joins the singing at the altar
T-26....... V.4:3 **E.** thing you look upon you saw but for an
T-26....... V.5:5 Yet in **e.** unforgiving act or thought, in
T-26..... V.13:1 **E.** day, and every minute in each day, and
T-26..... V.13:1 Each day, and every minute in **e.** day, and
T-26..... V.13:1 and every instant that **e.** minute holds,
T-26..... V.13:2 And so you die **e.** day to live again, until
T-26..... V.13:3 all. Such is **e.** life; a seeming interval from
T-26... VII.13:3 that **e.** idea the mind conceives but adds
T-26... VII.16:5 **E.** instant is the Son of God reborn until
T-26... VII.19:4 what can save **e.** one of us can save us all.
T-26... VII.19:7 And everything belongs to **e.** of them. No
T-26...... IX.4:4 grow ever brighter as **e.** one comes home.
T-26....... X.5:7 And **e.** unfairness that the world appears
T-27.........I.6:7 And **e.** has many voices, speaking to your
T-27.........I.7:2 The sick have reason for **e.** one of their
T-27..... II.16:7 And **e.** forgives the other, that he may
T-27....... V.3:2 **e.** one is born into this world as witness to
T-27..... V.10:4 and beyond **e.** one of them there are a
T-27..... V.10:5 **E.** one may seem to have a problem that is
T-27...... VI.2:5 **E.** one seems different because it has a
T-27...... VI.4:7 And for **e.** witness to the body's death He
T-27...... VI.4:8 **E.** miracle He brings is witness that the
T-27..... VII.4:4 For **e.** one thinks that if he does his part,
T-27... VIII.9:3 He bids you bring **e.** terrible effect to Him
T-27. VIII.12:2 He will teach you how **e.** one is caused.
T-27. VIII.13:7 is impossible is that you be unlike **e.** other
T-28....... II.3:6 of other bodies, **e.** with separate minds,
T-28...... III.7:5 pieces, **e.** concealed within a separate and
T-28...... IV.8:3 To **e.** He offers his Identity, which the
T-28...... IV.9:1 knowing You will come to close **e.** little
T-28...... IV.9:6 For the whole is in **e.** one. And every
T-28....... V.5:7 **e.** senseless scrap and shred of evidence,
T-28...... VI.6:1 Let this be your agreement with **e.** one;
T-29.........I.6:5 misuse **e.** circumstance and everyone you
T-29...... IV.4:8 And **e.** one represents some function that
T-29...... IV.6:6 **e.** dream becomes an offering of love. For
T-29....... V.7:5 **E.** form it takes in some way calls for
T-29....... V.7:6 **e.** with his tiny spear and rusted sword, to
T-29..... VII.1:2 fail, and you will weep **e.** time an idol falls
T-29..... VII.1:4 **E.** idol that you worship when God calls
T-29..... VII.3:2 And **e.** will fail him, all excepting one; for
T-29..... VII.5:4 Yet **e.** must fail and crumble and decay,
T-29... VIII.8:3 **e.** depending on the one of whom the
T-29... VIII.8:6 **E.** worshipper of idols harbors hope his
T-30.......in.1:4 **E.** one will help a little, every time it is
T-30.........I.1:5 set, adopted consciously **e.** time you wake
T-30...... IV.3:2 **e.** one seems to break the rules you set for
T-30..... VII.1:6 **e.** one be open to interpretation which is
T-31.........I.6:6 taught to you in every moment of **e.** day,
T-31.........I.7:2 **E.** has its outcome in a different world.
T-31.........I.7:3 **e.** world follows surely from its source.
T-31.........I.8:8 The soft eternal calling of **e.** part of God's
T-31.......I.10:3 that echoes past **e.** seeming call to death,
T-31.......I.10:3 that sings behind **e.** murderous attack
T-31.......I.10:4 Who calls to you beyond **e.** form of hate;
T-31.......I.10:4 beyond each form of hate; **e.** call to war.
T-31....... II.2:6 **e.** time you think you must decide on
T-31....... II.3:3 **e.** seeming to possess advantages you
T-31...... IV.2:9 And **e.** is but the means to gain that end,
T-31..... V.16:2 **E.** one will show the changes in your own
T-31..... V.16:6 And **e.** will seem to be accusing you. Yet
T-31..... VII.8:3 And to **e.** one has He allowed the grace to
T-31... VIII.3:2 **e.** perplexity Christ calls to you and gently
T-31. VIII.11:5 And as **e.** one elects to join with me, the
W-in..........3:2 **e.** day's exercises are planned around one
W-in..........4:2 will understand that **e.** of them is equally
W-pI....... 1.4:1 **E.** of the first three lessons should not be
W-pI....... 1.4:1 not be done more than twice a day **e.**,
W-pI....... 4.4:1 identify **e.** thought by the central figure or
W-pI....... 5.1:5 **e.** form becomes a proper subject for the
W-pI....... 5.1:6 day. Applying the same idea to **e.** of them
W-pI....... 5.7:2 Apply the idea for today to **e.** of them,
W-pI....... 6.2:2 the application of the idea to **e.** upsetting
W-pI....... 7.5:2 Glance briefly at **e.** subject, and then
W-pI....... 7.5:3 practice periods, **e.** to last a minute or so,
W-pI....... 8.4:4 there. Name **e.** one by the central figure or
W-pI....... 8.5:1 name **e.** of your thoughts specifically, for
W-pI....... 9.2:5 exercises. **E.** small step will clear a little of
W-pI..... 10.4:7 you. As **e.** one crosses your mind, say: *My*
W-pI..... 10.5:2 **e.** involving no more than a minute or so
W-pI..... 13.2:2 God and the ego "challenge" **e.** other as to
W-pI..... 13.4:1 more than a minute or so at most **e.** time,
W-pI..... 14.4:2 Name **e.** one as it occurs to you, and then
W-pI..... 14.5:2 In **e.** case, name the "disaster" quite
W-pI..... 15.4:5 to continue to look at **e.** subject while you
W-pI..... 15.4:6 should be repeated quite slowly **e.** time.
W-pI..... 16.5:1 and then as **e.** one crosses your mind hold
W-pI..... 17.2:3 on **e.** thing you note long enough to say: *I*
W-pI..... 18.3:1 your eyes on **e.** one long enough to say: *I*
W-pI..... 18.3:3 Conclude **e.** practice period by repeating
W-pI..... 18.3:5 will be sufficient for **e.** practice period.
W-pI..... 19.3:3 As you consider **e.** one, name it in terms
W-pI..... 19.4:1 now, and will no longer be repeated **e.** day
W-pI..... 21.1:3 are urged, allowing a full minute for **e.**.
W-pI..... 21.4:1 hold **e.** one in mind while you tell yourself
W-pI..... 22.3:1 times today, for at least a minute **e.** time.
W-pI..... 22.3:7 the end of **e.** practice period, ask yourself:
W-pI..... 23.3:2 **E.** of your perceptions of "external reality
W-pI..... 23.6:3 you. As **e.** one crosses your mind say: *I can*
W-pI..... 23.6:5 Hold **e.** attack thought in mind as you say
W-pI..... 24.3:2 honestly and carefully considered in **e.** of
W-pI..... 24.3:3 Two minutes are suggested for **e.** of the
W-pI..... 24.5:1 name **e.** situation that occurs to you, and
W-pI..... 24.5:2 form of **e.** application should be roughly
W-pI..... 24.7:1 **e.** unresolved situation that crosses your
W-pI..... 25.6:1 periods, **e.** of two-minutes duration, are
W-pI..... 25.6:2 **E.** practice period should begin with a
W-pI..... 25.6:3 eyes resting on **e.** subject you so select, say
W-pI..... 26.2:5 together. They contradict **e.** other.
W-pI..... 26.5:2 two minutes should be attempted for **e.** of
W-pI..... 26.6:4 than usual should be spent with **e.** one.
W-pI..... 26.7:3 referring to **e.** one quite specifically,
W-pI..... 26.8:1 available for **e.** situation you use, and
W-pI..... 26.8:3 outcomes for **e.** situation continues, you
W-pI..... 26.9:1 named **e.** outcome of which you are afraid
W-pI..... 26.9:3 Conclude **e.** practice period by repeating
W-pI..... 28.6:2 same request of **e.** subject that you use in
W-pI..... 28.6:3 to **e.** of them to let its purpose be revealed
W-pI..... 28.7:2 **e.** one should be accorded equal sincerity
W-pI..... 28.8:3 **E.** application should be made quite
W-pI..... 29.4:1 about you, naming **e.** one specifically. Try
W-pI..... 31.2:2 minutes for **e.** of these are recommended.
W-pI..... 31.3:1 **e.** to be considered for a moment, and
W-pI..... 34.3:1 are required for **e.** of the longer practice
W-pI..... 34.3:3 them arise in your mind, and let **e.** one go,
W-pI..... 35.4:1 For **e.** of the three five-minute practice
W-pI..... 35.7:4 After you have named **e.** one, add: *But my*
W-pI..... 35.9:1 idea in the form stated above to **e.** of them
W-pI..... 37.4:1 periods, **e.** to involve three to five minutes
W-pI..... 38.4:1 **e.** preferably to last a full five minutes,
W-pI..... 39.8:2 the idea for today to **e.** of them in this way
W-pI... 39.10:4 End **e.** practice period by repeating the
W-pI..... 44.4:1 today, **e.** lasting three to five minutes. A
W-pI..... 46.4:3 Mention **e.** one by name, and say: *God is*
W-pI..... 47.4:4 fear, dismissing **e.** one by telling yourself:
WpI... rI.in.1:2 **E.** of them will cover five of the ideas
WpI... rI.in.1:3 a few short comments after **e.** of the ideas,
WpI... rI.in.2:2 though **e.** one should be practiced at least
WpI... rI.in.2:3 two minutes or more to **e.** practice period,
WpI... rI.in.3:1 to cover the comments that follow **e.** idea
W-pI..... 61.5:1 **e.** one need not exceed a minute or two.
W-pI..... 62.3:1 while **e.** time you forgive you call upon the
W-pI..... 64.5:4 simple. **E.** one will lead to happiness or
W-pI..... 65.4:1 at approximately the same time **e.** day.
W-pI..... 65.5:4 uncover **e.** thought that arises to interfere

W-pI.....65.5:5 it. Note e. one as it comes to you, with as
W-pI.....65.5:5 dismissing e. one by telling yourself: *This*
W-pI.....68.6:2 all, thinking of e. one in turn as you do so:
W-pI.....70.6:1 e. of which should last some ten to fifteen
W-pI.....70.6:3 be a good time to lay aside for e. of them,
W-pI.....71.2:4 E. grievance you hold is a declaration, and
W-pI.....71.8:1 e. making equal contribution to the whole
W-pI.....73.3:1 and grievances increase with e. exchange.
W-pI.....76.1:2 be salvation. E. has imprisoned you with
W-pI.....78.1:1 yet quite clear to you that e. decision that
W-pI.....78.1:2 E. grievance stands like a dark shield of
W-pI.....78.3:1 in shining light where e. one stood before.
W-pI.....78.3:4 E. grievance made the darkness deeper,
W-pI...78.10:2 when we allow e. one we meet to save us,
W-pI.....79.4:2 problems, e. requiring a different answer.
W-pI.....79.9:2 today, e. one calling for an answer. Our
WpI..rII.in.1:2 review left off, and cover two ideas e. day.
WpI..rII.in.1:3 earlier part of e. day will be devoted to
WpI..rII.in.1:4 ones in which we practice e. of them.
WpI..rII.in.2:1 Take about fifteen minutes for e. of them,
WpI..rII.in.5:4 Be determined e. day not to leave your
W-pI...93.10:1 five minutes of e. hour for these exercises.
W-pI...93.10:3 to repeat these thoughts e. hour: *Light and*
W-pI.....94.3:1 the first five minutes of e. waking hour to
W-pI.....94.5:9 E. one you do will be a giant stride toward
W-pI...95.14:8 understand e. time you do so, someone
W-pI.....96.2:2 doubt, e. one as futile as the one before,
W-pI...96.12:1 E. time today you tell your frantic mind
W-pI.....97.3:2 E. time you practice, awareness is brought
W-pI.....97.5:1 five minutes of e. hour from your hands,
W-pI.....97.5:3 will increase in healing power e. time
W-pI.....97.6:1 Thus will e. gift to Him be multiplied a
W-pI.....97.8:1 Offer e. practice period today gladly to
W-pI.....98.5:1 minutes of your time e. hour to be able to
W-pI.....98.7:1 E. hour today give Him your tiny gift of
W-pI.....98.7:3 and make e. repetition of today's idea a
W-pI.....98.8:1 e. five minutes that you spend with Him,
W-pI.....98.9:6 you e. practice period you share with Him
W-pI...98.10:3 often, and do not forget e. time you do so,
W-pI...100.1:3 e. one of them is equally essential to them
W-pI...103.3:1 within your mind e. waking hour today.
W-pI...105.7:1 "enemies" a little while, and tell e. one, as
W-pI...105.9:1 thus with Him e. time you can today, but
W-pI...106.7:4 E. hour's exercises should begin with this
W-pI...106.9:2 For e. five minutes spent in listening, a
W-pI.107.11:2 E. time you tell yourself with confidence,
W-pI...108.9:1 Say e. one slowly and then pause a while,
W-pI.108.10:3 still faster and more sure e. time you say,
W-pI...109.6:1 E. hour that you take your rest today, a
W-pI...109.6:2 The world is born again e. time you rest,
W-pI...109.7:1 With e. five minutes that you rest today,
W-pI...109.9:2 E. brother comes to take his rest, and
W-pI...109.9:6 their resting place e. time we tell ourselves
W-pI.110.11:3 Son, our holy Self, the Christ in e. of us: *I*
WpI. rIII.in2:1 optimal e. day and every hour of the day.
WpI. rIII.in5:2 that are written down for e. day's exercise.
WpIrIII.in10:2 ideas a brief but serious review e. hour.
WpIrIII.in10:4 give more than just a moment to e. one.
WpIrIII.in11:2 you learn e. day to everything you do. Do
WpIrIII.in12:1 E. day's review assignments will conclude
WpIrIII.in12:1 restatement of the thought to use e. hour,
WpIrIII.in12:1 one to be applied on e. half hour as well.
WpIrIII.in12:3 This second chance with e. of these ideas
W-pI...121.7:1 E. unforgiving mind presents you with an
W-pI...121.7:2 E. one awaits release from hell through
W-pI.122.14:1 minute as e. quarter of an hour passes by.
W-pI...128.2:1 E. thing you value here is but a chain that
W-pI...132.6:4 e. one must go as far as he can let himself
W-pI...133.5:3 E. choice you make brings everything to
W-pI.133.13:3 of fifteen minutes e. begin with this: *I will*
W-pI.134.15:3 thought of him, and e. time ask yourself,
W-pI...135.3:2 fear, increasing fear as e. defense is made.
W-pI...136.2:5 The parts are seen as if e. one were whole
W-pI.138.12:1 that we have made e. hour in between.
W-pI.139.12:1 our dedication to our cause today e. hour,
WpI. rIV.in2:1 unifies e. step in the review we undertake,
WpI. rIV.in4:4 start e. practice period in this review with
WpI. rIV.in5:1 Begin e. day with time devoted to the
WpI. rIV.in5:1 of your mind to learn what e. idea you will
WpI. rIV.in6:2 e. one will bring the message of His Love
WpI. rIV.in7:1 merely read e. of the two ideas assigned to
WpI. rIV.in7:4 Let e. word shine with the meaning God
WpI. rIV.in7:5 Let e. idea which you review that day give
WpI. rIV.in8:1 E. hour of the day, bring to your mind
WpI. rIV.in9:3 E. day of practicing, as we review, we
W-pI. 151.11:2 see, and all occurrences, e. circumstance,
W-pI. 151.13:4 Let Him evaluate e. thought that comes to
W-pI. 151.14:2 And as e. thought is thus transformed, it
W-pI. 153.15:2 will begin e. day by giving our attention to
W-pI. 153.16:1 E. hour adds to our increasing peace, as
W-pI. 153.19:5 We call upon His strength e. time we feel
W-pI. 155.14:1 but that you think of Him a while e. day,
W-pI. 158.10:5 E. brother whom you meet today provides
W-pI...159.4:2 source, remaining with e. miracle you give
W-pI...162.3:3 what he receives e. time he practices the
W-pI. 166.11:4 He points to all the gifts you have e. time
W-pI...169.8:2 to all minds that e. one might determine,
W-pI. 169.11:5 salvation comes a little nearer e. uncertain
WpI...rV.in4:2 E. one but clarifies some aspect of this
WpI...rV.in7:1 My resurrection comes again e. time I
WpI...rV.in7:2 I am renewed e. time a brother learns
WpI...rV.in7:3 pain. I am reborn e. time a brother's mind
WpI.rV.in11:1 With this we start e. day of our review.
WpI.rV.in11:2 we start and end e. period of practice time
Wi181-200 3:4 go past all defenses for a little while e. day
W-pI...181.7:3 e. obstruction seems to block the vision of
W-pI. 182.10:1 Christ is reborn as but a little Child e.
W-pI...184.1:3 you see. E. one becomes a separate entity,
W-pI. 184.10:1 Thus what you need are intervals e. day
W-pI. 184.14:1 for e. awareness of an aspect of God's Son
W-pI...185.3:4 To e., the hero of the dream is different;
W-pI...185.4:8 e. to his gain and to another's loss.
W-pI...185.6:2 a form e. mind that seeks for it in honesty
W-pI. 186.11:1 the sun's return e. morning to dispel the
W-pI...187.5:7 for e. will have the thought in form most
W-pI...188.3:2 It pauses to caress e. living thing, and
W-pI...192.9:6 Thus does e. one who seems to tempt you
W-pI...193.3:3 E. lesson has a central thought, the same
W-pI...193.9:5 willed that laughter should replace e. one,
W-pI. 193.12:1 E. hour, spend a little time today, and in
W-pI...194.3:4 so e. instant given unto God in passing,
W-pI...194.5:3 Then is e. instant which was slave to time
W-pI...199.8:6 His Love and happiness e. time you say: *I*
W-pI...200.2:1 point to which e. one must come at last,
WpI rVI.in.1:1 this review we take but one idea e. day,
WpI rVI.in.1:3 E. of these ideas alone would be sufficient
WpI rVI.in.1:4 E. would be enough to give release to you
WpI rVI.in.2:2 lessons. E. contains the whole curriculum
WpI rVI.in.2:5 as e. contributes to the whole we learn.
WpI rVI.in.3:1 with which we start and end e. lesson. It is
WpI rVI.in.6:5 such special applications of e. day's idea,
WpI rVI.in.7:2 say and think, e. time you turn to Him.
WpI rVI.in.7:3 to you, e. time you call to Him to help you
WpI rVI.in.7:4 for the way e. practice period can best
W-pII ....in.2:6 time with Him e. morning and at night, as
W-pII ..in.11:3 thoughts should be reviewed e. day, each
W-pII ..in.11:3 e. one of them to be continued till the
W-pII . 240.1:8 fear in us, for we are e. a part of Love Itself
W-pII . 243.2:3 *one because e. part contains Your memory,*
W-pII . 260.2:3 And we who are His Sons are like e. other,
W-pII . 266.2:1 own, acknowledging our Self in e. of us;
W-pII . 267.1:5 E. heartbeat brings me peace; each breath
W-pII . 267.1:5 peace; e. breath infuses me with strength.
W-pII . 267.1:7 E. heartbeat calls His Name, and every
W-pII . 271.1:1 E. day, each hour, every instant, I am
W-pII . 271.1:1 Each day, e. hour, every instant, I am
W-pII ..... 8.2:1 for e. unhappy thought reflected in your
W-pII . 313.2:1 behold e. other in the sight of Christ. How
W-pII . 315.1:1 E. day a thousand treasures come to me
W-pII . 316.1:2 E. one allows a past mistake to go, and
W-pII . 329.2:1 our union with e. other and our Source.
W-pII . 338.1:5 and exchange e. fear thought for a happy
W-pII ... 13.3:4 E. lily of forgiveness offers all the world
W-pII ... 13.3:5 And e. is laid before the Word of God,
W-pII .... 349.h but give E. one a miracle of love instead.
W-pII . 349.1:5 *E. one that I accept gives me a miracle to give.*
W-ep ......... 5:3 for you e. time there is a choice to make.
W-ep ......... 5:4 e. choice you make brings Heaven nearer
M-1 ......... 2:12 E. one begins as a single light, but with
M-1 ......... 2:13 And e. one saves a thousand years of time
M-2 ........... 1:1 have been assigned to e. of God's teachers
M-2 ........... 4:3 finding e. other as if they had not met
M-2 ........... 5:5 e. one learns that giving and receiving are
M-3 ........... 1:2 E. teaching-learning situation involves a
M-3 ........... 1:5 contacts to be made for e. teacher of God.
M-3 ........... 1:8 relationship. They are ready for e. other.
M-3 ........... 2:4 E. of them has the potential for becoming
M-3 ........... 4:1 E. teaching-learning situation is maximal
M-3 ........... 4:1 that e. person involved will learn the most
M-3 ........... 4:5 e. has learned the most he can at the time.
M-3 ........... 5:2 which e. person is given a chosen learning
M-3 ........... 5:5 be quite hostile to e. other for some time,
M-4 ..... I.A.7:9 not e. step in this direction so heavily
M-4 ..... IX.1:9 Yet e. degree, however small, is worth
M-8 ........... 1:2 which e. thing seen competes with every
M-8 ........... 4:3 judging where e. sense datum fits best.
M-12 ......... 2:6 how could they be separate from e. other?
M-13 ......... 5:7 places, e. time believing it is there, and
M-13 ......... 5:7 there, and e. time disappointed in the end
M-13 ......... 8:1 and remember what e. decision you make
M-15 ............ h IS E. ONE TO BE JUDGED IN THE END?
M-15 ......... 1:5 One day e. one will welcome it, and on
M-16 ......... 1:2 no program, for the lessons change e. day.
M-16 ......... 2:4 although e. one must use them as best he
M-16 ....... 10:3 E. substitute he may accept as real can but
M-16 ....... 10:8 Yet e. temptation to accept magic as true
M-17 ......... 7:3 go. E. one says clearly to your frightened
M-20 ......... 1:5 consider e. of these questions separately,
M-20 ......... 1:5 e. reflects a different step along the way.
M-25 ......... 1:3 e. individual has many abilities of which
M-29 ......... 5:9 it. Prepare for this e. morning, remember
C-5 ............ 1:4 Beyond e. one there is a Thought of God,
C-ep .......... 1:8 Behind e. one there is reality and there is
P-2...........I.1:6 perhaps e. of them will enter into another
P-2...........I.1:7 of this; e. will progress. Retrogression is
P-2...........I.4:1 e. other and to receive the peace of God.
P-2..........II.7:3 the contrary, he listens patiently to e. one,
P-2..........II.8:4 E. one must share one goal with someone
P-2....... VII.1:7 E. patient who comes to a therapist offers
P-2....... VII.1:9 to heal from e. patient who comes to him.
P-3...........I.2:1 Who, then, decides what e. brother needs
P-3..........II.4:5 need for e. other implies a sense of lack. A
P-3........II.4:11 that any two should ever give e. other.
P-3..........II.6:8 will bring as much good as e. can accept
P-3..........II.8:4 as e. goal is reached another can be dimly
P-3........II.9:10 Yet at e. meeting there is One Who says,
S-1....... IV.1:2 point, e. one must ask for different things.
S-1....... IV.4:1 a newborn chance e. time you pray. And
S-2........ III.3:4 e. occasion then will be to you another
S-3........ IV.2:3 its merciful reprieve upon e. blade of

### eager 8

T-3 ....... VI.8:6 is, however, e. to undo it, not to punish
T-6 ........ I.19:3 will be as e. to share your learning as I am
T19 .IV.A.14:2 They are as e. to return to you what they
T-28 ..... III.6:3 gone and clutch them not with e. hands,
T-29 ..... IX.4:8 But they are e. to forget that they made
W-pI .. 162.6:2 e. to unite with one like him in holiness?
W-pI 196.11:1 perceived within you, e. for your death,
M-5 .........I.1:8 powerful, e. to keep all power for Himself.

### eagerly 2

T-4 .........V.4:3 This is the belief that the ego sponsors e..
T-29 ..... III.5:2 See how e. he comes, and steps aside from

### eagerness 1

T-17 .......II.8:3 The e. of the Holy Spirit to give you this is

### eagle 2

T-20 ..... IV.4:7 Ask not the sparrow how the e. soars, for
M-4 .........I.2:2 mighty power of an e. has been given him

### eagle's 1
T19...IV.A.9:2 Can it oppose an **e.** flight, or hinder the

### ear 1
P-2........VI.3:1 The **e.** translates; it does not hear. The

### earlier 20
T-1.......VII.4:3 on these **e.** sections not to require their
T-1.......VII.4:6 However, as you study these **e.** sections,
T-2.........V.1:8 level. To amplify an **e.** statement, spirit is
T-13.........I.1:1 **E.**, I said that the Holy Spirit shares the
T-14......X.12:4 **E.** I said this course will teach you how to
T-15......III.5:1 I asked you **e.**, "Would you be hostage to
T-16......III.2:2 I said **e.**, "By their fruits ye shall know
T-19.........I.4:1 Do not overlook our **e.** statement that
T-21.....II.10:4 **E.**, we spoke of your desire to create your
T-22.........I.2:1 have heard a very similar description **e.**,
T-24......IV.4:1 **E.** I said consider not the means by which
W-pI.....10.3:3 way of repeating our **e.** statement that
W-pI.....35.5:1 the **e.** part of the mind-searching period,
WpI. rII.in.1:3 The **e.** part of each day will be devoted to
W-pI...132.9:1 A lesson **e.** repeated once must now be
W-pI.161.10:1 practice in a form we have attempted **e.**.
M-16..........5:8 If it is expedient to spend this time **e.**, at
M-16..........8:5 this occurs he will return to **e.** attempts to
S-1.........II.8:3 Prayer in its **e.** forms is an illusion,
S-1........III.2:1 The **e.** forms of prayer, at the bottom of

### early 7
W-pI.....14.3:2 The **e.** steps in this exchange, which can
W-pI.....43.4:1 as **e.** and one as late as possible in the day.
W-pI...158.2:6 yesterday evoked a theme found **e.** in the
M-4.......IV.1:8 must learn,–and fairly **e.** in his training,
M-16..........3:3 of time is an essential **e.** emphasis which,
M-16..........5:2 time should be fairly **e.** in the evening, if it
C-in............5:1 issues in the course is brief and **e.**.

### earn 3
W-pI......197.h It can be but my gratitude I **e.**.
W-pI...197.9:7 **E.** now the gratitude you have denied
W-pI...217.1:1 (197) It can be but my gratitude I **e.**. *Who*

### earned 5
T-27......II.1:10 but add to all the guilt that he has really **e.**
W-pI...126.3:3 He has not **e.** your charitable tolerance,
W-pI...195.8:6 that everything has **e.** the right to love by
W-pII.....in.4:3 faithfulness **e.** Him the invitation that He
W-ep.........4:4 He has **e.** your trust by speaking daily to

### earnest 1
W-pI...164.9:5 Practice in **e.**, and the gift is yours. Would

### earnestly 1
W-pI...122.9:2 **E.** and gladly will we seek for it today,

### earnestness 1
W-pI.153.20:1 will now begin to take the **e.** of love, to

### earning 1
T-1........I.28:1 Miracles are a way of **e.** release from fear.

### ears 31
T-9........VI.1:2 with your eyes nor hear Him with your **e.**.
T-11.......II.4:2 willingness opens your **e.** to the Voice of
T-24.......II.4:6 strain your **e.** to hear its soundless voice,
T-24.......II.5:2 language and they fall on different **e.**. To
T-24.......V.3:5 He is your eyes, your **e.**, your hands, your
T-24.......V.5:1 no eyes with which to see; no **e.** to listen,
T-24.......V.7:3 that their **e.** may hear no more the sound
T-24.....VII.9:7 **e.** with which you listen to the sounds it
T-26.........I.7:3 and make your eyes and **e.** bear witness to
T-27......III.7:1 or **e.** have heard remains to be perceived.
T-27......VI.3:2 You use its eyes to see, its **e.** to hear, and
T-28.......V.4:3 the voices that its **e.** were made to hear.
T-28.......V.4:8 Its eyes are blind; its **e.** are deaf. It can not
T-28.......V.5:3 a dream; your **e.** bear witness to illusion.
T-28.......V.5:6 For eyes and **e.** are senses without sense,
T-28.......V.5:8 Let not the body's **e.** and eyes perceive
T-29......IX.8:5 of Heaven can be heard, not with the **e.**,
W-pI.72.10:12 to close our eyes and stop our **e.**.
W-pI...127.6:3 eyes that see and **e.** that hear love's Voice.
W-pI...151.3:5 faith in what your eyes and **e.** report. You
W-pI...151.7:2 nor what his body's mouth says to your **e.**
W-pII..237.2:1 *the* **e.** *that listen to the Voice for God today.*
W-pII......3.2:6 But eyes deceive, and **e.** hear falsely. Now
W-pII..268.2:1 nor let our **e.** attend to lying tongues.
W-pII..293.2:2 *let my* **e.** *be deaf to all the hymns of gratitude*
W-pII......9.5:2 needs your eyes and **e.** and hands and feet
W-pII....14.4:2 **e.** that hear the Voice for God proclaim
M-12.........4:2 God's Voice speak through it to human **e.**
M-12.........4:3 And these **e.** will carry to the mind of the
M-18.........2:5 can speak the Word of God to listening **e.**,
M-18.........3:3 eyes now "see"; its **e.** alone can "hear." Its

### earth 111
T-1........III.2:1 "Heaven and **e.** shall pass away" means
T-1.....VII.3:13 as a single "slave" remains to walk the **e.**,
T-2.........II.7:4 is meant by "the meek shall inherit the **e.**.
T-4.........I.12:4 the **e.** because their egos are humble, and
T-5.........II.8:4 God's Will is done on **e.** as it is in Heaven.
T-5.........II.8:5 Both Heaven and **e.** are in you, because
T-5.........II.9:2 that gave me all power in Heaven and **e.**.
T-5.........V.1:4 at its disposal to side with Heaven or **e.**,
T-11.....VII.1:4 speaks of a new Heaven and a new **e.**, yet
T-11... VIII.1:7 For as Heaven and **e.** become one, even
T-12.....VII.4:7 creation, so your function on **e.** is healing.
T-12.....VII.4:8 the Holy Spirit shares His with you on **e.**.
T-13......IV.1:4 that your function on **e.** is destruction,
T-13. VIII.10:5 you do on **e.** are lifted up to Heaven and
T-14......IV.3:7 On **e.** this is your only function, and you
T-14......IV.8:5 nothing on **e.** with which it can compare,
T-14......IX.5:4 **E.** can reflect Heaven or hell; God or the
T-14.......X.2:4 on **e.** have no conception of limitlessness,
T-15.......V.7:3 nothing in Heaven or **e.** that it resembles,
T-15.......V.8:1 on **e.** has formed special relationships,
T-20......IV.5:3 him. To each who walks this **e.** in seeming
T-21......IV.7:5 it sees that Heaven has come to **e.** at last,
T-21......IV.7:6 it found a home in your relationship on **e.**
T-21......IV.7:7 And **e.** can hold no longer what has been
T-22.......in.3:7 stand, but close enough not to return to **e.**
T-22.......I.11:9 home prepared for Them as **e.** is turned
T-22.....II.12:2 time and yet beyond, immortal yet on **e.**.
T-22.....II.12:4 will, and **e.** will be as it would have it be.
T-24...VII.1:10 child of **e.** on whom such love is lavished?
T-24.....VII.6:1 The test of everything on **e.** is simply this;
T-24...VII.11:1 and both appear to walk this **e.** without a
T-25. VIII.14:2 knows, and all the Holy Spirit brings to **e.**
T-26......VI.2:3 in Whom all power in **e.** and Heaven rests
T-26......IX.4:6 to it. The bloodied **e.** is cleansed, and the
T-26......IX.6:1 The holiest of all the spots on **e.** is where
T-26......IX.7:3 No one on **e.** but offers thanks to one who
T-26.......X.5:8 denied to every living thing upon the **e.**.
T-29.......II.7:5 Yet here on **e.** it has a double purpose, for
T-29......III.4:2 On **e.** this means forgive your brother,
T-30.......II.5:2 the **e.** but must depend on your decision,
T-30......III.9:2 depend on whether it is seen on **e.** or not.
T-30......III.9:3 is as far from **e.** as earth from Heaven. It is
T-30......III.9:3 is as far from earth as **e.** from Heaven. It is
T-30......III.9:4 the time that keeps this star invisible to **e.**
T-30.......V.3:5 little longer, with his feet still touching **e.**.
T-30... VIII.2:8 in Heaven or on **e.** could ever alter. But
T-31......VI.4:4 In Heaven as on **e.** this is forever true. It
T-31......VI.7:2 if you think you are in **e.** or Heaven. What
T-31. VIII.11:5 song of thanks from **e.** to Heaven grows
W-pI.....20.3:7 power is given him in Heaven and on **e.**.
W-pI.....60.1:5 It is the reflection of God's Love on **e.**. It
W-pI.....60.2:4 to see, I recognize His reflection on **e.**. I
W-pI.....61.3:2 step in accepting your real function on **e.**.
W-pI.....64.5:8 is impossible that any decision on **e.** can
W-pI.....98.9:5 that you have on **e.** as well as Heaven. He
W-pI.....99.3:1 meeting place at all where **e.** and Heaven
W-pI...100.4:2 on **e.** calls to all minds to let their sorrows
W-pI...106.5:1 which lifts the veil that lies upon the **e.**,
W-pI...131.7:4 and **e.** the other's sorry outcome which is
W-pI.153.14:1 to play our final, happy game upon this **e.**
W-pI...159.4:3 receiver are united in extension here on **e.**
W-pI...182.4:6 to **e.** the pure reflection of the light above,
W-pI...182.4:6 wherein are **e.** and Heaven joined as one.
W-pI...183.5:2 tiny, nameless things on **e.** slip into right
W-pI.183.11:3 The little things of **e.** have disappeared.
W-pI...184.8:3 in **e.** and Heaven is beyond your naming.
W-pI...186.1:5 of God is done on **e.** as well as Heaven. It
W-pI...186.1:6 It unites all wills on **e.** in Heaven's plan to
W-pI...191.9:1 power is given unto you in **e.** and Heaven.
W-pI.191.11:8 this, and **e.** and Heaven are one.
W-pI...192.2:6 on **e.**, you need the means to let illusions
W-pI...192.3:3 Forgiveness is the closest it can come to **e.**
W-pI.192.10:6 function here on **e.** is only to forgive him,
W-pI.193.13:5 Love of God the Father down to **e.** at last,
W-pI...194.1:4 How far are we progressing now from **e.**!
W-pI...198.6:3 all joy that ever can be found upon this **e.**.
W-pI.198.10:3 both on **e.** and in your holy home as well.
W-pI.198.11:3 is there tranquil light across the face of **e.**,
W-pI...208.1:2 *be still, and let the* **e.** *be still along with me.*
W-pI...219.1:5 *And then return to* **e.**, *without confusion as*
W-pII .....2.4:5 **E.** is being born again in new perspective.
W-pII .292.1:6 For God's Will is done in **e.** and Heaven.
W-pII .320.1:4 all the strength and love in **e.** and Heaven.
W-pII ...11.4:6 only to let God's Will be done on **e.**, only
W-pII .326.1:7 *And as it is in Heaven, so on* **e.**. *Your plan I*
W-pII .326.1:8 *Heaven of Your Love, where* **e.** *will vanish,*
W-pII .326.2:1 Let us today behold **e.** disappear, at first
W-pII .344.1:6 *me gifts beyond the worth of anything on* **e.**.
W-pII .345.1:6 *But here on* **e.**, *the miracle is closer to Your*
Wfl........in.4:1 It is our function to remember Him on **e.**,
M-11.......4:10 **e.** bows down before its gracious Presence
M-23.........5:6 the symbol of his Father here on **e.**. To
M-23.........6:1 No one on **e.** can grasp what Heaven is,
M-26.........3:3 be maintained for much of the time on **e.**.
M-28.........2:7 There is no sorrow still upon the **e.**. The
M-28.........4:5 now remain on **e.** to shelter sick illusions,
C-5............5:3 little life on **e.** was not enough to teach
C-6............1:1 upon the **e.** after he ascended into Heaven
C-6............1:3 He was "called down upon the **e.**" in the
C-6............2:3 All power in Heaven and **e.** is therefore
P-2..........I.4:2 for every "patient" on the face of this **e.**,
P-2........III.4:4 and too near to God to keep his feet on **e.**.
P-2........IV.3:2 now stalk the **e.** in unrelenting waves,
P-2.......VII.6:4 understands all power in **e.** and Heaven
P-3..........II.7:5 remain on **e.** until the closing of time.
S-1..........II.7:3 of you. The things of **e.** are left behind, all
S-2..........II.8:6 glow of Heaven shining on the face of **e.**,
S-3..........II.4:1 a kind forgiveness of the ways of **e.**, can
S-3........IV.2:3 wing and all the living things upon the **e.**.
S-3........IV.2:5 of prayer rest on the **e.** an instant, as the
S-3........IV.5:8 loss become the lot of everyone on **e.**,

### earthly 9
W-pI...98.11:1 you, be thankful and lay down all **e.** tasks,
W-pI...154.6:4 Like **e.** messengers, they did not write the
W-pI...154.7:1 An **e.** messenger fulfills his role by giving
W-pI.186.14:2 Forgiveness is an **e.** form of love, which as
W-pII .303.1:3 Let **e.** sounds be quiet, and the sights to
P-1............1:4 contributions an **e.** therapist can provide.
P-1............1:5 which an **e.** patient-therapist relationship
P-3........III.1:3 has some **e.** needs while he is here. Should
S-2........III.7:3 forgiveness, nor to set it in an **e.** frame.

### ease 8
T-2..........I.5:1 which can heal any of them with equal **e.**.
T-19.......I.14:5 of healing with equal **e.** to all of them. For
T-21......III.1:5 the "fairness" you attempt to **e.** the guilt
T-25......III.6:7 can, with equal **e.** and far more happiness

T-26..... VII.6:9 all must yield with equal e. to what God
T-30..... VII.2:4 the e. with which these labels change with
T-31....... V.9:1 some lack of e. at times and some distress
W-pI....... 2.2:3 with equal e. to a body or a button, a fly

**easier** 19

T-2......... II.3:2 The means are e. to understand after the
T-4........ IV.2:6 is much e. than trying to think against it.
T-6...... V.B.9:3 step is e. than the first because it follows.
T-19...... III.6:6 e. to believe that you have been mistaken
T-23..... II.21:5 another, nor that return from one is e..
T-24.... VI.13:1 believe it e. to see your brother's body
T-25...... VI.2:3 Dimness seems better; e. to see, and
T-25...... VI.2:4 and more obscure seems e. to look upon;
T-30......... I.9:1 what could be e. than to continue with:
T-30....... I.13:1 must be clear that it is e. to have a happy
T-31......... I.2:6 confused is e. to learn and understand.
W-pI....... 8.4:2 e. to recognize that no matter how vividly
W-pI..... 39.9:1 You may find these practice periods e. if
W-pI..... 39.9:4 first. It will become much e. as your mind
W-pI..... 63.4:1 will probably find it e. to let the related
W-pI. 122.10:2 point at which the road becomes far e..
M-9 ........... 2:3 This becomes e. and easier, as the teacher
M-9 ........... 2:3 This becomes easier and e., as the teacher
M-14 ......... 3:5 e. to forgive one sin than to forgive all of

**easiest** 5

T-7........ XI.1:3 Him is therefore the e. thing in the world,
T-14....... II.5:2 learn that what seemed hardest was the e.
T-16...... V.17:1 the e. decision that ever confronted you,
W-pI... 133.8:5 Here it is e. of all to be deceived. For what
M-17 ......... 3:1 It is e. to let error be corrected where it is

**easily** 93

T-2......... V.6:6 e. brought into alignment with a mind
T-4........ IV.7:1 God and His creations is e. made if you
T-4........ VI.2:5 then so small that knowledge can e. flow
T-5........ VI.7:1 sayeth the Lord" is e. reinterpreted if you
T-6....... II.11:1 it can so e. make the idea seem difficult.
T-6......... V.3:5 is perfectly clear, e. understood and very
T-6......... V.3:5 understood and very e. remembered.
T-7......... II.1:1 elements they share, can transfer e. to it.
T-7....... VII.3:4 very e. escape from this image by leaving
T-8......... II.8:5 Awakening runs e. and gladly through the
T-12....... II.8:5 will e. accomplish the goal of perfection
T-12.... VIII.8:6 perception is e. translated into knowledge
T-13...... IX.4:6 could as e. have freed him from the past,
T-14....... in.1:4 uses logic as e. and as well as does the ego
T-14....... III.1:3 The guiltless learner learns e. because his
T-14... VII.5:15 You will see how e. all that He asks can be
T-17....... II.7:1 the Son of God is lifted e. into his home.
T-17..... V.12:1 e. forgotten if you allow time to close over
T-17...... VI.1:3 simple is merely what is e. understood,
T-18...... II.9:6 of waking is e. transferred to its reality.
T-18....... V.1:4 from which you waken e. to knowledge.
T-18....... V.2:6 and make sure that you fulfill it e.. And
T-19....... I.12:1 Faith is as e. exchanged for knowledge as
T-19....... II.6:6 is a mistake, it can be undone e. by truth.
T-19....... II.8:1 e. escaped from that its whole correction
T19. IV.A.4:12 before their coming as e. as those that you
T19... IV.A.9:4 See but how e. this little wisp is lifted up
T19.... IV.B.5:5 How e. the gates are opened from within,
T-21....... II.7:1 in holiness and vision to see it e. enough.
T-21... VII.3:12 And love is turned to hate as e.. This is no
T-22...... III.3:5 Yet reason sees through it e., because it is
T-22...... IV.7:6 and you will learn how e. your fingers slip
T-22........ V.6:6 and so e. that you must be convinced, in
T-22...... VI.3:1 of means and end so e. in what God loves,
T-22.... VI.10:6 as vulnerable, frail and e. destroyed, and
T-22.... VI.11:2 frail and e. destroyed unless his Father is?
T-23..... II.22:7 Quite e.. How do you feel? Is peace in
T-23...... IV.5:7 you the battle is not real, and e. escaped.
T-24..... VII.8:1 to teach what cannot e. be learned. Its
T-25...... VI.7:4 you made can serve salvation e. and well.
T-27....... I.6:10 life; how e. destroyed is what you love.
T-27...... IV.2:7 must be simple and be e. resolved. It
T-27 .... VII.2:6 as hurting him, and also very e. removed.
T-27 . VIII.12:3 all of them are e. undone by but a single
T-28 ..... VI.2:6 is changed, it walks as e. another way. It
T-30 ...... V.5:2 the mind has learned how e. do idols go
T-30 ... VIII.2:6 any form, because it can so e. be changed.
T-31 ....... II.5:4 Herein is life as e. as death, for what you
T-31 ... VIII.2:2 How e. is this explained! You always
W-pI....... 2.2:1 glance e. and fairly quickly around you,
W-pI..... 32.1:3 You can give it up as e. as you made it up.
W-pI..... 70.9:1 e. walk on into the light of real salvation.
W-pI..... 73.5:5 that the barrier of grievances is e. passed,
W-pI..... 74.5:3 but the difference is e. detected. If you are
W-pI... 108.6:1 it can be tried so e. and seen as true. And
W-pI... 124.2:3 How e. do errors disappear, and death
W-pI... 124.6:2 as e. as in the ones who walk beside them
W-pI. 130.10:1 Dismiss temptation e. today whenever it
W-pI. 131.13:1 and see how e. the door swings open with
W-pI... 132.2:1 Yet is salvation e. achieved, for anyone is
W-pI. 133.12:5 you make choices e. and without pain.
W-pI... 134.2:1 of what forgiveness means is e. corrected,
W-pI... 135.4:2 that is very weak and e. assaulted. It must
W-pI... 137.9:2 teach how e. salvation can be yours; how
W-pI... 161.6:3 reason bodies e. become fear's symbols.
W-pI... 164.2:1 The world fades e. away before His sight.
W-pI... 164.3:3 How e. are all your seeming sins forgot,
W-pI... 182.6:3 He is so little that He seems so e. shut out,
W-pI... 183.4:3 and see how e. you will forget the names
W-pI... 188.2:3 e. be looked upon that arguments which
W-pI... 191.7:1 Be glad today how very e. is hell undone.
W-pI... 193.4:4 and yet is recognized as e. in all of them,
W-pI. 193.12:3 of time are e. unloosened in this way. Let
W-pI... 196.4:5 seem to need a thousand years can e. be
W-pI... 197.2:1 How e. are God and guilt confused by
W-pI... 200.3:1 you can ask as e. for love, for happiness,
W-pI... 200.3:6 a door that opens e. to welcome you?
W-pII ..... 1.2:3 more obscure; less e. accessible to doubt,
W-pII . 226.2:3 *dreams, when Heaven can so e. be mine?*
W-pII . 272.2:2 Heaven can be chosen just as e. as hell,
M-4 ........ X.1:1 is e. understood when its relation to
M-8 ........... 5:4 one? Will he dismiss more e. a whispered
M-11 ......... 4:3 How e., then, is your judgment of the
M-16 ......... 2:5 they e. become gods in their own right,
M-16 ......... 4:5 One can e. sit still an hour with closed
M-16 ......... 4:6 One can as e. give God only an instant,
M-16 ......... 7:1 How simply and how e. does time slip by
M-16 ......... 9:8 is the reason it can be so e. escaped. What
M-17 ......... 2:3 be e. concealed beneath a wish to help. It
M-17 ......... 3:6 is e. responded to with just one answer,
M-23 ......... 4:7 mind. God enters e., for these are the true
C-4 ............ 4:2 e. dispelled that it can last no longer than
P-2......... in.2:6 the impossible is e. accomplished, but

**easing** 1

S-3......... in.1:1 sure, e. the pain of fear and offering the

**Easter** 9

T19. IV.D.17:4 It is almost E., the time of resurrection.
T-20 ........ I.1:3 For E. is the sign of peace, not pain. A
T-20 ........ I.2:8 them. This E. I would have the gift of your
T-20 ........ I.4:1 E. is not the celebration of the *cost* of sin,
T-20 ........ I.4:6 The time of E. is a time of joy, and not of
T-20 ........ I.4:8 For E. is the time of your salvation, along
T-20 ....... II.6:1 This E., look with different eyes upon
T-20 ..... II.8:10 The song of E. is the glad refrain the Son
T-20 ..... II.10:1 the way to Heaven and to the peace of E.,

**Eastertide** 1

W-pI. 151.16:1 Such is your E.. And so you lay the gift of

**Eastertime** 3

W-pI. 135.25:3 For this is E. in your salvation. And you
W-pI. 135.26:4 stride, and celebrate your E. with you.
W-pI. 135.26:6 *This is my E.. And I would keep it holy. I will*

**easy** 55

T-4 .......... I.8:5 of your ego but within e. reach of spirit.
T-5 ....... II.11:4 is e. and my burden light" in this way;
T-7 ....... XI.1:3 in the world, and the only thing that is e.,
T-7 ....... XI.5:7 Nothing is so e. to recognize as truth.
T-9 ...... VII.1:3 have made it possible and e. to obtain it.
T-9 ..... VIII.8:1 It is e. to distinguish grandeur from
T-11 ..... VI.3:7 Learning of Christ is e., for to perceive
T-12 ....... II.4:4 It is e. to help an uncertain child, for he
T-13 ..... III.1:2 may also think that it would be e. enough
T-14 ..... IV.6:1 all decisions become as e. and as right as
T-14 .. VII.5:10 to Him it is so e. that it was accomplished
T-15 ....... X.9:5 *just as it is*, that makes the decision so e..
T-15 ....... X.9:6 God, and therefore very e. to understand.
T-17 ....... II.2:4 and this is so little and so e. to cross, that
T-18 ....... II.9:4 which awaking is so e. and so natural. For
T-18 ..... IV.7:1 the holy instant so e. and so natural. You
T-18 ..... IV.7:7 Salvation is e. just *because* it asks nothing
T-18 ..... IV.8:1 that is natural and e. for you impossible.
T-18 ..... IX.7:1 bank it is e. to see a whole world rising. A
T-21 ..... VI.3:6 Yet it is e. to leave the home of madness if
T-22 ..... IV.7:1 e. is it to offer this miracle to everyone!
T-22 ..... VI.3:5 as e. as is the shift from hate to gratitude
T-23 ....... II.3:3 same and equally untrue, it would be e.,
T-23 ..... III.4:1 is e. just because it makes no compromise
T-27 ........ I.4:6 Death seems an e. price, if they can say,
T-27 ... VIII.8:4 e. to perceive the jest when all around you
T-29 ....... II.1:3 Why does an e. path, so clearly marked it
T-30 ........ I.8:3 and paves the way for the next e. step.
T-30 ........ V.8:1 light and e. is the step across the narrow
T-31 ........ I.1:6 it could make such an e. lesson difficult.
T-31 ........ I.2:4 in e. steps that lead you gently from one
T-31 ........ I.4:1 maintain that lessons such as these are e.?
T-31 ....... V.9:1 Spirit's lesson plans arranged in e. steps,
W-pI .... 41.8:2 In fact it is very e., because it is the most
W-pI .... 44.4:3 e. one in the world for the trained mind,
W-pI .... 48.1:4 It is very e. to recognize this. But it is very
W-pI .... 68.5:2 Some of these will be quite e. to find.
W-pI .... 91.4:4 makes all miracles within your e. reach,
W-pI .. 109.7:3 the road that suddenly seems e. as they go
W-pI 133.12:2 obtain. Choosing is e. just because of this.
W-pI .. 135.4:3 must be something made e. prey, unable
W-pI 135.14:1 not e. to perceive that self-initiated plans
W-pI .. 160.2:3 And yet, how e. it would be to say, "This
W-pI .. 196.8:1 Our next steps will be e., if you take this
W-pI .. 200.8:4 Now the way is e., sloping gently toward
W-pII . 296.2:2 of e. reach and quick accomplishment.
W-pII . 296.2:3 us, to seek and find the e. path to God.
M-4 ..... I.A.6:8 And how e. to do! The teacher of God
M-4 ..... I.A.8:6 here, the way to Heaven is open and e.. In
M-4 ...... IV.2:2 that the function of salvation becomes e..
M-14 ......... 4:7 He does not judge it either as hard or e..
M-25 .......... 5:5 wish to be deceived, deception is made e..
S-1........ III.3:3 here it will be an e. step to the next levels.
S-1........ III.6:1 is not e. to realize that prayers for things,
S-2......... in.1:1 to make its rising e. and its progress swift.

**eaten** 1

T-3 ...... VII.3:5 forbidden it, or it could not have *been* e.. If

**eating** 1

T-3 ...... VII.4:1 E. of the fruit of the tree of knowledge is a

**eccentric** 1

W-pI .. 134.1:2 forgiveness must be seen as mere e. folly,

**eccentricity** 1

W-pI .. 126.5:2 It is an e., in which you sometimes choose

**echo** 12

T-17 ..... V.10:1 freedom heard, in joyous e. of your choice
T-18 ....... I.12:2 Their call is but an e. of the original error
T-26 ....... V.7:2 Is any e. from the past that he may hear a
T-31 . VIII.10:7 Salvation's song will e. through the world

T-7......VIII.5:6 all their e. will vanish from your mind and
T-9........IV.5:5 Holy Spirit the e. of error are nonexistent.
T-9........IV.5:6 and consistently cancelling out all its e.,
T-9.........V.4:3 attempts to dispel its e. by depreciating
T-9.........V.7:9 Its e. assure him it is there.
T-9........VI.1:1 of the Holy Spirit in you except by His e.?
T-11.......V.2:4 You are also learning that its e. can be
T-11.......V.2:5 that what has no e. does not exist. Laws
T-11.......V.4:2 cannot have any e. if its source is not real.
T-12.......V.3:1 that your attack on yourself has no e.. For
T-12......VII.2:3 if you see its e. you know it must be there.
T-14......III.9:4 Son can be separate or isolated in its e..
T-14....III.15:4 cannot happen can have no e. to fear. Be
T-14.......V.7:4 from the e. of this most holy lesson, which
T-14......XI.3:2 accomplished before its e. are manifest.
T-14......XI.7:8 the e. that only guiltlessness can bring,
T-14....XI.13:1 the e. of understanding are with them,
T-14....XI.15:4 of e. so powerful they could not be of you.
T-16......III.2:8 spoke for the cause of truth and its e..
T-16......IV.3:1 is an attempt to limit the destructive e. of
T-17.....V.12:6 instant, but to make it powerless in its e..
T-17.....V.15:1 will also accept the e. of the holy instant
T19... IV.A.9:3 Can it interfere with the e. of summer's
T-20.....VII.4:3 the result of letting the e. of sin be lifted,
T-20....VIII.2:5 As it was given you, so will be its e.. And
T-21.......II.2:7 and all e. of your mistakes will disappear.
T-21.....II.10:7 he seems to *be* the cause, producing real e..
T-21.....II.10:8 Nothing can have e. without a cause, and
T-21.....II.13:4 All its e. are gone, because its source has
T-21......III.2:3 imagine that you still experience its e., but
T-21.....VII.7:6 decision leads to its e. is not your problem
T-21.....VII.8:3 as you look on the e. of sin in any form, all
T-22.......in.1:7 the e. of what you both believed and saw.
T-22.....II.13:3 be released entirely from all e. of sin.
T-24......IV.3:5 the mind, and its e. are felt but where it is.
T-25......IV.2:4 that makes it what it is in its e. on you.
T-25......IV.2:5 chose it as a means to gain these same e.,
T-25......VI.2:1 to the dim e. perceived at twilight. And
T-25..VIII.14:1 complete deliverance from all e. of sin,
T-25......IX.1:3 you willing to be released from all e. of sin
T-26......VII.4:7 their e. but seem to be apart from them.
T-26.....VII.5:1 only there can its e. be utterly undone and
T-26.....VII.8:3 Illusions have no witnesses and no e..
T-26...VII.12:7 E. are seen as separate from their source,
T-26...VII.14:2 cause can merely shift e. to other forms.
T-26...VII.14:6 in its e. as is the whole idea of sacrifice. If
T-26...VII.17:3 So is attack deprived of its e., and hate is
T-26....VIII.3:2 is made yours and its e. will come to you.
T-26....VIII.4:6 now? A future cause as yet has no e.. And
T-26....VIII.5:3 Who can predict e. without a cause? And
T-26....VIII.5:4 fear e. unless he thought they had been
T-26....VIII.5:6 if its e. already have been judged as fearful
T-26....VIII.6:3 has in it all e. that you will see. They can
T-26....VIII.7:4 Why are not its e. apparent, then? Why in
T-26....VIII.9:6 the "reasoning" that would maintain e. of
T-26.......X.2:6 and cannot have e. of any kind. Their
T-27.........I.5:7 was ever done, or ever had e. of any kind.
T-27.......II.4:5 because they would entail e. that cannot
T-27.......II.7:6 a vain imagining, a foolish wish with no e.
T-27......IV.1:6 at all, for conflict has no limited e.. Yet if
T-27.......V.3:3 and demonstrates that war has no e.. For
T-27.....V.11:5 Your healing will be one of its e., as will
T-27.....V.11:6 you go, will you behold its multiplied e..
T-27......VI.5:2 proves that what they represent has no e..
T-27......VI.5:3 its own e. have come to take their place. It
T-27......VI.5:8 can deny, for it is the e. of life it brings.
T-27......VI.8:2 all sin if you but carry its e. with you. And
T-27.....VII.5:4 be changed by seeing it apart from its e..
T-27.....VII.5:5 The cause produces the e., which then
T-27.....VII.5:6 Look, then, beyond e.. It is not here the
T-27...VII.11:2 Who could be free to choose between e.,
T-27....VIII.4:5 as they are they have no more e. on him,
T-27....VIII.4:5 he understands he gave them their e. by
T-27....VIII.5:1 How willing are you to escape e. of all the
T-27....VIII.6:3 of both accomplishment and real e..
T-27....VIII.8:5 do its e. seem serious and sad indeed. Yet
T-27....VIII.9:1 perceive the cause, and looks not to e..
T-27....VIII.9:4 *You* judge e., but *He* has judged their cause
T-27....VIII.9:5 And by His judgment are e. removed.
T-28 ........I.1:5 in memory appears to have immediate e..
T-28 ........I.1:8 is gone, and what has truly gone has no e..
T-28 ........I.1:9 produce illusions of its presence, not e..
T-28 ........I.2:1 All the e. of guilt are here no more. For
T-28 ........I.2:4 to it in memory if you did not desire its e.
T-28 ........I.5:9 do their e. appear to be increased by time,
T-28 ........I.7:7 instead, the new e. of cause accepted *now*,
T-28 ........I.9:3 that were causeless and could never be e..
T-28 ......I.14:2 has made is causeless, having no e. at all.
T-28 .......II.1:1 Without a cause there can be no e., and
T-28 .......II.1:1 and yet without e. there is no cause. The
T-28 .......II.1:2 The cause a cause is *made* by its e.; the
T-28 .......II.1:3 Son. E. do not create their cause, but they
T-28 .......II.2:7 is. The body can be healed by its e., which
T-28 .....II.2:10 Only where its cause is given its e.. For
T-28 .....II.2:11 attempt to give e. to causelessness, and
T-28 .......II.3:5 is given no e. and none is seen. A mind
T-28 .......II.3:6 mind, creating with e. unlike yourself.
T-28 .......II.6:5 a dream, but never will you give it real e..
T-28 .......II.6:8 without a stable cause with guaranteed e..
T-28 .......II.7:8 As victim, he is suffering from its e., but
T-28 .....II.10:2 and shows you its e. are what you want. In
T-28 .....II.10:3 In His forgiving dreams are the e. of yours
T-28 .....II.10:5 hate, because you see that it has no e..
T-28 .....II.11:2 it also shows that, having no e., it is not
T-28 .....II.11:2 the function of causation is to have e..
T-28 .....II.11:3 And where e. are gone, there is no cause.
T-28 .....II.11:7 out its guilt caused nothing, and had no e.
T-28 .....II.12:4 glad e. of taking back the consequence of
T-28 ..... III.1:7 the dream will fade away without e.. For it
T-28 ..... III.2:5 the cause of sickness and perceived e..
T-28 ..... III.6:3 not. Let its e. be gone and clutch them not
T-28 ..... IV.1:4 Thus have they no e.. And you are free of
T-28 ..... IV.2:3 them as causing you, and giving you e..
T-28 ... IV.10:4 be a loss, and what is not of Him has no e.
T-28 ...... V.4:9 It can not think, and so it cannot have e..
T-28 ..... VI.5:3 agree that is your wish, it can have no e..
T-29 .......II.2:7 And its e. are there, though not yet seen.
T-29 .......II.3:4 Where they are causeless their e. are gone,
T-29 .......II.3:6 and loss, and all e. of hatred and attack.
T-29 .......II.3:7 and you should welcome the e. of love.
T-30 ......I.17:3 and gives it all e. that it will ever have. It
T-30 ..... IV.5:7 by a power that can have no real e. at all?
T-30 ... VI.10:2 mistakes that have been given no e.. But
T-30 ...VIII.2:8 and has no e. that anything in Heaven or
T-31 ........I.1:3 has not occurred, and can have no e.. And
W-pI........18.h alone in experiencing the e. of my seeing.
W-pI.....18.3:2 *not alone in experiencing the e. of how I see*
W-pI.....18.3:4 *not alone in experiencing the e. of my seeing.*
W-pI........19.h in experiencing the e. of my thoughts.
W-pI.....19.3:4 *in experiencing the e. of this thought about*
W-pI.....23.7:2 Their e. are exactly the same because they
W-pI.....26.1:4 e. through you must also have effects on
W-pI.....26.1:4 through you must also have e. on you. It is
W-pI.....41.2:3 e. cannot be cured because the problem is
W-pI.....53.3:8 I will escape all the e. of the world of fear,
W-pI.....53.4:5 from the e. of my own insane thoughts,
W-pI.....54.1:4 But thoughts cannot be without e.. As the
W-pI.....54.3:1 alone in experiencing the e. of my seeing.
W-pI.....54.4:1 in experiencing the e. of my thoughts. I
W-pI.....88.3:7 I am perfectly free of the e. of all laws save
W-pI... 132.1:4 are as strong in their e. as is the truth. A
W-pI... 132.1:6 be swayed by questioning his thoughts' e..
W-pI... 138.9:5 Now are they without e.. They cannot be
W-pI... 158.9:6 And all e. they seemed to have are gone
W-pI... 166.2:3 leads to opposite e. from those He wills.
W-pI... 169.4:3 mind that recognizes truth's e. on you.
W-pI... 184.7:3 results, the sooner does he question its e..
W-pI. 184.15:5 *from all e. our errors seemed to have. And we*
W-pI... 190.6:2 It has no e. at all. It merely represents
W-pI... 190.7:3 As an effect, it cannot make e.. As an
W-pI... 198.1:5 Then does illusion cease to have e., and
W-pI... 198.2:6 and its e. have not occurred at all. Yet
W-pII ......3.1:5 has gone, and its e. are gone as well.
W-pII . 293.1:4 love is obvious, and its e. apparent. All
W-pII . 309.1:6 Yet it has no e.. Within me is the Holiness
W-pII ... 10.3:1 them, and all e. they ever seemed to have.
W-pII . 314.1:3 its images, and being formless, it has no e.
W-pII . 326.1:8 *that You will gather Your e. into the tranquil*
W-pII . 359.1:6 *made mistakes which have no real e. on us.*
M-5 ........II.4:9 also go all the e. they seemed to cause.
M-10 ......... 3:4 to recognize in advance all the e. of his
M-10 ......... 4:9 He does know all the e. of His judgment
M-10 ......... 6:9 were but the e. of his mistaken choice,
M-16 ......... 9:4 They can have no e.; neither good nor bad
M-16 ......... 9:9 What has no e. can hardly terrify.
C-2 ............ 5:3 do, and cause and its e. must still be one.
C-5 ............ 4:1 forgiven because they carried no e. at all.
P-1............. 4:2 what he thought projected its e. on him
P-2....... VII.5:4 and of all the e. that may occur in them.
S-1........ IV.2:6 realize that you are asking for e. without
S-1........ IV.2:8 For no one can receive e. alone, asking a
S-3..........II.1:5 But the cause remains, and will not lack e.

## efficacy 4

T-2 ....... IV.5:3 means that a miracle, to attain its full e.,
T-3 ..... VI.5:10 the e. of judgment as a weapon of defense
T-5 .......V.7:12 a remedy whose e. is beyond doubt, how
W-in.......... 9:3 of this will matter, or decrease their e..

## effort 66

T-1 ....... III.4:4 This spares you needless e., because you
T-2 ....... III.5:3 do not involve any e. at all on their part.
T-2 ....... VI.6:1 under my guidance without conscious e.,
T-3 ........I.3:11 I have made every e. to use words that are
T-3 .........V.2:7 wasted e. even in its most ingenious form.
T-4 .........II.5:5 agreed to cooperate in the e. to become
T-4 .......II.8:10 creative e. can be turned to mythology. It
T-4 ....... IV.7:2 including yourself, is worth consistent e..
T-4 .......V.6:11 have made a decision about your future e.
T-5 .......II.3:10 It takes e. and great willingness to learn.
T-6 ... V.C.10:4 Vigilance does require e., but only until
T-6 ... V.C.10:4 until you learn that e. itself is unnecessary
T-6 ... V.C.10:5 have exerted great e. to preserve what you
T-6 ... V.C.10:6 you must now turn your e. against it.
T-6 ... V.C.10:7 it. Only this can cancel out the need for e.,
T-6 ... V.C.10:8 recognition is wholly without e. since it is
T-7 ....... IV.3:5 All you need do is make the e. to learn, for
T-7 ....... IV.3:5 Holy Spirit has a unified goal for the e.. If
T-8 ....... IX.6:5 even though it makes every e. to induce it.
T-9 ..........I.3:8 He is merely making every possible e.,
T-9 .....VIII.4:5 The ego will make every e. to recover and
T-11 .......V.4:3 which is so clearly senseless that any e. on
T-11 .......V.9:2 not its undoing, is the ego's constant e.,
T-12 .........I.3:2 it requires no e. at all on your part. Every
T-14 ... III.10:8 and gives them what they want without e.
T-14 ..... IV.6:2 There is no e., and you will be led as
T-14 .......V.6:4 Each e. made on its behalf is offered for
T-14 ..... VI.6:4 Yet even this strange and twisted e. to
T-15 ..... III.4:8 of God will support every e. you make on
T-16 ..... III.8:3 some little e. on behalf of bridging it. His
T-17 ..... VI.4:2 will therefore make every e. to overlook
T-18 ..... VII.4:8 Enormous e. is expended in the attempt
T-18 ..... VII.7:3 which you slip past centuries of e., and
T-20 ..... IV.8:4 will not arrange for you without your e..
T-24 ... VI.11:4 and e. that you never thought to cease.
T-24 ... VI.12:1 vigilance; with little e. and with little time
T-24 .... VII.1:6 No e. is too great, no cost too much, no
T-28 .........I.3:1 represents an e. to do anything at all. It is
W-in............ 7:2 This will require no e. on your part. The
W-pI .... 11.2:4 haste, and with no sense of urgency or e..
W-pI .... 20.1:2 them, minimal e. has been required, and
W-pI .... 20.2:2 it as an e. to exert force or pressure. You
W-pI .... 20.3:3 Do not mistake the little e. that is asked of
W-pI .... 20.5:2 to do so, but make a real e. to remember.
W-pI .... 27.4:6 you have saved yourself many years of e..
W-pI .... 35.8:3 nothing should be "dug out" with e..
W-pI .... 40.3:1 Today's exercises take little time and no e.
W-pI .... 41.6:4 Then make no e. to think of anything. Try
W-pI .... 50.4:5 without e. and in sure confidence. Tell
W-pI .... 65.6:2 not strain or make undue e. in doing this.
W-pI .... 67.1:6 We will make every e. today to reach this
W-pI .... 69.7:2 Your little e. and small determination call
W-pI .... 94.5:8 every e. to do the hourly exercises today.
W-pI .... 96.2:2 series of expenditures of time and e.,
W-pI .... 97.4:3 strength to every little e. that you make.

W-pI.133.12:1 or not worth the slightest **e.** to obtain.
W-pI...134.3:2 in an unfounded **e.** to deceive yourself by
W-pI...138.3:2 the aim of **e.** and expenditure of time.
W-pI...138.3:3 time is but a waste and **e.** dissipated. It is
W-pI.155.12:3 be holier, or more deserving of your **e.**, of
WpI.. rV.in1:2 time we are ready to give more **e.** and
WpI.. rV.in8:3 we devote our time and **e.** to them. And
W-pI...194.6:1 to give as much consistent **e.** as you can,
M-4...... X.2:11 makes no **e.** to exceed its legitimate goal.
M-7............2:2 this, he should not repeat his previous **e.**.
P-2......... V.7:2 In time no **e.** can be made in vain. It is not

## effortless 2

T-24.... VI.13:7 the means for **e.** accomplishment and rest
W-pI.....16.6:1 if you find them relatively **e.**. If strain is

## effortlessly 2

W-pI.....36.4:2 slowly, as **e.** and unhurriedly as possible.
W-pI.131.14:2 day, and through His aid slip **e.** past it, to

## efforts 20

T-1........IV.2:2 exert enormous **e.** to establish its reality.
T-4....... V.6:10 it is, it will direct your **e.** automatically.
T-7........ III.1:2 He maximizes all **e.** and all results. By
T-14....... V.7:1 Join your own **e.** to the power that cannot
T-16...... III.8:4 His little **e.** are powerfully supplemented
T-17..... V.11:3 also made enormous **e.** to help Him do
T-17..... V.11:7 you consistently appreciated the good **e.**,
W-pI.....42.1:2 in your **e.** to achieve the goal of the course
W-pI.....71.4:3 your **e.** in searching for it where it is not?
W-pI.....79.9:3 **e.** will be directed toward recognizing
W-pI.....91.4:1 Your **e.**, however little they may be, have
W-pI...91.10:1 the practice period, confident that your **e.**
WpI . rIII.in2:3 necessary that you make excessive **e.** to be
W-pI.186.10:3 Who could be constant in his **e.**, or direct
W-pII.....4.2:1 the mind made in its **e.** to deceive itself.
W-ep .........3:3 He will direct your **e.**, telling you exactly
M-15..........3:1 best **e.** meet with lack of appreciation and
M-25..........1:6 he is. Let all his learning and all his **e.** be
M-29..........8:7 *for you, And join your* **e.** *on behalf of God,*
P-2........ VI.4:9 To concentrate your healing **e.** here is but

## ego 930

*See also* ego-alien, ego-based, ego-body, ego-directed, ego-oriented

T-2......... II.2:5 in miscreation, the projections of the **e.**.
T-3...........IV.h Error and the **E.**
T-3........ IV.2:2 identified as the domain of the **e.**. The ego
T-3........ IV.2:3 **e.** is a wrong-minded attempt to perceive
T-3........ IV.3:1 The **e.** is the questioning aspect of the
T-3......... V.2:5 **e.** has invented many ingenious thought
T-3........ VI.7:4 Every symptom the **e.** makes involves a
T-3........ VI.7:4 is split between the **e.** and the Holy Spirit,
T-3........ VI.7:4 whatever the **e.** makes is incomplete and
T-4................h THE ILLUSIONS OF THE **E.**
T-4.........in.2:1 can speak from the spirit or from the **e.**,
T-4.........in.2:4 you speak from the **e.** you are disclaiming
T-4.........in.2:6 The **e.** may desire them, but spirit cannot
T-4.........in.3:5 the futile attempts of the **e.** at reparation,
T-4...........I.2:4 to enter into your **e.** you will find peace.
T-4...........I.2:6 Nothing can reach spirit from the **e.**, and
T-4...........I.2:6 and nothing can reach the **e.** from spirit.
T-4...........I.2:7 the **e.** nor reduce the conflict within it.
T-4...........I.2:8 it. The **e.** *is* a contradiction. Your self and
T-4........ I.2:11 cannot perceive and the **e.** cannot know.
T-4........ I.2:13 Nevertheless, the **e.** can learn, even
T-4...........I.3:1 need not be taught, but the **e.** must be.
T-4...........I.3:2 destruction, of the **e.** to the light of spirit.
T-4...........I.3:3 spirit. This is the change the **e.** must fear,
T-4...........I.3:5 I will never attack your **e.**, but I am trying
T-4...........I.3:6 your **e.** cannot but respond with fear.
T-4...........I.4:4 dream of a separated **e.** and believe in a
T-4...........I.5:3 It is impossible to convince the **e.** of this,
T-4...........I.5:5 is natural for the **e.** to try to protect itself
T-4...........I.5:6 The **e.** cannot make this choice because of
T-4...........I.6:2 as merely "a larger **e.**" you will be afraid,
T-4...........I.6:2 enlarge an **e.** would be to increase anxiety
T-4...........I.6:5 with the effect of his **e.** on other egos, and
T-4...........I.6:5 interaction as a means of **e.** preservation.
T-4...........I.7:8 Your **e.** is never at stake because God did
T-4...........I.8:1 **e.** tries to exploit all situations into forms
T-4...........I.8:5 of your **e.** but within easy reach of spirit.
T-4...........I.8:7 Do not let your **e.** dispute this, because
T-4...........I.8:7 because the **e.** cannot know what is as far
T-4...........I.9:6 Your **e.** has chosen to be afraid instead of
T-4.........I.9:10 The word "inevitable" is fearful to the **e.**,
T-4.........I.10:1 The **e.** is afraid of the spirit's joy, because
T-4.........I.10:1 will withdraw all protection from the **e.**,
T-4.........I.10:2 your **e.** rejoices when you witness to it.
T-4.........I.11:1 **e.** has built a shabby and unsheltering
T-4.........I.11:7 the perishable as the **e.** is of making the
T-4.........I.12:1 **e.** you can do nothing to save yourself or
T-4.........I.12:2 Humility is a lesson for the **e.**, not for the
T-4.........I.13:1 I will substitute for your **e.** if you wish,
T-4.........I.13:3 can protect the child's body and his **e.**,
T-4.........I.13:4 and your **e.** only because this enables you
T-4............ II.h The **E.** and False Autonomy
T-4......... II.1:1 the mind could ever have made the **e.**. In
T-4......... II.2:1 Everyone makes an **e.** or a self for himself
T-4......... II.2:2 makes an **e.** for everyone else he perceives
T-4......... II.2:5 Thinking about another **e.** is as effective
T-4......... II.2:6 that the **e.** is only an idea and not a fact.
T-4......... II.3:1 is a good example of how the **e.** was made
T-4......... II.4:4 your **e.** much as God does to His creations
T-4......... II.4:7 question is not how you respond to the **e.**,
T-4......... II.4:8 are. Belief is an **e.** function, and as long as
T-4......... II.4:8 you are regarding it from an **e.** viewpoint.
T-4....... II.4:10 idea of which **e.** thinking is capable. That
T-4....... II.4:11 of recognition that the **e.** is not the Self.
T-4......... II.6:3 To the **e.**, to give anything implies that
T-4......... II.6:5 to get" is an inescapable law of the **e.**,
T-4......... II.6:8 "Self-esteem" in **e.** terms means nothing
T-4......... II.6:8 the **e.** has deluded itself into accepting its
T-4......... II.7:1 The **e.** literally lives by comparisons.
T-4......... II.7:3 The **e.** never gives out of abundance,
T-4......... II.7:6 as it is of the so-called "higher **e.** needs."
T-4......... II.7:8 The **e.** regards the body as its home, and
T-4......... II.8:1 The **e.** believes it is completely on its own
T-4......... II.8:4 **e.** is the mind's belief that it is completely
T-4......... II.8:6 in its knowledge is unaware of the **e.**. It
T-4......... II.8:8 While the **e.** is equally unaware of spirit,
T-4......... II.8:9 self-esteem in **e.** terms must be delusional
T-4......... II.9:1 myths are usually related to **e.** origins,
T-4......... II.9:1 and magic to the powers the **e.** ascribes to
T-4......... II.9:4 to maintain that the **e.** existed before that
T-4......... II.9:5 to exist after a temporary lapse into **e.** life.
T-4....... II.10:3 The **e.** cannot survive without judgment,
T-4........ III.1:2 because it is not understandable to the **e.**,
T-4...... III.1:10 **e.** and your spirit will never be co-creators
T-4...... III.1:12 *and the* **e.** *will not prevail against it. Amen.*
T-4........ III.2:5 the **e.** has set up and can shine into your
T-4........ III.2:6 our united strength the **e.** cannot prevail.
T-4........ III.3:1 why the **e.** regards spirit as its "enemy."
T-4........ III.3:2 The **e.** arose from the separation, and its
T-4........ III.3:3 The **e.** must offer you some sort of reward
T-4........ III.3:7 of this can ever fully believe in the **e.** again
T-4........ III.4:1 with your **e.** cannot believe God loves you
T-4........ III.4:3 the **e.** has no allegiance to its maker. You
T-4........ III.4:5 onto the **e.** the decision to separate, and
T-4........ III.4:5 you feel for the **e.** because you made it.
T-4........ III.4:6 since no **e.** has experienced love without
T-4........ III.5:1 the **e.** can offer that you will never want to
T-4........ III.5:4 is not a condition as the **e.** sets conditions
T-4........ III.9:1 your own mind, though denied by the **e.**,
T-4........ III.9:3 This one fact means the **e.** does not exist,
T-4...... III.10:1 from the part of the mind the **e.** rules. The
T-4...... III.10:2 **e.** is desperate because it opposes literally
T-4...... III.10:3 been willing to exert to protect your **e.**,
T-4........ IV.1:2 your **e.** is demonstrated by your attitudes,
T-4........ IV.1:5 with schemes to save the face of your **e.**,
T-4........ IV.1:6 glass in which the **e.** seeks to see its face is
T-4........ IV.2:3 images your **e.** makes in a darkened glass.
T-4........ IV.2:8 otherwise has held your **e.** together, but
T-4........ IV.4:1 comes from the capriciousness of the **e.**,
T-4........ IV.5:1 the **e.** has indeed violated the laws of God,
T-4........ IV.5:2 Leave the "sins" of the **e.** to me. That is
T-4........ IV.5:4 mind about those whom your **e.** has hurt,
T-4........ IV.5:5 you feel guilty your **e.** is in command,
T-4........ IV.5:5 because only the **e.** can experience guilt.
T-4........ IV.6:1 your mind for the temptations of the **e.**,
T-4........ IV.6:4 demands of the **e.** to disengage yourself.
T-4........ IV.7:4 to me, but only the **e.** can *be* disheartened.
T-4........ IV.8:3 mine can unite in shining your **e.** away,
T-4........ IV.8:8 The **e.** *should* be brought to judgment and
T-4........ IV.8:9 protection and love, the **e.** cannot exist.
T-4........ IV.9:6 Your **e.** cannot prevent Him from shining
T-4...... IV.10:6 I assure you this is a mistake of your **e.**.
T-4...... IV.10:8 Your **e.** is trying to convince you that it is
T-4...... IV.11:1 I do not attack your **e.**. I do work with
T-4...... IV.11:2 just as your **e.** does with your lower mind,
T-4......... V.1:3 **e.** exerts maximal vigilance about what it
T-4......... V.1:4 **e.** is thrown further off balance because it
T-4......... V.1:5 **e.** has every reason to do this, according
T-4......... V.1:6 would inevitably judge against the **e.**, and
T-4......... V.1:6 and must be obliterated by the **e.** in the
T-4......... V.2:2 of God are unacceptable to the **e.**, because
T-4......... V.2:2 point to the nonexistence of the **e.** itself.
T-4......... V.2:3 The **e.** therefore either distorts them or
T-4......... V.2:6 threat, the **e.** perceives them as the same.
T-4......... V.2:7 **e.** attempts to save itself from being swept
T-4......... V.3:2 Yet this confusion is essential to the **e.**,
T-4......... V.3:3 since the idea of Him does dispel the **e.**.
T-4......... V.3:4 with which the **e.** identifies so closely,
T-4......... V.4:2 identification with which the **e.** feels safe,
T-4......... V.4:3 is the belief that the **e.** sponsors eagerly.
T-4......... V.4:4 the **e.** hates the body, because it cannot
T-4......... V.4:6 Being told by the **e.** that it is really part of
T-4......... V.4:7 go for protection?" to which the **e.** replies,
T-4......... V.4:8 reminds the **e.** that it has itself insisted
T-4......... V.4:9 The **e.** has no real answer to this because
T-4......... V.6:1 **e.** thinks it is an advantage not to commit
T-4......... V.6:2 Eternalness is the one function the **e.** has
T-4......... V.6:3 The **e.** compromises with the issue of the
T-4......... V.6:6 **e.** devices for impeding learning progress.
T-4........ VI.1:1 The **e.** does not recognize the real source
T-4........ VI.1:1 and if you associate yourself with the **e.**,
T-4........ VI.1:2 Only your allegiance to it gives the **e.** any
T-4........ VI.1:3 you. I have spoken of the **e.** as if it were a
T-4........ VI.1:6 The **e.** is nothing more than a part of your
T-4........ VI.3:1 to me instead of to your **e.** for guidance.
T-4........ VI.3:4 pain, because pain is an **e.** illusion, and
T-4........ VI.3:6 recognition is made by you and not the **e.**,
T-4........ VI.3:6 that you and your **e.** cannot be identical.
T-4........ VI.3:8 you must escape from the **e.** shows this;
T-4........ VI.3:8 escape from the **e.** by humbling it or
T-4........ VI.4:1 **e.** and the spirit do not know each other.
T-4........ VI.4:3 not because the **e.** is a separate thing, but
T-4........ VI.4:4 **e.** is a device for maintaining this belief,
T-4........ VI.5:6 misery with the **e.** and joy with the spirit.
T-4........ VI.5:8 really want the rewards of the **e.** in the
T-4........ VI.6:3 as to demonstrate that you are not an **e.**,
T-4....... VII.1:1 any particular **e.** illusion does not matter,
T-4....... VII.1:2 **E.** illusions are quite specific, although
T-4....... VII.1:4 splits. The concrete part believes in the **e.**,
T-4....... VII.1:4 because the **e.** depends on the concrete.
T-4....... VII.1:5 The **e.** is the part of the mind that believes
T-4....... VII.2:1 Everything the **e.** perceives is a separate
T-4....... VII.2:2 The **e.** is thus against communication,
T-4....... VII.2:3 the **e.** is based on its own thought system,
T-4....... VII.6:3 has no **e.** with which to accept such praise
T-5.........I.1:14 belief in the false association the **e.** makes
T-5..........II.3:2 When the **e.** was made, God placed in the
T-5..........II.3:3 that the **e.** always dissolves at Its sound.
T-5........ III.4:6 an ego-alien journey with the **e.** as guide.
T-5........ III.5:1 Delay is of the **e.**, because time is its
T-5........ III.5:3 the Holy Spirit is God's Answer to the **e.**.
T-5........ III.5:5 the task of undoing what the **e.** has made.
T-5........ III.5:6 at the same level on which the **e.** operates,
T-5........ III.6:2 So it is with the **e.** and the Holy Spirit;
T-5........ III.6:4 Time is a belief of the **e.**, so the lower
T-5........ III.7:1 of the **e.** and the knowledge of the spirit.
T-5........ III.7:4 of reinterpreting what the **e.** makes, not
T-5........ III.8:6 This vision frightens the **e.** because it is so

T-5........ III.8:8 The **e.** becomes strong in strife. If you
T-5....... III.8:10 The idea itself is an appeal to the **e.**. The
T-5....... III.8:11 is as vigilant as the **e.** to the call of danger,
T-5....... III.8:11 His strength just as the **e.** welcomes it.
T-5........ III.9:4 The **e.** is the symbol of separation, just as
T-5....... III.10:4 part, it is still much stronger than the **e.**,
T-5....... III.10:4 ego, although the **e.** does not recognize it.
T-5....... III.11:1 The **e.** made the world as it perceives it,
T-5....... III.11:1 the reinterpreter of what the **e.** made, sees
T-5....... IV.1:10 **e.** cannot prevail against the Kingdom
T-5....... IV.1:11 be as one, the **e.** fades away and is undone
T-5........ IV.2:1 What the **e.** makes it keeps to itself, and
T-5....... IV.2:13 cannot be limited to the self the **e.** sees.
T-5........ IV.3:4 **e.** can keep you in exile from the Kingdom
T-5........ IV.3:6 ideas of the **e.** can conflict because they
T-5......... V.1:2 The **e.** has a purpose, just as the Holy
T-5......... V.2:4 it invulnerable to the **e.** because its peace
T-5......... V.2:8 If the **e.** is the symbol of the separation, it
T-5....... V.2:11 meaningless concept except to the **e.**, but
T-5......... V.3:1 **e.** is the part of the mind that believes in
T-5......... V.3:4 The **e.** believes that this is what you did
T-5......... V.3:5 *is* you. If you identify with the **e.**, you must
T-5......... V.3:6 Whenever you respond to your **e.** you will
T-5......... V.3:7 The **e.** is quite literally a fearful thought.
T-5......... V.3:8 mind, never forget that the **e.** is not sane.
T-5......... V.4:3 If you enthrone the **e.** in your mind, your
T-5....... V.4:10 **e.** does not perceive sin as a lack of love,
T-5....... V.4:13 The **e.** regards this as doom, but you must
T-5......... V.5:6 The **e.** believes that by punishing itself it
T-5......... V.6:1 The **e.** cannot oppose the laws of God
T-5......... V.6:6 The Holy Spirit, like the **e.**, is a decision.
T-5......... V.6:8 and the **e.** are the only choices open to
T-5........ VI.2:4 It gives the **e.** a false sense of security by
T-5........ VI.2:9 Your **e.** cannot accept this freedom, and
T-5........ VI.3:5 for the **e.** always speaks first. Alternate
T-5........ VI.4:1 The **e.** speaks in judgment, and the Holy
T-5........ VI.4:3 the **e.** perceives is interpreted correctly.
T-5........ VI.4:4 does the **e.** cite Scripture for its purpose,
T-5........ VI.8:1 generation," as interpreted by the **e.**, is
T-5........ VI.9:2 a word the **e.** cannot even understand. To
T-5........ VI.9:3 **e.**, to be undone means to be destroyed.
T-5........ VI.9:4 The **e.** will not be destroyed because it is
T-5........ VI.9:5 the **e.** will merely return to the Kingdom,
T-6........... I.9:1 outrageous assault, as judged by the **e.**,
T-6......... I.16:7 between the **e.** and the Son of God. This
T-6......... II.3:3 is solely a device of the **e.** to make you feel
T-6......... II.3:4 The **e.** justifies this on the grounds that it
T-6......... II.3:7 The **e.** uses projection only to destroy
T-6......... II.4:2 Every ability of the **e.** has a better use,
T-6......... II.4:3 Holy Spirit extends and the **e.** projects. As
T-6......... II.7:4 it. The **e.** would prefer to believe that this
T-6....... II.10:8 The **e.** cannot prevail against this because
T-6....... II.10:8 statement that the **e.** never occurred.
T-6....... II.11:1 The **e.** can accept the idea that return is
T-6....... II.12:2 The **e.** projects to exclude, and therefore
T-6....... II.13:2 The **e.** is legion, but the Holy Spirit is One
T-6........ III.1:7 **e.** never was and never will be part of it,
T-6........ III.1:7 but through the **e.** you can hear and teach
T-6........ III.4:1 opposite of everything the **e.** believes.
T-6........ IV.1:2 The **e.** always speaks first. It is capricious
T-6........ IV.1:6 The **e.** does not regard itself as part of you
T-6........ IV.2:3 You made the **e.** without love, and so it
T-6........ IV.2:5 enables the **e.** to regard itself as separate
T-6........ IV.2:6 The **e.**, then, raised the first question that
T-6........ IV.2:8 **e.** has never answered any questions since
T-6........ IV.2:9 the **e.** have never done more than obscure
T-6........ IV.2:9 have the answer and *the e. is afraid of you.*
T-6........ IV.3:1 fact that the **e.** cannot know anything.
T-6........ IV.4:1 The **e.** cannot hear the Holy Spirit, but it
T-6........ IV.4:4 it, and the **e.** feels badly in need of allies,
T-6........ IV.4:5 mind, the **e.** turns to the body as its ally,
T-6........ IV.5:1 The **e.** uses the body to conspire against
T-6........ IV.5:1 **e.** realizes that its "enemy" can end them
T-6........ IV.5:3 The **e.**, which is not real, attempts to
T-6........ IV.6:1 the **e.** raises: You are a child of God, a
T-6...... IV.10:4 of "reasoning" in which the **e.** engages.
T-6...... V.A.1:1 and your **e.** and your dreams are gone,
T-6...... V.A.1:7 other impossible solution the **e.** attempts,
T-6...... V.A.2:5 He reinterprets what the **e.** uses as an
T-6 ..... V.A.5:3 **e.** uses the body for attack, for pleasure
T-6 ... V.B.3:10 Still strongly aware of the **e.** in yourself,
T-6 ... V.B.3:10 responding primarily to the **e.** in others,
T-6 ..... V.B.4:1 the **e.** perceives the first lesson as insane.
T-6 ..... V.B.6:3 The **e.** tries to persuade you that it is up to
T-6 ..... V.C.1:7 what the Holy Spirit rejects the **e.** accepts.
T-6 ..... V.C.4:2 can be as vigilant against the **e.** as for it.
T-6 ..... V.C.7:6 The **e.** speaks against His creation, and
T-7 .......... I.4:1 **e.**, on the other hand, always demands
T-7 ....... III.2:6 This is why the **e.** is insane; it teaches that
T-7 ..... III.2:10 though the **e.** does not know what it is.
T-7 ..... III.2:11 The **e.**, then, is always being undone, and
T-7 ..... III.2:12 cannot be unified in allegiance to the **e.**,
T-7 ..... III.2:13 "treacherous" to the **e.** is faithful to peace.
T-7 ....... III.3:1 because the **e.** perceives itself at war and
T-7 ....... IV.2:6 of God and forgetting the laws of the **e.**. I
T-7 ....... IV.3:1 The **e.** does not want to teach everyone
T-7 ....... IV.3:3 teaches you to use what the **e.** has made,
T-7 ....... IV.3:3 the opposite of what the **e.** has "learned."
T-7 ....... IV.5:2 The **e.** always seeks to divide and separate
T-7 ....... IV.6:2 The **e.** believes that it can, and that it can
T-7 ....... IV.7:7 sense of danger the **e.** has induced in you,
T-7 ........ V.2:2 Since the **e.** cannot obliterate the impulse
T-7 ........ V.2:3 The **e.** thus tries to teach you that the
T-7 ........ V.3:5 the service of the **e.** can hurt other bodies,
T-7 ........ V.7:7 it as long as you learn through the **e.**. This
T-7 ........ V.8:8 the change his **e.** thinks it has made in
T-7 ........ V.9:6 The **e.** is totally unable to understand this
T-7 ....... VI.1:5 depending on whether the **e.** or the Holy
T-7 ....... VI.3:1 ingeniousness of the **e.** to preserve itself is
T-7 ....... VI.3:1 the very power of the mind the **e.** denies.
T-7 ....... VI.3:2 that the **e.** attacks what is preserving it,
T-7 ....... VI.3:3 the **e.** never recognizes what it is doing. It
T-7 ....... VI.3:5 The **e.** draws upon the one source that is
T-7 ....... VI.3:8 the **e.** resolves this completely insane
T-7 ....... VI.4:1 The **e.** cannot afford to know anything.
T-7 ....... VI.4:2 and the **e.** does not believe in totality.
T-7 ....... VI.4:3 while the **e.** does not love you it *is* faithful
T-7 ....... VI.4:5 Produced by fear, the **e.** reproduces fear.
T-7 ....... VI.4:7 is your power, which the **e.** must deny. It
T-7 ....... VI.4:9 No one who has everything wants the **e.**.
T-7 ..... VI.4:11 decision the **e.** could possibly encounter,
T-7 ....... VI.5:1 The **e.** therefore opposes all appreciation,
T-7 ....... VI.8:1 that the **e.** does believe it can attack God,
T-7 ....... VI.8:2 **e.** proceeds perfectly logically to the belief
T-7 ....... VI.8:4 its weakness the **e.** wants your allegiance,
T-7 ....... VI.8:5 **e.** therefore wants to engage your mind in
T-7 ....... VI.8:6 of truth, because the **e.** itself is not true. If
T-7 ....... VI.9:6 The **e.** believes this totally, being fully
T-7 ....... VI.9:8 The **e.** therefore is totally committed to
T-7 ..... VI.11:4 That is all the world of the **e.** is. Nothing.
T-7 ....... VII.9:1 the **e.** is incapable of trust. Projecting its
T-7 .... VII.11:4 the **e.** are always experienced as sacrifices,
T-7 ..... VIII.1:5 To the **e.**, the law is perceived as a means
T-7 ..... VIII.1:8 To the **e.** it is the law of deprivation. It
T-7 ..... VIII.2:2 The **e.** always tries to preserve conflict. It
T-7 ..... VIII.2:4 The **e.** therefore tries to persuade you that
T-7 ..... VIII.2:4 lest you give the **e.** up and free yourself.
T-7 ..... VIII.2:5 the **e.** utilizes the power of the mind only
T-7 ..... VIII.4:4 that it can, an error the **e.** always makes,
T-7 ..... VIII.4:6 on your mind, because the **e.** is your belief
T-7 ..... VIII.4:7 The **e.** is a confusion in identification.
T-7 ..... VIII.5:1 *Do not be afraid of the e.*. It depends on
T-7 ..... VIII.6:2 **e.** can be completely forgotten at any time
T-7 ..... VIII.6:3 The more you learn about the **e.**, the
T-7 ..... VIII.7:1 that the **e.** is unbelievable and will forever
T-7 ..... VIII.7:2 made the **e.** by believing the unbelievable
T-7 ....... IX.1:4 Selfishness is of the **e.**, but Self-fullness is
T-7 ....... IX.1:5 that lies between the **e.** and the spirit,
T-7 ....... IX.1:6 To the **e.** this is partiality, and it responds
T-7 ....... IX.2:3 The **e.** cannot prevail against a totality
T-7 ......... X.3:6 What is joyful to you is painful to the **e.**,
T-7 ......... X.3:8 Spirit, and you will be giving up the **e.**.
T-7 ......... X.4:9 because the **e.** wishes for the impossible.
T-7 ......... X.5:5 asks for sacrifice, but the **e.** always does.
T-7 ......... X.7:1 which the **e.** guards so jealously, is not
T-7 ....... XI.1:7 **e.** perceives nothing as wholly desirable.
T-8 ........ I.1:10 so ready to throw it away when the **e.** asks
T-8 .......... I.2:1 The distractions of the **e.** may seem to
T-8 .......... I.2:1 **e.** has no power to distract you unless you
T-8 .......... I.3:1 Every response to the **e.** is a call to war,
T-8 ......... II.1:4 **e.** does not know what it is trying to teach
T-8 ......... II.1:8 then, the **e.** is totally confused and totally
T-8 ......... II.1:9 you could still learn nothing from the **e.**,
T-8 ......... II.1:9 the ego, because the **e.** knows nothing.
T-8 ......... II.2:4 **e.** has never given you a sensible answer
T-8 ......... II.2:6 Yet the **e.** has done more harm to your
T-8 ......... II.3:1 The **e.** cannot teach you anything as long
T-8 ......... II.3:3 That is why the **e.** is the denial of free will.
T-8 ......... II.3:7 undoing of everything the **e.** tries to teach
T-8 ......... II.4:1 **e.** tries to teach that you want to oppose
T-8 ....... III.5:6 The **e.** tries to find them in yourself alone,
T-8 ....... III.6:2 then, you cannot listen to the **e.**, whose
T-8 ....... III.6:3 The **e.** does not know this, because it does
T-8 ....... III.6:4 to look at what the **e.** would make of you.
T-8 ....... III.7:3 The **e.** teaches that your strength is in you
T-8 ......... V.4:1 with me you are uniting without the **e.**,
T-8 ......... V.4:1 because I have renounced the **e.** in myself
T-8 ......... V.4:2 the way to renounce the **e.** in you. The
T-8 ......... V.4:3 The truth in both of us is beyond the **e.**.
T-8 ......... V.4:4 transcending the **e.** is guaranteed by God,
T-8 ......... V.5:5 it is because the **e.** has attempted to join
T-8 ......... V.5:6 **e.** regards itself as rejected and becomes
T-8 ......... V.5:8 me as your companion *instead* of the **e.**.
T-8 ......... V.6:4 Never accord the **e.** the power to interfere
T-8 ......... V.6:6 all attempts of the **e.** to hold you back. I
T-8 ......... V.6:7 go before you because I am beyond the **e.**.
T-8 ......... V.6:8 because you want to transcend the **e.**. My
T-8 ...... VII.2:3 is. The **e.** separates through the body. The
T-8 ...... VII.9:3 Guided by the **e.**, it *is.* Guided by the Holy
T-8 ...... VII.9:6 to Him replaces devotion to the **e.**. In this
T-8 ..... VIII.1:5 it *is.* To the **e.** the body is to attack *with.*
T-8 ..... VIII.2:3 The **e.** makes a fundamental confusion
T-8 ..... VIII.2:4 **e.** has no real use for it because it is *not* an
T-8 ..... VIII.2:5 end that the **e.** has accepted as its own.
T-8 ..... VIII.2:7 is why the **e.** is forced to shift ceaselessly
T-8 ..... VIII.3:2 **e.** has a profound investment in sickness.
T-8 ..... VIII.4:4 want the **e.** are predisposed to defend it.
T-8 ..... VIII.4:6 The **e.** does not call upon witnesses who
T-8 ..... VIII.4:8 The **e.** as a judge gives anything but an
T-8 ..... VIII.4:9 When the **e.** calls on a witness, it has
T-8 ..... VIII.5:2 The **e.**, however, establishes it as an end
T-8 ..... VIII.5:3 is the purpose of everything the **e.** does.
T-8 ..... VIII.6:3 The **e.** uses this as its best argument for
T-8 ..... VIII.7:5 **e.** is incapable of knowing how you feel.
T-8 ..... VIII.7:6 I said that the **e.** does not know anything,
T-8 ..... VIII.7:6 one thing about the **e.** that is wholly true.
T-8 ..... VIII.7:7 if only knowledge has being and the **e.** has
T-8 ..... VIII.7:7 no knowledge, then the **e.** has no being.
T-8 ..... VIII.8:6 When you lay the **e.** aside, it will be gone.
T-8 ....... IX.1:3 **e.** does not know what a real question is,
T-8 ....... IX.1:4 as you learn to question the value of the **e.**
T-8 ....... IX.1:5 When the **e.** tempts you to sickness do
T-8 ....... IX.6:1 The **e.**, which always wants to weaken the
T-8 ....... IX.6:2 **e.** actually believes that it is protecting it.
T-8 ....... IX.6:3 the **e.** believes that mind is dangerous,
T-8 ....... IX.6:5 The **e.** despises weakness, even though it
T-8 ....... IX.6:6 it. The **e.** wants only what it hates. To the
T-8 ....... IX.6:7 it hates. To the **e.** this is perfectly sensible.
T-8 ....... IX.6:8 in the power of attack, the **e.** wants attack
T-9 .......... I.2:1 ego's, and that is why the **e.** is against you
T-9 ........ I.10:2 stems from the **e.** is a wish for nothing,
T-9 ........ I.10:5 **e.** cannot ask the Holy Spirit for anything,
T-9 ....... III.1:1 The alertness of the **e.** to the errors of
T-9 ....... III.2:1 To the **e.** it is kind and right and good to
T-9 ....... III.2:2 This makes perfect sense to the **e.**, which
T-9 ....... III.2:3 is. Errors are of the **e.**, and correction of
T-9 ....... III.2:3 errors lies in the relinquishment of the **e.**.
T-9 ....... III.2:5 certain that, if he is speaking from the **e.**,
T-9 ..... III.2:10 His **e.** is always wrong, no matter what it
T-9 ....... III.3:1 the errors of your brother's **e.** you must
T-9 ....... III.3:2 between the **e.** and the Holy Spirit. The
T-9 ....... III.3:3 The **e.** makes no sense, and the Holy
T-9 ....... III.3:4 knowing that nothing the **e.** makes means
T-9 ....... III.4:3 you are listening to your **e.** and making as
T-9 ....... III.7:8 this can only be the arrogance of the **e.**.
T-9 ....... IV.3:4 on your abilities through the eyes of the **e.**
T-9 ....... IV.4:1 The **e.**, too, has a plan of forgiveness

T-9 IV.4:3 situation, to which the **e.** always leads you
T-9 IV.4:7 the **e.** is forced to appeal to "mysteries,"
T-9 IV.5:6 that the **e.** does not exist and proves it.
T-9 IV.7:1 is so typical of the **e.** that you should be
T-9 IV.7:2 **e.** believes that all functions belong to it,
T-9 IV.7:4 that makes the **e.** likely to attack anyone
T-9 IV.7:5 at all. This is exactly what the **e.** does. It is
T-9 IV.8:2 the **e.** in a sound position as your guide.
T-9 IV.9:1 The **e.** literally lives on borrowed time,
T-9 IV.11:3 The symbols of fantasy are of the **e.**, and
T-9 V.1:2 healers, and is therefore of the **e.**. Let us
T-9 V.2:1 said that beliefs of the **e.** cannot be shared
T-9 V.3:6 have done is merely to identify with the **e.**
T-9 V.5:1 the mind, how can this build **e.** strength?
T-9 V.5:5 **e.** will always seek to get something from
T-9 V.7:1 situation" to which the **e.** always leads. It
T-9 VII.2:7 The **e.** is afraid of the obvious, since
T-9 VII.3:4 The **e.** is also in your mind, because you
T-9 VII.3:5 Spirit's, because the **e.** does not love you.
T-9 VII.3:7 **e.** is therefore capable of suspiciousness at
T-9 VII.4:4 The **e.** is deceived by everything you do,
T-9 VII.4:5 The **e.** is, therefore, particularly likely to
T-9 VII.4:6 The **e.** will attack your motives as soon as
T-9 VII.5:3 look to the **e.** to help you escape from a
T-9 VII.7:1 I have said that the **e.** does not know
T-9 VII.8:3 Remember this when the **e.** speaks, and
T-9 VIII.1:3 dimly, you abandon the **e.** automatically,
T-9 VIII.1:3 of the **e.** becomes perfectly apparent.
T-9 VIII.1:4 the **e.** believes that its "enemy" has struck
T-9 VIII.1:6 grandiosity of the **e.** is its alternative to
T-9 VIII.2:7 said before that the **e.** vacillates between
T-9 VIII.3:1 **e.** does not understand the difference
T-9 VIII.3:2 I told you that the **e.** is aware of threat to
T-9 VIII.3:4 When the **e.** experiences threat, its only
T-9 VIII.4:1 **e.** is immobilized in the presence of God's
T-9 VIII.4:2 literally drives the **e.** from your mind,
T-9 VIII.4:4 unless you do not allow the **e.** to attack it.
T-9 VIII.4:5 **e.** will make every effort to recover and
T-9 VIII.6:1 The **e.** depends solely on your willingness
T-9 VIII.6:2 and therefore you cannot want the **e.**.
T-9 VIII.6:3 Your grandeur is God's answer to the **e.**,
T-10 III.4:7 what the **e.** does perceive in a Son of God;
T-11 h GOD OR THE E.
T-11 in.1:1 Either God or the **e.** is insane. If you will
T-11 in.1:3 Neither God nor the **e.** proposes a partial
T-11 in.2:2 If you made the **e.**, how can the ego have
T-11 in.2:2 the ego, how can the **e.** have made you?
T-11 in.2:3 because the **e.** was made out of the wish
T-11 in.2:4 Him. The **e.**, then, is nothing more than a
T-11 in.2:6 **e.** never looks on what it does with perfect
T-11 in.2:8 And either the **e.**, which you made, *is* your
T-11 I.9:1 The projection of the **e.** makes it appear
T-11 II.5:5 Whenever you ask the **e.** to enter, you
T-11 II.7:1 you be hostage to the **e.** or host to God?
T-11 II.7:6 And the **e.** is nothing, whether you invite
T-11 IV.5:4 yourself, for only the **e.** blames at all. Self-
T-11 IV.5:5 Self-blame is therefore **e.** identification,
T-11 IV.5:5 as much an **e.** defense as blaming others.
T-11 V.h The "Dynamics" of the **E.**
T-11 V.1:5 of the **e.** will be our lesson for a while, for
T-11 V.3:1 Let us begin this lesson in "**e.** dynamics"
T-11 V.3:3 that the **e.** *has* the power to do anything.
T-11 V.3:4 **e.** is fearful to you because you believe
T-11 V.4:1 When we look at the **e.**, then, we are not
T-11 V.4:4 ego's goal is quite explicitly **e.** autonomy.
T-11 V.5:2 is. Everything that stems from the **e.** is the
T-11 V.6:7 The belief in **e.** autonomy is costing you
T-11 V.6:8 The **e.** sees all dependency as threatening,
T-11 V.7:1 **e.** always attacks on behalf of separation.
T-11 V.7:3 The **e.** is totally confused about reality,
T-11 V.8:1 the last thing the **e.** wishes you to realize
T-11 V.8:2 of it. For if the **e.** could give rise to fear, it
T-11 V.9:1 The **e.** can and does allow you to regard
T-11 V.10:1 how the **e.** wants you to experience it, is
T-11 V.10:1 it, is therefore the basic **e.** threat. Its
T-11 V.10:4 is the cost, and the **e.** cannot minimize it.
T-11 V.12:3 The **e.** believes that to accomplish its goal
T-11 V.12:6 this is what the **e.** would have you believe.
T-11 V.13:1 The **e.** analyzes; the Holy Spirit accepts.
T-11 V.13:3 approach of the **e.** to everything. The ego
T-11 V.13:4 The **e.** believes that power, understanding
T-11 V.13:5 the **e.** attacks everything it perceives by
T-11 V.13:6 The **e.** will always substitute chaos for
T-11 V.14:2 **e.** focuses on error and overlooks truth. It
T-11 V.14:6 **e.** proceeds to the next step in its thought
T-11 V.15:1 **e.** makes no attempt to understand this,
T-11 V.15:1 but the **e.** does make every attempt to
T-11 V.15:2 the **e.** succeeds in overlooking it and is left
T-11 V.16:6 the **e.** teach truly when it overlooks truth?
T-11 V.16:9 The **e.** looks straight at the Father and
T-11 V.17:4 see of His Son through the eyes of the **e.** is
T-11 V.18:1 becomes a witness for Christ or for the **e.**,
T-11 VI.1:6 complete triumph of Christ over the **e.**,
T-11 VI.1:7 does rise above the **e.** and all its works,
T-11 VII.3:1 The **e.** may see some good, but never
T-12 I.2:1 of **e.** motivation is very complicated, very
T-12 I.2:1 never without your own **e.** involvement.
T-12 I.8:5 as a crucial step in the undoing of the **e.**.
T-12 III.3:1 you are believing that the **e.** is to be saved,
T-12 III.4:7 Poverty is of the **e.**, and never of God. No
T-12 III.6:1 identify with the **e.** is to attack yourself
T-12 III.6:2 who identifies with the **e.** feels deprived.
T-12 III.6:5 its source as his own **e.** identification, and
T-12 III.7:5 attempt to maintain your **e.** identification
T-12 IV.1:1 The **e.** is certain that love is dangerous,
T-12 IV.1:2 everyone who believes that the **e.** is
T-12 IV.1:3 Yet the **e.**, though encouraging the search
T-12 IV.1:5 is the one promise the **e.** holds out to you,
T-12 IV.1:6 **e.** pursues its goal with fanatic insistence,
T-12 IV.2:1 The search the **e.** undertakes is therefore
T-12 IV.2:3 For the **e.** cannot love, and in its frantic
T-12 IV.2:4 search is inevitable because the **e.** is part
T-12 IV.2:4 of its source the **e.** is not wholly split off,
T-12 IV.2:6 the journey is on which the **e.** sets you.
T-12 IV.3:2 **e.** would be totally inadequate in love's
T-12 IV.3:4 The **e.** will therefore distort love, and
T-12 IV.3:4 calls forth the responses the **e.** *can* teach.
T-12 IV.4:1 Do you realize that the **e.** must set you on
T-12 VI.1:1 The **e.** is trying to teach you how to gain
T-12 VII.6:4 The **e.** finds what it seeks, and only that.
T-12 VII.14:1 The **e.** is not a traitor to God, to Whom
T-12 VII.14:4 you are listening to the voice of the **e.**,
T-12 VII.14:5 from God and not from the **e.** because, by
T-12 VII.14:5 because, by confusing yourself with the **e.**
T-13 I.2:4 of Christ is the proof that the **e.** never was
T-13 I.2:5 Without guilt the **e.** has no life, and God's
T-13 I.10:3 **e.** believes in atonement through attack,
T-13 I.10:4 but by identifying with the **e.** could you
T-13 I.11:1 **e.** teaches you to attack yourself because
T-13 II.1:2 the **e.** attempts to get rid of guilt from its
T-13 II.1:2 for much as the **e.** wants to retain guilt
T-13 II.1:3 if you are to retain guilt, as the **e.** insists,
T-13 II.1:4 the **e.** possibly induce you to project guilt,
T-13 II.2:4 it with a weird assortment of "**e.** ideals,"
T-13 II.2:4 which the **e.** claims you have failed. Yet
T-13 II.4:2 To the **e.**, *the guiltless are guilty*. Those who
T-13 II.4:4 while the **e.** can withstand your raising all
T-13 II.4:5 for the **e.** cannot protect you against truth
T-13 II.4:5 and in its presence the **e.** is dispelled.
T-13 II.5:6 For the **e.** does want to kill you, and if you
T-13 II.6:1 that the crucifixion is the symbol of the **e.**.
T-13 II.6:3 To the **e.**, the *ego* is God, and guiltlessness
T-13 II.6:3 To the ego, the ***e.*** is God, and guiltlessness
T-13 II.8:3 the futility of the **e.** and its offerings, but
T-13 III.1:9 if you did not believe that, without the **e.**,
T-13 III.5:4 You are more afraid of God than of the **e.**,
T-13 IV.1:4 The **e.** teaches that your function on earth
T-13 IV.4:1 The **e.** has a strange notion of time, and it
T-13 IV.4:2 The **e.** invests heavily in the past, and in
T-13 IV.4:5 For the **e.** regards the present only as a
T-13 IV.5:1 "Now" has no meaning to the **e.**. The
T-13 IV.5:3 **e.** cannot tolerate release from the past,
T-13 IV.5:3 over, the **e.** tries to preserve its image by
T-13 IV.6:6 The **e.** would preserve your nightmares,
T-13 IV.6:10 The **e.** teaches that you always encounter
T-13 IV.8:1 The **e.**, on the other hand, regards the
T-13 IV.8:1 **e.** interprets the goal of time as its own.
T-13 IV.8:2 the only purpose the **e.** perceives in time,
T-13 VII.10:11 The **e.** wants to have things for salvation,
T-13 VII.11:1 the **e.** tells you that you need will hurt you
T-13 VII.11:2 the **e.** urges you again and again to get, it
T-13 VII.11:4 the **e.** sees salvation it sees separation,
T-13 IX.2:3 The **e.** rewards fidelity to it with pain, for
T-13 IX.8:2 **e.** tells you all is black with guilt within
T-13 XI.11:2 reconciliation the **e.** would substitute for
T-13 XI.11:3 as the **e.** will not effect what it attempts.
T-13 XI.11:4 Failure is of the **e.**, not of God. From Him
T-14 in.1:4 logic as easily and as well as does the **e.**,
T-14 in.1:5 as the **e.** points to darkness and to death.
T-14 III.4:1 between the **e.** and the Holy Spirit. The
T-14 III.4:2 The **e.** is the choice for guilt; the Holy
T-14 IX.1:4 Bringing illusion to truth, or the **e.** to God
T-14 IX.2:1 the **e.** to God is but to bring error to truth
T-14 IX.5:4 can reflect Heaven or hell; God or the **e.**.
T-14 X.4:5 while others are motivated by the **e.**,
T-14 X.5:5 chaos shows you that you are not an **e.**,
T-14 X.5:5 and that more than an **e.** must be in you.
T-14 X.5:6 For the **e.** *is* chaos, and if it were all of you,
T-14 X.5:7 you impose upon your mind limits the **e.**,
T-14 X.7:6 of his offering by which the **e.** judges it.
T-14 X.8:1 **e.** is incapable of understanding content,
T-14 X.8:2 it. To the **e.**, if the form is acceptable the
T-14 X.8:4 something of the "dynamics" of the **e.**, let
T-14 X.8:6 of the **e.** is not the study of the mind. In
T-14 X.8:7 In fact, the **e.** enjoys studying itself, and
T-14 X.9:5 For no one alone can judge the **e.** truly.
T-14 X.9:6 **e.** can no longer defend its lack of content
T-14 XI.13:4 so by abandoning the **e.** on behalf of Him.
T-14 XI.13:5 Call not upon the **e.** for anything; it is
T-15 I.2:6 due but to your identification with the **e.**,
T-15 I.2:7 The **e.**, like the Holy Spirit, uses time to
T-15 I.2:8 To the **e.** the goal is death, which *is* its end.
T-15 I.3:1 The **e.** is an ally of time, but not a friend.
T-15 I.3:3 The **e.** wants *you* dead, but not itself. The
T-15 I.4:1 to those who identify with the **e.**. Their
T-15 I.4:3 The **e.** teaches that hell is in the future, for
T-15 I.4:5 **e.** aims at death and dissolution as an end
T-15 I.4:10 the **e.** must seem to keep fear from you to
T-15 I.4:12 Again the **e.** tries, and all too frequently
T-15 I.4:13 The **e.** teaches thus: Death is the end as
T-15 I.4:14 you and the **e.** cannot be separated, and
T-15 I.5:1 The **e.** teaches that Heaven is here and
T-15 I.5:4 The only time the **e.** allows anyone to
T-15 I.6:4 The **e.** does not advertise its final threat,
T-15 I.6:6 only way in which the **e.** allows the fear of
T-15 I.7:2 only what the **e.** has made of the present.
T-15 I.7:4 steadily to Heaven as the **e.** drives to hell.
T-15 I.7:5 the **e.** would make the present useless.
T-15 II.3:5 your brothers to your **e.** in an attempt to
T-15 II.4:1 by seeing them as sources of **e.** support.
T-15 II.4:2 they witness to the **e.** in your perception,
T-15 II.4:5 support the **e.** or the Holy Spirit in you.
T-15 III.5:1 you be hostage to the **e.** or host to God?"
T-15 III.5:6 make His Son hostage to the **e.**, cannot
T-15 IV.3:2 no plan of the **e.** before the plan of God.
T-15 IV.6:2 Complexity is of the **e.**, and is nothing
T-15 V.1:6 because you believe that without the **e.**,
T-15 V.1:7 Yet I assure you that without the **e.**, all
T-15 V.4:5 which you have chosen to support the **e.**,
T-15 VII.1:6 for any relationship in which the **e.** enters
T-15 VII.1:7 relationship on which the **e.** embarks *is*
T-15 VII.2:1 The **e.** establishes relationships only to
T-15 VII.2:3 It is impossible for the **e.** to enter into any
T-15 VII.2:3 the **e.** believes that anger makes friends.
T-15 VII.2:5 **e.** really believes that it can get and keep
T-15 VII.2:7 **e.** always seems to attract through love,
T-15 VII.4:1 We said before that the **e.** attempts to
T-15 VII.4:3 The **e.** wishes no one well. Yet its survival
T-15 VII.5:2 who cannot make himself host to the **e.**.
T-15 VII.5:3 at the relationships the **e.** contrives, and
T-15 VII.6:1 every relationship the **e.** makes is based
T-15 VII.6:4 the **e.** acknowledges "reality" as it sees it,
T-15 VII.7:7 for the **e.** believes that to forgive another
T-15 VII.7:8 that the **e.** can ensure the guilt that holds
T-15 VII.8:2 For relationships, to the **e.**, mean only
T-15 VII.8:3 It is always this that the **e.** demands, and
T-15 VII.8:5 To the **e.** the mind is private, and only the

T-15.....VII.9:1 with which the **e.** would "bless" all unions
T-15.....VII.9:7 what the **e.** really wants you do not realize
T-15...VII.10:1 relationship which the **e.** has "blessed,"
T-15...VII.10:3 attempt is the only basis the **e.** accepts for
T-15...VII.10:4 Guilt is the only need the **e.** has, and as
T-15...VII.12:4 For the **e.** will always teach that loneliness
T-15...... IX.1:1 the **e.** would limit your perception of your
T-15...... IX.2:3 The body is the symbol of the **e.**, as the
T-15...... IX.2:3 as the **e.** is the symbol of the separation.
T-15...... IX.3:2 is necessary to give up every use the **e.** has
T-15...... IX.3:2 accept the fact that the **e.** has no purpose
T-15...... IX.3:3 For the **e.** would limit everyone to a body
T-15...... IX.3:5 Yet you have surely recognized that the **e.**
T-15...... IX.4:1 between Heaven and hell, God and the **e.**,
T-15...... IX.4:3 Limits are demanded by the **e.**, and
T-15...... IX.5:5 the limits the **e.** would impose on them
T-15...... IX.7:2 and attack which the **e.** sees in it, you will
T-15....... X.1:4 them both, though not as the **e.** uses them
T-15....... X.4:4 For though the **e.** takes many forms, it is
T-15....... X.5:4 to be host to the **e.** or hostage to God.
T-15....... X.6:1 As host to the **e.**, you believe that you can
T-15....... X.6:3 yours. While it is obvious that the **e.** does
T-15....... X.6:4 You are unwilling to recognize that the **e.**,
T-15....... X.6:5 The **e.** will never let you perceive this,
T-15....... X.6:6 will not be deceived by any form the **e.**
T-15....... X.7:3 **e.** seems to demand less of you than God,
T-15....... X.9:1 succeed in being partial hostage to the **e.**,
T-16.........I.1:6 not relate through your **e.** to another ego.
T-16.........I.1:6 not relate through your ego to another **e.**.
T-16.........I.2:1 the **e.** uses it is destructive lies in the fact
T-16.........I.2:4 the **e.** sees itself and would increase itself
T-16.........I.2:5 the **e.** always empathizes to weaken, and
T-16....... V.2:2 For the **e.** would have you see Him, and
T-16....... V.3:2 The "dynamics" of the **e.** are clearest here
T-16....... V.4:3 the preservation of the **e.** that you believe
T-16....... V.4:4 For the **e.** would never have you see that
T-16....... V.5:2 both the **e.** and the Holy Spirit accept it.
T-16....... V.5:5 To the **e.** completion lies in triumph, and
T-16....... V.5:6 would remain to interfere with the **e.**.
T-16....... V.5:8 condition in which the **e.** cannot interfere
T-16....... V.6:1 **e.** device for joining hell and Heaven, and
T-16....... V.7:1 the **e.** fosters in the special relationship.
T-16....... V.8:1 self the **e.** seeks is always one that is more
T-16....... V.8:3 the **e.** sees "a union made in Heaven." For
T-16....... V.9:1 which the **e.** holds out to those who place
T-16....... V.9:5 For the **e.** is itself an illusion, and only
T-16...... VI.1:1 yourself with the **e.** and not with God. For
T-16...... VI.1:2 relationship has value only to the **e.**. To
T-16...... VI.1:3 To the **e.**, unless a relationship has special
T-16...... VI.3:3 **e.** has taught you that freedom lies in it.
T-16...... VI.5:7 special relationship the **e.** seeks does not
T-16...... VI.5:8 The **e.** wants but part of him, and sees
T-16.... VI.10:1 mockery of salvation the **e.** offered you,
T-16..... VII.3:3 For the **e.** remembers everything you have
T-16..... VII.3:5 For the **e.** holds the past against you, and
T-16..... VII.3:6 the **e.** could not hold you to the past. In
T-16..... VII.5:3 the one thing the **e.** never allows to reach
T-16... VII.10:3 Be an ally of God and not the **e.** in seeking
T-17...... III.2:1 that would make the **e.** holy in your sight,
T-17...... III.6:1 The **e.** seeks to "resolve" its problems,
T-17...... III.7:3 joined as one, the **e.** cannot put asunder.
T-17...... III.8:1 alliance with the **e.** against the present.
T-17...... III.9:5 choose except between God and the **e.**.
T-17...... IV.4:2 the **e.** did not understand what had been
T-17...... IV.4:3 The whole defense system the **e.** evolved
T-17...... IV.5:1 The **e.** is always alert to threat, and the
T-17...... IV.5:1 part of your mind into which the **e.** was
T-17...... IV.6:2 least in general terms, that the **e.** is insane
T-17...... IV.8:1 frame of all the defenses the **e.** uses. Its
T-17.... IV.11:8 thought system of the **e.** lies in its gifts, so
T-17....... V.4:1 temptation of the **e.** becomes extremely
T-17....... V.5:1 **e.** given time to reinterpret each slow step
T-17....... V.7:1 Now the **e.** counsels thus; substitute for
T-17....... V.8:4 and do not breathe life into your failing **e.**
T-17...... VI.2:7 **e.** does not know what it wants to come of
T-17...... VI.3:6 to make is whether or not the **e.** likes it; is
T-17...... VI.5:8 for the **e.** believes the situation brings the
T-17...... VI.6:9 this is so only from the viewpoint of the **e.**
T-17...... VI.6:9 **e.** believes in "solving" conflict through
T-17 ..... VI.7:1 the **e.** will attempt to take this aspect
T-18 ........I.1:6 strongest defense the **e.** has for separation
T-18 ........I.2:2 **e.** perceives one person as a replacement
T-18 ........I.2:8 relationships the **e.** sponsors to destroy.
T-18 ........II.1:5 you, and change it into a tribute to your **e.**
T-18 ........II.1:6 unless you saw yourself as one with the **e.**,
T-18 ........II.2:4 world, and changing it to suit the **e.** better
T-18 ..... IV.1:6 add the **e.** to Him and confuse the two. He
T-18 ... VIII.3:1 Within this kingdom the **e.** rules, and
T-19 ........I.2:2 every demand your **e.** would make of him.
T-19 ........II.5:1 sin as error is always indefensible to the **e.**
T-19 ........II.6:1 be said the **e.** made its world on sin. Only
T-19 ........II.6:5 an idea of God to an ideal the **e.** wants; a
T-19 ........II.7:2 To the **e.**, this is no mistake. For this is its
T-19 ........II.8:3 to agree with the **e.** that it is far better to
T-19 ..... III.1:7 part of what the **e.** thinks you are, you will
T-19 ..... III.2:1 The **e.** does not think it possible that love
T-19 ..... III.2:2 For the **e.** brings sin to fear, demanding
T19..IV.A.17:3 of you. To the **e.** sin means death, and so
T19IV.A.17:13 This is completion as the **e.** sees it. For
T19..IV.B.12:2 for it is one the **e.** sees as proof of sin. It is
T19..IV.B.14:8 **e.** and the Holy Spirit both recognize this,
T19IV.B.14:10 joy. The **e.** hides it, for it would keep you
T19..IV.B.16:2 Forget not that the **e.** has dedicated the
T19..IV.B.17:4 Like the **e.**, the Holy Spirit is both the
T19..IV.B.17:6 seeks. So does the **e.** find the death *it* seeks,
T19....IV.C.1:9 Made by the **e.**, its dark shadow falls
T19....IV.C.1:9 because the **e.** is the "enemy" of life.
T19..IV.C.2:15 is the result of the thought we call the **e.**,
T19....IV.C.3:1 From the **e.** came sin and guilt and death,
T19....IV.C.4:7 kill it. For what the **e.** loves, it kills for its
T19....IV.C.8:1 world the **e.** would lay the Son of God,
T19..IV.C.11:1 the **e.** has perceived it as a symbol of fear,
T19... IV.D.3:2 in secret to the **e.** never to lift this veil, not
T19... IV.D.3:3 the **e.** to keep what lies beyond the veil
T19... IV.D.4:4 are no more afraid of death than of the **e.**.
T19... IV.D.6:3 of the **e.** you swore in blood not to desert,
T19... IV.D.8:2 it was surely not the **e.** that led you here.
T-20 ..... III.2:1 Adjustments of any kind are of the **e.**. For
T-20 ..... III.2:4 The **e.** is the self-appointed mediator of
T-20 ..... III.5:6 of yourself is carefully preserved by the **e.**,
T-20 ..... III.6:2 as the world the **e.** looks upon is like itself
T-20 ...... V.3:2 Only the **e.** does this, but all it means is
T-20 ..... VI.4:7 **e.** seeks as many bodies as it can collect to
T-20 .... VII.4:6 with attributes of Christ or of the **e.**.
T-20 .... VII.5:1 body *is* the means by which the **e.** tries to
T-21 ........II.6:4 All that the **e.** is, is an idea that it is
T-21 ........II.9:1 is how the **e.** deals with what it wants, to
T-21 ..... IV.1:5 Fear in association with sin the **e.** deems
T-21 ..... IV.2:1 Remember that the **e.** is not alone. Its
T-21 ..... IV.2:3 Loudly the **e.** tells you not to look inward,
T-21 ..... IV.2:6 it. Loudly indeed the **e.** claims it is; too
T-21 ..... IV.2:7 proclamation, the **e.** is not certain it is so.
T-21 ..... IV.2:8 fear, and one which makes the **e.** tremble.
T-21 ..... IV.3:2 "fearful" question is one the **e.** never asks.
T-21 ..... IV.3:4 their belief that their identity lies in the **e.**
T-21 ..... IV.4:4 tells you now the **e.** would not hear. The
T-21 ..... IV.4:5 the part of your mind the **e.** knows not of.
T-21 ..... IV.5:4 that it was not the **e.** that joined the Holy
T-21 ..... IV.7:1 And now the **e.** *is* afraid. Yet what it hears
T-21 ..... IV.7:2 since first the **e.** came into your mind.
T-21 ..... IV.8:2 joined, and looks upon the **e.** unafraid.
T-21 ...... V.2:3 Listen to what the **e.** says, and see what it
T-21 ...... V.3:6 Miracles seem unnatural to the **e.** because
T-21 ...... V.5:9 reason's alien nature to the **e.** is proof you
T-21 ...... V.8:7 The **e.** never uses it, because it does not
T-21 .... V.10:2 asked the question the **e.** will never ask.
T-22 ........II.1:2 but truth. Only to the **e.**, to which truth is
T-22 ........II.5:1 Both reason and the **e.** will tell you this,
T-22 ........II.5:2 **e.** will assure you now that it is impossible
T-22 ........II.6:1 of you and the **e.** must be made complete.
T-22 ........II.6:4 Yet to the **e.** this must be impossible, and
T-22 ..... III.1:1 for reason and the **e.** are contradictory.
T-22 ... III.1:10 And here do reason and the **e.** separate,
T-22 ..... III.2:8 Thus does the **e.** damn, and reason save.
T-22 ..... III.4:1 Only the form of error attracts the **e.**.
T-22 ..... III.4:5 error in a special form the **e.** venerates. It
T-22 ...... V.2:1 Consider what the **e.** wants defenses for.
T-22 ... VI.15:4 to keep a little of the **e.** with this gift. For
T-22 ... VI.15:6 you that you cannot separate denies the **e.**
T-23 ........I.1:5 the **e.** has the power to be victorious. Why
T-23 ........I.1:7 it? Surely you realize the **e.** is at war with
T-23 ........I.2:6 The **e.** always marches to defeat, because
T-23 ........I.3:1 that it is impossible God and the **e.**, or
T-23 ........I.3:5 The **e.** joins with an illusion of yourself
T-23 ........I.3:9 The **e.** joins with nothing, being nothing.
T-23 ........II.8:6 Think not the **e.** will enable you to find
T-23 ........II.8:7 does not value what the **e.** cherishes.
T-23 ........II.9:1 The **e.** values only what it takes. This
T-24 ........II.1:1 Comparison must be an **e.** device, for
W-pI .... 13.2:2 in which God and the **e.** "challenge" each
W-pI .... 13.2:3 The **e.** rushes in frantically to establish its
W-pI .... 13.3:3 To the **e.** illusions are safety devices, as
W-pI .... 13.3:3 be to you who equate yourself with the **e.**.
W-pI .... 25.2:1 in it as meaningful in terms of **e.** goals.
W-pI .... 25.2:2 best interests, because the **e.** is not you.
W-pI .... 36.1:8 is related to His Holiness, not to your **e.**,
W-pI .... 44.6:1 stand aside from the **e.** by ever so little,
W-pI .... 50.2:3 They are songs of praise to the **e.**. Do not
W-pI .... 61.2:1 To the **e.**, today's idea is the epitome of
W-pI .... 61.2:2 But the **e.** does not understand humility,
W-pI .... 61.2:5 for you, and arrogance is always of the **e.**.
W-pI .... 64.3:2 only the arrogance of the **e.** that leads you
W-pI .... 64.3:2 only the fear of the **e.** that induces you to
W-pI .... 66.2:1 The **e.** does constant battle with the Holy
W-pI .... 66.2:4 The **e.** attacks and the Holy Spirit does
W-pI .... 66.3:4 the **e.** by listening to its attacks on truth.
W-pI .... 66.7:3 One is ruled by the **e.**, and is made up of
W-pI .... 66.7:5 but the fear that the **e.** always engenders,
W-pI .... 66.8:1 by the **e.** which you have made to replace
W-pI .... 66.8:3 to you, it must be the gift of the **e.**. Does
W-pI .... 66.8:4 Does the **e.** really have gifts to give, being
W-pI .... 66.9:7 from anything the **e.** ever proposed. Yet
W-pI .... 66.9:8 Yet the **e.** is the only alternative to the
W-pI .... 67.6:3 replacing everything that the **e.** tells you
W-pI .... 68.1:4 hold a grievance is to let the **e.** rule your
W-pI .... 71.1:1 You may not realize that the **e.** has set up
W-pI .... 72.1:2 which are actually associated with the **e.**,
W-pI .... 72.1:2 ego, while the **e.** appears to take on the
W-pI .... 72.2:2 the **e.** is the physical embodiment of that
W-pI .... 72.2:5 Yet the **e.** would have you believe that it is
W-pI .... 72.6:1 cannot enter, the **e.** comes to save you.
W-pI .. 72.11:5 no longer asking the **e.** what salvation is
W-pI .... 73.2:2 The wishes of the **e.** gave rise to it, and the
W-pI .... 73.2:3 the **e.** employs to traffic in grievances.
W-pI .... 73.7:6 Today it is the **e.** that stands powerless
W-pI .... 82.4:4 *This may threaten my* ***e.****, but cannot change*
W-pI .... 94.1:1 renders the **e.** silent and entirely undone.
W-pI .. 126.1:1 to the **e.** and the thinking of the world, is
W-pI .. 133.8:6 For what the **e.** wants it fails to recognize.
W-pI .. 151.9:4 What whispers of the **e.** can He hear?
W-pI .. 152.9:1 by which the **e.** seeks to prove it arrogant.
W-pI .. 152.9:2 Only the **e.** can be arrogant. But truth is
W-pI .. 153.4:1 of all the prices which the **e.** would exact.
W-pI .. 196.2:2 can never be escaped because the **e.**,
W-pI .. 196.3:1 teach your mind that you are not an **e.**.
W-pI .. 196.3:2 For the ways in which the **e.** would distort
W-pI .. 199.3:2 concerned that to the **e.** it is quite insane.
W-pI .. 199.3:3 **e.** holds the body dear because it dwells in
W-pII . 254.2:1 no **e.** thoughts direct our words or actions
W-pII . 319.1:3 up the space the **e.** left unoccupied by lies.
W-pII . 319.1:4 Only the **e.** can be limited, and therefore
W-pII . 319.1:5 The **e.** thinks that what one gains, totality
W-pII ...... 12.h What Is the **E.**?
W-pII ... 12.1:1 The **e.** is idolatry; the sign of limited and
W-pII ... 12.1:3 The **e.** is the "proof" that strength is weak
W-pII ... 12.2:1 The **e.** is insane. In fear it stands beyond
W-pII ... 12.4:1 reality is not to see the **e.** and its thoughts
W-pII . 332.1:1 The **e.** makes illusions. Truth undoes its
M-4 ......... I.2:3 in the shabby offerings of the **e.** when the
M-22 ......... 5:3 he has identified with another's **e.**, and
M-24 ......... 3:5 His **e.** will be enough for him to cope with
M-25 ......... 4:7 Yet the **e.** sees in these same strengths an
M-25 ......... 5:2 gifts, the **e.** has been seriously threatened.
M-25 ......... 6:5 which merely means to strengthen the **e.**.
C-in ........... 3:1 course remains within the **e.** framework,
C-in ........... 3:4 It is merely the **e.** that questions because
C-in ........... 3:4 because it is only the **e.** that doubts. The

| | |
|---|---|
| C-in 3:7 | These are attributes of the **e.**. *The course is* |
| C-in 4:1 | The **e.** will demand many answers that |
| C-in 4:3 | The **e.** may ask, "How did the impossible |
| C-1 2:4 | course *as if* it has two parts; spirit and **e.**. |
| C-1 6:1 | listens to the **e.** and makes illusions; |
| C-1 7:3 | or below; from the Holy Spirit or the **e.**. |
| C-2 h | THE **E.** – THE MIRACLE |
| C-2 1:4 | What is the ***e.***? But a dream of what you |
| C-2 2:1 | What is the **e.**? Nothingness, but in a |
| C-2 2:3 | world of form the **e.** cannot be denied for |
| C-2 2:5 | Who asks you to define the **e.** and explain |
| C-2 4:1 | really make a definition for what the **e.** is, |
| C-2 4:3 | from this that we deduce all that the **e.** is. |
| C-2 5:2 | we find all that is not the **e.** in this world. |
| C-2 5:3 | and here alone we look on what the **e.** was |
| C-2 6:2 | What is the **e.**? What the darkness was. |
| C-2 6:4 | Where is the **e.**? Where the darkness was. |
| C-2 6:10 | What is the **e.**? What the evil was. Where |
| C-2 6:12 | Where is the **e.**? In an evil dream that but |
| C-2 6:15 | What is the **e.**? Who has need to ask? |
| C-2 6:17 | Where is the **e.**? Who has need to seek for |
| C-2 8:1 | This was the **e.** –all the cruel hate, the |
| C-2 9:2 | Ask this instead of what the **e.** is, and you |
| C-2 9:2 | brightness cover up the world the **e.** made |
| C-2 10:1 | miracle forgives; the **e.** damns. Neither |
| C-3 7:3 | be so because the **e.** cannot be at peace. |
| P-2 I.2:2 | is one of the errors which the **e.** fosters; |
| P-2 I.2:6 | The changes the **e.** seeks to make are not |
| P-2 I.3:3 | of the **e.** on the therapeutic process. But |
| P-2 II.2:3 | is so obviously an **e.** attempt to reconcile |
| P-2 II.8:5 | the **e.** would impose upon the self. Only |

## ego's 244

| | |
|---|---|
| T-4 II.5:1 | Undermining the **e.** thought system must |
| T-4 II.6:9 | to any perceived threat to the **e.** existence. |
| T-4 II.7:4 | "getting" arose in the **e.** thought system. |
| T-4 II.7:5 | representing the **e.** need to confirm itself. |
| T-4 II.8:5 | **e.** ceaseless attempts to gain the spirit's |
| T-4 II.9:3 | is only the **e.** struggle to preserve itself, |
| T-4 III.1:8 | ceased to create because of the **e.** illusions |
| T-4 III.4:8 | is wholly without the **e.** "drive to get." |
| T-4 III.9:4 | In the **e.** language, "to have" and "to be" |
| T-4 IV.4:2 | vigilant against the **e.** dictates as for them |
| T-4 IV.9:2 | To the **e.** dark glass you need but say, "I |
| T-4 IV.10:2 | of the **e.** rule and the healing of the mind. |
| T-4 V.1:2 | no exceptions except in the **e.** judgment. |
| T-4 V.2:1 | major source of the **e.** off-balanced state is |
| T-4 V.3:3 | sense the **e.** fear of God is at least logical, |
| T-4 V.4:1 | body is the **e.** home by its own election. It |
| T-4 V.6:5 | mind. The **e.** characteristic busyness with |
| T-4 VII.2:6 | The specificity of the **e.** thinking, then, |
| T-5 III.4:6 | you because, by adopting the **e.** viewpoint |
| T-5 III.5:4 | is in direct opposition to the **e.** notions, |
| T-5 III.6:4 | so the lower mind, which is the **e.** domain |
| T-5 III.7:2 | with the **e.** beliefs in its own language. His |
| T-5 III.8:7 | Peace is the **e.** greatest enemy because, |
| T-5 III.10:4 | the **e.** attempts to conceal this part, it is |
| T-5 V.h | The **E.** Use of Guilt |
| T-5 V.1:1 | meaningful if the **e.** use of guilt is clarified |
| T-5 V.1:3 | The **e.** purpose is fear, because only the |
| T-5 V.1:4 | The **e.** logic is as impeccable as that of the |
| T-5 V.2:11 | the power of the **e.** belief in it. This is the |
| T-5 V.3:10 | Listening to the **e.** voice means that you |
| T-5 V.4:11 | is necessary to the **e.** survival because, as |
| T-5 VI.2:3 | This is the **e.** continuity. It gives the ego a |
| T-5 VI.4:2 | world. The **e.** decisions are always wrong, |
| T-5 VI.4:5 | Bible is a fearful thing in the **e.** judgment. |
| T-5 VI.5:1 | how the **e.** interpretations are misleading, |
| T-5 VI.8:2 | attempt to guarantee the **e.** own survival. |
| T-5 VI.11:2 | my reference to the **e.** dark glass, and |
| T-5 VII.3:4 | **e.** last-ditch defense of its own existence. |
| T-5 VII.3:5 | It reflects both the **e.** need to separate, |
| T-6 II.7:2 | **e.** perception has no counterpart in God, |
| T-6 II.12:1 | The difference between the **e.** projection |
| T-6 IV.4:6 | This makes the body the **e.** friend. It is an |
| T-6 IV.5:3 | that the mind is the **e.** learning device; |
| T-6 IV.6:5 | dreams contain many of the **e.** symbols |
| T-6 IV.10:6 | as the **e.** notion that it has affronted Him. |
| T-6 IV.12:6 | of communication arose as the **e.** voice. It |
| T-6 V.B.4:3 | The **e.** judgment, here as always, is |
| T-6 V.C.1:9 | The **e.** beliefs on this crucial issue vary, |
| T-7 III.2:14 | The **e.** "enemy" is therefore your friend. |
| T-7 III.3:1 | before that the **e.** friend is not part of you, |
| T-7 IV.5:1 | **e.** goal is as unified as the Holy Spirit's, |
| T-7 V.1:3 | effects of the **e.** decision in this matter are |
| T-7 V.3:3 | accept the **e.** confusion of mind and body. |
| T-7 VII.3:2 | yours. The **e.** picture of you is deprived, |
| T-7 VII.8:5 | the ultimate basis for all the **e.** projection. |
| T-7 VII.11:1 | of the **e.** thought system as wholly insane, |
| T-7 VIII.2:1 | The **e.** use of projection must be fully |
| T-7 VIII.5:4 | for the **e.** existence you will have laid |
| T-7 IX.3:4 | **e.** whole thought system blocks extension |
| T-7 X.1:2 | the **e.** reasoning to its logical conclusion, |
| T-7 X.1:5 | You are willing to look at the **e.** premises, |
| T-7 X.4:9 | His. The **e.** wishes do not mean anything, |
| T-7 X.4:11 | This is the **e.** weakness and your strength. |
| T-8 I.2:2 | so. The **e.** voice is an hallucination. You |
| T-8 V.6:1 | The **e.** way is not mine, but it is also not |
| T-8 VII.1:2 | this is the **e.** interpretation of the body. |
| T-8 VII.9:6 | The **e.** temple thus becomes the temple of |
| T-8 VIII.1:2 | The **e.** definitions of anything are childish |
| T-8 VIII.3:1 | to overcome the **e.** belief in the body as an |
| T-8 VIII.3:3 | object to the **e.** firm belief that you are not |
| T-8 VIII.3:4 | appealing argument from the **e.** point of |
| T-8 VIII.3:5 | not give this false witness to the **e.** stand. |
| T-8 VIII.4:3 | a strong witness on behalf of the **e.** views. |
| T-8 VIII.5:7 | **e.** interpretation of the body rests are true |
| T-8 VIII.7:3 | you have accepted the **e.** confusion, and |
| T-8 VIII.8:4 | the **e.** skill in building up false cases. Nor |
| T-8 IX.1:5 | to accept the **e.** belief that the body is the |
| T-8 IX.3:7 | reflect the **e.** distorted notions about what |
| T-9 I.2:1 | Your will is not the **e.**, and that is why the |
| T-9 IV.3:5 | their harmfulness lies in the **e.** judgment. |
| T-9 IV.4:2 | The **e.** plan, of course, makes no sense |
| T-9 IV.4:4 | **e.** plan is to have you see error clearly first |
| T-9 IV.8:3 | Let me repeat that the **e.** qualifications as |
| T-9 IV.9:2 | **e.** time is "borrowed" from your eternity. |
| T-9 V.1:1 | **e.** plan for forgiveness is far more widely |
| T-9 V.3:3 | All unhealed healers follow the **e.** plan for |
| T-9 V.4:1 | Some newer forms of the **e.** plan are as |
| T-9 V.4:2 | interpret the **e.** symbols in a nightmare, |
| T-9 V.4:6 | is a contradiction even in the **e.** terms, |
| T-9 V.7:1 | Both forms of the **e.** approach, then, |
| T-9 VII.4:9 | with the **e.** evaluation of what you are? |
| T-9 VII.6:8 | meaningless within the **e.** thought system |
| T-9 VII.7:3 | keep the **e.** whole thought system intact. |
| T-9 VII.7:6 | reality of the **e.** thought system merely |
| T-9 VIII.11:9 | He would have you replace the **e.** belief in |
| T-10 III.5:1 | at the logical conclusion of the **e.** thought |
| T-10 V.3:1 | to the denial of God is the **e.** religion. The |
| T-11 in.3:5 | the foundation of the **e.** thought system, |
| T-11 in.3:7 | the foundation of the **e.** thought system. |
| T-11 in.4:2 | at last looked at the **e.** foundation without |
| T-11 V.1:3 | at the **e.** thought system because together |
| T-11 V.4:3 | inappropriate if you recognize the **e.** goal, |
| T-11 V.4:4 | **e.** goal is quite explicitly ego autonomy. |
| T-11 V.5:5 | between the **e.** idle wishes and the Will of |
| T-11 V.6:4 | ascribe the **e.** arrogance to Him Who wills |
| T-11 V.9:2 | not its undoing, is the **e.** constant effort, |
| T-11 V.11:1 | If the **e.** goal of autonomy could be |
| T-11 V.11:3 | According to the **e.** teaching, *its* goal can |
| T-11 V.12:5 | Recognize only that the **e.** goal, which you |
| T-11 V.14:1 | The **e.** interpretations of the laws of |
| T-11 V.16:1 | appeal of the **e.** demonstrations to those |
| T-12 IV.2:6 | has the power to deny the **e.** existence, |
| T-12 IV.3:3 | would have to abandon the **e.** guidance, |
| T-12 V.7:1 | I have said that the **e.** rule is, "Seek and |
| T-12 VII.13:2 | The death penalty is the **e.** ultimate goal, |
| T-12 VII.13:3 | death penalty never leaves the **e.** mind, |
| T-13 in.3:4 | salvation, and this is the **e.** interpretation, |
| T-13 I.8:6 | in your mind to ensure the **e.** continuity. |
| T-13 I.8:7 | punished, the **e.** continuity is guaranteed. |
| T-13 I.8:8 | of your continuity is God's, not the **e.**. |
| T-13 I.10:2 | This is the **e.** plan, which it offers instead |
| T-13 I.11:2 | In the **e.** teaching, then, there is no escape |
| T-13 II.2:1 | strange a solution the **e.** arrangement is. |
| T-13 II.3:3 | for the **e.** destructive urge is so intense |
| T-13 II.4:1 | Much of the **e.** strange behavior is |
| T-13 II.4:4 | deepest cornerstone in the **e.** foundation, |
| T-13 II.7:4 | than you dismiss the **e.** thought system. |
| T-13 III.1:9 | look even upon the **e.** darkest cornerstone |
| T-13 III.2:1 | the **e.** dark foundation is the memory of |
| T-13 III.2:8 | For still deeper than the **e.** foundation, |
| T-13 III.4:4 | go into the blackness of the **e.** foundation, |
| T-13 IV.5:5 | if you follow the **e.** dictates you will react |
| T-13 IV.7:1 | of time is the exact opposite of the **e.**. The |
| T-13 VII.10:12 | its own sake is the **e.** fundamental creed, a |
| T-13 IX.1:2 | the future to the past as is the **e.** law. |
| T-13 IX.1:4 | The **e.** laws are strict, and breaches are |
| T-13 IX.2:1 | from guilt is the **e.** whole undoing. *Make* |
| T-13 IX.2:2 | obeying the **e.** harsh commandments you |
| T-13 XI.1:1 | and even death become the **e.** best advice |
| T-14 in.1:6 | We have followed much of the **e.** logic, |
| T-14 V.10:6 | Crucifixion is always the **e.** aim. It sees |
| T-14 X.9:1 | This is characteristic of the **e.** judgments. |
| T-14 X.9:4 | therefore remains the **e.** chosen condition |
| T-15 I.4:7 | the **e.** teaching is without the fear of death |
| T-15 I.4:9 | paradox in the **e.** thought system before, |
| T-15 I.4:15 | Such is the **e.** version of immortality. And |
| T-15 I.4:16 | it is this the **e.** version of time supports. |
| T-15 I.6:1 | bleak and despairing is the **e.** use of time! |
| T-15 I.7:6 | is no escape from fear in the **e.** use of time |
| T-15 I.14:5 | enough to transcend all of the **e.** making, |
| T-15 IV.6:2 | is nothing more than the **e.** attempt to |
| T-15 V.2:1 | The past is the **e.** chief learning device, |
| T-15 V.7:1 | **e.** use of relationships is so fragmented |
| T-15 VII.4:2 | For it is the **e.** fundamental doctrine that |
| T-15 VII.9:6 | The fury of those joined at the **e.** altar far |
| T-15 VII.12:1 | the **e.** plan to establish its own autonomy. |
| T-15 X.8:5 | To Him you ascribed the **e.** treachery, |
| T-16 I.1:2 | That is the **e.** interpretation of empathy, |
| T-16 I.4:7 | and yield not to the **e.** triumphant use of |
| T-16 III.2:4 | **e.** teaching produces immediate results, |
| T-16 III.2:6 | and effect are very clear in the **e.** thought |
| T-16 V.2:3 | The special love relationship is the **e.** chief |
| T-16 V.3:1 | relationship is the **e.** most boasted gift, |
| T-16 V.4:1 | from God, that the **e.** hatred triumphs. |
| T-16 V.6:5 | example could there be of the **e.** maxim, |
| T-16 V.8:4 | he will not interfere with the **e.** illusion of |
| T-16 V.9:4 | in strict accordance with the **e.** goals, is to |
| T-16 VII.3:1 | of the **e.** drive for vengeance on the past. |
| T-16 VII.3:9 | you while you pursue the **e.** goal as its ally |
| T-16 VII.6:1 | Against the **e.** insane notion of salvation |
| T-16 VII.6:3 | opposite of the **e.** fixed belief in salvation |
| T-16 VII.10:1 | the **e.** "atonement" that would destroy. |
| T-17 III.1:12 | unholy alliances to support the **e.** goals, |
| T-17 III.4:2 | For time *is* cruel in the **e.** hands, as it is |
| T-17 IV.4:1 | the special relationship was the **e.** answer |
| T-17 IV.6:4 | aspects of the **e.** thought system that you |
| T-17 VI.2:4 | In the **e.** procedure this is reversed. The |
| T-17 VI.5:8 | see the opposite of the **e.** way of looking, |
| T-18 II.2:5 | both of the **e.** inability to tolerate reality, |
| T-18 IX.5:2 | real foundation for the **e.** thought system. |
| T-19 II.2:6 | illusion underlying all the **e.** grandiosity. |
| T-19 II.4:1 | A major tenet in the **e.** insane religion is |
| T-19 II.5:3 | the most "holy" concept in the **e.** system; |
| T-19 II.7:1 | There is no stone in all the **e.** embattled |
| T-19 II.7:7 | And this would be the **e.** wish, which in |
| T19 IV.B.13:5 | all of the **e.** heavy investment in the body. |
| T19 IV.B.15:1 | The **e.** messages are always sent away |
| T19 IV.B.16:3 | in solemn celebration of the **e.** rule. Not |
| T19 IV.B.17:1 | It is not given to the **e.** disciples to realize |
| T19 IV.C.2:4 | "sinners," the **e.** mournful chorus, |
| T19 IV.C.2:13 | in place of the **e.** you renounced death, |
| T19 IV.C.6:5 | of communication, which is the **e.** goal. |
| T19 IV.C.7:6 | For in it lie hidden all the **e.** secrets, all its |
| T19 IV.C.7:7 | triumph of the **e.** making over creation, |
| T19 IV.C.8:1 | Himself is powerless before the **e.** might, |
| T19 IV.C.8:1 | created against the **e.** savage wish to kill. |
| T-20 III.2:2 | is the **e.** fixed belief that all relationships |
| T-20 VI.4:3 | body is the **e.** chosen weapon for seeking |
| T-20 VI.11:1 | The body is the **e.** idol; the belief in sin |
| T-20 VIII.10:6 | the **e.** purpose brought to your horrified |
| T-21 IV.2:5 | look. Yet this is not the **e.** hidden fear, nor |
| T-21 IV.3:3 | ask it now are threatening the **e.** whole |
| T-21 IV.6:3 | You have perceived the **e.** madness, and |

T-21......IV.7:3 The **e.** weakness is its strength. The song
T-21......IV.7:5 which the **e.** rule has kept it out so long.
T-21......IV.8:1 the **e.** weakness is revealed in both your
T-21....... V.1:6 all the **e.** raucous screams and senseless
T-21....... V.5:8 Yet such is clearly not the **e.** reasoning.
T-21..... V.7:12 reason is beyond the **e.** range of means.
T-22...... III.1:1 introduction of reason into the **e.** thought
T-22...... III.2:1 The **e.** whole continuance depends on its
T-22...... III.2:6 The **e.** opposition to correction leads to
T-23.........I.3:3 upon the body, the **e.** chosen home,
T-23..... II.12:8 Behold, unveiled, the **e.** secret gift, torn
T-25....... V.3:5 And yet, beneath the **e.** senseless shrieks,
W-pI.....44.5:6 Yet perceived through the **e.** eyes, it is loss
W-pI.....61.7:1 Today's idea goes far beyond the **e.** petty
W-pI.....66.9:2 to find salvation under the **e.** guidance.
W-pI.....71.1:3 plan in place of the **e.** is to be damned.
W-pI.....71.1:5 have considered just what the **e.** plan is,
W-pI.....71.2:1 The **e.** plan for salvation centers around
W-pI.....71.4:1 Such is the **e.** plan for your salvation.
W-pI.....71.4:2 in strict accord with the **e.** basic doctrine,
W-pI.....72.1:1 we have recognized that the **e.** plan for
W-pI.....72.2:1 **e.** fundamental wish is to replace God. In
W-pI.....73.1:2 This is not the same as the **e.** idle wishes,
W-pI.....73.1:4 in it. The **e.** idle wishes are unshared, and
W-pI.....73.2:2 rise to it, and the **e.** need for grievances,
W-pI.....73.4:5 The **e.** idle wishes have been withdrawn.
W-pI.....73.6:1 Forget the **e.** arguments which seek to
W-pI.....75.5:1 to see the **e.** shadow on the world today.
W-pI...106.1:1 If you will lay aside the **e.** voice, however
W-pI...133.9:4 that he has served the **e.** hidden goals.
W-pI.133.10:3 He who would still preserve the **e.** goals
W-pI.133.11:2 allowed the **e.** goals to come between the
W-pI...151.4:4 You merely can believe the **e.** judgments,
W-pI...151.7:4 light of what He sees do all the **e.** dreams
M-22 .........3:2 a central concept in the **e.** thought system
M-25 .........5:4 not seen through the **e.** defenses here,
C-2............1:3 It is the **e.** world because of this. What is
C-2............3:3 **e.** unreality is not denied by words nor is
C-2............5:1 The **e.** opposite in every way,–in origin,
C-2............5:3 Here is the **e.** opposite and here alone we
P-2...........I.2:3 we mean, but here is the **e.** last defense.

### ego-alien 2

T-5........ III.4:6 an **e.** journey with the ego as guide. This
T-9......VIII.3:1 miracle impulses and **e.** beliefs of its own.

### ego-based 2

T-4......... II.5:6 conflicted, because all attitudes are **e.**.
W-pI.....35.4:2 all the **e.** attributes which you ascribe to

### ego-body 1

T-4...........V.h The **E.** Illusion

### ego-directed 1

T-4........ VI.1:4 realize how much of your thinking is **e.**.

### ego-oriented 2

T-4...........I.6:4 is the opposite of the **e.** teacher's goal. He
T-4......... II.9:5 "religiously" **e.** may believe that the soul

### egocentric 2

T-2......VIII.1:2 are apt to forget this when you become **e.**,
T-4.........in.1:7 To be **e.** is to be dis-spirited, but to be Self-

### egocentricity 1

T-2......... V.2:4 because **e.** and fear usually occur together

### egoless 3

W-pII ... 12.3:1 The Son of God is **e.**. What can he know
P-2........ III.3:7 One wholly **e.** therapist could heal the
P-2........ III.4:4 the **e.** psychotherapist is an abstraction

### egos 10

T-4 ..........I.6:1 **E.** can clash in any situation, but spirit
T-4 ..........I.6:5 with the effect of his ego on other **e.**, and
T-4 .........I.12:4 the earth because their **e.** are humble, and
T-4 .........II.6:5 evaluates itself in relation to other **e.**. It is
T-4 .........II.6:7 whole perception of other **e.** as real is only
T-4 .........II.8:2 only turn to other **e.** and try to unite with
T-4 ...... VII.8:3 not protecting their **e.** and so nothing can
T-6 .....V.A.5:9 **E.** do join together in temporary
T-9 ....... III.1:1 ego to the errors of other **e.** is not the kind
T-9 ....... III.1:2 **E.** are critical in terms of the kind of

### egotistic 1

T-5 ........ V.1:3 is fear, because only the fearful can be **e.**.

### egotistically 1

T-4 ....... VI.2:3 Whenever you act **e.** towards another,

### Either 2

*either*

T-13 ...VIII.4:2 He is not separate from **E.**, being in the
T-28 .... VII.1:5 Father and the Son is not the Will of **E.**,

### either 96

*Either*

T-1 ........I.49:2 effective quite apart from **e.** the degree or
T-1 ...... VII.5:4 without **e.** over- or understating it. I am
T-2 ....... VI.5:2 things, **e.** simultaneously or successively.
T-3 ....... III.1:7 and time, it is subject to **e.** fear or love.
T-3 ..... VI.2:11 **E.** way you are placing your belief in the
T-3 ...... VII.1:2 It begins with **e.** a making or a creating, a
T-3 ...... VII.3:9 that any interpretation that sees **e.** God or
T-4 ........in.1:3 to a brother cannot set you back **e.**. It can
T-4 ..........I.6:7 as a teacher **e.** to be exalted or rejected,
T-4 ..........I.6:7 I do not accept **e.** perception for myself.
T-4 ........ V.2:3 therefore **e.** distorts them or refuses to
T-6 ........I.19:2 know that you cannot **e.** hurt or be hurt,
T-6 ..... V.C.4:8 still believe that you can choose **e.** one. By
T-7 ........ V.2:4 is not the level for **e.** teaching or learning,
T-7 ........ V.3:6 can be used **e.** for healing or for magic,
T-7 ....... VI.8:8 Commitment to **e.** must be total; they
T-8 ....... III.5:9 He will respond **e.** with pain or with joy,
T-9 ..........I.8:2 it can only decide **e.** that there is no God
T-9 ..........I.8:4 **E.** of these insane decisions will induce
T-9 ..........I.8:5 no one really wants **e.** abandonment or
T-9 ....... IV.2:3 to believe **e.** that you do not make them,
T-9 ........ V.1:6 but that it does not matter for **e.** of them.
T-10 . III.10:10 Yet fear is not due them **e.**, for nothing
T-11 ......in.1:1 **E.** God or the ego is insane. If you will
T-11 ......in.2:8 And **e.** the ego, which you made, *is* your
T-11 .......II.2:5 **e.** from your brother or in your own mind
T-11 ... VI.10:6 to His Will is **e.** great or small. What does
T-12 ....... V.5:5 **e.** for themselves or for anyone else. You
T-13 ..... VI.2:3 the past, **e.** his or yours as you perceived it
T-13 .... VII.2:4 yet **e.** one will seem as real to you as the
T-14 ..... III.2:3 You do not want **e.** alone, for without
T-14 ..... III.5:9 **E.** it is a penalty from which you suffer, or
T-14 .......X.7:2 much too confused **e.** to recognize love, or
T-15 .......II.3:6 to support **e.** their weakness or your own.
T-16 ........I.6:5 thing that would hurt **e.** him or you, for
T-16 ........I.6:8 you how to meet both without losing **e.**.
T-16 .......II.2:4 understand them, **e.** in part or in whole.
T-16 ...... V.6:2 and to the inability to perceive **e.** as it is.
T-18 ...... V.6:6 come to **e.** of you without the other. And
T-18 ...... V.6:7 it will come to both at the request of **e.**.
T19. IV.D.20:2 seen as **e.** the giver of guilt or of salvation,
T-20 ..... VI.8:2 They **e.** are or not. An unholy relationship
T-20 .... VII.4:7 **E.** must be an error, for both would place
T-20 .... VII.5:9 has no order. You **e.** see or not.
T-20 .... VII.7:5 **E.** is meaningless without the end for
T-20 ...VIII.2:7 not that you need make **e.** means or end.
T-21 ... VII.1:8 against him; **e.** you love him or attack him
T-22 .......II.5:4 an idea as what will make it **e.** true or false
T-22 ......II.6:10 Faith and belief can fall to **e.** side, but
T-22 .......II.7:3 **E.** you give each other life or death; either
T-22 .......II.7:3 **e.** you are each other's savior or his judge,
T-22 .......II.7:6 will **e.** escape from misery entirely or not
T-22 ..... IV.1:2 You must go **e.** one way or the other. For
T-22 ..... IV.3:4 **E.** you or your brother alone will see it as
T-22 ... VI.13:5 **E.** position is a logical conclusion. Either
T-22 ... VI.13:6 **E.** could be maintained, but never both.
T-23 ......I.12:7 be; where **e.** goes the other disappears. So
T-23 ..... IV.3:6 **E.** the Father and the Son are murderers,
T-25 ..... VI.6:5 He has the means for **e.**, as he always did.
T-25 .... VII.3:2 It must be so that **e.** God is mad, or is this
T-25 .... VII.6:3 and **e.** one perceives the other as insane
T-25 .. VII.11:7 understand that it must be **e.** God or this
T-25 .. VII.13:1 that **e.** God or you must lose to madness
T-27 .... VI.2:2 For **e.** witness is the same, and carries but
T-28 .... VII.3:1 **E.** there is a gap between you and your
T-29 ..... IV.1:7 some, for you are **e.** sleeping or awake.
T-31 .......II.3:1 is free, for it will have one outcome **e.** way.
T-31 .....V.11:4 go, if **e.** one were ever raised to doubt. The
T-31 .....V.13:4 Nor can this be explained by **e.** view. The
W-pI ...... 2.1:4 so that you include whatever is on **e.** side.
W-pI ...... 4.2:6 seeing impossible. You do not want **e.**.
W-pI .... 16.2:3 **e.** it extends the truth or it multiplies
W-pI .... 16.3:1 thought you have brings **e.** peace or war;
W-pI .... 16.3:1 brings either peace or war; **e.** love or fear.
W-pI .... 28.2:6 all. You **e.** see or not. When you have seen
W-pI .... 32.5:2 as you survey **e.** your inner or outer world
W-pI .... 46.7:1 shorter practice periods may consist **e.** of
WpI... rI.in.3:1 the comments that follow each idea **e.**.
W-pI .... 54.1:3 They will **e.** make a false world or lead me
W-pI .. 140.2:6 One **e.** sleeps or wakens. There is nothing
W-pI .. 163.6:3 total. **E.** all things die, or else they live and
W-pI .. 189.7:2 of everything it thinks is **e.** true or false, or
W-pII . 224.1:4 but this that can be **e.** given or received.
M-12 ....... 5:11 does not suffer **e.** in going or remaining.
M-14 ......... 4:7 He does not judge it **e.** as hard or easy. His
M-17 ......... 4:9 **E.** truth is apparent, or it is not. It cannot
M-19 ......... 5:4 In this lies **e.** Heaven or hell, as you elect.
M-24 ......... 1:2 has no meaning **e.** once or many times.
M-27 ......... 4:6 There is **e.** a god of fear or One of Love.
M-29 ......... 1:3 It is not a substitute for **e.**, but merely a
P-in ......... 1:8 **E.** way, the task is the same; the patient
P-2........... I.3:2 **E.** way, it sets a limit on psychotherapy
P-2........ III.2:5 may come from **e.** one at the beginning,
P-3..........II.9:6 **E.** they are equal or not. The attempts of
P-3........ III.4:7 There is no cost to **e.**. But thanks are due
S-1...........I.7:8 a specific problem will occur to **e.** of you;

### elaborate 3

T-17 ..... IV.7:5 The frame is very **e.**, all set with jewels,
T-17 ..... IV.8:2 heavy and so **e.** that the picture is almost
W-pI .. 135.3:5 as you **e.** your plans and make your armor

### elaboration 2

T-7 .........V.1:3 are so apparent that they need no **e.**, but
P-2..........II.2:3 that it hardly requires **e.** here. Religion is

### elapse 2

W-pI .... 90.3:3 time must **e.** before it can be worked out.
W-pI 137.11:2 does time **e.** between the instant they are

### elapsed 1

W-pII . 234.1:2 has **e.** between eternity and timelessness.

### elder 3

T-1 .........II.3:7 An **e.** brother is entitled to respect for his
T-1 .........II.4:5 as an **e.** brother to you on the one hand,
T-4 ........I.13:2 A father can safely leave a child with an **e.**

### elect 17

T-in ........... 1:5 *only that you can* **e.** *what you want to take at*
T-1 .........V.5:2 the mind can **e.** what it chooses to serve.
T-1 .........V.5:5 If it does not freely **e.** to do so, it retains
T-4 ..... IV.11:5 Your mind will **e.** to join with mine, and

T-20... VIII.9:4 see is merely how you **e.** to meet your goal
T-25...... IX.7:2 given specially to an **e.** and special group,
T-27...... VI.8:3 And no one will **e.** to suffer more. What
T-29......... I.4:3 separate till you and he **e.** to meet again.
W-pI...39.10:3 However you **e.** to use it, the idea should
W-pI...156.3:3 be of ice; the sea **e.** to be apart from water
W-pI...190.6:4 it will change entirely as you **e.** to change
W-pII.....284.h I can **e.** to change all thoughts that hurt.
W-pII..284.1:7 I can **e.** to change all thoughts that hurt.
W-pII..308.1:2 If I **e.** to reach past time to timelessness, I
W-pII..352.1:5 *I am redeemed when I e. to follow in this way*
M-19..........5:4 In this lies either Heaven or hell, as you **e.**.
P-3........ III.8:2 carrying the gift of healing, if you so **e.**.

### elected 4

T-5........ VI.1:4 have **e.** to be in time rather than eternity,
T-6...........I.9:1 I **e.**, for your sake and mine, to
T-7....... X.5:12 because he has **e.** to follow false guidance.
W-pI.153.11:2 done. God has **e.** all, but few have come to

### electing 1

T-3......... V.6:6 In **e.** perception instead of knowledge,

### election 5

T-4......... V.4:1 The body is the ego's home by its own **e.**.
T-5........ VI.1:5 Yet your **e.** is both free and alterable. You
T-24.........I.2:6 than you think, are there by your **e.**. Do
W-pI.153.10:6 of God, by His **e.** and their own as well?
M-5..........I.1:4 For sickness is an **e.**; a decision. It is the

### elects 7

T-1......... V.5:4 If it **e.** to do so, the mind can become the
T-5......... V.1:4 to side with Heaven or earth, as it **e.**. But
T-9........ IV.8:4 Anyone who **e.** a totally insane guide
T-25...... III.5:6 **e.** to see them elsewhere from their home,
T-31. VIII.11:5 And as each one **e.** to join with me, the
W-pI...152.1:2 pain except his choice **e.** this state for him
W-pI...167.9:2 When the mind **e.** to be what it is not,

### element 5

T-2... V.A.16:2 no **e.** of judgment at all. The statement
T-15... VIII.6:2 and by removing every **e.** of disagreement
T-16.........I.6:6 they always contain some **e.** of specialness
T-30..... VII.1:7 You add an **e.** into the script you write for
T-30..... VII.1:8 else. You take away another **e.**, and every

### elements 10

T-5...........I.7:1 of perception in which many **e.** are like
T-7......... II.1:1 of God, and because of the **e.** they share,
T-12...... VI.6:5 and more common **e.** in all situations, the
T-13... VIII.3:1 has many **e.** in common with knowledge,
T-15....... V.4:1 relationships have **e.** of fear in them. This
T-17...... III.8:4 those **e.** that fit the purpose of the unholy
T-27....... V.8:8 seen as one, for only common **e.** are there.
W-pI.151.11:1 will select the **e.** in them which represent
W-pI.151.13:3 to Him Who sees the **e.** of truth in them.
W-pI.151.13:4 comes to mind, remove the **e.** of dreams,

### elevator 2

M-3............2:2 of two apparent strangers in an **e.**, a child
M-3............2:5 seeming strangers in the **e.** will smile to

### eliminating 2

T-1......... II.6:9 it, thus **e.** certain intervals within it. It
T-7...... III.1:12 perception makes it meaningless by **e.** or

### else 323

### else's 4

### elsewhere 15

T-11...... IV.5:3 is why blame must be undone, not seen **e.**
T-14....... II.2:1 where you are but knowing you are **e.**,
T-14....... X.3:4 as something that must come from **e.**, not
T-17...... VI.7:1 the ego will attempt to take this aspect **e.**,
T-17..... VII.1:3 remove it from its source and place it **e.**.
T-17..... VII.1:7 To remove the problem **e.** is to keep it, for
T-17..... VII.2:3 For if you shift part of the problem **e.** the
T-17... VII.3:11 and seek not to have it made up to you **e.**,
T-19...... IV.1:3 Others will seem to arise from **e.**; from
T-20...... VI.1:2 If it were **e.** it would rest on contingency,
T-21...... III.8:4 desiring to place its power **e.** should
T-25...... III.5:6 If it elects to see them **e.** from their home,
T-26....... V.6:9 Yet can he still imagine he is **e.**, and in
T-29... VII.1:10 happiness abides, and seek no longer **e.**.
W-pI.155.13:2 Look not to ways that seem to lead you **e.**.

### elude 2

W-pI.....16.4:1 thought that may tend to **e.** the search.
W-pI...127.3:4 And it must **e.** the mind that thinks of it

### eludes 1

T-21..... VII.4:6 who always **e.** its murderous attack by

### elusive 2

T-21... VII.12:6 now an **e.** shadow attached to nothing, he
T-21... VII.13:1 **E.** happiness, or happiness in changing

### emaciated 1

T-20...... III.9:1 heavy chains for years, starved and **e.**,

### emanates 1

T-1......... II.1:7 Neither **e.** from consciousness, but both

### embark 3

T-4.........in.2:5 Do not **e.** on useless journeys, because
T-4.........in.2:6 but spirit cannot **e.** on them because it is
W-pI...157.8:1 Today we will **e.** upon a course you have

### embarked 1

W-pI...158.3:4 by him, although he has not yet **e.** on it.

### embarking 1

T-12..... II.10:1 We are therefore **e.** on an organized, well-

### embarks 2

T-15..... VII.1:7 relationship on which the ego **e.** *is* special.
T-15..... VII.4:6 And thus it **e.** on an endless, unrewarding

### embarrassing 1

M-21 .........5:3 situation that appears to be very **e.** to him

### embarrassment 1

M-7 ...........5:6 is a guilty **e.** stemming from false humility

### embattled 2

T-13...... XI.2:1 God would not have His Son **e.**, and so
T-19....... II.7:1 There is no stone in all the ego's **e.** citadel

### embodiment 2

W-pI.....72.2:2 fact, the ego is the physical **e.** of that wish.
W-pI...163.2:1 **E.** of fear, the host of sin, god of the guilty

### embrace 15

T-14....... V.8:5 everyone to its safe **e.** of love and union.
T-18.... VI.14:3 to you to be yourself, within its safe **e.**.
T-19...... IV.1:1 to **e.** all the Sonship and give it rest, it will
T-26....... VI.2:4 and forgiveness from your welcoming **e.**.
T-29....... V.2:4 peace surrounds you gently in its soft **e.**,
T-30...... IV.1:3 defensiveness entirely, and rush to its **e.**.
WpI... rI.in.5:1 there to **e.** any situation in which you are.
W-pI.....92.9:2 Self stands ready to **e.** you as Its Own.
W-pI.200.10:6 and you can feel its soft **e.** surround your
W-pII .244.1:3 *and loving, in the safety of Your Fatherly e.?*
W-pII ..... 9.2:1 it to **e.** the world and hold you safe within
W-pII .317.2:5 *And all my sorrows end in Your e., which*
P-2......... V.8:9 God returns to Heaven through its kind **e.**
S-3........ IV.2:5 Time remains only to let the last **e.** of
S-3........ IV.7:2 **e.** of everlasting Love and perfect peace.

### embraces 3

T-15...... XI.7:6 For communication **e.** everything, and in
T-30...... III.9:3 sky **e.** it and softly holds it in its perfect
T-31..... V.15:7 concept of the self **e.** all you look upon,

### embracing

*See* all-embracing

### embroider 1

W-pI...137.5:3 which dreams **e.** into pictures of the truth

### emerge 10

T-1..........II.6:4 and receiver both **e.** farther along in time
T-2...... VIII.2:8 you must **e.** from the conflict if you are to
T-15........X.5:1 **e.** in forms quite different from what it is.
T-16...... IV.2:3 unharmed, and will at last **e.** as yourself.
T-17..... V.7:12 will see the justification for your faith **e.**,
T-18.........I.5:3 from it a world of total unreality *had* to **e.**.
T-24......II.14:5 You but **e.** from an illusion of what you
T-25... VII.10:4 **e.** from deepest mourning into perfect joy
T-27..... VII.2:4 will **e.** in all its primitive simplicity. The
T-31........II.3:3 and the follower **e.** as separate roles, each

### emergencies 1

M-4 ..... I.A.8:3 counted on in all "**e.**" as well as tranquil

### emerges 2

T-15.........I.8:4 of God **e.** from the past into the present.
T-23........II.6:1 could not be more apparent than **e.** here.

### emerging 1

T-23......II.10:1 mechanisms of madness are seen **e.** here:

### eminence 1

W-pI...133.2:2 you buy, to **e.** as valued by the world, you

### emotion 14

T-14..... VII.7:5 into *one* meaning, *one* **e.** and *one* purpose.
T-18.........I.3:1 one **e.** in which substitution is impossible
T-18.........I.3:3 is both a fragmented and fragmenting **e.**.
T19. IV.A.12:2 And this depends on which **e.** was called
T19 IV.B.10:10 the home of the **e.** that calls them forth,
T-22.........I.4:7 fear. Here is the one **e.** that you made,
T-22.........I.4:8 to be. This is the **e.** of secrecy, of private
T-22.........I.4:9 This is the one **e.** that opposes love, and
T-22........I.4:10 Here is the one **e.** that keeps you blind,
W-pI....... 8.5:2 *[name of an object], about [name of an e.],*

W-pI.......8.6:3 any e. that the idea for today may induce,
W-pI.....13.1:1 that it is more specific as to the e. aroused
W-pI.....21.2:4 of the e. you experience does not matter.
W-pI...130.6:5 is all a piece because it stems from one e.,

### emotionally 3

T-11....... V.9:1 "lighthearted," distant, e. shallow, callous
T-12.........I.2:4 your reactions behaviorally, but not e..
W-pI.......3.1:6 see may have e. charged meaning for you.

### emotions 12

T-12.........I.9:5 Fear and love are the only e. of which you
T-13.......... V.h The Two E.
T-13.......... V.1:1 I have said you have but two e., love and
T-13.......... V.5:1 You have but two e., yet in your private
T-13.......... V.6:3 Your manifestations of e. are the opposite
T-13.......... V.6:3 are the opposite of what the e. are. You
T-13..... V.10:1 You have but two e., and one you made
T-18....... II.5:4 you realize that the e. the dream produces
W-pI.....34.6:1 the form of more generalized adverse e.,
W-pI...167.4:2 e. alternate because of causes you cannot
W-pI...186.8:5 in mood, and our e. raise us high indeed,
M-17 .........4:2 that gives rise to negative e., regardless of

### empathize 3

T-16.........I.1:1 To e. does not mean to join in suffering,
T-16.........I.1:3 capacity to e. is very useful to the Holy
T-16.........I.2:7 through you, you will e. with strength,

### empathizes 1

T-16.........I.2:5 maneuver; the ego always e. to weaken,

### empathizing 1

T-16.........I.2:6 You do not know what e. means. Yet of

### empathy 9

T-16............I.h True E.
T-16.........I.1:2 That is the ego's interpretation of e., and
T-16.........I.2:1 The clearest proof that e. as the ego uses
T-16.........I.3:4 All you have learned of e. is from the past.
T-16.........I.3:6 Do not use e. to make the past real, and
T-16.........I.4:1 True e. is of Him Who knows what it is.
T-16.........I.4:7 the ego's triumphant use of e. for its glory
T-16.........I.5:3 and the form of e. which would bring this
T-16.........I.5:8 anyone. Offer your e. to Him for it is *His*

### emphasis 21

T-2........ III.1:9 The e. on beautiful structures is a sign of
T-2........ IV.1:1 Our e. is now on healing. The miracle is
T-6............I.1:3 only e. laid upon it so far has been that it
T-13...... IV.4:3 Remember that its e. on guilt enables it to
T-13...... IV.7:5 His e. is therefore on the only aspect of
T-13... VII.13:2 supply them with no e. at all upon them.
T-14..... VII.4:1 Our e. has been on bringing what is
T-18.........I.3:7 with special e. on certain parts, and used
T-23...... II.16:5 the e. on form and disregard of content.
T-27..... VII.1:1 Suffering is an e. upon all that the world
W-pI.....10.2:4 The e. is now on the lack of reality of what
W-pI.....24.4:2 e. should be on uncovering the outcome
W-pI.....35.3:3 the e. for today is on the perceiver, rather
W-pI.....39.8:1 without undue e. on any one in particular
W-pI.....66.1:1 You have surely noticed an e. throughout
W-pI...129.1:3 Our e. is not on giving up the world, but
W-pI.135.15:3 Time becomes a future e., to be
W-pI...167.3:7 The e. this course has placed on that idea
M-16 .........3:3 of time is an essential early e. which,
M-24 .........6:1 e. of this course always remains the same;
C-in ...........5:1 will notice that the e. on structural issues

### emphasize 11

T-5......... V.8:2 e. the destructive results of the decision.
T-6 ........ V.3:2 He does not e. what you must avoid to
T-13 ...... IV.9:2 will e. only the aspect of time in which
T-21 .... VII.5:9 understand, he will but e. his helplessness
T-21 .... VII.6:4 We said this year would e. the sameness
W-pI.....18.2:2 for today e. this aspect of your perception
W-pI.....35.5:1 you will probably e. what you consider to
WpI... rI.in.3:2 Try, rather, to e. the central point, and
W-pI.....67.2:9 We are also trying to e. that you are part
WpI..rIII.in8:1 We e. the benefits to you if you devote
W-pI...127.4:1 to e. that there can never be a difference

### emphasized 31

T-1 ...... VII.5:3 also e. that awe is proper in the Presence
T-2 ........ V.6:1 It should be e. again that the body does
T-2 ....... VI.8:1 I have e. that the miracle, or the
T-2 .... VII.5:10 It should be e., however, that ultimately
T-2 ...... VII.7:7 and have e. that the only real mastery is
T-3 ....... IV.6:8 of correction because, as I have already e.,
T-4 .......II.11:1 It cannot be e. too often that correcting
T-5 ....... III.6:1 I have repeatedly e. that one level of the
T-6 ..........I.2:7 it. While I e. only the resurrection before,
T-6 ....... III.1:1 As we have already e., every idea begins
T-7 ....... IV.3:8 rather than their differences is e..
T-7 ........ V.2:5 learner because, as has been repeatedly e.,
T-7 ....... VI.8:1 I have repeatedly e. that the ego does
T-9 ..........I.5:1 I have e. many times that the Holy Spirit
T-12 .........I.8:5 repeatedly e. the need to recognize fear
T-18 .........I.3:7 The body is e., with special emphasis on
T-18 ...... IV.7:6 have e. that you need understand nothing
W-pI.......9.5:1 is e. again that while complete inclusion
W-pI.....29.2:4 Yet we e. yesterday that a table shares the
WpI... rI.in.4:1 is e. for practice periods at your stage of
W-pI.....72.1:1 e. that it is an active attack on His plan,
W-pI.....73.5:5 We have repeatedly e. that the barrier of
W-pI...135.7:2 This cannot be too often e.. It will be
W-pI...161.6:2 of our text, where it is often e.. This is the
M-4 ..... VII.1:6 e. throughout the text and the workbook,
M-16 .........3:3 learning process, becomes less and less e..
M-17 .........2:6 has it been e. that you give but to yourself
M-24 .........4:1 too strongly e. that this course aims at a
P-2........ IV.7:2 And as we have already e., correction
P-2...... IV.10:5 too strongly e. that the insane believe that
S-3.........in.1:3 importance should not be too strongly e.,

### emphasizes 11

T-3 ....... VI.2:5 never e. only the positive aspects of what
T-5 ....... VI.7:2 statement e. that vengeance cannot be
T-6 ..... V.C.3:4 e. the dichotomy between the desirable
T-9 .........II.3:1 The Bible e. that all prayer is answered,
T-16 ..... IV.3:3 contrary, it e. the guilt outside the haven
T-31 .... VII.1:8 concept e. treachery, and trust becomes
W-pI.....18.1:2 It also e. the idea that minds are joined,
W-pI...103.2:7 is fear. It also e. happiness belongs to you,
M-in ..........1:5 the other hand, e. that to teach *is* to learn,
M-in ..........1:6 also e. that teaching is a constant process;
M-2 ...........3:6 there. As the course e., you are not free to

### emphasizing 7

T-3 ....... III.1:1 We have been e. perception, and have
T-7 .........II.5:3 e. always that *these differences do not*
T-9 ........ V.6:3 light to remove it, while e. the distance?
W-pI.....10.3:2 Now we are e. that the presence of these
W-pI.....19.2:1 are again e. the fact that minds are joined.
WpI... rI.in.6:4 We are now e. the relationships among
W-pI...184.1:5 other things by e. space surrounding it.

### employ 7

T-20 .......II.1:4 e. this hated thing to draw your brother
T-25 ...... VI.7:5 the Holy Spirit cannot e. on his behalf,
T-28 .........I.3:4 can e. for healing have been given Him,
WpI..rIII.in6:6 and let the mind e. the thoughts you gave
W-pI...161.3:3 that He may e. them for a purpose which
W-pII .236.1:6 to the Holy Spirit to e. as He sees fit. I
W-pII .....7.3:3 He will e. the means you made for exile to

### employed 6

T-17 .... VII.9:3 And you will see the means you once e. to
T-20 .... VII.7:3 appropriate to the end for which it is e..
T-20 .... VII.7:4 one is a *choice* of purpose, e. on its behalf.
T-27 ..... III.1:3 and power used to weaken is e. to limit.
T-28 ........I.3:1 Nothing e. for healing represents an
T-28 .....II.11:4 sickness, and e. the body to be victim, or

### employs 4

T-30 ..... VI.4:1 the world e. to keep the sense of sin alive.
W-pI .... 73.2:3 the ego e. to traffic in grievances. They
W-pI 135.13:4 mind e. for this will function flawlessly,
C-5 ........... 1:6 go beyond the names the course itself e..

### emptied 1

T-30 ..... IV.8:8 The gap is e. of the toys of fear, and then

### emptiness 8

T-1 ....... IV.4:1 e. engendered by fear must be replaced by
T-2 ..........I.1:4 There is no e. in you. Because of your
T-2 ..........I.1:7 believe that some e. or lack exists in you,
T-2 ... V.A.14:4 then, is e.. Being without substantial
T-3 .........II.6:4 error and e. can never find lasting solace.
T-22 ..... III.3:6 cannot conceal its e. from reason's eyes.
T-26 ..... VI.3:2 its e. has left yours empty and unoccupied
T-28 .......V.7:6 behold the innocence and e. of sin that

### empty 33

T-1 ....... IV.2:9 perceives an e. shell and is unaware of the
T-1 .........V.1:4 You can make an e. shell, but you cannot
T-2 ... V.A.15:3 is an e. gesture unless it entails correction
T-4 ........I.11:4 to leave it e. by their own dispossession.
T-9 ... VIII.10:2 and while you leave your part of it e. your
T-11 ........I.3:4 there would be an e. place in God's Mind.
T-15 ..... IV.3:3 For you leave e. your place in His plan,
T-22 ..... VI.5:6 And every e. place in Heaven that you fill
T-23 ..... III.2:3 An e. box, however beautiful and gently
T-24 ... IV.3:15 and your treasure house barren and e.,
T-25 .......II.5:1 an e. frame upon a wall and stands before
T-26 ..... VI.3:2 has left yours e. and unoccupied? Make
T-27 ......I.10:1 Into this e. space, from which the goal of
T-27 ..... III.2:6 must stand for e. space and nothingness.
T-27 ..... III.2:7 Yet nothingness and e. space can not be
T-27 ..... III.3:8 the e. space it occupies be recognized as
T-27 ..... III.4:1 An e. space that is not seen as filled, an
T-28 .......II.5:1 An e. storehouse, with an open door,
T-28 ..... III.5:2 Yet separation is but e. space, enclosing
T-28 ..... III.5:2 unsubstantial as the e. place between the
T-28 ..... VII.1:3 An e. space, a little gap, would be a lack.
T-29 .......V.5:7 And being e. they receive, instead, a
T-30 ..... III.4:7 will could not be satisfied with e. forms,
W-pI .... 13.2:2 e. space that meaninglessness provides.
W-pI .. 126.7:3 Could He be satisfied with e. gestures,
W-pI 133.13:1 is reached with e. hands and open minds,
W-pI .. 161.4:6 What can they seem to be but e. sounds;
W-pI .. 189.7:2 E. your mind of everything it thinks is
W-pI .. 189.7:5 come with wholly e. hands unto your God
W-pII . 306.2:2 *with e. hands and open hearts and minds,*
W-pII . 344.1:3 *I found an e. place where nothing ever was or*
M-6 ........... 4:8 God's treasure house can never be e.. And
C-4 ............ 4:4 there is an e. place made clean and ready.

### emptying 1

W-pI .. 130.8:3 come to these five minutes e. your hands

### enable 21

T-1 ........I.15:2 The purpose of time is to e. you to learn
T-1 ........I.24:1 Miracles e. you to heal the sick and raise
T-2 ...... VII.1:8 it would take a miracle to e. you to do this
T-4 ..........I.4:1 because they e. you to change your mind
T-6 ........I.12:1 to e. the Sonship to know its Wholeness.
T-6 ... V.C.10:2 Holy Spirit will e. you to take this step, if
T-7 ....... III.1:6 does e. you to use it always and in all ways

T-11....... II.4:3 He will **e.** you to go far beyond the healing
T-12..... VII.2:6 in their existence as they **e.** you to act.
T-15..... VII.4:5 it, it will **e.** you to direct its anger outward
T-16...... VI.6:5 the only value the body has is to **e.** you to
T-17......... I.5:5 But to give illusions to truth is to **e.** truth
T-17......... I.5:5 and thus **e.** you to escape from them.
T-17.... III.1:10 hoping that their witness will **e.** you to
T-17.... III.10:3 to **e.** you to hurt yourself through them.
T-17..... V.12:5 and thus **e.** its results to be accepted and
T-23....... II.8:6 Son. Think not the ego will **e.** you to find
WpI ...rI.in.4:4 is to **e.** you to bring the quiet with you,
W-pI..... 95.8:4 for weakness will **e.** us to overlook it,
W-pI..... 98.9:2 He will **e.** you to understand your special
W-pI... 151.9:7 His lessons will **e.** you to bridge the gap

### enabled 3

T-17...... IV.4:3 it, and by His blessing **e.** it to be healed.
T-30....... V.8:6 for you have **e.** Him to rise from chains
W-pI..... 54.5:4 through me has **e.** love to replace fear,

### enables 30

T-1........ III.4:5 because it **e.** me to direct its application,
T-2........... I.4:4 which **e.** you to realize that your errors
T-2........ I.5:12 **e.** you to remain unshaken by lack of love
T-3........ VI.3:6 that **e.** recognition to replace perception.
T-4........ I.13:4 this **e.** you not to be concerned with them
T-4........ VI.4:4 to use the device that **e.** it to endure.
T-5........ III.7:2 His ability to deal with symbols **e.** Him to
T-5........ III.7:3 **e.** Him to understand the laws of God, for
T-6.......... II.8:3 Spirit **e.** you to perceive this wholeness
T-6........ IV.2:5 This **e.** the ego to regard itself as separate
T-6...... V.C.2:4 **e.** the mind to teach without judgment,
T-7...... IV.7:12 This **e.** you to remember what you are.
T-7..... VII.11:2 correction **e.** you to perceive any part of
T-11..... VII.4:1 denial of the opposite of goodness **e.** you
T-12..... VII.3:2 He **e.** you to do is clearly not of this world
T-12..... VII.3:3 Spirit **e.** you to do is clearly beyond all of
T-12..... VII.7:9 **e.** it to believe that it is pursuing one goal.
T-13...... IV.4:3 Remember that its emphasis on guilt **e.** it
T-13...... VI.5:1 miracle **e.** you to see your brother without
T-13...... VI.6:4 and thus **e.** them to reach each other. The
T-16....... II.4:4 of your gift **e.** Him to understand it, and
T-16...... IV.8:5 **e.** you to look on all your brothers with
T-17...... III.5:2 What forgiveness *is* **e.** Him to do so. If all
T-18.... IV.1:10 do so little that **e.** Him to give so much.
T-20....... II.5:4 And what **e.** Him to see His purpose shine
T-20... VIII.4:3 the vision that **e.** you to see the body not.
T-21...... II.10:3 seeming independence of effect **e.** it to be
M-26.......... 1:8 **e.** others to leave the world with them.
P-in............ 1:6 interpersonal relationships that **e.** him to
P-3......... II.9:3 This **e.** him to pass by many obstacles to

### enabling 4

T-6......... II.7:3 By **e.** you to use perception in a way that
T-13... VIII.5:4 into the darkness, and **e.** the world to see.
P-2........ VI.6:6 of his sins, **e.** him to let them go. Let him
S-1........ III.1:4 and **e.** you to recognize it is not he who is

### enact

*See* re-enact

### enacted 2

T-16..... V.11:4 is this ritual **e.** in the special relationship.
T-16..... V.11:6 Over and over and over this ritual is **e.**.

### enacts

*See* re-enacts

### enchant 1

T-17....... II.2:6 all ugliness into beauty that will **e.** you,

### enclose 1

T-17...... IV.9:8 system, for these aspects **e.** the whole,

### encloses 1

T-17...... IV.7:6 to divert your attention from what it **e.**.

### enclosing 1

T-28...... III.5:2 separation is but empty space, **e.** nothing,

### enclosure 2

T-17.. IV.12:10 of its enormous and disproportionate **e.**.
T-20...... VI.5:2 a meaningless **e.** carefully protected, yet

### encompass 8

T-1......... II.4:4 and man would be too great for you to **e.**.
T-10....... in.3:7 because, being in God, you **e.** everything.
T-14.... XI.14:4 His Creator must **e.** faith in His creation.
T-15....... II.3:4 The blessed instant reaches out to **e.** time,
T-15....... II.3:4 time, as God extends Himself to **e.** you.
T-17... VIII.2:4 it **e.** every situation and bring you peace.
T-18.... VI.11:4 else in which your mind enlarges to **e.** it.
T-19...... IV.3:6 in you has been extended to **e.** everyone,

### encompassed

*See* all-encompassed

### encompasses 15

T-4....... VII.5:1 God, Who **e.** all being, created beings
T-7..... V.10:11 everything because it **e.** all things within
T-8......... II.7:3 it **e.** all things because it created all things
T-8......... V.3:1 not separate, because His Oneness **e.** ours
T-11..... V.12:1 on Him, because His Autonomy **e.** yours,
T-12...... III.7:3 and the recognition that it **e.** completely
T-12... VIII.7:4 you is perfect in His sight, and **e.** all of it.
T-18...... VI.8:9 it. It **e.** everything. It encompasses you
T-18.... VI.8:10 It **e.** you entirely; you within it and it
T-18.... VI.10:7 limits can there be on you whom He **e.**?
T-19......... I.1:4 This faith **e.** everyone involved, for only
W-pI... 156.6:2 in you steps forward and **e.** the world. It
W-pI... 169.5:2 in His Being, He **e.** all things. No mind
W-pI... 194.1:2 So great the distance is that it **e.**, it sets
W-pII...... 9.2:1 advent, which **e.** all living things with you

### encompassing 2

*See also* all-encompassing, Self-encompassing, world-encompassing

T-18... VIII.8:3 **e.** only to preserve and keep complete
T-24....... II.9:5 and in peace so real and so **e.** that nothing

### encompassment

*See* love-encompassment

### encounter 15

*See also* Appendix C

T-7...... VI.4:11 the only decision the ego could possibly **e.**
T-8........... III.h The Holy **E.**
T-8........ III.4:1 you meet anyone, remember it is a holy **e.**
T-8........ III.6:8 And every holy **e.** in which you enter fully
T-8........ III.7:1 You can **e.** only part of yourself because
T-13...... IV.6:7 Would you recognize a holy **e.** if you are
T-13...... IV.6:8 of salvation, which makes the **e.** holy,
T-13...... IV.6:9 and the **e.** is holy because you are. The
T-13.... IV.6:10 ego teaches that you always **e.** your past,
T-19...... IV.1:1 and give it rest, it will **e.** many obstacles.
T-24... VII.11:1 earth without a meeting place and no **e.**.
W-pI..... 44.5:2 may find that you will **e.** strong resistance
W-pI. 135.19:2 and this life becomes a meaningful **e.** with
M-3........... 2:6 Even at the level of the most casual **e.**, it is
M-12......... 3:6 the fear that truth would **e.** in them. Do

### encounters 6

T-13...... IV.7:7 holy **e.** in which salvation can be found.
T19. IV.A.2:10 the peace in you **e.** in its going forth. This
M-3........... 2:2 consists of what seem to be very casual **e.**;
M-3........... 2:3 These are not chance **e.**. Each of them has
M-4..... I.A.4:5 events, **e.** and circumstances are helpful.
P-2........... I.4:1 psychotherapy is a series of holy **e.** in

### encouraged 2

T-3........... I.1:5 as if God permitted and even **e.** one of His
W-pI..... 39.5:1 and more frequent practice sessions are **e.**

### encourages 1

W-pI... 153.4:3 of threat the world **e.** is so much deeper,

### encouraging 2

T-12...... IV.1:3 though **e.** the search for love very actively,
W-pI. 152.11:2 its ways, **e.** our frightened minds with this

### encroach 2

T-14......... I.5:6 seem to **e.** upon deception and strike at it.
T-25...... III.8:9 But on His vision sin cannot **e.**, for sin has

### End 2

*end*

T-24..... VII.6:5 God is a Means as well as **E.**. In Heaven,
W-pII. 302.2:3 He the **E.** we seek, and He the Means by

### end 307

*End*

T-1......... I.15:3 a teaching device and a means to an **e.**.
T-1......... I.28:3 are thus a means and revelation is an **e.**.
T-1........ III.1:3 stand at the **e.** in case you fail temporarily
T-1....... VII.5:9 Healing is of God in the **e.**. The means are
T-1..... VII.5:11 may occasionally reveal the **e.** to you, but
T-2.......... II.6:9 the whole Atonement stands at time's **e.**.
T-2......... V.8:1 The fear of healing arises in the **e.** from
T-3........ III.6:5 and Omega, the beginning and the **e.**,"
T-3...... VI.2:10 In the **e.** it does not matter whether your
T-4...... IV.10:2 more than the **e.** of the ego's rule and the
T-6.......... II.7:5 Your perception will **e.** where it began.
T-6....... IV.5:1 ego realizes that its "enemy" can **e.** them
T-8........ IV.2:4 you always, even unto the **e.** of the world.
T-8......... VIII.h The Body as Means or **E.**
T-8...... VIII.2:3 between means and **e.** as it always does.
T-8...... VIII.2:4 Regarding the body as an **e.**, the ego has
T-8...... VIII.2:4 has no real use for it because it is *not* an **e.**.
T-8...... VIII.2:5 **e.** that the ego has accepted as its own.
T-8...... VIII.3:1 the ego's belief in the body as an **e.**,
T-8...... VIII.3:1 with the belief in attack as an **e.**. The ego
T-8...... VIII.5:1 no function of itself, because it is not an **e.**
T-8...... VIII.5:2 however, establishes it as an **e.** because, as
T-10......... IV.h The **E.** of Sickness
T-11......... I.2:1 but how can this be if infinity has no **e.**?
T-11......... I.5:5 There is no **e.** to God and His Son, for we
T-11......... I.7:4 Give, then, without limit and without **e.**,
T-11.... VIII.1:2 not feel you need a course which, in the **e.**,
T-11.... VIII.1:8 The **e.** of the world is not its destruction,
T-12........ II.5:5 is the **e.** of strife and this is the journey to
T-12.... III.10:1 its source, and where it begins it must **e.**.
T-12...... IV.2:2 which must **e.** in perceived self-defeat. For
T-12....... V.9:3 means and the **e.** are in complete accord.
T-12... VII.13:3 is what it always reserves for you in the **e.**.
T-12... VII.13:6 is the one **e.** toward which it works, and
T-12... VII.13:6 the only **e.** with which it will be satisfied.
T-13....... in.2:1 the acceptance of the Atonement is its **e.**.
T-13......... I.3:5 reach its **e.** it will roll up like a long carpet
T-13......... I.4:4 The Holy Spirit stands at the **e.** of time,
T-13...... IV.4:2 and in the **e.** believes that the past is the
T-13..... VII.7:3 and love surrounds him without **e.** or flaw
T-13... VII.13:4 for His sight is ever on the journey's **e.**,
T-13.... VIII.5:4 thus brings you nearer to the **e.** of time by
T-13........ X.6:2 The **e.** of guilt will never come as long as

C-1.....5:4 Here time and illusions e. together.
C-2.....1:11 like all dreams, can only e. in death?
C-4.....1:5 when all things visible will have an e..
C-4.....3:7 with the e. to lead to oneness far beyond
C-ep.....1:1 once this journey is begun the e. is certain
C-ep.....1:9 farther on the road where all illusions e.?
C-ep.....1:10 The e. *is* sure and guaranteed by God.
C-ep.....2:5 Long ago the e. was written in the stars
C-ep.....5:3 and the e. of all we thought we made. The
P-1.....5:7 There is no e. to the help that He begins
P-1.....5:8 all psychotherapy leads to God in the e..
P-2.....in.1:5 Its whole function, in the e., is to help the
P-2.....III.3:3 But in the e. there must be some success.
P-2.....III.4:4 stands at the e. of the process of healing,
P-2.....VII.1:2 In the e., everyone is both. He who needs
P-2.....VII.5:3 Yet who could experience the e. of guilt
P-3.....II.8:4 A goal marks the e. of a journey, not the
P-3.....III.3:9 Can this be how the dream of sin will e.?
S-1.....II.1:1 Prayer has no beginning and no e.. It is a
S-1.....II.8:1 prayer, giving it timelessness instead of e..
S-1.....V.4:4 you. Here will time e. forever. At this gate
S-2.....in.1:6 Illusion's e. will come with this. Unlike
S-2.....in.1:7 of its sister, prayer, forgiveness has an e..
S-2.....I.9:1 But to achieve this e. you first must learn,
S-2.....II.6:5 and how distorted is the e. it seeks. Have
S-2.....III.6:3 About the e. of sin and guilt and death.
S-3.....II.1:10 It merely signifies the e. has come for

## endanger 4

T-13.....XI.2:6 you made not a war that could e. freedom
T-24.....IV.3:10 This shift in purpose does "e." specialness
W-pII..338.1:3 frightens him, and nothing can e. him. He
P-2.....V.2:5 taught to those who think it will e. them.

## endangered 7

T-12.....III.7:3 A split mind is e., and the recognition
T-30.....IV.3:5 *you* are not e.. You can laugh at popping
W-pI.....35.6:5 *I see myself as e.. I see myself as helpless. I see*
W-pI.....76.5:2 body is e. by the mind that hurts itself.
W-pII..244.1:3 *doubt or fail to know he cannot suffer, be e.,*
P-2.....IV.6:1 of the self as weak, vulnerable, evil and e.,
P-2.....V.2:6 those who will attack because they feel e.,

## endangering 1

T-2.....V.4:1 his own readiness is e. his understanding.

## endeavors 1

W-pI...200.8:3 frantic, vain pursuits, and meaningless e..

## ended 11

T-29.....VI.4:6 Its purpose e., it is gone. And where it
T-31.....V.8:2 and e. with the single aim of teaching you
W-pI.153.14:3 So is the story e.. Let this day bring the
W-pI...156.8:2 a day, till certainty has e. doubting and
W-pI...158.4:5 the journey from the point at which it e.,
W-pI...169.8:2 from a point where time was e., when it is
W-pII..249.1:7 has e. in the light from which he came.
W-pII..337.2:3 *myself. Father, my dream is e. now. Amen.*
M-14.....1:9 How but in this way are all illusions e.?
C-4.....4:5 with time forever e. as the world spins
S-3.....II.3:3 from labor gladly done and gladly e..

## ending 39

*See also* never-ending

T-4.....III.3:4 own beginning and ends with its own e..
T19....IV.A.6:9 Such was the journey; such its e.. And in
T-26.....VII.8:6 the role forgiveness plays in e. death and
T-27....VII.11:6 away, and saw as if it were its start and e.,
T-27....VIII.7:1 circularity whose e. starts at its beginning
T-27....VIII.7:1 starts at its beginning, e. at its cause. The
T-28.....II.1:7 Its starting and its e. are the same. But in
T-28.....III.1:5 up to waking and the e. of the dream.
T-29.....VI.4:5 does not aim at keeping time, but at its e.,
T-30.....III.6:4 And in the Mind of God there is no e.,
T-31....IV.2:14 The choice is not what will the e. be, but
T-31. VIII.12:3 closes, e. at the place where it began. No
WpI...rI.in.1:2 with the first and e. with the fiftieth.
W-pI.....75.2:1 we celebrate the happy e. to your long
W-pI.122.10:4 indeed to the appointed e. of the dream.
W-pI...129.3:2 and know they have no e. and they will
W-pI...138.7:3 resolved, for e. opposition is to die. And
W-pI.138.10:1 is as sure as is the e. of the fear of hell,
W-pI...153.3:3 There seems to be no break nor e. in the
W-pI.155.10:1 at the journey's e. there will be no gap, no
W-pI.169.11:2 The e. must remain obscure to you until
WpI...rV.in5:1 that waits to meet us at the journey's e..
W-pI...200.3:1 and for eternal life in peace that has no e..
W-pII..292.1:5 Yet is the e. certain. For God's Will is
W-pII..324.2:4 And it is He Who makes the e. sure, and
W-pII..336.1:1 is the means appointed for perception's e.
W-pII..344.2:3 How close the e. of the dream of sin, and
Wfl.....in.2:2 it is this e. God Himself appointed. In the
Wfl.....in.3:4 It is His e. to the dream we seek, and not
M-1.....4:8 it. Yet time has an e., and it is this that the
M-14.....1:3 Yet will its e. be an illusion of mercy. The
M-14.....1:4 evil, concealing all sin and e. guilt forever.
M-14.....2:6 He brings the e. of the world with Him. It
M-14.....4:3 lesson, which brings the e. of the world,
M-17.....6:2 Its e. is inevitable, for its outcome must
M-27.....2:2 away, e. in dust and disappointment and
M-27.....2:4 Or if he waits, yet is the e. certain. Who
C-ep.....1:3 Yet is the e. sure. No one can fail to do
P-2.....II.3:5 lies the e. of the world and all it stands for

## endings 4

T-1.....I.13:1 Miracles are both beginnings and e., and
T-11.....I.2:3 There are no beginnings and no e. in God
T-11.....I.4:2 nor e. were created by the Eternal, Who
W-pII..292.2:2 *delay the happy e. You have promised us for*

## endless 38

T-1.....II.6:2 Sonship appears to involve almost e. time
T-3.....VI.7:1 at that level there is almost e. variation.
T-4.....in.3:6 are e. until they are voluntarily given up.
T-5.....VII.3:1 Why should you listen to the e. insane
T-8.....VIII.6:4 It dictates e. prescriptions for avoiding
T-8.....IX.1:3 question is, although it asks an e. number
T-12.....I.4:2 to engage in e. "battles" with reality, in
T-13.....VII.1:3 buy an e. list of things they do not need. It
T-13.....XI.1:5 ravaged and torn in e. battles if he himself
T-15.....VII.4:6 thus it embarks on an e., unrewarding
T-16.....IV.12:3 journey that seemed e. is almost complete
T-16.....IV.12:3 almost complete, for what *is* e. is very near
T-22.....II.12:1 the bright, e. circle that extends forever, is
T-24.....V.9:4 One with you, and that this Oneness is e.,
T-27.....I.10:6 it receive the power to represent an e. life,
T-29.....V.2:4 The still infinity of e. peace surrounds you
T-29.....V.3:5 wakening to peace eternal and to e. joy.
T-29.....VI.1:2 instead of e. strife and misery and pain?
T-29.....VII.8:1 what appeared to be an e. circle of despair
T-29....VIII.7:4 alcove separated off from what is e., *has* no
T-31.....II.11:5 and a sense of e. doubting as you stagger
W-pI.....50.1:3 and an e. list of forms of nothingness that
W-pI.....76.10:5 About the e. joy He offers you. About His
W-pI.....96.2:2 will attempt an e. list of goals you cannot
W-pI.139.10:2 and go your way rejoicing in the e. Love of
WpI. rIV.in9:2 to give us happiness and rest, and e. quiet
W-pI...153.8:2 not exchange for foolishness the e. joy our
W-pI...169.6:3 It returns the mind into the e. present,
W-pI...182.3:2 He goes uncertainly about in e. search,
W-pI...189.4:2 look out from the e. wells of joy within.
W-pII..249.1:5 of joy, abundance, charity and e. giving. It
W-pII..329.1:9 *I am safe, untroubled and serene, in e. joy,*
W-pII....13.3:5 in the light of perfect purity and e. joy.
M-27.....2:7 reigns and opposites make e. war. Where
P-2.....V.1:1 lost their way in e. mazes of complexity.
P-3.....III.8:4 He will give you e. opportunities to open
S-1.....in.1:3 E. the harmony, and endless, too, the
S-1.....in.1:3 Endless the harmony, and e., too, the

## endlessly 3

T-19.....III.2:6 must be eternal, and will be repeated e..
T-31.....I.3:1 went to practice and repeat the lessons e.,
W-pI...76.11:2 Thus is creation e. increased. His Voice

## endlessness 1

W-pI...163.4:3 for life, the e. of love and Heaven's perfect

## endow 12

T-4.....VII.3:11 e. itself with functions it was not given.
T-14.....IV.7:7 e. Him with attributes you understand.
T-15.....XI.4:6 for you e. it with fear and try to cast it out,
T-16.....V.11:3 think it safer to e. the little self you made
T-17.....III.9:3 choose you will e. with beauty and reality,
T-27.....III.3:2 hate, or to e. with power or to see as weak
T-29.....I.5:2 Thus do you e. it with a power that lies
T-30.....VII.3:1 can e. events with stable meaning. But it
W-pI.....13.3:2 it is certain that you will e. the world with
W-pI.....50.1:3 of nothingness that you e. with magical
M-5.....II.1:8 e. the body with non-mental motivators.
P-2.....IV.4:3 to heal the ills with which their minds e. it

## endowed 7

T-2.....V.6:2 but if it is falsely e. with self-initiative, it
T-14.....VII.4:8 a separate place can be e. with firm belief.
W-pI.....61.1:5 with which you have e. your idols. It
W-pI.....97.2:2 You are the spirit lovingly e. with all your
W-pI...135.6:3 Yet what e. the body with the right to
W-pI...170.5:3 it alone, love is e. with attributes of fear.
W-pII .321.1:6 *e. me with my freedom as Your holy Son will*

## endowing 2

T-2.....II.1:8 and by e. all thoughts with equal power
T-10.....IV.5:3 bring chaos; you are e. them with chaos,

## endowment 1

T-2.....I.2:8 requires God's e. of the Son with free will,

## ends 43

T-4.....III.3:4 own beginning and e. with its own ending
T-8.....VII.4:1 Communication e. separation. Attack
T-11.....V.16:4 For reasoning e. at its beginning, and no
T-13.....X.2:8 your own e. what you should have given
T-18....IX.11:4 Where learning e. there God begins, for
T-18....IX.11:4 learning e. before Him Who is complete
T-18....IX.12:3 learning e. when you have recognized all
T-20.....I.2:1 week begins with palms and e. with lilies,
T-25.....IX.5:1 solving is the way in which the problem e.
T-27.....II.11:2 has conflicting purposes and different e..
T-27.....IV.5:8 an honest answer where the conflict e..
W-pI.....91.6:6 question with which this statement e. is
W-pI...106.4:6 They will not fade when dreaming e..
W-pI...106.7:1 Thus does salvation start and thus it e.;
W-pI...110.5:6 This is the Word in which all sorrow e..
W-pI...129.7:5 until where one begins another e. loses all
W-pI...130.7:1 thought that e. all compromise and doubt
W-pI.140.12:8 This is the day when separation e., and
W-pI...158.6:3 reconciled, for here the journey e..
WpI...rV.in7:1 place at which the journey e. and is forgot
W-pI...188.2:7 There perception starts, and there it e.. It
W-pI...193.5:3 are the words with which temptation e.,
WpI rVI.in.3:6 The day begins and e. with this. And we
W-pII .237.1:4 see, aware it e. the bitter dream of death;
W-pII ....249.h Forgiveness e. all suffering and loss.
W-pII .....4.4:3 guilt, with but a little life that e. in death.
W-pII .270.1:4 *instant more of time which e. forever, as*
W-pII .....9.3:1 Coming e. the lessons that the Holy Spirit
W-pII .....9.3:1 in which learning e. in one last summary
W-pII ....10.1:2 the judgment is in which perception e.. At
W-pII ....10.2:4 There it was born, and there it e. as well.
W-pII ....333.h Forgiveness e. the dream of conflict here.
W-pII ....13.2:3 and thus it e. the strange distortions that
M-14.....1:5 So e. the world that guilt had made, for

M-19 .........2:7 the pathway ceases and time **e.** with it.
M-20 .........5:6 because you have decided death **e.** life.
M-25 .........3:5 used. Taking them as **e.** in themselves, no
M-28 .........1:7 It is the lesson in which learning **e.**, for it
M-28 .........3:1 Here the curriculum **e.**. From here on, no
C-in ...........2:7 possible because here alone uncertainty **e.**
S-1 ........... V.h The Ladder **E.**
S-1 ......... V.4:1 The ladder **e.** with this, for learning is no
S-3 ........ IV.8:1 that **e.** so soon it might as well have never

### **endure** 15

T-2......... V.8:4 cannot **e.** to see your own defiled altar.
T-4........ VI.4:4 to use the device that enables it to **e.**.
T-20.... VI.10:2 within it in the certainty it will **e.** forever.
T-25....... II.6:6 within a frame that will **e.** forever, when
T-27.........I.7:4 What pleasures could there be that will **e.**
T-28.........I.6:5 Yet change must have a cause that will **e.**,
T-30...... III.6:3 For thoughts **e.** as long as does the mind
W-pI... 182.4:4 with an innocence that will **e.** forever.
W-pI... 187.8:6 form of sacrifice and suffering can long **e.**
W-pII .... 300.h Only an instant does this world **e.**.
W-pII .327.1:4 This is the faith that will **e.**, and take me
M-26 ......... 3:2 world, it is almost impossible that this **e.**.
C-4............1:3 in the world you see that will **e.** forever.
C-4............3:3 It will not **e.**. But for the time it lasts it
P-2........ VI.4:3 Without protection it could not **e.**. Here

### **endured** 1

W-pI..... 70.8:6 in the cloud patterns you imagined that **e.**

### **endures** 3

W-pI... 129.3:1 losing is impossible; where love **e.** forever,
W-pI... 187.4:5 No form **e.**. It is the thought behind the
W-pII . 300.2:4 *thanks today the world* ***e.*** *but for an instant.*

### **enemies** 40

T-13....... II.4:3 who do not attack are its "**e.**" because, by
T-17...... III.1:4 would make immortal are "**e.**" of reality.
T19. IV.D.14:6 The "**e.**" of Christ, the worshippers of sin,
T-21... VII.5:13 *a world in which I have no* ***e.*** *and cannot sin?*
T-22....... II.9:4 not be the mind's extensions, but its **e.**.
T-23.......in.1:6 he has. Belief in **e.** is therefore the belief in
T-23....... II.2:5 them seem to be unlike, and therefore **e.**.
T-23....... II.5:4 Now are They different, and **e.**. And Their
T-23....... II.9:6 For **e.** do not give willingly to one another
T-23....... II.9:7 And what your **e.** would keep from you
T-23...... III.5:5 No one unites with **e.**, nor is at one with
T-24.........I.2:6 The secret **e.** of peace, your least decision
T-24.........I.3:5 Only the special could have **e.**, for they
T-24....... II.9:3 Your brother's specialness and yours *are* **e.**
T-24...... III.4:7 death between them, and makes them **e.**.
T-25....... V.2:2 you not be afraid with "**e.**" like these?
T-26... VII.14:9 and made Them both his **e.** in hate.
T-27....... V.7:7 the many friends he thought were **e.**.
T-27.... VIII.1:4 seeks for other bodies as its friends and **e.**
T-28..... II.10:3 and hated **e.** perceived as friends with
T-31...... III.5:3 the free, for they are **e.** which sin must kill
T-31...... III.6:6 not want to hold in guilt your chosen **e.**,
W-pI..... 51.5:4 I make all things my **e.**, so that my anger
W-pI..... 52.2:4 and everything, making them my **e.**.
W-pI..... 52.2:6 There will be no past, and therefore no **e.**.
W-pI... 105.7:1 Think of your "**e.**" a little while, and tell
W-pI... 170.6:4 their **e.** who are unreasonable and insane,
W-pI... 191.3:2 of dust against the legions of your **e.**.
W-pII ... 12.2:5 trembles at the figures in its dreams; its **e.**
W-pII . 338.1:4 him. He has no **e.**, and he is safe from all
S-1......... II.4:1 in terms known as "praying for one's **e.**."
S-1......... II.4:3 While you believe you have **e.**, you have
S-1......... II.4:4 yet, if you have **e.** you have need of prayer
S-1......... II.5:3 The prayer for **e.** thus becomes a prayer
S-1......... II.6:7 Pray truly for your **e.**, for herein lies your
S-1........ III.3:9 indeed to be a real advantage in having **e.**,
S-1........ III.3:9 gain must go, if **e.** are to be set free.
S-1........ III.6:5 kind, and prayer becomes requests for **e.**.
S-1........ IV.1:4 **E.** do not share a goal. It is in this their
S-1......... V.2:4 **E.** are useless now, because humility does

### **enemy** 126

T-4 ....... III.3:1 now why the ego regards spirit as its "**e.**"
T-5 ....... III.8:7 Peace is the ego's greatest **e.** because,
T-6 ....... IV.5:1 and because the ego realizes that its "**e.**"
T-7 ..... III.2:14 The ego's "**e.**" is therefore your friend.
T-9 ..... VIII.1:4 it, the ego believes that its "**e.**" has struck,
T-13 ..... XI.2:1 His Son's imagined "**e.**" is totally unreal.
T-14 ... III.13:5 You have no other "**e.**," and against this
T-18 ..... VI.6:5 fantasies have made your body your "**e.**";
T-18 ... VIII.3:6 The sun becomes the sunbeam's "**e.**" that
T-19 ........I.4:6 of it an "**e.**" of healing and the opposite of
T19..IV.B.15:3 that this is not so, but as the "**e.**" of peace,
T19....IV.C.1:9 things, because the ego is the "**e.**" of life.
T19. IV.D.13:3 Is this giver of salvation your friend or **e.**?
T19. IV.D.13:8 he is, and seek not to make of love an **e.**.
T19. IV.D.14:5 This "**e.**," this "stranger" still offers you
T-21 ..... IV.2:2 Its rule is tempered, and its unknown "**e.**,
T-21 .... VII.2:3 What can they be except his **e.**? And what
T-21 .... VII.3:2 Yet they know not their "**e.**," except they
T-21 .... VII.4:2 It has no weapons and it has no **e.**. Yes, it
T-21 .... VII.4:3 it can overrun the world and *seek* an **e.**.
T-21 .... VII.4:5 Yes, it can *dream* it found an **e.**, but this
T-21 .... VII.4:6 it caught a glimpse of the great **e.** who
T-21 .... VII.4:7 How treacherous does this **e.** appear, who
T-21 .... VII.5:2 There can be no faith in sin without an **e.**.
T-21 .... VII.5:3 in sin would dare believe he has no **e.**?
T-21 .... VII.5:9 let sin tell him that his **e.** must be himself.
T-21 .... VII.6:6 that truth may be the **e.** you yet may find.
T-21 .... VII.9:4 if you choose to see a world without an **e.**,
T-21 .. VII.10:8 let an "**e.**" tempt you to use the body's
T-22 .....II.10:3 His Son could be His **e.** does it seem
T-22 .....II.11:3 your savior as your **e.** and recognize him.
T-22 ...... V.4:3 This is your "**e.**,"–a frightened mouse
T-23 ......in.1:5 No one is strong who has an **e.**, and no
T-23 ......in.1:7 Being opposed to it, it is God's "**e.**." And
T-23 ......in.2:2 for sin can hurt you and become your **e.**.
T-23 ........I.1:8 Certain it is it has no **e.**. Yet just as certain
T-23 ........I.1:9 just as certain is its fixed belief it has an **e.**
T-23 ........I.4:4 This "**e.**" you fought as an intruder on
T-23 ........I.4:5 Your "**e.**" was God Himself, to Whom all
T-23 .......II.7:3 He has become the "**e.**" Who caused it, to
T-23 .......II.7:6 because the Savior has become the **e.**.
T-23 .....II.10:1 the "**e.**" made strong by keeping hidden
T-23 .....II.10:1 loss the **e.** must suffer to save yourself.
T-23 .....II.10:3 by the unscrupulous behavior of the **e.**,
T-23 .....II.11:2 this most treacherous and cunning **e.**? It
T-23 .....II.11:5 For it was taken from you by this **e.**, and
T-23 ..... III.5:6 no one compromises with an **e.** but hates
T-24 ........I.4:5 what would make them special *is* their **e.**.
T-24 ........I.6:4 You are his **e.** in specialness; his friend in
T-24 ......I.7:10 the "**e.**" that makes you and your brother
T-24 ........I.9:6 must he be your **e.** and not your friend.
T-24 .......II.5:6 Christ's vision is their "**e.**," for it sees not
T-24 .......II.8:2 He *is* the **e.** of specialness, but only friend
T-24 ..... III.2:3 And thus it stands against yourself; *your* **e.**
T-24 ..... IV.1:3 Everything else becomes your **e.**; feared
T-24 ..... IV.4:4 A sinless brother *is* its **e.**, while sin, if it
T-24 ..... IV.5:6 And so is specialness his "**e.**," and yours
T-25 ...... V.2:1 Attack makes Christ your **e.**, and God
T-25 ...... V.2:4 hurt yourself, and made your Self your "**e.**
T-25 ...... V.3:2 It is the "**e.**," confused with Christ, you
T-26 ...VIII.3:6 for time is not the **e.** that you perceive.
T-26 .......X.3:6 You have no **e.** except yourself, and you
T-26 .......X.3:6 and you are **e.** indeed to him because you
T-27 .. VII.12:1 separated from yourself, an ancient **e.**, a
T-27 .. VII.12:2 you become the murderer, the secret **e.**,
T-27 ...VIII.7:1 attack itself; a separate brother as an **e.**; a
T-27 .VIII.10:3 takes the role of **e.** and of attacker, still is
T-28 ...... V.3:7 upon your Self, which seems to be your **e.**;
T-29 ........I.3:4 had decided that your brother is your **e.**.
T-29 ........I.3:6 you and him, lest he turn again into an **e.**.
T-29 ........I.8:5 who learn their savior is their **e.** no more.
T-29 .......II.1:2 the truth instead of looking on it as an **e.**?
T-29 .....II.10:1 is the body asked to be God's **e.**, replacing
T-29 ...... V.7:1 he is your savior, not your **e.** in hate. A
T-29 ...VIII.4:8 Christ's **e.** is nowhere. He can take no
T-29 ..... IX.2:2 to hell, and God made **e.** unto His Son.
T-30 .....II.1:11 God is no **e.** to you. He asks no more than
T-30 .......II.3:1 Look once again upon your **e.**, the one
T-30 .....V.11:2 they joined, they thought He was their **e.**.
T-31 .......II.1:6 He has no **e.** in truth. And can he be
T-31 .......II.3:6 And every friend or **e.** becomes a means
T-31 .... VII.6:6 of the world, instead of as salvation's **e.**?
W-pI .... 13.5:2 because of the "vengeance" of the "**e.**."
W-pI .... 72.7:6 instead. It is your friend; He is your **e.**.
W-pI .... 76.5:5 It would not understand it is its own **e.**;
W-pI .... 78.5:4 He who was **e.** is more than friend when
W-pI .. 101.4:5 is real, salvation has become your bitter **e.**
W-pI .. 121.9:2 toward one whom you think of as an **e.**,
W-pI 121.12:2 to see around your former "**e.**" to him.
W-pI 121.13:1 let your "**e.**" and friend unite in blessing
W-pI 127.11:2 thought was made in hate to be love's **e.**.
W-pI .. 130.4:4 Love's **e.** has made them up. Yet love can
W-pI .. 130.4:5 Yet love can have no **e.**, and so they have
W-pI .. 161.6:4 of love's "**e.**" Christ's vision does not see.
W-pI .. 161.7:3 An **e.** must be perceived in such a form he
W-pI .. 161.9:5 Attack on him is **e.** to you, for you will not
W-pI 161.12:6 suddenly transformed from **e.** to savior;
W-pI .. 170.3:1 seems to be the **e.** without that you attack
W-pI .. 170.3:2 Yet your defense sets up an **e.** within; an
W-pI .. 170.3:3 For love now has an "**e.**," an opposite;
W-pI .. 170.5:1 attributes of love bestowed upon its "**e.**."
W-pI .. 170.6:1 With love as **e.**, must cruelty become a
W-pI 170.10:3 perceive their own confusion in fear's "**e.**"
W-pI .. 182.9:2 messages to those who think he is their **e.**.
W-pI 182.11:1 you raised against an **e.** without existence.
W-pI .. 184.4:2 Its **e.** is wholeness. It conceives of little
W-pI .. 194.9:6 No longer is the world our **e.**, for we have
W-pI .. 195.3:1 Your brother is your "**e.**" because you see
W-pI .. 196.5:5 could believe his Father is his deadly **e.**,
W-pI 196.10:4 seemed to be an **e.** outside you had to fear
W-pI 196.10:5 outside yourself became your mortal **e.**;
W-pII ... 12.1:2 is the "will" that sees the Will of God as **e.**
M-17 ......... 5:8 takes it for himself now has a deadly "**e.**."
M-17 ......... 6:8 not remember the immensity of the "**e.**,"
M-19 ......... 4:9 not see you hate and fear your Self as **e.**.
C-3 ........... 2:3 makes God appear to be an **e.** instead of
S-1..........II.5:1 **e.** is the symbol of an imprisoned Christ.
S-1..........II.6:3 The **e.** is you, as is the Christ. Before it can
S-1........ III.1:5 The poisonous thought that he *is* your **e.**,
S-1........ III.3:6 *have. Thus have I made of him my* ***e.***. It is
S-1........ III.4:7 to make a jailer of an **e.** seems to be safety
S-1........ III.5:4 This **e.** has come to bless you. Take his
S-1........ III.6:7 one who wants an **e.** will fail to find one.
S-1........ IV.1:3 the other as an **e.** has been questioned,
S-2..........II.5:3 offers one who could be savior, not an **e.**.
S-2..........II.5:4 But having been made **e.**, he must accept

### **energies** 2

T-9 .....VIII.4:5 and mobilize its **e.** against your release. It
W-pI 186.10:3 or direct his **e.** and concentrated drive

### **energy** 3

T-9 ........I.11:1 waste of **e.** you expend in denying truth.
W-pI .. 109.7:3 with hope reborn and **e.** restored to walk
C-1 ............ 1:1 agent of spirit, supplying its creative **e.**.

### **enervation** 1

W-pI .... 74.5:4 rather than a feeling of drowsiness and **e.**.

### **enfold** 1

T-16 .... VII.6:5 peace of *now* **e.** you in perfect gentleness.

### **enforce** 1

T-20 ... IV.2:10 them power to **e.** what God created not.

### **enforces** 1

T-31 ... III.3:11 orders, but **e.** orders on the prisoner.

### engage 9
T-2........III.1:4 in which minds **e.** arise from the distorted
T-3.........V.5:7 to **e.** in it when you are willing to let it go.
T-7........VI.8:5 ego therefore wants to **e.** your mind in its
T-7... VIII.3:12 they are forced to **e.** in constant activity in
T-12.........I.4:2 to **e.** in endless "battles" with reality, in
T-23....IV.5:10 as nothingness when you **e.** in it? How
W-pI.....66.3:2 not **e.** in senseless arguments about what
W-pI.135.26:5 you and tempt you to **e.** in weaving plans,
WpI.rIV.in5:2 and let this thought alone **e.** it fully, and

### engaged 6
T-6........I.11:4 and yours are constantly **e.** in justifying
T-12......IV.1:2 to be intensely **e.** in the search for love.
W-pI.....27.3:5 do this, even if you are **e.** in conversation,
W-pI.135.15:1 mind **e.** in planning for itself is occupied
W-pI...192.7:4 minds **e.** in worshipping what is not there
P-3.........II.1:2 profession be one in which everyone is **e.**?

### engages 2
T-6......IV.10:4 kind of "reasoning" in which the ego **e.**.
M-in..........1:4 one **e.** only a relatively small proportion

### engaging 2
T-2......IV.3:11 Those who do so are **e.** in a particularly
T-4........IV.7:1 habit of **e.** with God and His creations is

### engender 5
T-5...........I.7:4 that although it does not **e.** knowledge, it
T-7........VI.6:3 resolves the apparent conflict they **e.** by
T-15...... I.4:11 it must **e.** fear in order to maintain itself.
W-pI...107.4:3 the appearances the world presents **e.**.
M-4......I.A.5:2 the desirable, it will **e.** enormous conflict.

### engendered 2
T-1........IV.4:1 emptiness **e.** by fear must be replaced by
W-pI...163.3:1 apt to fail the hopes they once **e.**, and to

### engenders 14
T-2........III.3:4 An imprisoned will **e.** a situation which,
T-5.........V.2:7 Anything that **e.** fear is divisive because it
T-5.........V.4:7 This **e.** joy, not guilt, because it is natural.
T-6....V.C.1:10 point, and so the one mood He **e.** is joy.
T-6......V.C.7:6 His creation, and therefore **e.** doubt. You
T-14.......X.6:9 power of God, and not of you, **e.** miracles.
T-26... VIII.8:2 And this illusion is but one effect that it **e.**
W-pI........13.h A meaningless world **e.** fear.
W-pI.....13.4:7 *A meaningless world **e.** fear because I think I*
W-pI.....53.3:1 (13) A meaningless world **e.** fear. The
W-pI.....53.3:2 fear. The totally insane **e.** fear because it is
W-pI.....66.7:5 choice but the fear that the ego always **e.**,
W-pI...164.1:5 the sounds the senseless, busy world **e.**,
W-pII..259.1:3 What else but sin **e.** our attacks? What

### engine 1
T-20... VIII.4:8 can the **e.** of destruction be preferred, and

### enhance 1
T-27......III.4:2 that would **e.** the invitation's real appeal.

### enjoined 2
T-5.......II.12:1 I have **e.** you to behave as I behaved, but
T-8........IX.7:3 are **e.** to do the works of love because we

### enjoins 1
T-8........IX.7:1 The Bible **e.** you to be perfect, to heal all

### enjoy 2
T-27.........I.7:6 all of them, if they **e.** their benefits or not.
T-28......III.8:7 **e.** the feast of plenty set before them there

### enjoyed 1
S-1........IV.3:4 way. What was **e.** before, or seemed to be;

### enjoyment 2
T-18.....VII.1:2 comfort or protection or **e.** in some way?
T-30......IV.3:7 them as obeying rules he made for his **e.**.

### enjoys 1
T-14....... X.8:7 In fact, the ego **e.** studying itself, and

### enlarge 2
T-1.......VII.2:4 to help you **e.** your perception so you can
T-4...........I.6:2 because to **e.** an ego would be to increase

### enlarges 1
T-18....VI.11:4 in which your mind **e.** to encompass it. It

### enlighten 2
T-7.......V.10:6 that you can look into theirs and **e.** them,
T-7.......V.10:6 and enlighten them, as I can **e.** yours. I do

### enlightened 2
T-4.........in.1:8 truly inspired are **e.** and cannot abide in
T-12......VI.7:2 becomes so **e.** that light streams into it,

### enlightenment 4
T-8........III.1:4 want understanding and **e.** you will learn
T-12.......II.4:2 If they ask for **e.** and accept it, their fears
W-pI...106.7:4 should begin with this request for your **e.**:
W-pI...188.1:4 **E.** is but a recognition, not a change at all.

### enlivened 1
T-7.......VII.5:3 nothing live, since nothing cannot be **e.**.

### enmity 5
T-23... II.12:10 for love, born of your **e.** to your brother,
T-24.........I.4:6 Yet they protect its **e.** and call it "friend."
T-26.......IX.8:5 to replace an ancient **e.** that came to kill.
T-28..... II.10:4 Their **e.** is seen as causeless now, because
S-1........IV.1:5 It is in this their **e.** is kept. Their separate

### enormity 4
T-18.........I.5:6 to show you the **e.** of the original error,
T-19......III.2:4 it with respect and honoring its **e.**. What
T-21.....VII.1:5 it. **E.** has no appeal save to the little. And
T-31.........I.4:4 **e.** so great the Holy Spirit's Voice seems

### enormous 24
T-1........IV.2:2 you exert **e.** efforts to establish its reality.
T-2........III.3:3 and you are capable of **e.** procrastination,
T-2.......VII.7:9 may think this implies that an **e.** amount
T-4......... II.2:1 to **e.** variation because of its instability.
T-7........VI.3:1 of the ego to preserve itself is **e.**, but it
T-9.........I.11:1 not recognize the **e.** waste of energy you
T-12......VI.1:4 in the investment, but the cost to you is **e.**
T-17..IV.12:10 of its **e.** and disproportionate enclosure.
T-17.......V.11:3 made **e.** efforts to help Him do His work.
T-17.....VII.6:7 Nothing too small or too **e.**, too weak or
T-17... VIII.3:7 The strain of refusing faith to truth is **e.**,
T-18.....VII.4:8 sin. **E.** effort is expended in the attempt to
T-22....... V.2:6 in sin needs great defense, and at **e.** cost.
T-22....... V.5:3 body's eyes it looks like an **e.** solid body,
T-27...VII.11:3 is split between a tiny you and an **e.** world
W-pI.....19.2:2 carry with it an **e.** sense of responsibility,
W-pI.....92.6:4 limitations that but grow in darkness to **e.**
W-pI.138.11:4 no terror now, for what was made **e.**,
W-pI...158.9:4 they took, nor how **e.** they appeared to be
M-4.....I.A.5:2 the desirable, it will engender **e.** conflict.
M-5........II.1:7 it. The resistance to recognizing this is **e.**,
M-19.........2:6 grandeur of the scene and the **e.** opening
P-3..........II.9:1 that can save **e.** time if it is properly used.
P-3........III.2:8 where it rightfully belongs has **e.** cost.

### enough 86
T-1......... V.6:3 they are not deep **e.** to sustain you. The
T-2.......VII.1:7 do not guard your thoughts carefully **e.**.
T-3.......VII.3:2 is a system of thought real **e.** in time,
T-3.......VII.5:9 You have not yet gone back far **e.**, and
T-4........III.6:1 strong **e.** or worthy enough to guide you.
T-4........III.6:1 strong enough or worthy **e.** to guide you.
T-4......... V.4:4 cannot accept it as good **e.** to be its home.
T-4.......VII.7:2 Revelation is not **e.**, because it is only
T-5.........in.3:5 are beautiful **e.** to hold it by sharing it. It
T-5...........I.6:4 represents a state of mind close **e.** to One-
T-6......V.A.4:2 This is familiar **e.** to you by now, but it
T-7........IV.3:6 abilities are applied long **e.** to one goal,
T-9....... II.5:11 your faith in him strong **e.** to let you hear?
T-11.......in.3:6 little spark in your mind is **e.** to lighten it.
T-12.........I.8:2 recognize fear is not **e.** to escape from it,
T-13...... III.1:2 that it would be easy **e.** for the Holy Spirit
T-13........X.5:3 less, will be **e.** to free you from the past,
T-13...... XI.7:5 If that suffices Him, it is **e.** for you. You
T-14...... VI.6:4 not communicating holds **e.** of love to
T-14........X.9:3 For form is not **e.** for meaning, and the
T-15.......I.14:5 **e.** to transcend all of the ego's making,
T-15...... IV.8:4 to give it to you is not **e.** to make it yours,
T-16........II.5:6 understanding of the miracle be **e.** for you
T-18.........I.5:5 it? Its fragmented aspects are fearful **e.**, as
T-18...... III.2:5 be **e.** to remind you that your goal is light.
T-18...... IV.2:2 They are not **e.**. But trust implicitly your
T-18...... IX.4:3 to the surface, **e.** to hold its most external
T-18...... IX.6:4 It is not strong **e.** to stop a button's fall,
T19. IV.D.10:4 Yet merely to reach the place is not **e.**. A
T-20....VIII.1:1 but they will be **e.** to show you what is
T-21......II.4:10 is strong **e.** to make a world can let it go,
T-21........II.7:1 in holiness and vision to see it easily **e.**.
T-22.......in.3:7 stand, but close **e.** not to return to earth.
T-25.... IV.4:10 large **e.** to hold the world within its peace.
T-25..VIII.11:2 For just *one* witness is **e.**, if he sees truly.
T-27...... IV.6:9 the interval in which the mind is still **e.** to
T-30.........I.9:4 tiny opening will be **e.** to let you go ahead
T-31.........I.3:6 For your power to learn is strong **e.** to
T-31.........I.4:5 powerful **e.** to render God forgotten, and
T-31......II.10:1 be asking for, will be **e.** to let this happen.
W-pI........5.7:6 Three or four times during the day is **e.**.
W-pI.......7.5:3 each to last a minute or so, will be **e.**.
W-pI.....12.6:1 is **e.** for practicing the idea for today. Nor
W-pI.....16.6:2 If strain is experienced, three will be **e.**.
W-pI.....17.2:3 on each thing you note long **e.** to say: *I do*
W-pI.....18.3:1 your eyes on each one long **e.** to say: *I am*
W-pI.....44.9:1 form, pause long **e.** to repeat today's idea,
W-pI.....60.1:6 It will bring me near **e.** to Heaven that the
W-pI...71.9:10 **e.** to establish your claim to God's answer
W-pI...72.13:1 periods an hour will be **e.** for today, since
W-pI.....93.3:4 This is **e.** to prove that they are wrong,
W-pI...102.1:3 now, at least **e.** to let you question it, and
W-pI...108.5:2 wholly is **e.** to bring salvation to all minds
W-pI...110.1:2 one thought would be **e.** to save you and
W-pI...110.2:2 is **e.** to heal the past and make the future
W-pI...110.2:3 is **e.** to let the present be accepted as it is.
W-pI...110.2:4 It is **e.** to let time be the means for all the
W-pI.135.15:4 rests on the idea the past has taught **e.** to
W-pI.136.18:2 be **e.** to serve all truly useful purposes.
WpI. rIV.in5:4 this thought will be **e.** to set the day along
WpI. rIV.in8:2 time **e.** to see the gifts that they contain
W-pI...154.5:3 It is **e.** that he accept it, give it to the ones
W-pI...157.3:2 Yet you have come far **e.** along the way to
Wi181-200 3:6 will be **e.** to guarantee the rest will come.
W-pI...193.2:5 **e.** to let the light of Heaven shine upon it.
WpI rVI.in.1:4 Each would be **e.** to give release to you

| | |
|---|---|
| WpI rVI.in.2:3 | One is **e.**. But from that one, there must |
| M-1 ........... 1:5 | It may be a single light, but that is **e.**. He |
| M-3 ........... 2:7 | That moment will be **e.**. Salvation has |
| M-4 ..... X.2:13 | ultimately converges. It is indeed **e.**. |
| M-12 ......... 4:5 | This lesson is **e.** to let the thought of unity |
| M-16 ......... 8:7 | is not good **e.** for God's teacher, because |
| M-16 ......... 8:7 | teacher, because it is not **e.** for God's Son. |
| M-21 ......... 3:8 | It is **e.**. His words do not matter. Only the |
| M-21 ....... 3:12 | this Word stands for. And this, too, is **e.**. |
| M-24 ......... 3:5 | His ego will be **e.** for him to cope with, |
| M-25 ......... 5:3 | It may still be strong **e.** to rally under this |
| M-27 ......... 3:3 | is **e.** to show it cannot coexist with God. It |
| C-5............. 5:3 | His little life on earth was not **e.** to teach |
| P-2........ III.3:9 | His simple Presence is **e.** to heal. |
| P-2..... VII.9:10 | holiness **e.** to wake your memory of Him? |
| P-3......... II.3:5 | That "something" is **e.**. Sooner or later |
| P-3........ III.7:7 | long **e.** to think of this: You have perhaps |
| S-1........ III.3:2 | This is **e.**. From here it will be an easy step |
| S-1........ IV.3:1 | Even the joining, then, is not **e.**, if those |
| S-2........ III.7:1 | Still does He know, and that should be **e.**. |

## enraged 1

| | |
|---|---|
| W-pI... 195.4:1 | could you sanely be **e.** if he seems freer. |

## enshrined 1

| | |
|---|---|
| T-21....... II.6:7 | the mad idea you have **e.** upon your altars |

## enslave 6

| | |
|---|---|
| T-11.... VIII.7:6 | Nothing of God will **e.** His Son whom He |
| T-12......... I.1:7 | to attack you or desert you or **e.** you, you |
| T-19....... I.16:4 | You can **e.** a body, but an idea is free, |
| T-22....... II.9:1 | what you made has power to **e.** its maker. |
| T-31...... III.4:3 | It has no power to learn, to pardon, nor **e.** |
| W-pI... 199.6:6 | Without the power to **e.**, it is a worthy |

## enslaved 6

| | |
|---|---|
| T-6........ IV.9:7 | in itself demonstrates that you are not **e.**. |
| T-15....... I.13:3 | of freedom to all who are **e.** by time, and |
| T-22........ in.1:1 | Take pity on yourself, so long **e.**. Rejoice |
| T-29.... VIII.2:5 | has not **e.** himself to littleness and loss. |
| W-pI... 132.3:4 | You have **e.** the world with all your fears, |
| W-pI... 199.7:2 | who still believe they are **e.** within a body. |

## enslavement 2

| | |
|---|---|
| T-6........ IV.9:7 | the central place in your imagined **e.**, |
| W-pI. 135.13:1 | **E.** of the body to the plans the unhealed |

## ensure 22

| | |
|---|---|
| T-5........ VI.2:2 | thus **e.** that the future will be like the past. |
| T-9......... II.3:2 | been asked for anything will **e.** a response |
| T-13......... I.8:6 | in your mind to **e.** the ego's continuity. |
| T-13...... IV.4:3 | it to **e.** its continuity by making the future |
| T-13...... IV.9:6 | on to the past to **e.** a destructive future. |
| T-13... VII.13:3 | He will **e.** it never can become a dark spot, |
| T-15..... VII.7:8 | that the ego can **e.** the guilt that holds all |
| T-15.... VIII.4:1 | Sonship to you, to **e.** your perfect creation |
| T-26......... I.8:4 | special function to **e.** the door be opened, |
| T-26...... II.6:10 | can He **e.** that everyone receives it equally |
| T-27...... IV.1:2 | possible, and to **e.** no answer will be plain |
| T-29...... VI.4:1 | **e.** that only Heaven would not pass away. |
| W-pI..... 50.2:2 | are cherished to **e.** a body identification. |
| W-pI..... 70.4:2 | purpose was to **e.** that healing did not |
| W-pI..... 70.4:3 | occur. God's purpose was to **e.** that it did. |
| W-pI. 187.11:5 | And to **e.** this holy sight is ours, we offer it |
| W-pI... 193.9:3 | **e.** his holy rest remain untroubled and |
| W-pI... 197.1:5 | to **e.** that when He strikes He will not fail |
| W-pII ... 12.2:5 | to murder it before it can **e.** its safety by |
| M-4 ..... VII.2:9 | Why should he **e.** himself pain? But he |
| C-2............. 2:5 | seeks by definition to **e.** that its illusive |
| P-2......... II.8:1 | What must the teacher do to **e.** learning? |

## ensured 9

| | |
|---|---|
| T-25 . VIII.10:8 | Yet God **e.** that justice would be done |
| T-26 ...... V.9:6 | Father has **e.** must come to you. And from |
| T-30 ....... II.2:6 | God but **e.** that you would never lose your |
| W-pI..... 75.8:5 | began, and in which is the end of time **e.**. |
| W-pI..... 77.2:5 | It was **e.** in your creation, and guaranteed |
| W-pI..... 94.2:3 | **e.** your sinlessness must be the guarantee |
| W-pI... 121.1:4 | here the end of all uncertainty **e.** at last. |
| W-pI. 153.12:4 | in his winning is the gain to everyone **e.**. |
| W-pI. 169.14:4 | Its coming is **e.**. We ask for grace, and for |

## ensures 5

| | |
|---|---|
| T-1 ...... III.8:5 | of miracle-mindedness **e.** your grace, but |
| T-7 ..... VI.3:10 | This **e.** its continuance if you side with it, |
| T-31 ...... V.6:1 | lesson that **e.** your brother is condemned |
| W-pI..... 71.3:3 | **e.** that the fruitless search will continue, |
| W-pII . 337.1:1 | My sinlessness **e.** me perfect peace, |

## ensuring 1

| | |
|---|---|
| T-13 ... VI.13:3 | **e.** the real world for you when you awake. |

## entail 10

| | |
|---|---|
| T-2 ....... VI.4:4 | always **e.** a willingness to be separate. At |
| T-6 ..... V.C.4:1 | second may still **e.** conflict to some extent |
| T-16 .... V.10:2 | fearful nature, nor of the guilt it must **e.**, |
| T-25 ... VIII.6:2 | that their own belief in justice must **e.**. |
| T-25 ..... IX.1:4 | until you see all that the answer must **e.**. |
| T-27 ........ I.1:9 | all it would **e.** the whole of God's creation, |
| T-27 ....... II.4:5 | because they would **e.** effects that cannot |
| W-pI..... 26.3:2 | must **e.** the belief that you are vulnerable, |
| W-pI... 139.1:6 | is no conflict that does not **e.** the single, |
| S-1.......... II.3:1 | and so it must **e.** levels of learning. Here, |

## entailed 2

| | |
|---|---|
| T-27 ..... IV.6:9 | that is not **e.** within the question asked. It |
| W-pI....... 8.2:3 | what is actually **e.** in picturing the past or |

## entails 28

| | |
|---|---|
| T-1 ......... II.6:3 | miracle **e.** a sudden shift from horizontal |
| T-1 ........ IV.1:2 | hide. This step usually **e.** fear. Second, the |
| T-2 ....... IV.2:2 | because it always **e.** the belief that what is |
| T-2 ........ V.7:2 | This often **e.** fear, because you are afraid |
| T-2 ... V.A.15:3 | is an empty gesture unless it **e.** correction. |
| T-2 ....... VI.5:5 | consistent behavior, but **e.** great strain. In |
| T-2 ...... VII.2:2 | Miracle working **e.** a full realization of the |
| T-2 .... VII.3:12 | **e.** a set of Cause and Effect relationships |
| T-6 ... V.C.10:1 | **e.** a willingness to relinquish everything |
| T-14 ...... III.1:4 | **e.** the recognition that guilt is interference |
| T-15 ...... IX.1:3 | for you to learn just what this shift **e.**, so |
| T-17 ... VIII.3:8 | answer truth with faith **e.** no strain at all. |
| T-18 ........ I.1:2 | would but consider exactly what this **e.**, |
| T-18 ... VI.11:4 | what this "transportation" really **e.**, you |
| T-19 ....... II.2:1 | sin **e.** an arrogance which the idea of error |
| T-23 ...... III.1:8 | and escapes the guilt the thought **e.**. If the |
| T-30 ... VII.6:5 | All sacrifice **e.** the loss of your ability to |
| T-30 ... VIII.2:1 | cannot have the changelessness reality **e.**. |
| W-pI....... 1.4:2 | or so, unless that **e.** a sense of hurry. A |
| W-pI..... 65.1:5 | only function necessarily **e.** two phases; |
| W-pI..... 70.3:1 | that guilt is in your own mind **e.** the |
| W-pI... 105.1:6 | guilt. The truly given gift **e.** no loss. It is |
| W-pI... 134.1:1 | **e.** an unfair sacrifice of righteous wrath, a |
| W-pI... 154.3:2 | strength to understand it, do what it **e.**, |
| W-pII ... 12.4:1 | for its salvation, and the cost belief in it **e.** |
| M-13 ......... 3:2 | –and it is sacrifice indeed!–all this **e.**. |
| P-2......... in.2:3 | as it is, but without the suffering that it **e.**. |
| S-2........... I.5:4 | to everyone, for what he does **e.** your fate, |

## entente 1

| | |
|---|---|
| T-29 ........ I.3:9 | and your brother but shared a qualified **e.** |

## enter 167

| | |
|---|---|
| T-1 ....... IV.1:5 | you will not only be willing to **e.** into |
| T-3 ........... I.1:7 | Such anti-religious concepts **e.** into many |
| T-4 .......... I.2:4 | to **e.** into your ego you will find peace. |
| T-4 ........ I.11:5 | is ready for you when you choose to **e.** it. |
| T-4 ....... III.4:7 | Love will **e.** immediately into any mind |
| T-4 ....... III.5:2 | and hiding is why the light cannot **e.**. The |
| T-4 ....... III.8:3 | your mind for the Holy One to **e.**. We will |
| T-5 ......... II.4:1 | let the belief in darkness **e.** your mind and |
| T-5 ......... V.4:3 | your allowing it to **e.** makes it your reality |
| T-6 ........ I.16:2 | fear to **e.** into the thought system toward |
| T-6 ..... V.C.1:2 | to **e.** it in the light of what God put there. |
| T-6 ..... V.C.8:2 | in your mind because, if you let doubt **e.**, |
| T-6 ..... V.C.8:7 | about being must not **e.** your mind, or |
| T-7 ...... VI.12:1 | Allowing insanity to **e.** your mind means |
| T-8 ....... III.6:8 | you **e.** fully will teach you this is not so. |
| T-9 ....... IV.5:4 | let any belief in its realness **e.** your mind, |
| T-10 ....... V.4:1 | and death seemed to **e.** the mind of God's |
| T-11 ....... II.5:5 | Whenever you ask the ego to **e.**, you |
| T-11 ....... II.6:4 | mind, and let nothing that obscures it **e.**. |
| T-11 ..... III.6:2 | never let them **e.** the mind of God's Son, |
| T-11 ..... III.7:3 | may **e.** the temple and find it waiting for |
| T-11 ..... III.7:5 | what is unlike God cannot **e.** His Mind, |
| T-11 ..... III.7:8 | You cannot **e.** God's Presence with the |
| T-11 ..... III.7:8 | beside you, but you also cannot **e.** alone. |
| T-11 ..... III.7:9 | All your brothers must **e.** with you, for |
| T-11 ..... III.7:9 | you have accepted them *you* cannot **e.**. For |
| T-11 ...... IV.5:6 | ***e.*** *God's Presence if you attack His Son.* |
| T-11 ...... IV.6:2 | that the door is barred and you cannot **e.**. |
| T-11 ...... IV.6:3 | is impossible that you cannot **e.** the place |
| T-11 ...... IV.6:5 | You can refuse to **e.**, but you cannot bar |
| T-12 ........ V.1:3 | Before the idea of attack can **e.** your mind |
| T-13 ...... III.5:4 | love cannot **e.** where it is not welcome. |
| T-13 ...... III.9:4 | for love cannot **e.** where there is one spot |
| T-13 .... VII.5:9 | the past behind and **e.** into the world He |
| T-13 ..... X.11:1 | You cannot **e.** into real relationships with |
| T-13 ..... X.14:6 | where we will surely **e.** in our sinlessness. |
| T-14 ..... III.6:3 | to free his brother and **e.** light with him. |
| T-14 .... VII.5:1 | Light cannot **e.** darkness when a mind |
| T-14 .... VII.6:2 | Him **e.** the darkness and lighten it away. |
| T-14 ........ X.1:7 | **e.** into it they leave all reflections behind. |
| T-15 ........ V.2:4 | then, could guilt not **e.**? For separation is |
| T-15 .... VII.2:3 | to **e.** into any relationship without anger, |
| T-15 ...... XI.9:1 | lets Him **e.** and abide where He would be. |
| T-15 ...... XI.9:5 | them. And by allowing Him to **e.**, the |
| T-16 ......... I.1:7 | by delusional attempts to **e.** into it, and |
| T-16 ......... I.7:9 | you but ask Him to **e.** your relationships, |
| T-16 ...... IV.3:6 | Hatred can **e.**, and indeed is welcome in |
| T-16 ........ V.1:2 | despair, guilt and attack all **e.** into it, |
| T-16 ...... VI.5:6 | perfect faith, the universe would **e.** into it. |
| T-16 ...... VI.9:3 | Thought of your reality to **e.** your mind, |
| T-16 ...... VI.9:4 | and you could not **e.** into a relationship |
| T-16 ... VI.12:1 | you, **e.** with Him into a holy instant, and |
| T-16 .... VII.1:3 | all **e.** into the special relationship, which |
| T-16 .. VII.12:1 | *are no illusions, and where none can ever* ***e.***. |
| T-17 ... III.1:12 | why you should **e.** into unholy alliances to |
| T-17 ...... III.2:2 | into which they **e.** are totally insane. |
| T-17 ...... III.3:5 | The shadow figures **e.** more and more, |
| T-17 ...... III.4:4 | it is formed, doubt must **e.** in, because its |
| T-17 ...... III.4:5 | does not **e.** at all to "spoil" the dream. |
| T-17 ... III.10:1 | I would **e.** into all your relationships, and |
| T-17 ... III.10:8 | Let me **e.** in the Name of God and bring |
| T-17 ......... V.3:1 | the practical results of asking Him to **e.**. |
| T-17 ...... VI.7:6 | is not the condition in which truth can **e.**. |
| T-17 .... VII.5:4 | Let it **e.** and look upon it calmly, but do |
| T-17 .... VII.9:1 | **E.** each situation with the faith you give |
| T-17 .... VII.9:5 | to every situation in which you **e.**, or will |
| T-17 .... VII.9:5 | in which you enter, or will ever **e.**. And |
| T-17 ... VIII.2:6 | Let it **e.**, and it will call forth and secure |
| T-18 ......... I.9:4 | ground, in which no substitution can **e.**, |
| T-18 ...... III.1:4 | darkness, in which no ray of light could **e.** |
| T-18 ...... IV.2:3 | your willingness, whatever else may **e.**. |
| T-18 ...... IV.3:6 | believe He cannot **e.** where He wills to be, |
| T-18 ...... VI.7:2 | Son can **e.** an abode that harbors hate, |
| T-18 ... VIII.2:6 | it is your kingdom, where God can **e.** not. |
| T-18 ... VIII.8:5 | be there that you would call on love to **e.**? |
| T-18 ... VIII.9:6 | They **e.** one by one into this holy place, |
| T-18 . VIII.11:1 | to **e.** into your bleak and joyless kingdom, |
| T-19 ...... I.15:2 | calls on truth to **e.** and make lovely what |

| | |
|---|---|
| T-19 IV.2:6 | and e. into a relationship with Him? For it |
| T19 IV.B.12:5 | fear to e. and become your purpose. The |
| T19 IV.B.12:6 | The attraction of guilt *must* e. with it, and |
| T19 IV.C.10:3 | can e. and disturb the peace of sinlessness |
| T-20 III.9:6 | you shall this day e. with him to Paradise, |
| T-20 IV.2:1 | and can no more e. than can their source. |
| T-20 IV.6:6 | Each holy relationship must e. here, to |
| T-20 IV.6:7 | a new world rises in which sin can e. not, |
| T-20 IV.6:7 | Son of God can e. without fear and where |
| T-20 IV.6:8 | How can he e., to rest and to remember, |
| T-20 IV.7:3 | the hands of every two who e. here to rest. |
| T-20 VI.3:4 | in which they e. has lost its meaning. The |
| T-20 VI.5:5 | Here it is "safe," for here love cannot e.. |
| T-20 VI.7:10 | Where you are the body cannot e., for the |
| T-21 VI.2:9 | And how could thoughts that e. into what |
| T-22 I.10:7 | it is one with you who joined to let it e.. |
| T-22 II.8:2 | there one illusion you can e. Heaven with. |
| T-22 V.3:9 | Here can no weakness e., for here is no |
| T-23 III.3:5 | Let the idea of compromise but e., and |
| T-24 in.1:5 | Where He can e., there He is already. And |
| T-24 in.1:6 | it be He cannot e. where He wills to be? |
| T-24 II.13:2 | it demands a special place God cannot e., |
| T-24 III.6:4 | Ask not He e. this. The way is barred to |
| T-24 IV.3:15 | disturb your peace to e. and destroy. |
| T-25 III.2:5 | could not e. His Son's insanity with him, |
| T-25 VII.8:3 | but e. into it in quietness and show him |
| T-26 III.1:9 | how could strife e. in its simple presence, |
| T-27 III.4:1 | a silent invitation to the truth to e., and to |
| T-28 I.12:5 | and lets Them e. where They would abide |
| T-28 III.9:7 | Here can the lean years e. not, for time |
| T-29 II.4:3 | You did not hear Him e., for you did not |
| T-29 VIII.4:6 | voice could make demand He e. not? The |
| T-29 IX.7:7 | Only forgiving dreams can e. here, for |
| T-29 IX.7:8 | And the forms that e. in the dream are |
| T-30 VIII.6:2 | a dream allow uncertainty to e. here. Be |
| T-31 V.17:5 | is the truth left free to e. in its sanctuary, |
| W-pI 41.6:6 | Try to e. very deeply into your own mind, |
| W-pI 50.5:3 | Let no idle and foolish thoughts e. to |
| W-pI 56.3:3 | I see it now, truth cannot e. my awareness |
| W-pI 72.6:1 | animals seek for prey and mercy cannot e. |
| W-pI 97.1:5 | No chill of fear can e., for your mind has |
| W-pI 99.7:6 | your mistakes e. the darkened places of |
| W-pI 103.1:6 | there are gaps in love where sin can e., |
| W-pI 107.7:6 | count on it to e. into all the exercises that |
| W-pI 109.8:3 | bid them all e. here and rest with you. |
| W-pI 110.11:7 | lets you e. in the peace of God and His |
| W-pI 122.5:3 | bidding you to e. in and make yourself at |
| W-pI 131.11:7 | to the holy place where they can e. not. |
| W-pI 134.17:7 | *and yet no one can e. Heaven by himself.* |
| W-pI 136.14:1 | remain where truth has been allowed to e. |
| W-pI 137.9:1 | for a world where sadness cannot e., are |
| W-pI 138.2:5 | true in God's creation cannot e. here until |
| W-pI 152.2:5 | Can fear and sickness e. in a mind where |
| W-pI 157.h | Into His Presence would I e. now. |
| W-pI 157.9:1 | Into Christ's Presence will we e. now, |
| W-pI 167.9:2 | does not have, a foreign state it cannot e., |
| W-pI 174.1:1 | (157) Into His Presence would I e. now. |
| W-pI 181.5:7 | We e. in the time of practicing with one |
| W-pI 190.9:3 | Let no attack e. with you. Lay down the |
| W-pI 199.2:2 | Attack thoughts cannot e. such a mind, |
| W-pI 199.2:2 | and fear can never e. in a mind that has |
| W-pII in.1:4 | leave the world of pain, and go to e. peace |
| W-pII 228.2:2 | *not left that Source to e. in a body and to die.* |
| W-pII 3.2:4 | to be a place where God could e. not, and |
| W-pII 266.2:1 | This day we e. into Paradise, calling upon |
| W-pII 274.1:3 | *as well the truth will e. where illusions were,* |
| W-pII 307.1:5 | *e. into peace where conflict is impossible,* |
| W-pII 307.2:1 | And with this prayer we e. silently into a |
| W-pII 316.1:5 | and e. in where I am truly welcome and at |
| W-pII 332.1:6 | Forgiveness bids this presence e. in, and |
| W-pII 342.1:5 | *wondering if I should e. in and be at home.* |
| W-pII 14.5:5 | will e. in and disappear into the Heart of |
| M-3 4:3 | a time, two people e. into a fairly intense |
| M-8 4:1 | of the mind that errors in perception e.. |
| M-17 3:3 | intent. Attack can e. only if perception of |
| M-17 3:6 | and this answer will e. the teacher's mind |
| M-28 3:13 | it is asked to e. and envelop such a world! |
| C-5 1:1 | help to e. Heaven for you have never left. |
| P-1 2:1 | the Holy Spirit to e. into it and give it His |
| P-2 in.2:1 | Patients do not e. the therapeutic |
| P-2 I.1:6 | of them will e. into another commitment. |
| P-2 II.5:3 | God will e. into their relationship because |
| P-2 II.6:1 | invitation to God to e. into His Kingdom, |
| P-2 VI.1:4 | "God may not e. here" the sick repeat, |
| P-2 VII.2:3 | in a relationship which Christ can e.? This |
| P-3 II.3:8 | Spirit to e. the relationship and heal it. He |
| P-3 II.4:8 | dream a strange correction must e., for |
| P-3 III.8:3 | an invitation to e. and abide with you. He |
| S-3 II.6:4 | free to e. in the home that stands ready to |

## entered 41

| | |
|---|---|
| T-4 III.7:1 | It has never really e. your mind to give up |
| T-5 III.8:9 | the idea of danger has e. your mind. The |
| T-7 III.3:4 | the idea of competition has e. their minds |
| T-15 V.4:4 | And love, where fear has e., cannot be |
| T-17 V.11:2 | He could not have e. otherwise. Although |
| T-17 VII.3:4 | Some idea of bodies must have e., for |
| T-17 VII.8:8 | Cause has e. any situation that shares Its |
| T-18 I.9:6 | The original error has not e. here, nor |
| T-18 I.11:2 | Heaven has e. quietly, for all illusions |
| T-18 I.11:3 | and His whole creation have e. it together |
| T-18 VI.2:8 | You hate your mind, for guilt has e. into it |
| T-18 VIII.12:1 | this; love has e. your special relationship, |
| T-18 VIII.12:1 | and e. fully at your weak request. You do |
| T-19 IV.2:5 | answered you, and e. your relationship. |
| T19 IV.A.7:3 | Before the Holy Spirit e. to abide with you |
| T19 IV.C.1:1 | special relationship the Holy Spirit e., it is |
| T-20 III.1:5 | in which certainty is lost and doubt has e. |
| T-20 IV.6:5 | The ark of peace is e. two by two, yet the |
| T-22 I.8:6 | Where Christ has e. no one is alone, for |
| T-25 III.6:1 | Everyone here has e. darkness, yet no one |
| T-25 III.6:1 | darkness, yet no one has e. it alone. Nor |
| T-25 IV.5:11 | and all the thoughts that e. it and were |
| T-26 V.10:7 | of death, a vault God's Son e. an instant, |
| T-26 VI.1:5 | reality has e. all the world of sick illusions |
| T-26 IX.7:1 | of sin, and keep the light where it has e. in |
| T-27 V.11:4 | occurred within the instant that love e. in |
| T-29 II.1:8 | be present where their cause has e. in. |
| T-29 II.5:2 | e. in but waits for you to come where you |
| T-31 V.12:3 | that interaction must have e. in. There is |
| T-31 V.13:5 | e. in the choice by your decision. But this |
| W-pI 107.1:3 | Where truth has e. errors disappear. They |
| W-pI 140.5:4 | He is barred where sin has e.. Yet there is |
| W-pII 263.1:1 | *Mind created all that is, Your Spirit e. into it,* |
| M-1 1:4 | A light has e. the darkness. It may be a |
| M-1 1:6 | He has e. an agreement with God even if |
| M-2 2:6 | of separation e. the mind of God's Son, in |
| M-7 6:3 | about what you are has e. your mind, and |
| M-11 4:8 | here, because a Thought of God has e.. |
| M-17 3:3 | only if perception of separate goals has e.. |
| P-3 III.6:4 | have been before the Holy Spirit e. them, |
| S-3 III.6:6 | love has e. now where idols used to stand, |

## entering 7

| | |
|---|---|
| T-4 III.7:2 | of fear that prevent the Holy One from e.. |
| T-17 III.8:1 | the justification for e. into a continuing, |
| T-17 V.11:9 | Perhaps you are now e. upon a campaign |
| T-20 IV.h | E. the Ark |
| T-30 I.13:1 | if you prevent unhappiness from e. at all. |
| W-pI 44.10:1 | approaching, if not actually e. into light. |
| W-pI 135.22:1 | that blocks the truth from e. our minds. |

## enters 22

| | |
|---|---|
| T-2 VII.5:4 | Whenever light e. darkness, the darkness |
| T-7 II.7:8 | free, because nothing discordant ever e.. |
| T-7 III.5:7 | nothing questionable e. their minds. This |
| T-8 VII.1:2 | When attack in any form e. your mind |
| T-13 III.5:5 | for it e. of its own volition and cares not |
| T-13 VII.5:5 | judgment e. reality has slipped away. The |
| T-14 VII.6:3 | At your request He e. gladly. He brings |
| T-15 VII.1:6 | for any relationship in which the ego e.. |
| T-15 XI.9:5 | remembrance of the Father e. with Him, |
| T-16 IV.5:8 | conflict e. the instant the choice seems to |
| T-20 VI.2:4 | in which the body e. is based not on love, |
| T-21 V.8:4 | But reason e. not at all in this. For the |
| T-21 VI.5:6 | e. part be kept away from other parts? |
| T-22 I.10:7 | where fear is powerless love e. thankfully, |
| T-23 IV.1:6 | No difference e., and what is all the same |
| T-31 IV.2:12 | gaily for a while, before the bleakness e.. |
| W-pI 92.8:2 | none who e. its abode can leave without a |
| M-23 4:7 | mind. God e. easily, for these are the true |
| C-4 7:1 | wholly understandable, e. its kingdom. |
| C-ep 5:6 | quiet God has given him e. his home and |
| P-2 VII.2:6 | But once Christ e. in, what choice is there |
| P-3 II.1:3 | in every relationship in which he e.? Yet |

## entertain 2

| | |
|---|---|
| W-pI 79.8:3 | All that is necessary is to e. some doubt |
| W-pI 117.1:3 | *And so I choose to e. no substitutes for love.* |

## enthrone 1

| | |
|---|---|
| T-5 V.4:3 | real. If you e. the ego in your mind, your |

## enthroned 1

| | |
|---|---|
| T-24 IV.1:7 | Here is death e. as savior; crucifixion is |

## enthrones 1

| | |
|---|---|
| W-pI 170.9:4 | basic premise which e. the thought of fear |

## entire 1

| | |
|---|---|
| W-pI 22.1:5 | preoccupy him and people his e. world. |

## entirely 87

| | |
|---|---|
| T-2 III.1:2 | almost e. to defend *against* the Atonement |
| T-2 III.3:3 | you cannot depart e. from your Creator, |
| T-2 III.5:5 | and is e. worthy of receiving perfection. |
| T-2 VI.5:4 | should, but without e. wanting to do so. |
| T-2 VII.4:4 | rests e. on mastery through love. In the |
| T-3 I.3:8 | is, and how e. it arises from projection. |
| T-3 I.6:5 | The Atonement is e. unambiguous. It is |
| T-3 IV.5:9 | it could not e. separate itself from spirit, |
| T-3 IV.6:5 | the mind and e. inaccessible to the body. |
| T-3 V.9:5 | condition e. alien to the world's thinking. |
| T-4 II.8:12 | creative. Myths are e. perceptual, and so |
| T-4 II.11:4 | This removes the block e.. You may ask |
| T-5 IV.1:4 | but e. within your ability to accept. It |
| T-6 I.14:4 | speak of the crucifixion e. without anger, |
| T-6 V.C.1:5 | of accord e. He rejects by judging against. |
| T-7 VI.1:3 | and why it must be relinquished e.. If it is |
| T-7 VI.1:4 | relinquished e. it is not relinquished at all |
| T-7 VI.8:9 | must give up the idea of conflict e. and for |
| T-8 I.6:4 | teaching you e. different things in entirely |
| T-8 I.6:4 | you entirely different things in e. different |
| T-8 II.1:9 | if you could disregard the Holy Spirit e., |
| T-8 VII.2:6 | will change your mind e. about its value. |
| T-8 VII.12:4 | gives it over e. to the One Light in which |
| T-8 VIII.1:11 | Yet to know in part is to know e. because |
| T-8 VIII.4:1 | it is e. out of keeping with what you want. |
| T-11 VII.3:3 | It does not reject goodness e., for that you |
| T-14 VI.8:1 | Spirit's function is e. communication. He |
| T-15 V.1:2 | For its purpose is to suspend judgment e.. |
| T-16 IV.10:4 | and to be e. unwilling to settle for illusion |
| T-17 IV.15:5 | without value and e. deprived of meaning |
| T-17 V.7:3 | need not part e. if you choose not to do so |
| T-18 VI.8:10 | It encompasses you e.; you within it and it |
| T-18 VII.3:4 | Time controls it e., for sin is never wholly |
| T-19 I.3:3 | depends e. on how the mind perceives it, |
| T-19 II.8:1 | more than a mistake, e. correctable, and |
| T19 IV.D.1:5 | and the Son of God e. restored to sanity. |
| T-20 II.8:5 | began, nor have you ever failed e. to hear. |
| T-21 II.12:5 | depends e. upon the madness of its maker |
| T-21 IV.3:6 | now e. unwilling to look within and see it |
| T-21 V.1:9 | depends e. your whole belief in what you |
| T-21 V.8:6 | for it depends e. on reason's absence. The |
| T-22 I.3:1 | to understand what fails e. to reach you. |
| T-22 II.7:4 | This course will be believed e. or not at all |
| T-22 II.7:6 | either escape from misery e. or not at all. |
| T-22 II.13:3 | would be released e. from all effects of sin |

T-22...... VI.1:7 eclipsed **e.** when they are recognized as
T-24...... IV.5:2 in reality: When peace is not with you **e.**,
T-25...... III.2:4 He could not let Himself be separate **e.**.
T-26....... II.6:4 you wish to be preserved from sacrifice **e.**.
T-26..... VII.9:3 yet reached beyond the world of choice **e.**.
T-27....... II.4:5 that cannot be undone and overlooked **e.**.
T-27.... VIII.9:2 error, who have overlooked the cause **e.**?
T-28....... I.14:7 beyond fear, and past the world of sin **e.**.
T-28...... IV.8:2 This holy picture, healed **e.**, does He hold
T-30...... IV.1:3 of it you would forget defensiveness **e.**,
T-30...... VI.7:5 it. You must forgive God's Son **e.**. Or you
W-pI..... 46.3:5 You have forgiven them **e.** or not at all.
W-pI..... 72.5:7 It overlooks **e.** what your brother is. It
W-pI..... 94.1:1 renders the ego silent and **e.** undone. You
W-pI... 129.3:3 you go from there to where words fail **e.**,
W-pI. 133.12:1 all, **e.** desirable or not worth the slightest
W-pI... 134.6:3 feet of truth. And there they disappear **e.**.
W-pI... 152.2:7 for to do so is to contradict the truth **e.**.
W-pI... 152.4:3 that do not appear to be **e.** your own. And
W-pI... 163.6:5 contradicts one thought **e.** can not be true
W-pI... 168.1:6 He remains **e.** accessible. He loves His
W-pI... 169.1:2 for it leads beyond the world **e.**. It is past
W-pI... 169.9:2 for revelation is **e.** irrelevant to what must
W-pI... 185.1:4 awareness, memory of God **e.** restored,
W-pI... 190.6:4 will change **e.** as you elect to change your
W-pI... 196.6:3 that this, at least, must be **e.** impossible,
W-pII . 226.1:1 If I so choose, I can depart this world **e.**.
W-pII ..... 7.2:3 of love. And when this is **e.** accomplished,
W-pII . 326.2:1 forgiven, fade **e.** into God's holy Will.
W-pII . 336.1:2 gives way **e.** to what remains forever past
W-pII ... 13.2:2 because it fails **e.** to understand its ways.
M-2 ........... 2:4 for the Will of God is **e.** apart from time.
M-4 ..... I.A.3:5 which he can make the shift **e.** internally.
M-4 ..... I.A.5:3 teachers of God escape this distress **e.**.
M-4 ...... IX.1:6 is to reverse the thinking of the world **e.**.
M-5 ......... I.2:8 thus **e.** usurped the throne of his Creator.
M-19 ......... 4:7 an evaluation based **e.** on love,–you have
M-19 ......... 5:5 to Heaven just because it is **e.** impartial. It
M-20 ......... 2:5 It is a new thing **e.**. There is a contrast, yes
M-28 ......... 2:2 is all the thinking of the world reversed **e.**.
C-1............. 4:1 part of the mind is **e.** illusory and makes
P-3......... II.7:5 accepted the gift **e.** in order to stay and let

## entirety 2

T-17...... III.3:2 is not the central focus as it is, or in **e.**.
W-pI... 154.1:5 within a larger plan we cannot see in its **e.**

## entities 1

T-26......... I.1:8 All seeming **e.** can come a little nearer, or

## entitle 1

W-pI..... 89.1:5 only what the laws of God **e.** me to have,

## entitled 19

T-1......... II.3:7 is **e.** to respect for his greater experience,
T-1......... II.3:8 is also **e.** to love because he is a brother,
T-2........ III.5:1 The children of God are **e.** to the perfect
T-25...... IX.7:4 everyone is equally **e.** to His gift of healing
T-27......... I.7:5 frail **e.** to believe that every stolen scrap of
W-pI..... 37.1:6 And he is **e.** to everything because it is his
W-pI..... 40.1:1 of the happy things to which you are **e.**,
W-pI..... 47.6:1 which you need, and to which you are **e.**.
W-pI........ 77.h I am **e.** to miracles.
W-pI..... 77.1:1 are **e.** to miracles because of what you are.
W-pI..... 77.4:1 confidently that you are **e.** to miracles.
W-pI..... 77.7:3 *I am e. to miracles.* Ask for them whenever
W-pI..... 77.7:6 are fully **e.** to receive it whenever you ask.
W-pI..... 80.3:1 You are **e.** to peace today. A problem that
W-pI..... 89.1:1 (77) I am **e.** to miracles. I am entitled to
W-pI..... 89.1:2 I am **e.** to miracles because I am under no
W-pI..... 89.2:2 *Behind this is a miracle to which I am e.. Let*
W-pI... 195.9:3 it, we are not **e.** therefore to our bitterness
S-1........... I.5:3 fully **e.** to everything Love has to offer?

## entitles 3

T-1 ......... II.3:9 It is only my devotion that **e.** me to yours.
W-pI..... 74.5:1 the peace to which your reality **e.** you.
W-pI..... 75.7:1 that your forgiveness **e.** you to vision.

## entity 5

T-8 ...... VII.5:3 you look upon a brother as a physical **e.**,
T-8 .... VII.11:4 the body as a separate **e.** cannot but foster
T-26 ......... I.2:3 Around each **e.** is built a wall so seeming
W-pI... 184.1:3 Each one becomes a separate **e.**, identified
W-pII . 223.1:1 God, a separate **e.** that moved in isolation

## entrance 1

P-3........ III.8:8 Deny him **e.**, and you have denied the

## entrapped 1

C-6 ........... 4:8 your self **e.** in needs you do not have. It is

## entreat 2

S-1........... I.1:6 must avoid the pitfall of asking to **e.**. Ask,
S-1........... I.5:3 Why should holiness **e.**, being fully

## entreaty 2

S-1........... I.1:2 It is not merely a question or an **e.**. It
S-1........... I.7:2 ask that Christ be but Himself is not an **e.**.

## entrust 2

T-22 ........ I.9:1 God did not **e.** His Son to the unworthy.
T-25 .... VII.8:1 be madness to **e.** salvation to the insane.

## entrusted 13

T-4 ........ I.13:4 I can be **e.** with your body and your ego
T-19 ..... III.4:2 correct them all as God **e.** Him to do. But
T-22 ..... VI.4:3 all. Nothing **e.** to it can be misused, and
T-31 .... VII.8:2 life **e.** all salvation from the misery of hell.
T-31 .... VII.8:3 to the holy ones especially **e.** to his care.
T-31 .. VII.10:4 rest. To everyone has God **e.** all, because a
W-pI..... 99.6:5 Now are you **e.** with this plan, along with
W-pI...... 166.h I am **e.** with the gifts of God.
W-pI. 166.13:1 The gifts are yours, **e.** to your care, to
W-pI. 166.14:6 are **e.** with the world's release from pain.
W-pI. 166.15:3 God has **e.** all His gifts to you. Be witness
W-pI... 178.2:1 (166) I am **e.** with the gifts of God. God is
W-pI... 206.1:2 *I am e. with the gifts of God, because I am His*

## entrusts 2

W-pI. 166.15:6 For God **e.** the giving of His gifts to all
W-pI... 194.8:4 Who **e.** himself to God has also placed the

## entry 1

T-24 ... VI.11:3 itself, with every **e.** shut against intrusion,

## enumerate 1

W-pI..... 24.5:1 **e.** carefully as many goals as possible that

## envelop 6

T-10 ... IV.5:10 will **e.** you completely when you let them
T-16 .... VII.2:4 Shades of the past **e.** it, and make it what
W-pI.... 107.9:6 will **e.** you and give you peace so deep and
W-pI... 190.7:7 Your thoughts of death **e.** it in fear, while
M-28 ....... 3:13 as it is asked to enter and **e.** such a world!
C-4 ........... 8:1 if you only knew the peace that will **e.** you

## enveloping 1

T-16 ........ I.6:2 blesses it silently by **e.** it in healing wings.

## envelops 10

W-pI ....... 36.h My holiness **e.** everything I see.
W-pI .... 36.3:4 *My holiness e. that rug. My holiness*
W-pI .... 36.3:5 *rug. My holiness e. that wall. My holiness*
W-pI .... 36.3:6 *My holiness e. these fingers. My holiness*
W-pI .... 36.3:7 *My holiness e. that chair. My holiness*
W-pI .... 36.3:8 *chair. My holiness e. that body. My holiness*
W-pI .... 36.3:9 *body. My holiness e. this pen.* Several times
W-pI .... 58.1:1 (36) My holiness **e.** everything I see.
W-pII . 305.1:3 world departs in silence as this peace **e.** it,
W-pII .... 346.h Today the peace of God **e.** me, And I

## envious 1

T-25 . VIII.13:9 And so must he be **e.**, and try to take

## environment 9

T-7 ....... XI.2:2 his natural **e.** and does not function well.
T-7 ....... XI.2:3 not created for the **e.** that he has made.
T-7 ....... XI.2:7 the only **e.** in which he will not experience
T-7 ....... XI.2:8 It is also the only **e.** that is worthy of him,
T-7 ....... XI.3:6 is the only **e.** in which you can be happy.
T-7 ....... XI.6:1 Out of your natural **e.** you may well ask,
T-7 ....... XI.6:1 truth?" since truth is the **e.** by which and
W-pI .... 35.2:2 surround yourself with the **e.** you want.
W-pI .... 35.2:4 The image is part of this **e.**. What you see

## envy 5

T-21 .... VII.2:4 what can they do but **e.** him his power,
T-21 .... VII.2:4 by their **e.** make themselves afraid of it?
W-pI .. 163.1:2 and lack of trust; concern for bodies, **e.**,
W-pI .. 192.1:2 such a function mean within a world of **e.**,
S-1........ III.2:1 ladder, will not be free from **e.** and malice

## eons 1

W-pI .. 123.7:3 power to save the world **e.** more quickly

## ephemeral 7

T-10 ...... in.2:5 What can upset you except the **e.**, and
T-10 ...... in.2:5 **e.** be real if you are God's only creation
T-21 ... VIII.2:6 It sees not the **e.**, for it desires everything
T-27 ........ I.7:8 take pleasure in the quickly passing and **e.**
W-pI .. 107.3:4 liberating you from all beliefs in the **e.**.
W-pI .. 152.6:4 What can He know of the **e.**, the sinful
W-pI .. 188.3:4 all thoughts of the **e.** and valueless. It

## epilogue 2

W-ep........... h Epilogue
C-ep ............ h Epilogue

## episodes 1

W-pI .... 15.3:1 we go along, you may have many "light **e.**.

## epitaph 1

W-pI .. 163.5:2 be. His **e.**, which death itself has written,

## epitome 1

W-pI .... 61.2:1 today's idea is the **e.** of self-glorification.

## epitomizes 1

T-3 .......... I.7:2 **e.** harmlessness and sheds only blessing.

## equal 61

T-1 ....... III.6:6 neighbor are **e.** members of one family, as
T-2 .......... I.5:1 which can heal any of them with **e.** ease. It
T-2 ......... II.1:8 endowing all thoughts with **e.** power will
T-5 ........ II.3:11 God's Sons are as **e.** as learners as they are
T-6 ........ I.6:11 me, and we will become **e.** as teachers.

T-6........ I.10:1 We are still **e.** as learners, although we do
T-6........ I.10:1 we do not need to have **e.** experiences.
T-6......... II.5:4 the Holy Spirit perceives **e.** needs. This
T-6......... V.1:1 He teaches only to make you **e.** with Him.
T-6......V.A.4:7 Only one **e.** gift can be offered to the
T-6......V.A.4:7 gift can be offered to the **e.** Sons of God,
T-7........ III.3:3 Because God's **e.** Sons have everything,
T-7........ IX.2:2 equally whole and **e.** in perfection. The
T-8........ IV.6:8 God's Sons are **e.** in will, all being the
T-11....... VI.7:5 in which everyone has a part of **e.** value.
T-11.... VI.10:5 because all of God's Sons are of **e.** value,
T-12....... V.1:5 yourself and your brothers as **e.**, and
T-13.... VIII.6:1 same; all beautiful and **e.** in their holiness
T-14.... III.17:1 Whose **e.** Love is given equally to all alike!
T-14.... VII.4:5 them both alive and **e.** in their reality.
T-14..... X.6:11 gives **e.** blessing to all who share in it, and
T-15...... IV.8:6 is given and received with **e.** willingness,
T-18....... V.6:3 peace of one is an **e.** threat to the other.
T-19.........I.6:2 divided goal has given both an **e.** reality,
T-19...... I.14:5 brings the miracle of healing with **e.** ease
T-20.... VI.12:6 God as **e.** things are like unto each other.
T-21...... III.3:5 is impossible to place **e.** faith in opposite
T-21....... V.1:3 hold, perhaps, if other things were **e.**.
T-21....... V.1:4 They are not **e.**. For what you look for you
T-23..... II.19:5 **e.** in their inaccuracy and lack of meaning
T-23.... IV.1:12 of love because it seems to be of **e.** truth.
T-23..... IV.2:1 What can be **e.** to the truth, yet different?
T-24..... II.10:7 Himself to you and your brother in **e.** love
T-24.... VI.10:6 each part of Him with **e.** love and care.
T-25..... III.6:7 can, with **e.** ease and far more happiness,
T-25....... V.4:4 will give to each an **e.** strength to save the
T-25. VIII.13:5 since they are **e.** in the Holy Spirit's sight.
T-25...... IX.8:1 have an **e.** right to miracles with you, you
T-25...... IX.8:1 you were unjust to one with **e.** rights.
T-26..... VII.6:9 and all must yield with **e.** ease to what
T-27....... II.7:2 bestow an **e.** gift of full deliverance from
T-29...... IV.1:3 Their **e.** lack of truth becomes the basis
T-31....... II.7:1 Because he is your **e.** in God's Love, you
T-31....... II.7:5 you. Christ calls to all with **e.** tenderness,
T-31....... V.1:7 perfected it, to meet the world on **e.** terms
T-31..... V.13:6 But this gain is paid in almost **e.** loss, for
W-pI....... 2.2:3 exercise with **e.** ease to a body or a button
W-pI..... 12.2:6 rests on **e.** attention and equal time. This
W-pI..... 12.2:6 rests on equal attention and **e.** time. This
W-pI..... 12.2:7 step in learning to give them all **e.** value.
W-pI..... 28.7:2 each one should be accorded **e.** sincerity
W-pI..... 28.7:2 in an attempt to acknowledge the **e.** value
W-pI..... 33.2:1 your inner thoughts with **e.** casualness.
W-pI..... 38.2:6 It is **e.** in its power to help anyone because
W-pI..... 38.2:6 because it is **e.** in its power to save anyone
W-pI..... 71.8:1 each making **e.** contribution to the whole.
W-pI..... 99.2:1 Truth and illusions both are **e.** now, for
W-pI... 105.6:2 are their right under the **e.** laws of God.
W-pI... 124.3:2 with the **e.** love in which we were created,
P-3......... II.9:6 Either they are **e.** or not. The attempts of
S-2......... II.1:3 to separate and make what God created **e.**
W-pI... 126.3:3 lowered him beneath a true **e.** with you.
W-pII...... 9.4:3 In this **e.** is Christ restored as one Identity
P-3......... II.9:4 recognize the **e.** of himself and the patient
S-3........ III.2:6 in dreams, **e.** cannot be permanent. The

## equality 24

T-1......... II.6:2 the recognition of the **e.** of the members
T-1......... II.6:8 the underlying recognition of perfect **e.** of
T-1......... V.2:5 **E.** does not imply equality *now*. When
T-1......... V.2:5 Equality does not imply **e.** *now*. When
T-1....... VII.5:6 reaction to me because of our inherent **e.**.
T-3......... V.8:1 no judgments and nothing but perfect **e.**?
T-4......... II.7:2 **E.** is beyond its grasp, and charity
T-6........... I.5:1 fundamental **e.** can be demonstrated only
T-6......... II.3:4 obscuring your **e.** with them still further.
T-6......... II.5:4 Perceiving **e.**, the Holy Spirit perceives
T-6......... II.7:1 perfect **e.** of the Holy Spirit's perception is
T-6......... II.7:1 of the perfect **e.** of God's knowing. The
T-6......V.A.4:6 it, because it is a belief in perfect **e.**. Only
T-6......V.B.3:4 **e.** of *having* and *being* is not yet perceived.
T-8........ IV.6:7 and the perfect **e.** of all God's Sons cannot
T-11.... VI.10:5 equal value, and their **e.** is their oneness.
T-13.... III.10:6 attacked his own glorious **e.** with Him.
T-14.......... X.h The **E.** of Miracles
T-14....... X.2:7 being based not on differences but on **e.**.
T-15....... V.3:4 For it is the complete **e.** of the Atonement

## equalize 2

T-12....... V.1:5 attempt to "**e.**" the situation you made.
T-12....... V.2:8 no need to "**e.**" the situation to establish

## equally 72

T-1....... VII.3:9 will be **e.** strong in your belief in them.
T-3......... V.8:4 All of it is **e.** true, and knowing any part
T-4......... II.2:2 else he perceives, which is **e.** variable.
T-4......... II.8:2 them in an **e.** feeble show of strength. It is
T-4......... II.8:8 all. While the ego is **e.** unaware of spirit, it
T-5.........in.2:7 Every part benefits, and benefits **e.**.
T-5....... VII.2:5 that every mind God created is **e.** worthy
T-6.........in.1:4 the **e.** irrational conclusion that a brother
T-7......... V.7:2 receiving something **e.** desirable in return
T-7........ IX.2:2 creations **e.** whole and equal in perfection
T-7........ XI.5:5 God gives only **e.**. If you recognize His gift
T-8........ IV.7:9 He gives **e.** whatever is acceptable to Him.
T-9......... II.3:3 Yet it is **e.** certain that no response given
T-9......... V.1:6 more likely to start with the **e.** incredible
T-9...... VI.3:10 glory belongs to Him, but it is **e.** yours.
T-10.... III.11:8 is **e.** clear that it has everything to do with
T-11....... VI.1:1 but it is **e.** impossible to see what you do
T-12.........I.8:1 that His criteria are **e.** applicable to you.
T-13...... IV.7:2 The reason is **e.** clear, for they perceive
T-13..... X.11:1 Sons unless you love them all and **e.**. Love
T-14.... III.17:1 Whose equal Love is given **e.** to all alike!
T-14... VIII.2:4 there that is not **e.** worthy of Both, but
T-15..... V.10:6 He needs them all **e.**, and so do you. In
T-15...... VI.1:2 And it is **e.** impossible to condemn part of
T-15.... VI.6:10 the only need the Sons of God share **e.**,
T-16....... II.4:3 minds join as one and share one idea **e.**,
T-16....... III.3:3 is **e.** impossible that conviction be outside
T-18.......I.10:5 He loves you both, **e.** and as one. And as
T-18....... V.6:6 so is it **e.** impossible that the holy instant
T19..IV.B.16:5 yet within which is his death **e.** inevitable.
T-22....... II.3:9 not to other dreams that are but **e.** unreal.
T-23....... II.3:3 that they are all the same and **e.** untrue, it
T-23....... III.1:3 Attack in any form is **e.** destructive. Its
T-25..... II.11:5 nor apart from all God's Love as given **e.**.
T-25..... VII.6:5 But sin is **e.** insane within the sight of love
T-25...... IX.7:4 And everyone is **e.** entitled to His gift of
T-25.... IX.10:5 It is received and given **e.**. It is awareness
T-26...... II.6:10 can He ensure that everyone receives it **e.**.
T-26....... X.2:6 **e.** without a cause or consequence, and
T-26....... X.2:7 is your own and **e.** belongs to every living
T-27...... VI.1:7 Pleasure and pain are **e.** unreal, because
T-28...... III.9:5 before His Son, and shares it **e.** with him.
T-30.... IV.5:11 Yet this is **e.** forgotten in attack. God's
W-in.......... 4:2 of them is **e.** applicable to everyone and
W-pI....... 3.2:3 **e.** suitable and therefore equally useful.
W-pI....... 3.2:3 equally suitable and therefore **e.** useful.
W-pI....... 5.4:4 *are all* **e.** *disturbing to my peace of mind.*
W-pI....... 6.3:3 *are all* **e.** *disturbing to my peace of mind.*
W-pI....... 7.4:2 This is **e.** true of whatever you look at.
W-pI..... 16.3:3 you recognize them all as **e.** destructive,
W-pI..... 16.3:3 all as equally destructive, but **e.** unreal.
W-pI..... 29.4:3 any order you impose is **e.** alien to reality.
W-pI..... 30.5:4 without. Today's idea applies **e.** to both.
W-pI..... 32.3:3 Try to treat them both as **e.** as possible.
W-pI..... 33.2:2 Try to remain **e.** uninvolved in both, and
W-pI..... 35.4:3 All of them are **e.** unreal, because you do
W-pI..... 43.7:5 form is **e.** applicable to strangers as it is to
W-pI... 100.1:3 each one of them is **e.** essential to them all
WpI. rIII.in9:1 done throughout the day are **e.** important
W-pI... 140.9:3 between what is untrue and **e.** untrue.
W-pI... 154.2:2 **e.** aware of where they can be best applied
W-pI... 189.4:1 Yet is the world of hatred **e.** unseen and
W-pI... 195.2:2 **e.** insane to fail in gratitude to One Who
W-pII...... 9.4:2 now, is **e.** released from what he made. In
M-4 ...... III.1:8 judgment are all things **e.** acceptable, for
M-6 ........... 2:5 storehouse of treasures laid up **e.** for the
M-17 ......... 5:6 that it can be believed as fact is **e.** obvious
M-22 ......... 6:2 It is **e.** applicable to all individuals in all
M-22 ......... 7:6 Both are **e.** meaningless. Yet this will not
M-25 ......... 1:3 exist. It is **e.** obvious, however, that each
M-27 ....... 4:10 fear. Both are **e.** meaningless to Him.
S-3........ III.1:6 has, not **e.** bestowed on both as one. Here

## equals 6

T-1.......... II.3:4 is therefore a sign of love among **e.**.
T-1.......... II.3:5 **E.** should not be in awe of one another
T-1....... VII.5:2 experience awe in the presence of your **e.**.
T-5.......... II.9:1 like yours, because we were created as **e.**.
T-7........ III.3:2 as brothers, because only **e.** are at peace.
T-7........ III.3:4 as anything other than their perfect **e.**,

## equanimity 1

T-15......... I.5:4 anyone to look upon with **e.** is the past.

## equate 4

T-8....... VII.1:6 When you **e.** yourself with a body you will
T-8...... VIII.1:4 It does not **e.** it with what it *is*. To the ego
T-16...... VI.1:1 **e.** yourself with the ego and not with God.
W-pI..... 13.3:3 must also be to you who **e.** yourself with

## equated 4

T-6...... V.B.8:1 step, since *having* and *being* are still not **e.**.
T-9....... II.10:1 If paying is **e.** with getting, you will set
T-9......... V.4:5 Yet if the dreamer is **e.** with the mind, the
M-24 ......... 6:3 Atonement might be **e.** with total escape

## equates 2

T-8...... VIII.1:3 and **e.** what it sees with the function it
T-27... VII.10:2 world **e.** the body with the Self which God

## equating 4

T-6........... I.4:7 must be **e.** yourself with the destructible,
T-8....... VII.1:2 your mind you are **e.** yourself with a body
T-8...... VIII.1:6 **E.** you with the body, it teaches that *you*
T19..IV.B.12:4 result of **e.** yourself with the body, which

## equilibrium 2

T-1......... V.6:5 **e.** is temporarily experienced as unstable.
P-2.........in.2:4 Their whole **e.** rests on the insane belief

## equipment 2

W-pI..... 44.2:2 nor is the **e.** for seeing outside you. An
W-pI..... 44.2:3 An essential part of this **e.** is the light that

## equipped 1

T-8...... VIII.4:7 Spirit, and one He is perfectly **e.** to fulfill.

## equivalent 2

T-26...... IV.1:1 Forgiveness is this world's **e.** of Heaven's
C-1............. 3:3 It would, however, be an **e.** of "spirit,"

## era 1

W-pI..... 75.2:5 It is a new **e.**, in which a new world is

## eradicate 2

T-5......... V.6:9 God created one, and so you cannot **e.** it.
T-6...... IV.12:8 out, because to **e.** it would be to attack it.

## erase 1

T-3........ IV.7:7 but I can **e.** all misperceptions from your

**erased** 1

W-pI.....12.5:8 now, but when your words have been **e.**,

**erect** 1

W-pI.134.12:3 Nor need he **e.** the heavy walls of stone

**erected** 2

T-14.....VII.2:7 you have **e.** your insane system of belief,
T-16..... V.11:5 altar is **e.** in between two separate people,

**erratic** 4

T-2........ VI.5:9 and your behavior inevitably becomes **e.**.
T-3......... II.1:5 realize your thinking will be **e.** until a firm
T19... IV.A.8:3 be more **e.** and unpredictable than before
W-pI.....95.2:2 together by its **e.** and capricious maker, to

**erring** 1

W-pI...193.2:3 need for One Who can correct his **e.** sight,

**erroneous** 1

T-1.........I.37:2 a catalyst, breaking up **e.** perception and

**error** 193

T-1.........I.39:1 The miracle dissolves **e.** because the Holy
T-1.........I.39:1 Holy Spirit identifies **e.** as false or unreal.
T-1.........I.49:2 either the degree or the direction of the **e.**.
T-1........ III.1:6 to accept **e.** in yourself and others, you
T-1........ III.1:6 learn to undo **e.** and act to correct it. The
T-1........ III.5:1 **E.** cannot really threaten truth, which
T-1........ III.5:2 Only the **e.** is actually vulnerable. You are
T-1........ III.9:4 laws that govern the **e.** it aims to correct.
T-1........ IV.3:3 belief, from which only **e.** can proceed.
T-1........ VI.2:3 because, having made this fundamental **e.**
T-1........ VI.3:1 follows from the original **e.** that one can
T-1........ VI.3:1 before the **e.** of perceiving levels at all can
T-1.......VII.1:6 correction of the **e.** brings release from it.
T-2...........I.5:3 truth on the one hand, and **e.** on the other
T-2....... II.1:13 used to hide anything, but to correct **e.**. It
T-2....... II.1:14 It brings all **e.** into the light, and since
T-2....... II.1:14 and since **e.** and darkness are the same, it
T-2....... II.1:14 are the same, it corrects **e.** automatically.
T-2......... II.2:2 deny any belief that **e.** can hurt you. This
T-2......... II.2:5 it. Denial of **e.** is a strong defense of truth,
T-2......... II.2:6 right mind the denial of **e.** frees the mind,
T-2......... II.3:1 You can defend truth as well as **e.**. The
T-2........ III.4:1 Spiritual vision literally cannot see **e.**,
T-2........ III.4:4 over all others, looking past **e.** to truth.
T-2........ IV.1:6 kind of **e.** to which Atonement is applied
T-2........ IV.2:1 Atonement plan is to undo **e.** at all levels.
T-2........ IV.2:4 Only the mind is capable of **e.**. The body
T-2........ IV.2:6 the belief that it can, a fundamental **e.**,
T-2........ IV.2:9 This **e.** can take two forms; it can be
T-2......... V.1:6 introduces correction at the level of the **e.**.
T-2......... V.7:3 before that the Holy Spirit cannot see **e.**,
T-2......... V.8:2 nor can **e.** be corrected by any device that
T-2....V.A.13:2 Responding to any form of **e.** with
T-2....V.A.14:1 of this **e.** and an affirmation of the truth.
T-2....V.A.16:5 is no reference to the outcome of the **e.**.
T-2........ VI.4:7 not matter, but the fundamental **e.** does.
T-2...... VI.5:10 the **e.** from the first to the second type,
T-2........ VI.7:1 the **e.** is to know first that the conflict is
T-2.......VII.4:2 Yet any attempt to resolve the **e.** through
T-2.......VII.5:7 to concentrate on **e.** is only a further error
T-2.......VII.5:7 to concentrate on error is only a further **e.**
T-2.......VII.6:7 in **e.** or incompleteness if he so chooses.
T-2.......VII.6:9 The correction of this **e.** is the Atonement
T-2.......VII.7:7 fundamental **e.** that fear can be mastered,
T-3...........I.2:6 **e.** itself is no harder to correct than any
T-3...........I.3:9 This kind of **e.** is responsible for a host of
T-3......... II.6:4 Truth overcomes all **e.**, and those who
T-3......... II.6:4 and those who live in **e.** and emptiness
T-3........ III.7:1 If you attack **e.** in another, you will hurt
T-3...........IV.h **E.** and the Ego
T-3 ..... IV.3:10 and your creation is beyond your own **e.**.
T-3 ....... IV.6:7 Truth will always overcome **e.** in this way.
T-3 ....... IV.7:4 attempt to counteract **e.** with knowledge,
T-3 ....... IV.7:4 but to correct **e.** from the bottom up.
T-3 ........ V.5:2 always open to **e.** because it refers to the
T-3 ....... VI.8:4 This is the fundamental **e.** of all those
T-3 ..... VII.3:9 of destroying Their Own purpose is in **e.**.
T-4 ........in.3:7 make the pathetic **e.** of "clinging to the
T-5 ....... VI.4:2 based on the **e.** they were made to uphold
T-5 ...... VII.5:5 you will reinforce the **e.** rather than allow
T-5 ...... VII.6:5 to the point at which the **e.** was made,
T-6 ....... IV.1:7 Herein lies its primary **e.**, the foundation
T-6 ..... V.C.2:1 want you to teach **e.** and learn it yourself.
T-7 ..... VIII.3:6 The second **e.** is the idea that you can get
T-7 ..... VIII.4:4 that it can, an **e.** the ego always makes,
T-7 .........X.6:7 The whole separation lies in this **e.**. The
T-7 .........X.6:8 The only way out of the **e.** is to decide that
T-8 ..... VIII.6:8 *Any* way you handle **e.** results in nothing.
T-8 ....... IX.5:3 cannot distinguish among degrees of **e.**,
T-8 ....... IX.5:3 that one **e.** can be more real than another.
T-9 .......... III.h The Correction of **E.**
T-9 ....... III.2:8 level, because his **e.** is at another level. He
T-9 ....... IV.1:3 beyond **e.** and do not let your perception
T-9 ....... IV.2:3 merely be further **e.** to believe either that
T-9 ....... IV.4:4 ego's plan is to have you see **e.** clearly first
T-9 ....... IV.5:3 in looking beyond **e.** from the beginning,
T-9 ....... IV.5:5 Spirit the effects of **e.** are nonexistent. By
T-11 ...... V.1:6 We will undo this **e.** quietly together, and
T-11 .... V.14:2 The ego focuses on **e.** and overlooks truth
T-11 .... V.14:6 be true. Holding **e.** clearly in mind, and
T-11 .... V.14:6 system: **E.** is real and truth is error.
T-11 .... V.14:6 system: Error is real and truth is **e.**.
T-12 ........I.1:1 You have been told not to make **e.** real,
T-12 ........I.1:2 If you want to believe in **e.**, you would
T-12 ........I.1:7 done so, having made his **e.** real to you.
T-12 ........I.1:8 To interpret **e.** is to give it power, and
T-12 ......I.10:4 fear with love and translate **e.** into truth.
T-12 ...... III.2:4 and are making his **e.** real to both of you.
T-12 ... VIII.8:6 of **e.** and perception has never been.
T-13 ..... VI.1:2 sight, for reality leaves no room for any **e.**.
T-14 ... III.16:2 light, **e.** of any kind becomes impossible.
T-14 ..... IX.2:1 the ego to God is but to bring **e.** to truth,
T-14 ..... IX.8:1 of holiness to any form of **e.** is always the
T-17 .... VII.3:6 an **e.** in your thoughts about the situation
T-17 .... VII.3:7 You will make this **e.**, but be not at all
T-17 .... VII.3:8 that. The **e.** does not matter. Faithlessness
T-18 ........I.4:4 was. That one **e.**, which brought truth to
T-18 ........I.5:2 not realize the magnitude of that one **e.**. It
T-18 ........I.5:6 show you the enormity of the original **e.**,
T-18 ........I.6:1 was the first projection of **e.** outward. The
T-18 ........I.6:4 down arose from this projection of **e.**? It
T-18 ........I.7:1 of the original **e.** rising to frighten you,
T-18 ........I.7:5 truth is outside, and **e.** and guilt within.
T-18 ........I.9:6 The original **e.** has not entered here, nor
T-18 ......I.12:2 of the original **e.** that shattered Heaven.
T-18 ..... IX.1:2 told that **e.** must be corrected at its source
T-19 ......I.14:5 No **e.** interferes with its calm sight, which
T-19 ......... II.h Sin versus **E.**
T-19 .......II.1:1 essential that **e.** be not confused with sin,
T-19 .......II.1:2 For **e.** can be corrected, and the wrong
T-19 .......II.1:6 calls for punishment as **e.** for correction,
T-19 .......II.2:1 Sin is not an **e.**, for sin entails an
T-19 .......II.2:1 an arrogance which the idea of **e.** lacks.
T-19 .......II.4:1 religion is that sin is not **e.** but truth, and
T-19 .......II.5:1 sin as **e.** is always indefensible to the ego.
T-19 ...... III.1:1 attraction of guilt is found in sin, not **e.**.
T-19 ...... III.3:1 An **e.**, on the other hand, is not attractive
T-19 ...... III.3:6 the form of sin, granting that it was an **e.**,
T-19 ...... III.3:7 it is sin that calls for punishment, not **e.**.
T-19 ...... III.5:6 In **e.**, yes, for this can be corrected by the
T19..IV.B.11:7 Use not your **e.** as the justification for
T-20 .... VII.3:5 the **e.** of believing the means are difficult.
T-20 .... VII.4:7 Either must be an **e.**, for both would place
T-21 ..... VI.1:6 For uncorrected **e.** of any kind deceives
T-22 ......in.1:5 And each one seems to make a different **e.**
T-22 ........ III.h Reason and the Forms of **E.**
T-22 ..... III.2:5 and thus it must have been an **e.**. The
T-22 ..... III.3:5 sees through it easily, because it is an **e.**.
T-22 ..... III.4:1 Only the form of **e.** attracts the ego.
T-22 ..... III.4:3 can see is a mistake, an **e.** in perception, a
T-22 ..... III.4:5 but **e.** in a special form the ego venerates.
T-22 ..... III.5:1 form of **e.** is not what makes it a mistake.
T-22 ..... III.5:5 made to look on **e.** and not see past it.
T-22 ..... VI.5:2 sin. The form of **e.** is no longer seen, and
T-22 ..... VI.5:3 in your relationship corrects the **e.**, and
T-22 ..... VI.7:1 no **e.** is excluded and nothing kept hidden
T-22 ... VI.10:7 us look straight at how this **e.** came about
T-23 ...... in.3:6 every **e.** disappeared because they saw it
T-23 ........ I.3:4 at a mistake; an **e.** in your self-appraisal.
T-23 ....... II.4:3 one who makes the **e.** places him beyond
T-24 ..... III.1:4 he holds one **e.** to himself as lovely still.
T-25 ........ I.6:1 can be corrected where the **e.** lies. Because
T-25 ..... III.4:2 Corrected **e.** is the error's end. And thus
T-25 ..... III.4:3 has God protected still His Son, even in **e.**
T-25 ..... III.5:1 is another purpose in the world that **e.**
T-25 ..... III.5:6 the Maker of the world correct your **e.**,
T-25 ... III.8:10 And thus it must have been an **e.**, not a
T-25 ... III.8:13 it is to change its state from **e.** into truth.
T-25 ..... IX.3:6 And every **e.** is a perception in which one,
T-26 ....... II.2:3 was an **e.** in perception that now has been
T-26 ....... II.4:2 Every problem is an **e.**. It does injustice to
T-26 ..... V.11:3 an **e.** in the past that God remembers not,
T-26 .... VII.7:1 Sin is not **e.**, for it goes beyond correction
T-26 .. VII.12:1 Let us consider what the **e.** is, so it can be
T-26 .. VII.12:4 **e.** does the world of sin and sacrifice arise.
T-26 ... VIII.3:3 is the **e.** still obscured that is the source of
T-27 ..... II.13:3 what you would correct is only half the **e.**,
T-27 ... VIII.9:2 How else could He correct your **e.**, who
T-30 ..... VI.2:7 reaction to distress that rests on **e.**, and
T-30 ..... VI.5:6 be an **e.** that is more than a mistake; a
T-30 ..... VI.5:6 mistake; a special form of **e.** that remains
T-30 ... VI.10:1 an **e.** that could change the truth in him.
T-31 .... VII.9:1 they all are different names for just one **e.**;
W-pI .... 97.4:4 asks; replaces **e.** with the simple truth.
W-pI .. 103.2:3 basic **e.** we will try again to bring to truth
W-pI 133.10:4 it is **e.** to believe that sins are but mistakes
W-pI .. 138.2:7 be the **e.** truth can be brought to illusions.
W-pI .. 168.5:3 but He to Whom all **e.** is unknown is yet
W-pI 186.11:3 It comes from One Who knows no **e.**, and
W-pI .. 187.8:3 its very presence proves that **e.** has arisen
W-pI 191.10:2 made. In **e.** it began, but it will end in the
W-pI .. 192.7:3 we understand is but confusion born of **e.**
W-pII ..... 3.1:2 is born of **e.**, and it has not left its source.
W-pII ... 13.1:4 It undoes **e.**, but does not attempt to go
M-16 ......... 2:7 begin again, should the day begin with **e.**.
M-16 ....... 10:9 two aspects of one **e.** and no more, he
M-17 ......... 3:1 is easiest to let **e.** be corrected where it is
M-18 ......... 1:2 establish its **e.** or demonstrate its falsity,
M-19 ......... 1:4 exists in Heaven, for **e.** is impossible and
C-in ........... 1:4 the "original **e.**" or the "original sin." To
C-in ........... 1:5 the **e.** itself does not lead to correction, if
C-in ........... 1:5 indeed to succeed in overlooking the **e.**.
C-in ........... 3:2 what is beyond all **e.** because it is planned
C-3 ............ 1:4 it leads away from **e.** and not towards it.
P-2......... in.1:5 the patient deal with one fundamental **e.**;
P-2......... in.1:6 extent he comes to realize that this is an **e.**
P-2........ IV.5:2 **e.** lies in the belief that it can cure itself.
P-2........ IV.5:3 "degrees of **e.**" is a meaningful concept.
P-2........ IV.6:5 **e.** is accepted as real and dealt with by
P-3...........I.1:5 It would be an **e.**, however, to assume that
S-2...........I.2:3 Dear to its heart is **e.**, and mistakes loom
S-2...........I.3:3 *Do not see* **e.**. Do not make it real. Select
S-2...........I.6:8 eyes that look past **e.** to the Christ in you.

**error's** 1

T-25 ..... III.4:2 Corrected error is the **e.** end. And thus

**errors** 105

T-1 ........I.33:3 atone for your **e.** by freeing you from your
T-1 ....... III.1:4 all **e.** that you could not otherwise correct
T-1 ....... III.4:7 your **e.** and choose to abandon them by
T-1 ....... III.5:7 Atonement undoes all **e.** in this respect,
T-1 ....... III.5:9 you reinforce **e.** they have already made.
T-1 ....... IV.2:7 function of the mind and corrects its **e.**,
T-2 ..........I.4:4 realize that your **e.** never really occurred.
T-2 .......II.1:10 incapable of being shaken by **e.** of any

| | |
|---|---|
| T-2.........II.6:5 | It undoes your past **e.**, thus making it |
| T-2........IV.3:5 | in itself to introduce actual learning **e.**. |
| T-2.........V.1:5 | None of these **e.** is meaningful, because |
| T-2.......V.1:10 | device is not subject to **e.** of its own, |
| T-2.........V.5:2 | that its **e.** are healed by the Atonement. |
| T-3...........I.3:9 | error is responsible for a host of related **e.** |
| T-3........I.7:11 | are released from all **e.** if you believe this. |
| T-3........IV.7:2 | Truth cannot deal with **e.** that you want. |
| T-4.........II.1:3 | if the same **e.** were not being repeated in |
| T-5........IV.2:9 | You cannot cancel out your past **e.** alone. |
| T-5........IV.8:4 | purified them of the **e.** that hid their light, |
| T-5.........V.7:7 | for their **e.** without recognizing that, by |
| T-6.........V.4:1 | Holy Spirit never itemizes **e.** because He |
| T-7.....VIII.3:1 | are two major **e.** involved in this attempt. |
| T-7.....VIII.5:4 | to project responsibility for your own **e.**. |
| T-7.....VIII.5:5 | But having accepted the **e.** as yours, do |
| T-8........IX.7:1 | enjoins you to be perfect, to heal all **e.**, to |
| T-9........III.1:1 | The alertness of the ego to the **e.** of other |
| T-9........III.2:1 | good to point out **e.** and "correct" them. |
| T-9........III.2:2 | which is unaware of what **e.** are and what |
| T-9........III.2:3 | **E.** are of the ego, and correction of errors |
| T-9........III.2:3 | of **e.** lies in the relinquishment of the ego. |
| T-9........III.3:1 | point out the **e.** of your brother's ego you |
| T-9........III.3:1 | the Holy Spirit does not perceive his **e.**. |
| T-9........III.4:1 | When you react at all to **e.**, you are not |
| T-9........III.4:3 | as the brother whose **e.** you perceive. This |
| T-9........III.5:2 | If you perceive his **e.** and accept them, |
| T-9........III.5:4 | the one way in which you handle all **e.**, |
| T-9........III.5:4 | cannot understand how all **e.** are undone. |
| T-9........III.6:5 | His **e.** do not come from the truth that is |
| T-9........III.6:6 | His **e.** cannot change this, and can have |
| T-9........III.6:7 | To perceive **e.** in anyone, and to react to |
| T-9........III.7:1 | Your brother's **e.** are not of him, any |
| T-9........III.7:2 | of you. Accept his **e.** as real, and you have |
| T-9........III.7:5 | His **e.** are forgiven with yours. Atonement |
| T-9......III.8:11 | real to you, and all your **e.** will be forgiven |
| T-9........IV.2:2 | do not understand how to overlook **e.**, or |
| T-9........IV.2:4 | this Guide, your **e.** will not be corrected. |
| T-9........IV.2:6 | sense of limitation is where all **e.** arise. |
| T-13.....VI.5:2 | His **e.** are all past, and by perceiving him |
| T-13.....VII.6:6 | **e.** for the peace of God is but *your* will. |
| T-19.........I.9:5 | now. You freely choose to overlook his **e.**, |
| T-19......III.9:4 | **E.** are quickly recognized and quickly |
| T-20. VIII.10:7 | the **e.** which you made can be corrected. |
| T-21......IV.1:2 | **E.** He will correct, but this makes no one |
| T-21......VI.1:1 | Reason cannot see sin but can see **e.**, and |
| T-21......VI.7:7 | correction of his **e.** and make him whole. |
| T-22......III.2:2 | your **e.** and make way for their correction. |
| T-22......III.2:3 | For reason sees through **e.**, telling you |
| T-22......III.2:6 | to its fixed belief in sin and disregard of **e.** |
| T-22......III.4:6 | would preserve all **e.** and make them sins. |
| T-22......III.8:5 | sin? Beyond his **e.** is his holiness and your |
| T-22......III.9:7 | where both give **e.** gladly to correction, |
| T-23.......II.3:4 | **E.** of any kind can be corrected *because* |
| T-23.......II.4:2 | demand that **e.** call for punishment and |
| T-24......VI.8:2 | **e.** cannot withhold God's blessing from |
| T-25......III.7:2 | Let all your brother's **e.** be to you nothing |
| T-25......IX.1:1 | arrogance to think your little **e.** cannot be |
| T-25......IX.6:9 | justice if some **e.** are unforgivable, and |
| T-26.......II.4:1 | The miracle of justice can correct all **e.**. |
| T-26.....VII.7:2 | it is real has made some **e.** seem forever |
| T-27.........I.4:7 | and death would prove his **e.** must be sins |
| T-27.......II.4:6 | lies the proof that they are merely **e.**. Let |
| T-27.....II.13:4 | lest your **e.** and his own be seen as one. |
| T-31.......V.6:6 | where they cannot be perceived as **e.**, |
| W-pI.....47.6:1 | necessary step in the correction of your **e.**, |
| W-pI.....51.3:3 | is the projection of my own **e.** of thought. |
| W-pI.....54.1:5 | the world I see arises from my thinking **e.**, |
| W-pI.....54.1:5 | before my eyes as I let my **e.** be corrected. |
| W-pI....95.10:1 | Let all these **e.** go by recognizing them |
| W-pI....98.2:5 | For we have been absolved from **e.**. All |
| W-pI......107.h | Truth will correct all **e.** in my mind. |
| W-pI...107.1:2 | And what are **e.** but illusions that remain |
| W-pI...107.1:3 | Where truth has entered **e.** disappear. |
| W-pI...107.4:4 | when truth corrects the **e.** in your mind. |
| W-pI...107.9:1 | Truth will correct all **e.** in your mind |
| W-pI...107.9:5 | *Truth will correct all* **e.** *in my mind, And I* |
| W-pI.107.10:3 | and the **e.** that surround the world will be |
| W-pI.107.11:2 | "Truth will correct all **e.** in my mind," you |
| W-pI...115.1:2 | *to forgive the world for all the* **e.** *I have made.* |
| W-pI...119.1:1 | (107) Truth will correct all **e.** in my mind |
| W-pI...119.3:2 | Truth will correct all **e.** in my mind. On |
| W-pI...124.2:3 | How easily do **e.** disappear, and death |
| W-pI...158.7:3 | can be touched, a purity undimmed by **e.**, |
| W-pI...181.1:3 | You do not look beyond his **e.**. Rather, |
| W-pI.184.15:5 | *be absolved from all effects our* **e.** *seemed to* |
| W-pII......3.1:4 | world must disappear and all its **e.** vanish |
| W-pII....10.3:1 | the Correction He bestowed on all your **e.** |
| M-6 ..............1:4 | the correction of his **e.** in the mind of the |
| M-8 ...........4:1 | of the mind that **e.** in perception enter. |
| M-17 .........3:1 | and **e.** can be recognized by their results. |
| M-18 .........4:6 | means correction, or the undoing of **e.**. |
| P-2...........I.2:2 | This is one of the **e.** which the ego fosters; |
| P-2........IV.8:3 | Herein lies the basis of all **e.**, for all of |
| P-2.......VII.4:5 | patient's **e.** thus became his own failures, |
| P-3...........I.1:4 | There are no **e.** in God's plan. It would be |
| S-2........III.1:3 | evaluate the **e.** that it wants to overlook. It |

## escape 209

| | |
|---|---|
| T-1...........IV.h | The **E.** from Darkness |
| T-1........IV.1:1 | The **e.** from darkness involves two stages: |
| T-1........IV.1:4 | This step brings **e.** from fear. When you |
| T-2...........I.4:3 | Here is the real basis for your **e.** from fear. |
| T-2...........I.4:4 | **e.** is brought about by your acceptance of |
| T-3........IV.3:9 | This is why you cannot **e.** from fear until |
| T-3........IV.6:3 | to **e.** from the conflict you have induced. |
| T-3.........V.5:5 | a futile attempt to **e.** from an inescapable |
| T-3.......VII.1:8 | to **e.** from the prison you have made. |
| T-4........VI.2:1 | In learning to **e.** from illusions, your debt |
| T-4........VI.3:8 | that you believe you must **e.** from the ego |
| T-4........VI.3:8 | cannot **e.** from the ego by humbling it or |
| T-5........VI.2:4 | by believing that you cannot **e.** from it. |
| T-5.......VII.1:7 | to **e.** His care because that is not His Will, |
| T-6.........II.9:4 | Yet perception cannot **e.** the basic laws of |
| T-6.........V.3:2 | what you must avoid to **e.** from harm, but |
| T-6.........V.3:3 | instead, you will **e.** from harm and be safe |
| T-6......V.B.5:2 | thought system, and you cannot **e.** this, |
| T-7.......VII.3:4 | very easily **e.** from this image by leaving it |
| T-8.......VII.5:6 | belief in littleness, and thus **e.** from yours. |
| T-8.....VII.14:4 | learning should be to **e.** from limitations? |
| T-9...........I.3:5 | that it is impossible to **e.** from it without a |
| T-9.........II.1:4 | that its purpose is the **e.** from fear. |
| T-9........III.6:8 | You will not **e.** paying the price for this, |
| T-9.......VII.5:3 | to help you **e.** from a sense of inadequacy |
| T-9.......VII.5:4 | Can you **e.** from its evaluation of you by |
| T-10.......in.1:5 | but you cannot **e.** from them. They were |
| T-10.......V.5:2 | would be true, and you could never **e.**. It |
| T-11.......V.1:1 | No one can **e.** from illusions unless he |
| T-12.........I.8:2 | recognize fear is not enough to **e.** from it, |
| T-12.........I.8:2 | necessary to demonstrate the need for **e.**. |
| T-12.......II.7:4 | Our mission is to **e.** from crucifixion, not |
| T-12.......V.5:6 | which they can **e.** from their limitations. |
| T-13.......in.1:4 | punishing another, it will **e.** punishment. |
| T-13.......in.1:5 | to deny itself, and **e.** the penalty of denial. |
| T-13.........I.5:3 | seeking to **e.** from the prison he has made |
| T-13.......I.11:2 | teaching, then, there is no **e.** from guilt. |
| T-13.......IV.6:1 | the past are precisely what you must **e.**. |
| T-13.......IX.2:2 | will not **e.** the punishment it offers those |
| T-13......XI.1:3 | Believing this he must **e.**, for such a war |
| T-13......XI.2:2 | You are but trying to **e.** a bitter war from |
| T-14.........I.5:4 | nor **e.** the heavy burden of its dullness |
| T-14......III.2:2 | each representing an **e.** from what the |
| T-14......III.3:1 | **e.** the pain that only guiltlessness allays. |
| T-14....III.11:7 | try to **e.** the gift of God He so freely and so |
| T-14....III.13:4 | knows that all salvation is **e.** from guilt. |
| T-14.....IV.3:10 | Can you **e.** this guilt by failing to fulfill |
| T-14......XI.3:1 | Atonement teaches you how to **e.** forever |
| T-15.........I.6:4 | still believe that it can offer them **e.**. But |
| T-15.........I.7:6 | is no **e.** from fear in the ego's use of time. |
| T-15.......I.13:7 | give is your instantaneous **e.** from guilt. |
| T-15......III.3:5 | fulfilling it that you can **e.** from littleness. |
| T-15... VIII.3:8 | it calls to everyone to **e.** from loneliness, |
| T-16......IV.4:7 | love, to them, is only an **e.** from death. |
| T-16......IV.6:4 | to **e.** from one illusion into another must |
| T-16.....V.15:5 | and complete **e.** from all its consequences |
| T-16......VI.8:6 | and that **e.** from pain is really possible. |
| T-16.....VII.3:5 | and in your **e.** from the past it sees itself |
| T-16.....VII.5:7 | the **e.** from vengeance becomes your loss. |
| T-17.........I.5:5 | and thus enable you to **e.** from them. |
| T-17.......V.7:2 | **e.** from your distress only by getting rid of |
| T-18........II.4:3 | And yet the dream cannot **e.** its origin. |
| T-18......IV.6:3 | your plan for the **e.** from guilt has been to |
| T-18......VI.7:7 | it. But you would not **e.** from it, leaving it |
| T-18......VI.8:1 | Yet only thus *can* you **e.**. The home of |
| T-18....VI.11:3 | It is a sense of actual **e.** from limitations. |
| T-18....VI.13:1 | There is no violence at all in this **e.**. The |
| T-18.....VII.7:3 | past centuries of effort, and **e.** from time. |
| T-19........II.7:3 | is the "truth" from which **e.** will always be |
| T19. IV.A.14:4 | no little breath of love **e.** their notice. And |
| T19..IV.B.16:4 | the attraction of guilt is the **e.** from pain. |
| T19....IV.C.2:7 | him he can **e.** through your forgiveness. |
| T-20......VI.7:4 | Yet what you fear is but the herald of **e.**. |
| T-20.....VII.9:3 | not that his sinlessness is *your* **e.** from fear. |
| T-21........II.2:1 | from pain and the complete **e.** from sin, |
| T-21......VI.8:8 | behind insanity in order to **e.** from reason |
| T-22........II.2:3 | of misery and seek another is hardly an **e.**. |
| T-22........II.4:1 | only way to **e.** from misery is to recognize |
| T-22........II.5:3 | by which **e.** from guilt can be attained, |
| T-22........II.5:6 | **e.** from guilt was given to the Holy Spirit |
| T-22........II.7:6 | either **e.** from misery entirely or not at all. |
| T-23........II.8:1 | can be no release and no **e.**. Atonement |
| T-23........II.8:6 | enable you to find **e.** from what it wants. |
| T-23......III.6:1 | nor compromise for the **e.** from conflict. |
| T-24.......V.2:1 | the hope of peace and the **e.** from pain, in |
| T-24......VI.4:4 | will not **e.** its laws of violence and death. |
| T-24......VI.5:3 | law of death you bind him to will you **e.**. |
| T-24...VII.10:1 | beyond itself, and no **e.** within its sight. |
| T-25......II.11:5 | that **e.** from darkness into light be yours |
| T-25.....VII.9:5 | Nor is he left without **e.** from madness, |
| T-25.....VII.9:5 | for he has a special part in everyone's **e.**. |
| T-25....VIII.7:4 | **e.** has He for them except a door to hell |
| T-26......VI.1:7 | make one illusion real, and still **e.** the rest |
| T-26...VII.14:4 | less than full salvation and **e.** from guilt. |
| T-27.........I.1:4 | your brother and yourself will not **e.**. You |
| T-27.........I.2:6 | will not **e.** the death you made for him. |
| T-27.........I.4:3 | from which you swear he never will **e.**. |
| T-27......IV.4:7 | And which can bring **e.** from all the pain |
| T-27.....VII.1:7 | And he cannot **e.** because its source is |
| T-27.....VII.2:1 | Now you are being shown you *can* **e.**. All |
| T-27.....VII.4:2 | The world's **e.** from condemnation is a |
| T-27.....VII.6:1 | world from condemnation is your own **e.**. |
| T-27....VIII.5:1 | How willing are you to **e.** effects of all the |
| T-29.........I.1:9 | you can **e.** if there be need for you to flee. |
| T-29........II.3:2 | It has been futile to demand **e.** from sin |
| T-29......IV.1:3 | dreams are dreams; and that **e.** depends, |
| T-29......IX.3:5 | who judges him will not **e.** the penalty he |
| T-29......IX.5:8 | needs them that he may **e.** his thoughts, |
| T-30.......V.1:2 | goal, for the **e.** from guilt becomes its aim |
| T-30......VI.1:3 | It is here **e.** from fear begins, and will be |
| T-30......VI.5:6 | eternal, and beyond correction or **e.**. |
| T-30......VI.6:6 | pardon and a limited **e.** from guilt for you |
| T-30......VI.7:4 | And you could not **e.** all guilt, but only |
| T-30......VI.7:6 | within and find **e.** from every idol there. |
| T-30......VI.9:2 | if you think he does not merit the **e.** from |
| T-30.....VII.5:1 | **E.** from judgment simply lies in this; all |
| T-31......IV.1:1 | and **e.** from problems that its purpose is |
| T-31......IV.1:7 | you **e.** from them by leaving them behind |
| T-31......IV.2:5 | Seek not **e.** from problems here. The |
| T-31....IV.11:3 | You can not **e.** from what you are. For |
| T-31....IV.11:5 | is your **e.** from madness and from death. |
| T-31.......V.5:4 | and those who walk on them will not **e.**. |
| T-31.....V.14:3 | nothing more than the **e.** from concepts. |
| T-31......VI.1:7 | never will **e.** the body as your own reality, |
| T-31....VIII.1:2 | in what must die, unable to **e.** its frailty, |
| T-31....VIII.3:1 | thus **e.** all pain that what you chose before |
| W-pI.....21.3:1 | of anger **e.** you in the practice periods. |
| W-pI.....22.2:1 | this savage fantasy that you want to **e.**. Is |
| W-pI.....22.2:3 | a happy discovery to find that you can **e.**? |
| W-pI........23.h | I can **e.** from the world I see by giving up |
| W-pI.....23.4:2 | the world, but you can **e.** from its cause. |
| W-pI.....23.6:4 | say: *I can* **e.** *from the world I see by giving up* |
| W-pI.....31.2:5 | You will **e.** from both together, for the |
| W-pI.....44.6:2 | that to reach light is to **e.** from darkness, |
| W-pI.....53.3:8 | I will **e.** all the effects of the world of fear, |
| W-pI.....55.3:1 | (23) I can **e.** from this world by giving up |
| W-pI.....64.3:3 | it does the Son of God **e.** from all illusions |

W-pI.....65.3:2 you **e.** from all your perceived difficulties.
W-pI.....71.6:1 How can you **e.** all this? Very simply. The
W-pI.....72.5:5 be difficult indeed to **e.** this conclusion.
W-pI.....91.5:5 You can **e.** the body if you choose. You
W-pI.....97.8:4 and **e.** its sorry consequences if you yield
W-pI.....99.2:4 is the means by which you can **e.** illusions
W-pI...101.2:6 They would **e.** Him in their fear. And yet
W-pI...101.2:7 yet He will pursue, and they can not **e.**.
W-pI...101.7:2 Today **e.** from madness. You are set on
W-pI...110.2:4 for all the world to learn **e.** from time,
W-pI...121.4:5 hope. It wants **e.**, yet can conceive of none
W-pI...121.9:3 and see that their **e.** included yours.
W-pI...126.5:3 not **e.** the justified repayment for his sin.
W-pI...127.8:1 fifteen minutes twice today **e.** from every
W-pI...128.3:1 **E.** today the chains you place upon your
W-pI...128.7:3 every time you let your mind **e.** its chains.
W-pI...132.3:3 fears, you find **e.** and give it to the world.
W-pI...134.5:1 Pardon is no **e.** in such a view. It merely
W-pI.134.11:4 he cannot feel that all **e.** has been denied
W-pI.134.16:4 to experiencing the **e.** from all the heavy
W-pI...136.4:1 evaluates a threat, decides **e.** is necessary,
W-pI...138.3:1 is the obvious **e.** from what appears as
W-pI...153.2:6 to turn to find **e.** from its imaginings.
W-pI...153.3:1 until **e.** no longer can be hoped for nor
W-pI.153.11:4 you, and your **e.** has been accomplished.
W-pI.153.14:4 defense against a vengeance he can not **e.**,
W-pI.161.12:4 is your safe **e.** from anger and from fear.
W-pI...162.5:4 and for complete **e.** from sin and guilt?
W-pI...170.5:2 turn for solace and **e.** from doubts about
W-pI...170.9:1 do not think that fear is the **e.** from fear.
W-pI...183.9:2 You can **e.** all bondage of the world, and
W-pI.184.15:7 *is our salvation and* **e.** *from what we made.*
W-pI...185.4:3 form. The meaning must **e.** the dream, for
W-pI...191.3:1 not **e.** the madness which induced this
W-pI...191.5:2 safety and **e.** you will return and set it free
W-pI...192.8:4 He must be sure that he does not **e.**, and
W-pI...195.2:3 to **e.** a prison that they thought contained
W-pI...195.5:2 make room for all who will **e.** with you;
W-pI...196.5:1 and **e.** yourself has nailed you to the cross
W-pI...196.6:3 entirely impossible, how could there be **e.**
W-pI.196.10:1 so wholly that **e.** appears quite hopeless.
W-pI...199.7:3 can make use of your **e.** from bondage, to
W-pI...200.5:2 purpose of the world, if you would find **e.**.
W-pI...200.6:5 **e.** of God's beloved Son from evil dreams
W-pII .....5.4:2 made to fence him into hell without **e.**,
W-pII .289.1:1 my mind, the real world must **e.** my sight.
W-pII .293.2:1 *let not Your holy world* **e.** *my sight today.*
W-pII .296.1:4 *it I would set it free, that I may find* **e.**, *and*
W-pII .298.2:4 *and* **e.** *from everything that would obscure*
W-pII .330.1:6 thus **e.** forever from all things the dream
W-pII .357.1:1 *thus* **e.** *the prison house in which I think I live*
Wfl........in.1:5 the hope of trust and the **e.** from pain.
M-in..........4:2 There is no **e.** from it. How could it be
M-4 .....I.A.5:3 teachers of God **e.** this distress entirely.
M-13 .........3:4 Who can **e.** this self-condemnation? Only
M-15 .........1:2 No one can **e.** God's Final Judgment. Who
M-17 .........8:3 There is a way in which **e.** is possible. It
M-17 .........9:8 Now is **e.** impossible, until you see you
M-18 .........1:3 that it is their task to **e.** from what is real.
M-20 .........5:2 You see in death **e.** from what you made.
M-20 .........5:4 Death cannot be **e.**, because it is not life
M-24 .........2:2 would still be only to **e.** from them now. If
M-24 .........6:3 Atonement might be equated with total **e.**
M-26 .........4:2 It is your function to **e.** from them, but
M-29 .........3:8 Whom it belongs is thus the **e.** from fear.
P-2........IV.7:8 It will **e.** and take another form, being the
S-1........III.4:4 an illusion of **e.** ever brought a prisoner?
S-1........III.4:5 His real **e.** from guilt can lie only in the
S-1........III.4:7 Fear of **e.** makes it difficult to welcome
S-1........III.4:9 him your salvation and your **e.** from guilt.
S-1......III.4:10 Your investment in this **e.** is heavy, and
S-2.........II.7:3 Forgiveness is the means for your **e.**. How

## escaped 28

T-13......XI.2:2 escape a bitter war from which you *have* **e.**.
T-15.....VII.4:2 that what you do to others you have **e.**.
T-16...VI.10:1 glad you have **e.** the mockery of salvation
T-17.......II.2:6 little step, so small it has **e.** your notice, is
T-18 .VI.11:10 You have **e.** from fear to peace, asking no
T-19 .......II.8:1 easily **e.** from that its whole correction is
T-20 ..... VI.7:9 You have **e.** the body. Where you are the
T-23 ..... IV.5:7 you the battle is not real, and easily **e.**.
T-24 ........I.3:6 and a need to judge that cannot be **e.**.
T-25 ...VIII.3:2 sustained by someone else, but not **e.**.
T-27 ...... V.9:2 be solved as any one of them has been **e.**.
T-31 ..... III.6:5 see no one as prisoner to what you have **e.**
T-31 ..... IV.2:6 was made that problems could not *be* **e.**.
W-pI.....65.6:2 idle thoughts that **e.** your attention before
W-pI...101.2:1 then punishment is just and cannot be **e.**.
W-pI...101.3:2 cost of sin, and suffering can never be **e.**,
W-pI...127.8:3 be **e.** by anyone who does not hold it dear
W-pI.166.13:1 all who chose the lonely road you have **e.**.
W-pI...170.2:3 And thus is fear protected, not **e.**. Today
W-pI...194.7:6 **e.** all fear of future pain has found his way
W-pI...196.2:2 can never be **e.** because the ego, under
W-pII .278.1:2 which I perceive are real, and cannot be **e.**
W-pII .333.1:2 by deceit of any kind, if it would be **e.**. It
M-11 .........4:3 then, is your judgment of the world **e.**! It
M-13 .........4:5 No one who has **e.** the world and all its
M-16 .........9:8 is the reason it can be so easily **e.**. What
M-26 .........4:4 you must understand what needs to be **e.**.
S-1........ III.2:5 and then **e.** by him who asks for it. Only

## escapes 7

T19..IV.A.12:6 little shred of guilt **e.** their hungry eyes.
T-20 ..... VI.5:3 Here the unholy relationship **e.** reality,
T-23 ...... III.1:8 and **e.** the guilt the thought entails. If the
W-pI.....98.3:2 nor invent **e.** from fancied threats without
W-pI...194.5:2 becomes the instant in which time **e.** the
P-1............ 1:3 No one in this world **e.** fear, but everyone
P-3..........II.9:3 he **e.** the temptation to assume a function

## escaping 1

W-pI...107.6:1 then in that, evading capture and **e.** grasp

## especially 5

T-2 ...... VII.6:1 **e.** be noted that God has only *one* Son. If
T-9 ...... VII.4:4 **e.** when you respond to the Holy Spirit,
T-25 .. VII.10:3 this, in the alternative He chose **e.** for you.
T-31 .... VII.8:3 to the holy ones **e.** entrusted to his care.
W-pI.....26.8:3 **e.** those that occur to you toward the end,

## essence 3

T-3 ....... IV.3:7 this is the **e.** of the fear-prone condition,
T-9 .....VIII.2:5 The **e.** of grandiosity is competitiveness,
M-29 ......... 3:4 It is the **e.** of the Atonement. It is the core

## essential 69

T-1 ........I.26:3 The undoing of fear is an **e.** part of the
T-1 ....... III.4:5 nature of the miracle is an **e.** ingredient,
T-1 ....... VI.1:4 is, in fact, the **e.** difference between them.
T-2 ........ V.1:1 it is **e.** that they fully understand the fear
T-2 ........ V.1:7 is **e.** to remember that only the mind can
T-2 ........ V.3:5 It is **e.**, however, that the miracle worker
T-2 ........ V.9:7 Charity is **e.** to right-mindedness in the
T-2 ...V.A.12:1 what is created and what is made is **e.**. All
T-2 .....VIII.2:8 It is **e.**, however, that you free yourself
T-3 ..........I.2:9 **e.** that all such thinking be dispelled that
T-3 .........II.1:5 It is **e.** that you realize your thinking will
T-3 ........ V.7:8 Evaluation is an **e.** part of perception,
T-3 .....VII.1:8 It is **e.** to realize this, because otherwise
T-4 ........ V.3:2 Yet this confusion is **e.** to the ego, which
T-6 .... V.B.8:6 this step is **e.** for the ultimate decision, it
T-6 ..... V.C.6:5 **e.** to teach you that you must be included,
T-6 ..... V.C.8:6 This is why vigilance is **e.**. Doubts about
T-7 .........II.3:2 outside the Kingdom learning is **e.**. This
T-7 ....... VI.7:4 and vigilance has therefore become **e.**.
T-8 ....... IX.9:5 Yet your return to meaning is **e.** to His,
T-9 ...... VII.2:7 since obviousness is the **e.** characteristic
T-9 .....VIII.6:6 and extremes are its **e.** characteristic.
T-12 ..VII.14:3 is why the undoing of guilt is an **e.** part of
T-14 ..... III.1:2 is so **e.** to learning that it should never be
T-14 ..... XI.1:1 **e.** thing is learning that *you do not know.*
T-15 ..... III.2:4 It is **e.** that you accept the fact, and accept
T-15 .... VII.3:2 real to you, it is **e.** to look at it clearly, and
T-15 .......X.5:7 Sacrifice is so **e.** to your thought system
T-16 ..... IV.1:7 It is **e.** to bring it into sight, and to make
T-16 ..... IV.7:5 It is **e.** that we look very closely at exactly
T-16 .......V.4:3 It is **e.** to the preservation of the ego that
T-17 ..... IV.7:1 It is **e.** to realize that all defenses *do* what
T-17 ..... VI.1:7 it is **e.** at this point to use them in each
T-19 .......II.1:1 It is **e.** that error be not confused with sin
T-19 ..... III.1:7 an **e.** part of what the ego thinks you are,
T19 . IV.B.12:2 is **e.** that this relationship be understood,
T-22 . VI.12:11 its reality if it were not **e.** to attack to see
T-23 .......II.1:5 It is **e.** it be understood what they are for,
T-24 .... VII.8:5 is **e.** it be kept in mind that all perception
T-26 ..... III.4:7 The one **e.** thing to make a choice at all is
W-pI ...... 1.4:3 hurry. A comfortable sense of leisure is **e.**.
W-pI ...... 3.2:2 **e.** that you keep a perfectly open mind,
W-pI ...... 9.3:1 and the **e.** rule of excluding nothing. For
W-pI .... 13.3:1 **e.**, therefore, that you learn to recognize
W-pI .... 16.3:3 it is **e.** you recognize them all as equally
W-pI .... 17.3:1 it is **e.** to make no distinctions between
W-pI .... 19.4:2 all practice periods remains **e.** throughout
W-pI .... 33.1:3 though unhurried applications are **e.**.
W-pI .... 37.6:3 **e.** to use the idea if anyone seems to cause
W-pI .... 44.2:3 An **e.** part of this equipment is the light
W-pI .... 56.2:4 it is **e.** that I let this image of myself go. As
W-pI ..... 100.h My part is **e.** to God's plan for salvation.
W-pI .. 100.1:3 each one of them is equally **e.** to them all.
W-pI .. 100.2:4 is as **e.** to His plan as to your happiness.
W-pI .. 100.3:1 You are indeed **e.** to God's plan. Without
W-pI .. 100.4:1 You are indeed **e.** to God's plan. Just as
W-pI .. 100.5:2 fail to take the part that is **e.** to God's plan
W-pI 100.10:2 there. You are **e.** to His plan. You are His
W-pI 100.10:7 every time you tell yourself you are **e.** to
W-pI .. 115.2:1 My part is **e.** to God's plan for salvation.
W-pI .. 115.2:2 *I am* **e.** *to the plan of God for the salvation of*
W-pI .. 115.3:4 My part is **e.** to God's plan for salvation.
W-pI .. 181.1:1 your brothers is **e.** to establishing and
W-pI .. 184.5:3 its one **e.** goal by which communication is
W-pI .. 199.3:1 is **e.** for your progress in this course that
M-6 ........... 3:6 Trust is an **e.** part of giving; in fact, it is
M-16 ......... 3:3 The saving of time is an **e.** early emphasis
M-18 ......... 4:1 it thus becomes **e.** for the teacher of God
M-24 ......... 2:6 be regarded as **e.** to the curriculum. There

## essentially 6

T-2 ....... IV.1:7 All healing is **e.** the release from fear. To
T-2 ... V.A.15:4 Without this it is **e.** judgmental, rather
T-2 .... VII.5:11 nothing. Time is **e.** a device by which all
T-3 ...... VI.5:4 feel tired because it is **e.** disheartening.
T-6 ..... V.C.3:3 which is **e.** the identification of what is
C-in ........... 1:4 "individual consciousness" is **e.** irrelevant

## establish 61

*See also* re-establish

T-in ........... 1:4 *not mean that you can* **e.** *the curriculum. It*
T-1 ........I.34:2 atoning for lack they **e.** perfect protection
T-1 ....... III.5:3 free to **e.** your kingdom where you see fit,
T-1 ....... IV.2:2 you exert enormous efforts to **e.** its reality
T-1 ....... VI.1:9 to the particular order of needs you **e.**.
T-1 ..... VI.5:10 Only God can **e.** this solution, and this
T-3 ..........I.1:2 The crucifixion did not **e.** the Atonement;
T-3 .........V.1:4 now **e.** a distinction that will clarify some
T-3 ..... VI.10:2 he is not free to **e.** what his inheritance is.
T-4 ..........I.7:6 or make is necessary to **e.** your worth.
T-4 .........II.8:5 and thus **e.** its own existence are useless.
T-4 ...... VII.2:2 to **e.** separateness rather than to abolish it
T-4 ...... VII.3:2 it make any attempt to **e.** what is true. It
T-7 ....... III.1:6 Your vigilance does not **e.** it as yours, but
T-7 ....... IV.2:5 The laws of God **e.** this, and the Holy
T-7 ....... XI.7:4 Your creations cannot **e.** your reality, any
T-7 ....... XI.7:4 reality, any more than you can **e.** God's.
T-8 ....... IX.1:4 and thus **e.** your ability to evaluate its
T-9 ... VIII.11:2 not **e.** your value and it needs no defense.
T-11 .....V.12:2 can only **e.** your autonomy by identifying
T-11 .....V.13:4 to **e.** this belief it must attack. Unaware

| | |
|---|---|
| T-11.....VII.3:7 | To **e.** your personal autonomy you tried |
| T-12.......V.2:8 | need to "equalize" the situation to **e.** your |
| T-12.......V.5:6 | You would hardly turn to them to **e.** the |
| T-13......IV.2:3 | on demonstrating their reality to **e.** yours. |
| T-13....VII.17:5 | cannot **e.** its eternal reign where sorrow |
| T-13... VIII.9:1 | creations **e.** your fatherhood in Heaven. |
| T-13.......X.6:6 | to **e.** them as real and then forgive them. |
| T-14.......X.5:4 | together by a sense of order that you **e.**. |
| T-14......XI.8:1 | remain, **e.** for yourself your guiltlessness? |
| T-14....XI.10:7 | He would **e.** His bright teaching so firmly |
| T-15...VII.12:1 | of the ego's plan to **e.** its own autonomy. |
| T-15......IX.2:6 | by which you can **e.** real relationships, |
| T-16......VI.4:5 | The Great Rays would **e.** the total lack of |
| T-17.........I.5:6 | **e.** orders of reality that must imprison |
| T-17....III.6:11 | will learn to seek for and **e.** the conditions |
| T-18......IV.4:4 | is up to you to **e.** the conditions for peace. |
| T-18......VI.9:7 | things, and to **e.** different orders of reality |
| T-20......VI.4:7 | in, and so **e.** them as temples to itself. |
| T-23.........I.4:8 | Could nature possibly **e.** this, and make it |
| T-23...... I.11:6 | do battle only to **e.** which form is true. |
| T-24.....II.12:5 | that would **e.** sin love's substitute, and |
| T-26.....VII.7:6 | can not **e.** that the picture must be true. |
| T-27.......II.2:7 | forgiveness does not first **e.** sin and then |
| T-27......IV.4:6 | Which ones **e.** peace and offer joy? And |
| T-27......IV.4:9 | It asks but to **e.** sin is real, and answers in |
| T-28.......II.1:3 | their cause, but they **e.** its causation. Thus |
| T-29......VI.3:4 | you, and **e.** it as changeless and eternal. |
| T-29. VIII.9:10 | No idol can **e.** you as more than God. But |
| T-31.......II.2:5 | You would **e.** truth. And by your wish you |
| W-pI.....13.2:3 | The ego rushes in frantically to **e.** its own |
| W-pI.....31.3:2 | Try not to **e.** any kind of hierarchy among |
| W-pI...71.9:10 | enough to **e.** your claim to God's answer. |
| WpI . rIII.in3:4 | those that you **e.** to uphold a camouflage |
| W-pI...186.2:2 | We did not **e.** it. It is not our idea. The |
| W-pII..325.2:2 | *reflect, for Yours and Yours alone* ***e.*** *truth.* |
| M-4............1:3 | that will **e.** them as what they are. God |
| M-18..........1:2 | to **e.** its error or demonstrate its falsity, he |
| P-2.........in.1:2 | can hardly be expected to **e.** reality. That |
| P-3...........I.4:1 | of salvation, nor did he **e.** his part in it. |
| S-2........III.3:1 | Do not **e.** what the form should be that |

## established 85

*See also* re-established

| | |
|---|---|
| T-2.........II.3:2 | after the value of the goal is firmly **e.**. It is |
| T-2........III.3:7 | this recognition becomes more firmly **e.**, |
| T-3........III.6:1 | to His altars, which He **e.** in His Sons. |
| T-4...........I.7:1 | worth is not **e.** by teaching or learning. |
| T-4...........I.7:2 | Your worth is **e.** by God. As long as you |
| T-6......V.C.2:6 | God Himself has **e.** what you can extend |
| T-7........VI.9:3 | What you are is not **e.** by your perception |
| T-7.........X.1:8 | His thinking has **e.** them for you. They are |
| T-8...........I.5:1 | of the curriculum you have **e.** for yourself, |
| T-8.........V.1:7 | the Mind of God is **e.** in ours and as ours. |
| T-8.......VII.5:9 | His Voice which He has **e.** as part of you. |
| T-10.......in.1:6 | They were **e.** for your protection and are |
| T-10......IV.4:1 | His Will, and His laws are **e.** to uphold it. |
| T-10......IV.5:6 | manner of your creation **e.** you a creator. |
| T-10......IV.6:5 | by them He **e.** the universe as what it is. |
| T-11.....V.13:5 | Unaware that the belief cannot be **e.**, and |
| T-13....VI.10:8 | You have **e.** them as guides to peace, for |
| T-13... VIII.9:4 | are the miracles that you **e.** in His Name. |
| T-13......XI.3:3 | cannot be judged, for it has been **e.**. It is |
| T-13......XI.5:5 | will find the peace in which He has **e.** you, |
| T-14......IV.9:2 | The Atonement was **e.** as the means of |
| T-14....XI.10:7 | in what He has **e.** as holy by His Presence. |
| T-15......III.5:4 | creation, He **e.** you as host to Him forever |
| T-15......IX.2:6 | have no limits, having been **e.** by God. |
| T-16......IV.9:3 | of God and of His Son **e.** forever. Seek not |
| T-17.........I.4:2 | **e.** this order in reality by giving some of it |
| T-17......IV.1:1 | God **e.** His relationship with you to make |
| T-17.....V.13:1 | you may have **e.** a condition in which you |
| T-17.....VII.7:1 | the Holy Spirit's goal has been **e.** is so far |
| T-18....III.4:10 | of your relationship is **e.** in Heaven. You |
| T-18......IV.4:5 | God has **e.** them. They do not wait upon |
| T-18....IV.5:10 | *He Who* ***e.*** *His dwelling place in me created* |
| T-19.........I.4:3 | you have **e.** a condition in which uniting |
| T-19.........I.6:6 | nor **e.** remedy where sickness cannot be. |
| T19 .IV.D.19:2 | in the plan God has **e.** for salvation will be |
| T-20....IV.2:10 | of God in minds that have **e.** other laws, |
| T-20......IV.4:4 | thus their freedom is **e.** and maintained. |
| T-20.......V.4:3 | His worth has been **e.** by his Father, and |
| T-21.......V.5:1 | **e.** without your will and your consent. It |
| T-23.......II.6:3 | the truth of what has been **e.** for His belief |
| T-24.......II.1:3 | It is **e.** by a lack seen in another, and |
| T-24....VI.12:5 | the truth as God **e.** it no sacrifice is asked, |
| T-25......III.4:1 | that anything could be **e.** and maintained |
| T-27.......II.8:8 | innocence has been **e.** in your sight and |
| T-28.......V.4:2 | Here is a world **e.** that is sick, and this the |
| T-29......VI.4:7 | God **e.** for His Son in full awareness. Time |
| T-29... VIII.6:1 | An idol is **e.** by belief, and when it is |
| T-30.......II.3:2 | world, and thus the rule of fear **e.** there. |
| T-30.....VII.1:4 | as with one purpose, changelessly **e.**. And |
| T-30.....VII.6:1 | can communication really be **e.** while the |
| T-30... VIII.3:6 | You have **e.** limits. What you ask *is* given |
| T-31.........I.4:5 | from the home where God Himself **e.** him |
| T-31......VI.1:6 | depend, for here have you **e.** what you are |
| W-pI.....25.5:1 | up the goals you have **e.** for everything. |
| W-pI.....66.8:1 | function is **e.** by God through His Voice, |
| W-pI.....77.8:5 | *to me. God has* ***e.*** *miracles as my right.* |
| W-pI...123.3:5 | judgments of the one whom God **e.** as His |
| W-pI...127.6:5 | requests in your advance towards its **e.** |
| W-pI...131.8:3 | hell, when God Himself **e.** him in Heaven |
| W-pI.135.11:5 | greater plan **e.** for the good of everyone. |
| W-pI...156.8:2 | has ended doubting and **e.** peace. Today |
| W-pI.159.10:3 | God's Son, but follow in the way He has **e.** |
| W-pI.160.10:2 | may be complete and perfect as it was **e.**. |
| W-pI.167.3:11 | die. Its truth **e.** you as one with God. |
| W-pI.167.11:1 | home we strive to keep today as He **e.** it, |
| WpI rV.in10:4 | wholeness now complete, as God **e.** it. |
| W-pI...183.5:4 | you have **e.** there an altar which reaches |
| W-pI...184.2:4 | By this split you think you are **e.** as a unity |
| W-pI.185.12:1 | its Creator, and **e.** as His Own eternal gift. |
| W-pI.193.12:1 | in forgiveness in the form **e.** for the day. |
| W-pI...198.1:4 | and the right you have **e.** for yourself can |
| W-pII..279.1:3 | are gone, with truth **e.** in their place. And |
| W-pII..321.2:2 | through the certain way our Father has **e.**. |
| W-pII..326.1:4 | *Where You* ***e.*** *me I still abide. And all Your* |
| W-pII....14.1:3 | *fear impossible, and joy* ***e.*** *without opposite.* |
| M-1...........1:3 | his road is **e.** and his direction is sure. A |
| M-1.........2:10 | of this that the plan of the teachers was **e.**. |
| M-2...........2:4 | was **e.** and completed simultaneously, for |
| M-4......IX.1:3 | is limited, and his trust not yet firmly **e.**. |
| C-5............1:2 | Identity, which God alone **e.** in reality. |
| C-6............2:2 | **e.** Jesus as the leader in carrying out His |
| P-2........III.4:5 | he carries out the plan **e.** for salvation. |
| S-1.........II.2:6 | for you have **e.** what it is you want. |
| S-2...........I.9:6 | plan that God **e.** for returning be achieved |
| S-3........III.5:8 | Nothing else can heal as God **e.** healing. |

## establishes 25

*See also* re-establishes

| | |
|---|---|
| T-1.........I.47:2 | It **e.** an out-of-pattern time interval not |
| T-1........IV.2:7 | This **e.** the proper function of the mind |
| T-2.......VII.5:9 | **e.** a state of mind in which the Atonement |
| T-3.........II.5:6 | integration and **e.** the peace of God. Yet |
| T-3........III.3:3 | **e.** a seemingly stable state that is usually |
| T-4........VI.3:6 | the recognition itself **e.** that you and your |
| T-6.........II.5:3 | love for both, because it **e.** inclusion. |
| T-6......V.C.9:8 | **e.** you as a teacher who teaches like me. |
| T-8..... VIII.5:2 | The ego, however, **e.** it as an end because, |
| T-9..... VIII.4:1 | because His grandeur **e.** your freedom. |
| T-10.......in.2:6 | mind **e.** everything that happens to you. |
| T-12......III.4:2 | opposition **e.** that it does matter to you. It |
| T-13.........I.8:3 | guilt **e.** that you will be punished for what |
| T-14......XI.7:8 | thus **e.** the fact that guiltlessness must be. |
| T-15.....VII.2:1 | ego **e.** relationships only to get something |
| T-17......VI.6:5 | goal **e.** the fact that everyone involved in |
| T-18......VI.4:6 | from what the Holy Spirit **e.** it to be. The |
| T-23.......II.2:4 | Each one **e.** this for himself, and makes it |
| T-23.......II.3:2 | this **e.** degrees of truth among illusions, |
| T-28.......II.7:1 | The miracle **e.** you dream a dream, and |
| T-31... VIII.6:5 | you make **e.** your own identity as you will |
| W-pI.....35.3:2 | your Source it **e.** your Identity, and it |
| W-pI.....38.1:3 | power because it **e.** you as a Son of God, |
| W-pII..298.1:5 | I accept instead what God **e.** as mine, sure |
| W-pII..354.1:1 | *oneness with the Christ* ***e.*** *me as Your Son,* |

## establishing 13

*See also* re-establishing

| | |
|---|---|
| T-4.......VII.3:7 | to it, thus **e.** it forever as a channel for the |
| T-7........III.5:3 | undoes the question by **e.** the fact that to |
| T-8........III.2:6 | His power and glory and **e.** them as yours. |
| T-8......VI.5:14 | Himself with it and **e.** its value forever. |
| T-11.......V.6:8 | longing for God into a means of **e.** itself. |
| T-16......III.2:6 | toward **e.** the relationship between them. |
| T-17....VIII.3:4 | and continuous means for **e.** His purpose, |
| W-pI.....35.3:2 | **e.** your Source it establishes your Identity, |
| WpI. rIV.in2:4 | Son, **e.** the Son as co-creator with Himself |
| W-pI...181.1:1 | to **e.** and holding up your faith in your |
| W-pI...184.3:2 | them, **e.** perception as you wished to have |
| C-6............2:1 | **e.** our particular part in it and showing us |
| P-2........IV.7:2 | correction cannot be achieved by first **e.** |

## establishment 1

*See also* re-establishment

| | |
|---|---|
| T-2........VI.8:6 | The need for the remedy inspired its **e.**. |

## establishments 1

| | |
|---|---|
| W-pI...136.7:4 | go away and threaten your **e.** no more. |

## esteem 5

*See also* self-esteem

| | |
|---|---|
| T-9.........V.6:6 | an "unimportant mind" **e.** itself without |
| T-24........II.2:9 | To value specialness is to **e.** an alien will |
| T-25......II.11:4 | honor that you may **e.** yourself and him. |
| T-27.........I.7:3 | short and not **e.** the worth of passing joys |
| W-pI...129.5:5 | **E.** them, and they will seem real to you. |

## esteemed 1

| | |
|---|---|
| W-pII .325.1:3 | upon, **e.** as real and guarded as one's own. |

## esteems 3

| | |
|---|---|
| T-13...... XI.3:3 | the value of what God **e.** cannot be judged |
| T-29.......V.6:4 | If God **e.** him worthy of Himself, would |
| W-pI.186.10:4 | The functions which the world **e.** are so |

## estimate 1

| | |
|---|---|
| T-20.......V.4:1 | How can you **e.** the worth of him who |

## Eternal 5

*eternal*

| | |
|---|---|
| T-11.........I.4:2 | nor endings were created by the **E.**, Who |
| T-11........II.5:2 | The **E.** Guest remains, but His Voice |
| W-pI...131.8:4 | Could he lose what the **E.** Will has given |
| W-pI...190.2:5 | nightmare of abandonment by an **E.** Love, |
| C-5...........6:10 | *Nothing you can do can change* ***E.*** *Love.* |

## eternal 192

*Eternal*

| | |
|---|---|
| T-1........III.2:2 | life, shall not pass away because life is **e.**. |
| T-1.........V.5:1 | Whatever is true is **e.**, and cannot change |
| T-3.....IV.5:11 | God created and which is therefore **e.**. |
| T-4.........I.11:7 | perishable as the ego is of making the **e.**. |
| T-4......IV.11:7 | life is an **e.** attribute of everything that the |
| T-4.........V.6:1 | not to commit itself to anything that is **e.**, |
| T-4.........V.6:1 | because the **e.** must come from God. |
| T-4.........V.6:3 | ego compromises with the issue of the **e.**, |
| T-4........VI.3:5 | are immediately recognized as **e.**. Since |
| T-5...........I.5:6 | But what God creates is **e.**. The Holy |
| T-5........III.6:5 | The only aspect of time that is **e.** is *now.* |
| T-5.....III.10:8 | If peace is **e.**, you are at home only in |
| T-5........IV.8:6 | you, and we know what God creates is **e.**. |
| T-7...........I.3:9 | is yours, because He created you **e.**. |
| T-7...........I.5:6 | The **e.** are in peace and joy forever. |
| T-8........VI.3:2 | God can find joy in anything except the **e.**; |
| T-8........VI.3:3 | What God and His Sons create is **e.**, and |
| T-8........VI.5:8 | is no other gift that is **e.**, and therefore |

| | |
|---|---|
| T-9 IV.4:9 | because they speak of ideas that are e.. |
| T-9 VIII.10:2 | your e. place merely waits for your return. |
| T-10 in.2:5 | God's only creation and He created you e. |
| T-10 I.3:6 | Yet what has once been is so now, if it is e. |
| T-10 I.3:7 | will know that what you remember is e., |
| T-10 III.9:6 | He is therefore not e. and will be unmade |
| T-10 III.9:6 | your willingness to accept only the e.. |
| T-10 IV.7:6 | same spark. It is everywhere and it is e.. |
| T-10 V.9:1 | Only the e. can be loved, for love does not |
| T-10 V.10:10 | you in your creation, and His gifts are e.. |
| T-10 V.14:5 | eternity, you must look only on the e.. If |
| T-11 III.8:5 | from God if you use it on behalf of the e.. |
| T-11 VI.8:3 | to death whom God has given e. life. The |
| T-11 VII.1:2 | it. God created only the e., and everything |
| T-11 VII.1:4 | literally true, for the e. are not re-created. |
| T-11 VII.2:1 | thought that the Son of God ever had is e. |
| T-11 VII.2:4 | Yet they are e. because they are loving. |
| T-12 I.10:6 | attests to your e. knowledge that union is |
| T-12 II.5:6 | for the goal is inevitable because it is e.. |
| T-12 III.8:3 | world, in which everything reflects the e.. |
| T-12 IV.6:1 | you, that you might learn you have e. life. |
| T-12 IV.7:6 | The Holy Spirit guides you into life e., but |
| T-12 V.4:4 | tried to make the separation e., because |
| T-12 VI.7:5 | where everything e. in it has always been. |
| T-12 VII.15:4 | And would e. life have been given me of |
| T-12 VII.15:6 | will see only the e. as you look out upon a |
| T-13 in.4:3 | the e. fact that God's Son is not guilty. He |
| T-13 I.5:8 | for his e. guiltlessness is in the Mind of his |
| T-13 I.8:5 | You are immortal because you are e., and |
| T-13 I.9:4 | His Son, and being guiltless he is e.. |
| T-13 III.7:4 | Lay before His e. sanity all your hurt, and |
| T-13 V.1:2 | being offered by the e. to the eternal. In |
| T-13 V.1:2 | being offered by the eternal to the e.. In |
| T-13 VI.6:6 | In it are all things that are e., and they are |
| T-13 VII.17:5 | establish its e. reign where sorrow dwells. |
| T-14 V.6:4 | to the e. glory of God and His creation. |
| T-15 I.4:14 | it will pursue you still, because guilt is e.. |
| T-15 I.15:9 | instant of the e. sanctity of God's creation |
| T-15 I.15:10 | Give the e. instant, that eternity may be |
| T-15 II.1:2 | in you, it is e.. What holds remembrance |
| T-15 II.2:2 | of peace is e. *because* it is without fear. It |
| T-15 III.6:9 | Name of Christ, e. Host unto His Father. |
| T-15 IX.5:1 | would experience the attraction of the e.. |
| T-16 III.7:7 | nothing in Him that is not perfect and e.. |
| T-16 V.12:10 | delights you can bring death to the e.. Nor |
| T-16 VII.7:5 | mind. Yet the holy instant is e., and your |
| T-17 III.5:3 | have been forgotten, what remains is e.. |
| T-17 IV.10:5 | and the joy of His e. Spirit are marshalled |
| T-18 III.8:7 | and so make room for His e. Presence, in |
| T-18 IV.5:11 | *own awareness of my readiness, which is e..* |
| T-18 VI.8:3 | that is an e. property of mind. But the |
| T-18 IX.2:1 | little offering of darkness to the e. light. |
| T-19 I.16:1 | Let, then, your dedication be to the e., |
| T-19 I.16:2 | you think you do to the e. you do to *you.* |
| T-19 II.2:5 | Thus is creation seen as not e., and the |
| T-19 III.2:6 | And what is true must be e., and will be |
| T-19 III.8:3 | in e. opposition to Him and to each other. |
| T19 IV.B.4:1 | Peace is extended from you only to the e., |
| T19 IV.B.4:1 | and it reaches out from the e. in you. It |
| T19 IV.B.10:1 | Faith in the e. is always justified, for the |
| T19 IV.B.10:1 | always justified, for the e. is forever kind, |
| T19 IV.D.18:5 | knows no sin, no death, but only life e.. |
| T-20 III.8:7 | you recognize your brother as the e. gift of |
| T-20 III.11:8 | brother is the light of God's e. promise of |
| T-20 VI.9:3 | for the e. blessing of the holy instant and |
| T-21 V.5:4 | Will of God must be in you now, being e.. |
| T-22 II.3:4 | Joy is e.. You can be sure indeed that any |
| T-22 II.3:6 | turn to sorrow, for the e. cannot change. |
| T-22 II.3:7 | turned to joy, for time gives way to the e.. |
| T-22 II.5:3 | attained, then the belief in sin must be e.. |
| T-22 VI.5:6 | you fill again with the e. light you bring, |
| T-22 VI.6:7 | your remembrance of everything that is e. |
| T-23 I.1:2 | against itself remembers not e. gentleness |
| T-23 II.6:5 | belief that seems to make chaos e.. For if |
| T-23 II.19:7 | yet perceived as an e. barrier to Heaven. |
| T-24 II.14:4 | your death, but your awaking into life e.. |
| T-25 VII.6:6 | each defines the changeless and e. truth of |
| T-25 VII.12:4 | of truth can faith in God's e. saneness rest |
| T-25 VIII.14:1 | from all effects of sin, and to the life e., |
| T-26 V.5:1 | tiny instant you would keep and make e., |
| T-26 VII.4:3 | God's answer is e., though it works in |
| T-27 I.5:4 | It witnesses to the e. truth that you cannot |
| T-28 I.14:7 | Its Effects are changelessly e., beyond fear |
| T-29 I.1:4 | in His e. Love is quite impossible. For it |
| T-29 I.1:5 | attack, and His e. patience sometimes fail. |
| T-29 I.9:1 | happens when the gap is gone is peace e.. |
| T-29 V.3:3 | the changeless and e. that abide in him, |
| T-29 V.3:5 | wakening to peace e. and to endless joy. |
| T-29 V.8:4 | this is so, and seek not the e. in this world. |
| T-29 VI.2:7 | What *seems* e. all will have an end. The |
| T-29 VI.2:10 | time has set an end is not where the e. is. |
| T-29 VI.3:4 | you, and establish it as changeless and e.. |
| T-29 VI.4:1 | God gave to all that you would make e., to |
| T-29 VIII.5:4 | worthy of the gift of Heaven and e. peace. |
| T-29 VIII.6:2 | the infinite, a time transcending the e.. |
| T-30 III.8:4 | is like a star, unchangeable in an e. sky. So |
| T-30 III.9:1 | light, for He is the e. sky that holds it safe, |
| T-30 III.10:5 | and of its rest in its e. home, the Thought |
| T-30 III.11:3 | of? Outside you there is no e. sky, no |
| T-30 VI.5:6 | of error that remains unchangeable, e., |
| T-31 I.8:8 | The soft e. calling of each part of God's |
| W-pI 45.3:5 | What is thought by the Mind of God is e., |
| W-pI 45.6:6 | the truth in your mind, and reach to the e. |
| W-pI 49.4:3 | and obscure your e. link with God. Sink |
| W-pI 50.3:3 | can intrude upon the e. calm of the Son of |
| W-pI 50.4:3 | faith in the Love of God within you; e., |
| W-pI 87.3:4 | I believe that my e. safety is threatened. |
| W-pI 93.5:8 | creation, nor reduced e. sinlessness to sin, |
| W-pI 93.6:5 | touch it, or change what God created as e. |
| W-pI 93.7:4 | Creation is e. and unalterable. Your |
| W-pI 104.5:1 | joy and peace belong to us as His e. gifts. |
| W-pI 124.3:1 | is our e. gift to those who follow after, and |
| W-pI 132.9:3 | time that can bring change to your e. state |
| W-pI 135.18:4 | plans for death, He led you gently to e. life |
| W-pI 140.10:4 | illusions end, and peace returns to the e., |
| W-pI 151.3:7 | is witnessed to by the e. Voice for God |
| W-pI 151.14:1 | God wills His Son, as proof of His e. Love. |
| W-pI 152.9:3 | its changelessness and its e. wholeness, all- |
| W-pI 159.3:2 | for it reflects e. love and the rebirth of |
| W-pI 163.7:3 | over His, and so e. life gave way to death. |
| W-pI 163.9:4 | *We are not separate from Your e. life. There* |
| W-pI 165.1:2 | and the e. life your Father wills for you? |
| W-pI 167.6:5 | attributes it lacks, nor change its own e., |
| W-pI 167.10:5 | of life e. has been set by God Himself. |
| WpI rV.in5:4 | to return to the e. Self we thought we lost. |
| W-pI 182.4:4 | This childhood is e., with an innocence |
| W-pI 183.11:6 | In this e., still relationship, in which |
| W-pI 183.11:6 | words could possibly convey, is peace e.. |
| W-pI 185.7:6 | requesting the e. in the place of shifting |
| W-pI 185.12:1 | and established as His Own e. gift. How |
| W-pI 188.3:3 | What it gives must be e.. It removes all |
| W-pI 191.11:5 | They die till you accept your own e. life. |
| W-pI 193.1:2 | undisturbed; e. and forever gaining scope, |
| W-pI 193.9:3 | a care, in an e. home which cares for him. |
| W-pI 193.12:5 | unbound, in peace e. in the world of time. |
| W-pI 197.5:3 | you will never realize His gifts are sure, e., |
| W-pI 200.3:1 | and for e. life in peace that has no ending. |
| W-pII 234.2:2 | *help we have received, for Your e. patience,* |
| W-pII 4.3:3 | must have an end; e. life must die. And |
| W-pII 5.2:9 | there that God's e. Son can be destroyed? |
| W-pII 263.1:4 | *creation; all its purity, its joy, and its e.,* |
| W-pII 273.2:4 | *in quietness and in my own e. love for You.* |
| W-pII 7.2:4 | itself, to be replaced by the e. truth. |
| W-pII 297.2:2 | *grace. Thanks be to You for Your e. gifts, and* |
| W-pII 299.h | E. holiness abides in me. |
| W-pII 309.1:1 | Within me is e. innocence, because it is |
| W-pII 10.4:1 | return to the e. peace He shares with him. |
| W-pII 318.1:7 | Son, His one e. Love. I am salvation's |
| W-pII 11.4:2 | and unaware of our e. unity with Him. Yet |
| W-pII 323.1:1 | *him of pain, and giving him Your Own e. joy.* |
| W-pII 12.3:3 | and of suffering, when he lives in e. joy? |
| W-pII 331.1:9 | *Death is illusion; life, e. truth. There is no* |
| W-pII 334.2:1 | *I seek but the e.. For Your Son can be* |
| W-pII 337.1:1 | ensures me perfect peace, e. safety, |
| W-pII 348.1:6 | *afraid, when Your e. promise goes with me?* |
| W-pII 350.h | Miracles mirror God's e. Love. To offer |
| W-pII 14.1:2 | *creation sanctified and guaranteed e. life. In* |
| W-ep 4:2 | for He gives only the e. and the good. Let |
| M-4 X.3:2 | and e. truth do not appear in this context. |
| M-15 1:11 | *Holy are you, e., free and whole, at peace* |
| M-18 4:3 | Then let him turn within to his e. Guide, |
| M-24 1:6 | the recognition of the e. nature of life, it is |
| M-27 6:10 | and in Him all created things must be e.. |
| C-1 3:3 | being of God, it is e. and was never born. |
| C-3 3:5 | content is unchanging, as e. as its Creator. |
| C-3 6:9 | remains is peace e. and the Will of God. |
| C-4 1:2 | for what He creates must be e. as Himself. |
| C-6 1:2 | or spirit, is e. and has never changed. He |
| C-6 3:9 | Love of your Father to you in an e. shining |
| C-6 5:8 | to return to the e. formlessness of God. |
| S-2 III.6:8 | to come from His e. vigilance and Love. |
| S-3 IV.3:5 | His creation, for it lies in you as His e. gift. |
| S-3 IV.8:3 | your song is part of the e. harmony of love |
| S-3 IV.9:9 | the gift first of forgiveness, then e. peace. |

## eternally 25

| | |
|---|---|
| T-1 IV.2:8 | possessed by illusions, but spirit is e. free. |
| T-2 II.5:5 | The e. creative have nothing to learn. You |
| T-7 I.7:9 | there, because its being is e. changeless. It |
| T19 IV.D.19:4 | the peace of God, given to you e. by Him. |
| T-20 VI.10:3 | Its firm foundation is e. upheld by truth, |
| T-23 I.4:6 | He loves you perfectly, completely and e.. |
| T-23 IV.8:5 | the same, e. complete and wholly shared. |
| T-24 II.4:4 | to you e. in loving praise of what you are, |
| T-26 I.7:5 | Heaven, so must he be e. and everywhere. |
| T-30 III.6:9 | It is forever One, e. united and at peace. |
| T-31 V.6:1 | ensures your brother is condemned e.. |
| W-pI 58.5:8 | me forever. I am e. blessed as His Son. |
| W-pI 94.3:4 | *I am His Son e..* Now try to reach the Son of |
| W-pI 94.5:3 | *me. I am His Son e..* Tell yourself frequently |
| W-pI 94.5:7 | *You are His Son e..* Make every effort to do |
| W-pI 134.2:7 | can you forgive the sinless and e. benign? |
| W-pI 152.8:4 | be all that there ever was, e. as it is now. |
| W-pI 163.9:7 | *as ours, and our will is one with Yours e..* |
| W-pI 193.1:2 | e. expanding in the joy of full creation, |
| W-pI 193.1:2 | and e. open and wholly limitless in Him. |
| W-pII 262.1:8 | *Who are our Source, e. united in Your Love;* |
| W-pII 262.1:8 | *united in Your Love; e. the holy Son of God.* |
| W-pII 300.1:2 | than a passing cloud upon a sky e. serene. |
| W-pII 328.2:3 | *is Your Will that I be wholly safe, e. at peace.* |
| W-pII343.1:11 | *for I can only give, and everything is mine e..* |

## eternalness 1

| | |
|---|---|
| T-4 V.6:2 | E. is the one function the ego has tried to |

## eternity 125

| | |
|---|---|
| T-1 I.19:3 | Miracles therefore reflect the laws of e., |
| T-3 VII.3:2 | real enough in time, though not in e.. All |
| T-5 III.5:2 | Both time and delay are meaningless in e. |
| T-5 III.6:2 | ego and the Holy Spirit; with time and e.. |
| T-5 III.6:3 | E. is an idea of God, so the Holy Spirit |
| T-5 III.7:3 | to look beyond symbols into e. enables |
| T-5 III.8:3 | This is your life, your e. and your Self. It is |
| T-5 III.8:13 | E. and peace are as closely related as are |
| T-5 III.10:8 | is eternal, you are at home only in e.. |
| T-5 VI.h | Time and E. |
| T-5 VI.1:3 | Delay does not matter in e., but it is tragic |
| T-5 VI.1:4 | have elected to be in time rather than e., |
| T-5 VI.1:7 | time. Your place is only in e., where God |
| T-5 VI.2:6 | offers you the continuity of e. in exchange |
| T-5 VI.12:2 | the way in which time is exchanged for e.. |
| T-5 VI.12:6 | special function to return you to e. and |
| T-6 IV.7:5 | has given way to creation and to its e.. |
| T-6 V.1:6 | an ongoing process, not in time but in e.. |
| T-7 I.3:9 | E. is yours, because He created you |
| T-7 I.5:3 | forever, since joy and e. are inseparable. |
| T-7 I.5:5 | E. is the indelible stamp of creation. The |
| T-8 VI.2:6 | His creations, having created them for e.. |
| T-9 III.8:4 | God gave you the function to create in e.. |
| T-9 IV.9:2 | the ego's time is "borrowed" from your e.. |
| T-9 VI.6:1 | Miracles have no place in e., because they |
| T-9 VI.6:4 | first, though they are simultaneous in e., |
| T-9 VI.7:1 | E. is one time, its only dimension being |
| T-10 in.1:2 | Time and e. are both in your mind, and |

T-10.......in.1:2 time solely as a means to regain e.. You
T-10.....V.14:3 While this is not true in e. it *is* true in time,
T-10.....V.14:5 If you would remember e., you must look
T-10.....V.14:8 Time and e. cannot both be real, because
T-10.....V.14:9 begin to understand e. and make it yours.
T-11.........I.3:7 reality may arrest it in time, but not in e..
T-11.......III.8:4 will bless him in time, you will be in e..
T-13.........I.3:2 You are not guiltless in time, but in e..
T-13.........I.8:4 must deprive you of the appreciation of e.
T-13......IV.7:5 approximation of e. that this world offers.
T-13......IV.7:6 the beginning of the appreciation of e. lies
T-13......IV.8:1 as one of extending itself in place of e., for
T-13...VII.10:3 this is so, for what could you need in e.?
T-13...VII.17:6 You dwell not here, but in e.. You travel
T-13... VIII.1:5 unequivocally knows also it dwells in e.,
T-13... VIII.3:9 them as one with the final gift of e..
T-13... VIII.8:3 will all unite in the e. of God the Father.
T-13....XI.10:4 will remain unchanged throughout e..
T-14......IV.1:7 but the First in e. is God the Father, Who
T-14....... X.1:2 in time but bring e. nearer or farther. But
T-14....... X.1:3 But e. itself is beyond all time. Reach out
T-15...... I.11:5 ready to give you the remembrance of e..
T-15...... I.15:4 Holiness lies not in time, but in e.. There
T-15.... I.15:10 that e. may be remembered for you, in
T-15....... II.2:3 He has appointed to translate time into e.
T-15......IV.6:3 instant, beginning now and reaching to e.
T-15.....V.11:5 For the holy instant reaches to e., and to
T-15....... X.1:3 time nor season means anything in e.. But
T-16....IV.13:4 you across lifts you from time into e..
T-16....IV.13:5 Him Who gave e. to you in your creation.
T-17....... II.2:6 notice, is a stride through time into e.,
T-17....IV.11:4 The holy instant is a miniature of e.. It is a
T-17....IV.11:8 borrowed from e. and set in time for you.
T-17....IV.14:1 lightly framed, for time cannot contain e..
T-17....IV.14:3 The picture of Heaven and e. grows more
T-17....... V.9:5 a goal unchanged throughout e.? For you
T-19......III.5:3 of the difference between time and e..
T-19......III.5:4 when correction is completed, time *is* e..
T19. IV.C.10:6 ageless, born in time but nourished in e..
T-20..........V.h Heralds of E.
T-20....... V.1:6 miracle of joining is a mighty herald of e..
T-20....... V.2:1 of e. sings of the end of sin and fear. Each
T-20....... V.5:8 The little breath of e. that runs through
T-23.......in.5:2 beyond it, measureless and timeless as e..
T-24......VI.3:5 has no meaning in e. where He abides,
T-24......VI.7:3 e. is not regained by still one more denial
T-24.....VII.6:7 creation, found not within time, but in e..
T-25....... II.6:8 corruption, unchanged and perfect in e..
T-25......VI.7:7 and will remain in time and in e. alike.
T-25... VIII.3:7 triumph over e. and timelessness and life?
T-26....... V.2:2 For it is but a little hindrance to e., quite
T-26....... V.3:3 in your mind, with no effect upon e.. And
T-26.....V.12:1 do not change the laws of time nor of e..
T-27... VIII.6:2 Into e., where all is one, there crept a tiny,
T-27... VIII.6:4 that time cannot intrude upon e.. It is a
T-27... VIII.6:5 think that time can come to circumvent e.
T-28...... I.12:5 Son accepts gives welcome to e. and Him,
T-28...... I.13:4 of e. resound throughout the stillness, yet
T-28......III.7:4 a little gap perceived to tear e. apart, and
T-29....... V.1:2 time has left, and echoes of e. are heard.
T-29... VIII.7:3 a place where time can interrupt e.? A
T-30......III.8:6 and lovely will it shine through all e..
T-30....... V.4:3 has a purpose still beneath creation and e.
T-31. VIII.12:2 set for Him before time was, in calm e..
W-pI.....59.2:6 this day may help me to understand e..
W-pI.....94.2:6 in which you will remain throughout e..
W-pI...104.2:3 still be ours when time has passed into e..
W-pI...105.4:3 to the unlimited, e. to timelessness, and
W-pI...107.2:4 be extended to the end of time and to e..
W-pI.110.11:7 you enter in the peace of God and His e..
W-pI...129.4:1 plain as day, remains unlimited for all e..
W-pI...140.3:5 are gone. And thus they cure for all e..
W-pI...153.8:3 it for the Son of God; its tiny instant for e.
W-pI...157.1:3 this day, when echoes of e. are heard.
W-pI...157.3:2 above its laws, and walk into e. a while.
W-pI...164.1:4 past time, and sees e. as represented there
W-pI...165.2:7 E. and everlasting life shine in your mind,
W-pI...169.6:7 been at all. E. remains a constant state.
W-pI...169.8:2 when it is released to revelation and e..
W-pI...190.8:4 over love, and time replace e. and Heaven
W-pII...in.10:8 is complete. This year has brought us to e.
W-pII......2.5:2 are done, e. has shined away the world,
W-pII..234.1:2 has elapsed between e. and timelessness.
W-pII..300.2:5 *We would go beyond that tiny instant to e..*
W-pII..329.1:6 *That choice was made for all e.. It cannot*
W-pII..346.1:2 *the day I share with You as I will share e., for*
Wfl........in.6:5 there will be throughout all time and in e.
M-2 ...........4:8 What could delay the power of e.?
M-15 .......1:10 Time pauses as e. comes near, and silence
C-4.............8:3 into holiness; out of the world and to e.;
C-ep...........2:5 safe within e. and through all time as well
P-2......... II.1:5 be made perfect in time and restored to e.
S-1.........in.1:7 is what all prayer will be throughout e.,
S-1...........I.4:7 God answers only for e.. But still all little
S-1......... V.4:5 At this gate e. itself will join with you.
S-3.........III.5:3 It will remain to bless for all e.. It heals no
S-3.........IV.8:2 Let Me instead remind you of e., in which

### ethics 1

W-pI...135.2:4 its codes, its e. and its leaders and its gods

### evaded 1

W-pII..333.1:2 cannot be e., set aside, denied, disguised,

### evading 1

W-pI...107.6:1 in that, e. capture and escaping grasp. It

### evaluate 13

T-8...........I.2:5 to e. them in terms of their results to you.
T-8........IX.1:4 establish your ability to e. its questions.
T-9.......VII.6:1 e. an insane belief system from within it.
T-10......IV.2:4 and because of your ability to e. it truly,
T-14......III.15:1 is to e. his Father and judge against Him.
T-20....... V.7:1 Can you e. the giver of a gift like this?
T-26....... II.4:4 does not e. injustices as great or small, or
W-pI...126.7:3 e. such petty gifts as worthy of His Son?
W-pI.151.13:4 Him e. each thought that comes to mind,
M-6 ...........3:1 teachers to e. the outcome of their gifts. It
M-13 .........2:8 Yet a body cannot e.. By seeking after
P-1.............1:3 its causes and learn to e. them correctly.
S-2........ III.1:3 nor e. the errors that it wants to overlook.

### evaluated 6

T-7.....VII.11:1 and you have correctly e. all of it. This
T-9.......VII.4:5 because it has e. you as unloving and you
T-18....... V.1:6 deepest retreats you have e. as success.
T-20....... V.3:3 What is inestimable clearly cannot be e..
T-20...VII.8:10 attainment will be e. as worth the seeing,
T-26....... X.2:3 otherwise, how could some be e. as unfair

### evaluates 6

T-2.....V.A.16:3 what they do" in no way e. *what* they do. It
T-4......... II.6:5 always e. itself in relation to other egos. It
T-9.......VII.3:2 of what you are, and so He e. you truly.
T-15.......VII.8:7 these terms that it e. ideas as good or bad.
W-pI...136.4:1 Who but yourself e. a threat, decides
M-8 .........3:10 Only the mind e. their messages, and so

### evaluation 18

*See also* re-evaluation

T-1...........I.2:2 is their Source, which is far beyond e..
T-2...... VIII.3:5 might be called a process of right e.. It
T-3......... V.7:8 E. is an essential part of perception,
T-3.........VI.2:3 out that e. is its obvious prerequisite.
T-5....... II.8:10 call you answer now is an e. because it is a
T-6...........I.5:3 and did not share this e. for myself. And
T-9.......VII.3:2 His e. of you is based on His knowledge of
T-9.......VII.3:3 truly. And this e. must be in your mind,
T-9.......VII.3:5 it there. Its e. of you, however, is the exact
T-9.......VII.4:9 agreeing with the ego's e. of what you are?
T-9.......VII.5:4 Can you escape from its e. of you by using
T-9....VIII.10:9 that you believe your e. of yourself is truer
T-9.....VIII.11:1 your e. of yourself must *be* God's. You did
T-15...... III.2:1 is that your choice is your e. of yourself.
T-17...... VI.3:7 makes understanding doubtful and e.
T-20........II.3:1 gift is an e. of the receiver and the *giver.*
T-26...... III.4:2 ever make; the last e. that will be possible,
M-19 .........4:7 an e. based entirely on love,–you have

### evaluations 4

T-9........ VI.2:2 to you are your e. of His consistency.
T-9..........VII.h The Two E.
T-9.......VII.4:1 two conflicting e. of yourself in your mind
T-9.......VII.4:2 how completely different these e. are,

### evaluative 2

T-5..........II.5:2 Guidance is e., because it implies there is
T-6......V.C.1:1 We said before that the Holy Spirit is e.,

### even 305

T-1.........I.45:2 touch many people you have not e. met,
T-1.........I.45:2 situations of which you are not e. aware.
T-1......... III.7:2 e. without the awareness of the miracle
T-1........ IV.1:3 is nothing you want to hide e. if you could
T-1......... V.4:2 him, e. though he may be absent in spirit.
T-2......... V.9:4 e. if you cannot perceive it in yourself.
T-2......VIII.2:5 long period, and perhaps an e. longer one
T-3...........I.1:5 if God permitted and e. encouraged one
T-3...........I.4:3 e. as your Father in Heaven is merciful. It
T-3..........II.1:8 to deny truth totally, e. if he thinks he can
T-3........ III.5:11 thought. E. in its most spiritualized form
T-3........ IV.4:2 and e. this is subject to degrees, clearly
T-3....... IV.5:10 E. in miscreation the mind is affirming its
T-3......... V.2:7 effort e. in its most ingenious form. The
T-3....... VI.8:10 e. doubt whether you really exist at all.
T-3........ VI.9:5 your ability to identify it, or e. to place it.
T-3........VII.5:8 peace, e. though your mind is in conflict.
T-4.........I.2:13 e. though its maker can be misguided. He
T-4..........II.3:6 way, e. though it does work that way now.
T-4..........II.5:1 e. though this is anything but true. Babies
T-4..........II.5:6 attitudes e. toward this are necessarily
T-4..........II.9:6 life. Some e. believe that the soul will be
T-4.....VII.3:12 e. though it may refuse to utilize it on
T-5...........I.1:9 things, e. to the lower mind it is quite
T-5...........I.6:1 God honored e. the miscreations of His
T-5...........I.6:6 It might e. be more helpful here to use the
T-5..........II.3:9 It is possible e. in this world to hear only
T-5..........II.6:8 e. though they chose to leave Him. The
T-5..........II.7:6 remaining quiet e. in the midst of the
T-5......IV.2:12 I meant when I said it is possible e. in this
T-5......... V.5:7 Yet e. in this it is arrogant. It attributes to
T-5........ VI.4:4 but it e. interprets Scripture as a witness
T-5........ VI.9:2 a word the ego cannot e. understand. To
T-6...........I.4:2 can assault another, and can e. destroy it.
T-6........ II.11:2 the Holy Spirit tells you that e. return is
T-6......V.A.6:2 It is not e. necessary that you complete
T-6.......V.B.1:5 them, e. though it was apparent I was not.
T-7...........I.1:6 E. in this world there is a parallel. Parents
T-7........ III.2:10 e. though the ego does not know what it is
T-7........ IV.5:6 e. in a state of mind that is out of accord
T-7......... X.7:1 E. the relinquishment of your false
T-8...........I.5:9 relinquish the other, e. if it does not exist.
T-8..........II.1:9 E. if you could disregard the Holy Spirit
T-8........ IV.2:4 you always, e. unto the end of the world.
T-8........ VI.7:6 can e. imprison the mind of God's Son, if
T-8.......VII.9:1 not e. the body is perceived as whole. Its
T-8......VIII.8:2 of something you want, e. if it is not real?
T-8........ IX.3:2 All forms of sickness, e. unto death, are
T-8........ IX.6:5 e. though it makes every effort to induce
T-9...........I.8:5 e. though many may seek both. Can you
T-9.........I.12:2 goal e. though you do not want it. But
T-9..........II.2:3 achieved, e. when the state of healing is.
T-9........ IV.7:2 it, e. though it has no idea what they are.
T-9......... V.4:6 is a contradiction e. in the ego's terms,
T-9......... V.4:6 which it usually notes e. in its confusion.
T-9........ VI.1:4 e. though you are not experiencing joy
T-9........ VI.4:1 but not e. this would He keep from you.

T-9......VIII.1:4 e. though it does not understand it, the
T-9......VIII.4:2 E. the faintest hint of your reality literally
T-10.........I.2:5 e. though all the laws of what you awaken
T-10...... III.3:4 of a Son of God e. if he believes in it, for
T-11.......in.3:6 e. the little spark in your mind is enough
T-11.........I.9:6 E. in time you cannot live apart from Him
T-11...... III.5:1 e. though His Son would hide himself. Yet
T-11....... V.6:8 has twisted e. your longing for God into a
T-11....... V.9:1 callous, uninvolved and e. desperate, but
T-11....VIII.1:7 e. the real world will vanish from your
T-12...... III.5:4 allow yourself to believe, e. for an instant,
T-12...... III.6:5 E. if he is fully aware of anxiety he does
T-12...... III.9:2 to accept e. death to deny your Father.
T-12...... V.7:11 But perhaps you do not realize, e. yet,
T-12....VIII.5:4 e. control yourself should hardly aspire to
T-13....... II.3:3 You do not e. suspect this murderous but
T-13....... II.8:2 Yet e. when I interpret it for you, you may
T-13....... III.1:9 You could look e. upon the ego's darkest
T-13....... III.1:9 yourself something you fear e. more. You
T-13....... III.2:4 to look e. upon your savage wish to kill
T-13...... IV.3:1 wrong, e. apart from the fact that you
T-13...... IV.3:3 E. the past life that death might indicate,
T-13...... IV.3:6 it. And e. though you know not Heaven,
T-13....... V.9:7 extended your perception e. unto Him.
T-13.... VI.13:3 E. in sleep has Christ protected you,
T-13...... VII.3:5 ready to return to dust e. as you made it.
T-13..... VII.4:1 world has the power to touch you e. here,
T-13... VII.11:3 e. from the very hands that grasped it, it
T-13....VIII.2:6 E. the perception of the Holy Spirit, as
T-13....VIII.4:5 Yet e. Christ's vision is not His reality.
T-13....VIII.5:5 to make Christ's vision possible e. here.
T-13....... X.2:2 or e. hold one spot of it to mar its purity.
T-13....... X.5:3 A minute, e. less, will be enough to free
T-13..... X.13:2 e. unto the worth that God has placed
T-13..... X.14:2 that none of us alone can e. think of it.
T-13...... XI.1:1 Forgetfulness and sleep and e. death
T-13.... XI.3:13 brought e. a dim imagining of what it is.
T-13...... XI.9:5 Learn that e. the darkest nightmare that
T-14...... III.4:1 each hour and minute, e. each second,
T-14...... IV.1:6 received, e. as God gave it first to His Son.
T-14...... IV.8:6 e. give a blessing in perfect gentleness.
T-14...... VI.6:4 Yet e. this strange and twisted effort to
T-14....... X.4:1 which e. though they may conflict, can
T-14...... XI.2:2 in deepest sleep, could e. dream of it. Can
T-14...... XI.5:2 if all those who meet or e. think of you
T-15.........I.3:5 for you to find peace e. in death, it offers
T-15.........I.5:2 E. when it attacks so savagely that it tries
T-15.........I.5:2 is the only voice, it speaks of hell e. to him
T-15.........I.5:5 And e. there, its only value is that it is no
T-15........ II.3:5 days, hours and e. years in chaining your
T-15... III.12:6 above the stars and reaches e. to Heaven,
T-15....... V.7:1 that it frequently goes e. farther; one part
T-15...VII.13:3 that it can overcome e. this without fear.
T-15...... XI.7:2 unbroken e. if the body is destroyed,
T-16...... III.3:6 do not recognize It e. though It functions.
T-16....... V.3:3 judged to be acceptable and e. natural.
T-16....... V.3:4 and e. those who believe that hate is sin
T-16....... V.5:5 "victory" e. to the final triumph over God
T-16..... V.12:5 e. apart from its evident impossibility? If
T-16...... VI.5:7 does not include e. one whole individual.
T-16...... VI.8:7 You could not long find e. the illusion of
T-16..... VII.5:2 And e. when the hatred and the savagery
T-17....... II.1:5 you e. a little part of the happiness this
T-17....... II.5:5 e. what the Son of God made in insanity
T-17....... II.7:3 E. salvation will become a dream, and
T-17...... III.3:2 For e. the body of the other, already a
T-17...... III.4:7 of excluding e. the one with whom the
T-17...... IV.3:1 very real relationships e. in this world.
T-17....... V.3:3 disjunctive and e. quite distressing. The
T-17....... V.5:7 may e. become quite disorganized. And
T-17...... V.7:11 for faith a little longer, e. in bewilderment
T-17....VIII.2:5 Not e. faith is asked of you, for truth asks
T-18....... V.2:7 solid rock of faith, and rising e. to Heaven
T-18....... V.4:5 You do not e. realize you have accepted
T-18....... V.6:5 that this is necessary, or e. possible. Yet
T-18.... VI.12:3 and e. a general idea without specific
T-18....VIII.1:7 cannot e. think of God without a body, or
T-18....VIII.4:1 Yet neither sun nor ocean is e. aware of
T-18....VIII.4:3 E. that segment is not lost to them, for it
T-18 .... IX.10:1 e. forgiveness is not the end. Forgiveness
T-19 ........II.3:1 can e. turn the power of his mind against
T19..IV.A.11:5 What fear demands, love cannot e. see.
T19..IV.A.12:4 For fear is merciless e. to its friends. Its
T19..IV.B.15:2 And e. if you suffer, yet someone else will
T19..IV.C.10:4 What has been given you, e. in its infancy,
T19... IV.D.1:4 lies e. beyond them would you remember.
T19... IV.D.3:2 it, nor e. to suspect that it is there. This is
T19. IV.D.10:5 and e. when it is over it seems to make no
T-20 ...... V.3:4 your judgment you cannot e. see it? Judge
T-20 ..... VI.4:4 for what they are it does not e. see. It
T-20 ..... VI.6:4 E. the idols that are worshipped here are
T-21 ........II.3:7 and e. this He gives to you to give yourself
T-21 ..... IV.2:2 "enemy," Whom it cannot e. see, it fears.
T-21 .... VII.4:5 enemy, but this will shift e. as it attacks,
T-21 .... VII.4:7 changes so it is impossible e. to recognize
T-21 ...VIII.2:2 if you could e. imagine what it must be,
T-22 ..... IV.3:5 and peace has reached you e. here, before
T-22 ..... VI.2:4 Yet e. in this confusion, so profound it
T-23 ........II.6:3 not seen as e. necessary that He be asked
T-23 ..... IV.6:2 E. in forms you do not recognize, the
T-24 ........II.3:2 is impossible e. to imagine without this
T-24 ..... III.4:4 creeps or crawls, or e. lives at all. Nothing
T-24 ..... III.5:7 Salvation challenges not e. death. And
T-24 .. VII.10:8 Not identical, not e. like, but still a means
T-24 .. VII.11:4 nor where they go, nor e. what they do.
T-25 ..... III.4:3 God protected still His Son, e. in error.
T-25 ..... IV.2:6 E. in Heaven does this law obtain. The
T-26 ..... VI.1:9 same, and still maintain that e. one is best
T-27 ........II.9:7 Holy Spirit be deterred an instant, e. less,
T-27 .....II.14:1 your own mistakes you will not e. see.
T-27 ..... III.2:4 Yet e. this is quickly contradicted by the
T-27 ..... IV.5:2 It dictates the answer e. as it asks. Thus is
T-27 .. VII.12:4 little gap you do not e. see, the birthplace
T-27 ..VIII.2:3 it does not need and does not e. want. It
T-29 ...... V.8:2 e. though it was for this that every dream
T-29 ..... VI.5:2 For e. though it was a dream of death, you
T-29 ...VIII.8:8 or e. more affliction and more pain. But
T-30 .........I.8:1 receive you cannot e. let your question go,
T-30 ..... IV.8:6 And e. in illusions it but asks forgiveness
T-30 ...... V.4:3 itself. E. the real world has a purpose still
T-31 .........I.3:3 by it, and e. now depends on nothing else
T-31 .........I.3:6 to you, and e. you are someone else.
T-31 ...... V.2:7 smiles and charms and e. seems to love. It
T-31 ...... V.9:3 For e. though you do not yet perceive that
T-31 .... V.10:2 unlikely. E. if he did, who gave the face of
W-in.......... 9:1 them, and you need not e. welcome them.
W-pI..... 11.3:2 used in an unhurried, e. leisurely fashion.
W-pI..... 12.2:4 to keep a measured, e. tempo throughout.
W-pI..... 12.6:3 You may find e. this too long. Terminate
W-pI..... 13.6:2 and try not e. to think of it except during
W-pI..... 14.3:2 can be quite difficult and e. quite painful.
W-pI..... 17.4:1 benefit, e. if you experience resistance.
W-pI..... 18.3:5 minute or so, or e. less, will be sufficient
W-pI..... 19.2:2 and may e. be regarded as an "invasion of
W-pI..... 20.1:2 and not e. active cooperation and interest
W-pI..... 23.4:5 them, e. though they were made of hate.
W-pI..... 24.5:4 e. if some of them do not appear to be
W-pI..... 24.5:4 situation, or e. to be inherent in it at all.
W-pI..... 27.3:5 this, e. if you are engaged in conversation,
W-pI..... 29.2:2 senseless, funny and e. objectionable.
W-pI..... 30.1:3 you saw before be e. faintly visible to you.
W-pI..... 41.8:3 might e. say it is the only natural thing in
W-pI..... 41.8:5 results e. the first time it is attempted,
W-pI..... 42.4:2 the idea again, e. slower than before.
W-pI... 44.10:1 and e. a feeling that you are approaching,
W-pI..... 45.8:7 Yet e. with the little understanding you
W-pI..... 54.3:3 E. the mad idea of separation had to be
W-pI..... 66.4:3 happiness, e. if it appears to be different.
W-pI..... 66.5:5 e. if you do not yet accept the conclusion.
W-pI..... 67.5:3 five times an hour, and perhaps e. more,
W-pI..... 68.4:5 If you succeed e. by ever so little, there
W-pI..... 68.5:3 those you like and e. think you love. It
W-pI..... 74.6:5 e. if you do not experience the peace you
W-pI..... 76.8:4 Perhaps you e. think that there are laws
W-pI..... 78.4:5 Someone, perhaps, you fear and e. hate;
W-pI..... 78.6:4 think of his mistakes and e. of his "sins."
W-pI..... 79.1:2 E. if it is really solved already you will still
W-pI..... 79.2:4 E. if he is given the answer, he cannot see
W-pI .... 91.2:7 is useless to you then, e. though it is there
W-pI .. 93.10:1 You may not be willing or e. able to use
W-pI .. 107.2:3 a time,–perhaps a minute, maybe e. less
W-pI .. 108.1:4 E. that one will disappear, because the
WpI..rIII.in9:1 and perhaps of e. greater value. You have
W-pI .. 129.3:3 e. they will be exchanged at last for what
W-pI .. 133.8:7 does not e. tell the truth as it perceives it,
W-pI .. 136.3:4 In that second, e. less, in which the choice
W-pI .. 138.4:2 And e. this but seems to be a choice. Do
W-pI .. 151.2:3 e. though you learned a long while since
W-pI .. 151.2:4 last detail which they report is e. stranger,
W-pI 153.16:2 At times, perhaps, a minute, e. less, will
W-pI 153.18:3 e. though your time is spent in offering
W-pI .. 155.2:3 when they find their own reality is e. here,
W-pI .. 157.9:2 instant which transcends all vision, e. this
W-pI .. 163.7:1 e. the insane have difficulty in believing it
W-pI .. 166.4:4 where he goes, and e. who he really is.
W-pI .. 166.9:3 e. think the miserable self you thought
W-pI .. 167.2:6 and pain, e. a little sigh of weariness, a
W-pI 167.10:5 we let imagined opposites to life abide e.
W-pI .. 169.6:1 speak nor write nor e. think of this at all.
W-pI .. 170.6:3 ask if the demands are sensible or e. sane.
W-pI .. 181.4:3 thought that, e. if you should succeed,
W-pI 182.11:3 He has e. come to ask your help in letting
W-pI .. 183.1:5 are, e. within a world that does not know;
W-pI .. 183.1:5 e. though you have not remembered it.
W-pI 186.14:4 form you can fulfill your function e. here,
W-pI .. 192.3:1 cannot e. be conceived of in the world. It
W-pI .. 194.3:3 In no one instant can one e. die. And so
W-pI .. 194.3:4 from sadness, pain and e. death itself.
W-pI .. 195.2:3 Nor could the e. partly sane refuse to take
W-pI .. 195.8:6 to love by being loving, e. as your Self.
W-pI .. 196.6:5 its foolishness, or e. see that it is there, so
W-pI .. 199.8:5 increase of joy your practice brings e. to it
W-pII . 251.1:3 before I needed not, and did not e. want.
W-pII . 253.1:2 myself. E. in this world, it is I who rule my
W-pII . 273.1:2 we are content and e. more than satisfied
W-pII . 300.1:1 before they are possessed, or e. grasped.
W-pII . 334.1:2 dreams are gone e. while they are woven
W-pII . 345.1:3 *E. here, it takes a form which can be*
W-pII . 355.1:4 *it. E. now my fingers touch it. It is very close.*
M-1 .......... 1:6 God e. if he does not yet believe in Him.
M-2 .......... 3:6 or e. the form in which you will learn it.
M-2 .......... 4:1 past e. the possibility of remembering.
M-3 .......... 2:6 friends. E. at the level of the most casual
M-3 .......... 5:5 They may e. be quite hostile to each other
M-3 .......... 5:7 who falter and may e. seem to fail. No
M-4 ........II.2:3 one at one with himself can e. conceive of
M-4 .... VIII.1:8 E. so, the teacher of God is willing to
M-5 .... III.1:11 is. If they e. suspected it, they would be
M-6 .......... 1:7 the patient might e. try to destroy himself
M-10 ......... 1:6 e. the same person classifies the same
M-12 ......... 1:4 sees himself as a body, or e. as in a body.
M-12 ......... 3:3 all, and e. they cannot communicate His
M-14 ....... 2:11 be destroyed nor attacked nor e. touched.
M-15 ......... 3:1 with lack of appreciation and e. contempt
M-16 ....... 11:9 hour, and e. every minute and second,
M-17 ......... 4:4 too mild to be e. clearly recognized. Or it
M-17 ......... 8:7 Once this is e. dimly grasped, the way is
M-18 ......... 4:2 senses e. the faintest hint of irritation in
M-19 ......... 2:7 Yet e. these, whose splendor reaches
M-20 ......... 4:5 remember e. faintly now what happiness
M-21 ......... 2:2 E. when they seem most abstract, the
M-23 ......... 1:2 E. the most advanced of God's teachers
M-24 ......... 5:8 Yet e. this much is not required of the
M-25 ......... 1:5 Yet nothing he can do can compare e. in
M-25 ......... 5:1 E. those who no longer value the material
C-2 ........... 3:5 And yet there is an answer e. here.
C-2 ........... 8:4 and e. make the question meaningless?
C-3 ........... 7:2 E. the wished-for can become unwelcome.
P-in .......... 1:6 but e. then it is always some change in his
P-1............ 3:4 is sometimes e. willing to "sacrifice" his
P-2...........II.1:1 necessary to be religious or e. to believe in
P-2..........II.1:3 E. in this, complete consistency is not
P-2........ III.3:2 It is e. possible for the result to look like
P-2........ III.3:8 or talk to him or e. know of his existence.
P-2........ IV.9:6 of danger, to be attacked and e. killed.
P-2..........V.6:9 may e. seem to be a worsening and not a
P-3...........I.3:5 need you as much, and perhaps e. more,

| | |
|---|---|
| P-3 ......... II.3:1 | E. this the Holy Spirit can use, and will |
| P-3 ......... II.8:6 | E. those who have begun to understand |
| P-3 ........ III.1:3 | E. an advanced therapist has some earthly |
| P-3 ...... III.5:10 | they do this, a light goes out e. in Heaven. |
| S-1 ......... II.1:4 | appeal to God, or e. involve belief in Him. |
| S-1 ........ III.1:6 | goals, until it reaches e. up to God. |
| S-1 ........ III.6:6 | can be quite clearly recognized e. in this. |
| S-1 ........ IV.2:4 | is likely at first that what is asked for e. by |
| S-1 ........ IV.2:5 | E. together you may ask for things, and |
| S-1 ........ IV.3:1 | E. the joining, then, is not enough, if |
| S-2 .........in.1:2 | step, or e. to attempt to climb at all. |

## evening 21

| | |
|---|---|
| W-pI.......1.4:1 | a day each, preferably morning and e.. |
| W-pI.....32.3:1 | the morning and e. by repeating the idea |
| W-pI.....33.1:2 | to the morning and e. applications. In |
| W-pI.....34.2:2 | the morning and one in the e. are advised |
| W-pI.....50.5:1 | ten minutes, twice today, morning and e., |
| W-pI...92.11:1 | Morning and e. we will practice thus. |
| W-pI......111.h | For morning and e. review: |
| W-pI......112.h | For morning and e. review: |
| W-pI......113.h | For morning and e. review: |
| W-pI......114.h | For morning and e. review: |
| W-pI......115.h | For morning and e. review: |
| W-pI......116.h | For morning and e. review: |
| W-pI......117.h | For morning and e. review: |
| W-pI......118.h | For morning and e. review: |
| W-pI......119.h | For morning and e. review: |
| W-pI......120.h | For morning and e. review: |
| W-pI.122.10:1 | Morning and e. do we gladly give a |
| WpI rVI.in.1:2 | Besides the time you give morning and e., |
| W-pII..232.1:4 | *me. As e. comes, let all my thoughts be still of* |
| W-pII..346.2:1 | And when the e. comes today, we will |
| M-16..........5:2 | quiet time should be fairly early in the e., |

## evenly 2

| | |
|---|---|
| W-pI.....31.3:4 | to let the stream move on e. and calmly, |
| W-pI.....36.2:2 | Try to distribute them fairly e., and make |

## evens 1

| | |
|---|---|
| W-pI...101.2:5 | form that e. the account they owe to God. |

## event 14

| | |
|---|---|
| T-14......XI.3:8 | attempt to understand any e. or anything |
| T-20... VIII.5:7 | There is no problem, no e. or situation, |
| T-24......III.3:1 | or an e. that you did not anticipate upsets |
| T-25......III.6:5 | turned to an e. which justifies his love. He |
| T-29......IV.4:8 | you have assigned; some goal which an e., |
| W-in..........5:2 | with any person, situation or e., total |
| W-pI.......4.4:1 | by the central figure or e. it contains; for |
| W-pI.......5.1:1 | or e. you think is causing you pain. Apply |
| W-pI.....20.5:3 | any situation, person or e. that upsets you |
| W-pI.....34.6:4 | *this situation, personality or e.] with peace.* |
| W-pI.....38.6:2 | In that e., use the more specific form in |
| W-pI.....46.7:4 | In that e., tell him silently: *God is the Love* |
| W-pI.....71.2:2 | external circumstance or e. were changed, |
| W-pII.......9.4:1 | The Second Coming is the one e. in time |

## events 22

| | |
|---|---|
| T-21....... II.3:1 | God be merely driven by e. outside of him |
| T-21..... II.10:3 | serving as a cause of the e. and feelings its |
| T-27... VIII.3:3 | and e. wherein its "hero" finds itself, the |
| T-27... VIII.4:2 | and out of places and e. that it contrives. |
| T-28.........I.4:2 | Yet this is not a memory of past e., but |
| T-29....... II.7:7 | health, and with e. that seem to alter it. |
| T-30.....VII.3:1 | can endow e. with stable meaning. But it |
| T-30.....VII.4:5 | And so you offer it to all e., and let them |
| T-30.....VII.6:5 | your ability to see relationships among e.. |
| W-pI.....34.3:2 | situations, "offending" personalities or e., |
| W-pI.....35.7:2 | personalities and e. in which you figure |
| W-pI.....39.7:1 | e. or personalities you associate with |
| W-pI.....43.8:1 | various situations and e. that may occur, |
| W-pI.....70.7:5 | possessions, in various situations and e., |
| W-pI.135.15:3 | obtained from past e. and previous beliefs |
| W-pI.135.18:1 | knew that everything that happens, all e., |
| W-pI...158.7:5 | circumstance, all happenings and all e., |
| W-pI...167.9:3 | are substanceless, and all e. are nowhere. |
| W-pI...184.3:1 | the world becomes a series of discrete e., |
| W-pI...193.3:4 | with different circumstances and e.; with |
| W-pI...193.6:3 | which give you power over all e. that seem |
| M-4 .....I.A.4:5 | learning to understand that all things, e., |

## eventual 1

| | |
|---|---|
| T-26... VIII.2:7 | loss. You see e. salvation, not immediate |

## eventually 3

| | |
|---|---|
| T-2........ III.3:6 | E. everyone begins to recognize, however |
| T-3......IV.3:11 | you must e. choose to heal the separation. |
| W-pI.....41.1:1 | Today's idea will e. overcome completely |

## ever 182

*See also* ever-increasing, ever-present, ever-tightening

| | |
|---|---|
| T-3......... II.1:7 | is impossible. No one has e. lived who has |
| T-4......... II.1:1 | how the mind could e. have made the ego. |
| T-4..... II.11:10 | It is as true now as it e. was or ever will be, |
| T-4..... II.11:10 | It is as true now as it ever was or e. will be, |
| T-4........ III.3:7 | of this can e. fully believe in the ego again. |
| T-4........ III.7:1 | idea you e. had that opposes knowledge. |
| T-5........ IV.1:8 | Nothing that is not good was e. created, |
| T-5........ IV.8:3 | and every loving thought you e. had. I |
| T-6......... II.6:6 | You cannot change it now or e.. It is |
| T-6........ IV.2:6 | raised the first question that was e. asked, |
| T-7......... II.7:8 | free, because nothing discordant e. enters |
| T-7......... V.7:6 | device that was e. given him for change. |
| T-8...........I.3:3 | peace, and the only one you need e. make. |
| T-8........ VI.8:1 | but one you should e. ask of yourself;– |
| T-9...........I.1:1 | beliefs the human mind has e. made. It |
| T-9.........I.14:1 | possible, and nothing else will e. be. This |
| T-9......... II.1:1 | Everyone who e. tried to use prayer to |
| T-9......... II.3:3 | will e. be one that would increase fear. It |
| T-9........ IV.4:9 | They are as sensible now as they e. were, |
| T-10...... IV.5:5 | Nothing but the laws of God has e. been, |
| T-10...... IV.5:5 | been, and nothing but His Will will e. be. |
| T-11....... II.5:4 | Think like Him e. so slightly, and the little |
| T-11...... VI.4:7 | This is as true now as it will e. be, for the |
| T-11...... VI.4:9 | in the beginning, is now and e. shall be, |
| T-11..... VII.2:1 | that the Son of God e. had is eternal. The |
| T-12...... VI.3:3 | This gives it the only reality it will e. have. |
| T-13...... III.2:8 | and much stronger than it will e. be, is |
| T-13... VII.13:4 | for His sight is e. on the journey's end, |
| T-13... VIII.6:5 | miracle that e. was is God's most holy |
| T-13....... X.8:5 | that he e. thought his Father loved him |
| T-13... X.11:11 | *his Father that no guilt has e. touched him.* |
| T-13..... X.12:1 | No illusion that you have e. held against |
| T-13...... XI.2:7 | Nothing destructive e. was or will be. The |
| T-13.... XI.3:13 | so deep that no dream in this world has e. |
| T-14....... II.2:2 | This is the hardest lesson you will e. learn |
| T-14....... II.7:4 | What else could e. be, or ever was? This |
| T-14....... II.7:4 | What else could ever be, or e. was? This |
| T-14...... III.6:1 | No penalty is e. asked of God's Son |
| T-14...... III.9:5 | larger than anything you e. dreamed of. |
| T-14.... III.15:8 | that He could e. let His Son drop from the |
| T-14...... IV.4:4 | God will not fail, nor e. has in anything. |
| T-14...... IV.8:5 | and nothing you have e. felt apart from |
| T-14...... IV.8:5 | apart from Him resembles it e. so faintly. |
| T-14...... XI.3:5 | Nothing you have e. learned can help you |
| T-14...... XI.7:3 | not meet, if he but turn to Him e. so little. |
| T-14.... XI.14:6 | With your perfection e. in His sight, He |
| T-15...... III.2:4 | form of littleness that can e. content you. |
| T-15...... VI.7:7 | in full communication with all that e. was |
| T-15..... VII.3:5 | will be why it was you e. wanted it. You |
| T-15... VIII.4:3 | Nothing that e. was created but is yours. |
| T-15...... IX.7:5 | the only truth that you could e. want. All |
| T-15...... XI.9:5 | the only relationship they e. had, and ever |
| T-15...... XI.9:5 | they ever had, and e. want to have. |
| T-16....... II.9:1 | not solved for you, nor will you e. do so. |
| T-16.... III.5:10 | real has e. left the mind of its creator. And |
| T-16..... V.11:7 | never completed, nor e. will be completed |
| T-16..... V.17:1 | the easiest decision that e. confronted you |
| T-16... VII.12:1 | *are no illusions, and where none can e. enter* |
| T-17........II.1:2 | In no fantasy have you e. seen anything so |
| T-17........II.1:5 | that made your heart sing with joy has e. |
| T-17........II.3:1 | This step, the smallest e. taken, is still the |
| T-17........II.4:3 | Nothing will e. change; no shifts nor |
| T-17........II.7:5 | that there could e. be need of salvation? |
| T-17...... III.6:8 | be unwilling e. to lose the sight of it again. |
| T-17...... III.8:5 | all the truth the past could e. offer to the |
| T-17..... VII.9:5 | in which you enter, or will e. enter. And |
| T-18.........I.4:4 | and life to death, was all you e. made. |
| T-18.........I.4:6 | relationship that you have e. made is part |
| T-18.........I.9:6 | error has not entered here, nor e. will. |
| T-18........II.6:1 | Holy Spirit, e. practical in His wisdom, |
| T-18... III.4:15 | For you desire the only thing you e. had, |
| T-18... III.4:15 | the only thing you ever had, or e. were. |
| T-18... VI.8:11 | you. There is nothing else, anywhere or e. |
| T19. IV.A.16:1 | and a softly joyous whispering is e. heard. |
| T-20........II.8:5 | nor have you e. failed entirely to hear. |
| T-20....... V.6:3 | All that it e. held or will ever hold is here |
| T-20....... V.6:3 | ever held or will e. hold is here right now. |
| T-21.........I.9:6 | Nothing will e. be as dear to you as is this |
| T-21...... III.4:3 | is His direction; the only one He e. sees. |
| T-21... VII.12:6 | if he sees his happiness as e. changing, |
| T-22.........I.5:7 | Nor will it e. be made understandable by |
| T-22........II.6:4 | to do what holds no hope of e. being done |
| T-23.........I.3:1 | the ego, or yourself and it, will e. meet. |
| T-23...... IV.8:6 | happiness could e. suffer change of any |
| T-23...... IV.8:8 | touch of doubt can e. mar your certainty? |
| T-24.........I.3:1 | All that is e. cherished as a hidden belief, |
| T-24...... III.4:7 | is it possible the two can e. be the same, |
| T-24.... IV.3:12 | it. Yet what comfort has e. been in them, |
| T-25........II.1:6 | there is no exception, nor will there e. be. |
| T-25........II.2:6 | seek for hope where none is e. found. |
| T-25........II.7:4 | this face was e. darkened because you saw |
| T-25...... IV.5:3 | bird that e. sang will sing again in you. |
| T-25...... IV.5:4 | every flower that e. bloomed has saved its |
| T-25..... VII.3:7 | every Thought God e. had is an illusion. |
| T-26...... III.4:2 | the last comparison that he will e. make; |
| T-26....... V.2:1 | Nothing is e. lost but time, which in the |
| T-26....... V.3:6 | time was gone, for that was all it e. was. |
| T-26... VII.15:8 | thus it was created, and thus will it e. be. |
| T-26...... IX.4:4 | grow e. brighter as each one comes home. |
| T-27.........I.5:7 | his madness bid him do was e. done, or |
| T-27.........I.5:7 | ever done, or e. had effects of any kind. |
| T-27.........I.5:8 | he laid upon his heart was e. justified, and |
| T-27.........I.5:8 | and no attack can e. touch him with the |
| T-27........II.6:7 | last trumpet that the world will e. hear. |
| T-27...... III.7:1 | and nothing that the eyes have e. seen or |
| T-27...... IV.3:4 | a single, simple question is e. asked. The |
| T-27... VII.13:2 | No other cause it has, nor e. will. Nothing |
| T-27.... VIII.3:1 | of every dream the world has e. had. The |
| T-27.... VIII.5:1 | of all the dreams the world has e. had? Is |
| T-29.... VIII.4:9 | take no form in which he e. will be real. |
| T-30........I.17:3 | and gives it all effects that it will e. have. |
| T-30......II.1:10 | And not one Thought that God has e. had |
| T-30.........II.2:3 | else that e. should be called by freedom's |
| T-30...... III.8:7 | light grew dimmer or less perfect e. was. |
| T-30...... IV.7:3 | you forgive all things that no one e. did; |
| T-30.... IV.8:11 | him no single thing that he could e. want. |
| T-30....... V.9:3 | ahead is all you e. wanted in your heart. |
| T-30..... V.10:4 | *cost of pain, nor was it e. paid by you alone.* |
| T-30...... VI.3:6 | And this is all the world can e. give. It |
| T-30.... VIII.2:8 | in Heaven or on earth could e. alter. But |
| T-31.........I.3:1 | e. doubt the power of your learning skill. |
| T-31.........I.7:7 | safety you can make that e. will succeed. |
| T-31........I.12:1 | instant, and forget all things we e. learned |
| T-31........I.13:1 | good that e. crossed your mind of anyone. |
| T-31.........II.8:2 | all thought of what you e. learned before, |
| T-31...... IV.7:1 | Think not that happiness is e. found by |
| T-31..... V.11:4 | go, if either one were e. raised to doubt. |
| T-31...... VI.3:5 | Be not concerned how this could e. be. |
| T-31... VII.10:6 | to save from every concept that he e. held. |
| W-pI.....23.1:1 | only way out of fear that will e. succeed. |
| W-pI......29.3:7 | how you could e. have found it difficult. |
| W-pI......39.4:1 | to every question that was e. asked, is |
| W-pI......44.6:1 | can stand aside from the ego by e. so little |
| W-pI......66.9:7 | consider also whether it was e. reasonable |
| W-pI......66.9:7 | from anything the ego e. proposed. Yet |
| W-pI......68.4:5 | If you succeed even by e. so little, there |

W-pI.....68.4:5 never be a problem in motivation **e.** again
W-pI.....94.1:3 all the thoughts that this world **e.** held are
W-pI...106.4:4 **e.** dreamed or wished for in your dreams.
W-pI...109.2:5 everyone who **e.** came and yet will come
W-pI...121.1:3 hopes of **e.** finding quietness and peace.
W-pI...124.6:1 No miracle can **e.** be denied to those who
W-pI.124.10:3 thankfully aware no time was **e.** better
W-pI...130.9:4 that your eyes alone have **e.** seen before.
W-pI...132.2:2 you think or **e.** thought or yet will think.
W-pI...132.8:3 loose it from all things you **e.** thought it
W-pI...132.8:4 replace all thoughts you **e.** held of death.
W-pI.132.14:1 all the idle thoughts we **e.** held about it,
W-pI.135.18:3 blessing shine in every step you **e.** took.
W-pI.135.24:2 you will but wonder why you **e.** thought
W-pI...137.9:3 from everything that **e.** caused you pain.
W-pI.137.15:2 foolish thoughts that **e.** were imagined.
W-pI...152.8:4 then will be all that there **e.** was, eternally
W-pI...165.2:2 have you **e.** been apart from it an instant.
W-pI...182.3:7 for Heaven. All he **e.** made was hell.
W-pI.185.12:5 that **e.** seemed to take the place of truth.
W-pI...189.7:4 belief you **e.** learned before from anything
W-pI.190.11:1 make the only choice that **e.** can be made;
W-pI...195.6:2 And we rejoice that no exceptions **e.** can
W-pI.195.10:1 time by more than you could **e.** dream of.
W-pI...197.9:8 that He has **e.** ceased to offer thanks to
W-pI...198.6:3 joy that **e.** can be found upon this earth.
W-pI.198.11:6 and everything you **e.** thought you made
W-pII .231.1:3 *Your Love the only thing I seek, or* **e.** *sought.*
W-pII .231.1:4 *nothing else that I could* **e.** *really want to find*
W-pII .234.1:4 Nothing has **e.** happened to disturb the
W-pII .252.1:2 is any light that I have **e.** looked upon. Its
W-pII .281.1:4 *If* **e.** *I am sad or hurt or ill, I have forgotten*
W-pII .....9.4:2 For every one who **e.** came to die, or yet
W-pII ...10.3:1 and all effects they **e.** seemed to have. To
W-pII .344.1:3 *I found an empty place where nothing* **e.** *was*
Wfl........in.6:5 And more than that can no one **e.** have,
M-10 .........4:3 right, without **e.** realizing you were wrong
M-12 .........1:6 are joined with God's forever and **e.**. His
M-22 .........4:3 but it is rarely if **e.** consistently applied to
P-2.......VII.4:3 This confusion is rarely if **e.** in awareness,
P-2.......VII.6:2 way can **e.** doubt the power that is in him.
P-2.......VII.9:8 of pathways that can **e.** lead to peace. O
P-3........II.4:11 only message that any two should **e.** give
S-1........III.4:4 an illusion of escape **e.** brought a prisoner
S-2...........I.4:8 **e.** think you can see sin in anyone except
S-2........III.5:1 only thing you **e.** ask when help is needed

## ever-increasing 1

T-14....... V.7:7 And you will find **e.** confidence in your

## ever-present 1

W-pII .308.1:8 and love. And love is **e.**, here and now.

## ever-tightening 1

W-pI...153.3:3 to be no break nor ending in the **e.** grip of

## Everlasting 1

*everlasting*

T-20....VI.10:5 behind and resting in the **E.** Arms. Love's

## everlasting 24

*Everlasting*

T-2.....VII.5:14 but have **e.** life" needs only one slight
T-24.... II.13:3 safe from God and safe for conflict **e.**.
T-25.........I.1:7 whole and pure and worthy of His **e.** Love.
T-29.......III.4:4 he walks through darkness to the **e.** light.
T-29....... V.8:6 all dreams, unto the peace of **e.** life.
W-pI...124.2:3 disappear, and death give place to **e.** life.
W-pI.124.12:2 *and my Self, in* **e.** *holiness and peace.*
W-pI...134.5:4 If you sin, your guilt is **e.**. Those who are
W-pI...136.9:2 so the body is more powerful than **e.** life,
W-pI...151.8:3 rejoicing in His perfect, **e.** sinlessness.
W-pI.159.10:8 to our unlost and **e.** sanctity in God.
W-pI...165.2:7 Eternity and **e.** life shine in your mind,
W-pII .....3.5:5 was made to die can be restored to **e.** life.
W-pII .....4.4:4 and loves him with an **e.** Love which his
W-pII .261.1:7 In Him is **e.** peace. And only there will I
W-pII .264.1:7 *today, to be at peace within Your* **e.** *Love.*
W-pII ...12.3:4 all there is surrounding him is **e.** peace,
W-pII .337.1:1 me perfect peace, eternal safety, **e.** love,
W-pII .348.1:2 *Surrounding me is* **e.** *Love. I have no cause*
W-pII .351.1:5 *my* **e.** *Comforter and Friend beside me, and*
M-20 .........2:8 just slips away, and in its place is **e.** quiet.
M-28 .........4:1 for the time of **e.** things is now at hand.
S-3...........I.5:3 of the world or to the **e.** Love of God.
S-3........IV.7:2 embrace of **e.** Love and perfect peace. My

## every 584

T-1 ........ V.2:4 recognizes that **e.** collapse of time brings
T-1 ........ V.4:1 **e.** member of the family of God must
T-2 ....... VI.9:7 **E.** instant it is creating. It is hard to
T-2 ...... VII.6:2 **e.** one must be an integral part of the
T-3 ........I.3:11 I have made **e.** effort to use words that are
T-3 ....... IV.3:8 You have **e.** reason to feel afraid as you
T-3 ........ V.7:6 "less." At **e.** level it involves selectivity.
T-3 ....... VI.7:4 **E.** symptom the ego makes involves a
T-3 ...... VII.1:1 **E.** system of thought must have a starting
T-4 ..........I.5:1 **E.** good teacher hopes to give his
T-4 ....... III.7:1 your mind to give up **e.** idea you ever had
T-4 ....... IV.2:3 **e.** case you have thought wrongly about
T-4 ........ V.1:5 ego has **e.** reason to do this, according to
T-4 ...... VII.3:4 communication with **e.** aspect of creation,
T-4 ...... VII.3:7 created **e.** mind by communicating His
T-4 ...... VII.8:6 **E.** mind that is changed adds to this joy
T-5 ........in.2:7 **E.** part benefits, and benefits equally.
T-5 ........in.3:1 being blessed by **e.** beneficent thought of
T-5 ..........I.1:2 gladness calls to **e.** part of the Sonship to
T-5 ....... IV.3:1 **E.** loving thought held in any part of the
T-5 ....... IV.3:1 any part of the Sonship belongs to **e.** part.
T-5 ....... IV.4:3 irresistibly drawn to **e.** mind created by
T-5 ....... IV.8:3 and **e.** loving thought you ever had. I have
T-5 ........ V.6:3 answering it **e.** minute and every second,
T-5 ........ V.6:3 answering it every minute and **e.** second,
T-5 ........ V.7:5 **E.** disordered thought is attended by guilt
T-5 ....... VI.2:9 and will oppose it at **e.** possible moment
T-5 ....... VI.2:9 possible moment and in **e.** possible way.
T-5 ....... VI.9:2 **E.** loveless thought must be undone, a
T-5 ..... VI.10:3 and **e.** witness to guilt in God's creations
T-5 ..... VI.12:6 you of this in **e.** passing moment of time,
T-5 ...... VII.2:5 not learned that **e.** mind God created is
T-6 .........I.12:1 reawakening of **e.** Son of God is necessary
T-6 .........II.4:2 **E.** ability of the ego has a better use,
T-6 ........II.12:3 by recognizing Himself in **e.** mind, and
T-6 ....... III.1:1 **e.** idea begins in the mind of the thinker.
T-6 ..... III.1:10 it. **E.** lesson you teach you are learning.
T-6 ..... V.A.2:7 the body. **E.** miracle demonstrates this.
T-6 ..... V.B.1:9 and **e.** thought system centers on what
T-6 ..... V.C.1:2 teaches you to judge **e.** thought you allow
T-7 ...... IV.2:3 because **e.** part of creation is of one order.
T-7 ........ V.9:8 It literally believes that **e.** time it deprives
T-7 ...... VII.2:7 **E.** response you make is determined by
T-7 ...... VII.2:8 must determine **e.** response you make.
T-7 ...... VII.7:3 the inestimable worth of **e.** Son of God,
T-7 ...... VII.7:4 **E.** attack is a call for His patience, since
T-7 ...VIII.1:11 **E.** mind must project or extend, because
T-7 ...VIII.1:11 that is how it lives, and **e.** mind is life.
T-7 ....... IX.5:3 The creations of **e.** Son of God are yours,
T-7 ....... IX.5:3 since **e.** creation belongs to everyone,
T-7 .........X.8:6 **E.** miracle is thus a lesson in truth, and by
T-7 ....... XI.2:1 Grace is the natural state of **e.** Son of God
T-7 ....... XI.4:3 **E.** Son who returns to the Kingdom with
T-8 ...........I.3:1 **E.** response to the ego is a call to war, and
T-8 .........II.8:6 natural response of **e.** Son of God to the
T-8 ....... III.6:8 And **e.** holy encounter in which you enter
T-8 ....... III.7:8 and your brother from **e.** imprisoning
T-8 ....... VI.1:3 **E.** gain in our strength is offered for all, so
T-8 .....VIII.2:5 **e.** end that the ego has accepted as its own
T-8 ....... IX.6:5 even though it makes **e.** effort to induce it
T-9 ..........I.3:8 He is merely making **e.** possible effort,
T-9 ........ V.2:3 **E.** healer who searches fantasies for truth
T-9 ...... VII.1:6 **E.** minute and every second gives you a
T-9 ...... VII.1:6 Every minute and **e.** second gives you a
T-9 ...... VII.7:8 He judges **e.** belief you hold in terms of
T-9 ..... VIII.4:5 The ego will make **e.** effort to recover and
T-10 ...... in.2:7 **E.** response you make to everything you
T-10 ..... III.7:3 Yet **e.** Son of God has the power to deny
T-10 .......V.7:4 He calls to you from **e.** part of the Sonship
T-11 .......I.10:5 **E.** symptom of sickness and fear arises
T-11 .......II.1:2 **E.** attack is a step away from this, and
T-11 .......II.1:2 and **e.** healing thought brings it closer.
T-11 .......II.2:4 **E.** miracle that you accomplish speaks to
T-11 .......II.2:5 **E.** healing thought that you accept, either
T-11 .......II.2:6 In **e.** hurtful thought you hold, wherever
T-11 ..... IV.3:3 **E.** altar to God is part of you, because the
T-11 .......V.5:1 **E.** idea has a purpose, and its purpose is
T-11 .....V.14:3 It makes real **e.** mistake it perceives, and
T-11 .....V.15:1 does make **e.** attempt to demonstrate it,
T-11 .....V.18:1 **E.** brother you meet becomes a witness
T-11 .....V.18:4 **E.** brother has the power to release you, if
T-11 ... VI.10:6 whole power of God is in **e.** part of Him,
T-11 .... VII.2:1 **E.** loving thought that the Son of God
T-11 ...VIII.5:5 The Holy Spirit will answer **e.** specific
T-11 ...VIII.9:4 **e.** thought is as loving as the Thought of
T-12 ........I.3:3 **E.** loving thought is true. Everything else
T-12 ........I.7:4 **E.** appeal you answer in the Name of
T-12 ........I.7:5 then, hear **e.** call for help as what it is, so
T-12 ......I.10:1 than to recognize, in **e.** defense against it,
T-12 .......II.5:6 straight at **e.** image that rises to delay you
T-12 ..... III.4:3 and **e.** request of a brother is for you.
T-12 .......V.7:4 **E.** legitimate teaching aid, every real
T-12 .......V.7:4 legitimate teaching aid, **e.** real instruction
T-12 .......V.7:4 and **e.** sensible guide to learning will be
T-12 ..... VI.4:5 of Christ for **e.** Son of God who sleeps. In
T-12 ..... VI.6:1 **E.** child of God is one in Christ, for his
T-12 .... VII.1:6 In **e.** child of God His blessing lies, and in
T-12 .... VII.3:2 for miracles violate **e.** law of reality as this
T-12 .... VII.3:3 it. **E.** law of time and space, of magnitude
T-12 ...VIII.1:3 You attack the real world **e.** day and every
T-12 ...VIII.1:3 every day and **e.** hour and every minute,
T-12 ...VIII.1:3 every day and every hour and **e.** minute,
T-12 ...VIII.4:3 A Voice will answer **e.** question you ask,
T-13 ..... III.7:6 For He will heal **e.** little thought you have
T-13 ..... IV.5:7 of release that **e.** brother offers you *now.*
T-13 .....V.7:12 For **e.** Son of God is given you to whom
T-13 ..... VII.4:3 to it from **e.** part of this strange world you
T-13 .. VII.16:1 you have already overcome **e.** temptation
T-13 .. VII.17:2 until I have lifted **e.** voice with mine. And
T-13 .. VII.17:8 Give thanks to **e.** part of you that you
T-13 ...VIII.2:2 **E.** aspect is whole, and therefore no
T-13 ...VIII.5:2 **E.** miracle you offer to the Son of God is
T-13 ...VIII.5:3 Though **e.** aspect *is* the whole, you cannot
T-13 ...VIII.5:3 know this until you see that **e.** aspect is
T-13 ...VIII.6:4 And **e.** miracle you do contains them all,
T-13 ...VIII.6:4 **e.** aspect of reality you see blends quietly
T-13 ...VIII.8:4 in **e.** miracle you offered to your brothers,
T-13 ..... IX.6:2 In **e.** condemnation that you offer the Son
T-13 .......X.9:9 and He offers mercy to **e.** child of God, as
T-13 .....X.14:4 was. **E.** reaction you experience will be so
T-13 ..... XI.5:1 and **e.** trace of guilt that His dear Son has
T-14 ..... III.6:2 **E.** chance given him to heal is another
T-14 ..... III.9:5 **E.** decision is made for the whole Sonship
T-14 ... III.12:4 true. Peace abides in **e.** mind that quietly
T-14 ... III.13:3 it. **E.** decision you undertake alone but
T-14 ... III.14:7 not and He will make **e.** decision for you,
T-14 ... III.16:3 all knowledge lies behind **e.** decision the
T-14 ..... IV.6:4 in answering your **e.** question what to do.
T-14 .......V.4:3 it. Protect his purity from **e.** thought that
T-14 .......V.5:4 release from suffering of **e.** kind lie in it.
T-14 .......V.6:5 And **e.** teaching that points to this points
T-14 .... VII.6:1 bring to Him **e.** secret you have locked
T-14 .... VII.6:2 Open **e.** door to Him, and bid Him enter
T-14 ...VIII.1:2 All this lies hidden in **e.** darkened place,
T-14 .......X.6:3 the same response to **e.** call for help. It
T-14 .....X.6:13 it offers everything to **e.** call from anyone.
T-14 .....X.11:4 **E.** interpretation you would lay upon a
T-14 ..... XI.4:3 already learned for **e.** child of light by
T-14 ..... XI.4:7 **E.** dark lesson that you bring to Him Who
T-14 ..... XI.5:5 **E.** dark lesson teaches this, in one form or
T-14 ..... XI.9:4 And **e.** fear or pain or trial you have has
T-14 . XI.10:10 He offers you a miracle with **e.** one you let
T-14 ... XI.13:6 fill **e.** mind that so makes room for Him.

T-15......III.3:3 E. decision you make stems from what
T-15......III.4:8 The power of God will support e. effort
T-15......III.5:2 Holy Spirit e. time you make a decision.
T-15......III.5:3 For e. decision you make does answer this
T-15......III.5:7 E. decision you make is for Heaven or for
T-15......III.6:1 untouched by e. little gift the world of
T-15......IV.1:3 holy instant is this instant and e. instant.
T-15......IV.2:6 Give over e. plan you have made for your
T-15......IV.3:6 E. allegiance to a plan of salvation apart
T-15......IV.4:2 and gladly give over e. plan but His. For
T-15......IV.4:5 try to give over e. plan you have accepted
T-15......IV.8:1 E. thought you would keep hidden shuts
T-15.......V.4:6 e. relationship becomes a lesson in love.
T-15.....V.10:5 it. God loves e. brother as He loves you;
T-15.....VII.1:7 e. relationship on which the ego embarks
T-15.....VII.6:1 e. relationship the ego makes is based on
T-15... VIII.1:3 He must side with e. sign or token of your
T-15... VIII.5:4 God would respond to e. need, whatever
T-15... VIII.6:2 by removing e. element of disagreement,
T-15......IX.3:2 to give up e. use the ego has for the body,
T-15.......X.2:5 and e. sacrifice you ask of yourself you ask
T-16.......II.3:3 of the whole in e. part is perfectly natural,
T-16......IV.6:3 E. illusion is one of fear, whatever form it
T-16....IV.10:2 E. illusion you accept into your mind by
T-16....IV.10:3 E. fantasy, be it of love or hate, deprives
T-16....IV.11:6 and in e. fantasy that rises to delay you,
T-16.......V.9:2 of littleness lies in e. special relationship,
T-16.....V.13:3 For e. idol that you raise to place before
T-16.....V.15:5 Yet for e. learning that would hurt you,
T-16.....VII.1:5 past? E. such choice is made because of
T-17......III.3:4 of value. E. step taken in the making, the
T-17......III.7:4 hidden it may be, in e. relationship. For
T-17......IV.2:7 E. special relationship you have made is a
T-17......IV.3:3 E. special relationship you have made has
T-17......IV.7:4 E. defense operates by giving gifts, and
T-17......IV.9:8 enclose the whole, complete in e. aspect.
T-17....IV.16:6 It shines in e. part of Him, as in the whole
T-17.....V.13:4 You reinforce this e. time you attack your
T-17......VI.4:2 will therefore make e. effort to overlook
T-17.....VII.5:1 E. situation in which you find yourself is
T-17.....VII.6:6 and accomplish e. miracle needed for its
T-17...VII.8:11 in e. aspect and complete in every part.
T-17...VII.8:11 in every aspect and complete in e. part.
T-17.....VII.9:5 to e. situation in which you enter, or will
T-17.....VII.9:6 e. situation was thus made free of the past
T-17...VII.10:1 Him Who walks with you in e. situation.
T-17... VIII.1:1 of what e. situation is meant to be. The
T-17... VIII.1:2 has given it is also given to e. situation. It
T-17... VIII.1:4 of e. relationship and every situation,
T-17... VIII.1:4 of every relationship and e. situation,
T-17... VIII.1:5 whole. Faith has accepted e. aspect of the
T-17... VIII.2:4 it encompass e. situation and bring you
T-17... VIII.3:1 want to make a holy instant of e. situation
T-17... VIII.5:8 See only this in e. situation, and it will be
T-18.........I.4:6 and e. special relationship that you have
T-18...... I.13:2 and reaches out to e. broken fragment of
T-18......III.1:3 and e. fantasy that seemed to bring a light
T-18.......V.3:1 reborn and blessed in e. holy instant you
T-18....VI.12:4 in e. case, you join it without reservation
T-18.....VII.2:5 And e. instant that you spend without
T-18.....VII.8:3 of e. busy doing on which you are sent.
T-18... VIII.7:7 its happiness and deep content to e. part.
T-18......IX.9:4 of e. evil thought you laid upon it. Here
T-18....IX.14:2 cannot know until e. perception has been
T-19.........I.2:1 E. situation, properly perceived, becomes
T-19.........I.2:2 e. demand your ego would make of him.
T-19.......II.5:3 necessarily protected with e. defense at its
T-19......III.4:7 E. mistake *must* be a call for love. What,
T-19......IV.1:6 will quietly extend to e. aspect of your life,
T19... IV.A.5:2 this barrier, is e. miracle contained. There
T19... IV.A.6:8 E. miracle is but the end of an illusion.
T19. IV.A.11:2 and cherish e. scrap of evil and of sin that
T19... IV.C.4:2 damned by its maker and lamented by e.
T19... IV.C.5:7 the awareness of e. mind which heard His
T19... IV.C.9:3 from e. thought that would attack it, and
T19. IV.C.10:5 perfect safety, e. miracle you will perform
T19... IV.D.5:1 E. obstacle that peace must flow across is
T19. IV.D.15:3 as God created e. living thing and loves it.
T-20.......II.2:4 e. gift it offers depends on what it wants.
T-20.......II.5:4 from e. altar now is yours as well as His.
T-20......III.1:3 E. adjustment is therefore a distortion,
T-20......IV.7:3 the hands of e. two who enter here to rest.
T-21.......II.3:3 is the determiner of e. situation in which
T-22........I.11:9 as Both are drawn to e. holy relationship,
T-22.......II.1:5 E. illusion carries pain and suffering in
T-22.......II.4:2 are different from each other in e. way, in
T-22.......II.4:2 way, in e. instance and without exception.
T-22.....II.12:7 E. illusion brought to its forgiveness is
T-22......IV.5:1 E. mistake you and your brother make,
T-22......IV.6:3 as e. obstacle was finally surmounted that
T-22.......V.4:5 hymn of praise to its Creator that e. heart
T-22......VI.5:6 And e. empty place in Heaven that you fill
T-22......VI.8:9 He will use e. one of them for peace. Nor
T-22....VI.11:3 see that e. sin and every condemnation
T-22....VI.11:3 see that every sin and e. condemnation
T-22....VI.14:7 And e. thought in one brings gladness to
T-22....VI.14:9 anywhere in it, for e. thought is like itself.
T-23.......in.3:6 And e. error disappeared because they
T-23.......II.4:1 chaos, dear indeed to e. worshipper of sin
T-23.......II.7:4 e. aspect seems to be at war with Him,
T-23....IV.1:12 E. illusion is an assault on truth, and
T-23....IV.1:12 and e. one does violence to the idea of
T-24.......in.2:1 to question e. value that you hold. Not
T-24.......in.2:4 is neutral. E. one has the power to dictate
T-24.........I.6:3 not help him reach it in e. way you could,
T-24.........I.8:4 E. twinge of malice, or stab of hate or
T-24.......I.8:10 does not change with e. seeming blow,
T-24.......II.5:3 To e. special one a different message, and
T-24.......II.9:2 and e. vestige of the fear of God will melt
T-24......III.3:7 and turn and whirl about with e. breeze.
T-24.......V.9:2 And e. doubt must be about yourself.
T-24......VI.4:5 in e. way and every circumstance, in all
T-24......VI.4:5 in every way and e. circumstance, in all
T-24....VI.11:3 itself, with e. entry shut against intrusion,
T-24....VI.11:3 and e. window barred against the light.
T-25.........I.2:4 And e. body that you look upon reminds
T-25......IV.3:7 and e. wish to hurt and kill and die, will
T-25......IV.5:2 E. leaf that falls is given life in you. Each
T-25......IV.5:4 e. flower that ever bloomed has saved its
T-25......VI.5:6 and e. function of this world completed
T-25...VII.1:11 His creation, when it opposes it in e. way?
T-25.....VII.3:7 e. Thought God ever had is an illusion.
T-25...VII.11:5 For e. little gain must someone lose, and
T-25... VIII.9:7 And e. one that you accept brings joy to
T-25. VIII.12:2 You need not perceive, in e. circumstance
T-25. VIII.14:1 life eternal, joyous and complete in e. way
T-25......IX.3:6 And e. error is a perception in which one,
T-26.........I.4:5 e. sacrifice demands that they be separate
T-26.........I.5:4 add a limitless supply to e. meager scrap
T-26.........I.7:1 Yet e. instant can you be reborn, and
T-26.......II.1:3 E. problem is the same to Him, because
T-26.......II.2:1 from e. problem that you think you have.
T-26.......II.4:2 E. problem is an error. It does injustice to
T-26.......II.8:5 and e. bolt and barrier that seems to hold
T-26......III.2:5 e. thought made pure and wholly simple.
T-26......III.3:6 and e. choice has been already made.
T-26......III.6:5 this one lies the undoing of e. illusion, not
T-26......IV.2:2 and e. bird sings of the joy of Heaven.
T-26......IV.3:7 And here does e. light of Heaven come, to
T-26.......V.5:5 in e. judgment and in all belief in sin, is
T-26.....V.12:4 to illusion for all time and e. circumstance
T-26.....V.13:1 Each day, and e. minute in each day, and
T-26.....V.13:1 day, and e. instant that each minute holds
T-26.....VII.8:5 joy this world denies to e. aspect of God's
T-26...VII.10:6 And e. miracle is possible the instant that
T-26...VII.15:4 In e. miracle all healing lies, for God gave
T-26...VII.16:6 e. wish to hurt he chooses death instead
T-26...VII.16:7 Yet e. instant offers life to him because
T-26... VIII.2:3 believe that trust would settle e. problem
T-26......IX.4:4 up e. living thing and lifts it into Heaven,
T-26.......X.2:7 belongs to e. living thing along with you.
T-26.......X.5:8 denied to e. living thing upon the earth.
T-27.........I.2:2 But e. pain you suffer do you see as proof
T-27.........I.5:5 brother, who will see that e. scar is healed
T-27.........I.5:5 and e. tear is wiped away in laughter and
T-27.........I.7:5 to believe that e. stolen scrap of pleasure
T-27.....II.13:1 overlook the fact that e. thought extends
T-27......III.6:9 the place of e. learning aid will merely *be.*
T-27......IV.1:1 and is e. problem quietly resolved. In
T-27......IV.2:1 and e. problem can be answered *now.* Yet
T-27....VIII.1:3 It takes the central place in e. dream,
T-27....VIII.3:1 theme of e. dream the world has ever had.
T-27..VIII.11:4 the cause of e. form of sorrow and of pain.
T-27..VIII.12:1 Who knows that e. one is like the rest. He
T-28.......I.12:1 thanks for e. quiet instant given Him. For
T-28........II.6:1 e. dream that anyone has dreamed within
T-28......II.10:1 Like e. lesson that the Holy Spirit
T-28......II.12:2 next to e. dream of pain and suffering, of
T-28......II.12:7 of e. step in the descent to separation,
T-28......III.4:3 the seeds of pestilence and e. form of ill,
T-28......IV.8:2 does He hold out to e. separate piece that
T-28......IV.9:2 and perfect, lies in e. one of them. And
T-28......IV.9:7 And e. aspect of the Son of God is just the
T-28......IV.9:7 of God is just the same as e. other part.
T-28.......V.5:7 but you, who put together e. jagged piece,
T-28.......V.6:6 For it fills e. place and every time, and
T-28.......V.6:6 For it fills every place and e. time, and
T-28......VI.4:3 with e. brother who would walk apart.
T-28......VI.4:6 in consciousness is e. pledge to sickness.
T-28......VI.6:7 Yet God reminds him of it e. time he does
T-29........II.6:1 have life and e. living thing be part of him
T-29......IV.2:2 For e. dream is but a dream of fear, no
T-29......IV.3:3 or assault must be the theme of e. dream,
T-29......IV.5:1 role to e. figure which the dream contains
T-29......IV.6:5 He asks for help in e. dream he has, and
T-29.......V.3:5 And e. thought of love you offer him but
T-29.......V.5:6 their hold on e. vain illusion of the world.
T-29.......V.8:1 core of fear in e. dream that has been kept
T-29.......V.8:2 it was for this that e. dream was made.
T-29.....VII.3:5 This is the purpose e. idol has, for this the
T-29....VIII.9:8 also give the same to e. living thing as well
T-29....VIII.9:9 And thus is e. living thing a part of you, as
T-30.......in.1:3 alone; your willingness to practice e. step.
T-30.......in.1:4 will help a little, e. time it is attempted.
T-30.........I.1:4 become preoccupied with e. step you take
T-30......III.3:1 for e. idol lies the yearning for completion
T-30.......V.3:6 Yet is he glad to wait till e. hand is joined,
T-30.......V.3:6 and e. heart made ready to arise and go
T-30......VI.7:6 within and find escape from e. idol there.
T-30.....VII.1:6 it. For only if its aim could change with e.
T-30.....VII.1:6 which is different e. time you think of it.
T-30.....VII.1:7 script you write for e. minute in the day,
T-30.....VII.1:8 and e. meaning shifts accordingly.
T-30.....VII.2:7 with e. meaning shifting as they change.
T-31.........I.3:1 in e. form you could conceive of them,
T-31.........I.4:3 have continued, taking e. step, however
T-31.........I.4:4 And e. lesson that makes up the world
T-31.........I.6:6 taught to you in e. moment of each day,
T-31.......I.12:1 e. preconception that we hold of what
T-31.......I.12:4 Let e. image held of everyone be loosened
T-31........II.3:6 And e. friend or enemy becomes a means
T-31......II.11:7 e. step is made in certainty and sureness
T-31......III.1:3 and to e. situation that occurs. Learn this,
T-31......IV.3:1 There is no choice where e. end is sure.
T-31......IV.7:4 And e. road that leads the other way will
T-31......IV.9:4 e. road was made to separate the journey
T-31.......V.3:4 e. day a hundred little things make small
T-31.......V.9:6 what you should do in e. circumstance?
T-31.....V.16:3 be some confusion e. time there is a shift,
T-31.....V.17:5 When e. concept has been raised to doubt
T-31.....VII.8:2 To e. part of true creation has the Lord of
T-31...VII.10:6 to save from e. concept that he ever held.
T-31....VIII.3:2 you. In e. difficulty, all distress, and each
T-31....VIII.4:2 and let Christ's strength prevail in e.
T-31....VIII.4:2 circumstance and e. place you raised an
T-31....VIII.6:1 and so is e. living thing you look upon,
T-31....VIII.6:3 this, and you will see all pain, in e. form,
T-31....VIII.6:5 be, remembering that e. choice you make
T-31..VIII.10:7 the world with e. choice they make. For
T-31..VIII.11:1 to e. brother who would join with me in
W-in..........6:2 to e. situation in which you find yourself,
W-pI.......9.2:5 to lighten e. corner of the mind that has
W-pI.....16.2:3 E. thought you have contributes to truth
W-pI.....16.3:1 you also recognize that e. thought you
W-pI.....16.4:4 E. thought that occurs to you, regardless
W-pI.....20.5:1 today, attempting to do so e. half hour.
W-pI.....23.1:4 fail. E. thought you have makes up some

W-pI.....26.7:3 Then go over **e.** possible outcome that has
W-pI.....27.3:2 It should be used at least **e.** half hour, and
W-pI.....27.3:3 might try for **e.** fifteen or twenty minutes.
W-pI.....29.1:4 it explains **e.** idea we have used thus far,
W-pI.....38.1:2 It is beyond **e.** restriction of time, space,
W-pI.....39.4:1 answer to **e.** question that was ever asked,
W-pI.....39.8:1 search your mind for **e.** thought that
W-pI.....40.1:3 Once **e.** ten minutes would be highly
W-pI.....44.2:4 making vision possible in **e.** circumstance
W-pI.....44.7:2 letting go **e.** kind of interference and
W-pI.....45.5:3 There is **e.** reason to feel confident that
W-pI.....47.1:1 you have **e.** reason to be apprehensive,
W-pI.....47.3:1 God is your safety in **e.** circumstance. His
W-pI.....47.3:2 situations and in **e.** aspect of all situations
W-pI.....47.6:2 in **e.** respect and in all circumstances.
W-pI.....50.1:1 answer to **e.** problem that will confront
W-pI.....50.3:2 It will lift you out of **e.** trial, and raise you
W-pI.....51.3:6 it. But there is **e.** reason to let it go, and
W-pI.....54.4:6 power to change **e.** mind along with mine
W-pI.....56.4:2 Behind **e.** image I have made, the truth
W-pI.....56.4:3 Behind **e.** veil I have drawn across the face
W-pI.....62.3:1 Remember that in **e.** attack you call upon
W-pI........63.h peace to **e.** mind through my forgiveness.
W-pI.....63.1:1 have the power to bring peace to **e.** mind!
W-pI.....63.3:4 *peace to* **e.** *mind through my forgiveness. I*
W-pI.....64.4:4 **e.** time you choose whether or not to
W-pI.....67.1:6 We will make **e.** effort today to reach this
W-pI.....70.4:1 to do just the opposite, making **e.** attempt
W-pI.....72.5:6 **e.** grievance that you hold insists that the
W-pI.....74.7:5 A minute or two **e.** half an hour, with eyes
W-pI.....75.6:2 and clean of **e.** concept you have made.
W-pI.....75.9:2 Remind yourself **e.** quarter of an hour or
W-pI.....78.3:2 For **e.** grievance is a block to sight, and as
W-pI.....82.1:1 peace to **e.** mind through my forgiveness.
W-pI.....93.8:1 for the first five minutes of **e.** waking hour
W-pI.....94.5:1 for the first five minutes of **e.** hour, at
W-pI.....94.5:8 Make **e.** effort to do the hourly exercises
W-pI.....95.4:1 use of the first five minutes of **e.** waking
W-pI...95.10:2 Creator, at one with **e.** aspect of creation,
W-pI...95.11:2 *my Creator, at one with* **e.** *aspect of creation,*
W-pI...96.11:5 **E.** time you spend five minutes of the
W-pI.....97.4:3 all His strength to **e.** little effort that you
W-pI.....97.4:4 calls through His Voice to **e.** living thing;
W-pI.....97.8:3 Listen for His assurance **e.** time you speak
W-pI.....98.4:1 that they learned and **e.** gain they made.
W-pI.....98.6:1 you your full release from pain of **e.** kind,
W-pI.....98.9:6 exchanging **e.** instant of the time you
W-pI...100.4:2 increases **e.** light that shines in Heaven, so
W-pI.100.10:7 **e.** time you tell yourself you are essential
W-pI...101.4:2 and attempt in **e.** way he can to drown
W-pI...107.4:3 always was, to be depended on in **e.** need,
W-pI.107.10:3 with **e.** gift you give of five small minutes,
W-pI...108.5:3 law which holds for **e.** kind of learning, if
W-pI...108.6:2 works, in **e.** circumstance where it is tried
W-pI...109.9:5 those passed by, to **e.** Thought of God,
W-pI...110.2:4 and **e.** change that time appears to bring
WpI. rIII.in1:2 will review two recent lessons **e.** day for
WpI. rIII.in2:1 as optimal each day and **e.** hour of the day
W-pI...121.1:3 that appear to threaten you at **e.** turn, and
W-pI...121.3:1 waken or to go to sleep, afraid of **e.** sound
W-pI.121.13:4 happiness to **e.** unforgiving mind, with
W-pI.121.13:5 **E.** hour tell yourself: *Forgiveness is the key*
W-pI...123.7:3 to you in terms of years for **e.** second;
W-pI...124.9:4 with **e.** minute like a diamond set around
W-pI...125.9:5 true. As **e.** hour passes by today, be still a
W-pI...126.9:3 from **e.** bar to what forgiveness means,
W-pI...127.8:1 from **e.** law in which you now believe.
W-pI.127.10:4 dawns unlike the past in **e.** attribute.
W-pI...128.7:3 little, **e.** time you let your mind escape its
W-pI...131.3:4 beyond the world and **e.** worldly thought,
W-pI...131.7:4 which is Heaven's opposite in **e.** way.
W-pI.132.10:2 To free the world from **e.** kind of pain is
W-pI.132.11:5 creation is unlike the world in **e.** way.
W-pI.132.14:5 world this day from **e.** one of our illusions
W-pI.135.18:3 blessing shine in **e.** step you ever took.
W-pI.135.22:1 and from **e.** thought that blocks the truth
W-pI...136.6:1 **E.** defense takes fragments of the whole,
W-pI.137.15:4 be forgot as **e.** hour of the day slips by,
W-pI.138.12:3 As **e.** hour passed, we have declared our
W-pI.139.11:6 in truth, how much a part of us is **e.** mind,
W-pI.151.11:2 and **e.** happening that seems to touch on
W-pI.151.12:2 the world, past **e.** witness for unholiness,
W-pI...154.7:4 gain by **e.** message that they give away.
W-pI...155.5:1 road that leads away from loss of **e.** kind,
W-pI...157.3:3 will learn to do increasingly, as **e.** lesson,
W-pI...158.1:5 It was given as well to **e.** living thing, for
W-pI...158.2:8 Son are one will come in time to **e.** mind.
W-pI...158.7:5 it looks on everyone, on **e.** circumstance,
W-pI...161.4:2 **E.** mind contains all minds, for every
W-pI...161.4:2 contains all minds, for **e.** mind is one.
W-pI...163.8:5 death, and we renounce it now in **e.** form,
W-pI...165.8:3 His sureness lies beyond our **e.** doubt. His
W-pI...165.8:4 His Love remains beyond our **e.** fear. The
W-pI...166.2:4 but **e.** mind that looks upon the world
W-pI...166.7:2 defend against all reason, **e.** evidence, and
W-pI...168.4:3 and watch fear disappear from **e.** face as
W-pI...169.4:3 and speed its advent into **e.** mind that
W-pI...169.6:2 comes to **e.** mind when total recognition
WpI...rV.in5:2 **E.** step we take brings us a little nearer.
WpI.rV.in10:7 that it is free of all illusions **e.** time we say:
W-pI...183.2:2 and shelter you from **e.** worldly thought
W-pI...183.3:2 illusions. **E.** dream the world holds dear
W-pI...183.6:2 Become oblivious to **e.** name but His.
W-pI.184.12:4 **E.** gap is closed, and separation healed.
W-pI.184.15:6 *the truth You give, in place of* **e.** *one of them.*
W-pI...185.9:7 gone with **e.** twist and turning of the road
W-pI...185.9:7 forms which shift and change with **e.** step
W-pI.185.12:5 the gifts of God apart from **e.** dream that
W-pI.185.14:1 our desires with the need of **e.** heart, the
W-pI.185.14:1 the need of every heart, the call of **e.** mind
W-pI...186.1:1 day take all arrogance away from **e.** mind.
W-pI.186.13:4 which answer **e.** need His Son perceives,
W-pI...189.2:2 safe from **e.** form of danger and of pain. It
W-pI...189.7:2 or bad, of **e.** thought it judges worthy,
W-pI...189.9:8 Through **e.** opened door His Love shines
W-pI...191.3:3 snatch from your fingers **e.** scrap of hope,
W-pI...192.9:4 **E.** time you feel a stab of anger, realize
W-pI.193.13:4 To **e.** apprehension, every care and every
W-pI.193.13:4 **e.** care and every form of suffering, repeat
W-pI.193.13:4 every care and **e.** form of suffering, repeat
W-pI...194.8:3 **e.** living creature not respond with healed
W-pI...195.6:3 We give thanks for **e.** living thing, for
W-pI...196.4:2 taking **e.** step in its appointed sequence,
W-pI...197.5:1 God blesses **e.** gift you give to Him, and
W-pI...197.5:1 you give to Him, and **e.** gift is given Him,
W-pI...199.5:1 idea, and practice it today and **e.** day.
W-pI...199.5:2 it a part of **e.** practice period you take.
W-pI.200.11:8 home, and draw still nearer **e.** time we say
WpI rVI.in.1:4 and to the world from **e.** form of bondage
WpI rVI.in.3:7 And we repeat it **e.** time the hour strikes,
W-pI...203.1:2 *deliverance from* **e.** *thought of evil and of sin*
W-pI...207.1:3 *but turn to Him, and* **e.** *sorrow melts away,*
W-pII.....2.1:4 God's Word is given **e.** mind which thinks
W-pII.....2.2:4 power to heal the split became a part of **e.**
W-pII.232.1:2 *Let* **e.** *minute be a time in which I dwell with*
W-pII.232.2:1 is as **e.** day should be. Today, practice the
W-pII.236.2:1 *and closed today to* **e.** *thought but Yours. I*
W-pII....254.h Let **e.** voice but God's be still in me.
W-pII.....5.3:2 revert to fear, where **e.** dream is born. For
W-pII.264.1:2 *I hear, and* **e.** *hand that reaches for my own.*
W-pII.267.1:2 to me in **e.** heartbeat and in every breath;
W-pII.267.1:2 to me in every heartbeat and in **e.** breath;
W-pII.267.1:2 breath; in **e.** action and in every thought.
W-pII.267.1:2 breath; in every action and in **e.** thought.
W-pII.267.1:7 and **e.** one is answered by His Voice,
W-pII.270.1:6 *and* **e.** *thought except Your Own is gone.*
W-pII.....6.4:3 and peace has come to **e.** Son of God,
W-pII.271.1:1 Each day, each hour, **e.** instant, I am
W-pII.286.1:4 *In You is* **e.** *choice already made. In You has*
W-pII.286.1:5 *In You has* **e.** *conflict been resolved. In You is*
W-pII.292.1:4 we see, and **e.** situation that we meet. Yet
W-pII.292.2:2 *us for* **e.** *problem that we can perceive; for*
W-pII.292.2:2 *for* **e.** *trial we think we still must meet.*
W-pII.297.2:1 *how faithfully is* **e.** *step in my salvation set*
W-pII.....9.4:2 For **e.** one who ever came to die, or yet
W-pII...10.4:1 is as merciful as **e.** step in His appointed
W-pII.315.1:1 come to me with **e.** passing moment. I am
W-pII.315.2:1 *me today and* **e.** *day from every Son of God.*
W-pII.315.2:1 *me today and every day from* **e.** *Son of God.*
W-pII.316.1:1 As **e.** gift my brothers give is mine, so
W-pII.316.1:1 give is mine, so **e.** gift I give belongs to me
W-pII.316.1:3 His grace is given me in **e.** gift a brother
W-pII...11.3:2 creation is His Will complete in **e.** aspect,
W-pII...11.3:2 making **e.** part container of the whole. Its
W-pII.322.1:3 abides in **e.** gift that I receive of Him. And
W-pII.322.1:4 And **e.** dream serves only to conceal the
W-pII.324.1:2 *to take, and* **e.** *step in my appointed path. I*
W-pII.345.1:2 *And* **e.** *one I give returns to me, reminding*
W-pII....348.h And in **e.** need That I perceive, Your grace
W-pII...14.4:1 a world redeemed from **e.** thought of sin.
W-pII.354.1:1 *of time, and wholly free of* **e.** *law but Yours. I*
W-pII.356.1:5 *Your Name replaces* **e.** *thought of sin, and*
W-pII....357.h Truth answers **e.** call we make to God,
W-ep.........4:1 as Guide through **e.** difficulty and all pain
M-in..........1:6 process; it goes on **e.** moment of the day,
M-1...........3:1 There is a course for **e.** teacher of God.
M-4.....I.A.7:8 what he really wants in **e.** circumstance.
M-8...........1:2 with **e.** other in order to be recognized. A
M-16.........1:5 that his role should be, this day and **e.** day
M-16.......11:9 their training, **e.** day and every hour, and
M-16.......11:9 their training, every day and **e.** hour, and
M-16.......11:9 hour, and even **e.** minute and second,
M-19.........3:3 Selectively and arbitrarily is **e.** concept of
M-20.........2:2 in **e.** way it is totally unlike all previous
M-22.........1:8 and **e.** miracle has been accomplished. To
M-28.........2:6 Christ's face is seen in **e.** living thing, and
C-2............5:1 The ego's opposite in **e.** way,–in origin,
P-2..........I.4:2 to pass for **e.** "patient" on the face of this
P-2..........II.7:2 teacher uses one approach to **e.** pupil. On
P-2.........VII.1:9 And **e.** therapist must learn to heal from
P-3..........II.1:3 in **e.** relationship in which he enters? Yet
P-3..........II.5:1 from **e.** meeting of patient and therapist.
P-3.........III.8:5 is in **e.** circumstance and at all times.
S-1..........II.8:1 God is the goal of **e.** prayer, giving it
S-1........IV.3:5 from **e.** choice that stood for a mistake.
S-1..........V.2:6 Self, and this it sees in **e.** meeting, where
S-1..........V.2:6 where it gladly joins with **e.** Son of God,
S-1..........V.3:1 of things, of bodies, and of gods of **e.** kind
S-2.........I.10:2 you must choose between them **e.** instant
S-2..........II.8:1 and comparisons of **e.** kind are death. For
S-2.........III.3:2 the way to make of **e.** call a help to you, as
S-3..........I.2:4 Death stares at them as **e.** moment goes
S-3.........III.5:5 Now the cause of **e.** malady has been
S-3........IV.9:7 dear is **e.** gift to Me that you have made,

### everyone 313

T-1.........I.40:1 miracle acknowledges **e.** as your brother
T-1.......III.7:2 By being united this mind goes out to **e.**,
T-1.......IV.3:7 when you were created, just as **e.** was.
T-1.........V.2:4 **e.** closer to the ultimate release from time,
T-1.........V.2:6 **e.** recognizes that he has everything,
T-1.........V.3:3 and all His gifts are freely given to **e.** alike.
T-2.........II.3:4 *for.* **E.** defends his treasure, and will do so
T-2.......III.3:1 acceptance of the Atonement by **e.** is only
T-2.......III.3:6 limit. Eventually **e.** begins to recognize,
T-2.......VI.9:1 **E.** experiences fear. Yet it would take very
T-2......VII.3:4 You have been fearful of **e.** and everything
T-2.....VIII.3:6 It simply means that **e.** will finally come
T-2.....VIII.4:3 **E.** will ultimately look upon his own
T-3.....VI.10:2 of spirit. **E.** is free to refuse to accept his
T-3.....VI.10:3 is. The problem **e.** must decide is the
T-4.........II.2:1 **E.** makes an ego or a self for himself,
T-4.........II.2:2 also makes an ego for **e.** else he perceives,
T-4.......VI.7:5 of real recognition makes **e.** your brother
T-5.......II.10:8 **E.** will answer the Call of the Holy Spirit,
T-6........in.2:2 **E.** teaches, and teaches all the time. This
T-6.......IV.3:3 **E.** has called upon Him for help at one
T-6.......IV.3:4 which means that **e.** has the answer *now.*
T-6.....V.B.1:9 This is because **e.** identifies himself with
T-7.......IV.3:1 does not want to teach **e.** all it has learned
T-7.........V.3:1 Healing is the one ability **e.** can develop
T-7.........V.4:3 healer that **e.** else does not share with him
T-7.......V.11:6 Spirit, Who sees the altar of God in **e.**,
T-7....VII.10:5 See His abundance in **e.**, and you will
T-7.......IX.5:3 yours, since every creation belongs to **e.**,
T-7.......XI.1:2 This is His Will for **e.** because He speaks

W-pI...197.7:3 To **e.** who lives will Christ yet come, for
W-pI...197.7:3 come, for **e.** must live and move in Him.
W-pI...200.5:3 and **e.** made free of your mistakes and
W-pI...200.8:1 Peace is the bridge that **e.** will cross, to
W-pII.245.1:3 *It sheds its light on* **e.** *I meet. I bring it to the*
W-pII.247.2:1 *So would I look on* **e.** *today. My brothers are*
W-pII.269.1:5 *in which* **e.** *shows me the face of Christ, and*
W-pII.270.2:1 and through them peace will come to **e.**.
W-pII.....7.1:2 His gift to **e.** who turns to Him for truth.
W-pII.315.1:5 And **e.** who finds the way to God becomes
W-pII.338.1:2 thought is **e.** released at last from fear.
W-pII.339.1:5 **E.** will receive what he requests. But he
W-pII...14.3:4 We look on **e.** as brother, and perceive all
W-pII...14.5:1 His Word to **e.** whom He has sent to us,
Wfl........in.2:2 It is His way that **e.** must travel in the end,
M-in..........4:4 **E.** who follows the world's curriculum,
M-in..........4:4 and **e.** here does follow it until he changes
M-1...........2:9 **E.** will answer in the end, but the end can
M-3...........1:4 practical point of view he cannot meet **e.**,
M-3...........1:4 meet everyone, nor can **e.** find him.
M-10.........3:4 all the effects of his judgments on **e.** and
M-10.........3:5 judgment would be wholly fair to **e.** on
M-10.........4:9 on **e.** and everything involved in any way.
M-10.......4:10 And He is wholly fair to **e.**, for there is no
M-11.........1:1 This is a question **e.** must ask. Certainly
M-11.........3:3 And **e.** believes in what he made, for it
M-15.......1:10 the world that **e.** may hear this Judgment
M-25.........3:7 has any powers that are not available to **e.**
C-2............9:1 which asks of **e.** one question only: "Are
P-1............1:3 but **e.** can reconsider its causes and learn
P-1............1:4 correctly. God has given **e.** a Teacher
P-1............3:1 **E.** who needs help, regardless of the form
P-2......... II.8:3 the same requirement salvation asks of **e.**.
P-2.......VII.1:2 the end, **e.** is both. He who needs healing
P-3...........I.1:1 **E.** who is sent to you is a patient of yours.
P-3...........I.1:5 that you know what to offer **e.** who comes
P-3......... II.1:2 profession be one in which **e.** is engaged?
P-3......... II.1:3 which **e.** is both patient and therapist in
P-3........ III.1:7 last illusion be accepted by **e.** everywhere.
P-3...... III.6:11 **e.** must gain a blessing without cost.
S-1...........I.6:1 a level of prayer that **e.** can attain as yet.
S-1...........I.7:6 can be shared because it receives for **e.**.
S-1......... II.2:5 **E.** prays without ceasing. Ask and you
S-1......... V.3:8 to **e.** who comes to join in prayer with you
S-2...........I.5:4 You would be slave to **e.**, for what he does
S-3........ IV.5:8 grievous loss become the lot of **e.** on earth

## everyone's 6

T-1...........I.7:1 Miracles are **e.** right, but purification is
T-25..... VII.9:5 for he has a special part in **e.** escape. He
T-26..... II.6:10 For what you give to Him is **e.**, and by
W-pI.127.12:5 *no love but God's and yours and mine and* **e.**.
M-26.........1:2 His awareness is in **e.** memory, and His
M-26.........1:2 and His Word is written on **e.** heart. Yet

## everything 543

*See also* more-than-everything

T-1...........I.3:3 sense **e.** that comes from love is a miracle.
T-1..........I.24:3 **E.** else is your own nightmare, and does
T-1.........IV.3:5 they have **e.** have no needs of any kind.
T-1.........IV.3:6 of the Atonement is to restore **e.** to you;
T-1.........IV.3:7 You were given **e.** when you were created,
T-1......... V.2:6 When everyone recognizes that he has **e.**,
T-2...........I.2:3 **E.** God created is like Him. Extension, as
T-2......... V.7:7 **E.** that results from spiritual awareness is
T-2........VI.1:3 My control can take over **e.** that does not
T-2........VI.1:3 while my guidance can direct **e.** that does,
T-2.......VII.3:4 You have been fearful of everyone and **e.**.
T-2.......VII.5:1 Nothing and **e.** cannot coexist. To believe
T-2.......VII.5:3 other. Fear is really nothing and love is **e.**.
T-2.....VII.5:10 is possible between **e.** and nothing. Time
T-2......VIII.1:4 **e.** you create is necessarily a matter of will
T-2......VIII.5:6 and at any time to **e.** you have made, and
T-2....VIII.5:10 When **e.** you retain is lovable, there is no
T-3...........I.6:1 innocent mind has **e.** and strives only to
T-3...........I.7:5 however, perfectly aware of **e.** that is true.
T-3......... II.1:3 or **e.** and nothing as joint possibilities.
T-3.........II.3:4 The miracle perceives **e.** as it is. If nothing
T-3.........II.6:3 to accept what is true in **e.** you perceive,
T-3....... IV.2:5 can be sure of. **E.** else *is* open to question.
T-3........ V.6:3 those who have been forgiven have **e.**.
T-3........ V.9:6 The world believes that if anyone has **e.**,
T-3....... VI.4:1 very fearful of **e.** you have perceived but
T-3...... VII.2:6 in which **e.** is in direct opposition to God.
T-4..........I.7:3 you dispute this **e.** you do will be fearful,
T-4........I.12:1 you can do **e.** for the salvation of both.
T-4.....II.11:13 difference from **e.** else the mind can grasp
T-4....... III.9:2 *God has given you* **e.**. This one fact means
T-4....... III.9:5 that you both *have* **e.** and *are* everything.
T-4....... III.9:5 that you both *have* everything and *are* **e.**.
T-4....... IV.8:3 strength of God into **e.** you think and do.
T-4..... IV.11:7 attribute of **e.** that the living God created.
T-4........ V.5:7 **e.** you may want to learn has lasting value
T-4........ V.6:8 must learn to ask in connection with **e.**.
T-4...... VII.2:1 **E.** the ego perceives is a separate whole,
T-4...... VII.2:3 thought system, as is **e.** else it dictates. Its
T-4...... VII.2:7 specific ways to **e.** it perceives as related.
T-4...... VII.3:1 in the same way to **e.** it knows is true, and
T-4...... VII.3:3 that what is true is **e.** that God created. It
T-4...... VII.4:4 is in communication with **e.** that is real.
T-4...... VII.5:1 created beings who have **e.** individually,
T-4...... VII.5:6 irrelevant, because real creation gives **e.**,
T-4...... VII.5:8 the state of being the mind gives **e.** always
T-5..........I.1:8 is all. Having **e.**, spirit holds everything by
T-5..........I.1:8 everything, spirit holds **e.** by giving it,
T-5..........I.2:4 *E. is an idea. How, then, can giving and*
T-5....... III.5:4 **E.** of which the Holy Spirit reminds you is
T-5....... IV.1:3 reinterpret **e.** that you perceive as fearful,
T-5....... IV.2:5 **E.** that continues has already been born.
T-5....... IV.7:5 **E.** you think that is not through the Holy
T-5..... VI.10:4 Appeal **e.** you believe gladly to God's
T-5...... VII.4:3 for **e.** you made that is not in accord with
T-6........I.15:3 This is clearly the opposite of **e.** I taught.
T-6.........II.7:6 **E.** meets in God, because everything was
T-6.........II.7:6 **e.** was created by Him and in Him.
T-6.......II.10:2 it. Coming from God He uses **e.** for good,
T-6....... III.4:1 the exact opposite of **e.** the ego believes.
T-6....... III.4:8 **E.** you teach you are learning. Teach only
T-6....... IV.7:4 where **e.** lives in God without question.
T-6..... IV.10:3 **e.** need help and are therefore helpless.
T-6..... IV.11:3 and **e.** God created is faithful to His laws.
T-6..... V.A.1:3 **E.** is accomplished through life, and life is
T-6..... V.C.1:8 are in fundamental disagreement about **e.**
T-6... V.C.1:11 He protects it by rejecting **e.** that does not
T-6..... V.C.9:2 **E.** outside the Kingdom is illusion. When
T-6... V.C.10:1 entails a willingness to relinquish **e.** else.
T-7....... III.3:3 Because God's equal Sons have **e.**, they
T-7........ V.6:8 on. **E.** that is of God can be counted on,
T-7........ V.6:8 because **e.** of God is wholly real. Healing
T-7.... V.10:10 because only this is everywhere and in **e.**.
T-7.... V.10:11 It is **e.** because it encompasses all things
T-7....... VI.4:8 It must also deny **e.** this power gives you
T-7....... VI.4:8 this power gives you *because* it gives you **e.**
T-7....... VI.4:9 No one who has **e.** wants the ego. Its own
T-7...... VII.6:5 But love **e.** He created, of which you are a
T-7....... IX.2:4 God. **E.** He created is given all His power,
T-7.........X.1:2 which is total confusion about **e.**. If you
T-7.......X.3:10 On the contrary, you will be gaining **e.**. If
T-7.......X.5:11 betray, he believes that **e.** can betray him.
T-7.........X.6:9 **E.** has been given you by God's decision.
T-7....... XI.1:6 world perceives orders of difficulty in **e.**.
T-7....... XI.2:3 **E.** he does becomes a strain, because he
T-7..... XI.3:10 this, because they deny themselves **e.**.
T-7..... XI.3:11 to **e.** you see and touch and remember,
T-8..........I.6:2 who are in total disagreement about **e.**.
T-8.........II.3:7 is the undoing of **e.** the ego tries to teach.
T-8.........II.4:4 look beyond **e.** that would hold you back.
T-8....... III.7:1 because you are part of God, Who is **e.**.
T-8....... III.8:3 gives of Himself, and **e.** belongs to Him.
T-8....... IV.1:6 laws govern you because they govern **e.**.
T-8....... IV.1:8 because you are denying yourself **e.**.
T-8....... IV.2:1 a light into a world that does deny itself **e.**
T-8....... IV.2:2 this simply by dissociating itself from **e.**.
T-8..... IV.8:11 must be included in It, because It is **e.**.
T-8....... VI.4:1 squandered **e.** for nothing of any value,
T-8...... VII.2:2 Holy Spirit interprets **e.** you have made in
T-8..... VIII.5:3 This is the purpose of **e.** the ego does. Its
T-8..... VIII.5:4 aim is to lose sight of the function of **e.**.
T-8..... VIII.9:3 **E.** used in accordance with its function as
T-8..... VIII.9:4 **E.** used otherwise is. Do not allow the
T-8..... VIII.9:8 the natural state of **e.** when interpretation
T-8....... IX.1:2 He is the Answer to **e.**, because He knows
T-8....... IX.1:2 He knows what the answer to **e.** is. The
T-8....... IX.2:2 not. The reality of **e.** is totally harmless,
T-8....... IX.8:3 what I ask, and **e.** argues *for* your doing it.
T-9........I.10:6 Yet *you* can ask for **e.** of the Holy Spirit,
T-9........I.13:1 devotion to you created you devoted to **e.**,
T-9........I.13:3 Reality is **e.**, and you have everything
T-9........I.13:3 and you have **e.** because you are real. You
T-9.......II.12:3 Him nothing, and so you can share **e.**.
T-9....... III.8:1 The Holy Spirit forgives **e.** because God
T-9....... III.8:1 everything because God created **e.**. Do
T-9..... III.8:10 by learning how to look on **e.** without it.
T-9....... VI.3:8 **e.** for yourself because we are part of you,
T-9....... VI.3:8 of you, **e.** we do belongs to you as well.
T-9....... VI.7:6 **E.** else would be totally meaningless.
T-9...... VII.3:6 and wholly mistrustful of **e.** it perceives
T-9...... VII.4:4 you are. The ego is deceived by **e.** you do,
T-10...... in.2:4 is different because **e.** has always been.
T-10...... in.2:6 mind establishes **e.** that happens to you.
T-10...... in.2:7 to you. Every response you make to **e.** you
T-10...... in.3:7 because, being in God, you encompass **e.**.
T-10........I.1:4 **E.** that was created is therefore perfectly
T-10........I.2:4 instant you waken you realize that **e.** that
T-10........I.4:1 will remember **e.** the instant you desire it
T-10.......II.2:4 Give up gladly **e.** that would stand in the
T-10.......II.3:7 He will give you **e.** but for the asking.
T-10..... III.6:1 great appreciation for **e.** that God created
T-10... III.11:8 has **e.** to do with reality as you perceive it.
T-10..... IV.4:5 His. **E.** else is merely lawless and therefore
T-10..... IV.4:6 God Himself has protected **e.** He created
T-10..... IV.4:7 **E.** that is not under them does not exist.
T-10.......V.7:6 The Love of God is in **e.** He created, for
T-10......V.13:7 because His Fatherhood gave you **e.**. That
T-11.... in.3:10 and that **e.** of which you have been afraid
T-11...... in.4:3 you from our Father to offer you **e.** again.
T-11........I.6:5 **e.** He creates has the function of creating.
T-11........I.8:5 is. You must ask what God's Will is in **e.**,
T-11.......V.5:2 **E.** that stems from the ego is the natural
T-11.....V.13:3 contradictory approach of the ego to **e.**.
T-11.....V.13:5 attacks **e.** it perceives by breaking it into
T-11.....V.18:3 **E.** you perceive is a witness to the thought
T-11..... VI.6:3 The freedom to leave behind **e.** that hurts
T-11.... VII.1:2 the eternal, and **e.** you see is perishable.
T-11.... VII.3:8 Yet **e.** true *is* like Him. Perceiving only the
T-11... VIII.1:6 And then **e.** you made will be forgotten;
T-11... VIII.3:8 to question **e.** you learned of yourself, for
T-11... VIII.6:2 For what is yours is **e.**, and you share it
T-12........I.3:4 **E.** else is an appeal for healing and help,
T-12........I.8:7 and to regard **e.** else as an appeal for help,
T-12.....II.10:1 offer to the Holy Spirit **e.** you do not want
T-12..... III.7:5 **E.** you perceive as the outside world is
T-12..... III.8:3 real world, in which **e.** reflects the eternal.
T-12..... IV.6:4 treasure, you will sell **e.** else to purchase it
T-12..... IV.6:5 it, because you have sold **e.** else. Yet you
T-12.......V.9:5 **E.** else will be given you. For you really
T-12..... VI.6:6 you learn to apply it to everyone and **e.**,
T-12..... VI.7:5 where **e.** eternal in it has always been.
T-12.. VII.12:4 **E.** you behold without is a judgment of
T-12... VIII.4:3 will correct the perception of **e.** you see.
T-12... VIII.6:5 Him. **E.** you made has never been, and is
T-12... VIII.8:3 it. Its reality will make **e.** else invisible, for
T-13........I.4:5 already undone **e.** unworthy of the Son of
T-13... III.11:2 war he demanded **e.** and found nothing.
T-13.......V.4:3 private worlds, where **e.** is disordered,
T-13... VI.11:7 will **e.** remind you of your Father and His
T-13.... VII.7:2 God Himself, Who watches over him in **e.**
T-13.. VII.11:1 **E.** the ego tells you that you need will
T-13.. VII.12:6 He knows that **e.** you need is temporary,
T-13... VIII.1:7 that it is everywhere, just as it has **e.**, and
T-13... VIII.2:7 for the vision of Christ beholds **e.** in light.
T-13... VIII.3:8 of reality can be seen in **e.** and everywhere
T-13... VIII.4:4 is why Christ's vision looks on **e.** with love
T-13..... IX.4:1 brings a re-evaluation of **e.** you cherish,
T-13..... XI.3:7 In Heaven is **e.** God values, and nothing

| | |
|---|---|
| T-13......XI.3:9 | E. is clear and bright, and calls forth one |
| T-13....XI.11:1 | The Holy Spirit will undo for you e. you |
| T-14.........I.2:5 | And if you have and give and are e., and |
| T-14.........I.3:9 | knows it leads to nothing, for He knows e. |
| T-14........II.3:4 | *else is real, and e. beside it is not there. Let* |
| T-14........II.5:4 | will never learn how to make nothing e.. |
| T-14........II.6:1 | give e. you have learned to the Holy Spirit |
| T-14........II.8:4 | e. is clear, it is all holy. The quietness of |
| T-14........II.8:7 | everywhere, and His Son is in Him with e. |
| T-14....III.11:3 | gives you e. will simply offer it to you? He |
| T-14....III.11:6 | you are worthy of e. God wills for you. Do |
| T-14....III.12:2 | of the perfect purity of e. that He created, |
| T-14....III.12:6 | or where it lies, but ask the Holy Spirit e., |
| T-14....III.13:7 | decision to undo e. that would obscure |
| T-14....III.17:4 | with Him. In e. be led by Him, and do not |
| T-14....III.18:2 | with Him, and with e. that is within Him, |
| T-14....IV.10:5 | E. else that you have placed within your |
| T-14........V.1:9 | of value here, and e. of value there. Listen |
| T-14...V.10:11 | And e. you give to God is yours. Thus He |
| T-14......V.11:6 | for therein lies e. that makes it holy. |
| T-14......VI.3:8 | can live in light. E. else must disappear. |
| T-14......VI.7:6 | Yet if one means nothing and the other e., |
| T-14.....VII.1:5 | union, e. that is not real must disappear, |
| T-14.....VII.2:1 | out of e. that interferes with truth. Truth |
| T-14.....VII.5:8 | like e. you made, must be gently turned to |
| T-14.....VII.7:5 | the gentle fusing of e. into *one* meaning, |
| T-14... VIII.2:2 | E. that promises otherwise, great or small |
| T-14... VIII.4:7 | E. God created knows its Creator. For this |
| T-14......IX.3:1 | truth release you from e. that it is not. |
| T-14......IX.4:7 | Presence of Holiness lives in e. that lives, |
| T-14......X.6:13 | it offers e. to every call from anyone. |
| T-14.......X.7:2 | believe that e. else is nothing but a call for |
| T-14.....X.11:2 | for e. of Him is perfectly open and freely |
| T-14......XI.1:5 | it. E. you have taught yourself has made |
| T-14......XI.3:1 | how to escape forever from e. that you |
| T-14......XI.6:1 | from e. that you have taught yourself. |
| T-14......XI.6:4 | that e. you learned you do not want. Ask |
| T-14....XI.12:1 | and who have become willing to learn e., |
| T-15......III.1:5 | it. E. in this world is little because it is a |
| T-15....III.4:10 | that His Son be content with less than e.. |
| T-15....III.10:4 | remembering that e. I learned is yours. |
| T-15......IV.6:8 | to change nothing, but merely to accept e. |
| T-15......IV.8:3 | to let e. that interferes with it go forever?" |
| T-15.....VII.1:5 | wholly pure, everyone joined in it has e.. |
| T-15... VIII.1:2 | must use e. in this world for your release. |
| T-15......XI.3:1 | the Holy Spirit e. that would hurt you. Let |
| T-15......XI.7:6 | For communication embraces e., and in |
| T-16.........I.7:6 | He would share e. you give through Him. |
| T-16........II.8:6 | sure, and wholly kind to everyone and e.. |
| T-16........II.8:8 | will give you e. that makes for happiness. |
| T-16.......III.4:4 | Yet within you is e. you taught. What can |
| T-16......IV.2:2 | of love is without meaning if love is e.. |
| T-16......IV.2:6 | you on the other side, will give you e.. |
| T-16......IV.9:4 | is certain and where e. fails to satisfy. In |
| T-16........V.3:6 | e. here takes a direction exactly opposite |
| T-16......VI.7:2 | side, e. you see is grossly distorted and |
| T-16.....VII.3:3 | ego remembers e. you have done that has |
| T-16.....VII.6:6 | gentleness. E. is gone except the truth. |
| T-16.....VII.8:8 | e. the Holy Spirit teaches is to remind you |
| T-17.........I.5:7 | no order in reality, because e. there is true |
| T-17........II.2:2 | new, with e. sparkling under the open sun |
| T-17........II.2:3 | for e. has been forgiven and there are no |
| T-17........II.4:2 | for e. that has been used for learning will |
| T-17......IV.4:4 | holds within itself the truth about e.. And |
| T-17....IV.16:3 | gain e. by giving Him the power and the |
| T-17........V.1:2 | Like e. about salvation, the holy instant is |
| T-17......VI.4:2 | concentrate on e. that helps you meet it. |
| T-18.........I.2:8 | e. *seems* to come between the fragmented |
| T-18.........I.4:6 | it. E. you see reflects it, and every special |
| T-18.........I.6:4 | that a world in which e. is backwards and |
| T-18.........I.9:1 | He has taken charge of e. at your request, |
| T-18........II.3:4 | In dreams *you* arrange e.. People become |
| T-18.......III.8:7 | in which e. is radiant in the light. |
| T-18......IV.8:1 | it has been your decision to make e. that |
| T-18......IV.8:4 | E. God wills is not only possible, but has |
| T-18......VI.8:9 | it. It encompasses e.. It encompasses you |
| T-18... VIII.1:6 | idea? E. you recognize you identify with |
| T-18... VIII.5:3 | totally dependent on its one Creator for e. |
| T-18... VIII.8:1 | bodies, and reaches to e. created like itself |
| T-18. VIII.11:5 | Asking for e., you will receive it. And your |
| T-18......IX.3:4 | E. these messages relay to you is quite |
| T-18......IX.9:4 | e. is bright and shining with innocence, |
| T-18....IX.12:6 | transcend all learning that e. you learned |
| T-19........II.6:2 | in such a world could e. be upside down. |
| T-19......II.6:10 | and e. is brought to *it* for judgment. As a |
| T19... IV.A.8:5 | pervasive weakness, which extends to e.. |
| T19..IV.C.11:4 | And they may thus mean e. or nothing, |
| T19... IV.D.1:4 | Creator of life, the Source of e. that lives, |
| T19... IV.D.1:4 | e. that lies even beyond them would you |
| T-20........II.5:6 | that shines on e. He looks upon and loves. |
| T-20......IV.1:8 | are, the Holy Spirit merely gives e. to God |
| T-20......IV.8:8 | careless of e. except the only purpose that |
| T-20........V.6:5 | Here, then, is e.. Here is the loveliness of |
| T-20... VIII.6:1 | E. looked upon with vision falls gently |
| T-20... VIII.6:2 | end for e. He looks upon is always sure. |
| T-20... VIII.6:6 | any form and seeing it everywhere, in e.. |
| T-20... VIII.6:7 | and e. will stand condemned before you. |
| T-21.......in.1:10 | E. looked upon with vision is healed and |
| T-21.........I.4:9 | And e. they think is in it serves to remind |
| T-21.........I.8:1 | past e. you see and yet somehow familiar, |
| T-21.........I.8:4 | at all. The light expands and covers e., |
| T-21.........I.8:5 | Within it e. is joined in perfect continuity. |
| T-21........II.1:2 | the Holy Spirit for which He gives you e.; |
| T-21........II.2:5 | *And e. that seems to happen to me I ask for,* |
| T-21........II.4:3 | Give it away, and e. you see goes with it. |
| T-21......II.13:3 | grant that e. that seems to stand between |
| T-21... VIII.2:5 | looks on e. and sees it is the same. It sees |
| T-21... VIII.2:6 | ephemeral, for it desires e. be like itself, |
| T-22.........I.5:1 | along with e. that you can understand. |
| T-22.......II.3:8 | but e. in time can change with time. Yet if |
| T-22......III.4:3 | E. the body's eyes can see is a mistake, an |
| T-22......III.5:7 | distorted form of vision the outside of e., |
| T-22......IV.5:3 | e. that seems to rise between you both. So |
| T-22......V.1:12 | E. that needs defense you do not want, for |
| T-22........V.4:7 | Is it this tiny mouse or e. that God created |
| T-22......VI.6:7 | is your remembrance of e. that is eternal. |
| T-23.......in.2:2 | You will believe that e. you use for sin can |
| T-23.......in.3:3 | of the truth releases e. from the illusion of |
| T-23.......in.6:4 | and e. you once thought sinful now will |
| T-23.......I.10:6 | protecting you from e. that is not true. |
| T-23.......I.10:7 | e. is given those who would remember |
| T-23......IV.9:3 | For e. fought for on the battleground is of |
| T-23......IV.9:4 | that he has e. could seek for limitation, |
| T-23......IV.9:6 | What can conflict with e.? And what is |
| T-24.......in.2:5 | a conclusion based on e. that you believe. |
| T-24.........I.1:3 | Love offers e. forever. Hold back but one |
| T-24......II.10:6 | Not special, but possessed of e., including |
| T-24......III.4:4 | is attacked by e. that walks and breathes, |
| T-24.......IV.1:3 | E. else becomes your enemy; feared and |
| T-24....IV.3:15 | with an open door inviting e. that would |
| T-24......VI.5:6 | God in e. that lives and shares His Being. |
| T-24......VI.6:2 | It is His loveliness they see in e.. And it is |
| T-24.....VII.2:2 | all of creation, e. created and creating, |
| T-24.....VII.6:1 | The test of e. on earth is simply this; |
| T-25.......VI.1:1 | and e. they look on speaks of Him to the |
| T-25....VI.7:10 | Do this *one* thing, that e. be given you. |
| T-25.....VII.5:4 | For here is e. perceived as one, and no one |
| T-25.....VII.6:1 | Test e. that you believe against this one |
| T-25.....VII.6:1 | and understand that e. that meets this |
| T-25. VIII.10:1 | To him who merits e., how can it be that |
| T-25. VIII.13:7 | more or less is not aware that he has e.. |
| T-25......IX.9:2 | until they cover e. that you perceive and |
| T-26.........I.3:5 | to you are limits placed on e. outside, just |
| T-26.........I.3:5 | just as they are on e. you think is yours. |
| T-26........II.8:2 | He knows that e. that is belongs to Him, |
| T-26....III.1:12 | What is e. leaves room for nothing else. |
| T-26......III.2:6 | sin denied, and e. that *is* received instead. |
| T-26......IV.2:3 | is no parting here, for e. is totally forgiven |
| T-26......IV.3:5 | by e. created to the Source of its creation? |
| T-26........V.3:4 | and e. exactly as it was before the way to |
| T-26........V.8:2 | e. that points to it as real is but a wish |
| T-26........V.9:5 | e. that points the way in the direction of |
| T-26...VII.11:2 | He wills His Son have e.. And this He |
| T-26...VII.11:3 | He guaranteed when He created him *as* e.. |
| T-26...VII.11:8 | would sacrifice his own identity with e., |
| T-26...VII.14:5 | sacrifice, and thus denies that e. is his, |
| T-26...VII.19:7 | e. belongs to each of them. No wishes lie |
| T-26... VIII.6:6 | that e. brings good that comes from God. |
| T-26........X.3:4 | at the root of e. perceived to be unfair and |
| T-27........I.4:11 | And e. that it has shown to him have you |
| T-27........II.5:5 | And e. you say or do or think but testifies |
| T-27......III.4:6 | truth, for what can stand for more than e. |
| T-27........V.7:1 | Thus is your healing e. the world requires |
| T-27.....VII.7:3 | e. the world appeared to thrust upon you, |
| T-28........II.3:3 | cause of healing is the only Cause of e.. It |
| T-28.....VII.7:1 | and e. his Father promised him. No secret |
| T-29........II.5:1 | can give, because of e. you have received. |
| T-29......II.10:3 | For if He be the sum of e., then what is |
| T-29.....VII.2:2 | him. If e. is in him this cannot be so. And |
| T-29.....VII.2:3 | and seeks for something more than e., as |
| T-29....VIII.7:6 | an idol be, while God is e. and everywhere |
| T-29......IX.4:7 | e. their toys appear to do is in the minds |
| T-30........II.1:8 | your will, where e. created is for you. No |
| T-30........II.3:6 | you, and through your will created e.. Not |
| T-30......III.1:6 | It is as if you said, "I have no need of e.. |
| T-30......III.1:7 | thing I want, and it will be as e. to me." |
| T-30......III.1:8 | because it is your will that e. be yours. |
| T-30....III.1:10 | for loss. Decide for truth and e. is yours. |
| T-30........V.4:5 | of God knows e. his Father understands, |
| T-30........V.8:2 | Within your hand is e. you need to walk |
| T-30.....VII.4:2 | shared by everyone and e. you see. You |
| T-30.....VII.4:3 | learned one meaning has been given e., |
| T-30.....VII.5:2 | can be opposed to it, for it belongs to e., |
| T-30....VIII.1:4 | For e. you see will change, and yet you |
| T-31.........I.8:1 | and e. is lit with hope and sparkles with a |
| T-31.........I.8:4 | and e. within the world has always made, |
| T-31........II.6:4 | be still, forgetting e. we thought we heard |
| T-31......III.1:3 | a habit of response so typical of e. you do |
| T-31......V.14:6 | So it can learn that e. it thinks reflects the |
| T-31.....VII.7:3 | The light is kept from e. you see. At most, |
| T-31....VIII.2:6 | Christ in you is given charge of e. you do. |
| T-31....VIII.3:5 | mind from e. that hides His face from you |
| T-31..VIII.12:7 | forth from e. that lives and moves in You. |
| W-in..........4:1 | of everyone and e. in the world. The |
| W-in..........4:2 | applicable to everyone and e. you see. |
| W-in..........5:2 | total transfer to everyone and e. is certain |
| W-in..........6:2 | find yourself, and to everyone and e. in it. |
| W-in..........7:1 | ideas you will be practicing to include e.. |
| W-pI.......1.3:5 | Do not attempt to apply it to e. you see, |
| W-pI..........2.h | given e. I see in this room [on this street, |
| W-pI.......2.1:6 | to include e. you see in a given area, or |
| W-pI.......7.1:4 | It is the reason why you have given e. you |
| W-pI.......7.2:1 | because e. you believe is rooted in time, |
| W-pI.....14.1:3 | e. that does exist exists as He created it. |
| W-pI.....16.1:2 | E. you see is the result of your thoughts. |
| W-pI.....22.2:4 | e. that you hate and would attack and kill. |
| W-pI.....23.1:2 | else will work; e. else is meaningless. But |
| W-pI.....23.3:1 | and e. in it is a symbol of vengeance. Each |
| W-pI.....23.4:4 | replacement for e. you think you see now. |
| W-pI.....25.1:5 | E. is for your own best interests. That is |
| W-pI.....25.2:1 | You perceive the world and e. in it as |
| W-pI.....25.5:1 | up the goals you have established for e.. |
| W-pI........29.h | God is in e. I see. |
| W-pI.....29.1:1 | explains why you can see all purpose in e.. |
| W-pI........30.h | is in e. I see because God is in my mind. |
| W-pI.....30.3:2 | that the idea applies to e. you do see now, |
| W-pI........36.h | My holiness envelops e. I see. |
| W-pI.....37.1:6 | entitled to e. because it is his birthright as |
| W-pI.....38.3:1 | If you are holy, so is e. God created. You |
| W-pI.....41.3:1 | Deep within you is e. that is perfect, |
| W-pI.....44.5:4 | you leave behind e. that you now believe, |
| W-pI.....45.7:4 | were. E. you have thought since then will |
| W-pI.....50.1:2 | believe you are sustained by e. but God. |
| W-pI.....51.2:2 | I have judged e. I look upon, and it is this |
| W-pI.....51.5:5 | misused e. I see by assigning this role to it |
| W-pI.....52.2:4 | I hold the past against everyone and e., |
| W-pI.....52.2:5 | I am, I will bless everyone and e. I see. |
| W-pI.....53.4:3 | meaning, and e. that is real is in His Mind |
| W-pI.....54.3:5 | thoughts, which share e. with everyone. |
| W-pI.....54.4:3 | E. I think or say or do teaches all the |
| W-pI.....55.2:3 | It is a picture of attack on e. by everything |
| W-pI.....55.2:3 | It is a picture of attack on everything by e. |
| W-pI.....55.5:2 | purpose of e. is to prove that my illusions |
| W-pI.....55.5:3 | that I attempt to use everyone and e.. It is |
| W-pI.....56.4:1 | (29) God is in e. I see. Behind every |
| W-pI.....56.4:5 | God is still everywhere and in e. forever. |
| W-pI.....56.5:1 | is in e. I see because God is in my mind. |

W-pI.....57.3:3 I see e. upside down, and my thoughts are
W-pI.....58.1:1 (36) My holiness envelops e. I see. From
W-pI.....58.2:3 Everyone and e. I see in its light shares in
W-pI.....60.3:4 Everyone and e. I see will lean toward me
W-pI.....67.6:3 replacing e. that the ego tells you about
W-pI.....68.6:4 completely at peace with everyone and e.,
W-pI.....71.2:5 thus demanded of everyone and e. except
W-pI.....76.6:2 until you realize it applies to e. that you
W-pI.....85.3:7 e. I see will but reflect the light that shines
W-pI.....92.7:1 hates itself, and darkness covers e. it sees,
W-pI.....98.2:3 given e. we need with which to reach the
W-pI.....98.6:3 being asked for nothing in return for e..
W-pI...101.3:3 slowly, taking e. away before it grants the
W-pI...102.2:4 And e. you think it offers you is lacking in
W-pI...105.4:5 itself fulfill its aim of giving e. it has away,
W-pI...106.7:1 e. is yours and everything is given away, it
W-pI...106.7:1 everything is yours and e. is given away, it
W-pI...109.2:4 same truth in everyone and e. there is.
WpI. rIII.in4:5 But your practicing can offer e. to you.
WpIrIII.in11:2 what you learn each day to e. you do. Do
W-pI......122.h Forgiveness offers e. I want.
W-pI...122.4:1 other than the answer that will answer e.?
W-pI.122.13:1 Forgiveness offers e. you want. Today all
W-pI.122.14:3 *Forgiveness offers e. I want. Today I have*
W-pI...123.8:2 give Him thanks for e. He gave His Son,
W-pI...124.1:4 E. we touch takes on a shining light that
W-pI...124.2:2 And e. we see reflects the holiness within
W-pI...125.7:4 His Love is e. you are and that He is; the
W-pI...127.3:8 wholeness is the power holding e. as one,
W-pI...127.4:4 love but His, and what He is, is e. there is.
W-pI...128.2:2 e. must serve the purpose you have given
W-pI...130.4:1 Fear has made e. you think you see. All
W-pI...130.6:5 and reflects its source in e. you see.
W-pI.130.11:2 the place of e. that hell would show to you
W-pI...131.3:4 forgot, yet holding e. you really want.
W-pI...131.5:3 E. you seek but this will fall away. Yet not
W-pI...133.5:3 Each choice you make brings e. to you or
W-pI...133.5:4 you can distinguish e. from nothing, you
W-pI...133.7:2 is because, when you deny his right to e.,
W-pI.133.13:1 to find e. and claim it as their own. We
W-pI...134.2:3 It is irrelevant to e. except illusions. Truth
W-pI.134.17:6 In e. you do remember this: *No one is*
W-pI.135.13:4 e. the mind employs for this will function
W-pI.135.16:4 not see that here and now is e. it needs to
W-pI.135.18:1 if you but knew that e. that happens, all
W-pI.135.21:2 We will be sure that e. we need is given us
W-pI...137.9:3 you from e. that ever caused you pain.
W-pI.137.13:3 a small expense to offer for the gift of e.?
W-pI...141.2:1 (122) Forgiveness offers e. I want.
W-pI...151.9:6 Let Him be Judge as well of e. that seems
W-pI.151.12:3 In everyone and e. His Voice would speak
W-pI.151.12:4 So will you see the holy face of Christ in e.
W-pI.151.12:4 and hear in e. no sound except the echo of
W-pI...152.2:3 If you have the gift of e., can loss be real?
W-pI...154.3:2 to succeed in e. you do that is related to it.
W-pI.155.12:4 What way could give you more than e., or
W-pI...156.3:2 of His remains unshared by e. that lives.
W-pI...157.9:1 serenely unaware of e. except His shining
W-pI...161.2:3 does not look on e. as one. It sees instead
W-pI...161.3:4 of view, so we can see a different use in e..
W-pI...161.7:5 is insatiable, consuming e. its eyes behold
W-pI...161.7:5 eyes behold, seeing itself in e., compelled
W-pI...163.9:2 *reflection of Your Love which shines in e..*
W-pI...165.2:5 e. is one with you because it left you not.
W-pI...166.5:5 a treasure his so great that e. the world
W-pI...168.4:5 undone when your forgiveness rests on e.
W-pI...169.2:2 state so opposite to e. the world contains,
W-pI...183.6:6 the only Name of e. that we desire to see;
W-pI...183.6:6 to see; of e. that we would call our own.
W-pI...184.1:2 You have made up names for e. you see.
W-pI...185.1:2 But to mean these words is e.. If you
W-pI.186.12:4 bewildered, inconsistent and unsure of e.
W-pI.186.13:3 He knows that you have e. already. He has
W-pI.187.11:5 holy sight is ours, we offer it to e. we see.
W-pI...189.3:5 A world in which forgiveness shines on e.,
W-pI...189.7:2 mind of e. it thinks is either true or false,
W-pI...191.4:6 proclaimed to be forever part of e., the
W-pI...191.7:5 thought is e. you look on wholly changed.
W-pI...192.6:6 But we have indeed been given e. by God.
W-pI...193.6:4 these words apply to e. you see or any
W-pI.193.12:4 let e. that happened in its course go with
W-pI.193.13:1 There is a way to look on e. that lets it be
W-pI...195.8:6 will see that e. has earned the right to love
W-pI...195.9:2 We have been given e.. If we refuse to
W-pI.198.11:6 e. you ever thought you made completely
W-pI.198.12:4 Who could give him gifts when e. is his?
W-pI.198.13:1 still nearer to the end of e. that yet would
WpI rVI.in.3:8 of e. that clutters up the mind, and makes
W-pI...205.1:2 *The peace of God is e. I want. The peace of*
W-pI...209.1:3 *The Love of God is e. I am. The Love of God*
W-pII.....3.3:5 e. that they report is but illusion which is
W-pII.242.2:6 *And You will give us e. we need in helping us*
W-pII.251.1:7 Now have I e. that I could need. Now have
W-pII.251.1:8 Now have I e. that I could want. And now
W-pII.259.2:4 *are the Source of e. there is. And everything*
W-pII.259.2:5 *is. And e. that is remains with You, and You*
W-pII.283.1:8 *true Identity, when You created e. that is?*
W-pII.283.2:1 our only Source, and e. created part of us.
W-pII.286.1:6 *In You is e. I hope to find already given me.*
W-pII.292.1:2 joy can be the final outcome found for e..
W-pII.297.1:2 I want. And e. I give I give myself. This is
W-pII.298.2:4 *and escape from e. that would obscure my*
W-pII.....9.2:3 way, because it shines on e. as one. And
W-pII.339.2:2 *by myself, but hear Your Voice in e. I do;*
W-pII.343.1:2 *The gift of e. can be but gain. You only give.*
W-pII343.1:11 *for I can only give, and e. is mine eternally.*
W-pII.348.2:1 suffices us in e. that He would have us do.
W-ep.........6:3 answers, as we ask His Will in e. we do.
M-2...........4:7 God's Will in e. but seems to take time in
M-4....VIII.1:5 for e. that happens now or in the future.
M-6.........4:12 this holy exchange can receive less than e.
M-10.........3:4 and e. involved in them in any way. And
M-10.........4:9 on everyone and e. involved in any way.
M-12.........2:3 but e. internal now reflects only the Love
M-13.......4:10 chooses nothing as a substitute for e.?
M-13.........8:2 God, and e. is given you at no cost at all.
M-13.........8:3 at the expense of the awareness of e..
M-16.......11:7 and have learned that e. but this is magic.
M-17.......9:13 But His Love is Cause of e. beyond all fear
M-20.......2:11 gone. Quiet has reached to cover e..
M-20.........5:7 that e. that God created cannot have an
C-3............6:2 is. We can but go from nothingness to e.;
C-4............2:3 For e. they see not only will not last, but
C-4............2:4 guilt. While e. that God created is forever
P-2.......VII.2:7 is no need for more than this, for it is e..
P-3........III.1:2 part of His plan that e. in this world be
S-1...........I.5:3 being fully entitled to e. Love has to offer?
S-1...........I.7:5 asks nothing and receives e.. This prayer

## Everywhere 1

*everywhere*

W-pII...12.2:2 In fear it stands beyond the E., apart from

## everywhere 64

*Everywhere*

T-4........I.12:3 its radiance and gladly sheds its light e..
T-5........I.4:10 Knowledge is always ready to flow e., but
T-7....V.10:10 See only this Mind e., because only this is
T-7....V.10:10 because only this is e. and in everything.
T-7....VII.10:4 you will see it e. because it *is* everywhere.
T-7....VII.10:4 you will see it everywhere because it *is* e..
T-8.......III.7:2 power and glory are e., and you cannot be
T-8.......III.8:8 is. See this glory e. to remember what you
T-8.....IV.2:11 If my light goes with you e., you shine it
T-9.......IV.5:6 out all its effects, e. and in all respects, He
T-9.......VI.4:6 learn of your wholeness until you see it e..
T-9......VII.1:4 Your brothers are e.. You do not have to
T-10.....IV.7:6 by the same spark. It is e. and it is eternal.
T-10......V.7:6 in everything He created, for His Son is e..
T-11........I.2:2 because what has no limits must be e..
T-11.VIII.10:2 help, the Help of God goes with you e.. As
T-13......V.6:5 see only your own split mind e. you look.
T-13...VIII.1:7 to it. It knows that it is e., just as it has
T-13...VIII.2:7 can reach e. under His guidance, for the
T-13...VIII.3:8 of reality can be seen in everything and e..
T-13...VIII.7:2 Offer Christ's gift to everyone and e., for
T-13.......X.8:3 pain is pressing e. upon him from without
T-14.......II.8:7 else. God is e., and His Son is in Him with
T-15.....XI.7:5 is that sacrifice is nowhere and love is e..
T-17....VII.6:4 is holy unless its holiness goes with it e..
T-17....VII.6:5 in hand, so must its faith go e. with it. The
T-18...VIII.9:2 See how life springs up e.! The desert
T-19.....III.7:3 the proof of separation seems to be e..
T-20...VIII.6:6 to overlook it in any form and seeing it e.,
T-24.....VI.6:3 And it is He they look for e., and find no
T-25......in.2:1 Christ in him can fail to recognize Him e..
T-25.....III.2:2 Yet are His laws reflected e.. Not that the
T-26........I.7:5 in Heaven, so must he be eternally and e..
T-27.....IV.6:4 The answer is provided e.. Yet it is only
T-27.....V.11:6 E. you go, will you behold its multiplied
T-29....VII.7:2 and you see death and disappointment e..
T-29...VIII.4:4 place where what is e. has been excluded
T-29...VIII.7:6 an idol be, while God is everything and e..
T-30....VII.4:3 everything, and you are glad to see it e.. It
T-30....VII.4:4 change *because* you would perceive it e.,
T-31.....III.2:3 attack them e. except you hate yourself?
T-31..VII.11:3 within, and thus expect to see it e.. And so
T-31..VII.11:5 looks upon, and see his own salvation e..
WpI...rI.in.5:2 to where you are, so that your peace is e.,
W-pI....56.4:5 God is still e. and in everything forever.
W-pI..75.11:2 awareness of yourself and see it e. today,
W-pI....97.5:2 them e. He knows they will be welcome.
W-pI..103.1:4 has no limits, being e.. And therefore joy
W-pI..103.1:5 And therefore joy is e. as well. Yet can the
W-pI..107.3:6 can not be found, for truth is e. forever,
W-pI..121.4:5 of none because it sees the sinful e..
W-pI..124.1:5 thought that God Himself goes e. with us.
W-pI..132.3:5 Death strikes it e. because you hold the
W-pI 151.14:4 Thought that offers its perfection e..
W-pI..154.6:3 to give them e. that they were meant to be
W-pI..166.5:4 aware of the futility he sees about him e.,
W-pI..167.8:4 but yet within themselves, for they are e..
W-pI 187.11:2 we would extend, for we would see it e..
W-pI..189.4:3 look upon, and see its sure reflection e..
W-pII.264.1:1 *me, in the place I see myself, and e. I go. You*
W-pII...11.1:1 number infinite, and e. without all limit.
W-pII...13.5:4 And e. the signs of life spring up, to show
M-1...........2:5 goes on all the time e.. It calls for teachers
P-3.......III.1:7 last illusion be accepted by everyone e..

## evidence 13

T-11......in.1:2 will examine the e. on both sides fairly,
T-16.......II.6:1 No e. will convince you of the truth of
T-16.......II.6:8 clinging to it, and denying the e. for truth
T-21........I.1:2 infer what could be seen from e. forever
T-22........I.1:5 faith in this and see much e. on its behalf.
T-24..VII.10:1 no provisions made for e. beyond itself,
T-28.......V.5:7 piece, each senseless scrap and shred of e.
T-31.......V.9:1 of what seems to be the e. on its behalf.
W-pI..151.1:1 No one can judge on partial e.. That is
W-pI..151.7:1 must learn to doubt their e. will clear the
W-pI..155.3:2 The mad illusion will remain awhile in e.,
W-pI..166.7:2 defend against all reason, every e., and all
M-19.........5:6 It accepts all e. that is brought before it,

## evident 15

*See also* self-evident

T-3.........V.3:3 stable, and it is quite e. that you are not.
T-7.........V.4:5 quite e. that he does not understand God
T-9..........I.3:4 want. It is e., then, that you are judging
T-9.........V.5:2 e. inconsistencies account for why no one
T-13.....IV.7:1 It is e. that the Holy Spirit's perception of
T-15..VII.12:5 And despite the e. insanity of this lesson,
T-15..VII.14:1 making it e. that it is not impossible. In
T-16.....V.12:5 even apart from its e. impossibility? If it
T-17.....III.2:7 are central to all unholy relationships is e.
T-17.....VI.2:6 for this disorganized approach is e.. The
T-17...VIII.4:6 to give faith to truth, and see its e. reality.
T-25.......II.1:1 e. that what the body's eyes perceive fills
T-25.......II.1:4 it must be e. the outcome does not change
W-pI..166.3:2 God's gifts, however e. they may become,
M-27.........5:4 of illusions becomes more sharply e..

### evidently 1

T-3 VI.2:9 You **e.** do not believe this, or you would

### evil 108

*See also* good-and-evil

T-2 IV.4:4 such agents for corrective purposes is **e.**.
T-3 I.3:1 one assigns his own "**e.**" past to God. The
T-3 I.3:2 The "**e.**" past has nothing to do with God.
T-3 I.3:6 does not hold your "**e.**" deeds against you
T-3 I.7:4 is wisdom because it is unaware of **e.**, and
T-3 I.7:4 it is unaware of evil, and **e.** does not exist.
T-3 I.7:7 Good can withstand any form of **e.**, as
T-3 VI.7:3 This *is* "the root of all **e.**." Every symptom
T-11 III.1:7 Conflict is the root of all **e.**, for being
T-11 VII.2:8 For if you perceive both good and **e.**, you
T-15 VII.4:4 that you are exempt from its **e.** intentions
T-16 VII.1:5 "**e.**" in the past to which you cling, and
T-17 I.2:3 Yet by distorting it and devoting it to "**e.**,
T-17 III.1:9 represent the **e.** that you think was done
T-17 III.1:10 you only that you may return **e.** for evil,
T-17 III.1:10 you only that you may return evil for **e.**,
T-18 IX.9:4 of every **e.** thought you laid upon it. Here
T-19 III.1:6 is an idea of **e.** that cannot be corrected,
T-19 III.6:4 be split, and torn between good and **e.**;
T19 IV.A.11:2 scrap of **e.** and of sin that they can find,
T-22 V.3:3 and the material of **e.** dreams are nothing.
T-23 in.3:1 with your head held high, and fear no **e.**.
T-24 II.3:3 an **e.** flower with no roots at all. Here is
T-24 VII.10:5 it sinful and you hate its acts, judging it **e.**
T-25 I.2:4 of yourself; your sinfulness, your **e.** and,
T-25 IV.3:7 all their "**e.**" thoughts and "sinful" hopes,
T-25 IV.4:4 Your "**e.**" thoughts that haunt you now
T-25 VI.1:2 He can see no **e.**; nothing in the world to
T-25 VII.11:6 For otherwise would **e.** triumph, and
T-27 I.1:3 you will fear no **e.** and no shadows in the
T-27 II.2:7 truth. Good cannot *be* returned for **e.**, for
T-27 VII.6:2 to the world of **e.** cannot speak except for
T-27 VII.6:2 what has seen a need for **e.** in the world.
T-27 VII.9:4 of **e.** or a happy wakening and joy of life.
T-27 VIII.7:7 its **e.** deeds because you did not make it,
T-28 IV.1:9 depending on whose **e.** dream you share.
T-28 IV.1:10 be sure of just one thing; that you are **e.**,
T-28 IV.8:5 If you share not your brother's **e.** dream,
T-28 V.1:4 so the good is seen to be outside; the **e.**, in
T-28 V.1:5 off the self from good, and keeping **e.** in.
T-28 V.2:1 is the sharing of the **e.** dreams of hate and
T-28 V.3:1 no **e.** dreams if you forgive the dreamer,
T-28 V.3:3 separates the dreamer from the **e.** dream,
T-28 V.3:4 Remember if you share an **e.** dream, you
T-29 V.6:1 the touch of **e.** on it may appear to be. For
T-29 V.7:2 instead of dreaming **e.** separate dreams of
T-29 IX.2:9 you make yourself a part of **e.** dreams,
T-30 VI.9:5 of **e.** that can overcome the Will of God;
T-31 I.13:1 unaware of any thoughts of **e.** or of good
T-31 III.5:1 to the snarling dogs of hate and **e.**,
T-31 V.2:9 believes that it is good within an **e.** world.
T-31 V.10:9 If the world be **e.**, there is still no need to
T-31 V.15:3 you perceive a self that interacts with **e.**,
T-31 VI.3:8 is drawn across the **e.** and the good, and
T-31 VII.2:1 recognize your "**e.**" thoughts as long as
T-31 VII.2:6 "**e.**" thoughts have been forgiven with his,
T-31 VII.2:7 should be the sign of **e.** and of guilt in him
T-31 VII.5:2 you may not be frightened by your "**e.**"
W-pI 66.6:3 not. Love cannot give **e.**, and what is not
W-pI 66.6:3 give evil, and what is not happiness is **e.**.
W-pI 66.6:5 gives you only happiness, He must be **e.**.
W-pI 93.1:1 think you are the home of **e.**, darkness
W-pI 93.4:1 **e.** that you think you did was never done,
W-pI 93.6:6 The self you made, **e.** and full of sin, is
W-pI 93.7:2 Whatever **e.** you may think you did, you
W-pI 93.9:5 tiny idols of **e.** and sinfulness you have
W-pI 96.1:1 yourself as two; as both good and **e.**,
W-pI 96.3:2 and good and **e.** have no meeting place.
W-pI 110.1:3 God created was replaced by fear and **e.**,
W-pI 110.1:4 you fear has no meaning, **e.** is not real,
W-pI 122.2:3 eyelids so you see no dreams of fear and **e.**
W-pI 134.11:1 all dreams of **e.** and of hatred and attack
W-pI 134.15:3 all the **e.** things you thought of him, and
W-pI 151.6:2 to prove to you its **e.** is your own are false,
W-pI 190.7:6 Your strange desires bring it **e.** dreams.
W-pI 190.8:1 Pain is the thought of **e.** taking form, and
W-pI 191.3:3 Deny your own Identity, and look on **e.**,
W-pI 194.8:2 of sin and **e.** with the truth of love. Think
W-pI 200.6:5 Son from **e.** dreams that he imagines, yet
W-pI 203.1:2 *from every thought of **e.** and of sin, because*
W-pII 4.3:3 Sin "proves" God's Son is **e.**; timelessness
W-pII 4.4:3 has become a body, prey to **e.** and to guilt
W-pII 303.2:2 *has come to save me from the **e.** self I made.*
W-pII 332.1:2 undoes its **e.** dreams by shining them
W-pII 333.2:2 *No light but this can end our **e.** dream. No*
M-4 IV.2:8 have understood their **e.** thoughts came
M-4 X.1:4 judges the Son of God as **e.**, so open-
M-14 1:4 in gentleness, will cover it, hiding all **e.**,
M-28 6:2 any mind remains possessed of **e.** dreams,
M-29 6:3 attractive to you, He will respond with **e.**?
C-2 6:9 Where **e.** was there now is holiness. What
C-2 6:11 What the **e.** was. Where is the ego? In an
C-2 6:13 In an **e.** dream that but seemed real while
C-5 3:5 life in any way be changed by sin and **e.**,
P-2 IV.4:7 were the devil and must be found in **e.**.
P-2 IV.6:1 as weak, vulnerable, **e.** and endangered,
P-2 IV.6:6 becomes a threat and is perceived as **e.**.
P-2 VI.6:5 think of **e.** as besetting him here and now.
P-3 III.1:5 Money is not **e.**. It is nothing. But no one
S-1 III.1:5 that he *is* your enemy, your **e.** counterpart,
S-2 I.2:4 It carefully picks out all **e.** things, and
S-2 I.5:2 It always seems to be another who is **e.**,
S-2 I.5:6 And being **e.**, he can only give of what he
S-2 I.7:6 Who sees no **e.** in it sees like Him. For
S-2 I.9:4 cleansed from **e.** usages and hateful goals.
S-2 III.4:5 not real and makes illusions in its **e.** name
S-3 I.1:2 a shadow of an **e.** thought that seems to
S-3 II.6:3 upon God's substitute for **e.** dreams; a

### evil's 1

T-26 VIII.7:1 Why should the good appear in **e.** form?

### evils 2

T-15 X.7:3 of the two is judged as the lesser of two **e.**,
W-pI 153.7:3 you see at work in all the **e.** of the world?

### evoked 3

T-11 V.18:5 you have **e.** false witnesses against him. If
W-pI 153.14:5 dreams this story has **e.** in his confused,
W-pI 158.2:6 lesson yesterday **e.** a theme found early in

### evokes 1

T-12 I.6:5 to reality, for reality **e.** no conflict at all.

### evolution 1

T-2 II.6:1 **E.** is a process in which you seem to

### evolved 1

T-17 IV.4:3 whole defense system the ego **e.** to protect

### evolves 1

T-23 II.2:3 This principle **e.** from the belief there is a

### evolving 1

M-9 1:7 are given a slowly **e.** training program, in

### exacerbate 1

T-6 V.A.6:4 appear to **e.** conflict rather than resolve it,

### exact 12

T-6 III.4:1 salvation lies in teaching the **e.** opposite
T-9 II.11:8 the **e.** measure of the value you put upon
T-9 VII.3:5 is the **e.** opposite of the Holy Spirit's,
T-11 V.14:1 to be, the **e.** opposite of the Holy Spirit's.
T-13 IV.7:1 of time is the **e.** opposite of the ego's. The
T-17 V.2:6 shifted to the **e.** opposite of what it was.
T-25 VII.11:5 and pay **e.** amount in blood and suffering.
W-pI 65.6:5 You need not use these **e.** words, but try
W-pI 108.9:3 You will find you have **e.** return, for that
W-pI 153.4:1 of all the prices which the ego would **e.**. In
M-4 VII.1:8 the word means the **e.** opposite to the
M-5 II.1:1 Healing must occur in **e.** proportion to

### exacted 2

T-21 III.10:2 For sacrifice must be **e.** of a body, and by
T-31 III.7:3 penalty **e.** from your brother or yourself.

### exactly 70

T-6 V.B.7:3 Holy Spirit perceives the conflict **e.** as it is
T-7 II.5:1 purpose in translating is **e.** the opposite.
T-7 V.8:1 you heal, that is **e.** what you *are* learning.
T-7 VI.6:4 Holy Spirit perceives the conflict **e.** as it is
T-7 X.1:9 you. They are **e.** where they belong. They
T-8 IX.8:1 course, and one that means **e.** what it says
T-8 IX.8:3 can prevent you from doing **e.** what I ask,
T-9 IV.7:5 at all. This is **e.** what the ego does. It is
T-9 V.8:8 will tell you **e.** what to do to help anyone
T-10 III.4:7 And that is **e.** what the ego does perceive
T-11 IV.4:6 to realize that this is **e.** the same thing, for
T-12 I.4:1 for help as **e.** what they are except your
T-12 IV.2:6 will surely do so when you realize **e.** what
T-14 in.1:5 insane. They take a direction **e.** opposite,
T-14 X.6:3 The miracle offers **e.** the same response to
T-15 V.9:2 having always known you **e.** as He knows
T-15 IX.2:1 all the interference and seeing it **e.** as it is.
T-16 IV.7:5 we look very closely at **e.** what it is you
T-16 V.3:6 a direction **e.** opposite of what is true. In
T-16 V.11:4 See how **e.** is this ritual enacted in the
T-16 VII.8:7 Son will always be **e.** as he was created.
T-18 I.1:2 would but consider **e.** what this entails,
T-21 VI.6:3 you will learn of him **e.** what you taught.
T-25 in.2:7 does the Son of God abide **e.** where he is,
T-26 V.3:4 and everything **e.** as it was before the way
T-27 VII.3:5 who looks upon this "reasoning" **e.** as it is
T-27 VII.10:7 between **e.** as they are and where they are.
T-27 VIII.7:2 world you see depicts **e.** what you thought
T-27 VIII.8:1 to you **e.** what you think you did to them.
T-30 III.7:7 will always be **e.** as it was before the time
T-30 III.10:2 Thought God holds of you remains **e.** as it
T-31 I.1:9 told **e.** how to tell one from the other, and
T-31 V.9:5 And does he know **e.** what would happen
T-31 V.17:4 been laid by is truth revealed **e.** as it is.
T-31 VI.2:4 no one is **e.** as he was an instant previous,
W-pI 3.1:7 these things **e.** as you would anything else
W-pI 3.2:1 to see things **e.** as they appear to you now,
W-pI 23.7:2 Their effects are **e.** the same because they
W-pI 23.7:2 the same because they are **e.** the same.
W-pI 45.7:3 be in your mind, **e.** as they always were.
W-pI 47.3:2 telling you **e.** what to do to call upon His
W-pI 93.7:6 and will forever be **e.** as you were created.
W-pI 99.5:1 of God **e.** as it was received of Him within
W-pI 107.4:3 It stays **e.** as it always was, to be depended
W-pI 122.5:2 Be thankful it remains **e.** as He planned it.
W-pI 129.3:2 **e.** as you want them throughout time? Yet
W-pI 132.4:5 in truth you found **e.** what you looked for
W-pI 136.3:4 recognize **e.** what you would attempt to
W-pI 137.4:4 and always will remain **e.** as it has forever
W-pI 140.2:3 so his mind remains **e.** as it was before.
W-pI 154.2:2 Seeing your strengths **e.** as they are, and
W-pI 170.8:3 before this idol, seeing him **e.** as he is.
W-pI 186.12:4 Who knows all things **e.** as they are, or a
W-pII 1.4:5 must learn to welcome truth **e.** as it is.
W-pII 268.h Let all things be **e.** as they are.
W-pII 268.1:6 *me, when I let all things be **e.** as they are?*
W-pII 300.2:3 *and learned **e.** what to do to be restored to*
W-pII 11.1:5 Thoughts **e.** as they were and as they are,
W-pII 333.1:3 must be seen **e.** as it is, where it is thought
W-ep 3:3 your efforts, telling you **e.** what to do,

| | |
|---|---|
| T-20......IV.6:1 | you be concerned with anything **e.** the |
| T-20......IV.6:9 | **E.** you be there, he is not complete. And it |
| T-20......IV.8:8 | of everything **e.** the only purpose that you |
| T-20....... V.4:2 | What would you want **e.** his offering? His |
| T-20......VII.8:1 | be looked upon **e.** through judgment. To |
| T-21.... III.10:1 | sight; **e.** you do not realize you cannot see |
| T-21....... V.6:2 | He has no Thoughts **e.** the Self-extending, |
| T-21.....VII.2:3 | What can they be **e.** his enemy? And what |
| T-21.....VII.3:2 | know not their "enemy," **e.** they hate him. |
| T-21...VII.10:3 | the same as are the other three, **e.** in time. |
| T-21...VII.13:3 | be perceived **e.** through constant vision. |
| T-22.........I.1:7 | a plan of any kind **e.** to wander off, for |
| T-22.........I.4:3 | secrets be **e.** another "will" that is your |
| T-22.........I.7:5 | nor was received by anything **e.** yourself. |
| T-22.........I.7:6 | two brothers can unite **e.** through Christ, |
| T-22....... III.8:4 | attack **e.** what you associate with his body |
| T-22....... V.2:4 | can this be **e.** an invitation to insanity, to |
| T-22.... VI.12:7 | its value, **e.** in the desire to attack in safety |
| T-22.... VI.14:3 | mean **e.** your mind and your brother's are |
| T-23...... I.11:4 | And nothing is remembered **e.** illusions. |
| T-24......IV.1:1 | is a lack of trust in anyone **e.** yourself. |
| T-24......IV.1:7 | mean destruction of the world, **e.** yourself |
| T-24..... V.1:10 | itself. **E.** that one deludes; the other heals. |
| T-24....... V.8:4 | give a brother unto you **e.** he be as perfect |
| T-24.....VII.8:2 | **e.** to say that what is yours will come to |
| T-25.......in.2:2 | *E.* in bodies. And as long as he believes he |
| T-25.........I.2:1 | manifest the Christ in you **e.** to look on |
| T-25..... II.10:7 | has power over you **e.** His Will and yours, |
| T-25...... III.7:2 | you nothing **e.** a chance for you to see the |
| T-25...... III.9:3 | this be **e.** a misperception of himself? Is |
| T-25.....VII.2:6 | And what can share its attributes **e.** itself? |
| T-25...VII.10:1 | What is dependable **e.** God's Love? And |
| T-25...VII.10:2 | And where does sanity abide **e.** in Him? |
| T-25...VII.11:4 | belief **e.** a form of the more basic tenet, |
| T-25... VIII.7:3 | What could He be to them **e.** a devil, |
| T-25... VIII.7:4 | escape has He for them **e.** a door to hell |
| T-25......IX.1:2 | this mean **e.** that they are sins and not |
| T-26..... V.1:10 | road be made **e.** the way to Heaven. You |
| T-26....... V.9:8 | His, and nowhere can you go **e.** to Him. |
| T-26... VIII.3:7 | body is, **e.** in terms of what you see it for. |
| T-26... VIII.4:2 | can it be overlooked **e.** within the present. |
| T-26... VIII.4:5 | Who can feel desolation **e.** now? A future |
| T-26....... X.3:6 | You have no enemy **e.** yourself, and you |
| T-26....... X.5:5 | for the world is purposeless **e.** for this. To |
| T-27.....IV.4:17 | **e.** that what it states takes question's form |
| T-27......VI.2:6 | **E.** for this, the witnesses of sin are all alike |
| T-27......VII.6:2 | world of evil cannot speak **e.** for what has |
| T-27... VIII.7:3 | **E.** that now you think that what you did is |
| T-28......III.7:4 | What is the world **e.** a little gap perceived |
| T-28......III.7:5 | live within the world **e.** a picture of the |
| T-28..... V.1:10 | **E.** you share it, nothing can exist. And |
| T-29....... II.6:5 | is that **e.** the state confusion really means |
| T-29....... V.1:3 | still no sound **e.** a hymn to Heaven rises |
| T-29... VIII.7:5 | left no room for anything to be **e.** His Will |
| T-29......IX.6:6 | **E.** he judges this as does a child, who does |
| T-29......IX.7:2 | **E.** the figures have been changed. They |
| T-30....... II.3:8 | No light of Heaven shines **e.** for you, for it |
| T-30......IV.7:2 | What could it be **e.** a happy dream? It |
| T-30....IV.8:13 | be, **e.** a means to give him to Himself? |
| T-30..... V.10:1 | Do not look back **e.** in honesty. And |
| T-30..... V.10:3 | *brought you anything* **e.** *the "gift" of guilt.* |
| T-30..... V.10:4 | *Not one was bought* **e.** *at cost of pain, nor* |
| T-30......VI.6:7 | this be **e.** a false forgiveness of yourself, |
| T-30......VI.9:6 | is this **e.** a simple statement of the truth? |
| T-30.....VII.2:1 | scripts reflect **e.** your plans for what the |
| T-30.....VII.2:6 | **e.** to show there was no meaning there? |
| T-31......III.2:3 | them everywhere **e.** you hate yourself? |
| T-31......III.5:2 | ravages of fear **e.** in murder and in death. |
| T-31......IV.3:4 | way **e.** the pathways offered by the world. |
| T-31....... V.8:4 | be unlearned **e.** by lessons aimed to teach |
| T-31......VI.1:8 | more **e.** to heal and comfort and to bless. |
| T-31...VII.14:3 | dreams and no remaining hope **e.** to die, |
| W-pI.......7.3:5 | know about this cup **e.** what you learned |
| W-pI.......7.3:6 | what this cup is, **e.** for your past learning. |
| W-pI.....13.1:1 | one, **e.** that it is more specific as to the |
| W-pI.....13.6:2 | think of it **e.** during the practice periods. |
| W-pI.....26.4:2 | Nothing **e.** your thoughts can attack you. |
| W-pI.....26.4:3 | Nothing **e.** your thoughts can make you |
| W-pI.....26.4:4 | nothing **e.** your thoughts can prove to you |
| W-pI.....42.4:3 | try to think of nothing **e.** thoughts that |
| W-pI.....58.3:3 | What is there to be saved from **e.** illusions |
| W-pI.....58.3:4 | are all illusions **e.** false ideas about myself |
| W-pI.....61.1:1 | light of the world **e.** God's Son? This, then |
| W-pI.....70.1:2 | to come from anywhere **e.** from you. So, |
| W-pI.....71.2:5 | of everyone and everything **e.** yourself. |
| W-pI.....72.2:3 | unable to reach other minds **e.** through |
| W-pI.....76.6:1 | There are no laws **e.** the laws of God. This |
| W-pI.....94.4:1 | **e.** to lay all idols and self-images aside; go |
| W-pI...106.5:3 | who could reach God's Son **e.** his Father, |
| W-pI...108.1:3 | And what is light **e.** the resolution, born |
| W-pI...121.3:3 | behold **e.** the proof that all its sins are real |
| W-pI...132.1:2 | And what can save the world **e.** your Self? |
| W-pI.132.10:1 | lesson for today **e.** another way of saying |
| W-pI...134.2:3 | It is irrelevant to everything **e.** illusions. |
| W-pI...135.6:3 | right to serve you thus **e.** your own belief? |
| W-pI.135.11:4 | not depend upon itself for anything **e.** its |
| W-pI...139.1:3 | is choice **e.** uncertainty of what we are? |
| W-pI...139.2:1 | ask this question **e.** one who has refused |
| W-pI...139.3:3 | For what is life **e.** to be yourself, and what |
| W-pI...139.6:4 | What does this mean **e.** the world is mad? |
| W-pI.151.12:4 | hear in everything no sound **e.** the echo of |
| W-pI.151.13:1 | **e.** at the beginning of the time we spend |
| W-pI...152.1:2 | pain **e.** his choice elects this state for him. |
| W-pI...157.9:1 | serenely unaware of everything **e.** His |
| W-pI...159.7:6 | No one asks for anything of him **e.** the gift |
| W-pI...160.3:2 | What could the reason be **e.** that you had |
| W-pI...160.6:4 | **e.** a miracle will search him out and show |
| W-pI...161.6:7 | What else could be the seat of fear **e.** what |
| W-pI...165.1:1 | What makes this world seem real **e.** your |
| W-pI...165.1:3 | hide what cannot be concealed **e.** illusion |
| W-pI...165.1:4 | already have **e.** your choice to see it not, |
| WpI rV.in12:1 | **e.** at the beginning and the end of practice |
| W-pI...183.6:5 | No other word we use **e.** at the beginning, |
| W-pI...183.8:4 | Let all thoughts be still **e.** this one. And to |
| W-pI...191.4:1 | Yet what is it **e.** a game you play in which |
| W-pI...194.7:5 | And what can he regard **e.** with love? For |
| W-pI.195.10:6 | can walk no road **e.** the way of gratitude, |
| W-pI...196.8:3 | that you be hurt **e.** by your own thoughts, |
| W-pI...198.2:9 | **E.** one. Forgiveness is illusion that is |
| W-pI...199.4:3 | need of it **e.** the need the Holy Spirit sees. |
| W-pI.......200.h | There is no peace **e.** the peace of God. |
| W-pI...200.1:2 | will not find peace **e.** the peace of God. |
| W-pI...200.1:5 | nothing else for you to find **e.** the peace of |
| W-pI...200.7:1 | There is no peace **e.** the peace of God, |
| W-pI.200.11:9 | *There is no peace* **e.** *the peace of God, And I* |
| WpI rVI.in.3:8 | **e.** a deep relinquishment of everything |
| W-pI...220.1:1 | There is no peace **e.** the peace of God. *Let* |
| W-pII...... 1.1:5 | is sin, **e.** a false idea about God's Son? |
| W-pII..222.2:1 | *no words* **e.** *Your Name upon our lips and in* |
| W-pII...... 3.2:3 | And what is fear **e.** love's absence? Thus |
| W-pII..256.2:2 | *We have no goal* **e.** *to hear Your Voice, and* |
| W-pII..269.1:5 | *to me; that nothing is,* **e.** *Your holy Son.* |
| W-pII..270.1:6 | *and every thought* **e.** *Your Own is gone.* |
| W-pII...... 6.4:3 | for what remains to see **e.** Christ's face? |
| W-pII...... 6.5:3 | or of time, or anything **e.** the holy Self, |
| W-pII..277.1:6 | *because he knows no law* **e.** *the law of love.* |
| W-pII..277.2:2 | He is not bound **e.** by his beliefs. Yet what |
| W-pII..287.2:4 | **e.** *the memory of You could signify to me the* |
| W-pII..290.1:6 | look on nothing else **e.** the thing I seek. |
| W-pII...... 8.1:4 | real world cannot be perceived **e.** through |
| W-pII..312.2:1 | *I have no purpose for today* **e.** *to look upon a* |
| W-pII..322.2:2 | *And so I cannot sacrifice* **e.** *in dreams. As* |
| W-pII..322.2:5 | *What loss can I anticipate* **e.** *the loss of fear,* |
| W-pII..324.2:2 | stray **e.** an instant from His loving Hand. |
| W-pII..331.1:6 | *There is no will* **e.** *the Will of Love. Fear is a* |
| W-pII..335.2:1 | *to me,* **e.** *to see my brother's sinlessness? His* |
| W-pII.....346.h | me, And I forget all things **e.** His Love. |
| W-pII..346.1:5 | *time. I would forget all things* **e.** *Your Love. I* |
| W-pII..346.1:6 | *in You, and know no laws* **e.** *Your law of love.* |
| W-pII..346.2:2 | when we forget all things **e.** God's Love. |
| W-pII..348.1:3 | *I have no cause for anything* **e.** *the perfect* |
| W-pII..354.1:2 | *I have no self* **e.** *the Christ in me. I have no* |
| W-pII..354.1:6 | *is Christ* **e.** *Your Son as You created Him?* |
| W-pII..354.1:7 | *Him? And what am I* **e.** *the Christ in me?* |
| M-in ..........5:1 | **E.** for God's teachers there would be little |
| M-4 .... IV.1:11 | all, **e.** by those who realize that harm can |
| M-5 ...... III.1:4 | he has no function **e.** to rejoice with them, |
| M-8 ...........3:8 | eyes will never see **e.** through differences. |
| M-10 .........3:7 | **e.** in grandiose fantasies would claim this |
| M-13 .........2:7 | Could they mean anything **e.** to a body? |
| M-16 .......11:5 | the day **e.** to put your trust in magic, for it |
| M-17 .........7:8 | **E.** to kill. Here is salvation now. An angry |
| M-19 .........1:7 | **E.** in His judgment justice is impossible, |
| M-20 .........3:8 | For what **e.** attack will lead to war? And |
| M-28 ......... 1:6 | having no function **e.** communication. It |
| C-1.............3:2 | The term "soul" is not used **e.** in direct |
| C-2........... 1:11 | what could come of this **e.** a dream which, |
| C-2........... 10:2 | Neither need be defined **e.** by this. Yet |
| P-2............I.4:2 | **e.** a patient could possibly have come here |
| P-2...........II.9:7 | psychotherapy **e.** a help in just this same |
| P-2......... IV.1:6 | be **e.** an expression of sorrow and of guilt? |
| P-2......... IV.2:7 | what could its shadow be **e.** deformed? |
| P-2....... VII.2:3 | What is prayer **e.** the joining of minds in a |
| P-2....... VII.2:6 | what choice is there **e.** to have Him stay? |
| P-2....... VII.5:6 | he has such wisdom **e.** in madness. That |
| P-2....... VII.7:5 | will not succeed **e.** to some extent and for |
| P-3..........II.8:8 | The journey is not long **e.** in dreams. |
| P-3....... II.10:8 | **E.** in time. In time there can be a great lag |
| S-1 ..........II.5:2 | And who could He be **e.** yourself? The |
| S-2............I.4:8 | think you can see sin in anyone **e.** yourself |
| S-2 ..........II.4:4 | respond **e.** with silence and a gentle smile |
| S-2 ..........II.5:7 | **e.** to keep the witnesses of guilt away from |

## excepting 4

| | |
|---|---|
| T-26...... III.6:5 | the undoing of every illusion, not **e.** this. |
| T-29..... VI.4:4 | that time might be preserved, **e.** one. |
| T-29..... VII.1:3 | is not, and there can be no peace **e.** there. |
| T-29..... VII.3:2 | And each will fail him, all **e.** one; for he |

## exception 17

| | |
|---|---|
| T-4...... VII.3:9 | to any judgment, any **e.** or any alteration. |
| T-6...... V.C.8:1 | To teach the whole Sonship without **e.** |
| T-11...... IV.4:3 | and to oppose steadfastly, without **e.**. |
| T-17...... III.2:3 | Without **e.**, these relationships have as |
| T-18....VIII.7:8 | aspect that you think you set apart is no **e.** |
| T-22........II.4:2 | way, in every instance and without **e.**. To |
| T-22........II.4:3 | believe that one **e.** can exist is to confuse |
| T-25........II.1:6 | And there is no **e.**, nor will there ever be. |
| W-in.......... 3:2 | With the **e.** of the review periods, each |
| W-in.......... 5:3 | one **e.** held apart from true perception |
| W-pI..... 16.1:3 | There is no **e.** to this fact. Thoughts are |
| W-pI..... 86.2:3 | *This is no* **e.** *in God's plan for my salvation.* |
| W-pI... 166.1:4 | He gives without **e.**, holding nothing back |
| W-pI... 170.1:2 | This can have no **e.**. When you think that |
| WpI rVI.in.5:1 | is but one **e.** to this lack of structuring. |
| W-pII ..... 9.1:3 | all things without **e.** and without reserve. |
| M-25 ......... 6:2 | good. To this there is no **e.**. And the more |

## exceptions 25

| | |
|---|---|
| T-4......... V.1:2 | are no **e.** except in the ego's judgment. |
| T-6...... V.C.4:5 | in that it teaches there must be no **e.**, |
| T-6...... V.C.4:5 | that the temptation to make **e.** will occur. |
| T-7......... V.5:4 | By accepting **e.** and acknowledging that |
| T-7......... V.5:7 | Love is incapable of any **e.**. Only if there is |
| T-7......... V.5:8 | does the idea of **e.** seem to be meaningful. |
| T-7......... V.5:9 | **E.** are fearful because they are made by |
| T-7......... V.6:3 | Fear always makes **e.**. Healing never does. |
| T-7....... VII.2:5 | is the law of God, and it has no **e.**. What |
| T-7......... XI.4:2 | There are no **e.** to this lesson, because the |
| T-7......... XI.4:2 | lesson, because the lack of **e.** *is* the lesson. |
| T-11...... VI.4:7 | of God, which knows no time and no **e.**. |
| T-11....... VI.4:8 | But make no **e.** yourself, or you will not |
| T-21......VIII.2:3 | The constancy of happiness has no **e.**; no |
| T-22......II.12:6 | Its will has no **e.**, and what it wills is true. |
| W-in.......... 9:4 | allow yourself to make **e.** in applying the |
| W-pI..... 47.3:3 | are no **e.** because God has no exceptions. |
| W-pI..... 47.3:3 | are no exceptions because God has no **e.**. |
| W-pI..... 89.3:5 | I would make no **e.** and no substitutes. I |
| W-pI... 152.2:2 | Yet can truth have **e.**? If you have the gift |
| W-pI... 152.2:7 | Accept no opposites and no **e.**, for to do |
| W-pI... 195.6:2 | rejoice that no **e.** ever can be made which |
| WpI rVI.in.2:4 | from that one, there must be no **e.** made. |
| W-pII . 292.1:1 | God's promises make no **e.**. And He |
| M-13 ......... 7:5 | The Word of God has no **e.**. It is this that |

**excessive** 1

WpI. rIII.in2:3 it necessary that you make e. efforts to be

**exchange** 70

T-1 I.9:1 Miracles are a kind of e.. Like all
T-1 I.9:2 sense, the e. reverses the physical laws.
T-3 IV.6:2 perception involves an e. or translation,
T-5 VI.2:6 offers you the continuity of eternity in e..
T-5 VI.2:7 When you choose to make this e., you will
T-5 VI.2:7 you will simultaneously e. guilt for joy,
T-9 VII.8:7 He will give you all of Himself in e. for the
T-10 II.3:4 return in e. for yours is the exchange of
T-10 II.3:4 is the e. of knowledge for perception.
T-11 VIII.15:1 Would you not e. your fears for truth, if
T-11 VIII.15:1 for truth, if the e. is yours for the asking?
T-12 II.9:4 e. this awareness for the awareness of fear
T-12 III.6:3 he did was to e. Self-love for self-hate,
T-12 III.8:4 God gave you the real world in e. for the
T-12 VIII.8:1 you by God in loving e. for the world you
T-13 V.1:3 In this e. it is extended, for it increases as
T-13 VII.4:4 to give this world away in glad e. for what
T-13 VII.6:6 give this sad world over and e. your errors
T-13 VII.9:2 first e. of what you made for what you
T-13 VII.9:2 the e. of nightmares for the happy dreams
T-13 VII.16:9 Take it of me in glad e. for all the world
T-14 IV.4:12 Love, God will Himself e. your gift for His
T-14 V.5:6 have learned how to e. guilt for innocence
T-14 V.5:6 in this e. can freedom from pain be his.
T-14 VI.1:1 together is the e. of dark for light, of
T-14 XI.4:8 He will gladly e. each one for the bright
T-15 I.11:5 e. for this instant He stands ready to give
T-15 I.14:4 As long as it takes to e. hell for Heaven.
T-15 IV.2:6 made for your salvation in e. for God's.
T-15 IX.5:4 you not e. your little relationships for this
T-17 IV.15:5 of creation in e. for your little picture,
T-18 V.6:1 to let Him e. this instant for the holy one
T-20 II.2:6 And there they will e. their gifts, offering
T-20 V.7:2 Would you e. this gift for any other? This
T-20 VIII.2:2 not happily e. your doubts for certainty?
T-21 II.4:5 instant is this e. effected and maintained.
T-21 II.6:3 it the whole e. of separation for salvation.
T-21 VII.10:7 desire to e. your helplessness for power,
T-21 VII.11:2 if you are willing to e. the world of sin for
T-22 II.11:8 And would you not e., in gratitude, the
T-24 V.9:4 He will e. His certainty for all your doubts
T-27 III.5:6 Holy Spirit make e. of pictures possible,
T-28 II.5:8 you made the one you would e. for this.
T-30 VI.1:4 real world given in e. for dreams of terror.
T-31 V.8:5 asked to make e. of what you now believe
T-31 VIII.7:1 e. I lay before your feet the peace of God,
W-pI 14.3:2 The early steps in this e., which can truly
W-pI 51.3:7 I can e. what I see now for this merely by
W-pI 56.1:6 inheritance away in e. for the world I see.
W-pI 59.2:4 Let me be willing to e. my pitiful illusion
W-pI 73.3:1 and grievances increase with each e.. Can
W-pI 76.9:5 received. E. cannot be made; there are no
W-pI 98.6:2 You can e. a little of your time for peace of
W-pI 118.1:2 *glad e. for all the substitutes that I have made*
W-pI 129.4:6 when you e. it for the world you want.
W-pI 137.9:1 and the glad e. of all the world of sorrow
W-pI 153.8:2 and we would not e. for foolishness the
W-pI 164.9:4 can e. all suffering for joy this very day.
W-pI 165.5:4 What would you then e. for it? What
W-pI 170.1:5 And you mean that to attack is to e. the
W-pI.182.12:7 accept it in e. for all the toys of battle you
W-pI 187.5:7 And both must gain in this e., for each
WpI rVI.in.5:4 sure and quick e. for the idea we practice
W-pII in.6:2 world of sorrow in e. for its replacement,
W-pII 6.4:2 He will e. them for the final dream which
W-pII .338.1:5 them and e. each fear thought for a happy
M-6 4:12 holy e. can receive less than everything?
M-16 11:1 Is not this an e. that you would want?
P-3 III.3:3 can pay only for the e. of illusions. This,
S-3 II.1:1 a poor e. of one illusion for a "nicer" one;

**exchanged** 7

T-5 VI.12:2 is the way in which time is e. for eternity.
T-13 V.1:2 fear. One is changeless but continually e.,
T-19 I.12:1 easily e. for knowledge as is the real world
T-20 VI.10:4 the unholy instant is e. in gladness for the
W-pI 129.3:3 be e. at last for what we cannot speak of,
W-pI 165.5:6 For this sight proves that you have e. your
W-pII 5.4:2 of Heaven been e. for the pursuit of hell.

**exchanges** 1

T-28 II.5:7 happy dreams the miracle e. for your own

**exchanging** 5

T-17 VII.9:5 of your relationship by e. yours for His,
T19..IV.C.2:13 ego's you renounced death, e. it for life.
W-pI 98.9:6 e. every instant of the time you offer Him
W-pI 129.1:3 but on e. it for what is far more satisfying,
W-pI. 137.13:1 healing to the world, e. curse for blessing,

**exclude** 13

T-6 II.12:2 The ego projects to e., and therefore to
T-6 V.C.6:5 are not is the only thing that you must e..
T-7 VII.1:13 be able to e. yourself from your thoughts.
T-7 IX.4:3 E. any part of the Kingdom from yourself
T-8 IV.8:10 If you e. yourself from this union, you are
T-11 I.2:4 Can you e. yourself from the universe, or
T-15 VII.14:6 desire to e. anyone from your completion,
T-15 XI.4:4 guilt you e. your Father and your brothers
T-15 XI.4:6 What you e. from yourself seems fearful,
T-16 III.5:5 keeping one with you what you would e..
T-17 V.7:4 must e. major areas of fantasy from your
T-18 I.1:6 To fragment is to e., and substitution is
W-pI 188.6:4 E. the outer world, and let your thoughts

**excluded** 18

T-6 V.C.6:4 therefore e. yourself from it in your belief.
T-7 VIII.3:8 it outside you have e. it from within is a
T-7 IX.1:7 conceive of any part from which it is e..
T-8 III.7:2 and you cannot be e. from them. The ego
T-11 III.7:10 no part of the Son can be e. if he would
T-13 III.3:4 out God, and He does not will to be e..
T-13 IV.6:8 holy, would be e. from your sight. The
T-13 V.8:8 Yet for this, light must be e.. Dreams
T-14 V.8:2 of perfect purity, from which no one is e..
T-14 X.10:7 lonely journey fails because it has e. what
T-16 V.6:4 is a kind of union from which union is e.,
T-17 III.10:7 such dreams are cherished have e. me. Let
T-22 VI.7:1 no error is e. and nothing kept hidden,
T-28 I.15:9 that you be e. from the Will that is for you
T-29 VIII.4:4 has been e. and been kept apart? What
W-pI 1.3:6 sure that nothing you see is specifically e..
W-pI 2.2:5 but be sure that nothing is specifically e..
W-pI 39.4:4 whom your holiness belongs be e. from it

**excludes** 3

T-16 VI.5:4 for the separate union e. the universe. Far
T-22 II.4:7 belief e. one living thing and holds it out,
M-22 2:1 for a time e. some problem areas from it.

**excluding** 9

T-5 VII.3:4 E. yourself from the Atonement is the
T-6 II.2:2 You are e. yourself by the very judgment
T-6 II.3:8 process begins by e. something that exists
T-6 II.3:8 directly to e. you from your brothers.
T-8 I.3:7 give up peace, you are e. yourself from it.
T-17 III.4:7 of e. even the one with whom the union
W-pI 9.3:1 and the essential rule of e. nothing. For
W-pI 86.3:4 grievances, I am therefore e. my only
M-14 1:4 forgiveness, complete, e. no one, limitless

**exclusion** 14

T-1 V.3:5 does not stem from e. but from inclusion.
T-6 II.1:4 E. and separation are synonymous, as are
T-7 VII.1:12 Mind is too powerful to be subject to e..
T-15 VI.8:3 There is no e. in the holy instant because
T-15 VI.8:3 and with it goes the whole basis for e..
T-15 VI.8:4 Without its source e. vanishes. And this
T-16 V.3:8 love is perceived as separation and e..
T-16 V.6:4 basis for the attempt at union rests on e..
T-17 III.2:3 the e. of the truth about the other, and of
T-17 VIII.1:5 faithlessness has not forced any e. on it. It
W-pI 9.5:1 be attempted, specific e. must be avoided.
W-pI 43.5:1 without self-directed inclusion or e.. For
M-7 6:1 with the self to the e. of the patient. It is a
M-21 1:8 concentration and facilitating the e., or at

**exclusions** 1

W-pI 34.4:2 sure, however, not to make any specific e.

**exclusive** 2

T-6 V.C.4:7 coexist for long, since they are mutually e.
W-pI 28.4:4 seeing. It is not an e. commitment. It is a

**exclusively** 3

T-16 VI.6:2 For a time the body is still seen, but not e.
W-pI 72.4:2 e. concerned with what he does in a body.
M-in 3:1 determined e. by what you think you are,

**exclusiveness** 1

T-6 V.C.4:8 you are not recognizing this mutual e.,

**excuse** 4

T-2 VI.2:2 You would not e. insane behavior on your
T-14 XI.8:5 this fancied undependability as an e. for
T-29 I.8:1 is your e. for variable goals you hold, and
W-pI 95.7:3 as an e. not to return to it again as soon as

**executioner** 1

T-22 II.11:8 of an e. you gave him for the one he has in

**exemplify** 1

W-pII 14.2:5 and teach it, too, if we e. the words in us.

**exempt** 9

T-8 IV.1:7 You cannot e. yourself from His laws,
T-8 V.2:2 e. from it if you are to understand what it
T-13 III.9:2 But e. no one from your love, or you will
T-13 III.9:3 thus you will e. yourself from His healing
T-13 XI.9:2 It will not be possible to e. yourself from
T-14 V.7:4 not be e. from the effects of this most holy
T-15 VII.4:4 that you are e. from its evil intentions. It
W-pI 140.9:2 of healing, from which nothing is e.. We
W-pI 199.5:5 And would you be e. from the acceptance

**exempting** 1

T-8 V.2:3 you are e. yourself from the Will of God

**exercise** 30

T-2 VI.2:6 is only at this level that you can e. choice.
W-pI 1.3:2 applied. That is the purpose of the e.. The
W-pI 2.2:3 Try to apply the e. with equal ease to a
W-pI 4.3:1 This is a major e., and will be repeated
W-pI 16.6:3 The length of the e. period should also be
W-pI 32.4:2 can be utilized, if you find the e. restful.
W-pI 33.3:1 shorter e. periods should be as frequent
W-pI 34.5:3 awareness, the e. should take this form: *I*
W-pI 35.5:2 Toward the latter part of the e. period,
W-pI 35.8:1 During the longer e. periods, there will
W-pI 36.4:1 For the shorter e. periods, close your eyes
W-pI 37.4:1 Today's four longer e. periods, each to
W-pI 39.10:1 to introduce variety into the e. periods in
W-pI 40.2:1 need not close your eyes for the e. periods

W-pI.....41.8:5 e. can bring very startling results even the
W-pI.....43.5:1 of the e. period should be relatively short,
W-pI.....43.6:1 eyes, repeat the first phase of the e. period
W-pI.....44.3:2 we will use a form of e. which has been
W-pI.....44.5:2 quite ready to learn the form of e. we will
W-pI.....44.8:1 approach is advocated for this form of e.,
W-pI.....45.8:7 e. in holiness and an attempt to reach the
W-pI.....45.9:1 In the shorter e. periods for today, try to
WpI . rII.in.1:4 We will have one longer e. period, and
WpI . rII.in.3:1 Repeat the first phase of the e. period if
W-pI.....91.9:1 In the second phase of the e. period, try
W-pI.....93.8:1 In our longer e. periods today, which
WpI . rIII.in5:2 that are written down for each day's e..
W-pI...124.9:4 the mirror that this e. will offer you. And
WpI rVI.in.3:8 practice for the day, no form of e. is urged
W-pII.....in.2:1 to let the e. be merely a beginning. For we

## exercises 98

W-in..........1:1 make the e. in this workbook meaningful.
W-in..........1:2 the e. that will make the goal of the course
W-in..........2:1 e. are very simple. They do not require a
W-in..........2:5 The e. are numbered from 1 to 365. Do
W-in..........2:6 undertake to do more than one set of e. a
W-in..........3:2 day's e. are planned around one central
W-in..........4:2 The e. are planned to help you generalize
W-in..........6:1 the e. be practiced with great specificity,
W-in..........7:1 The overall aim of the e. is to increase
W-in..........7:3 The e. themselves meet the conditions
W-pI.......1.3:5 for these e. should not become ritualistic.
W-pI.......2.1:1 e. with this idea are the same as those for
W-pI.......3.1:4 These are not e. in judgment. Anything is
W-pI.......3.2:1 The point of the e. is to help you clear
W-pI.......4.1:1 e. do not begin with the idea for the day.
W-pI.......4.5:2 procedures to be followed for the e.. Do
W-pI.......4.6:1 since these e. are the first of their kind,
W-pI.......4.6:2 Do not repeat these e. more than three or
W-pI.......5.1:5 a proper subject for the e. for the day.
W-pI.......5.4:1 In these e., more than in the preceding
W-pI.......5.4:2 help to precede the e. with the statement:
W-pI.......5.6:4 *go. For the purposes of these e., then, I will*
W-pI.......6.1:1 The e. with this idea are very similar to
W-pI.......6.3:6 *go. For the purposes of these e., then, I will*
W-pI.......8.3:1 purpose of the e. for today is to begin to
W-pI.......8.4:1 The e. for today should be done with eyes
W-pI.......9.1:5 These e. are concerned with practice, not
W-pI.......9.2:4 that is required for these or any other e..
W-pI.......9.3:1 These e., for which three or four practice
W-pI.....10.4:1 Close your eyes for these e., and
W-pI.....10.4:4 The e. consist, as before, in searching
W-pI.....11.3:1 To do these e. for maximum benefit, the
W-pI.....11.3:5 On concluding the e., close your eyes and
W-pI.....12.2:1 These e. are done with eyes open. Look
W-pI.....12.3:6 these e. but remember that a "good world
W-pI.....12.3:7 mind are suitable subjects for today's e..
W-pI.....12.4:2 For the purposes of these e., there is no
W-pI.....12.5:9 That is the ultimate purpose of these e..
W-pI.....12.6:4 too long. Terminate the e. whenever you
W-pI.....13.4:1 The e. for today, which should be done
W-pI.....14.2:1 The e. for today are to be practiced with
W-pI.....15.3:6 These e. will not reveal knowledge to you.
W-pI.....18.2:2 the e. for today emphasize this aspect of
W-pI.....19.3:1 searching which today's e. require is to be
W-pI.....20.4:1 e. for today consist in reminding yourself
W-pI.....24.3:1 e. for today require much more honesty
W-pI.....24.3:3 the mind-searching periods which the e.
W-pI.....24.6:1 If these e. are done properly, you will
W-pI.....25.4:1 can make any sense out of the e. for today
W-pI.....26.8:1 you are doing the e. properly, you should
W-pI.....27.1:5 The purpose of today's e. is to bring the
W-pI.....28.4:2 purpose of these e. is to ask questions and
W-pI.....32.2:3 In today's e., try to introduce the thought
W-pI.....32.5:1 e. are also to be continued during the day,
W-pI.....34.2:1 periods are required for today's e.. One in
W-pI.....35.8:3 does occur should be omitted from the e.,
W-pI.....37.6:1 shorter e. consist of repeating the idea as
W-pI.....38.3:4 In today's e., we will apply the power of
W-pI.....38.5:4 you, but keep the e. focused on the theme
W-pI.....38.5:5 purpose of today's e. is to begin to instill
W-pI.....39.1:2 the ideas used for the e. are very simple,
W-pI.....39.3:6 Today's e. will apply to you, recognizing
W-pI.....39.3:7 As you apply the e. to your world, the
W-pI.....39.7:1 kind are suitable subjects for today's e.. It
W-pI.....40.3:1 Today's e. take little time and no effort.
W-pI.....42.6:1 thoughts is not appropriate for today's e..
W-pI.....43.6:3 the e. as often as necessary to prevent this
W-pI.....44.9:3 the e. with eyes closed as soon as possible.
W-pI...44.10:1 If you are doing the e. correctly, you
W-pI.....45.6:1 Begin the e. for today by repeating the
W-pI.....45.8:1 toward which the e. for today are directed
W-pI.....46.3:1 Today's e. require at least three full five-
W-pI.....46.4:1 If you are doing the e. well you should
WpI...rI.in.1:4 periods, the e. should be done as follows:
WpI...rI.in.3:3 e. should be done with your eyes closed
W-pI.....64.8:2 At times, do the e. with your eyes closed,
W-pI.....66.4:4 Today's e. are an attempt to go beyond
W-pI.....69.7:1 If you are doing the e. properly, you will
W-pI.....71.9:9 very fact that you are doing the e. proves
W-pI...72.13:2 These e. should begin with this: *Holding*
W-pI.....73.8:1 we undertake the e. for today in happy
W-pI.....74.1:1 toward which all our e. are directed.
W-pI.....74.2:1 and the e. for today are directed towards
W-pI.....75.3:1 Our e. for today will be happy ones, in
W-pI.....79.8:1 The e. for today will be successful to the
W-pI.....91.6:6 statement ends is needed for our e. today.
W-pI...93.10:1 first five minutes of each hour for these e..
W-pI.....94.5:8 every effort to do the hourly e. today.
W-pI.....95.3:2 again direct our e. towards reaching your
W-pI.....97.7:1 Begin these happy e. with the words the
W-pI...100.7:2 Begin the e. with the thought today's idea
W-pI...101.5:2 The e. teach sin is not real, and all that
W-pI...102.3:1 periods of practicing to e. planned to help
W-pI...106.7:4 it is. Each hour's e. should begin with this
W-pI...107.7:6 to enter into all the e. that we do this day.
W-pI.108.10:3 now. Think of the e. for today as quick
WpI . rIII.in9:1 The e. to be done throughout the day are
W-pI...132.8:1 this course, and in the e. that we do today

## exert 4

T-1........IV.2:2 e. enormous efforts to establish its reality.
T-2.......VI.9:10 believe that your thoughts cannot e. real
T-4......III.10:3 have been willing to e. to protect your ego
W-pI.....20.2:2 it as an effort to e. force or pressure. You

## exerted 2

T-6....V.C.10:5 You have e. great effort to preserve what
T-16......III.2:8 care you have e. in choosing its witnesses,

## exerts 2

T-4.........V.1:3 The ego e. maximal vigilance about what
T-23......IV.7:7 limits it e. on those in battle still are gone,

## exhausted 1

T-20......III.9:1 years, starved and emaciated, weak and e.

## exile 8

T-5........IV.3:4 ego can keep you in e. from the Kingdom,
T-10.........I.2:1 dreaming of e. but perfectly capable of
T-24.......II.3:5 never one, each one in e. from himself,
T-31.........I.4:5 in e. from the home where God Himself
W-pI...166.8:2 you then proclaim your poverty in e.? He
W-pI...182.1:5 could say with certainty you are an e. here
W-pII......7.3:3 the means you made for e. to restore your
W-pII..355.1:2 *keep Your Word You gave Your Son in e.. I*

## exiled 1

W-pI...160.5:4 Now is he e. of necessity, not knowing

## exist 128

T-1.........I.22:2 your physical eyes cannot see does not e..
T-1.........I.24:3 is your own nightmare, and does not e..
T-1..........II.4:1 except in time, and time does not really e.
T-1.........III.2:1 will not continue to e. as separate states.
T-1........IV.4:2 could demonstrate that death does not e..
T-1........VI.1:3 lack does not e. in the creation of God, it
T-1........VI.5:1 because they do not e. at the creative level
T-1........VI.5:1 level, and therefore do not e. at all. To
T-1........VI.5:8 *is fear, It produces a state that does not e..*
T-2..........I.2:2 the separation, nor does it actually e. now
T-2..........II.4:4 because belief in space and time did not e.
T-2........III.2:2 to fear, because fear did not e.. Both the
T-2.........V.1:5 miscreations of the mind do not really e..
T-2.........V.1:9 The body does not e. except as a learning
T-2....V.A.17:6 In time we e. for and with each other. In
T-2.......VII.1:3 I know it does not e., but you do not. If I
T-2.......VII.4:5 believe in the power of what does not e..
T-2.....VII.5:12 time itself involves intervals that do not e.
T-2......VIII.4:5 which, without belief, will no longer e..
T-3..........I.7:4 it is unaware of evil, and evil does not e..
T-3..........II.2:6 means that you never see what does not e.
T-3.........IV.1:5 did not e. until the separation introduced
T-3.........VI.2:8 that what you judged against does not e..
T-3......VI.5:10 This belief can e. only to the extent that
T-3......VI.8:10 even doubt whether you really e. at all.
T-4..........II.1:3 history would not e. if the same errors
T-4..........II.9:5 will continue to e. after a temporary lapse
T-4.........III.9:3 This one fact means the ego does not e.,
T-4.........IV.8:9 protection and love, the ego cannot e.. Let
T-6......IV.11:2 the Holy Spirit demonstrates does not e..
T-6......V.A.2:3 device, and therefore does not e.. The
T-7.........IV.1:7 to Him and therefore does not e., but
T-7........VI.6:2 all. They therefore do not e. for Him. He
T-7........VI.8:7 total, the untrue cannot e.. Commitment
T-7.......VI.11:7 It does not e.. Do not try to understand it
T-8...........I.5:9 relinquish the other, even if it does not e..
T-8.........I.5:10 teaches them that *all* directions e., and
T-8.......VII.7:3 orders of reality merely appear to e., just
T-8......VIII.8:1 that does not e. can be so insistent. Have
T-9..........IV.5:5 What has no effect does not e., and to the
T-9..........IV.5:6 that the ego does not e. and proves it.
T-9......VIII.9:5 transform to the Will of God does not e.
T-10.......in.2:2 What except Him can e.? Nothing beyond
T-10..........I.1:7 is not of God, and therefore does not e..
T-10......III.5:3 for which it stands, but which do not e..
T-10.....III.10:5 Yet they e. only because you honor them.
T-10......IV.4:7 that is not under them does not e.. "Laws
T-11.......V.2:5 that what has no effects does not e.. Laws
T-11.......V.17:4 a demonstration that His Son does not e.,
T-11.....VI.10:7 does not e. has no size and no measure.
T-11......VII.4:1 a condition in which opposites do not e..
T-12.........I.9:3 teach yourself that fear does not e. in you.
T-13....VIII.1:3 He teaches that the past does not e., a fact
T-14.......III.7:7 cause, and being without cause, cannot e..
T-14.....IV.10:5 have placed within your mind cannot e.,
T-14.....VII.3:6 a belief in something that does not e.. It is
T-14......XI.9:8 They do not e. in His Mind at all. For the
T-15.........I.8:2 of the past and future, which do not e..
T-15.......I.10:2 more than merely that hell does not e.. In
T-15.......V.7:2 a picture whose likeness does not e.. For
T-16........IV.2:1 of love play out a conflict that does not e..
T-16........IV.7:5 very real to you, but which does not e..
T-18.....VII.3:1 no single instant does the body e. at all. It
T-18....VIII.6:2 missing; it could not e. if it were separate,
T19. IV.A.10:8 what the other looks upon does not e..
T-21.....V.5:10 Yet if it must be so, it must e.. And if it
T-22........II.4:3 To believe that one exception can e. is to
T-23.......in.4:6 clean place where littleness does not e..
T-23.........I.8:2 e. between one power and nothingness.
T-26......III.4:3 "It has no meaning, and does not e.."
T-27........II.2:9 pardon and your hurt cannot e. together.
T-27.....VII.3:2 and you e. and think apart from me.
T-27....VIII.1:2 nor does it e. without the dream in which
T-28.....V.1:10 Except you share it, nothing can e.. And
T-28.....V.1:11 e. because God shared His Will with you,
T-28.......V.7:2 The world you see does not e., because
T-29.....II.10:3 then what is not in Him does not e., and
T-29......IV.4:5 the idea that they e. from which the fears
T-30....III.11:1 God holds of you e. but where you are? Is
T-31.....IV.10:5 A journey from yourself does not e.. How
T-31.......V.7:3 Apart from learning they do not e.. They

| | |
|---|---|
| W-pI.....13.3:2 | and crowd it with images that do not **e**.. |
| W-pI.....14.1:2 | What God did not create does not **e**.. And |
| W-pI.....14.1:3 | that does **e**. exists as He created it. The |
| W-pI.....14.1:5 | is of your own making, and it does not **e**.. |
| W-pI.....22.2:5 | and kill. All that you fear does not **e**.. |
| W-pI.....43.2:2 | has no function in God, and does not **e**.. |
| W-pI.....52.5:5 | They do not **e**., and so they mean nothing |
| W-pI.....53.3:8 | I am acknowledging that it does not **e**.. |
| W-pI.....53.4:2 | world **e**. if God did not create it? He is the |
| W-pI.....54.2:3 | If I did not think I would not **e**., because |
| W-pI.....76.6:4 | What it is meant to save does not **e**.. Only |
| W-pI.....80.7:2 | to be free of problems that do not **e**.. The |
| W-pI.....88.4:2 | *this shows me I believe in laws that do not* **e**.. |
| W-pI.....93.5:2 | Therefore, this self does not **e**. at all. And |
| W-pI.....96.3:4 | A mind and body cannot both **e**.. Make |
| W-pI.....96.6:6 | real, nor solve a problem that does not **e**.. |
| W-pI.....99.3:1 | within a mind where both of them **e**.? The |
| W-pI...102.2:3 | nothing, and does not **e**.. And everything |
| W-pI...110.1:4 | is not real, and misery and death do not **e**. |
| W-pI...129.3:1 | cannot **e**. and vengeance has no meaning? |
| W-pI...131.9:4 | believes that he abides in what does not **e**. |
| W-pI...132.7:4 | that the world does not **e**. because what |
| W-pI...132.8:2 | idea is true because the world does not **e**.. |
| W-pI...132.9:4 | How can a world of time and place **e**., if |
| W-pI.137.11:3 | What is opposed to God does not **e**., and |
| W-pI...140.9:4 | what does not **e**. is truer in some forms |
| W-pI...156.1:2 | guilt, and being causeless it does not **e**.. It |
| W-pI...160.4:8 | And if fear is real, then you do not **e**. at all |
| W-pI...167.1:6 | because an opposite to God does not **e**.. |
| W-pI...167.6:4 | What is alien to the mind does not **e**., |
| W-pII .223.1:2 | home, and I do not **e**. apart from Him. He |
| W-pII .258.1:2 | goals which offer nothing, and do not **e**.. |
| W-pII .....5.5:5 | Fear does not **e**.. Identify with love, and |
| M-3 ...........3:5 | that these levels cannot **e**. is simply to say |
| M-8 ...........3:5 | meaning does not **e**. in the world outside |
| M-8 ...........6:7 | place–for differences cannot **e**. within it |
| M-10 .........2:9 | "God's Son is guiltless, and sin does not **e**. |
| M-17 .......9:11 | This sword does not **e**.. The fear of God is |
| M-20 .........3:4 | and must believe that it cannot **e**.. In this |
| M-20 .........4:2 | that peace cannot **e**. will certainly return. |
| M-21 .........3:4 | not **e**. or seeks for illusions in his heart, all |
| M-25 .........1:2 | to make up a power that does not **e**.. It is |
| C-2............1:9 | a choice for options that do not **e**.. We |
| C-4............3:8 | world is saved from sin, for sin does not **e**. |
| P-1............4:3 | The world he sees does therefore not **e**.. |
| P-3......... II.4:4 | nor a perfect patient can possibly **e**.. Both |
| P-3..... II.10:11 | because time does not **e**. and the Will of |

## existed 3

| | |
|---|---|
| T-2...........I.2:2 | None of this **e**. before the separation, nor |
| T-4......... II.9:4 | that the ego **e**. before that point in time. |
| T-4......... II.9:5 | may believe that the soul **e**. before, and |

## existence 49

| | |
|---|---|
| T-1........ VI.4:4 | Belief produces the acceptance of **e**.. That |
| T-2...... IV.3:10 | is almost impossible to deny its **e**. in this |
| T-2....V.A.14:3 | what has no real effect has no real **e**.. Its |
| T-2.......VII.6:8 | so, he is believing in the **e**. of nothingness. |
| T-3......... II.3:6 | create with the same Will has any real **e**.. |
| T-3........VI.9:5 | Its **e**. does not depend on your ability to |
| T-4...........I.8:2 | doubtful as long as you believe in its **e**.. |
| T-4......... II.6:9 | to any perceived threat to the ego's **e**.. |
| T-4......... II.8:5 | and thus establish its own **e**. are useless. |
| T-4........ III.3:2 | continued **e**. depends on your continuing |
| T-4........ III.3:4 | All it can offer is a sense of temporary **e**., |
| T-4........ III.3:5 | you this life is your **e**. because it is its own. |
| T-4........ III.3:6 | Against this sense of temporary **e**. spirit |
| T-4........IV.1:7 | the trick of its **e**. except with mirrors? But |
| T-4.......VII.1:5 | believes your **e**. is defined by separation. |
| T-4.......VII.4:1 | **E**. as well as being rest on |
| T-4.......VII.4:2 | **E**., however, is specific in how, what and |
| T-4.......VII.5:7 | between *having* and *being,* as there is in **e**.. |
| T-5........IV.2:2 | Its **e**. is unshared. It does not die; it was |
| T-5.......VII.3:4 | is the ego's last-ditch defense of its own **e**. |
| T-7........IV.7:7 | by not recognizing its **e**. in your brother. |
| T-7........VI.3:5 | is totally inimical to its **e**. *for* its existence. |
| T-7........VI.3:5 | is totally inimical to its existence *for* its **e**.. |
| T-7 .......VI.3:7 | This threatens its own **e**., a state which it |
| T-7 .......VI.3:9 | It does not perceive *its* **e**. as threatened by |
| T-7 .....VI.11:9 | That would justify its **e**., which cannot be |
| T-7 ....VIII.4:6 | are. Yet its **e**. is dependent on your mind, |
| T-7 ....VIII.5:4 | for the ego's **e**. you will have laid aside all |
| T-9 ......VII.5:3 | produced, and must maintain for its **e**.? |
| T-9 .....VIII.3:2 | you that the ego is aware of threat to its **e**. |
| T-11 ...... V.8:5 | then, can its **e**. continue if you realize that |
| T-12 ........I.9:6 | the belief in what is denied for its own **e**.. |
| T-12 ..... IV.2:5 | mind that believes in it and gives **e**. to it. |
| T-12 ..... IV.2:6 | that has the power to deny the ego's **e**., |
| T-12 ....VII.2:6 | gain confidence in their **e**. as they enable |
| T-13 .......II.4:4 | for its **e**. depends on keeping this secret. |
| T-18 ...VIII.4:5 | being. Its whole **e**. still remains in them. |
| T19..IV.B.13:2 | guilt maintains the whole illusion of its **e**.. |
| T-26 .... V.12:2 | hinder not the true **e**. of the here and now |
| T-26 .... V.12:3 | are real, and have **e**. that can be perceived |
| W-pI.....99.3:3 | They have **e**. in that they are thoughts. |
| W-pI...102.2:4 | you think it offers you is lacking in **e**., like |
| W-pI...131.7:3 | its own **e**. and attacks itself is not of Him. |
| W-pI.138.11:2 | what has **e**. and what has nothing but an |
| W-pI.182.11:1 | you raised against an enemy without **e**.. |
| W-pI...191.4:6 | of its **e**. and its guarantee of immortality. |
| M-3 ...........5:3 | their **e**. implies that those involved have |
| M-5 ........II.1:7 | **e**. of the world as you perceive it depends |
| P-2........ III.3:8 | him or talk to him or even know of his **e**.. |

## existing 1

| | |
|---|---|
| T-28 ...... V.7:1 | in a world perceived to be **e**. here. The |

## exists 41

| | |
|---|---|
| T-in ...........2:3 | ***Nothing unreal e**.*. Herein lies the peace of |
| T-1 ....... III.9:3 | of size **e**. on a plane that is itself unreal. |
| T-1 ....... VI.5:5 | *If fear* **e**., Then *there is not perfect love.* But: |
| T-1 ....... VI.5:7 | But: *Only perfect love* **e**.. *If there is fear, It* |
| T-2 ..........I.1:7 | that some emptiness or lack **e**. in you, and |
| T-3 ..........I.6:6 | It is perfectly clear because it **e**. in light. |
| T-3 .........II.3:5 | If nothing but the truth **e**., right-minded |
| T-3 ....... IV.7:1 | therefore know that no miscreation **e**.. |
| T-4 ....... III.4:4 | the real relationship that **e**. between God |
| T-6 .........II.3:8 | that **e**. in you but which you do not want, |
| T-6 ........ IV.6:2 | Nothing else **e**. and only this is real. You |
| T-8 .....VIII.2:1 | body **e**. in a world that seems to contain |
| T-9 ......VII.6:3 | point where sanity **e**. and *see the contrast.* |
| T-10 ......in.2:1 | beside you and nothing beside you **e**., for |
| T-11 .... V.12:2 | fulfilling your function as it **e**. in truth. |
| T-12 .. VII.11:7 | only the real world **e**. and only the real |
| T-16 ..... III.8:2 | the gap he imagines **e**. between his selves. |
| T-21 ..... V.5:11 | And if it **e**. for you, and has your freedom |
| T-21 ...... V.8:7 | it, because it does not realize that it **e**.. |
| T-22 .......II.2:7 | where none **e**. will surely fail to make a |
| T-25 ... IX.10:7 | it sees no differences where none **e**.. And |
| T-27 .VIII.12:2 | He sees no differences where none **e**., and |
| T-28 .......II.6:2 | and no design **e**. that could be found and |
| T-28 ..... IV.6:1 | confused, for in the gap no stable self **e**.. |
| T-29 .. VII.10:2 | to prove there is no death, and only life **e**.. |
| T-30 ..... III.6:1 | Nothing that God knows not **e**.. And |
| T-30 ..... III.6:2 | not exists. And what He knows **e**. forever, |
| T-30 ..... III.6:8 | parts in what **e**. within God's Mind. It is |
| W-pI.....13.1:3 | Nothing without meaning **e**.. However, it |
| W-pI.....14.1:3 | everything that does exist **e**. as He created |
| W-pI.....66.4:4 | a common content where it **e**. in truth. |
| W-pI.....96.1:5 | you will never be compatible. But one **e**.. |
| W-pI...138.1:3 | If Heaven **e**. there must be hell as well, for |
| W-pI...140.1:3 | the body, where it thinks the mind **e**.. Its |
| Wi181-200 3:2 | of what **e**. beyond defensiveness remains |
| W-pII .227.1:3 | *Yet nothing that I thought apart from You* **e**. |
| W-pII .....2.5:2 | the world, and only Heaven now **e**. at all. |
| W-pII .....3.3:4 | its illusions but a solid base where truth **e**. |
| W-pII .307.1:4 | *can bring me happiness, and only Yours* **e**.. |
| M-19 .........1:4 | Neither justice nor injustice **e**. in Heaven, |
| M-20 .........3:3 | is, for anger must deny that peace **e**.. |

## exonerated 2

| | |
|---|---|
| T-3 ..........I.2:7 | hurts you," and feels **e**. in beating a child. |
| T-27 .......II.1:9 | He may be pitied for his guilt, but not **e**.. |

## expand 3

| | |
|---|---|
| T-18 ... VIII.9:8 | its beneficence your little garden will **e**., |
| T-19 ..... IV.2:2 | already lies deeply within must first **e**., |
| W-pI .... 72.2:4 | be the best means to **e**. communication. |

## expanding 1

| | |
|---|---|
| W-pI .. 193.1:2 | eternally **e**. in the joy of full creation, and |

## expands 1

| | |
|---|---|
| T-21 ........I.8:4 | at all. The light **e**. and covers everything, |

## expansion 1

| | |
|---|---|
| T-18 ... VI.14:2 | sudden **e**. of awareness that takes place |

## expect 24

| | |
|---|---|
| T-5 .........V.8:4 | you want you **e**.. This is not delusional. |
| T-5 ...... VII.5:2 | become defensive because you **e**. attack. |
| T-8 ..........I.2:3 | You cannot **e**. it to say "I am not real." |
| T-8 ....... VI.5:9 | or give anything else, and **e**. joy in return? |
| T-9 ..........I.8:6 | as these, and actually **e**. to receive them? |
| T-9 ....... IV.8:1 | how appropriately can you **e**. to react? |
| T-12 .......V.7:5 | itself, what can you **e**. but confusion? |
| T-12 .... VII.5:1 | You see what you **e**., and you expect what |
| T-12 .... VII.5:1 | you expect, and you **e**. what you invite. |
| T-13 .......X.4:5 | you **e**. to use your brothers as a means to |
| T-15 .... VII.6:6 | For the guilty **e**. attack, and having asked |
| T-18 .......II.3:3 | on awakening, you do not **e**. it to be gone. |
| T-18 ... IV.4:10 | and then **e**. one to be made *for* you? |
| T-29 .... VII.5:2 | and what would you **e**. but to perceive the |
| T-31 .. VII.11:3 | within, and thus **e**. to see it everywhere. |
| T-31 .. VII.11:4 | upon, that he may be what they **e**. of him. |
| W-pI .... 66.9:7 | to **e**. happiness from anything the ego |
| W-pI .. 103.3:2 | what you **e**. to take the place of pain. God, |
| W-pI .. 106.8:1 | Ask and **e**. an answer. Your request is |
| W-pII .... in.3:3 | and **e**. our Father to reveal Himself, as He |
| W-pII . 287.2:7 | *way but this could I* **e**. *to recognize my Self,* |
| C-4 ........... 6:6 | remedy can guilt **e**.? But seen within your |
| P-2....... VII.9:6 | now **e**. to see in him an answer that you |
| P-3..........II.5:6 | of this world do not **e**. this outcome, and |

## expectancy 2

| | |
|---|---|
| T19 ...IV.A.6:1 | There is a hush in Heaven, a happy **e**., a |
| W-pI .... 94.4:1 | yourself; and wait in silent **e**. for the truth |

## expectantly 1

| | |
|---|---|
| W-pII . 270.1:4 | *and waits* **e**. *the one remaining instant more* |

## expectation 2

| | |
|---|---|
| W-pI .. 103.3:4 | this **e**. frequently throughout the day, and |
| W-pII .... in.2:2 | we wait in quiet **e**. for our God and Father |

## expected 5

| | |
|---|---|
| T-6 ........ in.1:5 | **e**. from insane premises except an insane |
| T-26 .... VII.7:6 | insane picture an insane defense can be **e**. |
| T-28 .......II.6:3 | could be **e**. from a thing that has no cause |
| W-pI .... 13.5:3 | **e**. to believe the statement at this point, |
| P-2......... in.1:2 | can hardly be **e**. to establish reality. That |

## expecting 2

| | |
|---|---|
| W-pI .. 108.9:1 | a while, **e**. to receive the gift you gave. |
| W-pII . 285.1:1 | **e**. but the happy things of God to come to |

## expedient 3

| | |
|---|---|
| T-3 ....... VI.6:3 | Justice is a temporary **e**., or an attempt to |
| T-4 .......II.11:1 | perception is merely a temporary **e**.. It is |
| M-16 ......... 5:8 | If it is **e**. to spend this time earlier, at least |

### expediter 1
T-2.....VII.3:10 and effect principle now becomes a real e.

### expend 2
T-9........ I.11:1 waste of energy you e. in denying truth.
T-16......III.8:3 willing to e. some little effort on behalf of

### expended 3
T-11....... V.4:3 on its behalf is necessarily e. on nothing.
T-18.....VII.4:8 Enormous effort is e. in the attempt to
T-31....... II.1:3 that must be prepared; no time to be e.,

### expenditure 1
W-pI...138.3:2 become the aim of effort and e. of time.

### expenditures 1
W-pI.....96.2:2 a senseless series of e. of time and effort,

### expense 7
T-7......III.1:11 belonging to anyone at the e. of another.
T-15......III.1:8 always choose one at the e. of the other.
T-15......VI.1:1 at the e. of another and not to suffer guilt.
T-16.....V.12:2 take the place of God at the e. of content.
W-pI.137.13:3 a small e. to offer for the gift of everything
M-8............2:8 able to gratify its needs at the e. of others.
M-13..........8:3 at the e. of the awareness of everything.

### experience 173
T-1........ I.12:2 represent the lower or bodily level of e.,
T-1........ I.12:2 or the higher or spiritual level of e.. One
T-1......... II.2:3 Revelation induces only e.. Miracles, on
T-1......... II.2:7 because it is an e. of unspeakable love.
T-1......... II.3:3 and should e. awe only in the Presence of
T-1......... II.3:7 is entitled to respect for his greater e., and
T-1........III.4:5 lead to the highly personal e. of revelation
T-1........III.5:8 you e. God's reassurances as threat, it is
T-1.......VII.5:2 not e. awe in the presence of your equals.
T-1.......VII.5:8 the e. will be more traumatic than beatific
T-2...........I.4:5 fell upon Adam could he e. nightmares. If
T-2........IV.3:8 The body is merely part of your e. in the
T-3........III.4:5 the e. from the realm of knowledge. That
T-4...........I.2:3 the separation was their first e. of change.
T-4........III.5:1 a kind of e. so different from anything the
T-4........IV.5:5 because only the ego can e. guilt. *This*
T-4........VI.3:3 make. No one who learns from e. that one
T-4.......VII.6:6 it in His Own Being and its e. of His Son's
T-4.......VII.6:6 Being and its experience of His Son's e..
T-5...........I.1:3 mind can e. revelation with lasting effect,
T-5...........I.1:3 because revelation is an e. of pure joy. If
T-5........III.1:5 clarification, not in statement but in e..
T-5......... V.3:6 you respond to your ego you will e. guilt,
T-5......... V.8:3 the mind will affect both behavior and e..
T-6....... II.11:4 and you cannot e. perfection as a difficult
T-6......... V.3:3 confusion a child would e. if he were told,
T-7......... XI.2:7 environment in which he will not e. strain
T-8......... II.2:5 grounds of your own e. with its teaching,
T-8........III.2:2 is accomplished, then, there is no other e.
T-8........III.2:3 for other e. will block its accomplishment
T-8........III.2:3 upon you, being an e. of total willingness.
T-8........IV.1:1 joy, unless you e. only this you must be
T-8........IV.5:8 or join, and e. pain or joy accordingly. My
T-8......VI.9:10 conditions of truth, but the e. is of God.
T-8.......VII.1:6 with a body you will always e. depression.
T-9......... I.14:4 if you do distort reality you will e. anxiety,
T-10.........I.2:3 recognize from your own e. that what you
T-11......IV.2:4 What you e. when you deny your Father
T-11....... V.5:5 The real conflict you e., then, is between
T-11..... V.10:1 apart from how the ego wants you to e. it,
T-11......VI.1:2 Perceptions are built up on the basis of e.,
T-11......VI.1:2 basis of experience, and e. leads to beliefs.
T-11......VI.3:5 are learned *with* beliefs, and e. does teach.
T-11......VI.3:6 I am leading you to a new kind of e. that
T-12.......III.2:3 insist on refusing and e. a quick response
T-13....... II.2:3 You do e. the guilt, but you have no idea
T-13....... II.6:4 understand that any fear you may e. in
T-13......IV.2:2 the greatest threat you think you could e..
T-13......VI.2:1 consider it "natural" to use your past e. as
T-13......VI.4:7 the future on the basis of your past e., and
T-13..... X.14:4 Every reaction you e. will be so purified
T-14.......III.3:5 Son: *What I e. I will make manifest. If I am*
T-14.......IV.8:4 parallel in your e. of the world to help you
T-14....... V.4:2 him, or you will ask for guilt and will e. it.
T-15....... II.6:3 this single second, and to e. it as timeless,
T-15....... II.6:3 is to begin to e. yourself as not separate.
T-15....... V.1:3 for past e. is the basis on which you judge.
T-15....... V.2:7 e. yourself as alone is to deny the Oneness
T-15......VI.8:6 and you will e. the full communication of
T-15.VII.14:10 is that you e. yourself as you were created,
T-15......IX.5:1 you would e. the attraction of the eternal.
T-15......IX.7:3 and you e. only the attraction of God.
T-16..... V.15:4 system is a carefully contrived learning e.,
T-16.....VII.7:1 between your e. of truth and illusion. Yet
T-16.....VII.7:4 you will weaken the e. of Him for a while,
T-16.....VII.7:4 you from keeping the e. in your mind. Yet
T-17.......III.2:8 Your own e. has taught you this. But what
T-17....IV.16:1 will e. again the meaning of relationship
T-17....... V.1:4 fails. The e. of it is always felt. Yet without
T-17....... V.1:6 a constant reminder of the e. in which the
T-17..... V.12:1 The e. of an instant, however compelling
T-17......VI.5:6 If you e. peace, it is because the truth has
T-17......VI.5:8 the ego believes the situation brings the e.
T-17......VII.7:6 solutions bring but the illusion of e., and
T-18......III.7:5 that you and your brother e. is really past.
T-18....... V.6:4 for you or your brother to e. fear alone, or
T-18....VI.13:6 you e. much of what happens in the holy
T-18....VI.13:6 and space, the sudden e. of peace and joy,
T-20.....IV.4:1 choose freedom will e. only its results.
T-20......VI.2:1 the contrast better than the e. of both a
T-20.....VII.2:2 over. To the extent you still e. it, you are
T-21........ II.2:4 *I choose the feelings I e., and I decide upon*
T-21......III.2:3 may imagine that you still e. its effects,
T-21....... V.2:4 afraid. You will e. depression, a sense of
T-21... VIII.5:3 is the constant peace you could e. forever.
T-22....VI.13:9 natural and more in line with your e..
T-22....VI.14:2 one thinks, the other will e. with him.
T-25. VIII.12:3 need you look to your e. within the world,
T-27.........I.9:8 It stands apart from all e. of love or fear.
T-30.........I.4:1 to you, and the things you would e., and
T-30.....VII.2:4 made on different aspects of e.. And then,
W-pI.......5.7:2 perceive it, and of the feeling as you e. it.
W-pI.....10.5:3 half a minute or less if you e. discomfort.
W-pI.....12.6:4 exercises whenever you e. a sense of strain
W-pI.....17.4:1 benefit, even if you e. resistance. However
W-pI.....21.2:4 The degree of the emotion you e. does not
W-pI.....24.6:2 and that you must e. disappointment in
W-pI.....28.3:4 its meaning to your tiny e. of tables, nor
W-pI...29.5:11 e. a sense of restfulness as you do this.
W-pI.....34.4:1 If you begin to e. difficulty in thinking of
W-pI.....41.1:1 abandonment all the separated ones e..
W-pI...44.10:1 you should e. some sense of relaxation,
W-pI.....74.2:5 and e. the peace this recognition brings.
W-pI.....74.5:1 close your eyes and try to e. the peace to
W-pI.....74.6:2 By this e. will you recognize that you have
W-pI.....74.6:5 even if you do not e. the peace you seek.
W-pI...76.12:1 well as in response to any temptation to e.
W-pI.....82.3:4 will not e. the joy that God intends for me
W-pI.....84.1:3 suffer, I cannot e. loss and I cannot die. I
W-pI.....87.1:6 day I will e. the peace of true perception.
W-pI.....91.5:6 choose. You can e. the strength in you.
W-pI.....91.7:4 You need a real e. of something else,
W-pI.....91.9:1 try to e. these truths about yourself.
W-pI.....91.9:2 Concentrate particularly on the e. of
W-pI.....93.8:4 in trying to e. what God has given you, in
W-pI.....93.9:3 Try to e. the unity of your one Self. Try to
W-pI.....96.1:1 you are one Self, you e. yourself as two; as
W-pI...105.7:5 Now are you ready to e. the joy and peace
W-pI...124.7:5 we would e. ourselves at one with Him, so
W-pI...124.7:6 In our e. the world is freed. As we deny
W-pI...132.7:4 find it in e. that is not of this world, which
W-pI.135.15:3 be controlled by learning and e. obtained
W-pI.135.16:3 Its past e. directs its choice of what will
W-pI...157.1:4 This day is holy, for it ushers in a new e.; a
W-pI...157.2:2 a fresh e. that sheds a light on all that we
W-pI...157.5:3 For your e. today will so transform your
W-pI...157.6:1 of what you e. this day to light the world.
W-pI...157.6:2 We cannot give e. like this directly. Yet it
W-pI...157.6:3 the same e. in which the world is quietly
W-pI...157.7:1 As this e. increases and all goals but this
W-pI...157.8:2 with the e. this day holds out to you to be
W-pI...158.2:7 E. cannot be shared directly, in the way
W-pI...158.4:4 When e. will come to end your doubting
W-pI...158.5:1 A teacher does not give e., because he did
W-pI...158.6:4 E. –unlearned, untaught, unseen–is
W-pI...169.3:6 from e. with which it is familiarly at home
W-pI...169.4:3 the Word of God to hasten the e. of truth,
W-pI...169.7:1 This is beyond e. we try to hasten. Yet
W-pI.169.12:3 E. that grace provides will end in time, for
W-pI.169.13:2 you receive, through grace in your e., to
W-pI.169.14:5 grace, and for e. that comes from grace.
WpI.rV.in10:1 a time in which we share a new e. for you,
WpI.rV.in12:2 faith in the e. that comes from practice,
WpI.rV.in12:3 We wait for the e., and recognize that it is
Wi181-200 2:4 e. of freedom and of peace that comes as
Wi181-200 3:2 E. of what exists beyond defensiveness
W-pI...181.2:5 you e. the peace that comes from faith in
W-pI...181.9:6 we give our trust to the e. we ask for now.
W-pI...183.9:1 state in which you will e. the gift of grace.
W-pI.183.11:7 Name, we would e. this peace today. And
W-pI.184.13:2 E. must come to supplement the Word.
W-pI...186.5:5 to e. which might affront their stance. Yet
W-pI...186.8:5 change as we e. a thousand shifts in mood
W-pI...194.4:6 And you will see by your e. that you have
W-pI...194.7:3 cause him pain, or bring e. of loss to him?
W-pII ....in.1:3 For now we seek direct e. of truth alone.
W-pII ..in.11:2 deep e. which should come afterwards.
W-pII .244.1:3 *suffer, be endangered, or e. unhappiness,*
W-pII .310.1:2 *And what I will e. is not of time at all. The joy*
W-pII .327.1:3 me but learn from my e. that this is true,
W-pII .327.2:1 *that Your promises will never fail in my e., if I*
M-4 ........II.2:1 e. is largely due to their perfect honesty. It
M-10 ......... 4:2 Is there anyone who has not had this e.?
M-21 ......... 2:5 It always requests some kind of e., the
M-21 ......... 2:5 the desired e. in the opinion of the asker.
M-25 ......... 2:5 barriers to direct e. of the Holy Spirit,
M-26 ......... 3:1 have a brief e. of direct union with God.
C-in ........... 2:5 but a universal e. is not only possible but
C-in ........... 2:6 this e. toward which the course is directed
C-in ........... 4:4 Yet there is no answer; only an e.. Seek
P-2..........II.2:4 here. Religion is e.; psychotherapy is
P-2..........II.2:4 is experience; psychotherapy is e.. At the
P-2.......VII.5:3 Yet who could e. the end of guilt who feels

### experienced 33
T-1..........II.1:7 from consciousness, but both are e. there.
T-1......... V.6:5 equilibrium is temporarily e. as unstable.
T-2...........I.3:7 world has not yet e. any comprehensive
T-2........ III.3:9 of perception is usually e. as conflict,
T-3..........II.1:7 who has not e. *some* light and *some* thing.
T-4.........I.10:1 once you have e. it you will withdraw all
T-4........ III.3:7 No one who has e. the revelation of this
T-4........ III.4:6 and since no ego has e. love without
T-7.....VII.11:4 offer to the ego are always e. as sacrifices,
T-8........ III.2:1 it is the only function that can be fully e..
T-8........ VI.9:8 Truth can only be e.. It cannot be
T-9..........II.1:1 has e. what appears to be failure. This is
T-9......VIII.6:6 it is e. as shifting and extremes are its
T-10...... IV.6:1 When you have e. the protection of God,
T-15.........I.6:6 the fear of hell to be e. is to bring hell here
T-15...... VI.6:5 who has not yet e. the lifting of the veil,
T-16.....VII.2:3 No special relationship is e. in the present
T-17....... V.5:4 the situation is e. as very precarious.
T-17...... VI.5:9 it, and is e. according to the goal.
T-17...... VI.7:3 And peace will not be e. except in fantasy.
T-18.....VI.11:1 Everyone has e. what he would call a
T-18.....VII.3:2 or anticipated, but never e. just *now*. Only
T-18.....VII.3:5 guilt would be e. as pain and nothing else,
T-25.........I.6:3 as one, aware that it is one, and so e.. It is
T-25.........I.6:4 to teach you how this oneness is e., what
T-25.........I.6:4 what you must do that it can be e., and
T-26...... V.12:5 And then it was no more to be e. as there.

| | |
|---|---|
| W-pI.....16.6:2 | If strain is **e.**, three will be enough. The |
| W-pI...103.1:3 | it. Nor can it be **e.** where love is not. Love |
| W-pI...190.1:2 | When it is **e.** in any form, it is a proof of |
| W-pI...194.3:1 | felt, or pain **e.** or loss perceived. In no one |
| M-4 .........I.2:1 | When this power has once been **e.**, it is |
| M-4 .....I.A.3:2 | need not be painful, but it usually is so **e.**. |

## experiences 22

| | |
|---|---|
| T-2........ VI.9:1 | Everyone **e.** fear. Yet it would take very |
| T-4....... VII.2:4 | disrupt communication when it **e.** threat. |
| T-6.........I.10:1 | although we do not need to have equal **e.**. |
| T-6.........I.10:5 | in others you can learn from their **e.**, and |
| T-6.........I.11:2 | to repeat my **e.** because the Holy Spirit, |
| T-6.........I.11:3 | To use my **e.** constructively, however, you |
| T-9.....VIII.3:4 | When the ego **e.** threat, its only decision |
| T-11...... VI.3:4 | it. Yet different **e.** lead to different beliefs, |
| T-12...... III.6:3 | What he **e.** then is depression or anger, |
| T-14...... XI.6:5 | your **e.** to confirm what you have learned. |
| T-15....... V.4:5 | the ego, as learning **e.** that point to truth. |
| T-22.. VI.13:10 | it is necessary that you have other **e.**, |
| T-30..... V.9:11 | let not your **e.** here deceive in retrospect. |
| T-30..... VII.4:1 | given to the world and all **e.** here. In this |
| W-pI....... 7.3:2 | reviewing your past **e.** of picking up a cup |
| W-pI....... 7.3:3 | reactions to the cup, too, based on past **e.** |
| W-pI...96.11:4 | The joy your Self **e.** It will save for you, |
| W-pI...169.7:2 | brings with it the **e.** which bear witness |
| M-4 ........... 1:2 | their **e.** of the world vary greatly, and |
| M-20 .......... 2:2 | every way it is totally unlike all previous **e.** |
| M-21 ......... 2:6 | things themselves but stand for the **e.** that |
| M-21 ......... 3:1 | of this world will bring **e.** of this world. If |

## experiencing 16

| | |
|---|---|
| T-6.........I.10:5 | them without **e.** them directly yourself. |
| T-6......V.A.6:6 | step for a long time, **e.** very acute conflict. |
| T-7........ III.2:5 | meaning only by **e.** yourself as unreal. |
| T-9........ VI.1:4 | even though you are not **e.** joy yourself |
| T-15...... V.5:5 | in your mind, **e.** not loss but completion. |
| T-15...... XI.4:8 | hell, without **e.** himself as incomplete and |
| T-16..... VII.7:5 | being what it is, nor you from **e.** it as it is. |
| W-pI......... 18.h | am not alone in **e.** the effects of my seeing |
| W-pI..... 18.3:2 | *I am not alone in* **e.** *the effects of how I see–.* |
| W-pI..... 18.3:4 | *I am not alone in* **e.** *the effects of my seeing.* |
| W-pI......... 19.h | not alone in **e.** the effects of my thoughts. |
| W-pI..... 19.3:4 | *alone in* **e.** *the effects of this thought about–* |
| W-pI..... 54.3:1 | am not alone in **e.** the effects of my seeing |
| W-pI..... 54.4:1 | not alone in **e.** the effects of my thoughts. |
| W-pI. 134.16:4 | to **e.** the escape from all the heavy chains |
| Wi181-200 1:4 | It is **e.** this that makes it sure that you will |

## expert 1

| | |
|---|---|
| T-8......... II.1:6 | are. It is **e.** only in confusion. It does not |

## expiation 2

| | |
|---|---|
| T-13.........I.9:2 | in time, is always associated with **e.**, and |
| T-13.........I.9:2 | guilt could induce a sense of a need for **e.**. |

## explain 5

| | |
|---|---|
| T-7...........I.6:4 | to **e.** in words because words are symbols, |
| T-22.........I.3:8 | you, asking it to **e.** to you the world it sees |
| T-22.... VI.13:3 | Yet does the Holy Spirit **e.** this differently. |
| W-pI. 169.10:3 | listen to words which **e.** what is to come is |
| C-2............. 2:5 | ego and **e.** how it arose can be but he who |

## explained 10

| | |
|---|---|
| T-1..... VII.5:10 | The means are being carefully **e.** to you. |
| T-6............I.1:4 | however, can be **e.** in negative terms only. |
| T-7............I.6:4 | nothing that is true need be **e.**. However, |
| T-8........ VI.9:9 | It cannot be described and it cannot be **e.**. |
| T-9......... V.5:2 | really **e.** what happens in psychotherapy. |
| T-17....... V.8:1 | and let it be **e.** to you as you perceive its |
| T-23..... II.11:1 | vague unanswered question, not yet "**e.**." |
| T-31..... V.13:4 | Nor can this be **e.** by either view. The |
| T-31.... VIII.2:2 | How easily is this **e.**! You always choose |

| | |
|---|---|
| M-20 ......... 5:8 | In this one sentence is our course **e.**. In |

## explains 8

| | |
|---|---|
| T-22 .........I.3:6 | that sees, and as *not* you, **e.** its sight *to* you. |
| W-pI..... 25.1:2 | Today's idea **e.** why nothing you see |
| W-pI..... 29.1:1 | The idea for today **e.** why you can see all |
| W-pI..... 29.1:2 | It **e.** why nothing is separate, by itself or |
| W-pI..... 29.1:3 | it **e.** why nothing you see means anything. |
| W-pI..... 29.1:4 | fact, it **e.** every idea we have used thus far, |
| W-pI..... 42.1:2 | that **e.** why you cannot fail in your efforts |
| M-11 ......... 3:1 | text **e.** that the Holy Spirit is the Answer |

## explicit 5

| | |
|---|---|
| T-5 ...... VII.4:4 | I am making His plan perfectly **e.** to you, |
| T-6 ....... II.10:8 | **e.** statement that the ego never occurred. |
| T-17 ...... V.7:8 | Has He not been very **e.** in His answer? |
| T-17 .... V.7:10 | that He has given you a most **e.** statement |
| W-pI..... 13.6:1 | stating an **e.** cause and effect relationship |

## explicitly 3

| | |
|---|---|
| T-11 ...... V.4:4 | The ego's goal is quite **e.** ego autonomy. |
| T-13 ....... II.7:1 | This course has **e.** stated that its goal for |
| S-1........ III.6:4 | One need not ask **e.**. The goal of God is |

## exploit 1

| | |
|---|---|
| T-4 ..........I.8:1 | ego tries to **e.** all situations into forms of |

## exposed 2

| | |
|---|---|
| T-2 ....... IV.4:9 | If they are prematurely **e.** to a miracle, |
| T-17 ... IV.13:5 | from the frame in darkness is **e.** to light, it |

## express 7

| | |
|---|---|
| T-1 ........ V.1:4 | shell, but you cannot **e.** nothing at all. |
| T-17 .. V.11:10 | yourself unable to **e.** the holy instant, and |
| W-pI..... 78.8:8 | allowed the Holy Spirit to **e.** through him |
| W-pI..... 89.3:4 | By this idea do I **e.** my willingness to have |
| W-pI... 185.2:9 | these words **e.** the only thing they want. |
| C-in ........... 3:3 | and cannot **e.** what lies beyond symbols. |
| P-2........ III.4:6 | working through other patients to **e.** his |

## expressed 9

| | |
|---|---|
| T-1 ........I.11:3 | received, and through miracles love is **e.**. |
| T-1 ...... VII.2:3 | still be **e.** through one body to another, |
| T-2 ....... IV.5:1 | does not lie in the manner in which it is **e.** |
| T-2 ....... IV.5:2 | it will inevitably be **e.** in whatever way is |
| T-2 ....... IV.5:3 | must be **e.** in a language that the recipient |
| T-4 ...... VII.7:4 | actual revelation; its content cannot be **e.**, |
| T-5 ....... IV.7:3 | The full power of creation cannot be **e.** as |
| W-pI..... 97.7:3 | **E.** through you, the Holy Spirit will accept |
| W-pI... 130.9:3 | to see His thanks **e.** in tangible perception |

## expresses 1

| | |
|---|---|
| W-pI..... 27.1:1 | Today's idea **e.** something stronger than |

## expressing 3

| | |
|---|---|
| T-1 ....... IV.4:8 | Those who witness for me are **e.**, through |
| T-2 ..... VIII.1:3 | Who was **e.** the same Will in His creation. |
| T-14 ..... VI.6:5 | You who made it are but **e.** conflict, from |

## expression 25

| | |
|---|---|
| T-1 ........I.44:1 | The miracle is an **e.** of an inner awareness |
| T-1 ..... III.1:10 | is the potential, the achievement is its **e.**, |
| T-1 ....... III.7:4 | As an **e.** of what you truly are, the miracle |
| T-1 ........ V.1:3 | loveless and miraculous channels of **e.**. |
| T-2 ...... V.10:6 | The miracle, as an **e.** of charity, can only |
| T-2 ... V.A.13:2 | a desire to heal is an **e.** of this confusion. |
| T-2 ....... VI.7:1 | know first that the conflict is an **e.** of fear. |
| T-2 ....... VI.8:1 | that the miracle, or the **e.** of Atonement, |
| T-3 ...... VII.4:1 | **e.** for usurping the ability for self-creating |
| T-4 ....... IV.8:2 | the **e.** of his power as much as he chooses. |
| T-7 ....... IX.7:2 | Miracles are an **e.** of this confidence. They |
| T-9 .........II.2:5 | more fearful to him than its physical **e.**. In |
| T-12 .. VII.13:4 | kill you as the final **e.** of its feeling for you, |
| T-17 ....... V.1:1 | The holy relationship is the **e.** of the holy |
| T-17 ....... V.1:5 | Yet without **e.** it is not remembered. The |
| T-17 ..... V.13:3 | And by cutting yourself off from its **e.**, |
| T-19 ....... II.7:1 | the natural **e.** of what the Son of God has |
| T19 .IV.A.14:4 | act of charity, no tiny **e.** of forgiveness, no |
| T-20 ........ I.2:2 | the acceptance of the truth and its **e.**. This |
| T-26 .........I.1:6 | is the **e.** of a wish to see a little part of him |
| T-30 ..... III.1:3 | is content for its **e.** in the terms of form. |
| W-pI .... 74.1:6 | As an **e.** of the Will of God, you have no |
| W-pI .... 82.1:2 | the light of the world finds **e.** through me. |
| W-pI .... 96.4:1 | use of mind as means to find its Self **e.**. |
| P-2........ IV.1:6 | be except an **e.** of sorrow and of guilt? |

## expressions 12

| | |
|---|---|
| T-1 ..........I.1:4 | all the same. All **e.** of love are maximal. |
| T-1 ..........I.3:1 | Miracles occur naturally as **e.** of love. The |
| T-1 ..........I.9:2 | Like all **e.** of love, which are always |
| T-1 ........I.35:1 | Miracles are **e.** of love, but they may not |
| T-1 ....... III.8:4 | They are still **e.** of your own state of grace, |
| T-2 ..........I.5:6 | unaffected by all **e.** of lack of love. These |
| T-2 .........V.3:1 | already said that miracles are **e.** of miracle- |
| T-4 ... IV.11:11 | are natural, because they are **e.** of love. |
| T-8 .... VII.11:2 | Help and healing are the normal **e.** of a |
| T-8 ....... IX.3:2 | are physical **e.** of the fear of awakening. |
| T-14 ........I.4:5 | These are but indirect **e.** of the will to live, |
| WpI.rVI.in.6:5 | we will add but a few formal **e.** or specific |

## extend 75

| | |
|---|---|
| T-1 ....... III.9:2 | inevitable that they will **e.** them to others, |
| T-2 ..........I.1:1 | **e.** is a fundamental aspect of God which |
| T-2 ..........I.3:9 | to **e.** as God extended His Spirit to you. In |
| T-2 ..... VIII.2:5 | Last Judgment will **e.** over a similarly long |
| T-6 .........II.8:5 | You cannot **e.** His Kingdom until you |
| T-6 ......... III.2:9 | And what you project or **e.** you believe. |
| T-6 ..... V.C.2:5 | so that you will not project, instead of **e.**. |
| T-6 ..... V.C.2:6 | established what you can **e.** with perfect |
| T-7 ..........I.2:4 | this way can all creative power **e.** outward |
| T-7 ..........I.5:2 | as you, you can only **e.** yourself as He did. |
| T-7 ..........I.5:4 | are co-creator with Him **e.** His Kingdom |
| T-7 .........II.2:4 | What you project or **e.** is real for you. |
| T-7 .........II.3:6 | of being, know that what you **e.** you are. |
| T-7 .........II.7:5 | you share it and **e.** it as your Creator did. |
| T-7 ..... VI.12:5 | If you do not **e.** the Kingdom, you are not |
| T-7 ... VIII.1:11 | Every mind must project or **e.**, because |
| T-7 ..... IX.2:10 | to contain God, but wills to **e.** His Being. |
| T-8 ....... VI.5:4 | but they **e.** your creation as God extended |
| T-8 ....... VI.6:5 | you so that you can **e.** yourself as He did. |
| T-8 ....... VI.8:9 | Through our creations we **e.** our love, and |
| T-9 .........II.6:7 | the trust I have in you unless you **e.** it. |
| T-11 ..... IV.1:5 | you by your Creator that you might **e.** it. |
| T-12 ... III.10:9 | it, allowing the Holy Spirit to **e.** the real |
| T-12 .... VII.7:1 | before that what you project or **e.** is up to |
| T-12 .. VII.10:6 | Who wills to **e.** His peace through you. |
| T-12 .. VII.11:1 | accepted your mission to **e.** peace you will |
| T-13 ..... IV.7:5 | aspect of time that can **e.** to the infinite, |
| T-13 ....... V.9:6 | He sees within you, and He would **e.** it. |
| T-13 .. VII.13:7 | itself to let the rays **e.** in quiet to infinity. |
| T-15 ..... V.11:2 | judgment, out of His need to **e.** His Love. |
| T-15 ..... V.11:3 | in you, you have no need except to **e.** it. In |
| T-17 ..... IV.1:6 | but would **e.** happiness as its Creator did. |
| T-17 ..... V.15:2 | release, and Who would **e.** it through you. |
| T-18 ...... I.13:6 | brought you and him together must **e.**, as |
| T-18 ..... III.8:7 | the Great Rays **e.** back into darkness and |
| T-19 ..... IV.1:6 | will quietly **e.** to every aspect of your life, |
| T19 ...IV.A.1:2 | it. For it cannot **e.** unless you keep it. You |
| T19 .IV.A.5:11 | But let Him quietly **e.** the miracle of your |
| T-22 ...... in.3:3 | he would **e.** it by joining with another, |
| T-22 ...... in.4:6 | It must **e.**, as you extended when you and |
| T-22 ..... VI.9:5 | offer Him the tiny gifts He can **e.** forever. |
| T-23 ..... IV.4:3 | miracles you have the power to **e.** to all. |
| T-24 ....... V.1:9 | illusions as strongly as does love **e.** itself. |
| T-25 ..... III.7:8 | many chances to **e.** your own forgiveness. |

|  |  |
|---|---|
| T-25......IV.4:8 | And from you will the rest you found **e.**, |
| T-27..... II.13:1 | Consider how this self-perception must **e.** |
| T-27......III.5:7 | that can **e.** beyond the goal of learning. |
| T-27....... V.1:4 | its nature to **e.** itself the instant it is born. |
| T-27....... V.9:1 | Your healing will **e.**, and will be brought |
| T-29......III.4:1 | you did not create, but which you can **e.**. |
| W-in ..........7:1 | to increase your ability to **e.** the ideas you |
| W-pI .......9.4:1 | you, and then **e.** the range outward: *I do* |
| W-pI .....16.2:4 | nothing, but you will not **e.** it by doing so. |
| W-pI .....34.1:3 | your own thoughts, and then **e.** outward. |
| W-pI .....61.6:3 | find them helpful and want to **e.** them. |
| W-pI .....75.9:7 | that you will gladly **e.** today forever. |
| W-pI ...76.11:1 | and let His Will **e.** through us to Him. |
| W-pI .....82.2:2 | *Let peace e. from my mind to yours, [name].* |
| W-pI ...95.12:2 | may **e.** the allness and the unity of God. |
| W-pI ...108.6:3 | And from there it will **e.**, and finally |
| W-pI ...110.4:1 | saved to quietly **e.** into a timeless future. |
| W-pI ...121.9:3 | as one, we will **e.** the lesson to yourself, |
| W-pI.121.11:4 | try to let this light **e.** until it covers him, |
| W-pI ...137.9:3 | as you **e.** the little help He asks in freeing |
| W-pI ...156.4:4 | trees **e.** their arms to shield you from the |
| W-pI ...167.5:3 | They can **e.** all that their source contains. |
| W-pI ...167.8:4 | with the power to **e.** forever changelessly, |
| W-pI ...187.5:4 | Thoughts **e.** as they are shared, for they |
| W-pI.187.11:2 | What we have looked upon we would **e.**, |
| W-pI ...194.6:2 | you **e.** your learning to the world. And as |
| W-pI ...197.9:4 | the countless channels which **e.** this Self. |
| W-pII......9.3:1 | last summary that will **e.** beyond itself, |
| W-pII..320.2:1 | *then e. to all the world as well through me.* |
| M-26..........3:9 | laid the body down merely to **e.** their |
| C-2.............7:4 | see **e.** before you as you walk in gentleness |

## extended 41

|  |  |
|---|---|
| T-2...........I.1:2 | creation, God **e.** Himself to His creations |
| T-2...........I.3:9 | to extend as God **e.** His Spirit to you. In |
| T-7......VI.12:3 | divided state because only peace can be **e.** |
| T-7........IX.2:6 | Being *must* be **e.**. That is how it retains the |
| T-8......... II.8:4 | theirs, and through theirs yours is **e.**. |
| T-8........III.3:4 | His Own Fatherhood must be **e.** outward. |
| T-8........VI.5:4 | extend your creation as God **e.** Himself to |
| T-11.........I.3:8 | your creations have not ceased to be **e.**, |
| T-11...... I.10:2 | for otherwise His Will would not be **e.**. |
| T-13.........I.6:7 | for he has always **e.** the Love of his Father. |
| T-13....... V.1:3 | In this exchange it is **e.**, for it increases as |
| T-13....... V.9:7 | He has **e.** your perception even unto Him. |
| T-15.... VIII.1:1 | the holy instant has **e.** far beyond time. |
| T-16....... II.1:1 | see how it can be **e.** to include everyone. |
| T-17......VII.9:5 | the goal He placed there was **e.** to every |
| T-18....... II.7:3 | the Holy Spirit has laid upon it will be **e.**. |
| T-19......III.6:2 | the Creator must have **e.** Himself, and it is |
| T-19......IV.3:6 | in you has been **e.** to encompass everyone |
| T19....IV.B.4:1 | Peace is **e.** from you only to the eternal, |
| T19....IV.B.9:3 | be **e.** if you would have its limitless power |
| T-22.......in.4:6 | extend, as you **e.** when you and he joined. |
| T-22......VI.9:4 | that you give to Him that which can be **e.**. |
| T-23......IV.2:7 | How can a body be **e.** to hold the universe |
| T-23......IV.4:2 | yet, and so it cannot be **e.** to all creation. |
| T-24.........I.7:3 | to your brother that love might be **e.**, not |
| T-28....... II.2:2 | Love must be **e.**. Purity is not confined. It |
| W-pI .....10.5:3 | recommended that this time period be **e.**, |
| W-pI .....65.4:1 | to undertake the daily **e.** practice periods |
| W-pI .....68.5:1 | Begin today's **e.** practice period by |
| W-pI .....69.2:2 | this in our more **e.** practice period, let us |
| W-pI .....71.9:1 | the remainder of the **e.** practice periods to |
| W-pI .....95.4:2 | to wander, if it undertakes **e.** practice. |
| W-pI ...107.2:4 | be **e.** to the end of time and to eternity. |
| W-pI ...124.8:4 | This is our first attempt at an **e.** period for |
| W-pI.133.13:3 | two **e.** practice periods of fifteen minutes |
| W-pI ...199.4:5 | which helps forgiveness be **e.** to the all- |
| W-pII..253.2:2 | *assent to Yours, that it may be e. to Itself.* |
| W-pII..329.1:2 | *in truth is but Your Will, e. and extending.* |
| M-4........ X.1:5 | lets Christ's image be **e.** to him. Only the |
| P-in............1:7 | **e.** relationship with an "official" therapist |
| S-1 .........in.1:4 | And in this, creation is **e.**. God gives |

## extending 22

*See also* Self-extending

|  |  |
|---|---|
| T-1.........I.21:2 | accept God's forgiveness by **e.** it to others. |
| T-6......... II.8:1 | God created His Sons by **e.** His Thought, |
| T-6........ III.3:1 | The only safety lies in **e.** the Holy Spirit, |
| T-6.......... V.1:7 | God's **e.** outward, though not His |
| T-7...........I.5:2 | if God created you by **e.** Himself as you, |
| T-7.......... II.2:3 | unifies by increasing and integrates by **e.**. |
| T-7...... VI.13:7 | **e.** the joy in which it was created, and |
| T-7.......VII.5:4 | are not **e.** the gift you both *have* and *are,* |
| T-7.......VII.5:5 | All confusion comes from not **e.** life, |
| T-7........ IX.4:1 | forever **e.** because it is in the Mind of God |
| T-8........ III.3:2 | Their unity together by **e.** Their joint Will |
| T-8........ III.3:5 | the holy function of **e.** His Fatherhood by |
| T-9......... V.7:8 | **e.** it and accepting its acknowledgment. |
| T-12. VIII.7:11 | all things together by **e.** its wholeness. |
| T-13........IV.8:1 | time as one of **e.** itself in place of eternity, |
| T-13....... XI.8:6 | will teach you how to use it, and by **e.** it, |
| T-19.......IV.1:4 | them, **e.** past completely unencumbered. |
| T-21.........I.8:4 | **e.** to infinity forever shining and with no |
| W-pI ...192.1:1 | love created and in love preserved, **e.** love, |
| W-pI ...197.5:3 | **e.** love and adding to your never-ending |
| W-pII...314.1:5 | freed, **e.** its security and peace into a quiet |
| W-pII..329.1:2 | *am in truth is but Your Will, extended and e.* |

## extends 49

|  |  |
|---|---|
| T-6......... II.4:3 | The Holy Spirit **e.** and the ego projects. |
| T-6....... II.11:9 | **e.** outward only to what is true in other |
| T-6....... II.12:3 | Spirit **e.** by recognizing Himself in every |
| T-6........ III.1:2 | what **e.** from the mind is still in it, and |
| T-6........ III.1:2 | still in it, and from *what* it **e.** it knows itself |
| T-6........ III.3:6 | because it **e.** beneficence it is beneficent. |
| T-6.... V.B.1:10 | system is true, only truth **e.** from it. But if |
| T-7...........I.3:4 | Love **e.** outward simply because it cannot |
| T-7...........I.5:4 | are inseparable. God **e.** outward beyond |
| T-7........ IX.6:8 | Like His, It **e.** forever and in perfect peace. |
| T-7........ XI.5:2 | **e.** out into the darkness of other minds, |
| T-8........ VI.6:5 | and He **e.** His Fatherhood to you so that |
| T-8.....VII.10:5 | By reaching out, the mind **e.** itself. It does |
| T-8.....VII.12:7 | accomplished only if the mind **e.** to other |
| T-9......... II.6:4 | The Holy Spirit **e.** from your mind to his, |
| T-13......IV.9:5 | and **e.** the present rather than the past. |
| T-13...... VI.6:4 | **e.** to all aspects of the Sonship at the same |
| T-14.........I.3:3 | **e.** have all the power that he gives to them |
| T-15.........I.8:5 | the present **e.** forever. It is so beautiful |
| T-15....... II.3:4 | time, as God **e.** Himself to encompass you |
| T-15.......III.7:6 | little world but still in you, He **e.** forever. |
| T-16....... II.1:6 | you worry how the miracle **e.** to all the |
| T-16...VII.11:2 | miracle **e.** to bless everyone and to resolve |
| T-17.......III.5:6 | continuity **e.** the present by increasing its |
| T-18.........I.6:3 | For truth **e.** inward, where the idea of loss |
| T-18.... VI.11:8 | replaces it **e.** to what has freed you, and |
| T-19......IV.1:1 | As peace **e.** from deep inside yourself to |
| T19... IV.A.8:5 | weakness, which **e.** to everything. The |
| T-21..... V.10:6 | vision. Vision **e.** beyond itself, as does the |
| T-22.......in.4:8 | the sameness that you saw **e.** and finally |
| T-22....... II.12:1 | the bright, endless circle that **e.** forever, is |
| T-22..... VI.14:8 | love **e.** its being and creates more of itself. |
| T-23.......I.12:3 | Peace, looking on itself, **e.** itself. War is |
| T-25...... II.10:7 | His Will and yours, which but **e.** His Will. |
| T-25......IV.3:5 | you there is a vision that **e.** to all of them, |
| T-27...... II.13:1 | thought **e.** because that is its purpose, |
| T-27....... V.1:2 | The miracle **e.** without your help, but you |
| T-27...... V.1:12 | else. Yet by your listening His Voice **e.**, |
| W-pI .....16.2:3 | it **e.** the truth or it multiplies illusions. |
| W-pI .....36.1:1 | Today's idea **e.** the idea for yesterday |
| W-pI ...105.4:3 | **e.** the limitless to the unlimited, eternity |
| W-pI ...153.9:3 | ministry **e.** its holy blessing through the |
| W-pI ...188.3:1 | and from your heart **e.** around the world. |
| W-pI ...193.1:2 | Will **e.** to what He does not understand, |
| W-pI ...199.8:6 | God Himself **e.** His Love and happiness |
| W-pII......5.4:3 | of God **e.** his hand to reach his brother, |
| W-pII..330.1:4 | to spirit, and **e.** its freedom and its joy, as |
| S-1 ......... II.7:9 | all. So it **e.**, as it was meant to do. And for |
| S-3 ........IV.8:2 | love **e.** along with Mine beyond infinity, |

## extension 56

*See also* self-extension

|  |  |
|---|---|
| T-2...........I.1:7 | The inappropriate use of **e.**, or projection, |
| T-2...........I.2:4 | **E.**, as undertaken by God, is similar to the |
| T-5........IV.1:5 | It belongs to you because, as an **e.** of God, |
| T-6....... II.12:1 | and the Holy Spirit's **e.** is very simple. The |
| T-7.........II.5:6 | The **e.** of truth, which *is* the law of the |
| T-7..........II.7:6 | it does need **e.** because it *means* extension. |
| T-7..........II.7:6 | it does need extension because it *means* **e.**. |
| T-7...... VI.12:4 | mind is blocking the **e.** of the Kingdom, |
| T-7...... VI.12:4 | of the Kingdom, and its **e.** is your joy. If |
| T-7......VIII.1:1 | true that without **e.** there can be no love. |
| T-7......VIII.1:7 | To the Holy Spirit it is the law of **e.**. To |
| T-7......VIII.3:8 | is a complete distortion of the power of **e.** |
| T-7........... IX.h | The **E.** of the Kingdom |
| T-7........ IX.3:1 | **e.** of God's Being is spirit's only function. |
| T-7........ IX.3:3 | Fullness is **e.**. The ego's whole thought |
| T-7........ IX.3:4 | The ego's whole thought system blocks **e.**, |
| T-7........ IX.4:6 | selfishness impossible and **e.** inevitable. |
| T-7........ IX.7:3 | your identification is maintained by **e.**. |
| T-8..........II.7:3 | no boundaries because its **e.** is unlimited, |
| T-8..........II.8:6 | Voice for his creations and for his own **e.**. |
| T-8........ III.3:1 | Father and of the Son are One, by Their **e.** |
| T-8........ III.3:2 | Their **e.** is the result of Their Oneness, |
| T-8.....VII.11:3 | and by blocking its own **e.** beyond it, will |
| T-8.....VII.12:7 | minds, and does not arrest itself in its **e.**. |
| T-8.....VII.12:8 | because only **e.** is the mind's function. |
| T-8.....VII.16:7 | The power of wholeness is **e.**. Do not |
| T-11.......in.3:1 | make by projection, but God creates by **e.** |
| T-11.........I.3:5 | **E.** cannot be blocked, and it has no voids. |
| T-11.........I.7:9 | And being an **e.** of His Will, yours must |
| T-11....... IV.7:5 | is the **e.** of the Love and the loveliness of |
| T-11....... V.2:7 | If reality is recognized by its **e.**, what leads |
| T-11....... V.5:4 | the **e.** of His Will cannot be unlike itself. |
| T-12...... VI.3:5 | from the **e.** of loving thoughts outward. |
| T-12...... VI.6:3 | transfer to holiness is merely its natural **e.** |
| T-12...... VI.7:3 | loving the **e.** of Himself that is His Son. |
| T-14....... V.3:4 | Creation is the natural **e.** of perfect purity. |
| T-16........II.1:3 | yourself not with the **e.** of holiness, for |
| T-16........II.1:5 | It is their **e.**, far beyond the limits you |
| T-16....... V.5:4 | first in union, and then in the **e.** of union. |
| T-16....... V.5:5 | and in the **e.** of the "victory" even to the |
| T-16....... V.7:4 | union, for there is no increase and no **e.**. |
| T-19...... III.6:2 | If creation is **e.**, the Creator must have |
| T-19...... IV.1:5 | The **e.** of the Holy Spirit's purpose from |
| T19....IV.B.9:2 | the limits that would hold its **e.** back, and |
| T-22...... VI.9:2 | with charity? **E.** of forgiveness is the Holy |
| T-23...... IV.3:5 | Creation is the means for God's **e.**, and |
| T-24.........I.1:1 | Love is **e.**. To withhold the smallest gift is |
| T-28........I.11:3 | its radiant **e.** back into the Mind which |
| T-29.... VI.4:11 | to die. It must be life's **e.**, that it be as one |
| W-pI.....21.1:1 | continuation and **e.** of the preceding one. |
| W-pI.....92.1:1 | idea for today is an **e.** of the previous one. |
| W-pI... 159.4:3 | and receiver are united in **e.** here on earth |
| WpI.rV.in10:5 | His Son, completing His **e.** in your own. |
| W-pII .314.1:2 | now is recognized as but **e.** of the present. |
| W-pII ... 11.2:2 | For He would add to love by its **e.**. Thus |
| S-1 .........in.1:5 | God gives thanks to His **e.** in His Son. His |

## extensions 6

|  |  |
|---|---|
| T-6..........II.8:1 | the **e.** of His Thought in His Mind. All His |
| T-7........ IX.7:1 | your Identity and the **e.** which maintain It |
| T-9.....VIII.10:3 | God Himself keeps your **e.** safe within it. |
| T-12...... IV.6:8 | God is whole and all His **e.** are like Him. |
| T-15...... III.7:7 | Yet He brings all His **e.** to you, as host to |
| T-22........II.9:4 | true, thoughts would not be the mind's **e.**, |

## extent 45

|  |  |
|---|---|
| T-1..........II.6:5 | of abolishing time to the **e.** that it renders |
| T-1........ III.5:9 | but only to the **e.** to which you reinforce |
| T-1........ IV.4:6 | lets me, and to whatever **e.** he permits it. |
| T-1........ VI.5:2 | To whatever **e.** you are willing to submit |
| T-1........ VI.5:2 | to that **e.** are your perceptions corrected. |
| T-3...... VI.5:10 | This belief can exist only to the **e.** that you |
| T-4...... VII.4:5 | To whatever **e.** you permit this state to be |
| T-6..........I.4:5 | To the **e.** to which you believe that it does, |
| T-6...... V.C.4:1 | second may still entail conflict to some **e.**, |

| | |
|---|---|
| T-7........IV.5:1 | be reconciled in any way or to any e.. The |
| T-13....... II.7:5 | To some e., then, you must believe that |
| T-13...... III.1:1 | upon your hatred and realize its full e.. |
| T-14.........I.2:6 | do not underestimate the e. of its insanity |
| T-14...VII.5:14 | Him only to the small e. of believing that, |
| T-15...... IV.5:2 | And the e. to which you learn to accept |
| T-16...... IV.1:9 | The e. of the split that lies in this you do |
| T-16..... V.14:2 | They but seem to be fearful to the e. to |
| T-16..... V.14:2 | to the e. to which you *want* them to be true |
| T-16..... V.14:3 | And to the same e. you are denying truth, |
| T-18...... IV.1:4 | prepare your mind for it only to the e. of |
| T-20..... VII.2:2 | To the e. you still experience it, you are |
| T-21....... V.4:1 | You do not realize the whole e. to which |
| T-24..... VII.8:7 | that makes it hard to grasp the whole e. to |
| T-25...... III.1:1 | To the e. to which you value guilt, to that |
| T-25...... III.1:1 | that e. will you perceive a world in which |
| T-25...... III.1:2 | To the e. to which you recognize that guilt |
| T-25...... III.1:2 | to that e. you will perceive attack cannot |
| T-28..... VII.7:7 | nor more in worth than the e. to which it |
| W-pI..... 26.8:4 | treat them all alike to whatever e. you can |
| W-pI..... 43.3:3 | is real to the e. to which it shares the Holy |
| W-pI..... 65.7:1 | e. to which you really want salvation in |
| W-pI..... 79.8:1 | to the e. to which you do not insist on |
| W-pI..... 95.4:4 | the e. of your lack of mental discipline, |
| W-pI... 123.2:1 | e. of all the gains which you have made; |
| W-pI... 140.9:3 | will succeed to the e. to which we realize |
| W-pI... 196.7:1 | responsibility returned to some e. to you. |
| M-4 ..... I.A.4:6 | is only to the e. to which they are helpful |
| M-4 ...... IX.1:1 | The e. of the teacher of God's faithfulness |
| P-2.........in.1:6 | whatever e. he comes to realize that this is |
| P-2.........in.1:6 | this is an error, to that e. is he truly saved. |
| P-2.........in.3:3 | his self-concept to any significant e.. He |
| P-2......... II.1:1 | to believe in God to any recognizable e.. It |
| P-2........ III.2:4 | Now the e. of their success depends on |
| P-2....... VII.7:5 | except to some e. and for a little while. He |
| P-3........ III.2:1 | not succeed to the e. to which he values it. |

## external 24

| | |
|---|---|
| T-1....... VII.1:7 | God or to your brothers with anything e.. |
| T-2.........I.5:10 | Illness is some form of e. searching. |
| T-8......VIII.6:2 | extreme need to depend on e. guidance. |
| T-18...... IX.3:4 | these messages relay to you is quite e.. |
| T-18...... IX.4:3 | enough to hold its most e. manifestations |
| T-26..... VII.4:9 | out, and seems to be e. to the mind, is not |
| T-26....VIII.2:1 | because you still believe you are e. to him. |
| W-pI..... 23.3:2 | Each of your perceptions of "e. reality" is |
| W-pI..... 70.7:5 | reviewing some of the e. places where you |
| W-pI... 70.10:2 | You are free from all e. interference. You |
| W-pI..... 71.2:2 | if some e. circumstance or event were |
| W-pI... 136.4:3 | it, so it seems to be e. to your own intent; |
| W-pI... 161.8:2 | he beholds is his own fear e. to himself, |
| W-pI... 190.5:2 | pain. Nothing e. to your mind can hurt or |
| W-pI... 197.1:3 | you find e. gratitude and lavish thanks. |
| W-pII .338.1:4 | enemies, and he is safe from all e. things. |
| M-4 ..... I.A.3:6 | in what seem to be e. circumstances. |
| M-9 ........... 1:2 | not involve changes in the e. situation. |
| M-12 ......... 2:3 | Nothing e. alters, but everything internal |
| M-16 ......... 8:2 | when his mind is occupied with e. things? |
| P-1............. 3:6 | on, reacting to e. forces as they demand, |
| P-2........ IV.2:4 | for all e. things are only shadows of a |
| S-1........ III.6:1 | for human love, for e. "gifts" of any kind, |
| S-3...........I.1:3 | world. It is e. proof of inner "sins," and |

## externals 2

| | |
|---|---|
| T-18....VIII.1:6 | you recognize you identify with e., |
| T-22...... III.6:5 | eyes rest on e. and cannot go beyond. |

## extra 1

| | |
|---|---|
| W-pI..... 20.5:3 | The e. repetitions should be applied to |

## extracted 1

| | |
|---|---|
| T-16..... V.12:4 | strength is e. from the death of God, and |

## extraneous 1

| | |
|---|---|
| M-21 ......... 1:8 | or at least the control, of e. thoughts. Let |

## extravagant 1

| | |
|---|---|
| W-pI. 135.24:4 | is hell that makes e. demands for sacrifice |

## extreme 12

| | |
|---|---|
| T-2 ....... III.3:4 | will engenders a situation which, in the e., |
| T-6 ........in.2:1 | for learning, since an e. example is a |
| T-6 ..........I.2:1 | is nothing more than an e. example. Its |
| T-6 ..........I.6:7 | much less e. temptations to misperceive, |
| T-6 ........I.11:6 | to show this was true in an e. case, merely |
| T-6 ........I.11:6 | in to anger and assault would not be so e.. |
| T-7 ....... VI.3:2 | it, which must result in e. anxiety. That is |
| T-8 .....VIII.6:2 | e. need to depend on external guidance. |
| T-13 ......II.8:4 | In the e., you are afraid of redemption |
| T-17 ...VIII.1:1 | more than a special case, or an e. example |
| T-26 .... V.6:10 | In the e., he can delude himself that this is |
| W-pI... 152.2:1 | You may believe that this position is e., |

## extremely 11

| | |
|---|---|
| T-1 .........II.1:2 | involving the e. personal sense of creation |
| T-3 ...... VII.2:4 | to be e. powerful and extremely active. He |
| T-3 ...... VII.2:4 | to be extremely powerful and e. active. He |
| T-17 ..... V.4:1 | becomes e. intense with this shift in goals. |
| T-17 ..... VI.1:1 | of the Holy Spirit's purpose is e. simple, |
| T-18 ..... IV.7:4 | Holy Spirit's are so e. disproportionate. |
| T-18 .... VII.4:7 | It is e. difficult to reach Atonement by |
| T-18 ..... IX.2:3 | It is e. simple, being based on what this |
| T-25 ...VIII.6:1 | It is e. hard for those who still believe sin |
| W-pI... 122.6:7 | of this e. simple statement of the truth. |
| W-pI... 181.4:2 | quite preoccupied with how e. different |

## extremes 1

| | |
|---|---|
| T-9 .....VIII.6:6 | and e. are its essential characteristic. |

## eye 9

| | |
|---|---|
| T-1 ...... VII.2:4 | of which the physical e. is incapable. |
| T-2 ..........I.3:4 | an e. because it is merely a misperception. |
| T-2 ..... III.1:10 | cannot be seen with the physical e.. |
| T-2 ....... III.4:2 | All solutions the physical e. seeks dissolve |
| T-2 ........ V.8:2 | What the physical e. sees is not corrective |
| T-21 ..... IV.6:7 | still seem to shine and catch your e.. Yet |
| W-pI........ 7.4:3 | to whatever catches your e.. For example: |
| W-pI..... 25.6:2 | rest on whatever happens to catch your e. |
| P-2........ VI.3:2 | The e. reproduces; it does not see. Their |

## eyed

*See* open-eyed

## eyelids 4

| | |
|---|---|
| T-18 ..... III.3:4 | it. A little flicker of your e., closed so long, |
| W-pI..... 69.6:4 | forehead and e. as you go through them. |
| W-pI... 122.2:3 | rests upon your e. so you see no dreams |
| W-pI... 129.8:1 | to shine upon your e. as you rest beyond |

## eyes 376

| | |
|---|---|
| T-1 ........I.22:2 | your physical e. cannot see does not exist. |
| T-9 ........I.11:7 | If you hold your hands over your e., you |
| T-9 ....... IV.3:4 | on your abilities through the e. of the ego, |
| T-9 ....... VI.1:2 | with your e. nor hear Him with your ears. |
| T-11 .......I.5:10 | have your closed e. lost the ability to see. |
| T-11 .... V.17:4 | What you see of His Son through the e. of |
| T-11 ..... VI.8:4 | of crucifixion still lies heavy on your e., |
| T-12 .......II.4:7 | refusing to open your e. and look at them. |
| T-12 ..... VI.4:2 | open the e. of the blind is the Holy Spirit's |
| T-12 ..... VI.4:4 | Christ's e. are open, and He will look |
| T-12 .. VII.11:7 | Through the e. of Christ, only the real |
| T-13 ...... V.6:1 | you look with open e. upon your world, it |
| T-13 ...... V.8:3 | see in dreams although your e. are closed. |
| T-13 .......V.9:1 | Do not seek vision through your e., for |
| T-13 ...... VI.5:6 | where it is, and it will dawn on e. that see. |
| T-13 ... VI.12:6 | of isolation because your e. are closed. |
| T-15 ..... XI.1:6 | as simple as opening your e. to daylight |
| T-16 ..... IV.1:4 | before your open e. as you look on this. |
| T-17 .......II.6:1 | you look upon the world with forgiving e. |
| T-18 .......II.8:1 | not the dream take hold to close your e.. |
| T-18 .VIII.13:2 | to cloud your e. and keep you sightless. |
| T-18 ..... IX.2:4 | are seen only through the body's e.. Its |
| T-18 ..... IX.3:6 | Its e. perceive it not; its senses remain |
| T-18 ..... IX.4:6 | The body's e. will never look on it. Yet |
| T-19 ......I.11:3 | But through the e. of faith, the Son of |
| T-19 ......I.11:5 | you. It sees not through the body's e., nor |
| T-19 ......I.12:7 | you see, not through the body's e., but in |
| T-19 ... III.10:5 | your e. in faith to what you now can see. |
| T-19 ... III.11:1 | and let not sin arise again to blind your e.. |
| T19 .IV.A.12:6 | little shred of guilt escapes their hungry e. |
| T19 .. IV.D.6:2 | Your e. look down, remembering your |
| T19 .. IV.D.6:3 | all rise and bid you not to raise your e.. |
| T19 .. IV.D.7:1 | abandon you if you but raise your e.. Yet |
| T19 .. IV.D.8:6 | raise your e. you will be ready to look on |
| T19 .. IV.D.8:7 | lift up your e. and look on your brother in |
| T19 .. IV.D.8:7 | through the e. of faith that sees them not. |
| T19 IV.D.12:8 | and he will raise your e. in faith together, |
| T-20 .......II.1:2 | all the useless things made for its e. to see. |
| T-20 .......II.1:4 | to you, and to attract his body's e.? Learn |
| T-20 .......II.5:1 | You look still with the body's e., and they |
| T-20 .......II.6:1 | look with different e. upon your brother. |
| T-20 .......II.8:3 | You will not see it with the body's e.. Yet |
| T-20 .....II.8:11 | Let us lift up our e. together, not in fear |
| T-20 ..... III.5:1 | like; how it would look through happy e.? |
| T-20 ..... III.9:1 | and with e. so long cast down in darkness |
| T-20 ..... III.9:4 | raise your e. unto your strong companion |
| T-20 .... VII.8:9 | You closed your e. to shut him out. Such |
| T-20 ...VIII.6:5 | What can the body's e. perceive, with |
| T-20 ...VIII.6:6 | Its e. adjust to sin, unable to overlook it in |
| T-20 ...VIII.6:7 | Look through its e., and everything will |
| T-21 ........I.1:5 | but which stand open before unseeing e., |
| T-21 ........I.8:2 | all the circle fills with light before your e.. |
| T-21 ..... IV.2:3 | for if you do your e. will light on sin, and |
| T-21 .... VII.7:5 | whether to see him through the body's e., |
| T-21 .. VII.10:8 | the body's e. and change what you desire. |
| T-22 ........I.2:3 | that the world you see through e. that are |
| T-22 ........I.2:5 | of the e. that look upon the world. If this |
| T-22 ........I.3:8 | Yet if your e. are closed and you have |
| T-22 .......II.3:3 | in reason's e. can be confused with joy. |
| T-22 ..... III.3:4 | The body's e. behold it as solid granite, so |
| T-22 ..... III.3:6 | conceal its emptiness from reason's e.. |
| T-22 ..... III.4:3 | the body's e. can see is a mistake, an error |
| T-22 ..... III.5:3 | The body's e. see only form. They cannot |
| T-22 ..... III.6:1 | These e., made not to see, will never see. |
| T-22 ..... III.6:4 | For this the body's e. are perfect means, |
| T-22 ..... III.6:5 | See how the body's e. rest on externals |
| T-22 ..... III.8:2 | from you by what the body's e. can see. |
| T-22 ..... IV.4:6 | will bring to light the tired e. of those as |
| T-22 .......V.5:3 | body's e. it looks like an enormous solid |
| T-22 ..... VI.3:5 | from hate to gratitude before forgiving e.. |
| T-22 ..... VI.8:1 | see your value through your brother's e., |
| T-23 .....II.15:6 | And fear, with ashen lips and sightless e., |
| T-24 .....II.12:4 | from e. it veils but looks on sight of death. |
| T-24 ..... III.7:7 | Open your e. a little; see the savior God |
| T-24 .......V.3:5 | He is your e., your ears, your hands, your |
| T-24 .......V.4:7 | The sin its e. behold in him and love to |
| T-24 .......V.4:8 | from the bone and sightless holes for e., is |
| T-24 .......V.5:1 | Rejoice you have no e. with which to see; |
| T-24 .......V.7:3 | He gives them vision for their sightless e., |
| T-24 ..... VI.6:1 | sinlessness that e. that see can look upon. |
| T-24 ..... VI.6:5 | Let not your e. be blinded by the veil of |
| T-24 ... VI.11:3 | In its e. you are a separate universe, with |
| T-24 .... VII.9:7 | It gives the e. with which you look on it, |
| T-24 .. VII.10:2 | is sure, when seen through its own e.. It |
| T-25 .......II.1:1 | the body's e. perceive fills you with fear? |
| T-25 ..... III.8:2 | It is not there in His forgiving e.. And |
| T-25 ..... IV.3:2 | to all the weary e. and tired hearts that |
| T-25 .....V.2:10 | has not gone because your e. are closed. |
| T-25 .....V.2:11 | Savior, seeing Him through sightless e.? |
| T-25 ..... VI.1:1 | grace of God rests gently on forgiving e., |
| T-25 ..... VI.2:1 | E. become used to darkness, and the light |
| T-25 ..... VI.2:1 | to the e. grown long accustomed to the |

T-25......VI.2:4 less painful to the **e.** than what is wholly
T-25......VI.2:5 Yet this is not what **e.** are for, and who
T-25......VI.3:1 calls down the grace of God upon your **e.**,
T-25.....VII.6:5 gentle **e.** would look beyond the madness
T-25......IX.5:6 Not as it is seen through this world's **e.**,
T-26...... I.4:10 and sight of him replace the body's **e.**.
T-26.........I.7:3 and make your **e.** and ears bear witness to
T-26....... V.5:6 keep an ancient memory before your **e.**.
T-26......IX.1:6 Look with loving **e.** on him who carries
T-27.........I.3:2 a picture of your crucifixion before his **e.**,
T-27.........I.5:6 and with healed **e.** will look beyond it to
T-27....... II.3:7 not the proof of sin before his brother's **e.**
T-27......III.7:1 and nothing that the **e.** have ever seen or
T-27....... V.5:2 The **e.** of all the dying bring reproach,
T-27....... V.6:4 And suffering **e.** no longer will accuse, but
T-27....... V.6:5 holy instant's radiance will light your **e.**,
T-27....... V.7:6 which all **e.** look lovingly upon the Friend
T-27......VI.3:2 You use its **e.** to see, its ears to hear, and
T-27...VII.14:6 your sight, although your **e.** are closed. A
T-27... VIII.8:4 do your **e.** behold its heavy consequences,
T-28....... V.4:2 and this the world the body's **e.** perceive.
T-28....... V.4:8 Its **e.** are blind; its ears are deaf. It can not
T-28....... V.5:3 Let not your **e.** behold a dream; your ears
T-28....... V.5:6 For **e.** and ears are senses without sense,
T-28....... V.5:8 Let not the body's ears and **e.** perceive
T-29......III.5:6 and be sure his waking **e.** will rest on you.
T-31......VI.1:8 to touch your **e.** and bless your holy sight,
T-31......VI.2:7 the sight of those whose **e.** salvation has
T-31......VI.3:4 another world your **e.** could never find.
T-31......VI.5:4 change the world for **e.** that learn to see,
T-31......VI.6:4 so it looks on you with **e.** that see as yours
T-31.....VII.3:4 the sight your **e.** alone can offer you to see
T-31...VII.11:3 holiness is seen through holy **e.** that look
T-31...VII.11:6 his calm and open **e.** and what he sees. He
T-31...VII.15:3 beholding them with **e.** unopened. And
T-31...VII.15:4 see until he looks on them with seeing **e.**,
T-31... VIII.7:2 through the Christ in you unveil his **e.**,
T-31... VIII.8:4 your tired **e.** I bring a vision of a different
W-pI.......2.2:4 is merely that your **e.** have lighted on it.
W-pI.......8.4:1 for today should be done with **e.** closed.
W-pI.....10.4:1 Close your **e.** for these exercises, and
W-pI.....11.2:2 Begin with your **e.** closed, and repeat the
W-pI.....11.2:3 Then open your **e.** and look about, near
W-pI.....11.3:1 **e.** should move from one thing to another
W-pI.....11.3:5 close your **e.** and repeat the idea once
W-pI.....12.2:1 These exercises are done with **e.** open.
W-pI.....13.4:2 With **e.** closed, repeat today's idea to
W-pI.....13.4:3 Then open your **e.**, and look about you
W-pI.....13.4:6 Then close your **e.**, and conclude with: *A*
W-pI.....14.2:1 to be practiced with **e.** closed throughout.
W-pI.....14.4:1 With **e.** closed, think of all the horrors in
W-pI.....15.1:4 function you have given your body's **e.**. It
W-pI.....15.3:4 signs that you are opening your **e.** at last.
W-pI.....15.4:1 its name and letting your **e.** rest on it as
W-pI.....16.4:1 mind for a minute or so with **e.** closed,
W-pI.....17.2:1 today's idea, say to yourself, with **e.** open:
W-pI.....18.3:1 your **e.** on each one long enough to say: *I*
W-pI.....19.3:1 require is to be undertaken with **e.** closed.
W-pI.....21.2:2 Then close your **e.** and search your mind
W-pI.....22.3:2 **e.** move slowly from one object to another
W-pI.....23.6:2 and then close your **e.** and devote about a
W-pI.....24.4:1 by searching the mind, with closed **e.**, for
W-pI.....25.6:3 **e.** resting on each subject you so select,
W-pI.....25.6:7 without shifting your **e.** from the subject
W-pI.....26.3:2 effect is to weaken you in your own **e.**.
W-pI.....26.6:1 then closing your **e.** and reviewing the
W-pI.....28.8:1 of the subject your **e.** happen to light on,
W-pI.....28.8:1 you should rest your **e.** on it while saying:
W-pI.....30.5:1 it does not depend on the body's **e.** at all.
W-pI.....30.5:3 applying today's idea with your **e.** closed,
W-pI.....31.2:4 Then close your **e.**, and apply the same
W-pI.....32.3:2 your **e.** and look around your inner world
W-pI.....33.2:1 then close your **e.** and survey your inner
W-pI.....33.4:3 Closing your **e.** will probably help in this
W-pI.....34.2:3 should be done with your **e.** closed. It is
W-pI.....35.2:5 in it is seen through the **e.** of the image.
W-pI.....35.4:1 close your **e.** and search your mind for the
W-pI.....35.4:3 upon yourself through the **e.** of holiness.
W-pI.....35.9:2 repeat the idea to yourself, with closed **e.**.
W-pI.....36.3:1 close your **e.** and repeat the idea for today
W-pI.....36.3:2 your **e.** and look quite slowly about you,
W-pI...36.3:10 your **e.** and repeat the idea to yourself.
W-pI...36.3:11 open your **e.**, and continue as before.
W-pI.....36.4:1 periods, close your **e.** and repeat the idea;
W-pI.....36.4:1 one more repetition with your **e.** closed.
W-pI.....37.4:5 Then close your **e.** and apply the idea to
W-pI.....37.5:1 the practice period with your **e.** closed;
W-pI.....37.5:1 you may open your **e.** again and apply the
W-pI.....37.5:2 a repetition of the idea with your **e.** closed
W-pI.....37.5:2 following immediately, with your **e.** open.
W-pI.....38.4:1 repeat the idea for today, close your **e.**,
W-pI.....39.6:2 Then, with closed **e.**, search out your
W-pI.....40.2:1 not close your **e.** for the exercise periods,
W-pI.....40.2:2 closing your **e.** would not be feasible. Do
W-pI.....41.6:2 three to five minutes, with your **e.** closed.
W-pI.....41.9:1 it very slowly, preferably with **e.** closed.
W-pI.....42.4:1 idea for today slowly, with your **e.** open,
W-pI.....42.4:2 close your **e.** and repeat the idea again,
W-pI.....42.5:5 open your **e.** and repeat the thought once
W-pI.....42.5:5 while looking slowly about; close your **e.**,
W-pI.....42.6:3 slow repetitions of the idea with **e.** open,
W-pI.....42.6:3 idea with eyes open, then with **e.** closed,
W-pI.....43.4:3 the idea for today to yourself with **e.** open
W-pI.....43.5:2 the second and longer phase, close your **e.**
W-pI.....43.5:4 *I see through the* **e.** *of forgiveness. I see the*
W-pI.....43.6:1 unable to think of anything, open your **e.**,
W-pI.....44.5:6 Yet perceived through the ego's **e.**, it is
W-pI.....44.7:1 repeating today's idea with your **e.** open,
W-pI.....44.9:1 your **e.** closed unless you are aware of fear
W-pI.....44.9:2 it more reassuring to open your **e.** briefly.
W-pI.....44.9:3 to return to the exercises with **e.** closed as
W-pI...44.11:1 **e.** open or closed as seems better to you at
W-pI.....45.6:1 to yourself, closing your **e.** as you do so.
W-pI.....46.3:3 Close your **e.** as you do so, and spend a
W-pI.....47.4:3 Close your **e.** and begin, as usual, by
W-pI.....48.2:3 use it with your **e.** open at any time and in
W-pI.....48.2:4 to close your **e.** and repeat the idea slowly
W-pI.....49.5:2 Do so with your **e.** open when necessary,
W-pI.....49.5:3 you can, closing your **e.** on the world, and
WpI...rI.in.3:3 your **e.** closed and when you are alone in
W-pI.....54.1:5 the real world rise before my **e.** as I let my
W-pI.....58.1:5 me. Seen through understanding **e.**, the
W-pI.....59.2:3 Let me not look to my own **e.** to see today
W-pI.....59.3:7 when I try to see through the body's **e.**.
W-pI.....60.5:3 As I open my **e.**, His Love lights up the
W-pI.....61.5:6 your **e.** closed if the situation permits. Let
W-pI.....62.5:1 as you can, closing your **e.** if possible, say
W-pI.....63.4:1 If you close your **e.**, you will probably
W-pI.....64.1:4 It is this the body's **e.** look upon.
W-pI.....64.2:1 Nothing the body's **e.** seem to see can be
W-pI.....64.6:5 today to reflecting on this with closed **e.**.
W-pI.....64.8:2 times, do the exercises with your **e.** closed
W-pI.....64.8:3 your **e.** open after reviewing the thoughts,
W-pI.....65.5:2 day. Then close your **e.**, repeat the idea to
W-pI.....65.8:4 Sometimes close your **e.** as you practice
W-pI.....69.4:1 Very quietly now, with your **e.** closed, try
W-pI.....70.7:5 devote a few minutes, with your **e.** closed,
W-pI.72.10:12 used our grievances to close our **e.** and
W-pI...72.13:6 in silence, preferably with your **e.** closed,
W-pI.....74.5:1 close your **e.** and try to experience the
W-pI.....74.7:5 half an hour, with **e.** closed if possible,
W-pI.....75.9:6 the darkness of the past upon your **e.**, you
W-pI.....77.4:2 Closing your **e.**, remind yourself that you
W-pI.....78.1:3 And as you raise it up before your **e.**, you
W-pI.....78.2:3 our **e.** in silence to behold the Son of God.
W-pI.....78.7:4 The body's **e.** are closed, and as you think
W-pI...79.10:5 your **e.** for a moment and ask what it is.
W-pI.....80.5:2 Close your **e.**, and receive your reward.
WpI..rII.in.2:2 wish, and then close your **e.** and listen.
W-pI.....91.3:3 do not doubt that the body's **e.** can see.
W-pI.....91.6:3 *The body's* **e.** *do not perceive the light. But I*
W-pI...91.10:6 Their strength becomes your **e.**, that you
W-pI...91.11:5 *light. Let me not close my* **e.** *because of this.*
W-pI.....92.1:3 tied up with the body and its **e.** and brain.
W-pI.....92.1:4 putting little bits of glass before your **e.**.
W-pI.....92.1:5 you are a body, and the body's **e.** can see.
W-pI.....92.2:4 than to believe the body's **e.** can see; the
W-pI.....92.3:3 weakness that sees through the body's **e.**,
W-pI.....92.3:4 through **e.** that cannot see and cannot
W-pI.....92.8:2 can leave without a miracle before his **e.**,
W-pI.....92.9:1 the body's **e.** provide for self-deception.
W-pI...92.10:4 closing the body's **e.** and asking truth to
W-pI...93.10:6 to closing your **e.** and realizing that this is
W-pI...95.11:3 Then close your **e.** and tell yourself again,
W-pI...105.8:3 joy are mine," and close your **e.** a while,
W-pI...108.2:1 is not the light the body's **e.** behold. It is a
W-pI...108.8:4 Then close your **e.**, and for five minutes
W-pI...109.3:5 truth before the **e.** of you who rest in God.
W-pI...109.5:4 today. And as you close your **e.**, sink into
W-pI...121.4:2 It looks upon the world with sightless **e.**,
W-pI.121.11:1 close your **e.** and see him in your mind,
W-pI...122.2:2 It sparkles on your **e.** as you awake, and
W-pI...122.3:1 look with unforgiving **e.** upon the world.
W-pI...122.8:1 Open your **e.** today and look upon a
W-pI...122.8:3 quietness it rises up to greet your open **e.**,
W-pI...123.4:1 above despair, and raise our thankful **e.**,
W-pI...124.4:5 our **e.** behold His loveliness in all we look
W-pI.124.11:2 a sight too holy for the body's **e.** to see.
W-pI...125.9:2 and free your vision from the body's **e.**.
W-pI.126.10:1 close your **e.** upon the world that does not
W-pI...127.6:3 is perfectly apparent to the **e.** that see and
W-pI.127.10:4 we raise our **e.** upon a different present,
W-pI...128.7:2 And when your **e.** are opened afterwards,
W-pI...129.7:5 Then close your **e.** upon the world you see
W-pI...129.8:2 Here is light your **e.** can not behold. And
W-pI...130.9:4 kind of seeing that your **e.** alone have ever
W-pI.130.11:1 damned your **e.** and cursed your sight,
W-pI.131.11:5 mind and see, although your **e.** are closed,
W-pI...134.7:5 It looks on them with quiet **e.**, and merely
W-pI...137.4:5 **e.** accustomed to illusions must be shown
W-pI.138.12:1 Before we close our **e.** in sleep tonight, we
WpI. rIV.in7:2 Then close your **e.**, and say them slowly
W-pI...151.2:2 what is shown you through the body's **e.**.
W-pI...151.3:5 faith in what your **e.** and ears report. You
W-pI...151.7:2 be judged by what your **e.** behold in him,
W-pI...155.1:3 Your forehead is serene; your **e.** are quiet.
W-pI...155.6:3 illusion that you bring their **e.** to look on
W-pI...157.6:3 in our **e.** which we can offer everyone,
W-pI.158.11:3 practice seeing with the **e.** of Christ today.
W-pI...161.7:5 consuming everything its **e.** behold,
W-pI...161.9:1 the body's **e.** behold in one whom Heaven
W-pI.161.10:4 the witnesses your body's **e.** call forth.
W-pI.161.11:8 *I would behold you with the* **e.** *of Christ, and*
W-pI...163.2:2 all goals perceived but in its sightless **e.**.
W-pI...163.9:1 *Our Father, bless our* **e.** *today. We are Your*
W-pI...164.1:3 not in our sight, but in the **e.** of Christ. He
W-pI...164.5:4 unfold in perfect innocence before your **e.**
W-pI...164.5:5 Now will you see it with the **e.** of Christ.
W-pI...165.5:6 your blindness for the seeing **e.** of Christ;
W-pI...166.7:4 with **e.** cast down lest you might catch a
W-pI.167.10:3 Who changes life because he shuts his **e.**,
W-pI.170.11:6 by its weight; beheld not in its sightless **e.**,
W-pI.170.12:1 Now do your **e.** belong to Christ, and He
WpI...rV.in9:3 You are my voice, my **e.**, my feet, my
W-pI...181.6:2 and turn our **e.** upon our own mistakes,
W-pI...181.8:4 are the **e.** of Christ inevitably ours. And
W-pI...187.2:2 your body's **e.** will not perceive it yours.
W-pI...188.1:2 seek the light are merely covering their **e.**.
W-pI...188.6:1 Sit quietly and close your **e.**. The light
W-pI...189.1:2 And with its **e.** you will not see this light,
W-pI...189.1:3 Yet you have **e.** to see it. It is there for you
W-pI...189.3:2 through darkened **e.** of malice and of fear,
W-pI.191.10:1 from his sleep, and opening his holy **e.**,
W-pI...192.3:6 and **e.** already opening behold the joyful
W-pI...192.7:4 our **e.** shut tight against the light; our
W-pI...193.7:4 sees the pain through **e.** the mind directs.
W-pI...200.3:6 look with open **e.** to find that Heaven lies
W-pI.200.10:5 body's **e.** but serving for an instant longer
WpI rVI.in.4:3 We merely close our **e.**, and then forget
W-pI...218.1:2 *sightless* **e.** *I cannot see the vision of my glory*
W-pII ....in.6:4 and fix our **e.** upon the journey's end.
W-pII .237.2:1 *Christ is my* **e.** *today, and He the ears that*
W-pII ..... 3.2:6 But **e.** deceive, and ears hear falsely. Now
W-pII ..... 3.5:5 it must behold it through the **e.** of Christ,
W-pII ..... 4.1:4 Sin gave the body **e.**, for what is there the
W-pII .263.2:1 through holy vision and the **e.** of Christ.
W-pII ....270.h I will not use the body's **e.** today.

W-pII .270.1:1 *to translate all that the body's* **e.** *behold into*
W-pII .270.2:2 Christ is our **e.** today. And through His
W-pII .....6.2:4 by anything the body's **e.** perceive. For
W-pII .290.1:2 see. **E.** that begin to open see at last. And I
W-pII .....8.1:3 Your world is seen through **e.** of fear, and
W-pII .....8.1:4 except through **e.** forgiveness blesses, so
W-pII .....8.2:2 through quiet **e.** and with a mind at peace
W-pII .....8.4:2 His waking **e.** perceive the sure reflection
W-pII .293.2:4 *would see only this world before my* **e.** *today*
W-pII .295.1:1 Christ asks that He may use my **e.** today,
W-pII .295.2:2 *me. Help me to use the* **e.** *of Christ today, and*
W-pII .....9.5:2 needs your **e.** and ears and hands and feet
W-pII .301.1:4 *through happy* **e.** *forgiveness has released*
W-pII .302.1:1 *Father, our* **e.** *are opening at last. Your holy*
W-pII .304.1:5 by looking on it through the **e.** of Christ.
W-pII .313.1:4 *The* **e.** *of Christ look on a world forgiven. In*
W-pII ...13.3:2 The **e.** of Christ deliver them to all they
W-pII ...14.4:1 the **e.** through which Christ's vision sees a
W-pII .352.1:3 *will bind my* **e.** *and make me blind. Yet love,*
W-pII ....353.h My **e.**, my tongue, my hands, my feet
W-ep .........6:5 us how to behold him through His **e.**, and
M-4 ...........1:2 They do not look alike to the body's **e.**,
M-8 ...........1:6 What the body's **e.** behold is only conflict.
M-8 ...........3:3 the mind that judges what the **e.** behold.
M-8 ...........3:7 and it sends the body's **e.** to find it. The
M-8 ...........3:8 body's **e.** will never see except through
M-8 ...........4:3 mind classifies what the body's **e.** bring to
M-8 ...........6:1 body's **e.** will continue to see differences.
M-8 ...........6:3 the body's **e.** will report their changed
M-16 .........4:5 with closed **e.** and accomplish nothing.
M-16 .........5:8 which you close your **e.** and think of God.
M-18 .........2:5 and bring Christ's vision to **e.** that see.
M-18 .........3:3 The body's **e.** now "see"; its ears alone
M-19 .........3:2 is the lens which, held before the body's **e.**
M-23 .........5:5 But in his **e.** your loveliness is so complete
M-23 .........5:8 In his **e.** Christ's vision shines in perfect
C-4 ............2:1 The body's **e.** are therefore not the means
C-5 ............5:5 his vision, for the **e.** of Christ are shared.
P-2..........II.6:7 His **e.** is too fragmented to be meaningful.
P-2........ VI.7:4 their sinlessness to **e.** that still believe that
P-3...........I.3:3 for seeing is not limited to the body's **e.**.
P-3........ III.7:1 and in the **e.** of the world it would be so.
S-2...........I.6:4 Christ's vision does not use your **e.**, but
S-2...........I.6:8 **e.** that look past error to the Christ in you
S-2........ III.2:3 **e.** of Christ become the sight you choose.
S-2........ III.5:5 be His **e.** through which you look on him,
S-3..........II.5:1 for death is cruel in its frightened **e.** and

### eyes' 1

M-8 ...........3:4 the **e.** messages and gives them "meaning.

# F

### fabric 1

T-27..... II.6:11 his guilt is but the **f.** of a senseless dream.

### face 118

*See also* Appendix C

T-4........ IV.1:5 is filled with schemes to save the **f.** of your
T-4........ IV.1:5 ego, and you do not seek the **f.** of Christ.
T-4........ IV.1:6 the ego seeks to see its **f.** is dark indeed.
T-4......... V.2:6 its own preservation in the **f.** of threat,
T-6...........I.6:7 in the **f.** of much less extreme temptations
T-12.........I.8:5 to recognize fear and **f.** it without disguise
T-12.......I.9:11 across the **f.** of love has disappeared.
T-13.VII.16:10 like a veil of light across the world's sad **f.**,
T-15....VIII.1:6 In the **f.** of your fear of forgiveness, which
T19... IV.D.2:1 like a heavy veil before the **f.** of Christ. Yet
T19... IV.D.2:2 Yet as His **f.** rises beyond it, shining with
T19... IV.D.2:3 seems to make the **f.** of Christ Himself like
T19... IV.D.2:3 **f.** with glory appear as streams of blood,
T19... IV.D.4:6 the **f.** of Christ and join Him in His Father
T-20.........I.4:2 glimpses of the **f.** of Christ behind the veil
T-20.........I.4:2 behold your brother's **f.** and recognize it.
T-20...... IV.5:6 he is ready to look upon the **f.** of Christ,
T-20...... IV.7:4 the **f.** of Christ shines on them and they
T-20....... V.4:5 for who would see the **f.** of Christ and yet
T-20....... V.6:7 **f.** of Christ you yet will look upon already
T-20...... VI.5:7 sees the **f.** of Christ choose as His home
T-20.. VI.12:10 held back from looking on the **f.** of Christ
T-21....... II.2:6 helpless in the **f.** of what is done to you.
T-22...... IV.3:1 hangs between you and the **f.** of Christ.
T-22...... IV.3:7 The Love of Christ will light your **f.**, and
T-22....... V.2:2 in the **f.** of reason and makes no sense.
T-24...... VI.6:5 that hides the **f.** of Christ from him, and
T-25.........I.4:5 and nothing hides the **f.** of Christ from its
T-25....... II.7:3 the picture's **f.** which but reflects the light
T-25....... II.7:4 it to its Creator. Think not this **f.** was ever
T-26...... IV.3:2 And here you see the **f.** of Christ, arising
T-26...... IV.3:3 Who could behold the **f.** of Christ and not
T-26...... IX.2:2 the **f.** of Christ and memory of God. And
T-27....... V.6:5 all suffering and see Christ's **f.** instead.
T-27....... V.7:5 its witnesses to show the **f.** of Christ to
T-27...VII.14:7 has come to lighten up your sleeping **f.**.
T-29...... III.4:4 For it was in your **f.** he saw the light that
T-29....VIII.3:6 fall before His **f.** like a dark veil that seems
T-29....VIII.4:1 of idols *is* a veil across the **f.** of Christ,
T-30 ...... V.7:5 The **f.** of Christ is looked upon before the
T-31 ...... V.2:6 The first presents the **f.** of innocence, the
T-31 ...... V.2:7 **f.** that smiles and charms and even seems
T-31 ...... V.3:2 And so this **f.** is often wet with tears at the
T-31 ...... V.4:1 The **f.** of innocence the concept of the self
T-31 ...... V.4:2 makes a picture of himself omits this **f.**,
T-31 ...... V.5:1 Beneath the **f.** of innocence there is a
T-31 ...... V.5:2 a fear so devastating that the **f.** that smiles
T-31 ...... V.6:5 in the mists below the **f.** of innocence.
T-31 .... V.10:2 did, who gave the **f.** of innocence to you?
T-31 .... VII.8:6 single vision does he see the **f.** of Christ,
T-31 .... VII.9:1 The veil across the **f.** of Christ, the fear of
T-31 .. VII.13:7 the door held open for the **f.** of Christ to
T-31 ...VIII.3:5 everything that hides His **f.** from you. His
T-31 ...VIII.4:3 For what appears to hide the **f.** of Christ is
T-31 .VIII.12:5 to hide the **f.** of Christ from anyone. Thy
W-pI....... 7.4:9 *in that body. I see only the past in that* **f.**.
W-pI........ 9.4:4 *as it is now. I do not see that* **f.** *as it is now.*
W-pI...... 56.4:3 veil I have drawn across the **f.** of love, its
WpI..rII.in.4:1 to waver in the **f.** of distracting thoughts.
W-pI... 100.2:6 will see their function in your shining **f.**,
W-pI... 100.6:5 you and sees His message in your happy **f.**
W-pI... 107.5:1 love which does not falter in the **f.** of pain,
W-pI... 122.3:1 that hides the **f.** of Christ from those who
W-pI... 124.9:5 And you will see Christ's **f.** upon it, in
W-pI... 134.8:2 it becomes the undeceiver in the **f.** of lies;
W-pI... 151.8:1 that doubt is meaningless before Its **f.**.
W-pI... 151.8:4 before the rapture of Christ's holy **f.**.
W-pI. 151.10:2 the gentle **f.** of Christ in all of them. You
W-pI. 151.12:4 you see the holy **f.** of Christ in everything,
W-pI... 157.9:1 except His shining **f.** and perfect Love.
W-pI... 157.9:2 The vision of His **f.** will stay with you, but
W-pI. 161.11:3 See his **f.**, his hands and feet, his clothing.
W-pI... 168.4:3 and watch fear disappear from every **f.** as
W-pI... 169.6:4 time, forgiveness and the holy **f.** of Christ.
W-pI. 169.13:2 all who see the light that lingers in your **f.**.
W-pI. 169.13:3 What is the **f.** of Christ but his who went a
W-pI... 187.8:6 before the **f.** of one who has forgiven and
W-pI. 198.10:1 as the **f.** of Christ appears unveiled at last
W-pI. 198.10:4 shining upon you from the **f.** of Christ.
W-pI. 198.11:3 is there tranquil light across the **f.** of earth
W-pII .223.2:1 *us see the* **f.** *of Christ instead of our mistakes.*
W-pII .229.1:4 away no longer from the holy **f.** of Christ.
W-pII ....269.h sight goes forth to look upon Christ's **f.**.
W-pII .269.1:5 *in which everyone shows me the* **f.** *of Christ,*
W-pII . 269.2:2 upon the **f.** of Him Whose Self is ours. We
W-pII ..... 6.4:3 for what remains to see except Christ's **f.**?
W-pII ..... 6.5:1 And how long will this holy **f.** be seen,
W-pII ..... 6.5:2 to find Christ's **f.** and look on nothing else
M-4 ........X.2:7 No clouds remain to hide the **f.** of Christ.
M-13 ......... 4:4 the **f.** of Christ look back with longing on
M-22 ......... 4:5 the **f.** of Christ shining in front of him,
M-28 ......... 2:6 Christ's **f.** is seen in every living thing,
M-28 ......... 5:5 have seen the **f.** of Christ, His sinlessness,
M-28 ......... 6:3 the vision of Christ's **f.** to take the place of
C-3 ............... h FORGIVENESS – THE **F.** OF CHRIST
C-3 ............ 4:1 *The* **f.** *of Christ* has to be seen before the
C-3 ............ 4:3 Seeing the **f.** of Christ involves perception
C-3 ............ 4:5 But the **f.** of Christ is the great symbol of
C-3 ............ 7:6 This is the purpose of the **f.** of Christ. It is
C-4 ............ 4:1 world stands like a block before Christ's **f.**
C-4 ............ 4:5 destruction was perceived the **f.** of Christ
C-4 ............ 7:6 the **f.** of Christ has shone away time's final
C-5 ............ 2:1 who was a man but saw the **f.** of Christ in
C-6 ............ 3:5 in which the **f.** of Christ alone is seen. He
P-2...........I.4:2 for every "patient" on the **f.** of this earth,
P-2..........V.7:8 God, we will behold in him the **f.** of Christ
P-2....... VII.6:8 Christ's shining **f.** as it looks back at them
P-3.....II.10:10 This is the veil across the **f.** of Christ. Yet
S-1..........V.3:3 dream has veiled the **f.** of Christ from you
S-2...........I.3:5 sin by choosing in its place the **f.** of Christ
S-2...........I.6:5 instant only seem to hide the **f.** of Christ,
S-2...........I.8:1 when he could see the **f.** of Christ instead?
S-2..........II.5:2 It shows the **f.** of suffering and pain, in
S-2..........II.7:8 It is His **f.** forgiveness lets you see. It is His
S-2..........II.7:9 see. It is His **f.** in which you see your own.
S-2..........II.8:6 glow of Heaven shining on the **f.** of earth,
S-2........ III.7:7 silently open upon the shining **f.** of Christ
S-3...........I.3:3 overlook all shadows on the holy **f.** of

### faced 1

T-8 ...... VII.8:3 Being **f.** with an impossible learning

### faces 1

M-24 ......... 2:2 of the difficulties the individual **f.** now,

**faceted** 1
*See also* many-faceted
T-17......IV.8:4 and the tears are f. like diamonds and

**facets** 1
W-pI.....47.1:4 to be aware of all the f. of any problem,

**facilitate** 7
T-2........IV.3:3 Their purpose is merely to f. learning.
T-2........IV.3:4 device can do is to fail to f. learning. It has
T-2.........V.6:2 to the very learning it should f.. Only the
T19IV.C.11:10 *but let You use it for me, to f. its coming.*
W-pI.....32.4:3 restful. To f. this, select a time when few
WpI.rIV.in1:4 as will f. the readiness that we would now
M-7............1:7 And it is this he must f.. He is now the

**facilitates** 2
T-6...........I.2:2 lies solely in the kind of learning it f.. It
T-8.........II.2:7 and f. the development of what you have.

**facilitating** 4
T-1........I.15:4 when it is no longer useful in f. learning.
T-1.........V.1:1 that both are learning aids for f. a state in
T-12.......V.7:4 since they are all for f. the learning this
M-21..........1:8 concentration and f. the exclusion, or at

**facing** 1
W-pI.133.14:2 you see some difficult decisions f. you, be

**Fact** 2
*fact*
T-3...........I.8:2 God, for God is not symbolic; He is F..
T-6.........II.6:8 It is not a belief, but a F.. Anything that

**fact** 153
*Fact*
T-1........VI.1:4 It is, in f., the essential difference between
T-2........IV.5:2 In f., if it is used truly, it will inevitably be
T-2.........V.2:3 The very f. that you are afraid makes your
T-2.........V.3:4 In f., its purpose is to restore him *to* his
T-2.......VII.4:3 In f., it asserts the power of fear by the
T-3........III.2:1 the f. that you do not recognize yourself,
T-3........III.4:1 but it is still a correction rather than a f..
T-3........III.4:5 The f. that perception is involved at all
T-3.........V.9:5 f. that each one has this power completely
T-3........VI.3:3 In f., their meaning is lost to you precisely
T-4.........II.1:2 In f., it is the best question you could ask.
T-4.........II.2:6 that the ego is only an idea and not a f..
T-4.........II.4:6 In f., they resemble in many ways how
T-4........III.9:3 This one f. means the ego does not exist,
T-4........VI.3:8 The f. that you believe you must escape
T-6.........II.2:4 you try to keep the f. that you attacked
T-6........IV.3:1 f. that the ego cannot know anything. The
T-6........IV.8:6 In f., it is impossible. Remember, however
T-6......V.B.4:2 In f., this is its only alternative since the
T-7.........II.4:4 In f., his whole purpose is to change the
T-7........III.5:3 the question by establishing the f. that to
T-7........VI.9:4 at any level are not problems of f.. They
T-7.........X.3:4 you know what is joyful, and are, in f.,
T-8........IV.3:8 If you will accept the f. that I am with you,
T-8.......VII.8:4 In f., it is ultimately why the world itself is
T-9...........I.1:4 The very f. that the Will of God, which is
T-9.........I.11:5 f. that God is Love does not require belief,
T-9.........II.3:2 very f. that the Holy Spirit has been asked
T-10......III.8:6 them the fearful f. that you made them to
T-10....III.11:4 the god of sickness for your brothers; in f.,
T-10.......V.4:3 because he would not accept the f. that,
T-11......IV.4:3 denial of this simple f. takes many forms,
T-11......VI.6:2 in the f. that it represents what you want
T-12.........I.2:3 This is shown by the f. that you react to
T-12......I.10:5 dream of separation with the f. of unity.
T-13.......in.4:3 the eternal f. that God's Son is not guilty.
T-13......IV.3:1 apart from the f. that you were wrong?
T-13... VIII.1:3 exist, a f. which belongs to the sphere of
T-14....III.10:4 will fail to understand the simple f. that
T-14.....VII.4:8 Apart, this f. is lost from sight, for each in
T-14.....VII.4:9 the f. of their complete incompatibility is
T-14.......X.5:5 Yet the very f. that you can do this, and
T-14.......X.8:7 In f., the ego enjoys studying itself, and
T-14.......X.8:9 this f. behind impressive sounding words,
T-14.......X.9:7 The f. of union tells them it is not true.
T-14......XI.7:8 establishes the f. that guiltlessness must
T-15......III.2:4 It is essential that you accept the f., and
T-15......VI.2:1 to accept the f. that perfect love is in you.
T-15......VI.4:5 you find difficult to accept is the f. that,
T-15......IX.3:2 accept the f. that the ego has no purpose
T-15.......X.5:6 accept the f. that sacrifice gets nothing.
T-16.........I.2:1 uses it is destructive lies in the f. that it is
T-16.........I.4:4 to recognize and accept the f. that you do
T-16.........I.4:4 and accept the f. that He *does* know. You
T-16......III.3:1 Does not the f. that you have not learned
T-16......IV.4:2 is a f.. Where disillusionment is possible,
T-16......V.14:1 Salvation lies in the simple f. that
T-17....IV.14:6 but the f. that it is just a picture is brought
T-17......VI.1:2 In f., in order to be simple it *must* be
T-17......VI.6:5 The goal establishes the f. that everyone
T-17... VIII.3:6 Now it becomes a f., from which faith can
T-18.......II.2:3 on awaking because the f. that reality is so
T-18.......V.6:4 of joining its blessing lies in the f. that it is
T-19.........I.3:5 the "f." that separation has occurred. The
T-20......III.1:4 requires no adjustments and, in f., is lost
T-20... VIII.8:5 Once you accept this simple f. and take
T-21.......V.1:7 Perception is a choice and not a f.. But on
T-21......VI.6:6 That you are joined to him is but a f., not
T-21......VI.6:7 How can a f. be fearful unless it disagrees
T-21......VI.6:8 will tell you that this f. is your release.
T-22....VI.14:4 Look not with fear upon this happy f., and
T-23......III.5:4 to accept the f. their savage purpose is
T-25......IV.1:2 is so, seeing their safety in this happy f..
T-25.....VII.7:1 the special form in which the f. that God
T-26......III.4:5 It is but a simple statement of a simple f..
T-26.......V.6:8 is? For this is f., and does not change
T-26.......V.7:2 that he may hear a f. in what is there to
T-26... VIII.9:6 merely a denial of the f. that consequence
T-26.......X.2:6 And this denies the f. that *all* are senseless,
T-27.......II.8:3 the "f." that your salvation sacrifices his.
T-27.....II.13:1 overlook the f. that every thought extends
T-30.......I.14:6 but a simple statement of a simple f.. You
T-30.......I.16:1 The second rule as well is but a f.. For you
T-30.....VII.2:4 f. they have no meaning in themselves is
T-31......III.1:6 obscures the f. that you believe them to be
T-31.......V.4:1 a well-known f. the world deals harshly
W-pI.......8.1:6 cannot understand time, and cannot, in f.
W-pI.......9.1:4 In f., the recognition that you do not
W-pI.....10.4:6 In f., if you find it helpful to do so, you
W-pI.....12.1:1 importance of this idea lies in the f. that it
W-pI.....14.6:7 In recognition of this f., conclude the
W-pI.....16.1:3 There is no exception to this f.. Thoughts
W-pI.....19.2:1 emphasizing the f. that minds are joined.
W-pI.....19.2:3 it is a f. that there are no private thoughts.
W-pI.....28.5:1 You could, in f., gain vision from just that
W-pI.....29.1:4 In f., it explains every idea we have used
W-pI...39.10:3 the f. that your holiness is your salvation.
W-pI.....41.8:2 In f. it is very easy, because it is the most
W-pI.....42.5:2 may, in f., be astonished at the amount of
W-pI.....43.7:6 In f., try not to make distinctions of this
W-pI.....48.1:1 The idea for today simply states a f.. It is
W-pI.....48.1:2 is not a f. to those who believe in illusions,
W-pI.....53.5:4 The f. that I see a world in which there is
W-pI.....55.1:4 The very f. that I see such things is proof
W-pI.....66.4:1 acceptance of the f. that not only is there a
W-pI.....71.9:9 very f. that you are doing the exercises
W-pI.....72.2:2 In f., the ego is the physical embodiment
W-pI.....72.5:5 In f., if the body were real, it would be
W-pI.....77.6:2 You state a f. that cannot be denied. The
W-pI.....77.6:4 f. that you accepted must be so. There is
W-pI.....77.6:7 answer is a simple statement of a simple f.
W-pI.....77.7:1 be devoted to a reminder of a simple f..
W-pI.....80.1:8 Accept that f., and you are ready to take
W-pI.....96.2:1 The f. that truth and illusion cannot be
W-pI.131.15:4 world. If you forget this happy f., remind
W-pI.133.12:3 simple f. that no decision can be difficult.
W-pI...134.2:1 the f. that pardon is not asked for what is
W-pI...136.5:4 Mistake not this for f.. Defenses must
W-pI.136.13:1 It is this f. that demonstrates that time is
WpI. rIV.in2:3 That is a f., and represents the truth of
W-pI...187.1:2 In f., giving is proof of having. We have
W-pI...190.1:3 It is not a f. at all. There is no form it takes
W-pI...191.4:6 In this one f. is sinlessness proclaimed to
W-pI...196.2:2 It may, in f., appear to be a sign that
W-pI...200.1:3 Accept this f., and save yourself the agony
W-pII.304.1:3 Perception is a mirror, not a f.. And what
W-pII.359.1:7 *f. forgiveness rests upon a certain base more*
M-3...........5:4 that they necessarily recognize this; in f.,
M-4.........I.1:3 In f., perception *is* learning, because cause
M-4.....I.A.8:7 In f., it is here. Who would "go" anywhere
M-4.....VII.1:2 is not the usual meaning of the word; in f.,
M-6...........3:6 Trust is an essential part of giving; in f., it
M-10.........3:2 This is not an opinion but a f.. In order to
M-11.........1:9 What the world is, is but a f.. You cannot
M-13.........2:1 the f. that the world has nothing to give.
M-16.......10:2 f. that the teacher of God devotes his day.
M-17.........2:3 It can, in f., be easily concealed beneath a
M-17.........4:1 remember that no one can be angry at a f.
M-17.........5:5 That this can hardly be a f. is obvious. Yet
M-17.........5:6 it can be believed as f. is equally obvious.
M-17.........6:6 Accept it as a f., and then forget it. Do not
M-17.........8:6 comes from an interpretation and not a f.,
M-17.........9:7 witness that you do believe in it as f.. Now
M-18.........1:1 ceased to confuse interpretation with f.,
M-21.........5:3 problem as he perceives it, and may, in f.,
M-22.........5:5 He will, in f., be unable to recognize his
M-29.........1:2 raise. In f., it covers only a few of the more
C-1.............7:6 Yet the very f. that it has levels and can be
P-2.........in.3:4 He hopes, in f., to stabilize it sufficiently
P-2........III.4:2 But healing is a process, not a f.. The
P-2........IV.9:4 In f., this is his central task; the core of
P-3..........II.2:3 In f., it probably taught him how to make
S-2...........I.1:2 It has, in f., become a scourge; a curse

**factor** 3
T-1.........V.2:3 accepts the time-control f. gladly. He
T-23......II.12:5 missing f. in your madness that makes it
M-21.........1:2 The motivating f. is prayer, or asking.

**factors** 2
T-10.......in.1:3 to you is caused by f. outside yourself.
W-pI.....97.1:2 nor tries to weave opposing f. into unity.

**facts** 12
T-3......VI.11:5 Wishes are not f.. To wish is to imply that
T-9.........I.11:6 It is indeed possible for you to deny f.,
T-16........II.9:3 these f. together and made sense of them?
T-26......III.4:6 But in this world there are no simple f.,
T-26.....VII.9:6 F. are unchanged. Yet facts can be denied
T-26.....VII.9:7 Yet f. can be denied and thus unknown,
W-pI.....48.1:2 believe in illusions, but illusions are not f.
W-pI...136.5:5 Defenses must make f. unrecognizable.
M-5........II.1:3 this, one first must recognize certain f..
M-10.........4:1 knew all the "f." you needed for judgment
M-10.........4:8 He does know all the f.; past, present and
M-17.........4:2 seeming justification by what *appears* as f..

**faculties** 1
T-8........IX.3:4 by rendering the f. for seeing ineffectual.

**fade** 18
T-13.....VII.8:5 have lent yourself in time, and it will f..
T-17......III.4:3 to f. and to be questioned almost at once.
T-27......III.7:1 Forgiveness vanishes and symbols f., and
T-28......III.1:7 the dream will f. away without effects. For
T-29......VI.2:9 time and bloom and f. will not return.
T-30......IV.8:1 of separation start to f. and disappear.
T-30....VIII.6:5 There is no false appearance but will f., if

W-pI...106.4:6 They will not f. when dreaming ends.
W-pI.122.12:1 today the world will f. until it disappears,
W-pI...162.2:3 that will not f. away before their might.
W-pI...165.5:5 induce you now to let it f. away from your
W-pI...198.6:7 And as this one will f. away, the Word of
W-pII .....6.3:4 to f. before His glory and reveal your holy
W-pII ...10.2:6 now are useless, and will therefore f. away
W-pII .326.2:1 forgiven, f. entirely into God's holy Will.
M-2 ...........5:6 another, f. and grow dim and disappear.
M-13 .........1:2 and will ultimately f. into the nothingness
S-3........IV.9:3 See the shadows f. away in gentleness; the

### faded 1

T-18.....VII.2:2 It has perhaps f. at times from your sight,

### fades 9

T-5......IV.1:11 be as one, the ego f. away and is undone.
T-14.....VII.1:6 ignorance f. away when knowledge dawns
T-17.....IV.15:5 The frame f. gently and God rises to your
T19...IV.D.2:3 f. in the blazing light beyond it when the
T19...IV.D.5:3 the Holy Spirit from you f. in the presence
T-26......IX.3:1 hatred f. to let the grass grow green again,
W-pI...133.6:4 What f. and dies was never there, and
W-pI...164.2:1 The world f. easily away before His sight.
W-pI.167.12:3 perfectly it f. into what is reflected there.

### fading 2

T-27...VII.14:6 The dream of guilt is f. from your sight,
W-pI...158.7:5 without the slightest f. of the light it sees.

### fail 193

T-1........III.1:3 stand at the end in case you f. temporarily
T-2........IV.3:4 device can do is to f. to facilitate learning.
T-4........VI.6:7 My chosen channels cannot f., because I
T-9.........I.10:8 And could He f. to recognize it in His Son
T-11.......II.3:4 To deny meaning is to f. to understand.
T-12.........I.5:4 f. to recognize a call for help is to refuse
T-12.......II.8:4 You will not f. in your mission because I
T-12.......II.8:4 your mission because I did not f. in mine.
T-12.....II.10:6 Surely He will not f. to help you, since
T-13......XI.5:2 is impossible that this mission f.. Nothing
T-13......XI.6:8 Fear not the Holy Spirit will f. in what
T-13......XI.6:9 to do. The Will of God can f. in nothing.
T-14.....III.10:4 And they will f. to understand the simple
T-14.....III.14:3 will not f. to learn that what God wills for
T-14.....IV.4:4 God will not f., nor ever has in anything.
T-14....IV.4:10 Love. F. not in your function of loving in a
T-14....IV.4:11 F. not yourself, but instead offer to God
T-14.......V.5:8 of teaching is to f. to learn from them.
T-14.......V.6:6 fear that teaching this can f. to overcome.
T-14.......V.7:1 that cannot f. and must result in peace.
T-14.......V.9:9 F. not the only purpose to which my
T-14......VI.8:8 can f. to come where God has called him,
T-14......IX.6:5 to see, no one can f. to understand. It is
T-14......XI.1:7 of strength so pitiful that it must f. you.
T-15....VIII.3:5 He will not f. you, for He comes from One
T-15....VIII.3:5 for He comes from One Who cannot f..
T-16.......II.8:1 and deaf could f. to see and hear them.
T-16......IV.6:4 from one illusion into another must f.. If
T-16....IV.12:1 in you than you can f. to remember it.
T-16.....V.14:2 you f. to recognize them for what they are
T-16.....V.14:2 and you will f. to do this to the extent to
T-17......VI.6:7 No one will f. in anything. This seems to
T-17....VIII.5:6 F. him not now, for it has been given you
T-18.......II.5:9 you f. to recognize is that what caused the
T-18.......V.6:2 He will never f. in this. But forget not that
T-18..VIII.12:5 you not, or f. to recognize itself in you.
T19....IV.A.5:5 love. How can this f. to be accomplished,
T19....IV.B.9:9 of peace and happiness in what must f.?
T-21.........I.1:5 but f. to be aware you can go through the
T-21.........I.5:3 They try to reach each other, and they f.,
T-21.........I.5:3 each other, and they fail, and f. again.
T-21.......II.1:3 it cannot f. to be completely understood.
T-21.......II.8:1 what is really there you cannot f. to see.
T-21.....II.10:8 the two is merely to f. to understand them
T-21 .... V.10:4 cannot f. to lead to changed perception.
T-21 ...VIII.3:6 God Himself will never f. to answer. God
T-22 .......II.2:7 exists will surely f. to make a difference.
T-22 ..... VI.6:4 And who would f. to recognize a gift he
T-24 ......in.1:4 He will not f.. Where He can enter, there
T-24 .....II.14:2 will forever f. to bring you peace and joy
T-24 .... VII.3:2 How can you f. to know it in his holiness?
T-25 ......in.2:1 him can f. to recognize Him everywhere.
T-25 ...... V.2:7 f. to think he must be guilty to maintain
T-25 .... VII.9:1 nor f. completely to perceive at all. To
T-27 .... VII.3:5 it is could f. to see it does not follow and it
T-28 ......I.15:8 no fear that He will f. in what He wills.
T-29 ........I.1:5 and His eternal patience sometimes f.. All
T-29 .......II.9:4 can f. to be what you demanded that it be.
T-29 ..... III.1:9 could f. to understand this must be so.
T-29 .... IV.4:10 If it should f. you think the dream is sad.
T-29 ..... IV.5:2 No one can f. but your idea of him, and
T-29 .... VII.1:2 For it will f., and you will weep each time
T-29 .. VII.1:11 You will f.. But it is given you to know the
T-29 .... VII.3:2 And each will f. him, all excepting one;
T-29 .... VII.5:4 Yet each must f. and crumble and decay,
T-29 .... VII.7:2 dreams, in which all idols f. you, one by
T-30 ..... III.1:8 And this must f. to satisfy, because it is
T-30 ...VIII.1:3 and if you f. to see beyond appearances
T-31 ......I.10:3 How wrong are you who f. to hear the call
T-31 ...VIII.5:5 comes from God and that can never f..
T-31 ...VIII.8:1 f. to hear my voice and listen to my words
T-31 .VIII.11:3 And can You f. in what is but Your Will? I
W-pI.....23.1:3 But this way cannot f.. Every thought you
W-pI.....41.8:7 But it will never f. completely, and instant
W-pI.....42.1:2 you cannot f. in your efforts to achieve
W-pI.....45.5:2 f. in doing what He would have us do.
W-pI.....50.4:2 They will f. you. Put all your faith in the
W-pI.....69.7:4 You cannot f. because your will is His.
W-pI.....71.7:4 because of His plan, which cannot f..
W-pI.....75.7:3 Believe He will not f. you now. You have
W-pI.....75.8:1 you know you cannot f. because you trust
W-pI.....75.9:6 upon your eyes, you cannot f. to see today
W-pI.....76.5:3 mind will f. to see it is the victim of itself.
W-pI.....77.5:4 You cannot f. to be assured in this. You
W-pI.....80.4:2 be gone, because God's answer cannot f..
W-pI.....86.1:8 I will rejoice because His plan can never f.
W-pI.....94.4:4 You cannot f. because He cannot fail.
W-pI.....94.4:4 now. You cannot fail because He cannot f.
W-pI.....95.1:5 this, and you f. to realize it must be so,
W-pI.....95.5:3 time. You often f. to remember the short
W-pI.....95.9:1 f. to comply with the requirements of this
W-pI.....96.6:8 bring pain to him, and f. to set him free?
W-pI...96.11:1 Your Self knows that you cannot f. today.
W-pI...100.5:2 we f. to take the part that is essential to
W-pI...100.5:4 Thus do you f. to show the world how
W-pI...102.4:4 You cannot f. to find it when you learn it
W-pI...103.3:7 *today. I cannot f., because I seek the truth.*
W-pI...104.1:3 Who cannot f. to give you what He wills.
WpI..rIII.in6:4 the means the Holy Spirit uses will not f..
WpI..rIII.in7:3 It will not f.. It is the Holy Spirit's chosen
W-pI...122.5:1 your salvation cannot change, nor can it f.
W-pI...124.1:3 We can f. in nothing. Everything we
W-pI...124.8:5 as He sees fit today, certain He will not f..
W-pI...124.9:3 will you f. to recognize it when it dawns
W-pI...127.4:1 you really are could f. to emphasize that
W-pI...129.3:3 go from there to where words f. entirely,
W-pI...130.1:6 And no one can f. to look upon what he
W-pI...130.9:3 will you f. to see His thanks expressed in
W-pI......131.h one can f. who seeks to reach the truth.
W-pI...131.4:3 No one can f. to want this goal and reach
W-pI.131.10:2 No one can f. who seeks to reach the truth
W-pI.131.12:2 no one can f. who seeks to reach the truth
W-pI.131.14:1 You cannot f. today. There walks with
W-pI.131.15:7 *No one can f. who seeks to reach the truth.*
W-pI...135.4:5 body falters and must f. to serve the Son
W-pI...135.7:5 For it seems to f. your hopes, your needs,
W-pI.135.10:5 for you f. to see where hope must lie if it
W-pI.135.13:4 that has been given it and cannot f..
W-pI.137.12:4 inevitable to occur, and you will never f..
W-pI.138.10:3 Yet who can f. to make a choice between
W-pI...139.8:3 you know not what you cannot f. to know
W-pI...139.9:6 F. not your brothers, or you fail yourself.
W-pI...139.9:6 Fail not your brothers, or you f. yourself.
W-pI .. 140.6:5 which cannot f. to heal and heal forever.
W-pI .. 146.1:1 No one can f. who seeks to reach the truth
W-pI 151.15:4 No one can f. to listen, when you hear the
W-pI 153.11:3 And while you f. to teach what you have
W-pI 153.20:4 goal. The ministers of God can never f.,
W-pI 155.13:7 You will not f. your brothers nor your Self
W-pI .. 161.1:3 which can never f. to welcome in the
W-pI .. 162.6:2 Who could f. to welcome you into his
W-pI .. 163.3:1 apt to f. the hopes they once engendered,
W-pI .. 163.3:4 never f. to take all life as hostage to itself.
W-pI .. 164.9:7 Can His promise f.? Can you withhold so
W-pI .. 182.6:5 You will f. Him not. He will go home, and
W-pI .. 182.7:3 came because He knew you would not f..
W-pI 184.13:1 No one can f. who seeks the meaning of
W-pI 185.11:1 seeks the peace of God can f. to find it.
W-pI 185.12:2 gift. How can you f., when you but ask for
W-pI 185.14:2 can we f. today as we request the peace of
W-pI 186.11:6 but God's can never f. because He is its
W-pI .. 187.6:3 Nor can he f. to recognize the many forms
W-pI .. 191.7:4 *suffer loss, nor f. to do all that salvation asks.*
W-pI .. 193.8:6 Would you f. to learn the simple lessons
W-pI .. 194.8:3 love. Think you the world could f. to gain
W-pI .. 195.2:2 But it is equally insane to f. in gratitude to
W-pI .. 195.6:3 we f. to recognize the gifts of God to us.
W-pI .. 196.2:3 it f. to understand the truth it uses thus.
W-pI .. 197.1:5 that when He strikes He will not f. to kill.
W-pI .. 200.3:4 ask that what is false be true can only f..
WpI.rVI.in.7:3 He will not f. to be available to you, each
W-pII .... in.4:1 would not f. to take when we invited Him.
W-pII .... in.5:4 For now we cannot f.. Sit silently and wait
W-pII .... in.6:1 I am so close to you we cannot f.. Father,
W-pII .... in.7:7 Will created all that is, can f. in nothing.
W-pII .... in.7:8 which will not f. the Son who calls to You.
W-pII .... in.9:1 We had a wish that God would f. to have
W-pII . 244.1:3 *fear or doubt or f. to know he cannot suffer,*
W-pII . 246.1:3 Let me not f. to recognize myself, and still
W-pII . 284.2:2 *Let me not f. to trust in You today, accepting*
W-pII . 290.2:2 *You cannot f. to hear me, Father. What I ask*
W-pII . 312.1:4 f. to see what we have chosen to behold.
W-pII . 312.1:6 f. to look upon what Christ would have
W-pII . 327.2:1 *Your promises will never f. in my experience*
W-pII . 330.2:2 *but f. to know our one Identity we share with*
W-pII . 333.2:4 *For this alone will never f. in anything, being*
W-pII . 338.2:2 *Yours. All other plans will f.. And I will have*
W-pII . 338.2:4 *Mine alone will f., and lead me nowhere. But*
W-pII . 356.1:1 *You promised You would never f. to answer*
Wfl........in.3:5 not f. to recognize as part of God Himself.
M-3 ........... 5:7 who falter and may even seem to f.. No
M-3 ........... 5:8 No teacher of God can f. to find the Help
M-4 ........II.1:2 achieved, the others cannot f. to follow.
M-7 ........... 2:5 given the problem to One Who cannot f.,
M-16 ......... 7:4 He has a Guide Who will not f.. He need
M-18 ....... 4:10 there whom his forgiveness can f. to heal?
M-20 ......... 3:2 No one can f. to find it who but seeks out
M-23 ......... 3:7 it is likely that he will f. to keep them. Can
M-23 ......... 3:8 Can God f. His Son? And can one who is
C-4 ............ 4:4 is. And now it cannot f. to disappear, for
C-ep .......... 1:4 No one can f. to do what God appointed
P-2..........II.3:1 learns to forgive can f. to remember God.
P-2..........II.7:6 who believe they have found God will f..
P-2........ III.3:1 possible for psychotherapy to seem to f..
P-2....... VII.6:5 Whose Love is in him and Who cannot f..
P-2....... VII.9:2 But if you f. in this, you have denied that
P-3.........I.3:10 Spirit. It cannot f. to be accomplished.
S-1........ III.6:7 who wants an enemy will f. to find one.
S-2........ III.7:2 has a Teacher Who will f. in nothing. Rest
S-2........ III.7:5 nor f. to send His angels down to answer
S-3........ III.5:2 remedy that brings relief which cannot f..
S-3........ III.6:2 will never f. to bring His kindly remedy to
S-3........ IV.5:2 Nor will your judgment f. to reach to God

### failed 33

T-4 ....... III.6:4 He has never f. to answer this request,
T-4 .........V.6:2 but has systematically f. to achieve. The
T-7 ....... IX.6:1 f. to increase the inheritance of the Sons
T-7 ....... IX.6:1 thus have not f. to secure it for yourself.
T-12 .......V.2:7 attacks on yourself have f. to weaken you,
T-12 .......V.6:2 goals where yours have clearly f.. Your

| | |
|---|---|
| T-12....... V.6:5 | have f. to learn what learning aids are for? |
| T-13....... II.2:4 | ideals," which the ego claims you have f.. |
| T-14....... V.5:7 | those who have f. to learn need teaching, |
| T19..IV.B.11:6 | attack on what you think has f. you? Use |
| T-20....... II.8:5 | nor have you ever f. entirely to hear. You |
| T-22.........I.6:1 | you have received and f. to understand, |
| T-24..... II.14:2 | and the awareness that your plan has f., |
| T-24...... VI.3:2 | has He f. to lay before you lovingly, as |
| T-25....... II.3:3 | to uphold pursuit of what has always f., |
| T-25....... II.4:1 | past *has* f.. Be glad that it is gone within |
| T-27. VIII.10:6 | on you unless you f. to recognize it is your |
| T-29...... IV.4:1 | has f. to fill the function you allotted him? |
| T-30...... IV.2:3 | made for boxes and for bears have f. him, |
| T-31... VIII.3:1 | that you f. to learn presented once again, |
| W-pI.....52.2:7 | look with love on all that I f. to see before. |
| W-pI.....70.9:1 | Since all illusions of salvation have f. you, |
| W-pI.....71.3:3 | that, although this hope has always f., |
| W-pI.....79.7:4 | problem, which we have f. to recognize. |
| W-pI.....95.7:4 | you have already f. to do what is required. |
| W-pI...133.9:3 | not perceive that he has merely f. to gain. |
| W-pI.151.14:2 | and f. to be deceived by what was falsely |
| W-pI...154.9:3 | God has not f. to offer what you need, nor |
| W-pI...185.7:5 | that can succeed where all the rest have f.. |
| WpI rVI.in.4:4 | all we did not know and f. to understand. |
| W-pII..228.2:1 | *I f. to realize the Source from which I came. I* |
| W-pII......2.2:4 | was one, but f. to recognize its oneness. |
| Wfl .........in.5:7 | son because he f. to understand the truth? |

## failing 12

| | |
|---|---|
| T-13....... II.2:5 | no idea that you are f. the Son of God by |
| T-13....... II.2:6 | you do not realize that you are f. yourself. |
| T-14....IV.3:10 | this guilt by f. to fulfill your function here |
| T-16..... V.14:3 | are f. to make the simple choice between |
| T-17....... V.8:4 | and do not breathe life into your f. ego. |
| T-31...VII.14:3 | f. dreams and no remaining hope except |
| W-pI.....35.6:4 | *I see myself as f.. I see myself as endangered. I* |
| W-pI.....72.4:3 | more than f. to help in freeing him from |
| W-pI.....96.2:2 | before, and f. as the next one surely will. |
| W-pI...154.5:4 | f. to perform his proper part as bringer of |
| W-pI...193.7:1 | or someone else is f. to perceive the lesson |
| W-pII......2.3:1 | f. to support the world of dreams and |

## fails 19

| | |
|---|---|
| T-14....III.10:7 | nothing their will f. to provide that offers |
| T-14..... X.10:7 | lonely journey f. because it has excluded |
| T-16......IV.9:4 | certain and where everything f. to satisfy. |
| T-17....... V.1:3 | The holy instant never f.. The experience |
| T-21... VIII.3:4 | for it. For no one f. to ask for his desire of |
| T-22.........I.3:1 | understand what f. entirely to reach you. |
| T-23........ II.9:4 | thus it f. to recognize that you can never |
| T-29....IV.4:11 | But whether it succeeds or f. is not its core |
| T-29......IV.6:4 | And do not try to hurt him when he f. to |
| T-29. VIII.8:10 | And when one f. another takes its place, |
| W-pI.....60.4:3 | which His Voice f. to direct my thoughts, |
| W-pI.....75.7:2 | Understand that the Holy Spirit never f. |
| W-pI...133.8:6 | For what the ego wants it f. to recognize. |
| W-pI.160.10:2 | Not one He f. to give you to remember, |
| W-pI...191.2:5 | is no sight that f. to witness this to you. |
| W-pI...198.9:5 | that f. to hide an unforgiving thought. |
| W-pII..302.2:2 | He f. in nothing. He the End we seek, and |
| W-pII....13.2:2 | it f. entirely to understand its ways. A |
| M-22..........5:1 | When a teacher of God f. to heal, it is |

## failure 24

| | |
|---|---|
| T-3...........I.4:7 | the teacher offers. The result is learning f. |
| T-6......IV.12:5 | of perfection, but a f. in communication. |
| T-8...........I.4:4 | learning outcomes is a sign of learning f., |
| T-9........ I.10:5 | communication f. between them. Yet *you* |
| T-9......... II.1:1 | has experienced what appears to be f.. |
| T-12....... V.6:4 | ability to generalize is a crucial learning f. |
| T-13....XI.11:4 | F. is of the ego, not of God. From Him |
| T-14.......IV.3:9 | your guilt arises from your f. to fulfill |
| T-15... VIII.3:6 | Accept your sense of f. as nothing more |
| T-15... VIII.3:7 | For the holy host of God is beyond f., and |
| T-17......... V.8:2 | brother for the "f." of your relationship, |
| T-26...VII.12:6 | f. lies in that you still feel guilty, though |
| T-29....... II.9:5 | unmindful that the f. does not lie in that |
| T-29....... II.9:5 | be, but only in your f. to perceive that it is |
| W-pI.....71.5:4 | misery and a deep sense of f. and despair. |
| W-pI.....79.4:3 | must be inadequate, and f. is inevitable. |
| W-pI.....91.1:5 | absence is not the result of your f. to see. |
| W-pI.....91.2:5 | Denial of light leads to f. to perceive it. |
| W-pI.....91.2:6 | F. to perceive light is to perceive darkness |
| W-pI...131.1:1 | F. is all about you while you seek for |
| W-pI...200.6:6 | a choice to make between success and f.; |
| W-pII...... 1.4:4 | judge, for he must justify his f. to forgive. |
| M-7 ...........5:5 | Perhaps there is a fear of f. and shame |
| M-7 ...........6:2 | is a f. to recognize him as part of the Self, |

## failures 3

| | |
|---|---|
| T-18........ V.1:6 | greatest advances you have judged as f., |
| W-pI.....95.8:3 | f. to follow the instructions for practicing |
| P-2.......VII.4:5 | patient's errors thus became his own f., |

## faint 1

| | |
|---|---|
| T-11....... II.5:2 | but His Voice grows f. in alien company. |

## faintest 5

| | |
|---|---|
| T-9..... VIII.4:2 | Even the f. hint of your reality literally |
| T-18... VIII.3:3 | the f. ripple on the surface of the ocean. |
| W-pI...107.3:1 | not more than just the f. intimation of the |
| W-pI...127.7:1 | the f. glimmering of what love means |
| M-18 .........4:2 | If he senses even the f. hint of irritation in |

## faintly 6

| | |
|---|---|
| T-14......IV.8:5 | felt apart from Him resembles it ever so f. |
| W-pI.....30.1:3 | will what you saw before be even f. visible |
| W-pI...158.8:2 | that f. can compare with this in value; nor |
| W-pI...159.5:3 | shadows there; transparent, f. seen, at |
| W-pI...164.1:5 | world engenders, yet He hears them f.. |
| M-20 .........4:5 | remember even f. now what happiness |

## fair 19

| | |
|---|---|
| T-9....... II.11:3 | laws are always f. and perfectly consistent |
| T-25... VIII.5:4 | it well. For He is wholly f. to everyone. |
| T-25... VIII.5:6 | To be just is to be f., and not be vengeful. |
| T-25... VIII.8:2 | denied themselves because they are not f., |
| T-25. VIII.11:9 | For love is f., and cannot chasten without |
| T-25...... IX.2:7 | For God is f.. He does not fight against |
| T-25...... IX.9:2 | you perceive and leave you f. to no one. |
| T-26........ II.2:6 | attack be justified and vengeance f.. |
| T-26....... II.5:6 | Would it be f. to punish him because you |
| T-26....... II.5:8 | You deny the miracle of justice *can* be f.. |
| T-26....... II.6:2 | that some injustices are f. and good, and |
| T-26....... X.2:2 | be some forms in which you think it f.. |
| T-26....... X.6:4 | The world is f. because the Holy Spirit has |
| WpI. rIII.in9:3 | given your learning a f. chance to prove |
| W-pI...126.4:2 | nor is it f. that you should suffer when it |
| W-pI...165.4:7 | Yet God is f.. Sureness is not required to |
| M-10 ..........3:5 | so that his judgment would be wholly f. to |
| M-10 .......4:10 | And He is wholly f. to everyone, for there |
| M-23 .........1:3 | Would it be f. if their pupils were denied |

## fairly 16

| | |
|---|---|
| T-7........ XI.3:1 | you have made and judge its worth f.. Is it |
| T-11.......in.1:2 | will examine the evidence on both sides f. |
| T-16...... III.1:4 | Therefore He could look upon it f., and |
| T-24.........I.7:8 | Look f. at whatever makes you give your |
| T-25VIII.13:10 | and cannot f. see another's rights because |
| W-pI.......2.2:1 | glance easily and f. quickly around you, |
| W-pI.....11.3:1 | move from one thing to another f. rapidly |
| W-pI.....12.2:3 | involves a f. constant time interval. Do |
| W-pI.....36.2:2 | Try to distribute them f. evenly, and |
| W-pI.....45.6:2 | Then spend a f. short period in thinking a |
| W-pI.....66.9:7 | Remember the outcomes f., and consider |
| M-3 ...........4:3 | two people enter into a f. intense teaching- |
| M-4 ...... IV.1:8 | must learn,–and f. early in his training, |
| M-9 ...........2:4 | God's Voice, is usually a f. slow process, |
| M-16 .........5:2 | Perhaps your quiet time should be f. early |
| M-19 .........1:8 | If God's Son were f. judged, there would |

## fairness 8

| | |
|---|---|
| T-5........ VI.3:2 | me *is* in you, for God creates with perfect f. |
| T-5........ VI.3:3 | Holy Spirit remind you always of His f., |
| T-21...... III.1:4 | to keep the bargain in the name of "f.," |
| T-21...... III.1:5 | Thus in the "f." you attempt to ease the |
| T-25....VIII.5:7 | F. and vengeance are impossible, for each |
| T-27......II.10:2 | It belongs to One Who knows of f., not of |
| T-27......II.13:6 | His merit punishment, while yours, in f., |
| M-15 .........3:5 | be judged, and judged in f. and in honesty |

## fairy 1

| | |
|---|---|
| T-9...... IV.11:6 | F. tales can be pleasant or fearful, but no |

## faith 316

| | |
|---|---|
| T-1........ VI.4:3 | has perfect f. in His creations *because* He |
| T-1...... VI.5:10 | this solution, and this f. *is* His gift. |
| T-3..........II.6:1 | to withdraw your f. in them and invest it |
| T-5.......VII.2:2 | their f. because their faith was not whole. |
| T-5.......VII.2:2 | their faith because their f. was not whole. |
| T-6.........in.2:5 | it is still a form of f. and can be redirected |
| T-9..........II.4:2 | for your f. in him is your faith in yourself. |
| T-9..........II.4:2 | for your faith in him is your f. in yourself. |
| T-9..........II.4:3 | in me whose f. in you cannot be shaken. |
| T-9....... II.5:11 | f. in him strong enough to let you hear? |
| T-10...... III.7:8 | Your f. in it will make you whole when |
| T-10...... III.7:8 | make you whole when you have f. in me. |
| T-10...... IV.7:2 | likewise. It is an act of f., because it is the |
| T-10...... IV.8:7 | Put all your f. in it, and God Himself will |
| T-13.........I.7:2 | not, has kept f. with his Father for you. |
| T-13...VII.15:1 | f. that He will lead you safely through all |
| T-13...... IX.2:3 | fidelity to it with pain, for f. in it *is* pain. |
| T-13...... IX.2:4 | And f. can be rewarded only in terms of |
| T-13...... IX.2:4 | of the belief in which the f. was placed. |
| T-13...... IX.2:5 | F. makes the power of belief, and where it |
| T-13...... IX.2:6 | For f. is always given what is treasured, |
| T-13...... IX.3:1 | what you found in it and placed your f. in. |
| T-13...... IX.3:2 | your f. will be rewarded as you gave it. |
| T-13...... IX.3:3 | and if you place your f. in the past, the |
| T-13...... IX.5:5 | and the belief in one is f. in the other, |
| T-13...... IX.8:6 | is there, and what you put your f. in. |
| T-13...... IX.8:7 | sign of perfect f. your Father has in you. |
| T-13..... X.13:1 | my f. and my belief are centered on what I |
| T-13..... X.13:3 | and all my f. and my belief I offer unto it. |
| T-13..... X.13:4 | it. My f. in you is as strong as all the love I |
| T-13...... X.14:8 | then, lack f. in you and love Him perfectly |
| T-13...... XI.4:5 | He has perfect f. in your final judgment, |
| T-13...... XI.7:1 | Have f. in only this one thing, and it will |
| T-14........II.1:7 | Have f. in nothing and you will find the |
| T-14........II.3:6 | *Your f. in nothing is deceiving you. Offer* |
| T-14........II.3:7 | *Offer your f. to Me, and I will place it gently* |
| T-14.... III.15:5 | Be quiet in your f. in Him Who loves you, |
| T-14.... XI.14:3 | for His f. in you is His understanding. It is |
| T-14.... XI.14:4 | It is as firm as is His f. in His Creator, and |
| T-14.... XI.14:4 | and He knows that f. in His Creator must |
| T-14.... XI.14:4 | must encompass f. in His creation. In this |
| T-15....... VI.1:4 | Perfect f. in each one, for its ability to |
| T-15....... VI.1:4 | arises only from perfect f. in yourself. |
| T-15....... VI.2:1 | have so little f. in yourself because you are |
| T-15....... VI.2:3 | I offer you my perfect f. in you, in place of |
| T-15....... VI.2:4 | forget not that my f. must be as perfect in |
| T-15....... VI.2:5 | our f. in God's Son because we recognize, |
| T-15....... VI.4:4 | your f. in Him is strengthened by sharing. |
| T-15....... VI.6:5 | behind it, can have f. in love without fear. |
| T-15....... VI.6:6 | fear. Yet the Holy Spirit gives you this f., |
| T-15.... XI.10:2 | I have perfect f. in you to do all that you |
| T-16........II.5:1 | f. in reality be yours while you are bent on |
| T-16........II.8:4 | yet you have so little f. in what you heard, |
| T-16........II.8:4 | greater f. in the disaster you have made. |
| T-16........II.9:6 | for you to place your f. in them, and not |
| T-16........II.9:8 | Have f. in Him Who has faith in you. |
| T-16........II.9:8 | Have faith in Him Who has f. in you. |
| T-16...... III.2:7 | And would you not have f. in what you |
| T-16...... III.6:5 | to strengthen your f. in what you taught. |
| T-16....... V.9:1 | out to those who place their f. in littleness |

T-16...... VI.5:6 If one such union were made in perfect f.,
T-16.... VI.12:4 for your unwillingness by His perfect f.,
T-16.... VI.12:4 and it is His f. you share with Him there.
T-17.........I.3:3 your lack of f. in the power that heals all
T-17....... V.6:1 This is the time for *f.*. You let this goal be
T-17....... V.6:3 That was an act of f.. Do not abandon
T-17....... V.6:4 Do not abandon f., now that the rewards
T-17....... V.6:4 the rewards of f. are being introduced. If
T-17....... V.6:6 Have f. in your brother in what but seems
T-17....... V.7:6 Have f. in Him Who answered you. He
T-17..... V.7:11 Now He asks for f. a little longer, even in
T-17..... V.7:12 will see the justification for your f. emerge
T-17...... VI.6:1 The goal of truth requires f.. Faith is
T-17...... VI.6:2 F. is implicit in the acceptance of the Holy
T-17...... VI.6:2 Spirit's purpose, and this f. is all-inclusive
T-17...... VI.6:3 the goal of truth is set, there f. must be.
T-17...... VI.6:8 This seems to ask for f. beyond you, and
T-17.... VI.6:10 has f. in separation and not in wholeness.
T-17...... VI.7:4 has not come because f. has been denied,
T-17........VII.h The Call for F.
T-17..... VII.1:1 are the witnesses to your lack of f.. They
T-17..... VII.1:3 The problem *was* the lack of f., and it is
T-17..... VII.1:5 you not lacked f. that it could be solved,
T-17..... VII.2:1 is no problem in any situation that f. will
T-17..... VII.2:5 Yet f. must be where something has been
T-17..... VII.3:6 the justification for your lack of f.. You
T-17..... VII.3:9 to f. will never interfere with truth. But
T-17... VII.3:10 used *against* truth will always destroy f.. If
T-17... VII.3:11 If you lack f., ask that it be restored where
T-17..... VII.4:3 holiness cannot be seen except through f.,
T-17..... VII.4:3 relationship was not holy because your f.
T-17..... VII.4:4 Your f. must grow to meet the goal that
T-17..... VII.4:5 that peace and f. will not come separately.
T-17..... VII.4:6 What situation can you be in without f.,
T-17..... VII.6:1 closely tied to faithlessness as f. to truth.
T-17..... VII.6:2 If you lack f. in anyone to fulfill, and
T-17..... VII.6:5 As holiness and f. go hand in hand, so
T-17..... VII.6:5 hand, so must its f. go everywhere with it.
T-17..... VII.8:4 lack f. in him because of what you were.
T-17..... VII.8:7 for faithlessness, but there *is* Cause for f..
T-17..... VII.9:1 situation with the f. you give your brother
T-17..... VII.9:2 Your f. will call the others to share your
T-17..... VII.9:2 the same purpose called forth the f. in you
T-17..... VII.9:4 Truth calls for f., and faith makes room
T-17..... VII.9:4 calls for faith, and f. makes room for truth
T-17... VII.10:1 You call for f. because of Him Who walks
T-17... VII.10:5 come. Its call for f. is strong. Use not your
T-17.... VIII.1:3 that f. might answer to the call of truth.
T-17.... VIII.1:5 whole. F. has accepted every aspect of the
T-17.... VIII.2:5 Not even f. is asked of you, for truth asks
T-17.... VIII.2:6 secure for you the f. you need for peace.
T-17.... VIII.3:2 such is the gift of f., freely given wherever
T-17.... VIII.3:5 has been demonstrated has called for f.,
T-17.... VIII.3:6 from which f. can no longer be withheld.
T-17.... VIII.3:7 strain of refusing f. to truth is enormous,
T-17.... VIII.3:8 answer truth with f. entails no strain at all
T-17.... VIII.4:6 strain of refusing to give f. to truth, and
T-17.... VIII.5:6 your lack of f. in him must mean to you.
T-17.... VIII.6:2 you had f. in it for no one accepts what he
T-18.........I.9:9 Give Him but a little f. in your brother, to
T-18...... III.4:5 the gift of f. you offered to your brother.
T-18....... V.2:6 forgiven. On your little f., joined with His
T-18....... V.2:7 a ladder planted in the solid rock of f.,
T-18....... V.4:6 little f. it needed to change the purpose is
T-18..... VII.1:1 still have too much f. in the body as a
T-19...........I.h Healing and F.
T-19.........I.1:3 peace without f. will never be attained, for
T-19.........I.1:3 as its only goal is brought to truth *by* f..
T-19.........I.1:4 This f. encompasses everyone involved,
T-19.........I.1:5 else your f. is limited and your dedication
T-19.........I.2:2 he is healed *because* you offered f. to him,
T-19.........I.5:1 to realize that f. must be the opposite of
T-19.........I.5:3 f. would remove all limitations and make
T-19.........I.5:4 and separate; f. would unite and heal.
T-19.........I.5:5 f. would remove all obstacles that seem to
T-19.........I.5:6 dedicated to illusions; f. wholly to truth.
T-19.........I.8:3 withholding f. you see what is unworthy
T-19.........I.9:1 To have f. is to heal. It is the sign that you
T-19.........I.9:3 it. By f., you offer the gift of freedom from
T-19 .........I.9:6 in that one you see your f. is fully justified
T-19 .........I.9:7 for faithlessness, but f. is always justified.
T-19 .......I.10:1 F. is the opposite of fear, as much a part
T-19 .......I.10:2 F. is the acknowledgment of union. It is
T-19 .......I.10:6 makes f. forever justified in everyone.
T-19 .......I.11:1 F. is the gift of God, through Him Whom
T-19 .......I.11:3 But through the eyes of f., the Son of God
T-19 .......I.11:4 F. sees him only *now* because it looks not
T-19 .......I.12:1 F. is as easily exchanged for knowledge as
T-19 .......I.12:2 f. arises from the Holy Spirit's perception,
T-19 .......I.12:3 F. is a gift you offer to the Son of God
T-19 .......I.12:5 offers you f. to give unto your brother.
T-19 .......I.12:7 Yet f. unites you in the holiness you see,
T-19 .......I.13:5 together, that you may heal through f..
T-19 .......I.14:3 as it was made again through f.. And
T-19 .......I.14:4 that there is nothing f. cannot forgive. No
T-19 .......I.15:1 so will f. help the Holy Spirit prepare the
T-19 .......I.15:2 For f. brings peace, and so it calls on truth
T-19 .......I.15:3 Truth follows f. and peace, completing
T-19 .......I.15:4 For f. is still a learning goal, no longer
T-19 ......II.6:12 It is impossible to have f. in sin, for sin is
T-19 ......II.6:13 to have f. that a mistake can be corrected.
T-19 ... III.10:5 your eyes in f. to what you now can see.
T19....IV.A.9:5 when you had greater f. in its protection.
T19..IV.B.10:1 F. in the eternal is always justified, for the
T19..IV.B.11:4 body is the great seeming betrayer of f..
T19..IV.B.11:9 your mistake will give you grounds for f..
T19..IV.B.16:2 in it all its f. that this can be accomplished
T19... IV.D.8:7 through the eyes of f. that sees them not.
T19... IV.D.9:7 And let us join in f. that He Who brought
T19. IV.D.11:3 with perfect f. and love and tenderness.
T19. IV.D.12:8 and he will raise your eyes in f. together,
T19. IV.D.17:1 Give f. to your brother, for faith and
T19. IV.D.17:1 f. and hope and mercy are yours to give.
T19. IV.D.21:3 What you had f. in still is faithful, and
T19. IV.D.21:3 and watches over you in f. so gentle yet so
T-20 ......II.8:11 lift up our eyes together, not in fear but f..
T-20 ... III.11:2 Share, then, this f. with me, and know
T-20 ....... V.6:7 Here is the perfect f. that you will one day
T-20 ....... V.7:9 have f. that He Who sees the gift in you
T-20 ...VIII.7:6 Could you have f. in what you see, if you
T-21 ........II.6:8 that threatens this seems to attack your f.,
T-21 ........II.7:1 The Holy Spirit can give you f. in holiness
T-21 ........II.8:6 or not. F. and desire go hand in hand, for
T-21 ........II.9:2 the power of wanting, and therefore of f.,
T-21 ........II.9:3 F. in the unreal leads to adjustments of
T-21 ......II.11:4 and place your f. in its ability to do so,
T-21 ......... III.h F., Belief and Vision
T-21 ...... III.2:5 always with f. and with the persistence
T-21 ...... III.2:5 the persistence that f. inevitably brings.
T-21 ...... III.2:6 The power of f. is never recognized if it is
T-21 ...... III.3:1 to you that f. can move mountains? This
T-21 ...... III.3:3 For f. can keep the Son of God in chains
T-21 ...... III.3:4 withdrawing f. that they can hold him,
T-21 ...... III.3:5 is impossible to place equal f. in opposite
T-21 ...... III.3:6 What f. you give to sin you take away
T-21 ...... III.4:1 F. and belief and vision are the means by
T-21 ...... III.4:2 from all illusions where your f. was laid.
T-21 ...... III.4:5 f. and His belief and vision are all for you.
T-21 ...... III.4:7 f. and vision and belief are meaningful
T-21 ...... III.5:1 It is impossible that the Son of God lack f.
T-21 ...... III.5:2 Faithlessness is not a lack of f., but faith
T-21 ...... III.5:2 is not a lack of faith, but f. in nothing.
T-21 ...... III.5:3 F. given to illusions does not lack power,
T-21 ...... III.5:4 strong in f. in his illusions about himself.
T-21 ...... III.5:5 For f., perception and belief you made, as
T-21 ...... III.5:6 choice, and by your f. in what you chose,
T-21 ...... III.6:7 see. Then will you give your f. to holiness,
T-21 ...... III.7:1 F. and belief become attached to vision,
T-21 ...... III.7:4 so the body has your f. and your belief.
T-21 ...... III.8:3 the power of their belief and f. sees far
T-21 ...... III.8:4 their f. had limited their understanding of
T-21 ...... III.8:5 that follow this decision are also born of f.
T-21 ...... III.9:8 f. you give your brother can accomplish
T-21 ... III.10:1 f. in sacrifice has given it great power in
T-21 ... III.12:3 have f. in it to serve the Holy Spirit's goal,
T-21 ... III.12:5 The f. and the belief you gave it belongs
T-21 ... III.12:6 and belief and f. from mind to body. Let
T-21 ...... IV.1:7 It doubts not your belief and f. in sin. Its
T-21 ..... IV.1:9 Your f. that sin is there but witnesses to
T-21 ..... IV.4:3 Your f. is moving inward, past insanity
T-21 .......V.2:7 For this will be your f.. But never believe
T-21 .......V.2:8 never believe because it is your f. it makes
T-21 .......V.3:2 And if you place your f. in Them, you will
T-21 .......V.8:1 F. and perception and belief can be
T-21 .......V.8:3 end. F. and belief are strong in madness,
T-21 .....V.10:2 F. and belief have shifted, and you have
T-21 .....V.10:4 F. and belief, upheld by reason, cannot
T-21 .... VII.5:2 can be no f. in sin without an enemy.
T-22 ...... in.4:3 is the f. in differences shifted to sameness.
T-22 ........ I.1:5 f. in this and see much evidence on its
T-22 ........ I.3:5 and firm in f. that you are something else,
T-22 ...... I.11:6 for f. in another is always faith in Him.
T-22 ...... I.11:6 for faith in another is always f. in Him.
T-22 .......II.4:7 And f. in innocence is faith in sin, if the
T-22 .......II.4:7 And faith in innocence is f. in sin, if the
T-22 .......II.6:3 through their use will you gain f. in them.
T-22 .....II.6:10 F. and belief can fall to either side, but
T-22 ..... IV.4:7 Christ's forgiveness to dispel their f. in sin
T-22 ... VI.9:11 each quiet smile of f. and confidence with
T-23 .....II.20:7 And lack of f. in love, in any form, attests
T-23 .....II.21:1 belief in sin, the f. in chaos must follow. It
T-23 ..... III.6:9 protection stands against the f. in murder
T-24 ........ I.3:1 though unrecognized, is f. in specialness.
T-24 ..... IV.1:2 yourself. F. is invested in yourself alone.
T-24 .......V.1:7 wish for something and lack f. that it is so
T-25 .... VII.6:1 this one demand is worthy of your f.. But
T-25 .. VII.12:4 single rock of truth can f. in God's eternal
T-25 ... VIII.2:2 is it necessary that your f. in it be strong,
T-25 ... VIII.2:6 Have little f. that wisdom could be found
T-25 ... VIII.2:7 thankful that only little f. is asked of you.
T-25 ... VIII.2:8 a little f. remains to those who still believe
T-27 ........ I.3:4 you show yourself, and give it all your f..
T-28 ..... IV.4:4 by not supporting his illusions by your f.,
T-28 ..... IV.4:4 for if you do, you will have f. in yours.
T-28 ..... IV.4:5 With f. in yours, he will not be released,
T-30 ..... VI.7:7 Salvation rests on f. there cannot be some
T-31 .... VII.5:1 Have f. in him who walks with you, so
T-31 . VIII.10:2 My f. in them is Yours. I am as sure that
T-31 . VIII.12:5 Not one illusion is accorded f., and not
W-pI .... 47.2:3 can put his f. in weakness and feel safe?
W-pI .... 47.2:4 can put his f. in strength and feel weak?
W-pI .... 50.1:3 Your f. is placed in the most trivial and
W-pI .... 50.2:4 Do not put your f. in the worthless. It will
W-pI .... 50.4:1 Put not your f. in illusions. They will fail
W-pI .... 50.4:3 all your f. in the Love of God within you;
W-pI .... 91.3:5 Your f. lies in the darkness, not the light.
W-pI .... 91.5:3 a body. F. goes to what you want, and you
W-pI .... 91.7:3 need to feel something to put your f. in, as
W-pI .... 91.7:4 and more sure; more worthy of your f.,
W-pI .... 91.9:3 belief that is mistaken and deserves no f..
W-pI .... 91.9:4 Try to remove your f. from it, if only for a
W-pI .... 91.9:5 You will be accustomed to keeping f. with
W-pI .... 98.7:3 made in f. as perfect and as sure as His in
W-pI .... 98.8:1 to you all bright with f. and confidence so
W-pI .... 98.9:4 He will respond with all His f. and joy and
W-pI .... 99.6:2 because it lays no f. in what is not created
WpI..rIII.in6:2 Give it f. that it will use them wisely,
WpI..rIII.in6:4 Have f., in these reviews, the means the
WpI..rIII.in6:6 at the outset; then lean back in quiet f.,
WpI..rIII.in7:1 well; in perfect f. that you would see their
WpI..rIII.in7:2 in that same trust and confidence and f..
WpIrIII.in12:3 with firmer footsteps and with stronger f..
W-pI .. 122.9:1 our practicing today with hope and f. that
W-pI .. 124.4:2 our f. and our awareness of His Presence.
W-pI .. 126.8:4 Give Him your f. today, and ask Him that
W-pI .. 151.3:5 pathetic f. in what your eyes and ears
W-pI .. 151.6:3 f. in them is blind because you would not
W-pI 151.10:1 remove all f. that you have placed in pain,
W-pI 155.10:3 Step back in f. and let truth lead the way.
W-pI .. 168.5:2 us. Our f. lies in the Giver, not our own
W-pI .. 170.4:3 with perfect f. the split you made is real.
WpI...rV.in1:4 more sincere, with f. upheld more surely.
WpI.rV.in12:2 We place f. in the experience that comes
W-pI .. 181.1:1 your f. in your ability to transcend doubt
W-pI .. 181.2:5 peace that comes from f. in sinlessness.
W-pI .. 181.2:6 This f. receives its only sure support from
W-pII . 232.2:3 Have f. in Him Who is your Father. Trust

W-pII..240.2:3 *Give us f. today to recognize Your Son, and*
W-pII..255.1:3 me this day have f. in Him Who says I am
W-pII..277.2:3 is far beyond his f. in slavery or freedom.
W-pII..279.2:1 *Your promises today, and give my f. to them*
W-pII..327.1:1 on the basis of an unsupported f.. For
W-pII..327.1:3 and f. in Him must surely come to me.
W-pII..327.1:4 This is the f. that will endure, and take me
W-pII....12.4:2 the price for f. in it is so immense that
W-pII....13.4:1 The miracle is taken first on f., because to
W-pII....13.4:2 Yet f. will bring its witnesses to show that
W-pII....13.4:3 thus the miracle will justify your f. in it,
M-4..........I.2:3 And who would place his f. in the shabby
M-12..........6:5 but who would put his f. in dreams once
C-ep...........4:2 us arise and go in f. along the way to Him.
P-2........IV.2:3 f. is in the illness and not in salvation.
P-2........IV.3:4 could have f. in them once this is realized
P-2........IV.3:5 not have f. in them until he realizes this?
S-1.........in.3:3 F. in your goal will grow and hold you up
S-3......... II.6:3 overcome until all f. in it has been laid by,

### faithful 21

T-6......IV.11:3 everything God created is f. to His laws.
T-7......... II.4:6 mind cannot be f. to one meaning, and
T-7......III.2:13 is "treacherous" to the ego is f. to peace.
T-7........VI.4:3 while the ego does not love you it *is* f. to its
T-11.......in.1:8 you will be f. to the father you choose.
T-13....VI.13:2 and have been f. in your giving, for you
T-13......IX.3:2 Be f. unto darkness and you will not see,
T-14... VIII.1:8 To what He promised God He is wholly f.,
T-17.........I.2:4 You cannot be f. to two masters who ask
T-17.....VII.4:6 faith, and remain f. to your brother?
T-17.....VII.5:5 of illusion, and wholly f. to its master. Use
T19....IV.B.7:4 O come ye f. to the holy union of the
T19..IV.B.11:8 but you have been mistaken in what is f..
T19.IV.D.21:3 you had faith in still is f., and watches
T-25.........I.3:4 And always is it f. to your purpose, from
T-28......VI.5:4 his tiny oath to be forever f. unto death.
W-pI...109.8:2 you. You will be f. to your trust today,
W-pI.139.11:6 mind, how f. they have really been to us,
W-pI.153.16:1 to be f. to the Will we share with God. At
W-pII..248.1:2 Now let me be as f. in disowning falsity.
W-ep.........4:1 you in His hands, to be His f. follower,

### faithfully 4

T-24..... II.12:5 sin love's substitute, and serve it f.. And
W-pI...157.3:3 increasingly, as every lesson, f. rehearsed,
W-pI...194.3:2 be set upon a throne, and worshipped f..
W-pII..297.2:1 *f. is every step in my salvation set already,*

### faithfulness 13

T-25......VI.5:2 of special f. to one perceived as other than
WpI.rIV.in9:3 f. restored the world from darkness to the
W-pI...164.4:5 F. in practicing today will bring rewards
W-pII.....in.4:3 Has not His f. earned Him the invitation
M-4..........IX.h Faithfulness
M-4.......IX.1:1 The extent of the teacher of God's f. is the
M-4.......IX.1:4 F. is the teacher of God's trust in the
M-4.......IX.1:5 Generally, his f. begins by resting on just
M-4.......IX.1:7 And that alone is f.. Nothing but that
M-4.......IX.2:1 True f., however, does not deviate. Being
M-4.......IX.2:7 F., then, combines in itself the other
M-4.......IX.2:9 that f. in the true sense is always directed.
M-4.....IX.2:12 certainty on that alone to which all f. is

### faithless 5

T-17.....VII.5:2 See it as something else and you are f..
T-17.....VII.6:3 And so you have been f. to your brother,
T-17.....VII.9:1 or you are f. to your own relationship.
T-21........ II.6:9 Think not that you are f., for your belief
T-21......III.5:4 Thus is he f. to himself, but strong in faith

### faithlessness 41

T-17.....VII.3:5 The thought of bodies is the sign of f., for
T-17.....VII.3:9 F. brought to faith will never interfere
T-17...VII.3:10 f. used *against* truth will always destroy
T-17.....VII.5:3 Use not your f.. Let it enter and look upon
T-17.....VII.5:5 it. F. is the servant of illusion, and wholly
T-17.....VII.6:1 of illusion is as closely tied to f. as faith to
T-17.....VII.6:3 brother, and used your f. against him. No
T-17.....VII.7:3 them, your little f. can make it useless, if
T-17.....VII.7:3 it useless, if you would use the f. instead.
T-17.....VII.8:1 and learn the cause of f.: You think you
T-17.....VII.8:7 There is no cause for f., but there *is* Cause
T-17...VII.10:6 Use not your f. against it, for it calls you
T-17... VIII.1:3 It calls forth just the same suspension of f.
T-17... VIII.1:5 and f. has not forced any exclusion on it.
T-17... VIII.3:2 faith, freely given wherever f. is laid aside,
T-17... VIII.5:2 His f. did this to him. Think carefully
T-17... VIII.5:3 before you let yourself use f. against him.
T-19.........I.4:1 that f. leads straight to illusions. For
T-19.........I.4:2 f. is the perception of a brother as a body,
T-19.........I.4:4 f. to him has separated you from him, and
T-19.........I.4:5 Your f. has thus opposed the Holy Spirit's
T-19.........I.5:1 that faith must be the opposite of f.. Yet
T-19.........I.5:3 F. would always limit and attack; faith
T-19.........I.5:4 F. would destroy and separate; faith
T-19.........I.5:5 F. would interpose illusions between the
T-19.........I.5:6 F. is wholly dedicated to illusions; faith
T-19.........I.8:2 great the devastation wrought by your f.,
T-19.........I.8:2 for f. is an attack that seems to be justified
T-19.........I.9:7 There is no justification for f., but faith is
T-19.......I.11:2 F. looks upon the Son of God, and judges
T-19.......I.12:6 Your f. has driven you and him apart, and
T-19.......I.14:2 you. Lay f. aside, and come to it together.
T-19.......I.15:1 f. will keep your little kingdoms barren
T-19..... II.6:12 impossible to have faith in sin, for sin is f.
T19..IV.B.11:5 it lies disillusionment and the seeds of f.,
T19..IV.B.11:7 your error as the justification for your f..
T-21...... III.5:2 it be. F. is not a lack of faith, but faith in
T-28.....VII.3:3 A split allegiance is but f. to both, and
T-28.....VII.5:5 you tried to keep a promise to be true to f.
T-28.....VII.5:6 Yet f. is sickness. It is like the house set
W-pI...163.1:2 or doubt; as anger, f. and lack of trust;

### fall 34

T-1........ VI.1:6 which is the meaning of the "f.," nothing
T-3........VII.3:1 have discussed the f. or separation before,
T-17.......V.14:8 surely f. in place because the goal is sure.
T-18. VIII.13:7 with happy laughter, and it will f. away.
T-18......IX.6:4 is not strong enough to stop a button's f.,
T-18......IX.8:5 them to the light their shadows cannot f..
T19. IV.A.4:11 little wall will f. away so quietly beneath
T19. IV.A.4:12 barriers will f. away before their coming
T19... IV.A.5:7 your brother must f. away because of the
T19....IV.C.2:5 forgiveness, and watch the chains f. away,
T-21.........I.1:2 f. because of what they did not recognize,
T-21.........I.1:5 and so you stumble and f. down upon the
T-21....... V.8:5 For the perception would f. away at once,
T-22.... II.6:10 Faith and belief can f. to either side, but
T-24....... II.5:2 language and they f. on different ears. To
T-25......IV.4:8 can never f. away and leave you homeless.
T-26....... II.8:5 locked will merely f. away and disappear.
T-29.....VII.5:1 Idols must f. *because* they have no life,
T-29... VIII.3:6 And f. before His face like a dark veil that
T-29......IX.1:3 himself f. lower than the stones upon the
T-30......IV.4:5 But then they f. and cannot rise again.
T-31....... II.6:7 us, and we f. back if he does not advance.
T-31....... II.8:3 old will f. away before the new without
W-pI...131.5:3 Everything you seek but this will f. away.
W-pI...136.7:3 world appears to totter and prepare to f..
W-pI...188.9:2 gently bring them back to where they f. in
W-pI...192.9:5 And it will f. or be averted as you choose
W-pI...193.9:4 but waiting their appointed time to f.. For
W-pII..286.1:2 *How quietly do all things f. in place! This is*
W-pII.... 13.5:1 Miracles f. like drops of healing rain
M-10.........5:2 merely stagger and f. down beneath it.
M-19.........2:7 f. short indeed of all that wait when the
M-25.........2:6 would f. at the holy sound of His Voice.
S-3........IV.9:3 thorns f. softly from the bleeding brow of

### fallacious 1

W-pI.....21.3:3 f. grounds that they are more "obvious."

### fallacy 1

T-11....... V.3:3 whole separation f. lies in the belief that

### fallen 2

W-pI.200.10:3 f. from the trees of hopelessness you
M-10.........6:9 of his mistaken choice, have f. from him.

### fallible 2

T-14....... V.2:5 for your awaking is as perfect as yours is f.
W-pI.121.13:7 *the dream that I am mortal, f. and full of sin,*

### falling 1

T-31........II.9:4 and f. back when he would go ahead? For

### falls 8

T-5..........II.4:3 glory before which dissociation f. away,
T19....IV.C.1:9 its dark shadow f. across all living things,
T-20....VIII.6:1 upon with vision f. gently into place,
T-25...... IV.5:2 Every leaf that f. is given life in you. Each
T-26.....VII.9:5 Although it f. far short of giving you your
T-29.....VII.1:2 fail, and you will weep each time an idol f.
T-30....... V.5:1 The real world still f. short of this, for
W-pI...78.10:2 Temptation f. away when we allow each

### false 149

T-1.........I.37:1 introduced into f. thinking by me. It acts
T-1.........I.38:3 He separates the true from the f. by His
T-1.........I.39:1 Holy Spirit identifies error as f. or unreal.
T-1.........I.42:1 in releasing you from your f. sense of
T-1.........I.50:1 and rejecting what is out of accord as f..
T-1......... V.6:5 As these f. underpinnings are given up,
T-1........ VI.5:3 In sorting out the f. from the true, the
T-1.......VII.3:4 to control reality according to f. needs.
T-1.......VII.3:6 of making f. associations and attempting
T-1.......VII.3:7 although you can perceive f. associations,
T-2......VIII.4:1 a sorting out of the f. from the true. This
T-3..........II.1:4 They are all true or all f.. It is essential
T-4.........I.10:7 Do not present a f. and unworthy picture
T-4............ II.h The Ego and F. Autonomy
T-4.......... III.2:5 My role is to separate the true from the f.,
T-5.........I.1:14 the whole belief in the f. association the
T-5.........III.5:4 true and f. perceptions are themselves
T-5.........VI.2:4 It gives the ego a f. sense of security by
T-5......VI.10:3 is bearing f. witness to God Himself.
T-6...........I.4:5 accepting f. premises and teaching them
T-6...........I.6:7 accept them as f. justifications for anger.
T-6.......V.C.1:2 sorts out the true from the f. in your mind
T-7.......X.5:12 is only because he has elected to follow f.
T-7......... X.7:1 of your f. decision-making prerogative,
T-8.......VIII.3:5 not give this f. witness to the ego's stand.
T-8......VIII.4:1 is hard to perceive sickness as a f. witness,
T-8......VIII.8:4 the ego's skill in building up f. cases. Nor
T-8.........IX.5:3 to distinguish only between the f. and the
T-8.........IX.5:4 and the true, replacing the f. with the true
T-9...........I.4:2 sort out the true from the f. in your mind,
T-10......IV.6:6 it is. No f. gods you attempt to interpose
T-10......IV.7:1 a Son of God who has laid aside all f. gods
T-11..... V.10:3 though you may countenance a f. idea of
T-11..... V.11:2 the impossible and the f. from the true.
T-11..... V.18:5 accept f. witness of him unless you have
T-11..... V.18:5 you have evoked f. witnesses against him.
T-11.....VII.2:8 you are accepting both the f. and the true
T-11....VIII.1:6 the good and the bad, the f. and the true.
T-11..VIII.15:4 world in place of the f. one you have made
T-12.........I.9:6 One is f., for it was made out of denial;
T-12........II.4:7 in the darkness of your own f. certainty,
T-13.....VII.4:4 willingness to learn the one you made is f.
T-13.....VII.5:3 who judges what is true and what is f..
T-13.....VII.5:4 And what he judges f. he does not see.
T-13......IX.4:1 Spirit can separate the f. and the true,

T-14.....VII.2:5 or unrecognized, real or f. to you. If you
T-14...... XI.1:9 of God in you is but your learning of the f.
T-16...... IV.6:2 but it *is* necessary to seek for what is f..
T-17...... III.9:6 Thought systems are but true or f., and all
T-17...... VI.4:5 The f. becomes the useless from this point
T-20...... VI.9:4 and so invested in a f. attraction your
T-21.........I.2:5 will always give you f. directions, but
T-21....... II.9:6 And if its reality is f., you will uphold it by
T-22....... II.5:4 idea as what will make it either true or f..
T-22....... II.7:5 all. For it is wholly true or wholly f., and
T-24...... IV.4:7 All that is f. proclaims his sins as real. If
T-24.....VII.5:2 cannot touch it with the f. ideas you made
T-25.........I.7:5 truth, taking all f. ideas of what you are,
T-25.....VII.3:8 the world gives any meaning to are f., and
T-26.....VII.6:7 Illusions are illusions and are f.. Your
T-27..... II.2:10 One denies the other and must make it f..
T-28.....VII.1:7 Himself and what He is cannot be f..
T-29....VIII.3:1 An idol is a f. impression, or a false belief;
T-29....VIII.3:1 An idol is a false impression, or a f. belief;
T-30...... IV.1:7 You attack but f. ideas, and never truthful
T-30...... IV.1:8 All idols are the f. ideas you made to fill
T-30...... VI.4:1 This is the f. forgiveness which the world
T-30...... VI.6:7 this be except a f. forgiveness of yourself,
T-30....VIII.6:5 There is no f. appearance but will fade, if
T-31.........I.1:7 is it to see that what is f. can not be true,
T-31.........I.1:7 not be true, and what is true can not be f.
T-31.........I.1:8 you perceive no differences in f. and true.
T-31...... VI.1:3 If one is real the other must be f., for what
T-31....VIII.5:7 For in that choice are f. distinctions gone,
W-pI.......9.1:4 is a prerequisite for undoing your f. ideas.
W-pI.....16.1:5 They are merely true or f.. Those that are
W-pI.....16.1:7 likeness. Those that are f. make theirs.
W-pI.....25.2:3 This f. identification makes you incapable
W-pI.....26.3:5 f. image of yourself has come to take the
W-pI.....54.1:3 make a f. world or lead me to the real one.
W-pI.....54.1:6 My thoughts cannot be neither true nor f.
W-pI.....58.3:4 all illusions except f. ideas about myself?
W-pI.....66.5:6 are wrong that the conclusion could be f..
W-pI.....66.6:2 This could be f., of course, but in order to
W-pI.....66.6:2 order to be f. it is necessary to define God
W-pI.....67.5:2 mind is so preoccupied with f. self-images
W-pI.....72.5:3 full of f. promises and offering illusions in
W-pI...95.11:3 to sink into your mind, replacing f. ideas:
W-pI...103.2:6 corrects the f. belief that God is fear. It
W-pI.110.10:3 f. the images which you believed were you
W-pI.126.10:1 are changed and f. beliefs laid by. Repeat
W-pI...127.9:3 your mind wherever you give up a f. belief
W-pI.130.10:2 f. or true is what you see and only what
W-pI.132.11:5 If you are real the world you see is f., for
W-pI...134.2:2 true. It must be limited to what is f.. It is
W-pI...134.4:4 It says the truth is f., and smiles on the
W-pI...137.4:5 be shown that what they look upon is f..
W-pI...137.5:3 and f. ideas which dreams embroider into
W-pI...140.9:5 All of them are f., and can be cured
W-pI...151.4:4 the ego's judgments, all of which are f.. It
W-pI...151.6:2 to prove to you its evil is your own are f.,
W-pI...151.7:3 which merely bear f. witness to God's Son
W-pI...152.3:7 well as what is true, then part of truth is f.
W-pI...152.3:9 but the truth is true, and what is f. is false.
W-pI...152.3:9 but the truth is true, and what is false is f..
W-pI...152.5:1 with transitory states by definition f..
W-pI...152.5:3 and the f. kept separate from the truth, as
W-pI...152.9:1 abandoning the f. pretense by which the
W-pI.152.10:3 have been laid aside, and recognized as f..
W-pI.152.11:1 in glad acknowledgment that lies are f.,
W-pI...161.5:5 But fear attaches to specifics, being f..
W-pI...163.6:5 be true, unless its opposite is proven f..
W-pI...167.9:2 or a f. condition not within its Source, it
W-pI...170.2:7 *arms, and only then do you perceive it f..*
W-pI...186.4:1 All f. humility we lay aside today, that we
W-pI...186.5:1 to prove the f. is true has brought to you.
W-pI...189.7:2 of everything it thinks is either true or f.,
W-pI...190.2:2 Can they be anything but wholly f.? Pain
W-pI...200.3:4 To ask that what is f. be true can only fail.
W-pI.200.10:3 road is carpeted with leaves of f. desires,
W-pII .....1.1:5 is sin, except a f. idea about God's Son?
W-pII .228.1:3 I accept as true what He proclaims as f.?
W-pII .239.1:1 ourselves today be hidden by a f. humility
W-pII .....3.1:1 The world is f. perception. It is born of
W-pII .300.1:2 the idea that lets no f. perception keep us
W-pII .301.2:4 we have learned the world we saw was f.,
W-pII ... 10.1:1 for God proclaim that what is f. is false,
W-pII ... 10.1:1 for God proclaim that what is false is f.,
W-pII .334.1:2 out of thoughts that rest on f. perceptions
W-pII ... 13.1:3 reminds the mind that what it sees is f.. It
M-7 ........... 5:6 stemming from f. humility. The form of
C-4 ........... 3:1 is not the remedy for f. perception since,
C-4 ........... 3:2 for f. perception must be *true perception.*
C-4 ........... 7:2 Gone is perception, f. and true alike.
C-5 ........... 1:2 by f. beliefs of your Identity, which God
C-5 ........... 2:5 he saw the f. without accepting it as true.
C-5 ........... 3:4 obscure to you, between the f. and true.
P-1............ 5:2 as f. and to accept the truth as true. His
P-2.........in.3:2 as the patient may cherish f. self-concepts
P-2........ IV.7:4 make illusions true through f. perception.
S-3...........I.5:3 to kill, so healing can be f. as well as true;
S-3........... II.h F. versus True Healing
S-3..........II.1:1 F. healing merely makes a poor exchange
S-3..........II.1:3 Only f. healing can give way to fear, so
S-3..........II.1:4 F. healing can indeed remove a form of
S-3..........II.5:9 What is f. cannot be partly true. If you are
S-3..........II.6:1 F. healing rests upon the body's cure,
S-3........ III.1:1 F. healing heals the body in a part, but
S-3........ III.1:6 f., there is some power that another has,

## falsehood 1

W-pI... 152.5:3 which sets the truth apart from f., and the

## falsely 8

T-2 ........ V.6:2 but if it is f. endowed with self-initiative,
T-9 ....... IV.1:5 what you are, because you see him f..
W-pI..... 92.4:7 weakness is an idol f. worshipped and
W-pI. 151.14:2 failed to be deceived by what was f. added
W-pI... 154.1:1 today be neither arrogant nor f. humble.
W-pII ..... 3.2:6 But eyes deceive, and ears hear f.. Now
W-pII . 311.1:4 cannot see totality and therefore judges f..
W-pII . 323.2:1 and of images we worshipped f. –truth

## falser 1

W-pI... 151.3:3 Yet witness never f. was than this. But

## falsity 6

T-14 ..... VI.4:2 make the f. of its opposite perfectly clear.
T-17 ..... VI.4:3 Holy Spirit's sorting out of truth and f..
T19..IV.C.11:4 truth or f. of the idea which they reflect.
W-pII ..... 1.1:6 Son? Forgiveness merely sees its f., and
W-pII . 248.1:2 Now let me be as faithful in disowning f..
M-18 ......... 1:2 to establish its error or demonstrate its f.,

## falter 3

T-24 .......II.9:1 along the way of truth; too far to f. now.
W-pI... 107.5:1 love which does not f. in the face of pain,
M-3 ........... 5:7 teachers who f. and may even seem to fail.

## faltering 1

T-18 ..... III.5:4 little, f. footsteps that you may take can

## falters 2

T-28 ..... III.9:6 gap in which abundance f. and grows thin
W-pI... 135.4:5 body f. and must fail to serve the Son of

## fame 1

M-13 ......... 2:6 Power, f., money, physical pleasure; who

## familiar 10

T-5 .........II.1:3 of the time sequence should be quite f.,
T-6 .....V.A.4:2 This is f. enough to you by now, but it has
T-9 ....... IV.7:1 that you should be quite f. with it by now.
T-17 ...... V.9:4 a road far more f. than you now believe. Is
T-21 ........I.8:1 everything you see and yet somehow f., is
W-pI .... 15.2:2 the same f. objects which you see now.
W-pI .... 19.4:1 periods should be quite f. to you by now,
W-pI .... 29.4:1 for today should follow a now f. pattern:
W-pI .. 107.9:6 you will return to the f. world reluctantly.
W-pI 161.11:4 and see f. gestures which he makes so

## familiarly 1

W-pI .. 169.3:6 experience with which it is f. at home.

## family 3

T-1 ....... III.6:6 neighbor are equal members of one f., as
T-1 .........V.3:8 When this occurs the whole f. of God, or
T-1 .........V.4:1 member of the f. of God must return. The

## fanatic 1

T-12 ..... IV.1:6 the ego pursues its goal with f. insistence,

## fanatical 1

T-15 ........I.6:3 For underneath its f. insistence that the

## fancied 5

T-14 ..... XI.8:5 use this f. undependability as an excuse
T-24 ......I.8:10 blow, each slight, or f. judgment on itself?
W-pI .... 98.3:2 nor invent escapes from f. threats without
W-pI .. 122.3:5 What f. value, trivial effect or transient
W-pI .. 170.4:1 which your f. self-defense proceeds on its

## fancies 2

T-24 .... VII.5:3 Let not your foolish f. frighten you. What
T-25 .......II.1:5 Despite your hopes and f., always does

## fanciful 1

T-17 ..... IV.8:3 sorts of f. and fragmented illusions of love

## fancy 1

T-25 .......II.1:3 Perhaps you f. to attain some peace and

## fantasied 1

M-17 ......... 4:5 of violence, f. or apparently acted out. It

## fantasies 42

T-1 ...... VII.3:2 F. of any kind are distortions, because
T-1 ...... VII.3:6 destructively. F. are a means of making
T-1 .... VII.3:11 F. become totally unnecessary as the
T-2 ....... III.1:4 The many body f. in which minds engage
T-9 ..... IV.11:2 search for reality in f. you will not find it.
T-9 ..... IV.11:5 than the f. into which they are woven.
T-9 ..... IV.11:8 Yet when reality dawns, the f. are gone.
T-9 .........V.2:3 searches f. for truth must be unhealed,
T-16 ... IV.10:3 deprives you of knowledge for f. are the
T-16 ... IV.11:4 Hear not the call of hate, and see no f..
T-16 .......V.3:2 the f. that center around it are often quite
T-16 .......V.6:2 of both worlds has merely led to f. of both
T-16 .....V.16:4 is. For only f. make confusion in choosing
T-16 .... VII.3:4 The f. it brings to its chosen relationships
T-16 .... VII.3:4 act out its hate are f. of your destruction.
T-17 .........I.1:8 it. F. change reality. That is their purpose.
T-17 .......II.2:3 and there are no f. to hide the truth. The
T-17 .......II.3:5 F. are all undone, and no one and nothing
T-17 ..... III.3:3 What can be used for f. of vengeance, and
T-17 ..... III.4:8 it, and join with f. in uninterrupted "bliss.
T-17 ... III.10:1 and step between you and your f.. Let my
T-17 ... VIII.4:5 cold f. of fear and fiery dreams of hell.
T-18 ..... VI.3:5 make f. and direct the body to act them
T-18 ..... VI.3:7 the body is actually acting out its f., it will
T-18 ..... VI.5:2 from f. of vengeance to release from them
T-18 ..... VI.5:7 make f. in which your will conflicts with

T-18......VI.6:2 It is impossible to act out f.. For it is still
T-18......VI.6:3 For it is still the f. you want, and they
T-18......VI.6:5 For f. have made your body your "enemy"
W-pI.....35.5:3 of your f. about yourself does not matter.
WpI. rII.in.4:4 your will has power over all f. and dreams
W-pI.....93.2:3 and afraid of foolish f. and savage dreams
W-pI...109.5:5 that all its frantic f. were but the dreams
W-pI...137.7:1 so healing must replace the f. of sickness
W-pI...153.5:5 Son of God as but a victim to attack by f.,
W-pI...153.5:5 needful only of defense by still more f.,
W-pI...156.7:2 The past is gone, with all its f.. They keep
W-pI...181.8:1 Nor do we ask for f.. For what we seek to
W-pI...188.8:2 what you are, instead of f. and shadows.
W-pII..332.1:5 its presence is the mind recalled from f.,
M-10..........3:7 grandiose f. would claim this for himself?
C-5............1:8 of His Son while he believes his f. are true.

## fantastic 1

W-pI.....70.4:1 however distorted and f. it might be, to

## fantasy 36

T-1.......VII.3:1 F. is a distorted form of vision. Fantasies
T-1.......VII.3:4 they do. F. is an attempt to control reality
T-6.........V.4:3 Children *do* confuse f. and reality, and
T-9......IV.10:1 What can be fearful but f., and who turns
T-9......IV.10:1 and who turns to f. unless he despairs of
T-9......IV.10:2 that you will never find satisfaction in f.,
T-9......IV.11:1 The impossible can happen only in f..
T-9......IV.11:3 it. The symbols of f. are of the ego, and of
T-16....IV.10:3 Every f., be it of love or hate, deprives you
T-16....IV.10:4 is only needful to value truth beyond all f.
T-16....IV.11:6 hate, and in every f. that rises to delay you
T-16.....V.14:3 between truth and illusion; God and f..
T-16.....V.15:1 in the f. of destruction of love's meaning.
T-16.....V.15:4 to lead away from truth and into f.. Yet
T-16.....VII.2:6 How can you change the past except in f.?
T-16.....VII.4:2 is no f. that does not contain the dream of
T-17........... I.h Bringing F. to Truth
T-17.........I.2:5 What you use in f. you deny to truth. Yet
T-17.........I.2:6 give to truth to use for you is safe from f..
T-17.........I.3:3 to retain some aspects of reality for f.. If
T-17.........I.5:1 Think you that you can bring truth to f.,
T-17.........I.6:5 to solve his problems through f., you are
T-17....... II.1:2 In no f. have you ever seen anything so
T-17....... II.2:1 This loveliness is not a f.. It is the real
T-17....... V.7:4 must exclude major areas of f. from your
T-17......VI.7:3 peace will not be experienced except in f..
T-17......VI.7:6 For f. solutions bring but the illusion of
T-18....... II.4:7 you substitute the f. that reality is fearful,
T-18......III.1:1 in bringing truth to illusion, reality to f.,
T-18......III.1:3 and every f. that seemed to bring a light
W-pI.....22.2:1 this savage f. that you want to escape. Is it
W-pI.....23.3:4 Is not f. a better word for such a process,
W-pI.....70.9:4 And I assure you this will be no idle f..
W-pI.151.14:3 All the threads of f. are gone. And what
W-pI.153.14:4 can not escape, is but his own deluded f..
WfI........in.5:4 is mad, and vengeance merely foolish f..

## far 180

T-1...........I.2:2 Source, which is f. beyond evaluation.
T-2.........V.1:6 recognition is a f. better protective device
T-2.........V.9:6 that is f. beyond any form of charity you
T-2.......V.10:1 if he had already gone f. beyond his actual
T-3.......VII.5:9 You have not yet gone back f. enough,
T-4.........in.1:1 go with a brother twice as f. as he asks. It
T-4...........I.8:7 ego cannot know what is as f. beyond its
T-4........ I.12:5 beauty and dignity are f. beyond doubt,
T-4........ I.13:8 mind. Spirit is f. beyond the need of your
T-6...........I.1:3 The only emphasis laid upon it so f. has
T-6......... II.9:8 convergence seems to be f. in the future
T-6......V.C.3:3 It has advanced f. from the first lesson,
T-8.........V.1:6 f. beyond the power of its separate parts.
T-9.........V.1:1 is f. more widely used than God's. This is
T-9.......VII.1:5 You do not have to seek f. for salvation.
T-11....... II.4:3 He will enable you to go f. beyond the
T-11....... II.5:9 God. Yet you need f. more than patience.
T-12.... VIII.1:2 kept him f. away from your destructive
T-12.... VIII.2:3 Yet he is f. from you whose Self he is, for
T-13.... VIII.7:4 is f. beyond your individual concern. You
T-15.........I.2:1 Holy Spirit's teaching are f. in the future.
T-15.......I.4:13 Death is the end as f. as hope of Heaven
T-15.........I.6:3 hidden a f. more insidious threat to peace
T-15.......I.11:4 It takes f. longer to teach you to be willing
T-15....... II.1:9 Truth is so f. beyond time that all of it
T-15....... II.4:3 Yet they are f. stronger and much more
T-15......III.7:6 F. beyond your little world but still in you
T-15......IV.2:2 you is but as f. away as your desire for it.
T-15......IV.2:3 instead, by so much is it f. from you. By
T-15.....VII.9:6 ego's altar f. exceeds your awareness of it.
T-15.... VIII.1:1 holy instant has extended f. beyond time.
T-15.... VIII.4:5 f. beyond the petty sum of all the separate
T-16....... II.1:5 f. beyond the limits you perceive, that
T-16....... II.2:4 A better and f. more helpful way to think
T-16......III.6:4 taught this, and from f. off in the universe
T-16......VI.5:5 F. more is left outside than would be
T-16......VI.8:5 f. shorter than the time it took to fix your
T-16....VI.10:2 for you have come too f. to yield to the
T-17......IV.6:4 Yet we have looked at it f. closer than we
T-17....... V.9:4 to walk together along a road f. more
T-17......VI.1:7 understanding f. broader than you now
T-17.....VII.7:1 so f. beyond your little conception of the
T-17.... VIII.3:7 enormous, and f. greater than you realize.
T-17.... VIII.6:7 you have risen f. beyond any situation
T-18.........I.3:5 behavior, a f. more serious effect lies in
T-18.........I.8:1 turning till they disappear from sight, f.,
T-18.........I.8:1 disappear from sight, far, f. outside of you
T-18......IV.1:9 to make the holy instant f. greater than
T-18.....VI.11:2 feeling of liberation f. exceeds the dream
T-18.....VII.5:6 It would be f. more profitable now merely
T-18......IX.3:9 lead you safely through and f. beyond.
T-18....IX.12:6 you and yours of Him so f. transcend all
T-19....... II.8:3 it is f. better to be sinful than mistaken.
T19....IV.B.3:1 messengers are sent f. beyond the body,
T19....IV.D.8:1 Forget not that you came this f. together,
T19....IV.D.9:2 this f. unless his brother walked beside
T19.IV.D.21:1 came this f. because the journey was your
T19.IV.D.21:3 that it would lift you f. beyond the veil,
T-20....... V.2:2 Each speaks in time of what is f. beyond it
T-20....... V.3:4 what lies so f. beyond your judgment you
T-20......VI.9:7 them, and left them f. behind.
T-21......III.8:3 of their belief and faith sees f. beyond the
T-21....... V.1:5 look for you are f. more likely to discover
T-21....... V.1:8 depends f. more than you may realize as
T-21....... V.2:5 prey to forces f. beyond your own control,
T-21....... V.2:5 control, and f. more powerful than you.
T-21....... V.9:4 Knowledge is f. beyond attainment of any
T-22.......in.3:9 How f. from home can a relationship so
T-22......IV.1:4 The whole purpose of coming this f. was
T-22......IV.1:7 No one who reaches this f. can make the
T-22......VI.4:1 and blazing with a light f. brighter than
T-23.......in.4:6 destiny and purpose are f. beyond them,
T-23.........I.7:6 indivisible, and f. beyond their little reach
T-23.......I.12:9 Yet f. beyond this senseless war it shines,
T-24.........I.2:6 violence f. more inclusive than you think,
T-24....... II.9:1 You have come f. along the way of truth;
T-24....... II.9:1 along the way of truth; too f. to falter now
T-24....VI.12:1 pursue another goal with f. less vigilance;
T-25......III.6:7 with equal ease and f. more happiness,
T-25......III.8:8 He sees as f. beyond the chance of change.
T-25......IV.3:6 until it is but distant shadows, f. away,
T-25......IV.4:4 increasingly remote and f. away from you.
T-25......IV.4:6 twisted forms too f. away for recognition,
T-25.... VIII.4:8 with someone else by f. the greater part.
T-25.... VIII.9:3 You are not asked to trust Him f.. No
T-26.........I.7:7 and f. beyond the reach of any sacrifice of
T-26......IV.3:4 altar to rise and tower f. above the world,
T-26.....VII.9:5 it falls f. short of giving you your full
T-26...VII.11:7 of God ask not too much, but f. too little.
T-27....... II.6:6 This call has power f. beyond the weak
T-27..... V.11:7 will be f. less than all there really are.
T-28.........I.7:9 so ancient that It f. exceeds the span of
T-29....... II.1:3 rough and f. too difficult for you to follow
T-30......III.8:1 Thoughts of God are f. beyond all change,
T-30......III.9:3 is as f. from earth as earth from Heaven.
T-30......IV.6:2 will forever place you f. beyond deception
T-31.........I.6:5 and f. beyond all doubt and question?
T-31.........II.6:6 as near or f. away from what we want as
T-31.....VII.4:3 The contrast is f. greater than you think,
W-pI....... 1.3:7 excluded. One thing is like another as f. as
W-pI..... 11.2:3 your eyes and look about, near and f., up
W-pI..... 14.3:5 You will go f. beyond it. Our direction is
W-pI..... 20.1:1 casual about our practice periods thus f..
W-pI..... 25.6:2 happens to catch your eye, near or f.,
W-pI..... 29.1:4 it explains every idea we have used thus f.,
W-pI..... 30.4:1 limited to concepts such as "near" and "f.
W-pI..... 61.7:1 Today's idea goes f. beyond the ego's
W-pI..... 62.4:3 who seem to be f. away in space and time,
W-pI... 107.5:4 But the truth stands f. beyond illusions,
W-pI.108.10:2 be f. better understood from this time on,
W-pI... 109.8:3 let them come from f. across the world,
W-pI.122.10:2 point at which the road becomes f. easier.
W-pI... 123.1:4 which are f. greater than you realize.
W-pI... 123.3:5 Be thankful that your value f. transcends
W-pI... 128.6:1 and see how f. you rise above the world,
W-pI... 129.1:3 it for what is f. more satisfying, filled with
W-pI... 129.4:5 f. away from this are you who stay bound
W-pI... 131.6:7 as f. removed from time as is a tiny candle
W-pI... 132.6:4 it, and each one must go as f. as he can let
W-pI.132.16:1 to many brothers f. across the world, as
W-pI... 133.1:1 what seems theoretical and f. from what
W-pI... 133.2:1 not ask too much of life, but f. too little.
W-pI.133.12:5 It is f. more than merely letting you make
W-pI.134.16:3 been practicing thus f. in willingness and
W-pI... 135.6:4 its value f. beyond a little pile of dust and
W-pI.135.13:2 a plan which f. exceeds its own protection
W-pI... 136.5:3 force, as f. as your desires are concerned.
W-pI.136.14:1 Truth has a power f. beyond defense, for
W-pI... 139.8:3 It is so f. beyond all doubt and question
W-pI... 153.4:3 and so f. beyond the frenzy and intensity
W-pI... 157.3:2 Yet you have come f. enough along the
W-pI... 159.3:2 comes from f. beyond itself, for it reflects
W-pI... 162.1:3 It will mean f. more to you as you advance
W-pI... 164.2:3 dim. A melody from f. beyond the world
W-pI... 164.6:2 given you from f. beyond all things within
W-pI... 166.4:4 an outcast wandering so f. from home, so
W-pI... 167.5:4 In that, they can go f. beyond themselves.
W-pI.169.14:3 And revelation stands not f. behind. Its
WpI.rV.in12:4 meaning, which is f. beyond their sound.
W-pI... 182.6:2 He is f. from home. He is so little that He
W-pI... 182.9:4 they protect Him, for His home is f. away,
W-pI.183.11:6 communication f. transcends all words,
W-pI... 191.5:1 and you have risen f. above the world,
W-pI... 192.2:2 can understand a language f. beyond his
W-pI... 194.1:4 f. are we progressing now from earth!
W-pI... 194.9:5 for us that leaves temptation f. behind.
W-pI.198.13:2 And we are glad that we have come this f.,
W-pII ....in.2:5 We have come f. along the road, and now
W-pII ....in.5:7 have never come this f. unless you saw,
W-pII ..... 2.3:4 it, and the memory of God not f. behind.
W-pII .252.1:2 shimmering and perfect purity is f. more
W-pII .252.1:5 How f. beyond this world my Self must be
W-pII .277.2:3 is f. beyond his faith in slavery or freedom
W-pII .281.2:2 For I am f. beyond all pain. My Father
W-pII .286.2:1 travelled f. along it to a wholly certain
W-pII .299.1:1 My holiness is f. beyond my own ability
W-pII .315.1:2 in value f. beyond all things of which I can
W-pII .335.1:2 as he is, for that is f. beyond perception.
WfI........in.2:3 In the dream of time it seems to be f. off.
M-4 ... I.A.6:10 He has not yet come as f. as he thinks. Yet
M-4 ..... I.A.7:3 All that he really learned so f. was that he
M-4 ..... X.2:10 way for what goes f. beyond all learning.
M-4 ....... X.3:4 What God has given is so f. beyond our
M-9 ........... 1:7 f. the majority are given a slowly evolving
M-21 ......... 5:7 They are f. wiser than your own. God's
M-23 ......... 4:6 love cannot be f. behind a grateful heart
M-23 ......... 6:4 learning f. exceeds what we can learn.
M-25 ......... 6:9 hearts, and His holy sight not f. behind.
M-29 ......... 2:5 has come this f. without realizing that.
C-4............ 3:7 to lead to oneness f. beyond themselves.
C-6............ 4:6 seems to be a Guide through a f. country,
P-1............ 1:4 and help f. exceed whatever contributions
P-1............ 5:3 on from there, as f. as he is ready to go.
P-3...........I.4:8 of God. Who calls on him is f. beyond his
P-3.........II.1:8 be f. more able teachers outside of them.

S-1 ........ IV.3:6 What prayer can offer now so f. exceeds
S-1 ......... V.2:1 have goals so f. apart they cannot coexist,
S-2 .......... I.2:1 the world f. better than its true objective,
S-2 ......... II.2:2 so f. from love that arrogance could never
S-2 ........ III.1:8 His readiness to give lies f. beyond your

**farther** 13

T-1 ......... II.6:4 and receiver both emerge f. along in time
T-14 ....... X.1:2 in time but bring eternity nearer or f.. But
T-15 ....... V.7:1 fragmented that it frequently goes even f.;
T-15 ..... VII.8:6 they bring the body of another closer or f.
T-25 ...... IV.4:5 And they go f. and farther off, because the
T-25 ...... IV.4:5 And they go farther and f. off, because the
T-26 ......... I.1:8 can come a little nearer, or go a little f. off
W-pI ....... 1.2:1 look f. away from your immediate area,
W-pI ... 132.6:5 He will return and go still f., or perhaps
W-pI ... 140.8:3 It is not f. from us than ourselves. It is as
W-pII .327.1:4 and take me f. and still farther on the
W-pII .327.1:4 and still f. on the road that leads to Him.
C-ep .......... 1:9 His Love is but an instant f. on the road

**farthest** 1

M-23 ......... 6:8 and went beyond the f. reach of learning.

**fashion** 1

W-pI ..... 11.3:2 be used in an unhurried, even leisurely f..

**fast** 5

T-15 ...... IX.2:1 task is but to continue, as f. as possible,
T-28 ...... III.5:3 And covered just as f., as water rushes in
T-28 ... VII.5:10 lock the windows and make f. the bolts.
T-31 ...... IV.4:7 is none. Make f. your learning now, and
W-pI ... 153.3:1 is as if a circle held it f., wherein another

**faster** 4

W-pI ... 101.7:3 to go still f. to the waiting goal of peace.
W-pI. 108.10:2 and we will make much f. progress now.
W-pI. 108.10:3 made still f. and more sure each time you
M-4 .... VI.1:10 But he learns f. as his trust increases. It is

**fate** 2

T-27 .... VIII.7:7 its actions nor its purpose nor its f..
S-2 .......... I.5:4 everyone, for what he does entails your f.,

**Father** 697
*father*

T-1 ......... II.4:1 "No man cometh unto the F. but by me"
T-1 ......... II.4:7 the statement "I and my F. are one," but
T-1 ......... II.4:7 the statement in recognition that the F. is
T-1 ......... V.2:4 time, in which the Son and the F. are One.
T-1 ......... V.3:4 the Son in his true relationship with the F.
T-2 .......... I.2:4 the children of the F. inherit from Him.
T-2 .......... I.2:6 This is as true of the Son as of the F.. In
T-2 .... V.A.16:3 statement "F. forgive them for they know
T-3 .......... I.2:8 you believe our F. really thinks this way?
T-3 .......... I.4:3 even as your F. in Heaven is merciful. It
T-3 ......... II.4:6 the Will of the Sonship and the F. are One
T-3 ......... II.5:1 his spirit into the Hands of his F.. By
T-3 ......... V.6:6 your F. only by perceiving miraculously.
T-4 ........ III.4:3 Being made out of the denial of the F., the
T-4 ........ III.6:3 Let us ask the F. in my name to keep you
T-4 ........ III.7:6 I can help you only as our F. created us. I
T-4 ........ IV.2:9 both the glorious creations of a glorious F.
T-4 ........ VI.7:5 brother because each of them is of your F.
T-5 ......... in.3:4 to the F. for radiating His joy upon it.
T-5 .......... I.1:8 giving it, and thus creates as the F. created
T-5 .......... I.4:3 apart from the F. and from the Son. I
T-5 ......... II.1:7 of this union of Will between F. and Son.
T-5 ........ IV.7:4 the only creator that can create like the F.,
T-5 ...... VI.11:6 patience because my will is that of our F.,
T-6 ......... I.19:1 God the F. and His separated Sons. If you
T-7 ....... V.10:1 forget the F. because I am with you, and I
T-7 ...... V.10:8 the most holy children of a most holy F.?
T-7 ........ X.7:4 God, whose will must be the Will of the F.
T-7 ....... XI.7:9 Without your F. you will not know your
T-7 ..... XI.7:10 are as like the Sons as they are like the F..
T-8 ....... III.3:1 The Will of the F. and of the Son are One,
T-8 ....... III.3:4 The F. must give fatherhood to His Son,
T-8 ....... IV.3:4 with the Will of the F. by being aware of
T-8 ....... IV.6:8 equal in will, all being the Will of their F..
T-8 ....... IV.7:4 the F. and you are nothing without me,
T-8 ....... IV.7:4 by denying the F. you deny yourself. I will
T-8 ....... IV.8:5 identification with me and with the F..
T-8 ....... IV.8:6 is with the F. *and* with the Son. It cannot
T-8 ........ V.2:5 this likeness is to recognize the F.. If your
T-8 ........ V.3:7 witness to the Will of the F. for His Son,
T-8 ....... VI.2:1 blind the Sons to the F. if they behold it.
T-8 ....... VI.5:7 as you love your F. for the gift of creation.
T-9 ....... VI.5:5 to its reality as the Son does to the F..
T-10 ..... III.6:2 knows no idols, but he does know his F..
T-10 ..... III.9:5 him, because he is not the Will of the F..
T-10 ... III.10:7 It is your inheritance from your real F..
T-10 ... III.10:8 You cannot make your F., and the father
T-10 ...... V.4:4 Yet the Son *is* helpless without the F., Who
T-10 ...... V.5:4 because your F. did not create them. You
T-10 ...... V.7:1 Your F. has not denied you. He does not
T-10 ...... V.9:8 your F. is the acknowledgment of yourself
T-10 ...... V.9:9 Your F. created you wholly without sin,
T-10 .... V.11:2 what he had created in the Name of his F..
T-11 ...... in.4:3 from our F. to offer you everything again.
T-11 ...... in.4:7 I will lead you to your true F., Who hath
T-11 ........ I.2:5 I and my F. are one with you, for you are
T-11 ........ I.7:6 Your fatherhood and your F. are One.
T-11 ....... I.9:10 will death for himself because his F. is life,
T-11 ....... I.11:6 the Will of your F. is to know your own.
T-11 ....... II.1:3 Son of God *has* both F. and Son, because
T-11 ....... II.1:3 and Son, because he *is* both F. and Son. To
T-11 ..... III.5:7 your F. *is* your Creator, and you *are* like
T-11 ... III.7:10 if he would know the Wholeness of his F..
T-11 ..... III.8:1 and bless it with the light your F. gave it.
T-11 ..... IV.2:2 Can the Son deny the F. without believing
T-11 ..... IV.2:2 believing that the F. has denied him?
T-11 ..... IV.2:4 experience when you deny your F. is still
T-11 ..... IV.5:7 Creator, he will hear the Voice for his F..
T-11 ..... IV.6:4 of Christ, for so does your F. love you.
T-11 ..... IV.8:1 the Son of God whose radiance is of his F.,
T-11 ..... IV.8:1 wills to share as his F. shares it with him.
T-11 ..... IV.8:2 for there is no condemnation in the F..
T-11 ..... IV.8:3 Sharing the perfect Love of the F. the Son
T-11 ..... IV.8:3 he will not know the F. or the Son. Peace
T-11 ... V.16:9 ego looks straight at the F. and does not
T-11 ... V.17:1 Would *you* remember the F.? Accept His
T-11 ... V.17:4 exist, yet where the Son is the F. must be.
T-11 ... V.17:7 speaks to them of Himself and of His F..
T-11 ..... VI.1:7 and ascends to the F. and His Kingdom.
T-11 ..... VI.2:3 your prison and ascend to the F.? These
T-11 ..... VI.4:9 For we ascend unto the F. together, as it
T-11 ..... VI.4:9 nature of God's Son as his F. created him.
T-11 ..... VI.6:6 The F. has given you all that is His, and
T-11 ... VI.10:9 And to Christ it is given to be like the F..
T-11 ... VII.1:1 it cannot have been created by the F., for
T-11 ... VII.2:5 And being loving they are like the F., and
T-11 ... VII.3:7 you tried to create unlike your F.,
T-11 ... VIII.7:1 of God, you do not understand your F..
T-11 ... VIII.9:1 of God's Son and his F. will answer you,
T-11 ... VIII.9:1 for Christ is not deceived in His F. and His
T-11 ... VIII.9:1 Father and His F. is not deceived in Him.
T-11 ... VIII.9:3 Accept him as his F. accepts him and heal
T-11 ... VIII.9:4 Who is in no way separate from His F.,
T-11 ... VIII.9:4 of His F. by which He was created. Be not
T-11 ... VIII.9:6 in yourself you are deceived in your F., in
T-11 .VIII.11:5 he is one with himself and one with his F..
T-11 .VIII.11:6 Love him who is beloved of his F., and
T-11 .VIII.14:1 afraid of your brothers and of your F. and
T-11 .VIII.14:7 or your F. or yourself that frightens you.
T-11 .VIII.15:5 F. will lean down to you and take the last
T-12 ...... I.6:11 will recognize your own need for the F..
T-12 ........ I.7:4 of your F. closer to your awareness. For
T-12 ....... II.3:4 for your F. wills you to know your brother
T-12 ....... II.3:6 Love of Christ for His F. and for Himself.
T-12 ....... II.6:5 can withstand the Love of Christ for His F.
T-12 ....... II.7:5 walk with you as our F. walked with me.
T-12 ..... III.9:2 to accept even death to deny your F.. Yet
T-12 ..... IV.4:7 whom He loves with the Love of the F..
T-12 ..... IV.6:1 Behold the Guide your F. gave you, that
T-12 ..... IV.6:2 and whatever is true is the Will of the F..
T-12 ..... VI.2:5 F. never ceases to remind Him of His Son,
T-12 ..... VI.2:5 never ceases to remind His Son of the F..
T-12 ..... VI.2:7 You chose to forget your F. but you do not
T-12 ..... VI.4:8 Him your F. calls His Son to remember.
T-12 ... VI.4:10 For reality is one with the F. and the Son,
T-12 ..... VI.5:9 Spirit will lead everyone home to his F.,
T-12 ..... VI.6:2 Christ's Love for you is His Love for His F.
T-12 ..... VI.6:3 last led you to Christ at the altar to His F.,
T-12 ..... VI.7:2 Mind of the F. and becomes one with it.
T-12 .. VII.10:6 us. For we are there in the peace of the F.,
T-12 .. VII.14:2 that you have been treacherous to your F..
T-12 .. VII.15:4 of the F. unless He had also given it to you
T-12 ... VIII.1:2 The F. has hidden His Son safely within
T-12 ... VIII.1:2 know neither the F. nor the Son because
T-12 ... VIII.2:1 God's Son is as safe as his F., for the Son
T-12 ... VIII.2:3 he disappeared from your sight into his F.
T-12 ... VIII.2:5 all its works were not created by the F.,
T-12 ... VIII.7:5 you because He forgot not the F.. You
T-12 ... VIII.8:9 Your F. could not cease to love His Son.
T-13 ...... in.1:7 it is guilt that has obscured the F. to you,
T-13 ...... in.3:2 no F. could subject His children to this as
T-13 ...... in.3:6 was the F. Who drove him out of Paradise
T-13 ...... in.3:7 belief the knowledge of the F. was lost,
T-13 ........ I.1:2 that he may remember his F. in peace.
T-13 ........ I.1:3 the F. can be remembered only in peace.
T-13 ........ I.4:1 which his F. sets him is one of release and
T-13 ........ I.4:2 The F. is not cruel, and His Son cannot
T-13 ........ I.5:8 guiltlessness is in the Mind of his F., and
T-13 ........ I.6:7 he has always extended the Love of his F..
T-13 ........ I.7:2 not, has kept faith with his F. for you.
T-13 ....... II.9:3 you and the remembrance of your F., for
T-13 ..... III.2:6 your love for your F. would impel you to
T-13 ..... III.8:2 your F. as your Father calls you to Himself
T-13 ..... III.8:2 your Father as your F. calls you to Himself
T-13 ..... III.8:3 hidden, you will only to unite with the F.,
T-13 ..... III.9:1 the magnitude of your F. in peace and joy.
T-13 ... III.10:3 ask this of a F. Who truly loved His Son.
T-13 ... III.10:5 for he no longer understood his F.. He
T-13 ... III.10:6 made, but still more did he fear his real F.,
T-13 ... III.11:3 departing in peace and returning to the F.
T-13 ....... V.7:1 Little child, would you offer this to your F.
T-13 ..... V.7:11 The F. welcomes all of us in gladness, and
T-13 ....... V.9:7 He will not return unto the F. until He has
T-13 ....... V.9:8 He has returned you to the F. with Him.
T-13 ..... V.10:4 And seeing what He is, He knows His F..
T-13 ..... V.10:6 of love to you, given Him of the F. for you.
T-13 ..... V.11:4 the Son, they have risen in Him to the F..
T-13 ..... VI.8:8 Son is the witness that his light is of his F..
T-13 ... VI.11:7 will everything remind you of your F. and
T-13 ... VI.13:5 gave. God's Son is still as loving as his F..
T-13 ... VI.13:6 Continuous with his F., he has no past
T-13 .. VII.10:1 the F. for the perfect sanity of His most
T-13 .. VII.10:2 F. knoweth that you have need of nothing.
T-13 .. VII.17:9 God give thanks unto his F. for his purity.
T-13 ... VIII.4:1 Apart from the F. and the Son, the Holy
T-13 ... VIII.6:2 unto His F. as they were offered unto Him
T-13 ... VIII.6:5 created in the one reality that is his F..
T-13 ... VIII.7:5 all of it need only realize that it is of the F.
T-13 ... VIII.8:3 will all unite in the eternity of God the F..
T-13 ... VIII.8:5 be there with you, as you are in your F..
T-13 ..... IX.1:1 remains the only thing that hides the F.,
T-13 ..... IX.7:6 and in peace upon the altar to your F..
T-13 ..... IX.8:7 sign of perfect faith your F. has in you. He
T-13 ....... X.5:4 have yourself be welcome to your F., you
T-13 ....... X.8:4 will remember how much his F. loves him
T-13 ....... X.8:5 that he ever thought his F. loved him not,
T-13 ....... X.9:7 The altar to your F. is as pure as He Who
T-13 ..... X.10:5 have always loved your F. can have no fear
T-13 ..... X.11:11 *offer thanks unto his F. that no guilt has ever*
T-13 ..... X.12:6 I thank You, F., for the purity of Your
T-13 ..... X.13:4 you is as strong as all the love I give my F..
T-13 ..... X.13:6 I thank the F. for your loveliness, and for
T-13 ..... X.14:1 who make the F. One with His Own Son.
T-13 ..... X.14:4 is fitting as a hymn of praise unto your F..

T-13......XI.6:8 fail in what your F. has given Him to do.
T-14.........I.4:5 that your F. does not share with you. You
T-14......III.3:9 *Let me bring peace to God's Son from his F..*
T-14....III.15:1 is to evaluate his F. and judge against Him
T-14....III.17:3 your F. would have you share it with Him.
T-14......IV.1:7 but the First in eternity is God the F.,
T-14......IV.3:1 therefore stand in grace before your F., He
T-14......IV.5:6 of the joy of living with your God and F.,
T-14......IV.7:5 as guilty is denial of the F. so complete,
T-14......IV.8:4 understand how much your F. loves you,
T-14......IV.9:1 live in the light of the blessing of their F.,
T-14......IV.9:4 teach you what you are, or what your F. is.
T-14.......V.3:1 Blessed Son of a wholly blessing F., joy
T-14.......V.5:2 be restored between the F. and the Son.
T-14.......V.9:2 Our power comes not of us, but of our F..
T-14......VI.5:1 your communication with your F.. The
T-14... VIII.1:7 He has promised the F. that through Him
T-14... VIII.2:2 lay upon the altar to your F. and His Son.
T-14... VIII.2:4 by gifts wholly acceptable to F. and to Son
T-14. VIII.2:13 the unseparated F. and His Son lies in the
T-14. VIII.2:15 constantly between the F. and the Son, as
T-14... VIII.4:9 place are joined the F. and His creations,
T-14... VIII.5:1 The link with which the F. joins Himself
T-14... VIII.5:5 is worthy of the F. will be accepted by the
T-14......IX.1:5 Keep not your making from your F., for
T-14.......X.2:3 remembrance of his F. dawns on him, and
T-14.....X.10:4 If you would remember your F., let the
T-14......XI.5:4 for God's Son what his F. wills for him.
T-14......XI.5:6 you that you will with the F. and His Son.
T-14......XI.7:3 can make no needs his F. will not meet, if
T-14....XI.11:6 that you have always created like your F..
T-15...... I.14:5 the ego's making, and ascend unto your F.
T-15....III.4:11 be content with less than his F. has given
T-15......III.6:9 Name of Christ, eternal Host unto His F..
T-15......III.9:8 you. And you are of your F.. Let us join in
T-15....III.10:2 I will as my F. wills, knowing His Will is
T-15....III.10:5 What my F. loves I love as He does, and I
T-15......IV.4:1 altar on which your F. has placed Himself
T-15.......V.2:7 to deny the Oneness of the F. and His Son
T-15......VI.4:5 to accept is the fact that, like your F., *you*
T-15......VI.7:3 give yourself as your F. gives His Self, you
T-15......VII.1:1 powerful attraction of the F. for His Son.
T-15... VIII.3:2 of God's Son is the loneliness of his F..
T-15... VIII.4:6 Christ, where they become like to their F..
T-15... VIII.4:7 Christ knows of no separation from His F.
T-15... VIII.4:7 in which He gives as His F. gives to Him.
T-15......IX.6:5 attempted to separate the F. from the Son
T-15.......X.1:1 the perfect union of the F. and the Son.
T-15......XI.1:3 your F. have become very fearful to you.
T-15......XI.3:4 innocent as our relationship with our F.,
T-15......XI.4:4 your F. and your brothers from yourself.
T-15......XI.8:4 that you may give it and return it to the F.
T-15......XI.9:4 who receive the F. are one with Him,
T-15......XI.9:5 remembrance of the F. enters with Him,
T-16......III.7:6 and purity, and love Him as His F. does.
T-16....IV.10:2 and thus denies the Wholeness of your F..
T-16....IV.12:1 Your F. can no more forget the truth in
T-16...VII.12:1 *Forgive us our illusions, F., and help us to*
T-17....... II.1:7 look upon, and which He thanks the F. for
T-17....IV.16:2 Let us ascend in peace together to the F.,
T-17... VIII.6:1 as surely as your F. gave peace to you. For
T-18......VI.1:4 not his F. and dwells not apart from Him.
T-19...... I.10:3 everyone as a Son of your most loving F.,
T-19...... I.12:3 and wholly acceptable to his F. as to Him.
T-19....... II.4:3 of the Son of God as his F. created him,
T-19....... II.7:5 has somehow managed to corrupt his F.,
T-19......IV.3:9 And the F. will accept them in His Name.
T19....IV.B.4:8 And you want your F., not a little mound
T19....IV.B.7:2 the home you offered to my F. and to me.
T19....IV.B.7:3 in which the F. and the Son are joined.
T19....IV.B.7:4 holy union of the F. and the Son in you!
T19..IV.B.17:3 receiving from the F. and offering His
T19... IV.C.8:2 My brother, child of our F., this is a *dream*
T19...IV.D.1:3 simply, you would remember your F.. The
T19...IV.D.1:4 the F. of the universe and of the universe
T19...IV.D.4:6 the face of Christ and join Him in His F..
T19.IV.D.18:5 rise again to glad remembrance of his F.,
T19.IV.D.19:6 he is, and what his F. created him to be.
T19.IV.D.21:3 safely within the sure protection of his F..
T-20....III.11:5 look unto the Son to lead them to the F..
T-20....III.11:7 brother now will lead the other to the F.
T-20.......V.1:2 to find the certainty his F. has in him.
T-20.......V.4:3 His worth has been established by his F.,
T-20.......V.8:5 upon himself not as his F. knows him.
T-20......VI.1:4 relationship between him and his F.. His
T-20......VI.1:7 The one created by his F. is wholly Self-
T-20....VI.10:1 the Son of God has with his F. in reality.
T-20..VI.12:11 relationship with their F. from themselves
T-20... VIII.4:4 brother, you will see an altar to your F.,
T-21.........I.9:2 Here is the sight of him who knows his F..
T-21.........I.9:6 of love the Son of God sings to his F. still.
T-21...... II.11:5 what it wills, you are confusing Son and F.
T-21...... II.13:1 brother were both created by a loving F.,
T-21...... II.13:3 each other and separate from your F., you
T-21......VI.6:2 separate from you and from his F. forever,
T-21....VI.10:3 your F. gives you for completing Him.
T-21....VI.10:5 F. is as close to you as is your brother. Yet
T-22.......I.11:7 for here you will with Him and with His F.
T-22.......V.3:6 your F. Whom you would defend against.
T-22......VI.4:1 of your F. as a means for His Own plan. Be
T-22......VI.9:1 to look on what your F. loves with charity
T-22....VI.11:1 the Son of God and not attack his F.? How
T-22....VI.11:2 frail and easily destroyed unless his F. is?
T-22....VI.11:3 and justify *is* an attack upon your F.. And
T-22....VI.11:5 you think the F. and the Son are separate.
T-22....VI.12:5 without the whole, the Son without the F.;
T-23.........I.5:2 the memory of his F. must be forgotten. It
T-23.........I.9:4 Here will the F. never be remembered. Yet
T-23....... II.5:1 relationship between the F. and the Son.
T-23......IV.3:6 Either the F. and the Son are murderers,
T-23......IV.7:8 The body stands between the F. and the
T-24.........I.7:1 friend because his F. created him like you.
T-24.........I.8:7 and none your F. does not share with you.
T-24....... II.3:4 the "creator" who creates unlike the F.,
T-24....... II.6:2 so like his F. that the memory of Him
T-24....... II.6:3 creations, as like to him as he is to his F..
T-24......III.6:1 holiness, the perfect F. of a perfect Son,
T-24....III.8:13 your F. it was not His Will that you be
T-24....IV.3:12 would keep the gift your F. asks from Him
T-24.......V.1:3 that it is one with Him and with His F..
T-24......VI.1:9 F. waits for your acknowledgment that He
T-24......VI.2:1 a Heaven incomplete, a Son without a F..
T-24......VI.2:5 are not separate from him nor from his F..
T-24......VI.4:3 you will not know the F. nor yourself. For
T-24....VI.13:5 at all, for only what His F. wills is possible
T-24.....VII.1:7 son, beloved of you as you are to your F..
T-24.....VII.5:1 The F. keeps what He created safe. You
T-24.....VII.7:1 A co-creator with the F. must have a Son.
T-25.........I.1:7 meet and join and raise Him to His F.,
T-25.........I.5:3 F. and Son and Holy Spirit are as One, as
T-25.........I.5:4 and His F. never have been separate, and
T-25.........I.6:2 still is one with Both the F. and the Son,
T-25....... II.9:4 creation as the perfect F. that He is. And
T-25..... II.10:1 yourself from him nor from his F.. You
T-25..... II.10:3 as one, and thank his F. as He thanks you.
T-25..... II.10:6 He offers unto the F. and the Son alike.
T-25.....VII.4:4 sanity must lie apart from Both the F. and
T-25.....VII.4:8 *because* the F. and the Son are not insane.
T-25.....VII.6:7 a view of what the F. and the Son must be,
T-25.....VII.9:6 peace, than could the F. overlook His Son,
T-25. VIII.13:6 Their F. gave the same inheritance to both
T-26.........I.4:3 God's Son perceive himself without his F.
T-26.........I.4:4 And his F. be without His Son? Yet every
T-26......IV.3:3 Christ and not recall His F. as He really is?
T-26.......V.9:6 the justice your All-Loving F. has ensured
T-26...VII.14:9 He has forsworn his F. and himself, and
T-26...VII.16:6 death instead of what his F. wills for him.
T-26...VII.16:7 because his F. wills that he should live.
T-26...VII.17:5 of God because his F. willed that it be so.
T-26......IX.8:6 the F. and the Son return to what is Theirs
T-26.......X.6:6 *do I deny the Presence of the F. and the Son.*
T-27.........I.1:9 F. with the sacrifice of His beloved Son.
T-27....... II.6:7 The ancient calling of the F. to His Son,
T-27...VII.13:3 he has lost his innocence, denied his F.,
T-27...VII.15:7 He represents his F., Whom you see as
T-27...VII.16:2 the gifts you dream your F. gives to you.
T-28.......I.15:6 His F. wills that he be lifted up and gently
T-28....... II.1:2 by its effects; the F. *is* a Father by His Son.
T-28........II.1:2 by its effects; the Father *is* a F. by His Son.
T-28........II.8:1 dream the F. was deprived of His Effects,
T-28......III.8:6 place of welcome for your F. and your Self
T-28......III.9:5 Here is a feast the F. lays before His Son,
T-28......IV.7:7 And the F. comes to join His Son the Holy
T-28......IV.8:6 sin. And here the F. will receive His Son,
T-28......IV.9:1 I thank You, F., knowing You will come
T-28....IV.10:1 him, and where you join His Son the F. is.
T-28......VI.6:4 his. In his creation did his F. say, "You are
T-28.....VII.1:5 the F. and the Son is not the Will of Either
T-28.....VII.7:1 and everything his F. promised him. No
T-29......III.2:1 the F. lost Himself when He created you?
T-29......III.5:4 his F. lost not part of him in your creation
T-29.......V.1:3 up to gladden God the F. and the Son.
T-29.......V.5:1 There is no gift the F. asks of you but that
T-29.......V.5:2 perfect gift, in whom his F. shines forever,
T-29.......V.6:3 to him, created by his F. as His home? If
T-29......VI.2:4 killed. He is immortal as his F.. What he is
T-29...VII.10:6 Seek not outside your F. for your hope.
T-29...VIII.6:6 as perfect, sinless and as loving as his F.,
T-30......III.9:1 Who knows the F. knows this light, for
T-30....III.11:4 for there the Mind of F. and of Son joined
T-30.......V.4:5 God knows everything his F. understands,
T-30.......V.7:5 looked upon before the F. is remembered.
T-30......VI.9:4 *I thank You, F., for Your perfect Son, and in*
T-30....VI.10:6 Is his F. wrong about His Son? Or have
T-31......II.10:6 brother, must his F. be the same as yours,
T-31......VI.7:3 your F. wills of you can never change. The
T-31..VIII.10:1 I thank You, F., for these holy ones who
W-pI.....45.8:4 Heaven to God the F. and to God the Son.
W-pI.....50.5:5 resting place where your F. has placed you
W-pI.....56.4:4 is my will, united with the Will of my F..
W-pI.....58.5:6 am. My F. supports me, protects me, and
W-pI.....67.6:2 reminding you of your F. and of your Self.
W-pI.....69.8:1 Have confidence in your F. today, and be
W-pI...72.10:6 *What is salvation, F.? I do not know. Tell me,*
W-pI...72.11:2 "What is salvation, F.?" Ask and you will
W-pI...72.12:2 *What is salvation, F.? I do not know. Tell me,*
W-pI...72.13:5 *What is salvation, F.?* Then wait a minute
W-pI.....73.3:2 the Will the Son of God shares with his F.
W-pI.....73.9:3 you and your F. are in perfect accord. You
W-pI...76.10:4 About the Love your F. has for you. About
W-pI...76.12:3 is our acknowledgment that God is our F.,
W-pI.....77.2:4 It is implicit in what God your F. is. It was
W-pI...95.13:2 that Self; united with your F. in His Will.
W-pI...95.15:1 you are one Self, united with your F., is a
W-pI.....99.7:3 Your F. loves you. All the world of pain is
W-pI...99.10:2 You cannot lose the gifts your F. gave.
W-pI...100.1:1 Just as God's Son completes his F., so
W-pI...106.2:1 and hear your F. speak to you through His
W-pI...106.5:3 who could reach God's Son except his F.,
W-pI...107.6:8 Your F. wills these dreams be gone. Let
W-pI...107.8:3 your F. knows that You are Both the same
W-pI...117.2:3 *These are the gifts my F. gave to me. I would*
W-pI...120.2:3 *myself, and let my F. tell me Who I really am.*
W-pI...122.3:2 of your F. can arise across the threshold of
W-pI......123.h I thank my F. for His gifts to me.
W-pI...123.2:2 your F. has not left you to yourself, nor let
W-pI...123.8:2 world, remembering his F. and his Self.
W-pI...124.7:4 For we would keep the gifts our F. gave.
W-pI...124.7:7 As we deny our separation from our F., it
W-pI...125.1:2 Your F. wills you hear His Word today.
W-pI...125.4:1 Hear, holy Son of God, your F. speak. His
W-pI...125.8:3 in the single Mind of F. and of Son. In
W-pI...127.3:8 the link between the F. and the Son which
W-pI...127.9:1 Call to your F., certain that His Voice will
W-pI.132.12:4 from Him, and nowhere does the F. end,
W-pI.132.13:1 and made to separate the F. and the Son,
W-pI.132.14:4 For we are in the home our F. set for us,
W-pI...136.9:3 His Son is dust, the F. incomplete, and
W-pI...140.8:2 minds because our F. placed it there for us
W-pI.140.11:4 time when we can hear our F. speak to us.
W-pI.140.12:3 *Speak to us, F., that we may be healed.* And
WpI. rIV.in2:3 truth of What you are and What your F. is
WpI. rIV.in2:4 by which the F. gave creation to the Son,
WpI. rIV.in2:6 thoughts can dwell but those his F. shares
WpI. rIV.in9:2 and all our F. wills that we receive as the
W-pI...142.1:1 (123) I thank my F. for His gifts to me.
W-pI...151.9:3 knows the glory of the F. and the Son?

W-pI...152.8:5 to usurp the altar to the F. and the Son.
W-pI.152.12:2 for He speaks for you and for your F.. He
W-pI.153.13:1 are lost to hope, abandoned by your F.,
W-pI...154.4:1 the Voice for God, of F. and of Son, that
W-pI...158.2:8 The revelation that the F. and the Son are
W-pI...159.4:6 holiness was given by His F. and Himself.
W-pI...160.8:4 sure, that you are not a stranger to your F.
W-pI...163.4:4 the Will of F. and of Son defeated finally,
W-pI...163.7:4 And with the F. died the Son as well.
W-pI...163.9:1 *Our F., bless our eyes today. We are Your*
W-pI...165.1:2 and the eternal life your F. wills for you?
W-pI...167.1:7 death because the F. and the Son are One.
W-pI...168.6:7 *F., I come to You. And You will come to me*
W-pI...169.4:1 F. and the Son as One has been already set
W-pI...169.6:5 of God has merely disappeared into his F.,
W-pI...169.6:5 into his Father, as his F. has in him. The
W-pI.170.13:1 *F., we are like You. No cruelty abides in us,*
WpI...rV.in2:1 *Steady our feet, our F.. Let our doubts be*
WpI...rV.in4:5 Its constant state of union with Its F. and
WpI...rV.in9:8 me. Our F. wills His Son be one with Him.
W-pI...182.5:1 in you your F. knows as His Own Son. It is
W-pI...182.5:2 Son. It is this Child Who knows His F.. He
W-pI.183.10:5 He makes his claim to all his F. gave, is
W-pI.183.11:4 but the Son of God, who calls upon his F..
W-pI.184.15:1 *F., our Name is Yours. In It we are united*
W-pI...186.3:2 it says is that your F. still remembers you,
W-pI.187.10:2 here, before the altar to one God, one F.,
W-pI...188.7:3 Where God the F. and the Son are One.
W-pI...189.8:3 God the F. to be quietly removed forever.
W-pI.189.10:1 *F., we do not know the way to You. But we*
W-pI...190.3:7 in death, as mortal as the F. he has slain.
W-pI.193.13:5 and brings the Love of God the F. down to
W-pI...195.4:4 We offer thanks to God our F. that in us
W-pI...195.6:1 We thank our F. for one thing alone; that
W-pI...196.5:5 could believe his F. is his deadly enemy,
W-pI.196.11:4 Love, calling Him F. and yourself His Son.
W-pI...197.7:4 Him. His Being in His F. is secure, because
W-pI...198.3:7 of God awakens to his Self and to his F.,
W-pI...198.7:2 death is offered to God's Son and to his F.
W-pI.198.10:2 Spirit holds for you from God your F.. Let
W-pI.198.12:5 to perceive no more, and only know the F.
W-pI...200.9:6 The F. calls; the Son will hear. And that is
W-pI...201.1:3 *oneness with the universe and God, my F.,*
W-pI...219.1:5 *to what my F. loves forever as His Son.* I am
W-pII ....in.2:2 in quiet expectation for our God and F..
W-pII ....in.3:3 and expect our F. to reveal Himself, as He
W-pII ....in.5:5 Sit silently and wait upon your F.. He has
W-pII ....in.6:2 fail. F., we give these holy times to You, in
W-pII ....in.7:7 this. The F. and the Son, Whose holy Will
W-pII .221.1:1 *F., I come to You today to seek the peace that*
W-pII .221.1:4 *My F., speak to me today. I come to hear*
W-pII .222.2:1 *F., we have no words except Your Name*
W-pII .223.2:1 *Our F., let us see the face of Christ instead of*
W-pII ....224.h God is my F., and He loves His Son.
W-pII .224.1:3 It is the gift my F. gave to me; the one as
W-pII .224.2:1 *My Name, O F., still is known to You. I have*
W-pII .224.2:3 *Remind me, F., now, for I am weary of the*
W-pII ....225.h God is my F., and His Son loves Him.
W-pII .225.1:1 *F., I must return Your Love for me, for*
W-pII .226.2:1 *F., my home awaits my glad return. Your*
W-pII .227.1:1 *F., it is today that I am free, because my will*
W-pII .227.1:7 *release. F., I know my holiness is one with Yours.*
W-pII .228.1:1 My F. knows my holiness. Shall I deny
W-pII .228.2:1 *F., I was mistaken in myself, because I failed*
W-pII .229.1:5 lose, but which my F. has kept safe for me.
W-pII .229.2:1 *F., my thanks to You for what I am; for*
W-pII .230.1:4 How merciful is God my F., that when He
W-pII .230.2:1 *F., I seek the peace You gave as mine in my*
W-pII .....2.5:2 more to wait until his F. is remembered,
W-pII ....231.h F., I will but to remember You.
W-pII .231.1:1 *What can I seek for, F., but Your Love?*
W-pII .231.2:2 and with the One as well Who is our F..
W-pII ....232.h Be in my mind, my F., through the day.
W-pII .232.1:1 *Be in my mind, my F., when I wake, and*
W-pII .232.2:3 Have faith in Him Who is your F.. Trust
W-pII .233.1:1 *F., I give You all my thoughts today. I would*
W-pII ....234.h F., today I am Your Son again.
W-pII .234.1:4 the peace of God the F. and the Son. This
W-pII .234.2:1 *We thank You, F., that we cannot lose the*
W-pII .235.2:1 *F., Your Holiness is mine. Your Love*
W-pII .236.2:1 *F., my mind is open to Your Thoughts, and*
W-pII .237.1:3 which I hear as God my F. speaks to me.
W-pII .237.2:2 *F., I come to You through Him Who is Your*
W-pII .238.1:1 *F., Your trust in me has been so great, I must*
W-pII .238.2:1 pause to think how much our F. loves us.
W-pII ....239.h The glory of my F. is my own.
W-pII .239.1:2 be thankful for the gifts our F. gave us.
W-pII .239.2:1 *We thank You, F., for the light that shines*
W-pII .241.2:2 *F., Your Son, who never left, returns to*
W-pII .243.2:1 *F., today I leave creation free to be itself. I*
W-pII ....245.h Your peace is with me, F.. I am safe.
W-pII .245.1:1 *Your peace surrounds me, F.. Where I go,*
W-pII .245.1:6 *Send them to me, my F.. Let me bring Your*
W-pII ....246.h To love my F. is to love His Son.
W-pII .246.1:2 think that I can know his F. or my Self.
W-pII .246.1:3 that my awareness can contain my F., or
W-pII .246.1:3 my mind conceive of all the love my F. has
W-pII .246.2:1 *You choose for me to come to You, my F.. For*
W-pII .248.2:1 *F., my ancient love for You returns, and lets*
W-pII .248.2:2 *F., I am as You created me. Now is Your Love*
W-pII .249.2:1 *F., we would return our minds to You. We*
W-pII .250.2:1 *He is Your Son, my F.. And today I would*
W-pII .....4.4:4 But all the while his F. shines on him, and
W-pII .251.2:1 *And for that peace, our F., we give thanks.*
W-pII .252.2:1 *F., You know my true Identity. Reveal It*
W-pII .254.1:1 *F., today I would but hear Your Voice. In*
W-pII .255.1:6 I give today to finding what my F. wills for
W-pII .255.2:1 *And so, my F., would I pass this day with*
W-pII .256.2:1 *And so, our F., would we come to You in*
W-pII .257.2:1 *F., forgiveness is Your chosen means for our*
W-pII .259.2:1 *F., I would not be insane today. I would not*
W-pII .260.1:1 *F., I did not make myself, although in my*
W-pII .260.1:3 *Your Son, my F., calls on You today. Let me*
W-pII .261.2:2 *I would come, my F., home to You today. I*
W-pII .262.1:1 *F., You have one Son. And it is he that I*
W-pII .262.1:7 *Let me not see him as a stranger to his F., nor*
W-pII .263.1:1 *F., Your Mind created all that is, Your Spirit*
W-pII .264.1:1 *F., You stand before me and behind, beside*
W-pII .264.1:6 *F., Your Son is like Yourself. We come to You*
W-pII .266.1:1 *F., You gave me all Your Sons, to be my*
W-pII .267.2:2 *F., my heart is beating in the peace the Heart*
W-pII .270.1:1 *F., Christ's vision is Your gift to me, and it*
W-pII .270.1:4 *signifies Your Son acknowledges his F., lets*
W-pII .....6.2:5 His F. placed the means for your salvation
W-pII .....6.2:5 does He remain the Self Who, like His F.,
W-pII .271.1:4 live, remembering the F. and the Son;
W-pII .271.2:1 *F., Christ's vision is the way to You. What*
W-pII .272.1:1 *F., the truth belongs to me. My home is set*
W-pII .273.2:1 *F., Your peace is mine. What need have I to*
W-pII .274.1:1 *F., today I would let all things be as You*
W-pII .274.2:1 to us today, from Him Who is our F.. Give
W-pII .275.2:5 *F., Your Voice protects all things through*
W-pII .276.1:3 thus did God become the F. of the Son He
W-pII .276.1:6 be unsure of who we are, of Who our F. is,
W-pII .276.2:1 *F., Your Word is mine. And it is this that I*
W-pII .277.1:1 *Your Son is free, my F.. Let me not imagine I*
W-pII ....278.h If I am bound, my F. is not free.
W-pII .278.1:1 to die, then is my F. prisoner with me.
W-pII .278.1:3 any way, I do not know my F. nor my Self.
W-pII .278.2:1 *F., I ask for nothing but the truth. I have had*
W-pII .279.2:2 *My F. loves the Son Whom He created as His*
W-pII .280.1:6 God, whose F. willed that he be limitless,
W-pII .280.2:2 *F., I lay no limits on the Son You love and*
W-pII .....7.3:1 If you but knew how much your F. yearns
W-pII .281.1:1 *F., Your Son is perfect. When I think that I*
W-pII .281.2:3 My F. placed me safe in Heaven, watching
W-pII .282.1:2 as God Himself, my F. and my Source,
W-pII .282.2:1 *F., Your Name is Love and so is mine. Such is*
W-pII .283.1:1 *F., I made an image of myself, and it is this I*
W-pII .283.1:4 *I am he my F. loves. My holiness remains the*
W-pII .283.2:1 with God our F. as our only Source, and
W-pII .284.2:1 *F., what You have given cannot hurt, so*
W-pII .285.2:1 *F., my holiness is Yours. Let me rejoice in it,*
W-pII .286.1:1 *F., how still today! How quietly do all things*
W-pII ....287.h You are my goal, my F.. Only You.
W-pII .287.2:1 *You are my goal, my F.. What but You could*
W-pII .289.2:1 *F., let me not look upon a past that is not*
W-pII .290.2:2 *You cannot fail to hear me, F.. What I ask*
W-pII .291.2:5 *F., guide Your Son along the quiet path that*
W-pII .292.2:1 *We thank You, F., for Your guarantee of*
W-pII .293.2:1 *F., let not Your holy world escape my sight*
W-pII .294.2:1 *My body, F., cannot be Your Son. And what*
W-pII .295.2:1 *My F., Christ has asked a gift of me, and one I*
W-pII .297.2:1 *F., how certain are Your ways; how sure*
W-pII ....298.h I love You, F., and I love Your Son.
W-pII .298.2:1 *F., I come to You today, because I would not*
W-pII .298.2:4 *my love for God my F. and His holy Son.*
W-pII .299.1:2 my F., Who created it, acknowledges my
W-pII .299.2:1 *F., my holiness is not of me. It is not mine to*
W-pII .....9.4:4 And God the F. smiles upon His Son, His
W-pII .301.1:1 *F., unless I judge I cannot weep. Nor can I*
W-pII .301.1:7 *is gone. F., I will not judge Your world today.*
W-pII .302.1:1 *F., our eyes are opening at last. Your holy*
W-pII .303.2:1 *Your Son is welcome, F.. He has come to*
W-pII .304.2:3 *It is Your gift, my F., given me to offer to Your*
W-pII .305.2:1 *F., the peace of Christ is given us, because it*
W-pII .306.2:1 *so, our F., we return to You, remembering*
W-pII .307.1:1 *F., Your Will is mine, and only that. There is*
W-pII .308.2:1 *Thanks for this instant, F.. It is now I am*
W-pII .309.2:1 *step I take today, my F., is my sure release*
W-pII .310.1:1 *This day, my F., would I spend with You, as*
W-pII ... 10.5:3 to Me. I am your F. and you are My Son."
W-pII .311.2:1 *F., we wait with open mind today, to hear*
W-pII .312.2:2 *made. F., this is Your Will for me today, and*
W-pII .313.1:1 *F., there is a vision which beholds all things*
W-pII .314.2:1 *F., we were mistaken in the past, and choose*
W-pII .315.2:1 *I thank You, F., for the many gifts that come*
W-pII .316.1:2 no shadow on the holy mind my F. loves.
W-pII .316.2:1 *F., I would accept Your gifts today. I do not*
W-pII .317.2:1 *F., Your way is what I choose today. Where*
W-pII .318.2:1 *Let me today, my F., take the role You offer*
W-pII .319.2:1 *F., Your Will is total. And the goal which*
W-pII ....320.h My F. gives all power unto me.
W-pII .320.1:2 any attributes his F. gave in his creation.
W-pII .320.1:4 because his F. shines upon his mind, and
W-pII ... 11.5:1 Our F. calls to us. We hear His Voice, and
W-pII ....321.h F., my freedom is in You alone.
W-pII .321.1:2 *F., I have searched in vain until I heard Your*
W-pII .321.1:8 *F., my freedom is in You alone. Father, it is*
W-pII .321.1:9 *is in You alone. F., it is my will that I return.*
W-pII .321.2:2 the certain way our F. has established.
W-pII .322.2:1 *F., to You all sacrifice remains forever*
W-pII .324.1:1 *F., You are the One Who gave the plan for*
W-pII .325.2:1 *Our F., Your ideas reflect the truth, and*
W-pII .326.1:1 *F., I was created in Your Mind, a holy*
W-pII .327.2:1 *F., I thank You that Your promises will*
W-pII .328.1:4 This is not what our F. wills for us, nor is
W-pII .328.2:4 *happily I share that Will which You, my F.,*
W-pII .329.1:1 *F., I thought I wandered from Your Will,*
W-pII .329.1:8 *to itself. F., my will is Yours. And I am safe,*
W-pII .330.2:1 *F., Your Son can not be hurt. And if we think*
W-pII .331.1:1 *How foolish, F., to believe Your Son could*
W-pII .331.1:3 *You love me, F.. You could never leave me*
W-pII .332.2:4 *F., we would release it now. For as we offer*
W-pII .333.2:1 *F., forgiveness is the light You chose to*
W-pII .334.1:1 to find the treasures that my F. offers me.
W-pII .336.2:2 *Then let me, F., look within, and find Your*
W-pII .337.1:6 harm, to understand my F. loves His Son;
W-pII .337.1:6 His Son; to know I am the Son my F. loves
W-pII .337.2:3 *myself. F., my dream is ended now. Amen.*
W-pII .338.2:1 *Your plan is sure, my F., –only Yours. All*
W-pII .339.2:1 *F., this is Your day. It is a day in which I*
W-pII .340.1:1 *F., I thank You for today, and for the*
W-pII .340.1:5 *Thanks for today, my F.. I was born into this*
W-pII .340.2:4 Our F. has redeemed His Son this day.
W-pII .340.2:6 and none the F. will not gather to Himself
W-pII .341.1:1 *F., Your Son is holy. I am he on whom You*
W-pII .342.1:1 *I thank You, F., for Your plan to save me*
W-pII .344.1:1 *This is Your law, my F., not my own. I have*
W-pII .345.1:1 *F., a miracle reflects Your gifts to me, Your*
W-pII .345.1:5 *F., in Heaven it is different, for there, there*
W-pII .346.1:1 *F., I wake today with miracles correcting my*
W-pII .347.1:1 *F., I want what goes against my will, and do*
W-pII .347.1:2 *Straighten my mind, my F.. It is sick. But*
W-pII .348.1:1 *F., let me remember You are here, and I am*
W-pII .349.1:4 *F., Your gifts are mine. Each one that I accept*
W-pII .349.2:1 Our F. knows our needs. He gives us

W-pII..350.1:6 *Therefore, my F., I would turn to You. Only*
W-pII..351.1:6 *Choose, then, for me, my F., through Your*
W-pII..352.1:8 *it. F., I would hear Your Voice and find Your*
W-pII..353.1:1 *F., I give all that is mine today to Christ, to*
W-pII..354.1:4 *And He is like His F.. Thus must I be one with*
W-pII..355.1:1 *Why should I wait, my F., for the joy You*
W-pII..355.1:8 *Himself, and know You as his F. and Creator*
W-pII..356.1:1 *F., You promised You would never fail to*
W-pII..358.1:4 *Your Voice, my F., then is mine as well, and*
W-pII..359.1:1 *F., today we will forgive Your world, and let*
W-pII..360.1:1 *F., it is Your peace that I would give,*
Wfl........in.5:1 the gift our F. promised to His holy Son.
WpII361-5.1:5 He speaks for God my F. and His holy Son
W-ep .........4:4 of your F. and your brother and your Self.
M-5..........I.2:2 Son and the triumph of his F. over him. It
M-22..........5:5 at all, for his F. did not create bodies, and
M-22..........7:5 And to judge His Son is to limit his F..
M-23..........3:3 whole relationship of the Son to the F. lies
M-23..........5:5 that he sees in it an image of his F.. You
M-23..........5:6 become the symbol of his F. here on earth
M-27..........5:7 Him. He is not F., but destroyer. He is not
M-28........1:10 It is the single desire of the Son for the F..
M-29........6:11 more than this does your F. love His Son?
C-3...........8:4 Creator; the joining of the F. and the Son,
C-4............6:2 Son is set, and there his F. is remembered.
C-5............6:9 *no death because the Son of God is like his F..*
C-6............3:9 And He brings the Love of your F. to you
P-2......... V.5:5 distress can be but answered by his F.. Yet
P-2......... V.6:4 they must start their F. will complete. For
P-3......... II.5:4 like the relationship of the F. and the Son.
S-1 .........in.1:2 share; the song the Son sings to the F.,
S-1 .........in.2:4 to the truth of union in his F. and himself.
S-1 ...........I.7:1 because it is a gift of thanks to His F.. To
S-2 ...........I.3:9 You will hate his F. if you hate the Son He
S-2 ....... II.6:10 of God, and thank his F. for his holiness?
S-3 ...........I.4:4 to him in the Voice his F. placed in him.
S-3 ........IV.6:5 You are he your F. loves, who never left
S-3 ........IV.8:6 Listen, My child, your F. calls to you. Do
S-3 ......IV.10:7 your F. needs you and will call to you until

## father 30

*Father*

T-4........ I.13:2 A f. can safely leave a child with an elder
T-4........ I.13:3 himself with the f. because he does this. I
T-8........VI.4:1 This son of a loving f. left his home and
T-8........VI.4:2 time. He was ashamed to return to his f.,
T-8........VI.4:3 came home the f. welcomed him with joy,
T-10......III.8:6 You think they are your f., because you
T-10....III.10:8 and the f. you made did not make you.
T-11.......in.1:7 an answer to the question, "Who is my f.?
T-11.......in.1:8 you will be faithful to the f. you choose.
T-11.......in.2:3 out of the wish of God's Son to f. Him.
T-11.......in.2:4 system in which you made your own f..
T-11.......in.2:8 either the ego, which you made, *is* your f.,
T-13....III.10:4 Therefore you made of Him an unloving f.
T-13....III.10:4 of Him what only such a f. could give.
T-21....... II.10:4 own creator, and be f. and not son to him.
T-24...VII.10:8 a means to offer to the "f." what he wants.
T-28....... II.1:5 he is God's Son that he must also be a f.,
T-28....... II.3:7 And as their "f.," you must be like them.
T-29......IX.6:4 game, in which the child becomes the f.,
T-31....... I.10:2 For hate must f. fear, and look upon its
T-31...... I.10:2 father fear, and look upon its f. as itself.
WpI .. rV.in2:5 *a f. lead a little child along a way he does not*
WpI .. rV.in2:6 *he is safe because his f. leads the way for him.*
W-pI.182.11:4 beseech his f. for protection and for love.
W-pI ...183.1:3 own. A f. gives his son his name, and thus
Wfl ........in.5:7 is a f. angry at his son because he failed to
M-14..........1:6 f. of illusions is the belief that they have a
M-17........7:10 An angry f. pursues his guilty son. Kill or
M-29..........6:9 A loving f. does not let his child harm
M-29........6:10 for injury, but his f. will protect him still.

## Father's 118

*father's*

T-3......... V.1:3 by the union of my will with the F.. We
T-7......... X.7:4 the Father, because the F. Will *is* His Son.
T-8......... II.4:3 knowing that the Will of the Son is the F..
T-8........ IV.3:4 by being aware of the F. Will myself. This
T-8........IV.7:1 will were not mine it would not be our F..
T-8........VI.8:1 –"Do I want to know my F. Will for me?"
T-11....... II.6:1 can your will and your F. be wholly joined
T-11. VIII.11:6 and you will learn of the F. Love for you.
T-12....... II.6:5 for His Father, or His F. Love for Him.
T-12...... IV.6:2 For death is not your F. Will nor yours,
T-12......VI.5:6 because He knows of the F. Love for Him.
T-12......VI.5:8 peace He waits for you at His F. altar,
T-12......VI.5:8 holding out the F. Love to you in the quiet
T-12......VI.6:2 because He knows His F. Love for Him.
T-12... VIII.2:1 knows his F. protection and cannot fear.
T-12... VIII.2:2 His F. Love holds him in perfect peace,
T-12... VIII.4:1 of your F. Love you can never forget Him,
T-13..........I.1:2 this, for sharing the F. Love for His Son,
T-13.... VI.13:7 ceased to be his F. witness and his own.
T-13......VII.8:3 and His Son returns his F. Love forever.
T-13...VII.17:3 is my gift to you, so was it the F. gift to me
T-13... VIII.6:7 gift to you. His Being is His F. gift to Him.
T-13... VIII.7:1 bestow, and your F. gift you cannot lose.
T-13....... X.9:1 to yourself do not remember your F. Love.
T-13....... X.9:9 His Will is like His F., and He offers mercy
T-14....... V.9:6 your F. power that He has given him.
T-14...... VI.8:8 not the door himself upon his F. welcome.
T-14...... IX.4:3 the immortal assurance of their F. Love.
T19.... IV.B.4:9 In your holy relationship is your F. Son.
T19... IV.D.2:2 with joy because He is in His F. Love,
T19... IV.D.2:3 and the bright Rays of His F. Love that
T-20....... V.1:3 his F. laws to what was held outside them,
T-20....... V.4:3 it as you receive his F. gift through him.
T-20....... V.8:2 shares his F. certainty the universe rests in
T-20....... V.8:3 learn, to share his F. confidence in him.
T-21..... II.12:1 The Son's creations are like his F.. Yet in
T-21....... V.9:1 by your will in union with your F., to the
T-22.......I.11:8 This is your F. Will for you, and yours
T-22....... II.9:6 the Son of God could leave his F. Mind,
T-23.........I.5:1 that he is not himself, and *not* his F. Son.
T-23...... IV.8:1 is given those who share their F. purpose,
T-24...VII.11:3 The other rests within, his F. Son, within
T-24...VII.11:7 The Son of God retains his F. Will. The
T-25.........I.5:4 in the part of you that shares His F. Will.
T-25....... II.8:1 brother as his F. Mind shows him to you.
T-25..... II.9:10 will to make their F. happiness complete,
T-25...... IV.2:7 sharing his F. purpose in his own creation
T-25.....VII.4:1 is to deny your F. sanity and yours. For
T-25.....VII.4:4 is not his F. Son because the Son is mad,
T-25...VII.13:6 for if he could the loss would be his F.,
T-26.........I.8:2 reality, and sacrifice his F. Will for him?
T-26....... II.8:6 For it is not your F. Will that you should
T-26...... IV.4:4 Each reminds him of his F. Love as surely
T-26..... V.10:7 instantly restored unto his F. perfect Love
T-26...... X.3:7 to sacrifice his F. Love and yours as not
T-28.........I.8:5 F. Will that He be unremembered by His
T-28....... II.3:1 and not allow himself to be his F. Son. For
T-28.....VII.7:8 because it shares your F. Will with you.
T-29....... V.3:2 and you of him, because he is his F. Son,
T-29....... V.4:1 yourself; the mirror of his F. Love for you,
T-29....... V.4:1 the soft reminder of his F. Love by which
T-29....... V.6:2 and lead God's Son unto his F. house.
T-30...... III.2:2 can be a substitute for God the F. Love?
T-30....... V.8:5 as surely as His F. Love rests upon Him.
T-30....... V.8:6 and go with you, together, to His F. house
W-pI.....78.5:6 Such is his role in God your F. plan.
W-pI.....97.2:2 with all your F. Love and peace and joy.
W-pI...100.1:1 so your part in it completes your F. plan.
W-pI...100.4:4 all who will accept their F. gifts as theirs.
W-pI...100.7:1 in us according to our F. Will and ours.
W-pI...106.4:9 Today allow your F. ancient pledge to you
W-pI...106.6:3 One Who chose it in your F. Name for you
WpIrIII.in13:3 Do not forget your F. need of you, As you
W-pI...116.2:2 *I share my F. Will for me, His Son. What He*
W-pI...125.2:2 him surely to his F. house by his own will,
W-pI...125.9:4 Will of God the Son joins in his F. Will, at
W-pI.139.11:6 us, and how our F. Love contains them all.
W-pI.152.10:5 his perfect sinlessness, his F. Love, his
W-pI.152.11:4 *myself as what my F. Will created me to be.*
W-pI...153.7:2 the Christ and come to fear His F. anger.
W-pI...158.5:5 F. Will and His are joined in knowledge.
W-pI...162.2:1 by which the Son became his F. happiness
W-pI...164.2:4 are but your answer to your F. Call to you.
W-pI...182.4:3 is a Child in you Who seeks His F. house,
W-pI...182.5:4 again the holy air that fills His F. house.
W-pI...183.1:5 Your F. Name reminds you who you are,
W-pI.183.10:3 when God's Son calls on his F. Name. His
W-pI.183.10:4 His F. Thoughts become his own. He
W-pI.183.11:5 F. Voice gives answer in his Father's holy
W-pI.183.11:5 Voice gives answer in his F. holy Name. In
W-pI.183.11:7 In our F. Name, we would experience this
W-pI.187.10:5 shine in our reflection of our F. Love.
W-pI...188.8:1 your F. Voice when you refuse to listen.
W-pI...190.1:7 witnesses to God the F. hatred of His Son,
W-pI...192.1:1 F. holy Will that you complete Himself,
W-pI.192.10:5 His F. Love for him belongs to you. Your
W-pI.193.11:2 arise in haste and go unto our F. house.
W-pII .221.2:6 intent; to hear our F. answer to our call, to
W-pII .235.1:2 but keep in mind my F. Will for me is
W-pII .237.1:4 of death; aware it is my F. Call to me.
W-pII .255.1:6 it as mine, and giving it to all my F. Sons,
W-pII .263.2:2 walk together to our F. house as brothers
W-pII .277.2:4 He is free because he is his F. Son. And he
W-pII .280.1:3 No Thought of God has left its F. Mind.
W-pII ..... 7.4:3 memory of all your F. Love will not return
W-pII ..... 7.5:1 Accept your F. gift. It is a Call from Love
W-pII ..... 8.4:2 perceive the sure reflection of his F. Love;
W-pII ..... 9.5:6 we can reach our F. Love through Him.
W-pII .303.1:5 and see but sights that show His F. Love.
W-pII .309.1:3 For to deny my F. Will is to deny my own.
W-pII .317.1:4 go the way my F. plan appointed me to go
W-pII .320.1:6 in whom the power of my F. Will abides.
M-5 .........I.1:7 for placing God's Son on his F. throne.
M-13 ......... 4:9 Heaven and remembrance of his F. Love.
S-1.........in.1:6 in the song of his creating in his F. Name.
S-2......... III.3:2 in haste to go at last unto your F. house.
S-3...........I.4:3 and the remembrance of his F. Love. Yet
S-3...........I.4:5 The power to heal is now his F. gift, for

## father's 2

*Father's*

T-8........ VI.4:3 because the son himself *was* his f. treasure.
T-24...VII.10:7 the means to serve his "f." purpose. Not

## fathered 2

T-31...VII.12:3 the wish that f. it no longer is held dear.
S-3........ IV.6:2 which f. you in perfect sinlessness, and

## Fatherhood 23

*fatherhood*

T-3....... VII.5:2 to God, because it literally denies His F..
T-8......... III.3:4 His Own F. must be extended outward.
T-8......... III.3:5 His F. by placing no limits upon it. Let the
T-8........ VI.6:5 and He extends His F. to you so that you
T-10.... V.13:2 His is the only F., and it is yours only
T-10.... V.13:5 Yet the real F. must be acknowledged if
T-10.... V.13:7 Only if you accept the F. of God will you
T-10.... V.13:7 because His F. gave you everything. That
T-11............I.h The Gifts of F.
T-11..........I.5:8 to accept His F. has denied you yours. See
T-11.........II.2:4 accomplish speaks to you of the F. of God.
T-11.........II.2:6 the denial of God's F. and of your Sonship
T-11.........II.4:4 not accomplish with the F. of God in him?
T-13....VIII.9:2 You are the witness to the F. of God, and
T-18..VIII.11:8 No Son of God remains outside His F..
T-24..... VII.1:8 to you, that you might share the F. of God
T-28.........II.1:4 Thus, the Son gives F. to his Creator, and
T-28.........II.2:1 F. *is* creation. Love must be extended.
T-30....... V.4:1 a perfect Son and share His F. with him.
W-pI.132.12:3 shares His F. with you who are His Son,
W-pII .247.2:3 *Your F. created them, and gave them all to*
W-pII .276.1:5 Let us accept His F., and all is given us.
W-pII .341.1:3 *with You, in brotherhood and F. complete;*

**fatherhood** 7

*Fatherhood*

T-7........XI.7:9 your Father you will not know your f.. The
T-8........III.3:4 Father must give f. to His Son, because
T-11.........I.7:6 Your f. and your Father are One. God
T-13....VIII.9:1 your creations establish your f. in Heaven.
T-13....VIII.9:3 deny the witnesses to your f. in Heaven.
T-13......IX.6:9 where the witnesses to your f. rejoice.
W-pI.132.12:2 wait for this release to give you f., not of

**Fatherless** 3

*fatherless*

T-10.......V.4:2 on God" made His Son think he was F.,
T-11.......in.1:6 Nothing alive is F., for life is creation.
T-11....VI.3:10 Own, the Son of God will see himself as F.

**fatherless** 1

*Fatherless*

T-4........III.1:9 creations are no more f. than you are.

**Fatherly** 1

W-pII .244.1:3 *and loving, in the safety of Your F. embrace?*

**fathers** 1

T-5........VI.8:1 "I will visit the sins of the f. unto the

**fatigue** 4

T-4.........in.1:5 properly understood is the opposite of f..
T-4........IV.6:3 mind can focus and rise above f. and heal.
W-pI.....62.3:3 of weakness, strain and f. from your mind
W-pI.136.18:3 it is not limited by time, by weather or f.,

**fatigued** 1

T-4.........in.1:6 To be f. is to be dis-spirited, but to be

**fault** 1

T-31......III.3:5 must the body be at f. for what it does. It

**faultier** 1

M-8...........4:4 fits best. What basis could be f. than this?

**faults** 2

W-pI.....78.6:3 You will review his f., the difficulties you
W-pI...135.9:2 mind. For you have seen in it the f., the

**faulty** 9

T-1.........I.41:2 or atone for, the f. perception of lack.
T-2........IV.3:4 The worst a f. use of a learning device can
T-2.......V.10:2 Since his own thinking is f. he cannot see
T-13....VIII.3:5 is merely a f. formulation of reality, with
T-31....VIII.3:1 so where you made a f. choice before you
W-pI...151.2:4 they have been f. witnesses indeed! Why
W-pI...194.7:7 He is sure that his perception may be f.,
M-5 .......II.1:5 is but a f. problem-solving approach, it is
S-3...........I.5:1 true healing and its f. counterpart. The

**favor** 8

T-1........IV.4:8 in deprivation in f. of the abundance they
T-7........IX.1:5 between them always in f. of the spirit. To
T-11..VIII.13:2 own interpretations go in f. of reality,
T-13....III.10:2 were at peace until you asked for special f.
T-18.........I.1:3 aspect of the Sonship in f. of the other.
T19...IV.D.5:4 of the body is given up in f. of the spirit,
T-25......IX.1:5 of this world in f. of the peace of Heaven.
W-pI.....45.4:3 We will deny the world in f. of truth. We

**favorite** 1

T-4........V.6:6 incapable of solution are f. ego devices for

**favors** 2

M-25.........3:6 the "unseen," or "special" f. from God.
M-25.........3:7 God gives no special f., and no one has

**fear** 903

*See also* fear-prone, fear-weakened

T-in...........1:8 *The opposite of love is f., but what is all-*
T-1........I.22:1 Miracles are associated with f. only
T-1........I.26:1 Miracles represent freedom from f..
T-1........I.26:3 The undoing of f. is an essential part of
T-1........I.28:1 are a way of earning release from f..
T-1........I.28:2 in which f. has already been abolished.
T-1.........II.1:1 but temporary suspension of doubt and f.
T-1.........II.2:6 freedom from f. cannot be thrust upon
T-1.......III.5:7 respect, and thus uproots the source of f..
T-1.......IV.1:2 This step usually entails f.. Second, the
T-1.......IV.1:4 This step brings escape from f.. When
T-1.......IV.4:1 The emptiness engendered by f. must be
T-1.......VI.4:2 can never control the effects of f. yourself,
T-1.......VI.4:2 of fear yourself, because you made f., and
T-1.......VI.5:1 All aspects of f. are untrue because they
T-1.......VI.5:4 *Perfect love casts out f.. If fear exists, Then*
T-1.......VI.5:5 *If f. exists, Then there is not perfect love.* But:
T-1.......VI.5:8 *If there is f.,* It *produces a state that does not*
T-1......VII.5:1 because of the confusion between f. and
T-1......VII.5:8 or awe will be confused with f., and the
T-2..........I.2:1 in the separation, or the "detour into f.."
T-2..........I.4:1 All f. is ultimately reducible to the basic
T-2..........I.4:3 is the real basis for your escape from f..
T-2.........II.1:3 be performed in the spirit of doubt or f..
T-2.......III.1:9 structures is a sign of the f. of Atonement,
T-2.......III.2:2 the mind was invulnerable to f., because
T-2.......III.2:2 to fear, because f. did not exist. Both the
T-2.......III.2:3 exist. Both the separation and the f. are
T-2..........IV.h Healing as Release from F.
T-2.......IV.1:7 healing is essentially the release from f..
T-2.......IV.1:9 healing because of your own f.
T-2.......IV.4:7 or the sick, is an increase in f.. They are
T-2.......IV.5:3 the recipient can understand without f..
T-2.......IV.5:6 not to lower it by increasing f..
T-2........V.1:1 that they fully understand the f. of release
T-2........V.1:4 underlying f. that the mind can hurt itself
T-2........V.2:4 egocentricity and f. usually occur together
T-2........V.4:3 is always because f. has intruded on your
T-2........V.7:2 This often entails f., because you are
T-2........V.7:6 Nothing He perceives can induce f..
T-2........V.8:1 The f. of healing arises in the end from an
T-2..........VI.h F. and Conflict
T-2.......VI.1:4 F. cannot be controlled by me, but it can
T-2.......VI.1:5 be self-controlled. F. prevents me from
T-2.......VI.1:6 presence of f. shows that you have raised
T-2.......VI.4:1 The correction of f. *is* your responsibility.
T-2.......VI.4:2 When you ask for release from f., you are
T-2.......VI.4:3 conditions that have brought the f. about.
T-2.....VI.4:10 If you are sure that it is, there will be no f..
T-2.......VI.5:1 F. is always a sign of strain, arising
T-2.......VI.5:8 Whenever there is f., it is because you
T-2.....VI.5:10 second type, but will not obliterate the f..
T-2.......VI.6:7 Only your mind can produce f.. It does so
T-2.......VI.7:1 first that the conflict is an expression of f..
T-2.......VI.7:2 not to love, or the f. could not have arisen
T-2.......VI.7:5 Know first that this is f.. Fear arises from
T-2.......VI.7:6 fear. F. arises from lack of love. The only
T-2.......VI.8:8 the remedy, you have abolished the f..
T-2.......VI.9:1 Everyone experiences f.. Yet it would take
T-2.......VI.9:2 right thinking to realize why f. occurs.
T-2.......VI.9:4 hope to spare yourself from f. there are
T-2......VII.1:1 You may still complain about f., but you
T-2......VII.1:2 you cannot ask me to release you from f..
T-2......VII.3:1 Both miracles and f. come from thoughts
T-2......VII.3:3 choosing the miracle you *have* rejected f.,
T-2....VII.3:14 All f. is implicit in the second, and all love
T-2....VII.3:15 is therefore one between love and f..
T-2......VII.4:1 control f. because you yourself made it,
T-2......VII.4:2 attempting the mastery of f. is useless. In
T-2......VII.4:3 fact, it asserts the power of f. by the very
T-2......VII.5:3 F. is really nothing and love is everything.
T-2......VII.7:7 fundamental error that f. can be mastered
T-2.....VIII.2:8 that you free yourself from f. quickly,
T-2.....VIII.5:4 No one who lives in f. is really alive. Your
T-2...VIII.5:10 is no reason for f. to remain with you.
T-3..........I.1:1 before any residual f. still associated with
T-3..........I.4:2 It arises solely from f., and frightened
T-3.......III.1:7 and time, it is subject to either f. or love.
T-3.......III.1:8 love. Misperceptions produce f. and true
T-3.......III.3:3 to counteract an underlying f. that the
T-3.......III.3:4 f. inhibits the tendency to question at all.
T-3.......III.6:7 "F. God and keep His commandments"
T-3.......IV.3:9 is why you cannot escape from f. until you
T-3.......VI.5:9 You will also regard judgment with f.,
T-3.....VI.10:4 All f. comes ultimately, and sometimes by
T-3....VII.4:12 are filled with f. about what you make.
T-3....VII.5:10 you feel the f. of the destruction of your
T-3....VII.5:10 upon you as if it were the f. of death.
T-3......VII.6:5 You who f. salvation are choosing death.
T-4..........I.3:3 spirit. This is the change the ego must f.,
T-4..........I.3:6 your ego cannot but respond with f..
T-4..........I.9:1 God is not the author of f.. You are. You
T-4..........I.9:3 and have therefore made f. for yourself.
T-4........I.10:1 become totally without investment in f..
T-4........I.10:2 because f. is a witness to the separation,
T-4.......III.7:2 retain thousands of little scraps of f. that
T-4.......III.7:5 Watch your mind for the scraps of f., or
T-4.........V.3:3 sense the ego's f. of God is at least logical,
T-4.........V.3:4 ego. But f. of the body, with which the ego
T-5........in.2:2 If f. and love cannot coexist, and if it is
T-5.......III.4:7 ego as guide. This is bound to produce f..
T-5.......IV.1:1 What f. has hidden still is part of you.
T-5.......IV.1:2 Joining the Atonement is the way out of f.
T-5.........V.1:3 The ego's purpose is f., because only the
T-5.........V.2:7 Anything that engenders f. is divisive
T-5.........V.3:6 guilt, and you will f. punishment. The ego
T-5.......V.3:11 F. of retaliation from without follows,
T-5.......VI.8:3 thoughts from the ability to produce f..
T-5.......VI.9:4 be reinterpreted to release you from f..
T-5.......VI.9:6 cannot introduce the concept of f. into it.
T-5.....VI.10:1 not f. the Higher Court will condemn you.
T-6........in.1:1 relationship of anger to f. is not always so
T-6..........I.1:5 the crucifixion that is wholly devoid of f.,
T-6..........I.2:6 represents release from f. to anyone who
T-6..........I.2:8 life, and if you will consider it without f.,
T-6..........I.3:3 fosters assault, and assault promotes f..
T-6........I.14:3 and out of their own f. they spoke of the
T-6........I.16:2 I do not want you to allow any f. to enter
T-6........I.17:3 for f. makes appreciation impossible.
T-6.......IV.4:8 you are siding with an alliance of f..
T-6.........V.3:3 joy. Consider the f. and confusion a child
T-6.....V.A.5:6 Perhaps you think that f. as well as love
T-6.....V.A.5:8 communicate f. are promoting attack,
T-6.....V.B.1:1 a basic f. of retaliation and abandonment.
T-7.......IV.7:8 because it is a refusal to acknowledge f..
T-7.........V.5:8 exceptions. Only if there is f. does the idea
T-7.........V.5:9 are fearful because they are made by f..
T-7.........V.6:1 F. does not gladden. Healing does. Fear
T-7.........V.6:3 F. always makes exceptions. Healing
T-7.........V.6:5 does. F. produces dissociation, because it
T-7.........V.9:2 or an idol that you may worship out of f.,
T-7.......VI.1:5 F. and love make or create, depending on
T-7.......VI.4:5 Produced by f., the ego reproduces fear.
T-7.......VI.4:5 Produced by fear, the ego reproduces f..
T-7.......X.5:13 Unable to follow this guidance without f.,
T-7.......X.5:13 fear, he associates f. with guidance, and
T-7.......XI.3:4 Does it keep his heart untouched by f.,
T-8.......IV.2:3 maintained by f. of the same loneliness
T-8.........V.5:5 Whenever f. intrudes anywhere along the
T-8.......IX.3:2 expressions of the f. of awakening. They
T-8.......IX.3:3 to reinforce sleeping out of f. of waking.
T-8.......IX.5:1 Healing is release from the f. of waking
T-8.......IX.5:2 all healing involves replacing f. with love.
T-9..........I.1:1 F. of the Will of God is one of the
T-9..........I.2:2 seems to be the f. of God is really the fear
T-9..........I.2:2 of God is really the f. of your own reality.
T-9..........I.3:2 The association of truth and f., which

| | |
|---|---|
| T-9 I.4:5 | only source of f. in this process is what |
| T-9 I.9:4 | security of reality, f. is totally meaningless |
| T-9 I.9:6 | F. cannot be real without a cause, and |
| T-9 I.13:4 | reality is fearful, and f. cannot be created. |
| T-9 I.13:5 | As long as you believe that f. is possible, |
| T-9 II.1:4 | that its purpose is the escape from f.. |
| T-9 II.2:6 | he is not really asking for release from f., |
| T-9 II.3:3 | will ever be one that would increase f.. It |
| T-9 IV.5:1 | learned of me does not use f. to undo fear. |
| T-9 IV.5:1 | learned of me does not use fear to undo f.. |
| T-9 IV.9:2 | Do not f. the Last Judgment, but welcome |
| T-9 V.3:5 | appear retaliative, and f. His retribution. |
| T-9 V.5:1 | counteract f. is to reduce the importance |
| T-10 II.2:1 | reality brings more than merely lack of f.. |
| T-10 III.10:10 | Yet f. is not due them either, for nothing |
| T-10 III.10:11 | chosen to f. love because of its perfect |
| T-10 III.10:11 | f. you have been willing to give up your |
| T-11 I.10:4 | is your whole sickness and your whole f.. |
| T-11 I.10:5 | symptom of sickness and f. arises here, |
| T-11 III.4:4 | F. and grief are your guests, and they go |
| T-11 V.2:3 | you will be looking at is the source of f., |
| T-11 V.2:3 | are beginning to learn that f. is not real. |
| T-11 V.2:8 | Do not be afraid, then, to look upon f., for |
| T-11 V.4:2 | regard a delusional system without f., for |
| T-11 V.4:3 | F. becomes more obviously inappropriate |
| T-11 V.8:2 | For if the ego could give rise to f., it would |
| T-11 V.9:2 | Minimizing f., but not its undoing, is the |
| T-11 V.9:3 | without upholding it through f., and |
| T-11 V.10:1 | seems to separate you from God is only f., |
| T-11 V.10:3 | not accept the cost of f. if you recognize it. |
| T-11 V.10:5 | and you must f. unreality *because* you have |
| T-11 V.11:2 | Only by learning what f. is can you finally |
| T-11 V.12:5 | so diligently, has merely brought you f., |
| T-11 V.12:5 | difficult to maintain that f. is happiness. |
| T-11 V.12:6 | Upheld by f., this is what the ego would |
| T-11 V.12:9 | the insane would choose f. in place of love |
| T-11 V.12:10 | realize that only attack could produce f., |
| T-11 VIII.5:7 | f. of what you think it will demand of you. |
| T-11 VIII.7:7 | willing to ask the truth of God without f., |
| T-11 VIII.7:7 | learn that His answer is the release from f. |
| T-11 VIII.13:2 | in favor of reality, their f. goes with them. |
| T-11 VIII.13:3 | afraid, and laughs happily at his own f.. |
| T-11 VIII.14:4 | For f. lies not in reality, but in the minds |
| T-12 I.8:2 | recognize f. is not enough to escape from |
| T-12 I.8:3 | Spirit must still translate the f. into truth. |
| T-12 I.8:4 | If you were left with the f., once you had |
| T-12 I.8:5 | to recognize f. and face it without disguise |
| T-12 I.8:7 | you that f. itself is an appeal for help. This |
| T-12 I.8:8 | This is what recognizing f. really means. |
| T-12 I.8:11 | that f. and attack are inevitably associated |
| T-12 I.8:12 | If only attack produces f., and if you see |
| T-12 I.8:12 | it is, the unreality of f. must dawn on you. |
| T-12 I.8:13 | you. For f. *is* a call for love, in unconscious |
| T-12 I.9:1 | F. is a symptom of your own deep sense |
| T-12 I.9:2 | the loss, the basic cause of f. is removed. |
| T-12 I.9:3 | teach yourself that f. does not exist in you |
| T-12 I.9:5 | it. F. and love are the only emotions of |
| T-12 I.9:7 | By interpreting f. correctly as a positive |
| T-12 I.9:9 | If you raise what f. conceals to clear-cut |
| T-12 I.9:9 | predominance, f. becomes meaningless. |
| T-12 I.10:3 | Spirit's interpretation of f. does dispel it, |
| T-12 I.10:4 | Thus does the Holy Spirit replace f. with |
| T-12 II.8:1 | There is no f. in perfect love. We will but |
| T-12 II.8:3 | do not f. the unknown but the known. |
| T-12 II.9:1 | you who choose to banish f. must succeed |
| T-12 II.9:4 | this awareness for the awareness of f.? |
| T-12 II.9:5 | fear? When we have overcome f. –not by |
| T-12 II.10:7 | at the cause of f. and letting it go forever? |
| T-12 VIII.2:1 | his Father's protection and cannot f.. His |
| T-13 II.6:4 | You do not yet understand that any f. you |
| T-13 II.8:5 | no mistake about the depth of this f.. For |
| T-13 II.9:5 | for it is the recognition of love without f.. |
| T-13 III.h | The F. of Redemption |
| T-13 III.1:4 | one will countenance f. if he recognizes it. |
| T-13 III.1:5 | state of mind you are not afraid of f.. You |
| T-13 III.1:9 | without f. if you did not believe that, |
| T-13 III.1:9 | yourself something you f. even more. You |
| T-13 III.2:3 | Your f. of attack is nothing compared to |
| T-13 III.2:3 | is nothing compared to your f. of love. |

| | |
|---|---|
| T-13 III.7:5 | for any thoughts you may f. to uncover. |
| T-13 III.9:4 | Healing must be as complete as f., for love |
| T-13 III.9:4 | there is one spot of f. to mar its welcome. |
| T-13 III.10:6 | but still more did he f. his real Father, |
| T-13 V.1:1 | you have but two emotions, love and f.. |
| T-13 V.5:5 | And you react with f. to love, and draw |
| T-13 V.5:6 | Yet f. attracts you, and believing it is love, |
| T-13 V.5:7 | with figures of f. you have invited into it, |
| T-13 V.9:3 | Your "vision" comes from f., as His from |
| T-13 IX.7:5 | *The thing you f. is gone.* If you would look |
| T-13 X.8:6 | will not f. to look upon the Atonement |
| T-13 X.9:5 | F. not to look upon the lovely truth in you |
| T-13 X.10:4 | There is no f. in love, for love is guiltless. |
| T-13 X.10:5 | always loved your Father can have no f., |
| T-13 X.13:5 | without the f. that you will hear me not. I |
| T-13 XI.6:8 | this. F. not the Holy Spirit will fail in what |
| T-14 III.3:6 | *If I am guiltless, I have nothing to f.. I choose* |
| T-14 III.6:2 | darkness with light and f. with love. If he |
| T-14 III.15:4 | cannot happen can have no effects to f.. |
| T-14 V.6:6 | no trial, no f. that teaching this can fail to |
| T-14 V.10:8 | from f. and re-establish the reign of love. |
| T-14 VI.3:5 | and of ignorance look to them only for f., |
| T-14 VII.2:6 | you hid it and surrounded it with f.. |
| T-14 VII.2:7 | Under each cornerstone of f. on which |
| T-14 VII.2:8 | cannot know this, for by hiding truth in f. |
| T-14 VII.2:8 | the more you look at f. the less you see it, |
| T-14 VII.4:6 | joining thus becomes the source of f., for |
| T-14 VII.5:2 | ignorance, and love does not attack f.. |
| T-14 IX.4:4 | f. of death will be replaced with joy of life. |
| T-14 XI.5:2 | If you are wholly free of f. of any kind, |
| T-14 XI.9:4 | And every f. or pain or trial you have has |
| T-15 I.4:7 | ego's teaching is without the f. of death. |
| T-15 I.4:10 | ego must seem to keep f. from you to hold |
| T-15 I.4:11 | it must engender f. in order to maintain |
| T-15 I.6:6 | only way in which the ego allows the f. of |
| T-15 I.7:5 | uses it to undo the f. by which the ego |
| T-15 I.7:6 | no escape from f. in the ego's use of time. |
| T-15 I.8:2 | F. is not of the present, but only of the |
| T-15 I.8:3 | There is no f. in the present when each |
| T-15 I.9:7 | again you will go forth in time without f., |
| T-15 II.2:1 | and f. not the instant of holiness that will |
| T-15 II.2:1 | instant of holiness that will remove all f.. |
| T-15 II.2:2 | of peace is eternal *because* it is without f.. |
| T-15 II.6:4 | F. not that you will not be given help in |
| T-15 V.4:1 | relationships have elements of f. in them. |
| T-15 V.4:4 | And love, where f. has entered, cannot be |
| T-15 V.5:3 | removing as much f. as you will let Him. |
| T-15 VI.6:5 | behind it, can have faith in love without f. |
| T-15 VI.6:7 | F. not the holy instant will be denied you, |
| T-15 VII.9:3 | alliances, born of the f. of loneliness and |
| T-15 VII.11:1 | The Holy Spirit cannot teach through f.. |
| T-15 VII.13:3 | that it can overcome even this without f.. |
| T-15 VIII.1:6 | In the face of your f. of forgiveness, which |
| T-15 VIII.3:4 | F. not to give redemption over to your |
| T-15 X.4:5 | What is not love is always f., and nothing |
| T-15 X.5:1 | It is not necessary to follow f. through all |
| T-15 X.5:10 | this one idea, your f. of love would vanish. |
| T-15 X.6:7 | is therefore inseparable from attack and f. |
| T-15 X.6:8 | the price of love, which must be paid by f. |
| T-15 XI.1:1 | F. not to recognize the whole idea of |
| T-15 XI.2:9 | it. No f. can touch the Host Who cradles |
| T-15 XI.4:6 | you endow it with f. and try to cast it out, |
| T-16 II.6:3 | Regard this not with f., but with rejoicing. |
| T-16 II.6:6 | is true, just as you f., that to acknowledge |
| T-16 IX.2:2 | no f. that the attraction of those who |
| T-16 IV.4:9 | they find the f. of death is still upon them, |
| T-16 IV.4:10 | broken, f. rushes in and hatred triumphs. |
| T-16 IV.6:3 | Every illusion is one of f., whatever form |
| T-16 IV.7:2 | more than an attempt to bring love into f. |
| T-16 IV.7:2 | bring love into fear, and make it real in f.. |
| T-16 IV.9:2 | F. not to cross to the abode of peace and |
| T-16 IV.11:1 | Would you not go through f. to love? For |
| T-16 IV.11:9 | illusion, and therefore wholly without f.. |
| T-16 V.8:5 | Yet if all illusions are of f., and they can |
| T-16 V.8:5 | more than an "attractive" form of f., in |
| T-16 VI.7:5 | But f. it not, for it means only that you |
| T-16 VI.8:1 | F. not that you will be abruptly lifted up |
| T-17 III.9:4 | the real world or the world of guilt and f., |
| T-17 VIII.4:5 | fantasies of f. and fiery dreams of hell. |

| | |
|---|---|
| T-18 I.3:2 | F. involves substitution by definition, for |
| T-18 I.3:3 | F. is both a fragmented and fragmenting |
| T-18 I.3:7 | rejection for acting out a special form of f. |
| T-18 I.4:1 | that God is f. made but one substitution. |
| T-18 I.7:1 | to frighten you, say only, "God is not f., |
| T-18 II.4:4 | Anger and f. pervade it, and in an instant |
| T-18 II.6:3 | dreams of f. are changed to happy dreams |
| T-18 III.2:1 | retreating to the lesser forms of f., and |
| T-18 III.2:2 | your goal is the advance from f. to truth. |
| T-18 III.2:4 | F. seems to live in darkness, and when |
| T-18 III.3:2 | you have chosen, f. would be impossible. |
| T-18 III.3:8 | you retreat to the illusion your f. increases |
| T-18 III.3:9 | travel surely and very swiftly away from f. |
| T-18 III.4:4 | And f. must disappear before you now. Be |
| T-18 III.7:5 | for all the f. that you and your brother |
| T-18 III.7:7 | You have gone past f., for no two minds |
| T-18 IV.6:4 | And it is only f. that you will add, if you |
| T-18 V.1:4 | your dreams of f. to happy dreams, from |
| T-18 V.2:1 | remove all f. and hatred from your mind. |
| T-18 V.2:5 | to let Him remove all f. and hatred, and |
| T-18 V.5:5 | on thousands who believe that love is f., |
| T-18 V.6:1 | Holy Spirit your willingness, in spite of f., |
| T-18 V.6:4 | you or your brother to experience f. alone |
| T-18 VI.11:7 | awareness, and lost your f. of union. The |
| T-18 VI.11:10 | You have escaped from f. to peace, asking |
| T-18 IX.3:9 | to abandon Him at the outside ring of f., |
| T-18 IX.4:1 | of f. lies just below the level the body sees, |
| T-19 I.10:1 | Faith is the opposite of f., as much a part |
| T-19 I.10:1 | as much a part of love as f. is of attack. |
| T-19 III.1:3 | F. can become so acute that the sin is |
| T-19 III.1:8 | your own, could stamp it out through f.. |
| T-19 III.2:1 | does not think it possible that love, not f., |
| T-19 III.2:2 | For the ego brings sin to f., demanding |
| T-19 III.5:9 | held to the body by the f. of changed |
| T19 IV.A.4:4 | God. F. not this little obstacle. It cannot |
| T19 IV.A.10:1 | The attraction of guilt produces f. of love, |
| T19 IV.A.10:3 | As love must look past f., so must fear see |
| T19 IV.A.10:3 | look past fear, so must f. see love not. For |
| T19 IV.A.10:4 | end of guilt, as surely as f. depends on it. |
| T19 IV.A.10:6 | Overlooking guilt completely, it sees no f. |
| T19 IV.A.10:8 | F. is attracted to what love sees not, and |
| T19 IV.A.10:9 | exist. F. looks on guilt with just the same |
| T19 IV.A.11:2 | of f. are harshly ordered to seek out guilt, |
| T19 IV.A.11:4 | What f. would feed upon, love overlooks. |
| T19 IV.A.11:5 | What f. demands, love cannot even see. |
| T19 IV.A.11:6 | for f. is wholly absent from love's gentle |
| T19 IV.A.11:7 | love would look upon is meaningless to f., |
| T19 IV.A.12:4 | For f. is merciless even to its friends. Its |
| T19 IV.A.13:5 | For they are frantic with the pain of f., |
| T19 IV.A.14:1 | instead of those you trained through f.. |
| T19 IV.A.15:1 | but theirs, you will see f. no more. The |
| T19 IV.A.15:3 | The world contains no f. that you laid not |
| T19 IV.A.15:6 | given to replace the hungry dogs of f. you |
| T19 IV.A.15:7 | And they go forth to signify the end of f.. |
| T19 IV.B.2:9 | Here is the source of the idea that love is f. |
| T19 IV.B.3:3 | the messengers of f. that see the body, for |
| T19 IV.B.3:6 | But neither can it bring you f. of pain. |
| T19 IV.B.4:6 | You want communion, not the feast of f.. |
| T19 IV.B.12:5 | For it invites f. to enter and become your |
| T19 IV.B.12:6 | and whatever f. directs the body to do is |
| T19 IV.C.1:5 | to be the f. of death is really its attraction. |
| T19 IV.C.7:1 | Those who f. death see not how often and |
| T19 IV.C.9:1 | f. of death will go as its appeal is yielded |
| T19 IV.C.10:3 | What f. can enter and disturb the peace of |
| T19 IV.C.11:1 | anything seems to you to be a source of f., |
| T19 IV.C.11:1 | and the cold sweat of f. comes over it, |
| T19 IV.C.11:1 | the ego has perceived it as a symbol of f., |
| T19 IV.D.h | The Fourth Obstacle: The F. of God |
| T19 IV.D.1:1 | would you see without the f. of death? |
| T19 IV.D.2:3 | beyond it when the f. of death is gone. |
| T19 IV.D.3:4 | of your Self from you;–*the f. of God,* the |
| T19 IV.D.4:2 | this were gone, what could you f. but life? |
| T19 IV.D.4:6 | agreed never to let the f. of God be lifted, |
| T19 IV.D.5:1 | f. that raised it yields to the love beyond, |
| T19 IV.D.5:1 | to the love beyond, and so the f. is gone. |
| T19 IV.D.5:8 | wanting f. seemed to be holding them in |
| T19 IV.D.6:3 | the f. of vengeance of the ego you swore in |
| T19 IV.D.7:6 | no stab of f. nor the cold sweat of seeming |
| T19 IV.D.8:6 | be ready to look on terror with no f. at all. |

T19... IV.D.9:1 can look upon the f. of God unterrified,
T19. IV.D.11:1 the f. of God does need some preparation.
T19. IV.D.11:2 with pity and compassion, but not with f..
T19. IV.D.11:5 afraid of God *because* you f. your brother.
T19. IV.D.11:6 Those you do not forgive you f.. And no
T19. IV.D.11:7 no one reaches love with f. beside him.
T19. IV.D.12:6 that would heal it gives way to f.. Brother,
T-20......... I.2:5 the gift of love and not the "gift" of f.. You
T-20....... II.7:3 The f. of God is nothing to you now. Who
T-20....... II.8:9 There *is* no f. in love. The song of Easter is
T-20..... II.8:11 lift up our eyes together, not in f. but faith
T-20..... II.8:12 And there will be no f. in us, for in our
T-20........ II.9:4 We go beyond the veil of f., lighting each
T-20..... II.10:3 chill of f. and withering blight of sin alike.
T-20..... II.11:7 it to him shall you be led past f. to love.
T-20...... III.4:5 *is* frightened, and those who kill f. death.
T-20.... III.10:3 perfect, and without the veil of f. upon it?
T-20.... III.11:3 is no f. in perfect love *because* it knows no
T-20.... III.11:4 with charity within, what can it f. without
T-20.... III.11:9 as sinless, and there can *be* no f. in you.
T-20...... IV.6:7 without f. and where he rests a while, to
T-20....... V.2:1 of eternity sings of the end of sin and f..
T-20....... V.3:4 Do you recognize the f. that rises from the
T-20...... VI.1:6 broken into fragments and full of f.. The
T-20...... VI.6:8 realize is what you f. within your brother,
T-20...... VI.7:2 as it will surely do, and they retreat in f.,
T-20...... VI.7:4 Yet what you f. is but the herald of escape
T-20.... VI.12:8 Perhaps you f. your brother a little yet;
T-20.... VI.12:8 shadow of the f. of God remains with you.
T-20..... VII.9:3 that his sinlessness is *your* escape from f..
T-21...... III.7:2 limit to the body you hate because you f..
T-21...... III.7:5 free, removing hatred by removing f., not
T-21...... III.8:1 brothers from the body can have no f..
T-21......... IV.h The F. to Look Within
T-21...... IV.1:5 F. in association with sin the ego deems
T-21...... IV.1:6 It has no f. to let you feel ashamed. It
T-21.... IV.1:10 This merely seems to be the source of f..
T-21...... IV.2:5 Yet this is not the ego's hidden f., nor
T-21...... IV.2:8 Beneath your f. to look within because of
T-21...... IV.2:8 look within because of sin is yet another f.
T-21...... VI.8:1 the gift of Heaven, not the gift of f.. Does
T-22......... I.1:6 haunting f. of lack of meaning in yourself
T-22......... I.4:6 your f. of sin protect it from correction,
T-22......... I.4:6 for the attraction of guilt is only f.. Here is
T-22....... I.10:6 is to recognize that f. is meaningless. Into
T-22....... I.10:7 Into the holy home where f. is powerless
T-22....... II.3:5 happiness that does not last is really f..
T-22..... II.10:1 that it must be healed, and not with f..
T-22....... V.2:5 would you be saved from but what you f.?
T-22....... V.4:1 weak is f.; how little and how meaningless
T-22...... VI.5:7 The means of sinlessness can know no f.
T-22.... VI.10:7 that seems to keep the f. of God in place,
T-22.... VI.11:6 think that They are separate, because of f.
T-22.... VI.14:4 Look not with f. upon this happy fact,
T-22.... VI.15:3 Would you regret you cannot f. alone,
T-22.... VI.15:3 is there, which makes all f. impossible?
T-23....... in.1:3 The sinless cannot f., for sin of any kind is
T-23....... in.2:4 It is as certain you will f. what you attack
T-23....... in.2:6 with him there, protecting him from f..
T-23....... in.3:1 with your head held high, and f. no evil.
T-23....... in.3:4 sin and f. and happily returned to love.
T-23....... I.2:10 And f. will reign in madness, and will
T-23......... I.8:6 Conflict is fearful, for it is the birth of f..
T-23....... I.12:4 War is the condition in which f. is born,
T-23....... II.5:7 f. of God and of each other now appears
T-23....... II.7:1 See how the f. of God is reinforced by
T-23..... II.15:6 And f., with ashen lips and sightless eyes,
T-23..... II.15:7 lovely do the laws of f. make death appear
T-23..... II.15:8 who saved the Son of God for f. and death
T-23..... II.20:6 Certain it is illusions will bring f. because
T-23...... III.1:5 f. of punishment the murderer must feel?
T-23...... III.6:4 and the f. that haunts the place of death is
T-23...... IV.1:2 The f. of God is fear of life, and not of
T-23...... IV.1:2 The fear of God is f. of life, and not of
T-23...... IV.1:9 And it is this you f., and not the form.
T-24......... I.8:1 The f. of God and of your brother comes
T-24....... II.9:2 and every vestige of the f. of God will melt
T-24..... II.10:5 And it is this you f., for if He is not special
T-24....... V.6:3 His Love for God replaces all the f. you
T-24 ........ VI.h Salvation from F.
T-24 ..... VI.1:2 He is your savior from the dreams of f..
T-24 ..... VI.1:3 and f. that what you have will scatter with
T-24 ..... VI.6:6 let the f. of God no longer hold the vision
T-25 ....... II.1:1 the body's eyes perceive fills you with f.?
T-25 ....... II.2:2 but f. and guilt been your reward. How
T-25 ..... VI.1:2 can see no evil; nothing in the world to f.,
T-25 ... VIII.6:3 entail. And so they f. the Holy Spirit, and
T-25 ... VIII.6:6 deep suspicion and the chill of f. comes
T-25 . VIII.14:7 Let love decide, and never f. that you, in
T-25 ..... IX.2:3 God's justice warrants gratitude, not f..
T-26 ..... IV.3:4 is? Who could f. love, and stand upon the
T-26 VII.11:12 Is f. a treasure? Can uncertainty be what
T-26 ... VIII.3:3 error still obscured that is the source of f..
T-26 ... VIII.3:5 And it is here you f. the loss would lie. Do
T-26 ... VIII.3:6 Do not project this f. to time, for time is
T-26 ... VIII.4:3 Future loss is not your f.. But present
T-26 ... VIII.4:7 And therefore must it be that if you f.,
T-26 ... VIII.5:4 f. effects unless he thought they had been
T-26 ... VIII.5:5 Belief in sin arouses f., and like its cause,
T-26 ... VIII.5:9 of time that sin and f. have overlooked,
T-26 ... VIII.6:5 unfold in time and f. they may not come,
T-27 ........ I.1:3 will f. no evil and no shadows in the night
T-27 ........ I.5:8 the poisoned and relentless sting of f..
T-27 ........ I.9:8 apart from all experience of love or f.. For
T-27 ......... II.h The F. of Healing
T-27 ..... II.14:3 it, and hates it still as symbol of his f..
T-27 ..... III.5:9 interval it has a use that now you f., but
T-27 ..... III.7:4 The choice you f. to lose you never had.
T-27 ...... V.2:8 that is required for a healing is a lack of f..
T-27 ...... V.5:2 suffering whispers, "What is there to f.?"
T-27 ...... V.9:5 F. you not the way that you perceive them
T-27 ...... VI.5:6 them all as one, and called by name of f..
T-27 ...... VI.5:7 fear. As f. is witness unto death, so is the
T-27 .. VII.12:4 see, the birthplace of illusions and of f.,
T-27 .. VII.13:4 sweat of terror and a scream of mortal f.,
T-27 .. VII.13:4 his calmer mind to welcome, not to f., the
T-27 .. VII.13:5 and gave him means to waken without f..
T-27 .. VII.14:3 you dreamed in terror and in f. of death.
T-27 . VIII.5:10 the grounds for laughter, not a cause for f.
T-28 ............. h THE UNDOING OF F.
T-28 ...... I.10:4 would witness to is but the f. of God. He
T-28 ...... I.10:5 God. He has not done the thing you f.. No
T-28 ...... I.13:1 that has no f. to keep the memory away!
T-28 ...... I.13:5 And what is now remembered is not f.,
T-28 ...... I.13:5 but rather is the Cause that f. was made to
T-28 ...... I.14:7 Effects are changelessly eternal, beyond f.,
T-28 ...... I.15:8 no f. that He will fail in what He wills.
T-28 ....... II.7:4 f. was held in place because he did not see
T-28 ....... II.7:7 Thus does he f. his own attack, but sees it
T-28 ....... II.9:5 heard, because it seems to be the call to f..
T-28 ..... II.11:1 returns the cause of f. to you who made it.
T-28 ..... III.1:6 add your dream of f. to one that is already
T-28 ..... III.4:1 The end of dreaming is the end of f., and
T-28 ... IV.1:10 you are evil, for you share in dreams of f..
T-28 ..... IV.2:8 It is the dream you f., and not the mind.
T-28 ..... IV.4:3 on brotherhood, and not on dreams of f..
T-28 ..... IV.4:6 And dreams of f. will haunt the little gap,
T-28 ......... V.h The Alternate to Dreams of F.
T-28 ...... V.1:6 God is the Alternate to dreams of f.. Who
T-28 ...... V.2:3 The f. is gone from them because you did
T-28 ...... V.2:4 Where f. has gone there love must come,
T-28 ...... V.7:6 you have lost the f. of recognizing love.
T-28 ..... VI.3:1 thing you hate and f. and loathe and want
T-28 .... VII.6:1 in what was made for danger and for f.?
T-29 ........ I.2:1 Here is the f. of God most plainly seen.
T-29 ........ I.2:2 For love *is* treacherous to those who f.,
T-29 ........ I.2:2 fear, since f. and hate can never be apart.
T-29 ........ I.3:1 The f. of God! The greatest obstacle that
T-29 ........ I.6:3 and when to shrink more safely into f.. It
T-29 ........ I.7:2 But f. demands the sacrifice of love, for in
T-29 ........ I.7:2 love, for in love's presence f. cannot abide
T-29 ........ I.8:2 You do not f. its weakness, but its lack of
T-29 ........ I.8:7 of seeming f. around the happy message,
T-29 ........ I.9:3 Without the f. of God, what could induce
T-29 ....... II.3:3 and sin are one illusion, as are hate and f.,
T-29 ..... IV.2:1 as much as those in which the f. is seen.
T-29 ..... IV.2:2 For every dream is but a dream of f., no
T-29 ..... IV.2:3 The f. is seen within, without, or both. Or
T-29 ..... IV.2:5 the dream, for f. is the material of dreams
T-29 ..... IV.2:7 because you did not recognize the f.. You
T-29 ..... IV.3:3 of every dream, for they are made of f..
T-29 ..... IV.3:4 veils the heavy lump of f. that is their core
T-29 ..... IV.5:3 the Holy Spirit gives is never one of f..
T-29 ....... V.8:1 the core of f. in every dream that has been
T-29 ..... VI.6:2 How free from f., how filled with blessing
T-29 .... VII.4:6 and f. to look upon your devastation, but
T-29 .... VII.9:6 f. of God is but the fear of loss of idols. It
T-29 .... VII.9:6 fear of God is but the f. of loss of idols. It
T-29 .... VII.9:7 It is not the f. of loss of your reality. But
T-29 ... VIII.4:7 to make you tremble and to quail in f..
T-29 ..... IX.9:1 Whenever you feel f. in any form,–and
T-29 ..... IX.9:3 Your self-betrayal must result in f., for
T-29 ..... IX.9:3 must result in fear, for f. *is* judgment,
T-29 ... IX.10:4 the dreamer full release from dreams of f..
T-29 ... IX.10:5 f. his judgment for he has judged no one,
T-30 ...... in.1:5 to forgiving dreams and out of pain and f.
T-30 ........ I.2:6 produce confusion and uncertainty and f.
T-30 ........ I.3:4 This leads to f., because it contradicts
T-30 ........ I.4:3 will serve to let you be directed without f.,
T-30 ........ I.7:3 f. of being answered in a different way
T-30 ...... I.13:2 that will protect you from the ravages of f.
T-30 ....... II.3:2 and thus the rule of f. established there.
T-30 ....... II.3:3 your will to hate and be a prisoner to f., a
T-30 ... III.10:2 the myriad of forms that f. can take; quite
T-30 ..... IV.5:3 they bring f. *because* they hide the truth.
T-30 ..... IV.8:6 asks forgiveness be the substitute for f..
T-30 ..... IV.8:8 The gap is emptied of the toys of f., and
T-30 ....... V.1:2 F. is not its goal, for the escape from guilt
T-30 ....... V.1:4 to twist and fit into the dream of f..
T-30 ....... V.3:4 And f. has dropped away, because he is
T-30 ....... V.4:4 eternity. But f. is gone because its purpose
T-30 ....... V.7:1 brothers join in purpose in the world of f.
T-30 ....... V.8:1 the world of f. when you have recognized
T-30 ....... V.8:2 perfect confidence away from f. forever,
T-30 ....... V.9:2 And with it goes all hatred and all f.. Look
T-30 ..... V.10:8 beats in hope and does not pound in f..
T-30 ..... VI.1:3 It is here escape from f. begins, and will
T-30 ..... VI.3:2 F. cannot arise unless attack is justified,
T-30 ..... VI.4:3 Thus is the f. of God the sure result of
T-30 ..... VI.4:4 himself as guilty can avoid the f. of God.
T-30 .... VII.3:8 F. is a judgment never justified. Its
T-30 .. VII.3:10 thing you f. has fearful meaning in itself.
T-30 .... VII.7:4 state so seemingly unsafe that f. must rise
T-30 ... VIII.5:1 to you to see in happy form, devoid of f..
T-30 ... VIII.6:7 is. Why should you f. to see the Christ in
T-31 ........ I.8:1 guiltless is a world in which there is no f.,
T-31 ........ I.9:5 God were f. indeed if he whom He created
T-31 ...... I.10:1 f. of God results as surely from the lesson
T-31 ...... I.10:2 For hate must father f., and look upon its
T-31 ..... III.5:2 survive the ravages of f. except in murder
T-31 ....... V.5:2 and a f. so devastating that the face that
T-31 ....... V.7:5 hot with hatred and distortions born of f..
T-31 ..... V.16:7 you. Yet have no f. it will not be undone.
T-31 .... VII.7:5 guilty thoughts and concepts born of f..
T-31 .... VII.7:6 And what you see is hell, for f. *is* hell. All
T-31 .... VII.9:1 of Christ, the f. of God and of salvation,
T-31 .. VII.14:3 except to die, and end the dream of f..
T-31 ... VIII.5:6 And thus are miracles as natural as f. and
T-31 ... VIII.7:1 world uncertain, lonely, and in constant f.
W-pI ...... 5.1:3 you. The upset may seem to be f., worry,
W-pI ...... 6.1:2 to name both the form of upset (anger, f.,
W-pI ......... 13.h A meaningless world engenders f..
W-pI .... 13.3:1 the meaningless, and accept it without f..
W-pI .... 13.4:7 *A meaningless world engenders f. because I*
W-pI .... 13.5:4 of overt or covert f. which it may arouse.
W-pI .... 14.3:3 Some of them will lead you directly into f.
W-pI .... 14.5:4 attacks, or whatever may arouse f. in you.
W-pI .... 16.3:1 either peace or war; either love or f.. A
W-pI .... 16.3:3 to dismiss f. thoughts as unimportant,
W-pI .... 20.2:6 and sorrow, pleasure and pain, love and f.
W-pI .... 22.2:5 and kill. All that you f. does not exist.
W-pI .... 23.1:1 only way out of f. that will ever succeed.
W-pI .... 26.2:1 will be projected, you will f. attack. And if
W-pI .... 26.2:2 And if you f. attack, you must believe that
W-pI .... 26.6:2 worry, anger, a sense of imposition, f.,
W-pI .... 27.2:4 If f. of loss still persists, add further: *It can*
W-pI .... 34.3:2 Search your mind for f. thoughts, anxiety-

| | |
|---|---|
| W-pI.....39.6:2 | appear; uneasiness, depression, anger, f., |
| W-pI.....41.1:3 | misery, suffering and intense f. of loss. |
| W-pI.....41.3:2 | It will cure all sorrow and pain and f. and |
| W-pI....41.10:1 | can indeed afford to laugh at f. thoughts, |
| W-pI.....44.9:1 | your eyes closed unless you are aware of f. |
| W-pI.....46.2:2 | F. condemns and love forgives. |
| W-pI.....46.2:3 | Forgiveness thus undoes what f. has |
| W-pI.....46.6:5 | *No f. is possible in a mind beloved of God.* |
| W-pI.....47.2:2 | trust is unwarranted, and to justify f., |
| W-pI.....47.4:4 | your life which you have invested with f., |
| W-pI........48.h | There is nothing to f.. |
| W-pI.....48.1:3 | In truth there is nothing to f.. It is very |
| W-pI.....48.3:1 | The presence of f. is a sure sign that you |
| W-pI.....48.3:2 | to f. shows that somewhere in your mind, |
| W-pI.....48.3:3 | to do this there is indeed nothing to f.. |
| W-pI.....53.3:1 | (13) A meaningless world engenders f.. |
| W-pI.....53.3:2 | totally insane engenders f. because it is |
| W-pI.....53.3:8 | will escape all the effects of the world of f., |
| W-pI.....54.5:4 | through me has enabled love to replace f., |
| W-pI.....60.3:1 | (48) There is nothing to f.. How safe the |
| W-pI.....60.3:6 | be to f. in a world that I have forgiven, |
| W-pI.....62.3:4 | It will take away all f. and guilt and pain. |
| W-pI.....64.3:2 | and only the f. of the ego that induces you |
| W-pI.....66.7:5 | but the f. that the ego always engenders, |
| W-pI.....68.2:5 | Who can dream of hatred and not f. God? |
| W-pI.....78.4:3 | as we look out toward truth, away from f.. |
| W-pI.....78.4:5 | Someone, perhaps, you f. and even hate; |
| W-pI....93.11:1 | dispel the illusion of f. by repeating these |
| W-pI.....94.3:8 | This is the Self that knows no f., nor could |
| W-pI.....97.1:5 | No chill of f. can enter, for your mind has |
| W-pI.....98.3:1 | The guiltless have no f., for they are safe |
| W-pI.....99.9:8 | what you need to learn to lay all f. aside, |
| W-pI....99.11:1 | of doubt and f. forever from your mind. If |
| W-pI....99.12:5 | mind and let all f. be gently laid aside, |
| W-pI...100.6:3 | joy; no f. besets him to disturb his peace. |
| W-pI...101.2:6 | They would escape Him in their f.. And |
| W-pI...101.6:3 | F. not the Will of God. But turn to it in |
| W-pI...102.3:3 | Here is your peace, and here there is no f.. |
| W-pI...103.2:1 | F. is associated then with love, and its |
| W-pI...103.2:2 | in truth, bear witness to the f. of God, |
| W-pI...103.2:5 | *To f. Him is to be afraid of joy.* Begin your |
| W-pI...103.2:6 | corrects the false belief that God is f.. It |
| W-pI...103.3:2 | the happiness it brings as truth replaces f. |
| W-pI...105.3:2 | For giving has become a source of f., and |
| W-pI...107.3:2 | Without illusions there could be no f., no |
| W-pI...109.5:1 | pain, no f. of future and no past regrets. |
| W-pI...110.1:3 | God created was replaced by f. and evil, |
| W-pI...110.1:4 | as God created you f. has no meaning, |
| W-pI...110.3:1 | death be substitute for life, or f. for love. |
| W-pI...121.2:1 | The unforgiving mind is full of f., and |
| W-pI...122.2:3 | eyelids so you see no dreams of f. and evil, |
| W-pI...130.2:4 | F. must make blind, for this its weapon is: |
| W-pI...130.2:4 | is: That which you f. to see you cannot see |
| W-pI...130.2:5 | but f. obscures in darkness what is there. |
| W-pI...130.3:1 | What, then, can f. project upon the world |
| W-pI...130.3:3 | Truth is eclipsed by f., and what remains |
| W-pI...130.4:1 | F. has made everything you think you see |
| W-pI.134.12:4 | made to chain his mind to f. and misery. |
| W-pI...135.3:2 | It stems from f., increasing fear as each |
| W-pI...135.3:2 | fear, increasing f. as each defense is made. |
| W-pI...135.3:4 | speaks of f. made real and terror justified. |
| W-pI...135.5:1 | Yet it is not the body that can f., nor be a |
| W-pI...135.5:1 | the body that can fear, nor be a thing of f.. |
| W-pI...137.6:4 | while f. remains the one reality that can |
| W-pI...138.2:6 | where it could only be perceived with f.. |
| W-pI.138.10:1 | is as sure as is the ending of the f. of hell, |
| W-pI.138.11:4 | obscurity for f. to be invested there. Now |
| W-pI...152.1:3 | No one can grieve nor f. nor think him |
| W-pI...152.2:5 | Can f. and sickness enter in a mind where |
| W-pI...153.5:2 | You know not what you do, in f. of it. You |
| W-pI...153.7:2 | Christ and come to f. His Father's anger. |
| W-pI...153.9:2 | Now we cannot f., for we have left all |
| W-pI.153.12:2 | teach them that the game of f. is gone. His |
| W-pI.153.12:5 | The game of f. is gladly laid aside, when |
| W-pI......160.h | I am at home. F. is the stranger here. |
| W-pI...160.1:1 | F. is a stranger to the ways of love. |
| W-pI...160.1:2 | Identify with f., and you will be a stranger |
| W-pI...160.4:2 | it f. or you who are unsuited to the home |
| W-pI...160.4:3 | Is f. His Own, created in His likeness? Is it |
| W-pI...160.4:4 | it f. that love completes, and is completed |
| W-pI...160.4:5 | There is no home can shelter love and f.. |
| W-pI...160.4:7 | If you are real, then f. must be illusion. |
| W-pI...160.4:8 | And if f. is real, then you do not exist at |
| W-pI...161.1:3 | where f. and anger had prevailed before. |
| W-pI...161.5:2 | are but symbols for a concrete form of f.. |
| W-pI...161.5:3 | F. without symbols calls for no response, |
| W-pI...161.5:5 | But f. attaches to specifics, being false. |
| W-pI...161.6:7 | be the seat of f. except what thinks of fear |
| W-pI...161.6:7 | be the seat of fear except what thinks of f. |
| W-pI...161.7:5 | F. is insatiable, consuming everything its |
| W-pI...161.8:2 | beholds is his own f. external to himself, |
| W-pI...161.8:3 | intensity of rage projected f. must spawn. |
| W-pI...161.9:7 | Ask him not to symbolize your f.. Would |
| W-pI.161.12:4 | is your safe escape from anger and from f. |
| W-pI.161.12:5 | and perceive in him the symbol of your f.. |
| W-pI...163.1:2 | It may appear as sadness, f., anxiety or |
| W-pI...163.2:1 | Embodiment of f., the host of sin, god of |
| W-pI...165.8:4 | His Love remains beyond our every f.. |
| W-pI...166.9:1 | Your ancient f. has come upon you now, |
| W-pI.166.14:4 | f. but teaches them their fears are justified |
| W-pI...168.4:3 | and watch f. disappear from every face as |
| W-pI...169.2:1 | God within a world of seeming hate and f. |
| W-pI...169.2:2 | By grace alone the hate and f. are gone, |
| W-pI...169.2:2 | grace can not believe the world of f. is real |
| W-pI...170.1:5 | from dangerous invasion and from f.. |
| W-pI...170.2:1 | the idea that to defend from f. is to attack! |
| W-pI...170.2:2 | For here is f. begot and fed with blood, to |
| W-pI...170.2:3 | And thus is f. protected, not escaped. |
| W-pI...170.3:3 | now has an "enemy," an opposite; and f., |
| W-pI...170.5:2 | For f. becomes your safety and protector |
| W-pI...170.5:3 | love is endowed with attributes of f.. For |
| W-pI...170.9:1 | do not think that f. is the escape from fear |
| W-pI...170.9:1 | do not think that fear is the escape from f. |
| W-pI...170.9:3 | surmounting, is the f. of God Himself. |
| W-pI...170.9:4 | which enthrones the thought of f. as god. |
| W-pI...170.9:5 | For f. is loved by those who worship it, |
| W-pI.170.10:2 | not confused its attributes with those of f. |
| W-pI.170.10:3 | Yet must the worshippers of f. perceive |
| W-pI.170.11:4 | And so the f. of God returned with you. |
| W-pI.170.12:6 | Now has f. made way for love, as God |
| W-pI...175.2:2 | F. is the stranger here. God is but Love, |
| W-pI...182.8:3 | all words, untouched by f. and doubt, |
| W-pI...187.9:2 | could f. to look upon such lovely holiness |
| W-pI...187.9:3 | great illusion of the f. of God diminishes |
| W-pI.187.10:1 | are we one in thought, for f. has gone. |
| W-pI...189.2:1 | Who could feel f. in such a world as this? |
| W-pI...189.3:2 | through darkened eyes of malice and of f., |
| W-pI...190.3:2 | God is denied, confused with f., perceived |
| W-pI...190.3:6 | And f., denying love and using pain to |
| W-pI...190.7:7 | Your thoughts of death envelop it in f., |
| W-pI...190.8:4 | pain does f. appear to triumph over love, |
| W-pI...190.9:2 | Lay down all thoughts of danger and of f.. |
| W-pI...192.4:2 | is the means by which the f. of death is |
| W-pI...192.5:4 | the core of anguish and the seat of f.? |
| W-pI...193.5:4 | the dream of sin, and rid the mind of f.. |
| W-pI...194.7:4 | What can he f.? And what can he regard |
| W-pI...194.7:6 | escaped all f. of future pain has found his |
| W-pI...195.8:4 | The f. of God is now undone at last, and |
| W-pI...196.5:3 | merely stood for the belief the f. of God is |
| W-pI...196.5:5 | without the f. of hell upon his heart? |
| W-pI...196.6:4 | The f. of God is real to anyone who thinks |
| W-pI...196.7:1 | as will permit f. of retaliation to abate, |
| W-pI...196.7:3 | it is but your thoughts that bring you f., |
| W-pI...196.8:3 | thoughts, the f. of God must disappear. |
| W-pI...196.8:4 | then believe that f. is caused without. And |
| W-pI...196.9:2 | and need not f. its vengeance and pursuit. |
| W-pI...196.9:3 | deadly f. of God projection hides behind. |
| W-pI.196.10:2 | once and for all, that it is you you f., the |
| W-pI.196.10:4 | to be an enemy outside you had to f.. And |
| W-pI.196.10:5 | your mortal enemy; the source of f.. |
| W-pI.196.11:3 | For f. of God has disappeared. And you |
| W-pI.196.11:6 | Step back from f., and make advance to |
| W-pI.196.12:2 | When the f. of God is gone, there are no |
| W-pI...197.7:1 | with the end of this belief is f. forever over |
| W-pI...199.2:2 | and f. can never enter in a mind that has |
| W-pI...200.6:6 | between success and failure; love and f.? |
| W-pII..225.1:2 | *with f. behind and only peace ahead. How* |
| W-pII..232.2:2 | Today, practice the end of f.. Have faith in |
| W-pII ....240.h | F. is not justified in any form. |
| W-pII .240.1:1 | F. is deception. It attests that you have |
| W-pII .240.1:8 | There is no f. in us, for we are each a part |
| W-pII .....3.2:2 | It symbolizes f.. And what is fear except |
| W-pII .....3.2:3 | fear. And what is f. except love's absence? |
| W-pII .244.1:3 | *he f. or doubt or fail to know he cannot suffer* |
| W-pII .259.1:5 | And what but sin could be the source of f. |
| W-pII .259.1:5 | love the attributes of f. and of attack? |
| W-pII .....5.3:2 | but can quite suddenly revert to f., where |
| W-pII .....5.3:3 | creates in truth, and truth can never f.. |
| W-pII .....5.5:5 | F. does not exist. Identify with love, and |
| W-pII .265.1:5 | There is no f. in it. Let no appearance of |
| W-pII .272.2:2 | as hell, and love will happily replace all f.. |
| W-pII .273.2:2 | *What need have I to f. that anything can rob* |
| W-pII ....274.h | Today belongs to love. Let me not f.. |
| W-pII .274.2:2 | day to Him, and there will be no f. today, |
| W-pII .278.2:2 | *and have brought a dream of f. into my mind* |
| W-pII .278.2:4 | *to You instead of madness and instead of f..* |
| W-pII .....7.2:2 | from the witnesses of f. to those of love. |
| W-pII .282.2:4 | *The name of f. is simply a mistake. Let me* |
| W-pII .287.1:5 | And would I rather live with f. than love? |
| W-pII .....8.1:3 | Your world is seen through eyes of f., and |
| W-pII .....8.1:4 | and witnesses to f. can not be found. |
| W-pII .....8.2:1 | a sure correction for the sights of f. and |
| W-pII ....293.h | All f. is past and only love is here. |
| W-pII .293.1:1 | All f. is past, because its source is gone, |
| W-pII .293.1:3 | it, and showing me distorted forms of f.? |
| W-pII .293.2:2 | *world is singing underneath the sounds of f..* |
| W-pII .294.1:5 | for thoughts of f. are not invested there, |
| W-pII .295.1:7 | F. appears in many different forms, but |
| W-pII .298.1:1 | permits my love to be accepted without f.. |
| W-pII .298.1:5 | sure that I go through f. to meet my Love. |
| W-pII .302.1:6 | *for f. must disappear when love has come.* |
| W-pII .305.1:3 | it to truth, no more to be the home of f.. |
| W-pII .306.1:3 | Today I can go past all f., and be restored |
| W-pII ....309.h | I will not f. to look within today. |
| W-pII .309.1:5 | I f. to look within because I think I made |
| W-pII .310.2:4 | There is no room in us for f. today, for we |
| W-pII ...10.3:2 | To f. God's saving grace is but to fear |
| W-pII ...10.3:2 | but to f. complete release from suffering, |
| W-pII .313.1:1 | *all things as sinless, so that f. has gone, and* |
| W-pII .314.1:3 | so that f. has lost its idols and its images, |
| W-pII .322.2:5 | *loss can I anticipate except the loss of f., and* |
| W-pII ....323.h | I gladly make the "sacrifice" of f.. |
| W-pII .323.2:4 | for f. has gone and only love remains. |
| W-pII .330.1:6 | things the dream of f. appears to offer us. |
| W-pII ...12.2:2 | In f. it stands beyond the Everywhere, |
| W-pII ...12.3:4 | What can he know of f. and punishment, |
| W-pII .331.1:7 | *F. is a dream, and has no will that can conflict* |
| W-pII ....332.h | F. binds the world. Forgiveness sets it |
| W-pII .332.2:2 | *F. holds it prisoner. And yet Your Love has* |
| W-pII .338.1:2 | is everyone released at last from f.. Now |
| W-pII .338.1:5 | f. thought for a happy thought of love. He |
| W-pII .339.1:9 | confusing pain with joy, or f. with love. |
| W-pII .340.2:6 | Not one who will remain in f., and none |
| W-pII ...13.1:6 | f. must slip away under the gentle remedy |
| W-pII ....348.h | I have no cause for anger or for f., For |
| W-pII .348.1:4 | *You. What need have I for anger or for f.?* |
| W-pII .348.1:8 | *can I f., when You created me in holiness as* |
| W-pII ...14.1:3 | *In me is love perfected, f. impossible, and joy* |
| M-4 .....I.A.4:4 | will not generalize the lesson for f. of loss |
| M-4 .......V.1:2 | means that f. is now impossible, and what |
| M-4 ..VIII.1:10 | seen or yet to come can cause them f.. |
| M-5 .....II.4:11 | without distortion and without f., they re- |
| M-7 ...........2:5 | that his own uncertainty is not love but f., |
| M-7 ...........5:4 | there is a f. of weakness and vulnerability. |
| M-7 ...........5:5 | Perhaps there is a f. of failure and shame |
| M-10 .........6:6 | of sickening despair and f. of death; all |
| M-12 .........3:6 | the f. that truth would encounter in them. |
| M-12 .........3:7 | only where it is welcomed without f.. So |
| M-15 .........1:4 | until it is no longer associated with f.. |
| M-16 .........5:7 | of rest, and orients you away from f.. If it |
| M-16 .........6:8 | And it is this you f., and only this. How |
| M-16 .....11:10 | F. is withdrawn from them, and so they |
| M-17 .........1:3 | This strengthens f., and makes the magic |
| M-17 .........1:7 | pain, f. and disaster to come to him. Let |
| M-17 .........5:1 | magic thoughts is a basic cause of f.. |
| M-17 .........7:5 | the f. of God most starkly represented. |
| M-17 .......9:12 | The f. of God is causeless. But His Love is |

M-17 9:13 Love is Cause of everything beyond all f.,
M-18 3:12 *there is. F. is illusion, for you are like Him.*
M-19 4:3 it is this that overcomes the f. of death.
M-19 4:9 not see you hate and f. your Self as enemy
M-21 5:1 f. about the validity of what he hears. And
M-25 2:6 limits are placed out of f., for without
M-25 4:9 what is withheld from love is given to f.,
M-27 3:1 Death is the symbol of the f. of God. His
M-27 3:8 of life." God is insane, and f. alone is real.
M-27 4:6 There is either a god of f. or One of Love.
M-27 4:9 make death because He did not make f..
M-27 5:6 His Own creation must stand in f. of Him.
M-27 6:11 opposite, and f. would be as real as love?
M-28 4:4 And in his freedom is the end of f.. No
M-28 4:5 of f. and misperceptions of the universe.
M-29 3:6 of functions not your own is the basis of f.
M-29 3:7 you have done so, making f. inevitable.
M-29 3:8 it belongs is thus the escape from f.. And
M-29 7:9 your sense of frailty and your f. of harm,
C-2 8:1 of pain, the f. of dying and the urge to kill,
C-4 8:3 out of all f. and given back to love.
C-5 3:5 by sin and evil, malice, f. or death.
P-1 1:3 rests. No one in this world escapes f., but
P-2 IV.7:7 F. cannot long be hidden by illusions, for
P-2 VII.7:2 see in him because of this they f. indeed.
P-3 II.6:6 appeal and turn to dreams of f., which is
S-1 I.6:5 the goodness of God prays without f..
S-1 I.6:6 And one who prays without f. cannot but
S-1 II.8:8 the illusion of death and the f. of God.
S-1 III.2:3 made out of f. by those who cherish guilt.
S-1 III.4:2 time be followed by a deep retreat into f..
S-1 III.4:3 recognized they bring their f. with them.
S-1 III.4:7 F. of escape makes it difficult to welcome
S-1 III.4:8 released without an insane f. for yourself?
S-1 III.4:10 heavy, and your f. of letting it go is strong
S-1 III.5:5 your heart is lifted and your f. released.
S-3 in.1:1 sure, easing the pain of f. and offering the
S-3 I.2:5 they feel f. as bodies change and sicken.
S-3 II.1:3 Only false healing can give way to f., so
S-3 III.6:6 is no f. in one who has been truly healed,
S-3 III.6:6 stand, and f. has given way at last to God.
S-3 IV.2:4 F. has no haven here, for love has come in
S-3 IV.5:5 He Who is Love becomes the source of f.,
S-3 IV.5:5 of fear, for only f. can now be justified.
S-3 IV.8:1 of retribution and a little life beset with f.,

## fear's 7

T19. IV.A.12:3 F. messengers are trained through terror,
T19..IV.B.13:2 Under f. orders the body will pursue guilt,
T-21 IV.8:4 not held back by f. insane insistence that
W-pI 161.6:3 reason bodies easily become f. symbols.
W-pI 161.8:1 a brother as a body sees him as f. symbol.
W-pI. 170.10:3 perceive their own confusion in f. "enemy
S-1 III.4:3 For f. defenses are fearful in themselves,

## fear-prone 1

T-3 IV.3:7 and this is the essence of the f. condition,

## fear-weakened 1

T-2 IV.4:8 They are already in a f. state. If they are

## feared 35

T-13 III.10:6 He f. what he had made, but still more
T-13 IX.8:13 learn that what you f. was there has been
T-14 VI.1:9 cannot be loved, and so it must be f..
T-15 I.4:8 of merely as an end to pain, would it be f.
T-15 X.7:3 the lesser of two evils, one to be f. a little,
T-18 VIII.4:2 unaware that they are f. and hated by a
T19 IV.C.1:6 Guilt, too, is f. and fearful. Yet it could
T-23 in.1:8 And God is f. as an opposing will.
T-24 IV.1:3 else becomes your enemy; f. and attacked,
T-25 V.2:5 a "something" to be f. instead of loved.
T-26 II.8:1 until justice is loved instead of f.. He
T-26 IV.4:5 him that what he f. he loves the most.
T-26 IV.4:6 that he understands that love cannot be f.
T-26 V.8:4 was f. and made a symbol of your hate?
T-27 V.4:5 nothing within the world that could be f..
T-28 II.9:4 and while it lasts will wakening be f.. Nor
T-28 II.10:6 about as separate things need not be f..
T-29 I.1:2 There is nothing to be f.. There is no way
T-29 I.7:3 For hate to be maintained, love must be f.
T-29 VIII.1:5 obscure, and they are f. and worshipped,
T-29 VIII.5:3 to life, and given power that it may be f..
T-31 VI.6:8 in for a while, where nothing need be f.,
W-pI 101.3:3 Salvation must be f., for it will kill, but
W-pI 129.8:5 day we realize that what you f. to lose was
W-pI 164.6:5 your love, while nothing to be f. remains.
W-pI 190.4:5 no more to be f. than the insane illusions
W-pI 192.6:3 Is it to be f.? Or is it to be hoped for, met
W-pI 196.9:7 because you f. your strength and freedom
W-pII 265.1:3 deceived was I to think that what I f. was
M-12 2:4 God can no longer be f., for the mind sees
M-27 2:2 disappointment and despair, can but be f.
M-28 2:4 Love is no longer f., but gladly welcomed.
P-2 IV.6:7 Love becomes f. because reality is love.
S-3 II.5:3 could it be welcome when it must be f.?
S-3 III.6:5 more be f. because it has been understood

## fearful 167

T-1 IV.2:2 This deception makes you f. because you
T-1 VII.4:5 you may become much too f. of what is to
T-2 I.4:6 on while someone is dreaming a f. dream,
T-2 IV.1:8 undertake this you cannot be f. yourself.
T-2 VI.3:2 you are f., you have chosen wrongly. That
T-2 VI.8:7 need for the remedy, you will remain f..
T-2 VII.1:1 nevertheless persist in making yourself f..
T-2 VII.3:4 have been f. of everyone and everything.
T-2 VII.3:8 The f. *must* miscreate, because they
T-3 VI.4:1 very f. of everything you have perceived
T-3 VII.5:1 belief in separation very real and very f.,
T-3 VII.5:9 enough, and that is why you become so f..
T-4 I.2:2 Change is always f. to the separated,
T-4 I.7:3 dispute this everything you do will be f.,
T-4 I.8:4 reality, which is indeed a f. attempt, but
T-4 I.9:10 The word "inevitable" is f. to the ego, but
T-4 II.8:2 This is such a f. state that it can only turn
T-4 II.8:12 of them is not without f. connotations.
T-5 in.2:2 to be wholly f. and remain alive, the only
T-5 IV.1:3 everything that you perceive as f., and
T-5 V.1:3 is fear, because only the f. can be egotistic
T-5 V.3:7 The ego is quite literally a f. thought.
T-5 VI.4:5 Bible is a f. thing in the ego's judgment.
T-6 I.1:2 f. connotations you may associate with it.
T-6 I.2:4 because the f. are apt to perceive fearfully.
T-6 V.A.5:4 of this perception makes it a f. one indeed
T-7 V.5:9 are f. because they are made by fear. The
T-7 V.5:10 The "f. healer" is a contradiction in terms
T-7 VI.3:6 F. of perceiving the power of this source,
T-7 VII.8:4 must be f. if you believe that your brother
T-7 X.4:5 and one which is both f. and desirable.
T-7 X.5:4 mean except that you want to be f.? The
T-9 I.1:4 which is what you are, is perceived as f.,
T-9 I.2:4 and if you believe that what you are is f.,
T-9 I.3:1 is, why would you be so sure that it is f.?
T-9 I.8:2 there is no God or that God's Will is f..
T-9 I.9:5 To deny what is can only *seem* to be f..
T-9 I.12:1 Any attempt to deny what *is* must be f.,
T-9 I.13:4 unreal because the absence of reality is f.,
T-9 II.2:4 healing because he is f. of bodily harm. At
T-9 II.2:5 f. to him than its physical expression. In
T-9 IV.9:5 the return of sense. Can this possibly be f.
T-9 IV.10:1 What can be f. but fantasy, and who
T-9 IV.10:3 that reality is f. is wrong can God be right.
T-9 IV.11:6 Fairy tales can be pleasant or f., but no
T-9 V.3:4 condemnation and advocate a f. solution.
T-10 in.1:1 beyond yourself can make you f. or loving
T-10 II.1:3 has been forgotten then appears to be f.,
T-10 II.1:4 You are f. *because* you have forgotten. And
T-10 II.1:6 dissociated is accepted, it ceases to be f..
T-10 II.4:4 is God, you will realize why it is always f..
T-10 III.8:6 projecting onto them the f. fact that you
T-10 . III.10:10 due them either, for nothing cannot be f..
T-11 V.3:4 ego is f. to you because you believe this.
T-13 II.5:3 hidden him from you because it is very f.,
T-13 VII.9:6 In them you see nothing f., and because
T-13 IX.2:2 *Make no one f.,* for his guilt is yours, and by
T-13 X.1:3 is diverted, must be true; and must be f.,
T-13 X.1:3 guilt onto what you believed to be less f..
T-14 VI.1:2 Nothing you understand is f.. It is only in
T-14 VI.2:1 is hidden and therefore nothing is f..
T-14 VI.3:5 for fear, for what they keep obscure *is* f..
T-14 VI.3:6 go, and what was f. will be so no longer.
T-14 VI.8:4 teach you that, in the light, they are not f.,
T-15 X.7:1 How f., then, has God become to you,
T-15 X.8:2 so f. that you cannot accept it where it is.
T-15 XI.1:3 your Father have become very f. to you.
T-15 XI.4:6 What you exclude from yourself seems f.,
T-16 V.10:2 Let us not think of its f. nature, nor of the
T-16 V.11:2 f. has the truth become to you that unless
T-16 V.14:1 are not f. because they are not true. They
T-16 V.14:2 They but seem to be f. to the extent to
T-16 VI.10:4 wrought is ugly, f. and very dangerous.
T-17 I.2:1 only your wish to change reality that is f.,
T-17 IV.14:6 brought to light, is not perceived as f., but
T-18 I.5:5 Its fragmented aspects are f. enough, as
T-18 II.4:6 attempts to blot out reality are very f., but
T-18 II.4:7 you substitute the fantasy that reality is f.,
T-18 III.3:8 doubt that what you think it means *is* f..
T-18 IV.6:3 Atonement to it, and make salvation f..
T19 IV.C.1:6 Guilt, too, is feared and f.. Yet it could
T19 IV.D.11:3 For only if they share in it does it seem f.,
T19 IV.D.12:2 and your interpretation of him is very f..
T-20 III.4:6 All these are but the f. thoughts of those
T-20 III.4:6 to a world made f. by their adjustments.
T-20 III.5:8 it outside you, you should indeed be f..
T-20 VI.6:3 here is love made f. and hope abandoned.
T-20 VI.6:8 in him, is what makes God seem f. to you,
T-20 VI.12:1 You who are learning this may still be f.,
T-20 . VIII.10:4 the f. outcomes of imagined sin into the
T-21 II.9:4 of a f. world to justify its purpose. What
T-21 IV.1:2 He will correct, but this makes no one f..
T-21 IV.1:4 This you would not be f. to admit. Fear in
T-21 IV.3:2 "f." question is one the ego never asks.
T-21 VI.6:5 you. Yet think not this is f.. That you are
T-21 VI.6:7 fact be f. unless it disagrees with what you
T-21 VII.2:5 f. the power of the Son of God will strike
T-21 VII.6:2 For this one still seems f., and unlike the
T-22 I.9:7 a f. sight or sound that drew them gently
T-22 . VI.12:12 as if love could attack and become f..
T-23 in.5:7 Who can walk trembling in a f. world,
T-23 I.8:6 Conflict is f., for it is the birth of fear. Yet
T-25 V.2:3 And must you not be f. of yourself? For
T-26 V.8:4 And do you want that f. instant kept,
T-26 VIII.5:6 if its effects already have been judged as f.
T-27 V.2:9 The f. are not healed, and cannot heal.
T-27 V.4:6 blessing, will the world indeed seem f.,
T-27 .. VII.13:3 Nothing more f. than an idle dream has
T-27 .. VII.13:4 So f. is the dream, so seeming real, he
T-28 I.13:3 There is no past to keep its f. image in the
T-28 IV.2:2 part of f. dreams whatever form they take
T-28 V.3:5 Identity, because you think that It is f..
T-29 I.2:5 to hate, and so he thinks that love is f.;
T-29 I.3:3 make the way to light seem dark and f.,
T-29 VIII.4:2 A dark and f. purpose, yet a thought
T-29 IX.9:1 you *are* f. if you do not feel a deep content,
T-30 IV.5:7 made f. by a power that can have no real
T-30 V.9:8 bought at f. price in coins of suffering?
T-30 VI.4:8 you a f. judgment that your brother does
T-30 VII.3:9 meaning but to show you wrote a f. script
T-30 .. VII.3:10 the thing you fear has f. meaning in itself.
T-31 II.9:2 and release from all the f. images he holds
T-31 VII.2:3 And so they come in f. form, with content
T-31 VII.5:1 your f. concept of yourself may change.
T-31 VIII.4:2 Be never f. of temptation, then, but see it
W-pI 12.3:2 *I think I see a f. world, a dangerous world, a*
W-pI 13.2:3 f. that the void may otherwise be used to
W-pI 13.3:2 fear. If you are f., it is certain that you will
W-pI 39.6:3 take, they are unloving and therefore f..
W-pI 47.1:1 reason to be apprehensive, anxious and f..
W-pI 56.2:3 the f. nature of the self-image I have made
W-pI 56.3:2 world I see holds my f. self-image in place,
W-pI 68.2:4 has become f. to him in his dream of hate.

| | |
|---|---|
| W-pI.....87.1:3 | f. of shadows and afraid of things unseen |
| W-pI.....92.7:1 | it sees, leaving its dreams as f. as itself. No |
| W-pI...109.5:7 | No more f. dreams will come, now that |
| W-pI.133.11:3 | alternative you think you chose seems f., |
| W-pI...135.6:1 | Is not this picture f.? Can you be at peace |
| W-pI...153.7:3 | f. image you believe you see at work in all |
| W-pI...153.9:2 | for we have left all f. thoughts behind. |
| W-pI.153.12:2 | replace their f. toys with joyous games, |
| W-pI.153.13:1 | left alone in terror in a f. world made mad |
| W-pI...158.7:3 | f. thoughts of guilt from dreams of sin. It |
| W-pI...163.8:2 | And yet, can thoughts like these be f.? If |
| W-pI...170.9:3 | f. and beyond surmounting, is the fear of |
| W-pI.170.10:4 | more f. than the Heart of Love Itself? The |
| W-pI...189.5:4 | your heart, you will perceive a f. world, |
| W-pI...190.5:8 | And what was seen as f. now becomes a |
| W-pI...191.1:4 | it be but vicious and afraid, f. of shadows, |
| W-pI...192.7:4 | mists of shifting dreams and f. thoughts, |
| W-pI...196.6:1 | if you accept the f. thought you can attack |
| W-pII......5.3:4 | Made to be f., must the body serve the |
| W-pII..263.1:3 | *I would not perceive such dark and f. images* |
| W-pII......7.3:1 | for the f. images and dreams you made. |
| W-pII....12.1:3 | that strength is weak and love is f., life is |
| W-pII..351.1:2 | *Son of God; alone and friendless in a f. world* |
| M-4.......IV.1:9 | It will make him confused, f., angry and |
| M-16..........6:4 | from all the f. things you see in dreams. It |
| M-16..........9:4 | healing nor destructive, quieting nor f.. |
| M-16........10:8 | through his recognition, not that it is f., |
| M-25..........4:9 | to fear, and will be f. in consequence. |
| M-27..........5:9 | Terrible His Thoughts and f. His image. |
| P-2........VI.3:5 | the mind grows f. and begins to doubt its |
| P-2.......VII.7:3 | healer cannot but be f. of his patients, |
| S-1........III.4:3 | For fear's defenses are f. in themselves, |
| S-2.........II.6:5 | How f. has forgiveness now become, and |
| S-3...........I.2:3 | F. and frail it seems to be to those who |

## fearfully 6

| | |
|---|---|
| T-5........VI.4:6 | it as frightening, it interprets it f.. Being |
| T-6...........I.2:4 | because the fearful are apt to perceive f.. I |
| T-7........VI.1:7 | any of Them if he regards Them f.. He will |
| T-13.......X.7:1 | and show them to you f. to demonstrate |
| W-pI...163.5:4 | to the ground, they whisper f. that it is so. |
| W-pI...166.8:1 | cower f. lest you should feel Christ's touch |

## fearing 2

| | |
|---|---|
| T-12.....II.10:7 | reason for f. the world as you perceive it, |
| T-28.......V.3:5 | And f. it, you will not want to know your |

## fearlessly 2

| | |
|---|---|
| T-11.......in.3:7 | it. Bring this light f. with you, and bravely |
| T-16....IV.13:5 | and answer f. the Call of Him Who gave |

## fearlessness 3

| | |
|---|---|
| W-pII.....310.h | In f. and love I spend today. |
| W-pII..339.1:9 | only this, that we may spend this day in f. |
| M-4.......IX.2:4 | trust. Being based on f., it is gentle. Being |

## fears 32

| | |
|---|---|
| T-5........VI.2:2 | induce f. of retaliation or abandonment, |
| T-11. VIII.14:3 | too will laugh at your f. and replace them |
| T-11VIII.14:10 | you see you need reality to dispel your f.. |
| T-11. VIII.15:1 | Would you not exchange your f. for truth |
| T-12.......II.4:2 | and accept it, their f. vanish. But if they |
| T-13.........I.4:3 | he f. and that he sees will never touch him |
| T-13.......V.5:4 | what he loves, and recoils from what he f.. |
| T-14.......II.7:7 | the shapes and forms and f. of nothing. |
| T-15.........I.4:2 | and their f. are all associated with it. The |
| T-21......IV.2:2 | "enemy," Whom it cannot even see, it f.. |
| T-27.......II.9:1 | Who, then, f. healing? Only those to |
| T-28.....II.7:11 | f. is cause without the consequences that |
| T-29.........I.2:5 | He f. to love and loves to hate, and so he |
| T-29......IV.4:5 | idea that they exist from which the f. arise |
| T-29......IX.5:5 | because he f. his thoughts and gives them |
| W-pI.....44.6:1 | its opposition and its f. are meaningless. |
| W-pI.....92.7:1 | It f. and it attacks and hates itself, and |
| W-pI...103.3:4 | and quiet all your f. with this assurance, |
| W-pI...132.3:3 | release the future from your ancient f., |
| W-pI...132.3:4 | have enslaved the world with all your f., |
| W-pI...160.5:2 | Who f. has but denied himself and said, |
| W-pI...161.1:1 | f. may disappear and offer room to love. |
| W-pI.166.11:3 | all your f. with this one merciful reply, "It |
| W-pI.166.14:4 | fear but teaches them their f. are justified. |
| WpI...rV.in6:2 | I share your doubts and f. a little while, |
| WpI...rV.in6:2 | by which all f. and doubts are overcome. |
| W-pI...191.6:5 | your f. have laid the mark of death upon |
| W-pI...192.5:4 | f. could still assail those who have lost the |
| W-pI...199.7:4 | Let love replace their f. through you. |
| W-pII..240.2:1 | *How foolish are our f.! Would You allow* |
| W-pII....11.4:3 | Yet back of all our doubts, past all our f., |
| M-19.........3:1 | all f. of future states and all concerns |

## feasible 5

| | |
|---|---|
| T-29.........I.5:5 | to go there, what is f. for you to undertake |
| W-pI.....40.2:2 | when closing your eyes would not be f.. |
| W-pII..273.1:2 | If this is not yet f., we are content and |
| M-16.........5:2 | if it is not f. for you to take it just before |
| M-29.........5:9 | the Holy Spirit's help when it is f. to do so |

## feast 9

| | |
|---|---|
| T19. IV.A.12:5 | to f. only upon what they return to him. |
| T19. IV.A.13:1 | to f. upon it and to prey upon reality. For |
| T19. IV.A.16:1 | Love, too, would set a f. before you, on a |
| T19. IV.A.16:2 | is a f. that honors your holy relationship, |
| T19....IV.B.4:6 | You want communion, not the f. of fear. |
| T-28......III.8:7 | the f. of plenty set before them there. And |
| T-28......III.9:1 | f. unlike indeed to those the dreaming of |
| T-28......III.9:5 | Here is a f. the Father lays before His Son, |
| T-28......III.9:7 | enter not, for time waits not upon this f., |

## feat 2

| | |
|---|---|
| T-21......III.3:2 | This is indeed a little f. for such a power. |
| T-31.........I.2:7 | a giant learning f. it is indeed incredible. |

## feather 3

| | |
|---|---|
| T-18......IX.6:4 | stop a button's fall, nor hold a f.. Nothing |
| T19... IV.A.8:1 | This f. of a wish, this tiny illusion, this |
| T19... IV.A.9:1 | a little f. be before the great wings of truth |

## feather's 1

| | |
|---|---|
| T-28.....VII.6:4 | what will collapse beneath a f. weight? |

## feathered 1

| | |
|---|---|
| S-3........IV.2:3 | each blade of grass and f. wing and all the |

## feathers 1

| | |
|---|---|
| T-18.........I.7:6 | course like f. dancing insanely in the wind |

## feats 1

| | |
|---|---|
| W-pI.....39.1:3 | concerned with intellectual f. nor logical |

## features 1

| | |
|---|---|
| T-18.......II.5:7 | In dreams these f. are not obscure. You |

## fed 1

| | |
|---|---|
| W-pI...170.2:2 | For here is fear begot and f. with blood, to |

## feeble 4

| | |
|---|---|
| T-4.........II.8:2 | with them in a f. attempt at identification |
| T-4.........II.8:2 | them in an equally f. show of strength. It |
| T-22.......V.4:5 | be difficult to disregard its f. squeaks that |
| W-pI...118.2:2 | *Let my own f. voice be still, and let me hear* |

## feebly 2

| | |
|---|---|
| T-20......III.9:3 | You groped but f. in the dust and found |
| T-25....VIII.8:7 | save, while love stands f. by with helpless |

## feed 2

| | |
|---|---|
| T19. IV.A.11:4 | What fear would f. upon, love overlooks. |
| T19....IV.C.4:2 | to sin to f. upon and keep itself alive; a |

## feeds 1

| | |
|---|---|
| T19..IV.B.13:6 | that it keeps hidden, and yet f. upon. To |

## feel 147

| | |
|---|---|
| T-2........VI.1:7 | you f. personally responsible for them. |
| T-2........VI.3:3 | That is why you f. responsible for it. You |
| T-2.......VII.1:8 | You may f. that at this point it would take |
| T-3........IV.3:8 | reason to f. afraid as you perceive yourself |
| T-3........VI.5:1 | When you f. tired, it is because you have |
| T-3........VI.5:4 | All this makes you f. tired because it is |
| T-3......VI.11:1 | who does not f. that he is imprisoned in |
| T-3.....VII.5:10 | you f. the fear of the destruction of your |
| T-4..........II.4:1 | and the need they f. to protect them. That |
| T-4........III.4:5 | you f. for the ego because you made it. No |
| T-4........IV.5:1 | When you f. guilty, remember that the |
| T-4........IV.5:5 | you f. guilty your ego is in command, |
| T-5.........V.7:7 | makes them f. responsible for their errors |
| T-5.......VII.5:5 | If you allow yourself to f. guilty, you will |
| T-5.......VII.6:2 | to be wholly joyous if that is how you f.. |
| T-5.....VII.6:10 | *I do not f. guilty, because the Holy Spirit will* |
| T-6..........II.3:3 | the ego to make you f. different from your |
| T-7.......VII.1:1 | a blessing to a brother *you* will f. deprived, |
| T-7.......VII.8:3 | it. This makes you f. deprived of it, and by |
| T-8........IV.1:8 | if you do, you will f. lonely and helpless, |
| T-8......VIII.7:2 | It cannot tell you how you f.. You do not |
| T-8......VIII.7:3 | You do not know how you f. because you |
| T-8......VIII.7:3 | a learning device *can* tell you how you f.. |
| T-8......VIII.7:5 | ego is incapable of knowing how you f.. |
| T-9.........I.14:5 | When you f. these things, do not try to |
| T-10.........I.3:3 | the Holy Spirit you may f. better because |
| T-10.....V.12:3 | joyous, it is blasphemous to f. depressed. |
| T-11....VIII.1:2 | you do not f. you need a course which, in |
| T-12...VII.14:4 | as long as you f. guilty you are listening to |
| T-13.......in.1:1 | you did not f. guilty you could not attack, |
| T-13........X.3:1 | him or perceive his own, *you* will f. guilty. |
| T-14.....III.1:1 | The happy learner cannot f. guilty about |
| T-14....III.15:2 | you *will* f. guilty for this imagined crime, |
| T-14......IV.2:5 | can perhaps f. His Presence next to you, |
| T-14......IV.3:8 | You will f. guilty till you learn this. For in |
| T-15....VII.10:3 | an attempt to make someone f. guilty, |
| T-15....VII.10:6 | will f. guilty about communication and |
| T-16.......V.3:4 | believe that hate is sin merely f. guilty, |
| T-18.......V.6:1 | you f. the holiness of your relationship is |
| T19....IV.B.2:4 | "sacrifice" you f. to be too great to make, |
| T19....IV.C.5:2 | The body no more dies than it can f.. It |
| T19... IV.D.1:2 | What would you f. and think if death held |
| T-20.......V.8:1 | and f. the Holy Spirit watching over you |
| T-21......II.11:4 | made can tell you what you see and f., |
| T-21......IV.1:6 | It has no fear to let you f. ashamed. It |
| T-22.......V.6:1 | when you f. the need arise to be defensive |
| T-22.......V.6:2 | f. that you are weak because you are alone |
| T-23......II.22:8 | How do you f.? Is peace in your awareness |
| T-23......III.1:5 | fear of punishment the murderer must f.? |
| T-24.........I.4:5 | special ones f. weak and frail because of |
| T-24.....VII.9:4 | can f. it with your hands and hear it move |
| T-24.....VII.9:7 | which you look on it, the hands that f. it, |
| T-25......IV.1:1 | and recognize they are, can f. no guilt. For |
| T-25......IX.8:2 | Seek to deny and you will f. denied. Seek |
| T-26...VII.12:6 | Its failure lies in that you still f. guilty, |
| T-26....VIII.4:5 | Who can f. desolation except now? A |
| T-27......VI.4:5 | what it should f. and what its function is. |
| T-27..VIII.10:4 | the cause of any pain and suffering you f., |
| T-28......VI.1:9 | victimized, but cannot f. itself as victim. It |
| T-29.......II.9:3 | can be perceived and thought to f. and act |
| T-29......IX.4:6 | talk and think and f. and speak for them. |
| T-29......IX.9:1 | Whenever you f. fear in any form,–and |
| T-29......IX.9:1 | *are* fearful if you do not f. a deep content, a |
| T-30.........I.3:4 | what you perceive and so you f. attacked. |

T-30 I.5:3 you f. yourself unwilling to sit by and ask
T-30 I.8:2 *least I can decide I do not like what I f. now.*
T-30 I.9:1 that you do not like the way you f., what
T-30 I.9:3 because you do not like the way you f..
T-31 VI.4:6 nor what you choose to f. or think or wish
T-31 VIII.1:2 and bound by what it orders him to f.. It
W-pI 15.5:2 practice periods, if you begin to f. uneasy.
W-pI 15.5:3 you f. completely comfortable with it, and
W-pI 27.1:3 You may f. hesitant about using the idea,
W-pI 27.4:6 If only once during the day you f. that you
W-pI 32.4:3 when you yourself f. reasonably ready.
W-pI 34.5:1 made whenever you f. your peace of mind
W-pI 34.6:2 the idea until you f. some sense of relief. It
W-pI 35.7:3 you f. are applicable to your reactions to
W-pI 39.2:3 The hesitation you may f. in answering is
W-pI 39.10:1 should f. free to introduce variety into the
W-pI 42.3:2 by yourself, at a time when you f. ready,
W-pI 45.5:3 is every reason to f. confident that we will
W-pI 47.2:3 can put his faith in weakness and f. safe?
W-pI 47.2:4 can put his faith in strength and f. weak?
W-pI 47.7:2 reached it if you f. a sense of deep peace,
W-pI 60.2:5 because I f. the stirring of His strength in
W-pI 67.4:4 whether you f. you have succeeded or not.
W-pI 68.4:4 find out how you would f. without them.
W-pI 68.6:5 Try to f. safety surrounding you, hovering
W-pI 69.6:4 hand; f. them resting on your cheeks and
W-pI 69.7:1 you will begin to f. a sense of being lifted
W-pI 72.12:1 Whenever you f. your confidence wane
W-pI 74.5:2 Sink into it and f. it closing around you.
W-pI 74.5:4 will f. a deep sense of joy and an increased
W-pI 74.6:3 f. yourself slipping off into withdrawal,
W-pI 79.3:5 no time in which you f. completely free of
W-pI 91.4:3 to the attempt to let you f. this strength.
W-pI 91.4:5 awareness as you f. the strength in you.
W-pI 91.7:3 need to f. something to put your faith in,
W-pI 91.10:3 that you will f. the strength in you. They
W-pI 94.3:1 hour to the attempt to f. the truth in you.
W-pI 95.11:5 to f. the meaning that the words convey.
W-pI 95.13:3 F. this one Self in you, and let It shine
W-pI 95.13:5 it is given you to f. this Self within you,
W-pI 107.2:2 How it would f.? Try to remember when
W-pI.122.11:2 given you to f. the peace forgiveness offers
W-pI 124.4:4 We f. Him in our hearts. Our minds
W-pI.133.11:2 If you f. any guilt about your choice, you
W-pI 134.9:2 f. that you are tempted to accuse someone
W-pI.134.11:4 cannot f. that all escape has been denied
W-pI.136.17:2 well by this: The body should not f. at all.
W-pI 137.2:2 the rest, to suffer what the others do not f.
W-pI.140.12:4 And we will f. salvation cover us with soft
W-pI 153.1:1 who f. threatened by this changing world,
W-pI 153.5:3 who f. its iron grip upon your heart. You
W-pI.153.19:5 His strength each time we f. the threat of
W-pI 157.1:6 death. Today you learn to f. the joy of life.
W-pI 157.3:1 it will be given you to f. a touch of Heaven
W-pI 161.5:1 be the body that we f. limits our freedom,
W-pI 166.8:1 cower fearfully lest you should f. Christ's
W-pI 166.9:2 and you f. that you are not alone. You
W-pI.166.13:5 comes to those who f. the touch of Christ,
W-pI.166.15:4 accept His gifts, and f. the touch of Christ.
W-pI 169.5:5 part of mind sufficiently distinct to f. that
W-pI 182.1:4 you of. Yet still you f. an alien here, from
W-pI 189.h I f. the Love of God within me now.
W-pI 189.1:7 To f. the Love of God within you is to see
W-pI 189.2:1 Who could f. fear in such a world as this?
W-pI 189.4:1 to those who f. God's Love in them. Their
W-pI 189.5:3 will look upon that which you f. within. If
W-pI 189.5:5 If you f. the Love of God within you, you
W-pI 189.6:1 in us, and f. its all-embracing tenderness,
W-pI 192.9:4 Every time you f. a stab of anger, realize
W-pI 195.5:2 mourn a seeming loss or f. apparent pain,
W-pI.200.10:6 and you can f. its soft embrace surround
W-pI 209.1:1 (189) I f. the Love of God within me now.
W-pII in.10:3 Instead of words, we need but f. His Love.
W-pII .236.1:3 me what to think, and what to do and f..
W-pII .240.2:4 *f. the love for him which is Your Own as well.*
W-pII .301.1:2 *f. I am abandoned or unneeded in the world.*
W-pII .337.1:6 to f. God's Love protecting me from harm
M-6 2:7 No teacher of God should f. disappointed
M-15 3:1 sometimes f. your just due is not given
P-2 V.2:6 will attack because they f. endangered,
S-1 III.5:5 and f. how your heart is lifted and your
S-2 II.4:5 and do not show the bitter pain you f..
S-3 I.2:5 they f. fear as bodies change and sicken.

## feeling 23

T-12 VII.13:4 you as the final expression of its f. for you,
T-18 VI.11:2 This f. of liberation far exceeds the dream
T19 IV.B.14:3 just as certainly it has no f.. It transmits to
T19 IV.B.14:6 It has no f. for them. All of the feeling
T19 IV.B.14:7 All of the f. with which they are invested
T-20 VI.7:2 f. the seeming firm foundation of their
T-22 VI.12:5 or hurt yourself without the other f. pain.
T-27 I.6:5 or f. has a motivation other than this one.
T-28 VI.2:2 punishment you give because it has no f..
W-pI 5.1:2 using the description of the f. in whatever
W-pI 5.7:2 and of the f. as you experience it. Further
W-pI 7.3:2 a cup, f. the rim of a cup against your lips,
W-pI 44.10:1 and even a f. that you are approaching, if
W-pI 74.5:4 than a f. of drowsiness and enervation.
W-pI 100.7:1 by f. happiness arise in us according to
W-pI.134.16:3 your chest, a deep and certain f. of relief.
W-pI.136.17:3 will be no sense of f. ill or feeling well, of
W-pI.136.17:3 will be no sense of feeling ill or f. well, of
W-pI 152.5:2 false. And that includes all shifts in f.,
W-pI 157.1:4 a different kind of f. and awareness. You
W-pI 166.6:2 defeat and hopelessness as he is f. them.
W-pI 182.1:6 Just a persistent f., sometimes not more
P-3 I.3:8 or perhaps just a f. of reaching out to

## feelings 19

T-4 IV.1:2 your attitudes, your f. and your behavior.
T-4 IV.8:6 well you have done this by your own f.,
T-5 V.7:3 Guilt f. are always a sign that you do not
T-5 V.8:1 possible reason for continuing guilt f..
T-5 VI.2:1 Guilt f. are the preservers of time. They
T-7 VI.2:4 induces f. of unreality and results in utter
T-14 II.2:4 all the strange forms and f. and actions
T19 IV.B.14:4 It transmits to you the f. that you want.
T-21 II.2:4 *I see. I choose the f. I experience, and I decide*
T-21 II.10:3 events and f. its maker thinks it causes.
T-21 V.2:4 and f. of impermanence and unreality.
T-30 I.4:1 of day you want; the f. you would have,
W-pI 3.1:7 Try to lay such f. aside, and merely use
W-pI 34.6:4 *I can replace my f. of depression, anxiety or*
W-pI 47.5:2 is associated with f. of inadequacy, for
W-pI 96.1:2 induces f. of acute and constant conflict,
W-pI 167.2:4 one idea which underlies all f. that are not
S-1 II.2:1 involve f. of weakness and inadequacy,
S-2 I.5:4 for what he does entails your fate, your f.,

## feels 10

T-3 I.2:7 you," and f. exonerated in beating a child.
T-4 V.4:2 identification with which the ego f. safe,
T-6 IV.4:4 it, and the ego f. badly in need of allies,
T-12 III.6:2 who identifies with the ego f. deprived.
T-16 V.7:6 And he f. guilty for the "sin" of taking,
T-27 VI.3:2 to hear, and let it tell you what it is it f.. *It*
T-31 V.14:6 it f. about how it was made and what it is.
W-pI 181.8:5 Love He f. for us becomes our own as well
M-4 I.A.5:5 which the teacher of God f. called upon to
P-2 VII.5:3 the end of guilt who f. responsible for his

## feet 26

T-23 II.13:4 you walk in sanity with f. on solid ground,
T-23 II.13:5 the ground beneath your f. seem solid.
T-24 V.3:5 is your eyes, your ears, your hands, your f.
T-24 V.5:1 and no hands to hold nor f. to guide. Be
T-29 II.4:5 He has laid them at your f., and asks you
T-29 II.4:7 Guest will welcome everyone whose f.
T-29 VI.5:1 world will bind your f. and tie your hands
T-30 V.3:5 longer, with his f. still touching earth. Yet
T-31 VIII.7:1 I lay before your f. the peace of God, and
W-pI 60.4:3 thoughts, guide my actions and lead my f.
W-pI 134.6:2 and gently lays them at the f. of truth.
W-pI 154.11:4 He needs our f. to bring us where He wills
W-pI 155.13:1 Your f. are safely set upon the road that
W-pI 156.4:2 them in gratitude and gladness at your f..
W-pI 161.9:3 could scarce refrain from kneeling at his f.
W-pI 161.11:3 See his face, his hands and f., his clothing.
W-pI 166.6:1 f. that bleed a little from the rocky road
WpI rV.in2:1 *Steady our f., our Father. Let our doubts be*
WpI rV.in9:3 You are my voice, my eyes, my f., my
W-pII .227.1:5 *up, and lay them down before the f. of truth,*
W-pII 9.5:2 needs your eyes and ears and hands and f.
W-pII .324.1:5 *always call me back, and guide my f. aright.*
W-pII 353.h hands, my f. today Have but one purpose;
P-2 III.4:4 too near to God to keep his f. on earth.
S-2 in.1:4 to hold you up and keep your f. secure;
S-3 IV.6:5 in a savage world with f. that bleed, and

## fell 2

T-2 I.3:6 Bible says that a deep sleep f. upon Adam,
T-2 I.4:5 Only after the deep sleep f. upon Adam

## felt 15

T-6 I.15:2 love. If the Apostles had not f. guilty, they
T-14 IV.8:5 and nothing you have ever f. apart from
T-15 VI.6:5 and f. himself drawn irresistibly into the
T-17 III.8:3 dictates are not perceived nor f. as *now.*
T-17 V.1:4 fails. The experience of it is always f.. Yet
T-24 IV.3:5 mind, and its effects are f. but where it is.
T-27 VI.2:8 behind the pleasure will be f. no more.
T-31 IV.2:13 And on some the thorns are f. at once.
W-pI 91.4:4 When you have f. the strength in you,
W-pI 107.2:5 that you f. be multiplied a hundred times,
W-pI 166.6:2 and has f. defeat and hopelessness as he is
W-pI 169.13:3 he f. an instant back to bless the world?
W-pI 189.4:3 What they have f. in them they look upon
W-pI 194.3:1 In no one instant is depression f., or pain
P-2 V.1:6 self that holds in darkness what is truly f.,

## fence 6

T-18 VIII.2:5 The body is a tiny f. around a little part of
T-18 VIII.6:4 Nor does a f. surround it, preventing it
W-pII 5.1:1 a f. the Son of God imagines he has built,
W-pII 5.1:2 It is within this f. he thinks he lives, to die
W-pII 5.1:3 within this f. he thinks that he is safe from
W-pII 5.4:2 made to f. him into hell without escape,

## fenced

*See* fenced-off

## fenced-off 1

T-18 VIII.7:1 not accept this little, f. aspect as yourself.

## fences 2

T-26 I.3:1 little that the body f. off becomes the self,
W-pII 5.2:3 impermanence is "proof" his f. work, and

## fetid 1

T-27 I.10:3 sick of breathing in the f. scent of death.

## fever 1

W-pI 109.5:5 but the dreams of f. that has passed away.

## feverish 3

T-31 V.7:5 and many come from f. imaginations, hot
W-pI 101.6:4 sin has wrought in f. imagination. Say:
M-8 2:7 health a burden, it retreats into f. dreams.

## few 42

T-2 VI.9:3 F. appreciate the real power of the mind,
T-3 IV.7:12 are called but f. are chosen" should be,

T-3......IV.7:12 be, "All are called but f. choose to listen."
T-5..........I.2:1 with just a f. simple concepts: *Thoughts*
T-5........VI.5:1 but a f. will suffice to show how the Holy
T-15.......XI.1:4 with them for a f. special relationships, in
T-21......IV.6:7 A f. remaining trinkets still seem to shine
T-22......IV.2:1 first f. steps along the right way that seem
T-30.........I.9:4 you go ahead with just a f. more steps you
W-pI........8.2:3 Very f. have realized what is actually
W-pI.....24.3:2 using. A f. subjects, honestly and carefully
W-pI.....26.8:2 much more helpful to cover a f. situations
W-pI.....32.4:3 time when f. distractions are anticipated,
W-pI.....39.9:1 today's idea to yourself slowly a f. times.
W-pI.....39.9:2 to include a f. short intervals in which you
W-pI.....45.6:2 in thinking a f. relevant thoughts of your
WpI...rI.in.1:3 be a f. short comments after each of the
W-pI.....61.5:7 Let a f. related thoughts come to you, and
W-pI.....61.7:3 steps we will take in the next f. weeks. Try
W-pI.....64.3:1 review our last f. lessons, your function
W-pI.....65.6:2 longer, attempting to catch a f. of the idle
W-pI.....67.2:2 spend a f. minutes adding some relevant
W-pI.....70.7:5 Then devote a f. minutes, with your eyes
W-pI.....95.7:1 and urge you to omit as f. as possible.
W-pI.153.11:2 but f. have come to realize His Will is but
W-pI...163.6:1 and still select a f. you would not cherish
Wi181-200 1:1 Our next f. lessons make a special point
W-pI...182.5:4 for more than just a f. instants of respite;
W-pI...185.2:7 But f. indeed have meant them. You have
W-pI...185.2:8 around you to be sure how very f. they are
WpI rVI.in.6:5 we will add but a f. formal expressions or
W-pII.....in.7:8 we undertake these last f. steps to You,
W-pII..225.2:5 accomplish these f. final steps which end
M-1............2:7 Many hear It, but f. will answer. Yet it is
M-3............5:3 relationships are generally f., because
M-4......I.A.5:3 F. teachers of God escape this distress
M-12..........3:3 Only very f. can hear God's Voice at all,
M-13..........6:8 F. have heard it as yet, and they can but
M-26..........3:9 to those remaining behind are f. indeed.
M-29..........1:2 covers only a f. of the more obvious ones,
P-2........III.1:1 helps him to avoid a f. of the pitfalls along
P-3...........I.3:2 to you limited to the f. you actually see.

## fiction 1

C-3.............2:1 might be called a kind of happy f.; a way

## fidelity 5

T-6......IV.11:3 exist. F. to premises is a law of mind, and
T-6......IV.11:4 F. to other laws is also possible, however,
T-13......IX.1:3 law. F. to this law lets no light in, for it
T-13......IX.1:3 for it demands f. to darkness and forbids
T-13......IX.2:3 it. The ego rewards f. to it with pain, for

## fields 1

W-pI.....97.1:4 mind from conflict to the quiet f. of peace

## fierce 7

T19.IV.A.11:6 The f. attraction that guilt holds for fear is
T-20......III.7:8 This one wild thought, f. in its arrogance,
T-29......IX.5:4 grow large and dangerous and f. and wild
W-pI...190.2:4 is a dream of f. retaliation for a crime that
W-pI...192.4:2 it holds no f. attraction now and guilt is
W-pII..265.1:2 How f. they seemed! And how deceived
M-5..........I.1:8 God is seen as outside, f. and powerful,

## fiercer 1

M-4.......VI.1:7 f. and more powerful its defenses seem to

## fiery 1

T-17...VIII.4:5 cold fantasies of fear and f. dreams of hell

## fifteen 14

*See also* fifteen-minute, ten-to-fifteen-minute

W-pI.....27.3:3 might try for every f. or twenty minutes.
W-pI.....64.6:5 least once devote ten or f. minutes today
W-pI.....65.3:1 set aside ten to f. minutes for a more
W-pI.....70.6:1 which should last some ten to f. minutes.
WpI..rII.in.2:1 Take about f. minutes for each of them,
W-pI...123.7:1 yours to Him for f. minutes twice today.
W-pI...126.9:1 Give f. minutes twice today to the
W-pI...127.8:1 f. minutes twice today escape from every
W-pI.133.13:3 periods of f. minutes each begin with this:
W-pI.135.22:1 For f. minutes twice today we rest from
W-pI.151.15:1 Spend f. minutes thus when you awake,
W-pI.151.15:1 gladly give another f. more before you go
W-pI.153.15:4 Ten would be better; f. better still. And as
WpI rVI.in.1:2 which should not be less than f. minutes,

## fifteen-minute 1

W-pI.132.15:1 Begin the f. periods in which we practice

## fiftieth 1

WpI...rI.in.1:2 with the first and ending with the f..

## fifty 1

WpI...rI.in.6:4 the first f. of the ideas we have covered,

## fight 23

T-12.....V.7:10 so you f. against all learning and succeed,
T-18.....VII.5:7 and f. against the giving in to sin; when
T-18...VIII.3:2 of dust it bids you f. against the universe.
T-23.......in.2:3 you will f. against it, and try to weaken it
T-23.........I.7:3 Truth does not f. against illusions, nor do
T-23.........I.7:3 do illusions f. against the truth. Illusions
T-23......IV.1:7 asked to f. against your wish to murder.
T-24.........I.4:7 On its behalf they f. against the universe,
T-25......IX.2:8 f. against His Son's reluctance to perceive
T-28......III.3:6 F. not His coming with illusions, for it is
T-30.........I.1:7 *Do not f. yourself.* But think about the kind
T-30.......I.12:6 Nor will you f. against it, for you see that
T-30....... II.1:1 to oppose the Holy Spirit is to f. *yourself?*
T-30......IV.1:2 it up. You always f. illusions. For the truth
T-31......IV.6:2 To f. against this step is to defeat your
T-31.....VII.9:2 that it may f. to keep the space that holds
W-pI.134.12:1 He does not have to f. to save himself. He
W-pI...153.7:4 now, when it is but illusions that you f.?
W-pI...170.7:6 and no mighty warrior to f. for them.
W-pI...186.2:1 Let us not f. our function. We did not
P-1.............4:5 And he will f. against his freedom because
P-2...........I.3:3 Holy Spirit f. against the intrusions of the
P-3........III.4:1 to live is something no one need f. for. It

## fighting 4

T-3........VI.8:3 are literally f. you for your authorship.
T-4........IV.1:4 This is what you are f. to keep, and what
T-8.....VIII.2:1 to contain two voices f. for its possession.
T-18.....VII.4:7 to reach Atonement by f. against sin.

## figure 13

T-13....... V.3:6 in him a shadow f. in your private world.
T-27... VIII.1:1 the central f. in the dreaming of the world
T-27... VIII.4:3 does is true, for it is but a f. in a dream.
T-28....... II.7:4 of the dream, and not a f. in the dream.
T-28......IV.1:7 And you become a f. in his dream of pain,
T-28......IV.5:3 you become a passive f. in his dreams,
T-29......IV.5:1 role to every f. which the dream contains.
T-29......IV.5:6 shadow f. who attacks becomes a brother
W-pI.......4.4:1 by the central f. or event it contains; for
W-pI.......8.4:4 one by the central f. or theme it contains,
W-pI.....35.7:2 events in which you f. cross your mind.
W-pI...166.6:1 a sorry f.; weary, worn, in threadbare
M-12.........6:9 to behold a dream f. as sick and separate

## figured 1

T-17....IV.15:3 no f. representation of a thought system,

## figures 28

T-13......IV.6:1 shadowy f. from the past are precisely
T-13....... V.2:1 his world with f. from his individual past,
T-13....... V.2:2 Yet the f. that he sees were never real, for
T-13....... V.2:4 For these f. have no witnesses, being
T-13....... V.3:1 and shadowy f. that the insane relate to
T-13....... V.5:7 with f. of fear you have invited into it, and
T-17......III.1:4 shadow f. you would make immortal are
T-17......III.1:6 The shadow f. are the witnesses you bring
T-17......III.2:1 It is these shadow f. that would make the
T-17......III.2:2 The shadow f. always speak for vengeance
T-17......III.3:5 The shadow f. enter more and more, and
T-18........II.5:5 It is the f. in the dream and what they do
T-18......IX.7:3 F. stand out and move about, actions
T19....IV.C.3:5 The shrouded f. in the funeral procession
T-27....VIII.4:4 But who reacts to f. in a dream unless he
T-27..VIII.10:5 react at all to f. in a dream you knew that
T-28........II.8:4 so the f. in the dream have hated him. His
T-29...... IX.3:1 All f. in the dream are idols, made to save
T-29...... IX.7:2 Except the f. have been changed. They are
T-29.....IX.10:3 are kind to everyone who f. in the dream.
W-pI.....73.2:2 peoples it with f. that seem to attack you
W-pI.....73.2:3 These f. become the middlemen the ego
W-pI.136.16:3 There will be no dim f. from your dreams,
W-pI...153.8:3 we mistook the f. in it for the Son of God;
W-pI...158.4:1 vast illusion in which f. come and go as if
W-pII ...10.2:5 all the f. in the dream in which the world
W-pII ...12.2:5 and trembles at the f. in its dreams; its
M-12.........6:7 They watch the dream f. come and go,

## fill 25

T-2...........I.1:7 f. it with your own ideas instead of truth.
T-3......... V.2:4 you make something to f. a perceived lack
T-9....VIII.10:2 No one else can f. your part in it, and
T-14.... XI.13:6 f. every mind that so makes room for Him
T-15......IV.3:3 you must f. if you would join with me, by
T19IV.A.17:12 you would have calls upon pain to f. your
T-22...... VI.5:6 every empty place in Heaven that you f.
T-23.........I.8:8 battle. Why would you f. your world with
T-25...... VI.3:6 see no function in the world for them to f.
T-25...... VI.4:2 function in salvation he alone can f.; a
T-27...... III.4:3 For what you leave as vacant God will f.,
T-29...... IV.4:1 failed to f. the function you allotted him?
T-30...... III.4:7 made but to f. a gap that is not there. It is
T-30...... IV.1:8 the false ideas you made to f. the gap you
W-pI......35.8:2 think up specific things to f. the interval,
W-pI....98.11:2 He would have you take and help you f.,
W-pI...122.8:3 and f. your heart with deep tranquility as
W-pI...123.6:5 until they f. the world with gladness and
W-pI...135.7:3 abuse it by assigning it to roles it cannot f.
W-pI.190.11:2 gratitude unto our Teacher f. our hearts,
W-pI......192.h I have a function God would have me f..
W-pI...212.1:1 I have a function God would have me f.. *I*
W-pII .317.1:1 I have a special place to f.; a role for me
W-pII .319.1:3 f. up the space the ego left unoccupied by
W-pII .344.1:7 *brothers f. my store with Heaven's treasures*

## filled 21

T-1........ III.3:2 Being f. with spirit, they forgive in return.
T-3.....VII.4:12 why you cannot create and are f. with fear
T-4........IV.1:5 Your mind is f. with schemes to save the
T-11.........I.3:4 place in His Mind cannot be f. by anyone
T-11...... III.3:5 so f. with joy that it will leap into Heaven,
T-13....... V.5:7 private world is f. with figures of fear you
T-14.... XI.15:5 and you will find yourself so f. with power
T19. IV.A.13:3 return with gorges f. with things decayed
T-27...... III.4:1 An empty space that is not seen as f., an
T-29...... IV.4:3 the functions you have given have been f.;
T-29...... VI.6:2 how f. with blessing and with happiness!
T-30...... IV.3:1 not there is f. with toys in countless forms
W-pI........8.3:3 than believing that it is f. with real ideas,
W-pI......96.4:2 serves the spirit is at peace and f. with joy.
W-pI......98.3:4 f. completely in the perfect time and place
W-pI...129.1:3 for what is far more satisfying, f. with joy,
W-pI.184.12:3 all space is f. with truth's reflection. Every
W-pII .....4.1:9 And truth can be but f. with knowledge,
W-pII .266.2:3 f. the world with those who point to Him,

| | |
|---|---|
| W-pII .314.1:5 | and peace into a quiet future f. with joy? |
| M-4 ....... V.1:3 | open hands of gentleness are always f.. |

## filling 1

| | |
|---|---|
| T-11.........I.3:4 | you, and your f. it was your creation, |

## fills 8

| | |
|---|---|
| T-11....... II.5:4 | that f. your mind so that He becomes |
| T-21.........I.8:2 | all the circle f. with light before your eyes. |
| T-25.......in.3:4 | and f. it with the Holiness that shines |
| T-25....... II.1:1 | the body's eyes perceive f. you with fear? |
| T-28....... V.6:6 | For it f. every place and every time, and |
| T-29.... III.3:10 | and understand what really f. the gap so |
| W-pI... 182.5:4 | the holy air that f. His Father's house. You |
| W-pII .267.1:3 | Peace f. my heart, and floods my body |

## Final 7

*final*

| | |
|---|---|
| W-pII ... 10.4:1 | God's F. Judgment is as merciful as every |
| W-pII ... 10.5:1 | God's F. Judgment: "You are still My holy |
| M-15 ......... 1:2 | No one can escape God's F. Judgment. |
| M-15 ......... 1:4 | But the F. Judgment will not come until it |
| M-15 ......... 1:6 | as God's F. Judgment on him is received. |
| M-15 ......... 2:8 | yourself, and thus delay this F. Judgment. |
| M-28 ......... 6:6 | F. Judgment is restored the truth about |

## final 88

*Final*

| | |
|---|---|
| T-2......... II.5:2 | The Atonement is the f. lesson. Learning |
| T-2........ III.3:2 | of the inevitability of the f. decision, but |
| T-2........ IV.1:5 | The Atonement, or the f. miracle, is a |
| T-2......... V.7:4 | the discomfort is not the f. outcome of the |
| T-2......VIII.3:3 | It is a f. healing rather than a meting out |
| T-3...........I.7:9 | It is the f. demonstration that all the other |
| T-5....... II.3:11 | It is the f. lesson that I learned, and God's |
| T-6...... V.B.2:3 | It is also their last and f. one. Increasing |
| T-6...... V.B.8:6 | decision, it is clearly not the f. one. Lack |
| T-6...... V.C.5:7 | f. step will still be taken for you by God, |
| T-12... VII.13:4 | as the f. expression of its feeling for you, it |
| T-13.......in.4:6 | Atonement is the f. lesson he need learn, |
| T-13....... II.6:3 | as the f. guilt that fully justifies murder. |
| T-13...... IV.2:5 | destruction is the f. proof that you were |
| T-13.... VIII.3:9 | by crowning them as one with the f. gift of |
| T-13...... XI.4:5 | He has perfect faith in your f. judgment, |
| T-15.........I.6:4 | The ego does not advertise its f. threat, for |
| T-16....... V.5:5 | "victory" even to the f. triumph over God. |
| T-17....... II.3:7 | this f. blessing of God's Son upon himself, |
| T-18...... IX.9:6 | ready for the f. step in the journey inward. |
| T-18... IX.10:4 | Himself can take the f. step unhindered, |
| T19.... IV.C.6:5 | would be the f. and complete disruption |
| T19.... IV.C.7:7 | Here is the f. end of union, the triumph of |
| T19... IV.D.1:5 | peace must still surmount a f. obstacle, |
| T19... IV.D.3:4 | *fear of God*, the f. step in your dissociation. |
| T-20....... II.7:8 | the strength to look upon this f. obstacle, |
| T-21..... VII.6:5 | This f. question, which is indeed the last |
| T-21... VII.10:1 | Why is the f. question so important? |
| T-21... VII.11:5 | By answering the f. question "yes," you |
| T-21.... VIII.1:5 | the f. proof he valued the inconstant more |
| T-21.... VIII.2:8 | see the f. question is necessary to the rest, |
| T-21.... VIII.4:1 | how you would answer the f. question. |
| T-21.... VIII.4:3 | f. one that really asks if you are willing to |
| T-21.... VIII.5:5 | here the f. question is already answered, |
| T-23..... II.12:3 | a *f.* principle of chaos comes to the "rescue. |
| T-24....... II.9:4 | illusions that have reached this f. obstacle |
| T-26...... III.4:2 | possible, the f. judgment upon this world. |
| T-27...... III.6:7 | is God left free to take the f. step Himself. |
| T-28....... II.9:1 | is the separation's f. step, with which |
| T-28....... II.9:2 | f. step is an effect of what has gone before, |
| T-30.......I.12:1 | (7) This f. step is but acknowledgment of |
| T-30....... V.4:1 | The f. step is God's, because it is but God |
| T-31..............h | THE F. VISION |
| W-pI..... 23.5:4 | The f. one does not. Your images have |
| W-pI... 133.4:3 | and thus delay your f. choice until you |
| W-pI... 137.2:3 | body f. power to make the separation real, |
| W-pI... 138.6:5 | Here is the f. and the only choice in which |
| W-pI. 153.14:1 | but for a moment more, to play our f., |
| W-pI. 153.20:3 | no doubt that you will reach your f. goal. |
| W-pI. 155.11:4 | This is our f. journey, which we make for |
| W-pI... 168.3:2 | us up, taking salvation's f. step Himself. |
| W-pI... 169.3:2 | The f. step must go beyond all learning. |
| W-pI. 169.12:2 | for grace, the f. gift salvation can bestow. |
| W-pI... 170.9:3 | peace. The f. one, the hardest to believe is |
| W-pI. 184.12:2 | Name becomes the f. lesson that all things |
| W-pI. 193.13:6 | God will take this f. step Himself. Do not |
| W-pI... 194.1:3 | you await with certainty the f. step of God |
| W-pI... 200.2:1 | f. point to which each one must come at |
| W-pII .... in.2:3 | promised He will take the f. step Himself. |
| W-pII .... in.8:1 | start upon the f. part of this one holy year, |
| W-pII .. in.10:2 | For in this f. section, we will come to |
| W-pII . 225.2:5 | as we accomplish these few f. steps which |
| W-pII ..... 2.4:2 | Here we share our f. dream. It is a dream |
| W-pII ..... 6.4:2 | will exchange them for the f. dream which |
| W-pII . 289.2:4 | *And here am I made ready for Your f. step.* |
| W-pII ..... 8.5:2 | instant more for God to take His f. step, |
| W-pII . 292.1:2 | be the f. outcome found for everything. |
| W-pII . 297.2:1 | *are Your ways; how sure their f. outcome,* |
| W-pII ... 10.2:1 | The f. judgment on the world contains no |
| W-pII ... 14.2:2 | Yet in the f. days of this one year we gave |
| Wfl...............h | F. LESSONS. |
| Wfl.........in.1:1 | Our f. lessons will be left as free of words |
| M-4 ........X.2:9 | achieved. Forgiveness is the f. goal of the |
| M-5 ........II.4:6 | limit. The f. outcome of this lesson is the |
| M-14 ....... 3:10 | it is the f. lesson in which unity is restored |
| M-14 ......... 4:3 | The f. lesson, which brings the ending of |
| M-25 ......... 1:6 | directed toward this one great f. surprise, |
| M-27 ......... 6:5 | This is salvation's f. goal; the end of all |
| M-28 ......... 1:4 | awareness of the Holy Spirit's f. dream. It |
| M-28 ......... 1:8 | is the invitation to God to take His f. step. |
| C-1 ............ 5:3 | This is the f. vision, the last perception, |
| C-1 ............ 5:3 | in which God takes the f. step Himself. |
| C-3 .......... 4:11 | It is the f. step. And this we leave to God. |
| C-3 ............ 6:6 | to time. The f. step is also but a shift. As a |
| C-4 ............ 7:6 | of Christ has shone away time's f. instant, |
| C-5 ............ 3:5 | He offered you a f. demonstration that it |
| P-2...........I.2:3 | of "the saving illusion" or "the f. dream," |
| P-2......... VI.6:1 | realization is the f. goal of psychotherapy. |

## finally 46

| | |
|---|---|
| T-2 .....VIII.3:6 | simply means that everyone will f. come |
| T-3 ...... VII.4:8 | f. perceive correctly you can only be glad |
| T-4 ........in.3:5 | and f. the crucifixion of the body, or |
| T-4 ..........I.6:3 | absolve you f. from the need for a teacher. |
| T-5 ..........I.7:5 | F., it points the way beyond the healing |
| T-6 ..........I.9:2 | abandoned, beaten, torn, and f. killed. It |
| T-6 ....... IV.7:3 | Having f. been wholly answered, *it has* |
| T-6 ... V.C.4:10 | will f. liberate your mind from choice, |
| T-7 .........II.6:8 | so that you can f. *be* consistent. |
| T-7 .....VIII.2:1 | projection and anger can be f. undone. |
| T-9 .........II.4:8 | way you can hear it now, and f. know it. |
| T-9 ....... VI.7:2 | open Arms, and f. know His open Mind. |
| T-11 .... V.11:2 | what fear is can you f. learn to distinguish |
| T-12 .... VII.3:4 | where He must be, and f. know what He is |
| T-13 ..... XI.4:4 | will f. let Him judge the difference for you |
| T-17 ..... III.2:6 | And f., why all such relationships become |
| T-17 ... IV.13:6 | And f. you look upon the picture itself, |
| T-17 ........ V.5:3 | change develops and is f. accomplished, it |
| T-18 ..... VII.5:7 | or when the goal is f. achieved by anyone, |
| T-18 .... IX.14:2 | and purified, and f. removed forever. |
| T-22 ......in.4:8 | and f. removes all sense of differences, so |
| T-22 ..... IV.6:3 | as every obstacle was f. surmounted that |
| T-29 ...... V.8:6 | And leading f. beyond all dreams, unto |
| T-29 ... VIII.6:6 | a little while; to suffer pain and f. to die. |
| T-31 ...... V.7:9 | its ways and f. "maturing" in its thought. |
| W-pI....... 9.2:5 | and understanding will f. come to lighten |
| W-pI...... 23.7:5 | When you f. learn that thoughts of attack |
| WpI... rI.in.5:2 | And f. you will learn that there is no limit |
| W-pI...... 65.7:1 | F., repeat the idea for today once more, |
| W-pI... 108.6:3 | and f. arrive at the one Thought which |
| W-pI. 138.12:4 | sanity. And f., we close the day with this, |
| W-pI... 163.4:4 | is the Will of Father and of Son defeated f. |
| W-pI... 168.3:4 | But f. He comes Himself, and takes us in |
| W-pI. 169.13:4 | How could you f. attain to it forever, |
| W-pI... 198.4:1 | past all suffering, and f. away from death. |
| W-pII . 251.1:6 | hopes are f. fulfilled and dreams are gone. |
| W-pII . 284.1:6 | and more, and f. accepted as the truth. I |
| W-pII . 302.1:2 | *us, as our sight is f. restored and we can see.* |
| M-in.......... 4:8 | hope, their learning f. becomes complete. |
| M-4 ..... I.A.8:1 | And f., there is "a period of achievement. |
| M-4 ...... VI.1:8 | teacher of God f. agrees to look past them |
| M-13 ......... 1:5 | replaces the first, so both can f. disappear |
| M-24 ......... 4:2 | When this is f. accomplished, issues such |
| C-2 ............ 7:6 | you left behind at last and f. passed by. |
| P-2......... in.4:5 | They are f. given up in the minds of both. |
| P-2....... VII.3:6 | all sense of separation f. is overcome. |

## find 417

| | |
|---|---|
| T-1 ....... VI.1:1 | can f. it only by complete forgiveness. No |
| T-2 ..........I.5:9 | You cannot f. it outside. Illness is some |
| T-3 .........II.6:4 | and emptiness can never f. lasting solace. |
| T-3 ..... IV.7:15 | now, and they will f. rest unto their souls. |
| T-4 ..........I.2:4 | to enter into your ego you will f. peace. |
| T-4 ....... III.2:3 | will f. it very helpful if you understand it |
| T-4 ....... IV.1:8 | where you look to f. yourself is up to you. |
| T-4 .........V.5:2 | "Seek and ye shall f." does not mean that |
| T-5 ....... IV.6:2 | f. the way except by taking your brother |
| T-5 ..... VI.11:3 | still true that where you look to f. yourself |
| T-6 .........II.5:6 | which you can f. happiness in the world. |
| T-6 .........II.6:1 | else can you f. joy in a joyless place except |
| T-6 ....... IV.9:5 | both a Guide to f. it and a means to keep |
| T-6 ... IV.11:10 | only place where you can f. the sanity He |
| T-7 ....... IV.7:2 | this only, because you can f. nothing else. |
| T-7 ....... VI.7:2 | only reason you may f. this hard to accept |
| T-7 .....VIII.2:3 | because it does not want you to f. conflict |
| T-8 .........II.2:3 | a Son of God should turn to f. himself? |
| T-8 ....... III.4:5 | in him you will f. yourself or lose yourself. |
| T-8 ....... III.5:4 | you have another opportunity to f. them. |
| T-8 ....... III.5:6 | The ego tries to f. them in yourself alone, |
| T-8 ....... III.5:7 | only at yourself you cannot f. yourself, |
| T-8 ....... III.6:1 | are the Kingdom cannot f. yourself alone. |
| T-8 .........V.5:2 | me who know it for you and you will f. it. |
| T-8 ....... VI.3:2 | one created by God can f. joy in anything |
| T-8 ....... VI.6:4 | You cannot f. joy except as God does. His |
| T-8 ...... VII.1:8 | Since he can f. himself only in them, he |
| T-8 ....... IX.2:5 | and f. you when you meet its conditions. |
| T-9 .........II.6:1 | than you can f. joy for yourself alone. |
| T-9 ....... III.7:3 | If you would f. your way and keep it, see |
| T-9 ..... IV.10:2 | you will never f. satisfaction in fantasy, so |
| T-9 ..... IV.11:2 | for reality in fantasies you will not f. it. |
| T-9 ..... IV.11:3 | of the ego, and of these you will f. many. |
| T-9 .........V.6:3 | Can you f. light by analyzing darkness, as |
| T-9 ....... VI.7:8 | will f. your creations because he created |
| T-9 ...... VII.1:2 | He not have given you the means to f. it? |
| T-10 ... III.11:1 | Only at the altar of God will you f. peace. |
| T-11 ....... III.7:3 | enter the temple and f. it waiting for you. |
| T-11 .....V.10:8 | to f. what he believes would destroy him. |
| T-11 ..... VI.7:1 | will not f. peace until you have removed |
| T-12 ... III.10:9 | Yet to f. the place, you must relinquish |
| T-12 ..... IV.1:3 | actively, makes one proviso; do not f. it. |
| T-12 ..... IV.1:4 | summed up simply as: "Seek and do *not* f.. |
| T-12 ..... IV.2:3 | for love it is seeking what it is afraid to f.. |
| T-12 ..... IV.3:1 | wants to f. what would utterly defeat him. |
| T-12 ..... IV.4:2 | To seek and not to f. is hardly joyous. Is |
| T-12 ..... IV.4:5 | promise is always, "Seek and you *will* f.," |
| T-12 ........V.7:1 | that the ego's rule is, "Seek and do not f.." |
| T-12 .... VII.6:3 | you seek, for what you seek you will f.. |
| T-12 .... VII.6:5 | It does not f. love, for that is not what it is |
| T-12 .... VII.6:6 | if you seek for two goals you will f. them, |
| T-12 .... VII.7:4 | This is why you f. what you seek. What |
| T-12 .. VII.11:1 | mission to extend peace you will f. peace, |
| T-12 ...VIII.1:4 | in order to attack it, you will never f. it. |
| T-12 ...VIII.1:5 | how can you f. it except through itself? |
| T-12 ...VIII.7:7 | seeking the unreal, what else could you f.? |
| T-13 ........I.5:3 | and the way to f. release is not denied him |
| T-13 ........II.1:2 | wants to retain guilt *you* f. it intolerable, |
| T-13 ........II.5:2 | wish to crucify him if you could f. him. |
| T-13 ........II.5:3 | fearful, and so you are afraid to f. him. |
| T-13 ..... III.1:9 | f. within yourself something you fear even |
| T-13 ..... III.8:4 | You will f. this place of truth as you see it |
| T-13 . III.12:10 | But seek this place and you will f. it, for |
| T-13 ..... IV.6:5 | you could f. for release in the present. The |
| T-13 ..... VI.5:4 | and you will f. it if you seek it there. You |

T-13....VI.10:2 Yet you will f. it through its witnesses, for
T-13.....VI.11:5 you will lay aside the world and f. another
T-13.....VII.3:7 f. in it the road that leads away from it
T-13...VII.10:5 you f. yourself *because* you are lacking. Yet
T-13...VII.10:6 Yet can you f. yourself in such a world?
T-13...VII.16:4 peace of mind that we must f. together.
T-13... VIII.7:3 who are seeking you and where to f. them
T-13....... X.2:9 will f. it in that strange relationship. It is
T-13....... X.3:2 will you f. satisfaction and peace with him
T-13....... X.4:4 whom you f. no real relationships at all.
T-13....... X.4:8 the present, and hope to f. salvation now?
T-13....... X.6:1 where you would always f. Atonement.
T-13...... XI.5:5 You will f. the peace in which He has
T-13...... XI.6:4 you will f. the answer that makes the need
T-14....... II.1:7 you will f. the "treasure" that you seek.
T-14....... II.3:8 *You will f. no deception there, but only the*
T-14...... IV.6:7 tired will f. this is more restful than sleep.
T-14....... V.7:7 And you will f. ever-increasing confidence
T-14...... IX.6:7 for it, but knows not where to look to f. it.
T-14...... IX.7:4 and all their problems f. but healing there
T-14...... X.10:7 because it has excluded what it would f..
T-14.... XI.15:5 will f. yourself so filled with power that
T-15.........I.3:5 for you to f. peace even in death, it offers
T-15..... III.10:9 host of God needs not seek to f. anything.
T-15...... IV.1:8 past and future, where you will not f. it, it
T-15...... IV.2:5 Think not that you can f. salvation in
T-15...... IV.7:4 think you f. a way to keep what you would
T-15....... V.7:3 you cannot f. it because it is not real.
T-15...... VI.1:2 of a relationship and f. peace within it.
T-15...... VI.2:2 without for what you cannot f. without. I
T-15...... VI.4:1 f. it difficult to believe that when another
T-15...... VI.4:5 you f. difficult to accept is the fact that,
T-15...... VII.5:5 but you will become willing to f. out, if
T-15... VIII.3:9 are must everyone seek, and f. you there.
T-15...... XI.6:1 for love, you seek for sacrifice and f. it.
T-15...... XI.6:2 it. Yet you f. not love. It is impossible to
T-16.........I.6:1 to weakness, and hopes to f. love there.
T-16...... IV.4:9 they f. the fear of death is still upon them,
T-16...... IV.6:1 merely to seek and f. all of the barriers
T-16....... V.6:2 And the attempt to f. the imagined "best"
T-16....... V.6:5 be of the ego's maxim, "Seek but do not f.
T-16...... VI.2:5 will be unable to f. you and comfort you.
T-16...... VI.8:7 F. hope and comfort, rather than despair,
T-16...... VI.8:7 You could not long f. even the illusion of
T-16..... VII.4:1 you must return to the past to f. salvation
T-16... VII.11:1 Seek and *f.* His message in the holy instant
T-17....... V.6:9 you f. yourself in an insane relationship,
T-17....... V.8:2 You will f. many opportunities to blame
T-17..... V.11:9 of the situation in which you f. yourself.
T-17..... VII.5:1 Every situation in which you f. yourself is
T-18....... II.3:1 f. the differences between what you see in
T-18...... IV.7:3 You f. it difficult to accept the idea that
T-18..... VII.1:3 this always means you still f. sin attractive
T-18..... VII.6:1 everyone will one day f. in his own way, at
T-18. VIII.10:1 Go out and f. them, for they bring your
T-19...... III.7:2 you will f. guilt attractive and believe that
T19. IV.A.11:2 scrap of evil and of sin that they can f.,
T19..IV.B.12:1 pleasure through the body and not f. pain
T19..IV.B.17:6 seeks. So does the ego f. the death *it* seeks,
T-20....... II.9:6 So will we f. what we were meant to find
T-20....... II.9:6 we were meant to f. by Him Who leads us
T-20....... V.1:2 begins to f. the certainty his Father has in
T-20..... VII.1:4 or parts you f. more difficult than others,
T-20. VIII.10:2 meaning always looks within to f. itself,
T-21....... II.3:3 seems to f. himself by chance or accident.
T-21...... III.6:1 means for sin by which you sought to f. it.
T-21....... V.5:9 is proof you will not f. the answer there.
T-21..... V.5:11 purpose given it, you must be free to f. it.
T-21..... VII.4:4 But it can never f. what is not there. Yes,
T-21..... VII.4:5 so that it runs at once to f. another, and
T-21..... VII.5:5 him seek no longer what is not there to f..
T-21..... VII.6:6 truth may be the enemy you yet may f..
T-22.........I.8:6 never could He f. a home in separate ones
T-22...... IV.7:2 received it for himself could f. it difficult.
T-22...... VI.1:8 but yearns for freedom and tries to f. it.
T-22.... VI.1:10 the other serve his choice as means to f. it.
T-23....... II.8:6 enable you to f. escape from what it wants
T-23..... II.17:7 Who can f. safety from attack by turning
T-23...... III.6:7 But from within it you can f. no safety.
T-23...... IV.9:8 Love of God upholding him could f. the
T-24....... V.9:5 that He must go to f. Himself complete.
T-24....... VI.6:3 and f. no sight nor place nor time where
T-24.... VI.12:2 the two, it is this one you f. more difficult.
T-24.... VI.12:4 you f. a burden wearisome and tedious,
T-25....... II.1:2 think you f. a hope of satisfaction there.
T-25..... V.4:10 to him through you, that you may f. it,
T-25..... VII.7:3 place in which you think you f. yourself,
T-25... VIII.2:5 still against himself would f. impossible.
T-26....... II.5:4 *you* f. him guilty and would have him die.
T-26...... VI.1:8 f. the safety that the truth alone can give?
T-26... VII.11:8 to f. a little treasure of his own. And this
T-26.VII.11:10 This is the treasure he has sought to f..
T-26....... X.4:2 seek to f. an innocence that is not Theirs
T-27.........I.2:7 But in his innocence you f. your own.
T-27..... VII.6:8 is not where you should look to *f.* the truth
T-27..... VII.7:2 you f. the cause of your perspective on the
T-27... VII.10:6 and you will f. you have the peace of God.
T-28...... IV.2:3 You f. yourself by not accepting them as
T-29.........I.9:5 not afraid to f. a loss of self in finding God
T-29....... II.1:4 loss, to f. yourself in Heaven and in God?
T-29....... II.3:1 to attempt to f. the hope of peace upon a
T-29....... II.5:3 is no other place where He can f. His host,
T-29....... V.6:5 on Heaven itself, and hope to f. its peace?
T-29..... VII.1:5 and f. the happiness His answer brings.
T-29..... VII.2:5 in search of something that he cannot f.,
T-29..... VII.6:1 that you must f. what is outside yourself
T-30.........I.1:6 f. resistance strong and dedication weak,
T-30...... VI.7:6 within and f. escape from every idol there.
T-31.........I.7:8 that you can seek for here and hope to f..
T-31...... III.5:2 itself; a place where nothing can f. mercy,
T-31...... IV.6:3 come to learn to f. a road the world does
T-31...... IV.7:3 to f. this course to be too difficult to learn,
T-31....... V.8:3 Now must the Holy Spirit f. a way to help
T-31..... V.14:2 must f. the answer to the riddle of himself
T-31...... VI.3:4 see another world your eyes could never f.
T-31... VIII.9:1 f. so many chances to perceive another
W-in.......... 6:2 to every situation in which you f. yourself,
W-in.......... 8:1 presents you will f. hard to believe, and
W-pI....... 4.1:6 You will f., if you train yourself to look at
W-pI....... 4.6:1 you may f. the suspension of judgment in
W-pI....... 5.4:1 you may f. it hard to be indiscriminate,
W-pI....... 5.6:1 You may also f. yourself less willing to
W-pI....... 8.4:3 merely noting the thoughts you f. there.
W-pI....... 8.6:1 the day, unless you f. it irritates you. If
W-pI....... 8.6:2 If you f. it trying, three or four times is
W-pI....... 8.6:3 might f. it helpful, however, to include
W-pI..... 10.4:6 In fact, if you f. it helpful to do so, you
W-pI..... 12.6:3 You may f. even this too long. Terminate
W-pI..... 13.5:1 You may f. it difficult to avoid resistance,
W-pI..... 14.2:3 idea unless you f. them comfortable. If
W-pI..... 16.4:3 You will f. that it is still hard for you not
W-pI..... 16.6:1 if you f. them relatively effortless. If strain
W-pI..... 22.2:3 happy discovery to f. that you can escape?
W-pI..... 26.8:3 will probably f. some of them, especially
W-pI..... 29.2:1 will probably f. this idea very difficult to
W-pI..... 29.2:2 You may f. it silly, irreverent, senseless,
W-pI..... 32.4:2 be utilized, if you f. the exercise restful.
W-pI..... 33.1:3 be repeated as often as you f. comfortable
W-pI..... 34.6:2 f. you need more than one application of
W-pI..... 39.9:1 You may f. these practice periods easier if
W-pI..... 39.9:2 You may also f. it helpful to include a few
W-pI..... 40.2:1 will probably f. it more helpful if you do.
W-pI..... 41.7:1 you may repeat the idea if you f. it helpful
W-pI..... 42.2:2 in whatever circumstance you f. yourself.
W-pI..... 42.5:3 you f. your mind is merely wandering,
W-pI..... 42.6:3 If you f. this difficult, it is better to spend
W-pI..... 42.6:3 than it is to strain to f. suitable thoughts.
W-pI..... 43.6:1 If you f. your mind wandering; if you
W-pI..... 43.7:1 in which you f. yourself during the day.
W-pI..... 44.4:2 but only if you f. the time slipping by with
W-pI..... 44.5:2 you might f. that you will encounter strong
W-pI..... 44.6:2 You might f. it helpful to remind yourself,
W-pI..... 44.9:2 you will probably f. it more reassuring to
W-pI..... 45.6:5 *I would like to f. them.* Then try to go past
W-pI..... 55.4:4 to f. out what my own best interests are,
W-pI..... 61.6:3 f. them helpful and want to extend them.
W-pI..... 62.2:3 Your goal is to f. out who you are, having
W-pI..... 63.4:1 will probably f. it easier to let the related
W-pI..... 65.2:3 the only way in which you can f. peace of
W-pI..... 65.6:1 thoughts will become harder to f.. Try,
W-pI..... 66.3:5 will merely be glad that we can f. out what
W-pI..... 66.9:2 to f. salvation under the ego's guidance.
W-pI..... 66.9:3 Did you f. it? Were you happy? Did they
W-pI..... 67.3:3 in your mind It is there for you to f..
W-pI..... 67.4:1 You may f. it necessary to repeat the idea
W-pI..... 67.4:2 You may also f. that this is not sufficient,
W-pI..... 68.3:2 that those who forgive will f. peace. It is as
W-pI..... 68.4:4 to f. out how you would feel without them
W-pI..... 68.5:2 Some of these will be quite easy to f..
W-pI..... 70.8:2 f. it in the clouds that surround the light,
W-pI..... 71.4:2 ego's basic doctrine, "Seek but do not f."
W-pI..... 71.4:3 will not f. salvation than to channelize all
W-pI... 72.11:4 Seek and you will f.. We are no longer
W-pI... 72.11:5 the ego what salvation is and where to f. it
W-pI..... 73.8:1 that we will f. what it is your will to find,
W-pI..... 73.8:1 that we will find what it is your will to f.,
W-pI..... 74.7:4 Then try to f. what you are seeking. A
W-pI..... 76.2:2 salvation where it is not, and never f. it.
W-pI..... 77.7:6 not relying on yourself to f. the miracle,
W-pI..... 79.3:1 the position in which you f. yourself now.
WpI..rII.in.3:1 period if you f. your mind wandering, but
W-pI..... 83.3:5 makes me happy, if I would f. happiness.
W-pI..... 84.2:1 You might f. these specific forms helpful
W-pI..... 92.9:3 place we try today to f. and rest in, for the
W-pI... 92.10:4 how to f. the meeting place of self and Self
W-pI..... 96.4:1 of mind as means to f. its Self expression.
W-pI..... 96.8:1 We will attempt today to f. this thought,
W-pI..... 96.9:5 of dreams, to f. illusions in their place.
W-pI..... 96.9:7 have. Salvation is among them; f. it there.
W-pI... 99.12:5 that love may f. its rightful place in you
W-pI... 100.8:1 Now let us try to f. that joy that proves to
W-pI... 100.8:2 It is your function that you f. it here, and
W-pI... 100.8:2 you find it here, and that you f. it now.
W-pI. 100.10:4 you must f. what He would have you give.
W-pI... 101.2:5 seek them out and f. them somewhere,
W-pI... 101.6:8 and then attempt again to f. the joy these
W-pI... 102.4:4 fail to f. it when you learn it is your choice
W-pI... 104.4:2 come to f. what has been given us by Him.
W-pI... 108.9:3 You will f. you have exact return, for that
W-pI. 110.10:1 Seek Him today, and f. Him. He will be
W-pI. 110.10:3 For when you f. Him, you will understand
W-pI. 121.11:3 Try to f. some little spark of brightness
W-pI... 122.4:5 more. You will not f. another one instead.
W-pI. 124.10:2 When you are ready you will f. it there,
W-pI... 127.6:1 Seek not within the world to f. your Self.
W-pI... 129.3:1 a loss to f. a world instead where losing is
W-pI... 129.3:2 Is it loss to f. all things you really want,
W-pI... 130.8:6 *that I may f. my freedom and deliverance.*
W-pI... 131.1:3 the place to which he comes to f. stability
W-pI... 131.4:2 and must f. the goal you really want. No
W-pI... 131.5:2 You will f. Heaven. Everything you seek
W-pI... 131.9:4 while Heaven is the place he cannot f..
W-pI. 131.12:1 Seek for that door and f. it. But before
W-pI. 131.14:5 will f. the goal of all your searching here,
W-pI. 131.15:5 *Today I seek and f. all that I want. My single*
W-pI... 132.2:4 of seeking what you do not want to f..
W-pI... 132.3:3 you f. escape and give it to the world. You
W-pI... 132.7:4 Others f. it in experience that is not of this
W-pI... 132.8:1 And some will f. it in this course, and in
W-pI. 133.13:1 to f. everything and claim it as their own.
W-pI. 133.13:4 *value do I seek, for only that do I desire to f..*
W-pI... 134.3:1 major difficulty that you f. in genuine
W-pI... 134.9:1 way to f. the door to true forgiveness, and
W-pI... 140.8:2 will try today to f. the source of healing,
W-pI... 153.2:6 knows not where to turn to f. escape from
W-pI. 153.15:5 will f. that half an hour is too short a time
W-pI... 155.2:3 when they f. their own reality is even here
W-pI... 155.3:2 to f. they were mistaken in their choice.
W-pI... 155.9:2 And you may f. that you are tempted still
W-pI... 160.6:2 What can he f.? A stranger to himself can
W-pI... 160.6:3 to himself can f. no home wherever he
W-pI... 166.4:2 is the only safety he believes that he can f.
W-pI. 170.13:8 *see Your glory, and in them we f. our peace.*
WpI.rV.in12:6 of meaning. It is Here that we f. rest.
W-pI... 182.3:2 seeking in darkness what he cannot f.; not
W-pI... 182.4:1 childhood home that you would f. again.
W-pI... 183.3:2 and where it seemed to stand you f. a star;

W-pI...185.8:1 mind, to f. the dreams you cherish still.
W-pI.185.11:1 seeks the peace of God can fail to f. it. For
W-pI...186.8:1 And so we f. our peace. We will accept
W-pI...188.2:2 Why wait to f. it in the future, or believe it
W-pI...189.9:7 His Son to show Him how to f. His way.
W-pI.189.10:8 *Yours is the way that we would f. and follow.*
W-pI...191.5:1 But let today's idea f. a place among your
W-pI.191.11:3 of the world until you f. it in yourself.
W-pI...195.4:4 that in us all things will f. their freedom.
W-pI...195.7:3 direct them to the peace that we would f.,
W-pI...197.1:3 unless you f. external gratitude and lavish
W-pI...198.4:3 it, seek to f. a thousand ways in which it
W-pI...198.9:2 that you may f. the key to light and let the
W-pI...200.1:2 will not f. peace except the peace of God.
W-pI...200.1:5 else for you to f. except the peace of God,
W-pI...200.3:5 and seek no longer what you cannot f..
W-pI...200.3:6 open eyes to f. that Heaven lies before you
W-pI...200.4:5 it is given you to f. the means whereby the
W-pI...200.5:2 of the world, if you would f. escape. You
W-pI...200.7:2 What could he hope to f. in such a world?
W-pI...200.7:6 on it another way, and f. the peace of God
W-pI...208.1:3 *in that stillness we will f. the peace of God. It*
W-pI...217.1:3 *can I f. the Self to Whom my thanks are due?* I
W-pII ....in.1:5 f. the end toward which our practicing
W-pII ....in.7:2 We have sought to f. our way by following
W-pII .221.2:6 let our thoughts be still and f. His peace,
W-pII .225.2:1 Brother, we f. that stillness now. The way
W-pII .227.2:1 so today we f. our glad return to Heaven,
W-pII .229.1:1 Identity, and f. It in these words: "Love,
W-pII ....230.h Now will I seek and f. the peace of God.
W-pII .230.2:5 *I need but call on You to f. the peace You gave*
W-pII .....2.1:1 that you would f. your way to Him at last.
W-pII .231.1:4 *else that I could ever really want to f.. Let me*
W-pII .231.2:5 only this is what it will be given us to f..
W-pII .235.1:2 to f. that only happiness has come to me.
W-pII .....3.3:2 go to f. what has been given them to seek.
W-pII .242.2:6 *we need in helping us to f. the way to You.*
W-pII .246.1:1 me not think that I can f. the way to God,
W-pII .251.1:9 want. And now at last I f. myself at peace.
W-pII .256.1:3 have been to f. the way to where you are?
W-pII .256.2:2 *f. the way Your sacred Word has pointed out*
W-pII .260.2:1 and Therein we f. our true Identity at last.
W-pII .....5.5:8 home. Identify with love, and f. your Self.
W-pII .261.1:3 to f. my peace in murderous attack. I live
W-pII .261.1:5 In Him I f. my refuge and my strength. In
W-pII .261.2:3 *and f. the Son whom You created as my Self.*
W-pII .269.1:3 *It is given me to f. a new perception through*
W-pII .....6.5:2 to f. Christ's face and look on nothing else
W-pII .280.2:1 *to Your Son, for thus alone I f. the way to You*
W-pII .286.1:6 *is everything I hope to f. already given me.*
W-pII .287.1:4 treasure would I seek and f. and keep that
W-pII .289.2:5 *for Your Son to f. the loveliness You planned*
W-pII .292.1:4 we will not f. the end He has appointed as
W-pII .292.1:7 seek and we will f. according to His Will,
W-pII .296.1:4 *it I would set it free, that I may f. escape, and*
W-pII .296.2:3 us, to seek and f. the easy path to God.
W-pII .304.2:3 *Son, that he may f. again the memory of You,*
W-pII .309.1:4 To look within is but to f. my will as God
W-pII .309.2:3 *to my Self, and there I f. my true Identity.*
W-pII .318.1:4 salvation's purpose is to f. the sinlessness
W-pII .321.1:1 *what my freedom is, nor where to look to f. it*
W-pII .321.1:4 *nor understood the way to f. my freedom.*
W-pII .321.2:2 glad are we to f. our freedom through the
W-pII .322.1:2 illusions go I f. the gifts illusions tried to
W-pII .325.1:2 judges valuable, and therefore seeks to f..
W-pII .325.1:6 him, and f. the way to Heaven and to God
W-pII .328.1:3 Yet all we f. is sickness, suffering and loss
W-pII .328.1:5 To join with His is but to f. our own. And
W-pII .329.2:4 Through it we f. our way at last to God.
W-pII .331.2:2 today, that we may f. the peace of God.
W-pII .334.1:1 not wait another day to f. the treasures
W-pII .334.1:6 I go to f. the treasures God has given me.
W-pII .335.2:3 *In him I f. my Self, and in Your Son I find the*
W-pII .335.2:3 *in Your Son I f. the memory of You as well.*
W-pII .336.1:5 to f. what it has vainly sought without.
W-pII .336.2:2 *and f. Your promise of my sinlessness is kept*
W-pII .340.1:4 *him to f. Christ's vision through forgiveness*
W-pII ....343.h To f. the mercy and the peace of God.
W-pII .345.2:3 It will f. rest today, for we will offer what
W-pII .346.1:7 *I would f. the peace which You created for*
W-pII .349.1:2 *and give what I would f. and make my own. It*
W-pII .352.1:4 *have given me a way to f. Your peace again. I*
W-pII .352.1:8 *hear Your Voice and f. Your peace today. For*
W-pII .352.1:9 *own Identity, and f. in It the memory of You.*
W-pII .355.1:3 *me, and I need but reach out my hand to f. it.*
W-pII .357.1:4 *Voice instructing me to f. the way to You, as*
Wfl........in.2:1 way to f. the peace that God has given us.
Wfl........in.2:6 who are seeking for the way, but f. it not.
M-3 ........... 1:4 meet everyone, nor can everyone f. him.
M-3 ........... 5:8 No teacher of God can fail to f. the Help
M-4 ..... I.A.4:3 it. He will f. that many, if not most of the
M-8 ........... 3:7 and it sends the body's eyes to f. it. The
M-13 ......... 3:3 to know not what it really wants to f..
M-13 ......... 5:8 "Seek but do not f." remains this world's
M-16 ......... 1:6 who share that role with him will f. him,
M-16 ......... 4:7 or two after you begin to f. it difficult.
M-16 ......... 4:8 may f. that the difficulty will diminish
M-20 ......... 3:2 No one can fail to f. it who but seeks out
M-23 ......... 7:7 In him you f. God's Answer. Do you, then
C-in ........... 2:1 and those who seek controversy will f. it.
C-in ........... 2:2 who seek clarification will f. it as well.
C-2 ............ 5:2 we f. all that is not the ego in this world.
C-5 ............ 6:7 leave them both to f. the peace of God.
C-ep........... 3:7 Look up and f. your certain destiny the
P-2...........I.4:7 give for now. Yet both will f. sanity at last.
P-2..........II.2:7 What can be necessary to f. truth, which
P-2..........II.5:7 Together they can f. a pathway out, for no
P-2..........II.5:7 out, for no one will f. sanity alone.
P-2......... V.8:8 There is no other way to f. your Self. Holy
P-3........ III.2:2 it. Nor will he f. his healing in the process.
S-1........ III.6:7 one who wants an enemy will fail to f. one
S-2...........I.2:2 no guilt that it can seek and f. and "love."
S-2..........II.7:5 of God, and f. the peace He offers you.
S-3........ III.2:8 healed appears to be to f. a wiser one who
S-3........ III.3:2 his skill; to f. in him the remedy for pain.

## finding 28

T-9 ..... IV.10:1 he despairs of f. satisfaction in reality?
T-12 ........ IV.h Seeking and F.
T-12 .... VII.6:6 Yet seeking and f. are the same, and if you
T-13 ........ VI.h F. the Present
T-15 ..... III.3:5 is only by f. your function and fulfilling it
T-15 ..... IV.4:5 accepted for f. magnitude in littleness. *It is*
T-16 ..... IV.3:1 of hate by f. a haven in the storm of guilt.
T19..IV.B.17:5 itself along the way, and f. what it seeks.
T-20 ...... V.1:3 held outside them, and f. what was lost.
T-21 ..... III.5:5 as means for losing certainty and f. sin.
T-21 .... VII.6:7 to be the last remaining hope of f. sin,
T-28 ..... IV.2:1 is a way of f. certainty right here and now.
T-29 ..........I.9:5 not afraid to find a loss of self in f. God?
T-29 . VIII.8:10 with hope of f. more of something else. Be
T-30 ..... III.3:4 is missing. And by f. this, you will achieve
W-pI..... 46.4:1 well you should have no difficulty in f. a
W-pI..... 69.3:5 ancient search today by f. the light in us,
W-pI..... 74.2:1 for today are directed towards f. it. The
W-pI... 121.1:3 your hopes of ever f. quietness and peace.
W-pI... 130.7:2 devote our minds to f. only what is real.
W-pI... 185.6:2 is genuine, the means for f. it is given, in a
W-pI... 200.2:1 of f. happiness where there is none; of
W-pII . 255.1:6 I give today to f. what my Father wills for
M-2 ........... 4:3 f. each other as if they had not met before.
M-8 ........... 2:6 F. truth unacceptable, the mind revolts
M-8 ........... 2:7 victory. F. health a burden, it retreats into
M-13 ......... 3:3 mind condemned itself to seek without f.;
M-20 ......... 3:6 condition for f. the peace of God. More

## finds 28

T-7 ....... VI.3:7 existence, a state which it f. intolerable.
T-12 .... VII.6:4 The ego f. what it seeks, and only that. It
T-13 ........I.5:5 *When* he f. it is only a matter of time, and
T-13 ..... XI.1:5 No one f. himself ravaged and torn in
T-16 ...... V.7:3 Yet when it f. the special relationship in
T-17 ..... III.6:3 and f. the source of problems where it is,
T-20 ..... IV.5:6 each one f. his savior when he is ready to
T-20 ...... V.1:3 And there he f. his function of restoring
T-23 ......in.3:7 it not. Who looks for glory f. it where it is.
T-23 .....II.17:4 his savior powerless and f. salvation? Let
T-25 ..... VI.4:3 complete until he f. his special function,
T-26 .. VII.19:2 means whereby your brother f. the peace
T-27 .....V.10:3 by all the many different witnesses it f..
T-27 ... VIII.3:3 and events wherein its "hero" f. itself, the
T-31 ..... VI.3:8 so that perception f. no hiding place. How
W-pI .... 57.3:6 place where the Son of God f. his freedom
W-pI .... 82.1:2 of the world f. expression through me.
W-pI .. 128.6:1 it seek the level where it f. itself at home.
W-pI .. 131.4:5 When he is wrong, he f. correction. When
W-pI .. 155.8:7 As they step back, he f. himself again.
W-pI .. 189.5:4 If hatred f. a place within your heart, you
W-pI .. 199.7:6 that f. its full accomplishment in God.
W-pII . 305.1:1 but Christ's vision f. a peace so deep and
W-pII . 315.1:5 who f. the way to God becomes my savior
M-4 ..... I.A.5:8 he f. a happy lightheartedness instead;
M-4 ..... I.A.5:8 asked of him, he f. a gift bestowed on him
M-4 ...... VI.1:8 past them, he f. that nothing was there.
M-4 .... IX.2:10 Toward Them it looks, seeking until it f..

## finger 2

T-31 .......V.6:4 he does, for your accusing f. points to him
W-pI .... 29.5:5 *God is in this f.. God is in this lamp. God is in*

## fingers 7

T-22 ..... IV.7:6 easily your f. slip through its nothingness.
W-pI .... 36.3:6 *My holiness envelops these f.. My holiness*
W-pI .. 151.3:6 You think your f. touch reality, and close
W-pI .. 189.5:4 cruelly in death's sharp-pointed, bony f..
W-pI .. 191.3:3 snatch from your f. every scrap of hope,
W-pI .. 195.3:3 little left within his grasping f. as in yours.
W-pII . 355.1:4 *Even now my f. touch it. It is very close. I need*

## fingers' 1

W-pI .. 151.7:2 nor what your f. touch reports of him. He

## fingertips 1

W-pI .. 157.5:1 glow that travels from your f. to those you

## finish 2

P-2........ IV.4:5 It is ridiculous from start to f.. Yet having
P-2........ IV.4:6 Yet having started, it must f. thus. It is as

## finished 1

WpI.rV.in11:5 And thus, when we have f. this review, we

## finite 2

W-pI .. 187.2:2 it is sure that if you give a f. thing away,
P-2.........in.3:5 invulnerable and the f. limitless. The self

## fire 2

*See also* hell-fire

W-pI .. 170.7:2 blood, and f. seems to flame from him, he
W-pI 170.10:5 be upon His Lips; the f. comes from Him.

## fireflies 1

T-24 .......V.4:2 instant from the f. of sin and then go out,

## firefly 1

W-pI .... 97.6:2 the sun outshine the tiny gleam a f. makes

## fires 1

T-25 ... VIII.6:4 "f." of Heaven by God's Own angry Hand.

## firm 20

T-3 .........II.1:5 until a f. commitment to one or the other

T-3......... II.1:6 is made. A f. commitment to darkness or
T-5.......VII.6:4 Be very f. with yourself in this, and keep
T-8..... VIII.3:3 object to the ego's f. belief that you are
T-11... VIII.3:3 recognition of this is your f. beginning.
T-14....... II.6:2 on the f. foundation that truth is true. For
T-14.....VII.4:8 place can be endowed with f. belief. Bring
T-14.....XI.14:4 It is as f. as is His faith in His Creator, and
T-17..... V.14:8 Yet the goal is fixed, f. and unalterable,
T-19....... II.1:4 based on the f. conviction that minds, not
T-20...... VI.7:2 feeling the seeming f. foundation of their
T-20.... VI.10:3 f. foundation is eternally upheld by truth,
T-22.........I.3:5 and f. in faith that you are something else,
T-25.....VII.2:2 He did not make be f. and sure as Heaven.
T-26...VII.12:3 the f. conviction that ideas can leave their
T-28...... III.3:5 cherished, and upheld by f. belief, lest
W-pI.....61.7:4 build a f. foundation for these advances.
W-pI.....74.3:1 times, slowly and with f. determination to
W-pI.....98.1:4 two, but take a f. position with the One.
W-pI...132.9:1 contains the f. foundation for today's idea

## firmer 3

W-pI.....95.7:2 helpful, since it imposes f. structure. Do
WpIrIII.in12:3 with f. footsteps and with stronger faith.
WpI.. rV.in1:6 certainty, a f. purpose and a surer goal.

## firming 1

Wi181-200 1:1 of f. up your willingness to make your

## firmly 21

T-2......... II.3:2 after the value of the goal is f. established.
T-2....... III.3:7 recognition becomes more f. established,
T-14...... XI.8:1 so f. bound to guilt and committed so to
T-14.... XI.10:7 establish His bright teaching so f. in your
T-16....... II.7:3 accomplished in a mind f. convinced that
T-16...... III.9:1 you think, and your foot is planted f. on it
T-16.... IV.12:5 it. Turn with me f. away from all illusions
T-16...... VI.8:5 it took to fix your mind so f. on illusions.
T-17....... V.4:5 Set f. in the unholy relationship, there is
T-18...... I.10:3 so f. joined in truth that only God is there
T-18.... IX.13:1 shining and f. rooted in the world of light.
T-26....... X.3:1 so f. joined that where one is perceived
T-27....... II.1:4 stand f. in the way of trust and peace,
W-pI.....93.2:1 beliefs so f. fixed that it is difficult to help
W-pI...110.7:1 Then, with this statement f. in your mind
W-pI.122.14:1 but hold them f. in your mind by your
W-pI...162.1:1 This single thought, held f. in the mind,
W-pI...196.1:1 f. understood and kept in full awareness,
W-pI...199.1:4 f. tied to it and sheltered by its presence.
M-4....... IX.1:3 trust not yet f. established. Faithfulness is
M-27..........5:1 "reality" of death is f. rooted in the belief

## firmness 2

T-22....... V.5:2 weight, solidity and f. of foundation. Yes,
W-pI...73.10:1 yourself with gentle f. and quiet certainty:

## First 9

*first*

T-4......IV.10:1 F. Coming of Christ is merely another
T-4......IV.10:3 I was created like you in the F., and I have
T-7...........I.7:5 that He is the F. in the Holy Trinity Itself.
T-9........IV.9:3 was made for you as the F. was created.
T-14......IV.1:7 but the F. in eternity is God the Father,
T-14......IV.1:7 God the Father, Who is both F. and One.
T-14......IV.1:8 Beyond the F. there is no other, for there
T-14......IV.1:8 no second or third, and nothing but the F.
T-14......IV.2:1 You who belong to the F. Cause, created

## first 280

*First*

T-1...........I.7:1 right, but purification is necessary f..
T-1........IV.1:1 from darkness involves two stages: F., the
T-2...........I.1:9 F., you believe that what God created can
T-2...........I.5:5 remember the f. principle in this course;
T-2........ III.1:5 the f. step in correcting this distortion,
T-2........ IV.4:2 f. step in believing that the body makes its
T-2........ VI.5:2 This situation arises in two ways: F., you
T-2...... VI.5:10 the error from the f. to the second type,
T-2........ VI.7:1 f. corrective step in undoing the error is to
T-2........ VI.7:1 f. that the conflict is an expression of fear.
T-2........ VI.7:5 Know f. that this is fear. Fear arises from
T-2........ VI.9:9 It appears at f. glance that to believe such
T-2.....VII.3:14 in the second, and all love in the f.. The
T-2..... VIII.4:1 f. step toward freedom involves a sorting
T-3........ III.2:6 illusions is the f. step in undoing them.
T-3........ III.5:4 him. Until you f. perceive him as he is you
T-3........ IV.2:1 was the f. split introduced into the mind
T-3...... VI.11:8 of "Seek ye f. the Kingdom of Heaven" say
T-3...... VI.11:8 say, "*Will* ye f. the Kingdom of Heaven,"
T-4...........I.2:3 the separation was their f. experience of
T-4........ III.8:3 taken the f. step toward preparing your
T-4........ VI.8:5 Learn f. of them and you will be ready to
T-5...........I.4:6 Inspiration, taught me f. and foremost
T-5...........I.7:2 F., its universality is perfectly clear, and
T-5........ IV.7:2 devote themselves f. to healing because,
T-5......... V.8:6 any minute if it accepts the Atonement f..
T-5........ VI.3:5 for the ego always speaks f.. Alternate
T-5........ VI.3:6 unnecessary until the f. one was made.
T-5.......VII.6:3 the f. step in the undoing is to recognize
T-6...........I.7:5 of God, but f. believe that it is true for you
T-6........ IV.1:2 The ego always speaks f.. It is capricious
T-6........ IV.2:6 raised the f. question that was ever asked,
T-6........ IV.3:2 The Holy Spirit does not speak f., *but He*
T-6........ IV.7:2 because the f. question was never asked.
T-6......V.A.6:8 Having taken the f. step, however, they
T-6......V.B.2:2 for change is their f. and foremost goal. It
T-6......V.B.3:1 f. step in the reversal or undoing process
T-6......V.B.3:2 the Holy Spirit's f. lesson was "To have,
T-6......V.B.3:6 f. lesson seems to contain a contradiction,
T-6......V.B.3:9 the f. lesson is the hardest to learn. Still
T-6......V.B.4:1 the ego perceives the f. lesson as insane.
T-6......V.B.8:2 however, more advanced than the f. step,
T-6......V.B.9:3 step is easier than the f. because it follows.
T-6......V.C.3:3 It has advanced far from the f. lesson,
T-6......V.C.3:4 second as the second follows from the f.,
T-6......V.C.4:1 While the f. step seems to increase
T-6......V.C.6:1 You learn f. that *having* rests on giving,
T-7...........I.7:3 last, because He created f. and for always.
T-7...........I.7:4 It must be understood that the word "f."
T-7...........I.7:5 He is f. in the sense that He is the First in
T-7........ IV.7:1 Seek ye f. the Kingdom of Heaven,
T-7..... VIII.3:2 F., strictly speaking, conflict cannot be
T-8...........I.5:3 The f. change to be introduced is a change
T-8.......VII.5:4 but you must have attacked yourself f..
T-9........ IV.4:4 plan is to have you see error clearly f., and
T-9........ VI.6:4 In time the giving comes f., though they
T-10....... II.1:1 Unless you f. know something you
T-10....... II.4:5 why it is that you always attack yourself f..
T-10...... IV.8:5 the little light must be acknowledged f.,
T-11....... II.1:1 heal and to be healed is the f. step toward
T-11...... IV.4:6 difficult at f. to realize that this is exactly
T-11....... V.1:5 for we must look f. at this to see beyond it,
T-12...... III.2:6 The question is always twofold; f., *what* is
T-12....... V.3:4 you are always the f. point of your attack,
T-12...VII.12:3 see it without *because* you saw it f. within.
T-13....... V.3:7 And thus it is you must attack yourself f.,
T-13.....VII.9:1 You will f. dream of peace, and then
T-13.....VII.9:2 f. exchange of what you made for what
T-14.........I.1:4 blessing, it must have come f. to yourself.
T-14....... II.1:2 to misery must f. recognize that you are
T-14...... IV.1:6 Yet truth is offered f. to be received, even
T-14...... IV.1:6 received, even as God gave it f. to His Son.
T-14...... IV.1:7 The f. in time means nothing, but the
T-15...... III.3:2 The lesson may seem hard at f., but you
T-15....... V.6:5 Yet you had judged against yourself f., or
T-15.....VII.5:5 willing f. to perceive what you have made
T-16....... II.4:3 the f. link in the awareness of the Sonship
T-16....... V.1:1 it is necessary f. to realize that it involves
T-16....... V.5:4 knows that completion lies f. in union,
T-17...... III.7:9 But f., be sure you fully realize what you
T-17....... V.2:7 f. result of offering the relationship to the
T-17...... VI.2:1 you are uncertain, the f. thing to consider,
T-18.........I.6:1 was the f. projection of error outward.
T-18........II.6:3 I said before that the f. change, before
T-18.... IV.4:10 Would you f. make a miracle yourself,
T-18...... IV.5:6 to those who think that they must f. atone
T-19...... IV.2:2 already lies deeply within must f. expand,
T19...... IV.A.h F. Obstacle: The Desire to Get Rid of It
T19....IV.A.1:1 f. obstacle that peace must flow across is
T19. IV.A.2:10 the f. obstacle the peace in you encounters
T19....IV.B.1:1 We said that peace must f. surmount the
T19....IV.B.1:3 flow across, and closely related to the f., is
T19....IV.B.4:3 obstacle is no more solid than the f.. For
T19....IV.C.6:2 What better way to teach the f. and
T19....IV.C.6:2 to be the hardest can be accomplished f.?
T19.... IV.D.8:7 But f., lift up your eyes and look on your
T-20........II.4:5 you f. upon the altar in your chosen home
T-20...... III.3:4 deciding f. where they would have it be.
T-20...... VI.2:2 The f. is based on love, and rests on it
T-20....VIII.1:1 Vision will come to you at f. in glimpses,
T-21........II.4:8 of your wanting must f. be recognized.
T-21...... III.8:4 But f. they chose to recognize how much
T-21...... IV.7:2 hear since f. the ego came into your mind.
T-21.....VII.1:6 And only those who f. believe that they
T-21.....VII.5:6 f. he must be willing to perceive a world
T-21.....VII.6:1 have answered the f. three questions, but
T-22.......I.10:1 the f. direct perception that you can make
T-22...... IV.2:1 f. few steps along the right way that seem
T-23........II.2:1 *f.* chaotic law is that the truth is different
T-23........II.3:1 interfere with the f. principle of miracles.
T-23........II.4:2 This principle, closely related to the f., is
T-24...... IV.1:5 kill, and you are drawn to it to kill it f..
T-24....... V.4:6 not that it looked upon your brother f.,
T-24....... V.6:7 He looked upon you f., but recognized
T-25...... IX.4:7 can bring another problem added to the f.
T-25...... IX.7:7 unless you have decided f. to *be* unjust.
T-26....... V.3:5 of time in which the f. mistake was made,
T-26....... V.3:5 and all of them that came within the f..
T-27........II.2:7 forgiveness does not f. establish sin and
T-27...... III.4:8 And so the f. replacement for your picture
T-27...... IV.7:4 though they leave the f. unanswered. In
T-27...... V.10:4 Your brother f. among them will be seen,
T-27.....VII.6:3 And this is where your guilt was f. beheld.
T-27.....VII.6:4 was the f. attack upon yourself begun.
T-27....VIII.5:3 the second part, whose cause lies in the f..
T-28........II.8:8 Effect and cause are f. split off, and then
T-28........II.9:3 The miracle is the f. step in giving back to
T-28...... III.1:2 you have barely started to allow your f.,
T-29...... III.1:3 But he must learn he is a savior f., before
T-30.........I.3:3 not resolve the problem as you saw it f..
T-30.........I.3:7 it does occur at f., while you are learning
T-30.........I.4:3 for opposition will not f. arise and then
T-30.......I.13:5 again the very f. of the decisions which are
T-30.......I.14:6 all. The f. rule, then, is not coercion, but a
T-30....... V.1:6 that all things must be f. forgiven, and
T-30....... V.7:7 Yet is the Love of Christ accepted f.. And
T-30...... VI.5:5 it would be necessary f. there be some sin
T-31.........I.4:4 from the f. accomplishment of learning;
T-31........II.2:3 The f. is a decision that you make. But
T-31...... III.1:2 is f. one thing that must be overlearned. It
T-31...... III.1:3 your f. response to all temptation, and to
T-31....... V.2:6 The f. presents the face of innocence, the
T-31....... V.3:3 This aspect never makes the f. attack. But
T-31..... V.12:6 Yet who was it that did the choosing f.? If
T-31..... V.12:7 must have f. decided on the one to choose
T-31..... V.13:5 of the shifting to the second from the f. is
T-31.....VII.8:4 And this he learns when f. he looks upon
W-in.......... 3:1 the f. dealing with the undoing of the way
W-in.......... 3:2 around one central idea, which is stated f.
W-in.......... 6:1 to be observed throughout, then, are: F.,
W-pI....... 1.4:1 Each of the f. three lessons should not be
W-pI....... 2.1:1 idea are the same as those for the f. one.
W-pI....... 4.3:2 The aim here is to train you in the f. steps
W-pI....... 4.3:3 It is a f. attempt in the long-range purpose
W-pI....... 4.6:1 these exercises are the f. of their kind, you
W-pI....... 5.1:6 to each of them separately is the f. step in
W-pI....... 5.3:1 you f. search your mind for "sources" of
W-pI....... 5.6:2 If this occurs, think f. of this: *I cannot keep*
W-pI....... 7.1:1 idea is particularly difficult to believe at f..
W-pI....... 7.2:3 This f. time idea is not really so strange as
W-pI....... 7.2:3 not really so strange as it may sound at f..
W-pI....... 8.3:3 is the f. step to opening the way to vision.

W-pI.....11.1:1 the f. idea we have had that is related to a
W-pI.....13.6:1 f. attempt at stating an explicit cause and
W-pI.....15.4:1 the idea for today, repeat it f. to yourself,
W-pI.....16.5:1 periods, f. repeat the idea to yourself, and
W-pI.....17.1:3 It is always the thought that comes f.,
W-pI.....19.2:2 This is rarely a wholly welcome idea at f.,
W-pI.....19.3:2 The idea for today is to be repeated f., and
W-pI.....20.2:1 is our f. attempt to introduce structure.
W-pI.....23.5:2 This change requires, f., that the cause be
W-pI.....23.5:3 The f. two steps in this process require
W-pI.....23.5:6 By taking the f. two steps, you will see that
W-pI.....23.6:2 you, repeat the idea slowly to yourself f.,
W-pI.....26.3:1 thought that you always attack yourself f..
W-pI.....26.7:1 F., name the situation: *I am concerned*
W-pI.....28.7:1 in which the idea for the day is stated f.,
W-pI.....36.3:1 F., close your eyes and repeat the idea for
W-pI.....37.1:1 This idea contains the f. glimmerings of
W-pI.....39.9:3 concentration is very difficult at f.. It will
W-pI.....41.5:3 Today we will make our f. real attempt to
W-pI.....41.8:5 results even the f. time it is attempted,
W-pI.....43.6:1 repeat the f. phase of the exercise period,
W-pI.....43.6:3 Return to the f. phase of the exercises as
W-pI.....46.5:1 purpose of the f. phase of today's practice
WpI...rI.in.1:2 with the f. and ending with the fiftieth.
WpI...rI.in.6:4 the f. fifty of the ideas we have covered,
W-pI.....61.7:3 This is the f. of a number of giant steps we
W-pI.....64.7:2 This will be difficult, at f. particularly,
W-pI.....65.5:3 it. At f., make no attempt to concentrate
W-pI.....66.5:6 It is only if the f. two thoughts are wrong
W-pI.....66.6:1 The f. premise is that God gives you only
W-pI.....66.6:6 are believing if you do not accept the f.
W-pI.....71.8:3 at the second part; it is inherent in the f..
W-pI.....71.8:4 the f. is your full release from all your own
W-pI.....76.1:4 you must f. realize salvation lies not there.
W-pI.....78.6:2 in your mind, f. as you now consider him.
WpI..rII.in.3:1 Repeat the f. phase of the exercise period
W-pI.....90.3:3 I believe that the problem comes f., and
W-pI.....93.8:1 the f. five minutes of every waking hour,
W-pI...93.10:1 even able to use the f. five minutes of each
W-pI.....94.3:1 Today we will again devote the f. five
W-pI.....94.5:1 for the f. five minutes of every hour, at
W-pI.....95.4:1 use of the f. five minutes of every waking
W-pI.....95.7:2 Using the f. five minutes of the hour will
W-pI.....95.9:3 based on the f. and reinforcing it. It is this
W-pI.....97.3:4 Salvation is a miracle, the f. and last; the
W-pI.....97.3:4 the first and last; the f. that is the last, for
W-pI...106.6:5 miracles has need that you receive them f.
W-pI...108.4:1 does not depend on which is seen as f.,
WpI. rIII.in8:1 f. five minutes of the day to your reviews,
W-pI...124.5:4 see because we saw it f. within ourselves.
W-pI...124.8:4 is our f. attempt at an extended period for
W-pI...133.6:1 F., if you choose a thing that will not last
W-pI...134.5:5 pitifully mocked and twice condemned; f.,
W-pI...135.4:1 Let us consider f. what you defend. It
WpI. rIV.in9:3 repeating f. the thought that made the
W-pI...152.3:3 of it. Without the f., the second has no
W-pI...152.3:4 the second, is the f. no longer true. Truth
W-pI...154.6:2 that they deliver are intended f. for them.
W-pI...154.6:4 they become their f. receivers in the truest
W-pI...159.1:2 a thing requires f. you have it in your own
W-pI.161.11:2 See him f. as clearly as you can, in that
W-pI...168.4:2 will disappear, and vision f. will come,
W-pI...170.4:2 F., it is obvious ideas must leave their
W-pI...170.4:2 attack, and must have f. conceived of it.
Wi181-200 3:1 f. on what impedes your progress still.
W-pI...181.3:1 we f. let all such little focuses give way to
W-pI.184.13:3 f. you must accept the Name for all reality
W-pI...187.1:5 you must f. possess what you would give.
W-pI...187.3:1 Ideas must f. belong to you, before you
W-pI...187.3:2 world, you f. accept salvation for yourself.
W-pI...187.8:5 Given f. to you, it now is yours to give as
W-pI...196.2:1 at f. you will not understand how mercy,
W-pI...196.7:1 form must f. be changed at least as much
W-pII ..in.11:5 We give the f. of these instructions now.
W-pII .284.1:5 f. to be but said and then repeated many
W-pII .288.1:3 *I f. must recognize what You created one*
W-pII ...10.1:3 f. you see a world that has accepted this as
W-pII .326.2:1 behold earth disappear, at f. transformed,
W-pII ....328.h I choose the second place to gain the f..
W-pII .328.1:1 What seems to be the second place is f.,
W-pII .336.1:2 is restored after perception f. is changed,
W-pII ... 13.4:1 The miracle is taken f. on faith, because
W-pII ....357.h make to God, Responding f. with miracles
W-pII .357.1:2 *Son is pointed out to me, f. in my brother;*
M-3 ........... 4:4 As with the f. level, these meetings are not
M-4 ..... I.A.3:1 F., they must go through what might be
M-4 ...... VI.1:9 Slowly at f. he lets himself be undeceived.
M-5 ........II.1:3 this, one f. must recognize certain facts.
M-5 ........II.1:4 F., it is obvious that decisions are of the
M-7 ........... 3:4 Yet he must f. accept them. He need do no
M-7 ........... 4:4 appear unreasonable at f. to be told that
M-9 ........... 1:4 be the f. step in the newly made teacher of
M-13 ......... 1:5 another illusion that replaces the f., so
M-13 ......... 1:6 The f. illusion, which must be displaced
M-17 ......... 1:5 f. responsibility in this is not to attack it.
M-19 ......... 2:4 one is but the f. small step in the direction
M-20 ......... 2:1 F., how can the peace of God be
M-20 ......... 2:2 peace is recognized at f. by just one thing;
M-20 ....... 2:10 The contrast f. perceived has merely gone.
M-29 ......... 1:5 helpful for the pupil to read the manual f..
C-6 ........... 2:2 the f. to complete his own part perfectly.
P-2..........II.5:4 ascendance, f. through Christ's vision and
P-2......... III.1:1 pitfalls along the road by seeing them f..
P-2......... IV.7:2 correction cannot be achieved by f.
P-2......... V.1:5 F., it is ushered in by the belief that there
P-2......... VI.1:7 To hear it is the f. step in recovery. To
P-2......... VI.2:4 f. the willingness to question the "truth"
P-3..........II.2:1 F., the professional therapist is in an
P-3..........II.8:5 of the beginning stage of the f. journey.
S-1......... I.3:6 have sought f. the Kingdom of Heaven,
S-1........ IV.2:4 is likely at f. that what is asked for even by
S-2.......... I.1:4 Forgiveness' kindness is obscure at f.,
S-2...........I.9:1 But to achieve this end you f. must learn,
S-2..........II.2:1 In this group, f., there are the forms in
S-2..........II.3:1 still very like the f. if it is understood, does
S-3..........II.4:2 f. true healing must have come to bless
S-3......... IV.4:1 You f. forgive, then pray, and you are
S-3......... IV.9:9 will come the gift f. of forgiveness, then

## fish 1

T-24 .... VII.4:6 it for show, as bait to catch another f., to

## fit 22

T-1 ....... III.5:3 establish your kingdom where you see f.,
T-11 ..... III.4:6 are not f. companions for the Son of God,
T-12 ........I.3:7 his reality by interpreting it as you see f..
T-12 .......II.5:1 Christ, and so they are not f. gifts for you.
T-14 .... V.11:1 him f. for crucifixion or for redemption. If
T-16 .......II.4:4 have offered it to Him to use as He sees f.,
T-17 ...... III.8:4 elements that f. the purpose of the unholy
T-17 ... IV.13:1 f. the better picture into the wrong frame
T-17 ....... V.4:5 to change the relationship to f. the goal.
T-20 ..... III.6:4 not make adjustments to f. their orders.
T-21 ........II.9:3 of reality to make it f. the goal of madness
T-21 ...... V.8:2 nor can it be adjusted to f. its end. Faith
T-30 ...... V.1:4 to twist and f. into the dream of fear.
T-31 ..... VI.5:4 f. the picture as it was perceived before
W-pI... 124.8:5 God's Voice to speak as He sees f. today,
W-pII .236.1:6 to the Holy Spirit to employ as He sees f..
W-pII .263.1:4 *madman's dream is hardly f. to be my choice*
W-pII294.1:10 today; of service for a while and f. to serve
M-8 ........... 4:5 be given what will f. into these categories.
M-11 ......... 4:6 it and made it f. to welcome peace. And
M-22 ......... 3:5 as it sees f. could merely take the place of
M-29 ......... 2:8 is His, and He alone is f. to assume it. To

## fits 3

T-31 ...... V.1:2 It f. it well. For this an image is that suits
M-8 ........... 4:3 judging where each sense datum f. best.
S-2...........I.9:2 the key was made, and where alone it f.?

## fitting 6

T-7 ...... VII.6:1 Only honor is a f. gift for those whom
T-9 ...... VII.8:5 not offer to God as wholly f. for Him. You
T-12 .......II.5:1 for they are not f. offerings for Christ, and
T-13 .....X.14:4 is f. as a hymn of praise unto your Father.
W-pI 184.12:6 you made as f. tribute to the Son He loves
W-pI .. 197.3:5 who honor them and give them f. thanks,

## five 62

*See also* five-minute, five-minutes-an-hour, three-to-five-minute

W-pI ...... 8.6:1 be done four or f. times during the day,
W-pI .... 10.5:2 f. practice periods are recommended,
W-pI .... 11.4:2 more, as many as f. may be undertaken.
W-pI .... 16.6:1 or f. practice periods are recommended, if
W-pI .... 21.1:3 F. practice periods are urged, allowing a
W-pI .... 22.3:1 the world about you at least f. times today
W-pI .... 23.6:1 arises, f. practice periods are required in
W-pI .... 24.3:2 in each of the f. practice periods which
W-pI .... 26.8:1 you should have some f. or six distressing
W-pI .... 31.2:2 Three to f. minutes for each of these are
W-pI .... 32.4:1 three to f. minutes are recommended,
W-pI .... 32.4:2 More than f. can be utilized, if you find
W-pI .... 33.1:2 A full f. minutes should be devoted to the
W-pI .... 34.3:1 Some f. minutes of mind searching are
W-pI .... 37.4:1 to involve three to f. minutes of practice,
W-pI .... 38.4:1 each preferably to last a full f. minutes,
W-pI .... 39.5:1 A full f. minutes are urged for the four
W-pI .... 41.6:2 sit quietly for some three to f. minutes,
W-pI .... 43.4:5 Four or f. subjects for this phase of the
W-pI .... 44.4:1 today, each lasting three to f. minutes. A
W-pI .... 45.6:3 four or f. thoughts of your own to the idea
WpI... rI.in.1:2 will cover f. of the ideas already presented
WpI... rI.in.2:1 Begin the day by reading the f. ideas,
WpI... rI.in.2:5 If any one of the f. ideas appeals to you
W-pI .... 67.5:3 Four or f. times an hour, and perhaps
W-pI .. 76.12:1 today; at least four or f. times an hour, as
W-pI .. 91.11:1 F. or six times an hour, at reasonably
W-pI .... 93.8:1 the first f. minutes of every waking hour,
W-pI .. 93.10:1 f. minutes of each hour for these exercises
W-pI .... 94.3:1 the first f. minutes of each waking hour to
W-pI .... 94.5:1 for the first f. minutes of every hour, at
W-pI .... 95.4:1 use of the first f. minutes of every waking
W-pI .... 95.7:2 Using the first f. minutes of the hour will
W-pI .. 96.11:5 Every time you spend f. minutes of the
W-pI .... 97.5:1 Holy Spirit will be glad to take f. minutes
W-pI .... 98.5:1 worth f. minutes of your time each hour
W-pI .... 98.5:2 worth f. minutes hourly to recognize your
W-pI .... 98.5:3 f. minutes but a small request to make in
W-pI .... 98.7:1 give Him your tiny gift of but f. minutes.
W-pI .... 98.8:1 each f. minutes that you spend with Him,
W-pI .. 98.10:1 f. minutes you will spend again with Him.
W-pI .. 99.12:2 this between the times you give f. minutes
W-pI .. 101.7:1 Give these f. minutes gladly, to remove
W-pI .. 104.3:2 the hourly f. minutes given truth for your
W-pI .. 105.9:1 Spend your f. minutes thus with Him
W-pI .. 106.9:2 For each f. minutes spent in listening, a
W-pI 107.10:3 every gift you give of f. small minutes, and
W-pI .. 108.8:4 f. minutes think of what you would hold
W-pI .. 109.7:1 With each f. minutes that you rest today,
WpI..rIII.in5:1 is this: Devote f. minutes twice a day, or
WpI..rIII.in8:1 first f. minutes of the day to your reviews,
WpI..rIII.in8:1 and also give the last f. minutes of your
W-pI .. 130.7:1 we gladly give f. minutes to the thought
W-pI .. 130.8:3 come to these f. minutes emptying your
W-pI 138.11:1 and spend f. minutes making sure that we
W-pI 138.12:2 And now we give the last f. minutes of our
W-pI 139.11:1 F. minutes in the morning and at night
W-pI 140.11:1 speak to us f. minutes as the day begins,
W-pI 140.11:1 end the day by listening again f. minutes
WpI..rIV.in5:4 *God.* F. minutes with this thought will be
W-pI 152.11:2 and spend f. minutes practicing its ways,
W-pI 153.15:3 F. minutes now becomes the least we give

## five-minute 10

W-pI .... 35.4:1 each of the three f. practice periods today,
W-pI .... 43.4:1 Three f. practice periods are required
W-pI .... 45.4:1 Our three f. practice periods for today
W-pI .... 46.3:1 at least three full f. practice periods, and
W-pI .... 47.4:2 Four f. practice periods are necessary

W-pI.....49.3:1 need at least four f. practice periods today
W-pI.....96.8:2 Our hourly f. practicing will be a search
W-pI...100.7:1 for this today, in our f. practice periods,
W-pI...102.5:3 Besides these hourly f. rests, pause
W-pI...110.6:1 For your f. practice periods, begin with

**five-minutes-an-hour** 1
W-pI.....95.7:1 keep to the f. practice periods for a while,

**fix** 3
T-16......VI.8:5 took to f. your mind so firmly on illusions
T19... IV.A.9:6 greet the summer sun than f. your gaze
W-pII.....in.6:4 and f. our eyes upon the journey's end.

**fixed** 29
T-6....... II.11:7 the Holy Spirit, Whose Mind is f. on God.
T-10..... V.10:7 creation, f. forever in the Mind of God.
T-11......VI.1:3 beliefs are f. that perceptions stabilize. In
T-14......III.4:4 yours. What you can decide between is f.,
T-14....III.15:8 his abode was f. in perfect peace forever.
T-16......VI.8:3 your mind from its f. position here. This
T-16.....VII.6:3 opposite of the ego's f. belief in salvation
T-17....... II.6:2 your perception and f. it on the past. The
T-17..... V.14:8 Yet the goal is f., firm and unalterable,
T-18..... II.5:15 f. and insane idea that you can change it.
T-18......IV.3:3 f. conviction that you are not worthy of it.
T19... IV.A.7:3 the f. and unchangeable dedication to sin
T-20......III.2:2 it is the ego's f. belief that all relationships
T-22......III.2:6 its f. belief in sin and disregard of errors.
T-23.........I.1:9 Yet just as certain is its f. belief it has an
T-25....... II.3:3 Can it make sense to hold the f. belief that
T-25......III.8:4 is the f. belief perception cannot change.
T-25... VIII.2:3 You have no f. allegiance. But remember
T-29......VI.3:3 a blessing here, where purpose is not f.,
T-29......VI.4:3 because your function has been f. by God.
T-30......VI.6:4 about the meaning of a f. belief that some
T-31.........I.3:4 so overlearned and f. they rise like heavy
T-31.....VII.6:3 Yet it need not be f., unless you choose to
T-31. VIII.11:1 looks with f. determination toward the
W-pI.....93.2:1 are beliefs so firmly f. that it is difficult to
W-pI...167.4:3 is the f. belief ideas can leave their source,
W-pII.......1.2:4 come between a f. projection and the aim
M-27..........1:4 It is the one f., unchangeable belief of the
P-1.............1:2 in abandoning his f. delusional system,

**flame** 1
W-pI...170.7:2 with blood, and fire seems to f. from him,

**flaming** 1
T-24......III.4:7 while specialness stands like a f. sword of

**flash** 1
W-pI.136.16:1 Healing will f. across your open mind, as

**flashes** 1
S-3......... II.2:3 forms and clearly seen at most in lovely f..

**flaw** 1
T-13.....VII.7:3 and love surrounds him without end or f..

**flawless** 1
M-23..........5:5 eyes your loveliness is so complete and f.

**flawlessly** 1
W-pI.135.13:4 the mind employs for this will function f.,

**flaws** 1
W-pI.....78.6:4 will regard his body with its f. and better

**flee** 5
T-25... VIII.7:2 And f. the Holy Spirit as if He were a
T-29.........I.1:9 can escape if there be need for you to f..
T-29....... II.9:6 is your salvation, from which you would f.
W-pI...101.4:2 Who would not f. salvation, and attempt
M-15 .........1:3 Who could f. forever from the truth? But

**fleeting** 1
P-2........ VI.2:2 These f. awarenesses represent the many

**flesh** 17
T-8.......VII.7:1 says, "The Word (or thought) was made f.
T-8.......VII.7:4 Thought cannot be made into f. except by
T-8.....VII.14:1 the body, and thought cannot be made f..
T19. IV.A.13:2 bring you word of bones and skin and f..
T-20....VI.11:1 in sin made f. and then projected outward
T-20....VI.11:2 seems to be a wall of f. around the mind,
T-24....... V.4:8 with f. already loosened from the bone
T-24...... VI.9:5 glory in His Son, whom you mistook as f.,
T-25....... II.7:2 Mind that thought it, not in f. and bones,
T-31......VI.1:1 You see the f. or recognize the spirit.
T-31......VI.1:6 you are, as f. or spirit in your own belief.
T-31......VI.1:7 If you choose f., you never will escape the
T-31......VI.1:8 that you may see the world of f. no more
W-pI...107.8:2 are not made of f. and blood and bone,
W-pI...137.2:3 held in pieces by a solid wall of sickened f.
W-pI.161.12:3 you have seen as merely f. and bone, and
S-3......... II.3:2 be thrust down in pain upon unwilling f.,

**flicker** 3
T-18......III.3:4 A little f. of your eyelids, closed so long,
W-pI...72.12:1 and your hope of success f. and go out,
W-pI.....92.7:5 It does not change and f. and go out. It

**flickered** 1
T-17..... V.11:8 Or has your appreciation f. and grown

**flickers** 1
S-1......... II.7:6 The light no longer f., and will never go

**flies** 1
T-22....... V.2:2 f. in the face of reason and makes no

**flight** 1
T19... IV.A.9:2 Can it oppose an eagle's f., or hinder the

**flimsy** 2
T-29.... IV.4:11 fails is not its core, but just the f. covering
W-pI.138.11:3 is real, is f. and transparent in the light. It

**floating** 1
T19... IV.A.7:2 this little wish, uprooted and f. aimlessly,

**floods** 1
W-pII..267.1:3 heart, and f. my body with the purpose of

**floor** 2
T-18...... IX.6:1 this artificial f. that looks like rock, is like
W-pI.......2.2:3 ease to a body or a button, a fly or a f., an

**flourishes** 1
T-24...VII.10:3 It grows and withers, f. and dies. And you

**flow** 18
T-4........ VI.2:5 easily f. across it and obliterate it forever.
T-5...........I.4:9 God Himself can f. across the little gap.
T-5.........I.4:10 is always ready to f. everywhere, but it
T-13...... XI.6:6 truth, it will f. lightly over you without a
T-19...... IV.2:2 f. across the obstacles you placed before it
T19....IV.A.1:1 must f. across is your desire to get rid of it
T19....IV.A.4:6 God. Peace will f. across it, and join you
T19....IV.B.1:3 second obstacle that peace must f. across,
T19....IV.C.1:3 third obstacle that peace must f. across.
T19....IV.C.7:5 must f. across seems to be very great. For
T19... IV.D.5:1 Every obstacle that peace must f. across is
T-28.......I.15:3 to allow the memory of God to f. across it,
T-29.........I.3:2 that peace must f. across has not yet gone.
W-pI.....50.5:2 allow peace to f. over you like a blanket of
W-pI...96.10:3 it will again f. out from spirit to the spirit
W-pI...109.6:1 sing, a stream long dry begins to f. again.
W-pI...109.7:3 sing and see the stream begin to f. again,
W-pII ...12.4:2 and blood must f. before the altar where

**flower** 4
T-21...VII.3:11 A f. turns into a poisoned spear, a child
T-24........II.3:3 nothingness; an evil f. with no roots at all.
T-25...... IV.5:4 And every f. that ever bloomed has saved
T-26...... IV.2:2 see. Each f. shines in light, and every bird

**flowers** 4
T-26...... IX.3:1 and let the f. be all white and sparkling in
T-26...... IX.3:5 miracles sprung up as grass and f. on the
W-pI... 156.4:3 feet. The scent of f. is their gift to you. The
W-pI... 189.2:6 its own. It offers you its f. and its snow, in

**flows** 4
T-13...... XI.8:4 f. to you from Him Whose Will is peace.
T-14..VIII.2:15 and uninterrupted love f. constantly
T19....IV.B.4:2 It f. across all else. The second obstacle is
T19....IV.B.7:2 Salvation f. from deep within the home

**fluctuation** 1
T-8...........I.5:7 This leads to f., but not to change. The

**fluid** 1
W-pI.....76.3:3 or some f. pushed into your veins through

**flux** 1
T-30.....VII.3:7 Perception cannot be in constant f., and

**fly** 4
W-pI.......2.2:3 ease to a body or a button, a f. or a floor,
W-pI...128.6:4 and it will f. in sureness and in joy to join
W-pI...188.6:4 let your thoughts f. to the peace within.
M-4 .........I.2:2 Who would attempt to f. with the tiny

**focus** 26
T-2..........II.3:9 correct f. will shorten it immeasurably.
T-4........ IV.6:3 see how your mind can f. and rise above
T-7........ III.4:1 is merely to f. your full attention on it. As
T-16.........I.3:9 F. your mind only on this: *I am not alone,*
T-17...... III.3:2 of him, is not the central f. as it is, or in
T-17....IV.11:3 to f. all your attention on the picture. The
T-17....IV.11:6 If you f. on the picture, you will realize
T-17....IV.13:2 One is framed to be out of f. and not seen.
T19....IV.B.2:8 is the f. of the perception of Atonement as
T19....IV.B.8:5 will be the f. of the new perception that
T-26.........I.1:4 *lose.* Its f. on the body is apparent, for it is
T-27......II.14:2 f. of correction has been placed outside
T-27......II.14:4 is your brother, f. of your hate, unworthy
T-27.....VII.4:6 Vengeance must have a f.. Otherwise is
T-30.......in.1:1 now becomes the f. of the curriculum.
W-pI.....21.5:2 f. your anger on a particular attribute of a

W-pI.....65.7:1 to trying to f. on its importance to you,
W-pI...181.2:1 Perception has a f.. It is this that gives
W-pI...181.2:3 Change but this f., and what you behold
W-pI...181.2:5 Remove your f. on your brother's sins,
W-pI...181.5:3 against present change of f. in perception.
W-pI...181.6:2 us, our narrowed f. will restrict our sight,
W-pI...181.6:3 to our minds to change their f., as we say:
W-pI...181.7:3 from the misery the f. upon sin will bring,
W-pI...181.8:3 And as our f. goes beyond mistakes, we
M-4 ....... X.3:5 the f. properly belongs on the curriculum.

### focused 2

W-pI.....38.5:4 but keep the exercises f. on the theme,
W-pI...181.2:7 For their mistakes, if f. on, are witnesses

### focuses 4

T-11...... V.14:2 The ego f. on error and overlooks truth. It
T-21.....VII.5:9 For if he f. on what he cannot understand,
W-pI...140.6:7 It merely f. on what it is, and knows that
W-pI...181.3:1 we first let all such little f. give way to our

### focusing 2

T-27...... VI.1:3 it away from Him and f. upon itself. Its
T-31.....VII.3:3 well. By f. upon the good in him, the body

### fog 3

T-12....... II.2:1 of the density of the f. that obscures it. If
T-12....... II.2:2 no power to the f. to obscure the light, it
T-28....... V.7:3 The gap is carefully concealed in f., and

### folds 2

T-22....... II.1:5 the dark f. of the heavy garments in which
T-25.......in.3:4 His purpose f. the body in His light, and

### follow 124

T-1........ III.4:6 he does direct, leaving it up to you to f..
T-1......... V.6:2 is the natural result of choosing to f. Him.
T-2........ IV.4:4 It does not f., however, that the use of
T-2........ VI.5:7 rage, and projection is likely to f..
T-4........ IV.2:9 and urge you to f. my example as you look
T-4....... VII.8:8 whoever can f. my guidance through you.
T-5......... V.6:4 Its effects will f. automatically until the
T-6.........in.1:4 of attack rather than of love must f..
T-6...........I.6:7 You are merely asked to f. my example in
T-6...........I.8:7 and if the model they f. has chosen to save
T-6...........I.8:7 all respects, they are unwise not to f. him.
T-6.........I.11:3 still f. my example in how to perceive
T-6.........I.16:1 were not wholly ready to f. me at the time
T-6........ IV.9:6 to f. who will strengthen your command,
T-6...... V.B.9:4 Realizing that it *must* f. is a demonstration
T-6....V.C.10:2 enable you to take this step, if you f. Him.
T-7......... II.3:9 His Sons, who create like Him, f. it gladly,
T-7....... X.5:12 because he has elected to f. false guidance
T-7....... X.5:13 Unable to f. this guidance without fear, he
T-7....... X.5:13 and refuses to f. any guidance at all. If the
T-8...... IV.4:10 Only then will your mind choose to f. me.
T-9...........I.2:4 must f. that you will not learn this course.
T-9........ IV.2:4 And if you do not f. this Guide, your
T-9........ IV.6:1 F. the Holy Spirit's teaching in
T-9........ IV.6:3 to f. the Holy Spirit's plan of salvation,
T-9......... V.3:3 All unhealed healers f. the ego's plan for
T-11...... VI.5:8 only have you learn your will and f. it, not
T-12....... III.1:1 you have and give to the poor and f. me.
T-12...... IV.3:5 F. its teaching, then, and you will search
T-12....... V.9:2 if you f. the Teacher Who knows the way
T-13...... IV.5:5 if you f. the ego's dictates you will react to
T-13....... V.8:6 vision it does not f. you cannot see. But
T-13.... VI.11:3 forth to call you from the world and f. it.
T-13..... VII.6:4 As you f. Him, you will rejoice that you
T-13...VII.15:1 Then f. Him in joy, with faith that He will
T-13...... IX.1:6 who f. them believe that they are guilty,
T-14.......in.1:8 and f. the simple logic by which the Holy
T-14.... III.13:1 would have you f. can teach you what it is.
T-14 .... III.13:2 wisdom is capable of guiding you to f. it.
T-14 ... III.14:1 only Guide that you would f. to salvation.
T-15 .......X.5:1 is not necessary to f. fear through all the
T-16 . IV.13:11 The way to truth is open. F. it with me.
T-16 ..... V.16:1 to listen to this course and f. it is but the
T-17 .......II.5:3 real reason that He brings, as you f. Him,
T-18 ... VII.4:6 You may be attempting to f. a very long
T-18 ... IX.3:7 are willing to f. the Holy Spirit through
T-18 ... IX.13:2 there it calls to you to f. the course it took,
T19..IV.C.10:9 everyone who gives him shelter will f. him
T-20 ..... IV.3:7 Nor is it possible for those who f. them to
T-21 ..... III.2:5 it will f., grimly or happily, but always
T-21 ..... III.8:5 that f. this decision are also born of faith.
T-21 ..... IV.8:3 of sin, f. in gladness the way to certainty.
T-21 ..... IV.8:9 F. it happily, and question not what must
T-23 .....II.21:1 the belief in sin, the faith in chaos must f..
T-23 .....II.21:3 The steps to chaos do f. neatly from their
T-23 .....II.22:3 And they *will* f.. Attack in any form has
T-23 ..... III.1:2 must f. that you do not always recognize
T-24 ......in.2:6 suffering f. guilt and freedom sinlessness.
T-24 ...... V.4:1 specialness direct his way, and you will f..
T-24 ...... V.6:6 to see and hear and love and f. home? He
T-27 .... VII.3:5 to see it does not f. and it makes no sense.
T-27 ... VIII.8:6 Yet they but f.. And it is their cause that
T-28 ..... VI.2:5 It can but f. aimlessly the path on which it
T-29 .......II.1:3 rough and far too difficult for you to f.? Is
T-31 ... III.3:11 it. A jailer does not f. orders, but enforces
T-31 ... III.6:2 The body will but f.. It can never lead you
T-31 ...... V.8:2 that you will choose to f. this world's laws
W-pI.....13.1:4 not f. that you will not think you perceive
W-pI.....29.4:1 for today should f. a now familiar pattern:
WpI...rI.in.2:2 not necessary to f. any particular order in
WpI...rI.in.3:1 to cover the comments that f. each idea
W-pI.....55.4:4 I am willing to f. the Guide God has given
W-pI.....65.3:1 Today, and for a number of days to f., set
W-pI.....70.6:3 We will f. this practice for a number of
W-pI.....71.5:3 and you will attempt to f. two plans for
W-pI.....77.4:5 They merely f. from the laws of God.
WpI..rII.in.2:1 longer practice periods will f. this general
WpI..rII.in.6:2 which f. the statement of the ideas. These,
W-pI.....87.1:5 I will f. it where it leads me, and I will
W-pI.....95.8:3 and our failures to f. the instructions for
WpI..rIII.in1:3 are urged to f. just as closely as you can.
W-pI...124.2:5 who come to f. us will recognize the way
W-pI...124.3:1 is our eternal gift to those who f. after,
W-pI...134.8:4 Now are you free to f. in the way your true
W-pI. 134.12:5 to point the way to those who f. him.
W-pI. 134.14:3 will f. us to the reality we share with them
W-pI...137.9:1 which the Holy Spirit urges you to f. Him.
WpI. rIV.in1:2 on readiness for what will f. next. Such is
W-pI...155.6:4 way you call to them, that they may f. you
W-pI...155.9:3 to f. in your footsteps as you walk with
W-pI. 155.11:6 it goes before our brothers who will f. us.
W-pI. 159.10:3 Son, but f. in the way He has established.
WpI...rV.in2:6 *Yet does he f., sure that he is safe because his*
W-pI. 189.10:8 *Yours is the way that we would find and f..*
W-pI...195.2:3 and f. in the way He sets before them, to
W-pI...220.1:3 *But let me f. Him Who leads me home, and*
W-pII ....in.8:2 the choice to f. it as He would have us go.
W-pII .225.2:3 Now we f. it in peace together. You have
W-pII .233.1:6 *I will step back and merely f. You. Be You the*
W-pII ..... 3.4:3 F. His light, and see the world as He
W-pII .258.2:1 *goal is but to f. in the way that leads to You.*
W-pII .298.2:1 *because I would not f. any way but Yours.*
W-pII .....317.h I f. in the way appointed me.
W-pII .....324.h I merely f., for I would not lead.
W-pII .324.1:6 *My brothers all can f. in the way I lead them.*
W-pII .324.1:7 *Yet I merely f. in the way to You, as You*
W-pII .324.2:1 So let us f. One Who knows the way. We
W-pII .324.2:3 We walk together, for we f. Him. And it is
W-pII .326.1:8 *Your plan I f. here, and at the end I know that*
W-pII .334.1:4 God to all who hear and choose to f. Him.
W-pII .352.1:5 *I am redeemed when I elect to f. in this way.*
WfI........in.2:5 us together f. in the way that truth points
WpII ..361-5.h For I would f. You, Certain that Your
W-ep ......... 2:4 f. Him Whom you accepted as your voice,
M-in .......... 4:4 here does f. it until he changes his mind,
M-4 .......II.1:2 been achieved, the others cannot fail to f..
M-4 ..... V.1:11 They hold His gifts and f. in His way,
M-5 ........II.4:3 Does not this f. of necessity? Place cause
M-7 ........... 2:4 teacher of God has only one course to f..
M-22 ....... 6:14 All else must f. from this single purpose.
M-23 ....... 3:11 teacher be unavailable to those who f.
M-29 ......... 3:3 To f. the Holy Spirit's guidance is to let
C-5 ............ 3:2 He led the way for you to f. him. He leads
P-2...... IV.11:7 Given this single shift, all else will f..

### followed 11

T-13 ........I.6:7 Goodness and mercy have always f. him,
T-13 ... VI.13:2 have f. them through all your nightmares,
T-14 ......in.1:6 We have f. much of the ego's logic, and
W-in.......... 3:3 This is f. by a description of the specific
W-pI ...... 4.5:2 procedures to be f. for the exercises. Do
W-pI .... 24.4:1 today's idea, f. by searching the mind,
W-pI .... 25.6:2 f. by looking about you and letting your
W-pI .... 37.4:1 f. by a minute or so of looking about you
M-16 ......... 5:1 same procedures should be f. at night.
C-5 ............ 3:3 he saw the road before him, and he f. it.
S-1........ III.4:2 some time be f. by a deep retreat into fear

### follower 7

T-7 .........X.5:9 In this case, it always means that the f. is.
T-31 .......II.3:3 leader and the f. emerge as separate roles,
T-31 .......II.4:3 at times you want to let the f. in you arise,
T-31 .......II.5:7 the leader or the f. to you it matters not,
W-pII . 233.1:7 *and I the f. who questions not the wisdom of*
W-ep......... 4:1 you in His hands, to be His faithful f.,
P-2........ III.1:2 Ideally, he is also a f., for One should walk

### followers 4

T-6 ..........I.8:7 Disciples are f., and if the model they
T-31 .......II.7:5 tenderness, seeing no leaders and no f.,
W-pI 135.20:3 Your f. will join their light with yours,
W-pII ... 12.4:2 the altar where its sickly f. prepare to die.

### following 30

T-1 ....... III.4:7 to abandon them by f. my guidance."
T-2 ..........I.1:8 This process involves the f. steps: First,
T-5 ....... IV.6:2 By f. Him you are led back to God where
T-7 ....... XI.1:3 F. Him is therefore the easiest thing in the
T-8 ....... III.5:9 depending on which teacher you are f..
T-9 ..........II.8:5 By f. this way you are seeking the truth in
T-9 ....... III.6:8 f. the wrong guide and will therefore lose
T-9 ....... IV.4:3 f. its plan you will merely place yourself in
T-9 .........V.9:5 By f. the right Guide, you will learn the
T-12 ..... IV.5:7 your brothers home you are but f. Him.
T-13 ... VI.12:1 Awaking unto Christ is f. the laws of love
T-13 .... VII.6:2 and f. not the road that love points out.
T19 ...IV.C.3:6 they live. They are not f. His Will; they are
T-31 .....II.11:3 while you still insist on leading or on f.,
T-31 ..... IV.7:1 is ever found by f. a road away from it.
W-pI .... 16.5:5 The f. form is suggested for this purpose:
W-pI .... 37.5:2 eyes closed, and another, f. immediately,
W-pI .... 40.3:3 might, for example, consist of the f.: *I am*
W-pI ....... 51.h The review for today covers the f. ideas:
W-pI ....... 53.h Today we will review the f.:
W-pI ....... 55.h Today's review includes the f.:
W-pI ....... 56.h Our review for today covers the f.:
W-pI ....... 59.h The f. ideas are for review today:
W-pI .... 71.5:1 works simply because, by f. His direction,
WpI..rIV.in1:3 aim for this review, and for the lessons f..
W-pI .. 166.6:3 you see that he is f. the way he chose, and
Wi181-200 1:4 willingness to f. the way the course sets
W-pII .... in.7:2 our way by f. the Guide You sent to us.
M-4 ........... 2:2 teachers of God have the f. characteristics
M-29 ....... 3:10 think that f. the Holy Spirit's guidance is

### follows 44

T-1 ....... VI.3:1 which f. from the original error that one
T-2 .........V.6:2 a learning device it merely f. the learner,
T-2 .....VIII.1:5 It also f. that whatever you alone make is
T-5 ....... III.2:5 of other ideas because it f. the laws of the
T-5 .......V.3:11 you. Fear of retaliation from without f.,

T-6......V.B.9:3 step is easier than the first because it f..
T-6......V.C.3:4 which f. from the second as the second
T-6......V.C.3:4 the second as the second f. from the first,
T-10....... II.6:3 It f., then, that you want something other
T-11.........I.7:8 It f., then, that you will to create, since
T-11.........I.7:8 will to create, since your will f. from His.
T-15.........I.4:7 it unsatisfied. No one who f. the ego's
T-15......VI.5:6 From this it f. you can only give. And this
T-17...... III.9:8 that f. from them comes from what they
T-19.........I.5:2 though it f. directly from the fundamental
T-19...... I.15:3 Truth f. faith and peace, completing the
T-20......IV.3:6 What God has given f. His laws, and His
T-20.....VII.2:1 period of discomfort that f. the sudden
T-21......IV.5:6 it f. perfectly from what you have already
T-23..... II.21:2 f. that it seems to be a logical conclusion;
T-24.......in.2:6 and f. it as surely as does suffering follow
T-27... VIII.8:7 their cause that f. nothing and is but a jest
T-29....... II.6:3 Confusion f. on confusion here, for on
T-31.........I.7:3 And each world f. surely from its source.
T-31....... II.6:5 This brother neither leads nor f. us, but
T-31....... II.9:5 to walk with him, so neither leads nor f..
W-pI.......9.1:1 obviously f. from the two preceding ones.
W-pI.....18.2:3 are recommended should be done as f.:
W-pI.....24.5:2 each application should be roughly as f.:
W-pI.....26.6:5 one. Today's idea should be applied as f.:
W-pI.....35.6:1 applying the idea for today might be as f.:
WpI...rI.in.1:4 periods, the exercises should be done as f.
W-pI.....91.2:4 This f. from the premises from which the
W-pI...129.1:1 thought that f. from the one we practiced
W-pI.134.13:2 to any understanding of the laws it f., nor
W-pI...156.1:3 It f. surely from the basic thought so often
W-pI...166.6:2 comes here has pursued the path he f.,
W-pI.193.12:4 hour cast its shadow on the one that f.,
W-pII..312.1:1 Perception f. judgment. Having judged,
M-in ..........4:4 Everyone who f. the world's curriculum,
M-4.......IV.1:4 dishonest act that f. a dishonest thought.
M-9............2:2 and it is this he f. as his guide for action.
P-2........IV.3:1 hell f. step by step in an inevitable course,
P-3......... II.2:4 of the world's teaching f. a curriculum in

## folly 7

T-30....... V.2:3 The f. of pursuing guilt as goal is fully
W-pI...134.1:2 must be seen as mere eccentric f., and this
W-pI...135.1:2 And herein lies the f. of defense; it gives
W-pI.136.14:2 down its arms, and cease to play with f.. It
W-pI...153.6:4 it recognizes strength so great attack is f.,
W-pI...191.4:3 All else but this one thing is f. to believe.
M-24........1:11 In between, many kinds of f. are possible.

## food 2

W-pI.136.18:3 by weather or fatigue, by f. and drink, or
W-pII..222.1:2 I breathe, the f. by which I am sustained,

## fool

*See* fool-proof

## fool-proof 1

T-5......VI.10:6 The case may be f., but it is not God-proof

## foolish 49

T-3......... II.2:3 innocent are apt to be quite f. at times. It
T-14....... II.5:5 goal, and recognize how f. it has been. Be
T-16.........I.6:4 if a brother asks a f. thing of you to do it.
T-16.........I.6:5 certain that this does not mean to do a f.
T-16.........I.6:6 F. requests are foolish merely because
T-16.........I.6:6 are f. merely because they conflict, since
T-16.........I.6:7 recognizes f. needs as well as real ones.
T-21.........I.2:1 f. is it to attempt to judge what could be
T-24.....VII.5:3 Let not your f. fancies frighten you. What
T-27...... II.7:6 a vain imagining, a f. wish with no effects.
T-27......VI.6:3 How f. and insane it is to think a miracle
T-27... VIII.9:3 on its f. cause and laugh with Him a while
T-31....IV.10:6 How f. and insane it is to think that there
W-pI.....41.7:2 world and all the f. thoughts of the world.
W-pI.....50.5:3 surety. Let no idle and f. thoughts enter to
W-pI.....65.7:1 spite of your own f. ideas to the contrary.
W-pI.....76.9:2 Dismiss all f. magical beliefs today, and
W-pI...76.10:1 realize how f. are the "laws" you thought
W-pI.....92.2:4 no more f. than to believe the body's eyes
W-pI.....93.2:3 afraid of f. fantasies and savage dreams;
W-pI.....93.8:4 Then put away your f. self-images, and
W-pI...100.8:5 the little thoughts and f. goals you pass as
W-pI...100.9:5 What f. goal can keep you from success
W-pI.131.10:1 Leave f. thoughts like these behind today,
W-pI.131.10:3 to replace the f. images that we hold dear,
W-pI.134.11:2 the f. dreamer who believes in them. He
W-pI.135.26:5 the day, as f. little things appear to raise
W-pI.137.15:2 the f. thoughts that ever were imagined.
W-pI.138.11:5 Now it is recognized as but a f., trivial
W-pI.139.12:2 be cleared of all the f. cobwebs which the
W-pI...156.6:5 is seen. It is a f. thought, a silly dream, not
W-pI...156.7:1 many, many years on just this f. thought.
W-pI...170.5:4 ask you lay down all defense as merely f..
W-pI.184.14:3 all f. separations disappear which kept us
W-pI...189.6:4 snares the f. convolutions of the world's
W-pI...196.2:4 you can learn to see these f. applications,
W-pI...198.7:5 How f. to believe that They could die!
W-pI...198.7:6 die! How f. to believe you can attack! How
W-pI...200.3:6 be more f. than to seek and seek and seek
W-pII..229.2:1 *of all the thoughts of sin my f. mind made up.*
W-pII..240.2:1 *How f. are our fears! Would You allow Your*
W-pII..278.2:2 *I have had many f. thoughts about myself*
W-pII..331.1:1 *How f., Father, to believe Your Son could*
W-pII..346.1:7 *forgetting all the f. toys I made as I behold*
Wfl ........in.5:4 is mad, and vengeance merely f. fantasy.
M-4 ...... VI.1:6 are but f. guardians of mad illusions. The
M-15 .........3:1 even contempt; give up these f. thoughts!
M-16 .........6:9 How f. to be so afraid of nothing! Nothing
M-29 .........7:9 Forget your f. images, your sense of frailty

## foolishly 1

T-9........ III.2:7 tell him this verbally, if he is speaking f..

## foolishness 8

T-31..... V.10:6 Let us forget the concept's f., and merely
W-pI.....41.2:4 has the power to end all this f. forever.
W-pI.....41.2:5 And f. it is, despite the serious and tragic
W-pI...153.8:2 for f. the endless joy our function offers us
W-pI...154.1:2 We have gone beyond such f.. We cannot
W-pI...190.4:1 Peace to such f.! The time has come to
W-pI...196.6:5 And he will not perceive its f., or even see
W-pII..242.1:2 to try to lead my life alone must be but f..

## foot 5

T-16...... III.9:1 think, and your f. is planted firmly on it.
T-23..... II.22:4 your f. upon the twisted stairway that
W-pI.......1.1:5 *This f. does not mean anything. This pen*
W-pI.134.12:5 as he lifts his f. to stride ahead a star is left
W-pI...194.1:3 f. has reached the lawns that welcome you

## footprints 2

T-26...... IX.7:2 in. Your f. lighten up the world, for where
W-pI...124.2:4 Our shining f. point the way to truth, for

## footsteps 14

T-18...... III.5:4 faltering f. that you may take can separate
W-pI...107.7:4 shaky and unsteady f. of illusion are not
WpIrIII.in12:3 with firmer f. and with stronger faith.
W-pI...123.4:3 and walk with lightened f. as we go to do
W-pI.134.14:3 practicing becomes the f. lighting up the
W-pI.153.18:1 hear His loving Voice guiding your f. into
W-pI...155.5:4 and set their f. on the way that God has
W-pI...155.9:3 you, to follow in your f. as you walk with
W-pI...163.3:3 it will come with certain f. when the time
WpI...rV.in1:5 Our f. have not been unwavering, and
WpI...rV.in3:5 *Quicken our f. now, that we may walk more*
W-pI...200.9:4 God alone is sure, and He will guide our f.
Wfl ........in.1:3 Who leads the way and makes our f. sure.
S-2........ III.3:3 Now can He make your f. sure, your

## for 6605

## forbidden 3

T-3......VII.3:4 one tree was "f." in the symbolic garden.
T-3......VII.3:5 But God could not have f. it, or it could
T-3......VII.3:7 The "f. tree" was named the "tree of

## forbidding 1

T-13...... IV.5:6 the present, you are f. yourself to let it go.

## forbids 1

T-13...... IX.1:3 fidelity to darkness and f. awakening. The

## Force 2

*force*

T-22....... V.5:4 you is a F. that no illusions can resist. This
T-22....... V.5:5 immovable; this F. is irresistible in truth.

## force 17

*Force*

T-2........ VI.9:5 powerful, and never loses its creative f.. It
T-3.......VII.2:5 He is perceived as a f. in combat with God
T-4........ III.6:1 No f. except your own will is strong
T-7...... VI.10:6 powerful f. in the universe as if it were
T-9...........I.3:7 attempting to f. an alien will upon you.
T-13...... VI.4:2 unless you f. continuity on them. You can
T-18.........I.5:6 to f. you to make further substitutions.
T19....IV.C.9:2 grow into a mighty f. for God is very near.
T-22....... V.1:2 Surely not by f. or anger, nor by opposing
T-22...... VI.9:6 one and make of it a potent f. for peace.
T-29.........I.8:1 you hold, and f. the body to maintain.
W-pI.....20.2:2 it as an effort to exert f. or pressure. You
W-pI.....35.8:4 Neither f. nor discrimination should be
W-pI...125.2:3 He is not led by f., but only love. He is not
W-pI...131.4:4 not seek vainly, though he try to f. delay,
W-pI...136.5:3 sign that this decision still remains in f.,
W-pI...197.1:1 belief in outside f. pitted against your own

## forced 10

T-3...........I.3:9 and f. him out of the Garden of Eden. It is
T-7........ VI.3:6 of this source, it is f. to depreciate it. This
T-7........ VI.5:3 F., therefore, to detach itself from you, it
T-7....VIII.3:12 they are f. to engage in constant activity
T-8........ III.2:3 because God's Will cannot be f. upon you
T-8.......VIII.2:7 This is why the ego is f. to shift ceaselessly
T-9........ IV.4:7 where the ego is f. to appeal to "mysteries
T-17....VIII.1:5 faithlessness has not f. any exclusion on it
T-23......II.10:3 Were they not f. into this foul attack by
M-5 .........I.2:3 which the Son of God is f. to recognize. It

## forces 9

T-16........II.9:5 For the ideas are mighty f., to be used and
T19... IV.D.7:4 things beyond you, f. you cannot control,
T-21....... V.2:5 prey to f. far beyond your own control,
T-23.........I.8:1 Conflict must be between two f.. It
T-29....VIII.2:3 with f. massed against your confidence
P-1.............3:6 on, reacting to external f. as they demand,
P-2..........II.3:5 world has marshalled all its f. against this
P-2......... V.1:5 are f. to be overcome to be alive at all.
P-2......... V.1:6 seems as if these f. can be held at bay only

## foreboding 1

W-pI.....26.6:2 of imposition, fear, f. or preoccupation.

## forego 1

T-25...... IX.1:5 answer "yes" it means you will f. all values

## foreground 1

M-8 ........... 1:2 on uneven background and shifting f., on

## forehead 4

T-11...... VI.7:1 Son, and taken the last thorn from his f..
W-pI..... 69.6:4 and f. and eyelids as you go through them
W-pI... 122.2:3 It soothes your f. while you sleep, and
W-pI... 155.1:3 Your f. is serene; your eyes are quiet. And

## foreheads 1

W-pI... 163.5:4 and kneeling down with f. to the ground,

## foreign 3

W-pI... 160.2:1 who comes from an idea so f. to the truth
W-pI... 167.9:2 it does not have, a f. state it cannot enter,
W-pI... 200.4:2 your happiness in f. places and in alien

## foremost 3

T-5........... I.4:6 taught me first and f. that this Inspiration
T-6...... V.B.2:2 for change is their first and f. goal. It is
T-27.... VI.2:10 Yet which is f. makes no difference. Sin's

## foreshadows 1

W-pI. 169.12:3 will end in time, for grace f. Heaven, yet

## forest 1

T-24....... V.4:2 each intent, in the dark f. of the sightless,

## foretaste 1

T-15......... I.6:6 hell here, but always as a f. of the future.

## foretold 1

M-19 ......... 2:6 journey continues, be f. from the outset.

## forever 397

T-1........ III.5:4 *Spirit is in a state of grace f.. Your reality is*
T-1........ III.5:6 *you are in a state of grace f..* Atonement
T-4......... in.2:6 f. unwilling to depart from its Foundation
T-4......... I.11:5 Yet His home will stand f., and is ready
T-4......... I.12:5 stand f. as the mark of the Love of God for
T-4........ III.6:2 are as free as God, and must remain so f..
T-4........ III.7:3 and it is f. unwilling to destroy what you
T-4........ VI.2:5 can easily flow across it and obliterate it f.
T-4....... VII.3:7 thus establishing it f. as a channel for the
T-5........ VI.1:7 eternity, where God Himself placed you f.
T-6........... I.7:3 placed it there Himself, and so it is true f..
T-6......... II.6:7 It is f. true. It is not a belief, but a Fact.
T-6....... II.12:8 of the Kingdom shines in your mind f.,
T-6........ III.3:3 it, assuring it that it is perfectly safe f..
T-6......... V.4:7 God Himself, speaks only for what lasts f..
T-6...... V.A.1:1 gone, you will know that you will last f..
T-7........... I.3:6 stop. It creates f., but not in time. God's
T-7........... I.5:3 He did. Only joy increases f., since joy and
T-7........... I.5:4 extend His Kingdom f. and beyond limit.
T-7........... I.5:6 The eternal are in peace and joy f..
T-7........... I.7:8 beginning, is true now, and will be true f..
T-7......... I.7:10 because it was f. created to increase. If
T-7....... VII.3:1 God's blessing because that you have f.,
T-7...... VIII.7:1 is unbelievable and will f. be unbelievable
T-7........ IX.4:1 The Kingdom is f. extending because it is
T-7........ IX.6:2 Will of God to give it to you, He gave it f..
T-7........ IX.6:3 Since it was His Will that you have it f.,
T-7........ IX.6:8 Like His, It extends f. and in perfect peace
T-8........ IV.1:2 does not vacillate, being changeless f..
T-8...... VI.5:14 with it and establishing its value f..
T-8........ VI.7:8 to his Creator, it is f. knowable to him.
T-8........ VI.9:6 where you are always, and what you are f.
T-8........ IX.9:8 His Will must stand f. and in all things.
T-10....... V.9:2 What is of God is His f., and you are of
T-10 .... V.10:7 Son's creation, fixed f. in the Mind of God
T-11 ........ I.3:6 It continues f., however much it is denied.
T-11 ........ I.6:1 you a place in His Mind that is yours f..
T-11 ..... III.5:6 that it can sweep you out of all darkness f.
T-11 ..... III.8:3 God blessed His Son f.. If you will bless
T-11 ..... IV.6:6 while I live it cannot be shut, and I live f..
T-11 ..... VI.6:7 safely surrounded by what is yours f..
T-12 ..... II.10:7 at the cause of fear and letting it go f.?
T-12 ... VIII.4:8 no more past than future, being f. always.
T-12 ... VIII.8:7 to knowledge, which is f. the only reality.
T-13 ........ I.5:6 purity shines untouched f. in God's Mind.
T-13 ........ I.5:8 Mind of his Father, and protects him f..
T-13 ........ I.7:4 time, being f. unwilling to be without him
T-13 ....... VI.6:2 for it holds the only things that are f. true.
T-13 .... VII.1:7 Nothing is there but shines, and shines f..
T-13 .... VII.8:3 God loves His Son f., and His Son returns
T-13 .... VII.8:3 and His Son returns his Father's Love f..
T-13 ... VIII.1:7 just as it has everything, and f..
T-13 ... VIII.2:8 no perception, however holy, will last f..
T-13 ... VIII.5:1 is the miracle of creation; *that it is one f..*
T-13 ....... X.9:3 Yet it is f. true. In shining peace within
T-13 .. X.10:11 perfect purity that is f. within God's Son.
T-13 ..... X.12:5 for what you see will banish guilt f.. I
T-13 ..... X.12:6 Son, whom You have created guiltless f..
T-14 ........ I.3:2 system you made would be f. dark. The
T-14 ....... II.7:5 the dark door that you believe is locked f..
T-14 ... III.15:8 his abode was fixed in perfect peace f..
T-14 ..... IV.8:7 Would you know of One Who gives f.,
T-14 ...... V.1:6 This is f. changeless. Accept, then, the
T-14 ....... X.1:1 knowledge of creation must continue f..
T-14 ..... X.12:8 Himself, Who wills to be with His Son f..
T-14 ..... XI.2:1 and be glad that you are not bound to it f.
T-14 ..... XI.3:1 how to escape f. from everything that you
T-15 ........ I.7:7 demanding vengeance f..
T-15 ........ I.8:5 the present extends f.. It is so beautiful
T-15 ...... I.15:6 his purity remains f. beyond attack and
T-15 ...... I.15:9 of God's creation, it is transformed into f.
T-15 ....... II.3:2 where you have f. been and will forever be
T-15 ....... II.3:2 where you have forever been and will f. be
T-15 ....... II.3:3 All that you have, you have f.. The blessed
T-15 ..... III.5:4 He established you as host to Him f.. He
T-15 ..... III.7:6 little world but still in you, He extends f..
T-15 ..... III.9:9 you, who must remain f. beyond littleness
T-15 ... III.10:2 Will is constant and at peace f. with itself.
T-15 ... III.12:5 God's power is f. on the side of His host,
T-15 ..... IV.6:3 could live f. in the holy instant, beginning
T-15 ..... IV.8:3 let everything that interferes with it go f.?
T-15 ... VIII.3:8 You are f. in a relationship so holy that it
T-15 ..... IX.5:1 need your creations have to be with you f.
T-16 ..... IV.9:3 of God and of His Son established f.. Seek
T-16 ... IV.13:8 its center, and only there, you are safe f.,
T-16 ... IV.13:8 safe forever, because you are complete f..
T-17 ........ I.1:2 His reality is f. sinless. He need not be
T-17 ..... IV.1:3 relationships became f. "to make happy."
T-17 ... VIII.6:4 nothing that it needs to be f. changeless
T-18 ..... III.1:5 that you could hide from truth f., in
T-18 ..... III.4:7 gift is given f., for God Himself received it
T-18 ..... III.6:4 is offered to the light, and is removed f..
T-18 ..... III.8:2 one Ray that shines f. in the Mind of God
T-18 ..... VI.9:8 Yet love must be f. like itself, changeless
T-18 ..... VI.9:8 must be forever like itself, changeless f.,
T-18 ..... VI.9:8 forever, and f. without alternative. And so
T-18 ... IX.11:2 to speak of what must f. lie beyond words
T-18 ... IX.12:6 replaced f. by the knowledge of love and
T-18 ... IX.14:2 and purified, and finally removed f..
T-19 ...... I.5:10 is to set up a goal f. impossible to attain,
T-19 ........ I.7:2 This will remain f. true, however much
T-19 ...... I.10:6 what makes faith f. justified in everyone.
T-19 ...... I.15:5 has been learned. Yet truth will stay f..
T-19 ....... II.1:5 will f. so remain unless a mind not part of
T-19 ....... II.4:3 created him, and willed that he be f.. Is
T-19 ..... III.1:6 be corrected, and yet will be f. desirable.
T-19 ..... III.8:1 it must f. be beyond the hope of healing.
T-19 ..... IV.2:7 which it would have been f. impossible to
T19.... IV.B.7:7 and shows you that its power is gone f..
T19.... IV.B.9:8 you f. be a wanderer in search of peace?
T19.. IV.B.10:1 is always justified, for the eternal is f. kind
T19... IV.D.3:3 the veil f. blotted out and unremembered.
T19... IV.D.5:5 And the appeal of death is lost f. as love's
T19 .. IV.D.6:4 let the veil be lifted, *they* will be gone f.. All
T19 .. IV.D.7:2 will occur is you will leave the world f..
T-20 ...... V.1:4 can anything be lost, and never lost f.. So
T-20 ..... VI.1:3 And this is wholly loving and f.. Yet has
T-20 ... VI.10:2 within it in the certainty it will endure f..
T-20 ... VI.10:6 open to receive you, and give you peace f..
T-21 ........ I.1:2 could be seen from evidence f. indirect;
T-21 ........ I.8:4 extending to infinity f. shining and with
T-21 ....... II.6:5 will, a mad revolt against what must f. be.
T-21 ..... VI.6:2 separate from you and from his Father f.,
T-21 ... VIII.5:3 constant peace you could experience f..
T-22 ..... II.12:1 the bright, endless circle that extends f., is
T-22 ..... IV.6:2 And so they learn that it is theirs f.. All
T-22 ....... V.4:5 throughout the universe f. sings as one?
T-22 ..... VI.3:1 in what God loves, and would have free f..
T-22 ..... VI.9:5 offer Him the tiny gifts He can extend f..
T-23 ........ I.9:5 and drive Him out of what He loves f..
T-23 ........ I.9:6 He loves must be f. quiet and at peace
T-23 ..... III.4:8 your vision, f. clear and never out of sight,
T-23 ..... IV.8:4 and only love shines upon them f.. It is
T-23 ..... IV.8:9 mar your certainty? And that will last f.?
T-24 ........ I.1:3 Love offers everything f.. Hold back but
T-24 ....... II.6:6 nothing, and to receive the Love of God f.
T-24 ..... II.10:7 separate from what it is and must f. be.
T-24 ..... II.14:2 and will f. fail to bring you peace and joy
T-24 ..... III.4:6 be, and that you will oppose His Will f..
T-24 ..... III.6:6 Will it is you rest f. in the arms of peace,
T-24 ..... VI.3:2 to lay before you lovingly, as yours f.. And
T-24 ..... VI.7:6 of Him He set f. in your brother's holiness
T-25 ....... II.1:8 willing to relinquish it, and have it gone f.
T-25 ....... II.6:6 within a frame that will endure f., when
T-25 ..... III.2:5 not be lost f. in the madness of his wish.
T-25 ..... III.8:5 been damned is damned and damned f.,
T-25 ..... III.8:5 damned forever, being f. unforgivable. If,
T-25 ..... IV.4:6 far away for recognition, and are gone f..
T-25 ..... IX.1:2 sins and not mistakes, f. uncorrectable,
T-26 ........ I.7:6 He is the same f.. Born again each instant,
T-26 ....... II.7:4 to be f. undone and unremembered.
T-26 ....... II.8:2 to Him, and will f. be as He created it.
T-26 ..... V.10:8 since removed and gone f. from his mind?
T-26 ..... VII.5:3 truth. The laws of truth f. will be true, and
T-26 ..... VII.7:2 errors seem f. past the hope of healing,
T-26 .. VII.15:7 What God calls One will be f. One, not
T-26 .. VII.17:4 and from hell and death, all glory be f..
T-26 ... VIII.6:2 of the working out can seem to take f..
T-26 ..... IX.3:8 all the blight and withering have passed f.
T-26 ..... IX.8:6 Son return to what is Theirs, and will f. be
T-27 ...... I.10:6 to represent an endless life, f. unattacked.
T-27 ..... V.2:10 must be gone f. from your mind to heal.
T-27 ..... V.11:4 in without attack will stay with you f..
T-28 ........ I.9:4 miracle reminds you of a Cause f. present,
T-28 ...... I.15:5 left a stranded Son f. on a shore where he
T-28 ....... II.2:4 of the innocent to be f. uncontained,
T-28 ....... V.7:3 shapes, f. unsubstantial and unsure. Yet
T-28 ..... VI.5:4 his tiny oath to be f. faithful unto death.
T-28 ..... VI.6:4 "You are beloved of Me and I of you f.. Be
T-28 .... VII.7:4 wash away and yet this house will stand f.
T-28 .... VII.7:5 promise that His Son is safe f. in Himself.
T-29 ....... V.2:2 and where They are, f. must you be. The
T-29 ....... V.5:2 perfect gift, in whom his Father shines f.,
T-29 ... VI.4:11 extension, that it be as one f. and forever,
T-29 ... VI.4:11 extension, that it be as one forever and f.,
T-29 ... VIII.6:5 peace of God, f. given to all living things,
T-29 ... VIII.7:5 is beyond where God has set all things f.,
T-29 ..... IX.6:1 childhood should be passed and gone f..
T-29 ..... IX.8:5 that abides f. deep within the Son of God.
T-30 ...... I.13:3 dream of judgment has f. been undone.
T-30 ....... II.4:5 but keep your will f. and forever limitless.
T-30 ....... II.4:5 but keep your will forever and f. limitless.
T-30 ..... III.6:2 And what He knows exists f., changelessly
T-30 ..... III.6:9 It is f. One, eternally united and at peace.
T-30 ..... III.8:1 are far beyond all change, and shine f..
T-30 ..... III.9:1 it safe, f. lifted up and anchored sure. Its
T-30 ..... IV.6:2 that will f. place you far beyond deception
T-30 ....... V.8:2 with perfect confidence away from fear f.,
T-30 ..... V.11:1 of God f. lies in those whose hands are
T-30 .. VII.6:13 It must be f. unintelligible. This is not
T-31 ....... II.3:5 both these roles, f. split between the two.
T-31 ..... IV.9:6 die, without their Source f. in themselves.

T-31 V.5:2 face that smiles above it must f. look away
T-31 VI.4:4 In Heaven as on earth this is f. true. It
T-31 VII.6:1 remain f. unaccomplished and undone.
T-31. VIII.10:3 are sure of what they are, and will f. be.
W-pI 41.2:4 has the power to end all this foolishness f.
W-pI 43.1:4 have replaced knowledge f. in your mind.
W-pI 49.2:5 mind where stillness and peace reign f..
W-pI 50.4:3 you; eternal, changeless and f. unfailing.
W-pI 50.5:5 place where your Father has placed you f..
W-pI 56.4:5 is still everywhere and in everything f..
W-pI 56.5:2 attack, is the knowledge that all is one f.. I
W-pI 57.2:6 The Son of God must be f. free. He is as
W-pI 58.5:7 care for me is infinite, and is with me f.. I
W-pI 73.8:3 and end f. the insane belief that it is hell
W-pI 75.9:7 that you will gladly extend today f..
W-pI 76.2:2 you would f. seek salvation where it is not
W-pI 76.7:4 instead it is a truth that keeps us free f..
W-pI 76.9:6 else. God's laws f. give and never take.
W-pI 76.11:3 of Heaven which His laws keep limitless f.
W-pI 92.8:1 sure as love, f. glad to give itself away,
W-pI 93.7:6 and will f. be exactly as you were created.
W-pI 94.1:3 held are wiped away f. by this one idea.
W-pI 95.13:4 strength within you and His Love f. yours.
W-pI 96.3:3 two, and still be what It is and must f. be.
W-pI 99.4:1 with Mind and Thought which are f. One
W-pI 99.11:1 of doubt and fear f. from your mind. If
W-pI 105.4:5 it has away, securing it f. for itself.
W-pI 106.4:7 They end the dream instead; and last f.,
W-pI 106.7:1 is given away, it will remain with you f..
W-pI 107.3:6 not be found, for truth is everywhere f.,
W-pI 108.1:5 place. And now you are at peace f., for the
W-pI 110.8:1 world; the Savior Who has been f. saved,
W-pI 112.2:2 me. *I will remain f. as I was, created by the*
W-pI 114.2:2 *has created me for what I am and will f. be?*
W-pI 122.8:3 as ancient truths, f. newly born, arise in
W-pI 123.3:1 His Love f. will remain shining on you,
W-pI 123.3:1 remain shining on you, f. without change.
W-pI 125.2:2 f. in his mind and at his side to lead him
W-pI 125.2:2 house by his own will, f. free as God's. He
W-pI 125.4:3 place within the mind where He abides f.,
W-pI 127.3:8 which holds Them both f. as the same.
W-pI 129.3:1 losing is impossible; where love endures f.
W-pI 131.8:4 Will has given him to be his home f.? Let
W-pI 133.6:1 if you choose a thing that will not last f.,
W-pI 137.4:4 always will remain exactly as it has f. been
W-pI 137.8:6 to join with other minds, to be f. strong.
W-pI 139.8:2 It is set f. in the holy Mind of God, and in
W-pI 140.6:5 truth, which cannot fail to heal and heal f.
WpI. rIV.in2:8 from his awareness. Yet it is f. true.
WpIrIV.in10:2 in the peace wherein He wills you be f.,
W-pI.153.13:3 and childish thoughts of sin f. from the
W-pI 158.1:2 mind, in Mind and purely mind, sinless f.
W-pI 160.8:2 Son belongs where He has set His Son f..
W-pI 160.8:5 Whom God has joined remain f. one, at
W-pI 163.9:6 *things, to be like You and part of You f.. We*
W-pI 164.1:3 we come to look upon what is f. there; not
W-pI 165.6:5 His Son remain f. starved by his denial of
W-pI 167.8:4 F. unopposed by opposites of any kind,
W-pI 167.8:4 the Thoughts of God remain f. changeless
W-pI 167.8:4 with the power to extend f. changelessly,
W-pI.167.11:1 it, and wills it be f. and forever. He is Lord
W-pI.167.11:1 it, and wills it be forever and f.. He is Lord
W-pI.167.12:2 As we were, so are we now and will f. be.
W-pI 168.1:9 He will love His Son f.. When his mind
W-pI 168.2:2 For hope would be f. satisfied; despair of
W-pI 169.9:2 be a constant state, f. as it always was;
W-pI 169.9:2 as it always was; f. to remain as it is now.
W-pI.169.13:4 How could you finally attain to it f., while
W-pI.170.12:3 And now your heart remains at peace f..
WpI rV.in10:3 Name. Your glory undefiled f.. And your
W-pI 182.4:4 with an innocence that will endure f..
W-pI.183.10:5 Father gave, is giving still, and will f. give.
W-pI 184.9:1 symbols of the world, forgetting them f.;
W-pI 185.9:6 just as certainly, and to remain with you f.
W-pI 187.9:5 and leave instead the perfect gift f. there,
W-pI 187.9:5 the perfect gift forever there, f. to increase
W-pI 187.9:5 forever there, forever to increase, f. yours,
W-pI 187.9:5 to increase, forever yours, f. given away.
W-pI 188.3:2 with it that remains f. and forever. What
W-pI 188.3:2 with it that remains forever and f.. What
W-pI 189.8:3 God the Father to be quietly removed f..
W-pI 190.6:5 and unchangeable, f. and forever. And
W-pI 190.6:5 and unchangeable, forever and f.. And
W-pI 191.4:6 proclaimed to be f. part of everything, the
W-pI 192.1:1 Self shall be His sacred Son, f. pure as He,
W-pI 192.1:1 name, f. one with God and with your Self.
W-pI 193.1:2 undisturbed; eternal and f. gaining scope,
W-pI 193.2:6 and keeps his sinlessness f. safe.
W-pI 193.4:4 No one can hide f. from a truth so very
W-pI.196.12:1 and to go beyond it quickly, surely and f..
W-pI 197.3:3 of a thankful heart, released from hell f..
W-pI 197.5:3 eternal, changeless, limitless. f. giving out
W-pI 197.7:1 with the end of this belief is fear f. over.
W-pI.198.11:6 that God f. knows to be His only Son.
W-pI.198.12:6 and then you disappear f. into God.
W-pI 199.2:1 that serves the Holy Spirit is unlimited f.,
W-pI 199.8:2 In immortality you live f.. Would you not
W-pI 200.9:5 need, nor let him stray f. from his home.
W-pI 201.1:3 *of the whole that is my Self, f. One with me. I*
W-pI 204.1:2 *free in God, f. and forever one with Him.* I am
W-pI 204.1:2 *free in God, forever and f. one with Him.* I am
W-pI 219.1:5 *as to what my Father loves f. as His Son.* I am
W-pII 227.1:5 *feet of truth, to be removed f. from my mind.*
W-pII 230.1:4 when He created me He gave me peace f..
W-pII 230.1:6 can this be denied me, when it is f. true?
W-pII 234.1:3 in thoughts which are f. unified as one.
W-pII 235.1:3 Son and keeps his sinlessness f. perfect, to
W-pII 235.1:3 that I am saved and safe f. in His Arms. I
W-pII 235.2:2 *me, and made my sinlessness f. part of You. I*
W-pII 239.1:4 when He loves His Son f. and with perfect
W-pII 239.2:1 *You, Father, for the light that shines f. in us.*
W-pII 244.2:4 make afraid what will f. be a part of Him?
W-pII 4.3:4 Himself, His Will f. overcome by death,
W-pII 255.1:5 must remain f. in the peace of Heaven. In
W-pII 267.1:6 and held f. quiet and at peace within His
W-pII 268.1:5 *love was I created, and in love will I remain f.*
W-pII 270.1:4 *instant more of time which ends f., as Your*
W-pII 6.1:5 abides unchanged f. in the Mind of God.
W-pII 6.2:1 of despair, for hope f. will abide in Him.
W-pII 272.1:7 *am surrounded by Your Love, f. still, forever*
W-pII 272.1:7 *Love, forever still, f. gentle and forever safe.*
W-pII 272.1:7 *Love, forever still, forever gentle and f. safe.*
W-pII 280.1:5 No Thought of God but is f. pure. Can I
W-pII 7.1:4 There are sights and sounds f. laid aside.
W-pII 7.3:2 you would attain what is f. unattainable.
W-pII 282.1:3 truth remains f. living in the joy of love.
W-pII 293.1:2 state, whose Source is here f. and forever.
W-pII 293.1:2 state, whose Source is here forever and f..
W-pII 299.2:5 *It stands f. perfect and untouched. In it are*
W-pII 9.1:2 re-establishes what is f. and forever true.
W-pII 9.1:2 re-establishes what is forever and f. true.
W-pII 309.1:1 is God's Will that it be there f. and forever
W-pII 309.1:1 is God's Will that it be there forever and f.
W-pII 10.5:1 "You are still My holy Son, f. innocent,
W-pII 10.5:1 innocent, f. loving and forever loved, as
W-pII 10.5:1 innocent, forever loving and f. loved, as
W-pII 10.5:1 and completely changeless and f. pure.
W-pII 11.1:5 F. and forever are God's Thoughts exactly
W-pII 11.1:5 Forever and f. are God's Thoughts exactly
W-pII 11.2:4 God has willed to be f. One will still be
W-pII 11.3:3 Its oneness is f. guaranteed inviolate;
W-pII 11.3:3 inviolate; f. held within His holy Will,
W-pII 322.1:4 the Holy One Who still abides in Him f.,
W-pII 322.2:1 *to You all sacrifice remains f. inconceivable.*
W-pII 326.h I am f. an Effect of God.
W-pII 326.1:2 *I am f. Your Effect, and You forever and*
W-pII 326.1:2 *Effect, and You f. and forever are my Cause.*
W-pII 326.1:2 *Effect, and You forever and f. are my Cause.*
W-pII 329.1:5 *where my will became f. one with Yours.*
W-pII 330.1:6 thus escape f. from all things the dream of
W-pII 330.2:3 *to be made free f. from all our mistakes, and*
W-pII 12.3:4 peace, f. conflict-free and undisturbed, in
W-pII 12.5:2 peace will be restored f. to the holy minds
W-pII 336.1:2 to what remains f. past its highest reach.
W-pII 337.1:1 love, freedom f. from all thought of loss;
W-pII 340.1:4 *forgiveness, and be free f. from all suffering.*
W-pII 343.1:7 *so all things are given unto me f. and forever.*
W-pII 343.1:7 *so all things are given unto me forever and f..*
W-pII .355.1:6 *not wait an instant more to be at peace f.. It is*
W-pII .359.1:4 *You created sinless so abides f. and forever.*
W-pII .359.1:4 *You created sinless so abides forever and f..*
W-pII .360.1:2 *I am Your Son, f. just as You created me, for*
W-pII .360.1:2 *remain f. still and undisturbed within me. I*
M-in 5:1 for the world of sin would seem f. real.
M-in 5:7 remain a source of strength and truth f..
M-4 VII.2:12 generosity, protecting them f. for himself.
M-5 II.4:1 With this idea is pain f. gone. But with
M-12 1:6 thoughts are joined with God's f. and ever
M-12 1:9 He is f. one, because he is as God created
M-13 3:3 to be f. dissatisfied and discontented; to
M-14 1:4 evil, concealing all sin and ending guilt f..
M-15 1:3 Who could flee f. from the truth? But the
M-15 1:11 *and whole, at peace f. in the Heart of God.*
M-17 9:13 all fear, and thus f. real and always true.
M-18 3:10 *God reigns f., and His laws alone prevail*
M-19 1:9 thought of separation would have been f.
M-19 3:5 for not one "sin" but seems f. true.
M-19 4:5 It remains f. and forever like its Creator,
M-19 4:5 It remains forever and f. like its Creator,
M-22 7:10 my beloved Son, created perfect and f. so.
M-27 7:8 that the Son of God is guiltless now and f.
M-28 5:8 created us so will we be f. and forever,
M-28 5:8 created us so will we be forever and f.,
C-4 1:3 in the world you see that will endure f..
C-4 2:4 While everything that God created is f.
C-4 2:4 without sin and therefore is f. without
C-4 4:5 with time f. ended as the world spins into
C-4 6:4 forgiveness, for it seems to be f. sinful.
C-4 7:7 of guilt and death is there snuffed out f..
C-5 3:1 f. like Himself and One with Him–Jesus
C-ep 4:6 instant, though it seems to be unsung f..
C-ep 5:1 that the holiness of this rebirth will last f..
P-2 IV.8:4 to God that it must be f. inconceivable.
P-2 V.8:3 lay them down, to come away in peace f..
P-3 II.4:3 His creations do not change and last f., so
S-1 in.1:3 concord of the Love They give f. to Each
S-1 in.2:3 to separate is one f. in the Mind of God.
S-1 II.7:5 in Christ is fully recognized as set f.,
S-1 II.7:7 and clad f. in the pure sinlessness that is
S-1 V.4:4 Here will time end f.. At this gate eternity
S-2 I.9:5 treachery, and then let go f. and forever.
S-2 I.9:5 treachery, and then let go forever and f..
S-2 II.3:5 creation and the holiness that is His gift f.
S-3 III.5:4 It heals no part, but wholly and f.. Now
S-3 IV.6:4 Then arise and lay all dreaming down f..

## forevermore 2

T-24 III.4:6 It will f. be unforgiving, for that is what it
T-26 V.8:1 voice that calls from out a past f. gone by.

## forged 1

T-15 VII.4:6 f. out of anger and dedicated to but one

## forget 190

T-1 VII.2:2 Do not f. this. The Love of God, for a little
T-2 VIII.1:2 apt to f. this when you become egocentric
T-4 II.3:6 f. that the mind need not work that way,
T-4 VI.2:1 brother is something you must never f.. It
T-5 II.6:1 calls you both to remember and to f.. You
T-5 IV.5:3 I cannot f. my need to teach what I have
T-5 V.3:8 mind, never f. that the ego is not sane. It
T-6 III.2:8 not f. that what you teach is teaching you.
T-7 II.6:5 You f. in order to remember better. You
T-7 II.6:7 Therefore you must f. or relinquish one to
T-7 IV.6:7 you do not use it, you f. that you have it.
T-7 V.10:1 f. the Father because I am with you, and I
T-7 V.10:1 I am with you, and I cannot f. Him. To
T-7 V.10:2 f. me is to forget yourself and Him Who
T-7 V.10:2 is to f. yourself and Him Who created you
T-7 VII.5:7 and teach His way lest you f. yourself.
T-8 III.4:5 Never f. this, for in him you will find
T-8 III.5:11 you. Never f. your responsibility to him,
T-8 VI.1:5 F. not the Kingdom of God for anything
T-9 II.11:1 Never f., then, that you set the value on

T-9........ III.8:2 His function, or you will f. yours. Accept
T-9......VIII.5:4 When you f. this, you *will* despair and you
T-10............ II.h The Decision to F.
T-10........ II.1:2 is nothing more than a decision to f..
T-10....... V.2:1 Do not f., however, that to deny God will
T-11.......I.11:2 never f. that God did not will to be alone.
T-11...... IV.1:1 f. that the Sonship is your salvation, for
T-12...... VI.2:4 always, He cannot let you f. your worth.
T-12...... VI.2:7 You chose to f. your Father but you do
T-12....VIII.4:1 your Father's Love you can never f. Him,
T-12....VIII.4:1 no one can f. what God Himself placed in
T-14.... III.14:7 it. F. Him not and He will make every
T-14.... III.15:7 reality. Never f. the Love of God, Who has
T-15.... III.11:4 let no one f. what you would remember.
T-15.... III.12:4 F. not that his call is yours, and answer
T-15...... VI.2:4 But f. not that my faith must be as perfect
T-16..IV.11:13 to f. and your ability to remember. In
T-16.... IV.12:1 Your Father can no more f. the truth in
T-16...... VI.2:5 F. this not, or Love will be unable to find
T-17.........I.6:5 f. not this: When you become disturbed
T-17....... V.8:4 it. F. not now the misery you really found,
T-18...... IV.8:1 F. not that it has been your decision to
T-18....... V.6:3 But f. not that your relationship is one,
T-18.... VII.7:9 will remain when you f., and the body's
T-19.... III.10:5 F. what you have seen, and raise your eyes
T19.... IV.B.6:3 who he is, and f. what never was. I ask for
T19..IV.B.16:2 F. not that the ego has dedicated the body
T19... IV.D.7:6 mad desire, no trivial impulse to f. again,
T19... IV.D.8:1 F. not that you came this far together,
T-20....... II.3:7 F. not that it is your savior to whom the
T-20...... IV.6:7 to f. imprisonment and to remember
T-20...... IV.7:6 I could leave you, and f. part of myself.
T-20....... V.2:7 F. not Who has given you the gifts you
T-20.... VII.9:3 f. not that his sinlessness is *your* escape
T-21.........I.1:1 Never f. the world the sightless "see"
T-21.........I.3:3 happiness you want to learn and not f.. It
T-21...... III.1:3 F. not this; to bargain is to set a limit, and
T-21..... VII.7:1 F. not that the choice of sin or truth,
T-22....... V.6:1 F. not, when you feel the need arise to be
T-24.......in.1:1 F. not that the motivation for this course
T-24...... VI.4:1 F. not that the healing of God's Son is all
T-24.... VI.13:3 F. not that this judgment must apply to
T-25....... V.6:6 But f. not this; the role you give to him is
T-26....... V.9:1 F. the time of terror that has been so long
T-26...... IX.2:2 F. not that a shadow held between your
T-27.........I.4:3 you send lest he f. the injuries he gave,
T-27....... V.7:3 And then, when you f. it, will the world
T-27..... VII.6:2 F. not that the witness to the world of evil
T-27... VII.10:6 Awaken and f. all thoughts of death, and
T-28.........I.8:1 remembered for you, when you would f..
T-29...... III.4:3 your forgiveness, he will not f. his savior,
T-29..... VII.7:1 Let us f. the purpose of the world the past
T-29...... IX.4:8 But they are eager to f. that they made up
T-30.... III.11:8 F. not, then, that idols must keep hidden
T-30...... IV.1:3 you aware of it you would f. defensiveness
T-30..... V.11:5 can they f. for long that it is but their own
T-31.........I.6:2 God willed not His Son f. Him. And the
T-31........I.12:1 instant, and f. all things we ever learned,
T-31....... II.7:4 F. the dismal lessons that you learned
T-31....... II.9:5 For so do you f. the journey's goal, which
T-31.... IV.11:1 and f. all senseless journeys and all goal-
T-31..... V.10:6 so? Let us f. the concept's foolishness, and
T-31...... VI.5:1 be, f. not that no concept of yourself will
T-31....VIII.8:4 so new and clean and fresh you will f. the
W-pI..... 19.4:2 Do not f., however, that random selection
W-pI..... 20.5:2 Do not be distressed if you f. to do so, but
W-pI..... 40.1:4 If you f., try again. If there are long
W-pI... 44.10:3 And do not f. that they cannot hold you
W-pI... 44.11:2 But do not f.. Above all, be determined
W-pI... 44.11:3 Above all, be determined not to f. today.
W-pI..... 49.5:1 f. to repeat today's idea very frequently.
W-pI..... 60.2:6 I begin to remember the Love I chose to f.
W-pI..... 63.2:4 or you will f. your function and leave the
W-pI........ 64.h Let me not f. my function.
W-pI..... 64.6:2 *Let me not f. my function. Let me not try to*
W-pI..... 64.7:3 You may need to repeat "Let me not f. my
W-pI..... 68.1:2 To hold a grievance is to f. who you are.
W-pI..... 68.3:3 who hold grievances will f. who they are,
W-pI..... 73.6:1 F. the ego's arguments which seek to
W-pI..... 80.3:3 you do not f. that all problems are the
WpI..rII.in.4:4 Do not f. that your will has power over all
W-pI..... 82.3:1 (64) Let me not f. my function. I would
W-pI..... 82.3:2 I would not f. my function, because I
W-pI..... 82.3:3 I cannot fulfill my function if I f. it. And
W-pI..... 95.5:2 tend to f. about it for long periods of time
W-pI... 95.14:1 Do not f. today. We need your help; your
W-pI... 95.14:6 Do not f. today. Throughout the day do
W-pI... 95.14:7 Throughout the day do not f. your goal.
W-pI..... 97.6:3 nor will you be able to f. the way again.
W-pI... 98.10:3 it often, and do not f. each time you do so
W-pI. 100.10:5 Do not f. the idea for today between your
W-pI. 106.10:2 Do not f. today to reinforce your choice to
W-pI. 107.11:1 Do not f. your function for today. Each
WpIrIII.in12:2 F. them not. This second chance with
WpIrIII.in13:1 Do not f. how little you have learned. Do
WpIrIII.in13:2 Do not f. how much you can learn now.
WpIrIII.in13:3 Do not f. your Father's need of you, As
W-pI. 121.13:4 Do not f., throughout the day, the role
W-pI. 126.11:2 Do not let your mind f. this goal for long,
W-pI. 131.13:3 not quite f. in wandering away in dreams.
W-pI. 131.15:4 If you f. this happy fact, remind yourself
W-pI. 134.17:1 you f. its meaning and attack yourself.
W-pI... 136.4:3 plan requires that you must f. you made it
W-pI... 139.9:3 Let us not f. the goal that we accepted. It
W-pI. 153.16:3 Sometimes we will f.. At other times the
W-pI. 155.13:4 F. not He has placed His Hand in yours,
W-pI. 160.10:1 Not one does Christ f.. Not one He fails
WpI...rV.in3:3 *up. If we f. the way, we count upon Your sure*
WpI...rV.in3:4 *wander off, but You will not f. to call us back.*
W-pI... 183.4:3 see how easily you will f. the names of all
W-pI. 184.10:1 go into the sunlight and f. the darkness.
W-pI. 184.11:3 but He does not f. creation has one Name,
W-pI. 184.11:4 yet do not f. they share the Name of God
W-pI... 185.8:3 F. the words you use in making your
W-pI... 187.6:1 Never f. you give but to yourself. Who
W-pI... 189.5:3 But learn and do not let your mind f. this
W-pI... 189.7:5 F. this world, forget this course, and come
W-pI... 189.7:5 Forget this world, f. this course, and come
W-pI... 193.6:4 f. these words apply to everything you see
W-pI... 193.8:4 And God would have him not f. His Love,
W-pI... 194.9:3 If we f., we will be gently reassured. If we
W-pI... 198.9:5 Do not f. today that there can be no form
WpI rVI.in.4:3 and then f. all that we thought we knew
WpI rVI.in.7:4 us also not f. to Whom it has been given,
W-pI... 213.1:4 *I choose to learn His lessons and f. my own.* I
W-pII ....in.2:9 we f. our hourly remembrance in between
W-pII ....in.2:9 of Him as we are tempted to f. our goal.
W-pII ....in.7:3 not know the way, but You did not f. us.
W-pII ....in.7:4 And we know that You will not f. us now.
W-pII . 223.2:4 *Son. And we would not f. You longer. We are*
W-pII . 232.1:3 *And let me not f. my hourly thanksgiving*
W-pII . 257.1:1 I f. my goal I can be but confused, unsure
W-pII . 257.2:2 *us not f. today that we can have no will but*
W-pII . 266.1:3 *Let not Your Son f. Your holy Name. Let not*
W-pII . 266.1:4 *Let not Your Son f. his holy Source. Let not*
W-pII . 266.1:5 *Let not Your Son f. his Name is Yours.*
W-pII .... 288.h Let me f. my brother's past today.
W-pII . 306.1:2 Today I can f. the world I made. Today I
W-pII . 342.1:8 *at last, f. illusions in the blazing light of truth*
W-pII .... 346.h me, And I f. all things except His Love.
W-pII . 346.1:5 *time. I would f. all things except Your Love. I*
W-pII . 346.2:2 when we f. all things except God's Love.
W-pII . 358.1:6 *But let me not f. Your Love and care, keeping*
W-pII . 358.1:7 *Let me not f. myself is nothing, but my Self is*
Wfl........in.4:2 So let us not f. our goal is shared, for it is
M-5...... III.3:2 f. that all of them have the same purpose,
M-12......... 3:7 Do not f. that truth can come only where
M-13......... 7:1 Do not f. that sacrifice is total. There are
M-13......... 8:1 of God, do not f. the meaning of sacrifice,
M-16......... 5:8 be sure that you do not f. a brief period,–
M-16......... 8:6 F. not this is magic, and magic is a sorry
M-17......... 6:5 F. the battle. Accept it as a fact, and then
M-17......... 6:6 Accept it as a fact, and then f. it. Do not
M-21......... 1:9 Let us not f., however, that words are but
M-27....... 7:10 do not let yourself f. it is not less than this
M-29......... 6:1 Never f. that the Holy Spirit does not
M-29......... 7:9 F. your foolish images, your sense of
C-5.......... 6:11 *F. your dreams of sin and guilt, and come*
C-ep .......... 1:1 F. not once this journey is begun the end
C-ep .......... 1:5 do. When you f., remember that you walk
P-2.........V.4:8 us not f. that we are helpless of ourselves,
P-2....... VII.8:2 f. the world and all its little triumphs and
P-3........II.10:1 Do not f. that any form of specialness
P-3..... III.8:11 f. how very simple are the ways of God:
S-1...........I.4:1 is to f. the things you think you need. To
S-1........ III.5:2 Do not f. that it is you who did it, and
S-3........ IV.3:7 Do not f. the gratitude of God. Do not
S-3........ IV.3:8 Do not f. the holy grace of prayer. Do not
S-3........ IV.3:9 Do not f. forgiveness of God's Son.
S-3........ IV.5:1 Never f. this; it is you who are God's Son,

## forgetful 1

T-7 .......V.10:3 Our brothers are f.. That is why they need

## forgetfulness 4

T-12 .......II.2:6 not to remember, for his f. is yours. But
T-13 ..... XI.1:1 F. and sleep and even death become the
T-16 .. VII.12:4 *The sleep of f. is only the unwillingness to*
W-pI 122.14:1 not to let your gifts slip by and drift into f.

## forgets 8

T-9 ...... VII.4:3 you do, because He never f. what you are.
M-23 ......... 6:6 dedicated teacher of God f. his brothers.
C-6 ............ 3:6 He never f. the Creator or His creation.
C-6 ............ 3:7 He never f. the Son of God. He never
C-6 ............ 3:8 He never f. you. And He brings the Love
C-ep .......... 4:7 until the world is still an instant and f. all
P-3...........I.4:1 teacher of God, never f. one thing; he did
P-3..........II.6:1 instant that the therapist f. to judge the

## forgetting 24

T-7 .........II.6:4 that He teaches remembering and f., but
T-7 .........II.6:4 the f. is only to make the remembering
T-7 ....... IV.2:6 the laws of God and f. the laws of the ego.
T-7 ....... IV.2:7 ego. I said before that f. is merely a way of
T-7 ....... IV.4:4 Holy Spirit understands that your f. must
T-7 ....... IV.7:7 Healing is a way of f. the sense of danger
T-7 ..... IV.7:11 to it, you are merely f. what you are not.
T-9 ....... IV.4:8 f. that my words make perfect sense
T-11 ...... VI.8:8 f. of dreams and the awareness of Christ
T-12 .....II.2:10 God's Answer to your f. is but the way to
T-12 ..... VI.4:3 the sleep of f. to the remembering of God.
T-20 ..... IV.7:4 f. all the rest and yearning only to have
T-20 .......V.2:7 you give, and through your not f. this, will
T-25 ..... III.9:7 F. not that what he is to you will make
T-27 ...VIII.6:3 f. did the thought become a serious idea,
T-30 ..... III.7:6 of you is perfectly unchanged by your f..
T-31 .......II.6:4 be still, f. everything we thought we heard
W-pI .... 64.1:2 provide you with a justification for f. it. It
W-pI .. 103.2:2 witness to the fear of God, f. being Love,
W-pI .. 109.8:2 be faithful to your trust today, f. no one,
W-pI .. 136.5:1 It is this quick f. of the part you play in
W-pI .. 184.9:1 all symbols of the world, f. them forever;
W-pII . 346.1:7 *f. all the foolish toys I made as I behold Your*
M-17 ....... 6:11 Projecting your "f." onto Him, it seems to

## forgivable 1

T-25 ..... III.9:4 Is this a sin or a mistake, f. or not? Does

## forgive 170

T-1 ........I.27:2 It is the privilege of the forgiven to f..
T-1 ....... III.3:2 Being filled with spirit, they f. in return.
T-2 ... V.A.16:3 statement "Father f. them for they know
T-9 ....... IV.1:2 To f. is to overlook. Look, then, beyond
T-13 .......X.6:6 to establish them as real and then f. them.
T-14 ..... III.7:5 There is nothing to f.. No one can hurt
T-14 ..... IV.3:5 Ask, rather, to learn how to f., and to
T-15 .... VII.7:7 believes that to f. another is to lose him. It
T-15 .. VII.11:7 For bodies cannot f.. They can only do as
T-15 .. VIII.1:7 you recognize that there is nothing to f.,
T-16 .. VII.12:1 *F. us our illusions, Father, and help us to*

T-17.........I.6:5 to f. yourself for just this same attempt.
T-17.........I.6:7 As you f. him, you restore to truth what
T-17....... II.1:1 how beautiful those you f. will look to you
T-17...... III.1:1 f. is merely to remember only the loving
T-17...... III.1:5 Be willing to f. the Son of God for what he
T-19....... I.14:4 that there is nothing faith cannot f.. No
T19....IV.B.6:2 me. F. me all the sins you think the Son of
T19....IV.B.8:1 F. me your illusions, and release me from
T19... IV.C.8:5 upon it, and f. it what you ordered it to do
T19.IV.D.11:6 Those you do not f. you fear. And no one
T19.IV.D.13:5 He has in him the power to f. your sin, as
T19.IV.D.15:9 it. Whom you f. is free, and what you give
T19 IV.D15:10 F. the sins your brother thinks he has
T-21...... III.7:3 fear. In your refusal to f. him, you would
T-22....... V.6:7 If you f. your brother, this *must* happen.
T-24....... II.7:1 He has not lost the power to f. you all the
T-24....... II.8:5 it. Let him f. you all your specialness, and
T-24...... III.1:3 that is why it is impossible but partly to f.
T-24...... III.6:1 F. the great Creator of the universe, the
T-24...... III.6:7 F. the Holy One the specialness He could
T-24.... III.8:13 F. your Father it was not His Will that you
T-25....... II.10:1 F. your brother, and you cannot separate
T-25.... III.8:13 But to f. it is to change its state from error
T-25. VIII.9:11 Son of God the power to f. himself of sin.
T-26...... IV.1:6 which he learns he has done nothing to f..
T-26..... V.11:3 And will you not f. him now, because he
T-26..... V.14:1 F. the past and let it go, for it *is* gone. You
T-26... VIII.1:1 an interval between the time when you f.,
T-27....... II.1:8 To f. may be an act of charity, but not his
T-27..... II.1:10 And if you f. him his transgressions, you
T-27....... II.2:4 no one can f. a sin that he believes is real.
T-27....... II.2:7 does not first establish sin and then f. it.
T-27....... II.3:1 witness sin and yet f. it is a paradox that
T-27....... II.3:5 f. their brothers and themselves as well.
T-27..... II.10:4 No one can f. until he learns correction is
T-27..... II.10:4 until he learns correction is but to f., and
T-27... VII.15:5 F. him his illusions, and give thanks to
T-27. VIII.13:2 When you f. the world your guilt, you will
T-28....... I.9:10 When you f. It for your sins, It will no
T-28....... V.3:1 share no evil dreams if you f. the dreamer,
T-29...... III.3:5 So perfectly can you f. him his illusions he
T-29.... III.3:12 you f. is given power to forgive you your
T-29.... III.3:12 is given power to f. you your illusions. By
T-29...... III.4:2 On earth this means f. your brother, that
T-29...... VI.1:1 How willing are you to f. your brother?
T-30....... II.4:7 But you will not f. the world until you
T-30...... IV.7:3 that you f. all things that no one ever did;
T-30...... VI.1:7 mean that you f. a sin by overlooking
T-30...... VI.2:3 do not f. the unforgivable, nor overlook a
T-30...... VI.3:4 it must uphold the guilt you would "f.."
T-30...... VI.4:5 he is saved from this dilemma if he can f..
T-30...... VI.7:5 it. You must f. God's Son entirely. Or you
T-30...... VI.7:7 be some forms of guilt that you cannot f..
T-31....... II.9:1 F. your brother all appearances, that are
T-31.... IV.11:1 F. yourself your madness, and forget all
T-31...... VI.6:3 Do you f.? Then is the world forgiving, for
W-pI........46.h God is the Love in which I f..
W-pI.....46.1:1 not f. because He has never condemned.
W-pI.....46.1:4 who f. are thus releasing themselves from
W-pI.....46.1:5 only yourself, so do you f. only yourself.
W-pI.....46.2:1 Yet although God does not f., His Love is
W-pI.....46.4:4 *God is the Love in which I f. you, [name].*
W-pI.....46.5:1 is to put you in a position to f. yourself.
W-pI.....46.5:3 *God is the Love in which I f. myself.* Then
W-pI.....46.7:5 silently: *God is the Love in which I f. you.*
W-pI.....60.1:1 (46) God is the Love in which I f.. God
W-pI.....60.1:2 not f. because He has never condemned.
W-pI.....60.1:3 accepted their innocence see nothing to f.
W-pI.....60.2:2 is not my own strength through which I f.
W-pI.....60.2:3 in me, which I am remembering as I f.. As
W-pI.....60.2:5 I f. all things because I feel the stirring of
W-pI.....60.5:4 As I f., His Love reminds me that His Son
W-pI.....62.3:1 while each time you f. you call upon the
W-pI.....64.2:3 the world is a place where you learn to f.
W-pI.....64.6:4 *Let me f. and be happy.* At least once devote
W-pI.....68.3:2 is certain that those who f. will find peace.
W-pI.....68.3:3 is certain that those who f. will remember
W-pI.....82.1:5 Let me, then, f. the world, that it may be
W-pI.....95.8:3 to f. ourselves for our lapses in diligence,
W-pI.....97.7:2 *limits, safe and healed and whole, free to f.,*
W-pI.....99.7:5 F. yourself the thought He wanted this for
W-pI...99.10:1 F. all thoughts which would oppose the
W-pI...99.10:5 F. yourself the one you think you made.
W-pI...99.10:7 F. what you have made and you are saved.
W-pI...108.5:2 or that to f. one brother wholly is enough
W-pI...115.1:2 *is to f. the world for all the errors I have made*
W-pI...119.2:2 *I will f. all things today, that I may learn how*
W-pI...121.6:4 how to f. the self you think you made, and
W-pI...121.7:1 to teach your own how to f. itself. Each
W-pI...121.8:1 Today we practice learning to f.. If you
W-pI...122.6:3 F. and be forgiven. As you give you will
W-pI...126.3:1 When you "f." a sin, there is no gain to
W-pI...126.3:2 on a higher plane than he whom you f..
W-pI...126.4:3 sin that you f. is not your own. Someone
W-pI...134.1:1 Let us review the meaning of "f.," for it is
W-pI...134.2:7 can you f. the sinless and eternally benign
W-pI...134.3:1 that you still believe you must f. the truth,
W-pI...159.2:2 as accomplished in yourself when you f..
W-pI.161.11:5 sight of one who can f. you all your sins;
W-pI.186.14:5 of the world depends on you who can f..
W-pI.188.10:2 life. We will f. them all, absolving all the
W-pI.192.10:6 function here on earth is only to f. him,
W-pI.192.10:9 F. him now his sins, and you will see that
W-pI...193.3:7 It is this: *F., and you will see this differently.*
W-pI...193.5:1 *F., and you will see this differently.* These
W-pI...193.8:2 He would help you f. yourself. His Son
W-pI.193.13:3 *I will f., and this will disappear.* To every
W-pI...195.8:4 at last, and we f. without comparing.
W-pI...197.5:3 your never-ending joy while you f. but to
W-pI...198.2:2 F. and you are freed. Such is the law that
W-pI.198.10:4 as you f. the trespasses you thought Them
W-pI...200.3:5 F. yourself for vain imaginings, and seek
W-pI...216.1:4 *But if I f., salvation will be given me.* I am not
W-pII...... 1.4:4 He who would not f. must judge, for he
W-pII...... 1.4:4 judge, for he must justify his failure to f..
W-pII...... 1.4:5 But he who would f. himself must learn to
W-pII...... 1.5:3 His function, and f. whom He has saved,
W-pII..240.2:4 *free. Let us f. him in Your Name, that we may*
W-pII..241.1:7 will be united now, as you f. them all. For
W-pII..288.2:1 F. me, then, today. And you will know
W-pII..302.1:7 *Let me f. Your holy world today, that I may*
W-pII..304.2:2 *Let me f., and thus receive salvation for the*
W-pII.... 11.5:2 we f. creation in the Name of its Creator,
W-pII..342.1:7 *Let me f. all things, and let creation be as You*
W-pII..342.2:1 Brother, f. me now. I come to you to take
W-pII..344.1:6 *Yet he whom I f. will give me gifts beyond the*
W-pII..350.1:1 *we f. becomes a part of us, as we perceive*
W-pII..359.1:1 *Father, today we will f. Your world, and let*
W-pII..359.1:8 *Help us f., for we would be redeemed. Help*
W-pII..359.1:9 *Help us f., for we would be at peace.*
Wfl........in.3:2 Unto us the aim is given to f. the world. It
Wfl........in.3:5 all that we f. we will not fail to recognize
Wfl........in.4:3 And shall we not f. our brother, who can
M-4 ....... X.2:1 How do the open-minded f.? They have
M-14 .........3:5 to f. one sin than to forgive all of them.
M-14 .........3:5 to forgive one sin than to f. all of them.
M-20 .........5:7 life. F. the world, and you will understand
M-22 .........1:9 To f. is to heal. The teacher of God has
M-22 .........7:2 must remain beyond God's power to f.?
C-5.............5:8 F. him your illusions, and behold how
P-2.......... II.3:1 who learns to f. can fail to remember God
P-2.......... V.7:6 Let us help him to f. himself for all the
P-2........ VI.1:3 all this is but the grim refusal to f..
P-2........ VI.6:3 look at it, open it to re-evaluation and f. it
S-1...........I.4:2 the same as to look on sin and then f. it.
S-1 ......... II.6:8 F. them for your sins, and you will be
S-2...........I.3:1 Would you f. yourself for doing this?
S-2...........I.3:5 it real. Select the loving and f. the sin by
S-2...........I.4:2 It is impossible to f. another, for it is only
S-2...........I.4:6 Only in someone else can you f. yourself,
S-2......... II.2:3 Who can f. and yet despise? And who can
S-2......... II.3:2 one who would f. the other does not claim
S-2......... II.6:2 "I will f. you if you meet my needs, for in
S-2........ III.3:4 Let Him take charge of how you would f.,
S-2........ III.5:5 F. him as the Christ decides you should,
S-3...........I.5:3 ask amiss and seeming charity f. to kill, so
S-3...... IV.1:10 restored their wholeness so they can f.,
S-3........ IV.4:1 You first f., then pray, and you are healed
S-3........ IV.4:3 that you f. and pray but for yourself. And

## forgiven 116

T-1.........I.27:2 It is the privilege of the f. to forgive.
T-1........ III.3:1 The f. are the means of the Atonement.
T-3......... V.6:3 those who have been f. have everything.
T-5........ IV.7:2 f. must devote themselves first to healing
T-9........ III.7:5 His errors are f. with yours. Atonement is
T-9...... III.8:11 real to you, and all your errors will be f..
T-9......... IV.5:4 what you have made in order to be f..
T-14...... IV.3:4 Ask not to be f., for this has already been
T-16..... VII.9:2 All that must be f. are the illusions you
T-16..... VII.9:3 has no past, and only illusions can be f..
T-16..... VII.9:6 Thus will you learn that you have been f.,
T-16... VII.11:1 the holy instant, where all illusions are f..
T-17.........I.1:3 He need not be f. but awakened. In his
T-17.......... II.h The F. World
T-17........II.2:3 for everything has been f. and there are
T-17........II.7:1 From the f. world the Son of God is lifted
T-18....... V.2:5 remove all fear and hatred, and to be f..
T-18...... IX.9:3 Here are you f., for here you have forgiven
T-18...... IX.9:3 forgiven, for here you have f. everyone.
T-18.... IX.10:6 nothing perceived, f. nor transformed.
T-19.......I.11:3 of faith, the Son of God is seen already f.,
T19. IV.A.17:1 grace, which means you have at last f. me.
T-20........II.4:1 for lilies, for the Son of God has not f. me.
T-20........II.4:4 that I may be f. and you may look upon
T-20........II.6:2 You *have* f. me. And yet I cannot use your
T-22........in.1:6 same, and f. for its maker in the same way
T-24...... III.1:2 Only illusions can be f., and then they
T-24...... III.1:8 secret guilt would disappear, f. by himself
T-24...... III.6:6 you have f. Him Whose Will it is you rest
T-25...... III.8:6 If, then, it is f., sin's perception must have
T-25....... V.4:5 F. by you, your savior offers you salvation
T-26...... IV.1:5 and still believes that he has much to be f.
T-26...... IV.2:3 no parting here, for everything is totally f.
T-26...... IV.2:4 what has been f. must join, for nothing
T-26...... IX.2:1 to you, that you may be f. all your sins,
T-27........II.6:2 is healed, and has f. what he did not do.
T-29....... V.7:2 you have f. him for all his dreams of death
T-30........II.4:7 have f. Him Who gave your will to you.
T-30........II.5:4 And now is God f., for you chose to look
T-30....... V.1:6 recognized that all things must be first f.,
T-30...... VI.5:3 is how you learn that you must be f. too.
T-31...... III.2:1 did not believe they could not be f. in you
T-31...... VI.6:4 forgiving, for you have f. it its trespasses,
T-31..... VII.2:6 Your "evil" thoughts have been f. with his
W-pI.....46.3:3 mind for those whom you have not f.. It
W-pI.....46.3:4 matter "how much" you have not f. them.
W-pI.....46.3:5 You have f. them entirely or not at all.
W-pI.....46.4:1 a number of people you have not f.. It is a
W-pI.....46.6:4 *I have already been f.. No fear is possible in a*
W-pI.....46.6:6 *is no need to attack because love has f. me.*
W-pI.....52.2:5 have f. myself and remembered Who I am
W-pI.....58.1:3 Having f., I no longer see myself as guilty.
W-pI.....60.3:6 there be to fear in a world that I have f.,
W-pI.....60.3:6 that I have forgiven, and that has f. me?
W-pI.....75.5:5 *The light has come. I have f. the world.*
W-pI.....75.6:3 You have f. the world today. You can look
W-pI.....75.6:9 *The light has come. I have f. the world.*
W-pI.....75.7:4 You have f. the world. He will be with you
W-pI...75.7:11 The light has come. You have f. the world.
W-pI...75.10:3 *I have f. the world.* Should you be tempted,
W-pI...75.10:6 darkness: *The light has come. I have f. you.*
W-pI.....99.1:2 wrong; something to be saved from, f. for;
W-pI.121.13:3 Now have you been f. by yourself. Do not
W-pI...122.6:3 Forgive and be f.. As you give you will
W-pI...134.5:3 Guilt cannot be f.. If you sin, your guilt is
W-pI...134.5:5 Those who are f. from the view their sins
W-pI...158.9:1 Thus are his sins f. him, for Christ has
W-pI.158.10:4 in him, your sins have been f. by yourself.
W-pI.159.10:4 has dreamed the dream of a f. world. It is
W-pI...164.7:5 We stand f. in the sight of Christ, with all
W-pI...164.7:5 of Christ, with all the world f. in our own.
W-pI...187.8:6 of one who has f. and has blessed himself.
W-pI...192.8:1 but him who has f. everyone he sees or
W-pII ..... 1.1:4 And in that view are all your sins f.. What
W-pII ..... 1.5:2 He has f. you already, for such is His

W-pII .241.1:8 them all. For I will be f. by you today.
W-pII .241.2:1 *We have f. one another now, and so we*
W-pII .247.1:8 mine. You stand f., and I stand with you.
W-pII .256.1:8 can dream we have f. him in whom all sin
W-pII .269.1:5 *Today I choose to see a world f., in which*
W-pII .270.1:1 *body's eyes behold into the sight of a f. world*
W-pII .270.1:4 *world f. signifies Your Son acknowledges*
W-pII .288.2:2 And you will know you have f. me if you
W-pII .289.1:6 For what can be f. but the past, and if it is
W-pII .289.1:6 but the past, and if it is f. it is gone.
W-pII ..... 8.2:6 and sounds can reach the mind that has f.
W-pII ..... 8.5:4 And as we look upon a world f., it is He
W-pII .291.1:2 sight shows me all things f. and at peace,
W-pII .293.1:5 holy light, and I perceive a world f. at last.
W-pII .304.1:6 signs that all my sins have been f. me.
W-pII ... 10.2:2 For it sees the world as totally f., without
W-pII .313.1:4 *The eyes of Christ look on a world f.. In His*
W-pII .313.1:5 *His sight are all its sins f., for He sees no sin*
W-pII .326.2:1 at first transformed, and then, f., fade
W-pII .344.1:7 *Let my f. brothers fill my store with Heaven's*
Wfl ......... in.5:2 We are f. now. And we are saved from all
M-4 ......... I.1:7 the teachers of God look on a f. world.
M-14 ......... 3:7 One sin perfectly f. by one teacher of God
M-18 ......... 2:7 to Him. And now is guilt f., overlooked
M-18 ......... 4:8 His sins have been f. him, and he no
C-3............. 7:8 Son. But look on this and you have been f.
C-4............. 5:1 A world f. cannot last. It was the home of
C-5............. 4:1 all your sins have been f. because they
C-6............. 3:5 the light in which the f. world is perceived
P-1............. 2:7 in his healing is the therapist f. with him.
P-2....... V.8:10 for God, that all his sins have been f. him.
P-2........ VI.6:3 the patient all that he has not f. in himself
P-2....... VII.3:1 patient that all his sins have been f. him,
P-2....... VII.8:5 remains to be f. where there is no sin?
P-3....... II.4:10 be glad, for all your sins have been f. you.
P-3........ III.3:8 Can this be how he is f.? Can this be how
S-1......... II.6:8 for your sins, and you will be f. indeed.
S-1........ III.2:7 for hell. Those who have been f., and who
S-2........... I.4:7 Who but the sinful need to be f.? And do
S-2........... I.7:5 Christ has f. you, and in His sight the
S-2........... I.7:7 For what He has f. has not sinned, and

## forgiveness 495

*See also* forgiveness-for-salvation, forgiveness-to-destroy

T-1......... I.21:1 Miracles are natural signs of f.. Through
T-1......... I.21:2 miracles you accept God's f. by extending
T-1......... I.25:1 part of an interlocking chain of f. which,
T-1........ IV.4:1 engendered by fear must be replaced by f.
T-1........ VI.1:1 want peace can find it only by complete f.
T-2.... V.A.15:3 F. is an empty gesture unless it entails
T-2.... V.A.16:1 (6) Miracle-minded f. is *only* correction. It
T-3......... V.6:3 But the only meaningful prayer is for f.,
T-3......... V.6:4 Once f. has been accepted, prayer in the
T-3......... V.6:5 The prayer for f. is nothing more than a
T-3......... V.9:1 F. is the healing of the perception of
T-9........... IV.h The Holy Spirit's Plan of F.
T-9........ IV.4:1 a plan of f. because you are asking for one
T-9........ IV.5:1 F. that is learned of me does not use fear
T-9........ IV.5:3 F. through the Holy Spirit lies simply in
T-9........ IV.6:1 Follow the Holy Spirit's teaching in f.,
T-9........ IV.6:1 because f. is His function and He knows
T-9......... V.1:1 for f. is far more widely used than God's.
T-9......... V.3:3 ego's plan for f. in one form or another. If
T-14......... I.1:7 offer is complete f. you must have let guilt
T-15..... VII.7:7 well. F. becomes impossible, for the ego
T-15..... VII.7:8 It is only by attack without f. that the ego
T-15... VII.13:1 F. lies in communication as surely as
T-15... VII.14:6 There is complete f. here, for there is no
T-15.... VIII.1:6 In the face of your fear of f., which He
T-15.... VIII.1:6 as clearly as He knows f. is release, He will
T-15.... VIII.1:6 teach you to remember that f. is not loss,
T-15.... VIII.1:7 And that in complete f., in which you
T-16............. h THE F. OF ILLUSIONS
T-16... VII.12:3 *be in us that needs f. when Yours is perfect?*
T-16... VII.12:4 *to remember Your f. and Your Love. Let us*
T-17............. h F. AND THE HOLY RELATIONSHIP
T-17......... I.6:8 you will see f. where you have given it.
T-17 ....... II.3:5 and by your own f. you are free to see. Yet
T-17 ....... II.3:6 made, with the blessing of your f. on it.
T-17 ....... II.5:1 simply by the complete f. of the old, the
T-17 ....... II.5:1 of the old, the world you see without f..
T-17 ....... II.6:2 For f. literally transforms vision, and lets
T-17 ....... II.8:5 and into the real world of beauty and f..
T-17 ..... III.1:3 F. is a selective remembering, based not
T-17 ..... III.5:2 What f. *is* enables Him to do so. If all but
T-17 ..... III.8:2 present *is* f.. Therefore, the relationships
T-18 ..... IX.9:1 is the real world, where guilt meets with f.
T-18 ..... IX.9:4 with innocence, washed in the waters of f.
T-18 ... IX.10:1 Yet even f. is not the end. Forgiveness
T-18 ... IX.10:2 F. does make lovely, but it does not create
T-18 ... IX.10:5 A step beyond this holy place of f., a step
T-18 ... IX.13:1 the barriers of guilt, washed with f., and
T-18 ... IX.13:3 sent from beyond f. to remind you of all
T-18 ... IX.13:4 it is through f. that it will be remembered.
T-18 ... IX.14:1 place of f. you will remember nothing else
T-18 ... IX.14:3 F. removes only the untrue, lifting the
T-19 ...... I.11:2 of God, and judges him unworthy of f..
T19..IV.A.14:4 act of charity, no tiny expression of f., no
T19.... IV.B.6:3 of your f. he will remember who he is, and
T19.... IV.B.6:4 I ask for your f., for if you are guilty, so
T19.... IV.C.2:5 one of them with the gentle hands of f.,
T19.... IV.C.2:7 upon him he can escape through your f..
T19.. IV.C.10:7 a resting place by your f. of your brother,
T19... IV.D.8:7 born of complete f. of his illusions, and
T19... IV.D.9:3 complete f. of his brother in his heart.
T19. IV.D.11:4 complete f. you still stand unforgiving.
T19. IV.D.12:6 and f. that would heal it gives way to fear.
T19. IV.D.12:7 Brother, you need f. of your brother, for
T19. IV.D.14:4 Yet still He holds f. out to you, to share
T19. IV.D.15:2 Would you not offer him f., when only he
T-20 ........ I.1:5 symbol of the Son of God's f. on himself;
T-20 ........ I.2:8 the gift of your f. offered by you to me,
T-20 ...... I.2:10 be complete till your f. rests on Christ,
T-20 ........ I.4:5 In your f. of this stranger, alien to you
T-20 ....... II.4:2 I offer him f. when he offers thorns to me?
T-20 ....... II.9:2 within him where you laid the lilies of f..
T-20 ..... IV.7:2 Think not that your f. of your brother
T-20 ...... V.6:7 limitless f. you will give him already given
T-22 ....... II.4:7 thing and holds it out, apart from its f..
T-22 ..... II.12:7 its f. is gently overlooked and disappears.
T-22 ..... II.13:4 Would you have partial f. for yourself?
T-22 ..... III.8:2 the sight of which would show you your f.
T-22 ..... III.8:7 And yet, his holiness *is* your f.. Can you be
T-22 ..... IV.4:7 offering Christ's f. to dispel their faith in
T-22 ..... VI.7:1 upon your brother with complete f., from
T-22 ..... VI.9:2 charity? Extension of f. is the Holy Spirit's
T-23 ...... in.6:4 In kind f. will the world sparkle and shine
T-23 ...... I.10:3 and let f. sweep away all trace of the belief
T-23 ....... II.4:3 him beyond correction and beyond f..
T-23 ....... II.8:2 becomes a myth, and vengeance, not f., is
T-23 ..... III.2:5 Withhold f. from your brother and you
T-23 ..... III.4:5 F. cannot be withheld a little. Nor is it
T-23 ..... III.4:6 this and love for that and understand f..
T-23 ..... III.5:3 Could they accept f. side by side with the
T-23 ..... IV.4:2 f. of your brother is not complete as yet,
T-24 ....... II.8:6 for your f. only that he may return it unto
T-24 ........ III.h The F. of Specialness
T-24 ..... III.1:1 F. is the end of specialness. Only illusions
T-24 ..... III.1:3 F. is release from all illusions, and that is
T-24 ..... III.1:6 How can he then give his f. wholly, when
T-24 ..... III.5:1 God asks for your f.. He would have no
T-24 ..... III.8:6 his hands that he holds out for your f..
T-24 ...... V.3:1 Where could your peace arise *but* from f.?
T-24 ...... V.3:2 sees no condemnation that could need f..
T-24 ...... V.7:6 gift of life that your f. offers to your Self.
T-25 ..... II.10:2 You need no f., for the wholly pure have
T-25 ..... III.5:2 nothing is seen but justifies f. and the
T-25 ..... III.5:3 but is met with instant and complete f..
T-25 ..... III.6:7 ease and far more happiness, bestow f..
T-25 ..... III.7:8 and many chances to extend your own f..
T-25 ..... III.7:9 want to see peace and f. descend on them,
T-25 ...... V.6:4 f. will you understand His Love for you;
T-25 ..... VI.5:3 F. is the only function meaningful in time.
T-25 ..... VI.5:5 F. is for all. But when it rests on all it is
T-25 ..... IX.8:5 Only f. offers miracles. And pardon must
T-25 ..... IX.9:4 lost, condemns you as unworthy of f.. The
T-25 ..... IX.9:6 sole responsibility must be to take f. for
T-26 ..... IV.1:1 F. is this world's equivalent of Heaven's
T-26 ..... IV.1:3 Nothing in boundless love could need f..
T-26 ..... IV.1:6 F. thus becomes the means by which he
T-26 ..... IV.1:7 F. always rests upon the one who offers it,
T-26 ..... IV.1:8 of creating, which his f. offers him again.
T-26 ..... IV.2:1 F. turns the world of sin into a world of
T-26 ..... IV.4:1 F. brings no little miracles to lay before
T-26 ....... V.6:1 F. is the great release from time. It is the
T-26 ..... VI.2:4 and keeps His friendship and f. from your
T-26 .... VII.8:5 F. is the only function here, and serves to
T-26 .... VII.8:6 Perhaps you do not see the role f. plays in
T-26 .... VII.9:1 F. takes away what stands between your
T-26 .. VII.10:3 is f. but a willingness that truth be true?
T-26 .. VII.17:2 F. is the answer to attack of any kind. So
T-26 ... VIII.2:5 conceive of gaining what f. offers *now*. The
T-26 ... VIII.3:8 want a little time in which f. is withheld a
T-26 ... VIII.3:9 the time in which f. is withheld from you
T-26 ..... IX.7:2 for where you walk f. gladly goes with you
T-27 ........ I.5:6 And he will look on his f. there, and with
T-27 ....... II.2:6 F. is not pity, which but seeks to pardon
T-27 ....... II.2:7 for f. does not first establish sin and then
T-27 ....... II.3:6 no one in whom true f. rests can suffer.
T-27 ....... II.3:9 F. cannot be for one and not the other.
T-27 ....... II.4:1 F. is not real unless it brings a healing to
T-27 ....... II.4:5 guilt? Sins are beyond f. just because they
T-27 ....... II.5:9 tongues. For here is his f. proved to him.
T-27 ..... II.10:3 role, you lose the function of f.. No one
T-27 ..... II.16:1 knows correction and f. are the same.
T-27 ..... III.5:3 F. is not yet a power known as wholly free
T-27 ..... III.5:5 F. is the means by which the truth is
T-27 ..... III.7:1 F. vanishes and symbols fade, and
T-27 ..... III.7:8 all. Give welcome to the power beyond f.,
T-27 ..... VI.6:2 it stands for what is past f. and is true.
T-28 ..... III.8:4 The dream of healing in f. lies, and gently
T-28 ....... V.3:3 F. separates the dreamer from the evil
T-29 ..... III.4:3 light has come to him through your f., he
T-29 ....... V.6:1 knew the glorious goal that lies beyond f.,
T-29 ........ VI.h F. and the End of Time
T-29 ..... VI.1:4 F. is your peace, for herein lies the end of
T-29 ... VI.2:13 F. will not change him. Yet time waits
T-29 ... VI.2:14 Yet time waits upon f. that the things of
T-29 ..... VI.4:5 F. does not aim at keeping time, but at its
T-29 ..... VI.6:1 world whose purpose is f. of God's Son!
T-29 ..... IX.8:5 F., once complete, brings timelessness so
T-30 ..... IV.8:6 illusions it but asks f. be the substitute for
T-30 ....... V.1:1 only purpose of the world is seen to be f..
T-30 ....... V.1:3 value of f. is perceived and takes the place
T-30 ....... V.3:1 for the purpose of f. still remains. Yet
T-30 ....... V.3:2 everyone is certain he will go beyond f.,
T-30 ....... V.3:7 for the step in which is all f. left behind.
T-30 ....... V.4:4 But fear is gone because its purpose is f.,
T-30 ....... V.6:2 and what you are, f. washes joyfully away.
T-30 ....... V.7:6 has reached beyond f. to the Love of God.
T-30 ........ VI.h The Justification for F.
T-30 ..... VI.1:5 For it is on this f. rests, and is but natural.
T-30 ..... VI.2:6 your rights when you return f. for attack.
T-30 ..... VI.2:7 But you are merely asked to see f. as the
T-30 ..... VI.2:8 F. is the only sane response. It *keeps* your
T-30 ..... VI.3:3 basis of f. is quite real and fully justified.
T-30 ..... VI.3:5 Unjustified f. is attack. And this is all the
T-30 ..... VI.3:8 so they do not merit the f. that it gives.
T-30 ..... VI.4:1 false f. which the world employs to keep
T-30 ..... VI.4:7 learned f. is your right as much as his.
T-30 ..... VI.5:1 F. recognized as merited will heal. It
T-30 ..... VI.5:5 there be some sin that stands beyond f..
T-30 ..... VI.6:1 sickness and of joylessness f. cannot heal.
T-30 ..... VI.6:5 means you think f. must be limited. And
T-30 ..... VI.6:7 can this be except a false f. of yourself,
T-30 ..... VI.8:5 F. rests on recognizing this, and being
T-30 .... VII.7:8 with them f. has been given to us all, and
T-31 ........ I.5:6 simple lessons in f. have a power mightier
T-31 ....... II.5:8 calls for life, for hate or for f. and for help,
T-31 ....... V.6:3 For this is no f. possible. No longer does it
T-31 .... VII.2:5 upon your sight as wholly worthy of f.,
T-31 .... VII.4:5 For your f., offered unto him, has been
T-31 .... VII.5:6 you may have the gift of kind f. which you
T-31 .. VII.15:4 eyes, and offers them f. with his own. Can
W-pI .... 11.1:5 release made sure. The key to f. lies in it.

W-pI.....43.5:4 *I see through the eyes of f.. I see the world as*
W-pI.....46.1:2 be condemnation before f. is necessary.
W-pI.....46.1:3 F. is the great need of this world, but that
W-pI.....46.1:4 while those who withhold f. are binding
W-pI.....46.2:1 His Love is nevertheless the basis of f..
W-pI.....46.2:3 F. thus undoes what fear has produced,
W-pI.....46.2:4 this reason, f. can truly be called salvation
W-pI.....55.3:4 f. allows love to return to my awareness, I
W-pI.....57.5:4 I look upon has taken on the light of my f.
W-pI.....57.5:4 my forgiveness, and shines f. back at me.
W-pI.....60.1:4 f. is the means by which I will recognize
W-pI.....60.4:2 Voice ceases to call on my f. to save me.
W-pI........62.h F. is my function as the light of the world.
W-pI.....62.1:1 f. that will bring the world of darkness to
W-pI.....62.1:2 your f. that lets you recognize the light in
W-pI.....62.1:3 F. is the demonstration that you are the
W-pI.....62.1:4 f. does the truth about yourself return to
W-pI.....62.1:5 Therefore, in your f. lies your salvation.
W-pI.....62.2:2 That is why all f. is a gift to yourself. Your
W-pI.....62.2:5 For this attack must be replaced by f., so
W-pI.....62.3:2 to understand what f. will do for you? It
W-pI.....62.5:2 *F. is my function as the light of the world. I*
W-pI........63.h brings peace to every mind through my f..
W-pI.....63.3:4 *brings peace to every mind through my f.. I*
W-pI.....64.1:2 you see is to obscure your function of f.,
W-pI.....64.3:3 The world's salvation awaits your f.,
W-pI.....73.5:4 F. lifts the darkness, reasserts your will,
W-pI.....75.3:2 our sight and hide the world f. offers us.
W-pI.....75.4:1 looking at the world that our f. shows us.
W-pI.....75.7:1 Realize that your f. entitles you to vision.
W-pI.....75.9:4 power of f. to heal your sight completely.
W-pI.....78.7:1 our savior shining in the light of true f.,
W-pI.....81.3:1 (62) F. is my function as the light of the
W-pI.....81.3:4 function is, for I do not yet understand f..
W-pI.....81.4:2 *Let this help me learn what f. means. Let me*
W-pI.....82.1:1 brings peace to every mind through my f..
W-pI.....82.1:2 My f. is the means by which the light of
W-pI.....82.1:3 me. My f. is the means by which I become
W-pI.....82.1:4 My f. is the means by which the world is
W-pI.....82.2:4 *[name]. Through my f. I can see this as it is.*
W-pI.....90.1:6 to me through my f. of the grievance, and
W-pI.....92.5:7 will unite in purpose and f. and in love.
W-pI.....92.6:1 cannot see a purpose in f. and in love. It
W-pI.....99.1:1 Salvation and f. are the same. They both
W-pI.....99.2:2 impossible becomes the thing you need f.
W-pI.....99.9:7 *Salvation and f. are the same.* Then turn to
W-pI...99.10:6 F. and salvation are the same. Forgive
W-pI...99.12:5 Thus do you lay f. on your mind and let
W-pI......121.h F. is the key to happiness.
W-pI...121.4:4 It wants f., yet it sees no hope. It wants
W-pI...121.6:1 F. is acquired. It is not inherent in the
W-pI...121.6:3 yourself, f. must be learned by you as well
W-pI...121.7:5 your f. that it has been saved from hell.
W-pI...121.8:3 how to give f. and receive forgiveness, too
W-pI...121.8:3 how to give forgiveness and receive f., too
W-pI...121.9:2 they are one through practicing f. toward
W-pI.121.13:4 the role f. plays in bringing happiness to
W-pI.121.13:6 *F. is the key to happiness. I will awaken from*
W-pI......122.h F. offers everything I want.
W-pI...122.1:1 What could you want f. cannot give? Do
W-pI...122.1:3 F. offers it. Do you want happiness, a
W-pI...122.2:1 All this f. offers you, and more. It
W-pI...122.2:5 peace. All this f. offers you, and more.
W-pI...122.3:1 F. lets the veil be lifted up that hides the
W-pI...122.3:3 What would you want f. cannot give?
W-pI...122.3:5 can hold more hope than what f. brings?
W-pI...122.8:2 F. is the means by which it comes to take
W-pI...122.8:5 be described. Yet your f. offers it to you.
W-pI...122.9:1 Remembering the gifts f. gives, we
W-pI.122.11:2 will be given you to feel the peace f. offers,
W-pI.122.13:1 F. offers everything you want. Today all
W-pI.122.14:3 *F. offers everything I want. Today I have*
W-pI...126.1:2 there would be no problem in complete f.
W-pI...126.3:4 He has no claim on your f.. It holds out a
W-pI...126.4:1 Thus is f. basically unsound; a charitable
W-pI...126.5:1 true, f. has no grounds on which to rest
W-pI...126.6:1 You do not understand f.. As you see it, it
W-pI...126.7:5 And true f., as the means by which it is
W-pI...126.9:2 by which f. takes its proper place in your
W-pI...126.9:3 mind from every bar to what f. means,
W-pI.126.10:1 the world that does not understand f.,
W-pI......134.h Let me perceive f. as it is.
W-pI...134.1:2 f. must be seen as mere eccentric folly,
W-pI...134.2:1 view of what f. means is easily corrected,
W-pI...134.3:1 that you find in genuine f. on your part is
W-pI...134.4:2 of sin as true and not believe f. is a lie.
W-pI...134.4:3 Thus is f. really but a sin, like all the rest.
W-pI...134.6:1 is sin's unreality that makes f. natural and
W-pI...134.7:1 F. is the only thing that stands for truth
W-pI...134.8:4 in the way your true f. opens up to you.
W-pI...134.9:1 very simple way to find the door to true f.,
W-pI.134.10:4 F. stands between illusions and the truth;
W-pI.134.13:1 F. must be practiced, for the world
W-pI.134.14:1 Today we practice true f., that the time of
W-pI.134.14:4 Who understands the meaning of f., and
W-pI.134.14:6 Let us ask of Him: *Let me perceive f. as it is.*
W-pI.134.17:1 F. should be practiced through the day,
W-pI.134.17:3 *Let me perceive f. as it is. Would I accuse*
W-pI...137.5:2 Just as f. overlooks all sins that never were
W-pI...137.7:1 Just as f. shines away all sin and the real
W-pI...137.9:1 Healing, f., and the glad exchange of all
W-pI...140.3:2 The dreams f. lets the mind perceive do
WpI. rIV.in2:7 Lack of f. blocks this thought from his
WpI. rIV.in3:1 lack of true f. may be carefully concealed.
W-pI...141.1:1 (121) F. is the key to happiness.
W-pI...141.2:1 (122) F. offers everything I want.
W-pI...147.2:1 (134) Let me perceive f. as it is.
W-pI...158.6:2 the world made holy by f. and by love.
W-pI...158.9:2 all. In His f. are they gone. Unseen by One
W-pI...159.2:2 You accept f. as accomplished in yourself
W-pI...159.5:2 from this world into one made holy by f..
W-pI...159.8:1 in which the lilies of f. set their roots. This
W-pI...168.4:5 undone when your f. rests on everything?
W-pI...169.6:4 of time, f. and the holy face of Christ. The
W-pI...169.7:2 Yet f., taught and learned, brings with it
W-pI...169.7:3 from Him Who teaches what f. means.
W-pI.169.12:1 F. is the central theme that runs
W-pI.186.14:2 F. is an earthly form of love, which as it is
W-pI...189.3:5 A world in which f. shines on everything,
W-pI...190.7:7 it in fear, while in your kind f. does it live.
W-pI...191.8:3 and to give the world the gift of his f..
W-pI...192.2:3 F. represents your function here. It is not
W-pI...192.3:3 F. is the closest it can come to earth. For
W-pI...192.4:1 F. gently looks upon all things unknown
W-pI...192.4:2 F. is the means by which the fear of death
W-pI...192.4:3 F. lets the body be perceived as what it is;
W-pI...192.5:5 Only f. can relieve the mind of thinking
W-pI...192.5:6 Only f. can restore the peace that God
W-pI...192.5:7 Son. Only f. can persuade the Son to look
W-pI...192.7:1 do we need f. to perceive that this is so.
W-pI.193.12:1 in f. in the form established for the day.
W-pI...195.8:6 f. is complete you will have total gratitude
W-pI...197.1:2 You make attempts at kindness and f..
W-pI...197.6:2 learn to let f. take away the sins you think
W-pI.198.2:10 F. is illusion that is answer to the rest.
W-pI...198.3:1 F. sweeps all other dreams away, and
W-pI...198.3:4 F. is the end of dreams, because it is a
W-pI...198.4:1 F. is the only road that leads out of
W-pI...198.8:1 of any condemnation which could need f..
W-pI...198.9:4 *Only my own f. sets me free.* Do not forget
W-pI...198.9:6 can there be a form of pain f. cannot heal.
W-pI.198.12:5 offering f. to the Son of Sinlessness Itself,
W-pI...199.4:5 thus becomes a vehicle which helps f. be
W-pI...200.6:1 does f. do? In truth it has no function,
W-pII.........1.h What Is F.?
W-pII......1.1:1 F. recognizes what you thought your
W-pII......1.1:6 F. merely sees its falsity, and therefore
W-pII......1.4:1 F., on the other hand, is still, and quietly
W-pII......1.5:1 then, and let f. show you what to do,
W-pII......2.3:4 with the gifts of your f. laid before it, and
W-pII......3.1:4 has been changed to one of true f., will
W-pII......3.5:2 satisfied until f. has been made complete.
W-pII.....247.h Without f. I will still be blind.
W-pII..247.1:3 For f. is the only means whereby Christ's
W-pII.....249.h F. ends all suffering and loss.
W-pII..249.1:1 F. paints a picture of a world where
W-pII..256.1:1 The way to God is through f. here. There
W-pII..256.1:9 f. is the means by which our minds return
W-pII .257.2:1 *f. is Your chosen means for our salvation.*
W-pII .267.1:3 and floods my body with the purpose of f.
W-pII .....6.4:3 For when f. rests upon the world and
W-pII .....7.1:5 f. has made possible perception's tranquil
W-pII .....7.4:1 to you, to let f. rest upon your dreams,
W-pII .....7.4:2 Without f. will your dreams remain to
W-pII .283.2:2 world, which our f. has made one with us.
W-pII .285.2:2 *in it, and through f. be restored to sanity.*
W-pII .289.1:3 can I then perceive the world f. offers?
W-pII .....8.1:4 perceived except through eyes f. blesses,
W-pII .....8.2:4 for nothing there remains outside f.. And
W-pII .....8.5:4 Identity which our f. has restored to us.
W-pII .291.2:6 *Let my f. be complete, and let the memory of*
W-pII ....297.h F. is the only gift I give.
W-pII .297.1:1 F. is the only gift I give, because it is the
W-pII .298.1:3 intruded on my holy sight f. takes away.
W-pII .....9.1:3 willingness to let f. rest upon all things
W-pII .....9.2:3 F. lights the Second Coming's way,
W-pII .301.1:4 *happy eyes f. has released from all distortion*
W-pII .308.1:5 in this instant has f. come to set me free.
W-pII .330.1:1 us this day accept f. as our only function.
W-pII ...12.5:1 will one lily of f. change the darkness into
W-pII .331.2:1 F. shows us that God's Will is One, and
W-pII .331.2:2 look upon the holy sights f. shows today,
W-pII ....332.h Fear binds the world. F. sets it free.
W-pII .332.1:6 F. bids this presence enter in, and take its
W-pII .332.1:7 mind. Without f. is the mind in chains,
W-pII .332.1:8 f. does the light shine through the dream
W-pII ....333.h F. ends the dream of conflict here.
W-pII .333.2:1 *f. is the light You chose to shine away all*
W-pII ....334.h Today I claim the gifts f. gives.
W-pII .335.1:1 F. is a choice. I never see my brother as
W-pII ....336.h F. lets me know that minds are joined.
W-pII .336.1:1 F. is the means appointed for
W-pII .336.1:4 F. sweeps away distortions, and opens the
W-pII .336.2:1 *In quiet may f. wipe away my dreams of*
W-pII .340.1:4 *him to find Christ's vision through f., and be*
W-pII ...13.1:4 perception, nor exceed the function of f..
W-pII ...13.2:5 to the truth. Now is f. seen as justified.
W-pII ...13.3:1 F. is the home of miracles. The eyes of
W-pII ...13.3:4 Each lily of f. offers all the world the silent
W-pII ....342.h I let f. rest upon all things, For thus
W-pII ....342.h all things, For thus f. will be given me.
W-pII .345.1:7 *this gift alone today, which, born of true f.,*
W-pII .350.1:3 *Your memory depends on his f.. What he is,*
W-pII .350.1:8 *only my f. teaches me to let Your memory*
W-pII ...14.3:2 which through our joint f. is redeemed.
W-pII .352.1:1 *F. looks on sinlessness alone, and judges*
W-pII .352.1:4 *Yet love, reflected in f. here, reminds me You*
W-pII .357.1:1 *F., truth's reflection, tells me how to offer*
W-pII .359.1:7 *and on this fact f. rests upon a certain base*
Wfl........in.4:5 salvation, offered us through our f., given
M-4 ....... X.1:1 when its relation to f. is recognized. Open-
M-4 ....... X.2:2 have let go all things that would prevent f.
M-4 ....... X.2:9 F. is the final goal of the curriculum. It
M-4 ..... X.2:12 F. is its single aim, at which all learning
M-4 ....... X.3:8 glad tidings of complete f. to the world.
M-5 ...... III.2:5 ask the patient for f. for God's Son in his
M-14 ......... 1:4 The illusion of f., complete, excluding no
M-14 ......... 2:1 Until f. is complete, the world does have
M-14 ......... 2:2 It becomes the home in which f. is born,
M-14 ......... 5:7 complete f. brings all this to bless the
M-18 ....... 4:10 who is there whom his f. can fail to heal?
M-19 ......... 1:5 this world, however, f. depends on justice
M-19 ......... 3:5 F. has no place in such a scheme, for not
M-20 ......... 3:6 f. is the necessary condition for finding
M-20 ......... 3:7 than this, given f. there *must* be peace. For
M-22 ......... 3:1 That f. is healing needs to be understood,
M-22 ......... 6:9 It is your f. that must show him this.
M-28 ......... 2:6 held in darkness, apart from the light of f.
C-in ........... 1:3 The means of the Atonement is f.. The
C-3................h F. – THE FACE OF CHRIST
C-3............ 1:1 *F.* is for God and toward God but not of
C-3............ 1:2 of anything He created that could need f..
C-3............ 1:3 F., then, is an illusion, but because of its
C-3............ 2:1 F. might be called a kind of happy fiction;
C-3............ 4:5 the face of Christ is the great symbol of f..
C-3............ 5:1 F. is a symbol, too, but as the symbol of
C-4............ 3:6 F., salvation, Atonement, true perception,

| | |
|---|---|
| C-4 5:3 | bodies. But f. looks past bodies. This is its |
| C-4 5:6 | guilt as surely as f. takes all guilt away. |
| C-4 5:10 | F. proves it is impossible because it sees it |
| C-4 6:1 | seen within, and there f. lets it disappear. |
| C-4 6:4 | What is seen outside must lie beyond f., |
| C-4 6:7 | guilt and f. for an instant lie together, side |
| C-4 6:10 | come to claim His Own. F. is complete. |
| C-4 7:3 | Gone is f., for its task is done. And gone |
| P-1 2:6 | understood, teaches f. and helps the |
| P-2 II.1:2 | to teach f. rather than condemnation. |
| P-2 II.3:2 | God. F., then, is all that need be taught, |
| P-2 II.4:2 | for where there is f. truth must come. It |
| P-2 VI.1:1 | then, can be defined simply as f., for no |
| P-2 VI.5:5 | that only f. heals an unforgiveness, and |
| P-2 VI.7:4 | can but be seen as the bringers of f., for it |
| P-2 VII.3:2 | be the difference between healing and f.? |
| P-2 VII.5:1 | aim of therapy and the obvious aim of f.. |
| P-3 II.6:3 | of f. in which both will someday wake. |
| P-3 III.3:6 | F., the Holy Spirit's only dream, must |
| P-3 III.6:8 | teach the therapist how much he needs f., |
| S-1 II.3:4 | particularly for f. for the many sources of |
| S-1 II.8:4 | prayer is part of f. as long as forgiveness, |
| S-1 II.8:4 | prayer is part of forgiveness as long as f., |
| S-1 III.2:7 | been forgiven, and who accepted their f., |
| S-2 h | Forgiveness |
| S-2 in.1:1 | F. offers wings to prayer, to make its |
| S-2 in.1:3 | all. F. is prayer's ally; sister in the plan for |
| S-2 in.1:7 | nature of its sister, prayer, f. has an end. |
| S-2 I.h | F. of Yourself |
| S-2 I.1:1 | has been more misunderstood than has f. |
| S-2 I.1:5 | is used to hurt because f. is not wanted. |
| S-2 I.4:1 | for yourself, so is f. always given you. It is |
| S-2 I.4:4 | That is why f. of another is an illusion. |
| S-2 I.6:1 | F., truly given, is the way in which your |
| S-2 I.7:1 | Him how to learn f. as His vision lets it be |
| S-2 I.8:1 | F. is the call to sanity, for who but the |
| S-2 I.9:2 | F. is the key, but who can use a key when |
| S-2 I.10:4 | clear to you exactly what f. means to you, |
| S-2 II.2:2 | is. F. here rests on an attitude of gracious |
| S-2 II.6:5 | How fearful has f. now become, and how |
| S-2 II.7:3 | F. is the means for your escape. How |
| S-2 II.7:5 | there is a way to use f. for the goal of God, |
| S-2 II.7:8 | It is His face f. lets you see. It is His face in |
| S-2 II.8:1 | forms f. takes that do not lead away from |
| S-2 III.2:2 | His Voice will teach you what f. is, and |
| S-2 III.3:1 | the form should be that Christ's f. takes. |
| S-2 III.5:1 | ask when help is needed and f. sought. |
| S-2 III.5:3 | form in which f. comes to save God's Son. |
| S-2 III.6:4 | About the role f. has in Him. Do you but |
| S-2 III.6:6 | His Name, and places his f. in His hands. |
| S-2 III.6:7 | F. has been given Him to teach, to save it |
| S-2 III.6:8 | made free to save as true f. is allowed to |
| S-2 III.6:11 | morning, nor is His f. what you think it is. |
| S-2 III.7:2 | F. has a Teacher Who will fail in nothing. |
| S-2 III.7:3 | a while in this; do not attempt to judge f., |
| S-2 III.7:6 | beside the door to which f. is the only key. |
| S-3 I.3:1 | body can be healed as an effect of true f.. |
| S-3 I.3:3 | love. F. must be given by a mind which |
| S-3 II.1:2 | combining with f. kindly meant but not |
| S-3 II.4:1 | prayer, a kind f. of the ways of earth, can |
| S-3 II.4:4 | Now its f. comes to heal the world and it |
| S-3 II.5:11 | F. is the only gift you give and would |
| S-3 III.4:4 | and lets f. be what it is meant to be. You |
| S-3 IV.2:1 | As witness to f., aid to prayer, and the |
| S-3 IV.2:3 | F. shines its merciful reprieve upon each |
| S-3 IV.3:9 | of prayer. Do not forget f. of God's Son. |
| S-3 IV.9:9 | My gratitude will come the gift first of f., |

## forgiveness' 4

| | |
|---|---|
| S-2 I.1:4 | F. kindness is obscure at first, because |
| S-2 I.9:4 | F. role must be reversed, and cleansed |
| S-3 in.1:2 | F. witness and an aid to prayer, a giver of |
| S-3 in.1:3 | healing is a sign or symbol of f. strength, |

## forgiveness-for-salvation 3

| | |
|---|---|
| S-2 III.h | Forgiveness-for-salvation |
| S-2 III.1:1 | F. has one form, and only one. It does not |
| S-2 III.2:7 | F. is His task, and it is He Who will |

## forgiveness-to-destroy 9

| | |
|---|---|
| S-2 I.2:1 | F. will therefore suit the purpose of the |
| S-2 I.2:2 | F. will overlook no sin, no crime, no guilt |
| S-2 I.2:5 | F. *is* death, and this it sees in all it looks |
| S-2 I.7:3 | to Heaven while f. remains with you. |
| S-2 I.9:5 | F. must be unveiled in all its treachery, |
| S-2 II.h | Forgiveness-to-destroy |
| S-2 II.1:1 | F. has many forms, being a weapon of the |
| S-2 II.5:1 | F. will often hide behind a cloak like this. |
| S-2 II.6:1 | F. can also take the form of bargaining |

## forgives 16

| | |
|---|---|
| T-9 III.7:4 | Holy Spirit in you f. all things in you and |
| T-9 III.8:1 | The Holy Spirit f. everything because |
| T-22 in.1:7 | your relationship f. you and your brother, |
| T-26 IV.1:5 | No one f. unless he has believed in sin, |
| T-27 II.3:10 | Who f. is healed. And in his healing lies |
| T-27 II.16:7 | And each f. the other, that he may accept |
| T-27 VI.6:2 | The miracle f. because it stands for what |
| W-pI 43.2:7 | by which the Son of God f. his brother, |
| W-pI 43.2:7 | forgives his brother, and thus f. himself. |
| W-pI 46.2:2 | Fear condemns and love f.. Forgiveness |
| W-pI 99.6:2 | This is the Thought that saves and that f., |
| W-pI 188.5:4 | f. because he recognized the truth in him. |
| C-1 5:2 | listens to the Holy Spirit, f. the world, and |
| C-1 6:2 | right-mindedness merely overlooks, or f., |
| C-2 10:1 | The miracle f.; the ego damns. Neither |
| P-2 VII.3:3 | Only Christ f., knowing His sinlessness. |

## forgiving 22

| | |
|---|---|
| T-16 VII.9:5 | slavery of their illusions by f. them for the |
| T-17 II.6:1 | as you look upon the world with f. eyes. |
| T-22 VI.3:5 | shift from hate to gratitude before f. eyes. |
| T-25 III.8:2 | It is not there in His f. eyes. And therefore |
| T-25 VI.1:1 | The grace of God rests gently on f. eyes, |
| T-27 II.4:7 | Let yourself be healed that you may be f., |
| T-27 VII.14:4 | He brings f. dreams, in which the choice |
| T-28 II.5:6 | But in f. dreams is no one asked to be the |
| T-28 II.10:3 | f. dreams are the effects of yours undone, |
| T-29 V.8:5 | F. dreams are means to step aside from |
| T-29 IX.h | The F. Dream |
| T-29 IX.7:7 | Only f. dreams can enter here, for time is |
| T-29 IX.8:1 | F. dreams have little need to last. They |
| T-29 IX.10:1 | F. dreams remind you that you live in |
| T-29 IX.10:3 | attack. F. dreams are kind to everyone |
| T-30 in.1:5 | to f. dreams and out of pain and fear. |
| T-31 VI.6:4 | Then is the world f., for you have forgiven |
| W-pI 75.7:2 | never fails to give the gift of sight to the f.. |
| W-pI 164.7:6 | the freedom given us through His f. vision |
| W-pII 295.2:2 | *look upon, that His f. Love may rest on me.* |
| W-pII 325.1:6 | f. thoughts a gentle world comes forth, |
| M-28 3:8 | world, f. all things and replacing all attack |

## forgot 27

| | |
|---|---|
| T-12 II.2:10 | For you f. your brothers with Him, and |
| T-12 VIII.7:5 | you because He f. not the Father. You |
| T-13 X.2:5 | And you f. that real relationships are holy |
| T-16 IV.11:14 | and all the Love of God, Who f. you not. |
| T-18 III.1:6 | What you f. was simply that God cannot |
| T-29 VI.6:4 | Nor can it be f., in such a world, it *is* a little |
| T-29 IX.10:6 | all the while he is remembering what he f. |
| T-30 I.6:5 | *I f. what to decide.* This cancels out the |
| T-30 III.7:4 | Yet it did not die when you f. it. It was |
| T-30 III.7:7 | as it was before the time when you f., and |
| T-30 III.7:8 | the same within the interval when you f.. |
| T-31 IV.9:2 | But you f. His Presence and remembered |
| T-31 VII.10:5 | are; all those you saw an instant and f., |
| W-pI 131.3:4 | old yet new; an echo of a heritage f., yet |
| W-pI 136.5:2 | But what you have f. can be remembered, |
| W-pI 137.15:4 | this function be f. as every hour of the day |
| W-pI 157.6:3 | experience in which the world is quietly f. |
| W-pI 159.5:3 | there; transparent, faintly seen, at times f. |
| W-pI 161.10:6 | You are not f. in Heaven. Would you not |
| W-pI 164.3:3 | How easily are all your seeming sins f., |
| W-pI 168.3:6 | restores all memories the sleeping mind f. |
| WpI rV.in7:1 | place at which the journey ends and is f.. I |
| W-pI 183.9:3 | You can remember what the world f., and |
| W-pI 197.9:7 | you f. the function God has given you. |
| W-pII 302.1:4 | *But we had f. the Son whom You created.* |
| C-4 4:5 | appears, and in that instant is the world f. |
| S-3 I.3:5 | and f. that it is he who gave this role to it. |

## forgotten 71

| | |
|---|---|
| T-7 IV.4:4 | God. You have f. Him, but the Holy Spirit |
| T-7 VIII.6:2 | The ego can be completely f. at any time, |
| T-9 II.10:2 | You will have f., however, that to price is |
| T-9 IV.3:1 | given you because *you have f. how to do it.* |
| T-10 II.1:3 | has been f. then appears to be fearful, but |
| T-10 II.1:4 | You are fearful *because* you have f.. And |
| T-10 II.5:4 | you attack, you must have f. what you are. |
| T-10 III.3:4 | acknowledges the Love of God he has f.. |
| T-10 IV.8:2 | that the Rays can never be completely f.. |
| T-11 II.3:7 | Having f. your will, you do not know what |
| T-11 VI.8:7 | aware of dreams, and have not yet f. them |
| T-11 VIII.1:6 | And then everything you made will be f.; |
| T-12 II.2:8 | *This is what you have f..* To perceive the |
| T-12 VIII.3:8 | You who knew have f., and unless He had |
| T-14 III.1:2 | to learning that it should never be f.. The |
| T-14 III.14:6 | He has not f. it. Forget Him not and He |
| T-16 IV.11:11 | God has never f. what makes Him whole. |
| T-17 III.1:2 | All the rest must be f.. Forgiveness is a |
| T-17 III.5:3 | so. If all but loving thoughts have been f., |
| T-17 V.12:1 | is easily f. if you allow time to close over it |
| T-18 II.7:4 | Think not that He has f. anyone in the |
| T-18 II.7:5 | that He has f. you to whom He gave the |
| T-18 VII.2:1 | done; you have not utterly f. the body. It |
| T19 IV.D.3:4 | which the memory of God seems quite f.; |
| T-20 III.9:3 | to let it go or to take hold on life so long f. |
| T-20 V.7:4 | you prisoner to pain and death must be f.. |
| T-21 I.h | The F. Song |
| T-21 I.6:1 | catch a hint of an ancient state not quite f. |
| T-21 I.6:1 | like a song whose name is long f., and the |
| T-23 I.5:2 | this, the memory of his Father must be f.. |
| T-23 I.5:3 | It *is* f. in the body's life, and if you think |
| T-23 I.5:3 | are a body, you will believe you have f. it. |
| T-23 I.5:4 | Yet truth can never be f. by itself, and you |
| T-23 I.5:4 | by itself, and you have not f. what you are |
| T-24 VII.5:9 | from you, a sign that you have not f. them |
| T-26 V.10:4 | Let the dead and gone be peacefully f.. |
| T-26 V.11:10 | Once it is seen, this light can never be f.. |
| T-29 V.1:1 | in you where this whole world has been f.; |
| T-30 IV.1:6 | They were made that this might be f.. You |
| T-30 IV.5:11 | Yet this is equally f. in attack. God's Son |
| T-31 I.4:5 | lesson, powerful enough to render God f., |
| T-31 I.9:7 | But in guilt he has f. what he really is. |
| W-pI 42.8:1 | to you, and that you have not f. it. |
| W-pI 49.2:6 | you that your Creator has not f. His Son. |
| W-pI 56.5:3 | of Who I am because I have f. it. It has |
| W-pI 60.2:6 | I chose to forget, but which has not f. me. |
| W-pI 99.4:3 | and sins f. which were never real? |
| W-pI 136.6:4 | And yet you have f. that they stand but |
| W-pI 136.20:3 | *I have f. what I really am, for I mistook my* |
| W-pI 160.10:3 | has not f. you. But you will not remember |
| W-pI 166.4:4 | not realize he has f. where he came from, |
| W-pI 166.12:1 | you still of one thing more you had f.. For |
| WpI rV.in7:4 | I have f. no one. Help me now to lead you |
| W-pI 188.4:1 | mind reminds the world of what it has f., |
| W-pI 195.7:4 | a long f. Word re-echoes in our memory, |
| W-pI 195.8:2 | For hatred is f. when we lay comparisons |
| W-pI 198.10:1 | is remembered instantly; the world f., all |
| W-pI 198.10:1 | forgotten, all its weird beliefs f. with it, as |
| W-pII 224.2:2 | *I have f. It, and do not know where I am going* |
| W-pII 255.2:2 | *Your Son has not f. You. The peace You gave* |
| W-pII 281.1:2 | *in any way, it is because I have f. who I am,* |
| W-pII 281.1:4 | *am sad or hurt or ill, I have f. what You think* |
| W-pII 301.1:6 | *And all the tears I shed will be f., for their* |
| M-5 III.2:1 | another choice which they had f.. The |
| M-17 2:5 | Nor should it be f. that the outcome that |
| M-17 6:11 | onto Him, it seems to you He has f., too. |
| M-17 7:4 | Think not He has f.." Here we have the |
| M-17 8:11 | overlooked, and thus f. in the truest sense |

| | |
|---|---|
| M-22..........5:1 | to heal, it is because he has f. Who he is. |
| M-29........4:10 | Teacher Who knows the truth has not f. it |
| S-1 ......... II.6:1 | Let it never be f. that prayer at any level is |

## form 475

| | |
|---|---|
| T-1........ I.46:3 | When you return to your original f. of |
| T-1......... II.1:2 | reflects the original f. of communication |
| T-1.......VII.3:1 | Fantasy is a distorted f. of vision. |
| T-2........ I.5:10 | Illness is some f. of external searching. |
| T-2......IV.3:11 | in a particularly unworthy f. of denial. |
| T-2......... V.1:6 | device than any f. of level confusion, |
| T-2......... V.9:6 | any f. of charity you can conceive of as yet |
| T-2... V.A.13:2 | wrong-mindedness. Responding to any f. |
| T-2......VI.9:14 | All thinking produces f. at some level. |
| T-3........ I.2:11 | with this kind of distortion in any f.. |
| T-3...........I.7:7 | Good can withstand any f. of evil, as light |
| T-3......III.5:11 | most spiritualized f. perception involves |
| T-3........IV.6:3 | of perception, a distorted f. of creation, |
| T-3......... V.2:7 | wasted effort even in its most ingenious f. |
| T-4........ I.7:10 | and no f. of devotion is possible as long as |
| T-4....... II.8:12 | so ambiguous in f. and characteristically |
| T-4......... II.9:2 | this with its particular f. of magic. The so- |
| T-4......... III.2:1 | is written in the f. of a prayer because it is |
| T-5......... V.5:4 | I said before that illness is a f. of magic. It |
| T-5......... V.5:5 | to say that it is a f. of magical solution. |
| T-5....... V.7:11 | is to save the past in purified f. only. If |
| T-6.........in.2:5 | it is still a f. of faith and can be redirected. |
| T-6...........I.1:3 | been that it was not a f. of punishment. |
| T-6...........I.4:6 | to perceive any f. of assault in persecution |
| T-6........III.3:9 | attack in any f. and you have learned it, |
| T-6......IV.12:6 | A harsh and strident f. of communication |
| T-7......... II.3:2 | This is its teaching f., because outside the |
| T-7......... II.3:3 | f. implies that you will learn what you are |
| T-7......... II.3:7 | are. That f. of the law is not adapted at all, |
| T-7......... II.4:3 | he must alter the f. of what he translates, |
| T-7......... II.4:4 | whole purpose is to change the f. so that |
| T-7......... II.4:6 | change the meaning to preserve the f.. |
| T-7......... II.5:3 | idea that differences in f. are meaningful, |
| T-7......... V.3:2 | Spirit's f. of communication in this world, |
| T-8.......VII.1:2 | When attack in any f. enters your mind |
| T-8.....VII.15:8 | it must be unreal since it is a f. of attack, |
| T-8........IX.4:7 | Sleep is no more a f. of death than death |
| T-8........IX.4:7 | than death is a f. of unconsciousness. |
| T-8........IX.5:3 | if He taught that one f. of sickness is more |
| T-9........ I.10:3 | It is merely a denial in the f. of a request. |
| T-9........ I.10:4 | The Holy Spirit is not concerned with f., |
| T-9......... V.3:3 | plan for forgiveness in one f. or another. |
| T-9......... V.4:1 | f. does not matter and the content has not |
| T-9..... VIII.4:8 | are afraid of it because it is a f. of attack, |
| T-10......IV.1:9 | him in whatever f. he may appear to you, |
| T-11..... V.10:1 | regardless of the f. it takes and quite apart |
| T-12.........I.3:4 | and help, regardless of the f. it takes. Can |
| T-13......IX.5:4 | In any f., in anyone, *believe this not*. For sin |
| T-14......III.2:6 | To wish for guilt in any way, in any f., will |
| T-14......IV.3:9 | For in the end, whatever f. it takes, your |
| T-14......IX.8:1 | of holiness to any f. of error is always the |
| T-14....... X.7:3 | love. You are too bound to f., and not to |
| T-14....... X.7:5 | It is merely f., and nothing else. For you |
| T-14....... X.8:2 | if the f. is acceptable the content must be. |
| T-14....... X.8:3 | be. Otherwise it will attack the f.. If you |
| T-14....... X.8:8 | but study f. with meaningless content. |
| T-14....... X.9:3 | For f. is not enough for meaning, and the |
| T-14......XI.5:5 | lesson teaches this, in one f. or another. |
| T-15......III.2:4 | is no f. of littleness that can ever content |
| T-15... VIII.5:4 | respond to every need, whatever f. it takes |
| T-15....... X.6:6 | you will not be deceived by any f. the ego |
| T-15....... X.6:7 | Each f. will be recognized as but a cover |
| T-16.........I.1:2 | always used to f. a special relationship in |
| T-16.........I.5:3 | and the f. of empathy which would bring |
| T-16......IV.6:3 | illusion is one of fear, whatever f. it takes. |
| T-16....... V.1:4 | Whatever f. they take, they are always an |
| T-16....... V.8:5 | more than an "attractive" f. of fear, in |
| T-16....... V.8:5 | is buried deep and rises in the f. of "love." |
| T-16..... V.12:1 | Whenever any f. of special relationship |
| T-16..... V.12:1 | love is content, and not f. of any kind. |
| T-16..... V.12:2 | The special relationship is a ritual of f., |
| T-16..... V.12:2 | aimed at raising the f. to take the place of |
| T-16..... V.12:3 | There is no meaning in the f., and there |
| T-16..... V.12:4 | sign that f. has triumphed over content, |
| T-18.........I.3:4 | a different f. of acting out for satisfaction. |
| T-18.........I.3:7 | rejection for acting out a special f. of fear. |
| T-18.........I.7:1 | When you seem to see some twisted f. of |
| T-18.........I.7:9 | in f. are no real differences at all. None of |
| T-18..... II.5:11 | seem to waken to is but another f. of this |
| T-18... VIII.1:7 | or in some f. you think you recognize. |
| T-19...... III.2:3 | Yet punishment is but another f. of guilt's |
| T-19...... III.3:6 | For then you will but change the f. of sin, |
| T-20... VIII.6:3 | unadjusted f. and suited perfectly to meet |
| T-20... VIII.6:6 | it in any f. and seeing it everywhere, in |
| T-21.....VII.8:3 | as you look on the effects of sin in any f., |
| T-21...VII.13:1 | changing f. that shifts with time and place |
| T-22....... II.3:2 | f. in which they are accepted is irrelevant. |
| T-22....... II.3:3 | No f. of misery in reason's eyes can be |
| T-22....... II.9:5 | And here we see again another f. of the |
| T-22...... III.3:6 | f. it takes cannot conceal its emptiness |
| T-22...... III.4:1 | Only the f. of error attracts the ego. |
| T-22...... III.4:4 | And yet mistakes, regardless of their f., |
| T-22...... III.4:5 | but error in a special f. the ego venerates. |
| T-22...... III.5:1 | Reason will tell you that the f. of error is |
| T-22...... III.5:2 | If what the f. conceals is a mistake, the |
| T-22...... III.5:2 | mistake, the f. cannot prevent correction. |
| T-22...... III.5:3 | The body's eyes see only f.. They cannot |
| T-22...... III.5:6 | and stopping at the outside f. of nothing. |
| T-22...... III.5:7 | To this distorted f. of vision the outside of |
| T-22...... III.5:9 | It is held back by f., having been made to |
| T-22...... III.5:9 | that nothing else but f. will be perceived. |
| T-22...... III.6:6 | unable to go beyond the f. to meaning. |
| T-22...... III.6:7 | Nothing so blinding as perception of f.. |
| T-22...... III.6:8 | For sight of f. means understanding has |
| T-22...... III.7:2 | You can change f. *because* it is not true. It |
| T-22...... III.7:4 | you that if f. is not reality it must be an |
| T-22...... III.8:1 | Let not the f. of his mistakes keep you |
| T-22...... VI.4:4 | power to heal all pain, regardless of its f.. |
| T-22...... VI.5:2 | sin. The f. of error is no longer seen, and |
| T-22...... VI.7:2 | f. of suffering could block your sight, |
| T-22.... VI.12:3 | It is unjustified in any f., because it has no |
| T-23.........I.6:5 | And so it matters not what f. they take. |
| T-23.......I.11:6 | do battle only to establish which f. is true. |
| T-23..... II.16:5 | emphasis on f. and disregard of content. |
| T-23..... II.17:2 | Can an attack in any f. be love? What |
| T-23..... II.17:3 | What f. of condemnation is a blessing? |
| T-23..... II.17:5 | not the f. of the attack on him deceive you |
| T-23..... II.17:8 | it matter what the f. this madness takes? |
| T-23... II.17:10 | not deceived when madness takes a f. you |
| T-23..... II.18:4 | else could you perceive the f. they take, |
| T-23..... II.18:5 | Can any f. of this be tenable? Yet you |
| T-23..... II.18:6 | Yet you believe them *for* the f. they take, |
| T-23..... II.20:6 | the beliefs that they imply, not for their f.. |
| T-23..... II.20:7 | And lack of faith in love, in any f., attests |
| T-23..... II.21:4 | a different f. in the progression of truth's |
| T-23..... II.22:4 | Attack in any f. has placed your foot upon |
| T-23...... III.1:2 | If it is true attack in any f. will hurt you, |
| T-23...... III.1:2 | as in another f. that you *do* recognize, then |
| T-23...... III.1:3 | Attack in any f. is equally destructive. Its |
| T-23...... III.1:5 | and what f. of murder serves to cover the |
| T-23...... III.1:9 | intent is death, what matter the f. it takes |
| T-23...... III.2:1 | Is death in any f., however lovely and |
| T-23...... III.4:7 | assault upon your peace in any f., if only |
| T-23.... III.6:11 | the f. that murder takes can offer safety? |
| T-23...... IV.1:4 | and no illusion in any f. stalks Heaven. |
| T-23...... IV.1:8 | asked to realize the f. it takes conceals the |
| T-23...... IV.1:9 | And it is this you fear, and not the f.. |
| T-23...... IV.4:3 | Each f. of murder and attack that still |
| T-23...... IV.4:6 | that murder in any f. is not your will. The |
| T-24...... III.2:1 | Whatever f. of specialness you cherish, |
| T-24....... V.2:1 | hidden or disguised the f., however lovely |
| T-25....... II.4:3 | Take not the f. for content, for the form is |
| T-25....... II.4:3 | for the f. is but a means for content. And |
| T-25...... III.1:6 | This is perception's f., adapted to this |
| T-25...... III.4:1 | in some f. adapted to the need the Son of |
| T-25.....IV.5:10 | In any f.. This can you bring to all the |
| T-25....... V.3:4 | in content in whatever f. the call is made, |
| T-25...... VI.5:1 | the laws of God do not prevail in perfect f. |
| T-25.....VI.5:11 | His wish was not denied but changed in f. |
| T-25.....VII.4:6 | this belief depends upon the f. it takes. |
| T-25.....VII.4:7 | or is maintained by any f. of reason, |
| T-25.....VII.7:1 | Your special function is the special f. in |
| T-25.....VII.7:3 | The f. is suited to your special needs, and |
| T-25.....VII.7:5 | then the f. of sanity which makes it most |
| T-25.....VII.8:3 | given the choice of f. most suitable to him |
| T-25.....VII.9:1 | because the f. of the alternative is one |
| T-25...VII.11:4 | belief except a f. of the more basic tenet, |
| T-25....VIII.4:4 | that is vengeance in whatever f. it takes. |
| T-26........II.1:4 | whatever f. the problem seems to take. A |
| T-26........II.1:6 | to attempt to solve it in a special f.. It will |
| T-26........II.1:7 | all time and will not rise again in any f.. |
| T-26........II.2:2 | one, regardless of the f. it seems to take, is |
| T-26........II.3:1 | one mistake, in any f., has one correction. |
| T-26........II.7:2 | one, for pain in any f. you will not want. |
| T-26...VII.14:7 | If loss in any f. is possible, then is God's |
| T-26...VII.15:3 | justify a miracle whatever f. they took. In |
| T-26....VIII.3:3 | In this f. is the error still obscured that is |
| T-26....VIII.6:8 | disaster's f. is difficult to credit in advance |
| T-26....VIII.7:1 | Why should the good appear in evil's f.? |
| T-26....VIII.7:9 | as "good" some day but now in f. of pain. |
| T-26....VIII.8:2 | one f. in which its outcome is perceived. |
| T-26....VIII.8:3 | to be the f. in which the "good" appears, |
| T-26....VIII.9:4 | What profits freedom in a prisoner's f.? |
| T-26....VIII.9:8 | and so preserved because its f. is changed |
| T-26........X.1:7 | And its presence, in whatever f., will hide |
| T-26........X.3:3 | The belief you are is but another f. of the |
| T-27.........I.4:8 | death; a f. of vengeance not yet total. Yet |
| T-27.........I.7:1 | justified, is sickness in whatever f. it takes |
| T-27...... III.5:2 | Reality is ultimately known without a f., |
| T-27...... IV.4:3 | attesting the same thing in different f.. |
| T-27...... IV.4:8 | Whatever f. the question takes, its |
| T-27...... IV.4:9 | is real, and answers in the f. of preference. |
| T-27.... IV.4:17 | that what it states takes question's f.. |
| T-27...... IV.5:3 | the world a f. of propaganda for itself. |
| T-27..VIII.10:2 | No matter what the f. of the attack, this |
| T-27..VIII.11:1 | free from suffering, whatever f. it takes. |
| T-27..VIII.11:2 | of the f. of suffering that brings you pain. |
| T-27..VIII.11:4 | the cause of every f. of sorrow and of pain |
| T-27..VIII.11:5 | The f. affects His answer not at all, for He |
| T-27..VIII.11:5 | of all of them, no matter what their f.. |
| T-28...... III.4:3 | the seeds of pestilence and every f. of ill, |
| T-28...... IV.2:2 | of fearful dreams whatever f. they take, |
| T-28..... VII.4:7 | the choice cannot be made in terms of f.. |
| T-28..... VII.4:8 | The choice of sickness seems to be of f., |
| T-29...... IV.2:2 | fear, no matter what the f. it seems to take |
| T-29...... IV.2:4 | Or it can be disguised in pleasant f.. But |
| T-29...... IV.2:6 | Their f. can change, but they cannot be |
| T-29...... IV.3:1 | In simplest f., it can be said attack is a |
| T-29...... IV.6:7 | which lights whatever f. it takes with love. |
| T-29....... V.7:5 | Each f. it takes in some way calls for death |
| T-29...... VI.1:3 | questions are the same, in different f.. |
| T-29..... VII.3:3 | Its f. appears to be outside himself. Yet |
| T-29..... VII.5:3 | death, conceived as real and given living f. |
| T-29..... VII.5:4 | decay, because a f. of death cannot be life, |
| T-29....VIII.1:7 | may be replaced, no matter what their f.. |
| T-29....VIII.2:1 | Let not their f. deceive you. Idols are but |
| T-29....VIII.3:1 | or a false belief; some f. of anti-Christ, |
| T-29....VIII.3:2 | idol is a wish, made tangible and given f., |
| T-29....VIII.3:4 | is its f. apart from the idea it represents. |
| T-29....VIII.4:3 | Its f. is nowhere, for its source abides |
| T-29....VIII.4:9 | can take no f. in which he ever will be real |
| T-29....VIII.6:3 | this power and place and time are given f. |
| T-29...... IX.9:1 | Whenever you feel fear in any f., –and |
| T-30.........I.1:3 | to f. which sees you through the rest. It is |
| T-30.......I.16:4 | can be caused without some f. of union, |
| T-30...... III.1:3 | And so it has no f., nor is content for its |
| T-30...... III.1:3 | for its expression in the terms of f.. Idols |
| T-30...... III.2:1 | It is not f. you seek. What form can be a |
| T-30...... III.2:2 | f. can be a substitute for God the Father's |
| T-30...... III.2:3 | What f. can take the place of all the love |
| T-30...... III.2:9 | you decide upon the f. of what you want, |
| T-30.... III.2:10 | the idol, thus reducing it to a specific f.. |
| T-30...... III.3:2 | has no f. because it is unlimited. To seek a |
| T-30...... III.3:3 | mean that you believe some f. is missing. |
| T-30...... III.3:4 | will achieve completion in a f. you like. |
| T-30...... III.4:5 | God knows not f.. He cannot answer you |
| T-30...... III.5:5 | to any f. and limited to what is not in him |
| T-30.... III.5:11 | Not in any f. that would content you not, |
| T-30...... IV.5:2 | Dwell not on them in any f.. They but |
| T-30....... V.2:4 | as the sole cause of pain in any f.. No one |
| T-30...... VI.5:6 | mistake; a special f. of error that remains |

S-2 ........ III.5:2 f. the seeking takes you need not judge.
S-2 ........ III.5:3 let it not be you who sets the f. in which
S-3 ......... II.1:4 indeed remove a f. of pain and sickness.
S-3 ......... II.3:3 f. in which death comes when it is time to
S-3 ......... II.5:1 and takes the f. of punishment for sin.
S-3 ........ III.2:2 And yet it can be said of any f. of healing
S-3 ........ III.6:4 cause, it cannot come again in different f..

## formal 5

WpI rVI.in.6:5 we will add but a few f. expressions or
M-in .......... 3:2 to you. In the f. teaching situation, these
M-24.......... 3:4 to anyone, regardless of his f. beliefs. His
P-in............ 1:6 to start to open his mind without f. help,
P-2 ......... II.2:1 F. religion has no place in psychotherapy,

## formalize 1

P-2 ......... II.2:3 The attempt to f. religion is so obviously

## format 3

WpI. rIII.in1:3 a special f. for these practice periods, that
WpI. rIII.in5:1 The f. you should use for these reviews is
WpI. rIV.in7:6 will use no f. for our practicing but this:

## formed 6

T-15....... V.8:1 on earth has f. special relationships, and
T-15...VII.10:1 you can be sure that you have f. a special
T-17....... III.4:4 Once it is f., doubt must enter in, because
T-17....... III.4:8 For it was f. to get him out of it, and join
W-pI .....95.5:3 and you have not yet f. the habit of using
M-3............5:1 in relationships which, once they are f.,

## former 7

T-5........ VI.8:3 what f. generations had misunderstood,
T-9............I.8:3 The f. accounts for the atheist and the
T-17....... V.4:2 its f. goal completely without attraction,
T-17....... V.5:8 the f. organization of their perception no
T-17....... V.7:1 which your f. goal was quite appropriate.
W-pI.121.12:2 to see around your f. "enemy" to him.
M-10..........1:3 the f. and minimizing the latter. There is,

## formerly 1

M-4........ X.2:4 Nothing is now as it was f.. Nothing but

## formless 4

W-pI ...44.10:2 Try to think of light, f. and without limit,
W-pI ...192.3:5 power to translate in form the wholly f..
W-pII..314.1:3 lost its idols and its images, and being f.,
S-1 ......... II.1:3 with learning until it reaches its f. state,

## Formlessness 1

*formlessness*

W-pI.186.14:1 deceive, because they come from F. Itself.

## formlessness 3

*Formlessness*

W-pI.186.14:4 love will mean to you when f. has been
C-6.............5:8 form but to return to the eternal f. of God
S-2 ...........I.8:6 And thus is prayer restored to f., beyond

## forms 181

T-2........ IV.2:9 error can take two f.; it can be believed
T-2......... V.2:2 Physical medications are f. of "spells,"
T-2......... V.4:4 All f. of not-right-mindedness are the
T-2... V.A.12:2 All f. of healing rest on this fundamental
T-3...........I.2:7 In milder f. a parent says, "This hurts me
T-3...........I.7:7 of evil, as light abolishes f. of darkness.
T-4...........I.8:1 ego tries to exploit all situations into f. of
T-6........ I.18:3 that all f. of rejection are meaningless.
T-8........ IX.3:2 All f. of sickness, even unto death, are
T-8........ IX.8:7 All f. of sickness are signs that the mind is
T-9......... II.2:3 is why certain specific f. of healing are not
T-9......... V.4:1 Some newer f. of the ego's plan are as
T-9......... V.4:2 In one of the newer f., for example, a
T-9......... V.7:1 Both f. of the ego's approach, then, must
T-10...... III.4:3 f. of idolatry are caricatures of creation,
T-10....... V.1:6 as all f. of denial replace what is with what
T-10....... V.3:8 He has many f., but although he may
T-10..... V.12:4 many other f. that blasphemy may take,
T-11...... IV.4:3 the denial of this simple fact takes many f.
T-13....... V.1:4 The other has many f., for the content of
T-14....... II.2:4 all the strange f. and feelings and actions
T-14....... II.7:7 the shapes and f. and fears of nothing.
T-14....... V.3:5 to the denial of guilt in all its f.. To accuse
T-15...VII.10:2 Anger takes many f., but it cannot long
T-15....... X.4:4 For though the ego takes many f., it is
T-15....... X.5:1 emerge in f. quite different from what it is
T-18.........I.3:4 It seems to take many f., and each one
T-18.........I.4:2 It has taken many f., because it was the
T-18..... II.5:13 and your waking dreams have different f.,
T-18...... III.2:1 retreating to the lesser f. of fear, and
T-18...... IX.7:3 and f. appear and shift from loveliness to
T-22......... III.h Reason and the F. of Error
T-22....... III.7:1 Only mistakes have different f., and so
T-23.......I.11:5 can conflict, because their f. are different.
T-23..... II.16:7 Some f. it takes seem to have meaning,
T-23..... II.17:1 can some f. of murder not mean death?
T-23..... II.19:8 Illusions are but f.. Their content is never
T-23..... II.20:2 Their f. conflict, making it seem quite
T-23..... II.20:5 The seeming gentler f. of the attack are no
T-23...... III.1:1 recognize some of the f. attack can take?
T-23...... III.5:3 some f. by which their peace is saved?
T-23...... IV.5:8 battle, but the clash of f. is meaningless.
T-23...... IV.6:2 Even in f. you do not recognize, the signs
T-24.........I.3:2 This takes many f., but always clashes
T-25...... IV.4:6 in twisted f. too far away for recognition,
T-25. VIII.14:4 And you are safe from vengeance in all f..
T-26.......... II.h Many F.; One Correction
T-26....... II.1:5 A problem can appear in many f., and it
T-26..... VII.3:7 What is perceived takes many f., but none
T-26..... VII.4:2 of sickness, which applies to all its f..
T-26...VII.14:2 cause can merely shift effects to other f..
T-26... VIII.1:3 are one illusion, which takes different f..
T-26....... X.2:1 attack in certain f. to be unfair to you? It
T-26....... X.2:2 must be some f. in which you think it fair.
T-27....... V.8:1 are not specific but they take specific f.,
T-27....... V.8:7 are the same, despite their different f.. All
T-27... VIII.2:1 The dreaming of the world takes many f.,
T-27... VIII.3:3 Though the dream itself takes many f.,
T-27... VIII.7:1 mind within a body all are f. of circularity
T-27. VIII.12:1 all f. of suffering to Him Who knows that
T-28...... IV.9:5 f. the broken pieces seem to take mean
T-28....... V.7:3 vague uncertain f. and changing shapes,
T-28...... VII.4:7 No f. of sickness are immune, because the
T-29.... VIII.3:5 All f. of anti-Christ oppose the Christ.
T-29. VIII.8:11 not deceived by f. the "something" takes.
T-29...... IX.7:8 And the f. that enter in the dream are
T-30...... III.1:5 that there are f. that will bring happiness,
T-30...... III.4:7 will could not be satisfied with empty f.,
T-30.... III.10:2 the myriad of f. that fear can take; quite
T-30...... IV.3:1 not there is filled with toys in countless f..
T-30...... VI.6:1 than a belief there are some f. of sickness
T-30...... VI.7:1 true the miracle can heal all f. of sickness,
T-30...... VI.7:2 cannot be to judge which f. are real, and
T-30...... VI.7:7 be some f. of guilt that you cannot forgive
T-30...... VI.8:5 and being glad there cannot be some f. of
T-30...... VI.9:2 from guilt in all its consequences and its f.
T-30...... VI.9:5 joyful statement that there are no f. of evil
T-30... VIII.2:5 his perfect freedom from all f. of lack, and
T-30... VIII.3:3 Yet it is an assertion that some f. of idols
T-31.........I.8:6 been deceived by f. the call was hidden in.
T-31...... IV.6:4 is but the search for different f. of truth.
T-31...... IV.8:3 decision cannot lie in choosing different f.
T-31..... V.16:5 will appear in many places and in many f.
T-31.... VIII.1:1 has one lesson it would teach, in all its f.,
W-pI.......5.1:3 hatred, jealousy or any number of f., all of
W-pI.......5.3:1 and f. of upset which you think result.
W-pI.......5.7:1 of different f. of upset that are disturbing
W-pI.......9.2:2 with active resistance in any number of f..
W-pI.....15.3:2 They may take many different f., some of
W-pI.....16.3:4 in many f. before you really understand it
W-pI.....21.3:5 f. of attack are more justified than others.
W-pI.....21.4:1 As you search your mind for all the f. in
W-pI.....41.2:5 is, despite the serious and tragic f. it may
W-pI.....50.1:3 and an endless list of f. of nothingness
W-pI.....64.8:1 Two f. of shorter practice periods are
W-pI.....66.1:4 Their f. are different, but their content is
W-pI.....66.9:2 Think also about the many f. the illusion
W-pI.....79.5:2 varying f. and with such varied content,
W-pI.....80.3:4 Their many f. will not deceive you while
WpI..rII.in.6:1 and more specific f. when needed. Some
WpI..rII.in.6:2 needed. Some specific f. are included in
W-pI.....81.2:1 Some specific f. for applying this idea
W-pI.....81.4:1 f. for using this idea might include: *Let*
W-pI.....82.2:1 for specific f. for applying this idea are:
W-pI.....82.4:1 Suitable specific f. of this idea include:
W-pI.....83.2:1 of this idea might take these f.: *My*
W-pI.....83.4:1 Some useful f. for specific applications of
W-pI.....84.2:1 specific f. helpful in applying the idea: *Let*
W-pI.....84.4:1 specific f. for applying this idea would be
W-pI.....85.2:1 for this idea might be made in these f.: *Let*
W-pI.....85.4:1 f. of the idea are suitable for more specific
W-pI.....86.2:1 some suggested f. for applying this idea
W-pI.....86.4:1 for this idea might be in these f.: *I am*
W-pI.....87.2:1 f. of this idea would be helpful for specific
W-pI.....87.4:1 are some useful f. of this idea for specific
W-pI.....88.2:1 prove useful f. for specific applications of
W-pI.....88.4:1 For specific f. in applying this idea, these
W-pI.....89.4:1 specific f. for applying this idea would be:
W-pI.....90.2:1 of this idea might be in these f.: *This*
W-pI.....90.4:1 f. of the idea will be useful for specific
W-pI.....94.1:1 makes all f. of temptation powerless; the
W-pI...99.11:1 to remove all f. of doubt and fear forever
W-pI...124.6:2 power to heal all f. of suffering in anyone,
W-pI...134.7:2 the thousand f. in which they may appear
W-pI.135.14:3 some f. which these self-deceptions take,
W-pI...138.6:4 but conceal this one by taking different f..
W-pI...140.1:4 f. of healing thus must substitute illusion
W-pI...140.4:2 is not deceived by f. the dream may take.
W-pI...140.9:4 not exist is truer in some f. than others.
WpI. rIV.in3:1 understanding of the many f. in which the
W-pI...163.1:1 Death is a thought that takes on many f.,
W-pI...163.1:2 and all f. in which the wish to be as you
W-pI...167.2:3 that the idea of death takes many f.. It is
W-pI...170.8:6 it? For the god of cruelty takes many f..
W-pI...185.9:7 f. which shift and change with every step
W-pI.186.14:1 These are the f. which never can deceive,
W-pI...187.6:3 the many f. which sacrifice may take. He
W-pI...187.7:4 to all the f. that suffering appears to take.
W-pI...193.4:4 obvious that it appears in countless f.,
W-pI...200.4:2 in alien f. that have no meaning to you,
WpI rVI.in.4:1 and special f. of practicing for this review.
W-pII .262.1:4 *Why should I perceive a thousand f. in what*
W-pII .268.1:2 *Your creation, and distort it into sickly f..*
W-pII .293.1:3 it, and showing me distorted f. of fear?
W-pII .295.1:7 Fear appears in many different f., but love
M-1 ........... 4:2 There are many thousands of other f., all
M-5 ........II.2:2 this is so for healing in all f.. A patient
M-5 ...... III.3:1 teachers of God consider the f. of sickness
M-7 ........... 5:3 This illusion can take many f.. Perhaps
M-12 ......... 2:7 it matter if they then appear in many f.?
M-16 ......... 9:7 For magic of any kind, in all its f., simply
M-16 ....... 11:9 to recognize the f. of magic and perceive
M-22 ......... 4:3 applied to all specific f. of sickness, both
M-22 ......... 6:3 to heal all individuals of all f. of sickness.
M-28 ......... 5:5 His sinlessness, His Love behind all f.,
C-in ........... 4:3 happen?", and may ask this in many f..
C-5............. 1:3 reality. Helpers are given you in many f.,
C-5............. 6:3 Christ takes many f. with different names
P-2...........II.3:3 to the remembrance of God are f. of
P-2...........II.5:2 Some f. of religion have nothing to do
P-2...........II.5:2 some f. of psychotherapy have nothing to
P-2...........II.7:2 But both have many f., because no good
P-2........ VI.3:4 them into acceptable and pleasant f..
P-2........ VI.3:6 its slaves to change the f. they look upon;
P-2........ VI.5:1 Sickness takes many f., and so does

P-2........VI.5:2 The f. of one but reproduce the forms of
P-2........VI.5:2 of one but reproduce the f. of the other,
S-1.........II.2:1 These f. of prayer, or asking-out-of-need,
S-1.........II.2:2 sure of his Identity could pray in these f..
S-1.........II.3:4 to ask for things of this world in various f.
S-1.........II.8:3 Prayer in its earlier f. is an illusion,
S-1........III.2:1 The earlier f. of prayer, at the bottom of
S-2.........II.1:1 Forgiveness-to-destroy has many f.,
S-2.........II.1:3 Yet all the f. that it may seem to take have
S-2.........II.1:4 The difference is clear in several f. where
S-2.........II.2:1 there are the f. in which a "better" person
S-2.........II.8:1 All f. forgiveness takes that do not lead
S-3.........II.1:2 can occur at lower f. of prayer, combining
S-3.........II.2:3 and to reach the Christ in hidden f. and
S-3.........II.3:2 come in f. that seem to be thrust down in
S-3........III.2:3 These f. may heal the body, and indeed

## formula 3

W-pI...140.2:2 he found a magic f. to make him well. Yet
W-pII.297.1:3 This is salvation's simple f.. And I, who
P-2........III.3:5 This is the f. for salvation, and must heal.

## formulate 1

P-2.........II.7:3 one, and lets him f. his own curriculum;

## formulated 1

T-4.........V.5:4 goal must be f. clearly and kept in mind.

## formulation 1

T-13....VIII.3:5 separation is merely a faulty f. of reality,

## forsake 10

T-4........III.7:8 I will never f. you any more than God will,
T-4........III.7:8 wait as long as you choose to f. yourself.
T-5........IV.6:5 I will never leave you or f. you, because to
T-5........IV.6:5 to f. you would be to forsake myself and
T-5........IV.6:5 be to f. myself and God Who created me.
T-5........IV.6:6 You f. yourself and God if you forsake any
T-5........IV.6:6 forsake yourself and God if you f. any of
T-20.....II.11:2 not leave you, nor f. the savior in his pain.
T-22.......II.7:1 F. not now your brother. For you who are
W-pI.198.13:2 Who brought us here will not f. us now.

## forsworn 2

T-10.......V.1:3 Depression means that you have f. God.
T-26...VII.14:9 will. He has f. his Father and himself, and

## forth 82

T-5.........in.1:6 calls f. an integrated willingness to share
T-5.........in.1:7 joyous themselves call f. different kinds of
T-5...........I.4:8 is so close to knowledge that He calls it f.;
T-6.........I.15:7 called f. upon Judas was a similar mistake
T-12.......IV.3:4 calls f. the responses the ego *can* teach.
T-13.......V.7:7 come f. from your private world in peace.
T-13.......V.9:5 calling f. its witnesses and drawing them
T-13......VI.7:5 to shine on you *because you called them f.*.
T-13......VI.8:8 holy light that shines f. from God's Son is
T-13......VI.9:1 as you call f. the witnesses to His creation.
T-13....VI.11:3 it shines f. to call you from the world and
T-13......XI.3:9 clear and bright, and calls f. one response
T-14......IX.5:1 shines f. from you to all around you. You
T-14......IX.6:5 and the message that shines f. from what
T-14......IX.8:2 no contradiction in what holiness calls f..
T-15.........I.9:7 again you will go f. in time without fear,
T-15....III.12:1 Call f. in everyone only the remembrance
T-17.....VII.4:5 The goal's reality will call this f., for you
T-17.....VII.6:6 goal's reality will call f. and accomplish
T-17.....VII.9:2 the same purpose called f. the faith in you
T-17....VIII.1:3 It calls f. just the same suspension of
T-17....VIII.2:6 will call f. and secure for you the faith you
T-18......IX.3:3 For you sent f. these messengers to bring
T-18......IX.7:4 And back and f. they go, as long as you
T-19......I.11:6 sent f. to gather witnesses unto its coming
T-19......I.14:6 the altar from which they were sent f..
T19..IV.A.2:10 the peace in you encounters in its going f..
T19IV.A.10:10 each has messengers which it sends f.,
T19IV.A.10:10 the language in which their going f. was
T19..IV.A.13:5 f. by offering him what they hold dear.
T19..IV.A.14:3 If you send them f., they will see only the
T19..IV.A.15:1 you send f. only the messengers the Holy
T19..IV.A.15:7 And they go f. to signify the end of fear.
T19....IV.B.4:5 its going f. but barriers you place between
T19....IV.B.7:6 in Heaven. Send f. to all the world the
T19IV.B.10:10 the home of the emotion that calls them f.
T-20.......II.5:4 His purpose shine f. from every altar now
T-24.....III.7:2 to come f. and waken from their dream of
T-24.....VI.6:8 to you. He *is* set f. within his holiness.
T-24.....VI.7:6 set f. at last in terms you recognized and
T-24...VI.12:5 it no sacrifice is asked, no strain called f.,
T-24...VI.13:2 judging against the Christ and setting f.
T-25......in.2:7 as is his specialness set f. within his body.
T-25......in.3:3 it is here that Christ sets f. the remedy.
T-25.......II.8:2 step f. from darkness as you look on him,
T-25.......II.8:3 who brought him f. for you to look upon.
T-25.VIII.10:5 witnesses could they call f. to speak on his
T-26........I.8:4 that he may come f. to shine on you, and
T-26.......II.6:8 call f. will rest on you as surely as on him.
T-26....V.11:4 back and f. between the past and present.
T-27........I.6:6 witnesses that are called f. to be believed,
T-27......I.10:5 Then will it send f. the message it received
T-27......V.1:3 and it will go f. because of what it is. It is
T-27......V.7:5 It will call f. its witnesses to show the face
T-27.....VI.3:4 when you call f. the witnesses to its reality
T-27.....VI.6:6 Who sends f. miracles to bless the world,
T-28.....VI.3:2 it f. to seek for separation and be separate
T-29...III.3:11 God's witness has set f. the gentle way of
T-30...VIII.4:3 cannot come f. from you consistently. For
T-31..VII.11:4 they call it f. in everyone they look upon,
T-31.VIII.12:7 Your likeness does the light shine f. from
W-in..........1:4 to think along the lines the text sets f..
W-pI.....42.1:2 also sets f. a cause and effect relationship
W-pI.....58.2:5 holiness of the world shine f. for everyone
W-pI.....73.3:1 in which guilt is traded back and f., and
W-pI.....75.8:3 From this time f. you will see differently.
W-pI.....76.8:4 set f. what is God's and what is yours.
W-pI.....94.5:9 thought system which this course sets f..
W-pI...129.5:3 the world sets f. to keep you prisoner.
W-pI.137.12:6 this day go f. from what is healed to what
W-pI...155.2:6 and let the truth stand f. as what it is, is
W-pI...155.7:3 All this steps back as truth comes f. in you
W-pI.155.11:3 And we step f. toward this, as we progress
W-pI...157.5:1 From this day f., your ministry takes on a
W-pI.161.10:4 the witnesses your body's eyes call f..
WpI...rV.in1:5 and slowly on the road this course sets f..
Wi181-200 1:4 to following the way the course sets f..
W-pII....269.h sight goes f. to look upon Christ's face.
W-pII.325.1:6 thoughts a gentle world comes f., with
M-2...........2:1 the concept of time that the course sets f..
M-22.........4:4 of God calls f. the miracle of healing. He
M-23.........1:6 an invocation call f. any special power.

## fortress 1

T-13.....III.3:4 Spirit, then, seems to be attacking your f.,

## fortresses 1

S-1........IV.1:6 wishes are their arsenals; their f. in hate.

## fortunate 1

S-3........IV.1:9 can bestow unequal gifts on those less f..

## fortunately 1

T-3.......VI.9:3 F., to lose something does not mean that

## fortune 1

W-pI...153.1:1 world, its twists of f. and its bitter jests,

## forward 10

T-1........I.13:2 which seem to go back but really go f..
T-2.........II.6:2 your previous missteps by stepping f..
T-2.........II.6:3 terms, because you return as you go f..
T-18.....III.8:7 back into darkness and f. unto God, to
T-26...VIII.5:5 fear, and like its cause, is looking f.,
T-27.....VI.2:9 to name, as one steps f. and another back.
T-30.....V.10:8 Look f., then; in confidence walk with a
T-31.....II.11:5 back and f. in the darkness and alone. Yet
W-pI..129.5:2 Here can you but look f., never back to
W-pI..156.6:2 in you steps f. and encompasses the world

## foster 9

T-2.........V.1:2 Otherwise they may unwittingly f. the
T-2.......VI.2:1 I do not f. level confusion, but you must
T-2......VII.2:3 circular process that would not f. the time
T-3......III.1:8 produce fear and true perceptions f. love,
T-6...V.C.1:11 rejecting everything that does not f. joy,
T-8....VII.11:4 as a separate entity cannot but f. illness,
T-14.....III.8:4 to it, and do not f. belief in it in any mind.
T-16.....VI.3:4 must f. guilt and therefore must imprison
T-27......I.11:1 sure you knew its purpose was to f. guilt.

## fostered 1

S-3..........II.5:6 a viewpoint must be f. by the healing that

## fostering 1

T-8....VII.11:3 it, will induce illness by f. separation.

## fosters 5

T-6..........I.3:3 Projection means anger, anger f. assault,
T-16.......V.7:1 the ego f. in the special relationship. This
M-16.........4:2 that f. quiet thought as he awakes. If this
M-27.........6:9 the rituals the world f. in its vain attempts
P-2...........I.2:2 This is one of the errors which the ego f.;

## fought 3

T-23........I.4:4 This "enemy" you f. as an intruder on
T-23.....IV.9:3 everything f. for on the battleground is of
T-31.......II.1:2 nor f. against to lose to truth's appeal.

## foul 1

T-23.....II.10:3 Were they not forced into this f. attack by

## found 133

T-3.......VI.2:6 and rejected, or judged and f. wanting,
T-4.......IV.8:8 brought to judgment and f. wanting there
T-6..........I.8:6 it. I must f. His church on you, because
T-8.......III.6:1 The Kingdom cannot be f. alone, and you
T-11.....V.12:4 cannot be f. apart from Your joint Will.
T-12....VII.9:6 this decision that determined what you f.,
T-12...VIII.7:6 looked upon the unreal and f. despair.
T-13........I.5:2 sought his guiltlessness, and he has f. it.
T-13........I.5:4 Being in him, he has f. it. *When* he finds it
T-13...III.11:2 he demanded everything and f. nothing.
T-13.....IV.7:7 encounters in which salvation can be f..
T-13.....VI.5:5 where it is not, and therefore have not f. it
T-13.....VI.7:6 you looked for it in them and f. it there.
T-13....VII.6:4 will rejoice that you have f. His company,
T-13.....IX.3:1 what you f. in it and placed your faith in.
T-13.......X.4:6 Salvation is not f. by those who use their
T-14....VII.2:3 It can neither be lost nor sought nor f.. It
T-14...XI.12:4 go together and never can be f. alone.
T-15.....III.3:3 You who have sought and f. littleness,
T-17.......V.8:3 for satisfaction and thought you f. it.
T-17.......V.8:4 it. Forget not now the misery you really f.,
T-18.....III.8:6 You have f. your brother, and you will
T-19.......II.6:4 foundation seems to have is f. in this. For
T-19.....III.1:1 The attraction of guilt is f. in sin, not
T19.IV.A.14:5 return with all the happy things they f., to
T19 IV.D.10:3 Once he has f. his brother he *is* ready. Yet

T19.IV.D.19:1 beyond the veil, not to be lost but f.; not
T-20......III.9:3 groped but feebly in the dust and f. your
T-21......IV.7:6 it f. a home in your relationship on earth.
T-21.....VII.4:5 Yes, it can *dream* it f. an enemy, but this
T-22.......II.2:5 for how could joy be f. in misery? All that
T-22......VI.1:9 for it where he believes it is and can be f..
T-23.....II.11:3 It must be what you want but never f..
T-23.....II.11:4 "understand" the reason why you f. it not
T-23.....II.13:4 through a world where meaning can be f.,
T-24...VII.1:12 now that the host of God has f. another
T-24.....VII.6:7 state of true creation, f. not within time,
T-25.......II.2:6 would seek for hope where none is ever f..
T-25.......II.3:1 also true that you have f. some hope apart
T-25......IV.4:8 And from you will the rest you f. extend,
T-25......IV.4:9 to everyone have f. a home in Heaven the
T-25.......V.4:8 f. if he fulfilled the role God gave to him.
T-25...VIII.2:6 wisdom could be f. in such a state of mind
T-25.VIII.12:8 fulfilled. God's Son has f. a witness unto
T-27.....II.12:3 And so your own Identity is f.. Yet must
T-27......IV.3:3 there is no answer there that could be f..
T-27......VI.3:8 truth is f. in him if it is truth he represents
T-28.......II.2:6 Nor can it be f. where limitation is. The
T-28.......II.6:2 exists that could be f. and understood.
T-29.........I.9:6 God? Yet can your self be lost by being f.?
T-29.......II.7:3 the one in which you f. yourself before.
T-29.......V.3:4 The peace in you can but be f. in him.
T-29.......V.8:3 for here is not where changelessness is f..
T-29.....VII.1:3 Heaven cannot be f. where it is not, and
T-29.....VII.1:7 you want, insisting where it must be f..
T-29.....VII.2:3 off and f. where all the rest of it is not.
T-29.....VII.5:3 f. that represents a parody of life which,
T-29.....VII.8:3 see in it a place of idols f. outside yourself,
T-31.....II.5:10 him and in your answer is salvation f..
T-31......IV.4:2 believe there is another answer to be f..
T-31......IV.7:1 is ever f. by following a road away from it.
T-31......IV.7:4 way will not advance the purpose to be f..
T-31....IV.11:6 Nowhere but where He is can you be f..
W-pI.....29.3:7 how you could ever have f. it difficult.
W-pI.....70.8:6 also that you have never f. anything in the
W-pI.....73.5:2 light nor darkness can be f. without.
W-pI.....76.2:4 it waits for you, and there it will be f..
W-pI.....85.3:6 It is not f. outside and then brought in.
W-pI...96.10:1 has f. the function that it sought to lose.
W-pI...96.10:5 you are restored, for you have f. your Self.
W-pI...106.2:3 which tell you they have f. the source of
W-pI...107.3:6 They can not be f., for truth is everywhere
W-pI.124.10:2 within your mind and waiting to be f..
W-pI...127.6:2 Love is not f. in darkness and in death.
W-pI...128.4:5 of worth can not be f. in worthlessness.
W-pI...129.2:5 No lasting love is f., for none is here. This
W-pI...130.4:7 They can be sought, but they can not be f.
W-pI...130.4:8 this day in seeking what can not be f..
W-pI...132.4:5 in truth you f. exactly what you looked for
W-pI.136.14:3 folly. It is f. at any time; today, if you will
W-pI...140.2:2 dream he f. a magic formula to make him
W-pI...140.5:2 can not be f. where sin is cherished. God
W-pI...140.8:5 lose. We need but seek it and it must be f.
W-pI...158.2:6 yesterday evoked a theme f. early in the
W-pI...165.3:2 instantly prepare to go where they are f.,
W-pI...165.3:3 And having f. them, would he not make
W-pI...170.8:7 takes many forms. Another can be f..
W-pI...183.9:2 and give the world the same release you f.
W-pI...184.9:5 unity where true communication can be f.
W-pI...185.5:3 has looked on them, and f. them wanting.
W-pI...194.4:4 the lack of sequence really f. in time. You
W-pI...194.7:6 future pain has f. his way to present peace
W-pI.195.10:2 and where one is the other must be f.. For
W-pI...196.2:1 can be f. in the idea we practice for today.
W-pI...197.2:4 and claimed, and f. and fully recognized.
W-pI...198.6:3 all joy that ever can be f. upon this earth.
W-pI...199.1:3 in a body looks for it where it can not be f.
W-pI...199.3:4 sheltered it from being f. illusory itself.
W-pI...199.6:2 Him they have f. what they have sought.
W-pI...200.4:2 You have not f. your happiness in foreign
W-pI.200.11:2 Peace can not be f. in them. The peace of
W-pI.200.11:5 For we have f. a simple, happy way to
W-pII.....in.8:2 We have f. the way He chose for us, and
W-pII..251.1:1 I sought for many things, and f. despair.
W-pII..262.2:3 nowhere else can peace be sought and f..
W-pII..275.1:6 this the healing of the Voice for God is f..
W-pII..286.2:1 will give us hope that we have f. the way,
W-pII......8.1:4 and witnesses to fear can not be f..
W-pII..292.1:2 can be the final outcome f. for everything.
W-pII..321.2:3 learn our freedom can be f. in God alone.
W-pII..344.1:3 *I f. an empty place where nothing ever was or*
W-pII....14.2:2 I, we f. a single purpose that we shared.
W-pII..360.1:3 *for nowhere else can certainty be f.. Peace be*
Wfl.........in.5:3 belonged to God, and f. it was a dream.
M-1.........3:10 He has therefore f. his own salvation and
M-4....IX.2:12 And having f., it rests in quiet certainty
M-19.......5:11 What had been lost has now been f.. The
M-20.........1:3 How is it f.? And being found, how can it
M-20.........1:4 And being f., how can it be retained? Let
M-20.........3:1 How is this quiet f.? No one can fail to
M-20.........3:5 In this condition, peace cannot be f..
M-20.......3:11 apparent. Yet when peace is f., the war is
M-20.........4:1 is the peace of God retained, once it is f.?
M-24.........2:5 way to salvation can be f. by those who
M-28.........5:9 are lost, for unity of purpose has been f..
C-2............6:6 What is it now and where can it be f.?
C-ep...........5:2 We had lost our way but He has f. it for us
P-2.........in.4:3 in relationships that salvation can be f..
P-2.........II.6:4 for they have f. the way to call to Him. If
P-2.........II.7:6 who believe they have f. God will fail.
P-2........IV.4:7 if God were the devil and must be f. in evil
P-3.........II.3:7 help. He has himself f. a therapist. He has
S-2...........I.4:6 in him must your innocence now be f..

## Foundation 6

*foundation*

T-3.......VII.5:5 God is the only F. that cannot be shaken,
T-3.......VII.6:3 The light will shine from the true F. of life,
T-4.........in.2:6 it is forever unwilling to depart from its F.
T-28.....VII.7:2 instead has shaken the F. of his home.
W-pI.....45.7:4 F. on which it rests is wholly changeless.
W-pI.....45.8:1 It is this F. toward which the exercises for

## foundation 46

*Foundation*

T-1.......VII.5:1 A solid f. is necessary because of the
T-3.......VII.4:9 can is the f. stone in your thought system,
T-3.......VII.5:4 in the light of truth, because its f. is a lie.
T-4.........II.8:3 to question, because the premise is its f..
T-5........IV.2:7 I have come to give you the f., so your
T-6...........I.8:3 only you can be the f. of God's church. A
T-6........IV.1:7 error, the f. of its whole thought system.
T-6......V.A.4:5 It is a real f. stone of the thought system I
T-9.......VII.7:4 because it can be questioned only at its f..
T-9.......VII.7:5 it, because within it its f. does stand. The
T-9.......VII.7:6 merely because He knows its f. is not true.
T-11.......in.3:5 come to the f. of the ego's thought system,
T-11.......in.3:7 and bravely hold it up to the f. of the ego's
T-11.......in.4:2 have at last looked at the ego's f. without
T-11.........I.1:3 the f. on which God will help build again
T-11.......V.10:2 is shaken to its f. by this awareness. For
T-13.......II.4:4 and deepest cornerstone in the ego's f.,
T-13......III.2:1 Under the ego's dark f. is the memory of
T-13......III.2:8 this. For still deeper than the ego's f., and
T-13......III.4:4 you go into the blackness of the ego's f.,
T-13......III.6:1 because they do not rest on their own f..
T-14.........I.5:3 He merely looks at its f. and dismisses it.
T-14.......II.1:5 not realize that the f. on which this most
T-14.......II.6:2 quickly on the firm f. that truth is true.
T-18......IX.4:1 and seems to be the whole f. on which the
T-18......IX.5:2 and a real f. for the ego's thought system.
T-18......IX.6:5 rest upon it, for it is but an illusion of a f..
T-19.......II.6:4 that this world's f. seems to have is found
T-19......III.8:6 you do not realize that its f. has gone. Its
T-20......VI.7:2 feeling the seeming firm f. of their temple
T-20....VI.10:3 Its firm f. is eternally upheld by truth, and
T-22.......V.5:2 weight, solidity and firmness of f.. Yes, to
T-24......III.4:1 Without f. nothing is secure. Would God
T-25.....VII.1:8 a wish to make this world's f. sure as love,
T-25.....VII.5:1 f. of the world you see to something else; a
T-26...VII.6:11 go against His Will has no f. in the truth.
T-28.....VII.3:5 like this, because it lacks f. in the truth.
T-28.....VII.5:9 stability cannot be judged apart from its f.
T-30......VI.1:2 Attack has *no* f.. It is here escape from fear
T-30......VI.2:2 It has a sure f.. You do not forgive the
T-30......VI.3:2 if it had a real f. pardon would have none.
W-in..........1:1 A theoretical f. such as the text provides
W-pI.....11.3:4 It contains the f. for the peace, relaxation
W-pI.....61.7:4 begin to build a firm f. for these advances.
W-pI...132.9:1 for it contains the firm f. for today's idea.
M-4.........I.1:1 the f. on which their ability to fulfill their

## foundations 4

T-3.......VII.1:3 Their resemblance lies in their power as f.
T-4...........I.2:5 same thought system can stand on two f..
T-5........III.9:2 Those you accept are the f. of your beliefs.
T-11.......in.1:5 that their results are as different as their f.

## founded 1

M-29.......5:10 And your confidence will be well f. indeed

## four 26

W-pI.......4.6:2 more than three or f. times during the day
W-pI.......5.7:6 Three or f. times during the day is enough
W-pI.......6.2:2 the three or f. practice periods which are
W-pI.......7.5:3 Three or f. practice periods, each to last a
W-pI.......8.6:1 can be done f. or five times during the day
W-pI.......8.6:2 find it trying, three or f. times is sufficient
W-pI.......9.3:1 three or f. practice periods are sufficient,
W-pI.....12.6:1 Three or f. times is enough for practicing
W-pI.....13.4:1 about three or f. times for not more than
W-pI.....15.5:3 comfortable with it, and do not exceed f..
W-pI.....16.6:1 F. or five practice periods are
W-pI.....17.4:1 Three or f. specific practice periods are
W-pI.....18.2:3 The three or f. practice periods which are
W-pI.....19.5:2 if necessary. Do not attempt more than f..
W-pI.....36.2:1 F. three-to-five-minute practice periods
W-pI.....37.4:1 Today's f. longer exercise periods, each
W-pI.....38.4:1 In the f. longer practice periods, each
W-pI.....39.5:1 for the f. longer practice periods for today
W-pI...39.11:1 or f. times an hour and more if possible,
W-pI.....43.4:5 see. F. or five subjects for this phase of the
W-pI.....45.6:3 After you have added some f. or five
W-pI.....47.4:2 strength. F. five-minute practice periods
W-pI.....49.3:1 least f. five-minute practice periods today,
W-pI.....67.5:3 F. or five times an hour, and perhaps even
W-pI...76.12:1 today; at least f. or five times an hour, as
WpI..rII.in.2:2 or f. minutes to reading them over slowly,

## fourth 5

T-2.........I.1:12 F., you believe that you can create
T-5........VI.8:1 fathers unto the third and f. generation,"
T19......IV.D.h The F. Obstacle: The Fear of God
T19...IV.D.2:1 The f. obstacle to be surmounted hangs
T-23........II.9:2 This leads to the *f.* law of chaos, which, if

## fragile 5

T-18......IX.5:4 then you see it as a f. veil before the light.
W-pI...122.6:7 has spun of f. cobwebs disappear before
W-pI...135.9:4 conception of the mind as limited and f.,
W-pI.139.12:3 And learn the f. nature of the chains that
C-4............4:2 on it as nothing more than just a f. veil, so

## fragment 12

T-7......VIII.4:2 because it is impossible to f. the mind. To
T-7......VIII.4:3 To f. is to break into pieces, and mind
T-16........II.2:1 There is a tendency to f., and then to be
T-17.........I.4:4 To f. truth is to destroy it by rendering it
T-18.........I.1:6 To f. is to exclude, and substitution is the
T-18.......I.13:2 and reaches out to every broken f. of the
T-18.....VIII.3:3 This f. of your mind is such a tiny part of
T-18.....VIII.5:3 Each tiny f. seems to be self-contained,
T-22......III.4:3 a distorted f. of the whole without the
T-23.........I.7:5 Being fragmented, they f.. But truth is
W-pI...153.8:3 let our happiness slip by because a f. of a

W-pII ..... 2.2:4 of every f. of the mind that still was one,

**fragmentation** 3

T-17...... III.3:4 is a move toward further f. and unreality.
T-17...... VI.6:9 believes in "solving" conflict through f.,
T-18.........I.4:2 of illusion for truth; of f. for wholeness. It

**fragmented** 18

T-1........ VI.2:3 had already f. yourself into levels with
T-7........ VI.1:1 only as one, you can perceive it as f.. It is
T-8....... VII.9:2 purpose is seen as f. into many functions
T-8..... VII.10:3 or not mind, is a f. or sick interpretation.
T-11..... V.15:2 series of f. perceptions which it unifies on
T-15....... V.7:1 is so f. that it frequently goes even farther;
T-17...... IV.8:3 all sorts of fanciful and f. illusions of love,
T-18.........I.1:5 which the substitution occurred is thus f.,
T-18.........I.2:8 to come between the f. relationships the
T-18.........I.3:3 Fear is both a f. and fragmenting emotion
T-18.........I.3:5 the f. perception from which the behavior
T-18.........I.5:5 it? Its f. aspects are fearful enough, as you
T-18...... VI.3:3 that seems to be f. and private and alone.
T-18...... IX.2:5 limited, and so f. they are meaningless.
T-19...... III.8:3 each part of God's f. creation would have
T-22....... V.3:1 how can peace be so f.? It is still whole,
T-23.........I.7:5 Being f., they fragment. But truth is
P-2......... II.6:7 is unseen through His eyes is too f. to be

**fragmenting** 1

T-18.........I.3:3 Fear is both a fragmented and f. emotion.

**fragments** 6

T-20...... VI.1:6 broken into f. and full of fear. The one
T-28....... V.5:8 f. seen within the gap that you imagined,
W-pI... 136.6:1 Every defense takes f. of the whole,
W-pI... 161.2:4 It sees instead but f. of the whole, for only
M-19 ......... 4:2 f. you perceive as broken off and separate.
M-19 ......... 4:4 For separate f. must decay and die, but

**fragrance** 1

W-pI... 159.9:4 and to which they go again with added f..

**frail** 19

T-14...... IX.3:3 You are not f. with God beside you. Yet
T-20...... VI.9:2 their seeming power is f. as is a snowflake
T-22.... VI.10:6 as vulnerable, f. and easily destroyed, and
T-22.... VI.11:2 can God's Son be weak and f. and easily
T-24.........I.4:5 feel weak and f. because of differences, for
T-24...... III.3:2 Truth is not f.. Illusions leave it perfectly
T-24...... IV.2:2 makes it f. and helpless in its own defense
T-24...... IV.2:3 was conceived to make *you* f. and helpless.
T-27.......I.6:10 how f. and vulnerable is your life; how
T-27.........I.7:5 the f. entitled to believe that every stolen
T-27....... II.1:4 proclaiming that the f. can have no trust
T-28...... VI.3:8 And it is f. and little by your wish. It
W-pI..... 96.5:3 itself and hiding in the body's f. support.
W-pI... 136.9:2 everlasting life, Heaven more f. than hell,
W-pI... 163.2:3 eyes. The f., the helpless and the sick bow
W-pI... 190.5:5 power to make you ill or sad, or weak or f.
W-pI... 191.9:1 You who perceive yourself as weak and f.,
M-20 ......... 6:8 your tiny f. imaginings apart from Him?
S-3...........I.2:3 Fearful and f. it seems to be to those who

**frailties** 1

W-pII . 278.1:2 f. and the sins which I perceive are real,

**frailty** 12

T-8.....VIII.6:2 can be hurt. It is a witness to your f., your
T-23.......in.1:1 opposite of f. and weakness is sinlessness?
T-23.......in.1:4 would use to cover f. conceals it not, for
T-28...... VI.3:4 what it hears, and hate its f. and littleness
T-28..... VII.6:2 f. of the little gap of nothingness whereon
T-31 ... VIII.1:2 in what must die, unable to escape its f.,
W-pI..... 47.6:1 recognition of your own f. is a necessary
W-pI... 135.4:4 such f. that constant care and watchful,
W-pI... 191.2:6 not speak of f. within you and without; no
W-pII . 250.1:2 his strength diminished and reduced to f.;
M-17 ......... 6:8 do not think about your f. in comparison.
M-29 ......... 7:9 your sense of f. and your fear of harm,

**frame** 64

T-3 ..........I.2:2 a whole f. of reference in order to justify it
T-3 .........II.3:2 is hardly a miracle-based f. of reference. It
T-15 ...... V.9:3 thus removing the f. of reference you have
T-15 ...... V.9:4 Spirit substitutes His f. of reference for it.
T-15 ...... V.9:5 it. His f. of reference is simply God. The
T-16 ..... VI.7:5 hold on the distorted f. of reference that
T-16 ..... VI.7:6 f. of reference is built around the special
T-16 ..... VI.8:4 homeless and without a f. of reference.
T-17 ........I.4:5 a f. of reference for reality to which it
T-17 ........I.5:3 The f. of reference for its meaning must
T-17 ..... III.8:4 the f. of reference to which the present is
T-17 ..... IV.7:4 the defense protects, set in a golden f..
T-17 ..... IV.7:5 The f. is very elaborate, all set with jewels,
T-17 ..... IV.7:7 the f. without the picture you cannot have
T-17 ..... IV.8:1 f. of all the defenses the ego uses. Its
T-17 ..... IV.8:2 here, surrounded by a f. so heavy and so
T-17 ..... IV.8:3 Into the f. are woven all sorts of fanciful
T-17 ..... IV.9:2 Do not let the f. distract you. This gift is
T-17 ..... IV.9:4 cannot have the f. without the picture.
T-17 ..... IV.9:5 What you value is the f., for there you see
T-17 ..... IV.9:6 Yet the f. is only the wrapping for the gift
T-17 ..... IV.9:7 The f. is not the gift. Be not deceived by
T-17 ... IV.9:10 dwell on the hypnotic gleaming of the f..
T-17 ... IV.11:2 It is a picture, too, set in a f.. Yet if you
T-17 ... IV.11:3 accept this gift you will not see the f. at all
T-17 ... IV.11:5 a picture of timelessness, set in a f. of time
T-17 ... IV.11:6 the f. that made you think it *was* a picture.
T-17 ... IV.11:7 Without the f., the picture is seen as what
T-17 ... IV.12:4 their value by comparing a picture to a f..
T-17 ... IV.13:1 fit the better picture into the wrong f. and
T-17 ... IV.13:5 from the f. in darkness is exposed to light,
T-17 ... IV.13:6 seeing at last that, unprotected by the f.,
T-17 ... IV.15:5 The f. fades gently and God rises to your
T-24 ..... VI.6:4 the perfect f. for your salvation and the
T-24 .... VII.4:6 weave a f. of loveliness around your hate,
T-24 .... VII.4:8 rather, then, a f. of holiness around him,
T-25 ......in.1:8 Christ is within a f. of Holiness whose
T-25 ......in.1:9 that they may f. His Holiness in them.
T-25 .......II.4:4 f. is but a means to hold the picture up, so
T-25 .......II.4:5 A f. that hides the picture has no purpose.
T-25 .......II.4:6 be a f. if it is what you see. Without the
T-25 .......II.4:7 the picture is the f. without its meaning.
T-25 .......II.5:1 empty f. upon a wall and stands before it,
T-25 .......II.5:3 has set within this f. is all there is to see.
T-25 .......II.5:5 Yet what God has created needs no f., for
T-25 .......II.5:7 would you rather see the f. instead of this
T-25 .......II.6:1 The Holy Spirit is the f. God set around
T-25 .......II.6:2 Yet its f. is joined to its Creator, One with
T-25 .......II.6:3 not make the f. into the picture when you
T-25 .......II.6:4 The f. that God has given it but serves His
T-25 .......II.6:5 picture, and cherishes the f. instead of it.
T-25 .......II.6:6 within a f. that will endure forever, when
T-25 .......II.7:1 Accept God's f. instead of yours, and you
T-25 .......II.7:2 and bones, but in a f. as lovely as itself. Its
T-25 .......II.7:3 up the sinlessness the f. of darkness hides,
T-25 .......II.7:4 because you saw it in a f. of death. God
T-25 .......II.8:6 He is the f. in which your holiness is set,
T-25 .......II.8:7 in him and sees only a f. of darkness, it is
T-25 ..... III.3:5 specialness, it is the perfect f. to set it off;
W-pI... 108.3:3 based upon one f. of reference, from
W-pI... 108.4:3 perceived from the same f. of reference
W-pI. 124.12:1 Add further jewels to the golden f. that
W-pI. 151.11:2 in any way from His one f. of reference,
S-2........ III.7:3 forgiveness, nor to set it in an earthly f..

**framed** 8

T-17 . IV.12:11 The other is lightly f. and hung in light,
T-17 ... IV.13:1 pictures are each f. perfectly for what they
T-17 ... IV.13:2 One is f. to be out of focus and not seen.
T-17 ... IV.13:3 The other is f. for perfect clarity. The
T-17 ... IV.14:1 The other picture is lightly f., for time
T-25 ........I.2:8 F. in his body you will see your sinfulness,
T-25 ........I.4:3 Himself is f. in holiness and perfect purity
W-pI .. 124.9:4 This half an hour will be f. in gold, with

**frames** 1

T-25 .......II.5:5 created He supports and f. within Himself

**framework** 6

T-7 .........V.1:1 more than a f. for developing abilities,
W-in.......... 1:1 as the text provides is necessary as a f. to
W-pI .... 96.3:1 be resolved within the f. they are set. Two
W-pI .. 138.5:4 seek to teach within the f. of this course.
M-16 ......... 3:7 we are learning within the f. of our course
C-in ........... 3:1 This course remains within the ego f.,

**frankly** 1

T-6 ....... IV.4:7 It is an alliance f. based on separation. If

**frantic** 18

T-12 ..... IV.2:3 its f. search for love it is seeking what it is
T-14 ..... IV.5:6 Give up this f. and insane attempt that
T19 .IV.A.13:5 For they are f. with the pain of fear, and
T-21 ..... IV.2:7 this constant shout and f. proclamation,
T-21 .... VII.3:1 F. and loud and strong the dark ones
T-23 ..... III.1:5 and f. fear of punishment the murderer
T-29 ..... IX.9:3 to the f. search for idols and for death.
W-pI .... 49.2:3 part is a wild illusion, f. and distraught,
W-pI .... 49.4:4 the peace that waits for you beyond the f.,
W-pI .... 96.1:2 and leads to f. attempts to reconcile the
W-pI .. 96.12:1 Each time today you tell your f. mind
W-pI .. 109.5:5 your mind that all its f. fantasies were but
W-pI .. 124.5:2 We see it in the f., in the sad and the
W-pI 152.12:3 the peace of God for all your f. thoughts,
W-pI .. 161.8:4 and claws the air in f. hope it can reach to
W-pI 198.11:2 a f. rush of thoughts that made no sense.
W-pI .. 200.8:3 conflicting goals, to senseless journeys, f.,
W-pII ..... 1.3:2 In f. action it pursues its goal, twisting

**frantically** 2

T-14 ... III.16:3 so f. to anticipate all you cannot know,
W-pI .... 13.2:3 ego rushes in f. to establish its own ideas

**free** 387

*See also* conflict-free

T-in ........... 1:4 *F. will does not mean that you can establish*
T-1 .........II.1:9 You are f. to believe what you choose, and
T-1 ....... III.5:3 f. to establish your kingdom where you
T-1 ....... IV.2:8 by illusions, but spirit is eternally f.. If a
T-1 ....... VI.5:9 Believe this and you will be f.. Only God
T-2 ..........I.2:8 God's endowment of the Son with f. will,
T-2 ........I.3:10 your f. will was given you for your joy in
T-2 ..........I.4:9 that illuminates not only sets you f., but
T-2 ..........I.4:9 but also shows you clearly that you *are* f..
T-2 .........II.2:7 the will is really f. it cannot miscreate,
T-2 .........II.6:4 f. yourself from the past as you go ahead.
T-2 ....... III.3:2 may appear to contradict f. will because
T-2 ...... VII.3:2 If you are not f. to choose one, you would
T-2 ...... VII.3:2 would also not be f. to choose the other.
T-2 ..... VIII.2:8 that you f. yourself from fear quickly,
T-2 ..... VIII.3:8 vacillations between f. and imprisoned
T-3 ..........I.1:4 No one who is f. of the belief in scarcity
T-3 .........II.4:2 miscreate only when it believes it is not f..
T-3 .........II.4:3 mind is not f. because it is possessed, or
T-3 .........II.4:4 and the will is not f. to assert itself. To be
T-3 .........V.5:7 is *not* the truth that shall set you f., but
T-3 .........V.5:7 f. of the need to engage in it when you are
T-3 ..... VI.10:2 spirit. Everyone is f. to refuse to accept his
T-3 ..... VI.10:2 not f. to establish what his inheritance is.
T-3 ..... VI.11:2 result of his own f. will he must regard his
T-3 ..... VI.11:2 free will he must regard his will as not f.,

T-3......VI.11:3 F. will must lead to freedom. Judgment
T-3......VII.6:8 the oneness of knowledge is f. of conflict.
T-4.........in.3:3 you are also f. to join my resurrection.
T-4.........in.3:9 Until then you are f. to crucify yourself as
T-4......... I.13:6 together so we can be f. of them together.
T-4......... II.8:3 It is not f., however, to open the premise
T-4........ III.6:2 you. In this you are as f. as God, and must
T-4........ VI.5:8 You are still f. to choose, but can you
T-5......... II.6:4 In the holy state the will is f., so that its
T-5...... III.11:5 made truth, but truth can still set you f..
T-5........ IV.2:7 your own thoughts can make you really f..
T-5........ VI.1:5 Yet your election is both f. and alterable.
T-5........ VI.2:8 is only to unchain your will and set it f..
T-6...........I.5:2 f. to perceive yourself as persecuted if you
T-6........ III.4:2 you will learn the truth that will set you f.,
T-6........ III.4:2 will keep you f. as others learn it of you.
T-7......... II.7:8 It is totally f., because nothing discordant
T-7..... VIII.2:4 persuade you that *it* can f. you of conflict,
T-7..... VIII.2:4 lest you give the ego up and f. yourself.
T-8......... II.3:1 you anything as long as your will is f.,
T-8......... II.3:2 to be imprisoned because your will is f..
T-8......... II.3:3 That is why the ego is the denial of f. will.
T-8......... II.4:2 you afraid of your will *because* it is f.. The
T-8...... IV.5:12 you. Your will is as f. as mine, and God
T-8......... IV.7:2 imprisoned yours, and have not let it be f.
T-8...... IV.7:11 Sons. By offering freedom you will be f..
T-8...... VI.10:5 and f. the holy will of all those who are as
T-8..... VII.16:2 F. your mind from the belief that this is
T-10....... IV.5:1 You are not f. to give up freedom, but
T-10..... V.9:11 also deny what it creates because it is f..
T-10..... V.10:2 would not know His Son if he were not f..
T-11....... II.7:3 f. to determine who shall be your guest,
T-11..... V.18:4 to release you, if you choose to be f.. You
T-11...... VI.2:2 you condemn your brothers or f. them?
T-11... VIII.7:5 deny it to yourself, for it can only f. you.
T-11... VIII.7:6 whom He created f. and whose freedom is
T-13....... II.7:3 told again and again that it will set you f.,
T-13....... V.7:4 would release you from it and set you f..
T-13...... VI.4:8 between them, to f. you to be born again.
T-13...... VI.6:1 you, you will see that you are f. of them.
T-13...... VI.7:1 you with them, and f. you from the past.
T-13.... VI.12:1 is following the laws of love of your f. will,
T-13... VIII.8:1 having learned to f. yourself through Him
T-13...... IX.1:7 must intervene, if you would f. yourself.
T-13...... IX.6:3 have the Holy Spirit make you f. of it,
T-13....... X.5:3 will be enough to f. you from the past,
T-14....... II.7:2 Holy Spirit's plan to f. you from the past,
T-14....... II.8:1 and learn of them how to be f. of darkness
T-14...... III.1:3 learns easily because his thoughts are f..
T-14...... III.4:6 You are guilty or guiltless, bound or f.,
T-14...... III.5:3 that comes from choosing to be f. of guilt.
T-14...... III.6:3 to f. his brother and enter light with him.
T-14.... III.13:6 protector of the innocence that sets you f.
T-14....... V.5:5 Who is there but wishes to be f. of pain?
T-14...... XI.5:2 If you are wholly f. of fear of any kind,
T-14.... XI.10:1 from the past would teach you are f. of it.
T-14.... XI.10:4 He has made you f. of what you made.
T-15.........I.8:6 beautiful and so clean and f. of guilt that
T-15.........I.9:6 f. and wholly without condemnation.
T-15...... III.2:5 You are f. to try as many as you wish, but
T-15....... V.9:7 For in the holy instant, f. of the past, you
T-15..... VI.5:11 he is as f. as God would have him be. For
T-15... VIII.5:1 to f. you of what He does not understand.
T-15...... IX.6:7 the Holy Spirit must undo to set him f..
T-15...... IX.7:1 and your thoughts will be as f. as God's.
T-16...... III.2:1 but you have not learned how to be f.. I
T-16..... VII.8:6 it. When He willed that His Son be f., His
T-16..... VII.8:6 willed that His Son be free, His Son *was* f..
T-17....... II.3:5 by your own forgiveness you are f. to see.
T-17.... IV.12:7 on this basis are you really f. to choose.
T-17..... V.15:1 mistakes and f. you from their results.
T-17..... VII.9:6 situation was thus made f. of the past,
T-17... VIII.3:3 Holy Spirit's purpose is f. to use instead.
T-18....... II.1:5 are "f." to make over whatever seemed to
T-19.........I.2:3 Thus do you see him f., and in this vision
T-19...... I.11:3 f. of all the guilt he laid upon himself.
T-19...... I.16:4 You can enslave a body, but an idea is f.,
T19..IV.B.11:2 Here is your choice, and it *is* f.. But all that
T19..IV.B.15:3 all your messages of hate and f. yourself.
T19....IV.C.8:5 f. it from the merciless and unrelenting
T19.IV.D.15:9 it. Whom you forgive is f., and what you
T19.IV.D.17:7 And be you and your brother f. together,
T19.IV.D.18:1 F. your brother here, as I freed you. Give
T-20....... II.3:9 Offer him lilies and it is yourself you f..
T-20..... II.10:2 Now is he f., unlimited in his communion
T-20..... II.10:4 and his strong arm is f. to guide you safely
T-20..... II.11:1 and f. to lead you now where he would be.
T-20...... III.9:1 leap up in joy the instant they are made f..
T-20.... III.10:6 in separation are now made f. in Paradise.
T-20...... IV.1:7 Thus would He keep you f. of them. Being
T-20...... IV.3:4 He is as f. from this as you are, and in the
T-20...... IV.5:3 here is to release him, and so to f. himself.
T-20..... VII.9:7 and what he sees is f. of condemnation.
T-20... VIII.2:3 Would you not willingly be f. of misery,
T-21.......in.2:4 you joined the Will of God to set him f..
T-21....... II.8:1 to leave your altars f. of what you placed
T-21...... III.7:5 But holiness would set your brother f.,
T-21...... III.8:1 Those who would f. their brothers from
T-21...... IV.5:2 but to join with him and to be f. again, as
T-21..... V.5:11 purpose given it, you must be f. to find it.
T-21.... VI.11:3 lie but in himself, if he be f. already? And
T-21.... VI.11:9 he chooses to be merciful, there is he f..
T-21.. VI.11:10 chains his pardon on himself to set him f..
T-22...... VI.3:1 what God loves, and would have f. forever
T-23..... II.14:8 to hold love captive, and let sin go f..
T-24...... III.8:1 The slaves of specialness will yet be f..
T-25....... V.5:5 when he is f. to offer you the gift of sight
T-25....... V.6:2 is God made f. to let His Will be done. In
T-25..... VII.7:3 and where you can be f. of place and time,
T-25..... VII.7:6 whose problem is their choices are not f.,
T-25... VIII.8:2 In justice He is bound to set them f., and
T-26..... V.11:1 God created is as f. as God created him.
T-26... VII.18:2 all His Son's mistakes and set him f.. But
T-27.........I.2:5 and when it rests on him are you set f..
T-27.........I.9:9 mind made f. again to choose what it is
T-27.......I.10:1 removed, is Heaven f. to be remembered.
T-27....... II.9:4 to prove that he is slave, but they are f..
T-27....... II.9:5 they are f. *because* they hold him bound.
T-27..... II.15:3 in one unhealed and set the other f.. That
T-27...... III.5:3 yet a power known as wholly f. of limits.
T-27...... III.6:7 is God left f. to take the final step Himself.
T-27...... IV.5:8 in a conflict state is f. to ask this question,
T-27... VII.11:2 Who could be f. to choose between effects
T-27. VIII.11:1 learned will set you f. from suffering,
T-27. VIII.13:2 the world your guilt, you will be f. of it. Its
T-28.... II.12:6 mind is f. to make another choice instead.
T-28...... IV.1:5 And you are f. of dreams of pain because
T-28...... IV.6:4 your own away would he be f. of them,
T-28....... V.3:2 part of yours, from which you both are f..
T-29....... II.1:1 from suffering to learn that you are f.?
T-29....... II.3:6 You are f. of pain and sickness, misery
T-29...... III.2:6 the dream he made, that he be f. of it. He
T-29...... VI.6:2 How f. from fear, how filled with blessing
T-30.......I.15:4 grounds for opposition that you may be f.
T-30....... II.2:4 Unless you do your will you are not f..
T-30....... II.2:9 He joins with you in willing you be f.. And
T-30....... II.4:1 that merely waits your blessing to be f.? If
T-30....... II.4:2 then God Himself could not be f.. For
T-30....... II.4:6 when you have recognized that you are f..
T-30....... II.4:9 Nor can you be f. apart from Him Whose
T-30...... IV.6:5 Son of God declares that he is f. of idols.
T-30...... IV.6:6 that he is free of idols. And thus *is* he f..
T-30...... IV.7:5 asked to let yourself be f. of all the dreams
T-30..... V.9:12 were not f. from bitter cost and joyless
T-30..... V.11:3 they were f. to learn their will is one. And
T-30... VIII.6:6 There is no pain from which he is not f., if
T-30... VIII.6:9 As he is healed are you made f. of guilt,
T-31.......I.13:3 But you are f. to learn of him, and learn of
T-31.......I.13:5 him. Now is he f. to live as you are free,
T-31.......I.13:5 him. Now is he free to live as you are f.,
T-31....... II.3:1 a choice and gives but the illusion it is f.,
T-31...... III.5:3 and sin cannot abide the joyous and the f.
T-31..... V.17:5 is the truth left f. to enter in its sanctuary,
T-31..... V.17:5 enter in its sanctuary, clean and f. of guilt.
T-31... VII.13:1 is f. of any judgment made upon yourself.
T-31... VIII.9:7 And in this choice is everyone made f..
W-pI..... 29.5:1 be as f. of self-selection as possible. For
W-pI... 39.10:1 you should feel f. to introduce variety into
W-pI..... 57.2:3 All I need do is recognize this and I am f..
W-pI..... 57.2:6 The Son of God must be forever f.. He is
W-pI..... 57.3:5 is really a place where he can be set f.. I
W-pI... 70.10:2 You are f. from all external interference.
W-pI..... 71.8:4 attempts and mad proposals to f. yourself
W-pI..... 73.7:7 Your will is f., and nothing can prevail
W-pI..... 76.7:4 instead it is a truth that keeps us f. forever
W-pI..... 76.7:5 imprisons, but the laws of God make f..
W-pI..... 78.8:3 He would be f., and make his freedom
W-pI..... 78.8:5 you see through Him will f. you both. Be
W-pI..... 79.3:5 completely f. of problems and at peace.
W-pI..... 79.7:3 We will try to f. our minds of all the many
W-pI..... 80.5:4 that you are out of conflict; f. and at peace
W-pI..... 80.7:2 to be f. of problems that do not exist. The
W-pI..... 88.3:7 perfectly f. of the effects of all laws save
W-pI..... 96.6:8 bring pain to him, and fail to set him f.?
W-pI..... 96.8:4 do, restored to It and f. to serve Its Will.
W-pI..... 97.7:2 *Spirit am I, a holy Son of God, f. of all limits,*
W-pI..... 97.7:2 *safe and healed and whole, f. to forgive, and*
W-pI..... 97.7:2 *free to forgive, and f. to save the world.*
W-pI... 101.6:4 it will set you f. from all the consequences
W-pI... 102.2:6 you f. today to join the happy Will of God
W-pI... 105.7:3 and let your mind be f. of all that would
W-pI... 106.8:3 and which will f. the world from thinking
W-pI.107.11:2 release the world, as He would set you f..
W-pI... 110.2:2 to heal the past and make the future f.. It
W-pI... 110.3:3 to light the world and f. it from the past.
W-pI... 110.5:4 This is the truth that comes to set you f..
W-pI.110.11:6 This is the Word of God that sets you f..
W-pI... 125.2:2 this: The Son of God is f. to save himself,
W-pI... 125.2:2 house by his own will, forever f. as God's.
W-pI... 125.9:2 and f. your vision from the body's eyes.
W-pI... 127.6:4 Today we practice making f. your mind of
W-pI.127.11:3 Now are they all made f., along with us.
W-pI... 128.5:2 leave it f. of purposes we gave its aspects
W-pI... 128.6:2 It will be grateful to be f. a while. It knows
W-pI... 128.6:4 But f. its wings, and it will fly in sureness
W-pI... 131.3:4 you still are f. to choose a goal that lies
W-pI... 132.2:1 for anyone is f. to change his mind, and
W-pI... 132.2:3 f. the past from what you thought before.
W-pI... 132.2:4 f. the future from all ancient thoughts of
W-pI... 132.3:2 Here in the present is the world set f.. For
W-pI.132.10:2 To f. the world from every kind of pain is
W-pI.132.11:6 thoughts which made it and must set it f.,
W-pI.132.14:1 Today our purpose is to f. the world from
W-pI.132.14:5 one of our illusions, that we may be f..
W-pI... 134.8:4 Now are you f. to follow in the way your
W-pI.134.10:1 and keep your mind as f. of guilt and pain
W-pI.135.13:2 It is not f. to be the means of helping in a
W-pI.136.15:2 to ask the truth to come to us and set us f.
W-pI... 137.8:6 within a body f. to join with other minds,
W-pI.154.13:2 *the means by which to recognize that I am f..*
W-pI... 161.9:9 have it be revealed to you and set you f.?
W-pI.161.11:6 Ask this of him, that he may set you f.:
W-pI...... 163.h There is no death. The Son of God is f..
W-pI... 166.6:3 him and open up his treasures to be f.?
W-pI... 166.7:4 be released from self-deception and set f..
W-pI.170.13:9 *are we because Your Holiness has set us f..*
WpI.rV.in10:7 it is f. of all illusions every time we say:
W-pI... 177.1:2 The Son of God is f.. God is but Love, and
W-pI... 186.5:6 Yet are the humble f. to hear the Voice
W-pI... 190.8:2 ransom you have gladly paid not to be f..
W-pI.190.11:2 we are f. to choose our joy instead of pain,
W-pI... 191.4:4 In this one thought is everyone set f.. In
W-pI... 191.5:2 and escape you will return and set it f..
W-pI... 191.6:1 this and you are f.: You are the holy Son
W-pI... 191.6:4 it. You set it f. of your imprisonment. You
W-pI... 191.8:4 Son has come again at last to set it f.?
W-pI.191.11:2 They stay in chains till you are f.. They
W-pI.191.11:7 Remember this, and all the world is f..
W-pI... 192.8:2 could be set f. while he imprisons anyone
W-pI... 192.8:3 A jailer is not f., for he is bound together
W-pI... 192.9:2 instead of bind, for thus are you made f..
W-pI... 192.9:5 as you choose to be condemned or f..
W-pI... 193.9:5 each one, and that His Son be f. again.
W-pI.193.12:2 so that the next one is f. of the one before.
W-pI... 194.5:4 Now is he f., and all his glory shines upon
W-pI... 194.5:4 shines upon a world made f. with him, to
W-pI... 194.7:8 He is f. to choose again when he has been

W-pI...195.7:4 us. An ancient door is swinging f. again; a
W-pI...196.1:3 will be f. of the insane belief that to attack
W-pI...196.6:1 you can attack another and be f. yourself.
W-pI...196.9:6 And you are f., and glad of freedom. You
W-pI...197.1:1 Here is the second step we take to f. your
W-pI...197.9:2 Be you f. of all ingratitude to anyone who
W-pI...198.1:6 Then are you f., for freedom is your gift,
W-pI...198.9:4 *Only my own forgiveness sets me f..* Do not
W-pI......199.h I am not a body. I am f..
W-pI...199.1:4 mind can be made f. when it no longer
W-pI...199.4:2 is. Declare your innocence and you are f..
W-pI...199.7:1 Be f. today. And carry freedom as your
W-pI...199.7:3 Be you f., so that the Holy Spirit can make
W-pI...199.7:3 set f. the many who perceive themselves
W-pI...199.8:8 *I am f.. I hear the Voice that God has given*
W-pI...200.5:3 made f. of your mistakes and honored as
W-pI...200.5:5 as you f. the one, the other is accepted as
WpI rVI.in.3:4 *I am f.. For I am still as God created me.* The
W-pI......201.h I am f.. For I am still as God created me.
W-pI...201.1:5 I am f.. For I am still as God created me.
W-pI......202.h I am f.. For I am still as God created me.
W-pI...202.1:4 I am f.. For I am still as God created me.
W-pI......203.h I am f.. For I am still as God created me.
W-pI...203.1:4 I am f.. For I am still as God created me.
W-pI......204.h I am f.. For I am still as God created me.
W-pI...204.1:2 *rule the world of sick illusions, f. in God,*
W-pI...204.1:4 I am f.. For I am still as God created me.
W-pI......205.h I am f.. For I am still as God created me.
W-pI...205.1:5 I am f.. For I am still as God created me.
W-pI......206.h I am f.. For I am still as God created me.
W-pI...206.1:5 I am f.. For I am still as God created me.
W-pI......207.h I am f.. For I am still as God created me.
W-pI...207.1:5 I am f.. For I am still as God created me.
W-pI......208.h I am f.. For I am still as God created me.
W-pI...208.1:6 I am f.. For I am still as God created me.
W-pI......209.h I am f.. For I am still as God created me.
W-pI...209.1:5 *The Love of God within me sets me f..* I am
W-pI...209.1:7 I am f.. For I am still as God created me.
W-pI......210.h I am f.. For I am still as God created me.
W-pI...210.1:7 I am f.. For I am still as God created me.
W-pI......211.h I am f.. For I am still as God created me.
W-pI...211.1:4 I am f.. For I am still as God created me.
W-pI......212.h I am f.. For I am still as God created me.
W-pI...212.1:2 *me f. from all the vain illusions of the world.*
W-pI...212.1:6 I am f.. For I am still as God created me.
W-pI......213.h I am f.. For I am still as God created me.
W-pI...213.1:3 *I learn of Him becomes the way I am set f..*
W-pI...213.1:6 I am f.. For I am still as God created me.
W-pI......214.h I am f.. For I am still as God created me.
W-pI...214.1:7 I am f.. For I am still as God created me.
W-pI......215.h I am f.. For I am still as God created me.
W-pI...215.1:6 I am f.. For I am still as God created me.
W-pI......216.h I am f.. For I am still as God created me.
W-pI...216.1:6 I am f.. For I am still as God created me.
W-pI......217.h I am f.. For I am still as God created me.
W-pI...217.1:5 I am f.. For I am still as God created me.
W-pI......218.h I am f.. For I am still as God created me.
W-pI...218.1:5 I am f.. For I am still as God created me.
W-pI......219.h I am f.. For I am still as God created me.
W-pI...219.1:2 I am f.. *I am God's Son. Be still, my mind,*
W-pI...219.1:7 I am f.. For I am still as God created me.
W-pI......220.h I am f.. For I am still as God created me.
W-pI...220.1:5 I am f.. For I am still as God created me.
W-pII ......1.1:7 f. to take its place is now the Will of God.
W-pII .224.1:1 great, wholly beneficent and f. from guilt,
W-pII .227.1:1 *Father, it is today that I am f., because my*
W-pII .227.1:4 *And I am f. because I was mistaken, and did*
W-pII .236.1:8 And thus I set it f. to do the Will of God.
W-pII .240.2:3 *today to recognize Your Son, and set him f..*
W-pII .241.1:5 salvation dawns today upon a world set f..
W-pII .243.1:6 Thus do I f. myself and what I look upon,
W-pII .243.2:1 *Father, today I leave creation f. to be itself. I*
W-pII .268.2:2 Only reality is f. of pain. Only reality is
W-pII .268.2:3 Only reality is f. of loss. Only reality is
W-pII .277.1:1 *Son is f., my Father. Let me not imagine I*
W-pII .277.2:4 He is f. because he is his Father's Son.
W-pII ....278.h If I am bound, my Father is not f..
W-pII .278.1:5 For truth is f., and what is bound is not a
W-pII .280.1:1 Whom God created limitless is f.. I can
W-pII .289.2:2 *the past has left untouched and f. of sin. Here*
W-pII .296.1:4 *For having damned it I would set it f., that I*
W-pII .308.1:5 instant has forgiveness come to set me f..
W-pII .310.1:4 *to me, and that it is Your Will I be set f. today.*
W-pII .310.2:2 gave salvation to us, and Who set us f..
W-pII ... 10.4:6 your glad acceptance, which will set it f..
W-pII .312.2:1 *set f. from all the judgments I have made.*
W-pII .314.2:1 *past, and choose to use the present to be f..*
W-pII .321.1:1 *I did not understand what made me f., nor*
W-pII .330.2:3 *to be made f. forever from all our mistakes,*
W-pII ....332.h Fear binds the world. Forgiveness sets it f.
W-pII .332.2:3 *Your Love has given us the means to set it f..*
W-pII ....340.h I can be f. of suffering today.
W-pII .340.1:4 *and be f. forever from all suffering. Thanks*
W-pII .343.2:1 The mercy and the peace of God are f..
W-pII .350.1:7 *Only Your memory will set me f.. And only*
W-pII .354.1:1 *of time, and wholly f. of every law but Yours.*
Wfl........in.1:1 will be left as f. of words as possible. We
M-2 ........... 3:5 Because your will is f. you can accept what
M-2 ........... 3:6 you are not f. to choose the curriculum, or
M-2 ........... 3:7 You are f., however, to decide when you
M-4 .... IV.2:10 always was His Own, is f. to be itself.
M-10 ......... 5:2 Now are you f. of a burden so great that
M-13 ......... 4:6 must rejoice that he is f. of all the sacrifice
M-13 ......... 6:2 Son, and it is the course's aim to set him f.
M-15 ......... 1:6 setting it f. as God's Final Judgment on
M-15 ......... 1:8 This is the Judgment that will set him f..
M-15 ....... 1:11 *Holy are you, eternal, f. and whole, at peace*
M-15 ......... 3:3 God's Judgment waits for you to set you f.
M-18 ......... 2:6 Now is He f. to teach all minds the truth
M-28 ......... 4:3 The Son of God is f.. And in his freedom
M-28 ......... 5:6 because His Holiness has set us f. indeed!
M-28 ......... 6:8 f. because he let God's Voice proclaim the
P-2.........in.4:4 not completely f. of magical overtones.
S-1........ III.2:1 will not be f. from envy and malice. They
S-1........ III.3:7 advantage to himself in setting others f..
S-1........ III.3:9 gain must go, if enemies are to be set f..
S-1........ IV.4:2 to f. yourself from all of them at once? Do
S-2...........I.5:8 But you can f. him and yourself as well.
S-2.........I.10:4 and learn what it should be to set you f..
S-2..........II.8:8 Your wings are f., and prayer will lift you
S-2........ III.1:6 trust and willingness to learn how to be f..
S-2........ III.6:8 made f. to save as true forgiveness is
S-3..........II.1:3 fear, so sickness will be f. to strike again.
S-3..........II.6:4 and God's Son is f. to enter in the home

## freed 22

T-13 ..... IX.4:6 could as easily have f. him from the past,
T-14 .......II.7:9 the light has come and f. you from the
T-14 ... XI.10:1 He Who has f. you from the past would
T-18 ... VI.11:8 replaces it extends to what has f. you, and
T19. IV.D.18:1 Free your brother here, as I f. you. Give
T-20 .......II.8:8 ready to be unveiled and f. from all the
T-21 ... VI.11:6 And it is by his own desire that he is f..
T-26 .. VII.20:5 creation f. to call upon the Name of God
T-28 .....II.10:6 are you f. from this much of the dream;
W-pI..... 78.5:4 enemy is more than friend when he is f. to
W-pI... 124.7:6 In our experience the world is f.. As we
W-pI. 132.15:4 be changed so that the world is f., along
W-pI. 134.16:1 Let him be f. from all the thoughts you
W-pI... 191.6:2 learn as well that you have f. the world.
W-pI... 194.5:2 f. from its bequest of grief and misery, of
W-pI... 194.5:3 in God's Son is f. to bless the world. Now
W-pI... 198.2:2 Forgive and you are f.. Such is the law
W-pI... 214.1:3 *Now am I f. from both. For what God gives*
W-pII .314.1:5 or suffer when the present has been f.,
W-pII .321.2:1 the world, which will be f. along with us.
M-15 ......... 1:9 in which all things are f. with him. Time
M-16 ......... 6:2 limitless because all things are f. within it.

## freedom 228

T-1 ........I.26:1 Miracles represent f. from fear. "Atoning
T-1 .........II.2:6 because f. from fear cannot be thrust
T-2 .........II.2:6 mind, and re-establishes the f. of the will.
T-2 ..... VIII.4:1 The first step toward f. involves a sorting
T-3 ..... VI.11:3 Free will must lead to f.. Judgment always
T-5 .........II.6:5 F. to choose is the same power as freedom
T-5 .........II.6:5 to choose is the same power as f. to create
T-5 .......V.4:13 but you must learn to regard it as f..
T-5 ....... VI.2:9 Your ego cannot accept this f., and will
T-8 ...........II.h Difference between Imprisonment and F.
T-8 .........II.4:2 to learn it is a violation of your own f.,
T-8 .........II.4:4 leads you steadily along the path of f.,
T-8 .........II.5:2 difference between imprisonment and f..
T-8 .........II.5:3 taught yourself that imprisonment is f..
T-8 .........II.6:2 His direction is f. and His goal is God. Yet
T-8 .........II.6:5 This is f. and this is joy. Deny yourself
T-8 ............ IV.h The Gift of F.
T-8 ....... IV.6:6 How else can it be, if God's Kingdom is f.?
T-8 ....... IV.6:7 F. cannot be learned by tyranny of any
T-8 ....... IV.7:7 your f. because your freedom is in Him.
T-8 ....... IV.7:7 your freedom because your f. is in Him.
T-8 ..... IV.7:10 it is acceptable to Him it is the gift of f.,
T-8 ..... IV.7:11 all His Sons. By offering f. you will be free.
T-8 ....... IV.8:1 F. is the only gift you can offer to God's
T-8 ....... IV.8:2 is. F. is creation, because it is love. Whom
T-8 ...... VII.5:6 but give him f. from his belief in littleness
T-8 .... VII.16:5 F. from illusions lies only in not believing
T-8 ..... VIII.8:8 louder without violating your f. of choice,
T-9 ..... VIII.4:1 because His grandeur establishes your f..
T-10 ..... III.8:2 and offer them perfect f. from all illusions
T-10 ..... IV.4:2 it. His are the laws of f., but yours are the
T-10 ..... IV.4:3 Since f. and bondage are irreconcilable,
T-10 ..... IV.5:1 You are not free to give up f., but only to
T-11 .......II.7:4 Yet this is not real f., for it still depends
T-11 .......II.7:7 Real f. depends on welcoming reality, and
T-11 .......V.6:7 dependence on God, in which your f. lies.
T-11 ..... VI.5:3 is why his slavery is as complete as his f..
T-11 ..... VI.5:8 and submission, but in the gladness of f..
T-11 ..... VI.6:3 f. to leave behind everything that hurts
T-11 ... VIII.7:6 and whose f. is protected by His Being.
T-12 .... VII.9:1 remaining f. as a prisoner of this world.
T-13 ..... VI.5:7 will not see the f. that the present holds.
T-13 ... VIII.8:1 yourself through Him Who knows of f..
T-13 ..... IX.4:5 You have denied his f., and by so doing
T-13 ..... IX.4:7 And in his f. would have been your own.
T-13 ..... XI.1:4 he could look upon himself and see his f..
T-13 ..... XI.2:4 heard the hymn of f. rising unto Heaven.
T-13 ..... XI.2:6 Yet as you made not f., so you made not a
T-13 ..... XI.2:6 made not a war that could endanger f..
T-14 .......II.7:2 past, and open up the way to f. for you.
T-14 .......II.7:8 Accept this key to f. from the hands of
T-14 .......II.8:1 Behold your brothers in their f., and
T-14 ..... III.5:1 you have chosen guiltlessness, f. and joy.
T-14 ..... III.7:3 perfect f. from the belief that you can be
T-14 .......V.5:6 in this exchange can f. from pain be his.
T-15 ......I.10:7 in which you see yourself as bright with f.,
T-15 ......I.10:8 For remembering Him *is* to remember f..
T-15 ......I.13:3 of f. to all who are enslaved by time, and
T-15 ..... IV.3:5 would have His host abide in perfect f..
T-15 ..... IX.5:5 impose on them can offer you the gift of f.
T-15 .......X.3:6 is the time appointed for the gift of f.,
T-15 .......X.9:3 choose between total f. and total bondage
T-15 ... XI.10:7 *In the name of my f. I choose your release,*
T-15 ... XI.10:8 So will the year begin in joy and f.. There
T-16 ..... III.2:1 You may have taught f., but you have not
T-16 ..... III.3:4 have taught f. unless you did believe in it.
T-16 ..... IV.1:1 hate relationship, for f. lies in looking at it
T-16 .......V.5:6 In this it sees the ultimate f. of the self, for
T-16 ..... VI.2:1 Love is f.. To look for it by placing
T-16 ..... VI.2:3 union in separation, nor for f. in bondage
T-16 ..... VI.3:3 for the ego has taught you that f. lies in it.
T-17 ..... III.9:4 and fear, truth or illusion, f. or slavery–it
T-17 .....V.10:1 the Sonship is the song of f. heard, in
T-18 .......II.6:7 and guilt, but as a source of joy and f.. It
T-18 ... VI.11:2 the dream of f. sometimes hoped for in
T-18 ... VI.14:4 welcome you to openness of mind and f..
T-19 ........I.9:3 faith, you offer the gift of f. from the past,
T-19 ..... IV.1:7 of love and safety and f. to everyone who
T19 ... IV.B.8:2 So will you learn the f. that I taught by
T19 ... IV.B.8:2 I taught by teaching f. to your brother,
T19 ... IV.B.8:3 me behind the obstacles you raise to f.,
T19 . IV.B.15:4 and offering it to you as f. *from* attack.
T19 . IV.B.17:2 to death. F. is offered them but they have
T19 IV.D.17:6 gift of f. that I gave the Holy Spirit for you
T19 IV.D.18:4 Offer your brother f. and complete release

T-20..... II.11:4 the f. and the strength to lead you there.
T-20..... II.11:5 holy altar where the strength and f. wait,
T-20...... III.9:2 a while for them to understand what f. is.
T-20...... III.9:4 in whom the meaning of your f. lies. He
T-20...... IV.3:4 f. that you see in him you see your own.
T-20...... IV.4:1 choose f. will experience only its results.
T-20...... IV.4:4 thus their f. is established and maintained
T-20...... IV.4:6 of f. that you should ask what freedom is.
T-20...... IV.4:6 of freedom that you should ask what f. is.
T-20...... IV.6:7 forget imprisonment and to remember f..
T-20.... VI.11:7 the body, or let himself be given f. from it.
T-21...... III.3:4 hold him, and placing it in his f. instead.
T-21...... IV.5:3 It has been waiting for the birth of f.; the
T-21...... IV.7:4 The song of f., which sings the praises of
T-21....... V.3:1 and another Voice in which your f. lies,
T-21..... V.5:11 and has your f. as the purpose given it,
T-21.... VI.11:3 Where could his f. lie but in himself, if he
T-21.... VI.11:4 bind him but himself, if he deny his f.?
T-22...... III.4:7 bodies, believing the body's f. is their own
T-22...... IV.6:5 hope and f. and release from suffering to
T-22...... VI.1:1 Do you want f. of the body or of the mind
T-22...... VI.1:8 one but yearns for f. and tries to find it.
T-22...... VI.2:1 Where f. of the body has been chosen,
T-22...... VI.2:1 to contrive ways to achieve the body's f..
T-22...... VI.2:2 Yet f. of the body has no meaning, and so
T-22...... VI.3:3 This is the only service that leads to f.. To
T-23.......in.4:4 world of f. for a little sigh of seeming sin,
T-23.......in.6:7 For here is your salvation and your f..
T-24.......in.2:6 suffering follow guilt and f. sinlessness.
T-24...... III.7:2 F. and peace and joy stand there, beside
T-24...... VI.5:2 See in his f. yours, for such it is. Let not
T-25....... V.5:1 saved, for by his f. will you gain your own.
T-25....... V.5:6 you allow him f. to complete the task God
T-26.........I.8:4 give you back the gift of f. by receiving it
T-26... VIII.9:3 you have cause for f. *now*. What profits
T-26... VIII.9:4 What profits f. in a prisoner's form? Why
T-26...... IX.1:2 your own salvation, with his f. joined!
T-26...... IX.4:4 and f. lights up every living thing and lifts
T-29.... III.3:13 By your gift of f. is it given unto you.
T-30...... I.15:5 There is no f. from what must occur. And
T-30.......... II.h F. of Will
T-30....... II.2:2 For that is f.. There is nothing else that
T-30....... II.4:6 world awaits the f. you will give when you
T-30....... II.4:8 For it is by your will the world is given f..
T-30....... II.5:2 he shares your f. as he shares your will. It
T-30....... V.2:6 of f. has been grasped and welcomed, and
T-30... VIII.2:5 health, his perfect f. from all forms of lack
T-30... VIII.4:7 not been given f. to bestow His gifts upon
T-31...... III.7:2 see upholds their f. from imprisonment
W-pI..... 11.3:4 and f. from worry that we are trying to
W-pI..... 31.4:2 independence in the name of your own f..
W-pI..... 31.4:3 in your f. lies the freedom of the world.
W-pI..... 31.4:3 in your freedom lies the f. of the world.
W-pI..... 57.3:6 a place where the Son of God finds his f..
W-pI..... 57.4:2 When I see the world as a place of f., I
W-pI..... 73.7:5 the f. to remember Who you really are.
W-pI..... 76.3:1 Think of the f. in the recognition that you
W-pI... 76.12:2 of f. from all danger and all tyranny. It is
W-pI..... 78.8:3 He would be free, and make his f. yours.
W-pI..... 80.1:7 F. from conflict has been given you.
W-pI..... 88.3:2 Here is the perfect statement of my f.. I
W-pI..... 88.3:8 laws save God's. And His are the laws of f.
W-pI..... 99.7:2 for these are words in which your f. lies.
W-pI... 125.8:3 It is the Word of f. and of peace, of unity
W-pI... 128.5:4 that bar the door to f. from the world,
W-pI... 128.6:5 to be restored to sanity, to f. and to love.
W-pI... 130.8:6 *world, that I may find my f. and deliverance.*
W-pI.130.11:5 *I seek my f. and deliverance, and this is not a*
W-pI... 132.1:7 that the hope of f. comes to him at last.
W-pI.132.17:1 increase the f. sent through your ideas to
W-pI.134.14:2 meet with our reality in f. and in peace.
W-pI.134.16:2 And now you are prepared for f.. If you
W-pI... 137.8:1 Healing is f.. For it demonstrates that
WpI.rIV.in5:1 that day can offer you in f. and in peace.
W-pI... 161.5:1 to be the body that we feel limits our f.,
W-pI... 164.7:6 us, and offer it the f. given us through His
W-pI... 170.1:4 you believe to hurt another brings you f..
Wi181-200 2:4 But the experience of f. and of peace that
W-pI... 192.8:6 f. that the way to liberty depends for both
W-pI.192.10:3 asks that you accept the way to f. now.
W-pI... 194.2:2 chains that locked the door to f. on it.
W-pI... 195.4:4 that in us all things will find their f.. It
W-pI... 196.4:1 us from bondage to the state of perfect f..
W-pI... 196.9:6 And you are free, and glad of f.. You have
W-pI... 196.9:7 because you feared your strength and f..
W-pI... 197.2:4 f. and salvation are perceived as joined,
W-pI... 198.1:6 Then are you free, for f. is your gift, and
W-pI... 198.2:4 understands, for f. is a part of knowledge.
W-pI... 198.9:1 letting f. come to make its home with you.
W-pI... 199.1:1 F. must be impossible as long as you
W-pI... 199.1:3 Who would seek for f. in a body looks for
W-pI... 199.5:4 sound the call of f. round the world with
W-pI... 199.6:1 Spirit is the home of minds that seek for f.
W-pI... 199.6:5 mind with but the thought of f. as its goal,
W-pI... 199.6:6 a worthy servant of the f. which the mind
W-pI... 199.7:2 And carry f. as your gift to those who still
W-pI... 199.7:6 For He would give you perfect f., perfect
W-pI... 200.5:1 F. is given you where you beheld but
W-pI... 200.8:4 where f. lies within the peace of God.
WpI rVI.in.4:4 For thus is f. given us from all we did not
WpI rVI.in.6:1 to proclaim your f. from temptation, as
WpI rVI.in.7:4 best become a loving gift of f. to the world
W-pI... 212.1:3 *the function God has given me can offer f..*
W-pII...... 2.5:2 the call to all the world that f. is returned,
W-pII.. 277.2:1 make to hide the f. of the Son of God. He
W-pII.. 277.2:3 he is, is far beyond his faith in slavery or f.
W-pII..... 279.h Creation's f. promises my own.
W-pII.. 279.1:2 to be in prison, and awaits a future f., if it
W-pII.. 279.1:4 And now is f. his already. Should I wait in
W-pII.. 279.1:5 release, when God is offering me f. now?
W-pII.. 280.1:6 limitless, and like Himself in f. and in love
W-pII..... 321.h Father, my f. is in You alone.
W-pII.. 321.1:1 *what made me free, nor what my f. is, nor*
W-pII.. 321.1:4 *made nor understood the way to find my f..*
W-pII.. 321.1:6 *Who endowed me with my f. as Your holy*
W-pII.. 321.1:8 *Father, my f. is in You alone. Father, it is my*
W-pII.. 321.2:2 glad are we to find our f. through the
W-pII.. 321.2:3 we learn our f. can be found in God alone.
W-pII.. 330.1:4 to spirit, and extends its f. and its joy, as
W-pII.. 332.1:8 giving it the means to realize the f. that is
W-pII.. 332.2:5 *For as we offer f., it is given us. And we would*
W-pII.. 332.2:6 *prisoners, while You are holding f. out to us.*
W-pII.. 337.1:1 love, f. forever from all thought of loss;
W-pII.. 340.1:1 *today, and for the f. I am certain it will bring.*
W-pII.. 340.1:6 *it holds in joy and f. for Your holy Son and for*
W-pII.. 347.1:4 *But You have offered f., and I choose to claim*
W-pII.. 349.1:1 *things I see, and give to them the f. that I seek*
W-ep ......... 2:6 And thus He speaks of f. and of truth.
M-13 ......... 4:8 To them he sacrifices all his f.. And to
M-25 ......... 6:8 increased f. for greater imprisonment.
M-28 ......... 4:4 And in his f. is the end of fear. No hidden
C-1............. 7:1 only remaining f. is the freedom of choice
C-1............. 7:1 only remaining freedom is the f. of choice
P-1............. 4:5 his f. because he thinks that it is slavery.
S-1......... II.5:3 thus becomes a prayer for your own f..
S-1........ III.4:7 of escape makes it difficult to welcome f.,
S-2........... I.5:3 How could f. be possible if this were so?
S-2........... I.5:5 You have no f. unless he gives it to you.
S-2........... I.6:1 the way in which your only hope of f. lies.
S-2......... I.10:3 or you will not be able to attain your f..
S-2......... I.10:5 for here it waits its f. to ascend above the
S-2......... II.2:5 Who makes a slave to teach what f. is?
S-2........ III.1:4 nor promise f. while it asks for death.

## freedom's 2

T-30....... II.2:3 else that ever should be called by f. name.
W-pI... 101.7:3 You are set on f. road, and now today's

## freeing 4

T-1......... I.33:3 errors by f. you from your nightmares. By
W-pI..... 72.4:3 help in f. him from the body's limitations.
W-pI... 137.9:3 you extend the little help He asks in f. you
W-pII.... 10.3:1 on all your errors, f. you from them, and

## freely 20

T-1......... V.3:3 all His gifts are f. given to everyone alike.
T-1......... V.5:5 If it does not f. elect to do so, it retains its
T-2........... I.2:8 creation is f. given in one continuous line,
T-3....... VII.3:8 knowledge and gave it f. to His creations.
T-5........ IV.5:6 What I learned I give you f., and the Mind
T-5...... VI.12:8 Because He has been given you f. by God,
T-7...... IV.7:10 It comes f. to all the Sonship, being what
T-13...... VI.7:4 the light of perfect vision is f. given as it is
T-13...... VI.7:4 vision is freely given as it is f. received,
T-14.... III.11:7 of God He so f. and so gladly offers you.
T-14...... X.11:2 is perfectly open and f. accessible to all,
T-17...... V.15:1 gifts you have so f. given to your brother,
T-17.... VIII.3:2 f. given wherever faithlessness is laid
T-19......... I.9:5 now. You f. choose to overlook his errors,
T-20..VIII.2:10 Vision is f. given to those who ask to see.
T-25...... II.9:11 The gratitude of God Himself is f. offered
W-pI..... 62.5:5 Let related thoughts come f., for your
W-pII . 323.1:1 *and f. let Your Love come streaming in to his*
W-pII . 343.2:3 is a gift that must be f. given and received.
S-1........ IV.3:5 to let it be a f. chosen remedy from every

## freer 2

W-pI... 195.4:1 could you sanely be enraged if he seems f.
S-3.......... II.3:4 we go in peace to f. air and gentler climate

## frees 2

T-1...... III.5:11 their distortions and f. them from prison.
T-2.......... II.2:6 right mind the denial of error f. the mind,

## freezing 1

T-26...... IX.7:3 him from bitter winter and the f. cold.

## frenzy 1

W-pI... 153.4:3 so far beyond the f. and intensity of which

## frequency 1

M-29 ......... 3:1 to the Holy Spirit with increasing f..

## frequent 15

W-pI..... 31.1:4 and the other consisting of f. applications
W-pI..... 33.3:1 shorter exercise periods should be as f. as
W-pI..... 34.5:1 The shorter applications are to be f., and
W-pI..... 38.6:1 In the f. shorter applications, apply the
W-pI..... 39.5:1 more f. practice sessions are encouraged.
W-pI..... 40.1:2 today, but very f. short ones are necessary
W-pI..... 47.4:2 and longer and more f. ones are urged.
W-pI..... 48.2:1 will be very short, very simple and very f..
W-pI..... 64.7:1 f. applications of today's idea throughout
W-pI... 70.10:1 the short and f. practice periods today,
W-pI..... 77.7:1 Our shorter practice periods will be f.,
WpI..rII.in.1:4 and f. shorter ones in which we practice
W-pI..... 91.1:2 This needs repeating, and f. repeating. It
W-pI..... 95.5:1 F. but shorter practice periods have other
W-pI..... 95.6:1 planned to include f. reminders of your

## frequently 21

T-2........ IV.3:9 abilities can be and f. are overevaluated.
T-3........... I.2:4 Persecution f. results in an attempt to
T-6...... IV.11:7 I have f. said that what you teach you are.
T-15....... I.4:12 Again the ego tries, and all too f. succeeds
T-15....... V.4:2 This is why they shift and change so f..
T-15....... V.7:1 so fragmented that it f. goes even farther;
T-29......... I.7:5 f. you have demanded that love go away,
W-pI..... 36.2:2 and make the shorter applications f., to
W-pI..... 49.5:1 not forget to repeat today's idea very f..
W-pI..... 62.4:1 use it as f. as possible throughout the day.
W-pI..... 67.5:2 the truth about yourself as f. as possible,
W-pI..... 80.6:2 with deep conviction, as f. as possible.
W-pI..... 94.5:4 Tell yourself f. today that you are as God
W-pI..... 95.5:2 you are reminded of your purpose f., you

| | |
|---|---|
| W-pI...95.14:8 | Repeat today's idea as f. as possible, and |
| W-pI...102.5:3 | hourly five-minute rests, pause f. today, |
| W-pI...103.3:4 | Bolster this expectation f. throughout the |
| W-pI...151.2:4 | pause to recollect how f. they have been |
| W-pI...155.1:2 | appearance, though you smile more f.. |
| W-pI.161.11:4 | see familiar gestures which he makes so f.. |
| W-pI...182.9:1 | Rest with Him f. today. For He was |

## fresh 4

| | |
|---|---|
| T-31....VIII.8:4 | so new and clean and f. you will forget the |
| W-pI...157.2:2 | f. experience that sheds a light on all that |
| W-pI...200.8:2 | and leading from this f. perception to the |
| M-2...........3:4 | is looked upon as a new thought, a f. idea, |

## Friend 23

*friend*

| | |
|---|---|
| T-14....III.13:5 | Son of God the Holy Spirit is your only F.. |
| T19.IV.D.14:1 | Behold your F., the Christ Who stands |
| T19.IV.D.14:5 | still offers you salvation as His F.. The |
| T19.IV.D.15:5 | and receive from your most holy F.. Let |
| T19.IV.D.21:7 | you to see this purpose in your holy F., |
| T-20.........I.4:5 | alien to you and yet your ancient F., lies |
| T-20.........I.4:7 | Look on your risen F., and celebrate his |
| T-23...II.22:13 | Ask, then, your F. to join with you, and |
| T-26.........VI.h | The Appointed F. |
| T-26......VI.2:3 | Yet God has given him a better F., in |
| T-26......VI.3:2 | the throne that God appointed for your F. |
| T-26......VI.3:3 | of Him Whom God has called your F.. |
| T-26......VI.3:4 | And it is He Who is your only F. in truth. |
| T-27.......V.7:6 | the F. who brought them their release. |
| T-30....II.1:12 | more than that He hear you call Him "F.." |
| W-pI.....60.3:5 | I will recognize in everyone my dearest F.. |
| W-pI.....72.7:4 | the Voice of truth and welcome It as F.. |
| W-pI...123.5:2 | give thanks that in our solitude a F. has |
| W-pI...182.9:3 | that they may see He would be F. to them. |
| W-pII.274.1:1 | *the love of brother to his brother and his F..* |
| W-pII.351.1:5 | *my everlasting Comforter and F. beside me,* |
| W-ep.........1:2 | Your F. goes with you. You are not alone. |
| P-3........III.8:6 | reach you, holding out his hand to his F.. |

## friend 49

*Friend*

| | |
|---|---|
| T-6........IV.4:6 | This makes the body the ego's f.. It is an |
| T-7.....III.2:14 | The ego's "enemy" is therefore your f.. |
| T-7........III.3:1 | before that the ego's f. is not part of you, |
| T-15.........I.2:4 | it. Time is His f. in teaching. It does not |
| T-15.........I.3:1 | The ego is an ally of time, but not a f.. For |
| T-15.......I.13:3 | time, and thus make time their f. for them |
| T-15.......I.15:1 | Time is your f., if you leave it to the Holy |
| T19.IV.D.13:3 | Is this giver of salvation your f. or enemy? |
| T-20.......II.4:4 | him? Be you his f. for me, that I may be |
| T-20.....II.11:1 | Here is your savior and your f., released |
| T-20....III.10:7 | And here would I unite with you, my f., |
| T-21......IV.3:3 | for it to bother to pretend it is your f.. |
| T-23...II.17:11 | is intent on your destruction is not your f. |
| T-24.........I.4:6 | Yet they protect its enmity and call it "f.." |
| T-24.........I.6:4 | in specialness; his f. in a shared purpose. |
| T-24.........I.7:1 | Your brother is your f. because his Father |
| T-24.........I.9:6 | must he be your enemy and not your f.. |
| T-24.........I.9:8 | He is your f. *because* you are the same. |
| T-24.......II.8:1 | when you have looked on him as on a f.. |
| T-24.......II.8:2 | but only f. to what is real in you. Not one |
| T-24......IV.4:4 | sin, if it were possible, would be its f.. |
| T-25....VIII.7:2 | on them in the guise of a deliverer and f.. |
| T-26......VI.2:1 | solitude, with one illusion as your only f.. |
| T-26......VI.2:4 | one illusion that you think is f. obscures |
| T-26......VI.2:6 | Seek not another f. to take His place. |
| T-26......VI.2:7 | There *is* no other f.. What God appointed |
| T-26......VI.3:3 | Make no illusion f., for if you do, it can |
| T-27....IV.4:14 | It is your servant and also your f.. But tell |
| T-27...VII.13:4 | healed and where his brother was his f.. |
| T-29.........I.3:5 | Sometimes a f., perhaps, provided that |
| T-29.......II.3:7 | No more is pain your f. and guilt your god |
| T-29.......V.6:3 | Would you not want to be a f. to him, |
| T-30.......I.15:2 | how the f. whose counsel you have sought |
| T-30.......II.5:4 | chose to look upon your brother as a f.. |
| T-31........I.8:2 | but calls to you in soft appeal to be your f. |
| T-31........I.8:7 | had lost a f. who always wanted to be part |
| T-31.......II.3:6 | And every f. or enemy becomes a means |
| W-pI.....68.6:3 | do so: *I would see you as my f., that I may* |
| W-pI.....72.7:6 | instead. It is your f.; He is your enemy. |
| W-pI.....78.4:5 | who angered you; someone you call a f., |
| W-pI.....78.5:4 | He who was enemy is more than f. when |
| W-pI...121.9:2 | and one whom you consider as a f.. And |
| W-pI.121.12:1 | and turn your mind to one you call a f.. |
| W-pI.121.12:3 | Perceive him now as more than f. to you, |
| W-pI.121.13:1 | let your "enemy" and f. unite in blessing |
| W-pI...182.9:3 | of Heaven in His hand and calls them f., |
| W-pI.182.11:2 | Christ has called you f. and brother. He |
| W-pI...191.3:2 | you assail the universe alone, without a f., |
| W-pI...194.9:6 | for we have chosen that we be its f.. |

## friendless 4

| | |
|---|---|
| T-11.....III.2:3 | is lonely, and amid all his brothers he is f. |
| T-26.....VI.2:5 | Without Him you are f.. Seek not another |
| W-pII.351.1:2 | *a Son of God; alone and f. in a fearful world.* |
| M-29.........8:6 | *your holiness, for you are not Alone and f.. I* |

## friendliness 1

| | |
|---|---|
| T-31........I.8:1 | lit with hope and sparkles with a gentle f.. |

## friends 13

| | |
|---|---|
| T-15....VII.2:3 | for the ego believes that anger makes f.. |
| T19..IV.A.12:4 | him. For fear is merciless even to its f.. Its |
| T19...IV.D.4:5 | ego. These are your chosen f.. For in your |
| T19...IV.D.6:2 | remembering your promise to your "f.." |
| T19...IV.D.6:5 | All of your "f.," your "protectors" and |
| T-20.......II.5:5 | strangers; only dearly loved and loving f.. |
| T-27......V.7:7 | the many f. he thought were enemies. |
| T-27...VIII.1:4 | for other bodies as its f. and enemies. Its |
| T-28.....II.10:3 | perceived as f. with merciful intent. Their |
| T-31.....III.6:6 | a changing love, the ones you think are f.. |
| W-pI.....68.6:1 | now to see all these people as f.. Say to |
| W-pI...109.8:3 | your distant brothers and your closest f.; |
| M-3...........2:5 | him; perhaps the students will become f.. |

## friendship 5

| | |
|---|---|
| T-26.....VI.2:2 | This is no f. worthy of God's Son, nor one |
| T-26.....VI.2:4 | and keeps His f. and forgiveness from |
| T-29........I.3:5 | made your f. possible a little while. But |
| T-29........I.3:8 | A cautious f., and limited in scope and |
| W-pI.....76.8:3 | further; you believe in the "laws" of f., of |

## frighten 15

| | |
|---|---|
| T-5.......III.4:6 | alone your thoughts will f. you because, |
| T-6........V.2:1 | by a gentle Voice that will not f. them, but |
| T-6........V.4:1 | errors because He does not f. children, |
| T-12.......II.5:3 | Only the anticipation will f. you, for the |
| T-13.......X.7:1 | not keep illusions in your mind to f. you, |
| T-18........I.7:1 | form of the original error rising to f. you, |
| T-18.....IX.3:8 | For it is not His purpose to f. you, but |
| T-21.....VI.7:3 | reassure you, and seeks not to f. you. The |
| T-24....VII.5:3 | Let not your foolish fancies f. you. What |
| T-30.....IV.3:8 | that they can seem to break and f. him. |
| T-30.....IV.4:8 | But neither were they things to f. you, nor |
| W-pII.268.1:6 | *can f. me, when I let all things be exactly as* |
| W-pII.338.1:5 | His thoughts can f. him, but since these |
| W-pII.338.2:3 | *And I will have thoughts that will f. me, until* |
| W-pII.339.1:8 | it? He has asked for what will f. him, and |

## frightened 17

| | |
|---|---|
| T-3..........I.4:2 | from fear, and f. people can be vicious. |
| T-6........V.2:2 | that f. them so badly are not real, because |
| T-6........V.4:3 | are f. because they do not recognize the |
| T-11.VIII.14:6 | will ask for truth again when they are f.. It |
| T-18...VIII.3:5 | how alone and f. is this little thought, this |
| T-20.....III.4:2 | through constant dangers, alone and f., |
| T-20.....III.4:5 | A murderer *is* f., and those who kill fear |
| T-22......V.4:3 | a f. mouse that would attack the universe. |
| T-23......in.5:4 | of him. Leave him not f. and alone in his |
| T-30.....IV.2:2 | A child is f. when a wooden head springs |
| T-31....VII.5:2 | you may not be f. by your "evil" thoughts |
| W-pI 135.14:2 | They are the means by which a f. mind |
| W-pI 152.11:2 | ways, encouraging our f. minds with this: |
| W-pII.249.2:2 | *f. them with thoughts of violence and death.* |
| W-pII.334.2:3 | *offering to his bewildered mind and f. heart,* |
| M-17.........7:3 | go. Each one says clearly to your f. mind, |
| S-3..........II.5:1 | for death is cruel in its f. eyes and takes |

## frightening 23

| | |
|---|---|
| T-2....IV.4:10 | has induced the belief that miracles are f.. |
| T-2.....VIII.5:1 | The term "Last Judgment" is f. not only |
| T-3.......VI.8:5 | This belief is very f. to them, but hardly |
| T-3......VII.2:4 | "devil" is a f. concept because he seems to |
| T-4..........I.3:2 | be. Learning is ultimately perceived as f. |
| T-5.......VI.4:6 | Perceiving it as f., it interprets it fearfully. |
| T-7..........X.5:3 | Yet weakness is f.. What else, then, can |
| T-11.VIII.13:1 | Children perceive f. ghosts and monsters |
| T-12.......II.4:1 | about the f. perceptions of little children, |
| T-12.......II.5:3 | for the reality of nothingness cannot be f.. |
| T-14.....VI.1:3 | and in ignorance that you perceive the f., |
| T-14.....VI.1:5 | The obscure is f. because you do not |
| T-18.....III.4:6 | You will succeed only in f. yourself. The |
| T-27.......II.1:1 | healing f.? To many, yes. For accusation is |
| W-pI....12.1:2 | think that what upsets you is a f. world, |
| W-pI....52.1:2 | Reality is never f.. It is impossible that it |
| W-pI....55.5:6 | given the world has led to a f. picture of it. |
| W-pI..135.3:1 | Defense is f.. It stems from fear, |
| W-pI..156.6:5 | It is a foolish thought, a silly dream, not f. |
| W-pII.....4.4:1 | madman's dreams are f., and sin appears |
| W-pII.290.1:4 | sight I made is f. and painful to behold. |
| M-16.........9:3 | These attempts may indeed seem f., but |
| M-26.........2:4 | to whom such appearances would be f., |

## frightens 9

| | |
|---|---|
| T-5.......III.8:6 | This vision f. the ego because it is so calm. |
| T-11.....VI.6:3 | you and f. you cannot be thrust upon you, |
| T-11.VIII.14:5 | their lack of understanding that f. them, |
| T-11.VIII.14:7 | or your Father or yourself that f. you. You |
| T-13.....III.1:6 | not your desire to attack that really f. you. |
| T-13.....III.4:5 | is hidden there. *And it is this that f. you.* |
| T-20....VII.3:4 | hesitate, it is because the purpose f. you, |
| T-20.VIII.10:7 | you that it is not reality which f. you, and |
| W-pII.338.1:3 | Now has he learned that no one f. him, |

## from 2470

## front 1

| | |
|---|---|
| M-22.........4:5 | only the face of Christ shining in f. of him, |

## frown 1

| | |
|---|---|
| W-pI..167.2:6 | discomfort or the merest f., acknowledge |

## fruit 3

| | |
|---|---|
| T-3......VII.3:4 | The f. of only one tree was "forbidden" in |
| T-3......VII.4:1 | Eating of the f. of the tree of knowledge is |
| T-3......VII.6:1 | that bears no f. will be cut off and will |

## fruitless 1

| | |
|---|---|
| W-pI....71.3:3 | ensures that the f. search will continue, |

## fruits 2

| | |
|---|---|
| T-9........V.9:6 | *By their f. ye shall know them, and they shall* |
| T-16.....III.2:2 | earlier, "By their f. ye shall know them, |

## frustrating 1

| | |
|---|---|
| T-8......VII.8:1 | nothing so f. to a learner as a curriculum |

## fulfill 43

| | |
|---|---|
| T-1........IV.4:3 | I came to f. the law by reinterpreting it. |
| T-5.......VII.4:4 | your part in it, and how urgent it is to f. it |
| T-8........III.2:1 | To f. the Will of God perfectly is the only |
| T-8......IV.8:12 | in It and f. your function as part of It, the |
| T-8..... VIII.4:7 | and one He is perfectly equipped to f.. |
| T-9.........IV.6:1 | and He knows how to f. it perfectly. That |
| T-9......... V.8:6 | You can only let Him f. His function. He |
| T-11....... II.6:1 | rest until you know your function and f. it |
| T-14......IV.3:9 | to f. your function in God's Mind with all |
| T-14....IV.3:10 | you escape this guilt by failing to f. your |
| T-14...VII.5:11 | He can f. what God has given Him to do. |
| T-15.......IV.3:4 | I call you to f. your holy part in the plan |
| T-16.........I.7:9 | for He will f. it if you but ask Him to enter |
| T-17.......IV.1:5 | *else.* To f. this function you relate to your |
| T-17......IV.1:7 | Whatever does not f. this function cannot |
| T-17.....VII.6:2 | truth. If you lack faith in anyone to f., and |
| T-18....... V.2:6 | and make sure that you f. it easily. And |
| T-18....... V.5:6 | Let Him f. the function that He gave to |
| T19... IV.C.9:3 | and quietly made ready to f. the mighty |
| T-20......IV.8:4 | plan as the one function that you would f. |
| T-20......IV.8:8 | except the only purpose that you would f.. |
| T-25......VI.3:6 | no aim which only they can perfectly f.. |
| T-27....... I.9:10 | it may f. the function that it will receive. |
| T-27.......II.15:5 | rest assured that He will not f. a function |
| W-pI.....62.5:3 | *I would f. my function that I may be happy.* |
| W-pI.....64.4:4 | choose whether or not to f. your function, |
| W-pI.....69.3:3 | purpose here, and no other function to f.. |
| W-pI.....82.3:3 | I cannot f. my function if I forget it. And |
| W-pI.....82.3:4 | it. And unless I f. my function, I will not |
| W-pI.....82.4:3 | *use this as an opportunity to f. my function.* |
| W-pI.....98.2:3 | We have a mighty purpose to f., and have |
| W-pI...105.4:5 | f. its aim of giving everything it has away, |
| W-pI...123.3:4 | glad you have a function in salvation to f.. |
| W-pI.135.11:4 | its adequacy to f. the plans assigned to it. |
| W-pI...153.9:3 | sure we will f. our chosen purpose, as our |
| W-pI...154.5:3 | it is intended, and f. his role in its delivery |
| W-pI.186.14:4 | form you can f. your function even here, |
| W-pII......3.3:3 | Their aim is to f. the purpose which the |
| W-pII..285.1:4 | me, what purpose would my suffering f., |
| M-2............1:5 | Once he has chosen to f. his role, they are |
| M-2............1:5 | to fulfill his role, they are ready to f. theirs |
| M-4..........I.1:1 | on which their ability to f. their function |
| C-6.............3:2 | order to f. this special function the Holy |

## fulfilled 34

| | |
|---|---|
| T-13...VII.12:6 | and realize that all of them have been f.. |
| T-13...VII.16:6 | This is the only real need to be f. in time. |
| T-13......XI.4:6 | be to doubt that His mission will be f.. |
| T-13....XI.10:4 | mission of redemption will be f. as surely |
| T-15.........I.1:4 | He has not f. His teaching function until |
| T-16...VII.2:11 | it serves some purpose that you want f.. |
| T-16...VII.2:12 | this purpose could not be f. in the present |
| T-20......IV.6:7 | And as this purpose is f., a new world |
| T-20......IV.7:4 | perfectly f. in them and all their brothers. |
| T-21....... V.5:6 | Him arose, and was f. in the same instant. |
| T-24......VI.9:3 | Futility of function not f. will haunt you |
| T-25....... V.4:8 | found if he f. the role God gave to him. |
| T-25....... V.5:2 | be f. is but the means to let yours be. And |
| T-25......VI.7:1 | your special function, that His may be f.. |
| T-25......VI.7:9 | and let salvation be perfectly f. in you. Do |
| T-25...VII.13:3 | one can suffer for the Will of God to be f.. |
| T-25. VIII.12:7 | Holy Spirit's special function has been f.. |
| T-26....VII.3:3 | would see because perception is a wish f.. |
| T-26...VII.19:2 | finds the peace in which your wishes are f. |
| T-26......IX.4:2 | When They come, time's purpose is f.. |
| T-27..... II.15:2 | alone. And when it is f. as shared, it must |
| T-27.....VII.5:2 | by which this purpose seems to be f.. The |
| T-29......IV.4:4 | not matter if they be f. or merely wanted. |
| T-29.....VII.3:5 | to it, and this the role that cannot be f.. |
| T-30....... V.2:7 | a place where hope of happiness can be f.. |
| T-30....... V.5:1 | and yet completely shared and perfectly f. |
| T-31....... II.4:5 | f. the function that was given him by you. |
| W-pI...107.9:2 | to let His function be f. through you. To |
| W-pI...113.2:2 | *perfect plan for my salvation perfectly f..* |
| W-pI...169.9:3 | and fully recognized as perfectly f. by |
| W-pII.....in.5:1 | Now is the time of prophecy f.. Now are |
| W-pII..251.1:6 | hopes are finally f. and dreams are gone. |
| W-pII..344.1:8 | *Thus is the law of love f.. And thus Your Son* |
| M-12 .......5:10 | Voice will tell him when he has f. his role, |

## fulfilling 10

| | |
|---|---|
| T-4...........I.9:4 | peace because you are not f. your function |
| T-7...... VI.13:1 | f. your function as co-creator with God, |
| T-7........ IX.4:8 | Spirit is f. its function, and only complete |
| T-8........ III.8:5 | F. it perfectly will let you remember what |
| T-11...... V.12:2 | and f. your function as it exists in truth. |
| T-15...... III.3:5 | your function and f. it that you can escape |
| W-pI.....64.4:1 | Only by f. the function given you by God |
| W-pI.....66.1:1 | f. your function and achieving happiness. |
| W-pI.....83.3:4 | F. my function is my happiness because |
| W-pI.....96.4:3 | spirit, and it is f. happily its function here. |

## fulfillment 7

| | |
|---|---|
| T-2......... II.4:5 | necessary for its f. were planned. Then a |
| T-7........ IX.4:8 | its function, and only complete f. is peace. |
| T-7........ IX.5:2 | own being, because your f. includes them. |
| T-17......VII.6:6 | accomplish every miracle needed for its f.. |
| T-20......IV.8:9 | As that was given you, so will its f. be. |
| T-29...... VI.4:8 | set no end to its f. nor its changelessness. |
| W-pI.....56.1:5 | and complete f. are my inheritance. I have |

## fulfills 4

| | |
|---|---|
| T-8........ III.1:7 | His function perfectly He f. it perfectly, |
| T-12...... IV.5:6 | He f. His mission He will teach you yours, |
| T-25...... VI.4:3 | function, and f. the part assigned to him, |
| W-pI...154.7:1 | earthly messenger f. his role by giving all |

## full 62

| | |
|---|---|
| T-2........ IV.5:3 | that a miracle, to attain its f. efficacy, |
| T-2.......VII.2:2 | Miracle working entails a f. realization of |
| T-5........ IV.7:3 | f. power of creation cannot be expressed |
| T-5......... V.8:6 | and it will turn it back to f. creation at any |
| T-5......... V.8:7 | will also return to f. creation the instant it |
| T-6....... II.10:7 | The f. awareness of the Atonement, then, |
| T-6......V.A.4:7 | Sons of God, and that is f. appreciation. |
| T-7........ III.4:1 | is merely to focus your f. attention on it. |
| T-7........ IX.4:6 | f. appreciation of the mind's Self-fullness |
| T-10...... IV.2:5 | cannot dawn on a mind f. of illusions, |
| T-12....... II.9:5 | not by denying its f. import in any way– |
| T-13...... III.1:1 | upon your hatred and realize its f. extent. |
| T-13....... X.1:2 | your awareness the f. perception that it is |
| T-14....... V.5:2 | f. communication be restored between |
| T-15...... IV.7:5 | you wonder why it is that you are not in f. |
| T-15...... VI.7:7 | in f. communication with all that ever was |
| T-15...... VI.8:6 | the f. communication of ideas with ideas. |
| T-16..... VII.7:1 | hinder your f. awareness of the complete |
| T-17........... I.1:7 | Only in waking is the f. release from them |
| T19..IV.C.10:4 | is in f. communication with God and you. |
| T-20...... VI.1:6 | broken into fragments and f. of fear. The |
| T-26..... VII.9:5 | far short of giving you your f. inheritance, |
| T-26...VII.14:4 | than f. salvation and escape from guilt. |
| T-27....... II.7:2 | bestow an equal gift of f. deliverance from |
| T-28..... II.12:1 | This world is f. of miracles. They stand in |
| T-29...... VI.4:7 | established for His Son in f. awareness. |
| T-29.... IX.10:4 | the dreamer f. release from dreams of fear |
| W-pI.....21.1:3 | are urged, allowing a f. minute for each. |
| W-pI.....26.5:2 | A f. two minutes should be attempted for |
| W-pI.....28.5:2 | of infinite value, f. of happiness and hope. |
| W-pI.....33.1:2 | A f. five minutes should be devoted to the |
| W-pI.....37.1:5 | because it offers everyone his f. due. And |
| W-pI.....38.4:1 | each preferably to last a f. five minutes, |
| W-pI.....39.5:1 | A f. five minutes are urged for the four |
| W-pI.....46.3:1 | least three f. five-minute practice periods, |
| W-pI.....65.1:5 | The f. acceptance of salvation as your |
| W-pI.....69.3:1 | today with the f. realization that this is so, |
| W-pI.....71.8:4 | And in the first is your f. release from all |
| W-pI.....71.9:6 | Him f. charge of the rest of the practice |
| W-pI.....72.5:3 | f. of false promises and offering illusions |
| W-pI.....77.3:2 | promised f. release from the world you |
| W-pI.....93.6:6 | The self you made, evil and f. of sin, is |
| W-pI...96.11:4 | and it will yet be yours in f. awareness. |
| W-pI.....98.6:1 | your f. release from pain of every kind, |
| W-pI... 105.2:2 | return; a loan with interest to be paid in f. |
| W-pI... 121.2:1 | The unforgiving mind is f. of fear, and |
| W-pI. 121.13:7 | *dream that I am mortal, fallible and f. of sin,* |
| W-pI... 135.1:2 | folly of defense; it gives illusions f. reality, |
| W-pI. 155.12:3 | effort, of your love and of your f. intent? |
| W-pI... 185.1:4 | be completely given back to f. awareness, |
| W-pI... 193.1:2 | expanding in the joy of f. creation, and |
| W-pI... 193.6:4 | you hold these words in f. awareness, and |
| W-pI... 196.1:1 | understood and kept in f. awareness, you |
| W-pI... 199.7:6 | that finds its f. accomplishment in God. |
| W-pII ....in.6:5 | take that world to be the f. replacement of |
| W-pII . 225.1:2 | *return it, for I want it mine in f. awareness,* |
| W-pII . 284.1:8 | arrive at f. acceptance of the truth in them |
| W-pII . 316.1:4 | My treasure house is f., and angels watch |
| M-4 ..... I.A.8:4 | consistency of thought and f. transfer. |
| M-4 ...... IX.2:3 | Being unswerving, it is f. of trust. Being |
| M-6 ........... 4:9 | if one gift is missing, it would not be f.. |
| M-12 ......... 6:4 | with f. awareness of their consequences. |

## fullness 8

*See also* Self-fullness

| | |
|---|---|
| T-1.........I.34:1 | Miracles restore the mind to its f.. By |
| T-7........ IX.1:7 | it knows its f. and cannot conceive of any |
| T-7........ IX.2:2 | of its Creator is therefore spirit's own f., |
| T-7........ IX.3:2 | Its f. cannot be contained, any more than |
| T-7........ IX.3:2 | any more than can the f. of its Creator. |
| T-7........ IX.3:3 | F. is extension. The ego's whole thought |
| T-7........ IX.4:4 | A split mind cannot perceive its f., and |
| M-6 ......... 4:10 | full. Yet is its f. guaranteed by God. What |

## fully 64

| | |
|---|---|
| T-1......... V.3:4 | means that unless you f. recognize your |
| T-2...........I.1:3 | You have not only been f. created, but |
| T-2......... V.1:1 | that they f. understand the fear of release. |
| T-2......... VI.9:3 | no one remains f. aware of it all the time. |
| T-2......... VI.9:4 | things you must realize, and realize f.. |
| T-2.......VII.7:6 | cannot develop f. until mastery has been |
| T-4........ III.2:3 | find it very helpful if you understand it f.. |
| T-4........ III.3:7 | of this can ever f. believe in the ego again. |
| T-4.......VII.6:7 | created do not communicate f. with Him. |
| T-5.......VII.6:4 | yourself f. aware that the undoing process |
| T-5.......VII.6:6 | will respond f. to your slightest invitation: |
| T-6...........I.3:5 | and must be f. understood *as* impossible. |
| T-6........ III.3:2 | Once it can accept this f., it sees no need |
| T-6........ IV.3:1 | until you f. understand the basic fact that |
| T-6...... V.C.7:7 | go beyond belief until you believe f.. |
| T-7...........I.1:2 | You communicate f. with God, as He does |
| T-7.........I.7:15 | is f. shared be withheld and then revealed |
| T-7........ VI.9:6 | this totally, being f. committed to it. It is |
| T-7......VIII.2:1 | use of projection must be f. understood |
| T-8...........I.6:1 | a curriculum must be f. recognized before |
| T-8........ III.2:1 | only joy and peace that can be f. known, |
| T-8........ III.2:1 | only function that can be f. experienced. |
| T-8........ III.6:8 | you enter f. will teach you this is not so. |
| T-12.........I.3:8 | to your own mind is not yet f. apparent. If |
| T-12....... III.6:5 | f. aware of anxiety he does not perceive its |
| T-12...VII.13:2 | for it f. believes that you are a criminal, as |
| T-13.......I.10:3 | being f. committed to the insane notion |
| T-13........II.6:3 | as the final guilt that f. justifies murder. |
| T-14.... XI.13:4 | you f. realize that you know not, peace |
| T-15..... VII.1:3 | love that is f. given and fully returned. |
| T-15..... VII.1:3 | love that is fully given and f. returned. |
| T-17....... III.7:9 | be sure you f. realize what you have made |
| T-17....VIII.5:5 | and you are now f. responsible to him. |
| T-18..VIII.12:1 | and entered f. at your weak request. You |
| T-18...... IX.1:4 | The rest is f. in God's keeping, and needs |
| T-19.........I.9:6 | in that one you see your faith is f. justified |
| T-24.... VI.11:4 | furious, with anger always f. justified, you |
| T-25...... III.3:6 | perception; not one but can be f. justified. |
| T-27....... III.4:1 | of time not seen as spent and f. occupied, |
| T-30....... V.2:3 | of pursuing guilt as goal is f. recognized. |
| T-30....... VI.3:3 | of forgiveness is quite real and f. justified. |
| T-31...... VI.6:8 | is seen as stable, f. worthy of your trust; a |
| W-pI.....47.6:2 | in your real strength is f. justified in every |
| W-pI.....67.1:6 | this truth about you, and to realize f., if |
| W-pI.....68.1:5 | Perhaps you do not yet f. realize just what |
| W-pI.....77.7:6 | f. entitled to receive it whenever you ask. |

W-pI...91.10:1 are f. supported by the strength of God
W-pI.132.16:2 you may not f. understand as yet that you
W-pI.136.18:3 body's health is f. guaranteed, because it
W-pI...137.6:4 be seen and justified and f. understood.
WpI. rIV.in2:5 thought that f. guarantees salvation to the
WpI. rIV.in5:2 and let this thought alone engage it f.,
W-pI.153.10:4 surer that his happiness is f. guaranteed?
W-pI...169.9:3 and f. recognized as perfectly fulfilled by
W-pI.169.10:2 comes, it will be known and f. understood
W-pI...185.1:4 resurrection of all creation f. recognized.
W-pI...197.2:4 and claimed, and found and f. recognized
W-pII ....in.5:2 all ancient promises upheld and f. kept.
M-4 ..... I.A.8:5 for here is Heaven's state f. reflected.
M-4 ...... VI.1:6 until he f. understands that defenses are
M-10 ......... 3:3 rightly, one would have to be f. aware of
P-2...... IV.10:6 the belief that guilt is real and f. justified.
S-1 ...........I.5:3 being f. entitled to everything Love has to
S-1 ......... II.7:5 in Christ is f. recognized as set forever,

## function 460

T-1........ IV.2:7 the proper f. of the mind and corrects its
T-1........ VI.3:2 effectively while you f. on different levels.
T-2............ V.h The F. of the Miracle Worker
T-2.......... V.1:1 ready to undertake their f. in this world, it
T-3........ IV.5:6 to its proper f. only when it wills to know.
T-3........ IV.6:3 The interpretative f. of perception, a
T-3......... V.6:8 is your Source and your only real f..
T-4...........I.9:4 peace because you are not fulfilling your f.
T-4...........I.9:5 God gave you a very lofty f. that you are
T-4......... II.4:8 are. Belief is an ego f., and as long as your
T-4......... V.6:2 is the one f. the ego has tried to develop,
T-4......... VI.8:6 God. That is because the f. of love is one.
T-4..... VII.3:11 The mind can distort its f., but it cannot
T-5...........I.4:1 of the Holy Trinity that has a symbolic f..
T-5...........I.4:5 symbolic f. makes the Holy Spirit difficult
T-5........ III.7:4 perform the f. of reinterpreting what the
T-5....... V.6:15 The f. of thought comes from God and is
T-5...... VI.12:6 because it is His special f. to return you to
T-7........ III.5:5 His sole f. is to undo the questionable and
T-7...... VI.13:1 fulfilling your f. as co-creator with God,
T-7........ IX.3:1 extension of God's Being is spirit's only f..
T-7........ IX.3:4 extension, and thus blocks your only f.. It
T-7........ IX.4:8 Spirit is fulfilling its f., and only complete
T-7......... X.2:2 f. God Himself gave your mind through
T-7......... X.3:5 Holy Spirit's main f. is to teach you to tell
T-7......... XI.2:2 natural environment and does not f. well.
T-8........ III.1:7 Understanding His f. perfectly He fulfills
T-8........ III.2:1 is the only f. that can be fully experienced.
T-8........ III.3:5 You who belong in God have the holy f. of
T-8........ III.8:4 Giving of yourself is the f. He gave you.
T-8...... IV.8:12 place in It and fulfill your f. as part of It,
T-8...... VI.5:11 You made neither yourself nor your f..
T-8........ VI.6:1 f. is to add to God's treasure by creating
T-8........ VI.6:7 not accept his f. can understand what it is
T-8........ VI.6:7 no one can accept his f. unless he knows
T-8........ VI.7:7 choice does make the Son's f. unknown to
T-8........ VI.8:4 Our f. is to work together, because apart
T-8........ VI.8:4 apart from each other we cannot f. at all.
T-8....... VII.3:6 renders God on behalf of the f. He gives it
T-8..... VII.12:8 because only extension is the mind's f..
T-8...... VIII.1:3 what it sees with the f. it ascribes to it. It
T-8...... VIII.1:8 lies solely in your interpretation of its f..
T-8...... VIII.4:7 that judgment is the f. of the Holy Spirit,
T-8...... VIII.5:1 is still true that the body has no f. of itself,
T-8...... VIII.5:2 because, as such, its true f. is obscured.
T-8...... VIII.5:4 aim is to lose sight of the f. of everything.
T-8...... VIII.6:7 f. of truth is to collect information that is
T-8...... VIII.9:3 Everything used in accordance with its f.
T-8........ IX.5:4 His f. is to distinguish only between the
T-9...........I.4:2 I said that the Holy Spirit's f. is to sort out
T-9........ III.8:2 Do not undertake His f., or you will forget
T-9........ III.8:3 Accept only the f. of healing in time,
T-9........ III.8:4 God gave you the f. to create in eternity.
T-9........ IV.6:1 forgiveness is His f. and He knows how to
T-9........ IV.6:4 is. His work is not your f., and unless you
T-9........ IV.6:4 this you cannot learn what your f. is.
T-9......... V.8:6 You can only let Him fulfill His f.. He
T-9....... V.8:11 Trust Him, for help is His f., and He is of
T-11 ........I.6:5 He creates has the f. of creating. Love
T-11 ....... II.6:1 rest until you know your f. and fulfill it,
T-11 ....... II.6:3 God, for His f. became yours with His gift
T-11 ...... V.6:2 whole creative f. lies in your complete
T-11 ...... V.6:2 on God, Whose f. He shares with you. By
T-11 ..... V.12:2 and fulfilling your f. as it exists in truth.
T-11 ..... V.12:4 is given you to know that God's f. is yours
T-12 .... VII.4:6 Holy Spirit's work, for you share in His f..
T-12 .... VII.4:7 As your f. in Heaven is creation, so your
T-12 .... VII.4:7 is creation, so your f. on earth is healing.
T-12 .... VII.4:8 God shares His f. with you in Heaven, and
T-12 .. VII.12:5 will be wrong, for judgment is not your f..
T-12 .. VII.12:6 Spirit it will be right, for judgment *is* His f.
T-12 .. VII.12:7 share His f. only by judging as He does,
T-12 . VIII.7:11 the f. of love to unite all things unto itself,
T-13 ........ IV.h The F. of Time
T-13 ..... IV.1:3 told that your f. in this world is healing,
T-13 ..... IV.1:3 healing, and your f. in Heaven is creating.
T-13 ..... IV.1:4 that your f. on earth is destruction, and
T-13 ..... IV.1:4 and you have no f. at all in Heaven. It
T-13 ..... IV.7:4 He regards the f. of time as temporary,
T-13 ..... IV.7:4 as temporary, serving only His teaching f.
T-13 ..... IV.8:1 regards the f. of time as one of extending
T-13 ..... IV.9:1 the f. of time as you interpret yours. If you
T-13 ..... IV.9:2 accept your f. in the world of time as one
T-13 ..... IV.9:6 But if you interpret your f. as destruction,
T-13 ... VIII.3:6 miracle, without a f. in Heaven, is needful
T-13 ... VIII.4:1 and the Son, the Holy Spirit has no f.. He
T-14 ..... III.1:4 not salvation, and serves no useful f. at all
T-14 ........ IV.h Your F. in the Atonement
T-14 ..... IV.3:7 it. On earth this is your only f., and you
T-14 ..... IV.3:9 your f. in God's Mind with all of yours.
T-14 ... IV.3:10 this guilt by failing to fulfill your f. here?
T-14 ... IV.4:10 Fail not in your f. of loving in a loveless
T-14 ..... IV.5:1 have decided against your f. in Heaven,
T-14 ..... IV.5:2 f. here is only to decide against deciding
T-14 ..... IV.5:4 for God, and for your f. as He knows it. So
T-14 ...... V.2:3 that his true f. remains unfulfilled in him.
T-14 ..... VI.8:1 Holy Spirit's f. is entirely communication.
T-14 ..... IX.1:4 the ego to God, is the Holy Spirit's only f..
T-14 ....... X.2:6 The miracle, therefore, has a unique f.,
T-14 ....... X.5:9 Therefore it is not your f., but the Holy
T-15 ........ I.1:4 not fulfilled His teaching f. until you have
T-15 ..... III.3:5 For your f. is not little, and it is only by
T-15 ..... III.3:5 it is only by finding your f. and fulfilling it
T-15 ..... III.4:1 There is no doubt about what your f. is,
T-15 ...... V.4:5 In His f. as Interpreter of what you made,
T-15 .. VII.13:2 Holy Spirit's teaching f. to instruct those
T-15 .. VII.14:3 to disrupt communication, has no f. here.
T-15 ... VIII.6:2 It is His holy f. to accept them both, and
T-15 ... VIII.6:3 He will do this because it is His f.. Leave,
T-15 ....... X.1:4 it is the Holy Spirit's f. to use them both,
T-16 ........ I.7:4 them all to Him Whose f. is to meet them.
T-16 ........ I.7:5 That is His f., and not yours. He will not
T-16 ........ I.7:9 it. Leave Him His f., for He will fulfill it if
T-17 ....... II.4:2 has been used for learning will have no f..
T-17 ..... IV.1:2 God ascribed to anything is its only f..
T-17 ..... IV.1:3 the f. of relationships became forever "to
T-17 ..... IV.1:5 fulfill this f. you relate to your creations as
T-17 ..... IV.1:7 Whatever does not fulfill this f. cannot be
T-17 ..... IV.2:4 restore to them the f. given them by God.
T-17 ..... IV.2:5 The f. you have given them is clearly not
T-18 ...... I.13:1 to the most holy f. this world contains. It
T-18 ..... III.7:1 of salvation have the f. of bringing light to
T-18 ..... IV.6:6 yourself to Him Whose f. is release. Do
T-18 ..... IV.6:7 Do not assume His f. for Him. Give Him
T-18 ...... V.2:2 That is *its* f.. Never attempt to overlook
T-18 ...... V.2:4 That is *His* f.. Your part is only to offer
T-18 ...... V.3:3 could you prepare yourself for such a f.?
T-18 ...... V.5:4 the Holy Spirit, Who *has* a special f. here.
T-18 ...... V.5:6 Let Him fulfill the f. that He gave to your
T-18 ..... VI.4:6 clearly can misperceive the f. of the body,
T-18 ..... VI.4:6 it cannot change its f. from what the Holy
T-19 ..... IV.3:6 Holy Spirit's f. here will be accomplished.
T-20 ..... IV.5:3 whose special f. here is to release him,
T-20 ..... IV.6:6 learn its special f. in the Holy Spirit's plan
T-20 ..... IV.8:4 plan as the one f. that you would fulfill,
T-20 ...... V.1:3 And there he finds his f. of restoring his
T-20 ...... V.5:2 only as the Holy Spirit teaches, it has no f.
T-21 .......... V.h The F. of Reason
T-22 ....... II.8:5 Whose f. is to save, will save. *How* He will
T-22 ..... II.11:8 the f. of an executioner you gave him for
T-22 ..... IV.7:4 Such is the f. of a holy relationship; to
T-22 ..... VI.8:4 For you have asked what is your f. here,
T-22 ..... VI.9:2 of forgiveness is the Holy Spirit's f.. Leave
T-22 ... VI.14:1 This is the f. of your holy relationship.
T-23 ....... II.8:7 That is the f. of this course, which does
T-23 ..... II.14:3 the f. of insanity to take the place of truth.
T-23 ..... II.16:3 how it appears to f. many times before. In
T-23 ..... II.16:4 In truth it does not f., yet in dreams,
T-23 ..... IV.3:1 God does not share His f. with a body. He
T-23 ..... IV.3:2 gave the f. to create unto His Son because
T-23 ..... IV.3:3 to believe the f. of the Son is murder, but
T-23 ..... IV.3:4 What is the same can have no different f..
T-23 ..... IV.4:2 yet assume the holy f. God gave His Son,
T-24 ....... II.2:5 You have a f. in salvation. Its pursuit will
T-24 ....... II.7:1 and the f. of salvation given him for you.
T-24 ....... II.7:2 Nor will you change his f., any more than
T-24 ..... VI.9:3 Futility of f. not fulfilled will haunt you
T-24 ... VI.11:1 is the f. that you gave yourself. It stands
T-25 ........ I.6:4 It is the Holy Spirit's f. to teach you how
T-25 ....... II.8:7 still your only f. to behold in him what he
T-25 ....... V.4:8 If you decide against his proper f., the
T-25 ....... V.5:2 To let his f. be fulfilled is but the means to
T-25 ....... V.5:8 so do you define the f. he will have for you
T-25 ........ VI.h The Special F.
T-25 ..... VI.3:5 remain without the f. that He gave to him.
T-25 ..... VI.3:6 who see no f. in the world for them to fill;
T-25 ..... VI.4:2 a special f. in salvation he alone can fill; a
T-25 ..... VI.4:3 plan complete until he finds his special f.,
T-25 ..... VI.5:3 is the only f. meaningful in time. It is the
T-25 ..... VI.5:6 every f. of this world completed with it.
T-25 ..... VI.7:1 The Holy Spirit needs your special f., that
T-25 ..... VI.7:7 you see it as your special f. in the plan to
T-25 ..... VI.7:8 This is the f. given you for your brother.
T-25 .... VII.7:1 special f. is the special form in which the
T-25 .... VII.9:2 all. To each his special f. is designed to be
T-25 .... VII.9:6 without a special f. in the hope of peace,
T-25 .. VII.10:5 Accept the f. that has been assigned to
T-25 .. VII.12:7 plan in which your special f. has a part.
T-25 .. VII.12:8 For here your special f. is made whole,
T-25 .. VII.12:8 because it shares the f. of the whole.
T-25 ... VIII.9:6 It is His special f. to hold out to you the
T-25 . VIII.11:5 Each special f. He allots is but for this;
T-25 . VIII.12:5 Your special f. is a call to Him, that He
T-25 . VIII.12:7 Holy Spirit's special f. has been fulfilled.
T-25 . VIII.14:3 Your special f. shows you nothing else but
T-26 ........ I.5:2 Without your special f. has this world no
T-26 ........ I.8:4 special f. to ensure the door be opened,
T-26 ........ I.8:5 What is the Holy Spirit's special f. but to
T-26 ........ I.8:6 Could your f. be a task apart and separate
T-26 ....... II.6:5 Consider once again your special f.. One
T-26 ....... II.8:4 special f. opens wide the door beyond
T-26 ..... III.7:1 Is not this like your special f., where the
T-26 ..... IV.1:8 is he returned to his real f. of creating,
T-26 .... VII.8:5 Forgiveness is the only f. here, and serves
T-26 .. VII.11:5 miracle by which creation became your f.,
T-26 ....... X.5:7 without the f. that the Holy Spirit sees.
T-27 ........ I.9:1 f. is to show your brother sin can have no
T-27 ........ I.9:2 the proof that what your f. is can never be
T-27 ...... I.9:10 that it may fulfill the f. that it will receive.
T-27 ...... I.11:5 you made to hide your f. from yourself.
T-27 ...... I.11:6 hide the f. that the Holy Spirit gave. Let,
T-27 ...... I.11:7 its purpose and your f. both be reconciled
T-27 ..... II.10:1 Correction is not your f.. It belongs to
T-27 ..... II.10:3 role, you lose the f. of forgiveness. No one
T-27 ..... II.10:6 Identity and f. are the same, and by your
T-27 ..... II.10:6 and by your f. do you know yourself. And
T-27 ..... II.10:7 your f. with the function of Another, you
T-27 ..... II.10:7 your function with the f. of Another, you
T-27 ..... II.10:8 God's f. from Him and deny that it is His?
T-27 ..... II.11:2 can anyone perceive a f. unified which has
T-27 ..... II.11:5 This splits his f. off from yours, and gives
T-27 ..... II.11:6 with a single f. that would mean a shared
T-27 ..... II.12:1 because that is the f. given it *by* you. When
T-27 ..... II.12:6 Thus does your f. seem divided, with a
T-27 ..... II.13:2 necessary view of f. split between the two.
T-27 ..... II.14:7 does by giving you and him a f. that is one

T-27..... II.15:1 Correction is the f. given both, but
T-27..... II.15:5 He will not fulfill a f. that He does not see
T-27..... II.15:6 Your separate views of what your f. is. If
T-27..... II.15:7 is. If He upheld divided f., you were lost
T-27..... II.15:8 from the awareness of a f. not your own.
T-27..... II.16:3 and conceives a single f. as its only one.
T-27..... II.16:4 is the f. given it conceived to be its Own,
T-27..... II.16:5 In His acceptance of this f. lies the means
T-27...... III.7:3 There is no choice of f. anywhere. The
T-27...... VI.4:5 what it should feel and what its f. is. Yet
T-27...... VI.8:4 What better f. could you serve than this?
T-28....... II.9:3 in giving back to cause the f. of causation,
T-28..... II.11:2 the f. of causation is to have effects. And
T-28...... IV.8:1 The Holy Spirit's f. is to take the broken
T-28....... V.6:1 because it shares the f. all creation shares.
T-29....... II.3:2 to serve the f. of retaining sin and pain.
T-29...... IV.3:1 said attack is a response to f. unfulfilled as
T-29...... IV.3:1 function unfulfilled as you perceive the f..
T-29...... IV.4:1 has failed to fill the f. you allotted him?
T-29...... IV.4:8 represents some f. that you have assigned;
T-29...... IV.5:6 to help, if this becomes the f. of the dream
T-29...... IV.6:2 know, because your f. is obscure to you.
T-29...... IV.6:5 help to give him if you see the f. of the
T-29...... IV.6:5 of the dream as He perceives its f., Who
T-29...... IV.6:5 dreams as means to serve the f. given Him
T-29....... V.4:2 in him, and let It tell you what his f. is. He
T-29....... V.7:4 the Holy Spirit gives the dream its f., it
T-29....... V.8:1 Him Who sees a different f. for a dream.
T-29....... V.8:2 they lose the f. of attack and separation,
T-29...... VI.4:3 because your f. has been fixed by God. All
T-29...... VI.4:7 the f. God established for His Son in full
T-29...... VI.4:9 share the f. their Creator gave to them.
T-29.... VI.4:10 Life's f. cannot be to die. It must be life's
T-30...... III.5:1 Completion is the *f.* of God's Son. He has
T-31....... II.4:5 fulfilled the f. that was given him by you.
T-31..... VII.6:1 you hold would guarantee your f. here
T-31..... VII.6:4 it serve the f. given you to bring you peace
W-pI..... 15.1:4 is the f. you have given your body's eyes.
W-pI..... 37.1:1 glimmerings of your true f. in the world,
W-pI..... 43.1:6 That is its f. as the Holy Spirit sees it.
W-pI..... 43.1:7 sees it. Therefore, that is its f. in truth.
W-pI..... 43.2:2 Perception has no f. in God, and does not
W-pI..... 43.9:2 idea, and thus remembering your f..
W-pI..... 61.2:4 world if that is the f. God assigned to you.
W-pI..... 61.2:5 that would assert this f. cannot be for you
W-pI..... 61.3:2 step in accepting your real f. on earth. It is
W-pI..... 61.5:4 *That is my only f.. That is why I am here.*
W-pI..... 61.6:2 your f. and your only purpose here. These
W-pI........ 62.h Forgiveness is my f. as the light of the
W-pI..... 62.5:2 *Forgiveness is my f. as the light of the world. I*
W-pI..... 62.5:3 *I would fulfill my f. that I may be happy.*
W-pI..... 62.5:4 to considering your f. and the happiness
W-pI..... 63.2:1 the light of the world with such a f.. The
W-pI..... 63.2:4 you will forget your f. and leave the Son of
W-pI..... 63.3:1 Recognizing the importance of this f., we
W-pI........ 64.h Let me not forget my f..
W-pI..... 64.1:2 you see is to obscure your f. of forgiveness
W-pI..... 64.3:1 your f. here is to be the light of the world,
W-pI..... 64.3:1 light of the world, a f. given you by God.
W-pI..... 64.4:1 the f. given you by God will you be happy.
W-pI..... 64.4:2 That is because your f. is to be happy by
W-pI..... 64.4:4 choose whether or not to fulfill your f.,
W-pI..... 64.6:2 *Let me not forget my f.. Let me not try to*
W-pI..... 64.6:6 importance of your f. to you and to the
W-pI..... 64.7:3 my f." quite often to help you concentrate
W-pI..... 64.8:4 yourself: *This is the world it is my f. to save.*
W-pI........ 65.h My only f. is the one God gave me.
W-pI..... 65.1:2 you that you have no f. other than that.
W-pI..... 65.1:5 your only f. necessarily entails two phases
W-pI..... 65.1:5 the recognition of salvation as your f.,
W-pI..... 65.2:2 mean, "My only f. is the one God gave me
W-pI..... 65.5:6 *is preventing me from accepting my only f..*
W-pI..... 65.6:4 *clean slate let my true f. be written for me.*
W-pI..... 65.8:2 *My only f. is the one God gave me. I want no*
W-pI........ 66.h My happiness and my f. are one.
W-pI..... 66.1:1 fulfilling your f. and achieving happiness.
W-pI..... 66.2:1 fundamental question of what your f. is.
W-pI..... 66.2:5 He knows what your f. is. He knows that
W-pI..... 66.3:1 battle and arrive at the truth about your f.

W-pI..... 66.4:1 the f. God gave you and your happiness,
W-pI..... 66.4:3 the f. He gave you must be happiness,
W-pI..... 66.5:3 *He has given my f. to me. Therefore my*
W-pI..... 66.5:4 *Therefore my f. must be happiness.* Try to
W-pI..... 66.7:1 premise is that God has given you your f..
W-pI..... 66.8:1 must be that your f. is established by God
W-pI..... 66.8:3 Unless God gave your f. to you, it must be
W-pI..... 66.9:2 illusion of your f. has taken in your mind,
W-pI... 66.11:2 *My happiness and f. are one, because God*
W-pI..... 69.3:3 purpose here, and no other f. to fulfill.
WpI..rII.in.5:4 each day not to leave your f. unfulfilled.
W-pI..... 81.1:2 been given the f. of lighting up the world!
W-pI..... 81.3:1 (62) Forgiveness is my f. as the light of
W-pI..... 81.3:2 my f. that I will see the light in me. And in
W-pI..... 81.3:3 And in this light will my f. stand clear and
W-pI..... 81.3:4 depend on my recognizing what my f. is,
W-pI..... 81.4:3 *Let me not separate my f. from my will. I will*
W-pI..... 82.3:1 (64) Let me not forget my f.. I would not
W-pI..... 82.3:2 I would not forget my f., because I would
W-pI..... 82.3:3 Self. I cannot fulfill my f. if I forget it. And
W-pI..... 82.3:4 it. And unless I fulfill my f., I will not
W-pI..... 82.4:2 *Let me not use this to hide my f. from me. I*
W-pI..... 82.4:3 *use this as an opportunity to fulfill my f..*
W-pI..... 82.4:4 *my ego, but cannot change my f. in any way.*
W-pI..... 83.1:1 (65) My only f. is the one God gave me. I
W-pI..... 83.1:2 me. I have no f. but the one God gave me.
W-pI..... 83.1:5 that my only f. is the one God gave me.
W-pI..... 83.2:2 *My perception of this does not change my f..*
W-pI..... 83.2:3 *give me a f. other than the one God gave me.*
W-pI..... 83.2:4 *not use this to justify a f. God did not give me.*
W-pI..... 83.3:1 (66) My happiness and my f. are one. All
W-pI..... 83.3:4 Fulfilling my f. is my happiness because
W-pI..... 83.4:2 *cannot separate my happiness from my f..*
W-pI..... 83.4:3 *and my f. remains wholly unaffected by this.*
W-pI..... 83.4:4 *the illusion of happiness apart from my f..*
W-pI..... 89.1:5 that I may use it on behalf of the f. He has
W-pI..... 96.4:3 spirit, and it is fulfilling happily its f. here.
W-pI..... 96.4:5 Without its f. then it has no peace, and
W-pI..... 96.5:3 Dissociated from its f. now, it thinks it is
W-pI... 96.10:1 has found the f. that it sought to lose.
W-pI..... 97.2:3 Himself, and shares His f. as Creator. He
W-pI..... 98.3:4 they know their f. will be filled completely
W-pI..... 98.5:2 hourly to recognize your special f. here? Is
W-pI..... 98.9:2 enable you to understand your special f..
W-pI..... 98.9:5 then of Him Who knows the f. that you
W-pI........ 99.h Salvation is my only f. here.
W-pI..... 99.6:3 This is the Thought whose f. is to save by
W-pI..... 99.6:3 is to save by giving you its f. as your own.
W-pI..... 99.6:4 own. Salvation is your f., with the One to
W-pI..... 99.6:7 *Salvation is my only f. here. God still is Love,*
W-pI..... 99.9:6 *Salvation is my only f. here. Salvation and*
W-pI..... 99.9:8 turn to Him Who shares your f. here, and
W-pI... 99.10:4 You have no f. that is not of God. Forgive
W-pI... 99.11:3 *Salvation is my only f. here. God still is Love,*
W-pI... 99.12:1 only f. tells you you are one. Remind
W-pI... 99.12:4 *Salvation is my only f. here.* Thus do you lay
W-pI... 100.1:3 One f. shared by separate minds unites
W-pI... 100.2:6 They will see their f. in your shining face,
W-pI... 100.6:1 attempt to understand joy is our f. here. If
W-pI... 100.8:2 It is your f. that you find it here, and that
W-pI... 102.4:2 *for me, and I accept it as my f. now.* Then
W-pI... 102.4:3 Then seek this f. deep within your mind,
W-pI... 102.5:1 happy, for your only f. here is happiness.
W-pI... 102.5:3 now accepted happiness as your one f..
W-pI... 106.6:3 will learn your f. from the One Who chose
W-pI... 107.9:2 make your pledge to let His f. be fulfilled
W-pI... 107.9:3 you. To share His f. is to share His joy. His
W-pI. 107.11:1 Do not forget your f. for today. Each time
W-pI... 114.2:2 *can my f. be but to accept the Word of God,*
W-pI... 115.1:1 (99) Salvation is my only f. here. *My*
W-pI... 115.1:2 *My f. here is to forgive the world for all the*
W-pI... 115.3:2 Salvation is my only f. here. On the half
W-pI... 123.3:4 Be glad you have a f. in salvation to fulfill.
W-pI. 135.13:4 the mind employs for this will f. flawlessly
W-pI. 135.25:6 your f. from the Voice for God Himself?
W-pI... 137.6:1 not healing is unworthy of your f. here.
W-pI. 137.13:1 strikes, our f. is to let our minds be healed
W-pI. 137.15:4 Nor will we let this f. be forgot as every
W-pI... 153.8:2 foolishness the endless joy our f. offers us.

W-pI. 153.11:1 It is the f. of God's ministers to help their
W-pI... 154.1:4 off, and to delay commitment to our f.. It
W-pI... 154.2:1 God, Whose f. is to speak for you as well.
W-pI... 154.3:2 And that one Voice appoints your f., and
W-pI. 154.14:3 minds about ourselves, and what our f. is.
W-pI... 184.9:1 yet were asked to take a teaching f.. You
W-pI... 186.1:2 which holds no f. as your own but that
W-pI... 186.2:1 Let us not fight our f.. We did not
W-pI... 186.4:2 doubt our adequacy for the f. He will offer
W-pI... 186.8:2 We will accept the f. God has given us, for
W-pI. 186.10:1 serene, when you accept the f. given you.
W-pI. 186.11:1 truly given f. stands out clear and wholly
W-pI. 186.12:6 tells you of a f. given you by your Creator
W-pI. 186.14:4 this form you can fulfill your f. even here,
W-pI. 186.14:6 you who can forgive. Such is your f. here.
W-pI...... 192.h I have a f. God would have me fill.
W-pI... 192.1:2 can such a f. mean within a world of envy,
W-pI... 192.2:1 you have a f. in the world in its own terms
W-pI... 192.2:3 Forgiveness represents your f. here. It is
W-pI. 192.10:6 f. here on earth is only to forgive him,
W-pI... 195.6:2 nor impair or change our f. to complete
W-pI... 197.9:7 when you forgot the f. God has given you.
W-pI... 200.6:2 In truth it has no f., and does nothing. For
W-pI... 200.6:4 and where it must serve a mighty f.. Is not
WpI rVI.in.3:7 have a f. that transcends the world we see.
W-pI... 205.1:3 *end I seek, my purpose and my f. and my life,*
W-pI... 212.1:1 (192) I have a f. God would have me fill. *I*
W-pI... 212.1:2 *the f. that would set me free from all the vain*
W-pI... 212.1:3 *world. Only the f. God has given me can offer*
W-pII..... 1.5:2 has forgiven you already, for such is His f.
W-pII..... 1.5:3 Now must you share His f., and forgive
W-pII..... 3.5:3 And let us not attempt to change our f..
W-pII. 257.1:3 Nor can he f. without deep distress and
W-pII. 270.1:6 *Yours. His f. now is but Your Own, and every*
W-pII..... 7.5:4 refuse to take the f. of completing God,
W-pII... 10.2:3 and now without a f. in Christ's sight, it
W-pII... 11.4:6 our f. be only to let this memory return,
W-pII. 330.1:1 this day accept forgiveness as our only f..
W-pII... 13.1:4 nor exceed the f. of forgiveness. Thus it
W-pII. 343.1:9 *complete, having the f. of completing You. I*
W-pII... 14.2:5 Yet we can realize our f. here, and words
W-pII... 14.3:5 seek a f. that is past the gate of Heaven.
Wfl........ in.3:1 all our thoughts to serve the f. of salvation
Wfl........ in.4:1 It is our f. to remember Him on earth, as
M-1......... 2:11 Their f. is to save time. Each one begins as
M-4......... I.1:1 which their ability to fulfill their f. rests.
M-4...... IV.1:8 obliterates his f. from his awareness. It
M-4...... IV.2:2 this that the f. of salvation becomes easy.
M-4....... X.3:6 It is the f. of God's teachers to bring true
M-5......... III.h The F. of the Teacher of God
M-5...... III.1:4 he has no f. except to rejoice with them,
M-5...... III.1:5 a more specific f. for those who do not
M-5...... III.3:9 And this is the f. of God's teachers; to see
M-6........... 3:1 not the f. of God's teachers to evaluate the
M-6........... 3:2 It is merely their f. to give them. Once
M-12......... 4:2 that the body's f. is but to let God's Voice
M-12....... 5:10 his role, just as It tells him what his f. is.
M-12......... 6:6 of dreaming is the real f. of God's teachers
M-14......... 4:4 f. of the teacher of God in this concluding
M-14......... 5:9 hell into Heaven is the f. of God's teachers
M-15......... 2:5 is your f. to prepare yourself to hear this
M-15....... 3:10 It is your f. to make that end be soon. It is
M-15....... 3:11 It is your f. to hold it to your heart, and
M-16....... 11:4 f. to make sure that they have learned it.
M-22....... 1:10 the Atonement for himself as his only f..
M-22......... 2:3 the f. God has given him long before he
M-22......... 6:8 It is your f. to recognize for him that what
M-26......... 4:2 It is your f. to escape from them, but not
M-28......... 1:6 having no f. except communication. It is
M-28......... 6:5 by, and given Him Whose f. judgment is.
M-29......... 2:9 To do so is His f.. To refer the questions
M-29......... 3:8 To return the f. to the One to Whom it
C-in........... 3:9 It has one f. and one goal. Only in that
C-6............. 3:2 In order to fulfill this special f. the Holy
C-6............. 3:2 the Holy Spirit has assumed a dual f.. He
P-2......... in.1:3 That is not its f.. If it can make way for
P-2......... in.1:5 Its whole f., in the end, is to help the
P-2...... IV.10:7 the psychotherapist's f. to teach that guilt
P-2....... VII.4:3 devoting his life to the f. of true healing.

P-2 VII.5:4 a f. presupposes a knowledge that no one
P-2 VII.6:1 as insane not to accept a f. God has given
P-3 II.1:4 of one sort or another as their chief f..
P-3 II.9:3 to assume a f. that has not been given him
P-3 III.8:4 door to your salvation, for such is His f..
P-3 III.8:5 will also tell you exactly what your f. is in
S-2 III.5:8 Do not confuse His f. with your own. He

**functioning** 5

T-2 V.4:3 working inclinations are not f. properly,
T-10 IV.3:7 wrongly, you perceive it as f. wrongly.
T-27 II.16:3 f. as one because it is not split in purpose,
M-4 1:3 stages of their f. as teachers of God, have
S-3 II.1:10 the end has come for usefulness of body f.

**functionless** 4

T-22 VI.1:7 entirely when they are recognized as f..
T-27 III.5:8 its aim has been accomplished it is f.. Yet
W-pII .294.1:9 It is but f., unneeded and cast off. Let me
C-6 5:3 the Helper of God's Son for he alone is f..

**functions** 17

T-3 IV.1:2 All of your present f. are divided and
T-4 VII.3:11 endow itself with f. it was not given. That
T-5 V.5:9 usurp all the f. of God as it perceives them
T-8 VII.9:2 as fragmented into many f. with little or
T-8 VIII.1:9 F. are part of being since they arise from
T-9 IV.7:1 The confusion of f. is so typical of the ego
T-9 IV.7:2 The ego believes that all f. belong to it,
T-12 VII.4:9 As long as you believe you have other f.,
T-16 III.3:6 and do not recognize It even though It f..
T-16 III.3:7 What f. must be there. And it is only if
T-29 IV.4:3 the f. you have given have been filled; the
W-pI 49.1:3 the other part of your mind that f. in the
W-pI 135.6:4 gave the body all the f. that you see in it,
W-pI 184.2:4 a unity which f. with an independent will.
W-pI.186.10:4 The f. which the world esteems are so
M-28 1:6 is the dream in which the body f. perfectly
M-29 3:6 of f. not your own is the basis of fear. The

**fundamental** 45

T-1 VI.2:3 arose because, having made this f. error,
T-2 I.1:1 is a f. aspect of God which He gave to His
T-2 IV.2:6 create, and the belief that it can, a f. error,
T-2 V.A.12:2 forms of healing rest on this f. correction
T-2 VI.4:7 does not matter, but the f. error does. The
T-2 VII.1:4 of cause and effect; the most f. law there is
T-2 VII.3:13 f. conflict in this world, then, is between
T-2 VII.7:7 the f. error that fear can be mastered, and
T-3 II.1:2 Certain f. concepts cannot be understood
T-3 V.4:1 f. question you continually ask yourself
T-3 V.5:4 It is impossible to make so f. a confusion
T-3 VI.8:4 This is the f. error of all those who believe
T-3 VI.10:3 decide is the f. question of authorship. All
T-6 I.5:1 but our f. equality can be demonstrated
T-6 V.B.2:1 realize that only f. change will last, but
T-6 V.B.2:5 will inevitably produce f. change because
T-6 V.B.2:5 fundamental change because the mind *is* f.
T-6 V.B.4:4 f. change will still occur with the change
T-6 V.B.9:2 system, where the f. change will occur. At
T-6 V.C.1:8 are in f. disagreement about everything,
T-6 V.C.1:8 being in f. disagreement about what you
T-6 V.C.3:1 This is a major step toward f. change. Yet
T-7 VIII.1:2 These reflect a f. law of the mind, and
T-7 VIII.1:6 the Holy Spirit, it is the f. law of sharing,
T-8 VII.12:5 with a curriculum goal is a f. confusion
T-8 VIII.1:11 know entirely because of the f. difference
T-8 VIII.2:3 ego makes a f. confusion between means
T-13 III.6:3 is the f. illusion on which the others rest.
T-13.VII.10:12 for its own sake is the ego's f. creed, a
T-14 II.2:1 with the f. teaching that *truth* is true. This
T-15 VII.4:2 For it is the ego's f. doctrine that what you
T-16 IV.7:3 In f. violation of love's one condition, the
T-17 IV.3:3 you have made has, as its f. purpose, the
T-19 I.5:2 from the f. difference in what they are.
T-19 II.5:5 f. purpose of the special relationship in its
T19 IV.C.6:2 way to teach the first and f. principle in a
T-22 II.9:5 we see again another form of the same f.
T-25 III.1:3 with perception's f. law: You see what you
W-pI 30.2:5 f. difference between vision and the way
W-pI 66.2:1 on the f. question of what your function is
W-pI 72.2:1 The ego's f. wish is to replace God. In fact
W-pI 193.3:5 They are the same in f. content. It is this:
M-in 3:8 Its f. purpose is to diminish self-doubt.
P-2 in.1:5 is to help the patient deal with one f. error
P-2 VII.4:2 this f. confusion in one form or another,

**fundamentally** 3

T-4 I.2:11 They are f. irreconcilable, because spirit
T-11 in.1:5 and their f. irreconcilable natures cannot
W-pI 161.4:6 yet f. not understood nor understandable

**funeral** 3

T19 IV.C.2:6 the black robe he was wearing to his f.,
T19 IV.C.3:5 The shrouded figures in the f. procession
T19 IV.C.8:3 There is no f., no dark altars, no grim

**funny** 1

W-pI 29.2:2 senseless, f. and even objectionable.

**furious** 2

T-24 VI.11:4 Always attacked and always f., with anger
W-pII 1.3:4 sets about its f. attempts to smash reality,

**further** 57

T-2 VII.5:7 to concentrate on error is only a f. error.
T-3 I.1:1 f. point must be perfectly clear before any
T-3 V.5:4 increasing your overall confusion still f..
T-4 I.2:3 perceive it as a move toward f. separation,
T-4 V.1:4 The ego is thrown f. off balance because it
T-5 I.1:13 F., if the one to whom you give it accepts
T-6 II.3:4 obscuring your equality with them still f..
T-6 IV.5:3 mind is the ego's learning device; and f.,
T-6 V.B.3:3 and we can clarify this still f. now. At this
T-6 V.B.3:8 yet. F., the mind of the learner projects its
T-9 IV.2:3 merely be f. error to believe either that
T-10 II.4:5 you f. recognize that you are part of God,
T-12 III.3:4 asks for gifts, not for f. impoverishment.
T-14 VI.1:3 and shrink away from it to f. darkness.
T-15 IX.6:6 Seek not Atonement in f. separation. And
T-17 III.3:4 toward f. fragmentation and unreality.
T-17 VI.5:1 goal of truth has f. practical advantages. If
T-18 I.5:6 and to force you to make f. substitutions.
T-18 I.12:5 Would you still f. weaken and break apart
T-18 IX.8:4 world beyond them, still f. from the light.
T-18 IX.10:5 still f. inward but the one *you* cannot take,
T-28 VII.6:2 Why burden it with f. locks and chains
T-30 I.11:1 grain of wisdom will suffice to take you f..
W-pI 4.6:1 F., since these exercises are the first of
W-pI 5.7:3 it. F. examples are: *I am not worried*
W-pI 26.5:3 discomfort is too great. Do not reduce it f.
W-pI 27.2:4 If fear of loss still persists, add f.: *It can*
W-pI 76.8:3 Think f.; you believe in the "laws" of
W-pI 76.10:2 saw. Then listen f.. He will tell you more.
W-pI 102.2:1 we try to loose its weakened hold still f.,
W-pI.124.12:1 Add f. jewels to the golden frame that
W-pI 126.2:4 f. think that they can sin without affecting
W-pI 128.3:3 value greater in your sight limit you f.,
W-pI 134.5:2 merely is a f. sign that sin is unforgivable,
W-pI 153.2:5 Now are the weak still f. undermined, for
W-pI 154.6:3 that they become able to bring them f.,
W-pI.169.10:1 There is no need to f. clarify what no one
W-pI 185.1:3 no f. sorrow possible for you in any form;
W-pI 200.1:1 Seek you no f.. You will not find peace
W-pI 200.1:4 Seek you no f.. There is nothing else for
W-pI.200.10:2 Seek no f.. You have come to where the
W-pI.200.11:7 We seek no f.. We are close to home, and
W-pII ..in.11:1 One f. use for words we still retain. From
W-pII 1.2:3 to doubt, and f. kept from reason. What
W-pII .301.2:2 it, and bless it as a cause of f. joy in them.
W-ep 4:3 Let Him prepare you f.. He has earned
M-in 1:4 F., the act of teaching is regarded as a
M-2 2:4 was. F., the plan for this correction was
M-10 1:6 F., even the same person classifies the
M-25 6:8 It can be but f. limitations they lay upon
M-28 5:3 What f. sight is needed? What remains
P-1 3:4 up. F., he cherishes it, defends it, and is
P-2 I.1:3 It may be they will not get much f., for no
P-2 III.2:6 or go no f. than a step or two from hell.
S-1 IV.1:7 to rising f. still in prayer lies in this simple
S-2 II.6:4 in f. bargains which can give no hope, but
S-2 II.7:4 of it the means for f. slavery and pain.

**fury** 4

T-15 VII.9:6 The f. of those joined at the ego's altar far
T-18 IX.4:2 thoughts, all the insane attacks, the f., the
W-pI 21.2:5 is nothing but a veil drawn over intense f..
M-17 5:9 him safe from f. that can never be abated,

**fuse** 2

T-8 V.1:6 but together our minds f. into something
T-18 I.7:7 f. and merge and separate, in shifting and

**fuses** 2

T-12 VI.6:3 perception f. into knowledge because
S-1 II.1:3 and f. into total communication with God

**fusing** 1

T-14 VII.7:5 gentle f. of everything into *one* meaning,

**fusion** 1

T-31 II.3:4 So in their f. there appears to be the hope

**futile** 14

T-3 V.5:5 it is utilized in a f. attempt to escape from
T-4 in.3:5 the f. attempts of the ego at reparation,
T-12 IV.5:3 it is outside you the search will be f., for
T-13 IV.3:3 only have been f. if it must come to this,
T-22 IV.1:8 f. than standing where the road branches,
T-26 X.6:3 left without a purpose in a f. world. The
T-27 I.9:2 How f. must it be to see yourself a picture
T-29 II.3:2 It has been f. to demand escape from sin
T-29 VII.1:7 simply from a f. search for what you want
T-31 IV.9:4 it must have unless it be but f. wandering
W-pI 96.2:2 doubt, each one as f. as the one before,
W-pI 136.12:3 nor seek to prove how pitiful and f. your
W-pI .. 191.9:1 frail, with f. hopes and devastated dreams
W-pII . 287.2:4 *of dreams and f. substitutions for the truth?*

**futility** 9

T-12 IV.4:1 but lead to a sense of f. and depression?
T-13 II.8:3 the f. of the ego and its offerings, but
T-24 VI.9:3 F. of function not fulfilled will haunt you
T-27 I.7:1 The strongest witness to f., that bolsters
T-31 IV.5:1 world, unless he understood their real f.?
T-31 VII.6:2 to a bitter sense of deep depression and f..
W-pI .. 166.5:4 of the f. he sees about him everywhere,
W-pII . 332.1:7 the mind in chains, believing in its own f..
P-2 VI.4:9 your healing efforts here is but f.. Who

**future** 126

T-1 I.13:3 past in the present, and thus release the f.
T-3 III.3:1 in time, and therefore looks for f. answers
T-3 III.3:2 the f. and the present will be the same.
T-3 III.3:3 that the f. will be worse than the present.
T-4 V.6:11 have made a decision about your f. effort;
T-5 V.8:6 Your mind *does* make your f., and it will
T-5 VI.2:2 thus ensure that the f. will be like the past
T-6 II.9:8 to be far in the f. only because your mind
T-8 II.2:5 this alone disqualify it as your f. teacher?

T-12... VIII.4:8 It is no more past than f., being forever
T-13.........I.8:3 time, proceeding from past to f.. No one
T-13.........I.8:6 way of holding past and f. in your mind to
T-13.........I.9:1 and so the f. is needless and will not be.
T-13.........I.9:2 The f., in time, is always associated with
T-13......IV.4:3 continuity by making the f. like the past,
T-13......IV.4:4 the notion of paying for the past in the f.,
T-13......IV.4:4 the past becomes the determiner of the f.,
T-13......IV.4:5 present only as a brief transition to the f.,
T-13......IV.4:5 it brings the past to the f. by interpreting
T-13......IV.6:4 And this decision is one of f. pain. Unless
T-13......IV.6:5 choosing a f. of illusions and losing the
T-13....IV.6:10 dreams were not holy, the f. cannot be,
T-13......IV.7:6 in the reality of "now," without past or f.,
T-13......IV.8:2 The continuity of past and f., under its
T-13......IV.9:4 in the present to release the f.. This
T-13......IV.9:5 interpretation ties the f. to the present,
T-13......IV.9:6 on to the past to ensure a destructive f..
T-13......VI.4:2 Past, present and f. are not continuous,
T-13......VI.4:6 present and f. for your own purposes.
T-13......VI.4:7 the f. on the basis of your past experience,
T-13......VI.4:8 by doing so you are aligning past and f.,
T-13... VIII.3:2 redemption, which seems to be in the f.,
T-13......IX.1:2 linking the f. to the past as is the ego's law
T-13......IX.1:7 Between the f. and the past the laws of
T-13......IX.3:3 your faith in the past, the f. will be like it.
T-15.........I.2:1 the Holy Spirit's teaching are far in the f..
T-15.........I.4:3 it. The ego teaches that hell is in the f., for
T-15.........I.5:1 is here and now because the f. is hell.
T-15.........I.6:3 that the past and f. be the same is hidden
T-15.........I.6:6 here, but always as a foretaste of the f..
T-15.........I.8:2 of the present, but only of the past and f.,
T-15.........I.8:3 its shadow reaching out into the f.. Each
T-15.........I.9:2 For what is time without a past and f.? It
T-15......IV.1:8 For beyond the past and f., where you will
T-18.....VII.3:3 *now.* Only its past and f. make it seem real.
T-18.....VII.3:7 must be thought of in the past or in the f..
T-18.....VII.4:1 instant, you are willing to see no past or f.
T-18.....VII.4:2 prepare for it without placing it in the f..
T-18...VII.4:11 all of them look to the f. for release from a
T-18.....VII.7:5 here is time denied, and past and f. gone.
T-19....... II.7:4 This is his past, his present and his f.. For
T-20....... V.6:4 from it, and the f. will add no more. Here,
T-21... VIII.5:6 Here is the f. *now,* for time is powerless
T-23...... IV.8:5 It is their past, their present and their f.;
T-24..... VII.2:2 as yet, still in the f. or apparently gone by.
T-25....... II.2:4 gives no support to base your f. hopes,
T-25...... III.9:7 he is to you will make this choice your f.?
T-26... VIII.4:1 *now,* and cannot be perceived in f. time.
T-26... VIII.4:3 F. loss is not your fear. But present
T-26... VIII.4:6 now? A f. cause as yet has no effects. And
T-26... VIII.4:8 is *this* that needs correction, not a f. state.
T-26... VIII.5:1 make for safety all are laid within the f.,
T-26... VIII.7:5 Why in the f.? And you seek to be content
T-26... VIII.9:1 Be not content with f. happiness. It has
T-26... VIII.9:6 cause must be delayed until a f. time, is
T-28.........I.9:7 does not lie in the past, nor waits the f.. It
T-28.......I.14:6 It that could generate a different past or f.
T-29..... VII.7:2 For otherwise, the f. will be like the past,
T-31....... V.9:6 Can he see your f. and ordain, before it
W-pI.......8.2:3 picturing the past or in anticipating the f..
W-pI......28.1:3 them in the f. is not our concern here. If
W-pI......39.4:1 being asked now, or will be asked in the f.
W-pI...109.5:1 no pain, no fear of f. and no past regrets.
W-pI...110.2:2 to heal the past and make the f. free. It is
W-pI...110.4:1 saved to quietly extend into a timeless f..
W-pI...121.5:1 without the prospect of a f. which can
W-pI.127.10:1 Today the legion of the f. years of waiting
W-pI.127.10:2 today that we are spared a f. like the past.
W-pI.127.10:4 f. dawns unlike the past in every attribute
W-pI...131.6:3 is the great illusion it is past or in the f..
W-pI...132.2:4 You free the f. from all ancient thoughts
W-pI...132.3:3 and release the f. from your ancient fears,
W-pI...135.1:4 you do when you attempt to plan the f.,
W-pI.135.15:1 in setting up control of f. happenings. It
W-pI.135.15:3 Time becomes a f. emphasis, to be
W-pI.135.15:4 enough to let the mind direct its f. course.
W-pI.135.16:2 before becomes the basis for its f. goals.
W-pI.135.16:4 to guarantee a f. quite unlike the past,
W-pI.135.19:1 defense that promises a f. undisturbed,
W-pI.135.19:2 but your present trust direct the f., and
W-pI...158.3:7 it seems to have a f. still unknown to us.
W-pI...169.6:3 where the past and f. cannot be conceived
W-pI...181.3:3 We do not care about our f. goals. And
W-pI...181.4:1 involvement with your past and f. goals.
W-pI...181.5:2 For the past is gone; the f. but imagined.
W-pI...181.6:3 a little while, without regard to past or f.,
W-pI...188.2:2 Why wait to find it in the f., or believe it
W-pI......194.h I place the f. in the Hands of God.
W-pI...194.4:1 your f. as He holds your past and present.
W-pI...194.4:5 You are but asked to let the f. go, and
W-pI...194.4:6 and f. dread will now be meaningless.
W-pI...194.5:1 Release the f.. For the past is gone, and
W-pI...194.7:1 gives his f. to the loving Hands of God?
W-pI...194.7:6 escaped all fear of f. pain has found his
W-pI...194.8:1 Place, then, your f. in the Hands of God.
W-pI...195.9:3 a thought or care for us or for our f..
W-pI...214.1:1 (194) I place the f. in the Hands of God.
W-pI...214.1:2 *The past is gone; the f. is not yet. Now am I*
W-pII .279.1:2 to be in prison, and awaits a f. freedom, if
W-pII .308.1:3 cannot be to keep the past and f. one. The
W-pII .308.1:6 birth of Christ is now, without a past or f..
W-pII ....314.h I seek a f. different from the past.
W-pII .314.1:1 comes a f. very different from the past.
W-pII .314.1:2 The f. now is recognized as but extension
W-pII .314.1:4 Death will not claim the f. now, for life is
W-pII .314.1:5 and peace into a quiet f. filled with joy?
W-pII .314.2:2 *free. Now do we leave the f. in Your Hands,*
W-pII .314.2:2 *promises, and guide the f. in their holy light.*
M-4 ....VIII.1:5 everything that happens now or in the f..
M-10 .......... 3:5 on whom it rests now and in the f.. Who
M-19 .......... 3:1 of f. states and all concerns about the past
M-24 .......... 1:2 There is no past or f., and the idea of
M-24 .......... 2:3 If he is laying the groundwork for a f. life,
M-24 .......... 6:3 the past and total lack of interest in the f..
M-29 .......... 7:7 Not in the f. but immediately; now. God
P-2....... VII.5:4 have; a certainty of past, present and f.,

## futureless 1

W-pI...131.6:6 wills is now, without a past and wholly f..

---

# G

## gaily 1

T-31....IV.2:12 On some you travel g. for a while, before

## gain 84

T-4......... II.8:5 ego's ceaseless attempts to g. the spirit's
T-5...........I.7:2 that sharing it involves anything but g..
T-5....... II.7:11 profiteth it a man if he g. the whole world
T-6........ I.10:5 g. from them without experiencing them
T-7...........I.4:3 To g. you must give, not bargain. To
T-8....... VI.1:3 Every g. in our strength is offered for all,
T-12.........I.8:1 you will g. an increasing awareness that
T-12...... III.9:9 where it is will you g. control over it. For
T-12...... VI.1:1 ego is trying to teach you how to g. the
T-12...... VI.1:2 your soul and there is no g. in the world,
T-12.....VII.1:4 to all situations you will g. the real world.
T-12.....VII.2:6 but you g. confidence in their existence as
T-15...... VI.3:3 from another, and what you g. he loses.
T-15...... VI.4:6 wholly without loss and only with g..
T-15...... VI.5:2 For g. and loss are both accepted, and so
T-16.........I.2:7 will g. in strength and not in weakness.
T-16....... II.6:8 What g. is there to you in clinging to it,
T-16.... VI.11:1 new perspective you will g. from crossing
T-17.... IV.16:3 We will g. everything by giving Him the
T-20...... IV.1:4 Spirit, Who knows that as you give you g..
T-22....... II.6:3 through their use will you g. faith in them
T-23....... II.9:4 By this, another's loss becomes your g.,
T-23...... IV.9:2 could they g. but loss of their perfection?
T-25...... IV.2:5 you chose it as a means to g. these same
T-25....... V.5:1 for by his freedom will you g. your own.
T-25..... VII.5:4 and no one loses that each one may g..
T-25...VII.11:2 that one must g. *because* another lost. If
T-25...VII.11:5 For every little g. must someone lose, and
T-25...VII.11:6 be the total cost of any g. at all. You who
T-25...VII.12:1 the idea no one can lose for anyone to g..
T-25...VII.12:2 And everyone *must* g., if anyone would be
T-25... VIII.1:7 to the idea no one can lose for you to g..
T-25...... IX.2:1 To give reluctantly is not to g. the gift,
T-26....... II.2:2 and make a sacrifice that you might g..
T-26....... II.2:5 possible, and could result in g. for anyone
T-28..IV.10:10 And there will be no loss, but only g..
T-30.........I.7:3 of the question asks will g. momentum,
T-30.......I.10:1 will g. if what you have decided is not so.
T-30.....VII.2:2 success, advance, retreat, and g. and loss.
T-31...... III.2:9 What would be the g. to you? What could
T-31...... IV.2:9 And each is but the means to g. that end,
T-31...... IV.8:4 and you will g. as much as he will lose,
T-31..... V.13:6 But this g. is paid in almost equal loss, for
W-pI.....28.5:1 in fact, g. vision from just that table, if
W-pI.....39.2:6 at all. No one needs practice to g. what is
W-pI.....47.5:3 yourself that you will g. confidence. But
W-pI.....47.6:2 must also g. an awareness that confidence
W-pI.....74.6:5 definite g. in refusing to allow retreat into
W-pI.....98.4:1 that they learned and every g. they made.
W-pI.....98.6:5 lose. And what you g. is limitless indeed!
W-pI...105.1:7 that one can g. because another loses.
W-pI...124.9:2 may not be ready to accept the g. today.
W-pI...126.3:1 a sin, there is no g. to you directly. You
W-pI...131.2:3 and hope through them to g. in anything?
W-pI...133.7:4 deceived by the illusion loss can offer g..
W-pI...133.9:3 perceive that he has merely failed to g..
W-pI.133.12:4 What is the g. to you in learning this? It is
W-pI...138.3:5 There is no sense of g., for nothing is
W-pI...138.8:1 can g. unconscious hold of great intensity
W-pI...139.9:4 just our happiness alone we came to g..
W-pI.153.12:4 his winning is the g. to everyone ensured.

W-pI...154.7:4 g. by every message that they give away.
W-pI...155.8:4 There is no cost, but only g.. Illusion can
W-pI...163.3:1 quickly lost however hard to g., uncertain
W-pI...185.3:5 ratio of g. to loss and loss to gain takes on
W-pI...185.3:5 ratio of gain to loss and loss to g. takes on
W-pI...185.4:8 each to his g. and to another's loss.
W-pI.185.13:1 and everyone must g. whenever any gift
W-pI.186.10:5 What hope of g. can rest on goals like this
W-pI...187.5:2 You can only g. thereby. The thought
W-pI...187.5:7 And both must g. in this exchange, for
W-pI...194.8:3 you the world could fail to g. thereby, and
W-pI...199.5:3 not g. thereby in power to help the world,
W-pI...199.5:3 none which will not g. in added gifts to
W-pII ....328.h I choose the second place to g. the first.
W-pII .328.1:2 It seems that we will g. autonomy but by
W-pII .343.1:2 *The gift of everything can be but g.. You only*
M-4 .... IV.1:12 achieve nothing. No g. can come of it.
M-4 ..... VII.2:6 it. He could not g.. Therefore he does not
M-5 ....... II.1:2 no g. at all to me in this" and he is healed.
M-6 ........... 3:6 the giver will not lose, but only g.. Who
M-29 ......... 4:2 myself I can do nothing" is to g. all power
P-3...... III.6:11 everyone must g. a blessing without cost.
S-1 ........ III.3:9 enemies, and this imagined g. must go, if

### gained 10

T-6...... IV.11:5 What would be g. if God proved to you
T-11..... V.12:9 could believe that love can be g. by attack.
T-21....... V.9:3 have g. a means which cannot be applied
T-25....VIII.8:6 vengeance without love has g. in strength
T-30....... V.2:6 which it can be g. can now be understood.
W-pI.....45.8:7 little understanding you have already g.,
WpI. rIII.in9:3 a result, you have g. little reinforcement,
W-pI...184.7:5 can begin, a new perception can be g.,
W-pII .327.2:4 *and surety of Your abiding Love is g. at last.*
P-3........ III.7:3 How much is g. by striving for illusions?

### gainer 2

T-25...VII.12:2 *must* gain, if anyone would be a g.. Here is
W-pI...185.3:5 both. Loser and g. merely shift about in

### gaining 5

T-7....... X.3:10 On the contrary, you will be g. everything
T-18.....VI.13:5 You go where you would be, g., not losing
T-26.....VIII.2:5 of g. what forgiveness offers *now.* The
W-pI.....98.5:3 of g. a reward so great it has no measure?
W-pI...193.1:2 undisturbed; eternal and forever g. scope,

### gains 17

T-5....... II.7:10 No one g. from strife. What profiteth it a
T-5......... III.2:2 Being thought, the idea g. as it is shared.
T-15...... V.10:2 In the holy instant the Sonship g. as one,
T-15...... VI.3:2 power, and by sharing it, it g. in strength.
T-29....... II.1:6 the many g. your choice has offered you.
T-30.....VII.5:3 for the one who g. and him who loses.
T-31....... II.6:7 We make no g. he does not make with us,
T-31...... IV.8:5 lost, and what he g. is what is given *you.*
T-31..... V.13:1 Although this step has g., it does not yet
W-pI.....37.1:4 everyone g. through your holy vision. It
WpIrIII.in12:3 these reviews with learning g. so great we
W-pI...123.1:4 but you can well be grateful for your g.,
W-pI...123.2:1 extent of all the g. which you have made;
W-pI.135.10:4 of a kind from which it g. no benefit at all,
W-pII .319.1:5 The ego thinks that what one g., totality
W-pII .319.1:6 I learn that what one g. is given unto all.
M-4 ..... I.A.8:3 as merely shadows before become solid g.

### game 17

T-18...... IX.7:4 long as you would play the g. of children's
T-20....VIII.7:1 the idle g. of death in your imagination.
T-26....... X.4:7 Whatever way the g. of guilt is played,
T-26....... X.5:2 g. do you perceive one purpose for your
T-29...... IX.6:4 The dream of judgment is a children's g.,
W-pI.....45.8:7 to remind yourself that this is no idle g.,
W-pI...153.6:4 folly, or a silly g. a tired child might play,
W-pI.153.12:1 of as a g. that happy children play. It was
W-pI.153.12:2 teach them that the g. of fear is gone. His
W-pI.153.12:3 g. instructs in happiness because there is
W-pI.153.12:5 The g. of fear is gladly laid aside, when
W-pI.153.13:2 now. That g. is over. Now a quiet time has
W-pI.153.14:1 to play our final, happy g. upon this earth
W-pI...191.4:1 except a g. you play in which Identity can
W-pI...191.9:3 You play the g. of death, of being helpless
W-pII ..... 4.4:2 yet what sin perceives is but a childish g..
W-pII ..... 4.5:1 of God, will you maintain the g. of sin?

### games 5

T-13 ..... III.6:6 all the tricks and g. you offer it can heal it,
W-pI...153.8:1 We will not play such childish g. today.
W-pI.153.12:2 replace their fearful toys with joyous g.,
W-pI.153.14:2 truth abides and g. are meaningless. So is
W-pI...182.2:2 in g. they play to occupy their time, and

### gap 77

T-4 ....... VI.2:5 The g. is then so small that knowledge
T-4 ....... VI.7:1 my perception He can bridge the little g..
T-5 ..........I.4:9 God Himself can flow across the little g..
T-13 ..... IV.8:2 that no g. in its own continuity can occur.
T-16 ..... III.8:2 g. he imagines exists between his selves.
T-16 ..... III.8:3 which carries him across the g. as soon as
T-26 ..... V.13:2 cross the g. between the past and present,
T-26 ..... V.13:2 past and present, which is not a g. at all.
T-27 .. VII.11:4 The g. between reality and dreams lies
T-27 .. VII.12:4 The little g. you do not even see, the
T-28 ......I.15:3 better way to close the little g. between
T-28 ..... III.3:4 you have overlooked the g. between you,
T-28 ..... III.3:5 sickness, to preserve the little g. unhealed
T-28 ..... III.3:5 to bridge the little g. that leads to Him.
T-28 ..... III.4:2 The g. *is* little. Yet it holds the seeds of
T-28 ..... III.4:5 of the g. is all the cause that sickness has.
T-28 ..... III.5:3 as fast, as water rushes in to close the g.,
T-28 ..... III.5:4 Where is the g. between the waves when
T-28 ..... III.5:5 joined to close the little g. between them,
T-28 ..... III.7:4 a little g. perceived to tear eternity apart,
T-28 ..... III.8:2 the little g. was seen to stand between you
T-28 ..... III.9:6 And in Their sharing there can be no g. in
T-28 ..... IV.3:7 his dreams but seem to make a little g.,
T-28 ..... IV.4:1 yet, between your minds there is no g.. To
T-28 ..... IV.4:6 And dreams of fear will haunt the little g.,
T-28 ..... IV.5:2 to him to meet you in the g. between you,
T-28 ..... IV.6:1 confused, for in the g. no stable self exists.
T-28 ..... IV.7:1 One because there is no g. that separates
T-28 ..... IV.7:2 The g. between your bodies matters not,
T-28 ..... IV.8:5 the miracle will place within the little g.,
T-28 ..... IV.9:1 to close each little g. that lies between the
T-28 ... IV.10:5 then, would you perceive within the g.?
T-28 ... IV.10:7 insist on seeing in the g. what is not there.
T-28 ...... V.1:3 g. that is perceived between you and your
T-28 ...... V.4:1 conceived a little g. between illusions and
T-28 ...... V.5:8 seen within the g. that you imagined, and
T-28 ...... V.6:4 There is no g. that separates the truth
T-28 ...... V.7:1 is a little g. between you and your brother
T-28 ...... V.7:3 The g. is carefully concealed in fog, and
T-28 ...... V.7:4 Yet in the g. is nothing. And there are no
T-28 ...... V.7:6 Look at the little g., and you behold the
T-28 ..... VI.1:2 For here the little g. is seen, and yet it is
T-28 ..... VI.2:8 It perceives no g., because it does not hate
T-28 ..... VI.4:1 The body represents the g. between the
T-28 ..... VI.5:4 is no g. between my mind and yours" has
T-28 .... VII.1:3 An empty space, a little g., would be a
T-28 .... VII.1:5 a g. between the Father and the Son is not
T-28 .... VII.1:7 The promise that there is no g. between
T-28 .... VII.1:8 in Whose Wholeness there can be no g.?
T-28 .... VII.3:1 is a g. between you and your brother, or
T-28 .... VII.6:2 little g. of nothingness whereon it stands?
T-28 .... VII.7:6 What g. can interpose itself between the
T-29 ...........I.h The Closing of the G.
T-29 ........I.1:3 is no way in which a g. could be conceived
T-29 ........I.1:4 compromise the least and littlest g. would
T-29 ........I.1:6 a g. between your brother and yourself.
T-29 ........I.1:9 and leave a g. between you and His Love,
T-29 ........I.2:6 little g. must bring to those who cherish it
T-29 ........I.3:6 a g. perceived between you and him, lest
T-29 ........I.4:1 The g. between you and your brother is
T-29 ........I.8:4 there is no g. behind which you can hide?
T-29 ........I.9:1 that happens when the g. is gone is peace
T-29 ........I.9:4 What toys or trinkets in the g. could serve
T-29 ... III.3:10 understand what really fills the g. so long
T-29 ... VIII.3:1 a g. between the Christ and what you see.
T-29 ... VIII.7:3 Can there be a g. in what is infinite, a
T-30 ..... III.4:7 made but to fill a g. that is not there. It is
T-30 ..... IV.1:8 the false ideas you made to fill the g. you
T-30 ..... IV.3:1 The g. that is not there is filled with toys
T-30 ..... IV.8:2 For here the g. that is not there begins to
T-30 ..... IV.8:8 The g. is emptied of the toys of fear, and
T-30 .......V.6:4 The g. between your brother and yourself
W-pI .. 151.9:7 the g. between illusions and the truth.
W-pI 155.10:1 at the journey's ending there will be no g.,
W-pI 184.12:4 Every g. is closed, and separation healed.
W-pII ..... 7.1:2 bridge the g. between reality and dreams,
C-3 ............ 2:1 g. between their perception and the truth.

### gaps 1

W-pI .. 103.1:6 so, believing there are g. in love where sin

### garden 16

T-2 ..........I.3:1 The G. of Eden, or the pre-separation
T-3 ..........I.3:9 and forced him out of the G. of Eden. It is
T-3 ...... VII.3:4 tree was "forbidden" in the symbolic g..
T-6 ..........I.7:6 slept during the so-called "agony in the g.
T-18 ......VIII.h The Little G.
T-18 ...VIII.9:3 The desert becomes a g., green and deep
T-18 ...VIII.9:8 its beneficence your little g. will expand,
T-18 . VIII.10:2 And lead them gently to your quiet g.,
T-18 . VIII.10:4 and see your little g. gently transformed
T-18 . VIII.11:1 it into a g. of peace and welcome. Love's
T-18 . VIII.13:8 And walk into the g. love has prepared for
T-19 ......I.15:1 the most holy g. that He would make of it.
T19 ...IV.A.9:3 sun upon a g. covered by the snow? See
T19 .IV.A.16:1 cloth, set in a quiet g. where no sound but
T19 IV.D.18:4 here in the g. of seeming agony and death
W-pI .. 159.9:4 into a g. like the one they came from, and

### gardens 1

T-20 . VIII.11:1 to quiet views of g. under open skies, with

### garment 1

S-3........II.1:11 a choice, as one lays by a g. now outworn.

### garments 4

T-18 ..... IX.9:7 are the dark and heavy g. of guilt laid by,
T-22 .......II.1:5 heavy g. in which it hides its nothingness.
T-22 .......II.1:6 and heavy g. are those who seek illusions
T-26 ..... IX.4:6 the insane have shed their g. of insanity to

### gasp 1

T-13 .... in.2:10 wither and g. and are laid in the ground,

### gate 31

T-22 ..... III.3:2 Sin is a block, set like a heavy g., locked
T-25 ... VIII.7:4 to hell that seems to look like Heaven's g.
T-26 ..... III.2:4 is just beyond the g. of Heaven. Here is
T-26 ..... III.3:5 and only one continues past the g. where
T-26 ..... IV.1:2 g. behind which total lack of limits lies.
T-26 ..... IV.1:4 justice past the g. that opens into Heaven.
T-26 ..... IV.4:1 miracles to lay before the g. of Heaven.
T-26 ..... IV.6:1 back the happy opening of Heaven's g..
T-26 .......V.1:5 is a help or hindrance to the g. of Heaven.
T-26 .......V.2:4 the way to Heaven's g. is difficult at all.
T-26 .....V.14:3 reached the world that lies at Heaven's g..
T-27 ........I.3:2 closing off the g. and damning him to hell
T-30 .......V.8:2 and quickly reach the g. of Heaven itself.
W-pI 110.11:7 is the key that opens up the g. of Heaven,
W-pI 133.14:1 unencumbered, to the g. of Heaven,

W-pI.134.10:4 between the hell of guilt and Heaven's g..
W-pI.193.13:5 you hold the key that opens Heaven's g.,
W-pI...194.1:3 lawns that welcome you to Heaven's g.;
W-pI...200.8:2 to the g. of Heaven and the way beyond.
W-pII..263.2:1 we still remain outside the g. of Heaven,
W-pII..342.1:5 *I stand before the g. of Heaven, wondering if*
W-pII....14.3:5 a function that is past the g. of Heaven.
W-pII....14.5:5 the g. of Heaven stand open before him,
M-16......11:11 And thus the g. of Heaven is reopened,
C-3............4:9 to Heaven as is possible outside the g..
C-3...........4:10 this g. it is no more than just a step inside
S-1.........in.3:3 to the lawns of Heaven and the g. of peace
S-1.........V.4:2 Now you stand before the g. of Heaven,
S-1.........V.4:5 At this g. eternity itself will join with you.
S-3.........II.5:4 of what is merely opening the g. to higher
S-3.........II.6:4 At last the g. of Heaven opens and God's

### gates 8

T-13. VIII.10:6 know, and as they reach the g. of Heaven,
T-13.....X.14:6 we stand before the g. of Heaven where
T-14......VI.8:7 Its g. are open wide to greet His Son. No
T-18....IX.13:2 and gently placed before the g. of Heaven.
T19....IV.B.5:4 for we stand within the g. and not outside
T19....IV.B.5:5 How easily the g. are opened from within,
T-22......IV.4:4 The g. of Heaven, open now for you, will
T-24.....II.13:4 are the g. of hell you closed upon yourself,

### gather 11

T-8........VI.1:2 g. in our brothers as we continue together
T-13...VIII.3:9 Yet only God can g. them together, by
T-13...VIII.5:6 and let Him g. them into His quiet sight
T-19......I.11:6 sent forth to g. witnesses unto its coming,
T-19......IV.3:8 the Holy Spirit will g. all the thanks and
T-25......IX.9:2 And so they g. dust and grow, until they
T-26......IX.5:2 For They have come to g. in Their Own.
W-pI...125.4:3 We g. at the throne of God today, the
W-pII..326.1:8 *and at the end I know that You will g. Your*
W-pII..340.2:6 and none the Father will not g. to Himself
W-pII..350.2:1 And as we g. miracles from Him, we will

### gathered 2

T-16......III.6:4 to your teaching have g. to help you learn.
M-25..........3:1 may be g. on the way can be very helpful.

### gathering 1

T-17....III.2:10 g. to itself what it perceives as like itself.

### gathers 2

W-pI...195.7:4 and g. clarity as we are willing once again
M-4....I.A.6:12 rests a while, and g. them before going on

### gauge 1

T-24.......II.2:4 who can use him as the g. of littleness,

### gave 246

T-2...........I.1:1 aspect of God which He g. to His Son. In
T-2........III.5:8 He g. them His peace so they could not be
T-2.......VII.5:14 the world that he g. his only begotten Son
T-2.......VII.5:14 context; "He g. it *to* His only begotten Son.
T-3.......VII.3:8 knowledge and g. it freely to His creations
T-4...........I.9:5 God g. you a very lofty function that you
T-4.........II.6:6 with the belief in scarcity that g. rise to it.
T-4.........V.1:5 which g. rise to it and which it serves.
T-5.........II.5:6 When you chose to leave Him He g. you a
T-5.........II.9:2 that g. me all power in Heaven and earth.
T-5......VI.2:10 can do because you g. it the power to do it
T-5.......VII.2:7 He asks you only for what He g., knowing
T-5.......VII.4:3 God Himself g. you the perfect Correction
T-6.......II.12:6 one message God g. to Him and for which
T-6....IV.11:10 where you can find the sanity He g. you.
T-6....IV.12:10 He merely g. the Answer. His Answer is
T-7...........I.5:1 I g. only love to the Kingdom because I
T-7........IX.6:2 of God to give it to you, He g. it forever.
T-7........IX.6:3 He g. you the means for keeping it. *And*
T-7.........X.2:2 the function God Himself g. your mind
T-8........III.2:5 need Him, and why God g. Him to you.
T-8........III.8:4 of yourself is the function He g. you.
T-8........IV.6:2 God g. your will its power, which I can
T-8........VI.8:7 and g. him the power to create with Him.
T-9.........I.13:1 g. you what you are devoted *to.* Otherwise
T-9.........II.8:2 in them, for the sake of what God g. them
T-9.........III.8:4 is for. God g. you the function to create in
T-10.......in.3:3 g. you the power to create for yourself so
T-10.....V.9:10 own mind because of the power He g. it.
T-10...V.10:10 God g. Himself to you in your creation,
T-10.....V.13:7 because His Fatherhood g. you everything
T-11......III.5:2 and g. him the light that shines in him.
T-11......III.8:1 and bless it with the light your Father g. it
T-11......IV.2:5 only to the power that God g. to save you,
T-11...VIII.4:2 God will not refuse you the Answer He g..
T-12......III.8:1 that He g. it to His only begotten Son.
T-12......III.8:4 God g. you the real world in exchange for
T-12......IV.6:1 Behold the Guide your Father g. you, that
T-12......VI.4:7 the real world because God g. you Heaven
T-12.....VII.8:4 to you the messages you g. them. Love,
T-13.......II.6:2 and the reason it g. was that guiltlessness
T-13.....V.7:12 God is given you to whom God g. Himself
T-13....VI.10:6 And this they offer you who g. them joy.
T-13....VI.12:3 willing witnesses to the love you g. them,
T-13....VI.12:7 cannot look upon the light you g. to them
T-13....VI.13:4 for you, and given you the gifts He g..
T-13......IX.3:1 world can give you only what you g. it, for
T-13......IX.3:2 your faith will be rewarded as you g. it.
T-13......XI.5:1 this: God g. the Holy Spirit to you, and
T-13......XI.5:1 g. Him the mission to remove all doubt
T-14.....III.11:8 offers you but what God g. Him for you.
T-14.....III.14:5 is of Him to Whom God g. it for you. He
T-14......IV.1:6 received, even as God g. it first to His Son.
T-14...VIII.1:1 you have obscured the glory God g. you,
T-14......XI.4:3 child of light by Him to Whom God g. it.
T-15......III.5:4 God g. Himself to you in your creation,
T-15.....V.10:3 of love is the meaning God g. to it. Give to
T-15...VIII.4:1 instant on this: God g. the Sonship to you
T-15.......X.1:8 I can accept of you is the gift I g. to you.
T-15......XI.8:4 return it to the Father, Who g. it to me.
T-16....IV.13:5 Who g. eternity to you in your creation.
T-16......VI.1:5 as He would have it be, and g. it as it is.
T-16.....VI.11:4 that for all this you g. up *nothing!* The joy
T-16.....VII.8:5 He g. the holy instant to be given you,
T-16.....VII.8:5 that you receive it not *because* He g. it.
T-17......III.1:1 only the loving thoughts you g. in the past
T-17.....V.15:2 to Him Who g. you your release, and
T-17...VIII.6:1 as surely as your Father g. peace to you.
T-18.......II.7:5 has forgotten you to whom He g. the gift.
T-18......III.6:6 Would I not give you what you g. to me?
T-18.......V.5:6 Let Him fulfill the function that He g. to
T-19.........I.6:6 God g. healing not apart from sickness,
T-19....III.10:4 healed in the holy instant Heaven g. you.
T19.....IV.B.3:2 Such is the message that I g. them for you.
T19..IV.C.10:7 to whom you g. a resting place by your
T19.IV.D.17:6 freedom that I g. the Holy Spirit for you.
T19.IV.D.17:8 receive it of Him in return for what you g.
T-20.......II.7:6 For what God g. the Holy Spirit, you have
T-20.....II.11:7 the hands that g. it to him shall you be led
T-20......III.8:3 you look on is the answer that it g. you,
T-20.......V.2:7 Who g. the gifts to Him to give to you.
T-20...VIII.4:1 what God willed and g. you shall be yours
T-20...VIII.8:5 take unto yourself the power you g. them,
T-20. VIII.11:3 can behold the holiness God g. His Son.
T-21.......in.1:2 world you see is what you g. it, nothing
T-21.......II.3:6 and you g. the power of decision to Him
T-21.......II.5:3 in its testimony, and as it g. it back to you
T-21.......II.7:8 presence of what you thought you g. away
T-21....III.12:5 and the belief you g. it belongs beyond.
T-21....III.12:6 You g. perception and belief and faith
T-22.....II.11:6 g. the Holy Spirit to give to you *He gave.*
T-22.....II.11:6 gave the Holy Spirit to give to you *He g.*.
T-22.....II.11:8 function of an executioner you g. him for
T-22......III.8:6 You g. him not his holiness, but tried to
T-23......III.2:6 and receive of him but what you g..
T-23......IV.3:2 He g. the function to create unto His Son
T-23......IV.4:2 assume the holy function God g. His Son,
T-24.........I.3:2 and with the grandeur that He g. His Son.
T-24.........I.7:5 God g. you and your brother Himself,
T-24.........I.8:9 the goal of holiness that Heaven g. it?
T-24......II.10:7 remembering God g. Himself to you and
T-24......II.11:4 God's Love g. you to him and him to you
T-24......II.11:4 and him to you because He g. Himself.
T-24......II.14:1 key you threw away God g. your brother,
T-24......III.1:7 it wholly the instant that he g. it so. And
T-24......III.7:7 God g. to you that you might look on him
T-24....VI.11:1 is the function that you g. yourself. It
T-24.....VII.2:8 you g. to specialness but is his due. And
T-24.....VII.5:9 Its holy purpose g. it immortality, setting
T-24.VII.10:10 For as His Son's creation g. Him joy and
T-25........II.1:7 that you learn it g. you no rewards which
T-25........II.8:6 and what God g. him must be given you.
T-25......II.11:2 since He g. the same to both of you. His
T-25......III.6:7 will perceive that where he g. attack is but
T-25.......V.4:8 found if he fulfilled the role God g. to him
T-25.......V.5:5 you the gift of sight God g. to him for you!
T-25.......V.5:6 freedom to complete the task God g. to
T-25......VI.3:5 without the function that He g. to him.
T-25..VIII.13:6 Father g. the same inheritance to both.
T-26........II.8:6 you should offer or receive less than He g.
T-26.......V.3:1 God g. His Teacher to replace the one
T-26.......V.3:7 God g. answer to is answered and is gone.
T-26.......V.4:3 ago, before its unreality g. way to truth.
T-26.....VII.6:9 ease to what God g. as answer to them all.
T-26...VII.15:3 God g. to all illusions that were made
T-26...VII.15:4 lies, for God g. answer to them all as one.
T-26...VII.18:2 nor to make use of what He g. to answer
T-26...VII.18:3 arrogant to lay aside the power that He g.,
T-26..VIII.7:10 asks for what He g. without a cost at all.
T-27.........I.4:3 you send lest he forget the injuries he g.,
T-27........I.11:5 but g. illusions of a purpose to a thing you
T-27........I.11:6 hide the function that the Holy Spirit g..
T-27......IV.1:7 Yet if God g. an answer there must be a
T-27......IV.6:8 intact because it g. the answer to itself.
T-27.......V.6:4 but shine in thanks to you who blessing g.
T-27.......VI.3:4 tells you but the names you g. to it to use,
T-27...VII.11:6 but a part of your own dream you g. away
T-27...VII.13:5 and g. him means to waken without fear.
T-27...VII.14:1 Accept the dream He g. instead of yours.
T-27...VII.15:4 instead of counting up the hurts he g..
T-27...VII.15:5 thanks to him for all the helpfulness he g..
T-27....VIII.4:5 because he understands he g. them their
T-27....VIII.6:1 Let us return the dream he g. away unto
T-28.........I.2:7 the place of what God g. in your creation.
T-28........II.7:5 that he dreams he g. his brother. And it is
T-29......III.5:4 still because you g. your light to him, to
T-29......IV.5:1 you were not the one who g. the "proper"
T-29......VI.4:1 God g. to all that you would make eternal,
T-29......VI.4:9 the function their Creator g. to them.
T-29....VIII.9:7 God g. you all there is. And to be sure you
T-30........II.2:6 will when He g. you His perfect Answer.
T-30........II.4:7 forgiven Him Who g. your will to you. For
T-31.........I.5:1 is an ability you made and g. yourself. It
T-31........II.4:3 You hate the one you g. the leader's role
T-31........II.7:6 g. when God appointed Him His only Son
T-31.....V.10:2 did, who g. the face of innocence to you?
T-31.....V.13:3 done the learning which g. rise to them.
T-31..VIII.10:4 because You g. it me on their behalf. And
W-pI.....42.4:7 *me must be mine, because He g. them to me.*
W-pI.....49.3:5 His Voice. He g. It to you to be heard.
W-pI.....62.3:5 power God g. His Son to your awareness.
W-pI........65.h My only function is the one God g. me.
W-pI.....65.2:2 "My only function is the one God g. me."
W-pI.....65.8:2 *My only function is the one God g. me. I*
W-pI.....66.4:1 function God g. you and your happiness,
W-pI.....66.4:3 the function He g. you must be happiness
W-pI.....66.8:3 Unless God g. your function to you, it
W-pI.....72.6:7 get. God g. you nothing. The body is your
W-pI.....73.2:2 The wishes of the ego g. rise to it, and the
W-pI.....78.6:3 and all the little and the larger hurts he g..
W-pI.....78.8:8 role God g. Him that you might be saved.
W-pI.....83.1:1 My only function is the one God g. me. I
W-pI.....83.1:2 I have no function but the one God g. me.
W-pI.....83.1:5 my only function is the one God g. me.
W-pI.....83.2:3 *me a function other than the one God g. me.*

W-pI.....97.6:2 you g. as much as does the radiance of the
W-pI....99.10:2 You cannot lose the gifts your Father g..
W-pI....107.8:2 which g. the gift of life to Him as well. He
W-pI....108.9:1 while, expecting to receive the gift you g..
W-pI....108.9:2 to you in the amount in which you g. it.
W-pI....109.4:6 yours because you g. your voice to God,
WpI. rIII.in4:4 They g. you nothing. But your practicing
WpI. rIII.in6:2 by the One Who g. the thoughts to you.
WpI. rIII.in6:6 you g. as they were given you for it to use.
WpIrIII.in13:3 As you review these thoughts He g. to you
W-pI....115.2:3 *g. me His plan that I might save the world.*
W-pI....117.2:3 *it joy. These are the gifts my Father g. to me. I*
W-pI. 121.13:1 unite in blessing you with what you g..
W-pI....123.8:2 Him thanks for everything He g. His Son,
W-pI....124.3:2 on us and offers us the happiness we g..
W-pI....124.7:4 For we would keep the gifts our Father g..
W-pI. 124.10:3 thought to which you g. this half an hour,
W-pI....128.5:2 leave it free of purposes we g. its aspects
W-pI....132.8:3 the thoughts that g. it these appearances.
W-pI....135.6:4 It is your mind which g. the body all the
W-pI. 136.18:1 the body by the purposes you g. to it. As
W-pI....138.7:2 now transformed from the intent you g. it
W-pI. 139.11:4 the knowledge that God g. to us when He
WpI. rIV.in2:4 by which the Father g. creation to the Son
W-pI. 153.17:2 for all the gifts He g. us in the one gone by
W-pI....158.2:3 you give, for that is what creation g.. All
W-pI....161.3:3 is different from the one we g. to them.
W-pI....162.1:4 God g. in answer to the world you made.
W-pI....163.7:3 His, and so eternal life g. way to death.
W-pI. 166.10:5 understand, to which He g. an Answer.
W-pI....168.6:4 word He g. to us through His Own Voice,
W-pI....169.8:2 and g. it to all minds that each one might
W-pI....183.4:4 have lost the name of god you g. them.
W-pI....183.8:5 little names you g. your thoughts, not
W-pI. 183.10:5 He makes his claim to all his Father g., is
W-pI....184.3:2 You g. these names to them, establishing
W-pI. 184.12:5 Name of God is the inheritance He g. to
W-pI. 184.13:3 realize the many names you g. its aspects
W-pI....198.1:6 and you can now receive the gift you g..
W-pII .224.1:3 It is the gift my Father g. to me; the one as
W-pII .230.1:4 He created me He g. me peace forever.
W-pII .230.2:1 *seek the peace You g. as mine in my creation.*
W-pII .230.2:5 *need but call on You to find the peace You g..*
W-pII .230.2:6 *gave. It is Your Will that g. it to Your Son.*
W-pII .239.1:2 be thankful for the gifts our Father g. us.
W-pII .....3.1:3 the thought that g. it birth is cherished.
W-pII .247.2:3 *them, and g. them all to me as part of You,*
W-pII .....4.1:4 Sin g. the body eyes, for what is there the
W-pII .255.2:3 *The peace You g. him still is in his mind, and*
W-pII .263.1:1 *Spirit entered into it, Your Love g. life to it.*
W-pII .266.1:1 *Father, You g. me all Your Sons, to be my*
W-pII .269.1:3 *perception through the Guide You g. to me,*
W-pII .273.2:4 *so the peace You g. Your Son is with me still,*
W-pII .276.1:7 Who g. His Word to us in our creation, to
W-pII .279.2:3 *Would You withhold the gifts You g. to me?*
W-pII .310.2:2 and joy to Him Who g. salvation to us,
W-pII .316.2:3 *Yet I trust that You Who g. them will provide*
W-pII .320.1:2 any attributes his Father g. in his creation
W-pII .322.2:3 *created me, I can give up nothing You g. me.*
W-pII .324.1:1 *One Who g. the plan for my salvation to me.*
W-pII .328.2:4 *Will which You, my Father, g. as part of me.*
W-pII .338.2:5 *the Thought You g. me promises to lead me*
W-pII .347.1:5 *I give all judgment to the One You g. to me to*
W-pII ...14.2:2 of this one year we g. to God together,
W-pII .355.1:2 *You will keep Your Word You g. Your Son in*
M-2 ...........5:8 the one decision that g. his teacher to him
M-7 ...........3:7 Who g. the gift and Who received it. Thus
M-10 .........5:9 He g. himself to Him Whose judgment he
M-12 .........3:3 directly through the Spirit which g. them.
S-3...........I.3:5 forgot that it is he who g. this role to it.
S-3......... II.3:4 hard to see the gifts we g. were saved for

## gaze 5

T-13....VIII.4:6 His loving g. are partial glimpses of the
T-17....IV.9:10 gift. Let not your g. dwell on the hypnotic
T19... IV.A.9:6 fix your g. upon a disappearing snowflake
T-20....VIII.6:4 is turned to blessing under His gentle g..
W-pI.....92.4:2 steady g. upon the light that lies beyond

## geared 3

Wi181-200 2:1 lessons now are g. specifically to widening
W-pII ....in.1:5 which our practicing was always g..
M-4 ........... 1:6 which the teaching-learning situation is g.

## general 11

T-17 ..... IV.6:2 You recognize, at least in g. terms, that
T-17 ..... VI.1:4 The setting of the Holy Spirit's goal is g..
T-18 ... VI.12:3 even a g. idea without specific reference.
W-in.......... 6:1 only g. rules to be observed throughout,
W-pI..... 14.5:3 Do not use g. terms. For example, do not
W-pI..... 18.3:3 by repeating the more g. statement: *I am*
W-pI..... 45.4:1 the same g. form that we used in applying
WpI..rII.in.2:1 this g. form: Take about fifteen minutes
WpI..rII.in.6:1 form of the idea for g. applications, and
M-16 ......... 2:4 There are some g. rules which do apply,
P-3..........II.1:9 applications of the g. principles of healing

## generalizability 1

T-3 ........ V.2:3 made for a specific purpose has no true g.

## generalization 4

T-3 ........I.7:10 If you can accept this one g. now, there
T-4 ...... VII.2:6 results in spurious g. which is really not
T-12 .... VII.1:2 g. is demonstrated as you use it in more
M-16 ......... 4:7 Perhaps the one g. that can be made is

## generalizations 1

T-8 .....VIII.1:3 This is because it is incapable of true g.,

## generalize 5

T-12 ...... V.6:4 the ability to g. is a crucial learning failure
W-in.......... 4:2 are planned to help you g. the lessons, so
W-in.......... 6:2 This will help you to g. the ideas involved
M-4 ..... I.A.4:4 will not g. the lesson for fear of loss and
M-5 ........II.4:4 learning will g. and transform the world.

## generalized 3

T-12 ..... VI.6:5 guidance increases and becomes g..
W-pI..... 34.6:1 the form of more g. adverse emotions,
W-pI... 108.6:2 thought behind it can be g. to other areas

## generalizes 1

T-27 ...... V.8:6 instances, and g. to include them all. This

## generally 11

T-2 ....... III.1:3 is g. seen as a need to protect the body.
T-2 .....VIII.3:1 The Last Judgment is g. thought of as a
T-4 .........II.9:2 systems g. include some account of "the
W-pI..... 31.1:4 G. speaking, the form includes two
W-pI..... 69.4:1 that g. occupies your consciousness.
M-3 ........... 5:3 These relationships are g. few, because
M-3 ........... 5:4 recognize this; in fact, they g. do not.
M-4 ...... IX.1:5 G., his faithfulness begins by resting on
M-9 ........... 1:6 immediately, but these are g. special cases
S-1..........II.3:3 of identification has g. been reached, but
S-3......... III.2:3 the body, and indeed are g. limited to this

## generate 1

T-28 ......I.14:6 It that could g. a different past or future.

## generated 1

T-31 .... V.10:7 If one were g. by your brother, who was

## generation 1

T-5 ....... VI.8:1 of the fathers unto the third and fourth g.,

## generations 2

T-5 ....... VI.8:3 the statement means that in later g. He
T-5 ....... VI.8:3 what former g. had misunderstood, and

## generosity 4

M-4 ........ VII.h Generosity
M-4 ..... VII.1:1 term g. has special meaning to the teacher
M-4 ..... VII.1:4 g. means "giving away" in the sense of
M-4 ... VII.2:12 to him. These he can give away in true g.,

## generous 3

T-31 ....... V.3:2 to those who would be g. and good. This
M-4 ..... VII.1:3 without trust no one can be g. in the true
M-4 ..... VII.2:1 teacher of God is g. out of Self interest.

## gentle 62

T-6 .........V.2:1 by a g. Voice that will not frighten them,
T-14 ... III.12:6 and leave all decisions to His g. counsel.
T-14 ... VII.7:5 g. fusing of everything into *one* meaning,
T-14 ...VIII.4:3 through g. understanding which can lead
T-14 ..... IX.3:2 is so g. you need but whisper to it, and all
T-15 ..... XI.1:6 is nothing more than a g. awakening, and
T-16 ..... VI.8:2 keep g. pace with you in your transition.
T-18 ... VI.14:7 you, in answer to its g. call to be at peace.
T-19 ..... IV.3:2 with g. graciousness upon your brother,
T19 ...IV.A.5:4 Each is a g. winning over from the appeal
T19 .IV.A.11:6 is wholly absent from love's g. perception.
T19 .IV.A.14:3 and the beautiful, the g. and the kind.
T19 ...IV.C.2:5 Touch any one of them with the g. hands
T19 IV.D.21:3 and watches over you in faith so g. yet so
T-20 .......II.5:6 gleaming in the g. glow of peace that
T-20 .......V.8:2 rests in his g. hands in safety and in peace
T-20 ... VI.10:3 and love shines on it with the g. smile and
T-20 ...VIII.6:4 sin is turned to blessing under His g. gaze
T-20 . VIII.10:5 These g. sights and sounds are looked on
T-21 ........I.3:2 And g. lessons are acquired joyously, and
T-22 ......I.11:5 sweetness and His g. innocence protected
T-22 ..... VI.2:4 the Holy Spirit waits in g. patience, as
T-22 ..... VI.6:5 g. service that you give the Holy Spirit is
T-24 .......V.3:6 How g. are the sights He sees, the sounds
T-25 .... VII.6:5 g. eyes would look beyond the madness
T-26 .......II.7:3 resolved before the Holy Spirit's g. sight.
T-26 ..... IX.8:6 In g. gratitude do God the Father and the
T-27 ........I.1:3 Walk you the g. way, and you will fear no
T-27 ........I.5:1 Now in the hands made g. by His touch,
T-27 .. VII.14:3 and allow His g. dreams to take the place
T-27 ...VIII.9:1 g. laughter does the Holy Spirit perceive
T-28 ......I.13:6 The stillness speaks in g. sounds of love
T-29 ... III.3:11 forth the g. way of kindness to God's Son.
T-31 ........I.8:1 hope and sparkles with a g. friendliness.
W-pI .. 73.10:1 with g. firmness and quiet certainty: *I will*
W-pI .. 95.14:8 mind, the g. rustling of the wings of peace
W-pI .. 125.7:1 instead a g. listening to the Word of God.
W-pI .. 137.8:6 For by its g. hand is weakness overcome,
W-pI .. 137.9:2 His g. lessons teach how easily salvation
W-pI .. 140.3:4 They lead from sleep to g. waking, so that
W-pI 151.10:2 behold the g. face of Christ in all of them.
W-pI .. 156.5:5 transforming in Its g. light all things unto
W-pI .. 166.8:1 and perceive His g. hand directing you to
W-pI .. 182.7:7 He will wait until you hear His g. Voice
W-pI 186.13:1 His g. Voice is calling from the known to
W-pI .. 187.6:5 all, and in his g. laughter are they healed.
W-pI .. 189.2:3 you a warm and g. home in which to stay
W-pI .. 189.3:5 and peace offers its g. light to everyone, is
W-pII . 272.1:7 *Love, forever still, forever g. and forever safe*
W-pII ..... 8.2:5 And the sights are g.. Only happy sights
W-pII ..... 9.2:1 and hold you safe within its g. advent,
W-pII . 325.1:6 forgiving thoughts a g. world comes forth
W-pII ... 13.1:6 fear must slip away under the g. remedy it
W-pII . 347.2:2 and hear the g. Voice for God assuring
M-4 ...... IV.2:1 Therefore, God's teachers are wholly g..
M-4 ........V.1:4 The g. have no pain. They cannot suffer.
M-4 ...... IX.2:4 Being based on fearlessness, it is g.. Being
M-14 ......... 2:4 A g. Savior, born where sin was made and
S-2..........II.4:4 respond except with silence and a g. smile
S-3.........in.1:1 the steep ascent more g. and more sure,

S-3.........II.3:2 flesh, but as a g. welcome to release. If
S-3.........II.4:1 This g. passage to a higher prayer, a kind

## gentleness 50

T-6........III.3:1 as you see His g. in others your own mind
T-13....III.11:3 the g. of love respond to his demands,
T-14......IV.8:6 cannot even give a blessing in perfect g..
T-14.......V.2:7 His g. is yours, and all the love you share
T-14.....V.10:8 and in His g. He would release from fear
T-14.....V.10:9 The power of love is in His g., which is of
T-14......VI.8:4 them to Him and let His g. teach you that,
T-16.....VII.6:5 the peace of *now* enfold you in perfect g..
T-17.......II.5:5 spark of beauty that g. could release.
T-17......III.4:2 ego's hands, as it is kind when used for g..
T-18....IX.14:3 and carrying it, safe and sure within its g.,
T19.IV.A.11:1 and return with messages of love and g..
T19.IV.A.16:3 join in g. before the table of communion.
T-20.....II.8:12 and where we live in g. and peace, as one
T-20....III.10:4 with perfect g. upon each other and on
T-23.........I.1:2 against itself remembers not eternal g..
T-24......IV.1:4 Whatever g. it offers is but deception, but
T-24.......V.6:2 you there in g. and blessing all the way.
T-24......VI.1:1 peace descends on it in g. and blessing so
T-25.......in.3:6 Him not it carries Him in g. and love, to
T-25.........I.4:5 light. The veil is lifted through its g., and
T-25.......II.8:5 His g. becomes your strength, and both
T-25......III.8:1 The Maker of the world of g. has perfect
T-25......III.8:1 seems to stand between you and His g.. It
T-25......IV.3:5 of them, and covers them in g. and light.
T-25......VI.1:3 so he looks upon himself with love and g..
T-26.........I.8:1 God's justice rests in g. upon His Son,
T-29.........I.1:5 of hate, His g. turn sometimes to attack,
T-30......IV.1:3 them is so lovely and so still in loving g.,
W-pI...108.8:8 *I offer peace of mind. To everyone I offer g..*
W-pI...122.1:6 be disturbed, a g. that never can be hurt,
W-pI...127.9:5 In loving g. He will abide with you, as you
W-pI.152.10:5 humility the radiance of God's Son, his g.,
W-pI...189.4:2 g. and innocence they see surrounding
W-pII..250.2:2 *I would behold his g. instead of my illusions.*
W-pII.....265.h Creation's g. is all I see.
W-pII..265.1:4 the celestial g. with which creation shines.
W-pII265.1:10 God's. And so I can perceive creation's g..
W-pII..265.2:2 *they are the same, and I will see creation's g..*
M-4..........IV.h Gentleness
M-4.......IV.2:2 They need the strength of g., for it is in
M-4.......IV.2:7 and limitless strength of g.? The might of
M-4.......IV.2:8 might of God's teachers lies in their g., for
M-4........V.1:1 Joy is the inevitable result of g..
M-4........V.1:2 G. means that fear is now impossible, and
M-4........V.1:3 The open hands of g. are always filled.
M-4........V.1:8 with g. as surely as grief attends attack.
M-14..........1:4 complete, excluding no one, limitless in g.
C-2............7:4 see extend before you as you walk in g..
S-3........IV.9:3 See the shadows fade away in g.; the

## gentler 5

T-23.....II.20:5 The seeming g. forms of the attack are no
T-27...VII.13:4 unless a g. dream preceded his awaking,
T-27...VII.13:4 calls with love to waken him; a g. dream,
W-pI...123.1:2 to g. pathways and to smoother roads.
S-3.........II.3:4 we go in peace to freer air and g. climate,

## gently 78

T-4..........I.4:7 will correct it very g. and lead you back to
T-5....III.11:10 He holds this gladness g. in your mind,
T-7......VI.13:1 the Holy Spirit reminds you g. that you
T-12......VI.7:3 it. Very g. does God shine upon Himself,
T-14.......II.3:7 *place it g. in the holy place where it belongs.*
T-14......III.3:4 Say therefore, to yourself, g., but with the
T-14......IV.6:2 you will be led as g. as if you were being
T-14.....VII.5:8 must be g. turned to your own good,
T-14......IX.4:3 graciousness of God will take them g. in,
T-15.......II.1:6 in that instant you will awaken g. in Him.
T-15.......II.2:7 where He g. translates hell into Heaven.
T-16.........I.3:7 Step g. aside, and let healing be done for
T-16.....VII.6:1 the Holy Spirit g. lays the holy instant.
T-17.......II.6:2 reaching quietly and g. across chaos,
T-17....IV.15:5 The frame fades g. and God rises to your
T-17.....VII.6:7 will be g. turned to its use and purpose.
T-18.........I.8:3 The Holy Spirit takes you g. by the hand,
T-18.........I.8:3 you g. back to the truth and safety within.
T-18.......I.11:2 all illusions have been g. brought unto the
T-18.......II.9:4 the Holy Spirit has g. laid the real world;
T-18....VI.12:5 your body obeys and g. setting them aside
T-18. VIII.10:2 And lead them g. to your quiet garden,
T-18. VIII.10:4 and see your little garden g. transformed
T-18......IX.9:7 laid by, and g. replaced by purity and love
T-18....IX.13:2 and g. placed before the gates of Heaven.
T-19......IV.1:4 Yet peace will g. cover them, extending
T-19......IV.1:5 relationship to others, to bring them g. in
T-19......IV.3:8 and lay them g. before His Creator in the
T19...IV.A.1:4 place from which it g. reaches out, but
T19.IV.A.11:1 Love's messengers are g. sent, and return
T-20......III.6:5 They g. questioned it and whispered,
T-20....VI.10:5 the way to true relationships held g. open,
T-20... VIII.6:1 looked upon with vision falls g. into place
T-20... VIII.7:2 bringing them g. within the kindly sway
T-21......IV.8:1 Look g. on your brother, and remember
T-22.........I.9:7 sight or sound that drew them g. into one
T-22.....II.12:7 is g. overlooked and disappears. For at its
T-22......IV.5:1 the other will g. have corrected for you.
T-22....VI.9:11 and lays it g. in each quiet smile of faith
T-23......III.2:3 box, however beautiful and g. given, still
T-23......IV.6:6 all the lights of Heaven will g. lean to you,
T-25......VI.1:1 grace of God rests g. on forgiving eyes,
T-25......VI.7:9 Take it g., then, from your brother's hand
T-26.....V.14:5 Look g. on your brother, and behold the
T-26......IX.1:5 Regard him g.. Look with loving eyes on
T-27.......V.3:4 silent dead, are g. lifted up and comforted
T-27.......V.7:3 will the world remind you g. of what you
T-27...VII.13:5 God willed he waken g. and with joy, and
T-28.......I.11:2 It reaches g. from that quiet time, and
T-28.......I.15:6 that he be lifted up and g. carried over.
T-28......III.8:1 but let your world be g. lit by miracles.
T-28......III.8:4 and g. shows you that you never sinned.
T-29.......V.2:4 peace surrounds you g. in its soft embrace
T-30.......V.6:1 is the real world's purpose g. brought into
T-31.........I.2:4 steps that lead you g. from one to another
T-31... VIII.3:2 perplexity Christ calls to you and g. says,
W-pI.....45.6:3 idea, repeat it again and tell yourself g.:
W-pI.....78.2:3 lay it down and g. lift our eyes in silence
W-pI...99.12:5 your mind and let all fear be g. laid aside,
W-pI...107.9:6 *Self.* Then let Him lead you g. to the truth,
W-pI...134.6:2 laugh, and g. lays them at the feet of truth
W-pI.134.11:3 He has been g. wakened from his dream
W-pI.135.18:1 g. planned by One Whose only purpose is
W-pI.135.18:4 for death, He led you g. to eternal life.
W-pI...160.9:5 And He leads them g. home again, where
W-pI.166.11:3 One walks with you Who g. answers all
W-pI...169.1:4 it can be g. laid and willingly received; an
W-pI...188.8:2 you g. to accept His Word for what you
W-pI...188.9:2 and g. bring them back to where they fall
W-pI...192.4:1 Forgiveness g. looks upon all things
W-pI...194.9:3 If we forget, we will be g. reassured. If we
W-pI...200.8:4 easy, sloping g. toward the bridge where
WpI rVI.in.5:4 Then g. let the thought which you denied
W-pII..305.1:3 peace envelops it, and g. carries it to truth
W-pII....10.4:3 and g. waken from his dream of pain the
M-5....III.2:11 Very g. they call to their brothers to turn
M-11.........3:5 G. His Judgment substitutes for yours.
C-2............8:2 as g. as a loving mother sings her child to

## genuine 9

T-2.......VII.2:4 The miracle worker must have g. respect
T-4.........in.1:5 The result of g. devotion is inspiration, a
W-pI...134.3:1 you find in g. forgiveness on your part is
W-pI...157.5:1 your ministry takes on a g. devotion, and
W-pI...185.6:2 And when the wish for peace is g., the
W-pI...186.2:5 to do is to accept our part in g. humility,
M-25.........4:1 Nothing that is g. is used to deceive. The
M-25.........4:2 deception, and He can use only g. abilities
M-25.........5:6 Now the "power" is no longer a g. ability,

## genuinely 3

T-1..........II.1:4 Miracles, however, are g. interpersonal,
T-3...........I.2:3 applications and g. tragic on a wider scale
S-1...........I.7:9 both, if you are g. attuned to one another.

## gesture 1

T-2....V.A.15:3 is an empty g. unless it entails correction.

## gestures 2

W-pI...126.7:3 Could He be satisfied with empty g., and
W-pI.161.11:4 familiar g. which he makes so frequently.

## get 55

T-4..........II.6:5 "Giving to g." is an inescapable law of the
T-4........III.4:8 is wholly without the ego's "drive to g.."
T-6........IV.9:3 the point where they can g. you out of it.
T-6......V.A.5:9 always for what each one can g. *separately*
T-7.....VIII.3:3 Any attempt to keep part of it and g. rid
T-7.....VIII.3:6 second error is the idea that you can g. rid
T-8...........I.4:4 since it means that you did not g. what
T-8.......VII.1:4 attack can g. you something you want. If
T-9.......II.11:2 To believe that it is possible to g. much
T-9.......II.11:5 But to receive is to accept, not to g.. It is
T-9.........V.5:5 ego will always seek to g. something from
T-10........II.6:2 believe it can g. you something you want.
T-11....VIII.7:2 you believe that you can g. by taking. And
T-12.....III.7:10 not outside it before you can g. rid of it;
T-12.....III.7:10 and why you must g. rid of it before you
T-13........II.1:1 of projection is always to g. rid of guilt.
T-13........II.1:2 to g. rid of guilt from its viewpoint only,
T-13........II.2:2 is. You project guilt to g. rid of it, but you
T-13.VII.10:13 you lay all of the things it bids you g.,
T-13...VII.11:2 the ego urges you again and again to g., it
T-13...VII.11:2 for what you g. it will demand of you.
T-15.....VII.2:1 relationships only to g. something. And it
T-15.....VII.2:5 it can g. and keep *by making guilty.* This is
T-15.....X.5:12 someone must pay and someone must g..
T-16.......V.7:7 he would give away to g. a "better" one?
T-17......III.4:8 For it was formed to g. him out of it, and
T-18......VI.2:3 that you could give and g. something else,
T19.......IV.A.h First Obstacle: The Desire to G. Rid of It
T19....IV.A.1:1 flow across is your desire to g. rid of it.
T19....IV.A.7:1 little insane wish to g. rid of Him Whom
T19IV.A.17:10 believe that it can g. you what you want.
T19....IV.B.1:1 the obstacle of your desire to g. rid of it.
T19....IV.B.4:4 want neither to g. rid of peace nor limit it.
T19...IV.D.5:3 The desire to g. rid of peace and drive the
T-20.....VII.2:7 I do not want to learn the means to g. it?"
T-26...VII.19:9 To g. from one is to deprive them all. And
T-26........X.4:4 that your attack on him attempts to g.? Is
T-27....IV.4:13 body g. that you would want the most of
T-27....VIII.2:3 real. It works to g. them, doing senseless
T-29.........I.4:4 And then your bodies seem to g. in touch,
T-30.........I.7:3 which you g. *your* answer to *your* question.
T-30.........I.7:4 And you will not g. it, for it would destroy
T-30.......I.11:2 but merely hope to g. a thing you want.
W-pI.....16.4:2 is quite difficult until you g. used to it.
W-pI.....30.2:2 not attempting to g. rid of what we do not
W-pI.....30.4:2 To help you begin to g. used to this idea,
W-pI.....41.5:3 to g. past this dark and heavy cloud, and
W-pI.....41.6:2 morning, as soon as you g. up if possible,
W-pI.....41.6:5 instead, to g. a sense of turning inward,
W-pI.....65.6:5 but try to g. the sense of being willing to
W-pI.....69.2:3 literally attempting to g. in touch with the
W-pI.....72.6:6 Take the little you can g.. God gave you
WpI rVI.in.4:1 We will attempt to g. beyond all words
P-2.........in.3:3 The patient hopes to learn how to g. the
P-2...........I.1:3 It may be they will not g. much further,

## gets 2

T-15........X.5:6 accept the fact that sacrifice g. nothing.
T-29.........I.4:7 it g. away from total sacrifice and gives to

**getting** 16

T-4......... II.6:4 you are somehow g. something better,
T-4......... II.7:4 why the concept of "g." arose in the ego's
T-4......... II.7:5 system. Appetites are "g." mechanisms,
T-4........ III.9:6 is meaningful only when the idea of "g.,"
T-5...........I.1:7 spirit g. is meaningless and giving is all.
T-6...... V.B.3:1 process is the undoing of the g. concept.
T-6...... V.C.5:8 He is g. you ready for the translation of
T-6...... V.C.6:1 that *having* rests on giving, and not on g..
T-7......VIII.1:5 of g. rid of something it does not want. To
T-9......... II.10:1 If paying is equated with g., you will set
T-9......... II.10:5 The price for g. is to lose sight of value,
T-15...... IX.7:1 no value on it as a means of g. anything,
T-15..... X.5:13 is how much is the price, and for g. what.
T-17....... V.7:2 escape from your distress only by g. rid of
T-29..VIII.8:12 An idol is a means for g. more. And it is
W-pI.154.10:3 Voice the g. and the giving of God's Word

**ghost** 2

T-11..VIII.13:3 helped to translate his "g." into a curtain,
P-3...........I.4:6 on the savior of the world to let in a g.?

**ghostly** 1

W-pI...191.3:1 unnatural and g. thought that mocks

**ghosts** 2

T-11..VIII.13:1 frightening g. and monsters and dragons,
T-11..VIII.14:8 you perceive them as g. and monsters and

**giant** 10

T-6...... V.B.9:1 although it is a g. step toward the unified
T-21... VII.3:11 becomes a g. and a mouse roars like a lion
T-31.........I.2:7 taught yourself is such a g. learning feat it
W-pI..... 61.3:3 It is a g. stride toward taking your rightful
W-pI..... 61.7:3 first of a number of g. steps we will take in
W-pI... 66.10:5 us. Today's idea is another g. stride in the
W-pI..... 94.5:9 Each one you do will be a g. stride toward
W-pI... 130.9:2 will take this g. step with you in gratitude.
W-pI. 135.26:4 And all the world will take this g. stride,
W-pI... 194.1:1 quick salvation, and a g. stride it is indeed

**Gift** 1
*gift*

P-3...........I.4:6 Would he refuse this G. for a pebble, or

**gift** 378
*Gift*

T-1...... VI.5:10 this solution, and this faith *is* His g..
T-2........ III.5:4 Atonement is the only g. that is worthy of
T-3...........I.8:3 is the only appropriate g. for God's altar,
T-4.........I.12:6 to be a g. for a creation of God Himself.
T-4........ III.3:8 you prevail against the glorious g. of God
T-4........ VI.7:2 to your brother is the only g. I want. I will
T-5......... II.9:3 My only g. to you is to help you make the
T-6...... V.A.4:7 Only one equal g. can be offered to the
T-7........ IV.6:2 that it can offer you its own "will" as a g..
T-7........ IV.6:4 *it.* It is not a g.. It is nothing at all. God has
T-7........ IV.6:6 God has given you a g. that you both *have*
T-7......... V.4:4 he can offer as a g. to someone who does
T-7......... V.4:5 that the g. comes from God to him, but it
T-7....... V.11:4 because this is your proper g. to God. He
T-7....... VI.10:5 This limitless power is God's g. to you,
T-7....... VII.4:6 there is nothing there to receive your g..
T-7....... VII.5:1 The g. of life is yours to give, because it
T-7....... VII.5:2 of your g. because you do not give it. You
T-7....... VII.5:4 not extending the g. you both *have* and *are*
T-7....... VII.6:1 Only honor is a fitting g. for those whom
T-7....... VII.6:5 accept His g. for yourself and as yourself.
T-7........ XI.5:6 If you recognize His g. in anyone, you
T-8........ III.8:7 Glory is God's g. to you, because that is
T-8...........IV.h The G. of Freedom
T-8........ IV.7:9 This is our g. of gratitude to Him, which
T-8....... IV.7:10 is acceptable to Him it is the g. of freedom
T-8 ....... IV.8:1 is the only g. you can offer to God's Sons,
T-8 ....... VI.5:3 creations are your g. to the Holy Trinity,
T-8 ....... VI.5:7 you love your Father for the g. of creation.
T-8 ....... VI.5:8 There is no other g. that is eternal, and
T-8 ....... VI.5:8 therefore there is no other g. that is true.
T-10 ....... II.4:3 precludes the acceptance of God's g.,
T-10 ...... V.7:7 your heart in gratitude for your g. to Him.
T-10 ..... V.11:2 His Son removed himself from His g. by
T-11 ........I.7:2 heritage, because His one g. is Himself.
T-11 ........I.7:3 like Him if you would know His g. to you?
T-11 ....... II.6:3 for His function became yours with His g.
T-12 ..... VI.3:6 the real world is the g. of the Holy Spirit,
T-13 .... V.7:13 offer them, to recognize His g. to you.
T-13 .... V.10:6 Him, for His vision is His g. of love to you,
T-13 .... VII.8:6 yours, being the g. of God unto His Son.
T-13 .. VII.16:2 the way to quietness that is the g. of God.
T-13 .. VII.17:3 yet it is not mine, for as it is my g. to you,
T-13 .. VII.17:3 gift to you, so was it the Father's g. to me,
T-13 ... VIII.3:9 them as one with the final g. of eternity.
T-13 ... VIII.5:6 Help Him to give His g. of light to all who
T-13 ... VIII.6:6 Christ's vision is His g. to you. His Being
T-13 ... VIII.6:7 you. His Being is His Father's g. to Him.
T-13 ... VIII.7:1 healing, for Christ's g. you can bestow,
T-13 ... VIII.7:1 and your Father's g. you cannot lose.
T-13 ... VIII.7:2 Christ's g. to everyone and everywhere,
T-14 ... III.11:4 done to make you worthy of the g. of God
T-14 ... III.11:7 Do not try to escape the g. of God He so
T-14 ... IV.4:12 this small g. of appreciation for His Love,
T-14 ... IV.4:12 God will Himself exchange your g. for His
T-14 ... VIII.1:3 nothing can obscure the g. of God. It is
T-14 ... VIII.3:4 are joined in giving you the g. of oneness,
T-14 ... VIII.5:5 are brought together with the g. of God,
T-14 ..... IX.3:6 g. that you refused is held by Him in you.
T-14 ... XI.14:6 He gives the g. of peace to everyone who
T-15 ....... II.5:3 No g. of God is recognized in any other
T-15 ..... III.2:3 is much too poor a g. to satisfy you. It is
T-15 ..... III.6:1 untouched by every little g. the world of
T-15 ..... III.7:3 all your littleness to give the g. of God,
T-15 ..... VI.2:4 is in you, or it would be a limited g. to you
T-15 ... VIII.4:2 was His g., for as He withheld Himself not
T-15 ..... IX.4:4 from it, and you have denied his g. to you.
T-15 ..... IX.5:5 on them can offer you the g. of freedom.
T-15 ....... X.1:8 The only g. I can accept of you is the gift I
T-15 ....... X.1:8 only gift I can accept of you is the g. I gave
T-15 ....... X.2:3 What other g. can you offer me, when
T-15 ....... X.2:4 and offer everyone the g. you offer me.
T-15 ....... X.2:7 limited acceptance of the g. I offer you.
T-15 ....... X.3:4 The g. of union is the only gift that I was
T-15 ....... X.3:4 union is the only g. that I was born to give
T-15 ....... X.3:6 the time appointed for the g. of freedom,
T-16 ....... II.4:4 natural perception of your g. enables Him
T-16 ...... V.3:1 relationship is the ego's most boasted g.,
T-17 ..... IV.4:3 to the g. with which God blessed it, and
T-17 ..... IV.7:4 the g. is always a miniature of the thought
T-17 ..... IV.9:3 This g. is given you for your damnation,
T-17 ..... IV.9:6 is only the wrapping for the g. of conflict.
T-17 ..... IV.9:7 The frame is not the g.. Be not deceived
T-17 ..... IV.9:9 Death lies in this glittering g.. Let not
T-17 ... IV.10:2 against your acceptance of the g. of death.
T-17 ... IV.11:3 accept this g. you will not see the frame at
T-17 ... IV.11:3 the g. can only be accepted through your
T-17 ... IV.12:6 that it is the picture that is the g.. And
T-17 ... VIII.3:2 For such is the g. of faith, freely given
T-18 ...... I.10:9 His g. as our most holy and perfect reality
T-18 ....... II.7:5 has forgotten you to whom He gave the g.
T-18 ..... III.4:5 the g. of faith you offered to your brother.
T-18 ..... III.4:7 The g. is given forever, for God Himself
T-19 ........I.9:3 you offer the g. of freedom from the past,
T-19 ...... I.11:1 Faith is the g. of God, through Him
T-19 ...... I.12:3 Faith is a g. you offer to the Son of God
T-19 ..... IV.2:7 Who offered your relationship the g. of
T19. IV.D.13:2 sins against him, or accept his g. to you?
T19. IV.D.16:3 has been given the g. of holiness for you.
T19. IV.D.17:2 Into the hands that give, the g. is given.
T19. IV.D.17:3 in him the g. of God you would receive. It
T19. IV.D.17:6 Behold the g. of freedom that I gave the
T19. IV.D.17:7 as you offer to the Holy Spirit this same g.
T19. IV.D.18:2 Give him the selfsame g., nor look upon
T19. IV.D.19:6 Heaven is the g. you owe your brother,
T19 IV.D.20:1 you would look upon the giver of this g.,
T19 IV.D.20:1 on him so will the g. itself appear to be.
T-20 ........I.2:5 Offer your brother the g. of lilies, not the
T-20 ........I.2:5 the g. of love and not the "gift" of fear.
T-20 ........I.2:5 the gift of love and not the "g." of fear.
T-20 ........I.2:8 This Easter I would have the g. of your
T-20 ........I.3:6 But let the whiteness of your shining g. of
T-20 ........I.4:2 you have received and given as your g.,
T-20 ........I.4:4 Yet for your g. of lilies you will know. In
T-20 ..........II.h The G. of Lilies
T-20 ....... II.1:6 the g. proclaims his worthlessness to you,
T-20 ....... II.2:4 every g. it offers depends on what it wants
T-20 ....... II.3:1 Each g. is an evaluation of the receiver
T-20 ....... II.3:6 Here is your g. to both; your judgment on
T-20 ....... II.3:7 it is your savior to whom the g. is offered.
T-20 ....... II.6:3 use your g. of lilies while you see them not
T-20 ....... II.6:5 it. The Holy Spirit's vision is no idle g., no
T-20 .... II.10:4 Your g. has saved him from the thorns
T-20 ..... III.8:7 brother as the eternal g. of God to you?
T-20 ... III.11:1 Your g. unto your brother has given me
T-20 ....... V.2:6 and in your g. is everyone made glad.
T-20 ....... V.4:3 as you receive his Father's g. through him.
T-20 ....... V.7:1 Can you evaluate the giver of a g. like this
T-20 ....... V.7:2 Would you exchange this g. for any other
T-20 ....... V.7:3 This g. returns the laws of God to your
T-20 ....... V.7:5 is no g. your brother's body offers you.
T-20 ....... V.7:6 veil that hides the g. hides him as well. He
T-20 ....... V.7:7 He *is* the g., and yet he knows it not. No
T-20 ....... V.7:9 have faith that He Who sees the g. in you
T-20 . VIII.11:1 persuade you to accept the g. of vision?
T-21 ....... II.1:2 the little g. you offer to the Holy Spirit for
T-21 ....... II.3:7 is the little g. you offer to the Holy Spirit,
T-21 ....... II.3:8 For by this g. is given you the power to
T-21 ....... II.5:7 was your g. to you and to your brother. Be
T-21 ..... III.9:5 The g. that He has given you is more than
T-21 ..... VI.8:1 joined is your salvation; the g. of Heaven,
T-21 ..... VI.8:1 the gift of Heaven, not the g. of fear. Does
T-22 ..... VI.5:4 blessed are you who let this g. be given!
T-22 ..... VI.6:4 And who would fail to recognize a g. he
T-22 ..... VI.9:8 each little g. of love a source of healing for
T-22 ..... VI.9:9 Each little g. you offer to your brother
T-22 ... VI.15:4 to keep a little of the ego with this g.. For
T-23 ..... II.12:8 Behold, unveiled, the ego's secret g., torn
T-23 ..... II.12:8 hatred for the one to whom the g. belongs
T-23 ..... III.2:2 wrapping does not make the g. you give.
T-24 ........I.1:2 smallest g. is not to know love's purpose.
T-24 ....... II.8:3 g. that God would have him give to you.
T-24 ..... II.12:1 is the seal of treachery upon the g. of love.
T-24 ..... II.12:3 to kill. No g. that bears its seal but offers
T-24 ... IV.3:12 keep the g. your Father asks from Him,
T-24 ....... V.7:6 receiving from each one the g. of life that
T-24 .... VII.5:9 your creations recognize a g. from you, a
T-25 ....... II.9:6 This brother is His perfect g. to you. And
T-25 ..... II.10:5 it, you learn to understand His g. to you.
T-25 ....... V.5:5 you the g. of sight God gave to him for
T-25 ..... VI.3:1 and brings the g. of light that makes sight
T-25 ..... VI.5:2 he learns the g. was given to himself, and
T-25 ..... IX.2:1 To give reluctantly is not to gain the g.,
T-25 ..... IX.2:6 Each g. but adds to the supply. For God is
T-25 ..... IX.2:8 to perceive salvation as a g. from Him.
T-25 ..... IX.6:7 justice. It is not a special g. to some, to be
T-25 ..... IX.7:2 miracles, the Holy Spirit's g., were given
T-25 ..... IX.7:4 everyone is equally entitled to His g. of
T-26 ........I.8:4 the g. of freedom by receiving it of you.
T-26 ..... IV.4:2 g. that brings him nearer to his home.
T-26 .. VII.18:4 The g. of God to you is limitless. There is
T-26 .. VII.20:5 by this little g. of truth but let to be itself,
T-26 ... VIII.2:6 giving and receiving of the g. seems to be
T-26 ..... IX.5:1 this g. of what has been withheld so long.
T-27 ....... II.7:2 they bestow an equal g. of full deliverance
T-27 ..... V.11:9 He knows it is a g. of love unto His Son,
T-28 ....... II.1:4 and receives the g. that he has given Him.
T-29 ... III.3:13 By your g. of freedom is it given unto you.
T-29 ....... V.5:1 There is no g. the Father asks of you but
T-29 ....... V.5:1 but the shining glory of His g. to you.
T-29 ....... V.5:2 Behold His Son, His perfect g., in whom
T-29 ..... VI.4:1 Change is the greatest g. God gave to all
T-29 ... VIII.5:4 Its life and power are its believer's g., and
T-29 ... VIII.5:4 of the g. of Heaven and eternal peace. The

| | |
|---|---|
| T-29... VIII.8:5 | offer him a g. reality does not contain. |
| T-30...... III.2:8 | It will not bestow on you the g. you seek. |
| T-30..... V.10:3 | *you anything except the "g." of guilt. Not* |
| T-30..... VI.3:4 | While you regard it as a g. unwarranted, |
| T-31..... VII.4:4 | Born as a g. for someone not perceived to |
| T-31..... VII.5:6 | may have the g. of kind forgiveness which |
| T-31... VIII.7:1 | Deny me not the little g. I ask, when in |
| T-31... VIII.8:6 | To give this g. is how to make it yours. |
| T-31... VIII.9:1 | g. can once again be recognized as ours! |
| T-31. VIII.10:4 | be. They will accept the g. I offer them, |
| W-pI........42.h | God is my strength. Vision is His g.. |
| W-pI.....42.1:5 | And it is His g., rather than your own, |
| W-pI.....58.4:5 | is the g. of God to me and to the world. |
| W-pI.....59.2:2 | Vision is His g.. Let me not look to my |
| W-pI.....59.2:5 | Christ's vision is His g., and He has given |
| W-pI.....59.2:6 | Let me call upon this g. today, so that this |
| W-pI.....62.2:2 | is why all forgiveness is a g. to yourself. |
| W-pI.....66.8:3 | to you, it must be the g. of the ego. Does |
| W-pI.....75.7:2 | fails to give the g. of sight to the forgiving. |
| W-pI...92.10:3 | light in which the g. of sight is given you. |
| W-pI...96.12:2 | who asks for it, and will accept the g.. |
| W-pI.....97.6:1 | Thus will each g. to Him be multiplied a |
| W-pI.....97.6:2 | will surpass in might the little g. you gave |
| W-pI.....97.7:3 | this g. that you received of Him, increase |
| W-pI.....98.7:1 | give Him your tiny g. of but five minutes. |
| W-pI...105.1:4 | in which the giver loses as he gives the g.; |
| W-pI...105.1:6 | The truly given g. entails no loss. It is |
| W-pI...105.2:1 | No g. is given thus. Such "gifts" are but a |
| W-pI...105.2:2 | than was received by him who took the g.. |
| W-pI...105.3:3 | will learn a different way of looking at a g. |
| W-pI...105.4:1 | when you accept them as God's g. to you, |
| W-pI...105.5:6 | Receive His g. of joy and peace today, and |
| W-pI...105.5:6 | and He will thank you for your g. to Him. |
| W-pI...105.7:4 | Now are you ready to accept the g. of |
| W-pI...105.9:4 | to tempt you to deny God's g. to him, see |
| W-pI...107.5:1 | in its wings the g. of perfect constancy, |
| W-pI...107.5:2 | Here is the g. of healing, for the truth |
| W-pI...107.8:2 | which gave the g. of life to Him as well. |
| W-pI.107.10:3 | will increase with every g. you give of five |
| W-pI...108.9:1 | while, expecting to receive the g. you gave |
| W-pI...111.2:2 | *I see through strength, the g. of God to me.* |
| W-pI...111.2:3 | *My weakness is the dark His g. dispels, by* |
| W-pI...122.7:4 | It is the g. of God, and not the world. The |
| W-pI...124.3:1 | is our eternal g. to those who follow after, |
| W-pI.124.11:2 | Count this half hour as your g. to God, in |
| W-pI...126.3:3 | you bestow on one unworthy of the g., |
| W-pI...126.3:5 | It holds out a g. to him, but hardly to |
| W-pI...126.4:1 | yet undeserved, a g. bestowed at times, at |
| W-pI...126.4:5 | the g. is no more yours than was his sin. |
| W-pI...126.7:1 | having given Him the g. He asks of you, |
| W-pI...126.7:2 | He ask you for a g. unless it was for you? |
| W-pI...126.7:4 | Salvation is a better g. than this. And true |
| W-pI...127.8:4 | and let the g. of God replace them all. |
| W-pI...132.7:1 | But healing is the g. of those who are |
| W-pI...134.1:1 | wrath, a g. unjustified and undeserved, |
| W-pI...134.8:5 | if one brother has received this g. of you, |
| W-pI.137.10:4 | legions upon legions will receive the g. |
| W-pI.137.13:2 | worth the giving to receive a g. like this? |
| W-pI.137.13:3 | expense to offer for the g. of everything? |
| W-pI.137.14:1 | Yet must we be prepared for such a g.. |
| WpI.rIV.in7:5 | that day give you the g. that He has laid in |
| W-pI.151.16:2 | lay the g. of snow-white lilies on the world |
| W-pI...152.2:3 | If you have the g. of everything, can loss |
| W-pI...152.9:3 | God's perfect g. to His beloved Son. We |
| W-pI.154.12:3 | left no g. beyond what you already have; |
| W-pI...156.4:3 | The scent of flowers is their g. to you. The |
| W-pI...158.5:3 | time. But vision is his g.. This he can give |
| W-pI.158.11:2 | Yet time has still one g. to give, in which |
| W-pI...159.6:1 | This is the Holy Spirit's single g.; the |
| W-pI...159.7:6 | the g. of his acceptance of his welcoming. |
| W-pI.159.10:2 | give. Are you not worth the g., when God |
| W-pI.159.10:5 | It is His g., whereby a sweet transition can |
| W-pI.160.10:5 | and thus refusing to accept the g. of sight |
| W-pI...164.7:3 | Our practicing today becomes our g. of |
| W-pI...164.9:5 | Practice in earnest, and the g. is yours. |
| W-pI...165.4:3 | Nor need you perceive how great the g., |
| W-pI...168.3:1 | Today we ask of God the g. He has most |
| W-pI...168.3:2 | g. by which God leans to us and lifts us up |
| W-pI...168.3:5 | g. of grace is more than just an answer. It |
| W-pI...169.1:4 | received; an altar clean and holy for the g. |
| W-pI...169.2:2 | minds are lighted by the g. of grace can |
| W-pI.169.12:2 | for grace, the final g. salvation can bestow |
| WpI...rV.in9:1 | Let this review be then your g. to me. For |
| W-pI...183.9:1 | which you will experience the g. of grace. |
| W-pI.185.12:1 | and established as His Own eternal g.. |
| W-pI.185.12:4 | No g. of God can be unshared. It is this |
| W-pI.185.13:1 | and everyone must gain whenever any g. |
| W-pI.186.13:3 | though He is complete; a g. to you, |
| W-pI...187.9:5 | leave instead the perfect g. forever there, |
| W-pI...188.4:3 | To you, the giver of the g., does God |
| W-pI...188.6:3 | has power to give the g. of sight to you. |
| W-pI...189.6:1 | which is the g. its Love bestows on us. We |
| W-pI...191.5:4 | his salvation is the g. he gives to everyone, |
| W-pI...191.8:3 | to give the world the g. of his forgiveness. |
| W-pI...192.6:1 | that, for Christ's vision and the g. of sight, |
| W-pI...194.2:3 | salvation thus becomes the g. you give the |
| W-pI...197.5:1 | God blesses every g. you give to Him, and |
| W-pI...197.5:1 | give to Him, and every g. is given Him, |
| W-pI...198.1:6 | Then are you free, for freedom is your g., |
| W-pI...198.1:6 | and you can now receive the g. you gave. |
| W-pI...198.5:2 | and accept His g. with gratitude? And is it |
| W-pI.198.10:2 | This is the g. the Holy Spirit holds for you |
| W-pI.198.13:3 | For He would give to us the g. that God |
| W-pI...199.7:2 | carry freedom as your g. to those who still |
| W-pI...199.7:5 | Who calls to you to make this g. to Him. |
| WpI rVI.in.7:4 | best become a loving g. of freedom to the |
| W-pII..224.1:3 | It is the g. my Father gave to me; the one |
| W-pII..224.1:4 | is no g. but this that can be either given or |
| W-pII..233.1:7 | *but which is yet Your perfect g. to me.* |
| W-pII..236.2:3 | *it to You. Accept my g., for it is Yours to me.* |
| W-pII.....242.h | This day is God's. It is my g. to Him. |
| W-pII..270.1:1 | *Father, Christ's vision is Your g. to me, and* |
| W-pII...... 7.1:2 | g. to everyone who turns to Him for truth |
| W-pII...... 7.5:1 | Accept your Father's g.. It is a Call from |
| W-pII...... 7.5:3 | The Holy Spirit is His g., by which the |
| W-pII..287.1:3 | g. could I prefer before the peace of God? |
| W-pII..295.1:2 | this g. that He may offer peace of mind to |
| W-pII..295.2:1 | *My Father, Christ has asked a g. of me, and* |
| W-pII.....297.h | Forgiveness is the only g. I give. |
| W-pII..297.1:1 | Forgiveness is the only g. I give, because |
| W-pII..297.1:1 | gift I give, because it is the only g. I want. |
| W-pII..304.2:3 | *It is Your g., my Father, given me to offer to* |
| W-pII..305.2:2 | *Help us today but to accept Your g., and* |
| W-pII.....306.h | The g. of Christ is all I seek today. |
| W-pII...306.2:4 | *Son. But in Your Love the g. of Christ is his.* |
| W-pII.... 10.1:1 | Son of God this g.: to hear the Voice for |
| W-pII.... 10.3:1 | God's Judgment is the g. of the Correction |
| W-pII..311.1:5 | make a g. of it to Him Who has a different |
| W-pII..313.1:3 | *This vision is Your g.. The eyes of Christ look* |
| W-pII..315.1:4 | my mind receives this g. and takes it as its |
| W-pII..316.1:1 | As every g. my brothers give is mine, so |
| W-pII..316.1:1 | is mine, so every g. I give belongs to me. |
| W-pII..316.1:3 | His grace is given me in every g. a brother |
| W-pII..316.1:4 | its open doors that not one g. is lost, and |
| W-pII..322.1:3 | abides in every g. that I receive of Him. |
| W-pII..333.2:4 | *being Your g. to Your beloved Son.* |
| W-pII.... 13.2:1 | A miracle contains the g. of grace, for it is |
| W-pII..343.1:2 | *The g. of everything can be but gain. You* |
| W-pII..343.2:3 | a g. that must be freely given and received |
| W-pII.....344.h | that what I give my brother is my g. to me |
| W-pII..345.1:6 | *to Your gifts than any other g. that I can give.* |
| W-pII..345.1:7 | *Then let me give this g. alone today, which,* |
| W-pII..347.1:4 | *freedom, and I choose to claim Your g. today* |
| W-pII..349.1:3 | *I have chosen it as the g. I want to give. Father* |
| W-pII.... 14.3:3 | And this, our g., is therefore given us. We |
| Wfl ........in.5:1 | end this year without the g. our Father |
| M-4 ..... I.A.5:8 | of him, he finds a g. bestowed on him. |
| M-6 ........... 2:8 | to judge when his g. should be accepted. |
| M-6 ........... 3:3 | the outcome, for that is part of the g.. No |
| M-6 ........... 3:5 | giver nor the receiver would have the g.. |
| M-6 ........... 3:7 | Who gives a g. and then remains with it, |
| M-6 ........... 4:1 | about the g. that makes it truly given. |
| M-6 ........... 4:4 | mind of the giver Who gives the g. to him. |
| M-6 ........... 4:9 | And if one g. is missing, it would not be |
| M-7 ......... 1:10 | so he has not received the benefit of his g. |
| M-7 ........... 3:7 | let him remember Who gave the g. and |
| M-7 ........... 4:8 | not the g. and it is impossible to doubt its |
| M-8 ........... 6:5 | unreal. This is the g. of its Teacher; the |
| M-17 ......... 2:8 | Here is his g. most clearly given him. For |
| M-17 ....... 2:10 | And in this g. is his judgment upon the |
| M-20 ......... 4:8 | A tranquil mind is not a little g.. Would |
| M-20 ......... 6:6 | mighty Will of God Himself His g. to you. |
| C-3............. 7:4 | But Will is constant, as the g. of God. And |
| C-3............. 7:7 | It is the g. of God to save His Son. But |
| P-1............. 2:1 | it and give it His Own great g. of rejoicing |
| P-2........ IV.5:5 | by Him to the Holy Spirit as His g. to you |
| P-2......... V.5:4 | do for him becomes the g. we give to God. |
| P-2......... V.6:8 | does not seem to be a g. from Heaven. It |
| P-3.........I.2:11 | Or a greater g. to you? Would you rather |
| P-3..........II.5:3 | blessed by the Holy Spirit as a g. from |
| P-3..........II.7:5 | but they have not accepted the g. entirely |
| P-3........ III.3:5 | g. whereby all healing is accomplished. |
| P-3........ III.4:9 | Who would not be grateful for such a g.? |
| P-3........ III.7:9 | greater g. than this could you be given? |
| P-3...... III.7:10 | greater g. is there that you would give? |
| P-3........ III.8:2 | will come to you carrying the g. of healing |
| S-1.........in.1:1 | Prayer is the greatest g. with which God |
| S-1.........in.3:6 | is. This is the way. It is God's g. to you. |
| S-1...........I.3:2 | It is the song that is the g.. Along with it |
| S-1...........I.7:1 | because it is a g. of thanks to His Father. |
| S-1..........II.7:7 | sinlessness that is the g. of God to you, |
| S-2...........I.1:1 | No g. of Heaven has been more |
| S-2...........I.8:4 | need, and God holds out this g. to you. As |
| S-2..........II.3:5 | and the holiness that is His g. forever. |
| S-2........ III.6:2 | About salvation and the g. of peace. |
| S-2........ III.6:7 | death become again the holy g. of God. |
| S-2........ III.7:4 | to Christ, Who welcomes it as g. to Him. |
| S-3...........I.3:2 | is the g. of holiness and love. Forgiveness |
| S-3...........I.4:5 | The power to heal is now his Father's g., |
| S-3....... II.5:11 | is the only g. you give and would receive. |
| S-3........ III.4:5 | of the special g. that brings the healing. |
| S-3........ IV.3:5 | creation, for it lies in you as His eternal g.. |
| S-3........ IV.9:7 | dear is every g. to Me that you have made, |
| S-3........ IV.9:9 | will come the g. first of forgiveness, then |

## gifts 232

| | |
|---|---|
| T-1......... V.3:3 | all His g. are freely given to everyone alike |
| T-3....... VII.2:7 | souls in return for g. of no real worth. |
| T-4........ III.5:3 | to the immeasurable g. which are for you, |
| T-7................h | THE G. OF THE KINGDOM |
| T-7...........I.4:6 | God does not limit His g. in any way. You |
| T-7...........I.4:7 | You *are* His g., and so your gifts must be |
| T-7...........I.4:7 | His gifts, and so your g. must be like His. |
| T-7...........I.4:8 | Your g. to the Kingdom must be like His |
| T-7...........I.4:8 | to the Kingdom must be like His g. to you |
| T-7...........I.5:2 | you believe you are determines your g., |
| T-7..... VII.11:4 | this. The g. you offer to the ego are always |
| T-7..... VII.11:4 | but the g. you offer to the Kingdom are |
| T-7..... VII.11:4 | you offer to the Kingdom are g. to you. |
| T-7........ IX.1:3 | Do not withhold your g. to the Sonship, |
| T-8....... VII.6:4 | He has not withdrawn His g. from you, |
| T-9...........I.8:6 | ask the Holy Spirit for "g." such as these, |
| T-9..... VIII.1:4 | and attempts to offer g. to induce you to |
| T-10... V.10:10 | in your creation, and His g. are eternal. |
| T-10..... V.11:1 | Out of your g. to Him the Kingdom will |
| T-10..... V.13:3 | Your g. to yourself are meaningless, but |
| T-10..... V.13:3 | but your g. to your creations are like His, |
| T-11............I.h | The G. of Fatherhood |
| T-12........II.5:1 | Christ, and so they are not fit g. for you. |
| T-12...... III.3:4 | Their poverty asks for g., not for further |
| T-13.... VI.13:4 | for you, and given you the g. He gave. |
| T-13..... X.13:6 | and for the many g. that you will let me |
| T-14.... VIII.2:4 | will be replaced by g. wholly acceptable to |
| T-14.... VIII.2:7 | and g. to One are offered to the Other. |
| T-14.... VIII.5:4 | Lay no g. other than this upon your altars |
| T-14.... VIII.5:7 | Your little g. will vanish on the altar, |
| T-14.... XI.10:6 | He always gives His g. in place of yours. |
| T-15...... III.8:5 | have sought to purchase it with little g., |
| T-15.... III.10:7 | will make no more g. to offer to yourself, |
| T-15..... VII.9:1 | Suffering and sacrifice are the g. with |
| T-16..... VII.8:2 | For God's g. have no reality apart from |
| T-17...... IV.7:4 | Every defense operates by giving g., and |
| T-17.... IV.11:8 | thought system of the ego lies in its g., so |
| T-17.... IV.12:1 | Two g. are offered you. Each is complete, |
| T-17..... V.15:1 | begin to recognize and accept the g. you |
| T-20........II.2:1 | G. are not made through bodies, if they |

| | |
|---|---|
| T-20....... II.2:5 | making it ready to receive the g. it wants |
| T-20....... II.2:6 | it. And there they will exchange their g., |
| T-20....... V.2:7 | not Who has given you the g. you give, |
| T-20....... V.2:7 | Who gave the g. to Him to give to you. |
| T-21....... II.7:2 | unoccupied the altar where the g. belong. |
| T-21...... IV.6:6 | that all the g. it would withdraw from you |
| T-22...... VI.8:7 | Spirit does with g. you give your brother, |
| T-22...... VI.9:5 | Him the tiny g. He can extend forever. He |
| T-23...... IV.4:4 | your little g. and make them mighty. Also |
| T-24.... IV.3:14 | Offered to them, no g. can be returned. |
| T-25.... VIII.9:6 | out to you the g. the innocent deserve. |
| T-26.........I.7:8 | His g. can never suffer sacrifice and loss. |
| T-26...... VI.3:5 | He brings you g. that are not of this world |
| T-27... VII.15:6 | brush aside his many g. because he is not |
| T-27... VII.16:2 | Yet what you see as g. your brother offers |
| T-27... VII.16:2 | the g. you dream your Father gives to you. |
| T-27... VII.16:3 | Let all your brother's g. be seen in light of |
| T-27... VII.16:4 | of deep appreciation for his g. to you. |
| T-29....... II.4:4 | And yet His g. came with Him. He has |
| T-29....... II.4:7 | will be healed when you accept your g., |
| T-29....... II.4:7 | stand, and where His g. for them are laid. |
| T-29....... II.5:4 | And nowhere else His g. of peace and joy, |
| T-29....... II.5:6 | Guest, but you can see the g. He brought. |
| T-30....... V.1:3 | no longer, for their "g." are not held dear. |
| T-30.... VIII.4:7 | freedom to bestow His g. upon God's Son |
| W-pI..... 42.2:6 | is the strength of God. Such are His g.. |
| W-pI..... 42.4:7 | or: *God's g. to me must be mine, because He* |
| W-pI..... 66.8:4 | Does the ego really have g. to give, being |
| W-pI..... 66.8:4 | illusion and offering only the illusion of g. |
| W-pI..... 97.5:2 | that will accept the healing g. they bring, |
| W-pI..... 98.8:2 | chance to be the glad receiver of His g., |
| W-pI..... 98.9:3 | and peace and trust will be His g.; His |
| W-pI... 99.10:2 | You cannot lose the g. your Father gave. |
| W-pI... 100.4:4 | who will accept their Father's g. as theirs. |
| W-pI... 104.1:4 | be a place made ready to receive His g.. |
| W-pI... 104.1:5 | received the g. it made where His belong, |
| W-pI... 104.2:1 | and self-made g. which we have placed |
| W-pI... 104.2:1 | upon the holy altar where God's g. belong |
| W-pI... 104.2:2 | His are the g. that are our own in truth. |
| W-pI... 104.2:3 | the g. that we inherited before time was, |
| W-pI... 104.2:4 | His are the g. that are within us now, for |
| W-pI... 104.3:4 | other g. and other goals made of illusions, |
| W-pI... 104.4:2 | where His g. of peace and joy are welcome |
| W-pI... 104.5:1 | and peace belong to us as His eternal g.. |
| W-pI... 104.5:5 | *truth. God's g. of joy and peace are all I want.* |
| W-pI... 105.1:3 | these g. increase as we receive them. They |
| W-pI... 105.1:4 | are not like to the g. the world can give, in |
| W-pI... 105.1:5 | Such are not g., but bargains made with |
| W-pI... 105.2:2 | "g." are but a bid for a more valuable |
| W-pI... 105.2:4 | It strips all meaning from the g. you give, |
| W-pI... 105.3:4 | God's g. will never lessen when they are |
| W-pI... 105.7:3 | yourself to recognize God's g. to you, and |
| W-pI... 105.9:4 | let yourself receive the g. of God as yours. |
| W-pI... 106.1:1 | if you will not accept its petty g. that give |
| W-pI... 108.9:4 | to think of one to whom to give your g.. |
| WpI. rIII.in9:3 | prove how great are its potential g. to you |
| W-pI... 117.2:3 | *it joy. These are the g. my Father gave to me.* |
| W-pI... 122.3:4 | What g. but these are worthy to be sought |
| W-pI... 122.7:5 | The world can give no g. of any value to a |
| W-pI... 122.9:1 | Remembering the g. forgiveness gives, |
| W-pI. 122.12:2 | and we receive the g. that have been held |
| W-pI. 122.13:3 | Let not your g. recede throughout the day |
| W-pI. 122.13:4 | Retain your g. in clear awareness as you |
| W-pI. 122.14:1 | tempted not to let your g. slip by and drift |
| W-pI. 122.14:2 | precious are these g. with this reminder, |
| W-pI. 122.14:2 | power to hold your g. in your awareness |
| W-pI. 122.14:5 | *as true. Today I have received the g. of God.* |
| W-pI...... 123.h | I thank my Father for His g. to me. |
| W-pI... 123.2:1 | you have made; the g. you have received. |
| W-pI... 123.3:5 | your value far transcends your meager g. |
| W-pI... 123.6:3 | He receives your g. in loving gratitude, |
| W-pI... 123.6:4 | He will bless your g. by sharing them with |
| W-pI... 124.7:4 | For we would keep the g. our Father gave. |
| W-pI... 126.7:1 | asks of you, you cannot recognize His g., |
| W-pI... 126.7:3 | evaluate such petty g. as worthy of His |
| W-pI... 127.8:4 | upon its meager offerings and senseless g. |
| W-pI... 135.5:4 | or give it g. to make it beautiful or walls to |
| W-pI. 136.12:5 | it sighs a little when you throw away its g. |
| WpI. rIV.in8:2 | to see the g. that they contain for you, and |
| W-pI... 142.1:1 | (123) I thank my Father for His g. to me. |
| W-pI... 153.1:1 | the "g." it merely lends to take away again |
| W-pI... 153.1:3 | all its "g." of seeming safety are illusory |
| W-pI. 153.17:2 | for all the g. He gave us in the one gone by |
| W-pI. 153.20:5 | These are His g. to you. Defenselessness is |
| W-pI. 154.11:1 | have, that we may recognize His g. to us. |
| W-pI. 154.11:5 | be the true receivers of the g. He gives. |
| W-pI. 154.14:4 | our many g. from our Creator will spring |
| W-pI... 156.4:2 | All things that live bring g. to you, and |
| W-pI. 158.11:4 | And by the holy g. we give, Christ's vision |
| W-pI... 162.4:3 | God places all His g. and all His Love, to |
| W-pI... 164.3:4 | you who will today accept the g. He gives. |
| W-pI... 164.9:1 | Let not today slip by without the g. it |
| W-pI...... 166.h | I am entrusted with the g. of God. |
| W-pI... 166.1:5 | is one with His, His g. are not received. |
| W-pI... 166.3:1 | g. of God are not acceptable to anyone |
| W-pI... 166.3:2 | He must believe that to accept God's g., |
| W-pI... 166.5:1 | wanderings, God's g. go with him, all |
| W-pI... 166.8:1 | hand directing you to look upon your g.. |
| W-pI... 166.9:5 | Perhaps His g. to you are real. Perhaps He |
| W-pI. 166.11:4 | He points to all the g. you have each time |
| W-pI. 166.12:3 | The g. you have are not for you alone. |
| W-pI. 166.12:6 | you of all the g. that God has given you. |
| W-pI. 166.12:7 | your will when you accept these g., and |
| W-pI. 166.13:1 | The g. are yours, entrusted to your care, |
| W-pI. 166.13:5 | touch of Christ, and recognize God's g.. |
| W-pI. 166.14:5 | accepts God's g. can never suffer anything |
| W-pI. 166.15:3 | God has entrusted all His g. to you. Be |
| W-pI. 166.15:4 | becomes which chooses to accept His g., |
| W-pI. 166.15:6 | of His g. to all who have received them. |
| W-pI. 169.14:1 | and accept the g. that grace provided you. |
| W-pI... 178.2:1 | (166) I am entrusted with the g. of God. |
| W-pI. 185.12:5 | this attribute that sets the g. of God apart |
| W-pI... 188.3:6 | by. All of its g. are given everyone, and |
| W-pI... 188.4:2 | radiates with g. beyond all measure, given |
| W-pI... 188.4:4 | to the g. you have to offer to the world. |
| W-pI. 189.10:6 | *Our hands are open to receive Your g.. We* |
| W-pI... 193.8:4 | Love, and all the g. His Love brings with it |
| W-pI... 195.6:3 | we fail to recognize the g. of God to us. |
| W-pI... 197.1:4 | Your g. must be received with honor, lest |
| W-pI... 197.1:5 | so you think God's g. are loans at best; at |
| W-pI... 197.3:3 | Your gratitude is all your g. require, that |
| W-pI... 197.3:4 | you would undo by taking back your g., |
| W-pI... 197.3:5 | for it is you who have received the g.. |
| W-pI... 197.4:1 | matter if another thinks your g. unworthy |
| W-pI... 197.4:3 | matter if your g. seem lost and ineffectual |
| W-pI... 197.5:3 | Yet you will never realize His g. are sure, |
| W-pI... 197.6:1 | Withdraw the g. you give, and you will |
| W-pI... 197.6:2 | the g. of God are lent but for a little while, |
| W-pI. 198.12:4 | could give him g. when everything is his? |
| W-pI... 199.5:3 | will not gain in added g. to you as well. |
| W-pI... 199.5:5 | from the acceptance of the g. you give? |
| W-pI... 206.1:2 | *I am entrusted with the g. of God, because I* |
| W-pI... 206.1:3 | *give His g. where He intended them to be.* I |
| W-pII ...in.6:5 | Accept these little g. of thanks from us, as |
| W-pII ..... 2.3:4 | the g. of your forgiveness laid before it, |
| W-pII . 233.2:4 | a day of countless g. and mercies unto us. |
| W-pII . 234.2:2 | *thanks for all the g. You have bestowed on us* |
| W-pII . 239.1:2 | be thankful for the g. our Father gave us. |
| W-pII . 273.2:3 | *I cannot lose Your g. to me. And so the peace* |
| W-pII . 279.2:3 | *Would You withhold the g. You gave to me?* |
| W-pII . 284.2:2 | *today, accepting but the joyous as Your g.;* |
| W-pII . 297.2:2 | *Thanks be to You for Your eternal g., and* |
| W-pII . 298.2:4 | *grateful for Your holy g. of certain sanctuary* |
| W-pII . 306.2:1 | *went away; remembering Your holy g. to us.* |
| W-pII .... 315.h | All g. my brothers give belong to me. |
| W-pII . 315.1:2 | I am blessed with g. throughout the day, |
| W-pII . 315.2:1 | *many g. that come to me today and every day* |
| W-pII . 315.2:2 | *brothers are unlimited in all their g. to me.* |
| W-pII .... 316.h | All g. I give my brothers are my own. |
| W-pII . 316.1:5 | among the g. that God has given me. |
| W-pII . 316.2:1 | *Father, I would accept Your g. today. I do* |
| W-pII . 322.1:2 | illusions go I find the g. illusions tried to |
| W-pII . 330.1:4 | accept God's g. has been restored to spirit |
| W-pII .... 334.h | Today I claim the g. forgiveness gives. |
| W-pII . 334.1:3 | me not accept such meager g. again today |
| W-pII . 344.1:6 | *me g. beyond the worth of anything on earth* |
| W-pII . 345.1:1 | *Father, a miracle reflects Your g. to me,* |
| W-pII . 345.1:6 | *to Your g. than any other gift that I can give.* |
| W-pII . 349.1:4 | *Father, Your g. are mine. Each one that I* |
| WpII361-5.1:3 | mind, these are the g. I will receive of Him |
| M-4 ........... 1:4 | are. God gives special g. to His teachers, |
| M-4 ........... 1:6 | of time. These special g., born in the holy |
| M-4 ......... I.2:3 | when the g. of God are laid before him? |
| M-4 ...... V.1:11 | They hold His g. and follow in His way, |
| M-6 ........... 2:4 | And what is time before the g. of God? |
| M-6 ........... 2:5 | for the giver and the receiver of God's g.. |
| M-6 ........... 3:1 | to evaluate the outcome of their g.. It is |
| M-6 ......... 4:11 | of God have about what becomes of his g. |
| M-7 ........... 3:3 | because he gives the g. he has received. |
| M-7 ........... 3:9 | the g. of God could be withdrawn. That |
| M-15 ......... 3:4 | regardless of your judgments on its g., |
| M-23 ......... 1:1 | God's g. can rarely be received directly. |
| M-23 ......... 4:5 | for all the g. that God has given you. And |
| M-25 ......... 5:2 | withdrawn from the world's material g., |
| M-25 ......... 6:9 | The Holy Spirit needs these g., and those |
| M-26 ......... 2:9 | give all their g. to the teachers of God who |
| M-28 ......... 1:5 | It is the recognition of the g. of God. It is |
| M-29 ......... 5:2 | his Creator and accept His g.. And His |
| M-29 ......... 5:3 | And His g. have no limit. To ask the Holy |
| P-1............. 1:5 | which He offers His greater g. to both. |
| P-2.........V.5:1 | A brother seeking aid can bring us g. |
| P-2.........V.7:1 | all g. of God must be received. In time no |
| P-2....... VII.6:6 | he has the g. of God Himself to give away. |
| P-3...........I.3:2 | God will not have His g. to you limited to |
| S-1...........I.4:4 | There they become your g. to Him, for |
| S-1..........II.3:4 | also possible to ask for g. such as honesty |
| S-1........ III.6:1 | human love, for external "g." of any kind, |
| S-2........ III.1:4 | not offer g. in treachery, nor promise |
| S-2........ III.2:1 | You child of God, the g. of God are yours, |
| S-3..........II.3:4 | hard to see the g. we gave were saved for |
| S-3........ IV.1:5 | have no g. but those they have from God. |
| S-3........ IV.1:9 | bestow unequal g. on those less fortunate. |

## gilded 1

| | |
|---|---|
| T-17 ..... IV.8:3 | with g. threads of self-destruction. The |

## give 865

| | |
|---|---|
| T-1 ........I.16:1 | it is as blessed to g. as to receive. They |
| T-2 .......V.1:11 | then, that inducing the mind to g. up its |
| T-2 .........V.5:5 | The message you then g. to them is the |
| T-2 .....VIII.5:8 | to "g. you time" to achieve this judgment. |
| T-3 ..........I.2:6 | many have been unwilling to g. it up in |
| T-3 ....... VI.6:2 | received and that is what you should g.. |
| T-3 ....... VI.9:1 | Only those who g. over all desire to reject |
| T-4 ..........I.5:1 | Every good teacher hopes to g. his |
| T-4 .........II.6:3 | to g. anything implies that you will have |
| T-4 .........II.6:4 | you g. only because you believe that you |
| T-4 .........II.6:4 | can therefore do without the thing you g.. |
| T-4 ....... III.7:1 | mind to g. up every idea you ever had that |
| T-4 ....... VI.8:4 | only as you will g. Him to your brothers. |
| T-5 .........I.1:13 | the one to whom you g. it accepts it as his, |
| T-5 .........II.5:3 | By choosing one you g. up the other. The |
| T-5 .......II.12:6 | hear and g. away as you answer the Holy |
| T-5 ....... III.2:7 | in you as you g. it to your brother. Your |
| T-5 ....... IV.2:7 | I have come to g. you the foundation, so |
| T-5 ..... IV.3:11 | purified He lets you g. them away. The |
| T-5 ....... IV.5:6 | What I learned I g. you freely, and the |
| T-5 ....... IV.6:3 | complete until you join it and g. it away. |
| T-5 ....... IV.7:2 | idea of healing, they must g. it to hold it. |
| T-5 ..... IV.8:11 | hold it, and the hands are strong to g. it. |
| T-5 .........V.2:3 | giving rise to guilt, and must g. rise to joy. |
| T-5 ...... VI.7:3 | G. it therefore to the Holy Spirit, Who |
| T-5 ..... VI.12:7 | He is the only blessing you can truly g., |
| T-5 ..... VI.12:8 | you must g. Him as you received Him. |
| T-5 ...... VII.6:5 | and g. it over to the Atonement in peace. |
| T-6 .........I.11:6 | to g. in to anger and assault would not be |
| T-6 ........V.A.h | To Have, G. All to All |
| T-6 ... V.A.5:10 | only what each one can g. to all. He never |
| T-6 ... V.A.5:13 | begins with the lesson: *To have, g. all to all.* |
| T-6 ..... V.B.3:2 | first lesson was "To have, g. all to all." I |
| T-7 ..........I.1:7 | Parents g. birth to children, but children |
| T-7 ..........I.1:7 | but children do not g. birth to parents. |
| T-7 ..........I.1:8 | do, however, g. birth to their children, |
| T-7 ..........I.1:8 | and thus g. birth as their parents do. |
| T-7 ..........I.4:3 | To gain you must g., not bargain. To |

T-7.......V.9:10 joy that *is* the Kingdom lies in you to g..
T-7.......V.9:11 in you to give. Do you not want to g. it?
T-7.......V.11:5 He will accept it and g. it to the Sonship,
T-7.......VI.8:9 must g. up the idea of conflict entirely
T-7.......VII.1:5 but you can g. it the power of your mind,
T-7.......VII.5:1 The gift of life is yours to g., because it
T-7.......VII.5:2 of your gift because you do not g. it. You
T-7.......VII.5:8 G. only honor to the Sons of the living
T-7.......VII.6:2 G. them the appreciation God accords
T-7.......VII.7:7 G., therefore, of your abundance, and
T-7.......VIII.1:6 by which you g. what you value in order
T-7.......VIII.2:4 lest you g. the ego up and free yourself.
T-7.......VIII.5:6 G. them over quickly to the Holy Spirit to
T-7.......IX.6:2 Since it was the Will of God to g. it to you,
T-7.......XI.3:4 fear, and allow him to g. always, without
T-7.......XI.3:11 g. the Love of God to everything you see
T-8.......I.2:1 you unless you g. it the power to do so.
T-8.......I.3:5 How can you have what you g. up? You
T-8.......I.3:6 to have, but you do not g. it up yourself.
T-8.......I.3:7 When you g. up peace, you are excluding
T-8.......III.3:4 The Father must g. fatherhood to His Son
T-8.......III.5:12 G. him his place in the Kingdom and you
T-8.......IV.3:5 This is the awareness I came to g. you,
T-8.......IV.4:2 Do you not want to g. it to the world as
T-8.......IV.4:4 If you want to have it of me, you must g. it
T-8.......V.6:10 I g. it willingly and gladly, because I need
T-8.......VI.5:9 accept anything else or g. anything else,
T-8.......VII.4:5 If the body becomes a means you g. to the
T-8.......VII.5:6 but g. him freedom from his belief in
T-8.......VIII.3:5 not g. this false witness to the ego's stand.
T-8.......VIII.6:9 premises g. rise in order to judge them
T-8.......IX.4:2 To whom did you g. it? Under which
T-8.......IX.8:4 I g. you no limits because God lays none
T-9.......I.7:4 could not possibly g. you what you want.
T-9.......I.8:7 cannot g. you something you do not want
T-9.......II.11:1 you receive, and price it by what you g..
T-9.......II.11:8 What you g. is therefore the value you put
T-9.......II.12:1 g. to Him only where you recognize Him.
T-9.......III.5:3 want to g. yours over to the Holy Spirit,
T-9.......III.8:8 G. it to Him! You do not understand how
T-9.......V.1:4 he is trying to g. what he has not received.
T-9.......V.5:6 healer therefore does not know how to g.,
T-9.......VI.2:3 inconsistent you will not always g. rise to
T-9.......VII.8:7 will g. you all of Himself in exchange for
T-9.......VIII.4:2 because you will g. up all investment in it.
T-10.......II.2:1 to g. up the dissociation of reality brings
T-10.......II.2:4 G. up gladly everything that would stand
T-10.......II.3:7 will g. you everything but for the asking.
T-10.......III.6:6 When I said, "My peace I g. unto you," I
T-10..III.10:11 fear you have been willing to g. up your
T-10.......III.11:4 g. up the god of sickness for your brothers
T-10.......III.11:4 have to do so if you g. him up for yourself.
T-10.......IV.4:10 it from you, and you cannot g. it to them.
T-10.......IV.5:1 You are not free to g. up freedom, but
T-10.......V.2:2 you g. because it is the message you want.
T-10.......V.2:3 your brothers by the messages they g. you
T-10.......V.2:3 them by the message you g. to them. Do
T-11.......in.4:5 I g. you the lamp and I will go with you.
T-11.......I.6:7 To g. without limit is God's Will for you,
T-11.......I.7:3 g. except like Him if you would know His
T-11.......I.7:4 G., then, without limit and without end,
T-11.......I.7:5 on your willingness to g. as He gives.
T-11.......I.9:3 of you what you do not want to g., and
T-11.......III.7:2 He waits to g. you the peace that is yours.
T-11.......III.7:3 G. His peace, that you may enter the
T-11.......V.8:2 For if the ego could g. rise to fear, it would
T-11.......V.8:3 allegiance is that it can g. power to you.
T-11.......VI.9:5 unless you g. all that you have received
T-11... VIII.6:1 Holy Spirit will g. you only what is yours,
T-11... VIII.8:7 in him, to g. to anyone who asks it of him.
T-11. VIII.10:3 for It, you will g. It because you want It.
T-12.......I.1:8 To interpret error is to g. it power, and
T-12.......I.3:6 except the willingness to g. it to him, for
T-12.......I.5:3 are unwilling to g. help and to receive it.
T-12.......II.2:2 g. no power to the fog to obscure the light
T-12.......II.3:4 And to g. a brother what he really wants
T-12.......II.8:5 G. me but a little trust in the name of the
T-12.......III.1:1 you have and g. to the poor and follow me
T-12.......IV.4:6 the goal He sets before you He will g. you.
T-12.......VI.5:7 this, He would g. you what is yours. In
T-12.......VII.9:3 reality, for its reality is only what you g. it.
T-12.......VII.9:4 You cannot really g. anything but love to
T-12.......VII.9:5 to g. something else within yourself. It
T-12. VIII.7:10 God did not g. you has no power over you
T-13.......III.10:3 God did not g. it for the request was alien
T-13.......III.10:4 of Him what only such a father could g..
T-13.......III.12:8 hears His answer but will g. up insanity.
T-13.......VI.11:1 There is a light that this world cannot g..
T-13.......VI.11:2 Yet you can g. it, as it was given you. And
T-13.......VI.11:3 And as you g. it, it shines forth to call you
T-13.......VII.3:7 You could not g. it that, and so although
T-13.......VII.4:4 All that you need to g. this world away in
T-13.......VII.6:6 g. this sad world over and exchange your
T-13...VII.12:2 will g. you all things that do not block the
T-13...VII.16:8 My peace I g. you. Take it of me in glad
T-13...VII.17:8 G. thanks to every part of you that you
T-13...VII.17:9 Thus does the Son of God g. thanks unto
T-13... VIII.5:6 Help Him to g. His gift of light to all who
T-13.......IX.1:5 Therefore g. no obedience to its laws, for
T-13.......IX.3:1 world can g. you only what you gave it,
T-13.......X.5:3 and g. your mind in peace over to the
T-13.......X.7:3 G. no reality to guilt, and see no reason
T-13.......X.13:4 is as strong as all the love I g. my Father.
T-13.......XI.4:1 Nothing in this world can g. this peace,
T-14.......I.1:3 to bless, and cannot g. what you have not.
T-14.......I.1:5 as yours, for how else could you g. it away
T-14.......I.2:4 you decide to have and g. and be nothing
T-14.......I.2:5 And if you have and g. and are everything
T-14.......II.6:1 you must g. everything you have learned
T-14.......IV.3:1 He will g. Himself to you as He has always
T-14.......IV.5:6 G. up this frantic and insane attempt that
T-14.......IV.8:6 even g. a blessing in perfect gentleness.
T-14... V.10:11 And everything you g. to God is yours.
T-14.......VI.3:1 continue to g. imagined power to these
T-14...VII.6:11 and He will g. it to you as you join your
T-14.......X.10:4 your thoughts and g. only the answer
T-14.......X.12:2 must g. it to you because of what it is. But
T-14.......X.12:3 you must g. it because of what you are.
T-14.......XI.9:1 have you g. He would withhold from you?
T-15.......I.11:2 Could you not g. so short a time to the
T-15.......I.11:4 you to be willing to g. Him this than for
T-15.......I.11:5 to g. you the remembrance of eternity.
T-15.......I.12:1 You will never g. this holy instant to the
T-15.......I.12:2 to g. it to your brothers on behalf of theirs
T-15.......I.13:5 it. As you g. it, He offers it to you. Be not
T-15.......I.13:6 to g. what you would receive of Him, for
T-15.......I.13:7 crystal cleanness of the release you g. is
T-15.....I.15:10 G. the eternal instant, that eternity may
T-15.......III.1:3 Littleness is the offering you g. yourself.
T-15.......III.6:6 Neither g. littleness, nor accept it. All
T-15.......III.7:3 all your littleness to g. the gift of God, but
T-15.......III.7:4 For God would g. Himself *through* you. He
T-15.......III.8:7 offerings you g. slip into nothingness.
T-15.......III.9:1 holiness can content you and g. you peace
T-15.....III.10:8 But you will gladly g., having received.
T-15.......IV.2:6 it. G. over every plan you have made for
T-15.......IV.4:2 and gladly g. over every plan but His. For
T-15.......IV.4:5 practice, try to g. over every plan you
T-15.......IV.6:5 you receive and g. perfect communication
T-15.......IV.6:6 your mind is open, both to receive and g..
T-15.......IV.8:4 Holy Spirit's readiness to g. it to you is
T-15.......V.3:5 the Sonship can g. you more than others?
T-15.......V.10:4 G. to it any meaning apart from His, and
T-15.......VI.4:4 like Him, you can g. yourself completely,
T-15.......VI.5:6 From this it follows you can only g.. And
T-15.......VI.6:8 Spirit gives it unto you, as you will g. it.
T-15.......VI.7:3 g. yourself as your Father gives His Self,
T-15... VIII.3:4 Fear not to g. redemption over to your
T-15.......IX.3:2 to g. up every use the ego has for the body
T-15.......IX.4:2 Love would *always* g. increase. Limits are
T-15.......IX.4:5 you. His body cannot g. it. And seek it not
T-15.......X.3:1 We who are one cannot g. separately.
T-15.......X.3:4 union is the only gift that I was born to g..
T-15.......X.3:5 G. it to me, that you may have it. The
T-15.......X.6:1 believe that you can g. all your guilt away
T-15.......XI.2:8 Love must be total to g. Him welcome, for
T-15.......XI.3:1 Christmas g. the Holy Spirit everything
T-15.......XI.3:3 accepted it with me you will g. it with me.
T-15.......XI.8:4 I g. you that you may give it and return it
T-15.......XI.8:4 I give you that you may g. it and return it
T-15.......XI.10:5 *I g. you to the Holy Spirit as part of myself.*
T-16.......I.7:6 share everything you g. through Him.
T-16.......I.7:8 g. through Him is for the whole Sonship,
T-16.......II.8:8 and will g. you everything that makes for
T-16.......IV.2:6 on the other side, will g. you everything.
T-16.......V.7:7 he would g. away to get a "better" one?
T-16.......VI.10:7 to g. up nothing *because* it is nothing.
T-16.......VI.12:2 His perspective to g. it to you completely.
T-16.......VII.2:7 And who can g. you what you think the
T-16.......VII.8:4 You will receive *because* it is His Will to g..
T-16...VII.11:3 nothing that will not g. place to Him and
T-16...VII.11:4 their reality to g. over all illusions for the
T-17.......I.2:6 Yet what you g. to truth to use for you is
T-17.......I.3:6 Unless you g. it back, it is inevitable that
T-17.......I.5:5 to g. illusions to truth is to enable truth to
T-17.......I.6:1 to g. all you have held outside the truth to
T-17.......II.8:2 It will g. you the real world, trembling
T-17.......II.8:3 eagerness of the Holy Spirit to g. you this
T-17.......III.7:8 G. the past to Him Who can change your
T-17.......V.3:6 goal was all that seemed to g. it meaning.
T-17.......V.12:5 g. thanks to your brother is to appreciate
T-17.......VI.6:8 beyond you, and beyond what you can g..
T-17.......VII.9:1 with the faith you g. your brother, or you
T-17....VIII.4:6 strain of refusing to g. faith to truth, and
T-17....VIII.6:6 is certain. G. as you have received. And
T-18.......I.9:9 G. Him but a little faith in your brother,
T-18.......I.13:4 here, and you will g. as you have accepted
T-18.......III.3:4 sufficient to g. you confidence in yourself,
T-18.......III.6:6 Would I not g. you what you gave to me?
T-18.......III.8:4 great lights have joined with you to g. the
T-18.......IV.1:6 to g. the Holy Spirit what He does not ask
T-18.......IV.1:10 so little that enables Him to g. so much.
T-18.......IV.6:8 G. Him but what He asks, that you may
T-18.......IV.7:3 to accept the idea that you need g. so little
T-18.......IV.7:7 it asks nothing you cannot g. right now.
T-18.......IV.8:2 unwilling to g. place to One Who knows.
T-18.......VI.2:1 could God g. but knowledge of Himself?
T-18.......VI.2:2 What else is there to g.? The belief that
T-18.......VI.2:3 that you could g. and get something else,
T-18....VIII.5:3 needing the whole to g. it any meaning,
T-18....VIII.8:3 and keep complete what it would g.. In
T-18....VIII.9:4 G. them a place of refuge, prepared by
T-18..VIII.12:3 not be able to g. love welcome separately.
T-18..VIII.13:4 He has waited long to g. you this. Receive
T-18.......IX.1:7 G. it back to Heaven. Heaven has not lost
T-19.......I.12:5 offers you faith to g. unto your brother.
T-19.......II.1:5 a mind not part of it can g. it absolution.
T-19.......III.8:2 it; and g. His Son a will apart from His,
T-19.......III.9:5 that you g. it no power over your brother.
T-19.......IV.1:1 to embrace all the Sonship and g. it rest,
T-19.......IV.1:8 You will not wait to g. him this, for you
T-19.......IV.1:9 And you will draw him in and g. him rest,
T19IV.A.17:11 you believe that it can g. you pleasure,
T19....IV.B.5:7 The end of guilt is in your hands to g..
T19....IV.B.9:1 Your little part is but to g. the Holy Spirit
T19..IV.B.10:2 It will accept you wholly, and g. you peace
T19..IV.B.11:5 but only if you ask of it what it cannot g..
T19..IV.B.11:9 your mistake will g. you grounds for faith.
T19..IV.C.11:7 G. it to Him to judge for you, and say:
T19. IV.D.13:6 Neither can g. it to himself alone. And yet
T19. IV.D.15:3 For his redemption he will g. you yours,
T19. IV.D.15:4 And he will g. it truly, for it will be both
T19. IV.D.15:8 has been given you to g. your brother,
T19. IV.D.15:9 forgive is free, and what you g. you share.
T19. IV.D.17:1 G. faith to your brother, for faith and
T19. IV.D.17:1 faith and hope and mercy are yours to g..
T19. IV.D.17:2 Into the hands that g., the gift is given.
T19. IV.D.17:5 Let us g. redemption to each other and
T19. IV.D.18:2 G. him the selfsame gift, nor look upon
T19. IV.D.20:3 crucified g. pain because they are in pain.
T19. IV.D.20:4 redeemed g. joy because they have been
T-20.......I.2:6 lilies in the other, uncertain which to g..
T-20.......II.2:3 decides on what it would receive and g..
T-20.......II.7:5 of illusion that God Himself could g.. For
T-20.......II.11:4 G. joyously to your brother the freedom
T-20.......III.8:6 and g. him thanks for all the happiness
T-20....III.8:11 G. it no power to adjust the means and

T-20...... IV.1:1 you unless you g. it the power to do so.
T-20...... IV.1:2 Yet *you* g. power as the laws of this world
T-20...... IV.1:2 world interpret giving; as you g. you lose.
T-20...... IV.1:3 lose. It is not up to you to g. power at all.
T-20...... IV.1:4 Spirit, Who knows that as you g. you gain
T-20...... IV.3:1 and g. them power over you by accepting
T-20...... IV.4:2 they will g. it only to what God has given,
T-20...... IV.5:1 The sinless g. as they received. See, then,
T-20....... V.2:6 You g. to your brother for everyone, and
T-20....... V.2:7 not Who has given you the gifts you g.,
T-20....... V.2:7 Who gave the gifts to Him to g. to you.
T-20....... V.6:7 forgiveness you will g. him already given,
T-20...... VI.8:7 mad idea and g. it the illusion of reality.
T-20.... VI.10:6 to receive you, and g. you peace forever.
T-20.... VII.3:2 He asks no more to g. the means as well.
T-20.... VIII.3:3 may rise before your vision and g. you joy
T-20.. VIII.10:3 All meaning that you g. the world outside
T-21....... in.2:8 the power to g. it joy must lie within you.
T-21......... I.2:5 to light. Judgment will always g. you false
T-21........ II.3:7 even this He gives to you to g. yourself.
T-21........ II.3:8 savior, that he may g. salvation unto you.
T-21........ II.4:3 it. G. it away, and everything you see goes
T-21........ II.6:1 the need for you to g. this little offering.
T-21........ II.7:1 Holy Spirit can g. you faith in holiness
T-21........ II.7:4 tell you what must happen, you g. reality.
T-21....... III.3:6 you g. to sin you take away from holiness.
T-21....... III.6:7 Then will you g. your faith to holiness,
T-21....... III.9:8 you g. your brother can accomplish this.
T-21..... III.12:3 and g. it power to serve as means to help
T-21........ V.4:4 is, or grasp the information it would g.?
T-21....... VI.1:4 you will not believe that it is yours to g..
T-21....... VI.1:5 to give. And so you will not g. it, thus
T-21....... VI.9:6 must be given you to g. what It has given,
T-21....... VI.9:7 of what is given you to g. your brother,
T-21....... VI.9:8 To g. is no more blessed than to receive.
T-21..... VIII.3:8 Yet what he is uncertain of, God cannot g.
T-22........ II.3:9 imagined, illusions must g. way to truth,
T-22........ II.7:3 Either you g. each other life or death;
T-22...... II.11:6 gave the Holy Spirit to g. to you *He gave.*
T-22...... II.11:9 for you, not what you tried to g. yourself.
T-22....... III.4:3 the meaning that the whole would g..
T-22....... III.9:7 where both g. errors gladly to correction,
T-22....... IV.7:4 to receive together and g. as you received.
T-22....... VI.6:5 you g. the Holy Spirit is service to yourself
T-22....... VI.8:7 Spirit does with gifts you g. your brother,
T-22....... VI.9:4 you g. to Him that which can be extended
T-23....... in.4:4 g. up this world of freedom for a little sigh
T-23........ II.9:6 enemies do not g. willingly to one another
T-23...... II.12:9 that would g. meaning to your life. The
T-23...... II.15:8 G. thanks unto the hero on love's throne,
T-23.... II.22:13 you, and g. you certainty of where you go.
T-23....... III.2:2 wrapping does not make the gift you g..
T-23....... III.2:6 You g. him nothing, and receive of him
T-23....... III.3:2 you want; to take a little and g. up the rest
T-24......... I.7:8 you g. your brother only partial welcome,
T-24........ II.6:6 Is it a sacrifice to g. up nothing, and to
T-24........ II.8:3 gift that God would have him g. to you.
T-24........ II.8:4 need to g. it is as great as yours to have it.
T-24...... II.10:7 G. him but what he has, remembering
T-24....... III.1:6 How can he then g. his forgiveness wholly
T-24....... III.2:6 idol that seems to g. you power has taken
T-24....... III.6:7 Holy One the specialness He could not g.,
T-24....... III.7:7 on him, and g. him back his birthright. It
T-24..... IV.3:12 asks from Him, and g. it there instead?
T-24....... IV.4:5 and g. it meaning that the truth denies.
T-24........ V.2:4 nothing to the parts to g. them meaning.
T-24........ V.8:4 He g. a brother unto you except he be as
T-24.... VI.10:5 to save from pain and g. you happiness.
T-24.... VII.4:8 shine on him, and g. *you* safety from decay
T-24.... VII.6:3 yet you can g. reality to it, according to
T-25...... II.10:3 G., then, what He has given you, that you
T-25...... II.10:5 For what you g. is His, and giving it, you
T-25...... II.10:6 g. the Holy Spirit what He offers unto the
T-25...... II.11:4 but g. him honor that you may esteem
T-25........ V.4:4 it will g. to each an equal strength to save
T-25........ V.6:6 this; the role you g. to him is given you,
T-25.... VII.13:1 make you sane and g. you what you want;
T-25.... VIII.1:1 all that you g. to Him for your salvation.
T-25.... VIII.1:5 You need not g. it to Him wholly willingly

T-25 ... VIII.4:7 for all that you would keep, and not g. up.
T-25 ... VIII.8:2 and g. them all the honor they deserve
T-25 ... VIII.9:2 in your confusion you have much to g.?
T-25 ... VIII.9:4 you recognize you could not g. yourself.
T-25 . VIII.12:9 How little need you g. the Holy Spirit that
T-25 . VIII.13:5 To take from one to g. another must be
T-25 ..... IX.2:1 To g. reluctantly is not to gain the gift,
T-25 ..... IX.2:4 Nothing you g. is lost to you or anyone,
T-25 ..... IX.7:5 To g. a problem to the Holy Spirit to solve
T-25 ... IX.10:1 The miracle that you receive, you g.. Each
T-26 ........ I.8:4 and g. you back the gift of freedom by
T-26 ....... II.5:1 believe it safe to g. but some mistakes to
T-26 ..... II.6:10 For what you g. to Him is everyone's, and
T-26 ..... III.7:3 is so lies the ability to g. up all attempts to
T-26 ..... III.7:7 was never true, can it be hard to g. it up,
T-26 ..... V.12:4 for God to g. His Answer to illusion for all
T-26 ..... VI.1:8 find the safety that the truth alone can g.?
T-26 .... VII.8:8 time and place, and g. a little space to you
T-26 ..... IX.7:4 Son g. less in gratitude for so much more?
T-26 ..... IX.8:3 g. thanks that They are welcome made at
T-27 ........ I.3:4 you show yourself, and g. it all your faith.
T-27 ........ I.3:5 The Holy Spirit offers you, to g. to him, a
T-27 ..... III.6:2 you will g. it overwhelming preference.
T-27 ..... III.7:8 be at all. G. welcome to the power beyond
T-27 ...... V.6:3 Life is given you to g. the dying world.
T-27 ...... V.6:5 g. them sight to see beyond all suffering
T-27 .. VII.15:5 g. thanks to him for all the helpfulness he
T-28 ........ I.7:5 Let not the cause that you would g. them
T-28 ..... II.2:11 attempt to g. effects to causelessness, and
T-28 ....... II.6:5 dream, but never will you g. it real effects.
T-28 ..... III.4:4 And thus it seems to g. a cause to sickness
T-28 ..... IV.1:1 for yourself means not to g. support to
T-28 ...... V.2:3 because you did not g. them your support
T-28 ..... VI.2:2 the punishment you g. because it has no
T-29 ....... II.1:5 Until you realize you g. up nothing, until
T-29 ....... II.5:1 You do not see how much you now can g.
T-29 ..... III.1:7 Thus he learns it must be his to g.. Unless
T-29 ... III.1:10 For who could g. unless he has, and who
T-29 ..... III.3:7 as heavy shadows must g. way to light.
T-29 ..... IV.6:5 and you have help to g. him if you see the
T-29 ...... V.6:2 cost of holding anything God did not g. in
T-29 ..... VI.3:5 g. yourself a purpose that you do not have
T-29 .... VII.2:4 and g. him what would make himself
T-29 .... VII.4:3 To sacrifice is to g. up, and thus to be
T-29 .... VII.8:2 You g. it goals it does not have, and thus
T-29 .... VIII.6:5 given to all living things, g. way to chaos.
T-29 ... VIII.8:6 will g. him more than other men possess.
T-29 ... VIII.9:6 to g. you more than God bestowed upon
T-29 ... VIII.9:8 also g. the same to every living thing as
T-29 ..... IX.4:6 and g. their toys the power to move about
T-30 ...... I.17:6 and g. it to the world by having it yourself
T-30 ...... I.17:8 And as you have received, so must you g..
T-30 ....... II.4:6 you will g. when you have recognized that
T-30 ... III.4:10 to g. the Son of God what he already has?
T-30 ..... III.5:7 For can he g. a part of him away? What is
T-30 ... IV.5:10 G. them not your worship, for they are
T-30 ... IV.8:13 be, except a means to g. him to Himself?
T-30 ...... V.9:4 G. up the world! But not to sacrifice. You
T-30 ..... VI.3:6 And this is all the world can ever g.. It
T-30 ... VIII.3:4 obscure and g. to them reality instead.
T-30 ... VIII.6:4 g. it power to replace the changeless in
T-31 ...... I.10:5 Yet you will recognize Him as you g. Him
T-31 ...... I.11:6 all the world will g. you joy and peace. For
T-31 ....... II.4:3 arise, and g. away the role of leadership.
T-31 ....... II.6:2 *that I g. my brother is what I am asking for.*
T-31 ...... III.2:5 you are guilty, and must g. as you deserve
T-31 ...... III.2:7 it never would occur to you to g. attack to
T-31 .... III.3:10 and you g. its purpose to its prison house,
T-31 .... VII.2:4 You cannot g. yourself your innocence,
T-31 .... VII.2:8 as you g. your trust to what is good in him
T-31 .... VII.2:8 good in him, you g. it to the good in you.
T-31 .... VII.6:4 G. it instead to Him Who understands
T-31 .... VII.9:2 that you g. to the illusion of yourself, that
T-31 .. VII.10:2 g. rise to but an image of yourself that can
T-31 ... VIII.8:6 To g. this gift is how to make it yours.
T-31 . VIII.10:6 And I g. thanks for them. Salvation's song
T-31 . VIII.11:2 G. me my own, for they belong to You.
T-31 . VIII.11:4 I g. You thanks for what my brothers are.
W-in.......... 8:6 their use that will g. them meaning to you

W-pI ...... 5.7:1 the relative importance you may g. them.
W-pI .... 12.2:6 You teach yourself this as you g. whatever
W-pI .... 12.2:7 step in learning to g. them all equal value.
W-pI .... 18.1:1 the thoughts which g. rise to what you see
W-pI .... 20.1:6 if you g. in to resentment and opposition.
W-pI .... 25.5:1 to your learning to be willing to g. up the
W-pI .... 32.1:3 can g. it up as easily as you made it up.
W-pI .... 39.3:3 You cannot g. what you do not have. A
W-pI .... 39.7:3 them that will save you and g. you vision.
W-pI .... 43.2:6 Spirit g. it a meaning very close to God's.
W-pI .. 44.10:3 unless you g. them the power to do so.
W-pI .... 47.1:4 What would g. you the ability to be aware
W-pI .... 52.3:6 Let me learn to g. the past away, realizing
W-pI .... 55.2:5 attack thoughts that g. rise to this picture.
W-pI .... 55.2:6 g. me the peace God intended me to have.
W-pI .... 56.1:6 I have tried to g. my inheritance away in
W-pI .... 57.1:9 I would g. up my insane wishes and walk
W-pI .... 63.2:3 It is yours to g. him, for it belongs to you.
W-pI .... 63.2:6 accept salvation that it may be yours to g..
W-pI .... 66.6:3 is not. Love cannot g. evil, and what is not
W-pI .... 66.6:4 God cannot g. what He does not have,
W-pI .... 66.8:4 Does the ego really have gifts to g., being
W-pI .... 70.2:1 nothing outside yourself can g. you peace.
W-pI .... 71.9:6 *to whom?* G. Him full charge of the rest of
W-pI .... 74.2:3 Therefore it cannot g. rise to illusions.
W-pI .... 75.7:2 fails to g. the gift of sight to the forgiving.
W-pI .... 75.9:3 G. thanks for mercy and the Love of God.
W-pI .... 76.9:6 else. God's laws forever g. and never take.
W-pI .... 80.2:3 for the Holy Spirit to g. you God's answer.
W-pI .... 83.2:3 *This does not g. me a function other than the*
W-pI .... 83.2:4 *this to justify a function God did not g. me.*
W-pI .... 88.3:4 up other laws and g. them power over me.
W-pI .... 92.8:1 sure as love, forever glad to g. itself away,
W-pI .... 92.8:1 away, because it cannot g. but to itself.
W-pI .. 92.10:1 Let us g. twenty minutes twice today to
W-pI .... 95.8:4 than g. it power to delay our learning. If
W-pI .... 95.8:5 we g. it power to do this, we are regarding
W-pI .. 95.11:1 mind with all the certainty that you can g.
W-pI .. 95.15:2 be sure to g. the promise of today's idea
W-pI .. 96.10:2 Your Self will welcome it and g. it peace.
W-pI .. 96.12:3 how much is given unto you to g. this day
W-pI .... 97.3:3 which you g. are multiplied over and over
W-pI .... 97.4:2 G., then, these minutes willingly, and
W-pI .... 97.4:4 G. Him the minutes which He needs
W-pI .... 97.7:3 increase its power and g. it back to you.
W-pI .... 98.7:1 Each hour today g. Him your tiny gift of
W-pI .... 98.7:2 He will g. the words you use in practicing
W-pI .... 98.8:1 will accept your words and g. them back
W-pI .... 98.8:2 that you may g. them to the world today.
W-pI .... 98.9:1 G. Him the words, and He will do the
W-pI .. 99.12:2 this between the times you g. five minutes
W-pI 100.10:4 you must find what He would have you g..
W-pI .. 101.7:1 G. these five minutes gladly, to remove
W-pI .. 104.1:3 Who cannot fail to g. you what He wills.
W-pI .. 105.1:4 are not like to the gifts the world can g.,
W-pI .. 105.2:4 It strips all meaning from the gifts you g.,
W-pI .. 105.5:4 He cannot g. through loss. No more can
W-pI .. 105.9:1 worthless when you cannot g. Him more.
W-pI .. 105.9:2 call to Him to g. you what He wills to give,
W-pI .. 105.9:2 call to Him to give you what He wills to g.,
W-pI .. 106.1:1 that g. you nothing that you really want;
W-pI .. 106.7:6 *What does it mean to g. and to receive?*
W-pI 106.10:1 kept through your receiving it to g. away,
W-pI 106.10:4 *today, My voice is His, to g. what I receive.*
W-pI .. 107.6:6 G. truth its due, and it will give you yours.
W-pI .. 107.6:6 Give truth its due, and it will g. you yours.
W-pI .. 107.9:6 which will envelop you and g. you peace
W-pI 107.10:3 every gift you g. of five small minutes, and
W-pI ..... 108.h To g. and to receive are one in truth.
W-pI .. 108.7:3 To g. is to receive. Today we will attempt
W-pI .. 108.8:2 *To g. and to receive are one in truth. I will*
W-pI .. 108.9:4 to think of one to whom to g. your gifts.
W-pI .. 108.9:5 the others, and through him you g. to all.
W-pI 108.10:3 say, "To g. and to receive are one in truth.
W-pI .. 109.9:3 what we g. today we have received already
W-pI .. 109.9:4 is not the guardian of what we g. today.
W-pI .. 109.9:5 g. to those unborn and those passed by,
W-pI .. 110.2:1 and g. you perfect vision that will heal all
WpI..rIII.in3:1 the time to it that you are asked to g.. Do

WpI . rIII.in6:2 G. it faith that it will use them wisely,
WpI . rIII.in6:6 G. direction at the outset; then lean back
WpI . rIII.in8:1 and also g. the last five minutes of your
WpIrIII.in10:2 Attempt to g. your daily two ideas a brief
WpIrIII.in10:4 not g. more than just a moment to each
W-pI ...119.2:1 To g. and to receive are one in truth. *I will*
W-pI ...119.3:4 To g. and to receive are one in truth.
W-pI ...121.8:3 to g. forgiveness and receive forgiveness,
W-pI ...122.1:1 could you want forgiveness cannot g.? Do
W-pI ...122.3:3 would you want forgiveness cannot g.?
W-pI ...122.6:4 As you g. you will receive. There is no
W-pI ...122.7:5 The world can g. no gifts of any value to a
W-pI .122.10:1 Morning and evening do we gladly g. a
W-pI ...123.2:4 and His creation. G. Him thanks today.
W-pI ...123.3:1 G. thanks that He has not abandoned
W-pI ...123.3:2 G. thanks as well that you are changeless,
W-pI ...123.5:2 g. thanks that in our solitude a Friend has
W-pI ...123.6:2 of God today, as you g. thanks to Him.
W-pI ...123.6:3 For He would offer you the thanks you g.,
W-pI ...123.8:2 and g. Him thanks for everything He gave
W-pI ...124.1:1 again g. thanks for our Identity in God.
W-pI ...124.2:3 and death g. place to everlasting life. Our
W-pI ...124.7:3 We have accepted, and we now would g..
W-pI ...124.8:4 for which we g. no rules nor special words
W-pI ...125.4:2 His Voice would g. to you His holy Word,
W-pI ...125.5:1 your mind to Him to g. His Word to you.
W-pI ...125.7:1 g. ten minutes set apart from listening to
W-pI ......126.h All that I g. is given to myself.
W-pI ...126.3:2 You g. charity to one unworthy, merely to
W-pI ...126.5:2 to g. indulgently an undeserved reprieve.
W-pI ...126.6:3 It cannot g. you peace as you perceive it.
W-pI ...126.8:4 G. Him your faith today, and ask Him
W-pI ...126.9:1 G. fifteen minutes twice today to the
W-pI .126.11:3 *All that I g. is given to myself. The Help I need*
W-pI ...127.7:2 be glad to g. some time to God today, and
W-pI ...127.9:3 mind wherever you g. up a false belief, a
W-pI .127.10:2 Let us g. thanks today that we are spared
W-pI .127.12:3 mind, g. him this message from your Self:
W-pI ...128.1:1 anything at all that serves to g. you joy.
W-pI ...128.7:1 G. it ten minutes rest three times today.
W-pI ...129.8:4 grace is given you today, and we g. thanks
W-pI ...130.7:1 we gladly g. five minutes to the thought
W-pI ...131.3:3 you search, unless you g. it power to do so
W-pI ...132.3:3 you find escape and g. it to the world.
W-pI ...132.4:2 Your mind must g. it meaning. And what
W-pI ...132.4:4 waiting for your thoughts to g. it meaning
W-pI .132.12:2 wait for this release to g. you fatherhood,
W-pI ...133.5:2 It cannot g. you just a little, for there is no
W-pI .134.14:4 let us g. a quarter of an hour twice today,
W-pI ...135.5:4 or g. it gifts to make it beautiful or walls
W-pI .135.22:2 plan, that we may g. instead of organize.
W-pI .135.24:5 g. up nothing in these times today when,
W-pI .136.12:4 Truth merely wants to g. you happiness,
W-pI .136.15:2 we will g. a quarter of an hour twice to ask
W-pI .136.15:4 for just this invitation which we g. today.
W-pI .136.20:1 G. instant remedy, should this occur, by
W-pI .137.11:2 the grace of healing it is given them to g..
W-pI .137.14:2 and g. ten minutes to these thoughts with
W-pI .137.15:2 in quiet, be prepared to g. as you receive,
W-pI .137.15:2 as you receive, to hold but what you g.,
W-pI .138.12:2 And now we g. the last five minutes of our
WpI . rIV.in7:5 you review that day g. you the gift that He
WpI . rIV.in9:2 more than this to g. us happiness and rest
WpIrIV.in10:2 And as you g. your mind to the ideas for
W-pI ...143.2:1 (126) All that I g. is given to myself.
W-pI .151.13:4 and g. them back again as clean ideas that
W-pI .151.14:1 G. Him your thoughts, and He will give
W-pI .151.14:1 He will g. them back as miracles which
W-pI .151.15:1 and gladly g. another fifteen more before
W-pI .151.15:4 the Voice for God g. honor to God's Son.
W-pI .151.17:2 As we g. thanks, the world unites with us
W-pI .153.15:3 the least we g. to preparation for a day in
W-pI .153.15:6 Nor will we willingly g. less at night, in
W-pI .153.20:6 is all you need to g. Him in return. You
W-pI ...154.5:3 it, g. it to the ones for whom it is intended
W-pI ...154.6:3 and to g. them everywhere that they were
W-pI ...154.6:4 receiving to prepare themselves to g..
W-pI ...154.7:4 gain by every message that they g. away.
W-pI ...154.8:4 wait to g. the messages you have received.
W-pI .154.12:1 recognize what we receive until we g. it.
W-pI ...155.4:1 If truth demanded they g. up the world,
W-pI .155.12:4 way could g. you more than everything,
W-pI ...157.6:2 We cannot g. experience like this directly.
W-pI ......158.h Today I learn to g. as I receive.
W-pI ...158.2:3 It is not this knowledge which you g., for
W-pI ...158.2:5 What, then, are you to learn to g. today?
W-pI ...158.5:1 A teacher does not g. experience, because
W-pI ...158.5:4 gift. This he can g. directly, for Christ's
W-pI ...158.5:4 has a vision He can g. to anyone who asks
W-pI ...158.8:2 the world can not g. anything that faintly
W-pI ...158.8:3 this you g. today: See no one as a body.
W-pI .158.10:1 Thus do you learn to g. as you receive.
W-pI .158.11:2 Yet time has still one gift to g., in which
W-pI .158.11:4 And by the holy gifts we g., Christ's vision
W-pI ......159.h I g. the miracles I have received.
W-pI ...159.1:1 No one can g. what he has not received.
W-pI ...159.1:2 g. a thing requires first you have it in your
W-pI ...159.1:7 g. is how to recognize you have received.
W-pI ...159.2:1 that you are healed when you g. healing.
W-pI ...159.2:4 There is no miracle you cannot g., for all
W-pI ...159.4:2 remaining with each miracle you g., and
W-pI ...159.8:6 His messengers, who g. as they received.
W-pI .159.10:1 the store of miracles set out for you to g..
W-pI ...160.5:3 and g. him all I thought belonged to me."
W-pI ...160.9:4 as they g. Him welcome, they remember.
W-pI .160.10:2 Not one He fails to g. you to remember,
W-pI ......161.h G. me your blessing, holy Son of God.
W-pI ...161.3:3 We g. them to the Holy Spirit, that He
W-pI ...161.9:6 him but for this, and he will g. it to you.
W-pI .161.11:7 free: *G. me your blessing, holy Son of God.*
W-pI ...164.2:5 using your voice to g. His glad consent;
W-pI ...164.3:2 quiet is the time you g. to spend with Him
W-pI ...165.8:1 and not upon ourselves, to g. us certainty.
W-pI .166.12:4 to offer you, you now must learn to g..
W-pI .166.13:1 to g. to all who chose the lonely road you
W-pI ...167.2:5 It is the alarm to which you g. response of
W-pI ...167.5:5 not g. birth to what was never given them
W-pI ...167.5:7 they were born, so will they then g. birth.
W-pI ...167.6:5 are, and cannot g. them attributes it lacks
W-pI ...168.2:4 gladly g. the means by which His Will is
W-pI ...168.4:2 Son. Request Him now to g. the means by
W-pI .169.14:8 We do not look beyond what grace can g..
W-pI .169.14:9 can g. in the grace that has been given us.
W-pI .169.15:5 *released. By grace I g.. By grace I will release.*
W-pI .170.13:7 *g. thanks for them who render us complete.*
WpI 170.13:10 *has set us free. And we g. thanks. Amen.*
WpI ...rV.in1:2 This time we are ready to g. more effort
WpI ...rV.in2:3 *us. We have no words to g. to You. We would*
WpI ...rV.in9:2 words I speak, and g. them to the world.
W-pI ...174.2:1 (158) Today I learn to g. as I receive. God
W-pI ...175.1:1 (159) I g. the miracles I have received.
W-pI ...176.1:1 (161) G. me your blessing, holy Son of
Wi181-200 1:4 makes it sure that you will g. your total
Wi181-200 2:4 that comes as you g. up your tight control
W-pI ...181.2:4 shift, to g. support to the intent which has
W-pI ...181.3:1 we first let all such little focuses g. way to
W-pI ...181.9:6 And we g. our trust to the experience we
W-pI ...182.5:7 But g. Him just a little time to be Himself,
W-pI ...183.7:1 Thus do we g. an invitation which can
W-pI ...183.9:2 g. the world the same release you found.
W-pI .183.10:5 gave, is giving still, and will forever g.. He
W-pI ...184.1:6 all things to which you g. a different name
W-pI ...184.8:6 to take the name you g. him as his own.
W-pI .184.14:5 with blessings we can g. as we receive.
W-pI .184.15:5 *All our mistakes we g. to You, that we may be*
W-pI .184.15:6 *And we accept the truth You g., in place of*
W-pI ...185.4:6 bargain can g. them the peace of God?
W-pI .185.11:4 who requests an answer which is his to g.
W-pI .186.10:2 you make g. rise to but conflicting goals,
W-pI .186.13:5 For Love must g., and what is given in His
W-pI ...187.1:1 No one can g. unless he has. In fact,
W-pI ...187.1:5 you must first possess what you would g..
W-pI ...187.2:2 it is sure that if you g. a finite thing away,
W-pI ...187.2:4 lack for proof that when you g. ideas away
W-pI ...187.3:1 first belong to you, before you g. them. If
W-pI ...187.5:1 G. gladly. You can only gain thereby. The
W-pI ...187.5:6 who retains; another who will g. as well.
W-pI ...187.6:1 Never forget you g. but to yourself. Who
W-pI ...187.8:5 first to you, it now is yours to g. as well.
W-pI .187.10:3 stand in blessedness, and g. as we receive.
W-pI ...188.3:6 unites in giving thanks to you who g., and
W-pI ...188.4:3 of the gift, does God Himself g. thanks.
W-pI ...188.5:2 recognizes it within himself must g. it.
W-pI ...188.6:3 It alone has power to g. the gift of sight to
W-pI ...190.8:5 where sorrow rules and little joys g. way
W-pI ...191.8:3 to g. the world the gift of his forgiveness.
W-pI ...192.6:5 We are one, and therefore g. up nothing.
W-pI ...193.2:3 and g. him vision that will lead him back
W-pI ...193.6:3 These are words which g. you power over
W-pI .193.11:1 G. all you can, and give a little more. For
W-pI .193.11:1 Give all you can, and g. a little more. For
W-pI .193.11:5 Let us g. them all to Him Who knows the
W-pI .193.12:2 try to g. it application to the happenings
W-pI ...194.2:3 thus becomes the gift you g. the world,
W-pI ...194.6:1 to g. as much consistent effort as you can,
W-pI ...195.5:1 Therefore g. thanks, but in sincerity. And
W-pI ...195.6:3 We g. thanks for every living thing, for
W-pI .196.12:4 G. it welcome, as you should, for it is your
W-pI ...197.3:5 honor them and g. them fitting thanks,
W-pI ...197.5:1 God blesses every gift you g. to Him, and
W-pI ...197.6:1 Withdraw the gifts you g., and you will
W-pI ...197.9:1 G. thanks as you receive it. Be you free of
W-pI ...197.9:4 G. thanks for all the countless channels
W-pI .198.12:4 could g. him gifts when everything is his?
W-pI .198.13:3 For He would g. to us the gift that God
W-pI ...199.5:5 from the acceptance of the gifts you g.?
W-pI ...199.7:5 g. your mind to Him Who calls to you to
W-pI ...199.7:6 For He would g. you perfect freedom,
WpI rVI.in.1:2 the time you g. morning and evening,
WpI rVI.in.1:4 Each would be enough to g. release to you
WpI rVI.in.6:6 we g. these times of quiet to the Teacher
W-pI ...206.1:3 *I would g. His gifts where He intended them*
W-pI ...215.1:4 *I g. thanks to Him for showing me the way to*
W-pI ...217.1:2 *should g. thanks for my salvation but myself*
W-pII ....in.6:2 Father, we g. these holy times to You, in
W-pII ..in.11:5 We g. the first of these instructions now.
W-pII .221.1:1 *today to seek the peace that You alone can g..*
W-pII .224.1:1 guilt, that Heaven looks to It to g. it light.
W-pII .224.1:3 gave to me; the one as well I g. the world.
W-pII .227.1:5 *Now I g. them up, and lay them down before*
W-pII ..... 2.5:1 From here we g. salvation to the world,
W-pII ....233.h I g. my life to God to guide today.
W-pII .233.1:1 *Father, I g. You all my thoughts today.*
W-pII .233.1:3 *In place of them, g. me Your Own. I give You*
W-pII .233.1:4 *I g. You all my acts as well, that I may do*
W-pII .233.2:2 will g. this day to Him with no reserve at
W-pII .234.2:2 *g. thanks for all the gifts You have bestowed*
W-pII .236.1:6 Today I g. its service to the Holy Spirit to
W-pII .238.1:5 *g. Your Son to me in certainty that he is safe*
W-pII .240.2:3 *G. us faith today to recognize Your Son, and*
W-pII ..... 3.4:5 And let Him g. you peace and certainty,
W-pII .242.1:5 I g. this day to Him, for I would not delay
W-pII .242.2:1 *And so we g. today to You. We come with*
W-pII .242.2:4 *G. us what You would have received by us.*
W-pII .242.2:6 *will g. us everything we need in helping us to*
W-pII .245.1:5 *I g. Your peace to those who suffer pain, or*
W-pII .245.2:2 To all the world we g. the message that we
W-pII .251.2:1 *And for that peace, our Father, we g. thanks.*
W-pII .255.1:6 I g. today to finding what my Father wills
W-pII .262.1:5 *Why should I g. this one a thousand names,*
W-pII .270.1:3 *more will I perceive in it than sight can g..*
W-pII .273.1:3 If we g. way to a disturbance, let us learn
W-pII .274.1:1 *g. Your Son the honor due his sinlessness;*
W-pII .274.2:2 G. this day to Him, and there will be no
W-pII .275.2:3 *to think, what words to g. the world. The*
W-pII .279.2:1 *promises today, and g. my faith to them. My*
W-pII .280.2:1 *Today let me g. honor to Your Son, for thus*
W-pII .280.2:3 *The honor that I g. to him is Yours, and what*
W-pII .286.2:1 stillness of today will g. us hope that we
W-pII .295.2:1 *a gift of me, and one I g. that it be given me.*
W-pII ....297.h Forgiveness is the only gift I g..
W-pII .297.1:1 Forgiveness is the only gift I g., because it
W-pII .297.1:2 And everything I g. I give myself. This is
W-pII .297.1:2 And everything I give I g. myself. This is
W-pII .300.2:4 *g. thanks today the world endures but for an*
W-pII .306.2:2 *hearts and minds, asking but what You g..*
W-pII .307.1:5 *If I would have what only You can g., I must*

| | |
|---|---|
| W-pII .308.1:7 | has come to g. His present blessing to the |
| W-pII .10.4:5 | Salvation asks you g. it welcome. And the |
| W-pII ....315.h | All gifts my brothers g. belong to me. |
| W-pII ....316.h | All gifts I g. my brothers are my own. |
| W-pII .316.1:1 | As every gift my brothers g. is mine, so |
| W-pII .316.1:1 | is mine, so every gift I g. belongs to me. |
| W-pII ....322.h | I can g. up but what was never real. |
| W-pII .322.1:2 | readiness to g. God's ancient messages to |
| W-pII .322.2:3 | *created me, I can g. up nothing You gave me.* |
| W-pII .322.2:4 | *What You did not g. has no reality. What* |
| W-pII .323.1:1 | *Son; You ask him to g. up all suffering, all* |
| W-pII .327.1:5 | awaiting but my call to g. me all the help I |
| W-pII .327.2:4 | *You g. the means whereby conviction comes* |
| W-pII .330.1:2 | our minds, and g. them images of pain? |
| W-pII .334.2:3 | *to g. him certainty and bring him peace?* |
| W-pII .343.1:3 | *You only g.. You never take away. And You* |
| W-pII .343.1:6 | *I, too, must g.. And so all things are given* |
| W-pII343.1:11 | *cannot lose, for I can only g., and everything* |
| W-pII ....344.h | that what I g. my brother is my gift to me. |
| W-pII .344.1:6 | *Yet he whom I forgive will g. me gifts beyond* |
| W-pII .345.1:2 | *And every one I g. returns to me, reminding* |
| W-pII .345.1:4 | *miracles I g. are given back in just the form I* |
| W-pII .345.1:6 | *to Your gifts than any other gift that I can g..* |
| W-pII .345.1:7 | *Then let me g. this gift alone today, which,* |
| W-pII .347.1:5 | *And so I g. all judgment to the One You gave* |
| W-pII ....349.h | but g. Each one a miracle of love instead. |
| W-pII .349.1:1 | *I see, and g. to them the freedom that I seek.* |
| W-pII .349.1:2 | *and g. what I would find and make my own.* |
| W-pII .349.1:3 | *I have chosen it as the gift I want to g.. Father,* |
| W-pII .349.1:5 | *one that I accept gives me a miracle to g..* |
| W-pII .350.1:8 | *to me, and g. it to the world in thankfulness.* |
| W-pII .353.1:1 | *Father, I g. all that is mine today to Christ, to* |
| W-pII ....355.h | and joy, And all the miracles that I will g., |
| W-pII .357.1:3 | *to hear Your Word, and g. as I receive. And* |
| W-pII .358.1:3 | *what You g. me comes from God Himself.* |
| W-pII .360.1:1 | *Father, it is Your peace that I would g.,* |
| Wfl........in.1:4 | as to Him we g. our lives henceforth. For |
| WpII...361-5.h | This holy instant would I g. to You. Be |
| WpII361-5.1:1 | a word to help me, He will g. it to me. If I |
| WpII361-5.1:2 | If I need a thought, that will He also g.. |
| W-ep .........1:5 | has the answer, and will gladly g. it to you |
| W-ep .........4:2 | Nor will He g. you pleasures that will pass |
| M-in ..........2:6 | You cannot g. to someone else, but only |
| M-4 ..... I.A.5:7 | as he actually does g. up the valueless. |
| M-4 ..... I.A.6:6 | "G. up what you do not want, and keep |
| M-4 .....VII.2:3 | does not want anything he cannot g. away |
| M-4 ...VII.2:12 | These he can g. away in true generosity, |
| M-4 ...... IX.1:6 | To g. up all problems to one Answer is to |
| M-5 .........I.2:8 | given himself what God would g. to him, |
| M-5 .... II.2:8 | yet they but g. form to his own choice. He |
| M-5 .... III.2:10 | They merely g. what has been given them. |
| M-6 ...........3:2 | It is merely their function to g. them. |
| M-6 ...........3:4 | No one can g. if he is concerned with the |
| M-7 ...........3:6 | do. By accepting healing he can g. it. If he |
| M-9 ...........2:3 | of God learns to g. up his own judgment. |
| M-12 .........5:9 | g. the body another purpose from the one |
| M-13 .........1:6 | a sacrifice to g. up the things of this world |
| M-13 .........2:1 | the fact that the world has nothing to g.. |
| M-13 .........4:2 | Is it a sacrifice to g. up pain? Does an |
| M-13 .........7:3 | You cannot g. up Heaven partially. You |
| M-15 .........3:1 | contempt; g. up these foolish thoughts! |
| M-16 .........2:3 | must they do to learn to g. the day to God |
| M-16 .........4:6 | One can as easily g. God only an instant, |
| M-16 .........6:7 | What you g. up is merely the illusion of |
| M-16 .......10:9 | merely chooses to g. up all that he never |
| M-17 .........2:6 | emphasized that you g. but to yourself? |
| M-17 .........2:9 | For he will g. only what he has chosen for |
| M-17 .......8:10 | not really have the power to g. rise to guilt |
| M-17 .........9:5 | Can nothing g. rise to anger? Hardly so. |
| M-23 .........1:2 | will g. way to temptation in this world. |
| M-23 .........4:5 | name of Jesus Christ is to g. thanks for all |
| M-23 .........5:3 | love, but only that he might g. it to you. |
| M-26 .........2:4 | would be frightening, they g. their ideas. |
| M-26 .........2:9 | they g. all their gifts to the teachers of |
| M-29 .......7:11 | and I g. thanks for you that this is so. |
| M-29 .........8:7 | *I g. thanks for you, And join your efforts on* |
| C-in ...........4:1 | many answers that this course does not g. |
| P-1.............2:1 | it and g. it His Own great gift of rejoicing? |
| P-2.........in.4:3 | will learn to g. up their original goals, for |
| P-2...........I.4:6 | cannot take more than he can g. for now. |
| P-2..........II.8:6 | I, accept Atonement and learn to g. it as it |
| P-2........ III.1:2 | One should walk ahead of him to g. him |
| P-2......... V.3:6 | all he has to g. is worthy of the therapist. |
| P-2......... V.5:4 | do for him becomes the gift we g. to God. |
| P-2........ VI.5:5 | can possibly g. rise to sickness of any kind |
| P-2.......VII.6:6 | he has the gifts of God Himself to g. away. |
| P-2........VII.7:7 | answer can he g. to one who seems to be a |
| P-2.......VII.9:6 | him an answer that you have refused to g. |
| P-3........II.4:11 | that any two should ever g. each other. |
| P-3........ III.2:7 | To g. money where God's plan allots it |
| P-3...... III.2:10 | He cannot g. it, and so he does not have it |
| P-3........ III.3:2 | make demands, and so they cannot g.. |
| P-3........ III.5:2 | Because he has, he can g.. And because he |
| P-3........ III.5:6 | g. because they have heard His Word and |
| P-3........ III.6:6 | sent. Perhaps he was sent to g. his brother |
| P-3...... III.7:10 | greater gift is there that you would g.? |
| P-3........ III.8:4 | will g. you endless opportunities to open |
| P-3...... III.8:13 | *And then God sent His Son to g. it to you.* |
| S-1 .........in.1:3 | of the Love They g. forever to Each Other. |
| S-1 ........ IV.4:5 | thing can g. you more than this, in just |
| S-2...........I.5:6 | being evil, he can only g. of what he is. |
| S-2...........I.8:5 | As He would g., so must you give as well. |
| S-2...........I.8:5 | As He would give, so must you g. as well. |
| S-2..........II.6:4 | in further bargains which can g. no hope, |
| S-2..........II.6:8 | There is no giving but to g. like Him. All |
| S-2........ III.1:8 | His readiness to g. lies far beyond your |
| S-2........ III.2:2 | is, and how to g. it as He wills it be. Do |
| S-2........ III.2:4 | G. up all else, for there *is* nothing else. |
| S-2........ III.4:5 | Still will He g. the means to you to learn |
| S-2........ III.7:7 | G. it to Him to use instead of you, and |
| S-3...........I.3:2 | that can g. rememberance of immortality, |
| S-3..........II.1:3 | Only false healing can g. way to fear, so |
| S-3........II.5:11 | is the only gift you g. and would receive. |
| S-3........ III.2:5 | g. healing to the one who stands beneath |
| S-3........ IV.5:2 | you will g. the role to Him you see in His |
| S-3........ IV.6:6 | G. all your dreams to Christ and let Him |

**Given** 1

*given*

| | |
|---|---|
| T-24 .. VII.6:10 | Not till you go past learning to the G.; not |

**given** 825

*Given*

*See also* life-given

| | |
|---|---|
| T-in .......... 1:5 | *can elect what you want to take at a g. time.* |
| T-1 ........ IV.3:7 | were g. everything when you were created |
| T-1 ........ V.3:3 | all His gifts are freely g. to everyone alike. |
| T-1 ........ V.6:5 | As these false underpinnings are g. up, |
| T-2 ..........I.2:8 | creation is freely g. in one continuous line |
| T-2 .........I.3:10 | will was g. you for your joy in creating the |
| T-2 ....... IV.4:6 | the outside is temporarily g. healing belief |
| T-2 .... VII.5:11 | compromise in this respect can be g. up. |
| T-2 .....VIII.1:3 | will to create was g. you by your Creator, |
| T-3 ....... III.2:9 | at any g. time determines what you do, |
| T-3 ....... V.10:2 | the Atonement and g. themselves over to |
| T-3 ....... VI.8:7 | creations are g. their true Authorship, but |
| T-3 ......VII.3:9 | here has been g. many interpretations, |
| T-3 ......VII.6:9 | it was g. you from beyond this world. |
| T-4 ........in.3:6 | are endless until they are voluntarily g. up |
| T-4 ....... III.9:2 | *God has g. you everything.* This one fact |
| T-4 ....... IV.6:3 | you have g. up this voluntary dis-spiriting |
| T-4 .... VII.3:11 | endow itself with functions it was not g.. |
| T-5 ........I.1:12 | yours although all of it has been g. away. |
| T-5 ..........I.2:2 | *Thoughts increase by being g. away. The* |
| T-5 .........II.3:6 | But the other is g. you by God, Who asks |
| T-5 .........II.8:9 | divided devotion has g. you the two voices |
| T-5 ........ III.2:6 | It is strengthened by being g. away. It |
| T-5 ........ V.8:8 | Having g. up its disordered thought, the |
| T-5 ....... VI.3:4 | chance to claim it for yourself be g. you? |
| T-5 ....... VI.9:5 | The part of your mind that you have g. to |
| T-5 ..... VI.10:8 | g. to you to remind you of what you are. |
| T-5 ..... VI.12:8 | Because He has been g. you freely by God, |
| T-6 ........in.1:4 | G. these three wholly irrational premises, |
| T-6 .......II.13:1 | Spirit was g. you with perfect impartiality, |
| T-6 ....... IV.7:5 | has g. way to creation and to its eternity. |
| T-6 ..... V.C.9:5 | g. you a sick mind that must be healed. |
| T-7 ....... IV.4:1 | therefore be g. over to the Holy Spirit, |
| T-7 ....... IV.6:6 | has g. you a gift that you both *have* and *are.* |
| T-7 .........V.7:6 | device that was ever g. him for change. |
| T-7 ...... VII.5:1 | life is yours to give, because it was g. you. |
| T-7 ....... IX.2:4 | Everything He created is g. all His power, |
| T-7 .........X.5:7 | in motivation, and g. this confusion, trust |
| T-7 .........X.6:9 | has been g. you by God's decision. That is |
| T-7 ....... XI.4:3 | healed the Sonship and g. thanks to God. |
| T-7 ....... XI.5:6 | have acknowledged what He has g. you. |
| T-8 .........II.2:4 | never g. you a sensible answer to anything |
| T-8 ....... III.1:2 | Ask and it shall be g. you, because it has |
| T-8 ....... III.1:2 | be given you, because it has already *been* g. |
| T-8 ....... III.4:6 | they are g. another chance at salvation. |
| T-8 ....... III.7:7 | why He has g. you the means for undoing |
| T-8 ....... VI.8:3 | and learned of what He had already g.. |
| T-8 ..... VI.8:11 | G. this belief, you cannot understand |
| T-8 ..... VI.10:2 | He has g. His Will to His treasure, whose |
| T-8 ....... IX.4:4 | it was not g. to the Holy Spirit. Only when |
| T-8 ....... IX.8:3 | do. G. this, and given this quite literally, |
| T-8 ....... IX.8:3 | this, and g. this quite literally, nothing |
| T-9 ..........I.8:8 | cannot be g. because it was never created. |
| T-9 .........II.3:3 | it is equally certain that no response g. by |
| T-9 ....... IV.3:1 | which is g. you because *you have forgotten* |
| T-9 ....... VI.5:3 | you have g. them will teach you its value. |
| T-9 ...... VII.1:2 | He not have g. you the means to find it? If |
| T-10 ... III.1:10 | to help them, because He has g. it to you. |
| T-10 ... IV.4:10 | "g." your peace to the gods you made, but |
| T-10 .....V.12:4 | God has g. you the means for undoing |
| T-10 .....V.13:2 | it is yours only because He has g. it to you. |
| T-10 .....V.13:3 | like His, because they are g. in His Name. |
| T-11 ........I.6:1 | God has g. you a place in His Mind that is |
| T-11 ........I.6:2 | keep it only by giving it, as it was g. you. |
| T-11 ........I.6:3 | was g. you because God did not will to be |
| T-11 ........I.7:4 | end, to learn how much He has g. you. |
| T-11 ........I.9:5 | will is His life, which He has g. to you. |
| T-11 .......II.6:2 | be like Him, and He has g. Himself to you. |
| T-11 ..... IV.1:5 | g. you by your Creator that you might |
| T-11 .....V.12:4 | it is g. you to know that God's function is |
| T-11 ..... VI.6:6 | The Father has g. you all that is His, and |
| T-11 ..... VI.7:7 | Having g. Himself to him, how could it be |
| T-11 ..... VI.8:3 | assign to death whom God has g. eternal |
| T-11 ... VI.10:9 | And to Christ it is g. to be like the Father. |
| T-12 .......II.6:2 | For your purpose was g. you by God, and |
| T-12 .....II.10:4 | is g. Him that is not of God is gone. Yet |
| T-12 ..... III.1:4 | they are in need it is g. you to help them, |
| T-12 ..... IV.6:3 | pay no price for life for that was g. you, |
| T-12 .......V.9:5 | Everything else will be g. you. For you |
| T-12 .. VII.15:4 | And would eternal life have been g. me of |
| T-12 .. VII.15:4 | the Father unless He had also g. it to you? |
| T-12 ... VIII.3:8 | unless He had g. you a way to remember |
| T-12 ... VIII.8:1 | real world was g. you by God in loving |
| T-13 ......in.4:4 | only love because he has g. only love. He |
| T-13 ........I.4:5 | for such was His mission, g. Him by God. |
| T-13 ..... III.5:3 | is g. you is not so dear as what you made. |
| T-13 ... III.12:5 | Having g. you creation, He could not take |
| T-13 .......V.1:3 | it is extended, for it increases as it is g.. |
| T-13 .......V.7:7 | It is g. you to learn how to deny insanity, |
| T-13 .....V.7:12 | God is g. you to whom God gave Himself. |
| T-13 .....V.10:1 | and one you made and one was g. you. |
| T-13 .....V.10:3 | See through the vision that is g. you, for |
| T-13 .....V.10:6 | love to you, g. Him of the Father for you. |
| T-13 ..... VI.7:4 | the light of perfect vision is freely g. as it is |
| T-13 ... VI.10:2 | having g. light to them they will return it. |
| T-13 ... VI.11:2 | Yet you can give it, as it was g. you. And |
| T-13 ... VI.11:6 | is bright with love which you have g. it. |
| T-13 ... VI.13:4 | In your name He has g. for you, and given |
| T-13 ... VI.13:4 | given for you, and g. you the gifts He gave |
| T-13 ... VII.8:7 | Your one reality was g. you, and by it God |
| T-13 .. VII.17:3 | gift to me, g. me through His Spirit. The |
| T-13 ... VIII.4:3 | God has g. Him to you because He has no |
| T-13 ... VIII.9:2 | and He has g. you the power to create the |
| T-13 ..... IX.2:6 | For faith is always g. what is treasured, |
| T-13 .......X.2:8 | own ends what you should have g. Him, |
| T-13 .......X.8:1 | *Now* it is g. you to heal and teach, to make |
| T-13 ..... XI.6:8 | fail in what your Father has g. Him to do. |
| T-14 ........I.3:7 | him. But they can be g. up *by* him, for the |
| T-14 .......II.8:3 | vision of Christ is g. the very instant that |
| T-14 ..... III.6:2 | Every chance g. him to heal is another |
| T-14 ..... III.8:7 | The power that God has g. to His Son *is* his |

| | |
|---|---|
| T-14.III.10:6 | Yet will was g. them because it is holy, |
| T-14.III.17:1 | Whose equal Love is g. equally to all alike! |
| T-14.IV.3:3 | not cannot be, and therefore cannot be g.. |
| T-14.V.2:1 | message g. to each one is always the same; |
| T-14.V.4:1 | right of God's Son, g. him in his creation. |
| T-14.V.9:6 | your Father's power that He has g. him. |
| T-14.VII.5:10 | the instant it was g. Him for you. Do not |
| T-14.VII.5:11 | He can fulfill what God has g. Him to do. |
| T-14.VII.7:3 | with Him Whom God has g. you teaches |
| T-14.VIII.1:8 | the promise that was g. Him to share with |
| T-14.VIII.2:2 | will replace with the one promise g. unto |
| T-14.VIII.4:6 | can change the knowledge, g. you by God, |
| T-14.VIII.5:6 | To whom God gives Himself, He *is* g.. |
| T-14.X.6:15 | of difficulty here. A call for help is g. help. |
| T-14.X.10:6 | powerful that what you see is g. meaning. |
| T-14.XI.2:4 | And can His Son, g. all power by Him, |
| T-14.XI.6:10 | Guide Whom God has g. you will speak to |
| T-15.II.4:9 | because you have not g. complete release. |
| T-15.II.4:10 | g. a single instant completely to the Holy |
| T-15.II.5:6 | complete, accomplished and g. wholly. |
| T-15.II.6:4 | not that you will not be g. help in this. |
| T-15.III.4:11 | be content with less than his Father has g. |
| T-15.III.11:1 | for peace yourself, salvation will be g. you. |
| T-15.III.12:6 | even to Heaven, because of what is g. it. |
| T-15.IV.3:4 | in the plan that He has g. to the world for |
| T-15.IV.8:6 | is g. and received with equal willingness, |
| T-15.IV.9:4 | It is g. you the instant you would have it. |
| T-15.VII.1:3 | only love that is fully g. and fully returned |
| T-15.IX.1:4 | G. this willingness it will not leave you, |
| T-15.IX.3:1 | of relationships without limits is g. you. |
| T-15.IX.3:5 | do so with the strength that you have g. it. |
| T-15.IX.4:1 | is the only purpose for which it was g. you |
| T-15.X.8:3 | have g. God away rather than look at it. |
| T-15.XI.1:5 | and the Thought that has been g. you. |
| T-16.II.5:3 | Honor the truth that has been g. you, and |
| T-16.II.5:6 | witnesses that He has g. you to His reality. |
| T-16.II.8:2 | not to deny what has been g. you by God. |
| T-16.II.9:1 | never g. any problem to the Holy Spirit |
| T-16.II.9:4 | of the ideas that have been g. you. For the |
| T-16.IV.8:7 | specialness can offer you what God has g., |
| T-16.VI.12:5 | release, His perfect willingness is g. you. |
| T-16.VII.8:1 | What God has g. you is truly given, and |
| T-16.VII.8:1 | What God has given you is truly g., and |
| T-16.VII.8:5 | He gave the holy instant to be g. you, and |
| T-16.VII.8:8 | you have received what God has g. you. |
| T-16.VII.12:6 | *And let us receive only what You have g., and* |
| T-17.I.6:8 | will see forgiveness where you have g. it. |
| T-17.II.3:2 | All else is learned, but this is g., complete |
| T-17.II.8:2 | trembling with readiness to be g. you. The |
| T-17.III.1:1 | in the past, and those that were g. you. All |
| T-17.III.5:7 | is g. to Him Who gives it life and beauty. |
| T-17.IV.2:4 | to them the function g. them by God. The |
| T-17.IV.2:5 | have g. them is clearly not to make happy. |
| T-17.IV.9:3 | This gift is g. you for your damnation, and |
| T-17.IV.14:5 | And each is g. its rightful place when both |
| T-17.IV.16:5 | What He has g. is His. It shines in every |
| T-17.V.5:1 | ego g. time to reinterpret each slow step |
| T-17.V.7:10 | He has g. you a most explicit statement? |
| T-17.V.13:5 | recognize what has been g. and received |
| T-17.V.15:1 | gifts you have so freely g. to your brother, |
| T-17.VII.4:1 | have not g. can be lacking in any situation |
| T-17.VIII.1:2 | has g. it is also given to every situation. It |
| T-17.VIII.1:2 | has given it is also g. to every situation. It |
| T-17.VIII.3:2 | freely g. wherever faithlessness is laid |
| T-17.VIII.3:5 | has called for faith, and has been g. it. |
| T-17.VIII.5:6 | for it has been g. you to realize what your |
| T-18.I.1:2 | is with the goal the Holy Spirit has g. you, |
| T-18.I.13:5 | peace of God is g. you with the glowing |
| T-18.II.3:7 | a time it seems as if the world were g. you, |
| T-18.II.7:4 | anyone in the purpose He has g. you. And |
| T-18.III.4:7 | The gift is g. forever, for God Himself |
| T-18.III.6:2 | and this willingness has g. strength to |
| T-18.IV.5:2 | The answer is g.. Seek not to answer, but |
| T-18.IV.5:3 | but merely to receive the answer as it is g.. |
| T-18.VI.11:7 | really happens is that you have g. up the |
| T-18.VII.4:3 | Release is g. you the instant you desire it. |
| T-18.VII.5:7 | at last into the mind g. to contemplation; |
| T-18.VII.6:8 | than is g. to a century of contemplation, |
| T-19.I.2:4 | And since He shares it He has g. it, and so |
| T-19.I.6:2 | divided goal has g. both an equal reality, |
| T-19.I.6:7 | illusion; and g. up when brought to truth, |
| T-19.I.11:1 | God, through Him Whom God has g. you |
| T-19.I.13:1 | Grace is not g. to a body, but to a mind. |
| T-19.I.13:3 | There is the altar where the grace was g., |
| T-19.II.6:8 | But if the mistake is g. the status of truth, |
| T-19.III.9:4 | recognized and quickly g. to correction, |
| T-19.III.10:2 | of the grace that has been g. you. For sin |
| T-19.III.10:6 | who were sightless have been g. vision, |
| T-19.IV.1:9 | him in and give him rest, as it was g. you. |
| T19.IV.A.5:11 | to everyone contained in it as it was g.. |
| T19.IV.A.14:1 | Holy Spirit has g. you love's messengers |
| T19.IV.A.15:5 | The Holy Spirit has g. you His messengers |
| T19.IV.A.15:6 | They have been g. to replace the hungry |
| T19.IV.B.2:6 | the body really g. you that justifies your |
| T19.IV.B.10:6 | purpose of itself, but only what is g. to it. |
| T19.IV.B.14:5 | and sends the messages that it is g.. It has |
| T19.IV.B.14:7 | is g. by the sender and the receiver. The |
| T19.IV.B.17:1 | It is not g. to the ego's disciples to realize |
| T19.IV.B.17:2 | must also be received, to be truly g.. For |
| T19.IV.C.1:11 | it is g. to release and be released from the |
| T19.IV.C.6:1 | have been g. through your acceptance, the |
| T19.IV.C.9:3 | the mighty task for which it was g. you. |
| T19.IV.C.10:4 | What has been g. you, even in its infancy, |
| T19.IV.C.11:6 | g. to you to be the Source of judgment. |
| T19.IV.D.5:4 | of the body is g. up in favor of the spirit, |
| T19.IV.D.9:6 | where the purpose, g. in a holy instant, |
| T19.IV.D.15:8 | has been g. you to give your brother, and |
| T19.IV.D.16:3 | and has been g. the gift of holiness for you |
| T19.IV.D.17:2 | Into the hands that give, the gift is g.. |
| T19.IV.D.19:4 | peace of God, g. to you eternally by Him. |
| T19.IV.D.20:6 | by what he gives, and what is g. him. Nor |
| T19.IV.D.20:7 | Nor is it g. anything in hell or Heaven to |
| T19.IV.D.21:7 | Yet it is g. you to see this purpose in your |
| T-20.I.3:2 | of the resurrection, already g. him. Let |
| T-20.I.4:2 | lilies you have received and g. as your gift, |
| T-20.II.2:1 | bodies, if they be truly g. and received. |
| T-20.II.6:4 | you use what I have g. unless you share it. |
| T-20.II.7:2 | It has been g. you to see no thorns, no |
| T-20.II.7:8 | asked for and been g. the strength to look |
| T-20.III.8:3 | g. it power to adjust the world to make its |
| T-20.III.11:1 | Your gift unto your brother has g. me the |
| T-20.IV.1:4 | g. by Him and reawakened by the Holy |
| T-20.IV.1:8 | has already g. and received all that is true. |
| T-20.IV.1:9 | The untrue He has neither received nor g.. |
| T-20.IV.2:10 | and g. them power to enforce what God |
| T-20.IV.3:6 | What God has g. follows His laws, and |
| T-20.IV.4:2 | they will give it only to what God has g., |
| T-20.IV.5:3 | this earth in seeming solitude is a savior g. |
| T-20.IV.6:1 | the part that has been g. you to learn. For |
| T-20.IV.7:1 | This is the purpose g. you. Think not that |
| T-20.IV.8:9 | As that was g. you, so will its fulfillment |
| T-20.V.2:4 | unity of love proclaimed and g. welcome. |
| T-20.V.2:7 | not Who has g. you the gifts you give, and |
| T-20.V.3:6 | will be g. you to see your brother's worth |
| T-20.V.6:7 | forgiveness you will give him already g., |
| T-20.VI.11:2 | and g. but an instant in which to sigh and |
| T-20.VI.11:7 | it is g. him to choose to spend this instant |
| T-20.VI.11:7 | body, or let himself be g. freedom from it. |
| T-20.VI.12:9 | g. one true relationship beyond the body? |
| T-20.VII.3:6 | they be difficult if they are merely g. you? |
| T-20.VII.9:8 | he did not make, for it was g. him to see, |
| T-20.VIII.1:1 | is g. you who see your brother sinless. |
| T-20.VIII.2:5 | As it was g. you, so will be its effects. And |
| T-20.VIII.2:8 | All this is g. you who would but see your |
| T-20.VIII.2:9 | All this is g., waiting on your desire but to |
| T-20.VIII.2:10 | Vision is freely g. to those who ask to see. |
| T-20.VIII.3:1 | sinlessness is g. you in shining light, to |
| T-20.VIII.4:2 | vision that makes it yours is ready to be g. |
| T-21.II.2:1 | complete escape from sin, all to be g. you. |
| T-21.II.3:8 | is g. you the power to release your savior, |
| T-21.II.4:4 | Never was so much g. for so little. In the |
| T-21.II.4:7 | one you do is g. you because you want it. |
| T-21.II.5:6 | This was not g. you. This was your gift to |
| T-21.II.5:9 | in him, it will be g. you to see it in yourself |
| T-21.III.5:3 | Faith g. to illusions does not lack power, |
| T-21.III.8:4 | should another point of view be g. them. |
| T-21.III.8:6 | choose to look away from sin are g. vision, |
| T-21.III.9:5 | The gift that He has g. you is more than |
| T-21.III.10:1 | sacrifice has g. it great power in your sight |
| T-21.III.12:7 | to body. Let them now be g. back to what |
| T-21.IV.7:7 | longer what has been g. Heaven as its own |
| T-21.V.5:11 | and has your freedom as the purpose g. it, |
| T-21.VI.7:4 | is g. you because he must be one with you. |
| T-21.VI.7:6 | you it is g. you to change his whole mind, |
| T-21.VI.7:9 | is g. you to understand that this is so. For |
| T-21.VI.9:4 | This gracious plan was g. love by Love. |
| T-21.VI.9:6 | it must be g. you to give what It has given, |
| T-21.VI.9:6 | it must be given you to give what It has g., |
| T-21.VI.9:7 | of what is g. you to give your brother, and |
| T-21.VI.9:7 | with him what has been g. both of you. To |
| T-21.VII.9:4 | helpless, the means to see it will be g. you. |
| T-21.VII.13:4 | be g. only those who wish for constancy. |
| T-21.VIII.3:7 | God has already g. all that he really wants. |
| T-21.VIII.5:1 | to you to recognize what He has g. you? |
| T-21.VIII.5:5 | already answered, and what you ask for g. |
| T-22.I.5:1 | sight was g. you, along with everything |
| T-22.I.7:5 | He was not g. there, nor was received by |
| T-22.I.8:1 | Think what is g. you, my holy brother. |
| T-22.II.5:6 | escape from guilt was g. to the Holy Spirit |
| T-22.II.11:5 | has g. to your holy relationship is there. |
| T-22.II.11:7 | look upon the savior that has been g. you? |
| T-22.II.11:9 | of him what God has g. him for you, not |
| T-22.II.13:2 | Quickly and gladly is His vision g. anyone |
| T-22.III.3:1 | of mind in which salvation can be g. you. |
| T-22.IV.5:4 | message has not yet been g. everyone. For |
| T-22.IV.5:8 | joined with your brother's, is it safely g., |
| T-22.IV.6:1 | the grace is g. to be the givers of what they |
| T-22.IV.7:3 | it, he learned it was not g. him alone. |
| T-22.VI.4:3 | and nothing g. it but will be used. This |
| T-22.VI.5:4 | How blessed are you who let this gift be g. |
| T-22.VI.5:5 | part of Heaven that you bring is g. you. |
| T-22.VI.8:6 | This one was g. you, and only this. Accept |
| T-22.VI.9:8 | to it all the power that God has g. Him, to |
| T-22.VI.15:5 | gift. For it was g. you to be used, and not |
| T-23.in.6:3 | you come to understand all that is g. you. |
| T-23.I.10:7 | is g. those who would remember Him. |
| T-23.III.2:3 | box, however beautiful and gently g., still |
| T-23.IV.7:2 | where meaning can be g. what you see. |
| T-23.IV.8:1 | what is g. those who share their Father's |
| T-24.in.1:2 | G. this state the mind is quiet, and the |
| T-24.I.1:6 | it has g. it all the reality it seems to have. |
| T-24.I.2:3 | to become beliefs now g. power to direct |
| T-24.I.7:3 | You have been g. to your brother that love |
| T-24.II.7:1 | to your specialness, and g. it his place, |
| T-24.II.7:1 | the function of salvation g. him for you. |
| T-24.II.10:4 | not g. to His Son but kept for Him alone. |
| T-24.II.11:3 | has been g. him makes you complete, as it |
| T-24.II.12:2 | serves its purpose must be g. to kill. No |
| T-24.III.2:7 | you have g. your brother's birthright to it, |
| T-24.IV.3:13 | G. to Him, the universe is yours. Offered |
| T-24.IV.3:15 | What you have g. specialness has left you |
| T-24.IV.5:4 | the one whom God has g. you instead. So |
| T-24.V.5:4 | strength their purpose holds is g. them. |
| T-24.V.5:5 | see and hear and hold and lead is g. light, |
| T-24.VI.4:5 | g. you to be beyond its laws in all respects |
| T-24.VI.8:3 | delay, which it is g. you to take from him, |
| T-24.VI.9:4 | well, is g. you to save from condemnation, |
| T-24.VI.10:5 | g. you a part of Him to save from pain and |
| T-24.VI.12:5 | of truth itself is g. to provide the means, |
| T-24.VII.2:6 | All of the tribute you have g. specialness |
| T-24.VII.3:4 | is g. you to see his holiness *because* it is the |
| T-24.VII.11:12 | And it is g. you to make a different choice, |
| T-25.I.5:2 | link that has been g. you to join the truth |
| T-25.II.6:4 | that God has g. it but serves His purpose, |
| T-25.II.7:5 | on it, and see the holiness that He has g. it |
| T-25.II.8:6 | and what God gave him must be g. you. |
| T-25.II.10:3 | Give, then, what He has g. you, that you |
| T-25.II.10:4 | believe that all His praise is g. not to you. |
| T-25.II.11:5 | your brother is g. the power of salvation, |
| T-25.II.11:5 | apart from all God's Love as g. equally. |
| T-25.III.6:5 | chooses to avail himself of what is g. him, |
| T-25.III.7:2 | to see the workings of the Helper g. you to |
| T-25.IV.5:2 | Every leaf that falls is g. life in you. Each |
| T-25.V.3:5 | such is the call that God has g. him, that |
| T-25.V.6:6 | not this; the role you give to him is g. you, |
| T-25.VI.5:2 | he learns the gift was g. to himself, and so |
| T-25.VI.7:3 | You wanted it, and it is g. you. All that |

T-25......VI.7:8 is the function g. you for your brother.
T-25....VI.7:10 this *one* thing, that everything be g. you.
T-25.....VII.8:3 One is g. the choice of form most suitable
T-25..VIII.10:7 No justice would be g. him by you. Yet
T-25..VIII.12:9 Spirit that simple justice may be g. you.
T-25......IX.2:2 and you are willing it be g. you. God's
T-25......IX.2:4 treasures g. to God's Son are kept for him,
T-25......IX.2:5 Nor is the treasure less as it is g. out. Each
T-25......IX.7:2 g. specially to an elect and special group,
T-25....IX.10:5 alike. It is received and g. equally. It is
T-26.......I.4:10 Yet is it g. him to make the world recede
T-26.........I.6:4 nor see what it is g. him to witness to, that
T-26.........I.7:1 can you be reborn, and g. life again. His
T-26.........I.7:8 only one was g. him by One Who knows
T-26.......II.6:6 One is g. you to see in him his perfect
T-26.......II.8:5 wish that Heaven be g. you instead of hell,
T-26......VI.2:3 Yet God has g. him a better Friend, in
T-26......VI.3:5 to Whom they have been g. can make sure
T-26.....VII.4:2 God g. answer to the world of sickness,
T-26.....VII.6:2 it is possible that some are g. greater value
T-26...VII.17:4 To you to whom it has been g. to save the
T-26...VII.18:1 use the power God has g. you as He would
T-26....VIII.3:9 withheld from you and g. seem dangerous
T-26....VIII.5:2 No purpose has been g. it as yet, and what
T-26....VIII.7:9 G. a change of purpose for the good, there
T-26......IX.4:4 What hatred claimed is g. up to love, and
T-26......IX.5:3 what was held apart from light is g. up,
T-26.......X.2:4 are g. meaning and perceived as sensible.
T-26.......X.5:3 this you seek to add unto the purpose g. it
T-27.......I.9:10 but waiting for a purpose to be g., that it
T-27.......I.11:3 view, another purpose, can be g. it. You
T-27.......II.6:1 nothing less to him than it has g. unto you
T-27.....II.6:11 it is g. you to show him, by your healing,
T-27.......II.7:8 of sin. And what you wish is g. you to see.
T-27.....II.12:1 because that is the function g. it *by* you.
T-27.....II.12:4 Yet must He work with what is g. Him,
T-27.....II.15:1 Correction is the function g. both, but
T-27.....II.15:9 own. And thus is healing g. you and him.
T-27.....II.16:4 the function g. it conceived to be its Own,
T-27......III.6:1 picture of your brother g. you to occupy
T-27......IV.2:3 God must have g. you a way of reaching to
T-27......IV.6:3 so it can be g. you and also be received.
T-27.......V.6:3 Life is g. you to give the dying world. And
T-27.....V.11:2 And you will learn that peace is g. you
T-27.....V.11:9 His Son, and therefore is it g. unto Him.
T-27...VII.10:7 Yet if the choice is really g. you, then you
T-28.........I.3:4 can employ for healing have been g. Him,
T-28.........I.5:3 it receives, and does what it is g. it to do.
T-28.......I.12:1 He to Whom time is g. offers thanks for
T-28.......I.12:1 thanks for every quiet instant g. Him. For
T-28.......I.12:3 the one for whom He has been g. them!
T-28.......II.1:4 and receives the gift that he has g. Him. It
T-28.......II.2:10 Only where its cause is g. its effects. For
T-28.......II.3:5 is g. no effects and none is seen. A mind
T-28.......II.8:5 has g. it have they adopted as their own.
T-28....IV.10:4 What God has g. cannot be a loss, and
T-28.....VII.4:6 choice, and g. you the instant it is made.
T-29.......II.6:2 What you have g. "life" is not alive, and
T-29....III.3:12 you forgive is g. power to forgive you your
T-29....III.3:13 By your gift of freedom is it g. unto you.
T-29......IV.4:3 the functions you have g. have been filled;
T-29......IV.6:5 as means to serve the function g. Him.
T-29.......V.5:2 and to whom is all creation g. as his own.
T-29.......V.5:3 Because he has it is it g. you, and where it
T-29.......V.7:1 dream is g. you in which he is your savior,
T-29.......V.7:2 hate. A dream is g. you in which you have
T-29...VII.1:12 But it is g. you to know the truth, and not
T-29.....VII.5:3 death, conceived as real and g. living form
T-29.....VII.7:1 the purpose of the world the past has g. it.
T-29.....VII.8:4 wish, perceived as if it had been g. you.
T-29....VIII.3:2 idol is a wish, made tangible and g. form,
T-29....VIII.5:3 to life, and g. power that it may be feared.
T-29....VIII.6:3 this power and place and time are g. form
T-29....VIII.6:5 peace of God, forever g. to all living things
T-29....VIII.9:2 Who can have more, and who be g. less?
T-30.........I.4:2 *by myself, this is the day that will be g. me.*
T-30.........I.5:3 to sit by and ask to have the answer g. you
T-30.......II.4:8 it is by your will the world is g. freedom.
T-30......III.4:4 God's Will, and this is g. you by being His
T-30......V.6:3 again, that what is his be g. back to him.
T-30......VI.1:4 world g. in exchange for dreams of terror.
T-30....VI.10:2 mistakes that have been g. no effects. But
T-30....VI.10:7 in him who has been g. you to heal, for
T-30.....VII.3:3 If they are g. different meanings, it must
T-30.....VII.4:1 one interpretation g. to the world and all
T-30.....VII.4:3 one meaning has been g. everything, and
T-30.....VII.7:8 with them forgiveness has been g. to us all
T-30....VIII.3:5 be g. you to heal appearances you do not
T-30....VIII.3:7 What you ask *is* g. you, but not of God
T-30....VIII.4:6 is no miracle that can be g. you unless you
T-30....VIII.4:7 gives all miracles has not been g. freedom
T-30....VIII.5:2 be g. you to look upon your brother thus.
T-31.......II.2:4 But afterwards, the truth is g. you. You
T-31.......II.4:5 the function that was g. him by you. And
T-31.....II.11:4 light cannot be g. while you walk alone,
T-31......III.4:9 to suit the purpose g. by the mind. For
T-31......III.6:1 been g. you to change what you believe.
T-31......IV.1:5 a little time is g. you to use for you alone;
T-31......IV.2:7 by all the different names its roads are g..
T-31......IV.8:4 lose, and what you lose is what is g. him.
T-31......IV.8:5 lost, and what he gains is what is g. *you.*
T-31.......V.7:4 They are not g., so they must be made.
T-31.......V.8:3 if any peace of mind is to be g. you. Nor
T-31.....V.12:4 has meaning that was g. it by you. It also
T-31......VI.4:2 The means are g. you by which to see the
T-31.....VII.3:5 see without the Aid that God has g. you.
T-31.....VII.4:4 perceived to be yourself, it has been g. you
T-31.....VII.6:4 the function g. you to bring you peace,
T-31.....VII.7:7 All that is g. you is for release; the sight,
T-31..VII.10:5 The holy ones whom God has g. you to
T-31..VII.10:6 God has g. you His Son to save from every
T-31..VII.13:6 Then is the answer g.. And the door held
T-31..VII.15:1 Let not the world's light, g. unto you, be
T-31....VIII.2:5 your actions, you have g. it no power. And
T-31....VIII.2:6 in you is g. charge of everything you do.
T-31....VIII.2:7 and He has g. you His strength instead.
T-31....VIII.7:2 fear. For it is g. you to join with him, and
W-pI..........2.h I have g. everything I see in this room [on
W-pI.......2.1:6 to include everything you see in a g. area,
W-pI.......7.1:4 reason why you have g. everything you see
W-pI.....12.1:3 All these attributes are g. it by you. The
W-pI.....15.1:4 the function you have g. your body's eyes.
W-pI.....18.1:2 which will be g. increasing stress later on.
W-pI.....20.3:7 all power is g. him in Heaven and on earth
W-pI.....20.3:8 your determination to see is vision g. you.
W-pI.....25.1:8 this that what you see is g. meaning.
W-pI.....42.2:1 strength, and what He gives is truly g..
WpI....rI.in.6:1 are not g. in quite their original form. Use
WpI....rI.in.6:2 Use them as they are g. here. It is not
W-pI.....51.2:1 I have g. what I see all the meaning it has
W-pI.....52.1:6 upsetting because I have g. them reality,
W-pI.....53.3:6 I have g. it the illusion of reality, and have
W-pI.....55.4:4 to follow the Guide God has g. me to find
W-pI.....55.5:6 The purpose I have g. the world has led to
W-pI.....55.5:7 by withdrawing the one I have g. it, and
W-pI.....56.2:5 by truth, vision will surely be g. me. And
W-pI.....59.2:4 of seeing for the vision that is g. by God.
W-pI.....59.2:5 vision is His gift, and He has g. it to me.
W-pI.....59.3:8 of Christ has been g. me to replace them.
W-pI.....59.4:6 Now it is g. me to understand that God is
W-pI.....60.4:5 the only Guide that has been g. to His Son
W-pI.....60.5:5 the world with the vision He has g. me, I
W-pI.....61.3:4 of the power that is g. you to save others.
W-pI.....64.3:1 of the world, a function g. you by God. It
W-pI.....64.4:1 function g. you by God will you be happy.
W-pI.....66.5:3 *He has g. my function to me. Therefore my*
W-pI.....66.7:1 is that God has g. you your function. We
W-pI...66.11:2 *are one, because God has g. me both.* It will
W-pI.....69.8:2 that it is g. you and you will yet receive it.
W-pI.....75.3:4 We will be g. what we desire. We will to
W-pI.....75.4:5 Sight is g. us, now that the light has come.
W-pI.....76.9:4 God. Payment is neither g. nor received.
W-pI.....77.4:3 never taken from one and g. to another,
W-pI.....77.5:3 You have requested that you be g. the
W-pI.....78.7:1 in the light of true forgiveness, g. unto us.
W-pI...78.10:3 the past, allow the role of savior to be g.,
W-pI.....79.2:4 Even if he is g. the answer, he cannot see
W-pI.....79.8:4 trying to recognize that you have been g.
W-pI ....80.1:7 Freedom from conflict has been g. you.
W-pI ....80.5:1 that your acceptance brings be g. you.
W-pI ....81.1:2 g. the function of lighting up the world!
W-pI ....89.1:5 it on behalf of the function He has g. me.
W-pI ....90.4:3 *The answer to this problem is already g. me,*
W-pI ....92.5:1 and shines with light its Source has g. it;
W-pI ..92.10:3 the light in which the gift of sight is g. you
W-pI ....93.8:4 trying to experience what God has g. you,
W-pI ..95.13:5 and it is g. you to feel this Self within you,
W-pI ..96.12:2 And all of it is g. everyone who asks for it,
W-pI ..96.12:3 how much is g. unto you to give this day,
W-pI ..96.12:3 unto you to give this day, that it be g. you!
W-pI ....98.2:3 and have been g. everything we need with
W-pI ....98.3:3 that they will do what it is g. them to do.
W-pI ....98.5:1 accept the happiness that God has g. you?
W-pI ....99.6:4 with the One to Whom the plan was g..
W-pI ..100.2:3 to take in working out His plan is g. you
W-pI ..103.3:3 God, being Love, it will be g. you. Bolster
W-pI ..104.3:2 five minutes g. truth for your salvation,
W-pI ..104.4:1 as we ask to recognize what God has g. us.
W-pI ..104.4:2 come to find what has been g. us by Him.
W-pI ..105.1:6 guilt. The truly g. gift entails no loss. It is
W-pI ..105.2:1 No gift is g. thus. Such "gifts" are but a
W-pI ..105.3:4 will never lessen when they are g. away.
W-pI ..105.7:4 gift of peace and joy that God has g. you.
W-pI ..105.7:6 for you have g. what you would receive.
W-pI ..106.6:2 It is here, and will today be g. unto you.
W-pI ..106.7:1 is yours and everything is g. away, it will
W-pI ..106.9:3 who pause to ask that truth be g. them,
W-pI 106.10:2 g. to yourself as often as is possible today:
W-pI ..108.7:5 and in that peace is vision g. us, and we
WpI...rIII.in4:3 When you withdraw the value g. them,
WpI..rIII.in6:6 you gave as they were g. you for it to use.
WpI..rIII.in7:1 You have been g. them in perfect trust; in
WpI..rIII.in9:3 not g. your learning a fair chance to prove
W-pI ..116.2:3 *What He has g. me is all I want. What He has*
W-pI ..116.2:4 *is all I want. What He has g. me is all there is.*
W-pI ..121.7:7 Who was g. you to show the way to you.
W-pI ..122.4:2 perfect answer, g. to imperfect questions,
W-pI ..122.7:5 has received what God has g. as its own.
W-pI 122.11:2 will be g. you to feel the peace forgiveness
W-pI 122.13:2 Today all things you want are g. you. Let
W-pI ..123.6:3 thousand more than they were g.. He will
W-pI ..123.7:3 holy half an hour g. Him will be returned
W-pI ..125.2:2 g. the Word of God to be his Guide,
W-pI .....126.h All that I give is g. to myself.
W-pI ..126.7:1 Not having g. Him the gift He asks of you
W-pI ..126.7:1 gifts, and think He has not g. them to you.
W-pI ..126.7:6 remains as unreceived has not been g.,
W-pI ..126.7:6 what has been g. must have been received
W-pI 126.11:3 *All that I give is g. to myself. The Help I need*
W-pI ..128.2:2 must serve the purpose you have g. it,
W-pI ..128.5:1 thought of values we have g. to the world.
W-pI ..129.6:4 Let it be g. you today. It waits but for your
W-pI ..129.8:4 A day of grace is g. you today, and we give
W-pI ..131.8:4 what the Eternal Will has g. him to be his
W-pI 134.16:4 relief. The time remaining should be g. to
W-pI 135.13:4 strength that has been g. it and cannot fail
W-pI 135.21:2 we need is g. us for our accomplishment
W-pI 135.22:3 And we are g. truly, as we say: *If I defend*
W-pI ..136.5:2 g. willingness to reconsider the decision
W-pI 136.13:2 God has g. you is not the truth right now,
W-pI 137.11:2 all the grace of healing it is g. them to give
W-pI 140.12:6 be g. us as we attend in silence and in joy.
WpI..rIV.in7:4 shine with the meaning God has g. it, as it
WpI..rIV.in7:4 it, as it was g. to you through His Voice.
W-pI ..143.2:1 (126) All that I give is g. to myself.
W-pI ..154.7:3 roles that are not g. them by His authority
W-pI 154.12:3 But this is sure; until belief is g. it, you will
W-pI ..155.9:3 Your holy brothers have been g. you, to
W-pI 155.13:4 and g. you your brothers in His trust that
W-pI ..157.3:1 it will be g. you to feel a touch of Heaven,
W-pI ..157.4:2 day, what you are asking must be g. you.
W-pI ..157.8:2 truth, the holy Guide to Heaven g. you,
W-pI ..158.1:1 What has been g. you? The knowledge
W-pI ..158.1:4 This was g. you as knowledge which you
W-pI ..158.1:5 It was g. as well to every living thing, for
W-pI ..159.2:4 miracle you cannot give, for all are g. you.
W-pI ..159.4:6 holiness was g. by His Father and Himself

W-pI.159.10:2 the gift, when God appointed it be **g.** you?
W-pI...160.7:3 for you have **g.** him your rightful place.
W-pI...163.8:9 And it is **g.** us to look past death, and see
W-pI...164.6:2 **g.** you from far beyond all things within
W-pI...164.7:2 We will receive but what is **g.** us from
W-pI...164.7:6 it the freedom **g.** us through His forgiving
W-pI...165.4:4 Ask to receive, and it is **g.** you. Conviction
W-pI...165.6:1 end made certain, and salvation **g.** you.
W-pI...166.1:1 All things are **g.** you. God's trust in you is
W-pI...166.5:3 But he will not look at what is **g.** him. He
W-pI.166.10:7 this Answer **g.** you have need no more of
W-pI.166.12:6 you of all the gifts that God has **g.** you. He
W-pI...167.5:5 not give birth to what was never **g.** them.
W-pI......168.h Your grace is **g.** me. I claim it now.
W-pI...168.5:1 today, for we receive what has been **g.** us.
W-pI...168.6:5 *Your grace is* **g.** *me. I claim it now. Father, I*
W-pI...169.6:2 completely **g.** and received completely. It
W-pI.169.14:9 can give in the grace that has been **g.** us.
W-pI.169.15:2 gives the grace we ask, as it was **g.** Him?
W-pI.170.12:4 and your attributes, **g.** by your Creator,
WpI .. rV.in3:6 *we review the thoughts that You have* **g.** *us.*
WpI .. rV.in8:1 and knows the answer God has **g.** Him.
W-pI...179.2:1 (168) Your grace is **g.** me. I claim it now.
W-pI.183.10:1 of God for your release, and it is **g.** you.
W-pI.183.11:8 today. And in His Name, it shall be **g.** us.
W-pI...184.2:3 think that you have **g.** life in separation.
W-pI...184.3:3 The nameless things were **g.** names, and
W-pI...184.3:3 and thus reality was **g.** them as well. For
W-pI...184.3:4 For what is named is **g.** meaning and will
W-pI...184.4:1 purposefully set against the **g.** truth. Its
W-pI.184.10:2 Word, the Name which God has **g.** you;
W-pI.184.12:6 to let our minds accept what God has **g.** as
W-pI.184.14:1 have but one Name, which He has **g.** them
W-pI.184.14:4 we are **g.** strength to see beyond them.
W-pI...185.1:4 be completely **g.** back to full awareness,
W-pI...185.2:4 wants the peace of God, and it is **g.** him.
W-pI...185.6:2 is genuine, the means for finding it is **g.**,
W-pI...185.7:4 do not request another dream be **g.** us.
W-pI.185.10:6 Help has been **g.** you. And would you not
W-pI.185.12:1 was peace created, **g.** you by its Creator,
W-pI.185.14:2 as we request the peace of God be **g.** us?
W-pI...186.1:2 your own but that which has been **g.** you.
W-pI...186.2:4 The means are **g.** us by which it will be
W-pI...186.2:6 What is **g.** us to do, we have the strength
W-pI...186.8:2 We will accept the function God has **g.** us,
W-pI.186.10:1 when you accept the function **g.** you. The
W-pI.186.11:1 your truly **g.** function stands out clear and
W-pI.186.12:6 which tells you of a function **g.** you by
W-pI.186.13:5 and what is **g.** in His Name takes on the
W-pI.186.14:3 is needed here is **g.** here as it is needed. In
W-pI...187.1:7 Having had and **g.**, then the world asserts
W-pI...187.3:4 the idea of giving clarified and **g.** meaning
W-pI...187.8:5 it. **G.** first to you, it now is yours to give as
W-pI...187.9:5 to increase, forever yours, forever **g.** away.
W-pI...188.3:6 by. All of its gifts are **g.** everyone, and
W-pI...188.4:2 gifts beyond all measure, **g.** and returned.
W-pI...189.5:2 The choice is **g.** you. But learn and do not
W-pI.190.10:3 This is the day when it is **g.** you to realize
W-pI...191.9:1 power is **g.** unto you in earth and Heaven.
W-pI...192.6:6 we have indeed been **g.** everything by God
W-pI...193.6:3 that seem to have been **g.** power over you.
W-pI...194.3:4 so each instant **g.** unto God in passing,
W-pI...194.3:4 passing, with the next one **g.** Him already,
W-pI...195.9:2 We have been **g.** everything. If we refuse
W-pI...197.4:4 They are received where they are **g.**. In
W-pI...197.5:1 you give to Him, and every gift is **g.** Him,
W-pI...197.5:1 Him, because it can be **g.** only to yourself.
W-pI...197.6:1 you will think that what is **g.** you has been
W-pI...197.9:5 All that you do is **g.** unto Him. All that
W-pI...197.9:7 you forgot the function God has **g.** you.
W-pI.198.13:3 gift that God has **g.** us through Him today
W-pI...199.2:2 it has been **g.** to the Source of love, and
W-pI...199.8:9 *I hear the Voice that God has* **g.** *me, and it is*
W-pI...200.4:5 But it is **g.** you to find the means whereby
W-pI...200.5:1 Freedom is **g.** you where you beheld but
WpI rVI.in.4:4 For thus is freedom **g.** us from all we did
WpI rVI.in.5:4 let the thought which you denied be **g.** up,
WpI rVI.in.7:4 us also not forget to Whom it has been **g.**,
W-pI...202.1:2 *Himself has* **g.** *me His Voice to call me home?*

W-pI...212.1:3 *function God has* **g.** *me can offer freedom.*
W-pI...216.1:4 *But if I forgive, salvation will be* **g.** *me.* I am
W-pII.....in.3:2 conclude the year that we have **g.** God.
W-pII.....in.6:2 exchange for its replacement, **g.** us by You
W-pII...in.11:3 them to be continued till the next is **g.** you
W-pII......1.5:2 for such is His function, **g.** Him by God.
W-pII..224.1:4 but this that can be either **g.** or received.
W-pII..225.1:1 *same, and You have* **g.** *all Your Love to me.*
W-pII..230.1:3 It is not **g.** me to change my Self. How
W-pII..230.2:2 *What was* **g.** *then must be here now, for my*
W-pII......2.1:4 God's Word is **g.** every mind which thinks
W-pII......2.2:1 Thought of peace was **g.** to God's Son the
W-pII......2.2:2 before, for peace was **g.** without opposite,
W-pII......2.4:3 it holds a hint of all the glory **g.** us by God
W-pII..231.2:5 only this is what it will be **g.** us to find.
W-pII..234.2:2 *Word which You have* **g.** *us that we are saved*
W-pII..236.1:4 been **g.** me to serve whatever purpose I
W-pII......3.3:2 go to find what has been **g.** them to seek.
W-pII......3.4:2 all perception can be **g.** a new purpose by
W-pII..245.2:3 we share the Word that He has **g.** unto us.
W-pII......5.3:4 must the body serve the purpose **g.** it. But
W-pII..266.2:2 How many saviors God has **g.** us! How
W-pII..266.2:3 Him, and **g.** us the sight to look on them?
W-pII..267.1:4 and all I need to save the world is **g.** me.
W-pII..269.1:3 *is* **g.** *me to find a new perception through the*
W-pII......6.3:4 Yet will these dreams be **g.** unto Christ, to
W-pII..272.1:6 *I will accept no less than You have* **g.** *me. I am*
W-pII..273.1:4 peace that God Himself has **g.** to His Son.
W-pII..274.2:2 fear today, because the day is **g.** unto love.
W-pII..275.2:4 *The safety that I bring is* **g.** *me. Father, Your*
W-pII.....276.h The Word of God is **g.** me to speak.
W-pII..276.1:5 us accept His Fatherhood, and all is **g.** us.
W-pII..276.2:2 *brothers, who are* **g.** *me to cherish as my own*
W-pII......7.1:2 through the grace that God has **g.** Him, to
W-pII..284.2:1 *Father, what You have* **g.** *cannot hurt, so*
W-pII..286.1:6 *You is everything I hope to find already* **g.** *me*
W-pII..288.1:8 *Let me not attack the savior You have* **g.** *me.*
W-pII..290.2:3 *What I ask have You already* **g.** *me. And I am*
W-pII..291.1:6 And it is **g.** us to recognize it is a holiness
W-pII..295.2:1 *a gift of me, and one I give that it be* **g.** *me.*
W-pII......9.3:2 all minds are **g.** to the hands of Christ, to
W-pII..303.2:3 *He is the Self that You have* **g.** *me. He is but*
W-pII..304.2:3 *my Father,* **g.** *me to offer to Your holy Son,*
W-pII..305.2:1 *Father, the peace of Christ is* **g.** *us, because it*
W-pII..316.1:3 His grace is **g.** me in every gift a brother
W-pII..316.1:5 home, among the gifts that God has **g.** me
W-pII..317.1:4 already **g.** all my brothers and already
W-pII..319.1:6 I learn that what one gains is **g.** unto all.
W-pII..319.2:3 *salvation of the world could You have* **g.** *me?*
W-pII..320.1:5 I am he to whom all this is **g.**. I am he in
W-pII..320.2:3 *And so all power has been* **g.** *to Your Son.*
W-pII....11.2:1 God's Thoughts are **g.** all the power that
W-pII..332.2:3 *yet Your Love has* **g.** *us the means to set it free*
W-pII..332.2:5 *For as we offer freedom, it is* **g.** *us. And we*
W-pII..333.1:3 to be, in the reality which has been **g.** it,
W-pII..334.1:6 so I go to find the treasures God has **g.** me
W-pII..337.1:2 be my state, for only happiness is **g.** me.
W-pII..338.2:3 *me, until I learn that You have* **g.** *me the only*
W-pII....13.2:1 gift of grace, for it is **g.** and received as one
W-pII.....342.h things, For thus forgiveness will be **g.** me.
W-pII..342.1:3 **g.** *me the means to prove its unreality to me.*
W-pII..343.1:7 *all things are* **g.** *unto me forever and forever.*
W-pII..343.2:3 is a gift that must be freely **g.** and received
W-pII..345.1:4 *miracles I give are* **g.** *back in just the form I*
W-pII..349.1:3 *It will be* **g.** *me, because I have chosen it as*
W-pII....14.3:3 And this, our gift, is therefore **g.** us. We
W-pII..352.1:4 *have* **g.** *me a way to find Your peace again.*
W-pII.....353.h be **g.** Christ To use to bless the world with
Wfl ........in.2:1 way to find the peace that God has **g.** us.
Wfl ........in.3:2 Unto us the aim is **g.** to forgive the world.
Wfl ........in.3:3 It is the goal that God has **g.** us. It is His
Wfl ........in.3:6 Himself. And thus His memory is **g.** back,
Wfl ........in.4:1 **g.** us to be His Own completion in reality.
Wfl ........in.4:5 us through our forgiveness, **g.** unto him.
W-ep .........1:9 but ask it of Him, and it will be **g.** you.
W-ep .........3:4 His is the Word that God has **g.** you. His
M-1 .........4:10 Such was their choice, and it is **g.** them.
M-2 ...........2:6 in that same instant was God's Answer **g.**.
M-3 ...........5:2 which each person is **g.** a chosen learning

M-4 .........I.2:2 mighty power of an eagle has been **g.** him
M-4 ....... X.3:4 What God has **g.** is so far beyond our
M-4 ....... X.3:8 It is **g.** to the teachers of God to bring the
M-5 .........I.2:8 he **g.** himself what God would give to him,
M-5 ...... III.2:7 of the remedy God has already **g.** them. It
M-5 .... III.2:10 They merely give what has been **g.** them.
M-6 ...........2:3 healing has been **g.** it will be received.
M-6 ...........3:3 done that they have also **g.** the outcome,
M-6 ...........4:1 about the gift that makes it truly **g.**. And it
M-6 .........4:12 gifts? **G.** by God to God, who in this holy
M-7 ...........2:5 **g.** the problem to One Who cannot fail,
M-7 ...........5:1 of any problem that has been **g.** to God's
M-8 ...........4:5 to be **g.** what will fit into these categories.
M-9 ...........1:7 By far the majority are **g.** a slowly evolving
M-10 .........5:8 He has **g.** it away, along with judgment.
M-10 .........6:9 For he has **g.** up their cause, and they,
M-13 .........8:2 and everything is **g.** you at no cost at all.
M-15 .........1:5 it, and on that very day it will be **g.** him.
M-15 .........3:1 sometimes feel your just due is not **g.** you,
M-16 .........8:4 not of him, but will be **g.** him at any time,
M-17 .........2:8 Here is his gift most clearly **g.** him. For he
M-17 .........8:5 **G.** that, the lesson's manifest simplicity
M-20 .........3:7 this, **g.** forgiveness there *must* be peace.
M-20 .........5:9 is our practicing **g.** its one direction. And
M-21 .........3:2 this will be **g.** because this will be received
M-22 .........2:3 the function God has **g.** him long before
M-22 .........7:9 be **g.** and where it should be withheld.
M-23 .........4:5 thanks for all the gifts that God has **g.** you
M-25 .........3:2 **G.** to the Holy Spirit, and used under His
M-25 .........4:9 Yet what is not **g.** to the Holy Spirit must
M-25 .........4:9 to the Holy Spirit must be **g.** to weakness,
M-25 .........4:9 for what is withheld from love is **g.** to fear,
M-25 .........5:5 Yet, **g.** a remaining wish to be deceived,
M-28 .........6:5 and **g.** Him Whose function judgment is.
M-29 .........4:8 things because you have **g.** that belief to it
M-29 .........5:2 Yet to accept the power **g.** him by God is
M-29 .........5:8 wisdom will be **g.** you when you need it.
M-29 .........6:5 For God has **g.** Him the power to translate
M-29 .........7:5 He has **g.** you the means to prove it so.
M-29 .........7:6 of His Teacher, and all things are **g.** you.
M-29 .........8:4 *is* **g.** *you to be the means Through which His*
C-2........... 10:6 not go on a little while when it is **g.** him to
C-3.............3:3 having **g.** the content it is His Will that it
C-4.............8:3 eternity; out of all fear and **g.** back to love.
C-5.............1:3 reality. Helpers are **g.** you in many forms,
C-6.............2:3 and earth is therefore **g.** him and he will
C-6.............2:4 The Atonement principle was **g.** to the
C-ep...........5:6 and in the quiet God has **g.** him enters his
P-1.............1:4 God has **g.** everyone a Teacher Whose
P-2.........in.4:5 They are finally **g.** up in the minds of both
P-2........ III.2:3 all limitations has been **g.** them. Now the
P-2........ IV.5:5 **g.** by Him to the Holy Spirit as His gift to
P-2...... IV.11:7 **G.** this single shift, all else will follow.
P-2........ VI.2:2 **g.** us literally "to change our tune." The
P-2........ VI.6:3 and is thus **g.** another chance to look at it,
P-2....... VII.6:1 has **g.** you as to invent one He has not.
P-2....... VII.7:7 without the god who must be **g.** him?
P-3..........II.3:1 and will use, **g.** the slightest invitation.
P-3..........II.9:3 a function that has not been **g.** him. To
P-3........ III.1:4 Should he need money it will be **g.** him,
P-3...... III.1:10 he stays he will be **g.** what he needs to stay
P-3........ III.4:4 whatever one needs is **g.** by the other;
P-3........ III.5:1 been said that to him who hath shall be **g.**
P-3........ III.5:3 And because he gives, he shall be **g.**. This
P-3........ III.5:7 it. All that they need will thus be **g.** them.
P-3........ III.7:9 greater gift than this could you be **g.**?
S-1...........I.1:7 Ask, rather, to receive what is already **g.**;
S-1...........I.2:7 The form of the answer, if **g.** by God, will
S-1...........I.3:6 and all else has indeed been **g.** you.
S-1........ III.4:1 Guilt must be **g.** up, and not concealed.
S-1........ III.6:8 he lose the only true goal that is **g.** him.
S-2...........I.3:2 Then learn that God has **g.** you the means
S-2...........I.4:1 yourself, so is forgiveness always **g.** you. It
S-2...........I.6:1 Forgiveness, truly **g.**, is the way in which
S-2...........I.6:3 God Himself has **g.** all His Sons a remedy
S-2........ III.6:7 Forgiveness has been **g.** Him to teach, to
S-3...........I.3:3 Forgiveness must be **g.** by a mind which
S-3...........I.4:4 help is **g.** to him in the Voice his Father
S-3..........II.2:2 body, then, for all the service it has **g.** us.

S-3........III.6:6 stand, and fear has g. way at last to God.
S-3........IV.1:9 and g. up all separate dreams of special
S-3........IV.9:8 Arise and let My thanks be g. you. And

## Giver 5

*giver*

T-1..........I.4:1 mean life, and God is the G. of life. His
T-9..........I.8:8 the Universal G. for what you do not want
T-27.....II.16:4 that its G. keeps *because* it has been shared
W-pI...157.8:2 One, the G. of the happy dreams of life,
W-pI...168.5:2 us. Our faith lies in the G., not our own

## giver 31

*Giver*

T-1..........I.9:3 more love both to the g. *and* the receiver.
T-1........I.16:2 the g. and supply strength to the receiver.
T-1........II.6:4 which the g. and receiver both emerge
T-1........II.6:8 g. and receiver on which the miracle rests.
T-1.....VII.3:11 becomes apparent to both g. and receiver.
T-15.....VII.2:2 keep the g. bound to itself through guilt.
T-17....VIII.6:1 you became a g. of peace as surely as your
T19... IV.A.4:1 salvation away from the g. of salvation?
T19. IV.D.13:3 Is this g. of salvation your friend or enemy
T19. IV.D.20:1 you would look upon the g. of this gift, for
T19. IV.D.20:2 seen as either the g. of guilt or of salvation
T-20....... II.3:1 is an evaluation of the receiver and the g..
T-20....... V.7:1 Can you evaluate the g. of a gift like this?
T-23.........I.4:4 before your sight, into the g. of your peace
T-23...... III.2:4 And neither the receiver nor the g. is long
T-24...... II.12:3 seal but offers treachery to g. and receiver
W-pI...105.1:4 in which the g. loses as he gives the gift;
W-pI...126.6:5 become the joyous g. of what you received
W-pI...126.8:1 the truth that g. and receiver are the same
W-pI...159.4:3 It is the bond by which the g. and receiver
W-pI...163.1:3 of death as savior and as g. of release.
W-pI.166.14:5 hand becomes the g. of Christ's touch;
W-pI...187.5:5 There is no g. and receiver in the sense the
W-pI...187.5:6 There is a g. who retains; another who
W-pI...188.4:3 you, the g. of the gift, does God Himself
M-6 ...........2:5 for the g. and the receiver of God's gifts.
M-6 ...........3:5 the g. nor the receiver would have the gift.
M-6 ...........3:6 part that guarantees the g. will not lose,
M-6 ...........3:7 sure it is used as the g. deems appropriate
M-6 ...........4:4 mind of the g. Who gives the gift to him.
S-3.........in.1:2 a g. of assurance of success in ultimate

## givers 1

T-22......IV.6:1 to be the g. of what they have received.

## gives 232

T-4.........I.12:4 and this g. them truer perception. The
T-4........ II.7:3 ego never g. out of abundance, because it
T-4........ III.5:3 enter. The Bible g. many references to the
T-4........VI.1:2 to it g. the ego any power over you. I have
T-4.......VII.5:6 because real creation g. everything, since
T-4.......VII.5:8 of being the mind g. everything always.
T-5........IV.7:1 Atonement g. you the power of a healed
T-5........VI.2:4 It g. the ego a false sense of security by
T-7........VI.4:8 also deny everything this power g. you
T-7........VI.4:8 gives you *because* it g. you everything. No
T-7........XI.5:5 God g. only equally. If you recognize His
T-8.........I.5:10 exist, and g. them no rationale for choice.
T-8........III.8:3 God g. whatever belongs to Him because
T-8........III.8:3 belongs to Him because He g. of Himself,
T-8........IV.7:9 g. equally whatever is acceptable to Him.
T-8.......VII.3:6 God on behalf of the function He g. it.
T-8.....VII.12:4 and g. it over entirely to the One Light in
T-8......VIII.4:8 as a judge g. anything but an impartial
T-9...........I.7:5 it is, and this g. you the illusion of safety.
T-9......... II.5:1 message your brother g. you is up to you.
T-9.......VII.1:6 second g. you a chance to save yourself.
T-11..........I.7:5 on your willingness to give as He g.. Your
T-11........I.11:4 remember that what He g. He keeps, so
T-11........I.11:4 so that nothing He g. can contradict Him.
T-11....VIII.5:9 you. God g.; He does not take. When you
T-12........I.6:9 He g. them to you because they are *for* you
T-12.......II.2:3 only if the Son of God g. power to it. He
T-12 .....IV.2:5 mind that believes in it and g. existence to
T-12 .....VI.1:5 yours, and g. you nothing in return. You
T-12 .....VI.3:3 This g. it the only reality it will ever have.
T-12 ....VII.7:9 This g. it an illusion of integrity, and
T-12 ....VIII.8:7 Being corrected it g. place to knowledge,
T-13 ........I.4:6 God. And what God g. has always been.
T-13 ..VII.12:4 g. you all the things that you need have,
T-14 ........I.3:3 have all the power that he g. to them. The
T-14 .......II.7:8 from the hands of Christ Who g. it to you,
T-14 ... III.10:8 g. them what they want without effort,
T-14 ... III.11:3 g. you everything will simply offer it to
T-14 ... III.17:3 And so He g. you what is yours, because
T-14 ..... IV.8:7 Would you know of One Who g. forever,
T-14 ...VIII.5:1 those He g. the power to create can never
T-14 ...VIII.5:6 To whom God g. Himself, He *is* given.
T-14 .....X.6:11 reason why the miracle g. equal blessing
T-14 ..... XI.3:4 learning g. the present no meaning at all.
T-14 ... XI.10:6 He always g. His gifts in place of yours.
T-14 ... XI.14:6 He g. the gift of peace to everyone who
T-15 ......I.13:4 The Holy Spirit g. their blessed instant to
T-15 .......II.2:3 It will come, being the lesson God g. you,
T-15 ..... VI.6:6 fear. Yet the Holy Spirit g. you this faith,
T-15 ..... VI.6:8 through me the Holy Spirit g. it unto you,
T-15 ..... VI.7:3 give yourself as your Father g. His Self,
T-15 ...VIII.4:7 in which He g. as His Father gives to Him.
T-15 ...VIII.4:7 in which He gives as His Father g. to Him.
T-16 ........I.7:7 Him. That is why He g. it. What you give
T-16 ...... V.7:3 it can accomplish this it g. itself away,
T-17 ..... III.5:7 is given to Him Who g. it life and beauty.
T-18 ..... IV.6:5 the holy instant belongs to Him Who g. it
T-18 ... VII.2:5 awareness of it g. you a different view of it
T-18 ..... IX.6:3 It g. way softly to the mountain tops that
T19..IV.A.15:1 the messengers the Holy Spirit g. you,
T19....IV.B.9:2 And to accept the peace He g. instead,
T19....IV.B.9:3 g. must be extended if you would have its
T19..IV.C.10:9 who g. him shelter will follow him, not to
T19. IV.D.12:6 that would heal it g. way to fear. Brother,
T19. IV.D.20:5 Everyone g. as he receives, but he must
T19. IV.D.20:6 he will recognize his choice by what he g.,
T19. IV.D.21:4 Here is the only purpose that g. this world
T-20 ..... IV.1:5 He g. no power to sin, and therefore it has
T-20 ..... IV.1:6 and g. no power to their seeming source.
T-20 ..... IV.1:8 Holy Spirit merely g. everything to God,
T-20 ..... IV.2:6 Your savior g. you only love, but what
T-20 ...VIII.9:9 projection that g. the "nothing" all the
T-21 ........I.3:3 What g. you happiness you want to learn
T-21 ........I.3:7 vision g. you more than judgment does,
T-21 ......I.10:1 of their Creator g. praise to them as well.
T-21 .......II.1:2 Spirit for which He g. you everything; the
T-21 .......II.3:7 and even this He g. to you to give yourself
T-21 ... III.11:2 He g. not what it is His purpose to lead
T-21 ... III.11:7 Nor is it possible that what g. light be one
T-21 ..... VI.9:6 you to give what It has given, and g. still.
T-21 ... VI.10:3 your Father g. you for completing Him.
T-22 .......II.3:7 to joy, for time g. way to the eternal. Only
T-23 ..... III.3:3 Salvation g. up nothing. It is complete for
T-24 .......II.4:3 answer that the Holy Spirit g. can reach
T-24 .......II.7:4 It g. no different messages, and has one
T-24 ...... V.7:3 He g. them vision for their sightless eyes,
T-24 ... VII.9:7 It g. the eyes with which you look on it,
T-25 ......in.1:6 g. you life cannot be housed in death. No
T-25 ........I.3:4 nor g. the slightest witness unto anything
T-25 .......II.2:4 g. no support to base your future hopes,
T-25 ..... VI.4:2 each He g. a special function in salvation
T-25 .... VII.3:8 the world g. any meaning to are false, and
T-25 .. VII.12:7 the Holy Spirit g. meaning and direction
T-25 . VIII.9:11 g. the Son of God the power to forgive
T-25 ..... IX.5:6 is reflected in the sight the Holy Spirit g..
T-26 ........I.5:1 that g. it sense and makes it meaningful.
T-26 ........I.7:2 His holiness g. life to you, who cannot die
T-26 ..... IV.1:4 charity within the world g. way to simple
T-26 ... VII.6:8 Your preference g. them no reality. Not
T-26 ... VII.8:1 Nothing g. meaning where no meaning is
T-26 VII.19:10 to bless but one g. blessing to them all as
T-27 ....II.11:5 yours, and g. you both a different role.
T-27 .. VII.16:1 Brother, He g. but life. Yet what you see
T-27 .. VII.16:2 the gifts you dream your Father g. to you.
T-28 ........I.5:6 and g. you pictures of injustices and hurts
T-28 ......I.12:5 accepts g. welcome to eternity and Him,
T-28 .......II.1:4 the Son g. Fatherhood to his Creator, and
T-28 .......II.7:5 He g. himself the consequences that he
T-29 ........I.4:7 and g. to you the time in which to build
T-29 ..... III.1:6 who is savior but the one who g. salvation
T-29 ..... III.1:8 Unless he g. he will not know he has, for
T-29 ..... IV.5:3 the Holy Spirit g. is never one of fear. The
T-29 .......V.3:1 the role the Holy Spirit g. to you who wait
T-29 .......V.7:4 the Holy Spirit g. the dream its function,
T-29 ..... IX.5:5 thoughts and g. them to the toys instead.
T-30 ......I.17:3 and g. it all effects that it will ever have. It
T-30 .......II.3:7 Not one created thing but g. you thanks,
T-30 ..... III.4:9 Creation g. no separate person and no
T-30 ..... IV.6:4 not want whatever you believe an idol g..
T-30 ..... VI.3:8 they do not merit the forgiveness that it g.
T-30 ..... VI.5:2 It g. the miracle its strength to overlook
T-30 .... VII.6:2 Holy Spirit's goal g. one interpretation,
T-30 ...VIII.3:5 And Heaven g. no answer to the prayer,
T-30 ...VIII.4:7 g. all miracles has not been given freedom
T-31 .......II.3:1 a choice and g. but the illusion it is free,
T-31 ..... III.4:4 It g. no orders that the mind need serve,
T-31 .......V.7:6 which its maker g. a meaning of his own?
W-pI ... 16.2:2 What g. rise to the perception of a whole
W-pI .... 27.1:2 It g. vision priority among your desires.
W-pI .... 42.1:4 strength, not your own, that g. you power
W-pI .... 42.2:1 strength, and what He g. is truly given.
W-pI .... 42.4:6 *God g. truly,* or: *God's gifts to me must be*
W-pI .... 47.1:5 that g. you the recognition of the right
W-pI .... 65.3:4 g. you the answer to all the searching you
W-pI .... 66.4:2 God g. you only happiness. Therefore, the
W-pI .... 66.5:2 *God g. me only happiness. He has given my*
W-pI .... 66.6:1 premise is that God g. you only happiness
W-pI .... 66.6:5 Unless God g. you only happiness, He
W-pI .... 92.2:3 that lights the sun and g. it all its warmth;
W-pI .... 92.5:4 It g. its strength to everyone who asks, in
W-pI .... 92.5:6 And so it g. its light that all may see and
W-pI .... 97.8:5 else. The Holy Spirit g. you peace today.
W-pI .. 104.4:3 what belongs to us in truth is what He g..
W-pI .. 105.1:4 in which the giver loses as he g. the gift;
W-pI .. 122.2:2 and g. you joy with which to meet the day
W-pI .. 122.9:1 Remembering the gifts forgiveness g., we
W-pI .. 123.6:3 g. them back a thousand and a hundred
W-pI .. 124.5:1 of pain, and pain g. way to peace. We see
W-pI .. 126.7:5 it is attained, must heal the mind that g.,
W-pI 126.11:7 for what He g. will be received by you.
W-pI .. 129.2:4 It g. but to rescind, and takes away all
W-pI .. 135.1:2 folly of defense; it g. illusions full reality,
W-pI .. 137.2:3 It g. the body final power to make the
W-pI .. 137.3:5 and without the unity that g. It life. But
W-pI 151.10:2 g. you vision which can look beyond these
W-pI .. 153.2:1 The world g. rise but to defensiveness.
W-pI .. 154.8:6 understand he has received until he g..
W-pI 154.11:5 may be the true receivers of the gifts He g.
W-pI 159.10:8 His vision g. the means for a return to our
W-pI .. 162.3:3 g. the world what he receives each time he
W-pI .. 163.5:2 itself has written, g. no name to him, for
W-pI .. 164.2:3 an ancient call to which He g. an ancient
W-pI .. 164.3:1 Christ g. you His sight and hears for you,
W-pI .. 164.3:4 you who will today accept the gifts He g..
W-pI .. 164.9:3 see the value your acceptance g. the world
W-pI .. 166.1:4 He g. without exception, holding nothing
W-pI .. 167.8:2 His creations cannot share what He g. not
W-pI .. 168.6:2 has prepared for us He g. and we receive.
W-pI 169.15:2 this day of Him Who g. the grace we ask,
W-pI .. 181.2:2 is this that g. consistency to what you see.
W-pI .. 182.9:3 them friend, and g. His strength to them,
W-pI 182.12:7 Today He g. you His defenselessness, and
W-pI .. 183.1:3 A father g. his son his name, and thus
W-pI 183.11:5 Voice g. answer in his Father's holy Name
W-pI 185.13:2 God g. but to unite. To take away is
W-pI .. 187.2:6 Yet it must return to him who g.. Nor can
W-pI .. 187.7:4 thought of sacrifice g. rise to all the forms
W-pI .. 188.3:3 What it g. must be eternal. It removes all
W-pI .. 191.5:4 his salvation is the gift he g. to everyone,
W-pI .. 193.2:5 g. the means by which perception is made
W-pI .. 194.7:1 worry can beset the one who g. his future
W-pI 195.10:4 God g. thanks to you, His Son, for being
W-pI .. 197.7:2 and He g. thanks for you unto Himself.

W-pI...198.3:6 and g. direction with the certainty of God
W-pI...198.5:2 to thank the One Who g. salvation, and
W-pI...199.8:4 thought the Holy Spirit g. you for today.
WpI rVI.in.6:6 and g. our thoughts whatever meaning
W-pI...214.1:4 *For what God g. can only be for good. And I*
W-pI...214.1:5 *accept but what He g. as what belongs to me.*
W-pII....10.1:1 Christ's Second Coming g. the Son of
W-pII....10.1:4 perception g. a silent blessing and then
W-pII.....320.h My Father g. all power unto me.
W-pII.....334.h Today I claim the gifts forgiveness g..
W-pII..336.1:2 and then g. way entirely to what remains
W-pII..347.1:8 *g. the miracles my dreams would hide from*
W-pII..349.1:5 *Each one that I accept g. me a miracle to give.*
W-pII..349.2:2 He g. us grace to meet them all. And so
W-pII..351.1:7 *For He alone g. judgment in Your Name.*
W-pII..356.1:6 *Your Name g. answer to Your Son, because*
WpII.. 361-5.h Certain that Your direction g. me peace.
W-ep .........4:2 for He g. only the eternal and the good.
M-4............1:4 are. God g. special gifts to His teachers,
M-6............3:7 Who g. a gift and then remains with it, to
M-6............4:4 mind of the giver Who g. the gift to him.
M-7............3:3 because he g. the gifts he has received. Yet
M-7............4:9 This is the certainty that g. God's teachers
M-8............2:6 mind revolts against truth and g. itself an
M-8............3:4 the eyes' messages and g. them "meaning.
M-10..........2:3 He g. up an illusion; or better, he has an
M-13..........8:8 learning claims it and your learning g. it.
M-17..........2:7 of God g. to those who need his aid? Here
M-17..........4:2 an interpretation that g. rise to negative
M-19..........1:3 interpretations to which injustice g. rise,
M-20..........4:7 Which g. you more? A tranquil mind is
M-21..........4:7 are offered him, and g. as he receives. He
M-21..........5:9 And He Himself g. to the words they use
M-22..........3:3 This thought g. the body autonomy,
M-25..........3:7 God g. no special favors, and no one has
C-in............3:5 The course merely g. another answer,
C-3.............7:5 And what He g. is always like Himself.
C-ep...........5:5 offer thanks to Him, as He g. thanks to us.
P-2......... II.6:3 is it he who writes that g. the invitation?
P-2.......VII.6:8 as he g. it to them, they behold Christ's
P-3........III.5:3 And because he g., he shall be given. This
S-1.........in.1:5 God g. thanks to His extension in His Son
S-1.........in.1:6 His Son g. thanks for his creation, in the
S-1........ II.7:10 And for this giving God Himself g. thanks
S-2 ...........I.5:5 have no freedom unless he g. it to you.
S-2 ...........I.7:2 You are in need of what He g., and your
S-2......... II.4:5 the anger and the hurt another g., and do
S-2......... II.6:7 God g. and does not ask for recompense.
S-2........III.1:7 He g. His Teacher to whoever asks, and

## giving 195

*See also* life-giving

T-2........VI.1:5 Fear prevents me from g. you my control.
T-2........VI.2:8 the truth by "g." autonomy to behavior.
T-4......... II.1:3 no point in g. an answer in terms of the
T-4......... II.6:4 When you associate g. with sacrifice, you
T-4......... II.6:5 "G. to get" is an inescapable law of the
T-5...........I.1:7 spirit getting is meaningless and g. is all.
T-5...........I.1:8 everything, spirit holds everything by g. it
T-5........ I.1:14 ego makes between g. and losing is gone.
T-5...........I.2:5 *How, then, can g. and losing be associated?*
T-5......... II.9:5 It is made by g., and is therefore the one
T-5......... V.2:3 truly blessed is incapable of g. rise to guilt
T-5.......VII.2:7 gave, knowing that this g. will heal you.
T-6......... V.1:6 G. His joy is an ongoing process, not in
T-6.......V.B.3:5 is, *having* appears to be the opposite of g..
T-6.......V.C.6:1 You learn first that *having* rests on g., and
T-7...........I.4:4 To bargain is to limit g., and this is not
T-7......... V.7:2 he thinks he is g. something to them, and
T-7.......VII.2:4 is no way for you to have it except by g. it.
T-7.......VII.4:5 include them in it, you are g. life to them.
T-7.....VII.11:3 only, and g. this only you will *be* only this.
T-7..... VIII.2:3 intolerable that you will insist on g. it up.
T-7..... VIII.3:6 something you do not want by g. it away.
T-7..... VIII.3:7 G. it is how you *keep* it. The belief that by
T-7......... X.3:8 Holy Spirit, and you will be g. up the ego.
T-7........XI.3:5 Does it teach him that this g. is his joy,
T-7........XI.3:5 that God Himself thanks him for his g.?
T-8...........I.3:4 which you are g. up by attacking them.
T-8.........III.4:7 Do not leave anyone without g. salvation
T-8.........III.8:4 G. of yourself is the function He gave you.
T-9......... II.5:9 g. truth to his words and making you able
T-9....... II.10:3 If paying is associated with g. it cannot be
T-9....... II.10:3 of g. and receiving will be recognized. The
T-9....... II.11:4 By g. you receive. But to receive is to
T-9....... II.11:7 of having is the willingness for g., and
T-9....... II.12:1 of the Holy Spirit, then, only by g. to Him
T-9........III.4:6 It is the g. up of correction in yourself.
T-9........VI.2:4 cannot go beyond your offering in His g..
T-9........VI.2:5 This is not because He limits His g., but
T-9........VI.6:3 are a way of g. acceptance and receiving it
T-9........VI.6:4 In time the g. comes first, though they are
T-11...........I.6:2 Yet you can keep it only by g. it, as it was
T-12...........I.7:2 By g. help you are asking for it, and if you
T-12...........I.9:4 and you have demonstrated this by g. it.
T-12.........I.10:2 by answering the appeal for it by g. it?
T-13.... VI.12:2 willingly, and willingness is signified by g.
T-13.... VI.13:2 and have been faithful in your g., for you
T-14...... III.5:8 The cost of g. *is* receiving. Either it is a
T-14...... III.6:4 By g. power to nothing, he throws away
T-14...... IV.3:2 G. Himself is all He knows, and so it is all
T-14...... IV.8:7 and Who knows of nothing except g.?
T-14... VIII.3:4 are joined in g. you the gift of oneness,
T-14....... X.6:2 the Holy Spirit teaches by g. you the
T-14...... XI.3:3 by g. it whatever meaning it holds for you
T-15.........I.13:3 Practice g. this blessed instant of freedom
T-15.........I.13:4 blessed instant to you through your g. it.
T-15.........I.13:6 of Him, for you join with Him in g.. In the
T-15.......I.15:11 Spirit, and leave His g. it to you to Him.
T-15........ X.2:6 is nothing but a limitation imposed on g..
T-15...... XI.4:8 Heaven out and g. it the attributes of hell,
T-16...... II.5:2 truth for what it is, and g. thanks for it?
T-16...... IV.8:7 and what you are joined with Him in g..
T-16....... V.7:6 and of g. nothing of value in return. How
T-16....... V.9:3 of the g. of specialness as an act of love,
T-16.....VII.8:3 Your receiving completes His g.. You will
T-17...........I.4:2 this order in reality by g. some of it to one
T-17....... II.1:9 leads to seeing it and g. thanks with Him.
T-17...... IV.7:4 Every defense operates by g. gifts, and the
T-17.... IV.16:2 by g. Him ascendance in our minds. We
T-17.... IV.16:3 gain everything by g. Him the power and
T-18......VII.5:7 and fight against the g. in to sin; when the
T-18......VII.8:3 you, g. you rest in the midst of every busy
T-18... VIII.8:3 impartial in its g., encompassing only to
T-19...........I.2:2 g. him to the Holy Spirit and releasing
T19......IV.B.7:5 gratitude for g. peace its home in Heaven.
T19.IV.D.17:8 And g. it, receive it of Him in return for
T-20...... IV.1:2 as the laws of this world interpret g.; as
T-20...... IV.2:9 Salvation is a lesson in g., as the Holy
T-21...VII.13:2 by g. up the wish for the *inconstant*. Joy
T-21... VIII.3:4 out some promise of the power of g. it. He
T-21... VIII.3:9 God's g. must be incomplete unless it is
T-24...VII.11:9 his wish by g. it appearances of truth. Yet
T-25....... II.3:2 still be here prevents you still from g. up
T-25..... II.10:5 For what you give is His, and g. it, you
T-25..... IX.10:6 is awareness that g. and receiving are the
T-26...........I.1:5 a g. up of power in the name of saving just
T-26...........I.3:6 For g. and receiving are the same. And to
T-26..... II.6:10 g. it can He ensure that everyone receives
T-26......VII.9:5 far short of g. you your full inheritance, it
T-26... VIII.2:6 the g. and receiving of the gift seems to be
T-26....... X.4:3 innocence be purchased by the g. of your
T-27....... II.3:3 And by g. it, you grant your brother
T-27..... II.14:7 by g. you and him a function that is one,
T-28....... II.9:3 miracle is the first step in g. back to cause
T-28...... IV.2:3 them as causing you, and g. you effects.
T-28.... IV.10:6 and its g. up would be a sacrifice. But
T-29....... II.4:6 your help in g. them to all who walk apart
T-29...... III.1:8 know he has, for g. is the proof of having.
T-29.... III.1:10 lose by g. what must be increased thereby
T-29...... IV.5:6 becomes a brother g. you a chance to help
T-29......VII.4:4 And by this g. up is life renounced. Seek
T-31. VIII.11:5 redeemed from hell, and g. thanks to You
W-pI.........5.4:1 avoid g. greater weight to some subjects
W-pI.........23.h the world I see by g. up attack thoughts.
W-pI......23.6:4 *world I see by g. up attack thoughts about–.*
W-pI......28.1:1 we are really g. specific application to the
W-pI......47.6:1 in g. you the confidence which you need,
W-pI......47.8:3 are g. your trust to the strength of God.
W-pI......52.3:6 away, realizing that in so doing I am g. up
W-pI......55.3:1 from this world by g. up attack thoughts.
W-pI......99.6:3 to save by g. you its function as your own.
W-pI... 105.2:3 This strange distortion of what g. means
W-pI... 105.3:1 course has set is to reverse your view of g.,
W-pI... 105.3:2 For g. has become a source of fear, and so
W-pI... 105.4:2 True g. is creation. It extends the limitless
W-pI... 105.4:5 fulfill its aim of g. everything it has away,
W-pI... 106.7:3 Today we practice g., not the way you
W-pI... 106.8:3 the world from thinking g. is a way to lose
W-pI. 106.10:1 so you can teach the world what g. means
W-pI... 108.4:1 are both g. and receiving seen as different
W-pI... 108.6:1 learn that g. and receiving are the same
W-pI... 108.7:1 with the special case of g. and receiving.
W-pI... 108.8:3 *I will receive what I am g. now.* Then close
W-pI... 111.2:3 *by g. me His strength to take its place.*
W-pI... 121.9:1 believe that g. and receiving are the same.
W-pI... 126.4:5 gracious unto him by g. him what he does
W-pI... 126.7:5 the mind that gives, for g. is receiving.
W-pI... 129.1:3 Our emphasis is not on g. up the world,
W-pI. 136.14:3 choose to practice g. welcome to the truth
W-pI. 137.13:2 minute of the hour worth the g. to receive
W-pI. 152.11:5 we wait in silence, g. up all self-deceptions
W-pI. 153.15:2 will begin each day by g. our attention to
W-pI... 154.3:2 you, g. you the strength to understand it,
W-pI... 154.7:1 fulfills his role by g. all his messages away.
W-pI... 154.7:2 understand the messages by g. them away
W-pI... 154.8:7 For in the g. is his own acceptance of what
W-pI. 154.10:3 the getting and the g. of God's Word; the
W-pI. 154.10:3 Word; the g. and receiving of His Will.
W-pI. 154.11:1 We practice g. Him what He would have,
W-pI... 159.2:5 where they are laid, and g. them away.
W-pI... 162.4:3 to all the world, increased in g.; kept
W-pI. 166.12:5 This is the lesson that His g. holds, for He
W-pI. 166.15:6 For God entrusts the g. of His gifts to all
W-pI... 168.5:3 by g. us the means to lay them down, and
W-pI. 183.10:5 his claim to all his Father gave, is g. still,
W-pI... 187.1:2 fact, g. is proof of having. We have made
W-pI... 187.1:8 truth maintains that g. will increase what
W-pI... 187.2:5 thought seems to appear is changed in g..
W-pI... 187.3:4 the idea of g. clarified and given meaning.
W-pI... 187.3:5 that by your g. is your store increased.
W-pI... 187.4:1 you value by the act of g. them away, and
W-pI... 187.5:3 grows in strength as it is reinforced by g..
W-pI... 187.6:2 understands what g. means must laugh at
W-pI... 188.3:6 unites in g. thanks to you who give, and
W-pI... 188.5:3 means for g. it are in his understanding.
W-pI... 191.1:3 what you have done by g. to the world the
W-pI... 197.5:3 changeless, limitless, forever g. out,
W-pII .225.1:1 *Love for me, for g. and receiving are the same*
W-pII .249.1:5 of joy, abundance, charity and endless g..
W-pII .255.1:6 as mine, and g. it to all my Father's Sons,
W-pII .259.1:5 g. love the attributes of fear and of attack?
W-pII .282.2:3 *the truth be changed by merely g. it another*
W-pII .305.1:4 healed the world by g. it Christ's peace.
W-pII .311.1:6 mind by g. us God's Judgment of His Son.
W-pII .315.1:5 g. me his certainty that what he learned is
W-pII .323.1:1 *of pain, and g. him Your Own eternal joy.*
W-pII .332.1:8 and g. it the means to realize the freedom
W-pII .344.1:2 *I have not understood what g. means, and*
W-pII .349.1:6 *give. And g. as I would receive, I learn Your*
W-pII ... 14.3:7 concerned only with g. welcome to the
M-in ........... 1:3 teacher g. something to the learner rather
M-2 ........... 5:5 learns that g. and receiving are the same.
M-4 ..... I.A.5:2 If this is interpreted as g. up the desirable,
M-4 ..... VII.1:4 means "g. away" in the sense of "giving
M-4 ..... VII.1:4 "giving away" in the sense of "g. up." To
M-4 ..... VII.1:5 of God, it means g. away in order to keep.
M-6 ........... 3:4 give if he is concerned with the result of g.
M-6 ........... 3:5 That is a limitation on the g. itself, and
M-6 ........... 3:6 Trust is an essential part of g.; in fact, it is
M-6 ........... 3:8 Such is not g. but imprisoning.
M-6 ........... 4:2 And it is trust that makes true g. possible.
M-7 ......... 1:10 He lacked the trust that makes for g. truly
M-9 ........... 2:4 The g. up of judgment, the obvious
M-10 ......... 2:2 In g. up judgment, he is merely giving up
M-10 ......... 2:2 he is merely g. up what he did not have.

M-10 .........2:3 or better, he has an illusion of g. up. He
M-13 .........4:1 regret on g. up the pleasures of the world.
M-13 .........4:3 an adult resent the g. up of children's toys
M-13 .........6:4 always means the g. up of what you want.
M-19 .........4:7 g. God the lens of warped perception
C-6............2:1 as g. us the answer to the separation and
S-1...........I.5:5 a g. up of yourself to be at one with Love.
S-1....... II.7:10 And for this g. God Himself gives thanks.
S-1......... II.8:1 prayer, g. it timelessness instead of end.
S-2......... II.6:8 There is no g. but to give like Him. All
S-3........ III.4:8 There is no point in g. remedy apart from

## glad 113

T-3.......VII.4:8 you can only be g. that you cannot. Until
T-3.......VII.6:2 Be g.! The light will shine from the true
T-5...........I.1:1 perceive their oneness and become g..
T-5....... II.10:5 Holy Spirit is the Call to awaken and be g.
T-6.........I.10:2 Spirit is g. when you can learn from mine,
T-6........ IV.1:5 If it meant you well it would be g., as the
T-6........ IV.1:5 as the Holy Spirit will be g. when He has
T-9...... IV.10:5 Be g., then, that you have been wrong,
T-10.........I.4:2 but only the desire to waken and be g..
T-13.....VII.4:4 to give this world away in g. exchange for
T-13.....VII.9:8 and your g. response is your awakening to
T-13...VII.16:9 Take it of me in g. exchange for all the
T-13... XI.10:1 him the g. Call to waken and be glad? He
T-13... XI.10:1 him the glad Call to waken and be g.? He
T-14....... II.5:6 Be g. it is undone, for when you look at it
T-14....... V.5:4 Do not withhold this g. acknowledgment,
T-14...... XI.2:1 be g. that you are not bound to it forever.
T-15..... III.9:4 g. awareness of the glory that is in him.
T-15..... IV.1:9 into g. awareness while you do not want it
T-16....... II.5:3 you, and be g. you do not understand it.
T-16....... II.6:5 who bring you the g. tidings He has come.
T-16....... II.8:7 greater love than to accept this and be g..
T-16.... VI.10:1 Be g. you have escaped the mockery of
T-16.... VI.11:4 And you will think, in g. astonishment,
T-17.... IV.13:1 accept this and be g.: These pictures are
T-17..... V.14:4 you suffer, but which makes Heaven g.. If
T-18.......I.11:6 God Himself is g. that your relationship is
T-18....... V.7:1 be g. that he can pay his debt by bringing
T-18..VIII.11:3 no barriers to interfere with its g. coming.
T-19.......I.14:6 returning the g. tidings that it was done
T-19.... III.10:2 in g. acknowledgment of the grace that
T19.... IV.B.5:2 not g. that Heaven cannot be sacrificed,
T19. IV.D.18:5 let him rise again to g. remembrance of
T-20..... II.8:10 The song of Easter is the g. refrain the Son
T-20..... II.10:1 in which we join in g. awareness that the
T-20....... V.2:6 and in your gift is everyone made g..
T-20....... V.4:4 that you will merely love him and be g..
T-21...... VI.9:7 Spend but an instant in the g. acceptance
T-22..... II.10:6 Are you not g. to learn it is not true? Is it
T-24....... V.5:2 Be g. that only Christ can lend you His,
T-25....... II.4:2 Be g. that it is gone within your mind, to
T-25....... II.9:1 Lord of Heaven not be g. if you appreciate
T-25....... II.9:7 He is g. and thankful when you thank His
T-25...... IV.3:4 look upon, and where their hearts are g..
T-25...... VI.3:3 God is g. to have you look on him. He
T-27.....VII.9:3 Be g. indeed it is, for thus are you the one
T-28.........I.7:6 Be g. that it is gone, for this is what you
T-28.......I.13:3 the way of g. awakening to present peace.
T-28..... II.12:4 They are the g. effects of taking back the
T-29....... II.2:8 cause indeed for g. rejoicing and for hope
T-29...... III.5:7 you. And in his g. salvation you are saved.
T-29....... V.3:1 and would behold him waken and be g..
T-29....... V.8:4 Let us be g. indeed that this is so, and
T-29...VII.1:10 you g. that you are told where happiness
T-30....... II.1:9 life but was created with your g. consent,
T-30...... IV.8:4 Be g. indeed salvation asks so little, not so
T-30....... V.3:6 Yet is he g. to wait till every hand is joined
T-30...... VI.8:5 and being g. there cannot be some forms
T-30...... VI.9:5 the g. acknowledgment that guilt has not
T-30.....VII.4:3 and you are g. to see it everywhere. It
T-31...... III.6:1 us be g. that you will see what you believe,
T-31.....VII.5:5 and welcome the g. contrast offered you.
T-31....VIII.9:1 Let us be g. that we can walk the world,
W-pI.....11.1:4 g. indeed to practice the idea in its initial
W-pI.....62.4:1 Let us be g. to begin and end this day by
W-pI.....66.3:5 We will merely be g. that we can find out
W-pI.....72.6:4 Let us accept this and be g.. As a body, do
W-pI.....73.6:9 it with your blessing and your g. accord.
W-pI.....75.5:3 yourself the g. tidings of your release: *The*
W-pI.....76.2:1 Today we will be g. you cannot prove it.
W-pI.....92.8:1 sure as love, forever g. to give itself away,
W-pI.....97.5:1 Holy Spirit will be g. to take five minutes
W-pI.....98.8:2 chance to be the g. receiver of His gifts,
W-pI...98.10:2 wait for the g. time to come to you again.
W-pI. 107.10:1 will be g. to look again upon this world.
W-pI...108.3:2 to share it and be g. that they are one with
W-pI...109.6:1 today, a tired mind is suddenly made g., a
W-pI...118.1:2 *g. exchange for all the substitutes that I have*
W-pI...123.2:2 Be g. today, in loving thankfulness, your
W-pI...123.3:4 Be g. you have a function in salvation to
W-pI. 126.10:4 g. to hear the Voice of truth and healing
W-pI...127.7:2 be g. to give some time to God today, and
W-pI...131.4:1 Be g. that search you must. Be glad as
W-pI...131.4:2 g. as well to learn you search for Heaven,
W-pI...131.7:4 minds, with Heaven as the g. effect of one
W-pI...137.9:1 g. exchange of all the world of sorrow for
W-pI. 152.11:1 in g. acknowledgment that lies are false,
W-pI...164.2:5 using your voice to give His g. consent;
W-pI. 169.14:1 to return, as you were g. to go an instant,
W-pI. 184.15:4 *And we are g. and thankful we were wrong.*
W-pI...191.7:1 Be g. today how very easily is hell undone
W-pI...196.9:6 And you are free, and g. of freedom. You
W-pI...198.5:1 wiser to be g. you hold the answer to your
W-pI. 198.13:2 And we are g. that we have come this far,
W-pI. 200.11:9 *of God, And I am g. and thankful it is so.*
W-pI...218.1:3 *Yet today I can behold this glory and be g..* I
W-pII ....in.9:4 Now we are g. that this is all undone, and
W-pII . 226.2:1 *Father, my home awaits my g. return. Your*
W-pII . 227.2:1 so today we find our g. return to Heaven,
W-pII . 241.2:3 *g. are we to have our sanity restored to us,*
W-pII . 242.1:4 g. to make no choices for me but the ones
W-pII . 253.2:2 *own, which can but offer g. assent to Yours,*
W-pII ... 10.4:6 And the world awaits your g. acceptance,
W-pII . 321.2:2 g. are we to find our freedom through the
W-pII . 328.2:2 *I am g. that nothing I imagine contradicts*
W-pII . 340.2:1 Be g. today! Be glad! There is no room for
W-pII . 340.2:2 Be g.! There is no room for anything but
W-pII ... 14.5:3 We bring g. tidings to the Son of God,
M-4 ........X.3:8 the teachers of God to bring the g. tidings
M-28 .........1:4 and the g. awareness of the Holy Spirit's
M-29 .........2:12 g. you have a Teacher Who cannot make
P-3.......II.4:10 Awake and be g., for all your sins have
P-3........ III.8:9 the world, and the g. tidings of salvation.

## gladden 4

T-4 ........IV.8:1 opportunities you have had to g. yourself,
T-5 ........in.1:2 opportunities you have had to g. yourself,
T-7 ......... V.6:1 Fear does not g.. Healing does. Fear
T-29 ...... V.1:3 rises up to g. God the Father and the Son.

## gladdened 1

W-pII . 315.1:3 smiles upon another, and my heart is g..

## gladly 73

T-1 ........ V.2:3 accepts the time-control factor g.. He
T-4 .........I.12:3 radiance and g. sheds its light everywhere
T-5 ..... VI.10:4 you believe g. to God's Own Higher Court
T-7 .........II.3:9 His Sons, who create like Him, follow it g.
T-7 ......VII.5:8 God, and count yourself among them g..
T-7 .........X.5:8 No one g. obeys a guide he does not trust,
T-8 .........II.8:5 Awakening runs easily and g. through the
T-8 ...... V.6:10 I give it willingly and g., because I need
T-10 .........I.1:7 Recognize this g., for in this recognition
T-10 ........II.2:4 Give up g. everything that would stand in
T-11 ........II.6:7 so much that you will g. let it be increased
T-11 ..... VI.6:1 must compel your allegiance g., because it
T-12 ..... VI.2:3 you, He will g. teach you what He loves,
T-13 .... III.7:3 from His sight, but bring it g. to Him. Lay
T-13 .... VII.6:3 Love leads so g.! As you follow Him, you
T-14 ..... III.8:7 teaching the Holy Spirit would g. offer
T-14 ... III.11:7 of God He so freely and so g. offers you.
T-14 ... III.14:2 He knows the way, and leads you g. on it.
T-14 ..... IV.5:6 and of waking g. to His Love and Holiness
T-14 .....V.11:7 Come g. to the holy circle, and look out in
T-14 .... VII.6:3 At your request He enters g.. He brings
T-14 ..... XI.4:4 which He shares so g. with His Son. Learn
T-14 ..... XI.4:8 And He will g. exchange each one for the
T-15 ..... III.2:4 that you accept the fact, and accept it g.,
T-15 ... III.10:8 But you will g. give, having received. The
T-15 ..... IV.4:2 and g. give over every plan but His. For
T-15 ... VI.5:10 accepts the laws of God as what he g. wills
T-15 ... VII.5:4 at them, you will offer them g. to Him.
T-15 ...VIII.2:1 Hear Him g., and learn of Him that you
T-16 ..... III.5:8 they offer g. to your teaching of yourself,
T-16 ..... IV.4:8 in which it would g. come quietly to them
T-16 ... VI.10:7 Go on to meet them g., and learn how
T-17 ..... III.7:1 All this you will do g., if you but let Him
T-17 .....V.14:3 you not the goal itself will g. arrange the
T-17 .... VII.6:8 The universe will serve it g., as it serves
T-20 .....II.11:3 And g. will you and your brother walk the
T-21 ........I.3:2 joyously, and are remembered g.. What
T-22 .....II.13:2 Quickly and g. is His vision given anyone
T-22 ..... III.9:7 where both give errors g. to correction,
T-24 ... VI.10:1 not g. realize these laws are not for you?
T-25 .......II.8:5 strength, and both will g. look within,
T-26 ..... IX.7:2 you walk forgiveness g. goes with you. No
T-28 ......I.12:3 How g. does He offer them unto the one
T-29 ..... VI.1:5 asks, and g. offers peace instead of this.
W-pI .... 75.9:7 that you will g. extend today forever.
W-pI .... 97.8:1 each practice period today g. to Him. And
W-pI .... 98.4:1 the stand we take today will g. offer us all
W-pI .. 101.7:1 Give these five minutes g., to remove the
W-pI .. 104.1:5 They are not welcomed g. by a mind that
W-pI .. 122.9:2 Earnestly and g. will we seek for it today,
W-pI 122.10:1 Morning and evening do we g. give a
W-pI .. 130.7:1 we g. give five minutes to the thought that
W-pI 135.20:4 And g. will our brothers lay aside their
W-pI 151.15:1 g. give another fifteen more before you go
W-pI 153.12:5 The game of fear is g. laid aside, when
W-pI 155.14:2 we practice g. with this thought today:
W-pI .. 159.9:7 them. And they return them g. unto Him.
W-pI .. 168.2:4 Would He not g. give the means by which
W-pI .. 187.5:1 Give g.. You can only gain thereby. The
W-pI .. 190.8:2 the ransom you have g. paid not to be free
W-pII . 296.2:3 g. does the Holy Spirit come to rescue us
W-pII . 317.1:4 But when I willingly and g. go the way my
W-pII .... 323.h I g. make the "sacrifice" of fear.
W-pII . 323.1:2 *"sacrifice" You ask of me, and one I g. make;*
W-pII . 360.1:7 *And with this thought we g. say "Amen."*
W-ep ......... 1:5 has the answer, and will g. give it to you,
M-16 ....... 11:2 The world would g. make it, if it knew it
M-18 ......... 2:6 are, so they will g. be returned to Him.
M-28 ......... 2:4 Love is no longer feared, but g. welcomed
S-1..........V.1:5 be. All little gods it g. lays aside, not in
S-1..........V.2:6 where it g. joins with every Son of God,
S-3..........II.3:3 from labor g. done and gladly ended.
S-3..........II.3:3 from labor gladly done and g. ended.

## gladness 38

T-5 ..........I.1:2 This g. calls to every part of the Sonship
T-5 ... III.11:10 He holds this g. gently in your mind,
T-11 ..... VI.5:8 and submission, but in the g. of freedom.
T-13 .......II.8:3 not yet look upon the alternative with g..
T-13 .....V.7:11 The Father welcomes all of us in g., and
T-13 .....V.7:11 and g. is what we should offer Him. For
T-13 ..... VI.8:7 the hymn of g. and thanksgiving for the
T-13 ..... VI.9:3 of praise and g. rise to your Creator, He
T-13 .....X.12:5 and g. and appreciation for what you see
T-13 ..... XI.2:5 G. and joy belong to God for your release,
T-14 .......II.4:9 Because you taught them g. and release,
T-14 .......II.4:9 become your teachers in release and g..
T-15 .......II.6:8 universe bows to, in appreciation and g.?
T-17 .......II.8:5 Go out in g. to meet with your Redeemer,
T-17 .......V.8:1 with g. what you do not understand, and
T-17 .....V.14:5 outside you, you could not share in its g..
T-17 .....V.14:6 Yet because it is within, the g., too, is
T-17 .....V.14:9 will share the g. of the Sonship that it is so
T-17 .....V.15:2 and offer it in g. and thanksgiving to Him
T19 ...IV.A.6:1 a little pause of g. in acknowledgment of

T19...IV.A.9:4 never to return, and part with it in g., not
T19.IV.D.16:4 Join him in g., and remove all trace of
T-20....VI.10:4 in g. for the holy one of safe return. Here
T-21......IV.8:3 of sin, follow in g. the way to certainty. Be
T-21......VI.8:9 out for everyone to look upon with g..
T-22....VI.14:5 For when you have accepted it with g.,
T-22....VI.14:7 thought in one brings g. to the other
T-25........II.9:8 all His thanks and g. shine on you who
T-26......IV.2:6 in g. recognizing what is part of them has
W-pI.....75.4:4 Today the real world rises before us in g.,
W-pI.....98.1:8 In g. we accept it as it is, and take the part
W-pI.....98.8:1 they will light the world with hope and g..
W-pI...123.6:5 fill the world with g. and with gratitude.
W-pI.131.14:5 This is a day of g., for we come to the
W-pI.131.15:1 that today should be a time of special g.,
W-pI.151.16:4 we lift our resurrected minds in g. and in
W-pI...156.4:2 offer them in gratitude and g. at your feet.
S-1.........in.2:4 and turns in holy g. to the truth of union

## glance 11

T-2........VI.9:9 It appears at first g. that to believe such
T-24.....II.12:4 Not one g. from eyes it veils but looks on
W-pI.......2.1:2 the idea to whatever your g. rests on.
W-pI.......2.2:1 Merely g. easily and fairly quickly around
W-pI.......7.5:2 G. briefly at each subject, and then move
W-pI.....12.2:3 that the slow shifting of your g. from one
W-pI.....12.2:6 g. rests on equal attention and equal time
W-pI.....17.2:3 resting your g. on each thing you note
W-pI.....25.6:2 your g. rest on whatever happens to catch
W-pI.....33.2:1 Merely g. casually around the world you
W-pI.....43.4:4 Then g. around you for a short time,

## glass 10

T-4........IV.1:6 g. in which the ego seeks to see its face is
T-4........IV.2:3 images your ego makes in a darkened g..
T-4........IV.9:2 To the ego's dark g. you need but say, "I
T-5......VI.11:2 my reference to the ego's dark g., and
T-14.....II.1:10 A little piece of g., a speck of dust, a body
T-28.......V.6:2 It is not made of little bits of g., a piece of
W-pI.....92.1:4 by putting little bits of g. before your eyes
W-pI.124.10:1 see your own transfiguration in the g. this
W-pI.124.11:1 tomorrow, you will look into this g., and
W-pI...159.3:4 The darkened g. the world presents can

## gleam 4

T-17......IV.8:4 tears are faceted like diamonds and g. in
T-20.......II.4:6 thorns whose points g. sharply in a blood-
W-pI.....97.6:2 the tiny g. a firefly makes an uncertain
W-pI.121.11:2 a little g. which you had never noticed.

## gleaming 2

T-17....IV.9:10 gaze dwell on the hypnotic g. of the frame
T-20.......II.5:6 g. in the gentle glow of peace that shines

## gleams 1

T-24.......V.4:2 unlit but by the shifting tiny g. that spark

## glimmer 1

P-2.........V.3:3 the perfect psychotherapist is but a g. of a

## glimmering 3

T-25.......II.3:1 found some hope apart from this; some g.
T-31.....V.12:5 by you. It also shows some g. of sight into
W-pI...127.7:1 the faintest g. of what love means today,

## glimmerings 1

W-pI.....37.1:1 the first g. of your true function in the

## glimpse 7

T-21.....VII.4:6 thinking it caught a g. of the great enemy
T-28.......I.15:5 g. another shore that he can never reach.
T-31.....VII.7:4 you g. a shadow of what lies beyond. At
W-pI...126.8:5 only catch a tiny g. of the release that lies
W-pI...157.2:3 we catch a g. of what lies past the highest
W-pI...166.7:4 down lest you might catch a g. of truth,
S-1........III.4:2 and a g. of the merciful nature of this step

## glimpsed 1

M-13.........4:4 Does one whose vision has already g. the

## glimpses 4

T-13.....VII.6:1 some g. of the other world about him. Yet
T-13... VIII.4:6 g. of the Heaven that lies beyond them.
T-20.........I.4:2 see g. of the face of Christ behind the veil,
T-20... VIII.1:1 Vision will come to you at first in g., but

## glint 1

T-21...VII.10:7 same desire as a little g. of sin attracts you

## glisten 1

T-28......III.3:6 all things that seem to g. in the dream.

## glitter 3

T-17......IV.8:4 The g. of blood shines like rubies, and the
T19....IV.C.4:6 g. of guilt you laid upon the body would
T-25.....VII.1:5 and deceive with g. and with guile. Yet

## glittering 2

T-15.......II.5:5 so. Yet its shining and g. brilliance, which
T-17......IV.9:9 Death lies in this g. gift. Let not your gaze

## glorification

*See* self-glorification

## glorified 1

T-11......IV.5:8 glory is shared and They are g. together.

## glorifies 1

T-17......IV.2:7 and g. yours instead of His because of the

## glorify 3

T-8........VI.3:1 Let us g. Him Whom the world denies,
W-pI.....72.7:3 love the body, and try to g. and exalt it.
M-25.........4:7 same strengths an opportunity to g. itself.

## glorious 17

T-4........III.3:8 to you prevail against the g. gift of God?
T-4........III.5:5 It is the g. condition of what you are.
T-4........IV.2:9 both the g. creations of a glorious Father.
T-4........IV.2:9 both the glorious creations of a g. Father.
T-4.......VII.4:5 g. context of its real relationship to you.
T-9......VI.3:11 You cannot, then, be less g. than He is.
T-11.......III.5:2 hide his glory, for God wills him to be g.,
T-13....III.10:6 having attacked his own g. equality with
T-13.....X.14:3 it. Before the g. radiance of the Kingdom
T-18... VIII.2:5 a little part of a g. and complete idea. It
T-18... VIII.7:7 surrounding it with love is the g. whole,
T-29.......V.6:1 you but knew the g. goal that lies beyond
W-pI...163.9:2 *and we would look upon the g. reflection of*
W-pII..224.1:1 is so secure, so lofty, sinless, g. and great,
W-pII..270.1:2 *How g. and gracious is this world! Yet how*
M-4.......X.2:3 and in joy so g. they could never have
M-25.........1:5 the g. surprise of remembering Who he is

## glory 85

T-5.........II.4:3 the g. before which dissociation falls away
T-7.......V.9:10 The whole g. and perfect joy that *is* the
T-7.....VII.11:6 and g. are yours because the Kingdom is
T-7........XI.6:6 and you must have the g. you see in him.
T-8..........II.7:1 and g. are yours because the Kingdom is
T-8..........II.7:1 limit, and all power and g. lie within it. It
T-8..........II.7:7 are part of Him Who is all power and g.,
T-8..........II.8:1 To what else except all power and g. can
T-8........III.1:1 G. to God in the highest, and to you
T-8........III.2:6 and g. and establishing them as yours.
T-8........III.5:3 for the power and g. he thinks he has lost.
T-8........III.5:5 and g. are in him because they are yours.
T-8........III.7:2 His power and g. are everywhere, and you
T-8........III.7:8 Through His power and g. all your wrong
T-8........III.8:1 Power and g. belong to God alone. So do
T-8........III.8:7 G. is God's gift to you, because that is
T-8........III.8:8 this g. everywhere to remember what you
T-8.........V.3:5 G. be to the union of God and His holy
T-8.........V.3:6 All g. lies in Them *because* They are united
T-8........VI.2:1 and the g. of God and His holy Sons, but
T-8.......VII.5:3 and g. are "lost" to you and so are yours.
T-8.......VII.6:3 are has willed your power and g. for you,
T-9.......VI.3:9 is part of you and shares His g. with you.
T-9......VI.3:10 His g. belongs to Him, but it is equally
T-10........II.2:2 lie joy and peace and the g. of creation.
T-11.........I.5:11 Look upon the g. of His creation, and you
T-11.......III.5:2 Yet the Son of God cannot hide his g., for
T-11......IV.1:4 *from* anything, but you are saved *for* g..
T-11......IV.1:5 G. is your inheritance, given you by your
T-11......IV.5:8 Their g. is shared and They are glorified
T-11......IV.7:4 lives in His Creator and shines with His g.
T-11......IV.8:1 g. he wills to share as his Father shares it
T-14.......V.6:4 to the eternal g. of God and His creation.
T-14....VIII.1:1 you have obscured the g. God gave you,
T-14....VIII.1:5 let all that would hide your g. be brought
T-14....VIII.1:6 Whom He would save for g. *is* saved for it.
T-14....VIII.1:7 would be released from littleness to g.. To
T-14....VIII.3:7 God's g. and His Son's belong to you in
T-14.......XI.4:4 This lesson shines with God's g., for in it
T-15......III.1:6 yourself and blinding yourself to g..
T-15......III.1:7 Littleness and g. are the choices open to
T-15......III.6:5 power and the g. that lie in you from God
T-15......III.8:2 It is not sacrifice to wake to g.. But it is
T-15......III.8:3 is sacrifice to accept anything less than g..
T-15......III.9:4 the glad awareness of the g. that is in him.
T-16.........I.4:7 ego's triumphant use of empathy for its g.
T-16.....VII.5:5 you look not for g. in yourself. You have
T-17....IV.16:3 by giving Him the power and the g., and
T-19.....III.10:7 g. that has been restored for you to see.
T19...IV.D.2:3 face with g. appear as streams of blood,
T-23........in.3:1 Walk you in g., with your head held high,
T-23........in.3:7 not. Who looks for g. finds it where it is.
T-23........in.5:2 g. is beyond it, measureless and timeless
T-23........in.5:6 For who can know his g., and perceive the
T-23........in.5:7 and realize that Heaven's g. shines on him
T-24.......VI.9:5 And both shall see God's g. in His Son,
T-26.......IV.2:1 turns the world of sin into a world of g.,
T-26...VII.17:4 and from hell and death, all g. be forever.
T-26.......IX.1:6 may behold his g. and rejoice that Heaven
T-29....III.3:10 In g. will you see your brother then, and
T-29.......V.5:1 see in all creation but the shining g. of His
T-30.......VI.9:4 *perfect Son, and in his g. will I see my own.*
T-31....VIII.1:4 this, if Christ appeared to you in all His g.
W-pI.....94.2:5 cannot obscure the g. of God's Son. You
W-pI...126.8:5 for today, this is a day of g. for the world.
W-pI...151.9:3 knows the g. of the Father and the Son?
W-pI.170.13:8 *In them we see Your g., and in them we find*
WpI.rV.in10:3 g. undefiled forever. And your wholeness
W-pI...191.8:3 of God has come in g. to redeem the lost,
W-pI.191.10:5 Your g. is the light that saves the world.
W-pI...194.5:4 and all his g. shines upon a world made
W-pI...211.1:2 *In silence and in true humility I seek God's g.*
W-pI...218.1:2 *sightless eyes I cannot see the vision of my g..*
W-pI...218.1:3 *Yet today I can behold this g. and be glad.* I
W-pII.....2.4:3 it holds a hint of all the g. given us by God
W-pII.237.1:2 I will arise in g., and allow the light in me
W-pII....239.h The g. of my Father is my own.
W-pII.239.1:3 He shares His g. any trace of sin and guilt
W-pII.241.1:5 g. of salvation dawns today upon a world
W-pII.250.1:1 Son of God today, and witness to his g..

W-pII ..... 6.3:4 to fade before His g. and reveal your holy
W-pII ..... 6.5:3 else. As we behold His g., will we know we
W-pII . 326.1:8 *all separate thoughts unite in g. as the Son of*
W-pII . 346.1:7 *toys I made as I behold Your g. and my own.*
S-1 ......... V.3:2 how to understand your g. as God's Son,

## glow 3

T-20....... II.5:6 gleaming in the gentle g. of peace that
W-pI... 157.5:1 and a g. that travels from your fingertips
S-2 ......... II.8:6 the sunlight and the g. of Heaven shining

## glowing 3

T-18....... I.13:5 you with the g. purpose in which you join
T-19...... IV.1:6 and your brother with g. happiness and
T-20.... VIII.4:4 g. with radiant purity and sparkling with

## go 432

T-1......... I.13:2 seem to g. back but really go forward.
T-1......... I.13:2 seem to go back but really g. forward.
T-2......... II.6:3 because you return as you g. forward. The
T-2......... II.6:4 free yourself from the past as you g. ahead
T-3......... V.5:7 in it when you are willing to let it g..
T-4......... in.1:1 The Bible says that you should g. with a
T-4......... II.5:5 helpful, attributes that must g. together.
T-4......... V.4:7 "Where can I g. for protection?" to which
T-4......... V.5:1 be asked: "Where can I g. for protection?"
T-4........ VI.1:5 We cannot safely let it g. at that, however,
T-4........ VI.7:1 I will g. with you to the Holy One, and
T-5........... I.1:2 God g. out into them and through them.
T-5........... I.4:4 "If I g. I will send you another Comforter
T-5......... II.1:4 to heal the separation by letting it g..
T-5........ IV.8:8 g. with my blessing and for my blessing.
T-6...... V.A.6:3 Having chosen to g. that way, you place
T-6...... V.C.7:7 g. beyond belief until you believe fully.
T-8......... II.2:9 nature, and therefore cannot g. against it.
T-8...... IV.2:12 than darkness can abide wherever you g..
T-8...... IV.3:11 And I will g. to them with you, so we can
T-8...... IV.5:12 and God Himself would not g. against it. I
T-8......... V.5:9 or you will try to g. in different directions
T-8......... V.6:7 I g. before you because I am beyond the
T-8.... VII.10:4 if it uses the body to g. beyond itself. By
T-9........ VI.2:4 g. beyond your offering in His giving.
T-9.... VII.3:10 never g. beyond it because it can never *be*
T-9....... VII.6:3 You can only g. beyond it, look back from
T-10...... IV.2:4 your ability to evaluate it truly, to let it g..
T-10... IV.5:10 you completely when you let them g..
T-11........ in.4:5 I give you the lamp and I will g. with you.
T-11....... II.4:3 He will enable you to g. far beyond the
T-11....... II.5:7 you choose to take, He will g. with you,
T-11...... III.4:4 and they g. with you and abide with you
T-11.. VIII.13:2 own interpretations g. in favor of reality,
T-12..... II.10:7 at the cause of fear and letting it g. forever
T-13......... I.3:5 Time seems to g. in one direction, but
T-13....... II.4:3 they are in an excellent position to let it g.
T-13...... III.4:4 the deeper you g. into the blackness of the
T-13...... IV.5:6 you are forbidding yourself to let it g..
T-13....... V.4:2 die, yet they will not let condemnation g..
T-13....... V.8:5 let the darkness g. and all you made you
T-13...... VI.3:5 To be born again is to let the past g., and
T-13... VII.14:2 *me unto Christ, and where else would I g.?*
T-13....... X.3:5 they will not look within and let it g..
T-14......... I.1:7 forgiveness you must have let guilt g.,
T-14...... VI.3:6 But let them g., and what was fearful will
T-14... VII.4:10 One will g., because the other is seen in
T-14..... VII.5:1 believes in darkness, and will not let it g..
T-14..... XI.3:7 *Let it all g.*. Do not attempt to understand
T-14.... XI.12:4 peace and understanding g. together and
T-15......... I.9:7 you will g. forth in time without fear, and
T-15....... II.1:7 blessed instant you will let g. all your past
T-15....... II.4:2 to provide reasons for not letting it g.. Yet
T-15....... II.6:2 very specific instructions as you g. along.
T-15...... IV.2:1 your willingness to let all littleness g.. The
T-15...... IV.6:4 not to recognize it and not to let it g.. The
T-15...... IV.8:3 that interferes with it g. forever?" If the
T-15....... V.5:7 be afraid to let g. your imagined needs,
T-15..... VII.3:2 your investment in it, to learn to let it g..
T-15 ..... VII.3:3 choose to let g. what he believes has value
T-15 ....... X.5:3 and one you do not want, they g. together
T-16 ....... IV.1:3 solely to offset the hate, but not to let it g.
T-16 ...... IV.2:3 You will g. through this last undoing
T-16 ... IV.11:1 Would you not g. through fear to love?
T-16 ... IV.12:6 and then together we g. straight to God,
T-16 ...... VI.7:5 to let g. your hold on the distorted frame
T-16 ...... VI.9:4 where it could not g. with you, for you
T-16 ... VI.10:7 G. on to meet them gladly, and learn how
T-16 .... VII.1:1 It is impossible to let the past g. without
T-16 .. VII.2:10 really *not* let g. what has already gone. It
T-16 .... VII.4:3 Would you act out the dream, or let it g.?
T-17 ....... II.8:5 Him. G. out in gladness to meet with your
T-17 ...... III.2:5 you, and seems to g. by the name of love,
T-17 ...... III.2:9 that g. to make the relationship unholy.
T-17 ...... III.8:4 alliance are retained, and all the rest let g.
T-17 ...... III.8:5 And what is thus let g. is all the truth the
T-17 ...... III.9:2 that to choose one is to let the other g..
T-17 ...... IV.6:4 that you have been more willing to let g..
T-17 ...... IV.6:5 one remains, you will not let the others g..
T-17 ...... V.7:12 will g., and you will see the justification
T-17 .... VII.6:5 As holiness and faith g. hand in hand, so
T-17 .... VII.6:5 so must its faith g. everywhere with it.
T-18 ........ I.7:3 g. out into the mad world and so depart
T-18 ........ I.8:1 Let them all g., dancing in the wind,
T-18 ..... II.5:20 than in waking, you will not let g. of it.
T-18 ...... III.3:5 You g. toward love still hating it, and
T-18 ...... III.5:7 And where we g. we carry God with us.
T-18 ...... VI.8:7 It does not g. out. Within itself it has no
T-18 ... VI.13:5 You g. where you would be, gaining, not
T-18 ... VI.14:7 let g. the limits you have placed upon love
T-18 ... VIII.9:8 but has grown too weary to g. on alone.
T-18 . VIII.10:1 G. out and find them, for they bring your
T-18 . VIII.12:2 because you have not yet let g. of all the
T-18 ...... IX.7:4 And back and forth they g., as long as you
T-18 ... IX.11:3 world, beyond which learning cannot g.,
T-18 ... IX.11:3 learning cannot go, will g. beyond it, but
T-19 ...... III.1:4 will suffer, and not let g. of the idea of sin.
T-19 ...... III.2:7 is real you want, and will not let it g..
T-19 ...... III.3:5 repeat it; you will merely stop and let it g.,
T19.... IV.A.2:6 are not asked to let it g. for yourself alone.
T19.. IV.A.15:7 And they g. forth to signify the end of fear
T19.... IV.C.9:1 fear of death will g. as its appeal is yielded
T19.... IV.D.8:4 bid you look on them and g. beyond them
T-20 ........ I.3:4 Help him to g. in peace beyond it, with
T-20 ....... II.9:4 joy. We g. beyond the veil of fear, lighting
T-20 ...... III.9:3 uncertain whether to let it g. or to take
T-20 ... III.11:6 would they g. but where they will to be?
T-20 ...... IV.8:5 will g. before you making straight your
T-21 ........ I.1:5 but fail to be aware you can g. through
T-21 ........ I.2:5 but vision shows you where to g.. Why
T-21 ..... II.4:10 enough to make a world can let it g., and
T-21 ....... II.8:6 not. Faith and desire g. hand in hand, for
T-22 ....... II.4:1 is to recognize it *and g. the other way*. Truth
T-22 ... III.1:10 the ego separate, to g. their separate ways
T-22 ...... III.6:5 rest on externals and cannot g. beyond.
T-22 ...... III.6:6 unable to g. beyond the form to meaning.
T-22 ...... IV.1:1 is quite apparent, you cannot g. ahead.
T-22 ...... IV.1:2 You must g. either one way or the other.
T-22 ...... IV.1:3 For now if you g. straight ahead, the way
T-22 ...... IV.1:3 reached the branch, you will g. nowhere.
T-22 ...... IV.1:8 and not deciding on which way to g..
T-22 ...... IV.2:1 still may think you can g. back and make
T-22 ....... V.1:4 They g. against what must be true. The
T-23 ..... II.14:8 to hold love captive, and let sin g. free.
T-23 ... II.22:10 Are you certain which way you g.? And
T-23 ... II.22:13 and give you certainty of where you g..
T-24 ....... V.4:2 from the fireflies of sin and then g. out, to
T-24 ....... V.9:5 that He must g. to find Himself complete.
T-24 .... VII.5:8 Nor will that light g. out when it is gone.
T-24 .. VII.6:10 Not till you g. past learning to the Given;
T-24 .. VII.11:4 not lie in how they look, nor where they g.
T-25 ........ I.6:4 and where you should g. to do it.
T-25 ...... IV.4:5 you. And they g. farther and farther off,
T-25 .... VII.3:1 Let us g. back to what we said before, and
T-26 ........ I.1:8 a little nearer, or g. a little farther off, but
T-26 ...... III.5:5 set. It will not g. beyond this aim. Its only
T-26 ...... IV.5:2 to be complete, so will you g. with them.
T-26 ....... V.1:8 will g. along the way your chosen teacher
T-26 ..... V.1:11 but choose whether to g. toward Heaven,
T-26 ....... V.9:4 You can *not* g. back. And everything that
T-26 ....... V.9:8 and nowhere can you g. except to Him.
T-26 ..... V.14:1 Forgive the past and let it g., for it *is* gone.
T-26 .. VII.6:11 And any wish that seems to g. against His
T-27 ........ I.3:2 your blood and death, and g. before him,
T-27 ... IV.4:16 you what you want and where to g. for it.
T-27 ....... V.1:3 and it will g. forth because of what it is. It
T-27 ..... V.11:6 Everywhere you g., will you behold its
T-27 .... VII.3:7 to g. beyond the obvious in terms of cause
T-27 ... VIII.8:3 guilt outside yourself, but never letting g.!
T-28 ........ I.5:2 the past, but rather as a way to let it g..
T-28 ....... II.9:1 proceeds to g. the other way, begins. This
T-28 ...... IV.2:5 and join in one, but let the other g.. The
T-28 ...... IV.6:6 is no truth in yours, his dreams will g.,
T-28 ... IV.10:8 willingness to let illusions g. is all the
T-29 ........ I.4:5 for you and him to g. your separate ways.
T-29 ........ I.5:5 tells you where to g. and how to go there,
T-29 ........ I.5:5 tells you where to go and how to g. there,
T-29 ........ I.7:4 it seems to come and g. uncertainly, and
T-29 ........ I.7:5 you have demanded that love g. away,
T-29 ...... VI.2:9 All things that come and g., the tides, the
T-30 ........ I.8:1 you cannot even let your question g., you
T-30 ........ I.9:4 let you g. ahead with just a few more steps
T-30 ...... III.7:1 Thoughts seem to come and g.. Yet all
T-30 ....... V.3:2 is certain he will g. beyond forgiveness,
T-30 ....... V.3:6 heart made ready to arise and g. with him
T-30 ....... V.5:2 how easily do idols g. when they are still
T-30 ....... V.5:3 willingly the mind can let them g. when it
T-30 ....... V.8:2 from fear forever, and to g. straight on,
T-30 ....... V.8:6 Him to rise from chains and g. with you,
T-30 ...... VI.6:2 are not prepared, as yet, to let all idols g..
T-31 ....... II.6:9 And we g. separately along the way unless
T-31 ....... II.9:4 and falling back when he would g. ahead?
T-31 ....... II.9:6 Thus it is a way you g. together, not alone
T-31 ..... II.11:4 and so you cannot see which way you g..
T-31 ...... IV.1:8 What must g. with you, you will take with
T-31 ...... IV.2:9 start; however differently they seem to g..
T-31 ...... IV.3:7 must reach this point, and g. beyond it. It
T-31 ...... IV.4:7 but waste time unless you g. beyond what
T-31 ... IV.10:7 Where could it g.? And how could you be
T-31 ....... V.1:6 a self, and make one as you g. along. And
T-31 ....... V.8:2 and never seek to g. beyond its roads nor
T-31 ..... V.11:4 And both would g., if either one were ever
T-31 ..... V.12:7 on the one to choose, and let the other g..
T-31 ..... V.16:4 in the confidence that it will g. at last, and
T-31 ...... VI.2:7 because they chose to let it g. instead.
W-pI ....... 5.6:3 *keep this form of upset and let the others g.*.
W-pI ....... 6.3:5 *keep this form of upset and let the others g.*.
W-pI ..... 14.3:1 in learning to let g. the thoughts that you
W-pI ..... 14.3:5 You will g. far beyond it. Our direction is
W-pI ..... 15.3:1 we g. along, you may have many "light
W-pI ..... 23.5:2 that the cause be identified and then let g.
W-pI ..... 23.6:5 dismiss that thought and g. on to the next
W-pI ..... 23.7:5 you will be ready to let the cause g..
W-pI ..... 24.7:2 *in this situation,* and g. on to the next one.
W-pI ..... 26.7:3 g. over every possible outcome that has
W-pI ..... 31.3:3 come and g. as dispassionately as possible
W-pI ..... 34.3:3 arise in your mind, and let each one g., to
W-pI ....... 41.h God goes with me wherever I g..
W-pI ..... 41.4:1 its Source goes with you wherever you g..
W-pI ..... 41.4:2 of all joy goes with you wherever you g..
W-pI ..... 41.4:3 of all life goes with you wherever you g..
W-pI ..... 41.4:4 God goes with you wherever you g..
W-pI ..... 41.5:3 and to g. through it to the light beyond.
W-pI ..... 41.8:6 will g. into more detail about this kind of
W-pI ..... 41.8:6 about this kind of practice as we g. along.
W-pI .. 41.10:1 that God goes with you wherever you g..
W-pI ..... 42.3:1 as possible to the time you g. to sleep. It is
W-pI ..... 44.1:4 coexist, but light and life must g. together
W-pI ..... 44.7:2 letting g. every kind of interference and
W-pI ..... 45.6:6 Then try to g. past all the unreal thoughts
W-pI ..... 45.8:6 yet to realize how high you are trying to g.
W-pI ..... 47.7:3 Let g. all the trivial things that churn and
W-pI ..... 49.4:3 G. past all the raucous shrieks and sick
W-pI ..... 51.1:5 let it g. by realizing it has no meaning, so
W-pI ..... 51.3:6 it. But there is every reason to let it g., and
W-pI ..... 51.4:6 do not mean anything, and to let them g..
W-pI ..... 51.5:7 I no longer want. I am willing to let it g..

W-pI.....56.2:4 essential that I let this image of myself g..
W-pI.....59.1:1 (41) God goes with me wherever I g..
W-pI.....59.1:7 because God goes with me wherever I g..
W-pI.....60.4:5 There is nowhere else I can g., because
W-pI.....66.3:1 Today we will try to g. past this wholly
W-pI.....66.4:4 Today's exercises are an attempt to g.
W-pI.....68.4:2 not think you can let your grievances g..
W-pI.....68.6:9 *grievances g. I will know I am perfectly safe.*
W-pI.....69.4:1 closed, try to let g. of all the content that
W-pI.....69.5:4 to g. through them and past them, which
W-pI.....69.6:2 Determine to g. past the clouds. Reach
W-pI.....69.6:4 and eyelids as you g. through them. Go
W-pI.....69.6:5 them. G. on; clouds cannot stop you.
W-pI.....69.8:3 to g. through the clouds to the light, to
W-pI.....70.8:5 to g. through the clouds before you can
W-pI.....71.9:4 *Where would You have me g.? What would*
W-pI...72.12:1 your hope of success flicker and g. out,
W-pI.....73.6:4 a point beyond which illusions cannot g..
W-pI...73.11:7 This will help you let your grievances g.,
W-pI.....75.1:5 you bring peace with you wherever you g.
W-pI.....78.2:1 Today we g. beyond the grievances, to
W-pI.....79.8:2 in letting all your preconceived notions g.
W-pI.....85.1:5 Grievances and light cannot g. together,
W-pI.....91.1:1 and vision necessarily g. together. This
W-pI.....91.9:5 the more worthy in you as we g. along.
W-pI.....92.2:3 hand, securely bound until you let it g..
W-pI.....92.7:5 It does not change and flicker and g. out.
W-pI.....94.4:1 aside; g. past the list of attributes, both
W-pI.....95.8:2 only by your unwillingness to let them g..
W-pI...95.10:1 Let all these errors g. by recognizing
W-pI.....96.9:5 mind g. wandering in a world of dreams,
W-pI.....97.1:5 letting g. illusions of a split identity.
W-pI.....98.1:3 We side with truth and let illusions g..
W-pI.....98.7:4 will g. beyond their sound to what they
W-pI...100.1:2 separate lives and g. their separate ways.
W-pI...100.2:2 should you choose to g. against His Will?
W-pI...100.4:2 calls to all minds to let their sorrows g.,
W-pI...101.7:3 hope to g. still faster to the waiting goal of
W-pI...106.3:5 G. past all things which do not speak of
W-pI...107.1:7 From dust to dust they come and g., for
W-pI...107.4:2 nor come and g. and go and come again.
W-pI...107.4:2 nor come and go and g. and come again.
W-pI...107.6:1 does not come and g. nor shift nor change
W-pI...107.8:1 be in your awareness as you g. with Him.
W-pI...107.8:4 It is your Self you ask to g. with you, and
W-pI...109.7:2 too weary now to g. their way alone. And
W-pI...109.7:3 road that suddenly seems easy as they g..
W-pI.110.10:4 a great advance to truth by letting idols g.
WpI.rIII.in8:2 in the hour just before you g. to sleep.
WpI.rIII.in9:2 and then g. on your way to other things,
W-pI...121.3:1 weak and blustering, afraid to g. ahead,
W-pI...121.3:1 to stay, afraid to waken or to g. to sleep,
W-pI...123.4:3 as we g. to do what is appointed us to do.
W-pI...123.5:1 We do not g. alone. And we give thanks
W-pI...124.1:5 with the universe we g. our way rejoicing,
W-pI...128.5:1 Today we practice letting g. all thought
W-pI...128.5:4 g. beyond all little values and diminished
W-pI...129.2:2 loss in letting g. all thought of value here.
W-pI...129.3:3 g. from there to where words fail entirely,
W-pI...130.2:5 Love and perception thus g. hand in hand
W-pI...130.5:4 beyond which your decision cannot g..
W-pI...130.7:1 and doubt, and g. beyond them all as one.
W-pI...131.5:5 It will g. because you do not want it. You
W-pI.131.11:7 Then let them g., and sink below them to
W-pI.131.13:1 open with your one intent to g. beyond it.
W-pI...132.6:4 and each one must g. as far as he can let
W-pI...132.6:5 will return and g. still farther, or perhaps
W-pI...132.8:4 as you let g. all thoughts of sickness, and
W-pI.135.12:3 true, then is it healed, and lets the body g.
W-pI...136.7:4 that truth may g. away and threaten your
W-pI.137.12:6 thoughts of healing will this day g. forth
W-pI.139.10:2 and g. your way rejoicing in the endless
W-pI...140.9:2 g. beyond appearances today and reach
W-pI.140.11:1 five minutes more before we g. to sleep.
W-pI.151.15:1 fifteen more before you g. to sleep. Your
W-pI.153.14:2 And then we g. to take our rightful place
W-pI...155.8:2 accept the truth, and let it g. before you,
W-pI.155.10:4 way. You know not where you g.. But One
W-pI...157.2:4 us here an instant, and we g. beyond it,
W-pI...158.3:5 For time but seems to g. in one direction.
W-pI...158.4:1 which figures come and g. as if by magic.
W-pI...159.9:4 which they g. again with added fragrance.
W-pI...164.8:1 letting g. all things you think you want.
W-pI...165.3:2 not instantly prepare to g. where they are
W-pI...166.5:1 wanderings, God's gifts g. with him, all
W-pI...166.7:4 You g. on your appointed way, with eyes
W-pI...166.9:6 g. the way you chose without your Self.
W-pI.166.15:8 And now you g. to share it with the world
W-pI...167.5:4 In that, they can g. far beyond themselves
W-pI...167.9:2 it merely seems to g. to sleep a while. It
W-pI...169.3:2 The final step must g. beyond all learning
W-pI.169.10:4 and rise and work and g. to sleep by them
W-pI.169.14:1 return, as you were glad to g. an instant,
WpI...rV.in1:4 that we may g. on again more certain,
WpI...rV.in8:8 whole we g. together to our ancient home
WpI...rV.in9:5 own. To Him we g. together. Take your
WpI rV.in12:4 again to g. beyond them to their meaning
Wi181-200 3:4 So we now attempt to g. past all defenses
W-pI......182.h I will be still an instant and g. home.
W-pI...182.4:5 Where this Child shall g. is holy ground.
W-pI...182.5:3 to g. home so deeply, so unceasingly, His
W-pI...182.6:6 He will g. home, and you along with Him.
W-pI...182.7:7 you, calling you to let Him g. in peace,
W-pI.182.10:3 G. home with Him from time to time
W-pI.182.11:3 your help in letting Him g. home today,
W-pI.182.12:9 Be still an instant and g. home with Him,
W-pI...184.7:2 everyone who comes must g. through.
W-pI...184.9:1 to g. beyond all symbols of the world,
W-pI.184.10:1 a prison house from which you g. into the
W-pI...185.5:4 Now he seeks to g. beyond them,
W-pI...186.5:5 afraid to g. beyond them to experience
W-pI...186.6:2 and the holiness to g. beyond all images.
W-pI...186.7:3 Let it g.. Salvation of the world depends
W-pI.186.10:1 These unsubstantial images will g., and
W-pI...189.9:1 not choose the way in which we g. to Him
W-pI...192.2:6 you need the means to let illusions g..
W-pI.193.11:2 in haste and g. unto our Father's house.
W-pI.193.12:4 that happened in its course g. with it.
W-pI...194.4:5 You are but asked to let the future g., and
W-pI...195.5:3 All these g. with you. Let us not compare
W-pI.195.10:6 and thus we g. who walk the way to God.
W-pI...196.4:2 may quickly g. the way salvation shows us
W-pI...196.7:2 if you want to g. along this painful path.
W-pI...196.8:2 From there we g. ahead quite rapidly. For
W-pI.196.12:1 no Thought of God that does not g. with
W-pI.196.12:1 that instant, and to g. beyond it quickly,
W-pI...200.9:2 We g. to Heaven, and the path is straight.
WpI rVI.in.5:2 Permit no idle thought to g. unchallenged
WpI rVI.in.7:4 for us; allowing Him to teach us how to g.
W-pI...202.1:1 I will be still an instant and g. home. *Why*
W-pI...215.1:4 *thanks to Him for showing me the way to g..* I
W-pII.....in.1:4 the world of pain, and g. to enter peace.
W-pII.....in8:2 choice to follow it as He would have us g..
W-pII......1.1:6 sees its falsity, and therefore lets it g..
W-pII..228.2:5 *I let them g. today. And I stand ready to*
W-pII......2.3:2 Thus it lets illusions g.. By not supporting
W-pII......2.3:3 merely lets them quietly g. down to dust.
W-pII......3.3:2 And now they g. to find what has been
W-pII..245.1:2 *Where I g., Your peace goes there with me. It*
W-pII..245.2:1 And so we g. in peace. To all the world
W-pII..254.2:2 and look at them, and then we let them g.
W-pII..264.1:1 *in the place I see myself, and everywhere I g..*
W-pII..275.2:3 *Voice will tell me what to do and where to g.;*
W-pII......7.2:4 it, becomes the means to g. beyond itself,
W-pII..284.1:8 And I would g. beyond these words today
W-pII..287.1:1 Where would I g. but Heaven? What
W-pII..298.1:5 that I g. through fear to meet my Love.
W-pII..300.2:5 *g. beyond that tiny instant to eternity.*
W-pII..302.2:1 Our Love awaits us as we g. to Him, and
W-pII..302.2:3 and He the Means by which we g. to Him.
W-pII..306.1:3 made. Today I can g. past all fear, and be
W-pII....10.2:5 dream in which the world began g. with it
W-pII..316.1:2 Each one allows a past mistake to g., and
W-pII..317.1:4 But when I willingly and gladly g. the way
W-pII..317.1:4 way my Father's plan appointed me to g.,
W-pII..317.2:2 *Where it would lead me do I choose to g.;*
W-pII..322.1:2 illusions g. I find the gifts illusions tried
W-pII..323.2:1 a debt that merely is the letting g. of self-
W-pII.324.1:2 *You have set the way I am to g., the role to*
W-pII.324.1:7 *You, as You direct me and would have me g..*
W-pII.328.1:6 Him that we must g. to recognize our will.
W-pII.334.1:6 so I g. to find the treasures God has given
W-pII...13.1:4 does not attempt to g. beyond perception
W-pII.342.2:3 And as we g., the world goes with us on
W-pII.344.2:1 we are to one another, as we g. to God.
Wfl........in.1:2 remind us that we seek to g. beyond them
Wfl........in.2:4 us as gracious guidance in the way to g..
W-ep.........4:6 Him, as certain as is He of where you g.;
W-ep.........5:7 g. homeward to an open door which God
M-4.....I.A.3:1 must g. through what might be called "a
M-4.....I.A.4:1 must g. through "a period of sorting out."
M-4.....I.A.5:1 the teacher of God must g. can be called
M-4...I.A.6:11 Yet when he is ready to g. on, he goes
M-4...I.A.6:13 on. He will not g. on from here alone.
M-4.....I.A.8:8 Who would "g." anywhere, if peace of
M-4.......X.2:2 have let g. all things that would prevent
M-5.......II.4:9 also g. all the effects they seemed to cause
M-12.........6:7 watch the dream figures come and g.,
M-14.........4:3 the world and g. beyond its tiny reach.
M-14.........4:5 it; to be willing to g. in its direction. He
M-15.........2:6 and you will g. beyond belief to Certainty.
M-16.........7:6 and as he will be when he has let them g..
M-16.....11:10 is withdrawn from them, and so they g..
M-17.........7:2 which you have hidden but have not let g.
M-23.........6:9 take you with him, for he did not g. alone.
M-25.........6:9 offer them to Him and Him alone g. with
M-27.........4:1 that may g. on apart from what will die,
C-2..........10:6 g. on a little while when it is given him to
C-3............2:2 They cannot g. directly from perception
C-3............6:2 can but g. from nothingness to everything
C-5............1:6 but we will not g. beyond the names the
C-ep...........1:2 will come and g. and go to come again.
C-ep...........1:2 will come and go and g. to come again.
C-ep...........4:2 arise and g. in faith along the way to Him.
C-ep...........5:1 us g. out and meet the newborn world,
C-ep...........5:3 us. Let us g. and bid Him welcome Who
P-1............5:3 on from there, as far as he is ready to g..
P-2........III.2:6 reach almost to Heaven or g. no further
P-2........VI.6:6 of his sins, enabling him to let them g..
P-3..........II.8:2 reaches this in time he can g. towards it.
S-1...........I.4:3 them, and let them g. into God's Hands.
S-1...........I.5:1 Prayer is a stepping aside; a letting g., a
S-1...........I.5:4 And it is to Love you g. in prayer. Prayer
S-1..........II.7:6 no longer flickers, and will never g. out.
S-1........III.3:9 enemies, and this imagined gain must g.,
S-1......III.4:10 and your fear of letting it g. is strong.
S-1........III.5:2 who did it, and who can therefore let it g..
S-1........IV.1:8 change of mind: *We g. together, you and I.*
S-1.........V.3:9 *I cannot g. without you, for you are a part of*
S-2.........in.1:9 a purpose beyond which you cannot g.,
S-2.........in.1:9 you cannot go, nor have you need to g..
S-2...........I.9:1 before you reach where learning cannot g.
S-2...........I.9:5 and then let g. forever and forever. There
S-2........III.3:2 as you arise in haste to g. at last unto your
S-3..........II.3:4 ended. Now we g. in peace to freer air and

**goal** 360
*See also* goal-less
T-1.....VII.3:14 is the only g. of the miracle-minded.
T-2..........II.3:2 the value of the g. is firmly established. It
T-2.........VI.6:9 corrected only by accepting a unified g..
T-4...........I.5:2 This is the one true g. of the teacher. It is
T-4...........I.6:3 my g. will always be to absolve you finally
T-4...........I.6:4 opposite of the ego-oriented teacher's g..
T-4........IV.8:4 to accept anything but this as your g..
T-4.........V.5:4 g. must be formulated clearly and kept in
T-5.......II.11:2 As we share this g., we increase its power
T-6......V.B.2:2 for change is their first and foremost g.. It
T-7........IV.3:5 Holy Spirit has a unified g. for the effort.
T-7........IV.3:6 abilities are applied long enough to one g.
T-7........IV.5:1 ego's g. is as unified as the Holy Spirit's,
T-7.........X.3:2 would object to this g. if he recognized it.
T-8..........II.6:1 takes only *one* direction and has only *one* g.
T-8..........II.6:2 His direction is freedom and His g. is God
T-8........III.5:1 The g. of the curriculum, regardless of
T-8........III.6:2 To achieve the g. of the curriculum, then,

T-8........ III.6:2 ego, whose purpose is to defeat its own g..
T-8........ VI.9:7 a journey without distance to a g. that has
T-8........VII.7:7 thus to confuse the g. of His curriculum.
T-8........VII.8:6 the true g. of the curriculum has been lost
T-8.....VII.11:3 the mind believes the body is its g. it will
T-8.....VII.12:5 a learning device with a curriculum g. is a
T-8.....VII.14:6 He has accepted a learning g. in obvious
T-8......VIII.2:7 to shift ceaselessly from one g. to another,
T-9.........I.12:2 can be made into a very persistent g. even
T-11....... V.4:3 inappropriate if you recognize the ego's g.
T-11....... V.4:4 ego's g. is quite explicitly ego autonomy.
T-11....... V.7:2 because its g. of autonomy *is* nothing else.
T-11....... V.7:3 reality, but it does not lose sight of its g..
T-11..... V.11:1 If the ego's g. of autonomy could be
T-11..... V.11:3 *its* g. can be accomplished and God's
T-11..... V.12:3 that to accomplish its g. is happiness. But
T-11..... V.12:5 Recognize only that the ego's g., which
T-11..VIII.11:3 part of you as sick and achieve your g..
T-12....... II.5:6 for the g. is inevitable because it is eternal
T-12....... II.5:7 The g. of love is but your right, and it
T-12....... II.8:5 accomplish the g. of perfection together.
T-12....... IV.1:6 ego pursues its g. with fanatic insistence,
T-12....... IV.4:6 the g. He sets before you He will give you.
T-12....... V.6:3 Your learning g. has been *not* to learn, and
T-12....... V.7:3 The result of this curriculum g. is obvious
T-12....... V.7:8 A supplementary g. in this curriculum is
T-12....... V.8:2 possible that the way to achieve a g. is not
T-12....... V.9:3 g. is not divided and the means and the
T-12....VII.4:10 g. in direct opposition to the Holy Spirit's
T-12.....VII.6:8 it has one g. by making it seem to be one.
T-12.....VII.7:9 it to believe that it is pursuing one g.. Yet
T-12...VII.7:11 to be healed is to pursue one g., because
T-12...VII.13:2 The death penalty is the ego's ultimate g.,
T-13.........I.1:1 Spirit shares the g. of all good teachers,
T-13....... II.5:6 with it you must believe its g. is yours.
T-13....... II.7:1 that its g. for you is happiness and peace.
T-13...... IV.7:2 the g. of time as diametrically opposed.
T-13...... IV.8:1 the ego interprets the g. of time as its own
T-13...... IV.8:4 would share His g. of salvation for you.
T-13...VII.13:4 ever on the journey's end, which is His g..
T-14.........I.2:3 lead to nothing, for its g. is nothing. If
T-14....... II.1:5 g. depends means absolutely nothing. Yet
T-14....... II.5:5 Yet see that this has been your g., and
T-15.........I.2:7 inevitability of the g. and end of teaching.
T-15.........I.2:8 To the ego the g. is death, which *is* its end.
T-15.........I.2:9 But to the Holy Spirit the g. is life, which
T-15.........I.4:4 Hell is its g.. For although the ego aims at
T-15.........I.4:6 it. The g. of death, which it craves for you,
T-16.....VII.3:9 while you pursue the ego's g. as its ally.
T-17.... III.10:5 between you and your g. of madness. Be
T-17....... V.2:6 g. of the relationship is abruptly shifted
T-17....... V.3:2 At once His g. replaces yours. This is
T-17....... V.3:5 as it *is* is out of line with its own g., and
T-17....... V.3:6 g. was all that seemed to give it meaning.
T-17....... V.3:8 the pursuit of the old g. re-established in
T-17....... V.3:9 has accepted the g. of holiness, it can
T-17....... V.4:2 former g. completely without attraction,
T-17....... V.4:3 conflict between the g. and the structure
T-17....... V.4:4 Yet now the g. will not be changed. Set
T-17....... V.4:5 to change the relationship to fit the g..
T-17....... V.5:1 not be kinder to shift the g. more slowly,
T-17....... V.5:5 purposes, suddenly has holiness for its g..
T-17....... V.6:2 You let this g. be set for you. That was an
T-17....... V.6:7 The g. *is* set. And your relationship has
T-17....... V.6:9 recognized as such in the light of its g..
T-17....... V.7:1 your former g. was quite appropriate.
T-17....... V.9:5 that you will remember a g. unchanged
T-17....... V.9:6 For you have chosen but the g. of God,
T-17..... V.14:2 Here is the g., together with you. Think
T-17..... V.14:3 you. Think you not the g. itself will gladly
T-17..... V.14:8 Yet the g. is fixed, firm and unalterable,
T-17..... V.14:8 surely fall in place because the g. is sure.
T-17.........VI.h Setting the G.
T-17...... VI.1:4 setting of the Holy Spirit's g. is general.
T-17...... VI.2:3 of the g. belongs at the beginning, for it is
T-17...... VI.2:9 but only that. It has no positive g. at all.
T-17...... VI.3:1 Without a clear-cut, positive g., set at the
T-17...... VI.3:5 No g. was set with which to bring the
T-17...... VI.4:4 becomes what can be used to meet the g..
T-17 ..... VI.4:6 because the g. has made it meaningful.
T-17 ..... VI.5:1 The g. of truth has further practical
T-17 ..... VI.5:9 that the situation is as the g. determines it
T-17 ..... VI.5:9 it, and is experienced according to the g..
T-17 ..... VI.6:1 The g. of truth requires faith. Faith is
T-17 ..... VI.6:3 Where the g. of truth is set, there faith
T-17 ..... VI.6:5 The g. establishes the fact that everyone
T-17 ..... VI.7:2 unity, and must obscure the g. of truth.
T-17 ..... VI.7:5 the situation the g. of truth would bring.
T-17 .... VII.3:3 But if the g. is truth, this is impossible.
T-17 .... VII.4:2 g. of holiness was set for your relationship
T-17 .... VII.4:4 grow to meet the g. that has been set. The
T-17 .... VII.5:8 It interferes, not with the g., but with the
T-17 .... VII.5:8 goal, but with the value of the g. to you.
T-17 .... VII.6:1 The g. of illusion is as closely tied to
T-17 .... VII.7:1 you in whom the Holy Spirit's g. has been
T-17 .... VII.9:5 g. He placed there was extended to every
T-17 .. VII.10:4 relationship shares the Holy Spirit's g. are
T-17 ... VIII.6:1 truth as the g. for your relationship, you
T-17 ... VIII.6:2 g. of peace cannot be accepted apart from
T-18 ........I.1:2 with the g. the Holy Spirit has given you,
T-18 ..... III.1:4 Your g. was darkness, in which no ray of
T-18 ..... III.2:2 your g. is the advance from fear to truth.
T-18 ..... III.2:3 g. you accepted is the goal of knowledge,
T-18 ..... III.2:3 goal you accepted is the g. of knowledge,
T-18 ..... III.2:5 enough to remind you that your g. is light
T-18 ..... III.5:1 will teach you that this g. is possible, and
T-18 .... VII.1:4 for himself who still accepts sin as his g..
T-18 .... VII.4:6 very long road to the g. you have accepted
T-18 .... VII.5:7 when the g. is finally achieved by anyone,
T-19 ........I.1:3 its only g. is brought to truth *by* faith. This
T-19 ......I.5:10 to set up a g. forever impossible to attain,
T-19 ........I.6:2 divided g. has given both an equal reality,
T-19 ......I.15:4 For faith is still a learning g., no longer
T-19 ..... III.8:4 now, the g. of proving this is impossible.
T-19 ..... IV.1:5 which He will bring means and g. in line.
T19..IV.A.6:10 And in the g. of truth which you accepted
T19..IV.B.10:7 for reaching the g. that you assign to it.
T19..IV.B.16:2 ego has dedicated the body to the g. of sin
T19....IV.C.6:5 of communication, which is the ego's g..
T-20 .... VII.1:2 the Holy Spirit's g. will come from the
T-20 .... VII.2:3 You recognize you want the g.. Are you
T-20 .... VII.3:1 the g. the Holy Spirit indeed asks little.
T-20 .... VII.3:3 well. The means are second to the g.. And
T-20 .... VII.3:7 you? They guarantee the g., and they are
T-20 .... VII.3:9 For if a g. is possible to reach, the means
T-20 .... VII.4:2 perfectly consistent with the g. of holiness
T-20 .... VII.7:6 means seem real because the g. is valued.
T-20 .... VII.7:7 judgment has no value unless the g. is sin.
T-20 .... VII.9:4 fear. Salvation is the Holy Spirit's g.. The
T-20 ... VIII.9:4 is merely how you elect to meet your g..
T-20 ... VIII.9:5 serve to meet the g. of madness. They are
T-21 .......II.2:4 *and I decide upon the g. I would achieve.*
T-21 .......II.3:5 Suffer, and you decided sin was your g..
T-21 .......II.9:3 of reality to make it fit the g. of madness.
T-21 .......II.9:4 The g. of sin induces the perception of a
T-21 ..... III.1:1 special relationships have sin as their g..
T-21 ..... III.2:4 and protected as is a g. the mind accepts.
T-21 ..... III.4:1 by which the g. of holiness is reached.
T-21 ... III.12:3 have faith in it to serve the Holy Spirit's g.
T-21 .... V.7:11 and redirected from the g. of sin, as are
T-21 .. VI.7:10 away from madness toward the g. of truth
T-22 ..... III.1:3 For reason's g. is to make plain, and
T-22 ..... III.6:3 What was its maker's g. but not to see?
T-22 ..... VI.1:4 Which is your g.? For one you see as
T-22 ..... VI.3:4 as sinless, because the g. is sinlessness.
T-22 ..... VI.8:5 to change it, nor to substitute another g..
T-23 ...II.13:13 certain that you realize the g. is madness?
T-23 .....II.14:6 is the g. the laws of chaos serve. These are
T-23 .....II.15:5 g. of madness must be seen as sanity. And
T-23 ...II.22:11 you sure the g. of Heaven can be reached?
T-24 ............h THE G. OF SPECIALNESS
T-24 ........I.6:2 journey with him, to a g. that is the same?
T-24 ........I.6:6 reach them, or your g. is jeopardized. Can
T-24 ........I.6:7 have meaning where the g. is triumph?
T-24 ........I.8:9 now defeat the g. of holiness that Heaven
T-24 .......II.2:8 Here is a g. that would defeat salvation,
T-24 ..... IV.2:4 g. of separation is its curse. Yet bodies
T-24 ..... IV.2:5 Yet bodies have no g.. Purpose is of the
T-24 ... VI.11:4 you have pursued this g. with vigilance
T-24 ... VI.12:1 pursue another g. with far less vigilance;
T-24 VII.11:10 Yet can perception serve another g.. It is
T-25 ..... III.3:4 to serve the g. for which it is perceived.
T-25 ..... III.5:1 reconcile its g. with His Creator's purpose
T-25 ..... III.9:8 all time becomes a means to reach a g..
T-25 .......V.1:2 and is meaningless without the g. of sin.
T-26 ..... III.5:4 is the learning g. this course has set. It
T-26 .......V.2:3 reach a g. as high as learning can achieve?
T-26 .......X.5:6 add or take away from this one g. is but to
T-27 ........I.8:3 neutral and without a g. inherent in itself.
T-27 ......I.10:1 which the g. of sin has been removed, is
T-27 .....II.15:4 g. in which the Holy Spirit sees His Own.
T-27 .....II.15:8 inability to see His g. divided and distinct
T-27 ..... III.5:7 that can extend beyond the g. of learning.
T-27 ..... VI.1:8 for they have a g. without a meaning. And
T-29 ..... IV.4:8 have assigned; some g. which an event, or
T-29 .......V.6:1 glorious g. that lies beyond forgiveness,
T-29 ..... VI.3:4 can set a g. unlike God's purpose for you,
T-29 .... VII.4:1 Whenever you attempt to reach a g. in
T-30 ......in.1:2 The g. is clear, but now you need specific
T-30 ......I.11:6 the g. of being right when you are wrong.
T-30 .......V.1:2 Fear is not its g., for the escape from guilt
T-30 .......V.2:3 of pursuing guilt as g. is fully recognized.
T-30 .......V.6:1 to replace the g. of sin and guilt. And all
T-30 ..... VI.6:6 And you have set a g. of partial pardon
T-30 .... VII.5:6 change. In one united g. does this become
T-30 .... VII.6:2 Holy Spirit's g. gives one interpretation,
T-31 .......II.9:5 For so do you forget the journey's g.,
T-31 ..... IV.7:3 that to achieve a g. you must proceed in
T-31 ..... IV.9:3 Him, nor any worldly g. be one with His.
W-in.......... 1:2 will make the g. of the course possible. An
W-pI ...... 4.3:2 train you in the first steps toward the g. of
W-pI .... 20.3:3 an indication that our g. is of little worth.
W-pI .... 24.1:5 Yet they are your only g. in any situation
W-pI .... 42.1:2 your efforts to achieve the g. of the course
W-pI .... 42.8:1 the g. of the course is important to you,
W-pI .... 44.3:3 represents a major g. of mind training. It
W-pI .... 62.2:3 Your g. is to find out who you are, having
W-pI .... 65.5:6 *This thought reflects a g. that is preventing*
W-pI .... 69.3:4 Learning salvation is our only g.. Let us
W-pI .. 72.10:1 g. in the longer practice periods today is
W-pI .. 72.10:2 To achieve this g., we must replace attack
W-pI .. 74.1:6 of the Will of God, you have no g. but His
W-pI .... 75.4:3 single purpose makes our g. inevitable.
W-pI .... 94.4:1 reach this g. except to lay all idols and self-
W-pI .... 95.6:1 of your g. and regular attempts to reach it
W-pI .. 95.12:2 Son, one Self, with one Creator and one g.
W-pI .. 95.14:7 Throughout the day do not forget your g..
W-pI .... 98.2:3 we need with which to reach the g.. Not
W-pI .. 100.9:5 foolish g. can keep you from success when
W-pI .. 101.7:3 to go still faster to the waiting g. of peace.
W-pI .. 105.3:1 A major learning g. this course has set is
WpI..rIII.in2:4 are not our aim, and would defeat our g..
WpI..rIII.in4:1 have changed your mind about your g..
W-pI .. 126.1:2 in complete forgiveness, certainty of g.,
W-pI 126.11:1 can, remind yourself you have a g. today;
W-pI 126.11:2 not let your mind forget this g. for long,
W-pI .. 127.6:5 in your advance towards its established g.
W-pI .. 131.3:3 world can not dictate the g. for which you
W-pI .. 131.3:4 you still are free to choose a g. that lies
W-pI .. 131.4:2 and must find the g. you really want. No
W-pI .. 131.4:3 fail to want this g. and reach it in the end.
W-pI .. 131.5:6 it. You will reach the g. you really want as
W-pI 131.10:3 ten minutes to this g. three times today,
W-pI 131.12:4 now; no other g. is valued now nor sought
W-pI 131.14:5 will find the g. of all your searching here,
W-pI 135.11:5 accomplishment of any g. that serves the
W-pI .. 139.9:3 Let us not forget the g. that we accepted.
W-pI 153.15:3 in which salvation is the only g. we have.
W-pI 153.20:3 no doubt that you will reach your final g..
W-pI 155.13:6 your pathway certain and your g. secure.
W-pI .. 157.2:4 it, sure of our direction and our only g..
W-pI .. 158.6:5 This is beyond our g., for it transcends
W-pI .. 158.8:2 set up a g. that does not merely disappear
W-pI .. 169.1:3 It is past learning, yet the g. of learning,
W-pI .. 169.3:3 is not the g. this course aspires to attain.
W-pI 169.15:1 learning g. today does not exceed this
WpI...rV.in1:6 certainty, a firmer purpose and a surer g..

WpI.. rV.in5:3 we keep in mind that this remains our g.,
Wi181-200 2:1 limited to let you see the value of our g..
W-pI ...181.6:1 this g. if anger blocks our way in any form
W-pI ...184.5:3 one essential g. by which communication
W-pI ...185.4:3 for compromising is the g. of dreaming.
W-pI.186.11:5 All of them point to one g., and one you
W-pI ...194.1:2 with the g. in sight and obstacles behind.
W-pI ...194.1:5 How close are we approaching to our g.!
W-pI ...199.4:5 to the all-inclusive g. that it must reach,
W-pI ...199.6:4 in the ability to serve an undivided g.. In
W-pI ...199.6:5 with but the thought of freedom as its g.,
WpI rVI.in.7:4 day, advancing toward the g. He set for us
W-pI ...205.1:3 *The peace of God is my one g.; the aim of all*
W-pII.....in.1:5 Now we begin to reach the g. this course
W-pII.....in.2:9 of Him as we are tempted to forget our g..
W-pII......1.2:4 the aim that it has chosen as its wanted g.
W-pII......1.3:2 In frantic action it pursues its g., twisting
W-pII..226.1:4 want to keep as mine or search for as a g.,
W-pII......4.2:3 Yet can the g. of striving change. And
W-pII......4.2:5 as replacement for the g. of self-deception
W-pII.....256.h God is the only g. I have today.
W-pII..256.1:9 God is our g.; forgiveness is the means by
W-pII..256.2:2 *We have no g. except to hear Your Voice,*
W-pII..257.1:1 If I forget my g. I can be but confused,
W-pII.....258.h Let me remember that my g. is God.
W-pII..258.1:1 aims, and to remember that our g. is God.
W-pII..258.1:4 God is our only g., our only Love. We
W-pII..258.2:1 *g. is but to follow in the way that leads to You*
W-pII..258.2:2 *We have no g. but this. What could we want*
W-pII..259.1:1 makes the g. of God seem unattainable.
W-pII......5.4:2 yet has the g. of Heaven been exchanged
W-pII......6.5:1 g. of the Atonement has been reached at
W-pII......7.2:1 The g. the Holy Spirit's teaching sets is
W-pII......7.2:3 learning has achieved the only g. it has in
W-pII..286.2:1 travelled far along it to a wholly certain g.
W-pII.....287.h You are my g., my Father. Only You.
W-pII..287.2:1 *You are my g., my Father. What but You*
W-pII..287.2:5 *You are my only g.. Your Son would be as*
W-pII..288.1:1 *leads the way to You, and brings me to my g..*
W-pII......8.5:3 That instant is our g., for it contains the
W-pII..296.2:2 learning g. becomes an unconflicted one,
W-pII.....10.1:4 its g. accomplished and its mission done.
W-pII..312.1:5 Holy Spirit's purpose as his g. for seeing.
W-pII..312.2:2 *today, and therefore it must be my g. as well.*
W-pII..314.1:4 claim the future now, for life is now its g.,
W-pII..318.1:6 I am the g. the world is searching for. I
W-pII..319.2:2 *the g. which stems from it shares its totality.*
Wfl ........in.3:3 It is the g. that God has given us. It is His
Wfl ........in.4:2 So let us not forget our g. is shared, for it
W-ep .........4:6 proceed; as confident as He is of the g.,
M-2............5:7 same course share one interest and one g.
M-3............1:2 the ultimate g. is always the same; to
M-4......... X.2:8 Now is the g. achieved. Forgiveness is the
M-4......... X.2:9 is the final g. of the curriculum. It paves
M-4....... X.2:11 makes no effort to exceed its legitimate g..
M-9............2:5 training is directed toward achieving a g.
M-10...........3:1 unlike the g. of the world's learning, is the
M-14...........3:2 appears to be a long-range g. indeed. But
M-14...........3:3 still, and waits on the g. of God's teachers
M-15...........2:4 But this is still your g.; why you are here.
M-16...........1:7 is sent without a learning g. already set,
M-16...........9:6 and bring this g. nearer to recognition.
M-17...........3:5 divided g. of the pupil into one direction,
M-26...........3:4 that it cannot be considered a realistic g..
M-27...........6:5 This is salvation's final g.; the end of all
M-28...........3:5 g. of the curriculum has been achieved.
M-28...........6:3 God's teachers have the g. of wakening
C-in............3:9 It has one function and one g.. Only in
C-2...........10:6 the way is short and Heaven is his g.?
P-1.............2:2 What higher g. could there be for anyone
P-2.........in.2:1 relationship with this g. in mind. On the
P-2.........in.3:1 the patient's g. and the therapist's are at
P-2.............I.3:5 g. is wholly undivided always. Whatever
P-2......... II.4:1 a reasonable g. for psychotherapy. This
P-2......... II.5:3 if pupil and teacher join in sharing one g.,
P-2......... II.6:7 is impossible to share a g. not blessed by
P-2......... II.7:3 own curriculum; not the curriculum's g.,
P-2......... II.8:4 one must share one g. with someone else,
P-2......... II.9:8 g. that makes these processes the same,
P-2........ III.1:4 One be wholly absent if the g. is healing.
P-2......IV.11:1 single doctrine is the g. of all therapy.
P-2........VI.6:1 realization is the final g. of psychotherapy
P-3......... II.3:3 be uninterested in healing as his major g..
P-3......... II.5:7 Yet no therapist really sets the g. for the
P-3......... II.8:4 A g. marks the end of a journey, not the
P-3......... II.8:4 as each g. is reached another can be dimly
S-1 .........in.3:3 Faith in your g. will grow and hold you up
S-1 ......... II.8:1 God is the g. of every prayer, giving it
S-1 ......... II.8:2 because the g. has never changed. Prayer
S-1 ......... II.8:5 until the g. of learning has been reached.
S-1 ........ III.3:1 the learning g. must be to recognize that
S-1 ........ III.6:5 The g. of God is lost in the quest for lesser
S-1 ........ III.6:8 he lose the only true g. that is given him.
S-1 ........ IV.1:4 Enemies do not share a g.. It is in this
S-1 ........ IV.2:4 is not the g. that prayer should truly seek.
S-1 ........ IV.2:5 set up but an illusion of a g. you share.
S-1 ......... V.2:3 no g. but God because they need no idols,
S-2 ...........I.2:1 honest means by which this g. is reached.
S-2 ......... II.1:3 it may seem to take have but this single g.
S-2 ......... II.4:1 the g. is to separate from God the Son He
S-2 ......... II.4:2 This g. is also sought by those who seek
S-2 ......... II.7:5 a way to use forgiveness for the g. of God,
S-3 .........in.1:2 of success in ultimate attainment of the g.
S-3 .........in.1:3 of a change of mind about the g. of prayer
S-3 ........ IV.2:6 This instant is the g. of all true healers,

## goal's 3

T-17.....VII.4:5 The g. reality will call this forth, for you
T-17.....VII.6:6 g. reality will call forth and accomplish
T-24.....VI.12:5 and guarantee the g. accomplishment.

## goal-less 1

T-31....IV.11:1 all senseless journeys and all g. aims.

## goals 87

T-6......... II.4:4 As their g. are opposed, so is the result.
T-7........ IV.5:1 and it is because of this that their g. can
T-12......... V.6:2 try to set up curriculum g. where yours
T-12.....VII.6:6 if you seek for two g. you will find them,
T-12.....VII.7:7 for it represents the acceptance of two g.,
T-14....... V.6:2 is no unity of learning g. apart from this.
T-15...... IX.3:5 ego, whose g. are altogether unattainable,
T-16....... V.9:4 in strict accordance with the ego's g., is to
T-17.... III.1:12 unholy alliances to support the ego's g.,
T-17....... V.4:1 extremely intense with this shift in g.. For
T-21....... II.9:2 to make its g. seem real and possible.
T-23..... II.15:1 These do not seem to be the g. of chaos,
T-24.........I.6:5 it depends on g. that you alone can reach.
T-24.........I.8:8 has been made clean of special g.. And
T-29.........I.8:1 The body, innocent of g., is your excuse
T-29.........I.8:1 is your excuse for variable g. you hold,
T-29...... VI.4:4 All other g. are set in time and change
T-29.....VII.8:2 You give it g. it does not have, and thus
T-30.....VII.2:7 a meaning in the light of g. that change,
T-30.....VII.5:5 idea of different g. that makes perception
W-pI.....24.4:3 g. in mind as part of the desired outcome,
W-pI.....24.4:3 also that these g. are on different levels
W-pI.....24.5:1 as many g. as possible that you would like
W-pI.....24.6:2 that many of your g. are contradictory,
W-pI.....24.6:2 in connection with some of your g.,
W-pI.....24.7:1 list of as many hoped-for g. as possible,
W-pI.....25.1:7 this that your g. become unified. It is in
W-pI.....25.2:1 in it as meaningful in terms of ego g..
W-pI.....25.2:2 g. have nothing to do with your own best
W-pI.....25.2:5 to withdraw the g. you have assigned to
W-pI.....25.3:1 Another way of describing the g. you
W-pI.....25.3:2 your g. are really concerned with nothing.
W-pI.....25.3:3 them, therefore, you have no g. at all.
W-pI.....25.5:1 the g. you have established for everything
W-pI.....65.1:5 the relinquishment of all the other g. you
W-pI.....65.4:3 the trivial purposes and g. you will pursue
W-pI.....74.1:5 idea that you are torn by conflicting g.. As
W-pI.....83.1:3 it means I cannot have conflicting g..
W-pI.....96.2:2 you will attempt an endless list of g. you
W-pI...100.8:5 the little thoughts and foolish g. you pass
W-pI...104.3:4 other gifts and other g. made of illusions,
WpI. rIII.in4:2 if it interferes with g. you hold more dear.
W-pI...128.5:4 beyond all little values and diminished g..
W-pI...131.1:1 you seek for g. that cannot be achieved.
W-pI...131.2:1 G. that are meaningless are not attained.
W-pI...131.7:1 its shifting patterns and uncertain g., its
W-pI...133.8:7 protect its g. from tarnish and from rust,
W-pI...133.9:2 Its g. are obvious to anyone who cares to
W-pI...133.9:4 that he has served the ego's hidden g..
W-pI.133.10:3 still preserve the ego's g. and serve them
W-pI.133.11:2 allowed the ego's g. to come between the
W-pI.135.16:2 before becomes the basis for its future g..
W-pI...138.3:2 Decision lets one of conflicting g. become
W-pI...138.5:4 But knowledge is beyond the g. we seek to
W-pI...138.5:5 are teaching g., to be attained through
W-pI...157.7:1 and all g. but this become of little worth,
W-pI...163.2:2 all g. perceived but in its sightless eyes.
W-pI...164.8:5 sought above the world's unsatisfying g.?
Wi181-200 1:1 your scattered g. blend into one intent.
W-pI...181.3:3 We do not care about our future g.. And
W-pI...181.4:1 involvement with your past and future g..
W-pI...181.4:2 how extremely different the g. this course
W-pI...181.7:2 We do not seek for long-range g.. As each
W-pI.186.10:2 you make give rise to but conflicting g.,
W-pI.186.10:3 concentrated drive toward g. like these?
W-pI.186.10:5 What hope of gain can rest on g. like this?
W-pI...200.8:3 Peace is the answer to conflicting g., to
W-pI.200.11:5 and to replace our shifting g. and solitary
W-pII .233.1:4 *of seeking g. which cannot be obtained, and*
W-pII .257.1:2 serve contradicting g. and serve them well
W-pII .258.1:2 our pointless little g. which offer nothing,
M-13 .........5:8 pursues the world's g. can do otherwise.
M-16 .........2:5 the very g. for which they were set up.
M-17 .........3:3 if perception of separate g. has entered.
M-26 .........4:9 with g. for which you are not ready. God
P-2.........in.4:3 both will learn to give up their original g.,
P-2.........in.4:4 and therapists alike accept unrealistic g.
P-2...........I.3:6 in connection with their own divergent g.,
P-2........ III.3:6 heal. Divided g. alone can interfere with
S-1 .........in.2:4 separate g. and separate interests by, and
S-1 ........ III.1:6 of rising power and with ascending g.,
S-1 ........ III.6:2 are used for g. that substitute for God,
S-1 ........ III.6:5 is lost in the quest for lesser g. of any kind
S-1 ...... III.6:10 it well. All other g. are at the cost of God.
S-1 ......... V.2:1 and humility have g. so far apart they
S-2 ...........I.9:4 cleansed from evil usages and hateful g..
S-3 ........ III.1:2 Its separate g. become quite clear in this,

## God 3638

*god*

*See also* He, Him, His, Himself, I, Me, Mine, My, Myself, One, Our, Us, Who, Whom, Whose, You, Your, Yours, Yourself, God-created, God-destructive, God-proof; Appendix C

T-in ...........2:4 ***unreal exists***. Herein lies the peace of G..
T-1...........I.4:1 mean life, and G. is the Giver of life. His
T-1.........I.19:1 Miracles make minds one in G.. They
T-1.........I.19:2 Sonship is the sum of all that G. created.
T-1.........I.27:1 from G. through me to all my brothers. It
T-1.........I.29:1 Miracles praise G. through you. They
T-1.........I.31:2 should thank G. for what you really are.
T-1.........I.31:3 children of G. are holy and the miracle
T-1.........I.36:1 your perceptions with truth as G. created
T-1.........I.40:2 way of perceiving the universal mark of G.
T-1.........I.46:3 with G. by direct revelation, the need for
T-1..........II.1:2 between G. and His creations, involving
T-1..........II.1:5 Revelation unites you directly with G..
T-1....... II.3:11 have nothing that does not come from G..
T-1..........II.4:3 You stand below me and I stand below G.
T-1..........II.4:4 the distance between G. and man would
T-1..........II.4:5 one hand, and as a Son of G. on the other.
T-1..........II.5:3 keeping the direct channel from G. to you
T-1..........II.5:5 It proceeds from G. to you, but not from
T-1..........II.5:5 from God to you, but not from you to G..
T-1...... III.1:10 natural profession of the children of G., is
T-1........ III.2:3 You are the work of G., and His work is
T-1........ IV.2:5 you in communion with yourself and G..
T-1......... V.3:1 talents will be shared by all the Sons of G.

T-1 V.3:2 G. is not partial. All His children have His
T-1 V.3:4 your complete dependence on G., you
T-1 V.3:8 When this occurs the whole family of G.,
T-1 V.4:1 member of the family of G. must return.
T-1 V.4:3 "G. is not mocked" is not a warning but a
T-1 V.4:4 G. *would* be mocked if any of His creations
T-1 VI.1:3 lack does not exist in the creation of G., it
T-1 VI.2:1 A sense of separation from G. is the only
T-1 VI.3:1 error that one can be separated from G.,
T-1 VI.5:10 Only G. can establish this solution, and
T-1 VII.1:7 you can relate in peace to G. or to your
T-1 VII.2:1 Child of G., you were created to create
T-1 VII.2:3 The Love of G., for a little while, must still
T-1 VII.5:2 in connection with the Sons of G.,
T-1 VII.5:7 a more direct approach to G. Himself. It
T-1 VII.5:9 Healing is of G. in the end. The means are
T-2 I.1:1 aspect of G. which He gave to His Son. In
T-2 I.1:2 G. extended Himself to His creations and
T-2 I.1:6 No child of G. can lose this ability because
T-2 I.1:9 you believe that what G. created can be
T-2 I.1:11 that you can distort the creations of G.,
T-2 I.2:3 now. Everything G. created is like Him.
T-2 I.2:4 Extension, as undertaken by G., is similar
T-2 I.2:7 both the creation of the Son by G., and
T-2 I.3:9 to extend as G. extended His Spirit to you.
T-2 I.4:1 have the ability to usurp the power of G..
T-2 II.1:9 peace of G. which passeth understanding.
T-2 II.1:11 ability of anything not of G. to affect you.
T-2 II.7:2 Sons of G. make in one way or another. It
T-2 III.h The Altar of G.
T-2 III.3:10 acute. But the outcome is as certain as G..
T-2 III.5:1 children of G. are entitled to the perfect
T-2 III.5:4 worthy of being offered at the altar of G.,
T-2 III.5:6 G. and His creations are completely
T-2 III.5:11 G. is lonely without His Sons, and they
T-2 V.A.16:4 It is an appeal to G. to heal their minds.
T-2 V.A.17:5 direction, but timelessness belongs to G..
T-2 V.A.17:7 other. In timelessness we coexist with G..
T-2 VII.3:5 You are afraid of G., of me and of yourself
T-2 VII.3:11 is a term properly belonging to G., and
T-2 VII.5:14 The statement "For G. so loved the world
T-2 VII.6:1 be noted that "G. has only *one* Son. If all
T-2 VIII.1:5 own sight, though not in the Mind of G..
T-2 VIII.2:3 Judgment is not an attribute of G.. It was
T-2 VIII.3:1 of as a procedure undertaken by G..
T-2 VIII.4:3 just as G. Himself looked upon what He
T-2 VIII.5:1 because it has been projected onto G., but
T-3 I.1:5 it does appear as if G. permitted and even
T-3 I.1:6 led many people to be bitterly afraid of G.
T-3 I.1:9 likely that G. Himself would be capable of
T-3 I.2:4 the terrible misperception that G. Himself
T-3 I.3:1 one assigns his own "evil" past to G.. The
T-3 I.3:2 The "evil" past has nothing to do with G..
T-3 I.3:4 it. G. does not believe in retribution. His
T-3 I.3:9 including the belief that G. rejected Adam
T-3 I.4:1 Sacrifice is a notion totally unknown to G.
T-3 I.5:1 G. who taketh away the sins of the world,
T-3 I.5:4 they shall see G." is another way of saying
T-3 I.8:1 of G. is the true state of the mind of His
T-3 I.8:2 In this state your mind knows G., for God
T-3 I.8:2 mind knows God, for G. is not symbolic;
T-3 II.3:6 I have said that only what G. creates or
T-3 II.5:1 of G. who commends his spirit into the
T-3 II.5:4 The Son of G. is part of the Holy Trinity,
T-3 II.5:6 and establishes the peace of G.. Yet this
T-3 III.2:1 not recognize yourself, your brother or G.
T-3 III.4:4 A "vision of G." would be a miracle rather
T-3 III.5:2 Certainty is always of G.. When you love
T-3 III.5:5 clearly implying that you do not know G..
T-3 III.6:1 Right perception is necessary before G.
T-3 III.6:3 G. is not a stranger to His Sons, and His
T-3 III.6:7 "Fear G. and keep His commandments"
T-3 III.6:7 "Know G. and accept His certainty."
T-3 III.7:9 yours. G. knows His children with perfect
T-3 IV.5:11 mind belongs to spirit which G. created
T-3 IV.7:1 G. and His creations remain in surety,
T-3 IV.7:16 G. knows you only in peace, and this *is*
T-3 V.3:4 you are perfectly stable as G. created you.
T-3 V.6:7 that you yourself are a miracle of G..
T-3 V.7:1 The statement "G. created man in his
T-3 V.7:3 G. did create spirit in His Own Thought
T-3 V.9:3 Spirit knows G. completely. That is its
T-3 V.10:5 G. and His miracle are inseparable. How
T-3 V.10:6 the Thoughts of G. who live in His light!
T-3 VI.6:1 G. offers only mercy. Your words should
T-3 VI.8:4 believe they have usurped the power of G.
T-3 VI.8:5 to them, but hardly troubles G.. He is,
T-3 VI.9:2 You have not usurped the power of G.,
T-3 VI.10:5 The offense is never to G., but only to
T-3 VII.1:7 made by a child of G. is without power. It
T-3 VII.2:3 it, any more than you can weaken G.. The
T-3 VII.2:5 is perceived as a force in combat with G.,
T-3 VII.2:6 everything is in direct opposition to G..
T-3 VII.3:5 But G. could not have forbidden it, or it
T-3 VII.3:6 If G. knows His children, and I assure you
T-3 VII.3:8 G. created knowledge and gave it freely to
T-3 VII.3:9 that sees either G. or His creations as
T-3 VII.4:2 only sense in which G. and His creations
T-3 VII.5:2 destructive and clearly in opposition to G.
T-3 VII.5:5 creation by G. is the only Foundation that
T-3 VII.6:7 is to believe that G. and His Son can *not*.
T-4 in.2:2 chosen to "Be still and know that I am G..
T-4 I.4:7 it very gently and lead you back to G..
T-4 I.7:2 Your worth is established by G.. As long
T-4 I.7:8 never at stake because G. did not create it.
T-4 I.8:6 are afraid, be still and know that G. is real
T-4 I.9:1 G. is not the author of fear. You are. You
T-4 I.9:5 G. gave you a very lofty function that you
T-4 I.9:11 G. is inevitable, and you cannot avoid
T-4 I.10:5 Listen only to G., Who is as incapable of
T-4 I.11:4 strength. Only G. could make a home that
T-4 I.11:7 certain. G. is as incapable of creating the
T-4 I.12:5 mark of the Love of G. for His creations,
T-4 I.12:6 to be a gift for a creation of G. Himself.
T-4 II.4:4 your ego much as G. does to His creations
T-4 II.4:9 longer necessary you will merely know G..
T-4 II.5:8 that the outcome is as certain as G..
T-4 II.8:10 The creations of G. do not create myths,
T-4 III.3:8 you prevail against the glorious gift of G.?
T-4 III.4:1 with your ego cannot believe G. loves you.
T-4 III.4:4 that exists between G. and His creations
T-4 III.6:2 you. In this you are as free as G., and must
T-4 III.7:8 never forsake you any more than G. will,
T-4 III.9:2 *G. has given you everything.* This one fact
T-4 III.9:7 of G. and *being* the Kingdom of God.
T-4 III.9:7 of God and *being* the Kingdom of G..
T-4 IV.1:1 If you cannot hear the Voice for G., it is
T-4 IV.2:3 wrongly about some brother G. created,
T-4 IV.2:4 thought that G. would not have thought,
T-4 IV.2:4 not thought that G. would have you think
T-4 IV.5:1 the ego has indeed violated the laws of G.,
T-4 IV.7:1 The habit of engaging with G. and His
T-4 IV.8:2 is no limit to the power of a Son of G., but
T-4 IV.8:3 of G. into everything you think and do.
T-4 IV.9:1 in which G. Himself shines in perfect light
T-4 IV.10:1 for the creation, for Christ is the Son of G.
T-4 IV.11:7 of everything that the living G. created.
T-4 V.2:1 between the body and the Thoughts of G..
T-4 V.2:2 of G. are unacceptable to the ego, because
T-4 V.2:5 impulses, but also the Thoughts of G.,
T-4 V.3:1 confuses G. and the body must be insane.
T-4 V.3:3 sense the ego's fear of G. is at least logical,
T-4 V.4:2 best argument that you cannot be of G..
T-4 V.6:1 because the eternal must come from G..
T-4 VI.h The Rewards of G.
T-4 VI.3:5 effect. The rewards of G., however, are
T-4 VI.5:8 ego in the presence of the rewards of G.?
T-4 VI.7:3 I will bring it to G. for you, knowing that
T-4 VI.7:3 that to know your brother *is* to know G.. If
T-4 VI.7:4 you are grateful to G. for what He created.
T-4 VI.7:7 Kingdom of G. I can lead you back to your
T-4 VI.8:4 G. will come to you only as you will give
T-4 VI.8:5 of them and you will be ready to hear G..
T-4 VII.3:3 what is true is everything that G. created.
T-4 VII.3:5 This communication is the Will of G..
T-4 VII.3:7 G. created every mind by communicating
T-4 VII.3:10 G. created you by this and for this. The
T-4 VII.5:1 G., Who encompasses all being, created
T-4 VII.5:3 is why G. created you. Divine Abstraction
T-4 VII.6:1 states that you should praise G.. This
T-4 VII.7:1 G. has kept your Kingdom for you, but
T-4 VII.7:2 because it is only communication *from* G..
T-4 VII.7:3 G. does not need revelation returned to
T-4 VII.8:1 G. is praised whenever any mind learns
T-4 VII.8:4 Their helpfulness is their praise of G., and
T-4 VII.8:5 G. goes out to them and through them,
T-5 in.3:6 It is impossible for a child of G. to love his
T-5 I.1:2 and lets G. go out into them and through
T-5 I.1:6 and therefore honors only the laws of G..
T-5 I.4:9 so near to truth that G. Himself can flow
T-5 I.5:6 But what G. creates is eternal. The Holy
T-5 I.5:7 Spirit will remain with the Sons of G., to
T-5 I.6:1 G. honored even the miscreations of His
T-5 I.6:6 over," since the last step is taken by G..
T-5 II.h The Voice for G.
T-5 II.1:2 of G. were before healing was needed, and
T-5 II.1:5 in you because G. placed it in your mind,
T-5 II.1:6 it. G. Himself keeps your will alive by
T-5 II.2:2 Call to return with which G. blessed the
T-5 II.3:2 G. placed in the mind the Call to joy. This
T-5 II.3:5 made yourself, and that one is not of G..
T-5 II.3:6 But the other is given you by G., Who
T-5 II.5:1 G. does not guide, because He can share
T-5 II.5:4 for the Holy Spirit is the choice for G..
T-5 II.5:5 G. is not in you in a literal sense; you are
T-5 II.6:8 G. did not leave His children comfortless,
T-5 II.7:7 The Voice for G. is always quiet, because
T-5 II.8:2 the right choice, because He speaks for G..
T-5 II.8:3 is your remaining communication with G.
T-5 II.8:6 for G. comes from your own altars to Him
T-5 II.9:7 By deciding for G. I showed you that this
T-5 II.10:7 joyous one of waking it to the Call for G..
T-5 II.12:2 Holy Spirit, Whose Will is for G. always.
T-5 II.12:5 the Call for G. is the Call to the unlimited.
T-5 II.12:6 Child of G., my message is for you, to hear
T-5 III.2:3 Being the Call *for* G., it is also the idea *of*
T-5 III.2:3 the Call *for* God, it is also the idea *of* G..
T-5 III.2:4 are part of G. it is also the idea of yourself,
T-5 III.2:9 He may have dissociated the Call for G.,
T-5 III.2:10 become aware of the Call for G. in him,
T-5 III.6:3 Eternity is an idea of G., so the Holy Spirit
T-5 III.7:3 enables Him to understand the laws of G.,
T-5 III.7:7 Spirit to reinterpret you on behalf of G..
T-5 III.8:2 and the rightful place of the Sonship is G..
T-5 III.10:3 his mind, because part of it is still for G..
T-5 III.10:6 it is a place of peace, and peace is of G..
T-5 III.10:7 of G. are not at home except in His peace.
T-5 III.11:7 looks back to G. in remembrance of me.
T-5 III.11:8 He is in communion with G. always, and
T-5 IV.1:5 to you because, as an extension of G., you
T-5 IV.1:6 you are part of G. because He created you.
T-5 IV.2:13 you are part of G. and the Sonship is One,
T-5 IV.3:8 that are of G. and that He keeps for you.
T-5 IV.4:3 drawn to every mind created by G.,
T-5 IV.6:2 you are led back to G. where you belong,
T-5 IV.6:5 to forsake myself and G. Who created me.
T-5 IV.6:6 and G. if you forsake any of your brothers
T-5 IV.6:7 understand they belong to G. as you do.
T-5 IV.6:8 by rendering unto G. the things that are
T-5 IV.7:1 mind, but the power to create is of G..
T-5 IV.7:4 and the thinking of G. lacks nothing.
T-5 IV.8:6 and we know what G. creates is eternal.
T-5 IV.8:10 of G. in your heart and in your hands, to
T-5 IV.8:13 judgment is as strong as the wisdom of G.
T-5 IV.8:15 Sons. The Thoughts of G. are with you.
T-5 V.2:9 Guilt is more than merely not of G.. It is
T-5 V.2:10 It is the symbol of attack on G.. This is a
T-5 V.3:2 How could part of G. detach itself without
T-5 V.3:8 of attacking G. may be to the sane mind,
T-5 V.3:10 that you believe it is possible to attack G.,
T-5 V.4:5 that you must learn to think with G.. To
T-5 V.5:6 itself it will mitigate the punishment of G.
T-5 V.5:8 It attributes to G. a punishing intent, and
T-5 V.5:9 all the functions of G. as it perceives them
T-5 V.6:1 the laws of G. any more than you can, but
T-5 V.6:9 to you. G. created one, and so you cannot
T-5 V.6:11 Only what G. creates is irreversible and

T-5 V.6:12 because, when you do not think like G.,
T-5 V.6:15 of thought comes from G. and is in God.
T-5 V.6:15 of thought comes from God and is in G..
T-5 V.7:2 G. Himself orders your thought because
T-5 V.7:4 you believe you can think apart from G.,
T-5 VI.1:1 G. in His knowledge is not waiting, but
T-5 VI.1:2 the Sons of G. are waiting for your return,
T-5 VI.1:7 where G. Himself placed you forever.
T-5 VI.2:6 G. offers you the continuity of eternity in
T-5 VI.3:2 in you, for G. creates with perfect fairness.
T-5 VI.7:3 belong in your mind, which is part of G..
T-5 VI.10:3 There can be no case against a child of G.,
T-5 VI.10:3 is bearing false witness to G. Himself.
T-5 VI.11:5 Is not a child of G. worth patience? I have
T-5 VI.12:5 Holy Spirit, Who speaks for G. in time,
T-5 VI.12:8 He has been given you freely by G., you
T-5 VII.h The Decision for G.
T-5 VII.2:5 not learned that every mind G. created is
T-5 VII.2:5 of being healed *because* G. created it whole
T-5 VII.2:6 to return to G. the mind as He created it.
T-5 VII.3:1 you can know the Voice for G. is in you?
T-5 VII.3:2 G. commended His Spirit to you, and asks
T-5 VII.4:3 making. G. Himself gave you the perfect
T-5 VII.4:5 G. weeps at the "sacrifice" of His children
T-5 VII.6:4 within you because G. placed it there.
T-5 VII.6:11 *by allowing Him to decide for G. for me.*
T-6 I.3:4 of some of the Sons of G. upon another.
T-6 I.6:3 lesson a Son of G. should want to teach if
T-6 I.7:3 G. placed it there Himself, and so it is true
T-6 I.7:5 in the name of the Kingdom of G., but
T-6 I.8:5 the purpose for which G. intended it. I
T-6 I.9:2 these things, but not as G. knows them, I
T-6 I.11:7 will with G. that none of His Sons should
T-6 I.12:1 every Son of G. is necessary to enable the
T-6 I.14:3 "wrath of G." as His retaliatory weapon.
T-6 I.15:8 Judas was my brother and a Son of G., as
T-6 I.16:4 sins, and the Sons of G. are not sinners.
T-6 I.16:7 between the ego and the Son of G.. This
T-6 I.17:1 be grateful, or you cannot appreciate G..
T-6 I.18:1 of the Sons of G. is present all the time,
T-6 I.18:6 it. This is not as G. thinks, and you must
T-6 I.19:1 G. the Father and His separated Sons. If
T-6 II.1:2 The Wholeness of G., which is His peace,
T-6 II.6:2 cannot be anywhere G. did not put you,
T-6 II.6:2 you, and G. created you as part of Him.
T-6 II.6:9 that G. created is as true as He is. Its truth
T-6 II.7:2 ego's perception has no counterpart in G.,
T-6 II.7:6 it began. Everything meets in G., because
T-6 II.8:1 G. created His Sons by extending His
T-6 II.8:4 *now.* G. created you to create. You cannot
T-6 II.9:7 inspire perception and lead it toward G..
T-6 II.10:2 from G. He uses everything for good, but
T-6 II.10:4 only for this, because He speaks for G.. He
T-6 II.10:5 tells you to return your whole mind to G.,
T-6 II.11:6 the direct line of communication with G.,
T-6 II.11:7 Holy Spirit, Whose Mind is fixed on G..
T-6 II.12:6 is the one message G. gave to Him and for
T-6 II.12:7 The peace of G. lies in that message, and
T-6 II.12:7 message, and so the peace of G. lies in you
T-6 II.13:5 the Kingdom of G. together and as one.
T-6 III.1:4 no barrier to the communication of G..
T-6 III.3:3 The protection of G. then dawns upon it,
T-6 IV.2:1 G. created you He made you part of Him.
T-6 IV.2:5 are separate and outside the Mind of G..
T-6 IV.6:1 the ego raises: You are a child of G., a
T-6 IV.6:3 sleep is not real and G. calls you to awake.
T-6 IV.7:4 everything lives in G. without question.
T-6 IV.7:6 as G. because you are as true as He is, but
T-6 IV.9:2 is not true of anything that G. created,
T-6 IV.10:2 situation if G. showed you your perfection
T-6 IV.10:5 G., Who knows that His creations are
T-6 IV.11:3 everything G. created is faithful to His
T-6 IV.11:5 What would be gained if G. proved to you
T-6 IV.11:6 Can G. lose His Own certainty? I have
T-6 IV.11:8 have G. teach you that you have sinned? If
T-6 IV.12:1 G. does not teach. To teach is to imply a
T-6 IV.12:2 imply a lack, which G. knows is not there.
T-6 IV.12:3 G. is not conflicted. Teaching aims at
T-6 IV.12:4 but G. created only the changeless. The
T-6 IV.12:7 It could not shatter the peace of G., but it
T-6 IV.12:8 G. did not blot it out, because to eradicate
T-6 V.1:4 Would G. teach you that you had made a
T-6 V.1:5 G. does know is that His communication
T-6 V.4:7 shining with the light from G. Himself,
T-6 V.A.2:1 G. did not make the body, because it is
T-6 V.A.4:7 gift can be offered to the equal Sons of G.,
T-6 V.A.5:1 Holy Spirit, Who leads to G., translates
T-6 V.B.6:3 teaches you that truth was created by G.,
T-6 V.B.6:5 the Holy Spirit to decide for G. for you.
T-6 V.B.8:8 if G. Himself created you as a creator.
T-6 V.C.h Be Vigilant Only for G. and His Kingdom
T-6 V.C.1:2 to enter it in the light of what G. put there
T-6 V.C.2:6 G. Himself has established what you can
T-6 V.C.2:8 is: *Be vigilant only for G. and His Kingdom.*
T-6 V.C.5:4 have in your mind only what G. put there,
T-6 V.C.5:4 acknowledging your mind as G. created it
T-6 V.C.5:7 final step will still be taken for you by G.,
T-6 V.C.5:7 the Holy Spirit has prepared you for G..
T-6 V.C.7:1 where G. placed the altar to Himself.
T-6 V.C.7:2 but G. and His creations are beyond belief
T-6 V.C.7:3 Voice for G. speaks only for belief beyond
T-6 V.C.7:4 As long as belief in G. and His Kingdom is
T-6 V.C.8:8 Certainty is of G. for you. Vigilance is not
T-6 V.C.9:4 keep *only* the Kingdom of G. in your mind,
T-6 V.C.10:9 It is in the perfect safety of G.. Therefore,
T-7 I.1:1 power of G. and His creations is limitless,
T-7 I.1:2 You communicate fully with G., as He
T-7 I.1:3 share it, you are inspired to create like G..
T-7 I.1:4 you are not in a reciprocal relation to G.,
T-7 I.2:1 If you created G. and He created you, the
T-7 I.2:2 and you would not be co-creator with G..
T-7 I.2:8 vigilant only for G. and His Kingdom. By
T-7 I.3:1 belong in you, as you belong in G.. You
T-7 I.3:2 You are part of G., as your sons are part of
T-7 I.3:8 because you can create only as G. creates.
T-7 I.4:5 To will with G. is to create like Him. God
T-7 I.4:6 G. does not limit His gifts in any way. You
T-7 I.5:2 if G. created you by extending Himself as
T-7 I.5:4 G. extends outward beyond limits and
T-7 I.6:1 To think like G. is to share His certainty
T-7 I.6:2 because the Kingdom of G. is whole. I
T-7 I.6:3 reawakening of knowledge is taken by G..
T-7 I.7:1 G. does not take steps, because His
T-7 I.7:8 "last step" that G. will take was therefore
T-7 I.7:13 it. G. does not reveal this to you because it
T-7 II.1:1 world that resembles the Thought of G.,
T-7 II.1:4 Sickness and separation are not of G., but
T-7 II.1:5 you are perceiving what is not of G..
T-7 II.3:6 G. and His Sons, in the surety of being,
T-7 II.3:8 G. Himself created the law by creating *by* it
T-7 II.4:5 G. to those who do not understand them.
T-7 II.7:4 This meaning comes from G. and *is* God.
T-7 II.7:4 This meaning comes from God and *is* G..
T-7 II.7:9 That is why it is the Kingdom of G.. It
T-7 III.1:3 the power of the Kingdom of G. Himself,
T-7 III.5:1 G. has lit your mind Himself, and keeps
T-7 IV.1:2 certainty is of G. according to His laws.
T-7 IV.1:3 the Voice for G. and certainty comes from
T-7 IV.1:3 and certainty comes from the laws of G..
T-7 IV.1:4 Healing does not come directly from G.,
T-7 IV.1:5 whole. Yet healing is still of G., because it
T-7 IV.2:2 you are in G. because you are part of Him.
T-7 IV.2:5 The laws of G. establish this, and the Holy
T-7 IV.2:6 of G. and forgetting the laws of the ego. I
T-7 IV.4:3 of wholeness you learn to remember G..
T-7 IV.5:6 is therefore in accord with the laws of G.,
T-7 IV.6:1 think you can oppose the Will of G. is a
T-7 IV.6:6 G. has given you a gift that you both *have*
T-7 IV.6:9 thinking in accordance with the laws of G.
T-7 IV.7:1 that is where the laws of G. operate truly,
T-7 IV.7:4 G. is All in all in a very literal sense. All
T-7 V.4:5 believe that the gift comes from G. to him
T-7 V.4:5 he does not understand G. if he thinks he
T-7 V.5:6 of G. not be for all and for always? Love is
T-7 V.6:8 Everything that is of G. can be counted on
T-7 V.6:8 on, because everything of G. is wholly real
T-7 V.6:11 consistency because G. means consistency
T-7 V.6:14 G. cannot be out of accord with Himself,
T-7 V.7:5 for change that a Son of G. can recognize
T-7 V.7:7 changelessness of mind as G. created it,
T-7 V.9:5 That is how G. Himself created you; in
T-7 V.11:4 because this is your proper gift to G.. He
T-7 V.11:6 Who sees the altar of G. in everyone, and
T-7 V.11:6 calls upon you to love G. and His creation
T-7 VI.1:6 That includes his concept of G., of His
T-7 VI.7:1 for anything *but* G. and His Kingdom. The
T-7 VI.7:8 When you believe what G. does not know,
T-7 VI.8:1 that the ego does believe it can attack G.,
T-7 VI.9:8 Holy Spirit and to the knowledge of G..
T-7 VI.10:1 because your being *is* the knowledge of G..
T-7 VI.10:2 you, and will therefore obscure G. to you.
T-7 VI.10:3 since G. and His creation are not separate
T-7 VI.13:1 your function as co-creator with G., and
T-7 VII.2:5 it. This is the law of G., and it has no
T-7 VII.5:8 only honor to the Sons of the living G.,
T-7 VII.6:1 G. Himself created worthy of honor, and
T-7 VII.6:2 the appreciation G. accords them always,
T-7 VII.7:1 One child of G. is the only teacher
T-7 VII.7:3 the inestimable worth of every Son of G.,
T-7 VII.9:1 itself, and being without allegiance to G.,
T-7 VII.9:2 as you are, are out to take G. from you.
T-7 VII.9:5 If you choose to separate yourself from G.
T-7 VII.10:1 You *are* the Will of G.. Do not accept
T-7 VII.10:4 But see the Love of G. in you, and you will
T-7 VII.10:6 They are part of you, as you are part of G..
T-7 VII.10:7 this as G. Himself is lonely when His Sons
T-7 VII.10:8 The peace of G. is understanding this.
T-7 VII.11:5 will always be treasured by G. because
T-7 VIII.1:4 Kingdom, and keeps it in the Mind of G..
T-7 VIII.2:5 its own warped version of the laws of G.,
T-7 VIII.4:9 the laws of G. by distorted minds that are
T-7 IX.1:1 creative power, but G. wills to release it.
T-7 IX.1:3 withhold yourself from G.! Selfishness is
T-7 IX.1:4 of spirit because that is how G. created it.
T-7 IX.2:1 included in its own, as it is included in G..
T-7 IX.2:3 prevail against a totality that includes G.,
T-7 IX.2:3 God, and any totality *must* include G..
T-7 IX.2:10 It does not wish to contain G., but wills to
T-7 IX.3:6 but G. does not know unfulfillment and
T-7 IX.4:1 extending because it is in the Mind of G..
T-7 IX.5:3 The creations of every Son of G. are yours,
T-7 IX.6:1 increase the inheritance of the Sons of G.,
T-7 IX.6:2 Since it was the Will of G. to give it to you
T-7 X.1:6 the same thing with the premises of G.?
T-7 X.2:2 the function G. Himself gave your mind
T-7 X.4:6 Yet G. wills. He does not wish. Your will is
T-7 X.4:10 impossible, but you can will only with G..
T-7 X.6:2 G. Himself trusts you, and therefore your
T-7 X.6:4 it. I said before that you are the Will of G..
T-7 X.7:2 accomplished for you by the Will of G.,
T-7 X.7:4 is no confusion in the mind of a Son of G.,
T-7 X.8:1 Miracles are in accord with the Will of G.
T-7 XI.1:2 because He speaks for the Kingdom of G.,
T-7 XI.2:1 is the natural state of every Son of G..
T-7 XI.2:6 A Son of G. is happy only when he knows
T-7 XI.2:6 happy only when he knows he is with G..
T-7 XI.3:2 Is it worthy to be a home for a child of G.?
T-7 XI.3:5 that G. Himself thanks him for his giving?
T-7 XI.3:9 G. watches over His children and denies
T-7 XI.3:11 give the Love of G. to everything you see
T-7 XI.4:3 healed the Sonship and given thanks to G.
T-7 XI.5:3 The Majesty of G. is there, for you to
T-7 XI.5:4 Recognizing the Majesty of G. as your
T-7 XI.5:5 G. gives only equally. If you recognize His
T-7 XI.6:4 Sonship is worthy to be co-creator with G.
T-7 XI.6:7 He is a co-creator with G. with you. Deny
T-7 XI.6:8 denying yours and that of G. Who created
T-7 XI.7:7 Because G. shared His Being with you,
T-7 XI.7:10 Kingdom of G. includes all His Sons and
T-7 XI.7:11 Know, then, the Sons of G., and you will
T-8 I.1:5 This is not a bargain made by G., Who
T-8 II.2:3 teacher to whom a Son of G. should turn
T-8 II.3:4 It is never G. Who coerces you, because
T-8 II.4:3 any imprisoning of the will of a Son of G.,
T-8 II.6:2 His direction is freedom and His goal is G.
T-8 II.6:3 Yet He cannot conceive of G. without you,
T-8 II.6:6 this and you are denying G. His Kingdom,

T-8......... II.7:1 I meant: The Will of G. is without limit,
T-8......... II.7:5 Will of G. because that is how you were
T-8......... II.8:5 the Kingdom, in answer to the Call for G..
T-8......... II.8:6 Son of G. to the Voice for his Creator,
T-8........ III.1:1 Glory to G. in the highest, and to you
T-8........ III.2:1 fulfill the Will of G. perfectly is the only
T-8........ III.2:5 need Him, and why G. gave Him to you.
T-8........ III.2:7 yours. You share them as G. shares them,
T-8........ III.3:5 belong in G. have the holy function of
T-8........ III.3:6 know what it means only of G. Himself.
T-8........ III.4:6 Whenever two Sons of G. meet, they are
T-8........ III.7:1 part of yourself because you are part of G.
T-8........ III.7:4 all strength is in G. and *therefore* in you.
T-8........ III.7:5 G. wills no one suffer. He does not will
T-8........ III.8:1 Power and glory belong to G. alone. So
T-8........ III.8:3 G. gives whatever belongs to Him because
T-8........ IV.3:8 are denying the world and accepting G..
T-8...... IV.3:10 As G. sent me to you so will I send you to
T-8...... IV.5:10 not so the Sons of G. would be unequal.
T-8...... IV.5:12 and G. Himself would not go against it. I
T-8...... IV.5:13 I cannot will what G. does not will. I can
T-8........ IV.6:1 Nothing G. created can oppose your
T-8........ IV.6:1 as nothing G. created can oppose His Will
T-8........ IV.6:2 G. gave your will its power, which I can
T-8........ IV.7:6 of each other lies our remembrance of G..
T-8......... V.1:7 of G. is established in ours and as ours.
T-8......... V.2:1 creator, being wholly in the likeness of G.,
T-8......... V.2:3 from the Will of G. which *is* yourself. Yet
T-8......... V.2:7 of G. is the recognition of yourself. There
T-8......... V.2:8 is no separation of G. and His creation.
T-8....... V.2:10 Let the Love of G. shine upon you by your
T-8....... V.2:12 your awareness that the Will of G. is One.
T-8......... V.3:5 be to the union of G. and His holy Sons!
T-8......... V.4:4 transcending the ego is guaranteed by G.,
T-8......... V.5:1 Would you know the Will of G. for you?
T-8......... V.5:3 you nothing, as G. denies me nothing.
T-8......... V.5:4 the journey back to G. Who is our home.
T-8.......... VI.h The Treasure of G.
T-8........ VI.1:5 of G. for anything the world has to offer.
T-8........ VI.2:1 and the glory of G. and His holy Sons, but
T-8........ VI.2:2 cannot behold the world and know G..
T-8........ VI.2:6 Yet G. did not will the destruction of His
T-8........ VI.3:2 power. No one created by G. can find joy
T-8........ VI.3:3 What G. and His Sons create is eternal,
T-8........ VI.5:1 G. wants only His Son because His Son is
T-8........ VI.5:4 they extend your creation as G. extended
T-8........ VI.5:5 of G. Himself take joy in what is not real?
T-8........ VI.5:6 creations of G. and those that are created
T-8...... VI.5:13 because you are the treasure of G., and
T-8........ VI.6:4 You cannot find joy except as G. does. His
T-8........ VI.6:8 *he* is. Creation is the Will of G.. His Will
T-8........ VI.7:2 think you are unwilling to will with G.,
T-8........ VI.7:5 G. does not contradict Himself, and His
T-8........ VI.8:6 G. would not have us be alone because *He*
T-8........ VI.8:8 we are, and we are the Sons of G. Himself,
T-8........ VI.9:1 I share with G. the knowledge of the
T-8........ VI.9:4 Whom G. has joined cannot be separated,
T-8........ VI.9:4 G. has joined all His Sons with Himself.
T-8........ VI.9:6 journey to G. is merely the reawakening
T-8...... VI.9:10 but the experience is of G.. Together we
T-8...... VI.10:1 What G. has willed for you *is* yours. He
T-8...... VI.10:4 who are beloved of G. are wholly blessed.
T-8....... VII.1:7 child of G. thinks of himself in this way he
T-8....... VII.2:2 Link between G. and His separated Sons,
T-8....... VII.3:6 G. on behalf of the function He gives it.
T-8....... VII.5:9 To communicate with part of G. Himself
T-8....... VII.6:5 of G. remain hidden for His Name's sake,
T-8....... VII.9:7 the body does become a temple to G.; His
T-8..... VII.15:4 yourself, but condemnation is not of G..
T-8..... VII.16:8 you will open your mind to creation in G..
T-8......... IX.6:4 to make nothing out of what G. created.
T-8......... IX.8:4 no limits because G. lays none upon you.
T-8......... IX.9:4 for meaning, since meaning itself is of G..
T-9........... I.1:1 Fear of the Will of G. is one of the
T-9........... I.1:4 The very fact that the Will of G., which is
T-9........... I.1:5 the Will of G. of which you are afraid, but
T-9........... I.2:2 the fear of G. is really the fear of your own
T-9........... I.4:2 hidden and recognize the Will of G. there.
T-9........... I.8:2 there is no G. or that God's Will is fearful.
T-9 .......... I.8:3 who believes that G. demands sacrifices.
T-9 .......... I.8:4 martyr believes that G. is crucifying him.
T-9 .......... I.9:1 everyone must remember the Will of G.,
T-9 .......... I.9:6 without a cause, and G. is the only Cause.
T-9 .......... I.9:7 G. is Love and you do want Him. This *is*
T-9 ........ I.10:7 Would the Holy Spirit deny the Will of G.
T-9 ........ I.11:4 creation. G. could not will that happiness
T-9 ........ I.11:5 fact that G. is Love does not require belief,
T-9 ........ I.13:1 G. in His devotion to you created you
T-9 ........ I.14:7 *Christ is in me, and where He is G. must be,*
T-9 ......... II.4:1 are answered, never doubt a Son of G.. Do
T-9 ......... II.4:3 If you would know G. and His Answer,
T-9 ......... II.6:2 by the Holy Spirit under the laws of G..
T-9 ......... II.6:5 hear the Voice for G. in yourself alone,
T-9 ....... II.6:10 G. have created a Voice for you alone?
T-9 ......... II.7:1 I love you for the truth in you, as G. does.
T-9 ......... II.8:2 them, for the sake of what G. gave them.
T-9 ....... II.11:2 is to believe that you can bargain with G..
T-9 ....... III.2:9 He is still right, because he is a Son of G..
T-9 ....... III.7:9 Correction is of G., Who does not know
T-9 ....... III.8:1 everything because G. created everything.
T-9 ....... III.8:4 for. G. gave you the function to create in
T-9 ....... IV.3:3 what you have made into what G. created.
T-9 ....... IV.4:8 perfect sense because they come from G..
T-9 ..... IV.10:3 reality is fearful is wrong can G. be right.
T-9 ..... IV.10:4 And I assure you that G. *is* right. Be glad,
T-9 ..... IV.10:6 no more have been wrong than G. can.
T-9 ..... IV.12:2 It belongs to you and me and G., and is
T-9 ........ V.3:5 Projecting condemnation onto G., they
T-9 ........ V.6:2 When G. said, "Let there be light," there
T-9 ........ V.7:5 with G. that there is light *because* he sees it
T-9 ...... V.8:11 for help is His function, and He is of G..
T-9 ....... VI.3:5 G. has but one Son, knowing them all as
T-9 ....... VI.3:6 Only G. Himself is more than they but
T-9 ....... VI.3:9 Everyone G. created is part of you and
T-9 ....... VI.4:1 G. is more than you only because He
T-9 ....... VI.4:7 know yourself only as G. knows His Son,
T-9 ....... VI.4:7 His Son, for knowledge is shared with G..
T-9 ....... VI.7:9 you are co-creator with G. until you learn
T-9 ...... VII.1:8 G. wills you perfect happiness now. Is it
T-9 ...... VII.6:5 With the grandeur of G. in you, you have
T-9 ...... VII.7:9 If it comes from G., He knows it to be true
T-9 ...... VII.8:2 say: *G. Himself is incomplete without me.*
T-9 ...... VII.8:4 nothing unworthy of G. is worthy of you.
T-9 ...... VII.8:5 not offer to G. as wholly fitting for Him.
T-9 ..... VIII.1:1 Grandeur is of G., and only of Him.
T-9 ..... VIII.1:3 in the presence of the grandeur of G. the
T-9 ..... VIII.1:6 ego is its alternative to the grandeur of G..
T-9 ..... VIII.4:8 form of attack, but your grandeur is of G.,
T-9 ..... VIII.5:2 and keeping yourself in the Mind of G..
T-9 ..... VIII.5:3 be anywhere except in the Mind of G..
T-9 ..... VIII.8:5 G. wants you to behold what He created
T-9 ..... VIII.9:1 arrogant when G. Himself witnesses to it?
T-9 ..... VIII.9:5 transform to the Will of G. does not exist
T-9 ..... VIII.9:7 what G. has created cannot be replaced.
T-9 ..... VIII.9:8 G. is incomplete without you because His
T-9 ... VIII.10:1 altogether irreplaceable in the Mind of G.
T-9 ... VIII.10:3 G., through His Voice, reminds you of it,
T-9 ... VIII.10:3 and G. Himself keeps your extensions safe
T-9 ... VIII.10:6 G., Who knows your value, would not
T-9 ... VIII.10:8 accept yourself as G. created you cannot
T-9 ... VIII.11:6 of His answer, because it comes from G..
T-9 ... VIII.11:8 what you hear, for G. does not deceive. He
T-10 ...... in.2:1 G. created nothing beside you and
T-10 ...... in.3:1 G. does not change His Mind about you,
T-10 ...... in.3:5 Can anything exceed the Love of G.? Can
T-10 ...... in.3:7 you from beyond it because, being in G.,
T-10 ...... in.3:9 "Has G. changed His Mind about me?"
T-10 .... in.3:11 G. will never decide against you, or He
T-10 ........... I.h At Home in G.
T-10 ........ I.1:2 remember that *it is as impossible for G..*
T-10 ........ I.1:4 the laws of G. protect it by His Love. Any
T-10 ........ I.1:7 that your banishment is not of G., and
T-10 ........ I.2:1 You are at home in G., dreaming of exile
T-10 ....... II.2:3 for He retains the knowledge of G. and of
T-10 ....... II.2:4 remembering, for G. is in your memory.
T-10 ....... II.3:4 G. will do His part if you will do yours,
T-10 ....... II.4:4 always an attack on truth, and truth is G.,
T-10 ....... II.4:5 further recognize that you are part of G.,
T-10 ....... II.6:5 vigilant *against* G. and His Kingdom. And
T-10 ..... III.1:1 have not attacked G. and you do love Him
T-10 ..... III.1:8 worshippers are the Sons of G. in sickness
T-10 ..... III.1:9 G. would have them released from their
T-10 ..... III.2:1 of G. except His power through you?
T-10 ..... III.2:4 brothers simply by accepting G. for them.
T-10 ..... III.2:5 and G. has only one channel for healing
T-10 ..... III.3:1 To believe that a Son of G. can be sick is
T-10 ..... III.3:1 sick is to believe that part of G. can suffer.
T-10 ..... III.3:4 of a Son of G. even if he believes in it, for
T-10 ..... III.3:4 acceptance of G. in him acknowledges the
T-10 ..... III.3:4 the Love of G. he has forgotten. Your
T-10 ..... III.3:5 recognition of him as part of G. reminds
T-10 ..... III.3:6 denial of G. and thus lose sight of yourself
T-10 ..... III.4:1 To believe a Son of G. is sick is to worship
T-10 ..... III.4:2 G. created love, not idolatry. All forms of
T-10 ..... III.4:5 is impossible, because you are part of G.,
T-10 ..... III.4:7 what the ego does perceive in a Son of G.;
T-10 ..... III.6:1 for everything that G. created, because of
T-10 ..... III.6:7 Peace comes from G. through me to you.
T-10 ..... III.7:3 Yet every Son of G. has the power to deny
T-10 ..... III.8:4 G. is not jealous of the gods you make,
T-10 ..... III.8:6 fact that you made them to replace G.. Yet
T-10 ..... III.8:7 remember that nothing can replace G.,
T-10 ... III.10:1 If G. has but one Son, there is but one
T-10 ... III.10:1 God has but one Son, there is but one G..
T-10 ... III.11:1 Only at the altar of G. will you find peace.
T-10 ... III.11:2 this altar is in you because G. put it there.
T-10 ..... IV.1:4 If G. created you perfect, you *are* perfect. If
T-10 ..... IV.1:6 G. is not at war with the god of sickness
T-10 ..... IV.1:7 He is the symbol of deciding against G.,
T-10 ..... IV.4:4 The laws of G. work only for your good,
T-10 ..... IV.4:6 Yet G. Himself has protected everything
T-10 ..... IV.4:9 without meaning because it is without G..
T-10 ..... IV.5:2 it. You cannot do what G. did not intend,
T-10 ..... IV.5:5 Nothing but the laws of G. has ever been,
T-10 ..... IV.6:1 you have experienced the protection of G.
T-10 ..... IV.6:2 are no strange images in the Mind of G.,
T-10 ..... IV.6:7 all. Peace is yours because G. created you.
T-10 ..... IV.7:1 Son of G. who has laid aside all false gods,
T-10 ..... IV.7:5 the lamps of G. were lit by the same spark
T-10 ..... IV.8:2 Yet G. has kept the spark alive so that the
T-10 ..... IV.8:7 faith in it, and G. Himself will answer you.
T-10 .......... V.h The Denial of G.
T-10 ....... V.1:3 means that you have forsworn G.. Many
T-10 ....... V.1:5 to deny G. is to deny their own Identity,
T-10 ....... V.2:1 deny G. will inevitably result in projection
T-10 ....... V.2:5 brothers without it, you are denying G..
T-10 ....... V.3:1 Allegiance to the denial of G. is the ego's
T-10 ....... V.3:8 he is but one idea;–the denial of G..
T-10 ....... V.4:2 "attack on G." made His Son think he was
T-10 ....... V.6:1 Son of G., you have not sinned, but you
T-10 ....... V.6:2 this can be corrected and G. will help you,
T-10 ....... V.7:6 The Love of G. is in everything He created
T-10 ....... V.7:7 and G. will come rushing into your heart
T-10 ....... V.8:1 for healing but only to the G. of love, for
T-10 ....... V.8:5 without love on G. and His creation, from
T-10 ....... V.9:2 What is of G. is His forever, and you are
T-10 ....... V.9:2 is of God is His forever, and you are of G..
T-10 ....... V.9:5 you will accept yourself as G. created you,
T-10 ..... V.10:1 have denied yourself, and how much G.,
T-10 ..... V.10:3 be to attack Himself, and G. is not insane.
T-10 ..... V.10:6 G. will never cease to love His Son, and
T-10 ..... V.10:7 creation, fixed forever in the Mind of G..
T-10 ... V.10:10 G. gave Himself to you in your creation,
T-10 ..... V.11:6 G. has given you the means for undoing
T-10 ..... V.12:1 If G. knows His children as wholly sinless
T-10 ..... V.12:2 G. knows His children as wholly without
T-10 ..... V.12:3 G. knows His children to be wholly joyous
T-10 ..... V.12:5 If G. created His Son perfect, that is how
T-10 ..... V.13:1 perceive anything G. did not create or you
T-10 ..... V.13:6 images you perceive are the Sons of G..
T-10 ..... V.13:7 Fatherhood of G. will you have anything,
T-10 ..... V.14:2 the concept of choice, which is not of G.,
T-11 ............. h G. OR THE EGO
T-11 ...... in.1:1 Either G. or the ego is insane. If you will
T-11 ...... in.1:3 Neither G. nor the ego proposes a partial
T-11 ...... in.3:1 by projection, but G. creates by extension
T-11 ...... in.4:1 brother, you are part of G. and part of me.

T-11.........I.1:3 foundation on which **G.** will help build
T-11.........I.1:6 dwell in the Mind of **G.** with your brother
T-11.........I.1:6 for **G.** Himself did not will to be alone.
T-11.........I.2:3 are no beginnings and no endings in **G.**,
T-11.........I.2:4 universe, or from **G.** Who *is* the universe? I
T-11.........I.2:6 part of **G.** can be missing or lost to Him?
T-11.........I.3:1 If you were not part of **G.**, His Will would
T-11.........I.5:2 What holds for **G.** holds for you. If you
T-11.........I.5:3 If you believe you are absent from **G.**, you
T-11.........I.5:4 you, and you are meaningless without **G.**.
T-11.........I.5:5 There is no end to **G.** and His Son, for we
T-11.........I.5:6 **G.** is not incomplete, and He is not
T-11...... I.5:11 you will learn what **G.** has kept for you.
T-11.........I.6:1 **G.** has given you a place in His Mind that
T-11.........I.6:3 you because **G.** did not will to be alone?
T-11.........I.7:1 Could any part of **G.** be without His Love,
T-11.........I.7:2 **G.** is your heritage, because His one gift is
T-11.........I.7:7 **G.** wills to create, and your will is His. It
T-11.........I.9:3 **G.**, then, may seem to demand of you
T-11.........I.9:4 Would **G.**, Who wants only your will, be
T-11...... I.11:2 He is the Voice for **G.**, but never forget
T-11...... I.11:2 forget that **G.** did not will to be alone. He
T-11....... II.1:3 The Son of **G.** *has* both Father and Son,
T-11....... II.1:6 Yet when you attack any part of **G.** and
T-11....... II.2:4 speaks to you of the Fatherhood of **G.**.
T-11....... II.4:4 can the Son of **G.** not accomplish with the
T-11....... II.4:4 with the Fatherhood of **G.** in him? And
T-11....... II.5:8 patience, for He cannot leave a part of **G.**.
T-11....... II.6:3 You who have **G.** must be as God, for His
T-11....... II.6:3 You who have God must be as **G.**, for His
T-11....... II.6:5 Whom **G.** sent you will teach you how to
T-11....... II.7:1 you be hostage to the ego or host to **G.**?
T-11....... II.7:8 for the Comforter of **G.** is in you.
T-11...... III.1:6 **G.** is very quiet, for there is no conflict in
T-11...... III.1:8 Yet it always attacks the Son of **G.**, and
T-11...... III.1:8 the Son of God, and the Son of **G.** is you.
T-11...... III.2:3 At home in **G.** he is lonely, and amid all
T-11...... III.2:4 Would **G.** let this be real, when He did
T-11...... III.3:1 child, if you knew what **G.** wills for you,
T-11...... III.3:5 into Heaven, and into the Presence of **G.**.
T-11...... III.3:7 what **G.** wills for Himself He wills for you,
T-11...... III.4:2 way of pain, of which **G.** knows nothing.
T-11...... III.4:6 are not fit companions for the Son of **G.**,
T-11...... III.5:1 **G.** hides nothing from His Son, even
T-11...... III.5:2 Yet the Son of **G.** cannot hide his glory,
T-11...... III.5:2 his glory, for **G.** wills him to be glorious,
T-11...... III.5:3 will never lose your way, for **G.** leads you.
T-11...... III.7:4 But be holy in the Presence of **G.**, or you
T-11...... III.7:5 what is unlike **G.** cannot enter His Mind,
T-11...... III.8:3 **G.** blessed His Son forever. If you will
T-11...... III.8:5 you from **G.** if you use it on behalf of the
T-11...... IV.1:6 are looking on what **G.** created as yourself
T-11...... IV.2:1 Could you try to make **G.** homeless and
T-11...... IV.2:4 without the intervention of **G.** against it,
T-11...... IV.2:4 on your power is not the Will of **G.**,
T-11...... IV.2:5 only to the power that **G.** gave to save you
T-11...... IV.3:3 Every altar to **G.** is part of you, because
T-11...... IV.3:7 That is the law of **G.**, for the protection of
T-11...... IV.6:3 the place where **G.** would have you be.
T-11...... IV.6:7 **G.** is my life and yours, and nothing is
T-11...... IV.6:7 and nothing is denied by **G.** to His Son.
T-11...... IV.7:2 **G.** knows His Son as wholly blameless as
T-11...... IV.7:4 For Christ is the Son of **G.**, Who lives in
T-11...... IV.7:5 of the Love and the loveliness of **G.**, as
T-11...... IV.8:1 Blessed is the Son of **G.** whose radiance is
T-11...... IV.8:4 Peace be unto you who rest in **G.**, and in
T-11....... V.3:6 *All power is of* **G.**. *What is not of Him has no*
T-11....... V.5:3 I said before that to will contrary to **G.** is
T-11....... V.5:5 the ego's idle wishes and the Will of **G.**, ,
T-11....... V.6:2 lies in your complete dependence on **G.**,
T-11....... V.6:7 the knowledge of your dependence on **G.**,
T-11....... V.6:8 for **G.** into a means of establishing itself.
T-11..... V.10:1 seems to separate you from **G.** is only fear
T-11..... V.12:1 **G.** is as dependent on you as you are on
T-11... V.12:10 the Love of **G.** completely protects them.
T-11..... V.17:5 Accept what **G.** does not deny, and it will
T-11..... V.17:6 The witnesses for **G.** stand in His light
T-11.... VI.3:10 the Son of **G.** will see himself as Fatherless
T-11...... VI.4:2 You live in me because you live in **G.**. And
T-11...... VI.4:5 it in yourself and not perceive it in **G.**?
T-11...... VI.4:7 be, for the resurrection is the Will of **G.**,
T-11...... VI.5:2 god he made or the **G.** Who created him.
T-11...... VI.5:5 the Son of **G.** is born of sacrifice and pain.
T-11...... VI.5:6 The **G.** of resurrection demands nothing,
T-11...... VI.6:3 can be offered you through the grace of **G.**
T-11...... VI.6:4 by His grace, for **G.** is gracious to His Son,
T-11...... VI.6:7 for otherwise you will not awake in **G.**,
T-11...... VI.7:2 The Love of **G.** surrounds His Son whom
T-11...... VI.7:6 value. **G.** does not judge His guiltless Son.
T-11...... VI.8:2 God's Son, for the Will of **G.** cannot die.
T-11...... VI.8:3 assign to death whom **G.** has given eternal
T-11...... VI.8:5 you perceive the Son of **G.** as crucified,
T-11.... VI.10:6 whole power of **G.** is in every part of Him,
T-11.... VI.10:8 To **G.** all things are possible. And to
T-11..... VII.1:2 you see it. **G.** created only the eternal, and
T-11..... VII.2:1 that the Son of **G.** ever had is eternal. The
T-11..... VII.4:6 what you have made and what **G.** created,
T-11..... VII.4:8 can know **G.** because it is His Will to be
T-11... VIII.4:2 **G.** will not refuse you the Answer He gave
T-11... VIII.4:4 You made the problem **G.** has answered.
T-11... VIII.5:8 nothing of **G.** demands anything of you.
T-11... VIII.5:9 you. **G.** gives; He does not take. When you
T-11... VIII.6:2 is everything, and you share it with **G.**.
T-11... VIII.7:1 Little child of **G.**, you do not understand
T-11... VIII.7:6 Nothing of **G.** will enslave His Son whom
T-11... VIII.7:7 willing to ask the truth of **G.** without fear,
T-11... VIII.8:1 Beautiful child of **G.**, you are asking only
T-11... VIII.8:6 Ask for truth of any Son of **G.**, and you
T-11... VIII.9:4 Christ is the Son of **G.** Who is in no way
T-11. VIII.10:2 the Help of **G.** goes with you everywhere.
T-11. VIII.12:3 God's Son whom **G.** condemneth not. Let
T-11. VIII.12:5 you, for He wills to heal the Son of **G.**, in
T-11. VIII.15:2 For if **G.** is not deceived in you, you can be
T-11. VIII.15:3 Who will teach you that, as part of **G.**,
T-12........I.6:11 But hear his call for the Help of **G.**, and
T-12.........I.7:5 help as what it is, so **G.** can answer *you.*
T-12.......... II.h The Way to Remember **G.**
T-12....... II.2:3 only if the Son of **G.** gives power to it. He
T-12....... II.2:4 remembering that all power is of **G.**. You
T-12....... II.2:7 is his, for **G.** cannot be remembered alone
T-12....... II.2:9 yourself is thus the way to remember **G.**.
T-12....... II.6:1 still want what **G.** wills, and no nightmare
T-12....... II.6:1 can defeat a child of **G.** in his purpose. For
T-12....... II.6:2 For your purpose was given you by **G.**,
T-12..... II.10:4 is given Him that is not of **G.** is gone. Yet
T-12...... III.4:7 Poverty is of the ego, and never of **G.**. No
T-12...... III.8:1 I said before that **G.** so loved the world
T-12...... III.8:2 **G.** does love the real world, and those
T-12...... III.8:4 **G.** gave you the real world in exchange for
T-12...... III.8:5 yourself from the Mind of **G.** you would
T-12...... III.9:5 it is governed by the desire to be unlike **G.**
T-12.... III.10:3 altar of **G.** where Christ abideth is there.
T-12.... III.10:8 where **G.** and His Son dwell in peace and
T-12.... III.10:9 the real world to you from the altar of **G.**.
T-12...... IV.6:8 for **G.** is whole and all His extensions are
T-12....... V.9:1 is limitless because it will lead you to **G.**.
T-12...... VI.2:6 **G.** is in your memory because of Him.
T-12...... VI.4:3 of forgetting to the remembering of **G.**.
T-12...... VI.4:5 of Christ for every Son of **G.** who sleeps.
T-12...... VI.4:6 In His sight the Son of **G.** is perfect, and
T-12...... VI.4:7 real world because **G.** gave you Heaven.
T-12...... VI.6:1 Every child of **G.** is one in Christ, for his
T-12...... VI.6:1 his being is in Christ as Christ's is in **G.**.
T-12...... VI.6:7 they share the unification of the laws of **G.**
T-12...... VI.7:2 At the altar of **G.**, the holy perception of
T-12...... VI.7:3 Very gently does **G.** shine upon Himself,
T-12...... VI.7:4 as it blends into the purpose of **G.**. For the
T-12...... VI.7:6 join in perfect love of **G.** and of each other
T-12...... VI.7:7 and being in **G.** it must also be in you.
T-12..... VII.1:6 In every child of **G.** His blessing lies, and
T-12..... VII.1:6 of the children of **G.** is His blessing to you
T-12..... VII.4:8 **G.** shares His function with you in Heaven
T-12... VII.10:3 Coming only from **G.**, its power and
T-12... VII.13:2 as deserving of death as **G.** knows you are
T-12... VII.14:1 The ego is not a traitor to **G.**, to Whom
T-12... VII.14:4 to **G.** and therefore deserve death. You
T-12... VII.14:5 from **G.** and not from the ego because, by
T-12... VII.14:6 from what you want **G.** does not save you.
T-12.... VIII.1:1 believe that you can kill the Son of **G.**?
T-12.... VIII.4:1 what **G.** Himself placed in his memory.
T-12.... VIII.4:5 **G.** would reunite you with yourself, and
T-12.... VIII.5:2 memory of **G.** cannot shine in a mind that
T-12.... VIII.5:3 For the memory of **G.** can dawn only in a
T-12.... VIII.6:1 Son of **G.**, be not content with nothing!
T-12.... VIII.6:3 **G.** could not offer His Son what has no
T-12.. VIII.7:10 **G.** did not give you has no power over you
T-12.... VIII.8:1 real world was given you by **G.** in loving
T-13.... in.2:11 of them but has thought that **G.** is cruel.
T-13....... in.3:1 this were the real world, **G.** *would* be cruel.
T-13.........I.2:1 you have made the Son of **G.** *has* sinned.
T-13.........I.3:6 long as you believe the Son of **G.** is guilty
T-13.........I.4:1 Son of **G.** has set himself is useless indeed,
T-13.........I.4:5 everything unworthy of the Son of **G.**, for
T-13.........I.4:5 for such was His mission, given Him by **G.**
T-13.........I.4:6 God. And what **G.** gives has always been.
T-13.........I.5:1 me as you learn the Son of **G.** is guiltless.
T-13.........I.5:6 For the Son of **G.** is guiltless now, and the
T-13.........I.7:2 The Son of **G.**, who sleepeth not, has kept
T-13.........I.7:4 For **G.** waits not for His Son in time, being
T-13.........I.9:3 guiltlessness of the Son of **G.** as yours is
T-13.........I.9:4 For **G.** has never condemned His Son, and
T-13........I.11:5 As He looks upon the guiltless Son of **G.**,
T-13.......... II.h The Guiltless Son of **G.**
T-13........II.1:2 stands in the way of your remembering **G.**
T-13........II.2:5 the Son of **G.** by seeing him as guilty.
T-13........II.3:4 who the Son of **G.** is because it is blind.
T-13........II.6:2 that guiltlessness is blasphemous to **G.**.
T-13........II.6:3 To the ego, the *ego* is **G.**, and guiltlessness
T-13........II.9:7 son of man is the guiltless Son of **G.**, and
T-13...... III.2:1 ego's dark foundation is the memory of **G.**
T-13...... III.2:8 be, is your intense and burning love of **G.**,
T-13...... III.3:4 your fortress, for you would shut out **G.**,
T-13...... III.4:3 you have made a world **G.** would destroy;
T-13...... III.5:2 than a Son of **G.** in redemption. Your
T-13...... III.5:4 You are more afraid of **G.** than of the ego,
T-13...... III.7:6 restoring it to the magnitude of **G.**.
T-13.... III.10:3 And **G.** did not give it for the request was
T-13.... III.11:6 **G.** did not allow this to happen. Yet you
T-13.... III.12:2 **G.** did not do this to you. Could He set
T-13....... V.6:6 **G.** calls you and you do not hear, for you
T-13....... V.7:9 witnesses to the reality you share with **G.**.
T-13..... V.7:12 For every Son of **G.** is given you to whom
T-13..... V.7:12 is given you to whom **G.** gave Himself.
T-13..... V.7:13 And it is **G.** Whom you must offer them,
T-13..... VII.6:6 errors for the peace of **G.** is but *your* will.
T-13..... VII.6:7 Christ will always offer you the Will of **G.**,
T-13..... VII.7:2 He is as safe from pain as **G.** Himself,
T-13..... VII.7:3 because **G.** placed him in Himself where
T-13..... VII.8:1 peace of **G.** passeth your understanding
T-13..... VII.8:3 *now.* **G.** loves His Son forever, and His Son
T-13..... VII.8:6 yours, being the gift of **G.** unto His Son.
T-13..... VII.8:7 and by it **G.** created you as one with Him.
T-13... VII.15:3 a quiet journey to the peace of **G.**, where
T-13... VII.16:2 the way to quietness that is the gift of **G.**.
T-13... VII.17:9 Thus does the Son of **G.** give thanks unto
T-13.... VIII.2:3 of knowledge, being in the Mind of **G.**,
T-13.... VIII.3:2 Yet the last step must be taken by **G.**,
T-13.... VIII.3:2 was accomplished by **G.** in your creation.
T-13.... VIII.3:9 Yet only **G.** can gather them together, by
T-13.... VIII.4:3 He is a Thought of **G.**, and God has given
T-13.... VIII.4:3 and **G.** has given Him to you because He
T-13.... VIII.5:2 Every miracle you offer to the Son of **G.** is
T-13.... VIII.6:4 blends quietly into the one reality of **G.**.
T-13.... VIII.7:2 the Son of **G.** through the Holy Spirit,
T-13.... VIII.8:3 all unite in the eternity of **G.** the Father.
T-13.... VIII.9:2 are the witness to the Fatherhood of **G.**,
T-13.... VIII.9:4 The miracle that **G.** created is perfect, as
T-13.. VIII.10:2 **G.** knows it, but you do not, and so you
T-13.. VIII.10:4 **G.** waits your witness to His Son and to
T-13.. VIII.10:6 the gates of Heaven, **G.** will open them.
T-13....... IX.1:7 and the past the laws of **G.** must intervene
T-13....... IX.4:3 of **G.** is guiltless because you see the past,
T-13....... IX.5:3 idea that the guiltless Son of **G.** can attack
T-13....... IX.6:2 of **G.** lies the conviction of your own guilt.
T-13....... IX.6:5 to condemn the Son of **G.** in part. Those
T-13...... IX.8:11 where **G.** knows there is perfect innocence
T-13........X.7:4 Holy Spirit does what **G.** would have Him

T-13....... X.8:3 Son of G. believes that he is lost in guilt,
T-13....... X.9:9 and He offers mercy to every child of G.,
T-13..... X.10:2 as G. Himself has always loved His Son.
T-13..... X.10:7 reason because it is not in the Mind of G.,
T-13..... X.11:4 You can love only as G. loves. Seek not to
T-13..... X.11:7 himself as guiltless and in the peace of G..
T-13... X.11:10 say: *Behold the Son of G., and look upon his*
T-13..... X.13:2 is that I love *only* what G. loves with me,
T-13..... X.13:2 the worth that G. has placed upon you. I
T-13..... X.13:6 in honor of its wholeness that is of G..
T-13..... X.14:7 G. loves you. Could I, then, lack faith in
T-13...... XI.2:1 G. would not have His Son embattled,
T-13...... XI.2:5 Gladness and joy belong to G. for your
T-13...... XI.3:3 Value is where G. placed it, and the value
T-13...... XI.3:3 of what G. esteems cannot be judged, for
T-13...... XI.3:7 In Heaven is everything G. values, and
T-13...... XI.4:7 is this possible, when His mission is of G.?
T-13...... XI.5:1 this: G. gave the Holy Spirit to you, and
T-13...... XI.5:3 Nothing can prevent what G. would have
T-13...... XI.6:9 to do. The Will of G. can fail in nothing.
T-13...... XI.7:1 be sufficient: G. wills you be in Heaven,
T-13...... XI.7:3 prevail against the peace G. wills for you.
T-13...... XI.7:4 because insanity is not the Will of G.. If
T-13...... XI.7:6 not keep what G. would have removed,
T-13...... XI.8:1 Link that G. Himself placed within you,
T-13...... XI.8:2 G. would share with you is known. Yet
T-13...... XI.8:7 G. willed you Heaven, and will always will
T-13...... XI.8:9 Heaven will not be yours, for G. is sure,
T-13...... XI.9:3 Salvation is as sure as G.. His certainty
T-13...... XI.9:7 G. watches over him and light surrounds
T-13.... XI.10:1 when G. has placed within him the glad
T-13.... XI.10:7 Will of G. must be accepted as your will.
T-13.... XI.11:4 Failure is of the ego, not of G.. From Him
T-14......... I.2:8 is why G. placed the Holy Spirit in you,
T-14......... I.3:4 thoughts he shares with G. are beyond his
T-14....... II.4:2 Like G., He knows it to be true. He brings
T-14....... II.8:7 G. is everywhere, and His Son is in Him
T-14...... III.3:4 born of the Love of G. and of His Son:
T-14...... III.6:6 over the Son of G. is the happy lesson the
T-14...... III.7:6 No one can hurt the Son of G.. His guilt is
T-14...... III.8:1 G. is the only Cause, and guilt is not of
T-14...... III.8:2 that what is not of G. has power over you.
T-14...... III.8:6 and accept the Cause of G. as yours. The
T-14...... III.8:7 power that G. has given to His Son *is* his,
T-14.... III.11:4 done to make you worthy of the gift of G..
T-14.... III.11:6 are worthy of everything G. wills for you.
T-14.... III.11:7 gift of G. He so freely and so gladly offers
T-14.... III.11:8 offers you but what G. gave Him for you.
T-14.. III.11:10 you are deserving of it. G. knows you are.
T-14.... III.12:4 accepts the plan G. set for its Atonement,
T-14.... III.13:1 The One Who knows the plan of G. that
T-14.... III.13:1 knows the plan of God that G. would have
T-14.... III.13:5 of G. the Holy Spirit is your only Friend.
T-14.... III.14:3 learn that what G. wills for you *is* your will.
T-14.... III.14:5 is of Him to Whom G. gave it for you. He
T-14.... III.14:7 your salvation and the peace of G. in you.
T-14.... III.15:3 on the throne of G. is not a source of guilt.
T-14.... III.15:7 Never forget the Love of G., Who has
T-14.... III.16:2 decisions are reflections of what G. knows
T-14...... IV.1:6 received, even as G. gave it first to His Son
T-14...... IV.1:7 but the First in eternity is G. the Father,
T-14...... IV.2:3 this, must you attain, with G. beside you.
T-14...... IV.4:2 you. G. breaks no barriers; neither did He
T-14...... IV.4:4 G. will not fail, nor ever has in anything.
T-14...... IV.4:5 Decide that G. is right and you are wrong
T-14.... IV.4:11 offer to G. and you His blameless Son. For
T-14.... IV.4:12 G. will Himself exchange your gift for His.
T-14...... IV.5:4 decisions to the One Who speaks for G.,
T-14...... IV.5:5 upon yourself by loving not the Son of G.,
T-14...... IV.5:6 the joy of living with your G. and Father,
T-14...... IV.6:1 you have learned how to decide with G.,
T-14...... IV.7:1 you are guiltless you cannot know G.,
T-14...... IV.7:5 very mind where G. Himself has placed it.
T-14...... IV.8:3 yourself away and valued G. so little, hear
T-14...... IV.9:3 you the true condition of the Son of G.. It
T-14.... IV.10:3 G. can communicate only to the Holy
T-14.... IV.10:3 the knowledge of what you are with G..
T-14.... IV.10:4 only the Holy Spirit can answer G. for you
T-14.... IV.10:4 God for you, for only He knows what G. is
T-14 ... IV.10:5 communication with the Mind of G. has
T-14 ... IV.10:6 Communication with G. is life. Nothing
T-14 ...... V.1:1 is the part that links you still with G..
T-14 ...... V.1:3 *G. makes this possible.* Would you deny His
T-14 .... V.1:10 to the Holy Spirit, and to G. through Him.
T-14 .... V.1:12 for G. is blessed in His Son as the Son is
T-14 ...... V.2:4 but G. would not have you bound by it.
T-14 ...... V.2:7 all the love you share with G. He holds in
T-14 ...... V.3:2 Who can condemn whom G. has blessed?
T-14 ...... V.3:3 is nothing in the Mind of G. that does not
T-14 ...... V.3:7 that is the right of all that G. created.
T-14 ...... V.4:5 G. has hidden himself from his own sight.
T-14 ...... V.6:4 to the eternal glory of G. and His creation.
T-14 ...... V.6:5 straight to Heaven, and the peace of G..
T-14 ...... V.6:7 of G. Himself supports this teaching, and
T-14 ...... V.7:3 the power of G. if you teach only this. You
T-14 ...... V.8:3 is everyone whom G. created as His Son.
T-14 ...... V.8:5 The power of G. draws everyone to its safe
T-14 .... V.9:10 Restore to G. His Son as He created him,
T-14 .... V.10:9 G. and therefore cannot crucify nor suffer
T-14 .. V.10:11 And everything you give to G. is yours.
T-14 ..... VI.5:4 He knows you are not separate from G.,
T-14 ..... VI.8:8 Son. No one can fail to come where G. has
T-14 .... VII.3:3 Yet it is true because G. knows it. These
T-14 .... VII.3:5 are. To G., unknowing is impossible. It is
T-14 .... VII.5:5 G. knows it not. The Holy Spirit uses
T-14 .... VII.5:9 is mighty, but the power of G. is with Him
T-14 .. VII.5:11 He can fulfill what G. has given Him to do
T-14 .... VII.7:3 perception with Him Whom G. has given
T-14 .... VII.7:6 G. has one purpose which He shares with
T-14 .... VII.7:7 to accept what G. would have you have.
T-14 .... VII.7:9 through Him, and through Him unto G..
T-14 ... VIII.1:1 you have obscured the glory G. gave you,
T-14 ... VIII.1:3 because nothing can obscure the gift of G.
T-14 ... VIII.1:4 of the power of G. that shines in you.
T-14 ... VIII.1:8 what He promised G. He is wholly faithful
T-14 ... VIII.1:8 shares with G. the promise that was given
T-14 ... VIII.2:3 No altar stands to G. without His Son.
T-14 ... VIII.2:5 Can you offer guilt to G.? You cannot,
T-14 ... VIII.2:8 know not G. because you know not this.
T-14 ... VIII.2:9 And yet you do know G. and also this. All
T-14 . VIII.2:11 but in the meeting place where G., united
T-14 . VIII.2:14 the communication that G. Himself wills
T-14 ... VIII.3:3 will surely lead you to where G. and His
T-14 ... VIII.4:4 Where G. is, there are you. Such is the
T-14 ... VIII.4:6 change the knowledge, given you by G.,
T-14 ... VIII.4:7 Everything G. created knows its Creator.
T-14 ... VIII.5:3 Heaven remains the Will of G. for you.
T-14 ... VIII.5:5 are brought together with the gift of G.,
T-14 ... VIII.5:6 To whom G. gives Himself, He *is* given.
T-14 ..... IX.1:4 Bringing illusion to truth, or the ego to G.
T-14 ..... IX.2:1 the ego to G. is but to bring error to truth,
T-14 ..... IX.3:3 You are not frail with G. beside you. Yet
T-14 ..... IX.3:5 The Atonement offers you G.. The gift
T-14 ..... IX.3:8 you. G. has not left His altar, though His
T-14 ..... IX.4:3 graciousness of G. will take them gently in
T-14 ..... IX.4:5 For G. is life, and they abide in life. Life is
T-14 ..... IX.5:4 can reflect Heaven or hell; G. or the ego.
T-14 ..... IX.5:6 G. will shine upon it of Himself. Only the
T-14 ..... IX.6:3 reflection of G. needs no interpretation. It
T-14 ..... IX.7:1 power of healing that the reflection of G.,
T-14 ..... IX.8:6 G. is no image, and His creations, as part
T-14 ....... X.1:1 stands between G. and His creations, or
T-14 ....... X.2:2 the only perception the Son of G. accepts.
T-14 ....... X.6:9 simple. The power of G., and not of you,
T-14 ..... X.6:10 that you have the power of G. in you. That
T-14 ..... X.6:12 it. The power of G. is limitless. And being
T-14 ..... X.10:1 to remember G. in secret and alone. For
T-14 ..... X.11:1 As G. communicates to the Holy Spirit in
T-14 ..... X.11:2 G. has no secret communications, for
T-14 ..... X.12:8 And G. Himself, Who wills to be with His
T-14 ..... XI.1:2 is power, and all power is of G.. You who
T-14 ..... XI.1:9 G. in you is but your learning of the false,
T-14 ..... XI.2:2 yourself how to imprison the Son of G., a
T-14 ..... XI.2:3 Can G. learn how not to be God? And can
T-14 ..... XI.2:3 Can God learn how not to be G.? And can
T-14 ..... XI.4:2 Yet G. did not abandon you. And so you
T-14 ..... XI.4:3 child of light by Him to Whom G. gave it.
T-14 ..... XI.5:1 You have one test, as sure as G., by which
T-14 ... XI.6:10 Whom G. has given you will speak to you.
T-14 ..... XI.7:5 It is impossible that G. lose His Identity,
T-14 ... XI.10:8 Thank G. that He is there and works
T-14 ... XI.11:2 As we are held as one in G., so do we learn
T-14 ... XI.11:3 does G. proclaim His Oneness and His
T-14 ... XI.11:8 This is the Will of G. for all creation, and
T-14 ... XI.12:5 for it is the law of G. they be not separate.
T-14 ... XI.15:1 The power of G., from which they both
T-15 ........ I.8:4 Son of G. emerges from the past into the
T-15 ...... I.10:6 Heaven because there is no change in G..
T-15 ...... I.10:7 with freedom, you will remember G.. For
T-15 ...... I.14:2 love for everyone, for G. and for yourself.
T-15 ....... II.1:3 What holds remembrance of G. cannot be
T-15 ....... II.1:5 For unless G. is bound, you cannot be. An
T-15 ....... II.1:6 Holy Spirit is offered to G. on your behalf,
T-15 ....... II.2:3 It will come, being the lesson G. gives you
T-15 ....... II.2:8 only in Heaven that G. would have you be
T-15 ....... II.3:1 can it take to be where G. would have you
T-15 ....... II.3:4 as G. extends Himself to encompass you.
T-15 ....... II.4:7 Son of G. who has been released through
T-15 ....... II.5:3 gift of G. is recognized in any other way.
T-15 ....... II.6:6 it is the practice of the power of G. in you.
T-15 ..... III.4:8 The power of G. will support every effort
T-15 ... III.4:10 G. is not willing that His Son be content
T-15 ..... III.5:1 you be hostage to the ego or host to G.?"
T-15 ..... III.5:4 G. gave Himself to you in your creation,
T-15 ..... III.5:6 make little whom G. has joined with Him.
T-15 ..... III.6:3 Decide for G. through Him. For littleness,
T-15 ..... III.6:5 that lie in you from G. are for all who, like
T-15 ..... III.6:7 it. All honor is due the host of G.. Your
T-15 ..... III.7:2 the host whom G. appointed for Himself.
T-15 ..... III.7:3 all your littleness to give the gift of G., but
T-15 ..... III.7:4 For G. would give Himself *through* you. He
T-15 ..... III.9:1 Holy child of G., when will you learn that
T-15 ..... III.9:4 the host of G. to guilt and weakness with
T-15 ... III.10:9 host of G. needs not seek to find anything
T-15 ... III.11:1 to the plan of G. and unwilling to attempt
T-15 ... III.11:3 together that the Son of G. is host to Him.
T-15 ... III.12:1 in everyone only the remembrance of G.,
T-15 ..... IV.1:1 unless you believe that what G. wills takes
T-15 ..... IV.2:8 For peace is of G., and no one beside Him.
T-15 ..... IV.3:2 no plan of the ego before the plan of G..
T-15 ..... IV.3:5 G. would have His host abide in perfect
T-15 ..... IV.5:3 of the host of G. depends on willingness,
T-15 ..... IV.7:5 G. Who surrounds all of you together.
T-15 ... IV.9:10 to acknowledge that you are host to G.,
T-15 ....... V.3:2 you would love unlike to G., Who knows
T-15 ....... V.9:1 G. knows you *now*. He remembers
T-15 ....... V.9:5 it. His frame of reference is simply G.. The
T-15 ..... V.10:3 meaning of love is the meaning G. gave to
T-15 ..... V.10:5 it. G. loves every brother as He loves you;
T-15 ..... V.10:8 the holy instant you unite directly with G.
T-15 ... V.10:10 shares, as G. shares His Self with Christ.
T-15 ..... V.11:1 you that you can judge the Self of G.? God
T-15 ..... V.11:2 G. has created It beyond judgment, out of
T-15 ..... V.11:5 reaches to eternity, and to the Mind of G..
T-15 ........ VI.h The Holy Instant and the Laws of G.
T-15 ..... VI.4:1 that when another calls on G. for love,
T-15 ..... VI.4:2 do you think that when G. answers him,
T-15 ..... VI.4:4 however dimly, that G. is an idea, and so
T-15 ..... VI.5:7 this alone is natural under the laws of G..
T-15 ..... VI.5:8 In the holy instant the laws of G. prevail,
T-15 ... VI.5:10 Son of G. accepts the laws of God as what
T-15 ... VI.5:10 Son of God accepts the laws of G. as what
T-15 ... VI.5:11 he is as free as G. would have him be. For
T-15 ... VI.6:10 the only need the Sons of G. share equally
T-15 ..... VI.8:1 In the holy instant G. is remembered,
T-15 ..... VI.8:6 G. and the power of God will take Their
T-15 ..... VI.8:6 of G. will take Their rightful place in you,
T-15 .... VII.3:7 of G. can have no real investment here.
T-15 .... VII.5:1 this chain that binds the Son of G. to guilt
T-15 .... VII.5:2 belongs not around the chosen host of G.,
T-15 .. VII.13:3 power of G. in Him and you is joined in a
T-15 ... VIII.2:6 Behold the only need that G. and His Son
T-15 ... VIII.2:9 then, in peace from guilt to G. and them.
T-15 ... VIII.3:7 For the holy host of G. is beyond failure,
T-15 ... VIII.4:1 on this: G. gave the Sonship to you, to
T-15 ... VIII.4:5 this universe, being of G., is far beyond
T-15 ... VIII.4:6 its parts are joined in G. through Christ,

T-15... VIII.5:3 Holy Spirit asks you to respond as G. does
T-15... VIII.5:4 G. would respond to every need, whatever
T-15... VIII.5:6 G. does not understand your problem in
T-15... VIII.6:1 the awareness of what G. cannot know,
T-15... VIII.6:4 be possible because it is the Will of G..
T-15... VIII.6:5 only of G. teach you the only meaning of
T-15... VIII.6:6 For G. created the only relationship that
T-15.........IX.h The Holy Instant and the Attraction of G.
T-15......IX.1:1 them, so unlimited that they reach to G..
T-15......IX.1:5 that G. Himself plays in the Atonement,
T-15......IX.1:7 for it. G. is ready now, but you are not.
T-15......IX.2:6 no limits, having been established by G..
T-15......IX.4:1 between Heaven and hell, G. and the ego,
T-15......IX.5:1 Spirit tell you of the Love of G. for you,
T-15......IX.6:2 of guilt opposes the attraction of G.. His
T-15......IX.6:4 you invest in guilt you withdraw from G..
T-15......IX.7:3 you experience only the attraction of G..
T-15....... X.2:2 instant no guilt is laid upon the Son of G.,
T-15....... X.2:5 as incapable of receiving sacrifice as G. is,
T-15....... X.5:4 to be host to the ego or hostage to G..
T-15....... X.7:1 How fearful, then, has G. become to you,
T-15....... X.7:3 ego seems to demand less of you than G.,
T-15....... X.7:6 And this you think saves you from G.,
T-15....... X.8:3 have given G. away rather than look at it.
T-15....... X.8:4 if G. would demand total sacrifice of you,
T-15....... X.9:6 is simple, being of G., and therefore very
T-15....... X.9:8 demand for sacrifice and the peace of G..
T-15......XI.2:6 For He is Host to G.. And you need but
T-15......XI.2:9 Host Who cradles G. in the time of Christ,
T-15......XI.4:3 awareness of your relationship with G..
T-15......XI.6:6 joined in you it would be apart from G.,
T-15......XI.9:1 G. offers thanks to the holy host who
T-16.........I.6:2 lies in the strength of G. that hovers over
T-16....... II.3:3 natural, for it is the way G. thinks, and
T-16....... II.5:4 are natural to the One Who speaks for G..
T-16...... II.6:11 The Host of G. has called to you, and you
T-16....... II.7:7 G. wills you better. Could you not look
T-16....... II.7:8 on whom G. loves with perfect Love?
T-16....... II.8:2 to deny what has been given you by G..
T-16......III.5:2 Created by G., He left neither God nor His
T-16......III.5:2 God, He left neither G. nor His creation.
T-16......III.5:3 He is both G. and you, as you are God and
T-16......III.5:3 and you, as you are G. and Him together.
T-16......III.5:9 who are host to G. are also host to them.
T-16......III.6:2 What is beyond G.? If you who hold Him
T-16......IV.2:4 This is the last step in the readiness for G.
T-16......IV.8:7 can offer you what G. has given, and what
T-16......IV.9:1 completion, for you will be wholly in G.,
T-16......IV.9:3 of G. and of His Son established forever.
T-16......IV.9:5 In the Name of G., be wholly willing to
T-16......IV.9:6 and only this, there is G. completed, and
T-16....IV.10:1 for it was built with G. beside you, and
T-16..IV.11:10 Whom G. remembers must be whole.
T-16..IV.11:11 And G. has never forgotten what makes
T-16..IV.11:14 willingness to love and all the Love of G.,
T-16....IV.12:6 and then together we go straight to G., in
T-16....IV.13:2 interfere with G. must interfere with you.
T-16....IV.13:7 are directed straight to the Heart of G.. At
T-16....IV.13:9 the Love of G. in us together cannot lift.
T-16....... V.2:1 make guilty is always directed against G..
T-16....... V.4:1 the hidden wish for special love from G.,
T-16....... V.4:2 is the renunciation of the Love of G., and
T-16....... V.5:5 even to the final triumph over G.. In this
T-16..... V.10:1 special relationship as a triumph over G.,
T-16..... V.10:4 sacrifice is that G. must die so you can live
T-16..... V.12:2 the place of G. at the expense of content.
T-16..... V.12:4 strength is extracted from the death of G.,
T-16..... V.12:7 G. is not angry. He merely could not let
T-16... V.12:11 of G. have any influence at all upon it.
T-16..... V.14:3 between truth and illusion; G. and fantasy
T-16..... V.15:5 G. offers you correction and complete
T-16..... V.17:2 will recognize that G. is on the other side,
T-16......VI.1:1 yourself with the ego and not with G.. For
T-16......VI.1:4 unlike the relationship of G. and His Son,
T-16......VI.1:5 For G. created love as He would have it be
T-16......VI.2:3 it. For the Love of G., no longer seek for
T-16......VI.5:5 for G. is left without and *nothing* taken in.
T-16....VI.11:6 no longer, for the Love of G. and *you*. And
T-16.....VII.8:1 What G. has given you is truly given, and
T-16.....VII.8:8 you have received what G. has given you.
T-16.....VII.9:4 G. holds nothing against anyone, for He is
T-16...VII.10:2 The power of G. and all His Love, without
T-16...VII.10:3 Be an ally of G. and not the ego in seeking
T-16...VII.11:4 for the reality of your relationship with G.
T-16...VII.12:5 *temptation of the Son of G. is not Your Will.*
T-17.........I.1:1 of the Son of G. lies only in illusions, and
T-17.........I.1:4 betrayed himself, his brothers and his G..
T-17....... II.1:6 For you will see the Son of G.. You will
T-17....... II.4:4 will barely have time to thank G. for it.
T-17....... II.4:5 For G. will take the last step swiftly, when
T-17....... II.5:5 the Son of G. made in insanity could be
T-17....... II.7:1 the Son of G. is lifted easily into his home.
T-17...... III.1:5 the Son of G. for what he did not do. The
T-17...... III.7:3 One. Whom G. has joined as one, the ego
T-17...... III.9:5 choose except between G. and the ego.
T-17...... III.9:7 Only the Thoughts of G. are true. And all
T-17.... III.10:8 Let me enter in the Name of G. and bring
T-17...... IV.1:1 G. established His relationship with you
T-17...... IV.1:2 The purpose G. ascribed to anything is its
T-17...... IV.1:5 you relate to your creations as G. to His.
T-17...... IV.1:6 His. For nothing G. created is apart from
T-17...... IV.1:6 and nothing G. created but would extend
T-17...... IV.2:4 to them the function given them by G..
T-17...... IV.4:3 to the gift with which G. blessed it, and by
T-17...... IV.4:5 your relationship with G. restored to you.
T-17.... IV.10:5 The power of Heaven, the Love of G., the
T-17.... IV.15:5 gently and G. rises to your remembrance,
T-17.... IV.16:1 As G. ascends into His rightful place and
T-17..IV.16:10 For here is G., and where He is only the
T-17....... V.9:6 For you have chosen but the goal of G.,
T-17..... V.10:3 for G. Himself has blessed your holy
T-17... VII.10:3 For loneliness in G. must be a dream. You
T-17... VIII.5:1 Such was the crucifixion of the Son of G..
T-18.........I.2:7 Nothing can come between what G. has
T-18.........I.4:1 that G. is fear made but one substitution.
T-18.........I.7:1 to frighten you, say only, "G. is not fear,
T-18.........I.8:2 stillness dwells the living G. you never left
T-18.........I.9:5 abide. Here you are joined in G., as much
T-18.......I.10:3 firmly joined in truth that only G. is there.
T-18.......I.10:8 G. is with you, my brother. Let us join in
T-18.......I.11:3 G. and His whole creation have entered it
T-18.......I.11:6 G. Himself is glad that your relationship
T-18.......I.12:1 G. has called should hear no substitutes.
T-18.......I.13:5 peace of G. is given you with the glowing
T-18....... II.9:5 the truth of Heaven join in the Will of G..
T-18....... II.9:7 your will joined with the Will of G.. And
T-18...... III.1:6 forgot was simply that G. cannot destroy
T-18...... III.4:7 is given forever, for G. Himself received it.
T-18...... III.4:9 You have accepted G.. The holiness of
T-18.... III.4:14 The Will of G. is granted you. For you
T-18...... III.5:7 And where we go we carry G. with us.
T-18...... III.6:1 me in bringing Heaven to the Son of G.,
T-18...... III.8:2 in the Mind of G. but shines on you.
T-18...... III.8:4 of your desire the power of G. Himself,
T-18...... III.8:7 back into darkness and forward unto G.,
T-18...... IV.3:5 yourself? G. did not create His dwelling
T-18...... IV.4:5 G. has established them. They do not wait
T-18...... IV.5:7 Purification is of G. alone, and therefore
T-18...... IV.5:9 *I who am host to G. am worthy of Him. He*
T-18...... IV.8:4 Everything G. wills is not only possible,
T-18....... V.3:4 Yet it is possible, because G. wills it. Nor
T-18...... VI.1:3 For G. created only this, and He did not
T-18...... VI.1:4 is the dwelling place of the Son of G., who
T-18...... VI.2:1 could G. give but knowledge of Himself?
T-18...... VI.4:8 respecting what the Son of G. has made
T-18...... VI.5:5 What G. created is only what He would
T-18...... VI.7:1 This is the host of G. that *you* have made.
T-18...... VI.7:2 And neither G. nor His most holy Son can
T-18...... VI.9:3 is no barrier between G. and His Son, nor
T-18...... VI.9:5 is. Yet this could only be if G. were wrong.
T-18...... VI.9:6 G. would have had to create differently,
T-18.... VI.9:10 G. placed none between Himself and you.
T-18.... VI.10:4 Where G. is not? Is *He* a body, and did He
T-18... VIII.1:7 cannot even think of G. without a body,
T-18... VIII.2:3 G. cannot come into a body, nor can you
T-18... VIII.2:6 is your kingdom, where G. can enter not.
T-18... VIII.9:1 The Thought of G. surrounds your little
T-18. VIII.11:8 Son of G. remains outside His Fatherhood
T-18..VIII.12:4 You could no more know G. alone than
T-18...... IX.1:5 in its delusions, it thinks it is the Son of G.
T-18.... IX.1:10 is still a tiny segment of the Son of G.,
T-18...... IX.3:7 Yet G. can bring you there, if you are
T-18...... IX.9:5 Here there is no attack upon the Son of G.
T-18.... IX.10:4 led, that G. Himself can take the final step
T-18.... IX.11:4 Where learning ends there G. begins, for
T-18.... IX.14:1 And when the memory of G. has come to
T-19.........I.2:1 an opportunity to heal the Son of G.. And
T-19.........I.5:5 between the Son of G. and his Creator;
T-19.........I.6:6 G. gave healing not apart from sickness,
T-19.......I.11:1 Faith is the gift of G., through Him
T-19.......I.11:1 through Him Whom G. has given you.
T-19.......I.11:2 Faithlessness looks upon the Son of G.,
T-19.......I.11:3 the Son of G. is seen already forgiven, free
T-19.......I.12:3 is a gift you offer to the Son of G. through
T-19.......I.14:1 your brother stand before the altar G. has
T-19.......I.16:3 G. created as His Son is slave to nothing,
T-19........II.2:4 It assumes the Son of G. is guilty, and has
T-19........II.2:4 and making himself what G. created not.
T-19........II.2:5 Will of G. open to opposition and defeat.
T-19........II.2:7 by it G. Himself is changed, and rendered
T-19........II.3:1 The Son of G. can be mistaken; he can
T-19........II.4:3 of the Son of G. as his Father created him,
T-19........II.6:5 an idea of G. to an ideal the ego wants; a
T-19........II.7:1 what the Son of G. has made himself to be
T-19........II.7:6 Mourn, then, the death of G., Whom sin
T-19...... III.4:2 correct them all as G. entrusted Him to do
T-19...... III.5:1 sees the Son of G. can make mistakes. On
T-19...... III.6:1 this: If sin is real, Both G. and you are not.
T-19...... III.6:3 sin is real, G. must be at war with Himself
T-19...... III.7:4 And G. and His creation seem to be split
T-19...... III.7:5 For sin would prove what G. created holy
T-19...... III.7:6 sin. Sin is perceived as mightier than G.,
T-19...... III.7:6 God, before which G. Himself must bow,
T-19...... IV.1:8 recognizing in your call the Call for G..
T-19...... IV.3:8 When G. has taken the last step Himself,
T19....IV.A.1:5 how can it abide within the Son of G.? If it
T19. IV.A.2:11 of hatred would still oppose the Will of G.
T19....IV.A.3:3 You still oppose the Will of G., just by a
T19....IV.A.4:3 no more depart from you than from G..
T19....IV.A.4:5 It cannot contain the Will of G.. Peace
T19. IV.A.17:4 the Son of G. was killed instead of you.
T19....IV.B.6:2 sins you think the Son of G. committed.
T19....IV.C.2:9 It is the Will of G.. What is impossible to
T19..IV.C.2:15 as life is the result of the Thought of G..
T19....IV.C.3:1 innocence, and to the Will of G. Himself.
T19....IV.C.3:3 One thing is sure; G., Who created
T19....IV.C.4:3 the Son of G. to this *are* arrogant. But you
T19....IV.C.5:7 For G. has answered this insane idea with
T19....IV.C.7:2 the silencer of the Voice that speaks for G.
T19....IV.C.8:1 world the ego would lay the Son of G.,
T19....IV.C.8:1 orders, proof in his decay that G. Himself
T19....IV.C.8:7 insanity could look upon the defeat of G.,
T19....IV.C.9:2 to grow into a mighty force for G. is very
T19....IV.C.9:4 Holy Spirit and protected by G. Himself.
T19..IV.C.10:4 is in full communication with G. and you.
T19..IV.C.10:7 your brother, and see in it the Will of G..
T19...... IV.D.h The Fourth Obstacle: The Fear of G.
T19... IV.D.1:5 the Son of G. entirely restored to sanity.
T19... IV.D.3:4 the memory of G. seems quite forgotten;
T19... IV.D.3:4 of your Self from you;–*the fear of G.,* the
T19... IV.D.4:6 agreed never to let the fear of G. be lifted,
T19... IV.D.9:1 can look upon the fear of G. unterrified,
T19. IV.D.11:1 the fear of G. does need some preparation
T19. IV.D.11:5 afraid of G. *because* you fear your brother.
T19. IV.D.15:3 as G. created every living thing and loves
T19. IV.D.16:3 And offer thanks to G. that he is holy, and
T19. IV.D.17:3 see in him the gift of G. you would receive
T19. IV.D.19:2 nothing in the plan G. has established for
T19. IV.D.19:4 is the peace of G., given to you eternally
T19. IV.D.19:6 to the Son of G. in thanks for what he is,
T19. IV.D.21:3 and place the Son of G. safely within the
T-20.........I.2:1 and holy sign the Son of G. is innocent.
T-20.........I.2:4 honor the perfect purity of the Son of G.,
T-20.........I.3:1 journey the Son of G. has undertaken. He
T-20........II.3:6 judgment on the Son of G. for what he is.
T-20........II.4:1 for the Son of G. has not forgiven me.
T-20........II.4:4 you may look upon the Son of G. as whole

| | |
|---|---|
| T-20 II.7:3 | The fear of G. is nothing to you now. Who |
| T-20 II.7:5 | of illusion that G. Himself could give. For |
| T-20 II.7:6 | For what G. gave the Holy Spirit, you have |
| T-20 II.7:7 | Son of G. looks unto you for his release. |
| T-20 II.7:8 | thorns nor nails to crucify the Son of G., |
| T-20 II.8:10 | refrain the Son of G. was never crucified. |
| T-20 II.10:1 | that the Son of G. is risen from the past, |
| T-20 III.7:1 | make the Son of G. adjust to his insanity. |
| T-20 III.7:10 | ask, "How shall I look upon the Son of G.? |
| T-20 III.8:6 | brother with joy to bless the Son of G., |
| T-20 III.8:7 | brother as the eternal gift of G. to you? |
| T-20 III.9:6 | him to Paradise, and know the peace of G. |
| T-20 III.11:5 | the pure in heart see G. within His Son, |
| T-20 III.11:7 | as surely as G. created His Son holy, and |
| T-20 IV.1:4 | at all. Power is of G., given by Him and |
| T-20 IV.1:8 | Holy Spirit merely gives everything to G., |
| T-20 IV.2:10 | It is the reawakening of the laws of G. in |
| T-20 IV.2:10 | power to enforce what G. created not. |
| T-20 IV.3:6 | What G. has given follows His laws, and |
| T-20 IV.4:2 | Their power is of G., and they will give it |
| T-20 IV.4:2 | they will give it only to what G. has given, |
| T-20 IV.4:3 | their power according to the Will of G.. |
| T-20 IV.6:7 | the Son of G. can enter without fear and |
| T-20 IV.7:4 | them and they remember the laws of G., |
| T-20 IV.8:3 | ask yourself if it is possible that G. would |
| T-20 IV.8:12 | what can be more certain than a Son of G. |
| T-20 V.2:5 | to hold the unity of the Son of G. together |
| T-20 V.7:3 | the laws of G. to your remembrance. And |
| T-20 V.8:2 | He knows the Son of G., and shares his |
| T-20 V.8:6 | the confidence of G. should be misplaced. |
| T-20 VI.1:1 | meaning of the Son of G. lies solely in his |
| T-20 VI.1:4 | Yet has the Son of G. invented an unholy |
| T-20 VI.6:7 | What G. would have *not* be is here kept |
| T-20 VI.6:8 | him, is what makes G. seem fearful to you |
| T-20 VI.8:6 | with G. unholy seemed to be possible, all |
| T-20 VI.10:1 | the Son of G. has with his Father in reality |
| T-20 VI.11:4 | Here does the Son of G. stop briefly by, to |
| T-20 VI.12:6 | is as like your real relationship with G. as |
| T-20 VI.12:8 | shadow of the fear of G. remains with you |
| T-20 VIII.3:6 | bless the Son of G. in your relationship, |
| T-20 VIII.4:1 | that what G. willed and gave you shall be |
| T-20 VIII.11:3 | can behold the holiness G. gave His Son. |
| T-21 in.2:2 | see is what you did to hurt the Son of G.. |
| T-21 in.2:4 | you joined the Will of G. to set him free. |
| T-21 I.9:1 | This is the vision of the Son of G., whom |
| T-21 I.9:6 | love the Son of G. sings to his Father still. |
| T-21 I.10:3 | will look upon the vision of the Son of G., |
| T-21 II.3:1 | impossible the Son of G. be merely driven |
| T-21 II.3:4 | possible within the universe as G. created |
| T-21 II.3:6 | to Him Who must decide for G. for you. |
| T-21 II.6:4 | happen to the Son of G. without his will; |
| T-21 II.6:6 | G. powerless and so to take it for himself, |
| T-21 II.6:6 | without what G. has willed for him. This |
| T-21 III.3:3 | For faith can keep the Son of G. in chains |
| T-21 III.5:1 | is impossible that the Son of G. lack faith, |
| T-21 III.5:3 | the Son of G. believe that he is powerless. |
| T-21 IV.2:3 | light on sin, and G. will strike you blind. |
| T-21 V.1:6 | small Voice for G. is not drowned out by |
| T-21 V.5:2 | must have been accepted by the Son of G., |
| T-21 V.5:2 | for what G. wills for him he must receive. |
| T-21 V.5:3 | For G. wills not apart from him, nor does |
| T-21 V.5:3 | of G. wait upon time to be accomplished. |
| T-21 V.5:4 | joined the Will of G. must be in you now, |
| T-21 V.6:5 | plan of G. for your salvation is complete. |
| T-21 VI.3:1 | himself, as G. thinks not without His Son. |
| T-21 VI.6:1 | Son of G. to what can never be corrected. |
| T-21 VI.7:4 | The power to heal the Son of G. is given |
| T-21 VI.10:1 | The Son of G. is always blessed as one. |
| T-21 VI.11:1 | you have over the Son of G. is not a threat |
| T-21 VI.11:5 | G. is not mocked; no more His Son can be |
| T-21 VII.1:7 | Treachery to the Son of G. is the defense |
| T-21 VII.2:1 | one believes the Son of G. is powerless. |
| T-21 VII.2:2 | believe that they are not the Son of G.. |
| T-21 VII.2:5 | of the Son of G. will strike them dead, and |
| T-21 VIII.2:4 | as is the Love of G. for His creation. Sure |
| T-21 VIII.3:6 | whom G. Himself will never fail to answer |
| T-21 VIII.3:7 | G. has already given all that he really |
| T-21 VIII.3:8 | what he is uncertain of, G. cannot give. |
| T-22 in.1:2 | Rejoice whom G. hath joined have come |
| T-22 in.4:9 | circle where you recognize the Son of G.. |
| T-22 I.1:2 | whom G. would heal and hate the one He |
| T-22 I.3:10 | it. G. has no secrets. He does not lead you |
| T-22 I.9:1 | Be certain G. did not entrust His Son to |
| T-22 I.11:9 | to Christ is drawn to G. as surely as Both |
| T-22 II.9:6 | Son of G. could leave his Father's Mind, |
| T-22 II.11:4 | him for what he is, if G. would have it so. |
| T-22 II.11:5 | G. has given to your holy relationship is |
| T-22 II.11:9 | of him what G. has given him for you, not |
| T-22 II.12:1 | holy relationship, beloved of G. Himself. |
| T-22 II.13:6 | of perfect purity, and G. created it for you |
| T-22 IV.6:1 | To all who share the Love of G. the grace |
| T-22 V.3:5 | G. holds your hands, and what can |
| T-22 V.3:8 | G. rests with you in quiet, undefended |
| T-22 V.4:7 | tiny mouse or everything that G. created? |
| T-22 V.4:8 | by this mouse, but by the Will of G.. And |
| T-22 V.4:9 | can a mouse betray whom G. has joined? |
| T-22 VI.3:1 | means and end so easily in what G. loves, |
| T-22 VI.7:4 | G. would let nothing interfere with those |
| T-22 VI.9:8 | He will join to it all the power that G. has |
| T-22 VI.10:3 | Think you the Will of G. is powerless? Is |
| T-22 VI.10:7 | that seems to keep the fear of G. in place, |
| T-22 VI.11:1 | can attack the Son of G. and not attack his |
| T-22 VI.12:1 | one with G. and recognized this oneness, |
| T-23 in.1:6 | and what is weak is not the Will of G.. |
| T-23 in.1:8 | And G. is feared as an opposing will. |
| T-23 I.1:1 | memory of G. comes to the quiet mind. It |
| T-23 I.1:7 | you realize the ego is at war with G.. |
| T-23 I.2:1 | war against yourself would be a war on G. |
| T-23 I.2:4 | The death of G., if it were possible, would |
| T-23 I.2:7 | And G. thinks otherwise. This is no war; |
| T-23 I.2:8 | of G. can be attacked and overthrown. |
| T-23 I.3:1 | certain that it is impossible G. and the ego |
| T-23 I.4:5 | Your "enemy" was G. Himself, to Whom |
| T-23 I.4:7 | The Son of G. at war with his Creator is a |
| T-23 I.5:1 | teach the Son of G. that he is not himself, |
| T-23 I.7:2 | For you must be as G. created you. Truth |
| T-23 I.7:10 | untouched and quiet in the peace of G.. |
| T-23 I.8:5 | that G. created with anything but love. |
| T-23 I.8:9 | turn in peace to the rememberance of G., |
| T-23 I.10:3 | keeps G. homeless and His Son with Him. |
| T-23 I.10:4 | You are not a stranger in the house of G.. |
| T-23 I.10:5 | G. has set him in serenity and peace, and |
| T-23 I.11:1 | can the resting place of G. turn on itself, |
| T-23 I.11:2 | the house of G. perceives itself divided. |
| T-23 I.12:8 | So is the memory of G. obscured in minds |
| T-23 II.4:4 | G. Himself is powerless to overcome. Sin |
| T-23 II.4:5 | being the belief the Son of G. can make |
| T-23 II.5:7 | fear of G. and of each other now appears |
| T-23 II.5:7 | made real by what the Son of G. has done |
| T-23 II.6:6 | For if G. cannot be mistaken, He must |
| T-23 II.7:1 | of G. is reinforced by this third principle. |
| T-23 II.7:5 | made inevitable, beyond the help of G.. |
| T-23 II.8:2 | not forgiveness, is the Will of G.. From |
| T-23 II.8:5 | And G. Himself seems to be siding with it, |
| T-23 II.13:3 | Nor will G. end His vengeance upon both, |
| T-23 II.14:7 | which the laws of G. appear to be reversed |
| T-23 II.15:8 | saved the Son of G. for fear and death! |
| T-23 II.19:2 | Where G. created life, there life must be. |
| T-23 III.2:1 | for G. speaks through you to your brother |
| T-23 IV.1:2 | The fear of G. is fear of life, and not of |
| T-23 IV.3:1 | G. does not share His function with a |
| T-23 IV.4:1 | of your relationship is like the Love of G.. |
| T-23 IV.4:2 | assume the holy function G. gave His Son, |
| T-23 IV.6:6 | G. Himself and all the lights of Heaven |
| T-23 IV.6:7 | the peace of G. together with His Son. |
| T-23 IV.9:1 | strength of G. in their awareness could |
| T-23 IV.9:8 | Who with the Love of G. upholding him |
| T-24 in.1:2 | in which G. is remembered is attained. It |
| T-24 in.1:9 | G. does not wait upon illusions to let Him |
| T-24 in.2:8 | What G. creates has no alternative. The |
| T-24 I.4:1 | What G. created cannot be attacked, for |
| T-24 I.7:5 | G. gave you and your brother Himself, |
| T-24 I.8:1 | The fear of G. and of your brother comes |
| T-24 I.8:3 | And G. Himself must honor it or suffer |
| T-24 I.9:2 | but an attack upon the Will of G.? You |
| T-24 II.2:8 | and thus run counter to the Will of G.. To |
| T-24 II.4:4 | in the melody that pours from G. to you |
| T-24 II.4:6 | the Call of G. Himself is soundless to you. |
| T-24 II.5:1 | will you hear the Voice for G. beside it. |
| T-24 II.6:2 | The shining radiance of the Son of G., so |
| T-24 II.6:6 | and to receive the Love of G. forever? |
| T-24 II.8:3 | gift that G. would have him give to you. |
| T-24 II.8:7 | It is not G. Who has condemned His Son, |
| T-24 II.9:2 | of the fear of G. will melt away in love. |
| T-24 II.9:4 | which seems to make G. and His Heaven |
| T-24 II.10:3 | You are alike to G. as God is to Himself. |
| T-24 II.10:3 | You are alike to God as G. is to Himself. |
| T-24 II.10:7 | remembering G. gave Himself to you and |
| T-24 II.11:5 | What is the same as G. is one with Him. |
| T-24 II.11:6 | make the truth of G. and you as one seem |
| T-24 II.13:1 | it seem possible G. made the body as the |
| T-24 II.13:2 | it demands a special place G. cannot enter |
| T-24 II.13:3 | illusions; safe from G. and safe for conflict |
| T-24 II.13:4 | your special kingdom, apart from G., |
| T-24 II.14:1 | key you threw away G. gave your brother, |
| T-24 II.14:5 | acceptance of yourself as G. created you. |
| T-24 III.2:2 | all your puny might against the Will of G.. |
| T-24 III.2:4 | So does it seem to split you off from G., |
| T-24 III.2:5 | You would protect what G. created not. |
| T-24 III.4:2 | Would G. have left His Son in such a state |
| T-24 III.4:6 | secret vow that what G. wants for you will |
| T-24 III.5:1 | G. asks for your forgiveness. He would |
| T-24 III.5:8 | And G. Himself, Who knows that death is |
| T-24 III.7:5 | curse G. because He did not make their |
| T-24 III.7:6 | Curse G. and die, but not by Him Who |
| T-24 III.7:7 | see the savior G. gave to you that you |
| T-24 III.8:2 | free. Such is the Will of G. and of His Son. |
| T-24 III.8:3 | Would G. condemn Himself to hell and to |
| T-24 III.8:5 | G. calls to you from him to join His Will |
| T-24 III.8:7 | G. asks your mercy on His Son and on |
| T-24 IV.5:1 | in which G. is bereft of what He loves, and |
| T-24 IV.5:4 | the one whom G. has given you instead. |
| T-24 V.6:3 | His Love for G. replaces all the fear you |
| T-24 V.6:9 | that each might offer you the Love of G.. |
| T-24 VI.1:4 | In him is your assurance G. is here, and |
| T-24 VI.1:5 | that G. is knowable and will be known to |
| T-24 VI.2:1 | Without you there would be a lack in G., |
| T-24 VI.2:3 | For what G. wills is whole, and part of |
| T-24 VI.2:5 | you that G. is One with him and you; that |
| T-24 VI.3:2 | Nothing that G. created has He failed to |
| T-24 VI.3:5 | G. changes not His Mind about His Son |
| T-24 VI.5:6 | Voice that speaks for G. in everything that |
| T-24 VI.6:6 | let the fear of G. no longer hold the vision |
| T-24 VI.7:6 | And where is G. Himself but in that part |
| T-24 VI.10:3 | part of G. holds not for all the rest. You |
| T-24 VI.10:5 | how great the Love of G. for you must be, |
| T-24 VI.10:6 | will disappear before the Will of G., Who |
| T-24 VI.12:1 | and with the power of G. maintaining it, |
| T-24 VI.12:4 | But a tiny willingness, a nod to G., a |
| T-24 VI.12:5 | the truth as G. established it no sacrifice |
| T-24 VII.1:8 | that you might share the Fatherhood of G. |
| T-24 VII.1:12 | now that the host of G. has found another |
| T-24 VII.2:1 | memory of G. shines not alone. What is |
| T-24 VII.6:5 | G. is a Means as well as End. In Heaven, |
| T-24 VII.11:7 | The Son of G. retains his Father's Will. |
| T-25 h | THE JUSTICE OF G. |
| T-25 in.2:7 | the Son of G. abide exactly where he is, |
| T-25 I.4:1 | *You* are the means for G.; not separate, |
| T-25 I.6:2 | knows the Will of G. and what you really |
| T-25 II.5:3 | masterpiece that G. has set within this |
| T-25 II.5:5 | Yet what G. has created needs no frame, |
| T-25 II.6:1 | Holy Spirit is the frame G. set around the |
| T-25 II.6:4 | that G. has given it but serves His purpose |
| T-25 II.6:6 | G. has set His masterpiece within a frame |
| T-25 II.6:8 | G. creates is safe from all corruption, |
| T-25 II.7:5 | G. kept it safe that you might look on it, |
| T-25 II.8:6 | and what G. gave him must be given you. |
| T-25 II.9:4 | G. cherishes creation as the perfect Father |
| T-25 II.9:11 | gratitude of G. Himself is freely offered to |
| T-25 II.11:1 | brother are the same, as G. Himself is One |
| T-25 III.4:1 | link that kept it still within the laws of G.; |
| T-25 III.4:1 | itself upholds the universe as G. created it |
| T-25 III.4:1 | to the need the Son of G. believes he has. |
| T-25 III.4:3 | And thus has G. protected still His Son, |
| T-25 III.9:1 | The Son of G. could never sin, but he can |
| T-25 IV.2:7 | The Son of G. creates to bring him joy, |
| T-25 IV.4:1 | Would you not do this for the Love of G.? |

| | |
|---|---|
| T-25......IV.5:5 | supersede the Will of G. and of His Son, |
| T-25.......V.1:1 | perceive the Son of G. as other than he is. |
| T-25.......V.2:1 | your enemy, and G. along with Him. |
| T-25.......V.2:8 | Son of G. as innocent and wish him dead? |
| T-25.......V.3:5 | such is the call that G. has given him, that |
| T-25.......V.3:5 | answer by returning unto G. what is His |
| T-25.......V.4:1 | The Son of G. asks only this of you; that |
| T-25.......V.4:8 | if he fulfilled the role G. gave to him. But |
| T-25.......V.5:5 | you the gift of sight G. gave to him for you |
| T-25.......V.5:6 | to complete the task G. gave to him. |
| T-25.......V.5:8 | be what G. appointed that he be to you. |
| T-25.......V.6:1 | the Son of G. may cherish toward himself, |
| T-25.......V.6:1 | is G. believed to be without the power to |
| T-25.......V.6:2 | is G. made free to let His Will be done. In |
| T-25.......V.6:3 | in what the Will of G. must be for you. In |
| T-25......VI.1:1 | grace of G. rests gently on forgiving eyes, |
| T-25......VI.1:8 | And being in accord with what G. wills, |
| T-25......VI.1:8 | on with the grace of G. upon his sight. |
| T-25......VI.3:1 | calls down the grace of G. upon your eyes, |
| T-25......VI.3:3 | G. is glad to have you look on him. He |
| T-25......VI.5:1 | laws of G. do not prevail in perfect form, |
| T-25......VI.6:6 | he chose to hurt himself did G. appoint to |
| T-25......VI.7:5 | The Son of G. can make no choice the |
| T-25......VI.7:7 | plan to save the Son of G. from all attack, |
| T-25.....VII.1:8 | as Heaven, and as strong as G. Himself. |
| T-25...VII.1:11 | possible what G. created not should share |
| T-25.....VII.2:8 | nothing is changeless but the Will of G., |
| T-25.....VII.3:2 | It must be so that either G. is mad, or is |
| T-25.....VII.3:7 | every Thought G. ever had is an illusion. |
| T-25...VII.3:12 | make. The rest is up to G., and not to you. |
| T-25.....VII.4:2 | For G. and His beloved Son do not think |
| T-25.....VII.5:2 | would lead the Son of G. to sanity and joy. |
| T-25.....VII.7:1 | the fact that G. is not insane appears most |
| T-25.....VII.7:4 | The Son of G. cannot be bound by time |
| T-25.....VII.7:4 | nor place nor anything G. did not will. |
| T-25.....VII.8:2 | Because He is not mad has G. appointed |
| T-25...VII.11:1 | the underlying tenet G. must be insane. |
| T-25...VII.11:3 | If this were true, then G. is mad indeed! |
| T-25...VII.11:7 | all. You who believe that G. is mad, look |
| T-25...VII.11:7 | it must be either G. or this must be insane |
| T-25...VII.13:1 | either G. or you must lose to madness |
| T-25...VII.13:3 | can suffer for the Will of G. to be fulfilled. |
| T-25...VII.13:5 | alone, but for the Self that is the Son of G. |
| T-25... VIII.5:2 | G. knows not of this. But justice does He |
| T-25... VIII.6:3 | and perceive the "wrath" of G. in Him. |
| T-25... VIII.6:8 | the "threat" of what G. knows as justice to |
| T-25... VIII.9:9 | G. rejoices as His Son receives what loving |
| T-25. VIII.9:11 | of G. the power to forgive himself of sin. |
| T-25. VIII.10:3 | G. knows of no injustice. He would not |
| T-25. VIII.10:8 | Yet G. ensured that justice would be done |
| T-25. VIII.12:1 | the Son of G. could merit vengeance. You |
| T-25. VIII.14:1 | way, as G. appointed for His holy Son. |
| T-25. VIII.14:6 | what justice must accord the Son of G.. |
| T-25......IX.2:7 | For G. is fair. He does not fight against |
| T-25......IX.3:7 | is justice not accorded to the Son of G.. |
| T-25......IX.5:6 | G. knows it and as knowledge is reflected |
| T-26.........I.4:6 | The memory of G. must be denied if any |
| T-26.........I.7:2 | die because his sinlessness is known to G.; |
| T-26.........I.7:3 | to the death of G. and of His holy Son, |
| T-26.........I.7:3 | make of Them what G. willed not They be |
| T-26.........I.8:5 | the holy Son of G. from the imprisonment |
| T-26....... II.2:6 | If this were true, then G. would be unfair; |
| T-26....... II.3:5 | on what you see can limit G. in any way. |
| T-26....... II.4:3 | It does injustice to the Son of G., and |
| T-26....... II.4:6 | from which the Son of G. is suffering, but |
| T-26....... II.5:3 | Son of G. is guilty then is he condemned, |
| T-26....... II.5:3 | deserves no mercy from the G. of justice. |
| T-26....... II.5:4 | But ask not G. to punish him because *you* |
| T-26....... II.5:5 | him die. G. offers you the means to see his |
| T-26....... II.6:1 | G. is just, then can there be no problems |
| T-26....... II.7:7 | place the Love of G. can be remembered, |
| T-26....... II.8:1 | G. cannot be remembered until justice is |
| T-26...... III.1:1 | Complexity is not of G.. How could it be, |
| T-26...... III.4:1 | the Son of G. believes can be destroyed. |
| T-26......IV.4:2 | Son of G. Himself comes to receive each |
| T-26......IV.6:3 | join the mighty chorus to the Love of G.! |
| T-26....... V.3:1 | G. gave His Teacher to replace the one |
| T-26....... V.3:7 | G. gave answer to is answered and is gone |
| T-26....... V.5:2 | of the Son of G. can hardly still be there, |
| T-26....... V.8:4 | to disappear and G. was feared and made |
| T-26....... V.9:2 | Can sin withstand the Will of G.? Can it |
| T-26..... V.10:1 | Would G. allow His Son to lose his way |
| T-26..... V.11:1 | whom G. created is as free as God created |
| T-26..... V.11:1 | whom God created is as free as G. created |
| T-26..... V.11:3 | error in the past that G. remembers not, |
| T-26..... V.12:4 | the time it took for G. to give His Answer |
| T-26..... V.14:4 | There is no hindrance to the Will of G., |
| T-26...... VI.2:3 | Yet G. has given him a better Friend, in |
| T-26...... VI.2:8 | What G. appointed has no substitute, for |
| T-26...... VI.3:1 | loneliness is not the Will of G.. Would |
| T-26...... VI.3:2 | throne that G. appointed for your Friend, |
| T-26...... VI.3:3 | take the place of Him Whom G. has called |
| T-26..... VII.3:3 | The Son of G. perceived what he would |
| T-26..... VII.4:2 | G. given answer to the world of sickness, |
| T-26..... VII.4:4 | Yet because it is of G., the laws of time do |
| T-26..... VII.6:9 | ease to what G. gave as answer to them all |
| T-26..... VII.7:4 | powers, until G. becomes impatient, |
| T-26... VII.10:6 | the Son of G. perceives his wishes and the |
| T-26... VII.10:6 | his wishes and the Will of G. are one. |
| T-26... VII.11:1 | What is the Will of G.? He wills His Son |
| T-26... VII.11:5 | became your function, sharing it with G.. |
| T-26... VII.11:7 | Here does the Son of G. ask not too much, |
| T-26... VII.13:2 | G. wills you learn what always has been |
| T-26... VII.13:6 | possible in trying to deceive the Son of G.. |
| T-26... VII.15:3 | G. gave to all illusions that were made |
| T-26... VII.15:4 | lies, for G. gave answer to them all as one. |
| T-26... VII.15:7 | What G. calls One will be forever One, |
| T-26... VII.16:3 | Heaven is shining on the Son of G.. Deny |
| T-26... VII.16:5 | Each instant is the Son of G. reborn until |
| T-26... VII.17:4 | has been given to save the Son of G. from |
| T-26... VII.17:5 | power to save the Son of G. because his |
| T-26... VII.18:1 | To use the power G. has given you as He |
| T-26... VII.18:4 | The gift of G. to you is limitless. There is |
| T-26... VII.19:1 | in peace, where G. would have you be. |
| T-26... VII.19:5 | is no difference among the Sons of G.. |
| T-26... VII.20:2 | your brother's name and G. will answer, |
| T-26... VII.20:5 | itself, the Son of G. allowed to be himself, |
| T-26... VII.20:5 | freed to call upon the Name of G. as One. |
| T-26... VIII.6:6 | brings good that comes from G.. And yet |
| T-26...... IX.1:1 | for G. calls lovingly unto your brother, |
| T-26...... IX.1:3 | you wish he be condemned, G. is in him. |
| T-26...... IX.2:2 | the face of Christ and memory of G.. And |
| T-26...... IX.8:1 | Now is the temple of the living G. rebuilt |
| T-26...... IX.8:6 | In gentle gratitude do G. the Father and |
| T-26....... X.2:8 | G. limits not. And what is limited cannot |
| T-26....... X.3:5 | yourself, in deep injustice to the Son of G. |
| T-26....... X.4:5 | own attack upon the Son of G. you seek? |
| T-27...... III.4:3 | For what you leave as vacant G. will fill, |
| T-27...... III.6:7 | is G. left free to take the final step Himself |
| T-27...... IV.1:7 | Yet if G. gave an answer there must be a |
| T-27...... IV.2:3 | G. must have given you a way of reaching |
| T-27...... V.11:9 | G. thanks you for your healing, for He |
| T-27...... VI.3:9 | call him by the holy Name of G. Himself. |
| T-27...... VI.4:5 | Nor could it tell a part of G. Himself what |
| T-27.... VI.6:11 | G. Himself has guaranteed the strength of |
| T-27... VII.10:2 | the body with the Self which G. created. |
| T-27... VII.10:6 | and you will find you have the peace of G.. |
| T-27... VII.13:5 | G. willed he waken gently and with joy, |
| T-27... VIII.6:2 | the Son of G. remembered not to laugh. |
| T-27... VIII.7:1 | real; a part of G. that can attack itself; a |
| T-27... VIII.9:7 | Him say, "My brother, holy Son of G., |
| T-28.........I.2:7 | the place of what G. gave in your creation. |
| T-28.........I.4:1 | use of memory, for G. Himself is there. |
| T-28........I.10:4 | would witness to is but the fear of G.. He |
| T-28........I.11:4 | when the memory of G. returns to them. |
| T-28........I.12:2 | to offer all its treasures to the Son of G., |
| T-28........I.12:6 | instant does the Son of G. do nothing that |
| T-28........I.13:1 | How instantly the memory of G. arises in |
| T-28........I.13:6 | the Son of G. remembers from before his |
| T-28........I.14:1 | Now is the Son of G. at last aware of |
| T-28........I.15:2 | of G. has come to take the place of loss? |
| T-28........I.15:3 | allow the memory of G. to flow across it, |
| T-28........I.15:4 | For G. has closed it with Himself. His |
| T-28....... II.1:5 | be a father, who creates as G. created him. |
| T-28....... II.3:1 | of G. attempt to make himself his cause, |
| T-28...... III.3:5 | lest G. should come to bridge the little |
| T-28...... III.6:1 | G. builds the bridge, but only in the |
| T-28...... III.7:5 | a picture of the Son of G. in broken pieces |
| T-28...... IV.8:1 | of G. and put the pieces into place again. |
| T-28...... IV.9:7 | of G. is just the same as every other part. |
| T-28.... IV.10:4 | What G. has given cannot be a loss, and |
| T-28....... V.1:6 | G. is the Alternate to dreams of fear. Who |
| T-28..... V.1:11 | exist because G. shared His Will with you, |
| T-28....... V.5:1 | What is there G. created to be sick? And |
| T-28...... VI.6:2 | it is the one that he has made to G., as |
| T-28...... VI.6:2 | has made to God, as G. has made to him. |
| T-28...... VI.6:3 | G. keeps His promises; His Son keeps his. |
| T-28...... VI.6:7 | Yet G. reminds him of it every time he |
| T-28...... VI.6:8 | vows are powerless before the Will of G., |
| T-28...... VI.6:9 | who has made promise of himself to G.. |
| T-28..... VII.1:1 | G. asks for nothing, and His Son, like |
| T-28..... VII.1:5 | A space where G. is not, a gap between |
| T-28..... VII.2:1 | of you because it is a part of G. Himself. |
| T-28..... VII.3:6 | help you reach the home where G. abides. |
| T-29.........I.1:1 | time, no place, no state where G. is absent |
| T-29.........I.2:1 | Here is the fear of G. most plainly seen. |
| T-29.........I.2:3 | love, and therefore must he be afraid of G. |
| T-29.........I.3:1 | The fear of G.! The greatest obstacle that |
| T-29.........I.8:7 | around the happy message, "G. is Love." |
| T-29.........I.9:3 | Without the fear of G., what could induce |
| T-29.........I.9:5 | afraid to find a loss of self in finding G.? |
| T-29........II.1:4 | loss, to find yourself in Heaven and in G.? |
| T-29........II.6:1 | Such is the promise of the living G.; His |
| T-29........II.8:4 | it asks that G. be less than all He really is. |
| T-29.....II.10:5 | He lives in G., and it is this that makes |
| T-29...... III.1:9 | Only those who think that G. is lessened |
| T-29...... III.3:1 | created in the dark, where G. still shines. |
| T-29...... III.3:6 | light where G. abides within the darkness, |
| T-29...... III.3:6 | see that G. Himself is where his body is. |
| T-29...... III.5:1 | Son of G. can be your savior in the midst |
| T-29....... V.1:3 | up to gladden G. the Father and the Son. |
| T-29....... V.2:4 | intrude upon the sacred Son of G. within. |
| T-29....... V.3:1 | gives to you who wait upon the Son of G., |
| T-29....... V.4:1 | This sacred Son of G. is like yourself; the |
| T-29....... V.6:2 | cost of holding anything G. did not give in |
| T-29....... V.6:4 | If G. esteems him worthy of Himself, |
| T-29...... VI.2:1 | Swear not to die, you holy Son of G.! You |
| T-29...... VI.4:1 | Change is the greatest gift G. gave to all |
| T-29...... VI.4:3 | your function has been fixed by G.. All |
| T-29...... VI.4:7 | the function G. established for His Son in |
| T-29..... VII.1:4 | that you worship when G. calls will never |
| T-29..... VII.6:3 | G. dwells within, and your completion |
| T-29..... VII.9:5 | Your holy mind is altar unto G., and |
| T-29..... VII.9:6 | fear of G. is but the fear of loss of idols. It |
| T-29... VII.10:4 | An idol cannot take the place of G.. Let |
| T-29.... VIII.4:3 | within your mind where G. abideth not. |
| T-29.... VIII.6:5 | the changeless change; the peace of G., |
| T-29.... VIII.6:6 | And the Son of G., as perfect, sinless and |
| T-29.... VIII.7:5 | beyond where G. has set all things forever |
| T-29.... VIII.7:6 | be, while G. is everything and everywhere. |
| T-29.... VIII.9:1 | G. has not many Sons, but only One. |
| T-29.... VIII.9:3 | In Heaven would the Son of G. but laugh, |
| T-29.... VIII.9:6 | to give you more than G. bestowed upon |
| T-29.... VIII.9:7 | G. gave you all there is. And to be sure |
| T-29..VIII.9:10 | No idol can establish you as more than G. |
| T-29...... IX.1:3 | holy Son of G. that this could be his wish; |
| T-29...... IX.2:1 | mind that G. created perfect as Himself. |
| T-29...... IX.2:2 | to hell, and G. made enemy unto His Son. |
| T-29...... IX.3:6 | G. knows of justice, not of penalty. But in |
| T-29...... IX.8:5 | abides forever deep within the Son of G.. |
| T-30.......I.14:8 | For they are made with idols or with G.. |
| T-30.......I.16:4 | a dream of judgment or the Voice for G.. |
| T-30........II.1:5 | G. *asks* you do your will. He joins with *you.* |
| T-30......II.1:10 | not one Thought that G. has ever had but |
| T-30......II.1:11 | G. is no enemy to you. He asks no more |
| T-30........II.2:5 | And would G. leave His Son without what |
| T-30........II.2:6 | G. but ensured that you would never lose |
| T-30........II.2:8 | G. would not have His Son made prisoner |
| T-30........II.3:3 | Now hear G. speak to you, through Him |
| T-30........II.3:5 | in you has joined with G. Himself in all |
| T-30........II.4:2 | then G. Himself could not be free. For |
| T-30........II.4:3 | whom G. so loves is done to God Himself. |
| T-30........II.4:3 | whom God so loves is done to G. Himself. |
| T-30........II.5:1 | G. turns to you to ask the world be saved, |
| T-30........II.5:4 | And now is G. forgiven, for you chose to |
| T-30...... III.2:2 | What form can be a substitute for G. the |
| T-30...... III.2:3 | of all the love in the Divinity of G. the Son |

T-30...... III.4:5 G. knows not form. He cannot answer
T-30...... III.4:9 thing the power to complete the Son of G.
T-30...... III.4:10 to give the Son of G. what he already has?
T-30...... III.5:5 in him, he would not be as G. created him
T-30...... III.5:11 completely lovely Thought G. holds of
T-30...... III.6:1 Nothing that G. knows not exists. And
T-30...... III.6:4 And in the Mind of G. there is no ending,
T-30...... III.7:6 The Thought G. holds of you is perfectly
T-30...... III.8:1 Thoughts of G. are far beyond all change,
T-30...... III.8:4 The Thought G. holds of you is like a star,
T-30.... III.10:1 all idols is the Thought G. holds of you.
T-30.... III.10:2 Thought G. holds of you remains exactly
T-30.... III.10:4 worships idols, and that knows not G.. In
T-30.... III.10:5 the Thought G. holds of you has never left
T-30.... III.11:1 Thought G. holds of you exist but where
T-30.... III.11:7 idol *or* the Thought G. holds of you is your
T-30.... III.11:8 what you are, not from the Mind of G.,
T-30.. III.11:10 But you, the holy Son of G. Himself, are
T-30...... IV.4:1 Reality observes the laws of G., and not
T-30...... IV.6:5 thus the Son of G. declares that he is free
T-30...... IV.7:5 strength of idle wishes for the Will of G..
T-30.... IV.8:10 the Son of G. can have no need of them.
T-30....... V.4:1 because it is but G. Who could create a
T-30....... V.4:5 to remember that the Son of G. knows
T-30....... V.6:3 Yet G. need not create His Son again, that
T-30....... V.6:5 Son of G. knew in creation he must know
T-30....... V.7:6 beyond forgiveness to the Love of G.. Yet
T-30..... V.11:1 The Will of G. forever lies in those whose
T-30..... V.11:4 Will of G. must reach to their awareness.
T-30...... VI.4:2 alive. And recognizing G. is just, it seems
T-30...... VI.4:3 Thus is the fear of G. the sure result of
T-30...... VI.4:4 himself as guilty can avoid the fear of G..
T-30...... VI.4:8 Nor will you think that G. intends for you
T-30...... VI.5:7 could replace it and destroy the Will of G.
T-30...... VI.9:5 of evil that can overcome the Will of G.;
T-30.... VI.10:3 idol of the Son of G. you will not pardon.
T-30..... VII.1:1 Would G. have left the meaning of the
T-30.... VIII.3:7 you, but not of G. Who knows no limits.
T-31......... I.4:5 powerful enough to render G. forgotten,
T-31......... I.4:5 home where G. Himself established him.
T-31......... I.4:6 taught yourself the Son of G. is guilty, say
T-31......... I.5:2 It was not made to do the Will of G., but
T-31......... I.5:6 call from G. and from your Self to you.
T-31......... I.6:2 G. willed not His Son forget Him. And the
T-31......... I.6:5 What outcome is inevitable, sure as G.,
T-31....... I.7:10 that reflects the Love of G. is stronger still
T-31......... I.9:3 The Christ in you remembers G. with all
T-31......... I.9:5 For G. were fear indeed if he whom He
T-31....... I.10:1 fear of G. results as surely from the lesson
T-31....... I.10:6 and you will know in Him that G. is Love.
T-31....... II.7:4 about this Son of G. who calls to you.
T-31....... II.7:6 when G. appointed Him His only Son.
T-31...... III.7:4 G. has said there *is* no sacrifice that can be
T-31.... IV.11:4 For G. is merciful, and did not let His Son
T-31....... V.2:3 take the place of your reality as Son of G..
T-31.... VI.3:11 the universe that G. created that must still
T-31...... VI.4:7 For G. Himself has said, "Your will be
T-31...... VI.5:1 the Son of G. as you would have him be,
T-31...... VI.7:1 Your will be done, you holy child of G.. It
T-31..... VII.3:5 see without the Aid that G. has given you.
T-31..... VII.5:7 changed to one that brings the peace of G.
T-31..... VII.9:1 of Christ, the fear of G. and of salvation,
T-31... VII.10:4 To everyone has G. entrusted all, because
T-31... VII.10:5 The holy ones whom G. has given you to
T-31... VII.10:6 For G. has given you His Son to save from
T-31... VII.11:1 could you be the savior of the Son of G.?
T-31... VII.15:5 Can you to whom G. says, "Release My
T-31.... VIII.1:2 persuade the holy Son of G. he is a body,
T-31.... VIII.3:4 from you whom G. created altar unto joy.
T-31.... VIII.3:7 is the Self that G. created as His only Son.
T-31.... VIII.4:1 what G. Himself would have you be. Be
T-31.... VIII.4:5 joined in all the power of the Will of G..
T-31.... VIII.5:2 *I am as G. created me. His Son can suffer*
T-31.... VIII.5:5 that comes from G. and that can never fail
T-31.... VIII.6:1 You *are* as G. created you, and so is every
T-31.... VIII.7:1 I lay before your feet the peace of G., and
T-31.... VIII.8:7 And G. ordained, in loving kindness, that
T-31.... VIII.9:5 G. has ordained I cannot call in vain, and
W-pI..... 12.5:7 your words is written the Word of G.. The
W-pI..... 13.2:2 represents a situation in which G. and the
W-pI..... 13.4:7 *because I think I am in competition with G..*
W-pI........ 14.h G. did not create a meaningless world.
W-pI..... 14.1:2 What G. did not create does not exist.
W-pI..... 14.3:1 and see the Word of G. in their place. The
W-pI..... 14.4:3 G. did not create it, and so it is not real.
W-pI..... 14.4:5 *G. did not create that war, and so it is not real*
W-pI..... 14.4:6 *G. did not create that airplane crash, and so*
W-pI..... 14.4:7 *G. did not create that disaster [specify], and*
W-pI..... 14.5:4 do not say, "G. did not create illness," but
W-pI..... 14.5:4 illness," but, "G. did not create cancer,"
W-pI..... 14.6:5 G. did not create can only be in your own
W-pI..... 14.6:8 idea: *G. did not create a meaningless world.*
W-pI..... 14.7:4 *G. did not create a meaningless world. He*
W-pI..... 19.2:5 be possible because it is the Will of G..
W-pI..... 20.3:6 G. has one Son, and he is the resurrection
W-pI........ 29.h G. is in everything I see.
W-pI..... 29.2:3 Certainly G. is not in a table, for example,
W-pI..... 29.5:3 *G. is in this coat hanger. God is in this*
W-pI..... 29.5:4 *G. is in this magazine. God is in this finger.*
W-pI..... 29.5:5 *G. is in this finger. God is in this lamp.*
W-pI..... 29.5:6 *G. is in this lamp. God is in that body. God*
W-pI..... 29.5:7 *G. is in that body. God is in that door. God*
W-pI..... 29.5:8 *G. is in that door. God is in that waste basket*
W-pI..... 29.5:9 *G. is in that waste basket.* In addition to the
W-pI........ 30.h G. is in everything I see because God is in
W-pI........ 30.h everything I see because G. is in my mind.
W-pI..... 37.1:6 because it is his birthright as a Son of G..
W-pI..... 38.1:3 because it establishes you as a Son of G.,
W-pI..... 38.2:1 holiness the power of G. is made manifest
W-pI..... 38.2:2 holiness the power of G. is made available
W-pI..... 38.2:3 is nothing the power of G. cannot do.
W-pI..... 38.3:1 you are holy, so is everything G. created.
W-pI..... 38.5:3 *cannot do because the power of G. lies in it.*
W-pI..... 39.4:5 G. does not know unholiness. Can it be
W-pI........ 40.h I am blessed as a Son of G..
W-pI..... 40.3:2 you associate with being a Son of G.,
W-pI..... 40.3:4 *I am blessed as a Son of G.. I am happy,*
W-pI..... 40.3:7 *I am blessed as a Son of G.. I am calm, quiet,*
W-pI..... 40.3:9 that you are blessed as a Son of G. will do.
W-pI........ 41.h G. goes with me wherever I go.
W-pI..... 41.4:4 because G. goes with you wherever you go
W-pI..... 41.8:1 It is quite possible to reach G.. In fact it is
W-pI... 41.10:1 that G. goes with you wherever you go.
W-pI........ 42.h G. is my strength. Vision is His gift.
W-pI..... 42.1:3 You will see because it is the Will of G.. It
W-pI..... 42.2:1 G. is indeed your strength, and what He
W-pI..... 42.2:5 Such is the strength of G.. Such are His
W-pI..... 42.4:6 *G. gives truly,* or: *God's gifts to me must be*
W-pI........ 43.h G. is my Source. I cannot see apart from
W-pI..... 43.1:1 Perception is not an attribute of G.. His is
W-pI..... 43.1:4 Without this link with G., perception
W-pI..... 43.1:5 With this link with G., perception will
W-pI..... 43.2:1 In G. you cannot see. Perception has no
W-pI..... 43.2:2 see. Perception has no function in G., and
W-pI..... 43.2:4 by the Son of G. for an unholy purpose, it
W-pI..... 43.2:7 which the Son of G. forgives his brother,
W-pI..... 43.3:1 see apart from G. because you cannot be
W-pI..... 43.3:1 God because you cannot be apart from G.
W-pI..... 43.3:3 then you cannot see apart from G..
W-pI..... 43.4:7 *G. is my Source. I cannot see this desk apart*
W-pI..... 43.4:9 *G. is my Source. I cannot see that picture*
W-pI..... 43.7:3 *G. is my Source. I cannot see you apart from*
W-pI..... 43.8:3 *G. is my Source. I cannot see this apart from*
W-pI........ 44.h G. is the light in which I see.
W-pI..... 44.6:3 G. is the light in which you see. You are
W-pI........ 45.h G. is the Mind with which I think.
W-pI..... 45.2:1 You think with the Mind of G.. Therefore
W-pI..... 45.2:5 you think with the Mind of G. leave your
W-pI..... 45.2:6 your thoughts are in the Mind of G., as
W-pI..... 45.3:5 is thought by the Mind of G. is eternal,
W-pI..... 45.4:5 what G. would have us do is impossible.
W-pI..... 45.4:6 only what G. would have us do is possible.
W-pI..... 45.5:1 only what G. would have us do is what we
W-pI..... 45.5:4 we will succeed today. It is the Will of G..
W-pI..... 45.7:1 that you thought with G. in the beginning
W-pI..... 45.8:2 is your mind joined with the Mind of G..
W-pI..... 45.8:4 to G. the Father and to God the Son. For
W-pI..... 45.8:4 to God the Father and to G. the Son. For
W-pI .... 45.9:1 holiness of the mind that thinks with G..
W-pI ....... 46.h G. is the Love in which I forgive.
W-pI .... 46.1:1 G. does not forgive because He has never
W-pI .... 46.2:1 Yet although G. does not forgive, His
W-pI .... 46.2:3 returning the mind to the awareness of G.
W-pI .... 46.4:4 *G. is the Love in which I forgive you, [name].*
W-pI .... 46.5:3 *G. is the Love in which I forgive myself.* Then
W-pI .... 46.5:5 *G. is the Love with which I love myself. God*
W-pI .... 46.5:6 *myself. G. is the Love in which I am blessed.*
W-pI .... 46.6:3 *I cannot be guilty because I am a Son of G.. I*
W-pI .... 46.6:5 *No fear is possible in a mind beloved of G..*
W-pI .... 46.7:5 silently: *G. is the Love in which I forgive you.*
W-pI ....... 47.h G. is the strength in which I trust.
W-pI .... 47.3:1 G. is your safety in every circumstance.
W-pI .... 47.3:3 exceptions because G. has no exceptions.
W-pI .... 47.4:5 yourself: *G. is the strength in which I trust.*
W-pI .... 47.5:4 of G. in you is successful in all things.
W-pI .... 47.7:6 in you where the strength of G. abides.
W-pI .... 47.8:3 are giving your trust to the strength of G..
W-pI .... 48.3:2 recognize as yet, you have remembered G.
W-pI .... 49.1:2 is in constant communication with G.,
W-pI .... 49.2:1 that is listening to the Voice for G. is calm
W-pI .... 49.3:3 we are joining our will with the Will of G..
W-pI .... 49.4:3 and obscure your eternal link with G..
W-pI .... 49.4:8 truly welcome. We are trying to reach G..
W-pI ....... 50.h I am sustained by the Love of G..
W-pI .... 50.1:2 you are sustained by everything but G..
W-pI .... 50.2:1 are your replacements for the Love of G..
W-pI .... 50.3:1 of G. will protect you in all circumstances.
W-pI .... 50.3:3 upon the eternal calm of the Son of G..
W-pI .... 50.4:3 all your faith in the Love of G. within you;
W-pI .... 50.4:5 Through the Love of G. within you, you
W-pI .... 50.5:3 to disturb the holy mind of the Son of G..
W-pI .... 51.4:2 because I am trying to think without G..
W-pI .... 51.4:4 thoughts are the thoughts I think with G..
W-pI .... 51.4:8 lies in the thoughts I think with G..
W-pI .... 52.3:5 that I am trying to use time against G.. Let
W-pI .... 53.4:1 (14) G. did not create a meaningless
W-pI .... 53.4:2 world exist if G. did not create it? He is
W-pI .... 54.4:4 of G. cannot think or speak or act in vain.
W-pI .... 54.4:6 with mine, for mine is the power of G..
W-pI .... 54.5:5 me that my will and the Will of G. are one
W-pI .... 55.1:3 be what G. created for His beloved Son.
W-pI .... 55.1:4 is proof that I do not understand G..
W-pI .... 55.2:4 of the Love of G. and the Love of His Son.
W-pI .... 55.2:6 give me the peace G. intended me to have.
W-pI .... 55.4:4 I am willing to follow the Guide G. has
W-pI .... 56.1:7 G. has kept my inheritance safe for me.
W-pI .... 56.3:4 it to the world that reflects the Love of G..
W-pI .... 56.4:1 (29) G. is in everything I see. Behind
W-pI .... 56.4:5 G. is still everywhere and in everything
W-pI .... 56.5:1 (30) G. is in everything I see because God
W-pI .... 56.5:1 everything I see because G. is in my mind.
W-pI .... 56.5:4 It has been kept for me in the Mind of G.,
W-pI .... 57.2:4 it is possible to imprison the Son of G.. I
W-pI .... 57.2:6 The Son of G. must be forever free. He is
W-pI .... 57.2:7 He is as G. created him, and not what I
W-pI .... 57.2:8 He is where G. would have him be, and
W-pI .... 57.3:6 see it as a place where the Son of G. finds
W-pI .... 57.4:2 that it reflects the laws of G. instead of the
W-pI .... 58.3:6 holiness, which I share with G. Himself,
W-pI .... 58.4:5 is the gift of G. to me and to the world.
W-pI .... 58.5:1 (40) I am blessed as a Son of G.. Herein
W-pI .... 58.5:3 I am blessed as a Son of G.. All good
W-pI .... 58.5:4 mine, because G. intended them for me. I
W-pI .... 59.1:1 (41) G. goes with me wherever I go. How
W-pI .... 59.1:2 I be alone when G. always goes with me?
W-pI .... 59.1:7 because G. goes with me wherever I go.
W-pI .... 59.2:1 (42) G. is my strength. Vision is His gift.
W-pI .... 59.2:4 of seeing for the vision that is given by G..
W-pI .... 59.3:1 (43) G. is my Source. I cannot see apart
W-pI .... 59.3:3 Him. I can see what G. wants me to see. I
W-pI .... 59.4:1 (44) G. is the light in which I see. I cannot
W-pI .... 59.4:3 G. is the only light. Therefore, if I am to
W-pI .... 59.4:6 that G. is the light in which I see. Let me
W-pI .... 59.5:1 (45) G. is the Mind with which I think. I
W-pI .... 59.5:2 I have no thoughts I do not share with G..
W-pI .... 60.1:1 (46) G. is the Love in which I forgive. God
W-pI .... 60.1:2 G. does not forgive because He has never

W-pI.....60.1:6 that the Love of G. can reach down to me
W-pI.....60.2:1 (47) G. is the strength in which I trust. It
W-pI.....60.2:3 It is through the strength of G. in me,
W-pI.....60.5:1 (50) I am sustained by the Love of G.. As
W-pI.....61.1:6 It refers to you as you were created by G..
W-pI.....61.2:4 world if that is the function G. assigned to
W-pI.....61.7:6 G. has built His plan for the salvation of
W-pI.....62.3:5 power G. gave His Son to your awareness.
W-pI.....62.4:2 as happy for you as G. wants you to be.
W-pI.....63.2:2 Son of G. looks to you for his redemption.
W-pI.....63.2:4 function and leave the Son of G. in hell.
W-pI.....63.3:5 *I am the means G. has appointed for the*
W-pI.....64.1:3 temptation to abandon G. and His Son by
W-pI.....64.3:1 of the world, a function given you by G..
W-pI.....64.3:2 of the task assigned to you by G. Himself.
W-pI.....64.3:3 the Son of G. escape from all illusions,
W-pI.....64.3:4 from all temptation. The Son of G. is you.
W-pI.....64.4:1 given you by G. will you be happy. That is
W-pI........65.h My only function is the one G. gave me.
W-pI.....65.2:2 "My only function is the one G. gave me."
W-pI.....65.4:3 so that you have set apart the time for G.,
W-pI.....65.8:2 *My only function is the one G. gave me. I*
W-pI.....66.4:1 function G. gave you and your happiness,
W-pI.....66.4:2 G. gives you only happiness. Therefore,
W-pI.....66.5:2 *G. gives me only happiness. He has given my*
W-pI.....66.6:1 is that G. gives you only happiness. This
W-pI.....66.6:2 to define G. as something He is not. Love
W-pI.....66.6:4 G. cannot give what He does not have,
W-pI.....66.6:5 Unless G. gives you only happiness, He
W-pI.....66.7:1 is that G. has given you your function. We
W-pI.....66.8:1 is established by G. through His Voice, or
W-pI.....66.8:3 Unless G. gave your function to you, it
W-pI...66.10:4 For G. Himself shares it with us. Today's
W-pI...66.11:2 *are one, because G. has given me both.* It will
W-pI.....67.1:3 is why G. appointed you as the world's
W-pI.....67.1:4 Son of G. looks to you for his salvation.
W-pI.....67.2:7 which is in accord with G. as He defines
W-pI.....67.2:8 of G. and replace it with His Own. We are
W-pI.....67.6:2 This is the Voice for G., reminding you of
W-pI.....67.6:3 with the simple truth about the Son of G..
W-pI.....68.2:5 Who can dream of hatred and not fear G.
W-pI.....68.3:1 will redefine G. in their own image, as it is
W-pI.....68.3:1 certain that G. created them like Himself,
W-pI.....69.7:2 G. Himself will raise you from darkness
W-pI.....69.8:5 what you undertake with G. must succeed
W-pI.....69.8:6 power of G. work in you and through you,
W-pI.....70.3:2 G. would not have put the remedy for the
W-pI.....70.5:2 G. wants us to be healed, and we do not
W-pI.....70.5:3 today, we are really in agreement with G..
W-pI.....71.5:2 are to succeed, as G. promises you will,
W-pI.....71.7:3 All things are possible to G.. Salvation
W-pI.....71.9:1 to asking G. to reveal His plan to us. Ask
W-pI.....72.1:2 G. is assigned the attributes which are
W-pI.....72.1:2 ego appears to take on the attributes of G.
W-pI.....72.2:1 ego's fundamental wish is to replace G..
W-pI.....72.4:5 Herein is G. attacked, for if His Son is
W-pI.....72.5:1 If G. is a body, what must His plan for
W-pI.....72.5:4 makes this view of G. quite convincing. In
W-pI.....72.5:9 be death, projecting this attack onto G.,
W-pI.....72.6:2 G. made you a body. Very well. Let us
W-pI.....72.6:7 G. gave you nothing. The body is your
W-pI.....72.6:9 It is the death of G. and your salvation.
W-pI.....72.9:1 of truth is in us, where it was placed by G.
W-pI.....73.1:1 are considering the will you share with G..
W-pI.....73.1:3 will you share with G. has all the power of
W-pI.....73.3:2 Will the Son of G. shares with his Father?
W-pI.....73.3:3 G. create disaster for His Son? Creation is
W-pI.....73.3:5 Would G. create a world that kills Himself
W-pI.....73.4:2 because it does not oppose the Will of G..
W-pI.....73.9:4 of G. from hell and from all idle wishes.
W-pI...73.10:4 the power of G. and united with your Self.
W-pI.....74.1:6 As an expression of the Will of G., you
W-pI.....74.3:9 *one. G. wills peace for His Son.* During this
W-pI.....75.9:3 Give thanks for mercy and the Love of G..
W-pI...75.11:1 serenity in which G. would have you be.
W-pI.....76.6:1 There are no laws except the laws of G..
W-pI.....76.7:1 The laws of G. can never be replaced. We
W-pI.....76.7:5 imprisons, but the laws of G. make free.
W-pI.....76.9:3 says there is no loss under the laws of G..
W-pI...76.12:3 our acknowledgment that G. is our Father
W-pI.....77.1:2 will receive miracles because of what G. is.
W-pI.....77.1:3 offer miracles because you are one with G.
W-pI.....77.2:4 It is implicit in what G. your Father is. It
W-pI.....77.2:5 creation, and guaranteed by the laws of G.
W-pI.....77.3:3 that the Kingdom of G. is within you, and
W-pI.....77.4:5 They merely follow from the laws of G..
W-pI.....77.5:5 are but asking that the Will of G. be done.
W-pI.....77.8:5 *me. G. has established miracles as my right.*
W-pI.....78.2:3 our eyes in silence to behold the Son of G.
W-pI.....78.3:2 it lifts you see the Son of G. where he has
W-pI.....78.5:6 Such is his role in G. your Father's plan.
W-pI.....78.7:1 this Son of G. in his reality and truth, that
W-pI.....78.7:2 in the holy Name of G. and of His Son, as
W-pI.....78.8:8 role G. gave Him that you might be saved.
W-pI.....78.9:1 G. thanks you for these quiet times today
W-pI.....78.9:2 one Thought of G. but must rejoice as you
W-pI.....82.3:4 will not experience the joy that G. intends
W-pI.....83.1:1 My only function is the one G. gave me. I
W-pI.....83.1:2 I have no function but the one G. gave me
W-pI.....83.1:5 my only function is the one G. gave me.
W-pI.....83.2:3 *me a function other than the one G. gave me.*
W-pI.....83.2:4 *this to justify a function G. did not give me.*
W-pI.....83.3:2 one. All things that come from G. are one.
W-pI.....87.4:2 *this in accordance with the Will of G.. It is*
W-pI.....88.4:3 *I see only the laws of G. at work in this. Let me*
W-pI.....89.1:5 what the laws of G. entitle me to have,
W-pI.....89.3:6 and only Heaven, as G. wills me to have.
W-pI.....90.3:5 yet realize that G. has placed the answer
W-pI...91.10:1 by the strength of G. and all His Thoughts
W-pI.....92.4:7 darkness rule where G. appointed that
W-pI.....92.9:3 in, for the peace of G. is where your Self,
W-pI.....93.4:2 yourself cannot withstand the Will of G..
W-pI.....93.5:1 The self you made is not the Son of G..
W-pI.....93.5:6 It does not battle with the Son of G.. It
W-pI.....93.5:9 when it would contradict the Will of G.?
W-pI.....93.6:1 Your sinlessness is guaranteed by G..
W-pI.....93.6:4 Your sinlessness is guaranteed by G..
W-pI.....93.6:5 it, or change what G. created as eternal.
W-pI.....93.6:7 Your sinlessness is guaranteed by G., and
W-pI.....93.7:1 one thought;–you are as G. created you,
W-pI.....93.7:2 think you did, you are as G. created you.
W-pI.....93.7:5 Your sinlessness is guaranteed by G.. You
W-pI.....93.7:7 abide in you because G. put them there.
W-pI.....93.8:3 *My sinlessness is guaranteed by G..* Then
W-pI.....93.8:4 to experience what G. has given you, in
W-pI.....93.9:1 are what G. created or what you made.
W-pI.....93.9:5 with the Self which G. created as you, by
W-pI...93.10:5 *My sinlessness is guaranteed by G..* Then try
W-pI...93.11:4 *Your sinlessness is guaranteed by G..* You
W-pI...93.11:6 in salvation that G. has assigned to you.
W-pI........94.h I am as G. created me.
W-pI.....94.1:2 You are as G. created you. The sounds of
W-pI.....94.2:2 If you remain as G. created you, you must
W-pI.....94.2:4 well. You are as G. created you. Darkness
W-pI.....94.3:3 *I am as G. created me. I am His Son eternally.*
W-pI.....94.3:5 Now try to reach the Son of G. in you.
W-pI.....94.3:7 home in G. to walk the world uncertainly.
W-pI.....94.4:2 G. has Himself promised that it will be
W-pI.....94.5:2 *I am as G. created me. I am His Son eternally.*
W-pI.....94.5:4 today that you are as G. created you. And
W-pI.....94.5:6 *You are as G. created you. You are His Son*
W-pI.....95.1:1 accurately describes you as G. created you
W-pI.....95.2:2 many warring parts, separate from G.,
W-pI.....95.2:5 does not understand you are the Son of G.
W-pI...95.12:2 may extend the allness and the unity of G.
W-pI...95.13:2 are one Self, the holy Son of G., united
W-pI...95.13:4 This is your Self, the Son of G. Himself,
W-pI.....96.7:1 within your mind and in the Mind of G..
W-pI.....96.7:3 Salvation is a thought you share with G.,
W-pI.....97.2:1 Self, the holy Son of G. Who rests in you,
W-pI.....97.7:2 *Spirit am I, a holy Son of G., free of all limits,*
W-pI.....97.8:2 that you are spirit, one with Him and G.,
W-pI.....98.1:5 today, and to salvation as G. planned it be
W-pI.....98.1:8 is, and take the part assigned to us by G..
W-pI.....98.5:1 the happiness that G. has given you? Is it
W-pI.....99.1:2 apart or different from the Will of G..
W-pI.....99.3:4 thinks these thoughts is separate from G..
W-pI.....99.4:3 but a Thought of G. could be this plan, by
W-pI.....99.5:1 Holy Spirit holds this plan of G. exactly as
W-pI.....99.5:1 within the Mind of G. and in your own. It
W-pI.....99.5:5 one thing must still be true; G. is still Love
W-pI.....99.6:8 *here. G. still is Love, and this is not His Will.*
W-pI.....99.8:1 This part belongs to G., as does the rest.
W-pI...99.10:4 You have no function that is not of G..
W-pI...99.11:4 *here. G. still is Love, and this is not His Will.*
W-pI...99.12:5 and show you that you are the Son of G..
W-pI...100.2:6 and hear G. calling to them in your happy
W-pI...100.3:4 the light that G. Himself appointed as the
W-pI...100.4:4 They are the proof that G. wills perfect
W-pI...100.5:3 of what has been assigned to you by G..
W-pI...100.6:3 G. asks you to be happy, so the world can
W-pI...100.9:5 when He Who calls to you is G. Himself?
W-pI...101.2:5 that evens the account they owe to G..
W-pI...101.4:5 curse of G. upon you who have crucified
W-pI...101.6:3 Fear not the Will of G.. But turn to it in
W-pI...102.2:6 you free today to join the happy Will of G.
W-pI......103.h G., being Love, is also happiness.
W-pI...103.2:2 in truth, bear witness to the fear of G.,
W-pI...103.2:4 *G., being Love, is also happiness. To fear*
W-pI...103.2:6 corrects the false belief that G. is fear. It
W-pI...103.3:3 pain. G., being Love, it will be given you.
W-pI...103.3:5 *G., being Love, is also happiness. And it is*
W-pI...104.1:3 They come to you from G., Who cannot
W-pI...104.3:1 we but unite our will with what G. wills,
W-pI...104.4:1 we ask to recognize what G. has given us.
W-pI...105.6:2 are their right under the equal laws of G..
W-pI...105.7:4 gift of peace and joy that G. has given you.
W-pI...105.9:4 let yourself receive the gifts of G. as yours.
W-pI...106.4:7 for they come from G. to His dear Son,
W-pI...106.5:2 G. calls to them through you. He needs
W-pI.106.10:1 Today the holy Word of G. is kept
W-pI.106.10:4 *I am the messenger of G. today, My voice is*
W-pI......109.h I rest in G..
W-pI...109.2:1 "I rest in G.." This thought will bring to
W-pI...109.2:3 "I rest in G.." This thought has power to
W-pI...109.2:6 the thought in which the Son of G. is born
WpI...109.3:1 "I rest in G.." Completely undismayed,
W-pI...109.3:2 death, and onward to the certainty of G..
W-pI...109.3:5 truth before the eyes of you who rest in G.
W-pI...109.4:2 You rest in G., and while the world is torn
W-pI...109.4:5 and come to you because you rest in G..
W-pI...109.4:6 yours because you gave your voice to G.,
W-pI...109.5:7 dreams will come, now that you rest in G.
W-pI...109.6:2 to bring the peace of G. into the world,
W-pI...109.8:1 You rest within the peace of G. today,
W-pI...109.9:1 You rest within the peace of G. today,
W-pI...109.9:5 those passed by, to every Thought of G.,
WpI...109.9:6 each time we tell ourselves, "I rest in G.."
W-pI......110.h I am as G. created me.
W-pI...110.1:3 that what G. created was replaced by fear
W-pI...110.1:4 you remain as G. created you fear has no
W-pI...110.3:1 remain as G. created you, appearances
W-pI...110.3:2 occurred, if you remain as G. created you.
W-pI...110.4:2 If you are as G. created you, then there
W-pI...110.5:5 This is the truth that G. has promised you
W-pI...110.6:2 *I am as G. created me. His Son can suffer*
W-pI...110.7:1 the Self Who is the holy Son of G. Himself
W-pI...110.8:1 the Son of G. and brother to the world;
W-pI...110.9:1 You are as G. created you. Today honor
W-pI...110.9:3 to be the Son of G. instead of what he is
W-pI.110.10:4 hands and hearts and minds to G. today.
W-pI.110.11:4 us: *I am as G. created me.* Let us declare this
W-pI.110.11:6 This is the Word of G. that sets you free.
W-pI.110.11:7 enter in the peace of G. and His eternity.
WpIrIII.in11:6 Son, acceptable to G. and to your Self.
W-pI...111.2:2 *I see through strength, the gift of G. to me.*
W-pI...112.1:3 *welcome them into the home I share with G.,*
W-pI...112.2:1 (94) I am as G. created me. *I will remain*
W-pI...112.3:4 On the half hour: I am as G. created me.
W-pI...113.1:2 *whole, at one with all creation and with G..*
W-pI...114.1:2 *I am the Son of G.. No body can contain my*
W-pI...114.1:3 *impose on me a limitation G. created not.*
W-pI...114.2:2 *my function be but to accept the Word of G.,*
W-pI...115.2:2 *to the plan of G. for the salvation of the world*
W-pI...117.1:1 (103) G., being Love, is also happiness.
W-pI...117.3:2 G., being Love, is also happiness. On the
W-pI...119.1:3 *whose Self rests safely in the Mind of G..*

W-pI...120.1:1 (109) I rest in G.. *I rest in God today, and*
W-pI...120.1:2 *I rest in G. today, and let Him work in me and*
W-pI...120.2:1 (110) I am as G. created me. *I am God's*
W-pI...120.3:2 I rest in G.. On the half hour: I am as God
W-pI...120.3:4 On the half hour: I am as G. created me.
W-pI.121.13:7 *of sin, and know I am the perfect Son of G..*
W-pI...122.3:2 It lets you recognize the Son of G., and
W-pI...122.6:5 but this for the salvation of the Son of G..
W-pI...122.7:4 It is the gift of G., and not the world. The
W-pI...122.7:5 has received what G. has given as its own.
W-pI...122.7:6 G. wills salvation be received today, and
W-pI.122.14:5 *as true. Today I have received the gifts of G..*
W-pI...123.3:5 the one whom G. established as His Son.
W-pI...123.4:2 in honor of the Self that G. has willed to
W-pI...123.5:2 come to speak the saving Word of G. to us
W-pI...123.6:2 Receive the thanks of G. today, as you
W-pI......124.h Let me remember I am one with G..
W-pI...124.1:1 again give thanks for our Identity in G..
W-pI...124.1:5 At one with G. and with the universe we
W-pI...124.1:5 that G. Himself goes everywhere with us.
W-pI...124.2:2 the mind at one with G. and with itself.
W-pI...124.2:4 for G. is our Companion as we walk the
W-pI...124.3:2 And G., Who loves us with the equal love
W-pI...124.6:1 those who know that they are one with G.
W-pI...124.7:1 as we say that we are one with G.. For in
W-pI...124.8:3 to the thought that you are one with G..
W-pI.124.11:2 Count this half hour as your gift to G., in
W-pI.124.12:2 *Let me remember I am one with G., at one*
W-pI...125.2:2 this: The Son of G. is free to save himself,
W-pI...125.2:2 given the Word of G. to be his Guide,
W-pI...125.3:3 the world has laid upon the Son of G.. It
W-pI...125.3:5 but wait in silence for the Word of G..
W-pI...125.4:1 Hear, holy Son of G., your Father speak.
W-pI...125.4:3 We gather at the throne of G. today, the
W-pI...125.7:1 a gentle listening to the Word of G.. He
W-pI...125.8:4 let Him tell you G. has never left His Son,
W-pI...125.9:4 of G. the Son joins in his Father's Will, at
W-pI...125.9:5 day; in quiet to receive the Word of G..
W-pI...126.6:6 It is not what G. intended it to be for you.
W-pI...127.1:7 It is the Heart of G., and also of His Son.
W-pI...127.2:6 perceive the Son of G. in separate parts.
W-pI...127.4:2 is your own, and shared by G. Himself.
W-pI...127.7:2 be glad to give some time to G. today, and
W-pI...127.8:4 gifts, and let the gift of G. replace them all
W-pI.127.12:4 *I bless you, brother, with the Love of G.,*
W-pI...129.4:2 And G. Himself speaks to His Son, as His
W-pI...130.8:4 You wait for G. to help you, as you say: *It*
W-pI...130.8:6 *Let me accept the strength G. offers me and*
W-pI...130.9:1 G. will be there. For you have called upon
W-pI...131.5:6 certainly as G. created you in sinlessness.
W-pI...131.6:4 be, if it is where G. wills His Son to be.
W-pI...131.6:5 How could the Will of G. be in the past, or
W-pI...131.7:2 G. made no contradictions. What denies
W-pI...131.8:1 G. does not suffer conflict. Nor is His
W-pI...131.8:3 G. Himself established him in Heaven?
W-pI...131.9:2 Son of G. make time to take away the Will
W-pI...131.9:2 make time to take away the Will of G.? He
W-pI.131.14:4 Today G. keeps His ancient promise to
W-pI...132.9:2 You are as G. created you. There is no
W-pI...132.9:4 exist, if you remain as G. created you?
W-pI.132.11:1 if you are as G. created you, you cannot
W-pI.132.11:6 know the Thoughts you share with G..
W-pI.132.12:2 not of illusions, but as G. in truth. God
W-pI.132.12:3 G. shares His Fatherhood with you who
W-pI.132.13:1 because it is a thought apart from G., and
W-pI.132.13:1 and break away a part of G. Himself and
W-pI.132.15:2 *I who remain as G. created me would loose*
W-pI.134.10:1 and pain as G. Himself intended it to be,
W-pI...135.4:5 fail to serve the Son of G. as worthy host?
W-pI.135.25:5 the part for you within the plan of G..
W-pI.135.25:6 function from the Voice for G. Himself?
W-pI.135.26:8 *Son of G. needs no defense against the truth*
W-pI.136.10:2 with G. made blind by your illusions,
W-pI.136.11:1 G. knows not of your plans to change His
W-pI.136.12:5 what G. wills for you must be received.
W-pI.136.13:2 For time lets you think what G. has given
W-pI.136.13:3 Thoughts of G. are quite apart from time.
W-pI.137.11:3 What is opposed to G. does not exist, and
W-pI.137.13:1 for joy, and separation for the peace of G..
W-pI.137.15:2 and to receive the Word of G. to take the
W-pI...139.1:2 to accept ourselves as G. created us. And
W-pI...139.8:2 It is set forever in the holy Mind of G.,
W-pI.139.10:2 way rejoicing in the endless Love of G.. It
W-pI.139.11:3 *for myself, For I remain as G. created me.* We
W-pI.139.11:4 not lost the knowledge that G. gave to us
W-pI.139.12:2 would weave around the holy Son of G..
W-pI.139.12:4 *for myself, For I remain as G. created me.*
W-pI...140.5:1 be to you who have been cured in G., and
W-pI...140.5:3 G. abides in holy temples. He is barred
W-pI.140.10:2 as one, restoring saneness to the Son of G.
W-pI.140.10:4 returns to the eternal, quiet home of G..
WpI. rIV.in2:2 *My mind holds only what I think with G..*
WpI. rIV.in4:1 mind holds only what you think with G..
WpI. rIV.in5:3 *My mind holds only what I think with G..*
WpI. rIV.in5:4 day along the lines which G. appointed,
WpI. rIV.in7:4 shine with the meaning G. has given it, as
WpIrIV.in10:1 G. offers thanks to you who practice thus
W-pI......141.h My mind holds only what I think with G.
W-pI......142.h My mind holds only what I think with G..
W-pI...142.2:1 (124) Let me remember I am one with G..
W-pI......143.h My mind holds only what I think with G..
W-pI......144.h My mind holds only what I think with G..
W-pI......145.h My mind holds only what I think with G..
W-pI......146.h My mind holds only what I think with G..
W-pI......147.h My mind holds only what I think with G..
W-pI......148.h My mind holds only what I think with G..
W-pI......149.h My mind holds only what I think with G..
W-pI......150.h My mind holds only what I think with G..
W-pI......151.h All things are echoes of the Voice for G..
W-pI...151.3:7 to by the eternal Voice for G. Himself.
W-pI...151.7:1 and let the Voice for G. alone be Judge of
W-pI...151.7:4 He recognizes only what G. loves, and in
W-pI...151.8:3 The Voice for G. can only honor Him,
W-pI.151.10:3 can come to you who are beloved of G.,
W-pI.151.13:1 beginning of the time we spend with G..
W-pI.151.13:4 ideas that do not contradict the Will of G.
W-pI.151.14:1 and the happiness G. wills His Son, as
W-pI.151.15:3 teach the Son of G. the holy lesson of his
W-pI.151.15:4 the Voice for G. give honor to God's Son.
W-pI.151.17:3 truth has no illusions, and the peace of G.,
W-pI...152.5:1 As G. created you, you must remain
W-pI...152.6:2 G. made it not. Of this you can be sure.
W-pI...152.7:1 To think that G. made chaos, contradicts
W-pI...152.7:3 And can you see what G. created not? To
W-pI...152.7:4 you can perceive what G. willed not to be.
W-pI.152.10:2 are, and humbly recognize the Son of G..
W-pI.152.11:6 grateful to restore His home to G., as it
W-pI.152.12:3 peace of G. for all your frantic thoughts,
W-pI.152.12:3 the truth of G. for self-deceptions, and
W-pI...153.5:4 the holy peace of G. by your defensiveness
W-pI...153.5:5 of G. as but a victim to attack by fantasies,
W-pI...153.8:3 mistook the figures in it for the Son of G.;
W-pI.153.10:6 who are among the chosen ones of G., by
W-pI.153.11:2 G. has elected all, but few have come to
W-pI.153.13:3 of Heaven's children and the Son of G..
W-pI.153.15:5 hour is too short a time to spend with G..
W-pI.153.16:1 to be faithful to the Will we share with G..
W-pI.153.16:4 a little while, and turn our thoughts to G..
W-pI.153.17:1 will observe our trust as ministers of G.,
W-pI.153.20:4 The ministers of G. can never fail, because
W-pI......154.h I am among the ministers of G..
W-pI...154.2:1 may be, it was selected by the Voice for G.
W-pI...154.3:3 G. has joined His Son in this, and thus His
W-pI...154.4:1 It is this joining, through the Voice for G.
W-pI...154.4:2 in the mind that G. created sinless. Now
W-pI...154.4:4 in which its will and that of G. are joined.
W-pI...154.7:2 The messengers of G. perform their part
W-pI...154.8:1 Would you receive the messages of G.?
W-pI...154.9:1 You who are now the messenger of G.,
W-pI...154.9:3 G. has not failed to offer what you need,
W-pI...154.9:5 received for you the messages of G. would
W-pI.154.12:3 but will not know that G. Himself has left
W-pI.154.13:2 *I am among the ministers of G., and I am*
W-pI...155.5:4 on the way that G. has opened up to you,
W-pI...155.8:5 seem to hold in chains the holy Son of G..
W-pI.155.11:1 the holy Son of G. will make no journeys.
W-pI.155.12:1 We walk to G.. Pause and reflect on this.
W-pI.155.12:4 less and still content the holy Son of G.?
W-pI 155.12:5 God? We walk to G.. The truth that walks
W-pI 155.13:1 upon the road that leads the world to G..
W-pI ..... 156.h I walk with G. in perfect holiness.
W-pI .. 156.1:4 be true, how can you be apart from G.?
W-pI .. 156.2:4 You cannot walk the world apart from G.,
W-pI .. 156.5:4 holiness, saluting you as savior and as G..
W-pI .. 156.6:5 to G. Himself for such a senseless whim?
W-pI .. 156.7:4 The approach to G. is near. And in the
W-pI .. 156.8:4 cease. G. speaks for you in answering
W-pI .. 156.8:5 *I walk with G. in perfect holiness. I light the*
W-pI .. 156.8:6 *all the minds which G. created one with me.*
W-pI .. 157.5:3 touchstone for the holy Thoughts of G..
W-pI .. 158.7:2 mistake it for the Son whom G. created. It
W-pI .. 158.8:4 a body. Greet him as the Son of G. he is,
W-pI 158.10:5 on you, and offer you the peace of G..
W-pI .. 159.3:3 G. created perfect can be mirrored there.
W-pI 159.10:2 gift, when G. appointed it be given you?
W-pI 159.10:8 our unlost and everlasting sanctity in G..
W-pI .. 160.4:2 the home which G. provided for His Son?
W-pI .. 160.7:4 as certain of Its Own as G. is of His Son.
W-pI .. 160.8:5 Whom G. has joined remain forever one,
W-pI ..... 161.h Give me your blessing, holy Son of G..
W-pI .. 161.1:5 Here is the answer of the Voice for G..
W-pI .. 161.9:1 the angels love and G. created perfect.
W-pI 161.11:7 *me your blessing, holy Son of G.. I would*
W-pI 161.12:2 For He will hear the Voice for G. in you,
W-pI ..... 162.h I am as G. created me.
W-pI .. 162.1:4 words G. gave in answer to the world you
W-pI .. 162.1:6 words are spoken. For they come from G..
W-pI .. 162.4:3 G. places all His gifts and all His Love, to
W-pI .. 162.4:4 And thus you learn to think with G..
W-pI .. 162.6:3 You are as G. created you. These words
W-pI .. 162.6:6 For you have recognized the Son of G.,
W-pI ..... 163.h There is no death. The Son of G. is free.
W-pI .. 163.4:2 is the strength and might of G. Himself
W-pI .. 163.4:3 of G. proclaimed as lord of all creation,
W-pI .. 163.4:4 upon the body of the holy Son of G..
W-pI .. 163.5:3 but this: "Here lies a witness G. is dead."
W-pI .. 163.7:1 idea of the death of G. is so preposterous
W-pI .. 163.7:2 For it implies that G. was once alive and
W-pI .. 163.8:6 G. made not death. Whatever form it
W-pI .. 164.1:6 Heaven, and the Voice for G. more clear,
W-pI .. 164.9:6 Would G. deceive you? Can His promise
W-pI ..... 165.h Let not my mind deny the Thought of G..
W-pI .. 165.2:1 The Thought of G. created you. It left you
W-pI .. 165.2:6 The Thought of G. protects you, cares for
W-pI .. 165.2:7 because the Thought of G. has left you not
W-pI .. 165.4:7 Yet G. is fair. Sureness is not required to
W-pI .. 165.5:6 the Thought of G. as your inheritance.
W-pI .. 165.6:5 Would G. consent to let His Son remain
W-pI .. 165.7:3 doubts are meaningless, for G. is certain.
W-pI .. 165.8:1 We count on G., and not upon ourselves,
W-pI ..... 166.h I am entrusted with the gifts of G..
W-pI .. 166.2:2 This world is not the Will of G., and so it
W-pI .. 166.2:5 in one, himself alone. But never in one G..
W-pI .. 166.3:1 gifts of G. are not acceptable to anyone
W-pI .. 166.5:5 and poverty, alone though G. is with him,
W-pI .. 166.8:5 make for him whom G. intended only joy
W-pI 166.10:3 It is not G. you have imprisoned in your
W-pI 166.12:5 sought to make in which to hide from G..
W-pI 166.12:6 you of all the gifts that G. has given you.
W-pI 166.15:3 G. has entrusted all His gifts to you. Be
W-pI 166.15:6 For G. entrusts the giving of His gifts to
W-pI ..... 167.h There is one life, and that I share with G..
W-pI .. 167.1:3 in which all that G. created share. Like all
W-pI .. 167.1:5 no death because what G. created shares
W-pI .. 167.1:6 because an opposite to G. does not exist.
W-pI 167.3:11 Its truth established you as one with G..
W-pI .. 167.8:1 G. creates only mind awake. He does not
W-pI .. 167.8:4 Thoughts of G. remain forever changeless
W-pI 167.10:5 of life eternal has been set by G. Himself.
W-pI .. 168.1:1 G. speaks to us. Shall we not speak to
W-pI .. 168.3:1 Today we ask of G. the gift He has most
W-pI .. 168.3:2 gift by which G. leans to us and lifts us up,
W-pI .. 168.4:1 G. loves His Son. Request Him now to
W-pI .. 169.1:1 Grace is an aspect of the Love of G. which
W-pI .. 169.2:1 Love of G. within a world of seeming hate
W-pI .. 169.4:3 of G. to hasten the experience of truth,
W-pI .. 169.5:1 Oneness is simply the idea G. is. And in
W-pI .. 169.5:4 Him. We say "G. is," and then we cease to

W-pI...169.6:5 Son of G. has merely disappeared into his
W-pI.169.11:5 that does not beat as yet in tune with G..
W-pI......170.h There is no cruelty in G. and none in me.
W-pI...170.9:3 surmounting, is the fear of G. Himself.
W-pI.170.10:6 all who acknowledge Him to be their G..
W-pI.170.11:4 And so the fear of G. returned with you.
W-pI.170.12:2 your voice belongs to G. and echoes His.
W-pI.170.12:5 The Call for G. is heard and answered.
W-pI.170.12:6 for love, as G. Himself replaces cruelty.
WpI.. rV.in4:3 *G. is but Love, and therefore so am I.* This
WpI.. rV.in8:1 and knows the answer G. has given Him.
WpI.. rV.in8:5 G. would not have Heaven incomplete. It
WpI rV.in10:4 now complete, as G. established it. You
WpI rV.in10:8 we say: *G. is but Love, and therefore so am I.*
W-pI......171.h G. is but Love, and therefore so am I.
W-pI...171.1:1 All things are echoes of the Voice for G..
W-pI...171.1:2 G. is but Love, and therefore so am I.
W-pI...171.2:2 G. is but Love, and therefore so am I.
W-pI......172.h G. is but Love, and therefore so am I.
W-pI...172.1:2 lies. G. is but Love, and therefore so am I.
W-pI...172.2:1 (154) I am among the ministers of G..
W-pI...172.2:2 G. is but Love, and therefore so am I.
W-pI......173.h G. is but Love, and therefore so am I.
W-pI...173.1:2 way. G. is but Love, and therefore so am I.
W-pI...173.2:1 (156) I walk with G. in perfect holiness.
W-pI...173.2:2 G. is but Love, and therefore so am I.
W-pI......174.h G. is but Love, and therefore so am I.
W-pI...174.1:2 G. is but Love, and therefore so am I.
W-pI...174.2:2 G. is but Love, and therefore so am I.
W-pI......175.h G. is but Love, and therefore so am I.
W-pI...175.1:2 G. is but Love, and therefore so am I.
W-pI...175.2:3 G. is but Love, and therefore so am I.
W-pI......176.h G. is but Love, and therefore so am I.
W-pI...176.1:1 Give me your blessing, holy Son of G..
W-pI...176.1:2 G. is but Love, and therefore so am I.
W-pI...176.2:1 (162) I am as G. created me. God is but
W-pI...176.2:2 me. G. is but Love, and therefore so am I.
W-pI......177.h G. is but Love, and therefore so am I.
W-pI...177.1:2 The Son of G. is free. God is but Love, and
W-pI...177.1:3 free. G. is but Love, and therefore so am I.
W-pI...177.2:2 G. is but Love, and therefore so am I.
W-pI......178.h G. is but Love, and therefore so am I.
W-pI...178.1:1 Let not my mind deny the Thought of G..
W-pI...178.1:2 G. is but Love, and therefore so am I.
W-pI...178.2:1 (166) I am entrusted with the gifts of G..
W-pI...178.2:2 G. is but Love, and therefore so am I.
W-pI......179.h G. is but Love, and therefore so am I.
W-pI...179.1:1 There is one life, and that I share with G..
W-pI...179.1:2 G. is but Love, and therefore so am I.
W-pI...179.2:3 G. is but Love, and therefore so am I.
W-pI......180.h G. is but Love, and therefore so am I.
W-pI...180.1:3 G. is but Love, and therefore so am I.
W-pI...180.2:1 There is no cruelty in G. and none in me.
W-pI...180.2:2 me. G. is but Love, and therefore so am I.
W-pI...181.9:7 Our sinlessness is but the Will of G.. This
W-pI...183.4:1 Repeat the Name of G., and little names
W-pI...183.4:5 the Name of G. replace their little names,
W-pI...183.5:1 Repeat the Name of G., and call upon
W-pI...183.5:3 Those who call upon the Name of G. can
W-pI...183.5:3 grace, nor bodies for the holy Son of G..
W-pI...183.5:4 reaches to G. Himself and to His Son.
W-pI...183.7:2 And G. will come, and answer it Himself.
W-pI.183.10:1 Turn to the Name of G. for your release,
W-pI.183.10:6 place the holy Name of G. becomes his
W-pI.183.11:4 consists of nothing but the Son of G., who
W-pI......184.h The Name of G. is my inheritance.
W-pI.184.10:2 Word, the Name which G. has given you;
W-pI.184.11:4 they share the Name of G. along with you.
W-pI.184.12:1 G. has no name. And yet His Name
W-pI.184.12:5 The Name of G. is the inheritance He gave
W-pI.184.12:6 our minds accept what G. has given as the
W-pI.184.13:1 who seeks the meaning of the Name of G..
W-pI......185.h I want the peace of G..
W-pI...185.1:4 memory of G. entirely restored, the
W-pI...185.2:4 He wants the peace of G., and it is given
W-pI...185.3:1 that what they will becomes the Will of G.
W-pI...185.4:6 bargain can give them the peace of G.?
W-pI...185.5:1 the peace of G. is to renounce all dreams.
W-pI...185.7:2 We want the peace of G.. This is no idle
W-pI...185.8:8 in place of Heaven and the peace of G.?"
W-pI.185.10:1 You want the peace of G.. And so do all
W-pI.185.11:1 seeks the peace of G. can fail to find it. For
W-pI.185.11:5 is his to give? The peace of G. is yours.
W-pI.185.12:4 No gift of G. can be unshared. It is this
W-pI.185.12:5 this attribute that sets the gifts of G. apart
W-pI.185.13:1 gift of G. has been requested and received
W-pI.185.13:2 G. gives but to unite. To take away is
W-pI.185.14:1 but which still remains as G. created it.
W-pI.185.14:2 as we request the peace of G. be given us?
W-pI...186.1:5 of G. is done on earth as well as Heaven. It
W-pI...186.3:7 that would deny the Call for G. Himself.
W-pI...186.6:2 Voice for G. assures you that you have the
W-pI...186.6:5 can come not near the holy home of G..
W-pI...186.7:1 All this the Voice for G. relates to you.
W-pI...186.7:5 What can it tell the holy Son of G.? Why
W-pI...186.8:2 will accept the function G. has given us,
W-pI...186.9:1 Is this the Son of G.? Could He create
W-pI...187.9:3 great illusion of the fear of G. diminishes
W-pI.187.10:2 And here, before the altar to one G., one
W-pI.187.10:2 we stand together as one Son of G.. Not
W-pI.187.10:4 The Name of G. is on our lips. And as we
W-pI.187.11:3 it shining with the grace of G. in everyone
W-pI......188.h The peace of G. is shining in me now.
W-pI...188.3:1 The peace of G. is shining in you now,
W-pI...188.4:3 of the gift, does G. Himself give thanks.
W-pI...188.5:1 The peace of G. can never be contained.
W-pI...188.5:5 The peace of G. is shining in you now,
W-pI...188.6:6 the holy messengers of G. Himself.
W-pI...188.7:3 Where G. the Father and the Son are One.
W-pI...188.8:4 For as the peace of G. is shining in you, it
W-pI...188.9:2 line with all the thoughts we share with G.
W-pI.188.10:1 that the peace of G. still shines in us, and
W-pI.188.10:6 *The peace of G. is shining in me now. Let all*
W-pI......189.h I feel the Love of G. within me now.
W-pI...189.1:7 feel the Love of G. within you is to see the
W-pI...189.3:1 This is the world the Love of G. reveals. It
W-pI...189.5:5 If you feel the Love of G. within you, you
W-pI...189.7:1 thoughts of what you are and what G. is;
W-pI...189.7:5 with wholly empty hands unto your G..
W-pI...189.8:3 the Son and G. the Father to be quietly
W-pI...189.8:4 forever. G. will do His part in joyful and
W-pI...189.8:6 to G. by which He should appear to you.
W-pI...189.9:6 G. knows His Son, and knows the way to
W-pI......190.h I choose the joy of G. instead of pain.
W-pI...190.1:5 For pain proclaims G. cruel. How could it
W-pI...190.1:7 to G. the Father's hatred of His Son, the
W-pI...190.3:2 It demonstrates G. is denied, confused
W-pI...190.3:3 If G. is real, there is no pain. If pain is real,
W-pI...190.3:4 pain is real, there is no G.. For vengeance
W-pI...190.3:6 and using pain to prove that G. is dead,
W-pI...190.3:7 The body is the Son of G., corruptible in
W-pI...190.6:4 the joy of G. as what you really want.
W-pI...190.8:3 In pain is G. denied the Son He loves. In
W-pI.190.10:2 Here does the joy of G. belong to you.
W-pI.190.11:2 of sin, the peace of G. instead of conflict,
W-pI......191.h I am the holy Son of G. Himself.
W-pI...191.1:3 the world the role of jailer to the Son of G.
W-pI...191.3:1 that mocks creation and that laughs at G..
W-pI...191.4:2 You are as G. created you. All else but this
W-pI...191.6:1 free: You are the holy Son of G. Himself.
W-pI...191.7:3 *I am the holy Son of G. Himself. I cannot*
W-pI...191.8:3 of G. has come in glory to redeem the lost,
W-pI.191.10:1 let the Son of G. awaken from his sleep,
W-pI.191.11:6 life. You are the holy Son of G. Himself.
W-pI......192.h I have a function G. would have me fill.
W-pI...192.1:1 forever one with G. and with your Self.
W-pI...192.3:5 Yet G. created One Who has the power to
W-pI...192.4:1 which the Word of G. can now replace the
W-pI...192.5:6 peace that G. intended for His holy Son.
W-pI...192.6:6 have indeed been given everything by G..
W-pI.192.10:2 The Son of G. deserves your mercy. It is
W-pI.192.10:7 He is as G. created him. And you are what
W-pI......193.h things are lessons G. would have me learn
W-pI...193.1:1 G. does not know of learning. Yet His
W-pI...193.2:1 G. sees no contradictions. Yet His Son
W-pI...193.2:4 G. does not perceive at all. Yet it is He
W-pI...193.3:1 are the lessons G. would have you learn.
W-pI...193.8:1 G. would not have you suffer thus. He
W-pI...193.8:4 G. would have him not forget His Love,
W-pI...193.8:6 and G. may be remembered by His Son?
W-pI...193.9:1 are lessons G. would have you learn. He
W-pI...193.9:5 G. has willed that laughter should replace
W-pI.193.11:7 His are the lessons G. would have us learn
W-pI.193.13:1 lesson G. would have you learn: There is a
W-pI.193.13:5 Love of G. the Father down to earth at last
W-pI.193.13:6 G. will take this final step Himself. Do not
W-pI......194.h I place the future in the Hands of G..
W-pI...194.1:3 await with certainty the final step of G..
W-pI...194.3:4 so each instant given unto G. in passing,
W-pI...194.4:1 G. holds your future as He holds your
W-pI...194.7:1 gives his future to the loving Hands of G.?
W-pI...194.8:1 then, your future in the Hands of G.. For
W-pI...194.8:4 entrusts himself to G. has also placed the
W-pI...195.4:1 not offer G. your gratitude because your
W-pI...195.4:4 offer thanks to G. our Father that in us all
W-pI...195.6:3 we fail to recognize the gifts of G. to us.
W-pI...195.8:4 The fear of G. is now undone at last, and
W-pI...195.9:5 G. has cared for us, and calls us Son. Can
W-pI.195.10:4 G. gives thanks to you, His Son, for being
W-pI.195.10:6 and thus we go who walk the way to G..
W-pI...196.4:5 done in just one instant by the grace of G.
W-pI...196.5:3 stood for the belief the fear of G. is real.
W-pI...196.6:4 fear of G. is real to anyone who thinks this
W-pI...196.8:3 thoughts, the fear of G. must disappear.
W-pI...196.8:5 G., Whom you had thought to banish,
W-pI...196.9:3 deadly fear of G. projection hides behind.
W-pI.196.11:3 For fear of G. has disappeared. And you
W-pI.196.12:1 is no Thought of G. that does not go with
W-pI.196.12:2 When the fear of G. is gone, there are no
W-pI.196.12:2 between you and the holy peace of G..
W-pI...197.2:1 How easily are G. and guilt confused by
W-pI...197.4:5 acknowledged by the Heart of G. Himself.
W-pI...197.5:1 G. blesses every gift you give to Him, and
W-pI...197.5:2 And what belongs to G. must be His Own.
W-pI...197.6:2 the gifts of G. are lent but for a little while
W-pI...197.7:2 for this, for He is grateful only unto G.,
W-pI...197.8:1 Thanks be to you, the holy Son of G.. For
W-pI...197.8:3 And you are still as G. created you. Nor
W-pI...197.8:5 In your heart the Heart of G. is laid. He
W-pI...197.9:6 sharing with Him the holy Thoughts of G.
W-pI...197.9:7 you forgot the function G. has given you.
W-pI...198.3:6 direction with the certainty of G. Himself.
W-pI...198.3:7 of G. awakens to his Self and to his Father
W-pI...198.4:2 when this one is the plan of G. Himself?
W-pI...198.6:4 His words are born in G., and come to
W-pI...198.6:7 the Word of G. will come to take its place,
W-pI...198.7:7 and that the holy Son of G. can die!
W-pI.198.10:2 Spirit holds for you from G. your Father.
W-pI.198.11:4 now the Word of G. alone remains upon
W-pI.198.11:6 that G. forever knows to be His only Son.
W-pI.198.12:6 and then you disappear forever into G..
W-pI.198.13:3 that G. has given us through Him today.
W-pI...199.2:3 It rests in G.. And who can be afraid who
W-pI...199.7:6 that finds its full accomplishment in G..
W-pI...199.8:6 it. And G. Himself extends His Love and
W-pI...199.8:9 *I hear the Voice that G. has given me, and it is*
W-pI......200.h There is no peace except the peace of G..
W-pI...200.1:2 will not find peace except the peace of G..
W-pI...200.1:5 else for you to find except the peace of G.,
W-pI...200.7:1 There is no peace except the peace of G.,
W-pI...200.7:6 it another way, and find the peace of G..
W-pI...200.8:4 where freedom lies within the peace of G..
W-pI...200.9:4 G. alone is sure, and He will guide our
W-pI...200.9:7 what appears to be a world apart from G.,
W-pI.200.11:3 The peace of G. is ours, and only this will
W-pI.200.11:6 For peace is union, if it be of G.. We seek
W-pI.200.11:9 *There is no peace except the peace of G., And*
WpI rVI.in.1:4 invite the memory of G. to come again.
WpI rVI.in.3:5 *free. For I am still as G. created me.* The day
WpI rVI.in.4:2 path to the serenity and peace of G.. We
W-pI......201.h I am free. For I am still as G. created me.
W-pI...201.1:3 *with oneness with the universe and G., my*
W-pI...201.1:6 I am free. For I am still as G. created me.
W-pI......202.h I am free. For I am still as G. created me.
W-pI...202.1:2 *when G. Himself has given me His Voice to*
W-pI...202.1:5 I am free. For I am still as G. created me.
W-pI......203.h I am free. For I am still as G. created me.

W-pI...203.1:2 *The Name of G. is my deliverance from every*
W-pI...203.1:5 I am free. For I am still as G. created me.
W-pI......204.h I am free. For I am still as G. created me.
W-pI...204.1:1 (184) The Name of G. is my inheritance.
W-pI...204.1:2 *rule the world of sick illusions, free in G.,*
W-pI...204.1:5 I am free. For I am still as G. created me.
W-pI......205.h I am free. For I am still as G. created me.
W-pI...205.1:1 (185) I want the peace of G.. *The peace of*
W-pI...205.1:2 *The peace of G. is everything I want. The*
W-pI...205.1:3 *The peace of G. is my one goal; the aim of all*
W-pI...205.1:6 I am free. For I am still as G. created me.
W-pI......206.h I am free. For I am still as G. created me.
W-pI...206.1:2 *I am entrusted with the gifts of G., because I*
W-pI...206.1:6 I am free. For I am still as G. created me.
W-pI......207.h I am free. For I am still as G. created me.
W-pI...207.1:6 I am free. For I am still as G. created me.
W-pI......208.h I am free. For I am still as G. created me.
W-pI...208.1:1 The peace of G. is shining in me now. *I will*
W-pI...208.1:3 *in that stillness we will find the peace of G.. It*
W-pI...208.1:4 *my heart, which witnesses to G. Himself.* I
W-pI...208.1:7 I am free. For I am still as G. created me.
W-pI......209.h I am free. For I am still as G. created me.
W-pI...209.1:1 (189) I feel the Love of G. within me now.
W-pI...209.1:2 *The Love of G. is what created me. The Love*
W-pI...209.1:3 *The Love of G. is everything I am. The Love*
W-pI...209.1:4 *The Love of G. proclaimed me as His Son.*
W-pI...209.1:5 *The Love of G. within me sets me free.* I am
W-pI...209.1:8 I am free. For I am still as G. created me.
W-pI......210.h I am free. For I am still as G. created me.
W-pI...210.1:1 I choose the joy of G. instead of pain. *Pain*
W-pI...210.1:3 *It is not a Thought of G., but one I thought*
W-pI...210.1:8 I am free. For I am still as G. created me.
W-pI......211.h I am free. For I am still as G. created me.
W-pI...211.1:1 (191) I am the holy Son of G. Himself. *In*
W-pI...211.1:5 I am free. For I am still as G. created me.
W-pI......212.h I am free. For I am still as G. created me.
W-pI...212.1:1 (192) I have a function G. would have me
W-pI...212.1:3 *function G. has given me can offer freedom.*
W-pI...212.1:7 I am free. For I am still as G. created me.
W-pI......213.h I am free. For I am still as G. created me.
W-pI...213.1:1 things are lessons G. would have me learn
W-pI...213.1:2 *A lesson is a miracle which G. offers to me, in*
W-pI...213.1:7 I am free. For I am still as G. created me.
W-pI......214.h I am free. For I am still as G. created me.
W-pI...214.1:1 (194) I place the future in the Hands of G.
W-pI...214.1:4 *For what G. gives can only be for good. And I*
W-pI...214.1:8 I am free. For I am still as G. created me.
W-pI......215.h I am free. For I am still as G. created me.
W-pI...215.1:7 I am free. For I am still as G. created me.
W-pI......216.h I am free. For I am still as G. created me.
W-pI...216.1:7 I am free. For I am still as G. created me.
W-pI......217.h I am free. For I am still as G. created me.
W-pI...217.1:6 I am free. For I am still as G. created me.
W-pI......218.h I am free. For I am still as G. created me.
W-pI...218.1:6 I am free. For I am still as G. created me.
W-pI......219.h I am free. For I am still as G. created me.
W-pI...219.1:8 I am free. For I am still as G. created me.
W-pI......220.h I am free. For I am still as G. created me.
W-pI...220.1:1 There is no peace except the peace of G..
W-pI...220.1:3 *home, and peace is certain as the Love of G..* I
W-pI...220.1:6 I am free. For I am still as G. created me.
W-pII ....in.2:2 in quiet expectation for our G. and Father
W-pII ....in.2:9 calling to G. when we have need of Him as
W-pII ....in.3:2 conclude the year that we have given G..
W-pII ....in.8:1 together in the search for truth and G.,
W-pII ....in.9:1 We had a wish that G. would fail to have
W-pII ....in.9:2 We wanted G. to change Himself, and be
W-pII ....in.9:5 The memory of G. is shimmering across
W-pII ..in.10:2 to understand that we need only call to G.
W-pII ..... 1.1:7 free to take its place is now the Will of G..
W-pII ..... 1.5:2 for such is His function, given Him by G..
W-pII ..... 1.5:3 and whom He honors as the Son of G..
W-pII .221.2:2 G. is here, because we wait together. I am
W-pII ....222.h G. is with me. I live and move in Him.
W-pII .222.1:1 G. is with me. He is my Source of life, the
W-pII ....223.h G. is my life. I have no life but His.
W-pII .223.1:1 when I thought I lived apart from G., a
W-pII ....224.h G. is my Father, and He loves His Son.
W-pII ....225.h G. is my Father, and His Son loves Him.
W-pII .227.2:2 Son of G. this day lays down his dreams.
W-pII .227.2:3 The Son of G. this day comes home again,
W-pII ....228.h G. has condemned me not. No more do I.
W-pII ....230.h Now will I seek and find the peace of G..
W-pII .230.1:4 How merciful is G. my Father, that when
W-pII ..... 2.1:1 Salvation is a promise, made by G., that
W-pII ..... 2.3:4 Name of G. whereon His Word is written,
W-pII ..... 2.3:4 it, and the memory of G. not far behind.
W-pII ..... 2.4:3 holds a hint of all the glory given us by G..
W-pII ....233.h I give my life to G. to guide today.
W-pII .234.1:4 the peace of G. the Father and the Son.
W-pII ....235.h G. in His mercy wills that I be saved.
W-pII .235.1:1 myself, "G. wills that I be saved from this,
W-pII .235.1:5 saved because G. in His mercy wills it so.
W-pII .236.1:8 And thus I set it free to do the Will of G..
W-pII ....237.h Now would I be as G. created me.
W-pII .237.1:3 which I hear as G. my Father speaks to me
W-pII .237.2:1 *the ears that listen to the Voice for G. today.*
W-pII .240.1:7 We are the Sons of G.. There is no fear in
W-pII ..... 3.2:1 The world was made as an attack on G..
W-pII ..... 3.2:4 to be a place where G. could enter not,
W-pII ..... 3.4:2 Sounds become the call for G., and all
W-pII ..... 3.4:2 Whom G. appointed Savior to the world.
W-pII .242.1:4 choices for me but the ones that lead to G.
W-pII .242.1:5 and it is He Who knows the way to G..
W-pII .243.1:6 look upon, to be in peace as G. created us.
W-pII .244.2:3 In G. we are secure. For what can come to
W-pII .244.2:4 For what can come to threaten G. Himself
W-pII .245.2:3 thus we come to hear the Voice for G.,
W-pII .246.1:1 me not think that I can find the way to G.,
W-pII .248.1:7 deceits and lies about the holy Son of G..
W-pII .248.1:8 to accept him back as G. created him, and
W-pII .249.1:7 the journey which the Son of G. began has
W-pII .250.1:1 Let me behold the Son of G. today, and
W-pII ..... 4.3:4 And G. Himself has lost the Son He loves,
W-pII ..... 4.4:3 Son of G. may play he has become a body,
W-pII ..... 4.5:1 How long, O Son of G., will you maintain
W-pII ..... 4.5:8 How long, O holy Son of G., how long?
W-pII ....252.h The Son of G. is my Identity.
W-pII .252.1:4 from the boundless Love of G. Himself.
W-pII .252.1:5 and yet how near to me and close to G.!
W-pII .254.2:6 G. speaks to us and tells us of our will, as
W-pII .255.1:2 yet, my G. assures me that His Son is like
W-pII ....256.h G. is the only goal I have today.
W-pII .256.1:1 The way to G. is through forgiveness here
W-pII .256.1:6 holiness of him whom G. created sinless?
W-pII .256.1:9 G. is our goal; forgiveness is the means by
W-pII .257.1:4 only what G. would have us do this day.
W-pII ....258.h Let me remember that my goal is G..
W-pII .258.1:1 aims, and to remember that our goal is G.
W-pII .258.1:4 G. is our only goal, our only Love. We
W-pII .259.1:1 makes the goal of G. seem unattainable.
W-pII ....260.h Let me remember G. created me.
W-pII ..... 5.1:1 a fence the Son of G. imagines he has built
W-pII ..... 5.4:3 Son of G. extends his hand to reach his
W-pII ....261.h G. is my refuge and security.
W-pII .261.1:4 I live in G.. In Him I find my refuge and
W-pII .262.1:8 *in Your Love; eternally the holy Son of G..*
W-pII .263.2:2 house as brothers and the holy Sons of G..
W-pII ....264.h I am surrounded by the Love of G..
W-pII .266.2:1 in each of us; united in the holy Love of G.
W-pII .266.2:2 How many saviors G. has given us! How
W-pII ....267.h My heart is beating in the peace of G..
W-pII .267.1:1 is all the life that G. created in His Love. It
W-pII .267.1:6 I am a messenger of G., directed by His
W-pII .269.2:3 one because of Him Who is the Son of G.;
W-pII .270.2:3 the holy Son whom G. created whole; the
W-pII .270.2:3 whole; the holy Son whom G. created One
W-pII ..... 6.1:2 us with one another, and with G. as well.
W-pII ..... 6.1:5 unchanged forever in the Mind of G..
W-pII ..... 6.2:1 is the link that keeps you one with G., and
W-pII ..... 6.3:1 the Holy Spirit, and at home in G. alone,
W-pII ..... 6.4:2 which G. appointed as the end of dreams.
W-pII ..... 6.4:3 and peace has come to every Son of G.,
W-pII ..... 6.5:3 the Christ Whom G. created as His Son.
W-pII .272.2:2 and ask ourselves if we, the Sons of G.,
W-pII ....273.h The stillness of the peace of G. is mine.
W-pII .273.1:4 "The stillness of the peace of G. is mine,"
W-pII .273.1:4 that G. Himself has given to His Son.
W-pII .275.1:1 Let us today attend the Voice for G.,
W-pII .275.1:4 For the Voice for G. tells us of things we
W-pII .275.1:6 the healing of the Voice for G. is found.
W-pII ....276.h The Word of G. is given me to speak.
W-pII .276.1:1 What is the Word of G.? "My Son is pure
W-pII .276.1:3 thus did G. become the Father of the Son
W-pII .277.2:1 make to hide the freedom of the Son of G.
W-pII .277.2:5 and G. can will that He deceive Himself.
W-pII .279.1:5 when G. is offering me freedom now?
W-pII .280.1:1 Whom G. created limitless is free. I can
W-pII .280.1:3 Thought of G. has left its Father's Mind.
W-pII .280.1:4 No Thought of G. is limited at all. No
W-pII .280.1:5 No Thought of G. but is forever pure. Can
W-pII .280.1:6 Can I lay limits on the Son of G., whose
W-pII ..... 7.1:2 through the grace that G. has given Him,
W-pII ..... 7.4:1 where He has been placed by G., the Holy
W-pII ..... 7.5:4 to take the function of completing G.,
W-pII .282.1:2 insane, and to accept myself as G. Himself
W-pII .282.1:4 Self Whom G. created as the Son He loves
W-pII .283.1:1 *of myself, and it is this I call the Son of G.. Yet*
W-pII .283.1:5 *the light of Heaven and the Love of G.. Is not*
W-pII .283.2:1 with G. our Father as our only Source,
W-pII .285.1:1 but the happy things of G. to come to me.
W-pII .286.2:2 end which G. Himself has promised us.
W-pII .287.1:3 gift could I prefer before the peace of G.?
W-pII ..... 8.5:2 instant more for G. to take His final step,
W-pII ..... 8.5:3 our goal, for it contains the memory of G..
W-pII .291.1:6 we share; it is the Holiness of G. Himself.
W-pII .294.1:1 I am a Son of G.. And can I be another
W-pII .294.1:3 Did G. create the mortal and corruptible?
W-pII .296.2:3 us, to seek and find the easy path to G..
W-pII .298.1:5 instead what G. establishes as mine, sure
W-pII .298.2:4 *my love for G. my Father and His holy Son.*
W-pII .299.1:2 know. Yet G., my Father, Who created it,
W-pII ..... 9.1:1 Second Coming, which is sure as G., is
W-pII ..... 9.3:1 extend beyond itself, and reaches up to G.
W-pII ..... 9.3:2 name of true creation and the Will of G..
W-pII ..... 9.4:3 of G. acknowledge that they all are one.
W-pII ..... 9.4:4 And G. the Father smiles upon His Son,
W-pII ..... 9.5:6 Behold, the Son of G. is one in us, and we
W-pII ....301.h And G. Himself shall wipe away all tears.
W-pII .306.1:4 of loving kindness and the peace of G..
W-pII .309.1:4 is but to find my will as G. created it, and
W-pII .309.1:7 Within me is the Holiness of G.. Within
W-pII ... 10.1:1 the Son of G. this gift: to hear the Voice
W-pII ... 10.1:1 for G. proclaim that what is false is false,
W-pII ... 10.2:6 away, because the Son of G. is limitless.
W-pII ... 10.4:3 the Son whom G. acknowledges as His. Be
W-pII .315.1:5 finds the way to G. becomes my savior,
W-pII .315.2:1 *me today and every day from every Son of G.*
W-pII .316.1:5 among the gifts that G. has given me.
W-pII .318.1:4 the sinlessness that G. has placed in me. I
W-pII .319.1:6 And yet it is the Will of G. I learn that
W-pII .320.1:1 The Son of G. is limitless. There are no
W-pII ... 11.2:4 What G. has willed to be forever One will
W-pII ... 11.3:2 Creation is the holy Son of G., for in
W-pII ... 11.4:1 We are creation; we the Sons of G.. We
W-pII ... 11.4:6 to sanity, and to be but as G. created us.
W-pII .321.2:3 our freedom can be found in G. alone.
W-pII .325.1:6 forth, with mercy for the holy Son of G.,
W-pII .325.1:6 and find the way to Heaven and to G..
W-pII ....326.h I am forever an Effect of G..
W-pII .326.1:6 *Let me know that I am an Effect of G., and so*
W-pII .326.1:8 *thoughts unite in glory as the Son of G..*
W-pII .327.1:2 For G. has promised He will hear my call,
W-pII .328.1:1 down until we listen to the Voice for G.. It
W-pII .329.2:4 Through it we find our way at last to G..
W-pII .330.1:3 G. holds out His power and His Love, and
W-pII .330.1:4 as is the Will of G. united with its own.
W-pII .330.1:5 The Self which G. created cannot sin, and
W-pII ... 12.1:2 "will" that sees the Will of G. as enemy,
W-pII ... 12.1:3 death, and what opposes G. alone is true.
W-pII ... 12.2:3 it has become a victor over G. Himself.
W-pII ... 12.2:4 it "sees" the Will of G. has been destroyed
W-pII ... 12.3:1 The Son of G. is egoless. What can he
W-pII ... 12.3:2 he know of madness and the death of G.,
W-pII ... 12.4:2 G. is offered daily at its darkened shrine,
W-pII ... 12.5:2 holy minds which G. created as His Son,
W-pII .331.2:2 today, that we may find the peace of G..

M-22 2:3 the function G. has given him long before
M-22 2:9 was required, would G. withhold the rest?
M-22 3:1 if the teacher of G. is to make progress.
M-22 3:5 of G. and prove salvation is impossible.
M-22 4:4 of G. calls forth the miracle of healing. He
M-22 4:8 It is true of all things that G. created. In it
M-22 5:1 When a teacher of G. fails to heal, it is
M-22 5:7 Step back now, teacher of G.. You have
M-22 6:4 Not to believe this is to be unfair to G.,
M-22 6:5 perceives himself as separate from G..
M-22 7:1 Who can limit the power of G. Himself?
M-22 7:8 his judgment from the Son of G.,
M-22 7:8 of God, accepting him as G. created him.
M-22 7:9 No longer does he stand apart from G.,
M-22 7:10 Now can he say with G., "This is my
M-23 2:4 He has become the risen Son of G.. He has
M-23 2:6 has recognized himself as G. created him,
M-23 2:7 on his power, because it is the power of G.
M-23 2:8 So has his name become the Name of G.,
M-23 3:2 Jesus you are remembering G.. The whole
M-23 3:8 Can G. fail His Son? And can one who is
M-23 3:9 can one who is one with G. be unlike Him
M-23 4:4 the shining symbol for the Word of G., so
M-23 4:5 for all the gifts that G. has given you. And
M-23 4:6 gratitude to G. becomes the way in which
M-23 4:7 G. enters easily, for these are the true
M-23 6:6 teacher of G. forgets his brothers. Yet
M-23 7:4 Would G. leave anyone without a very
M-24 3:2 teacher of G. should be as helpful to those
M-24 4:4 The teacher of G. is, therefore, wise to
M-24 5:1 that the teacher of G. should not believe
M-25 3:6 the "unseen," or "special" favors from G..
M-25 3:7 G. gives no special favors, and no one has
M-26 h CAN G. BE REACHED DIRECTLY?
M-26 1:1 G. indeed can be reached directly, for
M-26 1:10 But in their joining is the power of G..
M-26 2:1 are those who have reached G. directly,
M-26 2:9 teachers of G. who look to them for help,
M-26 3:1 Sometimes a teacher of G. may have a
M-26 3:1 a brief experience of direct union with G..
M-26 3:8 If G. were reached directly in sustained
M-26 4:10 G. takes you where you are and welcomes
M-27 1:6 path,–all this is taken as the Will of G..
M-27 2:1 perception of the universe as G. created it,
M-27 3:1 Death is the symbol of the fear of G.. His
M-27 3:3 enough to show it cannot coexist with G..
M-27 3:4 holds an image of the Son of G. in which
M-27 3:8 of life." G. is insane, and fear alone is real.
M-27 4:1 proclaim a loving G. nor re-establish any
M-27 4:8 because not one could be acceptable to G.
M-27 5:2 And if G. created bodies, death would
M-27 5:3 But G. would not be loving. There is no
M-27 5:5 Death is indeed the death of G., if He is
M-27 6:8 But what is born of G. and still can die?
M-27 6:10 G. is, and in Him all created things must
M-27 7:1 Teacher of G., your one assignment could
M-27 7:8 the Son of G. is guiltless now and forever.
M-28 1:5 It is the recognition of the gifts of G.. It is
M-28 1:8 the invitation to G. to take His final step.
M-28 2:5 of G. shines unimpeded across the world.
M-28 3:10 is left to contradict the Word of G.. There
M-28 4:3 The Son of G. is free. And in his freedom
M-28 5:8 As G. created us so will we be forever and
M-28 6:6 the truth about the holy Son of G.. He is
M-28 6:9 as he prepares with them to meet his G..
M-29 2:5 Surely no teacher of G. has come this far
M-29 4:4 As G. created you, you *have* all power. The
M-29 5:2 Yet to accept the power given him by G. is
M-29 5:9 remember G. when you can throughout
M-29 6:5 G. has given Him the power to translate
M-29 6:8 G. would be cruel if He let your words
M-29 7:8 G. does not wait, for waiting implies time
M-29 7:10 G. knows but His Son, and as he was
M-29 8:2 *G. turns to you for help to save the world.*
M-29 8:3 *Teacher of G., His thanks He offers you, And*
M-29 8:7 *for you, And join your efforts on behalf of G.*
M-29 8:7 *And for all those who walk to G. with me.*
C-1 1:2 term is capitalized it refers to G. or Christ
C-1 1:2 (i.e., the Mind of G. or the Mind of Christ).
C-1 1:3 is the Thought of G. which He created like
C-1 2:1 split, the Sons of G. appear to be separate.
C-1 3:1 in contact with G. through the Holy Spirit
C-1 3:3 with the understanding that, being of G.,
C-1 4:3 unabated because that is the Will of G..
C-1 5:3 in which G. takes the final step Himself.
C-3 1:1 is for G. and toward God but not of Him.
C-3 1:1 is for God and toward G. but not of Him.
C-3 2:3 makes G. appear to be an enemy instead
C-3 3:2 G. knows what His Son needs before he
C-3 4:1 seen before the memory of G. can return.
C-3 4:12 It is the final step. And this we leave to G.
C-3 6:9 is peace eternal and the Will of G..
C-3 7:4 But Will is constant, as the gift of G.. And
C-3 7:7 It is the gift of G. to save His Son. But look
C-3 8:5 G. is not seen but only understood. His
C-4 1:2 G. did not create it, for what He creates
C-4 2:4 guilt. While everything that G. created is
C-4 6:9 G. has come to claim His Own.
C-4 7:4 light upon the altar to the Son of G.. God
C-4 7:5 G. knows it is His Own, as it is his. And
C-4 8:1 safe and pure and lovely in the Mind of G.
C-5 1:2 which G. alone established in reality.
C-5 1:4 Beyond each one there is a Thought of G.,
C-5 1:7 G. does not help because He knows no
C-5 1:9 Thank G. for them for they will lead you
C-5 2:1 in all his brothers and remembered G.. So
C-5 2:2 a man no longer, but at one with G.. The
C-5 3:1 with the Christ–the perfect Son of G.,
C-5 3:3 to G. because he saw the road before him,
C-5 5:4 to lead you from the hell you made to G..
C-5 5:9 at last and carry it with you unto your G..
C-5 6:4 Christ's single message of the Love of G..
C-5 6:7 leave them both to find the peace of G..
C-5 6:9 *death because the Son of G. is like his Father.*
C-6 1:1 Christ, the Son of G. as He created Him.
C-6 1:4 His is the Voice for G., and has therefore
C-6 1:5 which G. alone knows along with Christ,
C-6 3:1 Link between G. and His separated Sons.
C-6 3:3 He knows because He is part of G.; He
C-6 3:7 He never forgets the Son of G.. He never
C-6 3:9 be obliterated because G. has put it there.
C-6 4:3 He speaks for G. and also for you, being
C-6 5:7 place the hymn to G. is heard a little while
C-6 5:8 to return to the eternal formlessness of G.
C-ep 1:4 to do what G. appointed him to do. When
C-ep 1:8 each one there is reality and there is G..
C-ep 1:10 end? The end *is* sure and guaranteed by G..
C-ep 3:7 would hide but G. would have you see.
C-ep 4:4 alone. For G. is here, and with Him all our
C-ep 5:4 G. is welcomed and His Son with Him.
C-ep 5:6 and in the quiet G. has given him enters
P-1 1:4 G. has given everyone a Teacher Whose
P-1 2:2 learn to call upon G. and hear His Answer
P-1 2:3 the truth and the life, and to remember G.
P-1 5:1 patient need not think of truth as G. in
P-1 5:8 all psychotherapy leads to G. in the end.
P-2 I.4:1 each other and to receive the peace of G..
P-2 I.4:3 somewhat more specialized teacher of G..
P-2 II.1:1 To be a teacher of G., it is not necessary
P-2 II.1:1 to believe in G. to any recognizable extent
P-2 II.3:1 learns to forgive can fail to remember G..
P-2 II.3:3 All blocks to the remembrance of G. are
P-2 II.4:1 not the awareness of G. that constitutes a
P-2 II.4:3 would be unfair indeed if belief in G. were
P-2 II.4:4 is belief in G. a really meaningful concept,
P-2 II.4:4 concept, for G. can be but known. Belief
P-2 II.4:5 but knowledge of G. has no true opposite.
P-2 II.4:6 Not to know G. is to have no knowledge,
P-2 II.5:2 of religion have nothing to do with G.,
P-2 II.5:3 goal, G. will enter into their relationship
P-2 II.5:4 restores the place of G. to ascendance,
P-2 II.5:4 then through the memory of G. Himself.
P-2 II.6:1 invitation to G. to enter into His Kingdom
P-2 II.6:4 G. comes to those who would restore His
P-2 II.7:4 the teacher does not think of G. as part of
P-2 II.7:5 understand that healing comes from G..
P-2 II.7:6 who believe they have found G. will fail.
P-2 III.4:4 too near to G. to keep his feet on earth.
P-2 IV.1:2 It is a judgment on the Son of G., and
P-2 IV.4:7 if G. were the devil and must be found in
P-2 IV.5:5 understand this without the Word of G.,
P-2 IV.8:4 to G. that it must be forever inconceivable
P-2 V.3:7 For G. Himself holds out his brother as
P-2 V.4:3 two come very close to G. in this attempt,
P-2 V.4:4 two have joined for healing, G. is there.
P-2 V.5:3 What he asks is asked by G. through him.
P-2 V.5:4 do for him becomes the gift we give to G..
P-2 V.5:8 holy interaction is the plan of G. Himself,
P-2 V.7:1 all gifts of G. must be received. In time no
P-2 V.7:8 the veil of guilt that shrouds the Son of G.
P-2 V.8:5 It will be G. to Whom you answer, for you
P-2 V.8:9 Son of G. returns to Heaven through its
P-2 V.8:10 For healing tells him, in the Voice for G.,
P-2 VI.1:4 "G. may not enter here" the sick repeat,
P-2 VII.1:11 G. does not know of separation. What He
P-2 VII.1:14 G. comes to him who calls, and in Him he
P-2 VII.4:1 in no way confuses himself with G.. All
P-2 VII.4:3 would instantly become a teacher of G.,
P-2 VII.6:1 as insane not to accept a function G. has
P-2 VII.6:6 he has the gifts of G. Himself to give away.
P-2 VII.7:1 The insane, thinking they are G., are not
P-2 VII.7:8 Behold your G. in him, for what you see
P-2 VII.9:2 this, you have denied that G. created you,
P-2 VII.9:9 patient in, for he has come to you from G.
P-3 I.1:9 of yourself is to demand a sacrifice of G.,
P-3 I.2:8 Would G. send His Son to you and not be
P-3 I.2:9 Think what G. is telling you; He needs
P-3 I.2:12 or hear the Voice of Him Who is G. in you
P-3 I.3:1 for you to serve them in the Name of G..
P-3 I.3:2 G. will not have His gifts to you limited to
P-3 I.4:1 holy therapist, an advanced teacher of G.,
P-3 I.4:5 They come bearing G.. Would he refuse
P-3 I.4:7 Let him not betray the Son of G.. Who
P-3 II.4:1 G. is said to have looked on all He created
P-3 II.4:7 the way G. chose for the return of His Son
P-3 II.7:7 They are the Saints of G.. They are the
P-3 II.10:2 therapist has the strength of G. with him,
P-3 II.10:5 Because it is the Will of G. that he take his
P-3 II.10:6 Because it is the Will of G. that his patient
P-3 II.10:11 Will of G. has always been exactly as it is.
P-3 III.1:1 healing is of G. and He asks for nothing. It
P-3 III.4:2 It is promised him, and guaranteed by G..
P-3 III.5:4 This is the law of G., and not of the world.
P-3 III.5:8 that all they have comes only from G.. If
P-3 III.6:4 place of Christ and home of G. Himself.
P-3 III.7:4 How much is lost by throwing G. away?
P-3 III.8:10 of G. for the restoration of joy and peace.
P-3 III.8:11 forget how very simple are the ways of G.:
P-3 III.8:13 *And then G. sent His Son to give it to you.*
S-1 in.1:1 which G. blessed His Son at his creation.
S-1 in.1:5 G. gives thanks to His extension in His
S-1 in.2:3 G. created one must recognize its oneness
S-1 in.2:3 separate is one forever in the Mind of G..
S-1 in.3:1 down your dreams, you holy Son of G.,
S-1 in.3:1 of God, and rising up as G. created you,
S-1 I.1:1 way offered by the Holy Spirit to reach G..
S-1 I.1:5 to pray for idols and hope to reach G..
S-1 I.2:7 The form of the answer, if given by G.,
S-1 I.4:7 G. answers only for eternity. But still all
S-1 I.5:7 That nothingness becomes the altar of G..
S-1 I.6:3 another mediates between you and G..
S-1 I.6:5 the goodness of G. prays without fear.
S-1 II.1:3 fuses into total communication with G..
S-1 II.1:4 and often does not, make appeal to G., or
S-1 II.2:1 of G. who knows Who he is. No one, then,
S-1 II.3:2 may be addressed to G. in honest belief,
S-1 II.5:6 it acknowledges the Son of G. as he was
S-1 II.7:7 sinlessness that is the gift of G. to you, His
S-1 II.7:10 for this giving G. Himself gives thanks.
S-1 II.8:1 G. is the goal of every prayer, giving it
S-1 II.8:6 unblemished into the Mind of G.. Being
S-1 II.8:8 the illusion of death and the fear of G..
S-1 III.1:6 goals, until it reaches even up to G..
S-1 III.5:7 He is a Son of G., along with you. He is no
S-1 III.6:2 are used for goals that substitute for G.,
S-1 III.6:5 The goal of G. is lost in the quest for lesser
S-1 III.6:10 it well. All other goals are at the cost of G.

| | |
|---|---|
| S-1 ........IV.3:1 | ask, before all else, what is the Will of **G.**. |
| S-1 ........IV.4:4 | Prayer can bring the peace of **G.**. What |
| S-1 ........V.1:3 | the ground where it begins to rise to **G.**, |
| S-1 ........V.2:3 | no goal but **G.** because they need no idols, |
| S-1 ........V.2:5 | it is, knowing creation is the Will of **G.**. Its |
| S-1 ........V.2:6 | where it gladly joins with every Son of **G.**, |
| S-2 ........in.1:5 | Behold the greatest help that **G.** ordained |
| S-2 ..........I.1:2 | grace, a parody upon the holy peace of **G.**. |
| S-2 ..........I.3:2 | learn that **G.** has given you the means by |
| S-2 ..........I.3:6 | How otherwise can prayer return to **G.**? |
| S-2 ........I.3:10 | and as you see yourself is **G.** to you. |
| S-2 ..........I.6:3 | Yet **G.** Himself has given all His Sons a |
| S-2 ..........I.8:3 | **G.** calls on you to save His Son from death |
| S-2 ..........I.8:4 | need, and **G.** holds out this gift to you. As |
| S-2 ..........I.8:6 | song that all creation sings unto its **G.**. |
| S-2 ..........I.9:6 | plan that **G.** established for returning be |
| S-2 ........II.1:3 | separate and make what **G.** created equal, |
| S-2 ........II.2:4 | sin, and yet perceive him as the Son of **G.**? |
| S-2 ........II.3:3 | deserve the retribution of the wrath of **G.**. |
| S-2 ........II.4:1 | the goal is to separate from **G.** the Son He |
| S-2 ........II.6:7 | **G.** gives and does not ask for recompense. |
| S-2 ......II.6:10 | try to strike a bargain with the Son of **G.**, |
| S-2 ........II.7:5 | a way to use forgiveness for the goal of **G.**, |
| S-2 ........II.8:5 | You do not want to be afraid of **G.**. You |
| S-2 ........II.8:6 | redeemed from sin and in the Love of **G.**. |
| S-2 ........II.8:8 | you home where **G.** would have you be. |
| S-2 ........III.1:5 | Would **G.** deceive you? He but asks for |
| S-2 ........III.1:7 | and seeks to understand the Will of **G.**. |
| S-2 ........III.2:1 | You child of **G.**, the gifts of God are yours |
| S-2 ........III.2:1 | You child of God, the gifts of **G.** are yours |
| S-2 ........III.4:2 | **G.** did not choose this sorry path for you. |
| S-2 ........III.4:3 | for prayer is merciful and **G.** is just. His is |
| S-2 ........III.6:7 | death become again the holy gift of **G.**. |
| S-2 ......III.6:10 | to **G.** you turn to hear what you should do |
| S-2 ........III.7:8 | the door; the Son of **G.** as He created him. |
| S-3 ..........I.1:3 | that injure and would hurt the Son of **G.**. |
| S-3 ..........I.2:1 | cause is unforgiveness of the Son of **G.**. It |
| S-3 ..........I.3:4 | brother, and the Son of **G.** upon himself. |
| S-3 ..........I.5:3 | the world or to the everlasting Love of **G.**. |
| S-3 ........II.2:1 | Son of **G.** along the way he goes to God. |
| S-3 ........II.2:1 | Son of God along the way he goes to **G.**. |
| S-3 ........II.3:5 | sustained in us; His Voice, the Word of **G.** |
| S-3 ........II.6:2 | to take its vengeance on the Son of **G.**. Yet |
| S-3 ........III.1:8 | to obscure the unity that is the Son of **G.**. |
| S-3 ........III.5:1 | are Sons of **G.** who recognize their Source |
| S-3 ........III.5:6 | place is written now the holy Word of **G.**. |
| S-3 ........III.5:8 | else can heal as **G.** established healing. |
| S-3 ........III.6:6 | stand, and fear has given way at last to **G.**. |
| S-3 ........IV.1:3 | voice, through whom He speaks for **G.**, |
| S-3 ........IV.1:5 | have no gifts but those they have from **G.**. |
| S-3 ......IV.1:10 | sing of their union and their thanks to **G.**. |
| S-3 ........IV.3:3 | **G.** thanks His healers, for He knows the |
| S-3 ........IV.3:7 | Do not forget the gratitude of **G.**. Do not |
| S-3 ........IV.4:2 | Your prayer has risen up and called to **G.**, |
| S-3 ........IV.4:6 | and no desire to attack the Son of **G.**. |
| S-3 ........IV.5:1 | him so are you to yourself, and **G.** to you. |
| S-3 ........IV.5:2 | Nor will your judgment fail to reach to **G.**, |
| S-3 ........IV.9:3 | brow of him who is the holy Son of **G.**. |

## god 39

*God*

| | |
|---|---|
| T-10........III.h | The **G.** of Sickness |
| T-10......III.4:6 | A sick **g.** must be an idol, made in the |
| T-10......III.4:7 | does perceive in a Son of God; a sick **g.**, |
| T-10......III.9:3 | You will hear the **g.** you listen to. You |
| T-10......III.9:4 | to. You made the **g.** of sickness, and by |
| T-10....III.11:4 | up the **g.** of sickness for your brothers; in |
| T-10....III.11:5 | For if you see the **g.** of sickness anywhere, |
| T-10....III.11:7 | belief that you can choose which **g.** is real. |
| T-10......IV.1:6 | God is not at war with the **g.** of sickness |
| T-10.......V.1:1 | rituals of the **g.** of sickness are strange and |
| T-10.......V.3:2 | The **g.** of sickness obviously demands the |
| T-10.......V.3:7 | is the offering your **g.** demands because, |
| T-10.......V.4:2 | depression he made the **g.** of depression. |
| T-10.......V.8:1 | look to the **g.** of sickness for healing but |
| T-11......VI.5:1 | the power the **g.** he worships has over him |
| T-11......VI.5:2 | For he places himself at the altar of his **g.**, |
| T-11......VI.5:2 | whether it be the **g.** he made or the God |
| T-11......VI.5:3 | for he will obey only the **g.** he accepts. The |
| T-11......VI.5:4 | **g.** of crucifixion demands that he crucify, |
| T-11......VI.7:2 | Son whom the **g.** of crucifixion condemns |
| T-29.......II.3:7 | more is pain your friend and guilt your **g.**, |
| T-29.......II.8:8 | what is gone from Him becomes your **g.**, |
| T-29.......II.9:1 | that is asked to be a **g.** will be attacked, |
| W-pI...153.7:3 | now from your delusion of an angry **g.**, |
| W-pI...163.2:1 | **g.** of the guilty and the lord of all illusions |
| W-pI...170.6:1 | love as enemy, must cruelty become a **g.**. |
| W-pI...170.7:1 | we look upon this cruel **g.** dispassionately. |
| W-pI...170.8:6 | it? For the **g.** of cruelty takes many forms. |
| W-pI...170.9:4 | which enthrones the thought of fear as **g.**. |
| W-pI.170.11:2 | stone you made, and call it **g.** no longer. |
| W-pI.170.11:3 | chosen that this cruel **g.** remain with you |
| W-pI...183.4:4 | have lost the name of **g.** you gave them. |
| W-pI.196.10:5 | And thus a **g.** outside yourself became |
| M-27 .........2:5 | Who loves such a **g.** knows not of love, |
| M-27 .........4:6 | There is either a **g.** of fear or One of Love. |
| P-2.........in.3:6 | The self he sees is his **g.**, and he seeks only |
| P-2........VII.7:7 | without the **g.** who must be given him? |
| P-3.........I.2:12 | you rather choose who would be **g.**, or |
| S-1 ........III.2:4 | They call upon a vengeful **g.**, and it is he |

## God's 936

*See also* His, Mine, My, Our, Whose, Your, Yours

| | |
|---|---|
| T-1.........I.21:2 | miracles you accept **G.** forgiveness by |
| T-1.........I.38:2 | both **G.** creations and your illusions. He |
| T-1........III.3:4 | salvation or release of all of **G.** creations. |
| T-1........III.5:8 | you experience **G.** reassurances as threat, |
| T-1.........V.3:5 | The specialness of **G.** Sons does not stem |
| T-1........VII.1:4 | real pleasure comes from doing **G.** Will. |
| T-2...........I.2:8 | requires **G.** endowment of the Son with |
| T-2........VI.6:4 | no strain in doing **G.** Will as soon as you |
| T-3...........I.8:3 | is the only appropriate gift for **G.** altar, |
| T-3.........II.4:1 | afraid of **G.** Will because you have used |
| T-3........III.7:7 | There are no strangers in **G.** creation. To |
| T-3........IV.7:7 | I cannot unite your will with **G.** for you, |
| T-3.........V.2:8 | of the abstract creativity of **G.** creations. |
| T-3.........V.3:5 | disagreeing with **G.** idea of your creation. |
| T-3.........V.8:9 | To know **G.** miracle is to know Him. |
| T-3.........V.9:7 | **G.** miracles are as total as His Thoughts |
| T-3........VI.8:7 | unhappy. **G.** creations are given their true |
| T-4...........I.2:9 | Your self and **G.** Self *are* in opposition. |
| T-4......III.10:1 | The calm being of **G.** Kingdom, which in |
| T-4........IV.2:5 | then change your mind to think with **G.**. |
| T-4........IV.2:7 | it. Your mind is one with **G.**. Denying this |
| T-4........VI.6:3 | and I do not choose **G.** channels wrongly. |
| T-4........VII.8:7 | The truly helpful are **G.** miracle workers, |
| T-5.........in.3:5 | upon it. Only **G.** holy children are worthy |
| T-5...........I.4:6 | As a man and also one of **G.** creations, my |
| T-5.........II.2:5 | Holy Spirit is **G.** Answer to the separation |
| T-5........II.3:11 | and **G.** Sons are as equal as learners as |
| T-5.........II.8:4 | Holy Spirit is the way in which **G.** Will is |
| T-5........III.1:4 | Mind is partly yours and also partly **G.**. |
| T-5........III.5:3 | the Holy Spirit is **G.** Answer to the ego. |
| T-5........IV.3:3 | Sharing is **G.** way of creating, and also |
| T-5........IV.4:3 | because **G.** Wholeness is the Wholeness |
| T-5........IV.5:5 | because my name is the Name of **G.** Son. |
| T-5........IV.6:8 | rendering unto God the things that are **G.** |
| T-5........IV.7:3 | of **G.** ideas is withheld from the Kingdom. |
| T-5.........V.3:3 | on the concept of usurping **G.** power. The |
| T-5.......VI.10:3 | and every witness to guilt in **G.** creations |
| T-5.......VI.10:4 | believe gladly to **G.** Own Higher Court, |
| T-5.......VII.1:1 | can make a voice that can drown out **G.**? |
| T-5.......VII.5:1 | with a lack of love to one of **G.** creations. |
| T-6...........I.8:3 | you can be the foundation of **G.** church. A |
| T-6.........II.1:2 | recognizes the Wholeness of **G.** creation. |
| T-6.........II.7:1 | of the perfect equality of **G.** knowing. The |
| T-6.........II.9:2 | is as true of **G.** Thinking as it is of yours. |
| T-6........II.11:5 | in which you must perceive **G.** creations, |
| T-6........IV.8:2 | in the presence of **G.** accomplishments, |
| T-6.........V.1:7 | **G.** extending outward, though not His |
| T-6.......V.B.7:2 | up to you to decide what **G.** creations are. |
| T-6.......V.B.9:1 | perception that reflects **G.** knowing. As |
| T-6.......V.C.7:5 | is why you must be vigilant on **G.** behalf. |
| T-7...........I.2:3 | **G.** creative Thought proceeds from Him |
| T-7...........I.2:5 | **G.** accomplishments are not yours, but |
| T-7...........I.3:7 | **G.** creations have always been, because |
| T-7...........I.4:4 | is to limit giving, and this is not **G.** Will. |
| T-7..........II.5:5 | **G.** law of creation does not involve the |
| T-7........III.2:1 | **G.** meaning waits in the Kingdom, |
| T-7........III.2:4 | **G.** meaning perceive yourself as absent |
| T-7........III.3:3 | Because **G.** equal Sons have everything, |
| T-7........IV.2:4 | This is **G.** Will and yours. The laws of |
| T-7.......VI.10:2 | from this will obscure **G.** Voice in you, |
| T-7.......VI.10:5 | This limitless power is **G.** gift to you, |
| T-7.......VI.11:1 | your part in it, **G.** creation is seen as weak |
| T-7.......VI.13:2 | This is not **G.** choice but yours. If your |
| T-7.......VI.13:3 | your mind could be out of accord with **G.**, |
| T-7.......VI.13:4 | Yet because **G.** Will is unchangeable, no |
| T-7.......VI.13:6 | not separation, is your will *because* it is **G.**, |
| T-7.......VII.3:1 | need **G.** blessing because that you have |
| T-7........IX.3:1 | The extension of **G.** Being is spirit's only |
| T-7........IX.6:5 | Disobeying **G.** Will is meaningful only to |
| T-7........IX.6:7 | Your Self-fullness is as boundless as **G.**. |
| T-7.........X.2:5 | Truth is **G.** Will. Share His Will and you |
| T-7.........X.4:3 | opposite of **G.** Will can be better for you. |
| T-7.........X.4:4 | it is possible to *do* the opposite of **G.** Will. |
| T-7.........X.6:9 | has been given you by **G.** decision. That is |
| T-7.........X.8:3 | are **G.** Will and do not accept His Will, |
| T-7........XI.1:5 | nature, being out of accord with **G.** laws. |
| T-7........XI.7:4 | any more than you can establish **G.**. But |
| T-8..........II.3:6 | The lesson is that your will and **G.** cannot |
| T-8..........II.4:1 | to teach that you want to oppose **G.** Will. |
| T-8..........II.6:3 | because it is not **G.** Will to *be* without you. |
| T-8..........II.6:4 | you have learned that your will is **G.**, you |
| T-8..........II.8:1 | Holy Spirit appeal to restore **G.** Kingdom |
| T-8........III.2:3 | **G.** Will cannot be forced upon you, being |
| T-8........III.2:6 | His teaching will release your will to **G.**, |
| T-8........III.8:7 | Glory is **G.** gift to you, because that is |
| T-8........IV.1:1 | **G.** Will for you is complete peace and joy, |
| T-8........IV.3:1 | You were in darkness until **G.** Will was |
| T-8.......IV.5:14 | it and thereby violating **G.** Will for you. |
| T-8........IV.6:6 | else can it be, if **G.** Kingdom is freedom? |
| T-8........IV.6:7 | perfect equality of all **G.** Sons cannot be |
| T-8........IV.6:8 | **G.** Sons are equal in will, all being the |
| T-8........IV.8:1 | is the only gift you can offer to **G.** Sons, |
| T-8.........V.3:1 | **G.** Oneness and ours are not separate, |
| T-8.........V.4:5 | I bring **G.** peace back to all His children |
| T-8.........V.4:6 | because nothing can prevail against **G.**. |
| T-8.........V.6:3 | one for which **G.** Voice speaks in all of us. |
| T-8........VI.1:4 | **G.** welcome waits for us all, and He will |
| T-8........VI.4:1 | and learn what **G.** treasure is and yours: |
| T-8.......VI.5:14 | its value lies in **G.** sharing Himself with it |
| T-8........VI.6:1 | is to add to **G.** treasure by creating yours. |
| T-8........VI.7:3 | thinking. **G.** Will *is* Thought. It cannot be |
| T-8........VI.7:6 | can even imprison the mind of **G.** Son, if |
| T-8........VI.8:5 | The whole power of **G.** Son lies in all of us |
| T-8.......VI.8:10 | because you who are **G.** Own treasure do |
| T-8.......VII.3:5 | This is **G.** way of making unlimited what |
| T-8......VII.13:2 | be listening to **G.** joyous Teacher and |
| T-8......VII.15:1 | purpose, and unified purpose is only **G.**. |
| T-8........IX.7:3 | The Name of **G.** Son is One, and you are |
| T-9...........I.5:2 | this is not **G.** Will because it is not yours. |
| T-9...........I.5:3 | is no difference between your will and **G.**. |
| T-9...........I.7:8 | your salvation because it is the same as **G.** |
| T-9...........I.8:1 | can believe that its will is stronger than **G.** |
| T-9...........I.8:2 | there is no God or that **G.** Will is fearful. |
| T-9...........I.9:2 | recognition that his will and **G.** are one. |
| T-9.........I.14:1 | then, that **G.** Will is already possible, and |
| T-9........II.6:11 | except as He answers all of **G.** Sons? Hear |
| T-9..........II.7:5 | my brothers in whom **G.** Voice speaks. |
| T-9..........II.8:7 | Hear only **G.** Answer in His Sons, and you |
| T-9........II.11:3 | God. **G.** laws are always fair and perfectly |
| T-9........II.12:6 | *myself. I see you as G. Son and my brother.* |
| T-9.........V.1:1 | is far more widely used than **G.**. This is |
| T-9........VI.4:3 | this. Neither **G.** light nor yours is dimmed |
| T-9........VI.5:4 | as you were created witnesses to **G.**. Yet |
| T-9........VI.7:2 | to you until you remember **G.** open Arms |
| T-9........VI.7:7 | **G.** meaning is incomplete without you, |
| T-9.......VII.1:1 | **G.** Will is your salvation. Would He not |
| T-9......VIII.4:1 | in the presence of **G.** grandeur, because |
| T-9......VIII.6:3 | Your grandeur is **G.** answer to the ego, |
| T-9....VIII.10:7 | Your value is in **G.** Mind, and therefore |
| T-9....VIII.10:9 | evaluation of yourself is truer than **G.**. |
| T-9....VIII.11:1 | your evaluation of yourself must *be* **G.**. |
| T-10.......in.1:5 | can violate **G.** laws in your imagination, |

T-10.......in.2:5 the ephemeral be real if you are G. only
T-10....... II.4:3 reality precludes the acceptance of G. gift,
T-10....... II.5:5 And if your reality is G., when you attack
T-10...... III.2:6 G. remaining Communication Link with
T-10...... III.6:2 G. Son knows no idols, but he does know
T-10...... III.6:5 you, because the value of G. Son is one.
T-10...... III.8:1 I do not bring G. message with deception
T-10.... III.11:6 because he was made as G. replacement.
T-10...... IV.1:7 he cannot be reconciled with G. Will. If
T-10...... IV.3:4 removed part of your mind from G. Will.
T-10...... IV.4:1 G. laws will keep your mind at peace
T-10...... IV.7:4 the miracle worker has heard G. Voice, he
T-10....... V.4:1 enter the mind of G. Son against His Will.
T-10...... V.11:3 created as the dwelling place of G. Son.
T-11.......in.2:3 ego was made out of the wish of G. Son to
T-11.......in.3:2 The cornerstone of G. creation is you, for
T-11.........I.1:5 the mind of G. Son you restore this reality
T-11.........I.3:4 would be an empty place in G. Mind.
T-11.........I.6:4 G. Mind cannot be lessened. It can only
T-11.........I.6:7 To give without limit is G. Will for you,
T-11.........I.8:3 know." G. Will is that you are His Son. By
T-11.........I.8:5 must ask what G. Will is in everything,
T-11.........I.8:7 Him, therefore, what G. Will is for you,
T-11.........I.9:1 it appear as if G. Will is outside yourself,
T-11.........I.9:2 possible for G. Will and yours to conflict.
T-11.......I.9:10 G. Son cannot will death for himself
T-11.......I.10:2 It is immutable by G. Will and yours, for
T-11.......I.10:3 You are afraid to know G. Will, because
T-11.......I.11:8 be so. G. Will is that His Son be One, and
T-11....... II.2:5 mind, teaches you that you are G. Son. In
T-11....... II.2:6 it, lies the denial of G. Fatherhood and of
T-11....... II.3:5 yourself, for only G. Son needs healing.
T-11...... III.1:4 way, for that is not G. Will for His Son.
T-11...... III.2:1 G. Son is indeed in need of comfort, for
T-11...... III.3:3 comes and you have said, "G. Will is mine
T-11...... III.4:5 the dark journey is not the way of G. Son.
T-11...... III.6:2 never let them enter the mind of G. Son,
T-11...... III.7:1 Only G. Comforter can comfort you. In
T-11...... III.7:8 You cannot enter G. Presence with the
T-11.........IV.h The Inheritance of G. Son
T-11...... IV.1:2 As G. creation It is yours, and belonging
T-11...... IV.2:3 G. laws hold only for your protection,
T-11...... IV.5:6 *enter G. Presence if you attack His Son.*
T-11...... IV.6:1 Christ is at G. altar, waiting to welcome
T-11...... IV.7:1 G. altar Christ waits for the restoration of
T-11..... V.11:1 G. purpose could be defeated, and this is
T-11..... V.11:3 goal can be accomplished and G. purpose
T-11..... V.11:4 *only* G. purpose can be accomplished, and
T-11..... V.12:4 it is given you to know that G. function is
T-11..... V.12:7 Yet G. Son is not insane, and cannot
T-11..... V.17:7 is the sign that they have beheld G. Son,
T-11...... VI.3:9 little beliefs that are unworthy of G. Son.
T-11...... VI.4:9 nature of G. Son as his Father created him
T-11...... VI.5:1 the power of the devotion of G. Son, nor
T-11...... VI.7:1 the nails from the hands of G. Son, and
T-11...... VI.7:5 undoing of the crucifixion of G. Son is the
T-11...... VI.8:2 Yet you cannot crucify G. Son, for the
T-11.... VI.10:1 G. Son *is* saved. Bring only this awareness
T-11.... VI.10:5 because all of G. Sons are of equal value,
T-11....VIII.8:5 G. Sons have nothing they do not share.
T-11....VIII.9:1 of G. Son and his Father will answer you,
T-11....VIII.9:5 Be not deceived in G. Son, for thereby
T-11..VIII.10:5 disappear in the Presence of G. Answer?
T-11..VIII.11:5 Be not deceived in G. Son, for he is one
T-11..VIII.12:3 G. Son whom God condemneth not. Let
T-11..VIII.12:4 all offenses of G. Son against himself and
T-12.........I.5:7 you will not recognize G. Answer to you.
T-12.........I.6:4 How simple, then, is G. plan for salvation
T-12.........I.7:3 recognize G. Answer as you want It to be,
T-12..... II.2:10 and G. Answer to your forgetting is but
T-12...... III.7:1 thoughts of G. Son are the world's reality,
T-12...... IV.4:7 will never deceive G. Son whom He loves
T-12....... V.9:6 can oppose the decision of G. Son. His
T-12...... VI.7:2 the holy perception of G. Son becomes so
T-12...... VI.7:2 spirit of G. Son shines in the Mind of the
T-12....VII.10:2 your mind is the loveliest of G. creations.
T-12....VIII.2:1 G. Son is as safe as his Father, for the Son
T-12....VIII.3:6 The definition of reality is G., not yours.
T-12....VIII.7:2 G. Son can be seen because his vision is
T-12 ...VIII.7:9 And you who share G. Being with Him
T-13 ......in.2:1 the mind of G. Son was the beginning of
T-13 ......in.3:4 and this is the ego's interpretation, not G.
T-13 ......in.4:1 *is* a picture of the crucifixion of G. Son.
T-13 ......in.4:2 realize that G. Son cannot be crucified,
T-13 ......in.4:3 the eternal fact that G. Son is not guilty.
T-13 ........I.1:5 the denial of the blamelessness of G. Son.
T-13 ........I.2:5 ego has no life, and G. Son *is* without guilt.
T-13 ........I.5:6 shines untouched forever in G. Mind.
T-13 ........I.5:7 G. Son will always be as he was created.
T-13 ........I.6:1 you will realize there is no guilt in G. Son.
T-13 ........I.6:4 you cannot know that you are G. Son.
T-13 ........I.7:6 Let the holiness of G. Son shine away the
T-13 ........I.8:8 Yet the guarantee of your continuity is G.,
T-13 ........I.9:3 G. way of reminding you of His Son, and
T-13 .......I.11:7 then, are saved because G. Son is guiltless
T-13 .......II.3:2 G. Son by condemning him to death. You
T-13 .......II.3:3 of G. Son can ultimately satisfy it. It does
T-13 .......II.5:1 that you believe you have crucified G. Son
T-13 .......II.6:2 of G. Son it did attempt to kill him, and
T-13 ..... III.2:4 even upon your savage wish to kill G. Son
T-13 ..... III.4:1 you would be helpless in G. Presence, and
T-13 ..... III.6:6 it, for here is the real crucifixion of G. Son
T-13 ..... III.8:6 For grandeur is the right of G. Son, and
T-13 .... III.10:5 And the peace of G. Son was shattered,
T-13 .... V.10:5 dreams He sees G. guiltless Son within
T-13 ..... VI.3:6 that obscures G. Son to you *is* the past,
T-13 ..... VI.8:4 G. guiltless Son is only light. There is no
T-13 ..... VI.8:8 holy light that shines forth from G. Son is
T-13 ... VI.13:5 gave. G. Son is still as loving as his Father.
T-13 .... VII.7:1 G. Will that nothing touch His Son except
T-13 .. VII.13:5 G. Son is not a traveller through outer
T-13 .. VII.17:4 sorrow from the mind of G. most holy
T-13 ...VIII.6:5 miracle that ever was is G. most holy Son,
T-13 ...VIII.8:2 the power of G. Son will move in us, and
T-13 .. X.10:11 the perfect purity that is forever within G.
T-13 .....X.11:1 of G. Sons unless you love them all and
T-13 ..... XI.5:4 thoughts may occur to you, G. Will *is* done
T-13 ..... XI.9:5 G. sleeping Son holds no power over him.
T-13 ... XI.10:1 Can G. Son lose himself in dreams, when
T-14 ........I.3:3 The thoughts the mind of G. Son projects
T-14 ..... III.3:9 *Let me bring peace to G. Son from his Father*
T-14 ..... III.6:1 No penalty is ever asked of G. Son except
T-14 ..... III.9:4 No thought of G. Son can be separate or
T-14 ... III.12:1 Would you deny the truth of G. decision,
T-14 ... III.12:2 Nothing can shake G. conviction of the
T-14 ... III.15:1 worth of G. Son whom He created holy,
T-14 ..... IV.3:9 your function in G. Mind with all of yours
T-14 ...... V.1:2 into a radiant message of G. Love, to
T-14 ...... V.2:1 one is always the same; *G. Son is guiltless.*
T-14 ...... V.4:1 of the Kingdom is the right of G. Son,
T-14 ...... V.7:4 to restore what is the right of G. creation.
T-14 ..... VI.8:6 are no hidden chambers in G. temple. Its
T-14 ...VIII.3:7 G. glory and His Son's belong to you in
T-14 ..... IX.5:3 mirror that would hold G. reflection in it.
T-14 ..... XI.4:4 This lesson shines with G. glory, for in it
T-14 ..... XI.5:2 be sure that you have learned G. lesson,
T-14 ..... XI.5:4 you do not will for G. Son what his Father
T-14 ..... XI.7:3 G. Son can make no needs his Father will
T-14 ... XI.11:1 G. Son will always be indivisible. As we
T-14 ... XI.13:3 G. Teacher is as like to His Creator as is
T-15 ........I.1:3 G. Teacher cannot be satisfied with His
T-15 .......I.15:2 little to restore G. whole power to you. He
T-15 .......I.15:5 in which G. Son could lose his purity. His
T-15 .......I.15:9 of the eternal sanctity of G. creation, it is
T-15 .......II.2:4 Blessed is G. Teacher, Whose joy it is to
T-15 .......II.2:4 joy it is to teach G. holy Son his holiness.
T-15 .......II.2:7 Through Him you stand before G. altar,
T-15 .......II.6:5 G. Teacher and His lesson will support
T-15 ... III.12:5 G. power is forever on the side of His host
T-15 ..... IV.2:6 for your salvation in exchange for G.. His
T-15 ..... VI.2:5 our faith in G. Son because we recognize,
T-15 .. VII.14:8 understand that your completion is G.,
T-15 ...VIII.2:5 is. G. Son has such great need of your
T-15 ...VIII.3:2 of G. Son is the loneliness of his Father.
T-15 ...VIII.5:1 The Holy Spirit is G. attempt to free you
T-15 ..... IX.6:7 limit not your vision of G. Son to what
T-15 ..... IX.7:1 and your thoughts will be as free as G.. As
T-16 .......II.8:1 Do not interpret against G. Love, for you
T-16 ..... III.5:4 G. Answer to the separation added more
T-16 ..... III.6:5 gratitude has joined with yours and G. to
T-16 ... IV.13:1 of any kind would hinder G. completion,
T-16 ... IV.13:3 in G. completion seem to be possible. The
T-16 .... VII.8:2 For G. gifts have no reality apart from
T-17 .......II.3:1 of all in G. plan of Atonement. All else is
T-17 .......II.3:7 this final blessing of G. Son upon himself,
T-17 .......II.6:3 a blade of grass a sign of G. perfection.
T-17 ..... III.7:2 G. Son is One. Whom God has joined as
T-17 ..... IV.2:6 the holy relationship shares G. purpose,
T-17 ..... IV.2:7 you have made is a substitute for G. Will,
T-17 ..... IV.4:1 Who was G. Answer to the separation.
T-17 ..... IV.4:7 preserved, to serve G. purpose for you.
T-18 ......I.10:2 Your reality was G. creation, and has no
T-18 ..... IV.4:2 with the unlimited power of G. Will. You
T-18 ..... IV.5:5 That is but to confuse your role with G..
T-18 ..... VI.6:8 it to be the dwelling place of G. Son, and
T-18 ..... IX.1:4 The rest is fully in G. keeping, and needs
T-19 ..... III.8:2 For there would be a power beyond G.,
T-19 ..... III.8:3 And each part of G. fragmented creation
T19 ...IV.A.3:5 whole. G. Will is One, not many. It has no
T19 ... IV.B.9:3 power, and use it for the Son of G. release
T19 ... IV.C.7:4 Only G. Answer is its end. The obstacle of
T19 IV.D.18:5 the way unto the resurrection of G. Son,
T-20 ........I.1:2 brooding on the crucifixion of G. Son, but
T-20 ........I.1:5 of the Son of G. forgiveness on himself;
T-20 ... III.11:8 of G. eternal promise of your immortality
T-20 ... IV.8:10 be. G. guarantee will hold against all
T-20 .......V.1:1 G. Son comes closest to himself in a holy
T-20 .......V.1:5 the parts of G. Son gradually join in time,
T-20 ... VIII.4:6 is a better home, a safer shelter for G. Son
T-21 .......II.6:5 is the Son of G. replacement for his will, a
T-21 .......V.5:1 G. plan for your salvation could not have
T-21 .......V.6:1 G. plan is simple; never circular and
T-21 .. VII.13:5 The power of the Son of G. desire remains
T-21 .. VIII.3:9 and G. giving must be incomplete unless
T-21 ... VIII.4:1 complete G. Will and are His happiness,
T-21 ... VIII.5:1 What is the holy instant but G. appeal to
T-22 ........I.4:1 What could be secret from G. Will? Yet
T-22 ..... IV.5:6 received. G. offer still is open, yet it waits
T-22 ... VI.11:2 How can G. Son be weak and frail and
T-23 ......in.1:7 Being opposed to it, it is G. "enemy." And
T-23 ......in.5:1 let littleness lead G. Son into temptation.
T-23 ..... IV.2:4 they be to those who see G. Son a body.
T-23 ..... IV.3:5 Creation is the means for G. extension,
T-24 ........I.3:2 with the reality of G. creation and with
T-24 .....II.11:4 G. Love gave you to him and him to you
T-24 ..... III.2:3 against yourself; *your* enemy, not G.. So
T-24 ..... VI.1:8 See in him G. creation. For in him his
T-24 ..... VI.4:1 the healing of G. Son is all the world is for
T-24 ..... VI.4:5 all belief G. Son can suffer pain because
T-24 ..... VI.8:2 cannot withhold G. blessing from himself
T-24 ..... VI.9:5 And both shall see G. glory in His Son,
T-24 .. VII.1:11 parody of G. creation that takes the place
T-24 .. VII.10:9 Such is the travesty on G. creation. For as
T-25 .......II.7:1 Accept G. frame instead of yours, and
T-25 .....II.11:5 apart from all G. Love as given equally.
T-25 ..... III.1:6 to this world, of G. more basic law; that
T-25 ..... III.2:1 G. laws do not obtain directly to a world
T-25 ..... IV.2:7 might be increased, and G. along with his
T-25 .... VII.2:1 death is just as strong as is G. Will for life.
T-25 .. VII.10:1 What is dependable except G. Love? And
T-25 .. VII.10:4 It is G. Will that you remember this, and
T-25 .. VII.10:5 you in G. Own plan to show His Son that
T-25 .. VII.12:4 single rock of truth can faith in G. eternal
T-25 .. VII.13:1 a mad belief that G. insanity would make
T-25 .. VIII.5:5 Vengeance is alien to G. Mind *because* He
T-25 ... VIII.6:4 "fires" of Heaven by G. Own angry Hand.
T-25 ... VIII.7:2 work G. vengeance on them in the guise
T-25 ... VIII.9:5 G. Own justice does He recognize all you
T-25 . VIII.9:11 same does mercy stand at G. right Hand,
T-25 . VIII.12:8 fulfilled. G. Son has found a witness unto
T-25 . VIII.14:5 replace G. justice with a version of its own
T-25 . VIII.14:7 will deprive yourself of what G. justice
T-25 ..... IX.2:3 G. justice warrants gratitude, not fear.
T-25 ..... IX.2:4 treasures given to G. Son are kept for him
T-25 ..... IX.7:1 Salvation cannot seek to help G. Son be
T-25 . IX.10:10 *What is G. belongs to everyone, and* ***is his***
T-26 ........I.4:3 than that G. Son perceive himself without

T-26.........I.4:7 What witness to the Wholeness of G. Son
T-26.........I.7:4 G. Son is not imprisoned in a body, nor is
T-26.........I.8:1 G. justice rests in gentleness upon His
T-26....... II.4:9 hurt G. Son must be unfair and therefore
T-26..... V.10:7 death, a vault G. Son entered an instant,
T-26...... VI.2:2 This is no friendship worthy of G. Son,
T-26..... VII.4:3 G. answer is eternal, though it works in
T-26..... VII.5:1 G. answer lies where the belief in sin
T-26... VII.6:10 G. Will is One. And any wish that seems
T-26..... VII.7:4 Then would G. Will be split in two, and
T-26..... VII.8:5 of G. Son where sin was thought to rule.
T-26..... VII.9:4 state, and not in opposition to G. Will.
T-26... VII.14:4 G. Son could never be content with less
T-26... VII.14:7 G. Son made incomplete and not himself.
T-27.........I.1:9 all it would entail the whole of G. creation
T-27.........I.3:1 your brother of attack upon G. Son. You
T-27....... II.8:9 G. Son remembered that he *is* God's Son.
T-27....... II.8:9 God's Son remembered that he *is* G. Son.
T-27..... II.10:8 separation but a wish to take G. function
T-27...... VI.4:1 G. Witness sees no witnesses against the
T-27... VII.13:3 than an idle dream has terrified G. Son,
T-28...... I.12:2 For in that instant is G. memory allowed
T-28...... II.1:5 he is G. Son that he must also be a father,
T-28...... IV.9:4 part of the completed picture of G. Son!
T-28.... IV.10:8 go is all the Healer of G. Son requires. He
T-28...... VI.5:4 my mind and yours" has kept G. promise,
T-28..... VII.1:6 G. promise is a promise to Himself, and
T-28..... VII.4:4 do. It serves to help the healing of G. Son,
T-28..... VII.7:5 resting on G. promise that His Son is safe
T-28..... VII.7:7 be used to liberate G. Son unto his home.
T-29..... II.10:1 "something" is the body asked to be G.
T-29.........III.h G. Witnesses
T-29.... III.3:11 G. witness has set forth the gentle way of
T-29.... III.3:11 forth the gentle way of kindness to G. Son
T-29....... V.4:2 Be very still and hear G. Voice in him, and
T-29....... V.4:3 complete can be a part of G. completion,
T-29....... V.6:2 and lead G. Son unto his Father's house.
T-29.... VI.2:11 is. G. Son can never change by what men
T-29...... VI.3:4 can set a goal unlike G. purpose for you,
T-29...... VI.5:1 think that it was made to crucify G. Son.
T-29...... VI.6:1 whose purpose is forgiveness of G. Son!
T-29..... VII.3:4 Yet does he seek to kill G. Son within, and
T-29... VIII.4:5 hand could be held up to block G. way?
T-29. VIII.8:13 more. And it is this that is against G. Will
T-29...... IX.2:3 How can G. Son awaken from the dream?
T-29...... IX.3:5 Judgment is an injustice to G. Son, and it
T-30...... III.4:4 Your will to be complete is but G. Will,
T-30...... III.5:1 Completion is the *function* of G. Son. He
T-30...... III.6:8 parts in what exists within G. Mind. It is
T-30.... IV.5:12 in attack. G. Son needs no defense against
T-30.... IV.8:13 What could G. plan for his salvation be,
T-30....... V.4:1 The final step is G., because it is but God
T-30....... V.5:1 short of this, for this is G. Own purpose;
T-30...... VI.7:5 You must forgive G. Son entirely. Or you
T-30...... VI.7:8 that have replaced the truth about G. Son
T-30...... VI.9:1 G. Son is perfect, or he cannot be God's
T-30...... VI.9:1 Son is perfect, or he cannot be G. Son.
T-30... VIII.4:7 freedom to bestow His gifts upon G. Son.
T-31.........I.7:4 that G. Son is guilty is the world you see.
T-31...... I.7:11 And you will learn G. Son is innocent,
T-31.........I.8:1 The outcome of the lesson that G. Son is
T-31.........I.8:8 calling of each part of G. creation to the
T-31.........I.9:6 G. perfect Son remembers his creation.
T-31....... I.10:1 that His Son is guilty as G. Love must be
T-31....... II.7:1 Because he is your equal in G. Love, you
T-31... VIII.6:4 A miracle has come to heal G. Son, and
T-31... VIII.9:1 situation where G. gift can once again be
W-pl........35.h My mind is part of G.. I am very holy.
W-pl.....35.7:5 *But my mind is part of G.. I am very holy.*
W-pl.....36.1:2 are holy because your mind is part of G..
W-pl.....36.1:7 mind is part of G. you must be sinless, or
W-pl.....42.4:7 *G. gifts to me must be mine, because He gave*
W-pl.....43.2:6 Spirit give it a meaning very close to G..
W-pl.....43.5:7 *I see my own thoughts, which are like G..* Any
W-pl........49.h G. Voice speaks to me all through the day
W-pl.....49.1:1 It is quite possible to listen to G. Voice all
W-pl.....49.2:6 Try to hear G. Voice call to you lovingly,
W-pl.....49.3:2 We will try actually to hear G. Voice
W-pl.....49.5:3 realizing that you are inviting G. Voice to

W-pl.....52.1:7 Nothing in G. creation is affected in any
W-pl.....53.5:5 see. Yet G. way is sure. The images I have
W-pl.....57.3:4 I see the world as a prison for G. Son. It
W-pl.....57.5:1 (35) My mind is part of G.. I am very
W-pl.....60.1:5 It is the reflection of G. Love on earth. It
W-pl.....60.4:1 (49) G. Voice speaks to me all through
W-pl.....60.4:2 There is not a moment in which G. Voice
W-pl.....60.4:5 G. Voice is the only Voice and the only
W-pl.....60.5:2 As I listen to G. Voice, I am sustained by
W-pl.....61.1:1 is the light of the world except G. Son?
W-pl.....61.3:1 it is G. Voice which tells you it is true.
W-pl.....63.4:4 that G. Son looks to you for his salvation.
W-pl.....64.6:3 *Let me not try to substitute mine for G.. Let*
W-pl.....69.2:5 tears of G. Son disappear in the sunlight.
W-pl.....69.8:4 that you are at last joining your will to G..
W-pl.....70.4:3 G. purpose was to ensure that it did.
W-pl.....70.5:1 Today we practice realizing that G. Will
W-pl........71.h Only G. plan for salvation will work.
W-pl.....71.1:1 up a plan for salvation in opposition to G.
W-pl.....71.1:3 Since it is the opposite of G., you also
W-pl.....71.1:3 you also believe that to accept G. plan in
W-pl.....71.5:1 G. plan for salvation works simply
W-pl.....71.6:4 Only G. plan for salvation will work.
W-pl.....71.6:5 no possible alternative to G. plan that will
W-pl.....71.8:2 G. plan for your salvation will work, and
W-pl.....71.8:5 and anger; but G. plan will succeed. It will
W-pl....71.9:10 to establish your claim to G. answer.
W-pl....71.10:1 yourself often that G. plan for salvation,
W-pl....71.10:3 *is the opposite of G. plan for salvation. And*
W-pl........72.h is an attack on G. plan for salvation.
W-pl.....72.1:1 plan for salvation is the opposite of G., we
W-pl.....72.3:1 is an attack on G. plan for salvation. But
W-pl.....72.7:4 you are attacking G. plan for salvation,
W-pl.....72.9:5 to end the attack on G. plan for salvation,
W-pl...72.10:1 today is to become aware that G. plan for
W-pl...72.10:3 cannot understand what G. plan for us is.
W-pl...72.10:5 aside, and ask what G. plan for us is:
W-pl.72.10:10 We have attacked G. plan for salvation
W-pl...72.13:3 *is an attack on G. plan for salvation. Let me*
W-pl.....73.7:2 to accept G. plan because you share in it.
W-pl.....73.9:1 the recognition that G. plan for salvation,
W-pl...73.10:3 *the light that reflects G. Will and mine.* Then
W-pl........74.h There is no will but G..
W-pl.....74.1:2 G. is the only Will. When you have
W-pl.....74.3:2 *There is no will but G.. I cannot be in conflict*
W-pl.....74.3:7 *My will is G.. My will and God's are one. God*
W-pl.....74.3:8 *My will and G. are one. God wills peace for*
W-pl....74.3:12 *is no will but G.. These conflict thoughts are*
W-pl.....74.4:3 *There is no will but G.. I share it with Him.*
W-pl.....74.7:2 *There is no will but G.. I seek His peace today*
W-pl........76.h I am under no laws but G..
W-pl.....76.6:2 you have made in opposition to G. Will.
W-pl.....76.8:4 set forth what is G. and what is yours.
W-pl.....76.9:1 There are no laws but G.. Dismiss all
W-pl.....76.9:6 else. G. laws forever give and never take.
W-pl...76.11:1 Let us today open G. channels to Him,
W-pl...76.11:4 and understood there are no laws but G..
W-pl...76.11:6 concludes: *I am under no laws but G..*
W-pl.....78.4:1 Today we will attempt to see G. Son. We
W-pl.....78.5:2 of whom we ask G. Son be shown to you.
W-pl.....78.8:4 to you, seeing no separation in G. Son.
W-pl...78.10:1 assigned to us as part of G. salvation plan,
W-pl.....80.1:8 your rightful place in G. plan for salvation
W-pl.....80.2:3 for the Holy Spirit to give you G. answer.
W-pl.....80.4:2 be gone, because G. answer cannot fail.
W-pl.....86.1:1 (71) Only G. plan for salvation will work.
W-pl.....86.1:7 Only G. plan for salvation will work. And
W-pl.....86.2:2 *G. plan for salvation will save me from my*
W-pl.....86.2:3 *is no exception in G. plan for my salvation.*
W-pl.....86.2:4 *this only in the light of G. plan for salvation.*
W-pl.....86.3:1 is an attack on G. plan for salvation.
W-pl.....86.3:2 that G. plan for salvation will not work.
W-pl.....86.3:6 I would accept G. plan for salvation, and
W-pl.....87.3:1 (74) There is no will but G.. I am safe
W-pl.....87.3:2 safe today because there is no will but G..
W-pl.....87.3:6 I am safe because there is no will but G..
W-pl.....87.4:3 *It is G. Will you are His Son, [name], and*
W-pl.....87.4:4 *This is part of G. Will for me, however I may*
W-pl.....88.3:1 (76) I am under no laws but G.. Here is

W-pl.....88.3:3 freedom. I am under no laws but G.. I am
W-pl.....88.3:7 free of the effects of all laws save G.. And
W-pl.....88.4:4 *Let me allow G. laws to work in this, and not*
W-pl.....89.1:2 because I am under no laws but G.. His
W-pl.....89.3:4 according to G. plan for my salvation. I
W-pl.....92.3:1 It is G. strength in you that is the light in
W-pl.....93.3:2 thoughts are not according to G. Will.
W-pl.....94.2:5 cannot obscure the glory of G. Son. You
W-pl.....95.2:1 as a ridiculous parody on G. creation;
W-pl.....95.12:2 peace. You are G. Son, one Self, with one
W-pl.....96.6:8 G. plan for the release of His dear Son
W-pl........98.h accept my part in G. plan for salvation.
W-pl.....98.7:6 *I will accept my part in G. plan for salvation.*
W-pl.....99.9:2 It is G. Will your mind be one with His. It
W-pl.....99.9:3 It is G. Will that He has but one Son. It is
W-pl.....99.9:4 Son. It is G. Will that His one Son is you.
W-pl...99.12:2 with Him Who shares G. plan with you.
W-pl......100.h part is essential to G. plan for salvation.
W-pl...100.1:1 Just as G. Son completes his Father, so
W-pl...100.2:1 G. Will for you is perfect happiness. Why
W-pl...100.3:1 are indeed essential to G. plan. Without
W-pl...100.4:1 You are indeed essential to G. plan. Just
W-pl...100.4:2 and take their place beside you in G. plan.
W-pl...100.4:3 G. messengers are joyous, and their joy
W-pl...100.5:2 to take the part that is essential to G. plan
W-pl...100.6:4 You are G. messenger today. You bring
W-pl...100.7:4 to take his place among G. messengers.
W-pl...100.7:7 You but receive according to G. plan, and
W-pl...100.8:1 to us and all the world G. Will for us. It is
W-pl. 100.10:7 to G. plan for the salvation of the world.
W-pl......101.h G. Will for me is perfect happiness.
W-pl...101.1:5 that sin is real, and that G. Son can sin.
W-pl...101.5:3 that you have made a devil of G. Son.
W-pl...101.6:1 G. Will for you is perfect happiness
W-pl...101.6:6 *G. Will for me is perfect happiness. There is*
W-pl...101.7:6 *G. Will for me is perfect happiness. This is*
W-pl......102.h I share G. Will for happiness for me.
W-pl...102.3:1 the happiness G. Will has placed in you.
W-pl...102.4:1 with this acceptance of G. Will for you: *I*
W-pl...102.4:2 *I share G. Will for happiness for me, and I*
W-pl...102.4:4 is your choice, and that you share G. Will.
W-pl...102.5:2 to be less loving to G. Son than He Whose
W-pl...102.5:4 you are joining with G. Will in doing this.
W-pl...104.2:1 upon the holy altar where G. gifts belong.
W-pl...104.5:5 *truth. G. gifts of joy and peace are all I want.*
W-pl......105.h G. peace and joy are mine.
W-pl...105.1:1 G. peace and joy are yours. Today we will
W-pl...105.3:3 Accept G. peace and joy, and you will
W-pl...105.3:4 G. gifts will never lessen when they are
W-pl...105.4:1 when you accept them as G. gift to you, so
W-pl...105.5:1 Today accept G. peace and joy as yours.
W-pl...105.7:2 *That I may have G. peace and joy as mine.*
W-pl...105.7:3 yourself to recognize G. gifts to you, and
W-pl...105.7:6 you can say, "G. peace and joy are mine,"
W-pl...105.8:3 tell yourself, "G. peace and joy are mine,"
W-pl...105.9:4 seems to tempt you to deny G. gift to him
W-pl...105.9:6 *That I may have G. peace and joy as mine.*
W-pl...106.4:1 Today the promise of G. Word is kept.
W-pl...106.5:3 who could reach G. Son except his Father,
WplrIII.in11:6 day and make it holy, worthy of G. Son,
W-pl...113.2:2 *mind, I see G. perfect plan for my salvation*
W-pl...114.2:1 accept my part in G. plan for salvation.
W-pl...114.3:4 accept my part in G. plan for salvation.
W-pl...115.2:1 part is essential to G. plan for salvation. *I*
W-pl...115.3:4 part is essential to G. plan for salvation.
W-pl...116.1:1 (101) G. Will for me is perfect happiness.
W-pl...116.1:2 *G. Will is perfect happiness for me. And I*
W-pl...116.2:1 I share G. Will for happiness for me. *I*
W-pl...116.3:2 G. Will for me is perfect happiness. On
W-pl...116.3:4 I share G. Will for happiness for me.
W-pl...118.1:1 (105) G. peace and joy are mine. *Today I*
W-pl...118.1:2 *Today I will accept G. peace and joy, in glad*
W-pl...118.2:2 *for Truth Itself assure me that I am G. perfect*
W-pl...118.3:2 G. peace and joy are mine. On the half
W-pl...119.1:3 *I am G. Son, whose Self rests safely in the*
W-pl...120.2:2 me. *I am G. Son. Today I lay aside all sick*
W-pl...122.5:1 G. plan for your salvation cannot change,
W-pl...124.8:5 will trust G. Voice to speak as He sees fit
W-pl......125.h In quiet I receive G. Word today.

| | |
|---|---|
| W-pI...125.2:2 | for G. plan is simply this: The Son of God |
| W-pI...125.2:2 | house by his own will, forever free as G.. |
| W-pI...125.3:1 | In stillness we will hear G. Voice today |
| W-pI......127.h | There is no love but G.. |
| W-pI...127.3:5 | There is no love but G., and all of love is |
| W-pI.127.11:4 | Now are they all our brothers in G. Love. |
| W-pI.127.12:5 | *but G. and yours and mine and everyone's.* |
| W-pI...130.9:5 | will know G. strength upheld you as you |
| W-pI...131.4:4 | G. Son can not seek vainly, though he try |
| W-pI...131.8:5 | an alien will upon G. single purpose. He is |
| W-pI.132.11:5 | G. creation is unlike the world in every |
| W-pI...134.2:4 | Truth is G. creation, and to pardon that is |
| W-pI...136.9:2 | and G. design for the salvation of His Son |
| W-pI...137.3:6 | to attack the universal Oneness of G. Son. |
| W-pI.137.12:1 | Would you not offer shelter to G. Will? |
| W-pI.137.14:4 | *be banished from the mind of G. one Son,* |
| W-pI...138.2:5 | true in G. creation cannot enter here until |
| W-pI.139.10:1 | and demonstrates the Oneness of G. Son |
| W-pI...143.1:1 | (125) In quiet I receive G. Word today. |
| W-pI...144.1:1 | (127) There is no love but G.. |
| W-pI...151.7:3 | which merely bear false witness to G. Son |
| W-pI.151.12:4 | no sound except the echo of G. Voice. |
| W-pI.151.15:4 | the Voice for God give honor to G. Son. |
| W-pI...152.9:3 | G. perfect gift to His beloved Son. We lay |
| W-pI.152.10:3 | To recognize G. Son implies as well that |
| W-pI.152.10:5 | And in humility the radiance of G. Son, |
| W-pI.152.12:2 | G. Voice will answer, for He speaks for |
| W-pI.152.12:3 | and G. Son for your illusions of yourself. |
| W-pI.153.10:2 | G. ministers have chosen that the truth |
| W-pI.153.11:1 | It is the function of G. ministers to help |
| W-pI.153.14:5 | G. ministers have come to waken him |
| W-pI.153.14:6 | G. Son can smile at last, on learning that |
| W-pI.154.10:3 | the getting and the giving of G. Word; the |
| W-pI.155.10:2 | keep the truth apart from G. completion, |
| W-pI.155.13:3 | a worthy guide for you who are G. Son. |
| W-pI.159.10:3 | Judge not G. Son, but follow in the way |
| W-pI...160.8:1 | G. certainty suffices. Who He knows to |
| W-pI...161.7:4 | as G. Voice proclaims there is no death. |
| W-pI...163.4:3 | all creation, stronger than G. Will for life, |
| W-pI...165.6:6 | deprivation cannot cut him off from G. |
| W-pI...166.1:2 | G. trust in you is limitless. He knows His |
| W-pI...166.3:2 | He must believe that to accept G. gifts, |
| W-pI...166.5:1 | wanderings, G. gifts go with him, all |
| W-pI...166.9:4 | Perhaps G. Word is truer than your own. |
| W-pI.166.10:1 | G. Will does not oppose. It merely is. It is |
| W-pI.166.13:5 | the touch of Christ, and recognize G. gifts |
| W-pI.166.14:5 | accepts G. gifts can never suffer anything. |
| W-pI...169.3:5 | It is not shut tight against G. Voice. It has |
| W-pI...169.6:2 | its will is G. has been completely given |
| WpI...rV.in6:6 | G. Son is crucified until you walk along |
| W-pI......183.h | I call upon G. Name and on my own. |
| W-pI...183.1:1 | G. Name is holy, but no holier than yours |
| W-pI...183.2:1 | G. Name can not be heard without |
| W-pI...183.3:1 | Repeat G. Name, and all the world |
| W-pI...183.4:2 | and unwanted thing before G. Name. |
| W-pI...183.5:4 | repeat G. Name along with him within |
| W-pI...183.6:1 | repeat G. Name slowly again and still |
| W-pI...183.6:6 | then G. Name becomes our only thought, |
| W-pI...183.8:1 | Repeat G. Name, and you acknowledge |
| W-pI...183.8:5 | and see G. Name replace the thousand |
| W-pI.183.10:3 | when G. Son calls on his Father's Name. |
| W-pI.184.14:1 | for each awareness of an aspect of G. Son, |
| W-pI...185.9:4 | You choose G. peace, or you have asked |
| W-pI...185.9:6 | Yet will G. peace come just as certainly, |
| W-pI.185.11:2 | by denying to himself what is G. Will. |
| W-pI...186.4:1 | that we may listen to G. Voice reveal to us |
| W-pI...186.5:4 | G. Voice assures you that salvation needs |
| W-pI.186.11:6 | G. can never fail because He is its Source. |
| W-pI.186.12:1 | Do as G. Voice directs. And if It asks a |
| W-pI...188.7:4 | G. peace is shining on them, but they |
| W-pI...188.7:4 | your mind, as yours was born in G.. They |
| W-pI...189.4:1 | to those who feel G. Love in them. Their |
| W-pI...191.8:4 | G. Son has come again at last to set it free |
| W-pI...192.2:4 | It is not G. creation, for it is the means by |
| W-pI...194.4:5 | let the future go, and place it in G. Hands. |
| W-pI...194.5:3 | in G. Son is freed to bless the world. Now |
| W-pI...194.9:2 | For in G. Hands we rest untroubled, sure |
| W-pI...197.1:5 | And so you think G. gifts are loans at best |
| W-pI...198.7:2 | is offered to G. Son and to his Father. You |
| W-pI.198.10:1 | there is no condemnation in G. Son, and |
| W-pI...199.4:5 | that it must reach, according to G. plan. |
| W-pI...199.8:1 | You are G. Son. In immortality you live |
| W-pI...199.8:5 | along with you, G. Son will weep no more |
| W-pI...200.6:5 | not the escape of G. beloved Son from evil |
| W-pI...200.7:1 | in opposition to G. Will and to his own, |
| W-pI...203.1:1 | I call upon G. Name and on my own. *The* |
| W-pI...204.1:2 | *G. Name reminds me that I am His Son, not* |
| W-pI...207.1:2 | *G. blessing shines upon me from within my* |
| W-pI...211.1:2 | *In silence and in true humility I seek G. glory* |
| W-pI...219.1:3 | *I am G. Son. Be still, my mind, and think a* |
| W-pII ....in.9:7 | and we who are G. Sons are safely home, |
| W-pII ..in.10:6 | We will accept the way G. plan will end, |
| W-pII ..... 1.1:5 | is sin, except a false idea about G. Son? |
| W-pII .223.1:2 | Now I know my life is G., I have no other |
| W-pII ..... 2.1:4 | well. G. Word is given every mind which |
| W-pII ..... 2.2:1 | Thought of peace was given to G. Son the |
| W-pII ..... 2.5:2 | and G. Son has but an instant more to |
| W-pII .235.1:3 | And I need but remember that G. Love |
| W-pII ....242.h | This day is G.. It is my gift to Him. |
| W-pII .246.1:2 | Let me not try to hurt G. Son, and think |
| W-pII ..... 4.3:3 | Sin "proves" G. Son is evil; timelessness |
| W-pII ....254.h | Let every voice but G. be still in me. |
| W-pII .255.1:3 | have faith in Him Who says I am G. Son. |
| W-pII .255.1:5 | says. G. Son can have no cares, and must |
| W-pII .258.1:3 | to allow G. grace to shine in unawareness, |
| W-pII .259.1:5 | the source of fear, obscuring G. creation; |
| W-pII ..... 5.2:3 | For the Son of G. impermanence is "proof |
| W-pII ..... 5.2:9 | "proof" is there that G. eternal Son can be |
| W-pII ..... 5.4:1 | means by which G. Son returns to sanity. |
| W-pII .265.1:7 | What is reflected there is in G. Mind. The |
| W-pII .265.1:9 | Yet is my mind at one with G.. And so I |
| W-pII ....266.h | My holy Self abides in you, G. Son. |
| W-pII .266.2:1 | calling upon G. Name and on our own, |
| W-pII ..... 6.1:1 | Christ is G. Son as He created Him. He is |
| W-pII ..... 6.2:3 | He is the part in which G. Answer lies; |
| W-pII .271.1:2 | would have me see, to listen to G. Voice, |
| W-pII .271.1:2 | witnesses to what is true in G. creation. In |
| W-pII .271.1:3 | sight, the world and G. creation meet, |
| W-pII ....272.h | How can illusions satisfy G. Son? |
| W-pII .272.1:8 | *safe. G. Son must be as You created him.* |
| W-pII ....275.h | G. healing Voice protects all things today |
| W-pII .277.2:5 | cannot be bound unless G. truth can lie, |
| W-pII .279.1:1 | G. Son is not abandoned by His Love. |
| W-pII ....280.h | What limits can I lay upon G. Son? |
| W-pII ..... 7.5:3 | of Heaven is restored to G. beloved Son. |
| W-pII .290.1:4 | I perceive without G. Own Correction for |
| W-pII ..... 8.4:1 | guilt is over, and G. Son no longer sleeps. |
| W-pII .292.1:1 | G. promises make no exceptions. And He |
| W-pII .292.1:6 | For G. Will is done in earth and Heaven. |
| W-pII .294.1:4 | use has G. beloved Son for what must die |
| W-pII ..... 9.1:3 | to G. Word to take illusion's place; the |
| W-pII ..... 9.2:2 | brings, as G. creation must be limitless. |
| W-pII ..... 9.5:5 | Let us rejoice that we can do G. Will, and |
| W-pII .301.2:1 | G. world is happy. Those who look on it |
| W-pII .301.2:4 | and we will look upon G. world today. |
| W-pII .303.1:2 | Let all G. holy Thoughts surround me, |
| W-pII .307.2:1 | because we join our holy will with G., in |
| W-pII .309.1:1 | it is G. Will that it be there forever and |
| W-pII ... 10.3:1 | You who believed that G. Last Judgment |
| W-pII ... 10.3:1 | G. Judgment is the gift of the Correction |
| W-pII ... 10.3:2 | have. To fear G. saving grace is but to fear |
| W-pII ... 10.4:1 | G. Final Judgment is as merciful as every |
| W-pII ... 10.5:1 | G. Final Judgment: "You are still My holy |
| W-pII .311.1:6 | mind by giving us G. Judgment of His Son |
| W-pII .318.1:1 | In me, G. holy Son, are reconciled all |
| W-pII .318.1:4 | I am the means by which G. Son is saved, |
| W-pII .318.1:7 | I am G. Son, His one eternal Love. I am |
| W-pII ... 11.1:1 | Creation is the sum of all G. Thoughts, in |
| W-pII ... 11.1:5 | G. Thoughts exactly as they were and as |
| W-pII ... 11.2:1 | G. Thoughts are given all the power that |
| W-pII ... 11.4:5 | G. memory is in our holy minds, which |
| W-pII ... 11.4:6 | only to let G. Will be done on earth, only |
| W-pII .322.1:2 | readiness to give G. ancient messages to |
| W-pII .322.1:4 | to conceal the Self which is G. only Son, |
| W-pII .326.2:1 | forgiven, fade entirely into G. holy Will. |
| W-pII .328.1:2 | independence from the rest of G. creation |
| W-pII .330.1:4 | accept G. gifts has been restored to spirit, |
| W-pII .331.2:1 | Forgiveness shows us that G. Will is One, |
| W-pII .334.1:4 | G. Voice is offering the peace of God to all |
| W-pII .337.1:6 | to feel G. Love protecting me from harm, |
| W-pII .346.2:2 | when we forget all things except G. Love. |
| W-pII .348.2:1 | G. grace suffices us in everything that He |
| W-pII .... 350.h | Miracles mirror G. eternal Love. To offer |
| W-pII ... 14.1:1 | *I am G. Son, complete and healed and* |
| W-pII .... 355.h | that I will give, When I accept G. Word. |
| W-pII .... 359.h | G. answer is some form of peace. All pain |
| W-ep ......... 6:4 | do. He loves G. Son as we would love him. |
| W-ep ......... 6:7 | G. angels hover near and all about. His |
| M-in .......... 5:1 | Except for G. teachers there would be |
| M-1 ............. h | WHO ARE G. TEACHERS? |
| M-1 ............ 3:5 | theme is always, "G. Son is guiltless, and |
| M-2 ........... 1:1 | have been assigned to each of G. teachers, |
| M-2 ........... 2:6 | of separation entered the mind of G. Son, |
| M-2 ........... 2:6 | in that same instant was G. Answer given. |
| M-2 ........... 4:7 | G. Will in everything but seems to take |
| M-2 ........... 5:3 | G. Teacher speaks to any two who join |
| M-3 ........... 3:5 | situation is part of G. plan for Atonement |
| M-3 ........... 3:7 | G. teachers work at different levels, but |
| M-4 ............. h | CHARACTERISTICS OF G. TEACHERS? |
| M-4 ........... 1:1 | surface traits of G. teachers are not at all |
| M-4 ........II.1:1 | other traits of G. teachers rest on trust. |
| M-4 ........II.2:6 | the trust on which G. teachers rest secure |
| M-4 ...... III.1:1 | G. teachers do not judge. To judge is to |
| M-4 ...... III.1:6 | of the teacher of G. whole thought system |
| M-4 ...... IV.1:1 | Harm is impossible for G. teachers. They |
| M-4 ...... IV.1:7 | the absence of G. curriculum, and its |
| M-4 .... IV.1:11 | Nor can G. Teacher be heard at all, except |
| M-4 ...... IV.2:1 | Therefore, G. teachers are wholly gentle. |
| M-4 ...... IV.2:8 | of G. teachers lies in their gentleness, for |
| M-4 ...... IV.2:8 | came neither from G. Son nor his Creator |
| M-4 ........V.1:9 | G. teachers trust in Him. And they are |
| M-4 ......V.1:11 | G. Voice directs them in all things. Joy is |
| M-4 ...... VI.1:1 | G. teachers have learned how to be |
| M-4 ..... VII.1:3 | Like all the other attributes of G. teachers |
| M-4 ...... IX.1:1 | extent of the teacher of G. faithfulness is |
| M-4 ...... IX.1:4 | Faithfulness is the teacher of G. trust in |
| M-4 ...... IX.2:7 | in itself the other attributes of G. teachers |
| M-4 ........X.1:3 | shuts the mind against G. Teacher, so |
| M-4 ........X.3:1 | attributes of G. teachers does not include |
| M-4 ........X.3:1 | things that are the Son of G. inheritance. |
| M-4 ........X.3:6 | is the function of G. teachers to bring true |
| M-5 .........I.1:7 | for placing G. Son on his Father's throne. |
| M-5 .........I.2:2 | It symbolizes the defeat of G. Son and the |
| M-5 ...... III.2:1 | To them G. teachers come, to represent |
| M-5 ...... III.2:4 | As G. messengers, His teachers are the |
| M-5 ...... III.2:5 | forgiveness for G. Son in his own Name. |
| M-5 ...... III.2:7 | With G. Word in their minds they come |
| M-5 ...... III.3:3 | They seek for G. Voice in this brother |
| M-5 ...... III.3:3 | himself as to believe G. Son can suffer. |
| M-5 ...... III.3:9 | And this is the function of G. teachers; to |
| M-5 ...... III.3:9 | their own, nor theirs as separate from G.. |
| M-6 ........... 2:5 | for the giver and the receiver of G. gifts. |
| M-6 ........... 3:1 | the function of G. teachers to evaluate the |
| M-6 ........... 4:8 | G. treasure house can never be empty. |
| M-7 ........... 4:9 | This is the certainty that gives G. teachers |
| M-7 ........... 5:1 | that has been given to G. Teacher for |
| M-9 ............. h | THE LIFE SITUATION OF G. TEACHERS |
| M-9 ........... 1:1 | are required in the *minds* of G. teachers. |
| M-9 ........... 1:3 | and chance plays no part in G. plan. It is |
| M-9 ........... 1:4 | in the newly made teacher of G. training. |
| M-9 ........... 2:4 | obvious prerequisite for hearing G. Voice, |
| M-10 ......... 2:9 | is, and it is only one: "G. Son is guiltless, |
| M-11 ......... 1:7 | G. Word has promised that peace is |
| M-11 ......... 2:6 | G. Word assures you that He loves the |
| M-11 ......... 4:6 | has G. Judgment on this distorted world |
| M-12 ......... 1:6 | are joined with G. forever and ever. His |
| M-12 ......... 1:7 | of himself is based upon G. Judgment, |
| M-12 ......... 1:8 | Thus does he share G. Will, and bring His |
| M-12 ......... 2:5 | G. teachers appear to be many, for that is |
| M-12 ......... 3:3 | Only very few can hear G. Voice at all, |
| M-12 ......... 3:8 | So do G. teachers need a body, for their |
| M-12 ......... 4:1 | makes G. teachers is their recognition of |
| M-12 ......... 4:2 | G. Voice speak through it to human ears. |
| M-12 ....... 5:10 | it holy. G. Voice will tell him when he has |
| M-12 ......... 6:2 | G. teachers choose to look on dreams a |
| M-12 ......... 6:6 | is the real function of G. teachers. They |
| M-12 ....... 6:11 | And it is this G. teachers acknowledge as |

M-13..........3:5 through G. Word could this be possible.
M-13..........4:1 G. teachers can have no regret on giving
M-13..........6:2 hold dear the things that crucify G. Son,
M-13........6:10 other voice in all the world that echoes G.
M-14..........2:7 It is His Call G. teachers answer, turning
M-14..........3:3 still, and waits on the goal of G. teachers.
M-14..........4:6 if G. Voice tells him it is a lesson he can
M-14..........5:9 into Heaven is the function of G. teachers,
M-15..........1:2 No one can escape G. Final Judgment.
M-15..........1:6 as G. Final Judgment on him is received.
M-15..........3:3 G. Judgment waits for you to set you free.
M-16..........8:7 It is not good enough for G. teacher,
M-16..........8:7 because it is not enough for G. Son.
M-16..........9:2 attempt to substitute another will for G..
M-16........11:3 G. teachers who must teach it that it can.
M-16........11:6 "There is no will but G.." His teachers
M-16........11:9 must G. teachers learn to recognize the
M-17............h DO G. TEACHERS DEAL WITH MAGIC
M-17..........1:6 any form, G. teacher can be sure that he is
M-18..........2:1 G. teachers' major lesson is to learn how
M-18..........2:7 completely in His sight and in G. Word.
M-18..........3:2 is taken as replacement for G. Word. The
M-18..........4:5 The sole responsibility of G. teacher is to
M-19..........1:8 If G. Son were fairly judged, there would
M-19..........4:1 Salvation is G. justice. It restores to your
M-19..........4:6 G. Judgment is His justice. Onto this,–a
M-19..........5:1 Pray for G. justice, and do not confuse
M-19..........5:5 G. justice points to Heaven just because it
M-20..........2:2 G. peace is recognized at first by just one
M-20..........3:3 G. peace can never come where anger is,
M-20..........4:6 you want, or is G. peace the better choice?
M-20........6:12 G. peace is the condition for His Will.
M-21..........5:1 G. fear about the validity of what he hears
M-21..........5:8 G. teachers have God's Word behind
M-21..........5:8 have G. Word behind their symbols. And
M-22..........4:6 result of the recognition, by G. teacher, of
M-22..........7:2 must remain beyond G. power to forgive?
M-22..........7:4 up to G. teachers to set limits upon Him,
M-22..........7:7 will not be understood until G. teacher
M-23..........1:1 G. gifts can rarely be received directly.
M-23..........1:2 the most advanced of G. teachers will give
M-23..........7:7 In him you find G. Answer. Do you, then,
M-24..........6:8 lead to this is of concern to G. teachers.
M-26..........1:5 Here, then, is the role of G. teachers. They
M-26........3:10 by their awakening can G. Voice be heard
M-27..........4:8 Not one can be acceptable to G. teachers,
M-27..........5:1 rooted in the belief that G. Son is a body.
M-28..........4:7 And we, G. children, rise up from the
M-28..........6:3 G. teachers have the goal of wakening the
M-28..........6:7 he has heard G. Word and understood its
M-28..........6:8 because he let G. Voice proclaim the truth
C-1.............1:4 The unified spirit is G. one Son, or Christ.
C-1.............4:2 for creating, but its Will, which is G.,
C-1.............6:3 Christ Mind, Whose Will is One with G..
C-2.............2:4 Yet could G. Son as He created him abide
C-2...........6:14 there was crucifixion stands G. Son.
C-2.............9:1 no answer, being made to still G. Voice,
C-3.............6:1 G. Will is all there is. We can but go from
C-4.............7:1 now G. *knowledge*, changeless, certain,
C-4.............7:7 For where G. memory has come at last
C-5.............3:5 that it is impossible to kill G. Son; nor can
C-5.............6:1 Is he G. only Helper? No, indeed. For
C-5...........6:11 *instead to share the resurrection of G. Son.*
C-6.............4:5 in that form He speaks G. Word to you.
C-6.............5:3 of G. Son for he alone is functionless. But
P-2........IV.2:1 Once G. Son is seen as guilty, illness
P-2.........V.5:5 The sacred calling of G. holy Son for help
P-2.........V.6:2 And now G. promises are kept by Him.
P-2.........V.8:1 Let us stand silently before G. Will, and
P-2.......VII.6:7 His patients are G. saints, who call upon
P-2.......VII.7:1 are not afraid to offer weakness to G. Son.
P-3...........I.1:4 There are no errors in G. plan. It would
P-3........III.2:7 money where G. plan allots it has no cost.
P-3........III.3:7 if it does, it merely crucifies G. Son again.
P-3........III.5:5 So it is with G. healers. They give because
P-3......III.5:11 Where G. Son turns against himself, he
S-1.........in.2:4 by which G. Son leaves separate goals and
S-1.........in.3:6 is. This is the way. It is G. gift to you.
S-1...........I.4:3 see them, and let them go into G. Hands.
S-1.........II.8:8 if peace is to be restored to G. Son, who
S-1.........V.3:2 how to understand your glory as G. Son,
S-2...........I.2:6 G. mercy has become a twisted knife that
S-2...........I.7:4 G. mercy would remove this withering
S-2.........II.3:5 love for G. creation and the holiness that
S-2........III.4:8 G. Will is truth, and you are one with
S-2........III.5:3 in which forgiveness comes to save G. Son
S-3...........I.4:1 he has done now must G. Son undo. But
S-3.........II.6:3 placed upon G. substitute for evil dreams;
S-3.........II.6:4 gate of Heaven opens and G. Son is free to
S-3........III.6:1 G. Voice alone can tell you how to heal.
S-3........IV.1:3 Whose Voice He is,–such are G. healers.
S-3........IV.3:9 Do not forget forgiveness of G. Son.
S-3........IV.5:1 forget this; it is you who are G. Son, and

## God-created 1

P-2.......VII.4:2 themselves as self-created rather than G..

## God-destructive 1

T-10.......V.3:5 Blasphemy, then, is *self-destructive*, not G.

## God-proof 1

T-5......VI.10:6 case may be fool-proof, but it is not G..

## Godlike 1

T-6........III.1:6 Your G. mind can never be defiled. The

## gods 31

T-4........III.6:6 Thou shalt have no other g. before Him
T-10......III.8:3 other g. before Him or you will not hear.
T-10......III.8:4 God is not jealous of the g. you make, but
T-10....III.10:3 To accept other g. before Him is to place
T-10....III.10:4 not realize how much you listen to your g.
T-10....III.11:3 when you place no other g. before Him.
T-10......IV.1:5 sick, you have placed other g. before Him.
T-10......IV.3:4 If you perceive other g. your mind is split,
T-10....IV.4:10 "given" your peace to the g. you made,
T-10......IV.5:3 g. do not bring chaos; you are endowing
T-10......IV.6:6 it is. No false g. you attempt to interpose
T-10......IV.7:1 a Son of God who has laid aside all false g.
T-10.......V.3:4 are sick you cannot keep the g. you made,
T-10.......V.5:4 Your g. are nothing, because your Father
T-11......III.6:3 there *are* no other g. to place before Him,
T-14......IX.3:8 His worshippers placed other g. upon it.
T-14......IX.5:3 reflections of the images of other g. must
T-16.....V.13:1 attempt to raise other g. before Him, and
T-30......IV.2:1 dissatisfying g. you made are blown-up
W-pI.....53.5:7 and I will place no other g. before Him.
W-pI...135.2:4 codes, its ethics and its leaders and its g.,
W-pI...170.6:2 And g. demand that those who worship
W-pI.170.10:1 the totally insane belief in g. of vengeance
W-pI.182.11:5 and take illusions as your g. no more.
W-pI...183.4:3 forget the names of all the g. you valued.
W-pI...183.4:5 them worshipfully, naming them as g..
M-16 .........2:5 they easily become g. in their own right,
M-23 .........4:3 names of all the g. to which you pray. It
S-1 ...........I.4:4 that you would have no g. before Him; no
S-1 .........V.1:5 be. All little g. it gladly lays aside, not in
S-1 .........V.3:1 things, of bodies, and of g. of every kind,

## goes 93

T-1........III.7:2 being united this mind g. out to everyone,
T-2....V.A.18:5 *He wishes, knowing He g. there with me. I*
T-4...........I.5:3 because it g. against all of its own laws.
T-4.......VII.8:5 God g. out to them and through them,
T-6......V.C.5:3 g. beyond them towards real integration.
T-7........XI.1:5 The world g. against your nature, being
T-8.......IV.2:11 If my light g. with you everywhere, you
T-8.....VII.14:2 if it g. beyond it and does not interpret it
T-11. VIII.10:2 the Help of God g. with you everywhere.
T-11. VIII.13:2 in favor of reality, their fear g. with them.
T-12.......II.7:7 mean that peace g. with *us* on the journey?
T-13......IV.1:6 satisfied with you, as its reasoning g., it
T-14.........I.4:1 the Holy Spirit leads you not, g. nowhere.
T-15.......I.4:13 is the end as far as hope of Heaven g.. Yet
T-15.......V.7:1 that it frequently g. even farther; one part
T-15......VI.8:3 with it g. the whole basis for exclusion.
T-15.....VII.8:3 object where the mind g. or what it thinks
T-16......IV.3:7 love. If the illusion g., the relationship is
T-17.....VII.6:4 unless its holiness g. with it everywhere.
T-17.....VII.7:1 how great the strength that g. with you.
T-18......III.8:1 Not one light in Heaven but g. with you.
T19IV.A.17:15 kind of completion, which g. beyond guilt
T19IV.A.17:15 guilt, because it g. beyond the body.
T-20......IV.6:5 beginning of another world g. with them.
T-21........II.4:3 it away, and everything you see g. with it.
T-21.....VI.10:2 gratitude g. out to you who blessed him,
T-21....VIII.1:5 He g. from life to death, the final proof he
T-22.......V.2:2 Always to justify what g. against the truth
T-23.......I.12:7 be; where either g. the other disappears.
T-26.....VII.2:2 When the separation is denied, it g.. For
T-26.....VII.7:1 it g. beyond correction to impossibility.
T-26......IX.7:2 you walk forgiveness gladly g. with you.
T-29......IV.1:8 And dreaming g. with only one of these.
T-29......IX.9:1 a calm assurance Heaven g. with you,–be
T-30.......V.9:2 And with it g. all hatred and all fear. Look
T-31.........I.2:4 merely g. from one apparent lesson to the
T-31.....V.16:1 concepts of the self as learning g. along.
W-pI........41.h God g. with me wherever I go.
W-pI.....41.4:1 its Source g. with you wherever you go.
W-pI.....41.4:2 of all joy g. with you wherever you go.
W-pI.....41.4:3 of all life g. with you wherever you go.
W-pI.....41.4:4 because God g. with you wherever you go.
W-pI...41.10:1 that God g. with you wherever you go.
W-pI.....59.1:1 (41) God g. with me wherever I go. How
W-pI.....59.1:2 I be alone when God always g. with me?
W-pI.....59.1:7 because God g. with me wherever I go.
W-pI.....61.7:1 Today's idea g. far beyond the ego's petty
W-pI.....91.5:3 body. Faith g. to what you want, and you
W-pI.....97.6:2 makes an uncertain moment and g. out.
W-pI...98.11:1 the hour g. and He is there once more to
W-pI...107.8:1 Begin by asking Him Who g. with you
W-pI.107.10:2 that g. with you will carry to the world.
W-pI...109.5:2 time g. by without its touch upon you, for
W-pI...124.1:5 that God Himself g. everywhere with us.
W-pI...128.7:5 and where it g. to rest when you release it
W-pI...138.3:4 in return, and time g. by without results.
W-pI.153.18:2 you will know that Heaven g. with you.
W-pI...155.9:4 It g. before you now, that they may see
W-pI.155.10:5 But One Who knows g. with you. Let Him
W-pI.155.11:6 For as truth g. before us, so it goes before
W-pI.155.11:6 g. before our brothers who will follow us.
W-pI...162.3:1 bringing them with him as he g. to sleep.
W-pI...166.4:4 where he came from, where he g., and
W-pI...166.5:4 but dwindles, as he g. ahead to nowhere.
W-pI...181.8:3 And as our focus g. beyond mistakes, we
W-pI...182.3:2 He g. uncertainly about in endless search,
W-pI.193.12:4 the one that follows, and when that one g.
W-pI.195.10:2 Gratitude g. hand in hand with love, and
W-pII .245.1:2 *Where I go, Your peace g. there with me. It*
W-pII .....269.h sight g. forth to look upon Christ's face.
W-pII .....8.5:2 taking perception with it as it g., and
W-pII .342.2:3 the world g. with us on our way to God.
W-pII .347.1:1 *Father, I want what g. against my will, and*
W-pII .348.1:6 *when Your eternal promise g. with me?*
W-ep .........1:2 end. Your Friend g. with you. You are not
M-in .........1:6 process; it g. on every moment of the day,
M-1 ...........2:5 It g. on all the time everywhere. It calls for
M-2 ...........4:1 g. backward to an instant so ancient that
M-4 .....I.A.3:8 that much, he g. on to the second stage.
M-4 ...I.A.6:11 he g. with mighty companions beside him
M-4 ......III.1:7 Let this be lost, and all his learning g..
M-4 .......V.1:8 Joy g. with gentleness as surely as grief
M-4 .....V.1:10 they are sure His Teacher g. before them,
M-4 .....X.2:10 It paves the way for what g. far beyond all
M-5 ........II.4:2 idea g. also all confusion about creation.
M-14 .......3:11 It g. against all the thinking of the world,
M-19 .........2:5 becomes quite different as one g. along.
C-3............6:4 No, not in truth, for truth g. nowhere. But
P-3.........II.5:8 this, and then g. on from there.
P-3.....III.5:10 they do this, a light g. out even in Heaven.
S-3...........I.2:4 as every moment g. irrevocably past their

S-3......... II.2:1 Son of God along the way he g. to God.
S-3......... III.3:2 this wiser one another g. to profit by his

## going 26

T-4.....VII.6:7 The constant g. out of His Love is blocked
T-5...... III.10:3 learner without g. counter to his mind,
T-6......... II.1:5 defense, or the device that keeps it g.. The
T-6......... II.3:2 only purpose is to keep the separation g..
T-9......... II.8:6 g. beyond yourself but toward yourself.
T-9.......VII.4:5 and you are g. against its judgment. The
T19. IV.A.2:10 the peace in you encounters in its g. forth.
T19IV.A.10:10 language in which their g. forth was asked
T19....IV.B.4:5 its g. forth but barriers you place between
T-20...... VI.9:1 and leave no trace behind their g.. The
T-21...... VI.3:7 not leave insanity by g. somewhere else.
T-22.......in.1:8 their g. is the need for sin gone with them
T-24....... V.6:2 He knows where you are g., and He leads
T-26....... V.2:3 in it, why should you waste it g. nowhere,
W-pI..... 10.4:6 an oddly assorted procession g. by, which
W-pI..... 44.3:1 Today we are g. to attempt to reach that
W-pI..... 67.4:3 perhaps you will succeed in g. past that,
W-pI..... 72.8:5 Now we are g. to try to see this differently
W-pI... 72.10:5 Now we are g. to try to lay judgment aside
WpI. rIV.in4:3 change the coming and the g. of the tides,
W-pII .224.2:2 *forgotten It, and do not know where I am g.,*
M-3 ........... 2:2 he is g. running into an adult "by chance,
M-4 ... I.A.6:12 a while, and gathers them before g. on.
M-12 ....... 5:11 does not suffer either in g. or remaining.
M-16 ......... 5:2 for you to take it just before g. to sleep. It
M-16 ......... 5:6 just before g. to sleep is a desirable time

## gold 2

T-28...... III.7:2 mistook for g. the shining of a pebble,
W-pI... 124.9:4 This half an hour will be framed in g.,

## golden 13

T-1........ III.6:2 The G. Rule asks you to do unto others as
T-1........ III.6:4 The G. Rule is the rule for appropriate
T-1......... V.6:4 on which the reverse of the G. Rule rests.
T-13....VIII.4:6 The g. aspects of reality that spring to
T-14....... II.2:7 are kings with g. crowns because of them.
T-17...... IV.7:4 the defense protects, set in a g. frame. The
T-20....... V.5:8 through time like g. light is all the same;
T-21.........I.8:1 an arc of g. light that stretches as you look
T-22.......in.4:9 Here is the g. circle where you recognize
T-22...... II.12:1 the g. light that reaches it from the bright,
T-28...... III.7:1 then, the silver miracles and g. dreams of
W-pI.124.12:1 Add further jewels to the g. frame that
W-pI... 159.6:5 unmet within this g. treasury of Christ.

## gone 202

T-1...........I.6:2 they do not occur something has g. wrong
T-2....... V.10:1 if he had already g. far beyond his actual
T-3........ VI.9:3 something does not mean that it has g.. It
T-3.......VII.5:9 You have not yet g. back far enough, and
T-5.........I.1:14 ego makes between giving and losing is g.
T-5........ IV.8:2 All your past except its beauty is g., and
T-6.......V.A.1:1 and your ego and your dreams are g., you
T-7.......VII.1:6 use it to deny reality, reality is g. for you.
T-8........ IV.2:6 loneliness of the world, the loneliness is g.
T-8......VIII.8:6 When you lay the ego aside, it will be g..
T-9........ IV.6:2 they do not occur something has g. wrong
T-9...... IV.11:8 when reality dawns, the fantasies are g..
T-9...... IV.11:9 Reality has not g. in the meanwhile. The
T-10....... II.5:6 This is not because He is g., but because
T-12..... II.10:4 is given Him that is not of God is g.. Yet
T-13...... VI.3:6 past, and if you would have it past and g.,
T-13...... VI.3:7 in your illusions, it has not g. from you,
T-13...... IX.7:5 *The thing you fear is g.*. If you would look
T-13....... X.7:2 What He has saved you from is g.. Give
T-13...... XI.2:3 The war is g.. For you have heard the
T-13...... XI.2:8 past are g. as one into the unreality from
T-14...... IV.4:3 When you release them they are g.. God
T-15....... V.9:4 Once this is g., the Holy Spirit substitutes
T-15...... VI.8:3 in the holy instant because the past is g.,
T-15 ..... VII.8:9 communicate, and so he would be "g.."
T-15 ..... IX.4:7 and the loneliness in Heaven is g..
T-16 ...... V.1:2 by periods in which they seem to be g..
T-16 .... VII.2:9 for deprivation on it, for the past is g..
T-16 .. VII.2:10 cannot really *not* let go what has already g.
T-16 .. VII.2:11 the illusion that it has not g. because you
T-16 .... VII.4:1 The past is g.; seek not to preserve it in
T-16 .... VII.6:4 instant it is understood that the past is g.,
T-16 .... VII.6:6 Everything is g. except the truth.
T-17 .... VII.1:5 could be solved, the problem would be g..
T-18 ....... II.3:3 awakening, you do not expect it to be g..
T-18 ....... II.5:6 the illusion of satisfaction would be g.. In
T-18 ....... II.5:8 You seem to waken, and the dream is g..
T-18 ....... II.5:9 what caused the dream has not g. with it.
T-18 ...... III.1:2 For you have g. from waking to sleeping,
T-18 ...... III.3:3 and cruel, and you have g. deep into it. A
T-18 ...... III.7:7 You have g. past fear, for no two minds
T-18 ...... IV.8:5 And that is why the past has g.. It never
T-18 ..... VII.7:5 is time denied, and past and future g..
T-18 ... VIII.4:6 Without the sun the sunbeam would be g.
T-19 ..... III.8:6 do not realize that its foundation has g..
T19.... IV.B.7:7 and shows you that its power is g. forever.
T19.... IV.B.7:8 can guilt be, when the belief in sin is g.?
T19.... IV.C.2:3 They but walk past and it is g.. But what
T19... IV.D.2:3 light beyond it when the fear of death is g.
T19... IV.D.4:2 For if this were g., what could you fear
T19... IV.D.5:1 to the love beyond, and so the fear is g..
T19... IV.D.6:4 let the veil be lifted, *they* will be g. forever.
T-20 ....... II.4:7 And yet the thorns are g.. Look you still
T-20 ... VIII.8:3 Believe them not and they are g.. And all
T-21 ..... II.13:4 All its effects are g., because its source has
T-21 ..... III.2:2 The *source* of sin is g.. You may imagine
T-21 ...... V.7:9 disregard them, and you have g. past this.
T-22 ...... in.1:8 going is the need for sin g. with them.
T-22 ...... V.5:7 is quietly passed through and g. beyond?
T-23 ....... II.1:7 merely looked upon and g. beyond.
T-23 ..... III.1:7 in nightmares where the smiles are g.,
T-23 ..... IV.7:7 it exerts on those in battle still are g., and
T-24 ......... I.1:4 but one belief, one offering, and love is g.,
T-24 .... VII.2:2 yet, still in the future or apparently g. by.
T-24 .... VII.5:8 Nor will that light go out when it is g.. Its
T-24 .... VII.9:3 And without a light it seems that it is g..
T-25 ....... II.1:8 to relinquish it, and have it g. forever.
T-25 ....... II.4:2 Be glad that it is g. within your mind, to
T-25 ..... IV.4:6 away for recognition, and are g. forever.
T-25 ...... V.1:1 this: The whole desire to attack is g., and
T-25 ...... V.1:2 for guilt is g. because it has no purpose,
T-25 .... V.2:10 He has not g. because your eyes are closed
T-26 ....... II.2:3 out so no one loses is the problem g.,
T-26 ....... II.7:6 Sacrifice is g.. And in its place the Love of
T-26 ...... V.3:6 And in that tiny instant time was g., for
T-26 ...... V.3:7 God gave answer to is answered and is g..
T-26 ...... V.4:1 you live in time and know not it is g., the
T-26 ...... V.4:1 in time, though it has long since g.. You
T-26 ...... V.6:6 a place and time that have long since g. by
T-26 ...... V.8:1 calls from out a past forevermore g. by.
T-26 ...... V.8:2 it as real is but a wish that what is g. could
T-26 ...... V.8:3 this a hindrance to the truth the past is g.,
T-26 .... V.10:1 a road long since a memory of time g. by?
T-26 .... V.10:4 the dead and g. be peacefully forgotten.
T-26 .... V.10:8 removed and g. forever from his mind?
T-26 .... V.12:2 They come from what is past and g., and
T-26 .... V.13:3 of an instant g. by long ago that cannot be
T-26 .... V.14:1 Forgive the past and let it go, for it *is* g..
T-26 .... V.14:3 You have g. on, and reached the world
T-26 .... VII.2:3 g. as soon as the idea that brought it has
T-26 .... IX.3:8 The shadow of an ancient hate has g., and
T-27 ..... III.2:4 it cancelled out, and so they both are g..
T-27 .... V.2:10 must be g. forever from your mind to heal
T-28 ........ I.1:5 And what it takes away is long since g.,
T-28 ........ I.1:8 The miracle but shows the past is g., and
T-28 ........ I.1:8 gone, and what has truly g. has no effects.
T-28 ........ I.6:4 be made possible because its cause has g..
T-28 ........ I.7:3 appear, remember that their cause is g..
T-28 ........ I.7:6 Be glad that it is g., for this is what you
T-28 ........ I.9:9 They but remind you that It has not g..
T-28 ....... I.13:2 Its own remembering has g.. There is no
T-28 ....... I.15:5 His memory has not g. by, and left a
T-28 ....... II.9:2 final step is an effect of what has g. before
T-28 ..... II.11:3 And where effects are g., there is no cause
T-28 ..... II.12:7 the steps have been retraced, the ladder g.
T-28 ..... III.6:3 Let its effects be g. and clutch them not
T-28 ..... IV.7:5 are g. if someone wills to be united with
T-28 ....... V.2:3 The fear is g. from them because you did
T-28 ....... V.2:4 Where fear has g. there love must come,
T-29 ........ I.3:2 that peace must flow across has not yet g..
T-29 ........ I.7:3 only sometimes present, sometimes g..
T-29 ........ I.9:1 that happens when the gap is g. is peace
T-29 ....... II.3:4 they are causeless their effects are g., and
T-29 ....... II.8:8 what is g. from Him becomes your god,
T-29 ..... III.3:9 The coming of the light means it is g.. In
T-29 ..... VI.4:6 Its purpose ended, it is g.. And where it
T-29 ..... IX.6:1 should be passed and g. forever. Seek not
T-30 ....... V.4:4 is g. because its purpose is forgiveness,
T-31 ..... V.13:2 have g. before these concepts of the self.
T-31 ..... V.17:2 come a time when images have all g. by,
T-31 ..... VI.3:7 For if you did, it would be g.. The veil of
T-31 ... VIII.5:7 For in that choice are false distinctions g.,
T-31 ... VIII.9:2 hell, the secret sins and hidden hates be g.
W-pI .... 23.4:3 is the world you see when its cause is g.?
W-pI .... 67.3:1 have g. over several such related thoughts
W-pI .... 74.1:4 The belief that conflict is possible has g..
W-pI .... 80.4:2 The problem must be g., because God's
W-pI .... 88.1:8 the darkness, and the darkness has g..
W-pI .... 96.3:6 your mind is g. from your self-concept,
W-pI .... 98.2:2 that doubt is g. and surety has come. We
W-pI .... 99.1:2 both imply that something has g. wrong;
W-pI .. 102.1:4 It has not g. as yet, but lacks the roots
W-pI .. 107.1:5 They are g. because, without belief, they
W-pI .. 107.6:8 Your Father wills these dreams be g.. Let
W-pI .. 124.6:2 in times g. by and times as yet to come, as
W-pI .. 133.1:1 particularly after you have g. through
W-pI .. 140.3:4 to gentle waking, so that dreams are g..
W-pI .. 140.4:7 For sickness now is g., with nothing left to
W-pI 151.14:3 All the threads of fantasy are g.. And what
W-pI 153.12:2 teach them that the game of fear is g.. His
W-pI 153.17:2 for all the gifts He gave us in the one g. by
W-pI .. 154.1:2 We have g. beyond such foolishness. We
W-pI 155.10:2 you travelled will be g. from you as well,
W-pI .. 156.6:4 In lightness and in laughter is sin g.,
W-pI .. 156.7:2 The past is g., with all its fantasies. They
W-pI .. 158.4:5 again; reviewing mentally what has g. by.
W-pI .. 158.9:2 In His forgiveness are they g.. Unseen by
W-pI .. 158.9:6 they seemed to have are g. with them,
W-pI .. 169.2:2 By grace alone the hate and fear are g., for
W-pI .. 181.5:2 For the past is g.; the future but imagined.
W-pI .. 183.3:2 the world holds dear has suddenly g. by,
W-pI .. 185.9:7 will not be g. with every twist and turning
W-pI 187.10:1 Now are we one in thought, for fear has g.
W-pI .. 191.4:5 In this one truth are all illusions g.. In this
W-pI .. 192.4:2 no fierce attraction now and guilt is g..
W-pI .. 192.6:1 With anger g., you will indeed perceive
W-pI 193.11:3 We have been g. too long, and we would
W-pI .. 194.5:2 For the past is g., and what is present,
W-pI 196.12:2 When the fear of God is g., there are no
W-pI .. 214.1:2 *The past is g.; the future is not yet. Now am I*
W-pII ..... 2.4:6 Night has g., and we have come together
W-pII . 234.1:1 time when dreams of sin and guilt are g.,
W-pII ..... 3.1:5 Now its source has g., and its effects are
W-pII ..... 3.1:5 has gone, and its effects are g. as well.
W-pII ..... 3.2:7 quite possible, for certainty has g..
W-pII . 241.1:4 when sorrows pass away and pain is g..
W-pII . 249.1:2 Attack is g., and madness has an end.
W-pII . 251.1:6 are finally fulfilled and dreams are g..
W-pII . 270.1:6 *and every thought except Your Own is g..*
W-pII . 279.1:3 Yet in reality his dreams are g., with truth
W-pII . 288.1:5 *mine, and I am saved because the past is g..*
W-pII . 289.1:6 but the past, and if it is forgiven it is g..
W-pII . 293.1:1 All fear is past, because its source is g.,
W-pII . 293.1:1 is gone, and all its thoughts g. with it.
W-pII . 295.1:3 that seemed to settle on the world are g..
W-pII . 300.1:1 their joys are g. before they are possessed,
W-pII . 301.1:6 *I shed will be forgotten, for their source is g..*
W-pII . 313.1:1 *all things as sinless, so that fear has g., and*
W-pII . 323.2:4 for fear has g. and only love remains.
W-pII . 334.1:2 dreams are g. even while they are woven
M-4 ........ X.2:6 are all things welcoming, for threat is g..
M-5 ........ II.4:1 With this idea is pain forever g.. But with

| | |
|---|---|
| W-pI......168.h | Your **g.** is given me. I claim it now. |
| W-pI...168.2:3 | His **g.** His answer is to all despair, for in it |
| W-pI...168.2:5 | His **g.** is yours by your acknowledgment. |
| W-pI...168.3:5 | His gift of **g.** is more than just an answer. |
| W-pI...168.4:3 | For in **g.** you see a light that covers all the |
| W-pI...168.6:5 | *Your* **g.** *is given me. I claim it now. Father, I* |
| W-pI......169.h | By **g.** I live. By grace I am released. |
| W-pI......169.h | By grace I live. By **g.** I am released. |
| W-pI...169.1:1 | **G.** is an aspect of the Love of God which |
| W-pI...169.1:3 | **g.** cannot come until the mind prepares |
| W-pI...169.1:4 | **G.** becomes inevitable instantly in those |
| W-pI...169.2:1 | **G.** is acceptance of the Love of God |
| W-pI...169.2:2 | By **g.** alone the hate and fear are gone, for |
| W-pI...169.2:2 | gone, for **g.** presents a state so opposite to |
| W-pI...169.2:2 | minds are lighted by the gift of **g.** can not |
| W-pI...169.3:1 | **G.** is not learned. The final step must go |
| W-pI...169.3:3 | **G.** is not the goal this course aspires to |
| W-pI...169.3:4 | prepare for **g.** in that an open mind can |
| W-pI.169.12:2 | sure. And now we ask for **g.**, the final gift |
| W-pI.169.12:3 | that **g.** provides will end in time, for grace |
| W-pI.169.12:3 | end in time, for **g.** foreshadows Heaven, |
| W-pI.169.13:2 | you receive, through **g.** in your experience |
| W-pI.169.14:1 | and accept the gifts that **g.** provided you. |
| W-pI.169.14:5 | We ask for **g.**, and for experience that |
| W-pI.169.14:5 | and for experience that comes from **g.**. |
| W-pI.169.14:8 | We do not look beyond what **g.** can give. |
| W-pI.169.14:9 | can give in the **g.** that has been given us. |
| W-pI.169.15:2 | this day of Him Who gives the **g.** we ask, |
| W-pI.169.15:3 | *By* **g.** *I live. By grace I am released. By grace* |
| W-pI.169.15:4 | *By* **g.** *I am released. By grace I give. By grace* |
| W-pI.169.15:5 | *released. By* **g.** *I give. By grace I will release.* |
| W-pI.169.15:6 | *released. By grace I give. By* **g.** *I will release.* |
| W-pI...179.2:1 | (168) Your **g.** is given me. I claim it now. |
| W-pI...180.1:1 | (169) By **g.** I live. By grace I am released. |
| W-pI...180.1:2 | By **g.** I am released. God is but Love, and |
| W-pI...183.3:2 | to stand you find a star; a miracle of **g.**. |
| W-pI...183.5:3 | the nameless for the Name, nor sin for **g.**, |
| W-pI...183.9:1 | in which you will experience the gift of **g.**. |
| W-pI.187.11:3 | it shining with the **g.** of God in everyone. |
| W-pI...196.4:5 | done in just one instant by the **g.** of God. |
| W-pII .258.1:3 | to allow God's **g.** to shine in unawareness, |
| W-pII .....7.1:2 | through the **g.** that God has given Him, to |
| W-pII .297.2:1 | *set already, and accomplished by Your* **g.**. |
| W-pII .310.1:4 | *holy Son, the sign Your* **g.** *has come to me,* |
| W-pII ...10.3:2 | have. To fear God's saving **g.** is but to fear |
| W-pII .316.1:3 | His **g.** is given me in every gift a brother |
| W-pII ...13.2:1 | A miracle contains the gift of **g.**, for it is |
| W-pII ....348.h | need That I perceive, Your **g.** suffices me. |
| W-pII .348.2:1 | God's **g.** suffices us in everything that He |
| W-pII .349.2:2 | He gives us **g.** to meet them all. And so we |
| M-29 .........8:3 | *all the world stands silent in the* **g.** *You bring* |
| S-1......... V.1:3 | to **g.** the mind that thought it was alone |
| S-2...........I.1:2 | was meant to bless, a cruel mockery of **g.**, |
| S-3........IV.3:8 | Do not forget the holy **g.** of prayer. Do |

## gracious 14

| | |
|---|---|
| T-11...... VI.6:4 | it by His grace, for God is **g.** to His Son, |
| T-14....... II.6:4 | open up before you in all its **g.** simplicity. |
| T-14.... III.17:1 | How **g.** it is to decide all things through |
| T-17..... V.12:2 | shining and **g.** in your awareness of time, |
| T-19.......I.10:3 | It is the **g.** acknowledgment of everyone |
| T-21...... VI.9:4 | This **g.** plan was given love by Love. And |
| T-26...VII.18:5 | which is not resolved within its **g.** light. |
| T-28...... IV.8:6 | Son, because His Son was **g.** to himself. |
| W-pI...126.4:5 | And if you then are **g.** unto him by giving |
| W-pII .270.1:2 | *How glorious and* **g.** *is this world! Yet how* |
| W-pII .310.1:4 | *You, Your* **g.** *calling to Your holy Son, the* |
| Wfl ........in.2:4 | serving us as **g.** guidance in the way to go. |
| M-11 .......4:10 | earth bows down before its **g.** Presence, |
| S-2......... II.2:2 | on an attitude of **g.** lordliness so far from |

## graciousness 4

| | |
|---|---|
| T-4........ VI.2:3 | you are throwing away the **g.** of your |
| T-14...... IX.4:3 | The **g.** of God will take them gently in, |
| T-19...... IV.2:6 | Would you not now return His **g.**, and |
| T-19...... IV.3:2 | you look with gentle **g.** upon your brother |

## gradual 1

| | |
|---|---|
| T-7 ..........I.7:1 | because His accomplishments are not **g.**. |

## gradually 4

| | |
|---|---|
| T-4 ....... VI.5:5 | It **g.** becomes desirable as he changes his |
| T-12 ..... VI.6:6 | **G.** you learn to apply it to everyone and |
| T-20 ...... V.1:5 | do the parts of God's Son **g.** join in time, |
| M-21 .........4:5 | way. **G.**, he learns how to let his words be |

## grain 2

| | |
|---|---|
| T-28 ..... IV.9:4 | How holy is the smallest **g.** of sand, when |
| T-30 ......I.11:1 | (6) This tiny **g.** of wisdom will suffice to |

## grand 2

| | |
|---|---|
| T-19 .......II.2:6 | Sin is the **g.** illusion underlying all the |
| T-24 ........I.5:2 | Here is the **g.** illusion of what you are and |

## grandeur 33

| | |
|---|---|
| T-9 ......VII.6:5 | the **g.** of God in you, you have chosen to |
| T-9 ........VIII.h | **G.** versus Grandiosity |
| T-9 .....VIII.1:1 | **G.** is of God, and only of Him. Therefore |
| T-9 .....VIII.1:3 | because in the presence of the **g.** of God |
| T-9 .....VIII.1:6 | the ego is its alternative to the **g.** of God. |
| T-9 .....VIII.3:1 | the difference between **g.** and grandiosity, |
| T-9 .....VIII.4:1 | is immobilized in the presence of God's **g.** |
| T-9 .....VIII.4:1 | because His **g.** establishes your freedom. |
| T-9 .....VIII.4:3 | in it. **G.** is totally without illusions, and |
| T-9 .....VIII.4:6 | and argue that **g.** cannot be a real part of |
| T-9 .....VIII.4:7 | Yet your **g.** is not delusional because you |
| T-9 .....VIII.4:8 | it is a form of attack, but your **g.** is of God |
| T-9 .....VIII.5:1 | From your **g.** you can only bless, because |
| T-9 .....VIII.5:1 | bless, because your **g.** is your abundance. |
| T-9 .....VIII.6:2 | to look upon your **g.** you cannot despair, |
| T-9 .....VIII.6:3 | ego. Your **g.** is God's answer to the ego, |
| T-9 .....VIII.6:4 | Littleness and **g.** cannot coexist, nor is it |
| T-9 .....VIII.7:1 | denials of each other because **g.** is truth. |
| T-9 .....VIII.7:3 | When **g.** slips away from you, you have |
| T-9 .....VIII.7:6 | Your **g.** will never deceive you, but your |
| T-9 .....VIII.8:1 | is easy to distinguish **g.** from grandiosity, |
| T-9 .....VIII.8:4 | They attest to your **g.**, but they cannot |
| T-9 .....VIII.9:1 | your **g.** be arrogant when God Himself |
| T-9 .....VIII.9:6 | because it is used to replace your **g.**. Yet |
| T-9 .....VIII.9:8 | without you because His **g.** is total, and |
| T-12 ..VII.10:3 | power and **g.** could only bring you peace *if* |
| T-13 ..... III.4:2 | lies in defiance, and that attack is **g.**. You |
| T-13 ..... III.8:4 | you they long for the **g.** that is in them. |
| T-13 ..... III.8:6 | For **g.** is the right of God's Son, and no |
| T-15 ..... III.9:5 | My birth in you is your awakening to **g.**. |
| T-18 ....VIII.2:2 | you will not see the **g.** that surrounds you. |
| T-24 ........I.3:2 | and with the **g.** that He gave His Son. |
| M-19 .........2:6 | **g.** of the scene and the enormous opening |

## grandiose 2

| | |
|---|---|
| W-pI.....35.4:2 | desirable or undesirable, **g.** or debased. |
| M-10 .........3:7 | except in **g.** fantasies would claim this for |

## grandiosity 15

| | |
|---|---|
| T-9 ....... IV.7:4 | of **g.** and confusion that makes the ego |
| T-9 ........VIII.h | Grandeur versus **G.** |
| T-9 .....VIII.1:6 | The **g.** of the ego is its alternative to the |
| T-9 .....VIII.2:1 | **G.** is always a cover for despair. It is |
| T-9 .....VIII.2:4 | Without this belief **g.** is meaningless, and |
| T-9 .....VIII.2:5 | it. The essence of **g.** is competitiveness, |
| T-9 .....VIII.3:1 | the difference between grandeur and **g.**, |
| T-9 .....VIII.3:5 | its offer of **g.** it will attack immediately. If |
| T-9 .....VIII.4:8 | You made **g.** and are afraid of it because it |
| T-9 .....VIII.6:5 | Littleness and **g.** can and must alternate, |
| T-9 .....VIII.7:4 | in littleness; perhaps it is the belief in **g.**. |
| T-9 .....VIII.8:1 | It is easy to distinguish grandeur from **g.**, |
| T-9 .....VIII.9:6 | all. **G.** is delusional, because it is used to |
| T-13 ..... III.8:1 | Beneath all the **g.** you hold so dear is |
| T-19 .......II.2:6 | grand illusion underlying all the ego's **g.**. |

## granite 2

| | |
|---|---|
| T-22 ..... III.3:4 | it. The body's eyes behold it as solid **g.**, so |
| T-22 ..... III.5:6 | unable to look beyond the **g.** block of sin, |

## grant 4

| | |
|---|---|
| T-14 ..... IV.1:5 | **G.** it to him, and you will see the truth of |
| T-16 .....V.11:1 | How can you **g.** unlimited power to what |
| T-21 .....II.13:3 | But **g.** that everything that seems to stand |
| T-27 .......II.3:3 | you **g.** your brother mercy but retain the |

## granted 8

| | |
|---|---|
| T-9 ...... VII.6:7 | is taken for **g.** there and you do not ask, |
| T-9 ...... VII.6:7 | there and you do not ask, "Who **g.** it?" |
| T-18 ... III.4:14 | The Will of God is **g.** you. For you desire |
| T-26 .... VII.3:1 | asks for punishment, and its request is **g.**. |
| T-30 ... III.5:10 | Your will *is* **g.**. Not in any form that would |
| T-30 ... VI.1:10 | by being **g.** where it is not due. |
| W-pI .... 77.5:1 | for the assurance that your request is **g.**. |
| W-pI .... 77.6:3 | but assure you that your request is **g.**. The |

## granting 1

| | |
|---|---|
| T-19 ..... III.3:6 | the form of sin, **g.** that it was an error, but |

## grants 1

| | |
|---|---|
| W-pI .. 101.3:3 | taking everything away before it **g.** the |

## grasp 29

| | |
|---|---|
| T-4 .........II.7:2 | Equality is beyond its **g.**, and charity |
| T-4 .....II.11:13 | from everything else the mind can **g.**. |
| T-14 .......X.3:4 | What is more difficult to **g.** is the lack of |
| T-15 ... III.11:1 | and unwilling to attempt to **g.** for peace |
| T-18 ..... IX.6:6 | to **g.** it and your hands hold nothing. |
| T-21 .......V.4:4 | is, or **g.** the information it would give? All |
| T-24 .... IV.3:2 | oft repeated, but is difficult to **g.** as yet. |
| T-24 .......V.9:4 | within your **g.** because your hands are His |
| T-24 .... VII.8:7 | And it is this that makes it hard to **g.** the |
| T-28 .... VII.3:3 | to **g.** uncertainly at any straw that seems |
| T-29 .......II.9:3 | and hold you in its **g.** as prisoner to itself. |
| T-29 .......V.5:5 | are not hands that **g.** in dreams of pain. |
| T-31 ........I.2:8 | judge it hard to learn or too complex to **g.** |
| T-31 ..... IV.4:8 | and perfectly within your learning **g.**. |
| T-31 .....V.16:3 | world is loosening its **g.** upon your mind. |
| T-31 ...VIII.1:3 | he has; his **g.** cannot exceed its tiny reach. |
| W-pI ...... 8.1:5 | Your mind cannot **g.** the present, which is |
| W-pI .... 29.2:1 | this idea very difficult to **g.** at this point. |
| W-pI .. 107.6:1 | in that, evading capture and escaping **g.**. |
| W-pI .. 127.5:1 | obeys can help you **g.** love's meaning. |
| W-pI .. 155.6:3 | their eyes to look on and their minds to **g.** |
| W-pI .. 161.4:7 | itself to think specifically can no longer **g.** |
| W-pI .. 163.2:2 | all hopes and wishes in its blighting **g.**; all |
| W-pI .. 192.2:2 | a language far beyond his simple **g.**? |
| W-pII . 243.1:2 | what must remain beyond my present **g.**. |
| W-pII ..... 4.1:6 | What would they hear or reach to **g.**? |
| M-2 ........... 2:1 | is necessary to **g.** the concept of time that |
| M-23 ......... 6:1 | No one on earth can **g.** what Heaven is, |
| S-2........ III.1:8 | your understanding and your simple **g.**. |

## grasped 6

| | |
|---|---|
| T-13 .. VII.11:3 | And even from the very hands that **g.** it, it |
| T-26 ... III.1:14 | anything that cannot be immediately **g.**. |
| T-30 .......V.2:6 | of freedom has been **g.** and welcomed, |
| W-pII . 300.1:1 | gone before they are possessed, or even **g.** |
| M-14 ......... 4:3 | cannot be **g.** by those not yet prepared to |
| M-17 ......... 8:7 | Once this is even dimly **g.**, the way is open |

## grasping 2

| | |
|---|---|
| W-pI .. 195.3:3 | little left within his **g.** fingers as in yours. |
| S-3...........I.2:4 | goes irrevocably past their **g.** hands, |

**grass** 8

T-17....... II.6:3 a blade of g. a sign of God's perfection.
T-26...... IX.3:1 hatred fades to let the g. grow green again
T-26...... IX.3:5 miracles sprung up as g. and flowers on
T-29... VIII.4:2 to change one blade of g. from something
W-pI ...134.4:4 as if they were as blameless as the g.; as
W-pI ...156.3:3 g. to grow with roots suspended in the air
W-pII......2.4:4 The g. is pushing through the soil, the
S-3 ........IV.2:3 blade of g. and feathered wing and all the

**grateful** 27

T-4........ VI.7:4 God. If you are g. to your brother, you are
T-4........ VI.7:4 you are g. to God for what He created.
T-6........ I.17:1 to develop your weakened ability to be g.,
T-7......... V.7:1 from his brothers, but he is not g. to them
T-9......... II.9:4 cannot be g. for what you do not value.
T-13.... VI.10:5 The sick, who ask for love, are g. for it,
T-17..... V.11:6 you been similarly g. to your brother?
T-20....... V.4:4 will shine so brightly in your g. vision that
T-22...... I.10:7 g. that it is one with you who joined to let
T-22...... VI.3:2 But be you rather g. that you can be the
T-26...... IX.5:1 Heaven is g. for this gift of what has been
W-pI .....53.2:6 I am g. that this world is not real, and
W-pI ...123.1:4 but you can well be g. for your gains,
W-pI ...123.2:3 Be g. He has saved you from the self you
W-pI ...123.3:3 Be g. you are saved. Be glad you have a
W-pI ...128.6:2 It will be g. to be free a while. It knows
W-pI ...129.9:2 last, and we are g. that the choice is made.
W-pI.152.11:6 awareness, g. to restore His home to God,
W-pI.154.13:2 *and I am g. that I have the means by which to*
W-pI.169.14:1 Be g. to return, as you were glad to go an
W-pI ...197.7:2 Self for this, for He is g. only unto God,
W-pII..298.2:4 *am g. for Your holy gifts of certain sanctuary*
W-pII..350.2:1 miracles from Him, we will indeed be g..
M-23..........4:6 far behind a g. heart and thankful mind.
M-23..........5:2 Why would you not be g. to him? He has
P-3 ...........I.4:4 could he be but g. for them and to them?
P-3 ........III.4:9 Who would not be g. for such a gift? Yet

**gratefully** 2

W-pI.135.20:1 Heaven g. acknowledges to be its own.
W-pI ...197.4:6 them back, when He has g. accepted them

**gratification** 1

T-15...... IX.2:2 without g. what you think you want. The

**gratify** 2

M-8............2:8 and able to g. its needs at the expense of
M-14..........1:6 they serve a need or g. a want. Perceived

**gratifying** 1

T-15...... VI.3:3 seek for satisfaction in g. your needs as

**grating** 1

W-pI ...182.6:3 amid the g. sounds and harsh and rasping

**gratitude** 98

T-1........ I.31:1 Miracles should inspire g., not awe. You
T-4........ VI.7:2 g. to your brother is the only gift I want. I
T-4........ VI.7:5 your g. you come to know your brother,
T-5.........in.3:2 want to bless them in return, out of g..
T-6........ I.17:1 I do not need g., but you need to develop
T-7......... V.7:1 healer wants g. from his brothers, but he
T-7....... V.11:3 and by our g. to them make them aware
T-8........ IV.7:9 This is our gift of g. to Him, which He will
T-8........ VI.5:3 Trinity, created in g. for your creation.
T-9........ VI.5:3 their g. and their appreciation of what
T-10....... V.7:7 into your heart in g. for your gift to Him.
T-12.........I.6:2 G. is due him for both his loving thoughts
T-13.... VI.11:9 them in g. because they brought you here.
T-16...... III.5:8 and their power and g. to you for their
T-16...... III.6:5 Their g. has joined with yours and God's
T-16...... III.7:4 learner, who offers it to the teacher in g.,
T-16...... III.7:5 As you learn, your g. to your Self, Who
T-16...... IV.8:5 you to look on all your brothers with g.,
T-16.. IV.11:12 and His g. to you for His completion. In
T-17... V.11:10 lack of thanks and g. you make yourself
T-18....... I.10:9 Let us join in Him in peace and g., and
T-18....... II.7:8 If you but recognized His g.! Or mine
T-18....... V.7:1 to the other and how much g. is due him,
T-19...... IV.3:1 The g. you owe to Him He asks but that
T-19...... IV.3:8 thanks and g. that you have offered Him,
T-19.... IV.3:10 is there of seeing, in the presence of His g.
T19.... IV.B.7:5 in g. for giving peace its home in Heaven.
T19. IV.D.19:6 the debt of g. you offer to the Son of God
T-21.... VI.10:2 as his g. goes out to you who blessed him,
T-21.... VI.10:3 g. he offers you reminds you of the thanks
T-22.... II.11:8 And would you not exchange, in g., the
T-22...... VI.3:5 shift from hate to g. before forgiving eyes.
T-25...... II.9:11 The g. of God Himself is freely offered to
T-25...... IX.2:3 you. God's justice warrants g., not fear.
T-26...... IV.3:5 What is Heaven but a song of g. and love
T-26...... IV.5:1 there, and sing their song of g. and praise.
T-26...... IX.6:6 grow, in g. for what has been restored.
T-26...... IX.7:4 His Son give less in g. for so much more?
T-26...... IX.8:6 gentle g. do God the Father and the Son
T-29...... III.5:2 him, and shines on you in g. and love. He
T-30....... V.8:6 His g. to you is past your understanding,
T-31...... III.7:1 innocent release in g. for their release.
W-pI .....80.2:2 to yourself today, with g. and conviction.
W-pI ...110.5:3 Practice today's idea with g.. This is the
W-pI ...123.2:1 day devoted now to g. will add the benefit
W-pI ...123.4:1 in g. we lift our hearts above despair, and
W-pI ...123.6:3 since He receives your gifts in loving g.,
W-pI ...123.6:5 fill the world with gladness and with g..
W-pI ...123.8:1 care for you, how perfect is His g. to you.
W-pI ...130.7:1 Six times today, in thanks and g., we
W-pI ...130.9:2 will take this giant step with you in g..
WpIrIV.in10:2 His g. surrounds you in the peace wherein
W-pI.151.16:4 and in g. to Him Who has restored our
W-pI.153.15:6 willingly give less at night, in g. and joy.
W-pI ...156.4:2 offer them in g. and gladness at your feet.
W-pI ...168.5:3 down, and rise to Him in g. and love.
W-pI.190.11:2 Let our g. unto our Teacher fill our hearts,
W-pI ...191.5:4 in g. to Him Who pointed out the way to
W-pI......195.h Love is the way I walk in g..
W-pI ...195.1:1 G. is a lesson hard to learn for those who
W-pI ...195.1:7 Your g. is due to Him alone Who made all
W-pI ...195.2:2 But it is equally insane to fail in g. to One
W-pI ...195.4:1 offer God your g. because your brother is
W-pI ...195.4:3 And g. can only be sincere if it be joined
W-pI ...195.5:2 And let your g. make room for all who
W-pI ...195.8:1 Walk, then, in g. the way of love. For
W-pI ...195.8:6 is complete you will have total g., for you
W-pI ...195.9:1 we learn to think of g. in place of anger,
W-pI ...195.9:4 future. G. becomes the single thought we
W-pI.195.10:1 Our g. will pave the way to Him, and
W-pI.195.10:2 of. G. goes hand in hand with love, and
W-pI.195.10:3 For g. is but an aspect of the Love which is
W-pI.195.10:5 Your g. to Him is one with His to you. For
W-pI.195.10:6 love can walk no road except the way of g.
W-pI......197.h It can be but my g. I earn.
W-pI ...197.1:3 you find external g. and lavish thanks.
W-pI ...197.3:3 Your g. is all your gifts require, that they
W-pI ...197.4:5 In your g. are they accepted universally,
W-pI ...197.7:5 g. to all They have created has no end, for
W-pI ...197.7:5 has no end, for g. remains a part of love.
W-pI ...197.8:7 All g. belongs to you, because of what you
W-pI ...197.9:7 Earn now the g. you have denied yourself
W-pI ...198.5:2 gives salvation, and accept His gift with g.
W-pI ...215.1:1 (195) Love is the way I walk in g.. *The*
W-pI ...217.1:1 (197) It can be but my g. I earn. *Who*
W-pII.....in.6:2 in g. to Him Who taught us how to leave
W-pII..293.2:2 *hymns of g. the world is singing underneath*
W-pII..298.1:1 My g. permits my love to be accepted
W-pII..306.2:2 *In g. and thankfulness we come, with empty*
W-pII..315.1:4 Someone speaks a word of g. or mercy,
W-pII..315.2:3 *that g. to them may lead me on to my Creator*
M-10 .........5:1 down, not with regret but with a sigh of g.
M-23 .........4:6 And g. to God becomes the way in which
M-25 .........6:9 alone go with Christ's g. upon their hearts
C-ep...........4:1 and kneel down an instant in our g. to
P-3........ III.4:6 The therapist repays the patient in g., as
S-3........ IV.3:7 Do not forget the g. of God. Do not forget
S-3........ IV.9:9 And with My g. will come the gift first of

**grave** 2

T-15.........I.3:4 that it can pursue you beyond the g.. And
T-27.........I.8:1 end alike within the termination of the g..

**graven** 2

T-30.... VI.10:4 to you a g. image and a sign of death. Is
W-pI ...110.9:3 Let g. images you made to be the Son of

**gravity** 1

W-pI ...140.6:6 an illusion by its size, its seeming g., or

**Great** 10
*great*

T-10...... IV.8:1 remains, for the G. Rays are obscured. Yet
T-10...... IV.8:6 the spark is still as pure as the G. Light,
T-11...... III.4:7 G. Light always surrounds you and shines
T-15...... IX.1:1 let you see the G. Rays shining from them
T-15...... IX.3:1 the G. Rays replace the body in awareness
T-15.. XI.10:10 long left unfulfilled, in the G. Awakening.
T-16...... VI.4:5 The G. Rays would establish the total lack
T-16...... VI.6:3 holds the G. Rays within it is also visible,
T-18...... III.8:7 light will the G. Rays extend back into
W-pII .360.1:2 *me, for the G. Rays remain forever still and*

**great** 125
*Great*

T-1..........II.4:4 would be too g. for you to encompass. I
T-1........ III.1:6 you must join the g. crusade to correct it;
T-2........ VI.5:5 consistent behavior, but entails g. strain.
T-4.........I.10:2 Your investment is g. now because fear is
T-4....... VII.8:5 there is g. joy throughout the Kingdom.
T-5....... II.3:10 It takes effort and g. willingness to learn.
T-6....... II.12:8 The g. peace of the Kingdom shines in
T-6........ IV.2:8 since, although it has raised a g. many.
T-6........ IV.6:8 created there will have g. reality for you,
T-6.... V.C.10:5 You have exerted g. effort to preserve
T-7........ IV.5:7 strength of right perception is so g. that it
T-10...... III.6:1 but there is g. appreciation for everything
T-11...... III.5:6 you is part of a light so g. that it can sweep
T-11.... VI.10:6 to His Will is either g. or small. What
T-11....VIII.3:5 Instruction in perception is your g. need,
T-13.........II.9:6 be g. joy in Heaven on your homecoming,
T-13...... IX.6:9 release from guilt g. is the joy in Heaven,
T-14....VIII.2:2 that promises otherwise, g. or small,
T-14........X.4:1 can occur together and in g. numbers.
T-15...... IV.3:1 Be humble before Him, and yet g. *in* Him.
T-15....VIII.2:5 is. God's Son has such g. need of your
T-15....VIII.2:5 this that you cannot conceive of need so g.
T-15...... IX.6:3 your power, being His, is as g. as His, you
T-15........X.7:1 and how g. a sacrifice do you believe His
T-15........X.8:3 this has been so g. that you have given
T-16....... V.1:1 realize that it involves a g. amount of pain
T-16... VII.11:2 problems, be they perceived as g. or small
T-17........II.5:2 The g. Transformer of perception will
T-17..... VII.7:1 how g. the strength that goes with you.
T-17..... VII.7:3 so g. it reaches past the stars and to the
T-18...... III.8:4 When such g. lights have joined with you
T-18...... IV.6:8 how little is your part, and how g. is His.
T-19.........I.8:2 not see how g. the devastation wrought by
T-19...... III.2:4 is always the g. preserver of sin, treating it
T19.... IV.A.9:1 feather be before the g. wings of truth?
T19.... IV.B.2:4 "sacrifice" you feel to be too g. to make,
T19.... IV.B.7:9 when its g. advocate is heard no more?
T19.. IV.B.11:4 body is the g. seeming betrayer of faith. In
T19.. IV.B.15:3 g. deceiver recognizes that this is not so,
T19.... IV.C.7:2 the g. dark savior from the light of truth,
T19.... IV.C.7:5 peace must flow across seems to be very g.
T19... IV.D.3:4 the g. amnesia in which the memory of

T-20....... II.4:1 I have g. need for lilies, for the Son of
T-20..... VII.1:5 And this produces g. discomfort. This
T-21......... I.8:1 as you look into a g. and shining circle.
T-21.... III.10:1 has given it g. power in your sight; except
T-21....... V.8:1 and serve the g. deceiver's needs as well as
T-21..... VII.4:6 it caught a glimpse of the g. enemy who
T-21.... VIII.5:2 you? Here is the g. appeal to reason; the
T-22.... II.10:1 Behold the g. projection, but look on it
T-22.... II.12:3 How g. the power that lies in it. Time
T-22....... V.2:6 fear? Belief in sin needs g. defense, and at
T-22.... VI.11:7 to attack the g. Creator of the universe,
T-23.... II.15:1 for by the g. reversal they appear to be the
T-24......... I.5:1 Specialness is the g. dictator of the wrong
T-24....... II.8:4 need to give it is as g. as yours to have it.
T-24.... II.12:6 and the g. defender of all illusions from
T-24..... III.6:1 Forgive the g. Creator of the universe, the
T-24.... VI.10:5 how g. the Love of God for you must be,
T-24..... VII.1:6 No effort is too g., no cost too much, no
T-25....... V.5:5 it! And how g. will be your joy, when he is
T-25.. VIII.12:4 so g. and holy that He could not doubt
T-26....... II.4:4 does not evaluate injustices as g. or small,
T-26....... II.5:7 has no resolution, you have made it g.,
T-26....... II.6:3 you think are g. and cannot be resolved.
T-26....... II.7:1 how g. your own release will be when you
T-26...... IV.6:3 g. will be the joy in Heaven when you join
T-26....... V.6:1 Forgiveness is the g. release from time. It
T-26.... VIII.3:2 believing that the risk of loss is g. between
T-27.... VIII.3:3 and seems to show a g. variety of places
T-29....... V.6:2 For you would understand how g. the cost
T-31......... I.4:4 an enormity so g. the Holy Spirit's Voice
T-31..... II.10:1 old ideas of who your g. companion is and
T-31...... IV.5:4 The g. release of power must begin with
T-31..... V.14:1 been the g. preoccupation of the world.
W-in.......... 2:2 They do not require a g. deal of time, and
W-in.......... 6:1 exercises be practiced with g. specificity,
W-pI..... 20.2:8 apart. And g. indeed will be your reward.
W-pI..... 26.5:2 to a minute if the discomfort is too g.. Do
W-pI..... 27.2:1 There may be a g. temptation to believe
W-pI..... 46.1:3 Forgiveness is the g. need of this world,
W-pI..... 66.9:6 We need g. honesty today. Remember the
W-pI..... 74.2:1 There is g. peace in today's idea, and the
W-pI..... 91.4:2 Did you but realize how g. this strength,
W-pI..... 98.5:3 gaining a reward so g. it has no measure?
W-pI... 100.5:4 how g. the happiness He wills for you.
W-pI... 110.5:2 g. restorer of the truth to the awareness of
W-pI. 110.10:4 you. Today we make a g. advance to truth
WpI. rIII.in9:3 prove how g. are its potential gifts to you.
WpIrIII.in12:3 g. we will continue on more solid ground,
W-pI... 130.9:2 For you have called upon the g. unfailing
W-pI... 131.6:3 is the g. illusion it is past or in the future.
W-pI... 134.8:2 of lies; the g. restorer of the simple truth.
W-pI. 137.10:2 nor realize how g. your offering to all the
W-pI... 138.8:1 can gain unconscious hold of g. intensity,
W-pI... 151.8:1 because it rests on Certainty so g. that
W-pI... 153.6:4 it recognizes strength so g. attack is folly,
W-pI. 155.14:1 His Love, reminding you how g. His trust;
W-pI... 164.4:5 so g. and so completely different from all
W-pI... 165.4:3 Nor need you perceive how g. the gift,
W-pI... 166.5:5 and a treasure his so g. that everything
W-pI... 181.3:1 way to our g. need to let our sinlessness
W-pI... 187.9:3 g. illusion of the fear of God diminishes to
W-pI... 194.1:2 So g. the distance is that it encompasses,
W-pII .224.1:1 so secure, so lofty, sinless, glorious and g.,
W-pII .238.1:1 *Father, Your trust in me has been so g., I*
W-pII .257.1:3 without deep distress and g. depression.
M-4..... I.A.4:5 It takes g. learning to understand that all
M-4..... V.1:14 need of them is just as g. as theirs of Him.
M-10......... 5:2 Now are you free of a burden so g. that
M-13......... 2:1 It takes g. learning both to realize and to
M-17....... 6:10 of Who your g. "opponent" really is.
M-25......... 1:6 directed toward this one g. final surprise,
M-25......... 6:6 is also a g. channel of hope and healing in
C-3............ 4:5 of Christ is the g. symbol of forgiveness. It
C-6............ 3:4 is the g. correction principle; the bringer
P-1............ 2:1 it and give it His Own g. gift of rejoicing?
P-2......... V.1:2 This is the g. illusion. In its wake comes
P-3......... II.9:2 there is g. temptation to misuse his role.
P-3....... II.10:9 In time there can be a g. lag between the
P-3........ III.3:4 must demand payment, and the cost is g..
S-1.......... II.4:4 you have need of prayer, and g. need, too.
S-2........... I.5:1 This is the g. deception of the world, and
S-2........... I.5:1 world, and you the g. deceiver of yourself.
S-3........ IV.5:7 His. His g. destroyer, death. And sickness,

## greater 50

T-1......... II.3:7 is entitled to respect for his g. experience,
T-1......... II.3:7 and obedience for his g. wisdom. He is
T-1......... II.4:7 in recognition that the Father is g..
T-2.......... I.5:4 seem to be of g. magnitude than others.
T-4......... II.8:8 being rejected by something g. than itself.
T-4....... VI.6:1 you is g. than yours in me at the moment,
T-10..... IV.8:3 little spark you will learn of the g. light,
T-12..... II.10:7 Do you not have g. reason for fearing the
T-14....... X.6:6 consider which call is louder or g. or more
T-16....... II.7:8 look with g. charity on whom God loves
T-16....... II.8:4 still g. faith in the disaster you have made.
T-16....... II.8:7 no g. love than to accept this and be glad.
T-17.... VIII.3:7 is enormous, and far g. than you realize.
T-17.... VIII.4:1 to His Call seems to be g. than before.
T-18...... IV.1:9 instant far g. than you can understand. It
T19.... IV.A.9:5 stood for nothing when you had g. faith
T19.. IV.A.17:7 Mine was of no g. value than yours; no
T-20.... VI.12:2 The holy instant is of g. value now to you
T-25.... VIII.4:8 you, with someone else by far the g. part.
T-25.... VIII.4:9 in the total cost, the g. his the less is yours
T-25..... IX.1:8 truth has g. value now than all illusions.
T-25..... IX.3:3 but has added to it and made it g., harder
T-26........ I.4:3 g. sacrifice could be demanded than that
T-26....... II.1:2 g. difficulty in resolving some than others
T-26.... VII.6:2 it is possible that some are given g. value,
T-27....... II.5:8 with power g. than a thousand tongues.
T-28........ IV.h The G. Joining
T-31........ I.3:2 There is no g. power in the world. The
T-31...... V.8:5 of self, and g. terror would arise in you.
T-31.... VII.4:3 The contrast is far g. than you think, for
W-pI....... 5.4:1 giving g. weight to some subjects than to
W-pI..... 63.1:3 have that would bring you g. happiness?
WpI..rIII.in9:1 important, and perhaps of even g. value.
W-pI... 123.1:4 gains, which are far g. than you realize.
W-pI... 128.3:3 value g. in your sight limit you further,
W-pI. 135.11:5 that serves the g. plan established for the
W-pI... 153.2:5 treachery without and still a g. treachery
WpI... rV.in1:6 hasten on, for we approach a g. certainty,
W-pI. 186.14:4 has been restored to you is g. still.
W-pII294.1:10 serve, and then to be replaced for g. good.
M-4..... VII.1:7 curriculum. Its g. strangeness lies merely
M-5......... I.1:3 price to pay for something of g. worth.
M-25......... 6:3 the power, the g. its potential usefulness.
M-25......... 6:8 increased freedom for g. imprisonment.
P-1............ 1:5 through which He offers His g. gifts to
P-3......... I.2:11 Or a g. gift to you? Would you rather
P-3....... III.7:9 What g. gift than this could you be given?
P-3..... III.7:10 What g. gift is there that you would give?
S-2......... II.6:4 give no hope, but only g. pain and misery.
S-3........ IV.8:2 in which your joy grows g. as your love

## greatest 13

T-4.......... I.4:1 and learning are your g. strengths now,
T-5....... III.8:7 calm. Peace is the ego's g. enemy because,
T-13..... IV.2:2 real Heaven is the g. threat you think you
T-17....... II.3:1 still the g. accomplishment of all in God's
T-18...... V.1:6 of your g. advances you have judged as
T-20....... II.7:5 your vision has become the g. power for
T-29........ I.3:2 g. obstacle that peace must flow across
T-29..... VI.4:1 Change is the g. gift God gave to all that
T-31..... IV.3:6 they could have learned their g. lesson.
W-pI..... 56.2:2 I am, I realize that vision is my g. need.
M-23....... 3:11 the g. teacher be unavailable to those who
S-1......... in.1:1 Prayer is the g. gift with which God
S-2......... in.1:5 Behold the g. help that God ordained to

## greatly 4

T-2..... VIII.2:6 can, however, be g. shortened by miracles
T-13...... V.1:4 content of individual illusions differs g..
M-1........... 3:2 The form of the course varies g.. So do the
M-4........... 1:2 their experiences of the world vary g., and

## greatness 5

T-15..... III.8:7 Before the g. that lives in you, your poor
T-15... III.12:3 but only his call for Heaven and g.. Forget
T-16..... V.13:1 them to obscure their tininess and His g..
T-18..... IV.1:8 It is He Who adds the g. and the might.
T-18..... IV.3:2 with less than g. that comes not of you.

## green 4

T-18... VIII.9:3 becomes a garden, g. and deep and quiet,
T-26..... IX.3:1 hatred fades to let the grass grow g. again,
W-pI.... 76.3:2 of g. paper strips and piles of metal discs.
W-pII... 13.5:3 Now the world is g.. And everywhere the

## greet 10

T-14..... VI.8:7 Its gates are open wide to g. His Son. No
T19... IV.A.9:6 Would you not rather g. the summer sun
T-20..... II.10:5 savior from illusions has come to g. you,
W-pI.. 122.8:3 quietness it rises up to g. your open eyes,
W-pI.. 158.8:4 as a body. G. him as the Son of God he is,
WpI.rV.in11:3 words upon our lips, to g. another day.
W-pI.. 186.8:4 and g. the day with welcome or with tears
W-pII. 312.1:5 must the real world come to g. the holy
M-27......... 3:4 where worms wait to g. him and to last a
S-3........ IV.9:2 Lift up your hearts to g. its advent. See

## greeted 1

W-pI.. 184.1:6 time; all bodies which are g. by a name.

## greeting 2

T-3.......... I.6:3 honor is the natural g. of the truly loved
T-24... VI.12:4 a nod to God, a g. to the Christ in you,

## grew 1

T-30..... III.8:7 its light g. dimmer or less perfect ever was

## grief 17

T-11..... III.4:4 Fear and g. are your guests, and they go
T-27...... I.4:10 your brother *you* have looked upon in g..
T-29..... VI.1:4 of madness and of murder, g. and loss.
T-31..... III.5:1 attack; of pain and age, of g. and suffering
W-pI.... 99.5:4 death, on g. and separation and on loss.
WpI..rIV.in9:3 from darkness to the light, from g. to joy,
W-pI.. 152.2:4 Can pain be part of peace, or g. of joy?
W-pI.. 162.5:4 to all as remedy for g. and misery, all
W-pI.. 164.3:4 On this day is g. laid by, for sights and
W-pI.. 187.6:4 well at pain and loss, at sickness and at g.,
W-pI.. 194.5:2 freed from its bequest of g. and misery, of
W-pII. 284.1:3 There is no g. with any cause at all. And
W-pII. 284.2:1 *hurt, so g. and pain must be impossible. Let*
W-pII. 285.1:4 and how would g. and loss avail me if
M-4..... I.A.5:8 he learns that where he anticipated g., he
M-4........ V.1:8 gentleness as surely as g. attends attack.
S-2.......... II.2:6 There is no union here, but only g.. This

## grievance 19

W-pI.... 68.1:2 To hold a g. is to forget who you are. To
W-pI.... 68.1:3 To hold a g. is to see yourself as a body.
W-pI.... 68.1:4 hold a g. is to let the ego rule your mind
W-pI.... 68.7:1 whenever any thought of g. arises against
W-pI.... 69.9:8 *If I hold this g. the light of the world will be*
W-pI.... 71.2:4 Each g. you hold is a declaration, and an
W-pI.... 72.5:6 And every g. that you hold insists that the
W-pI.. 73.11:6 you are tempted to hold a g. of any kind.
W-pI.... 78.1:1 make is one between a g. and a miracle.
W-pI.... 78.1:2 Each g. stands like a dark shield of hate
W-pI.... 78.3:2 For every g. is a block to sight, and as it
W-pI.... 78.3:4 Each g. made the darkness deeper, and
W-pI.... 89.2:3 *Let me not hold a g. against you, [name], but*
W-pI.... 89.4:2 *not hold this g. apart from my salvation. Let*

W-pI.....90.1:2 some form of **g.** that I would cherish. Let
W-pI.....90.1:3 miracle with which I let the **g.** be replaced
W-pI.....90.1:5 The problem is a **g.**; the solution is a
W-pI.....90.1:6 to me through my forgiveness of the **g.**,
W-pI.....90.2:3 *miracle behind this* **g.** *will resolve it for me.*

## grievances 75

T-17......III.2:5 reminds you of your past **g.** attracts you,
W-pI........68.h Love holds no **g.**.
W-pI.....68.1:1 itself can hold no **g.** and know your Self.
W-pI.....68.1:5 just what holding **g.** does to your mind. It
W-pI.....68.2:2 Can all this arise from holding **g.**? Oh, yes
W-pI.....68.2:4 holds **g.** denies he was created by love,
W-pI.....68.3:1 sure that those who hold **g.** will redefine
W-pI.....68.3:2 that those who hold **g.** will suffer guilt, as
W-pI.....68.3:3 those who hold **g.** will forget who they are
W-pI.....68.4:1 your **g.** if you believed all this were so?
W-pI.....68.4:2 you do not think you can let your **g.** go.
W-pI.....68.5:1 you hold what you regard as major **g.**.
W-pI.....68.5:3 Then think of the seemingly minor **g.** you
W-pI.....68.5:4 whom you do not cherish **g.** of some sort.
W-pI.....68.6:8 yourself: *Love holds no* **g.**. *When I let all my*
W-pI.....68.6:9 *let all my* **g.** *go I will know I am perfectly safe.*
W-pI.....68.7:2 *Love holds no* **g.**. *Let me not betray my Self.*
W-pI.....68.7:5 *Love holds no* **g.**. *I would wake to my Self by*
W-pI.....68.7:6 *laying all my* **g.** *aside and wakening in Him.*
W-pI........69.h My **g.** hide the light of the world in me.
W-pI.....69.1:1 one can look upon what your **g.** conceal.
W-pI.....69.1:2 **g.** are hiding the light of the world in you,
W-pI.....69.1:3 But as the veil of your **g.** is lifted, you are
W-pI.....69.9:1 remind yourself that your **g.** are hiding
W-pI.....69.9:4 *My* **g.** *hide the light of the world in me. I*
W-pI.....71.2:1 for salvation centers around holding **g.**. It
W-pI...71.10:2 Be alert to all temptation to hold **g.** today,
W-pI...71.10:3 *Holding* **g.** *is the opposite of God's plan for*
W-pI........72.h Holding **g.** is an attack on God's plan for
W-pI.....72.3:1 why holding **g.** is an attack on God's plan
W-pI.....72.3:2 kinds of things you are apt to hold **g.** for.
W-pI.....72.7:4 and holding your **g.** against Him and His
W-pI.72.10:11 We have shouted our **g.** so loudly that we
W-pI.72.10:12 our **g.** to close our eyes and stop our ears.
W-pI...72.13:3 *Holding* **g.** *is an attack on God's plan for*
W-pI.....73.2:1 Idle wishes and **g.** are partners or co-
W-pI.....73.2:2 gave rise to it, and the ego's need for **g.**,
W-pI.....73.2:3 the ego employs to traffic in **g.**. They
W-pI.....73.3:1 forth, and **g.** increase with each exchange.
W-pI.....73.5:3 **G.** darken your mind, and you look out
W-pI.....73.5:5 that the barrier of **g.** is easily passed, and
W-pI...73.11:7 This will help you let your **g.** go, instead
W-pI.....77.8:3 *I will not trade miracles for* **g.**. *I want only*
W-pI........78.h Let miracles replace all **g.**.
W-pI.....78.1:4 in light, but you behold your **g.** instead.
W-pI.....78.2:1 Today we go beyond the **g.**, to look upon
W-pI.....78.3:1 He waits for you behind your **g.**, and as
W-pI.....78.4:2 blind to him; we will not look upon our **g.**
W-pI.....78.4:4 person you have used as target for your **g.**
W-pI.....78.4:4 and lay the **g.** aside and look at him.
W-pI.....78.5:3 the **g.** that you have held against him, you
W-pI.....78.7:4 be shown the light in him beyond your **g.**.
W-pI.....78.8:7 No dark **g.** obscure the sight of him. You
W-pI...78.10:2 and refuse to hide his light behind our **g.**.
W-pI...78.10:5 as well, we pray: *Let miracles replace all* **g.**.
W-pI.....80.7:1 us be determined not to collect **g.** today.
W-pI.....84.3:1 (68) Love holds no **g.**. Grievances are
W-pI.....84.3:2 **G.** are completely alien to love.
W-pI.....84.3:3 **G.** attack love and keep its light obscure.
W-pI.....84.3:4 hold **g.** I am attacking love, and therefore
W-pI.....85.1:1 My **g.** hide the light of the world in me.
W-pI.....85.1:2 me. My **g.** show me what is not there, and
W-pI.....85.1:3 this, what do I want my **g.** for? They keep
W-pI.....85.1:5 **G.** and light cannot go together, but light
W-pI.....85.1:6 To see, I must lay **g.** aside. I want to see,
W-pI.....86.3:1 Holding **g.** is an attack on God's plan for
W-pI.....86.3:2 Holding **g.** is an attempt to prove that
W-pI.....86.3:4 By holding **g.**, I am therefore excluding
W-pI.....86.4:3 *If I see grounds for* **g.** *in this, I will not see the*
W-pI.....88.1:4 Attack and **g.** are not there to choose.
W-pI.....89.1:3 laws release me from all **g.**, and replace
W-pI.....89.1:4 accept the miracles in place of the **g.**,
W-pI.....89.3:1 (78) Let miracles replace all **g.**. By this
W-pI.....89.4:3 *Let our* **g.** *be replaced by miracles, [name].*
W-pI.....89.4:4 *is the miracle by which all my* **g.** *are replaced.*

## grieve 5

T-20....VI.11:2 sigh and **g.** and die in honor of its master.
T-30......IV.4:6 but toys, my child, so do not **g.** for them.
W-pI...152.1:3 No one can **g.** nor fear nor think him sick
W-pII..245.1:5 *peace to those who suffer pain, or* **g.** *for loss,*
W-pII..314.1:5 can **g.** or suffer when the present has been

## grieved 1

W-pI.....78.7:4 and as you think of him who **g.** you, let

## grieves 1

W-pII..248.1:4 What **g.** is not myself. What is in pain is

## grievous 1

S-3........IV.5:8 suffering and **g.** loss become the lot of

## grim 10

T19....IV.C.2:4 procession that honors their **g.** master,
T19....IV.C.8:3 no **g.** commandments nor twisted rituals
T-24....VI.11:5 And all this **g.** determination was for this;
W-pI.151.10:2 can look beyond these **g.** appearances,
W-pI...153.4:2 In them lies madness in a form so **g.** that
W-pI.153.11:3 holds the world in **g.** imprisonment. Nor
M-17.........9:9 Let this **g.** sword be taken from you now.
C-4.............7:7 and the **g.** appeal of guilt and death is
P-2........IV.3:2 together and sometimes in **g.** succession.
P-2........VI.1:3 all this is but the **g.** refusal to forgive.

## grimly 1

T-21......III.2:5 This it will follow, **g.** or happily, but

## grimness 1

M-27.........3:3 The **g.** of the symbol is enough to show it

## grip 4

W-pI...138.8:1 and **g.** the mind with terror and anxiety
W-pI...153.3:3 **g.** of the imprisonment upon the mind.
W-pI...153.5:3 who feel its iron **g.** upon your heart. You
W-pI.196.10:1 instant in which terror seems to **g.** your

## grope 2

W-pI.....87.1:3 It is not my will to **g.** about in darkness,
W-pI...192.7:2 Without its kindly light we **g.** in darkness,

## groped 1

T-20......III.9:3 **g.** but feebly in the dust and found your

## grossly 1

T-16......VI.7:2 everything you see is **g.** distorted and

## grotesque 3

T-18......IX.7:3 appear and shift from loveliness to the **g.**.
M-4 ......VI.1:7 The more **g.** the dream, the fiercer and
P-2........IV.2:6 **g.** and ugly since it mimics deformity. If a

## ground 30

T-13.....in.2:10 wither and gasp and are laid in the **g.**, and
T-14.......V.9:5 with me, and stand with me on holy **g.**.
T-18.........I.9:4 Here is holy **g.**, in which no substitution
T-18... VIII.9:1 come inside and shine upon the barren **g.**.
T-19.......I.15:1 the Holy Spirit prepare the **g.** for the most
T-22.......II.7:7 there is no middle **g.** where you can pause
T-23......II.13:4 you walk in sanity with feet on solid **g.**,
T-23......II.13:5 make the **g.** beneath your feet seem solid.
T-24.........I.9:5 **g.** of battle which you wage against him.
T-25...... IX.4:2 Holy Spirit's perception leaves no **g.** for
T-26...... IV.3:4 and stand upon the **g.** where sin has left a
T-26...... V.14:2 You stand no longer on the **g.** that lies
T-26...... IX.2:4 The **g.** whereon you stand is holy ground
T-26...... IX.2:4 stand is holy **g.** because of Them Who,
T-26...... IX.3:5 and flowers on the barren **g.** that hate had
T-26...... IX.3:7 you stand on **g.** so holy Heaven leans to
T-26...... IX.4:6 to join Them on the **g.** whereon you stand
T-28....... V.3:6 alien **g.** which your Creator did not make,
T-28..... V.3:11 A middle **g.**, where you can be a thing
T-28.....VII.2:7 is no middle **g.** in any aspect of salvation.
T-29........II.4:7 touched the holy **g.** whereon you stand,
T-29...... IX.1:3 fall lower than the stones upon the **g.**, and
WpIrIII.in12:3 so great we will continue on more solid **g.**,
W-pI... 156.4:4 on the **g.** that you may walk in softness,
W-pI... 159.8:1 Christ's vision is the holy **g.** in which the
W-pI... 163.5:4 kneeling down with foreheads to the **g.**,
W-pI... 182.4:5 Where this Child shall go is holy **g.**. It is
W-pI... 183.2:2 to surround the **g.** on which you stand,
W-pI... 186.8:5 or dash us to the **g.** in hopelessness.
S-1......... V.1:3 leave the **g.** where it begins to rise to God,

## grounds 26

T-6..........II.3:4 ego justifies this on the **g.** that it makes
T-8..........II.2:5 Simply on the **g.** of your own experience
T-16....... IV.3:7 unsatisfying on the **g.** of disillusionment.
T19..IV.B.11:6 mistake be reasonable **g.** for depression
T19..IV.B.11:9 of your mistake will give you **g.** for faith.
T-23.........I.3:2 alliances on **g.** that have no meaning. For
T-24.........I.4:4 serves as **g.** from which attack on those
T-25........II.3:1 warranted on **g.** that are not in this world
T-25........II.3:3 **g.** that it will suddenly succeed and bring
T-25...... IX.4:6 deprived, and thus with **g.** for vengeance.
T-26..... VII.7:2 hope of healing, and the lasting **g.** for hell.
T-27.........I.9:6 No **g.** are offered that it may be judged in
T-27........II.1:4 that the damaged have no **g.** for peace.
T-27........II.9:3 the **g.** on which they justify his pain. The
T-27..VIII.5:10 And we will see the **g.** for laughter, not a
T-28...... III.5:5 Where are the **g.** for sickness when the
T-30.......I.15:4 nor **g.** for opposition that you may be free
W-pI.....21.3:3 fallacious **g.** that they are more "obvious.
W-pI.....27.1:3 **g.** that you are not sure you really mean it
W-pI.....53.3:2 undependable, and offers no **g.** for trust.
W-pI.....71.3:3 there is still **g.** for hope in other places
W-pI.....86.4:3 *If I see* **g.** *for grievances in this, I will not see*
W-pI.....86.4:3 *in this, I will not see the* **g.** *for my salvation.*
W-pI... 126.5:1 forgiveness has no **g.** on which to rest
W-pI... 186.3:6 the specious **g.** that modesty is outraged.
M-27.........4:1 God nor re-establish any **g.** for trust. If

## groundwork 1

M-24.........2:3 If he is laying the **g.** for a future life, he

## group 3

T-25...... IX.7:2 given specially to an elect and special **g.**,
W-pI... 186.9:5 an instant, break apart to **g.** again, and
S-2..........II.2:1 In this **g.**, first, there are the forms in

## grow 32

T-11........II.6:5 the little spark and are willing to let it **g.**.
T-13....VIII.8:2 **g.** in strength the power of God's Son will
T-14........X.5:2 of Heaven last but a moment and **g.** dim,
T-16........II.7:1 increase and peace will **g.** with its increase
T-16........III.7:5 He is, will **g.** and help you honor Him.
T-17.....VII.4:4 must **g.** to meet the goal that has been set.
T-18..VIII.10:3 So will it **g.** and stretch across the desert,
T19....IV.C.9:2 to **g.** into a mighty force for God is very
T-25...... IX.9:2 And so they gather dust and **g.**, until they
T-26...... IX.3:1 hatred fades to let the grass **g.** green again
T-26...... IX.4:4 lights **g.** ever brighter as each one comes

T-26 IX.6:6 And all the lights in Heaven brighter g., in
T-28 III.5:5 where the seeds of sickness seemed to g.?
T-29 IX.5:4 Or can a toy g. large and dangerous and
T-31 II.11:8 but cannot make the way itself g. dark.
T-31 V.3:1 This aspect can g. angry, for the world is
W-pI 92.6:4 that but g. in darkness to enormous size.
W-pI 105.4:1 so does the joy of your Creator g. when
W-pI 123.6:5 And so they g. in power and in strength,
W-pI 127.11:2 we will watch it g. in health and strength,
W-pI 156.3:3 grass to g. with roots suspended in the air
W-pI 159.8:3 never g. in its unnourishing and shallow
W-pI 164.2:2 Its sounds g. dim. A melody from far
W-pI 170.2:2 blood, to make it g. and swell and rage.
W-pI 187.4:4 will change and g. unrecognizable in time
M-2 5:6 another, fade and g. dim and disappear.
C-ep 4:7 will g. in life and strength and hope, until
P-2 III.2:5 as the other shares it, it will g.. Progress
P-3 II.3:6 or later that something will rise and g.; a
S-1 in.3:3 Faith in your goal will g. and hold you up
S-1 II.1:3 and g. with learning until it reaches its
S-2 I.2:3 and mistakes loom large and g. and swell

## growing 4

T-6 V.B.9:4 demonstration of a g. awareness that the
T-31 V.7:9 g. in its ways and finally "maturing" in its
W-pI 96.12:1 you lay another treasure in your g. store.
M-10 6:6 loss; of passing time and g. hopelessness;

## grown 5

T-11 III.1:3 if you did you could never have g. weary.
T-17 V.11:8 and g. dim in what seemed to be the light
T-18 VIII.9:8 water, but has g. too weary to go on alone
T-25 VI.2:1 to the eyes g. long accustomed to the dim
T-27 I.10:3 a breath of immortality to those g. sick of

## grows 21

T-11 II.5:2 but His Voice g. faint in alien company.
T-13 VII.1:5 There is no day that brightens and g. dim.
T-15 IX.6:5 your sight g. weak and dim and limited,
T-17 II.5:4 Each spot His reason touches g. alive with
T-17 IV.13:4 of death g. less convincing as you search it
T-17 IV.14:3 picture of Heaven and eternity g. more
T-17 V.5:3 it g. increasingly beneficent and joyous.
T-23 I.11:3 The altar disappears, the light g. dim, the
T-23 I.12:4 fear is born, and g. and seeks to dominate
T-24 VII.10:3 It g. and withers, flourishes and dies. And
T-26 X.6:2 The world g. dim and threatening, not a
T-28 III.9:6 in which abundance falters and g. thin.
T-31 III.4:7 And it g. old and dies, because that mind
T-31 VII.3:3 body g. decreasingly persistent in your
T-31 VIII.11:5 to Heaven g. from tiny scattered threads
WpI.rV.in12:5 The sound g. dim and disappears, as we
W-pI 187.5:3 g. in strength as it is reinforced by giving.
M-14 2:2 and where it g. and becomes stronger and
P-2 VI.3:5 mind g. fearful and begins to doubt its
S-1 V.1:2 and g. in strength and love and holiness.
S-3 IV.8:2 in which your joy g. greater as your love

## growth 2

T-13 in.2:6 Their g. is attended by suffering, and they
P-2 I.2:4 its interpretation of progress and g..

## guarantee 27

T-2 III.5:13 is the g. that they will ultimately succeed.
T-5 III.8:7 of reality, war is the g. of its survival. The
T-5 IV.1:9 is the g. of the safety of the Kingdom, and
T-5 VI.8:2 becomes merely an attempt to g. the ego's
T-6 V.B.2:4 is all that a teacher need do to g. change.
T-8 VII.11:1 is the only way to g. help and healing.
T-13 I.8:8 Yet the g. of your continuity is God's, not
T-17 III.6:2 thus it seeks to g. there will be no solution
T-20 IV.3:1 made to g. that you would make mistakes
T-20 IV.8:10 God's g. will hold against all obstacles, for
T-20 VII.3:7 They g. the goal, and they are perfectly in
T-22 III.5:9 having been made to g. that nothing else
T-24 VI.12:5 means, and g. the goal's accomplishment.
T-27 V.10:1 will g. that they remain unviolated and
T-29 II.8:2 Its nothingness is g. that it can *not* be sick.
T-30 I.17:2 to g. the joy they asked for will be wholly
T-30 IV.4:2 set. It is His laws that g. your safety. All
T-31 VII.6:1 that now you hold would g. your function
W-pI 47.1:5 and the g. that it will be accomplished?
W-pI 71.4:3 could more surely g. that you will not find
W-pI 94.2:3 be the g. of strength and light as well. You
W-pI 135.16:4 it needs to g. a future quite unlike the past
Wi181-200 3:6 It will be enough to g. the rest will come.
W-pI 191.4:6 of its existence and its g. of immortality.
W-pI 193.1:4 His Will provides the means to g. that it is
W-pII 292.2:1 *Your g. of only happy outcomes in the end.*
M-4 VII.2:7 he could keep, because that is a g. of loss.

## guaranteed 26

T-8 V.4:4 in transcending the ego is g. by God, and
T-13 I.8:7 will be punished, the ego's continuity is g.
T-26 VII.11:3 He g. when He created him *as* everything.
T-27 VI.6:11 And God Himself has g. the strength of
T-28 II.6:8 but without a stable cause with g. effects.
W-pI 77.2:5 your creation, and g. by the laws of God.
W-pI 80.5:7 It is because of this that it is g. to work.
W-pI 93.6:1 Your sinlessness is g. by God. Over and
W-pI 93.6:4 Your sinlessness is g. by God. Nothing
W-pI 93.6:7 Your sinlessness is g. by God, and light
W-pI 93.7:5 Your sinlessness is g. by God. You are
W-pI 93.8:3 *My sinlessness is g. by God.* Then put away
W-pI 93.10:5 *me. My sinlessness is g. by God.* Then try to
W-pI 93.11:4 *Your sinlessness is g. by God.* You can do
W-pI 96.8:1 whose presence in your mind is g. by Him
W-pI 122.10:1 to the search in which the end of hell is g..
W-pI 124.1:2 home is safe, protection g. in all we do,
W-pI 136.18:3 The body's health is fully g., because it is
W-pI 153.10:4 be surer that his happiness is fully g.?
W-pII 11.3:3 Its oneness is forever g. inviolate; forever
W-pII 14.1:2 *is His creation sanctified and g. eternal life.*
M-6 4:10 be full. Yet is its fullness g. by God. What
M-15 3:9 His promises have g. His Judgment, and
C-ep 1:10 The end *is* sure and g. by God. Who stands
P-2 V.4:5 g. that He will hear and answer them in
P-3 III.4:2 promised him, and g. by God. Therefore

## guaranteeing 2

T-7 VI.3:10 g. that you will not know your own safety.
W-pI 98.6:1 offer g. you your full release from pain of

## guarantees 13

T-14 V.6:7 this teaching, and g. its limitless results.
T-20 VIII.4:1 The Holy Spirit g. that what God willed
T-31 V.5:4 it g. the pathways of the world are safely
W-pI 56.3:2 self-image in place, and g. its continuance
WpI. rIV.in2:5 thought that fully g. salvation to the Son.
W-pII 222.1:3 Thoughts, and g. my safety from all pain.
W-pII 2.1:3 It g. that time will have an end, and all the
W-pII 6.2:1 and g. that separation is no more than an
W-pII 292.1:2 And He g. that only joy can be the final
W-pII 292.1:7 to His Will, which g. that our will is done.
W-pII 324.2:4 ending sure, and g. a safe returning home
M-6 3:6 the part that g. the giver will not lose, but
M-23 3:4 completed learning g. your own success.

## guard 6

T-2 VII.1:7 do not g. your thoughts carefully enough.
T-4 I.2:1 Many stand g. over their ideas because
T-11 III.7:7 G. carefully His temple, for He Himself
T-11 VI.6:7 them. G. them in their resurrection, for
T-14 VI.8:4 serve to g. the dark doors behind which
T-31 III.6:4 be. It does not g. your sleep, nor interfere

## guarded 4

T-18 IX.1:9 g. by attack and reinforced by hate.
T19 IV.C.9:3 infancy of salvation is carefully g. by love,
W-pI 135.5:4 so unsafe it must be g. with your very life.
W-pII 325.1:3 esteemed as real and g. as one's own.

## guardian 5

T-4 I.4:7 willing to renounce the role of g. of your
T-22 IV.5:8 it have become its willing g. and protector
W-pI 109.9:4 Time is not the g. of what we give today.
W-pI 170.7:6 who see in him their safety have no g., no
W-pI 189.2:4 the night as silent g. of your holy sleep. It

## guardians 3

T-14 VI.2:5 and you who made these g. of illusion out
T-14 VI.3:5 As g. of darkness and of ignorance look to
M-4 VI.1:6 are but foolish g. of mad illusions. The

## guards 4

T-7 X.7:1 prerogative, which the ego g. so jealously,
T-13 II.4:4 question, it g. this one secret with its life,
T-31 III.5:1 it chose and g. and holds itself at bay, a
W-pI 194.9:5 we will appeal to Him Who g. our rest to

## guess 1

T-21 I.2:6 you where to go. Why should you g.?

## Guest 8

*guest*

T-11 II.5:2 The Eternal G. remains, but His Voice
T-11 II.5:4 mind so that He becomes your only G..
T-11 II.6:5 The G. Whom God sent you will teach
T-16 I.3:10 *and I would not intrude the past upon my G.*
T-29 II.h The Coming of the G.
T-29 II.4:1 Your G. *has* come. You asked Him, and
T-29 II.4:7 G. will welcome everyone whose feet have
T-29 II.5:6 You cannot see your G., but you can see

## guest 4

*Guest*

T-11 II.4:5 you invite as your g. will abide with you.
T-11 II.7:3 are free to determine who shall be your g.,
T-15 X.8:7 partial sacrifice will appease this savage g.
T19 IV.A.16:2 everyone is welcomed as an honored g..

## Guests 4

*guests*

T-26 X.5:4 Presence of your holy G. be known to you.
T-28 III.8:8 will meet with your invited G. the miracle
T-28 III.9:3 The G. have brought unlimited supply
T-28 III.9:8 seemed to keep your G. apart from you.

## guests 2

*Guests*

T-11 II.7:7 and of your g. only the Holy Spirit is real.
T-11 III.4:4 Fear and grief are your g., and they go

## guidance 49

T-1 III.4:5 under my g. miracles lead to the highly
T-1 III.4:7 to abandon them by following my g.."
T-2 VI.1:3 my g. can direct everything that does, if
T-2 VI.2:9 as you place what you think under my g..
T-2 VI.3:5 do not need g. except at the mind level.
T-2 VI.6:1 under my g. without conscious effort, but
T-3 IV.7:7 your mind if you will bring it under my g.
T-4 III.2:4 your own Guide and therefore need g..
T-4 VI.3:1 often to me instead of to your ego for g..
T-4 VII.8:8 to whoever can follow my g. through you.
T-5 II.4:4 Before the separation you did not need g..
T-5 II.5:2 G. is evaluative, because it implies there is
T-6 IV.1:5 you home and you no longer need His g..
T-7 X.5:2 As long as you avoid His g. in any way,

| | |
|---|---|
| T-13...... IV.4:3 | its emphasis on g. enables it to ensure its |
| T-13...... VI.3:3 | is as He was created, there is no g. in Him. |
| T-13...... VI.3:4 | No cloud of g. has risen to obscure Him, |
| T-13......... IX.h | The Cloud of G. |
| T-13...... IX.1:1 | G. remains the only thing that hides the |
| T-13...... IX.1:1 | Father, for g. is the attack upon His Son. |
| T-13...... IX.2:1 | from g. is the ego's whole undoing. *Make* |
| T-13...... IX.2:2 | *Make no one fearful,* for his g. is yours, and |
| T-13...... IX.4:2 | and g. has become as true for you as |
| T-13...... IX.4:6 | mind the cloud of g. that binds him to it. |
| T-13...... IX.5:1 | Lay not his g. upon him, for his guilt lies |
| T-13...... IX.5:1 | for his g. lies in his secret thought that he |
| T-13...... IX.6:2 | of God lies the conviction of your own g.. |
| T-13...... IX.6:6 | guilty become the witnesses to g. in you, |
| T-13...... IX.6:7 | G. is always in your mind, which has |
| T-13...... IX.6:9 | release from g. great is the joy in Heaven, |
| T-13...... IX.7:1 | G. makes you blind, for while you see one |
| T-13...... IX.7:1 | for while you see one spot of g. within you |
| T-13...... IX.7:2 | seems dark, and shrouded in your g.. You |
| T-13...... IX.8:2 | ego tells you all is black with g. within you |
| T-13...... IX.8:3 | your brothers, and see the g. in them. Yet |
| T-13.... IX.8:11 | Can you see g. where God knows there is |
| T-13.......... X.h | Release from G. |
| T-13....... X.1:2 | is to hide the real source of g., and keep |
| T-13....... X.1:3 | by the illusion that the source of g., from |
| T-13....... X.1:3 | displaced the g. onto what you believed to |
| T-13....... X.2:2 | No real relationship can rest on g., or |
| T-13....... X.2:3 | For all relationships that g. has touched |
| T-13....... X.2:3 | are used but to avoid the person *and* the g. |
| T-13....... X.2:7 | If you displace your g. upon them, the |
| T-13....... X.3:1 | in which you seek to lay your g. upon him |
| T-13....... X.3:3 | will see g. in that relationship because |
| T-13....... X.3:4 | is inevitable that those who suffer g. will |
| T-13....... X.3:7 | is to perceive the source of g. outside |
| T-13....... X.4:1 | but the source of your g. lies in the past, |
| T-13....... X.5:4 | to your Father, you will see no g. in you. |
| T-13....... X.5:5 | within you all the while you dreamed of g. |
| T-13....... X.6:1 | you believe that g. is justified in any way, |
| T-13....... X.6:2 | The end of g. will never come as long as |
| T-13....... X.6:3 | must learn that g. is always totally insane, |
| T-13....... X.6:5 | If g. were real, Atonement would not be. |
| T-13....... X.7:3 | Give no reality to g., and see no reason for |
| T-13....... X.8:3 | Son of God believes that he is lost in g., |
| T-13....... X.8:6 | The moment that you realize g. is insane, |
| T-13....... X.9:6 | the cloud of g. that dims your vision, and |
| T-13..... X.10:1 | Release from g. as you would be released. |
| T-13..... X.10:7 | Your g. is without reason because it is not |
| T-13..... X.11:3 | imposing g. on all your relationships and |
| T-13... X.11:11 | *his Father that no g. has ever touched him.* |
| T-13..... X.12:2 | wholly untouched by g. and wholly loving |
| T-13..... X.12:5 | for what you see will banish g. forever. I |
| T-13..... X.14:3 | radiance of the Kingdom g. melts away, |
| T-13...... XI.1:1 | and harsh intrusion of g. on peace. Yet no |
| T-13...... XI.2:8 | The war, the g., the past are gone as one |
| T-13...... XI.5:1 | whose mind is darkened by doubt and g., |
| T-13...... XI.5:1 | g. that His dear Son has laid upon himself |
| T-14......... I.1:7 | complete forgiveness you must have let g. |
| T-14...... III.1:4 | the recognition that g. is interference, not |
| T-14...... III.2:1 | merely to offset the pain of g., and do not |
| T-14...... III.2:2 | that g. and guiltlessness are both of value, |
| T-14...... III.2:6 | To wish for g. in any way, in any form, |
| T-14...... III.3:1 | no compromise that you can make with g. |
| T-14...... III.3:3 | Whenever the pain of g. seems to attract |
| T-14...... III.4:2 | The ego is the choice for g.; the Holy |
| T-14...... III.5:3 | that comes from choosing to be free of g.. |
| T-14...... III.7:7 | His g. is wholly without cause, and being |
| T-14...... III.8:1 | is the only Cause, and g. is not of Him. |
| T-14...... III.8:7 | imposing on himself the penalty of g., in |
| T-14.... III.10:2 | believe they are guilty will respond to g., |
| T-14.... III.10:3 | that increasing g. is self-protection. And |
| T-14.... III.13:4 | knows that all salvation is escape from g.. |
| T-14.... III.15:3 | on the throne of God is not a source of g.. |
| T-14...... IV.3:9 | your g. arises from your failure to fulfill |
| T-14.... IV.3:10 | you escape this g. by failing to fulfill your |
| T-14...... IV.5:5 | and trying to teach him g. instead of love. |
| T-14...... IV.6:8 | For you can bring your g. into sleeping, |
| T-14..... V.1:12 | There is no g. in you, for God is blessed in |
| T-14....... V.2:4 | The burden of g. is heavy, but God would |
| T-14....... V.3:5 | to the denial of g. in all its forms. To |
| T-14 ...... V.4:2 | or you will ask for g. and will experience it |
| T-14 ...... V.4:5 | but shine away the heavy veils of g. within |
| T-14 ...... V.5:6 | learned how to exchange g. for innocence, |
| T-14 ...... V.6:4 | for the single purpose of release from g., |
| T-14 ...... V.7:5 | whom you accord release from g. you will |
| T-14 ...... V.8:4 | with no one left outside to suffer g. alone. |
| T-14 ...... V.8:7 | it, as a teacher of Atonement, not of g.. |
| T-14 .... V.10:3 | of the release from g. by guiltlessness. |
| T-14 ..... VI.4:2 | of guiltlessness shines g. away because, |
| T-14 ..... VI.4:3 | Keep not g. and guiltlessness apart, for |
| T-14 ... VIII.1:2 | in g. and in the dark denial of innocence. |
| T-14 ... VIII.2:5 | Can you offer g. to God? You cannot, |
| T-14 ....... X.1:5 | holiness calls everyone to lay all g. aside. |
| T-14 ..... XI.8:1 | bound to g. and committed so to remain, |
| T-14 ... XI.10:7 | no dark lesson of g. can abide in what He |
| T-15 ...... I.4:14 | will pursue you still, because g. is eternal. |
| T-15 ........ I.6:5 | belief in g. must lead to the belief in hell, |
| T-15 ........ I.7:7 | g. until it becomes all-encompassing, |
| T-15 ........ I.8:6 | of g. that nothing but happiness is there. |
| T-15 ...... I.13:7 | give is your instantaneous escape from g.. |
| T-15 ..... III.9:4 | the host of God to g. and weakness with |
| T-15 ...... V.2:2 | is to bring g. into your relationships, and |
| T-15 ...... V.2:4 | then, could g. not enter? For separation is |
| T-15 ...... V.2:5 | For separation is the source of g., and to |
| T-15 ...... V.4:1 | Because of g., all special relationships |
| T-15 ...... V.5:5 | All the g. in it arises from your use of it. |
| T-15 ..... VI.1:1 | expense of another and not to suffer g.. |
| T-15 ..... VI.1:5 | this you cannot have while g. remains. |
| T-15 ..... VI.1:6 | be g. as long as you accept the possibility, |
| T-15 .... VII.2:2 | keep the giver bound to itself through g.. |
| T-15 .... VII.2:7 | who perceives that it attracts through g.. |
| T-15 .... VII.3:1 | of g. must be recognized for what it is. For |
| T-15 .... VII.3:4 | Yet the attraction of g. has value to you |
| T-15 .... VII.4:1 | ego attempts to maintain and increase g., |
| T-15 .... VII.5:1 | this chain that binds the Son of God to g., |
| T-15 .... VII.7:6 | accept the g. and sacrifice himself as well. |
| T-15 .... VII.7:8 | g. that holds all its relationships together. |
| T-15 .... VII.8:8 | guilty and holds him through g. is "good. |
| T-15 .... VII.8:9 | releases him from g. is "bad," because he |
| T-15 .... VII.9:3 | relief from g. by increasing it in the other. |
| T-15 .... VII.9:4 | each believes that this decreases g. in him |
| T-15 .. VII.10:2 | who will learn that love brings no g. at all, |
| T-15 .. VII.10:2 | brings g. cannot be love and *must* be anger |
| T-15 .. VII.10:4 | G. is the only need the ego has, and as |
| T-15 .. VII.10:4 | with it, g. will remain attractive to you. |
| T-15 .. VII.12:2 | your brother in his body, held there by g.. |
| T-15 .. VII.12:3 | safety in g. and danger in communication |
| T-15 .. VII.12:4 | teach that loneliness is solved by g., and |
| T-15 .. VII.13:1 | as surely as damnation lies in g.. It is the |
| T-15 .. VII.14:2 | In the holy instant g. holds no attraction, |
| T-15 .. VII.14:3 | And g., whose only purpose is to disrupt |
| T-15 ... VIII.2:9 | then, in peace from g. to God and them. |
| T-15 ..... IX.6:2 | of g. opposes the attraction of God. His |
| T-15 ..... IX.6:4 | you invest in g. you withdraw from God. |
| T-15 ....... X.1:2 | attraction of g. does stand between them. |
| T-15 ....... X.2:2 | instant no g. is laid upon the Son of God, |
| T-15 ....... X.3:2 | as real, g. will hold no attraction for you. |
| T-15 ..... X.5:11 | G. cannot last when the idea of sacrifice |
| T-15 ....... X.6:1 | give all your g. away whenever you want, |
| T-15 ....... X.6:8 | And that g. is the price of love, which |
| T-15 ..... XI.4:2 | sacrifice brings g. as surely as love brings |
| T-15 ..... XI.4:3 | G. is the condition of sacrifice, as peace is |
| T-15 ..... XI.4:4 | Through g. you exclude your Father and |
| T-16 ..... IV.3:1 | hate by finding a haven in the storm of g.. |
| T-16 ..... IV.3:3 | it emphasizes the g. outside the haven by |
| T-16 ..... IV.4:5 | trying to live with g. rather than die of it. |
| T-16 ..... IV.8:5 | Your relationship with them is without g. |
| T-16 ...... V.1:2 | despair, g. and attack all enter into it, |
| T-16 ...... V.3:1 | appeal to those unwilling to relinquish g.. |
| T-16 ...... V.8:5 | in which the g. is buried deep and rises in |
| T-16 ...... V.9:1 | hell lies only in the terrible attraction of g. |
| T-16 .... V.10:2 | fearful nature, nor of the g. it must entail, |
| T-16 ..... VI.3:2 | in protecting you from the attraction of g. |
| T-16 ..... VI.3:4 | foster g. and therefore must imprison. |
| T-16 ..... VI.8:8 | recognize the g. of self-betrayal for what it |
| T-16 ... VI.10:2 | illusion of the beauty and holiness of g.. |
| T-16 ... VI.10:4 | What g. has wrought is ugly, fearful and |
| T-17 ..... III.9:4 | the real world or the world of g. and fear, |
| T-18 ........ I.6:8 | Invest it not with g., for guilt implies it |
| T-18 ........ I.6:8 | g. implies it was accomplished in reality. |
| T-18 ........ I.7:5 | truth is outside, and error and g. within. |
| T-18 ....... II.4:8 | would do to it. And thus is g. made real. |
| T-18 ....... II.5:6 | for if you did the g. would not be theirs, |
| T-18 ....... II.6:7 | will remain, not as a source of pain and g. |
| T-18 ....... II.7:1 | means for undoing g. in everyone blessed |
| T-18 ..... IV.6:3 | Remember you made g., and that your |
| T-18 ..... IV.6:3 | from g. has been to bring Atonement to it |
| T-18 ....... V.2:3 | your g. before you ask the Holy Spirit's |
| T-18 ..... VI.2:5 | your g. to your body from your mind. Yet |
| T-18 ..... VI.2:8 | hate your mind, for g. has entered into it, |
| T-18 ..... VI.3:4 | Its g., which keeps it separate, is projected |
| T-18 ..... VI.3:7 | increasing the projection of its g. upon it. |
| T-18 ..... VI.4:5 | It can project its g., but it will not lose it |
| T-18 ..... VI.6:1 | to use the body as the scapegoat for g., |
| T-18 ..... VI.6:7 | and the perceived source of your g.. You |
| T-18 ..... VI.7:3 | thing you made to serve your g. stands |
| T-18 ..... VI.7:7 | it unharmed, without your g. upon it. |
| T-18 ... VII.3:5 | the attraction of g. would be experienced |
| T-18 ..... IX.1:1 | darkness to the light, and g. to holiness. |
| T-18 ..... IX.4:2 | that were made to keep the g. in place, so |
| T-18 ..... IX.5:1 | directs as long as you believe that g. is real |
| T-18 ..... IX.5:2 | For the reality of g. is the illusion that |
| T-18 ..... IX.8:1 | So should it be with the dark clouds of g., |
| T-18 ..... IX.9:1 | world, where g. meets with forgiveness. |
| T-18 ..... IX.9:2 | anew, without the shadow of g. upon it. |
| T-18 ..... IX.9:7 | the dark and heavy garments of g. laid by, |
| T-18 ... IX.13:1 | safely brought through the barriers of g., |
| T-19 ...... I.10:5 | in your purpose to be released from g.. |
| T-19 ...... I.11:3 | free of all the g. he laid upon himself. |
| T-19 ....... II.2:3 | that attack is real and g. is justified. It |
| T-19 ....... II.6:3 | clouds of g. seem heavy and impenetrable |
| T-19 ..... III.1:1 | The attraction of g. is found in sin, not |
| T-19 ..... III.1:4 | while the g. remains attractive the mind |
| T-19 ..... III.1:5 | For g. still calls to it, and the mind hears |
| T-19 ..... III.3:5 | stop and let it go, unless the g. remains. |
| T-19 ..... III.7:2 | you will find g. attractive and believe that |
| T19 ... IV.A.5:4 | from the appeal of g. to the appeal of love. |
| T19 ... IV.A.5:6 | G. can raise no real barriers against it. |
| T19 .... IV.A.i.h | The Attraction of G. |
| T19 . IV.A.10:1 | The attraction of g. produces fear of love, |
| T19 . IV.A.10:1 | love, for love would never look on g. at all |
| T19 . IV.A.10:4 | For love contains the end of g., as surely |
| T19 . IV.A.10:6 | Overlooking g. completely, it sees no fear. |
| T19 . IV.A.10:9 | exist. Fear looks on g. with just the same |
| T19 . IV.A.11:2 | of fear are harshly ordered to seek out g., |
| T19 . IV.A.11:6 | The fierce attraction that g. holds for fear |
| T19 . IV.A.12:5 | steal guiltily away in hungry search of g., |
| T19 . IV.A.12:6 | little shred of g. escapes their hungry eyes |
| T19 . IV.A.15:2 | cleansed of all g. and softly brushed with |
| T19IV.A.17:14 | For g. creeps in where happiness has been |
| T19IV.A.17:15 | kind of completion, which goes beyond g. |
| T19 ... IV.B.1:2 | it. Where the attraction of g. holds sway, |
| T19 ... IV.B.1:4 | of g. made manifest in the body, and seen |
| T19 ... IV.B.4:7 | You want salvation, not the pain of g.. |
| T19 ... IV.B.5:7 | The end of g. is in your hands to give. |
| T19 ... IV.B.5:8 | stop now to look for g. in your brother? |
| T19 ... IV.B.6:1 | me be to you the symbol of the end of g., |
| T19 ... IV.B.6:5 | I surmounted g. and overcame the world, |
| T19 ... IV.B.6:6 | me the symbol of g. or of the end of guilt, |
| T19 ... IV.B.6:6 | me the symbol of guilt or of the end of g., |
| T19 ... IV.B.7:6 | world the joyous message of the end of g., |
| T19 ... IV.B.7:8 | Where can g. be, when the belief in sin is |
| T19 . IV.B.10:9 | and g. are both conditions of the mind, to |
| T19 . IV.B.12:6 | The attraction of g. *must* enter with it, and |
| T19 . IV.B.13:2 | fear's orders the body will pursue g., |
| T19 . IV.B.13:2 | serving its master whose attraction to g. |
| T19 . IV.B.15:1 | g. will someone other than yourself suffer |
| T19 . IV.B.16:4 | the attraction of g. is the escape from pain |
| T19 ... IV.C.1:6 | G., too, is feared and fearful. Yet it could |
| T19 ... IV.C.3:1 | From the ego came sin and g. and death, |
| T19 ... IV.C.4:5 | The arrogance of sin, the pride of g., the |
| T19 ... IV.C.4:6 | of g. you laid upon the body would kill it. |
| T19 .. IV.D.6:3 | of sin, the delicate appeal of g., the "holy" |
| T19 IV.D15:10 | and all the g. you think you see in him. |
| T19 IV.D.16:4 | remove all trace of g. from his disturbed |
| T19 IV.D.20:2 | as either the giver of g. or of salvation, so |
| T-20 ..... II.10:3 | the lilies of his innocence untouched by g. |
| T-21 ..... III.1:5 | ease the g. that comes from the accepted |

| | |
|---|---|
| T-22.........I.4:6 | for the attraction of g. is only fear. Here is |
| T-22........II.3:1 | Illusions carry only g. and suffering, |
| T-22........II.5:2 | impossible for you to see no g. in anyone. |
| T-22........II.5:3 | by which escape from g. can be attained, |
| T-22........II.5:6 | if escape from g. was given to the Holy |
| T-23.......in.4:2 | can be no attraction of g. in innocence. |
| T-23.....II.11:6 | in his body, making it the cover for his g., |
| T-23.......III.1:5 | to cover the massive g. and frantic fear of |
| T-23.......III.1:8 | and escapes the g. the thought entails. If |
| T-23.....III.6:12 | Can g. be absent from a battlefield? |
| T-23.......IV.6:3 | There is a stab of pain, a twinge of g., and |
| T-24.......in.2:6 | follow g. and freedom sinlessness. There |
| T-24.......III.1:8 | And thus his secret g. would disappear, |
| T-25........II.2:2 | but fear and g. been your reward. How |
| T-25.......III.1:1 | To the extent to which you value g., to |
| T-25.......III.1:2 | you recognize that g. is meaningless, to |
| T-25.......IV.1:1 | and recognize they are, can feel no g.. For |
| T-25.......IV.3:7 | their dreams of g. and merciless revenge, |
| T-25........V.1:2 | for g. is gone because it has no purpose, |
| T-26.....VII.3:1 | G. asks for punishment, and its request is |
| T-26.....VII.8:6 | and all beliefs that rise from mists of g.. |
| T-26...VII.14:4 | less than full salvation and escape from g. |
| T-26........X.4:2 | alone, and at the cost of someone else's g.. |
| T-26........X.4:3 | by the giving of your g. to someone else? |
| T-26........X.4:7 | Whatever way the game of g. is played, |
| T-27.........I.2:6 | to make yourself a living symbol of his g., |
| T-27.........I.3:6 | And what was martyred to his g. becomes |
| T-27.........I.4:3 | you but represents your brother's g.; the |
| T-27.........I.4:7 | For sickness is the witness to his g., and |
| T-27.......I.4:11 | to the g. in him which you perceived and |
| T-27.........I.6:1 | Attest his innocence and not his g.. Your |
| T-27.........I.6:4 | Its only purpose is to prove g. real. No |
| T-27.........I.6:9 | show how lovely are the witnesses for g.. |
| T-27.........I.8:4 | the sign of g. whose consequences still are |
| T-27.......I.11:1 | sure you knew its purpose was to foster g. |
| T-27........II.1:9 | due. He may be pitied for his g., but not |
| T-27......II.1:10 | add to all the g. that he has really earned. |
| T-27........II.2:3 | the consequences of the g. they overlook. |
| T-27........II.4:4 | unless his sins have no effect to warrant g. |
| T-27........II.6:6 | weak and miserable cry of death and g.. |
| T-27......II.6:11 | g. is but the fabric of a senseless dream. |
| T-27........II.7:2 | from g. upon your brother and yourself. |
| T-27........II.7:7 | nor g. upon his heart made heavy with |
| T-27........II.9:4 | The constant sting of g. he suffers serves |
| T-27......II.10:2 | to One Who knows of fairness, not of g.. |
| T-27.....VII.6:3 | And this is where your g. was first beheld. |
| T-27.....VII.7:4 | to you, your g. was not among them. Nor |
| T-27...VII.14:6 | The dream of g. is fading from your sight, |
| T-27....VIII.7:4 | g. for what you thought is being placed |
| T-27....VIII.8:2 | because you *want* the g. to rest on them. |
| T-27....VIII.8:3 | innocence by pushing g. outside yourself, |
| T-27. VIII.13:2 | When you forgive the world your g., you |
| T-27. VIII.13:3 | it. Its innocence does not demand your g., |
| T-28.........I.2:1 | All the effects of g. are here no more. For |
| T-28.........I.2:2 | more. For g. is over. In its passing went its |
| T-28.........I.4:7 | of time where g. appears to linger still. |
| T-28......II.11:7 | sick; projecting out its g. caused nothing, |
| T-28......II.12:2 | dream of pain and suffering, of sin and g.. |
| T-28.......III.2:3 | other mind cannot project its g. without |
| T-28.......III.6:2 | and the shame of g. He cannot bridge, for |
| T-28.......III.8:5 | The miracle would leave no proof of g. to |
| T-29........II.3:3 | as are hate and fear, attack and g. but one |
| T-29........II.3:7 | more is pain your friend and g. your god, |
| T-29.......IX.2:9 | laid in terror and in g. upon yourself. |
| T-29.......IX.9:2 | that it will save you lie the g. and pain of |
| T-30........V.1:2 | for the escape from g. becomes its aim. |
| T-30........V.2:3 | of pursuing g. as goal is fully recognized. |
| T-30........V.2:4 | g. is understood as the sole cause of pain |
| T-30........V.5:4 | can g. and sin be seen without a purpose, |
| T-30........V.6:1 | to replace the goal of sin and g.. And all |
| T-30.....V.10:3 | *brought you anything except the "gift" of g.* |
| T-30.......VI.3:4 | it must uphold the g. you would "forgive. |
| T-30.......VI.6:6 | and a limited escape from g. for you. |
| T-30.......VI.7:4 | And you could not escape all g., but only |
| T-30.......VI.7:7 | some forms of g. that you cannot forgive. |
| T-30.......VI.9:2 | g. in all its consequences and its forms. |
| T-30.......VI.9:5 | the glad acknowledgment that g. has not |
| T-30....VIII.6:9 | As he is healed are you made free of g., for |
| T-31.........I.9:5 | He created innocent could be a slave to g.. |

| | |
|---|---|
| T-31.........I.9:7 | But in g. he has forgotten what he really is |
| T-31.......III.5:2 | of sacrifice preserved, for here g. rules, |
| T-31.......III.6:6 | want to hold in g. your chosen enemies, |
| T-31......V.13:6 | now you stand accused of g. for what your |
| T-31......V.13:7 | is. And you must share his g., because you |
| T-31......V.17:5 | enter in its sanctuary, clean and free of g.. |
| T-31.......VI.2:7 | from looking at the cost of keeping g., |
| T-31.....VII.2:7 | should be the sign of evil and of g. in him. |
| T-31.....VII.9:1 | of salvation, and the love of g. and death, |
| W-pI.....39.1:1 | If g. is hell, what is its opposite? Like the |
| W-pI.....39.2:1 | If g. is hell, what is its opposite? This is |
| W-pI.....39.2:4 | But do you believe that g. is hell? If you |
| W-pI.....39.4:2 | Your holiness means the end of g., and |
| W-pI....39.10:5 | and adding: *If g. is hell, what is its opposite?* |
| W-pI.....58.4:2 | Since my holiness saves me from all g., |
| W-pI.....62.3:4 | It will take away all fear and g. and pain. |
| W-pI.....68.3:2 | those who hold grievances will suffer g., |
| W-pI.....70.1:3 | So, too, does the source of g.. You see |
| W-pI.....70.1:4 | You see neither g. nor salvation as in your |
| W-pI.....70.1:5 | all g. is solely an invention of your mind, |
| W-pI.....70.1:5 | you also realize that g. and salvation must |
| W-pI.....70.3:1 | clear to you why the recognition that g. is |
| W-pI.....73.3:1 | in which g. is traded back and forth, and |
| W-pI...105.1:5 | are not gifts, but bargains made with g.. |
| W-pI.133.11:2 | If you feel any g. about your choice, you |
| W-pI...134.5:3 | G. cannot be forgiven. If you sin, your |
| W-pI...134.5:4 | If you sin, your g. is everlasting. Those |
| W-pI...134.7:4 | shrieks of sinners mad with g.. It looks on |
| W-pI...134.8:3 | which has been blocked by dreams of g.. |
| W-pI.134.10:1 | and keep your mind as free of g. and pain |
| W-pI.134.10:4 | between the hell of g. and Heaven's gate. |
| W-pI.138.10:3 | a but imagined source of g. and pain? |
| W-pI...140.4:3 | Sickness where g. is absent cannot come, |
| W-pI...140.4:3 | come, for it is but another form of g.. |
| W-pI...140.4:5 | takes away the g. that makes the sickness |
| W-pI...151.4:5 | black with sin, how wretched in your g.. |
| W-pI...151.5:5 | It is within itself it sees the g.. It is its own |
| W-pI...151.8:4 | Whom He has judged can only laugh at g. |
| W-pI.151.16:3 | redeemed, and joyfully released from g.. |
| W-pI.153.13:1 | in a fearful world made mad by sin and g. |
| W-pI.153.13:3 | come, in which we put away the toys of g., |
| W-pI...154.4:2 | g. abolished in the mind that God created |
| W-pI...156.1:2 | It promises there is no cause for g., and |
| W-pI...158.7:3 | fearful thoughts of g. from dreams of sin. |
| W-pI...162.5:4 | and for complete escape from sin and g.? |
| W-pI...192.4:2 | no fierce attraction now and g. is gone. |
| W-pI...193.5:3 | with which temptation ends, and g., |
| W-pI...194.2:1 | sin, and devastation brought about by g.. |
| W-pI...197.2:1 | How easily are God and g. confused by |
| W-pI...197.2:4 | until g. and salvation are not seen as one, |
| W-pII..223.2:3 | *for g. proclaims that we are not Your Son.* |
| W-pII..224.1:1 | great, wholly beneficent and free from g., |
| W-pII..234.1:1 | time when dreams of sin and g. are gone, |
| W-pII..235.2:3 | *I have no g. nor sin in me, for there is none in* |
| W-pII..239.1:3 | He shares His glory any trace of sin and g. |
| W-pII......4.4:3 | has become a body, prey to evil and to g., |
| W-pII..259.1:4 | else but sin could be the source of g., |
| W-pII..289.2:3 | *sin. Here is the end of g.. And here am I made* |
| W-pII......8.4:1 | that the dream of sin and g. is over, and |
| W-pII.....12.3:4 | of fear and punishment, of sin and g., of |
| M-4.......IV.1:5 | It is a verdict of g. upon a brother, and |
| M-4........X.1:5 | of g. upon him would send him to hell, so |
| M-5......II.3:11 | Herein is the release from g. and sickness |
| M-5........II.4:7 | What do g. and sickness, pain, disaster |
| M-14..........1:4 | concealing all sin and ending g. forever. |
| M-14..........1:5 | So ends the world that g. had made, for |
| M-14..........2:4 | where sin was made and g. seemed real. |
| M-17..........5:7 | And herein lies the birthplace of g.. Who |
| M-17..........7:2 | They can but reawaken sleeping g., which |
| M-17..........7:6 | For in that thought has g. already raised |
| M-17........8:10 | not really have the power to give rise to g. |
| M-18..........2:7 | Him. And now is g. forgiven, overlooked |
| M-18..........3:1 | Anger but screeches, "G. is real!" Reality |
| M-29..........3:3 | is to let yourself be absolved of g.. It is the |
| M-29........4:12 | And therefore incapable of arousing g.. |
| C-1.............6:1 | sin and justifying anger, and seeing g., |
| C-4.............2:3 | but lends itself to thoughts of sin and g.. |
| C-4.............2:4 | sin and therefore is forever without g.. |
| C-4.............5:6 | From sin comes g. as surely as forgiveness |

| | |
|---|---|
| C-4.............5:6 | as surely as forgiveness takes all g. away. |
| C-4.............5:7 | once all g. is gone what more remains to |
| C-4.............6:6 | What remedy can g. expect? But seen |
| C-4.............6:7 | mind, g. and forgiveness for an instant lie |
| C-4.............7:7 | appeal of g. and death is there snuffed out |
| C-5...........6:11 | *Forget your dreams of sin and g., and come* |
| P-2........IV.1:6 | except an expression of sorrow and of g.? |
| P-2........IV.3:1 | the decision that g. is real has been made. |
| P-2......IV.10:6 | the belief that g. is real and fully justified. |
| P-2......IV.10:7 | function to teach that g., being unreal, |
| P-2......IV.11:2 | insane burden of g. it carries so wearily, |
| P-2.........V.7:8 | the veil of g. that shrouds the Son of God, |
| P-2........VI.1:3 | The hanging-on to g., its hugging-close |
| P-2.......VII.4:5 | his own failures, and g. became the cover, |
| P-2.......VII.4:6 | G. is inevitable in those who use their |
| P-2.......VII.4:7 | G. is impossible in those through whom |
| P-2.......VII.5:1 | passing of g. is the true aim of therapy |
| P-2.......VII.5:3 | the end of g. who feels responsible for his |
| P-2.......VII.8:3 | can be remembered of the world of g.. |
| S-1...........II.3:4 | for the many sources of g. that inevitably |
| S-1...........II.3:5 | need. Without g. there is no scarcity. The |
| S-1.........III.1:4 | your projections of g. from your brother, |
| S-1.........III.1:5 | before *you* can be saved from g.. For this |
| S-1.........III.2:3 | made out of fear by those who cherish g.. |
| S-1.........III.4:1 | G. must be given up, and not concealed. |
| S-1.........III.4:5 | His real escape from g. can lie only in the |
| S-1.........III.4:5 | in the recognition that the g. has gone. |
| S-1.........III.4:9 | your salvation and your escape from g.. |
| S-1.........III.6:1 | made to set up jailers and to hide from g.. |
| S-2............I.1:6 | G. becomes salvation, and the remedy |
| S-2............I.2:2 | no g. that it can seek and find and "love." |
| S-2............I.7:7 | has not sinned, and g. can be no more. |
| S-2...........II.3:4 | induce a rivalry in sinfulness and g.. It is |
| S-2...........II.5:2 | silent proof of g. and of the ravages of sin. |
| S-2...........II.5:4 | he must accept the g. and heavy-laid |
| S-2...........II.5:6 | who needs salvation from the pain of g.? |
| S-2...........II.5:7 | to keep the witnesses of g. away from love |
| S-2...........II.6:4 | And you will seek to rid yourself of g. in |
| S-2...........II.7:2 | try to reinforce his g. and thus your own? |
| S-2.........III.6:3 | About the end of sin and g. and death. |
| S-3.........IV.5:4 | is blamed for your deception and your g.. |

## guilt's 5

| | |
|---|---|
| T-18......IX.5:1 | The body will remain g. messenger, and |
| T-19......III.2:3 | is but another form of g. protection, for |
| T-23.......in.4:4 | sin, nor for a tiny stirring of g. attraction. |
| T-24.......IV.1:6 | And such is g. attraction. Here is death |
| P-2........IV.2:6 | Illness can be but g. shadow, grotesque |

## guiltily 3

| | |
|---|---|
| T-15.......V.9:7 | love g. from where you thought it was. |
| T-17....III.1:10 | think g. of another and not harm yourself |
| T19. IV.A.12:5 | steal g. away in hungry search of guilt, for |

## guiltless 46

| | |
|---|---|
| T-5.........V.5:1 | The g. mind cannot suffer. Being sane, |
| T-11......VI.7:6 | God does not judge His g. Son. Having |
| T-13..............h | THE G. WORLD |
| T-13.........I.3:1 | be tempted to wonder how you can be g.. |
| T-13.........I.3:2 | Yet consider this: You are not g. in time, |
| T-13.........I.5:1 | see me as you learn the Son of God is g.. |
| T-13.........I.5:6 | For the Son of God is g. now, and the |
| T-13.........I.6:2 | him as g. can you understand his oneness. |
| T-13.........I.8:1 | You are invulnerable because you are g.. |
| T-13.........I.9:4 | His Son, and being g. he is eternal. |
| T-13.......I.11:5 | As He looks upon the g. Son of God, He |
| T-13.......I.11:7 | then, are saved because God's Son is g.. |
| T-13..........II.h | The G. Son of God |
| T-13........II.4:2 | To the ego, *the g. are guilty.* Those who do |
| T-13........II.9:3 | Father, for you will remember His g. Son, |
| T-13........II.9:7 | redeemed son of man is the g. Son of God |
| T-13......V.10:5 | dreams He sees God's g. Son within you, |
| T-13.......VI.8:4 | God's g. Son is only light. There is no |
| T-13.......IX.4:3 | Son of God is g. because you see the past, |
| T-13.......IX.5:3 | The idea that the g. Son of God can attack |
| T-13......X.10:4 | There is no fear in love, for love is g.. You |

T-13..... X.11:7 see himself as g. and in the peace of God.
T-13..... X.11:8 If he is g. and in peace and sees it not, he
T-13..... X.12:6 Son, whom You have created g. forever.
T-14.........I.1:7 for yourself and learning you are g.. How
T-14...... III.1:3 The g. learner learns easily because his
T-14...... III.3:6 *If I am g., I have nothing to fear. I choose to*
T-14...... III.4:6 true. You are guilty or g., bound or free,
T-14...... III.7:3 can be harmed shows him that he is g..
T-14...... IV.2:1 and part of Him, are more than merely g..
T-14...... IV.7:1 Unless you are g. you cannot know God,
T-14...... IV.7:2 Therefore, you *must* be g.. Yet if you do
T-14.... IV.10:1 The g. and the guilty are totally incapable
T-14....... V.2:1 one is always the same; *God's Son is g.*.
T-14....... V.9:3 we know Him, as He knows us g.. I stand
T-14..... V.10:5 guiltlessness to whomever you see as g..
T-14....VIII.1:1 the power He bestowed upon His g. Son.
T-15.......I.10:5 by those who cannot see themselves as g..
T19..IV.C.10:2 What can attack the g.? What fear can
T19. IV.D.18:3 kind. See him as g. as I look on you, and
T-27....... II.4:3 How else could he be g.? And how could
T-31.........I.8:1 is g. is a world in which there is no fear,
W-pI.....98.3:1 The g. have no fear, for they are safe and
M-1 ........... 3:5 central theme is always, "God's Son is g.,
M-10 ......... 2:9 is, and it is only one: "God's Son is g., and
M-27 ......... 7:8 that the Son of God is g. now and forever.

**guiltlessness** 41

T-13............I.h G. and Invulnerability
T-13.........I.5:2 He has always sought his g., and he has
T-13.........I.5:8 his eternal g. is in the Mind of his Father,
T-13.........I.9:1 your g. you learn that the past has never
T-13.........I.9:3 Accepting the g. of the Son of God as
T-13....... II.3:5 Yet let it perceive g. anywhere, and it will
T-13....... II.6:2 confronted with the real g. of God's Son it
T-13....... II.6:2 it gave was that g. is blasphemous to God.
T-13....... II.6:3 and g. must be interpreted as the final
T-13....... II.7:6 that it is only your g. that *can* protect you.
T-13...... IX.6:1 will affirm the truth of g. unto yourself. In
T-13..... X.12:4 For in love of him is your g.. But look
T-14.........III.h The Decision for G.
T-14...... III.2:1 using g. merely to offset the pain of guilt,
T-14...... III.2:2 believe that guilt and g. are both of value,
T-14...... III.2:4 Yet you are whole only in your g., and
T-14...... III.2:4 and only in your g. can you be happy.
T-14...... III.2:6 lose appreciation of the value of your g.,
T-14...... III.3:1 and escape the pain that only g. allays.
T-14...... III.3:8 *my g. by making it manifest and sharing it.*
T-14...... III.4:2 for guilt; the Holy Spirit the choice for g..
T-14...... III.5:1 teaches you that you have chosen g.,
T-14...... III.7:1 lesson is merely this: G. is invulnerability.
T-14.... III.19:5 teach you quietly how to perceive your g.,
T-14...... IV.1:1 you accept a brother's g. you will see the
T-14...... IV.1:3 the symbol of your brother's g. shining
T-14...... IV.1:4 His g. is *your* Atonement. Grant it to him,
T-14 ..... IV.2:2 state of g. is only the condition in which
T-14 ..... IV.7:4 g. is the condition for knowing Him.
T-14 ..... IV.9:2 restoring g. to minds that have denied it,
T-14 ...... V.5:3 The miracle acknowledges the g. that
T-14 ...... V.9:3 g. we know Him, as He knows us guiltless.
T-14 .... V.10:3 the symbol of the release from guilt by g..
T-14 .... V.10:5 Yet you restore g. to whomever you see as
T-14 .... V.10:8 The Holy Spirit sees only g., and in His
T-14 ..... VI.4:2 The light of g. shines guilt away because,
T-14 ..... VI.4:3 Keep not guilt and g. apart, for your belief
T-14 ..... XI.7:8 brings the effects that only g. can bring,
T-14 ..... XI.7:8 thus establishes the fact that g. must be.
T-14 ..... XI.8:1 to remain, establish for yourself your g.?
T-27 .VIII.13:3 your guilt, nor does your g. rest on its sins

**guilty** 83

T-4 ....... IV.5:1 When you feel g., remember that the ego
T-4 ....... IV.5:5 While you feel g. your ego is in command,
T-5 ........ V.3:5 the ego, you must perceive yourself as g..
T-5 ...... VII.5:5 If you allow yourself to feel g., you will
T-5 .... VII.6:10 *I do not feel g., because the Holy Spirit will*
T-6 ........I.15:2 If the Apostles had not felt g., they never
T-10 .... V.12:1 it is blasphemous to perceive them as g..
T-12 .. VII.14:4 long as you feel g. you are listening to the
T-13 ......in.1:1 If you did not feel g. you could not attack,
T-13 ......in.3:5 this, for only the g. could conceive of it.
T-13 ......in.4:3 the eternal fact that God's Son is not g..
T-13 ........I.3:6 God is g. you will walk along this carpet,
T-13 ......I.11:1 you to attack yourself because you are g.,
T-13 .......II.2:5 failing the Son of God by seeing him as g..
T-13 .......II.4:2 To the ego, *the guiltless are g.*. Those who
T-13 .......II.9:2 Your "g. secret" is nothing, and if you will
T-13 ..... IX.1:2 The g. always condemn, and having done
T-13 ..... IX.1:6 who follow them believe that they are g.,
T-13 ..... IX.4:4 saying, "I who was g. choose to remain so.
T-13 ..... IX.5:3 himself and make himself g. is insane. In
T-13 ..... IX.6:1 See no one, then, as g., and you will
T-13 ..... IX.6:6 as g. become the witnesses to guilt in you,
T-13 ..... IX.8:5 g. in the dark in which they shroud them,
T-13 .......X.3:1 him or perceive his own, *you* will feel g..
T-13 .......X.4:1 maintain that you are g. but the source of
T-14 ..... III.1:1 learner cannot feel g. about learning. This
T-14 ..... III.4:6 You are g. or guiltless, bound or free,
T-14 ... III.10:2 believe they are g. will respond to guilt,
T-14 ... III.15:2 you *will* feel g. for this imagined crime,
T-14 ..... IV.3:8 You will feel g. till you learn this. For in
T-14 ..... IV.7:5 as g. is denial of the Father so complete,
T-14 ... IV.10:1 guiltless and the g. are totally incapable of
T-14 .... V.10:4 you perceive as g. you would crucify. Yet
T-14 .... V.10:7 ego's aim. It sees everyone as g., and by its
T-15 ........I.3:7 for you. How can the g. hope for Heaven?
T-15 ...... V.2:6 To be alone *is* to be g.. For to experience
T-15 .... VII.2:5 that it can get and keep *by making* g.. This
T-15 .... VII.6:5 Yet to make g. *is* direct attack, although it
T-15 .... VII.6:6 For the g. expect attack, and having asked
T-15 .... VII.8:8 another g. and holds him through guilt is
T-15 .. VII.10:3 than an attempt to make someone feel g.,
T-15 .. VII.10:6 you will feel g. about communication and
T-16 .......V.1:4 an attack on the self to make the other g..
T-16 .......V.2:1 to make g. is always directed against God.
T-16 .......V.2:2 have you see Him, and Him alone, as g.,
T-16 .......V.3:4 who believe that hate is sin merely feel g.,
T-16 .......V.7:6 And he feels g. for the "sin" of taking, and
T-18 ..... VI.2:6 Yet a body cannot be g., for it can do
T-19 .......II.1:5 And thus the mind is g., and will forever
T-19 .......II.2:4 It assumes the Son of God is g., and has
T-19 .......II.3:3 reality in any way, nor make him really g..
T19 ... IV.B.6:4 I ask for your forgiveness, for if you are g.,
T19 IV.B.14:12 accuse, make g. and condemn himself?
T-21 ..... VI.2:4 looks upon himself as g. and sees a sinless
T-23 .....II.10:2 yourself. Thus do the g. ones protest their
T-25 .......V.2:7 think he must be g. to maintain the wish,
T-26 .......II.5:3 Son of God is g. then is he condemned,
T-26 .......II.5:4 *you* find him g. and would have him die.
T-26 .. VII.12:6 Its failure lies in that you still feel g.,
T-27 ........I.2:2 do you see as proof that he is g. of attack.
T-27 .....II.11:4 different from you in that he is more g.,
T-27 ... VIII.7:4 a g. world that dreams your dreams and
T-27 . VIII.13:6 learn that both of you are innocent or g..
T-30 ..... VI.4:4 who sees himself as g. can avoid the fear
T-30 ... VIII.6:3 made g. and afraid when you are tempted
T-31 ........I.4:6 have taught yourself the Son of God is g.,
T-31 ........I.7:4 that God's Son is g. is the world you see.
T-31 ......I.10:1 the lesson that His Son is g. as God's Love
T-31 ..... III.2:5 for by attack do you assert that you are g.,
T-31 .....V.15:6 see a g. world is but the sign your learning
T-31 .... VII.1:5 In this world's concepts are the g. "bad";
T-31 .... VII.7:5 g. thoughts and concepts born of fear.
W-pI .... 46.6:3 *I cannot be g. because I am a Son of God. I*
W-pI .... 58.1:3 forgiven, I no longer see myself as g.. I can
W-pI .. 152.6:4 of the ephemeral, the sinful and the g.,
W-pI .. 152.9:4 says that we are sinners, g. and afraid,
W-pI .. 163.2:1 god of the g. and the lord of all illusions
W-pI 198.10:4 the trespasses you thought Them g. of,
M-7 ........... 5:6 Perhaps there is a g. embarrassment
M-17 ....... 7:10 An angry father pursues his g. son. Kill or
P-2........ IV.2:1 Once God's Son is seen as g., illness
S-1........ III.3:9 To the g. there seems indeed to be a real
S-2...........I.4:6 for you have called him g. of your sins,

**guise** 1

T-25 ... VIII.7:2 on them in the g. of a deliverer and friend

**guns** 1

T-23 ..... III.6:4 return because the g. are stilled an instant

# H

**habit** 9
T-4........IV.7:1 The **h.** of engaging with God and His
T-14....III.18:1 taught yourself the most unnatural **h.** of
T-19.......III.8:8 Only the **h.** of looking for it still remains.
T-31......III.1:3 It must become a **h.** of response so typical
T-31... VIII.5:1 the happy **h.** of response to all temptation
W-pI.....95.5:3 yet formed the **h.** of using the idea as an
WpIrIII.in11:2 help you form the **h.** of applying what you
W-pI...194.6:2 a **h.** in your problem-solving repertoire, a
M-29..........5:8 it a **h.** to ask for help when and where you

**habits** 2
T-1...........I.5:1 Miracles are **h.**, and should be
T-30.......in.1:8 We seek to make them **h.** now, so you will

**had** 138

**hails** 1
T-18... VIII.3:4 imperceptible ripple **h.** itself as the ocean.

**half** 44
*See also* half-lit
T-21.........I.7:4 the world you learned is **h.** so dear as this.
T-27..... II.12:4 and you allow Him only **h.** your mind.
T-27..... II.12:5 And thus He represents the other **h.**, and
T-27..... II.12:6 divided, with a **h.** in opposition to a half.
T-27..... II.12:6 divided, with a half in opposition to a **h.**.
T-27..... II.13:3 you would correct is only **h.** the error,
T-27..... II.14:4 and thus outside yourself; the other **h.**,
T-27..... II.14:6 To this remaining **h.** the Holy Spirit must
T-27..... II.14:6 **h.** until you recognize it *is* the other half.
T-27..... II.14:6 half until you recognize it *is* the other **h.**.
T-27..... II.16:2 With **h.** a mind this is not understood.
T-27..... II.16:7 he may accept his other **h.** as part of him.
T-27......III.2:3 **h.** is cancelled out by the remaining half.
T-27......III.2:3 half is cancelled out by the remaining **h.**.
T-27......III.2:4 quickly contradicted by the **h.** it cancelled
T-27......III.6:5 it is but **h.** the picture and is incomplete,
T-27......III.6:6 The other **h.** of what it represents remains
T-28..... II.11:5 Yet **h.** the lesson will not teach the whole.
W-pI.....10.5:3 and it should be reduced to **h.** a minute or
W-pI.....20.5:1 today, attempting to do so every **h.** hour.
W-pI.....27.3:2 It should be used at least every **h.** hour,
W-pI...71.10:6 no better way to spend a **h.** minute or less
W-pI.....74.7:5 A minute or two every **h.** an hour, with
WpIrIII.in10:3 hour, and the other one a **h.** an hour later.
WpIrIII.in12:1 one to be applied on each **h.** hour as well.
W-pI...111.3:3 On the **h.** hour: Miracles are seen in light,
W-pI...112.3:3 On the **h.** hour: I am as God created me.
W-pI...113.3:3 On the **h.** hour: Salvation comes from my
W-pI...114.3:3 On the **h.** hour: I will accept my part in
W-pI...115.3:3 On the **h.** hour: My part is essential to
W-pI...116.3:3 On the **h.** hour: I share God's Will for
W-pI...117.3:3 On the **h.** hour: I seek but what belongs to
W-pI...118.3:3 On the **h.** hour: Let me be still and listen
W-pI...119.3:3 On the **h.** hour: To give and to receive are
W-pI...120.3:3 On the **h.** hour: I am as God created me.
W-pI...123.7:3 This holy **h.** an hour given Him will be
W-pI...124.8:3 devote a **h.** an hour to the thought that
W-pI...124.8:6 Abide with Him this **h.** an hour. He will
W-pI...124.9:4 This **h.** an hour will be framed in gold,
W-pI.124.10:1 this holy **h.** an hour will hold out to you,
W-pI.124.10:3 thought to which you gave this **h.** an hour
W-pI.124.11:2 Count this **h.** hour as your gift to God, in
W-pI.153.15:5 we will find that **h.** an hour is too short a
M-13 .........7:2 There are no **h.** sacrifices. You cannot

**half-lit** 1
W-ep .........2:1 it has set, and in the **h.** hours in between.

**halfhearted** 1
W-pI...122.4:2 requests, **h.** willingness to hear, and less

**halfway** 2
W-pI...122.4:2 and less than **h.** diligence and partial trust
P-3......... II.9:5 There is no **h.** point in this. Either they

**hallowed** 4
WpI rV.in10:2 still. **H.** your Name. Your glory undefiled
W-pII..244.2:2 No storms can come into the **h.** haven of
W-pII..254.2:6 And in the stillness, **h.** by His Love, God
C-4.............8:2 **H.** your Name and His, for they are joined

**hallucinates** 1
T-26..... V.11:7 You are like to one who still **h.**, but lacks

**hallucination** 5
T-8...........I.2:2 do so. The ego's voice is an **h.**. You cannot
T-20... VIII.7:3 What if you recognized this world is an **h.**
T-26..... V.12:3 part of the **h.** time and death are real, and
W-pI.....23.3:4 **h.** a more appropriate term for the result?
M-8 ...........5:2 in a larger **h.** as opposed to a smaller one?

**hallucinations** 5
T-8...........I.2:4 you are not asked to dispel your **h.** alone.
T-20... VIII.8:1 **H.** disappear when they are recognized
T-20... VIII.8:6 One thing is sure; **h.** serve a purpose, and
T-20... VIII.9:5 **H.** serve to meet the goal of madness.
T-20. VIII.10:4 your wild **h.** that show you all the fearful

**halo** 2
W-pI...133.8:7 for it needs to keep the **h.** which it uses to
W-pI.133.10:1 though he tries to keep its **h.** clear within

**halves** 2
T-27..... II.12:7 two **h.** appear to represent a split within a
T-27..... II.16:6 the **h.** of you that you perceive as separate

**hamper** 2
W-pI...70.10:1 your own thoughts can **h.** your progress.
M-4 .....I.A.4:2 they increase the helpfulness or **h.** it. He

**hampered** 2
WpI. rIII.in2:2 Learning will not be **h.** when you miss a
WpI. rIII.in3:1 But learning will be **h.** when you skip a

**Hand** 8
*hand*
T-25... VIII.6:4 "fires" of Heaven by God's Own angry **H.**.
T-25. VIII.9:11 same does mercy stand at God's right **H.**,
W-pI...106.3:5 Who holds your happiness within His **H.**,
W-pI. 155.13:4 Forget not He has placed His **H.** in yours,
W-pI...164.9:8 when His **H.** holds out complete salvation
W-pII ....in.8:3 His **H.** has held us up. His Thoughts have
W-pII .324.2:2 stray except an instant from His loving **H.**
S-2........ III.6:8 Prayer is His Own right **H.**, made free to

**hand** 96
*Hand*
T-1..........II.2:4 Miracles, on the other **h.**, induce action.
T-1..........II.4:5 as an elder brother to you on the one **h.**,
T-2...........I.5:3 to distinguish between truth on the one **h.**
T-2...... III.1:11 Spiritual sight, on the other **h.**, cannot see
T-3......... V.7:5 Perception, on the other **h.**, is impossible
T-7...........I.4:1 The ego, on the other **h.**, always demands
T-8......... V.6:8 my **h.** because you want to transcend the
T-12....VIII.8:2 Only take it from the **h.** of Christ and look
T-13...... IV.8:1 The ego, on the other **h.**, regards the
T-17......... V.9:4 And take his **h.**, to walk together along a
T-17..... VII.6:5 As holiness and faith go **h.** in hand, so
T-17..... VII.6:5 As holiness and faith go hand in **h.**, so
T-18.........I.8:3 The Holy Spirit takes you gently by the **h.**,
T-18...... III.4:1 who hold your brother's **h.** also hold mine
T-18...... III.5:5 I hold your **h.** as surely as you agreed to
T-18.... VI.10:1 stretch out your **h.** and reach to Heaven.
T-18.... VI.10:2 **h.** is joined with your brother's have
T-19...... III.3:1 An error, on the other **h.**, is not attractive
T-20.........I.2:6 thorns in one **h.** and lilies in the other,
T-20...... III.9:3 in the dust and found your brother's **h.**,
T-21.........II.8:6 or not. Faith and desire go **h.** in hand, for
T-21.........II.8:6 or not. Faith and desire go hand in **h.**, for
T-21...... III.9:6 The instant for its recognition is at **h.**. Join
T-22...... IV.5:8 Into your **h.**, joined with your brother's, is
T-22...... IV.7:6 But hold out your **h.**, joined with your
T-24.........II.7:6 brother with the key to Heaven in his **h.**,
T-24........ V.3:7 beautiful His **h.** that holds His brother's,
T-24........ V.6:4 you Himself in him whose **h.** you hold,
T-24........ V.7:1 that same **h.** that holds your brother's in
T-24........ V.7:2 own. Christ's **h.** holds all His brothers in
T-24........ V.7:4 reaches through them, holding out His **h.**,
T-24........ V.7:9 The **h.** of Christ is all there is to hold.
T-25..... VI.7:9 it gently, then, from your brother's **h.**,
T-25...... IX.2:4 out his **h.** in willingness they be received.
T-26........ V.2:5 holding your brother's **h.** and keeping
T-26....VIII.7:8 until the time of liberation is at **h.**. Given
T-27.........I.4:6 say, "Behold me, brother, at your **h.** I die.
T-27........I.10:7 be, "Behold me, brother, at your **h.** I live."
T-27..... VII.4:7 is the avenger's knife in his own **h.**, and
T-27..... VII.4:8 And he must see it in another's **h.**, if he
T-28.........I.6:2 It works **h.** in hand with all the other
T-28.........I.6:2 It works hand in **h.** with all the other
T-29........ V.5:7 a brother's **h.** in which completion lies.
T-29........ V.6:2 in minds that can direct the **h.** to bless,
T-29........ V.6:6 brother thinks he holds the **h.** of death.
T-29....VIII.4:5 **h.** could be held up to block God's way?
T-30........ V.3:6 Yet is he glad to wait till every **h.** is joined,
T-30........ V.7:4 their hands it was Christ's **h.** they took,
T-30........ V.7:4 they will look on Him Whose **h.** they hold
T-30........ V.8:1 you have recognized Whose **h.** you hold!
T-30........ V.8:2 Within your **h.** is everything you need to
T-30........ V.8:3 For He Whose **h.** you hold was waiting
T-30..... V.10:7 not perceive Whose loving **h.** you hold.
T-31........II.6:8 Take not his **h.** in anger but in love, for in
T-31..... VII.5:6 Hold out your **h.**, that you may have the
T-31..VIII.11:1 In joyous welcome is my **h.** outstretched
W-in..........5:3 On the other **h.**, one exception held apart
W-pI........1.1:4 *This* **h.** *does not mean anything. This foot*
W-pI........7.4:7 *I see only the past in this* **h.**. *I see only the past*
W-pI.....25.6:6 *for. I do not know what this* **h.** *is for.* Say this

W-pI.....69.6:4 Brush them aside with your **h.**; feel them
W-pI.....70.9:3 think of me holding your **h.** and leading
W-pI.....92.2:3 or that you held the world within your **h.**,
W-pI.....93.1:3 you would rush to death by your own **h.**,
W-pI...125.7:3 His Voice is closer than your **h.**. His Love
W-pI...130.2:5 Love and perception thus go **h.** in hand,
W-pI...130.2:5 Love and perception thus go hand in **h.**,
W-pI.131.13:1 Put out your **h.**, and see how easily the
W-pI...137.8:6 For by its gentle **h.** is weakness overcome,
W-pI...158.4:1 Time is a trick, a sleight of **h.**, a vast
W-pI...161.9:4 Yet you will take his **h.** instead, for you
W-pI...163.2:2 all living things within its withered **h.**; all
W-pI...166.8:1 and perceive His gentle **h.** directing you to
W-pI...166.9:2 Christ's **h.** has touched your shoulder,
W-pI.166.14:5 **h.** becomes the giver of Christ's touch;
W-pI...169.7:2 to abandon all but this is now at **h.**. We
WpI...rV.in9:6 Take your brother's **h.**, for this is not a
W-pI...182.9:3 of Heaven in His **h.** and calls them friend,
W-pI.195.10:2 Gratitude goes **h.** in hand with love, and
W-pI.195.10:2 Gratitude goes hand in **h.** with love, and
W-pI...198.5:1 the answer to your problems in your **h.**? Is
W-pII .....1.4:1 Forgiveness, on the other **h.**, is still, and
W-pII .225.2:4 You have reached your **h.** to me, and I will
W-pII .....5.4:3 of God extends his **h.** to reach his brother,
W-pII .264.1:2 *I hear, and every* **h.** *that reaches for my own.*
W-pII .288.1:4 *is the* **h.** *that leads me on the way to You. His*
W-pII .342.1:4 *The key is in my* **h.**, *and I have reached the*
W-pII .355.1:3 *me, and I need but reach out my* **h.** *to find it.*
M-in ..........1:5 The course, on the other **h.**, emphasizes
M-27 .........2:3 He holds your little life in his **h.** but by a
M-28 .........4:1 the time of everlasting things is now at **h.**.
P-2......... II.9:3 but he cannot hold out his **h.** to receive it.
P-2......... V.5:6 a **h.** to reach His Son and touch his heart.
P-3........ III.8:6 reach you, holding out his **h.** to his Friend
S-1........ III.5:3 Hold out your **h.**. This enemy has come to
S-2......... II.4:2 who seek the role of martyr at another's **h.**

## handicap 1

T-12....... V.6:1 the meaning of love, and that is your **h.**.

## handicapped 1

T-12....... V.5:7 is beyond them, they would not be **h.**.

## handicaps 1

T-12....... V.5:1 You have learning **h.** in a very literal

## handle 4

T-8......VIII.6:8 *Any* way you **h.** error results in nothing.
T-9........ III.5:4 the one way in which you **h.** all errors,
T-12...... III.6:5 always tries to **h.** it by making some sort
W-pI...135.1:2 and then attempts to **h.** them as real. It

## handled 1

T-13....... II.5:4 You have **h.** this wish to kill yourself by

## Hands 13

*hands*

T-3......... II.5:1 his spirit into the **H.** of his Father. By
T-5.....IV.8:13 in Whose Heart and **H.** we have our being
W-pI......194.h I place the future in the **H.** of God.
W-pI...194.4:5 let the future go, and place it in God's **H.**.
W-pI...194.4:6 laid the past and present in His **H.** as well,
W-pI...194.7:1 gives his future to the loving **H.** of God?
W-pI...194.8:1 Place, then, your future in the **H.** of God.
W-pI...194.8:4 the world within the **H.** to which he has
W-pI...194.9:2 For in God's **H.** we rest untroubled, sure
W-pI...214.1:1 (194) I place the future in the **H.** of God.
W-pII .314.2:2 *free. Now do we leave the future in Your* **H.**,
M-29 .......7:11 In confidence I place you in His **H.**, and I
S-1...........I.4:3 see them, and let them go into God's **H.**.

## hands 69

*Hands*

T-5 ..... IV.8:10 peace of God in your heart and in your **h.**,
T-5 ..... IV.8:11 to hold it, and the **h.** are strong to give it.
T-9 ........I.11:7 If you hold your **h.** over your eyes, you
T-11 ...... VI.7:1 the nails from the **h.** of God's Son, and
T-13 .. VII.11:3 And even from the very **h.** that grasped it,
T-14 .......II.7:8 from the **h.** of Christ Who gives it to you,
T-14 ..... XI.4:6 joyously laid down by **h.** open to receive,
T-16 ..... IV.8:1 creations are holding out their **h.** to help
T-17 ..... III.4:2 For time *is* cruel in the ego's **h.**, as it is kind
T-18 ..... IX.6:6 to grasp it and your **h.** hold nothing.
T19....IV.B.5:7 The end of guilt is in your **h.** to give.
T19....IV.C.2:5 of them with the gentle **h.** of forgiveness,
T19..IV.C.10:5 In its tiny **h.** it holds, in perfect safety,
T19. IV.D.12:4 Yet in his **h.** is your salvation. You see his
T19. IV.D.17:2 Into the **h.** that give, the gift is given. Look
T-20 .....II.11:7 And by the **h.** that gave it to him shall you
T-20 ..... IV.7:3 the **h.** of every two who enter here to rest.
T-20 ...... V.8:2 rests in his gentle **h.** in safety and in peace
T-22 ...... V.3:5 God holds your **h.**, and what can separate
T-24 .....II.14:1 whose holy **h.** would offer it to you when
T-24 ..... III.8:6 the print of nails upon his **h.** that he holds
T-24 ... III.8:12 The print of nails is on your **h.** as well.
T-24 ...... V.3:5 He is your eyes, your ears, your **h.**, your
T-24 ...... V.5:1 listen, and no **h.** to hold nor feet to guide.
T-24 ...... V.9:4 within your grasp because your **h.** are His.
T-24 .... VII.9:4 you still can feel it with your **h.** and hear it
T-24 .... VII.9:7 which you look on it, the **h.** that feel it,
T-25 ... VIII.8:7 love stands feebly by with helpless **h.**,
T-26 .. VII.17:6 And in your **h.** does all salvation lie, to be
T-27 ........I.5:1 Now in the **h.** made gentle by His touch,
T-27 .....II.6:10 He thinks your blood is on his **h.**, and so
T-27 .......II.7:7 your brother with no blood upon his **h.**,
T-28 .......II.7:7 his own attack, but sees it at another's **h.**.
T-28 ..... III.6:3 be gone and clutch them not with eager **h.**
T-29 ...... V.5:4 in which your **h.** are joined in innocence.
T-29 ...... V.5:5 are not **h.** that grasp in dreams of pain.
T-29 ...... V.6:4 would you attack him with the **h.** of hate?
T-29 ...... V.6:5 Who would lay bloody **h.** on Heaven itself
T-29 ...... VI.5:1 and tie your **h.** and kill your body only if
T-30 ...... V.7:4 their **h.** it was Christ's hand they took,
T-30 .... V.11:1 forever lies in those whose **h.** are joined.
W-pI.....65.3:3 have closed upon yourself, in your own **h.**.
W-pI.....97.5:1 five minutes of each hour from your **h.**,
W-pI.110.10:4 our **h.** and hearts and minds to God today
W-pI...122.9:2 aware we hold the key within our **h.**,
W-pI...130.8:3 **h.** of all the petty treasures of this world.
W-pI.133.13:1 is reached with empty **h.** and open minds,
W-pI.140.12:1 With nothing in our **h.** to which we cling,
W-pI.153.11:6 As they take it from your **h.**, so will you
W-pI.154.11:3 He needs our **h.** to hold His messages, and
W-pI.154.14:4 spring to our sight and leap into our **h.**,
W-pI...161.9:5 you will not perceive that in his **h.** is your
W-pI.161.11:3 See his face, his **h.** and feet, his clothing.
W-pI.161.11:5 whose sacred **h.** can take away the nails
WpI...rV.in9:3 feet, my **h.** through which I save the world
W-pI...189.7:5 and come with wholly empty **h.** unto your
W-pI.189.10:6 *Our* **h.** *are open to receive Your gifts. We*
W-pII .238.1:3 *yet You placed Your Son's salvation in my* **h.**
W-pII .....9.3:2 all minds are given to the **h.** of Christ, to
W-pII .....9.5:2 It needs your eyes and ears and **h.** and feet
W-pII .306.2:2 *with empty* **h.** *and open hearts and minds,*
W-pII ....353.h My eyes, my tongue, my **h.**, my feet today
W-ep .........4:1 And now I place you in His **h.**, to be His
M-1 ...........4:9 For time is in their **h.**. Such was their
M-4 ....... V.1:3 The open **h.** of gentleness are always filled
M-5 ..... III.2:8 It is not their **h.** that heal. It is not their
P-3...........I.3:9 The joining is in the **h.** of the Holy Spirit.
S-2........ III.6:6 Name, and places his forgiveness in His **h.**
S-3...........I.2:4 goes irrevocably past their grasping **h.**,

## hang 1

T-20 .......II.1:1 all the trinkets made to **h.** upon the body,

## hanger 1

W-pI.....29.5:3 *God is in this coat* **h.**. *God is in this magazine*

## hanging

*See* hanging-on

## hanging-on 1

P-2........ VI.1:3 The **h.** to guilt, its hugging-close and

## hangs 3

T19 .. IV.D.2:1 to be surmounted **h.** like a heavy veil
T-22 ..... IV.3:1 that **h.** between you and the face of Christ
T-25 .......II.5:1 **h.** an empty frame upon a wall and stands

## happen 53

T-4 .........II.3:3 only recognize it to see that it does **h.**. If
T-9 ..... IV.11:1 The impossible can **h.** only in fantasy.
T-9 .........V.6:1 What, then, should **h.**? When God said,
T-10 ......in.2:3 Nothing beyond Him can **h.**, because
T-10 ........I.2:4 to **h.** in the dream did not happen at all.
T-10 ........I.2:4 to happen in the dream did not **h.** at all.
T-10 ..... IV.5:2 what He did not intend does not **h.**. Your
T-13 ... III.11:6 not. God did not allow this to **h.**. Yet you
T-13 ... III.11:7 happen. Yet you demanded that it **h.**, and
T-14 ... III.11:1 It will never **h.** that you must make
T-14 ... III.15:4 What cannot **h.** can have no effects to fear
T-16 .....V.12:8 merely could not let this **h.**. You cannot
T-17 ..... VI.3:1 the outset, the situation just seems to **h.**,
T-17 ..... VI.3:4 past, but you have no idea what should **h.**
T-17 ..... VI.4:1 what you want to **h.** is simply that you
T-17 ..... VI.4:1 the situation as a means to *make* it **h.**. You
T-18 .... VII.2:3 to let this **h.** for more than an instant, yet
T-21 .......II.2:5 *everything that seems to* **h.** *to me I ask for,*
T-21 .......II.6:4 it is possible that things could **h.** to the
T-21 .......II.7:4 which seems to tell you what must **h.**, you
T-21 .......II.7:8 interference with what will **h.** of itself;
T-22 ..... IV.3:6 veil. Think what will **h.** after. The Love of
T-22 .......V.5:6 then, must **h.** when they come together?
T-22 .......V.6:7 If you forgive your brother, this *must* **h.**.
T-26 ... VIII.5:2 as yet, and what will **h.** has as yet no cause
T-29 ..... IX.6:7 heal. And bad things seem to **h.**, and he is
T-30 ........I.1:8 in which this very day can **h.** just like that.
T-30 ........I.3:6 There are rules by which this will not **h.**.
T-30 ........I.4:1 have, the things you want to **h.** to you,
T-30 ......I.16:3 agreement that permits all things to **h.**.
T-31 .....II.10:1 be asking for, will be enough to let this **h.**.
T-31 .......V.9:5 And does he know exactly what would **h.**?
T-31 .....V.11:2 And what would **h.** to the world you see,
W-pI .... 12.3:2 whatever descriptive terms **h.** to occur to
W-pI .... 14.5:1 anything you are afraid might **h.** to you,
W-pI .... 24.5:3 *I would like_to* **h.**, *and_to happen,* and so
W-pI .... 24.5:3 *I would like_to happen, and_to* **h.**, and so
W-pI .... 26.7:4 specifically, saying: *I am afraid_will* **h.**.
W-pI .... 28.8:1 of the subject your eyes **h.** to light on, and
W-pI .... 38.3:4 in any form that you **h.** to think of, in
W-pI .. 101.5:2 believe must come from sin will never **h.**,
W-pI .. 131.6:5 the Will of God be in the past, or yet to **h.**
W-pI 135.16:3 directs its choice of what will **h.**. And it
W-pI .. 151.9:6 that seems to **h.** to you in this world. His
W-pI .. 167.9:3 what seems to **h.** never has occurred, the
W-pII . 253.1:4 does not occur is what I do not want to **h.**.
M-4 .... VIII.1:6 as well as him to whom it seemed to **h.**.
M-13 ....... 7:12 A split that cannot **h.**. Yet a split in which
M-13 ....... 7:14 situation the impossible can seem to **h.**. It
M-13 ....... 7:15 It seems to **h.** at the "sacrifice" of truth.
M-22 ......... 5:3 In allowing this to **h.**, he has identified
M-26 ......... 3:6 be it. If it does not **h.**, so be it as well. All
C-in ........... 4:3 occur?", "To what did the impossible **h.**?"

## happened 30

T-3 ...... VII.5:7 seen since then, but nothing has really **h.**.
T-6 .......II.11:2 because what never **h.** cannot be difficult.
T-9 .........V.5:4 Nothing real has **h.** to the unhealed healer
T-10 ........I.3:1 to reconcile what **h.** in conflicting dreams
T-11 ..... III.3:2 what He wills has **h.**, for it was always
T-11 .......V.2:6 and what leads to nothing has not **h.**. If
T-12 ..... III.7:6 Yet consider what has **h.**, for thoughts do
T-12 .......V.2:3 be demonstrating that nothing really **h.**.

T-15.........I.1:5 When this has **h.**, you will no longer need
T-15.......II.5:1 The holy instant has not yet **h.** to you.
T-17......VI.3:1 and makes no sense until it has already **h.**
T-18......IV.8:4 is not only possible, but has already **h.**.
T-18......IV.8:6 It never **h.** in reality. Only in your mind,
T-22.....VI.11:4 And that is why it has not **h.**, nor could be
T-28.......II.4:1 Nothing at all has **h.** but that you have
T-29... VIII.6:3 the world where the impossible has **h.**.
T-29......IX.1:3 What **h.** to the holy Son of God that this
T-30.........I.5:3 Be certain this has **h.** if you feel yourself
W-pI.....99.2:1 both are equal now, for both have **h.**. The
W-pI...137.4:3 sickness would impose has never really **h.**
W-pI...153.8:3 of a senseless dream **h.** to cross our minds
W-pI...182.4:2 hold a picture of a past that never **h.**. Yet
W-pI.193.12:4 everything that **h.** in its course go with it.
W-pII..234.1:4 Nothing has ever **h.** to disturb the peace
M-2............2:7 In time this **h.** very long ago. In reality it
M-2............2:8 very long ago. In reality it never **h.** at all.
M-2............3:2 **h.** long ago seems to be happening now.
M-2............3:5 has already **h.** at any time you choose,
C-1.............6:2 overlooks, or forgives, what never **h.**.
P-3.........II.3:4 Yet something **h.** to him, however slight it

## happening 9

T-9........IV.8:1 no idea what is **h.**, how appropriately can
T-10.......in.1:3 as long as you believe that anything **h.** to
T-24.......V.2:2 believes that what he made is **h.** to him.
T-25. VIII.12:3 of all that is really **h.** within yourself. The
W-pI...135.2:1 you must protect yourself from what is **h.**
W-pI...136.4:3 intent; a **h.** beyond your state of mind, an
W-pI.151.11:2 every **h.** that seems to touch on you in any
M-2............3:2 happened long ago seems to be **h.** now.
M-3............2:2 two students "**h.**" to walk home together.

## happenings 9

T-21.......II.3:2 impossible that **h.** that come to him were
T-31......VI.2:2 things, and **h.** that make no sense at all.
W-pI.135.15:1 occupied in setting up control of future **h.**
W-pI.151.10:3 are beloved of God, for He will judge all **h.**
W-pI...158.7:5 every circumstance, all **h.** and all events,
W-pI...184.1:6 name; all **h.** in terms of place and time; all
W-pI.193.12:2 it application to the **h.** the hour brought,
WpI rVI.in.2:2 to all the seeming **h.** throughout the day.
W-pII..335.1:4 much I seem to be impelled by outside **h.**.

## happens 25

T-3.........V.5:5 always **h.** when method and content are
T-3.........V.8:1 What **h.** to perceptions if there are no
T-9.........V.5:2 really explained what **h.** in psychotherapy
T-10.......in.2:6 mind establishes everything that **h.** to you
T-14.......IV.2:7 to the condition in which it **h.** of itself.
T-14. VIII.4:10 in the oneness out of which creation **h.**.
T-15.......II.1:9 so far beyond time that all of it **h.** at once.
T-15......VI.6:1 nothing **h.** that has not always been. Only
T-18.....VI.11:7 What really **h.** is that you have given up
T-18.....VI.13:6 much of what **h.** in the holy instant; the
T-18.....VII.2:3 instant that the miracle of Atonement **h.**.
T-21.....VII.9:2 It is irrelevant to how it **h.**, but not to why
T-22.........I.3:4 Think, then, what **h.**. Denying what you
T-23.........I.7:8 of two illusions is a state where nothing **h.**
T-23.......I.11:2 And think what **h.** when the house of God
T-29.........I.9:1 all that **h.** when the gap is gone is peace
T-29.......II.2:3 is not a separate thing that **h.** suddenly,
T-30.....VII.1:7 and all that **h.** now means something else.
W-pI.....25.6:2 rest on whatever **h.** to catch your eye,
W-pI...124.9:1 not be less if you believe that nothing **h.**.
W-pI.135.18:1 if you but knew that everything that **h.**, all
W-pI...136.7:2 not a thing that **h.** to you, quite unsought,
W-pII..253.1:3 What **h.** is what I desire. What does not
M-4.... VIII.1:5 for everything that **h.** now or in the future
M-26..........3:5 If it **h.**, so be it. If it does not happen, so

## happier 1

T-3........VI.4:3 in what seem to be your **h.** dreams

## happiest 2

W-pI.....44.8:2 Salvation is your **h.** accomplishment. It is
W-pI.....49.3:3 We will approach this **h.** and holiest of

## happily 19

T-11. VIII.13:3 afraid, and laughs **h.** at his own fear.
T-14.......II.1:1 His mission can be **h.** accomplished. You
T-20.........I.1:2 but **h.** in the celebration of his release. For
T-20.... VIII.2:2 not **h.** exchange your doubts for certainty
T-20. VIII.10:5 gentle sights and sounds are looked on **h.**,
T-20. VIII.11:1 life-giving water running **h.** beside them
T-21.......III.2:5 it will follow, grimly or **h.**, but always
T-21......IV.8:9 Follow it **h.**, and question not what must
T-21......VI.9:3 Reason speaks **h.** indeed of this. This
T-22.......III.9:7 that both may **h.** be healed as one.
T-23.......in.3:4 from sin and fear and **h.** returned to love.
T-27.......V.7:7 And **h.** your brother will perceive the
W-pI.....96.4:3 and it is fulfilling **h.** its function here. Yet
W-pI.151.17:2 with us and **h.** accepts our holy thoughts,
W-pII..232.1:5 *of Your care, and* **h.** *aware I am Your Son.*
W-pII..272.2:2 as hell, and love will **h.** replace all fear.
W-pII..314.1:4 and all the needed means are **h.** provided.
W-pII..328.2:4 *And* **h.** *I share that Will which You, my*
M-10.........6:3 down **h.** the instant he recognizes its cost.

## happiness 204

T-6.........II.5:6 way in which you can find **h.** in the world.
T-9.........I.11:4 God could not will that **h.** depended on
T-9.........I.11:9 and the laws of **h.** were created for you,
T-9.......VII.1:8 God wills you perfect **h.** now. Is it
T-11.....V.12:3 believes that to accomplish its goal is **h.**.
T-11.....V.12:4 and **h.** cannot be found apart from Your
T-11.....V.12:5 difficult to maintain that fear is **h.**.
T-13.......II.7:1 stated that its goal for you is **h.** and peace.
T-14.......II.1:3 contrast, for you believe that misery *is* **h.**.
T-14.......III.3:3 to it, you are deciding against your **h.**,
T-14.......III.5:3 attesting to your **h.** that comes from
T-14.......V.5:4 for hope of **h.** and release from suffering
T-14......XI.4:5 Learn of His **h.**, which is yours. But to
T-15.........I.8:6 free of guilt that nothing but **h.** is there.
T-15.........I.9:4 of time as a teaching aid to **h.** and peace.
T-16.......II.8:8 will give you everything that makes for **h.**.
T-17.......II.1:5 part of the **h.** this sight will bring you. For
T-17......IV.1:6 For nothing God created is apart from **h.**,
T-17......IV.1:6 but would extend **h.** as its Creator did.
T-18.......I.12:6 Is it here that you would look for **h.**? Or
T-18.......V.5:5 who believe that love is fear, not **h.**. Let
T-18.......V.7:1 he can pay his debt by bringing **h.** to both
T-18.... VIII.7:7 all its **h.** and deep content to every part.
T-19......IV.1:6 and your brother with glowing **h.** and the
T19IV.A.17:12 and to limit the **h.** that you would have
T19IV.A.17:14 guilt creeps in where **h.** has been removed
T19....IV.B.7:7 Think of your **h.** as everyone offers you
T19....IV.B.9:9 invest your hope of peace and **h.** in what
T19..IV.B.13:7 it teaches that the body's pleasure is **h.**.
T-20.......III.8:6 for all the **h.** that he held out to you? Did
T-21.........I.3:3 you **h.** you want to learn and not forget. It
T-21.........II.2:1 only thing that you need do for vision, **h.**,
T-21...VII.12:5 No one decides against his **h.**, but he may
T-21...VII.12:6 it. And if he sees his **h.** as ever changing,
T-21...VII.13:1 Elusive **h.**, or happiness in changing form
T-21...VII.13:1 **h.** in changing form that shifts with time
T-21...VII.13:2 H. must be constant, because it is
T-21... VIII.1:6 Surely he thought he wanted **h.**. Yet he
T-21... VIII.2:3 The constancy of **h.** has no exceptions; no
T-21... VIII.2:5 **h.** looks on everything and sees it is the
T-21... VIII.3:1 that you cannot ask for **h.** inconstantly.
T-21... VIII.3:2 you desire you receive, and **h.** is constant,
T-21... VIII.4:1 who complete God's Will and are His **h.**,
T-21... VIII.5:2 to see, the **h.** that could be always yours.
T-22.......II.3:5 seeming **h.** that does not last is really fear.
T-23......IV.8:6 know it is impossible their **h.** could ever
T-24.....VI.10:5 of Him to save from pain and give you **h.**.
T-25......II.9:10 will to make their Father's **h.** complete,
T-25......III.6:7 he can, with equal ease and far more **h.**,
T-26.........I.5:4 tiny crumb of **h.** that you allot yourself.
T-26.... VIII.9:1 Be not content with future **h.**. It has no
T-26..VIII.9:10 yours. Should not His **h.** be yours as well?
T-27......VI.8:1 the world awaits your healing and your **h.**
T-27......VII.8:5 as thoughtless of his peace and **h.** as is the
T-28......III.7:1 silver miracles and golden dreams of **h.** as
T-28....IV.10:3 he has received the simple **h.** of health?
T-28......VII.7:1 upon your brother's health, upon his **h.**,
T-29........II.5:4 and joy, and all the **h.** His Presence brings
T-29......III.1:5 On saving you depends his **h.**. For who is
T-29......IV.6:3 that you imagine would bring **h.** to you.
T-29......VI.6:2 fear, how filled with blessing and with **h.**!
T-29......VII.1:5 and find the **h.** His answer brings. Seek
T-29...VII.1:10 you glad that you are told where **h.** abides
T-29......VII.2:1 that will bring **h.** and peace to him. If
T-29...VII.10:7 your hope. For hope of **h.** is *not* despair.
T-30.......I.10:2 you will believe your **h.** depends on being
T-30.......I.15:2 counsel you have sought perceives your **h.**
T-30.......I.17:1 needs but two who would have **h.** this day
T-30......III.1:5 that there are forms that will bring **h.**,
T-30.......V.2:7 a place where hope of **h.** can be fulfilled.
T-30.......V.3:5 hope of **h.** in him so sure and constant he
T-30.......V.9:7 **h.** have you sought here that did not
T-30.....V.9:10 right, and what you pay for is not **h.**. Be
T-31.........I.7:6 Nor is there hope of **h.** in it. There is no
T-31......III.1:4 for it is here delay of **h.** is shortened by a
T-31......IV.4:8 point will learning lead to heights of **h.**, in
T-31......IV.7:1 Think not that **h.** is ever found by
W-pI.....28.5:2 and of infinite value, full of **h.** and hope.
W-pI.....62.4:3 space and time, to share this **h.** with you.
W-pI.....62.5:4 and the **h.** and release it will bring you.
W-pI.....63.1:3 you have that would bring you greater **h.**?
W-pI.....64.4:2 means by which **h.** becomes inevitable.
W-pI.....64.5:4 Each one will lead to **h.** or unhappiness.
W-pI........66.h My **h.** and my function are one.
W-pI.....66.1:1 fulfilling your function and achieving **h.**.
W-pI.....66.2:2 with the Holy Spirit about what your **h.** is
W-pI.....66.2:6 function is. He knows that it is your **h.**.
W-pI.....66.3:3 become hopelessly involved in defining **h.**
W-pI.....66.4:1 the function God gave you and your **h.**,
W-pI.....66.4:2 God gives you only **h.**. Therefore, the
W-pI.....66.4:3 the function He gave you must be **h.**, even
W-pI.....66.5:2 *God gives me only* **h.** *He has given my*
W-pI.....66.5:4 *Therefore my function must be* **h.** Try to see
W-pI.....66.6:1 first premise is that God gives you only **h.**
W-pI.....66.6:3 cannot give evil, and what is not **h.** is evil.
W-pI.....66.6:5 Unless God gives you only **h.**, He must be
W-pI.....66.9:7 **h.** from anything the ego ever proposed.
W-pI...66.11:2 *My* **h.** *and function are one, because God*
W-pI.....69.9:1 of today's idea to you and your **h.**, remind
W-pI.....73.6:5 Suffering is not **h.**, and it is happiness you
W-pI.....73.6:5 not happiness, and it is **h.** you really want
W-pI.....83.3:1 (66) My **h.** and my function are one. All
W-pI.....83.3:4 Fulfilling my function is my **h.** because
W-pI.....83.3:5 what makes me happy, if I would find **h.**.
W-pI.....83.4:2 *cannot separate my* **h.** *from my function.*
W-pI.....83.4:3 *oneness of my* **h.** *and my function remains*
W-pI.....83.4:4 *the illusion of* **h.** *apart from my function.*
W-pI.....92.5:3 only will for **h.** and peace for everyone. It
W-pI...95.14:2 little part in bringing **h.** to all the world.
W-pI.....96.4:5 no peace, and **h.** is alien to its thoughts.
W-pI.....98.5:1 to accept the **h.** that God has given you?
W-pI.....98.9:3 He will open up the way to **h.**, and peace
W-pI...100.2:1 God's Will for you is perfect **h.**. Why
W-pI...100.2:4 is as essential to His plan as to your **h.**.
W-pI...100.4:4 proof that God wills perfect **h.** for all who
W-pI...100.5:4 world how great the **h.** He wills for you.
W-pI...100.6:5 You bring His **h.** to all you look upon; His
W-pI...100.7:1 by feeling **h.** arise in us according to our
W-pI......101.h God's Will for me is perfect **h.**.
W-pI...101.1:1 we will continue with the theme of **h.**.
W-pI...101.2:3 If sin is real, then **h.** must be illusion, for
W-pI...101.6:1 you is perfect **h.** because there is no sin,
W-pI...101.6:6 *God's Will for me is perfect* **h.** *There is no*
W-pI...101.7:6 *God's Will for me is perfect* **h.** *This is the*
W-pI......102.h I share God's Will for **h.** for me.
W-pI...102.3:1 reach the **h.** God's Will has placed in you.
W-pI...102.4:2 *I share God's Will for* **h.** *for me, and I accept*
W-pI...102.5:1 happy, for your only function here is **h.**.
W-pI...102.5:3 now accepted **h.** as your one function.
W-pI......103.h God, being Love, is also **h.**.

W-pI...103.1:1 **H.** is an attribute of love. It cannot be
W-pI...103.1:7 strange belief would limit **h.** by redefining
W-pI...103.2:4 *God, being Love, is also* **h.**. *To fear Him is to*
W-pI...103.2:7 fear. It also emphasizes **h.** belongs to you,
W-pI...103.3:2 all the **h.** it brings as truth replaces fear,
W-pI...103.3:5 *being Love, is also* **h.**. *And it is happiness I*
W-pI...103.3:6 *And it is* **h.** *I seek today. I cannot fail, because*
W-pI...106.3:5 Him Who holds your **h.** within His Hand,
W-pI...109.1:3 We ask for safety and for **h.**, although we
W-pI...109.2:2 and the safety and the **h.** you seek. "I rest
W-pI...116.1:1 (101) God's Will for me is perfect **h.**.
W-pI...116.1:2 *God's Will is perfect* **h.** *for me. And I can*
W-pI...116.2:1 (102) I share God's Will for **h.** for me. *I*
W-pI...116.3:2 God's Will for me is perfect **h.**. On the
W-pI...116.3:4 half hour: I share God's Will for **h.** for me.
W-pI...117.1:1 (103) God, being Love, is also **h.**. *Let me*
W-pI...117.1:2 *Let me remember love is* **h.**, *and nothing else*
W-pI...117.3:2 God, being Love, is also **h.**. On the half
W-pI...118.1:2 *substitutes that I have made for* **h.** *and peace*
W-pI......121.h Forgiveness is the key to **h.**.
W-pI...121.8:2 you can learn today to take the key to **h.**,
W-pI.121.13:4 in bringing **h.** to every unforgiving mind,
W-pI.121.13:6 *Forgiveness is the key to* **h.**. *I will awaken*
W-pI...122.1:4 Do you want **h.**, a quiet mind, a certainty
W-pI...122.2:4 it offers you another day of **h.** and peace.
W-pI.122.11:1 into **h.** as you begin these practice periods
W-pI...124.3:2 smiles on us and offers us the **h.** we gave.
W-pI...133.2:2 the world, you ask for sorrow, not for **h.**.
W-pI.135.20:2 for your **h.** according to the ancient plan,
W-pI.135.26:2 For you can not conceive of all the **h.** that
W-pI.136.12:4 it. Truth merely wants to give you **h.**, for
W-pI...139.9:4 is more than just our **h.** alone we came to
WpI. rIV.in9:2 no more than this to give us **h.** and rest,
WpI. rIV.in9:3 a special time of blessing and of **h.** for us;
W-pI...141.1:1 (121) Forgiveness is the key to **h.**.
W-pI.151.14:1 wholeness and the **h.** God wills His Son,
W-pI...153.8:3 We would not let our **h.** slip by because a
W-pI.153.10:4 be surer that his **h.** is fully guaranteed?
W-pI.153.12:3 instructs in **h.** because there is no loser.
W-pI...155.7:3 of death, and set them on the way to **h.**.
W-pI...159.6:1 the things that can contribute to your **h.**.
W-pI...162.2:1 by which the Son became his Father's **h.**,
W-pI...165.1:2 and death obscure the perfect **h.** and the
W-pI...165.2:6 way, lighting your mind with **h.** and love.
W-pI...166.1:4 back that can contribute to your **h.**. And
W-pI.166.13:5 Teach them by showing them the **h.** that
W-pI.166.15:4 Be witness in your **h.** to how transformed
W-pI...185.8:4 believe will comfort you, and bring you **h.**
W-pI...191.5:4 out the way to **h.** that changed his whole
W-pI...193.1:2 in that He wills the **h.** His Son inherited of
W-pI...195.2:2 replaced with laughter and with **h.**. Nor
W-pI...199.8:6 extends His Love and **h.** each time you say
W-pI...200.2:1 all hope of finding **h.** where there is none;
W-pI...200.3:1 Yet you can ask as easily for love, for **h.**,
W-pI...200.4:2 not found your **h.** in foreign places and in
W-pII .235.1:2 in mind my Father's Will for me is only **h.**
W-pII .235.1:2 to find that only **h.** has come to me. And I
W-pII .245.1:5 *loss, or think they are bereft of hope and* **h.**.
W-pII .....5.3:2 dreams it sometimes seems to picture **h.**,
W-pII .272.1:4 *Can illusions bring me* **h.**? *What but Your*
W-pII .281.1:3 *Your Thoughts can only bring me* **h.**. *If ever I*
W-pII .287.1:2 What could be a substitute for **h.**? What
W-pII ....290.h My present **h.** is all I see.
W-pII .290.1:1 what is not there, my present **h.** is all I see
W-pII .290.1:6 This the day I seek my present **h.**, and
W-pII .290.2:4 *me. And I am sure that I will see my* **h.** *today.*
W-pII .307.1:4 *Your Will alone can bring me* **h.**, *and only*
W-pII ...10.3:2 suffering, return to peace, security and **h.**,
W-pII .337.1:2 And only **h.** can be my state, for only
W-pII .337.1:2 can be my state, for only **h.** is given me.
W-pII .339.1:3 No one would avoid his **h.**. But he can
M-20 .........4:5 faintly now what **h.** was yours without it,
C-5.............3:1 Son of God, His one creation and His **h.**,
P-2.......VII.2:8 Healing is here, and **h.** and peace. These

## happy 150

*See also* Appendix C

T-5.........in.1:1 To heal is to make **h.**. I have told you to
T-5 ........in.2:1 To be wholehearted you must be **h.**. If
T-7 ....... XI.2:6 Son of God is **h.** only when he knows he is
T-7 ....... XI.3:6 only environment in which you can be **h.**.
T-8 ..........I.4:1 simply because it has not made you **h.**.
T-9 ........I.11:3 the impossible in order to be **h.** is totally
T-9 ......VII.5:1 see yourself as unloving you will not be **h.**
T-11 ......I.10:1 be **h.** unless you do what you will truly,
T-13 ....VII.9:2 of nightmares for the **h.** dreams of love.
T-14 ......... II.h The H. Learner
T-14 .......II.1:1 The Holy Spirit needs a **h.** learner, in
T-14 .......II.1:2 that you are miserable and not **h.**. The
T-14 .......II.1:4 that unless you learn it you will not be **h.**.
T-14 .......II.4:5 They will be **h.** learners of the lesson this
T-14 .......II.5:3 Learn to be a **h.** learner. You will never
T-14 .......II.6:1 If you would be a **h.** learner, you must
T-14 .......II.7:1 The **h.** learner meets the conditions of
T-14 ..... III.1:1 The **h.** learner cannot feel guilty about
T-14 ..... III.2:3 not see yourself as whole and therefore **h.**.
T-14 ..... III.2:4 only in your guiltlessness can you be **h.**.
T-14 ..... III.3:3 happiness, and will not learn how to be **h.**
T-14 ..... III.4:6 or guiltless, bound or free, unhappy or **h.**.
T-14 ..... III.5:9 the **h.** purchase of a treasure to hold dear.
T-14 ..... III.6:6 is the **h.** lesson the Holy Spirit teaches,
T-14 ..... III.8:7 place of all the **h.** teaching the Holy Spirit
T-14 ... III.18:3 and learn of all the **h.** communication
T-14 ...... V.2:8 teach you nothing except how to be **h.**.
T-14 ...... V.3:7 The **h.** learners of the Atonement become
T-16 .......II.8:8 For love asks only that you be **h.**, and will
T-17 ..... IV.1:1 His relationship with you to make you **h.**,
T-17 ..... IV.1:3 relationships became forever "to make **h.**.
T-17 ..... IV.2:2 Yet it *is* possible to make **h.**. I have said
T-17 ..... IV.2:5 have given them is clearly not to make **h.**.
T-17 ...... V.1:7 holy relationship a **h.** song of praise to the
T-17 ...... V.4:6 Until this **h.** solution is seen and accepted
T-18 .......II.6:3 dreams of fear are changed to **h.** dreams.
T-18 .......II.7:2 It will be a **h.** dream, and one which you
T-18 .......II.9:4 laid the real world; the world of **h.** dreams
T-18 ......... V.h The H. Dream
T-18 ...... V.1:4 change your dreams of fear to **h.** dreams,
T-18 ...... V.4:1 **H.** dreams come true, not because they
T-18 ...... V.4:1 are dreams, but only because they are **h.**.
T-18 ...... V.5:5 will become the **h.** dream through which
T-18 .... VII.5:7 always comes with just one **h.** realization;
T-18 .VIII.13:7 Blow on it lightly and with **h.** laughter,
T19....IV.A.6:1 is a hush in Heaven, a **h.** expectancy, a
T19..IV.A.14:5 they will return with all the **h.** things they
T19IV.A.17:12 and **h.** with so little is to hurt yourself,
T19. IV.D.16:5 toss it lightly and with **h.** laughter away
T-20 ..... III.5:1 like; how it would look through **h.** eyes?
T-20 ..... III.8:5 How **h.** did it make you? Did you meet
T-20 ..... VI.3:6 the sunlight and **h.** in the body's darkness
T-20 ...VIII.2:6 which its **h.** end is yours is also not of you.
T-20 .VIII.10:4 your nightmares into **h.** dreams; your
T-21 .........I.3:7 You are not a **h.** learner yet because you
T-21 .......II.3:6 Be **h.**, and you gave the power of decision
T-22 ..... IV.4:3 How **h.** you will be to be together, after
T-22 ... VI.14:4 Look not with fear upon this **h.** fact, and
T-23 ......in.4:3 Think what a **h.** world you walk, with
T-23 ......in.6:5 it is to walk, clean and redeemed and **h.**,
T-25 ..... IV.1:2 this is so, seeing their safety in this **h.** fact.
T-26 ..... IV.6:1 back the **h.** opening of Heaven's gate.
T-26 ...... V.2:5 certain purpose and high resolve and **h.**
T-26 .......X.6:2 a trace of all the **h.** sparkle that salvation
T-27 ..... III.7:5 and single thoughts, complete and **h.**,
T-27 .... VII.9:4 of evil or a **h.** wakening and joy of life.
T-27 .. VII.14:8 is peaceful now, for these are **h.** dreams.
T-28 ........I.7:9 they bring will be the **h.** consequences of
T-28 .......II.5:7 **h.** dreams the miracle exchanges for your
T-28 .......II.6:8 of himself as sick or well, depressed or **h.**,
T-29 ........I.8:7 of seeming fear around the **h.** message,
T-29 ..... IV.5:1 **h.** would your dreams become if you were
T-29 ...... V.5:4 and from this quiet come the **h.** dreams in
T-29 ..... VI.6:3 is to dwell a little while in such a **h.** place!
T-29 .... VII.1:9 Do you prefer that you be right or **h.**? Be
T-29 .... VII.6:1 is outside yourself to be complete and **h.**.
T-30 ........I.7:5 the rules that promise you a **h.** day. Yet
T-30 ......I.13:1 clear that it is easier to have a **h.** day if you
T-30 ......I.14:1 We said you can begin a **h.** day with the
T-30 ......I.17:7 the world by your decision for a **h.** day.
T-30 ..... IV.7:2 What could it be except a **h.** dream? It
T-30 ..... IV.8:7 Such is the only rule for **h.** dreams. The
T-30 .....V.10:8 confidence walk with a **h.** heart that beats
T-30 ...VIII.2:5 The **h.** dream about him takes the form of
T-30 ...VIII.5:1 and offer them to you to see in **h.** form,
T-31 .....V.16:4 and **h.** in the confidence that it will go at
T-31 ..... VI.6:8 your trust; a **h.** place to rest in for a while,
T-31 .... VII.5:3 you be willing that this **h.** change occur.
T-31 ...VIII.5:1 the **h.** habit of response to all temptation
W-pI .... 12.5:3 you, it would make you indescribably **h.**.
W-pI .... 17.3:3 that is really true, and therefore really **h.**.
W-pI .... 20.2:4 You want to be **h.**. You want peace. You
W-pI .... 22.2:3 a **h.** discovery to find that you can escape?
W-pI .... 24.1:1 the outcome that would make you **h.**.
W-pI .... 40.1:1 of the **h.** things to which you are entitled,
W-pI .... 40.3:5 *I am* **h.**, *peaceful, loving and contented.*
W-pI .... 59.4:7 Let me welcome vision and the **h.** world it
W-pI .... 62.4:2 day as **h.** for you as God wants you to be.
W-pI .... 62.5:3 *I would fulfill my function that I may be* **h.**.
W-pI .... 62.5:7 *remember this because I want to be* **h.**.
W-pI .... 63.3:1 will be **h.** to remember it very often today.
W-pI .... 64.4:1 function given you by God will you be **h.**.
W-pI .... 64.4:2 function is to be **h.** by using the means by
W-pI .... 64.4:4 really choosing whether or not to be **h.**.
W-pI .... 64.6:4 *Let me forgive and be* **h.**. At least once
W-pI .... 66.9:4 Were you **h.**? Did they bring you peace?
W-pI .... 73.8:1 the exercises for today in **h.** confidence,
W-pI .... 75.2:1 Today we celebrate the **h.** ending to your
W-pI .... 75.3:1 Our exercises for today will be **h.** ones, in
W-pI .... 83.3:5 learn to recognize what makes me **h.**, if I
W-pI .... 86.3:6 accept God's plan for salvation, and be **h.**.
W-pI .... 97.7:1 Begin these **h.** exercises with the words
W-pI .... 98.2:1 How **h.** to be certain! All our doubts we
W-pI .. 98.10:1 let your time be spent in **h.** preparation
W-pI .. 98.10:3 let your mind be readied for the **h.** time to
W-pI .. 98.11:1 ideas, and spend a **h.** time again with Him
W-pI .. 100.2:6 hear God calling to them in your **h.** laugh.
W-pI .. 100.6:3 God asks you to be **h.**, so the world can
W-pI .. 100.6:5 you and sees His message in your **h.** face.
W-pI .. 100.7:3 Then realize your part is to be **h.**. Only
W-pI .. 102.2:6 you free today to join the **h.** Will of God.
W-pI .. 102.5:1 Be **h.**, for your only function here is
W-pI .. 106.4:4 as **h.** and as wonderful as those you ever
W-pI .. 107.7:3 own. Today we practice on the **h.** note of
W-pI .. 122.8:1 upon a **h.** world of safety and of peace.
W-pI 131.15:4 If you forget this **h.** fact, remind yourself
W-pI .. 140.3:1 The **h.** dreams the Holy Spirit brings are
W-pI .. 140.3:3 His **h.** dreams are heralds of the dawn of
W-pI 153.12:1 thought of as a game that **h.** children play
W-pI 153.13:1 made mad by sin and guilt; be **h.** now.
W-pI 153.14:1 to play our final, **h.** game upon this earth.
W-pI .. 157.8:2 One, the Giver of the **h.** dreams of life,
W-pI .. 162.3:2 His dreams are **h.** and his rest secure, his
W-pI .. 167.2:4 all feelings that are not supremely **h.**. It is
W-pI .. 183.3:5 the tears of pain are dried as **h.** laughter
W-pI 200.11:5 **h.** way to leave the world of ambiguity,
W-pII .... in.2:6 and at night, as long as makes us **h.**. We
W-pII .... in.4:3 the invitation that He seeks to make us **h.**
W-pII . 285.1:1 but the **h.** things of God to come to me. I
W-pII ..... 8.2:6 Only **h.** sights and sounds can reach the
W-pII .... 292.h A **h.** outcome to all things is sure.
W-pII . 292.2:1 *guarantee of only* **h.** *outcomes in the end.*
W-pII . 292.2:2 *delay the* **h.** *endings You have promised us*
W-pII . 301.1:4 *through* **h.** *eyes forgiveness has released*
W-pII . 301.2:h God's world is **h.**. Those who look on it
W-pII . 338.1:5 each fear thought for a **h.** thought of love.
M-4 ..... I.A.5:8 he finds a **h.** lightheartedness instead;
C-2 ............ 7:5 **h.** in the certainty of Heaven and the
C-3 ............ 2:1 might be called a kind of **h.** fiction; a way
S-2...........I.4:5 Yet it is the only **h.** dream in all the world;

## harbor 4

T-11 ..... IV.4:5 there is a strong tendency to **h.** it within.
T-15 ..... IV.7:3 you can **h.** thoughts you would not share,
T-29 ........I.1:5 mean His Love could **h.** just a hint of hate,
W-pI 136.19:2 If you let your mind **h.** attack thoughts,

### harboring 1

W-pI.....34.3:2 about which you are **h.** unloving thoughts

### harbors 3

T-18......VI.7:2 holy Son can enter an abode that **h.** hate,
T-29... VIII.8:6 Each worshipper of idols **h.** hope his
W-pI...107.5:1 truth has come it **h.** in its wings the gift of

### hard 46

T-1.......VII.1:1 making it **h.** for them to reach your own
T-2.........II.7:3 **h.** to believe a defense that cannot attack
T-2........VI.9:8 is **h.** to recognize that thought and belief
T-3...........I.4:4 **h.** for many Christians to realize that this
T-4.........II.9:4 **h.** to maintain that the ego existed before
T-4........III.1:1 **h.** to understand what "The Kingdom of
T-4........IV.2:6 This may seem **h.** to do, but it is much
T-7...........I.6:4 **h.** to explain in words because words are
T-7........VI.7:2 only reason you may find this **h.** to accept
T-8..... VIII.4:1 is **h.** to perceive sickness as a false witness
T-11......III.4:1 The way is not **h.**, but it *is* very different.
T-11......III.4:3 That way is **h.** indeed, and very lonely.
T-14......IV.6:3 own volition seems to make deciding **h.**.
T-15......III.3:2 The lesson may seem **h.** at first, but you
T-17..IV.12:10 **h.** to see at all beneath the heavy shadows
T-17....IV.13:1 You who have tried so **h.**, and are still
T-18......IV.7:4 And it is very **h.** for you to realize it is not
T-22...... I.2:12 long and **h.** you tried to understand its
T-22......IV.2:1 few steps along the right way that seem **h.**
T-23......IV.9:8 choice of miracles or murder **h.** to make?
T-24.....VII.8:7 And it is this that makes it **h.** to grasp the
T-25.........I.1:1 is **h.** to do the task that Christ appointed
T-25... VIII.6:1 extremely **h.** for those who still believe sin
T-26......III.7:7 was never true, can it be **h.** to give it up,
T-26....... V.2:6 do. But it is **h.** indeed to wander off, alone
T-26....... V.4:5 that it is **h.** indeed to hold it to your heart,
T-28.........I.4:3 is **h.** for you to realize it is a skill that can
T-29....... V.7:3 hate. Why does it seem so **h.** to share this
T-30.........I.7:5 This can be very **h.** to realize, when once
T-31.........I.1:5 **h.** to learn by anyone who wants it to be
T-31.........I.1:7 **h.** is it to see that what is false can not be
T-31.........I.2:8 to judge it **h.** to learn or too complex to
T-31.........I.5:4 Its lessons are not true; too **h.** to learn,
W-in..........8:1 presents you will find **h.** to believe, and
W-pI.......5.4:1 you may find it **h.** to be indiscriminate,
W-pI.....16.4:3 You will find that it is still **h.** for you not
W-pI.....78.4:5 you see as difficult at times or **h.** to please,
W-pI...163.3:1 quickly lost however **h.** to gain, uncertain
W-pI...184.5:2 It is **h.** to teach the mind a thousand alien
W-pI...187.1:4 seems to make it **h.** to credit is not this.
W-pI...195.1:1 Gratitude is a lesson **h.** to learn for those
M-4......I.A.7:9 heavily reinforced, it would be **h.** indeed!
M-14..........4:7 He does not judge it either as **h.** or easy.
P-3...........I.3:2 This may be **h.** to remember, but God will
S-3......... II.3:4 where it is not **h.** to see the gifts we gave
S-3........IV.6:5 heavy heart made **h.** against the love that

### harder 12

T-1...........I.1:2 One is not "h." or "bigger" than another.
T-3...........I.2:6 the error itself is no **h.** to correct than any
T-4......IV.11:8 Why do you believe it is **h.** for me to
T-8..... VIII.6:9 become the **h.** it may be to recognize their
T-13......III.3:1 not **h.** for you to say "I love" than "I hate"
T-23....... II.3:2 of them are **h.** to overcome than others. If
T-25......IX.3:3 it greater, **h.** to resolve and more unfair. It
T-30......VI.6:4 are **h.** to look past than others are. It
T-30... VIII.3:3 that makes them **h.** to resist than those
W-pI.....65.6:1 thoughts will become **h.** to find. Try,
M-8............5:2 Is it **h.** to dispel the belief of the insane in
P-3......... II.7:3 He has learned that it is no **h.** to wake a

### hardest 6

T-6......V.B.3:9 respects, the first lesson is the **h.** to learn.
T-14....... II.2:2 This is the **h.** lesson you will ever learn,
T-14....... II.5:2 learn that what seemed **h.** was the easiest.
T19... IV.C.6:2 to be the **h.** can be accomplished first?
W-pI.133.11:1 for choice that is the **h.** to believe, because
W-pI...170.9:3 The final one, the **h.** to believe is nothing,

### hardly 47

T-2......VI.9:12 of it, but you are **h.** likely to respect it.
T-2.......VII.1:5 is. I would **h.** help you if I depreciated the
T-3......... II.3:2 is **h.** a miracle-based frame of reference. It
T-3......... V.3:6 but you would **h.** want to do it if you were
T-3........VI.8:5 frightening to them, but **h.** troubles God.
T-4......... II.3:5 though **h.** to something that occurs with
T-4.......VII.6:2 This **h.** means that you should tell Him
T-6......V.C.2:2 He would **h.** be consistent if He allowed
T-7........III.4:4 but seeming and reality are **h.** the same.
T-7....... X.5:14 decision is confusion, this is **h.** surprising.
T-10.......IV.5:7 unworthy of you that you could **h.** want it
T-11..... V.16:8 to its denial, but **h.** to what it has denied.
T-12......IV.4:2 To seek and not to find is **h.** joyous. Is this
T-12....... V.5:6 You would **h.** turn to them to establish
T-12... VIII.5:4 even control yourself should **h.** aspire to
T-14.......XI.4:1 **h.** judge the truth and value of this course
T-16....... II.3:5 attributes could **h.** cause you perplexity.
T-20.... VI.12:4 confusion, but **h.** discouragement. You
T-22....... II.2:3 of misery and seek another is **h.** an escape
T-23....... II.1:2 Chaotic laws are **h.** meaningful, and
T-25....... II.2:3 in this respect is **h.** worth delaying change
T-25...VII.11:7 God or this must be insane, but **h.** both.
T-26....... V.5:2 of the Son of God can **h.** still be there, for
W-pI.....16.2:2 of a whole world can **h.** be called idle.
W-pI.....17.1:6 its highly variable nature, this is **h.** likely.
W-pI.....47.6:1 but it is **h.** a sufficient one in giving you
W-pI.....55.2:2 is **h.** the representation of loving thoughts
W-pI.....70.3:3 the way your mind has worked, but **h.** His
W-pI...126.3:5 holds out a gift to him, but **h.** to yourself.
W-pI...132.4:4 **h.** waiting for your thoughts to give it
W-pI...135.8:2 valueless and **h.** worth the least defense,
W-pI...139.3:1 so vast, its magnitude can **h.** be conceived
W-pI...182.1:6 tiny throb, at other times **h.** remembered,
W-pI...192.4:3 but **h.** changing him who learns at all.
W-pII..263.1:4 *A madman's dream is **h.** fit to be my choice,*
M-7 .........3:10 was a mistake, but **h.** one to stay with.
M-11 .........1:7 what He promises can **h.** be impossible.
M-16 .........9:9 What has no effects can **h.** terrify.
M-17 .........5:5 That this can **h.** be a fact is obvious. Yet
M-17 .........9:6 **H.** so. Remember, then, teacher of God,
M-22 .........5:4 **h.** offer it to his brother in Christ's Name.
M-29 .........5:7 That would **h.** be practical, and it is the
M-29 .........6:4 **H.!** For God has given Him the power to
P-2.........in.1:2 but psychotherapy can **h.** be expected to
P-2......... II.2:3 to reconcile the irreconcilable that it **h.**
P-3...........I.1:8 This could **h.** be true. To demand sacrifice
P-3......... II.7:6 could **h.** be called professional therapists.

### harken 1

T-27...... VI.4:2 Neither does He **h.** to the witnesses by

### harm 30

T-2......... V.1:3 belief that **h.** can be limited to the body.
T-4......... II.5:2 they may well **h.** themselves if you do not.
T-6......... V.3:2 what you must avoid to escape from **h.**,
T-6......... V.3:3 you will escape from **h.** and be safe, and
T-8......... II.2:6 the ego has done more **h.** to your learning
T-9......... II.2:4 healing because he is fearful of bodily **h.**.
T-17.... III.1:10 guiltily of another and not **h.** yourself.
T-19.........I.6:3 This will not **h.** the body, but it *will* keep
T-22......IV.5:2 salvation, which he would protect from **h.**
T-23..... II.17:6 You cannot seek to **h.** him and be saved.
T-24.....VII.4:5 in that choice lie both its health and **h.**.
T-25.......VI.4:1 of what you made, to heal instead of **h.**.
T-26......VI.1:6 in sin, in power of attack, in hurt and **h.**,
W-pI.....68.6:6 that nothing can **h.** you in any way. At the
W-pI...196.1:1 you will not attempt to **h.** yourself, nor
W-pII.....11.3:3 His holy Will, beyond all possibility of **h.**,
W-pII.....337.h My sinlessness protects me from all **h.**.
W-pII..337.1:6 to feel God's Love protecting me from **h.**,
M-4 ......IV.1:1 **H.** is impossible for God's teachers. They
M-4 ......IV.1:2 They can neither **h.** nor be harmed. Harm
M-4 ...... IV.1:3 **H.** is the outcome of judgment. It is the
M-4 .... IV.1:11 that **h.** can actually achieve nothing. No
M-4 ...... IV.2:3 easy. To those who would do **h.**, it is
M-4 ...... IV.2:4 To those to whom **h.** has no meaning, it is
M-4 ...... IV.2:7 come from **h.** in place of the unfailing, all-
M-4 ..... V.1:10 making sure no **h.** can come to them.
M-29 .........6:9 father does not let his child **h.** himself, or
M-29 .........7:9 your sense of frailty and your fear of **h.**,
P-2......... V.2:2 What they believe will help can only **h.**;
P-2......... V.2:2 what they believe will **h.** alone can help.

### harmed 3

T-6...........I.9:3 I had not **h.** anyone and had healed many
T-14...... III.7:3 can be **h.** shows him that he is guiltless.
M-4 ...... IV.1:2 They can neither harm nor be **h.**. Harm is

### harmful 9

T-7......... V.3:6 involves the belief that healing is **h.**. This
T-8.......VII.3:1 you use the body for attack, it is **h.** to you.
T-8.......VII.4:3 or ugly, peaceful or savage, helpful or **h.**,
T-9..........II.1:2 with specific things that might be **h.**, but
T-23.......in.3:3 Nothing they see is **h.**, for their awareness
T-23.......in.3:4 seemed **h.** now stands shining in their
T-24...... IV.3:6 must it be that **h.** purpose hurts the mind
T-25...... IV.2:3 is **h.** or beneficent apart from what you
W-pI.......4.5:1 thought that you recognize as **h.**. This

### harmfulness 3

T-9........ IV.3:5 All their **h.** lies in the ego's judgment. All
T-23.......in.3:3 releases everything from the illusion of **h.**.
M-4 ...... IV.1:8 that **h.** completely obliterates his function

### harmless 6

T-4..........II.5:5 the effort to become both **h.** and helpful,
T-4.......VII.8:2 is impossible without being wholly **h.**,
T-6........ III.3:1 own mind perceives itself as totally **h.**,
T-8........ IX.2:2 not. The reality of everything is totally **h.**,
T-21...... III.1:6 to make it useful to Him and **h.** to you.
T-31...... VI.6:2 Then the world is **h.** in your sight. Do you

### harmlessness 4

T-3...........I.7:2 epitomizes **h.** and sheds only blessing. It
T-8........ IX.2:2 total **h.** is the condition of its reality. It is
T-10.. III.10:11 to fear love because of its perfect **h.**, and
W-pI... 190.5:7 As you perceive the **h.** in them, they will

### harmonics 1

S-1 ...........I.3:3 Along with it come the overtones, the **h.**,

### harmony 6

T-7......... V.6:6 Healing always produces **h.**, because it
T-11..... V.13:6 for if separation is salvation, **h.** is threat.
T-20....... V.6:6 with means and end in perfect **h.** already.
W-pI...95.13:1 are one Self, in perfect **h.** with all there is,
S-1 .........in.1:3 Son. Endless the **h.**, and endless, too, the
S-3........ IV.8:3 your song is part of the eternal **h.** of love.

### harsh 6

T-6...... IV.12:6 A **h.** and strident form of communication
T-13...... IX.2:2 obeying the ego's **h.** commandments you
T-13...... XI.1:1 and **h.** intrusion of guilt on peace. Yet no
W-pI... 170.6:3 **H.** punishment is meted out relentlessly
W-pI... 182.6:3 and **h.** and rasping noises of the world.
S-3........ IV.7:5 Underneath the sounds of **h.** and bitter

### harshly 2

T19. IV.A.11:2 messengers of fear are **h.** ordered to seek
T-31....... V.4:1 world deals **h.** with defenseless innocence

**has** 2453

**haste** 3

W-pI.....11.2:4 to yourself, being sure to do so without **h.**
W-pI.193.11:2 arise in **h.** and go unto our Father's house.
S-2........III.3:2 in **h.** to go at last unto your Father's house

**hasten** 7

W-pI...169.4:3 Word of God to **h.** the experience of truth
W-pI...169.7:1 This is beyond experience we try to **h.**.
W-pI...169.7:3 We do not **h.** it, in that what you will offer
WpI...rV.in1:6 But now we **h.** on, for we approach a
WpI rVI.in.5:3 deny its hold and **h.** to assure your mind
WpI rVI.in.6:1 are tempted, **h.** to proclaim your freedom
W-pII ....226.h My home awaits me. I will **h.** there.

**hastening** 1

T-28.......I.11:4 miracle delay in **h.** to all unquiet minds,

**hastily** 1

M-29 .........7:3 But do not read this **h.** or wrongly. If His

**hate** 139

*See also* self-hate; Appendix C

T-10...... III.1:4 a sure sign that you **h.** what you *think* you
T-11......IV.1:6 it. Yet if you **h.** part of your Self all your
T-13......III.3:1 harder for you to say "I love" than "I **h.**"?
T-16......IV.1:1 to look upon the special **h.** relationship,
T-16......IV.1:3 is undertaken solely to offset the **h.**, but
T-16......IV.1:5 this. You cannot limit **h.**. The special love
T-16......IV.1:8 is the attempt to balance **h.** with love that
T-16......IV.2:1 The symbols of **h.** against the symbols of
T-16......IV.3:1 **h.** by finding a haven in the storm of guilt
T-16......IV.4:3 is possible, there was not love but **h.**. For
T-16......IV.4:4 For **h.** *is* an illusion, and what can change
T-16......IV.5:2 love. Only **h.** is at all concerned with the
T-16......IV.5:3 of love can triumph over the illusion of **h.**,
T-16....IV.10:3 Every fantasy, be it of love or **h.**, deprives
T-16....IV.11:3 calls, but **h.** would have you stay. Hear
T-16....IV.11:4 stay. Hear not the call of **h.**, and see no
T-16....IV.11:6 See in the call of **h.**, and in every fantasy
T-16....... V.3:4 it bizarre to love and **h.** together, and
T-16....... V.3:4 believe that **h.** is sin merely feel guilty, but
T-16.....VII.3:4 out its **h.** are fantasies of your destruction
T-17....... V.1:7 hymn of **h.** in praise of its maker, so is the
T-18......VI.2:7 think you **h.** your body deceive yourself.
T-18......VI.2:8 You **h.** your mind, for guilt has entered
T-18......VI.6:5 worthy of the **h.** that you invest in it. How
T-18......VI.6:7 You have identified with this thing you **h.**
T-18......VI.7:2 Son can enter an abode that harbors **h.**,
T-18......VI.7:6 You **h.** this prison you have made, and
T-18......VI.8:2 place you set aside to house your **h.** is not
T-18......IX.1:9 guarded by attack and reinforced by **h.**.
T19..IV.B.15:3 all your messages of **h.** and free yourself.
T19.IV.D.12:5 which you **h.** because you share it. And all
T-20....... II.1:3 made to make seem lovely what you **h.**.
T-21.........I.4:8 **h.** the world they learned through pain.
T-21......III.1:3 you have a limited relationship, you **h.**.
T-21......III.7:2 limit to the body you **h.** because you fear.
T-21......III.9:4 you will **h.** Him because you are afraid.
T-21....III.10:7 a means for limitation, and thus for **h.**.
T-21.....VII.2:7 with him, they know not whom they **h.**.
T-21.....VII.3:2 not their "enemy," except they **h.** him. In
T-21...VII.3:12 And love is turned to **h.** as easily. This is
T-21.....VII.5:1 Yet **h.** must have a target. There can be
T-22.........I.1:2 God would heal and **h.** the one He loves,
T-22......VI.3:5 from **h.** to gratitude before forgiving eyes.
T-22......VI.3:7 to **h.** what serves whom you would heal.
T-23....... II.6:6 Son's belief in what he is, and **h.** him for it
T-24.........I.3:4 who could **h.** someone whose Self is his,
T-24.........I.6:1 possible for you to **h.** your brother if you
T-24.........I.8:4 stab of **h.** or wish to separate arises here.
T-24....... II.9:3 and bound in **h.** to kill each other and
T-24......III.7:5 They **h.** the call that would awaken them,
T-24 ..... IV.1:4 it offers is but deception, but its **h.** is real.
T-24 ....VII.4:6 a frame of loveliness around your **h.**, and
T-24 ..VII.10:5 it. You brand it sinful and you **h.** its acts,
T-25 ..... III.8:1 the world of violence and **h.** that seems to
T-25 ...... V.3:3 And **h.** because there is no sin in him for
T-25 ..... VI.6:8 His special **h.** became his special love.
T-25 ...VIII.3:7 without insanity where love means **h.**,
T-25 ..... IX.7:8 and peace be scattered by the winds of **h.**.
T-26 ...... V.8:4 was feared and made a symbol of your **h.**?
T-26 ... V.14:5 world in which perception of your **h.** has
T-26 ..VII.14:9 and made Them both his enemies in **h.**.
T-26 ..VII.17:3 and **h.** is answered in the name of love. To
T-26 ..... IX.2:3 would you trade Them for an ancient **h.**?
T-26 ..... IX.3:5 **h.** had scorched and rendered desolate.
T-26 ..... IX.3:6 What **h.** has wrought have They undone.
T-26 ..... IX.3:8 The shadow of an ancient **h.** has gone,
T-27 .....III.14:4 This is your brother, focus of your **h.**,
T-27 ..... III.3:2 nothing to attack or to deny; to love or **h.**,
T-27 ..... IV.4:2 question asked in **h.** cannot be answered,
T-27 ..VII.12:4 fear, the time of terror and of ancient **h.**,
T-28 .........I.5:6 if it seems to serve to cherish ancient **h.**,
T-28 .........I.7:3 When ancient memories of **h.** appear,
T-28 .......II.8:6 **h.** it for the vengeance it would offer them
T-28 .....III.10:5 can accept the role of maker of their **h.**,
T-28 ...... V.2:1 is the sharing of the evil dreams of **h.** and
T-28 ...... V.3:7 your brother, as a part of what you **h.**.
T-28 ..... VI.2:8 It perceives no gap, because it does not **h.**.
T-28 ..... VI.2:9 It can be used for **h.**, but it cannot be
T-28 ..... VI.3:1 thing you **h.** and fear and loathe and want
T-28 ..... VI.3:3 And then you **h.** it, not for what it is, but
T-28 ..... VI.3:4 it hears, and **h.** its frailty and littleness.
T-28 ..... VI.4:2 You **h.** it, yet you think it is your self, and
T-29 .........I.1:5 His Love could harbor just a hint of **h.**,
T-29 .........I.2:2 fear, since fear and **h.** can never be apart.
T-29 .........I.2:5 He fears to love and loves to **h.**, and so he
T-29 .........I.2:5 so he thinks that love is fearful; **h.** is love.
T-29 .........I.7:3 For **h.** to be maintained, love must be
T-29 .......II.3:3 and sin are one illusion, as are **h.** and fear.
T-29 .......II.9:5 it be. And you will **h.** it for its littleness,
T-29 .....II.10:2 you love, or look upon it as a thing you **h.**.
T-29 ...... V.6:4 you attack him with the hands of **h.**? Who
T-29 ...... V.7:1 he is your savior, not your enemy in **h.**. A
T-29 ...... V.7:2 of dreaming evil separate dreams of **h.**.
T-29 ...... V.7:4 the dream its function, it was made for **h.**,
T-29 ...VIII.6:6 as his Father, come to **h.** a little while; to
T-30 .......II.3:1 the one you chose to **h.** instead of love.
T-30 .......II.3:3 your will to **h.** and be a prisoner to fear, a
T-30 ...... V.9:1 An ancient **h.** is passing from the world.
T-31 ......I.10:2 For **h.** must father fear, and look upon its
T-31 ......I.10:4 Who calls to you beyond each form of **h.**;
T-31 .......II.4:3 You **h.** the one you gave the leader's role
T-31 .......II.4:3 **h.** as well his not assuming it at times you
T-31 .......II.5:8 life, for **h.** or for forgiveness and for help,
T-31 ..... III.1:5 You never **h.** your brother for his sins, but
T-31 ..... III.2:3 them everywhere except you **h.** yourself?
T-31 ..... III.5:1 prisoner to the snarling dogs of **h.** and
T-31 ..VII.12:6 Yet it can look with love or look with **h.**,
W-pI..... 22.2:4 that you **h.** and would attack and kill. All
W-pI..... 23.4:5 them, even though they were made of **h.**.
W-pI..... 68.2:4 become fearful to him in his dream of **h.**.
W-pI..... 72.7:2 see. Some **h.** the body, and try to hurt and
W-pI..... 78.1:2 of **h.** before the miracle it would conceal.
W-pI..... 78.2:3 We will not wait before the shield of **h.**,
W-pI..... 78.4:5 Someone, perhaps, you fear and even **h.**;
W-pI..... 92.7:2 miracles are here, but only **h.**. It separates
W-pI..... 93.5:8 eternal sinlessness to sin, and love to **h.**.
W-pI... 109.4:2 the world is torn by winds of **h.** your rest
W-pI... 127.2:3 he can love at times, and **h.** at other times
W-pI. 127.11:2 was made in **h.** to be love's enemy. Now
W-pI... 129.2:3 you, quick to avenge and pitiless with **h.**.
W-pI... 129.3:1 **h.** cannot exist and vengeance has no
W-pI... 130.2:1 Yet who can really **h.** and love at once?
W-pI. 138.11:4 made enormous, vengeful, pitiless with **h.**
W-pI. 151.11:3 And you will see the love beyond the **h.**,
W-pI... 161.7:1 **H.** is specific. There must be a thing to be
W-pI... 169.2:1 within a world of seeming **h.** and fear. By
W-pI... 169.2:2 By grace alone the **h.** and fear are gone,
W-pI. 185.14:1 brotherhood that **h.** has sought to sever,
W-pI... 191.1:4 lacking all reason, blind, insane with **h.**?
W-pII ..... 4.3:4 overcome by death, love slain by **h.**, and
M-7 ........... 2:5 is not love but fear, and therefore **h.**. His
M-7 ........... 2:6 offering **h.** to one to whom he offered love
M-7 ........... 4:7 And **h.** must be the opposite of love,
M-19 ......... 4:9 not see you **h.** and fear your Self as enemy
C-2 ............ 8:1 This was the ego–all the cruel **h.**, the
S-1........ IV.1:6 are their arsenals; their fortresses in **h.**.
S-2...........I.3:8 remember Him and **h.** what He created?
S-2...........I.3:9 will **h.** his Father if you hate the Son He
S-2...........I.3:9 hate his Father if you **h.** the Son He loves.

**hated** 11

T-18 .... VII.4:8 to make holy what is **h.** and despised. Nor
T-18 ... VIII.4:2 and **h.** by a tiny segment of themselves.
T-20 .......II.1:4 this **h.** thing to draw your brother to you,
T-24 ..... IV.1:3 **h.** and worthy only of destruction.
T-24 .......V.4:6 first, nor **h.** him before it hated you. The
T-24 .......V.4:6 first, nor hated him before it **h.** you. The
T-27 .....II.14:3 be returned to its accuser, who had **h.** it,
T-28 .......II.8:4 And as he **h.** his Creator, so the figures in
T-28 .......II.8:4 so the figures in the dream have **h.** him.
T-28 .....II.10:3 and **h.** enemies perceived as friends with
T-31 .......V.6:8 still your brother for the **h.** thing you are.

**hateful** 8

T-10 ..... III.1:6 What you think you are can be very **h.**,
T-16 .......V.9:3 as an act of love, would make love **h.**. The
T-27 ..... III.1:9 such as "weakened power" or "**h.** love"?
T-27 ..... III.2:1 your brother is a symbol for a "**h.** love," a
T-27 .VIII.10:6 them be as **h.** and as vicious as they may,
T-28 ..... VI.2:9 for hate, but it cannot be **h.** made thereby
S-2...........I.2:4 plague; a **h.** thing of danger and of death.
S-2...........I.9:4 cleansed from evil usages and **h.** goals.

**hates** 11

T-4 .........V.4:4 Yet the ego **h.** the body, because it cannot
T-8 ....... IX.6:6 The ego wants only what it **h.**. To the ego
T-15 .... VII.7:2 something to the other, and **h.** him for it.
T-23 ..... III.5:6 with an enemy but **h.** him still, for what
T-25 .......V.6:4 through your attack believe He **h.** you,
T-27 .....III.14:3 it, and **h.** it still as symbol of his fear. This
T-29 .........I.2:3 No one who **h.** but is afraid of love, and
T-31 ... VIII.9:2 hell, the secret sins and hidden **h.** be gone
W-pI .... 92.7:1 It fears and it attacks and **h.** itself, and
W-pI .. 161.6:5 for attack, for no one thinks he **h.** a mind.
S-2...........I.2:5 and this it sees in all it looks upon and **h.**.

**hath** 3

T-11 ......in.4:7 to your true Father, Who **h.** need of you,
T-22 ......in.1:2 Rejoice whom God **h.** joined have come
P-3........ III.5:1 well been said that to him who **h.** shall be

**hating** 4

T-16 .....V.10:8 **h.** it you have made it little and unworthy,
T-18 ..... III.3:5 You go toward love still **h.** it, and terribly
T-20 ..... VI.3:6 **h.** the sunlight and happy in the body's
W-pI .... 96.1:1 two; as both good and evil, loving and **h.**,

**hatred** 53

T-4 ....... III.4:4 because of your **h.** for the self you made.
T-8 ...... VII.4:9 lead you to **h.** and attack and loss of peace
T-12 .......II.3:3 health is to recognize in **h.** the call for love
T-12 .......II.5:4 of **h.** will not leave you without help, and
T-12 .......II.6:5 Do not let your **h.** stand in the way of love
T-12 ... III.7:10 you must realize that your **h.** is in your
T-12 .. VII.13:5 live, but its **h.** is not satisfied until you die
T-13 ..... III.1:1 upon your **h.** and realize its full extent.
T-13 ..... III.3:2 love with weakness and **h.** with strength,
T-13 ..... III.5:5 But **h.** can, for it enters of its own volition
T-13 .......V.5:3 If you see your own **h.** as your brother,
T-16 ..... IV.3:4 a place of safety from which **h.** is split off
T-16 ..... IV.3:6 **H.** can enter, and indeed is welcome in
T-16 ... IV.4:10 broken, fear rushes in and **h.** triumphs.

T-16......IV.5:4 As long as the illusion of h. lasts, so long
T-16......IV.6:5 can be certain that you perceive h. within,
T-16.......V.4:1 love from God, that the ego's h. triumphs.
T-16.....VII.5:2 h. and the savagery break briefly through,
T-17......III.5:7 relationship where h. is remembered; yet
T-18.......V.2:1 to remove all fear and h. from your mind.
T-18.......V.2:5 to let Him remove all fear and h., and to
T19.IV.A.2:11 little wall of h. would still oppose the Will
T19IV.B.14:11 send messages of h. and attack if he but
T-21......III.7:5 free, removing h. by removing fear, not as
T-21.....VII.3:3 In h. they have come together, but have
T-21.....VII.3:4 had they done so h. would be impossible.
T-23.....II.12:8 in h. for the one to whom the gift belongs.
T-23.....II.14:6 illusions true, attack a kindness, h. love,
T-25.......V.6:1 Against the h. that the Son of God may
T-26......IX.3:1 of h. fades to let the grass grow green
T-26......IX.4:4 What h. claimed is given up to love, and
T-26......IX.6:1 an ancient h. has become a present love.
T-26......IX.6:5 What h. has released to love becomes the
T-28......VI.3:9 thus deserve your h. for the limitations
T-29.........I.6:2 in "love," with intervals of h. in between.
T-29........II.3:6 and loss, and all effects of h. and attack.
T-30.......II.3:2 For thus was h. born into the world, and
T-30.......V.9:2 And with it goes all h. and all fear. Look
T-31.......V.7:5 hot with h. and distortions born of fear.
W-pI........5.1:3 fear, worry, depression, anxiety, anger, h.
W-pI.....68.2:5 Who can dream of h. and not fear God?
W-pI.134.11:1 evil and of h. and attack brought silently
W-pI...161.7:4 When h. rests upon a thing, it calls for
W-pI...189.3:5 who see a world of h. rising from attack,
W-pI...189.4:1 Yet is the world of h. equally unseen and
W-pI...189.5:4 If h. finds a place within your heart, you
W-pI...190.1:7 to God the Father's h. of His Son, the
W-pI...192.1:2 within a world of envy, h. and attack?
W-pI...195.5:2 walk the way of h. and the path of death.
W-pI...195.8:2 h. is forgotten when we lay comparisons
W-pII..246.1:1 the way to God, if I have h. in my heart.
W-pII....12.3:4 of sin and guilt, of h. and attack, when all
S-3........IV.4:6 attained until there is no h. in your heart,

**haunt** 6

T-17.......V.8:3 A sense of aimlessness will come to h. you
T-24......VI.1:1 to h. you in the darkness of the night. He
T-24......VI.9:3 will h. you while your brother lies asleep,
T-25......IV.4:4 Your "evil" thoughts that h. you now will
T-28......IV.4:6 And dreams of fear will h. the little gap,
W-pI.....79.5:5 and rise to h. you from time to time, only

**haunting** 3

T-22.........I.1:6 h. fear of lack of meaning in yourself arise
W-pI...136.8:4 h. thought that you might be something
W-pI...182.1:3 A memory of home keeps h. you, as if

**haunts** 2

T-23......III.6:4 that h. the place of death is not apparent.
W-pI...198.7:1 separate h. where mercy has no meaning,

**have** 3003

**haven** 6

T-16......IV.3:1 hate by finding a h. in the storm of guilt.
T-16......IV.3:3 it emphasizes the guilt outside the h. by
WpI...rI.in.4:5 and seeking a h. of isolation for yourself.
W-pI.137.11:3 a h. where the weary can remain to rest.
W-pII..244.2:2 come into the hallowed h. of our home. In
S-3........IV.2:4 Fear has no h. here, for love has come in

**having** 13
• noun
*verb*

T-4........III.9:7 is why we make no distinction between *h.*
T-4.......VII.5:7 there is no difference between *h.* and *being*
T-5...........I.1:5 knows no difference between *h.* and *being.*
T-6.......V.B.3:4 equality of *h.* and *being* is not yet perceived
T-6.......V.B.3:5 it is, *h.* appears to be the opposite of *giving.*
T-6.......V.B.8:1 since *h.* and *being* are still not equated
T-6.......V.C.5:8 getting you ready for the translation of *h.*
T-6.......V.C.6:1 You learn first that *h.* rests on giving, and
T-7........III.4:7 how *h.* and *being* are ultimately reconciled,
T-9........II.11:7 of h. is the willingness for giving, and only
T-11........II.1:4 unite *h.* and *being* is to unite your will with
T-29.......III.1:8 know he has, for giving is the proof of h..
W-pI...187.1:2 In fact, giving is proof of h.. We have

**having** 87
• verb
*noun*

T-1.........I.48:2 it, h. nothing to do with time at all.
T-1........VI.2:3 because, h. made this fundamental error,
T-2........VI.8:4 loveless, h. chosen without love. This is
T-3......IV.6:10 be remembered, never h. been destroyed.
T-4........VI.4:3 H. done this, it denies all truly natural
T-5...........I.1:8 H. everything, spirit holds everything by
T-5...........I.1:9 of thinking is totally alien to h. things,
T-5........IV.2:8 but h. made them you did not realize how
T-5........IV.7:2 because, h. received the idea of healing,
T-5.........V.8:8 so. H. given up its disordered thought, the
T-6........IV.7:3 H. finally been wholly answered, *it has*
T-6.........V.1:2 wrongly, h. believed what was not true.
T-6......V.A.6:3 H. chosen to go that way, you place
T-6......V.A.6:8 H. taken the first step, however, they will
T-7.....VIII.4:8 Never h. had a consistent model, it never
T-7.....VIII.5:5 But h. accepted the errors as yours, do not
T-8........III.6:7 H. made this choice you will understand
T-8........VI.2:6 His creations, h. created them for eternity
T-9.........V.4:3 H. made it real, he then attempts to dispel
T-10.......V.3:7 h. made him out of your insanity, he is
T-11.........I.4:4 know your creations, h. denied infinity?
T-11.......II.3:7 H. forgotten your will, you do not know
T-11......VI.7:7 H. given Himself to him, how could it be
T-11......VI.8:6 crucify him, you are only h. nightmares.
T-12.........I.1:7 done so, h. made his error real to you. To
T-12.........I.1:8 and h. done this you will overlook truth.
T-12.........I.8:7 then. H. taught you to accept only loving
T-12.......II.1:7 Yet h. obscured it, the light in another
T-12......III.2:1 Suppose a brother insists on h. you do
T-12.....VII.8:3 opposition there, h. sought it there. But
T-13.......in.4:6 for it teaches him that, never h. sinned, he
T-13.....III.10:6 h. attacked his own glorious equality with
T-13.....III.12:5 H. given you creation, He could not take it
T-13.....VI.10:2 h. given light to them they will return it.
T-13.....VI.10:7 for h. received it of you they would keep it
T-13.....VIII.8:1 h. learned to free yourself through Him
T-13......IX.1:2 and h. done so they will still condemn,
T-14.......in.1:7 And h. seen them, we have realized that
T-14......III.2:1 do not look upon it as h. value in itself.
T-14......XI.9:5 to light, h. accepted them instead of you,
T-14.....XI.11:7 h. the holy stamp of immortality upon it.
T-15.....III.10:8 But you will gladly give, h. received. The
T-15.......V.9:2 h. always known you exactly as He knows
T-15.....VII.3:2 it is. For h. been made real to you, it is
T-15.....VII.6:6 and h. asked for it they are attracted to it.
T-15......IX.2:6 no limits, h. been established by God.
T-16.........I.2:4 itself. H. identified with what it thinks it
T19....IV.B.9:4 be rid of, and h. it you cannot limit it. If
T-22......III.5:9 h. been made to guarantee that nothing
T-23.......II.9:7 would keep from you must be worth h.,
T-23......II.22:2 For h. taken one, you will not recognize
T-28........I.14:2 has made is causeless, h. no effects at all.
T-28......II.11:2 it also shows that, h. no effects, it is not
T-28......III.1:5 And h. started, will the way be made
T-30.........I.9:1 (5) H. decided that you do not like the
T-30........I.17:6 and give it to the world by h. it yourself.
T-30....VI.10:3 But what you see as h. power to make an
W-pI........7.3:2 against your lips, h. breakfast and so on?
W-pI.....22.1:2 H. projected his anger onto the world, he
W-pI.....58.1:3 H. forgiven, I no longer see myself as
W-pI.....62.2:3 are, h. denied your Identity by attacking
W-pI.....80.4:3 H. recognized one, you have recognized
W-pI...126.7:1 Not h. given Him the gift He asks of you,
W-pI...157.4:2 And h. joined your will with His this day,
W-pI...165.3:3 And h. found them, would he not make
W-pI...187.1:7 H. had and given, then the world asserts
W-pII.296.1:4 *For h. damned it I would set it free, that I may*
W-pII.312.1:2 H. judged, we therefore see what we
W-pII.335.1:7 h. chosen to behold my brother in its holy
W-pII.343.1:9 *complete, h. the function of completing You*
M-4.....I.A.4:2 h. learned that the changes in his life are
M-4....IX.2:12 And h. found, it rests in quiet certainty on
M-5........II.4:8 H. no purpose, they are gone. And with
M-6...........1:5 H. accepted the Atonement for himself,
M-6...........1:8 H. nothing to live for, he may ask for
M-7...........2:8 H. offered love, only love can be received.
M-8...........4:6 And h. done so, it concludes that the
M-16.........5:5 H. gone through the workbook, you must
M-22.........2:9 And h. done what was required, would
M-22.......6:12 H. been received, it must be accepted. It is
M-28.........1:6 h. no function except communication. It
C-2..........10:4 here, and h. met at last the choice is clear.
C-3............3:3 but h. given the content it is His Will that
P-2........IV.4:3 real in their own minds, and h. done so,
P-2........IV.4:6 Yet h. started, it must finish thus. It is as if
S-1........III.3:9 to be a real advantage in h. enemies, and
S-2..........II.5:4 But h. been made enemy, he must accept

**havoc** 2

T-10........II.6:1 If you realized the complete h. this makes
W-pI...190.8:1 form, and working h. in your holy mind.

**hazard** 1

W-pI...181.4:1 major h. to success has been involvement

**hazardous** 1

T-12.........I.1:6 the motives of others is h. to you. If you

**He** 938
• God
*Christ/Self*
*Holy Spirit*
*he*

T-1........VI.4:3 in His creations *because* H. created them.
T-2...........I.1:1 aspect of God which H. gave to His Son.
T-2.........III.5:7 H. depends on them *because* He created
T-2.........III.5:7 on them *because* H. created them perfect.
T-2.........III.5:8 H. gave them His peace so they could not
T-2.....VII.5:14 world that h. gave his only begotten Son,
T-2.....VII.5:14 "H. gave it *to* His only begotten Son."
T-2.....VIII.4:3 just as God Himself looked upon what H.
T-3...........I.3:3 God. H. did not create it and He does not
T-3...........I.3:3 not create it and H. does not maintain it.
T-3...........I.3:6 H. does not hold your "evil" deeds against
T-3...........I.3:7 likely that H. would hold them against me
T-3...........I.8:2 God, for God is not symbolic; H. is Fact.
T-3..........II.4:1 H. created in the likeness of His Own, to
T-3.........III.6:1 altars, which H. established in His Sons.
T-3.........III.6:2 There H. can communicate His certainty,
T-3.........III.7:8 create as H. created you can create only
T-3......III.7:10 H. created them by knowing them. He
T-3......III.7:11 H. recognizes them perfectly. When they
T-3........VI.8:6 H. is, however, eager to undo it, not to
T-3........VI.8:6 only because H. knows that it makes them
T-3.......VII.3:6 children, and I assure you that H. does,
T-3.......VII.3:6 would H. have put them in a position
T-4...........I.7:9 spirit is never at stake because H. did.
T-4...........I.8:6 beloved Son in whom H. is well pleased.
T-4..........I.9:11 Him any more than H. can avoid you.
T-4..........I.10:5 of deception as is the spirit H. created.
T-4........III.6:4 H. has never failed to answer this request,
T-4........III.6:4 it asks only for what H. has already willed.
T-4........III.8:4 for this together, for once H. has come,
T-4........VI.7:1 my perception H. can bridge the little gap
T-4........VI.7:4 are grateful to God for what H. created.
T-4.......VII.6:2 you should tell Him how wonderful H. is.
T-4.......VII.6:3 H. has no ego with which to accept such
T-4.......VII.6:5 And this H. does know. He knows it in
T-4.......VII.6:6 H. knows it in His Own Being and its

T-4.......VII.6:7 **H.** is lonely when the minds He created
T-4.......VII.6:7 lonely when the minds **H.** created do not
T-4.......VII.7:1 but **H.** cannot share His joy with you until
T-4.......VII.7:3 but **H.** does want it brought to others.
T-4.......VII.8:4 **H.** will return their praise of Him because
T-5..........I.6:2 **H.** also blessed His children with a way of
T-5.........II.5:1 **H.** can share only perfect knowledge.
T-5.........II.5:6 When you chose to leave Him **H.** gave you
T-5........IV.1:6 as you are part of God because **H.** created
T-5........IV.3:8 that are of God and that **H.** keeps for you.
T-5.......VII.1:3 for your safety and joy better than **H.** can?
T-5.......VII.1:4 cares upon Him because **H.** careth for you
T-5.......VII.1:5 You are His care because **H.** loves you. His
T-5.......VII.1:7 of His care for all those **H.** created by it.
T-5.......VII.2:6 to return to God the mind as **H.** created it.
T-5.......VII.2:7 it. **H.** asks you only for what He gave,
T-5.......VII.2:7 it. He asks you only for what **H.** gave,
T-5.......VII.3:3 Him. **H.** wills to keep it in perfect peace,
T-6........I.17:2 **H.** does not need your appreciation, but
T-6........I.18:6 as **H.** thinks if you are to know Him again.
T-6.........II.6:9 that God created is as true as **H.** is. Its
T-6........IV.2:1 God created you **H.** made you part of Him
T-6........IV.6:1 which **H.** created as part of Him. Nothing
T-6........IV.7:6 as God because you are as true as **H.** is,
T-6......IV.11:9 **H.** confronted the self you made with the
T-6......IV.11:9 made with the truth **H.** created for you,
T-6....IV.11:10 where you can find the sanity **H.** gave you.
T-6......IV.12:9 Being questioned, **H.** did not question. He
T-6....IV.12:10 **H.** merely gave the Answer. His Answer is
T-6.........V.1:4 when **H.** knows your mind only as whole?
T-6.........V.1:5 **H.** cannot impart His joy and know that
T-6.........V.1:8 So **H.** thought, "My children sleep and
T-7..........I.1:2 fully with God, as **H.** does with you. This
T-7..........I.1:4 God, since **H.** created you but you did not
T-7..........I.2:1 If you created God and **H.** created you,
T-7..........I.2:6 **H.** created the Sonship and you increase it
T-7..........I.3:7 always been, because **H.** has always been.
T-7..........I.3:9 is yours, because **H.** created you eternal.
T-7..........I.5:2 you can only extend yourself as **H.** did.
T-7..........I.6:1 share the perfect Love **H.** shares with you.
T-7..........I.7:2 **H.** does not teach, because His creations
T-7..........I.7:3 **H.** does nothing last, because He created
T-7..........I.7:3 because **H.** created first and for always. It
T-7..........I.7:5 **H.** is first in the sense that He is the First
T-7..........I.7:5 first in the sense that **H.** is the First in the
T-7..........I.7:6 Itself. **H.** is the Prime Creator, because He
T-7..........I.7:6 **H.** created His co-creators. Because He
T-7..........I.7:7 Because **H.** did, time applies neither to
T-7..........I.7:7 neither to Him nor to what **H.** created.
T-7........III.2:1 because that is where **H.** placed it. It does
T-7.......V.11:5 **H.** will accept it and give it to the Sonship,
T-7......VI.12:5 your Creator and creating as **H.** created.
T-7.......VII.6:1 worthy of honor, and whom **H.** honors.
T-7.......VII.6:2 beloved Sons in whom **H.** is well pleased.
T-7.......VII.6:5 But love everything **H.** created, of which
T-7........IX.1:2 **H.** no more wills you to deprive yourself
T-7........IX.1:2 than **H.** wills to deprive Himself of His.
T-7........IX.2:4 Everything **H.** created is given all His
T-7........IX.6:2 of God to give it to you, **H.** gave it forever.
T-7........IX.6:3 **H.** gave you the means for keeping it. *And*
T-7.........X.2:6 His Will and you share what **H.** knows.
T-7.........X.4:7 **H.** does not wish. Your will is as powerful
T-7........XI.5:6 have acknowledged what **H.** has given you
T-7........XI.7:8 But you must also know all **H.** created, to
T-8.........II.3:4 you, because **H.** shares His Will with you.
T-8.........II.6:4 Him than **H.** could will to be without you.
T-8.........II.6:6 Kingdom, because **H.** created you for this.
T-8.........II.7:7 and are therefore as unlimited as **H.** is.
T-8........III.1:1 and to you because **H.** has so willed it.
T-8........III.7:6 **H.** does not will anyone to suffer for a
T-8........III.7:7 is why **H.** has given you the means for
T-8........III.8:3 to Him because **H.** gives of Himself, and
T-8........III.8:4 of yourself is the function **H.** gave you.
T-8........III.8:7 gift to you, because that is what **H.** is. See
T-8........IV.1:4 Yet **H.** is All in all. His peace is complete,
T-8........IV.7:8 praise of Him and you whom **H.** created.
T-8........IV.7:9 which **H.** will share with all His creations,
T-8........IV.7:9 **H.** gives equally whatever is acceptable to
T-8........IV.8:1 of what they are and what **H.** is. Freedom
T-8........VI.1:4 **H.** will welcome us as I am welcoming you
T-8........VI.2:8 of yourself. **H.** has saved you *for* yourself.
T-8........VI.5:2 You want your creations as **H.** wants His.
T-8......VI.5:13 of God, and what **H.** values is valuable.
T-8........VI.6:3 **H.** would not withhold creation from you
T-8........VI.6:5 and **H.** extends His Fatherhood to you so
T-8........VI.6:5 so that you can extend yourself as **H.** did.
T-8......VI.6:10 from His, and so you must will as **H.** wills.
T-8........VI.8:2 **H.** will not hide it. He has revealed it to
T-8........VI.8:3 **H.** has revealed it to me because I asked it
T-8........VI.8:3 and learned of what **H.** had already given.
T-8........VI.8:6 alone because ***H.*** does not will to be alone.
T-8........VI.8:7 That is why **H.** created His Son, and gave
T-8........VI.8:8 the Sons of God Himself, as holy as **H.** is.
T-8........VI.9:1 knowledge of the value **H.** puts upon you.
T-8......VI.10:2 **H.** has given His Will to His treasure,
T-8.......VII.3:6 God on behalf of the function **H.** gives it.
T-8.......VII.6:3 **H.** of Whom you are has willed your
T-8.......VII.6:4 **H.** has not withdrawn His gifts from you,
T-8........IX.9:7 **H.** cannot lose this, but you *can* not know
T-9.........I.10:8 could **H.** fail to recognize it in His Son?
T-9........VI.3:6 than they but they are not less than **H.** is.
T-9......VI.3:11 cannot, then, be less glorious than **H.** is.
T-9........VI.4:1 than you only because **H.** created you, but
T-9........VI.4:1 but not even this would **H.** keep from you.
T-9........VI.4:2 Therefore you can create as **H.** did, and
T-9.......VII.1:2 **H.** not have given you the means to find it
T-9.......VII.1:3 it? If **H.** wills you to have it, He must have
T-9.......VII.1:3 **H.** must have made it possible and easy to
T-9.......VII.8:7 **H.** will give you all of Himself in exchange
T-9......VIII.8:5 you to behold what **H.** created because it
T-9....VIII.11:9 **H.** would have you replace the ego's belief
T-10.......in.2:5 only creation and **H.** created you eternal?
T-10.......in.3:1 you, for **H.** is not uncertain of Himself.
T-10.......in.3:2 what **H.** knows can be known, because He
T-10.......in.3:2 **H.** does not know it only for Himself. He
T-10.......in.3:3 **H.** created you for Himself, but He gave
T-10.......in.3:3 but **H.** gave you the power to create for
T-10.....in.3:11 or **H.** would be deciding against Himself.
T-10........II.3:7 **H.** will give you everything but for the
T-10........II.5:6 Him. This is not because **H.** is gone, but
T-10.....III.1:10 **H.** will not limit your power to help them,
T-10.....III.1:10 help them, because **H.** has given it to you.
T-10.......III.2:2 where in the Sonship **H.** is accepted. He is
T-10.......III.2:3 **H.** is always accepted for all, and when
T-10.......III.2:5 for healing because **H.** has but one Son.
T-10.....III.11:3 **H.** will be heard when you place no other
T-10.......IV.4:6 protected everything **H.** created by His
T-10.......IV.5:2 what **H.** did not intend does not happen.
T-10.......IV.6:5 **H.** established the universe as what it is.
T-10.......IV.6:8 created you. And **H.** created nothing else.
T-10........V.5:5 any more than **H.** could have created a
T-10........V.6:4 love Him, and that you know **H.** loves you
T-10........V.7:2 **H.** does not retaliate, but He does call to
T-10........V.7:2 retaliate, but **H.** does call to you to return.
T-10........V.7:3 you think **H.** has not answered your call,
T-10........V.7:4 His. **H.** calls to you from every part of the
T-10........V.7:5 hear His message **H.** has answered you,
T-10........V.7:6 Love of God is in everything **H.** created,
T-10........V.8:2 acknowledge Him you will know that **H.**
T-10........V.8:5 from which **H.** cannot be separated.
T-10........V.9:3 Would **H.** allow Himself to suffer? And
T-10........V.9:4 And would **H.** offer His Son anything that
T-10......V.9:10 own mind because of the power **H.** gave it
T-10......V.10:2 it so. Yet **H.** would not interfere with you,
T-10......V.10:2 because **H.** would not know His Son if he
T-10......V.13:2 yours only because **H.** has given it to you.
T-11.........I.1:4 **H.** wills His Son to be and where he is. In
T-11.........I.4:3 you have tried to limit what **H.** created,
T-11.........I.5:3 you will believe that **H.** is absent from you
T-11.........I.5:6 is not incomplete, and **H.** is not childless.
T-11.........I.5:7 Because **H.** did not will to be alone, He
T-11.........I.5:7 to be alone, **H.** created a Son like Himself.
T-11.........I.6:5 everything **H.** creates has the function of
T-11.........I.6:7 is His and that **H.** wills to share with you.
T-11.........I.7:4 end, to learn how much **H.** has given you.
T-11.........I.7:5 on your willingness to give as **H.** gives.
T-11.........I.9:5 will is His life, which **H.** has given to you.
T-11.........I.9:8 What **H.** created can sleep, but cannot die
T-11.......I.11:3 **H.** shares His Will with you; He does not
T-11.......I.11:3 with you; **H.** does not thrust it upon you.
T-11.......I.11:4 remember that what **H.** gives He keeps, so
T-11.......I.11:4 remember that what He gives **H.** keeps, so
T-11.......I.11:4 that nothing **H.** gives can contradict Him.
T-11........II.1:4 will with His, for **H.** wills you Himself.
T-11........II.6:2 like Him, and **H.** has given Himself to you
T-11.......III.1:5 for **H.** knows no attack and His peace
T-11.......III.2:4 when **H.** did not will to be alone Himself?
T-11.......III.3:2 And what **H.** wills has happened, for it
T-11.......III.3:7 God wills for Himself **H.** wills for you, and
T-11.......III.3:7 for you, and what **H.** wills for you is yours
T-11.......III.7:2 **H.** waits to give you the peace that is
T-11.......III.7:7 for **H.** Himself dwells there and abides in
T-11.......IV.1:7 And since what **H.** created is part of Him,
T-11.......IV.3:3 the light **H.** created is one with Him.
T-11.......IV.7:2 as Himself, and **H.** is approached through
T-11........V.6:2 God, Whose function **H.** shares with you.
T-11........V.6:3 it, **H.** became as dependent on you as you
T-11........V.6:5 **H.** has included you in His Autonomy.
T-11......V.17:6 in His light and behold what **H.** created.
T-11.......VI.5:6 nothing, for **H.** does not will to take away.
T-11.......VI.5:7 away. **H.** does not require obedience, for
T-11.......VI.5:8 **H.** would only have you learn your will
T-11.......VI.6:6 is His, and **H.** Himself is yours with them.
T-11....VIII.4:2 will not refuse you the Answer **H.** gave.
T-11....VIII.5:9 God gives; **H.** does not take. When you
T-11....VIII.7:6 His Son whom **H.** created free and whose
T-12.......III.8:1 that **H.** gave it to His only begotten Son.
T-12.......III.9:3 Yet **H.** would not have it so, and so it is
T-12.......VI.2:5 and **H.** never ceases to remind His Son of
T-12...VII.15:4 Father unless **H.** had also given it to you?
T-12....VIII.3:7 **H.** created it, and He knows what it is.
T-12....VIII.3:7 He created it, and **H.** knows what it is.
T-12....VIII.3:8 and unless **H.** had given you a way to
T-13.......III.3:4 God, and **H.** does not will to be excluded.
T-13.....III.12:3 Could **H.** set you apart, knowing that your
T-13.....III.12:4 **H.** denied you only your request for pain,
T-13.....III.12:5 creation, **H.** could not take it from you.
T-13.....III.12:6 **H.** could but answer your insane request
T-13.....III.12:7 And this **H.** did. No one who hears His
T-13........V.7:3 to Him. And **H.** will not return it, for it is
T-13........V.7:4 Yet **H.** would release you from it and set
T-13.......VI.9:3 **H.** will return your thanks in His clear
T-13...VII.15:3 where **H.** would have you be in quietness.
T-13....VIII.4:3 you because **H.** has no Thoughts He does
T-13....VIII.4:3 He has no Thoughts **H.** does not share.
T-13....VIII.9:2 and **H.** has given you the power to create
T-13..VIII.10:7 never would **H.** leave His Own beloved
T-13.......IX.8:8 you. **H.** does not value you as you do. He
T-13.......IX.8:9 **H.** knows Himself, and knows the truth in
T-13.....IX.8:10 **H.** knows there is no difference, for He
T-13.....IX.8:10 difference, for **H.** knows not of differences
T-13.....IX.8:13 then, upon the light **H.** placed within you,
T-13........X.9:7 is as pure as **H.** Who raised it to Himself.
T-13......X.13:3 I love all that **H.** created, and all my faith
T-13......X.14:5 only praise of Him in what **H.** has created,
T-13......X.14:5 for **H.** will never cease His praise of you.
T-13.......XI.5:5 the peace in which **H.** has established you,
T-13.......XI.5:5 because **H.** does not change His Mind. He
T-13.......XI.5:6 **H.** is invariable as the peace in which you
T-13.......XI.7:6 you with whom **H.** would communicate.
T-13.......XI.8:9 sure, and what **H.** wills is as sure as He is.
T-13.......XI.8:9 sure, and what He wills is as sure as **H.** is.
T-14.....III.12:2 purity of everything that **H.** created, for it
T-14.....III.15:1 worth of God's Son whom **H.** created holy
T-14.....III.15:8 quite impossible that **H.** could ever let His
T-14.......IV.3:1 **H.** will give Himself to you as He has
T-14.......IV.3:1 give Himself to you as **H.** has always done.
T-14.......IV.3:2 Giving Himself is all **H.** knows, and so it is
T-14.......IV.3:3 For what **H.** knows not cannot be, and
T-14.......IV.4:2 no barriers; neither did **H.** make them.
T-14.......IV.4:6 **H.** created you out of Himself, but still
T-14.......IV.4:7 **H.** knows what you are. Remember that
T-14.......IV.7:3 Him, though **H.** is all around you. He
T-14.......IV.7:4 **H.** cannot be known without His Son,
T-14........V.1:5 You yearn for Him, as **H.** for you. This is
T-14........V.9:3 we know Him, as **H.** knows us guiltless. I
T-14........V.9:6 your Father's power that **H.** has given him

| | |
|---|---|
| T-14.....V.9:10 | Restore to God His Son as H. created him, |
| T-14...V.10:12 | yours. Thus H. creates, and thus must you |
| T-14.....VII.7:6 | has one purpose which H. shares with you |
| T-14... VIII.1:1 | power H. bestowed upon His guiltless Son |
| T-14... VIII.5:1 | the Father joins Himself to those H. gives |
| T-14... VIII.5:6 | To whom God gives Himself, H. *is* given. |
| T-14... VIII.5:7 | on the altar, where H. has placed His Own |
| T-14.....X.12:8 | His Son with all the Love H. holds for him |
| T-14......XI.4:4 | which H. shares so gladly with His Son. |
| T-14......XI.7:4 | Yet H. cannot compel His Son to turn to |
| T-14......XI.7:5 | that God lose His Identity, for if H. did, |
| T-14......XI.7:6 | being yours H. cannot change Himself, |
| T-15....... II.2:3 | through the Teacher H. has appointed to |
| T-15.....III.4:11 | For H. is not content without His Son, |
| T-15......III.5:4 | H. established you as host to Him forever. |
| T-15......III.5:5 | H. has not left you, and you have not left |
| T-15......III.7:5 | you. H. reaches from you to everyone and |
| T-15......III.7:6 | world but still in you, H. extends forever. |
| T-15......III.7:7 | Yet H. brings all His extensions to you, as |
| T-15.....III.10:5 | What my Father loves I love as H. does, |
| T-15.....III.10:5 | accept it as what it is not, than H. can. |
| T-15.....III.12:5 | protects only the peace in which H. dwells |
| T-15......IV.3:4 | in the plan that H. has given to the world |
| T-15....... V.9:2 | H. remembers nothing, having always |
| T-15....... V.9:2 | known you exactly as H. knows you now. |
| T-15.....V.10:5 | God loves every brother as H. loves you; |
| T-15.....V.10:6 | H. needs them all equally, and so do you. |
| T-15... VIII.4:2 | for as H. withheld Himself not from you, |
| T-15... VIII.4:2 | from you, H. withheld not His creation. |
| T-15... VIII.5:1 | free you of what H. does not understand. |
| T-15... VIII.5:5 | H. keeps this channel open to receive His |
| T-15... VIII.5:6 | for H. does not share it with you. It is only |
| T-15......IX.1:5 | for it is the only step in it H. understands. |
| T-15......XI.8:5 | H. joins us in the celebration of His Son's |
| T-15......XI.9:1 | Him enter and abide where H. would be. |
| T-15......XI.9:2 | your welcome does H. welcome you into |
| T-16....... II.8:3 | that is the only reason H. has called to you |
| T-16......III.6:3 | Him and whom H. holds are the universe, |
| T-16......III.8:1 | for what H. is Who created you as you are |
| T-16.....IV.11:7 | H. not answer you whose completion is |
| T-16.....IV.11:8 | H. loves you, wholly without illusion, as |
| T-16.....IV.13:4 | The bridge that H. would carry you across |
| T-16....... V.4:2 | for the self the specialness that H. denied. |
| T-16.....V.12:8 | H. merely could not let this happen. You |
| T-16......VI.1:5 | God created love as H. would have it be, |
| T-16.....VII.8:5 | H. gave the holy instant to be given you, |
| T-16.....VII.8:5 | that you receive it not *because* H. gave it. |
| T-16.....VII.8:6 | When H. willed that His Son be free, His |
| T-16.....VII.9:4 | for H. is incapable of illusions of any kind. |
| T-17....IV.16:5 | What H. has given is His. It shines in |
| T-17..IV.16:10 | H. is only the perfect and complete can be |
| T-18...... I.10:4 | And H. would never accept something |
| T-18...... I.10:5 | H. loves you both, equally and as one. |
| T-18...... I.10:6 | And as H. loves you, so you are. You are |
| T-18......IV.3:6 | believe H. cannot enter where He wills to |
| T-18......IV.3:6 | He cannot enter where H. wills to be, you |
| T-18....IV.5:10 | *H. Who established His dwelling place in* |
| T-18....IV.5:10 | *place in me created it as H. would have it be.* |
| T-18....... V.3:5 | it. Nor will H. change His Mind about it. |
| T-18....... V.3:9 | H. will provide the means to anyone who |
| T-18......VI.1:3 | and H. did not depart from it nor leave it |
| T-18......VI.5:5 | created is only what H. would have it be, |
| T-18......VI.9:7 | H. would have had to create different |
| T-18....VI.10:5 | Is *H.* a body, and did He create you as He |
| T-18....VI.10:5 | a body, and did H. create you as He is not, |
| T-18....VI.10:5 | a body, and did He create you as H. is not, |
| T-18....VI.10:5 | you as He is not, and where H. cannot be? |
| T-18....VI.10:7 | there be on you whom H. encompasses? |
| T-18. VIII.12:4 | than H. knows you without your brother. |
| T-18....IX.11:4 | Him Who is complete where H. begins, |
| T-19......III.6:4 | H. must be split, and torn between good |
| T-19......III.6:5 | For H. must have created what wills to |
| T19....IV.B.9:6 | H. Who is our home is homeless with us. |
| T19... IV.C.8:1 | unable to protect the life that H. created |
| T-20......IV.1:9 | untrue H. has neither received nor given. |
| T-21....... V.6:2 | self-defeating. H. has no Thoughts except |
| T-21... VIII.2:5 | vision as its Creator is in what H. knows, |
| T-21... VIII.5:1 | to you to recognize what H. has given you |
| T-22.........I.1:2 | God would heal and hate the one H. loves, |
| T-22........I.3:11 | H. does not lead you through a world of |
| T-22........I.3:11 | the journey's end, why H. did this to you. |
| T-22....... II.5:6 | Whom nothing H. wills can be impossible |
| T-22..... II.11:6 | For what H. gave the Holy Spirit to give to |
| T-22..... II.11:6 | gave the Holy Spirit to give to you *H. gave*. |
| T-22....... V.3:5 | whom H. has joined as one with Him? It is |
| T-23.........I.4:6 | H. loves you perfectly, completely and |
| T-23.........I.9:5 | drive Him out of what H. loves forever. |
| T-23.........I.9:6 | And what H. loves must be forever quiet |
| T-23....... II.6:2 | H. must think and what He must believe; |
| T-23....... II.6:2 | He must think and what H. must believe; |
| T-23....... II.6:2 | must believe; and how H. must respond, |
| T-23....... II.6:3 | It is not seen as even necessary that H. be |
| T-23....... II.6:4 | and H. has but the choice whether to take |
| T-23....... II.6:6 | H. must accept His Son's belief in what he |
| T-23....... II.7:3 | For now H. has become the "enemy" Who |
| T-23..... II.13:3 | madness H. must have this substitute for |
| T-23.......IV.1:3 | Yet H. remains the only place of safety. In |
| T-23.......IV.3:2 | H. gave the function to create unto His |
| T-23.......IV.6:7 | to remain where H. would have you, and |
| T-23.......IV.7:8 | the Heaven H. created for His Son *because* |
| T-24.......in.1:4 | H. will not fail. Where He can enter, there |
| T-24.......in.1:5 | Where H. can enter, there He is already. |
| T-24.......in.1:5 | Where He can enter, there H. is already. |
| T-24.......in.1:6 | it be H. cannot enter where He wills to be |
| T-24.......in.1:6 | it be He cannot enter where H. wills to be |
| T-24.......in.2:9 | The truth arises from what H. knows. |
| T-24.....in.2:10 | in His Mind *because* of what H. knows. |
| T-24.........I.3:2 | with the grandeur that H. gave His Son. |
| T-24..... II.10:4 | H. is not special, for He would not keep |
| T-24..... II.10:4 | for H. would not keep one part of what He |
| T-24..... II.10:4 | keep one part of what H. is unto Himself, |
| T-24..... II.10:5 | it is this you fear, for if H. is not special, |
| T-24..... II.10:5 | then H. willed His Son to be like Him, and |
| T-24..... II.11:4 | and him to you because H. gave Himself. |
| T-24......III.5:2 | H. would have no separation, like an alien |
| T-24......III.5:2 | what H. wills for you and what you will. |
| T-24......III.6:3 | H. chose not this for you. Ask not He |
| T-24......III.6:4 | Ask not H. enter this. The way is barred |
| T-24......III.6:7 | One the specialness H. could not give, and |
| T-24......III.7:5 | God because H. did not make their dream |
| T-24......IV.5:1 | in which God is bereft of what H. loves, |
| T-24....... V.8:3 | H. Who willed not to be without His Son |
| T-24....... V.8:4 | H. give a brother unto you except he be as |
| T-24......VI.1:6 | H. could never leave His Own creation. |
| T-24......VI.1:9 | acknowledgment that H. created you as |
| T-24......VI.3:2 | that God created has H. failed to lay |
| T-24......VI.3:4 | as lovingly as H. conceived of you before |
| T-24......VI.3:4 | world began, and as H. knows you still. |
| T-24......VI.3:5 | no meaning in eternity where H. abides, |
| T-24......VI.3:6 | Your brother *is* as H. created him. And it is |
| T-24......VI.3:7 | you from a world that H. created not. |
| T-24......VI.6:3 | And it is H. they look for everywhere, and |
| T-24......VI.6:3 | sight nor place nor time where H. is not. |
| T-24......VI.7:6 | in that part of Him H. set forever in your |
| T-24....VI.10:5 | H. has given you a part of Him to save |
| T-24.....VII.5:1 | The Father keeps what H. created safe. |
| T-25....... II.5:5 | for what H. has created He supports and |
| T-25....... II.5:5 | created H. supports and frames within |
| T-25....... II.5:6 | His masterpiece H. offers you to see. And |
| T-25....... II.7:5 | it, and see the holiness that H. has given it |
| T-25....... II.9:2 | What could H. do but offer thanks to you |
| T-25....... II.9:2 | thanks to you who love His Son as H. does |
| T-25....... II.9:3 | H. not make known to you His Love, if |
| T-25....... II.9:3 | you but share His praise of what H. loves? |
| T-25....... II.9:4 | creation as the perfect Father that H. is. |
| T-25....... II.9:7 | H. is glad and thankful when you thank |
| T-25..... II.10:3 | Give, then, what H. has given you, that |
| T-25..... II.10:3 | and thank his Father as H. thanks you. |
| T-25..... II.11:2 | since H. gave the same to both of you. His |
| T-25......III.2:4 | and from His Son's belief H. could not let |
| T-25......III.2:5 | H. could not enter His Son's insanity with |
| T-25......III.2:5 | but H. could be sure His sanity went there |
| T-25....... V.6:1 | save what H. created from the pain of hell |
| T-25....... V.6:4 | through your attack believe H. hates you, |
| T-25......VI.3:4 | on him. H. does not will your savior be |
| T-25......VI.3:5 | Nor does H. will that he remain without |
| T-25......VI.3:5 | without the function that H. gave to him. |
| T-25.....VII.2:2 | Nor can the basis of a world H. did not |
| T-25.....VII.2:4 | what H. did not will cannot be changed? |
| T-25.....VII.8:2 | Because H. is not mad has God appointed |
| T-25.....VII.8:2 | God appointed One as sane as H. to raise |
| T-25....VII.10:3 | the alternative H. chose especially for you. |
| T-25....VIII.5:3 | But justice does H. know, and knows it |
| T-25....VIII.5:4 | it well. For H. is wholly fair to everyone. |
| T-25....VIII.5:5 | to God's Mind *because* H. knows of justice. |
| T-25..VIII.10:4 | H. would not allow His Son be judged by |
| T-25..VIII.10:8 | would be done unto the Son H. loves, and |
| T-25.......IX.2:8 | is fair. H. does not fight against His Son's |
| T-26........II.8:2 | feared. H. cannot be unjust to anyone or |
| T-26........II.8:2 | because H. knows that everything that is |
| T-26........II.8:2 | Him, and will forever be as H. created it. |
| T-26........II.8:3 | Nothing H. loves but must be sinless and |
| T-26........II.8:6 | should offer or receive less than H. gave, |
| T-26........II.8:6 | gave, when H. created you in perfect love. |
| T-26...... III.1:2 | How could it be, when all H. knows is One |
| T-26...... III.1:3 | H. knows of one creation, one reality, one |
| T-26.......IV.3:3 | and not recall His Father as H. really is? |
| T-26....... V.3:2 | what H. would replace has been replaced. |
| T-26....... V.9:7 | to yourself has H. protected you. You |
| T-26.....VII.7:5 | Thus has H. lost His Mind, proclaiming |
| T-26...VII.11:2 | H. wills His Son have everything. And this |
| T-26...VII.11:3 | And this H. guaranteed when He created |
| T-26...VII.11:3 | when H. created him *as* everything. It is |
| T-26...VII.13:2 | true: that H. created you as part of Him, |
| T-26...VII.18:1 | you as H. would have it used is natural. It |
| T-26...VII.18:2 | It is not arrogant to be as H. created you, |
| T-26...VII.18:2 | to make use of what H. gave to answer all |
| T-26...VII.18:2 | to lay aside the power that H. gave, and |
| T-26...VII.18:3 | senseless wish instead of what H. wills. |
| T-26...VII.20:3 | Could H. refuse to answer when He has |
| T-26...VII.20:3 | Could He refuse to answer when H. has |
| T-26.......IX.1:4 | And never will you know H. is in you as |
| T-26.......IX.8:2 | Where H. dwells, His Son dwells with |
| T-27......III.4:3 | where H. is there must the truth abide. |
| T-27......III.7:9 | H. would merely be, and so He merely is. |
| T-27......III.7:9 | He would merely be, and so H. merely is. |
| T-27.......IV.1:7 | for what H. wills already has been done. |
| T-27.......V.11:9 | H. knows it is a gift of love unto His Son, |
| T-27...VII.14:1 | the dream H. gave instead of yours. It is |
| T-27...VII.16:1 | Brother, H. gives but life. Yet what you |
| T-28.........I.8:5 | Father's Will that H. be unremembered |
| T-28.......I.10:1 | is not H. Who laid a judgment on His Son |
| T-28.......I.10:5 | H. has not done the thing you fear. No |
| T-28.......I.12:4 | H. would not be deprived of His Effects. |
| T-28.......I.15:7 | H. has built the bridge, and it is He Who |
| T-28.......I.15:7 | is H. Who will transport His Son across it. |
| T-28.......I.15:8 | no fear that H. will fail in what He wills. |
| T-28.......I.15:8 | no fear that He will fail in what H. wills. |
| T-28........II.8:1 | them since H. was no longer their Creator |
| T-28...... III.6:2 | and the shame of guilt H. cannot bridge, |
| T-28...... III.6:2 | for H. can not destroy the alien will that |
| T-28...... III.6:2 | destroy the alien will that H. created not. |
| T-28....... V.5:2 | And what that H. created not can be? Let |
| T-28.....VII.1:6 | to what H. wills as part of what He is. The |
| T-28.....VII.1:6 | to what He wills as part of what H. is. The |
| T-28.....VII.1:7 | Himself and what H. is cannot be false. |
| T-29.........I.1:8 | For H. must be deceptive in His Love. Be |
| T-29........II.8:4 | it asks that God be less than all H. really is |
| T-29........II.8:6 | For H. is told that part of Him belongs to |
| T-29........II.8:7 | H. must sacrifice your self, and in His |
| T-29........II.8:7 | more and H. is lessened by the loss of you. |
| T-29......II.10:1 | what H. is with littleness and limit and |
| T-29......II.10:3 | For if H. be the sum of everything, then |
| T-29...... III.2:1 | Father lost Himself when H. created you? |
| T-29...... III.2:2 | Was H. made weak because He shared |
| T-29...... III.2:2 | made weak because H. shared His Love? |
| T-29...... III.2:3 | H. made incomplete by your perfection? |
| T-29...... III.2:4 | the proof that H. is perfect and complete? |
| T-29.....VII.9:5 | God, and where H. is no idols can abide. |
| T-29....VIII.4:6 | voice could make demand H. enter not? |
| T-29....VIII.9:8 | H. also give the same to every living thing |
| T-30........II.1:6 | will. H. joins with *you*. He did not set His |
| T-30........II.1:7 | H. did not set His Kingdom up alone. And |
| T-30......II.1:12 | H. asks no more than that He hear you |
| T-30......II.1:12 | than that H. hear you call Him "Friend." |
| T-30........II.2:6 | will when H. gave you His perfect Answer. |
| T-30........II.2:9 | H. joins with you in willing you be free. |

T-30....... II.4:4 Think not H. wills to bind you, Who has
T-30....... II.4:5 H. would but keep your will forever and
T-30...... III.4:6 H. cannot answer you in terms that have
T-30...... III.6:2 exists. And what H. knows exists forever,
T-30...... III.9:1 for H. is the eternal sky that holds it safe,
T-30....... V.7:6 For H. must be unremembered till His
T-30..... V.11:2 joined, they thought H. was their enemy.
T-30..... VII.1:2 If H. had, it *has* no meaning. For it cannot
T-31.........I.9:4 only if His Son is innocent can H. be Love.
T-31.........I.9:5 if he whom H. created innocent could be a
T-31...... IV.9:1 H. has not left His Thoughts! But you
T-31...... IV.9:6 Yet has H. never left His Thoughts to die,
T-31.... IV.10:1 H. has not left His Thoughts! He could no
T-31.... IV.10:2 H. could no more depart from them than
T-31.... IV.11:5 For what H. is be thankful, for in that is
T-31.... IV.11:6 but where H. is can you be found. There *is*
T-31..... VII.8:3 And to each one has H. allowed the grace
T-31... VII.15:5 that it is you for whom H. asks release?
W-pI..... 14.1:3 that does exist exists as H. created it. The
W-pI..... 14.7:5 *H. did not create [specify the situation*
W-pI..... 38.3:2 holy because all things H. created are holy
W-pI..... 38.3:3 things H. created are holy because you are
W-pI..... 39.4:6 Can it be H. does not know His Son?
W-pI..... 42.2:1 strength, and what H. gives is truly given.
W-pI..... 42.4:7 *must be mine, because H. gave them to me.*
W-pI..... 43.1:3 Yet H. has created the Holy Spirit as the
W-pI..... 45.2:2 with Him, as H. shares His with you. They
W-pI..... 45.2:7 They are in your mind as well, where H. is
W-pI..... 45.5:2 fail in doing what H. would have us do.
W-pI..... 45.9:4 for the Thoughts H. is thinking with you.
W-pI..... 46.1:1 forgive because H. has never condemned.
W-pI..... 47.3:4 which speaks for Him thinks as H. does.
W-pI..... 49.3:4 H. wants you to hear His Voice. He gave It
W-pI..... 49.3:5 His Voice. H. gave It to you to be heard.
W-pI..... 53.4:3 it? H. is the Source of all meaning, and
W-pI..... 53.4:4 mind too, because H. created it with me.
W-pI..... 59.1:4 when H. rests in me in absolute peace?
W-pI..... 59.2:5 vision is His gift, and H. has given it to me
W-pI..... 60.1:2 forgive because H. has never condemned.
W-pI..... 60.5:5 the world with the vision H. has given me,
W-pI..... 66.4:3 function H. gave you must be happiness,
W-pI..... 66.5:3 *H. has given my function to me. Therefore*
W-pI..... 66.6:2 to define God as something H. is not.
W-pI..... 66.6:4 God cannot give what H. does not have,
W-pI..... 66.6:4 have, and H. cannot have what He is not.
W-pI..... 66.6:4 have, and He cannot have what H. is not.
W-pI..... 66.6:5 gives you only happiness, H. must be evil.
W-pI..... 67.2:7 H. defines Himself is appropriate for use.
W-pI..... 68.1:7 makes you believe that H. is like what you
W-pI..... 69.8:1 that H. has heard you and answered you.
W-pI..... 70.3:4 H. wants you to be healed, so He has kept
W-pI..... 70.3:4 H. has kept the Source of healing where
W-pI..... 70.5:4 H. does not want us to be sick. Neither do
W-pI..... 70.5:6 do we. H. wants us to be healed. So do we.
W-pI..... 71.9:7 H. will answer in proportion to your
W-pI..... 72.4:5 Son is only a body, so must H. be as well.
W-pI..... 72.5:3 not of death, H. is a liar and a deceiver,
W-pI..... 72.7:6 It is your friend; H. is your enemy.
W-pI... 72.12:5 H. will answer. Be determined to hear.
W-pI..... 89.1:5 on behalf of the function H. has given me.
W-pI..... 93.3:3 weird beliefs H. does not share with you.
W-pI..... 94.2:3 H. Who ensured your sinlessness must be
W-pI..... 94.4:4 You cannot fail because H. cannot fail.
W-pI..... 95.8:2 mistakes. H. can be held back only by
W-pI... 95.15:4 *you because of What I am, and What H. is,*
W-pI..... 97.2:4 H. is with you always, as you are with Him
W-pI..... 97.4:3 H. will offer all His strength to every little
W-pI..... 97.4:4 Him the minutes which H. needs today,
W-pI..... 98.7:2 minutes. H. will give the words you use in
W-pI..... 98.8:1 H. will accept your words and give them
W-pI..... 98.9:1 Him the words, and H. will do the rest.
W-pI..... 98.9:2 H. will enable you to understand your
W-pI..... 98.9:3 H. will open up the way to happiness, and
W-pI..... 98.9:4 H. will respond with all His faith and joy
W-pI..... 98.9:6 H. will be with you each practice period
W-pI... 98.11:1 And when the hour goes and H. is there
W-pI... 98.11:2 H. would have you take and help you fill,
W-pI... 98.11:2 and H. will make you sure you want this
W-pI... 98.11:2 H. has made with you and you with Him.
W-pI..... 99.7:5 the thought H. wanted this for you. Then
W-pI..... 99.7:6 Then let the Thought with which H. has
W-pI..... 99.8:3 upon no obstacle to what H. wills for you.
W-pI..... 99.9:3 It is God's Will that H. has but one Son. It
W-pI... 100.2:3 The part that H. has saved for you to take
W-pI... 100.2:3 you might be restored to what H. wills.
W-pI... 100.2:5 by those to whom H. sends you. They will
W-pI... 100.5:4 how great the happiness H. wills for you.
W-pI... 100.6:3 world can see how much H. loves His Son,
W-pI... 100.9:5 when H. Who calls to you is God Himself?
W-pI. 100.10:1 H. will be there. You are essential to His
W-pI. 100.10:4 must find what H. would have you give.
W-pI... 101.2:7 And yet H. will pursue, and they can not
W-pI... 102.5:2 to God's Son than H. Whose Love created
W-pI... 103.2:2 forgetting being Love, H. must be joy.
W-pI... 103.2:7 belongs to you, because of what H. is.
W-pI... 104.1:3 Who cannot fail to give you what H. wills.
W-pI... 104.4:3 belongs to us in truth is what H. gives.
W-pI... 104.5:2 to seek for them where H. has laid them.
W-pI... 105.5:2 Himself as H. defines completion. You
W-pI... 105.5:4 H. cannot give through loss. No more can
W-pI... 105.5:6 and H. will thank you for your gift to Him
W-pI... 105.9:2 to Him to give you what H. wills to give,
W-pI... 105.9:3 not to interfere today with what H. wills.
W-pI... 106.4:3 H. would speak to you. He comes with
W-pI... 106.4:4 H. comes with miracles a thousand times
W-pI... 106.5:3 H. needs your voice to speak to them, for
W-pI... 106.5:4 to hear the Word that H. will speak today.
WpIrIII.in13:3 you review these thoughts H. gave to you.
W-pI... 112.2:3 *And I am one with Him, and H. with me.*
W-pI... 115.2:3 *For H. gave me His plan that I might save the*
W-pI... 116.2:3 *What H. has given me is all I want. What He*
W-pI... 116.2:4 *I want. What H. has given me is all there is.*
W-pI... 122.5:2 thankful it remains exactly as H. planned
W-pI... 123.2:3 Be grateful H. has saved you from the self
W-pI... 123.3:1 thanks that H. has not abandoned you,
W-pI... 123.3:2 the Son H. loves is changeless as Himself.
W-pI... 123.6:3 H. would offer you the thanks you give,
W-pI... 123.6:3 give, since H. receives your gifts in loving
W-pI... 123.6:4 H. will bless your gifts by sharing them
W-pI... 123.7:2 H. thanks as you are thanking Him. This
W-pI... 123.8:1 how lovingly H. holds you in His Mind,
W-pI... 123.8:2 give Him thanks for everything H. gave
W-pI... 124.8:2 one with your Creator, as H. is with you.
W-pI... 124.8:5 God's Voice to speak as H. sees fit today,
W-pI... 124.8:5 as He sees fit today, certain H. will not fail
W-pI... 124.8:7 Him this half an hour. H. will do the rest.
W-pI... 125.1:3 H. calls to you from deep within your
W-pI... 125.1:3 deep within your mind where H. abides.
W-pI... 125.4:3 within the mind where H. abides forever,
W-pI... 125.4:3 the holiness that H. created and will never
W-pI... 125.5:1 H. has not waited until you return your
W-pI... 125.5:2 H. has not hid Himself from you, while
W-pI... 125.5:3 H. does not cherish the illusions which
W-pI... 125.5:4 H. knows His Son, and wills that he
W-pI... 125.6:1 Today H. speaks to you. His Voice awaits
W-pI... 125.7:2 H. speaks from nearer than your heart to
W-pI... 125.7:4 Love is everything you are and that H. is;
W-pI... 125.7:4 the same as you, and you the same as H..
W-pI... 125.8:1 to which you listen as H. speaks to you. It
W-pI... 125.8:2 It is your word H. speaks. It is the Word
W-pI... 126.7:1 having given Him the gift H. asks of you,
W-pI... 126.7:1 and think H. has not given them to you.
W-pI... 126.7:2 H. ask you for a gift unless it was for you?
W-pI... 126.7:3 Could H. be satisfied with empty gestures,
W-pI... 127.4:3 For what you are is what H. is. There is no
W-pI... 127.4:4 There is no love but His, and what H. is, is
W-pI... 127.9:2 H. Himself has promised this. And He
W-pI... 127.9:3 And H. Himself will place a spark of truth
W-pI... 127.9:4 H. will shine through your idle thoughts
W-pI... 127.9:5 loving gentleness H. will abide with you,
W-pI... 127.9:6 And H. will bless the lesson with His Love
W-pI... 131.6:6 What H. wills is now, without a past and
W-pI... 131.7:4 H. did not make two minds, with Heaven
W-pI... 131.8:6 H. is here because He wills to be, and
W-pI... 131.8:6 He is here because H. wills to be, and
W-pI... 131.8:6 to be, and what H. wills is present now,
W-pI. 132.12:3 for H. makes no distinctions in what is
W-pI. 132.12:4 What H. creates is not apart from Him,
W-pI 132.14:5 And we who are as H. created us would
W-pI 135.25:1 H. has remembered you. Today we will
W-pI 136.13:5 Yet what H. wills is here, and you remain
W-pI 136.13:5 is here, and you remain as H. created you.
W-pI 139.11:4 gave to us when H. created us like Him.
W-pI .. 140.5:4 H. is barred where sin has entered. Yet
W-pI .. 140.5:5 Yet there is no place where H. is not. And
WpI..rIV.in6:3 be yours, as H. Himself has willed it be.
WpI..rIV.in6:4 so will H. join with you who are complete
WpI..rIV.in6:4 as you unite with Him, and H. with you.
WpI..rIV.in7:5 H. has laid in it for you to have of Him.
WpIrIV.in10:2 the peace wherein H. wills you be forever,
W-pI .. 152.6:4 What can H. know of the ephemeral, the
W-pI .. 152.6:5 think H. made a world where such things
W-pI .. 152.6:6 H. is not mad. Yet only madness makes a
W-pI 153.17:2 and learn what H. would have us do the
W-pI 153.17:2 all the gifts H. gave us in the one gone by.
W-pI 153.18:4 Think you H. will not make this possible,
W-pI 155.12:6 and leads us to where H. has always been.
W-pI 155.13:4 not H. has placed His Hand in yours, and
W-pI 155.13:5 H. cannot be deceived. His trust has made
W-pI 155.14:1 now H. asks but that you think of Him a
W-pI 155.14:1 that H. may speak to you and tell you of
W-pI .. 156.2:5 H. is what your life is. Where you are He
W-pI .. 156.2:6 is. Where you are H. is. There is one life.
W-pI .. 156.3:1 Yet where H. is, there must be holiness as
W-pI 159.10:3 but follow in the way H. has established.
W-pI .. 160.7:5 H. cannot be confused about creation. He
W-pI .. 160.7:6 H. is sure of what belongs to Him. No
W-pI .. 160.7:8 H. does not know of strangers. He is
W-pI .. 160.7:9 of strangers. H. is certain of His Son.
W-pI .. 160.8:2 H. knows to be His Son belongs where He
W-pI .. 160.8:2 belongs where H. has set His Son forever.
W-pI .. 160.8:3 H. has answered you who ask, "Who is
W-pI .. 166.1:3 H. knows His Son. He gives without
W-pI .. 166.1:4 Son. H. gives without exception, holding
W-pI .. 166.2:3 to opposite effects from those H. wills.
W-pI .. 166.9:6 Perhaps H. has not wholly been outwitted
W-pI 166.10:4 H. does not know about a plan so alien to
W-pI 166.10:5 There was a need H. did not understand,
W-pI 166.10:5 understand, to which H. gave an Answer.
W-pI 166.15:7 H. has shared His joy with you. And now
W-pI .. 167.8:2 H. does not sleep, and His creations
W-pI .. 167.8:2 creations cannot share what H. gives not,
W-pI .. 167.8:2 make conditions which H. does not share
W-pI 167.11:1 strive to keep today as H. established it,
W-pI 167.11:2 H. is Lord of what we think today. And in
W-pI 167.11:3 whom H. created in a unity of life that
W-pI 167.12:1 the holy minds which H. created perfect.
W-pI .. 168.1:3 H. is not distant. He makes no attempt to
W-pI .. 168.1:4 H. makes no attempt to hide from us. We
W-pI .. 168.1:6 H. remains entirely accessible. He loves
W-pI .. 168.1:7 H. loves His Son. There is no certainty but
W-pI .. 168.1:9 H. will love His Son forever. When his
W-pI 168.1:10 mind remains asleep, H. loves him still.
W-pI 168.1:11 H. loves him with a never-changing Love.
W-pI .. 168.2:4 H. not gladly give the means by which His
W-pI .. 168.3:1 Today we ask of God the gift H. has most
W-pI .. 168.3:4 But finally H. comes Himself, and takes us
W-pI .. 168.5:3 but H. to Whom all error is unknown is
W-pI .. 168.6:1 And H. descends to meet us, as we come
W-pI .. 168.6:2 For what H. has prepared for us He gives
W-pI .. 168.6:2 prepared for us H. gives and we receive.
W-pI .. 168.6:3 Such is His Will, because H. loves His Son
W-pI .. 168.6:4 returning but the word H. gave to us
W-pI .. 169.5:2 in His Being, H. encompasses all things.
W-pI 170.10:6 And H. is terrible above all else, cruel
W-pI .. 183.7:3 Think not H. hears the little prayers of
W-pI .. 183.7:5 H. cannot hear requests that He be not
W-pI .. 183.7:5 hear requests that H. be not Himself, or
W-pI 184.12:5 Name of God is the inheritance H. gave to
W-pI 184.12:6 made as fitting tribute to the Son H. loves
W-pI 184.14:1 but one Name, which H. has given them.
W-pI .. 185.4:8 H. means is lost to sleeping minds intent
W-pI 185.12:2 when you but ask for what H. wills for you
W-pI 185.13:4 share one Will with Him, and H. with you
W-pI .. 186.3:2 trust H. holds in you who are His Son. It
W-pI .. 186.4:1 reveal to us what H. would have us do.
W-pI .. 186.4:2 adequacy for the function H. will offer us.

W-pI...186.4:3 certain only that H. knows our strengths,
W-pI...186.4:4 And if H. deems us worthy, so we are. It is
W-pI...186.9:2 H. create such instability and call it Son?
W-pI...186.9:3 it Son? H. Who is changeless shares His
W-pI.186.11:6 can never fail because H. is its Source.
W-pI.186.13:2 H. would comfort you, although He
W-pI.186.13:2 you, although H. knows no sorrow. He
W-pI.186.13:3 H. would make a restitution, though He is
W-pI.186.13:3 make a restitution, though H. is complete;
W-pI.186.13:3 to you, although H. knows that you have
W-pI.186.13:4 H. has Thoughts which answer every need
W-pI.186.13:4 Son perceives, although H. sees them not.
W-pI...189.8:1 Is it not H. Who knows the way to you?
W-pI...189.8:6 to God by which H. should appear to you.
W-pI...189.9:7 H. does not need His Son to show Him
W-pI...190.1:7 of His Son, the sinfulness H. sees in him,
W-pI...190.8:3 In pain is God denied the Son H. loves. In
W-pI...192.1:1 shall be His sacred Son, forever pure as H.
W-pI...193.1:2 extends to what H. does not understand,
W-pI...193.1:2 H. wills the happiness His Son inherited
W-pI...193.2:5 Yet it is H. Who gives the means by which
W-pI...193.2:6 It is H. Who answers what His Son would
W-pI...193.3:2 His loving kindness to the Son H. loves.
W-pI...193.8:2 H. would help you forgive yourself. His
W-pI...193.9:2 learn. H. would not leave an unforgiving
W-pI...193.9:3 way. H. would ensure his holy rest remain
W-pI...193.9:4 H. would have all tears be wiped away,
W-pI.193.13:7 the little steps H. asks you take to Him.
W-pI...194.4:1 future as H. holds your past and present.
W-pI...195.2:3 refuse to take the steps which H. directs,
W-pI...195.2:3 and follow in the way H. sets before them,
W-pI...196.8:5 back within the holy mind H. never left.
W-pI...197.1:5 that when H. strikes He will not fail to kill
W-pI...197.1:5 that when He strikes H. will not fail to kill
W-pI...197.4:6 when H. has gratefully accepted them?
W-pI...197.6:2 before H. snatches them away again in
W-pI...197.8:6 is laid. H. holds you dear, because you are
W-pI...197.9:8 But never think that H. has ever ceased to
W-pI...200.7:1 because H. has one Son who cannot make
W-pI...200.9:4 is sure, and H. will guide our footsteps.
W-pI...200.9:5 H. will not desert His Son in need, nor let
W-pI...206.1:3 *And I would give His gifts where H. intended*
W-pI...207.1:2 *me from within my heart, where H. abides.*
W-pI...211.1:2 *it in the Son whom H. created as my Self.* I am
W-pI...214.1:5 *but what H. gives as what belongs to me.* I am
W-pII.....in.2:3 H. has promised He will take the final
W-pII.....in.2:3 has promised H. will take the final step
W-pII.....in.3:3 to reveal Himself, as H. has promised. We
W-pII.....in.3:4 and H. has promised that His Son will not
W-pII.....in.4:1 to take the step to us that H. has told us,
W-pII.....in.4:1 H. would not fail to take when we invited
W-pII.....in.4:2 H. has not left His Son in all his madness,
W-pII.....in.4:3 invitation that H. seeks to make us happy
W-pII.....in.5:6 H. has willed to come to you when you
W-pII.....in.5:6 have recognized it is your will H. do so.
W-pII.....in.8:2 We have found the way H. chose for us,
W-pII.....in.8:2 choice to follow it as H. would have us go.
W-pII.....in.9:1 the Son whom H. created for Himself. We
W-pII.....in.9:7 safely home, where H. would have us be.
W-pII..221.2:3 I am sure that H. will speak to you, and
W-pII..222.1:2 H. is my Source of life, the life within, the
W-pII..222.1:3 H. is my home, wherein I live and move;
W-pII..222.1:4 H. covers me with kindness and with care,
W-pII..222.1:4 and holds in love the Son H. shines upon,
W-pII..222.1:5 knows the truth of what H. speaks today!
W-pII..223.1:3 H. has no Thoughts that are not part of
W-pII.....224.h God is my Father, and H. loves His Son.
W-pII..228.1:3 I accept as true what H. proclaims as false
W-pII..228.1:4 for what I am, since H. is my Creator, and
W-pII..230.1:4 H. created me He gave me peace forever.
W-pII..230.1:4 He created me H. gave me peace forever.
W-pII..235.1:4 I am the Son H. loves. And I am saved
W-pII..239.1:3 Can we see in those with whom H. shares
W-pII..239.1:4 when H. loves His Son forever and with
W-pII..239.1:4 knowing he is as H. created him?
W-pII..245.2:3 share the Word that H. has given unto us.
W-pII......4.3:4 God Himself has lost the Son H. loves,
W-pII..266.2:3 when H. has filled the world with those
W-pII......6.1:1 Christ is God's Son as H. created Him. He
W-pII..276.1:3 become the Father of the Son H. loves, for
W-pII..277.2:5 and God can will that H. deceive Himself.
W-pII..279.2:2 *loves the Son Whom H. created as His Own.*
W-pII......7.5:4 when all H. wills is that you be complete?
W-pII..281.2:4 And I would not attack the Son H. loves,
W-pII..281.2:4 for what H. loves is also mine to love.
W-pII..282.1:4 Whom God created as the Son H. loves,
W-pII......8.5:4 it is H. Who calls to us and comes to take
W-pII..292.1:2 And H. guarantees that only joy can be
W-pII..292.1:4 we will not find the end H. has appointed
W-pII..302.2:2 H. fails in nothing. He the End we seek,
W-pII..302.2:3 H. the End we seek, and He the Means by
W-pII..302.2:3 and H. the Means by which we go to Him.
W-pII....10.3:1 Correction H. bestowed on all your errors
W-pII....10.4:1 to the eternal peace H. shares with him.
W-pII....11.2:2 For H. would add to love by its extension.
W-pII..322.1:4 in Him forever, as H. still abides in me.
W-pII..324.2:4 And it is H. Who makes the ending sure,
W-pII..327.1:2 For God has promised H. will hear my call
W-pII..327.1:5 For thus I will be sure that H. has not
W-pII..344.2:2 God. How near is H. to us. How close the
W-pII..347.2:2 H. has judged you as the Son He loves.
W-pII..347.2:2 He has judged you as the Son H. loves.
W-pII..348.2:1 us in everything that H. would have us do.
W-pII..349.2:2 H. gives us grace to meet them all. And so
W-pII....14.5:1 Word to everyone whom H. has sent to us
W-pII.....354.h And in Him Is His Creator, as H. is in me.
Wfl........in.6:2 Would H. hurt His Son? Or would He
Wfl........in.6:3 Or would H. rush to answer him, and say,
Wfl........in.6:4 Be certain H. will answer thus, for these
M-5 .........I.1:9 His death can H. be conquered by His Son
M-11 .........1:6 Word assures us that H. loves the world.
M-11 .........1:7 H. promises can hardly be impossible.
M-11 .........2:6 Word assures you that H. loves the world;
M-13 .......8:11 Word to you, for H. has need of teachers.
M-17 .......6:11 Him, it seems to you H. has forgotten, too
M-17 .........7:4 Think not H. has forgotten." Here we
M-20 .........5:7 end, and nothing H. did not create is real.
M-20 .........6:7 H. does not seek to keep it for Himself.
M-21 .........5:9 H. Himself gives to the words they use the
M-23 .........4:6 the way in which H. is remembered, for
M-27 .........4:9 H. did not make death because He did not
M-27 .........4:9 make death because H. did not make fear.
M-27 .........5:5 is indeed the death of God, if H. is Love.
M-27 .........5:7 H. is not Father, but destroyer. He is not
M-27 .........5:8 H. is not Creator, but avenger. Terrible
M-27 .......6:11 not see that otherwise H. has an opposite,
M-29 .........6:8 cruel if H. let your words replace His Own
M-29 .........7:5 H. has given you the means to prove it so.
M-29 .........7:8 for waiting implies time and H. is timeless
M-29 .........8:3 *Teacher of God, His thanks H. offers you,*
M-29 .........8:4 *You are the Son H. loves, And it is given you*
C-1.............1:3 of God which H. created like Himself. The
C-2.............1:6 and a wish to be what H. created not. It is
C-2.............2:4 Yet could God's Son as H. created him
C-3.............1:2 It is impossible to think of anything H.
C-3.............2:3 to be an enemy instead of what H. really is
C-3.............3:3 H. is not at all concerned with form, but
C-3.............7:5 And what H. gives is always like Himself.
C-4.............1:2 H. creates must be eternal as Himself. Yet
C-4.............8:3 Here H. leans down to lift you up to Him,
C-5.............1:7 does not help because H. knows no need.
C-5.............1:8 But H. creates all Helpers of His Son while
C-5...........6:12 *bring with you all those whom H. has sent to*
C-6.............1:1 Christ, the Son of God as H. created Him.
C-ep...........2:2 to Him Who loves you as H. loves Himself
C-ep...........3:6 H. has set your Name along with His.
C-ep...........5:5 thanks to Him, as H. gives thanks to us.
P-1...........5:10 for H. would have us all be healed in Him.
P-2.........II.5:3 because H. has been invited to come in. In
P-2.........II.6:5 If any two are joined, H. must be there. It
P-2.........V.4:5 And H. has guaranteed that He will hear
P-2.........V.4:5 guaranteed that H. will hear and answer
P-2.........V.4:6 be sure that healing is a process H. directs
P-2.........V.5:6 H. needs a voice through which to speak
P-2.........V.6:5 For H. has never asked for more than just
P-2.........V.6:7 And H. will send His Answer through the
P-2.....VII.1:12 H. knows is only that He has one Son. His
P-2.....VII.1:12 He knows is only that H. has one Son. His
P-2.......VII.6:1 has given you as to invent one H. has not.
P-3...........I.1:9 of God, and H. knows nothing of sacrifice.
P-3.........I.1:10 ask of Perfection that H. be imperfect?
P-3...........I.2:9 you; H. needs your voice to speak for Him
P-3..........II.4:1 on all H. created and pronounced it good.
P-3..........II.4:2 No, H. declared it perfect, and so it was.
P-3........III.1:1 healing is of God and H. asks for nothing.
S-1...........I.6:7 Him. H. can therefore also reach His Son,
S-2...........I.2:6 that would destroy the holy Son H. loves.
S-2...........I.3:7 H. loves His Son. Can you remember Him
S-2...........I.3:8 remember Him and hate what H. created?
S-2...........I.3:9 his Father if you hate the Son H. loves. For
S-2...........I.8:5 As H. would give, so must you give as well
S-2..........II.4:1 is to separate from God the Son H. loves,
S-2..........II.7:5 of God, and find the peace H. offers you.
S-2........III.1:6 H. but asks for trust and willingness to
S-2........III.1:7 H. gives His Teacher to whoever asks, and
S-2........III.1:9 H. has willed you learn the way to Him,
S-2........III.2:2 is, and how to give it as H. wills it be. Do
S-2........III.4:4 His is a justice H. can understand, but you
S-2........III.4:5 Still will H. give the means to you to learn
S-2........III.7:1 Still does H. know, and that should be
S-2........III.7:5 H. will not leave you comfortless, nor fail
S-2........III.7:6 Name. H. stands beside the door to which
S-2........III.7:8 door; the Son of God as H. created him.
S-3...........I.4:5 H. still can reach His Son, reminding him
S-3........IV.1:6 they know that this is what H. wills. They
S-3........IV.3:3 H. knows the Cause of healing is Himself,
S-3........IV.5:3 and H. is then no longer Cause but only
S-3........IV.5:4 H. is blamed for your deception and your
S-3........IV.5:5 H. Who is Love becomes the source of
S-3........IV.5:8 which H. abandoned to the devil's care,
S-3........IV.5:8 care, swearing H. will deliver it no more.

## He 240

- Christ/Self
  - *God*
  - *Holy Spirit*
  - *he*

T-9.........I.14:7 *Christ is in me, and where H. is God must be,*
T-11....VIII.9:4 of His Father by which H. was created. Be
T-12......VI.4:4 and H. will look upon whatever you see
T-12......VI.5:5 H. is waiting to be seen, for He has never
T-12......VI.5:5 be seen, for H. has never lost sight of you.
T-12......VI.5:6 H. looks quietly on the real world, which
T-12......VI.5:6 which H. would share with you because
T-12......VI.5:6 share with you because H. knows of the
T-12......VI.5:7 this, H. would give you what is yours. In
T-12......VI.5:8 peace H. waits for you at His Father's altar
T-12......VI.6:2 H. knows because He knows His Father's
T-12......VI.6:2 He knows because H. knows His Father's
T-13.......V.9:4 And H. sees for you, as your witness to
T-13.......V.9:5 H. is the Holy Spirit's manifestation,
T-13.......V.9:6 H. loves what He sees within you, and He
T-13.......V.9:6 He loves what H. sees within you, and He
T-13.......V.9:6 sees within you, and H. would extend it.
T-13.......V.9:7 H. will not return unto the Father until
T-13.......V.9:7 the Father until H. has extended your
T-13.......V.9:8 for H. has returned you to the Father with
T-13.....V.10:3 Christ's vision H. beholds Himself. And
T-13.....V.10:4 And seeing what H. is, He knows His
T-13.....V.10:4 seeing what He is, H. knows His Father.
T-13.....V.10:5 Beyond your darkest dreams H. sees
T-13.....V.11:3 for H. is no more alone than they are.
T-13......VI.3:2 you now has no past, for H. is changeless,
T-13......VI.3:3 For if H. is as He was created, there is no
T-13......VI.3:3 For if He is as H. was created, there is no
T-13......VI.3:4 and H. stands revealed in everyone you
T-13....VI.13:4 In your name H. has given for you, and
T-13....VI.13:4 for you, and given you the gifts H. gave.
T-13.....VII.5:9 H. lives within you in the quiet present,
T-13.....VII.5:9 into the world H. holds out to you in love.
T-13....VIII.6:2 And H. will offer them unto His Father as
T-13........X.9:9 and H. offers mercy to every child of God,
T-13........X.9:9 child of God, as H. would have you do.
T-15....VIII.4:7 which H. gives as His Father gives to Him.
T-15......XI.2:3 come. H. comes demanding nothing. No
T-15......XI.2:6 For H. is Host to God. And you need but

T-15...... XI.2:9 the perfect Innocence which H. protects,
T-16...... III.7:5 to your Self, Who teaches you what H. is,
T19... IV.A.2:8 H. would bring peace to everyone, and
T19... IV.A.2:8 how can H. do this except through you?
T19... IV.D.2:2 with joy because H. is in His Father's Love
T19. IV.D.14:2 How holy and how beautiful H. is! You
T19. IV.D.14:3 You thought H. sinned because you cast
T19. IV.D.14:4 Yet still H. holds forgiveness out to you,
T-22.........I.8:6 for never could H. find a home in separate
T-22.........I.8:7 must H. be reborn into His ancient home,
T-22.........I.8:7 so seeming new and yet as old as H., a
T-22.......I.11:2 For H. is always drawn unto Himself.
T-22.......I.11:6 And here can H. return in confidence, for
T-22...... IV.3:8 this holy place H. will return with you,
T-24....... V.1:2 H. looks on what He loves, and knows it
T-24....... V.1:2 He looks on what H. loves, and knows it
T-24....... V.1:3 And thus does H. rejoice at what He sees,
T-24....... V.1:3 And thus does He rejoice at what H. sees,
T-24....... V.1:3 because H. knows that it is one with Him
T-24....... V.3:3 H. is at peace *because* He sees no sin.
T-24....... V.3:3 is at peace *because* H. sees no sin. Identify
T-24....... V.3:4 Him, and what has H. that you have not?
T-24....... V.3:5 H. is your eyes, your ears, your hands,
T-24....... V.3:6 feet. How gentle are the sights H. sees, the
T-24....... V.3:6 are the sights He sees, the sounds H. hears
T-24....... V.3:7 and how lovingly H. walks beside him,
T-24....... V.6:2 H. knows where you are going, and He
T-24....... V.6:2 and H. leads you there in gentleness and
T-24....... V.6:7 H. looked upon you first, but recognized
T-24....... V.6:8 And so H. sought for your completion in
T-24....... V.6:8 living thing that H. beholds and loves.
T-24....... V.7:1 Yet is H. quiet, for He knows that love is
T-24....... V.7:1 quiet, for H. knows that love is in you now
T-24....... V.7:3 H. gives them vision for their sightless
T-24....... V.7:4 H. reaches through them, holding out His
T-24....... V.7:5 And H. rejoices that these sights are yours
T-24....... V.7:6 perfect lack of specialness H. offers you,
T-24....... V.9:4 H. will exchange His certainty for all your
T-24....... V.9:4 if you agree that H. is One with you, and
T-24....... V.9:5 H. is within you, yet He walks beside you
T-24....... V.9:5 you, yet H. walks beside you and before,
T-24....... V.9:5 that H. must go to find Himself complete.
T-24...... VI.6:8 to you. H. *is* set forth within his holiness.
T-24.... VI.10:8 you decide against the holiness H. sees?
T-25.......in.1:2 Yet H. is in you. And thus it must be that
T-25.......in.1:8 is that H. may be made manifest to those
T-25.......in.1:8 that H. may call to them to come to Him
T-25.......in.2:3 a body, where he thinks he is H. cannot be
T-25.......in.2:5 he does not recognize Him where H. is.
T-25.........I.1:1 you to do, since it is H. Who does it. And
T-25....... V.2:10 H. has not gone because your eyes are
T-25..VIII.12:4 so great and holy that H. could not doubt
T-25..VIII.12:5 H. may smile on you whose sinlessness He
T-25..VIII.12:5 smile on you whose sinlessness H. shares.
T-26...... VI.3:4 it is H. Who is your only Friend in truth.
T-26...... VI.3:5 H. brings you gifts that are not of this
T-26...... VI.3:5 only H. to Whom they have been given
T-26...... VI.3:6 H. will place them on your throne, when
T-30....... V.8:3 For H. Whose hand you hold was waiting
T-30....... V.8:4 would H. delay in showing you the way
T-30....... V.8:4 you the way that H. must walk with you?
T-30....VIII.5:9 And when H. has appeared to you, you
T-30....VIII.5:9 for H. is the changeless in your brother
T-31.........I.9:3 certainty with which H. knows His Love.
T-31.......I.10:5 Him answer in the language that H. calls.
T-31.......I.10:6 H. will appear when you have answered
T-31....... II.7:6 Because H. hears one Voice, He cannot
T-31....... II.7:6 H. cannot hear a different answer from
T-31....... II.7:6 the one H. gave when God appointed Him
T-31..... II.11:9 And H. Who travels with you *has* the light.
T-31....VIII.1:6 For H. *has* come, and He *is* asking this.
T-31....VIII.1:6 For He *has* come, and H. *is* asking this.
T-31....VIII.2:7 and H. has given you His strength instead
T-31....VIII.3:3 H. would not leave one source of pain
T-31....VIII.3:4 H. would remove all misery from you
T-31....VIII.3:5 H. would not leave you comfortless, alone
T-31....VIII.3:6 Holiness is yours because H. is the only
T-31....VIII.3:7 His strength is yours because H. is the Self
T-31....VIII.4:6 And what they will is only what H. wills.

W-pI... 100.9:1 H. will be there. And you can reach Him
W-pI... 107.8:1 upon this undertaking that H. be in your
W-pI... 107.8:3 H. is your Brother, and so like to you your
W-pI... 107.8:4 how could H. be absent where you are?
W-pI. 107.11:2 release the world, as H. would set you free
W-pI... 110.9:5 yourself while H. is unacknowledged and
W-pI. 110.10:2 H. will be your Savior from all idols you
W-pI. 152.11:5 ask our Self that H. reveal Himself to us.
W-pI. 152.11:6 And H. Who never left will come again to
W-pI. 153.19:4 that H. remains beside us through the day
W-pI. 153.19:6 We will pause a moment, as H. tells us, "I
W-pI... 157.4:1 H. will direct your practicing today, for
W-pI... 157.4:1 for what you ask for now is what H. wills.
W-pI... 158.5:4 H. has a vision He can give to anyone who
W-pI... 158.5:4 a vision H. can give to anyone who asks.
W-pI... 159.8:5 the love with which H. looks on them.
W-pI... 160.9:5 And H. leads them gently home again,
W-pI. 160.10:2 Not one H. fails to give you to remember,
W-pI. 160.10:3 H. has not forgotten you. But you will not
W-pI. 160.10:4 Him until you look on all as H. does. Who
W-pI. 161.12:1 H. will answer Whom you called upon.
W-pI. 161.12:2 For H. will hear the Voice for God in you,
W-pI... 164.1:4 H. looks past time, and sees eternity as
W-pI... 164.1:5 H. hears the sounds the senseless, busy
W-pI... 164.1:5 engenders, yet H. hears them faintly. For
W-pI... 164.1:6 them all H. hears the song of Heaven, and
W-pI... 164.2:3 call to which H. gives an ancient answer.
W-pI... 164.3:1 answers in your name the Call H. hears!
W-pI... 164.3:4 who will today accept the gifts H. gives.
W-pI... 164.8:3 H. has need of your most holy mind to
W-pI... 166.8:3 in exile? H. would make you laugh at this
W-pI. 166.11:4 H. points to all the gifts you have each
W-pI. 166.12:1 H. reminds you still of one thing more
W-pI. 166.12:4 What H. has come to offer you, you now
W-pI. 166.12:5 for H. has saved you from the solitude you
W-pI. 166.12:6 H. has reminded you of all the gifts that
W-pI. 166.12:7 H. speaks as well of what becomes your
W-pI. 170.12:1 to Christ, and H. looks through them.
W-pI... 181.8:5 Love H. feels for us becomes our own as
W-pI... 182.4:3 house, and knows that H. is alien here.
W-pI... 182.5:3 H. desires to go home so deeply, so
W-pI... 182.5:4 H. does not ask for more than just a few
W-pI... 182.5:4 just an interval in which H. can return to
W-pI... 182.5:6 H. will return. But give Him just a little
W-pI... 182.6:2 H. is far from home. He is so little that He
W-pI... 182.6:3 H. is so little that He seems so easily shut
W-pI... 182.6:3 is so little that H. seems so easily shut out,
W-pI... 182.6:4 Yet does H. know that in you still abides
W-pI... 182.6:6 H. will go home, and you along with Him.
W-pI... 182.7:2 H. trusts in you. He came because He
W-pI... 182.7:3 H. came because He knew you would not
W-pI... 182.7:3 came because H. knew you would not fail.
W-pI... 182.7:4 H. whispers of His home unceasingly to
W-pI... 182.7:5 For H. would bring you back with Him,
W-pI... 182.7:5 with Him, that H. Himself might stay,
W-pI... 182.7:5 return again where H. does not belong,
W-pI... 182.7:5 and where H. lives an outcast in a world
W-pI... 182.7:7 H. will wait until you hear His gentle
W-pI... 182.7:7 to where H. is at home and you with Him.
W-pI... 182.8:2 So poignantly H. calls to you that you will
W-pI... 182.8:3 that instant H. will take you to His home,
W-pI... 182.9:2 For H. was willing to become a little Child
W-pI... 182.9:3 H. holds the might of Heaven in His hand
W-pI... 182.9:3 they may see H. would be Friend to them.
W-pI... 182.9:4 H. asks that they protect Him, for His
W-pI... 182.9:4 far away, and H. will not return to it alone
W-pI. 182.10:4 You are as much an alien here as H..
W-pI. 182.11:3 H. has even come to ask your help in
W-pI. 182.11:4 H. has come as does a little child, who
W-pI. 182.11:5 H. rules the universe, and yet He asks
W-pI. 182.11:5 H. asks unceasingly that you return with
W-pI. 182.12:7 Today H. gives you His defenselessness,
W-pI... 197.7:2 for this, for H. is grateful only unto God,
W-pI... 197.7:2 and H. gives thanks for you unto Himself.
W-pII . 237.2:1 *and H. the ears that listen to the Voice for*
W-pII . 238.1:5 *of You, and yet is mine, because H. is my Self.*
W-pII ..... 6.1:2 H. is the Self we share, uniting us with
W-pII ..... 6.1:3 well. H. is the Thought which still abides
W-pII ..... 6.1:4 H. has not left His holy home, nor lost the

W-pII ..... 6.1:4 the innocence in which H. was created.
W-pII ..... 6.1:5 H. abides unchanged forever in the Mind
W-pII ..... 6.2:3 H. is the part in which God's Answer lies;
W-pII ..... 6.2:4 H. remains untouched by anything the
W-pII ..... 6.2:5 yet does H. remain the Self Who, like His
W-pII . 271.1:4 for nothing that H. looks on but must live
W-pII . 271.2:2 *What H. beholds invites Your memory to be*
W-pII . 295.1:1 asks that H. may use my eyes today, and
W-pII . 295.1:2 H. asks this gift that He may offer peace of
W-pII . 295.1:2 He asks this gift that H. may offer peace of
W-pII . 303.1:4 Christ be welcomed where H. is at home.
W-pII . 303.1:5 let Him hear the sounds H. understands,
W-pII . 303.1:6 here, for H. is born again in me today.
W-pII . 303.2:2 *H. has come to save me from the evil self I*
W-pII . 303.2:3 *H. is the Self that You have given me. He is*
W-pII . 303.2:4 *H. is but what I really am in truth. He is the*
W-pII . 303.2:5 *H. is the Son You love above all things. He is*
W-pII . 303.2:6 *H. is my Self as You created me. It is not*
W-pII . 308.1:7 H. has come to give His present blessing
W-pII . 313.1:5 *for H. sees no sin in anything He looks upon.*
W-pII . 313.1:5 *for He sees no sin in anything H. looks upon.*
W-pII . 330.1:6 us choose today that H. be our Identity,
W-pII . 353.1:2 *alone, for H. and I have joined in purpose.*
W-pII . 354.1:4 *And H. is like His Father. Thus must I be one*
M-14 ......... 2:6 H. brings the ending of the world with
C-5 ............ 2:6 And Christ needed his form that H. might
C-6 ............ 5:5 H. offers thanks to you as well as him for
C-ep .......... 5:2 had lost our way but H. has found it for us
S-1..........II.5:2 And who could H. be except yourself? The
S-2...........I.6:7 H. does not know of shadows. His the
S-2...........I.7:2 be. You are in need of what H. gives, and
S-2...........I.7:7 For what H. has forgiven has not sinned,
S-2..........II.7:7 Christ is for all because H. is in all. It is
S-2........ III.2:5 any form, H. is the One to answer for you.
S-2........ III.2:7 and it is H. Who will respond for you.
S-2........ III.3:2 H. knows the way to make of every call a
S-2........ III.3:3 Now can H. make your footsteps sure,
S-2........ III.5:6 H. knows the need; the question and the
S-2........ III.5:7 H. will say exactly what to do, in words
S-2........ III.5:9 H. is the Answer. You the one who hears.
S-2........ III.6:1 And what is it H. speaks to you about?
S-2........ III.6:6 For H. will be heard by anyone who calls
S-3........ IV.7:1 H. comes for Me and speaks My Word to

## He 779

• Holy Spirit
*God*
*Christ/Self*
*he*

T-1 ........I.38:2 H. recognizes both God's creations and
T-1 ........I.38:3 H. separates the true from the false by His
T-2 .........V.7:5 H. also looks immediately toward the
T-2 .........V.7:6 Nothing H. perceives can induce fear.
T-2 ... V.A.18:4 *to do, because H. Who sent me will direct me*
T-2 ... V.A.18:5 *me. I am content to be wherever H. wishes,*
T-2 ... V.A.18:5 *He wishes, knowing H. goes there with me. I*
T-5 ..........I.3:3 is in your right mind, as H. was in mine.
T-5 ..........I.4:2 H. is referred to as the Healer, the
T-5 ..........I.4:3 Guide. H. is also described as something
T-5 ..........I.4:4 Comforter and h. will abide with you."
T-5 ..........I.4:8 so close to knowledge that H. calls it forth
T-5 ..........I.5:2 H. came into being with the separation as
T-5 ..........I.6:4 Atonement. H. represents a state of mind
T-5 .........II.2:2 H. is the Call to return with which God
T-5 .........II.5:6 for Him because H. could no longer share
T-5 .........II.8:2 H. is in the part of your mind that always
T-5 .........II.8:2 right choice, because H. speaks for God.
T-5 .........II.8:3 H. is your remaining communication with
T-5 .......II.12:3 H. teaches you how to keep me as the
T-5 ....... III.1:4 H. is part of the Holy Trinity, because His
T-5 ....... III.5:6 H. undoes it at the same level on which
T-5 ....... III.7:3 the laws of God, for which H. speaks. He
T-5 ....... III.7:4 H. can therefore perform the function of
T-5 ....... III.7:6 in light because H. is in you who are light,
T-5 ..... III.10:2 H. uses only what your mind already
T-5 ..... III.10:5 the place in the mind where H. is at home.
T-5 ..... III.11:3 H. must work through opposites, because
T-5 ..... III.11:3 H. must work with and for a mind that is

T-5......III.11:6 looks, and understand as H. understands.
T-5......III.11:8 H. is in communion with God always, and
T-5......III.11:8 with God always, and H. is part of you. He
T-5......III.11:9 H. is your Guide to salvation, because He
T-5......III.11:9 H. holds the remembrance of things past
T-5....III.11:10 H. holds this gladness gently in your
T-5......IV.3:11 purified H. lets you give them away. The
T-5........VI.6:1 ye reap" H. interprets to mean what you
T-5........VI.8:3 in later generations H. can still reinterpret
T-5......VI.10:7 hear it, because H. can only witness truly.
T-5......VI.10:8 because H. was given to you to remind
T-5......VI.12:6 H. reminds you of this in every passing
T-5......VI.12:7 H. is the only blessing you can truly give,
T-5......VI.12:7 can truly give, because H. is truly blessed.
T-5......VI.12:8 H. has been given you freely by God, you
T-6.........II.5:2 is shared H. recognizes it in others, thus
T-6.........II.9:7 well. H. can inspire perception and lead it
T-6.......II.10:2 Coming from God H. uses everything for
T-6.......II.10:2 but H. does not believe in what is not true
T-6.......II.10:4 only for this, because H. speaks for God.
T-6.......II.10:5 H. tells you to return your whole mind to
T-6.......II.11:9 H. perceives only what is true in your
T-6.......II.12:5 Wherever H. looks He sees Himself, and
T-6.......II.12:5 Wherever He looks H. sees Himself, and
T-6.......II.12:5 H. is united He offers the whole Kingdom
T-6.......II.12:5 He is united H. offers the whole Kingdom
T-6.......II.12:6 gave to Him and for which H. must speak,
T-6.......II.12:6 He must speak, because that is what H. is.
T-6........III.1:4 nothing, H. presents no barrier to the
T-6........IV.1:5 as the Holy Spirit will be glad when H. has
T-6........IV.3:2 does not speak first, *but H. always answers.*
T-6........IV.3:4 answers truly H. answers for all time,
T-6.........V.1:1 but H. teaches only to make you equal
T-6.........V.4:1 because H. does not frighten children,
T-6.........V.4:2 Yet H. always answers their call, and His
T-6.........V.4:5 H. merely shines them away. His light is
T-6......V.A.2:5 H. reinterprets what the ego uses as an
T-6......V.A.3:2 H. always tells you that only the mind is
T-6......V.A.5:1 just as H. ultimately translates perception
T-6... V.A.5:11 H. never takes anything back, because He
T-6... V.A.5:11 back, because H. wants you to keep it.
T-6......V.C.1:2 H. sorts out the true from the false in your
T-6......V.C.1:3 is in accord with this light H. retains, to
T-6......V.C.1:4 in accord with it H. accepts and purifies.
T-6......V.C.1:5 entirely H. rejects by judging against. This
T-6......V.C.1:6 is how H. keeps the Kingdom perfectly
T-6....V.C.1:10 and so the one mood H. engenders is joy.
T-6....V.C.1:11 H. protects it by rejecting everything that
T-6....V.C.1:11 so H. alone can keep you wholly joyous.
T-6......V.C.2:1 H. does not want you to teach error and
T-6......V.C.2:2 yourself. H. would hardly be consistent if
T-6......V.C.2:2 hardly be consistent if H. allowed you to
T-6......V.C.2:3 of the thinker, then, H. *is* judgmental
T-6......V.C.5:8 H. is getting you ready for the translation
T-7...........I.6:6 H. can therefore tell you something about
T-7.........II.5:2 H. translates only to preserve the original
T-7.........II.5:3 H. opposes the idea that differences in
T-7.........II.6:4 I said before that H. teaches remembering
T-7........III.1:2 H. maximizes all efforts and all results. By
T-7........III.1:3 H. teaches you that all power is yours. Its
T-7........IV.2:1 work *through* you to teach you H. is *in* you.
T-7........IV.4:2 H. uses them only for healing, because He
T-7........IV.4:2 because H. knows you only as whole. By
T-7.........V.3:2 in this world, and the only one H. accepts.
T-7.........V.3:3 H. recognizes no other, because He does
T-7.........V.3:3 H. does not accept the ego's confusion of
T-7........V.11:6 H. calls upon you to love God and His
T-7........VI.6:1 because H. cannot perceive them at all.
T-7........VI.6:3 H. resolves the apparent conflict they
T-7........VI.6:5 conflict; H. wants you to realize that,
T-7.......VII.7:2 and H. teaches the same lesson to all. He
T-7.......VII.7:3 all. H. always teaches you the inestimable
T-7.......VII.7:3 of the infinite Love for which H. speaks.
T-7.........X.3:3 you want to listen to what H. says. You no
T-7........XI.1:2 Will for everyone because H. speaks for
T-8.........II.5:2 That is the same as saying H. teaches you
T-8.........II.6:3 H. cannot conceive of God without you,
T-8........III.1:6 is no limit on His teaching because H. was
T-8........III.1:7 function perfectly H. fulfills it perfectly,
T-8.........V.6:2 minds, and the one H. taught me is yours.
T-8.......VII.2:2 you have made in the light of what H. is.
T-8.......VII.3:6 H. knows the only reality of anything is
T-8.......VII.5:9 which H. has established as part of you.
T-8.......VIII.4:7 and one H. is perfectly equipped to fulfill.
T-8.......VIII.9:1 so H. can teach His message through you.
T-8........IX.1:2 H. is the Answer to everything, because
T-8........IX.1:2 H. knows what the answer to everything
T-8........IX.5:3 for if H. taught that one form of sickness
T-8........IX.5:3 H. would be teaching that one error can
T-9...........I.3:7 H. is not attempting to force an alien will
T-9...........I.3:8 H. is merely making every possible effort,
T-9...........I.4:2 I meant that H. has the power to look into
T-9...........I.4:3 it real to you because H. is in your mind,
T-9...........I.4:3 mind, and therefore H. is your reality. If,
T-9...........I.4:4 H. *is* helping you to remember what you
T-9...........I.8:7 H. cannot give you something you do not
T-9.........I.10:1 Spirit for what would hurt you H. cannot
T-9.......II.6:11 as H. answers all of God's Sons? Hear of
T-9.......II.12:3 H. will deny you nothing because you
T-9........III.3:4 Since H. does not understand it, He does
T-9........III.3:4 not understand it, H. does not judge it,
T-9........III.4:2 H. has merely disregarded them, and if
T-9......III.8:10 it. H. will teach you how to see yourself
T-9........IV.3:3 H. translates what you have made into
T-9........IV.5:6 H. teaches that the ego does not exist and
T-9........IV.6:1 and H. knows how to fulfill it perfectly.
T-9.........V.8:5 H. makes healing clear in any situation in
T-9.........V.8:5 in any situation in which H. is the Guide.
T-9.........V.8:7 H. needs no help for this. He will tell you
T-9.........V.8:8 H. will tell you exactly what to do to help
T-9.........V.8:8 to help anyone H. sends to you for help,
T-9.......V.8:11 for help is His function, and H. is of God.
T-9........VI.2:4 H. cannot go beyond your offering in His
T-9........VI.2:5 This is not because H. limits His giving,
T-9.......VII.3:1 Spirit looks with love on all H. perceives,
T-9.......VII.3:1 all He perceives, H. looks with love on you
T-9.......VII.3:2 you are, and so H. evaluates you truly.
T-9.......VII.3:3 must be in your mind, because H. is. The
T-9.......VII.4:3 is. H. is not deceived by anything you do,
T-9.......VII.4:3 do, because H. never forgets what you are.
T-9.......VII.7:6 because H. knows its foundation is not
T-9.......VII.7:8 H. judges every belief you hold in terms of
T-9.......VII.7:9 it comes from God, H. knows it to be true.
T-9.....VII.7:10 does not, H. knows that it is meaningless.
T-9.....VIII.9:5 What H. cannot transform to the Will of
T-9... VIII.11:6 *is.* Ask the Holy Spirit what it is and H. will
T-10.......II.2:3 for H. retains the knowledge of God and
T-11.........I.8:7 Will is for you, and H. will tell you yours.
T-11.......I.11:1 Holy Spirit only because H. speaks for you
T-11.......I.11:2 H. is the Voice for God, but never forget
T-11.......II.4:3 H. will enable you to go far beyond the
T-11.......II.4:3 your small willingness to make whole H.
T-11.......II.5:1 host, because H. will not be heard. The
T-11.......II.5:3 H. needs your protection, only because
T-11.......II.5:4 mind so that H. becomes your only Guest.
T-11.......II.5:6 H. will remain, but you have allied
T-11.......II.5:7 you choose to take, H. will go with you,
T-11.......II.5:8 for H. cannot leave a part of God. Yet you
T-11.......II.6:7 H. will lighten it so much that you will
T-11.......II.7:5 although H. cannot help you without your
T-11... VIII.2:4 it, H. will restore to you what you have
T-11. VIII.12:4 H. would save you from all condemnation
T-11. VIII.12:5 power and use it for all H. sends you, for
T-11. VIII.12:5 you, for H. wills to heal the Son of God, in
T-11. VIII.12:5 Son of God, in whom H. is not deceived.
T-11. VIII.14:9 it, and H. will tell you what they are. For
T-12.........I.6:7 it is. H. does not change His Mind about
T-12.........I.6:9 H. gives them to you because they are *for*
T-12.........I.8:7 H. has taught you that fear itself is an
T-12.........I.8:9 you do not protect it, H. will reinterpret it
T-12.......II.9:3 in the peace out of which H. was created.
T-12.......II.9:7 Spirit will judge, and H. will judge truly.
T-12.......II.9:8 Yet H. cannot shine away what you keep
T-12.......II.9:8 it to Him and H. cannot take it from you.
T-12.....II.10:2 H. knows what to do with it. You do not
T-12.....II.10:3 understand how to use what H. knows.
T-12.....II.10:6 Surely H. will not fail to help you, since
T-12......IV.4:6 goal H. sets before you He will give you.
T-12......IV.4:6 goal He sets before you H. will give you.
T-12......IV.4:7 For H. will never deceive God's Son whom
T-12......IV.4:7 whom H. loves with the Love of the Father
T-12......IV.5:5 H. will guide you to your home because
T-12......IV.5:6 As H. fulfills His mission He will teach
T-12......IV.5:6 fulfills His mission H. will teach you yours
T-12.......V.5:3 H. becomes your Resource because of
T-12......VI.2:1 Holy Spirit is your strength because H.
T-12......VI.2:2 you. H. is perfectly aware that you do not
T-12......VI.2:3 Because H. loves you, He will gladly teach
T-12......VI.2:3 H. will gladly teach you what He loves, for
T-12......VI.2:3 He will gladly teach you what H. loves, for
T-12......VI.2:3 you what He loves, for H. wills to share it.
T-12......VI.2:4 H. cannot let you forget your worth. For
T-12......VI.4:2 for H. knows that they have not lost their
T-12......VI.4:3 H. would awaken them from the sleep of
T-12......VI.4:6 and H. longs to share His vision with you.
T-12......VI.4:7 H. will show you the real world because
T-12.....VII.3:1 them you will learn that H. is there. What
T-12.....VII.3:2 What H. enables you to do is clearly not
T-12.....VII.3:4 you will understand where H. must be,
T-12.....VII.3:4 He must be, and finally know what H. is.
T-12.....VII.4:2 you do, you will not realize H. is there.
T-12.....VII.6:2 For H. will send you His witnesses if you
T-12...VII.12:7 His function only by judging as H. does,
T-12...VII.12:8 against yourself, but H. will judge *for* you.
T-12....VIII.6:6 it. Yet what H. does see is yours to behold,
T-12....VIII.7:5 H. has remembered you because He forgot
T-12....VIII.7:5 you because H. forgot not the Father. You
T-13.........I.1:2 H. seeks to remove all guilt from his mind
T-13.........I.4:4 where you must be because H. is with you
T-13.........I.4:5 you. H. has already undone everything
T-13.......I.11:5 As H. looks upon the guiltless Son of God,
T-13.......I.11:5 Son of God, H. knows that this is true.
T-13......III.7:6 For H. will heal every little thought you
T-13......IV.7:4 unnecessary. H. regards the function of
T-13...VII.10:9 H. knows what you have need of and what
T-13...VII.12:2 For H. will give you all things that do not
T-13...VII.12:4 H. gives you all the things that you need
T-13...VII.12:5 H. will take nothing from you as long as
T-13...VII.12:6 yet H. knows that everything you need is
T-13...VII.12:7 Therefore H. has no investment in the
T-13...VII.12:7 investment in the things that H. supplies,
T-13...VII.12:8 H. knows that you are not at home there,
T-13...VII.12:8 H. wills no delay to wait upon your joyous
T-13...VII.13:2 H. will supply them with no emphasis at
T-13...VII.13:3 H. will ensure it never can become a dark
T-13...VII.15:1 faith that H. will lead you safely through
T-13....VIII.1:3 H. teaches that the past does not exist, a
T-13....VIII.4:2 H. is not separate from either, being in
T-13....VIII.4:3 One. H. is a Thought of God, and God has
T-13........X.2:8 Him, H. cannot use it for your release. No
T-13........X.7:1 demonstrate what H. has saved you from.
T-13........X.7:2 What H. has saved you from is gone. Give
T-13........X.7:5 so. H. has seen separation, but knows of
T-13........X.7:6 H. teaches healing, but He also knows of
T-13........X.7:6 healing, but H. also knows of creation. He
T-13........X.7:7 H. would have you see and teach as He
T-13........X.7:7 would have you see and teach as H. does,
T-13........X.7:8 Yet what H. knows you do not know,
T-13..... X.10:9 H. would remove only illusions. All else
T-13... X.10:10 All else H. would have you see. And in
T-13... X.10:11 And in Christ's vision H. would show you
T-13......XI.4:5 H. has perfect faith in your final judgment
T-13......XI.4:5 H. knows that He will make it for you. To
T-13......XI.4:5 He knows that H. will make it for you. To
T-13.....XI.11:3 and one H. will effect as surely as the ego
T-14.........I.3:9 leads to nothing, for H. knows everything.
T-14.........I.4:2 Anything you deny that H. knows to be
T-14.........I.4:2 H. must therefore teach you not to deny it
T-14.........I.5:2 H. must introduce the simple truth into a
T-14.........I.5:3 H. merely looks at its foundation and
T-14........II.4:2 Like God, H. knows it to be true. He
T-14........II.4:3 true. H. brings the light of truth into the
T-14.... III.11:3 when H. Who gives you everything will
T-14.... III.11:4 H. will never ask what you have done to
T-14.... III.11:6 answer, for H. knows that you are worthy
T-14.... III.11:7 God H. so freely and so gladly offers you.
T-14.... III.11:8 H. offers you but what God gave Him for

T-14.... III.13:6 Friend. H. is the strong protector of the
T-14.... III.14:2 H. knows the way, and leads you gladly
T-14.... III.14:6 H. has not forgotten it. Forget Him not
T-14.... III.14:7 and H. will make every decision for you,
T-14.... III.17:2 H. leaves you no one outside you. And so
T-14.... III.17:3 you. And so H. gives you what is yours,
T-14.... III.19:2 *H. leadeth me and knows the way, which I*
T-14.... III.19:3 *H. will never keep from me what He would*
T-14.... III.19:3 *will never keep from me what H. would have*
T-14.... III.19:4 *to me all that H. knows for me.* Then let Him
T-14...... IV.5:4 God, and for your function as H. knows it.
T-14...... IV.5:5 So will H. teach you to remove the awful
T-14...... IV.6:5 H. knows. And He will tell you, and then
T-14...... IV.6:6 And H. will tell you, and then do it for
T-14.... IV.10:3 because only H. shares the knowledge of
T-14.... IV.10:4 for you, for only H. knows what God is.
T-14..... V.1:11 H. speaks of you to *you.* There is no guilt in
T-14....... V.2:6 you do, but H. Who knows is with you.
T-14....... V.2:7 share with God H. holds in trust for you.
T-14....... V.2:8 H. would teach you nothing except how
T-14..... V.10:8 gentleness H. would release from fear and
T-14...... VI.5:4 H. knows you are not separate from God,
T-14...... VI.5:4 but H. perceives much in your mind that
T-14...... VI.5:5 nothing else would H. separate from you.
T-14...... VI.5:6 H. would teach you how to use on your
T-14...... VI.6:7 H. will interpret it to you with perfect
T-14...... VI.6:7 H. knows with Whom you are in perfect
T-14...... VI.7:3 H. will not attempt to communicate the
T-14...... VI.7:4 H. will separate out all that has meaning,
T-14...... VI.8:2 H. therefore must remove whatever
T-14...... VI.8:3 sight, for H. will not attack your sentinels.
T-14... VII.5:11 to peace by wondering how H. can fulfill
T-14... VII.5:14 asked to do the little H. suggests you do,
T-14... VII.5:14 small extent of believing that, if H. asks it,
T-14... VII.5:15 will see how easily all that H. asks can be
T-14..... VII.6:3 away. At your request H. enters gladly. He
T-14..... VII.6:4 H. brings the light to darkness if you
T-14..... VII.6:5 But what you hide H. cannot look upon.
T-14..... VII.6:6 H. sees for you, and unless you look with
T-14..... VII.6:6 unless you look with Him H. cannot see.
T-14..... VII.6:9 H. holds the light, and you the darkness.
T-14... VII.6:11 and H. will give it to you as you join your
T-14.... VIII.1:6 H. would save for glory *is* saved for it. He
T-14.... VIII.1:7 H. has promised the Father that through
T-14.... VIII.1:8 H. promised God He is wholly faithful, for
T-14.... VIII.1:8 He promised God H. is wholly faithful, for
T-14.... VIII.1:8 for H. shares with God the promise that
T-14.... VIII.2:1 H. shares it still, for you. Everything that
T-14.... VIII.2:2 H. will replace with the one promise given
T-14.. VIII.2:11 H. shines not in division, but in the
T-14.... VIII.3:3 H. will surely lead you to where God and
T-14..... X.10:4 the answer with which H. answers you.
T-14...... XI.4:7 Who teaches light H. will accept from you
T-14...... XI.4:8 And H. will gladly exchange each one for
T-14...... XI.4:8 the bright lesson H. has learned for you.
T-14.... XI.6:11 you. H. will take His rightful place in your
T-14...... XI.9:1 you give H. would withhold from you?
T-14...... XI.9:2 have no problems that H. cannot solve by
T-14...... XI.9:5 H. has brought all of them to light, having
T-14...... XI.9:6 are no dark lessons H. has not already
T-14...... XI.9:7 lessons you would teach yourself H. has
T-14.... XI.9:10 H. does not see time as you do. And each
T-14.... XI.9:11 miracle H. offers you corrects your use of
T-14.... XI.10:1 H. Who has freed you from the past
T-14.... XI.10:2 of it. H. would but have you accept His
T-14.... XI.10:2 as yours, because H. did them for you.
T-14.... XI.10:3 And because H. did, they *are* yours. He has
T-14.... XI.10:4 H. has made you free of what you made.
T-14.... XI.10:6 H. always gives His gifts in place of yours.
T-14.... XI.10:7 H. would establish His bright teaching so
T-14.... XI.10:7 H. has established as holy by His Presence
T-14.... XI.10:8 that H. is there and works through you.
T-14.. XI.10:10 H. offers you a miracle with every one you
T-14.... XI.11:5 For H. teaches the miracle of oneness, and
T-14.... XI.14:3 desert Him but H. will never reciprocate,
T-14.... XI.14:4 and H. knows that faith in His Creator
T-14.... XI.14:5 His Holiness which H. cannot abandon,
T-14.... XI.14:6 H. gives the gift of peace to everyone who
T-14.... XI.15:3 mighty works that H. will do through you,

T-15 ........I.1:4 H. has not fulfilled His teaching function
T-15 ......I.11:3 H. asks no more, for He has no need of
T-15 ......I.11:3 asks no more, for H. has no need of more.
T-15 ......I.11:5 exchange for this instant H. stands ready
T-15 ......I.13:5 it, H. offers it to you. Be not unwilling to
T-15 ......I.15:2 H. needs but very little to restore God's
T-15 ......I.15:3 to you. H. Who transcends time for you
T-15 .......II.2:7 H. gently translates hell into Heaven. For
T-15 ..... III.6:2 side against Him in what H. wills for you.
T-15 ..... IV.9:9 to the readiness for purity H. offers you.
T-15 ... IV.9:10 offers you. Thus will H. make you ready to
T-15 ...... V.5:2 Yet H. also perceives that you have made
T-15 ...... V.5:2 H. would purify and not let you destroy.
T-15 ...... V.5:3 be, H. can translate them into holiness by
T-15 ..... VI.6:6 H. offered it to me and I accepted it. Fear
T-15 .... VII.5:5 H. can make of them you do not know,
T-15 .. VII.11:2 And how can H. communicate with you,
T-15 .. VII.13:3 And H. will do so, for the power of God in
T-15 ... VIII.1:2 H. must use everything in this world for
T-15 ... VIII.1:3 H. must side with every sign or token of
T-15 ... VIII.1:4 be. H. is swift to utilize whatever you offer
T-15 ... VIII.1:6 which H. perceives as clearly as He knows
T-15 ... VIII.1:6 clearly as H. knows forgiveness is release,
T-15 ... VIII.1:6 is release, H. will teach you to remember
T-15 ... VIII.3:5 H. will not fail you, for He comes from
T-15 ... VIII.3:5 for H. comes from One Who cannot fail.
T-15 ... VIII.5:3 for H. would teach you what you do not
T-15 ... VIII.5:8 yet H. understands it because you made it
T-15 ... VIII.6:3 H. will do this because it is His function.
T-16 ........I.1:5 H. does not understand suffering, and
T-16 ........I.1:6 When H. relates through you, He does
T-16 ........I.1:6 H. does not relate through your ego to
T-16 ........I.1:7 H. does not join in pain, understanding
T-16 ......I.3:11 *I have invited Him, and H. is here. I need do*
T-16 ........I.4:3 H. will not desert you, but be sure that
T-16 ........I.4:4 and accept the fact that H. *does* know. You
T-16 ........I.4:5 You are not sure that H. will do His part,
T-16 ........I.5:6 You are the learner; H. the Teacher. Do
T-16 ........I.6:8 And H. will teach you how to meet both
T-16 ........I.7:6 H. will not meet them secretly, for He
T-16 ........I.7:6 for H. would share everything you give
T-16 ........I.7:7 That is why H. gives it. What you give
T-16 ........I.7:9 H. will fulfill it if you but ask Him to enter
T-16 .......II.4:4 have offered it to Him to use as H. sees fit,
T-16 .......II.5:6 the witnesses that H. has given you to His
T-16 .......II.6:5 bring you the glad tidings H. has come. It
T-16 .......II.9:1 the Holy Spirit H. has not solved for you,
T-16 ..... III.1:4 Therefore H. could look upon it fairly,
T-16 ..... III.1:5 H. must have done so from the basis of a
T-16 ..... III.1:6 For certainly what H. has taught, and
T-16 ..... III.1:6 with what you taught before H. came.
T-16 ..... III.5:2 God, H. left neither God nor His creation.
T-16 ..... III.5:3 H. is both God and you, as you are God
T-16 ..... III.5:5 H. protected both your creations and you
T-16 ... VI.12:2 H. needs only your willingness to share
T-17 ........I.6:4 H. will accomplish it; not you. But forget
T-17 .......II.1:7 upon, and which H. thanks the Father for.
T-17 .......II.1:8 H. was created to see this for you, until
T-17 .......II.5:1 the light of the real reason that H. brings,
T-17 .......II.5:3 H. will show you that there is no reason
T-17 .......II.8:3 you this is so intense H. would not wait,
T-17 .......II.8:3 not wait, although H. waits in patience.
T-17 ..... III.6:3 H. seeks and finds the source of problems
T-17 ..... III.6:5 H. is not at all confused by any "reasons"
T-17 ..... III.6:6 All H. perceives in separation is that it
T-17 ..... III.7:6 because H. knows that only this is true.
T-17 ..... IV.2:4 that is meant by that is that H. will restore
T-17 ...... V.6:5 still believe that H. is there to purify what
T-17 ...... V.6:5 what H. has taken under His guidance?
T-17 ...... V.7:7 H. heard. Has He not been very explicit in
T-17 ...... V.7:8 H. not been very explicit in His answer?
T-17 .... V.7:10 deny that H. has given you a most explicit
T-17 .... V.7:11 Now H. asks for faith a little longer, even
T-17 .... V.11:2 H. could not have entered otherwise.
T-17 .... V.11:4 H. has not been lacking in appreciation
T-17 .... V.11:5 Nor does H. see the mistakes at all. Have
T-17 ..... VI.1:5 Now H. will work with you to make it
T-17 ..... VI.1:6 guidelines H. provides for any situation,
T-17 .... VII.9:5 the goal H. placed there was extended to

T-18 ........I.2:3 H. does not judge between them, knowing
T-18 ........I.8:4 H. brings all your insane projections and
T-18 ........I.8:5 Thus H. reverses the course of insanity
T-18 ........I.9:1 where H. has taken charge of everything
T-18 ........I.9:1 H. has set the course inward to the truth
T-18 .......II.6:5 H. does not destroy it, nor snatch it away
T-18 .......II.6:6 But H. does use it differently, as a help to
T-18 .......II.7:4 Think not that H. has forgotten anyone in
T-18 .......II.7:4 anyone in the purpose H. has given you.
T-18 .......II.7:5 And think not that H. has forgotten you
T-18 .......II.7:5 forgotten you to whom H. gave the gift.
T-18 .......II.7:6 gift. H. uses everyone who calls on Him as
T-18 .......II.7:7 And H. will waken everyone through you
T-18 ..... IV.1:6 give the Holy Spirit what H. does not ask,
T-18 ..... IV.1:7 H. asks but little. It is He Who adds the
T-18 ..... IV.1:8 H. Who adds the greatness and the might
T-18 ..... IV.1:9 H. joins with you to make the holy instant
T-18 ..... IV.6:8 Give Him but what H. asks, that you may
T-18 .......V.2:6 H. will build your part in the Atonement
T-18 .......V.5:5 which H. can spread joy to thousands on
T-18 .......V.5:6 Let Him fulfill the function that H. gave to
T-18 .......V.5:6 would make of it what H. would have it be
T-18 .......V.6:2 H. will never fail in this. But forget not
T-18 .... VII.7:9 H. will remain when you forget, and the
T-18 . VIII.13:3 H. Whom you welcomed has come to you
T-18 . VIII.13:4 you. H. has waited long to give you this.
T-18 . VIII.13:5 of Him, for H. would have you know Him.
T-18 ..... IX.3:9 but H. would lead you safely through and
T-18 ..... IX.8:3 nature as H. leads you past them, for
T-19 ........I.2:4 And since H. shares it He has given it, and
T-19 ........I.2:4 And since He shares it H. has given it, and
T-19 ........I.2:4 has given it, and so H. heals through you.
T-19 ......I.15:1 holy garden that H. would make of it. For
T-19 ..... III.4:2 sin. Mistakes H. recognizes, and would
T-19 ..... III.4:3 to do. But sin H. knows not, nor can He
T-19 ..... III.4:3 nor can H. recognize mistakes that cannot
T-19 ... III.11:1 what H. would show you in your brother,
T-19 ..... IV.1:5 which H. will bring means and goal in line
T-19 ..... IV.1:6 The peace H. lay, deep within you and
T-19 ..... IV.2:5 Him. H. answered you, and entered your
T-19 ..... IV.2:7 For it is H. Who offered your relationship
T-19 ..... IV.3:1 to Him H. asks but that you receive for
T-19 ..... IV.3:3 For you are looking where H. *is,* and not
T19 ... IV.A.5:8 H. Who answered you would call. His
T19 ... IV.B.3:7 Holy Spirit asks, and this H. *would* remove
T19 ... IV.B.9:2 And to accept the peace H. gives instead,
T19 ... IV.B.9:3 For what H. gives must be extended if you
T19 .. IV.D.9:7 let us join in faith that H. Who brought us
T19 IV.D.17:9 H. leadeth you and me together, that we
T-20 .......II.5:5 H. sees no strangers; only dearly loved
T-20 .......II.5:6 H. sees no thorns but only lilies, gleaming
T-20 .......II.5:6 on everything H. looks upon and loves.
T-20 ..... III.6:6 And H. Who watches over all perception
T-20 ..... IV.1:7 Thus would H. keep you free of them.
T-20 ..... IV.6:2 For H. Who knows the rest will see to it
T-20 ..... IV.6:3 But think not that H. does not need your
T-20 ..... IV.8:5 H. will go before you making straight
T-20 .......V.7:9 have faith that H. Who sees the gift in you
T-20 .......V.8:1 and perfect confidence in what H. sees.
T-20 .......V.8:2 H. knows the Son of God, and shares his
T-20 ..... VI.5:7 H. Who sees the face of Christ choose as
T-20 .... VII.3:2 H. asks no more to give the means as well.
T-20 ... VIII.4:8 Spirit offers, where H. will dwell with you
T-20 ... VIII.6:2 everything H. looks upon is always sure.
T-20 . VIII.10:4 sights with which H. would replace them.
T-21 .......II.1:2 Spirit for which H. gives you everything;
T-21 .......II.3:7 even this H. gives to you to give yourself.
T-21 ..... III.4:3 is His direction; the only one H. ever sees.
T-21 ..... III.4:4 wander, H. reminds you there is but one.
T-21 ..... III.6:2 as H. uses them they lead away from sin,
T-21 ..... III.6:3 H. sees the means you use, but not the
T-21 ..... III.6:4 H. would not take them from you, for He
T-21 ..... III.6:4 for H. sees their value as a means for what
T-21 ..... III.6:4 value as a means for what H. wills for you.
T-21 ..... III.9:3 H. makes no bargains. And if you seek to
T-21 ..... III.9:5 The gift that H. has given you is more
T-21 ..... III.9:9 For H. Who loves the world is seeing it for
T-21 ... III.11:2 H. gives not what it is His purpose to lead
T-21 ... III.11:3 think H. would deprive you for your good

T-21......IV.1:2 Errors H. will correct, but this makes no
T-21....... V.5:5 the Holy Spirit can abide, and where H. is.
T-21....... V.5:6 is. H. must have been there since the need
T-21......VI.8:7 the means by which H. would direct you
T-22....... II.8:6 will save. *How* H. will do it is beyond your
T-22......VI.2:4 certain of the outcome as H. is sure of His
T-22......VI.2:5 H. knows this mad decision was made by
T-22......VI.3:1 all to think how H. can change the role of
T-22......VI.6:6 now His means must love all that H. loves
T-22......VI.8:7 your brother, to whom H. offers them,
T-22......VI.8:8 Him. H. will bestow them where they are
T-22......VI.8:9 H. will use every one of them for peace.
T-22......VI.9:5 Save no dark secrets that H. cannot use,
T-22......VI.9:5 Him the tiny gifts H. can extend forever.
T-22......VI.9:6 H. will take each one and make of it a
T-22......VI.9:7 H. will withhold no blessing from it, nor
T-22......VI.9:8 H. will join to it all the power that God
T-23......IV.4:5 mighty. Also H. understands how your
T-25.........I.6:2 H. knows the Will of God and what you
T-25..... II.10:6 And give the Holy Spirit what H. offers
T-25...... III.7:2 to see the world H. made instead of yours.
T-25...... III.8:8 sees what H. sees as far beyond the chance
T-25......VI.4:2 To each H. gives a special function in
T-25... VIII.1:2 But H. cannot use what you withhold, for
T-25... VIII.1:2 H. cannot take it from you without your
T-25... VIII.1:3 if H. did, you would believe He wrested it
T-25... VIII.1:3 believe H. wrested it from you against
T-25... VIII.1:6 But this H. needs; that you prefer He take
T-25... VIII.1:6 prefer H. take it than that you keep it for
T-25... VIII.5:9 Yet how could H. be just if He condemns
T-25... VIII.5:9 Yet how could He be just if H. condemns
T-25. VIII.5:10 justice be if H. demanded of the ones
T-25... VIII.6:2 believe H. shares their own confusion,
T-25... VIII.7:2 Spirit as if H. were a messenger from hell,
T-25... VIII.7:3 What could H. be to them except a devil,
T-25... VIII.7:4 And what escape has H. for them except a
T-25... VIII.8:2 In justice H. is bound to set them free,
T-25... VIII.9:2 Could H., in justice and in love, believe in
T-25... VIII.9:4 No more than what you see H. offers you,
T-25... VIII.9:5 In God's Own justice does H. recognize all
T-25... VIII.9:8 H. knows that Heaven is richer made by
T-25. VIII.11:5 special function H. allots is but for this;
T-25......IX.3:2 because H. asks no sacrifice of anyone. An
T-25......IX.4:3 attack, and loss of any kind H. cannot see.
T-25......IX.7:2 deserving, then is H. ally to specialness.
T-25......IX.7:3 H. cannot perceive He bears no witness to
T-25......IX.7:3 He cannot perceive H. bears no witness to
T-26....... II.1:2 H. has not greater difficulty in resolving
T-26....... II.4:7 And so H. takes the thorns and nails away
T-26....... II.4:8 H. does not pause to judge whether the
T-26....... II.4:9 H. makes but one judgment; that to hurt
T-26..... II.6:10 it can H. ensure that everyone receives it
T-26. VIII.7:10 asks for what H. gave without a cost at all.
T-27..... II.12:4 Yet must H. work with what is given Him,
T-27..... II.12:5 And thus H. represents the other half,
T-27..... II.14:7 And this H. does by giving you and him a
T-27..... II.15:5 And you can rest assured that H. will not
T-27..... II.15:5 that H. does not see and recognize as His.
T-27..... II.15:6 For only thus can H. keep yours preserved
T-27..... II.15:7 is. If H. upheld divided function, you were
T-27..... V.1:11 H. does not speak to someone else. Yet by
T-27..... V.1:12 because you have accepted what H. says.
T-27..... V.10:2 merely to apply what H. has taught you to
T-27..... V.10:2 you to yourself, and H. will do the rest.
T-27......VI.4:2 Neither does H. harken to the witnesses
T-27......VI.4:3 H. knows it is not real. For nothing could
T-27......VI.4:6 Yet must H. love whatever you hold dear.
T-27......VI.4:7 each witness to the body's death H. sends
T-27......VI.4:8 Each miracle H. brings is witness that the
T-27......VI.4:9 Its pains and pleasures does H. heal alike,
T-27...VII.14:4 H. brings forgiving dreams, in which the
T-27...VII.14:5 dreams H. brings there is no murder and
T-27... VIII.9:2 How else could H. correct your error, who
T-27... VIII.9:3 H. bids you bring each terrible effect to
T-27... VIII.9:4 judge effects, but *H.* has judged their cause
T-27. VIII.11:3 Whatever hurt you bring to Him H. will
T-27. VIII.11:5 H. would teach you but the single cause of
T-27. VIII.12:2 H. sees no differences where none exists,
T-27. VIII.12:2 H. will teach you how each one is caused.

T-28.........I.5:2 H. does not seek to use it as a means to
T-28.........I.8:2 because H. let It not be unremembered. It
T-28.........I.8:3 never was a time in which H. did not keep
T-28.......I.12:1 H. to Whom time is given offers thanks
T-28.......I.12:3 gladly does H. offer them unto the one for
T-28.......I.12:3 the one for whom H. has been given them
T-28..... II.10:2 what H. would have you learn, and shows
T-28......IV.7:1 and H. is One because there is no gap that
T-28......IV.8:2 does H. hold out to every separate piece
T-28......IV.8:3 To each H. offers his Identity, which the
T-28....IV.10:9 H. will place the miracle of healing where
T-29....... II.4:2 You asked Him, and H. came. You did not
T-29....... II.4:5 H. has laid them at your feet, and asks
T-29....... II.4:6 H. needs your help in giving them to all
T-29....... II.5:2 Yet H. Who entered in but waits for you
T-29....... II.5:3 no other place where H. can find His host,
T-29....... II.5:5 where H. is Who brought them with Him,
T-29....... II.5:6 but you can see the gifts H. brought. And
T-29......IV.6:5 of the dream as H. perceives its function,
T-29......IV.6:6 Because H. loves the dreamer, not the
T-30....... II.1:2 H. tells you but your will; He speaks for
T-30....... II.1:2 tells you but your will; H. speaks for you.
T-30....... II.1:4 And all H. knows is but your knowledge,
T-30... VIII.4:7 and H. Who gives all miracles has not
T-31..... V.11:6 So H. merely asks if just a little question
W-pI.....64.2:2 therefore H. sees another purpose in them
W-pI.....65.4:4 it consistently for the purpose H. shares
W-pI.....66.2:5 H. knows what your function is. He
W-pI.....66.2:6 is. H. knows that it is your happiness.
W-pI.....75.7:3 Believe H. will not fail you now. You have
W-pI.....75.7:5 H. will be with you as you watch and wait.
W-pI.....75.7:6 H. will show you what true vision sees. It
W-pI.....75.7:9 H. will be there. The light has come. You
W-pI.....75.8:2 to look upon the world H. promised you.
W-pI...76.10:3 H. will tell you more. About the Love your
W-pI...76.10:5 you. About the endless joy H. offers you.
W-pI.....97.5:2 H. will not overlook one open mind that
W-pI.....97.5:2 H. will lay them everywhere He knows
W-pI.....97.5:2 will lay them everywhere H. knows they
W-pI.....97.8:2 And H. will speak to you, reminding you
W-pI.....97.8:3 you speak the words H. offers you today,
W-pI.....99.5:5 does H. know one thing must still be true;
W-pI.....99.6:6 Him. H. has one answer to appearances;
W-pI...126.8:4 Him that H. share your practicing in truth
W-pI.126.10:4 you will understand the words H. speaks,
W-pI.126.10:4 recognize H. speaks your words to you.
W-pI.126.11:7 for what H. gives will be received by you.
W-pI.134.15:1 Then choose one brother as H. will direct
W-pI.135.18:2 plan, for H. would never offer pain to you.
W-pI.135.18:4 for death, H. led you gently to eternal life.
W-pI...137.9:3 as you extend the little help H. asks in
W-pI...151.7:2 H. will not tell you that your brother
W-pI...151.7:3 H. passes by such idle witnesses, which
W-pI...151.7:4 H. recognizes only what God loves, and in
W-pI...151.7:4 and in the holy light of what H. sees do all
W-pI...151.7:4 are vanish before the splendor H. beholds
W-pI...151.8:1 for H. has certainty in which there is no
W-pI...151.8:4 H. has judged can only laugh at guilt,
W-pI...151.9:1 thus H. judges you. Accept His Word for
W-pI...151.9:2 are, for H. bears witness to your beautiful
W-pI...151.9:4 What whispers of the ego can H. hear?
W-pI.151.10:1 H. will remove all faith that you have
W-pI.151.10:2 loss. H. gives you vision which can look
W-pI.151.10:3 of God, for H. will judge all happenings,
W-pI.151.11:1 H. will select the elements in them which
W-pI.151.11:2 And H. will reinterpret all you see, and all
W-pI.151.14:1 H. will give them back as miracles which
W-pI.151.15:5 which H. has retranslated in your mind.
W-pI.152.12:2 for H. speaks for you and for your Father.
W-pI.152.12:3 H. will substitute the peace of God for all
W-pI...154.2:2 H. chooses and accepts your part for you.
W-pI...154.2:3 you. H. does not work without your own
W-pI...154.2:4 But H. is not deceived in what you are,
W-pI...154.9:5 H. Who has received for you the messages
W-pI.154.10:3 Him. H. alone can speak to us and for us,
W-pI.154.11:1 practice giving Him what H. would have,
W-pI.154.11:2 us. H. needs our voice that He may speak
W-pI.154.11:2 our voice that H. may speak through us.
W-pI.154.11:3 H. needs our hands to hold His messages,

W-pI.154.11:3 carry them to those whom H. appoints.
W-pI.154.11:4 H. needs our feet to bring us where He
W-pI.154.11:4 needs our feet to bring us where H. wills,
W-pI.154.11:5 H. needs our will united with His Own,
W-pI.154.11:5 be the true receivers of the gifts H. gives.
W-pI...161.3:3 H. may employ them for a purpose which
W-pI...161.3:4 Yet H. can use but what we made, to
W-pI...169.8:2 H. recognized all that time holds, and
W-pI.184.11:3 H. does not forget creation has one Name,
W-pI...186.7:2 And as H. speaks, the image trembles and
W-pI...192.3:6 What H. makes are dreams, but of a kind
W-pI...198.5:3 learn the simple lessons H. would teach,
W-pI.198.13:2 and recognize that H. Who brought us
W-pI.198.13:3 For H. would give to us the gift that God
W-pI...199.7:6 For H. would give you perfect freedom,
WpI rVI.in.7:3 H. will not fail to be available to you, each
WpI rVI.in.7:4 advancing toward the goal H. set for us;
W-pI...215.1:3 *H. walks with me in love. And I give thanks*
W-pII ..... 1.5:2 H. has forgiven you already, for such is
W-pII ..... 1.5:3 function, and forgive whom H. has saved,
W-pII ..... 1.5:3 He has saved, whose sinlessness H. sees,
W-pII ..... 1.5:3 and whom H. honors as the Son of God.
W-pII .236.1:6 to the Holy Spirit to employ as H. sees fit.
W-pII ..... 3.4:3 light, and see the world as H. beholds it.
W-pII .242.1:4 And H. is glad to make no choices for me
W-pII .242.1:5 and it is H. Who knows the way to God.
W-pII .255.1:4 bear witness to the truth of what H. says.
W-pII ..... 6.4:2 H. will exchange them for the final dream
W-pII ..... 7.1:2 Since H. must bridge the gap between
W-pII ..... 7.1:3 Across the bridge that H. provides are
W-pII ..... 7.2:4 guides it to the outcome H. perceives for
W-pII ..... 7.3:3 H. will employ the means you made for
W-pII ..... 7.4:1 where H. has been placed by God, the
W-pII ..... 8.5:2 Now H. waits but that one instant more
W-pII .311.1:6 it. H. will relieve us of the agony of all the
W-pII .347.1:6 *H. sees what I behold, and yet He knows the*
W-pII .347.1:6 *what I behold, and yet H. knows the truth.*
W-pII .347.1:7 *H. looks on pain, and yet He understands it*
W-pII .347.1:7 *on pain, and yet H. understands it is not real,*
W-pII .347.1:8 *H. gives the miracles my dreams would hide*
W-pII347.1:10 *know my will, but H. is sure it is Your Own.*
W-pII347.1:11 *Own. And H. will speak for me, and call Your*
W-pII .351.1:7 *For H. alone gives judgment in Your Name.*
WpII361-5.1:1 a word to help me, H. will give it to me. If
WpII361-5.1:2 If I need a thought, that will H. also give.
WpII361-5.1:4 H. is in charge by my request. And He will
WpII361-5.1:5 And H. will hear and answer me, because
WpII361-5.1:5 because H. speaks for God my Father and
W-ep ......... 1:5 you, be certain that H. has the answer,
W-ep ......... 1:6 H. will not withhold all answers that you
W-ep ......... 1:7 H. knows the way to solve all problems,
W-ep ......... 2:6 thus H. speaks of freedom and of truth.
W-ep ......... 3:3 H. will direct your efforts, telling you
W-ep ......... 4:2 will H. give you pleasures that will pass
W-ep ......... 4:2 for H. gives only the eternal and the good.
W-ep ......... 4:4 H. has earned your trust by speaking daily
W-ep ......... 4:5 H. will continue. Now you walk with Him,
W-ep ......... 4:6 Him, as certain as is H. of where you go;
W-ep ......... 4:6 as sure as H. of how you should proceed;
W-ep ......... 4:6 proceed; as confident as H. is of the goal,
W-ep ......... 5:4 H. will speak for God and for your Self,
W-ep ......... 6:4 H. loves God's Son as we would love him.
W-ep ......... 6:5 H. teaches us how to behold him through
W-ep ......... 6:5 through His eyes, and love him as H. does
M-10 ......... 4:8 H. does know all the facts; past, present
M-10 ......... 4:9 come. H. does know all the effects of His
M-10 ....... 4:10 way. And H. is wholly fair to everyone, for
M-14 ......... 4:8 trusts that H. will show him how to learn
M-16 ......... 7:5 for H. to Whom he turns with all of them
M-18 ......... 2:4 of God. Now H. can remind the world of
M-18 ......... 2:5 Now H. can speak the Word of God to
M-18 ......... 2:6 Now is H. free to teach all minds the truth
M-25 ......... 4:2 and H. can use only genuine abilities.
M-25 ......... 4:4 what H. uses cannot be used for magic.
M-29 ......... 2:7 guidance. Ask and H. will answer. The
M-29 ......... 2:8 is His, and H. alone is fit to assume it. To
M-29 ......... 6:2 H. understands the requests of your heart
M-29 ......... 6:3 attractive to you, H. will respond with evil

M-29 ......... 6:6 H. understands that an attack is a call for
M-29 ......... 6:7 And H. responds with help accordingly.
C-6............ 1:3 H. was "called down upon the earth" in
C-6............ 2:2 is. H. has established Jesus as the leader in
C-6............ 3:3 H. knows because He is part of God; He
C-6............ 3:3 He knows because H. is part of God; He
C-6............ 3:3 H. perceives because He was sent to save
C-6............ 3:3 because H. was sent to save humanity. He
C-6............ 3:4 H. is the great correction principle; the
C-6............ 3:5 H. is the light in which the forgiven world
C-6............ 3:6 seen. H. never forgets the Creator or His
C-6............ 3:7 H. never forgets the Son of God. He never
C-6............ 3:8 H. never forgets you. And He brings the
C-6............ 3:9 And H. brings the Love of your Father to
C-6............ 4:2 H. represents your Self and your Creator,
C-6............ 4:3 H. speaks for God and also for you, being
C-6............ 4:4 therefore it is H. Who proves Them One.
C-6............ 4:5 H. seems to be a Voice, for in that form
C-6............ 4:5 in that form H. speaks God's Word to you
C-6............ 4:6 you. H. seems to be a Guide through a far
C-6............ 4:7 H. seems to be whatever meets the needs
C-6............ 4:8 But H. is not deceived when you perceive
C-6............ 4:9 It is from these H. would deliver you. It is
C-6........... 4:10 is from these that H. would make you safe
P-1............ 1:5 which H. offers His greater gifts to both.
P-1............ 5:5 Holy Spirit uses time as H. thinks best,
P-1............ 5:5 as He thinks best, and H. is never wrong.
P-1............ 5:6 is one of the means H. uses to save time,
P-1............ 5:7 to the help that H. begins and He directs.
P-1............ 5:7 to the help that He begins and H. directs.
P-1............ 5:8 directs. By whatever routes H. chooses, all
P-2........ I.3:4 H. will wait, and His patience is infinite.
P-2........ III.1:5 H. may, however, not be recognized. And
P-3........ III.2:4 will be those from whom H. does not ask.
P-3........ III.8:4 H. will give you endless opportunities to
P-3........ III.8:5 H. will also tell you exactly what your
P-3........ III.8:6 Whoever H. sends you will reach you,
S-3........ III.6:2 kindly remedy to those H. sends to you,
S-3........ IV.1:3 voice, through whom H. speaks for God,
S-3........ IV.1:3 He speaks for God, Whose Voice H. is,–

## he 43

• Jesus
*noise word*
*He*

T-3........... I.1:5 of His Sons to suffer because h. was good.
T-3....... II.5:10 "When h. shall appear (or be perceived)
T-3....... II.5:10 be like him, for we shall see him as h. is."
M-23 ......... 3:5 Is h. still available for help? What did he
M-23 ......... 3:6 What did h. say about this? Remember
M-23 ......... 3:7 it is likely that h. will fail to keep them.
M-23 ......... 5:3 H. has asked for love, but only that he
M-23 ......... 5:3 love, but only that h. might give it to you.
M-23 ......... 5:5 that h. sees in it an image of his Father.
M-23 ......... 5:7 To you h. looks for hope, because in you
M-23 ......... 5:7 h. sees no limit and no stain to mar your
M-23 ......... 5:9 H. has remained with you. Would you not
M-23 ....... 5:11 when h. has made the journey for you?
M-23 ......... 6:9 H. will take you with him, for he did not
M-23 ......... 6:9 take you with him, for h. did not go alone.
M-23 ......... 7:8 then, teach with him, for h. is with you; he
M-23 ......... 7:8 him, for he is with you; h. is always here.
C-5............ 2:2 So h. became identified with *Christ*, a man
C-5............ 2:3 for h. seemed to be a separate being,
C-5............ 2:5 Jesus remains a Savior because h. saw the
C-5............ 3:2 H. led the way for you to follow him. He
C-5............ 3:3 H. leads you back to God because he saw
C-5............ 3:3 you back to God because h. saw the road
C-5............ 3:3 the road before him, and h. followed it.
C-5............ 3:4 H. made a clear distinction, still obscure
C-5............ 3:5 H. offered you a final demonstration that
C-5............ 5:1 Is h. the Christ? O yes, along with you.
C-5............ 5:3 mighty lesson that h. learned for all of you
C-5............ 5:4 H. will remain with you to lead you from
C-5............ 5:6 since you were born, for such indeed h. is.
C-5............ 5:8 behold how dear a brother h. would be to
C-5............ 5:9 For h. will set your mind at rest at last and
C-5............ 6:1 Is h. God's only Helper? No, indeed. For
C-5............ 6:7 Yet h. would help you yet a little more if
C-5............ 6:8 most of all that h. would have you learn,
C-6............ 1:1 Whom h. called down upon the earth
C-6............ 1:1 the earth after h. ascended into Heaven,
C-6............ 2:2 His plan since h. was the first to complete
C-6............ 2:3 is therefore given him and h. will share it
C-6............ 5:3 Alone h. cannot be the Helper of God's
C-6............ 5:3 of God's Son for h. alone is functionless.
C-6............ 5:4 joined with you h. is the shining Savior of
C-6............ 5:5 with him when h. began to save the world

## he 2240

• noise word
*Jesus*
*He*

## head 9

T-11 ..... VI.8:1 a crown of thorns upon your own h.. Yet
T-12 ....... II.4:6 you are hiding your h. under the cover of
T-23 ...... in.3:1 Walk you in glory, with your h. held high
T-29 ... VIII.2:6 his little self for strength to raise his h.,
T-30 ..... IV.2:2 when a wooden h. springs up as a closed
W-pI....... 2.1:4 Turn your h. so that you include whatever
W-pI... 156.4:4 sinks to a whisper round your holy h..
W-pI. 161.11:5 you have placed upon your bleeding h..
W-pI... 192.9:4 realize you hold a sword above your h..

## heading 1

T-9 ........ V.7:2 help someone to point out where he is h.,

## heads 2

T-30 ..... IV.3:6 laugh at popping h. and squeaking toys,
W-pI... 195.7:1 let our brothers lean their tired h. against

## headstone 1

W-pI... 163.4:4 and laid to rest beneath the h. death has

## heal 185

T-1 ........ I.17:3 from the bodily level. That is why they h..
T-1 ........ I.24:1 Miracles enable you to h. the sick and
T-1 ........ I.29:3 h. because they deny body-identification
T-2 .......... I.5:1 which can h. any of them with equal ease.
T-2 ......... II.4:9 is not a two-edged sword. It can only h..
T-2 ....... IV.4:3 to h. it through non-creative agents. It
T-2 ........ V.2:2 but if you are afraid to use the mind to h.,
T-2 ........ V.5:3 you accept this, your mind can only h.. By
T-2 ... V.A.13:2 to h. is an expression of this confusion.
T-2 ... V.A.16:4 It is an appeal to God to h. their minds.
T-2 ... V.A.18:6 *I will be healed as I let Him teach me to h..*
T-3 ..... IV.3:11 eventually choose to h. the separation.
T-4 ....... IV.6:3 can focus and rise above fatigue and h..
T-4 ....... IV.8:7 used to attack or protect; to hurt or to h..
T-5 ........ in.1:1 To h. is to make happy. I have told you to
T-5 ........ in.1:3 you that you have refused to h. yourself.
T-5 ........ in.1:7 attempt to h. without being wholly joyous
T-5 ........ in.2:5 h. or to make joyous is therefore the same
T-5 ......... II.1:4 to h. the separation by letting it go. Your
T-5 ....... II.11:1 call on me to remind you how to h. by
T-5 ...... VII.2:1 many healers who did not h. themselves.
T-5 ...... VII.2:7 gave, knowing that this giving will h. you.
T-6 ..... V.A.2:6 If the mind can h. the body, but the body
T-6 ..... V.A.2:6 body, but the body cannot h. the mind,
T-6 ..... V.C.9:6 against this sickness is the way to h. it.
T-7 ......... II.1:1 To h. is the only kind of thinking in this
T-7 ......... II.2:1 To h., then, is to correct perception in
T-7 ....... IV.2:6 it. When you h., you are remembering the
T-7 ....... IV.5:3 Holy Spirit always seeks to unify and h..
T-7 ....... IV.5:4 As you h. you are healed, because the
T-7 ........ V.5:4 he can sometimes h. and sometimes not,
T-7 ........ V.8:1 When you h., that is exactly what you *are*
T-7 ....... IX.4:4 of its wholeness to dawn upon it and h. it.
T-7 ....... XI.6:5 you h. a brother by recognizing his worth,
T-8 ........ V.2:4 Yet to h. is still to make whole. Therefore,
T-8 ........ V.2:5 h. is to unite with those who are like you,
T-8 ..... VIII.9:2 This will h. them and therefore heal you.
T-8 ..... VIII.9:2 This will heal them and therefore h. you.
T-8 ....... IX.1:5 do not ask the Holy Spirit to h. the body,
T-8 ....... IX.6:3 and that to make mindless is to h.. But to
T-8 ....... IX.7:1 enjoins you to be perfect, to h. all errors,
T-8 ....... IX.9:3 a chaotic thought system *is* the way to h. it.
T-9 ....... III.5:1 you can h. him only by perceiving the
T-9 ......... V.8:1 A therapist does not h.; *he lets healing be.*
T-10 ..... III.2:4 H. your brothers simply by accepting
T-10 ..... III.2:7 aware of this is to h. them because it is the
T-10 ..... III.6:5 sick, but my value of you can h. you,
T-10 ..... III.7:4 I can h. you because I know you. I know
T-10 ..... III.7:7 I will h. you merely because I have only
T-10 ..... IV.8:4 Perceiving the spark will h., but knowing
T-11 ....... II.1:1 the decision to h. and to be healed is the
T-11 ....... II.3:5 You can h. only yourself, for only God's
T-11 ... VIII.9:2 that his mind is split you will h. yours.
T-11 ... VIII.9:3 accepts him and h. him unto Christ, for
T-11 . VIII.11:3 To love yourself is to h. yourself, and you
T-11 . VIII.11:4 we h. together as we live together and
T-11 . VIII.12:2 H. in Christ and be not offended by Him,
T-11 . VIII.12:5 you, for He wills to h. the Son of God, in
T-12 ....... II.1:2 If to love oneself is to h. oneself, those
T-12 ....... II.1:3 are asking for the love that would h. them
T-12 ....... II.1:6 The sick must h. themselves, for the truth
T-13 ..... III.6:6 the tricks and games you offer it can h. it,
T-13 ..... III.7:4 sanity all your hurt, and let Him h. you.
T-13 ..... III.7:6 will h. every little thought you have kept
T-13 ..... IV.3:5 h. and be healed if you did question it.
T-13 ..... VI.9:2 whom you h. bear witness to your healing
T-13 ....... X.8:1 *Now* it is given you to h. and teach, to
T-14 ..... III.6:2 Every chance given him to h. is another
T-16 ........ I.3:2 choose neither to hurt it nor to h. it in
T-16 .. VII.10:1 that would h. and the ego's "atonement"
T-18 ...... I.12:7 you not prefer to h. what has been broken
T-19 ........ I.2:1 an opportunity to h. the Son of God. And
T-19 ........ I.3:1 The body cannot h., because it cannot
T-19 ........ I.5:4 and separate; faith would unite and h..
T-19 ...... I.5:11 The other part would h., and therefore
T-19 ........ I.9:1 To have faith is to h.. It is the sign that
T-19 ...... I.13:5 together, that you may h. through faith.
T19 IV.D.12:6 that would h. it gives way to fear. Brother,
T-21 ..... VI.7:4 The power to h. the Son of God is given
T-21 .... VII.7:1 is the choice of whether to attack or h..
T-21 .... VII.7:3 Whom you attack you *cannot* want to h..
T-21 ... VIII.2:8 those who choose to h. and not to judge.
T-22 ........ I.1:2 God would h. and hate the one He loves,
T-22 ..... VI.3:7 to hate what serves whom you would h..
T-22 ..... VI.4:4 relationship has the power to h. all pain,
T-24 ... IV.2:12 See it as means to h., and it is healed.
T-24 ..... IV.3:4 Yet to those who wish to h. and not attack
T-25 ...... in.3:6 in gentleness and love, to h. their minds.
T-25 ..... VI.1:7 For he would only h. and only bless. And
T-25 ..... VI.1:8 he has the power to h. and bless all those
T-25 ..... VI.4:1 of what you made, to h. instead of harm.
T-27 ....... V.1:1 The only way to h. is to be healed. The
T-27 ....... V.2:5 If you wish only to be healed, you h.. Your
T-27 ....... V.2:9 The fearful are not healed, and cannot h..
T-27 ...... V.2:10 be gone forever from your mind to h.. For
T-27 ....... V.4:1 sadness where a miracle has come to h..
T-27 ..... VI.4:9 Its pains and pleasures does He h. alike,
T-27 ..... VI.8:5 Be healed that you may h., and suffer not
T-28 ........ I.2:9 It can be used to h. and not to hurt, if you
T-28 .... VII.2:2 help, the Call to healing and the Call to h.
T-29 ....... II.2:2 the power to h. must also now be yours.
T-29 ..... IX.6:6 not know what hurts and what will h..
T-30 ....... II.5:3 It *is* your will to h. him, and because you
T-30 ..... VI.5:1 Forgiveness recognized as merited will h.
T-30 ..... VI.6:1 and of joylessness forgiveness cannot h..
T-30 ..... VI.7:1 the miracle can h. all forms of sickness, or
T-30 ..... VI.7:1 heal all forms of sickness, or it cannot h..
T-30 ..... VI.8:3 h. is to make whole. And what is whole
T-30 ..... VI.8:5 the miracle must lack the power to h..
T-30 ... VI.10:7 in him who has been given you to h., for
T-30 ... VIII.3:5 a miracle be given you to h. appearances
T-30 ... VIII.4:4 be withheld from power to h. all dreams.
T-30 ... VIII.4:7 Choose what you would h., and He Who
T-30 ... VIII.5:1 already there to h. all things that change,

T-31......VI.1:8 except to **h.** and comfort and to bless.
T-31... VIII.6:4 A miracle has come to **h.** God's Son, and
W-pI.....41.3:2 and loss because it will **h.** the mind that
WpI...rI.in.4:4 with you, and to **h.** distress and turmoil.
W-pI.....58.3:2 holiness is unlimited in its power to **h.**,
W-pI.....75.1:2 You are healed and you can **h.**. The light
W-pI.....75.9:4 of forgiveness to **h.** your sight completely.
W-pI.....97.5:3 them as his thoughts, and uses them to **h.**
W-pI...108.3:1 and vision, being healed, has power to **h.**.
W-pI...109.3:3 There is no suffering it cannot **h.**. There is
W-pI...110.2:1 to let complete correction **h.** your mind,
W-pI...110.2:1 and give you perfect vision that will **h.** all
W-pI...110.2:2 to **h.** the past and make the future free. It
W-pI...124.6:2 to **h.** all forms of suffering in anyone, in
W-pI...124.7:2 that we can save and **h.** accordingly. We
W-pI...126.7:5 it is attained, must **h.** the mind that gives,
W-pI.135.10:5 You do not **h.**, but merely take away the
W-pI...136.1:1 No one can **h.** unless he understands
W-pI...140.1:3 When it tries to **h.** the mind, it sees no
W-pI...140.4:4 Atonement does not **h.** the sick, for that is
W-pI...140.6:3 Nor does it seek to **h.** what is not sick,
W-pI...140.6:5 which cannot fail to **h.** and heal forever. It
W-pI...140.6:5 which cannot fail to heal and **h.** forever. It
W-pI...165.6:2 in your mind, to **h.** as you were healed.
W-pI...167.3:8 It is the reason you can **h.**. It is the cause
W-pI...198.9:6 be a form of pain forgiveness cannot **h.**.
W-pII......2.2:4 Thought that has the power to **h.** the split
W-pII......5.4:5 holy. Now it serves to **h.** the mind that it
W-pII....10.4:3 For it alone can **h.** all sorrow, wipe away
W-pII..349.2:3 and **h.** our minds as we return to Him.
M-5.......III.2:7 not to **h.** the sick but to remind them of
M-5.......III.2:8 It is not their hands that **h.**. It is not their
M-7............1:3 is healed, what remains to **h.** him from?
M-18..........4:1 In order to **h.**, it thus becomes essential
M-18........4:10 there whom his forgiveness can fail to **h.**?
M-22..........1:9 To forgive is to **h.**. The teacher of God has
M-22........1:11 What is there, then, he cannot **h.**? What
M-22..........3:6 What, then, is left to **h.**? The body has
M-22..........5:1 When a teacher of God fails to **h.**, it is
M-22..........5:6 and distorted perception does not **h.**.
M-22..........6:3 power to **h.** all individuals of all forms of
M-22..........6:7 It is your task to **h.** the sense of separation
M-23..........1:6 magic? A name does not **h.**, nor does an
M-23..........2:1 Atonement for himself can **h.** the world.
C-4.............3:4 But for the time it lasts it comes to **h.**. For
P-2........III.3:5 is the formula for salvation, and must **h.**.
P-2........III.3:7 therapist could **h.** the world without a
P-2........III.3:9 His simple Presence is enough to **h.**.
P-2........IV.3:7 **h.** the sick is but to bring this realization
P-2........IV.4:3 seek for magic by which to **h.** the ills with
P-2........IV.7:5 cannot **h.**, for it opposes truth. Perhaps
P-2.........V.7:3 that is asked in our attempts to **h.**. We are
P-2.......VII.1:3 He who needs healing must **h.**. Physician,
P-2.......VII.1:4 Physician, **h.** thyself. Who else is there to
P-2.......VII.1:5 Who else is there to **h.**? And who else is in
P-2.......VII.1:7 therapist offers him a chance to **h.** himself
P-2.......VII.1:9 to **h.** from each patient who comes to him
P-2.......VII.7:4 He tries to **h.**, and thus at times he may.
P-2.......VII.9:7 **H.** and be healed. There is no other choice
P-3.........II.3:8 Spirit to enter the relationship and **h.** it.
P-3........III.2:1 healer would try to **h.** for money, and he
P-3........III.8:1 healer, therapist, teacher, **h.** thyself.
S-2...........I.1:5 was meant to **h.** is used to hurt because
S-3...........I.4:5 The power to **h.** is now his Father's gift,
S-3...........I.5:2 for what in Heaven could there be to **h.**?
S-3.........II.4:4 Now its forgiveness comes to **h.** the world
S-3........III.2:3 These forms may **h.** the body, and indeed
S-3........III.5:8 else can **h.** as God established healing.
S-3........III.6:1 God's Voice alone can tell you how to **h.**.
S-3........III.6:2 those He sends to you, to let Him **h.** them,
S-3........IV.3:1 what it means to help the Christ to **h.**!

## healed 206

T-1........ I.37:3 principle, where perception is **h.**. Until
T-2...........I.2:7 the Son's creations when his mind is **h.**.
T-2.........V.5:2 that its errors are **h.** by the Atonement.
T-2... V.A.18:6 *me. I will be* **h.** *as I let Him teach me to heal.*
T-4......IV.10:9 Christ has come into your mind and **h.** it.
T-5...........I.1:3 them. Only the **h.** mind can experience
T-5...........I.5:5 is **h.** there will be no Call to return. But
T-5......... II.1:2 and will be when they have been **h.**. This
T-5.......III.2:10 This dissociation is **h.** in both of you as
T-5.......IV.7:1 gives you the power of a **h.** mind, but the
T-5.........V.5:2 mind heals the body because *it* has been **h.**
T-5.......VII.2:3 Some of them have **h.** the sick at times,
T-5.......VII.2:5 of being **h.** *because* God created it whole.
T-5.......VII.3:6 means that you do not want to be **h.**.
T-6...........I.9:3 had not harmed anyone and had **h.** many.
T-6......V.C.9:5 and given you a sick mind that must be **h.**
T-6......V.C.9:7 it. Once your mind is **h.** it radiates health,
T-7........IV.5:4 As you heal you are **h.**, because the Holy
T-7.........V.3:1 develop and must develop if he is to be **h.**.
T-7.......V.11:2 and as we see them truly they will be **h.**.
T-7........XI.4:3 **h.** the Sonship and given thanks to God.
T-8......IV.4:11 this choice you could not be **h.** because
T-9.........II.2:5 At the same time, if he were **h.** physically,
T-9.........V.6:6 sinner" cannot be **h.** without magic, nor
T-10......III.9:2 And in that awareness you are **h.**. You
T-11.......II.1:1 the decision to heal and to be **h.** is the
T-11.......II.2:2 have than those who have been **h.** by it?
T-12.........I.7:2 but one need in yourself you will be **h.**.
T-12...VII.7:10 perceive the world as split, you are not **h.**.
T-12...VII.7:11 For to be **h.** is to pursue one goal, because
T-12... VIII.6:6 through His vision your perception is **h.**.
T-13......III.2:5 you do not want the separation **h.**. You
T-13......III.9:3 total love you will not be **h.** completely.
T-13......IV.3:5 could heal and be **h.** if you did question it.
T-13... VIII.5:4 **h.** and healing sight into the darkness,
T-15......XI.3:2 Let yourself be **h.** completely that you
T-17......IV.4:3 it, and by His blessing enabled it to be **h.**.
T-17.........V.h The **H.** Relationship
T-19.........I.2:2 he is **h.** *because* you offered faith to him,
T-19.........I.2:7 body is **h.** because you came without it,
T-19.........I.4:4 and kept you both apart from being **h.**.
T-19.........I.6:1 is the belief that the body must be **h.**, and
T-19.........I.7:5 separation is, and where it must be **h.**.
T-19.......I.10:6 **h.** because you look on what makes faith
T-19.......I.13:2 and sees the holy place where it was **h.**.
T-19.......I.13:5 And be you **h.** by grace together, that you
T-19......III.9:4 and quickly given to correction, to be **h.**,
T-19......III.9:5 You will be **h.** of sin and all its ravages the
T-19....III.10:4 Your perception was **h.** in the holy instant
T19.IV.D.20:4 give joy because they have been **h.** of pain
T-20.........I.1:5 he looks upon himself as **h.** and whole.
T-21......in.1:10 looked upon with vision is **h.** and holy.
T-21......VI.7:2 other being blessed by it, and **h.** of pain.
T-21......VI.7:8 that you choose to let yourself be **h.**, in
T-21......VII.7:4 And whom you would have **h.** must be
T-22......II.10:1 on it with the decision that it must be **h.**,
T-22......III.9:7 that both may happily be **h.** as one.
T-22......VI.4:8 healing is the Sonship **h.** *because* your will
T-24....IV.2:12 is hurt. See it as means to heal, and it is **h.**
T-25....IX.10:2 must be done to all, if anyone is to be **h.**.
T-26.....VII.2:3 as the idea that brought it has been **h.**,
T-26......IX.8:4 and ancient scars are **h.** within His sight.
T-27.........I.5:5 brother, who will see that every scar is **h.**,
T-27.........I.5:6 and with **h.** eyes will look beyond it to the
T-27.......II.3:10 Who forgives is **h.**. And in his healing lies
T-27.......II.4:7 yourself be **h.** that you may be forgiving,
T-27.......II.5:1 body shows the mind has not been **h.**. A
T-27.......II.6:2 does your healing show your mind is **h.**,
T-27.......II.6:3 was never lost, and **h.** along with you.
T-27.......II.7:3 you are **h.** because you wished him well.
T-27.......V.1:1 The only way to heal is to be **h.**. The
T-27.......V.1:6 No one can ask another to be **h.**. But he
T-27.......V.1:7 But he can let *himself* be **h.**, and thus offer
T-27.......V.2:4 No one is **h.** through double messages. If
T-27.......V.2:5 If you wish only to be **h.**, you heal. Your
T-27.......V.2:9 The fearful are not **h.**, and cannot heal.
T-27.......V.4:3 In that one instant you are **h.**, and in that
T-27.......V.5:1 back because he was afraid of being **h.**?
T-27.......V.5:5 from attack upon yourself, that it be **h.**.
T-27.......V.6:1 Come to the holy instant and be **h.**, for
T-27.......V.7:1 the world requires, that it may be **h.**. It
T-27.......V.7:4 who let yourself be **h.** that it might live. It
T-27......VI.7:3 But there *is* need that you be **h.**, because
T-27......VI.8:5 Be **h.** that you may heal, and suffer not
T-27...VII.13:4 his suffering was **h.** and where his brother
T-27..VIII.13:9 learn. And it will be no secret you are **h.**.
T-28.......I.10:8 You need no healing to be **h.**. In quietness
T-28.......I.11:2 and from the mind it **h.** in quiet then, to
T-28........II.2:7 is. The body can be **h.** by its effects, which
T-28......II.11:4 Thus is the body **h.** by miracles because
T-28......II.11:6 if you learn but that the body can be **h.**,
T-28...... IV.8:2 This holy picture, **h.** entirely, does He
T-28...... VI.5:5 death. And by his healing is his brother **h.**
T-28...... VI.6:7 sick, but lets his mind be **h.** and unified.
T-28......VII.4:1 With *this* as purpose is the body **h.**. It is
T-29........II.2:1 cause, and so it must be you are **h.**. And
T-29........II.2:2 And being **h.**, the power to heal must also
T-29........II.4:7 They will be **h.** when you accept your gifts
T-30........II.5:1 be saved, for by your own salvation is it **h.**
T-30........II.5:3 you have decided with him, he is **h.**. And
T-30...... VI.5:8 withstand the miracle, and not be **h.** by it.
T-30...... VI.8:2 him outside your willingness that he be **h.**
T-30....VIII.5:4 you would not have him **h.** and whole.
T-30....VIII.6:9 As he is **h.** are you made free of guilt, for
W-pI.....43.2:7 **H.** perception becomes the means by
W-pI.....70.3:4 He wants you to be **h.**, so He has kept the
W-pI.....70.5:2 this. God wants us to be **h.**, and we do not
W-pI.....70.5:6 do we. He wants us to be **h.**. So do we.
W-pI.....75.1:2 You are **h.** and you can heal. The light has
W-pI.....82.1:4 is the means by which the world is **h.**,
W-pI.....82.1:5 the world, that it may be **h.** along with me
W-pI...95.12:3 are one Self, complete and **h.** and whole,
W-pI.....97.7:2 *God, free of all limits, safe and* **h.** *and whole,*
W-pI...108.3:1 shows no opposites, and vision, being **h.**,
W-pI.121.12:3 savior, saved and saving, **h.** and whole.
W-pI...124.7:2 we say as well that we are saved and **h.**;
W-pI...124.7:7 from our Father, it is **h.** along with us.
W-pI...132.8:4 sick are **h.** as you let go all thoughts of
W-pI.135.11:1 A **h.** mind does not plan. It carries out
W-pI.135.12:1 A **h.** mind is relieved of the belief that it
W-pI.135.12:3 it has accepted this as true, then is it **h.**,
W-pI.136.15:7 *I am, and let my mind be wholly* **h.** *today.*
W-pI.136.16:4 It will be **h.** of all the sickly wishes that it
W-pI.136.17:1 Now is the body **h.**, because the source of
W-pI.136.20:2 not be confused about what must be **h.**,
W-pI......137.h When I am **h.** I am not healed alone.
W-pI......137.h When I am healed I am not **h.** alone.
W-pI...137.3:2 It is impossible that anyone be **h.** alone.
W-pI...137.4:4 **h.** is merely to accept what always was the
W-pI.137.10:1 And as you let yourself be **h.**, you see all
W-pI.137.10:1 no contact with you, **h.** along with you.
W-pI.137.10:3 But you are never **h.** alone. And legions
W-pI.137.10:4 the gift that you receive when you are **h.**.
W-pI.137.11:1 are **h.** become the instruments of healing.
W-pI.137.11:2 elapse between the instant they are **h.**,
W-pI.137.12:6 what is **h.** to what must yet be healed,
W-pI.137.12:6 what is healed to what must yet be **h.**,
W-pI.137.13:1 our function is to let our minds be **h.**, that
W-pI.137.14:3 *When I am* **h.** *I am not healed alone. And I*
W-pI.137.14:3 *When I am healed I am not* **h.** *alone. And I*
W-pI.137.15:5 *When I am* **h.** *I am not healed alone. And I*
W-pI.137.15:5 *When I am healed I am not* **h.** *alone. And I*
W-pI.137.15:6 *my brothers, for I would be* **h.** *with them, as*
W-pI.137.15:6 *be healed with them, as they are* **h.** *with me.*
W-pI...140.2:1 He is not **h.**. He merely had a dream that
W-pI.140.12:3 *Speak to us, Father, that we may be* **h.**. And
W-pI...149.1:1 When I am **h.** I am not healed alone.
W-pI...149.1:1 When I am healed I am not **h.** alone.
W-pI...159.2:1 understand that you are **h.** when you give
W-pI...159.6:5 There is no sickness not already **h.**, no
W-pI...159.7:3 where the suffering are **h.** and welcome.
W-pI...162.3:2 secure, his safety certain and his body **h.**,
W-pI...165.6:2 in your mind, to heal as you were **h.**. For
W-pI...183.3:3 The sick arise, **h.** of their sickly thoughts.
W-pI.184.12:4 Every gap is closed, and separation **h.**.
W-pI...185.2:1 one can mean these words and not be **h.**.
W-pI...187.6:5 all, and in his gentle laughter are they **h.**.
W-pI...194.8:3 creature not respond with **h.** perception?
W-pI...195.2:2 the certain means whereby all pain is **h.**,
W-pI...196.1:4 is your own, and in his healing you are **h.**.
W-pII ..in.10:5 we need but be still and let all things be **h.**
W-pII .247.1:4 the simple truth, and I am **h.** completely.
W-pII .267.1:4 Now my mind is **h.**, and all I need to save

| | |
|---|---|
| W-pII .299.2:6 | *In it are all things* **h.**, *for they remain as You* |
| W-pII .305.1:4 | **h.** the world by giving it Christ's peace. |
| W-pII .347.1:7 | *it is not real, and in His understanding it is* **h.** |
| W-pII ...14.1:1 | *I am God's Son, complete and* **h.** *and whole,* |
| W-pII .357.1:5 | *be: "Behold his sinlessness, and be you* **h.**." |
| W-pII ....359.h | All pain Is **h.**; all misery replaced with joy. |
| M-5 .........I.2:5 | "life." If he is **h.**, he is responsible for his |
| M-5 ....... II.1:2 | is no gain at all to me in this" and he is **h.**. |
| M-5 ....... II.2:4 | decides against recovery, he will not be **h.**. |
| M-5 ...... III.1:1 | must change his mind in order to be **h.**, |
| M-5 .... III.1:11 | If they even suspected it, they would be **h.** |
| M-7 ........... 1:3 | If the patient is **h.**, what remains to heal |
| M-7 ........... 1:6 | of God himself whose mind needs to be **h.** |
| M-8 ........... 6:2 | be **h.** will no longer acknowledge them. |
| M-8 ........... 6:4 | **h.** mind will put them all in one category; |
| M-18 ......... 4:4 | So is he **h.**, and in his healing is his pupil |
| M-18 ......... 4:4 | and in his healing is his pupil **h.** with him. |
| M-22 ......... 1:5 | Accept Atonement and you are **h.**. |
| M-22 ......... 4:9 | that God created. In it are all illusions **h.**. |
| M-22 ....... 5:10 | to your Teacher, and let yourself be **h.**. |
| M-22 ......... 7:2 | then, can say which one can be **h.** of what, |
| P-in............ 1:2 | mind can be sick, only the mind can be **h.** |
| P-1........... 5:10 | for He would have us all be **h.** in Him. |
| P-2......... II.1:4 | and the **h.** have no need for a therapist. |
| P-2......... V.5:7 | In such a process, who could not be **h.**? |
| P-2........ VI.4:7 | is not the "something else" that can be **h.**. |
| P-2........ VI.7:1 | No one is **h.** alone. This is the joyous |
| P-2....... VII.9:7 | Heal and be **h.**. There is no other choice |
| P-3......... II.7:2 | necessary understanding for the **h.** healer. |
| P-3........ III.4:5 | made holy, for herein both are **h.**. The |
| S-3........... I.3:1 | can be **h.** as an effect of true forgiveness. |
| S-3........ II.5:10 | If you are **h.** your healing is complete. |
| S-3........ III.2:8 | **h.** appears to be to find a wiser one who, |
| S-3........ III.4:8 | is, for never thus can it be truly **h.**. |
| S-3........ III.5:7 | separation must be **h.** by love and union. |
| S-3........ III.6:6 | is no fear in one who has been truly **h.**, for |
| S-3........ IV.1:1 | How holy are the **h.**! For in their sight |
| S-3...... IV.1:10 | which the **h.** sing of their union and their |
| S-3........ IV.4:1 | first forgive, then pray, and you are **h.**. |
| S-3........ IV.4:4 | And in this understanding you are **h.**. In |
| S-3........ IV.7:3 | who does not understand that he is **h.**, |
| S-3........ IV.7:6 | Hear this an instant and you will be **h.**. |
| S-3........ IV.9:7 | **h.** My Son and took him from the cross. |

## Healer 3

*healer*

| | |
|---|---|
| T-5........... I.4:2 | He is referred to as the **H.**, the Comforter |
| T-13.... VIII.1:2 | That is why the Holy Spirit is the only **H.**. |
| T-28.... IV.10:8 | to let illusions go is all the **H.** of God's Son |

## healer 28

*Healer*

| | |
|---|---|
| T-2......... V.4:1 | The **h.** who relies on his own readiness is |
| T-5....... VII.2:4 | Unless the **h.** heals himself, he cannot |
| T-7......... V.1:4 | clarification. The unhealed **h.** obviously |
| T-7......... V.4:3 | Healing perceives nothing in the **h.** that |
| T-7......... V.4:4 | always sees something "special" in the **h.**, |
| T-7......... V.5:2 | Unless the **h.** always heals by Him the |
| T-7......... V.5:4 | **h.** is obviously accepting inconsistency. |
| T-7....... V.5:10 | "fearful **h.**" is a contradiction in terms, |
| T-7......... V.7:1 | The unhealed **h.** wants gratitude from his |
| T-9............ V.h | The Unhealed **H.** |
| T-9......... V.1:3 | ego. Let us consider the unhealed **h.** more |
| T-9......... V.1:5 | If an unhealed **h.** is a theologian, for |
| T-9......... V.2:3 | Every **h.** who searches fantasies for truth |
| T-9......... V.3:2 | The unhealed **h.** cannot do this because |
| T-9......... V.5:4 | real has happened to the unhealed **h.**, and |
| T-9......... V.5:6 | unhealed **h.** therefore does not know how |
| T-9......... V.7:3 | The unhealed **h.** cannot do this for him, |
| T-9......... V.7:4 | the **h.** can make is to present an example |
| T-9......... V.7:6 | acknowledgment the **h.** knows it is there. |
| P-2....... VII.4:3 | the unhealed **h.** would instantly become a |
| P-2....... VII.5:8 | No unhealed **h.** can be wholly sane. |
| P-2....... VII.7:3 | unhealed **h.** cannot but be fearful of his |
| P-3......... II.3:2 | The unhealed **h.** may be arrogant, selfish, |
| P-3......... II.3:4 | it may have been, when he chose to be a **h.** |
| P-3......... II.7:2 | necessary understanding for the healed **h.** |
| P-3........ III.2:1 | unhealed **h.** would try to heal for money, |
| P-3........ III.2:9 | who would do this loses the name of **h.**, |
| P-3........ III.8:1 | Physician, **h.**, therapist, teacher, heal |

## healer's 1

| | |
|---|---|
| T-5 ........in.3:7 | That is why the **h.** prayer is: *Let me know* |

## healers 10

| | |
|---|---|
| T-5 ...... VII.2:1 | many **h.** who did not heal themselves. |
| T-9 ........ V.1:2 | is because it is undertaken by unhealed **h.** |
| T-9 ........ V.3:3 | All unhealed **h.** follow the ego's plan for |
| P-2........ IV.5:1 | "**h.**" of the world may recognize the mind |
| P-2........ VII.4:2 | All "unhealed **h.**" make this fundamental |
| P-3........ III.5:5 | So it is with God's **h.**. They give because |
| S-3........ III.5:1 | **H.** there are, for they are Sons of God |
| S-3........ IV.1:3 | Whose Voice He is,–such are God's **h.**. |
| S-3........ IV.2:6 | This instant is the goal of all true **h.**, |
| S-3........ IV.3:3 | this? God thanks His **h.**, for He knows the |

## healing 473

*See also* healing-to-separate

| | |
|---|---|
| T-1 .......... I.8:1 | are **h.** because they supply a lack; they are |
| T-1 ........ I.20:2 | that leads to the **h.** power of the miracle. |
| T-1 ........ I.23:2 | **h.** because sickness comes from confusing |
| T-1 ...... VII.5:9 | **H.** is of God in the end. The means are |
| T-2 ......... II.1:2 | are natural, corrective, **h.** and universal. |
| T-2 ..... III.5:12 | the world as a means of **h.** the separation. |
| T-2 .......... IV.h | **H.** as Release from Fear |
| T-2 ....... IV.1:1 | Our emphasis is now on **h.**. The miracle |
| T-2 ....... IV.1:2 | is the principle, and **h.** is the result. To |
| T-2 ....... IV.1:3 | speak of "a miracle of **h.**" is to combine |
| T-2 ....... IV.1:4 | **H.** is not a miracle. The Atonement, or |
| T-2 ....... IV.1:5 | is a remedy and any type of **h.** is a result. |
| T-2 ....... IV.1:7 | All **h.** is essentially the release from fear. |
| T-2 ....... IV.1:9 | understand **h.** because of your own fear. |
| T-2 ....... IV.4:6 | the outside is temporarily given **h.** belief. |
| T-2 ........ V.2:4 | to misunderstand any **h.** that might occur |
| T-2 ........ V.2:4 | unable to accept the real Source of the **h.**. |
| T-2 ........ V.2:5 | to rely temporarily on physical **h.** devices, |
| T-2 ........ V.4:5 | those who need **h.** are simply those who |
| T-2 ........ V.4:5 | not realized that right-mindedness *is* **h.**. |
| T-2 ........ V.8:1 | The fear of **h.** arises in the end from an |
| T-2 ........ V.8:1 | accept unequivocally that **h.** is necessary. |
| T-2 ........ V.9:1 | **H.** is an ability that developed after the |
| T-2 ........ V.9:3 | **h.** is needed as a means of protection. |
| T-2 ........ V.9:4 | This is because **h.** rests on charity, and |
| T-2 ... V.A.12:2 | All forms of **h.** rest on this fundamental |
| T-2 ... V.A.15:1 | induces the right perception for **h.**. Until |
| T-2 ... V.A.15:2 | has occurred **h.** cannot be understood. |
| T-2 ... V.A.15:4 | it is essentially judgmental, rather than **h.** |
| T-2 ... V.A.18:1 | behalf of your own **h.** and that of others if |
| T-2 ....... VI.3:1 | outcome of misthought can result in **h.**. |
| T-2 ....... VI.8:9 | the fear. This is how true **h.** occurs. |
| T-2 ..... VIII.3:3 | It is a final **h.** rather than a meting out of |
| T-3 ......... II.6:7 | This is the **h.** that the miracle induces. |
| T-3 ........ V.9:1 | is the **h.** of the perception of separation. |
| T-3 ...... V.10:3 | that anyone who perceives at all needs **h.**. |
| T-4 .......... I.2:2 | of it as a move towards **h.** the separation. |
| T-4 .......... I.4:3 | dreaming is not really **h.** his split mind. |
| T-4 ........ I.13:7 | teachers who share my aim of **h.** the mind |
| T-4 ..... IV.10:2 | of the ego's rule and the **h.** of the mind. I |
| T-5 ............... h | **H.** AND WHOLENESS |
| T-5 ........ in.2:6 | what part of the Sonship the **h.** is offered. |
| T-5 .......... I.1:1 | **H.** is a thought by which two minds |
| T-5 .......... I.5:3 | Before that there was no need for **h.**, for |
| T-5 .......... I.7:5 | the way beyond the **h.** that it brings, and |
| T-5 ......... II.1:1 | **H.** is not creating; it is reparation. The |
| T-5 ......... II.1:2 | The Holy Spirit promotes **h.** by looking |
| T-5 ......... II.1:2 | of God were before **h.** was needed, and |
| T-5 ........ III.1:3 | ways of thinking would not be open to **h.**. |
| T-5 ........ III.2:1 | The Holy Spirit is the idea of **h.**. Being |
| T-5 .......... IV.h | Teaching and **H.** |
| T-5 ....... IV.5:2 | Teaching should be **h.**, because it is the |
| T-5 ....... IV.7:2 | must devote themselves first to **h.** because |
| T-5 ....... IV.7:2 | because, having received the idea of **h.**, |
| T-6 ..... V.C.9:7 | it radiates health, and thereby teaches **h.**. |
| T-7 .......... IV.h | **H.** as the Recognition of Truth |
| T-7 ....... IV.1:4 | **H.** does not come directly from God, |
| T-7 ....... IV.1:5 | Yet **h.** is still of God, because it proceeds |
| T-7 ....... IV.4:2 | He uses them only for **h.**, because He |
| T-7 ....... IV.4:3 | By **h.** you learn of wholeness, and by |
| T-7 ....... IV.5:4 | Holy Spirit sees no order of difficulty in **h.** |
| T-7 ....... IV.5:5 | healing. **H.** is the way to undo the belief in |
| T-7 ....... IV.6:9 | you are. **H.**, then, is a way of approaching |
| T-7 ....... IV.7:7 | His. **H.** is a way of forgetting the sense of |
| T-7 ............V.h | **H.** and the Changelessness of Mind |
| T-7 .........V.1:3 | with **h.** that it does need clarification. The |
| T-7 .........V.2:7 | If you teach both sickness *and* **h.**, you are |
| T-7 .........V.3:1 | **H.** is the one ability everyone can develop |
| T-7 .........V.3:2 | be healed. **H.** is the Holy Spirit's form of |
| T-7 .........V.3:6 | too, can be used either for **h.** or for magic, |
| T-7 .........V.3:6 | involves the belief that **h.** is harmful. This |
| T-7 .........V.4:1 | **H.** only strengthens. Magic always tries |
| T-7 .........V.4:3 | **H.** perceives nothing in the healer that |
| T-7 .........V.5:1 | chance, and **h.** that is of Him *always* works |
| T-7 .........V.5:3 | vary. Yet **h.** itself is consistent, since only |
| T-7 .........V.6:2 | **H.** does. Fear always makes exceptions. |
| T-7 .........V.6:4 | **H.** never does. Fear produces dissociation |
| T-7 .........V.6:6 | **H.** always produces harmony, because it |
| T-7 .........V.6:9 | real. **H.** can be counted on because it is |
| T-7 .......V.6:10 | **h.** is consistent it cannot be inconsistently |
| T-7 .........V.7:4 | **h.** lesson is limited by his own ingratitude |
| T-8 ....... IV.4:5 | **H.** does not come from anyone else. You |
| T-8 ....... IV.4:8 | That is why **h.** is a collaborative venture. I |
| T-8 ..... IV.4:11 | you would have decided against **h.**, and |
| T-8 ..... IV.4:11 | my decision for you makes **h.** impossible. |
| T-8 ....... IV.5:1 | **H.** reflects our joint will. This is obvious |
| T-8 ....... IV.5:2 | obvious when you consider what **h.** is for. |
| T-8 ....... IV.5:3 | **H.** is the way in which the separation is |
| T-8 .... VII.10:1 | **H.** is the result of using the body solely |
| T-8 .... VII.11:1 | is the only way to guarantee help and **h.**. |
| T-8 .... VII.11:2 | Help and **h.** are the normal expressions of |
| T-8 .......... IX.h | **H.** as Corrected Perception |
| T-8 ....... IX.1:5 | that the body is the proper aim of **h.**. Ask, |
| T-8 ....... IX.5:1 | **H.** is release from the fear of waking and |
| T-8 ....... IX.5:2 | all **h.** involves replacing fear with love. |
| T-8 ....... IX.9:1 | then, is the Holy Spirit's only way of **h.**. |
| T-8 ....... IX.9:2 | the only level at which **h.** means anything. |
| T-8 ....... IX.9:6 | Your **h.**, then, is part of His health, since |
| T-9 .........II.2:3 | specific forms of **h.** are not achieved, even |
| T-9 .........II.2:3 | not achieved, even when the state of **h.** is. |
| T-9 .........II.2:4 | is. An individual may ask for physical **h.** |
| T-9 .........II.2:7 | This request is, therefore, not for **h.** at all. |
| T-9 ....... III.8:3 | Accept only the function of **h.** in time, |
| T-9 .........V.2:3 | not have the answer to the problem of **h.**. |
| T-9 .........V.4:4 | be a **h.** approach if the dreamer were also |
| T-9 .........V.6:4 | **H.** is not mysterious. Nothing will change |
| T-9 .........V.8:1 | A therapist does not heal; *he lets* **h.** *be.* He |
| T-9 .........V.8:5 | makes **h.** clear in any situation in which |
| T-9 ....... VI.6:2 | Yet while you still need **h.**, your miracles |
| T-10 ..... III.2:5 | for **h.** because He has but one Son. God's |
| T-10 .......V.8:1 | sickness for **h.** but only to the God of love, |
| T-10 .......V.8:1 | love, for **h.** is the acknowledgment of Him |
| T-11 ........ I.1:1 | You have learned your need of **h.**. Would |
| T-11 ........ I.1:2 | recognizing your need of **h.** for yourself? |
| T-11 ...... I.11:9 | why **h.** is the beginning of the recognition |
| T-11 ..........II.h | The Invitation to **H.** |
| T-11 .......II.1:2 | this, and every **h.** thought brings it closer. |
| T-11 .......II.2:1 | **H.** thus becomes a lesson in |
| T-11 .......II.2:3 | to join them is your **h.** accomplished. |
| T-11 .......II.2:5 | Every **h.** thought that you accept, either |
| T-11 .......II.3:5 | only yourself, for only God's Son needs **h.** |
| T-11 .......II.4:1 | **H.** is a sign that you want to make whole. |
| T-11 .......II.4:3 | go far beyond the **h.** you would undertake |
| T-11 .......V.2:1 | **h.** but the removal of all that stands in the |
| T-11 ... VIII.9:3 | unto Christ, for Christ is his **h.** and yours. |
| T-11 . VIII.10:4 | It. Nothing will be beyond your **h.** power, |
| T-11 . VIII.11:1 | you will not accept your **h.** without his. |
| T-11 . VIII.11:2 | as you share Heaven, and his **h.** is yours. |
| T-11 . VIII.12:5 | His **h.** power and use it for all He sends |
| T-12 ........ I.3:4 | Everything else is an appeal for **h.** and |
| T-12 ........ I.4:2 | the reality of the need for **h.** by making it |
| T-12 .......II.2:9 | To perceive the **h.** of your brother as the |
| T-12 .......II.2:9 | your brother as the **h.** of yourself is thus |
| T-12 .......II.3:6 | **H.** is the Love of Christ for His Father and |

T-12.....VII.4:7 is creation, so your function on earth is h.
T-13......III.6:5 that its need of h. cannot be denied. Not
T-13......III.7:2 Here is both his pain and his h., for the
T-13......III.9:3 will exempt yourself from His h. power,
T-13......III.9:4 H. must be as complete as fear, for love
T-13......IV.1:3 told that your function in this world is h.,
T-13......IV.9:2 function in the world of time as one of h.,
T-13......IV.9:2 the aspect of time in which h. can occur.
T-13......IV.9:3 H. cannot be accomplished in the past. It
T-13......VI.6:3 All h. lies within it because its continuity
T-13......VI.9:2 whom you heal bear witness to your h.,
T-13...VII.17:5 abide. H. in time is needed, for joy cannot
T-13... VIII.1:1 All h. is release from the past. That is
T-13... VIII.5:4 healed and h. sight into the darkness, and
T-13... VIII.7:1 Be you content with h., for Christ's gift
T-13... VIII.9:5 They need no h., nor do you, when you
T-13.......X.7:6 teaches h., but He also knows of creation.
T-14......III.5:4 guilt. Everyone you offer h. to returns it.
T-14.......V.5:3 been denied to produce the need of h.. Do
T-14......VI.2:4 apart from love cannot share its h. power,
T-14......IX.7:1 the power of h. that the reflection of God,
T-14......IX.7:4 their different problems to its h. light,
T-14......IX.7:4 and all their problems find but h. there.
T-14......IX.8:3 Its one response is h., without regard for
T-14......IX.8:4 Those who have learned to offer only h.,
T-15......XI.3:2 that you may join with Him in h., and let
T-16.........I.1:7 in pain, understanding that h. pain is not
T-16.........I.3:3 You do not know what h. is. All you have
T-16.........I.3:7 gently aside, and let h. be done for you.
T-16.........I.6:2 it silently by enveloping it in h. wings. Let
T-17....IV.16:9 For here is only h., already complete and
T-18...... I.13:2 the Sonship with h. and uniting comfort.
T-18....IX.10:3 create. It is the source of h., but it is the
T-19.......... I.h H. and Faith
T-19.........I.2:6 And this *is* h.. The body is healed because
T-19.........I.2:7 and joined the Mind in which all h. rests.
T-19.........I.3:2 sick. It *needs* no h.. Its health or sickness
T-19.........I.4:6 have made of it an "enemy" of h. and the
T-19.........I.6:4 Here, then, is h. needed. And it is here
T-19.........I.6:5 And it is here that h. *is*. For God gave
T-19.........I.6:6 For God gave h. not apart from sickness,
T-19...... I.14:5 brings the miracle of h. with equal ease to
T-19......III.8:1 it must forever be beyond the hope of h..
T-19....III.11:3 Your relationship is now a temple of h.; a
T-19......IV.1:7 unto your temple, where h. waits for him.
T-20... VIII.8:2 are. This is the h. and the remedy. Believe
T-21......VI.6:1 If you choose sin instead of h., you would
T-21.....VII.7:2 heal. For h. comes of power, and attack of
T-22......VI.4:6 all. Only in your joint will does h. lie. For
T-22......VI.4:7 lie. For here your h. is, and here will you
T-22......VI.4:8 h. is the Sonship healed *because* your will
T-22......VI.9:8 gift of love a source of h. for everyone.
T-23......IV.4:3 is, limits the h. and the miracles you have
T-24......IV.3:9 merely change of purpose from hurt to h..
T-24......VI.1:3 He is the h. of your sense of sacrifice and
T-24......VI.4:1 the h. of God's Son is all the world is for.
T-24......VI.4:3 Until you see the h. of the Son as all you
T-25.......in.3:1 The body needs no h.. But the mind that
T-25......IX.6:3 H. must be for everyone, because he does
T-25......IX.6:7 more condemned, and thus apart from h.
T-25......IX.6:9 vengeance in place of h. and return of
T-25......IX.7:4 to His gift of h. and deliverance and peace
T-26....... II.5:7 made it great, and past the hope of h..
T-26........VII.h The Laws of H.
T-26.....VII.1:2 the laws of h. must be understood before
T-26.....VII.1:3 all that must occur for h. to be possible.
T-26.....VII.6:2 less willingly offered to truth for h. and
T-26.....VII.7:2 errors seem forever past the hope of h.,
T-26...VII.14:2 h. of effect without the cause can merely
T-26...VII.15:4 In every miracle all h. lies, for God gave
T-26...VII.17:1 for h. is not needed where there is no pain
T-26... VIII.5:7 is it protected and kept separate from h..
T-27..............h THE H. OF THE DREAM
T-27.........I.6:2 h. is his comfort and his health because it
T-27....... I.10:2 and perfect h. take the place of death. The
T-27....... I.10:4 Let it have h. as its purpose. Then will it
T-27.......... II.h The Fear of H.
T-27....... II.1:1 Is h. frightening? To many, yes. For
T-27..... II.3:11 And in his h. lies the proof that he has
T-27....... II.4:1 it brings a h. to your brother and yourself
T-27....... II.5:2 A miracle of h. proves that separation is
T-27....... II.5:7 h. can it offer him mute testimony of his
T-27....... II.6:2 So does your h. show your mind is healed
T-27..... II.6:11 Yet it is given you to show him, by your h.
T-27....... II.7:3 Your h. saves him pain as well as you, and
T-27....... II.7:4 obeys; that h. sees no specialness at all. It
T-27....... II.8:4 knows your h. is the witness unto his, and
T-27....... II.8:7 Show him your h., and he will consent no
T-27....... II.9:1 Who, then, fears h.? Only those to whom
T-27....... II.9:8 And need your h. be delayed because you
T-27..... II.15:9 own. And thus is h. given you and him.
T-27......... V.h The H. Example
T-27....... V.1:3 Accept the miracle of h., and it will go
T-27....... V.2:7 But if you are afraid of h., then it cannot
T-27....... V.2:8 The only thing that is required for a h. is a
T-27..... V.2:11 if it were, there were no need for h. then.
T-27....... V.4:3 and in that single instant is all h. done.
T-27....... V.6:6 H. replaces suffering. Who looks on one
T-27....... V.7:1 is your h. everything the world requires,
T-27....... V.8:6 is. But h. is apparent in specific instances,
T-27....... V.9:1 Your h. will extend, and will be brought
T-27....... V.9:4 All h. must proceed in lawful manner, in
T-27..... V.11:1 Peace be to you to whom is h. offered.
T-27..... V.11:2 you when you accept the h. for yourself.
T-27..... V.11:5 Your h. will be one of its effects, as will
T-27..... V.11:9 God thanks you for your h., for He knows
T-27..... VI.6:6 itself are but a single sound; a call for h.,
T-27..... VI.8:1 world awaits your h. and your happiness,
T-27..... VI.8:1 you may demonstrate the h. of the world.
T-28.........I.3:1 Nothing employed for h. represents an
T-28.........I.3:4 can employ for h. have been given Him,
T-28.......I.10:8 You need no h. to be healed. In quietness,
T-28....... II.2:8 must all h. come about because the mind
T-28....... II.2:8 is quite apart from it, and where all h. is.
T-28....... II.2:9 Where, then, is h.? Only where its cause is
T-28....... II.3:3 cause of h. is the only Cause of everything
T-28....... II.4:4 you wish for dreams of h., or for dreams
T-28...... III.2:6 H. is the effect of minds that join, as
T-28...... III.8:4 The dream of h. in forgiveness lies, and
T-28.... IV.10:9 place the miracle of h. where the seeds of
T-28...... VI.5:5 death. And by his h. is his brother healed.
T-28..... VII.2:2 of help, the Call to h. and the Call to heal?
T-28..... VII.2:3 Your savior waits for h., and the world
T-28..... VII.2:5 For h. will be one or not at all, its oneness
T-28..... VII.2:5 at all, its oneness being where the h. is.
T-28..... VII.4:4 It serves to help the h. of God's Son, and
T-30...... VI.7:3 appearance must remain apart from h.,
T-30... VIII.4:5 you cannot have when you desire h.. But
W-pI.....70.3:4 kept the Source of h. where the need for
W-pI.....70.3:4 of healing where the need for h. lies.
W-pI.....70.4:1 to separate h. from the sickness for which
W-pI.....70.4:2 was to ensure that h. did not occur. God's
W-pI.....97.5:2 that will accept the h. gifts they bring,
W-pI.....97.5:3 And they will increase in h. power each
W-pI....107.5:2 Here is the gift of h., for the truth needs
W-pI....109.5:6 Let it be still and thankfully accept its h..
W-pI....110.5:1 The h. power of today's idea is limitless.
W-pI.126.10:4 to hear the Voice of truth and h. speak to
W-pI....132.7:1 h. is the gift of those who are prepared to
W-pI.132.16:1 need not realize that h. comes to many
W-pI.135.10:1 These are the thoughts in need of h., and
W-pI.135.10:5 heal, but merely take away the hope of h.,
W-pI....136.1:4 this is seen, h. is automatic. It dispels this
W-pI.136.15:5 We introduce it with a h. prayer, to help
W-pI.136.16:1 H. will flash across your open mind, as
W-pI....137.1:2 h. is the opposite of all the world's ideas
W-pI....137.3:1 serves, but h. operates apart from them.
W-pI....137.3:4 But h. is his own decision to be one again,
W-pI....137.3:6 But h. is accomplished as he sees the body
W-pI....137.4:2 But h. demonstrates that truth is true.
W-pI....137.4:6 So h., never needed by the truth, must
W-pI....137.5:1 H. might thus be called a counter-dream,
W-pI....137.5:2 h. but removes illusions that have not
W-pI....137.5:3 all, h. but offers restitution for imagined
W-pI....137.6:1 not h. is unworthy of your function here.
W-pI....137.7:1 h. must replace the fantasies of sickness
W-pI....137.8:1 H. is freedom. For it demonstrates that
W-pI....137.8:3 H. is shared. And by this attribute it
W-pI... 137.8:5 H. is strength. For by its gentle hand is
W-pI....137.9:1 H., forgiveness, and the glad exchange of
W-pI.137.10:2 all the world, when you let h. come to you
W-pI.137.11:1 are healed become the instruments of h..
W-pI.137.11:2 all the grace of h. it is given them to give.
W-pI.137.12:6 that thoughts of h. will this day go forth
W-pI.137.13:1 healed, that we may carry h. to the world,
W-pI.137.14:4 *And I would share my h. with the world, that*
W-pI.137.15:1 Let h. be through you this very day. And
W-pI....140.1:4 forms of h. thus must substitute illusion
W-pI....140.6:3 sick, unmindful where the need for h. is.
W-pI....140.7:2 H. must be sought but where it is, and
W-pI....140.8:2 We will try today to find the source of h.,
W-pI....140.9:2 today and reach the source of h., from
W-pI.140.10:2 will be still and listen for the Voice of h.,
W-pI.140.12:6 And we will say our prayer for h. hourly,
W-pI.140.12:7 This is the day when h. comes to us. This
W-pI.151.14:2 it takes on h. power from the Mind which
W-pI....159.2:1 that you are healed when you give h.. You
W-pI....164.6:3 becomes the h. and salvation of the world
W-pI....165.3:1 his joy, his h. and his peace of mind, his
W-pI.166.14:3 If you are sick, you but withhold their h..
W-pI....167.3:9 It is the cause of h.. It is why you cannot
W-pI.193.11:4 settle by ourselves, and kept apart from h.
W-pI....196.1:4 is your own, and in his h. you are healed.
W-pII ..... 2.2:3 the mind is split there is a need of h.. So
W-pII .270.2:3 we offer h. to the world through Him, the
W-pII ....275.h God's h. Voice protects all things today.
W-pII .275.1:6 in this the h. of the Voice for God is found
W-pII .275.2:1 *Your h. Voice protects all things today, and*
W-pII .323.1:1 *streaming in to his awareness, h. him of pain*
W-pII ... 13.5:1 Miracles fall like drops of h. rain from
W-pII .349.1:6 *I learn Your h. miracles belong to me.*
W-pII ....356.h sin. H. is but another name for God. The
M-5 .............h HOW IS H. ACCOMPLISHED?
M-5 ........... 1:1 H. involves an understanding of what the
M-5 ........... 1:2 is for. H. is impossible without this.
M-5 .........I.1:1 H. is accomplished the instant the
M-5 .........I.2:1 this insane conviction, does h. stand for?
M-5 ........II.1:1 H. must occur in exact proportion to
M-5 ........II.2:1 it would use the body, is the basis of h..
M-5 ........II.2:2 And this is so for h. in all forms. A patient
M-5 ...... III.1:5 those who do not understand what h. is.
M-6 ..............h IS H. CERTAIN?
M-6 ........... 1:1 H. is always certain. It is impossible to let
M-6 ........... 1:6 way of life, believing h. is the way to death
M-6 ........... 1:7 so, a sudden h. might precipitate intense
M-6 ........... 1:9 death. H. must wait, for his protection.
M-6 ........... 2:1 H. will always stand aside when it would
M-6 ........... 2:3 h. has been given it will be received. And
M-6 ........... 2:7 if he has offered h. and it does not appear
M-6 ........... 4:3 H. is the change of mind that the Holy
M-7 ..............h SHOULD H. BE REPEATED?
M-7 ........... 1:2 H. cannot be repeated. If the patient is
M-7 ........... 1:4 And if the h. is certain, as we have already
M-7 ........... 1:5 the result of h. is to limit the healing. It is
M-7 ........... 1:5 the result of healing is to limit the h.. It is
M-7 ........... 2:1 to be a channel for h. he has succeeded.
M-7 ........... 3:6 By accepting h. he can give it. If he doubts
M-7 ........... 4:1 to doubt a h. because of the appearance
M-7 ........... 6:5 If you are offering only h., you cannot
M-8 ........... 5:1 no order of difficulty in h. merely because
M-8 ........... 5:8 And so it is with h.. The properties of
M-8 ........... 6:8 one answer to sickness of any kind is h..
M-16 ......... 9:4 demanding sacrifice, h. nor destructive,
M-18 ......... 4:4 and in his h. is his pupil healed with him.
M-21 ............h WHAT IS THE ROLE OF WORDS IN H.?
M-21 ......... 1:1 speaking, words play no part at all in h..
M-21 ......... 2:3 and thus cannot help the h. process. The
M-22 ............h ARE H. AND ATONEMENT RELATED?
M-22 ......... 1:1 H. and Atonement are not related; they
M-22 ......... 3:1 forgiveness is h. needs to be understood,
M-22 ......... 4:4 of God calls forth the miracle of h.. He
M-22 ......... 4:5 all mistakes and h. all perception. Healing
M-22 ......... 4:6 H. is the result of the recognition, by
M-22 ......... 4:6 teacher, of who it is that is in need of h..
M-22 ....... 6:10 H. is very simple. Atonement is received
M-22 ....... 6:13 It is in the receiving, then, that h. lies. All
M-22 ......... 7:9 determining where h. should be given

M-23 ............h JESUS HAVE A SPECIAL PLACE IN **H.**?
M-23 .........1:3 their pupils were denied **h.** because of this
M-23 .........1:9 Why is the appeal to him part of **h.**?
M-25 .........6:6 of hope and **h.** in the Holy Spirit's service.
C-4.............6:8 single remedy joined in one **h.** brightness.
P-in............1:3 Only the mind is in need of **h.**. This does
P-1.............2:7 in his **h.** is the therapist forgiven with him
P-2...........I.1:2 with the realization that **h.** is of the mind,
P-2......... II.5:2 psychotherapy have nothing to do with **h.**
P-2......... II.6:1 **h.** is an invitation to God to enter into His
P-2......... II.7:5 not understand that **h.** comes from God.
P-2......... II.8:2 must the therapist do to bring **h.** about?
P-2........ III.1:4 this One be wholly absent if the goal is **h.**.
P-2........ III.2:1 **H.** is limited by the limitations of the
P-2........ III.3:6 goals alone can interfere with perfect **h.**.
P-2........ III.4:2 Christ. But **h.** is a process, not a fact. The
P-2........ III.4:4 that stands at the end of the process of **h.**,
P-2........ IV.3:6 **H.** is therapy or correction, and we have
P-2........ IV.4:2 cure, and not one of them understands **h.**.
P-2...... IV.11:2 carries so wearily, and **h.** is accomplished.
P-2............ V.h The Process of **H.**
P-2......... V.4:1 **H.** is holy. Nothing in the world is holier
P-2......... V.4:4 Where two have joined for **h.**, God is
P-2......... V.4:6 can be sure that **h.** is a process He directs,
P-2......... V.6:3 count as nothing, for the **h.** has begun.
P-2......... V.7:4 already, if we think there is a need of **h.**.
P-2......... V.7:7 His **h.** is our own. And as we see the
P-2......... V.8:9 Holy is **h.**, for the Son of God returns to
P-2....... V.8:10 For **h.** tells him, in the Voice for God, that
P-2........... VI.h The Definition of **H.**
P-2........ VI.1:1 forgiveness, for no **h.** can be anything else
P-2........ VI.1:5 **H.** occurs as a patient begins to hear the
P-2........ VI.2:3 The sound of **h.** can be heard instead. But
P-2........ VI.4:9 To concentrate your **h.** efforts here is but
P-2....... VII.1:3 He who needs **h.** must heal. Physician,
P-2....... VII.1:6 heal? And who else is in need of **h.**? Each
P-2....... VII.2:1 whom you pray, and who is in need of **h.**.
P-2....... VII.2:2 is prayer, and **h.** is its aim and its result.
P-2....... VII.2:8 **H.** is here, and happiness and peace.
P-2....... VII.3:2 the difference between **h.** and forgiveness
P-2....... VII.4:3 devoting his life to the function of true **h.**.
P-2....... VII.8:5 **H.** is done, for what is perfect needs no
P-2....... VII.8:5 is done, for what is perfect needs no **h.**,
P-3......... II.1:4 devote themselves primarily to **h.** of one
P-3......... II.1:9 applications of the general principles of **h.**
P-3......... II.2:1 that there is no order of difficulty in **h.**.
P-3......... II.2:2 or nothing about the real principles of **h.**.
P-3......... II.2:3 taught him how to make **h.** impossible.
P-3......... II.3:3 He may be uninterested in **h.** as his major
P-3......... II.6:1 forgets to judge the patient that **h.** occurs.
P-3......... II.7:1 it is when judgment ceases that **h.** occurs,
P-3......... II.7:1 that there is no order of difficulty in **h.**.
P-3......... II.8:1 order of difficulty in **h.** is meaningless.
P-3......... II.8:7 laws of **h.** can be theirs in just an instant.
P-3......... II.9:4 there is no order of difficulty in **h.**, he
P-3......... II.9:8 at their shrine, and this they regard as **h.**.
P-3....... II.10:9 the offering and the acceptance of **h.**. This
P-3........ III.1:1 for **h.** is of God and He asks for nothing.
P-3........ III.2:2 it. Nor will he find his **h.** in the process.
P-3........ III.2:9 for he could never understand what **h.** is.
P-3........ III.3:5 only gift whereby all **h.** is accomplished.
P-3........ III.8:2 will come to you carrying the gift of **h.**, if
S-3..................h Healing
S-3.........in.1:2 in ultimate attainment of the goal, is **h.**.
S-3.........in.1:3 for **h.** is a sign or symbol of forgiveness'
S-3...........I.1:4 **H.** the body is impossible, and this is
S-3...........I.1:5 its **h.** but delays its turning back to dust,
S-3...........I.5:1 between true **h.** and its faulty counterpart
S-3...........I.5:3 to kill, so **h.** can be false as well as true; a
S-3............ II.h False versus True **H.**
S-3......... II.1:1 False **h.** merely makes a poor exchange of
S-3......... II.1:3 yet. Only false **h.** can give way to fear, so
S-3......... II.1:4 False **h.** can indeed remove a form of pain
S-3......... II.3:3 If there has been true **h.**, this can be the
S-3......... II.4:2 Yet first true **h.** must have come to bless
S-3......... II.5:4 What **h.** has occurred in such a view of
S-3......... II.5:6 by the **h.** that the world cannot conceive.
S-3......... II.5:7 There is no partial **h.**. What but shifts
S-3....... II.5:10 true. If you are healed your **h.** is complete.
S-3.........II.6:1 False **h.** rests upon the body's cure,
S-3........ III.1:1 False **h.** heals the body in a part, but
S-3........ III.1:5 For it is this that makes true **h.** possible.
S-3........ III.1:8 here the meaning of true **h.** has been lost,
S-3........ III.2:2 be said of any form of **h.** that is based on
S-3........ III.2:5 can give **h.** to the one who stands beneath
S-3........ III.2:6 The **h.** of the body can be done by this
S-3........ III.3:1 the aim of **h.** as the world conceives of it.
S-3........ III.3:4 be? True **h.** cannot come from inequality
S-3........ III.4:1 Is there a role for **h.**, then, that one can
S-3........ III.4:5 bearer of the special gift that brings the **h.**
S-3........ III.5:8 else can heal as God established **h.**.
S-3........ III.5:9 Without Him there is no **h.**, for there is
S-3........ III.6:3 body's **h.** will occur because its cause has
S-3.......... IV.h The Holiness of **H.**
S-3........ IV.1:2 sight their brothers share their **h.** and
S-3...... IV.1:10 Their **h.** has restored their wholeness so
S-3........ IV.2:1 effect of mercy truly taught, **h.** is blessing.
S-3........ IV.3:3 for He knows the Cause of **h.** is Himself,
S-3........ IV.3:4 Do not ask partial **h.**, nor accept an idol
S-3........ IV.5:4 Now **h.** is impossible, for He is blamed for
S-3........ IV.6:3 Dream now of **h.**. Then arise and lay all
S-3........ IV.6:6 to Christ and let Him be your Guide to **h.**,

## healing's 3

T-29 .......II.2:1 You have accepted **h.** cause, and so it
S-3...........I.5:2 The world of opposites is **h.** place, for
S-3........ III.6:2 all those who serve with Him in **h.** name.

## healing-to-separate 1

S-3........ III.2:1 **H.** may seem to be a strange idea. And

## heals 24

T-2 ....... III.2:4 This **h.** the separation by placing within
T-3 ....... IV.4:4 because it **h.** misperception, and this is
T-5 .........II.2:5 means by which the Atonement **h.** until
T-5 .........II.7:8 Peace is stronger than war because it **h.**.
T-5 ........ V.5:2 the mind **h.** the body because *it* has been
T-5 ...... VII.2:4 Unless the healer **h.** himself, he cannot
T-7 ........ V.5:2 always **h.** by Him the results will vary. Yet
T-8 .... VII.10:2 Since this is natural it **h.** by making whole
T-8 ....... IX.3:1 Wholeness **h.** because it is of the mind.
T-9 ..... IV.12:3 Only this awareness **h.**, because it is the
T-14 ..... IX.7:1 image of the holiness that **h.** the world.
T-17 ........I.3:3 your lack of faith in the power that **h.** all
T-19 ........I.2:4 He has given it, and so He **h.** through you.
T-24 .... V.1:10 Except that one deludes; the other **h.**.
W-pI... 100.4:3 and their joy **h.** sorrow and despair. They
W-pI... 108.3:3 that **h.** because it brings single perception
W-pI... 124.1:4 on a shining light that blesses and that **h.**.
W-pI... 140.4:1 Atonement **h.** with certainty, and cures
C-4 ........... 5:4 This is its holiness; this is how it **h.**. The
P-2..........II.7:1 religion **h.**, so must true psychotherapy
P-2........ VI.5:5 that only forgiveness **h.** an unforgiveness,
P-2....... VII.3:4 His vision **h.** perception and sickness
S-3........ III.1:1 False healing **h.** the body in a part, but
S-3........ III.5:4 It **h.** no part, but wholly and forever. Now

## health 37

*See also* health-inducing

T-2 ........I.5:11 **H.** is inner peace. It enables you to remain
T-6 ..... V.C.9:7 it. Once your mind is healed it radiates **h.**,
T-8 ... VII.13:4 **H.** is therefore nothing more than united
T-8 .... VIII.1:7 body, then, is not the source of its own **h.**.
T-8 .... VIII.2:2 other, making the concepts of both **h.** and
T-8 .... VIII.9:8 to attack. **H.** is seen as the natural state of
T-8 .... VIII.9:9 anything. **H.** is the result of relinquishing
T-8 ... VIII.9:10 body lovelessly. **H.** is the beginning of the
T-8 ....... IX.9:6 Your healing, then, is part of His **h.**, since
T-10 ..... III.6:3 **H.** in this world is the counterpart of
T-10 ...... V.3:2 obviously demands the denial of **h.**,
T-10 ...... V.3:2 because **h.** is in direct opposition to its
T-12 .......II.3:3 perceive in sickness the appeal for **h.** is to
T-19 ........I.3:3 Its **h.** or sickness depends entirely on how
T-24 .... VII.4:5 For in that choice lie both its **h.** and harm
T-27 ........I.6:2 healing is his comfort and his **h.** because
T-27 .......I.10:5 and by its **h.** and loveliness proclaim the
T-27 .......II.7:7 Your **h.** is a result of your desire to see
T-27 .......V.2:1 **H.** is the witness unto health. As long as
T-27 .......V.2:1 Health is the witness unto **h.**. As long as
T-28 ... IV.10:3 he has received the simple happiness of **h.**
T-28 .......V.1:3 your brother, and what is now seen as **h.**?
T-28 .... VII.2:2 deny yourself your wholeness and your **h.**
T-28 .... VII.7:1 Your home is built upon your brother's **h.**
T-29 ........I.5:6 do. It dictates what its **h.** can tolerate, and
T-29 .......II.7:7 change with time, with sickness or with **h.**
T-30 ... VIII.2:5 form of the appearance of his perfect **h.**,
W-pI .... 76.4:3 of medicine, of economics and of **h.**.
W-pI .. 110.3:1 the truth, **h.** cannot turn to sickness, nor
W-pI 127.11:2 we will watch it grow in **h.** and strength,
W-pI 135.10:1 body will respond with **h.** when they have
W-pI 135.13:3 while. In this capacity is **h.** assured. For
W-pI 136.18:3 The body's **h.** is fully guaranteed, because
M-5 .........I.1:6 strength is seen as threat and **h.** as danger
M-8 ........... 2:7 Finding **h.** a burden, it retreats into
P-2........ IV.7:6 Perhaps an illusion of **h.** is substituted for
S-3.........II.1:1 one; a dream of sickness for a dream of **h.**.

## health-inducing 1

W-pI .. 135.5:3 structures of defense, no **h.** medicine, no

## healthy 3

W-pI .. 135.7:3 will be strong and **h.** if the mind does not
W-pI .. 135.8:2 quite apart from you, and it becomes a **h.**,
M-12 ......... 6:9 real than to regard it as **h.** and beautiful.

## heap 1

T-28 ..... III.7:2 stored a **h.** of snow that shone like silver.

## hear 286

T-4 ....... IV.1:1 If you cannot **h.** the Voice for God, it is
T-4 ....... VI.8:5 of them and you will be ready to **h.** God.
T-5 .........II.3:4 choose to **h.** one of two voices within you.
T-5 .........II.3:9 in this world to **h.** only that Voice and no
T-5 .....II.10:10 it whole? **H.** only this through the Holy
T-5 .......II.12:6 **h.** and give away as you answer the Holy
T-5 ....... III.4:3 increased in strength before you can **h.** It.
T-5 ....... III.4:4 It is impossible to **h.** It in yourself while It
T-5 ....... III.4:5 It is limited by your unwillingness to **h.** It.
T-5 ..... IV.1:11 presence of those who **h.** the Holy Spirit's
T-5 ....... IV.4:2 to share It in order to **h.** It yourself. The
T-5 ....... IV.5:6 was in me rejoices as you choose to **h.** it.
T-5 ...... VI.10:7 The Holy Spirit will not **h.** it, because He
T-6 .........I.8:1 share my decision to **h.** only one Voice,
T-6 ........I.10:4 **h.** only one Voice you are never called on
T-6 ........I.10:5 being able to **h.** the Holy Spirit in others
T-6 ........I.19:2 to help them **h.** this for themselves. When
T-6 ....... III.1:7 ego you can **h.** and teach and learn what
T-6 ....... IV.4:1 The ego cannot **h.** the Holy Spirit, but it
T-6 ....... IV.6:1 **H.**, then, the one answer of the Holy
T-6 ....... IV.6:4 left of your dream when you **h.** Him,
T-7 .........V.9:1 As you can **h.** two voices, so you can see
T-8 ....... IV.3:9 and your decision to **h.** me is the decision
T-8 ....... IV.3:9 to **h.** His Voice and abide in His Will. As
T-9 .........II.4:7 As you **h.** him you will hear me. Listening
T-9 .........II.4:7 As you hear him you will **h.** me. Listening
T-9 .........II.4:8 to truth is the only way you can **h.** it now,
T-9 .........II.5:9 his words and making you able to **h.** them
T-9 .......II.5:11 faith in him strong enough to let you **h.**?
T-9 .........II.6:5 **h.** the Voice for God in yourself alone,
T-9 .........II.6:8 that it is for you unless you **h.** it in others.
T-9 .......II.6:11 **h.** His answer except as He answers all of
T-9 .......II.6:12 **H.** of your brother what you would have
T-9 .......II.6:12 what you would have me **h.** of you, for
T-9 .........II.7:4 you. I **h.** only the Holy Spirit in you, Who
T-9 .........II.7:5 If you would **h.** me, hear my brothers in
T-9 .........II.7:5 me, **h.** my brothers in whom God's Voice
T-9 .........II.7:7 as you **h.** the answer in everyone. Do not
T-9 .........II.7:8 to anything else or you will not **h.** truly.
T-9 .........II.8:7 **H.** only God's Answer in His Sons, and

| | |
|---|---|
| T-9........III.4:3 | If you do not **h.** Him, you are listening to |
| T-9........VI.1:2 | with your eyes nor **h.** Him with your ears. |
| T-9........VII.8:3 | the ego speaks, and you will not **h.** it. The |
| T-9... VIII.11:8 | Listen and do not question what you **h.**, |
| T-10.........I.3:3 | When you **h.** the Holy Spirit you may feel |
| T-10......III.8:3 | other gods before Him or you will not **h.**. |
| T-10......III.9:3 | You will **h.** the god you listen to. You |
| T-10......III.9:4 | him you made yourself able to **h.** him. Yet |
| T-10....... V.7:5 | you **h.** His message He has answered you, |
| T-10....... V.7:5 | and you will learn of Him if you **h.** aright. |
| T-11...... I.11:6 | Blessed are you who learn that to **h.** the |
| T-11......IV.5:7 | Creator, he will **h.** the Voice for his Father |
| T-11..... V.18:7 | You **h.** but your own voice, and if Christ |
| T-11..... V.18:7 | speaks through you, you will **h.** Him. |
| T-12....... I.6:11 | But **h.** his call for the Help of God, and |
| T-12.........I.7:5 | then, **h.** every call for help as what it is, so |
| T-12...VII.11:3 | nor **h.** the answer that you sought. That is |
| T-13....... V.6:2 | there, and you **h.** what makes no sound. |
| T-13....... V.6:6 | God calls you and you do not **h.**, for you |
| T-13......VII.4:3 | or not to **h.** the cries of pain that rise to it |
| T-13...... X.13:5 | without the fear that you will **h.** me not. I |
| T-14......IV.8:3 | **h.** me speak for Him and for yourself. You |
| T-15...... II.4:12 | of Him that you will **h.** and understand. |
| T-15...... II.4:13 | will doubt until you **h.** one witness whom |
| T-15....III.12:3 | **H.** not his appeal to hell and littleness, |
| T-15...VII.10:6 | and will be afraid to **h.** the Holy Spirit, |
| T-15... VIII.2:1 | **H.** Him gladly, and learn of Him that you |
| T-15.......IX.5:2 | No one can **h.** Him speak of this and long |
| T-16....... II.8:1 | and deaf could fail to see and **h.** them. |
| T-16....IV.11:4 | stay. **H.** not the call of hate, and see no |
| T-17......III.1:7 | Because you bring them, you will **h.** them. |
| T-17....III.1:11 | with keeping separation could **h.** them. |
| T-17......IV.3:3 | completely that you will not **h.** the call of |
| T-17....... V.7:5 | *H. not this now!* Have faith in Him Who |
| T-18.........I.5:1 | may be surprised to **h.** how very different |
| T-18...... I.12:1 | God has called should **h.** no substitutes. |
| T19..IV.B.16:1 | **H.** not its madness, and believe not the |
| T19... IV.C.2:6 | to his funeral, and **h.** him laugh at death. |
| T-20....... II.6:6 | Listen and **h.** this carefully, nor think it |
| T-20....... II.8:5 | nor have you ever failed entirely to **h.**. |
| T-21......IV.4:4 | reason tells you now the ego would not **h.** |
| T-21......IV.7:2 | the song it longed to **h.** since first the ego |
| T-21....... V.1:6 | senseless ravings to those who want to **h.** |
| T-21....... V.1:9 | For on the voice you choose to **h.**, and on |
| T-22.... II.10:7 | Is it not welcome news to **h.** not one of |
| T-24....... II.4:6 | strain your ears to **h.** its soundless voice, |
| T-24....... II.5:1 | never will you **h.** the Voice for God beside |
| T-24....... II.5:5 | special messages the special **h.** convince |
| T-24....... II.6:5 | never was, nor **h.** what makes no sound. |
| T-24......III.7:3 | Yet they **h.** nothing. They are lost in |
| T-24....... V.3:7 | see nothing and there is no sound to **h.**. |
| T-24....... V.5:5 | see and **h.** and hold and lead is given light |
| T-24....... V.6:6 | Christ is there to see and **h.** and love and |
| T-24....... V.7:3 | that their ears may **h.** no more the sound |
| T-24....... V.7:8 | The song of Christ is all there is to **h.**. The |
| T-24......VII.9:4 | can feel it with your hands and **h.** it move. |
| T-25......III.6:6 | He will **h.** plainly that the calls to war he |
| T-25....... V.3:4 | to see. Nor do you **h.** his plaintive call, |
| T-25....... V.3:5 | that you might **h.** in him His Call to you, |
| T-26.........I.6:3 | **H.**, then, the song your brother sings to |
| T-26.........I.6:4 | will **h.** no song of liberation for yourself, |
| T-26....... V.7:2 | Is any echo from the past that he may **h.** a |
| T-26....... V.7:2 | fact in what is there to **h.** where he is now |
| T-27....... II.6:7 | last trumpet that the world will ever **h.**. |
| T-27......IV.6:9 | the mind is still enough to **h.** an answer |
| T-27.....VI.2:11 | Sin's witnesses **h.** but the call of death. |
| T-27......VI.3:2 | You use its eyes to see, its ears to **h.**, and |
| T-27... VIII.9:7 | But **h.** Him say, "My brother, holy Son of |
| T-28....... V.4:3 | the voices that its ears were made to **h.**. |
| T-28....... V.4:5 | It cannot see nor **h.**. It does not know |
| T-28....... V.5:4 | to **h.** the voices that can make no sound. |
| T-28....... V.5:6 | and what they see and **h.** they but report. |
| T-28....... V.5:7 | It is not they that **h.** and see, but you, who |
| T-28......VI.2:1 | you do not like, although it cannot **h.**. It |
| T-29....... II.4:3 | You did not **h.** Him enter, for you did not |
| T-29....... V.4:2 | Be very still and **h.** God's Voice in him, |
| T-29......IX.1:4 | up? **H.**, then, your story in the dream you |
| T-30.........I.3:3 | **h.** may not resolve the problem as you |
| T-30.........I.3:7 | at first, while you are learning how to **h.**. |
| T-30..... II.1:12 | He asks no more than that He **h.** you call |
| T-30....... II.2:7 | **H.** It now, that you may be reminded of |
| T-30....... II.3:3 | Now **h.** God speak to you, through Him |
| T-31.........I.8:7 | in. And so you did not **h.** it, and had lost a |
| T-31.......I.10:3 | How wrong are you who fail to **h.** the call |
| T-31.......I.11:4 | **H.** not the call for this within yourself. |
| T-31.......I.11:7 | For as you **h.**, you answer. And behold! |
| T-31....... II.5:9 | **H.** the one, and you are separate from |
| T-31.... II.5:10 | But **h.** the other, and you join with him |
| T-31.... II.5:11 | The voice you **h.** in him is but your own. |
| T-31.... II.5:14 | see an image of yourself and **h.** your voice |
| T-31....... II.7:6 | He cannot **h.** a different answer from the |
| T-31....... II.8:5 | wish to **h.** a call that never has been made |
| T-31....... II.8:8 | But as you **h.** it, you will understand you |
| T-31....... II.9:2 | **H.** but his call for mercy and release from |
| T-31...... V.17:6 | the world is more afraid to **h.** than this: *I* |
| T-31... VIII.8:1 | fail to **h.** my voice and listen to my words. |
| T-31... VIII.9:4 | **H.** me, my brothers, hear and join with |
| T-31... VIII.9:4 | me, my brothers, **h.** and join with me. |
| T-31... VIII.9:6 | For you *will* **h.**, and you *will* choose again. |
| W-pI.....22.2:2 | it not joyous news to **h.** that it is not real? |
| W-pI.....49.2:6 | Try to **h.** God's Voice call to you lovingly, |
| W-pI.....49.3:2 | We will try actually to **h.** God's Voice |
| W-pI.....49.3:4 | He wants you to **h.** His Voice. He gave It |
| W-pI....66.10:1 | You will listen to madness or **h.** the truth |
| W-pI.....67.5:2 | You need to **h.** the truth about yourself as |
| W-pI.....67.5:4 | itself. **H.** the truth about yourself in this. |
| W-pI.....71.9:7 | to your willingness to **h.** His Voice. Refuse |
| W-pI.....71.9:8 | Refuse not to **h.**. The very fact that you |
| W-pI.....72.7:4 | that you may not **h.** the Voice of truth |
| W-pI.72.10:10 | salvation without waiting to **h.** what it is. |
| W-pI....72.11:1 | Now we would see and **h.** and learn. |
| W-pI....72.12:6 | He will answer. Be determined to **h.**. |
| W-pI.....76.9:2 | hold your mind in silent readiness to **h.** |
| W-pI....76.10:1 | **H.** Him Who tells you this, and realize |
| W-pI.....95.2:3 | It does not **h.** your prayers, for it is deaf. |
| W-pI.....95.3:1 | to be aware only of what can **h.** and see, |
| W-pI.....98.4:3 | While those as yet unborn will **h.** the call |
| W-pI....100.2:6 | and **h.** God calling to them in your happy |
| W-pI....106.1:1 | then you will **h.** the mighty Voice of truth, |
| W-pI....106.2:1 | and **h.** your Father speak to you through |
| W-pI....106.3:3 | **H.** them not. Be still today and listen to |
| W-pI....106.3:6 | **H.** only Him today, and do not wait to |
| W-pI....106.3:7 | to reach Him longer. **H.** one Voice today. |
| W-pI....106.4:2 | **H.** and be silent. He would speak to you. |
| W-pI....106.5:1 | **H.** Him today, and listen to the Word |
| W-pI....106.5:4 | **H.** Him today, and offer Him your voice |
| W-pI....106.5:4 | to **h.** the Word that He will speak today. |
| W-pI....106.6:4 | you will **h.** a Voice which will resound |
| W-pI....106.9:2 | and they will **h.** the holy Word you hear. |
| W-pI....106.9:2 | and they will hear the holy Word you **h.**. |
| W-pI.106.10:2 | today to reinforce your choice to **h.** and to |
| W-pI....109.4:5 | and they will **h.** and come to you because |
| W-pI....109.4:6 | They will not **h.** another voice than yours |
| W-pI....109.7:3 | will **h.** the bird begin to sing and see the |
| W-pI....118.2:2 | *let me h. the mighty Voice for Truth Itself* |
| W-pI....122.4:2 | requests, halfhearted willingness to **h.**, |
| W-pI....125.1:2 | Your Father wills you **h.** His Word today. |
| W-pI....125.1:4 | **H.** Him today. No peace is possible until |
| W-pI....125.1:5 | **h.** to usher in the quiet time of peace. |
| W-pI....125.3:1 | In stillness we will **h.** God's Voice today |
| W-pI....125.4:1 | **H.**, holy Son of God, your Father speak. |
| W-pI....125.6:4 | mind to **h.** the Voice for its Creator speak. |
| W-pI....125.9:4 | You will **h.** the Word in which the Will of |
| W-pI.126.10:4 | glad to **h.** the Voice of truth and healing |
| W-pI.126.11:7 | And what you **h.** of Him you will believe, |
| W-pI....127.6:3 | eyes that see and ears that **h.** love's Voice. |
| W-pI.140.10:4 | Today we **h.** a single Voice which speaks |
| W-pI.140.11:4 | when we can **h.** our Father speak to us. |
| W-pI.140.11:5 | We **h.** Him now. We come to Him today. |
| W-pI.140.12:6 | to **h.** the answer to our prayer be given us |
| W-pI....151.6:1 | **H.** not its voice. The witnesses it sends to |
| W-pI....151.9:4 | Son? What whispers of the ego can He **h.**? |
| W-pI.151.12:4 | and **h.** in everything no sound except the |
| W-pI.151.15:4 | when you **h.** the Voice for God give honor |
| W-pI.153.18:1 | **h.** His loving Voice guiding your footsteps |
| W-pI....154.3:1 | It is through His ability to **h.** one Voice |
| W-pI.154.10:2 | it is but our voice we **h.** as we attend Him. |
| W-pI....155.6:3 | it is not illusion that they **h.** you speak of, |
| W-pI...160.8:4 | **H.** His Voice assure you, quietly and sure, |
| W-pI...161.2:6 | to your mind the sounds it wants to **h.**. |
| W-pI.161.12:2 | For He will **h.** the Voice for God in you, |
| W-pI...162.2:6 | and **h.** this sound will never look on death |
| W-pI...169.3:4 | an open mind can **h.** the Call to waken. It |
| WpI...rV.in9:2 | I need; that you will **h.** the words I speak, |
| W-pI...182.7:7 | He will wait until you **h.** His gentle Voice |
| W-pI...182.8:1 | restless mind, then will you **h.** His Voice. |
| W-pI.182.12:4 | This is the voice you **h.**, and this the call |
| W-pI...183.3:4 | The blind can see; the deaf can **h.**. The |
| W-pI...183.6:3 | His. **H.** nothing else. Let all your thoughts |
| W-pI...183.7:5 | cannot **h.** requests that He be not Himself |
| W-pI...186.5:6 | the humble free to **h.** the Voice which tells |
| W-pI.186.12:6 | **H.** instead a certain Voice, which tells you |
| W-pI...191.9:1 | **h.** this: All power is given unto you in |
| W-pI...195.7:4 | clarity as we are willing once again to **h.**. |
| W-pI...198.5:3 | a kindness to yourself to **h.** His Voice and |
| W-pI...198.6:5 | Those who **h.** His words have heard the |
| W-pI...199.8:9 | *I h. the Voice that God has given me, and it is* |
| W-pI...200.9:6 | The Father calls; the Son will **h.**. And that |
| W-pII .221.1:5 | *I come to h. Your Voice in silence and in* |
| W-pII .221.1:5 | *love, sure You will h. my call and answer me.* |
| W-pII .221.2:3 | that He will speak to you, and you will **h.**. |
| W-pII .221.2:6 | to **h.** our Father's answer to our call, to let |
| W-pII .221.2:6 | to **h.** Him speak to us of what we are, and |
| W-pII .226.2:2 | *Your Arms are open and I h. Your Voice.* |
| W-pII .232.1:3 | *be there to h. my call to You and answer me.* |
| W-pII .237.1:3 | which I **h.** as God my Father speaks to me |
| W-pII ..... 3.2:6 | But eyes deceive, and ears **h.** falsely. Now |
| W-pII ..... 3.4:4 | it. **H.** His Voice alone in all that speaks to |
| W-pII .245.2:3 | And thus we come to **h.** the Voice for God |
| W-pII ..... 4.1:6 | What would they **h.** or reach to grasp? |
| W-pII .254.1:1 | *Father, today I would but h. Your Voice. In* |
| W-pII .254.1:2 | *to h. Your Voice and to receive Your Word. I* |
| W-pII .256.2:2 | *We have no goal except to h. Your Voice, and* |
| W-pII .264.1:2 | *in all the things I look upon, the sounds I h.,* |
| W-pII .271.1:1 | to look upon, the sounds I want to **h.**, the |
| W-pII .272.2:2 | And if we **h.** temptation call to us to stay |
| W-pII .275.1:2 | will seek and **h.** and learn and understand |
| W-pII .290.2:2 | *You cannot fail to h. me, Father. What I ask* |
| W-pII .296.1:1 | *Your Voice, and h. Your Word through me. I* |
| W-pII .296.1:4 | *and h. the Word Your holy Voice will speak* |
| W-pII .303.1:5 | let Him **h.** the sounds He understands, |
| W-pII ... 10.1:1 | **h.** the Voice for God proclaim that what is |
| W-pII .311.2:1 | *to h. Your Judgment of the Son You love. We* |
| W-pII ... 11.5:2 | We **h.** His Voice, and we forgive creation |
| W-pII .327.1:2 | For God has promised He will **h.** my call, |
| W-pII .334.1:4 | to all who **h.** and choose to follow Him. |
| W-pII .339.2:2 | *myself, but h. Your Voice in everything I do;* |
| W-pII .340.1:4 | *For he will h. Your Voice directing him to* |
| W-pII .347.2:2 | and **h.** the gentle Voice for God assuring |
| W-pII ... 14.4:2 | ears that **h.** the Voice for God proclaim |
| W-pII .352.1:8 | *I would h. Your Voice and find Your peace* |
| W-pII .357.1:3 | *instructs me patiently to h. Your Word, and* |
| W-pII .357.1:4 | *I h. Your Voice instructing me to find the* |
| WpII361-5.1:5 | And He will **h.** and answer me, because |
| W-ep .........3:2 | **h.** but the Voice for God and for your Self |
| M-1 ...........2:7 | Many **h.** It, but few will answer. Yet it is |
| M-12 .........3:3 | Only very few can **h.** God's Voice at all, |
| M-15 ......... 1:6 | will **h.** his sinlessness proclaimed around |
| M-15 ....... 1:10 | may **h.** this Judgment of the Son of God: |
| M-15 ........2:5 | function to prepare yourself to **h.** this |
| M-15 .......2:10 | and **h.** the Voice of Judgment in yourself? |
| M-18 .........3:3 | eyes now "see"; its ears alone can "**h.**." Its |
| M-21 .........4:3 | words, being as yet unable to **h.** in silence. |
| C-2.............8:3 | Is not a song like this what you would **h.**? |
| C-6.............1:3 | to accept Him and to **h.** His Voice. His is |
| C-ep...........4:1 | called to us and helped us **h.** His Call. |
| P-1.............2:2 | learn to call upon God and **h.** His Answer |
| P-2......... V.4:5 | that He will **h.** and answer them in truth. |
| P-2......... V.8:4 | **H.** a brother call for help and answer him. |
| P-2......... V.8:6 | There is no other way to **h.** His Voice. |
| P-2........ VI.1:5 | as a patient begins to **h.** the dirge he sings |
| P-2........ VI.1:7 | To **h.** it is the first step in recovery. To |
| P-2........ VI.2:1 | to **h.** this song of death only an instant, |
| P-2........ VI.3:1 | The ear translates; it does not **h.**. The eye |
| P-2........ VI.3:6 | forms they look upon; the sounds they **h.**. |
| P-2........ VI.7:2 | song salvation sings to all who **h.** its Voice |
| P-3...........I.2:7 | What you **h.** is true. Would God send His |

P-3 I.2:12 or **h.** the Voice of Him Who is God in you
P-3 I.4:9 to **h.** the call and understand that it is his?
P-3 II.10:3 He does not see and he does not **h.**. How,
P-3 II.10:7 Because his inability to see and **h.** does
S-1 I.3:4 In true prayer you **h.** only the song. All
S-2 III.6:10 to God you turn to **h.** what you should do
S-3 IV.7:6 **H.** this an instant and you will be healed.
S-3 IV.7:7 **H.** this an instant and you have been
S-3 IV.8:7 Do not refuse to **h.** the Call for Love. Do

## heard 79

T-2 I.3:2 "lies of the serpent," all he **h.** was untruth
T-5 IV.4:1 I **h.** one Voice because I understood that I
T-9 II.3:4 is possible that His answer will not be **h.**.
T-9 II.3:6 have already received but have not yet **h.**.
T-10 III.8:2 all illusions because you **h.** His Voice. But
T-10 III.11:3 and He will be **h.** when you place no other
T-10 IV.7:4 the miracle worker has **h.** God's Voice, he
T-11 II.5:1 host, because He will not be **h.**. The
T-11 VIII.6:5 You *have* **h.** the answer, but you have
T-12 VII.11:3 I have **h.** your call and I have answered it,
T-12 VIII.4:4 what you have not **h.** is the only Answer.
T-13 III.3:3 response to the call of love if you **h.** it, and
T-13 V.1:6 are not seen, and sounds that are not **h.**.
T-13 XI.2:4 have **h.** the hymn of freedom rising unto
T-13 XI.7:7 would communicate. His Voice *will* be **h.**.
T-16 II.6:11 of God has called to you, and you have **h.**.
T-16 II.8:4 yet you have so little faith in what you **h.**,
T-16 II.9:9 Think what you have really seen and **h.**,
T-17 V.7:7 He **h.**. Has He not been very explicit in
T-17 V.10:1 the Sonship is the song of freedom **h.**, in
T-18 I.12:3 what became of peace in those who **h.**?
T19. IV.A.16:1 and a softly joyous whispering is ever **h.**.
T19 IV.B.7:9 when its great advocate is **h.** no more?
T19 IV.C.5:7 which **h.** His Answer and accepted It.
T19 IV.D.5:9 you **h.** the Voice of Love beyond them,
T-20 II.8:6 You **h.**, but knew not how to look, nor
T-20 VIII.10:5 are looked on happily, and **h.** with joy.
T-21 I.6:1 which you **h.** completely unremembered.
T-21 I.6:3 how wonderful the setting where you **h.** it
T-21 VI.5:4 you see it, if you **h.** the voice of reason.
T-22 I.2:1 have **h.** a very similar description earlier,
T-24 V.3:7 showing him what can be seen and **h.**,
T-24 VI.13:2 Here is the voice of specialness **h.** clearly,
T-25 III.6:6 war he **h.** before are really calls to peace.
T-26 I.4:9 his song of union and of love be **h.** at all.
T-26 V.11:6 from the past are **h.** and then are doubted
T-27 III.7:1 or ears have **h.** remains to be perceived. A
T-27 IV.6:5 Yet it is only here it can be **h.**. An honest
T-28 II.9:5 will the call to wakening be **h.**, because it
T-28 V.5:5 that *can* be seen and **h.** and understood.
T-29 V.1:2 time has left, and echoes of eternity are **h.**
T-29 IX.8:4 a melody is **h.** that everyone remembers,
T-29 IX.8:4 he has not **h.** it since before all time began
T-29 IX.8:5 so close the song of Heaven can be **h.**, not
T-29 IX.8:6 song again, he knows he never **h.** it not.
T-31 I.8:8 the whole is **h.** throughout the world this
T-31 I.9:2 have **h.** its calling as the ancient call to life
T-31 II.6:4 forgetting everything we thought we **h.**;
W-pI 49.3:5 hear His Voice. He gave It to you to be **h.**.
W-pI 69.8:1 certain that He has **h.** you and answered
W-pI 79.10:6 You will be **h.** and you will be answered.
W-pI 98.4:3 as yet unborn will hear the call we **h.**, and
W-pI 123.5:4 His Word is soundless if it be not **h.**. In
W-pI 123.6:1 Thanks be to you who **h.**, for you become
W-pI 125.1:5 until His Word is **h.** around the world;
W-pI 125.6:2 not be **h.** until your mind is quiet for a
W-pI 152.3:2 This you have **h.** before, but may not yet
W-pI 154.12:2 it. You have **h.** this said a hundred ways, a
W-pI 157.1:3 this day, when echoes of eternity are **h.**.
W-pI 161.7:3 a form he can be touched and seen and **h.**,
W-pI 170.12:5 The Call for God is **h.** and answered. Now
W-pI 183.2:1 Name can not be **h.** without response,
W-pI 196.9:1 be **h.** in the idea we practice for today. If it
W-pI 198.6:5 His words have **h.** the song of Heaven. For
W-pII 8.2:4 There are no cries of pain and sorrow **h.**,
W-pII 321.1:2 *I have searched in vain until I* **h.** *Your Voice*
M-1 3:7 who the teacher was before he **h.** the Call.
M-4 IV.1:11 Nor can God's Teacher be **h.** at all, except
M-13 6:8 Few have **h.** it as yet, and they can but
M-15 2:12 to be quiet, for His Voice is **h.** in stillness.
M-26 3:10 by their awakening can God's Voice be **h.**.
M-26 4:3 If you would be **h.** by those who suffer,
M-28 6:7 for he has **h.** God's Word and understood
M-29 8:4 *which His Voice is* **h.** *around the world, To*
C-6 5:7 place the hymn to God is **h.** a little while.
P-2 VI.2:3 The sound of healing can be **h.** instead.
P-2 VI.2:6 are **h.** instead of loud discordant shrieks.
P-3 III.5:6 they have **h.** His Word and understood it.
S-2 III.6:6 be **h.** by anyone who calls upon His Name

## hearer 1

M-12 4:3 the **h.** messages that are not of this world,

## hearing 9

T-9 III.4:2 if you attend to them you are not **h.** Him.
T-11 VIII.14:3 the Teacher of reality, and **h.** His answer,
T-19 I.3:6 **h.** what truth has never said and behaving
T-31 II.7:5 **h.** but one answer to them all. Because He
W-pI 140.11:1 We waken **h.** Him, and let Him speak to
W-pI 161.2:6 All **h.** but brings to your mind the sounds
W-pII 275.1:3 Join me in **h.**. For the Voice for God tells
M-9 2:4 obvious prerequisite for **h.** God's Voice, is
M-25 2:5 Whose Voice is available but for the **h.**.

## hears 32

T-5 II.10:2 because it **h.** only one Voice and answers
T-13 III.12:8 one who **h.** His answer but will give up
T-13 V.3:4 And no one **h.** their answer save him who
T-19 III.1:5 to it, and the mind **h.** it and yearns for it,
T-21 IV.7:2 Yet what it **h.** in terror, the other part
T-21 IV.7:2 the other part **h.** as the sweetest music;
T-22 I.6:4 sounds a baby makes and what he **h.** are
T-22 I.6:5 he **h.** nor sights he sees are stable yet. But
T-22 I.6:6 But what he **h.** and does not understand
T-24 V.3:6 are the sights He sees, the sounds He **h.**.
T-24 VII.1:5 while it calls to him he **h.** no other Voice.
T-26 IV.5:3 no one **h.** the song of Heaven and remains
T-28 V.4:3 Here are the sounds it **h.**; the voices that
T-28 VI.3:4 shrink from what it sees and what it **h.**,
T-28 VI.3:7 It **h.** your voice. And it is frail and little by
T-29 IX.8:6 And when he **h.** this song again, he knows
T-31 II.7:6 Because He **h.** one Voice, He cannot hear
W-pI 95.14:8 you do so, someone **h.** the voice of hope,
W-pI 164.1:5 He **h.** the sounds the senseless, busy
W-pI 164.1:5 world engenders, yet He **h.** them faintly.
W-pI 164.1:6 beyond them all He **h.** the song of Heaven
W-pI 164.3:1 Christ gives you His sight and **h.** for you,
W-pI 164.3:1 and answers in your name the Call He **h.**!
W-pI 183.7:3 Think not He **h.** the little prayers of those
M-8 5:3 voice he **h.** than to that of a softer one?
M-21 4:9 speaking. He listens and **h.** and speaks.
M-21 5:1 God's fear about the validity of what he **h.**
M-21 5:2 what he **h.** may indeed be quite startling.
P-2 III.3:4 another **h.** and tries to answer in the form
P-2 VI.1:6 Until he **h.** it, he cannot understand that
S-2 III.5:10 He is the Answer. You the one who **h.**.
S-3 IV.4:2 and called to God, Who **h.** and answers.

## Heart 12

*heart*

T-5 IV.8:13 Whose **H.** and Hands we have our being.
T-16 IV.13:7 you are directed straight to the **H.** of God.
T-26 IV.3:4 the universe to touch the **H.** of all creation
W-pI 127.1:7 It is the **H.** of God, and also of His Son.
W-pI 170.10:4 becomes more fearful than the **H.** of Love
W-pI 197.4:5 acknowledged by the **H.** of God Himself.
W-pI 197.8:5 In your heart the **H.** of God is laid. He
W-pII 267.2:2 *is beating in the peace the* **H.** *of Love created.*
W-pII 340.2:6 awake in Heaven in the **H.** of Love.
W-pII 14.5:5 enter in and disappear into the **H.** of God.
M-15 1:11 *and whole, at peace forever in the* **H.** *of God.*
S-3 IV.9:6 lovingly I hold you in My **H.** and in My

## heart 82

*Heart*

T-1 III.2:4 how a man must think of himself in his **h.**,
T-1 IV.2:2 you realize in your **h.** it *is* a deception, and
T-2 II.1:5 Remember that where your **h.** is, there is
T-3 I.5:4 "Blessed are the pure in **h.** for they shall
T-5 IV.8:10 peace of God in your **h.** and in your hands
T-5 IV.8:11 The **h.** is pure to hold it, and the hands
T-7 XI.3:4 Does it keep his **h.** untouched by fear, and
T-7 XI.4:3 the Kingdom with this lesson in his **h.** has
T-8 VI.10:3 Your **h.** lies where your treasure is, as His
T-10 V.7:7 your **h.** in gratitude for your gift to Him.
T-11 III.3:5 and your **h.** will be so filled with joy that it
T-11 III.3:6 this will be like, for your **h.** is not ready.
T-12 V.8:1 learn what you do not want should take **h.**
T-15 VIII.2:3 cast aside, but still desire with all your **h.**.
T-17 II.1:5 your **h.** sing with joy has ever brought you
T19 IV.D.9:3 forgiveness of his brother in his **h.**. Stand
T-20 III.11:5 and the pure in **h.** see God within His Son
T-21 IV.6:5 its ranting strikes no terror in your **h.**. For
T-22 V.4:5 to its Creator that every **h.** throughout the
T-26 V.4:5 that it is hard indeed to hold it to your **h.**,
T-27 I.5:8 he laid upon his **h.** was ever justified, and
T-27 II.7:7 nor guilt upon his **h.** made heavy with the
T-30 V.3:6 every **h.** made ready to arise and go with
T-30 V.9:3 lies ahead is all you ever wanted in your **h.**
T-30 V.10:8 in confidence walk with a happy **h.** that
T-31 VI.6:9 Who is unwelcome to the kind in **h.**? And
W-pI 14.5:4 "God did not create cancer," or **h.** attacks,
W-pI 62.5:5 for your **h.** will recognize these words,
W-pI 92.8:2 and strength and light abiding in his **h.**.
W-pI 122.8:3 your **h.** with deep tranquility as ancient
W-pI 122.13:4 you see the changeless in the **h.** of change;
W-pI 125.7:2 He speaks from nearer than your **h.** to you
W-pI 131.2:7 while in your **h.** you pray for danger and
W-pI 135.2:5 but must have terror striking at his **h.**.
W-pI 136.8:5 suffer, twist your limbs and stop your **h.**,
W-pI 153.5:3 who feel its iron grip upon your **h.**. You
W-pI 162.6:2 fail to welcome you into his **h.** with loving
W-pI 164.4:2 an ancient peace you carry in your **h.** and
W-pI 169.11:5 each uncertain **h.** that does not beat as yet
W-pI 170.12:3 And now your **h.** remains at peace forever
W-pI 185.8:2 What do you ask for in your **h.**? Forget
W-pI 185.14:1 our desires with the need of every **h.**, the
W-pI 188.3:1 from your **h.** extends around the world. It
W-pI 189.5:4 If hatred finds a place within your **h.**, you
W-pI 191.6:5 have laid the mark of death upon its **h.**.
W-pI 191.10:8 Is not your **h.** willing to bring your weary
W-pI 196.5:5 without the fear of hell upon his **h.**?
W-pI 197.3:3 they be a lasting offering of a thankful **h.**,
W-pI 197.8:5 In your **h.** the Heart of God is laid. He
W-pI 200.10:6 feel its soft embrace surround your **h.** and
W-pI 207.1:2 *blessing shines upon me from within my* **h.**,
W-pI 208.1:4 *It is within my* **h.**, *which witnesses to God*
W-pII 221.1:3 *In the quiet of my* **h.**, *the deep recesses of my*
W-pII 246.1:1 the way to God, if I have hatred in my **h.**.
W-pII 267.h My **h.** is beating in the peace of God.
W-pII 267.1:3 Peace fills my **h.**, and floods my body with
W-pII 267.2:2 *my* **h.** *is beating in the peace the Heart of*
W-pII 286.h The hush of Heaven holds my **h.** today.
W-pII 286.1:8 *My* **h.** *is quiet, and my mind at rest. Your*
W-pII 288.1:6 *Let me not cherish it within my* **h.**, *or I will*
W-pII 315.1:3 upon another, and my **h.** is gladdened.
W-pII 334.2:3 *to his bewildered mind and frightened* **h.**, *to*
W-pII 336.2:2 *my mind, Your Love is still abiding in my* **h.**.
M-15 3:11 It is your function to hold it to your **h.**,
M-21 1:4 But this refers to the prayer of the **h.**, not
M-21 2:4 The prayer of the **h.** does not really ask for
M-21 3:2 If the prayer of the **h.** asks for this, this
M-21 3:3 the prayer of the **h.** remain unanswered in
M-21 3:4 not exist or seeks for illusions in his **h.**, all
M-23 4:6 behind a grateful **h.** and thankful mind.
M-26 1:2 and His Word is written on everyone's **h.**.
M-29 6:2 He understands the requests of your **h.**,
M-29 6:5 your prayers of the **h.** into His language.
C-ep 1:5 Him and with His Word upon your **h.**.
P-2 V.5:6 a hand to reach His Son and touch his **h.**.
P-2 VII.3:1 the therapist in his **h.** tells the patient that
P-3 II.3:6 rise and grow; a patient will touch his **h.**,

S-1 .........in.3:2 and bless you as you lift your h. to Him in
S-1 ........III.5:5 your h. is lifted and your fear released. Do
S-2 ...........I.2:3 Dear to its h. is error, and mistakes loom
S-3 ........IV.4:6 attained until there is no hatred in your h.
S-3 ........IV.6:5 and with a heavy h. made hard against the

## heart's 1

W-pI.182.12:3 This is your h. desire. This is the voice

## heartbeat 4

T-20....... V.2:4 And in that single h. is the unity of love
W-pII..267.1:2 calls to me in every h. and in every breath;
W-pII..267.1:5 me. Each h. brings me peace; each breath
W-pII..267.1:7 Each h. calls His Name, and every one is

## heartens 1

M-24..........2:4 and if it h. them its value is self-evident. It

## hearth 1

W-pI...159.7:3 center of redemption and the h. of mercy,

## hearts 28

T-3......... II.5:8 Because their h. are pure, the innocent
T-20....... V.2:3 raised together call to the h. of everyone,
T-25......IV.3:2 h. that look on sin and beat its sad refrain
T-25......IV.3:4 to look upon, and where their h. are glad.
W-pI.....57.4:4 the h. of all who share this place with me.
W-pI.110.10:4 our hands and h. and minds to God today
W-pI.110.11:1 day with thankful h. and loving thoughts
W-pI...123.4:1 in gratitude we lift our h. above despair,
W-pI...124.4:4 We feel Him in our h.. Our minds contain
W-pI.140.12:1 with lifted h. and listening minds we pray
W-pI...152.9:4 and lift our h. in true humility instead to
W-pI...168.3:1 most carefully preserved within our h.,
W-pI...168.4:3 as h. rise up and claim the light as theirs.
WpI.. rV.in5:4 Let us raise our h. from dust to life, as we
W-pI...188.3:5 It brings renewal to all tired h., and lights
W-pI...189.9:4 And in our quiet h. and open minds, His
W-pI.190.11:2 our gratitude unto our Teacher fill our h.,
W-pII.....in.4:1 but His Word upon our minds and h.,
W-pII..270.2:1 The quiet of today will bless our h., and
W-pII..306.2:2 *with empty hands and open h. and minds,*
W-pII..310.2:4 for we have welcomed love into our h..
W-pII..345.2:1 Peace to all seeking h. today. The light
W-pII....14.5:1 to us, we learn that it is written on our h..
M-25..........6:9 go with Christ's gratitude upon their h.,
M-28..........4:1 All living h. are tranquil with a stir of
S-3 ...........I.2:6 the heavy scent of death upon their h..
S-3 ........IV.6:1 such twisted thoughts upon your h.. You
S-3 ........IV.9:2 Lift up your h. to greet its advent. See the

## heat 2

T-24......III.6:6 without the h. and malice of one thought
W-pI...156.4:4 their arms to shield you from the h., and

## Heaven 557

*heaven*
*See also* Heaven-born

T-1........III.2:1 "H. and earth shall pass away" means
T-3...........I.4:3 even as your Father in H. is merciful. It
T-3......... II.4:6 Father are One, their perfect accord is H..
T-3......VI.11:8 of "Seek ye first the Kingdom of H." say,
T-3......VI.11:8 say, "*Will* ye first the Kingdom of H.," and
T-4......... I.12:5 The Kingdom of H. is the spirit's right,
T-4........III.1:1 of H. is within you" really means. This is
T-4........III.1:4 The Kingdom of H. *is* you. What else *but*
T-5...........I.7:1 are like those in the Kingdom of H. itself:
T-5......... II.4:1 You *are* the Kingdom of H., but you have
T-5......... II.4:3 of H. breaks through into its own. Before
T-5......... II.8:4 God's Will is done on earth as it is in H..
T-5......... II.8:5 Both H. and earth are in you, because the
T-5......... II.9:2 that gave me all power in H. and earth.
T-5........IV.3:9 And of such is the Kingdom of H.. The
T-5......... V.1:4 at its disposal to side with H. or earth, as
T-5......... V.2:1 H. there is no guilt, because the Kingdom
T-7........IV.7:1 Seek ye first the Kingdom of H., because
T-7.......VII.8:4 you to tear the Kingdom of H. from you.
T-7...... XI.3:11 are literally denying H. to yourself.
T-10......III.6:3 world is the counterpart of value in H.. It
T-10..... V.11:3 H. waits for his return, for it was created
T-11...... III.3:5 so filled with joy that it will leap into H.,
T-11.....VII.1:4 Bible speaks of a new H. and a new earth,
T-11.....VII.3:9 the real world will lead you to the real H.,
T-11... VIII.1:7 For as H. and earth become one, even the
T-11... VIII.1:8 its destruction, but its translation into H..
T-11... VIII.8:3 The Kingdom of H. *is* within you. Believe
T-11. VIII.11:2 you share the real world as you share H.,
T-12......IV.6:6 Yet you cannot sell the Kingdom of H..
T-12......VI.4:7 the real world because God gave you H..
T-12......VI.7:5 the real world has slipped quietly into H.,
T-12......VI.7:7 H. is your home, and being in God it must
T-12.....VII.4:7 As your function in H. is creation, so your
T-12.....VII.4:8 God shares His function with you in H.,
T-13....... II.9:6 be great joy in H. on your homecoming,
T-13......III.2:6 you to answer His Call and leap into H..
T-13......IV.1:3 and your function in H. is creating. The
T-13......IV.1:4 and you have no function at all in H.. It
T-13......IV.2:1 nor hell is as unacceptable to you as H..
T-13......IV.2:2 Your definition of H. *is* hell and oblivion,
T-13......IV.2:2 real H. is the greatest threat you think you
T-13......IV.3:4 You question H., but you do not question
T-13......IV.3:6 And even though you know not H., might
T-13...VII.10:3 In H. this is so, for what could you need in
T-13... VIII.2:6 be, is without meaning in H.. Perception
T-13... VIII.3:6 The miracle, without a function in H., is
T-13... VIII.4:6 glimpses of the H. that lies beyond them.
T-13... VIII.9:1 creations establish your fatherhood in H..
T-13... VIII.9:3 the witnesses to your fatherhood in H..
T-13. VIII.10:5 do on earth are lifted up to H. and to Him
T-13. VIII.10:6 know, and as they reach the gates of H.,
T-13.......IX.6:9 you release from guilt great is the joy in H.
T-13...... X.14:6 before the gates of H. where we will surely
T-13.........XI.h The Peace of H.
T-13......XI.2:4 heard the hymn of freedom rising unto H.
T-13......XI.3:1 When we are all united in H., you will
T-13......XI.3:7 value. In H. is everything God values, and
T-13......XI.3:8 H. is perfectly unambiguous. Everything
T-13......XI.6:1 will not remember change and shift in H..
T-13......XI.7:1 it will be sufficient: God wills you be in H.
T-13......XI.8:7 God willed you H., and will always will
T-13......XI.8:9 is no chance that H. will not be yours, for
T-13....XI.10:5 to know that H. is yours to make it so. It *is*
T-13....XI.11:8 only truth, in which the peace of H. lies.
T-14.......in.1:5 pointing as clearly to H. as the ego points
T-14......III.3:2 is living here, as creating is being in H..
T-14....III.15:2 in this world or H. could possibly commit
T-14......IV.5:1 have decided against your function in H.,
T-14......IV.9:1 The children of H. live in the light of the
T-14......IV.9:2 it, and thus denied H. to themselves.
T-14....... V.1:8 of death behind, and return quietly to H..
T-14....... V.6:5 that points to this points straight to H.,
T-14... VIII.5:2 H. itself is union with all of creation, and
T-14... VIII.5:3 And H. remains the Will of God for you.
T-14......IX.5:2 You can reflect H. here. Yet no reflections
T-14......IX.5:4 it. Earth can reflect H. or hell; God or the
T-14......IX.8:4 holiness in them, are ready at last for H..
T-14....... X.1:6 Reflect the peace of H. here, and bring
T-14....... X.1:6 Heaven here, and bring this world to H..
T-14....... X.2:1 In H. reality is shared and not reflected.
T-14....... X.4:5 For some are reflections of H., while
T-14....... X.5:2 of H. last but a moment and grow dim, as
T-15.........I.3:6 It speaks to you of H., but assures you
T-15.........I.3:6 but assures you that H. is not for you.
T-15.........I.3:7 for you. How can the guilty hope for H.?
T-15.......I.4:13 Death is the end as far as hope of H. goes.
T-15.........I.5:1 The ego teaches that H. is here and now
T-15.........I.7:4 as steadily to H. as the ego drives to hell.
T-15.......I.10:3 In this redeeming instant lies H.. And
T-15.......I.10:4 And H. will not change, for the birth into
T-15.......I.10:6 in H. because there is no change in God.
T-15.......I.11:4 tiny instant to offer you the whole of H..
T-15.......I.14:4 As long as it takes to exchange hell for H..
T-15........II.2:7 where He gently translates hell into H..
T-15........II.2:8 is only in H. that God would have you be.
T-15.... III.5:7 decision you make is for H. or for hell,
T-15.... III.12:1 of God, and of the H. that is in him. For
T-15.... III.12:3 but only his call for H. and greatness.
T-15.... III.12:6 above the stars and reaches even to H.,
T-15....... V.7:3 is nothing in H. or earth that it resembles,
T-15....... V.8:1 and although this is not so in H., the Holy
T-15....... V.8:1 how to bring a touch of H. to them here.
T-15...... IX.4:1 divide your strength between H. and hell,
T-15...... IX.4:7 accepted and the loneliness in H. is gone.
T-15...... IX.5:3 For it is your will to be in H., where you
T-15...... XI.2:2 yourself, but shining in the H. within, and
T-15...... XI.4:8 try to resolve the "conflict" of H. and hell
T-15...... XI.4:8 H. out and giving it the attributes of hell,
T-15...... XI.5:3 For who could thrust H. and its Creator
T-16...... III.8:4 supplemented by the strength of H., and
T-16...... III.8:4 united will of all who make H. what it is,
T-16...... IV.8:1 H. waits silently, and your creations are
T-16....... V.2:3 chief weapon for keeping you from H.. It
T-16....... V.3:6 For this world *is* the opposite of H., being
T-16....... V.3:7 In H., where the meaning of love is known
T-16....... V.4:3 believe this specialness is not hell, but H..
T-16....... V.4:4 being the one condition in which H. could
T-16....... V.5:1 To everyone H. is completion. There can
T-16....... V.5:7 This is its idea of H.. And therefore union,
T-16....... V.6:1 ego device for joining hell and H., and
T-16....... V.8:3 other, the ego sees "a union made in H.."
T-16....... V.8:4 not interfere with the ego's illusion of H.,
T-16....... V.8:4 which it offered him to interfere with H..
T-16....... V.8:5 the illusion of H. is nothing more than an
T-16..... V.11:8 arises not from death, nor H. from hell.
T-16.... VI.11:1 will be the understanding of where H. *is.*
T-16.... VI.11:5 joy of H., which has no limit, is increased
T-16.... VI.12:6 Call upon Him, for H. is at His Call. And
T-16.... VI.12:7 His Call. And let Him call on H. for you.
T-16..... VII.9:7 time, to bring you the true condition of H.
T-17........II.7:5 Who, awake in H., could dream that there
T-17.... IV.10:5 The power of H., the Love of God, the
T-17.... IV.11:1 The holy instant is a miniature of H., sent
T-17.... IV.11:1 is a miniature of Heaven, sent you *from* H..
T-17.... IV.11:8 gifts, so the whole of H. lies in this instant
T-17.... IV.14:3 The picture of H. and eternity grows more
T-17..... V.14:4 make you suffer, but which makes H. glad
T-17..... V.14:5 If H. were outside you, you could not
T-18.........I.5:6 error, which seemed to cast you out of H.,
T-18.........I.9:9 you made for H. can keep you from it.
T-18.......I.11:1 H. is restored to all the Sonship through
T-18.......I.11:2 H. has entered quietly, for all illusions
T-18.......I.11:5 H. beholds it, and rejoices that you have
T-18.......I.11:8 H. looks with love on what is joined in it,
T-18.......I.12:2 of the original error that shattered H..
T-18.......I.12:4 Return with me to H., walking together
T-18........II.9:1 H. is sure. This is no dream. Its coming
T-18........II.9:5 and the truth of H. join in the Will of God
T-18.... III.4:10 of your relationship is established in H..
T-18...... III.6:1 with me in bringing H. to the Son of God,
T-18...... III.8:1 Not one light in H. but goes with you.
T-18...... III.8:3 H. is joined with you in your advance to
T-18...... III.8:3 is joined with you in your advance to H..
T-18....... V.2:7 solid rock of faith, and rising even to H..
T-18....... V.2:8 Nor will you use it to ascend to H. alone.
T-18....... V.3:1 thousands will rise to H. with you. Can
T-18....... VI.1:2 that the Kingdom of H. is restored to you.
T-18....... VI.1:4 Kingdom of H. is the dwelling place of the
T-18....... VI.1:5 H. is not a place nor a condition. It is
T-18....... VI.2:3 the awareness of H. and of your Identity.
T-18.... VI.10:1 can stretch out your hand and reach to H.
T-18....VIII.2:6 small, around a very little segment of H.,
T-18....VIII.9:5 will bring love with him from H. for you.
T-18..VIII.10:4 transformed into the Kingdom of H., with
T-18..VIII.11:6 tried to hide from H. straight to Heaven.
T-18..VIII.11:6 tried to hide from Heaven straight to H..
T-18....... IX.1:6 the little part you think you stole from H..
T-18....... IX.1:7 Give it back to H.. Heaven has not lost it,
T-18....... IX.1:8 H. has not lost it, but *you* have lost sight of
T-18....... IX.1:8 has not lost it, but *you* have lost sight of H.
T-18.... IX.13:2 and gently placed before the gates of H..

| | |
|---|---|
| T-19....... II.8:5 | not lightly, for it is the choice of hell or H. |
| T-19...... III.8:5 | H. has smiled upon it, and the belief in sin |
| T-19.... III.10:1 | will see the smile of H. shining on both |
| T-19.... III.10:3 | against a union H. has smiled upon. Your |
| T-19.... III.10:4 | was healed in the holy instant H. gave you |
| T-19.... III.10:6 | to H. will disappear before your holy sight |
| T19... IV.A.3:8 | little wall would hide the purpose of H., |
| T19... IV.A.3:8 | purpose of Heaven, and keep it *from* H.. |
| T19... IV.A.6:1 | There is a hush in H., a happy expectancy |
| T19... IV.A.6:2 | end. For H. knows you well, as you know |
| T19... IV.A.6:2 | Heaven knows you well, as you know H.. |
| T19....IV.B.5:2 | you not glad that H. cannot be sacrificed, |
| T19....IV.B.7:5 | gratitude for giving peace its home in H.. |
| T19....IV.C.3:2 | madness and set against the peace of H.? |
| T19. IV.D.12:7 | will share in madness or in H. together. |
| T19. IV.D.15:5 | grace of H. that you cannot offer to your |
| T19. IV.D.19:6 | H. is the gift you owe your brother, the |
| T19. IV.D.20:7 | in hell or H. to interfere with his decision. |
| T-20..... II.8:12 | only a pathway to the open door of H., the |
| T-20..... II.10:1 | is the way to H. and to the peace of Easter, |
| T-20..... II.11:3 | door of H. and recognize the home that |
| T-20.... III.10:3 | limit. For what is H. but union, direct and |
| T-20...... IV.2:1 | Sin has no place in H., where its results |
| T-20...... IV.2:3 | In him *is* H.. See sin in him instead, and |
| T-20...... IV.2:4 | sin in him instead, and H. is lost to you. |
| T-20.....VIII.4:4 | will see an altar to your Father, holy as H., |
| T-21...... III.4:8 | In H. they are unknown. Yet Heaven is |
| T-21...... III.4:9 | Yet H. is reached through them. |
| T-21...... III.9:5 | than anything that stands this side of H.. |
| T-21...... III.9:9 | makes the sight of it as beautiful as H.. |
| T-21...... IV.6:8 | Yet you would not "sell" H. to have them. |
| T-21...... IV.7:5 | For it remembers H., and now it sees that |
| T-21...... IV.7:5 | it sees that H. has come to earth at last, |
| T-21...... IV.7:6 | H. has come because it found a home in |
| T-21...... IV.7:7 | longer what has been given H. as its own. |
| T-21...... VI.8:1 | are joined is your salvation; the gift of H., |
| T-21...... VI.8:2 | Does H. seem to be a burden to you? In |
| T-21...... VI.8:5 | Reason assures you H. is what you want, |
| T-22.......in.3:7 | Just under H. does he stand, but close |
| T-22.......in.3:9 | home can a relationship so like to H. be? |
| T-22.......I.11:9 | for Them as earth is turned to H.. |
| T-22....... II.7:7 | the joy of H. and the misery of hell. Until |
| T-22....... II.7:8 | Until you choose H., you *are* in hell and |
| T-22....... II.8:1 | no part of H. you can take and weave into |
| T-22....... II.8:2 | is there one illusion you can enter H. with |
| T-22..... II.13:5 | reach H. while a single sin still tempts you |
| T-22..... II.13:6 | H. is the home of perfect purity, and God |
| T-22...... IV.2:3 | of H. to uphold it cannot be undone. Your |
| T-22...... IV.4:4 | The gates of H., open now for you, will |
| T-22...... VI.5:3 | the error, and lays a part of H. in its place. |
| T-22...... VI.5:5 | Each part of H. that you bring is given you |
| T-22...... VI.5:6 | And every empty place in H. that you fill |
| T-22...... VI.6:4 | a gift he let be laid in H. through himself? |
| T-23.......in.4:5 | meaningless distractions, lay H. aside? |
| T-23.......in.6:2 | on it lovingly, and see the light of H. in it. |
| T-23.......in.6:4 | now will be reinterpreted as part of H.. |
| T-23..... II.13:8 | hold in place the substitute for H. which |
| T-23..... II.19:1 | There is no life outside of H.. Where God |
| T-23..... II.19:3 | In any state apart from H. life is illusion. |
| T-23..... II.19:6 | Life not in H. is impossible, and what is |
| T-23..... II.19:6 | and what is not in H. is not anywhere. |
| T-23..... II.19:7 | Outside of H., only the conflict of illusion |
| T-23..... II.19:7 | yet perceived as an eternal barrier to H.. |
| T-23..... II.21:6 | whole descent from H. lies in each one. |
| T-23..... II.22:4 | the twisted stairway that leads from H.. |
| T-23..... II.22:6 | chose the stairs to H. or the way to hell? |
| T-23... II.22:11 | are you sure the goal of H. can be reached |
| T-23...... IV.1:4 | and no illusion in any form stalks H.. |
| T-23...... IV.1:5 | H. is wholly true. No difference enters, |
| T-23...... IV.6:6 | all the lights of H. will gently lean to you, |
| T-23...... IV.7:8 | and the H. He created for His Son *because* |
| T-24.........I.8:9 | defeat the goal of holiness that H. gave it? |
| T-24....... II.3:7 | instead of H. and instead of peace, and |
| T-24....... II.7:6 | brother with the key to H. in his hand, |
| T-24....... II.9:4 | H. so remote that They cannot be reached |
| T-24..... II.11:6 | God and you as one seem anything but H. |
| T-24....... V.7:3 | sightless eyes, and sings to them of H., |
| T-24....... V.8:1 | Lord of H. has Himself come down to you |
| T-24...... VI.2:1 | would be a lack in God, a H. incomplete, a |
| T-24 ... VI.12:5 | and all the power of H. and the might of |
| T-24 .... VII.5:9 | it immortality, setting another light in H., |
| T-24 .... VII.6:6 | In H., means and end are one, and one |
| T-25 ........I.5:1 | H. presents itself to you as separate, too. |
| T-25 .......II.9:1 | How could the Lord of H. not be glad if |
| T-25 ..... III.5:5 | lamps of H. are not for mind to choose to |
| T-25 ..... IV.2:6 | Even in H. does this law obtain. The Son |
| T-25 ..... IV.4:9 | a home in H. the world cannot destroy. |
| T-25 ..... IV.5:1 | In you is all of H.. Every leaf that falls is |
| T-25 ..... IV.5:5 | that H. be restored to him for whom it |
| T-25 ... IV.5:12 | to bring the light of H. with you, as you |
| T-25 ...... V.4:9 | But think not H. is lost to him alone. Nor |
| T-25 ...... V.5:3 | And so you walk toward H. or toward hell |
| T-25 ...... V.6:4 | He hates you, thinking H. must be hell. |
| T-25 ...... V.6:5 | that he is the way to H. or to hell, as you |
| T-25 .... VII.1:8 | foundation sure as love, dependable as H. |
| T-25 .... VII.2:2 | He did not make be firm and sure as H.. |
| T-25 .... VII.2:3 | could it be that hell and H. are the same? |
| T-25 .. VII.10:5 | His Son that hell and H. are different, not |
| T-25 .. VII.10:6 | same. And that in H. *They* are all the same, |
| T-25 .. VII.10:6 | made a hell of H. and a heaven of hell, |
| T-25 ... VIII.2:9 | know of H. and the justice of the saved? |
| T-25 ... VIII.6:4 | "fires" of H. by God's Own angry Hand. |
| T-25 ... VIII.6:5 | They *do* believe that H. is hell, and *are* |
| T-25 ... VIII.9:8 | knows that H. is richer made by each one |
| T-25 .VIII.14:2 | This is the only justice H. knows, and all |
| T-25 ........ IX.h | The Justice of H. |
| T-25 ..... IX.1:5 | of this world in favor of the peace of H.. |
| T-25 ..... IX.2:4 | but cherished and preserved in H., where |
| T-26 ........I.5:3 | house as rich and limitless as H. itself. No |
| T-26 ........I.7:4 | In H., God's Son is not imprisoned in a |
| T-26 ........I.7:5 | And as he is in H., so must he be eternally |
| T-26 .......II.8:5 | wish that H. be given you instead of hell, |
| T-26 ..... III.2:1 | that stands between this world and H.. It |
| T-26 ..... III.2:4 | borderland is just beyond the gate of H.. |
| T-26 ..... III.5:1 | Salvation stops just short of H., for only |
| T-26 ..... III.5:2 | H. was never lost, and so cannot be saved. |
| T-26 ..... III.5:3 | wish for H. and the wish for hell unless he |
| T-26 ..... IV.1:4 | justice past the gate that opens into H.. |
| T-26 ..... IV.2:2 | light, and every bird sings of the joy of H.. |
| T-26 ..... IV.3:5 | is H. but a song of gratitude and love and |
| T-26 ..... IV.3:7 | And here does every light of H. come, to |
| T-26 ..... IV.4:1 | little miracles to lay before the gate of H.. |
| T-26 ..... IV.5:1 | and you will join the lights of H. there, |
| T-26 ..... IV.5:3 | no one hears the song of H. and remains |
| T-26 ..... IV.6:2 | that withholds the wealth of H. from you. |
| T-26 ..... IV.6:3 | And how great will be the joy in H. when |
| T-26 ...... V.1:5 | is a help or hindrance to the gate of H.. |
| T-26 ..... V.1:10 | road be made except the way to H.. You |
| T-26 ..... V.1:11 | You but choose whether to go toward H., |
| T-26 ...... V.5:1 | passed away in H. too soon for anything |
| T-26 ...... V.8:4 | when H. seemed to disappear and God |
| T-26 ..... VI.2:3 | in Whom all power in earth and H. rests. |
| T-26 .... VII.7:3 | would H. be opposed by its own opposite, |
| T-26 .... VII.9:5 | have placed between the H. where you are |
| T-26 .. VII.10:1 | there; a little sigh that speaks for H. as a |
| T-26 .. VII.10:2 | you, to replace the world you see with H., |
| T-26 .. VII.16:3 | H. is shining on the Son of God. Deny |
| T-26 ..... IX.1:6 | rejoice that H. is not separate from you. |
| T-26 ..... IX.3:7 | on ground so holy H. leans to join with it, |
| T-26 ..... IX.4:4 | up every living thing and lifts it into H., |
| T-26 ..... IX.5:1 | H. is grateful for this gift of what has |
| T-26 ..... IX.5:3 | between the light of H. and the world. |
| T-26 ..... IX.6:3 | There is no place in H. holier. And They |
| T-26 ..... IX.6:6 | And all the lights in H. brighter grow, in |
| T-26 ..... IX.7:4 | And shall the Lord of H. and His Son give |
| T-26 .......X.2:9 | And what is limited cannot be H.. So it |
| T-27 ........I.3:2 | his sins are writ in H. in your blood and |
| T-27 ........I.3:3 | hell. Yet this is writ in hell and not in H., |
| T-27 ......I.10:1 | removed, is H. free to be remembered. |
| T-27 .. VII.15:2 | dream the Lord of H. will Himself awaken |
| T-29 .......II.1:4 | any loss, to find yourself in H. and in God |
| T-29 .......II.7:4 | in immortality, and H. knows it not. Yet |
| T-29 ...... V.1:3 | so still no sound except a hymn to H. rises |
| T-29 ...... V.1:5 | And where They are is H. and is peace. |
| T-29 ...... V.2:3 | be. The changelessness of H. is in you, so |
| T-29 ...... V.6:5 | Who would lay bloody hands on H. itself, |
| T-29 ..... VI.4:1 | ensure that only H. would not pass away. |
| T-29 .... VII.1:3 | H. cannot be found where it is not, and |
| T-29 ... VIII.5:4 | worthy of the gift of H. and eternal peace. |
| T-29 ... VIII.9:3 | In H. would the Son of God but laugh, if |
| T-29 ... VIII.9:5 | For more than H. can you never have. If |
| T-29 ... VIII.9:6 | If H. is within, why would you seek for |
| T-29 ... VIII.9:6 | seek for idols that would make of H. less, |
| T-29 ..... IX.2:2 | And in that dream was H. changed to hell, |
| T-29 ..... IX.8:5 | so close the song of H. can be heard, not |
| T-29 ..... IX.9:1 | of help, a calm assurance H. goes with you |
| T-30 .......II.1:8 | And H. itself but represents your will, |
| T-30 .......II.3:8 | No light of H. shines except for you, for it |
| T-30 .......II.3:8 | for you, for it was set in H. by your will. |
| T-30 ..... III.8:5 | So high in H. is it set that those outside of |
| T-30 ..... III.8:5 | those outside of H. know not it is there. |
| T-30 ..... III.9:3 | which is as far from earth as earth from H. |
| T-30 ... III.11:4 | The mind of Heaven's Son in H. is, for |
| T-30 .......V.3:1 | Not yet is H. quite remembered, for the |
| T-30 .......V.4:2 | one outside of H. knows how this can be, |
| T-30 .......V.4:2 | can be, for understanding this is H. itself. |
| T-30 .......V.8:2 | on, and quickly reach the gate of H. itself. |
| T-30 ... VIII.2:8 | anything in H. or on earth could ever alter |
| T-30 ... VIII.3:5 | And H. gives no answer to the prayer, nor |
| T-31 ..... VI.1:8 | and all H. bends to touch your eyes and |
| T-31 ..... VI.4:1 | that you must make the way to H. plain. |
| T-31 ..... VI.4:4 | In H. as on earth this is forever true. It |
| T-31 ..... VI.7:2 | matter if you think you are in earth or H.. |
| T-31 .. VII.14:9 | is hell or H., and of these you choose but |
| T-31 ... VIII.8:3 | inclusive it is but a step from there to H.. |
| T-31 ... VIII.9:3 | appear like lawns of H. to our sight, to lift |
| T-31 .VIII.11:5 | the song of thanks from earth to H. grows |
| W-pI .... 20.3:7 | all power is given him in H. and on earth. |
| W-pI .... 45.8:4 | H. to God the Father and to God the Son. |
| W-pI .... 45.8:7 | an attempt to reach the Kingdom of H.. |
| W-pI .... 47.7:3 | and below them to the Kingdom of H.. |
| W-pI .... 50.5:4 | Such is the Kingdom of H.. Such is the |
| W-pI .... 60.1:6 | will bring me near enough to H. that the |
| W-pI .... 73.4:3 | It is not H., but the light of Heaven shines |
| W-pI .... 73.4:3 | Heaven, but the light of H. shines on it. |
| W-pI .... 73.6:1 | which seek to prove all this is really H.. |
| W-pI .... 73.8:3 | it is hell in place of H. that you choose. |
| W-pI .. 76.11:3 | as well as of the joys of H. which His laws |
| W-pI .... 78.9:2 | The world and H. join in thanking you, |
| W-pI .... 89.3:6 | I want all of H. and only Heaven, as God |
| W-pI .... 89.3:6 | I want all of Heaven and only H., as God |
| W-pI .. 95.14:3 | H. looks to you in confidence that you will |
| W-pI .... 98.9:5 | that you have on earth as well as H.. He |
| W-pI .... 99.3:1 | all where earth and H. can be reconciled |
| W-pI .. 100.4:2 | increases every light that shines in H., so |
| W-pI 110.11:7 | is the key that opens up the gate of H., |
| W-pI .. 121.7:2 | to you imploringly for H. here and now. It |
| W-pI .. 122.6:2 | stand outside while all of H. waits for you |
| W-pI .. 126.5:4 | Think you the Lord of H. would allow the |
| W-pI .. 129.8:1 | Today the lights of H. bend to you, to |
| W-pI 130.10:3 | choice, and hell or H. comes to you as one |
| W-pI 130.11:2 | Yet the release of H. still remains within |
| W-pI .. 131.4:2 | Be glad as well to learn you search for H., |
| W-pI .. 131.5:2 | You will find H.. Everything you seek but |
| W-pI .. 131.6:1 | Why wait for H.? It is here today. Time is |
| W-pI .. 131.7:1 | H. remains your one alternative to this |
| W-pI .. 131.7:4 | minds, with H. as the glad effect of one, |
| W-pI .. 131.8:3 | when God Himself established him in H.? |
| W-pI .. 131.9:4 | He thinks he made a hell opposing H., |
| W-pI .. 131.9:4 | exist, while H. is the place he cannot find. |
| W-pI 131.14:2 | walks with you the Spirit H. sent you, that |
| W-pI 131.15:3 | Today is set by H. itself to be a time of |
| W-pI 133.13:1 | H. itself is reached with empty hands and |
| W-pI 133.14:1 | reaches, unencumbered, to the gate of H., |
| W-pI 134.17:7 | *and yet no one can enter H. by himself.* |
| W-pI 135.20:1 | you become a light which H. gratefully |
| W-pI 135.24:3 | H. asks nothing. It is hell that makes |
| W-pI .. 136.9:2 | everlasting life, H. more frail than hell, |
| W-pI 136.10:2 | that H. quails before such mad attacks as |
| W-pI 136.11:3 | And H. has not bowed to hell, nor life to |
| W-pI ..... 138.h | H. is the decision I must make. |
| W-pI .. 138.1:1 | In this world H. is a choice, because here |
| W-pI .. 138.1:3 | If H. exists there must be hell as well, for |
| W-pI .. 138.2:3 | that makes the choice of H. seem to be the |
| W-pI .. 138.6:1 | H. appears to take the form of choice, |
| W-pI .. 138.9:1 | H. is chosen consciously. The choice |
| W-pI 138.10:1 | The conscious choice of H. is as sure as is |

W-pI.138.11:1 We make the choice for **H.** as we wake,
W-pI.138.12:5 ***H.*** *is the decision I must make. I make it now,*
W-pI...149.2:1 (138) **H.** is the decision I must make.
W-pI.151.17:2 which **H.** has corrected and made pure.
W-pI.152.10:5 Love, his right to **H.** and release from hell,
W-pI.153.18:2 For you will know that **H.** goes with you.
W-pI...154.1:6 Our part is cast in **H.**, not in hell. And
W-pI...157.1:3 It is a time **H.** has set apart to shine upon,
W-pI...157.3:1 it will be given you to feel a touch of **H.**,
W-pI...157.6:3 forgot, and **H.** is remembered for a while.
W-pI...157.7:1 of time; a little more like **H.** in its ways; a
W-pI...157.8:2 into truth, the holy Guide to **H.** given you,
W-pI...159.1:3 Here the laws of **H.** and the world agree.
W-pI...159.3:3 Christ's vision pictures **H.**, for it sees a
W-pI...159.3:3 for it sees a world so like to **H.** that what
W-pI...159.4:3 here on earth, as they are one in **H.**. Christ
W-pI...161.1:4 passed safely by and **H.** now restored.
W-pI...161.9:1 eyes behold in one whom **H.** cherishes,
W-pI.161.10:6 You are not forgot in **H.**. Would you not
W-pI...164.1:6 beyond them all He hears the song of **H.**,
W-pI...165.4:1 Deny not **H.**. It is yours today, but for the
W-pI...168.4:4 What now remains that **H.** be delayed an
W-pI.169.12:3 will end in time, for grace foreshadows **H.**
WpI.. rV.in8:5 God would not have **H.** incomplete. It
W-pI...182.3:6 There is no substitute for **H.**. All he ever
W-pI...182.4:6 It is His Holiness that lights up **H.**, and
W-pI...182.4:6 wherein are earth and **H.** joined as one.
W-pI...182.9:3 might of **H.** in His hand and calls them
W-pI...184.8:3 in earth and **H.** is beyond your naming.
W-pI.184.12:5 of the world to take the place of **H.**. In our
W-pI...185.1:4 **H.** would be completely given back to full
W-pI...185.8:8 have, in place of **H.** and the peace of God?
W-pI...186.1:5 Will of God is done on earth as well as **H.**.
W-pI.186.14:2 of love, which as it is in **H.** has no form.
W-pI.187.10:5 see the purity of **H.** shine in our reflection
W-pI...188.1:1 Why wait for **H.**? Those who seek the
W-pI.189.10:9 *in the world, that it become a part of* ***H.*** *now.*
W-pI...190.8:4 love, and time replace eternity and **H.**.
W-pI.190.11:1 the truth, or pain and joy, or hell and **H.**.
W-pI.190.11:2 light of **H.** for the darkness of the world.
W-pI...191.9:1 power is given unto you in earth and **H.**.
W-pI.191.11:8 Remember this, and earth and **H.** are one.
W-pI...192.2:5 And who would pardon **H.**? Yet on earth,
W-pI...192.4:1 looks upon all things unknown in **H.**, sees
W-pI...193.2:5 enough to let the light of **H.** shine upon it.
W-pI.193.13:5 down to earth at last, to raise it up to **H.**.
W-pI...194.1:2 it sets you down just short of **H.**, with the
W-pI...198.6:5 hear His words have heard the song of **H.**.
W-pI.198.10:1 Son, and **H.** is remembered instantly; the
W-pI...199.8:5 and **H.** offers thanks for the increase of
W-pI...200.2:1 of chaos, joy of pain, and **H.** out of hell.
W-pI...200.3:6 to look with open eyes to find that **H.** lies
W-pI...200.6:3 For it is unknown in **H.**. It is only hell
W-pI...200.8:2 to the gate of **H.** and the way beyond.
W-pI...200.9:2 We go to **H.**, and the path is straight.
W-pI.200.10:5 And you look up and on toward **H.**, with
W-pII..223.2:5 *We are lonely here, and long for* ***H.****, where*
W-pII..224.1:1 guilt, that **H.** looks to It to give it light. It
W-pII..226.2:3 *dreams, when* ***H.*** *can so easily be mine?*
W-pII..227.2:1 so today we find our glad return to **H.**,
W-pII......2.5:2 the world, and only **H.** now exists at all.
W-pII..231.2:3 To remember Him is **H.**. This we seek.
W-pII......3.4:5 away, but **H.** has preserved for you in Him
W-pII..241.2:2 *who never left, returns to* ***H.*** *and his home.*
W-pII..249.1:6 It is now so like to **H.** that it quickly is
W-pII......4.5:7 Would you still hold return to **H.** back?
W-pII..252.2:2 *in You, and know that* ***H.*** *is restored to me.*
W-pII..253.1:6 **H.** where my holy Self abides with them
W-pII..255.1:5 must remain forever in the peace of **H.**. In
W-pII......5.4:2 goal of **H.** been exchanged for the pursuit
W-pII..263.2:1 we still remain outside the gate of **H.**, let
W-pII..265.1:6 the light of **H.** shining on the world. What
W-pII......6.3:1 at peace within the **H.** of your holy mind.
W-pII..272.1:2 *My home is set in* ***H.*** *by Your Will and mine.*
W-pII..272.2:2 **H.** can be chosen just as easily as hell, and
W-pII......7.5:3 of **H.** is restored to God's beloved Son.
W-pII..281.2:3 My Father placed me safe in **H.**, watching
W-pII..283.1:5 *remains the light of* ***H.*** *and the Love of God.*
W-pII..283.1:7 *Is not the light of* ***H.*** *infinite? Is not Your Son*
W-pII.....286.h The hush of **H.** holds my heart today.
W-pII..286.1:9 *rest. Your Love is* ***H.****, and Your Love is mine.*
W-pII..287.1:1 Where would I go but **H.**? What could be
W-pII..292.1:6 For God's Will is done in earth and **H.**.
W-pII..300.2:3 *do to be restored to* ***H.*** *and our true Identity.*
W-pII..306.1:1 **H.** that an ancient memory returns to me?
W-pII..310.1:3 *nor hours, for it comes from* ***H.*** *to Your Son.*
W-pII..320.1:4 it all the strength and love in earth and **H.**
W-pII..325.1:6 him, and find the way to **H.** and to God.
W-pII..326.1:7 *And as it is in* ***H.****, so on earth. Your plan I*
W-pII..326.1:8 *effects into the tranquil* ***H.*** *of Your Love,*
W-pII..340.2:6 Himself, awake in **H.** in the Heart of Love.
W-pII....13.5:1 rain from **H.** on a dry and dusty world,
W-pII..342.1:5 *I stand before the gate of* ***H.****, wondering if I*
W-pII..345.1:5 *Father, in* ***H.*** *it is different, for there, there*
W-pII....14.1:5 *I am the* ***H.*** *where His Love resides. I am His*
W-pII....14.3:5 seek a function that is past the gate of **H.**.
W-pII....14.5:5 sees the gate of **H.** stand open before him,
Wfl........in.4:2 the way to Him and to the **H.** of His peace.
W-ep.........5:4 each choice you make brings **H.** nearer to
M-4.....I.A.8:6 From here, the way to **H.** is open and easy
M-4......IV.2:6 hell when he perceives a way to **H.**? And
M-5.....II.4:11 and without fear, they re-establish **H.**.
M-11.........4:9 turns hell to **H.** merely by being what it is
M-13.........4:9 **H.** and remembrance of his Father's Love.
M-13.........7:3 You cannot give up **H.** partially. You
M-14.......3:11 the thinking of the world, but so does **H.**.
M-14.........5:9 into **H.** is the function of God's teachers,
M-14.........5:9 teach are lessons in which **H.** is reflected.
M-16.....10:10 "sacrifice" is **H.** restored to his awareness.
M-16.....11:11 And thus the gate of **H.** is reopened, and
M-19.........1:4 Neither justice nor injustice exists in **H.**,
M-19.........5:4 In this lies either **H.** or hell, as you elect.
M-19.........5:5 God's justice points to **H.** just because it is
M-21.........3:6 Herein lie hell and **H.**. The sleeping Son of
M-21.........5:9 meaningless symbols to the Call of **H.**
M-22.........1:4 areas of hell in **H.** are inconceivable.
M-23.........6:1 No one on earth can grasp what **H.** is, or
M-24.........6:4 **H.** is here. There is nowhere else. Heaven
M-24.........6:6 else. **H.** is now. There is no other time. No
M-28.........2:8 the earth. The joy of **H.** has come upon it.
M-28.........3:6 Thoughts turn to **H.** and away from hell.
M-28.........4:8 The song of **H.** sounds around the world,
C-2............7:5 the certainty of **H.** and the surety of peace
C-2..........10:6 understand the way is short and **H.** is his
C-3............4:9 near to **H.** as is possible outside the gate.
C-3............5:3 the world in part, and yet the bridge to **H.**
C-3............6:2 nothingness to everything; from hell to **H.**
C-5............1:1 for help to enter **H.** for you have never left
C-6............1:1 upon the earth after he ascended into **H.**,
C-6............2:3 All power in **H.** and earth is therefore
P-2........III.2:6 it can reach almost to **H.** or go no further
P-2.........V.6:8 answer does not seem to be a gift from **H.**.
P-2.........V.8:9 Son of God returns to **H.** through its kind
P-2.......VII.6:4 and **H.** belongs to him because of who he
P-3......III.5:10 if they do this, a light goes out even in **H.**.
S-1.........in.3:3 to the lawns of **H.** and the gate of peace.
S-1...........I.3:6 You have sought first the Kingdom of **H.**,
S-1..........II.7:1 Prayer is a ladder reaching up to **H.**. At
S-1.........V.3:6 You have come almost to **H.**. There is
S-1.........V.4:2 Now you stand before the gate of **H.**, and
S-2...........I.1:1 gift of **H.** has been more misunderstood
S-2...........I.7:3 Prayer cannot be released to **H.** while
S-2.........II.8:6 the glow of **H.** shining on the face of earth
S-2.........III.3:4 be to you another step to **H.** and to peace.
S-3...........I.5:2 for what in **H.** could there be to heal? As
S-3.........II.6:4 At last the gate of **H.** opens and God's Son
S-3........IV.8:9 Own. **H.** is here and Heaven is your home.
S-3........IV.8:9 Own. Heaven is here and **H.** is your home.

## heaven 1

*Heaven*

T-25...VII.10:6 made a hell of Heaven and a **h.** of hell,

## Heaven's 45

T-19......III.9:1 yet you look with **H.** smile upon your lips,
T-19......III.9:1 your lips, and **H.** blessing on your sight.
T-20....VIII.7:2 gently within the kindly sway of **H.** laws.
T-22.......in.3:8 For this relationship has **H.** Holiness.
T-23.......in.5:7 and realize that **H.** glory shines on him?
T-25......III.6:3 For he has come with **H.** Help within him,
T-25....VIII.7:4 to hell that seems to look like **H.** gate?
T-25......IX.1:1 errors cannot be undone by **H.** justice?
T-26......IV.1:1 is this world's equivalent of **H.** justice. It
T-26......IV.3:4 for **H.** altar to rise and tower far above the
T-26......IV.6:1 back the happy opening of **H.** gate. How
T-26.......V.2:4 Think not the way to **H.** gate is difficult at
T-26.......V.2:5 hand and keeping step to **H.** song, is
T-26.......V.5:4 that not one note in **H.** song was missed.
T-26.....V.14:3 and reached the world that lies at **H.** gate.
T-26.....VII.9:4 Yet is this wish in line with **H.** state, and
T-26......IX.4:5 **H.** joy has been increased because what is
T-26......IX.6:5 becomes the brightest light in **H.** radiance
T-29.........I.9:5 allow the body to say "no" to **H.** calling,
T-30....III.11:4 The mind of **H.** Son in Heaven is, for
T-30.......V.4:5 And so is **H.** Son prepared to be himself,
W-pI.....75.5:2 it we see **H.** reflection lie across the world.
W-pI.....76.8:6 would not save but damn in **H.** name. Yet
W-pI...105.4:1 As **H.** peace and joy intensify when you
W-pI...122.9:2 accepting **H.** answer to the hell we made,
W-pI...131.7:4 outcome which is **H.** opposite in every
W-pI.134.10:4 between the hell of guilt and **H.** gate.
W-pI...138.9:3 to be judged again, this time with **H.** help.
W-pI.151.11:3 in sin, and only **H.** blessing on the world.
W-pI.153.13:3 minds of **H.** children and the Son of God.
W-pI...154.6:1 difference in the role of **H.** messengers,
W-pI...159.3:5 The real world pictures **H.** innocence.
W-pI...163.4:3 life, the endlessness of love and **H.** perfect
W-pI...186.1:6 wills on earth in **H.** plan to save the world
W-pI...186.1:6 to save the world, restoring it to **H.** peace.
W-pI...190.9:1 where **H.** peace holds all things still at last
W-pI...193.8:6 simple lessons **H.** Teacher sets before you,
W-pI.193.13:5 then you hold the key that opens **H.** gate,
W-pI...194.1:3 the lawns that welcome you to **H.** gate;
W-pI...198.6:4 and come to you with **H.** love upon them.
W-pII.303.1:2 and be still with me while **H.** Son is born.
W-pII.318.1:1 reconciled all parts of **H.** plan to save the
W-pII.344.1:7 *brothers fill my store with* ***H.*** *treasures,*
M-4.....I.A.8:5 peace, for here is **H.** state fully reflected.
S-3........IV.8:3 wait in sorrow **H.** melody is incomplete,

## Heaven-born 1

W-pI...192.3:4 For being **H.**, it has no form at all. Yet

## Heavens 1

C-ep...........2:5 and set into the **H.** with a shining Ray

## heavily 6

T-1.......VII.4:3 the later parts of the course rest too **h.** on
T-13......IV.4:2 The ego invests **h.** in the past, and in the
T-19........II.7:1 **h.** defended than the idea that sin is real;
T19....IV.C.2:4 chorus, plodding so **h.** away from life,
W-pI.....95.6:3 who remain **h.** defended against learning.
M-4.....I.A.7:9 each step in this direction so **h.** reinforced

## heavy 50

*See also* heavy-laid, heavy-seeming

T-11......VI.8:4 of crucifixion still lies **h.** on your eyes, but
T-12........II.4:6 **h.** blankets you have laid upon yourself.
T-12......IV.6:3 do pay a price for death, and a very **h.** one
T-14.........I.5:4 nor escape the **h.** burden of its dullness
T-14........II.4:6 The **h.** chains that seem to bind them to
T-14.......V.2:4 The burden of guilt is **h.**, but God would
T-14.......V.4:5 but shine away the **h.** veils of guilt within
T-16....IV.10:4 To lift the veil that seems so dark and **h.**,
T-17......IV.8:2 here, surrounded by a frame so **h.** and so
T-17..IV.12:10 hard to see at all beneath the **h.** shadows
T-18......IX.4:4 its intensity is veiled by its **h.** coverings,
T-18......IX.5:2 that seems to make it **h.** and opaque,
T-18......IX.9:7 the dark and **h.** garments of guilt laid by,
T-19........II.6:3 clouds of guilt seem **h.** and impenetrable.
T19..IV.B.13:5 all of the ego's **h.** investment in the body.

T19...IV.D.2:1 like a **h.** veil before the face of Christ. Yet
T19.IV.D.16:5 Help him to lift the **h.** burden of sin you
T-20...... III.9:1 Prisoners bound with **h.** chains for years,
T-22....... II.1:5 the dark folds of the **h.** garments in which
T-22....... II.1:6 dark and **h.** garments are those who seek
T-22....... III.3:2 Sin is a block, set like a **h.** gate, locked
T-22....... III.4:7 its **h.** anchor in the shifting world it made
T-22....... V.6:5 to stand, **h.** and solid and immovable,
T-22.... VI.10:7 for here lies buried the **h.** anchor that
T-22.... VI.14:4 think not that it lays a **h.** burden on you.
T-24.... VI.12:3 nor do you deem this cost too **h.**. But a
T-24.... VI.12:4 and tedious, too **h.** to be borne. Yet to the
T-27....... II.7:7 nor guilt upon his heart made **h.** with the
T-27..... VII.2:3 obscured by **h.** clouds of complication,
T-27.... VIII.8:4 do your eyes behold its **h.** consequences,
T-28..... VII.6:2 further locks and chains and **h.** anchors,
T-29...... III.3:7 as **h.** shadows must give way to light. The
T-29...... III.5:2 from **h.** shadows that have hidden him,
T-29...... IV.3:4 veils the **h.** lump of fear that is their core.
T-31......... I.3:4 they rise like **h.** curtains to obscure the
W-pI..... 41.5:2 under a **h.** cloud of insane thoughts,
W-pI..... 41.5:3 attempt to get past this dark and **h.** cloud,
W-pI..... 69.4:2 a vast circle, surrounded by a layer of **h.**,
W-pI... 101.7:1 remove the **h.** load you lay upon yourself
W-pI.134.12:3 Nor need he erect the **h.** walls of stone
W-pI.134.16:4 the escape from all the **h.** chains you
W-pI... 135.2:4 doubts, its penalties and **h.** armaments,
W-pI... 153.3:2 in **h.** bands of steel with iron overlaid,
W-pI... 194.2:2 the **h.** chains that locked the door to
W-pII.256.1:6 in **h.** clouds of doubt about the holiness
M-20......... 4:2 form, will drop the **h.** curtain once again,
S-1...... III.4:10 Your investment in this escape is **h.**, and
S-3........... I.2:6 the **h.** scent of death upon their hearts.
S-3........ IV.6:5 and with a **h.** heart made hard against the
S-3........ IV.9:1 time to lift the **h.** burden from the world.

## heavy-laid 1

S-2......... II.5:4 and **h.** reproach that thus is put upon him

## heavy-seeming 2

T-18...... IX.6:1 This **h.** barrier, this artificial floor that
T-22...... IV.7:6 your brother's, and touch this **h.** block,

## heed 4

T-27..VIII.12:6 Yet to its witnesses you pay no **h.** at all.
W-pI... 134.7:4 **h.** the self-accusing shrieks of sinners mad
W-pI... 166.7:3 not you. You **h.** them not. You go on your
W-pI... 188.8:1 **h.** your Father's Voice when you refuse to

## heeding 1

W-pI.135.19:1 set in time, but **h.** only immortality. Let

## heeds 1

T-25..VIII.11:1 paid, the Holy Spirit **h.** not who looks on

## heels 1

T-26..... VII.7:5 brought His Love at last to vengeance's **h.**

## height 1

W-pI.183.11:6 exceeds in depth and **h.** whatever words

## heights 4

T-31...... IV.4:8 point will learning lead to **h.** of happiness
M-8........... 1:2 unequal **h.** and diverse sizes, on varying
M-19......... 2:7 reaches indescribable **h.** as one proceeds,
P-2......... V.5:1 beyond the **h.** perceived in any dream. He

## held 82

*See also* long-held

T-3......... II.4:3 not free because it is possessed, or **h.** back
T-4....... IV.2:8 otherwise has **h.** your ego together, but
T-5....... IV.3:1 Every loving thought **h.** in any part of the
T-13..... X.12:1 No illusion that you have ever **h.** against
T-14..... IX.3:6 gift that you refused is **h.** by Him in you.
T-14....... X.5:4 that still remains is **h.** together by a sense
T-14... XI.11:2 As we are **h.** as one in God, so do we learn
T-15.. VII.12:2 your brother in his body, **h.** there by guilt
T-16....... II.9:5 forces, to be used and not **h.** idly by. They
T-16..... IV.3:6 it is still **h.** together by the illusion of love.
T-16.... VII.9:2 you have **h.** against your brothers. Their
T-17......... I.6:1 to give all you have **h.** outside the truth to
T-19....... III.5:9 **h.** to the body by the fear of changed
T19..IV.C.10:5 miracle you will perform, **h.** out to you.
T19... IV.D.1:2 and think if death **h.** no attraction for you
T-20..... III.8:6 for all the happiness that he **h.** out to you
T-20...... V.1:3 Father's laws to what was **h.** outside them
T-20...... V.6:3 ever **h.** or will ever hold is here right now.
T-20...... V.7:4 the laws that **h.** you prisoner to pain and
T-20..... VI.6:6 perceived in awe and **h.** in reverence.
T-20..... VI.8:8 to have a home that **h.** together for a little
T-20... VI.10:5 way to true relationships **h.** gently open,
T-20. VI.12:10 long **h.** back from looking on the face of
T-20.... VII.6:4 hold about him are not **h.** up to his reality
T-20... VIII.8:6 purpose is no longer **h.** they disappear.
T-21........ I.7:5 you knew so long ago and **h.** more dear
T-21..... IV.8:4 Be not **h.** back by fear's insane insistence
T-21. VI.11:10 condemn instead, there is he **h.** a prisoner
T-22..... III.5:9 It is **h.** back by form, having been made to
T-23...... in.3:1 you in glory, with your head **h.** high, and
T-24....... II.6:4 and all the sins he **h.** in its defense against
T-24....... II.7:6 key to Heaven in his hand, **h.** out to you.
T-24...... V.7:1 and safely **h.** in you by that same hand
T-24.... VII.7:3 **h.** to limits or uncertainties of any kind.
T-26...... V.3:5 **h.** also the Correction for that one, and all
T-26..... IX.2:2 Forget not that a shadow **h.** between your
T-26..... IX.5:3 what was **h.** apart from light is given up,
T-27.... VII.1:4 he has no reason to be **h.** responsible. He
T-28........ I.4:7 only you have **h.** it to a part of time where
T-28........ I.6:7 past. Only the past is **h.** in memory as you
T-28....... II.7:4 fear was **h.** in place because he did not see
T-29..... VI.4:7 And where it once **h.** seeming sway is now
T-29... VIII.4:5 hand could be **h.** up to block God's way?
T-30...... V.1:3 no longer, for their "gifts" are not **h.** dear.
T-31...... I.12:4 know. Let every image **h.** of everyone be
T-31.... VII.4:2 can be interchanged but never jointly **h.**.
T-31.. VII.10:6 to save from every concept that he ever **h.**.
T-31.. VII.12:3 wish that fathered it no longer is **h.** dear.
T-31.. VII.13:7 the door **h.** open for the face of Christ to
T-31.. VII.13:7 and ancient concepts **h.** so long and dear
W-in.......... 5:3 hand, one exception **h.** apart from true
W-pI..... 78.5:3 grievances that you have **h.** against him,
W-pI..... 92.2:3 It is as if you thought you **h.** the match
W-pI..... 92.2:3 or that you **h.** the world within your hand
W-pI..... 94.1:3 this world ever **h.** are wiped away forever
W-pI..... 95.2:2 and tenuously **h.** together by its erratic
W-pI..... 95.8:2 **h.** back only by your unwillingness to let
W-pI... 106.3:5 **h.** out to you in welcome and in love.
W-pI.122.12:2 gifts that have been **h.** in store for us since
W-pI... 132.8:4 replace all thoughts you ever **h.** of death.
W-pI.132.14:1 all the idle thoughts we ever **h.** about it,
W-pI... 137.2:3 split apart and **h.** in pieces by a solid wall
W-pI... 153.3:1 is as if a circle **h.** it fast, wherein another
W-pI... 162.1:1 This single thought, **h.** firmly in the mind
W-pI... 181.2:4 which has replaced the one you **h.** before.
W-pI... 181.4:2 is advocating are from those you **h.** before
W-pI... 189.5:4 world, **h.** cruelly in death's sharp-pointed,
W-pI... 196.2:1 limitless and with all things **h.** in its sure
W-pII.... in.8:3 His Hand has **h.** us up. His Thoughts have
W-pII.249.2:2 *them,* **h.** *them in a vise of bitterness, and*
W-pII.267.1:6 and **h.** forever quiet and at peace within
W-pII... 11.3:3 inviolate; forever **h.** within His holy Will,
W-ep......... 5:7 which God has **h.** unclosed to welcome us
M-4.... VIII.1:6 The past as well **h.** no mistakes; nothing
M-19......... 3:2 the lens which, **h.** before the body's eyes,
M-27......... 3:2 like a shield **h.** up to obscure the sun. The
M-28......... 2:6 living thing, and nothing is **h.** in darkness
C-ep........... 2:5 that **h.** it safe within eternity and through
P-2........... I.1:4 there will be a relationship **h.** out to them
P-2.......... II.9:3 It is **h.** out to him, but he cannot hold out
P-2.......... V.1:6 it seems as if these forces can be **h.** at bay
S-3.......... II.6:2 It can be **h.** at bay a little while, and there

## hell 164

*See also* hell-fire

T-13..... IV.1:7 it becomes overtly savage, it offers you **h.**.
T-13..... IV.2:1 neither oblivion nor **h.** is as unacceptable
T-13..... IV.2:2 definition of Heaven *is* **h.** and oblivion,
T-13..... IV.2:3 **h.** and oblivion are ideas that you made
T-14..... IX.5:4 Earth can reflect Heaven or **h.**; God or the
T-15........ I.3:5 in death, it offers you immortality in **h.**. It
T-15........ I.4:1 The belief in **h.** is inescapable to those
T-15........ I.4:3 it. The ego teaches that **h.** is in the future,
T-15........ I.4:4 **H.** is its goal. For although the ego aims at
T-15........ I.5:1 is here and now because the future is **h.**.
T-15........ I.5:2 the only voice, it speaks of **h.** even to him.
T-15........ I.5:3 For it tells him **h.** is here as well, and bids
T-15........ I.5:3 and bids him leap from **h.** into oblivion.
T-15........ I.6:5 belief in guilt must lead to the belief in **h.**,
T-15........ I.6:6 **h.** to be experienced is to bring hell here,
T-15........ I.6:6 hell to be experienced is to bring **h.** here,
T-15........ I.6:7 himself as deserving of **h.** can believe that
T-15........ I.7:1 Holy Spirit teaches thus: There is no **h.**.
T-15........ I.7:2 **H.** is only what the ego has made of the
T-15........ I.7:3 The belief in **h.** is what prevents you from
T-15........ I.7:4 steadily to Heaven as the ego drives to **h.**.
T-15...... I.10:2 more than merely that **h.** does not exist.
T-15...... I.14:4 long as it takes to exchange **h.** for Heaven.
T-15....... II.2:7 where He gently translates **h.** into Heaven
T-15..... III.5:7 decision you make is for Heaven or for **h.**,
T-15... III.12:3 Hear not his appeal to **h.** and littleness,
T-15..... IX.4:1 your strength between Heaven and **h.**,
T-15..... XI.4:8 the "conflict" of Heaven and **h.** in him by
T-15..... XI.4:8 out and giving it the attributes of **h.**,
T-16....... V.4:3 that you believe this specialness is not **h.**,
T-16....... V.5:8 the ego cannot interfere, must be **h.**.
T-16....... V.6:1 ego device for joining **h.** and Heaven, and
T-16....... V.8:4 one will recognize that he has asked for **h.**
T-16....... V.9:1 The appeal of **h.** lies only in the terrible
T-16..... V.11:8 not from death, nor Heaven from **h.**.
T-17... VIII.4:5 fantasies of fear and fiery dreams of **h.**.
T-19....... II.8:5 lightly, for it is the choice of **h.** or Heaven.
T19 IV.D.20:7 Nor is it given anything in **h.** or Heaven to
T-22....... II.7:7 the joy of Heaven and the misery of **h.**.
T-22....... II.7:8 choose Heaven, you *are* in **h.** and misery.
T-23..... II.22:1 take not one step in the descent to **h.**. For
T-23..... II.22:6 chose the stairs to Heaven or the way to **h.**
T-24..... II.13:4 the gates of **h.** you closed upon yourself,
T-24..... III.6:2 Here is the **h.** you chose to be your home.
T-24..... III.6:6 release your brother from the depths of **h.**
T-24..... III.8:3 condemn Himself to **h.** and to damnation
T-24..... III.8:5 to join His Will to save you both from **h.**.
T-24..... VI.5:4 you see in him but keeps you both in **h.**.
T-25....... V.5:3 so you walk toward Heaven or toward **h.**,
T-25....... V.6:1 save what He created from the pain of **h.**.
T-25....... V.6:4 He hates you, thinking Heaven must be **h.**
T-25....... V.6:5 that he is the way to Heaven or to **h.**, as
T-25.... VII.2:3 it be that **h.** and Heaven are the same?
T-25.. VII.10:5 His Son that **h.** and Heaven are different,
T-25.. VII.10:6 made a **h.** of Heaven and a heaven of hell,
T-25.. VII.10:6 made a hell of Heaven and a heaven of **h.**,
T-25... VIII.6:5 They *do* believe that Heaven is **h.**, and *are*
T-25... VIII.7:2 Spirit as if He were a messenger from **h.**,
T-25... VIII.7:4 to **h.** that seems to look like Heaven's gate
T-26....... II.8:5 that Heaven be given you instead of **h.**,
T-26..... III.5:3 and the wish for **h.** unless he recognizes
T-26.... VII.7:2 of healing, and the lasting grounds for **h.**.
T-26.. VII.17:4 from crucifixion and from **h.** and death,
T-26..... X.2:10 cannot be Heaven. So it must be **h.**.
T-27........ I.3:2 off the gate and damning him to **h.**. Yet
T-27........ I.3:3 Yet this is writ in **h.** and not in Heaven,
T-29....... II.1:4 see it as the road to **h.** instead of looking
T-29..... IX.2:2 in that dream was Heaven changed to **h.**,
T-31.... VII.7:6 And what you see is **h.**, for fear *is* hell. All
T-31.... VII.7:6 And what you see is hell, for fear *is* **h.**. All
T-31.... VII.7:7 out of **h.** with those you love beside you,
T-31.... VII.8:2 all salvation from the misery of **h.**. And to
T-31.. VII.10:1 but the wish to stay in **h.** and misery?

T-31...VII.10:2 miserable, and remain in **h.** and torment?
T-31...VII.11:1 Yet while you wish to stay in **h.**, how
T-31...VII.14:9 There is **h.** or Heaven, and of these you
T-31... VIII.1:5 *saviors of the world, or would remain in* ***h.***,
T-31... VIII.3:5 you comfortless, alone in dreams of **h.**,
T-31... VIII.6:2 to perceive yourself defenseless and in **h.**.
T-31... VIII.8:3 There is no place for **h.** within a world
T-31... VIII.9:2 And thus will all the vestiges of **h.**, the
T-31. VIII.10:8 one in purpose, and the end of **h.** is near.
T-31. VIII.11:5 chorus from a world redeemed from **h.**,
W-pI.....14.6:3 and others are part of your personal **h.**. It
W-pI.....39.1:1 If guilt is **h.**, what is its opposite? Like the
W-pI.....39.2:1 If guilt is **h.**, what is its opposite? This is
W-pI.....39.2:4 But do you believe that guilt is **h.**? If you
W-pI.....39.4:2 end of guilt, and therefore the end of **h.**.
W-pI.....39.8:3 *thoughts about_are keeping me in* ***h.***. *My*
W-pI...39.10:5 adding: *If guilt is* ***h.***, *what is its opposite?*
W-pI.....44.5:5 speaking, this is the release from **h.**. Yet
W-pI.....44.5:6 it is loss of identity and a descent into **h.**.
W-pI.....63.2:4 function and leave the Son of God in **h.**.
W-pI.....69.1:4 stood beside you when you were in **h.**. He
W-pI.....73.5:7 Do you really want to be in **h.**? Do you
W-pI.....73.8:3 it is **h.** in place of Heaven that you choose.
W-pI.....73.9:4 of God from **h.** and from all idle wishes.
W-pI...76.10:6 creation; denied to Him by his belief in **h.**.
W-pI.....89.3:3 By this idea do I accept my release from **h.**
W-pI...121.7:2 one awaits release from **h.** through you,
W-pI...121.7:5 forgiveness that it has been saved from **h.**.
W-pI...122.8:2 by which it comes to take the place of **h.**.
W-pI...122.9:2 Heaven's answer to the **h.** we made, but
W-pI.122.10:1 in which the end of **h.** is guaranteed.
W-pI.130.10:3 and **h.** or Heaven comes to you as one.
W-pI.130.11:1 Accept a little part of **h.** as real, and you
W-pI.130.11:1 and what you will behold is **h.** indeed. Yet
W-pI.130.11:2 take the place of everything that **h.** would
W-pI.130.11:3 to you. All you need say to any part of **h.**,
W-pI...131.4:4 himself and think that it is **h.** he seeks.
W-pI...131.5:1 No one remains in **h.**, for no one can
W-pI...131.8:3 How could it be His Son could be in **h.**,
W-pI...131.9:4 He thinks he made a **h.** opposing Heaven,
W-pI.134.10:4 between the **h.** of guilt and Heaven's gate.
W-pI.135.24:4 It is **h.** that makes extravagant demands
W-pI...136.9:2 everlasting life, Heaven more frail than **h.**,
W-pI.136.11:3 And Heaven has not bowed to **h.**, nor life
W-pI...138.1:3 If Heaven exists there must be **h.** as well,
W-pI...138.2:3 to be the same as the relinquishment of **h.**
W-pI...138.7:2 it be a means for demonstrating **h.** is real,
W-pI.138.10:1 is as sure as is the ending of the fear of **h.**,
W-pI.152.10:5 his right to Heaven and release from **h.**,
W-pI...154.1:6 Our part is cast in Heaven, not in **h.**. And
W-pI...182.3:7 for Heaven. All he ever made was **h.**.
W-pI...185.2:3 He cannot make a **h.** and think it real. He
W-pI.190.11:1 truth, or pain and joy, or **h.** and Heaven.
W-pI...191.7:1 glad today how very easily is **h.** undone.
W-pI...194.2:1 you have passed all anxiety, all pits of **h.**,
W-pI...196.5:4 real. And what is that but **h.**? Who could
W-pI...196.5:5 without the fear of **h.** upon his heart?
W-pI...197.3:3 a thankful heart, released from **h.** forever.
W-pI...200.2:1 of chaos, joy of pain, and Heaven out of **h.**
W-pI...200.3:6 to seek and seek and seek again for **h.**,
W-pI...200.6:4 It is only **h.** where it is needed, and where
W-pII......5.4:2 made to fence him into **h.** without escape,
W-pII......5.4:2 been exchanged for the pursuit of **h.**. The
W-pII..272.2:2 Heaven can be chosen just as easily as **h.**,
W-pII..296.2:3 the Holy Spirit come to rescue us from **h.**,
W-pII....10.3:1 condemn the world to **h.** along with you,
W-pII..342.1:1 *for Your plan to save me from the* ***h.*** *I made.*
W-ep .........5:4 making sure that **h.** will claim you not,
M-in ..........5:3 And what else is **h.**? This is a manual for
M-4.......IV.2:6 chooses **h.** when he perceives a way to
M-4......... X.1:5 of guilt upon him would send him to **h.**,
M-11...........4:9 else but a Thought of God turns **h.** to
M-13.........6:11 would sacrifice the truth, they stay in **h.**.
M-13..........7:4 You cannot be a little bit in **h.**. The Word
M-14..........5:9 To turn **h.** into Heaven is the function of
M-19..........5:4 In this lies either Heaven or **h.**, as you
M-21..........3:6 Herein lie **h.** and Heaven. The sleeping
M-22..........1:4 areas of **h.** in Heaven are inconceivable.
M-28..........2:3 and misery of any kind perceived as **h.**.
M-28 .........3:6 turn to Heaven and away from **h.**. All
M-28 .........6:2 of evil dreams, the thought of **h.** is real.
M-29 ........3:11 It is the way out of **h.** for you.
C-2...........10:5 Who chooses **h.** when it is recognized?
C-3............6:2 to everything; from **h.** to Heaven. Is this a
C-5.............5:4 to lead you from the **h.** you made to God.
P-2........ III.2:6 go no further than a step or two from **h.**.
P-2........IV.3:1 The descent into **h.** follows step by step
P-2........IV.8:3 compromise by seeing just a little bit of **h.**
S-1........ III.2:5 **H.** cannot be asked for another, and then
S-1........ III.2:6 Only those who are in **h.** can ask for hell.
S-1........ III.2:6 Only those who are in hell can ask for **h.**.

## hell-fire 1

T-1........IV.4:5 who brought the "**h.**" concept into it. I

## Help 13
*help*

T-10..III.10:11 helpfulness and your own perfect **H.**.
T-10....... V.4:4 without the Father, Who alone is his **H.**.
T-11. VIII.10:2 the **H.** of God goes with you everywhere.
T-11. VIII.10:3 become willing to accept this **H.** by asking
T-12.......I.6:11 But hear his call for the **H.** of God, and
T-12......... II.5:4 not leave you without help, and **H.** is here.
T-14.... III.11:2 of help, and **H.** that knows the answer.
T-25....... III.6:3 he has come with Heaven's **H.** within him,
W-pI...126.8:3 But the **H.** you need is there. Give Him
W-pI.126.11:4 ***H.*** *I need to learn that this is true is with me*
W-pI.185.10:6 **H.** has been given you. And would you
W-pI.185.14:2 it. With **H.** like this beside us, can we fail
M-3 ...........5:8 of God can fail to find the **H.** he needs.

## help 282
*Help*

T-1.......VII.2:4 use your body best to **h.** you enlarge your
T-2.........IV.4:7 thing that can **h.** the non-right-minded,
T-2....... V.10:3 both an acknowledgment that he needs **h.**
T-2.....V.A.18:1 of others if, in a situation calling for **h.**,
T-2........ VI.2:2 on your part by saying you could not **h.** it.
T-2........ VI.4:3 for **h.** in the conditions that have brought
T-2........ VI.4:5 At that level you *can* **h.** it. You are much
T-2.......VII.1:5 I would hardly **h.** you if I depreciated the
T-2.......VII.2:1 or you will not be able to **h.** me. Miracle
T-2..... VIII.3:2 be undertaken by my brothers with my **h.**
T-3......IV.7:11 I can **h.** you make your own right choice.
T-4.......in.3:11 they will **h.** prepare you to undertake it.
T-4...........I.4:1 your mind and **h.** others to change theirs.
T-4........ III.2:4 The reason you need my **h.** is because you
T-4........ III.7:6 I can **h.** you only as our Father created us.
T-4........ III.8:4 to **h.** me make other minds ready for Him.
T-5......... II.9:3 to you is to **h.** you make the same decision
T-5........IV.1:3 The Holy Spirit will **h.** you reinterpret
T-6...........I.2:8 it will **h.** you understand your own role as
T-6...........I.5:6 you will believe it, you will **h.** me teach it.
T-6...........I.7:5 **H.** me to teach it to our brothers in the
T-6.........I.19:2 to **h.** them hear this for themselves. When
T-6........IV.3:3 Everyone has called upon Him for **h.** at
T-6.......IV.10:3 need **h.** and are therefore helpless. This is
T-6.......V.B.5:4 called upon the Voice for peace to **h.** you.
T-7......... V.8:8 **h.** him undo the change his ego thinks it
T-7.....VII.1:11 it can **h.** you recognize part of reality, and
T-8......IV.5:11 decision, but mine alone cannot **h.** you.
T-8........IV.6:3 His. If you want to be like me I will **h.** you,
T-8......... V.1:5 **H.** them by offering them your unified
T-8.....VII.11:1 the only way to guarantee **h.** and healing.
T-8.....VII.11:2 **H.** and healing are the normal expressions
T-9...........I.2:4 is to **h.** you remember what you are, and if
T-9...........I.4:1 where it remains, but cannot **h.** you.
T-9......... V.7:2 It may **h.** someone to point out where he
T-9......... V.8:7 He needs no **h.** for this. He will tell you
T-9......... V.8:8 do to **h.** anyone He sends to you for help,
T-9......... V.8:8 do to help anyone He sends to you for **h.**,
T-9......... V.8:9 helping, and the wrong choice will not **h.**.
T-9....... V.8:11 Trust Him, for **h.** is His function, and He
T-9.......VII.5:3 look to the ego to **h.** you escape from a
T-10.... III.1:10 He will not limit your power to **h.** them,
T-10....... V.6:2 this can be corrected and God will **h.** you,
T-11.........I.1:3 the foundation on which God will **h.** build
T-11........II.7:5 He cannot **h.** you without your invitation.
T-11..VIII.10:2 and because no one is without your **h.**, the
T-12.........I.3:4 else is an appeal for healing and **h.**,
T-12.........I.3:5 with anger to a brother's plea for **h.**? No
T-12.........I.3:9 believe that an appeal for **h.** is something
T-12.........I.4:1 for **h.** as exactly what they are except your
T-12.........I.5:3 to perceive an appeal for **h.** as what it is, it
T-12.........I.5:3 are unwilling to give **h.** and to receive it.
T-12.........I.5:4 to recognize a call for **h.** is to refuse help.
T-12.........I.5:4 to recognize a call for help is to refuse **h.**.
T-12.........I.5:7 be helped. Deny him your **h.** and you will
T-12.........I.5:8 need your **h.** in interpreting motivation,
T-12.........I.6:2 his loving thoughts and his appeals for **h.**,
T-12........I.6:10 not attempt to "**h.**" a brother in your way,
T-12........I.6:10 in your way, for you cannot **h.** yourself.
T-12.........I.7:2 By giving **h.** you are asking for it, and if
T-12.........I.7:5 then, hear every call for **h.** as what it is, so
T-12.........I.8:7 regard everything else as an appeal for **h.**,
T-12.........I.8:7 you that fear itself is an appeal for **h.**. This
T-12.......I.8:12 if you see attack as the call for **h.** that it is,
T-12.........II.4:4 It is easy to **h.** an uncertain child, for he
T-12.........II.5:4 of hatred will not leave you without **h.**,
T-12.........II.7:5 Trust in my **h.**, for I did not walk alone,
T-12......II.10:6 Surely He will not fail to **h.** you, since help
T-12......II.10:6 to help you, since **h.** is His only purpose.
T-12...... III.1:4 they are in need it is given you to **h.** them,
T-12...... III.3:5 You who could **h.** them are surely acting
T-13...... III.8:1 you hold so dear is your real call for **h.**.
T-13..... VII.4:3 answers, being unable to deny a call for **h.**
T-13....VIII.5:6 **H.** Him to give His gift of light to all who
T-13..... XI.6:7 to **h.** you realize that this is what you want
T-14.... III.11:2 You are not bereft of **h.**, and Help that
T-14...... IV.8:4 of the world to **h.** you understand it.
T-14........X.1:4 touch it, with the **h.** of its reflection in you
T-14........X.6:3 the same response to every call for **h.**. It
T-14..... X.6:15 difficulty here. A call for **h.** is given help.
T-14..... X.6:15 of difficulty here. A call for help is given **h.**
T-14...... XI.3:5 can **h.** you understand the present, or
T-15........II.6:4 not that you will not be given **h.** in this.
T-16...... III.6:4 teaching have gathered to **h.** you learn.
T-16...... III.7:5 He is, will grow and **h.** you honor Him.
T-16...... IV.8:1 hands to **h.** you cross and welcome them.
T-16.... IV.11:6 call for **h.** that rises ceaselessly from you
T-16...... VI.3:1 way in which the Holy Spirit asks your **h.**,
T-16.... VI.12:1 The Holy Spirit asks only this little **h.** of
T-16...VII.10:4 to you. His **h.** suffices, for His Messenger
T-16...VII.12:1 *and* ***h.*** *us to accept our true relationship with*
T-17..... V.11:3 also made enormous efforts to **h.** Him do
T-18.........I.9:9 to **h.** Him show you that no substitute you
T-18........II.6:6 as a **h.** to make His purpose real to you.
T-18...... III.7:6 Time has been readjusted to **h.** us do,
T-18....... V.2:3 guilt before you ask the Holy Spirit's **h.**.
T-18...... IX.1:5 and delusional thought needs **h.** because,
T-19.......I.15:1 so will faith **h.** the Holy Spirit prepare the
T-19...... III.4:9 a call for **h.** that you would keep unheard
T-19...... III.9:6 And you will **h.** him overcome mistakes
T19... IV.D.8:3 peace can be surmounted through its **h.**.
T19. IV.D.16:5 **H.** him to lift the heavy burden of sin you
T-20.........I.3:4 **H.** him to go in peace beyond it, with the
T-20........ IV.6:2 the rest will see to it without your **h.**. But
T-20........ IV.6:3 not need your part to **h.** Him with the rest
T-20....VIII.5:2 Can such a savior **h.** you? Would you turn
T-20....VIII.5:3 distress and need for **h.** unto the helpless?
T-21.... III.12:3 to serve as means to **h.** the blind to see.
T-21....... V.2:2 But your awareness of it needs your **h.**,
T-21....... V.3:5 are the obvious response to calls for **h.**,
T-21...... VI.1:3 when you think you sin, you call for **h.**.
T-21...... VI.1:4 if you will not accept the **h.** you call for,
T-21....VIII.4:2 it possible to **h.** you be already partly sane
T-22...... III.3:3 the **h.** of reason would try to pass it. The
T-23.......in.5:4 but **h.** him rise above it and perceive the
T-23........II.7:2 impossible to turn to Him for **h.** in misery
T-23........II.7:5 made inevitable, beyond the **h.** of God.
T-23........II.8:3 there is no sight of **h.** that can succeed.
T-24.........I.6:3 not **h.** him reach it in every way you could
T-25...... III.6:4 he chooses can be any time, for **h.** is there,
T-25...... III.9:5 Does he need **h.** or condemnation? Is it

T-25....VIII.8:7 what but vengeance now can **h.** and save,
T-25...... IX.7:1 Salvation cannot seek to **h.** God's Son be
T-25...... IX.7:6 it for yourself to solve without His **h.** is to
T-26....... V.1:5 is a **h.** or hindrance to the gate of Heaven.
T-26..... VII.6:2 offered to truth for healing and for **h.**. No
T-27....... V.1:2 The miracle extends without your **h.**, but
T-27...... VI.6:6 and a plaintive cry for **h.** within a world of
T-28...... IV.1:6 be. Unless you **h.** him, you will suffer pain
T-28..... VII.2:2 and your health, the Source of **h.**, the Call
T-28..... VII.3:6 merely as an aid to **h.** you reach the home
T-28..... VII.4:4 It serves to **h.** the healing of God's Son,
T-29....... II.4:6 He needs your **h.** in giving them to all who
T-29...... III.5:6 the dream; that you can **h.** him waken,
T-29...... IV.5:6 a brother giving you a chance to **h.**, if this
T-29...... IV.6:5 He asks for **h.** in every dream he has, and
T-29...... IV.6:5 and you have **h.** to give him if you see the
T-29...... IX.9:1 not feel a deep content, a certainty of **h.**, a
T-30.......in.1:4 Each one will **h.** a little, every time it is
T-30.........I.9:3 reminds you that **h.** is not being thrust
T-30.......I.14:9 And you ask **h.** of anti-Christ or Christ,
T-30...... VI.2:7 that rests on error, and thus calls for **h.**.
T-31....... II.3:6 a means to **h.** you save yourself from this.
T-31....... II.5:8 life, for hate or for forgiveness and for **h.**,
T-31....... V.8:3 to **h.** you see this concept of the self must
T-31...... VI.3:3 For you can see the body without **h.**, but
W-in..........4:2 planned to **h.** you generalize the lessons,
W-in..........6:2 will **h.** you to generalize the ideas involved
W-pI.......3.2:1 The point of the exercises is to **h.** you
W-pI.......5.4:2 might **h.** to precede the exercises with the
W-pI.....10.4:3 *idea will **h.** to release me from all that I now*
W-pI.....10.5:5 *idea will **h.** to release me from all that I now*
W-pI.....26.4:1 Practice with today's idea will **h.** you to
W-pI.....30.4:2 To **h.** you begin to get used to this idea,
W-pI.....33.4:3 Closing your eyes will probably **h.** in this
W-pI.....34.6:2 one application of today's idea to **h.** you
W-pI.....34.6:3 will **h.** you if you tell yourself specifically: *I*
W-pI.....38.2:6 equal in its power to **h.** anyone because it
W-pI.....50.5:2 come to **h.** you recognize its truth, and
W-pI.....59.2:6 this day may **h.** me to understand eternity
W-pI.....62.4:2 It will **h.** to make the day as happy for you
W-pI.....62.4:3 And it will **h.** those around you, as well as
W-pI.....64.6:6 Related thoughts will come to **h.** you, if
W-pI.....64.7:3 forget my function" quite often to **h.** you
W-pI.....69.7:2 call on the power of the universe to **h.** you
W-pI.....70.3:2 remedy for the sickness where it cannot **h.**
W-pI.....72.4:3 You are doing more than failing to **h.** in
W-pI...73.11:7 This will **h.** you let your grievances go,
W-pI.....81.4:2 *Let this **h.** me learn what forgiveness means.*
W-pI.....93.2:1 **h.** you see that they are based on nothing.
W-pI...95.14:2 today. We need your **h.**; your little part in
W-pI.....97.4:4 to **h.** you understand with Him you are
W-pI...98.11:2 He would have you take and **h.** you fill,
W-pI...102.3:1 to **h.** you reach the happiness God's Will
WpIrIII.in10:6 and let it serve to **h.** you keep your peace
WpIrIII.in11:2 to **h.** you form the habit of applying what
WpIrIII.in11:5 and whenever you need **h.** of any kind.
W-pI...125.6:4 to **h.** make ready your most holy mind to
W-pI...126.2:3 for **h.** are not in any way related to your
W-pI...126.8:2 You will need **h.** to make this meaningful,
W-pI.126.10:2 ask for **h.** in understanding what it really
W-pI...127.5:1 No law the world obeys can **h.** you grasp
W-pI...127.9:4 and **h.** you understand the truth of love.
W-pI...130.8:4 You wait for God to **h.** you, as you say: *It is*
W-pI.136.15:5 prayer, to **h.** us rise above defensiveness,
W-pI...137.9:3 extend the little **h.** He asks in freeing you
W-pI...138.7:1 choice that time was made to **h.** us make.
W-pI...138.9:3 judged again, this time with Heaven's **h.**.
W-pI.153.11:1 the function of God's ministers to **h.** their
W-pI.153.20:1 to **h.** you keep your mind from wandering
WpI...rV.in7:5 **H.** me now to lead you back to where the
W-pI...182.6:3 His call for **h.** almost unheard amid the
W-pI.182.11:3 even come to ask your **h.** in letting Him go
W-pI.185.10:5 it, and where to turn for **h.** in the attempt.
W-pI...193.8:2 He would **h.** you forgive yourself. His Son
W-pI.196.12:1 go with you to **h.** you reach that instant,
W-pI...199.5:3 not gain thereby in power to **h.** the world,
WpI rVI.in.7:3 you, each time you call to Him to **h.** you.
W-pII .234.2:2 *on us, for all the loving **h.** we have received,*
W-pII .....5.4:3 to **h.** him walk along the road with him.
W-pII .292.2:2 ***H.** us not interfere, and so delay the happy*
W-pII .294.2:3 *then, use this dream to **h.** Your plan that we*
W-pII .295.2:2 *me. **H.** me to use the eyes of Christ today, and*
W-pII .305.2:2 ***H.** us today but to accept Your gift, and judge*
W-pII .325.1:6 and **h.** his brothers walk ahead with him,
W-pII .327.1:5 to give me all the **h.** I need to come to Him
W-pII .345.1:4 *I need to **h.** me with the problems I perceive.*
W-pII .359.1:8 ***H.** us forgive, for we would be redeemed.*
W-pII .359.1:9 ***H.** us forgive, for we would be at peace.*
Wfl........in.6:1 and ask Him to **h.** us to learn His lessons,
WpII361-5.1:1 And if I need a word to **h.** me, He will
M-17.........2:3 be easily concealed beneath a wish to **h.**.
M-17.........2:4 wish that makes the **h.** of little value, and
M-17.........2:7 better shown than in the kinds of **h.** the
M-17.........3:5 the call for **h.** becoming his one appeal.
M-17.........6:4 Magic again must **h.**. Forget the battle.
M-21.........2:3 and thus cannot **h.** the healing process.
M-23.........3:5 Is he still available for **h.**? What did he say
M-23.........7:4 a very present **h.** in time of trouble; a
M-26.........2:9 teachers of God who look to them for **h.**,
M-26.........4:8 All the **h.** you can accept will be provided,
M-29.........5:8 to ask for **h.** when and where you can, you
M-29.........5:9 Holy Spirit's **h.** when it is feasible to do so
M-29.........6:6 understands that an attack is a call for **h.**.
M-29.........6:7 And He responds with **h.** accordingly.
M-29.........8:2 *God turns to you for **h.** to save the world.*
C-2..........1:10 We name it but to **h.** us understand that it
C-2............9:1 you ready yet to **h.** Me save the world?"
C-3............3:1 an illusion of **h.** because they are helpless;
C-5............1:1 is no need for **h.** to enter Heaven for you
C-5............1:2 But there is need for **h.** beyond yourself as
C-5............1:7 does not **h.** because He knows no need.
C-5............6:7 Yet he would **h.** you yet a little more if you
C-6............4:6 a far country, for you need that form of **h.**.
C-ep...........2:3 Ask but my **h.** to roll the stone away, and
P-in...........1:6 start to open his mind without formal **h.**,
P-1.............1:4 and **h.** far exceed whatever contributions
P-1.............2:4 To **h.** in this is the proper purpose of
P-1.............3:1 Everyone who needs **h.**, regardless of the
P-1.............5:7 to the **h.** that He begins and He directs. By
P-2.........in.1:5 **h.** the patient deal with one fundamental
P-2.........in.2:2 little to them, or they would not need **h.**.
P-2..........II.9:7 except a **h.** in just this same direction? It
P-2........ III.3:4 One asks for **h.**; another hears and tries to
P-2........ III.3:4 hears and tries to answer in the form of **h.**
P-2........ III.4:5 he can **h.** through those in need of help,
P-2........ III.4:5 he can help through those in need of **h.**,
P-2........ IV.2:3 to seek for remedies that cannot **h.**,
P-2......... V.2:1 who come to us for **h.** are bitterly afraid.
P-2......... V.2:2 What they believe will **h.** can only harm;
P-2......... V.2:2 what they believe will harm alone can **h.**.
P-2......... V.4:2 is holier than helping one who asks for **h.**.
P-2......... V.4:7 to guide us, as we try to **h.** our brothers.
P-2......... V.5:5 of God's holy Son for **h.** in his perceived
P-2......... V.6:6 To ask for **h.**, whatever form it takes, is
P-2......... V.6:9 even seem to be a worsening and not a **h.**.
P-2......... V.7:6 Let us **h.** him to forgive himself for all the
P-2......... V.8:4 Hear a brother call for **h.** and answer him.
P-2....... VII.2:9 with which the patient came to ask for **h.**.
P-2....... VII.3:6 needs the **h.** of a very advanced therapist,
P-3..........II.1:5 that a large number of others turn for **h.**.
P-3..........II.3:6 the therapist will silently ask him for **h.**.
P-3..........II.5:6 be able to accept **h.** from them if they did.
P-3........II.7:10 other images, and **h.** with kindly dreams.
P-3........ III.1:2 Holy Spirit to **h.** in carrying out the plan.
P-3........ III.1:4 to **h.** him better serve the plan. Money is
P-3........ III.7:8 look. Whoever asks your **h.** can show you
S-1...........I.6:2 not reached it still need your **h.** in prayer
S-1...........I.6:3 **H.** in prayer does not mean that another
S-1........ IV.2:1 Now it is possible to **h.** in prayer, and so
S-2.........in.1:5 Behold the greatest **h.** that God ordained
S-2...........I.7:1 Ask, then, His **h.**, and ask Him how to
S-2........ III.2:5 When someone calls for **h.** in any form,
S-2........ III.3:2 the way to make of every call a **h.** to you,
S-2........ III.5:1 when **h.** is needed and forgiveness sought.
S-3...........I.4:4 **h.** is given to him in the Voice his Father
S-3..........II.2:1 body has been kindly used to **h.** the Son of
S-3........ III.3:4 and used to **h.** restore the wounded and
S-3........ III.4:1 one can use to offer **h.** for someone else?
S-3........ III.4:6 your oneness with the one who calls for **h.**
S-3........ IV.3:1 what it means to **h.** the Christ to heal! Can
S-3........ IV.8:1 **H.** Me to wake My children from the

### helped 12

T-6 .....V.A.6:8 the first step, however, they will be **h.**.
T-9 .........V.7:2 unless he is also **h.** to change his direction
T-11 .VIII.13:3 is **h.** to translate his "ghost" into a curtain
T-12 ........I.5:6 only by answering his appeal *can* you be **h.**
T-30 ........I.9:4 more steps you need to let yourself be **h.**.
T-30 ......I.12:1 of lack of opposition to be **h.**. It is a
T-30 ......I.12:6 you see that it is you who will be **h.** by it.
WpI..rIII.in6:2 being **h.** in its decisions by the One Who
C-ep ..........4:1 Who called to us and **h.** us hear His Call.
P-in ...........1:8 the patient must be **h.** to change his mind
P-2..........V.3:5 they are sick, they can and must be **h.**. No
P-3........II.10:6 is the Will of God that his patient be **h.** to

### Helper 3

*helper*

T-25 ..... III.7:2 see the workings of the **H.** given you to see
C-5 ............ 6:1 Is he God's only **H.**? No, indeed. For
C-6 ............ 5:3 Alone he cannot be the **H.** of God's Son

### helper 1

*Helper*

T-14 .... VII.1:8 rather than a **h.** in the search for truth.

### Helpers 2

*helpers*

C-5 ............ 1:3 **H.** are given you in many forms, although
C-5 ............ 1:8 But He creates all **H.** of His Son while he

### helpers 4

*Helpers*

M-26 ....... 3:10 need **h.** who are still in bondage and still
C-2 ............ 7:5 Look at the **h.** all along the way you travel,
P-3..........II.1:7 These are therefore "officially" **h.**. They
S-3........ III.4:3 in humility there is indeed a place for **h.**.

### helpful 55

T-2 ....... IV.5:2 in whatever way is most **h.** to the receiver.
T-2 ... V.A.18:2 way: *I am here only to be truly **h.**. I am here to*
T-2 ...... VII.1:7 It is much more **h.** to remind you that you
T-2 ...... VII.7:1 some additional points might be **h.** here.
T-4 .........II.5:5 the effort to become both harmless and **h.**
T-4 ........ III.2:3 find it very **h.** if you understand it fully.
T-4 ...... VII.1:1 correction is more **h.** in a specific context.
T-4 ...... VII.8:1 whenever any mind learns to be wholly **h.**
T-4 ...... VII.8:3 The truly **h.** are invulnerable, because
T-4 ...... VII.8:7 it. The truly **h.** are God's miracle workers,
T-4 ...... VII.8:8 direct you to wherever you can be truly **h.**
T-5 ..........I.6:6 It might even be more **h.** here to use the
T-6 ........in.2:1 example is a particularly **h.** learning
T-7 .........II.4:1 be communicated if they are to be **h.**. In
T-8 ...... VII.4:3 or ugly, peaceful or savage, **h.** or harmful,
T-16 .......II.2:4 A better and far more **h.** way to think of
T-16 ....... VI.3:2 His. The holy instant is His most **h.** aid in
T-31 .... VII.1:2 as yet too alien to your thinking to be **h.**,
W-pI ...... 8.6:3 You might find it **h.**, however, to include
W-pI .... 10.4:6 fact, if you find it **h.** to do so, you might
W-pI .... 24.3:2 will be more **h.** than a more cursory
W-pI .... 26.8:2 is much more **h.** to cover a few situations
W-pI .... 37.6:2 It is particularly **h.** to apply it silently to
W-pI .... 39.9:2 You may also find it **h.** to include a few
W-pI .. 39.11:2 arise, a particularly **h.** form of the idea is:
W-pI .... 40.2:1 you will probably find it more **h.** if you do
W-pI .... 41.7:1 you may repeat the idea if you find it **h.**.
W-pI .... 44.6:2 You might find it **h.** to remind yourself,
W-pI .... 61.6:3 find them **h.** and want to extend them.
W-pI .. 66.11:1 most **h.** today if undertaken twice an hour
W-pI .... 67.2:5 *kind. Helpfulness created me **h.**. Perfection*
W-pI .... 67.5:1 It will be particularly **h.** today to practice

W-pI.....84.2:1 specific forms **h.** in applying the idea: *Let*
W-pI.....84.4:1 forms for applying this idea would be **h.**:
W-pI.....87.2:1 idea would be **h.** for specific applications:
W-pI...91.11:3 form would be **h.** for this special purpose:
W-pI.....95.7:2 minutes of the hour will be particularly **h.**
W-pI...108.9:4 It might be **h.**, too, to think of one to
W-pI...187.5:7 have the thought in form most **h.** to him.
M-4......I.A.3:7 These changes are always **h.**. When the
M-4......I.A.4:2 that the changes in his life are always **h.**,
M-4......I.A.4:5 encounters and circumstances are **h.**. It is
M-4......I.A.4:6 to the extent to which they are **h.** that any
M-17..........4:1 Perhaps it will be **h.** to remember that no
M-21..........1:8 Words can be **h.**, particularly for the
M-24..........1:4 question should be, "Is the concept **h.**?"
M-24..........1:6 of the eternal nature of life, it is **h.** indeed.
M-24..........3:1 it would not be **h.** to take any definite
M-24..........3:2 A teacher of God should be as **h.** to those
M-24..........4:6 to any concept or belief that will be **h.**, he
M-25..........3:1 be gathered on the way can be very **h.**.
M-26..........2:3 when and where it is **h.** for them to do so.
M-29..........1:5 be **h.** for the pupil to read the manual first
P-3...........I.3:6 way can be most **h.** to both of you. It does
P-3...........I.3:8 will be sent in whatever form is most **h.**; a

### helpfulness 7

T-4.......VII.8:4 Their **h.** is their praise of God, and He will
T-9........IV.3:6 their **h.** lies in the judgment of the Holy
T-10..III.10:11 own perfect **h.** and your own perfect Help
T-27...VII.15:5 give thanks to him for all the **h.** he gave.
W-pI.....67.2:5 *H. created me helpful. Perfection created*
M-4......I.A.4:2 whether they increase the **h.** or hamper it.
M-26..........3:9 their **h.** to those remaining behind are

### helping 9

T-9...........I.4:4 He *is* **h.** you to remember what you are.
T-9.........V.8:9 that you choose the guide for **h.**, and the
W-pI.....30.5:3 aid in **h.** you to become more accustomed
W-pI.135.13:2 free to be the means of **h.** in a plan which
W-pII..242.2:6 *everything we need in* ***h.*** *us to find the way to*
M-21..........1:8 in **h.** concentration and facilitating the
P-2.........II.9:6 but an aid in **h.** him to see that this is so?
P-2.........V.3:4 yet be done in **h.** the insane within the
P-2.........V.4:2 is holier than **h.** one who asks for help.

### helpless 33

T-6......IV.10:3 everything need help and are therefore **h.**.
T-8........IV.1:8 only if you do, you will feel lonely and **h.**,
T-10.......V.4:4 Yet the Son *is* **h.** without the Father, Who
T-13.....III.4:1 think you would be **h.** in God's Presence,
T-16.......V.11:3 truth, triumphing over it and leaving it **h.**
T-16.......V.12:6 you would have made yourself **h.**. God is
T-20... VIII.5:3 distress and need for help unto the **h.**? Is
T-21.......II.2:6 are **h.** in the face of what is done to you.
T-21.......V.2:5 will believe that you are **h.** prey to forces
T-21.....VII.1:2 Being **h.** is the cost of sin. Helplessness is
T-21.....VII.1:4 Only the **h.** could believe in it. Enormity
T-21.....VII.2:2 And those who see themselves as **h.** must
T-21...VII.5:12 *a world where I am powerful instead of* ***h.****?*
T-21.....VII.9:4 an enemy, in which you are not **h.**, the
T-21...VII.13:5 that he is wrong who sees himself as **h.**.
T-24......IV.2:2 makes it frail and **h.** in its own defense. It
T-24......IV.2:3 It was conceived to make *you* frail and **h.**.
T-25... VIII.8:7 while love stands feebly by with **h.** hands,
T-27.....VII.8:4 make. **H.** he stands, a victim to a dream
W-pI.....35.6:6 *I see myself as* ***h.***. *I see myself as victorious. I*
W-pI.....91.8:5 *I am not* ***h.***, *but all powerful. I am not limited*
W-pI.....92.3:3 the dying, those in need, the **h.** and afraid
W-pI.....96.5:2 its Source of strength, and sees itself as **h.**,
W-pI...151.4:5 how weak you are; how **h.** and afraid,
W-pI...153.5:5 he has made; yet **h.** in their presence,
W-pI...163.2:3 **h.** and the sick bow down before its image
W-pI...186.6:4 You are not ignorant and **h.**. Sin can not
W-pI...191.8:3 in glory to redeem the lost, to save the **h.**,
W-pI...191.9:3 You play the game of death, of being **h.**,
W-pI...199.7:3 themselves as bound and **h.** and afraid.
C-3.............3:1 an illusion of help because they are **h.**; a
P-1.............3:6 and **h.** midst the power of the world.
P-2.........V.4:8 us not forget that we are **h.** of ourselves,

### helplessness 8

T-21.....VII.1:3 **H.** is sin's condition; the one requirement
T-21.....VII.2:5 dead, and raising up their **h.** against him.
T-21.....VII.5:9 understand, he will but emphasize his **h.**,
T-21.....VII.7:1 that the choice of sin or truth, **h.** or power
T-21.....VII.7:2 healing comes of power, and attack of **h.**.
T-21...VII.10:7 can desire to exchange your **h.** for power,
T-27.......II.9:3 **h.** and weakness represent the grounds
W-pI.....41.1:3 So are anxiety, worry, a deep sense of **h.**,

### helps 11

T-17......VI.4:2 on everything that **h.** you meet it. It is
T-27.........I.7:1 that bolsters all the rest and **h.** them paint
T-29......IX.6:5 What hurts him is destroyed; what **h.** him
W-pI.....61.4:3 to the truth, and **h.** you depart in peace,
W-pI.....70.9:3 you. If it **h.** you, think of me holding your
WpI...rV.in4:2 this thought, or **h.** it be more meaningful,
W-pI...199.4:5 which **h.** forgiveness be extended to the
P-1.............2:6 and **h.** the patient to recognize and accept
P-2........III.1:1 **h.** him to avoid a few of the pitfalls along
S-1...........I.6:4 beside you and **h.** to raise you up to Him.
S-3........III.4:4 It is like the role that **h.** in prayer, and lets

### hence 1

T-31......VI.2:4 he be the same as he is now an instant **h.**.

### henceforth 2

Wfl........in.1:4 lessons, as to Him we give our lives **h.**. For
W-ep.........3:2 **H.**, hear but the Voice for God and for

### her 1

C-2............8:2 as a loving mother sings **h.** child to rest. Is

### herald 4

T-20.......V.1:6 of joining is a mighty **h.** of eternity. No
T-20.......V.2:1 Each **h.** of eternity sings of the end of sin
T-20......VI.7:4 Yet what you fear is but the **h.** of escape.
P-2........VI.2:6 of the universe," "the **h.** angel's song," all

### heralds 3

T-20..........V.h **H.** of Eternity
W-pI...140.3:3 are **h.** of the dawn of truth upon the mind
W-pI...156.6:3 It **h.** not the end of sin in punishment and

### Here 1

*here*

WpI rV.in12:6 of meaning. It is **H.** that we find rest.

### here 684

*Here*

T-2...........I.4:3 **H.** is the real basis for your escape from
T-2.......IV.3:12 The term "unworthy" **h.** implies only that
T-2....V.A.18:2 *I am* ***h.*** *only to be truly helpful. I am here to*
T-2....V.A.18:3 *I am* ***h.*** *to represent Him Who sent me. I do*
T-2.......VI.2:4 There is a confusion **h.** that you would do
T-2........VI.6:5 own. The lesson **h.** is quite simple, but
T-2.......VII.7:1 additional points might be helpful **h.**.
T-3.......VII.3:9 The symbolism **h.** has been given many
T-4.........V.4:5 **H.** is where the mind becomes actually
T-4........VI.1:5 necessarily conflicted as long as you are **h.**
T-4........VI.1:5 or as long as you believe that you are **h.**.
T-4........VI.2:4 The term "holy" can be used **h.** because,
T-5...........I.6:6 might even be more helpful **h.** to use the
T-5.........V.2:2 word "create" is appropriate **h.** because,
T-6........III.1:3 The word "knows" is correct **h.**, because
T-6......V.B.4:3 judgment, **h.** as always, is predetermined
T-6......V.C.4:6 **H.**, then, your consistency is called on
T-9......IV.12:1 Behold, my child, reality is **h.**. It belongs
T-11........I.10:5 symptom of sickness and fear arises **h.**,
T-11.....III.4:10 for the light is **h.** and the way is clear.
T-11.....VII.4:5 it. Truth is not absent **h.**, but it is obscure.
T-12........II.5:4 not leave you without help, and Help is **h.**.
T-13......III.6:6 for **h.** is the real crucifixion of God's Son.
T-13......III.7:2 **H.** is both his pain and his healing, for the
T-13......IV.1:5 thus destroy you **h.** and bury you here,
T-13......IV.1:5 thus destroy you here and bury you **h.**,
T-13......IV.7:7 lies. For only "now" is **h.**, and only "now"
T-13.......V.8:4 And it is **h.** that what you see you made.
T-13....VI.11:7 And **h.** will everything remind you of your
T-13....VI.11:9 in gratitude because they brought you **h.**.
T-13.....VII.4:1 world has the power to touch you even **h.**,
T-13.....VII.8:2 Yet **h.** it *is*, and you can understand it *now*.
T-13...VII.16:7 Salvation from the world lies only **h.**. My
T-13...VII.17:6 You dwell not **h.**, but in eternity. You
T-13....VIII.3:6 function in Heaven, is needful **h.**. Aspects
T-13....VIII.5:5 to make Christ's vision possible even **h.**.
T-13....VIII.9:3 His. Deny a brother **h.**, and you deny the
T-13.......XI.3:1 you will value nothing that you value **h.**.
T-13.......XI.3:2 that you value **h.** do you value wholly, and
T-13.......XI.6:2 have need of contrast only **h.**. Contrast
T-14........II.7:1 meets the conditions of learning **h.**, as he
T-14......III.2:5 There is no conflict **h.**. To wish for guilt in
T-14......III.3:2 Learning is living **h.**, as creating is being
T-14....IV.3:10 guilt by failing to fulfill your function **h.**?
T-14......IV.5:1 whether you want to make decisions **h.**.
T-14......IV.5:2 Your function **h.** is only to decide against
T-14......IV.8:2 It is **h.** without your making, but not
T-14.......V.1:9 Heaven. There is nothing of value **h.**, and
T-14.......V.3:5 Your only calling **h.** is to devote yourself,
T-14.......V.5:1 We are all joined in the Atonement **h.**,
T-14.....V.11:8 out, for **h.** is what he seeks along with you
T-14..VIII.2:14 wills with His Son is quite impossible **h.**.
T-14.....VIII.5:5 with it. **H.** your little offerings are brought
T-14......IX.5:2 you. You can reflect Heaven **h.**. Yet no
T-14......IX.8:5 of what was but reflected to them **h.**. God
T-14........X.1:6 Reflect the peace of Heaven **h.**, and bring
T-14........X.2:2 sharing its reflection **h.**, its truth becomes
T-14........X.3:4 must come from elsewhere, not from **h.**.
T-14.....X.6:14 There is no order of difficulty **h.**. A call for
T-14.....XI.11:6 Teach like Him **h.**, and you will remember
T-15.........I.4:9 system before, but never so clearly as **h.**.
T-15.........I.5:1 is **h.** and now because the future is hell.
T-15.........I.5:3 For it tells him hell is **h.** as well, and bids
T-15.........I.6:6 of hell to be experienced is to bring hell **h.**
T-15.........I.9:6 Nothing can reach you **h.** out of the past,
T-15.........I.9:6 it is **h.** that you are completely absolved,
T-15........II.5:6 And **h.** it is, all in this instant, complete,
T-15.......V.8:1 to bring a touch of Heaven to them **h.**. In
T-15.......V.9:6 The Holy Spirit's timelessness lies only **h.**.
T-15......VI.4:7 Herein lies peace, for **h.** there *is* no conflict
T-15.....VII.3:7 of God can have no real investment **h.**.
T-15...VII.14:3 communication, has no function **h.**. Here
T-15...VII.14:4 here. **H.** there is no concealment, and no
T-15...VII.14:6 There is complete forgiveness **h.**, for there
T-15.VII.14:10 And **h.** it is that you experience yourself as
T-15......IX.5:2 of this and long remain willing to linger **h.**
T-15......IX.7:6 that you could ever want. All truth *is* **h.**.
T-15........X.1:4 But **h.** it is the Holy Spirit's function to
T-16.......I.3:11 *I have invited Him, and He is* ***h.***. *I need do*
T-16.......V.3:2 The "dynamics" of the ego are clearest **h.**,
T-16.......V.3:3 overt. **H.** they are usually judged to be
T-16.......V.3:6 and everything **h.** takes a direction exactly
T-16.......V.3:8 **H.**, where the illusion of love is accepted
T-16.....V.16:2 For **h.** is truth, separated from illusion
T-16.....V.17:2 on the other side, and nothing at all is **h.**.
T-16......VI.6:2 seen, but not exclusively, as it is seen **h.**.
T-16......VI.7:7 be no meaning you would still seek **h.**.
T-16......VI.8:3 your mind from its fixed position **h.**. This
T-16......VI.8:7 of love in any special relationship **h.**. For
T-17........II.1:3 Nothing you see **h.**, sleeping or waking,
T-17........II.2:3 Nothing is hidden **h.**, for everything has
T-17........II.5:3 show you that there is no reason **h.** at all.
T-17......IV.8:2 ego uses. Its thought system is offered **h.**,
T-17....IV.14:2 There is no distraction **h.**. The picture of
T-17....IV.16:9 For **h.** is only healing, already complete
T-17..IV.16:10 For **h.** is God, and where He is only the

T-17....... V.2:6 For h., the goal of the relationship is
T-17..... V.14:2 H. is the goal, together with you. Think
T-17...... VI.5:8 H. again you see the opposite of the ego's
T-18.........I.9:4 love. H. is holy ground, in which no
T-18.........I.9:5 abide. H. you are joined in God, as much
T-18.........I.9:6 The original error has not entered h., nor
T-18.........I.9:7 H. is the radiant truth, to which the Holy
T-18.........I.9:8 Let Him bring it h., where *you* would have
T-18.......I.12:6 Is it h. that you would look for happiness?
T-18.......I.13:4 Accept it h., and you will give as you have
T-18....... II.1:5 H., you are "free" to make over whatever
T-18....... II.5:3 Yet h. is a world, clearly within your mind
T-18....... V.5:4 Holy Spirit, Who *has* a special function h..
T-18..... VII.6:1 H. is the ultimate release which everyone
T-18..... VII.7:3 H. is the quick and open door through
T-18..... VII.7:5 For h. is time denied, and past and future
T-18...... IX.4:2 H. are all the illusions, all the twisted
T-18...... IX.9:2 H. the world outside is seen anew,
T-18...... IX.9:3 it. H. are you forgiven, for here you have
T-18...... IX.9:3 for h. you have forgiven everyone. Here is
T-18...... IX.9:4 everyone. H. is the new perception, where
T-18...... IX.9:5 H. there is no attack upon the Son of God,
T-18...... IX.9:6 H. is your innocence, waiting to clothe
T-18...... IX.9:7 H. are the dark and heavy garments of
T-18.... IX.10:4 H. you are led, that God Himself can take
T-18.... IX.10:4 for h. does nothing interfere with love,
T-18.... IX.10:6 H. is the Source of light; nothing
T-19.........I.6:4 H., then, is healing needed. And it is here
T-19.........I.6:5 And it is h. that healing *is*. For God gave
T-19....... II.5:4 For h. lies its "best" defense, which all the
T-19....... II.5:5 H. is its armor, its protection, and the
T-19..... III.11:4 H. is the rest that waits for all, after the
T-19....... IV.3:6 Spirit's function h. will be accomplished.
T19.... IV.B.1:4 h. is the attraction of guilt made manifest
T19.... IV.B.2:8 death? H. is the focus of the perception of
T19.... IV.B.2:9 H. is the source of the idea that love is fear
T19.. IV.B.11:2 H. is your choice, and it *is* free. But all that
T19.. IV.B.14:8 both also recognize that h. the sender and
T19.... IV.C.7:7 H. is the final end of union, the triumph
T19.. IV.C.10:8 H. is the babe of Bethlehem reborn. And
T19... IV.D.1:6 to sanity. For h. your world *does* end.
T19... IV.D.3:4 H. is your promise never to allow union to
T19... IV.D.8:2 it was surely not the ego that led you h..
T19... IV.D.8:6 Guide Who brought you h. remains with
T19... IV.D.9:4 Stand you h. a while and tremble not. You
T19... IV.D.9:6 instant, h. in this place where the purpose
T19... IV.D.9:7 He Who brought us h. together will offer
T19. IV.D.10:7 H., with the journey's end before you, you
T19. IV.D.10:8 h. you choose whether to look upon it or
T19. IV.D.16:1 H. is the holy place of resurrection, to
T19. IV.D.17:9 that we might meet h. in this holy place,
T19. IV.D.18:1 Free your brother h., as I freed you. Give
T19. IV.D.18:4 sin, h. in the garden of seeming agony and
T19. IV.D.19:4 H. is the peace of God, given to you
T19. IV.D.19:5 H. is the rest and quiet that you seek, the
T19. IV.D.21:4 H. is the only purpose that gives this
T-20....... II.3:5 H. is the value that you lay upon your
T-20....... II.3:6 H. is your gift to both; your judgment on
T-20..... II.11:1 H. is your savior and your friend,
T-20.... III.10:2 H. there is only holiness and joining
T-20.... III.10:4 it? H. are we one, looking with perfect
T-20.... III.10:5 H. all thoughts of any separation between
T-20.... III.10:7 And h. would I unite with you, my friend,
T-20...... IV.5:3 whose special function h. is to release him
T-20...... IV.6:6 Each holy relationship must enter h., to
T-20...... IV.7:3 hands of every two who enter h. to rest.
T-20....... V.6:3 ever held or will ever hold is h. right now.
T-20....... V.6:5 more. H., then, is everything. Here is the
T-20....... V.6:6 H. is the loveliness of your relationship,
T-20....... V.6:7 H. is the perfect faith that you will one
T-20....... V.6:7 and h. the limitless forgiveness you will
T-20...... VI.5:3 H. the unholy relationship escapes reality,
T-20...... VI.5:4 H. it would drag its brothers, holding
T-20...... VI.5:4 brothers, holding them h. in its idolatry.
T-20...... VI.5:5 H. it is "safe," for here love cannot enter.
T-20...... VI.5:5 Here it is "safe," for h. love cannot enter.
T-20...... VI.6:3 condemnation. For h. is love made fearful
T-20...... VI.6:4 idols that are worshipped h. are shrouded
T-20...... VI.6:6 return. H. is the "mystery" of separation

T-20..... VI.6:7 have *not* be is h. kept "safe" from Him. But
T-20... VI.10:4 H. the unholy instant is exchanged in
T-20... VI.10:5 H. is the way to true relationships held
T-20... VI.11:4 H. does the Son of God stop briefly by, to
T-20... VI.11:5 And h. he is more dead than living. Yet it
T-20... VI.11:6 Yet it is also h. he makes his choice again
T-20... VI.11:7 H. it is given him to choose to spend this
T-20... VI.11:8 H. he can accept the holy instant, offered
T-20... VI.11:9 And h. can he learn relationships are his
T-20.... VII.5:3 But the *purpose* h. is sin. It cannot be
T-20.... VII.6:4 is h. that the illusions you hold about him
T-20.... VII.6:5 H. are illusions and reality kept separated.
T-20.... VII.6:6 H. are illusions never brought to truth,
T-20.... VII.6:7 it. And h., in darkness, is your brother's
T-21........I.9:2 well. H. is the sight of him who knows his
T-21........I.9:3 H. is the memory of what you are; a part
T-21.......II.2:2 for h. the power of salvation lies: *I am*
T-21.......II.4:6 H. is the world you do not want brought
T-21.......II.4:7 h. the one you do is given you because you
T-21.......II.6:8 to attack your faith, for h. is it invested.
T-21...... V.7:7 part. H. is the part you can accept. What
T-21...... V.9:2 H. was the Holy Spirit's purpose accepted
T-21... VI.7:11 And h. you will lay down the burden of
T-21... VI.10:4 And h. alone does reason tell you that you
T-21.... VII.6:7 find. H., then, would seem to be the last
T-21... VIII.5:2 you? H. is the great appeal to reason; the
T-21... VIII.5:3 yours. H. is the constant peace you could
T-21... VIII.5:4 H. is what denial has denied revealed to
T-21... VIII.5:5 h. the final question is already answered,
T-21... VIII.5:6 H. is the future *now*, for time is powerless
T-22......in.4:2 H. is belief in differences undone. Here is
T-22......in.4:3 H. is the faith in differences shifted to
T-22......in.4:4 And h. is sight of differences transformed
T-22......in.4:9 apparent. H. is the golden circle where
T-22.......I.4:7 fear. H. is the one emotion that you made,
T-22.......I.4:10 H. is the one emotion that keeps you
T-22......I.10:1 H. is the first direct perception that you
T-22......I.11:5 you. H. are His sweetness and His gentle
T-22......I.11:6 And h. can He return in confidence, for
T-22......I.11:7 h. you will with Him and with His Father.
T-22.......II.6:1 h. the separation of you and the ego must
T-22.......II.9:5 And h. we see again another form of the
T-22.....II.12:5 H. is no separate will, nor the desire that
T-22 ...II.12:10 as well? No misery is h., but only joy.
T-22.....II.13:1 in quiet h. with Christ is share His vision.
T-22..... III.1:5 for h. is the beginning of a vision that has
T-22 ... III.1:10 And h. do reason and the ego separate, to
T-22..... III.4:7 For h. is its own stability, its heavy anchor
T-22..... IV.3:1 your brother stand, h. in this holy place,
T-22..... IV.3:5 and peace has reached you even h., before
T-22..... IV.5:5 For you are h. to let it be received. God's
T-22...... V.3:9 H. can no weakness enter, for here is no
T-22...... V.3:9 h. is no attack and therefore no illusions.
T-22..... VI.4:7 For h. your healing is, and here will you
T-22..... VI.4:7 is, and h. will you accept Atonement. And
T-22..... VI.8:4 you have asked what is your function h.,
T-22... VI.10:7 h. lies buried the heavy anchor that seems
T-23......in.6:7 For h. is your salvation and your freedom.
T-23........I.4:3 not now accept the peace offered you h.?
T-23........I.4:4 intruder on your peace is h. transformed,
T-23........I.9:4 H. will the Father never be remembered.
T-23.......II.1:6 H. are the laws that rule the world you
T-23.......II.6:1 not be more apparent than emerges h..
T-23.......II.6:2 H. is a principle that would define what
T-23.....II.10:1 of madness are seen emerging h.: the
T-23.....II.12:3 And h. a *final* principle of chaos comes to
T-23.....II.12:7 H. is what makes your vengeance justified
T-23.....II.13:6 And it *is* h. you look for meaning. These
T-23.....II.14:8 H. do the laws of sin appear to hold love
T-23... III.6:10 H. stands the body, torn between the
T-23..... IV.5:3 H. in the midst of it, it does seem real.
T-23..... IV.5:4 H. you have chosen to be part of it. Here
T-23..... IV.5:5 H. murder is your choice. Yet from above,
T-24........I.5:2 H. is the grand illusion of what you are
T-24........I.5:3 And h. is what must make the body dear
T-24........I.8:4 stab of hate or wish to separate arises h..
T-24........I.8:5 h. the purpose that you and your brother
T-24........I.9:5 H. is the ground of battle which you wage
T-24........I.9:6 H. must he be your enemy and not your

T-24.......II.2:8 H. is a goal that would defeat salvation,
T-24.......II.3:4 H. is the self-made "savior," the "creator"
T-24.......II.7:6 H. stands your brother with the key to
T-24.......II.9:5 H. in this holy place does truth stand
T-24.....II.10:1 H. is your savior *from* your specialness.
T-24.....II.13:3 Nothing is sacred h. but unto you, and
T-24.....II.13:4 H. are the gates of hell you closed upon
T-24..... III.6:2 H. is the hell you chose to be your home.
T-24..... IV.1:7 H. is death enthroned as savior;
T-24.......V.2:2 for h. the maker of the dream believes
T-24.......V.2:3 not realize he picked a thread from h., a
T-24..... VI.1:4 In him is your assurance God is h., and
T-24.... VI.13:2 H. is the voice of specialness heard clearly
T-24.... VII.6:4 H. you are but means, along with it. God
T-24.... VII.6:8 To no one h. is this describable. Nor is
T-24.... VII.7:4 H. do the means and end unite as one,
T-24.... VII.8:3 ready. H. are the means and the purpose
T-24.... VII.9:5 move. H. is an image that you want to be
T-24.. VII.10:6 whispers, "H. is my own beloved son, in
T-25......in.3:3 it is h. that Christ sets forth the remedy.
T-25........I.1:7 H. is the meeting of the holy Christ unto
T-25.......II.3:2 hope that they may still be h. prevents
T-25..... III.6:1 Everyone h. has entered darkness, yet no
T-25..... VI.5:1 H., where the laws of God do not prevail
T-25..... VI.7:2 Think not you lack a special value h.. You
T-25.... VII.3:7 If one belief so deeply valued h. were true,
T-25.... VII.5:4 For h. is everything perceived as one, and
T-25.. VII.12:3 H. is sanity restored. And on this single
T-25.. VII.12:5 for all insane beliefs can be corrected h..
T-25.. VII.12:8 h. your special function is made whole,
T-25... VIII.2:1 H. is the only principle salvation needs.
T-26........I.5:4 itself. No instant passes h. in which your
T-26..... III.2:3 H. is the meeting place where thoughts
T-26..... III.2:5 H. is every thought made pure and wholly
T-26..... III.2:6 H. is sin denied, and everything that *is*
T-26..... III.3:3 And yet there is a contradiction h., in that
T-26..... III.7:5 There is no conflict h.. No sacrifice is
T-26..... IV.2:3 is no sadness and there is no parting h.,
T-26..... IV.3:2 And h. you see the face of Christ, arising
T-26..... IV.3:7 And h. does every light of Heaven come,
T-26..... IV.3:8 For h. is what was lost restored to them,
T-26..... IV.4:2 Heaven. H. the Son of God Himself comes
T-26.......V.8:2 made real again and seen as h. and now,
T-26.......V.8:2 now, in place of what is *really* now and h..
T-26.....V.11:9 H. the shadow of the past remains, but
T-26.....V.12:2 not the true existence of the h. and now.
T-26.....V.13:4 belief that what is over is still h. and now.
T-26.... VII.8:5 Forgiveness is the only function h., and
T-26.. VII.11:7 H. does the Son of God ask not too much,
T-26.. VII.12:3 H. is the firm conviction that ideas can
T-26... VIII.3:5 And it is h. you fear the loss would lie. Do
T-26... VIII.5:5 back, but overlooking what is h. and now.
T-26... VIII.5:6 Yet only h. and now its cause must be, if
T-26... VIII.5:9 *now*. It stands already h., in present grace,
T-26... VIII.7:3 Its cause is h., if it appears at all. Why are
T-27........I.5:7 H. is the proof that he has never sinned;
T-27......I.10:2 H. its peace can come, and perfect healing
T-27.......II.5:9 For h. is his forgiveness proved to him.
T-27.....II.16:4 H. is the function given it conceived to be
T-27..... IV.2:5 It is h. that all your problems should be
T-27..... IV.2:6 H. they belong, for here their answer is.
T-27..... IV.2:6 Here they belong, for h. their answer is.
T-27..... IV.6:3 H. is it possible to separate your wishes
T-27..... IV.6:5 Yet it is only h. it can be heard. An honest
T-27..... IV.7:3 H. are the answers that will solve your
T-27..... VI.2:2 and carries but one message: "You are h.,
T-27.... VII.1:2 you. H. is the world's demented version of
T-27.... VII.5:7 h. the cause of suffering and sin must lie.
T-27.... VII.7:2 h. you find the cause of your perspective
T-27.. VII.12:3 H. is the cause of suffering, the space
T-27.. VII.12:4 hate, the instant of disaster, all are h..
T-27.. VII.12:5 H. is the cause of unreality. And it is here
T-27.. VII.12:6 And it is h. that it will be undone.
T-28........I.2:1 All the effects of guilt are h. no more. For
T-28........I.7:7 cause accepted *now*, with consequences *h.*.
T-28.....II.12:7 Beginning h., salvation will proceed to
T-28..... III.1:4 H. is where we must begin. And having
T-28..... III.9:2 For h., the more that anyone receives, the
T-28..... III.9:5 H. is a feast the Father lays before His Son

T-28......III.9:7 **H.** can the lean years enter not, for time
T-28......IV.2:1 way of finding certainty right **h.** and now.
T-28......IV.8:6 And **h.** the Father will receive His Son,
T-28....... V.4:2 **H.** is a world established that is sick, and
T-28....... V.4:3 **H.** are the sounds it hears; the voices that
T-28....... V.7:1 do not see that it is **h.** you are as prisoners
T-28....... V.7:1 in a world perceived to be existing **h.**. The
T-28......VI.1:2 For **h.** the little gap is seen, and yet it is
T-28......VI.1:2 the little gap is seen, and yet it is not **h.**. It
T-28......VII.7:7 From **h.** the body can be seen as what it is,
T-29.........I.2:1 **H.** is the fear of God most plainly seen.
T-29....... II.6:3 Confusion follows on confusion **h.**, for on
T-29....... II.7:5 Yet **h.** on earth it has a double purpose,
T-29....... V.3:1 **H.** is the role the Holy Spirit gives to you
T-29....... V.8:3 **h.** is not where changelessness is found.
T-29......VI.3:3 only thing that can be made a blessing **h.**,
T-29......VI.5:4 nothing **h.** but is defined as what you see
T-29......VII.2:1 No one who comes **h.** but must still have
T-29... VIII.6:3 **H.** the world of idols has been set by the
T-29... VIII.6:4 **H.** the deathless come to die, the all-
T-29... VIII.6:5 **H.** does the changeless change; the peace
T-29... VIII.9:4 and tells you idols have no purpose **h.**.
T-29......IX.7:7 Only forgiving dreams can enter **h.**, for
T-30....... I.13:5 first of the decisions which are offered **h.**.
T-30....... I.15:4 you can see there cannot be coercion **h.**,
T-30.....III.10:2 of birth and death that **h.** are dreamed,
T-30.....III.10:4 peace. **H.** is your one reality kept safe,
T-30......IV.8:1 **H.** does the dream of separation start to
T-30......IV.8:2 For **h.** the gap that is not there begins to
T-30....... V.2:1 **H.**, it is thought that understanding is
T-30....... V.9:7 happiness have you sought **h.** that did not
T-30..... V.9:11 your experiences **h.** deceive in retrospect.
T-30......VI.1:3 It is **h.** escape from fear begins, and will
T-30......VI.1:4 **H.** is the real world given in exchange for
T-30......VI.9:5 **H.** is the joyful statement that there are no
T-30.....VII.4:1 given to the world and all experiences **h.**.
T-30... VIII.6:2 a dream allow uncertainty to enter **h.**. Be
T-31.........I.7:8 is no joy that you can seek for **h.** and hope
T-31......III.1:4 for it is **h.** delay of happiness is shortened
T-31......III.5:2 **H.** are the thoughts of sacrifice preserved,
T-31......III.5:2 of sacrifice preserved, for **h.** guilt rules,
T-31......III.5:3 For **h.** are you made sin, and sin cannot
T-31......IV.2:5 Seek not escape from problems **h.**. The
T-31......IV.2:9 end, for it is **h.** that all its roads will lead,
T-31......IV.6:2 this step is to defeat your purpose **h.**. You
T-31....... V.1:4 **H.** it walks at home, where what it sees is
T-31....... V.4:4 it is **h.** the learning of the world has set its
T-31....... V.4:4 for it is **h.** the world's "reality" is set, to
T-31....... V.6:1 **H.** is the central lesson that ensures your
T-31....... V.8:1 for no one **h.** can see what it is for, and
T-31......VI.1:6 for **h.** have you established what you are,
T-31.....VII.1:6 no one **h.** but holds a concept of himself
T-31.....VII.6:1 guarantee your function **h.** remain forever
W-pI.......4.3:2 The aim **h.** is to train you in the first steps
W-pI.......8.2:1 can hold about the past is that it is not **h.**.
W-pI.....23.2:6 **H.** you are changing the cause. The effect
W-pI.....28.1:3 them in the future is not our concern **h.**. If
W-pI.....37.1:1 function in the world, or why you are **h.**.
W-pI.....45.8:2 **H.** is your mind joined with the Mind of
W-pI.....45.8:3 **H.** are your thoughts one with His. For
W-pI.....49.4:5 You do not live **h.**. We are trying to reach
W-pI.....50.1:1 **H.** is the answer to every problem that
WpI ...rI.in.6:2 Use them as they are given **h.**. It is not
W-pI.....61.5:5 *That is why I am* ***h.***. Then think about these
W-pI.....61.6:2 your function and your only purpose **h.**.
W-pI.....64.3:1 function **h.** is to be the light of the world,
W-pI.....69.3:3 There is no other purpose **h.**, and no
W-pI.....72.3:1 that a body would impose is obvious **h.**, it
W-pI.....72.4:1 are not dealing **h.** with what the person is.
W-pI.....73.9:3 It is the one purpose **h.** on which you and
W-pI.....88.3:2 **H.** is the perfect statement of my freedom.
W-pI.....92.7:2 itself. No miracles are **h.**, but only hate. It
W-pI.....93.9:7 **H.** you are; This is You. And light and joy
W-pI.....94.1:4 idea. **H.** is salvation accomplished. Here is
W-pI.....94.1:5 accomplished. **H.** is sanity restored.
W-pI.....96.4:3 and it is fulfilling happily its function **h.**.
W-pI.....96.9:6 **H.** are your thoughts, the only ones you
W-pI.....98.5:2 to recognize your special function **h.**? Is
W-pI.....98.6:1 **H.** is an offer guaranteeing you your full
W-pI.....98.6:4 **H.** is a bargain that you cannot lose. And
W-pI........99.h Salvation is my only function **h.**.
W-pI.....99.6:7 *Salvation is my only function* ***h.***. *God still is*
W-pI.....99.9:6 *Salvation is my only function* ***h.***. *Salvation*
W-pI.....99.9:8 turn to Him Who shares your function **h.**,
W-pI...99.11:3 *Salvation is my only function* ***h.***. *God still is*
W-pI...99.12:4 *Salvation is my only function* ***h.***. Thus do
W-pI...100.6:1 to understand joy is our function **h.**. If
W-pI...100.8:2 It is your function that you find it **h.**, and
W-pI...102.3:2 **H.** is your home, and here your safety is.
W-pI...102.3:2 Here is your home, and **h.** your safety is.
W-pI...102.3:3 **H.** is your peace, and here there is no fear.
W-pI...102.3:3 Here is your peace, and **h.** there is no fear.
W-pI...102.3:4 no fear. **H.** is salvation. Here is rest at last.
W-pI...102.3:5 no fear. Here is salvation. **H.** is rest at last.
W-pI...102.5:1 for your only function **h.** is happiness.
W-pI...105.6:3 **H.** you denied them to yourself. And here
W-pI...105.6:4 And **h.** you must return to claim them as
W-pI...106.6:2 It is **h.**, and will today be given unto you.
W-pI...107.5:2 sure. **H.** is the gift of healing, for the truth
W-pI...108.4:1 **H.** are both giving and receiving seen as
W-pI...108.4:2 place. **H.** it is understood that both occur
W-pI...109.2:5 **H.** is the end of suffering for all the world,
W-pI...109.2:6 **H.** is the thought in which the Son of God
W-pI...109.8:3 bid them all enter **h.** and rest with you.
W-pI...109.9:3 We rest together **h.**, for thus our rest is
WpI. rIII.in2:1 what is suggested **h.** as optimal each day
WpI. rIII.in9:4 to you. **H.** is another chance to use it well.
W-pI...115.1:1 (99) Salvation is my only function **h.**. *My*
W-pI...115.1:2 *function* ***h.*** *is to forgive the world for all the*
W-pI...115.3:2 Salvation is my only function **h.**. On the
W-pI...121.1:1 **H.** is the answer to your search for peace.
W-pI...121.1:2 **H.** is the key to meaning in a world that
W-pI...121.1:3 sense. **H.** is the way to safety in apparent
W-pI...121.1:4 **H.** are all questions answered; here the
W-pI...121.1:4 **h.** the end of all uncertainty ensured at
W-pI...121.7:2 to you imploringly for Heaven **h.** and now
W-pI...122.4:2 **H.** is the perfect answer, given to
W-pI...122.4:3 **H.** is the answer! Seek for it no more. You
W-pI...122.6:1 **H.** is the answer! Would you stand
W-pI...122.6:6 that this is so, for **h.** we have an answer,
W-pI...122.7:1 **H.** is the answer! Do not turn away in
W-pI...128.2:1 Each thing you value **h.** is but a chain that
W-pI...128.3:1 your mind when you perceive salvation **h.**
W-pI...128.4:2 Nothing is **h.** to cherish. Nothing here is
W-pI...128.4:3 Nothing **h.** is worth one instant of delay
W-pI...129.2:2 no loss in letting go all thought of value **h.**
W-pI...129.2:5 No lasting love is found, for none is **h.**.
W-pI...129.5:2 **H.** can you but look forward, never back
W-pI...129.5:3 **H.** is the world that comes to take its place
W-pI...129.7:4 *of this, for* ***h.*** *is nothing that I really want.*
W-pI...129.8:2 **H.** is light your eyes can not behold. And
W-pI...131.3:1 Yet searching is inevitable **h.**. For this you
W-pI...131.6:2 It is **h.** today. Time is the great illusion it
W-pI...131.8:6 He is **h.** because He wills to be, and what
W-pI.131.14:5 will find the goal of all your searching **h.**,
W-pI...132.3:2 **H.** in the present is the world set free. For
W-pI...133.8:5 **H.** it is easiest of all to be deceived. For
W-pI...133.9:3 **H.** is deception doubled, for the one who
W-pI.135.16:4 see that **h.** and now is everything it needs
W-pI.136.13:5 Yet what He wills is **h.**, and you remain as
W-pI...137.6:1 healing is unworthy of your function **h.**.
W-pI.137.11:4 For **h.** is truth bestowed, and here are all
W-pI.137.11:4 and **h.** are all illusions brought to truth.
W-pI...138.1:1 **h.** we believe there are alternatives to
W-pI...138.2:2 But **h.** is opposition part of being "real." It
W-pI...138.2:5 in God's creation cannot enter **h.** until it
W-pI...138.6:5 forms. **H.** is the final and the only choice
W-pI...139.1:1 **H.** is the end of choice. For here we come
W-pI...139.1:2 For **h.** we come to a decision to accept
W-pI...139.1:4 There is no doubt that is not rooted **h.**.
W-pI...139.6:5 sad belief that what is universal **h.** is true?
W-pI...139.9:1 We have a mission **h.**. We did not come
W-pI...140.9:4 **H.** there are no degrees, and no beliefs
W-pI...152.1:6 **H.** is your world, complete in all details.
W-pI...152.1:7 **H.** is its whole reality for you. And it is
W-pI...152.1:8 for you. And it is only **h.** salvation is.
W-pI.153.19:6 pause a moment, as He tells us, "I am **h.**."
W-pI...155.1:1 a way of living in the world that is not **h.**,
W-pI...155.2:3 when they find their own reality is even **h.**
W-pI...157.2:4 leaves us **h.** an instant, and we go beyond
W-pI...158.6:1 **H.** is the joining of the world of doubt
W-pI...158.6:2 **H.** is a quiet place within the world made
W-pI...158.6:3 **H.** are all contradictions reconciled, for
W-pI...158.6:3 reconciled, for **h.** the journey ends.
W-pI...159.1:3 **H.** the laws of Heaven and the world agree
W-pI...159.1:4 **h.** they also separate. The world believes
W-pI...159.4:3 are united in extension **h.** on earth, as
W-pI...159.5:3 quite solid **h.** are merely shadows there;
W-pI...159.6:2 All are laid **h.** already. All can be received
W-pI...159.6:4 **H.** the door is never locked, and no one is
W-pI...159.7:1 **H.** does the world remember what was
W-pI...159.7:2 For **h.** it is repaired, made new again, but
W-pI...159.8:3 can be brought from **h.** back to the world,
W-pI......160.h I am at home. Fear is the stranger **h.**.
W-pI...160.2:4 **H.** I belong, and will not leave because a
W-pI...160.5:2 himself and said, "I am the stranger **h.**.
W-pI...161.1:2 love. **H.** is salvation in the simple words in
W-pI...161.1:3 **H.** is the answer to temptation which can
W-pI...161.1:4 **H.** is Atonement made complete, the
W-pI...161.1:5 **H.** is the answer of the Voice for God.
W-pI...162.2:1 **H.** is the Word by which the Son became
W-pI...162.2:2 **H.** creation is proclaimed, and honored as
W-pI...163.4:2 this? **H.** is the strength and might of God
W-pI...163.4:3 **H.** is the opposite of God proclaimed as
W-pI...163.4:4 constancy. **H.** is the Will of Father and of
W-pI...163.5:3 but this: "**H.** lies a witness God is dead."
W-pI...163.6:5 For **h.** again we see an obvious position,
W-pI...164.4:5 that you will know that **h.** your treasure is
W-pI...164.4:5 that here your treasure is, and **h.** your rest
W-pI...166.2:1 **H.** is the paradox that underlies the
W-pI...166.4:1 **H.** is the only home he thinks he knows.
W-pI...166.4:2 **H.** is the only safety he believes that he
W-pI...166.4:4 not realize that it is **h.** he is afraid indeed,
W-pI...166.6:2 comes **h.** has pursued the path he follows,
W-pI...169.9:1 For oneness must be **h.**. Whatever time
W-pI.169.13:2 is **h.** that miracles are laid; to be returned
W-pI...170.2:2 For **h.** is fear begot and fed with blood, to
W-pI...170.9:4 **H.** is the basic premise which enthrones
WpI.rV.in12:3 recognize that it is only **h.** conviction lies.
W-pI...175.2:2 Fear is the stranger **h.**. God is but Love,
W-pI...182.1:4 you of. Yet still you feel an alien **h.**, from
W-pI...182.1:5 say with certainty you are an exile **h.**. Just
W-pI...182.4:3 house, and knows that He is alien **h.**. This
W-pI.182.10:4 today. You are as much an alien **h.** as He.
W-pI.184.10:2 **H.** you understand the Word, the Name
W-pI...186.1:1 **H.** is the statement that will one day take
W-pI...186.1:2 **H.** is the thought of true humility, which
W-pI.186.14:3 is needed **h.** is given here as it is needed.
W-pI.186.14:3 is needed here is given **h.** as it is needed.
W-pI.186.14:4 form you can fulfill your function even **h.**,
W-pI.186.14:6 who can forgive. Such is your function **h.**.
W-pI...187.9:3 before the purity that you will look on **h.**.
W-pI.187.10:2 And **h.**, before the altar to one God, one
W-pI...188.1:5 bear the light in you are alien **h.** as well.
W-pI.190.10:1 **H.** will you understand there is no pain.
W-pI.190.10:2 **H.** does the joy of God belong to you. This
W-pI...191.1:1 **H.** is your declaration of release from
W-pI...191.1:2 And **h.** as well is all the world released.
W-pI...192.2:3 Forgiveness represents your function **h.**.
W-pI...192.3:2 It has no meaning **h.**. Forgiveness is the
W-pI.192.10:6 function **h.** on earth is only to forgive him
W-pI.193.11:3 too long, and we would linger **h.** no more.
W-pI...197.1:1 **H.** is the second step we take to free your
W-pI.198.13:2 brought us **h.** will not forsake us now. For
W-pI...199.4:1 **H.** does it hide, and here it can be seen as
W-pI...199.4:1 it hide, and **h.** it can be seen as what it is.
W-pI...200.4:4 You are a stranger **h.**. But it is given you
W-pI...200.7:4 Is it **h.** that he would seek for peace? Or
W-pI...205.1:3 *God is my one goal; the aim of all my living* ***h.***
W-pII .221.2:2 God is **h.**, because we wait together. I am
W-pII .223.2:5 *We are lonely* ***h.***, *and long for Heaven, where*
W-pII .230.2:2 *What was given then must be* ***h.*** *now, for my*
W-pII .....2.4:2 **H.** we share our final dream. It is a dream
W-pII .....2.5:1 From **h.** we give salvation to the world,
W-pII .....2.5:1 world, for it is **h.** salvation was received.
W-pII .....3.2:5 **H.** was perception born, for knowledge
W-pII .256.1:1 The way to God is through forgiveness **h.**.

W-pII .256.1:7 **H.** we can but dream. But we can dream
W-pII .289.2:3 *sin. H. is the end of guilt. And here am I made*
W-pII .289.2:4 *And h. am I made ready for Your final step.*
W-pII ....293.h All fear is past and only love is **h.**.
W-pII .293.1:2 whose Source is **h.** forever and forever.
W-pII .300.1:1 are the certain lot of all who come **h.**, for
W-pII .303.1:6 Let Him no longer be a stranger **h.**, for He
W-pII .308.1:8 And love is ever-present, **h.** and now.
W-pII .317.1:4 will I recognize salvation is already **h.**,
W-pII .319.1:1 **H.** is a thought from which all arrogance
W-pII .323.1:1 *H. is the only "sacrifice" You ask of Your*
W-pII .326.1:8 *Your plan I follow h., and at the end I know*
W-pII ....333.h Forgiveness ends the dream of conflict **h.**.
W-pII .336.1:6 For **h.**, and only here, is peace of mind
W-pII .336.1:6 For here, and only **h.**, is peace of mind
W-pII .345.1:3 *h., it takes a form which can be recognized*
W-pII .345.1:6 *But h. on earth, the miracle is closer to Your*
W-pII .348.1:1 *Father, let me remember You are h., and I*
W-pII ...14.2:5 Yet we can realize our function **h.**, and
W-pII .352.1:4 *Yet love, reflected in forgiveness h., reminds*
Wfl ........in.2:4 And yet, in truth, it is already **h.**; already
M-in .......... 4:4 and everyone **h.** does follow it until he
M-in .......... 5:5 are not perfect, or they would not be **h.**.
M-in .......... 5:6 Yet it is their mission to become perfect **h.**
M-4 ... I.A.6:13 going on. He will not go on from **h.** alone.
M-4 ..... I.A.8:2 It is **h.** that learning is consolidated. Now
M-4 ..... I.A.8:5 for **h.** is Heaven's state fully reflected.
M-4 ..... I.A.8:6 From **h.**, the way to Heaven is open and
M-4 ..... I.A.8:7 In fact, it is **h.**. Who would "go" anywhere
M-4 ....... X.3:3 They would be most inappropriate **h.**.
M-8 ........... 4:2 And it is **h.** correction must be made. The
M-11 ......... 1:2 Certainly peace seems to be impossible **h.**.
M-11 ......... 1:7 has promised that peace is possible **h.**,
M-11 ......... 3:9 of God what is reflected **h.** is only peace.
M-11 ......... 4:8 Peace now belongs **h.**, because a Thought
M-11 ....... 4:12 it not impossible that peace be absent **h.**?
M-13 ....... 7:10 For it is **h.** the split with God occurs. A
M-13 ......... 8:6 For it is **h.** that your concern should be.
M-14 ......... 2:3 **H.** is it nourished, for here it is needed. A
M-14 ......... 2:3 Here is it nourished, for **h.** it is needed. A
M-14 ......... 2:5 **H.** is His home, for here there is need of
M-14 ......... 2:5 home, for **h.** there is need of Him indeed.
M-14 ......... 3:9 No; it is meaningless to anyone **h.**. Yet it
M-15 ......... 2:4 But this is still your goal; why you are **h.**.
M-17 ......... 2:8 **H.** is his gift most clearly given him. For
M-17 ......... 7:5 **H.** we have the fear of God most starkly
M-17 ......... 7:9 kill. **H.** is salvation now. An angry father
M-17 ....... 7:11 Kill or be killed, for **h.** alone is choice.
M-19 ......... 3:2 **H.** is the lens which, held before the
M-19 ......... 5:8 **H.** all attack and condemnation becomes
M-20 ....... 3:10 **H.** the initial contrast stands out clear and
M-23 ......... 5:6 the symbol of his Father **h.** on earth. To
M-23 ......... 7:8 him, for he is with you; he is always **h.**.
M-24 ......... 6:4 Heaven is **h.**. There is nowhere else.
M-25 ......... 4:6 **H.** are strengths which the Holy Spirit
M-25 ......... 5:4 not seen through the ego's defenses **h.**,
M-25 ......... 6:6 Yet **h.** is also a great channel of hope and
M-26 ......... 1:5 **H.**, then, is the role of God's teachers.
M-28 ......... 3:1 **H.** the curriculum ends. From here on, no
M-28 ......... 3:2 From **h.** on, no directions are needed.
M-29 ......... 4:1 **H.** again is the paradox often referred to
C-in ........... 2:7 **H.** alone consistency becomes possible
C-in ........... 2:7 possible because **h.** alone uncertainty
C-1............. 5:4 **H.** time and illusions end together.
C-2............. 3:5 And yet there is an answer even **h.**.
C-2............. 5:2 And **h.** we find all that is not the ego in
C-2............. 5:3 **H.** is the ego's opposite and here alone we
C-2............. 5:3 the ego's opposite and **h.** alone we look on
C-2............. 5:3 was, for **h.** we see all that it seemed to do,
C-2........... 10:4 Problem and answer lie together **h.**, and
C-4............. 6:3 **H.** are all illusions brought to truth and
C-4............. 7:6 his. And **h.** They join, for here the face of
C-4............. 7:6 **h.** the face of Christ has shone away time's
C-4............. 8:2 for they are joined **h.** in this holy place.
C-4............. 8:3 **H.** He leans down to lift you up to Him,
C-ep........... 2:1 You *are* a stranger **h.**. But you belong to
C-ep........... 4:1 Let us wait **h.** in silence, and kneel down
C-ep........... 4:4 alone. For God is **h.**, and with Him all our
C-ep........... 4:7 is **h.** begun will grow in life and strength
P-2........... I.2:3 we mean, but **h.** is the ego's last defense.
P-2........... I.3:1 as defined **h.** can be characteristic of a
P-2........... I.4:2 a patient could possibly have come **h.**?
P-2.......... II.2:3 that it hardly requires elaboration **h.**.
P-2.......... II.5:6 are all insane or they would not be **h.**.
P-2........ IV.5:1 and the word is perhaps questionable **h.**,
P-2........ VI.1:4 "God may not enter **h.**" the sick repeat,
P-2........ VI.4:4 **H.** is all sickness cherished, but without
P-2........ VI.4:9 your healing efforts **h.** is but futility. Who
P-2........ VI.6:4 as gone into a past that is no longer **h.**.
P-2........ VI.6:5 think of evil as besetting him **h.** and now.
P-2....... VII.2:8 Healing is **h.**, and happiness and peace.
P-2....... VII.5:4 a knowledge that no one **h.** can have; a
P-3........ III.1:3 has some earthly needs while he is **h.**.
P-3........ III.1:7 But no one **h.** can live with no illusions,
P-3........ III.1:9 He stays **h.** but for this. And while he
S-1......... in.3:4 For this is prayer, and **h.** salvation is. This
S-1........... I.2:4 There are decisions to make **h.**, and they
S-1.......... II.3:2 **H.**, the asking may be addressed to God
S-1........ III.3:3 **h.** it will be an easy step to the next levels.
S-1......... V.1:2 And **h.** again it rises slowly up, and grows
S-1......... V.4:3 **h.** the place appointed for the time when
S-1......... V.4:4 you. **H.** will time end forever. At this gate
S-2......... I.10:5 for **h.** it waits its freedom to ascend above
S-2.......... II.2:2 is. Forgiveness **h.** rests on an attitude of
S-2.......... II.2:6 There is no union **h.**, but only grief. This
S-2.......... II.3:3 that **h.** is one whose sinfulness he shares,
S-2.......... II.4:1 **H.** the goal is to separate from God the
S-2.......... II.4:3 **H.** must the aim be clearly seen, for this
S-2.......... II.8:7 From **h.** is prayer released, along with you
S-2........ III.4:9 Will and purpose. **H.** all dreams are done.
S-3........ III.1:7 **H.** is the separation shown. And here the
S-3........ III.1:8 And **h.** the meaning of true healing has
S-3........ IV.2:4 Fear has no haven **h.**, for love has come in
S-3........ IV.8:9 Heaven is **h.** and Heaven is your home.

## herein 24

T-in ........... 2:4 ***unreal exists.*** **H.** lies the peace of God.
T-6 ....... IV.1:7 **H.** lies its primary error, the foundation
T-13 ...... in.1:3 But **h.** lies the split. For the mind that
T-15 ..... VI.4:7 **H.** lies peace, for here there *is* no conflict.
T-26 ..... III.4:8 **h.** lies the difference between the worlds.
T-29 ........ I.5:3 And **h.** lies its power over you. For now
T-29 ..... VI.1:4 for **h.** lies the end of separation and the
T-31 ....... II.5:4 **H.** is life as easily as death, for what you
W-pI..... 55.3:2 **H.** lies salvation, and nowhere else.
W-pI..... 58.5:2 **H.** lies my claim to all good and only good
W-pI..... 72.4:5 **H.** is God attacked, for if His Son is only a
W-pI... 132.5:1 you wish, and **h.** lies your ultimate release
W-pI... 135.1:2 And **h.** lies the folly of defense; it gives
W-pI... 187.3:4 **H.** is the idea of giving clarified and given
M-in .......... 4:5 **H.** is the purpose of the world. What else,
M-5 ...... II.3:11 **H.** is the release from guilt and sickness
M-17 ......... 5:7 And **h.** lies the birthplace of guilt. Who
M-21 ......... 3:6 **H.** lie hell and Heaven. The sleeping Son
M-22 ......... 7:8 **H.** does he receive Atonement, for he
P-2........ IV.8:3 **H.** lies the basis of all errors, for all of
P-3........ III.4:5 **H.** is the relationship made holy, for
P-3........ III.4:5 made holy, for **h.** both are healed. The
S-1........... I.7:4 are. **H.** lies the power of prayer. It asks
S-1.......... II.6:7 enemies, for **h.** lies your own salvation.

## heritage 7

T-3 ..... VI.10:1 Peace is a natural **h.** of spirit. Everyone is
T-11 ........ I.7:2 God is your **h.**, because His one gift is
W-pI... 103.2:1 results become the **h.** of minds that think
W-pI... 117.2:2 *Love is my h., and with it joy. These are the*
W-pI... 131.3:4 old yet new; an echo of a **h.** forgot, yet
W-pI. 167.10:1 of the truth, and not deny our holy **h.**.
M-20 ....... 6:10 This is your **h.**. The universe beyond the

## hero 7

T-23 ..... II.15:8 Give thanks unto the **h.** on love's throne,
T-27 ...... VIII.h The "**H.**" of the Dream
T-27 ... VIII.3:2 The "**h.**" of this dream will never change,
T-27 ... VIII.3:3 and events wherein its "**h.**" finds itself,
T-28 ..... IV.3:4 dreams, nor is his body, "**h.**" of the dream
W-pI .. 185.3:4 To each, the **h.** of the dream is different;
M-13 ......... 2:6 the "**h.**" to whom all these things belong?

## hesitance 1

W-pI .. 123.1:4 some small objections and a little **h.**, but

## hesitant 1

W-pI ..... 27.1:3 You may feel **h.** about using the idea, on

## hesitate 5

T-16 ..... IV.5:7 Seen in these terms, no one would **h.**. But
T-20 .... VII.3:4 goal. And when you **h.**, it is because the
W-pI .. 126.1:3 to you, and would not **h.** to use it now.
W-pI 138.10:5 this? And shall we **h.** to choose today?
W-pI .. 194.6:1 you will not **h.** to give as much consistent

## hesitates 1

W-pI 138.10:4 Who **h.** to make a choice like this? And

## hesitation 1

W-pI .... 39.2:3 **h.** you may feel in answering is not due to

## hid 6

T-5 ....... IV.8:4 them of the errors that **h.** their light, and
T-14 .... VII.2:6 you **h.** it and surrounded it with fear.
T-18 ..... III.6:1 to the Son of God, who **h.** in darkness.
T-23 ..... II.11:6 He **h.** it in his body, making it the cover
W-pI .. 125.5:2 He has not **h.** Himself from you, while
W-pII ..... 2.3:4 And what they **h.** is now revealed; an altar

## hidden 107

T-1 ........ I.31:3 holiness, which can be **h.** but never lost.
T-1 ....... IV.2:1 can never be really **h.** in darkness, but you
T-5 ....... IV.1:1 fear has **h.** still is part of you. Joining the
T-6 .......... I.8:5 that does not inspire love has a **h.** altar
T-7 ........ I.7:13 reveal this to you because it was never **h.**.
T-8 ...... VII.6:5 Son of God remain **h.** for His Name's sake
T-9 .......... I.4:2 **h.** and recognize the Will of God there.
T-9 ..... VIII.8:3 reality. Truth is not obscure nor **h.**, but its
T-10 ..... III.5:3 yours. And you are willing to keep it **h.**, to
T-11 ...... in.2:7 carefully **h.** in the dark cornerstone of its
T-11 ...... in.4:4 it in order to keep a dark cornerstone **h.**,
T-12 ....... II.7:1 me, for I am not **h.** because *you* are hiding.
T-12 ....... II.9:8 He cannot shine away what you keep **h.**,
T-12 ... VIII.1:2 has **h.** His Son safely within Himself, and
T-12 ... VIII.1:7 But offer attack and love will remain **h.**,
T-13 ....... II.3:1 darkest of your **h.** cornerstones holds
T-13 ....... II.3:3 murderous but insane idea lies **h.** there,
T-13 ....... II.5:3 the wish has **h.** him from you because it is
T-13 ..... III.1:8 keep it **h.** because you are more afraid of
T-13 ..... III.4:4 you come to the Love that is **h.** there. *And*
T-13 ..... III.6:1 upon your illusions and not keep them **h.**,
T-13 ..... III.6:4 them, and concealed as long as they are **h.**
T-13 ..... III.7:5 leave any spot of pain **h.** from His light,
T-13 ..... III.8:3 In that place which you have **h.**, you will
T-13 .. VII.13:3 **h.** in your mind and kept to hurt you.
T-14 ....... V.4:5 Never allow purity to remain **h.**, but shine
T-14 ....... V.4:5 of God has **h.** himself from his own sight.
T-14 ..... VI.1:4 And yet it is only the **h.** that can terrify,
T-14 ..... VI.1:7 Nothing has **h.** value, for what is hidden
T-14 ..... VI.1:7 value, for what is **h.** cannot be shared,
T-14 ..... VI.1:8 The **h.** is kept apart, but value always lies
T-14 ..... VI.2:1 is **h.** and therefore nothing is fearful.
T-14 ..... VI.2:2 love if it is brought to love, not **h.** from it.
T-14 ..... VI.8:6 There are no **h.** chambers in God's temple
T-14 .... VII.2:7 insane system of belief, the truth lies **h.**.
T-14 ... VIII.1:2 All this lies **h.** in every darkened place,
T-14 ..... IX.5:5 of **h.** darkness you have drawn upon it.
T-15 ........ I.6:3 is **h.** a far more insidious threat to peace.
T-15 ..... IV.8:1 would keep **h.** shuts communication off,
T-15 ..... IV.9:7 For what you would hide *is* **h.** from you. In

T-16....... II.5:5 it represents, and which is **h.** to you. Let
T-16...... IV.1:3 in which the meaning of love is **h.**, is
T-16.... IV.10:3 are the veil behind which truth is **h.**. To
T-16....... V.4:1 of the **h.** wish for special love from God,
T-17....... II.2:3 sun. Nothing is **h.** here, for everything has
T-17....... II.5:5 in insanity could be without a **h.** spark of
T-17...... III.5:7 is the spark of beauty **h.** in the ugliness of
T-17...... III.6:7 Let Him uncover the **h.** spark of beauty in
T-17.... III.6:10 unwilling to let it be **h.** from you. And you
T-17...... III.7:4 must be safe, however **h.** it may be, in
T-18...... IX.4:2 the world could rise from it and keep it **h.**.
T-18...... IX.4:4 apart from what was made to keep it **h.**.
T-19...... III.4:9 it be but a mistake you would keep **h.**; a
T-19...... III.9:4 given to correction, to be healed, not **h.**.
T19 .. IV.B.13:6 is this insane relationship that it keeps **h.**,
T19 ... IV.C.7:6 For in it lie **h.** all the ego's secrets, all its
T-20....... II.8:8 freed from all the terror that kept it **h.**.
T-20...... VI.3:6 and keep their secrets **h.** along with them.
T-20...... VI.4:1 are kept obscure and **h.** from the sun. It
T-20...... VI.5:2 speck of darkness; a **h.** secret room, a tiny
T-20..... VII.6:6 brought to truth, and always **h.** from it.
T-21...... IV.2:5 Yet this is not the ego's **h.** fear, nor yours
T-22......... I.4:4 this is no secret that need be **h.** as a sin.
T-22....... II.1:6 covered, and **h.** from the joy of truth.
T-22...... VI.7:1 no error is excluded and nothing kept **h.**,
T-23....... in.1:4 it not, for how can the unreal be **h.**? No
T-23....... II.9:7 because they keep it **h.** from your sight.
T-23..... II.10:1 "enemy" made strong by keeping **h.** the
T-23..... II.11:2 this priceless pearl, this **h.** secret treasure,
T-23..... II.11:5 and **h.** where you would not think to look.
T-23..... II.12:8 **h.** there in malice and in hatred for the
T-24....... in.2:2 Not one can be kept **h.** and obscure but it
T-24......... I.2:3 decisions have been made and kept **h.**, to
T-24......... I.2:4 of these **h.** warriors to disrupt your peace.
T-24......... I.3:1 All that is ever cherished as a **h.** belief, to
T-24....... V.2:1 **h.** or disguised the form, however lovely it
T-26..... VII.2:4 in a relationship kept **h.** from awareness
T-28......... I.5:7 history of all the body's past is **h.** there.
T-28....... V.4:1 Self is safely **h.** by what you have made.
T-29...... III.5:2 from heavy shadows that have **h.** him,
T-30.... III.11:8 then, that idols must keep **h.** what you are
T-31......... I.8:6 been deceived by forms the call was **h.** in.
T-31..... V.10:8 from whom must something be kept **h.**?
T-31... VII.15:1 given unto you, be **h.** from the world. It
T-31... VIII.9:2 hell, the secret sins and **h.** hates be gone.
W-pI..... 28.5:3 **H.** under all your ideas about it is its real
W-pI..... 41.5:2 you, when the truth is **h.** deep within,
W-pI..... 57.5:5 what my illusions about myself kept **h.**. I
W-pI..... 69.5:1 there is a brilliant light **h.** by the clouds.
W-pI..... 69.9:5 *I cannot see what I have* **h.**. *Yet I want to let it*
W-pI..... 69.9:8 *the light of the world will be* **h.** *from me,* if
W-pI..... 78.5:3 you will learn that what lay **h.** while you
W-pI..... 79.5:5 time, only to be **h.** again but still unsolved
W-pI... 102.1:4 the dark and **h.** secret places of your mind
W-pI... 133.9:4 that he has served the ego's **h.** goals.
W-pI... 151.5:3 Yet underneath remains the **h.** doubt that
W-pI... 184.8:5 His true Identity is **h.** from you by what
W-pI... 189.1:5 in you to be kept **h.** from your sight. This
W-pI... 194.5:3 the light that was kept **h.** in God's Son is
W-pII.. 239.1:1 ourselves today be **h.** by a false humility.
W-pII.. 258.1:2 His memory is **h.** in our minds, obscured
W-pII.. 333.1:2 another name, or **h.** by deceit of any kind,
W-pII.. 336.1:4 and opens the **h.** altar to the truth. Its
M-17.......... 7:2 which you have **h.** but have not let go.
M-28.......... 4:5 fear. No **h.** places now remain on earth to
P-2........ IV.7:7 Fear cannot long be **h.** by illusions, for it
S-3......... II.2:3 to reach the Christ in **h.** forms and clearly

## hiddenness 1

T-14...... VI.1:4 can terrify, not for what it is, but for its **h.**

## hide 89

T-1........ I.22:1 because of the belief that darkness can **h.**.
T-1........ IV.1:1 the recognition that darkness cannot **h.**.
T-1........ IV.1:3 nothing you want to **h.** even if you could.
T-1........ IV.1:5 you have become willing to **h.** nothing,
T-2....... II.1:13 denial. It is not used to **h.** anything, but to
T-4........ III.5:1 you will never want to cover or **h.** it again.
T-4........ III.8:2 for we must **h.** nothing from each other. If
T-4......... V.6:4 it hopes to **h.** the real question and keep it
T-8......... VI.8:2 He will not **h.** it. He has revealed it to me
T-11....... I.10:6 Believing this you **h.** in darkness, denying
T-11....... III.5:1 even though His Son would **h.** himself.
T-11....... III.5:2 Yet the Son of God cannot **h.** his glory,
T-12....... II.4:3 **h.** their nightmares they will keep them.
T-13....... III.2:9 for you. This is what you really want to **h.**.
T-13....... III.7:3 Do not **h.** suffering from His sight, but
T-13. VII.16:10 which we **h.** our brothers from the world,
T-13....... X.1:2 is to **h.** the real source of guilt, and keep
T-14..... VII.2:6 you. If you **h.** it, it becomes unreal to you
T-14..... VII.6:5 But what you **h.** He cannot look upon. He
T-14... VIII.1:5 let all that would **h.** your glory be brought
T-14...... X.11:3 would **h.** from the Holy Spirit is nothing.
T-15...... IV.9:6 as long as you would **h.** it from yourself.
T-15...... IV.9:7 For what you would **h.** *is* hidden from you.
T-16...... IV.1:7 into sight, and to make no attempt to **h.** it
T-17....... II.2:3 and there are no fantasies to **h.** the truth.
T-18......... I.6:2 The world arose to **h.** it, and became the
T-18....... III.1:5 that you could **h.** from truth forever, in
T-18. VIII.11:6 to **h.** from Heaven straight to Heaven. No
T19 ... IV.A.3:8 little wall would **h.** the purpose of Heaven
T19. IV.D.14:3 veil of sin upon Him to **h.** His loveliness.
T-20...... VI.2:6 nothing that it would keep apart and **h.**.
T-20...... VI.3:6 can **h.** and keep their secrets hidden along
T-21...... VI.8:8 **H.** not behind insanity in order to escape
T-25..... VII.1:5 seem to **h.** the pain of sin from sinners,
T-25...... IX.9:1 you keep and **h.** become your secret sins,
T-26....... X.1:7 in whatever form, will **h.** Their Presence.
T-27....... I.11:5 made to **h.** your function from yourself.
T-27....... I.11:6 thing without a purpose cannot **h.** the
T-29......... I.8:4 there is no gap behind which you can **h.**?
T-30...... IV.5:3 they bring fear *because* they **h.** the truth.
T-31..... V.10:9 is still no need to **h.** what you are made of.
T-31... VIII.4:3 For what appears to **h.** the face of Christ is
T-31. VIII.12:5 to **h.** the face of Christ from anyone. Thy
W-pI........ 69.h grievances **h.** the light of the world in me.
W-pI..... 69.9:4 *My grievances* **h.** *the light of the world in me.*
W-pI..... 75.3:2 and **h.** the world forgiveness offers us.
W-pI..... 76.5:4 mind holds up to **h.** what really suffers. It
W-pI..... 76.6:5 Only what it is meant to **h.** will save you.
W-pI..... 76.7:3 It is no longer a truth that we would **h.**.
W-pI... 78.10:2 to **h.** his light behind our grievances. To
W-pI..... 82.4:2 *me not use this to* **h.** *my function from me. I*
W-pI..... 85.1:1 grievances **h.** the light of the world in me.
W-pI..... 85.1:2 there, and **h.** from me what I would see.
W-pI..... 85.1:4 They keep me in darkness and **h.** the light
W-pI..... 87.2:2 *This cannot* **h.** *the light I will to see. You*
W-pI..... 89.1:4 but illusions that **h.** the miracles beyond.
W-pI..... 92.6:4 In darkness it remains to **h.** itself, and
W-pI... 107.6:2 It does not **h.**. It stands in open light, in
W-pI... 122.7:6 no longer **h.** their nothingness from you.
W-pI... 127.5:2 believes was made to **h.** love's meaning,
W-pI... 128.3:3 limit you further, **h.** your worth from you,
W-pI. 131.11:8 completely lock to **h.** what lies beyond.
W-pI. 135.22:5 *strong, and I will learn what my defenses* **h.**.
W-pI... 136.2:3 like all the rest, its purpose is to **h.** reality,
W-pI... 140.5:6 home in which to **h.** from His beneficence
W-pI... 151.2:6 you would **h.** with show of certainty?
W-pI... 164.5:2 which appeared to **h.** it merely sink away.
W-pI... 165.1:3 could **h.** what cannot be concealed except
W-pI. 166.12:5 sought to make in which to **h.** from God.
W-pI... 168.1:4 He makes no attempt to **h.** from us. We
W-pI... 168.1:5 We try to **h.** from Him, and suffer from
W-pI. 185.14:1 beyond despair, the love attack would **h.**,
W-pI... 189.6:4 apparent reasoning but serve to **h.**.
W-pI... 190.9:4 with which you seek to **h.** your holiness.
W-pI... 193.4:4 No one can **h.** forever from a truth so very
W-pI... 196.9:3 Nor need you **h.** in terror from the deadly
W-pI... 198.9:5 that fails to **h.** an unforgiving thought.
W-pI... 199.4:1 Here does it **h.**, and here it can be seen as
W-pII.. 277.2:1 make to **h.** the freedom of the Son of God.
W-pII.. 289.1:4 This the past was made to **h.**, for this the
W-pII.. 322.1:2 go I find the gifts illusions tried to **h.**,
W-pII.. 347.1:8 *gives the miracles my dreams would* **h.** *from*
M-4....... X.2:7 No clouds remain to **h.** the face of Christ.
M-5......... I.2:4 would **h.** from himself to protect his "life.
C-ep........... 3:7 would **h.** but God would have you see.
S-1........ III.6:1 made to set up jailers and to **h.** from guilt.
S-1......... V.2:5 not **h.** in shame because it is content with
S-2........... I.6:5 instant only seem to **h.** the face of Christ,
S-2.......... II.5:1 will often **h.** behind a cloak like this. It

## hides 21

T-11...... III.5:1 God **h.** nothing from His Son, even
T-13......... I.1:5 Guilt **h.** Christ from your sight, for it is
T-13...... IX.1:1 remains the only thing that **h.** the Father,
T-15........ X.5:1 burrows underground and **h.** in darkness,
T-15........ X.6:7 for the one idea that **h.** behind them all;
T19 IV.B.14:10 joy. The ego **h.** it, for it would keep you
T-20....... V.7:6 The veil that **h.** the gift hides him as well.
T-20....... V.7:6 The veil that hides the gift **h.** him as well.
T-22........ II.1:5 garments in which it **h.** its nothingness.
T-24...... VI.6:5 that **h.** the face of Christ from him, and
T-25......... I.4:5 and nothing **h.** the face of Christ from its
T-25........ II.4:5 frame that **h.** the picture has no purpose.
T-25........ II.7:3 the sinlessness the frame of darkness **h.**,
T-31....... V.5:2 away, lest it perceive the treachery it **h.**.
T-31..... VII.7:1 before the truth, and **h.** it from your sight
T-31.... VIII.3:5 from everything that **h.** His face from you.
W-pI..... 91.4:5 of weakness **h.** will leap into awareness as
W-pI... 122.3:1 that **h.** the face of Christ from those who
W-pI. 133.12:3 **h.** the very simple fact that no decision
W-pI... 196.9:3 deadly fear of God projection **h.** behind.
S-1........ III.4:6 recognized as long as he **h.** it in another,

## hiding 21

T-4........ III.5:2 and **h.** is why the light cannot enter. The
T-12........ II.4:6 **h.** your head under the cover of the heavy
T-12........ II.4:7 are **h.** your nightmares in the darkness of
T-12........ II.7:1 me, for I am not hidden because *you* are **h.**
T-12........ II.9:5 we have overcome fear–not by **h.** it, not
T-13....... III.9:2 will be **h.** a dark place in your mind where
T-14..... VII.2:8 cannot know this, for by **h.** truth in fear,
T-14...... IX.1:5 for **h.** it has cost you knowledge of Him
T-19......... I.7:8 protecting the body by **h.** this connection,
T-20...... VI.5:2 carefully protected, yet **h.** nothing. Here
T-23..... II.11:6 guilt, the **h.** place for what belongs to you.
T-24..... II.13:2 and a **h.** place where none is welcome but
T-31...... VI.3:8 so that perception finds no **h.** place. How
W-pI..... 69.1:2 grievances are **h.** the light of the world in
W-pI..... 69.9:1 that your grievances are **h.** the light of the
W-pI... 73.11:7 cherishing them and **h.** them in darkness.
W-pI..... 93.9:5 by **h.** Its majesty behind the tiny idols of
W-pI..... 96.5:3 itself and **h.** in the body's frail support.
W-pI..... 99.8:2 and make them real by **h.** them from Him
W-pI... 193.7:4 And there remains an unforgiveness **h.** in
M-14......... 1:4 in gentleness, will cover it, **h.** all evil,

## hierarchy 5

T-20.. VIII.8:10 is no order; only a seeming **h.** of values.
T-23........ II.2:3 from the belief there is a **h.** of illusions;
T-26..... VII.6:5 at all. All that a **h.** of illusions can show is
W-pI..... 31.3:2 to establish any kind of **h.** among them.
M-8........... 3:7 Its **h.** of values is projected outward, and

## high 18

T-2....... III.3:5 Tolerance for pain may be **h.**, but it is not
T-5........... I.6:2 so **h.** they could reach almost back to Him
T-9....... II.10:1 set the price low but demand a **h.** return.
T-9....... II.10:4 The price will then be set **h.**, because of
T-12...... VI.1:3 yourself, and the overhead is **h.**. Not only
T-18.... VIII.7:7 Arched **h.** above it and surrounding it
T-18.... IX.13:2 lifted **h.** above the darkness and gently
T-23....... in.3:1 Walk you in glory, with your head held **h.**
T-23...... IV.6:5 they occur leave not your place on **h.**, but
T-26....... V.2:3 reach a goal as **h.** as learning can achieve?
T-26....... V.2:5 and **h.** resolve and happy confidence,
T-30...... III.8:5 So **h.** in Heaven is it set that those outside
T-31.... VIII.9:3 to lift us **h.** above the thorny roads we
W-pI..... 45.8:6 yet to realize how **h.** you are trying to go.
W-pI..... 50.3:2 and raise you **h.** above all the perceived

W-pI...186.8:5 and our emotions raise us h. indeed, or
S-1...in.3:2 until both h. and low have disappeared.
S-1...V.3:5 H. has the ladder risen. You have come

## Higher 3
*higher*

T-5...VI.4:7 you do not appeal to the H. Court because
T-5...VI.10:1 not fear the H. Court will condemn you. It
T-5...VI.10:4 you believe gladly to God's Own H. Court,

## higher 17
*Higher*

T-1...I.12:2 or the h. or spiritual level of experience.
T-1...II.4:4 I am h. because without me the distance
T-1...II.5:3 mediates h. to lower communication,
T-4...II.7:6 as it is of the so-called "h. ego needs."
T-4...IV.11:2 I do work with your h. mind, the home of
T-5...I.1:6 The h. mind thinks according to the laws
T-5...I.4:9 I have spoken before of the h. or "true"
T-5...IV.2:6 unhealed part of your mind to the h. part,
T-5...VI.4:1 its decision, much as a h. court has the
T-23...IV.5:1 up, and from a h. place look down upon it
W-pI...126.3:2 on a h. plane than he whom you forgive.
P-1...2:2 h. goal could there be for anyone than to
S-1...in.3:2 song that reaches h. and then higher still,
S-1...in.3:2 song that reaches higher and then h. still,
S-1...II.3:1 also possible to reach a h. form of asking-
S-3...II.4:1 This gentle passage to a h. prayer, a kind
S-3...II.5:4 gate to h. prayer and kindly justice done?

## highest 8

T-1...I.46:1 Spirit is the h. communication medium.
T-2...IV.5:4 necessarily mean that this is the h. level of
T-2...IV.5:5 that it is the h. level of communication of
T-8...III.1:1 Glory to God in the h., and to you
W-pI...157.2:3 past the h. reaches it can possibly attain.
W-pII.336.1:2 to what remains forever past its h. reach.
C-1...7:5 its h. it becomes aware of the real world,
P-2...II.2:5 At the h. levels they become one. Neither

## highly 12

T-1...III.4:5 to the h. personal experience of revelation
T-3...V.2:8 The h. specific nature of invention is not
T-9...I.3:2 fear, which would be h. artificial at most,
T-18...II.1:6 as under attack and h. vulnerable to it.
T-22...I.6:4 makes and what he hears are h. unreliable
W-pI...17.1:6 In view of its h. variable nature, this is
W-pI...40.1:3 every ten minutes would be h. desirable,
W-pI...44.4:2 A longer time is h. recommended, but
W-pI...49.1:4 distracted, disorganized and h. uncertain.
M-9...1:5 since training is always h. individualized.
M-29...2:6 The curriculum is h. individualized, and
C-1...3:2 because of its h. controversial nature. It

## Him 868
• God
*Christ/Self*
*Holy Spirit*
*him*

T-1...I.29:2 They praise H. by honoring His creations,
T-2...I.2:3 now. Everything God created is like H..
T-2...I.2:4 the children of the Father inherit from H..
T-2...III.5:11 His Sons, and they are lonely without H..
T-3...III.7:12 each other, they do not recognize H..
T-3...V.8:9 To know God's miracle is to know H..
T-3...VI.10:5 to God, but only to those who deny H.. To
T-3...VII.2:5 battling H. for possession of His creations
T-4...I.9:3 You have chosen to create unlike H., and
T-4...I.9:11 avoid H. any more than He can avoid you.
T-4...I.12:5 are wholly worthy of H. and only of Him.
T-4...I.12:5 are wholly worthy of Him and only of H..
T-4...III.6:3 of His Love for you and yours for H.. He
T-4...III.6:6 gods before H. because there *are* none.
T-4...III.8:4 to help me make other minds ready for H.
T-4...III.8:5 How long will you deny H. His Kingdom?
T-4...IV.9:6 cannot prevent H. from shining on you,
T-4...IV.9:6 prevent you from letting H. shine through
T-4...V.3:3 since the idea of H. does dispel the ego.
T-4...VI.8:4 only as you will give H. to your brothers.
T-4...VII.3:8 communicate with H. and like Him. This
T-4...VII.3:8 communicate with Him and like H.. This
T-4...VII.6:2 hardly means that you should tell H. how
T-4...VII.6:7 created do not communicate fully with H.
T-4...VII.7:3 does not need revelation returned to H.,
T-4...VII.8:4 their praise of H. because they are like
T-4...VII.8:4 praise of Him because they are like H.,
T-5...I.6:2 high they could reach almost back to H..
T-5...II.5:5 in you in a literal sense; you are part of H..
T-5...II.5:6 When you chose to leave H. He gave you a
T-5...II.5:6 Voice to speak for H. because He could no
T-5...II.6:8 even though they chose to leave H.. The
T-5...II.8:6 for God comes from your own altars to H.
T-5...IV.1:5 extension of God, you created it with H..
T-5...V.3:2 itself without believing it is attacking H.?
T-5...V.3:10 a part of H. has been torn away by you.
T-5...V.4:6 To think with H. is to think like Him. This
T-5...V.4:6 To think with Him is to think like H.. This
T-5...V.6:16 Thought, you *cannot* think apart from H..
T-5...V.7:2 because your thought was created by H..
T-5...VI.10:4 it speaks for H. and therefore speaks truly
T-5...VII.1:2 system that can separate you from H.? Do
T-5...VII.1:4 cares upon H. because He careth for you.
T-5...VII.3:2 and asks that you commend yours to H..
T-5...VII.3:3 you are of one mind and spirit with H..
T-5...VII.4:5 children who believe they are lost to H..
T-6...I.18:6 as He thinks if you are to know H. again.
T-6...II.6:2 you, and God created you as part of H..
T-6...II.6:10 inclusion in H. Who alone is perfect. To
T-6...II.6:11 To deny this is to deny yourself and H.,
T-6...II.7:6 everything was created by H. and in Him.
T-6...II.7:6 everything was created by Him and in H..
T-6...II.10:5 mind to God, because it has never left H..
T-6...II.10:6 Him. If it has never left H., you need only
T-6...IV.2:1 God created you He made you part of H..
T-6...IV.6:1 Kingdom, which He created as part of H..
T-6...IV.6:4 left of your dream when you hear H.,
T-6...IV.10:6 as the ego's notion that it has affronted H.
T-6...V.1:5 channels are not open to H., so that He
T-6...V.1:7 does not communicate with H. as one. So
T-7...I.1:4 He created you but you did not create H..
T-7...I.2:3 creative Thought proceeds from H. to you
T-7...I.4:5 To will with God is to create like H.. God
T-7...I.5:4 co-creator with H. extend His Kingdom
T-7...I.6:1 and to create like H. is to share the perfect
T-7...I.7:4 as applied to H. is not a time concept. He
T-7...I.7:7 neither to H. nor to what He created. The
T-7...II.3:9 And His Sons, who create like H., follow it
T-7...II.7:10 It belongs to H. and is therefore like Him.
T-7...II.7:10 It belongs to Him and is therefore like H..
T-7...IV.1:6 in a state of mind that does not know H..
T-7...IV.1:7 state is unknown to H. and therefore does
T-7...IV.2:2 you are in God because you are part of H..
T-7...IV.4:4 You have forgotten H., but the Holy Spirit
T-7...IV.7:5 All being is in H. Who is all Being. You
T-7...IV.7:6 are therefore in H. since your being is His.
T-7...V.6:14 and you cannot be out of accord with H..
T-7...V.10:1 I am with you, and I cannot forget H.. To
T-7...V.10:2 forget me is to forget yourself and H. Who
T-7...V.10:4 your remembrance of me and of H. Who
T-7...V.11:5 acceptable to H. and therefore to His Sons
T-7...VI.7:8 makes it appear as if you are attacking H..
T-7...VII.5:6 You can do nothing apart from H., and
T-7...VII.5:6 Him, and you *do* do nothing apart from H.
T-7...VII.6:3 them because you are not apart from H..
T-7...VII.10:5 will know that you are in H. with them.
T-7...VII.10:7 is lonely when His Sons do not know H..
T-7...VII.11:5 to His beloved Sons, who belong to H.. All
T-7...IX.2:4 part of H. and shares His Being with Him.
T-7...IX.2:4 part of Him and shares His Being with H..
T-7...XI.3:10 when they deny H. they do not know this,
T-7...XI.6:4 only the whole Sonship can create like H..
T-7...XI.7:7 His Being with you, you can know H.. But
T-8...II.6:4 no more will to be without H. than He
T-8...II.7:6 creates only like Himself, you are like H..
T-8...II.7:7 are part of H. Who is all power and glory,
T-8...III.8:3 whatever belongs to H. because He gives
T-8...III.8:3 of Himself, and everything belongs to H..
T-8...III.8:5 will let you remember what you *have* of H.,
T-8...III.8:5 you will remember also what you *are* in H..
T-8...IV.1:3 because you do not believe you are in H..
T-8...IV.2:13 of yourself, and of H. Who sent me to you
T-8...IV.7:7 freedom because your freedom is in H..
T-8...IV.7:8 in praise of H. and you whom He created.
T-8...IV.7:9 This is our gift of gratitude to H., which
T-8...IV.7:9 gives equally whatever is acceptable to H..
T-8...IV.7:10 is acceptable to H. it is the gift of freedom,
T-8...V.2:6 If your perfection is in H. and only in Him
T-8...V.2:6 If your perfection is in Him and only in H.
T-8...V.2:6 can you know it without recognizing H.?
T-8...V.3:4 As we unite, we unite with H.. Glory be to
T-8...V.4:5 children because I received it of H. for us
T-8...VI.3:1 Let us glorify H. Whom the world denies,
T-8...VI.6:6 this because you do not understand H..
T-8...VI.7:5 Himself, and His Sons, who are like H.,
T-8...VI.7:5 Him, cannot contradict themselves or H..
T-8...VI.8:3 revealed it to me because I asked it of H.,
T-8...VI.8:7 and gave him the power to create with H..
T-8...VI.9:2 My devotion to you is of H., being born of
T-8...VI.9:2 born of my knowledge of myself and H..
T-8...VII.6:4 believe you have withdrawn them from H.
T-9...I.9:7 God is Love and you do want H.. This *is*
T-9...I.14:7 *He is God must be, for Christ is part of H..*
T-9...V.3:5 onto God, they make H. appear retaliative
T-9...VI.3:10 His glory belongs to H., but it is equally
T-9...VI.4:8 When you awake in H. you will know
T-9...VI.7:3 Like H., *you* are "always"; in His Mind and
T-9...VII.8:5 not offer to God as wholly fitting for H..
T-9...VII.8:7 Return your part to H., and He will give
T-9...VII.8:7 belongs to H. and renders Him complete.
T-9...VII.8:7 belongs to Him and renders H. complete.
T-9...VIII.1:1 Grandeur is of God, and only of H..
T-10...in.2:1 beside you exists, for you are part of H..
T-10...in.2:2 Him. What except H. can exist? Nothing
T-10...in.2:3 Nothing beyond H. can happen, because
T-10...in.2:3 happen, because nothing except H. is real.
T-10...in.2:4 Your creations add to H. as you do, but
T-10...in.3:3 create for yourself so you would be like H.
T-10...II.2:5 you are part of H. when you are willing to
T-10...II.2:5 H. and know your own reality again. Let
T-10...II.2:6 this world delay your remembering of H.,
T-10...II.3:6 But signify your will to remember H., and
T-10...II.5:5 you attack you are not remembering H..
T-10...II.5:6 are actively choosing not to remember H..
T-10...II.6:6 that makes you afraid to remember H..
T-10...III.1:1 have not attacked God and you do love H.
T-10...III.2:3 mind receives H. the remembrance of
T-10...III.2:3 of H. awakens throughout the Sonship.
T-10...III.2:6 joins them together, and them to H.. To
T-10...III.6:1 knowledge that each one is part of H..
T-10...III.8:3 other gods before H. or you will not hear.
T-10...III.10:2 You share reality with H., because reality
T-10...III.10:3 To accept other gods before H. is to place
T-10...III.11:3 when you place no other gods before H..
T-10...IV.1:5 sick, you have placed other gods before H.
T-10...IV.6:2 of one mind and that mind belongs to H..
T-10...IV.6:3 It is yours *because* it belongs to H., for to
T-10...IV.6:3 to Him, for to H. ownership is sharing.
T-10...IV.6:4 And if it is so for H., it is so for you. His
T-10...V.5:5 have created a Son who was unlike H.. If
T-10...V.6:2 knowing that you could not sin against H.
T-10...V.6:3 You denied H. because you loved Him,
T-10...V.6:3 You denied Him because you loved H.,
T-10...V.6:3 that if you recognized your love for H.,
T-10...V.6:3 your love for Him, you could not deny H..
T-10...V.6:4 of H. therefore means that you love Him,
T-10...V.6:4 of Him therefore means that you love H.,
T-10...V.7:5 and you will learn of H. if you hear aright.
T-10...V.7:7 your heart in gratitude for your gift to H..
T-10...V.8:1 for healing is the acknowledgment of H..
T-10...V.8:2 When you acknowledge H. you will know
T-10...V.9:4 Son anything that is not acceptable to H.?
T-10...V.9:6 you must acknowledge H. as your Creator

| | |
|---|---|
| T-10.....V.9:10 | If you deny H. you bring sin, pain and |
| T-10.....V.10:4 | When you deny H. *you* are insane. Would |
| T-10.....V.10:5 | Would you have H. share your insanity? |
| T-10.....V.10:6 | and His Son will never cease to love H.. |
| T-10...V.10:11 | eternal. Would you deny yourself to H.? |
| T-10.....V.11:1 | Out of your gifts to H. the Kingdom will |
| T-10.....V.13:1 | God did not create or you are denying H.. |
| T-10.....V.13:8 | That is why to deny H. is to deny yourself. |
| T-11.......in.2:3 | out of the wish of God's Son to father H.. |
| T-11.........I.1:3 | the thought system you share with H.. |
| T-11.........I.1:4 | you place upon it but will be blessed by H. |
| T-11.........I.2:6 | part of God can be missing or lost to H.? |
| T-11.........I.4:2 | creation or upon those who create like H.. |
| T-11.........I.5:8 | Himself. Do not deny H. His Son, for your |
| T-11.........I.5:9 | Son, for yours were created in honor of H. |
| T-11.........I.7:3 | like H. if you would know His gift to you? |
| T-11.........I.7:5 | Your ability to accept H. depends on your |
| T-11.........I.9:6 | in time you cannot live apart from H.. |
| T-11.......I.9:10 | his Father is life, and His Son is like H.. |
| T-11.......I.11:4 | so that nothing He gives can contradict H. |
| T-11.......I.11:7 | For it is your will to be like H., Whose |
| T-11.......I.11:8 | One, and united with H. in His Oneness. |
| T-11.......II.1:5 | And you will yourself to H. because, in |
| T-11.......II.1:5 | in your perfect understanding of H., you |
| T-11.......II.6:2 | To have H. is to be like Him, and He has |
| T-11.......II.6:2 | To have Him is to be like H., and He has |
| T-11......III.1:5 | Pain is not of H., for He knows no attack |
| T-11......III.1:6 | is very quiet, for there is no conflict in H.. |
| T-11......III.2:5 | be true of you, because it is not true of H.. |
| T-11......III.5:7 | Father *is* your Creator, and you *are* like H.. |
| T-11......III.6:3 | tempted to deny H. remember that there |
| T-11......III.6:3 | there *are* no other gods to place before H., |
| T-11......III.7:5 | and therefore does not belong to H.. And |
| T-11......III.8:2 | be worthy to dwell in the temple with H., |
| T-11......IV.1:7 | And since what He created is part of H., |
| T-11......IV.1:7 | are denying H. His place in His Own altar. |
| T-11......IV.3:3 | the light He created is one with H.. Would |
| T-11......IV.7:5 | as His Creator and at peace with H.. |
| T-11......IV.8:3 | the Son must share what belongs to H., |
| T-11.......V.3:7 | *is not of H. has no power to do anything.* |
| T-11.......V.6:3 | as dependent on you as you are on H.. Do |
| T-11.......V.6:4 | not ascribe the ego's arrogance to H. Who |
| T-11.......V.6:6 | autonomy is meaningful apart from H.? |
| T-11.....V.12:1 | is as dependent on you as you are on H., |
| T-11.....V.12:2 | your autonomy by identifying with H., |
| T-11.....V.16:9 | straight at the Father and does not see H., |
| T-11.....V.17:2 | Accept His Son and you will remember H. |
| T-11....VI.10:6 | whole power of God is in every part of H., |
| T-11.....VII.3:7 | you made is capable of being unlike H.. |
| T-11.....VII.3:8 | Yet everything true *is* like H.. Perceiving |
| T-12.......II.2:10 | For you forgot your brothers with H., and |
| T-12.......II.7:6 | not know that I walked with H. in peace? |
| T-12......III.9:4 | You still cannot will against H., and that |
| T-12......IV.6:8 | is whole and all His extensions are like H.. |
| T-12.......V.9:2 | You can teach the way to H. and learn it, |
| T-12.......V.9:2 | knows the way to H. and understands His |
| T-12...VIII.2:5 | and could not live in the knowledge of H.. |
| T-12...VIII.4:1 | Father's Love you can never forget H., for |
| T-12...VIII.4:6 | You are waiting only for H., and do not |
| T-12...VIII.6:4 | instant you thought you had deserted H.. |
| T-12...VIII.7:9 | share God's Being with H. could never be |
| T-13.......in.3:7 | who do not understand H. could believe it |
| T-13......III.4:3 | God would destroy; and by loving H., |
| T-13......III.8:3 | the Father, in loving remembrance of H.. |
| T-13....III.10:3 | not give it for the request was alien to H., |
| T-13....III.10:4 | of H. an unloving father, demanding of |
| T-13....III.10:4 | of H. what only such a father could give. |
| T-13....III.10:6 | attacked his own glorious equality with H. |
| T-13.......V.7:2 | offer it to yourself, you *are* offering it to H.. |
| T-13.......V.7:3 | of you because it is unworthy of H.. Yet |
| T-13.....V.7:11 | and gladness is what we should offer H.. |
| T-13.......V.9:7 | extended your perception even unto H.. |
| T-13......VI.9:1 | for you will remember H. as you call forth |
| T-13......VI.9:4 | called upon H. and remained unanswered |
| T-13......VI.9:5 | His Call to you is but your call to H.. And |
| T-13......VI.9:6 | And in H. you are answered by His peace. |
| T-13....VI.13:6 | his Father, he has no past apart from H.. |
| T-13.....VII.6:7 | in recognition that you share it with H.. |
| T-13.....VII.8:7 | and by it God created you as one with H.. |
| T-13. VIII.10:3 | Nor do you witness unto H., for reality is |
| T-13. VIII.10:5 | on earth are lifted up to Heaven and to H. |
| T-13.......X.9:2 | do not remember how much you love H.. |
| T-13......X.10:3 | *And as His Son loves H.*. There is no fear in |
| T-13......X.11:5 | Seek not to love unlike H., for there is no |
| T-13......X.14:5 | only praise of H. in what He has created, |
| T-13......X.14:8 | lack faith in you and love H. perfectly? |
| T-13......XI.7:5 | If that suffices H., it is enough for you. |
| T-13......XI.8:3 | be wholly closed and separated from H.. |
| T-13......XI.8:4 | flows to you from H. Whose Will is peace. |
| T-13....XI.11:5 | From H. you cannot wander, and there is |
| T-14.......II.8:7 | and His Son is in H. with everything. Can |
| T-14......III.8:1 | is the only Cause, and guilt is not of H. |
| T-14....III.12:3 | against it, for being of H. it must be true. |
| T-14....III.15:1 | evaluate his Father and judge against H.. |
| T-14....III.18:2 | remain in close communication with H., |
| T-14....III.18:2 | and with everything that is within H., as it |
| T-14......IV.2:1 | by H. like unto Himself and part of Him, |
| T-14......IV.2:1 | by Him like unto Himself and part of H., |
| T-14......IV.2:4 | still think that you are separate from H.. |
| T-14......IV.2:5 | but cannot know that you are one with H. |
| T-14......IV.4:6 | you out of Himself, but still within H.. He |
| T-14......IV.4:8 | Remember that there is no second to H.. |
| T-14......IV.5:6 | the truth in you, making you one with H.. |
| T-14......IV.7:1 | God, Whose Will is that you know H.. |
| T-14......IV.7:3 | the necessary conditions for knowing H., |
| T-14......IV.7:3 | have denied H. and do not recognize Him |
| T-14......IV.7:3 | have denied Him and do not recognize H. |
| T-14......IV.7:4 | is the condition for knowing H.. |
| T-14......IV.7:7 | endow H. with attributes you understand. |
| T-14......IV.7:8 | H. not, and anything you understand is |
| T-14......IV.7:8 | and anything you understand is not of H.. |
| T-14......IV.8:3 | hear me speak for H. and for yourself. |
| T-14......IV.8:5 | apart from H. resembles it ever so faintly. |
| T-14......IV.9:8 | Remembrance of reality is in H., and |
| T-14.......V.1:2 | all the lonely ones who have denied H.? |
| T-14.......V.1:5 | You yearn for H., as He for you. This is |
| T-14.....V.1:12 | in His Son as the Son is blessed in H.. |
| T-14.......V.9:3 | In guiltlessness we know H., as He knows |
| T-14......IX.1:5 | cost you knowledge of H. and of yourself. |
| T-14......IX.3:4 | you. Yet without H. you are nothing. The |
| T-14......IX.3:6 | gift that you refused is held by H. in you. |
| T-14......IX.8:6 | no image, and His creations, as part of H., |
| T-14......IX.8:6 | as part of Him, hold H. in them in truth. |
| T-14......X.10:2 | remembering H. means you are not alone, |
| T-14......X.11:2 | for everything of H. is perfectly open and |
| T-14......XI.2:4 | And can His Son, given all power by H., |
| T-14......XI.4:3 | so you have another lesson sent from H., |
| T-14......XI.7:3 | not meet, if he but turn to H. ever so little. |
| T-14......XI.7:4 | His Son to turn to H. and remain Himself. |
| T-14....XI.11:2 | as one in God, so do we learn as one in H.. |
| T-14....XI.15:2 | You think you know H. not, only because, |
| T-14....XI.15:2 | alone, it is impossible to know H.. Yet see |
| T-14....XI.15:3 | be convinced you did them through H.. It |
| T-14....XI.15:5 | you. Leave room for H., and you will find |
| T-15.......I.10:8 | remembering H. *is* to remember freedom. |
| T-15.......II.1:6 | that instant you will awaken gently in H.. |
| T-15......III.5:4 | He established you as host to H. forever. |
| T-15......III.5:5 | has not left you, and you have not left H.. |
| T-15......III.5:6 | make little whom God has joined with H.. |
| T-15......III.6:8 | magnitude is of H. Who dwells in you, |
| T-15......III.7:7 | all His extensions to you, as host to H.. |
| T-15......III.8:4 | in you in honor of H. Whose host you are. |
| T-15......III.8:6 | love dwells in you, for you are host to H.. |
| T-15....III.11:3 | together that the Son of God is host to H.. |
| T-15......IV.2:8 | For peace is of God, and no one beside H.. |
| T-15......IV.3:1 | Be humble before H., and yet great *in* Him |
| T-15......IV.3:1 | Be humble before Him, and yet great *in* H. |
| T-15......IV.3:6 | of salvation apart from H. diminishes the |
| T-15......IV.3:7 | yet it is your mind that is the host to H.. |
| T-15......VI.4:4 | faith in H. is strengthened by sharing. |
| T-15......VI.4:6 | an idea. And like H., you can give yourself |
| T-15......VI.8:1 | all your brothers is remembered with H.. |
| T-15......VI.8:7 | is, and what His creation is along with H.. |
| T-15.....VII.5:3 | in the Name of H. Who would release him |
| T-15...VIII.5:5 | communication to you, and yours to H.. |
| T-15......IX.7:4 | it as undivided you join H. wholly, in an |
| T-15......IX.7:4 | place no limits on your union with H.. |
| T-15.......X.8:4 | to project H. outward and away from you, |
| T-15........X.8:4 | and away from you, and not be host to H.. |
| T-15........X.8:5 | To H. you ascribed the ego's treachery, |
| T-15........X.8:5 | it to take His place to protect you from H.. |
| T-15......XI.2:7 | need but invite H. in Who is there already |
| T-15......XI.2:7 | to His Oneness can abide with H. there. |
| T-15......XI.2:8 | Love must be total to give H. welcome, for |
| T-15......XI.6:6 | to be without H. *is* to be without meaning. |
| T-15......XI.9:1 | to the holy host who would receive H., |
| T-15......XI.9:1 | lets H. enter and abide where He would |
| T-15......XI.9:2 | you who welcome H. is returned to Him. |
| T-15......XI.9:2 | you who welcome Him is returned to H.. |
| T-15......XI.9:3 | as we welcome H. into ourselves. Those |
| T-15......XI.9:4 | who receive the Father are one with H., |
| T-15......XI.9:4 | Him, being host to H. Who created them. |
| T-15......XI.9:5 | them. And by allowing H. to enter, the |
| T-15......XI.9:5 | remembrance of the Father enters with H. |
| T-15......XI.9:5 | H. they remember the only relationship |
| T-16........II.3:3 | and what is natural to H. is natural to you |
| T-16.......III.6:3 | who hold H. and whom He holds are the |
| T-16......III.7:7 | in H. that is not perfect and eternal. All |
| T-16......IV.8:7 | and what you are joined with H. in giving. |
| T-16......IV.9:1 | special, but only to be wholly like to H., |
| T-16......IV.9:1 | Him, completing H. by your completion. |
| T-16......IV.9:6 | is God completed, and His Son with H.. |
| T-16....IV.10:1 | to H. where your completion rests, wholly |
| T-16..IV.11:11 | has never forgotten what makes H. whole. |
| T-16..IV.11:14 | H. are joined your willingness to love and |
| T-16....IV.12:2 | The Holy Spirit is the Bridge to H., made |
| T-16....IV.12:2 | to unite with H. and created by His joy in |
| T-16....IV.13:5 | and answer fearlessly the Call of H. Who |
| T-16.......V.2:2 | For the ego would have you see H., and |
| T-16.......V.2:2 | would have you see Him, and H. alone, as |
| T-16......V.13:1 | attempt to raise other gods before H., and |
| T-16......V.13:3 | raise to place before H. stands before *you*, |
| T-16...VII.10:4 | in salvation in your relationship with H.. |
| T-16...VII.11:3 | nothing that will not give place to H. and |
| T-16...VII.11:4 | To join in close relationship with H. is to |
| T-16...VII.11:5 | your relationship with H. and to no other. |
| T-17.......II.3:3 | No one but H. Who planned salvation |
| T-17.......II.4:5 | world and have been made ready for H.. |
| T-17....IV.16:2 | by giving H. ascendance in our minds. We |
| T-17....IV.16:3 | by giving H. the power and the glory, and |
| T-17....IV.16:6 | His. It shines in every part of H., as in the |
| T-17....IV.16:7 | whole reality of your relationship with H. |
| T-18.........I.9:5 | God, as much together as you are with H.. |
| T-18.......I.10:9 | Let us join in H. in peace and gratitude, |
| T-18.......I.10:9 | and perfect reality, which we share in H.. |
| T-18......IV.3:5 | create His dwelling place unworthy of H.. |
| T-18......IV.4:3 | that it is needful to prepare yourself for H. |
| T-18......IV.5:8 | than seek to prepare yourself for H., try to |
| T-18......IV.5:9 | *I who am host to God am worthy of H.. He* |
| T-18....IV.5:11 | *It is not needful that I make it ready for H.*, |
| T-18.......V.3:6 | means and purpose both belong to H.. |
| T-18......VI.1:4 | his Father and dwells not apart from H.. |
| T-18....VI.10:6 | be? You are surrounded only by H.. What |
| T-18....VIII.2:3 | into a body, nor can you join H. there. |
| T-18....VIII.2:4 | on love will always seem to shut H. out, |
| T-18....VIII.2:4 | shut Him out, and keep you apart from H. |
| T-18....IX.11:4 | ends before H. Who is complete where He |
| T-18....IX.12:6 | of you and yours of H. so far transcend all |
| T-19.......I.10:3 | most loving Father, loved by H. like you, |
| T-19......III.6:2 | what is part of H. is totally unlike the rest. |
| T-19......III.6:5 | have created what wills to destroy H., and |
| T-19......III.8:3 | eternal opposition to H. and to each other |
| T19..IV.B.4:10 | He has not lost communion with H., nor |
| T19....IV.C.5:7 | His Own; an Answer which left H. not, |
| T19. IV.D.19:4 | peace of God, given to you eternally by H. |
| T-20......IV.1:4 | by H. and reawakened by the Holy Spirit, |
| T-20......VI.6:7 | have *not* be is here kept "safe" from H.. |
| T-21....VI.10:3 | your Father gives you for completing H.. |
| T-22.........I.9:2 | Nothing but what is part of H. is worthy |
| T-22.........I.9:3 | that anything not part of H. *can* join. |
| T-22.......II.10:4 | His joy to misery, and make H. different. |
| T-22.......V.3:5 | whom He has joined as one with H.? It is |
| T-22....VI.15:2 | And in H. is all creation joined. Would |
| T-23.........I.9:5 | and drive H. out of what He loves forever. |
| T-23.......I.10:1 | You who are beloved of H. are no illusion |
| T-23.......I.10:2 | certainty of H. and of yourself is home to |
| T-23.......I.10:3 | keeps God homeless and His Son with H.. |

| | |
|---|---|
| T-23 I.10:7 | is given those who would remember H.. |
| T-23 II.6:4 | His Son can tell H. this, and He has but |
| T-23 II.7:2 | impossible to turn to H. for help in misery |
| T-23 II.7:4 | every aspect seems to be at war with H., |
| T-23 IV.1:4 | In H. is no attack, and no illusion in any |
| T-24 in.1:3 | It is not necessary to tell H. what to do. |
| T-24 in.1:9 | wait upon illusions to let H. be Himself. |
| T-24 II.3:4 | His Son like to itself and not like unto H.. |
| T-24 II.3:5 | himself, and H. of Whom they are a part. |
| T-24 II.3:6 | which created them as one with H.. They |
| T-24 II.6:2 | memory of H. springs instantly to mind. |
| T-24 II.10:4 | not given to His Son but kept for H. alone |
| T-24 II.10:5 | then He willed His Son to be like H., and |
| T-24 II.10:7 | the universe with H. Who chose that love |
| T-24 II.11:5 | What is the same as God is one with H.. |
| T-24 II.13:1 | prison house that keeps His Son from H.. |
| T-24 III.2:4 | make you separate from H. as its defender |
| T-24 III.4:3 | No, His Son is safe, resting on H.. It is |
| T-24 III.6:6 | you have forgiven H. Whose Will it is you |
| T-24 III.7:6 | die, but not by H. Who made not death; |
| T-24 IV.3:12 | keep the gift your Father asks from H., |
| T-24 IV.3:13 | Given to H., the universe is yours. Offered |
| T-24 V.8:4 | as like to H. in holiness as you must be? |
| T-24 VI.1:9 | that He created you as part of H.. |
| T-24 VI.2:3 | and part of H. because His Will is One. |
| T-24 VI.2:4 | Nothing alive that is not part of H., and |
| T-24 VI.2:4 | of Him, and nothing is but is alive in H.. |
| T-24 VI.3:5 | eternity where He abides, and you with H. |
| T-24 VI.6:4 | the shining memory of H. in Whom your |
| T-24 VI.7:6 | God Himself but in that part of H. He set |
| T-24 VI.10:5 | that He has given you a part of H. to save |
| T-24 VI.10:6 | each part of H. with equal love and care. |
| T-24 VII.1:8 | Fatherhood of God, not snatch it from H.. |
| T-24 VII.6:6 | means and end are one, and one with H.. |
| T-24.VII.10:10 | For as His Son's creation gave H. joy and |
| T-25 II.6:1 | part of H. that you would see as separate. |
| T-25 II.6:2 | One with H. and with His masterpiece. |
| T-25 II.9:5 | when any part of H. joins in His praise, to |
| T-25 II.9:8 | would complete His joy, along with H.. |
| T-25 VI.1:1 | they look on speaks of H. to the beholder. |
| T-25 VII.10:2 | And where does sanity abide except in H. |
| T-25 VII.10:3 | One Who speaks for H. can show you this |
| T-25 VII.13:6 | his Father's, and in H. no loss is possible. |
| T-25 IX.2:8 | to perceive salvation as a gift from H.. Yet |
| T-26 II.8:2 | that everything that is belongs to H., and |
| T-26 III.1:5 | then, could there be complexity in H.? |
| T-26 V.9:8 | His, and nowhere can you go except to H.. |
| T-26 VII.7:5 | His reality from H. and brought His Love |
| T-26 VII.11:6 | It is not understood apart from H., and |
| T-26 VII.13:2 | true: that He created you as part of H., |
| T-26 VII.15:5 | And what is one to H. must be the same. |
| T-26 VII.20:2 | and God will answer, for on H. you call. |
| T-26 VII.20:3 | has already answered all who call on H.? |
| T-26 IX.8:1 | host again to H. by Whom it was created. |
| T-26 IX.8:2 | Where He dwells, His Son dwells with H., |
| T-27 II.10:8 | function from H. and deny that it is His? |
| T-27 V.11:9 | His Son, and therefore is it given unto H.. |
| T-27 VI.4:7 | to your life in H. Who knows no death. |
| T-28 I.10:2 | You would deny H. His Effects, yet have |
| T-28 I.12:5 | accepts gives welcome to eternity and H., |
| T-28 II.1:4 | and receives the gift that he has given H.. |
| T-28 III.3:5 | to bridge the little gap that leads to H.. |
| T-28 III.6:4 | thus make room for H. Who wills to come |
| T-28 IV.10:4 | a loss, and what is not of H. has no effects. |
| T-28 V.1:7 | Who shares in them can never share in H. |
| T-28 V.1:8 | his mind from sharing them *is* sharing H.. |
| T-28 VII.1:1 | God asks for nothing, and His Son, like H. |
| T-29 I.1:7 | How could you trust H., then? For He |
| T-29 I.1:9 | Be wary, then; let H. not come too close, |
| T-29 I.9:3 | what could induce you to abandon H.? |
| T-29 II.8:6 | that part of H. belongs to Him no longer. |
| T-29 II.8:6 | that part of Him belongs to H. no longer. |
| T-29 II.8:8 | what is gone from H. becomes your god, |
| T-29 II.8:8 | god, protecting you from being part of H.. |
| T-29 II.10:3 | then what is not in H. does not exist, and |
| T-29 III.2:5 | Deny H. not His witness in the dream His |
| T-29 VII.6:3 | within, and your completion lies in H.. |
| T-29 VII.10:5 | Let H. remind you of His Love for you, |
| T-29 VIII.9:6 | your brother and on you, as one with H.? |

| | |
|---|---|
| T-30 II.1:12 | than that He hear you call H. "Friend." |
| T-30 II.2:10 | to oppose H. is to make a choice against |
| T-30 II.3:6 | Remember H. Who has created you, and |
| T-30 II.4:4 | co-creator of the universe along with H.. |
| T-30 II.4:7 | forgiven H. Who gave your will to you. |
| T-30 II.4:9 | apart from H. Whose holy Will you share. |
| T-30 V.4:5 | and understands it perfectly with H.. |
| T-31 I.6:2 | God willed not His Son forget H.. And the |
| T-31 I.6:3 | His Will is in the Voice that speaks for H.. |
| T-31 IV.9:3 | No pathway in the world can lead to H., |
| T-31 IV.10:2 | from them than they could keep H. out. |
| T-31 IV.10:3 | out. In unity with H. do they abide, and in |
| T-31 IV.10:4 | There is no road that leads away from H.. |
| T-31 IV.11:4 | and did not let His Son abandon H.. For |
| T-31 IV.11:7 | There *is* no path that does not lead to H.. |
| W-pI 43.h | is my Source. I cannot see apart from H.. |
| W-pI 43.3:2 | Whatever you do you do in H., because |
| W-pI 43.4:8 | *I cannot see this desk apart from H.. God is* |
| W-pI 43.4:10 | *I cannot see that picture apart from H..* |
| W-pI 43.7:4 | *I cannot see you apart from H..* This form is |
| W-pI 43.8:4 | *my Source. I cannot see this apart from H..* |
| W-pI 44.6:4 | you see. You are attempting to reach H.. |
| W-pI 45.2:2 | you share your thoughts with H., as He |
| W-pI 45.9:3 | are unworthy of H. Whose host you are. |
| W-pI 45.9:4 | thank H. for the Thoughts He is thinking |
| W-pI 47.3:2 | Voice speaks for H. in all situations and in |
| W-pI 47.3:4 | which speaks for H. thinks as He does. |
| W-pI 49.3:2 | reminding you of H. and of your Self. We |
| W-pI 53.5:6 | H. because it is not my will that they do so |
| W-pI 53.5:7 | and I will place no other gods before H.. |
| W-pI 56.4:6 | we who are part of H. will yet look past all |
| W-pI 56.5:5 | them, am one with them and one with H.. |
| W-pI 59.1:3 | myself when perfect certainty abides in H. |
| W-pI 59.1:5 | love and joy surround me through H.? Let |
| W-pI 59.3:2 | I cannot see apart from H.. I can see what |
| W-pI 59.3:6 | when I think I can see apart from H.. It is |
| W-pI 59.4:4 | if I am to see, it must be through H.. I |
| W-pI 59.5:3 | I have no thoughts apart from H., because |
| W-pI 60.1:6 | reach down to me and raise me up to H.. |
| W-pI 66.6:6 | definition of H. you are believing if you do |
| W-pI 66.8:1 | ego which you have made to replace H.. |
| W-pI 68.1:6 | from your Source and make you unlike H. |
| W-pI 68.3:1 | Himself, and defined them as part of H.. |
| W-pI 71.9:2 | Ask H. very specifically: *What would You* |
| W-pI 71.9:6 | *to whom?* Give H. full charge of the rest of |
| W-pI 71.9:6 | and let H. tell you what needs to be done |
| W-pI 72.5:9 | God, and holding H. responsible for it. |
| W-pI 72.7:4 | grievances against H. and His creation, |
| W-pI 74.4:4 | *I share it with H.. My conflicts about* _ |
| W-pI 76.10:6 | creation; denied to H. by his belief in hell. |
| W-pI 76.11:1 | Let us today open God's channels to H., |
| W-pI 76.11:1 | and let His Will extend through us to H.. |
| W-pI 95.1:2 | are one within yourself, and one with H.. |
| W-pI 97.2:4 | He is with you always, as you are with H.. |
| W-pI 97.4:2 | and count on H. Who promised to lay |
| W-pI 97.4:4 | Give H. the minutes which He needs |
| W-pI 97.4:4 | help you understand with H. you are the |
| W-pI 97.4:4 | Him you are the spirit that abides in H., |
| W-pI 98.7:1 | give H. your tiny gift of but five minutes. |
| W-pI 98.7:5 | Today you practice with H., as you say: *I* |
| W-pI 98.8:1 | each five minutes that you spend with H., |
| W-pI 98.9:1 | Give H. the words, and He will do the |
| W-pI 98.9:5 | then of H. Who knows the function that |
| W-pI 98.9:6 | each practice period you share with H., |
| W-pI 98.9:6 | you offer H. for timelessness and peace. |
| W-pI 98.10:1 | five minutes you will spend again with H.. |
| W-pI 98.11:1 | and spend a happy time again with H.. |
| W-pI 98.11:2 | Tell H. once more that you accept the part |
| W-pI 98.11:2 | He has made with you and you with H.. |
| W-pI 99.8:2 | make them real by hiding them from H.. |
| W-pI 101.2:6 | They would escape H. in their fear. And |
| W-pI 103.2:5 | *To fear H. is to be afraid of joy.* Begin your |
| W-pI 104.4:2 | come to find what has been given us by H. |
| W-pI 104.5:1 | So do we clear the way for H. today by |
| W-pI 105.5:2 | Let H. complete Himself as He defines |
| W-pI 105.5:3 | that what completes H. must complete |
| W-pI 105.5:6 | and He will thank you for your gift to H.. |
| W-pI 105.9:1 | thus with H. each time you can today, but |
| W-pI 105.9:1 | worthless when you cannot give H. more. |

| | |
|---|---|
| W-pI 105.9:2 | call to H. to give you what He wills to give, |
| W-pI 106.3:5 | which do not speak of H. Who holds your |
| W-pI 106.3:6 | Hear only H. today, and do not wait to |
| W-pI 106.3:6 | today, and do not wait to reach H. longer. |
| W-pI 106.5:1 | Hear H. today, and listen to the Word |
| W-pI 106.5:4 | Hear H. today, and offer Him your voice |
| W-pI 106.5:4 | and offer H. your voice to speak to all the |
| W-pI 106.10:1 | means by listening and learning it of H.. |
| W-pI 109.4:6 | rest in H. and let Him speak through you. |
| W-pI 109.4:6 | rest in Him and let H. speak through you. |
| W-pI 109.5:1 | In H. you have no cares and no concerns, |
| W-pI 110.11:1 | We will remember H. throughout the day |
| W-pI 110.11:2 | For it is thus that we remember H.. And |
| W-pI 112.1:3 | *I share with God, because I am a part of H..* |
| W-pI 112.2:3 | *And I am one with H., and He with me.* |
| W-pI 120.1:2 | *today, and let H. work in me and through me* |
| W-pI 120.1:2 | *I rest in H. in quiet and in perfect certainty.* |
| W-pI 123.2:3 | to take the place of H. and His creation. |
| W-pI 123.2:4 | and His creation. Give H. thanks today. |
| W-pI 123.4:2 | has willed to be our true Identity in H.. |
| W-pI 123.6:2 | of God today, as you give thanks to H.. |
| W-pI 123.7:1 | to H. for fifteen minutes twice today. And |
| W-pI 123.7:2 | Whom He thanks as you are thanking H.. |
| W-pI 123.7:3 | This holy half an hour given H. will be |
| W-pI 123.7:3 | eons more quickly for your thanks to H.. |
| W-pI 123.8:2 | Remember hourly to think of H., and give |
| W-pI 123.8:2 | give H. thanks for everything He gave His |
| W-pI 124.4:3 | are one with H. today in recognition and |
| W-pI 124.4:4 | feel H. in our hearts. Our minds contain |
| W-pI 124.7:5 | would experience ourselves at one with H. |
| W-pI 124.8:6 | Abide with H. this half an hour. He will |
| W-pI 125.1:4 | Hear H. today. No peace is possible until |
| W-pI 125.5:1 | your mind to H. to give His Word to you. |
| W-pI 125.5:2 | have wandered off a little while from H.. |
| W-pI 125.5:4 | as part of H. regardless of his dreams; |
| W-pI 126.7:1 | having given H. the gift He asks of you, |
| W-pI 129.4:2 | speaks to His Son, as His Son speaks to H. |
| W-pI 131.7:3 | existence and attacks itself is not of H.. He |
| W-pI 131.14:4 | Son, as does His Son remember his to H.. |
| W-pI 132.11:1 | you, you cannot think apart from H., nor |
| W-pI 132.11:3 | Does it create like H.? Unless it does, it is |
| W-pI 132.12:4 | What He creates is not apart from H., and |
| W-pI 132.12:4 | Son begin as something separate from H.. |
| W-pI 134.2:5 | All truth belongs to H., reflects His laws |
| W-pI 135.25:2 | Today we will remember H.. For this is |
| W-pI 139.11:4 | God gave to us when He created us like H. |
| W-pI 140.11:1 | We waken hearing H., and let Him speak |
| W-pI 140.11:1 | and let H. speak to us five minutes as the |
| W-pI 140.11:5 | We hear H. now. We come to Him today. |
| W-pI 140.11:6 | We hear Him now. We come to H. today. |
| WpI.rIV.in6:1 | alone, for they will all be shared with H.. |
| WpI.rIV.in6:2 | to you, returning messages of yours to H.. |
| WpI.rIV.in6:4 | And as His Own completion joins with H. |
| WpI.rIV.in6:4 | who are complete as you unite with H., |
| WpI.rIV.in7:5 | that He has laid in it for you to have of H.. |
| WpI.rIV.in9:2 | receive as the inheritance we have of H.. |
| W-pI 152.6:5 | You but accuse H. of insanity, to think He |
| W-pI 152.7:2 | see at once these things are not of H.. And |
| W-pI 152.9:4 | to H. Who has created us immaculate, |
| W-pI 152.10:2 | And we accept of H. that which we are, |
| W-pI 152.12:1 | patience wait for H. throughout the day, |
| W-pI 152.12:1 | and hourly invite H. with the words with |
| W-pI 153.17:2 | by and wait on H. and listen to His Voice, |
| W-pI 153.17:2 | while thanking H. for all the gifts He gave |
| W-pI 153.18:1 | you will never cease to think of H., and |
| W-pI 153.18:3 | keep your mind away from H. a moment, |
| W-pI 153.20:4 | them to all their brothers come from H.. |
| W-pI 153.20:6 | is all you need to give H. in return. You |
| W-pI 154.3:3 | becomes His messenger of unity with H.. |
| W-pI 154.12:4 | until you have identified with H. and with |
| W-pI 155.h | I will step back and let H. lead the way. |
| W-pI 155.10:6 | with you. Let H. lead you with the rest. |
| W-pI 155.12:6 | that walks before us now is one with H., |
| W-pI 155.14:1 | but that you think of H. a while each day, |
| W-pI 155.14:3 | *I will step back and let H. lead the way, For I* |
| W-pI 155.14:3 | *way, For I would walk along the road to H..* |
| W-pI 156.2:4 | God, because you could not be without H. |
| W-pI 156.2:8 | That life you share with H.. Nothing can |
| W-pI 156.2:9 | Nothing can be apart from H. and live. |

W-pI...156.7:5 and mistake **H.** for the senseless, ancient
W-pI...160.7:6 is sure of what belongs to **H.**. No stranger
W-pI...160.8:5 joined remain forever one, at home in **H.**,
W-pI...163.7:2 by those who did not want **H.** to survive.
W-pI......164.h are we one with **H.** Who is our Source.
W-pI...165.7:4 And the Thought of **H.** is never absent.
W-pI...165.7:5 must abide within you who are host to **H.**.
W-pI...165.7:6 between **H.** and your certainty of Him.
W-pI...165.7:6 between Him and your certainty of **H.**.
W-pI...165.8:5 Thought of **H.** is still beyond all dreams
W-pI.167.11:3 there is one life, and that we share with **H.**
W-pI...168.1:2 Shall we not speak to **H.**? He is not distant
W-pI...168.1:5 We try to hide from **H.**, and suffer from
W-pI...168.2:6 And memory of **H.** awakens in the mind
W-pI...168.2:6 the means of **H.** whereby its sleep is done.
W-pI...168.4:2 Son. Request **H.** now to give the means by
W-pI...168.5:3 down, and rise to **H.** in gratitude and love
W-pI...168.6:1 He descends to meet us, as we come to **H.**.
W-pI...168.6:4 To **H.** we pray today, returning but the
W-pI...169.5:3 No mind holds anything but **H.**. We say
W-pI.170.10:5 be upon His Lips; the fire comes from **H.**.
W-pI.170.10:6 all who acknowledge **H.** to be their God.
W-pI.170.12:4 You have chosen **H.** in place of idols, and
WpI.. rV.in9:8 Our Father wills His Son be one with **H.**.
W-pI...173.1:1 I will step back and let **H.** lead the way.
W-pI...177.2:1 (164) Now are we one with **H.** Who is our
W-pI...183.7:3 little prayers of those who call on **H.** with
W-pI...183.7:4 They cannot reach **H.** thus. He cannot
W-pI...183.8:1 acknowledge **H.** as sole Creator of reality.
W-pI...183.8:2 also that His Son is part of **H.**, creating in
W-pI.183.10:6 He calls on **H.** to let all things he thought
W-pI.185.13:3 To take away is meaningless to **H.**. And
W-pI.185.13:4 can be sure you share one Will with **H.**,
W-pI.186.12:6 and urges that you now remember **H.**.
W-pI.187.10:3 Not separate from **H.** Who is our Source;
W-pI...188.1:7 with you from **H.** Who is your Source. It
W-pI...188.7:1 These thoughts you think with **H.**. They
W-pI...189.8:2 You need not know the way to **H.**. Your
W-pI...189.8:7 way to reach **H.** is merely to let Him be.
W-pI...189.8:7 way to reach Him is merely to let **H.** be.
W-pI...189.9:1 not choose the way in which we go to **H.**.
W-pI...189.9:2 But we do choose to let **H.** come. And
W-pI...189.9:7 His Son to show **H.** how to find His way.
W-pI...193.1:2 His Son inherited of **H.** be undisturbed;
W-pI...193.1:2 eternally open and wholly limitless in **H.**.
W-pI.193.13:1 that lets it be to you another step to **H.**,
W-pI.193.13:7 deny the little steps He asks you take to **H.**
W-pI...194.3:4 with the next one given **H.** already, is a
W-pI...194.4:2 They are one to **H.**, and so they should be
W-pI...194.8:2 you call the memory of **H.** to come again,
W-pI...194.9:5 we will appeal to **H.** Who guards our rest
W-pI...195.1:7 gratitude is due to **H.** alone Who made all
W-pI...195.6:1 no living thing, and therefore one with **H.**.
W-pI.195.10:1 Our gratitude will pave the way to **H.**,
W-pI.195.10:4 and the Source of love, along with **H.**.
W-pI.195.10:5 gratitude to **H.** is one with His to you. For
W-pI.196.11:4 on **H.** to save you from illusions by His
W-pI.196.11:4 calling **H.** Father and yourself His Son.
W-pI...197.5:1 God blesses every gift you give to **H.**, and
W-pI...197.5:1 you give to Him, and every gift is given **H.**
W-pI.198.12:5 Itself, so like to **H.** Whose Son he is, that
W-pI...204.1:2 *free in God, forever and forever one with **H.**.*
W-pI...207.1:3 *I need but turn to **H.**, and every sorrow melts*
W-pI...210.1:3 *I thought apart from **H.** and from His Will.*
W-pI...213.1:3 *I learn of **H.** becomes the way I am set free.*
W-pII.....in.2:5 far along the road, and now we wait for **H.**
W-pII.....in.2:6 will continue spending time with **H.** each
W-pII.....in.2:9 of **H.** as we are tempted to forget our goal.
W-pII.....in.3:4 have called on **H.**, and He has promised
W-pII.....in.4:1 Now do we come to **H.** with but His
W-pII.....in.4:1 and wait for **H.** to take the step to us that
W-pII.....in.4:1 would not fail to take when we invited **H.**.
W-pII.....in.4:2 his madness, nor betrayed his trust in **H.**.
W-pII.....in.4:3 faithfulness earned **H.** the invitation that
W-pII.....in.4:5 So our times with **H.** will now be spent.
W-pII.....in.4:6 and then we wait for **H.** to come to us.
W-pII.....in.9:2 and be what we would make of **H.**. And
W-pII..221.2:6 to hear **H.** speak to us of what we are, and
W-pII.....222.h God is with me. I live and move in **H.**.
W-pII..222.1:4 He shines upon, who also shines on **H.**.
W-pII..223.1:2 home, and I do not exist apart from **H.**.
W-pII..223.1:3 and I have none but those which are of **H.**.
W-pII.....225.h God is my Father, and His Son loves **H.**.
W-pII......2.1:1 that you would find your way to **H.** at last.
W-pII..231.2:3 To remember **H.** is Heaven. This we seek.
W-pII..232.2:3 fear. Have faith in **H.** Who is your Father.
W-pII..232.2:4 Trust all things to **H.**. Let Him reveal all
W-pII..232.2:5 Let **H.** reveal all things to you, and be you
W-pII..233.2:2 give this day to **H.** with no reserve at all.
W-pII..238.2:2 Love, remains to **H.** Whose Love is made
W-pII......3.2:4 and where His Son could be apart from **H.**
W-pII.....242.h This day is God's. It is my gift to **H.**.
W-pII..244.2:4 afraid what will forever be a part of **H.**?
W-pII..246.1:3 me, and all the love which I return to **H.**.
W-pII..253.1:6 with them and **H.** Who has created me.
W-pII..254.2:6 will, as we have chosen to remember **H.**.
W-pII..256.1:9 by which our minds return to **H.** at last.
W-pII..258.1:5 We have no aim but to remember **H.**.
W-pII..260.2:3 Sons are like each other, and alike to **H.**.
W-pII..261.1:5 In **H.** I find my refuge and my strength. In
W-pII..261.1:6 In **H.** is my Identity. In Him is everlasting
W-pII..261.1:7 In **H.** is everlasting peace. And only there
W-pII..266.2:3 How can we lose the way to **H.**, when He
W-pII..266.2:3 the world with those who point to **H.**, and
W-pII..267.1:6 by His Voice, sustained by **H.** in love, and
W-pII..267.1:7 His Voice, assuring me I am at home in **H.**
W-pII..274.2:1 to us today, from **H.** Who is our Father.
W-pII..274.2:2 Give this day to **H.**, and there will be no
W-pII..276.1:4 the Word His Son did not create with **H.**,
W-pII..276.1:7 we need but to acknowledge **H.** Who gave
W-pII..276.1:7 to remember **H.** and so recall our Self.
W-pII..286.2:3 We trust in **H.**, and in our Self, Who still
W-pII..286.2:3 and in our Self, Who still is One with **H.**.
W-pII..302.2:1 Our Love awaits us as we go to **H.**, and
W-pII..302.2:3 and He the Means by which we go to **H.**.
W-pII..309.1:8 of God. Within me is the memory of **H.**.
W-pII..310.2:2 and joy to **H.** Who gave salvation to us,
W-pII.... 11.4:2 and unaware of our eternal unity with **H.**.
W-pII..322.1:3 abides in every gift that I receive of **H.**.
W-pII..324.2:3 We walk together, for we follow **H.**. And
W-pII..327.1:3 and faith in **H.** must surely come to me.
W-pII..327.1:4 still farther on the road that leads to **H.**.
W-pII..327.1:5 give me all the help I need to come to **H.**.
W-pII..328.1:6 **H.** that we must go to recognize our will.
W-pII.... 12.3:2 the death of God, when he abides in **H.**?
W-pII.... 12.5:2 completely His, completely one with **H.**.
W-pII..334.1:4 to all who hear and choose to follow **H.**.
W-pII..341.1:3 *Son, a universe of Thought completing **H.**.*
W-pII..349.2:3 trust in **H.** to send us miracles to bless the
W-pII..349.2:3 and heal our minds as we return to **H.**.
W-pII.....350.h To offer them is to remember **H.**, And
W-pII..350.2:1 And as we gather miracles from **H.**, we
W-pII..350.2:2 For as we remember **H.**, His Son will be
W-pII.... 14.5:1 holy messengers of God who speak for **H.**,
W-pII.....356.h for God. The miracle is thus a call to **H.**.
Wfl........in.1:3 Let us turn to **H.** Who leads the way and
Wfl........in.1:4 To **H.** we leave these lessons, as to Him we
Wfl........in.1:4 as to **H.** we give our lives henceforth. For
Wfl........in.4:1 is our function to remember **H.** on earth,
Wfl........in.4:2 way to **H.** and to the Heaven of His peace.
Wfl........in.6:1 and ask **H.** to help us to learn His lessons,
W-ep .........2:3 of those whom God has called to **H.**.
M-1 ...........1:6 God even if he does not yet believe in **H.**.
M-2 ...........2:5 So is all reality, being of **H.**. The instant
M-4 ...... IV.2:9 thoughts with **H.** Who is their Source.
M-4 ....... V.1:9 God's teachers trust in **H.**. And they are
M-7 ...........4:9 for they have put their trust in **H.**.
M-13 .........8:3 at all. Decide against **H.**, and you choose
M-16 .........4:6 in that instant join with **H.** completely.
M-17 .......6:11 is. Projecting your "forgetting" onto **H.**, it
M-18 .......3:12 *is. Fear is illusion, for you are like **H.**.*
M-19 .........4:5 forever like its Creator, being one with **H.**.
M-19 .........4:8 Now it belongs to **H.** and not to you. You
M-19 .........4:9 You are afraid of **H.**, and do not see you
M-20 .........6:8 your tiny frail imaginings apart from **H.**?
M-20 .......6:13 Attain His peace, and you remember **H.**.
M-21 .........4:6 "I will step back and let **H.** lead the way."
M-22 .........6:4 unfair to God, and thus unfaithful to **H.**.
M-22 .........7:4 up to God's teachers to set limits upon **H.**,
M-23 .........2:8 no longer sees himself as separate from **H.**
M-23 .........3:9 can one who is one with God be unlike **H.**
M-26 .........1:1 is no distance between **H.** and His Son.
M-27 .........2:1 be impossible to think of **H.** as loving. For
M-27 .......4:10 fear. Both are equally meaningless to **H.**.
M-27 .........5:6 His Own creation must stand in fear of **H.**
M-27 .......6:10 in **H.** all created things must be eternal.
M-29 .........8:3 *stands silent in the grace You bring from **H.**.*
C-3.............1:1 is for God and toward God but not of **H.**.
C-3.............2:4 to rise up and to return to **H.** in peace.
C-4.............8:1 but rush to meet **H.** where His altar is.
C-4.............8:3 Here He leans down to lift you up to **H.**,
C-5.............3:1 forever like Himself and One with **H.** –
C-6.............1:2 with **H.** and in His likeness or spirit, is
C-6.............1:5 Christ, His real Son, Who is part of **H.**.
C-ep...........1:5 remember that you walk with **H.** and with
C-ep...........2:2 to **H.** Who loves you as He loves Himself.
C-ep...........4:1 our gratitude to **H.** Who called to us and
C-ep...........4:2 arise and go in faith along the way to **H.**.
C-ep...........4:4 God is here, and with **H.** all our brothers.
C-ep...........5:4 God is welcomed and His Son with **H.**.
C-ep...........5:5 We who complete **H.** offer thanks to Him,
C-ep...........5:5 We who complete Him offer thanks to **H.**,
P-1.............5:9 end. But that is up to **H.**. We are all His
P-1...........5:10 for He would have us all be healed in **H.**.
P-2..........II.6:4 for they have found the way to call to **H.**.
P-2........ IV.5:5 by **H.** to the Holy Spirit as His gift to you?
P-2......... V.6:2 And now God's promises are kept by **H.**.
P-2......... V.6:6 whatever form it takes, is but to call on **H.**
P-2......... V.8:5 Whom you answer, for you called on **H.**.
P-2.....VII.1:14 who calls, and in **H.** he recognizes Himself
P-2.....VII.9:10 enough to wake your memory of **H.**?
P-3...........I.2:9 you; He needs your voice to speak for **H.**.
P-3.........I.2:12 or hear the Voice of **H.** Who is God in you
S-1.........in.1:2 returns the thanks it offers **H.** unto the
S-1.........in.3:1 dispense with idols and remember **H.**.
S-1.........in.3:2 as you lift your heart to **H.** in rising song
S-1...........I.4:4 There they become your gifts to **H.**, for
S-1...........I.4:4 they tell **H.** that you would have no gods
S-1...........I.4:4 that you would have no gods before **H.**;
S-1...........I.4:5 answer be but your remembrance of **H.**?
S-1...........I.5:8 the altar of God. It disappears in **H.**.
S-1...........I.6:4 beside you and helps to raise you up to **H.**
S-1...........I.6:6 prays without fear cannot but reach **H.**.
S-1...........II.1:4 appeal to God, or even involve belief in **H.**
S-2.........in.1:5 to be with you until you reach to **H.**.
S-2...........I.3:2 by which you can return to **H.** in peace.
S-2...........I.3:8 remember **H.** and hate what He created?
S-2..........II.3:6 condemn himself and still remember **H.**?
S-2..........II.6:8 There is no giving but to give like **H.**. All
S-2........ III.1:9 Yet He has willed you learn the way to **H.**,
S-2........ III.4:5 He give the means to you to learn of **H.**,
S-2........ III.4:8 you are one with **H.** in Will and purpose.
S-2........ III.7:4 to Christ, Who welcomes it as gift to **H.**.
S-2........ III.7:7 Give it to **H.** to use instead of you, and
S-3........ III.5:9 Without **H.** there is no healing, for there
S-3........ IV.1:4 but speak for **H.** and never for themselves.
S-3........ IV.3:3 to share with **H.** creation's holy joy. Do
S-3........ IV.3:4 idol for rememberance of **H.** Whose Love
S-3........ IV.3:5 dear to **H.** as is the whole of His creation,
S-3........ IV.5:2 give the role to **H.** you see in His creation.
S-3...... IV.10:7 you until you come to **H.** in peace at last.

## Him 182

- Christ/Self
  - *God*
  - *Holy Spirit*
  - *him*

T-1......... V.6:2 the natural result of choosing to follow **H.**
T-11...... IV.7:3 waits for your acceptance of **H.** as yourself
T-11..... V.18:7 speaks through you, you will hear **H.**.
T-11...... VI.3:7 perceive with **H.** involves no strain at all.
T-11.....VIII.9:1 and His Father is not deceived in **H.**. Do
T-11..VIII.12:1 offended by Christ and are deceived in **H.**.
T-11..VIII.12:2 Heal in Christ and be not offended by **H.**,
T-11..VIII.12:2 by Him, for there is no offense in **H.**. If
T-12........II.6:5 for His Father, or His Father's Love for **H.**.

T-12...... VI.5:6 He knows of the Father's Love for H.. And
T-12...... VI.6:2 He knows His Father's Love for H.. When
T-13....... V.9:8 He has returned you to the Father with H.
T-13..... V.10:6 And this *you* will see as you look with H.,
T-13..... V.10:6 love to you, given H. of the Father for you.
T-13..... V.11:2 And all who would behold H. can see Him
T-13..... V.11:2 And all who would behold Him can see H.
T-13..... V.11:3 Nor will they see H. alone, for He is no
T-13..... V.11:4 Son, they have risen in H. to the Father.
T-13..... V.11:5 the Christ in them, and recognized H.. In
T-13...... VI.3:3 is as He was created, there is no guilt in H.
T-13...... VI.3:4 No cloud of guilt has risen to obscure H.,
T-13...... VI.3:4 meet because you see H. through Himself.
T-13..... VII.5:7 is still there, although you know H. not.
T-13..... VII.6:4 As you follow H., you will rejoice that you
T-13..... VII.6:4 and learned of H. the joyful journey home
T-13... VII.14:3 *I go? What need have I but to awake in H.?*
T-13.... VIII.5:6 Help H. to give His gift of light to all who
T-13.... VIII.5:6 and let H. gather them into His quiet
T-13.... VIII.6:2 His Father as they were offered unto H..
T-13.... VIII.6:7 to you. His Being is His Father's gift to H..
T-14....... II.7:8 join H. in the holy task of bringing light.
T-15.... VIII.4:7 in which He gives as His Father gives to H.
T-15...... XI.2:4 of any kind, of anyone, is asked by H.. In
T-15...... XI.2:9 protects, and Whose power protects H..
T-16...... III.7:5 He is, will grow and help you honor H..
T-16...... III.7:6 and purity, and love H. as His Father does
T19... IV.D.2:2 brush the veil aside and run to meet H.,
T19... IV.D.2:2 to meet Him, and to join with H. at last.
T19... IV.D.4:6 the face of Christ and join H. in His Father
T19. IV.D.14:3 veil of sin upon H. to hide His loveliness.
T-20...... IV.5:6 upon the face of Christ, and see H. sinless.
T-22......... I.8:7 holiness of your relationship to let H. live.
T-22........ I.11:3 What is as like H. as a holy relationship?
T-22........ I.11:4 your brother together draws H. to you.
T-22........ I.11:6 for faith in another is always faith in H..
T-22........ I.11:7 here you will with H. and with His Father.
T-22...... IV.3:9 His messenger, returning H. unto Himself
T-22...... IV.4:1 that you will see, who walk with H.! And
T-24....... V.1:3 that it is one with H. and with His Father.
T-24....... V.3:4 Identify with H., and what has He that
T-24....... V.6:4 hand you hold, and whom you lead to H..
T-24....... V.7:5 to look upon with H. and share His joy.
T-24...... V.7:10 There is no journey but to walk with H..
T-24.... VI.13:5 To H. this judgment makes no sense at all
T-24.... VI.13:5 and there is no alternative for H. to see.
T-25....... in.1:8 made manifest to those who know H. not,
T-25....... in.1:8 He may call to them to come to H. and see
T-25....... in.1:8 H. where they thought their bodies were.
T-25....... in.2:1 in him can fail to recognize H. everywhere
T-25....... in.2:4 And so he carries H. unknowingly, and
T-25....... in.2:4 and does not make H. manifest. And thus
T-25....... in.2:5 thus he does not recognize H. where He is
T-25....... in.3:4 it with the Holiness that shines from H..
T-25....... in.3:5 body says or does but makes H. manifest.
T-25....... in.3:6 To those who know H. not it carries Him
T-25....... in.3:6 not it carries H. in gentleness and love, to
T-25......... I.1:5 the body through the mind at one with H.
T-25......... I.1:7 meet and join and raise H. to His Father,
T-25......... I.2:1 to look on holiness and see H. there?
T-25......... I.4:6 and your brother stand before H. now, to
T-25......... I.4:6 to let H. draw aside the veil that seems to
T-25....... V.2:1 your enemy, and God along with H..
T-25...... V.2:11 Savior, seeing H. through sightless eyes?
T-25.. VIII.12:5 Your special function is a call to H., that
T-26...... VI.2:5 Without H. you are friendless. Seek not
T-26...... VI.3:3 take the place of H. Whom God has called
T-26...... VI.3:6 when you make room for H. on His.
T-29.... VIII.3:6 veil that seems to shut you off from H.,
T-30....... V.7:4 will look on H. Whose hand they hold.
T-30....... V.8:3 hold was waiting but for you to join H..
T-30....... V.8:5 surely as His Father's Love rests upon H..
T-30....... V.8:6 enabled H. to rise from chains and go
T-30.... VIII.5:8 in him because you let H. come to you.
T-30.... VIII.5:9 to you, you will be certain you are like H.,
T-31........ I.10:5 Yet you will recognize H. as you give Him
T-31........ I.10:5 as you give H. answer in the language that
T-31........ I.10:6 will appear when you have answered H.,
T-31........ I.10:6 and you will know in H. that God is Love.
T-31 ....... II.7:6 when God appointed H. His only Son.
T-31 ... VIII.2:7 you have brought your weakness unto H.,
T-31 ... VIII.4:4 The saviors of the world, who see like H.,
T-31 ... VIII.4:4 of their own weakness, seen apart from H.
T-31 . VIII.12:2 the abode You set for H. before time was,
W-pI..... 68.7:6 *all my grievances aside and wakening in H..*
W-pI... 100.9:2 And you can reach H. now. What could
W-pI... 100.9:3 look upon in place of H. Who waits that
W-pI... 100.9:3 Him Who waits that you may look on H.?
W-pI. 100.10:7 And it is H. you answer, every time you
W-pI... 107.8:1 Begin by asking H. Who goes with you
W-pI... 107.8:1 He be in your awareness as you go with H.
W-pI... 107.8:2 which gave the gift of life to H. as well. He
W-pI... 107.9:1 which tell you you could be apart from H..
W-pI... 107.9:2 You speak to H. today, and make your
W-pI... 107.9:5 *mind, And I will rest in H. Who is my Self.*
W-pI... 107.9:6 Then let H. lead you gently to the truth,
W-pI. 107.11:2 speak for all the world and H. Who would
W-pI... 110.8:1 Seek H. within you Who is Christ in you,
W-pI... 110.8:1 with power to save whoever touches H.,
W-pI... 110.8:1 Word that tells him he is brother unto H..
W-pI. 110.10:1 Seek H. today, and find Him. He will be
W-pI. 110.10:1 Seek Him today, and find H.. He will be
W-pI. 110.10:3 have made. For when you find H., you will
W-pI... 121.6:5 your mind as one to H. Who is your Self,
W-pI... 125.8:4 let H. tell you God has never left His Son,
W-pI... 151.8:3 The Voice for God can only honor H.,
W-pI. 151.12:3 and your Creator, Who is One with H.. So
W-pI... 153.6:3 your own weakness, seen apart from H..
W-pI... 159.9:7 And they return them gladly unto H..
W-pI. 159.10:6 Let us an instant dream with H.. His
W-pI... 160.9:1 to search the world for what belongs to H.
W-pI... 160.9:3 They see H. as a stranger, for they do not
W-pI... 160.9:4 as they give H. welcome, they remember.
W-pI. 160.10:4 will not remember H. until you look on all
W-pI. 160.10:5 Who denies his brother is denying H.,
W-pI... 164.3:2 quiet is the time you give to spend with H.
W-pI... 164.5:3 of judgment left to H. Who judges true.
WpI...rV.in9:5 To H. we go together. Take your brother's
W-pI... 182.5:3 voice cries unto you to let H. rest a while.
W-pI... 182.5:7 But give H. just a little time to be Himself,
W-pI... 182.6:5 You will fail H. not. He will go home, and
W-pI... 182.6:6 He will go home, and you along with H..
W-pI... 182.7:5 For He would bring you back with H.,
W-pI... 182.7:7 you, calling you to let H. go in peace,
W-pI... 182.7:7 to where He is at home and you with H..
W-pI... 182.8:2 to you that you will not resist H. longer.
W-pI... 182.8:3 you will stay with H. in perfect stillness,
W-pI... 182.9:1 Rest with H. frequently today. For He
W-pI... 182.9:2 might learn of H. how strong is he who
W-pI... 182.9:4 He asks that they protect H., for His home
W-pI. 182.10:3 Go home with H. from time to time today
W-pI. 182.11:3 ask your help in letting H. go home today,
W-pI. 182.11:5 asks unceasingly that you return with H.,
W-pI. 182.12:9 Be still an instant and go home with H.,
W-pI... 197.7:3 for everyone must live and move in H..
W-pI... 197.9:5 All that you do is given unto H.. All that
W-pI... 197.9:6 sharing with H. the holy Thoughts of God
W-pII . 237.2:2 *I come to You through H. Who is Your Son,*
W-pII . 269.2:2 we look upon the face of H. Whose Self is
W-pII . 269.2:3 one because of H. Who is the Son of God;
W-pII . 269.2:3 of God; of H. Who is our own Identity.
W-pII . 270.2:3 we offer healing to the world through H.,
W-pII ..... 6.1:1 Christ is God's Son as He created H.. He
W-pII ..... 6.2:1 despair, for hope forever will abide in H..
W-pII ..... 6.2:5 though in H. His Father placed the means
W-pII ..... 9.5:6 can reach our Father's Love through H..
W-pII . 303.1:5 let H. hear the sounds He understands,
W-pII . 303.1:6 Let H. no longer be a stranger here, for He
W-pII . 322.1:4 Holy One Who still abides in H. forever,
W-pII . 353.1:1 *will serve the purpose that I share with H..*
W-pII . 353.1:4 *A while I work with H. to serve His purpose.*
W-pII .... 354.h And in H. Is His Creator, as He is in me.
W-pII . 354.1:5 *Thus must I be one with You as well as H..*
W-pII . 354.1:6 *is Christ except Your Son as You created H.?*
M-4 ..... V.1:14 need of them is just as great as theirs of H.
M-14 ......... 2:5 home, for here there is need of H. indeed.
M-14 ......... 2:6 He brings the ending of the world with H.
M-14 ......... 2:7 to H. in silence to receive His Word. The
C-6 ............ 1:1 Christ, the Son of God as He created H..
C-ep .......... 5:3 for us. Let us go and bid H. welcome Who
P-2....... VII.2:4 into which psychotherapy invites H..
P-2....... VII.2:6 what choice is there except to have H. stay
S-2........... I.6:4 look through His and learn to see like H..
S-2........... I.7:1 and ask H. how to learn forgiveness as His
S-2........... I.7:2 your salvation rests on learning this of H..
S-2........... I.7:6 Who sees no evil in it sees like H.. For
S-2......... III.3:4 Let H. take charge of how you would
S-2......... III.5:5 you look on him, and speak for H. as well.
S-2......... III.6:4 About the role forgiveness has in H.. Do
S-2......... III.6:7 Forgiveness has been given H. to teach, to
S-3.......... II.2:4 Now we can behold H. without blinders,
S-3......... IV.2:6 to see His likeness and to teach like H..
S-3......... IV.6:6 Christ and let H. be your Guide to healing

**Him** 442
• Holy Spirit
*God*
*Christ/Self*
*him*

T-2 ... V.A.18:3 *I am here to represent H. Who sent me. I do*
T-2 ... V.A.18:6 *I will be healed as I let H. teach me to heal.*
T-5 .......... I.3:2 but I can bring H. to you only at your own
T-5 ....... III.3:4 mind, and you will recognize H. in yours.
T-5 ....... III.7:2 ability to deal with symbols enables H. to
T-5 ....... III.7:3 enables H. to understand the laws of God,
T-5 ....... IV.6:2 By following H. you are led back to God
T-5 ..... VI.12:8 you must give H. as you received Him.
T-5 ..... VI.12:8 you must give Him as you received H..
T-5 .... VII.6:10 *of my wrong decision if I will let H.. I choose*
T-5 .... VII.6:11 *I choose to let H., by allowing Him to decide*
T-5 .... VII.6:11 *by allowing H. to decide for God for me.*
T-6 ........ II.12:6 gave to H. and for which He must speak,
T-6 ........ II.13:1 and only by recognizing H. impartially
T-6 ........ II.13:1 impartially can you recognize H. at all.
T-6 ....... III.2:2 from the Holy Spirit and teach only by H..
T-6 ....... IV.3:3 Everyone has called upon H. for help at
T-6 ......... V.1:1 teaches only to make you equal with H..
T-6 ..... V.C.5:8 nature of the steps you must take with H..
T-6 ... V.C.10:2 you to take this step, if you follow H..
T-6 ... V.C.10:3 is the sign that you *want* H. to guide you.
T-7 ......... V.5:1 and healing that is of H. *always* works.
T-7 ......... V.5:2 always heals by H. the results will vary.
T-7 ........ VI.6:2 all. They therefore do not exist for H.. He
T-7 ....... IX.5:1 your awareness whenever you will let H..
T-7 ....... XI.1:3 Following H. is therefore the easiest thing
T-8 ......... II.1:3 of the curriculum, you must learn it of H..
T-8 ......... II.5:3 make this distinction without H. because
T-8 ....... III.2:5 That is why you need H., and why God
T-8 ....... III.2:5 need Him, and why God gave H. to you.
T-8 ...... VII.9:6 to H. replaces devotion to the ego. In this
T-8 ....... IX.3:8 on behalf of waking if you will let H..
T-9 .......... I.3:8 effort, within the limits you impose on H.,
T-9 ......... I.10:6 because your requests to H. are real,
T-9 ......... II.3:3 that no response given by H. will ever be
T-9 ........ II.12:1 the Holy Spirit, then, only by giving to H.,
T-9 ........ II.12:1 give to H. only where you recognize Him.
T-9 ........ II.12:1 give to Him only where you recognize H..
T-9 ........ II.12:2 If you recognize H. in everyone, consider
T-9 ........ II.12:2 how much you will be asking of H., and
T-9 ........ II.12:3 because you have denied H. nothing, and
T-9 ....... III.4:2 you attend to them you are not hearing H.
T-9 ....... III.4:3 If you do not hear H., you are listening to
T-9 ....... III.8:8 Give it to H.! You do not understand how
T-9 ....... IV.3:4 this through H. you cannot look on your
T-9 ......... V.8:6 You can only let H. fulfill His function. He
T-9 ........ V.8:11 Trust H., for help is His function, and He
T-9 ........ V.8:12 other minds to the Holy Spirit through H.
T-9 ....... VI.1:2 You cannot see H. with your eyes nor hear
T-9 ....... VI.1:2 with your eyes nor hear H. with your ears.
T-9 ....... VI.1:3 How, then, can you perceive H. at all? If
T-9 ....... VI.2:4 you offer to your brother you offer to H.,
T-11 ......... I.8:7 Ask H., therefore, what God's Will is for
T-11 ........ II.5:3 your care is a sign that you want H..
T-11 ........ II.5:4 Think like H. ever so slightly, and the
T-11 ........ II.5:6 but you have allied yourself against H..
T-11 ........ II.6:7 If you will merely offer H. a little place, He

| | |
|---|---|
| T-11... VIII.2:4 | for you, and if you will let **H.** interpret it, |
| T-11... VIII.2:5 | you will see no need to ask it of **H.**. |
| T-11... VIII.3:8 | willingness to learn of **H.** depends on your |
| T-12....... I.10:5 | thus will you learn of **H.** how to replace |
| T-12....... II.9:8 | offered it to **H.** and He cannot take it from |
| T-12..... II.10:4 | is given **H.** that is not of God is gone. Yet |
| T-12...... IV.5:7 | brothers home you are but following **H.**. |
| T-12...... VI.2:5 | never ceases to remind **H.** of His Son, and |
| T-12...... VI.2:6 | God is in your memory because of **H.**. |
| T-12...... VI.4:8 | **H.** your Father calls His Son to remember. |
| T-12..... VII.6:1 | me it will be because you have invited **H.**. |
| T-13......... I.4:5 | for such was His mission, given **H.** by God |
| T-13...... III.7:3 | from His sight, but bring it gladly to **H.**. |
| T-13...... III.7:4 | sanity all your hurt, and let **H.** heal you. |
| T-13... VII.10:8 | because of **H.** the answer is a joyous *yes!* As |
| T-13... VII.13:1 | Leave, then, your needs to **H.**. He will |
| T-13... VII.13:3 | What comes to you of **H.** comes safely, for |
| T-13... VII.15:1 | Then follow **H.** in joy, with faith that He |
| T-13... VIII.4:3 | and God has given **H.** to you because He |
| T-13... VIII.8:1 | through **H.** Who knows of freedom. Unite |
| T-13....... X.2:8 | own ends what you should have given **H.**, |
| T-13....... X.7:4 | Spirit does what God would have **H.** do, |
| T-13....... X.7:7 | see and teach as He does, and through **H.**. |
| T-13...... XI.4:4 | finally let **H.** judge the difference for you, |
| T-13...... XI.4:4 | allowing **H.** to demonstrate which must |
| T-13...... XI.5:1 | gave **H.** the mission to remove all doubt |
| T-13...... XI.6:8 | fail in what your Father has given **H.** to do |
| T-14...... III.6:6 | and would have you teach with **H.**. It is |
| T-14.... III.11:8 | offers you but what God gave **H.** for you. |
| T-14.... III.14:1 | Let **H.**, therefore, be the only Guide that |
| T-14.... III.14:3 | **H.** you will not fail to learn that what God |
| T-14.... III.14:5 | is of **H.** to Whom God gave it for you. He |
| T-14.... III.14:7 | it. Forget **H.** not and He will make every |
| T-14.... III.15:5 | Be quiet in your faith in **H.** Who loves you |
| T-14.... III.17:1 | it is to decide all things through **H.** Whose |
| T-14.... III.17:3 | Father would have you share it with **H.**. In |
| T-14.... III.17:4 | In everything be led by **H.**, and do not |
| T-14.... III.17:5 | Trust **H.** to answer quickly, surely, and |
| T-14.... III.19:4 | *And so I trust H. to communicate to me all* |
| T-14.... III.19:5 | let **H.** teach you quietly how to perceive |
| T-14..... V.1:10 | to the Holy Spirit, and to God through **H.**. |
| T-14...... VI.5:3 | All things you made have use to **H.**, for |
| T-14...... VI.5:7 | to crucify yourself must learn of **H.** how to |
| T-14...... VI.6:6 | Leave what you would communicate to **H.** |
| T-14...... VI.8:4 | to **H.** and let His gentleness teach you that |
| T-14..... VII.5:9 | is mighty, but the power of God is with **H.** |
| T-14... VII.5:10 | to **H.** it is so easy that it was accomplished |
| T-14... VII.5:10 | the instant it was given **H.** for you. Do not |
| T-14... VII.5:11 | He can fulfill what God has given **H.** to do |
| T-14... VII.5:12 | Leave that to **H.** Who knows. You are not |
| T-14... VII.5:14 | do, trusting **H.** only to the small extent of |
| T-14..... VII.6:1 | bring to **H.** every secret you have locked |
| T-14..... VII.6:1 | secret you have locked away from **H.**. |
| T-14..... VII.6:2 | Open every door to **H.**, and bid Him enter |
| T-14..... VII.6:2 | bid **H.** enter the darkness and lighten it |
| T-14..... VII.6:4 | if you make the darkness open to **H.**. But |
| T-14..... VII.6:6 | unless you look with **H.** He cannot see. |
| T-14..... VII.6:7 | The vision of Christ is not for **H.** alone, |
| T-14..... VII.6:7 | is not for Him alone, but for **H.** with you. |
| T-14..... VII.6:8 | all your dark and secret thoughts to **H.**, |
| T-14..... VII.6:8 | to Him, and look upon them with **H.**. He |
| T-14..... VII.7:1 | Joining with **H.** in seeing is the way in |
| T-14..... VII.7:1 | in which you learn to share with **H.** the |
| T-14..... VII.7:3 | Sharing perception with **H.** Whom God |
| T-14..... VII.7:5 | with **H.** will show you that all meaning, |
| T-14..... VII.7:9 | All honor to you through **H.**, and through |
| T-14..... VII.7:9 | through Him, and through **H.** unto God. |
| T-14... VIII.1:7 | promised the Father that through **H.** you |
| T-14... VIII.1:8 | promise that was given **H.** to share with |
| T-14... VIII.2:2 | the one promise given unto **H.** to lay upon |
| T-14. VIII.2:11 | His Son, speaks to His Son through **H.**. |
| T-14...... XI.4:3 | child of light by **H.** to Whom God gave it. |
| T-14...... XI.4:7 | that you bring to **H.** Who teaches light He |
| T-14...... XI.4:9 | learned apart from **H.** means anything. |
| T-14.... XI.6:11 | instant you abandon it, and offer it to **H.**. |
| T-14...... XI.8:5 | Thus would you make **H.** undependable, |
| T-14...... XI.8:5 | for keeping certain dark lessons from **H.**. |
| T-14...... XI.9:9 | For the past binds **H.** not, and therefore |
| T-14.... XI.10:5 | You can deny **H.**, but you cannot call on |
| T-14.... XI.10:5 | Him, but you cannot call on **H.** in vain. |
| T-14.. XI.10:10 | with every one you let **H.** do through you. |
| T-14.... XI.11:4 | and do not raise your voice against **H.**. |
| T-14.... XI.11:6 | Teach like **H.** here, and you will |
| T-14.... XI.13:4 | for you will have invited **H.** to do so by |
| T-14.... XI.13:4 | so by abandoning the ego on behalf of **H.**. |
| T-14.... XI.13:6 | fill every mind that so makes room for **H.**. |
| T-14.... XI.14:3 | desert **H.** but He will never reciprocate, |
| T-15......... I.1:4 | learner that you learn only of **H.**. When |
| T-15......... I.2:5 | It does not waste **H.**, as it does you. And |
| T-15....... I.11:4 | you to be willing to give **H.** this than for |
| T-15....... I.11:4 | than for **H.** to use this tiny instant to offer |
| T-15....... I.13:6 | to give what you would receive of **H.**, for |
| T-15....... I.13:6 | of Him, for you join with **H.** in giving. In |
| T-15..... I.15:11 | Spirit, and leave His giving it to you to **H.**. |
| T-15....... II.2:7 | Through **H.** you stand before God's altar, |
| T-15..... II.4:12 | the witness to **H.** will speak so clearly of |
| T-15..... II.4:12 | of **H.** that you will hear and understand. |
| T-15...... III.4:2 | it reaches you through **H.** *from* Magnitude. |
| T-15...... III.6:2 | side against **H.** in what He wills for you. |
| T-15...... III.6:3 | Decide for God through **H.**. For littleness, |
| T-15...... IV.8:4 | for you are not ready to share it with **H.**. |
| T-15....... V.5:3 | removing as much fear as you will let **H.**. |
| T-15....... V.5:4 | if you offer **H.** your willingness to have it |
| T-15..... VII.5:4 | at them, you will offer them gladly to **H.**. |
| T-15... VII.13:3 | power of God in **H.** and you is joined in a |
| T-15... VIII.1:3 | to learn of **H.** what the truth must be. He |
| T-15... VIII.1:4 | whatever you offer **H.** on behalf of this. |
| T-15... VIII.2:1 | Hear **H.** gladly, and learn of Him that you |
| T-15... VIII.2:1 | and learn of **H.** that you have need of no |
| T-15... VIII.6:4 | to **H.** Who knows it must be possible |
| T-15... VIII.6:5 | And let **H.** Whose teaching is only of God |
| T-15...... IX.5:2 | No one can hear **H.** speak of this and long |
| T-15....... X.1:7 | and let me celebrate *your* birth through **H.** |
| T-15...... XI.3:2 | that you may join with **H.** in healing, and |
| T-16......... I.1:3 | provided you let **H.** use it in His way. His |
| T-16....... I.3:11 | *I have invited H., and He is here. I need do* |
| T-16......... I.4:1 | empathy is of **H.** Who knows what it is. |
| T-16......... I.4:2 | if you let **H.** use your capacity for strength |
| T-16......... I.4:3 | you, but be sure that you desert not **H.**. |
| T-16......... I.5:5 | Attempt to teach **H.** not. You are the |
| T-16......... I.5:8 | anyone. Offer your empathy to **H.** for it is |
| T-16......... I.5:9 | And let **H.** offer you His strength and His |
| T-16......... I.7:4 | all to **H.** Whose function is to meet them. |
| T-16......... I.7:6 | share everything you give through **H.**. |
| T-16......... I.7:8 | give through **H.** is for the whole Sonship, |
| T-16......... I.7:9 | Leave **H.** His function, for He will fulfill it |
| T-16......... I.7:9 | you but ask **H.** to enter your relationships |
| T-16....... II.4:4 | have offered it to **H.** to use as He sees fit, |
| T-16....... II.4:4 | of your gift enables **H.** to understand it, |
| T-16....... II.6:2 | Yet your relationship with **H.** is real. |
| T-16....... II.6:5 | Bid **H.** welcome, and honor the witnesses |
| T-16....... II.6:6 | to acknowledge **H.** is to deny all that you |
| T-16....... II.9:8 | Have faith in **H.** Who has faith in you. |
| T-16...... III.1:6 | and what you have taught through **H.**, |
| T-16...... III.5:3 | and you, as you are God and **H.** together. |
| T-16.... VI.12:1 | you, enter with **H.** into a holy instant, and |
| T-16.... VI.12:1 | a holy instant, and there let **H.** release you |
| T-16.... VI.12:4 | and it is His faith you share with **H.** there. |
| T-16.... VI.12:6 | Call upon **H.**, for Heaven is at His Call. |
| T-16.... VI.12:7 | Call. And let **H.** call on Heaven for you. |
| T-16..... VII.7:3 | Spirit will prevail, because you joined **H.**. |
| T-16..... VII.7:4 | weaken the experience of **H.** for a while, |
| T-17......... I.3:5 | away from **H.** Who would release you. |
| T-17......... I.6:1 | the truth to **H.** Who knows the truth, and |
| T-17....... II.1:9 | to seeing it and giving thanks with **H.**. |
| T-17....... II.5:3 | reason that He brings, as you follow **H.**, |
| T-17....... II.8:4 | your impatience at delay in meeting **H.**. |
| T-17....... II.8:5 | and walk with **H.** in trust out of this world |
| T-17...... III.5:2 | What forgiveness *is* enables **H.** to do so. If |
| T-17...... III.5:7 | is given to **H.** Who gives it life and beauty. |
| T-17...... III.6:7 | Let **H.** uncover the hidden spark of beauty |
| T-17...... III.7:1 | if you but let **H.** hold the spark before you |
| T-17...... III.7:8 | Give the past to **H.** Who can change your |
| T-17...... IV.4:5 | **H.** is your relationship with God restored |
| T-17...... IV.4:6 | with **H.** has never been broken, because |
| T-17...... IV.4:7 | **H.** have all your holy relationships been |
| T-17....... V.3:1 | the practical results of asking **H.** to enter. |
| T-17....... V.7:6 | Have faith in **H.** Who answered you. He |
| T-17..... V.7:13 | Abandon **H.** not now, nor your brother. |
| T-17..... V.11:3 | enormous efforts to help **H.** do His work. |
| T-17..... V.11:4 | appreciation for all you have done for **H.**. |
| T-17..... V.15:2 | to **H.** Who gave you your release, and |
| T-17... VII.10:1 | call for faith because of **H.** Who walks |
| T-17.... VIII.6:7 | keep you separate from **H.** Whose Call you |
| T-18......... I.9:8 | Let **H.** bring it here, where *you* would have |
| T-18......... I.9:9 | Give **H.** but a little faith in your brother, |
| T-18......... I.9:9 | help **H.** show you that no substitute you |
| T-18........ II.7:6 | uses everyone who calls on **H.** as means |
| T-18........ II.7:7 | you who offered your relationship to **H.**. |
| T-18...... II.7:10 | one purpose, being of one mind with **H.**. |
| T-18...... IV.1:6 | will add the ego to **H.** and confuse the two |
| T-18.... IV.1:10 | so little that enables **H.** to give so much. |
| T-18...... IV.6:5 | holy instant belongs to **H.** Who gives it. |
| T-18...... IV.6:6 | yourself to **H.** Whose function is release. |
| T-18...... IV.6:7 | Do not assume His function for **H.**. Give |
| T-18...... IV.6:8 | Give **H.** but what He asks, that you may |
| T-18....... V.2:5 | part is only to offer **H.** a little willingness |
| T-18....... V.2:5 | to let **H.** remove all fear and hatred, and |
| T-18....... V.2:7 | with **H.**, you will build a ladder planted in |
| T-18....... V.5:6 | Let **H.** fulfill the function that He gave to |
| T-18....... V.6:1 | to let **H.** exchange this instant for the holy |
| T-18.. VIII.13:5 | Receive it now of **H.**, for He would have |
| T-18.. VIII.13:5 | of Him, for He would have you know **H.**. |
| T-18...... IX.3:7 | trusting **H.** not to abandon you and leave |
| T-18...... IX.3:9 | are severely tempted to abandon **H.** at the |
| T-19......... I.2:5 | joining **H.** in a united purpose that makes |
| T-19....... I.11:1 | through **H.** Whom God has given you. |
| T-19....... I.12:2 | and is the sign you share it with **H.**. Faith |
| T-19....... I.12:3 | you offer to the Son of God through **H.**, |
| T-19....... I.12:3 | wholly acceptable to his Father as to **H.**. |
| T-19....... I.12:7 | but in the sight of **H.** Who joined you, |
| T-19...... III.4:2 | correct them all as God entrusted **H.** to do |
| T-19...... III.4:4 | cannot be corrected is meaningless to **H.**. |
| T-19...... IV.2:4 | Holy Spirit asks that you offer **H.** a resting |
| T-19...... IV.2:4 | a resting place where you will rest in **H.**. |
| T-19...... IV.2:6 | and enter into a relationship with **H.?** For |
| T-19...... IV.3:1 | to **H.** He asks but that you receive for Him |
| T-19...... IV.3:1 | to Him He asks but that you receive for **H.** |
| T-19...... IV.3:2 | upon your brother, you are beholding **H.**. |
| T-19...... IV.3:3 | looking where He *is*, and not apart from **H.** |
| T-19...... IV.3:8 | and gratitude that you have offered **H.**, |
| T19. IV.A.5:10 | to stand between **H.** and His holy purpose |
| T19. IV.A.5:11 | But let **H.** quietly extend the miracle of |
| T19... IV.A.7:1 | little insane wish to get rid of **H.** Whom |
| T19... IV.A.7:1 | in and push **H.** out *must* produce conflict. |
| T19... IV.B.8:5 | in **H.** it *is* possible that our communion, |
| T19.. IV.B.17:5 | what is sent through **H.** returns to Him, |
| T19.. IV.B.17:5 | what is sent through Him returns to **H.**, |
| T19.. IV.C.11:7 | Give it to **H.** to judge for you, and say: |
| T19... IV.D.5:3 | of the quiet recognition that you love **H.**. |
| T19. IV.D.17:8 | receive it of **H.** in return for what you gave |
| T-20........ II.5:4 | And what enables **H.** to see His purpose |
| T-20........ II.9:6 | we were meant to find by **H.** Who leads us |
| T-20...... IV.6:3 | not need your part to help **H.** with the rest |
| T-20....... V.2:7 | Who gave the gifts to **H.** to give to you. |
| T-20..... VII.2:2 | means to **H.** Who changed the purpose. |
| T-20..... VII.8:4 | from **H.** Who would undo your teaching. |
| T-20.... VIII.3:1 | vision and to rejoice in along with **H.**. For |
| T-20.... VIII.3:2 | and at one with **H.** on what salvation is. |
| T-20.... VIII.5:9 | it the laws beloved of **H.** Whose sight it is. |
| T-21........ II.3:6 | to **H.** Who must decide for God for you. |
| T-21...... III.1:6 | make it useful to **H.** and harmless to you. |
| T-21...... III.9:4 | And if you seek to limit **H.**, you will hate |
| T-21...... III.9:4 | you will hate **H.** because you are afraid. |
| T-21....... V.5:6 | been there since the need for **H.** arose, |
| T-21...... VI.8:6 | Listen to **H.** Who speaks with reason, and |
| T-22...... VI.8:7 | them, and where and when, is up to **H.**. |
| T-22...... VI.9:3 | Leave this to **H.**. Let your concern be only |
| T-22...... VI.9:4 | you give to **H.** that which can be extended |
| T-22...... VI.9:5 | but offer **H.** the tiny gifts He can extend |
| T-22...... VI.9:8 | to it all the power that God has given **H.**, |
| T-22.... VI.9:11 | be dispelled by **H.** Who knows the light, |
| T-25.... VIII.1:1 | all that you give to **H.** for your salvation. |
| T-25.... VIII.1:5 | You need not give it to **H.** wholly willingly |
| T-25.... VIII.1:5 | for if you could you had no need of **H.**. |
| T-25.... VIII.6:3 | and perceive the "wrath" of God in **H.**. |
| T-25.... VIII.6:4 | they trust **H.** not to strike them dead with |

T-25....VIII.9:3 You are not asked to trust **H.** far. No more
T-25....VIII.9:7 you accept brings joy to **H.** as well as you.
T-25..... IX.3:5 To **H.**, what is unfair must be corrected
T-26....... II.1:3 Every problem is the same to **H.**, because
T-26....... II.2:2 They are the same to **H.** because each one,
T-26....... II.2:4 for **H.** to bring to truth than is another.
T-26....... II.4:5 They have no properties to **H.**. They are
T-26..... II.6:10 For what you give to **H.** is everyone's, and
T-27..... II.12:4 Yet must He work with what is given **H.**,
T-27..... II.12:4 and you allow **H.** only half your mind.
T-27...... VI.1:3 it away from **H.** and focusing upon itself.
T-27....VIII.9:3 you bring each terrible effect to **H.** that
T-27....VIII.9:3 its foolish cause and laugh with **H.** a while
T-27....VIII.9:7 But hear **H.** say, "My brother, holy Son of
T-27..VIII.11:3 Whatever hurt you bring to **H.** He will
T-27..VIII.12:1 all forms of suffering to **H.** Who knows
T-28.........I.3:4 employ for healing have been given **H.**,
T-28.......I.12:1 thanks for every quiet instant given **H.**.
T-28...... IV.7:2 not, for what is joined in **H.** is always one.
T-29....... II.4:2 You asked **H.**, and He came. You did not
T-29....... II.4:3 You did not hear **H.** enter, for you did not
T-29....... II.4:3 enter, for you did not wholly welcome **H.**.
T-29....... II.4:4 And yet His gifts came with **H.**. He has
T-29....... II.5:2 you to come where you invited **H.** to be.
T-29....... II.5:3 host, nor where His host can meet with **H.**
T-29....... II.5:5 where He is Who brought them with **H.**,
T-29...... IV.6:5 as means to serve the function given **H.**.
T-29....... V.8:1 that has been kept apart from use by **H.**
T-30....... II.1:4 you that you may do your will through **H.**.
T-30....... II.3:3 **H.** Who is His Voice and yours as well,
T-31..... VII.6:4 Give it instead to **H.** Who understands
W-pI..... 75.7:7 It is His Will, and you have joined with **H.**
W-pI..... 75.7:8 Wait patiently for **H.**. He will be there.
W-pI..... 75.8:1 Tell **H.** you know you cannot fail because
W-pI..... 75.8:1 you cannot fail because you trust in **H.**.
W-pI... 76.10:1 Hear **H.** Who tells you this, and realize
W-pI..... 78.7:1 Then let us ask of **H.** Who knows this Son
W-pI..... 78.7:2 ask **H.** in the holy Name of God and of His
W-pI..... 78.8:5 you see through **H.** will free you both. Be
W-pI..... 78.8:8 role God gave **H.** that you might be saved.
W-pI..... 90.3:6 Spirit will teach me this, if I will let **H.**.
W-pI..... 96.8:1 **H.** Who speaks to you from your one Self.
W-pI..... 96.8:2 will be a search for **H.** within your mind.
W-pI..... 96.8:3 from this one Self through **H.** Who is the
W-pI..... 96.8:4 and let **H.** speak to you about your Self,
W-pI... 96.11:5 seeking **H.** Who joins your mind and Self,
W-pI... 96.11:5 offer **H.** another treasure to be kept for
W-pI..... 97.6:1 Thus will each gift to **H.** be multiplied a
W-pI..... 97.7:1 let them echo round the world through **H.**
W-pI..... 97.7:3 will accept this gift that you received of **H.**
W-pI..... 97.8:1 each practice period today gladly to **H.**.
W-pI..... 97.8:2 that you are spirit, one with **H.** and God,
W-pI..... 97.8:3 let **H.** tell your mind that they are true.
W-pI..... 97.8:6 Receive His words, and offer them to **H.**.
W-pI..... 99.5:1 as it was received of **H.** within the Mind of
W-pI..... 99.6:5 entrusted with this plan, along with **H.**.
W-pI..... 99.9:8 turn to **H.** Who shares your function here,
W-pI..... 99.9:8 let **H.** teach you what you need to learn to
W-pI... 99.12:2 with **H.** Who shares God's plan with you.
W-pI... 121.6:4 Through **H.** you learn how to forgive the
W-pI... 123.5:3 And thanks to you for listening to **H.**. His
W-pI... 123.5:5 thanking **H.** the thanks are yours as well.
W-pI... 126.8:4 Give **H.** your faith today, and ask Him
W-pI... 126.8:4 and ask **H.** that He share your practicing
W-pI. 126.11:5 *And I will trust in* **H.**. Then spend a quiet
W-pI. 126.11:7 And what you hear of **H.** you will believe,
W-pI... 128.7:7 Open your mind to **H.**. Be still and rest.
W-pI. 134.14:5 to teach it. Let us ask of **H.**: *Let me perceive*
W-pI. 135.19:1 Your present trust in **H.** is the defense
W-pI... 137.9:1 the Holy Spirit urges you to follow **H.**. His
W-pI... 151.8:1 Let **H.** be Judge of what you are, for He
W-pI... 151.9:3 body mean to **H.** Who knows the glory of
W-pI... 151.9:5 could convince **H.** that your sins are real?
W-pI... 151.9:6 Let **H.** be Judge as well of everything that
W-pI. 151.13:3 appealing silently to **H.** Who sees the
W-pI. 151.13:4 Let **H.** evaluate each thought that comes
W-pI. 151.14:1 Give **H.** your thoughts, and He will give
W-pI. 151.16:4 to **H.** Who has restored our sanity to us.
W-pI. 151.17:1 will hourly remember **H.** Who is salvation
W-pI... 154.9:6 you identify with **H.** and claim your own.
W-pI. 154.10:2 minds apart from **H.** Who speaks for us,
W-pI. 154.10:2 it is but our voice we hear as we attend **H.**.
W-pI. 154.11:1 practice giving **H.** what He would have,
W-pI... 169.7:3 **H.** Who teaches what forgiveness means.
W-pI... 169.9:3 as perfectly fulfilled by **H.** Who wrote
W-pI. 169.15:2 this day of **H.** Who gives the grace we ask,
W-pI. 169.15:2 gives the grace we ask, as it was given **H.**?
WpI...rV.in8:1 to you from **H.** Who sees your bitter need,
WpI...rV.in8:1 and knows the answer God has given **H.**.
W-pI... 191.5:4 gratitude to **H.** Who pointed out the way
W-pI. 193.11:5 Let us give them all to **H.** Who knows the
W-pI. 198.13:3 that God has given us through **H.** today.
W-pI... 199.6:2 **H.** they have found what they have sought
W-pI... 199.7:5 give your mind to **H.** Who calls to you to
W-pI... 199.7:5 Who calls to you to make this gift to **H.**.
WpI rVI.in.7:1 To **H.** I offer this review for you. I place
WpI rVI.in.7:2 let **H.** teach you what to do and say and
WpI rVI.in.7:2 say and think, each time you turn to **H.**.
WpI rVI.in.7:3 you, each time you call to **H.** to help you.
WpI rVI.in.7:4 us offer **H.** the whole review we now begin
WpI rVI.in.7:4 for us; allowing **H.** to teach us how to go,
WpI rVI.in.7:4 trusting **H.** completely for the way each
W-pI... 215.1:4 *thanks to* **H.** *for showing me the way to go.* I
W-pII... 220.1:3 *But let me follow* **H.** *Who leads me home,*
W-pII ....in.6:2 in gratitude to **H.** Who taught us how to
W-pII ..... 1.5:1 to do, through **H.** Who is your Guide,
W-pII ..... 1.5:2 for such is His function, given **H.** by God.
W-pII ..... 3.4:5 And let **H.** give you peace and certainty,
W-pII ..... 3.4:5 but Heaven has preserved for you in **H.**.
W-pII . 242.1:5 I give this day to **H.**, for I would not delay
W-pII . 255.1:3 have faith in **H.** Who says I am God's Son.
W-pII ..... 6.4:1 your dreams, and bids them come to **H.**,
W-pII ..... 7.1:2 through the grace that God has given **H.**,
W-pII ..... 7.1:2 gift to everyone who turns to **H.** for truth.
W-pII ..... 7.3:3 if you offer them to **H.**, He will employ the
W-pII . 311.1:5 gift of it to **H.** Who has a different use for
W-pII . 347.1:9 *Let* **H.** *judge today. I do not know my will,*
WpII361-5.1:3 these are the gifts I will receive of **H.**. He is
W-ep ......... 1:4 No one who calls on **H.** can call in vain.
W-ep ......... 1:5 if you simply turn to **H.** and ask it of Him.
W-ep ......... 1:5 if you simply turn to Him and ask it of **H.**.
W-ep ......... 1:9 You need but ask it of **H.**, and it will be
W-ep ......... 2:4 follow **H.** Whom you accepted as your
W-ep ......... 3:3 mind, and when to come to **H.** in silence,
W-ep ......... 4:1 with **H.** as Guide through every difficulty
W-ep ......... 4:3 Let **H.** prepare you further. He has earned
W-ep ......... 4:6 Now you walk with **H.**, as certain as is He
W-ep ......... 5:5 And so we walk with **H.** from this time on,
W-ep ......... 5:5 and turn to **H.** for guidance and for peace
W-ep ......... 6:1 We trust our ways to **H.** and say "Amen."
W-ep ......... 6:2 in His way, and trust all things to **H.**. In
M-4 ........X.1:3 so open-mindedness invites **H.** to come in
M-10 ......... 5:9 He gave himself to **H.** Whose judgment he
M-15 ....... 2:11 you still attempt to take His role from **H.**?
M-15 ....... 2:13 aside in quiet listening, and wait for **H.**.
M-18 ......... 2:6 are, so they will gladly be returned to **H.**.
M-18 ......... 4:3 let **H.** judge what the response should be.
M-25 ......... 4:3 What is used for magic is useless to **H.**.
M-25 ......... 6:9 and those who offer them to **H.** and Him
M-25 ......... 6:9 and **H.** alone go with Christ's gratitude
M-28 ......... 6:5 and given **H.** Whose function judgment is
M-29 ....... 2:10 To refer the questions to **H.** is yours.
M-29 ......... 5:5 say anything without consulting **H.**? No,
M-29 ......... 5:9 so, and thank **H.** for His guidance at night
M-29 ......... 6:5 God has given **H.** the power to translate
C-6 ............ 1:3 to accept **H.** and to hear His Voice. His is
S-3........ III.6:2 those He sends to you, to let **H.** heal them,
S-3........ III.6:2 those who serve with **H.** in healing's name

## him 27

• Jesus
*noise word*
*Him*

T-2 .... VII.5:14 that whosoever believeth in **h.** should not
T-3 .......II.5:10 (or be perceived) we shall be like **h.**, for
T-3 .......II.5:10 be like him, for we shall see **h.** as he is."
T-13 .......II.6:2 of God's Son it did attempt to kill **h.**, and
M-23 ......... 1:9 Why is the appeal to **h.** part of healing?
M-23 ......... 3:3 of the Son to the Father lies in **h.**. His part
M-23 ....... 3:11 be unavailable to those who follow **h.**?
M-23 ......... 5:2 Why would you not be grateful to **h.**? He
M-23 ......... 6:9 He will take you with **h.**, for he did not go
M-23 ....... 6:10 And you were with **h.** then, as you are
M-23 ......... 7:1 This course has come from **h.** because his
M-23 ......... 7:7 In **h.** you find God's Answer. Do you, then
M-23 ......... 7:8 Do you, then, teach with **h.**, for he is with
C-5 ............ 3:2 be. He led the way for you to follow **h.**. He
C-5 ............ 3:3 to God because he saw the road before **h.**,
C-5 ............ 4:3 dreams. Arise with **h.** who showed you
C-5 ............ 4:3 this because you owe **h.** this who shared
C-5 ............ 5:6 shared. Walking with **h.** is just as natural
C-5 ............ 5:7 of **h.** who would be only brother to the
C-5 ............ 5:8 Forgive **h.** your illusions, and behold how
C-5 ............ 6:6 them without accepting **h.** into your life.
C-5 ............ 6:7 you will share your pains and joys with **h.**,
C-6 ............ 2:3 therefore given **h.** and he will share it with
C-6 ............ 5:2 calls to you to be His Voice along with **h.**.
C-6 ............ 5:5 He offers thanks to you as well as **h.** for
C-6 ............ 5:5 with **h.** when he began to save the world.
C-6 ............ 5:6 And you will be with **h.** when time is over

## him 1526

• noise word
*Jesus*
*Him*

## Himself 302

• God
*Christ/Self*
*Holy Spirit*
*himself*

T-1 ...... VII.5:7 involve a more direct approach to God **H.**
T-2 ..........I.1:2 God extended **H.** to His creations and
T-2 ..... VIII.4:3 just as God **H.** looked upon what He had
T-3 ..........I.1:9 likely that God **H.** would be capable of the
T-3 ..........I.2:4 that God **H.** persecuted His Own Son on
T-4 ........I.12:6 to be a gift for a creation of God **H.**.
T-4 ....... IV.9:1 in which God **H.** shines in perfect light.
T-5 ..........I.4:9 that God **H.** can flow across the little gap.
T-5 .........II.1:6 obliterate it. God **H.** keeps your will alive
T-5 .........V.7:2 God **H.** orders your thought because your
T-5 ....... VI.1:7 eternity, where God **H.** placed you forever
T-5 ..... VI.10:3 is bearing false witness to God **H.**. Appeal
T-5 ..... VII.4:3 God **H.** gave you the perfect Correction
T-6 ..........I.7:3 it. God placed it there **H.**, and so it is true
T-6 .........V.4:7 Spirit, shining with the light from God **H.**,
T-6 ..... V.B.8:8 difficult if God **H.** created you as a creator
T-6 ..... V.C.2:6 God **H.** has established what you can
T-6 ..... V.C.7:1 center, where God placed the altar to **H.**.
T-7 ..........I.5:2 if God created you by extending **H.** as you
T-7 .........II.3:8 God **H.** created the law by creating *by* it.
T-7 ....... III.1:3 the power of the Kingdom of God **H.**, He
T-7 ....... III.5:1 God has lit your mind **H.**, and keeps your
T-7 .......V.6:14 God cannot be out of accord with **H.**, and
T-7 .........V.9:5 love. That is how God **H.** created you; in
T-7 ...... VII.6:1 whom God **H.** created worthy of honor,
T-7 .... VII.10:7 this as God **H.** is lonely when His Sons do
T-7 ....... IX.1:2 than He wills to deprive **H.** of His. Do not
T-7 .........X.2:2 Yet the function God **H.** gave your mind
T-7 .........X.6:2 are. God **H.** trusts you, and therefore your
T-7 ....... XI.3:5 and that God **H.** thanks him for his giving
T-8 .........II.7:6 Because your Creator creates only like **H.**,
T-8 ....... III.3:6 can know what it means only of God **H.**.
T-8 ....... III.8:3 belongs to Him because He gives of **H.**,
T-8 ..... IV.5:12 mine, and God **H.** would not go against it.
T-8 ....... VI.5:4 your creation as God extended **H.** to you.
T-8 ....... VI.5:5 creations of God **H.** take joy in what is not
T-8 ..... VI.5:14 its value lies in God's sharing **H.** with it
T-8 ....... VI.7:5 God does not contradict **H.**, and His Sons
T-8 ....... VI.8:8 as we are, and we are the Sons of God **H.**,
T-8 ....... VI.9:4 and God has joined all His Sons with **H.**.
T-8 ...... VII.5:9 To communicate with part of God **H.** is to
T-9 ....... VI.3:6 Only God **H.** is more than they but they
T-9 ...... VII.8:2 say: *God* **H.** *is incomplete without me.*

| | |
|---|---|
| T-9.......VII.8:7 | and He will give you all of **H.** in exchange |
| T-9..... VIII.9:1 | be arrogant when God **H.** witnesses to it? |
| T-9... VIII.10:3 | God **H.** keeps your extensions safe within |
| T-10.......in.3:1 | about you, for He is not uncertain of **H.**. |
| T-10.......in.3:2 | because He does not know it only for **H.**. |
| T-10.......in.3:3 | He created you for **H.**, but He gave you |
| T-10.... in.3:11 | you, or He would be deciding against **H.**. |
| T-10......IV.4:6 | Yet God **H.** has protected everything He |
| T-10......IV.8:7 | faith in it, and God **H.** will answer you. |
| T-10....... V.9:3 | Would He allow **H.** to suffer? And would |
| T-10.....V.10:3 | interfere with you would be to attack **H.**, |
| T-10... V.10:10 | God gave **H.** to you in your creation, and |
| T-11.........I.1:6 | for God **H.** did not will to be alone. |
| T-11.........I.2:3 | no endings in God, Whose universe is **H.**. |
| T-11.........I.5:7 | will to be alone, He created a Son like **H.**. |
| T-11.........I.7:2 | is your heritage, because His one gift is **H.** |
| T-11....... II.1:4 | your will with His, for He wills you **H.**. |
| T-11....... II.6:2 | to be like Him, and He has given **H.** to you |
| T-11......III.2:4 | real, when He did not will to be alone **H.**? |
| T-11......III.3:7 | that what God wills for **H.** He wills for you |
| T-11......III.7:7 | for He **H.** dwells there and abides in peace |
| T-11......IV.7:2 | knows His Son as wholly blameless as **H.**, |
| T-11......VI.6:6 | that is His, and He **H.** is yours with them. |
| T-11......VI.7:7 | Having given **H.** to him, how could it be |
| T-11. VIII.15:5 | last step for you, by raising you unto **H.**. |
| T-12......VI.7:3 | it. Very gently does God shine upon **H.**, |
| T-12......VI.7:3 | loving the extension of **H.** that is His Son. |
| T-12... VIII.1:2 | has hidden His Son safely within **H.**, and |
| T-12... VIII.4:1 | forget what God **H.** placed in his memory. |
| T-13......III.8:2 | your Father as your Father calls you to **H.**. |
| T-13......V.7:12 | of God is given you to whom God gave **H.**. |
| T-13.....VII.7:1 | Will that nothing touch His Son except **H.** |
| T-13.....VII.7:2 | He is as safe from pain as God **H.**, Who |
| T-13.....VII.7:3 | God placed him in **H.** where pain is not, |
| T-13. VIII.10:4 | waits your witness to His Son and to **H.**. |
| T-13. VIII.10:7 | beloved Son outside them, and beyond **H.** |
| T-13......IX.8:9 | He knows **H.**, and knows the truth in you. |
| T-13....... X.9:7 | Father is as pure as He Who raised it to **H.** |
| T-13..... X.10:2 | surely as God **H.** has always loved His Son |
| T-13......XI.8:1 | Link that God **H.** placed within you, |
| T-14......IV.2:1 | by Him like unto **H.** and part of Him, are |
| T-14......IV.3:1 | will give **H.** to you as He has always done. |
| T-14......IV.3:2 | Giving **H.** is all He knows, and so it is all |
| T-14......IV.4:6 | He created you out of **H.**, but still within |
| T-14....IV.4:12 | God will **H.** exchange your gift for His. |
| T-14......IV.7:5 | the very mind where God **H.** has placed it. |
| T-14....... V.6:7 | power of God **H.** supports this teaching, |
| T-14. VIII.2:14 | in the communication that God **H.** wills |
| T-14... VIII.5:1 | The link with which the Father joins **H.** to |
| T-14... VIII.5:6 | To whom God gives **H.**, He *is* given. Your |
| T-14......IX.5:6 | it. God will shine upon it of **H.**. Only the |
| T-14......IX.5:7 | reflection of **H.** can be perceived upon it. |
| T-14...... X.12:8 | It. And God **H.**, Who wills to be with His |
| T-14......XI.7:4 | His Son to turn to Him and remain **H.**. It |
| T-14......XI.7:6 | And being yours He cannot change **H.**, for |
| T-15....... II.3:4 | as God extends **H.** to encompass you. You |
| T-15......III.5:4 | God gave **H.** to you in your creation, He |
| T-15......III.7:2 | to the host whom God appointed for **H.**. |
| T-15......III.7:4 | For God would give **H.** *through* you. He |
| T-15......IV.4:1 | altar on which your Father has placed **H.**? |
| T-15... VIII.4:2 | gift, for as He withheld **H.** not from you, |
| T-15......IX.1:5 | part that God **H.** plays in the Atonement, |
| T-15......XI.9:2 | welcome does He welcome you into **H.**, |
| T-17......III.7:5 | has left no part of it without **H.**. This is |
| T-17..... V.10:3 | God **H.** has blessed your holy relationship |
| T-18...... I.11:6 | And God **H.** is glad that your relationship |
| T-18......III.1:6 | was simply that God cannot destroy **H.**. |
| T-18......III.4:7 | gift is given forever, for God **H.** received it |
| T-18......III.8:4 | spark of your desire the power of God **H.**, |
| T-18......VI.1:3 | from it nor leave it separate from **H.**. The |
| T-18......VI.2:1 | What could God give but knowledge of **H.** |
| T-18......VI.9:3 | be separated from **H.** except in illusions. |
| T-18......VI.9:6 | separated **H.** from His Son to make this |
| T-18.....VI.9:10 | God placed none between **H.** and you. |
| T-18....IX.10:4 | God **H.** can take the final step unhindered |
| T-19...... I.14:1 | God has raised unto **H.** and both of you. |
| T-19....... II.2:7 | For by it God **H.** is changed, and rendered |
| T-19......III.6:2 | the Creator must have extended **H.**, and it |
| T-19......III.6:3 | If sin is real, God must be at war with **H.**. |
| T-19...... III.7:6 | than God, before which God **H.** must bow |
| T-19...... IV.3:8 | When God has taken the last step **H.**, the |
| T19....IV.C.3:1 | and innocence, and to the Will of God **H.**. |
| T19....IV.C.8:1 | his decay that God **H.** is powerless before |
| T19....IV.C.9:4 | the Holy Spirit and protected by God **H.**. |
| T-20....... II.7:5 | undoing of illusion that God **H.** could give |
| T-21... VIII.3:6 | made by one whom God **H.** will never fail |
| T-22..... II.12:1 | your holy relationship, beloved of God **H.** |
| T-23.........I.4:5 | Your "enemy" was God **H.**, to Whom all |
| T-23.......I.10:1 | no illusion, being as true and holy as **H.**. |
| T-23....... II.4:4 | which God **H.** is powerless to overcome. |
| T-23....... II.8:5 | And God **H.** seems to be siding with it, to |
| T-23...... IV.6:6 | And God **H.** and all the lights of Heaven |
| T-24.......in.1:9 | not wait upon illusions to let Him be **H.**. |
| T-24.........I.7:5 | God gave you and your brother **H.**, and to |
| T-24.........I.8:3 | God **H.** must honor it or suffer vengeance. |
| T-24....... II.4:6 | yet the Call of God **H.** is soundless to you. |
| T-24..... II.10:3 | You are alike to God as God is to **H.**. He is |
| T-24..... II.10:4 | not keep one part of what He is unto **H.**, |
| T-24..... II.10:7 | remembering God gave **H.** to you and |
| T-24..... II.11:4 | to him and him to you because He gave **H.** |
| T-24..... III.5:8 | And God **H.**, Who knows that death is |
| T-24...... III.8:3 | condemn **H.** to hell and to damnation? |
| T-24...... III.8:7 | asks your mercy on His Son and on **H.**. |
| T-24....... V.8:1 | Lord of Heaven has **H.** come down to you, |
| T-24...... VI.7:6 | And where is God **H.** but in that part of |
| T-24..... VII.7:2 | must this Son have been created like **H.**. A |
| T-25.........I.4:3 | Each aspect of **H.** is framed in holiness |
| T-25....... II.5:5 | created He supports and frames within **H.** |
| T-25...... II.9:11 | The gratitude of God **H.** is freely offered |
| T-25..... II.11:1 | brother are the same, as God **H.** is One |
| T-25...... III.2:4 | He could not let **H.** be separate entirely. |
| T-25..... VII.1:8 | as Heaven, and as strong as God **H.**. The |
| T-26...... IV.4:2 | Here the Son of God **H.** comes to receive |
| T-26..... VII.7:4 | world apart, and relegates attack unto **H.**. |
| T-27...... III.6:7 | is God left free to take the final step **H.**. |
| T-27...... VI.3:9 | call him by the holy Name of God **H.**. |
| T-27...... VI.4:5 | Nor could it tell a part of God **H.** what it |
| T-27.... VI.6:11 | And God **H.** has guaranteed the strength |
| T-27... VII.15:2 | of Heaven will **H.** awaken His beloved Son |
| T-28.........I.4:1 | make use of memory, for God **H.** is there. |
| T-28.......I.15:4 | God has closed it with **H.**. His memory |
| T-28..... III.6:4 | and bridge His Son's returning to **H.**. |
| T-28..... VII.1:6 | God's promise is a promise to **H.**, and |
| T-28..... VII.1:7 | between **H.** and what He is cannot be false |
| T-28..... VII.2:1 | a part of you because it is a part of God **H.** |
| T-28..... VII.7:5 | promise that His Son is safe forever in **H.**. |
| T-29...... III.2:1 | the Father lost **H.** when He created you? |
| T-29...... III.3:6 | will see that God **H.** is where his body is. |
| T-29....... V.6:4 | If God esteems him worthy of **H.**, would |
| T-29... VIII.9:9 | is every living thing a part of you, as of **H.**. |
| T-29...... IX.2:1 | the mind that God created perfect as **H.**. |
| T-30...... II.3:5 | joined with God **H.** in all creation's birth. |
| T-30....... II.4:2 | prisoner, then God **H.** could not be free. |
| T-30....... II.4:3 | whom God so loves is done to God **H.**. |
| T-30..III.11:10 | But you, the holy Son of God **H.**, are |
| T-30.... IV.8:13 | be, except a means to give him to **H.**? |
| T-31.........I.4:5 | the home where God **H.** established him. |
| T-31...... VI.4:7 | For God **H.** has said, "Your will be done." |
| T-31... VIII.4:1 | against what God **H.** would have you be. |
| W-pI......58.3:6 | of my holiness, which I share with God **H.** |
| W-pI......64.3:2 | of the task assigned to you by God **H.**. The |
| W-pI.....66.10:4 | For God **H.** shares it with us. Today's idea |
| W-pI......67.2:7 | as He defines **H.** is appropriate for use. |
| W-pI......67.2:9 | that you are part of His definition of **H.**. |
| W-pI......68.3:1 | it is certain that God created them like **H.**, |
| W-pI......69.7:2 | God **H.** will raise you from darkness into |
| W-pI......72.5:3 | trying to present **H.** as the Author of life |
| W-pI....72.12:1 | of infinity, Who created you like **H.**: *What* |
| W-pI......73.3:5 | Would God create a world that kills **H.**? |
| W-pI......78.7:2 | of God and of His Son, as holy as **H.**: *Let* |
| W-pI......94.4:2 | truth. God has **H.** promised that it will be |
| W-pI.....95.13:4 | is your Self, the Son of God **H.**, sinless as |
| W-pI......97.2:3 | You are the spirit which completes **H.**, |
| W-pI....100.3:4 | light that God **H.** appointed as the means |
| W-pI....100.9:5 | when He Who calls to you is God **H.**? |
| W-pI....102.5:2 | Whose Love created him as loving as **H.**. |
| W-pI....105.5:2 | yours. Let Him complete **H.** as He defines |
| W-pI....110.7:1 | the Self Who is the holy Son of God **H.**. |
| W-pI... 112.2:2 | *as I was, created by the Changeless like **H.**.* |
| W-pI... 123.3:2 | for the Son He loves is changeless as **H.**. |
| W-pI... 124.1:5 | the thought that God **H.** goes everywhere |
| W-pI... 125.5:2 | He has not hid **H.** from you, while you |
| W-pI... 127.4:2 | is your own, and shared by God **H.**. For |
| W-pI... 127.4:5 | There is no limit placed upon **H.**, and so |
| W-pI... 127.9:2 | He **H.** has promised this. And He Himself |
| W-pI... 127.9:3 | **H.** will place a spark of truth within your |
| W-pI... 129.4:2 | And God **H.** speaks to His Son, as His Son |
| W-pI... 131.8:3 | when God **H.** established him in Heaven? |
| W-pI. 132.12:3 | in what is **H.** and what is still Himself. |
| W-pI. 132.12:3 | in what is Himself and what is still **H.**. |
| W-pI. 132.13:1 | break away a part of God **H.** and thus |
| W-pI. 134.10:1 | guilt and pain as God **H.** intended it to be, |
| W-pI. 135.25:6 | your function from the Voice for God **H.**? |
| WpI. rIV.in2:4 | establishing the Son as co-creator with **H.**. |
| WpI. rIV.in6:3 | Hosts be yours, as He **H.** has willed it be. |
| W-pI... 151.3:7 | to by the eternal Voice for God **H.**. |
| W-pI... 152.9:4 | like to **H.** in power and in love. |
| W-pI. 154.12:3 | but will not know that God **H.** has left no |
| W-pI. 155.10:2 | apart from God's completion, holy as **H.**. |
| W-pI... 156.3:3 | What lives is holy as **H.**, because what |
| W-pI... 156.6:5 | to God **H.** for such a senseless whim? |
| W-pI... 160.8:5 | one, at home in Him, no stranger to **H.**. |
| W-pI... 163.4:2 | strength and might of God **H.** perceived |
| W-pI. 167.10:5 | of life eternal has been set by God **H.**. |
| W-pI... 168.3:2 | lifts us up, taking salvation's final step **H.**. |
| W-pI... 168.3:4 | But finally He comes **H.**, and takes us in |
| W-pI... 170.9:3 | surmounting, is the fear of God **H.**. Here |
| W-pI. 170.12:6 | way for love, as God **H.** replaces cruelty. |
| W-pI... 183.5:4 | which reaches to God **H.** and to His Son. |
| W-pI... 183.7:2 | And God will come, and answer it **H.**. |
| W-pI... 183.7:5 | He cannot hear requests that He be not **H.** |
| W-pI... 186.3:7 | pride that would deny the Call for God **H.** |
| W-pI... 188.4:3 | giver of the gift, does God **H.** give thanks. |
| W-pI... 188.6:6 | become the holy messengers of God **H.**. |
| W-pI... 190.3:2 | as mad, and seen as traitor to **H.**. If God is |
| W-pI......191.h | I am the holy Son of God **H.**. |
| W-pI... 191.6:1 | are free: You are the holy Son of God **H.**. |
| W-pI... 191.7:3 | *I am the holy Son of God **H.**. I cannot suffer,* |
| W-pI. 191.11:6 | life. You are the holy Son of God **H.**. |
| W-pI... 192.1:1 | Father's holy Will that you complete **H.**, |
| W-pI. 193.13:6 | God will take this final step **H.**. Do not |
| W-pI... 195.6:2 | complete the One Who is **H.** completion. |
| W-pI... 197.4:5 | acknowledged by the Heart of God **H.**. |
| W-pI... 197.8:6 | He holds you dear, because you are **H.**. All |
| W-pI... 198.3:6 | direction with the certainty of God **H.**. It |
| W-pI... 198.4:2 | way, when this one is the plan of God **H.**? |
| W-pI... 199.8:6 | God **H.** extends His Love and happiness |
| W-pI... 202.1:2 | *God **H.** has given me His Voice to call me* |
| W-pI... 208.1:4 | *within my heart, which witnesses to God **H.**.* |
| W-pI... 211.1:1 | (191) I am the holy Son of God **H.**. *In* |
| W-pII ....in.2:3 | promised He will take the final step **H.**. |
| W-pII ....in.3:3 | and expect our Father to reveal **H.**, as He |
| W-pII ....in.9:1 | to have the Son whom He created for **H.**. |
| W-pII ....in.9:2 | We wanted God to change **H.**, and be |
| W-pII . 221.2:6 | we are, and to reveal **H.** unto His Son. |
| W-pII . 244.2:4 | For what can come to threaten God **H.**, or |
| W-pII ..... 4.3:4 | And God **H.** has lost the Son He loves, |
| W-pII ..... 4.3:4 | loves, with but corruption to complete **H.**, |
| W-pII . 252.1:4 | but from the boundless Love of God **H.**. |
| W-pII . 255.1:2 | my God assures me that His Son is like **H.** |
| W-pII . 273.1:4 | peace that God **H.** has given to His Son. |
| W-pII . 277.2:5 | lie, and God can will that He deceive **H.**. |
| W-pII . 280.1:6 | and like **H.** in freedom and in love? |
| W-pII . 282.1:2 | be insane, and to accept myself as God **H.**, |
| W-pII . 286.2:2 | the end which God **H.** has promised us. |
| W-pII . 291.1:6 | we share; it is the Holiness of God **H.**. |
| W-pII .....301.h | And God **H.** shall wipe away all tears. |
| W-pII . 322.1:4 | which is God's only Son, the likeness of **H.** |
| W-pII . 327.1:2 | He will hear my call, and answer me **H.**. |
| W-pII ... 12.2:3 | thinks it has become a victor over God **H.**. |
| W-pII . 336.1:6 | for this the dwelling place of God **H.**. |
| W-pII . 340.2:6 | and none the Father will not gather to **H.**, |
| W-pII ... 14.1:4 | *I am the holy home of God **H.**. I am the* |
| W-pII .....352.h | The other comes the peace of God **H.**. |
| W-pII . 358.1:3 | *And what You give me comes from God **H.**.* |
| Wfl........in.2:2 | it is this ending God **H.** appointed. In the |
| Wfl........in.3:5 | will not fail to recognize as part of God **H.** |

M-5 .........I.1:8 powerful, eager to keep all power for **H.**.
M-17 .........7:6 raised madness to the throne of God **H.**.
M-17 .........8:2 They bring the light of hope from God **H.**.
M-20 .........6:6 the mighty Will of God **H.** His gift to you.
M-20 .........6:7 He does not seek to keep it for **H.**. Why
M-21 .........5:9 And He **H.** gives to the words they use the
M-22 .........7:1 Who can limit the power of God **H.**?
M-23 .........7:4 of trouble; a savior who can symbolize **H.**
C-1.............1:3 Thought of God which He created like **H.**.
C-1.............5:3 in which God takes the final step **H.**. Here
C-3.............7:5 And what He gives is always like **H.**. This
C-4.............1:2 for what He creates must be eternal as **H.**.
C-5.............3:1 forever like **H.** and One with Him–Jesus
C-ep...........2:2 to Him Who loves you as He loves **H.**. Ask
P-2......... II.5:4 and then through the memory of God **H.**.
P-2......... V.3:7 God **H.** holds out his brother as his savior
P-2......... V.5:8 This holy interaction is the plan of God **H.**
P-2.......VII.6:6 he has the gifts of God **H.** to give away.
P-3........ III.6:4 place of Christ and home of God **H.**.
S-1....... II.7:10 And for this giving God **H.** gives thanks.
S-2...........I.6:3 God **H.** has given all His Sons a remedy
S-3........IV.3:3 for He knows the Cause of healing is **H.**,

## Himself 27

• Christ/Self
*God*
*Holy Spirit*
*himself*

T-11......IV.7:1 waits for the restoration of **H.** in you. God
T-11..... V.17:7 for Christ speaks to them of **H.** and of His
T-12....... II.3:6 Love of Christ for His Father and for **H.**.
T-13..... V.10:3 for through Christ's vision He beholds **H.**.
T-13...... VI.3:4 you meet because you see Him through **H.**
T19... IV.A.2:7 Christ asks it of you for **H.**. He would
T19... IV.D.2:3 make the face of Christ **H.** like to a leper's,
T-22.......I.11:1 Christ comes to what is like **H.**; the same,
T-22.......I.11:2 For He is always drawn unto **H.**. What is
T-22...... IV.3:9 His messenger, returning Him unto **H.**.
T-24....... V.1:2 on what He loves, and knows it as **H.**. And
T-24....... V.6:4 you **H.** in him whose hand you hold, and
T-24....... V.7:2 Christ's hand holds all His brothers in **H.**.
T-24....... V.9:5 way that He must go to find **H.** complete.
T-25.........I.1:7 is the meeting of the holy Christ unto **H.**;
T-25.........I.2:9 the Christ in him proclaims **H.** as you.
W-pI...151.8:2 Christ cannot doubt **H.**. The Voice for
W-pI.152.11:5 ask our Self that He reveal **H.** to us. And
W-pI...159.4:6 holiness was given by His Father and **H.**.
W-pI.166.12:2 His touch on you has made you like **H.**.
W-pI...182.5:7 But give Him just a little time to be **H.**,
W-pI...182.7:5 you back with Him, that He **H.** might stay
W-pI...197.7:2 God, and He gives thanks for you unto **H.**.
W-pII .355.1:8 *Your Son would be H., and know You as his*
P-2.....VII.1:14 who calls, and in Him he recognizes **H.**.
S-1...........I.7:2 that Christ be but **H.** is not an entreaty. It
S-2...........I.7:5 His sight the world becomes as holy as **H.**.

## Himself 3

• Holy Spirit
*God*
*Christ/Self*
*himself*

T-6....... II.12:3 extends by recognizing **H.** in every mind,
T-6....... II.12:5 same. Wherever He looks He sees **H.**, and
T-14.... XI.13:6 The Holy Spirit will, of **H.**, fill every mind

## himself 1

• Jesus
*noise word*
*Himself*

C-5............2:3 to be a separate being, walking by **h.**,

## himself 353

• noise word
*Jesus*
*Himself*

## hinder 8

T-4 ....... IV.8:5 for any beliefs that **h.** its accomplishment,
T-14 ..... XI.5:3 lessons in your mind that hurt and **h.** you
T-16 ... IV.13:1 of any kind would **h.** God's completion,
T-16 .... VII.7:1 to **h.** your full awareness of the complete
T-18 ..... III.7:6 what your separate pasts would **h.**. You
T19....IV.A.9:2 flight, or **h.** the advance of summer? Can
T-26 .... V.12:2 and **h.** not the true existence of the here
M-4 ..... I.A.4:3 before will merely **h.** his ability to transfer

## hindrance 13

T-5 .........II.5:6 share His knowledge with you without **h.**.
T19....IV.A.4:6 will flow across it, and join you without **h.**
T-26 ..... IV.6:2 little is the **h.** that withholds the wealth of
T-26 ......... V.h The Little **H.**
T-26 ...... V.1:1 A little **h.** can seem large indeed to those
T-26 ...... V.1:5 All learning is a help or **h.** to the gate of
T-26 ...... V.2:2 For it is but a little **h.** to eternity, quite
T-26 ...... V.6:7 a **h.** can this dream be to where he really
T-26 ...... V.7:1 Is this a **h.** to the place whereon he stands
T-26 ...... V.8:3 Is this a **h.** to the truth the past is gone,
T-26 .... V.14:4 There is no **h.** to the Will of God, nor any
W-pI..... 95.4:5 this, for it is indeed a **h.** to your advance.
M-21 ......... 5:1 A major **h.** in this aspect of his learning is

## hint 8

T-4 .......II.4:11 contains a **h.** of recognition that the ego is
T-9 .....VIII.4:2 Even the faintest **h.** of your reality literally
T-21 ........I.6:1 you catch a **h.** of an ancient state not
T-24 .... VII.1:6 the whispered doubt, the **h.** of threat, or
T-29 ........I.1:5 His Love could harbor just a **h.** of hate,
W-pI... 107.3:1 And now you have a **h.**, not more than
W-pII ..... 2.4:3 holds a **h.** of all the glory given us by God.
M-18 ......... 4:2 senses even the faintest **h.** of irritation in

## hints 1

T-26 ...VIII.7:8 clearly **h.** at punishment until the time of

## hires 1

T-27 ...VIII.2:4 It **h.** other bodies, that they may protect it

## His 1674

• God
*Christ/Self*
*Holy Spirit*
*his*

T-1 ..........I.4:2 **H.** Voice will direct you very specifically.
T-1 ........I.29:2 praise Him by honoring **H.** creations,
T-1 .........II.1:2 between God and **H.** creations, involving
T-1 ....... III.2:3 and **H.** work is wholly lovable and wholly
T-1 ........ V.3:3 All **H.** children have His total Love, and
T-1 ........ V.3:3 All His children have **H.** total Love, and
T-1 ........ V.3:3 all **H.** gifts are freely given to everyone
T-1 ........ V.4:4 if any of **H.** creations lacked holiness. The
T-1 ....... VI.4:3 has perfect faith in **H.** creations *because* He
T-1 ..... VI.5:10 this solution, and this faith *is* **H.** gift.
T-2 ..........I.1:1 aspect of God which He gave to **H.** Son. In
T-2 ..........I.1:2 God extended Himself to **H.** creations and
T-2 ..........I.3:9 extend as God extended **H.** Spirit to you.
T-2 ....... III.5:6 God and **H.** creations are completely
T-2 ....... III.5:8 He gave them **H.** peace so they could not
T-2 ..... III.5:11 God is lonely without **H.** Sons, and they
T-2 .... VII.3:11 to God, and **H.** "Effect" is His Son. This
T-2 .... VII.3:11 to God, and His "Effect" is **H.** Son. This
T-2 .... VII.5:14 world that he gave **h.** only begotten Son,
T-2 .... VII.5:14 "He gave it *to* **H.** only begotten Son."
T-2 ...... VII.6:2 If all **H.** creations are His Sons, every one
T-2 ...... VII.6:2 If all His creations are **H.** Sons, every one
T-2 ..... VIII.1:3 expressing the same Will in **H.** creation.
T-3 ..........I.1:5 of **H.** Sons to suffer because he was good.
T-3 ..........I.1:9 the kind of thinking which **H.** Own words
T-3 ..........I.1:9 have clearly stated is unworthy of **H.** Son?
T-3 ..........I.2:4 **H.** Own Son on behalf of salvation. The
T-3 ..........I.3:5 **H.** Mind does not create that way. He
T-3 ..........I.8:1 God is the true state of the mind of **H.** Son
T-3 ..........I.8:3 Knowing **H.** Son as he is, you realize that
T-3 .........II.4:1 He created in the likeness of **H.** Own, to
T-3 ....... III.6:1 can communicate directly to **H.** altars,
T-3 ....... III.6:1 altars, which He established in **H.** Sons.
T-3 ....... III.6:2 There He can communicate **H.** certainty,
T-3 ....... III.6:2 **H.** knowledge will bring peace without
T-3 ....... III.6:3 God is not a stranger to **H.** Sons, and His
T-3 ....... III.6:3 **H.** Sons are not strangers to each other.
T-3 ....... III.6:7 "Fear God and keep **H.** commandments"
T-3 ....... III.6:7 "Know God and accept **H.** certainty."
T-3 ....... III.7:9 knows **H.** children with perfect certainty.
T-3 ....... IV.7:1 God and **H.** creations remain in surety,
T-3 .........V.7:3 God did create spirit in **H.** Own Thought
T-3 .........V.7:3 Thought and of a quality like to **H.** Own.
T-3 .........V.9:7 God's miracles are as total as **H.** Thoughts
T-3 .........V.9:7 Thoughts because they *are* **H.** Thoughts.
T-3 .......V.10:5 God and **H.** miracle are inseparable. How
T-3 .......V.10:6 the Thoughts of God who live in **H.** light!
T-3 ....... VI.8:6 to undo it, not to punish **H.** children, but
T-3 ..... VI.10:6 To deny **H.** Authorship is to deny yourself
T-3 ...... VII.2:5 Him for possession of **H.** creations. The
T-3 ...... VII.3:6 If God knows **H.** children, and I assure
T-3 ...... VII.3:8 and gave it freely to **H.** creations. The
T-3 ...... VII.3:9 either God or **H.** creations as capable of
T-3 ...... VII.4:2 in which God and **H.** creations are not co-
T-3 ...... VII.5:2 because it literally denies **H.** Fatherhood.
T-3 ...... VII.6:7 is to believe that God and **H.** Son can *not*.
T-4 ..........I.8:6 and you are **H.** beloved Son in whom He
T-4 ........I.11:4 a home that is worthy of **H.** creations,
T-4 ........I.11:5 Yet **H.** home will stand forever, and is
T-4 ........I.12:5 mark of the Love of God for **H.** creations,
T-4 .........II.4:4 ego much as God does to **H.** creations,–
T-4 ....... III.1:5 and what else *but* you is **H.** Kingdom? This
T-4 ....... III.4:4 and **H.** creations because of your hatred
T-4 ....... III.6:3 of **H.** Love for you and yours for Him. He
T-4 ....... III.8:5 How long will you deny Him **H.** Kingdom
T-4 ....... IV.7:1 God and **H.** creations is easily made if you
T-4 ....... IV.9:4 **H.** Mind shone on you in your creation
T-4 ....... IV.9:5 **H.** Mind still shines on you and must
T-4 ....... VI.6:4 my will is never out of accord with **H.**.
T-4 ...... VII.3:7 mind by communicating **H.** Mind to it,
T-4 ...... VII.3:7 for the reception of **H.** Mind and Will.
T-4 ...... VII.3:8 **H.** creations naturally communicate with
T-4 ...... VII.6:4 **H.** joy is not complete because yours is
T-4 ...... VII.6:6 He knows it in **H.** Own Being and its
T-4 ...... VII.6:6 and its experience of **H.** Son's experience.
T-4 ...... VII.6:7 constant going out of **H.** Love is blocked
T-4 ...... VII.6:7 is blocked when **H.** channels are closed,
T-4 ...... VII.7:1 but He cannot share **H.** joy with you until
T-5 ........in.3:4 to the Father for radiating **H.** joy upon it.
T-5 ........in.3:5 are worthy channels of **H.** beautiful joy,
T-5 ..........I.6:1 God honored even the miscreations of **H.**
T-5 ..........I.6:2 He also blessed **H.** children with a way of
T-5 .........II.1:6 **H.** Mind to yours as long as there is time.
T-5 .........II.2:2 blessed the minds of **H.** separated Sons.
T-5 .........II.5:6 Him because He could no longer share **H.**
T-5 .........II.6:8 God did not leave **H.** children comfortless
T-5 .........II.6:9 their minds was not the Voice for **H.** Will,
T-5 ....... III.2:4 of yourself, as well as of all **H.** creations.
T-5 ..... III.10:7 of God are not at home except in **H.** peace
T-5 ....... IV.4:3 Wholeness is the Wholeness of **H.** Son.
T-5 ..... IV.8:14 **H.** quiet children are His blessed Sons.
T-5 ..... IV.8:14 His quiet children are **H.** blessed Sons.
T-5 .......V.6:16 As part of **H.** Thought, you *cannot* think
T-5 ....... VI.1:1 God in **H.** knowledge is not waiting, but
T-5 ....... VI.1:1 but **H.** Kingdom is bereft while *you* wait.
T-5 ....... VI.3:3 Spirit remind you always of **H.** fairness,
T-5 ..... VI.11:7 **H.** Voice was in me as It is in you,
T-5 ...... VII.1:5 You are **H.** care because He loves you. His
T-5 ...... VII.1:6 **H.** Voice reminds you always that all hope
T-5 ...... VII.1:6 that all hope is yours because of **H.** care.
T-5 ...... VII.1:7 escape **H.** care because that is not His Will

T-5.......VII.1:7 escape His care because that is not H. Will
T-5.......VII.1:7 but you can choose to accept H. care and
T-5.......VII.1:7 of H. care for all those He created by it.
T-5.......VII.3:2 God commended H. Spirit to you, and
T-5.......VII.4:3 that is not in accord with H. holy Will.
T-5.......VII.4:4 making H. plan perfectly explicit to you,
T-5.......VII.4:5 "sacrifice" of H. children who believe they
T-6...........I.8:6 I must found H. church on you, because
T-6........ I.11:7 will with God that none of H. Sons should
T-6........ I.14:3 "wrath of God" as H. retaliatory weapon.
T-6........ I.19:1 God the Father and H. separated Sons. If
T-6......... II.1:2 The Wholeness of God, which is H. peace,
T-6......... II.8:1 God created H. Sons by extending His
T-6......... II.8:1 His Sons by extending H. Thought, and
T-6......... II.8:1 the extensions of H. Thought in His Mind
T-6......... II.8:1 the extensions of His Thought in H. Mind
T-6......... II.8:2 All H. Thoughts are thus perfectly united
T-6......... II.8:5 You cannot extend H. Kingdom until you
T-6....... II.11:6 God, and lets your mind converge with H.
T-6........IV.6:1 of God, a priceless part of H. Kingdom,
T-6......IV.10:5 Who knows that H. creations are perfect,
T-6......IV.11:3 God created is faithful to H. laws. Fidelity
T-6......IV.11:6 Can God lose H. Own certainty? I have
T-6....IV.12:11 the Answer. H. Answer is your Teacher.
T-6......... V.1:5 God does know is that H. communication
T-6......... V.1:5 so that He cannot impart H. joy and know
T-6......... V.1:5 joy and know that H. children are wholly
T-6......... V.1:6 Giving H. joy is an ongoing process, not
T-6......... V.1:7 outward, though not H. completeness, is
T-6.........V.C.h Vigilant Only for God and H. Kingdom
T-6......V.C.2:8 is: *Be vigilant only for God and H. Kingdom.*
T-6......V.C.7:2 God and H. creations are beyond belief
T-6......V.C.7:4 As long as belief in God and H. Kingdom
T-6......V.C.7:4 mind, H. perfect accomplishment is not
T-6......V.C.7:6 The ego speaks against H. creation, and
T-7...........I.1:1 power of God and H. creations is limitless
T-7...........I.1:5 your creative power differs from H.. Even
T-7...........I.2:5 are not yours, but yours are like H.. He
T-7...........I.2:8 vigilant only for God and H. Kingdom. By
T-7...........I.3:2 of God, as your sons are part of H. Sons.
T-7...........I.4:6 God does not limit H. gifts in any way.
T-7...........I.4:7 You *are* H. gifts, and so your gifts must be
T-7...........I.4:7 His gifts, and so your gifts must be like H.
T-7...........I.4:8 the Kingdom must be like H. gifts to you.
T-7...........I.5:4 co-creator with Him extend H. Kingdom
T-7...........I.6:1 to share H. certainty of what you are, and
T-7...........I.7:1 H. accomplishments are not gradual. He
T-7...........I.7:2 teach, because H. creations are changeless
T-7...........I.7:6 He created H. co-creators. Because He did
T-7........ I.7:14 H. light was never obscured, because it is
T-7........ I.7:14 obscured, because it is H. Will to share it.
T-7......... II.3:6 God and H. Sons, in the surety of being,
T-7......... II.3:9 And H. Sons, who create like Him, follow
T-7......... II.5:5 use of truth to convince H. Sons of truth.
T-7........III.5:1 keeps your mind lit by H. light because
T-7........III.5:1 light because H. light is what your mind is
T-7........IV.1:2 certainty is of God according to H. laws.
T-7........IV.1:4 knows H. creations as perfectly whole. Yet
T-7........IV.1:5 it proceeds from H. Voice and from His
T-7........IV.1:5 from His Voice and from H. laws. It is
T-7........IV.5:6 state of mind that is out of accord with H..
T-7........IV.5:7 it brings the mind into accord with H.,
T-7........IV.5:7 His, because it serves H. Voice, which is in
T-7........IV.7:6 therefore in Him since your being is H..
T-7......... V.6:9 on because it is inspired by H. Voice, and
T-7......... V.6:9 His Voice, and is in accord with H. laws.
T-7....... V.6:12 Since that is H. meaning, it is also yours.
T-7....... V.6:13 meaning cannot be out of accord with H.,
T-7....... V.6:13 meaning comes from H. and is like His.
T-7....... V.6:13 meaning comes from His and is like H..
T-7....... V.6:15 created you by sharing H. Being with you.
T-7....... V.11:5 to Him and therefore to H. Sons. This is
T-7....... V.11:6 upon you to love God and H. creation.
T-7........VI.1:6 of God, of H. creations and of his own. He
T-7........VI.7:1 for anything *but* God and H. Kingdom.
T-7........VI.7:8 your thought seems to contradict H., and
T-7......VI.10:3 Unless you perceive H. creation truly you
T-7......VI.10:3 God and H. creation are not separate. The
T-7.......VII.5:7 Keep H. way to remember yourself, and
T-7.......VII.5:7 and teach H. way lest you forget yourself.
T-7.......VII.6:2 are H. beloved Sons in whom He is well
T-7.......VII.6:4 in H. Love and protect your rest by loving
T-7.......VII.6:5 learn of H. peace and accept His gift for
T-7.......VII.6:5 accept H. gift for yourself and as yourself.
T-7.....VII.10:5 See H. abundance in everyone, and you
T-7.....VII.10:7 is lonely when H. Sons do not know Him.
T-7.....VII.11:5 because they belong to H. beloved Sons,
T-7.....VII.11:6 glory are yours because the Kingdom is H.
T-7........ IX.1:2 than He wills to deprive Himself of H.. Do
T-7........ IX.2:4 He created is given all H. power, because
T-7........ IX.2:4 part of Him and shares H. Being with Him
T-7...... IX.2:10 contain God, but wills to extend H. Being.
T-7........ IX.6:3 it was H. Will that you have it forever, He
T-7........ IX.6:8 Like H., It extends forever and in perfect
T-7......... X.1:7 are the logical outcome of H. premises.
T-7......... X.1:8 H. thinking has established them for you.
T-7....... X.1:10 as part of your identification with H., but
T-7......... X.2:2 gave your mind through H. you may deny
T-7......... X.2:6 Share H. Will and you share what He
T-7......... X.2:7 Deny H. Will as yours, and you are
T-7......... X.2:7 you are denying H. Kingdom *and* yours.
T-7......... X.4:8 will is as powerful as H. because it *is* His.
T-7......... X.4:8 will is as powerful as His because it *is* H..
T-7......... X.6:5 God. H. Will is not an idle wish, and your
T-7......... X.6:5 identification with H. Will is not optional,
T-7......... X.6:6 Sharing H. Will with me is not really open
T-7....... X.6:10 That is H. Will, and you cannot undo it.
T-7......... X.7:3 H. Voice will teach you how to distinguish
T-7......... X.7:4 Father, because the Father's Will *is* H. Son.
T-7......... X.8:3 are God's Will and do not accept H. Will,
T-7........ XI.3:9 over H. children and denies them nothing
T-7........ XI.5:6 If you recognize H. gift in anyone, you
T-7........ XI.7:7 Because God shared H. Being with you,
T-7...... XI.7:10 Kingdom of God includes all H. Sons and
T-8...........I.1:6 result of your misuse of H. laws on behalf
T-8...........I.1:6 behalf of an imaginary will that is not H..
T-8...........I.1:7 Knowledge *is* H. Will. If you are opposing
T-8...........I.1:8 If you are opposing H. Will, how can you
T-8......... II.3:4 you, because He shares H. Will with you.
T-8......... II.3:5 H. Voice teaches only in accordance with
T-8......... II.3:5 teaches only in accordance with H. Will,
T-8......... II.6:6 and you are denying God H. Kingdom,
T-8......... II.7:1 glory are yours because the Kingdom is H.
T-8........ III.2:6 uniting it with H. power and glory and
T-8........ III.3:4 Father must give fatherhood to H. Son,
T-8........ III.3:4 H. Own Fatherhood must be extended
T-8........ III.3:5 of extending H. Fatherhood by placing no
T-8........ III.7:2 H. power and glory are everywhere, and
T-8........ III.7:8 it. Through H. power and glory all your
T-8........IV.1:1 must be refusing to acknowledge H. Will.
T-8........IV.1:2 His Will. H. Will does not vacillate, being
T-8........IV.1:5 all. H. peace is complete, and you must be
T-8........IV.1:6 H. laws govern you because they govern
T-8........IV.1:7 You cannot exempt yourself from H. laws,
T-8........IV.3:9 My will is H., and your decision to hear
T-8........IV.3:9 to hear H. Voice and abide in His Will. As
T-8........IV.3:9 to hear His Voice and abide in H. Will. As
T-8........IV.6:1 nothing God created can oppose H. Will.
T-8........IV.6:2 I can only acknowledge in honor of H.. If
T-8........IV.7:9 which He will share with all H. creations,
T-8......IV.7:10 freedom, which is H. Will for all His Sons.
T-8......IV.7:10 freedom, which is His Will for all H. Sons.
T-8......... V.2:8 is no separation of God and H. creation.
T-8....... V.2:11 me. My reality is yours and H.. By joining
T-8......... V.3:1 because H. Oneness encompasses ours.
T-8......... V.3:2 join with me is to restore H. power to you
T-8......... V.3:3 only the recognition of H. power in you,
T-8......... V.3:5 be to the union of God and H. holy Sons!
T-8......... V.3:7 to the Will of the Father for H. Son, and
T-8......... V.3:7 to our joy in uniting with H. Will for us.
T-8......... V.4:5 I bring God's peace back to all H. children
T-8........VI.2:1 and the glory of God and H. holy Sons,
T-8........VI.2:6 not will the destruction of H. creations,
T-8........VI.2:7 H. Will has saved you, not from yourself
T-8........VI.3:1 over H. Kingdom the world has no power.
T-8........VI.3:3 What God and H. Sons create is eternal,
T-8........VI.5:1 God wants only H. Son because His Son
T-8........VI.5:1 Son because H. Son is His only treasure.
T-8........ VI.5:1 Son because His Son is H. only treasure.
T-8........ VI.5:2 You want your creations as He wants H..
T-8........ VI.5:6 of God and those that are created like H.?
T-8........ VI.6:2 H. Will *to* you is His Will *for* you. He would
T-8........ VI.6:2 His Will *to* you is H. Will *for* you. He would
T-8........ VI.6:3 creation from you because H. joy is in it.
T-8........ VI.6:5 H. joy lay in creating you, and He extends
T-8........ VI.6:5 and He extends H. Fatherhood to you so
T-8........ VI.6:9 H. Will created you to create. Your will
T-8...... VI.6:10 will was not created separate from H., and
T-8........ VI.7:5 does not contradict Himself, and H. Sons,
T-8........ VI.8:7 That is why He created H. Son, and gave
T-8........ VI.9:4 God has joined all H. Sons with Himself.
T-8...... VI.10:2 He has given H. Will to His treasure,
T-8...... VI.10:2 He has given His Will to H. treasure,
T-8...... VI.10:3 lies where your treasure is, as H. does.
T-8.......VII.2:2 Link between God and H. separated Sons,
T-8.......VII.5:9 H. Voice which He has established as part
T-8.......VII.6:3 perfectly accomplish H. holy Will for you
T-8.......VII.6:4 He has not withdrawn H. gifts from you,
T-8.......VII.6:5 of God remain hidden for H. Name's sake
T-8.......VII.6:5 Name's sake, because H. Name is yours.
T-8.......VII.9:7 H. Voice abides in it by directing the use
T-8.....VII.15:2 When yours is unified it is H.. Believe you
T-8.....VII.15:3 Believe you can interfere with H. purpose,
T-8........ IX.9:5 your return to meaning is essential to H.,
T-8........ IX.9:5 to His, because your meaning is part of H.
T-8........ IX.9:6 Your healing, then, is part of H. health,
T-8........ IX.9:6 health, since it is part of H. wholeness.
T-8........ IX.9:8 Yet it is still H. Will for you, and His Will
T-8........ IX.9:8 and H. Will must stand forever and in all
T-9...........I.8:2 believes that its will is different from H., it
T-9.........I.10:8 And could He fail to recognize it in H. Son
T-9.........I.13:1 God in H. devotion to you created you
T-9..........II.4:3 If you would know God and H. Answer,
T-9........ II.6:11 hear H. answer except as He answers all of
T-9..........II.8:7 Hear only God's Answer in H. Sons, and
T-9......... V.3:5 appear retaliative, and fear H. retribution.
T-9........ VI.3:9 is part of you and shares H. glory with you
T-9...... VI.3:10 H. glory belongs to Him, but it is equally
T-9........ VI.4:7 know yourself only as God knows H. Son,
T-9........ VI.4:8 by accepting H. limitlessness as yours.
T-9........ VI.7:2 Arms, and finally know H. open Mind.
T-9........ VI.7:3 in H. Mind and with a mind like His. In
T-9........ VI.7:3 in His Mind and with a mind like H.. In
T-9.......VIII.4:1 H. grandeur establishes your freedom.
T-9.......VIII.4:8 is of God, Who created it out of H. Love.
T-9.......VIII.8:5 what He created because it is H. joy.
T-9.......VIII.9:8 without you because H. grandeur is total,
T-9....VIII.10:3 God, through H. Voice, reminds you of it,
T-9....VIII.11:9 H. Own exalted Answer to what you are,
T-10.......in.3:1 God does not change H. Mind about you,
T-10.......in.3:9 "Has God changed H. Mind about me?"
T-10.....in.3:10 Then accept H. decision, for it is indeed
T-10.........I.1:4 the laws of God protect it by H. Love. Any
T-10........II.2:5 H. Voice will tell you that you are part of
T-10........II.3:4 God will do H. part if you will do yours,
T-10........II.3:4 and H. return in exchange for yours is the
T-10........II.3:5 Nothing is beyond H. Will for you. But
T-10........II.6:5 vigilant *against* God and H. Kingdom. And
T-10...... III.1:9 their sickness and returned to H. Mind.
T-10...... III.2:1 of God except H. power through you?
T-10...... III.2:6 with all H. children joins them together,
T-10...... III.8:2 all illusions because you heard H. Voice.
T-10.... III.11:3 H. Voice still calls you to return, and He
T-10...... IV.4:1 mind at peace because peace is H. Will,
T-10...... IV.4:1 and H. laws are established to uphold it.
T-10...... IV.4:2 H. are the laws of freedom, but yours are
T-10...... IV.4:4 and there are no other laws beside H..
T-10...... IV.4:6 has protected everything He created by H.
T-10...... IV.5:5 been, and nothing but H. Will will ever be
T-10...... IV.5:6 created through H. laws and by His Will,
T-10...... IV.5:6 created through His laws and by H. Will,
T-10...... IV.6:2 what is not in H. Mind cannot be in yours
T-10...... IV.6:5 H. definitions *are* His laws, for by them He
T-10...... IV.6:5 His definitions *are* H. laws, for by them He
T-10....... V.4:1 the mind of God's Son against H. Will.
T-10....... V.4:2 made H. Son think he was Fatherless, and
T-10....... V.7:3 your call, you have not answered H.. He

T-10....... V.7:4 Sonship, because of **H.** Love for His Son.
T-10....... V.7:4 Sonship, because of His Love for **H.** Son.
T-10....... V.7:5 you hear **H.** message He has answered you
T-10....... V.7:6 He created, for **H.** Son is everywhere.
T-10....... V.8:2 **H.** acknowledgment of you lies your being
T-10....... V.8:5 without love on God and **H.** creation,
T-10....... V.9:2 What is of God is **H.** forever, and you are
T-10....... V.9:4 And would He offer **H.** Son anything that
T-10..... V.10:1 yourself, and how much God, in **H.** Love,
T-10..... V.10:2 would not know **H.** Son if he were not free
T-10..... V.10:6 God will never cease to love **H.** Son, and
T-10..... V.10:6 and **H.** Son will never cease to love Him.
T-10..... V.10:7 was the condition of **H.** Son's creation,
T-10... V.10:10 in your creation, and **H.** gifts are eternal.
T-10..... V.11:1 the Kingdom will be restored to **H.** Son.
T-10..... V.11:2 **H.** Son removed himself from His gift by
T-10..... V.11:2 His Son removed himself from **H.** gift by
T-10..... V.12:1 God knows **H.** children as wholly sinless,
T-10..... V.12:2 knows **H.** children as wholly without pain
T-10..... V.12:3 knows **H.** children to be wholly joyous, it
T-10..... V.12:5 If God created **H.** Son perfect, that is how
T-10..... V.13:2 **H.** is the only Fatherhood, and it is yours
T-10..... V.13:3 but your gifts to your creations are like **H.**
T-10..... V.13:3 His, because they are given in **H.** Name.
T-10..... V.13:4 is why your creations are as real as **H.**. Yet
T-10..... V.13:7 **H.** Fatherhood gave you everything. That
T-11.......in.3:2 is you, for **H.** thought system is light.
T-11.......in.3:4 approach the center of **H.** thought system,
T-11.........I.1:4 the holy dwelling place of **H.** Son, where
T-11.........I.1:4 He wills **H.** Son to be and where he is. In
T-11.........I.3:1 part of God, **H.** Will would not be unified.
T-11.........I.3:3 Can part of **H.** Mind contain nothing? If
T-11.........I.3:4 If your place in **H.** Mind cannot be filled
T-11.........I.4:2 Who placed no limits on **H.** creation or
T-11.........I.5:5 There is no end to God and **H.** Son, for we
T-11.........I.5:8 deny Him **H.** Son, for your unwillingness
T-11.........I.5:8 to accept **H.** Fatherhood has denied you
T-11.........I.5:9 See **H.** creations as His Son, for yours
T-11.........I.5:9 See His creations as **H.** Son, for yours
T-11.......I.5:11 Look upon the glory of **H.** creation, and
T-11.........I.6:1 a place in **H.** Mind that is yours forever.
T-11.........I.6:7 is **H.** and that He wills to share with you.
T-11.........I.6:8 love is as boundless as **H.** because it *is* His.
T-11.........I.6:8 love is as boundless as His because it *is* **H.**.
T-11.........I.7:1 any part of God be without **H.** Love, and
T-11.........I.7:1 could any part of **H.** Love be contained?
T-11.........I.7:2 heritage, because **H.** one gift is Himself.
T-11.........I.7:3 like Him if you would know **H.** gift to you
T-11.........I.7:7 God wills to create, and your will is **H.**. It
T-11.........I.7:8 to create, since your will follows from **H.**.
T-11.........I.7:9 And being an extension of **H.** Will, yours
T-11.........I.8:3 God's Will is that you are **H.** Son. By
T-11.........I.9:5 Your will is **H.** life, which He has given to
T-11.........I.9:9 Immortality is **H.** Will for His Son, and
T-11.........I.9:9 Immortality is His Will for **H.** Son, and
T-11.........I.9:9 for His Son, and **H.** Son's will for himself.
T-11.......I.9:10 his Father is life, and **H.** Son is like Him.
T-11.......I.9:11 Him. Creation is your will *because* it is **H.**.
T-11.......I.10:2 otherwise **H.** Will would not be extended.
T-11.......I.11:3 He shares **H.** Will with you; He does not
T-11.......I.11:5 who share **H.** life must share it to know it,
T-11.......I.11:8 so. God's Will is that **H.** Son be One, and
T-11.......I.11:8 One, and united with Him in **H.** Oneness.
T-11.......I.11:9 of the recognition that your will is **H.**.
T-11....... II.1:4 and *being* is to unite your will with **H.**, for
T-11....... II.1:6 attack any part of God and **H.** Kingdom
T-11....... II.6:3 for **H.** function became yours with His gift
T-11....... II.6:3 for His function became yours with **H.** gift
T-11...... III.1:4 way, for that is not God's Will for **H.** Son.
T-11...... III.1:5 and **H.** peace surrounds you silently. God
T-11...... III.2:5 if your will is **H.** it cannot be true of you,
T-11...... III.3:4 joy you will create beauty in **H.** Name, for
T-11...... III.3:4 joy could no more be contained than **H.**.
T-11...... III.5:1 God hides nothing from **H.** Son, even
T-11...... III.5:1 even though **H.** Son would hide himself.
T-11...... III.6:2 Son, for they have no place in **H.** temple.
T-11...... III.6:3 Him, and accept **H.** Will for you in peace.
T-11...... III.7:2 In the quiet of **H.** temple, He waits to give
T-11...... III.7:5 what is unlike God cannot enter **H.** Mind,
T-11 ..... III.7:5 not **H.** Thought and therefore does not
T-11 ..... III.7:6 And your mind must be as pure as **H.**, if
T-11 ..... III.7:7 Guard carefully **H.** temple, for He Himself
T-11 ..... III.8:3 God blessed **H.** Son forever. If you will
T-11 ..... IV.1:2 It is yours, and belonging to you It is **H.**.
T-11 ..... IV.1:7 denying Him **H.** place in His Own altar.
T-11 ..... IV.1:7 denying Him His place in **H.** Own altar.
T-11 ..... IV.2:5 that it is yours *because* it is **H.**, and join
T-11 ..... IV.2:5 and join with your brothers in **H.** peace.
T-11 ..... IV.3:7 the protection of the Wholeness of **H.** Son
T-11 ..... IV.5:6 *enter God's Presence if you attack* **H.** *Son.*
T-11 ..... IV.5:7 When **H.** Son lifts his voice in praise of his
T-11 ..... IV.5:8 Creator cannot be praised without **H.** Son
T-11 ..... IV.6:1 at God's altar, waiting to welcome **H.** Son.
T-11 ..... IV.6:7 and nothing is denied by God to **H.** Son.
T-11 ..... IV.7:2 God knows **H.** Son as wholly blameless as
T-11 ..... IV.7:2 through the appreciation of **H.** Son.
T-11 ..... IV.7:4 in His Creator and shines with **H.** glory.
T-11 ...... V.5:4 **H.** Will is One *because* the extension of His
T-11 ...... V.5:4 of **H.** Will cannot be unlike itself. The real
T-11 ...... V.6:3 By **H.** willingness to share it, He became
T-11 ...... V.6:5 He has included you in **H.** Autonomy.
T-11 .... V.12:1 because **H.** Autonomy encompasses yours
T-11 .... V.16:9 does not see Him, for it has denied **H.** Son
T-11 .... V.17:2 Accept **H.** Son and you will remember
T-11 .... V.17:3 can demonstrate that **H.** Son is unworthy,
T-11 .... V.17:4 What you see of **H.** Son through the eyes
T-11 .... V.17:4 demonstration that **H.** Son does not exist,
T-11 .... V.17:6 in **H.** light and behold what He created.
T-11 ..... VI.1:7 ascends to the Father and **H.** Kingdom.
T-11 ..... VI.6:4 And you can accept it by **H.** grace, for
T-11 ..... VI.6:4 His grace, for God is gracious to **H.** Son,
T-11 ..... VI.6:4 him without question as **H.** Own. Who,
T-11 ..... VI.6:6 The Father has given you all that is **H.**,
T-11 ..... VI.7:2 The Love of God surrounds **H.** Son whom
T-11 ..... VI.7:6 God does not judge **H.** guiltless Son.
T-11 ..... VI.8:3 **H.** Son has been redeemed from his own
T-11 ... VI.10:6 nothing contradictory to **H.** Will is either
T-11 .... VII.4:8 can know God because it is **H.** Will to be
T-11 ... VIII.7:6 Nothing of God will enslave **H.** Son whom
T-11 ... VIII.7:6 whose freedom is protected by **H.** Being.
T-11 ... VIII.7:7 can you learn that **H.** answer is the release
T-12 ....... II.6:2 must accomplish it because it is **H.** Will.
T-12 ..... III.8:1 that He gave it to **H.** only begotten Son.
T-12 ... III.10:8 where God and **H.** Son dwell in peace and
T-12 ..... IV.6:8 for God is whole and all **H.** extensions are
T-12 ...... V.9:2 understands **H.** curriculum for learning it.
T-12 ..... VI.2:5 never ceases to remind Him of **H.** Son,
T-12 ..... VI.2:5 He never ceases to remind **H.** Son of the
T-12 ..... VI.4:8 your Father calls **H.** Son to remember.
T-12 ..... VI.4:9 The awakening of **H.** Son begins with his
T-12 ..... VI.7:3 the extension of Himself that is **H.** Son.
T-12 .... VII.1:6 In every child of God **H.** blessing lies, and
T-12 .... VII.1:6 the children of God is **H.** blessing to you.
T-12 .... VII.4:8 shares **H.** function with you in Heaven,
T-12 .. VII.10:6 Who wills to extend **H.** peace through you
T-12 ... VIII.1:2 has hidden **H.** Son safely within Himself,
T-12 ... VIII.4:7 Yet **H.** memory shines in your mind and
T-12 ... VIII.6:3 could not offer **H.** Son what has no value,
T-12 ... VIII.6:3 has no value, nor could **H.** Son receive it.
T-12 ... VIII.8:9 Father could not cease to love **H.** Son.
T-13 ...... in.3:2 For no Father could subject **H.** children to
T-13 ........ I.1:2 for sharing the Father's Love for **H.** Son,
T-13 ........ I.4:2 not cruel, and **H.** Son cannot hurt himself
T-13 ........ I.7:4 For God waits not for **H.** Son in time,
T-13 ........ I.9:3 God's way of reminding you of **H.** Son,
T-13 ........ I.9:4 For God has never condemned **H.** Son,
T-13 ....... II.9:3 for you will remember **H.** guiltless Son,
T-13 ..... III.2:6 to answer **H.** Call and leap into Heaven.
T-13 ..... III.2:8 and burning love of God, and **H.** for you.
T-13 ..... III.4:1 and you would save yourself from **H.** Love
T-13 ... III.10:3 this of a Father Who truly loved **H.** Son.
T-13 ... III.12:3 that your peace lies in **H.** Oneness? He
T-13 ... III.12:4 for pain, for suffering is not of **H.** creation
T-13 ... III.12:8 No one who hears **H.** answer but will give
T-13 ... III.12:9 **H.** answer is the reference point beyond
T-13 ...... V.7:5 **H.** sane Answer tells you what you have
T-13 ...... V.7:5 but **H.** offering to you has never changed.
T-13 .... V.7:13 offer them, to recognize **H.** gift to you.
T-13 ..... VI.9:1 you call forth the witnesses to **H.** creation.
T-13 ..... VI.9:3 thanks in **H.** clear Answer to your call. For
T-13 ..... VI.9:4 never be that **H.** Son called upon Him and
T-13 ..... VI.9:5 **H.** Call to you is but your call to Him. And
T-13 ..... VI.9:6 And in Him you are answered by **H.** peace
T-13 ... VI.11:7 you of your Father and **H.** holy Son. Light
T-13 .... VII.7:1 that nothing touch **H.** Son except Himself
T-13 .... VII.8:3 God loves **H.** Son forever, and His Son
T-13 .... VII.8:3 **H.** Son returns his Father's Love forever.
T-13 .... VII.8:6 yours, being the gift of God unto **H.** Son.
T-13 .. VII.10:1 for the perfect sanity of **H.** most holy Son.
T-13 .. VII.17:3 gift to me, given me through **H.** Spirit.
T-13 ... VIII.9:2 the witnesses to yours, which is as **H.**.
T-13 ... VIII.9:4 miracles that you established in **H.** Name.
T-13 . VIII.10:2 and so you do not share **H.** witness to it.
T-13 . VIII.10:4 God waits your witness to **H.** Son and to
T-13 . VIII.10:7 He leave **H.** Own beloved Son outside
T-13 ..... IX.1:1 Father, for guilt is the attack upon **H.** Son.
T-13 ... IX.8:12 You can deny **H.** knowledge, but you
T-13 ..... X.10:2 as God Himself has always loved **H.** Son.
T-13 ..... X.10:3 *And as* **H.** *Son loves Him.* There is no fear in
T-13 ..... X.11:5 Him, for there is no love apart from **H.**.
T-13 ..... X.14:1 make the Father One with **H.** Own Son.
T-13 ..... X.14:5 for He will never cease **H.** praise of you.
T-13 ..... XI.2:1 God would not have **H.** Son embattled,
T-13 ..... XI.2:1 so **H.** Son's imagined "enemy" is totally
T-13 ..... XI.5:1 that **H.** dear Son has laid upon himself. It
T-13 ..... XI.5:5 you, because He does not change **H.** Mind
T-13 ..... XI.7:7 communicate. **H.** Voice *will* be heard.
T-13 ..... XI.8:1 within you, joining your mind with **H.**,
T-13 ..... XI.8:3 Yet **H.** channels of reaching out cannot be
T-13 ..... XI.8:4 Peace will be yours because **H.** peace still
T-13 ..... XI.8:8 The Holy Spirit knows only of **H.** Will.
T-13 ..... XI.9:4 **H.** certainty suffices. Learn that even the
T-14 ....... II.8:7 and **H.** Son is in Him with everything.
T-14 ..... III.3:4 born of the Love of God and of **H.** Son:
T-14 ..... III.8:7 power that God has given to **H.** Son *is* his,
T-14 ..... III.8:7 and nothing else can **H.** Son see or choose
T-14 ... III.12:1 **H.** calm and unswerving value of His Son?
T-14 ... III.12:1 His calm and unswerving value of **H.** Son?
T-14 ... III.15:8 that He could ever let **H.** Son drop from
T-14 ..... IV.1:6 even as God gave it first to **H.** Son. The
T-14 ..... IV.2:5 can perhaps feel **H.** Presence next to you,
T-14 ..... IV.4:9 therefore, be anyone without **H.** Holiness,
T-14 ..... IV.4:9 nor anyone unworthy of **H.** perfect Love.
T-14 ... IV.4:11 instead offer to God and you **H.** blameless
T-14 ... IV.4:12 this small gift of appreciation for **H.** Love,
T-14 ... IV.4:12 will Himself exchange your gift for **H.**.
T-14 ..... IV.5:6 of waking gladly to **H.** Love and Holiness
T-14 ..... IV.7:4 you. He cannot be known without **H.** Son,
T-14 ..... IV.7:5 Accepting **H.** Son as guilty is denial of the
T-14 ...... V.1:4 Would you deny **H.** yearning to be known
T-14 ..... V.1:12 for God is blessed in **H.** Son as the Son is
T-14 ....... V.2:5 **H.** plan for your awaking is as perfect as
T-14 ....... V.3:3 that does not share **H.** shining innocence.
T-14 ....... V.6:4 the eternal glory of God and **H.** creation.
T-14 ....... V.8:3 is everyone whom God created as **H.** Son.
T-14 ....... V.9:7 that you cannot teach **H.** perfect peace.
T-14 ..... V.9:10 Restore to God **H.** Son as He created him,
T-14 ..... VI.8:7 Its gates are open wide to greet **H.** Son.
T-14 .... VII.7:8 Behold your will, accepting it as **H.**, with
T-14 .... VII.7:8 it as His, with all **H.** Love as yours. All
T-14 ... VIII.1:1 power He bestowed upon **H.** guiltless Son
T-14 ... VIII.2:2 upon the altar to your Father and **H.** Son.
T-14 ... VIII.2:3 No altar stands to God without **H.** Son.
T-14 ... VIII.2:6 You cannot, then, offer it to **H.** Son. For
T-14 . VIII.2:11 place where God, united with **H.** Son,
T-14 . VIII.2:11 His Son, speaks to **H.** Son through Him.
T-14 . VIII.2:13 **H.** Son lies in the Holy Spirit and in you.
T-14 . VIII.2:14 wills with **H.** Son is quite impossible here.
T-14 ... VIII.3:3 God and **H.** Son await your recognition.
T-14 ... VIII.3:7 glory and **H.** Son's belong to you in truth.
T-14 ... VIII.4:8 by the Creator and by **H.** creations. In the
T-14 ... VIII.4:9 are joined the Father and **H.** creations,
T-14 ... VIII.4:9 creations of **H.** Son with Them together.
T-14 ... VIII.5:7 on the altar, where He has placed **H.** Own.
T-14 ..... IX.3:8 you. God has not left **H.** altar, though His
T-14 ..... IX.3:8 though **H.** worshippers placed other gods
T-14 ..... IX.8:6 God is no image, and **H.** creations, as part

| | |
|---|---|
| T-14.X.1:1 | stands between God and H. creations, or |
| T-14.X.1:1 | or between H. children and their own, the |
| T-14.X.12:8 | Who wills to be with H. Son forever, will |
| T-14.X.12:8 | will bless each recognition of H. Son with |
| T-14.X.12:9 | will the power of all H. Love be absent |
| T-14.X.12:9 | from any miracle you offer to H. Son. |
| T-14.XI.2:4 | And can H. Son, given all power by Him, |
| T-14.XI.4:4 | with God's glory, for in it lies H. power, |
| T-14.XI.4:4 | which He shares so gladly with H. Son. |
| T-14.XI.4:5 | Learn of H. happiness, which is yours. But |
| T-14.XI.5:6 | that you will with the Father and H. Son. |
| T-14.XI.7:4 | compel H. Son to turn to Him and remain |
| T-14.XI.7:5 | It is impossible that God lose H. Identity, |
| T-14.XI.7:7 | miracle acknowledges H. changelessness |
| T-14.XI.7:7 | by seeing H. Son as he always was, and |
| T-14.XI.11:3 | is as like to His Creator as is H. Son, and |
| T-14.XI.11:3 | through H. Teacher does God proclaim |
| T-14.XI.11:3 | God proclaim H. Oneness and His Son's. |
| T-14.XI.11:3 | God proclaim His Oneness and H. Son's. |
| T-14.XI.14:4 | must encompass faith in H. creation. In |
| T-15.III.4:8 | effort you make on behalf of H. dear Son. |
| T-15.III.4:9 | the little, and you deny yourself H. power. |
| T-15.III.4:10 | God is not willing that H. Son be content |
| T-15.III.4:11 | For He is not content without H. Son, and |
| T-15.III.4:11 | and H. Son cannot be content with less |
| T-15.III.5:6 | All your attempts to deny H. magnitude, |
| T-15.III.5:6 | and make H. Son hostage to the ego, |
| T-15.III.7:5 | beyond everyone to H. Son's creations, |
| T-15.III.7:7 | Yet He brings all H. extensions to you, as |
| T-15.III.10:2 | knowing H. Will is constant and at peace |
| T-15.III.10:3 | will be content with nothing but H. Will. |
| T-15.III.11:2 | not you can substitute your plan for H.. |
| T-15.III.11:3 | Rather, join with me in H., that we may |
| T-15.III.12:5 | power is forever on the side of H. host, for |
| T-15.III.12:6 | Lay not littleness before H. holy altar, |
| T-15.IV.1:2 | delay the recognition that H. Will is so. |
| T-15.IV.2:7 | H. will content you, and nothing else can |
| T-15.IV.3:3 | For you leave empty your place in H. plan, |
| T-15.IV.3:3 | by your decision to join in any plan but H. |
| T-15.IV.3:5 | God would have H. host abide in perfect |
| T-15.IV.3:6 | value of H. Will for you in your own mind |
| T-15.IV.4:2 | and gladly give over every plan but H.. |
| T-15.V.2:7 | the Oneness of the Father and H. Son, |
| T-15.V.9:3 | The holy instant reflects H. knowing by |
| T-15.V.10:4 | Give to it any meaning apart from H., and |
| T-15.V.10:10 | shares, as God shares H. Self with Christ. |
| T-15.V.11:2 | out of H. need to extend His Love. With |
| T-15.V.11:2 | out of His need to extend H. Love. With |
| T-15.VI.7:3 | give yourself as your Father gives H. Self, |
| T-15.VI.8:7 | is, and what H. creation is along with Him |
| T-15.VII.1:1 | attraction of the Father for H. Son. There |
| T-15.VII.14:9 | makes you H. in your awareness. And |
| T-15.VIII.2:6 | the only need that God and H. Son share, |
| T-15.VIII.4:2 | was H. gift, for as He withheld Himself |
| T-15.VIII.4:2 | from you, He withheld not H. creation. |
| T-15.VIII.5:5 | open to receive H. communication to you, |
| T-15.VIII.6:6 | and that is H. relationship with you. |
| T-15.IX.6:3 | H. attraction for you remains unlimited, |
| T-15.IX.6:3 | but because your power, being H., is as |
| T-15.IX.6:3 | your power, being His, is as great as H., |
| T-15.X.7:1 | sacrifice do you believe H. Love demands! |
| T-15.X.8:5 | to take H. place to protect you from Him. |
| T-15.XI.2:7 | by recognizing that H. Host is One, and |
| T-15.XI.2:7 | no thought alien to H. Oneness can abide |
| T-15.XI.8:5 | us in the celebration of H. Son's creation. |
| T-15.XI.9:3 | And we but celebrate H. Wholeness as we |
| T-16.II.8:4 | H. Voice has spoken clearly, and yet you |
| T-16.III.5:2 | God, He left neither God nor H. creation. |
| T-16.IV.9:3 | of God and of H. Son established forever. |
| T-16.IV.9:6 | is God completed, and H. Son with Him. |
| T-16.IV.10:1 | rests, wholly compatible with H.. Every |
| T-16.IV.11:7 | not answer you whose completion is H.? |
| T-16.IV.11:12 | lie the memory of H. Wholeness and His |
| T-16.IV.11:12 | H. gratitude to you for His completion. In |
| T-16.IV.11:12 | His gratitude to you for H. completion. In |
| T-16.IV.11:13 | In H. link with you lie both His inability |
| T-16.IV.11:13 | In His link with you lie both H. inability |
| T-16.IV.12:2 | and created by H. joy in union with you. |
| T-16.IV.12:6 | to God, in joyous answer to H. Call for His |
| T-16.IV.12:6 | answer to His Call for H. completion. |
| T-16.V.12:4 | and invested in H. killer as the sign that |
| T-16.V.12:9 | You cannot change H. Mind. No rituals |
| T-16.V.13:1 | to obscure their tininess and H. greatness. |
| T-16.VI.1:4 | unlike the relationship of God and H. Son |
| T-16.VI.1:6 | except as its Creator defined it by H. Will. |
| T-16.VII.8:3 | Your receiving completes H. giving. You |
| T-16.VII.8:4 | will receive *because* it is H. Will to give. He |
| T-16.VII.8:6 | When He willed that H. Son be free, His |
| T-16.VII.8:6 | willed that His Son be free, H. Son *was* free |
| T-16.VII.8:7 | In the holy instant is H. reminder that His |
| T-16.VII.8:7 | is His reminder that H. Son will always be |
| T-16.VII.10:2 | power of God and all H. Love, without |
| T-16.VII.10:2 | plan of Atonement arising from H. Love. |
| T-16.VII.10:4 | to you. H. help suffices, for His Messenger |
| T-16.VII.10:4 | H. Messenger understands how to restore |
| T-16.VII.11:1 | and *find* H. message in the holy instant, |
| T-16.VII.11:3 | not give place to Him and to H. Majesty. |
| T-17.IV.1:1 | God established H. relationship with you |
| T-17.IV.1:1 | that does not share H. purpose can be real |
| T-17.IV.1:3 | of H. reason for creating His relationship |
| T-17.IV.1:3 | for creating H. relationship with you, the |
| T-17.IV.1:5 | you relate to your creations as God to H.. |
| T-17.IV.2:7 | glorifies yours instead of H. because of the |
| T-17.IV.4:3 | and by H. blessing enabled it to be healed. |
| T-17.IV.16:1 | As God ascends into H. rightful place and |
| T-17.IV.16:4 | They are in us, through H. ascendance. |
| T-17.IV.16:5 | What He has given is H.. It shines in every |
| T-17.V.10:4 | Join in H. blessing, and withhold not |
| T-18.I.10:9 | and accept H. gift as our most holy and |
| T-18.I.11:3 | God and H. whole creation have entered |
| T-18.III.8:7 | and so make room for H. eternal Presence |
| T-18.IV.3:5 | create H. dwelling place unworthy of Him |
| T-18.IV.3:6 | be, you must be interfering with H. Will. |
| T-18.IV.3:7 | to come from you, but only from H. Will. |
| T-18.IV.5:10 | *He Who established H. dwelling place in me* |
| T-18.IV.5:11 | *but only that I do not interfere with H. plan* |
| T-18.IV.5:12 | *I need add nothing to H. plan. But to receive* |
| T-18.V.3:5 | Nor will He change H. Mind about it. The |
| T-18.V.3:9 | means to anyone who shares H. purpose. |
| T-18.VI.5:5 | what He would have it be, being H. Will. |
| T-18.VI.5:6 | You cannot make H. Will destructive. |
| T-18.VI.5:7 | in which your will conflicts with H., but |
| T-18.VI.7:2 | And neither God nor H. most holy Son |
| T-18.VI.9:3 | is no barrier between God and H. Son, |
| T-18.VI.9:3 | nor can H. Son be separated from Himself |
| T-18.VI.9:6 | separated Himself from H. Son to make |
| T-18. VIII.11:8 | of God remains outside H. Fatherhood. |
| T-19.I.10:4 | is H. Love that joins you and your brother |
| T-19.I.10:4 | and for H. Love you would keep no one |
| T-19.I.16:3 | God created as H. Son is slave to nothing, |
| T-19.II.7:5 | Father, and change H. Mind completely. |
| T-19.III.7:4 | And God and H. creation seem to be split |
| T-19.III.7:6 | and offer H. creation to its conqueror. Is |
| T-19.III.8:2 | that could attack H. Will and overcome it; |
| T-19.III.8:2 | it; and give H. Son a will apart from His, |
| T-19.III.8:2 | it; and give His Son a will apart from H., |
| T-19.III.8:3 | would have a different will, opposed to H. |
| T-19.IV.3:8 | Creator in the Name of H. most holy Son. |
| T-19.IV.3:10 | of seeing, in the presence of H. gratitude? |
| T19..IV.B.17:3 | and offering H. messages unto the Son. |
| T19..IV.C.2:10 | to you who chose H. Will as yours? What |
| T19.IV.C.3:6 | They are not following H. Will; they are |
| T19.IV.C.5:7 | answered this insane idea with H. Own; |
| T19.IV.C.5:7 | which heard H. Answer and accepted It. |
| T-20.III.11:5 | the pure in heart see God within H. Son, |
| T-20.III.11:7 | as surely as God created H. Son holy, and |
| T-20.IV.3:6 | What God has given follows H. laws, and |
| T-20.IV.3:6 | has given follows His laws, and H. alone. |
| T-20.IV.7:4 | the rest and yearning only to have H. laws |
| T-20.IV.8:4 | work. Once you accept H. plan as the one |
| T-20..VI.12:11 | keep remembrance of H. Love apart from |
| T-20. VIII.11:3 | can behold the holiness God gave H. Son. |
| T-21.V.6:3 | of you that knows H. Will and shares it. It |
| T-21.VI.3:1 | himself, as God thinks not without H. Son |
| T-21.VI.11:5 | no more H. Son can be imprisoned save |
| T-21.VIII.2:4 | as is the Love of God for H. creation. Sure |
| T-21.VIII.4:1 | complete God's Will and are H. happiness |
| T-21.VIII.4:1 | happiness, whose will is powerful as H., a |
| T-22.I.1:3 | Yet if you *are* H. Will, what you must then |
| T-22.I.4:3 | "will" that is your own, apart from H.? |
| T-22.I.9:1 | did not entrust H. Son to the unworthy. |
| T-22.I.11:8 | Father's Will for you, and yours with H.. |
| T-22.II.9:6 | himself different and oppose H. Will, |
| T-22.II.10:2 | Creator, and with a will opposed to H.. |
| T-22.II.10:3 | only if you would believe H. Son could be |
| T-22.II.10:3 | His Son could be H. enemy does it seem |
| T-22.II.10:4 | You would condemn H. joy to misery, |
| T-22.VI.4:1 | your Father as a means for H. Own plan. |
| T-22.VI.7:4 | interfere with those whose wills are H., |
| T-22.VI.7:4 | and they will recognize their wills are H., |
| T-22.VI.7:4 | wills are His, *because* they serve H. Will. |
| T-22.VI.12:1 | you would know H. power is yours. But |
| T-22.VI.14:5 | of the union of the Creator and H. Son. |
| T-23.I.9:5 | no illusion can invade H. home and drive |
| T-23.I.9:6 | quiet and at peace *because* it is H. home. |
| T-23.I.10:3 | Open the door of H. most holy home, and |
| T-23.I.10:3 | keeps God homeless and H. Son with Him |
| T-23.I.10:8 | Over H. home the Holy Spirit watches, |
| T-23.II.6:3 | of what has been established for H. belief. |
| T-23.II.6:4 | H. Son can tell Him this, and He has but |
| T-23.II.6:6 | must accept H. Son's belief in what he is, |
| T-23.II.8:5 | to be siding with it, to overcome H. Son. |
| T-23.II.13:3 | will God end H. vengeance upon both, for |
| T-23.II.13:3 | H. madness He must have this substitute |
| T-23.IV.3:1 | does not share H. function with a body. |
| T-23.IV.3:2 | create unto H. Son because it is His Own. |
| T-23.IV.3:2 | create unto His Son because it is H. Own. |
| T-23.IV.3:5 | and what is H. must be His Son's as well. |
| T-23.IV.3:5 | and what is His must be H. Son's as well. |
| T-23.IV.4:2 | the holy function God gave H. Son, for |
| T-23.IV.6:7 | the peace of God together with H. Son. |
| T-23.IV.7:8 | for H. Son *because* it has no purpose. |
| T-24.in.1:7 | Peace will be yours *because* it is H. Will. |
| T-24.in.1:10 | No more H. Son. They *are*. And what |
| T-24.in.2:10 | rose in H. Mind *because* of what He knows |
| T-24.I.3:2 | with the grandeur that He gave H. Son. |
| T-24.II.3:4 | made H. Son like to itself and not like |
| T-24.II.8:7 | It is not God Who has condemned H. Son |
| T-24.II.9:4 | God and H. Heaven so remote that They |
| T-24.II.10:4 | given to H. Son but kept for Him alone. |
| T-24.II.10:5 | then He willed H. Son to be like Him, and |
| T-24.II.13:1 | prison house that keeps H. Son from Him |
| T-24.II.14:1 | you were ready to accept H. plan for your |
| T-24.III.4:2 | God have left H. Son in such a state, |
| T-24.III.4:3 | No, H. Son is safe, resting on Him. It is |
| T-24.III.4:6 | and that you will oppose H. Will forever. |
| T-24.III.8:2 | Such is the Will of God and of H. Son. |
| T-24.III.8:5 | to join H. Will to save you both from hell. |
| T-24.III.8:7 | your mercy on H. Son and on Himself. |
| T-24.III.8:13 | it was not H. Will that you be crucified. |
| T-24.V.8:2 | H. is yours because in your completion is |
| T-24.V.8:2 | because in your completion is H. Own. He |
| T-24.V.8:3 | He Who willed not to be without H. Son |
| T-24.VI.1:6 | For He could never leave H. Own creation |
| T-24.VI.2:3 | and part of Him because H. Will is One. |
| T-24.VI.3:3 | And no Thought within H. Mind is absent |
| T-24.VI.3:4 | It is H. Will you share His Love for you, |
| T-24.VI.3:4 | It is His Will you share H. Love for you, |
| T-24.VI.3:5 | God changes not H. Mind about His Son |
| T-24.VI.3:5 | God changes not His Mind about H. Son |
| T-24.VI.5:6 | everything that lives and shares H. Being. |
| T-24.VI.6:1 | It is H. sinlessness that eyes that see can |
| T-24.VI.6:2 | It is H. loveliness they see in everything. |
| T-24.VI.9:5 | And both shall see God's glory in H. Son, |
| T-24.VII.10:10 | For as H. Son's creation gave Him joy and |
| T-24.VII.10:10 | to H. Love and shared His purpose, so |
| T-24.VII.10:10 | to His Love and shared H. purpose, so |
| T-25.I.1:7 | pure and worthy of H. everlasting Love. |
| T-25.I.4:1 | not separate, nor with a life apart from H. |
| T-25.I.4:2 | H. life is manifest in you who are His Son. |
| T-25.I.4:2 | His life is manifest in you who are H. Son. |
| T-25.II.5:6 | H. masterpiece He offers you to see. And |
| T-25.II.6:2 | One with Him and with H. masterpiece. |
| T-25.II.6:4 | God has given it but serves H. purpose, |
| T-25.II.6:4 | His purpose, not yours apart from H.. It is |
| T-25.II.6:6 | Yet God has set H. masterpiece within a |
| T-25.II.9:1 | be glad if you appreciate H. masterpiece? |

T-25....... II.9:2 thanks to you who love H. Son as He does
T-25....... II.9:3 He not make known to you H. Love, if you
T-25....... II.9:3 if you but share H. praise of what He loves
T-25....... II.9:5 And so H. joy is made complete when any
T-25....... II.9:5 when any part of Him joins in H. praise,
T-25....... II.9:5 of Him joins in His praise, to share H. joy.
T-25....... II.9:6 This brother is H. perfect gift to you. And
T-25....... II.9:7 thank H. perfect Son for being what he is.
T-25....... II.9:8 And all H. thanks and gladness shine on
T-25....... II.9:8 shine on you who would complete H. joy,
T-25..... II.9:10 complete, and theirs along with H.. The
T-25..... II.9:11 to everyone who shares H. purpose. It is
T-25..... II.9:12 It is not H. Will to be alone. And neither
T-25..... II.10:3 given you, that you may see H. Son as one
T-25..... II.10:4 that all H. praise is given not to you. For
T-25..... II.10:5 For what you give is H., and giving it, you
T-25..... II.10:5 it, you learn to understand H. gift to you.
T-25..... II.10:7 power over you except H. Will and yours,
T-25..... II.10:7 Will and yours, which but extends H. Will
T-25..... II.11:1 Himself is One and not divided in H. Will
T-25..... II.11:3 H. Will is brought together as you join in
T-25...... III.2:2 Yet are H. laws reflected everywhere. Not
T-25...... III.2:4 all. Only because H. Son believes it is, and
T-25...... III.2:4 and from H. Son's belief He could not let
T-25...... III.2:5 not enter H. Son's insanity with him, but
T-25...... III.2:5 be sure H. sanity went there with him, so
T-25...... III.4:3 And thus has God protected still H. Son,
T-25...... IV.5:5 supersede the Will of God and of H. Son,
T-25....... V.3:5 by returning unto God what is H. Own.
T-25....... V.6:2 is God made free to let H. Will be done. In
T-25....... V.6:4 will you understand H. Love for you;
T-25... VII.1:11 should share the attributes of H. creation,
T-25..... VII.2:5 What is immutable besides H. Will? And
T-25..... VII.2:7 What wish can rise against H. Will, and
T-25..... VII.3:3 Not one Thought of H. makes any sense
T-25..... VII.3:4 as true has any meaning in H. Mind at all.
T-25..... VII.3:8 And if but one Thought of H. is true, then
T-25..... VII.4:2 For God and H. beloved Son do not think
T-25..... VII.7:5 Yet if H. Will is seen as madness, then the
T-25..... VII.9:6 than could the Father overlook H. Son,
T-25... VII.10:5 H. Son that hell and Heaven are different,
T-25... VII.13:4 Salvation is H. Will *because* you share it.
T-25.... VIII.9:9 And God rejoices as H. Son receives what
T-25.. VIII.10:4 He would not allow H. Son be judged by
T-25.. VIII.14:1 way, as God appointed for H. holy Son.
T-25...... IX.2:8 not fight against H. Son's reluctance to
T-25...... IX.2:9 Yet would H. justice not be satisfied until
T-26......... I.4:4 And his Father be without H. Son? Yet
T-26......... I.7:3 to the death of God and of H. holy Son,
T-26......... I.7:8 H. gifts can never suffer sacrifice and loss.
T-26......... I.8:1 justice rests in gentleness upon H. Son,
T-26....... II.8:4 is the memory of H. Love kept perfectly
T-26....... V.3:1 gave H. Teacher to replace the one you
T-26....... V.9:8 your way because there is no way but H.,
T-26..... V.10:1 Would God allow H. Son to lose his way
T-26..... V.12:4 the time it took for God to give H. Answer
T-26... VII.6:11 wish that seems to go against H. Will has
T-26..... VII.7:5 Thus has He lost H. Mind, proclaiming
T-26..... VII.7:5 proclaiming sin has taken H. reality from
T-26..... VII.7:5 H. Love at last to vengeance's heels. For
T-26... VII.11:2 He wills H. Son have everything. And this
T-26... VII.15:8 H. Kingdom is united; thus it was created,
T-26... VII.18:2 all H. Son's mistakes and set him free. But
T-26...... IX.1:4 as well while you attack H. chosen home,
T-26...... IX.1:4 His chosen home, and battle with H. host.
T-26...... IX.7:4 And shall the Lord of Heaven and H. Son
T-26...... IX.8:2 Where He dwells, H. Son dwells with Him
T-27......... I.1:9 the Father with the sacrifice of H. beloved
T-27....... II.6:7 ancient calling of the Father to H. Son,
T-27..... II.10:8 function from Him and deny that it is H.?
T-27..... II.10:9 Yet if it is not H. it is not yours, for you
T-27..... V.11:9 He knows it is a gift of love unto H. Son,
T-27... VII.15:2 will Himself awaken H. beloved Son.
T-28......... I.8:5 Will that He be unremembered by H. Son
T-28....... I.10:1 is not He Who laid a judgment on H. Son.
T-28....... I.10:2 You would deny Him H. Effects, yet have
T-28....... I.10:3 There was no time in which H. Son could
T-28....... I.10:3 what was causeless and against H. Will.
T-28....... I.12:4 He would not be deprived of H. Effects.
T-28 ...... I.12:5 The instant's silence that H. Son accepts
T-28 ...... I.15:5 H. memory has not gone by, and left a
T-28 ...... I.15:7 is He Who will transport H. Son across it.
T-28 ....... II.1:2 its effects; the Father *is* a Father by H. Son.
T-28 ....... II.8:1 the Father was deprived of H. Effects, and
T-28 ..... III.3:6 Fight not H. coming with illusions, for it
T-28 ..... III.3:6 for it is H. coming that you want above all
T-28 ..... III.6:4 and bridge H. Son's returning to Himself.
T-28 ..... III.9:5 is a feast the Father lays before H. Son,
T-28 ..... IV.7:7 the Father comes to join H. Son the Holy
T-28 ..... IV.8:6 And here the Father will receive H. Son,
T-28 ..... IV.8:6 because H. Son was gracious to himself.
T-28 ... IV.10:1 and where you join H. Son the Father is.
T-28 .... V.1:11 because God shared H. Will with you,
T-28 .... V.1:11 with you, that H. creation might create.
T-28 ..... VI.6:3 God keeps H. promises; His Son keeps his
T-28 ..... VI.6:3 God keeps His promises; H. Son keeps his
T-28 ..... VI.6:6 H. Son remembers not that he replied "I
T-28 .... VII.1:1 God asks for nothing, and H. Son, like
T-28 .... VII.7:5 that H. Son is safe forever in Himself.
T-29 ........ I.1:3 conceived of in the Wholeness that is H..
T-29 ........ I.1:4 in H. eternal Love is quite impossible. For
T-29 ........ I.1:5 mean H. Love could harbor just a hint of
T-29 ........ I.1:5 H. gentleness turn sometimes to attack,
T-29 ........ I.1:5 and H. eternal patience sometimes fail.
T-29 ........ I.1:8 For He must be deceptive in H. Love. Be
T-29 ........ I.1:9 and leave a gap between you and H. Love,
T-29 ........ I.9:4 to hold you back an instant from H. Love?
T-29 ....... II.6:1 H. Son have life and every living thing be
T-29 ....... II.8:7 and in H. sacrifice are you made more and
T-29 ..... II.10:2 H. loss you celebrate when you behold the
T-29 ..... II.10:3 and H. completion is its nothingness.
T-29 ..... III.2:2 He made weak because He shared H. Love
T-29 ..... III.2:5 Deny Him not H. witness in the dream
T-29 ..... III.2:5 in the dream H. Son prefers to his reality.
T-29 ...... V.5:1 but the shining glory of H. gift to you.
T-29 ...... V.5:2 Behold H. Son, His perfect gift, in whom
T-29 ...... V.5:2 Behold His Son, H. perfect gift, in whom
T-29 ...... V.6:3 to him, created by his Father as H. home?
T-29 ..... VI.4:7 established for H. Son in full awareness.
T-29 .... VII.1:4 God calls will never answer in H. place.
T-29 .... VII.1:5 and find the happiness H. answer brings.
T-29 .... VII.6:4 No idol takes H. place. Look not to idols.
T-29 .. VII.10:5 Let Him remind you of H. Love for you,
T-29 .. VII.10:5 seek to drown H. Voice in chants of deep
T-29 ... VIII.7:5 no room for anything to be except H. Will
T-29 ..... IX.2:2 to hell, and God made enemy unto H. Son
T-30 ....... II.1:7 He did not set H. Kingdom up alone. And
T-30 ....... II.2:5 And would God leave H. Son without
T-30 ....... II.2:6 will when He gave you H. perfect Answer.
T-30 ....... II.2:7 reminded of H. Love and learn your will.
T-30 ....... II.2:8 will. God would not have H. Son made
T-30 ....... II.3:3 Him Who is H. Voice and yours as well,
T-30 ..... III.4:4 Will, and this is given you by being H..
T-30 ..... III.6:4 time in which H. Thoughts were absent or
T-30 ..... IV.4:2 It is H. laws that guarantee your safety.
T-30 ...... V.4:1 Son and share H. Fatherhood with him.
T-30 ...... V.5:1 for this is God's Own purpose; only H.,
T-30 ...... V.6:3 Yet God need not create H. Son again,
T-30 ...... V.7:6 For He must be unremembered till H. Son
T-30 ..... VI.4:2 seems impossible H. pardon could be real
T-30 ... VI.10:6 Is his Father wrong about H. Son? Or
T-31 ........ I.4:5 forgotten, and H. Son an alien to himself,
T-31 ........ I.6:2 God willed not H. Son forget Him. And
T-31 ........ I.6:3 of H. Will is in the Voice that speaks for
T-31 ........ I.9:3 certainty with which He knows H. Love.
T-31 ........ I.9:4 only if H. Son is innocent can He be Love.
T-31 ...... I.10:1 the lesson that H. Son is guilty as God's
T-31 ....... II.7:6 when God appointed Him H. only Son.
T-31 ..... IV.9:1 He has not left H. Thoughts! But you
T-31 ..... IV.9:2 forgot H. Presence and remembered not
T-31 ..... IV.9:2 Presence and remembered not H. Love.
T-31 ..... IV.9:3 Him, nor any worldly goal be one with H..
T-31 ..... IV.9:6 Yet has He never left H. Thoughts to die,
T-31 ... IV.10:1 He has not left H. Thoughts! He could no
T-31 ... IV.11:4 and did not let H. Son abandon Him. For
T-31 .. VII.10:6 God has given you H. Son to save from
T-31 ... VIII.3:7 is the Self that God created as H. only Son
T-31 ... VIII.5:3 *H. Son can suffer nothing. And I* ***am His Son***
T-31 ... VIII.5:4 *And I* ***am*** *H. Son.* Thus is Christ's strength
T-31 ... VIII.9:5 in vain, and in H. certainty I rest content.
W-pI .... 12.5:8 words have been erased, you will see H..
W-pI .... 14.6:5 only be in your own mind apart from H..
W-pI .... 36.1:7 or a part of H. Mind would be sinful.
W-pI .... 36.1:8 Your sight is related to H. Holiness, not to
W-pI .... 39.4:6 Can it be He does not know H. Son?
W-pI ....... 42.h God is my strength. Vision is H. gift.
W-pI .... 42.1:4 It is H. strength, not your own, that gives
W-pI .... 42.1:5 And it is H. gift, rather than your own,
W-pI .... 42.2:6 is the strength of God. Such are H. gifts.
W-pI .... 43.1:2 H. is the realm of knowledge. Yet He has
W-pI .... 43.3:2 you think, you think with H. Mind. If
W-pI .... 45.2:2 with Him, as He shares H. with you. They
W-pI .... 45.2:8 is. As you are part of H. Mind, so are your
W-pI .... 45.2:8 so are your thoughts part of H. Mind.
W-pI .... 45.8:3 Here are your thoughts one with H.. For
W-pI .... 46.2:1 forgive, H. Love is nevertheless the basis
W-pI .... 47.3:2 H. Voice speaks for Him in all situations
W-pI .... 47.3:2 call upon H. strength and His protection.
W-pI .... 47.3:2 call upon His strength and H. protection.
W-pI .... 48.3:2 and let H. strength take the place of your
W-pI .... 49.2:6 your Creator has not forgotten H. Son.
W-pI .... 49.3:4 He wants you to hear H. Voice. He gave It
W-pI .... 53.4:3 and everything that is real is in H. Mind.
W-pI .... 53.5:7 so. My will is H., and I will place no other
W-pI .... 55.1:3 be what God created for H. beloved Son.
W-pI .... 55.1:5 I also do not understand H. Son. What I
W-pI .... 55.2:4 of the Love of God and the Love of H. Son.
W-pI .... 56.5:4 of God, Who has not left H. Thoughts.
W-pI .... 58.5:7 H. care for me is infinite, and is with me
W-pI .... 58.5:8 forever. I am eternally blessed as H. Son.
W-pI .... 59.2:2 Vision is H. gift. Let me not look to my
W-pI .... 59.2:5 Christ's vision is H. gift, and He has given
W-pI .... 59.3:5 else. Beyond H. Will lie only illusions. It is
W-pI .... 59.5:3 because I have no mind apart from H.. As
W-pI .... 59.5:4 As part of H. Mind, my thoughts are His
W-pI .... 59.5:4 my thoughts are H. and His Thoughts are
W-pI .... 59.5:4 my thoughts are His and H. Thoughts are
W-pI .... 60.2:4 to see, I recognize H. reflection on earth.
W-pI .... 60.2:5 I feel the stirring of H. strength in me.
W-pI .... 60.4:3 which H. Voice fails to direct my thoughts
W-pI .... 60.4:5 only Guide that has been given to H. Son.
W-pI .... 60.5:2 to God's Voice, I am sustained by H. Love
W-pI .... 60.5:3 H. Love lights up the world for me to see.
W-pI .... 60.5:4 forgive, H. Love reminds me that His Son
W-pI .... 60.5:4 Love reminds me that H. Son is sinless.
W-pI .... 60.5:5 given me, I remember that I am H. Son.
W-pI .... 61.7:6 God has built H. plan for the salvation of
W-pI .... 61.7:6 plan for the salvation of H. Son on you.
W-pI .... 62.3:5 power God gave H. Son to your awareness
W-pI .... 63.4:5 And Who but your Self must be H. Son?
W-pI .... 64.1:3 temptation to abandon God and H. Son
W-pI .... 66.8:1 is established by God through H. Voice,
W-pI .... 67.2:8 of God and replace it with H. Own. We
W-pI .... 67.2:9 you are part of H. definition of Himself.
W-pI .... 69.7:3 light. You are in accord with H. Will. You
W-pI .... 69.7:4 You cannot fail because your will is H..
W-pI .... 69.8:2 You may not recognize H. answer yet, but
W-pI .... 69.8:6 you, that H. Will and yours be done.
W-pI .... 70.3:3 way your mind has worked, but hardly H.
W-pI .... 71.5:1 simply because, by following H. direction,
W-pI .... 71.6:6 H. is the only plan that is certain in its
W-pI .... 71.6:7 H. is the only plan that must succeed.
W-pI .... 71.7:4 must be yours because of H. plan, which
W-pI .... 71.9:1 to asking God to reveal H. plan to us. Ask
W-pI .... 71.9:6 done by you in H. plan for your salvation.
W-pI .... 71.9:7 to your willingness to hear H. Voice.
W-pI .. 71.10:1 that God's plan for salvation, and only H.,
W-pI .. 71.10:4 *salvation. And only H. plan will work.* Try to
W-pI .... 72.1:1 that it is an active attack on H. plan, and a
W-pI .... 72.4:5 God attacked, for if H. Son is only a body,
W-pI .... 72.5:1 body, what must H. plan for salvation be?
W-pI .... 72.7:4 grievances against Him and H. creation,
W-pI .... 72.7:5 Your chosen savior takes H. place instead.
W-pI .... 72.9:6 And wherever H. plan is accepted, it is
W-pI .. 72.10:9 Then we will wait in quiet for H. answer.
W-pI 72.10:11 that we have not listened to H. Voice. We
W-pI .. 72.13:6 your eyes closed, and listen for H. answer.

W-pI.....73.3:3 God create disaster for **H.** Son? Creation
W-pI.....73.9:1 that God's plan for salvation, and only **H.**,
W-pI.....74.1:3 you have recognized that your will is **H.**.
W-pI.....74.1:6 the Will of God, you have no goal but **H.**.
W-pI.....74.3:9 *one. God wills peace for* **H.** *Son.* During this
W-pI.....74.7:3 *I seek* **H.** *peace today.* Then try to find what
W-pI.....76.7:6 has come because there are no laws but **H.**
W-pI...76.10:6 you. About **H.** yearning for His only Son,
W-pI...76.10:6 you. About His yearning for **H.** only Son,
W-pI...76.10:6 Son, created as **H.** channel for creation;
W-pI...76.11:1 and let **H.** Will extend through us to Him.
W-pI...76.11:3 **H.** Voice will speak of this to us, as well as
W-pI...76.11:3 which **H.** laws keep limitless forever. We
W-pI...76.12:3 is our Father, and that **H.** Son is saved.
W-pI.....78.7:2 in the holy Name of God and of **H.** Son, as
W-pI.....86.1:8 will rejoice because **H.** plan can never fail.
W-pI.....86.3:3 Yet only **H.** plan will work. By holding
W-pI.....87.4:3 *It is God's Will you are* **H.** *Son, [name], and*
W-pI.....88.3:8 God's. And **H.** are the laws of freedom.
W-pI.....89.1:3 **H.** laws release me from all grievances,
W-pI...91.10:1 the strength of God and all **H.** Thoughts.
W-pI.....92.3:1 see, as it is **H.** Mind with which you think.
W-pI.....92.3:2 **H.** strength denies your weakness. It is
W-pI.....92.9:3 peace of God is where your Self, **H.** Son, is
W-pI.....94.3:4 *I am* **H.** *Son eternally.* Now try to reach the
W-pI.....94.5:3 *me. I am* **H.** *Son eternally.* Tell yourself
W-pI.....94.5:7 *You are* **H.** *Son eternally.* Make every effort
W-pI...95.13:2 Self; united with your Father in **H.** Will.
W-pI...95.13:4 with **H.** strength within you and His Love
W-pI...95.13:4 strength within you and **H.** Love forever
W-pI.....96.6:8 release of **H.** dear Son bring pain to him,
W-pI.....96.7:3 **H.** Voice accepted it for you and answered
W-pI.....97.2:3 and shares **H.** function as Creator. He is
W-pI.....97.4:3 He will offer all **H.** strength to every little
W-pI.....97.4:4 that calls through **H.** Voice to every living
W-pI.....97.4:4 offers **H.** sight to everyone who asks;
W-pI.....98.7:3 **H.** words will join with yours, and make
W-pI.....98.7:3 in faith as perfect and as sure as **H.** in you.
W-pI.....98.7:4 **H.** confidence in you will bring the light
W-pI.....98.8:2 chance to be the glad receiver of **H.** gifts,
W-pI.....98.9:3 and peace and trust will be **H.** gifts; His
W-pI.....98.9:3 will be His gifts; **H.** answer to your words.
W-pI.....98.9:4 He will respond with all **H.** faith and joy
W-pI.....99.5:5 God is still Love, and this is not **H.** Will.
W-pI.....99.6:8 *God still is Love, and this is not* **H.** *Will.*
W-pI.....99.7:4 you. All the world of pain is not **H.** Will.
W-pI.....99.7:6 the thoughts that never were **H.** Will.
W-pI.....99.9:2 It is God's Will your mind be one with **H.**.
W-pI.....99.9:4 It is God's Will that **H.** one Son is you.
W-pI...99.11:4 *God still is Love, and this is not* **H.** *Will.*
W-pI...100.2:2 should you choose to go against **H.** Will?
W-pI...100.2:3 for you to take in working out **H.** plan is
W-pI...100.2:4 essential to **H.** plan as to your happiness.
W-pI...100.2:5 Your joy must be complete to let **H.** plan
W-pI...100.3:2 Without your joy, **H.** joy is incomplete.
W-pI...100.6:3 world can see how much He loves **H.** Son,
W-pI...100.6:5 bring **H.** happiness to all you look upon;
W-pI...100.6:5 **H.** peace to everyone who looks on you
W-pI...100.6:5 and sees **H.** message in your happy face.
W-pI.100.10:2 You are essential to **H.** plan. You are His
W-pI.100.10:3 You are **H.** messenger today. And you
W-pI...101.4:5 God upon you who have crucified **H.** Son.
W-pI...104.1:4 be a place made ready to receive **H.** gifts.
W-pI...104.1:5 received the gifts it made where **H.** belong
W-pI...104.2:2 **H.** are the gifts that are our own in truth.
W-pI...104.2:3 **H.** are the gifts that we inherited before
W-pI...104.2:4 **H.** are the gifts that are within us now, for
W-pI...104.4:2 place within our minds before **H.** altar,
W-pI...104.4:2 **H.** gifts of peace and joy are welcome, and
W-pI...104.5:1 recognizing that **H.** Will is done already,
W-pI...104.5:1 and peace belong to us as **H.** eternal gifts.
W-pI...105.4:1 you accept **H.** joy and peace as yours.
W-pI...105.5:3 Him must complete **H.** Son as well. He
W-pI...105.5:6 Receive **H.** gift of joy and peace today, and
W-pI...105.8:3 and let **H.** Voice assure you that the words
W-pI...106.2:1 speak to you through **H.** appointed Voice,
W-pI...106.3:5 holds your happiness within **H.** Hand,
W-pI...106.4:5 **H.** miracles are true. They will not fade
W-pI...106.4:7 for they come from God to **H.** dear Son,
W-pI.106.10:4 *the messenger of God today, My voice is* **H.**,
W-pI...110.4:2 been no separation of your mind from **H.**,
W-pI...110.6:3 **H.** *Son can suffer nothing. And I am His Son.*
W-pI...110.6:4 *His Son can suffer nothing. And I am* **H.** *Son.*
W-pI.110.11:3 say, that we may be reminded of **H.** Son,
W-pI.110.11:7 enter in the peace of God and **H.** eternity.
W-pI...111.2:3 *My weakness is the dark* **H.** *gift dispels, by*
W-pI...111.2:3 *by giving me* **H.** *strength to take its place.*
W-pI...115.2:3 *gave me* **H.** *plan that I might save the world.*
W-pI...116.1:3 *the belief there is another will apart from* **H.**.
W-pI...116.2:2 *share my Father's Will for me,* **H.** *Son. What*
W-pI......123.h I thank my Father for **H.** gifts to me.
W-pI...123.2:3 to take the place of Him and **H.** creation.
W-pI...123.3:1 **H.** Love forever will remain shining on
W-pI...123.3:5 the one whom God established as **H.** Son.
W-pI...123.6:1 messenger who brings **H.** Voice with you,
W-pI...123.7:1 Receive **H.** thanks and offer yours to Him
W-pI...123.8:1 Receive **H.** thanks, and you will
W-pI...123.8:1 how lovingly He holds you in **H.** Mind,
W-pI...123.8:1 how deep and limitless **H.** care for you,
W-pI...123.8:1 for you, how perfect is **H.** gratitude to you
W-pI...123.8:2 thanks for everything He gave **H.** Son,
W-pI...124.4:1 Today we will not doubt **H.** Love for us,
W-pI...124.4:1 nor question **H.** protection and His care.
W-pI...124.4:1 nor question His protection and **H.** care.
W-pI...124.4:2 faith and our awareness of **H.** Presence.
W-pI...124.4:5 Our minds contain **H.** Thoughts; our eyes
W-pI...124.4:5 behold **H.** loveliness in all we look upon.
W-pI.124.11:2 in certainty that **H.** return will be a sense
W-pI...125.1:2 Your Father wills you hear **H.** Word today
W-pI...125.1:5 until **H.** Word is heard around the world;
W-pI...125.3:1 without all judgment of **H.** holy Word.
W-pI...125.4:2 **H.** Voice would give to you His holy Word
W-pI...125.4:2 His Voice would give to you **H.** holy Word
W-pI...125.5:1 your mind to Him to give **H.** Word to you.
W-pI...125.5:4 knows **H.** Son, and wills that he remain as
W-pI...125.6:2 you. **H.** Voice awaits your silence, for His
W-pI...125.6:2 for **H.** Word can not be heard until your
W-pI...125.6:3 Await **H.** Word in quiet. There is peace
W-pI...125.7:3 **H.** Voice is closer than your hand. His
W-pI...125.7:4 **H.** Love is everything you are and that He
W-pI...125.8:4 let Him tell you God has never left **H.** Son,
W-pI...126.5:5 not **H.** care for you be small indeed, if
W-pI...126.7:1 asks of you, you cannot recognize **H.** gifts,
W-pI...126.7:3 such petty gifts as worthy of **H.** Son?
W-pI...127.1:7 It is the Heart of God, and also of **H.** Son.
W-pI...127.3:5 is no love but God's, and all of love is **H.**.
W-pI...127.4:4 There is no love but **H.**, and what He is, is
W-pI...127.9:1 Father, certain that **H.** Voice will answer.
W-pI...127.9:5 allow **H.** Voice to teach love's meaning to
W-pI...127.9:6 And He will bless the lesson with **H.** Love.
W-pI...129.4:2 And God Himself speaks to **H.** Son, as His
W-pI...129.4:2 to His Son, as **H.** Son speaks to Him.
W-pI...130.9:3 will you fail to see **H.** thanks expressed in
W-pI...131.5:1 abandon his Creator, nor affect **H.** perfect
W-pI...131.6:4 be, if it is where God wills **H.** Son to be.
W-pI...131.8:2 Nor is **H.** creation split in two. How could
W-pI...131.8:3 How could it be **H.** Son could be in hell,
W-pI.131.14:4 keeps **H.** ancient promise to His holy Son,
W-pI.131.14:4 keeps His ancient promise to **H.** holy Son,
W-pI.131.14:4 Son, as does **H.** Son remember his to Him
W-pI.132.11:1 make what does not share **H.** timelessness
W-pI.132.11:6 **H.** Thought by which you were created, so
W-pI.132.12:3 shares **H.** Fatherhood with you who are
W-pI.132.12:3 His Fatherhood with you who are **H.** Son,
W-pI.132.13:1 Himself and thus destroy **H.** Wholeness.
W-pI...134.2:5 reflects **H.** laws and radiates His Love.
W-pI...134.2:5 reflects His laws and radiates **H.** Love.
W-pI...136.9:2 salvation of **H.** Son opposed by a decision
W-pI...136.9:2 by a decision stronger than **H.** Will. His
W-pI...136.9:3 **H.** Son is dust, the Father incomplete, and
W-pI...136.9:3 and chaos sits in triumph on **H.** throne.
W-pI.136.11:1 knows not of your plans to change **H.** Will
W-pI.139.12:1 Name of its Creator and **H.** Oneness with
W-pI...140.5:6 in which to hide from **H.** beneficence.
WpI. rIV.in5:4 and to place **H.** Mind in charge of all the
WpI. rIV.in6:2 will bring the message of **H.** Love to you,
WpI. rIV.in6:4 as **H.** Own completion joins with Him, so
WpI. rIV.in7:4 it, as it was given to you through **H.** Voice.
WpIrIV.in10:1 who practice thus the keeping of **H.** Word
WpIrIV.in10:2 **H.** gratitude surrounds you in the peace
W-pI...142.1:1 (123) I thank my Father for **H.** gifts to me
W-pI.151.14:1 and the happiness God wills **H.** Son, as
W-pI.151.14:1 wills His Son, as proof of **H.** eternal Love.
W-pI...152.7:1 that God made chaos, contradicts **H.** Will
W-pI...152.9:3 God's perfect gift to **H.** beloved Son. We
W-pI.153.10:6 God, by **H.** election and their own as well?
W-pI.153.11:2 but few have come to realize **H.** Will is but
W-pI.153.12:2 designed by One Who loves **H.** children,
W-pI.153.12:3 **H.** game instructs in happiness because
W-pI.153.17:1 remembrance of our mission and **H.** Love.
W-pI.153.17:2 by and wait on Him and listen to **H.** Voice
W-pI.153.18:1 and hear **H.** loving Voice guiding your
W-pI.153.18:4 for you who chose to carry out **H.** plan for
W-pI.153.20:5 These are **H.** gifts to you. Defenselessness
W-pI...154.3:3 it. God has joined **H.** Son in this, and thus
W-pI...154.3:3 and thus **H.** Son becomes His messenger
W-pI...154.3:3 becomes **H.** messenger of unity with Him.
W-pI...154.4:3 it, and of **H.** lasting union with itself. So is
W-pI...154.7:2 of **H.** messages as for themselves, and
W-pI...154.7:3 that are not given them by **H.** authority.
W-pI...154.8:2 For thus do you become **H.** messenger.
W-pI...154.9:1 messenger of God, receive **H.** messages.
W-pI.154.10:3 Word; the giving and receiving of **H.** Will.
W-pI.154.11:1 have, that we may recognize **H.** gifts to us.
W-pI.154.11:3 He needs our hands to hold **H.** messages,
W-pI.154.11:5 He needs our will united with **H.** Own,
W-pI.154.12:3 denied the tiniest of blessings to **H.** Son.
W-pI.154.12:4 identified with Him and with **H.** Own?
W-pI.155.13:4 not He has placed **H.** Hand in yours, and
W-pI.155.13:4 and given you your brothers in **H.** trust
W-pI.155.13:4 that you are worthy of **H.** trust in you. He
W-pI.155.13:6 **H.** trust has made your pathway certain
W-pI.155.14:1 may speak to you and tell you of **H.** Love,
W-pI.155.14:1 Love, reminding you how great **H.** trust;
W-pI.155.14:1 how great His trust; how limitless **H.** Love
W-pI.155.14:2 In your Name and **H.** Own, which are the
W-pI...156.3:2 No attribute of **H.** remains unshared by
W-pI...156.3:3 what shares **H.** life is part of Holiness, and
W-pI...160.4:2 the home which God provided for **H.** Son
W-pI...160.4:3 Is fear **H.** Own, created in His likeness? Is
W-pI...160.4:3 Is fear His Own, created in **H.** likeness? Is
W-pI...160.7:4 as certain of Its Own as God is of **H.** Son.
W-pI...160.7:7 No stranger can be interposed between **H.**
W-pI...160.7:7 His knowledge and **H.** Son's reality. He
W-pI...160.7:9 know of strangers. He is certain of **H.** Son.
W-pI...160.8:2 knows to be **H.** Son belongs where He has
W-pI...160.8:2 belongs where He has set **H.** Son forever.
W-pI...160.8:4 Hear **H.** Voice assure you, quietly and
W-pI...162.2:1 happiness, **H.** Love and His completion.
W-pI...162.2:1 happiness, His Love and **H.** completion.
W-pI...162.4:3 God places all **H.** gifts and all His Love, to
W-pI...162.4:3 God places all His gifts and all **H.** Love, to
W-pI...163.7:3 Their stronger will could triumph over **H.**
W-pI...164.9:7 Can **H.** promise fail? Can you withhold so
W-pI...164.9:8 **H.** Hand holds out complete salvation to
W-pI...164.9:8 holds out complete salvation to **H.** Son?
W-pI...165.6:5 Would God consent to let **H.** Son remain
W-pI...165.8:2 And in **H.** Name we practice as His Word
W-pI...165.8:2 we practice as **H.** Word directs we do. His
W-pI...165.8:3 **H.** sureness lies beyond our every doubt.
W-pI...165.8:4 **H.** Love remains beyond our every fear.
W-pI...165.8:5 and in our minds, according to **H.** Will.
W-pI...166.1:3 knows **H.** Son. He gives without exception
W-pI...166.1:5 And yet, unless your will is one with **H.**,
W-pI...166.1:5 is one with His, **H.** gifts are not received.
W-pI...166.1:6 you think there is another will than **H.**?
W-pI...166.9:5 Perhaps **H.** gifts to you are real. Perhaps
W-pI...166.9:6 your plan to keep **H.** Son in deep oblivion,
W-pI.166.10:4 not know about a plan so alien to **H.** Will.
W-pI.166.15:3 God has entrusted all **H.** gifts to you. Be
W-pI.166.15:4 becomes which chooses to accept **H.** gifts,
W-pI.166.15:6 of **H.** gifts to all who have received them.
W-pI.166.15:7 He has shared **H.** joy with you. And now
W-pI...167.1:4 Like all **H.** Thoughts, it has no opposite.
W-pI...167.1:5 because what God created shares **H.** life.
W-pI...167.8:2 and **H.** creations cannot share what He
W-pI.167.11:1 **H.** holy home we strive to keep today as

W-pI.167.11:3 in H. Thoughts, which have no opposite,
W-pI...168.1:7 He loves H. Son. There is no certainty but
W-pI...168.1:9 He will love H. Son forever. When his
W-pI...168.2:1 If you but knew the meaning of H. Love,
W-pI...168.2:3 H. grace His answer is to all despair, for in
W-pI...168.2:3 His grace H. answer is to all despair, for in
W-pI...168.2:3 for in it lies remembrance of H. Love.
W-pI...168.2:4 the means by which H. Will is recognized
W-pI...168.2:5 is recognized? H. grace is yours by your
W-pI...168.3:3 but this we learn, instructed by H. Voice.
W-pI...168.3:4 and takes us in H. Arms and sweeps away
W-pI...168.3:5 sleep. H. gift of grace is more than just an
W-pI...168.4:1 God loves H. Son. Request Him now to
W-pI...168.6:3 Such is H. Will, because He loves His Son.
W-pI...168.6:3 Such is His Will, because He loves H. Son.
W-pI...168.6:4 word He gave to us through H. Own Voice
W-pI...168.6:4 to us through His Own Voice, H. Word,
W-pI...168.6:4 His Own Voice, His Word, H. Love: *Your*
W-pI...169.5:2 is. And in H. Being, He encompasses all
W-pI.170.10:5 The blood appears to be upon H. Lips; the
W-pI.170.12:2 your voice belongs to God and echoes H..
WpI...rV.in9:8 Our Father wills H. Son be one with Him.
WpI.rV.in10:5 You are H. Son, completing His extension
WpI.rV.in10:5 Son, completing H. extension in your own
W-pI...181.9:8 This instant is our willing one with H..
W-pI...182.5:1 in you your Father knows as H. Own Son.
W-pI...183.1:2 To call upon H. Name is but to call upon
W-pI...183.2:2 Say H. Name, and you invite the angels to
W-pI...183.4:3 Repeat H. Name, and see how easily you
W-pI...183.5:1 call upon your Self, Whose Name is H..
W-pI...183.5:2 is His. Repeat H. Name, and all the tiny,
W-pI...183.5:4 reaches to God Himself and to H. Son.
W-pI...183.6:2 Become oblivious to every name but H..
W-pI...183.7:5 H. Son receive another name than His.
W-pI...183.7:5 His Son receive another name than H..
W-pI...183.8:2 also that H. Son is part of Him, creating in
W-pI...183.8:2 Son is part of Him, creating in H. Name.
W-pI...183.8:3 let H. Name become the all-encompassing
W-pI.183.11:8 And in H. Name, it shall be given us.
W-pI.184.12:2 H. Name becomes the final lesson that all
W-pI...185.4:7 Illusions come to take H. place. And what
W-pI.185.12:1 and established as H. Own eternal gift.
W-pI...186.3:2 trust He holds in you who are H. Son. It
W-pI...186.9:3 shares H. attributes with His creation. All
W-pI...186.9:3 shares His attributes with H. creation. All
W-pI...186.9:4 All the images H. Son appears to make
W-pI.186.11:3 and H. Voice is certain of Its messages.
W-pI.186.13:1 H. gentle Voice is calling from the known
W-pI.186.13:4 which answer every need H. Son perceives
W-pI.186.13:5 and what is given in H. Name takes on the
W-pI.187.11:6 in us and offers us H. Holiness as ours.
W-pI...188.4:4 And in H. blessing does the light in you
W-pI...188.8:2 gently to accept H. Word for what you are
W-pI...189.8:4 forever. God will do H. part in joyful and
W-pI...189.9:4 H. Love will blaze its pathway of itself.
W-pI...189.9:6 God knows H. Son, and knows the way to
W-pI...189.9:7 need H. Son to show Him how to find His
W-pI...189.9:7 His Son to show Him how to find H. way.
W-pI...189.9:8 way. Through every opened door H. Love
W-pI...190.1:7 to God the Father's hatred of H. Son, the
W-pI...190.1:7 H. insane desire for revenge and death.
W-pI...192.1:1 and that your Self shall be H. sacred Son,
W-pI...192.5:6 peace that God intended for H. holy Son.
W-pI...193.1:2 Yet H. Will extends to what He does not
W-pI...193.1:2 the happiness H. Son inherited of Him be
W-pI...193.1:3 in Him. That is H. Will. And thus His Will
W-pI...193.1:4 And thus H. Will provides the means to
W-pI...193.2:2 Yet H. Son believes he sees them. Thus he
W-pI...193.2:6 answers what H. Son would contradict,
W-pI...193.3:2 H. Will reflects them all, and they reflect
W-pI...193.3:2 reflect H. loving kindness to the Son He
W-pI...193.8:3 H. Son does not remember who he is.
W-pI...193.8:4 God would have him not forget H. Love,
W-pI...193.8:4 and all the gifts H. Love brings with it.
W-pI...193.8:6 and God may be remembered by H. Son?
W-pI...193.9:2 or nail to hurt H. holy Son in any way. He
W-pI...193.9:5 each one, and that H. Son be free again.
W-pI...194.4:6 the past and present in H. Hands as well,
W-pI.195.10:4 God gives thanks to you, H. Son, for
W-pI.195.10:4 are; H. Own completion and the Source of
W-pI.195.10:5 gratitude to Him is one with H. to you.
W-pI.196.11:4 Him to save you from illusions by H. Love
W-pI.196.11:4 calling Him Father and yourself H. Son.
W-pI...197.5:2 what belongs to God must be H. Own. Yet
W-pI...197.5:3 Yet you will never realize H. gifts are sure,
W-pI.198.11:6 that God forever knows to be H. only Son.
W-pI...199.8:6 it. And God Himself extends H. Love and
W-pI...200.7:1 and to his own, which is the same as H..
W-pI...200.9:5 He will not desert H. Son in need, nor let
W-pI...202.1:2 *has given me H. Voice to call me home?* I am
W-pI...203.1:2 *and of sin, because it is my own as well as H..*
W-pI...204.1:2 *God's Name reminds me that I am H. Son,*
W-pI...206.1:2 *with the gifts of God, because I am H. Son.*
W-pI...206.1:3 *And I would give H. gifts where He intended*
W-pI...207.1:3 *away, as I accept H. boundless Love for me.*
W-pI...209.1:4 *The Love of God proclaimed me as H. Son.*
W-pI...210.1:3 *I thought apart from Him and from H. Will.*
W-pI...210.1:4 *H. Will is joy, and only joy for His beloved*
W-pI...210.1:4 *Will is joy, and only joy for H. beloved Son.*
W-pI...213.1:4 *to learn H. lessons and forget my own.* I am
W-pI...219.1:5 *as to what my Father loves forever as H. Son.*
W-pII ....in.2:4 And we are sure H. promises are kept. We
W-pII ....in.3:4 and He has promised that H. Son will not
W-pII ....in.3:4 unanswered when he calls H. Name.
W-pII ....in.4:1 but H. Word upon our minds and hearts,
W-pII ....in.4:1 us that He has told us, through H. Voice,
W-pII ....in.4:2 He has not left H. Son in all his madness,
W-pII ....in.4:3 H. faithfulness earned Him the invitation
W-pII ....in.4:6 words of invitation that H. Voice suggests
W-pII ....in.8:3 go. H. Hand has held us up. His Thoughts
W-pII ....in.8:4 H. Thoughts have lit the darkness of our
W-pII ....in.8:5 H. Love has called to us unceasingly since
W-pII ..in.10:3 Instead of words, we need but feel H. Love
W-pII ..in.10:4 of prayers, we need but call H. Name.
W-pII .221.2:6 let our thoughts be still and find H. peace,
W-pII .221.2:6 we are, and to reveal Himself unto H. Son.
W-pII ....223.h God is my life. I have no life but H..
W-pII ....224.h God is my Father, and He loves H. Son.
W-pII ....225.h God is my Father, and H. Son loves Him.
W-pII .228.1:2 Shall I deny H. knowledge, and believe in
W-pII .228.1:2 in what H. knowledge makes impossible?
W-pII .228.1:4 Or shall I take H. Word for what I am,
W-pII .228.1:4 Who knows the true condition of H. Son?
W-pII ..... 2.3:4 Name of God whereon H. Word is written
W-pII .232.2:5 you undismayed because you are H. Son.
W-pII .233.2:3 at all. This is H. day. And so it is a day of
W-pII ....235.h God in H. mercy wills that I be saved.
W-pII .235.1:3 that God's Love surrounds H. Son and
W-pII .235.1:3 I am saved and safe forever in H. Arms.
W-pII .235.1:5 saved because God in H. mercy wills it so.
W-pII .238.2:2 us. And how dear H. Son, created by His
W-pII .238.2:2 how dear His Son, created by H. Love,
W-pII .239.1:3 shares H. glory any trace of sin and guilt?
W-pII .239.1:4 He loves H. Son forever and with perfect
W-pII ..... 3.2:4 where H. Son could be apart from Him.
W-pII .245.2:3 Who speaks to us as we relate H. Word;
W-pII ....246.h To love my Father is to love H. Son.
W-pII ..... 4.3:4 H. Will forever overcome by death, love
W-pII .254.2:6 And in the stillness, hallowed by H. Love,
W-pII .255.1:2 assures me that H. Son is like Himself. Let
W-pII .255.1:6 In H. Name, I give today to finding what
W-pII .258.1:2 God. H. memory is hidden in our minds,
W-pII .260.2:3 we who are H. Sons are like each other,
W-pII .267.1:1 is all the life that God created in H. Love.
W-pII .267.1:6 a messenger of God, directed by H. Voice,
W-pII .267.1:6 quiet and at peace within H. loving Arms.
W-pII .267.1:7 Each heartbeat calls H. Name, and every
W-pII .267.1:7 and every one is answered by H. Voice,
W-pII ..... 6.5:3 the Christ Whom God created as H. Son.
W-pII .273.1:4 that God Himself has given to H. Son.
W-pII .276.1:4 the Word H. Son did not create with Him,
W-pII .276.1:4 Him, because in this H. Son was born. Let
W-pII .276.1:5 Let us accept H. Fatherhood, and all is
W-pII .276.1:6 us. Deny we were created in H. Love and
W-pII .276.1:7 Who gave H. Word to us in our creation,
W-pII .279.1:1 God's Son is not abandoned by H. Love.
W-pII .279.2:2 *loves the Son Whom He created as H. Own.*
W-pII ..... 7.3:1 you would not let H. Voice appeal in vain,
W-pII ..... 7.3:1 nor turn away from H. replacement for
W-pII ..... 7.5:3 The Holy Spirit is H. gift, by which the
W-pII ..... 8.5:2 instant more for God to take H. final step,
W-pII .292.1:3 let an alien will appear to be opposing H..
W-pII .292.1:7 seek and we will find according to H. Will
W-pII .298.2:4 *my love for God my Father and H. holy Son.*
W-pII .299.1:2 it, acknowledges my holiness as H.. Our
W-pII ..... 9.4:4 And God the Father smiles upon H. Son,
W-pII ..... 9.4:4 His Son, H. one creation and His only joy.
W-pII ..... 9.4:4 His Son, His one creation and H. only joy.
W-pII .309.1:2 I, H. Son, whose will is limitless as is His
W-pII .309.1:2 Son, whose will is limitless as is H. Own,
W-pII ... 10.4:1 step in H. appointed plan to bless His Son
W-pII ... 10.4:1 step in His appointed plan to bless H. Son
W-pII ... 10.4:3 the Son whom God acknowledges as H..
W-pII .311.1:6 by giving us God's Judgment of H. Son.
W-pII .315.2:3 *lead me on to my Creator and H. memory.*
W-pII .316.1:3 H. grace is given me in every gift a brother
W-pII .318.1:7 I am God's Son, H. one eternal Love. I am
W-pII ... 11.2:3 Thus H. Son shares in creation, and must
W-pII ... 11.3:2 in creation is H. Will complete in every
W-pII ... 11.3:3 inviolate; forever held within H. holy Will
W-pII ... 11.5:2 We hear H. Voice, and we forgive creation
W-pII ... 11.5:2 Whose Holiness H. Own creation shares;
W-pII .322.1:3 me. H. memory abides in every gift that I
W-pII .324.2:2 except an instant from H. loving Hand.
W-pII .328.1:4 for us, nor is there any second to H. Will.
W-pII .328.1:5 To join with H. is but to find our own.
W-pII .328.1:6 And since our will is H., it is to Him that
W-pII .329.2:2 We have no will apart from H., and all of
W-pII .329.2:2 all of us are one because H. Will is shared
W-pII .330.1:3 God holds out H. power and His Love,
W-pII .330.1:3 God holds out His power and H. Love,
W-pII ... 12.5:2 holy minds which God created as H. Son,
W-pII ... 12.5:2 God created as His Son, H. dwelling place
W-pII ... 12.5:2 as His Son, His dwelling place, H. joy, His
W-pII ... 12.5:2 Son, His dwelling place, His joy, H. love,
W-pII ... 12.5:2 place, His joy, His love, completely H.,
W-pII .337.1:6 to understand my Father loves H. Son; to
W-pII .338.1:7 God has planned that H. beloved Son will
W-pII .340.2:4 Our Father has redeemed H. Son this day.
W-pII .341.1:3 *Lord of Sinlessness conceives us as H. Son, a*
W-pII ....346.h me, And I forget all things except H. Love.
W-pII .348.2:2 that we choose to be our will as well as H..
W-pII ....350.h through H. memory to save the world.
W-pII .350.2:2 H. Son will be restored to us in the reality
W-pII ... 14.1:1 *whole, shining in the reflection of H. Love.*
W-pII ... 14.1:2 *me is H. creation sanctified and guaranteed*
W-pII ... 14.1:5 *I am the Heaven where H. Love resides. I am*
W-pII ... 14.1:6 *I am H. holy Sinlessness Itself, for in my*
W-pII ... 14.1:6 *Itself, for in my purity abides H. Own.*
W-pII ... 14.5:1 and carrying H. Word to everyone whom
W-pII ....358.h be sure; H. answer is the one I really want.
Wfl........in.3:4 It is H. ending to the dream we seek, and
Wfl........in.3:6 thus H. memory is given back, completely
Wfl........in.4:1 us to be H. Own completion in reality. So
Wfl........in.4:2 way to Him and to the Heaven of H. peace
Wfl........in.5:1 gift our Father promised to H. holy Son.
Wfl........in.6:1 and ask Him to help us to learn H. lessons
Wfl........in.6:1 through the Voice of H. Own Teacher.
Wfl........in.6:2 Would He hurt H. Son? Or would He rush
Wfl........in.6:4 thus, for these are H. Own words to you.
WpII361-5.1:5 He speaks for God my Father and H. holy
W-ep......... 6:8 H. Love surrounds you, and of this be
M-in.......... 4:7 despair and death, God sends H. teachers.
M-in.......... 4:8 as they teach H. lessons of joy and hope,
M-2........... 5:4 send H. Spirit into any holy relationship.
M-3........... 3:5 and H. plan can have no levels, being a
M-3........... 3:5 no levels, being a reflection of H. Will.
M-3........... 4:7 holy. God is not mistaken in H. Son.
M-4........... 1:4 are. God gives special gifts to H. teachers,
M-4........... 1:4 a special role in H. plan for Atonement.
M-4..... IV.2:10 so their will, which always was H. Own, is
M-4......V.1:10 they are sure H. Teacher goes before them
M-4......V.1:11 They hold H. gifts and follow in His way,
M-4......V.1:11 They hold His gifts and follow in H. way,
M-4... VII.2:10 that are of God, and therefore for H. Son.
M-4...... IX.2:8 Word of God and H. definition of His Son
M-4...... IX.2:8 Word of God and His definition of H. Son

| | |
|---|---|
| M-4........X.1:4 | judged by the Voice for God on **H.** behalf. |
| M-5..........I.1:9 | by **H.** death can He be conquered by His |
| M-5..........I.1:9 | His death can He be conquered by **H.** Son. |
| M-5.......III.2:4 | **H.** teachers are the symbols of salvation. |
| M-11..........1:4 | **H.** Word has promised peace. It has also |
| M-11..........1:6 | and yet **H.** Word assures us that He loves |
| M-11..........1:8 | if **H.** promises are to be accepted. What |
| M-11..........3:4 | has sent **H.** Judgment to answer yours. |
| M-11..........3:5 | Gently **H.** Judgment substitutes for yours. |
| M-12..........1:8 | bring **H.** Thoughts to still deluded minds. |
| M-12..........3:3 | cannot communicate **H.** messages directly |
| M-13........8:11 | God holds out **H.** Word to you, for He has |
| M-13........8:12 | What other way is there to save **H.** Son? |
| M-14........5:11 | say you cannot learn **H.** Own curriculum. |
| M-14........5:12 | **H.** Word says otherwise. His Will be done |
| M-14........5:13 | **H.** Will be done. It cannot be otherwise. |
| M-15..........3:7 | **H.** promises are sure. Only remember |
| M-15..........3:9 | that. **H.** promises have guaranteed His |
| M-15..........3:9 | promises have guaranteed **H.** Judgment, |
| M-15..........3:9 | guaranteed His Judgment, and **H.** alone, |
| M-16..........7:1 | of God who has accepted **H.** protection! |
| M-16........11:7 | **H.** teachers know that this is so, and have |
| M-17..........8:1 | hopeless situation God sends **H.** teachers. |
| M-17..........9:13 | But **H.** Love is Cause of everything beyond |
| M-18........3:10 | *H. laws alone prevail upon you and upon the* |
| M-18........3:11 | *H. Love remains the only thing there is. Fear* |
| M-19..........4:6 | God's Judgment is **H.** justice. Onto this,– |
| M-19..........5:1 | confuse **H.** mercy with your own insanity. |
| M-20..........6:2 | the simple understanding that **H.** Will is |
| M-20..........6:3 | is no thought that contradicts **H.** Will, yet |
| M-20..........6:4 | The contrast between **H.** Will and yours |
| M-20..........6:5 | there was no conflict, for **H.** Will is yours. |
| M-20..........6:6 | mighty Will of God Himself **H.** gift to you. |
| M-20........6:12 | God's peace is the condition for **H.** Will. |
| M-20........6:13 | Attain **H.** peace, and you remember Him. |
| M-21..........5:9 | the words they use the power of **H.** Spirit, |
| M-22..........1:7 | Accept **H.** Word and what remains to |
| M-22..........1:8 | Accept **H.** Word and every miracle has |
| M-22..........7:4 | it is not up to them to judge **H.** Son. And |
| M-22..........7:5 | And to judge **H.** Son is to limit his Father. |
| M-23..........3:8 | Can God fail **H.** Son? And can one who is |
| M-26..........1:1 | is no distance between Him and **H.** Son. |
| M-26..........1:2 | **H.** awareness is in everyone's memory, |
| M-26..........1:2 | **H.** Word is written on everyone's heart. |
| M-27..........3:2 | **H.** Love is blotted out in the idea, which |
| M-27..........5:6 | And now **H.** Own creation must stand in |
| M-27..........5:9 | Terrible **H.** Thoughts and fearful His |
| M-27..........5:9 | His Thoughts and fearful **H.** image. To |
| M-27........5:10 | image. To look on **H.** creations is to die. |
| M-28..........1:8 | the invitation to God to take **H.** final step. |
| M-28..........5:8 | we wish for nothing but **H.** Will to be our |
| M-29..........5:2 | his Creator and accept **H.** gifts. And His |
| M-29..........5:3 | And **H.** gifts have no limit. To ask the |
| M-29..........6:8 | cruel if He let your words replace **H.** Own. |
| M-29........6:11 | than this does your Father love **H.** Son? |
| M-29..........7:1 | Remember you are **H.** completion and |
| M-29..........7:1 | you are His completion and **H.** Love. |
| M-29..........7:2 | Remember your weakness is **H.** strength. |
| M-29..........7:4 | If **H.** strength is in you, what you perceive |
| M-29..........7:6 | it so. Ask all things of **H.** Teacher, and all |
| M-29........7:10 | God knows but **H.** Son, and as he was |
| M-29........7:11 | is. In confidence I place you in **H.** Hands, |
| M-29..........8:3 | *Teacher of God, H. thanks He offers you,* |
| M-29..........8:4 | *which H. Voice is heard around the world,* |
| C-3.............3:2 | knows what **H.** Son needs before he asks. |
| C-3.............3:3 | content it is **H.** Will that it be understood. |
| C-3.............5:1 | of **H.** Will alone it cannot be divided. And |
| C-3.............5:2 | the unity that it reflects becomes **H.** Will. |
| C-3.............7:7 | It is the gift of God to save **H.** Son. But |
| C-3.............8:6 | **H.** Son is not attacked but recognized. |
| C-4.............6:9 | God has come to claim **H.** Own. |
| C-4.............7:5 | God knows it is **H.** Own, as it is his. And |
| C-4.............8:1 | but rush to meet Him where **H.** altar is. |
| C-4.............8:2 | Hallowed your Name and **H.**, for they are |
| C-5.............1:8 | But He creates all Helpers of **H.** Son while |
| C-5.............3:1 | God, **H.** one creation and His happiness, |
| C-5.............3:1 | God, His one creation and **H.** happiness, |
| C-6.............1:2 | with Him and in **H.** likeness or spirit, is |
| C-6.............1:5 | knows along with Christ, **H.** real Son, |
| C-6.............3:1 | Link between God and **H.** separated Sons. |
| C-6.............3:6 | never forgets the Creator or **H.** creation. |
| C-ep...........1:5 | Him and with **H.** Word upon your heart. |
| C-ep...........1:9 | when **H.** Love is but an instant farther on |
| C-ep...........2:3 | away, and it is done according to **H.** Will. |
| C-ep...........3:6 | Look up and see **H.** Word among the stars |
| C-ep...........3:6 | He has set your Name along with **H.**. Look |
| C-ep...........4:1 | called to us and helped us hear **H.** Call. |
| C-ep...........5:4 | God is welcomed and **H.** Son with Him. |
| P-1.............2:2 | to call upon God and hear **H.** Answer? |
| P-1...........5:10 | We are all **H.** psychotherapists, for He |
| P-2.........II.6:1 | to God to enter into **H.** Kingdom, what |
| P-2.........II.6:4 | to those who would restore **H.** world, for |
| P-2.........IV.5:5 | by Him to the Holy Spirit as **H.** gift to you |
| P-2.........V.4:6 | directs, because it is according to **H.** Will. |
| P-2.........V.4:7 | We have **H.** Word to guide us, as we try to |
| P-2.........V.5:6 | through which to speak **H.** holy Word; a |
| P-2.........V.5:6 | hand to reach **H.** Son and touch his heart. |
| P-2.........V.5:8 | of God Himself, by which **H.** Son is saved. |
| P-2.........V.6:5 | the tiniest of whispers of **H.** Name. To ask |
| P-2.........V.6:7 | And He will send **H.** Answer through the |
| P-2.........V.6:7 | can serve **H.** Son in all his present needs. |
| P-2.........V.8:6 | There is no other way to hear **H.** Voice. |
| P-2.........V.8:7 | There is no other way to seek **H.** Son. |
| P-2.....VII.1:13 | Son. **H.** knowledge is reflected in the ideal |
| P-2.......VII.9:2 | and so you will not know you are **H.** Son. |
| P-3...........I.2:8 | Would God send **H.** Son to you and not |
| P-3...........I.3:2 | God will not have **H.** gifts to you limited |
| P-3.........II.4:3 | And since **H.** creations do not change and |
| P-3.........II.4:7 | way God chose for the return of **H.** Son. |
| P-3.........II.5:3 | gift from their Creator as a sign of **H.** Love |
| P-3........III.1:2 | part of **H.** plan that everything in this |
| P-3........III.5:6 | have heard **H.** Word and understood it. |
| P-3......III.8:13 | *And then God sent H. Son to give it to you.* |
| S-1.........in.1:1 | which God blessed **H.** Son at his creation. |
| S-1.........in.1:5 | gives thanks to **H.** extension in His Son. |
| S-1.........in.1:5 | gives thanks to His extension in **H.** Son. |
| S-1.........in.1:6 | **H.** Son gives thanks for his creation, in |
| S-1...........I.2:8 | is merely an echo of the reply of **H.** Voice. |
| S-1...........I.4:4 | have no gods before Him; no Love but **H.**. |
| S-1...........I.4:5 | **H.** answer be but your remembrance of |
| S-1...........I.6:7 | Him. He can therefore also reach **H.** Son, |
| S-1.........II.7:7 | that is the gift of God to you, **H.** Son, |
| S-2...........I.3:7 | He loves **H.** Son. Can you remember Him |
| S-2...........I.6:3 | Yet God Himself has given all **H.** Sons a |
| S-2...........I.8:3 | God calls on you to save **H.** Son from |
| S-2.........II.3:5 | and the holiness that is **H.** gift forever. |
| S-2.........II.3:6 | Can **H.** Son condemn himself and still |
| S-2........III.1:7 | He gives **H.** Teacher to whoever asks, and |
| S-2........III.1:8 | **H.** readiness to give lies far beyond your |
| S-2........III.1:9 | Him, and in **H.** willing there is certainty. |
| S-2........III.2:1 | not by your plans but by **H.** holy Will. His |
| S-2........III.2:2 | **H.** Voice will teach you what forgiveness |
| S-2........III.4:4 | **H.** is a justice He can understand, but you |
| S-2........III.6:8 | Prayer is **H.** Own right Hand, made free |
| S-2........III.6:8 | come from **H.** eternal vigilance and Love. |
| S-2......III.6:11 | **H.** answer will be clear as morning, nor is |
| S-2......III.6:11 | nor is **H.** forgiveness what you think it is. |
| S-2........III.7:5 | nor fail to send **H.** angels down to answer |
| S-2........III.7:5 | down to answer you in **H.** Own Name. He |
| S-3...........I.4:5 | **H.** Voice He still can reach His Son, |
| S-3...........I.4:5 | He still can reach **H.** Son, reminding him |
| S-3........IV.3:3 | God thanks **H.** healers, for He knows the |
| S-3........IV.3:3 | the Cause of healing is Himself, **H.** Love, |
| S-3........IV.3:3 | of healing is Himself, His Love, **H.** Son, |
| S-3........IV.3:3 | restored as **H.** completion and returned |
| S-3........IV.3:5 | dear to Him as is the whole of **H.** creation, |
| S-3........IV.3:5 | creation, for it lies in you as **H.** eternal gift |
| S-3........IV.5:2 | give the role to Him you see in **H.** creation |
| S-3........IV.5:3 | that it is you who are creator in **H.** place, |
| S-3........IV.5:6 | Vengeance is **H.**. His great destroyer, |
| S-3........IV.5:7 | **H.** great destroyer, death. And sickness, |

## His 237

• Christ/Self
*God*
*Holy Spirit*
*his*

| | |
|---|---|
| T-1.........I.44:1 | and the acceptance of **H.** Atonement. |
| T-11......IV.7:3 | as yourself, and of **H.** Wholeness as yours. |
| T-11......IV.7:4 | in **H.** Creator and shines with His glory. |
| T-11......IV.7:5 | as perfect as **H.** Creator and at peace with |
| T-11.....V.17:7 | to them of Himself and of **H.** Father. They |
| T-11.....V.17:8 | to them, and it is **H.** words they speak. |
| T-11......VI.3:8 | at all. **H.** perceptions are your natural |
| T-11....VI.3:10 | For until Christ comes into **H.** Own, the |
| T-11....VIII.9:1 | for Christ is not deceived in **H.** Father and |
| T-11....VIII.9:1 | and **H.** Father is not deceived in Him. Do |
| T-11....VIII.9:4 | Who is in no way separate from **H.** Father |
| T-11....VIII.9:4 | of **H.** Father by which He was created. Be |
| T-12........II.3:6 | Healing is the Love of Christ for **H.** Father |
| T-12........II.6:5 | withstand the Love of Christ for **H.** Father |
| T-12........II.6:5 | His Father, or **H.** Father's Love for Him. |
| T-12......VI.4:4 | with love if you accept **H.** vision as yours. |
| T-12......VI.4:6 | In **H.** sight the Son of God is perfect, and |
| T-12......VI.4:6 | and He longs to share **H.** vision with you. |
| T-12......VI.5:8 | peace He waits for you at **H.** Father's altar, |
| T-12......VI.6:2 | Love for you is **H.** Love for His Father, |
| T-12......VI.6:2 | Love for you is His Love for **H.** Father, |
| T-12......VI.6:2 | knows because He knows **H.** Father's Love |
| T-12......VI.6:3 | led you to Christ at the altar to **H.** Father, |
| T-13.......V.9:3 | "vision" comes from fear, as **H.** from love. |
| T-13.....V.10:4 | seeing what He is, He knows **H.** Father. |
| T-13.....V.10:6 | Him, for **H.** vision is His gift of love to you |
| T-13.....V.10:6 | Him, for His vision is **H.** gift of love to you |
| T-13.....V.11:6 | the sanity of **H.** vision they looked upon |
| T-13......VI.3:2 | and in **H.** changelessness lies your release. |
| T-13......VI.7:5 | you look at Christ and call **H.** witnesses to |
| T-13.....VII.5:8 | not. **H.** Being does not depend upon your |
| T-13.....VII.6:4 | rejoice that you have found **H.** company, |
| T-13....VIII.4:5 | Yet even Christ's vision is not **H.** reality. |
| T-13....VIII.4:6 | that spring to light under **H.** loving gaze |
| T-13....VIII.5:6 | Help Him to give **H.** gift of light to all who |
| T-13....VIII.5:6 | into **H.** quiet sight that makes them one. |
| T-13....VIII.6:2 | He will offer them unto **H.** Father as they |
| T-13....VIII.6:6 | Christ's vision is **H.** gift to you. His Being |
| T-13....VIII.6:7 | you. **H.** Being is His Father's gift to Him. |
| T-13....VIII.6:7 | you. His Being is **H.** Father's gift to Him. |
| T-13........X.9:9 | **H.** Will is like His Father's, and He offers |
| T-13........X.9:9 | His Will is like **H.** Father's, and He offers |
| T-15......III.6:9 | of Christ, eternal Host unto **H.** Father. |
| T-15....VIII.4:7 | knows of no separation from **H.** Father, |
| T-15....VIII.4:7 | His Father, Who is **H.** one relationship, in |
| T-15....VIII.4:7 | which He gives as **H.** Father gives to Him. |
| T-15......XI.2:5 | In **H.** Presence the whole idea of sacrifice |
| T-16......III.7:6 | learn **H.** power and strength and purity, |
| T-16......III.7:6 | purity, and love Him as **H.** Father does. |
| T-16......III.7:7 | **H.** Kingdom has no limits and no end, |
| T-17....IV.10:5 | joy of **H.** eternal Spirit are marshalled to |
| T-19......IV.3:9 | the Father will accept them in **H.** Name. |
| T19...IV.D.2:2 | Yet as **H.** face rises beyond it, shining with |
| T19...IV.D.2:2 | with joy because He is in **H.** Father's Love, |
| T19...IV.D.2:3 | bright Rays of **H.** Father's Love that light |
| T19...IV.D.2:3 | of His Father's Love that light **H.** face with |
| T19...IV.D.4:6 | face of Christ and join Him in **H.** Father. |
| T19. IV.D.14:3 | veil of sin upon Him to hide **H.** loveliness. |
| T19. IV.D.14:4 | out to you, to share **H.** Holiness. This |
| T19. IV.D.14:5 | still offers you salvation as **H.** Friend. The |
| T-22.........I.8:7 | must He be reborn into **H.** ancient home, |
| T-22.......I.11:5 | are **H.** sweetness and His gentle innocence |
| T-22.......I.11:5 | are His sweetness and **H.** gentle innocence |
| T-22.......I.11:7 | on your brother as **H.** chosen home, for |
| T-22.......I.11:7 | you will with Him and with **H.** Father. |
| T-22.......II.12:8 | light **H.** home with vision that overlooks |
| T-22.......II.13:1 | in quiet here with Christ is share **H.** vision |
| T-22.......II.13:2 | Quickly and gladly is **H.** vision given |
| T-22......IV.3:9 | You will become **H.** messenger, returning |
| T-24.......V.1:3 | that it is one with Him and with **H.** Father |
| T-24.......V.3:7 | beautiful **H.** hand that holds His brother's |
| T-24.......V.3:7 | beautiful His hand that holds **H.** brother's |
| T-24.......V.5:2 | Be glad that only Christ can lend you **H.**, |
| T-24.......V.6:3 | **H.** Love for God replaces all the fear you |

T-24....... V.6:4 H. Holiness shows you Himself in him
T-24....... V.7:2 hand holds all H. brothers in Himself. He
T-24....... V.7:4 through them, holding out H. hand, that
T-24....... V.7:5 to look upon with Him and share H. joy.
T-24....... V.7:6 H. perfect lack of specialness He offers
T-24....... V.9:3 and from H. certainty His quiet comes.
T-24....... V.9:3 and from His certainty H. quiet comes.
T-24....... V.9:4 exchange H. certainty for all your doubts,
T-24....... V.9:4 your grasp because your hands are H.. He
T-24....... V.9:6 H. quietness becomes your certainty. And
T-24.... VI.13:5 for only what H. Father wills is possible,
T-24.... VI.13:6 see. Out of H. lack of conflict comes your
T-24.... VI.13:7 H. purpose comes the means for effortless
T-25.......in.1:9 that they may frame H. Holiness in them.
T-25.......in.3:4 H. purpose folds the body in His light,
T-25.......in.3:4 His purpose folds the body in H. light,
T-25.........I.1:3 it. For the Mind is H.. And so it must be
T-25.........I.1:5 H. Holiness directs the body through the
T-25.........I.1:7 stand between the aspects of H. Holiness,
T-25.........I.1:7 meet and join and raise Him to H. Father,
T-25.........I.5:4 and H. Father never have been separate,
T-25.........I.5:4 part of you that shares H. Father's Will.
T-25.........I.6:2 Because H. purpose still is one with Both
T-25....... V.3:5 that you might hear in him H. Call to you,
T-25..VIII.12:4 that He could not doubt H. innocence.
T-25..VIII.12:6 H. understanding will be yours. And so
T-26...... IV.3:3 and not recall H. Father as He really is?
T-26...... VI.2:4 obscures H. grace and majesty from you,
T-26...... VI.2:4 and keeps H. friendship and forgiveness
T-26...... VI.2:6 Seek not another friend to take H. place.
T-26...... VI.3:6 when you make room for Him on H..
T-26...... IX.8:4 ancient scars are healed within H. sight.
T-27....... II.6:7 to His Son, and of the Son unto H. Own,
T-29....VIII.3:6 And fall before H. face like a dark veil that
T-30....... V.8:5 H. blessing lies on you as surely as His
T-30....... V.8:5 surely as H. Father's Love rests upon Him.
T-30....... V.8:6 Him. H. gratitude to you is past your
T-30....... V.8:6 with you, together, to H. Father's house.
T-31....VIII.1:4 if Christ appeared to you in all H. glory,
T-31....VIII.2:7 and He has given you H. strength instead.
T-31....VIII.3:5 everything that hides H. face from you.
T-31....VIII.3:6 H. Holiness is yours because He is the
T-31....VIII.3:7 H. strength is yours because He is the Self
T-31....VIII.4:3 of Christ is powerless before H. majesty,
T-31....VIII.4:3 and disappears before H. holy sight. The
T-31....VIII.4:4 are merely those who choose H. strength
W-pI...107.9:2 to let H. function be fulfilled through you.
W-pI...107.9:3 To share H. function is to share His joy.
W-pI...107.9:3 To share His function is to share H. joy.
W-pI...107.9:4 joy. H. confidence is with you, as you say:
W-pI...151.8:3 only honor Him, rejoicing in H. perfect,
W-pI.152.11:6 grateful to restore H. home to God, as it
W-pI...153.7:2 Christ and come to fear H. Father's anger.
W-pI.153.19:3 remember that H. strength abides in us.
W-pI.153.19:4 our weakness unsupported by H. strength
W-pI.153.19:5 We call upon H. strength each time we
W-pI.153.20:7 to look on Christ and see H. sinlessness.
W-pI......157.h Into H. Presence would I enter now.
W-pI...157.4:2 having joined your will with H. this day,
W-pI...157.9:1 except H. shining face and perfect Love.
W-pI...157.9:2 The vision of H. face will stay with you,
W-pI...158.5:5 Will and H. are joined in knowledge. Yet
W-pI...158.9:2 In H. forgiveness are they gone. Unseen
W-pI...159.4:5 And in H. sight the sinless are as one.
W-pI...159.4:6 Their holiness was given by H. Father and
W-pI...159.8:6 And they become H. messengers, who
W-pI...159.9:1 Take from H. storehouse, that its
W-pI...159.9:2 H. lilies do not leave their home when
W-pI.159.10:5 It is H. gift, whereby a sweet transition
W-pI.159.10:7 H. dream awakens us to truth. His vision
W-pI.159.10:8 H. vision gives the means for a return to
W-pI...160.9:2 H. vision sees no strangers, but beholds
W-pI...160.9:2 beholds H. Own and joyously unites with
W-pI...164.2:1 world fades easily away before H. sight.
W-pI...164.2:5 using your voice to give H. glad consent;
W-pI...164.3:1 gives you H. sight and hears for you, and
W-pI...164.5:4 And in H. judgment will a world unfold in
W-pI...164.7:6 the freedom given us through H. forgiving
W-pI...166.8:1 and perceive H. gentle hand directing you

W-pI.166.11:4 and speaks of H. Companionship when
W-pI.166.12:2 For H. touch on you has made you like
W-pI.166.12:5 This is the lesson that H. giving holds, for
W-pI...174.1:1 (157) Into H. Presence would I enter now
W-pI...182.4:3 Child in you Who seeks H. Father's house,
W-pI...182.4:6 It is H. Holiness that lights up Heaven,
W-pI...182.5:2 It is this Child Who knows H. Father. He
W-pI...182.5:3 H. voice cries unto you to let Him rest a
W-pI...182.5:4 the holy air that fills H. Father's house.
W-pI...182.5:5 You are H. home as well. He will return.
W-pI...182.5:7 Himself, within the peace that is H. home,
W-pI...182.6:3 shut out, H. tiny voice so readily obscured
W-pI...182.6:3 H. call for help almost unheard amid the
W-pI...182.6:4 that in you still abides H. sure protection.
W-pI...182.7:4 whispers of H. home unceasingly to you.
W-pI...182.7:6 H. patience has no limits. He will wait
W-pI...182.7:7 He will wait until you hear H. gentle Voice
W-pI...182.8:1 restless mind, then will you hear H. Voice.
W-pI...182.8:3 that instant He will take you to H. home,
W-pI...182.9:3 holds the might of Heaven in H. hand and
W-pI...182.9:3 friend, and gives H. strength to them, that
W-pI...182.9:4 they protect Him, for H. home is far away,
W-pI.182.12:6 H. home is yours. Today He gives you His
W-pI.182.12:7 Today He gives you H. defenselessness,
W-pI...197.7:4 H. Being in His Father is secure, because
W-pI...197.7:4 His Being in H. Father is secure, because
W-pI...197.9:6 that you think can only be H. Thoughts,
W-pII.247.1:4 Let me accept what H. sight shows me as
W-pII.270.2:3 And through H. sight we offer healing to
W-pII.....6.1:3 abides within the Mind that is H. Source.
W-pII.....6.1:4 He has not left H. holy home, nor lost the
W-pII.....6.2:2 Your mind is part of H., and His of yours.
W-pII.....6.2:2 Your mind is part of His, and H. of yours.
W-pII.....6.2:5 For though in Him H. Father placed the
W-pII.....6.2:5 He remain the Self Who, like H. Father,
W-pII.....6.3:4 before H. glory and reveal your holy Self,
W-pII.....6.5:3 As we behold H. glory, will we know we
W-pII.271.1:4 H. kindly sight redeems the world from
W-pII.291.1:2 H. sight shows me all things forgiven and
W-pII.303.1:5 see but sights that show H. Father's Love.
W-pII.304.1:2 looks upon, unless it is H. vision that I use
W-pII.308.1:7 to give H. present blessing to the world,
W-pII.313.1:5 *In H. sight are all its sins forgiven, for He sees*
W-pII.313.1:6 *Now let H. true perception come to me, that*
W-pII....13.3:3 Perception stands corrected in H. sight,
W-pII.353.1:4 *A while I work with Him to serve H. purpose.*
W-pII....354.h And in Him Is H. Creator, as He is in me.
W-pII.354.1:3 *I have no purpose but H. Own. And He is like*
W-pII.354.1:4 *And He is like H. Father. Thus must I be one*
M-4..... V.1:14 H. need of them is just as great as theirs of
M-14......... 2:5 Here is H. home, for here there is need of
M-14......... 2:7 Him. It is H. Call God's teachers answer,
M-14......... 2:7 to Him in silence to receive H. Word. The
M-14......... 2:8 have been rightly judged by H. judgment.
M-25......... 6:9 hearts, and H. holy sight not far behind.
M-28......... 5:5 have seen the face of Christ, H. sinlessness
M-28......... 5:5 His sinlessness, H. Love behind all forms,
M-28......... 5:6 because H. Holiness has set us free indeed
M-28......... 5:7 And we accept H. Holiness as ours; as it is
P-2..........II.6:7 for what is unseen through H. eyes is too
P-2....... VII.2:4 can enter? This is H. home, into which
P-2....... VII.3:3 Christ forgives, knowing H. sinlessness.
P-2....... VII.3:4 H. vision heals perception and sickness
S-1...........I.7:1 because it is a gift of thanks to H. Father.
S-1..........II.5:5 Christ and a recognition of H. sinlessness.
S-1......... V.3:4 Now can you look upon H. sinlessness.
S-2...........I.6:4 look through H. and learn to see like Him.
S-2...........I.6:6 H. constancy remains in tranquil silence
S-2...........I.6:8 H. the eyes that look past error to the
S-2...........I.7:1 Ask, then, H. help, and ask Him how to
S-2...........I.7:1 to learn forgiveness as H. vision lets it be.
S-2...........I.7:5 and in H. sight the world becomes as holy
S-2..........II.7:8 It is H. face forgiveness lets you see. It is
S-2..........II.7:9 It is H. face in which you see your own.
S-2........ III.2:7 Forgiveness-for-salvation is H. task, and it
S-2........ III.3:3 with your own sincerity, but with H. Own
S-2........ III.5:5 H. eyes through which you look on him,
S-2........ III.5:8 not confuse H. function with your own.
S-2........ III.6:6 heard by anyone who calls upon H. Name

S-2........ III.6:6 and places his forgiveness in H. hands.
S-3..........II.3:5 now; H. vision more sustained in us; His
S-3..........II.3:5 His vision more sustained in us; H. Voice,
S-3........ IV.2:6 to see H. likeness and to teach like Him.
S-3........ IV.8:8 Do not deny to Christ what is H. Own.

## His 435

• Holy Spirit
*God*
*Christ/Self*
*his*

T-1 ........I.38:3 the false by H. ability to perceive totally
T-5 ..........I.4:5 H. symbolic function makes the Holy
T-5 .........II.3:8 H. is the Voice that calls you back to
T-5 .........II.4:3 H. is the glory before which dissociation
T-5 ....... III.1:2 were related, because in H. Mind they are.
T-5 ....... III.1:3 relationship must be in H. Mind because,
T-5 ....... III.1:4 because H. Mind is partly yours and also
T-5 ....... III.7:2 H. ability to deal with symbols enables
T-5 ....... III.7:3 H. ability to look beyond symbols into
T-5 ..... III.8:11 opposing it with H. strength just as the
T-5 ..... III.10:5 because it is H. Own dwelling place; the
T-5 ..... III.11:7 H. understanding looks back to God in
T-5 ... III.11:10 that you increase it in H. Name by sharing
T-5 ... III.11:10 by sharing it to increase H. joy in you.
T-5 ....... VI.5:1 can reinterpret them in H. Own light.
T-5 ..... VI.10:8 H. verdict will always be "thine is the
T-5 ..... VI.12:6 because it is H. special function to return
T-6 .........I.10:6 inevitably led to demonstrate H. way for
T-6 .........I.19:2 If you will listen to H. Voice you will know
T-6 ....... III.1:3 mind through H. impartial perception. By
T-6 ....... III.3:1 because as you see H. gentleness in others
T-6 ....... IV.1:5 and you no longer need H. guidance. The
T-6 .........V.4:2 and H. dependability makes them more
T-6 .........V.4:6 H. light is always the Call to awaken,
T-6 ... V.A.5:12 H. teaching begins with the lesson: *To*
T-6 ..... V.B.7:4 H. second lesson is: *To have peace, teach*
T-7 .........II.5:4 meaning of H. message is always the same
T-7 .........II.6:6 You will not understand H. translations
T-7 ....... III.5:5 questions. H. sole function is to undo the
T-7 .........V.8:4 Spirit in him that never changes H. Mind.
T-7 ...... VII.7:4 Every attack is a call for H. patience, since
T-7 ...... VII.7:4 since H. patience can translate attack into
T-7 .....VIII.6:1 is beyond belief and H. perception is true.
T-7 .........X.5:2 long as you avoid H. guidance in any way,
T-7 ........ XI.1:1 guide you truly, because your joy is H..
T-7 ........ XI.1:2 is H. Will for everyone because He speaks
T-8 .........II.6:2 H. direction is freedom and His goal is
T-8 .........II.6:2 direction is freedom and H. goal is God.
T-8 .........II.8:2 H. appeal, then, is merely to what the
T-8 ....... III.1:6 There is no limit on H. teaching because
T-8 ....... III.1:7 Understanding H. function perfectly He
T-8 ....... III.1:7 perfectly, because that is H. joy and yours.
T-8 ....... III.2:6 Only H. teaching will release your will to
T-8 .........V.6:3 lose sight of H. direction through illusions
T-8 ...... VII.7:7 thus to confuse the goal of H. curriculum.
T-8 .... VII.13:2 joyous Teacher and learning H. lessons.
T-8 .....VIII.9:1 so He can teach H. message through you.
T-8 ....... IX.4:5 you utilized sleep according to H. purpose
T-8 ....... IX.5:4 H. function is to distinguish only between
T-9 ..........I.4:3 H. recognition of this Will can make it
T-9 ..........I.4:4 H. perception of your mind brings its
T-9 .........II.3:4 possible that H. answer will not be heard.
T-9 .........II.5:5 and H. Voice speaks to you through him.
T-9 .........II.6:6 And H. answer is only for what you are.
T-9 .......II.12:4 way, and the only way to have H. answer,
T-9 .......II.12:4 H. answer is all you can ask for and want.
T-9 ....... III.8:2 Do not undertake H. function, or you will
T-9 ....... IV.6:1 because forgiveness is H. function and He
T-9 ....... IV.6:4 H. work is not your function, and unless
T-9 .........V.8:6 You can only let Him fulfill H. function.
T-9 .......V.8:11 Trust Him, for help is H. function, and He
T-9 ....... VI.1:1 the Holy Spirit in you except by H. effects
T-9 ....... VI.2:2 you are your evaluations of H. consistency
T-9 ....... VI.2:3 will not always recognize H. consistency.
T-9 ....... VI.2:4 go beyond your offering in H. giving. This
T-9 ....... VI.2:5 This is not because He limits H. giving,
T-9 ...... VII.3:2 you. H. evaluation of you is based on His

T-9.......VII.3:2 is based on H. knowledge of what you are,
T-9... VIII.11:6 tell you, but do not be afraid of H. answer,
T-11....... II.4:3 He will lay H. Own complete Will and
T-11....... II.5:2 but H. Voice grows faint in alien company
T-11....... II.5:5 the ego to enter, you lessen H. welcome.
T-11....... II.5:8 You can safely trust H. patience, for He
T-11....... II.6:6 need not be perfect, because H. is. If you
T-11......III.7:3 Give H. peace, that you may enter the
T-11... VIII.5:6 H. answer is both many and one, as long
T-11... VIII.5:7 You may be afraid of H. specificity, for
T-11... VIII.6:4 question you must ask to learn H. answer
T-11. VIII.12:4 perceive no one but through H. guidance,
T-11. VIII.12:5 Accept H. healing power and use it for all
T-11. VIII.14:3 Teacher of reality, and hearing H. answer,
T-12.........I.5:8 motivation, but you do need H..
T-12.........I.6:7 He does not change H. Mind about reality
T-12.........I.6:8 divided state, H. remain consistently true.
T-12.........I.8:1 that H. criteria are equally applicable to
T-12...... II.10:5 otherwise H. knowledge remains useless
T-12...... II.10:6 to help you, since help is H. only purpose.
T-12......IV.4:5 For H. promise is always, "Seek and you
T-12......IV.4:5 and under H. guidance you cannot be
T-12......IV.4:6 H. is the journey to accomplishment, and
T-12......IV.5:5 to your home because that is H. mission.
T-12......IV.5:6 fulfills H. mission He will teach you yours,
T-12......IV.5:6 yours, for your mission is the same as H..
T-12.....VII.3:1 but you can see the results of H. Presence,
T-12.....VII.3:4 Perceiving H. results, you will understand
T-12.....VII.4:1 Spirit, but you can see H. manifestations.
T-12.....VII.4:3 Miracles are H. witnesses, and speak for
T-12.....VII.4:3 His witnesses, and speak for H. Presence.
T-12.....VII.4:6 Spirit's work, for you share in H. function
T-12.....VII.4:8 Holy Spirit shares H. with you on earth.
T-12.....VII.6:2 For He will send you H. witnesses if you
T-12...VII.12:6 will be right, for judgment *is* H. function.
T-12...VII.12:7 share H. function only by judging as He
T-12... VIII.6:6 H. vision your perception is healed. You
T-12... VIII.7:4 is invisible to you is perfect in H. sight,
T-13.........I.4:5 the Son of God, for such was H. mission,
T-13......III.7:2 vision is merciful and H. remedy is quick.
T-13......III.7:3 Do not hide suffering from H. sight, but
T-13......III.7:4 Lay before H. eternal sanity all your hurt,
T-13......III.7:5 any spot of pain hidden from H. light,
T-13......III.9:3 exempt yourself from H. healing power,
T-13......IV.7:4 serving only H. teaching function, which
T-13......IV.7:5 H. emphasis is therefore on the only
T-13......IV.8:4 it. It is H. interpretation of the means of
T-13......IV.8:4 would share H. goal of salvation for you.
T-13...VII.13:4 Under H. guidance you will travel light
T-13...VII.13:4 for H. sight is ever on the journey's end,
T-13...VII.13:4 ever on the journey's end, which is H. goal
T-13... VIII.2:7 can reach everywhere under H. guidance,
T-13... VIII.4:4 H. message speaks of timelessness in time
T-13... VIII.8:2 me under the holy banner of H. teaching,
T-13......IX.6:3 accept H. offer of Atonement for all your
T-13......XI.4:6 to doubt that H. mission will be fulfilled.
T-13......XI.4:7 is this possible, when H. mission is of God
T-13....XI.11:3 kind of reconciliation in H. Mind for you,
T-14.......in.1:4 except that H. conclusions are not insane.
T-14.........I.5:1 must begin H. teaching by showing you
T-14.........I.5:2 H. message is not indirect, but He must
T-14....... II.1:1 H. mission can be happily accomplished.
T-14....... II.2:1 begins H. lesson in simplicity with the
T-14......III.6:7 It is H. joy to teach it, as it will be yours.
T-14....III.11:6 Instead, accept H. answer, for He knows
T-14....III.12:6 leave all decisions to H. gentle counsel.
T-14....III.13:2 Only H. wisdom is capable of guiding you
T-14....III.13:7 And it is H. decision to undo everything
T-14....III.14:4 Without H. guidance you will think you
T-14....III.16:2 For H. decisions are reflections of what
T-14....III.16:4 Learn of H. wisdom and His Love, and
T-14....III.16:4 Learn of His wisdom and H. Love, and
T-14....III.16:4 and teach H. answer to everyone who
T-14....III.18:3 isolation through H. loving guidance, and
T-14....III.19:1 should do, think of H. Presence in you,
T-14......IV.9:6 H. memory is yours. If you remember
T-14....... V.2:7 H. gentleness is yours, and all the love you
T-14.....V.10:8 H. gentleness He would release from fear
T-14.....V.10:9 The power of love is in H. gentleness,

T-14...... VI.5:3 use to Him, for H. most holy purpose. He
T-14...... VI.8:3 no source of interference from H. sight,
T-14...... VI.8:4 Him and let H. gentleness teach you that,
T-14.....VII.5:7 H. perception of them, according to His
T-14.....VII.5:7 of them, according to H. purpose, merely
T-14.....VII.5:9 H. task is mighty, but the power of God is
T-14...VII.6:11 H. judgment must prevail, and He will
T-14...VII.6:11 it to you as you join your perception to H.
T-14..... X.11:1 translate H. communications through you
T-14.....XI.6:11 you. He will take H. rightful place in your
T-14...... XI.9:8 They do not exist in H. Mind at all. For
T-14.....XI.9:11 corrects your use of time, and makes it H..
T-14....XI.10:2 you accept H. accomplishments as yours,
T-14....XI.10:6 He always gives H. gifts in place of yours.
T-14....XI.10:7 establish H. bright teaching so firmly in
T-14....XI.10:7 He has established as holy by H. Presence.
T-14....XI.10:9 And all H. works are yours. He offers you
T-14....XI.11:3 God's Teacher is as like to H. Creator as is
T-14....XI.11:5 and before H. lesson division disappears.
T-14....XI.14:3 for H. faith in you is His understanding. It
T-14....XI.14:3 for His faith in you is H. understanding. It
T-14....XI.14:4 It is as firm as is H. faith in His Creator,
T-14....XI.14:4 It is as firm as is His faith in H. Creator,
T-14....XI.14:4 and He knows that faith in H. Creator
T-14....XI.14:5 this consistency lies H. Holiness which He
T-14....XI.14:5 abandon, for it is not H. Will to do so.
T-14....XI.14:6 With your perfection ever in H. sight, He
T-14....XI.15:1 both arise, is yours as surely as it is H..
T-15.........I.1:3 God's Teacher cannot be satisfied with H.
T-15.........I.1:4 He has not fulfilled H. teaching function
T-15.........I.2:3 the Holy Spirit uses time in H. Own way,
T-15.........I.2:4 Time is H. friend in teaching. It does not
T-15.......I.12:5 time to the Holy Spirit for H. use of it.
T-15......I.15:11 and leave H. giving it to you to Him.
T-15....... II.2:5 H. joy is not contained in time. His
T-15....... II.2:6 H. teaching is for you because His joy is
T-15....... II.2:6 teaching is for you because H. joy is yours.
T-15....... II.4:4 Spirit. And they support H. strength. It is,
T-15....... II.6:5 God's Teacher and H. lesson will support
T-15....... V.4:5 In H. function as Interpreter of what you
T-15....... V.4:6 Under H. teaching, every relationship
T-15....... V.5:4 place any relationship under H. care and
T-15....... V.5:4 willingness to have it serve no need but H.
T-15....... V.5:6 it. All the love from H. Do not, then, be
T-15....... V.5:8 the relationship. Your only need is H..
T-15....... V.6:1 been offered to the Holy Spirit for H. use.
T-15....... V.9:4 substitutes H. frame of reference for it.
T-15....... V.9:5 H. frame of reference is simply God. The
T-15...VII.10:6 recognizing in H. Voice your own need to
T-15... VIII.1:2 For a teaching assignment such as H., He
T-15... VIII.1:5 H. concern and care for you are limitless.
T-15... VIII.6:2 It is H. holy function to accept them both,
T-15... VIII.6:3 He will do this because it is H. function.
T-16.........I.1:3 provided you let Him use it in H. way. His
T-16.........I.2:1 way. H. way is very different. He does not
T-16.........I.4:2 will learn H. interpretation of it if you let
T-16.........I.4:5 You are not sure that He will do H. part,
T-16.........I.5:7 Do not confuse your role with H., for this
T-16.........I.5:8 Offer your empathy to Him for it is *H.*
T-16.........I.5:8 and *H.* strength that you would share. And
T-16.........I.5:9 offer you H. strength and His perception,
T-16.........I.5:9 offer you His strength and H. perception,
T-16.........I.7:5 That is H. function, and not yours. He will
T-16.........I.7:6 Leave Him H. function, for He will fulfill
T-16....... II.4:4 H. natural perception of your gift enables
T-16....... II.4:4 to use H. understanding on your behalf. It
T-16....... II.5:5 For H. task is to translate the miracle into
T-16....... II.5:6 Let H. understanding of the miracle be
T-16....... II.5:6 the witnesses that He has given you to H.
T-16....... II.7:5 you listened to H. interpretation the
T-16.......VI.3:1 Spirit asks your help, if you would have H.
T-16.......VI.3:2 The holy instant is H. most helpful aid in
T-16....VI.12:2 needs only your willingness to share H.
T-16....VI.12:3 not be complete because H. is perfect. It is
T-16....VI.12:4 H. task to atone for your unwillingness by
T-16....VI.12:4 for your unwillingness by H. perfect faith,
T-16....VI.12:4 and it is H. faith you share with Him there
T-16....VI.12:5 release, H. perfect willingness is given you
T-16....VI.12:6 Call upon Him, for Heaven is at H. Call.

T-17........II.1:9 And all H. teaching leads to seeing it and
T-17........II.5:4 spot H. reason touches grows alive with
T-17........II.8:4 Meet H. patience with your impatience at
T-17...... III.5:1 Holy Spirit bring H. interpretation of the
T-17...... III.6:3 make H. resolutions complete and perfect
T-17...... III.6:4 each step in H. undoing is the separation
T-17....... V.2:7 to the Holy Spirit, to use for H. purposes.
T-17....... V.3:2 At once H. goal replaces yours. This is
T-17....... V.6:5 what He has taken under H. guidance?
T-17....... V.7:8 He not been very explicit in H. answer?
T-17...... V.11:3 enormous efforts to help Him do H. work.
T-17......VII.9:5 relationship by exchanging yours for H.,
T-17....VIII.3:4 means for establishing H. purpose, and
T-17....VIII.4:1 to H. Call seems to be greater than before.
T-18........II.6:1 Holy Spirit, ever practical in H. wisdom,
T-18........II.6:6 as a help to make H. purpose real to you.
T-18........II.7:8 If you but recognized H. gratitude! Or
T-18........II.7:9 Or mine through H.! For we are joined as
T-18...... III.5:4 desire from H. Will and from His strength
T-18...... III.5:4 desire from His Will and from H. strength
T-18...... IV.6:7 Do not assume H. function for Him. Give
T-18...... IV.6:8 how little is your part, and how great is H.
T-18....... V.2:4 That is *H.* function. Your part is only to
T-18....... V.2:6 little faith, joined with H. understanding,
T-18....... V.7:6 *Spirit, that H. blessing may descend on us,*
T-18...... IX.3:8 For it is not H. purpose to frighten you,
T-19...... III.5:2 On this you share H. vision. Yet you do
T-19...... III.5:3 Yet you do not share H. recognition of the
T-19...... IV.2:6 you not now return H. graciousness, and
T-19...... IV.3:8 and lay them gently before H. Creator in
T19....IV.A.5:9 H. home is in your holy relationship. Do
T19. IV.A.5:10 stand between Him and H. holy purpose,
T19. IV.A.15:5 Holy Spirit has given you H. messengers
T19... IV.D.9:7 that you will accept it for my love and H..
T-20........II.5:3 purpose as their own share also H. vision.
T-20........II.5:4 And what enables Him to see H. purpose
T-20........II.5:4 from every altar now is yours as well as H.
T-20...... IV.6:6 plan, now that it shares H. purpose. And
T-20..... V.7:10 And through H. vision will you see it, and
T-20..... V.7:10 and through H. understanding recognize
T-20...... VI.5:6 Spirit does not build H. temples where
T-20...... VI.5:7 sees the face of Christ choose as H. home
T-20.... VI.7:10 for the Holy Spirit has set H. temple there
T-20...... VI.9:6 And from H. holy temple, look you not
T-20.....VII.1:2 from the same Source as does H. purpose.
T-20.....VII.8:2 Holy Spirit offers you to serve H. purpose.
T-20.....VII.8:5 H. vision cannot see the body because it
T-20....VIII.6:1 brought to it by H. calm and certain sight.
T-20....VIII.6:3 sure. For it will meet H. purpose, seen in
T-20....VIII.6:4 is turned to blessing under H. gentle gaze.
T-20..VIII.10:6 H. substitutes for all the terrifying sights
T-21...... III.4:3 This is H. direction; the only one He ever
T-21...... III.4:5 H. faith and His belief and vision are all
T-21...... III.4:5 and H. belief and vision are all for you.
T-21...... III.6:2 H. purpose lies in the opposite direction.
T-21.... III.11:2 not what it is H. purpose to lead you *from.*
T-21...... VI.8:6 and brings your reason into line with H..
T-22........II.5:6 was given to the Holy Spirit as H. purpose
T-22...... IV.6:5 carrying H. message of hope and freedom
T-22...... VI.2:4 outcome as He is sure of H. Creator's Love
T-22...... VI.2:5 as dear to H. Creator as love is to itself.
T-22...... VI.3:2 that you can be the means to serve H. end
T-22...... VI.6:6 now H. means must love all that He loves.
T-25...... III.5:1 its goal with H. Creator's purpose. In His
T-25...... III.5:2 In H. perception of the world, nothing is
T-25...... III.8:1 to stand between you and H. gentleness.
T-25...... III.8:2 It is not there in H. forgiving eyes. And
T-25...... III.8:9 But on H. vision sin cannot encroach, for
T-25...... III.8:9 for sin has been corrected by H. sight.
T-25...... VI.4:1 of specialness; H. use of what you made,
T-25...... VI.7:1 special function, that H. may be fulfilled.
T-25....VIII.9:6 It is H. special function to hold out to you
T-25...... IX.7:4 And everyone is equally entitled to H. gift
T-25...... IX.7:6 for yourself to solve without H. help is to
T-26.........I.6:2 nor keep the Holy Spirit from H. task of
T-26.........I.8:6 be a task apart and separate from H. Own
T-26........II.7:4 For all of them *are* little in H. sight, and
T-26..VIII.9:10 Should not H. happiness be yours as well?
T-27.........I.5:1 in the hands made gentle by H. touch, the

| | |
|---|---|
| T-27..... II.15:4 | goal in which the Holy Spirit sees **H.** Own. |
| T-27..... II.15:5 | that He does not see and recognize as **H.**. |
| T-27..... II.15:8 | **H.** inability to see His goal divided and |
| T-27..... II.15:8 | His inability to see **H.** goal divided and |
| T-27..... II.16:5 | In **H.** acceptance of this function lies the |
| T-27..... II.16:6 | **H.** single purpose unifies the halves of you |
| T-27..... V.1:12 | Yet by your listening **H.** Voice extends, |
| T-27...... VI.1:2 | and keep **H.** words from your awareness. |
| T-27...... VI.4:9 | alike, for all sin's witnesses do **H.** replace. |
| T-27... VII.14:3 | and allow **H.** gentle dreams to take the |
| T-27.... VIII.9:5 | And by **H.** judgment are effects removed. |
| T-27.... VIII.9:8 | and your brother's joined with **H.**. |
| T-27.. VIII.11:5 | The form affects **H.** answer not at all, for |
| T-28....... I.12:4 | them! And **H.** Creator shares His thanks, |
| T-28....... I.12:4 | them! And His Creator shares **H.** thanks, |
| T-28..... II.10:3 | In **H.** forgiving dreams are the effects of |
| T-28...... IV.7:1 | gap that separates **H.** Oneness from Itself. |
| T-29....... II.4:4 | And yet **H.** gifts came with Him. He has |
| T-29....... II.4:7 | stand, and where **H.** gifts for them are laid |
| T-29....... II.5:3 | no other place where He can find **H.** host, |
| T-29....... II.5:3 | nor where **H.** host can meet with Him. |
| T-29....... II.5:4 | And nowhere else **H.** gifts of peace and joy |
| T-29....... II.5:4 | and all the happiness **H.** Presence brings, |
| T-29....... II.5:7 | you will believe **H.** Presence must be there |
| T-29....... II.5:8 | the love and grace **H.** Presence holds. |
| T-29...... IV.6:7 | For at its center is **H.** Love for you, which |
| T-30....... II.1:3 | In **H.** Divinity is but your own. And all He |
| T-30..... VII.7:7 | through **H.** use of symbols are we joined, |
| T-30.... VIII.4:7 | to bestow **H.** gifts upon God's Son. When |
| T-31......... I.5:6 | **H.** simple lessons in forgiveness have a |
| T-31..... VII.3:6 | And in **H.** sight there *is* another world. |
| W-pI..... 75.7:7 | It is **H.** Will, and you have joined with |
| W-pI..... 95.8:1 | delayed in **H.** teaching by your mistakes. |
| W-pI..... 97.8:3 | Listen for **H.** assurance every time you |
| W-pI..... 97.8:6 | Receive **H.** words, and offer them to Him. |
| W-pI..... 99.8:4 | Open your secrets to **H.** kindly light, and |
| W-pI..... 99.9:1 | Practice **H.** Thought today, and let His |
| W-pI..... 99.9:1 | and let **H.** light seek out and lighten up all |
| WpI. rIII.in7:5 | Since it has **H.** trust, His means must |
| WpI. rIII.in7:5 | **H.** means must surely merit yours as well. |
| W-pI... 123.5:4 | **H.** Word is soundless if it be not heard. In |
| W-pI. 126.11:6 | your mind to **H.** correction and His Love. |
| W-pI. 126.11:6 | your mind to His correction and **H.** Love. |
| W-pI. 131.14:2 | and through **H.** aid slip effortlessly past it, |
| W-pI. 135.18:2 | Perhaps you have misunderstood **H.** plan, |
| W-pI. 135.18:3 | your defenses did not let you see **H.** loving |
| W-pI... 137.9:2 | Him. **H.** gentle lessons teach how easily |
| W-pI... 137.9:2 | you need undertake to let **H.** laws replace |
| W-pI... 137.9:3 | **H.** life becomes your own, as you extend |
| W-pI... 140.3:3 | **H.** happy dreams are heralds of the dawn |
| W-pI... 151.9:2 | Accept **H.** Word for what you are, for He |
| W-pI... 151.9:7 | **H.** lessons will enable you to bridge the |
| W-pI. 151.11:2 | in any way from **H.** one frame of reference |
| W-pI. 151.12:3 | everyone and everything **H.** Voice would |
| W-pI... 154.2:4 | are, and listens only to **H.** Voice in you. |
| W-pI... 154.3:1 | It is through **H.** ability to hear one Voice |
| W-pI... 154.3:1 | ability to hear one Voice which is **H.** Own |
| W-pI... 169.8:1 | All learning was already in **H.** Mind, |
| W-pI... 169.9:3 | salvation's script in **H.** Creator's Name, |
| W-pI... 169.9:3 | and in the Name of **H.** Creator's Son. |
| W-pI. 193.11:6 | Truth is **H.** message; truth His teaching is. |
| W-pI. 193.11:6 | Truth is His message; truth **H.** teaching is. |
| W-pI. 193.11:7 | is. **H.** are the lessons God would have us |
| W-pI... 198.5:2 | and accept **H.** gift with gratitude? And is |
| W-pI... 198.5:3 | kindness to yourself to hear **H.** Voice and |
| W-pI... 198.5:3 | instead of trying to dismiss **H.** words, and |
| W-pI... 198.5:3 | and substitute your own in place of **H.**? |
| W-pI... 198.6:1 | **H.** words will work. His words will save. |
| W-pI... 198.6:2 | **H.** words will save. His words contain all |
| W-pI... 198.6:3 | **H.** words contain all hope, all blessing |
| W-pI... 198.6:4 | **H.** words are born in God, and come to |
| W-pI... 198.6:5 | who hear **H.** words have heard the song of |
| WpI rVI.in.7:2 | you. I place you in **H.** charge, and let Him |
| W-pII ..... 1.5:2 | you already, for such is **H.** function, given |
| W-pII ..... 1.5:3 | Now must you share **H.** function, and |
| W-pII ..... 3.4:3 | Follow **H.** light, and see the world as He |
| W-pII ..... 3.4:4 | Hear **H.** Voice alone in all that speaks to |
| W-pII . 269.1:3 | ***H.** lessons to surpass perception and return* |
| W-pII ..... 7.1:2 | **H.** gift to everyone who turns to Him for |
| W-pII ..... 8.5:1 | of time when it has served **H.** purpose. |
| W-pII . 295.2:2 | *upon, that **H.** forgiving Love may rest on me.* |
| W-pII . 296.2:3 | allow **H.** teaching to persuade the world, |
| W-pII . 347.1:7 | *not real, and in **H.** understanding it is healed* |
| Wfl........ in.2:1 | **H.** is the only way to find the peace that |
| Wfl........ in.2:2 | is **H.** way that everyone must travel in the |
| W-ep......... 1:8 | **H.** certainty is yours. You need but ask it |
| W-ep......... 2:5 | **H.** is the Voice for God and also yours. |
| W-ep......... 3:3 | for **H.** sure direction and His certain |
| W-ep......... 3:3 | His sure direction and **H.** certain Word. |
| W-ep......... 3:4 | **H.** is the Word that God has given you. |
| W-ep......... 3:5 | **H.** is the Word you chose to be your own. |
| W-ep......... 4:1 | And now I place you in **H.** hands, to be |
| W-ep......... 4:1 | in His hands, to be **H.** faithful follower, |
| W-ep......... 6:2 | In peace we will continue in **H.** way, and |
| W-ep......... 6:3 | In confidence we wait **H.** answers, as we |
| W-ep......... 6:3 | as we ask **H.** Will in everything we do. He |
| W-ep......... 6:5 | us how to behold him through **H.** eyes, |
| M-9........... 2:2 | he asks his Teacher for **H.** answer, and it |
| M-10......... 4:9 | know all the effects of **H.** judgment on |
| M-10....... 4:10 | for there is no distortion in **H.** perception. |
| M-15....... 2:11 | you still attempt to take **H.** role from Him |
| M-15....... 2:12 | be quiet, for **H.** Voice is heard in stillness. |
| M-15....... 2:13 | And **H.** Judgment comes to all who stand |
| M-18......... 2:7 | completely in **H.** sight and in God's Word |
| M-19......... 1:7 | in **H.** judgment justice is impossible, for |
| M-25......... 2:6 | would fall at the holy sound of **H.** Voice. |
| M-25......... 3:2 | Holy Spirit, and used under **H.** direction, |
| M-28......... 6:6 | And in **H.** Final Judgment is restored the |
| M-29......... 2:8 | The responsibility is **H.**, and He alone is |
| M-29......... 2:9 | it. To do so is **H.** function. To refer the |
| M-29....... 2:13 | **H.** answers are always right. Would you |
| M-29....... 4:11 | it. **H.** decisions bring benefit to all, being |
| M-29......... 5:9 | and thank Him for **H.** guidance at night. |
| M-29......... 6:5 | your prayers of the heart into **H.** language |
| C-6........... 1:3 | to accept Him and to hear **H.** Voice. His is |
| C-6........... 1:4 | **H.** is the Voice for God, and has therefore |
| C-6........... 1:5 | This form is not **H.** reality, which God |
| C-6........... 2:2 | the leader in carrying out **H.** plan since he |
| C-6........... 5:1 | You are **H.** manifestation in this world. |
| C-6........... 5:2 | calls to you to be **H.** Voice along with him. |
| P-1............ 1:5 | which He offers **H.** greater gifts to both. |
| P-1............ 2:1 | it and give it **H.** Own great gift of rejoicing |
| P-1............ 5:6 | Psychotherapy under **H.** direction is one |
| P-1............ 5:6 | to prepare additional teachers for **H.** work |
| P-2.......... I.3:4 | He will wait, and **H.** patience is infinite. |
| P-2.......... I.3:5 | **H.** goal is wholly undivided always. |
| P-2.......... I.3:6 | reconciled as one until they join with **H.**. |
| P-3........ III.2:3 | Spirit asks some payment for **H.** purpose. |
| P-3........ III.6:4 | them, they are always **H.** potential temple |
| P-3........ III.8:4 | to your salvation, for such is **H.** function. |
| S-3........ III.6:2 | and you will never fail to bring **H.** kindly |

## his 21

- Jesus

*noise word*

*His*

| | |
|---|---|
| M-23......... 1:8 | What does calling on **h.** name confer? |
| M-23......... 3:4 | **H.** part in the Sonship is also yours, and |
| M-23......... 3:4 | and **h.** completed learning guarantees |
| M-23......... 3:7 | Remember **h.** promises, and ask yourself |
| M-23......... 5:5 | **h.** eyes your loveliness is so complete and |
| M-23......... 5:5 | that he sees in it an image of **h.** Father. |
| M-23......... 5:6 | the symbol of **h.** Father here on earth. To |
| M-23......... 5:8 | In **h.** eyes Christ's vision shines in perfect |
| M-23....... 5:10 | the lesson of salvation through **h.** learning |
| M-23......... 7:1 | because **h.** words have reached you in a |
| C-5........... 2:1 | in all **h.** brothers and remembered God. |
| C-5........... 2:3 | that appeared to hold **h.** self from Self, as |
| C-5........... 2:6 | And Christ needed **h.** form that He might |
| C-5........... 3:1 | **h.** complete identification with the Christ |
| C-5........... 3:5 | nor can **h.** life in any way be changed by |
| C-5........... 5:3 | **H.** little life on earth was not enough to |
| C-5........... 5:5 | And when you join your will with **h.**, your |
| C-5........... 5:5 | will with his, your sight will be **h.** vision, |
| C-5........... 6:6 | It is possible to read **h.** words and benefit |
| C-5........... 6:8 | Yet still it is **h.** lesson most of all that he |
| C-6........... 2:2 | the first to complete **h.** own part perfectly. |

## his 1591

- noise word

*Jesus*

*His*

## history 2

| | |
|---|---|
| T-4......... II.1:3 | and **h.** would not exist if the same errors |
| T-28........ I.5:7 | **h.** of all the body's past is hidden there. |

## hold 262

| | |
|---|---|
| T-1......... V.6:4 | can be deepened, and thus made to **h.**, is |
| T-2....... IV.4:5 | the illness has a sufficiently strong **h.** over |
| T-3.......... I.3:6 | does not **h.** your "evil" deeds against you. |
| T-3.......... I.3:7 | it likely that He would **h.** them against me |
| T-5........ in.3:5 | are beautiful enough to **h.** it by sharing it. |
| T-5....... IV.4:5 | hurt you and **h.** nothing against him, or |
| T-5....... IV.4:5 | against him, or you **h.** it against yourself. |
| T-5....... IV.7:2 | idea of healing, they must give it to **h.** it. |
| T-5....... IV.8:9 | **H.** it and share it, that it may always be |
| T-5..... IV.8:10 | heart and in your hands, to **h.** and share. |
| T-5..... IV.8:11 | The heart is pure to **h.** it, and the hands |
| T-6..... V.B.9:2 | As you take this step and **h.** this direction, |
| T-6..... V.C.8:2 | to **h.** its oneness in your mind because, if |
| T-8......... II.4:4 | look beyond everything that would **h.** you |
| T-8......... V.5:9 | Do not attempt to **h.** on to both, or you |
| T-8......... V.6:6 | all attempts of the ego to **h.** you back. I go |
| T-9........ I.11:7 | If you **h.** your hands over your eyes, you |
| T-9...... VII.7:8 | you **h.** in terms of where it comes from. If |
| T-9..... VIII.5:2 | you **h.** it in your mind, protecting it from |
| T-11...... in.3:7 | and bravely **h.** it up to the foundation of |
| T-11....... II.2:6 | In every hurtful thought you **h.**, wherever |
| T-11..... IV.2:3 | God's laws **h.** only for your protection, |
| T-11..... IV.2:3 | your protection, and they never **h.** in vain |
| T-11..... IV.6:6 | Come unto me who **h.** it open for you, for |
| T-11... VIII.3:2 | Not one thought you **h.** is wholly true. |
| T-12. VIII.7:11 | and to **h.** all things together by extending |
| T-13...... in.1:6 | to relinquish denial, but to **h.** on to it. For |
| T-13........ I.2:3 | guilt that you accepted, and you **h.** it dear |
| T-13........ I.8:2 | can **h.** on to the past only through guilt. |
| T-13...... I.10:4 | could you **h.** dear what you do not want? |
| T-13..... III.8:1 | the grandiosity you **h.** so dear is your real |
| T-13..... IV.6:2 | and have no **h.** over you unless you bring |
| T-13..... IV.9:6 | sight of the present and **h.** on to the past |
| T-13..... VI.7:2 | you, then, **h.** the past against them? For if |
| T-13... VI.12:3 | them, and it is they who **h.** it out to you. |
| T-13.... VII.2:4 | you as the amount to which you **h.** it dear. |
| T-13.... VII.3:5 | it. **H.** it not dear, for it is old and tired and |
| T-13.. VII.11:6 | value that this world can really **h.** for you. |
| T-13.. VII.16:1 | every temptation that would **h.** you back. |
| T-13.. VII.16:3 | **H.** me dear, for what except your brothers |
| T-13..... IX.3:4 | Whatever you **h.** dear you think is yours. |
| T-13....... X.2:2 | or even **h.** one spot of it to mar its purity. |
| T-13....... X.5:2 | Use no relationship to **h.** you to the past, |
| T-14..... III.5:9 | happy purchase of a treasure to **h.** dear. |
| T-14..... IX.5:3 | mirror that would **h.** God's reflection in it |
| T-14..... IX.8:6 | as part of Him, **h.** Him in them in truth. |
| T-14....... X.9:2 | Separately, they seem to **h.**, but put them |
| T-14..... X.10:3 | for no thought you **h.** *is* for yourself. If you |
| T-15...... I.4:10 | keep fear from you to **h.** your allegiance. |
| T-15..... III.4:5 | **h.** your magnitude in perfect awareness in |
| T-15..... III.6:1 | The Holy Spirit can **h.** your magnitude, |
| T-15..... VI.5:5 | to **h.** all of your brothers in your mind, |
| T-15..... VI.5:9 | laws of this world cease to **h.** any meaning |
| T-15.... VII.2:6 | so weak that it would have no **h.** at all, |
| T-15....... X.3:2 | as real, guilt will **h.** no attraction for you. |
| T-16..... III.6:3 | If you who **h.** Him and whom He holds |
| T-16..... VI.7:5 | to let go your **h.** on the distorted frame of |
| T-16..... VI.7:5 | that seemed to **h.** your world together. |
| T-16.... VII.3:6 | the ego could not **h.** you to the past. In |
| T-16.... VII.9:1 | is nothing you can **h.** against reality. All |
| T-17....... II.1:4 | you value like unto this, nor **h.** so dear. |
| T-17..... III.7:1 | if you but let Him **h.** the spark before you, |
| T-17.... VII.8:1 | think you **h.** against your brother what he |
| T-17.... VII.8:3 | not his past but yours you **h.** against him. |
| T-17... VIII.6:7 | any situation that could **h.** you back, and |
| T-18..... II.5:19 | is your determination to keep your **h.** on |
| T-18....... II.8:1 | not the dream take **h.** to close your eyes. |

T-18......III.4:1 h. your brother's hand also hold mine, for
T-18......III.4:1 hold your brother's hand also h. mine, for
T-18......III.5:5 I h. your hand as surely as you agreed to
T-18......VI.3:4 attacked to h. the separation in the mind,
T-18. VIII.12:2 yet let go of all the barriers you h. against
T-18......IX.4:3 the surface, enough to h. its most external
T-18......IX.6:3 and has no power at all to h. back anyone
T-18......IX.6:4 to stop a button's fall, nor h. a feather.
T-18......IX.6:6 to grasp it and your hands h. nothing.
T19...IV.A.3:7 h. back the universe and its Creator. This
T19.IV.A.13:5 forth by offering him what they h. dear.
T19.IV.A.14:2 to you what they h. dear as are the others.
T19....IV.B.9:2 the limits that would h. its extension back
T19...IV.C.1:7 have no h. at all except on those who are
T19.IV.D.13:2 Would you h. his sins against him, or
T-20.........I.3:5 H. him not back with thorns and nails
T-20.......II.2:2 neither offer nor accept; h. out nor take.
T-20......III.9:3 it go or to take h. on life so long forgotten.
T-20......III.9:4 Strengthen your h. and raise your eyes
T-20.....IV.8:10 guarantee will h. against all obstacles, for
T-20.......V.2:5 to h. the unity of the Son of God together.
T-20.......V.6:3 ever held or will ever h. is here right now.
T-20.....VII.6:4 illusions you h. about him are not held up
T-20...VIII.8:8 world seems to h. out many purposes,
T-21.........I.4:4 believing this, they h. those lessons dear,
T-21......III.3:4 withdrawing faith that they can h. him,
T-21......IV.7:7 And earth can h. no longer what has been
T-21.......V.1:3 of size and shape and brightness would h.
T-21......VI.6:7 with what you h. more dear than truth?
T-21.....VII.6:5 still seems to h. a threat the rest have lost
T-22......IV.7:6 But h. out your hand, joined with your
T-23.......II.2:5 and those who h. them seem to be unlike,
T-23.....II.13:8 They h. in place the substitute for Heaven
T-23.....II.14:8 the laws of sin appear to h. love captive,
T-23......IV.2:7 can a body be extended to h. the universe
T-23......IV.6:6 will gently lean to you, and h. you up. For
T-24.......in.1:8 Can you believe a shadow can h. back the
T-24.......in.2:1 to question every value that you h.. Not
T-24.........I.1:4 H. back but one belief, one offering, and
T-24......IV.2:9 what they h. as purpose can be changed,
T-24.......V.5:1 and no hands to h. nor feet to guide. Be
T-24.......V.5:5 see and hear and h. and lead is given light
T-24.......V.6:4 you Himself in him whose hand you h.,
T-24.......V.7:9 The hand of Christ is all there is to h..
T-24......VI.6:6 let the fear of God no longer h. the vision
T-24.....VI.11:3 power to h. itself complete within itself,
T-25.......II.1:7 The only value that the past can h. is that
T-25.......II.3:3 Can it make sense to h. the fixed belief
T-25.......II.4:4 frame is but a means to h. the picture up,
T-25......III.1:5 from this, to h. it up and offer it support.
T-25.....IV.4:10 enough to h. the world within its peace.
T-25...VIII.9:6 It is His special function to h. out to you
T-25......IX.1:7 will you h. dear that sin be kept in place.
T-26.......II.8:5 every bolt and barrier that seems to h. the
T-26.......V.4:5 that it is hard indeed to h. it to your heart
T-27.........I.3:2 You h. a picture of your crucifixion before
T-27.....II.3:11 h. against himself or any living thing.
T-27.......II.9:5 they are free *because* they h. him bound.
T-27......VI.4:6 is. Yet must He love whatever you h. dear.
T-27.....VII.4:9 he does not h. has made upon himself.
T-28.........I.6:7 it is a way to h. the past against the now.
T-28......IV.8:2 h. out to every separate piece that thinks
T-28......VI.2:1 a senseless point of view to h. responsible
T-28.....VII.3:3 that seems to h. some promise of relief.
T-29.........I.8:1 is your excuse for variable goals you h.,
T-29.........I.9:4 to h. you back an instant from His Love?
T-29.......II.9:3 and h. you in its grasp as prisoner to itself
T-29......IV.2:1 you think you like would h. you back as
T-29.......V.5:6 They h. no sword, for they have left their
T-29.......V.5:6 their h. on every vain illusion of the world
T-29.......V.6:1 you would not keep h. on any thought,
T-29......IX.2:7 will h. the judgment off from resting on
T-30......IV.2:2 bear begins to squeak as he takes h. of it.
T-30.......V.7:4 will look on Him Whose hand they h..
T-30.......V.8:1 you have recognized Whose hand you h.!
T-30.......V.8:3 you h. was waiting but for you to join
T-30.....V.10:7 not perceive Whose loving hand you h..
T-30...VIII.6:1 h. in place of what your brother really is.
T-31......I.12:1 and every preconception that we h. of
T-31......III.6:6 want to h. in guilt your chosen enemies,
T-31......VI.1:5 all you see and think is real and h. as true.
T-31.....VII.5:5 now you h. has brought you in its wake,
T-31.....VII.5:6 H. out your hand, that you may have the
T-31.....VII.6:1 concept of yourself that now you h. would
T-31.....VII.6:3 unless you choose to h. it past the hope of
T-31.....VII.9:3 Yet while you h. this sword, you must
T-31...VIII.1:5 *remain in hell, and h. your brothers there.*
W-pI.......8.2:1 can h. about the past is that it is not here.
W-pI.....16.5:1 as each one crosses your mind h. it in
W-pI.....21.4:1 themselves, h. each one in mind while
W-pI.....23.6:5 H. each attack thought in mind as you say
W-pI...44.10:3 And do not forget that they cannot h. you
W-pI.....45.4:4 let the thoughts of the world h. us back.
W-pI.....52.2:4 seeing. I h. the past against everyone and
W-pI.....57.2:8 not where I thought to h. him prisoner.
W-pI.....58.1:5 I can picture only the thoughts I h. about
W-pI.....65.1:4 you h. while you still cherish others. The
W-pI.....68.1:1 can h. no grievances and know your Self.
W-pI.....68.1:2 To h. a grievance is to forget who you are.
W-pI.....68.1:3 h. a grievance is to see yourself as a body.
W-pI.....68.1:4 h. a grievance is to let the ego rule your
W-pI.....68.3:1 It is as sure that those who h. grievances
W-pI.....68.3:2 those who h. grievances will suffer guilt,
W-pI.....68.3:3 who h. grievances will forget who they are
W-pI.....68.5:1 h. what you regard as major grievances.
W-pI.....68.5:3 of the seemingly minor grievances you h.
W-pI.....69.8:3 light, to h. this confidence in your mind.
W-pI.....69.9:8 *If I h. this grievance the light of the world will*
W-pI.....69.9:8 tempted to h. anything against anyone
W-pI...70.10:7 *me. Nothing outside of me can h. me back.*
W-pI.....71.2:4 Each grievance you h. is a declaration,
W-pI...71.10:2 to all temptation to h. grievances today,
W-pI.....72.3:2 of things you are apt to h. grievances for.
W-pI.....72.4:4 actively trying to h. him to it by confusing
W-pI.....72.5:6 every grievance that you h. insists that the
W-pI...73.11:6 are tempted to h. a grievance of any kind.
W-pI.....74.3:1 what they mean, and to h. them in mind:
W-pI.....76.8:7 you h. must be obeyed to make you safe.
W-pI.....76.9:2 and h. your mind in silent readiness to
W-pI.....78.6:2 You will attempt to h. him in your mind,
W-pI.....79.5:1 all the problems the world appears to h..
W-pI.....84.3:4 If I h. grievances I am attacking love, and
W-pI.....89.2:3 *Let me not h. a grievance against you, [name*
W-pI.....89.4:2 *I would not h. this grievance apart from my*
W-pI.....99.4:2 What plan could h. the truth inviolate,
W-pI...100.9:4 little thought has power to h. you back?
W-pI...102.2:1 try to loose its weakened h. still further,
W-pI...108.8:4 of what you would h. out to everyone, to
WpI. rIII.in4:2 if it interferes with goals you h. more dear
W-pI.121.11:3 the ugly picture that you h. of him. Look
W-pI...122.3:5 can h. more hope than what forgiveness
W-pI...122.9:2 aware we h. the key within our hands,
W-pI.122.11:1 they h. out the sure rewards of questions
W-pI.122.14:1 but h. them firmly in your mind by your
W-pI.122.14:2 which has power to h. your gifts in your
W-pI.124.10:1 this holy half an hour will h. out to you, to
W-pI...125.5:3 the illusions which you h. about yourself.
W-pI...127.8:3 The world that seems to h. you prisoner
W-pI...127.8:3 be escaped by anyone who does not h. it
W-pI...128.4:1 holds anything you want to h. you back.
W-pI...128.5:3 We h. it purposeless within our minds,
W-pI.131.10:3 replace the foolish images that we h. dear,
W-pI...132.1:4 The thoughts you h. are mighty, and
W-pI...132.3:5 it everywhere because you h. the bitter
W-pI...134.3:3 the h. that the idea of sin retains as yet
W-pI...137.7:1 which you h. before the simple truth.
W-pI...137.7:2 of all the laws that h. it cannot but be real,
W-pI...137.8:4 unlike the ones which h. that sickness is
W-pI...137.9:2 made to h. yourself a prisoner to death.
W-pI.137.15:2 as you receive, to h. but what you give,
W-pI...138.8:1 can gain unconscious h. of great intensity,
WpI. rIV.in3:3 h. correction off through self-deceptions
W-pI...154.1:4 These are but attempts to h. decision off,
W-pI.154.11:3 He needs our hands to h. His messages,
W-pI...155.8:5 seem to h. in chains the holy Son of God.
W-pI...163.2:2 For it seems to h. all living things within
WpI rV.in11:4 the thoughts to h. it up before our minds,
W-pI...182.4:2 h. a picture of a past that never happened
W-pI...189.7:1 world; all images you h. about yourself.
W-pI...189.7:3 H. onto nothing. Do not bring with you
W-pI...190.9:4 judgment that you h. against your throat,
W-pI...191.2:6 no hope you h. but will dissolve in tears.
W-pI...191.5:1 all the worldly thoughts that h. it prisoner
W-pI...191.8:2 For time has lost its h. upon the world.
W-pI.191.11:4 pain until you have denied its h. on you.
W-pI...192.9:1 Therefore, h. no one prisoner. Release
W-pI...192.9:4 realize you h. a sword above your head.
W-pI...193.6:4 when you h. these words in full awareness
W-pI.193.10:3 not try to h. it off another day, another
W-pI.193.13:5 you h. the key that opens Heaven's gate,
W-pI...198.5:1 wiser to be glad you h. the answer to your
W-pI...199.3:1 accept today's idea, and h. it very dear. Be
WpI rVI.in.5:3 one, deny its h. and hasten to assure your
W-pII .....4.5:7 Would you still h. return to Heaven back?
W-pII .290.2:1 *and ask Your strength to h. me up today,*
W-pII .300.1:2 lets no false perception keep us in its h.,
W-pII .....9.2:1 and h. you safe within its gentle advent,
M-4 ..... V.1:11 They h. His gifts and follow in His way,
M-13 .........1:6 another thought system can take h., is
M-13 .........6:1 requires sacrifice of all you really h. dear.
M-13 .........6:2 h. dear the things that crucify God's Son,
M-15 .........3:4 free. What can the world h. out to you,
M-15 .......3:11 It is your function to h. it to your heart,
C-4.............8:1 you and h. you safe and pure and lovely in
C-5.............2:3 body that appeared to h. his self from Self
P-2..........II.9:3 but he cannot h. out his hand to receive it
P-3..........II.7:4 No professional therapist can h. this
S-1.........in.3:3 Faith in your goal will grow and h. you up
S-1........III.5:3 H. out your hand. This enemy has come
S-1........III.5:6 Do not h. on to it, nor onto him. He is a
S-1........IV.1:3 once the need to h. the other as an enemy
S-2.........in.1:4 Both must come to h. you up and keep
S-2...........I.8:6 with nothing of the past to h. it back from
S-3...........I.2:4 hands, which cannot h. them back. And
S-3........IV.9:6 lovingly I h. you in My Heart and in My

## holding 45

T-3........VI.5:8 you will insist on h. on to judgment. You
T-8........III.3:2 h. Their unity together by extending
T-11.....V.14:6 H. error clearly in mind, and protecting
T-12......VI.5:8 h. out the Father's Love to you in the
T-13.........I.8:6 way of h. past and future in your mind to
T-13......VI.2:5 with you, and by h. it in your mind, see it
T-14......III.5:5 it and cherishes it by h. it against you.
T-14..VIII.4:10 h. Them in the oneness out of which
T-14......IX.6:6 Spirit is h. to the mirror that is in him. He
T-15.......I.4:12 using dissociation for h. its contradictory
T-15......VI.5:4 By h. it within itself, there *is* no loss. The
T-16......IV.8:1 and your creations are h. out their hands
T-17.........I.6:6 h. both of you away from truth and from
T-18....VIII.3:5 h. itself apart against the universe. The
T19...IV.D.5:8 fear seemed to be h. them in place. Yet
T-20......VI.5:4 its brothers, h. them here in its idolatry.
T-24.......V.7:4 reaches through them, h. out His hand,
T-26......IV.6:1 and your brother still is h. back the happy
T-26.......V.2:5 h. your brother's hand and keeping step
T-29.......V.6:2 how great the cost of h. anything God did
W-pI.....19.3:3 and h. it in your mind as you do so, say: *I*
W-pI.....68.1:5 just what h. grievances does to your mind
W-pI.....68.2:2 Can all this arise from h. grievances? Oh,
W-pI.....68.6:5 you, hovering over you and h. you up. Try
W-pI.....69.3:5 h. it up for everyone who searches with us
W-pI.....70.9:3 think of me h. your hand and leading you.
W-pI.....71.2:1 for salvation centers around h. grievances
W-pI...71.10:3 *H. grievances is the opposite of God's plan*
W-pI........72.h H. grievances is an attack on God's plan
W-pI.....72.3:1 so apparent why h. grievances is an attack
W-pI.....72.5:9 onto God, and h. Him responsible for it.
W-pI.....72.7:4 and h. your grievances against Him and
W-pI...72.13:3 *H. grievances is an attack on God's plan for*
W-pI.....86.3:1 (72) H. grievances is an attack on God's
W-pI.....86.3:2 H. grievances is an attempt to prove that
W-pI.....86.3:4 By h. grievances, I am therefore excluding
W-pI...127.3:8 is the power h. everything as one, the link
W-pI...131.3:4 forgot, yet h. everything you really want.
W-pI...165.2:5 It is your Source of life, h. you one with it,

| | |
|---|---|
| W-pI...166.1:4 | **h.** nothing back that can contribute to |
| W-pI.169.12:1 | **h.** all its parts in meaningful relationships |
| W-pI...181.1:1 | to establishing and **h.** up your faith in |
| W-pI...184.3:1 | kept apart and **h.** bits of mind as separate |
| W-pII .332.2:6 | *while You are **h.** freedom out to us.* |
| P-3........III.8:6 | reach you, **h.** out his hand to his Friend. |

## holds 191

| | |
|---|---|
| T-1.........V.6:7 | Nor can anything that **h.** it upside down |
| T-4.........V.1:3 | not the way a balanced mind **h.** together. |
| T-5...........I.1:8 | spirit **h.** everything by giving it, and thus |
| T-5.....III.11:9 | because He **h.** the remembrance of things |
| T-5....III.11:10 | He **h.** this gladness gently in your mind, |
| T-6........III.1:3 | because the Holy Spirit still **h.** knowledge |
| T-7........III.5:8 | This **h.** them in perfect serenity, because |
| T-8........III.7:8 | thought any part of the Sonship **h.**. |
| T-9........IV.1:3 | you will believe what your perception **h.**. |
| T-11.........I.5:2 | What **h.** for God holds for you. If you |
| T-11.........I.5·2 | What holds for God **h.** for you. If you |
| T-11......IV.6:5 | cannot bar the door that Christ **h.** open. |
| T-12......IV.1:5 | is the one promise the ego **h.** out to you, |
| T-12....VIII.2:2 | His Father's Love **h.** him in perfect peace, |
| T-12....VIII.6:7 | invisible the only truth that this world **h.**. |
| T-13....... II.3:1 | of your hidden cornerstones **h.** your belief |
| T-13...... VI.5:7 | not see the freedom that the present **h.**. |
| T-13...... VI.6:2 | it **h.** the only things that are forever true. |
| T-13.....VII.5:9 | into the world He **h.** out to you in love. |
| T-13...VII.13:6 | world outside himself **h.** his inheritance. |
| T-13...... XI.9:5 | God's sleeping Son **h.** no power over him. |
| T-14....... II.7:5 | This simple lesson **h.** the key to the dark |
| T-14....... V.2:7 | you share with God He **h.** in trust for you. |
| T-14...... VI.6:4 | not communicating **h.** enough of love to |
| T-14.....VII.6:9 | He **h.** the light, and you the darkness. |
| T-14...... IX.3:7 | The Holy Spirit **h.** it there for you. God |
| T-14...... IX.6:5 | what the mirror **h.** out for everyone to see |
| T-14..... X.11:6 | Neither his mind nor yours **h.** more than |
| T-14..... X.12:8 | of His Son with all the Love He **h.** for him. |
| T-14..... XI.3:3 | giving it whatever meaning it **h.** for you. |
| T-15....... II.1:3 | What **h.** remembrance of God cannot be |
| T-15......IV.1:9 | for it **h.** the whole release from littleness. |
| T-15......IV.8:2 | breaking communication **h.** value to you. |
| T-15.....VII.7:8 | guilt that **h.** all its relationships together. |
| T-15.....VII.8:8 | guilty and **h.** him through guilt is "good." |
| T-15...VII.14:2 | In the holy instant guilt **h.** no attraction, |
| T-15...... XI.6:5 | away **h.** all the meaning of the universe, |
| T-15...... XI.6:5 | **h.** the universe together in its meaning. |
| T-16...... III.6:3 | Him and whom He **h.** are the universe, all |
| T-16....... V.9:1 | which the ego **h.** out to those who place |
| T-16...... VI.6:3 | little spark that **h.** the Great Rays within |
| T-16.....VII.3:5 | For the ego **h.** the past against you, and in |
| T-16.....VII.9:4 | God **h.** nothing against anyone, for He is |
| T-17......IV.4:4 | blessing **h.** within itself the truth about |
| T-18.......I.12:4 | loveliness and joy the other **h.** within it. |
| T-18....VI.14:2 | the irresistible appeal the holy instant **h.**. |
| T19. IV.A.11:6 | The fierce attraction that guilt **h.** for fear |
| T19....IV.B.1:2 | it. Where the attraction of guilt **h.** sway, |
| T19..IV.C.10:5 | In its tiny hands it **h.**, in perfect safety, |
| T19. IV.D.14:4 | Yet still He **h.** forgiveness out to you, to |
| T-20....VIII.3:4 | which **h.** him to illusions of what he is. It |
| T-20....VIII.9:9 | the "nothing" all the meaning that it **h.**. |
| T-21...... VI.8:9 | the Holy Spirit still **h.** out for everyone to |
| T-21....VIII.3:4 | his desire of something he believes **h.** out |
| T-22....... II.4:7 | excludes one living thing and **h.** it out, |
| T-22....... II.6:4 | to do what **h.** no hope of ever being done. |
| T-22....... V.3:5 | God **h.** your hands, and what can |
| T-23.........I.6:7 | Madness **h.** out no menace to reality, and |
| T-23..... II.12:4 | It **h.** there is a substitute for love. This is |
| T-24.......in.1:8 | back the Will that **h.** the universe secure? |
| T-24..... II.12:6 | And no relationship that **h.** its purpose |
| T-24...... III.1:4 | for he **h.** one error to himself as lovely still |
| T-24...... III.8:6 | hands that he **h.** out for your forgiveness. |
| T-24....... V.3:7 | beautiful His hand that **h.** His brother's, |
| T-24....... V.5:4 | strength their purpose **h.** is given them. |
| T-24....... V.7:1 | hand that **h.** your brother's in your own. |
| T-24....... V.7:2 | own. Christ's hand **h.** all His brothers in |
| T-24.....VI.10:3 | governs part of God **h.** not for all the rest. |
| T-25....... II.5:4 | to see. The body **h.** it for a while, without |
| T-25...... IX.2:4 | offered anyone who but **h.** out his hand in |
| T-26 ..... V.13:1 | day, and every instant that each minute **h.** |
| T-26 .. VII.10:4 | a unity which **h.** all things within itself? |
| T-27 ........II.3:7 | **h.** not the proof of sin before his brother's |
| T-27 ..... IV.7:2 | place that **h.** the answer lovingly for you. |
| T-27 ..... VI.3:1 | **h.** all your memories and all your hopes. |
| T-27 ..... VI.4:4 | contain what you believe it **h.** within. Nor |
| T-28 ........I.4:3 | believe that memory **h.** only what is past, |
| T-28 ........I.5:3 | Memory **h.** the message it receives, and |
| T-28 ........II.1:8 | in itself it **h.** the universe of all creation, |
| T-28 ........II.5:1 | door, **h.** all your shreds of memories and |
| T-28 ..... III.4:3 | Yet it **h.** the seeds of pestilence and every |
| T-29 ........II.5:8 | the love and grace His Presence **h.**. |
| T-29 ...... V.6:6 | brother thinks he **h.** the hand of death. |
| T-30 ... III.5:11 | completely lovely Thought God **h.** of you. |
| T-30 ..... III.7:6 | it. The Thought God **h.** of you is perfectly |
| T-30 ..... III.8:4 | The Thought God **h.** of you is like a star, |
| T-30 ..... III.9:1 | for He is the eternal sky that **h.** it safe, |
| T-30 ..... III.9:3 | embraces it and softly **h.** it in its perfect |
| T-30 ... III.10:1 | all idols is the Thought God **h.** of you. |
| T-30 ... III.10:2 | God **h.** of you remains exactly as it always |
| T-30 ... III.10:5 | the Thought God **h.** of you has never left |
| T-30 ... III.11:1 | God **h.** of you exist but where you are? Is |
| T-30 ... III.11:7 | the Thought God **h.** of you is your reality. |
| T-31 ........II.9:2 | **h.** of what he is and of what you must be. |
| T-31 ......II.11:7 | to you is One Who **h.** the light before you, |
| T-31 ..... III.4:5 | It **h.** in prison but the willing mind that |
| T-31 ..... III.5:1 | it chose and guards and **h.** itself at bay, a |
| T-31 .... VII.1:6 | no one here but **h.** a concept of himself in |
| T-31 .... VII.9:1 | of yourself that **h.** him off from you, and |
| T-31 .... VII.9:2 | to keep the space that **h.** your brother off |
| T-31 .... VII.9:3 | who **h.** the mirror to another view of what |
| T-31 .. VII.11:6 | **h.** no concept of himself between his calm |
| T-31 .. VII.13:3 | to look on only what the present **h.**. It |
| W-pI..... 22.1:1 | the way anyone who **h.** attack thoughts in |
| W-pI..... 23.4:4 | gone? Vision already **h.** a replacement for |
| W-pI..... 45.1:1 | idea **h.** the key to what your real thoughts |
| W-pI..... 53.3:4 | It **h.** out no safety and no hope. But such a |
| W-pI..... 56.3:2 | I see **h.** my fearful self-image in place, and |
| W-pI..... 57.1:7 | Nothing **h.** me in this world. Only my |
| W-pI....... 68.h | Love **h.** no grievances. |
| W-pI..... 68.2:4 | For he who **h.** grievances denies he was |
| W-pI..... 68.6:8 | *Love **h.** no grievances. When I let all my* |
| W-pI..... 68.7:2 | *Love **h.** no grievances. Let me not betray my* |
| W-pI..... 68.7:5 | *Love **h.** no grievances. I would wake to my* |
| W-pI..... 76.5:4 | the mind **h.** up to hide what really suffers. |
| W-pI..... 84.3:1 | (68) Love **h.** no grievances. Grievances |
| W-pI..... 96.7:2 | The Holy Spirit **h.** salvation in your mind, |
| W-pI..... 96.7:4 | your Self **h.** dear and cherishes for you. |
| W-pI..... 99.5:1 | Holy Spirit **h.** this plan of God exactly as |
| W-pI... 106.3:5 | Who **h.** your happiness within His Hand, |
| W-pI... 108.5:3 | law which **h.** for every kind of learning, if |
| W-pI. 122.11:2 | the joy the lifting of the veil **h.** out to you. |
| W-pI... 123.8:1 | will understand how lovingly He **h.** you in |
| W-pI. 124.12:1 | that **h.** the mirror offered you today, by |
| W-pI... 126.3:5 | **h.** out a gift to him, but hardly to yourself. |
| W-pI... 127.3:8 | which **h.** Them both forever as the same. |
| W-pI...... 128.h | The world I see **h.** nothing that I want. |
| W-pI... 128.1:1 | world you see **h.** nothing that you need to |
| W-pI... 128.2:5 | world you see **h.** nothing that you want. |
| W-pI... 128.4:1 | to believe the world **h.** anything you want |
| W-pI... 128.8:4 | *The world I see **h.** nothing that I want.* |
| W-pI... 129.6:3 | world **h.** nothing that you really want, but |
| W-pI... 129.9:4 | this: *The world I see **h.** nothing that I want.* |
| W-pI. 138.11:4 | It **h.** no terror now, for what was made |
| WpI. rIV.in2:2 | *My mind **h.** only what I think with God.* That |
| WpI. rIV.in4:1 | mind **h.** only what you think with God. |
| WpI. rIV.in5:3 | *My mind **h.** only what I think with God.* Five |
| W-pI...... 141.h | My mind **h.** only what I think with God |
| W-pI...... 142.h | My mind **h.** only what I think with God. |
| W-pI...... 143.h | My mind **h.** only what I think with God. |
| W-pI...... 144.h | My mind **h.** only what I think with God. |
| W-pI... 144.2:1 | The world I see **h.** nothing that I want. |
| W-pI...... 145.h | My mind **h.** only what I think with God. |
| W-pI...... 146.h | My mind **h.** only what I think with God. |
| W-pI...... 147.h | My mind **h.** only what I think with God. |
| W-pI...... 148.h | My mind **h.** only what I think with God. |
| W-pI...... 149.h | My mind **h.** only what I think with God. |
| W-pI...... 150.h | My mind **h.** only what I think with God. |
| W-pI. 153.11:3 | salvation waits and darkness **h.** the world |
| W-pI .. 157.8:2 | the experience this day **h.** out to you to be |
| W-pI .. 164.9:1 | by without the gifts it **h.** for you receiving |
| W-pI .. 164.9:8 | His Hand **h.** out complete salvation to His |
| W-pI .. 166.3:1 | to anyone who **h.** such strange beliefs. He |
| W-pI 166.12:5 | This is the lesson that His giving **h.**, for |
| W-pI .. 169.5:3 | No mind **h.** anything but Him. We say |
| W-pI .. 169.8:2 | He recognized all that time **h.**, and gave it |
| W-pI .. 182.9:3 | He **h.** the might of Heaven in His hand |
| W-pI .. 183.3:2 | the world **h.** dear has suddenly gone by, |
| W-pI .. 183.8:3 | idea that **h.** your mind completely. Let all |
| W-pI 183.10:2 | is necessary, for it **h.** them all within it. |
| W-pI .. 186.1:2 | which **h.** no function as your own but that |
| W-pI .. 186.3:2 | perfect trust He **h.** in you who are His Son |
| W-pI .. 190.9:1 | Heaven's peace **h.** all things still at last. |
| W-pI .. 192.4:2 | because it **h.** no fierce attraction now and |
| W-pI .. 194.4:1 | God **h.** your future as He holds your past |
| W-pI .. 194.4:1 | God holds your future as He **h.** your past |
| W-pI .. 197.8:6 | He **h.** you dear, because you are Himself. |
| W-pI 198.10:2 | gift the Holy Spirit **h.** for you from God |
| W-pI .. 199.3:3 | ego **h.** the body dear because it dwells in |
| W-pII . 222.1:4 | and **h.** in love the Son He shines upon, |
| W-pII ..... 2.4:3 | it **h.** a hint of all the glory given us by God |
| W-pII . 241.1:3 | today **h.** out the instant to the darkened |
| W-pII . 252.1:3 | an intensity that **h.** all things within it, in |
| W-pII . 264.1:5 | *without the Love which **h.** all things within* |
| W-pII .... 286.h | The hush of Heaven **h.** my heart today. |
| W-pII ..... 8.2:1 | The real world **h.** a counterpart for each |
| W-pII . 293.2:3 | *real world which the present **h.** safe from all* |
| W-pII . 330.1:3 | when God **h.** out His power and His Love, |
| W-pII . 332.2:2 | *Fear **h.** it prisoner. And yet Your Love has* |
| W-pII . 338.2:5 | *because it **h.** Your promise to Your Son.* |
| W-pII . 340.1:6 | ***h.** in joy and freedom for Your holy Son and* |
| M-13 ....... 8:11 | God **h.** out His Word to you, for He has |
| M-19 ......... 3:2 | that made the lens and **h.** it very dear. |
| M-22 ......... 2:3 | all that his acceptance **h.** out to him. It is |
| M-27 ......... 2:3 | He **h.** your little life in his hand but by a |
| M-27 ......... 3:2 | which **h.** it from awareness like a shield |
| M-27 ......... 3:4 | It **h.** an image of the Son of God in which |
| C-ep .......... 2:6 | And **h.** it still; unchanged, unchanging |
| P-2..........V.1:6 | of self that **h.** in darkness what is truly felt |
| P-2..........V.3:7 | For God Himself **h.** out his brother as his |
| S-2...........I.8:4 | your need, and God **h.** out this gift to you. |

## holes 1

| | |
|---|---|
| T-24 .......V.4:8 | from the bone and sightless **h.** for eyes, is |

## holier 10

| | |
|---|---|
| T-26 ..... IX.6:3 | There is no place in Heaven **h.**. And They |
| W-pI 153.10:3 | Who is **h.** than they? Who could be surer |
| W-pI 155.12:3 | Could any way be **h.**, or more deserving of |
| W-pI .. 183.1:1 | God's Name is holy, but no **h.** than yours |
| W-pII . 288.2:3 | than can I, and you can not be **h.** than he. |
| P-1............. 2:5 | Could anything be **h.**? For psychotherapy, |
| P-2...........I.1:5 | in the same relationship, making it **h.**. Or |
| P-2..........V.4:2 | is **h.** than helping one who asks for help. |
| P-3.........I.2:10 | Could anything be **h.**? Or a greater gift to |
| S-3........ IV.3:2 | Can anything be **h.** than this? God thanks |

## Holies 1

| | |
|---|---|
| C-ep ........ 1:11 | Holy of the **H.** opens up an ancient door |

## holiest 4

| | |
|---|---|
| T-26 ..... IV.3:6 | The **h.** of altars is set where once sin was |
| T-26 ..... IX.6:1 | The **h.** of all the spots on earth is where |
| W-pI .... 49.3:3 | approach this happiest and **h.** of thoughts |
| W-pI .. 157.9:2 | transcends all vision, even this, the **h.**. |

## Holiness 41

*holiness*

| | |
|---|---|
| T-14 ..... IV.4:9 | therefore, be anyone without His **H.**, nor |
| T-14 ..... IV.5:6 | waking gladly to His Love and **H.** that join |
| T-14 ..... IX.3:9 | for the Presence that dwells within it *is* **H.**. |
| T-14 ..... IX.4:1 | **H.** waits quietly for the return of them |
| T-14 ..... IX.4:6 | is as holy as the **H.** by which it was created |

T-14......IX.4:7 The Presence of **H.** lives in everything that
T-14......IX.4:7 in everything that lives, for **H.** created life,
T-14......IX.5:1 **H.** of your Creator shines forth from you
T-14....XI.14:5 lies His **H.** which He cannot abandon, for
T-15......XI.2:8 of **H.** creates the holiness that surrounds
T19.IV.D.14:4 forgiveness out to you, to share His **H.**.
T-22.......in.3:8 For this relationship has Heaven's **H.**.
T-24.......V.6:4 **H.** shows you Himself in him whose hand
T-25.......in.1:8 Christ is within a frame of **H.** whose only
T-25.......in.1:9 away, that they may frame His **H.** in them
T-25.........I.1:5 His **H.** directs the body through the mind
T-25.........I.1:7 to stand between the aspects of His **H.**,
T-28......IV.9:2 Your **H.**, complete and perfect, lies in
T-31...VIII.3:6 **H.** is yours because He is the only power
W-pI.....36.1:8 Your sight is related to His **H.**, not to your
W-pI.....93.9:4 Try to appreciate Its **H.** and the love from
W-pI...156.3:3 because what shares His life is part of **H.**,
W-pI...156.5:5 their reverence, for it is due to **H.** Itself,
W-pI.167.12:7 is one that knows its Source, its Self, its **H.**
W-pI.170.13:9 *Holy are we because Your **H.** has set us free.*
W-pI...182.4:6 It is His **H.** that lights up Heaven, and that
W-pI.187.11:6 dwells in us and offers us His **H.** as ours.
W-pII..235.2:1 *Father, Your **H.** is mine. Your Love created*
W-pII..285.2:5 *part of You. And what can alter **H.** Itself?*
W-pII..291.1:6 we share; it is the **H.** of God Himself.
W-pII..299.2:8 *For **H.** Itself created me, and I can know my*
W-pII..309.1:7 Within me is the **H.** of God. Within me is
W-pII....11.5:2 the Name of its Creator, **H.** Itself, Whose
W-pII....11.5:2 Itself, Whose **H.** His Own creation shares;
W-pII....11.5:2 shares; Whose **H.** is still a part of us.
W-pII..341.1:2 *smiles back on You, and shares Your **H.**.*
M-28..........5:6 we because His **H.** has set us free indeed!
M-28..........5:7 And we accept His **H.** as ours; as it is. As
P-2.......VII.4:5 for what should be the **H.** of Christ. Guilt
S-3........IV.6:2 still are holy with the **H.** which fathered
S-3........IV.9:4 How lovely are you, child of **H.**! How like

## holiness 294

*Holiness*

T-1........I.31:3 are holy and the miracle honors their **h.**,
T-1........I.32:2 They intercede for your **h.** and make your
T-1........III.6:7 of your own **h.** to the holiness of others.
T-1........III.6:7 of your own holiness to the **h.** of others.
T-1........IV.2:1 **H.** can never be really hidden in darkness
T-1.........V.4:4 mocked if any of His creations lacked **h.**.
T-1.........V.4:5 is whole, and the mark of wholeness is **h.**.
T-2........III.1:8 true **h.** lies at the inner altar around which
T-12......VI.6:3 to **h.** is merely its natural extension. Love
T-13.........I.7:6 Let the **h.** of God's Son shine away the
T-13...VIII.6:1 same; all beautiful and equal in their **h.**.
T-13.....X.10:5 any reason, to look within and see your **h.**
T-13...X.11:11 *In quiet look upon his **h.**, and offer thanks*
T-14.......V.8:6 with you in the safety of its peace and **h.**.
T-14.....V.11:6 him. **H.** must be shared, for therein lies
T-14.........IX.h The Reflection of **H.**
T-14......IX.1:3 It merely brings unholiness to **h.**; or what
T-14......IX.7:1 the image of the **h.** that heals the world.
T-14......IX.7:2 image of **h.** that shines in your mind is
T-14......IX.8:1 The response of **h.** to any form of error is
T-14......IX.8:2 is no contradiction in what **h.** calls forth.
T-14......IX.8:4 because of the reflection of **h.** in them, are
T-14......IX.8:5 There, **h.** is not a reflection, but rather the
T-14.......X.1:5 you. And you will turn from time to **h.**, as
T-14.......X.1:5 as the reflection of **h.** calls everyone to lay
T-15.........I.9:7 From this holy instant wherein **h.** was
T-15......I.10:1 without change, yet **h.** does not change.
T-15......I.12:2 For the instant of **h.** is shared, and cannot
T-15......I.13:8 guilt. You must be holy if you offer **h.**.
T-15......I.15:4 **H.** lies not in time, but in eternity. There
T-15......I.15:7 Time stands still in his **h.**, and changes
T-15.......II.2:1 fear not the instant of **h.** that will remove
T-15.......II.2:4 joy it is to teach God's holy Son his **h.**. His
T-15......III.7:1 celebrates the birth of **h.** into this world,
T-15......III.7:1 join with me who decided for **h.** for you. It
T-15......III.9:1 will you learn that only **h.** can content you
T-15......III.9:6 not into a manger, but into the altar to **h.**,
T-15......III.9:6 holiness, where **h.** abides in perfect peace.
T-15.......V.5:3 can translate them into **h.** by removing as
T-15......VI.2:5 of his worth we cannot doubt his **h.**. And
T-15......VI.3:1 All separation vanishes as **h.** is shared.
T-15......VI.3:2 For **h.** is power, and by sharing it, it gains
T-15......XI.2:8 Holiness creates the **h.** that surrounds it.
T-16..........II.h The Power of **H.**
T-16.......II.1:1 think that **h.** is impossible to understand,
T-16.......II.1:3 yourself not with the extension of **h.**, for
T-16.......II.7:2 power of **h.** and the weakness of attack are
T-16.......II.7:3 that **h.** is weakness and attack is power.
T-16......IV.9:2 cross to the abode of peace and perfect **h.**.
T-16....VI.10:2 to the illusion of the beauty and **h.** of guilt
T-16...VII.12:2 *Our **h.** is Yours. What can there be in us that*
T-17....III.2:10 seeks to reinforce itself, as **h.** does, by
T-17......III.7:4 The spark of **h.** must be safe, however
T-17.......V.3:9 relationship has accepted the goal of **h.**, it
T-17.......V.5:5 purposes, suddenly has **h.** for its goal. As
T-17.....VII.4:2 the goal of **h.** was set for your relationship
T-17.....VII.4:3 because **h.** cannot be seen except through
T-17.....VII.6:4 holy unless its **h.** goes with it everywhere.
T-17.....VII.6:5 As **h.** and faith go hand in hand, so must
T-18.......II.6:9 its **h.** will become an offering to everyone.
T-18....III.4:10 The **h.** of your relationship is established
T-18......IV.4:4 to make arrogant preparations for **h.**, and
T-18.......V.6:1 When you feel the **h.** of your relationship
T-18......IX.1:1 the darkness to the light, and guilt to **h.**.
T-19.......I.12:7 Yet faith unites you in the **h.** you see, not
T-19.......II.4:2 of the self as sinful is perceived as **h.**. And
T-19.......II.6:9 The "**h.**" of sin is kept in place by just this
T-19......IV.2:7 offered your relationship the gift of **h.**,
T19.IV.D.16:3 and has been given the gift of **h.** for you.
T-20.............h THE VISION OF **H.**
T-20.........I.4:7 Friend, and celebrate his **h.** along with me
T-20.......II.9:5 The **h.** that leads us is within us, as is our
T-20......III.3:2 is within the truth they recognize their **h.**,
T-20......III.8:8 Did you see the **h.** that shone in both you
T-20......III.9:6 his **h.** remained untouched and perfect,
T-20...III.10:2 there is only **h.** and joining without limit.
T-20....VII.2:1 from sin to **h.** may now be almost over.
T-20....VII.4:2 not perfectly consistent with the goal of **h.**
T-20....VII.4:3 **h.** is merely the result of letting the effects
T-20....VII.4:4 for **h.** is positive and the body is merely
T-20...VIII.9:2 And one is sin, the other **h.**. Nothing is in
T-20. VIII.11:3 you can behold the **h.** God gave His Son.
T-21.......in.2:4 If you see **h.** and hope, you joined the Will
T-21.......II.7:1 in **h.** and vision to see it easily enough.
T-21......III.3:6 faith you give to sin you take away from **h.**
T-21......III.3:7 you offer **h.** has been removed from sin.
T-21......III.4:1 means by which the goal of **h.** is reached.
T-21......III.6:7 to see. Then will you give your faith to **h.**,
T-21......III.7:1 served sin are redirected now toward **h.**.
T-21......III.7:5 belief. But **h.** would set your brother free,
T-21......III.8:3 desire to look upon their brothers in **h.**,
T-21......III.8:6 from sin are given vision, and are led to **h.**
T-21...VIII.5:7 that nothing stand between the **h.** of your
T-21...VIII.5:7 relationship and your *awareness* of its **h.**.
T-22.......in.1:7 The **h.** of your relationship forgives you
T-22.........I.8:7 the **h.** of your relationship to let Him live.
T-22......III.8:1 keep you from him whose **h.** is yours. Let
T-22......III.8:2 Let not the vision of his **h.**, the sight of
T-22......III.8:5 his errors is his **h.** and your salvation. You
T-22......III.8:6 You gave him not his **h.**, but tried to see
T-22......III.8:7 And yet, his **h.** *is* your forgiveness. Can you
T-22......III.8:8 sinful the one whose **h.** is your salvation?
T-22......III.9:1 newly born, must value **h.** above all else.
T-24.........I.8:9 now defeat the goal of **h.** that Heaven gave
T-24......III.6:1 universe, the Source of life, of love and **h.**,
T-24.......V.7:4 may bless all living things, and see their **h.**
T-24.......V.8:4 just as like to Him in **h.** as you must be?
T-24......VI.1:1 Before your brother's **h.** the world is still,
T-24......VI.1:7 yourself may disappear before his **h.**. See
T-24......VI.2:5 Your brother's **h.** shows you that God is
T-24......VI.5:5 release you both, for **h.** is quite impartial,
T-24......VI.6:4 not. Within your brother's **h.**, the perfect
T-24......VI.6:8 Christ to you. He *is* set forth within his **h.**.
T-24......VI.7:1 his body or his **h.** as what you want to see,
T-24......VI.7:5 Where is your peace but in his **h.**? And
T-24......VI.7:6 of Him He set forever in your brother's **h.**,
T-24......VI.8:1 brother's **h.** is sacrament and benediction
T-24......VI.8:7 The Christ in you beholds his **h.**. Your
T-24....VI.10:8 Would you decide against the **h.** He sees?
T-24....VI.13:1 to see your brother's body than his **h.**, be
T-24.....VII.2:4 The **h.** in you belongs to him. And by
T-24.....VII.3:2 How can you fail to know it in his **h.**? Seek
T-24.....VII.3:4 it is given you to see his **h.** *because* it is the
T-24.....VII.4:8 rather, then, a frame of **h.** around him,
T-24.....VII.5:7 as means for truth shares in its **h.**, and
T-25.......in.2:7 he is, and walks with him within his **h.**, as
T-25.......in.3:4 fills it with the **H.** that shines from Him.
T-25.........I.2:1 except to look on **h.** and see Him there?
T-25.........I.2:9 Set in his **h.**, the Christ in him proclaims
T-25.........I.4:3 Himself is framed in **h.** and perfect purity,
T-25........II.7:3 Its **h.** lights up the sinlessness the frame of
T-25........II.7:5 on it, and see the **h.** that He has given it.
T-25........II.8:5 and see the **h.** that must be there because
T-25........II.8:6 He is the frame in which your **h.** is set,
T-25..VIII.10:2 unfair indeed to all the **h.** that is in him,
T-26.........I.5:4 in which your brother's **h.** cannot be seen,
T-26.........I.6:5 not his **h.** a sacrifice to your belief in sin.
T-26.........I.7:2 His **h.** gives life to you, who cannot die
T-26......IX.3:4 Presence which has lifted **h.** again to take
T-28.....VII.7:8 purpose is it made a home of **h.** a little
T-29......IX.8:5 the **h.** that never left the altar that abides
T-31...VII.11:2 his **h.** while you see him apart from yours
T-31...VII.11:3 For **h.** is seen through holy eyes that look
T-31....VIII.5:6 to be before the choice for **h.** was made.
W-pI.....29.3:6 shown you the **h.** that lights up the world,
W-pI.....35.4:3 look upon yourself through the eyes of **h.**.
W-pI........36.h My **h.** envelops everything I see.
W-pI.....36.3:4 *My **h.** envelops that rug. My holiness*
W-pI.....36.3:5 *rug. My **h.** envelops that wall. My holiness*
W-pI.....36.3:6 *My **h.** envelops these fingers. My holiness*
W-pI.....36.3:7 *My **h.** envelops that chair. My holiness*
W-pI.....36.3:8 *My **h.** envelops that body. My holiness*
W-pI.....36.3:9 *body. My **h.** envelops this pen.* Several times
W-pI........37.h My **h.** blesses the world.
W-pI.....37.1:2 is to see the world through your own **h.**.
W-pI.....37.2:6 **h.** blesses him by asking nothing of him.
W-pI.....37.3:1 Your **h.** is the salvation of the world. It
W-pI.....37.3:2 **h.** are all things blessed along with you.
W-pI.....37.4:2 *My **h.** blesses this chair. My holiness blesses*
W-pI.....37.4:3 *My **h.** blesses that window. My holiness*
W-pI.....37.4:4 *My **h.** blesses this body.* Then close your
W-pI.....37.4:6 and saying: *My **h.** blesses you, [name].*
W-pI.....37.6:4 him the blessing of your **h.** immediately,
W-pI........38.h There is nothing my **h.** cannot do.
W-pI.....38.1:1 Your **h.** reverses all the laws of the world.
W-pI.....38.1:3 **h.** is totally unlimited in its power because
W-pI.....38.2:1 **h.** the power of God is made manifest.
W-pI.....38.2:2 **h.** the power of God is made available.
W-pI.....38.2:4 Your **h.**, then, can remove all pain, can
W-pI.....38.3:4 apply the power of your **h.** to all problems
W-pI.....38.4:5 *myself, there is nothing that my **h.** cannot do*
W-pI.....38.4:6 *himself, there is nothing my **h.** cannot do.*
W-pI.....38.5:3 *nothing my **h.** cannot do because the power*
W-pI.....38.5:4 theme, "There is nothing my **h.** cannot do
W-pI........39.h My **h.** is my salvation.
W-pI.....39.3:1 that your **h.** is the salvation of the world.
W-pI.....39.4:1 **h.** is the answer to every question that was
W-pI.....39.4:2 **h.** means the end of guilt, and therefore
W-pI.....39.4:3 Your **h.** is the salvation of the world, and
W-pI.....39.4:4 your **h.** belongs be excluded from it? God
W-pI.....39.8:4 *keeping me in hell. My **h.** is my salvation.*
W-pI...39.10:3 is the fact that your **h.** is your salvation.
W-pI...39.11:3 the idea is: *My **h.** is my salvation from this.*
W-pI.....41.4:1 be deprived of your perfect **h.** because its
W-pI.....41.9:3 on the **h.** that they imply about you; on
W-pI.....43.2:4 the restoration of his **h.** to his awareness.
W-pI.....45.8:7 exercise in **h.** and an attempt to reach the
W-pI.....45.9:1 the **h.** of the mind that thinks with God.
W-pI.....45.9:2 the day, to appreciate your mind's **h.**.
W-pI.....57.5:6 to understand the **h.** of all living things,
W-pI.....58.1:1 (36) My **h.** envelops everything I see.
W-pI.....58.1:2 From my **h.** does the perception of the
W-pI.....58.1:5 eyes, the **h.** of the world is all I see, for I
W-pI.....58.2:1 (37) My **h.** blesses the world. The
W-pI.....58.2:2 The perception of my **h.** does not bless me
W-pI.....58.2:4 there is nothing that does not share my **h.**
W-pI.....58.2:5 As I recognize my **h.**, so does the holiness

W-pI.....58.2:5 so does the **h.** of the world shine forth for
W-pI.....58.3:1 (38) There is nothing my **h.** cannot do.
W-pI.....58.3:2 My **h.** is unlimited in its power to heal,
W-pI.....58.3:5 My **h.** undoes them all by asserting the
W-pI.....58.3:6 In the presence of my **h.**, which I share
W-pI.....58.4:1 (39) My **h.** is my salvation. Since my
W-pI.....58.4:2 Since my **h.** saves me from all guilt,
W-pI.....58.4:2 guilt, recognizing my **h.** is recognizing my
W-pI.....58.4:4 Once I have accepted my **h.**, nothing can
W-pI.....67.2:3 as: *H. created me holy. Kindness created me*
W-pI.....81.1:3 Let me be still before my **h.**. In its calm
W-pI...111.1:3 *Let the light of **h.** and truth light up my mind*
W-pI.121.12:3 in that light his **h.** shows you your savior,
W-pI...124.2:2 everything we see reflects the **h.** within
W-pI.124.12:2 *and my Self, in everlasting **h.** and peace.*
W-pI...125.4:3 the **h.** that He created and will never leave
W-pI...140.5:2 For cure must come from **h.**, and holiness
W-pI...140.5:2 **h.** can not be found where sin is cherished
W-pI...140.5:7 There is no place where **h.** is not, and
WpI. rIV.in9:3 to joy, from pain to peace, from sin to **h.**.
W-pI...152.2:5 in a mind where love and perfect **h.** abide
W-pI......156.h I walk with God in perfect **h.**.
W-pI...156.3:1 He is, there must be **h.** as well as life. No
W-pI...156.5:4 And thus they see in you their **h.**, saluting
W-pI...156.8:5 *I walk with God in perfect **h.**. I light the*
W-pI...158.8:4 that he is one with you in **h.**.
W-pI...158.9:3 because a vision of the **h.** that lies beyond
W-pI.158.11:2 so accurate its image shares its unseen **h.**;
W-pI...159.4:6 **h.** was given by His Father and Himself.
W-pI...159.5:4 **H.** has been restored to vision, and the
W-pI...162.5:2 is the right to perfect **h.** you now accept.
W-pI...162.5:3 sin when **h.** like this has blessed the world
W-pI...162.6:2 eager to unite with one like him in **h.**?
W-pI...164.4:3 There is a sense of **h.** in you the thought of
W-pI...164.7:4 our joy, because its **h.** reflects our own.
W-pI...173.2:1 (156) I walk with God in perfect **h.**. God
W-pI...183.2:2 thought that would intrude upon your **h.**.
W-pI...186.4:3 our strengths, our wisdom and our **h.**.
W-pI...186.6:2 and the **h.** to go beyond all images. You
W-pI...187.9:2 could fear to look upon such lovely **h.**?
W-pI...188.9:7 restore to them the **h.** of their inheritance.
W-pI...190.5:8 becomes a source of innocence and **h.**.
W-pI...190.9:4 with which you seek to hide your **h.**.
W-pI.190.11:2 joy instead of pain, our **h.** in place of sin,
W-pI.191.10:2 but it will end in the reflection of his **h.**.
W-pI...192.5:7 the Son to look again upon his **h.**.
W-pI...194.5:4 world made free with him, to share his **h.**.
W-pI.198.12:2 in him. He is perfect in his **h.**. He needs no
W-pII .227.2:3 again, released from sin and clad in **h.**,
W-pII .228.1:1 My Father knows my **h.**. Shall I deny His
W-pII .228.2:3 *My **h.** remains a part of me, as I am part of*
W-pII .238.1:5 *And I must be steadfast in **h.** as well, that You*
W-pII .240.2:4 *Your Name, that we may understand his **h.**,*
W-pII .252.1:1 the thoughts of **h.** of which I now conceive
W-pII .256.1:6 the **h.** of him whom God created sinless?
W-pII .264.1:5 *this, and nothing is that does not share its **h.***
W-pII .283.1:5 *My **h.** remains the light of Heaven and the*
W-pII ....285.h My **h.** shines bright and clear today.
W-pII .285.1:3 joyous things the instant I accept my **h.**.
W-pII .285.1:4 from me today, and I accept my **h.** instead
W-pII .285.2:1 *Father, my **h.** is Yours. Let me rejoice in it,*
W-pII .285.2:4 *My **h.** is part of me, and also part of You. And*
W-pII .288.2:2 you behold your brother in the light of **h.**.
W-pII .291.1:5 What **h.** we see surrounding us! And it is
W-pII .291.1:6 us to recognize it is a **h.** in which we share
W-pII ....299.h Eternal **h.** abides in me.
W-pII .299.1:1 My **h.** is far beyond my own ability to
W-pII .299.1:2 created it, acknowledges my **h.** as His.
W-pII .299.2:1 *Father, my **h.** is not of me. It is not mine to be*
W-pII .299.2:7 *And I can know my **h.**. For Holiness Itself*
W-pII .302.1:7 *I may look upon its **h.** and understand it but*
W-pII .304.2:1 *from the darkness to the light; from sin to **h.**.*
W-pII .306.1:3 and be restored to love and **h.** and peace.
W-pII .310.2:3 We are restored to peace and **h.**. There is
W-pII .335.2:2 *His **h.** reminds me that he was created one*
W-pII .348.1:8 *You created me in **h.** as perfect as Your Own?*
W-pII .360.1:5 *In **h.** were we created, and in holiness do we*
W-pII .360.1:5 *were we created, and in **h.** do we remain.*
M-13 .........7:7 It is its **h.** that points to God. It is its
M-13 .........7:8 It is its **h.** that makes you safe. It is denied
M-14 .........2:9 will end with the benediction of **h.** upon it
M-29 .........8:6 *and in your light the world Reflects your **h.**,*
C-2 ............6:9 Where evil was there now is **h.**. What is
C-4 ............5:4 This is its **h.**; this is how it heals. The
C-4 ............8:3 lift you up to Him, out of illusions into **h.**;
C-ep...........5:1 that the **h.** of this rebirth will last forever.
P-2..... VII.9:10 **h.** enough to wake your memory of Him?
S-1...........I.5:2 it is a way of remembering your **h.**. Why
S-1...........I.5:3 Why should **h.** entreat, being fully
S-1......... V.1:2 up, and grows in strength and love and **h.**.
S-1......... V.3:1 of every kind, and you can rest in **h.** at last
S-2..........II.3:5 creation and the **h.** that is His gift forever.
S-2........II.6:10 of God, and thank his Father for his **h.**?
S-3...........I.3:2 is the gift of **h.** and love. Forgiveness must
S-3...........IV.h The **H.** of Healing
S-3........ IV.1:9 They have chosen **h.**, and given up all
S-3........ IV.7:3 unison with all creation, in the **h.** of Love.

## Holy 20

*Holy Spirit*
*Holy Spirit's*
*holy*
*See also* Appendix C

C-ep.........1:11 the **H.** of the Holies opens up an ancient
T-3 .........II.5:4 Son of God is part of the **H.** Trinity, but
T-4 ....... III.7:2 fear that prevent the **H.** One from entering
T-4 ....... III.8:3 your mind for the **H.** One to enter. We will
T-4 ....... IV.9:3 Then let the **H.** One shine on you in peace,
T-4 ....... VI.6:4 The **H.** One shares my trust, and accepts
T-4 ....... VI.7:1 I will go with you to the **H.** One, and
T-5 ..........I.4:1 **H.** Trinity that has a symbolic function.
T-5 ....... III.1:4 is part of the **H.** Trinity, because His Mind
T-7 ..........I.7:5 that He is the First in the **H.** Trinity Itself
T-8 ....... IV.8:9 The **H.** Trinity is holy *because* It is One. If
T-8 ..... IV.8:10 are perceiving the **H.** Trinity as separated.
T-8 ..... IV.8:12 part of It, the **H.** Trinity is as bereft as you
T-8 ....... VI.5:3 creations are your gift to the **H.** Trinity,
T-8 ....... VI.8:9 and thus increase the joy of the **H.** Trinity
T-23 ......I.11:3 of the **H.** One becomes a house of sin. And
T-24 ..... III.6:7 Forgive the **H.** One the specialness He
W-pI. 151.12:2 witness for unholiness, within the **H.**,
W-pI... 157.8:2 of. But the **H.** One, the Giver of the happy
W-pII . 322.1:4 **H.** One Who still abides in Him forever,

## Holy Spirit 758

*Holy*
*Holy Spirit's*
*See also* He, Him, Himself, His, I, Me, My, One, Who, Whom, Whose, You, Your

T-1 ........I.38:1 The **H. S.** is the mechanism of miracles.
T-1 ........I.39:1 the **H. S.** identifies error as false or unreal.
T-1 ........I.46:1 The **H. S.** is the highest communication
T-1 .........II.5:1 by me because I am close to the **H. S.**, and
T-1 .........II.5:3 themselves. The **H. S.** mediates higher to
T-1 ....... III.3:4 in which minds that serve the **H. S.** unite
T-1 ....... IV.2:6 placing the mind in the service of the **H. S.**
T-2 ....... III.5:9 and your mind cannot serve the **H. S.**.
T-2 ........ V.7:3 said before that the **H. S.** cannot see error,
T-2 ........ V.7:5 When the **H. S.** is permitted to look upon
T-2 ....... VI.6:2 The **H. S.** cannot ask more than you are
T-3 ....... VI.7:4 mind is split between the ego and the **H. S.**
T-3 .... VII.4:11 mind is split with the **H. S.** on this point,
T-4 ........II.10:1 is not the One-mindedness of the **H. S.**,
T-4 ....... III.9:4 different, but they are identical to the **H. S.**
T-4 ....... III.9:5 **H. S.** knows that you both *have* everything
T-4 ..... IV.11:2 your higher mind, the home of the **H. S.**,
T-5 ............I.h The Invitation to the **H. S.**
T-5 ..........I.3:1 This is the invitation to the **H. S.**. I have
T-5 ..........I.3:2 reach up and bring the **H. S.** down to you,
T-5 ..........I.3:3 The **H. S.** is in your right mind, as He was
T-5 ..........I.4:1 **H. S.** is the only part of the Holy Trinity
T-5 ..........I.4:5 makes the **H. S.** difficult to understand,
T-5 ..........I.4:6 the **H. S.** or the Universal Inspiration,
T-5 ..........I.4:8 because the **H. S.** is so close to knowledge
T-5 ..........I.5:1 **H. S.** is the Christ Mind which is aware of
T-5 ..........I.5:4 Voice of the **H. S.** is the Call to Atonement
T-5 ..........I.5:7 **H. S.** will remain with the Sons of God, to
T-5 ..........I.6:3 The **H. S.** is the Mind of the Atonement.
T-5 ..........I.7:1 The **H. S.**, the shared Inspiration of all
T-5 .........II.1:2 **H. S.** promotes healing by looking beyond
T-5 .........II.1:4 The **H. S.** is the motivation for miracle-
T-5 .........II.2:1 The **H. S.** is the spirit of joy. He is the Call
T-5 .........II.2:5 **H. S.** is God's Answer to the separation;
T-5 .........II.3:7 The **H. S.** is in you in a very literal sense.
T-5 .........II.4:2 The **H. S.** is the radiance that you must let
T-5 .........II.5:4 choice for the **H. S.** is the choice for God.
T-5 .........II.6:1 The **H. S.** calls you both to remember and
T-5 .........II.6:7 The **H. S.** is one way of choosing. God did
T-5 .........II.6:9 for His Will, for which the **H. S.** speaks.
T-5 .........II.7:1 The Voice of the **H. S.** does not command
T-5 .........II.8:1 The **H. S.** is your Guide in choosing. He is
T-5 .........II.8:4 The **H. S.** is the way in which God's Will is
T-5 .......II.10:5 **H. S.** is the Call to awaken and be glad.
T-5 .......II.10:8 Everyone will answer the Call of the **H. S.**,
T-5 .....II.10:10 only this through the **H. S.** within you,
T-5 .......II.12:2 This Mind is the **H. S.**, Whose Will is for
T-5 .......II.12:6 away as you answer the **H. S.** within you.
T-5 ....... III.1:1 brother is by recognizing the **H. S.** in him.
T-5 ....... III.1:2 I have already said that the **H. S.** is the
T-5 ....... III.2:1 The **H. S.** is the idea of healing. Being
T-5 ....... III.2:5 The idea of the **H. S.** shares the property
T-5 ....... III.2:8 be aware of the **H. S.** in himself or in you
T-5 ....... III.3:4 See him through the **H. S.** in his mind,
T-5 ....... III.4:1 The Voice of the **H. S.** is weak in you.
T-5 ....... III.4:6 make the mistake of looking for the **H. S.**
T-5 ....... III.5:3 that the **H. S.** is God's Answer to the ego.
T-5 ....... III.5:4 Everything of which the **H. S.** reminds
T-5 ....... III.5:5 **H. S.** has the task of undoing what the ego
T-5 ....... III.6:2 So it is with the ego and the **H. S.**; with
T-5 ....... III.6:3 God, so the **H. S.** understands it perfectly.
T-5 ....... III.7:1 The **H. S.** is the Mediator between the
T-5 ....... III.7:6 The **H. S.** is in light because He is in you
T-5 ....... III.7:7 of the **H. S.** to reinterpret you on behalf of
T-5 ....... III.8:4 It is of this that the **H. S.** reminds you. It is
T-5 ....... III.8:5 It is this that the **H. S.** sees. This vision
T-5 ..... III.8:11 **H. S.** is as vigilant as the ego to the call of
T-5 ..... III.8:12 **H. S.** counters this welcome by welcoming
T-5 ....... III.9:4 just as the **H. S.** is the symbol of peace.
T-5 ....... III.9:6 but the **H. S.** lets your mind reinterpret its
T-5 ..... III.10:1 The **H. S.** is the perfect Teacher. He uses
T-5 ..... III.10:3 The **H. S.** can deal with a reluctant learner
T-5 ..... III.10:5 The **H. S.** recognizes it perfectly because it
T-5 ..... III.11:1 the world as it perceives it, but the **H. S.**,
T-5 ..... III.11:2 home. The **H. S.** must perceive time, and
T-5 ..... III.11:6 Look as the **H. S.** looks, and understand
T-5 ....... IV.1:3 **H. S.** will help you reinterpret everything
T-5 ....... IV.1:7 can be lost because it comes from the **H. S.**
T-5 ..... IV.3:10 The rest remains with you until the **H. S.**
T-5 ....... IV.6:1 The **H. S.** atones in all of us by undoing,
T-5 ....... IV.7:5 that is not through the **H. S.** *is* lacking.
T-5 ....... IV.8:6 They came from the **H. S.** within you, and
T-5 .........V.1:2 ego has a purpose, just as the **H. S.** has.
T-5 .........V.1:4 logic is as impeccable as that of the **H. S.**,
T-5 .........V.2:2 you have made is undone by the **H. S.**, the
T-5 .........V.6:6 **H. S.**, like the ego, is a decision. Together
T-5 .........V.6:8 The **H. S.** and the ego are the only choices
T-5 ....... VI.3:3 Let the **H. S.** remind you always of His
T-5 ....... VI.4:1 and the **H. S.** reverses its decision, much
T-5 ....... VI.5:1 but a few will suffice to show how the **H. S.**
T-5 ....... VI.7:3 Give it therefore to the **H. S.**, Who will
T-5 ....... VI.8:3 To the **H. S.**, the statement means that in
T-5 ..... VI.10:7 The **H. S.** will not hear it, because He can
T-5 ..... VI.12:5 The **H. S.**, Who speaks for God in time,
T-5 ...... VII.6:6 remembering that the **H. S.** will respond
T-5 .... VII.6:10 ***H. S.** will undo all the consequences of my*
T-6 ........I.10:2 The **H. S.** is glad when you can learn from
T-6 ........I.10:5 by being able to hear the **H. S.** in others
T-6 ........I.10:6 That is because the **H. S.** is One, and
T-6 ........I.11:2 to repeat my experiences because the **H. S.**
T-6 ........I.11:5 the judgment of the **H. S.** can be justified.
T-6 ........I.19:1 that the **H. S.** is the Communication Link
T-6 .........II.4:3 The **H. S.** extends and the ego projects. As
T-6 .........II.5:1 **H. S.** begins by perceiving you as perfect.
T-6 .........II.5:4 equality, the **H. S.** perceives equal needs.
T-6 .........II.7:2 but the **H. S.** remains the Bridge between

T-6........II.7:4 yet it is *your* perception the H. S. guides.
T-6........II.8:3 The H. S. enables you to perceive this
T-6........II.9:6 it and the H. S. can therefore use it well.
T-6........II.10:1 The H. S. uses time, but does not believe
T-6........II.10:3 Since the H. S. is in your mind, your mind
T-6........II.10:4 The H. S. can speak only for this, because
T-6........II.11:2 Yet the H. S. tells you that even return is
T-6........II.11:5 into the one line the H. S. sees. This line is
T-6........II.11:7 that all perception is guided by the H. S.,
T-6........II.11:8 God. Only the H. S. can resolve conflict,
T-6........II.11:8 because only the H. S. is conflict-free. He
T-6........II.12:3 The H. S. extends by recognizing Himself
T-6........II.12:4 what the H. S. perceives is all the same.
T-6........II.13:1 The H. S. was given you with perfect
T-6........II.13:2 The ego is legion, but the H. S. is One. No
T-6........III.1:3 because the H. S. still holds knowledge
T-6........III.2:2 only from the H. S. and teach only by Him
T-6........III.3:1 The only safety lies in extending the H. S.
T-6........IV.1:1 Remember that the H. S. is the Answer,
T-6........IV.1:5 H. S. will be glad when He has brought
T-6........IV.3:2 The H. S. does not speak first, *but He*
T-6........IV.3:4 Since the H. S. answers truly He answers
T-6........IV.4:1 The ego cannot hear the H. S., but it does
T-6........IV.6:1 then, the one answer of the H. S. to all the
T-6........IV.11:1 That is why the H. S. never commands.
T-6........IV.11:2 the H. S. demonstrates does not exist.
T-6........V.h The Lessons of the H. S.
T-6........V.1:1 the H. S. knows more than you do now,
T-6........V.4:1 The H. S. never itemizes errors because
T-6........V.4:4 H. S. makes no distinction among dreams
T-6........V.4:7 lasting lies in dreams, and the H. S.,
T-6........V.A.2:4 The H. S., as always, takes what you have
T-6........V.A.3:1 have said that the H. S. is the motivation
T-6........V.A.4:1 To the H. S., there is no order of difficulty
T-6........V.A.5:1 The H. S., Who leads to God, translates
T-6........V.A.5:5 The H. S. sees the body only as a means of
T-6...V.A.5:10 The H. S. communicates only what each
T-6........V.B.6:3 but the H. S. teaches you that truth was
T-6........V.B.6:5 allow the H. S. to decide for God for you.
T-6........V.B.7:3 H. S. perceives the conflict exactly as it is.
T-6........V.B.9:4 awareness that the H. S. will lead you on.
T-6........V.C.1:1 We said before that the H. S. is evaluative
T-6........V.C.1:7 that what the H. S. rejects the ego accepts.
T-6....V.C.1:10 The H. S. never varies on this point, and
T-6........V.C.2:1 H. S. does not teach you to judge others,
T-6........V.C.4:9 the H. S. will ultimately teach you that
T-6........V.C.5:1 Choosing through the H. S. will lead you
T-6........V.C.5:7 step the H. S. has prepared you for God.
T-6....V.C.10:2 The H. S. will enable you to take this step,
T-7........I.6:2 To this the H. S. leads you, that your joy
T-7........I.6:5 the H. S. has the task of translating the
T-7........II.2:1 and yourself by sharing the H. S. with him
T-7........II.4:5 The H. S. is the Translator of the laws of
T-7........III.1:1 The H. S. teaches one lesson, and applies
T-7........III.5:4 That is why the H. S. never questions. His
T-7........IV.1:2 Inspiration is of the H. S., and certainty is
T-7........IV.2:1 The H. S. must work *through* you to teach
T-7........IV.2:3 The miracles the H. S. inspires can have
T-7........IV.2:5 this, and the H. S. reminds you of it.
T-7........IV.3:3 The H. S. teaches you to use what the ego
T-7........IV.3:5 the H. S. has a unified goal for the effort.
T-7........IV.4:1 should therefore be given over to the H. S.
T-7........IV.4:4 the H. S. understands that your forgetting
T-7........IV.5:3 The H. S. always seeks to unify and heal.
T-7........IV.5:4 H. S. sees no order of difficulty in healing.
T-7........IV.7:8 This strengthens the H. S. in both of you,
T-7........V.5:1 The H. S. does not work by chance, and
T-7........V.8:3 That is how you perceive the H. S. in him.
T-7........V.8:4 is only the H. S. in him that never changes
T-7........V.11:6 This is true communion with the H. S.,
T-7........VI.1:5 ego or the H. S. begets or inspires them,
T-7........VI.6:1 H. S. undoes illusions without attacking
T-7........VI.6:4 I have said before that the H. S. perceives
T-7........VI.6:5 H. S. does not want you to understand
T-7........VI.7:1 keep in mind what the H. S. offers you,
T-7........VI.7:6 by the H. S. if you had not believed the
T-7........VI.9:8 to the H. S. and to the knowledge of God.
T-7........VI.10:1 perceived with meaning only by the H. S.
T-7........VI.13:1 In this depressing state the H. S. reminds
T-7........VII.1:11 But in the service of the H. S., it can help
T-7........VIII.1:6 To the H. S., it is the fundamental law of
T-7........VIII.1:7 To the H. S. it is the law of extension. To
T-7........VIII.5:6 Give them over quickly to the H. S. to be
T-7........VIII.6:1 H. S. will teach you to perceive beyond
T-7........IX.1:5 H. S. is in the part of the mind that lies
T-7........IX.5:1 are protected for you because the H. S.,
T-7........X.3:1 H. S. will direct you only so as to avoid
T-7........X.3:3 is not whether what the H. S. says is true,
T-7........X.3:8 Obey the H. S., and you will be giving up
T-7........X.5:1 The H. S. always sides with you and with
T-7........X.5:5 The H. S. never asks for sacrifice, but the
T-7........X.6:1 The H. S. is perfectly trustworthy, as you
T-7........XI.1:1 The H. S. will always guide you truly,
T-7........XI.4:4 because he has learned it of the H. S..
T-8........II.1:9 if you could disregard the H. S. entirely,
T-8........II.4:3 The H. S. opposes any imprisoning of the
T-8........II.4:4 H. S. leads you steadily along the path of
T-8........II.5:1 We have said that the H. S. teaches you
T-8........II.8:1 and glory can the H. S. appeal to restore
T-8........III.2:4 The H. S. understands how to teach this,
T-8........III.3:6 Let the H. S. teach you how to do this, for
T-8........III.5:7 The H. S. teaches you that if you look only
T-8........III.7:4 The H. S. teaches that all strength is in
T-8........V.6:2 The H. S. has one direction for all minds,
T-8........VII.2:1 Remember that the H. S. interprets the
T-8........VII.2:2 H. S. interprets everything you have made
T-8........VII.2:4 The H. S. reaches through it to others.
T-8........VII.2:5 perceive your brothers as the H. S. does,
T-8........VII.3:6 The H. S. does not see the body as you do,
T-8........VII.4:5 you give to the H. S. to use on behalf of
T-8........VII.4:8 from the H. S. and you will mistrust it.
T-8........VII.9:4 Guided by the H. S., it is not. It becomes a
T-8........VII.9:6 thus becomes the temple of the H. S.,
T-8........VIII.4:6 disagree with its case, nor does the H. S.. I
T-8........VIII.4:7 that judgment is the function of the H. S.,
T-8........VIII.6:5 The H. S., perfectly aware of the same
T-8........VIII.8:8 of choice, which the H. S. seeks to restore,
T-8........VIII.9:1 H. S. teaches you to use your body only to
T-8........VIII.9:3 function as the H. S. sees it cannot be sick.
T-8........VIII.9:8 when interpretation is left to the H. S.,
T-8........IX.1:1 I said before that the H. S. is the Answer.
T-8........IX.1:5 do not ask the H. S. to heal the body, for
T-8........IX.1:6 H. S. teach you the right *perception* of the
T-8........IX.3:8 is. Yet the H. S., too, has use for sleep, and
T-8........IX.4:4 dispiritedly, it was not given to the H. S..
T-8........IX.5:3 H. S. cannot distinguish among degrees of
T-9........I.4:6 the H. S. sees that you can possibly have.
T-9........I.5:1 that the H. S. will never call upon you to
T-9........I.5:2 the H. S. must remind you that this is not
T-9........I.7:1 insist that the H. S. does not answer you,
T-9........I.8:6 you ask the H. S. for "gifts" such as these,
T-9........I.10:1 ask the H. S. for what would hurt you He
T-9........I.10:4 The H. S. is not concerned with form,
T-9........I.10:5 The ego cannot ask the H. S. for anything,
T-9........I.10:6 Yet *you* can ask for everything of the H. S.,
T-9........I.10:7 Would the H. S. deny the Will of God?
T-9........II.2:1 ask of the H. S. is what you really want,
T-9........II.3:2 The very fact that the H. S. has been asked
T-9........II.4:4 Can you ask of the H. S. truly, and doubt
T-9........II.5:5 Remember that the H. S. is in him, and
T-9........II.6:2 directed by the H. S. under the laws of
T-9........II.6:4 The H. S. extends from your mind to his,
T-9........II.6:8 You will not trust the guidance of the H. S.
T-9........II.7:4 I hear only the H. S. in you, Who speaks
T-9........II.12:1 You can ask of the H. S., then, only by
T-9........III.1:1 the H. S. would have you maintain. Egos
T-9........III.1:4 To the H. S. it makes no sense at all.
T-9........III.3:1 the H. S. does not perceive his errors. This
T-9........III.3:2 between the ego and the H. S.. The ego
T-9........III.3:3 the H. S. does not attempt to understand
T-9........III.4:1 to errors, you are not listening to the H. S.
T-9........III.5:3 If you want to give yours over to the H. S.,
T-9........III.7:4 The H. S. in you forgives all things in you
T-9........III.8:1 The H. S. forgives everything because
T-9........IV.3:2 H. S. merely reminds you of the natural
T-9........IV.3:6 helpfulness lies in the judgment of the H.S.
T-9........IV.5:3 Forgiveness through the H. S. lies simply
T-9........IV.5:5 H. S. the effects of error are nonexistent.
T-9........V.4:5 power through the H. S. is denied. This is
T-9........V.8:4 The H. S. is the only Therapist. He makes
T-9........V.8:12 awaken other minds to the H. S. through
T-9........VI.1:1 of the H. S. in you except by His effects?
T-9........VI.2:1 It seems to you that the H. S. does not
T-9........VI.5:2 the H. S. teaches you to awaken others. As
T-9........VII.3:1 is perfectly obvious that if the H. S. looks
T-9........VII.4:4 especially when you respond to the H. S.,
T-9........VII.7:6 The H. S. judges against the reality of the
T-9........VIII.9:4 good can come of it the H. S. cannot use it
T-9....VIII.11:6 *is*. Ask the H. S. what it is and He will tell
T-10........I.3:3 hear the H. S. you may feel better because
T-10........II.2:3 Offer the H. S. only your willingness to
T-10........IV.7:3 it. It is a call to the H. S. in his mind, a call
T-11........I.8:6 it is, but the H. S. remembers it for you.
T-11........I.8:9 the H. S. tells you appears to be coercive,
T-11........I.11:1 the H. S. only because He speaks for you.
T-11........II.4:2 opens your ears to the Voice of the H. S.,
T-11........II.5:1 H. S. cannot speak to an unwelcoming
T-11........II.7:5 it. The H. S. is there, although He cannot
T-11........II.7:7 and of your guests only the H. S. is real.
T-11........V.13:1 The ego analyzes; the H. S. accepts. The
T-11........VII.4:9 real world is all that the H. S. has saved
T-11....VIII.2:4 the H. S. has saved its meaning for you,
T-11....VIII.5:5 H. S. will answer every specific problem
T-11....VIII.6:1 The H. S. will give you only what is yours,
T-11....VIII.6:4 the H. S., Who wills only to restore, be
T-11....VIII.6:6 of the H. S. is to ask for deprivation.
T-11..VIII.12:4 Let the H. S. remove all offenses of God's
T-11..VIII.15:3 the truth about yourself from the H. S.,
T-12........I.h The Judgment of the H. S.
T-12........I.5:8 you. The H. S. does not need your help in
T-12........I.8:3 The H. S. must still translate the fear into
T-12........I.10:4 Thus does the H. S. replace fear with love
T-12........II.9:7 If you will look, the H. S. will judge, and
T-12........II.10:1 to the H. S. everything you do not want.
T-12....III.10:9 allowing the H. S. to extend the real world
T-12........IV.4:4 The H. S. offers you another promise, and
T-12........IV.5:5 Yet the H. S. remembers it for you, and
T-12........IV.7:6 The H. S. guides you into life eternal, but
T-12........VI.1:2 The H. S. teaches that you cannot lose
T-12........VI.2:1 H. S. is your strength because He knows
T-12........VI.3:6 for the real world is the gift of the H. S.,
T-12........VI.4:5 The H. S. keeps the vision of Christ for
T-12........VI.4:10 H. S. blesses the real world in Their Name
T-12........VI.5:9 For the H. S. will lead everyone home to
T-12........VI.6:3 H. S. has at last led you to Christ at the
T-12........VII.1:5 the H. S. sends you for your blessing. In
T-12........VII.3:1 The H. S. is invisible, but you can see the
T-12........VII.3:3 H. S. enables you to do is clearly beyond
T-12........VII.4:1 You cannot see the H. S., but you can see
T-12........VII.4:8 and the H. S. shares His with you on earth
T-12........VII.6:1 I am the manifestation of the H. S., and
T-12....VII.12:6 is the judgment of the H. S. it will be right
T-12....VIII.3:2 for the H. S. sees it with perfect clarity. It
T-12....VIII.3:5 What can be seen is what the H. S. sees.
T-12....VIII.6:5 invisible because the H. S. does not see it.
T-12....VIII.7:3 H. S. looks upon him, and sees nothing
T-13........I.1:1 that the H. S. shares the goal of all good
T-13........I.1:2 The H. S. wants only this, for sharing the
T-13........I.4:3 believes in it the H. S. knows it is not true.
T-13........I.4:4 The H. S. stands at the end of time, where
T-13........I.11:4 H. S. dispels it simply through the calm
T-13........III.1:2 easy enough for the H. S. to show it to you
T-13........III.3:4 The H. S., then, seems to be attacking
T-13........III.9:2 your mind where the H. S. is not welcome
T-13........IV.6:9 The H. S. teaches that you always meet
T-13........IV.7:3 The H. S. interprets time's purpose as
T-13........IV.8:1 itself in place of eternity, for like the H. S.,
T-13........IV.8:3 while the H. S. would release you from it.
T-13........V.11:1 H. S. is the light in which Christ stands
T-13........V.11:6 seeing themselves as the H. S. sees them.
T-13........VII.9:3 for the H. S. corrects the world of dreams,
T-13....VII.10:7 Without the H. S. the answer would be no
T-13....VII.12:1 Only the H. S. knows what you need. For
T-13....VII.14:2 *The H. S. leads me unto Christ, and where*
T-13....VII.16:5 The H. S. will teach you to awaken unto
T-13....VIII.1:2 That is why the H. S. is the only Healer.
T-13....VIII.2:6 the perception of the H. S., as perfect as

T-13....VIII.4:1 and the Son, the **H. S.** has no function. He
T-13....VIII.7:2 offered the Son of God through the **H. S.**,
T-13....VIII.7:3 **H. S.** knows your part in the redemption,
T-13...... IX.4:1 means by which the **H. S.** can separate the
T-13...... IX.6:3 would have the **H. S.** make you free of it,
T-13....... X.2:6 They are used only by the **H. S.**, and it is
T-13....... X.2:7 upon them, the **H. S.** cannot use them.
T-13....... X.6:4 The **H. S.** seeks not to dispel reality. If
T-13....... X.7:1 The **H. S.** does not keep illusions in your
T-13....... X.7:4 **H. S.** does what God would have Him do,
T-13..... X.10:8 which the **H. S.** would restore to you. He
T-13...... XI.4:4 The **H. S.** points quietly to the contrast,
T-13...... XI.5:1 remember this: God gave the **H. S.** to you,
T-13...... XI.5:6 dwell, and of which the **H. S.** reminds you
T-13...... XI.6:8 Fear not the **H. S.** will fail in what your
T-13...... XI.7:4 The **H. S.** will restore your sanity because
T-13...... XI.8:6 The **H. S.** will teach you how to use it, and
T-13...... XI.8:8 The **H. S.** knows only of His Will. There is
T-13...... XI.9:2 from what the **H. S.** wants to teach you.
T-13.... XI.11:1 The **H. S.** will undo for you everything
T-13.... XI.11:3 The **H. S.** has a very different kind of
T-13.... XI.11:5 no possibility that the plan the **H. S.** offers
T-14.......in.1:4 The **H. S.** uses logic as easily and as well as
T-14.......in.1:8 follow the simple logic by which the **H. S.**
T-14.........I.2:8 That is why God placed the **H. S.** in you,
T-14.........I.4:1 lead you where the **H. S.** leads you not,
T-14.........I.5:1 The **H. S.**, therefore, must begin His
T-14....... II.1:1 **H. S.** needs a happy learner, in whom His
T-14....... II.1:3 **H. S.** cannot teach without this contrast,
T-14....... II.2:1 **H. S.**, seeing where you are but knowing
T-14....... II.3:1 All this the **H. S.** sees, and teaches, simply
T-14....... II.3:2 that it is not nothing, the **H. S.** says, with
T-14....... II.4:1 Like you, the **H. S.** did not make truth.
T-14....... II.6:1 everything you have learned to the **H. S.**,
T-14...... III.4:1 between the ego and the **H. S.**. The ego is
T-14...... III.4:2 guilt; the **H. S.** the choice for guiltlessness.
T-14...... III.6:6 God is the happy lesson the **H. S.** teaches,
T-14...... III.8:7 teaching the **H. S.** would gladly offer him.
T-14.... III.10:8 the **H. S.** quietly understands it for them,
T-14.... III.12:6 where it lies, but ask the **H. S.** everything,
T-14.... III.13:4 **H. S.** knows that all salvation is escape
T-14.... III.13:5 Son of God the **H. S.** is your only Friend.
T-14.... III.15:3 The **H. S.** teaches only that the "sin" of
T-14.... III.16:1 Say to the **H. S.** only, "Decide for me,"
T-14.... III.16:3 every decision the **H. S.** makes for you?
T-14...... IV.6:4 The **H. S.** will not delay in answering your
T-14...... IV.9:5 The **H. S.**, Who remembers this for you,
T-14.... IV.10:3 God can communicate only to the **H. S.** in
T-14.... IV.10:4 only the **H. S.** can answer God for you, for
T-14..... V.1:10 Listen to the **H. S.**, and to God through
T-14..... V.10:8 The **H. S.** sees only guiltlessness, and in
T-14...... VI.2:1 The quiet light in which the **H. S.** dwells
T-14...... VI.5:2 The **H. S.** reinterprets it as a means of re-
T-14...... VI.6:5 from which the **H. S.** would release you.
T-14........VII.h Sharing Perception with the **H. S.**
T-14..... VII.5:6 The **H. S.** uses defenses on behalf of truth
T-14..... VII.5:8 translated by the **H. S.** from means of self-
T-14..... VII.6:1 The **H. S.** asks of you but this; bring to
T-14..... VII.7:7 The single vision which the **H. S.** offers
T-14....VIII.1:5 be brought to the judgment of the **H. S.**,
T-14..VIII.2:10 is safe within you, where the **H. S.** shines.
T-14..VIII.2:13 and His Son lies in the **H. S.** and in you.
T-14...... IX.3:7 The **H. S.** holds it there for you. God has
T-14...... IX.6:6 It is the message that the **H. S.** is holding
T-14....... X.6:2 This lesson the **H. S.** teaches by giving you
T-14..... X.10:4 let the **H. S.** order your thoughts and give
T-14..... X.11:1 As God communicates to the **H. S.** in you
T-14..... X.11:1 the **H. S.** translate His communications
T-14..... X.11:3 you would hide from the **H. S.** is nothing.
T-14..... X.11:5 Let the **H. S.** show him to you, and teach
T-14...... XI.5:6 which the **H. S.** will replace the dark ones
T-14...... XI.8:4 that the guidance of the **H. S.** is limited.
T-14...... XI.9:1 think that what the **H. S.** would have you
T-14.... XI.13:6 The **H. S.** will, of Himself, fill every mind
T-15.........I.2:3 For the **H. S.** uses time in His Own way,
T-15.........I.2:7 ego, like the **H. S.**, uses time to convince
T-15.........I.2:9 But to the **H. S.** the goal is life, which *has*
T-15.........I.7:1 The **H. S.** teaches thus: There is no hell.
T-15.........I.7:4 **H. S.** leads as steadily to Heaven as the

T-15 ........I.7:5 to hell. For the **H. S.**, Who knows only the
T-15 ........I.8:1 The **H. S.** would undo all of this *now*. Fear
T-15 .......I.11:2 short a time to the **H. S.** for your salvation
T-15 .......I.12:1 will never give this holy instant to the **H. S.**
T-15 .......I.12:5 to offer time to the **H. S.** for His use of it.
T-15 .......I.13:4 The **H. S.** gives their blessed instant to
T-15 .......I.15:1 friend, if you leave it to the **H. S.** to use.
T-15 .....I.15:11 of the holy instant through the **H. S.**, and
T-15 ........II.1:6 the **H. S.** is offered to God on your behalf,
T-15 ........II.1:7 the **H. S.** will quickly offer you the whole
T-15 ........II.4:3 more compelling witnesses for the **H. S.**.
T-15 ........II.4:5 they support the ego or the **H. S.** in you.
T-15 ........II.4:7 the **H. S.** in a brother is always recognized
T-15 ......II.4:10 a single instant completely to the **H. S.**.
T-15 ......II.4:13 you have wholly released through the **H. S.**
T-15 ...... III.4:1 function is, for the **H. S.** knows what it is.
T-15 ...... III.5:2 the **H. S.** every time you make a decision.
T-15 ...... III.6:1 The **H. S.** can hold your magnitude, clean
T-15 ....... V.4:5 made, the **H. S.** uses special relationships,
T-15 ....... V.5:1 The **H. S.** knows no one is special. Yet He
T-15 ....... V.6:1 not been offered to the **H. S.** for His use.
T-15 ....... V.8:1 the **H. S.** knows how to bring a touch of
T-15 ....... V.9:4 **H. S.** substitutes His frame of reference
T-15 ..... V.10:7 and let the **H. S.** bring to you those who
T-15 ...... VI.6:6 Yet the **H. S.** gives you this faith, because
T-15 ...... VI.6:8 through me the **H. S.** gives it unto you, as
T-15 ..... VII.5:1 the **H. S.** would remove from his holy
T-15 ..... VII.5:3 and let the **H. S.** judge them truly. For it is
T-15 .. VII.10:6 and will be afraid to hear the **H. S.**,
T-15 .. VII.11:1 The **H. S.** cannot teach through fear. And
T-15 ... VIII.1:1 for the **H. S.** must not leave you as your
T-15 ... VIII.5:1 The **H. S.** is God's attempt to free you of
T-15 ... VIII.5:3 **H. S.** asks you to respond as God does, for
T-15 ... VIII.5:8 **H. S.** knows that it is not understandable,
T-15 ... VIII.6:1 **H. S.** alone lies the awareness of what God
T-15 ...... IX.1:1 so would the **H. S.** release your vision and
T-15 ...... IX.5:1 let the **H. S.** tell you of the Love of God for
T-15 ...... IX.6:7 what the **H. S.** must undo to set him free.
T-15 ...... IX.7:2 As you let the **H. S.** teach you how to use
T-15 ........X.1:7 do it. Let the **H. S.** teach you, and let me
T-15 ...... XI.3:1 the **H. S.** everything that would hurt you.
T-15 ... XI.10:5 *I give you to the H. S. as part of myself. I know*
T-16 .........I.1:3 to empathize is very useful to the **H. S.**,
T-16 .........I.2:7 by and let the **H. S.** relate through you,
T-16 .........I.6:7 Only the **H. S.** recognizes foolish needs as
T-16 ........II.4:4 made this joining as the **H. S.** bids you,
T-16 ........II.9:1 to the **H. S.** He has not solved for you, nor
T-16 ...... III.5:1 done this, for the **H. S.** is part of you.
T-16 ...... III.5:8 communicate to you through the **H. S.**,
T-16 ... IV.12:2 The **H. S.** is the Bridge to Him, made from
T-16 ....... V.5:2 both the ego and the **H. S.** accept it. They
T-16 ....... V.5:4 The **H. S.** knows that completion lies first
T-16 ...... VI.3:1 is a way in which the **H. S.** asks your help,
T-16 ... VI.12:1 The **H. S.** asks only this little help of you:
T-16 ..... VII.6:1 the **H. S.** gently lays the holy instant. We
T-16 ..... VII.6:2 before that the **H. S.** must teach through
T-16 ..... VII.7:3 instant the power of the **H. S.** will prevail,
T-16 ..... VII.8:8 everything the **H. S.** teaches is to remind
T-17 ........II.1:7 will behold the beauty the **H. S.** loves to
T-17 ........II.8:3 The eagerness of the **H. S.** to give you this
T-17 ...... III.5:1 **H. S.** bring His interpretation of the body
T-17 ...... III.6:3 **H. S.** wants only to make His resolutions
T-17 ...... III.7:6 only part of the relationship the **H. S.** sees
T-17 ...... IV.2:3 I have said repeatedly that the **H. S.** would
T-17 ...... IV.4:1 ego's answer to the creation of the **H. S.**,
T-17 ...... IV.4:3 the **H. S.** was in response to the gift with
T-17 ...... IV.4:5 the **H. S.** is in close relationship with you,
T-17 ...... IV.4:6 because the **H. S.** has not been separate
T-17 ....... V.2:7 of offering the relationship to the **H. S.**, to
T-17 ....... V.3:1 **H. S.** wastes no time in introducing the
T-17 ....... V.6:5 believed the **H. S.** was there to accept the
T-17 ..... V.11:1 to invite the **H. S.** into your relationship.
T-17 ...... VI.5:9 The **H. S.** knows that the situation is as
T-17 ...... VI.6:4 be. The **H. S.** sees the situation as a whole.
T-17 ..... VII.9:5 When the **H. S.** changed the purpose of
T-17 ... VIII.2:1 simple courtesy is all the **H. S.** asks of you.
T-18 .........I.1:2 is with the goal the **H. S.** has given you,
T-18 .........I.2:1 The **H. S.** never uses substitutes. Where
T-18 .........I.2:2 the **H. S.** sees them joined and indivisible.

T-18 .........I.2:7 has joined and what the **H. S.** sees as one.
T-18 .........I.8:3 The **H. S.** takes you gently by the hand,
T-18 .........I.9:7 the **H. S.** has committed your relationship
T-18 ........II.6:1 The **H. S.**, ever practical in His wisdom,
T-18 ........II.6:4 the **H. S.** does in the special relationship.
T-18 ........II.7:3 the **H. S.** has laid upon it will be extended.
T-18 ........II.9:4 the **H. S.** has gently laid the real world;
T-18 ...... IV.1:6 to give the **H. S.** what He does not ask, or
T-18 ........V.5:4 Yet it is very useful to the **H. S.**, Who *has* a
T-18 ........V.6:1 and offer the **H. S.** your willingness, in
T-18 ........V.7:6 *this instant as the one to offer to the H. S.*,
T-18 ...... VI.4:6 function from what the **H. S.** establishes it
T-18 ..... VII.7:8 Into this place the **H. S.** comes, and there
T-18 ...... IX.1:3 split off and separate, the **H. S.** needs. The
T-18 ...... IX.1:9 Let the **H. S.** remove it from the withered
T-18 ...... IX.3:7 to follow the **H. S.** through seeming terror
T-19 .........I.2:2 giving him to the **H. S.** and releasing him
T-19 .........I.2:3 and in this vision does the **H. S.** share.
T-19 .......I.15:1 so will faith help the **H. S.** prepare the
T-19 ...... III.4:1 The **H. S.** cannot punish sin. Mistakes He
T-19 ...... III.5:1 **H. S.** clearly sees the Son of God can make
T-19 ...... III.5:5 The **H. S.** can teach you how to look on
T-19 ...... IV.2:3 with the **H. S.** remains unfinished. You
T-19 ...... IV.2:4 **H. S.** asks that you offer Him a resting
T-19 ...... IV.3:4 You cannot see the **H. S.**, but you can see
T-19 ...... IV.3:8 the **H. S.** will gather all the thanks and
T19 .IV.A.4:10 one you asked the **H. S.** to share with you.
T19 ...IV.A.7:3 Before the **H. S.** entered to abide with you
T19 .IV.A.14:1 The **H. S.** has given you love's messengers
T19 .IV.A.15:1 only the messengers the **H. S.** gives you,
T19 .IV.A.15:5 The **H. S.** has given you His messengers to
T19 ... IV.B.3:5 The **H. S.** does not demand you sacrifice
T19 ... IV.B.3:7 Pain is the only "sacrifice" the **H. S.** asks,
T19 ... IV.B.9:1 to give the **H. S.** the whole idea of sacrifice
T19 . IV.B.14:8 The ego and the **H. S.** both recognize this,
T19 . IV.B.14:9 The **H. S.** tells you this with joy. The ego
T19 . IV.B.17:3 For the **H. S.**, too, is a communication
T19 . IV.B.17:4 **H. S.** is both the sender and the receiver.
T19 ... IV.C.1:1 special relationship the **H. S.** entered, it is
T19 ... IV.C.9:4 the **H. S.** and protected by God Himself. It
T19 .. IV.D.5:3 the **H. S.** from you fades in the presence of
T19 IV.D.13:1 of Atonement, for the **H. S.** is in him.
T19 IV.D.17:6 of freedom that I gave the **H. S.** for you.
T19 IV.D.17:7 as you offer to the **H. S.** this same gift.
T-20 ........II.7:6 For what God gave the **H. S.**, you have
T-20 ...... III.7:3 before the shining light the **H. S.** offered,
T-20 ...... IV.1:4 given by Him and reawakened by the **H. S.**
T-20 ...... IV.1:6 occurred because the **H. S.** sees them not,
T-20 ...... IV.1:8 the **H. S.** merely gives everything to God,
T-20 ...... IV.2:9 a lesson in giving, as the **H. S.** interprets it
T-20 ...... IV.8:4 there will be nothing else the **H. S.** will
T-20 ........V.5:2 When it is used only as the **H. S.** teaches,
T-20 ........V.8:1 and feel the **H. S.** watching over you in
T-20 .........VI.h The Temple of the **H. S.**
T-20 ...... VI.5:6 **H. S.** does not build His temples where
T-20 ... VI.7:10 for the **H. S.** has set His temple there.
T-20 ... VI.10:2 The **H. S.** rests within it in the certainty it
T-20 .... VII.3:1 obtain the goal the **H. S.** indeed asks little.
T-20 .... VII.8:2 the **H. S.** offers you to serve His purpose.
T-20 ... VIII.3:2 shared with the **H. S.** and at one with Him
T-20 ... VIII.4:1 **H. S.** guarantees that what God willed
T-20 ... VIII.4:8 to replace the holy home the **H. S.** offers,
T-20 . VIII.10:4 Vision is the means by which the **H. S.**
T-21 ........II.1:2 little gift you offer to the **H. S.** for which
T-21 ........II.3:7 This is the little gift you offer to the **H. S.**,
T-21 ........II.7:1 The **H. S.** can give you faith in holiness
T-21 ...... III.1:6 And that is why the **H. S.** must change its
T-21 ...... III.4:2 them the **H. S.** leads you to the real world,
T-21 ...... III.6:1 **H. S.** has a use for all the means for sin by
T-21 ...... III.6:6 The **H. S.** sees perception as a means to
T-21 ...... III.9:1 sin must think the **H. S.** asks for sacrifice,
T-21 ...... III.9:2 **H. S.** knows that sacrifice brings nothing.
T-21 ... III.11:1 you the **H. S.** is concerned with this? He
T-21 ...... IV.1:1 The **H. S.** will never teach you that you
T-21 ...... IV.6:1 no inconsistency in what the **H. S.** teaches
T-21 ........V.5:5 aside a place in which the **H. S.** can abide,
T-21 ...... VI.8:9 the **H. S.** still holds out for everyone to
T-21 .. VII.11:2 the world of sin for what the **H. S.** sees,
T-22 ........II.5:6 guilt was given to the **H. S.** as His purpose

T-22..... II.11:6 He gave the **H. S.** to give to you *He gave.*
T-22....... V.2:7 All that the **H. S.** offers must be defended
T-22...... VI.2:4 **H. S.** waits in gentle patience, as certain of
T-22...... VI.6:5 you give the **H. S.** is service to yourself.
T-22...... VI.8:7 **H. S.** does with gifts you give your brother
T-22.... VI.13:3 Yet does the **H. S.** explain this differently.
T-23...... I.10:8 Over His home the **H. S.** watches, sure
T-23...... IV.4:4 the **H. S.** understand how to increase your
T-24....... II.4:3 answer that the **H. S.** gives can reach you,
T-24...... VI.4:2 is the only purpose the **H. S.** sees in it, and
T-25.........I.5:3 Father and Son and **H. S.** are as One, as all
T-25.........I.5:5 The **H. S.** links the other part–the tiny,
T-25.........I.6:1 **H. S.** serves Christ's purpose in your mind
T-25....... II.6:1 The **H. S.** is the frame God set around the
T-25..... II.10:6 And give the **H. S.** what He offers unto the
T-25...... III.8:8 The **H. S.**, too, sees what He sees as far
T-25...... VI.5:4 It is the means the **H. S.** uses to translate
T-25...... VI.7:1 The **H. S.** needs your special function,
T-25...... VI.7:5 the **H. S.** cannot employ on his behalf,
T-25..... VII.1:1 **H. S.** can commute each sentence that you
T-25..... VII.5:1 **H. S.** has the power to change the whole
T-25... VII.12:7 vantage point from which the **H. S.** gives
T-25... VIII.1:1 The **H. S.** can use all that you give to Him
T-25... VIII.6:3 And so they fear the **H. S.**, and perceive
T-25... VIII.7:2 the **H. S.** as if He were a messenger from
T-25. VIII.11:1 **H. S.** heeds not who looks on innocence at
T-25. VIII.11:4 Of each one does the **H. S.** ask if he will be
T-25. VIII.12:9 little need you give the **H. S.** that simple
T-25. VIII.14:2 knows, and all the **H. S.** brings to earth.
T-25...... IX.3:1 to a problem the **H. S.** solves will always
T-25...... IX.3:4 impossible the **H. S.** could see unfairness
T-25...... IX.5:6 is reflected in the sight the **H. S.** gives.
T-25...... IX.7:5 To give a problem to the **H. S.** to solve for
T-26.........I.6:2 keep the **H. S.** from His task of showing
T-26....... II.1:1 ask the **H. S.** to solve all problems for you.
T-26....... II.2:1 The **H. S.** offers you release from every
T-26....... II.4:4 The **H. S.** does not evaluate injustices as
T-26....... II.6:9 will the **H. S.** be content until it is received
T-26....... V.4:1 the **H. S.** still guides you through the
T-26... VIII.6:3 The change of purpose the **H. S.** brought
T-26. VIII.7:10 be the cost the **H. S.** asks for what He gave
T-26....... X.5:7 without the function that the **H. S.** sees.
T-26....... X.6:4 world is fair because the **H. S.** has brought
T-27.........I.3:5 The **H. S.** offers you, to give to him, a
T-27.........I.5:1 the **H. S.** lays a picture of a different you.
T-27...... I.11:6 hide the function that the **H. S.** gave. Let,
T-27....... II.8:2 "price" the **H. S.** and the world interpret
T-27....... II.8:4 **H. S.** knows your healing is the witness
T-27....... II.9:7 could the **H. S.** be deterred an instant,
T-27..... II.14:6 remaining half the **H. S.** must represent
T-27..... II.15:4 the goal in which the **H. S.** sees His Own.
T-27...... III.5:6 It lets the **H. S.** make exchange of pictures
T-27...... V.1:10 The **H. S.** speaks to *you.* He does not speak
T-27...... VI.1:2 shrieks would silence what the **H. S.** says,
T-27... VII.14:3 Rest in the **H. S.**, and allow His gentle
T-27... VIII.9:1 laughter does the **H. S.** perceive the cause,
T-27. VIII.11:2 **H. S.** will repeat this one inclusive lesson
T-28.........I.3:4 truth. All things the **H. S.** can employ for
T-28.........I.4:1 **H. S.** can indeed make use of memory, for
T-28.........I.8:1 Cause the **H. S.** has remembered for you,
T-28..... II.10:1 Like every lesson that the **H. S.** requests
T-28...... IV.7:1 The **H. S.** is in both your minds, and He
T-28...... IV.7:7 comes to join His Son the **H. S.** joined.
T-29...... IV.5:3 dreams the **H. S.** gives is never one of fear.
T-29....... V.3:1 Here is the role the **H. S.** gives to you who
T-29....... V.7:4 the **H. S.** gives the dream its function, it
T-29... VIII.9:4 It is for him the **H. S.** speaks, and tells you
T-30....... II.1:1 to oppose the **H. S.** is to fight *yourself?* He
T-30..... VII.1:4 The **H. S.** looks upon the world as with
T-31.........I.5:5 skill the **H. S.** sees in all the world. His
T-31....... V.8:3 Now must the **H. S.** find a way to help you
T-31....... V.11:5 The **H. S.** does not seek to throw you into
W-pI.....43.1:3 created the **H. S.** as the Mediator between
W-pI.....43.1:6 That is its function as the **H. S.** sees it.
W-pI.....43.2:6 **H. S.** give it a meaning very close to God's.
W-pI.....64.2:2 learned that the **H. S.** has another use for
W-pI.....64.2:3 To the **H. S.**, the world is a place where
W-pI.....64.5:9 That is the only choice the **H. S.** sees.
W-pI.....65.4:4 so that the **H. S.** can use it consistently for
W-pI.....66.2:1 the **H. S.** on the fundamental question of
W-pI.....66.2:2 the **H. S.** about what your happiness is. It
W-pI.....66.2:4 attacks and the **H. S.** does not respond.
W-pI.....66.7:4 The other is the home of the **H. S.**, where
W-pI.....66.7:5 love that the **H. S.** always offers to replace
W-pI.....75.7:2 Understand that the **H. S.** never fails to
W-pI.....77.6:3 The **H. S.** cannot but assure you that your
W-pI.....78.5:4 the holy role the **H. S.** has assigned to him
W-pI.....78.8:4 The **H. S.** leans from him to you, seeing
W-pI.....78.8:8 allowed the **H. S.** to express through him
W-pI.....78.9:1 of love the **H. S.** showed you in their place
W-pI.....80.2:3 way for the **H. S.** to give you God's answer
W-pI.....90.3:6 The **H. S.** will teach me this, if I will let
W-pI.....91.7:2 need to be aware of what the **H. S.** uses to
W-pI.....95.8:1 The **H. S.** is not delayed in His teaching
W-pI.....96.7:2 The **H. S.** holds salvation in your mind,
W-pI.....97.5:1 The **H. S.** will be glad to take five minutes
W-pI.....97.7:1 with the words the **H. S.** speaks to you,
W-pI.....97.7:3 **H. S.** will accept this gift that you received
W-pI.....97.8:5 The **H. S.** gives you peace today. Receive
W-pI.....99.5:1 The **H. S.** holds this plan of God exactly
W-pI.....99.5:4 Unshaken does the **H. S.** look on what you
WpI. rIII.in6:4 the means the **H. S.** uses will not fail. The
W-pI...137.9:1 the means by which the **H. S.** urges you to
W-pI...140.3:1 The happy dreams the **H. S.** brings are
W-pI...158.5:6 is a vision which the **H. S.** sees because the
W-pI...161.3:3 We give them to the **H. S.**, that He may
W-pI.184.11:3 The **H. S.** uses all of them, but He does
W-pI...193.5:2 the **H. S.** speaks in all your tribulations,
W-pI.198.10:2 gift the **H. S.** holds for you from God your
W-pI...199.2:1 that serves the **H. S.** is unlimited forever,
W-pI...199.4:3 no need of it except the need the **H. S.** sees
W-pI...199.6:1 The **H. S.** is the home of minds that seek
W-pI...199.6:6 which the mind within the **H. S.** seeks.
W-pI...199.7:3 so that the **H. S.** can make use of your
W-pI...199.8:4 the thought the **H. S.** gives you for today.
WpI rVI.in.2:1 carefully review the thoughts the **H. S.** has
W-pI...215.1:2 *The **H. S.** is my only Guide. He walks with me*
W-pII..236.1:6 to the **H. S.** to employ as He sees fit. I thus
W-pII...... 6.3:1 Home of the **H. S.**, and at home in God
W-pII...... 6.4:1 The **H. S.** reaches from the Christ in you
W-pII.........7.h What Is the **H. S.**?
W-pII...... 7.1:1 The **H. S.** mediates between illusions and
W-pII...... 7.2:4 as the **H. S.** guides it to the outcome He
W-pII...... 7.3:2 **H. S.** understands the means you made,
W-pII...... 7.4:1 been placed by God, the **H. S.** calls to you,
W-pII...... 7.5:3 Itself. The **H. S.** is His gift, by which the
W-pII...... 8.5:1 The **H. S.** has no need of time when it has
W-pII.....295.h The **H. S.** looks through me today.
W-pII.....296.h The **H. S.** speaks through me today.
W-pII..296.1:1 *The **H. S.** needs my voice today, that all the*
W-pII..296.2:3 does the **H. S.** come to rescue us from hell,
W-pII...... 9.3:1 ends the lessons that the **H. S.** teaches,
M-6 ........... 4:3 is the change of mind that the **H. S.** in the
M-6 ........... 4:4 And it is the **H. S.** in the mind of the giver
M-7 ........... 2:3 the **H. S.** so accepted it and so used it.
M-11 .......... 3:1 text explains that the **H. S.** is the Answer
M-18 .......... 2:3 the **H. S.** can now speak of the reality of
M-21 ........ 3:11 **H. S.** alone understands what this Word
M-22 .......... 3:8 to the **H. S.** unless the body is killed? And
M-25 .......... 2:5 barriers to direct experience of the **H. S.**,
M-25 .......... 3:2 Given to the **H. S.**, and used under His
M-25 .......... 4:2 The **H. S.** is incapable of deception, and
M-25 .......... 4:6 which the **H. S.** wants and needs. Yet the
M-25 .......... 4:9 to the **H. S.** must be given to weakness,
M-25 .......... 6:4 the world would destroy the **H. S.** would
M-25 .......... 6:9 The **H. S.** needs these gifts, and those who
M-29 .......... 3:1 –in referring decisions to the **H. S.** with
M-29 .......... 4:6 The **H. S.** knows the truth about you. The
M-29 .......... 5:4 ask the **H. S.** to decide for you is simply to
M-29 .......... 6:1 the **H. S.** does not depend on your words.
C-1............. 3:1 still in contact with God through the **H. S.**
C-1............. 5:2 *Right-mindedness* listens to the **H. S.**,
C-1............. 7:3 above or below; from the **H. S.** or the ego.
C-6.................h THE **H. S.**
C-6............. 1:1 Jesus is the manifestation of the *H. S.*,
C-6............. 1:2 The **H. S.**, being a creation of the one
C-6............. 2:1 **H. S.** is described throughout the course
C-6............. 2:4 the **H. S.** long before Jesus set it in motion
C-6............. 3:1 The **H. S.** is described as the remaining
C-6............. 3:2 the **H. S.** has assumed a dual function. He
C-6............. 4:1 The **H. S.** abides in the part of your mind
P-1............. 2:1 than to invite the **H. S.** to enter into it and
P-1............. 5:5 The **H. S.** uses time as He thinks best, and
P-2........... I.3:3 **H. S.** fight against the intrusions of the
P-2.......... II.1:5 are still the temple of the **H. S.**, and they
P-2........ IV.5:5 by Him to the **H. S.** as His gift to you?
P-2....... VII.4:7 in those through whom the **H. S.** speaks.
P-3........... I.3:9 The joining is in the hands of the **H. S.**. It
P-3.......... II.3:1 Even this the **H. S.** can use, and will use,
P-3.......... II.3:8 asked the **H. S.** to enter the relationship
P-3.......... II.5:3 blessed by the **H. S.** as a gift from their
P-3....... II.10:7 hear does not limit the **H. S.** in any way.
P-3........ III.1:2 the **H. S.** to help in carrying out the plan.
P-3........ III.2:3 will be those of whom the **H. S.** asks some
P-3........ III.6:4 have been before the **H. S.** entered them,
P-3........ III.8:3 The **H. S.** never refuses an invitation to
S-1........... I.1:1 is a way offered by the **H. S.** to reach God.
S-1........... I.2:1 told to ask the **H. S.** for the answer to any

## Holy Spirit's 139

*Holy*
*Holy Spirit*
*See also* His, My, Whose, Your

T-5...... IV.1:11 those who hear the **H. S.** Call to be as one,
T-6.......... II.7:1 perfect equality of the **H. S.** perception is
T-6....... II.12:1 and the **H. S.** extension is very simple.
T-6...... V.B.3:2 the **H. S.** first lesson was "To have, give all
T-6...... V.B.4:5 increasing clarity of the **H. S.** Voice makes
T-6...... V.B.6:4 realize the quiet power of the **H. S.** Voice,
T-6...... V.C.2:7 Therefore, the **H. S.** third lesson is: *Be*
T-7.......... II.5:1 The **H. S.** purpose in translating is exactly
T-7.......... II.6:3 is why the **H. S.** teaching is a lesson in
T-7........ IV.5:1 The ego's goal is as unified as the **H. S.**,
T-7......... V.1:3 but the **H. S.** decision to use the body only
T-7......... V.3:2 to be healed. Healing is the **H. S.** form of
T-7...... VI.13:5 is the **H. S.** perfectly consistent teaching.
T-7......... X.3:5 The **H. S.** main function is to teach you to
T-8.......... II.3:5 **H. S.** lesson because that is what you *are.*
T-8.......... II.6:1 **H. S.** teaching takes only *one* direction and
T-8....... VII.7:7 is to lose sight of the **H. S.** purpose, and
T-8....... VII.8:5 The **H. S.** curriculum is never depressing,
T-8...... VIII.8:7 **H. S.** Voice is as loud as your willingness
T-8........ IX.9:1 then, is the **H. S.** only way of healing. This
T-9........... I.4:2 I said that the **H. S.** function is to sort out
T-9....... II.5:10 His words are the **H. S.** answer to you. Is
T-9........ III.8:7 This is the **H. S.** use of an ability that you
T-9........... IV.h The **H. S.** Plan of Forgiveness
T-9........ IV.6:1 Follow the **H. S.** teaching in forgiveness,
T-9........ IV.6:3 willingness to follow the **H. S.** plan of
T-9....... VII.3:5 however, is the exact opposite of the **H. S.**,
T-9....... VII.4:2 understand how lofty the **H. S.** perception
T-11..... V.11:4 *not.* According to the **H. S.** teaching, *only*
T-11..... V.14:1 have to be, the exact opposite of the **H. S.**.
T-12..............h THE **H. S.** CURRICULUM
T-12......... I.3:2 **H. S.** judgment it requires no effort at all
T-12......... I.8:1 By applying the **H. S.** interpretation of
T-12......... I.8:6 of the ego. Consider how well the **H. S.**
T-12....... I.10:3 **H. S.** interpretation of fear does dispel it,
T-12....... V.4:1 The **H. S.** Love is your strength, for yours
T-12...... VI.4:2 the eyes of the blind is the **H. S.** mission,
T-12...... VI.5:8 you in the quiet light of the **H. S.** blessing.
T-12...... VI.6:5 the transfer of training under the **H. S.**
T-12..... VII.4:6 Do the **H. S.** work, for you share in His
T-12... VII.4:10 in direct opposition to the **H. S.** purpose.
T-12... VII.14:3 is an essential part of the **H. S.** teaching.
T-13...... III.7:2 **H. S.** vision is merciful and His remedy is
T-13...... IV.7:1 It is evident that the **H. S.** perception of
T-13....... V.9:5 He is the **H. S.** manifestation, looking
T-13...... XI.5:4 your reactions to the **H. S.** Voice may be,
T-14........ II.7:2 in the **H. S.** plan to free you from the past,
T-14...... VI.8:1 **H. S.** function is entirely communication.
T-14...... IX.1:4 the ego to God, is the **H. S.** only function.
T-14........ X.5:9 it is not your function, but the **H. S.**.
T-14........ X.7:1 the **H. S.** one division into two categories;
T-15......... I.2:1 of the **H. S.** teaching are far in the future.
T-15......... I.9:4 Begin to practice the **H. S.** use of time as a

| | |
|---|---|
| T-15......IV.8:4 | then the **H. S.** readiness to give it to you is |
| T-15......IV.9:9 | Let the **H. S.** purity shine them away, and |
| T-15.......V.1:1 | The holy instant is the **H. S.** most useful |
| T-15.......V.9:6 | The **H. S.** timelessness lies only here. For |
| T-15......VI.1:3 | Under the **H. S.** teaching all relationships |
| T-15...VII.13:2 | It is the **H. S.** teaching function to instruct |
| T-15.......X.1:4 | it is the **H. S.** function to use them both, |
| T-17......VI.1:1 | of the **H. S.** purpose is extremely simple, |
| T-17......VI.1:4 | The setting of the **H. S.** goal is general. |
| T-17......VI.4:3 | to the **H. S.** sorting out of truth and falsity |
| T-17......VI.6:2 | in the acceptance of the **H. S.** purpose, |
| T-17......VII.7:1 | The power set in you in whom the **H. S.** |
| T-17...VII.10:4 | You whose relationship shares the **H. S.** |
| T-17....VIII.1:2 | The meaning that the **H. S.** purpose has |
| T-17....VIII.3:3 | of the **H. S.** purpose is free to use instead. |
| T-18......III.5:3 | accord with all the power of the **H. S.** Will |
| T-18......IV.7:4 | **H. S.** are so extremely disproportionate. |
| T-18.......V.1:3 | the holy relationship, the **H. S.** teaching, |
| T-18.......V.2:3 | your guilt before you ask the **H. S.** help. |
| T-18.......V.4:5 | accepted the **H. S.** purpose as your own, |
| T-19.........I.4:5 | has thus opposed the **H. S.** purpose, and |
| T-19.......I.12:2 | For faith arises from the **H. S.** perception, |
| T-19......IV.1:5 | The extension of the **H. S.** purpose from |
| T-19......IV.3:6 | **H. S.** function here will be accomplished. |
| T19...IV.A.3:1 | **H. S.** purpose rests in peace within you. |
| T19....IV.B.3:1 | The **H. S.** messengers are sent far beyond |
| T19..IV.C.2:13 | When you accepted the **H. S.** purpose in |
| T-20.......II.5:3 | who accept the **H. S.** purpose as their own |
| T-20.......II.6:5 | share it. The **H. S.** vision is no idle gift, no |
| T-20......IV.6:6 | learn its special function in the **H. S.** plan, |
| T-20......VI.5:1 | The **H. S.** temple is not a body, but a |
| T-20......VI.6:1 | cannot make the body the **H. S.** temple, |
| T-20......VI.7:8 | **H. S.** purpose lies safe in your relationship |
| T-20.....VII.1:2 | also said the means to meet the **H. S.** goal |
| T-20.....VII.9:4 | Salvation is the **H. S.** goal. The means is |
| T-20....VIII.3:1 | to look on with the **H. S.** vision and to |
| T-21....III.12:3 | can have faith in it to serve the **H. S.** goal, |
| T-21......IV.4:5 | **H. S.** purpose was accepted by the part of |
| T-21......IV.4:9 | willing to see the **H. S.** purpose as its own |
| T-21......IV.5:4 | not the ego that joined the **H. S.** purpose, |
| T-21.....V.7:10 | serves the **H. S.** purpose in its own right. |
| T-21.......V.9:2 | **H. S.** purpose accepted and accomplished |
| T-22.......II.6:2 | to let the **H. S.** purpose be accomplished, |
| T-22......VI.9:2 | of forgiveness is the **H. S.** function. Leave |
| T-25.........I.6:4 | is the **H. S.** function to teach you how this |
| T-25......VI.4:1 | is the **H. S.** kind perception of specialness; |
| T-25....VIII.5:8 | It is impossible for you to share the **H. S.** |
| T-25....VIII.6:1 | to understand the **H. S.** justice. They must |
| T-25..VIII.12:7 | **H. S.** special function has been fulfilled. |
| T-25..VIII.13:5 | since they are equal in the **H. S.** sight. |
| T-25......IX.4:2 | The **H. S.** perception leaves no ground for |
| T-25......IX.5:1 | **H. S.** problem solving is the way in which |
| T-25......IX.7:2 | the **H. S.** gift, were given specially to an |
| T-26.........I.8:5 | What is the **H. S.** special function but to |
| T-26.......II.7:3 | hurt resolved before the **H. S.** gentle sight. |
| T-26....VIII.9:9 | The **H. S.** purpose now is yours. Should |
| T-26......IX.8:7 | Now is the **H. S.** purpose done. For They |
| T-26.......X.5:4 | The **H. S.** purpose is to let the Presence of |
| T-27.........I.9:3 | The **H. S.** picture changes not the body |
| T-27.....II.12:2 | know the **H. S.** Mind and yours are One. |
| T-28.........I.5:1 | The **H. S.** use of memory is quite apart |
| T-28......IV.8:1 | The **H. S.** function is to take the broken |
| T-30.....VII.6:2 | The **H. S.** goal gives one interpretation, |
| T-31.........I.4:4 | enormity so great the **H. S.** Voice seems |
| T-31.......V.9:1 | are the **H. S.** lesson plans arranged in easy |
| W-pI......43.3:3 | extent to which it shares the **H. S.** purpose |
| W-pI.....66.9:8 | is the only alternative to the **H. S.** Voice. |
| W-pI.....89.3:2 | this idea do I unite my will with the **H. S.**, |
| WpI. rIII.in7:4 | the **H. S.** chosen means for your salvation. |
| W-pI...159.6:1 | This is the **H. S.** single gift; the treasure |
| W-pII .....7.2:1 | The goal the **H. S.** teaching sets is just this |
| W-pII .295.2:2 | *thus allow the **H. S.** Love to bless all things* |
| W-pII .312.1:5 | the **H. S.** purpose as his goal for seeing. |
| M-4 ....IV.1:10 | make the **H. S.** lessons impossible to learn |
| M-19 .........1:6 | Justice is the **H. S.** verdict upon the world. |
| M-20 .......5:10 | in this one sentence is the **H. S.** whole |
| M-25 .........6:6 | of hope and healing in the **H. S.** service. |
| M-28 .........1:3 | acceptance of the **H. S.** interpretation of |
| M-28 .........1:4 | glad awareness of the **H. S.** final dream. It |
| M-29 .........2:6 | the **H. S.** particular care and guidance. |
| M-29 .........3:3 | follow the **H. S.** guidance is to let yourself |
| M-29 .......3:10 | think that following the **H. S.** guidance is |
| M-29 .........5:9 | the **H. S.** help when it is feasible to do so, |
| C-3 ............1:3 | because of its purpose, which is the **H. S.**, |
| P-3........III.3:6 | Forgiveness, the **H. S.** only dream, must |
| S-3........IV.1:3 | of peace,–the **H. S.** voice, through whom |

**holy** 694
*Holy*
*See also* Appendix C

| | |
|---|---|
| T-1 ........I.31:3 | of God are **h.** and the miracle honors their |
| T-1 ........I.32:2 | holiness and make your perceptions **h.**. |
| T-1 ......VII.2:1 | create the good, the beautiful and the **h.**. |
| T-3 .......III.4:6 | That is why visions, however **h.**, do not |
| T-4 .......VI.2:3 | and the **h.** perception it would produce. |
| T-4 .......VI.2:4 | The term "**h.**" can be used here because, |
| T-5 ........in.3:5 | it. Only God's **h.** children are worthy |
| T-5 .........II.6:4 | In the **h.** state the will is free, so that its |
| T-5 .......IV.8:1 | How can you who are so **h.** suffer? All |
| T-5 ......VII.4:3 | that is not in accord with His **h.** Will. I am |
| T-6 ..........I.8:4 | of the altar is what makes the church **h.**. A |
| T-7 ......V.10:8 | the most **h.** children of a most holy Father |
| T-7 ......V.10:8 | the most holy children of a most **h.** Father |
| T-8 ..........III.h | The **H.** Encounter |
| T-8 .......III.3:5 | who belong in God have the **h.** function of |
| T-8 .......III.4:1 | anyone, remember it is a **h.** encounter. As |
| T-8 .......III.6:8 | every **h.** encounter in which you enter |
| T-8 .......IV.8:9 | The Holy Trinity is **h.** *because* It is One. If |
| T-8 ........V.3:5 | be to the union of God and His **h.** Sons! |
| T-8 .......VI.2:1 | and the glory of God and His **h.** Sons, but |
| T-8 .......VI.8:8 | Our creations are as **h.** as we are, and we |
| T-8 .......VI.8:8 | are the Sons of God Himself, as **h.** as He is |
| T-8 .....VI.10:5 | and free the **h.** will of all those who are as |
| T-8 ......VII.5:7 | As part of you, he is **h.**. As part of me, you |
| T-8 ......VII.6:3 | perfectly accomplish His **h.** Will for you |
| T-9 .........II.5:6 | can so **h.** a brother tell you except truth? |
| T-10 .......in.2:6 | Your **h.** mind establishes everything that |
| T-10 .......in.3:4 | That is why your mind is **h.**. Can anything |
| T-11 ........I.1:4 | restoring the **h.** dwelling place of His Son, |
| T-11 .....III.7:4 | But be **h.** in the Presence of God, or you |
| T-12 .....VI.6:3 | so **h.** that its transfer to holiness is merely |
| T-12 .....VI.7:2 | the **h.** perception of God's Son becomes |
| T-12 ....VII.1:5 | this **h.** perception you will be made whole |
| T-12 ..VII.11:2 | Its **h.** witnesses will surround you because |
| T-13 ........I.7:1 | the **h.** companions who travel with you, |
| T-13 .....IV.6:7 | recognize a **h.** encounter if you are merely |
| T-13 .....IV.6:8 | salvation, which makes the encounter **h.**, |
| T-13 .....IV.6:9 | and the encounter is **h.** because you are. |
| T-13 ...IV.6:10 | and because your dreams were not **h.**, the |
| T-13 .....IV.7:7 | the opportunities for the **h.** encounters in |
| T-13 .....VI.8:8 | The **h.** light that shines forth from God's |
| T-13 ...VI.10:5 | and in their joy they shine with **h.** thanks. |
| T-13 ...VI.11:7 | remind you of your Father and His **h.** Son. |
| T-13 ..VII.10:1 | for the perfect sanity of His most **h.** Son. |
| T-13 ..VII.13:6 | However **h.** his perception may become, |
| T-13 ..VII.17:4 | from the mind of God's most **h.** Son, |
| T-13 ...VIII.2:8 | Yet no perception, however **h.**, will last |
| T-13 ...VIII.6:5 | miracle that ever was is God's most **h.** Son |
| T-13 ...VIII.8:2 | me under the **h.** banner of His teaching, |
| T-13 ...VIII.8:4 | The **h.** light you saw outside yourself, in |
| T-13 .....IX.8:7 | Within you is the **h.** sign of perfect faith |
| T-13 .......X.2:5 | you forgot that real relationships are **h.**, |
| T-13 .......X.9:6 | to the **h.** place where you will see the light. |
| T-13 ......X.12:6 | Father, for the purity of Your most **h.** Son, |
| T-14 .......II.3:7 | *place it gently in the **h.** place where it belongs* |
| T-14 .......II.7:8 | join Him in the **h.** task of bringing light. |
| T-14 .......II.8:4 | Where everything is clear, it is all **h.**. The |
| T-14 ...III.10:6 | Yet will was given them because it is **h.**, |
| T-14 ...III.15:1 | worth of God's Son whom He created **h.**, |
| T-14 .....IV.3:1 | in your most **h.** mind be undone for you, |
| T-14 .......V.7:4 | from the effects of this most **h.** lesson, |
| T-14 .......V.8:3 | Within its **h.** circle is everyone whom God |
| T-14 .......V.9:5 | with me, and stand with me on **h.** ground. |
| T-14 .....V.11:1 | within the **h.** circle of Atonement or leave |
| T-14 .....V.11:6 | for therein lies everything that makes it **h.** |
| T-14 .....V.11:7 | Come gladly to the **h.** circle, and look out |
| T-14 .....V.11:9 | the **h.** place of peace which is for all of us, |
| T-14 .....VI.5:3 | have use to Him, for His most **h.** purpose. |
| T-14 .....VI.5:7 | to apply it to the **h.** cause of restoration. |
| T-14 ......VIII.h | The **H.** Meeting Place |
| T-14 .VIII.2:13 | The **h.** meeting place of the unseparated |
| T-14 ...VIII.4:9 | **h.** meeting place are joined the Father and |
| T-14 .....IX.1:1 | The Atonement does not make **h.**. You |
| T-14 .....IX.1:2 | You were created **h.**. It merely brings |
| T-14 .....IX.3:9 | The temple still is **h.**, for the Presence that |
| T-14 .....IX.4:6 | is as **h.** as the Holiness by which it was |
| T-14 .....IX.4:7 | and leaves not what It created **h.** as Itself. |
| T-14 ...XI.10:7 | He has established as **h.** by His Presence. |
| T-14 ...XI.11:7 | the **h.** stamp of immortality upon it. This |
| T-15 .............h | THE **H.** INSTANT |
| T-15 .........I.9:7 | From this **h.** instant wherein holiness was |
| T-15 .......I.10:4 | birth into the **h.** present is salvation from |
| T-15 .......I.10:7 | In the **h.** instant, in which you see yourself |
| T-15 .......I.12:1 | You will never give this **h.** instant to the |
| T-15 .......I.13:8 | guilt. You must be **h.** if you offer holiness. |
| T-15 .....I.15:11 | miracle of the **h.** instant through the Holy |
| T-15 ........II.2:4 | joy it is to teach God's **h.** Son his holiness. |
| T-15 ........II.3:6 | In this **h.** instant you will unchain all your |
| T-15 ........II.5:1 | **h.** instant has not yet happened to you. |
| T-15 ........II.5:4 | practice the mechanics of the **h.** instant, |
| T-15 ........II.6:1 | little part in separating out the **h.** instant. |
| T-15 ......III.9:1 | **H.** child of God, when will you learn that |
| T-15 ...III.12:6 | Lay not littleness before His **h.** altar, |
| T-15 .........IV.h | Practicing the **H.** Instant |
| T-15 ......IV.1:3 | **h.** instant is this instant and every instant. |
| T-15 ......IV.3:4 | I call you to fulfill your **h.** part in the plan |
| T-15 ......IV.4:1 | and immaculate is the **h.** altar on which |
| T-15 ......IV.4:2 | This you will recognize in the **h.** instant, |
| T-15 ......IV.4:4 | You can claim the **h.** instant any time and |
| T-15 ......IV.4:7 | Use the **h.** instant only to recognize that |
| T-15 ......IV.5:1 | I stand within the **h.** instant, as clear as |
| T-15 ......IV.5:2 | time in which the **h.** instant will be yours. |
| T-15 ......IV.5:3 | you to make the **h.** instant yours at once, |
| T-15 ......IV.6:3 | You could live forever in the **h.** instant, |
| T-15 ......IV.6:5 | **h.** instant is a time in which you receive |
| T-15 ......IV.7:2 | that makes the **h.** instant what it is. You |
| T-15 ......IV.8:6 | **h.** instant is given and received with equal |
| T-15 ......IV.9:1 | The necessary condition for the **h.** instant |
| T-15 ...........V.h | The **H.** Instant and Special Relationships |
| T-15 ........V.1:1 | **h.** instant is the Holy Spirit's most useful |
| T-15 ........V.3:7 | Yet the **h.** instant teaches you it is not so. |
| T-15 ........V.8:2 | In the **h.** instant no one is special, for your |
| T-15 ........V.8:5 | them. In the **h.** instant, you see in each |
| T-15 ........V.9:3 | The **h.** instant reflects His knowing by |
| T-15 ........V.9:7 | For in the **h.** instant, free of the past, you |
| T-15 ......V.10:1 | relationships are blessed in the **h.** instant, |
| T-15 ......V.10:2 | In the **h.** instant the Sonship gains as one, |
| T-15 ......V.10:8 | the **h.** instant you unite directly with God, |
| T-15 ......V.11:4 | the **h.** instant there is no conflict of needs, |
| T-15 ......V.11:5 | For the **h.** instant reaches to eternity, and |
| T-15 .........VI.h | The **H.** Instant and the Laws of God |
| T-15 ......VI.2:5 | **h.** instant we share our faith in God's Son |
| T-15 ......VI.5:3 | In the **h.** instant you recognize the idea of |
| T-15 ......VI.5:5 | **h.** instant thus becomes a lesson in how to |
| T-15 ......VI.5:8 | In the **h.** instant the laws of God prevail, |
| T-15 ......VI.6:1 | In the **h.** instant nothing happens that |
| T-15 ......VI.6:7 | Fear not the **h.** instant will be denied you, |
| T-15 ....VI.6:10 | For in the **h.** instant you will recognize the |
| T-15 ......VI.8:1 | In the **h.** instant God is remembered, and |
| T-15 ......VI.8:3 | in the **h.** instant because the past is gone, |
| T-15 .....VII.3:6 | such as this belongs not in your **h.** mind. |
| T-15 .....VII.5:1 | Spirit would remove from his **h.** mind. |
| T-15 ..VII.13:3 | in a real relationship so **h.** and so strong, |
| T-15 ..VII.14:1 | **h.** instant that what seems impossible is |
| T-15 ..VII.14:2 | In the **h.** instant guilt holds no attraction, |
| T-15 ...VIII.1:1 | The **h.** instant does not replace the need |
| T-15 ...VIII.1:1 | **h.** instant has extended far beyond time. |
| T-15 ...VIII.2:4 | in making the **h.** instant all that there is, |
| T-15 ...VIII.3:7 | For the **h.** host of God is beyond failure, |
| T-15 ...VIII.3:8 | You are forever in a relationship so **h.** that |
| T-15 ...VIII.6:2 | It is His **h.** function to accept them both, |
| T-15 .........IX.h | The **H.** Instant and the Attraction of God |
| T-15 ......IX.1:2 | that is accomplished in the **h.** instant. Yet |
| T-15 ......IX.3:1 | In the **h.** instant, where the Great Rays |
| T-15 ......IX.7:3 | In the **h.** instant there are no bodies, and |
| T-15 ........X.2:1 | The **h.** instant is truly the time of Christ. |

T-15.......X.4:1 It is in your power to make this season **h.**,
T-15......XI.2:9 the Host is as **h.** as the perfect Innocence
T-15......XI.7:1 the **h.** instant the condition of love is met,
T-15......XI.9:1 to the **h.** host who would receive Him,
T-15..XI.10:10 Accept the **h.** instant as this year is born,
T-15..XI.10:12 all your relationships be made **h.** for you.
T-16.......II.1:2 told that it must include everyone to *be* **h.**.
T-16......III.8:1 most **h.** Self all praise is due for what you
T-16......VI.3:2 The **h.** instant is His most helpful aid in
T-16....VI.11:7 may the **h.** instant speed you on the way,
T-16....VI.12:1 you, enter with Him into a **h.** instant, and
T-16.....VII.6:1 the Holy Spirit gently lays the **h.** instant.
T-16.....VII.6:3 The **h.** instant is the opposite of the ego's
T-16.....VII.6:4 In the **h.** instant it is understood that the
T-16.....VII.7:1 to bring illusions into the **h.** instant, to
T-16.....VII.7:3 **h.** instant the power of the Holy Spirit will
T-16.....VII.7:5 Yet the **h.** instant is eternal, and your
T-16.....VII.8:5 He gave the **h.** instant to be given you,
T-16.....VII.8:7 In the **h.** instant is His reminder that His
T-16.....VII.9:7 the **h.** instant this is done for you in time,
T-16...VII.11:1 and *find* His message in the **h.** instant,
T-17.............h AND THE **H.** RELATIONSHIP
T-17......III.2:1 that would make the ego **h.** in your sight,
T-17......III.9:8 as is the **h.** Source from which they came.
T-17....III.10:1 My **h.** brother, I would enter into all your
T-17....III.10:6 and let not the **h.** purpose of Atonement
T-17......IV.2:6 the **h.** relationship shares God's purpose,
T-17......IV.4:7 all your **h.** relationships been carefully
T-17....IV.10:1 That is why the **h.** instant is so important
T-17....IV.11:1 The **h.** instant is a miniature of Heaven,
T-17....IV.11:4 The **h.** instant is a miniature of eternity. It
T-17....IV.16:8 **h.** instant shines alike on all relationships,
T-17.......V.1:1 The **h.** relationship is the expression of
T-17.......V.1:1 of the **h.** instant in living in this world.
T-17.......V.1:2 **h.** instant is a practical device, witnessed
T-17.......V.1:3 The **h.** instant never fails. The experience
T-17.......V.1:6 The **h.** relationship is a constant reminder
T-17.......V.1:7 so is the **h.** relationship a happy song of
T-17.......V.2:1 The **h.** relationship, a major step toward
T-17.......V.2:3 **h.** relationship is a phenomenal teaching
T-17.....V.7:14 This relationship has been reborn as **h.**.
T-17.......V.8:1 its purpose work in it to make it **h.**. You
T-17.....V.10:2 have joined with many in the **h.** instant,
T-17.....V.10:3 Himself has blessed your **h.** relationship.
T-17...V.11:10 yourself unable to express the **h.** instant,
T-17.....V.12:5 brother is to appreciate the **h.** instant,
T-17.....V.13:1 You *have* received the **h.** instant, but you
T-17.....V.14:1 brother stand together in the **h.** presence
T-17.....V.15:1 will also accept the effects of the **h.** instant
T-17.....VII.4:3 and your relationship was not **h.** because
T-17.....VII.6:4 No relationship is **h.** unless its holiness
T-17...VII.8:12 outside it and keep the situation **h.**. For it
T-17... VIII.1:1 **h.** instant is nothing more than a special
T-17... VIII.1:4 The **h.** instant is the shining example, the
T-17... VIII.3:1 you not want to make a **h.** instant of every
T-18.........I.8:2 where in **h.** stillness dwells the living God
T-18.........I.9:4 love. Here is **h.** ground, in which no
T-18......I.10:7 Thought so **h.** and so perfect that illusions
T-18......I.10:7 the **h.** place in which you stand together.
T-18......I.10:9 His gift as our most **h.** and perfect reality,
T-18......I.11:4 lovely and how **h.** is your relationship,
T-18......I.13:1 the most **h.** function this world contains.
T-18......I.13:3 This is offered you, in your **h.** relationship
T-18......I.13:6 The **h.** light that brought you and him
T-18.......II.7:1 blessed through your **h.** relationship. It
T-18....III.4:13 That wish was the desire to be **h.**. The
T-18......III.6:5 me in the **h.** light of your relationship, is
T-18......III.7:3 the **h.** instant to which you brought it. We
T-18......IV.1:1 The **h.** instant is the result of your
T-18......IV.1:1 the result of your determination to be **h.**.
T-18......IV.1:9 He joins with you to make the **h.** instant
T-18......IV.2:6 them you would not need the **h.** instant.
T-18......IV.2:8 The miracle of the **h.** instant lies in your
T-18......IV.3:3 Your difficulty with the **h.** instant arises
T-18......IV.4:1 The **h.** instant does not come from your
T-18......IV.5:4 In preparing for the **h.** instant, do not
T-18......IV.5:4 attempt to make yourself **h.** to be ready to
T-18......IV.6:5 preparation for the **h.** instant belongs to
T-18......IV.7:1 the **h.** instant so easy and so natural. You
T-18......IV.8:2 believe the **h.** instant is difficult for you, it
T-18.......V.1:3 The **h.** instant, the holy relationship, the
T-18.......V.1:3 The holy instant, the **h.** relationship, the
T-18.......V.2:1 Never approach the **h.** instant after you
T-18.......V.3:1 Through your **h.** relationship, reborn and
T-18.......V.3:1 reborn and blessed in every **h.** instant you
T-18.......V.5:2 Nor is your **h.** relationship a dream. All
T-18.......V.6:1 for the **h.** one that you would rather have.
T-18.......V.6:6 is it equally impossible that the **h.** instant
T-18.......V.7:3 *I desire this* **h.** *instant for myself, that I may*
T-18......VI.7:2 And neither God nor His most **h.** Son can
T-18....VI.13:6 much of what happens in the **h.** instant;
T-18....VI.14:2 the irresistible appeal the **h.** instant holds.
T-18.....VII.4:1 the **h.** instant without reservation unless,
T-18.....VII.4:8 to make **h.** what is hated and despised.
T-18.....VII.5:2 A **h.** relationship is a means of saving time
T-18... VIII.9:6 They enter one by one into this **h.** place,
T-18. VIII.11:1 The **h.** instant is your invitation to love to
T-18. VIII.11:4 In the **h.** instant, you ask of love only
T-18....IX.1:10 the Son of God, complete and **h.**, serene
T-18....IX.10:5 A step beyond this **h.** place of forgiveness,
T-18....IX.13:3 **h.** instant in which you and your brother
T-18....IX.14:1 to you in the **h.** place of forgiveness you
T-19.......I.10:5 just as he is perceived in the **h.** instant,
T-19.......I.12:5 Your **h.** relationship, with its new purpose
T-19.......I.13:2 and sees the **h.** place where it was healed.
T-19.......I.14:1 In the **h.** instant, you and your brother
T-19.......I.15:1 most **h.** garden that He would make of it.
T-19.......II.5:3 the most "**h.**" concept in the ego's system;
T-19......III.7:5 God created **h.** could not prevail against it
T-19......III.8:4 Your **h.** relationship has, as its purpose
T-19....III.10:1 In the **h.** instant, you will see the smile of
T-19....III.10:4 healed in the **h.** instant Heaven gave you.
T-19....III.10:6 Heaven will disappear before your **h.** sight
T-19......IV.3:8 Creator in the Name of His most **h.** Son.
T19... IV.A.5:2 For in the miracle of your **h.** relationship,
T19... IV.A.5:9 His home is in your **h.** relationship. Do
T19. IV.A.5:10 to stand between Him and His **h.** purpose
T19. IV.A.10:2 it would unite in **h.** union and completion
T19. IV.A.16:2 is a feast that honors your **h.** relationship,
T19. IV.A.16:3 in a **h.** instant grace is said by everyone
T19....IV.B.3:1 the mind to join in **h.** communion and be
T19....IV.B.4:9 your **h.** relationship is your Father's Son.
T19....IV.B.5:3 in your **h.** relationship I am there already.
T19....IV.B.7:1 **h.** relationship truth proclaims the truth,
T19....IV.B.7:4 O come ye faithful to the **h.** union of the
T19....IV.B.8:3 I am within your **h.** relationship, yet you
T19....IV.C.5:1 as long as it is useful for your **h.** purpose.
T19..IV.C.11:6 Remember the **h.** Presence of the One
T19....IV.D.6:3 of guilt, the "**h.**" waxen image of death,
T19....IV.D.9:6 Let us join together in a **h.** instant, here in
T19....IV.D.9:6 where the purpose, given in a **h.** instant,
T19. IV.D.14:2 you. How **h.** and how beautiful He is! You
T19. IV.D.15:5 and receive from your most **h.** Friend. Let
T19. IV.D.16:1 Here is the **h.** place of resurrection, to
T19. IV.D.16:3 And offer thanks to God that he is **h.**, and
T19. IV.D.17:9 that we might meet here in this **h.** place,
T19. IV.D.21:7 you to see this purpose in your **h.** Friend,
T-20...........I.h **H.** Week
T-20.........I.1:2 Let us not spend this **h.** week brooding on
T-20.........I.2:1 and **h.** sign the Son of God is innocent.
T-20.........I.3:1 yet this **h.** week is the symbol of the whole
T-20.......II.9:1 not have your **h.** brother lead you there?
T-20.......II.9:2 and shining from the **h.** altar within him
T-20......II.11:5 And come before his **h.** altar where the
T-20......III.2:5 recognize your **h.** relationship for what it
T-20......III.3:1 The **h.** do not interfere with truth. They
T-20......III.6:1 a **h.** relationship can long remain unholy?
T-20......III.6:2 The world the **h.** see is one with them, just
T-20......III.6:3 The world the **h.** see is beautiful because
T-20......III.8:9 That is the purpose of your **h.** relationship
T-20....III.11:7 Father as surely as God created His Son **h.**.
T-20......IV.6:6 Each **h.** relationship must enter here, to
T-20.......V.1:1 closest to himself in a **h.** relationship.
T-20.......V.2:5 Peace to your **h.** relationship, which has
T-20.......V.5:4 serves the purpose of a **h.** relationship.
T-20.......V.5:6 Why should it take so many **h.** instants to
T-20.......V.6:1 each **h.** instant as a different point in time
T-20......VI.2:1 of both a **h.** and an unholy relationship.
T-20......VI.9:3 **h.** instant and its unlimited beneficence?
T-20......VI.9:4 your preference to the **h.** instant, which
T-20......VI.9:6 And from His **h.** temple, look you not
T-20....VI.10:1 The **h.** relationship reflects the true
T-20....VI.10:4 in gladness for the **h.** one of safe return.
T-20....VI.11:8 Here he can accept the **h.** instant, offered
T-20....VI.12:2 The **h.** instant is of greater value now to
T-20.....VII.1:1 must be brought in line before your **h.**
T-20.....VII.8:3 can a **h.** relationship achieve its purpose
T-20.....VII.8:7 Your **h.** brother, sight of whom is your
T-20....VIII.1:3 Open the **h.** place that you closed off by
T-20....VIII.2:4 Your **h.** relationship offers all this to you.
T-20....VIII.2:6 as its **h.** purpose was not made by you, the
T-20....VIII.4:4 see an altar to your Father, **h.** as Heaven,
T-20....VIII.4:8 replace the **h.** home the Holy Spirit offers,
T-20....VIII.6:9 Your **h.** relationship, the source of your
T-20....VIII.6:9 its most **h.** purpose bereft of means for its
T-21.....in.1:10 looked upon with vision is healed and **h.**.
T-21........II.4:5 In the **h.** instant is this exchange effected
T-21........II.8:2 The **h.** instant is not an instant of creation
T-21......III.6:6 of a **h.** relationship is all you *want* to see.
T-21......IV.3:5 A **h.** relationship is one in which you join
T-21....VIII.5:1 What is the **h.** instant but God's appeal
T-22.............h AND THE **H.** RELATIONSHIP
T-22.......in.3:1 A **h.** relationship starts from a different
T-22.......in.4:1 Think what a **h.** relationship can teach!
T-22.....in.4:10 born into a **h.** relationship can never end.
T-22...........I.h The Message of the **H.** Relationship
T-22.........I.7:1 So in each **h.** relationship is the ability to
T-22.........I.7:2 Yet a **h.** relationship, so recently reborn
T-22.........I.8:1 Think what is given you, my **h.** brother.
T-22.......I.10:7 Into the **h.** home where fear is powerless
T-22.......I.11:3 What is as like Him as a **h.** relationship?
T-22.......I.11:9 as Both are drawn to every **h.** relationship
T-22......II.11:5 has given to your **h.** relationship is there.
T-22......II.12:1 extends forever, is your **h.** relationship,
T-22......II.12:9 you not have this **h.** home be yours as well
T-22......II.13:7 you. Look on your **h.** brother, sinless as
T-22......III.9:1 A **h.** relationship, however newly born,
T-22......III.9:7 reason sees a **h.** relationship as what it is;
T-22......IV.3:1 your brother stand, here in this **h.** place,
T-22......IV.3:8 from this **h.** place He will return with you,
T-22......IV.7:4 Such is the function of a **h.** relationship;
T-22......IV.7:8 and the **h.** Self you share together.
T-22.........VI.h The Light of the **H.** Relationship
T-22......VI.4:1 **h.** relationship, lovely in its innocence,
T-22......VI.4:4 This **h.** relationship has the power to heal
T-22......VI.5:1 Before a **h.** relationship there is no sin.
T-22....VI.14:1 is the function of your **h.** relationship. For
T-23.......I.10:1 illusion, being as true and **h.** as Himself.
T-23.......I.10:3 Open the door of His most **h.** home, and
T-23.......IV.4:2 assume the **h.** function God gave His Son,
T-24........II.9:5 in this **h.** place does truth stand waiting to
T-24......II.14:1 **h.** hands would offer it to you when you
T-24.......V.8:1 The **h.** Lord of Heaven has Himself come
T-24.....VII.5:9 Its **h.** purpose gave it immortality, setting
T-24...VII.6:10 not till you make again a **h.** home for your
T-25.........I.1:6 you are manifest unto your **h.** brother, as
T-25.........I.1:7 the meeting of the **h.** Christ unto Himself;
T-25..VIII.12:4 great and **h.** that He could not doubt His
T-25..VIII.14:1 way, as God appointed for His **h.** Son.
T-26.........I.7:3 to the death of God and of His **h.** Son,
T-26.........I.8:5 the **h.** Son of God from the imprisonment
T-26......IV.3:1 The **h.** place on which you stand is but
T-26......IX.1:1 Think but how **h.** you must be from
T-26......IX.1:2 And think how **h.** he must be when in him
T-26......IX.2:4 stand is **h.** ground because of Them Who,
T-26......IX.3:7 ground so **h.** Heaven leans to join with it,
T-26........X.5:4 of your **h.** Guests be known to you. And
T-27......IV.2:4 Such is the **h.** instant. It is here that all
T-27......IV.3:1 but within the **h.** instant's surety. For
T-27......IV.6:1 Only within the **h.** instant can an honest
T-27......IV.6:9 The **h.** instant is the interval in which the
T-27......IV.7:5 the **h.** instant, you can bring the question
T-27.......V.3:1 **h.** instant is the miracle's abiding place.
T-27.......V.4:4 the blessing that the **h.** instant brings? Be
T-27.......V.6:1 Come to the **h.** instant and be healed, for
T-27.......V.6:5 **h.** instant's radiance will light your eyes,
T-27......VI.3:9 call him by the **h.** Name of God Himself.

T-27......VI.8:2 The **h.** instant will replace all sin if you
T-27...VII.15:1 who unites with you in **h.** innocence. And
T-27....VIII.9:7 hear Him say, "My brother, **h.** Son of God
T-27....VIII.9:8 will leave the **h.** instant with your laughter
T-28......IV.8:2 This **h.** picture, healed entirely, does He
T-28......IV.9:1 between the broken pieces of Your **h.** Son.
T-28......IV.9:4 How **h.** is the smallest grain of sand, when
T-28....VII.7:8 **h.** purpose is it made a home of holiness a
T-29....... II.4:7 touched the **h.** ground whereon you stand
T-29...... III.5:1 How **h.** are you, that the Son of God can
T-29...... VI.2:1 Swear not to die, you **h.** Son of God! You
T-29.....VII.9:5 Your **h.** mind is altar unto God, and
T-29...... IX.1:3 to the **h.** Son of God that this could be his
T-30....... II.4:9 apart from Him Whose **h.** Will you share.
T-30...... III.5:3 all. Beyond all idols stands his **h.** will to be
T-30..III.11:10 But you, the **h.** Son of God Himself, are
T-31....... II.8:6 Nothing will hurt you in this **h.** place, to
T-31...... VI.1:8 to touch your eyes and bless your **h.** sight,
T-31...... VI.7:1 Your will be done, you **h.** child of God. It
T-31.....VII.8:3 the **h.** ones especially entrusted to his care
T-31...VII.10:5 The **h.** ones whom God has given you to
T-31...VII.11:3 For holiness is seen through **h.** eyes that
T-31....VIII.1:2 persuade the **h.** Son of God he is a body,
T-31....VIII.4:3 and disappears before His **h.** sight. The
T-31..VIII.10:1 for these **h.** ones who are my brothers as
T-31..VIII.10:5 And as I would but do Your **h.** Will, so
W-pI.....29.3:5 Its **h.** purpose stands beyond your little
W-pI........35.h My mind is part of God's. I am very **h.**.
W-pI.....35.7:6 *But my mind is part of God's. I am very* ***h.*.**
W-pI.....36.1:2 are **h.** because your mind is part of God's.
W-pI.....36.1:3 And because you are **h.**, your sight must
W-pI.....36.1:3 you are holy, your sight must be **h.** as well
W-pI.....37.1:4 everyone gains through your **h.** vision. It
W-pI.....38.3:1 If you are **h.**, so is everything God created
W-pI.....38.3:2 **h.** because all things He created are holy.
W-pI.....38.3:2 holy because all things He created are **h.**.
W-pI.....38.3:3 things He created are **h.** because you are.
W-pI.....44.8:1 that you are attempting something very **h.**
W-pI.....50.5:3 to disturb the **h.** mind of the Son of God.
W-pI.....57.5:2 I am very **h.**. As I share the peace of the
W-pI.....63.1:1 How **h.** are you who have the power to
W-pI.....67.2:3 *Holiness created me* ***h.*.** *Kindness created*
W-pI.....78.5:4 **h.** role the Holy Spirit has assigned to him
W-pI.....78.7:2 in the **h.** Name of God and of His Son, as
W-pI.....78.7:2 of God and of His Son, as **h.** as Himself:
W-pI.....78.7:3 *to lead me to the* ***h.*** *light in which he stands,*
W-pI.....81.1:2 How **h.** am I, who have been given the
W-pI.....93.4:1 you are as pure and **h.** as you were created
W-pI...95.13:2 are one Self, the **h.** Son of God, united
W-pI...95.13:5 Mind that is this Self, the **h.** truth in you.
W-pI.....97.2:1 Self, the **h.** Son of God Who rests in you,
W-pI.....97.7:2 *Spirit am I, a* ***h.*** *Son of God, free of all limits,*
W-pI...104.2:1 upon the **h.** altar where God's gifts belong
W-pI...104.4:2 a **h.** place within our minds before His
W-pI...106.9:2 and they will hear the **h.** Word you hear.
W-pI.106.10:1 Today the **h.** Word of God is kept
W-pI...109.8:2 peace, the **h.** sanctuary where you rest.
W-pI...110.7:1 the Self Who is the **h.** Son of God Himself.
W-pI...110.9:4 Deep in your mind the **h.** Christ in you is
W-pI.110.11:3 may be reminded of His Son, our **h.** Self,
WpIrIII.in11:6 in the business of the day and make it **h.**,
W-pI...123.7:3 **h.** half an hour given Him will be returned
W-pI...124.2:1 How **h.** are our minds! And everything
W-pI.124.10:1 this **h.** half an hour will hold out to you, to
W-pI.124.11:2 a sight too **h.** for the body's eyes to see.
W-pI...125.3:1 and without all judgment of His **h.** Word.
W-pI...125.4:1 Hear, **h.** Son of God, your Father speak.
W-pI...125.4:2 His Voice would give to you His **h.** Word,
W-pI...125.4:2 of salvation and the **h.** time of peace. We
W-pI...125.6:4 to help make ready your most **h.** mind to
W-pI...128.6:4 sureness and in joy to join its **h.** purpose.
W-pI.131.11:7 to the **h.** place where they can enter not.
W-pI.131.14:4 keeps His ancient promise to His **h.** Son,
W-pI.135.19:1 increases, as this life becomes a **h.** instant,
W-pI.135.26:7 *And I would keep it* ***h.*.** *I will not defend*
W-pI...138.7:2 Such is its **h.** purpose, now transformed
W-pI...139.8:2 It is set forever in the **h.** Mind of God, and
W-pI...139.8:5 Let us not allow our **h.** minds to occupy
W-pI.139.12:1 that would distract us from our **h.** aim.
W-pI.139.12:2 would weave around the **h.** Son of God.
W-pI...140.5:3 God abides in **h.** temples. He is barred
W-pI...151.7:4 the **h.** light of what He sees do all the ego's
W-pI...151.8:4 before the rapture of Christ's **h.** face.
W-pI.151.12:2 unholiness, within the Holy, **h.** as Itself.
W-pI.151.12:4 you see the **h.** face of Christ in everything,
W-pI.151.15:3 Son of God the **h.** lesson of his sanctity.
W-pI.151.17:2 us and happily accepts our **h.** thoughts,
W-pI...153.5:4 the **h.** peace of God by your defensiveness
W-pI...153.9:3 extends its **h.** blessing through the world.
W-pI.153.10:1 in silence think how **h.** is your purpose,
W-pI.153.13:3 from the pure and **h.** minds of Heaven's
W-pI.154.14:1 minds, and realize these **h.** words are true
W-pI...155.8:5 seem to hold in chains the **h.** Son of God.
W-pI...155.9:3 Your **h.** brothers have been given you, to
W-pI.155.10:2 from God's completion, **h.** as Himself.
W-pI.155.11:1 the **h.** Son of God will make no journeys.
W-pI.155.12:4 less and still content the **h.** Son of God?
W-pI...156.3:3 What lives is **h.** as Himself, because what
W-pI...156.4:1 whose presence is so **h.** that the world is
W-pI...156.4:4 sinks to a whisper round your **h.** head.
W-pI...157.1:4 heard. This day is **h.**, for it ushers in a new
W-pI...157.3:3 swiftly to this **h.** place and leaves you, for
W-pI...157.5:3 touchstone for the **h.** Thoughts of God.
W-pI...157.8:2 truth, the **h.** Guide to Heaven given you,
W-pI...158.6:2 world made **h.** by forgiveness and by love.
W-pI.158.11:4 And by the **h.** gifts we give, Christ's vision
W-pI...159.5:2 world into one made **h.** by forgiveness.
W-pI...159.8:1 Christ's vision is the **h.** ground in which
W-pI......161.h Give me your blessing, **h.** Son of God.
W-pI...161.9:3 form so **h.** and so beautiful that you could
W-pI.161.11:7 *me your blessing,* ***h.*** *Son of God. I would*
W-pI...162.3:1 **H.** indeed is he who makes these words
W-pI...163.4:4 has placed upon the body of the **h.** Son of
W-pI...164.3:1 How **h.** is your practicing today, as Christ
W-pI...164.8:3 of your most **h.** mind to save the world. Is
W-pI.167.10:1 of the truth, and not deny our **h.** heritage.
W-pI.167.11:1 His **h.** home we strive to keep today as He
W-pI.167.12:1 in the **h.** minds which He created perfect.
W-pI...168.5:1 is a new and **h.** day today, for we receive
W-pI...169.1:4 received; an altar clean and **h.** for the gift.
W-pI...169.6:4 time, forgiveness and the **h.** face of Christ.
W-pI.169.13:2 be returned by you from **h.** instants you
W-pI.170.13:9 ***H.*** *are we because Your Holiness has set us*
WpI...rV.in2:2 *our doubts be quiet and our* ***h.*** *minds be still,*
WpI...rV.in4:2 more descriptive of the **h.** Self we share
W-pI...176.1:1 Give me your blessing, **h.** Son of God.
W-pI...181.9:2 of the **h.** Self which knows no sin, and
W-pI...182.4:5 Where this Child shall go is **h.** ground. It
W-pI...182.5:4 the **h.** air that fills His Father's house. You
W-pI.182.12:5 The **h.** Child remains with you. His home
W-pI...183.1:1 God's Name is **h.**, but no holier than
W-pI...183.5:3 for grace, nor bodies for the **h.** Son of God
W-pI.183.10:6 and in their place the **h.** Name of God
W-pI.183.11:5 gives answer in his Father's **h.** Name. In
W-pI...186.6:5 misery can come not near the **h.** home of
W-pI...186.7:5 What can it tell the **h.** Son of God? Why
W-pI.187.11:5 And to ensure this **h.** sight is ours, we
W-pI...188.6:6 become the **h.** messengers of God Himself
W-pI...189.2:4 night as silent guardian of your **h.** sleep. It
W-pI...190.5:7 they will accept your **h.** will as theirs. And
W-pI...190.6:1 My **h.** brother, think of this awhile: The
W-pI...190.6:5 want. Your Self is radiant in this **h.** joy,
W-pI...190.8:1 form, and working havoc in your **h.** mind.
W-pI......191.h I am the **h.** Son of God Himself.
W-pI...191.6:1 One **h.** thought like this and you are free:
W-pI...191.6:1 free: You are the **h.** Son of God Himself.
W-pI...191.6:2 And with this **h.** thought you learn as well
W-pI...191.7:3 *I am the* ***h.*** *Son of God Himself. I cannot*
W-pI.191.10:1 from his sleep, and opening his **h.** eyes,
W-pI.191.11:6 life. You are the **h.** Son of God Himself.
W-pI...192.1:1 is your Father's **h.** Will that you complete
W-pI...192.5:6 peace that God intended for His **h.** Son.
W-pI...193.9:2 one thorn or nail to hurt His **h.** Son in any
W-pI...193.9:3 his **h.** rest remain untroubled and serene,
W-pI...194.5:3 slave to time transformed into a **h.** instant
W-pI...196.8:5 be welcomed back within the **h.** mind He
W-pI.196.12:2 between you and the **h.** peace of God.
W-pI...197.8:1 Thanks be to you, the **h.** Son of God. For
W-pI .. 197.9:6 sharing with Him the **h.** Thoughts of God.
W-pI .. 198.7:7 and that the **h.** Son of God can die!
W-pI 198.10:3 both on earth and in your **h.** home as well
W-pI .. 211.1:1 (191) I am the **h.** Son of God Himself. *In*
W-pII .... in.3:2 the remaining **h.** instants which conclude
W-pII .... in.6:2 Father, we give these **h.** times to You, in
W-pII .... in.7:7 the Son, Whose **h.** Will created all that is,
W-pII .... in.8:1 start upon the final part of this one **h.** year
W-pII .. in.11:4 while, preceding one of the **h.** and blessed
W-pII . 223.2:2 *For we who are Your* ***h.*** *Son are sinless. We*
W-pII .... 227.h This is my **h.** instant of release.
W-pII . 227.1:6 *This is my* ***h.*** *instant of release. Father, I*
W-pII . 229.1:4 I will turn away no longer from the **h.** face
W-pII ..... 2.3:4 an altar to the **h.** Name of God whereon
W-pII ..... 2.4:1 Let us come daily to this **h.** place, and
W-pII . 234.1:1 we have reached the **h.** peace we never left
W-pII .... 241.h This **h.** instant is salvation come.
W-pII . 248.1:7 deceits and lies about the **h.** Son of God.
W-pII . 250.1:2 me not try to obscure the **h.** light in him,
W-pII ..... 4.5:8 How long, O **h.** Son of God, how long?
W-pII . 252.1:1 My Self is **h.** beyond all the thoughts of
W-pII . 253.1:6 in Heaven where my **h.** Self abides with
W-pII . 260.2:2 **H.** indeed are we, because our Source can
W-pII ..... 5.4:4 Now is the body **h.**. Now it serves to heal
W-pII . 262.1:8 *in Your Love; eternally the* ***h.*** *Son of God.*
W-pII .... 263.h My **h.** vision sees all things as pure.
W-pII . 263.2:1 through **h.** vision and the eyes of Christ.
W-pII . 263.2:2 house as brothers and the **h.** Sons of God.
W-pII .... 266.h My **h.** Self abides in you, God's Son.
W-pII . 266.1:1 *in sight; the bearers of Your* ***h.*** *Voice to me.*
W-pII . 266.1:3 *Let not Your Son forget Your* ***h.*** *Name. Let*
W-pII . 266.1:4 *Let not Your Son forget his* ***h.*** *Source. Let not*
W-pII . 266.2:1 in each of us; united in the **h.** Love of God.
W-pII . 269.1:5 *to me; that nothing is, except Your* ***h.*** *Son.*
W-pII . 270.2:3 Him, the **h.** Son whom God created whole
W-pII . 270.2:3 whole; the **h.** Son whom God created One
W-pII ..... 6.1:4 He has not left His **h.** home, nor lost the
W-pII ..... 6.3:1 peace within the Heaven of your **h.** mind.
W-pII ..... 6.3:4 before His glory and reveal your **h.** Self,
W-pII ..... 6.5:1 And how long will this **h.** face be seen,
W-pII ..... 6.5:3 or of time, or anything except the **h.** Self,
W-pII . 276.1:2 "My Son is pure and **h.** as Myself." And
W-pII . 288.2:3 He cannot be less **h.** than can I, and you
W-pII . 293.1:5 the world shines in reflection of its **h.** light
W-pII . 293.2:1 *let not Your* ***h.*** *world escape my sight today.*
W-pII . 296.1:4 *Word Your* ***h.*** *Voice will speak to me today.*
W-pII . 298.1:3 on my **h.** sight forgiveness takes away.
W-pII . 298.2:4 *grateful for Your* ***h.*** *gifts of certain sanctuary*
W-pII . 298.2:4 *my love for God my Father and His* ***h.*** *Son.*
W-pII . 300.2:1 *We seek Your* ***h.*** *world today. For we, Your*
W-pII ..... 9.5:5 Will, and join together in its **h.** light.
W-pII . 302.1:2 *Your* ***h.*** *world awaits us, as our sight is finally*
W-pII . 302.1:7 *Let me forgive Your* ***h.*** *world today, that I*
W-pII .... 303.h The **h.** Christ is born in me today.
W-pII . 303.1:2 Let all God's **h.** Thoughts surround me,
W-pII . 304.1:1 I can obscure my **h.** sight, if I intrude my
W-pII . 304.1:2 I behold the **h.** sights Christ looks upon,
W-pII . 304.2:3 *my Father, given me to offer to Your* ***h.*** *Son,*
W-pII . 306.2:1 *went away; remembering Your* ***h.*** *gifts to us.*
W-pII . 307.1:5 *the* ***h.*** *truth that I remain as You created me.*
W-pII . 307.2:1 because we join our **h.** will with God's, in
W-pII . 309.2:3 *It is the* ***h.*** *altar to my Self, and there I find my*
W-pII . 310.1:4 *You, Your gracious calling to Your* ***h.*** *Son,*
W-pII ... 10.1:4 And with this **h.** sight, perception gives a
W-pII ... 10.3:1 accept this **h.** truth: God's Judgment is the
W-pII ... 10.5:1 Final Judgment: "You are still My **h.** Son,
W-pII . 312.1:5 the real world come to greet the **h.** sight of
W-pII . 313.1:6 *undefiled upon the altar to Your* ***h.*** *Son, the*
W-pII . 313.2:3 How **h.** and how loving! Brother, come
W-pII . 313.2:6 vision it becomes as **h.** as the light in us.
W-pII . 314.2:2 *and guide the future in their* ***h.*** *light.*
W-pII . 316.1:2 shadow on the **h.** mind my Father loves.
W-pII . 318.1:1 In me, God's **h.** Son, are reconciled all
W-pII . 320.1:4 His **h.** will can never be denied, because
W-pII ... 11.3:2 truth. Creation is the **h.** Son of God, for in
W-pII ... 11.3:3 inviolate; forever held within His **h.** Will,
W-pII ... 11.4:5 God's memory is in our **h.** minds, which
W-pII . 321.1:6 *freedom as Your* ***h.*** *Son will not be lost to me.*
W-pII . 325.1:6 forth, with mercy for the **h.** Son of God, to

W-pII..326.1:1 *Mind, a* ***h.*** *Thought that never left its home. I*
W-pII..326.2:1 forgiven, fade entirely into God's **h.** Will.
W-pII....12.5:2 peace will be restored forever to the **h.**
W-pII..331.2:2 the **h.** sights forgiveness shows today, that
W-pII..335.1:7 chosen to behold my brother in its **h.** light
W-pII..340.1:2 *This day is* ***h.****, for today Your Son will be*
W-pII..340.1:6 *joy and freedom for Your* ***h.*** *Son and for the*
W-pII..341.1:1 *Father, Your Son is* ***h.****. I am he on whom You*
W-pII..341.1:3 *How pure, how safe, how* ***h.****, then, are we,*
W-pII....14.1:4 *I am the* ***h.*** *home of God Himself. I am the*
W-pII....14.1:6 *I am His* ***h.*** *Sinlessness Itself, for in my purity*
W-pII....14.5:1 **h.** messengers of God who speak for Him,
W-pII..351.1:1 *Who is my brother but Your* ***h.*** *Son? And if I*
W-pII..351.1:4 *also see my brother sinless, as Your* ***h.*** *Son.*
W-pII..357.1:2 *Your* ***h.*** *Son is pointed out to me, first in my*
W-pII..359.1:3 *have not made sinners of the* ***h.*** *Sons of God.*
W-pII.....360.h Peace be to me, the **h.** Son of God. Peace
Wfl ........in.5:1 the gift our Father promised to His **h.** Son
WpII.. 361-5.h This **h.** instant would I give to You. Be
WpII361-5.1:5 speaks for God my Father and His **h.** Son.
M-2............5:4 relationship is **h.** because of that purpose,
M-2............5:4 to send His Spirit into any **h.** relationship.
M-3............1:2 make of the relationship a **h.** relationship,
M-3............1:7 have the potential for a **h.** relationship.
M-3............4:6 destiny of all relationships to become **h.**.
M-4............1:6 born in the **h.** relationship toward which
M-6..........4:12 who in this **h.** exchange can receive less
M-12..........5:4 who have it not, and the body becomes **h.**.
M-12..........5:5 Because it is **h.** it cannot be sick, nor can it
M-12..........5:9 purpose from the one that keeps it **h.**.
M-13..........7:6 that makes it **h.** and beyond the world. It
M-15..........1:11 ***H.*** *are you, eternal, free and whole, at peace*
M-15..........3:2 to occupy your **h.** mind an instant longer.
M-17........2:10 is his judgment upon the **h.** Son of God.
M-25..........2:6 would fall at the **h.** sound of His Voice.
M-25..........6:9 hearts, and His **h.** sight not far behind.
M-28..........5:6 **H.** are we because His Holiness has set us
M-28..........6:6 the truth about the **h.** Son of God. He is
M-29..........8:6 *there.* ***H.*** *are you, and in your light the world*
C-3.............8:3 Now you are **h.** and perceive it so. And
C-4.............8:2 for they are joined here in this **h.** place.
P-2...........I.4:1 psychotherapy is a series of **h.** encounters
P-2......... V.4:1 Healing is **h.**. Nothing in the world is
P-2......... V.5:5 The sacred calling of God's **h.** Son for help
P-2......... V.5:6 voice through which to speak His **h.** Word
P-2......... V.5:8 **h.** interaction is the plan of God Himself,
P-2......... V.8:9 **H.** is healing, for the Son of God returns
P-2.......VII.3:6 capable of joining with the patient in a **h.**
P-3...........I.4:1 A **h.** therapist, an advanced teacher of
P-3......... II.8:3 Many **h.** instants can be his along the way
P-3........ III.4:4 If their relationship is to be **h.**, whatever
P-3........ III.4:5 Herein is the relationship made **h.**, for
S-1 .........in.2:4 turns in **h.** gladness to the truth of union
S-1 .........in.3:1 down your dreams, you **h.** Son of God,
S-1 ......... II.5:6 now it has become **h.**, for it acknowledges
S-1 ......... II.6:4 Before it can become **h.**, then, prayer
S-2 ...........I.1:2 grace, a parody upon the **h.** peace of God.
S-2 ...........I.2:6 that would destroy the **h.** Son He loves.
S-2 ...........I.7:4 and poisoned thinking from your **h.** mind
S-2 ...........I.7:5 sight the world becomes as **h.** as Himself.
S-2 ........III.2:1 not by your plans but by His **h.** Will. His
S-2 ........III.5:1 Your **h.** Son?" should be the only thing
S-2 ........III.6:7 and death become again the **h.** gift of God
S-3 ...........I.3:3 overlook all shadows on the **h.** face of
S-3 ...........I.4:3 his **h.** sinlessness and the remembrance of
S-3 ........III.5:6 place is written now the **h.** Word of God.
S-3 ........IV.1:1 How **h.** are the healed! For in their sight
S-3 ........IV.1:8 They are **h.**. They have chosen holiness,
S-3 ........IV.2:4 for love has come in all its **h.** oneness.
S-3 ........IV.3:3 to share with Him creation's **h.** joy. Do
S-3 ........IV.3:8 Do not forget the **h.** grace of prayer. Do
S-3 ........IV.6:2 You still are **h.** with the Holiness which
S-3 ........IV.9:3 brow of him who is the **h.** Son of God.
S-3 ......IV.10:1 So now return your **h.** voice to Me. The

**home** 261

T-4........ I.11:1 built a shabby and unsheltering **h.** for you
T-4........ I.11:4 make a **h.** that is worthy of His creations,
T-4.........I.11:5 Yet His **h.** will stand forever, and is ready
T-4......... II.7:8 The ego regards the body as its **h.**, and
T-4......IV.11:2 higher mind, the **h.** of the Holy Spirit,
T-4......IV.11:2 does with your lower mind, which is its **h.**
T-4......... V.4:1 body is the ego's **h.** by its own election. It
T-4......... V.4:4 accept it as good enough to be its **h.**. Here
T-4.......VII.4:8 it. It is your real **h.**, your real temple and
T-5...... III.10:5 the place in the mind where He is at **h.**.
T-5...... III.10:6 You are at **h.** there, too, because it is a
T-5...... III.10:7 of God are not at **h.** except in His peace. If
T-5...... III.10:8 is eternal, you are at **h.** only in eternity.
T-5...... III.11:1 as a teaching device for bringing you **h.**.
T-6........ IV.1:5 **h.** and you no longer need His guidance.
T-7........ XI.3:2 Is it worthy to be a **h.** for a child of God?
T-8......... V.5:4 the journey back to God Who is our **h.**.
T-8........ VI.4:1 This son of a loving father left his **h.** and
T-8........ VI.4:3 came **h.** the father welcomed him with joy
T-10............I.h At **H.** in God
T-10..........I.2:1 You are at **h.** in God, dreaming of exile
T-10..... V.11:4 You are not at **h.** anywhere else, or in any
T-11...... III.2:3 At **h.** in God he is lonely, and amid all his
T-11...... IV.2:1 homeless and know that you are at **h.**?
T-12...... IV.5:1 because you are not at **h.** in this world.
T-12...... IV.5:2 *will* search for your **h.** whether you realize
T-12...... IV.5:4 for you do not believe your **h.** is there. Yet
T-12...... IV.5:5 you to your **h.** because that is His mission
T-12...... IV.5:7 By guiding your brothers **h.** you are but
T-12...... VI.5:9 Spirit will lead everyone **h.** to his Father,
T-12...... VI.7:7 Heaven is your **h.**, and being in God it
T-13.... VI.10:9 And seeing it, its beauty calls you **h.**.
T-13...... VII.6:4 and learned of Him the joyful journey **h.**.
T-13...VII.12:8 He knows that you are not at **h.** there, and
T-13...VII.17:7 You travel but in dreams, while safe at **h.**.
T-15...... III.2:6 only in magnitude, which is your **h.**.
T-16...... III.5:8 your teaching of yourself, who is their **h.**.
T-17....... II.7:1 the Son of God is lifted easily into his **h.**.
T-17.... IV.14:6 that it is just a picture is brought **h.** at last
T-18...... III.8:5 and your brother are coming **h.** together,
T-18...... VI.8:2 The **h.** of vengeance is not yours; the
T19... IV.A.1:4 You are its **h.**; its tranquil dwelling place
T19... IV.A.5:9 His **h.** is in your holy relationship. Do not
T19....IV.B.2:3 for which you would deny a **h.** to peace.
T19....IV.B.4:8 not a little mound of clay, to be your **h.**.
T19....IV.B.7:2 the **h.** you offered to my Father and to me
T19....IV.B.7:5 gratitude for giving peace its **h.** in Heaven
T19....IV.B.9:6 And He Who is our **h.** is homeless with us
T19IV.B.10:10 the **h.** of the emotion that calls them forth
T19.... IV.D.6:5 "protectors" and your "**h.**" will vanish.
T-20....... II.2:5 It will adorn its chosen **h.** most carefully,
T-20....... II.2:5 to those who come unto its chosen **h.**, or
T-20....... II.3:2 No one but sees his chosen **h.** as an altar
T-20....... II.4:5 you first upon the altar in your chosen **h.**,
T-20....... II.4:6 light, the body is your chosen **h.** and it is
T-20....... II.8:1 chosen **h.** is on the other side, beyond the
T-20....... II.8:5 Your **h.** has called to you since time began
T-20..... II.8:12 the **h.** we share in quietness and where we
T-20....... II.9:5 that leads us is within us, as is our **h.**. So
T-20..... II.10:5 to greet you, and lead you **h.** with him.
T-20..... II.11:3 and recognize the **h.** that called to you.
T-20..... II.11:5 the bright awareness that leads you **h.**.
T-20....... III.7:2 the **h.** of truth and who will wander off.
T-20....... VI.5:7 sees the face of Christ choose as His **h.** the
T-20....... VI.6:2 It is the **h.** of the idolater, and of love's
T-20....... VI.7:5 This place of darkness is not your **h.**.
T-20....... VI.8:8 seemed to have a **h.** that held together for
T-20... VIII.4:6 Why do you think the body is a better **h.**,
T-20... VIII.4:8 and chosen to replace the holy **h.** the Holy
T-21...... IV.7:6 it found a **h.** in your relationship on earth
T-21...... VI.3:5 The **h.** of madness cannot be the home of
T-21...... VI.3:5 of madness cannot be the **h.** of reason.
T-21...... VI.3:6 leave the **h.** of madness if you see reason.
T-22.......in.3:9 far from **h.** can a relationship so like to
T-22..........I.6:7 recognize his **h.** and see them there with
T-22..........I.8:6 never could He find a **h.** in separate ones.
T-22..........I.8:7 Yet must He be reborn into His ancient **h.**
T-22.......I.10:7 Into the holy **h.** where fear is powerless
T-22.......I.11:7 looking on your brother as His chosen **h.**,
T-22.......I.11:9 **h.** prepared for Them as earth is turned to
T-22...... II.12:8 light His **h.** with vision that overlooks the
T-22......II.12:9 you not have this holy **h.** be yours as well?
T-22......II.13:6 Heaven is the **h.** of perfect purity, and
T-23.........I.3:3 upon the body, the ego's chosen **h.**, which
T-23.........I.9:5 no illusion can invade His **h.** and drive
T-23.........I.9:6 quiet and at peace *because* it is His **h.**.
T-23.......I.10:2 Him and of yourself is **h.** to Both of You,
T-23.......I.10:3 Open the door of His most holy **h.**, and
T-23.......I.10:5 Welcome your brother to the **h.** where
T-23.......I.10:8 Over His **h.** the Holy Spirit watches, sure
T-24...... III.6:2 Here is the hell you chose to be your **h.**.
T-24....... V.6:6 to see and hear and love and follow **h.**?
T-24...VII.6:10 holy **h.** for your creations is it understood
T-25...... III.5:6 elects to see them elsewhere from their **h.**,
T-25...... IV.4:9 to everyone have found a **h.** in Heaven the
T-25...... IV.5:5 him for whom it was created as his only **h.**
T-25...... VI.6:1 than a reminder this world is not your **h.**.
T-26...... IV.4:2 each gift that brings him nearer to his **h.**.
T-26...... IX.1:4 you as well while you attack His chosen **h.**
T-26...... IX.4:4 grow ever brighter as each one comes **h.**.
T-26...... IX.6:2 where a **h.** for Them has been set up.
T-26...... IX.7:3 thanks to one who has restored his **h.**,
T-27...... III.4:1 the truth to enter, and to make itself at **h.**.
T-28..... VII.3:4 Yet who can build his **h.** upon a straw,
T-28..... VII.3:5 The body can be made a **h.** like this,
T-28..... VII.3:6 it does, it can be seen as not your **h.**, but
T-28..... VII.3:6 to help you reach the **h.** where God abides
T-28..... VII.6:4 Would you build your **h.** upon what will
T-28..... VII.7:1 **h.** is built upon your brother's health,
T-28..... VII.7:2 has shaken the Foundation of his **h.**. The
T-28..... VII.7:7 be used to liberate God's Son unto his **h.**.
T-28..... VII.7:8 holy purpose is it made a **h.** of holiness a
T-29....... V.6:3 to him, created by his Father as His **h.**? If
T-30.... III.10:5 and of its rest in its eternal **h.**, the
T-31.........I.4:5 the **h.** where God Himself established
T-31....... V.1:4 Here it walks at **h.**, where what it sees is
T-31..VIII.12:8 where all of us are one, and we are **h.**,
W-pI.....49.4:6 We are trying to reach your real **h.**. We
W-pI.....53.4:5 when the perfection of creation is my **h.**?
W-pI.....66.7:4 The other is the **h.** of the Holy Spirit,
W-pI.....93.1:1 You think you are the **h.** of evil, darkness
W-pI.....94.3:7 Self that never left Its **h.** in God to walk
W-pI... 102.3:2 Here is your **h.**, and here your safety is.
W-pI... 112.1:2 in me. *I am the* ***h.*** *of light and joy and peace.*
W-pI... 112.1:3 *I welcome them into the* ***h.*** *I share with God,*
W-pI... 122.5:3 you to enter in and make yourself at **h.**,
W-pI... 124.1:2 Our **h.** is safe, protection guaranteed in
W-pI... 128.6:1 it seek the level where it finds itself at **h.**.
W-pI... 131.8:4 Will has given him to be his **h.** forever?
W-pI. 132.14:4 For we are in the **h.** our Father set for us,
W-pI... 135.5:4 but say your **h.** is open to the thief of time
W-pI... 135.6:2 be at peace with such a concept of your **h.**
W-pI. 137.12:2 You but invite your Self to be at **h.**. And
W-pI... 139.7:2 a place whose purpose is to be a **h.** where
W-pI... 140.5:6 can have no **h.** in which to hide from His
W-pI. 140.10:4 returns to the eternal, quiet **h.** of God.
W-pI. 152.11:6 grateful to restore His **h.** to God, as it was
W-pI... 159.7:3 What was to be the **h.** of sin becomes the
W-pI... 159.7:4 one will be turned away from this new **h.**,
W-pI... 159.8:2 This is their **h.**. They can be brought from
W-pI... 159.9:2 His lilies do not leave their **h.** when they
W-pI......160.h I am at **h.**. Fear is the stranger here.
W-pI... 160.2:2 and yet maintains his **h.** belongs to him,
W-pI... 160.2:2 to him, while he is alien now who is at **h.**.
W-pI... 160.2:3 easy it would be to say, "This is my **h.**.
W-pI... 160.3:3 were another **h.** more suited to his tastes.
W-pI... 160.4:2 to the **h.** which God provided for His Son
W-pI... 160.4:5 There is no **h.** can shelter love and fear.
W-pI... 160.5:3 so I leave my **h.** to one more like me than
W-pI... 160.5:4 and that his **h.** has been denied to him.
W-pI... 160.6:3 to himself can find no **h.** wherever he may
W-pI... 160.6:6 For in his **h.** his Self remains. It asked no
W-pI... 160.8:5 joined remain forever one, at **h.** in Him,
W-pI... 160.9:5 And He leads them gently **h.** again, where
W-pI. 160.10:2 that your **h.** may be complete and perfect
W-pI. 160.10:5 his **h.** remembered and salvation come.
W-pI... 165.6:6 God's sustaining Love and from his **h.**.
W-pI... 166.4:1 Here is the only **h.** he thinks he knows.
W-pI... 166.4:4 too; an outcast wandering so far from **h.**,
W-pI. 167.11:1 His holy **h.** we strive to keep today as He

W-pI...169.3:6 experience with which it is familiarly at **h.**
WpI...rV.in8:8 whole we go together to our ancient **h.**,
W-pI...175.2:1 (160) I am at **h.**. Fear is the stranger here.
W-pI......182.h I will be still an instant and go **h.**.
W-pI...182.1:1 world you seem to live in is not **h.** to you.
W-pI...182.1:3 A memory of **h.** keeps haunting you, as if
W-pI...182.3:1 who walks this world, for he is not at **h.**.
W-pI...182.3:5 The **h.** he seeks can not be made by him.
W-pI...182.4:1 childhood **h.** that you would find again.
W-pI...182.5:3 Father. He desires to go **h.** so deeply, so
W-pI...182.5:5 You are His **h.** as well. He will return. But
W-pI...182.5:7 be Himself, within the peace that is His **h.**
W-pI...182.6:2 He is far from **h.**. He is so little that He
W-pI...182.6:6 He will go **h.**, and you along with Him.
W-pI...182.7:4 He whispers of His **h.** unceasingly to you.
W-pI...182.7:7 to where He is at **h.** and you with Him.
W-pI...182.8:3 In that instant He will take you to His **h.**,
W-pI...182.8:3 doubt, sublimely certain that you are at **h.**
W-pI...182.9:4 they protect Him, for His **h.** is far away,
W-pI.182.10:1 each time a wanderer would leave his **h.**.
W-pI.182.10:3 Go **h.** with Him from time to time today.
W-pI.182.11:3 ask your help in letting Him go **h.** today,
W-pI.182.12:6 His **h.** is yours. Today He gives you His
W-pI.182.12:9 Be still an instant and go **h.** with Him,
W-pI...186.6:5 can come not near the holy **h.** of God.
W-pI.187.11:6 altar, making it a **h.** for Innocence Itself,
W-pI...188.1:6 light came with you from your native **h.**,
W-pI...188.1:8 It shines in you because it lights your **h.**,
W-pI...188.1:8 to where it came from and you are at **h.**.
W-pI...188.7:2 They recognize their **h.**. And they point
W-pI...188.9:4 within our minds direct them to come **h.**.
W-pI...189.2:3 you a warm and gentle **h.** in which to stay
W-pI...189.9:8 Love shines outward from its **h.** within,
W-pI...192.5:5 mind of thinking that the body is its **h.**.
W-pI...193.9:3 care, in an eternal **h.** which cares for him.
W-pI...197.2:3 as bound, and bars become your **h.**. Nor
W-pI...198.9:1 freedom come to make its **h.** with you.
W-pI.198.10:3 both on earth and in your holy **h.** as well.
W-pI...199.3:3 lives united with the **h.** that it has made.
W-pI...199.6:1 Holy Spirit is the **h.** of minds that seek for
W-pI...200.4:1 Come **h.**. You have not found your
W-pI...200.9:5 need, nor let him stray forever from his **h.**
W-pI.200.11:8 We are close to **h.**, and draw still nearer
W-pI...202.1:1 (182) I will be still an instant and go **h.**.
W-pI...202.1:2 *Himself has given me His Voice to call me* ***h.****?*
W-pI...205.1:3 *my life, while I abide where I am not at* ***h.****.* I
W-pI...220.1:3 *But let me follow Him Who leads me* ***h.****, and*
W-pII ....in.9:7 and we who are God's Sons are safely **h.**,
W-pII .222.1:3 He is my **h.**, wherein I live and move; the
W-pII .223.1:2 I know my life is God's, I have no other **h.**,
W-pII .223.2:5 *and long for Heaven, where we are at* ***h.****.*
W-pII ....226.h My **h.** awaits me. I will hasten there.
W-pII .226.2:1 *Father, my* ***h.*** *awaits my glad return. Your*
W-pII .227.2:3 The Son of God this day comes **h.** again,
W-pII .229.1:4 So still It waited for my coming **h.**, that I
W-pII .241.2:2 *who never left, returns to Heaven and his* ***h.****.*
W-pII .242.1:5 Him, for I would not delay my coming **h.**,
W-pII .244.2:2 come into the hallowed haven of our **h.**.
W-pII .....4.3:1 Sin is the **h.** of all illusions, which but
W-pII .....4.5:3 How soon will you be ready to come **h.**?
W-pII .....5.5:7 Identify with love, and you are **h.**. Identify
W-pII .261.2:2 *I would come, my Father,* ***h.*** *to You today. I*
W-pII .262.2:2 We would come **h.**, and rest in unity. For
W-pII .263.1:4 *its joy, and its eternal, quiet* ***h.*** *in You.*
W-pII .267.1:7 His Voice, assuring me I am at **h.** in Him.
W-pII .267.2:3 *It is there and only there that I can be at* ***h.****.*
W-pII .....6.1:4 He has not left His holy **h.**, nor lost the
W-pII .....6.3:1 **H.** of the Holy Spirit, and at home in God
W-pII .....6.3:1 of the Holy Spirit, and at **h.** in God alone,
W-pII .272.1:2 *My* ***h.*** *is set in Heaven by Your Will and mine*
W-pII .....7.3:3 restore your mind to where it truly is at **h.**
W-pII .....8.5:4 Who calls to us and comes to take us **h.**,
W-pII .301.1:3 *This is my* ***h.*** *because I judge it not, and*
W-pII .303.1:4 Let Christ be welcomed where He is at **h.**.
W-pII .305.1:3 it to truth, no more to be the **h.** of fear.
W-pII .316.1:5 in where I am truly welcome and at **h.**,
W-pII .324.2:4 sure, and guarantees a safe returning **h.**.
W-pII .325.1:6 to offer him a kindly **h.** where he can rest
W-pII .326.1:1 *Mind, a holy Thought that never left its* ***h.****. I*
W-pII .338.2:5 *You gave me promises to lead me* ***h.****, because*
W-pII ...13.3:1 Forgiveness is the **h.** of miracles. The eyes
W-pII .342.1:5 *wondering if I should enter in and be at* ***h.****.*
W-pII .342.2:2 I come to you to take you **h.** with me. And
W-pII ...14.1:4 *I am the holy* ***h.*** *of God Himself. I am the*
W-ep .........2:1 You are as certain of arriving **h.** as is the
M-3 ...........2:2 students "happening" to walk **h.** together
M-14 .........2:2 the **h.** in which forgiveness is born, and
M-14 .........2:5 Here is His **h.**, for here there is need of
C-4 ............5:2 It was the **h.** of bodies. But forgiveness
C-5 ............1:9 God for them for they will lead you **h.**.
C-ep...........5:6 him enters his **h.** and is at peace at last.
P-2.......VII.2:4 This is His **h.**, into which psychotherapy
P-2.......VII.9:4 saint can come to take you **h.** with him?
P-3.......III.6:4 place of Christ and **h.** of God Himself.
S-2...........I.6:2 illusion of a world appears to be your **h.**.
S-2..........II.8:8 you **h.** where God would have you be.
S-3...........I.4:5 him the body may become his chosen **h.**,
S-3...........I.4:5 home, but it will never be his **h.** in truth.
S-3..........II.6:4 the **h.** that stands ready to welcome him,
S-3........IV.6:5 he your Father loves, who never left his **h.**
S-3........IV.8:9 Heaven is here and Heaven is your **h.**.

### homecoming 4

T-13 .......II.9:6 will be great joy in Heaven on your **h.**,
T-13 ..VII.12:8 wills no delay to wait upon your joyous **h.**
T-15 .....III.2:5 all you will be doing is to delay your **h.**.
M-23 .........4:7 these are the true conditions for your **h.**.

### homeless 15

T-11 .....III.2:2 Kingdom is his, and yet he wanders **h.**. At
T-11 .....IV.2:1 try to make God **h.** and know that you are
T-15 .......X.6:5 since this recognition would make it **h.**.
T-16 .....VI.8:4 will not leave you **h.** and without a frame
T19....IV.A.1:5 If you would make it **h.**, how can it abide
T19....IV.A.2:1 Why would you want peace **h.**? What do
T19....IV.B.2:2 that it would dispossess, and leave you **h.**.
T19....IV.B.9:5 If peace is **h.**, so are you and so am I. And
T19....IV.B.9:6 And He Who is our home is **h.** with us. Is
T-20 .....III.7:4 stranger is made **h.** and *you* are welcome.
T-20 .....VI.4:7 **H.**, the ego seeks as many bodies as it can
T-23 ......I.10:3 that keeps God **h.** and His Son with Him.
T-25 .....IV.4:8 peace can never fall away and leave you **h.**
W-pI...166.4:3 he made is he an outcast; **h.** and afraid.
W-pI...166.4:4 that it is here he is afraid indeed, and **h.**,

### homes 2

T-13 ....VII.3:2 The **h.** you built have never sheltered you.
W-pI...182.3:3 seeks. A thousand **h.** he makes, yet none

### homeward 1

W-ep.........5:7 go **h.** to an open door which God has held

### honest 23

T-4 .......III.8:2 for. Be very **h.** with yourself in this, for we
T-8 .....VIII.4:4 A more **h.** statement would be that those
T-12 ......V.8:5 It is merely the result of an **h.** appraisal of
T-13 .....IV.3:8 An open mind is more **h.** than this.
T-14 ....VII.2:1 search for truth is but the **h.** searching out
T-24 .......II.1:6 you stand as tall and stately, clean and **h.**,
T-25 .VIII.10:5 What **h.** witnesses could they call forth to
T-27 .....IV.5:6 An **h.** question is a learning tool that asks
T-27 .....IV.5:8 *want* an **h.** answer where the conflict ends.
T-27 .....IV.6:1 can an **h.** question honestly be asked.
T-27 .....IV.6:6 An **h.** answer asks no sacrifice because it
T-27 ..VII.11:3 An **h.** choice could never be perceived as
W-pI.......9.5:2 Be sure you are **h.** with yourself in making
W-pI.133.13:2 and with an **h.** willingness to value but
W-pI...188.6:6 For **h.** thoughts, untainted by the dream
W-pII .243.1:1 I will be **h.** with myself today. I will not
M-4 ......I.A.8:4 is their result; the outcome of **h.** learning,
M-4 ........II.1:7 Such are the truly **h.**. At no level are they
M-4 ........II.2:8 In this, as in all things, they are **h.**. They
M-4 ......IX.2:2 Being consistent, it is wholly **h.**. Being
M-10 .........2:4 He has actually merely become more **h.**.
S-1..........II.3:2 may be addressed to God in **h.** belief,
S-2..........I.2:1 the **h.** means by which this goal is reached

### honestly 10

T-4 .......IV.2:4 Think **h.** what you have thought that God
T-11 .......V.1:4 this, for we are merely looking **h.** for truth
T-13 ........I.3:1 upon yourself and judge what you do **h.**,
T-15 .....IV.8:3 Ask yourself **h.**, "Would I want to have
T-16 .......II.7:6 considering **h.** what they have been? God
T-27 .....IV.6:1 can an honest question **h.** be asked. And
W-pI ....24.3:2 **h.** and carefully considered in each of the
W-pI ....24.5:4 kinds of outcomes as may **h.** occur to you,
W-pI ..153.2:2 attack seem reasonable, **h.** provoked, and
M-23 .........3:7 ask yourself **h.** whether it is likely that he

### honesty 27

T-11 ......in.2:6 insane when it is stated with perfect **h.**,
T-11 ......in.2:6 looks on what it does with perfect **h.**. Yet
T-11 ......in.3:8 Be willing to judge it with perfect **h.**.
T-13 .....III.3:1 In **h.**, is it not harder for you to say "I
T-14 .......II.5:6 for when you look at it in simple **h.**, it *is*
T-24 .......II.9:6 place, to which you come in hope and **h.**.
T-30 ......I.11:3 want. And you can say in perfect **h.**: *I want*
T-30 .....V.9:11 Be speeded on your way by **h.**, and let not
T-30 .....V.10:1 Do not look back except in **h.**. And when
W-pI ....24.3:1 more **h.** than you are accustomed to using
W-pI ....66.9:6 We need great **h.** today. Remember the
W-pI ....80.7:3 The means is simple **h.**. Do not deceive
W-pI ....91.8:2 Ask this in **h.**, and then devote several
W-pI ..134.8:1 The strength of pardon is its **h.**, which is
W-pI 134.16:3 practicing thus far in willingness and **h.**,
W-pI ..182.2:5 who, in simple **h.**, without defensiveness
W-pI ..185.6:2 that seeks for it in **h.** can understand.
Wfl........in.6:1 We come in **h.** to God and say we did not
M-4 ...........II.h Honesty
M-4 ........II.1:3 Only the trusting can afford **h.**, for only
M-4 ........II.1:4 **H.** does not apply only to what you say.
M-4 ........II.2:1 is largely due to their perfect **h.**. It is only
M-4 ......II.2:12 They choose in perfect **h.**, sure of their
M-4 .....III.1:10 Judgment destroys **h.** and shatters trust.
M-15 .........3:5 judged, and judged in fairness and in **h.**.
S-1..........II.3:4 to ask for gifts such as **h.** or goodness, and
S-1..........V.1:5 **h.** and recognition that they do not serve.

### honor 44

T-1 ........I.33:1 Miracles **h.** you because you are lovable.
T-3 ..........I.6:3 It can only **h.** other minds, because honor
T-3 ..........I.6:3 **h.** is the natural greeting of the truly loved
T-4 .......III.7:7 I will love you and **h.** you and maintain
T-7 ......VII.5:8 Give only **h.** to the Sons of the living God,
T-7 ......VII.6:1 Only **h.** is a fitting gift for those whom
T-7 ......VII.6:1 whom God Himself created worthy of **h.**,
T-8 .......IV.6:2 which I can only acknowledge in **h.** of His.
T-10 ... III.10:5 Yet they exist only because you **h.** them.
T-10 ... III.10:6 Place **h.** where it is due, and peace will be
T-10 ... III.10:9 **H.** is not due to illusions, for to honor
T-10 ... III.10:9 for to **h.** them is to honor nothing. Yet
T-10 ... III.10:9 for to honor them is to **h.** nothing. Yet
T-11 ........I.5:9 Son, for yours were created in **h.** of Him.
T-13 .....X.13:6 Kingdom in **h.** of its wholeness that is of
T-14 ....VII.7:9 All **h.** to you through Him, and through
T-15 .....III.6:7 it. All **h.** is due the host of God. Your
T-15 .....III.8:4 born in you in **h.** of Him Whose host you
T-16 .......II.5:3 **H.** the truth that has been given you, and
T-16 .......II.6:5 and **h.** the witnesses who bring you the
T-16 .....III.7:5 what He is, will grow and help you **h.** Him
T19 ...IV.C.3:5 march not in **h.** of their Creator, Whose
T-20 ........I.2:4 we **h.** the perfect purity of the Son of God,
T-20 ... VI.11:2 sigh and grieve and die in **h.** of its master.
T-21 ......I.10:1 for that same song they sing in **h.** of their
T-24 ........I.8:3 will. And God Himself must **h.** it or suffer
T-24 .......II.4:5 vast song of **h.** and of love for what you
T-25 .....II.11:4 him **h.** that you may esteem yourself and
T-25 ...VIII.8:2 and give them all the **h.** they deserve and
W-pI ..95.15:4 *I* ***h.*** *you because of What I am, and What He*

W-pI....110.9:2 Today **h.** your Self. Let graven images you
W-pI....123.4:2 in **h.** of the Self that God has willed to be
W-pI....151.8:3 Voice for God can only **h.** Him, rejoicing
W-pI.151.15:4 the Voice for God give **h.** to God's Son.
W-pI....162.5:1 We **h.** you today. Yours is the right to
W-pI....197.1:4 Your gifts must be received with **h.**, lest
W-pI....197.3:5 who **h.** them and give them fitting thanks,
W-pII..239.2:2 *us. And we* **h.** *it, because You share it with us.*
W-pII..243.2:2 *I* **h.** *all its parts, in which I am included. We*
W-pII..247.2:4 *Today I* **h.** *You through them, and thus I*
W-pII..274.1:1 *and give Your Son the* **h.** *due his sinlessness;*
W-pII..280.2:1 *Today let me give* **h.** *to Your Son, for thus*
W-pII..280.2:3 *The* **h.** *that I give to him is Yours, and what is*
W-pII..288.1:9 *But let me* **h.** *him who bears Your Name, and*

## honored 7

T-5...........I.6:1 God **h.** even the miscreations of His
T-7.......VII.6:6 **h.** all those who were created like you.
T19.IV.A.16:2 everyone is welcomed as an **h.** guest. And
W-pI....162.2:2 Here creation is proclaimed, and **h.** as it is
W-pI....197.3:4 back your gifts, because they were not **h.**?
W-pI....200.5:3 made free of your mistakes and **h.** as he is
M-24........6:11 beliefs that lead to progress should be **h.**.

## honoring 4

T-1........I.29:2 you. They praise Him by **h.** His creations,
T-15......III.9:9 Let us join in **h.** you, who must remain
T-19......III.2:4 it with respect and **h.** its enormity. What
T19... IV.C.4:4 him are but **h.** the Will of his Creator. The

## honors 7

T-1........I.31:3 are holy and the miracle **h.** their holiness,
T-1.........V.4:2 to return because it blesses and **h.** him,
T-5...........I.1:6 and therefore **h.** only the laws of God. To
T-7.......VII.6:1 worthy of honor, and whom He **h.**. Give
T19.IV.A.16:2 is a feast that **h.** your holy relationship,
T19... IV.C.2:4 slow procession that **h.** their grim master,
W-pII......1.5:3 sees, and whom He **h.** as the Son of God.

## hope 154

T-2........VI.9:4 if you **h.** to spare yourself from fear there
T-4......IV.11:3 are too confused to recognize your own **h.**
T-5.......VII.1:6 that all **h.** is yours because of His care.
T-8.....VII.16:3 impossibility lies your only **h.** for release.
T-8.....VII.16:4 what other **h.** would you want? Freedom
T-8..... VIII.2:7 you will continue to **h.** it can yet offer you
T-9......IV.10:2 your only **h.** is to change your mind about
T-9..... VIII.2:2 It is without **h.** because it is not real. It is
T-13....... X.4:8 the present, and **h.** to find salvation now?
T-14....... V.5:4 **h.** of happiness and release from suffering
T-15.........I.3:7 you. How can the guilty **h.** for Heaven?
T-15...... I.4:13 is the end as far as **h.** of Heaven goes. Yet
T-15......VI.4:2 him, your **h.** of answer is diminished. On
T-16......VI.8:7 Find **h.** and comfort, rather than despair,
T-19......III.8:1 must forever be beyond the **h.** of healing.
T19....IV.B.3:5 you sacrifice the **h.** of the body's pleasure;
T19....IV.B.3:5 the body's pleasure; it *has* no **h.** of pleasure
T19....IV.B.9:9 Would you invest your **h.** of peace and
T19.IV.D.17:1 faith and **h.** and mercy are yours to give.
T-20......VI.6:3 is love made fearful and **h.** abandoned.
T-21.......in.2:4 If you see holiness and **h.**, you joined the
T-21......IV.7:4 of another world, brings to it **h.** of peace.
T-21......VI.6:2 Father forever, without a **h.** of safe return.
T-21.....VII.6:7 to be the last remaining **h.** of finding sin,
T-22....... II.6:4 to do what holds no **h.** of ever being done.
T-22.......IV.6:5 carrying His message of **h.** and freedom
T-23......III.6:4 lingered there in cowering **h.** that it will
T-24....... II.9:6 to which you come in **h.** and honesty.
T-24..... II.11:6 with the **h.** of peace at last in sight.
T-24..... II.13:1 **h.** of specialness makes it seem possible
T-24....... V.2:1 the **h.** of peace and the escape from pain,
T-25....... II.1:2 think you find a **h.** of satisfaction there.
T-25....... II.2:1 **h.** of satisfaction from the world you see?
T-25....... II.2:5 where no **h.** lies must make you hopeless.
T-25....... II.2:6 while you would seek for **h.** where none is
T-25....... II.3:1 you have found some **h.** apart from this;
T-25....... II.3:2 And yet your **h.** that they may still be here
T-25...... IV.1:7 the **h.** of change unless the aim is changed
T-25.....VII.9:4 him and whatever **h.** he has of being sane.
T-25.....VII.9:6 a special function in the **h.** of peace, than
T-26....... II.5:7 made it great, and past the **h.** of healing.
T-26......VII.7:2 errors seem forever past the **h.** of healing,
T-29.........I.2:6 think that it is their salvation and their **h.**.
T-29....... II.2:8 for glad rejoicing and for **h.** of peace.
T-29....... II.3:1 hopeless to attempt to find the **h.** of peace
T-29....... V.6:5 on Heaven itself, and **h.** to find its peace?
T-29....... V.7:2 death; a dream of **h.** you share with him,
T-29....... V.8:3 without the **h.** of change and betterment,
T-29.....VII.2:1 one who comes here but must still have **h.**
T-29.....VII.6:2 is vain to worship idols in the **h.** of peace.
T-29.....VII.8:1 and open up a road of **h.** and of release in
T-29...VII.10:6 Seek not outside your Father for your **h.**.
T-29...VII.10:7 hope. For **h.** of happiness is *not* despair.
T-29... VIII.8:6 Each worshipper of idols harbors **h.** his
T-29. VIII.8:10 with **h.** of finding more of something else.
T-29.......IX.9:2 For beneath your **h.** that it will save you
T-30.........I.9:2 *And so I* **h.** *I have been wrong.* This works
T-30.......I.11:2 but merely **h.** to get a thing you want.
T-30....... V.2:7 The world becomes a place of **h.**, because
T-30....... V.2:7 where **h.** of happiness can be fulfilled.
T-30....... V.2:8 no one stands outside this **h.**, because the
T-30....... V.2:8 share, if **h.** be more than just a dream.
T-30....... V.3:5 There is a **h.** of happiness in him so sure
T-30...... V.10:8 beats in **h.** and does not pound in fear.
T-30.... VI.10:1 Look on your brother with this **h.** in you,
T-30.... VIII.4:3 the **h.** of change is that the miracle cannot
T-31.........I.7:6 Nor is there **h.** of happiness in it. There is
T-31.........I.7:8 that you can seek for here and **h.** to find.
T-31.........I.8:1 everything is lit with **h.** and sparkles with
T-31....... II.3:4 to be the **h.** of satisfaction and of peace.
T-31...... IV.3:5 learning they led nowhere, lost their **h.**.
T-31...... IV.4:3 there is no **h.** of answer in the world. But
T-31...... IV.4:6 No longer look for **h.** where there is none.
T-31......VII.6:3 unless you choose to hold it past the **h.** of
T-31...VII.14:3 dreams and no remaining **h.** except to die
W-pI.....28.5:2 of infinite value, full of happiness and **h.**.
W-pI.....53.3:4 It holds out no safety and no **h.**. But such
W-pI.....71.3:3 that, although this **h.** has always failed,
W-pI.....71.3:3 for **h.** in other places and in other things.
W-pI....72.12:1 and your **h.** of success flicker and go out,
W-pI.....86.3:4 only **h.** of salvation from my awareness. I
W-pI.....95.3:3 In patience and in **h.** we try again today.
W-pI....95.14:8 you do so, someone hears the voice of **h.**,
W-pI.....96.6:7 Perhaps you **h.** it can. Yet would you have
W-pI.....98.8:1 will light the world with **h.** and gladness.
W-pI....101.7:3 and **h.** to go still faster to the waiting goal
W-pI....107.7:5 sure we live and **h.** and breathe and think.
W-pI....109.7:3 with **h.** reborn and energy restored to
W-pI....121.2:2 the **h.** of respite and release from pain. It
W-pI....121.4:4 It wants forgiveness, yet it sees no **h.**. It
W-pI....121.7:3 It has no **h.**, but you become its hope.
W-pI....121.7:3 It has no hope, but you become its **h.**.
W-pI....121.7:4 And as its **h.**, do you become your own.
W-pI....122.3:5 more **h.** than what forgiveness brings?
W-pI....122.9:1 our practicing today with **h.** and faith
W-pI....128.2:3 to perceive some **h.** where there is none.
W-pI....129.1:2 see that there is something else to **h.** for,
W-pI....131.2:3 and **h.** through them to gain in anything?
W-pI....131.2:5 achieve that offers any **h.** of being real?
W-pI....132.1:7 the **h.** of freedom comes to him at last.
W-pI.135.10:5 but merely take away the **h.** of healing, for
W-pI.135.10:5 see where **h.** must lie if it be meaningful.
W-pI.135.25:5 Now is the light of **h.** reborn in you, for
W-pI....138.7:2 hell is real, **h.** changes to despair, and life
W-pI....153.4:2 lies madness in a form so grim that **h.** of
W-pI.153.13:1 who have played that you are lost to **h.**,
W-pI.159.10:5 death to life; from hopelessness to **h.**. Let
W-pI....161.8:4 and claws the air in frantic **h.** it can reach
W-pI....165.7:1 Practice today in **h.**. For hope indeed is
W-pI....165.7:2 For **h.** indeed is justified. Your doubts are
W-pI....168.2:1 Love, **h.** and despair would be impossible.
W-pI....168.2:2 For **h.** would be forever satisfied; despair
W-pI....170.5:2 strength, and **h.** of rest in dreamless quiet
W-pI....185.7:5 try to make another bargain in the **h.** that
W-pI.185.14:1 mind, the **h.** that lies beyond despair, the
W-pI.186.10:5 What **h.** of gain can rest on goals like this
W-pI... 189.1:7 anew, shining in innocence, alive with **h.**,
W-pI... 191.2:6 no **h.** you hold but will dissolve in tears.
W-pI... 191.3:3 snatch from your fingers every scrap of **h.**
W-pI... 195.3:1 relentless that there is no **h.** remaining.
W-pI... 196.6:2 Until this form is changed, there is no **h.**.
W-pI... 198.6:3 His words contain all **h.**, all blessing and
W-pI... 199.7:6 and **h.** that finds its full accomplishment
W-pI....200.2:1 lay aside all **h.** of finding happiness where
W-pI....200.6:6 could **h.** for more, while there appears to
W-pI....200.7:2 What could he **h.** to find in such a world?
W-pII ..... 1.5:1 your Savior and Protector, strong in **h.**,
W-pII .241.1:6 is the time of **h.** for countless millions.
W-pII .245.1:5 *or think they are bereft of* **h.** *and happiness.*
W-pII .247.2:4 *and thus I* **h.** *this day to recognize my Self.*
W-pII ..... 6.2:1 of despair, for **h.** forever will abide in Him
W-pII .286.1:6 *is everything I* **h.** *to find already given me.*
W-pII .286.2:1 will give us **h.** that we have found the way,
W-pII .332.1:8 the dream of darkness, offering it **h.**, and
Wfl........in.1:5 the **h.** of trust and the escape from pain.
M-in .......... 4:8 as they teach His lessons of joy and **h.**,
M-in .......... 5:1 there would be little **h.** of salvation, for
M-1 ........... 4:5 It is old and worn and without **h.**. There
M-4 .... III.1:11 teacher of God can judge and **h.** to learn.
M-13 ......... 4:9 to possess them must he sacrifice his **h.** of
M-13 ......... 6:9 no other **h.** in all the world that they can
M-17 ......... 7:7 And now there is no **h.**. Except to kill.
M-17 ......... 8:2 bring the light of **h.** from God Himself.
M-23 ......... 5:7 To you he looks for **h.**, because in you he
M-25 ......... 6:6 is also a great channel of **h.** and healing in
C-4............ 6:5 Where is **h.** while sin is seen as outside?
C-ep........... 1:6 Who could despair when **h.** like this is his
C-ep........... 4:7 will grow in life and strength and **h.**, until
S-1...........I.1:5 to pray for idols and **h.** to reach God.
S-1........ IV.2:3 The way is open, and **h.** is justified. Yet it
S-2...........I.5:4 your fate, your feelings, your despair or **h.**
S-2...........I.6:1 way in which your only **h.** of freedom lies.
S-2.........II.6:4 in further bargains which can give no **h.**,
S-3.........in.1:1 the comfort and the promises of **h.**.

## hoped 4

*See also* hoped-for

T-18.... VI.11:2 sometimes **h.** for in special relationships.
W-pI... 153.3:1 until escape no longer can be **h.** for nor
W-pI... 192.6:4 Or is it to be **h.** for, met with thanks and
M-21 ......... 2:6 stand for the experiences that are **h.** for.

## hoped-for 1

W-pI.....24.7:1 the list of as many **h.** goals as possible, for

## hopefully 1

P-2.........in.4:3 H., both will learn to give up their

## hopefulness 3

T-25........II.3:1 **h.** is warranted on grounds that are not in
W-pI.....96.2:2 of time and effort, **h.** and doubt, each one
W-pI. 122.10:2 Begin in **h.**, for we have reached the

## hopeless 10

T-18.......I.12:5 break apart what is already broken and **h.**
T19. IV.D.16:6 nor nail him to it, unredeemed and **h.**.
T-22...... IV.1:8 the journey that seems more **h.** and futile
T-25........II.2:5 where no hope lies must make you **h.**. Yet
T-25........II.3:2 **h.** and unrewarding task you set yourself.
T-29........II.3:1 It has been **h.** to attempt to find the hope
W-pI... 196.5:1 **h.** thought that you can make attacks on
W-pI. 196.10:1 so wholly that escape appears quite **h.**.
M-in .......... 4:7 Into this **h.** and closed learning situation,
M-17 ......... 8:1 this **h.** situation God sends His teachers.

## hopelessly 1

W-pI.....66.3:3 will not become **h.** involved in defining

**hopelessness** 9

T-25....... II.2:6 Yet is this **h.** your choice, while you would
T-27....... II.6:5 And **h.** and death must disappear before
W-pI.135.25:4 from what was seeming death and **h.**.
W-pI.159.10:5 made from death to life; from **h.** to hope.
W-pI...166.6:2 has felt defeat and **h.** as he is feeling them.
W-pI...186.8:5 indeed, or dash us to the ground in **h.**.
W-pI...200.1:3 despair, and sense of icy **h.** and doubt.
W-pI.200.10:3 from the trees of **h.** you sought before.
M-10 .........6:6 of loss; of passing time and growing **h.**; of

**hopes** 21

T-4...........I.5:1 Every good teacher **h.** to give his students
T-4......... V.6:4 it **h.** to hide the real question and keep it
T-16.........I.6:1 to weakness, and **h.** to find love there.
T-25....... II.1:5 Despite your **h.** and fancies, always does
T-25....... II.2:4 gives no support to base your future **h.**,
T-25....... II.2:5 To place your **h.** where no hope lies must
T-25...... IV.3:7 all their "evil" thoughts and "sinful" **h.**,
T-27...... VI.3:1 holds all your memories and all your **h.**.
W-pI.....56.1:4 All my **h.** and wishes and plans appear to
W-pI...121.1:3 bring uncertainty to all your **h.** of ever
W-pI...128.1:2 **h.** that turn to bitter ashes of despair. No
W-pI...135.7:5 it. For it seems to fail your **h.**, your needs,
W-pI.153.14:4 of terrifying destiny, defeat of all his **h.**,
W-pI...163.2:2 all **h.** and wishes in its blighting grasp; all
W-pI...163.3:1 apt to fail the **h.** they once engendered,
W-pI.166.14:1 Your sighs will now betray the **h.** of those
W-pI...191.9:1 frail, with futile **h.** and devastated dreams
W-pII .251.1:6 all **h.** are finally fulfilled and dreams are
W-pII ...12.4:1 its laws and its beliefs, its dreams, its **h.**,
P-2.........in.3:3 patient **h.** to learn how to get the changes
P-2.........in.3:4 He **h.**, in fact, to stabilize it sufficiently to

**hoping** 2

T-17.... III.1:10 **h.** that their witness will enable you to
T-20...... III.4:2 **h.** at most that death will wait a little

**horizon** 1

M-17 .........8:5 an intense white light against a black **h.**,

**horizons** 2

Wi181-200 2:1 now are geared specifically to widening **h.**
W-pII ....in.9:5 is shimmering across the wide **h.** of our

**horizontal** 3

T-1......... II.4:2 in terms of a vertical rather than a **h.** axis.
T-1......... II.6:2 longitudinal or **h.** plane the recognition of
T-1......... II.6:3 shift from **h.** to vertical perception. This

**horrified** 2

T-20..VIII.10:6 purpose brought to your **h.** awareness.
T-23...... III.1:7 to meet his **h.** awareness and pursue him

**horror** 1

W-pI.....93.1:3 struck with **h.** so intense that you would

**horrors** 2

W-pI.....14.4:1 the **h.** in the world that cross your mind.
W-pI.....14.6:1 repertory of **h.** at which you are looking.

**hospital** 1

W-pI...190.6:6 inheritance, and keep it as a **h.** for pain; a

**Host** 7
*host*

T-1........ III.7:5 the **H.** within and the stranger without.
T-15...... III.6:9 of Christ, eternal **H.** unto His Father.
T-15 ..... XI.2:6 For He is **H.** to God. And you need but
T-15 ..... XI.2:7 already, by recognizing that His **H.** is One
T-15 ..... XI.2:9 it. No fear can touch the **H.** Who cradles
T-15 ..... XI.2:9 the **H.** is as holy as the perfect Innocence
T-16 .....II.6:11 The **H.** of God has called to you, and you

**host** 43
*Host*

T-3 ..........I.3:9 is responsible for a **h.** of related errors,
T-11 .......II.5:1 Spirit cannot speak to an unwelcoming **h.**
T-11 .......II.7:1 you be hostage to the ego or **h.** to God?
T-15 ..... III.5:1 you be hostage to the ego or **h.** to God?"
T-15 ..... III.5:4 He established you as **h.** to Him forever.
T-15 ..... III.6:7 it. All honor is due the **h.** of God. Your
T-15 ..... III.7:2 the **h.** whom God appointed for Himself.
T-15 ..... III.7:7 all His extensions to you, as **h.** to Him.
T-15 ..... III.8:4 in you in honor of Him Whose **h.** you are.
T-15 ..... III.8:6 love dwells in you, for you are **h.** to Him.
T-15 ..... III.9:4 the **h.** of God to guilt and weakness with
T-15 ... III.10:9 **h.** of God needs not seek to find anything.
T-15 ... III.11:3 together that the Son of God is **h.** to Him.
T-15 ... III.12:5 power is forever on the side of His **h.**, for
T-15 ..... IV.3:5 God would have His **h.** abide in perfect
T-15 ..... IV.3:7 yet it is your mind that is the **h.** to Him.
T-15 ..... IV.5:3 of the **h.** of God depends on willingness,
T-15 ... IV.9:10 to acknowledge that you are **h.** to God,
T-15 ... VII.3:7 **h.** of God can have no real investment
T-15 ... VII.4:5 counsels, therefore, that if you are **h.** to it,
T-15 ... VII.5:2 belongs not around the chosen **h.** of God,
T-15 ... VII.5:2 who cannot make himself **h.** to the ego. In
T-15 ...VIII.3:7 For the holy **h.** of God is beyond failure,
T-15 .......X.5:4 to be **h.** to the ego or hostage to God. This
T-15 .......X.6:1 As **h.** to the ego, you believe that you can
T-15 .......X.6:4 only to those who think they are its **h.**.
T-15 .......X.8:4 and away from you, and not be **h.** to Him.
T-15 .......X.9:2 Nor can you be partial **h.** to it. You must
T-15 ..... XI.9:1 to the holy **h.** who would receive Him,
T-15 ..... XI.9:4 Him, being **h.** to Him Who created them.
T-16 ..... III.5:9 who are **h.** to God are also host to them.
T-16 ..... III.5:9 who are host to God are also **h.** to them.
T-18 ..... IV.5:9 *I who am* **h.** *to God am worthy of Him. He*
T-18 ..... VI.7:1 This is the **h.** of God that *you* have made.
T-24 ..VII.1:12 now that the **h.** of God has found another
T-26 ..... IX.1:4 His chosen home, and battle with His **h.**.
T-26 ..... IX.8:1 **h.** again to Him by Whom it was created.
T-29 .......II.5:3 is no other place where He can find His **h.**,
T-29 .......II.5:3 host, nor where His **h.** can meet with Him
W-pI.....45.9:3 are unworthy of Him Whose **h.** you are.
W-pI...135.4:5 fail to serve the Son of God as worthy **h.**?
W-pI...163.2:1 Embodiment of fear, the **h.** of sin, god of
W-pI...165.7:5 must abide within you who are **h.** to Him.

**hostage** 7

T-11 .......II.7:1 you be **h.** to the ego or host to God? You
T-15 ..... III.5:1 you be **h.** to the ego or host to God?" Let
T-15 ..... III.5:6 and make His Son **h.** to the ego, cannot
T-15 ... IV.9:10 to God, and **h.** to no one and to nothing.
T-15 .......X.5:4 possible to be host to the ego or **h.** to God
T-15 .......X.9:1 not succeed in being partial **h.** to the ego,
W-pI...163.3:4 will never fail to take all life as **h.** to itself.

**hostile** 3

W-pI.....12.3:2 *fearful world, a dangerous world, a* **h.** *world,*
W-pI.....72.3:6 "betrays" his **h.** thoughts in his behavior.
M-3 ...........5:5 be quite **h.** to each other for some time,

**hostility** 1

T-13 ..... III.1:7 are not seriously disturbed by your **h.**.

**Hosts** 1

WpI. rIV.in6:3 communion with the Lord of **H.** be yours,

**hot** 1

T-31 .......V.7:5 **h.** with hatred and distortions born of

**hour** 96
*See also* five-minutes-an-hour

T-12 ... VIII.1:3 every day and every **h.** and every minute,
T-14 ..... III.4:1 Each day, each **h.** and minute, even each
T-29 ... VI.2:12 nor set the **h.** of his birth and death.
W-pI .... 20.5:1 and positively at least twice an **h.** today,
W-pI .... 20.5:1 today, attempting to do so every half **h.**.
W-pI .... 27.3:2 It should be used at least every half **h.**,
W-pI .. 29.5:10 the idea for today at least once an **h.**,
W-pI .. 39.11:1 or four times an **h.** and more if possible,
W-pI .... 65.8:1 should be undertaken at least once an **h.**,
W-pI .. 66.11:1 helpful today if undertaken twice an **h.**,
W-pI .... 67.5:3 Four or five times an **h.**, and perhaps even
W-pI .... 68.7:4 the idea several times an **h.** in this form:
W-pI .. 71.10:5 today's idea some six or seven times an **h.**.
W-pI .. 72.13:1 periods an **h.** will be enough for today,
W-pI .. 73.11:5 should be repeated several times an **h.**. It
W-pI .... 74.7:5 A minute or two every half an **h.**, with
W-pI .... 75.9:2 Remind yourself every quarter of an **h.** or
W-pI .. 76.12:1 today; at least four or five times an **h.**, as
W-pI .. 91.11:1 Five or six times an **h.**, at reasonably
W-pI .... 93.8:1 the first five minutes of every waking **h.**,
W-pI .. 93.10:1 five minutes of each **h.** for these exercises.
W-pI .. 93.10:3 to repeat these thoughts each **h.**: *Light and*
W-pI .... 94.3:1 **h.** to the attempt to feel the truth in you.
W-pI .... 94.5:1 for the first five minutes of every **h.**, at
W-pI .... 95.4:1 minutes of every waking **h.** for practicing
W-pI .... 95.7:2 of the **h.** will be particularly helpful, since
W-pI .. 96.11:5 minutes of the **h.** seeking Him Who joins
W-pI .... 97.5:1 five minutes of each **h.** from your hands,
W-pI .... 98.5:1 worth five minutes of your time each **h.** to
W-pI .... 98.7:1 Each **h.** today give Him your tiny gift of
W-pI .. 98.10:1 Throughout the **h.**, let your time be spent
W-pI .. 98.11:1 the **h.** goes and He is there once more to
W-pI .. 103.3:1 within your mind each waking **h.** today.
W-pI .. 106.9:3 And when the **h.** is past, you will again
W-pI .. 109.6:1 Each **h.** that you take your rest today, a
WpI..rIII.in2:1 optimal each day and every **h.** of the day.
WpI..rIII.in8:2 other in the **h.** just before you go to sleep.
WpIrIII.in10:2 ideas a brief but serious review each **h.**.
WpIrIII.in10:3 Use one on the **h.**, and the other one a
WpIrIII.in10:3 hour, and the other one a half an **h.** later.
WpIrIII.in12:1 restatement of the thought to use each **h.**,
WpIrIII.in12:1 one to be applied on each half **h.** as well.
W-pI .. 111.3:1 On the **h.**: Miracles are seen in light. On
W-pI .. 111.3:3 On the half **h.**: Miracles are seen in light,
W-pI .. 112.3:1 On the **h.**: Light and joy and peace abide
W-pI .. 112.3:3 On the half **h.**: I am as God created me.
W-pI .. 113.3:1 On the **h.**: I am one Self, united with my
W-pI .. 113.3:3 On the half **h.**: Salvation comes from my
W-pI .. 114.3:1 On the **h.**: I am spirit. On the half hour: I
W-pI .. 114.3:3 On the half **h.**: I will accept my part in
W-pI .. 115.3:1 On the **h.**: Salvation is my only function
W-pI .. 115.3:3 On the half **h.**: My part is essential to
W-pI .. 116.3:1 On the **h.**: God's Will for me is perfect
W-pI .. 116.3:3 On the half **h.**: I share God's Will for
W-pI .. 117.3:1 the **h.**: God, being Love, is also happiness.
W-pI .. 117.3:3 On the half **h.**: I seek but what belongs to
W-pI .. 118.3:1 On the **h.**: God's peace and joy are mine.
W-pI .. 118.3:3 On the half **h.**: Let me be still and listen to
W-pI .. 119.3:1 On the **h.**: Truth will correct all errors in
W-pI .. 119.3:3 On the half **h.**: To give and to receive are
W-pI .. 120.3:1 On the **h.**: I rest in God. On the half hour:
W-pI .. 120.3:3 On the half **h.**: I am as God created me.
W-pI 121.13:5 Every **h.** tell yourself: *Forgiveness is the key*
W-pI 122.10:1 quarter of an **h.** to the search in which the
W-pI 122.14:1 minute as each quarter of an **h.** passes by.
W-pI .. 123.7:3 holy half an **h.** given Him will be returned
W-pI .. 124.8:3 devote a half an **h.** to the thought that you
W-pI .. 124.8:6 Abide with Him this half an **h.**. He will do
W-pI .. 124.9:4 This half an **h.** will be framed in gold,
W-pI 124.10:1 this holy half an **h.** will hold out to you, to
W-pI 124.10:3 thought to which you gave this half an **h.**,
W-pI 124.11:2 Count this half **h.** as your gift to God, in
W-pI .. 125.9:5 true. As every **h.** passes by today, be still a

W-pI.127.12:2 least three times an **h.** think of one who
W-pI.134.14:4 let us give a quarter of an **h.** twice today,
W-pI.136.15:2 will give a quarter of an **h.** twice to ask the
W-pI.137.13:1 We will remember, as the **h.** strikes, our
W-pI.137.13:2 Is not a minute of the **h.** worth the giving
W-pI.137.15:4 be forgot as every **h.** of the day slips by,
W-pI.138.12:1 that we have made each **h.** in between.
W-pI.138.12:3 As every **h.** passed, we have declared our
W-pI.139.12:1 our dedication to our cause today each **h.**,
W-pI.140.12:6 hourly, and take a minute as the **h.** strikes
WpI.rIV.in8:1 Each **h.** of the day, bring to your mind
W-pI.153.15:5 will find that half an **h.** is too short a time
W-pI.153.16:1 Each **h.** adds to our increasing peace, as
W-pI.153.16:2 the most that we can offer as the **h.** strikes
W-pI.153.17:2 have us do the **h.** that is yet to come;
W-pI.186.10:4 ten times an **h.** at their most secure. What
W-pI.193.12:1 Each **h.**, spend a little time today, and in
W-pI.193.12:2 to the happenings the **h.** brought, so that
W-pI.193.12:4 no one **h.** cast its shadow on the one that
WpI rVI.in.3:7 And we repeat it every time the **h.** strikes,
W-pII..271.1:1 Each day, each **h.**, every instant, I am
M-16..........4:5 One can easily sit still an **h.** with closed
M-16........11:9 their training, every day and every **h.**, and

### hour's 1

W-pI...106.7:4 Each **h.** exercises should begin with this

### hourly 19

W-pI.....94.5:1 of every hour, at least remind yourself **h.**:
W-pI.....94.5:8 every effort to do the **h.** exercises today.
W-pI.....96.8:2 **h.** five-minute practicing will be a search
W-pI.....98.5:2 five minutes **h.** to recognize your special
W-pI.100.10:5 today between your **h.** practice periods. It
W-pI...102.5:3 Besides these **h.** five-minute rests, pause
W-pI...104.3:2 the **h.** five minutes given truth for your
W-pI...105.9:2 least remember **h.** to say the words which
W-pI...109.6:2 and **h.** remember that you came to bring
W-pI...123.8:2 Remember **h.** to think of Him, and give
W-pI.124.12:1 you today, by **h.** repeating to yourself: *Let*
W-pI...129.9:3 Remember your decision **h.**, and take a
W-pI.140.12:6 And we will say our prayer for healing **h.**,
W-pI.151.17:1 And we will **h.** remember Him Who is
W-pI.152.12:1 **h.** invite Him with the words with which
W-pI.153.17:1 in **h.** remembrance of our mission and
WpI rVI.in.1:2 **h.** remembrances you make throughout
W-pII.....in.2:9 we forget our **h.** remembrance in between
W-pII..232.1:3 *And let me not forget my* **h.** *thanksgiving*

### hours 5

T-15....... II.3:5 days, **h.** and even years in chaining your
W-pI...153.3:2 become the circles of the **h.** and the days
W-pI.169.10:4 convey to those who count the **h.** still,
W-pII..310.1:3 *The joy that comes to me is not of days nor* **h.**
W-ep .........2:1 it has set, and in the half-lit **h.** in between.

### house 33

T-4........ I.11:2 try to make this impoverished **h.** stand.
T-18......VI.8:2 place you set aside to **h.** your hate is not a
T-18... VIII.5:2 Each body seems to **h.** a separate mind, a
T-20......VI.8:7 and bodies made to **h.** the mad idea and
T-20......VI.8:9 **h.** this mad idea against reality but for an
T-23...... I.10:4 You are not a stranger in the **h.** of God.
T-23...... I.11:2 the **h.** of God perceives itself divided. The
T-23...... I.11:3 of the Holy One becomes a **h.** of sin. And
T-24..... II.13:1 prison **h.** that keeps His Son from Him.
T-24....IV.3:15 and your treasure **h.** barren and empty,
T-24.....VII.4:6 fish, to **h.** your specialness in better style,
T-26.........I.5:3 become a treasure **h.** as rich and limitless
T-28.....VII.5:7 It is like the **h.** set upon straw. It seems to
T-28.....VII.7:4 away and yet this **h.** will stand forever, for
T-29....... V.6:2 and lead God's Son unto his Father's **h.**.
T-30....... V.8:6 go with you, together, to His Father's **h.**.
T-31.....III.3:10 and you give its purpose to its prison **h.**,
T-31......III.5:1 sin, to keep it in the prison **h.** it chose and
W-pI...125.2:2 surely to his Father's **h.** by his own will,
W-pI...159.6:1 the treasure **h.** to which you can appeal
W-pI...182.4:3 a Child in you Who seeks His Father's **h.**,
W-pI...182.5:4 again the holy air that fills His Father's **h.**.
W-pI.184.10:1 a prison **h.** from which you go into the
W-pI...192.9:6 your savior from the prison **h.** of death.
W-pI.193.11:2 arise in haste and go unto our Father's **h.**.
W-pI...197.2:4 Nor will you leave the prison **h.**, or claim
W-pI...200.4:5 seems to be a prison **h.** or jail for anyone.
W-pII..263.2:2 and walk together to our Father's **h.** as
W-pII..316.1:4 My treasure **h.** is full, and angels watch its
W-pII..357.1:1 *escape the prison* **h.** *in which I think I live.*
M-6 ...........4:8 God's treasure **h.** can never be empty.
M-13 .........4:4 look back with longing on a slaughter **h.**?
S-2........ III.3:2 in haste to go at last unto your Father's **h.**.

### housed 2

T-25.......in.1:6 What gives you life cannot be **h.** in death.
W-pII..223.1:1 unattached, and **h.** within a body. Now I

### hover 2

T-26...... IX.7:1 Around you angels **h.** lovingly, to keep
W-ep .........6:7 God's angels **h.** near and all about. His

### hovering 1

W-pI.....68.6:5 you, **h.** over you and holding you up. Try

### hovers 1

T-16.........I.6:2 lies in the strength of God that **h.** over it

### how 852

### however 230

### howling 1

W-pI...161.8:2 to attack, and **h.** to unite with him again.

### hugging

*See* hugging-close

### hugging-close 1

P-2........VI.1:3 hanging-on to guilt, its **h.** and sheltering,

### human 7

T-9...........I.1:1 beliefs the **h.** mind has ever made. It
W-pI.....25.6:2 or "unimportant," "**h.**" or "nonhuman."
W-pI...127.6:4 that you think are part of **h.** destiny.
W-pII..317.1:3 I am the slave of time and **h.** destiny. But
M-12 .........4:2 let God's Voice speak through it to **h.** ears
M-21 .......3:10 that which has no **h.** symbols at all. The
S-1 ........ III.6:1 prayers for things, for status, for **h.** love,

### humanity 1

C-6.............3:3 perceives because He was sent to save **h.**.

### humble 8

T-4.........I.12:4 inherit the earth because their egos are **h.**,
T-15...... IV.3:1 Be **h.** before Him, and yet great *in* Him.
W-pI...152.8:1 Let us today be truly **h.**, and accept what
W-pI...152.9:3 is **h.** in acknowledging its mightiness, its
W-pI...154.1:1 us today be neither arrogant nor falsely **h.**
W-pI...186.5:6 Yet are the **h.** free to hear the Voice which
S-1 ......... V.2:3 truly **h.** have no goal but God because
S-2 ......... II.3:4 This can appear to be a **h.** thought, and

### humbles 1

T-11...... VI.6:3 you and **h.** you and frightens you cannot

### humbling 1

T-4........ VI.3:8 from the ego by **h.** it or controlling it or

### humbly 2

W-pI.152.10:2 we are, and **h.** recognize the Son of God.
W-pI.152.11:5 **h.** ask our Self that He reveal Himself to

### humiliate 1

W-pI.....72.7:2 hate the body, and try to hurt and **h.** it.

### humility 31

T-4.........I.12:2 **H.** is a lesson for the ego, not for the spirit
T-4.........I.12:3 Spirit is beyond **h.**, because it recognizes
T-4...... IV.10:7 ego. Do not mistake it for **h.**. Your ego is
T-16.........I.4:4 **H.** is strength in this sense only; that to
T-18...... IV.3:1 **H.** will never ask that you remain content
T-19........II.4:4 Is this **h.**? Or is it, rather, an attempt to
T-19...... III.7:7 to its conqueror. Is this **h.** or madness?
T-22.... VI.10:4 Is this **h.**? You do not see what this belief
W-pI.....61.2:2 ego does not understand **h.**, mistaking it
W-pI.....61.2:3 self-debasement. **H.** consists of accepting
W-pI.....61.2:4 **h.** to insist you cannot be the light of the
W-pI.....61.3:1 True **h.** requires that you accept today's
W-pI...152.7:2 **H.** would see at once these things are not
W-pI...152.9:1 Today we practice true **h.**, abandoning
W-pI...152.9:4 and lift our hearts in true **h.** instead to
W-pI.152.10:5 And in **h.** the radiance of God's Son, his
W-pI...186.1:2 Here is the thought of true **h.**, which
W-pI...186.2:5 to do is to accept our part in genuine **h.**,
W-pI...186.3:4 What could **h.** request but this? And what
W-pI...186.4:1 All false **h.** we lay aside today, that we
W-pI...211.1:2 *In silence and in true* **h.** *I seek God's glory, to*
W-pII .239.1:1 ourselves today be hidden by a false **h.**.
M-7 ...........5:6 embarrassment stemming from false **h.**.
M-14 .......5:10 And now sit down in true **h.**, and realize
S-1 ......... V.1:1 Prayer is a way to true **h.**. And here again
S-1 ......... V.1:3 true **h.** will come at last to grace the mind
S-1 ......... V.1:4 **H.** brings peace because it does not claim
S-1 ......... V.2:1 Illusions and **h.** have goals so far apart
S-1 ......... V.2:4 useless now, because **h.** does not oppose.
S-1 ......... V.3:2 at last. **H.** has come to teach you how to
S-3 ........ III.4:3 in **h.** there is indeed a place for helpers. It

### hundred 7

T-26...... IX.4:1 What is a **h.** or a thousand years to Them
T-31....... V.3:4 But every day a **h.** little things make small
W-pI...107.2:5 quiet that you felt be multiplied a **h.** times
W-pI...107.2:5 and then be multiplied another **h.** more.
W-pI...123.6:3 them back a thousand and a **h.** thousand
W-pI.154.12:2 it. You have heard this said a **h.** ways, a
W-pI.154.12:2 heard this said a hundred ways, a **h.** times

### hung 1

T-17..IV.12:11 The other is lightly framed and **h.** in light,

### hunger 2

T19. IV.A.13:4 they seem to allay their savage pangs of **h.**
W-pI...195.5:2 feel apparent pain, who suffer cold or **h.**,

### hungry 3

T19. IV.A.12:5 steal guiltily away in **h.** search of guilt, for
T19. IV.A.12:6 little shred of guilt escapes their **h.** eyes.
T19. IV.A.15:6 the **h.** dogs of fear you sent instead. And

### hurl 1

T-24....... V.4:2 to a nameless precipice and **h.** him over it

### hurled 2

T-13...VII.11:3 it, it will be wrenched and **h.** into the dust
T-16......VI.8:1 be abruptly lifted up and **h.** into reality.

### hurls 1

T-24......III.3:1 upsets your world, and **h.** it into chaos.

### hurry 4

W-pI.......1.4:2 or so, unless that entails a sense of **h.**. A
W-pI.....28.8:4 as thoughtfully as possible. There is no **h.**.
W-pI.....31.3:5 as you care to, but with no sense of **h.**.
WpI. rIV.in7:3 There is no **h.** now, for you are using time

### hurt 127

T-2......... II.1:4 are acknowledging its power to **h.** you.
T-2......... II.2:2 deny any belief that error can **h.** you. This
T-2......... V.1:4 underlying fear that the mind can **h.** itself
T-2......... V.5:5 and their miscreations cannot **h.** them. By
T-3........ III.7:1 error in another, you will **h.** yourself. You
T-3.......VII.2:2 will **h.** you because you really understand
T-4......... II.5:4 need precisely what would **h.** you most.
T-4........ IV.5:4 mind about those whom your ego has **h.**,
T-4........ IV.8:7 used to attack or protect; to **h.** or to heal.
T-4.......VII.8:3 their egos and so nothing can **h.** them.
T-5........ IV.4:4 You cannot be **h.**, and do not want to
T-5........ IV.4:5 Show him that he cannot **h.** you and hold
T-6.........I.19:2 know that you cannot either **h.** or be hurt,
T-6.........I.19:2 know that you cannot either hurt or be **h.**,
T-6......... II.3:1 projection will always **h.** you. It reinforces
T-6......... III.3:9 and you have learned it, and it will **h.** you.
T-6......... V.3:3 it will **h.** you and make you unsafe; but if
T-7......... V.3:4 can communicate, but they cannot **h.**.
T-7......... V.3:5 the service of the ego can **h.** other bodies,
T-7....VIII.3:10 their projections will return and **h.** them.
T-8........ VI.4:2 father, because he thought he had **h.** him.
T-8.....VII.13:3 is to limit your mind and to **h.** yourself.
T-8......VIII.6:1 a way of demonstrating that you can be **h.**
T-9.........I.10:1 ask the Holy Spirit for what would **h.** you
T-9.........I.10:1 answer because nothing can **h.** you, and
T-11...... III.1:1 are weary, remember you have **h.** yourself
T-11...... III.1:4 Unless you **h.** yourself you could never
T-13.......in.2:7 its powers to decline if their bodies are **h.**.
T-13.........I.4:2 not cruel, and His Son cannot **h.** himself.
T-13...... III.7:4 Lay before His eternal sanity all your **h.**,
T-13...... III.7:6 to **h.** you and cleanse it of its littleness,
T-13...VII.10:9 you have need of and what will not **h.** you
T-13...VII.11:1 the ego tells you that you need will **h.** you.
T-13...VII.11:5 and your advice to yourself will **h.** you.
T-13...VII.13:3 hidden in your mind and kept to **h.** you.
T-14...... III.7:4 He can do nothing that can **h.** you, and by
T-14...... III.7:6 No one can **h.** the Son of God. His guilt is
T-14...... III.8:2 Teach no one he has **h.** you, for if you do,
T-14...... III.9:2 It will **h.** you because of the concept of
T-14... III.10:4 that what they do not want must **h.** them.
T-14...... XI.5:3 are dark lessons in your mind that **h.** and
T-15...... XI.3:1 Holy Spirit everything that would **h.** you.
T-16.........I.3:2 choose neither to **h.** it nor to heal it in
T-16.........I.6:5 thing that would **h.** either him or you, for
T-16.........I.6:5 for what would **h.** one will hurt the other.
T-16.........I.6:5 for what would hurt one will **h.** the other.
T-16....... II.3:1 to **h.** your mind has made it so unnatural
T-16..... V.15:5 Yet for every learning that would **h.** you,
T-16...... VI.8:6 Delay will **h.** you now more than before,
T-17 ... III.10:3 to enable you to **h.** yourself through them
T-18 ..... VI.4:2 what it does to **h.** the body to prove it can
T-19 ........I.8:1 strange concealment has **h.** your mind,
T19IV.A.17:12 and happy with so little is to **h.** yourself,
T-20 ..... IV.1:1 Nothing can **h.** you unless you give it the
T-21 ......in.2:2 all you see is what you did to **h.** the Son of
T-22 ... VI.12:5 **h.** yourself without the other feeling pain.
T-23 ......in.2:2 sin can **h.** you and become your enemy.
T-23 ..... III.1:2 If it is true attack in any form will **h.** you,
T-24 ........I.6:8 can be made for this that will not **h.** you?
T-24 ... IV.2:11 See it as means to **h.**, and it is hurt. See it
T-24 ... IV.2:11 See it as means to hurt, and it is **h.**. See it
T-24 ..... IV.3:1 You can but **h.** yourself. This has been oft
T-24 ..... IV.3:9 change of purpose from **h.** to healing.
T-24 .... VII.4:3 And much you think you save, you **h.**.
T-25 ..... III.9:1 but he can wish for what would **h.** him.
T-25 ..... III.9:2 he has the power to think he can be **h.**.
T-25 ..... IV.3:7 and every wish to **h.** and kill and die, will
T-25 ...... V.2:4 For you have **h.** yourself, and made your
T-25 ..... VI.6:6 The specialness he chose to **h.** himself did
T-26 .......II.4:8 to judge whether the **h.** be large or little.
T-26 .......II.4:9 that to **h.** God's Son must be unfair and
T-26 .......II.7:3 will see each little **h.** resolved before the
T-26 ..... VI.1:1 valuable and worth striving for can **h.** you
T-26 ..... VI.1:2 so. Not because it has the power to **h.**, but
T-26 ..... VI.1:6 in sin, in power of attack, in **h.** and harm,
T-26 .. VII.16:6 every wish to **h.** he chooses death instead
T-27 ........I.5:4 to the eternal truth that you cannot be **h.**,
T-27 .......II.2:8 the better of the two, I pardon you my **h.**.
T-27 .......II.2:9 pardon and your **h.** cannot exist together.
T-27 .......II.6:9 your brother that you had no **h.** of him.
T-27 ...... V.3:4 For all the **h.** that war has sought to bring,
T-27 ..... VI.2:2 here, within this body, and you can be **h.**.
T-27 ..... VI.2:7 Call pleasure pain, and it will **h.**. Call pain
T-27 ...VIII.2:7 slave of bodies that would **h.** and torture
T-27 .VIII.11:3 Whatever **h.** you bring to Him He will
T-28 ........I.2:9 It can be used to heal and not to **h.**, if you
T-28 ..... VI.4:7 it is a promise to another to be **h.** by him,
T-29 ..... IV.6:4 And do not try to **h.** him when he fails to
T-31 .......II.1:5 Who could be **h.** in such a war, unless he
T-31 .......II.8:6 Nothing will **h.** you in this holy place, to
T-31 ... V.15:8 If you can be **h.** by anything, you see a
T-31 ... VI.6:10 And what could **h.** the truly innocent?
W-pI.....51.2:6 My judgments have **h.** me, and I do not
W-pI.....51.5:6 to defend a thought system that has **h.** me
W-pI.....70.2:2 that nothing outside yourself can **h.** you,
W-pI.....72.7:2 the body, and try to **h.** and humiliate it.
W-pI.....93.5:7 It does not **h.** him, nor attack his peace. It
W-pI... 119.1:2 *mistaken when I think I can be **h.** in any way.*
W-pI... 122.1:6 a gentleness that never can be **h.**, a deep,
W-pI. 136.20:1 your defensiveness to **h.** you longer. Do
W-pI... 158.9:4 to be, nor who seemed to be **h.** by them.
W-pI... 170.1:1 No one attacks without intent to **h.**. This
W-pI... 170.1:4 believe to **h.** another brings you freedom.
W-pI... 190.5:2 your mind can **h.** or injure you in any way
W-pI... 193.9:2 one thorn or nail to **h.** His holy Son in any
W-pI... 196.8:3 you be **h.** except by your own thoughts,
W-pI... 196.9:2 you you crucify, you did not **h.** the world,
W-pI... 200.2:1 none; of being saved by what can only **h.**;
W-pI... 213.1:2 *to me, in place of thoughts I made that **h.** me.*
W-pII . 235.1:1 look upon all things that seem to **h.** me,
W-pII . 246.1:2 Let me not try to **h.** God's Son, and think
W-pII .... 281.h I can be **h.** by nothing but my thoughts.
W-pII . 281.1:2 *When I think that I am **h.** in any way, it is*
W-pII . 281.1:4 *If ever I am sad or **h.** or ill, I have forgotten*
W-pII . 281.1:5 *I can be **h.** by nothing but my thoughts. The*
W-pII . 281.2:1 I will not **h.** myself today. For I am far
W-pII .... 284.h I can elect to change all thoughts that **h.**.
W-pII . 284.1:7 I can elect to change all thoughts that **h.**.
W-pII . 284.2:1 *Father, what You have given cannot **h.**, so*
W-pII . 294.1:8 aside. It is not sick nor old nor **h.**. It is but
W-pII .... 330.h I will not **h.** myself again today.
W-pII . 330.2:1 *Father, Your Son can not be **h.**. And if we*
Wfl........in.6:2 Would He **h.** His Son? Or would He rush
M-17......... 1:2 teacher of God has **h.** himself and has also
S-2...........I.1:5 to **h.** because forgiveness is not wanted.
S-2...........II.4:5 the anger and the **h.** another gives, and
S-3...........I.1:3 that injure and would **h.** the Son of God.

### hurtful 3

T-11 .......II.2:6 In every **h.** thought you hold, wherever
T-27 ...VIII.1:7 and avoid the things that would be **h.**.
S-3..........II.1:9 It does not come because of **h.** thoughts

### hurting 3

T-27 .... VII.2:6 problem be resolved if it is seen as **h.** him,
T-27 .... VII.3:6 it looks as if the world were **h.** you. And
S-1........ III.1:4 you to recognize it is not he who is **h.** you.

### hurts 12

T-3 ..........I.2:7 says, "This **h.** me more than it hurts you,"
T-3 ..........I.2:7 says, "This hurts me more than it **h.** you,"
T-11 ..... VI.6:3 to leave behind everything that **h.** you
T-13 ..... IV.5:2 The present merely reminds it of past **h.**,
T-24 ..... IV.3:6 that harmful purpose **h.** the mind as one.
T-27 .. VII.15:4 instead of counting up the **h.** he gave.
T-28 ........I.5:6 of injustices and **h.** that you were saving,
T-29 ..... IX.6:5 What **h.** him is destroyed; what helps him
T-29 ..... IX.6:6 does not know what **h.** and what will heal.
T-31 .......II.1:5 be hurt in such a war, unless he **h.** himself
W-pI .... 76.5:2 is endangered by the mind that **h.** itself.
W-pI .... 78.6:3 and all the little and the larger **h.** he gave.

### hush 2

T19 ...IV.A.6:1 is a **h.** in Heaven, a happy expectancy, a
W-pII .... 286.h The **h.** of Heaven holds my heart today.

### hymn 9

T-13 ..... VI.8:7 the **h.** of gladness and thanksgiving for
T-13 .. VII.17:1 We cannot sing redemption's **h.** alone.
T-13 .....X.14:4 is fitting as a **h.** of praise unto your Father
T-13 ..... XI.2:4 have heard the **h.** of freedom rising unto
T-17 .......V.1:7 is a continuing **h.** of hate in praise of its
T-21 ........I.9:6 you as is this ancient **h.** of love the Son of
T-22 .......V.4:5 and would drown out the **h.** of praise to
T-29 .......V.1:3 still no sound except a **h.** to Heaven rises
C-6 ............ 5:7 place the **h.** to God is heard a little while.

### hymns 2

T-13 ..... VI.9:3 And as your **h.** of praise and gladness rise
W-pII . 293.2:2 *let my ears be deaf to all the **h.** of gratitude*

### hypnotic 1

T-17 ... IV.9:10 dwell on the **h.** gleaming of the frame.

# I

**I** 9
• God
*Christ*
*Holy Spirit*
*Jesus*
*noise word*

T-4.........in.2:2 to “Be still and know that **I.** am God.”
T-5........VI.8:1 “**I.** will visit the sins of the fathers unto
T-28......VI.6:4 are beloved of Me and **I.** of you forever. Be
W-pII....10.5:3 **I.** am your Father and you are My Son.”
Wfl........in.6:3 say, “This is My Son, and all **I.** have is his”
S-3........IV.7:2 **I.** would recall My weary Son to Me from
S-3........IV.7:3 My Arms are open to the Son **I.** love, who
S-3........IV.9:6 lovingly **I.** hold you in My Heart and in
S-3......IV.10:5 **I.** ask but this; that you be comforted and

**I** 2
• Christ
*God*
*Holy Spirit*
*Jesus*
*noise word*

T-28......VI.6:6 Son remembers not that he replied “**I.** will
W-pI.153.19:6 a moment, as He tells us, “**I.** am here.”

**I** 1
• Holy Spirit
*God*
*Christ*
*Jesus*
*noise word*

T-14.......II.3:7 *I. will place it gently in the holy place where it*

**I** 537
• Jesus
*God*
*Christ*
*Holy Spirit*
*noise word*

T-1........I.32:1 **I.** inspire all miracles, which are really
T-1.......II.3:11 **I.** have nothing that does not come from
T-1.......II.3:12 difference between us now is that **I.** have
T-1.........II.4:1 that **I.** am in any way separate or different
T-1.........II.4:3 stand below me and **I.** stand below God.
T-1.........II.4:4 up,” **I.** am higher because without me the
T-1.........II.4:5 **I.** bridge the distance as an elder brother
T-1.........II.4:6 **I.** render complete because I share it. This
T-1.........II.4:6 I render complete because **I.** share it. This
T-1.........II.4:7 the statement “**I.** and my Father are one,”
T-1.........II.5:1 me because **I.** am close to the Holy Spirit,
T-1.........II.5:2 **I.** can thus bring down to them more than
T-1........III.1:1 **I.** am in charge of the process of
T-1........III.1:1 Atonement, which **I.** undertook to begin.
T-1........III.1:3 you come before me is that **I.** do not need
T-1........III.1:3 but **I.** stand at the end in case you fail
T-1........III.1:8 **I.** will provide the opportunities to do
T-1........III.4:1 **I.** am the only one who can perform
T-1........III.4:1 because **I.** am the Atonement. You have a
T-1........III.4:2 role in the Atonement which **I.** will dictate
T-1........III.8:5 only **I.** am in a position to know where
T-1........IV.4:2 and why **I.** could demonstrate that death
T-1........IV.4:3 **I.** came to fulfill the law by reinterpreting
T-1........IV.4:6 **I.** assure you that I will witness for anyone
T-1........IV.4:6 that **I.** will witness for anyone who lets me
T-1.......VII.5:1 and awe to which **I.** have already referred,
T-1.......VII.5:2 **I.** have said that awe is inappropriate in
T-1.......VII.5:4 **I.** have been careful to clarify my role in
T-1.......VII.5:5 it. **I.** am also trying to do the same with
T-1.......VII.5:6 yours. **I.** have stressed that awe is not an
T-2.........II.1:1 You can do anything **I.** ask. I have asked
T-2.........II.1:2 **I.** have asked you to perform miracles,
T-2.........V.3:1 **I.** have already said that miracles are
T-2.........V.7:3 **I.** said before that the Holy Spirit cannot
T-2.......V.10:5 world. **I.** said before that only revelation
T-2....V.A.11:3 **I.** will arrange both time and space to
T-2........VI.1:2 **I.** have said already that only constructive
T-2........VI.2:1 **I.** do not foster level confusion, but you
T-2........VI.6:6 **I.** will therefore repeat it, urging you to
T-2........VI.8:1 **I.** have emphasized that the miracle, or
T-2.......VII.1:2 **I.** have already indicated that you cannot
T-2.......VII.1:3 **I.** know it does not exist, but you do not.
T-2.......VII.1:4 **I.** intervened between your thoughts and
T-2.......VII.1:4 **I.** would be tampering with a basic law of
T-2.......VII.1:5 **I.** would hardly help you if I depreciated
T-2.......VII.1:5 I would hardly help you if **I.** depreciated
T-2.......VII.2:1 **I.** cannot let you leave your mind
T-2.......VII.7:1 **I.** have already briefly spoken about
T-3........I.2:10 **I.** was not “punished” because *you* were
T-3........I.3:10 time to time that **I.** am misdirecting you. I
T-3........I.3:11 **I.** have made every effort to use words
T-3..........I.5:1 **I.** have been correctly referred to as “the
T-3..........I.7:9 that all the other lessons **I.** taught are true
T-3.........II.1:1 **I.** have stated that the basic concepts
T-3.........II.3:6 **I.** have said that only what God creates or
T-3........III.6:5 the end,” and “Before Abraham was **I.** am
T-3........IV.6:8 because, as **I.** have already emphasized,
T-3........IV.7:3 **I.** was a man who remembered spirit and
T-3........IV.7:4 As a man **I.** did not attempt to counteract
T-3........IV.7:5 **I.** demonstrated both the powerlessness
T-3........IV.7:6 **I.** naturally remembered spirit and its real
T-3........IV.7:7 **I.** cannot unite your will with God’s for
T-3........IV.7:7 but **I.** can erase all misperceptions from
T-3......IV.7:11 **I.** cannot choose for you, but I can help
T-3......IV.7:11 but **I.** can help you make your own right
T-3.........V.1:1 **I.** have said that the abilities you possess
T-3.........V.1:3 since. **I.** have also made it clear that the
T-3........VI.2:3 **I.** have discussed this before in terms of
T-3........VI.7:1 **I.** have spoken of different symptoms,
T-3.......VII.3:6 children, and **I.** assure you that He does,
T-3.......VII.4:8 And, as **I.** said before, when you finally
T-4.......in.3:10 is not the gospel **I.** intended to offer you.
T-4..........I.3:4 and because **I.** learned it I can teach it. I
T-4..........I.3:4 and because I learned it **I.** can teach it. I
T-4..........I.3:5 it. **I.** will never attack your ego, but I am
T-4..........I.3:5 **I.** am trying to teach you how its thought
T-4..........I.3:6 When **I.** remind you of your true creation,
T-4..........I.4:7 **I.** will correct it very gently and lead you
T-4..........I.6:3 **I.** will teach with you and live with you if
T-4..........I.6:6 **I.** would not be able to devote myself to
T-4..........I.6:6 myself to teaching if **I.** believed this, and
T-4..........I.6:7 it. **I.** am constantly being perceived as a
T-4..........I.6:7 but **I.** do not accept either perception for
T-4..........I.7:5 **I.** am willing to do this, because I have no
T-4..........I.7:5 **I.** have no right to set your learning limits
T-4........I.13:1 **I.** will substitute for your ego if you wish,
T-4........I.13:4 **I.** can be entrusted with your body and
T-4........I.13:5 **I.** could not understand their importance
T-4........I.13:5 to you if **I.** had not once been tempted to
T-4........I.13:7 **I.** need devoted teachers who share my
T-4......I.13:10 *because I. have overcome the world. That is*
T-4........III.7:4 through a wall, but **I.** can step around it.
T-4........III.7:6 **I.** can help you only as our Father created
T-4........III.7:7 us. **I.** will love you and honor you and
T-4........III.7:7 but **I.** will not uphold it unless it is true. I
T-4........III.7:8 **I.** will never forsake you any more than
T-4........III.7:8 but **I.** must wait as long as you choose to
T-4........III.7:9 **I.** wait in love and not in impatience, you
T-4......III.7:10 truly. **I.** will come in response to a single
T-4........IV.2:1 **I.** have said that you cannot change your
T-4........IV.2:1 your behavior, but **I.** have also said, and
T-4........IV.2:9 brother **I.** am deeply concerned with your
T-4......IV.10:3 **I.** was created like you in the First, and I
T-4......IV.10:3 and **I.** have called you to join with me in
T-4......IV.10:4 **I.** am in charge of the Second Coming,
T-4......IV.10:5 believe **I.** was mistaken in choosing you. I
T-4......IV.10:6 **I.** assure you this is a mistake of your ego.
T-4......IV.10:8 convince you that it is real and **I.** am not,
T-4......IV.10:8 it is real and I am not, because if **I.** am real
T-4......IV.10:8 I am real, **I.** am no more real than you are.
T-4......IV.10:9 and **I.** assure you that it *is* knowledge,
T-4......IV.11:1 **I.** do not attack your ego. I do work with
T-4......IV.11:2 **I.** do work with your higher mind, the
T-4......IV.11:3 **I.** am your vigilance in this, because you
T-4......IV.11:4 **I.** am not mistaken. Your mind will elect
T-4......IV.11:7 **I.** raised the dead by knowing that life is
T-4......IV.11:9 **I.** do not believe that there is an order of
T-4....IV.11:10 do. **I.** have called and you will answer. I
T-4....IV.11:11 **I.** understand that miracles are natural,
T-4........VI.1:3 **I.** have spoken of the ego as if it were a
T-4........VI.5:6 **I.** am teaching you to associate misery
T-4........VI.6:3 **I.** do not choose God’s channels wrongly.
T-4........VI.6:5 **I.** have said before that I am in charge of
T-4........VI.6:5 I have said before that **I.** am in charge of
T-4........VI.6:6 only because **I.** completed my part in it as
T-4........VI.6:7 because **I.** will lend them my strength as
T-4........VI.7:1 **I.** will go with you to the Holy One, and
T-4........VI.7:2 to your brother is the only gift **I.** want. I
T-4........VI.7:3 **I.** will bring it to God for you, knowing
T-4........VI.7:7 of God **I.** can lead you back to your own
T-4........VI.8:1 withdraw from him **I.** become distant to
T-4.......VII.8:7 whom **I.** direct until we are all united in
T-4.......VII.8:8 **I.** will direct you to wherever you can be
T-5.........in.1:2 make happy. **I.** have told you to think how
T-5..........I.3:2 **I.** have said already that I can reach up
T-5..........I.3:2 I have said already that **I.** can reach up
T-5..........I.3:2 but **I.** can bring Him to you only at your
T-5..........I.3:6 It asks that you may think as **I.** thought,
T-5..........I.4:4 Son. **I.** myself said, “If I go I will send you
T-5..........I.4:4 “If **I.** go I will send you another Comforter
T-5..........I.4:4 “If I go **I.** will send you another Comforter
T-5..........I.4:7 for all. **I.** could not have It myself without
T-5..........I.4:9 **I.** have spoken before of the higher or
T-5.......II.3:11 It is the final lesson that **I.** learned, and
T-5..........II.9:6 **I.** am your model for decision. By
T-5..........II.9:7 By deciding for God **I.** showed you that
T-5.......II.10:1 **I.** have assured you that the Mind that
T-5.....II.10:10 brothers to listen as **I.** am teaching you.
T-5.......II.12:1 **I.** have enjoined you to behave as I
T-5.......II.12:1 have enjoined you to behave as **I.** behaved
T-5........III.1:2 **I.** have already said that the Holy Spirit is
T-5........III.5:3 **I.** have said before that the Holy Spirit is
T-5........III.6:1 **I.** have repeatedly emphasized that one
T-5........IV.2:7 **I.** have come to give you the foundation,
T-5......IV.2:12 **I.** meant when I said it is possible even in
T-5......IV.2:12 I meant when **I.** said it is possible even in
T-5........IV.4:1 **I.** heard one Voice because I understood
T-5........IV.4:1 I heard one Voice because **I.** understood
T-5........IV.4:1 that **I.** could not atone for myself alone.
T-5........IV.5:3 **I.** cannot forget my need to teach what I
T-5........IV.5:3 my need to teach what **I.** have learned,
T-5........IV.5:3 which arose in me *because* **I.** learned it. I
T-5........IV.5:4 it. **I.** call upon you to teach what you have
T-5........IV.5:6 What **I.** learned I give you freely, and the
T-5........IV.5:6 What I learned **I.** give you freely, and the

T-5 IV.6:5 **I.** will never leave you or forsake you,
T-5 IV.8:3 **I.** have saved all your kindnesses and
T-5 IV.8:4 **I.** have purified them of the errors that
T-5 IV.8:7 because **I.** have loved you as I loved myself
T-5 IV.8:7 because I have loved you as **I.** loved myself
T-5 IV.8:10 **I.** place the peace of God in your heart
T-5 V.4:5 **I.** said before that you must learn to think
T-5 V.5:4 **I.** said before that illness is a form of
T-5 V.7:8 for himself, and **I.** assure you that it is,
T-5 VI.11:1 **I.** said "I am come as a light into the world
T-5 VI.11:1 I said "**I.** am come as a light into the world
T-5 VI.11:1 **I.** meant that I came to share the light
T-5 VI.11:1 that **I.** came to share the light with you.
T-5 VI.11:2 dark glass, and remember also that **I.** said
T-5 VI.11:6 **I.** have shown you infinite patience
T-5 VI.11:6 from Whom **I.** learned of infinite patience
T-5 VII.4:2 yourself because, as **I.** told you before, the
T-5 VII.4:4 **I.** am making His plan perfectly explicit to
T-6 I.1:2 **I.** did not dwell on it before because of the
T-6 I.2:5 **I.** have already told you that you can
T-6 I.2:6 **I.** have also told you that the crucifixion
T-6 I.2:7 While **I.** emphasized only the resurrection
T-6 I.3:6 **I.** cannot serve as a model for learning.
T-6 I.5:1 **I.** have made it perfectly clear that I am
T-6 I.5:1 that **I.** am like you and you are like me,
T-6 I.5:3 that **I.** was persecuted as the world judges,
T-6 I.5:4 And because **I.** did not share it, I did not
T-6 I.5:4 I did not share it, **I.** did not strengthen it.
T-6 I.5:5 not strengthen it. **I.** therefore offered a
T-6 I.5:5 and one which **I.** want to share with you.
T-6 I.6:1 As **I.** have said before, "As you teach so
T-6 I.7:2 **I.** am the model for rebirth, but rebirth
T-6 I.7:4 **I.** believed in it, and therefore accepted it
T-6 I.7:6 **I.** could not be angry with them because I
T-6 I.7:6 because **I.** knew I could not *be* abandoned.
T-6 I.7:6 because I knew **I.** could not *be* abandoned.
T-6 I.8:1 **I.** am sorry when my brothers do not
T-6 I.8:2 Yet **I.** know they cannot really betray
T-6 I.8:2 still on them that **I.** must build my church
T-6 I.8:6 **I.** must found His church on you, because
T-6 I.9:1 **I.** elected, for your sake and mine, to
T-6 I.9:2 not as God knows them, **I.** was betrayed,
T-6 I.9:3 since **I.** had not harmed anyone and had
T-6 I.10:3 only way in which **I.** can be perceived as
T-6 I.11:1 You are not persecuted, nor was **I.**. You
T-6 I.11:5 lesson, which **I.** must teach as I learned it,
T-6 I.11:5 lesson, which I must teach as **I.** learned it,
T-6 I.11:6 **I.** undertook to show this was true in an
T-6 I.11:7 **I.** will with God that none of His Sons
T-6 I.15:2 "**I.** come not to bring peace but a sword."
T-6 I.15:3 the opposite of everything **I.** taught. Nor
T-6 I.15:5 **I.** could not have said, "Betrayest thou the
T-6 I.15:5 with a kiss?" unless **I.** believed in betrayal.
T-6 I.15:6 the crucifixion was simply that **I.** did not.
T-6 I.15:7 "punishment" **I.** was said to have called
T-6 I.15:9 Was it likely that **I.** would condemn him
T-6 I.15:9 that I would condemn him when **I.** was
T-6 I.16:1 remember that **I.** told them myself that
T-6 I.16:2 **I.** do not want you to allow any fear to
T-6 I.16:2 system toward which **I.** am guiding you. I
T-6 I.16:3 **I.** do not call for martyrs but for teachers.
T-6 I.17:1 **I.** do not need gratitude, but you need to
T-6 I.19:3 be as eager to share your learning as **I.** am
T-6 III.2:4 **I.** said before that the message of the
T-6 IV.11:7 **I.** have frequently said that what you
T-6 V.A.1:5 you can overcome death because **I.** did.
T-6 V.A.3:1 **I.** have said that the Holy Spirit is the
T-6 V.A.4:5 system **I.** teach and want you to teach.
T-6 V.B.1:5 Many thought **I.** was attacking them, even
T-6 V.B.1:5 even though it was apparent **I.** was not.
T-6 V.B.3:3 **I.** said that this is apt to increase conflict
T-6 V.B.6:5 That is why **I.** suggested before that you
T-6 V.C.4:2 **I.** have already told you that you can be as
T-7 I.1:5 **I.** have already told you that only in this
T-7 I.5:1 **I.** gave only love to the Kingdom because
T-7 I.5:1 because **I.** believed that was what I was.
T-7 I.5:1 because I believed that was what **I.** was.
T-7 I.6:3 whole. **I.** have said that the last step in the
T-7 II.2:8 **I.** assure you that you must obey them,
T-7 II.6:4 in remembering. **I.** said before that He
T-7 III.1:7 When **I.** said "I am with you always," I
T-7 III.1:7 When I said "**I.** am with you always," I
T-7 III.1:7 am with you always," **I.** meant it literally.
T-7 III.1:8 literally. **I.** am not absent to anyone in any
T-7 III.1:9 Because **I.** am always with you, *you* are the
T-7 III.1:10 not make this power, any more than **I.** did
T-7 III.3:1 **I.** said before that the ego's friend is not
T-7 IV.2:7 **I.** said before that forgetting is merely a
T-7 V.9:9 **I.** have spoken often of the increase of the
T-7 V.10:1 forget the Father because **I.** am with you,
T-7 V.10:1 I am with you, and **I.** cannot forget Him.
T-7 V.10:5 about themselves, as **I.** can change yours.
T-7 V.10:6 enlighten them, as **I.** can enlighten yours.
T-7 V.10:7 yours. **I.** do not want to share my body in
T-7 V.10:8 Would **I.** try to share an illusion with the
T-7 V.10:9 Yet **I.** do want to share my mind with you
T-7 VI.6:4 **I.** have said before that the Holy Spirit
T-7 VI.6:6 As **I.** have already said, understanding
T-7 VI.8:1 **I.** have repeatedly emphasized that the
T-7 X.6:4 **I.** said before that you are the Will of God.
T-7 XI.4:1 **I.** call upon you to remember that I have
T-7 XI.4:1 I call upon you to remember that **I.** have
T-7 XI.6:4 **I.** have already said that only the whole
T-8 I.1:9 **I.** have told you what knowledge offers
T-8 II.7:1 When **I.** said, "All power and glory are
T-8 II.7:1 **I.** meant: The Will of God is without limit,
T-8 III.4:8 For **I.** am always there with you, in
T-8 IV.2:1 **I.** am come as a light into a world that
T-8 IV.2:4 **I.** said that I am with you always, even
T-8 IV.2:4 I said that **I.** am with you always, even
T-8 IV.2:5 That is why **I.** am the light of the world. If
T-8 IV.2:6 If **I.** am with you in the loneliness of the
T-8 IV.2:9 **I.** do not attack it, but my light must
T-8 IV.3:5 This is the awareness **I.** came to give you,
T-8 IV.3:6 this sense **I.** *am* the salvation of the world.
T-8 IV.3:8 will accept the fact that **I.** am with you,
T-8 IV.3:10 God sent me to you so will **I.** send you to
T-8 IV.3:11 And **I.** will go to them with you, so we can
T-8 IV.4:9 **I.** can tell you what to do, but you must
T-8 IV.4:9 believing that **I.** know what you should do
T-8 IV.5:13 it. **I.** cannot will what God does not will. I
T-8 IV.5:14 **I.** can offer my strength to make yours
T-8 IV.5:14 **I.** cannot oppose your decision without
T-8 IV.6:2 **I.** can only acknowledge in honor of His.
T-8 IV.6:3 If you want to be like me **I.** will help you,
T-8 IV.6:4 **I.** will wait until you change your mind. I
T-8 IV.6:5 **I.** can teach you, but only you can choose
T-8 IV.6:9 This is the only lesson **I.** came to teach.
T-8 IV.7:4 **I.** am nothing without the Father and you
T-8 IV.7:5 **I.** will always remember you, and in my
T-8 V.1:5 **I.** am offering you mine on behalf of yours
T-8 V.3:3 it. **I.** offer you only the recognition of His
T-8 V.4:1 **I.** have renounced the ego in myself and
T-8 V.4:4 and **I.** share this confidence for both of us
T-8 V.4:5 of us. **I.** bring God's peace back to all His
T-8 V.4:5 because **I.** received it of Him for us all.
T-8 V.5:3 it. **I.** will deny you nothing, as God denies
T-8 V.5:7 to its retaliation because **I.** am with you.
T-8 V.6:7 **I.** go before you because I am beyond the
T-8 V.6:7 before you because **I.** am beyond the ego.
T-8 V.6:10 so. **I.** give it willingly and gladly, because I
T-8 V.6:10 **I.** need you as much as you need me.
T-8 VI.1:4 will welcome us as **I.** am welcoming you.
T-8 VI.2:4 **I.** am come to tell you that the choice of
T-8 VI.8:3 has revealed it to me because **I.** asked it of
T-8 VI.9:1 **I.** share with God the knowledge of the
T-8 VI.9:10 **I.** can make you aware of the conditions of
T-8 VIII.4:7 **I.** have said that judgment is the function
T-8 VIII.7:6 When **I.** said that the ego does not know
T-8 VIII.7:6 **I.** said the one thing about the ego that is
T-8 IX.1:1 **I.** said before that the Holy Spirit is the
T-8 IX.8:2 **I.** would not ask you to do things you
T-8 IX.8:2 it is impossible that **I.** could do things you
T-8 IX.8:3 you from doing exactly what **I.** ask, and
T-8 IX.8:4 it. **I.** give you no limits because God lays
T-9 I.4:2 **I.** said that the Holy Spirit's function is to
T-9 I.4:2 **I.** meant that He has the power to look
T-9 I.5:1 **I.** have emphasized many times that the
T-9 II.3:7 **I.** assure you that they are waiting for you.
T-9 II.6:7 the trust **I.** have in you unless you extend
T-9 II.7:1 **I.** love you for the truth in you, as God
T-9 II.7:3 what you are, **I.** cannot doubt you. I hear
T-9 II.7:4 **I.** hear only the Holy Spirit in you, Who
T-9 II.8:1 in your brothers because **I.** believe in you,
T-9 IV.6:2 That is what **I.** meant when I said that
T-9 IV.6:2 when **I.** said that miracles are natural, and
T-9 IV.8:6 You realize it because **I.** realize it, and you
T-9 IV.8:6 judged it by the same standard **I.** have.
T-9 IV.10:4 And **I.** assure you that God *is* right. Be glad
T-9 V.2:1 **I.** have repeatedly said that beliefs of the
T-9 VII.7:1 **I.** have said that the ego does not know
T-9 VIII.3:2 **I.** told you that the ego is aware of threat
T-10 III.6:4 that **I.** contribute to you but my love, for
T-10 III.6:6 When **I.** said, "My peace I give unto you,"
T-10 III.6:6 When I said, "My peace **I.** give unto you,"
T-10 III.6:6 "My peace I give unto you," **I.** meant it.
T-10 III.7:4 **I.** can heal you because I know you. I
T-10 III.7:4 I can heal you because **I.** know you. I
T-10 III.7:5 **I.** know your value for you, and it is this
T-10 III.7:7 **I.** will heal you merely because I have only
T-10 III.7:7 I will heal you merely because **I.** have only
T-10 III.8:1 **I.** do not bring God's message with
T-10 V.5:1 **I.** said before that of yourself you can do
T-11 in.4:3 **I.** come to you from our Father to offer
T-11 in.4:5 **I.** give you the lamp and I will go with you
T-11 in.4:5 I give you the lamp and **I.** will go with you
T-11 in.4:7 **I.** will lead you to your true Father, Who
T-11 in.4:7 Father, Who hath need of you, as **I.** have.
T-11 I.2:5 **I.** and my Father are one with you, for you
T-11 III.3:6 **I.** cannot tell you what this will be like, for
T-11 III.3:7 Yet **I.** can tell you, and remind you often,
T-11 IV.6:6 for you, for while **I.** live it cannot be shut,
T-11 IV.6:6 I live it cannot be shut, and **I.** live forever.
T-11 V.5:3 **I.** said before that to will contrary to God
T-11 VI.1:5 *do* see. That is what **I.** meant when I said,
T-11 VI.1:5 *do* see. That is what I meant when **I.** said,
T-11 VI.3:6 teach. **I.** am leading you to a new kind of
T-11 VI.4:1 **I.** am *your* resurrection and *your* life. You
T-11 VI.7:3 Teach not that **I.** died in vain. Teach
T-11 VI.7:4 in vain. Teach rather that **I.** did not die by
T-11 VI.7:4 die by demonstrating that **I.** live in you.
T-11 VI.9:2 If **I.** live in you, you are awake. Yet you
T-11 VI.9:3 you must see the works **I.** do through you,
T-11 VI.9:3 perceive that **I.** have done them unto you.
T-11 VI.9:4 on what you believe **I.** can do through you
T-11 VI.9:4 you will not accept what **I.** can do *for* you.
T-11 VIII.8:1 are asking only for what **I.** promised you.
T-11 VIII.8:2 Do you believe **I.** would deceive you? The
T-11 VIII.8:4 truth is in me, for **I.** know that it is in you.
T-12 II.7:1 **I.** am not hidden because *you* are hiding. I
T-12 II.7:2 **I.** will awaken you as surely as I awakened
T-12 II.7:2 you as surely as **I.** awakened myself, for I
T-12 II.7:2 as I awakened myself, for **I.** awoke for you
T-12 II.7:5 Trust in my help, for **I.** did not walk alone
T-12 II.7:5 **I.** will walk with you as our Father walked
T-12 II.7:6 know that **I.** walked with Him in peace?
T-12 II.8:4 mission because **I.** did not fail in mine.
T-12 II.8:5 name of the complete trust **I.** have in you,
T-12 III.1:1 **I.** once asked you to sell all you have and
T-12 III.1:2 **I.** meant: If you have no investment in
T-12 III.8:1 **I.** said before that God so loved the world
T-12 V.7:1 **I.** have said that the ego's rule is, "Seek
T-12 VII.6:1 **I.** am the manifestation of the Holy Spirit
T-12 VII.7:1 **I.** said before that what you project or
T-12 VII.11:3 to you. **I.** have heard your call and I have
T-12 VII.11:3 to you. I have heard your call and **I.** have
T-12 VII.11:5 Yet as **I.** become more real to you, you will
T-12 VII.15:1 for death, *remember that **I.** did not die.* You
T-12 VII.15:3 **I.** have overcome death for myself alone?
T-13 I.1:1 **I.** said that the Holy Spirit shares the goal
T-13 II.6:1 **I.** have said that the crucifixion is the
T-13 II.8:2 Yet even when **I.** interpret it for you, you
T-13 V.1:1 **I.** have said you have but two emotions,
T-13 V.7:10 **I.** am with them as I am with you, and we
T-13 V.7:10 I am with them as **I.** am with you, and we
T-13 VI.8:6 as **I.** am calling you to join with me. Each
T-13 VII.16:8 My peace **I.** give you. Take it of me in glad

T-13...VII.17:2 until I. have lifted every voice with mine.
T-13.....X.11:9 To him I. say: *Behold the Son of God, and*
T-13.....X.12:6 I. thank You, Father, for the purity of
T-13.....X.13:1 my belief are centered on what I. treasure.
T-13.....X.13:2 is that I. love *only* what God loves with me,
T-13.....X.13:2 and because of this I. treasure you beyond
T-13.....X.13:3 I. love all that He created, and all my faith
T-13.....X.13:3 all my faith and my belief I. offer unto it.
T-13.....X.13:4 as strong as all the love I. give my Father.
T-13.....X.13:6 I. thank the Father for your loveliness,
T-13.....X.14:8 Could I., then, lack faith in you and love
T-14.......II.5:7 I. said before, "Be not content with
T-14.......V.9:4 I. stand within the circle, calling you to
T-14.....X.12:4 Earlier I. said this course will teach you
T-15.....III.5:1 I. asked you earlier, "Would you be
T-15.....III.9:2 not for yourself alone, no more than I. did
T-15.....III.9:3 I. learned for you that you can learn of me
T-15.....III.9:4 I. would but teach you what is yours, so
T-15....III.10:2 I. will as my Father wills, knowing His
T-15....III.10:4 remembering that everything I. learned is
T-15....III.10:5 What my Father loves I. love as He does,
T-15....III.10:5 I. can no more accept it as what it is not,
T-15......IV.3:4 I. call you to fulfill your holy part in the
T-15......IV.5:1 I. stand within the holy instant, as clear
T-15......IV.5:3 I. call to you to make the holy instant
T-15.......V.1:7 Yet I. assure you that without the ego, all
T-15.....V.10:7 been told to offer miracles as I. direct, and
T-15......VI.2:3 I. offer you my perfect faith in you, in
T-15......VI.6:6 He offered it to me and I. accepted it. Fear
T-15......VI.6:7 will be denied you, for I. denied it not.
T-15.......X.1:8 gift I. can accept of you is the gift I gave to
T-15.......X.1:8 I can accept of you is the gift I. gave to you
T-15.......X.1:9 Release me as I. choose your own release.
T-15.......X.2:3 me, when only this I. choose to offer you?
T-15.......X.2:5 I. am as incapable of receiving sacrifice as
T-15.......X.2:7 limited acceptance of the gift I. offer you.
T-15.......X.3:4 is the only gift that I. was born to give.
T-15......XI.7:5 The lesson I. was born to teach, and still
T-15......XI.8:2 for so you offer me the love I. offer you.
T-15......XI.8:4 which I. give you that you may give it and
T-15....XI.10:2 I. have perfect faith in you to do all that
T-16.......I.6:4 I. have said that if a brother asks a foolish
T-16......III.2:2 free. I. said earlier, "By their fruits ye shall
T-16.......V.1:5 I. have spoken of this before, but there are
T-17....III.10:1 I. would enter into all your relationships,
T-17....III.10:5 truth that I. would interpose between you
T-17......IV.2:3 I. have said repeatedly that the Holy Spirit
T-18.......II.6:3 I. said before that the first change, before
T-18......III.4:2 Do you believe that I. would leave you in
T-18......III.5:5 I. hold your hand as surely as you agreed
T-18......III.5:6 for I. stand with you and walk with you in
T-18......III.6:6 I. not give you what you gave to me? For
T19. IV.A.16:4 And I. will join you there, as long ago I
T19. IV.A.16:4 as long ago I. promised and promise still.
T19. IV.A.16:5 new relationship am I. made welcome.
T19. IV.A.16:6 And where I. am made welcome, there I
T19. IV.A.16:6 where I am made welcome, there I. am.
T19. IV.A.17:1 I. am made welcome in the state of grace,
T19. IV.A.17:2 For I. became the symbol of your sin, and
T19. IV.A.17:2 sin, and so I. had to die instead of you. To
T19. IV.A.17:5 you. Yet would I. offer you my body, you
T19. IV.A.17:5 I offer you my body, you whom I. love,
T19. IV.A.17:6 I. teach that bodies cannot keep us apart?
T19....IV.B.3:2 is the message that I. gave them for you. It
T19....IV.B.5:3 your holy relationship I. am there already.
T19....IV.B.6:4 I. ask for your forgiveness, for if you are
T19....IV.B.6:4 for if you are guilty, so must I. be. But if I
T19....IV.B.6:5 But if I. surmounted guilt and overcame
T19....IV.B.6:6 that what I. signify to you you see within
T19....IV.B.8:1 punishment for what I. have not done. So
T19....IV.B.8:2 will you learn the freedom that I. taught
T19....IV.B.8:3 I. am within your holy relationship, yet
T19....IV.B.9:5 peace is homeless, so are you and so am I..
T19. IV.D.17:6 gift of freedom that I. gave the Holy Spirit
T19. IV.D.18:1 Free your brother here, as I. freed you.
T19. IV.D.18:3 See him as guiltless as I. look on you, and
T-20.........I.2:8 This Easter I. would have the gift of your
T-20.........I.4:3 I. was a stranger and you took me in, not
T-20.........I.4:3 you took me in, not knowing who I. was.
T-20.......II.4:1 I. have great need for lilies, for the Son of
T-20.......II.4:2 And can I. offer him forgiveness when he
T-20.......II.4:4 that I. may be forgiven and you may look
T-20.......II.6:3 I. cannot use your gift of lilies while you
T-20.......II.6:4 use what I. have given unless you share it.
T-20....III.10:7 And here would I. unite with you, my
T-20.....IV.7:6 of them outside than I. could leave you,
T-24.....IV.4:1 Earlier I. said consider not the means by
T-28.....IV.9:1 I. thank You, Father, knowing You will
T-31... VIII.7:1 Deny me not the little gift I. ask, when in
T-31... VIII.7:1 exchange I. lay before your feet the peace
T-31... VIII.8:2 I. ask for nothing but your own release.
T-31... VIII.8:4 eyes I. bring a vision of a different world,
T-31... VIII.9:5 God has ordained I. cannot call in vain,
T-31... VIII.9:5 in vain, and in His certainty I. rest content
T-31. VIII.10:1 I. thank You, Father, for these holy ones
T-31. VIII.10:3 I. am as sure that they will come to me as
T-31. VIII.10:4 be. They will accept the gift I. offer them,
T-31. VIII.10:5 And as I. would but do Your holy Will, so
T-31. VIII.10:6 And I. give thanks for them. Salvation's
T-31. VIII.11:4 I. give You thanks for what my brothers
W-pI.....70.9:4 I. assure you this will be no idle fantasy.
WpI...rV.in6:1 I. take the journey with you. For I share
WpI...rV.in6:2 For I. share your doubts and fears a little
WpI...rV.in6:4 I. must understand uncertainty and pain,
WpI...rV.in6:4 although I. know they have no meaning.
WpI...rV.in7:1 again each time I. lead a brother safely to
WpI...rV.in7:2 I. am renewed each time a brother learns
WpI...rV.in7:3 I. am reborn each time a brother's mind
WpI...rV.in7:4 I. have forgotten no one. Help me now to
WpI...rV.in8:1 again the thoughts I. brought to you from
WpI...rV.in8:6 It waits for you, as I. do. I am incomplete
WpI...rV.in8:7 I. am incomplete without your part in me.
WpI...rV.in8:8 as I. am made whole we go together to our
WpI...rV.in9:2 For this alone I. need; that you will hear
WpI...rV.in9:2 need; that you will hear the words I. speak
WpI...rV.in9:3 my hands through which I. save the world
WpI...rV.in9:4 from which I. call to you is but your own.
WpI...rV.in9:7 In him I. walk with you, and you with me.
WpI rVI.in.7:1 To Him I. offer this review for you. I place
WpI rVI.in.7:2 I. place you in His charge, and let Him
W-pII.....in.6:1 I. am so close to you we cannot fail.
W-pII..221.2:3 I. am sure that He will speak to you, and
W-pII..225.2:4 hand to me, and I. will never leave you.
W-pII..288.2:3 He cannot be less holy than can I., and
W-pII..310.2:1 We spend this day together, you and I..
W-pII..342.2:2 I. come to you to take you home with me.
W-pII....14.2:2 year we gave to God together, you and I.,
W-pII....14.2:3 with me, so what I. am are you as well.
W-ep .........4:1 And now I. place you in His hands, to be
W-ep .........6:8 that I. will never leave you comfortless.
M-29 .......7:11 In confidence I. place you in His Hands,
M-29 .......7:11 and I. give thanks for you that this is so.
M-29 .........8:7 *I. give thanks for you, And join your efforts*
C-5...........6:12 *He has sent to you to care for as I. care for you.*
P-2......... II.8:6 pupil, therapist and patient, you and I.,

**I** 2015
• noise word
*God*
*Christ*
*Holy Spirit*
*Jesus*

**ice** 1
W-pI...156.3:3 than the sun could choose to be of i.; the

**icy** 1
W-pI...200.1:3 and sense of i. hopelessness and doubt.

**idea** 603
T-1........VI.2:3 The i. of order of needs arose because,
T-1........VI.3:1 The i. of orders of need, which follows
T-3.........V.3:5 disagreeing with God's i. of your creation.
T-3.........V.4:8 i. of "changing your image" recognizes
T-3........VI.3:1 You have no i. of the tremendous release
T-3........VI.5:3 only because you cannot tolerate the i. of
T-3.....VII.6:10 the i. of an authority problem meaningful
T-4..........II.2:6 that the ego is only an i. and not a fact.
T-4.......II.4:10 loftiest i. of which ego thinking is capable.
T-4..........II.7:9 But the i. that this is possible is a decision
T-4........III.7:1 i. you ever had that opposes knowledge.
T-4........III.9:6 is meaningful only when the i. of "getting,
T-4.........V.3:3 since the i. of Him does dispel the ego.
T-5.........I.1:11 If you share an i., however, you do not
T-5..........I.2:4 *Everything is an i.. How, then, can giving*
T-5..........II.4:2 that you must let banish the i. of darkness
T-5.......II.10:6 very tired, because it is the i. of weariness.
T-5........III.2:1 The Holy Spirit is the i. of healing. Being
T-5........III.2:2 Being thought, the i. gains as it is shared.
T-5........III.2:3 the Call *for* God, it is also the i. *of* God.
T-5........III.2:4 are part of God it is also the i. of yourself,
T-5........III.2:5 i. of the Holy Spirit shares the property of
T-5........III.6:3 Eternity is an i. of God, so the Holy Spirit
T-5........III.8:9 the i. of danger has entered your mind.
T-5.......III.8:10 The i. itself is an appeal to the ego. The
T-5........IV.7:2 because, having received the i. of healing,
T-5.........V.3:8 ridiculous the i. of attacking God may be
T-6..........I.16:5 reinforces the i. that blame is justified.
T-6..........II.9:8 is not in perfect alignment with the i., and
T-6.......II.11:1 The ego can accept the i. that return is
T-6.......II.11:1 it can so easily make the i. seem difficult.
T-6.......II.11:3 *make* the i. of return both necessary and
T-6........III.1:1 every i. begins in the mind of the thinker.
T-6........III.4:6 An i. that you share you must have. It
T-7..........II.5:3 opposes the i. that differences in form are
T-7........III.3:4 i. of competition has entered their minds.
T-7........III.3:5 your need to be vigilant *against* this i.,
T-7.........V.5:8 the i. of exceptions seem to be meaningful
T-7........VI.8:9 the i. of conflict entirely and for all time.
T-7......VIII.3:6 The second error is the i. that you can get
T-7......VIII.7:3 thus dispelling the i. of separation and
T-7.........X.3:7 is the cause of the whole i. of sacrifice.
T-8.......VII.1:5 i. of attack would have no appeal for you.
T-8....VIII.1:14 The i. of part-whole relationships has
T-9.........IV.7:2 it, even though it has no i. what they are.
T-9.........IV.7:6 because it has no i. of what it perceives.
T-9.........IV.8:1 If you have no i. what is happening, how
T-10.......V.3:7 him out of your insanity, he is an insane i.
T-10.......V.3:8 be many different things he is but one i.;
T-11.......V.5:1 Every i. has a purpose, and its purpose is
T-11......V.10:3 countenance a false i. of independence,
T-12.......V.1:3 the i. of attack can enter your mind, you
T-13.........I.6:3 i. of guilt brings a belief in condemnation
T-13.........II.2:3 the guilt, but you have no i. why. On the
T-13.........II.2:5 Yet you have no i. that you are failing the
T-13.........II.3:3 murderous but insane i. lies hidden there,
T-13.......IX.5:3 i. that the guiltless Son of God can attack
T-13.....X.11:6 is true, you will have no i. what love is like
T-15......VI.4:4 however dimly, that God is an i., and so
T-15......VI.4:5 the fact that, like your Father, *you* are an i..
T-15......VI.5:3 instant you recognize the i. of love in you,
T-15......VI.5:3 unite this i. with the Mind that thought it,
T-15......VI.7:2 Join me in the i. of peace, for in ideas
T-15......VI.7:7 If you were not an i., and nothing but an
T-15......VI.7:7 were not an idea, and nothing but an i.,
T-15.....VII.6:1 is based on the i. that by sacrificing itself,
T-15......IX.6:1 no i. of all the loveliness that you could
T-15.........X.4:4 takes many forms, it is always the same i..
T-15.........X.5:3 as different manifestations of the same i.,
T-15.........X.5:4 i. is simply this: You believe it is possible
T-15.....X.5:10 If you would accept but this one i., your
T-15.....X.5:11 when the i. of sacrifice has been removed.
T-15.........X.6:7 for the one i. that hides behind them all;
T-15......XI.1:1 not to recognize the whole i. of sacrifice
T-15......XI.2:5 the whole i. of sacrifice loses all meaning.
T-16.........II.4:3 minds join as one and share one i. equally
T-16.......V.5:7 ego. This is its i. of Heaven. And therefore
T-17.........I.5:6 Reserve not one i. aside from truth, or
T-17.....IV.10:3 truth accept an i. so dangerous to truth,
T-17......VI.3:4 but you have no i. what should happen.
T-17.....VII.3:4 Some i. of bodies must have entered, for
T-17.....VII.7:1 that you have no i. how great the strength
T-18.........I.6:3 i. of loss is meaningless and only increase

T-18..... II.5:15 fixed and insane **i.** that you can change it.
T-18...... IV.7:3 to accept the **i.** that you need give so little,
T-18.... VI.12:3 a general **i.** without specific reference. Yet
T-18....VIII.1:5 within a body know yourself as an **i.**?
T-18....VIII.2:5 a little part of a glorious and complete **i.**.
T-18....VIII.6:3 ruled by an **i.** of separation from the rest.
T-19.........I.7:6 of an **i.** is never separate from its source.
T-19.........I.7:7 The **i.** of separation produced the body
T-19.......I.16:4 You can enslave a body, but an **i.** is free,
T-19....... II.2:1 an arrogance which the **i.** of error lacks.
T-19....... II.3:5 insanity inherent in the whole **i.** of sin, it
T-19....... II.5:2 **i.** of sin is wholly sacrosanct to its thought
T-19....... II.6:5 an **i.** of God to an ideal the ego wants; a
T-19....... II.7:1 defended than the **i.** that sin is real; the
T-19...... III.1:4 will suffer, and not let go of the **i.** of sin.
T-19...... III.1:6 Sin is an **i.** of evil that cannot be corrected
T19....IV.B.2:9 Here is the source of the **i.** that love is fear
T19....IV.B.9:1 the Holy Spirit the whole **i.** of sacrifice.
T19..IV.B.13:4 seeking it dutifully and obeying the **i.** that
T19..IV.B.13:5 this **i.** that underlies all of the ego's heavy
T19..IV.C.2:14 We know that an **i.** leaves not its source.
T19....IV.C.5:6 mad **i.** of corruption that can be corrected
T19....IV.C.5:7 has answered this insane **i.** with His Own;
T19..IV.C.11:4 truth or falsity of the **i.** which they reflect.
T-20...... VI.8:6 The instant that the mad **i.** of making
T-20...... VI.8:7 to house the mad **i.** and give it the illusion
T-20...... VI.8:9 mad **i.** against reality but for an instant?
T-21....... II.6:4 is an **i.** that it is possible that things could
T-21....... II.6:7 the mad **i.** you have enshrined upon your
T-21...... III.2:1 accepted the **i.** of making room for truth.
T-21....... V.4:1 realize the whole extent to which the **i.** of
T-22.........I.2:2 you. But still this strange **i.** which it does
T-22....... II.5:4 reason sees the source of an **i.** as what will
T-22....... II.5:5 This must be so, if the **i.** is like its source.
T-22....... II.9:3 It is the meaningless **i.** that thoughts can
T-22...... III.6:2 For the **i.** they represent left not its maker
T-22...... VI.2:3 chooses this has no **i.** of what is valuable.
T-23...... III.3:5 Let the **i.** of compromise but enter, and
T-23.... IV.1:12 and every one does violence to the **i.** of
T-24....... II.3:1 Specialness is the **i.** of sin made real. Sin
T-24.VII.10:10 does the body testify to the **i.** that made it
T-25...VII.12:1 the **i.** no one can lose for anyone to gain.
T-25....VIII.1:7 to the **i.** no one can lose for you to gain.
T-25..VIII.5:10 the **i.** of punishment that they lay it aside,
T-26.........I.1:1 "dynamics" of attack is sacrifice a key **i.**. It
T-26....... II.2:5 mistake; the whole **i.** that loss is possible,
T-26.....VII.2:3 gone as soon as the **i.** that brought it has
T-26...VII.13:3 that each **i.** the mind conceives but adds
T-26...VII.14:6 in its effects as is the whole **i.** of sacrifice.
T-26....VIII.6:9 advance. Nor is there really sense in this **i.**
T-26....... X.3:3 another form of the **i.** you are deprived by
T-27..... II.13:2 is. From an **i.** of self as two, there comes a
T-27...... III.1:8 does it join to the **i.** a something it is not,
T-27....VIII.6:2 where all is one, there crept a tiny, mad **i.**,
T-27....VIII.6:3 did the thought become a serious **i.**, and
T-29....... II.8:3 it be more than this lies the **i.** of sickness.
T-29...... IV.4:5 It is the **i.** that they exist from which the
T-29...... IV.5:2 No one can fail but your **i.** of him, and
T-29....VIII.3:4 is its form apart from the **i.** it represents.
T-29....VIII.6:2 **i.** there is a power past omnipotence, a
T-29....VIII.6:3 world of idols has been set by the **i.** this
T-30...... III.3:7 sin is the **i.** you are alone and separated
T-30.....VII.5:4 no thought of sacrifice apart from this **i.**.
T-30.....VII.5:5 **i.** of different goals that makes perception
W-in.......... 3:2 are planned around one central **i.**, which
W-in.......... 3:3 by which the **i.** for the day is to be applied
W-pI....... 1.1:1 this **i.** very specifically to whatever you see
W-pI....... 1.2:1 area, and apply the **i.** to a wider range:
W-pI....... 1.3:4 As you practice the **i.** for the day, use it
W-pI....... 1.3:7 as the application of the **i.** is concerned.
W-pI....... 2.1:1 exercises with this **i.** are the same as those
W-pI....... 2.1:2 apply the **i.** to whatever your glance rests
W-pI....... 2.1:5 and apply the **i.** to what was behind you.
W-pI....... 2.2:4 The sole criterion for applying the **i.** to
W-pI....... 3.1:1 this **i.** in the same way as the previous
W-pI....... 3.1:2 a proper subject for applying the **i.**. Be
W-pI....... 3.1:3 of anything for application of the **i.**. These
W-pI....... 3.2:2 to which the **i.** for the day is to be applied.
W-pI....... 4.1:1 exercises do not begin with the **i.** for the
W-pI....... 4.1:3 Then apply the **i.** to them. If you are
W-pI....... 4.1:4 thoughts, use them as subjects for the **i.**.
W-pI....... 4.2:1 subjects for the application of today's **i.**,
W-pI....... 4.4:1 for application of the **i.** for today, identify
W-pI....... 4.5:1 can also use the **i.** for a particular thought
W-pI....... 5.1:1 This **i.**, like the preceding one, can be
W-pI....... 5.1:6 day. Applying the same **i.** to each of them
W-pI....... 5.2:1 When using the **i.** for today for a specific
W-pI....... 5.6:1 to apply today's **i.** to some perceived
W-pI....... 5.7:2 Apply the **i.** for today to each of them,
W-pI....... 6.1:1 exercises with this **i.** are very similar to
W-pI....... 6.1:2 specifically for any application of the **i.**.
W-pI....... 6.2:1 Today's **i.** is useful for application to
W-pI....... 6.2:2 the application of the **i.** to each upsetting
W-pI....... 6.3:1 resist applying the **i.** to some upsetting
W-pI....... 7.1:1 **i.** is particularly difficult to believe at first.
W-pI....... 7.2:3 This first time **i.** is not really so strange as
W-pI....... 7.3:6 You would have no **i.** what this cup is,
W-pI....... 7.4:3 Acknowledge this by applying the **i.** for
W-pI....... 8.1:1 This **i.** is, of course, the reason why you
W-pI....... 8.6:3 emotion that the **i.** for today may induce,
W-pI....... 9.1:1 This **i.** obviously follows from the two
W-pI....... 9.2:2 This **i.** can be quite disturbing, and may
W-pI....... 9.3:1 the **i.** for the day to whatever you see,
W-pI..... 10.1:1 **i.** applies to all the thoughts of which you
W-pI..... 10.1:2 reason the **i.** is applicable to all of them is
W-pI..... 10.2:1 second time we have used this kind of **i.**.
W-pI..... 10.2:3 This time the **i.** is introduced with "My
W-pI..... 10.3:1 of the correction process began with the **i.**
W-pI..... 10.4:1 the **i.** for today quite slowly to yourself.
W-pI..... 10.4:3 ***i.*** *will help to release me from all that I now*
W-pI..... 10.5:4 the **i.** slowly before applying it specifically
W-pI..... 10.5:5 ***i.*** *will help to release me from all that I now*
W-pI..... 11.1:1 the first **i.** we have had that is related to a
W-pI..... 11.1:3 Today's **i.** introduces the concept that
W-pI..... 11.1:4 indeed to practice the **i.** in its initial form,
W-pI..... 11.1:4 for in this **i.** is your release made sure.
W-pI..... 11.2:1 The practice periods for today's **i.** are to
W-pI..... 11.2:2 closed, and repeat the **i.** slowly to yourself
W-pI..... 11.2:4 in using the **i.** merely repeat it to yourself,
W-pI..... 11.3:3 The introduction to this **i.**, in particular,
W-pI..... 11.3:5 repeat the **i.** once more slowly to yourself.
W-pI..... 12.1:1 importance of this **i.** lies in the fact that it
W-pI..... 12.4:1 today's **i.** to what you think is pleasant
W-pI..... 12.6:1 is enough for practicing the **i.** for today.
W-pI..... 13.1:1 Today's **i.** is really another form of the
W-pI..... 13.4:2 eyes closed, repeat today's **i.** to yourself.
W-pI..... 14.1:1 The **i.** for today is, of course, the reason
W-pI..... 14.2:3 **i.** unless you find them comfortable. If
W-pI..... 14.3:1 **i.** for today is another step in learning to
W-pI..... 14.5:1 of today's **i.** also include anything you are
W-pI..... 14.6:7 practice periods by repeating today's **i.**:
W-pI..... 14.7:1 The **i.** for today can, of course, be applied
W-pI..... 15.2:1 introductory **i.** to the process of image
W-pI..... 15.4:1 In practicing the **i.** for today, repeat it
W-pI..... 15.4:4 subjects for the application of today's **i.**. It
W-pI..... 15.4:5 subject while you repeat the **i.** to yourself.
W-pI..... 15.4:6 The **i.** should be repeated quite slowly
W-pI..... 15.5:1 to apply the **i.** to very many things during
W-pI..... 15.5:3 for today's **i.** unless you feel completely
W-pI..... 15.5:4 **i.** can be applied as needed throughout
W-pI..... 16.1:1 The **i.** for today is a beginning step in
W-pI..... 16.3:4 will practice this **i.** in many forms before
W-pI..... 16.4:1 In applying the **i.** for today, search your
W-pI..... 16.4:4 is a suitable subject for applying today's **i.**
W-pI..... 16.5:1 periods, first repeat the **i.** to yourself, and
W-pI..... 16.5:4 use today's **i.** whenever you are aware of a
W-pI..... 17.1:1 This **i.** is another step in the direction of
W-pI..... 17.2:1 In applying today's **i.**, say to yourself,
W-pI..... 18.1:1 **i.** for today is another step in learning
W-pI..... 18.1:2 emphasizes the **i.** that minds are joined,
W-pI..... 18.2:1 Today's **i.** does not refer to what you see
W-pI..... 18.3:1 of the **i.** for today as randomly as possible
W-pI..... 19.1:1 The **i.** for today is obviously the reason
W-pI..... 19.2:2 This is rarely a wholly welcome **i.** at first,
W-pI..... 19.2:4 Despite your initial resistance to this **i.**,
W-pI..... 19.3:2 The **i.** for today is to be repeated first, and
W-pI..... 19.5:1 the "as needed" application of today's **i.**,
W-pI..... 20.4:2 to see. Today's **i.** also tacitly implies the
W-pI .... 20.4:3 Therefore, as you repeat the **i.**, you are
W-pI .... 20.5:1 Repeat today's **i.** slowly and positively at
W-pI .... 21.1:1 **i.** for today is obviously a continuation
W-pI .... 21.1:2 in addition to applying the **i.** to particular
W-pI .... 21.2:1 begin by repeating the **i.** to yourself. Then
W-pI .... 22.1:1 Today's **i.** accurately describes the way
W-pI .... 23.1:1 The **i.** for today contains the only way out
W-pI .... 23.5:1 The **i.** for today introduces the thought
W-pI .... 23.6:1 periods are required in applying today's **i.**
W-pI .... 23.6:2 you, repeat the **i.** slowly to yourself first,
W-pI .... 24.2:3 The **i.** for today is a step toward opening
W-pI .... 24.4:1 should begin with repeating today's **i.**,
W-pI .... 24.5:1 In applying the **i.** for today, name each
W-pI .... 25.1:2 Today's **i.** explains why nothing you see
W-pI .... 25.5:3 The **i.** for today is a step in this direction.
W-pI .... 25.6:2 with a slow repetition of the **i.** for today,
W-pI .... 25.6:8 subject, and apply today's **i.** as before.
W-pI .... 26.3:1 The **i.** for today introduces the thought
W-pI .... 26.4:1 Practice with today's **i.** will help you to
W-pI .... 26.5:1 periods are required in applying today's **i.**
W-pI .... 26.6:1 begin with repeating the **i.** for today, then
W-pI .... 26.6:5 Today's **i.** should be applied as follows:
W-pI .... 26.9:3 repeating today's **i.** to yourself once more.
W-pI .... 27.1:1 Today's **i.** expresses something stronger
W-pI .... 27.1:3 You may feel hesitant about using the **i.**,
W-pI .... 27.1:5 the **i.** will be wholly true a little nearer.
W-pI .... 27.3:1 The **i.** for today needs many repetitions
W-pI .... 27.3:4 for using the **i.** when you wake or shortly
W-pI .... 27.4:2 much do you want today's **i.** to be true?
W-pI .... 27.4:6 while you were repeating today's **i.**, you
W-pI .... 28.1:1 specific application to the **i.** for yesterday.
W-pI .... 28.6:1 as a subject for applying the **i.** for today,
W-pI .... 28.7:1 in which the **i.** for the day is stated first,
W-pI .... 28.7:2 equal sincerity as today's **i.** is applied to it
W-pI .... 29.1:1 The **i.** for today explains why you can see
W-pI .... 29.1:4 it explains every **i.** we have used thus far,
W-pI .... 29.1:5 Today's **i.** is the whole basis for vision.
W-pI .... 29.2:1 this **i.** very difficult to grasp at this point.
W-pI .... 29.3:6 you will understand today's **i.** perfectly.
W-pI .... 29.4:1 Begin with repeating the **i.** to yourself,
W-pI .... 29.4:2 with today's **i.** because of its wholly alien
W-pI .. 29.5:10 the **i.** for today at least once an hour,
W-pI .... 30.1:1 **i.** for today is the springboard for vision.
W-pI .... 30.1:2 this **i.** will the world open up before you,
W-pI .... 30.3:1 Today's **i.** should be applied as often as
W-pI .... 30.3:2 and trying to realize that the **i.** applies to
W-pI .... 30.4:2 To help you begin to get used to this **i.**,
W-pI .... 30.4:2 can actually see, as you apply today's **i.**.
W-pI .... 30.5:3 become more accustomed to this **i.** as well
W-pI .... 30.5:3 applying today's **i.** with your eyes closed,
W-pI .... 30.5:4 Today's **i.** applies equally to both.
W-pI .... 31.1:1 Today's **i.** is the introduction to your
W-pI .... 31.1:2 the **i.** should be applied to both the world
W-pI .... 31.1:3 In applying the **i.**, we will use a form of
W-pI .... 31.1:4 you apply the **i.** on a more sustained basis
W-pI .... 31.1:4 applications of the **i.** throughout the day.
W-pI .... 31.2:1 practice with the **i.** for today are needed,
W-pI .... 31.2:3 while repeating the **i.** two or three times.
W-pI .... 31.2:4 and apply the same **i.** to your inner world.
W-pI .... 31.3:5 today's **i.** to yourself as often as you care
W-pI .... 31.4:1 repeat the **i.** for today as often as possible
W-pI .... 31.5:1 **i.** for today is also a particularly useful
W-pI .... 32.2:1 The **i.** for today, like the preceding ones,
W-pI .... 32.3:1 and evening by repeating the **i.** for today
W-pI .... 32.3:4 Repeat the **i.** for today unhurriedly as
W-pI .... 32.5:2 consist of repeating the **i.** slowly, as you
W-pI .... 32.6:1 The **i.** for today should also be applied
W-pI .... 32.6:2 you. Apply the **i.** by telling yourself: *I have*
W-pI .... 33.1:1 Today's **i.** is an attempt to recognize that
W-pI .... 33.1:3 the **i.** should be repeated as often as you
W-pI .... 33.2:2 as you repeat the **i.** throughout the day.
W-pI .... 33.3:2 Specific applications of today's **i.** should
W-pI .... 33.4:1 Remember to apply today's **i.** the instant
W-pI .... 33.4:2 and repeat the **i.** to yourself several times.
W-pI .... 34.1:1 The **i.** for today begins to describe the
W-pI .... 34.2:4 applications of today's **i.** should be made.
W-pI .... 34.3:3 repeating the **i.** for today slowly as you
W-pI .... 34.4:1 the **i.** to yourself in an unhurried manner,
W-pI .... 34.6:1 or worry, use the **i.** in its original form. If

## ideal 13



## ideally 2



## ideals 1



## ideas 151



## identical 5

## identification 31

*See also* body-identification, spirit-identification

T-4......II.8:2 to unite with them in a feeble attempt at **i.**
T-4......V.4:2 is the only **i.** with which the ego feels safe,
T-6......V.C.3:3 essentially the **i.** of what is more desirable
T-7......VI.9:2 **i.** with the Kingdom is totally beyond
T-7......VI.9:4 in **i.** at any level are not problems of fact.
T-7......VIII.4:7 The ego is a confusion in **i.**. Never having
T-7......VIII.7:3 and affirming your true **i.** with the whole
T-7......VIII.7:4 **i.** is as beyond doubt as it is beyond belief
T-7......IX.7:3 of both your proper **i.** with your brothers,
T-7......IX.7:3 that your **i.** is maintained by extension.
T-7......X.1:10 in your mind as part of your **i.** with His,
T-7......X.6:5 and your **i.** with His Will is not optional,
T-8......IV.8:5 your true **i.** with me and with the Father.
T-8......IV.8:6 Your **i.** is with the Father *and* with the Son.
T-8......V.1:1 be separated from your **i.** and be at peace
T-8......IX.7:2 not my name alone, for ours is a shared **i.**.
T-10......II.5:3 be what you are, it is an attack on your **i.**.
T-10......II.5:4 is thus the way in which your **i.** is lost,
T-11......IV.5:5 at all. Self-blame is therefore ego **i.**, and as
T-12......III.6:5 not perceive its source as his own ego **i.**,
T-12......III.7:5 your attempt to maintain your ego **i.**, for
T-12......III.7:5 for everyone believes that **i.** is salvation.
T-12......IV.2:2 And since it also teaches that it is your **i.**,
T-15......I.2:6 with it is due but to your **i.** with the ego,
T-19......I.7:7 it sick because of the mind's **i.** with it. You
T-19......I.7:8 your **i.** safe from the "attack" of truth.
T-19......I.8:1 your own **i.** has become because of it! You
W-pI......25.2:3 you. This false **i.** makes you incapable of
W-pI......50.2:2 things are cherished to ensure a body **i.**.
C-5......3:1 In his complete **i.** with the Christ–the
S-1......II.3:3 sense of **i.** has generally been reached, but

## identified 14

T-3......IV.2:2 is correctly **i.** as the domain of the ego.
T-4......V.4:8 has itself insisted that it is **i.** with the body
T-9......V.4:4 if the dreamer were also **i.** as unreal. Yet if
T-16......I.2:4 itself. Having **i.** with what it thinks it
T-18......VI.6:7 You have **i.** with this thing you hate, the
T-22......V.6:1 you have **i.** yourself with an illusion. And
W-pI......23.5:2 first, that the cause be **i.** and then let go,
W-pI......80.2:6 answer, because the problem has been **i.**.
W-pI.154.12:4 you have **i.** with Him and with His Own?
W-pI...166.6:2 No one but has **i.** with him, for everyone
W-pI...184.1:3 a separate entity, **i.** by its own name. By
M-22......5:3 to happen, he has **i.** with another's ego,
C-5......2:2 So he became **i.** with *Christ*, a man no
C-6......1:1 or became completely **i.** with the Christ,

## identifies 7

T-1......I.39:1 the Holy Spirit **i.** error as false or unreal.
T-4......V.3:4 the body, with which the ego **i.** so closely,
T-6......V.B.1:9 everyone **i.** himself with his thought
T-12......III.6:2 who **i.** with the ego feels deprived. What
W-pI......97.1:1 Today's idea **i.** you with your one Self. It
W-pI...183.1:3 his name, and thus **i.** the son with him.
C-5......2:4 and then **i.** them as what they are? Jesus

## identify 35

T-3......VI.9:5 does not depend on your ability to **i.** it, or
T-4......III.4:1 You who **i.** with your ego cannot believe
T-5......V.3:5 If you **i.** with the ego, you must perceive
T-6......V.B.5:2 If you **i.** with your thought system, and
T-6......V.C.7:1 allowing you to **i.** only with the center,
T-7......V.9:4 what you understand you can **i.** with, and
T-8......IV.8:4 not love him and you cannot **i.** with him.
T-9......V.3:6 they have done is merely to **i.** with the ego
T-12......III.6:1 To **i.** with the ego is to attack yourself
T-13......II.5:6 **i.** with it you must believe its goal is yours
T-15......I.4:1 is inescapable to those who **i.** with the ego
T-15...VII.10:4 the ego has, and as long as you **i.** with it,
T-18......VI.7:4 *are* joined, but you do not **i.** with them.
T-18...VIII.1:6 Everything you recognize you **i.** with
T-21......IV.4:7 And yet this part, with which you now **i.**,
T-21......VII.1:7 defense of those who do not **i.** with him.
T-23......I.1:6 Why else would you **i.** with it? Surely you
T-23......I.2:9 You may **i.** with this belief, but never will
T-24......V.3:4 **I.** with Him, and what has He that you
W-pI......4.4:1 **i.** each thought by the central figure or
W-pI......5.7:1 and try to **i.** a number of different forms
W-pI......35.7:3 **i.** the descriptive term or terms you feel
W-pI......38.4:3 **I.** the situation specifically, and also the
W-pI......49.2:5 Try to **i.** with the part of your mind where
W-pI......74.4:2 **i.** the particular person or persons and
W-pI...154.9:6 do you **i.** with Him and claim your own.
W-pI...155.9:4 may see something with which they can **i.**
W-pI...160.1:2 **I.** with fear, and you will be a stranger to
W-pII..250.2:4 *truly, that this day I may at last* **i.** *with him.*
W-pII......5.5:1 will **i.** with what you think will make you
W-pII......5.5:6 **I.** with love, and you are safe. Identify
W-pII......5.5:7 **I.** with love, and you are home. Identify
W-pII......5.5:8 are home. **I.** with love, and find your Self.
W-pII..261.1:1 I will **i.** with what I think is refuge and
W-pII..313.1:6 *Your holy Son, the Self with which I would* **i.**.

## identifying 8

T-6......V.C.6:3 is the condition for **i.** with the Kingdom,
T-7......VI.13:7 and **i.** itself with both its Creator and its
T-11......V.12:2 establish your autonomy by **i.** with Him,
T-13......I.10:4 for how else but by **i.** with the ego could
T-13......II.5:4 who you are, and **i.** with something else.
W-pI......17.1:1 in the direction of **i.** cause and effect as it
W-pI......23.7:4 stage of **i.** the cause of the world you see.
W-pII......5.1:4 **I.** with his safety, he regards himself as

## Identity 71

*identity*

T-7......IX.7:1 that you have never lost your **I.** and the
T-9......IV.1:6 Remember always that your **I.** is shared,
T-10......V.1:5 that to deny God is to deny their own **I.**,
T-14......X.12:4 what you are, restoring to you your **I.**. We
T-14......X.12:5 have already learned that this **I.** is shared.
T-14......X.12:7 your **I.** wherever It is not recognized, you
T-14......XI.7:5 It is impossible that God lose His **I.**, for if
T-14......XI.7:6 change Himself, for your **I.** is changeless.
T-18......VI.2:3 the awareness of Heaven and of your **I.**.
T-18......VI.3:4 in the mind, and let it not know its **I.**.
T-18....VI.10:2 yourself, to reach your shared **I.** together.
T-18....VI.11:9 this lasts you are not uncertain of your **I.**,
T-20...VIII.2:1 Do you not want to know your own **I.**?
T-21......V.7:3 Your **I.**, as much a true Effect of this same
T-27......II.12:3 And so your own **I.** is found. Yet must He
T-28......IV.3:2 himself, for your **I.** depends on his reality.
T-28......IV.8:3 To each He offers his **I.**, which the whole
T-28......V.3:5 it, you will not want to know your own **I.**,
T-29......V.2:2 For your **I.** abides in Them, and where
T-29......V.3:3 that abide in him, for your **I.** is there. The
W-pI......35.3:2 your Source it establishes your **I.**, and it
W-pI......62.2:3 are, having denied your **I.** by attacking
W-pI......77.1:5 It is merely a statement of your true **I.**. It
W-pI...123.4:2 God has willed to be our true **I.** in Him.
W-pI...124.1:1 we will again give thanks for our **I.** in God
W-pI...166.9:3 you thought was you may not be your **I.**.
W-pI...184.8:5 His true **I.** is hidden from you by what you
W-pI.184.10:2 you; the one **I.** which all things share; the
W-pI...191.2:3 see? Deny your own **I.**, and this is what
W-pI...191.3:1 Deny your own **I.**, and you will not
W-pI...191.3:2 God. Deny your own **I.**, and you assail the
W-pI...191.3:3 Deny your own **I.**, and look on evil, sin
W-pI...191.4:1 a game you play in which **I.** can be denied
W-pI...191.5:3 he who can accept his true **I.** is truly saved
W-pI.192.10:6 that you may accept him back as your **I.**.
W-pII..224.1:1 My true **I.** is so secure, so lofty, sinless,
W-pII..229.1:1 I seek my own **I.**, and find It in these
W-pII..229.1:5 attests the truth of the **I.** I sought to lose,
W-pII..229.2:1 *am; for keeping my* **I.** *untouched and sinless*
W-pII......2.2:5 itself, and thought its own **I.** was lost.
W-pII......252.h The Son of God is my **I.**.
W-pII..252.2:1 *Father, You know my true* **I.**. *Reveal It now*
W-pII..258.2:4 *You? What could we seek but our* **I.***?*
W-pII..260.1:5 *me. Let me remember my* **I.**. *And let my*
W-pII..260.2:1 and Therein we find our true **I.** at last.
W-pII.261.1:6 In Him is my **I.**. In Him is everlasting
W-pII.269.2:3 the Son of God; of Him Who is our own **I.**
W-pII.282.1:4 Son He loves, and Who remains my one **I.**
W-pII....283.h My true **I.** abides in You.
W-pII.283.1:8 *Is not Your Son my true* **I.***, when You created*
W-pII.283.2:1 Now are we One in shared **I.**, with God
W-pII.287.1:4 and keep that can compare with my **I.**?
W-pII.287.2:7 *recognize my Self, and be at one with my* **I.***?*
W-pII......8.5:4 us home, reminding us of our **I.** which our
W-pII.297.2:2 *eternal gifts, and thanks to You for my* **I.**.
W-pII.300.2:3 *to do to be restored to Heaven and our true* **I.**
W-pII......9.4:3 In this equality is Christ restored as one **I.**,
W-pII.309.2:3 *altar to my Self, and there I find my true* **I.**.
W-pII...10.3:2 happiness, and union with your own **I.**.
W-pII.330.1:6 Let us choose today that He be our **I.**, and
W-pII.330.2:2 *but fail to know our one* **I.** *we share with You.*
W-pII.352.1:9 *For I would love my own* **I.***, and find in It the*
W-pII.353.1:5 *Then I lose myself in my* **I.***, and recognize*
W-pII.355.1:7 *It is You I choose, and my* **I.** *along with You.*
M-13......2:9 obscuring its **I.** and losing sight of what it
M-26......2:1 and remembering their own **I.** perfectly.
C-5......1:2 circumscribed by false beliefs of your **I.**,
S-1......II.2:2 is sure of his **I.** could pray in these forms.
S-1......II.2:3 of his **I.** can avoid praying in this way.
S-1......II.4:6 lose the recognition of your own **I.**. Be
S-1......II.7:5 lack. **I.** in Christ is fully recognized as set

## identity 20

*Identity*

T-21......IV.3:4 from their belief that their **i.** lies in the ego
T-26......I.2:5 they joined each one would lose its own **i.**,
T-26......I.3:2 incomplete to keep its own **i.** intact. In
T-26...VII.11:8 would sacrifice his own **i.** with everything,
T-27......II.10:6 **I.** and function are the same, and by your
T-27......II.11:1 a split mind, **i.** must seem to be divided.
T-27......II.11:6 would mean a shared **i.** with but one end.
T-28......IV.1:8 both become illusions, and without **i.**.
T-28......IV.2:2 form they take, for you will lose **i.** in them
T-28......IV.5:4 **I.** in dreams is meaningless because the
T-29......IX.2:9 evil dreams, where idols are your "true" **i.**,
T-31....VIII.6:5 own **i.** as you will see it and believe it is.
W-pI......44.5:6 eyes, it is loss of **i.** and a descent into hell.
W-pI......97.1:2 It accepts no split **i.**, nor tries to weave
W-pI......97.1:5 madness, letting go illusions of a split **i.**.
W-pI...136.8:4 Thus is your "true" **i.** preserved, and the
W-pI.136.19:2 a bodily **i.** which will attack the body, for
W-pI...183.1:4 in a bond to which they turn for their **i.**.
M-7......6:2 Self, and thus represents a confusion in **i.**.
M-13......3:6 self-condemnation is a decision about **i.**,

## idle 42

T-2......VI.9:13 it. There *are* no **i.** thoughts. All thinking
T-7......X.6:5 God. His Will is not an **i.** wish, and your
T-11......V.5:5 is between the ego's **i.** wishes and the Will
T-13......X.4:8 you impose your **i.** wishes on the present,
T-20......II.6:5 it. The Holy Spirit's vision is no **i.** gift, no
T-20....VIII.7:1 the senseless means to play the **i.** game of
T-21......II.5:1 is but the **i.** witness that you were right.
T-27......VII.8:7 conceived within the **i.** dreaming of the
T-27...VII.13:3 than an **i.** dream has terrified God's Son,
T-27....VIII.9:7 holy Son of God, behold your **i.** dream, in
T-30......IV.7:5 strength of **i.** wishes for the Will of God.
W-pI......16.2:1 concept than that of "**i.** thoughts." What
W-pI......16.2:2 of a whole world can hardly be called **i.**.
W-pI......16.3:1 recognizing that thoughts are never **i.**,
W-pI......41.6:5 past all the **i.** thoughts of the world. Try
W-pI......45.8:7 to remind yourself that this is no **i.** game,
W-pI......50.5:3 Let no **i.** and foolish thoughts enter to
W-pI......63.2:5 is no **i.** request that is being asked of you.
W-pI......65.6:2 to catch a few of the **i.** thoughts that
W-pI......70.9:4 And I assure you this will be no **i.** fantasy.
W-pI......73.1:2 This is not the same as the ego's **i.** wishes,
W-pI......73.1:4 it. The ego's **i.** wishes are unshared, and
W-pI......73.1:5 Its wishes are not **i.** in the sense that they
W-pI......73.1:6 But they are **i.** indeed in terms of creation.
W-pI......73.2:1 **I.** wishes and grievances are partners or
W-pI......73.4:5 The ego's **i.** wishes have been withdrawn.

| | |
|---|---|
| W-pI.....73.8:2 | No **i.** wishes can detain us, nor deceive us |
| W-pI.....73.9:4 | of God from hell and from all **i.** wishes. |
| W-pI.....86.1:6 | I will undertake no more **i.** seeking. Only |
| W-pI.....92.9:1 | so you do not dwell on **i.** shadows that the |
| W-pI.....93.3:1 | which such **i.** thoughts are meaningless. |
| W-pI...104.1:1 | that joy and peace are not but **i.** dreams. |
| W-pI...127.9:4 | will shine through your **i.** thoughts today, |
| W-pI.132.14:1 | all the **i.** thoughts we ever held about it, |
| W-pI...140.5:1 | been cured in God, and not in **i.** dreams. |
| W-pI...151.7:3 | He passes by such **i.** witnesses, which |
| W-pI.151.11:1 | those aspects which reflect but **i.** dreams. |
| W-pI...153.4:2 | hope of sanity seems but to be an **i.** dream |
| W-pI...185.7:3 | This is no **i.** wish. These words do not |
| W-pI...190.7:5 | Your **i.** wishes represent its pains. Your |
| WpI rVI.in.5:2 | Permit no **i.** thought to go unchallenged. |
| W-pII .309.2:1 | *is my sure release from* **i.** *dreams of sin. Your* |

## idly 8

| | |
|---|---|
| T-16....... II.9:5 | forces, to be used and not held **i.** by. They |
| T-24.....in.1:12 | illusion that **i.** seems to drift between |
| T-26...VII.13:4 | of what is **i.** wished as what is truly willed, |
| T-27...... III.3:8 | to its seeing be perceived as **i.** spent, a |
| T-27....VIII.4:2 | And so you wander **i.** in and out of places |
| T-28....VII.4:3 | Nor is it **i.** blamed for what it did not do. |
| T-30....... V.1:4 | No rules are **i.** set, and no demands are |
| WpIrIII.in10:1 | **i.** by between your longer practice periods |

## idol 58

| | |
|---|---|
| T-7......... V.9:2 | or an **i.** that you may worship out of fear, |
| T-10...... III.4:1 | is sick is to worship the same **i.** he does. |
| T-10...... III.4:6 | A sick god must be an **i.**, made in the |
| T-10...... III.4:8 | Is this the **i.** you would worship? Is this |
| T-10...... III.5:3 | protect an **i.** you think will save you from |
| T-16..... V.13:3 | For every **i.** that you raise to place before |
| T-20.... VI.11:1 | The body is the ego's **i.**; the belief in sin |
| T-24...... III.2:6 | **i.** that seems to give you power has taken |
| T-24...... III.2:7 | misery, before the **i.** that can save you not |
| T-29.....VII.1:2 | fail, and you will weep each time an **i.** falls |
| T-29.....VII.1:4 | Each **i.** that you worship when God calls |
| T-29.....VII.3:2 | understand the **i.** that he seeks *is* but his |
| T-29.....VII.3:5 | This is the purpose every **i.** has, for this |
| T-29.....VII.5:3 | than an **i.** found that represents a parody |
| T-29.....VII.6:4 | No **i.** takes His place. Look not to idols. |
| T-29.....VII.9:8 | But you have made of your reality an **i.**, |
| T-29.....VII.9:9 | the means by which this **i.** can be saved. |
| T-29...VII.10:4 | An **i.** cannot take the place of God. Let |
| T-29....VIII.1:1 | What is an **i.**? Do you think you know? |
| T-29....VIII.1:6 | An **i.** is an image of your brother that you |
| T-29....VIII.3:1 | An **i.** is a false impression, or a false belief |
| T-29....VIII.3:2 | An **i.** is a wish, made tangible and given |
| T-29....VIII.5:1 | is an **i.**? Nothing! It must be believed |
| T-29....VIII.6:1 | An **i.** is established by belief, and when it |
| T-29....VIII.6:1 | and when it is withdrawn the **i.** "dies." |
| T-29....VIII.7:1 | Where is an **i.**? Nowhere! Can there be a |
| T-29....VIII.7:5 | **i.** is beyond where God has set all things |
| T-29....VIII.7:6 | Nothing and nowhere must an **i.** be, while |
| T-29....VIII.8:1 | What purpose has an **i.**, then? What is it |
| T-29....VIII.8:9 | But more of something is an **i.** for. And |
| T-29..VIII.8:12 | An **i.** is a means for getting more. And it |
| T-29..VIII.9:10 | No **i.** can establish you as more than God. |
| T-29...... IX.3:3 | an **i.** keep the dream alive and terrible, for |
| T-29...... IX.3:4 | And this the **i.** represents, and so its |
| T-29...... IX.9:1 | goes with you,–be sure you made an **i.**, |
| T-30...... III.2:4 | What **i.** can make two of what is one? |
| T-30...... III.2:6 | You do not want an **i.**. It is not your will |
| T-30.... III.2:10 | So you see your will within the **i.**, thus |
| T-30...... III.3:1 | every **i.** lies the yearning for completion. |
| T-30...... III.3:5 | This is the purpose of an **i.**; that you will |
| T-30...... III.4:1 | It never is the **i.** that you want. But what |
| T-30.... III.4:10 | What **i.** can be called upon to give the Son |
| T-30...... III.5:6 | What **i.** can he need to be himself? For |
| T-30.... III.11:7 | **i.** *or* the Thought God holds of you is your |
| T-30...... IV.6:4 | not want whatever you believe an **i.** gives. |
| T-30....... V.7:2 | and think they see an **i.** that they want. |
| T-30..... V.10:2 | And when an **i.** tempts you, think of this: |
| T-30..... V.10:3 | *never was a time an* **i.** *brought you anything* |
| T-30..... V.10:6 | And do not choose an **i.** thoughtlessly, |
| T-30..... VI.7:6 | within and find escape from every **i.** there |
| T-30 ... VI.10:3 | see as having power to make an **i.** of the |
| T-31 ...... V.2:3 | It is an **i.**, made to take the place of your |
| T-31 ...... V.4:4 | "reality" is set, to see to it the **i.** lasts. |
| W-pI..... 92.4:7 | weakness is an **i.** falsely worshipped and |
| W-pI... 163.4:2 | perceived within an **i.** made of dust. Here |
| W-pI... 170.8:3 | You make a choice, standing before this **i.** |
| W-pI... 170.8:5 | Or will you make another **i.** to replace it? |
| S-3........ IV.3:4 | nor accept an **i.** for rememberance of Him |

## idolater 2

| | |
|---|---|
| T-20 ..... VI.6:2 | love. It is the home of the **i.**, and of love's |
| T-20 ..... VI.7:7 | You are an **i.** no longer. The Holy Spirit's |

## idolaters 2

| | |
|---|---|
| T-10 ..... III.6:1 | There are no **i.** in the Kingdom, but there |
| T-20 ..... VI.7:1 | **I.** will always be afraid of love, for |

## idolatrous 1

| | |
|---|---|
| T-10 ..... III.7:6 | A whole mind is not **i.**, and does not |

## idolatry 11

| | |
|---|---|
| T-10 ..... III.4:2 | God created love, not **i.**. All forms of |
| T-10 ..... III.4:3 | All forms of **i.** are caricatures of creation, |
| T-10 ..... III.4:4 | Sickness is **i.**, because it is the belief that |
| T-20 ..... VI.2:4 | body enters is based not on love, but on **i.** |
| T-20 ..... VI.5:4 | its brothers, holding them here in its **i.**. |
| T-20 ... VI.11:6 | his choice again between **i.** and love. Here |
| T-20 ... VI.12:7 | **I.** is past and meaningless. Perhaps you |
| T-30 ...... V.4:4 | because its purpose is forgiveness, not **i.**. |
| T-30 ..... VI.6:1 | no surer proof **i.** is what you wish than a |
| W-pII . 277.2:1 | nor believe in any law **i.** would make to |
| W-pII ... 12.1:1 | ego is **i.**; the sign of limited and separated |

## idols 98

| | |
|---|---|
| T-10 ............h | THE **I.** OF SICKNESS |
| T-10 ..... III.1:7 | those who make **i.** do worship them. The |
| T-10 ..... III.1:8 | The **i.** are nothing, but their worshippers |
| T-10 ..... III.6:2 | God's Son knows no **i.**, but he does know |
| T-10 ..... IV.6:1 | the making of **i.** becomes inconceivable. |
| T-20 ..... VI.3:1 | But **i.** do not share. Idols accept, but |
| T-20 ..... VI.3:2 | **I.** accept, but never make return. They |
| T-20 ..... VI.4:5 | for the offerings on which its **i.** thrive. The |
| T-20 ..... VI.4:7 | bodies as it can collect to place its **i.** in, |
| T-20 ..... VI.6:4 | Even the **i.** that are worshipped here are |
| T-20 ..... VI.9:1 | **I.** must disappear, and leave no trace |
| T-20 ... VI.11:4 | his devotion to death's **i.** and then pass on |
| T-21 .......II.7:3 | you have set up your **i.** to something else. |
| T-29 .... VII.3:1 | will impel him to seek out a thousand **i.**, |
| T-29 .... VII.5:1 | **I.** must fall *because* they have no life, and |
| T-29 .... VII.6:1 | All **i.** of this world were made to keep the |
| T-29 .... VII.6:2 | is vain to worship **i.** in the hope of peace. |
| T-29 .... VII.6:5 | place. Look not to **i.**. Do not seek outside |
| T-29 .... VII.7:2 | depressing dreams, in which all **i.** fail you, |
| T-29 .... VII.8:3 | in it a place of **i.** found outside yourself, |
| T-29 .... VII.8:5 | Your **i.** do what you would have them do, |
| T-29 .... VII.9:4 | And speed the end of **i.** in a world made |
| T-29 .... VII.9:4 | world made sad and sick by seeing **i.** there |
| T-29 .... VII.9:5 | unto God, and where He is no **i.** can abide |
| T-29 .... VII.9:6 | The fear of God is but the fear of loss of **i.**. |
| T-29 .. VII.10:5 | in chants of deep despair to **i.** of yourself. |
| T-29 ...VIII.1:3 | For **i.** are unrecognized as such, and never |
| T-29 ...VIII.1:7 | **I.** are made that he may be replaced, no |
| T-29 ...VIII.2:2 | **I.** are but substitutes for your reality. In |
| T-29 ...VIII.2:5 | have. No one believes in **i.** who has not |
| T-29 ...VIII.4:1 | world of **i.** *is* a veil across the face of Christ, |
| T-29 ...VIII.6:3 | Here the world of **i.** has been set by the |
| T-29 ...VIII.8:4 | The world believes in **i.**. No one comes |
| T-29 ...VIII.8:6 | Each worshipper of **i.** harbors hope his |
| T-29 ...VIII.9:3 | laugh, if **i.** could intrude upon his peace. |
| T-29 ...VIII.9:4 | and tells you **i.** have no purpose here. For |
| T-29 ...VIII.9:6 | seek for **i.** that would make of Heaven less |
| T-29 ..... IX.1:1 | slave of **i.** is a willing slave. For willing he |
| T-29 ..... IX.1:3 | and look to **i.** that they raise him up? |
| T-29 ..... IX.2:7 | not, for he who judges will have need of **i.**, |
| T-29 ..... IX.2:9 | dreams, where **i.** are your "true" identity, |
| T-29 ..... IX.3:1 | All figures in the dream are **i.**, made to |
| T-29 ..... IX.3:7 | condemned; and wish to be the slave of **i.**, |
| T-29 ..... IX.4:2 | For **i.** must be part of it, to save you from |
| T-29 ..... IX.4:4 | **i.** are the toys you dream you play with. |
| T-29 ..... IX.7:3 | They are not seen as **i.** which betray. It is a |
| T-29 ..... IX.9:3 | to the frantic search for **i.** and for death. |
| T-29 ... IX.10:2 | not another try to worship **i.** and to keep |
| T-30 ......I.14:8 | For they are made with **i.** or with God. |
| T-30 ........ III.h | Beyond All **I.** |
| T-30 ..... III.1:1 | **I.** are quite specific. But your will is |
| T-30 ..... III.1:4 | **I.** are limits. They are the belief that there |
| T-30 ..... III.1:9 | Decide for **i.** and you ask for loss. Decide |
| T-30 ..... III.5:3 | all **i.** stands his holy will to be but what he |
| T-30 ..... III.9:5 | seek for **i.** cannot know the star is there. |
| T-30 ... III.10:1 | Beyond all **i.** is the Thought God holds of |
| T-30 ... III.10:4 | unaware of all the world that worships **i.**, |
| T-30 ... III.11:8 | that **i.** must keep hidden what you are, |
| T-30 ..... IV.1:5 | And this you knew when you made **i.**. |
| T-30 ..... IV.1:8 | All **i.** are the false ideas you made to fill |
| T-30 ..... IV.5:9 | they are **i.** which but dance to vain desires |
| T-30 ... IV.5:13 | His **i.** do not threaten him at all. His one |
| T-30 ..... IV.6:5 | the Son of God declares that he is free of **i.** |
| T-30 .......V.1:3 | is perceived and takes the place of **i.**, |
| T-30 .......V.2:4 | And **i.** are not wanted there, for guilt is |
| T-30 .......V.5:2 | the mind has learned how easily do **i.** go |
| T-30 .......V.5:3 | that **i.** are nothing and nowhere, and are |
| T-30 .......V.7:3 | surely set away from **i.** toward reality. For |
| T-30 ..... VI.6:2 | means that you prefer to keep some **i.**, |
| T-30 ..... VI.6:2 | and are not prepared, as yet, to let all **i.** go |
| T-30 ... VIII.3:3 | some forms of **i.** have a powerful appeal |
| T-31 .....V.7:10 | They are ideas of **i.**, painted with the |
| W-pI .... 50.4:7 | declaration of release from the belief in **i.**. |
| W-pI .... 58.3:6 | I share with God Himself, all **i.** vanish. |
| W-pI .... 61.1:5 | with which you have endowed your **i.**. It |
| W-pI .... 70.9:1 | in the clouds, looking vainly for **i.** there, |
| W-pI .... 84.1:6 | I will worship no **i.**, nor raise my own self- |
| W-pI .... 93.2:3 | and have bowed down to **i.** made of dust, |
| W-pI .... 93.9:5 | by hiding Its majesty behind the tiny **i.** of |
| W-pI .... 94.4:1 | except to lay all **i.** and self-images aside; |
| W-pI 110.10:2 | be your Savior from all **i.** you have made. |
| W-pI 110.10:3 | will understand how worthless are your **i.** |
| W-pI 110.10:4 | a great advance to truth by letting **i.** go, |
| W-pI .. 163.4:1 | Would you bow down to **i.** such as this? |
| W-pI 170.12:4 | You have chosen Him in place of **i.**, and |
| W-pI .. 183.7:3 | with names of **i.** cherished by the world. |
| W-pI 200.11:1 | Today we seek no **i.**. Peace can not be |
| W-pII . 261.2:1 | *Let me not seek for* **i.**. *I would come, my* |
| W-pII . 277.2:1 | Let us not worship **i.**, nor believe in any |
| W-pII . 283.1:3 | *Let me not worship* **i.**. *I am he my Father* |
| W-pII . 314.1:3 | it, so that fear has lost its **i.** and its images |
| M-28 ......... 2:5 | welcomed. **I.** have disappeared, and the |
| C-5 ............ 5:7 | is. Some bitter **i.** have been made of him |
| S-1.........in.3:1 | you, dispense with **i.** and remember Him. |
| S-1...........I.1:5 | to pray for **i.** and hope to reach God. True |
| S-1..........V.2:3 | no goal but God because they need no **i.**, |
| S-3........ III.1:8 | **i.** have arisen to obscure the unity that is |
| S-3........ III.6:6 | has entered now where **i.** used to stand, |

## i.e. 1

| | |
|---|---|
| C-1 ............ 1:2 | God or Christ (**i. e.**, the Mind of God or |

## if 1560

## ignorance 11

| | |
|---|---|
| T-14 ..... VI.1:1 | of dark for light, of **i.** for understanding. |
| T-14 ..... VI.1:3 | and in **i.** that you perceive the frightening, |
| T-14 ..... VI.3:5 | As guardians of darkness and of **i.** look to |
| T-14 .... VII.1:2 | or darkness, knowledge or **i.** are yours, |
| T-14 .... VII.1:6 | so **i.** fades away when knowledge dawns. |
| T-14 .... VII.1:7 | by which **i.** is brought to knowledge. Yet |
| T-14 .... VII.1:8 | it becomes the messenger of **i.** rather than |
| T-14 .... VII.5:2 | go. Truth does not struggle against **i.**, and |
| T-31 ..... VI.3:8 | of **i.** is drawn across the evil and the good, |
| W-pI .. 151.1:3 | merely an opinion based on **i.** and doubt. |

M-29..........4:8 Yet, despite its obvious and complete i.,

### ignorant 1

W-pI...186.6:4 You are not i. and helpless. Sin can not

### ill 4

T-28......III.4:3 seeds of pestilence and every form of i.,
W-pI.136.17:3 will be no sense of feeling i. or feeling well
W-pI...190.5:5 that has the power to make you i. or sad,
W-pII..281.1:4 *If ever I am sad or hurt or i., I have forgotten*

### illness 27

T-2........I.5:10 I. is some form of external searching.
T-2........IV.2:7 Physical i. represents a belief in magic.
T-2........IV.4:2 believing that the body makes its own i..
T-2........IV.4:5 Sometimes the i. has a sufficiently strong
T-5.........V.5:3 sane mind cannot conceive of i. because it
T-5.........V.5:4 I said before that i. is a form of magic. It
T-8.....VII.11:3 it, will induce i. by fostering separation.
T-8.....VII.11:4 as a separate entity cannot but foster i.,
T-8.....VII.12:8 This arrest is the cause of all i., because
W-pI.....14.5:4 do not say, "God did not create i.," but,
W-pI.....56.1:3 Pain, i., loss, age and death seem to
P-2...........IV.h The Process of I.
P-2........IV.1:1 is psychotherapy, so all i. is mental illness
P-2........IV.1:1 is psychotherapy, so all illness is mental i.
P-2........IV.1:6 can i. be except an expression of sorrow
P-2........IV.2:1 Son is seen as guilty, i. becomes inevitable
P-2........IV.2:3 all who ask for i. have now condemned
P-2........IV.2:3 their faith is in the i. and not in salvation.
P-2........IV.2:6 I. can be but guilt's shadow, grotesque
P-2........IV.5:1 may recognize the mind as the source of i.
P-2........IV.5:4 temporary, or another i. rise instead, for
P-2........IV.6:1 I. of any kind may be defined as the
P-2........IV.7:1 I. is therefore a mistake and needs
P-2........IV.7:3 i. is real it cannot be overlooked in truth,
P-2........IV.8:1 is insanity because all sickness is mental i.
P-2........IV.8:2 real is the belief that i. varies in intensity;
S-3.........II.6:1 leaving the cause of i. still unchanged,

### ills 5

T-2........IV.4:1 i. are restatements of magic principles.
W-pI.....41.2:1 they believe to be "the i. of the world."
W-pI.140.10:2 of healing, which will cure all i. as one,
M-13..........4:5 its i. looks back on it with condemnation.
P-2........IV.4:3 the i. with which their minds endow it.

### illuminate 1

T-14......XI.3:9 at all in darkness to i. your understanding

### illuminated 1

T-2.........V.6:4 Spirit is already i. and the body in itself is

### illuminates 1

T-2...........I.4:9 knowledge that i. not only sets you free,

### illumination 2

T-2.........V.6:3 Only the mind is capable of i.. Spirit is
T-2.........V.6:5 can bring its i. to the body by recognizing

### illusion 335

T-1.........V.6:4 The i. that shallow roots can be deepened
T-1...........VI.h The I. of Needs
T-4............V.h The Ego-Body I.
T-4........VI.3:4 through pain, because pain is an ego i.,
T-4.......VII.1:1 of any particular ego i. does not matter,
T-6.......V.C.9:2 Everything outside the Kingdom is i..
T-7.......V.10:8 Would I try to share an i. with the most
T-7......VIII.4:1 perpetuate an i. about another without
T-8........IV.2:3 is therefore an i. of isolation, maintained
T-8........IV.2:3 by fear of the same loneliness that *is* its i..
T-8........IV.2:7 maintain the i. of loneliness if you are not
T-8........VI.2:7 from yourself but from your i. of yourself.
T-9...........I.7:5 it is, and this gives you the i. of safety. Yet
T-9... VIII.2:10 it offers you the i. of attack as a "solution.
T-10......III.7:2 The acceptance of peace is the denial of i.,
T-10......III.7:2 the denial of illusion, and sickness *is* an i..
T-11.....VII.3:4 to the real, thus confusing i. and reality.
T-11.....VII.3:6 If you believe in truth and i., you cannot
T-12.....VII.7:9 This gives it an i. of integrity, and enables
T-13..........I.5:5 only a matter of time, and time is but an i.
T-13......III.6:3 fundamental i. on which the others rest.
T-13......IV.6:5 Unless you learn that past pain is an i.,
T-13.......X.1:3 by the i. that the source of guilt, from
T-13.....X.12:1 No i. that you have ever held against him
T-14......III.4:4 are no alternatives except truth and i..
T-14......VI.2:5 of i. out of nothing are now afraid of them
T-14......IX.1:4 Bringing i. to truth, or the ego to God, is
T-14......IX.1:8 past, and the present was dedicated to i..
T-15........I.10:5 Change is an i., taught by those who
T-15...VII.12:1 The i. of the autonomy of the body and
T-16...III.4:10 seeming conflict between truth and i. can
T-16...III.4:10 yourself from the i. and not from truth.
T-16.........IV.h The I. and the Reality of Love
T-16......IV.2:6 For the i. of love will never satisfy, but its
T-16......IV.3:6 but it is still held together by the i. of love.
T-16......IV.3:7 If the i. goes, the relationship is broken or
T-16......IV.4:1 Love is not an i.. It is a fact. Where
T-16......IV.4:4 For hate *is* an i., and what can change was
T-16......IV.4:9 love relationship loses the i. that it is what
T-16......IV.5:3 i. of love can triumph over the illusion of
T-16......IV.5:3 of love can triumph over the i. of hate,
T-16......IV.5:4 As long as the i. of hatred lasts, so long
T-16......IV.5:4 lasts, so long will love be an i. to you. And
T-16......IV.5:5 remaining possible is which i. you prefer.
T-16......IV.5:6 conflict in the choice between truth and i.
T-16......IV.6:3 Every i. is one of fear, whatever form it
T-16......IV.6:4 escape from one i. into another must fail.
T-16......IV.6:6 peace will never come from the i. of love,
T-16......IV.7:1 is to be distinguished from i.: The special
T-16......IV.7:4 How but in i. could this be done? It is
T-16......IV.8:4 what makes you whole in truth, not in i..
T-16......IV.9:4 Seek not for this in the bleak world of i.,
T-16....IV.10:2 His. Every i. you accept into your mind by
T-16....IV.10:4 unwilling to settle for i. in place of truth.
T-16....IV.11:8 He loves you, wholly without i., as you
T-16....IV.11:9 For love *is* wholly without i., and therefore
T-16.......V.3:8 the i. of love is accepted in love's place,
T-16.......V.8:4 not interfere with the ego's i. of Heaven,
T-16.......V.8:5 the i. of Heaven is nothing more than an
T-16.......V.9:4 is to destroy reality and substitute i.. For
T-16.......V.9:5 the ego is itself an i., and only illusions
T-16.....V.14:3 the simple choice between truth and i.;
T-16.....V.15:1 core of the separation i. lies simply in the
T-16.....V.16:1 it is but the choice between truth and i..
T-16.....V.16:2 separated from i. and not confused with it
T-16......VI.7:7 Without this i. there could be no meaning
T-16......VI.8:7 long find even the i. of love in any special
T-16....VI.10:2 to the i. of the beauty and holiness of guilt
T-16....VI.10:5 See no i. of truth and beauty there. And
T-16...VII.2:11 that you are maintaining the i. that it has
T-16.....VII.5:2 the i. of love is not profoundly shaken.
T-16.....VII.7:1 between your experience of truth and i..
T-16...VII.10:1 you always choose between truth and i.;
T-17..........I.1:6 what they are *because* of their i. of reality.
T-17..........I.4:1 so long will the i. of an order of difficulty
T-17..........I.5:2 Truth *has* no meaning in i.. The frame of
T-17......III.8:4 is referred for meaning is an *i.* of the past,
T-17......III.9:1 you to choose to join with truth or with i..
T-17......III.9:4 or the world of guilt and fear, truth or i.,
T-17......IV.2:7 because of the i. that they are different.
T-17......VI.7:6 solutions bring but the i. of experience,
T-17......VI.7:6 and the i. of peace is not the condition in
T-17.....VII.5:5 it. Faithlessness is the servant of i., and
T-17.....VII.5:9 Accept not the i. of peace it offers, but
T-17.....VII.5:9 look upon its offering and recognize it *is* i..
T-17.....VII.6:1 goal of i. is as closely tied to faithlessness
T-18..........I.4:2 it was the substitution of i. for truth; of
T-18..........I.4:4 That one error, which brought truth to i.,
T-18........II.4:4 instant the i. of satisfaction is invaded by
T-18........II.4:4 satisfaction is invaded by the i. of terror.
T-18........II.5:6 and the i. of satisfaction would be gone.
T-18......III.1:1 have spent your life in bringing truth to i.,
T-18......III.3:8 you retreat to the i. your fear increases,
T-18.......V.1:2 the difference between truth and i., the
T-18......VI.8:2 hate is not a prison, but an i. of yourself.
T-18....VI.11:7 have given up the i. of a limited awareness
T-18....VIII.3:5 is this little thought, this infinitesimal i.,
T-18......IX.5:2 reality of guilt is the i. that seems to make
T-18......IX.6:2 impenetrable appearance is wholly an i..
T-18......IX.6:5 upon it, for it is but an i. of a foundation.
T-19.........I.3:6 body thus becomes the instrument of i.,
T-19.........I.5:8 Truth is the absence of i.; illusion the
T-19.........I.5:8 absence of illusion; i. the absence of truth.
T-19.........I.6:7 to keep both truth and i. in the mind,
T-19.........I.6:7 must be, are recognized as dedication to i.
T-19.........I.7:1 Truth and i. have no connection. This
T-19........II.2:6 Sin is the grand i. underlying all the ego's
T-19........II.6:3 strange i. that makes the clouds of guilt
T19....IV.A.6:8 Every miracle is but the end of an i.. Such
T19....IV.A.8:1 This feather of a wish, this tiny i., this
T19..IV.B.12:7 the i. of pleasure will be the same as pain.
T19..IV.B.13:2 maintains the whole i. of its existence.
T-20........II.7:5 undoing of i. that God Himself could give.
T-20......IV.1:8 Being without i. of what you are, the Holy
T-20......VI.8:7 the mad idea and give it the i. of reality.
T-20.....VII.5:4 It cannot be attained but in i., and so the
T-20.....VII.5:4 so the i. of a brother as a body is quite in
T-20.....VII.8:7 sight of whom is your release, is no i..
T-21...VII.13:1 and place, is an i. that has no meaning.
T-22.........I.7:2 ancient than the old i. it has replaced, is
T-22.......I.10:4 else" you thought was you is an i.. And
T-22........II.1:5 Every i. carries pain and suffering in the
T-22........II.4:4 One i. cherished and defended against the
T-22........II.6:6 between yourself and an i. of yourself.
T-22........II.8:2 is there one i. you can enter Heaven with.
T-22........II.9:1 Let us look closer at the whole i. that
T-22........II.9:5 i. we have seen many times before. Only if
T-22......II.12:7 true. Every i. brought to its forgiveness is
T-22......III.7:4 that if form is not reality it must be an i.,
T-22......IV.7:8 only an i. stands between you and your
T-22.......V.5:7 i. of immovability be long defended from
T-22.......V.6:1 you have identified yourself with an i..
T-22.......V.6:8 and defends the i. of its immovability.
T-22......VI.6:9 timeless. And no i. can disturb the peace
T-22......VI.7:3 i. could there be you will not recognize as
T-23.......in.3:3 everything from the i. of harmfulness.
T-23.........I.3:5 ego joins with an i. of yourself you share
T-23.........I.5:5 are. Only a strange i. of yourself, a wish to
T-23.........I.7:8 One i. about yourself can battle with
T-23.........I.9:2 the vanquisher of the i. that was less real,
T-23.........I.9:2 that was less real, made an i. by defeat.
T-23.........I.9:5 Yet no i. can invade His home and drive
T-23.......I.10:1 You who are beloved of Him are no i.,
T-23.......I.12:1 I. meets illusion; truth, itself. The
T-23.......I.12:1 Illusion meets i.; truth, itself. The
T-23......II.18:9 be content with an i. that you are living?
T-23......II.19:3 In any state apart from Heaven life is i..
T-23......II.19:7 of Heaven, only the conflict of i. stands;
T-23......III.6:9 Not one i. of protection stands against the
T-23......IV.1:4 and no i. in any form stalks Heaven.
T-23....IV.1:12 Every i. is an assault on truth, and every
T-23......IV.6:7 no i. can attack the peace of God together
T-24.....in.1:12 i. that idly seems to drift between Them
T-24.........I.5:2 Here is the grand i. of what you are and
T-24.........I.5:6 become to keep your specialness *is* an i..
T-24........II.5:6 the specialness they think they see is an i..
T-24......II.14:3 you travel now, yet it is but i. of despair.
T-24......II.14:5 You but emerge from an i. of what you
T-24......III.1:4 clings to one i. can see himself as sinless,
T-25.......V.1:3 Attack and sin are bound as one i., each
T-25.....VII.3:7 then every Thought God ever had is an i..
T-26.........I.5:1 truth instead of to i. merely ask that they
T-26......III.4:3 It is the judgment of the truth upon i., of
T-26......III.6:4 That there is choice is an i.. Yet within
T-26......III.6:5 within this one lies the undoing of every i.
T-26......III.7:6 of an i. recognized as such. Where all
T-26.......V.4:4 one i. still remains unanswered in your

T-26..... V.12:4 This terrible i. was denied in but the time
T-26..... V.12:4 to i. for all time and every circumstance.
T-26...... VI.1:2 just because you have denied it is but an i.
T-26...... VI.1:7 For no one can make one i. real, and still
T-26...... VI.2:1 in solitude, with one i. as your only friend
T-26...... VI.2:4 one i. that you think is friend obscures
T-26...... VI.2:8 for what i. can replace the truth?
T-26...... VI.3:3 Make no i. friend, for if you do, it can but
T-26..... VII.5:4 be corrected where the i. of reversal lies.
T-26..... VII.6:1 impossible that one i. be less amenable to
T-26..... VII.6:3 No i. has any truth in it. Yet it appears
T-26.... VIII.1:3 For time and space are one i., which takes
T-26.... VIII.8:1 Yet this i. has a cause which, though
T-26.... VIII.8:2 this i. is but one effect that it engenders,
T-27.... VIII.5:6 seen at once that these ideas are one i.,
T-28..... IV.2:6 The dream is but i. in the mind. And with
T-28.... IV.2:10 real and what is but i. in yourself you do
T-28..... IV.3:2 Share not in his i. of himself, for your
T-28....... V.3:9 You are your Self or an i.. What can be
T-28..... V.3:10 What can be between i. and the truth? A
T-28....... V.5:3 a dream; your ears bear witness to i..
T-29....... II.3:3 For pain and sin are one i., as are hate
T-29....... V.1:1 no memory of sin and of i. lingers still.
T-29....... V.5:6 left their hold on every vain i. of the world
T-29..... VII.2:1 but must still have hope, some lingering i.
T-29..... VII.3:1 The lingering i. will impel him to seek
T-30..... IV.5:8 What could it be but an i., making things
T-30..... VI.7:3 from healing, one i. must be part of truth.
T-31....... II.3:1 is not a choice and gives but the i. it is free
T-31...... III.6:6 keep in chains, to the i. of a changing love
T-31...... IV.2:1 Real choice is no i.. But the world has
T-31...... IV.8:3 is still the same i. and the same mistake.
T-31..... VII.9:1 kept apart by an i. of yourself that holds
T-31..... VII.9:2 weapon that you give to the i. of yourself,
T-31.. VIII.12:5 Not one i. is accorded faith, and not one
W-pI..... 16.2:3 you have contributes to truth or to i.;
W-pI..... 49.2:3 is. The other part is a wild i., frantic and
W-pI..... 51.2:4 It is merely an i. of reality, because my
W-pI..... 52.1:6 reality, and thus regard reality as an i..
W-pI..... 53.3:6 I have given it the i. of reality, and have
W-pI..... 55.1:7 than those which show me an i. of myself.
W-pI..... 59.2:4 to exchange my pitiful i. of seeing for the
W-pI..... 66.8:4 an i. and offering only the illusion of gifts
W-pI..... 66.8:4 an illusion and offering only the i. of gifts
W-pI..... 66.9:2 Think also about the many forms the i. of
W-pI..... 71.3:3 will continue, for the i. persists that,
W-pI..... 73.8:2 us, nor deceive us with an i. of strength.
W-pI..... 83.4:4 *the i. of happiness apart from my function.*
W-pI..... 84.2:2 *Let me not see an i. of myself in this. As I look*
W-pI..... 88.1:5 why I always choose between truth and i.;
W-pI..... 91.8:8 *I am not an i., but a reality. I cannot see in*
W-pI... 93.11:1 quickly dispel the i. of fear by repeating
W-pI..... 96.2:1 fact that truth and i. cannot be reconciled
W-pI..... 99.2:3 borderland between the truth and the i..
W-pI... 101.2:3 If sin is real, then happiness must be i.,
W-pI... 107.7:4 footsteps of i. are not our approach today.
W-pI... 127.9:3 a dark i. of your own reality and what love
W-pI... 131.6:3 is the great i. it is past or in the future. Yet
W-pI... 133.7:4 been deceived by the i. loss can offer gain.
W-pI... 134.3:2 to deceive yourself by making an i. true.
W-pI. 134.17:2 to see through this i. as you tell yourself:
W-pI... 136.1:5 It dispels this meaningless i. by the same
W-pI. 136.13:1 fact that demonstrates that time is an i..
W-pI... 140.1:4 healing thus must substitute i. for illusion
W-pI... 140.1:4 healing thus must substitute illusion for i.
W-pI... 140.6:6 not a thought that judges an i. by its size,
W-pI... 140.6:7 what it is, and knows that no i. can be real
W-pI... 140.7:6 how can one i. differ from another but in
W-pI. 140.12:4 so deep that no i. can disturb our minds,
W-pI... 155.2:1 The world is an i.. Those who choose to
W-pI... 155.2:6 But to let i. sink behind the truth and let
W-pI... 155.3:2 The mad i. will remain awhile in evidence
W-pI... 155.3:4 look beyond i. to the simple truth in them
W-pI... 155.6:1 I. still appears to cling to you, that you
W-pI... 155.6:3 And it is not i. that they hear you speak of
W-pI... 155.6:3 nor i. that you bring their eyes to look on
W-pI... 155.6:4 illusions, for the road leads past i. now,
W-pI... 155.7:4 Their suffering is but i.. Yet they need a
W-pI... 155.7:5 out of it, for they mistake i. for the truth.
W-pI... 155.8:2 lighting up the path of ransom from i.. It
W-pI... 155.8:5 I. can but seem to hold in chains the holy
W-pI. 155.11:2 be no wish to be i. rather than the truth.
W-pI... 158.4:1 a vast i. in which figures come and go as if
W-pI... 160.4:7 If you are real, then fear must be i.. And if
W-pI... 162.2:3 no thought of sin and no i. which the
W-pI... 163.8:7 form it takes must therefore be i.. This
W-pI... 165.1:3 hide what cannot be concealed except i.?
WpI.rV.in10:6 knew before i. seemed to claim the world.
W-pI... 182.2:4 will maintain that what we speak of is i.,
W-pI... 184.6:6 What denies that it is true is but i., for it
W-pI... 187.7:1 I. recognized must disappear. Accept not
W-pI... 187.9:3 The great i. of the fear of God diminishes
W-pI... 190.7:4 As an i., it is what you wish. Your idle
W-pI. 190.10:4 It is this: Pain is i.; joy, reality. Pain is but
W-pI... 198.1:2 yet i. makes illusion. If you can condemn,
W-pI... 198.1:2 yet illusion makes i.. If you can condemn,
W-pI... 198.1:5 Then does i. cease to have effects, and
W-pI... 198.2:8 I. makes illusion. Except one. Forgiveness
W-pI... 198.2:8 Illusion makes i.. Except one. Forgiveness
W-pI. 198.2:10 Forgiveness is i. that is answer to the rest.
W-pI. 198.10:1 Accept the one i. which proclaims there
W-pI... 199.3:4 is a part of the i. that has sheltered it from
W-pII ..... 3.3:1 mechanisms of i. have been born instead.
W-pII ..... 3.3:5 is but i. which is kept apart from truth.
W-pII . 248.1:5 What is in pain is but i. in my mind.
W-pII . 269.1:4 *for the i. which transcends all those I made.*
W-pII ..... 6.2:1 is no more than an i. of despair, for hope
W-pII . 331.1:9 *Death is i.; life, eternal truth. There is no*
W-pII . 344.1:5 *And what can an i. offer me? Yet he whom I*
M-2 ........... 3:1 The world of time is the world of i.. What
M-3 ........... 3:2 i. of one permits the illusion of the other.
M-3 ........... 3:2 illusion of one permits the i. of the other.
M-3 ........... 3:4 it. We have covered the i. of time already,
M-3 ........... 3:4 but the i. of levels of teaching seems to be
M-4 ..... I.A.4:6 be accorded them in this world of i.. The
M-5 ........... 1:1 of what the i. of sickness is for. Healing is
M-7 ........... 5:3 This i. can take many forms. Perhaps
M-8 ........... 2:3 an i. is an attempt to make something
M-8 ........... 2:6 truth and gives itself an i. of victory.
M-8 ........... 5:1 in healing merely because all sickness is i..
M-10 ......... 2:3 He gives up an i.; or better, he has an
M-10 ......... 2:3 or better, he has an i. of giving up. He has
M-10 ......... 5:3 And it was all i.. Nothing more. Now can
M-12 ......... 3:1 Why is the i. of many necessary? Only
M-12 ......... 4:6 God appear to share the i. of separation,
M-12 ......... 4:6 not believe in the i. despite appearances.
M-13 ......... 1:4 Like all lessons it is an i., for in reality
M-13 ......... 1:5 i. must be replaced by a corrective device;
M-13 ......... 1:5 device; another i. that replaces the first,
M-13 ......... 1:6 The first i., which must be displaced
M-13 ......... 1:7 What could this be but an i., since this
M-14 ......... 1:2 The world will end in an i., as it began.
M-14 ......... 1:3 Yet will its ending be an i. of mercy. The
M-14 ......... 1:4 The i. of forgiveness, complete, excluding
M-14 ......... 3:6 The i. of orders of difficulty is an obstacle
M-16 ......... 6:7 up is merely the i. of protecting illusions.
M-16 ....... 11:8 maintained by just one simple-minded i.;
M-18 ......... 1:1 interpretation with fact, or i. with truth.
M-18 ....... 3:12 *thing there is. Fear is i., for you are like Him.*
M-20 ......... 5:3 you made death, and it is but i. of an end.
M-21 ......... 1:7 minds to keep them in the i. of separation
M-27 ......... 7:3 but been misperceived and carried to i..
M-27 ......... 7:4 task to let the i. be carried to the truth. Be
M-28 ......... 3:8 last i. spreads across the world, forgiving
M-29 ......... 3:7 see reflects the i. that you have done so,
M-29 ......... 7:4 you perceive as your weakness is but i..
C-2 .......... 6:18 to seek for an i. now that dreams are gone
C-2 ............ 8:1 the brotherless i. and the self that seemed
C-3 ............ 1:3 Forgiveness, then, is an i., but because of
C-3 ............ 3:1 so they need an i. of help because they are
C-4 ............ 1:1 The world you see is an i. of a world. God
C-5 ............ 2:3 The man was an i., for he seemed to be a
P-1............ 5:2 he must begin to separate truth from i.,
P-2......... in.2:8 paid this price. Now he wants a "better" i.
P-2........... I.2:3 of "the saving i." or "the final dream,"
P-2........ IV.7:6 Perhaps an i. of health is substituted for a
P-2......... V.1:2 This is the great i.. In its wake comes the
P-2........ VI.5:2 forms of the other, for they are the same i.
P-3...... II.10:11 Yet it can be but an i., because time does
P-3........ III.1:7 yet strive to have the last i. be accepted by
S-1.......... II.8:3 Prayer in its earlier forms is an i., because
S-1.......... II.8:4 as long as forgiveness, itself an i., remains
S-1.......... II.8:8 lives now with the i. of death and the fear
S-1........ III.4:4 has an i. of escape ever brought a prisoner
S-1........ IV.2:5 thus set up but an i. of a goal you share.
S-2........... I.4:4 That is why forgiveness of another is an i..
S-2........... I.6:2 this i. of a world appears to be your home
S-3.......... II.1:1 a poor exchange of one i. for a "nicer" one

## illusion's 3

W-pII . 224.1:6 and only this. This is i. end. It is the truth.
W-pII ..... 9.1:3 invitation to God's Word to take i. place;
S-2......... in.1:6 I. end will come with this. Unlike the

## illusions 468

T-1 ......... I.33:2 They dispel i. about yourself and perceive
T-1 ......... I.33:4 mind from the imprisonment of your i.,
T-1 ......... I.38:2 both God's creations and your i.. He
T-1 ....... IV.2:5 It thus dispels i. about yourself, and puts
T-1 ....... IV.2:8 Your mind can be possessed by i., but
T-1 ...... VII.1:6 of Self. Denial of Self results in i., while
T-2 .......... I.4:8 This release does not depend on i.. The
T-3 ....... III.2:6 Questioning i. is the first step in undoing
T-3 ....... VI.2:7 One of the i. from which you suffer is the
T-4 .............. h THE I. OF THE EGO
T-4 ....... III.1:8 not ceased to create because of the ego's i.
T-4 ....... VI.2:1 In learning to escape from i., your debt to
T-4 ...... VII.1:2 Ego i. are quite specific, although the
T-5 ......... V.4:4 is capable of creating reality or making i..
T-6 ..... V.C.8:9 for truth, but it is necessary against i..
T-6 ..... V.C.9:1 Truth is without i. and therefore within
T-7 ....... VI.5:5 The mind can, however, make up i., and if
T-7 ....... VI.6:1 Spirit undoes i. without attacking them,
T-7 ...... VII.3:7 you. All i. about the Sonship are dispelled
T-7 ...... VII.4:1 I. are investments. They will last as long
T-7 ...... VII.4:4 The only way to dispel i. is to withdraw all
T-7 ...... VII.7:8 Do not share their i. of scarcity, or you
T-8 ......... V.1:4 perceive their i. which block knowledge.
T-8 ......... V.6:3 not lose sight of His direction through i.,
T-8 ......... V.6:3 only i. of another direction can obscure
T-8 ......... V.6:6 Leave all i. behind, and reach beyond all
T-8 .... VII.16:5 Freedom from i. lies only in not believing
T-8 ....... IX.3:7 Dreams are i. of joining, because they
T-9 .......... I.1:3 cannot "threaten" anything except i.,
T-9 ..... VIII.4:3 in it. Grandeur is totally without i., and
T-9 ..... VIII.5:2 protecting it from i. and keeping yourself
T-9 ..... VIII.7:6 never deceive you, but your i. always will.
T-9 ..... VIII.7:7 I. are deceptions. You cannot triumph,
T-10 ..... III.7:3 to deny i. anywhere in the Kingdom,
T-10 ..... III.8:2 from all i. because you heard His Voice.
T-10 ... III.10:9 Honor is not due to i., for to honor them
T-10 ..... IV.2:5 cannot dawn on a mind full of i., because
T-10 ..... IV.2:5 because truth and i. are irreconcilable.
T-10 ..... V.12:4 All of these i., and the many other forms
T-11 ..... III.5:5 dark companions, the dark way, are all i..
T-11 ....... V.1:1 can escape from i. unless he looks at them
T-11 ....... V.1:2 There is no need to shrink from i., for
T-11 ....... V.2:2 else can one dispel i. except by looking at
T-13 ..... III.6:1 You must look upon your i. and not keep
T-13 ..... III.8:6 and no i. can satisfy him or save him from
T-13 ..... III.9:1 Save him from his i. that you may accept
T-13 ... III.12:9 answer is the reference point beyond i.,
T-13 ..... IV.6:5 you are choosing a future of i. and losing
T-13 ....... V.1:4 the content of individual i. differs greatly.
T-13 ..... VI.1:2 for this no i. can rise to meet your sight,
T-13 ..... VI.1:6 In your questioning of i., ask yourself if it
T-13 ..... VI.3:7 If you see it now in your i., it has not gone
T-13 ....... X.6:6 The purpose of Atonement is to dispel i.,
T-13 ....... X.7:1 Spirit does not keep i. in your mind to
T-13 ..... X.10:9 you. He would remove only i.. All else He
T-14 ...... in.1:7 that they cannot be seen except in i., for
T-16 ............ h THE FORGIVENESS OF I.
T-16 ...... II.5:2 reality of i. than you would be in joyously
T-16 ..... III.4:9 I. are but beliefs in what is not there. And
T-16 ..... IV.5:3 but always at the price of making both i..

| | |
|---|---|
| T-16......IV.5:8 | the choice seems to be one between **i.**, but |
| T-16......IV.9:5 | of God, be wholly willing to abandon all **i.** |
| T-16....IV.12:5 | Turn with me firmly away from all **i.** now, |
| T-16.......V.8:5 | Yet if all **i.** are of fear, and they can be of |
| T-16.......V.9:5 | only **i.** can be the witnesses to its "reality. |
| T-16.....V.14:1 | Salvation lies in the simple fact that **i.** are |
| T-16......VI.8:5 | it took to fix your mind so firmly on **i.**. |
| T-16........VII.h | The End of **I.** |
| T-16.....VII.7:1 | time you may attempt to bring **i.** into the |
| T-16.....VII.7:4 | The **i.** you bring with you will weaken the |
| T-16.....VII.7:5 | and your **i.** of time will not prevent the |
| T-16.....VII.9:2 | the **i.** you have held against your brothers |
| T-16.....VII.9:3 | has no past, and only **i.** can be forgiven. |
| T-16.....VII.9:4 | He is incapable of **i.** of any kind. Release |
| T-16.....VII.9:5 | their **i.** by forgiving them for the illusions |
| T-16.....VII.9:5 | them for the **i.** you perceive in them. Thus |
| T-16.....VII.9:6 | forgiven, for it is you who offered them **i.**. |
| T-16...VII.11:1 | the holy instant, where all **i.** are forgiven. |
| T-16...VII.11:4 | to give over all **i.** for the reality of your |
| T-16...VII.12:1 | *Forgive us our* **i.**, *Father, and help us to* |
| T-16...VII.12:1 | *with You, in which there are no* **i.**, *and where* |
| T-17.........I.1:1 | betrayal of the Son of God lies only in **i.**, |
| T-17.........I.5:1 | truth means from the perspective of **i.**? |
| T-17.........I.5:4 | When you try to bring truth to **i.**, you are |
| T-17.........I.5:4 | to illusions, you are trying to make **i.** real, |
| T-17.........I.5:5 | But to give **i.** to truth is to enable truth to |
| T-17.........I.5:5 | enable truth to teach that the **i.** are unreal |
| T-17.......II.6:2 | removing all **i.** that had twisted your |
| T-17......IV.8:3 | sorts of fanciful and fragmented **i.** of love, |
| T-17....IV.16:3 | glory, and keeping no **i.** of where they are. |
| T-17.....VII.5:6 | Use it, and it will carry you straight to **i.**. |
| T-17.....VII.9:3 | you to **i.** transformed to means for truth. |
| T-18......I.10:7 | You are not joined together in **i.**, but in |
| T-18......I.10:7 | so perfect that **i.** cannot remain to darken |
| T-18......I.11:2 | for all **i.** have been gently brought unto |
| T-18.......II.2:2 | can be utilized to substitute **i.** for truth. |
| T-18.......II.8:6 | last, the choice between the truth and *all* **i.**. |
| T-18......III.3:7 | and away from all **i.** in which you have |
| T-18......VI.4:8 | has made and using it to save him from **i.**. |
| T-18......VI.9:3 | be separated from Himself except in **i.**. |
| T-18......IX.4:2 | Here are all the **i.**, all the twisted thoughts |
| T-19.........I.4:1 | that faithlessness leads straight to **i.**. For |
| T-19.........I.4:5 | the Holy Spirit's purpose, and brought **i.**, |
| T-19.........I.5:5 | Faithlessness would interpose **i.** between |
| T-19.........I.5:6 | Faithlessness is wholly dedicated to **i.**; |
| T-19.........I.7:3 | But **i.** are always connected, as is truth. |
| T19...IV.A.6:3 | No **i.** stand between you and your brother |
| T19...IV.A.6:7 | by shadows from the light in which **i.** end. |
| T19.IV.A.6:10 | truth which you accepted must all **i.** end. |
| T19....IV.B.5:1 | You have paid very dearly for your **i.**, and |
| T19....IV.B.8:1 | Forgive me your **i.**, and release me from |
| T19..IV.B.12:7 | It will share the pain of all **i.**, and the |
| T19...IV.D.8:7 | born of complete forgiveness of his **i.**, and |
| T19...IV.D.9:1 | the Atonement and learned **i.** are not real. |
| T-20.......II.7:1 | You have the vision now to look past all **i.** |
| T-20.......II.7:4 | Who is afraid to look upon **i.**, knowing |
| T-20.....II.8:12 | no fear in us, for in our vision will be no **i.** |
| T-20.......II.9:3 | Let him be to you the savior from **i.**, and |
| T-20.....II.10:5 | the savior from **i.** has come to greet you, |
| T-20......VI.9:7 | For no **i.** can attract the mind that has |
| T-20.....VII.6:4 | and it is here that the **i.** you hold about |
| T-20.....VII.6:5 | Here are **i.** and reality kept separated. |
| T-20.....VII.6:6 | Here are **i.** never brought to truth, and |
| T-20...VIII.3:4 | body, which holds him to **i.** of what he is. |
| T-21......III.4:2 | away from all **i.** where your faith was laid. |
| T-21......III.5:3 | Faith given to **i.** does not lack power, for |
| T-21......III.5:4 | but strong in faith in his **i.** about himself. |
| T-21...VIII.4:1 | as His, a power that is not lost in your **i.**, |
| T-22......I.10:6 | It is denial of **i.** that calls on truth, for to |
| T-22......I.10:6 | for to deny **i.** is to recognize that fear is |
| T-22.......II.1:1 | of **i.** is not disillusionment but truth. Only |
| T-22.......II.1:6 | garments are those who seek **i.** covered, |
| T-22.......II.2:1 | is the opposite of **i.** because it offers joy. |
| T-22.......II.2:4 | To change **i.** is to make no change. The |
| T-22.......II.3:1 | **I.** carry only guilt and suffering, sickness |
| T-22.......II.3:9 | not imagined, **i.** must give way to truth, |
| T-22.......II.4:4 | all truth meaningless, and all **i.** real. Such |
| T-22.......II.8:1 | of Heaven you can take and weave into **i.**. |
| T-22.....II.10:7 | of the **i.** that you made replaced the truth |
| T-22......III.5:6 | perception, for they can see only **i.**, |
| T-22......III.7:6 | and must perceive **i.** as the truth. Could it, |
| T-22......IV.6:5 | let **i.** be lifted from their minds are this |
| T-22.......V.1:1 | How does one overcome **i.**? Surely not by |
| T-22.......V.1:8 | Only **i.** need defense because of weakness. |
| T-22.......V.3:9 | for here is no attack and therefore no **i.**. |
| T-22.......V.5:2 | by the **i.** it presents of size and thickness, |
| T-22.......V.5:4 | within you is a Force that no **i.** can resist. |
| T-22.......V.6:3 | This is the cost of all **i.**. Not one but rests |
| T-22......VI.2:2 | and so the mind is dedicated to serve **i.**. |
| T-23.........I.3:6 | And yet **i.** cannot join. They are the same, |
| T-23.........I.6:1 | against yourself is but the battle of two **i.**, |
| T-23.........I.6:8 | it. **I.** cannot triumph over truth, nor can |
| T-23.........I.7:3 | Truth does not fight against **i.**, nor do |
| T-23.........I.7:3 | illusions, nor do **i.** fight against the truth. |
| T-23.........I.7:4 | **I.** battle only with themselves. Being |
| T-23.........I.7:8 | of two **i.** is a state where nothing happens. |
| T-23.........I.8:4 | *by* attacking it you make two **i.** of yourself, |
| T-23.........I.9:1 | how the conflict of **i.** disappears when it is |
| T-23.........I.9:3 | Thus, conflict is the choice between **i.**, |
| T-23.......I.10:6 | him. **I.** have no place where love abides, |
| T-23.......I.11:4 | sin. And nothing is remembered except **i.**. |
| T-23.......I.11:5 | **I.** can conflict, because their forms are |
| T-23.......I.12:2 | The meeting of **i.** leads to war. Peace, |
| T-23.......II.2:3 | from the belief there is a hierarchy of **i.**; |
| T-23.......II.3:2 | this establishes degrees of truth among **i.**, |
| T-23.....II.14:6 | around, with madness sanity, **i.** true, |
| T-23.....II.19:8 | **I.** are but forms. Their content is never |
| T-23.....II.20:1 | The laws of chaos govern all **i.**. Their |
| T-23.....II.20:6 | Certain it is **i.** will bring fear because of |
| T-24.......in.1:9 | not wait upon **i.** to let Him be Himself. |
| T-24.........I.5:5 | **I.** can attack it, and they do. For what |
| T-24.......I.7:10 | you and your brother **i.** to each other? |
| T-24.........I.9:1 | special must defend **i.** against the truth. |
| T-24.......II.2:9 | **i.** of yourself are dearer than the truth. |
| T-24.......II.9:4 | Yet it is not **i.** that have reached this final |
| T-24.......II.9:6 | Leave all **i.** of yourself outside this place, |
| T-24.....II.12:6 | defender of all **i.** from the "threat" of love. |
| T-24.....II.13:3 | safe from all intrusions of sanity upon **i.**; |
| T-24.....III.1:2 | Only **i.** can be forgiven, and then they |
| T-24......III.1:3 | Forgiveness is release from all **i.**, and that |
| T-24......III.3:3 | not frail. **I.** leave it perfectly unmoved and |
| T-24......III.5:5 | They are powerless to make attack upon **i.** |
| T-24......III.5:6 | They wait for all **i.** to be brought to Them, |
| T-24......III.6:1 | perfect Son, for your **i.** of your specialness |
| T-24....IV.3:10 | in the sense that all **i.** are "threatened" by |
| T-24.......V.1:9 | power of a wish upholds **i.** as strongly as |
| T-24.......V.5:3 | They are **i.**, too, as much as yours. And |
| T-25.........I.7:5 | use all learning to transfer **i.** to the truth, |
| T-25......III.3:5 | perfect shelter for **i.** which it would make |
| T-25......IX.1:8 | that truth has greater value now than all **i.** |
| T-26......III.2:3 | and all **i.** are laid down beside the truth, |
| T-26......III.7:2 | All **i.** are but one. And in the recognition |
| T-26.......V.7:3 | And how much can his own **i.** about time |
| T-26.....V.10:7 | No past **i.** have the power to keep you in a |
| T-26......VI.1:5 | reality has entered all the world of sick **i.**. |
| T-26......VI.1:9 | Who can believe **i.** are the same, and still |
| T-26.....VII.3:2 | in the world of shadows and **i.** built on sin |
| T-26.....VII.6:5 | at all. All that a hierarchy of **i.** can show is |
| T-26.....VII.6:7 | truth? **I.** are illusions and are false. Your |
| T-26.....VII.6:7 | truth? Illusions are **i.** and are false. Your |
| T-26.....VII.8:3 | **I.** have no witnesses and no effects. Who |
| T-26...VII.13:5 | leave their source is to invite **i.** to be true, |
| T-26...VII.15:1 | **I.** serve the purpose they were made to |
| T-26...VII.15:3 | God gave to all **i.** that were made another |
| T-27.........I.6:2 | his health because it proves **i.** are not true |
| T-27.......I.11:5 | gave **i.** of a purpose to a thing you made |
| T-27......IV.4:5 | It is this: "Of these **i.**, which of them *is* true |
| T-27.....VII.7:6 | This is how all **i.** came about. The one |
| T-27...VII.12:4 | even see, the birthplace of **i.** and of fear, |
| T-27...VII.15:5 | Forgive him his **i.**, and give thanks to him |
| T-28.........I.1:9 | a cause can but produce **i.** of its presence, |
| T-28.......I.15:3 | the little gap between **i.** and reality than |
| T-28.......II.6:8 | sleeps. He sees **i.** of himself as sick or well, |
| T-28.......II.7:2 | This is a crucial step in dealing with **i.**. No |
| T-28......III.3:6 | Fight not His coming with **i.**, for it is His |
| T-28......IV.1:2 | to separate, and let him turn **i.** on himself |
| T-28......IV.1:8 | do you and your brother both become **i.**, |
| T-28......IV.3:3 | of him as a mind in which **i.** still persist, |
| T-28......IV.4:4 | is, by not supporting his **i.** by your faith, |
| T-28......IV.4:6 | gap, inhabited but by **i.** which you have |
| T-28....IV.10:8 | willingness to let **i.** go is all the Healer of |
| T-28.......V.4:1 | little gap between **i.** and the truth to be |
| T-28.......V.6:4 | the truth from dreams and from **i.**. Truth |
| T-29......III.3:5 | So perfectly can you forgive him his **i.** he |
| T-29....III.3:12 | is given power to forgive you your **i.**. By |
| T-29......IV.1:1 | you believe that truth can be but some **i.**? |
| T-30.........IV.h | The Truth behind **I.** |
| T-30......IV.1:2 | You always fight **i.**. For the truth behind |
| T-30......IV.4:3 | All **i.** that you believe about yourself obey |
| T-30......IV.5:5 | Attack has power to make **i.** real. Yet |
| T-30....IV.5:15 | them real. What can the power of **i.** do? |
| T-30......IV.8:6 | **i.** it but asks forgiveness be the substitute |
| T-30....IV.8:12 | He is delivered from **i.** by his will, and but |
| T-30......VI.5:2 | the miracle its strength to overlook **i.**. |
| T-30......VI.9:5 | succeeded by your wish to make **i.** real. |
| T-30....VIII.3:1 | is temptation but a wish to make **i.** real? |
| T-31......IV.1:3 | among **i.** seems to be the only choice. And |
| T-31.......V.1:3 | is that suits a world of shadows and **i.**. |
| W-pI.......8.2:2 | about it at all is therefore to think about **i.** |
| W-pI......13.3:3 | To the ego **i.** are safety devices, as they |
| W-pI.....14.6:3 | Some of them are shared **i.**, and others |
| W-pI.....15.1:7 | place of seeing, replacing vision with **i.**. |
| W-pI.....16.2:3 | it extends the truth or it multiplies **i.**. You |
| W-pI.....35.5:4 | **I.** have no direction in reality. They are |
| W-pI.....46.1:3 | that is because it is a world of **i.**. Those |
| W-pI.....46.1:4 | are thus releasing themselves from **i.**, |
| W-pI.....46.2:5 | It is the means by which **i.** disappear. |
| W-pI.....48.1:2 | It is not a fact to those who believe in **i.**, |
| W-pI.....48.1:2 | believe in illusions, but **i.** are not facts. In |
| W-pI.....48.1:5 | to recognize it for those who want **i.** to be |
| W-pI.....50.4:1 | Put not your faith in **i.**. They will fail you. |
| W-pI.....52.1:5 | I have replaced reality with **i.** I made up. |
| W-pI.....52.1:6 | The **i.** are upsetting because I have given |
| W-pI.....55.4:3 | merely bind me closer to the world of **i.**. I |
| W-pI.....55.5:2 | is to prove that my **i.** about myself are real |
| W-pI.....57.5:5 | see what my **i.** about myself kept hidden. |
| W-pI.....58.3:3 | What is there to be saved from except **i.**? |
| W-pI.....58.3:4 | are all **i.** except false ideas about myself? |
| W-pI.....59.1:6 | Let me not cherish **i.** about myself. I am |
| W-pI.....59.3:5 | Beyond His Will lie only **i.**. It is these I |
| W-pI.....61.4:2 | today. It is the perfect answer to all **i.**, and |
| W-pI.....62.2:1 | **I.** about yourself and the world are one. |
| W-pI.....64.2:2 | another use for all the **i.** you have made, |
| W-pI.....64.3:3 | it does the Son of God escape from all **i.**, |
| W-pI.....65.6:5 | your **i.** of purpose be replaced by truth. |
| W-pI.....66.7:3 | is ruled by the ego, and is made up of **i.**. |
| W-pI...66.10:6 | On one side stand all **i.**. All truth stands |
| W-pI.....68.2:1 | weaves **i.** in its sleep appears to be awake. |
| W-pI.....70.9:1 | Since all **i.** of salvation have failed you, |
| W-pI.....72.5:3 | promises and offering **i.** in place of truth. |
| W-pI.....73.1:5 | **i.** in which your belief can be very strong. |
| W-pI.....73.6:4 | is a point beyond which **i.** cannot go. |
| W-pI.....74.2:3 | true. Therefore it cannot give rise to **i.**. |
| W-pI.....74.2:4 | Without **i.** conflict is impossible. Let us |
| W-pI.....77.2:1 | does not lie in your **i.** about yourself. It |
| WpI..rII.in.5:2 | into detours, **i.** and thoughts of death. |
| W-pI.....89.1:4 | are but **i.** that hide the miracles beyond. |
| W-pI.....89.3:4 | to have all my **i.** be replaced with truth, |
| W-pI.....95.9:4 | you would defend **i.** against the truth. |
| W-pI...95.13:3 | It shine away all your **i.** and your doubts. |
| W-pI...95.13:5 | all your **i.** out of the one Mind that is this |
| W-pI.....96.6:6 | Salvation cannot make **i.** real, nor solve a |
| W-pI.....96.9:5 | a world of dreams, to find **i.** in their place. |
| W-pI.....97.1:5 | madness, letting go **i.** of a split identity. |
| W-pI.....98.1:3 | We side with truth and let **i.** go. We will |
| W-pI.....99.2:1 | Truth and **i.** both are equal now, for both |
| W-pI.....99.2:4 | it is the means by which you can escape **i.**. |
| W-pI.....99.3:2 | The mind that sees **i.** thinks them real. |
| W-pI.....99.4:2 | inviolate, yet recognize the need **i.** bring, |
| W-pI.....99.6:1 | is the Thought that brings **i.** to the truth, |
| W-pI...104.3:4 | offer other gifts and other goals made of **i.** |
| W-pI...107.1:1 | What can correct **i.** but the truth? And |
| W-pI...107.1:2 | errors but **i.** that remain unrecognized for |
| W-pI...107.2:1 | imagine what a state of mind without **i.** is |
| W-pI...107.3:2 | Without **i.** there could be no fear, no |
| W-pI...107.5:3 | **I.** can be brought to truth to be corrected. |
| W-pI...107.5:4 | But the truth stands far beyond **i.**, and |

W-pI...120.2:3 *Today I lay aside all sick* **i.** *of myself, and let*
W-pI...125.5:3 the **i.** which you hold about yourself. He
W-pI...125.9:4 with no **i.** interposed between the wholly
W-pI...130.8:2 You do not want **i.**. And you come to
W-pI...132.1:4 and **i.** are as strong in their effects as is
W-pI.132.12:2 release to give you fatherhood, not of **i.**,
W-pI.132.13:4 Deny **i.**, but accept the truth. Deny you
W-pI.132.14:5 the world this day from every one of our **i.**
W-pI...134.2:3 It is irrelevant to everything except **i.**.
W-pI...134.3:1 you must forgive the truth, and not **i.**.
W-pI...134.6:2 It does not countenance **i.**, but collects
W-pI...134.7:1 that stands for truth in the **i.** of the world.
W-pI...134.8:1 so uncorrupted that it sees **i.** as illusions,
W-pI...134.8:1 so uncorrupted that it sees illusions as **i.**,
W-pI.134.10:4 stands between **i.** and the truth; between
W-pI...135.1:2 the folly of defense; it gives **i.** full reality,
W-pI...135.1:3 as real. It adds **i.** to illusions, thus making
W-pI...135.1:3 as real. It adds illusions to **i.**, thus making
W-pI...136.6:1 constructs **i.** of a whole that is not there.
W-pI.136.10:2 as these, with God made blind by your **i.**,
W-pI.136.10:3 believes **i.** but the one who made them up
W-pI.136.14:1 for no **i.** can remain where truth has been
W-pI...137.4:5 Yet eyes accustomed to **i.** must be shown
W-pI...137.5:2 but removes **i.** that have not occurred.
W-pI.137.11:4 and here are all **i.** brought to truth.
W-pI...138.2:7 be the error truth can be brought to **i.**.
W-pI...140.7:4 brings **i.** to the truth is really changed.
W-pI...140.8:1 of sickness, for we seek a cure for all **i.**,
W-pI.140.10:4 speaks to us of truth, where all **i.** end, and
WpI. rIV.in3:2 Because they are **i.**, they are not perceived
W-pI...151.9:7 to bridge the gap between **i.** and the truth
W-pI.151.17:3 world the joyous news that truth has no **i.**
W-pI.152.12:3 and God's Son for your **i.** of yourself.
W-pI...153.5:5 by dreams, and by **i.** he has made; yet
W-pI...153.5:5 dreams by which **i.** of his safety comfort
W-pI...153.7:4 What but **i.** could defend you now, when
W-pI...153.7:4 you now, when it is but **i.** that you fight?
W-pI...155.2:2 seeking for a place where they can be **i.**,
W-pI...155.2:5 To let **i.** walk ahead of truth is madness.
W-pI...155.6:4 ahead of you, speak to them through **i.**,
W-pI...155.8:6 It is but from **i.** he is saved. As they step
W-pI...155.9:2 ahead of truth, and let **i.** be your guide.
W-pI.155.10:2 And all **i.** walking in the way you travelled
W-pI...162.1:5 **i.** vanish as these words are spoken. For
W-pI...163.2:1 guilty and the lord of all **i.** and deceptions
WpI.rV.in10:7 that it is free of all **i.** every time we say:
W-pI.182.11:5 Him, and take **i.** as your gods no more.
W-pI...183.3:1 all the world responds by laying down **i.**.
W-pI...184.8:2 **I.**, yes! But what is true in earth and
W-pI...185.4:7 **I.** come to take His place. And what He
W-pI...185.5:2 no one means these words who wants **i.**,
W-pI...185.5:2 therefore seeks the means which bring **i.**.
W-pI...185.7:6 these words acknowledges **i.** are in vain,
W-pI...185.8:5 But be you not dismayed by lingering **i.**,
W-pI...186.8:2 for all **i.** rest upon the weird belief that we
W-pI...189.6:1 Today we pass **i.**, as we seek to reach to
W-pI...190.3:1 Pain is a sign **i.** reign in place of truth. It
W-pI...190.4:5 feared than the insane **i.** which it shields,
W-pI.190.11:1 made; we choose between **i.** and the truth
W-pI...191.4:5 In this one truth are all **i.** gone. In this one
W-pI...192.2:6 on earth, you need the means to let **i.** go.
W-pI...194.5:2 the bondage of **i.** where it runs its pitiless,
W-pI...194.8:5 the sick **i.** of the world along with his, and
W-pI.196.11:4 on Him to save you from **i.** by His Love,
W-pI...197.3:1 you when you offer it release from your **i.**.
W-pI...198.3:2 others. All **i.** save this one must multiply a
W-pI...198.3:3 But this is where **i.** end. Forgiveness is the
W-pI...198.8:3 bridge to it that brings **i.** to the other side
W-pI...204.1:2 *by laws which rule the world of sick* **i.**, *free in*
W-pI...212.1:2 *set me free from all the vain* **i.** *of the world.*
W-pII ....in.9:4 all undone, and we no longer think **i.** true
W-pII .226.1:5 have not sought for **i.** to replace the truth.
W-pII .227.1:4 *did not affect my own reality at all by my* **i.**.
W-pII .....2.3:2 Thus it lets **i.** go. By not supporting them,
W-pII .240.1:5 It witnesses but to your own **i.** of yourself.
W-pII .....3.3:4 in its **i.** but a solid base where truth exists,
W-pII .250.2:2 *would behold his gentleness instead of my* **i.**
W-pII .....4.1:2 and seeks to let **i.** take the place of truth.
W-pII .....4.1:3 mad, it sees **i.** where the truth should be,
W-pII .....4.3:1 Sin is the home of all **i.**, which but stand
W-pII ....272.h How can **i.** satisfy God's Son?
W-pII .272.1:4 *Can* **i.** *bring me happiness? What but Your*
W-pII .272.2:1 Today we pass **i.** by. And if we hear
W-pII .274.1:3 *this as well the truth will enter where* **i.** *were,*
W-pII .280.1:2 imprisonment for him, but only in **i.**, not
W-pII .....7.1:1 Spirit mediates between **i.** and the truth.
W-pII .299.2:4 **I.** *can obscure it, but can not put out its*
W-pII ... 11.3:1 Creation is the opposite of all **i.**, for
W-pII .322.1:1 I sacrifice **i.**; nothing more. And as
W-pII .322.1:2 **i.** go I find the gifts illusions tried to hide,
W-pII .322.1:2 illusions go I find the gifts **i.** tried to hide,
W-pII ... 12.5:1 the altar to **i.** to the shrine of Life Itself.
W-pII .332.1:1 The ego makes **i.**. Truth undoes its evil
W-pII .334.1:2 **I.** are all vain, and dreams are gone even
W-pII .342.1:8 *at last, forget* **i.** *in the blazing light of truth,*
M-1 ........... 4:7 But time, with its **i.** of change and death,
M-2 ........... 2:2 forth. Atonement corrects **i.**, not truth.
M-4 ...... VI.1:6 are but foolish guardians of mad **i.**. The
M-5 ...... III.3:5 They recognize **i.** can have no effect. The
M-5 ...... III.3:6 brothers, so that **i.** are not reinforced.
M-6 ........... 1:2 is impossible to let **i.** be brought to truth
M-6 ........... 1:2 be brought to truth and keep the **i.**. Truth
M-6 ........... 1:3 Truth demonstrates **i.** have no value. The
M-8 ........... 2:1 **I.** are always illusions of differences. How
M-8 ........... 2:1 Illusions are always **i.** of differences. How
M-8 ........... 2:5 **I.** are travesties of creation; attempts to
M-8 ........... 5:7 realizes they are all **i.** they will disappear.
M-8 ........... 5:9 The properties of **i.** which seem to make
M-8 ........... 6:7 it–so too are **i.** without distinctions. The
M-8 ........... 6:9 healing. The one answer to all **i.** is truth.
M-10 ......... 1:1 by which the world of **i.** is maintained, is
M-13 ......... 5:2 It is the cost of believing in **i.**. It is the
M-14 ......... 1:6 of **i.** is the belief that they have a purpose;
M-14 ......... 1:9 How but in this way are all **i.** ended? They
M-16 ......... 6:7 up is merely the illusion of protecting **i.**.
M-16 ......... 7:6 was before **i.** were accepted into his mind,
M-17 ....... 4:11 is unaware of truth must look upon **i.**.
M-18 ......... 1:6 Magic thoughts are but **i.**. Otherwise
M-21 ......... 3:4 does not exist or seeks for **i.** in his heart,
M-22 ......... 4:9 that God created. In it are all **i.** healed.
M-27 ......... 1:1 the central dream from which all **i.** stem.
M-27 ......... 5:4 world of **i.** becomes more sharply evident.
M-27 ......... 6:5 is salvation's final goal; the end of all **i.**.
M-27 ......... 6:6 And in death are all **i.** born. What can be
M-28 ......... 4:5 now remain on earth to shelter sick **i.**,
M-28 ......... 5:9 **I.** of another will are lost, for unity of
C-1 ........... 4:1 mind is entirely illusory and makes only **i.**
C-1 ........... 5:4 Himself. Here time and **i.** end together.
C-1 ........... 6:1 listens to the ego and makes **i.**; perceiving
C-1 ........... 6:2 and the real world are **i.** because right-
C-2 ........... 1:1 **I.** will not last. Their death is sure and
C-3 ........... 1:4 Unlike all other **i.** it leads away from error
C-3 ........... 6:5 But **i.** shift from place to place; from time
C-4 ........... 2:1 for the **i.** that they look upon must lead to
C-4 ........... 2:1 look upon must lead to more **i.** of reality.
C-4 ........... 6:3 all **i.** brought to truth and laid upon the
C-4 ........... 8:3 lift you up to Him, out of **i.** into holiness;
C-5 ........... 2:3 to hold his self from Self, as all **i.** do. Yet
C-5 ........... 2:4 save unless he sees **i.** and then identifies
C-5 ........... 2:6 to men and save them from their own **i.**.
C-5 ........... 5:8 Forgive him your **i.**, and behold how dear
C-ep........... 1:7 **I.** of despair may seem to come, but learn
C-ep........... 1:9 would you wait for this and trade it for **i.**,
C-ep........... 1:9 farther on the road where all **i.** end? The
P-in ........... 1:8 change his mind about the "reality" of **i.**.
P-1............. 5:2 to see **i.** as false and to accept the truth as
P-2.........in.2:6 In **i.** the impossible is easily accomplished
P-2.........in.2:6 but only at the cost of making **i.** true. The
P-2...........I.2:9 or different. **I.** are illusions; truth is truth.
P-2...........I.2:9 or different. Illusions are **i.**; truth is truth.
P-2........ IV.3:3 things, however real they seem, are but **i.**.
P-2........ IV.6:5 is accepted as real and dealt with by **i.**.
P-2........ IV.6:6 Truth being brought to **i.**, reality now
P-2........ IV.7:4 to make **i.** true through false perception.
P-2........ IV.7:7 Fear cannot long be hidden by **i.**, for it is
P-2........ IV.7:8 another form, being the source of all **i.**.
P-2........ IV.8:2 degrees. One of the **i.** by which sickness is
P-2........ IV.9:1 A madman will defend his own **i.** because
P-2..........V.1:6 truly felt, and seeks to raise **i.** to the light.
P-3........ III.1:7 But no one here can live with no **i.**, for he
P-3........ III.3:3 can pay only for the exchange of **i.**. This,
P-3........ III.7:3 How much is gained by striving for **i.**?
S-1.........in.2:3 rejoice that what **i.** seemed to separate is
S-1...........I.2:4 must be made whether they be **i.** or not.
S-1........ IV.3:4 to love,–all these are but **i.** from the past.
S-1........ IV.3:5 the present from its chains of past **i.**; to let
S-1..........V.2:1 **I.** and humility have goals so far apart
S-2...........I.6:3 a remedy for all **i.** that they think they see.
S-2........ III.4:5 is not real and makes **i.** in its evil name.
S-2........ III.4:7 **I.** are untrue. God's Will is truth, and you
S-3..........II.5:8 What but shifts **i.** has done nothing.

## illusions' 1

T-23 ......I.12:8 minds that have become **i.** battleground.

## illusive 1

C-2 ............ 2:5 that its **i.** nature is concealed behind the

## illusory 9

T-31 ... VIII.5:7 distinctions gone, **i.** alternatives laid by,
W-pI .. 153.1:3 "gifts" of seeming safety are **i.** deceptions.
W-pI .. 199.3:4 has sheltered it from being found **i.** itself.
M-7 ........... 5:2 that trust has been placed in an **i.** self, for
M-8 ......... 3:11 decides whether what is seen is real or **i.**,
M-8 ........... 5:9 for their properties are as **i.** as they are.
M-26 ......... 3:7 All worldly states must be **i.**. If God were
C-1 ........... 2:3 joined. In this **i.** state, the concept of an
C-1 ........... 4:1 is entirely **i.** and makes only illusions.

## illustrates 1

W-pII ... 13.2:2 it **i.** the law of truth the world does not

## illustration 1

T-25 ... IX.10:2 give. Each one becomes an **i.** of the law on

## image 75

*See also* self-image

T-3 .........V.4:5 You have no **i.** to be perceived. The word
T-3 .........V.4:6 word "**i.**" is always perception-related,
T-3 .........V.4:8 idea of "changing your **i.**" recognizes the
T-3 .........V.7:1 created man in his own **i.** and likeness"
T-3 .........V.7:2 "**I.**" can be understood as "thought," and
T-3 ...... VII.4:3 tendency of the self to make an **i.** of itself.
T-3 .... VII.4:10 believe you are an **i.** of your own making.
T-7 .........V.9:2 One way shows you an **i.**, or an idol that
T-7 ...... VII.3:4 very easily escape from this **i.** by leaving it
T-7 ...... VII.3:9 **i.** of yourself as long as perception lasts.
T-8 ..... VIII.9:6 an **i.** of your own perception of littleness.
T-10 ..... III.1:6 this strange **i.** makes you do can be very
T-10 ..... III.1:7 the destruction is no more real than the **i.**,
T-10 ..... III.4:6 made in the **i.** of what its maker thinks he
T-10 ..... III.4:9 Is this the **i.** you would be vigilant to save?
T-12 .......II.5:6 straight at every **i.** that rises to delay you,
T-13 ..... IV.5:3 its **i.** by responding as if it were present. It
T-13 ..... VI.1:5 you see but an **i.** of him that you made
T-14 ..... IX.7:1 the **i.** of the holiness that heals the world.
T-14 ..... IX.7:2 **i.** of holiness that shines in your mind is
T-14 ..... IX.8:6 God is no **i.**, and His creations, as part of
T19 .. IV.D.6:3 of guilt, the "holy" waxen **i.** of death, and
T-20 ..... III.5:6 the ego, whose **i.** it is and which it loves,
T-24 .. VII.8:10 of a wish; an **i.** that you wanted to be true.
T-24 .... VII.9:5 Here is an **i.** that you want to be yourself.
T-28 ......I.13:3 There is no past to keep its fearful **i.** in the
T-29 ... VIII.1:6 An idol is an **i.** of your brother that you
T-30 .......V.6:2 that stood between your **i.** of yourself and
T-30 ..... VI.7:6 will keep an **i.** of yourself that is not whole
T-30 ... VI.10:4 to you a graven **i.** and a sign of death. Is
T-31 .......I.12:4 Let every **i.** held of everyone be loosened
T-31 .....II.5:14 because you see an **i.** of yourself and hear
T-31 .......V.1:3 an **i.** is that suits a world of shadows and
T-31 .....V.13:7 you chose it for him in the **i.** of your own.

T-31...VII.10:2 but an **i.** of yourself that can be miserable,
T-31...VII.12:4 the self whose **i.** has the wish begot of you
T-31... VIII.3:3 unhealed, nor any **i.** left to veil the truth.
T-31... VIII.4:2 place you raised an **i.** of yourself before.
W-pI.....15.1:6 It is **i.** making. It takes the place of seeing,
W-pI.....15.2:1 to the process of **i.** making that you call
W-pI.....15.4:2 *This_is an **i.** that I have made. That_is an*
W-pI.....15.4:3 *That_is an **i.** that I have made.* It is not
W-pI.....23.4:1 but you do not see yourself as the **i.** maker
W-pI.....26.3:5 A false **i.** of yourself has come to take the
W-pI.....35.2:3 the **i.** of yourself that you have made. The
W-pI.....35.2:4 The **i.** is part of this environment. What
W-pI.....35.2:5 are in it is seen through the eyes of the **i.**.
W-pI.....56.2:4 it is essential that I let this **i.** of myself go.
W-pI.....56.4:2 see. Behind every **i.** I have made, the truth
W-pI.....68.3:1 will redefine God in their own **i.**, as it is
W-pI.....91.7:2 to replace the **i.** of a body in your mind.
W-pI.....93.4:2 **i.** of yourself cannot withstand the Will of
W-pI.....94.3:6 sinned, nor made an **i.** to replace reality.
W-pI...128.8:2 value in an aspect or an **i.** of the world,
W-pI...153.7:3 fearful **i.** you believe you see at work in all
W-pI.158.11:2 accurate its **i.** shares its unseen holiness;
W-pI...163.2:3 and the sick bow down before its **i.**,
W-pI...186.6:1 makes an **i.** of yourself that is not real. It
W-pI...186.6:2 this **i.** which quails and retreats in terror,
W-pI...186.6:3 You are not weak, as is the **i.** of yourself.
W-pI...186.7:2 **i.** trembles and seeks to attack the threat
W-pI.186.12:4 as they are, or a distorted **i.** of yourself,
W-pI...191.6:5 see a devastating **i.** of yourself walking the
W-pII..283.1:1 *Father, I made an **i.** of myself, and it is this I*
W-pII..325.1:2 the mind makes up an **i.** of the thing the
M-4........ X.1:5 lets Christ's **i.** be extended to him. Only
M-23..........5:5 that he sees in it an **i.** of his Father. You
M-26..........2:2 visible, their **i.** can yet be called upon.
M-27..........3:4 It holds an **i.** of the Son of God in which
M-27..........5:9 Terrible His Thoughts and fearful His **i.**.
M-29..........4:5 The **i.** you made of yourself has none. The
M-29..........4:7 The **i.** you made does not. Yet, despite its
M-29..........4:8 this **i.** assumes it knows all things because
C-ep.........1:11 Who stands before a lifeless **i.** when a step
P-3......... II.7:9 **i.** remains, because they have chosen that

## images 50

*See also* self-images

T-3......... V.4:7 **I.** are symbolic and stand for something
T-3.......VII.4:4 **I.** are perceived, not known. Knowledge
T-4........IV.2:3 and are perceiving **i.** your ego makes in a
T-4........IV.9:2 there because I know these **i.** are not true.
T-7......VI.11:3 Therefore they make up **i.**, perceive them
T-10.....III.10:3 Him is to place other **i.** before yourself.
T-10......IV.6:2 are no strange **i.** in the Mind of God, and
T-10..... V.13:6 that the sick **i.** you perceive are the Sons
T-13....... V.3:2 only those who remind them of these **i.**,
T-14......IX.5:3 no reflections of the **i.** of other gods must
T-14......IX.5:5 clear of all the **i.** of hidden darkness you
T-31....... II.8:2 before, and put aside all **i.** you made. The
T-31....... II.9:2 and release from all the fearful **i.** he holds
T-31..... V.17:1 no **i.** of you unless you want to learn them
T-31..... V.17:2 will come a time when **i.** have all gone by,
T-31.....VII.7:2 All things you see are **i.**, because you look
T-31... VIII.4:1 The **i.** you make cannot prevail against
T-31... VIII.6:1 you look upon, regardless of the **i.** you see
W-pI.....13.3:2 and crowd it with **i.** that do not exist. To
W-pI........15.h My thoughts are **i.** that I have made.
W-pI.....15.1:1 you think you think appear as **i.** that you
W-pI.....23.4:5 now. Loveliness can light your **i.**, and so
W-pI.....23.5:5 Your **i.** have already been replaced. By
W-pI.....32.3:4 watch the **i.** your imagination presents to
W-pI.....35.2:7 image. This is not vision. **I.** cannot see.
W-pI.....53.5:1 (15) My thoughts are **i.** that I have made.
W-pI.....53.5:6 The **i.** I have made cannot prevail against
W-pI.....61.4:3 It brings all the **i.** you have made about
W-pI.....67.3:1 and then try to reach past all your **i.** and
W-pI.....78.9:1 times today in which you laid your **i.** aside
W-pI.....91.3:4 not doubt the **i.** they show you are reality.
W-pI...103.2:2 These **i.**, with no reality in truth, bear
W-pI...110.9:3 Let graven **i.** you made to be the Son of
W-pI.110.10:3 false the **i.** which you believed were you.
W-pI.131.10:3 to replace the foolish **i.** that we hold dear,
W-pI...159.3:4 can show but twisted **i.** in broken parts.
W-pI...186.6:2 and the holiness to go beyond all **i.**. You
W-pI...186.9:4 All the **i.** His Son appears to make have
W-pI.186.10:1 These unsubstantial **i.** will go, and leave
W-pI.186.10:2 **i.** you make give rise to but conflicting
W-pI...189.7:1 the world; all **i.** you hold about yourself.
W-pII..263.1:3 *I would not perceive such dark and fearful **i.**.*
W-pII..265.1:8 The **i.** I see reflect my thoughts. Yet is my
W-pII...... 7.3:1 for the fearful **i.** and dreams you made.
W-pII..314.1:3 it, so that fear has lost its idols and its **i.**,
W-pII..323.2:1 and of **i.** we worshipped falsely–truth
W-pII..325.1:3 find. These **i.** are then projected outward,
W-pII..330.1:2 attack our minds, and give them **i.** of pain
M-29 .........7:9 Forget your foolish **i.**, your sense of frailty
P-3....... II.7:10 They take the place of other **i.**, and help

## imaginary 3

T-8...........I.1:6 laws on behalf of an **i.** will that is not His.
T-11........ II.7:8 and do not be satisfied with **i.** comforters,
T-18.....VII.3:7 Its whole attraction is **i.**, and therefore

## imagination 8

T-10.......in.1:5 You can violate God's laws in your **i.**, but
T-18.......IX.7:2 range, a lake, a city, all rise in your **i.**, and
T-18.......IX.7:5 regardless of how much **i.** you bring to it,
T-20... VIII.7:1 to play the idle game of death in your **i.**.
T-21..........I.4:7 the world they learned to "see" in their **i.**,
W-pI.....32.2:3 the thought that both are in your own **i.**.
W-pI.....32.3:4 images your **i.** presents to your awareness
W-pI...101.6:4 sin has wrought in feverish **i.**. Say: *God's*

## imaginations 1

T-31....... V.7:5 is true, and many come from feverish **i.**,

## imagine 19

T-6......... II.2:4 thus **i.** that you have made yourself safe.
T-15.........I.1:1 Can you **i.** what it means to have no cares
T-17....... II.1:1 you **i.** how beautiful those you forgive will
T-20.....VII.1:8 It is impossible to **i.** one that asks so little,
T-21.........I.2:2 necessary to **i.** what the world must look
T-21.........I.8:6 to **i.** that anything could be outside, for
T-21....... III.2:3 may **i.** that you still experience its effects,
T-21... VIII.2:2 Yet if you could even **i.** what it must be,
T-24....... II.3:2 is impossible even to **i.** without this base.
T-26....... V.6:9 Yet can he still **i.** he is elsewhere, and in
T-29......IV.6:3 that you **i.** would bring happiness to you.
W-pI.....10.4:6 might **i.** that you are watching an oddly
W-pI.....60.3:3 not look anything like what I **i.** I see now.
W-pI...107.2:1 **i.** what a state of mind without illusions is
W-pI.167.10:2 Our life is not as we **i.** it. Who changes life
W-pI...170.2:4 needless misery than you can possibly **i.**.
W-pII..277.1:2 *Let me not **i.** I have bound him with the laws I*
W-pII..328.2:2 *I **i.** contradicts what You would have me be.*
P-3......III.4:10 could possibly **i.** that it could be bought?

## imagined 30

T-6........IV.9:7 the central place in your **i.** enslavement,
T-8.....VII.16:1 to suffer from **i.** results of what is not true
T-12..........I.4:1 they are except your own **i.** need to attack
T-13.......XI.2:1 so His Son's **i.** "enemy" is totally unreal.
T-14.....III.15:2 And you *will* feel guilty for this **i.** crime,
T-14.......VI.3:1 to give **i.** power to these strange ideas of
T-15....... V.2:3 and look to them to meet your **i.** needs,
T-15....... V.5:7 not, then, be afraid to let go your **i.** needs,
T-15....... V.6:5 would never have **i.** that you needed your
T-16....... V.6:2 And the attempt to find the **i.** "best" of
T-16.....VII.1:3 it. **I.** slights, remembered pain, past
T-20.....VII.6:4 He can but be **i.** in the darkness, and it is
T-20.....VII.6:7 is your brother's reality **i.** as a body, in
T-20. VIII.10:4 all the fearful outcomes of **i.** sin into the
T-21.........I.1:1 the world the sightless "see" must be **i.**,
T-21.....VII.6:6 And this **i.** difference attests to your belief
T-22....... II.3:9 time. Yet if the change be real and not **i.**,
T-28....... V.5:8 fragments seen within the gap that you **i.**,
W-pI.....70.8:6 in the cloud patterns you **i.** that endured,
W-pI...130.3:3 by fear, and what remains is but **i.**. Yet
W-pI...131.2:6 Pursuit of the **i.** leads to death because it
W-pI...137.5:3 healing but offers restitution for **i.** states
W-pI.137.15:2 of all the foolish thoughts that ever were **i.**
W-pI.138.10:3 thing, a but **i.** source of guilt and pain?
W-pI.167.10:5 Nor will we let **i.** opposites to life abide
W-pI...170.4:1 fancied self-defense proceeds on its **i.** way
W-pI...181.5:2 For the past is gone; the future but **i.**.
W-pII ..... 4.3:1 all illusions, which but stand for things **i.**,
M-29 ......... 3:6 The **i.** usurping of functions not your own
S-1 ........ III.3:9 having enemies, and this **i.** gain must go,

## imagines 4

T-16...... III.8:2 the gap he **i.** exists between his selves.
W-pI...192.8:1 forgiven everyone he sees or thinks of or **i.**
W-pI...200.6:5 beloved Son from evil dreams that he **i.**,
W-pII ..... 5.1:1 is a fence the Son of God **i.** he has built, to

## imagining 8

T-13.... XI.3:13 ever brought even a dim **i.** of what it is.
T-17.........I.1:1 and all his "sins" are but his own **i.**. His
T-20..... VII.7:1 difference between this vain **i.** and vision.
T-26..... V.6:10 from mere **i.** into belief and into madness,
T-27.........II.7:6 would prove all suffering is but a vain **i.**, a
W-pI...132.8:3 And if it is indeed your own **i.**, then you
W-pI...158.4:5 back on it, **i.** we make it once again;
W-pII . 302.1:5 *Now we see that darkness is our own **i.**, and*

## imaginings 14

T-13...... XI.7:2 wildest misperceptions, your weird **i.**,
T-17....VIII.4:5 and pain, darkness and dim **i.** of terror,
T19....IV.C.7:6 deception, all its sick ideas and weird **i.**.
T-20..... VII.8:8 for your **i.** about him will seem real there.
T-28....... V.5:8 them persuade their maker his **i.** are real.
T-31..... VII.7:5 and perceive the terrified **i.** that come
W-pI.....49.4:3 the raucous shrieks and sick **i.** that cover
W-pI...130.3:4 what can be real in blind **i.** of panic born?
W-pI. 136.16:1 arise to take the place of war and vain **i.**.
W-pI...153.2:6 where to turn to find escape from its **i.**.
W-pI...164.5:1 is the day when vain **i.** part like a curtain,
W-pI...200.3:5 Forgive yourself for vain **i.**, and seek no
W-pII .233.1:4 *be obtained, and wasting time in vain **i.**.*
M-20 ......... 6:8 to keep your tiny frail **i.** apart from Him?

## imbued 1

T-2...........I.1:2 His creations and **i.** them with the same

## immaculate 3

T-15...... IV.4:1 Would you learn how perfect and **i.** is the
W-pI...152.9:4 instead to Him Who has created us **i.**, like
WpI...rV.in8:8 and kept unchanged by time, **i.** and safe,

## immeasurable 2

T-2......VIII.2:7 this shortening process can be virtually **i.**.
T-4........ III.5:3 references to the **i.** gifts which are for you,

## immeasurably 2

T-2..........II.3:9 unduly. The correct focus will shorten it **i.**
WpI...rV.in5:3 This review will shorten time **i.**, if we keep

## immediacy 1

T-26.......VIII.h The **I.** of Salvation

## immediate 12

T-1.........I.48:1 at your **i.** disposal for controlling time.
T-2....... VII.5:8 an indication that **i.** correction is needed.
T-5...... VI.12:1 only infinite patience produces **i.** effects.
T-7........ XI.5:8 This is the recognition that is **i.**, clear and

T-15...... IV.1:1 This course is not beyond **i.** learning,
T-16...... III.2:4 The ego's teaching produces **i.** results,
T-26....VIII.2:7 You see eventual salvation, not **i.** results.
T-26....VIII.3:1 Salvation *is* **i.**. Unless you so perceive it,
T-28.........I.1:5 kept in memory appears to have **i.** effects.
W-pI.......1.2:1 Then look farther away from your **i.** area,
W-pI.....25.4:4 who is not physically in your **i.** vicinity.
W-pI...189.8:4 will do His part in joyful and **i.** response.

**immediately** 18
T-2........ III.4:3 and recognizes **i.** that the altar has been
T-2......... V.7:5 He also looks **i.** toward the Atonement.
T-4........ III.4:7 enter **i.** into any mind that truly wants it,
T-4........ VI.3:5 God, however, are **i.** recognized as eternal
T-9......VIII.3:5 its offer of grandiosity it will attack **i.**. If
T-16...... III.2:4 its decisions are **i.** accepted as your choice
T-17....... V.3:1 This invitation is accepted **i.**, and the
T-26.... III.1:14 on anything that cannot be **i.** grasped.
W-pI.....32.6:1 for today should also be applied **i.** to any
W-pI.....33.3:2 of today's idea should also be made **i.**,
W-pI.....37.5:2 eyes closed, and another, following **i.**,
W-pI.....37.6:4 Offer him the blessing of your holiness **i.**,
W-pI.....48.2:5 important that you use the idea **i.**, should
W-pI...73.11:6 to apply today's idea in this form **i.** you
W-pI...74.3:11 Tell yourself **i.**: *There is no will but God's.*
W-pII .319.1:3 is no arrogance the truth will come **i.**, and
M-9 ........... 1:6 to change their life situation almost **i.**, but
M-29 ......... 7:7 Not in the future but **i.**; now. God does

**immense** 1
W-pII ... 12.4:2 price for faith in it is so **i.** that crucifixion

**immensity** 1
M-17 ......... 6:8 Do not remember the **i.** of the "enemy,"

**immobilized** 2
T-9......VIII.4:1 ego is **i.** in the presence of God's grandeur
T-20.... VI.12:1 this may still be fearful, but you are not **i.**.

**immortal** 14
T-4....... II.11:9 Spirit is **i.**, and immortality is a constant
T-6...... III.3:10 Yet this learning is not **i.**, and you can
T-13.........I.8:5 You are **i.** because you are eternal, and
T-13....... II.9:3 Son, who did not die because he is **i.**. And
T-14...... IX.4:3 the **i.** assurance of their Father's Love.
T-15.......I.14:3 your **i.** creations who share it with you. As
T-17...... III.1:4 would make **i.** are "enemies" of reality. Be
T-19...... II.3:6 of sin *is* death, and how can the **i.** die?
T19..IV.B.10:3 what already is at peace in you, **i.** as itself.
T-22..... II.12:2 in time and yet beyond, **i.** yet on earth.
T-24..... VII.5:4 What is **i.** cannot be attacked; what is but
T-29...... VI.2:4 He is **i.** as his Father. What he is cannot
W-pI.158.11:2 holiness; its likeness shines with its **i.** love
M-19 ......... 4:4 must decay and die, but wholeness is **i.**. It

**immortality** 21
T-4....... II.11:9 is immortal, and **i.** is a constant state. It is
T-11.........I.9:9 **I.** is His Will for His Son, and His Son's
T-13.........I.8:9 And **i.** is the opposite of time, for time
T-13.........I.8:9 for time passes away, while **i.** is constant.
T-13.........I.9:1 the Atonement teaches you what **i.** is, for
T-14.... XI.11:7 having the holy stamp of **i.** upon it. This
T-15.........I.3:5 peace even in death, it offers you **i.** in hell.
T-15.......I.4:15 Such is the ego's version of **i.**. And it is
T-15.........I.8:7 is remembered, and **i.** and joy are now.
T-15.......I.14:3 As long as it takes to remember **i.**, and
T-20.... III.11:8 light of God's eternal promise of your **i.**.
T-24..... VII.5:9 Its holy purpose gave it **i.**, setting another
T-27.......I.10:3 and a breath of **i.** to those grown sick of
T-29....... II.7:4 There is no change in **i.**, and Heaven
W-pI...131.1:2 **i.** within the darkness of the dream of
W-pI.135.19:1 instant, set in time, but heeding only **i.**.
W-pI...191.4:6 core of its existence and its guarantee of **i.**

W-pI...199.8:2 Son. In **i.** you live forever. Would you not
W-pII ... 13.5:4 born can never die, for what has life has **i.**
C-2 .......... 1:10 ancient thought that what is made has **i.**.
S-3...........I.3:2 Only that can give rememberance of **i.**,

**immovability** 2
T-22 ...... V.5:7 illusion of **i.** be long defended from what
T-22 ...... V.6:8 and defends the illusion of its **i.**.

**immovable** 4
T-22 ...... V.5:3 enormous solid body, **i.** as is a mountain.
T-22 ...... V.5:5 This body only seems to be **i.**; this Force is
T-22 ...... V.6:5 not seem to stand, heavy and solid and **i.**,
T-22 ... VI.10:7 fear of God in place, **i.** and solid as a rock.

**immune** 1
T-28 .... VII.4:7 No forms of sickness are **i.**, because the

**immunity** 1
T-6 ..........I.6:4 Rather, teach your own perfect **i.**, which

**immunization** 1
W-pI.....76.8:2 for example, the "laws" of nutrition, of **i.**,

**immutable** 8
T-7 .........II.2:5 This is an **i.** law of the mind in this world
T-11 ......I.10:1 and you cannot change this because it is **i.**
T-11 ......I.10:2 **i.** by God's Will and yours, for otherwise
T-14 ...... V.1:7 Accept, then, the **i.**. Leave the world of
T-25 .... VII.1:3 It is **i.**. And on its changelessness the
T-25 .... VII.2:5 What is **i.** besides His Will? And what can
T-25 .... VII.2:7 wish can rise against His Will, and be **i.**?
T-25 .... VII.6:6 Each sees a world **i.**, as each defines the

**impair** 1
W-pI... 195.6:2 nor **i.** or change our function to complete

**impaired** 4
T-1 ........ V.3:8 or the Sonship, is **i.** in its relationships.
T-12 ..... IV.1:6 and its judgment, though severely **i.**, is
T-12 ...... V.5:2 your learning skills that are so **i.** that you
T-20 ..... III.1:6 this **i.** condition *are* adjustments necessary

**impairment** 1
T-12 ...... V.6:4 and the **i.** of the ability to generalize is a

**impart** 1
T-6 ........ V.1:5 so that He cannot **i.** His joy and know that

**impartial** 6
T-6 ....... III.1:3 in your mind through His **i.** perception.
T-8 .....VIII.4:8 a judge gives anything but an **i.** judgment.
T-18 ...VIII.8:3 meaning. It is completely **i.** in its giving,
T-24 ..... VI.5:5 release you both, for holiness is quite **i.**,
T-25VIII.13:10 judges. He is not **i.**, and cannot fairly see
M-19 ......... 5:5 to Heaven just because it is entirely **i.**. It

**impartiality** 2
T-6 .......II.13:1 Holy Spirit was given you with perfect **i.**,
T-25 .VIII.13:1 Without **i.** there is no justice. How can

**impartially** 1
T-6 .......II.13:1 Him **i.** can you recognize Him at all. The

**impasse** 2
T-3 .........V.5:5 attempt to escape from an inescapable **i.**.
T-9 .........V.7:1 ego's approach, then, must arrive at an **i.**;

**impatience** 2
T-4 ....... III.7:9 Because I wait in love and not in **i.**, you
T-17 .......II.8:4 Meet His patience with your **i.** at delay in

**impatient** 1
T-26 .... VII.7:4 opposing powers, until God becomes **i.**,

**impeccable** 1
T-5 .........V.1:4 ego's logic is as **i.** as that of the Holy Spirit

**impede** 1
W-pI 135.11:5 that obstacles can not **i.** its progress to

**impedes** 1
Wi181-200 3:1 by concentrating first on what **i.** your

**impeding** 1
T-4 .........V.6:6 ego devices for **i.** learning progress. In all

**impel** 2
T-13 ..... III.2:6 your love for your Father would **i.** you to
T-29 .... VII.3:1 lingering illusion will **i.** him to seek out a

**impelled** 2
W-pI .... 12.5:4 you are **i.** to write upon it what you would
W-pII . 335.1:4 I seem to be **i.** by outside happenings. I

**impels** 1
T-22 ..... III.9:4 other what **i.** him to sin against his will.

**impenetrable** 6
T-18 ..... IX.5:2 seems to make it heavy and opaque, **i.**,
T-18 ..... IX.6:2 Its **i.** appearance is wholly an illusion. It
T-18 ..... IX.8:1 guilt, no more **i.** and no more substantial.
T-19 .......II.6:3 the clouds of guilt seem heavy and **i.**. The
T-22 .......V.6:8 you and your brother that makes it look **i.**
W-pI .. 170.9:3 with the appearance of a solid block, **i.**,

**imperative** 1
W-pI .... 39.7:2 It is **i.** for your salvation that you see them

**imperceptible** 1
T-18 ...VIII.3:4 almost **i.** ripple hails itself as the ocean.

**imperfect** 4
T-2 ........I.1:10 is perfect can be rendered **i.** or lacking.
T-6 ........I.14:3 Their own **i.** love made them vulnerable
W-pI .. 122.4:2 is the perfect answer, given to **i.** questions
P-3.........I.1:10 Who could ask of Perfection that He be **i.**

**imperfection** 1
W-pII ... 11.3:3 **i.** and of any spot upon its sinlessness.

**impermanence** 2
T-21 .......V.2:4 and feelings of **i.** and unreality. You will
W-pII ..... 5.2:3 Son of God's **i.** is "proof" his fences work,

### impermanent 2
W-pI...131.1:2 You look for permanence in the **i.**, for
W-pI.186.10:2 rise to but conflicting goals, **i.** and vague,

### impersonal 4
T-1........III.4:5 The **i.** nature of the miracle is an essential
T-1........III.7:3 The **i.** nature of miracles is because the
T-1........III.8:5 **i.** nature of miracle-mindedness ensures
T-4.........II.1:4 because knowledge is completely **i.**, and

### impervious 1
W-pI...132.6:1 from yourself, **i.** to what you think, and

### implacable 2
T-31.........I.5:4 stand **i.** before the Voice of truth, and
W-pI...123.1:3 back, and no **i.** resistance to the truth. A

### implications 1
T-1.......VII.4:6 to see some of the **i.** that will be amplified

### implicit 4
T-2.....VII.3:14 All fear is **i.** in the second, and all love in
T-3.......VII.4:3 that they are is **i.** in the "self-concept," or
T-17......VI.6:2 Faith is **i.** in the acceptance of the Holy
W-pI.....77.2:4 It is **i.** in what God your Father is. It was

### implicitly 2
T-18......IV.2:3 But trust **i.** your willingness, whatever
W-pI...151.2:5 Why would you trust them so **i.**? Why but

### implied 1
T-6......V.C.5:3 brings together the lessons **i.** in the others

### implies 40
T-1.........II.3:5 of one another because awe **i.** inequality.
T-1........VI.1:5 Lack **i.** that you would be better off in a
T-2......IV.3:12 term "unworthy" here **i.** only that it is not
T-2........VI.6:1 but this **i.** a willingness that you have not
T-2.......VII.7:9 You may think this **i.** that an enormous
T-3.........V.4:3 This **i.** that the answer is not only one you
T-3.........V.4:8 also **i.** that there is nothing stable to know
T-3......VI.2:12 because it **i.** the belief that reality is yours
T-4.........II.6:3 to give anything **i.** that you will have to do
T-4.....II.11:10 ever will be, because it **i.** no change at all.
T-4........III.9:6 when the idea of "getting," which **i.** a lack
T-5.........II.5:2 because it **i.** there is a right way and also a
T-5........IV.4:2 Listening to one Voice **i.** the decision to
T-5.......VII.5:4 in the usual sense, because this **i.** guilt. If
T-6......V.B.8:5 still **i.** that the desirable has degrees.
T-6......V.C.3:2 since it **i.** that there is something you
T-7.........II.3:3 This form **i.** that you will learn what you
T-7........VI.9:5 since their presence **i.** a belief that what
T-11.......V.3:3 "Dynamics" **i.** the power to do something
T-11......VI.5:7 obedience, for obedience **i.** submission.
T-18.........I.6:8 for guilt **i.** it was accomplished in reality.
T-21...VII.10:5 **i.** a state where vacillations are impossible
T-29.....VII.4:6 The search **i.** you are not whole within
W-pI.....12.3:6 that a "good world" **i.** a "bad" one, and a
W-pI.....12.3:6 world" **i.** an "unsatisfying" one. All terms
W-pI.....20.4:2 Today's idea also tacitly **i.** the recognition
W-pI...105.1:8 loses. This **i.** a limit and an insufficiency.
W-pI...105.4:4 more, for that **i.** that it was less before. It
W-pI.152.10:3 To recognize God's Son **i.** as well that all
W-pI...163.7:2 it **i.** that God was once alive and somehow
W-pII....13.4:1 because to ask for it **i.** the mind has been
M-3...........5:3 their existence **i.** that those involved have
M-4.......II.2:6 God. Challenge **i.** doubt, and the trust on
M-4.......III.1:4 Judgment **i.** that you have been deceived
M-4.......III.1:6 Judgment **i.** a lack of trust, and trust
M-4.......IX.2:8 **i.** acceptance of the Word of God and His
M-7...........5:2 And that necessarily **i.** that trust has been
M-29.........7:8 wait, for waiting **i.** time and He is timeless
P-2..........II.4:5 Belief **i.** that unbelief is possible, but
P-3.........II.4:5 very need for each other **i.** a sense of lack.

### imploringly 1
W-pI...121.7:2 turns to you **i.** for Heaven here and now.

### imply 13
T-1.........V.2:5 Equality does not **i.** equality *now*. When
T-2.......V.10:4 perceptions clearly **i.** their dependence on
T-2.......VII.7:5 state does not **i.** more than a potential for
T-3......VI.11:6 wish is to **i.** that willing is not sufficient.
T-4.......VII.2:1 without the relationships that **i.** being.
T-6......IV.12:2 To teach is to **i.** a lack, which God knows
T-23.........I.1:5 you must **i.** that you believe the ego has
T-23.....II.20:6 fear because of the beliefs that they **i.**, not
T-26.......III.3:3 here, in that the words **i.** a limited reality,
W-pI.....41.9:3 on the holiness that they **i.** about you; on
W-pI.....64.5:7 of form does not **i.** complexity of content.
W-pI.....99.1:2 both **i.** that something has gone wrong;
W-pI.....99.1:3 Thus do both terms **i.** a thing impossible

### implying 6
T-1.........II.3:2 **i.** that one of a lesser order stands before
T-2........VI.4:2 release from fear, you are **i.** that it is not.
T-3........III.2:2 to "know again," **i.** that you knew before.
T-3........III.5:5 are clearly **i.** that you do not know God.
T-3.........V.2:4 are tacitly **i.** that you believe in separation
T-11.....VII.1:5 is merely to perceive again, **i.** that before,

### import 1
T-12.......II.9:5 it, and not by denying its full **i.** in any way

### importance 20
T-4.........I.13:5 I could not understand their **i.** to you if I
T-9.........V.4:3 by depreciating the **i.** of the dreamer. This
T-9.........V.5:1 fear is to reduce the **i.** of the mind, how
T-14.......X.8:7 would "analyze" it, thus approving its **i.**.
T-17.......III.3:5 in whom they seem to be decreases in **i.**.
T-22.......VI.1:6 increasing its **i.** by diminishing its own.
W-pI.......2.2:1 color, material, or relative **i.** to you. Take
W-pI.......5.7:1 regardless of the relative **i.** you may give
W-pI.....12.1:1 The **i.** of this idea lies in the fact that it
W-pI.....20.1:4 lost sight of the crucial **i.** of the reversal of
W-pI.....42.1:1 very powerful thoughts, both of major **i.**.
W-pI.....44.8:1 is a sense of the **i.** of what you are doing;
W-pI.....63.3:1 Recognizing the **i.** of this function, we
W-pI.....64.6:6 remember the crucial **i.** of your function
W-pI.....65.7:1 period to trying to focus on its **i.** to you,
W-pI.....69.6:1 After you have thought about the **i.** of
W-pI.....69.9:1 as possible in view of the **i.** of today's idea
W-pII..318.1:3 or one of more or less **i.** than the rest? I
M-8...........2:3 real that is regarded as of major **i.**, but is
S-3.........in.1:3 **i.** should not be too strongly emphasized,

### important 22
T-1.........II.2:6 working miracles is **i.** because freedom
T-4.........II.2:4 is **i.** to realize that this alteration can and
T-12.......V.2:1 is so **i.** to the restoration of your sanity.
T-14.......X.4:3 some of your thoughts as more **i.**, larger
T-14.......X.6:6 which call is louder or greater or more **i.**.
T-17....IV.10:1 holy instant is so **i.** in the defense of truth.
T-21.......in.1:4 Therefore, to you it is **i.**. It is the witness
T-21...VII.10:1 Why is the final question so **i.**? Reason
W-pI.....25.6:2 eye, near or far, "**i.**" or "unimportant,"
W-pI.....28.2:1 You may wonder why it is **i.** to say, for
W-pI.....28.2:2 In itself it is not **i.** at all. Yet what is by
W-pI.....42.8:1 that the goal of the course is **i.** to you, and
W-pI.....45.9:1 try to remember how **i.** it is to you to
W-pI.....48.2:5 It is particularly **i.** that you use the idea
W-pI...73.11:6 It is most **i.**, however, to apply today's
W-pI.....91.1:1 is **i.** to remember that miracles and vision
WpI. rIII.in9:1 be done throughout the day are equally **i.**,
M-7...........5:7 The form of the mistake is not **i.**. What is
M-7...........5:8 **i.** is only the recognition of a mistake as a
M-16.........3:3 it remains **i.** throughout the learning
M-25.........3:4 only **i.** consideration is how they are used.
M-29.........3:1 is another advantage,–and a very **i.** one,

### impose 20
T-9...........I.3:8 effort, within the limits you **i.** on Him, to
T-13........X.4:8 you **i.** your idle wishes on the present, and
T-14........X.5:7 though the order you **i.** upon your mind
T-15.......IX.5:5 see without the limits the ego would **i.** on
T-19......IV.1:2 Some of them you will try to **i.**. Others
T-26.........I.3:7 is to **i.** these limits on each brother whom
T-26........II.3:5 Think not the limits you **i.** on what you
T-26.....VII.8:7 you **i.** between your brother and yourself.
T-27......III.1:7 and **i.** an opposite that contradicts the
T-27......III.5:4 Yet it sets no limits you have chosen to **i.**.
T-28.........I.4:4 as vast as those you let the world **i.** on you
T-29....IX.10:5 judgment from what judgment must **i.**.
W-pI.....29.4:3 Remember that any order you **i.** is equally
W-pI.....72.3:1 that a body would **i.** is obvious here, it is
W-pI...114.1:3 *nor **i.** on me a limitation God created not.*
W-pI...131.8:5 Let us not try longer to **i.** an alien will
W-pI...135.9:4 And you will **i.** upon the body all the pain
W-pI.136.10:2 to laws which your defenses would **i.** on it
W-pI...137.4:3 would **i.** has never really happened. To be
P-2..........II.8:5 boundaries the ego would **i.** upon the self.

### imposed 4
T-15........X.2:6 is nothing but a limitation **i.** on giving.
T-18......VI.8:3 The body is a limit **i.** on the universal
T-25......VI.6:2 Its laws are not **i.** on you, its values are
W-pI.....35.6:2 *I see myself as **i.** on. I see myself as depressed.*

### imposes 4
T-24.........I.3:6 difference of any kind **i.** orders of reality,
T-28.........I.4:4 the world **i.** on it are as vast as those you
W-pI.....95.7:2 helpful, since it **i.** firmer structure. Do not
W-pI...136.6:2 It is this process that **i.** threat, and not

### imposing 5
T-8.....VII.14:3 the body, you are **i.** this limit on yourself.
T-13.....X.11:3 you are **i.** guilt on all your relationships
T-14......III.8:7 without **i.** on himself the penalty of guilt,
T-17......IV.8:1 the most **i.** and deceptive frame of all the
T-17......IV.8:2 is almost obliterated by its **i.** structure.

### imposition 1
W-pI.....26.6:2 of depression, worry, anger, a sense of **i.**,

### impossibility 4
T-8.....VII.16:3 complete **i.** lies your only hope for release.
T-16.....V.12:5 be possible, even apart from its evident **i.**?
T-26.....VII.7:1 error, for it goes beyond correction to **i.**.
C-2............1:9 is. A symbol of **i.**; a choice for options that

### impossible 372
T-1.........I.37:4 knowledge of the Divine Order is **i.**.
T-1..........II.2:2 any attempt to describe it in words is **i.**.
T-2...........I.3:8 Such a rebirth is **i.** as long as you continue
T-2........III.1:6 that Atonement in physical terms is **i.**.
T-2......IV.3:10 it is almost **i.** to deny its existence in this
T-3...........I.3:8 how utterly **i.** this assumption is, and how
T-3.........I.3:11 to use words that are almost **i.** to distort,
T-3..........II.1:3 It is **i.** to conceive of light and darkness or
T-3..........II.1:6 to darkness or nothingness, however, is **i.**.
T-3......IV.5:11 be. This is **i.**, because the mind belongs to
T-3.........V.3:2 literally **i.** for you to know anything.
T-3.........V.5:4 is **i.** to make so fundamental a confusion
T-3.........V.7:5 is **i.** without a belief in "more" and "less."
T-3.........V.8:2 Perception becomes **i.**. Truth can only be

T-3......... V.8:6 because partial knowledge is **i.**. It is all
T-3........ VI.9:1 can know that their own rejection is **i.**.
T-4...........I.5:3 It is **i.** to convince the ego of this, because
T-4......... II.7:2 beyond its grasp, and charity becomes **i.**.
T-4....... VII.7:3 to Him, which would clearly be **i.**, but He
T-4....... VII.8:2 This is **i.** without being wholly harmless,
T-5.........in.2:2 is **i.** to be wholly fearful and remain alive,
T-5.........in.3:6 is **i.** for a child of God to love his neighbor
T-5........ III.4:4 **i.** to hear It in yourself while It is so weak
T-5........ IV.3:7 *It is **i.** to share opposing thoughts.* You can
T-6...........I.3:5 This, of course, is **i.**, and must be fully
T-6...........I.3:5 must be fully understood *as* **i.**. Otherwise,
T-6...........I.4:3 Yet if destruction itself is **i.**, anything that
T-6.........I.15:9 to demonstrate that condemnation is **i.**?
T-6.........I.17:3 appreciate, for fear makes appreciation **i.**.
T-6......... II.3:6 Anger without projection is **i.**. The ego
T-6....... II.6:11 it is **i.** to accept one without the other.
T-6......... II.7:4 prefer to believe that this memory is **i.**,
T-6........ IV.2:2 is why attack within the Kingdom is **i.**.
T-6........ IV.8:6 In fact, it is **i.**. Remember, however, that
T-6........ IV.8:7 put yourself in an **i.** situation you believe
T-6........ IV.8:7 situation you believe that the **i.** *is* possible.
T-6........ IV.9:3 In an **i.** situation, you can develop your
T-6...... IV.10:1 an **i.** situation only because you think it is
T-6...... IV.10:2 *would* be in an **i.** situation if God showed
T-6...... IV.10:6 **i.** as the ego's notion that it has affronted
T-6......V.A.1:7 any other **i.** solution the ego attempts, *it*
T-6......V.A.5:8 breaks communication, making it **i.**. Egos
T-6...... V.B.4:5 makes it **i.** for the learner not to listen.
T-6...... V.B.5:2 disagreement, peace of mind is **i.**. If you
T-7......... II.6:2 Learning is **i.** without memory since it
T-7......... III.2:7 That is so contradictory it is clearly **i.**. It is
T-7......... III.3:6 therefore you have accepted the **i.** as true.
T-7......... VI.1:2 It is **i.**, however, to see something in part
T-7....... VII.1:2 It is as **i.** to deny part of the Sonship as it
T-7......VIII.4:2 this, because it is **i.** to fragment the mind.
T-7........ IX.4:6 selfishness **i.** and extension inevitable.
T-7........ IX.6:6 In truth it is **i.**. Your Self-fullness is as
T-7......... X.4:5 believe that an **i.** choice is open to you,
T-7......... X.4:9 anything, because the ego wishes for the **i.**
T-7....... X.4:10 You can wish for the **i.**, but you can will
T-7......... X.5:7 and given this confusion, trust becomes **i.**
T-8...........I.6:3 curriculum presents an **i.** learning task.
T-8......... II.1:9 the Holy Spirit entirely, which is **i.**, you
T-8........ IV.3:7 the world *is* the belief that love is **i.**. If you
T-8...... IV.4:11 of my decision for you makes healing **i.**.
T-8....... VII.5:2 Loss of any kind is **i.**. But when you look
T-8....... VII.7:2 Strictly speaking this is **i.**, since it seems
T-8....... VII.8:3 Being faced with an **i.** learning situation is
T-8........ IX.4:8 Complete unconsciousness is **i.**. You can
T-8........ IX.6:4 But to make mindless is **i.**, since it would
T-8........ IX.8:2 is **i.** that I could do things you cannot do.
T-9...........I.2:3 It is **i.** to learn anything consistently in a
T-9...........I.3:5 up this strange situation so that it is **i.** to
T-9...........I.6:1 It is **i.** to communicate in alien tongues.
T-9.........I.11:2 someone who persists in attempting the **i.**
T-9.........I.11:3 belief that you must have the **i.** in order to
T-9.........I.11:6 although it is **i.** for you to change them. If
T-9.........I.12:2 Willing against reality, though **i.**, can be
T-9......... II.3:5 It is **i.**, however, that it will be lost. There
T-9....... II.11:6 It is **i.** not to have, but it is possible not to
T-9........ IV.4:3 merely place yourself in an **i.** situation, to
T-9...... IV.11:1 The **i.** can happen only in fantasy. When
T-9......... V.7:1 the characteristic "**i.** situation" to which
T-10.........I.1:1 and to attack what you have created is **i.**.
T-10.........I.1:2 But remember that *it is as **i.** for God.* The
T-10.........I.4:3 will be **i.** because you will want only truth,
T-10....... III.4:5 Yet this is **i.**, because you are part of God,
T-11.......in.1:4 all respects so that partial allegiance is **i.**.
T-11....... IV.6:3 and it is **i.** that you cannot enter the place
T-11..... V.11:1 purpose could be defeated, and this is **i.**.
T-11..... V.11:2 from the **i.** and the false from the true.
T-11....... VI.1:1 It is **i.** not to believe what you see, but it
T-11....... VI.1:1 is equally **i.** to see what you do not believe
T-11..VIII.15:3 you that, as part of God, deceit in you is **i.**
T-12....... V.5:4 situation in which you placed yourself is **i.**
T-12...VII.14:1 a traitor to God, to Whom treachery is **i.**.
T-13........I.11:6 yourself, for without guilt attack is **i.**. You
T-13.....VIII.1:4 indeed be **i.** to be in the world with this
T-13 ..... IX.6:5 that it is **i.** to condemn the Son of God in
T-13 ..... XI.5:2 It is **i.** that this mission fail. Nothing can
T-14 .......II.8:5 will realize it is **i.** to deny the simple truth.
T-14 ...... III.5:7 is **i.** to offer what you do not want without
T-14 ... III.10:8 **i.** burden of deciding what they want and
T-14 ... III.15:8 For it is quite **i.** that He could ever let His
T-14 ... III.16:2 in this light, error of any kind becomes **i.**.
T-14 ..... IV.7:6 would but listen, and learn how **i.** this is!
T-14 .... VII.3:5 To God, unknowing is **i.**. It is therefore
T-14 .... VII.4:4 their joint acceptance becomes **i.**. But if
T-14 .VIII.2:14 Himself wills with His Son is quite **i.** here.
T-14 ..... IX.2:3 stand when its **i.** nature is clearly revealed
T-14 .......X.3:5 From the world's viewpoint, this is **i.**.
T-14 .......X.9:3 lack of content makes a cohesive system **i.**
T-14 .....X.10:1 is **i.** to remember God in secret and alone.
T-14 ... XI.3:10 a condition in which seeing becomes **i.**.
T-14 ..... XI.7:5 It is **i.** that God lose His Identity, for if He
T-14 ..... XI.8:2 That is **i.**. But be sure that you are willing
T-14 ..... XI.8:3 you are willing to acknowledge that it *is* **i.**.
T-14 ... XI.15:2 only because, alone, it is **i.** to know Him.
T-14 ... XI.15:4 It is **i.** to deny the Source of effects so
T-15 ..... IV.8:2 is **i.** to recognize perfect communication
T-15 ...... V.1:4 Judgment becomes **i.** without the past, for
T-15 ..... V.10:4 from His, and it is **i.** to understand it.
T-15 ..... VI.1:1 **i.** to use one relationship at the expense of
T-15 ..... VI.1:2 And it is equally **i.** to condemn part of a
T-15 ..... VI.5:1 love has no meaning and peace is **i.**. For
T-15 ... VI.5:10 he gladly wills, it is **i.** that he be bound, or
T-15 .... VII.2:3 guilt. It is **i.** for the ego to enter into any
T-15 .... VII.7:7 well. Forgiveness becomes **i.**, for the ego
T-15 .. VII.14:1 the holy instant that what seems **i.** is
T-15 .. VII.14:1 making it evident that it is not **i.**. In the
T-15 ...VIII.6:4 Leave, then, what seems to you to be **i.**, to
T-15 ..... IX.2:2 For it is **i.** to recognize as wholly without
T-15 ..... IX.2:4 communication, and thereby to make it **i.**
T-15 ..... IX.4:1 **i.** to divide your strength between Heaven
T-15 ..... IX.5:3 loving relationships that any limit is **i.**.
T-15 ..... XI.6:3 **i.** to deny what love is and still recognize
T-16 .......II.1:1 still think that holiness is **i.** to understand
T-16 .......II.2:7 Yet it is still **i.** to accomplish what you do
T-16 .......II.3:4 order of difficulty in miracles is quite **i.**,
T-16 .......II.4:5 is **i.** to convince you of the reality of what
T-16 ..... III.3:3 it is **i.** to teach successfully wholly without
T-16 ..... III.3:3 is equally **i.** that conviction be outside of
T-16 ..... IV.1:2 be **i.** not to know the meaning of love,
T-16 ..... IV.7:3 love relationship would accomplish the **i.**.
T-16 .... V.17:3 It is **i.** not to make the natural decision as
T-16 ..... VI.1:7 **i.** to define it otherwise and understand it
T-16 .... VII.1:1 **i.** to let the past go without relinquishing
T-16 .... VII.8:5 **i.** that you receive it not *because* He gave it.
T-16 .. VII.11:2 perceived as great or small, possible or **i.**.
T-17 ........I.1:6 is **i.** to convince the dreamer that this is so
T-17 ..... III.4:4 must enter in, because its purpose is **i.**.
T-17 ..... IV.2:1 this world it is **i.** to create. Yet it *is* possible
T-17 .... V.13:5 it is **i.** to deny yourself, and to recognize
T-17 ..... VI.3:7 understanding doubtful and evaluation **i.**.
T-17 .... VII.2:2 of the problem but will make solution **i.**.
T-17 .... VII.3:3 But if the goal is truth, this is **i.**. Some
T-18 ........I.3:1 emotion in which substitution is **i.** is love.
T-18 ........I.4:3 now almost **i.** to perceive it once was one,
T-18 ..... III.3:2 that you have chosen, fear would be **i.**.
T-18 ..... IV.4:4 It is **i.** to make arrogant preparations for
T-18 ..... IV.8:1 that is natural and easy for you **i.**. If you
T-18 ...... V.4:4 is an undertaking **i.** for you to understand
T-18 ...... V.6:4 in the fact that it is now **i.** for you or your
T-18 ...... V.6:6 just as this is **i.**, so is it equally impossible
T-18 ...... V.6:6 it equally **i.** that the holy instant come to
T-18 ..... VI.6:2 It is **i.** to act out fantasies. For it is still the
T-18 .... VII.4:1 It is **i.** to accept the holy instant without
T-19 ........I.4:3 in which uniting with him becomes **i.**.
T-19 ........I.5:7 truth. Partial dedication is **i.**. Truth is the
T-19 .......I.5:10 both is to set up a goal forever **i.** to attain,
T-19 .......II.3:5 inherent in the whole idea of sin, it is **i.**.
T-19 .....II.6:12 truth. It is **i.** to have faith in sin, for sin is
T-19 .......II.7:3 from which escape will always be **i.**. This
T-19 ..... III.6:2 **i.** that what is part of Him is totally unlike
T-19 ..... III.8:4 purpose now, the goal of proving this is **i.**.
T-19 ..... IV.2:7 been forever **i.** to appreciate your brother.
T19..IV.B.12:1 is **i.** to seek for pleasure through the body
T19 .IV.B.16:1 its madness, and believe not the **i.** is true.
T19 .IV.C.2:10 is **i.** to you who chose His Will as yours?
T-20 ... III.10:5 of any separation between us become **i.**.
T-20 ..... IV.8:2 Perhaps this seems **i.** to you. But ask
T-20 .......V.3:1 is **i.** to overestimate your brother's value.
T-20 .......V.8:6 yet it is **i.** the confidence of God should be
T-20 .... VII.1:8 It is **i.** to imagine one that asks so little, or
T-20 .... VII.3:8 remember that if you think they are **i.**,
T-20 .... VII.4:1 It *is* **i.** to see your brother as sinless and
T-20 .... VII.4:4 To see a sinless body is **i.**, for holiness is
T-21 .......II.3:1 It is **i.** the Son of God be merely driven by
T-21 .......II.3:2 It is **i.** that happenings that come to him
T-21 ..... III.3:5 It is **i.** to place equal faith in opposite
T-21 ..... III.5:1 It is **i.** that the Son of God lack faith, but
T-21 ... VI.2:10 what *is* yours? If minds are joined, this is **i.**
T-21 .... VII.3:4 For had they done so hatred would be **i.**.
T-21 .... VII.4:7 changes so it is **i.** even to recognize him.
T-21 .. VII.10:5 implies a state where vacillations are **i.**.
T-22 ........I.3:1 realized it is **i.** to understand what fails
T-22 .......II.5:2 you now that it is **i.** for you to see no guilt
T-22 .......II.5:6 One to Whom nothing He wills can be **i.**,
T-22 .......II.6:4 Yet to the ego this must be **i.**, and no one
T-22 .....II.11:1 Only *your* thoughts have been **i.**.
T-22 .....II.11:3 be. It *is* **i.** to look upon your savior as your
T-22 ..... III.9:6 And so it must become **i.** for each to see
T-22 .......V.3:7 Yet it remains **i.** to keep love out. God
T-22 ..... VI.2:3 a situation so contradictory and so **i.** that
T-22 ..... VI.3:7 it will be **i.** for you to hate what serves
T-22 ... VI.12:9 It is **i.**. And this is so because the universe
T-22 ... VI.15:3 of love is there, which makes all fear **i.**?
T-23 ........I.1:4 is **i.** unless belief in victory is cherished.
T-23 ........I.3:1 Be certain that it is **i.** God and the ego, or
T-23 .......II.7:2 Now it becomes **i.** to turn to Him for help
T-23 .......II.7:6 of God. For now salvation must remain **i.**,
T-23 .....II.19:6 Life not in Heaven is **i.**, and what is not in
T-23 .....II.19:7 stands; senseless, **i.** and beyond all reason
T-23 ..... III.3:6 for compromise is the belief salvation is **i.**
T-23 ..... III.4:4 that salvation is **i.** cannot uphold a quiet,
T-23 ..... III.4:7 if only thus does it become **i.** that you lose
T-23 ..... IV.8:6 They know it is **i.** their happiness could
T-24 ........I.2:1 other because conflicting outcomes are **i.**.
T-24 .......II.3:2 Sin is **i.** even to imagine without this base.
T-24 ..... III.1:3 and that is why it is **i.** but partly to forgive
T-24 ..... IV.3:3 To minds intent on specialness it is **i.**. Yet
T-25 .. VII.12:6 And sin must be **i.**, if this is true. This is
T-25 ...VIII.2:5 divided still against himself would find **i.**.
T-25 ...VIII.5:7 Fairness and vengeance are **i.**, for each
T-25 ...VIII.5:8 **i.** for you to share the Holy Spirit's justice
T-25 .VIII.11:8 And love without justice is **i.**. For love is
T-25 .VIII.12:1 is **i.** the Son of God could merit vengeance
T-25 ..... IX.3:4 It is **i.** the Holy Spirit could see unfairness
T-25 ..... IX.4:1 sight of innocence makes punishment **i.**,
T-26 ..... III.4:9 In this one, choice is made **i.**. In the real
T-26 .... VII.6:1 It is **i.** that one illusion be less amenable
T-26 .. VII.11:4 It is **i.** that anything be lost, if what you
T-26 ...VIII.2:2 him. This makes trust **i.**. And you cannot
T-27 ..... IV.2:2 that, in your state of mind, solution is **i.**.
T-27 .VIII.13:7 that is **i.** is that you be unlike each other;
T-28 .......II.3:2 For this **i.** desire, he does not believe that
T-29 ........I.1:4 represent in His eternal Love is quite **i.**.
T-29 .......II.1:3 so clearly marked it is **i.** to lose the way,
T-29 ...VIII.6:3 the world where the **i.** has happened.
T-30 .... VI.4:2 is just, it seems **i.** His pardon could be real
T-30 .... VII.5:6 In one united goal does this become **i.**, for
T-31 ........I.1:3 The **i.** has not occurred, and can have no
T-31 ..... IV.7:5 understand, then is this course **i.** to learn.
T-31 ..... VI.5:2 Undoing truth would be **i.**. But concepts
T-31 .... VII.1:8 treachery, and trust becomes **i.**. Nor
W-in.......... 5:3 makes its accomplishments anywhere **i.**.
W-pI ...... 4.2:5 are blocks to sight, and make seeing **i.**.
W-pI .... 13.1:2 Actually, a meaningless world is **i.**.
W-pI .... 14.1:1 the reason why a meaningless world is **i.**.
W-pI .... 16.3:2 result is **i.** because a neutral thought is
W-pI .... 16.3:2 impossible because a neutral thought is **i.**.
W-pI .... 45.4:5 us that what God would have us do is **i.**.
W-pI .... 47.7:5 There is a place in you where nothing is **i.**.
W-pI .... 52.1:3 It is **i.** that it could upset me. Reality
W-pI .... 54.1:2 thoughts are **i.** because all thoughts have
W-pI .... 64.5:8 It is **i.** that any decision on earth can have

W-pI.....74.2:4 Without illusions conflict is **i.**. Let us try
W-pI.....79.5:2 that they confront you with an **i.** situation
W-pI.....90.3:7 I will understand it is **i.** that I could have a
W-pI.....91.3:7 For you it is **i.**, but you are not alone in
W-pI.....93.1:3 hand, living on after seeing this being **i.**.
W-pI.....95.1:4 Your perfect unity makes change in you **i.**
W-pI.....99.1:3 a thing **i.** but yet which has occurred,
W-pI.....99.2:2 **i.** becomes the thing you need forgiveness
W-pI...105.1:7 **i.** that one can gain because another loses.
W-pI...107.6:4 It is **i.** that anyone could seek it truly, and
WpI. rIII.in2:1 it may be **i.** for you to undertake what is
WpI. rIII.in2:2 because it is **i.** at the appointed time. Nor
W-pI...127.2:2 does not see that changing love must be **i.**
W-pI...129.3:1 to find a world instead where losing is **i.**;
W-pI......130.h It is **i.** to see two worlds.
W-pI...130.5:1 It is **i.** to see two worlds which have no
W-pI...130.8:5 *It is **i.** to see two worlds. Let me accept the*
W-pI.130.11:4 *It is **i.** to see two worlds. I seek my freedom*
W-pI...134.4:2 is **i.** to think of sin as true and not believe
W-pI.136.18:4 to make it well, for sickness has become **i.**
W-pI...137.3:2 It is **i.** that anyone be healed alone. In
W-pI.139.5:11 it part of you, then certainty would be **i.**.
W-pI...139.7:3 and they learn it is **i.** to doubt yourself,
W-pI...140.8:4 our own thoughts; so close it is **i.** to lose.
W-pI...145.2:1 (130) It is **i.** to see two worlds.
W-pI...155.7:2 for defeat, and aims that will remain **i.**.
W-pI...156.1:1 truth that makes the thought of sin **i.**. It
W-pI...160.6:3 he may look, for he has made return **i.**.
W-pI...163.6:1 It is **i.** to worship death in any form, and
W-pI...166.2:4 **I.** indeed; but every mind that looks upon
W-pI...168.2:1 of His Love, hope and despair would be **i.**.
W-pI.186.11:6 Your plan may be **i.**, but God's can never
W-pI.186.12:2 if It asks a thing of you which seems **i.**,
W-pI...192.5:3 Anger becomes **i.**, and where is terror
W-pI...196.6:3 see that this, at least, must be entirely **i.**,
W-pI...196.8:3 For once you understand it is **i.** that you
W-pI...198.1:1 Injury is **i.**. And yet illusion makes
W-pI...198.2:5 To condemn is thus **i.** in truth. What
W-pI...199.1:1 Freedom must be **i.** as long as you
W-pII..228.1:2 believe in what His knowledge makes **i.**?
W-pII..240.1:2 therefore look upon a world which is **i.**.
W-pII..249.1:1 loss becomes **i.** and anger makes no sense
W-pII..253.1:1 It is **i.** that anything should come to me
W-pII..256.1:8 forgiven him in whom all sin remains **i.**,
W-pII..284.1:2 Pain is **i.**. There is no grief with any cause
W-pII..284.2:1 *cannot hurt, so grief and pain must be **i.**. Let*
W-pII......8.1:4 so they see a world where terror is **i.**, and
W-pII..307.1:5 *me, and enter into peace where conflict is **i.**,*
W-pII..312.1:4 It is **i.** to overlook what we would see, and
W-pII..343.1:5 *so sacrifice becomes **i.** for me as well as You. I*
W-pII....14.1:3 *is love perfected, fear **i.**, and joy established*
W-pII..359.1:7 *us. Sin is **i.**, and on this fact forgiveness rests*
M-in ..........3:3 is **i.** not to use the content of any situation
M-4..........I.2:1 **i.** to trust one's own petty strength again.
M-4......I.A.5:6 how wholly **i.** such a demand would be.
M-4......I.A.7:5 system, had made it **i.** for him to judge.
M-4......I.A.7:7 that may remain **i.** to reach for a long,
M-4........ II.1:9 Therefore it is **i.** for them to be in conflict
M-4........ II.2:6 God's teachers rest secure makes doubt **i.**.
M-4.......III.1:3 Judgment without self-deception is **i.**.
M-4.......IV.1:1 Harm is **i.** for God's teachers. They can
M-4......IV.1:10 make the Holy Spirit's lessons **i.** to learn.
M-4.......IV.2:3 To those who would do harm, it is **i.**. To
M-4........ V.1:2 Gentleness means that fear is now **i.**, and
M-5............1:2 sickness is for. Healing is **i.** without this.
M-6............1:2 It is **i.** to let illusions be brought to truth
M-7............2:7 This is **i.**. Having offered love, only love
M-7............4:6 Yet love without trust is **i.**, and doubt and
M-7............4:8 not the gift and it is **i.** to doubt its result.
M-7............6:9 of what you want, and doubt becomes **i.**.
M-10..........2:5 that judgment was always **i.** for him, he
M-10..........3:1 that judgment in the usual sense is **i.**. This
M-11..........1:2 Certainly peace seems to be **i.** here. Yet
M-11..........1:3 of God promises other things that seem **i.**
M-11..........1:7 and what He promises can hardly be **i.**.
M-11..........4:1 Peace is **i.** to those who look on war.
M-11..........4:4 is not the world that makes peace seem **i.**.
M-11..........4:5 It is the world you see that is **i.**. Yet has
M-11........4:12 "Is it not **i.** that peace be absent here?"
M-12 ........5:12 or remaining. Sickness is now **i.** to him.
M-13 ........3:1 it becomes **i.** for the mind to understand
M-13 ........7:11 split that is **i.**. A split that cannot happen.
M-13 ........7:13 you have set up a situation that is **i.**. And
M-13 ........7:14 in this situation the **i.** can seem to happen
M-17 .........6:7 Do not remember the **i.** odds against you.
M-17 .........9:8 Now is escape **i.**, until you see you have
M-18 .........1:4 is real. And this can only be **i.**. Reality is
M-18 .........1:7 age-old **i.** dream in but another form. Yet
M-19 .........1:4 for error is **i.** and correction meaningless.
M-19 .........1:7 Except in His judgment justice is **i.**, for no
M-21 .........3:3 It is **i.** that the prayer of the heart remain
M-21 .........3:4 If he asks for the **i.**, if he wants what does
M-22 .........3:4 body could be sick Atonement would be **i.**
M-22 .........3:5 the place of God and prove salvation is **i.**.
M-24 .........1:1 In the ultimate sense, reincarnation is **i.**.
M-25 .........2:4 It would be **i.** to do so. The limits the
M-26 .........3:2 this world, it is almost **i.** that this endure.
M-27 .........2:1 it, it would be **i.** to think of Him as loving.
M-27 .........2:8 war. Where there is death is peace **i.**.
C-in ...........2:5 A universal theology is **i.**, but a universal
C-in ...........4:2 of a question to which an answer is **i.**. The
C-in ...........4:3 The ego may ask, "How did the **i.** occur?",
C-in ...........4:3 occur?", "To what did the **i.** happen?",
C-3.............1:2 It is **i.** to think of anything He created that
C-4.............5:9 it could not remain where separation is **i.**.
C-4...........5:10 Forgiveness proves it is **i.** because it sees it
C-5.............3:5 that it is **i.** to kill God's Son; nor can his
P-2.........in.2:5 because to the sane mind it is so clearly **i.**,
P-2.........in.2:6 In illusions the **i.** is easily accomplished,
P-2......... II.6:7 It is **i.** to share a goal not blessed by Christ
P-2......... II.9:1 Communion is **i.** alone. No one who
P-2........ III.1:4 **i.** that this One be wholly absent if the
P-2........ IV.6:2 were really the self, defense would be **i.**.
P-2......... V.2:3 Progress becomes **i.** until the patient is
P-2.......VII.4:7 Guilt is **i.** in those through whom the
P-3......... II.2:3 taught him how to make healing **i.**. Most
P-3........ III.7:6 nothing, and to attempt to do what is **i.**.
S-1 ...........I.1:5 **i.** to pray for idols and hope to reach God.
S-2 ...........I.4:2 you. It is **i.** to forgive another, for it is only
S-3 ...........I.1:4 Healing the body is **i.**, and this is shown
S-3 ........ IV.5:4 Now healing is **i.**, for He is blamed for

### impotence 1
W-pI.....13.2:3 to demonstrate its own **i.** and unreality.

### impotent 2
T-2...... VI.9:11 but at the cost of perceiving the mind as **i.**
T-19...... III.5:9 could change perception is thus kept **i.**,

### impoverish 2
T-12...... III.4:5 For to do so is to deny yourself and **i.** both
T-12...... VI.1:3 without profit is surely to **i.** yourself, and

### impoverished 1
T-4.........I.11:2 Do not try to make this **i.** house stand. Its

### impoverishment 1
T-12...... III.3:4 poverty asks for gifts, not for further **i.**.

### impractical 2
P-3........ III.7:1 This view of payment may well seem **i.**,
P-3........ III.7:6 Surely it is **i.** to strive for nothing, and to

### impression 1
T-29... VIII.3:1 An idol is a false **i.**, or a false belief; some

### impressive 1
T-14....... X.8:9 this fact behind **i.** sounding words, but

### imprison 19
T-1........ III.5:9 you project this to others you **i.** them, but
T-8..........II.2:8 learning because your learning will **i.** you.
T-8........ IV.8:3 Whom you seek to **i.** you do not love.
T-8........ IV.8:4 Therefore, when you seek to **i.** anyone,
T-8........ IV.8:5 When you **i.** yourself you are losing sight
T-8........ VI.7:6 they can even **i.** the mind of God's Son, if
T-13........II.7:3 sometimes react as if it is trying to **i.** you.
T-13...... VI.4:1 Time can release as well as **i.**, depending
T-14...... XI.2:2 taught yourself how to **i.** the Son of God,
T-15.... XI.10:6 *released, unless I want to use you to **i.** myself.*
T-16.........I.5:3 that it would **i.** what it would release. The
T-16...... VI.3:4 it must foster guilt and therefore must **i.**.
T-17.........I.5:6 establish orders of reality that must **i.** you
T19.....IV.B.8:3 yet you would **i.** me behind the obstacles
T-20...... IV.4:5 upheld through all temptation to **i.** and to
W-pI.....57.2:4 believing it is possible to **i.** the Son of God
W-pI.....72.2:3 through the body that was made to **i.** it.
S-1 ..........II.4:6 may not seek to **i.** Christ and thereby lose
S-1 ........ IV.4:2 you stifle and **i.** it in ancient prisons,

### imprisoned 19
T-2........ III.3:4 An **i.** will engenders a situation which, in
T-2.......VIII.3:8 the vacillations between free and **i.** will
T-3..........II.4:3 free. An "**i.**" mind is not free because it is
T-3...... VI.11:1 who does not feel that he is **i.** in some way
T-6...... V.C.9:5 What you made has **i.** your will, and given
T-8..........II.3:2 your will to be **i.** because your will is free.
T-8...... III.5:10 He will be **i.** or released according to your
T-8........ IV.7:2 This would mean you have **i.** yours, and
T-8...... IV.8:13 of It can be **i.** if Its truth is to be known.
T-9...........I.4:1 **i.** your will beyond your own awareness,
T-15...... IX.6:8 him free. For his belief in limits *has* **i.** him.
T-19.........I.3:6 and behaving insanely, being **i.** *by* insanity
T-20...... IV.4:5 all temptation to imprison and to be **i.**. It
T-21...... VI.11:5 no more His Son can be **i.** save by his own
T-26.........I.7:4 In Heaven, God's Son is not **i.** in a body,
W-pI.....76.1:2 has **i.** you with laws as senseless as itself.
W-pI.166.10:3 you have **i.** in your plan to lose your Self.
C-1............. 4:2 to be **i.** while the mind is not unified.
S-1 ..........II.5:1 An enemy is the symbol of an **i.** Christ.

### imprisoning 3
T-8..........II.4:3 opposes any **i.** of the will of a Son of God,
T-8........ III.7:8 **i.** thought any part of the Sonship holds.
M-6 ...........3:8 appropriate? Such is not giving but **i.**.

### imprisonment 19
T-1.........I.33:4 By releasing your mind from the **i.** of your
T-2......... V.1:2 foster the belief that release is **i.**, a belief
T-8............ II.h The Difference between **I.** and Freedom
T-8..........II.5:2 the difference between **i.** and freedom.
T-8..........II.5:3 have taught yourself that **i.** is freedom.
T-8...... III.7:10 The **i.** they seem to produce is no more
T-20...... IV.6:7 to forget **i.** and to remember freedom.
T-26.........I.8:5 **i.** he made to keep himself from justice?
T-31...... III.6:5 Release your body from **i.**, and you will
T-31...... III.7:2 upholds their freedom from **i.** and death.
W-pI... 153.3:3 the ever-tightening grip of the **i.** upon the
W-pI.153.11:3 and darkness holds the world in grim **i.**.
W-pI... 186.5:1 released from the **i.** your plan to prove the
W-pI... 191.6:4 You set it free of your **i.**. You will not see a
W-pI... 194.2:2 released the world from all **i.** by loosening
W-pII .280.1:2 is free. I can invent **i.** for him, but only in
M-25 ......... 6:8 their increased freedom for greater **i.**. The
P-3........ III.4:8 for the release from long **i.** and doubt.
S-2........ III.4:1 Are you not weary of **i.**? God did not

### imprisons 4
T-1......... V.5:6 As a result it **i.**, because such are the
T-3...... VI.11:4 Judgment always **i.** because it separates
W-pI.....76.7:5 Magic **i.**, but the laws of God make free.
W-pI... 192.8:2 Who could be set free while he **i.** anyone?

**improperly** 1
T-7........IV.2:9 Perceived **i.**, it induces a perception of

**improve** 1
T-2......... II.5:6 You can learn to **i.** your perceptions, and

**improvement** 1
P-2.........in.3:2 perceptions of "**i.**" still must differ. The

**impulse** 4
T-5.........in.1:6 promotes the mind's natural **i.** to respond
T-7......... V.2:2 Since the ego cannot obliterate the **i.** to
T-7......... V.2:2 because it is also the **i.** to create, it can
T19... IV.D.7:6 No mad desire, no trivial **i.** to forget again

**impulses** 10
T-1..........VII.h Distortions of Miracle **I.**
T-1.......VII.1:1 produce a dense cover over miracle **i.**,
T-1.......VII.1:2 The confusion of miracle **i.** with physical
T-1.......VII.1:2 with physical **i.** is a major perceptual
T-1.......VII.1:3 **i.** are misdirected miracle impulses. All
T-1.......VII.1:3 impulses are misdirected miracle **i.**. All
T-4......... V.2:5 conceal not only "unacceptable" body **i.**,
T-4........ VI.4:3 done this, it denies all truly natural **i.**, not
T-9......VIII.3:1 miracle **i.** and ego-alien beliefs of its own.
W-pII .252.1:4 from burning **i.** which move the world,

**in** 8264

**inability** 5
T-16..IV.11:13 link with you lie both His **i.** to forget and
T-16....... V.6:2 and to the **i.** to perceive either as it is. The
T-18....... II.2:5 both of the ego's **i.** to tolerate reality, and
T-27..... II.15:8 His **i.** to see His goal divided and distinct
P-3....... II.10:7 **i.** to see and hear does not limit the Holy

**inaccessible** 4
T-2........IV.4:5 a person temporarily **i.** to the Atonement.
T-3...........I.6:7 it **i.** to those who do not choose to see.
T-3........IV.6:5 This makes spirit almost **i.** to the mind
T-3........IV.6:5 to the mind and entirely **i.** to the body.

**inaccuracy** 1
T-23..... II.19:5 life, equal in their **i.** and lack of meaning.

**inadequacies** 1
M-29 .......3:10 is necessary merely because of your own **i.**

**inadequacy** 6
T-9.......VII.5:3 escape from a sense of **i.** it has produced,
T-18...VII.4:11 a state of present unworthiness and **i.**.
W-pI.....47.5:1 concerns related to your own sense of **i.**.
W-pI.....47.5:2 concern is associated with feelings of **i.**,
M-7 ...........5:5 and shame associated with a sense of **i.**.
S-1......... II.2:1 always involve feelings of weakness and **i.**,

**inadequate** 4
T-6......IV.10:3 demonstrate that the perfect are **i.** to
T-9.......VII.5:2 and must therefore regard yourself as **i.**.
T-12.......IV.3:2 ego would be totally **i.** in love's presence,
W-pI.....79.4:3 in which your problem solving must be **i.**,

**inanimate** 1
W-pI.....17.3:1 what you believe to be animate or **i.**;

**inapplicable** 1
W-in.......... 6:3 or things to which the ideas are **i.**. This

**inappropriate** 10
T-1 .........II.3:6 It is therefore an **i.** reaction to me. An
T-1 ......VII.5:2 is **i.** in connection with the Sons of God,
T-2 ..........I.1:7 The **i.** use of extension, or projection,
T-2 ...... III.5:2 themselves more comfortable by **i.** means
T-9 ..........I.3:2 particularly **i.** in the minds of those who
T-11 ...... V.4:3 obviously **i.** if you recognize the ego's goal
T-12 ......I.3:10 response will therefore be **i.** to reality as it
T-30 ... VI.1:10 And thus is pardon **i.**, by being granted
T-30 ..... VI.2:4 responses which are **i.** to what is real.
M-4 ........X.3:3 They would be most **i.** here. What God

**inappropriately** 3
T-2 ..........I.1:6 he is, but he can use it **i.** by projecting.
T-2 ....... IV.1:3 is to combine two orders of reality **i.**.
T-2 ......VII.5:6 and to deny it is merely to use denial **i.**.

**inappropriateness** 1
T-17 ...... V.4:2 of its **i.** for meeting its new purpose. The

**incapable** 31
T-1 ......VII.2:4 real vision, of which the physical eye is **i.**.
T-2 .......II.1:10 This peace is totally **i.** of being shaken by
T-3 ..........I.6:1 Innocence is **i.** of sacrificing anything,
T-3 ....... IV.1:3 them, and are therefore **i.** of knowledge.
T-3 ....... IV.1:4 You are also **i.** of knowledge because you
T-3 ....... IV.6:4 loss of power, because it is **i.** of darkness.
T-4 ........I.10:5 **i.** of deception as is the spirit He created.
T-4 ........I.11:7 God is as **i.** of creating the perishable as
T-4 ........ V.6:6 to be **i.** of solution are favorite ego devices
T-5 ..........I.7:3 it is **i.** of attack and is therefore truly open
T-5 .........II.7:1 command, because It is **i.** of arrogance. It
T-5 ........ V.2:3 is truly blessed is **i.** of giving rise to guilt,
T-7 ........ V.5:7 Love is **i.** of any exceptions. Only if there
T-7 ......VII.9:1 allegiance to God, the ego is **i.** of trust.
T-7 ......VII.9:2 brothers, who are as **i.** of this as you are,
T-8 .....VIII.1:3 is because it is **i.** of true generalizations,
T-8 .....VIII.7:5 The ego is **i.** of knowing how you feel.
T-9 .....VIII.3:3 it **i.** of judgment except in terms of attack.
T-10 ...... V.9:5 created you, you will be **i.** of suffering. Yet
T-14 ... IV.10:1 totally **i.** of understanding one another.
T-14 .......X.8:1 The ego is **i.** of understanding content,
T-15 .......X.2:5 I am as **i.** of receiving sacrifice as God is,
T-16 ....VII.9:4 anyone, for He is **i.** of illusions of any kind
T-18 ..... VI.7:5 **i.** of reaching out as being reached. You
T-19 .......I.16:4 **i.** of being kept in prison or limited in any
T-21 ..... VI.4:4 Reason would be **i.** of this. And if you
T-24 ........I.4:2 "better," someone **i.** of being like what he
W-pI.....23.2:4 **i.** of change because it is merely an effect.
W-pI.....25.2:3 This false identification makes you **i.** of
M-25 ......... 4:2 The Holy Spirit is **i.** of deception, and He
M-29 ....... 4:12 attack. And therefore **i.** of arousing guilt.

**inception** 1
T-5 ........ V.7:5 thought is attended by guilt at its **i.**, and

**inclination** 1
W-pI..... 11.4:2 or no uneasiness and an **i.** to do more, as

**inclinations** 1
T-2 ........ V.4:3 working **i.** are not functioning properly, it

**inclined** 3
T-14 .......II.2:5 and nothing are you less **i.** to listen to.
T-15 ..... VI.4:3 more **i.** to regard his success as witness to
WpI..rIII.in9:2 **i.** to practice only at appointed times, and

**include** 31
T-4 .........II.9:2 generally **i.** some account of "the creation
T-5 ....... IV.3:6 also **i.** opposite thoughts at the same level
T-7 ...... VII.4:5 While you **i.** them in it, you are giving life
T-7 ....... IX.2:3 includes God, and any totality *must* **i.** God
T-13 .......V.2:2 do not **i.** their reactions to him. Therefore
T-16 .......II.1:1 see how it can be extended to **i.** everyone.
T-16 .......II.1:2 told that it must **i.** everyone to *be* holy.
T-16 ..... VI.5:7 does not **i.** even one whole individual.
T-27 .......V.8:6 instances, and generalizes to **i.** them all.
W-in.......... 7:1 you will be practicing to **i.** everything.
W-pI ...... 2.1:4 so that you **i.** whatever is on either side. If
W-pI ...... 2.1:6 to **i.** everything you see in a given area, or
W-pI ...... 2.2:5 Make no attempt to **i.** anything particular
W-pI ...... 8.6:3 it helpful, however, to **i.** your irritation, or
W-pI .... 12.3:3 rather than negative occur to you, **i.** them
W-pI .... 14.5:1 idea also **i.** anything you are afraid might
W-pI .... 15.4:4 It is not necessary to **i.** a large number of
W-pI .... 23.7:1 sure to **i.** both your thoughts of attacking
W-pI .... 28.8:1 the applications should **i.** the name of the
W-pI .... 29.5:2 For example, a suitable list might **i.**: *God is*
W-pI .... 32.2:2 periods for today will again **i.** two phases,
W-pI .... 35.4:2 **I.** all the ego-based attributes which you
W-pI .... 38.5:2 like, for example, to **i.** thoughts such as:
W-pI .... 39.9:2 You may also find it helpful to **i.** a few
W-pI .... 68.7:1 short practice periods should **i.** a quick
W-pI .... 76.8:2 These would **i.**, for example, the "laws" of
W-pI .... 81.4:1 Specific forms for using this idea might **i.**
W-pI .... 82.4:1 Suitable specific forms of this idea **i.**: *Let*
W-pI .... 95.6:1 planned to **i.** frequent reminders of your
M-4 ........X.3:1 of attributes of God's teachers does not **i.**
P-2......... in.3:4 to stabilize it sufficiently to **i.** within it the

**included** 15
T-6 ..... V.C.6:5 essential to teach you that you must be **i.**,
T-7 ....... IX.2:1 of all its brothers is **i.** in its own, as it is
T-7 ....... IX.2:1 is included in its own, as it is **i.** in God.
T-7 ....... IX.7:5 in the lesson, you have **i.** the whole.
T-8 ....... IV.1:5 peace is complete, and you must be **i.** in it
T-8 ..... IV.8:11 must be **i.** in It, because It is everything.
T-11 .......V.6:5 He has **i.** you in His Autonomy. Can you
T-21 .......V.6:2 and in this your will must be **i.**. Thus,
W-pI .... 19.4:1 it will occasionally be **i.** as a reminder. Do
W-pI .... 42.7:2 and nothing is **i.** that is contradictory or
WpI... rI.in.2:1 the five ideas, with the comments **i.**.
WpI.. rII.in.2:1 comments that are **i.** in the assignments.
WpI.. rII.in.6:2 needed. Some specific forms are **i.** in the
W-pI .. 121.9:3 yourself, and see that their escape **i.** yours
W-pII . 243.2:2 *I honor all its parts, in which I am* **i.**. *We are*

**includes** 11
T-2 ..........I.2:7 sense the creation **i.** both the creation of
T-4 ....... VI.2:4 to the whole Sonship, which **i.** me, you
T-7 ....... VI.1:6 **i.** his concept of God, of His creations and
T-7 ....... IX.2:3 prevail against a totality that **i.** God, and
T-7 ....... IX.5:2 being, because your fulfillment **i.** them.
T-7 ..... XI.7:10 of God **i.** all His Sons and their children,
W-pI .... 31.1:4 speaking, the form **i.** two aspects, one in
W-pI ....... 55.h Today's review **i.** the following:
W-pI .. 152.5:2 And that **i.** all shifts in feeling, alterations
M-3 ........... 1:5 plan **i.** very specific contacts to be made
M-19 ......... 2:3 itself, justice **i.** nothing that opposes truth

**including** 11
T-2 ........I.1:11 distort the creations of God, **i.** yourself.
T-3 ..........I.3:9 **i.** the belief that God rejected Adam and
T-4 ....... IV.7:2 it is the belief that no one, **i.** yourself, is
T-7 ....... IX.7:5 By **i.** any part of totality in the lesson, you
T-8 ....... III.7:6 to suffer for a wrong decision, **i.** you. That
T-8 ....... IV.8:4 you seek to imprison anyone, **i.** yourself,
T-14 .... VII.7:5 will show you that all meaning, **i.** yours,
T-14 ..... XI.6:7 *I do not know what anything,* **i.** *this, means.*
T-24 .....II.10:6 but possessed of everything, **i.** you. Give
W-pI .... 57.5:6 the holiness of all living things, **i.** myself,
W-pI .... 83.4:4 *Nothing,* **i.** *this, can justify the illusion of*

### inclusion 9

| | |
|---|---|
| T-1......... V.3:5 | does not stem from exclusion but from **i.**. |
| T-6......... II.5:3 | love for both, because it establishes **i.**. |
| T-6......... II.6:5 | It is total **i.**. You cannot change it now or |
| T-6....... II.6:10 | truth lies only in its perfect **i.** in Him Who |
| T-6..V.C.10:10 | **i.** is total and creation is without limit. |
| T-9......... II.6:2 | Prayer is the restatement of **i.**, directed by |
| T-14....... V.7:7 | your safe **i.** in the circle with everyone you |
| W-pI........9.5:1 | again that while complete **i.** should not be |
| W-pI.....43.5:1 | without self-directed **i.** or exclusion. For |

### inclusive 5

*See also* all-inclusive

| | |
|---|---|
| T-24.........I.2:6 | and to violence far more **i.** than you think |
| T-27. VIII.11:2 | Holy Spirit will repeat this one **i.** lesson of |
| T-31... VIII.8:3 | so **i.** it is but a step from there to Heaven. |
| T-31. VIII.11:5 | threads of melody to one **i.** chorus from a |
| W-pI...152.2:1 | position is extreme, and too **i.** to be true. |

### inclusiveness 2

*See also* all-inclusiveness

| | |
|---|---|
| M-22..........2:1 | whether he recognizes the Atonement's **i.**, |
| M-22..........2:5 | necessary realization of **i.** may reach him. |

### incoherent 1

| | |
|---|---|
| T-14....... X.9:2 | from joining them is **i.** and utterly chaotic |

### incompatibility 1

| | |
|---|---|
| T-14.....VII.4:9 | of their complete **i.** is instantly apparent. |

### incompatible 3

| | |
|---|---|
| T-23......IV.2:2 | Murder and love are **i.**. Yet if they both |
| T-27.........I.1:2 | Who can combine the wholly **i.**, and |
| W-pI.135.17:2 | disregard what you consider **i.** with your |

### incomplete 27

| | |
|---|---|
| T-3........VI.7:4 | the ego makes is **i.** and contradictory. |
| T-4.......VII.6:4 | His joy is not complete because yours is **i.**. |
| T-9........VI.7:7 | God's meaning is **i.** without you, and you |
| T-9........VI.7:7 | you, and you are **i.** without your creations |
| T-9.......VII.8:2 | *God Himself is* **i.** *without me.* Remember |
| T-9...... VIII.9:8 | be replaced. God is **i.** without you because |
| T-11.........I.5:6 | God is not **i.**, and He is not childless. |
| T-11..... V.12:1 | yours, and is therefore **i.** without it. You |
| T-15......XI.4:8 | experiencing himself as **i.** and lonely? |
| T-19.........I.1:5 | faith is limited and your dedication **i.**. |
| T-19....... II.2:7 | God Himself is changed, and rendered **i.**. |
| T-21.........I.4:9 | them that they are **i.** and bitterly deprived |
| T-21......IV.4:1 | still is only partial; still limited and **i.**, yet |
| T-21... VIII.3:9 | giving must be **i.** unless it is received. |
| T-24......VI.2:1 | there would be a lack in God, a Heaven **i.**, |
| T-26.........I.3:2 | part, remaining **i.** to keep its own identity |
| T-26...VII.14:7 | then is God's Son made **i.** and not himself |
| T-26......IX.4:5 | home. The **i.** is made complete again, and |
| T-27......III.6:5 | Though it is but half the picture and is **i.**, |
| T-29......III.2:3 | Was He made **i.** by your perfection? Or |
| T-30......III.3:5 | to the source of the belief that you are **i.**. |
| W-pI...100.3:2 | Without your joy, His joy is **i.**. Without |
| W-pI...136.9:3 | His Son is dust, the Father **i.**, and chaos |
| WpI.. rV.in8:5 | God would not have Heaven **i.**. It waits |
| WpI.. rV.in8:7 | I am **i.** without your part in me. And as I |
| M-28..........3:7 | for what remains unanswered or **i.**? The |
| S-3 .........IV.8:3 | you wait in sorrow Heaven's melody is **i.**, |

### incompleteness 1

| | |
|---|---|
| T-2.......VII.6:7 | can believe in error or **i.** if he so chooses. |

### incompletion 2

| | |
|---|---|
| T-21....... V.6:6 | because its Source knows not of **i.**. |
| T-25......VI.4:3 | complete within a world where **i.** rules. |

### incomprehensible 1

| | |
|---|---|
| T-2......... II.6:3 | process is actually **i.** in temporal terms, |

### inconceivable 16

| | |
|---|---|
| T-3........VI.7:5 | it accepts the one **i.** thought as its premise |
| T-3........VI.7:5 | can produce only ideas that are **i.**. |
| T-3.....VII.4:11 | you believe the one thing that is literally **i.** |
| T-8..... VIII.5:8 | Without these premises sickness is **i.**. |
| T-10......IV.6:1 | of God, the making of idols becomes **i.**. |
| T-15.......I.10:1 | Time is **i.** without change, yet holiness |
| T-18....... V.3:8 | such as this, without the means, is **i.**. He |
| T-18... VIII.4:6 | be gone; the ripple without the ocean is **i.**. |
| T-23......IV.8:3 | Sorrow of any kind is **i.**. Only the light |
| W-pI.....72.4:6 | A creator wholly unlike his creation is **i.**. |
| W-pI...189.3:5 | is **i.** to those who see a world of hatred |
| W-pI...189.4:1 | world of hatred equally unseen and **i.** to |
| W-pII..322.2:1 | *Father, to You all sacrifice remains forever* **i.** |
| M-19 .........1:9 | of separation would have been forever **i.**. |
| M-22 .........1:4 | as special areas of hell in Heaven are **i.**. |
| P-2........IV.8:4 | so alien to God that it must be forever **i.**. |

### inconceivably 1

| | |
|---|---|
| M-10 .........3:3 | be fully aware of an **i.** wide range of things |

### incongruities 1

| | |
|---|---|
| T-3......... V.5:3 | **i.** are the result of attempts to regard |

### inconsistencies 3

| | |
|---|---|
| T-9......... V.5:2 | Such evident **i.** account for why no one |
| T-20.....VII.1:4 | The seeming **i.**, or parts you find more |
| M-27 .........6:9 | The **i.**, the compromises and the rituals |

### inconsistency 3

| | |
|---|---|
| T-7......... V.5:4 | not, the healer is obviously accepting **i.**. |
| T-11..... V.14:5 | truth is meaningless, **i.** must be true. |
| T-21......IV.6:1 | is no **i.** in what the Holy Spirit teaches. |

### inconsistent 8

| | |
|---|---|
| T-7......... V.2:6 | **i.** lesson will be poorly taught and poorly |
| T-8...........I.5:4 | A meaningful curriculum cannot be **i.**. If |
| T-9........VI.2:3 | are **i.** you will not always give rise to joy, |
| T-20.....VII.2:5 | If you are not, let us admit that *you* are **i.**. |
| W-pI.....95.6:3 | however, for those whose motivation is **i.**, |
| W-pI...156.2:1 | **i.** in the thoughts that we present in our |
| W-pI.186.12:4 | bewildered, **i.** and unsure of everything? |
| M-10 .........1:8 | himself may well be **i.** in what he believes. |

### inconsistently 1

| | |
|---|---|
| T-7....... V.6:10 | is consistent it cannot be **i.** understood. |

### inconstant 3

| | |
|---|---|
| T-21...VII.13:2 | is attained by giving up the wish for the *i.*. |
| T-21... VIII.1:5 | the final proof he valued the **i.** more than |
| T-25....... II.3:1 | apart from this; some glimmering,– **i.**, |

### inconstantly 1

| | |
|---|---|
| T-21... VIII.3:1 | you that you cannot ask for happiness **i.**. |

### incorporates 2

| | |
|---|---|
| T-7......... V.9:7 | It **i.** to take away. It literally believes that |
| W-pII..350.1:2 | *The Son of God* **i.** *all things within himself as* |

### incorrect 1

| | |
|---|---|
| T-7........IV.2:9 | something else, as all **i.** perception does. |

### incorrectly 1

| | |
|---|---|
| T-9..........II.1:3 | latter in particular might be **i.** interpreted |

### incorruptible 5

| | |
|---|---|
| T19.....IV.C.i.h | The **I.** Body |
| T19....IV.C.5:1 | that would keep the body **i.** and perfect as |
| T19....IV.C.5:4 | Of itself it is neither corruptible nor **i.**. It *is* |
| T19....IV.C.6:1 | are dedicated to the **i.** have been given |
| S-1 ..........II.7:5 | as set forever, beyond all change and **i.**. |

### increase 52

| | |
|---|---|
| T-1.........I.16:2 | They simultaneously **i.** the strength of the |
| T-2......... IV.4:7 | the sick, is an **i.** in fear. They are already |
| T-4...........I.6:2 | would be to **i.** anxiety about separation. I |
| T-4...........I.9:9 | attempt to **i.** its believableness is merely |
| T-4........ VI.3:1 | will **i.** as you turn more and more often to |
| T-4....... VII.5:1 | but who want to share it to **i.** their joy. |
| T-5...........I.2:2 | *Thoughts* **i.** *by being given away. The more* |
| T-5..........II.7:9 | War is division, not **i.**. No one gains from |
| T-5....... II.11:2 | **i.** its power to attract the whole Sonship, |
| T-5.... III.11:10 | asking only that you **i.** it in His Name by |
| T-5.... III.11:10 | His Name by sharing it to **i.** His joy in you |
| T-5........ IV.2:6 | It will **i.** as you are willing to return the |
| T-5........ IV.2:8 | of unshared ideas that are too weak to **i.**, |
| T-5........ VI.7:1 | that ideas **i.** only by being shared. The |
| T-6...... V.B.3:3 | that this is apt to **i.** conflict temporarily, |
| T-6...... V.C.4:1 | While the first step seems to **i.** conflict |
| T-7...........I.2:1 | the Kingdom could not **i.** through its own |
| T-7...........I.2:6 | He created the Sonship and you **i.** it. You |
| T-7.........I.7:10 | It does not change by **i.**, because it was |
| T-7.........I.7:10 | because it was forever created to **i.**. If you |
| T-7..........II.3:9 | that the **i.** of the Kingdom depends on it, |
| T-7......... V.9:9 | of the **i.** of the Kingdom by your creations |
| T-7........ IX.6:1 | to **i.** the inheritance of the Sons of God, |
| T-8........ VI.8:9 | and thus **i.** the joy of the Holy Trinity. |
| T-9..........II.3:3 | by Him will ever be one that would **i.** fear. |
| T-11........II.6:8 | increased. And by this **i.**, you will begin to |
| T-13.......I.11:1 | you are guilty, and this must **i.** the guilt, |
| T-15..... VII.4:1 | the ego attempts to maintain and **i.** guilt, |
| T-15...... IX.4:2 | you. Love would *always* give **i.**. Limits are |
| T-16.........I.2:4 | would **i.** itself by sharing what is like itself |
| T-16........II.7:1 | listening will **i.** and peace will grow with |
| T-16........II.7:1 | increase and peace will grow with its **i.**. |
| T-16....... V.7:4 | union, for there is no **i.** and no extension. |
| T-18.........I.6:3 | is meaningless and only **i.** is conceivable. |
| T-23....... IV.4:4 | how to **i.** your little gifts and make them |
| W-in.......... 7:1 | the exercises is to **i.** your ability to extend |
| W-pI....... 2.1:3 | on. Then **i.** the range outward. Turn your |
| W-pI.....73.3:1 | and grievances **i.** with each exchange. Can |
| W-pI.....97.5:3 | And they will **i.** in healing power each |
| W-pI.....97.7:3 | Him, **i.** its power and give it back to you. |
| W-pI.....98.3:5 | and thus **i.** it by accepting it ourselves. |
| W-pI...105.1:3 | these gifts **i.** as we receive them. They are |
| W-pI...105.3:5 | they are given away. They but **i.** thereby. |
| W-pI. 107.10:3 | They will **i.** with every gift you give of five |
| W-pI. 132.17:1 | **i.** the freedom sent through your ideas to |
| W-pI...159.9:1 | His storehouse, that its treasures may **i.**. |
| W-pI...164.7:4 | All that we see will but **i.** our joy, because |
| W-pI...187.1:8 | maintains that giving will **i.** what you |
| W-pI...187.9:5 | the perfect gift forever there, forever to **i.**, |
| W-pI...199.8:5 | the **i.** of joy your practice brings even to it |
| M-4 ..... I.A.4:2 | they **i.** the helpfulness or hamper it. He |
| M-6 ...........2:6 | Not one is lost, for they can but **i.**. No |

### increased 19

| | |
|---|---|
| T-1......... V.6:7 | it upside down be conducive to **i.** stability |
| T-4.......VII.5:2 | Nothing real can be **i.** except by sharing. |
| T-5.......... III.4:3 | be **i.** in strength before you can hear It. It |
| T-7......... V.9:8 | deprives someone of something, it has **i.**. |
| T-9.......VII.4:7 | to viciousness, since its uncertainty is **i.**. |
| T-11.........I.6:5 | It can only be **i.**, for everything He creates |
| T-11........II.6:7 | it so much that you will gladly let it be **i.**. |
| T-16.... VI.11:5 | is **i.** with each light that returns to take its |
| T-25.......IV.2:7 | his own creation, that his joy might be **i.**, |
| T-26.......IV.3:7 | come, to be rekindled and **i.** in joy. For |
| T-26.......IX.4:5 | and Heaven's joy has been **i.** because what |

T-28.........I.5:9 do their effects appear to be **i.** by time,
T-29.... III.1:10 lose by giving what must be **i.** thereby?
W-pI.....74.5:4 feel a deep sense of joy and an **i.** alertness,
W-pI...76.11:2 Thus is creation endlessly **i.**. His Voice
W-pI.135.20:3 be **i.** until the world is lighted up with joy.
W-pI...162.4:3 be distributed to all the world, **i.** in giving
W-pI...187.3:5 that by your giving is your store **i.**.
M-25.........6:8 their **i.** freedom for greater imprisonment

### increases 12

T-5.........I.1:13 he reinforces it in your mind and thus **i.** it
T-5.........III.2:7 It **i.** in you as you give it to your brother.
T-7...........I.5:3 Only joy **i.** forever, since joy and eternity
T-9.......VII.4:4 because at such times its confusion **i.**. The
T-12...... VI.6:5 guidance **i.** and becomes generalized.
T-13....... V.1:3 it is extended, for it **i.** as it is given. The
T-18...... III.3:8 you retreat to the illusion your fear **i.**, for
W-pI...100.4:2 Just as your light **i.** every light that shines
W-pI.135.19:1 of sorrow, and with joy that constantly **i.**,
W-pI...157.7:1 As this experience **i.** and all goals but this
M-4 .... VI.1:10 But he learns faster as his trust **i.**. It is not
M-25 .........1:4 As his awareness **i.**, he may well develop

### increasing 18

*See also* ever-increasing
T-2........IV.5:6 communication, not to lower it by **i.** fear.
T-3......... V.5:4 **i.** your overall confusion still further.
T-6...... V.B.2:4 **I.** motivation for change in the learner is
T-6...... V.B.4:5 **i.** clarity of the Holy Spirit's Voice makes
T-7.........I.7:11 perceive it as not **i.** you do not know what
T-7......... II.2:3 it unifies by **i.** and integrates by extending
T-12.........I.8:1 will gain an **i.** awareness that His criteria
T-14.... III.10:3 They believe that **i.** guilt is self-protection.
T-15.....VII.9:3 seeks relief from guilt by **i.** it in the other.
T-17...... III.5:6 the present by **i.** its reality and its value in
T-18...... VI.3:7 the body by **i.** the projection of its guilt
T-22...... VI.1:6 **i.** its importance by diminishing its own.
W-pI.....18.1:2 which will be given **i.** stress later on.
W-pI...135.3:2 from fear, **i.** fear as each defense is made.
W-pI.153.16:1 Each hour adds to our **i.** peace, as we
M-9 ...........2:1 he learns one lesson with **i.** thoroughness.
M-25 .........5:7 "power's" uncertainties with **i.** deception.
M-29 .........3:1 to the Holy Spirit with **i.** frequency.

### increasingly 15

T-2........ III.4:6 and makes it **i.** unable to tolerate delay,
T-2........ III.4:7 the mind becomes **i.** sensitive to what it
T-4........ VI.3:2 The results will convince you **i.** that this
T-9........ VI.1:1 How can you become **i.** aware of the Holy
T-13....... II.6:4 will become **i.** convinced that this is so.
T-17.... III.6:10 become **i.** unwilling to let it be hidden
T-17....... V.5:3 it grows **i.** beneficent and joyous. But at
T-25...... IV.4:4 will seem **i.** remote and far away from you
W-pI.....21.2:5 will become **i.** aware that a slight twinge
W-pI.....22.1:4 This becomes an **i.** vicious circle until he
W-pI.....44.3:2 before, and which we will utilize **i.**. It is a
W-pI...157.3:3 This you will learn to do **i.**, as every lesson
W-pI...164.2:3 the world is **i.** more and more distinct; an
C-1.............7:5 real world, and can be trained to do so **i.**.
P-1.............5:2 and becoming **i.** willing to see illusions as

### incredible 10

T-4...........I.9:7 to understand this, because it is literally **i.**
T-4...........I.9:8 *Do not believe the* **i.** *now.* Any attempt to
T-7......VIII.6:2 at any time, because it is a totally **i.** belief,
T-7......VIII.6:4 The **i.** cannot be understood because it is
T-9......... V.1:6 the equally **i.** belief that attack is real for
T-13....... X.8:5 And it will seem **i.** that he ever thought
T-18.........I.5:3 so vast and so completely **i.** that from it a
T-18....... II.8:3 It is the *wish* to make it that is **i.**. Your
T-31.........I.2:7 is such a giant learning feat it is indeed **i.**.
T-31.........I.6:6 strange in outcome and **i.** in difficulty will

### indebted 1

T-4 ....... VI.2:4 how much you are **i.** to the whole Sonship

### indebtedness 2

T-4 ....... VI.2:3 the graciousness of your **i.** and the holy
T-18 ...... V.7:1 how deep is his **i.** to the other and how

### indeed 177

T-3 ...... IV.4:4 and this is **i.** a miracle in view of how you
T-3 ...... V.10:6 How beautiful **i.** are the Thoughts of God
T-4 ........in.2:5 journeys, because they are **i.** in vain. The
T-4 ........in.3:4 Until you do so your life is **i.** wasted. It
T-4 .........I.8:4 reality, which is **i.** a fearful attempt, but to
T-4 ....... IV.1:6 the ego seeks to see its face is dark **i.**. How
T-4 ....... IV.5:1 remember that the ego has **i.** violated the
T-4 ........ V.5:8 **I.**, many of the things you want to learn
T-5 ....... IV.8:7 You can **i.** depart in peace because I have
T-6 ....... III.2:8 If that is true, and it is true **i.**, do not
T-6 ..... V.A.5:4 of this perception makes it a fearful one **i.**.
T-8 ....... IX.4:6 You can **i.** be "drugged" by sleep, if you
T-9 ........I.11:6 It is **i.** possible for you to deny facts,
T-9 .........II.3:1 all prayer is answered, and this is **i.** true.
T-10 ....in.3:10 accept His decision, for it is **i.** changeless,
T-11 ..... III.2:1 God's Son is **i.** in need of comfort, for he
T-11 ..... III.4:3 That way is hard **i.**, and very lonely. Fear
T-11 ...... V.9:2 is **i.** a skill at which it is very ingenious.
T-12 ..... III.1:3 invested wrongly, and they are poor **i.**!
T-12 ...... V.8:1 you set yourself is depressing **i.**, it is
T-13 ........I.4:1 the Son of God has set himself is useless **i.**
T-13 ...VIII.1:4 **i.** be impossible to be in the world with
T-14 .......in.1:1 Yes, you are blessed **i.**. Yet in this world
T-14 .......X.4:2 You may **i.** be so used to this that it causes
T-16 ..... IV.3:6 and **i.** is welcome in some aspects of the
T-17 ..... III.4:1 is **i.** unkind to the unholy relationship.
T-18 ..... IV.1:5 It is not necessary that you do more; **i.**, it
T-18 ....VII.4:4 have **i.** achieved their instants of success.
T-19 .......II.6:1 **i.** be said the ego made its world on sin.
T-19 ..... IV.2:4 **i.** be sure of nothing you see outside you,
T-20 ..... III.5:8 it outside you, you should **i.** be fearful.
T-20 .....VII.3:1 the goal the Holy Spirit **i.** asks little. He
T-20 ....VII.7:1 There is **i.** a difference between this vain
T-21 .......II.6:9 for your belief and trust in this is strong **i.**
T-21 ..... III.3:2 This is **i.** a little feat for such a power. For
T-21 ..... IV.1:3 **i.** afraid to look within and see the sin you
T-21 ..... IV.2:6 it. Loudly **i.** the ego claims it is; too loudly
T-21 ..... VI.9:3 Reason speaks happily **i.** of this. This
T-21 ....VII.2:8 hate. They are **i.** a sorry army, each one as
T-21 ....VII.4:1 The army of the powerless is weak **i.**. It
T-21 ....VII.6:5 which is **i.** the last you need decide, still
T-22 .........I.1:4 You can **i.** believe this, and you do. And
T-22 .........I.4:5 But a mistake **i.**! Let not your fear of sin
T-22 .......I.11:7 **i.** correct in looking on your brother as
T-22 .......II.3:5 be sure **i.** that any seeming happiness that
T-22 ..... III.5:6 Theirs is **i.** a strange perception, for they
T-23 ......in.2:1 How strange **i.** becomes this war against
T-23 .......II.4:1 chaos, dear **i.** to every worshipper of sin,
T-24 ....VII.3:3 truth, for if it were you would be lost **i.**. Be
T-25 ......in.3:2 the mind that thinks it is a body is sick **i.**!
T-25 ..VII.11:3 If this were true, then God is mad **i.**! But
T-25 .VIII.10:2 unfair **i.** to all the holiness that is in him,
T-26 .........I.3:3 the body's loss would be a sacrifice **i.**. For
T-26 ...... V.1:1 little hindrance can seem large **i.** to those
T-26 ...... V.2:6 But it is hard **i.** to wander off, alone and
T-26 ...... V.4:5 that it is hard **i.** to hold it to your heart, as
T-26 ..... VI.3:1 Who dwells with shadows is alone **i.**, and
T-26 .......X.3:6 and you are enemy **i.** to him because you
T-27 .....II.15:7 upheld divided function, you were lost **i.**.
T-27 ...... V.4:6 blessing, will the world **i.** seem fearful, for
T-27 ....VII.4:1 There is **i.** a need. The world's escape
T-27 ....VII.8:5 Careless **i.** of him this mind must be, as
T-27 ....VII.9:3 Be glad **i.** it is, for thus are you the one
T-27 ...VIII.8:5 cause do its effects seem serious and sad **i.**
T-28 .........I.4:1 Holy Spirit can **i.** make use of memory,
T-28 .........I.8:4 mind. Its consequences will **i.** seem new,
T-28 ..... III.9:1 a feast unlike **i.** to those the dreaming of
T-28 ..... VI.2:1 It is **i.** a senseless point of view to hold
T-29 .......II.2:8 cause **i.** for glad rejoicing and for hope of
T-29 ..... IV.2:7 miracle were treacherous **i.** if it allowed
T-29 .......V.8:4 Let us be glad **i.** that this is so, and seek
T-30 ..... III.4:2 you want **i.** and have the right to ask for.
T-30 ..... IV.7:1 Salvation is a paradox **i.**! What could it
T-30 ..... IV.8:4 Be glad **i.** salvation asks so little, not so
T-31 .........I.2:7 such a giant learning feat it is **i.** incredible
T-31 .........I.9:5 God were fear **i.** if he whom He created
T-31 .....II.11:8 A blindfold can **i.** obscure your sight, but
T-31 ..... IV.3:8 true **i.** there is no choice at all within the
T-31 .. VII.15:2 It needs the light, for it is dark **i.**, and men
W-pI ...... 9.1:7 **i.** be circular to aim at understanding,
W-pI ..... 11.1:4 Be glad **i.** to practice the idea in its initial
W-pI ..... 16.2:4 You can **i.** multiply nothing, but you will
W-pI ..... 20.2:8 apart. And great **i.** will be your reward.
W-pI ..... 23.2:5 But there is **i.** a point in changing your
W-pI .. 41.10:1 can **i.** afford to laugh at fear thoughts,
W-pI ..... 42.2:1 God is **i.** your strength, and what He
W-pI ..... 48.3:3 willing to do this there is **i.** nothing to fear
W-pI ..... 63.2:1 You are **i.** the light of the world with such
W-pI ..... 69.8:2 but you can **i.** be sure that it is given you
W-pI ..... 72.5:5 be difficult **i.** to escape this conclusion.
W-pI ..... 73.1:6 But they are idle **i.** in terms of creation.
W-pI .. 93.11:7 mind that the idea for the day is true **i.**.
W-pI ..... 95.4:5 for it is **i.** a hindrance to your advance.
W-pI ..... 98.6:5 lose. And what you gain is limitless **i.**!
W-pI .. 100.3:1 are **i.** essential to God's plan. Without
W-pI .. 100.4:1 You are **i.** essential to God's plan. Just as
W-pI .. 100.7:6 You have **i.** been wrong in your belief that
W-pI 122.10:4 are close **i.** to the appointed ending of the
W-pI .. 126.5:5 Would not His care for you be small **i.**, if
W-pI .. 129.2:3 The world you see is merciless **i.**, unstable
W-pI .. 129.6:3 but what you choose instead you want **i.**!
W-pI 130.11:1 sight, and what you will behold is hell **i.**.
W-pI .. 132.1:3 Belief is powerful **i.**. The thoughts you
W-pI .. 132.8:3 And if it is **i.** your own imagining, then
W-pI .. 133.3:4 The choosing you can do; **i.**, you must.
W-pI 135.17:3 Yet what remains is meaningless **i.**. For it
W-pI 135.23:3 nor **i.** the answers to the problems which
W-pI .. 140.4:6 And that is cure **i.**. For sickness now is
W-pI .. 151.2:4 they have been faulty witnesses **i.**! Why
W-pI .. 155.5:3 be distinct from them, although you are **i.**
W-pI .. 162.3:1 Holy **i.** is he who makes these words his
W-pI .. 165.7:2 For hope **i.** is justified. Your doubts are
W-pI .. 166.2:4 Impossible **i.**; but every mind that looks
W-pI .. 166.4:4 not realize that it is here he is afraid **i.**,
W-pI .. 170.5:5 your arms **i.** would crumble into dust. For
W-pI .. 184.9:1 It would **i.** be strange if you were asked to
W-pI .. 185.2:7 But few **i.** have meant them. You have but
W-pI .. 186.8:5 mood, and our emotions raise us high **i.**,
W-pI .. 192.6:1 With anger gone, you will **i.** perceive that
W-pI .. 192.6:6 we have **i.** been given everything by God.
W-pI .. 194.1:1 quick salvation, and a giant stride it is **i.**!
W-pI .. 194.9:1 Now are we saved **i.**. For in God's Hands
W-pI 196.12:5 is **i.** but you your mind can try to crucify.
W-pI .. 199.1:5 the truth, the mind were vulnerable **i.**!
W-pII . 238.1:4 *I must be beloved of You* **i.**. *And I must be*
W-pII ..... 4.4:1 frightening, and sin appears **i.** to terrify.
W-pII . 260.2:2 Holy **i.** are we, because our Source can
W-pII . 265.1:1 I have **i.** misunderstood the world,
W-pII . 269.2:1 Today our sight is blessed **i.**. We share
W-pII . 339.1:6 be confused **i.** about the things he wants;
W-pII . 350.2:1 miracles from Him, we will **i.** be grateful.
W-ep ......... 2:2 **I.**, your pathway is more certain still. For
M-4 ..... I.A.7:1 The next stage is **i.** "a period of unsettling
M-4 ..... I.A.7:9 so heavily reinforced, it would be hard **i.**!
M-4 ..... I.A.8:4 times. **I.**, the tranquility is their result; the
M-4 ......X.2:13 ultimately converges. It is **i.** enough.
M-4 ........X.3:9 world. Blessed **i.** are they, for they are the
M-10 ......... 6:2 But it is difficult **i.** to try to keep it. The
M-11 ....... 1:12 you would see it. **I.**, you *must* choose this.
M-13 ......... 3:2 But what a sacrifice,–and it is sacrifice **i.**!
M-14 ......... 2:5 His home, for here there is need of Him **i.**.
M-14 ......... 3:2 appears to be a long-range goal **i.**. But
M-15 ......... 1:1 **I.**, yes! No one can escape God's Final
M-16 ......... 3:4 to starting the day right does **i.** save time.
M-16 ......... 9:3 These attempts may **i.** seem frightening,
M-17 ......... 3:4 And this must **i.** have been the case if the
M-19 ......... 2:7 proceeds, fall short **i.** of all that wait when
M-21 ......... 4:2 No, **i.**! There are many who must be

M-21..........5:2 what he hears may **i.** be quite startling. It
M-22..........7:3 This is insanity **i.**. It is not up to God's
M-23..........2:2 **I.**, he has already done so. Temptation
M-24..........1:6 of the eternal nature of life, it is helpful **i.**.
M-25..........4:8 turned to weakness are tragedy **i.**. Yet
M-26..........1:1 God **i.** can be reached directly, for there
M-26..........3:9 to those remaining behind are few **i.**. And
M-27..........5:2 created bodies, death would be real. But
M-27..........5:5 Death is **i.** the death of God, if He is Love.
M-28..........5:6 we because His Holiness has set us free **i.**!
M-29..........5:6 No, **i.**! That would hardly be practical,
M-29........5:10 your confidence will be well founded **i.**.
C-in............1:5 are **i.** to succeed in overlooking the error.
C-5.............5:6 knew since you were born, for such **i.** he is
C-5.............6:2 No, **i.**. For Christ takes many forms with
P-in............1:4 manifestations of this world seem real **i.**.
P-2.........II.4:3 It would be unfair **i.** if belief in God were
P-2.......VII.7:2 they see in him because of this they fear **i.**.
P-3.........II.6:4 The good is saved; **i.** is cherished. But
P-3.........II.9:7 compromise in this respect are strange **i.**.
P-3........III.3:1 therapists of this world are **i.** useless to
P-3........III.3:4 This, **i.**, must demand payment, and the
S-1...........I.3:6 Heaven, and all else has **i.** been given you.
S-1.........II.6:8 for your sins, and you will be forgiven **i.**.
S-1........III.3:9 To the guilty there seems **i.** to be a real
S-2.........II.3:4 may **i.** induce a rivalry in sinfulness and
S-3.........II.1:4 can **i.** remove a form of pain and sickness.
S-3........III.2:3 body, and **i.** are generally limited to this.
S-3........III.4:3 in humility there is **i.** a place for helpers.

## indefensible 2

T-19.......II.5:1 sin as error is always **i.** to the ego. The
M-19..........5:8 becomes meaningless and **i.**. Perception

## indelible 1

T-7...........I.5:5 Eternity is the **i.** stamp of creation. The

## independence 8

T-4........III.2:2 It is a declaration of **i.**. You will find it
T-11.......V.6:1 is the **i.** of creation, not of autonomy.
T-11.......V.8:2 diminish your **i.** and weaken your power.
T-11.....V.10:3 you may countenance a false idea of **i.**,
T-21......II.10:3 This seeming **i.** of effect enables it to be
T-21......II.13:5 its seeming **i.** of its source that keeps you
W-pI.....31.4:2 of **i.** in the name of your own freedom.
W-pII..328.1:2 **i.** from the rest of God's creation is the

## independent 7

T-11.......V.4:5 itself and **i.** of any power except its own.
T-11.......V.6:4 to Him Who wills not to be **i.** of you. He
T-21.......II.8:4 and wholly **i.** of inference and judgment.
T-21......II.12:2 delude himself that he is **i.** of his Source.
T-21......II.13:6 same mistake as thinking you are **i.** of the
T-22.........I.2:5 is wholly **i.** of the eyes that look upon the
W-pI...184.2:4 as a unity which functions with an **i.** will.

## indescribable 1

M-19..........2:7 whose splendor reaches **i.** heights as one

## indescribably 1

W-pI.....12.5:3 it for you, it would make you **i.** happy.

## indicate 1

T-13......IV.3:3 life. Even the past life that death might **i.**,

## indicated 3

T-2.......VII.1:2 I have already **i.** that you cannot ask me
W-in..........6:1 with great specificity, as will be **i.**. This
W-pI.....31.1:3 used more and more, with changes as **i.**.

## indicates 1

T19...IV.A.8:6 little remnant induces merely **i.** its limited

## indication 3

T-2.......VII.5:8 an **i.** that immediate correction is needed.
T-8.....VII.14:5 result, is a clear-cut **i.** of a poor learner.
W-pI.....20.3:3 you for an **i.** that our goal is of little worth

## indications 1

T-20.....VII.1:4 are merely **i.** of areas where means and

## indirect 5

T-14.........I.2:1 **I.** proof of truth is needed in a world
T-14.........I.4:3 Undoing *is* **i.**, as doing is. You were created
T-14.........I.4:5 are but **i.** expressions of the will to live,
T-14.........I.5:2 learn. His message is not **i.**, but He must
T-21.........I.1:2 could be seen from evidence forever **i.**;

## indirectly 1

T-1.........II.5:1 Revelations are **i.** inspired by me because

## indiscriminate 3

W-pI.......2.1:6 you. Remain as **i.** as possible in selecting
W-pI.......5.4:1 ones, you may find it hard to be **i.**, and to
W-pI.......9.3:1 the need for its **i.** application, and the

## indiscriminately 5

T-1........III.4:1 the only one who can perform miracles **i.**,
T-13.......II.5:5 You have projected guilt blindly and **i.**,
W-pI.......1.3:4 the idea for the day, use it totally **i.**. Do
W-pI.......7.4:3 for today **i.** to whatever catches your eye.
W-pI.....43.5:1 the subjects for this phase of practice **i.**,

## indiscriminateness 2

T-1.........I.49:3 the direction of the error. This is its true **i.**
W-pI.....19.4:1 The requirement of as much **i.** as possible

## indistinguishable 3

T-16.......V.6:1 hell and Heaven, and making them **i.**.
T-23......IV.2:3 they be the same, and **i.** from one another
W-pII..326.1:5 *like his Cause that Cause and Its Effect are* ***i.***.

## individual 18

T-1.........V.2:6 **i.** contributions to the Sonship will no
T-4.......VII.8:6 this joy with its **i.** willingness to share in it
T-9.........II.2:4 An **i.** may ask for physical healing because
T-13.......III.5:3 Your **i.** death seems more valuable than
T-13.......V.1:4 the content of **i.** illusions differs greatly.
T-13.......V.2:1 his world with figures from his **i.** past,
T-13...VIII.7:4 Knowledge is far beyond your **i.** concern.
T-13.......X.2:9 his **i.** salvation will find it in that strange
T-16......VI.5:7 seeks does not include even one whole **i.**.
T-22.......in.1:4 Sin is a strictly **i.** perception, seen in the
M-10.........1:3 term, an **i.** is capable of "good" and "bad"
M-16.........3:8 **i.** need becomes the chief consideration.
M-24.........2:2 for some of the difficulties the **i.** faces now
M-25.........1:3 that each **i.** has many abilities of which he
M-25.........5:7 the **i.** changes his mind about its purpose,
C-in...........1:4 The structure of "**i.** consciousness" is
C-1............2:3 of an "**i.** mind" seems to be meaningful. It
P-in............1:5 an **i.** can begin to question their reality.

## individual's 1

M-22.........4:3 both in the **i.** perception of himself and of

## individualized 2

M-9...........1:5 pattern, since training is always highly **i.**.
M-29.........2:6 that. The curriculum is highly **i.**, and all

## individually 3

T-4.......VII.5:1 created beings who have everything **i.**,
T-5.........in.3:3 You need not know them **i.**, or they you.
T-18.........I.7:8 To judge them **i.** is pointless. Their tiny

## individuals 5

T-7........III.1:1 and applies it to all **i.** in all situations.
T-16......VI.5:3 When two **i.** seek to become one, they are
T-17.......V.5:5 undertaken by two **i.** for their unholy
M-22.........6:2 applicable to all **i.** in all circumstances.
M-22.........6:3 power to heal all **i.** of all forms of sickness

## indivisible 7

T-9........VI.4:6 Wholeness is **i.**, but you cannot learn of
T-9....VIII.11:1 if truth is **i.**, your evaluation of yourself
T-14....XI.11:1 God's Son will always be **i.**. As we are
T-18.........I.2:2 the Holy Spirit sees them joined and **i.**.
T-23.........I.7:6 But truth is **i.**, and far beyond their little
T-28.......V.6:6 and every time, and makes them wholly **i.**
W-pI...125.9:4 interposed between the wholly **i.** and true

## induce 19

T-1.........I.10:1 use of miracles as spectacles to **i.** belief is
T-1..........II.2:4 Miracles, on the other hand, **i.** action.
T-2.........V.7:6 Nothing He perceives can **i.** fear.
T-4........VI.3:4 can never **i.** more than a temporary effect.
T-5........VI.2:2 **i.** fears of retaliation or abandonment,
T-8.....VII.11:3 it, will **i.** illness by fostering separation.
T-8........IX.6:5 even though it makes every effort to **i.** it.
T-9...........I.8:4 of these insane decisions will **i.** panic,
T-9.........I.12:1 and if the attempt is strong it will **i.** panic.
T-9......VIII.1:4 gifts to **i.** you to return to its "protection."
T-13.........I.9:2 could **i.** a sense of a need for expiation.
T-13.........II.1:4 the ego possibly **i.** you to project guilt,
T-17.......V.5:2 Only a radical shift in purpose could **i.** a
T-29.........I.9:3 God, what could **i.** you to abandon Him?
W-pI.......8.6:3 any emotion that the idea for today may **i.**
W-pI...138.4:3 the doubts that myriad decisions would **i.**
W-pI...140.3:2 perceive do not **i.** another form of sleep,
W-pI...165.5:5 What would **i.** you now to let it fade away
S-2..........II.3:4 indeed **i.** a rivalry in sinfulness and guilt.

## induced 4

T-2......IV.4:10 **i.** the belief that miracles are frightening.
T-3........IV.6:3 to escape from the conflict you have **i.**.
T-7........IV.7:7 the sense of danger the ego has **i.** in you,
W-pI...191.3:1 escape the madness which **i.** this weird,

## induces 19

T-1.........I.28:2 fear. Revelation **i.** a state in which fear has
T-1..........II.1:1 Revelation **i.** complete but temporary
T-1..........II.1:8 Consciousness is the state that **i.** action,
T-1..........II.2:3 Revelation **i.** only experience. Miracles,
T-2....V.A.15:1 miracle **i.** the right perception for healing.
T-3..........II.6:7 This is the healing that the miracle **i.**.
T-3......III.5:10 result of revelation and **i.** only thought.
T-3........IV.4:3 state of mind that **i.** accurate perception.
T-3......IV.7:10 Sane perception **i.** sane choosing. I
T-5...........I.7:1 **i.** a kind of perception in which many
T-7........IV.2:9 **i.** a perception of conflict with something
T-7.........V.6:5 dissociation, because it **i.** separation.
T-7........VI.2:4 **i.** feelings of unreality and results in utter
T19....IV.A.8:6 the little remnant **i.** merely indicates its
T-21........II.9:4 goal of sin **i.** the perception of a fearful
W-pI.....64.3:2 and only the fear of the ego that **i.** you to
W-pI.....96.1:2 of being split into opposites **i.** feelings of
M-4.........I.2:4 What is it that **i.** them to make the shift?
M-24.......1:10 At worst, it **i.** inertia in the present. In

**inducing** 1
*See also* health-inducing
T-2....... V.1:11 i. the mind to give up its miscreations is

**indulge** 1
W-pI..... 66.3:4 it. We will not i. the ego by listening to its

**indulgences** 1
T-29.........I.6:2 It will allow but limited i. in "love," with

**indulgently** 1
W-pI... 126.5:2 choose to give i. an undeserved reprieve.

**ineffectual** 8
T-2...... VI.9:12 think is i. you may cease to be afraid of it,
T-5......... V.6:3 is a judgment that is anything but i.. Its
T-8........ IX.3:4 see by rendering the faculties for seeing i..
T-15...... IX.4:3 its demands to make little and i.. Limit
W-pI. 133.10:2 His i. mistakes appear as sins to him,
W-pI... 197.4:3 not matter if your gifts seem lost and i..
M-6 ........... 4:6 How can it be i.? How can it be wasted?
M-27 ......... 6:9 are mindless magic, i. and meaningless.

**inept** 1
W-pI... 136.2:3 reality, attack it, change it, render it i.,

**inequality** 4
T-1......... II.3:5 awe of one another because awe implies i.
T-6...... IV.11:2 To command is to assume i., which the
S-3........ III.2:2 of healing that is based on i. of any kind.
S-3........ III.3:4 healing cannot come from i. assumed and

**inertia** 1
M-24 ....... 1:10 At worst, it induces i. in the present. In

**inescapable** 6
T-3......... V.5:5 attempt to escape from an i. impasse.
T-4......... II.6:5 "Giving to get" is an i. law of the ego,
T-5......... V.7:6 Guilt is i. by those who believe they order
T-15.........I.4:1 is i. to those who identify with the ego.
T-21.... III.10:6 body an i. belief of those who value sin.
W-pI... 170.2:6 *by your own defense against it is it real and i.*

**inestimable** 3
T-7....... VII.7:3 always teaches you the i. worth of every
T-20....... V.3:3 What is i. clearly cannot be evaluated. Do
W-pI..... 44.8:1 of what you are doing; its i. value to you,

**inevitability** 2
T-2........ III.3:2 will because of the i. of the final decision,
T-15.........I.2:7 of the i. of the goal and end of teaching.

**inevitable** 61
T-1........ III.5:3 the right choice is i. if you remember this:
T-1........ III.9:2 it i. that they will extend them to others, a
T-2........ VI.6:8 producing i. strain because wanting and
T-2....... VII.4:5 interim, however, the sense of conflict is i.
T-2...... VIII.1:2 where a belief in magic is virtually i.. Your
T-4...........I.9:9 is merely to postpone the i.. The word
T-4.........I.9:10 The word "i." is fearful to the ego, but
T-4.........I.9:11 God is i., and you cannot avoid Him any
T-4........ II.11:3 of right perception lies in the i. realization
T-4.... IV.11:12 you is as natural as your answer, and as i..
T-6...... V.C.3:5 It therefore makes the ultimate choice i..
T-7...... VIII.2:1 the i. association between projection and
T-7........ IX.4:6 selfishness impossible and extension i..
T-9....... II.10:5 making it i. that you will not value what
T-9 ...... VII.6:6 that dictated this choice the lament is i..
T-12 ....... II.5:6 you, for the goal is i. because it is eternal.
T-12 ..... IV.2:4 is i. because the ego is part of your mind,
T-13 ....... X.3:4 i. that those who suffer guilt will attempt
T-17 ........I.3:6 it is i. that your perspective on reality be
T-17 ..... VI.6:6 This is i.. No one will fail in anything.
T-18 ........I.6:5 It was i.. For truth brought to this could
T-18 . VIII.11:2 Love's answer is i.. It will come because
T-19 ........I.1:1 been dedicated wholly to truth, peace is i.
T-19 ........I.6:1 The i. compromise is the belief that the
T19..IV.B.12:4 It is but the i. result of equating yourself
T19..IV.B.13:1 Is not this i.? Under fear's orders the
T19..IV.B.16:5 yet within which is his death equally i..
T-21 ..... II.10:1 confusion of cause and effect becomes i..
T-23 ....... II.4:5 for which his own destruction becomes i..
T-23 ....... II.7:5 And now is conflict made i., beyond the
T-23 ..... II.10:1 and the i. loss the enemy must suffer to
T-25 ..... IV.1:7 is seen that makes the choice of means i.,
T-31 ........I.6:5 What outcome is i., sure as God, and far
W-pI..... 24.1:4 It is i., then, that you will not serve your
W-pI..... 41.1:2 is an i. consequence of separation. So are
W-pI..... 64.4:2 the means by which happiness becomes i.
W-pI..... 75.4:3 Our single purpose makes our goal i..
W-pI..... 79.4:3 must be inadequate, and failure is i..
W-pI..... 79.5:3 and depression are i. as you regard them.
W-pI... 131.3:1 Yet searching is i. here. For this you came
W-pI... 137.8:4 that sickness is i. are more potent than
W-pI. 137.12:4 Ask the i. to occur, and you will never fail.
W-pI... 163.2:3 its image, thinking it alone is real, i.,
W-pI... 169.1:4 Grace becomes i. instantly in those who
W-pI... 194.5:2 where it runs its pitiless, i. course. Then is
M-in .......... 4:1 This is i.. There is no escape from it. How
M-2 ........... 4:5 place. This is i., because he made the right
M-2 ........... 4:6 made an i. choice out of an ancient past.
M-4 ........ II.2:4 Conflict is the i. result of self-deception,
M-4 ....... V.1:1 Joy is the i. result of gentleness.
M-11 ......... 2:5 sees but death as the i. end of life. God's
M-11 ......... 4:2 Peace is i. to those who offer peace. How
M-17 ......... 6:2 Its ending is i., for its outcome must be
M-18 ......... 1:3 Depression is then i., for he has "proved,"
M-25 ......... 5:7 It is almost i. that, unless the individual
M-29 ......... 3:7 that you have done so, making fear i.. To
P-2......... in.4:4 i. that patients and therapists alike accept
P-2........ IV.2:1 Son is seen as guilty, illness becomes i.. It
P-2........ IV.3:1 hell follows step by step in an i. course,
P-2......... V.1:3 In its wake comes the i. belief that, to be
P-2....... VII.4:6 Guilt is i. in those who use their judgment

**inevitably** 19
T-2 .........II.1:8 understanding will then i. value wrongly,
T-2 .........II.1:8 with equal power will i. destroy peace.
T-2 ....... IV.5:2 it will i. be expressed in whatever way is
T-2 ....... VI.5:9 and your behavior i. becomes erratic.
T-2 ..... VIII.4:5 the same time the mind will i. disown its
T-4 ........ V.1:6 judgment would i. judge against the ego,
T-6 ........ in.2:3 This is a responsibility you i. assume the
T-6 ........I.10:6 is i. led to demonstrate His way for all.
T-6 .........II.3:5 Projection and attack are i. related,
T-6 ..... V.B.2:5 this will i. produce fundamental change
T-10 ...... V.2:1 to deny God will i. result in projection,
T-12 ......I.8:11 that fear and attack are i. associated. If
T-14 ...... V.7:5 from guilt you will i. learn your innocence
T-17 ...... V.5:6 of this new purpose, they are i. appalled.
T-21 ..... III.2:5 with the persistence that faith i. brings.
W-pI..... 37.2:2 Any other way of seeing will i. demand
W-pI... 181.4:3 succeed, you will i. lose your way again.
W-pI... 181.8:4 perception, are the eyes of Christ i. ours.
S-1..........II.3:4 of guilt that i. underlie any prayer of need

**inexperienced** 2
W-pI....... 4.5:4 You are too i. as yet to avoid a tendency
W-pI..... 13.6:1 kind which you are very i. in recognizing.

**inextricably** 1
P-2........ VI.2:5 distortions woven i. into the self-concept,

**infancy** 3
T19 ... IV.C.9:3 i. of salvation is carefully guarded by love,
T19 . IV.C.10:4 What has been given you, even in its i., is
W-pI 127.11:1 The world in i. is newly born. And we

**infant** 2
T19 . IV.C.10:7 Behold this i., to whom you gave a resting
T-22 ........I.7:3 in this i. is your vision returned to you,

**infer** 1
T-21 ........I.1:2 must i. what could be seen from evidence

**inference** 2
T-21 ........I.1:5 see. Your cues for i. are wrong, and so you
T-21 .......II.8:4 wholly independent of i. and judgment.

**inferences** 1
T-21 ........I.1:2 and reconstruct their i. as they stumble

**inferiority** 1
T-4 ..........I.7:3 itself to the belief in superiority and i..

**Infinite** 2
*infinite*
W-pII . 233.1:7 *who questions not the wisdom of the I., nor*
W-pII ... 12.2:2 apart from All, in separation from the I..

**infinite** 19
*Infinite*
T-5 ..... VI.11:6 I have shown you i. patience because my
T-5 ..... VI.11:6 from Whom I learned of i. patience. His
T-5 ..... VI.12:1 Now you must learn that only i. patience
T-5 ..... VI.12:3 I. patience calls upon infinite love, and by
T-5 ..... VI.12:3 Infinite patience calls upon i. love, and by
T-5 ...... VII.1:7 His care and use the i. power of His care
T-7 ...... VII.7:3 teaching it with i. patience born of the
T-7 ...... VII.7:3 born of the i. Love for which He speaks.
T-13 ..... IV.7:5 aspect of time that can extend to the i., for
T-17 .... VII.7:1 little conception of the i. that you have no
T19 . IV.B.10:1 kind, i. in its patience and wholly loving.
T-29 ... VIII.6:2 past omnipotence, a place beyond the i., a
T-29 ... VIII.7:3 Can there be a gap in what is i., a place
W-pI .... 28.5:2 beautiful and clean and of i. value, full of
W-pI .... 58.5:7 care for me is i., and is with me forever. I
W-pI .. 72.12:1 you are asking of the i. Creator of infinity,
W-pII . 283.1:7 *Is not the light of Heaven i.? Is not Your Son*
W-pII ... 11.1:1 sum of all God's Thoughts, in number i.,
P-2...........I.3:4 But He will wait, and His patience is i..

**infinitely** 2
T-18 ... VIII.2:6 It draws a circle, i. small, around a very
T-26 .......V.4:1 still guides you through the i. small and

**infinitesimal** 1
T-18 ... VIII.3:5 this little thought, this i. illusion, holding

**infinity** 12
T-7 ..... VIII.7:5 has no limits because being is i..
T-11 ........I.2:1 To be alone is to be separated from i., but
T-11 ........I.2:1 but how can this be if i. has no end? No
T-11 ........I.4:4 you know your creations, having denied i.
T-11 ........I.5:4 I. is meaningless without you, and you are
T-13 .. VII.13:7 itself to let the rays extend in quiet to i..
T-18 ........I.4:4 which brought truth to illusion, i. to time,
T-21 .........I.8:4 extending to i. forever shining and with
T-27 .....V.11:8 are. I. cannot be understood by merely
T-29 .......V.2:4 The still i. of endless peace surrounds you
W-pI .. 72.12:1 you are asking of the infinite Creator of i.,

S-3 ........IV.8:2 love extends along with Mine beyond **i.**,

## inflated 1
P-2 .........V.1:6 bay only by an **i.** sense of self that holds in

## inflating
*See* self-inflating

## inflation
*See* self-inflation

## influence 9
T-2 ......VI.9:10 **i.** because you are actually afraid of them.
T-6 ........ I.18:2 Their **i.** on each other is without limit,
T-14 ......XI.3:3 but its **i.** determines the present by giving
T-16 ... V.12:11 Wholeness of God have any **i.** at all upon
T-21 ...... II.11:3 not by your Creator has any **i.** over you.
T-21 ....... V.3:6 how separate minds can **i.** each other.
T-23 .........I.6:7 no menace to reality, and has no **i.** upon it
W-pI .....50.1:3 pills, money, "protective" clothing, **i.**,
W-pI ...198.2:6 seems to be its **i.** and its effects have not

## influenced 1
T-7 ........VI.9:3 your perception, and is not **i.** by it at all.

## influencing 1
T-14 ......III.9:5 and **i.** a constellation larger than anything

## inform 1
T-6 .........V.2:2 You do not **i.** them that the nightmares

## information 2
T-8 ..... VIII.6:7 function of truth is to collect **i.** that is true
T-21 ....... V.4:4 reason is, or grasp the **i.** it would give? All

## infuses 1
W-pII..267.1:5 me peace; each breath **i.** me with strength

## ingenious 6
T-3 ......... V.2:5 ego has invented many **i.** thought systems
T-3 ......... V.2:7 is wasted effort even in its most **i.** form.
T-3 ......... V.5:5 Your mind may have become very **i.**, but
T-3 ......... V.5:7 **I.** thinking is *not* the truth that shall set
T-7 ..... VIII.2:3 It is very **i.** in devising ways that seem to
T-11 ....... V.9:2 and is indeed a skill at which it is very **i.**.

## ingeniousness 1
T-7 ........VI.3:1 **i.** of the ego to preserve itself is enormous,

## ingenuity 3
T-3 ......... V.5:6 **I.** is totally divorced from knowledge,
T-3 ......... V.5:6 because knowledge does not require **i.**.
C-in ............3:6 attempt to resort to inventiveness or **i.**.

## ingratitude 2
T-7 ......... V.7:4 His healing lesson is limited by his own **i.**,
W-pI ...197.9:2 Be you free of all **i.** to anyone who makes

## ingredient 2
T-1 ........III.4:5 nature of the miracle is an essential **i.**,
T-23 ..... II.12:9 deprive you of the secret **i.** that would

## inhabited 2
T-18 ... VIII.5:1 those in a world **i.** by bodies seem to be.
T-28 ......IV.4:6 gap, **i.** but by illusions which you have

## inhabits 1
T-25 .......in.1:1 The Christ in you **i.** not a body. Yet He is

## inherent 18
T-1 .......VII.5:6 reaction to me because of our **i.** equality.
T-2 ...........I.1:6 this ability because it is **i.** in what he is,
T-2 ......... II.4:7 is the **i.** characteristic of other defenses.
T-6 ......V.C.5:3 way to remember it is **i.** in the third step,
T-17 .....VII.2:3 to the problem is **i.** in its meaning. Is it
T-19 ....... II.3:5 the wild insanity **i.** in the whole idea of sin
T-27 .........I.8:3 as neutral and without a goal **i.** in itself.
T-29 .........I.5:7 "**i.**" weaknesses set up the limitations on
W-pI .....24.5:4 to the situation, or even to be **i.** in it at all.
W-pI .....71.8:3 angry at the second part; it is **i.** in the first
W-pI .....77.2:3 It is **i.** in the truth of what you are. It is
W-pI .....80.4:4 The solution is **i.** in the problem. You are
W-pI ...121.6:2 It is not **i.** in the mind, which cannot sin.
W-pI.132.11:2 Are these **i.** in the world you see? Does it
W-pI ...135.2:2 is an acknowledgment of an **i.** weakness; a
W-pI ...184.3:4 of true effect, with consequence **i.** in itself.
M-19 .........2:4 is no **i.** conflict between justice and truth;
C-6 .............3:4 the **i.** power of the vision of Christ. He is

## inherently 3
T-2 ......... II.7:6 A two-way defense is **i.** weak precisely
T-2 ........IV.3:7 it is not **i.** open to misinterpretation. The
T-3 ......... V.1:1 that perception, which is **i.** judgmental,

## inherit 3
T-2 ...........I.2:4 the children of the Father **i.** from Him. Its
T-2 ......... II.7:4 is meant by "the meek shall **i.** the earth."
T-4 .........I.12:4 meek shall **i.** the earth because their egos

## inheritance 39
T-in ...........1:7 *of love's presence, which is your natural* ***i.****.*
T-3 ......VI.10:2 Everyone is free to refuse to accept his **i.**,
T-3 ......VI.10:2 but he is not free to establish what his **i.** is
T-3 ......VI.11:8 "I know what I am and I accept my own **i.**.
T-7 ......... II.5:7 is your **i.** and requires no learning at all,
T-7 ........ IX.6:1 failed to increase the **i.** of the Sons of God
T-7 ........ XI.5:4 as your brother is to accept your own **i.**.
T-10 .... III.10:7 It is your **i.** from your real Father. You
T-11 .........IV.h The **I.** of God's Son
T-11 .......IV.1:5 Glory is your **i.**, given you by your Creator
T-11 ... VIII.3:6 not accept it, for understanding is your **i.**.
T-12 ......IV.6:7 Your **i.** can neither be bought nor sold.
T-12 ......IV.7:5 Your **i.** awaits only the recognition that
T-13 ......IV.1:5 leaving you no **i.** except the dust out of
T-13 ...VII.13:6 no world outside himself holds his **i.**.
T-14 ....... V.4:1 **i.** of the Kingdom is the right of God's
T-23 ..... II.10:1 the valuable **i.** that should be yours; your
T-25. VIII.13:6 Their Father gave the same **i.** to both.
T-26 .....VII.9:5 it falls far short of giving you your full **i.**,
T-31 ..... II.11:1 Together is your joint **i.** remembered and
W-pI .....56.1:5 and complete fulfillment are my **i.**. I have
W-pI .....56.1:6 to give my **i.** away in exchange for the
W-pI .....56.1:7 But God has kept my **i.** safe for me. My
W-pI ...104.3:3 *to me in truth, And joy and peace are my* ***i.****.*
WpI. rIV.in9:2 that we receive as the **i.** we have of Him.
WpIrIV.in10:2 are learning now to claim again as your **i.**.
W-pI ...165.5:6 and accept the Thought of God as your **i.**.
W-pI ......184.h The Name of God is my **i.**.
W-pI ...184.6:1 the sum of the **i.** the world bestows. And
W-pI.184.12:5 Name of God is the **i.** He gave to those
W-pI.184.12:6 to the pitiful **i.** you made as fitting tribute
W-pI.184.15:8 *us in the oneness which is our* ***i.*** *and peace.*
W-pI ...188.9:7 We restore to them the holiness of their **i.**
W-pI ...190.6:6 deny a little corner of your mind its own **i.**
W-pI ...204.1:1 (184) The Name of God is my **i.**. *God's*
W-pII..332.1:8 means to realize the freedom that is its **i.**.

M-4 ....... X.3:1 include things that are the Son of God's **i.**.
M-11 .........1:5 must occur, and that rebirth is man's **i.**.
M-29 .........5:4 for you is simply to accept your true **i.**.

## inherited 2
W-pI ... 104.2:3 His are the gifts that we **i.** before time was
W-pI ... 193.1:2 His Son **i.** of Him be undisturbed; eternal

## inhibits 1
T-3 ........ III.3:4 This fear **i.** the tendency to question at all.

## inimical 1
T-7 ........ VI.3:5 is totally **i.** to its existence *for* its existence.

## initial 4
T-2 .......VII.5:8 The **i.** corrective procedure is to recognize
W-pI ..... 11.1:4 indeed to practice the idea in its **i.** form,
W-pI ..... 19.2:4 Despite your **i.** resistance to this idea, you
M-20 ....... 3:10 **i.** contrast stands out clear and apparent.

## initially 2
T-2 ...........I.4:6 he may **i.** interpret the light itself as part
M-4 ..... I.A.3:3 it is rarely understood **i.** that their lack of

## initiated
*See* self-initiated

## initiative
*See* self-initiative

## injunction 2
T-2 ....V.A.17:1 **i.** "Be of one mind" is the statement for
T-3 ...........I.4:3 way is a violation of my **i.** that you should

## injure 4
T-27 ..... VII.1:1 upon all that the world has done to **i.** you.
W-pI ... 190.5:2 to your mind can hurt or **i.** you in any way
W-pI ... 198.1:4 For you have believed that you can **i.**, and
S-3 ...........I.1:3 that **i.** and would hurt the Son of God.

## injured 4
T-27 ........II.1:5 Who has been **i.** by his brother, and could
T-27 ........II.2:8 and mean, "My brother, you have **i.** me,
W-pI ... 198.1:3 If you can condemn, you can be **i.**. For
S-2 ...........I.5:2 is evil, and in his sin you are the **i.** one.

## injures 3
W-pI ...... 198.h Only my condemnation **i.** me.
W-pI ... 198.9:3 *Only my condemnation* ***i.*** *me. Only my own*
W-pI ... 218.1:1 (198) Only my condemnation **i.** me. *My*

## injuries 1
T-27 .........I.4:3 that you send lest he forget the **i.** he gave,

## injury 2
W-pI ... 198.1:1 **I.** is impossible. And yet illusion makes
M-29 ....... 6:10 may ask for **i.**, but his father will protect

## injustice 20
T-3 ........ VI.6:4 only because you are capable of **i.**.
T-25..VIII.10:2 For that would be **i.**, and unfair indeed to
T-25..VIII.10:3 God knows of no **i.**. He would not allow
T-25..VIII.13:5 give another must be an **i.** to them both,
T-25...... IX.7:6 and lasting in its power of **i.** and attack.

T-26.........I.8:1 keeps him safe from all **i.** the world would
T-26....... II.4:3 It does **i.** to the Son of God, and therefore
T-26.......... X.h The End of **I.**
T-26....... X.3:5 of yourself, in deep **i.** to the Son of God.
T-26....... X.6:1 this **i.** does to you who judge unfairly, and
T-26....... X.6:4 Spirit has brought **i.** to the light within,
T-26....... X.6:5 If you perceive **i.** anywhere, you need but
T-26....... X.6:7 *And I would rather know of Them than see* **i.**
T-29....... IX.3:5 Judgment is an **i.** to God's Son, and it *is*
M-19 ......... 1:1 Justice is the divine correction for **i.**.
M-19 ......... 1:2 **I.** is the basis for all the judgments of the
M-19 ......... 1:3 the interpretations to which **i.** gives rise,
M-19 ......... 1:4 Neither justice nor **i.** exists in Heaven, for
M-19 ......... 3:1 all concerns about the past, stem from **i.**.
M-19 ......... 4:7 on love,–you have projected your **i.**,

## injustices 6

T-16.....VII.1:3 perceived **i.** and deprivations all enter
T-26....... II.4:4 Holy Spirit does not evaluate **i.** as great or
T-26....... II.6:2 you believe that some **i.** are fair and good,
T-28.........I.5:6 gives you pictures of **i.** and hurts that you
T-31....... V.3:2 face is often wet with tears at the **i.** the
M-19 ......... 1:7 just interpretations and laying all **i.** aside.

## ink 1

P-2......... II.6:2 Does the paper matter, or the **i.**, or the

## inner 19

T-1.........I.44:1 is an expression of an **i.** awareness of
T-2...........I.2:4 similar to the **i.** radiance that the children
T-2.........I.5:11 Health is **i.** peace. It enables you to
T-2........ III.1:1 within you by releasing the **i.** light. Since
T-2........ III.1:8 Its true holiness lies at the **i.** altar around
T-2........ III.2:1 belongs at the center of the **i.** altar, where
T-21....... VIII.h The **I.** Shift
T-31.....VII.7:7 vision and the **i.** Guide all lead you out of
W-pI.....31.2:4 and apply the same idea to your **i.** world.
W-pI.....31.2:5 for the **i.** is the cause of the outer.
W-pI.....31.3:1 As you survey your **i.** world, merely let
W-pI.....32.2:1 ones, applies to your **i.** and outer worlds,
W-pI.....32.3:2 your eyes and look around your **i.** world.
W-pI.....32.5:2 as you survey either your **i.** or outer world
W-pI.....33.1:1 the world in both its outer and **i.** aspects.
W-pI.....33.1:4 surveying your outer and **i.** perceptions,
W-pI.....33.2:1 your **i.** thoughts with equal casualness.
W-pI.....34.2:4 your **i.** world to which the applications of
S-3...........I.1:3 world. It is external proof of **i.** "sins," and

## Innocence 3

*innocence*

T-15...... XI.2:9 as holy as the perfect **I.** which He protects,
W-pI. 187.11:6 our altar, making it a home for **I.** Itself,
W-pI... 199.2:4 And who can be afraid who lives in **I.**, and

## innocence 125

*Innocence*

T-3...........I.5:2 a very simple symbol that speaks of my **i.**.
T-3...........I.5:3 that strength and **i.** are not in conflict, but
T-3...........I.5:6 not confuse destruction with **i.** because it
T-3...........I.5:6 because it associates **i.** with strength, not
T-3...........I.6:1 **I.** is incapable of sacrificing anything,
T-3...........I.6:4 the world" in the sense that the state of **i.**,
T-3...........I.7:3 this if it arose from anything but perfect **i.**
T-3...........I.7:4 **I.** is wisdom because it is unaware of evil,
T-3...........I.8:1 The **i.** of God is the true state of the mind
T-3......... II.2:1 **I.** is not a partial attribute. It is not real
T-3......... II.2:4 It is not until their **i.** becomes a viewpoint
T-13...... IX.4:2 and guilt has become as true for you as **i.**.
T-13.... IX.8:11 guilt where God knows there is perfect **i.?**
T-13...... X.12:1 against him has touched his **i.** in any way.
T-14.... III.13:6 strong protector of the **i.** that sets you free
T-14.... III.13:7 obscure your **i.** from your unclouded
T-14....... V.3:3 of God that does not share His shining **i.**.
T-14....... V.3:7 **i.** that is the right of all that God created.
T-14 ...... V.4:4 Bring **i.** to light, in answer to the call of
T-14 ...... V.5:6 have learned how to exchange guilt for **i.**,
T-14 ...... V.6:1 Teachers of **i.**, each in his own way, have
T-14 ...... V.7:5 from guilt you will inevitably learn your **i.**.
T-14 .... V.9:10 as He created him, by teaching him his **i.**.
T-14 ... VIII.1:2 in guilt and in the dark denial of **i.**.
T-15 ..... IV.9:3 **I.** is not of your making. It is given you the
T-18 ..... IX.9:4 everything is bright and shining with **i.**,
T-18 ..... IX.9:6 Here is your **i.**, waiting to clothe you and
T-19 ........II.2:4 and has thus succeeded in losing his **i.** and
T-19 ........II.4:1 but truth, and it is **i.** that would deceive.
T19.... IV.C.3:1 guilt and death, in opposition to life and **i.**
T19... IV.D.8:7 and look on your brother in **i.** born of
T19... IV.D.9:7 here together will offer you the **i.** you need
T-20 ........I.3:4 light of his own **i.** lighting his way to his
T-20 ........II.9:2 His **i.** will light your way, offering you its
T-20 .... II.10:3 are the lilies of his **i.** untouched by guilt,
T-20 .... II.11:3 your brother walk the way of **i.** together,
T-20 ..... III.6:3 is beautiful because they see their **i.** in it.
T-21 ..... III.9:9 and in the **i.** that makes the sight of it as
T-22 ........I.11:5 His sweetness and His gentle **i.** protected
T-22 ........II.4:7 And faith in **i.** is faith in sin, if the belief
T-22 ..... VI.4:1 This holy relationship, lovely in its **i.**,
T-23 ......in.1:2 **I.** is strength, and nothing else is strong.
T-23 ......in.3:2 are safe because they share their **i.**.
T-23 ......in.3:4 harmful now stands shining in their **i.**,
T-23 ......in.3:5 strength of love *because* they looked on **i.**.
T-23 ......in.4:2 There can be no attraction of guilt in **i.**.
T-23 ......in.5:5 Your **i.** will light the way to his, and so is
T-23 ......in.6:5 redemption that your **i.** bestows upon it!
T-23 ......II.10:2 Thus do the guilty ones protest their "**i.**."
T-25 ..... IV.1:3 Their joy is in the **i.** they see. And thus
T-25 ..... IV.4:7 stand in quiet, in **i.** and wholly unafraid.
T-25 ...... V.2:7 to maintain the wish, while wanting **i.?**
T-25 ...... V.3:4 him, and join with him in **i.** and peace.
T-25 . VIII.11:1 Spirit heeds not who looks on **i.** at last,
T-25VIII.11:12 vengeance. For that would be unjust to **i.**.
T-25 . VIII.12:4 and holy that He could not doubt His **i.**.
T-25 ..... IX.4:1 sight of **i.** makes punishment impossible,
T-26 ........I.6:6 You sacrifice your **i.** with his, and die each
T-26 ........II.5:5 die. God offers you the means to see his **i.**.
T-26 .. VII.12:5 This world is an attempt to prove your **i.**,
T-26 ..... IX.2:4 have blessed it with Their **i.** and peace.
T-26 ........X.2:7 veil that stands between Their shining **i.**,
T-26 ........X.4:2 you seek to find an **i.** that is not Theirs but
T-26 ........X.4:3 Can **i.** be purchased by the giving of your
T-26 ........X.4:4 *is* it **i.** that your attack on him attempts to
T-26 ........X.4:6 of this, and victimized despite your **i.?**
T-26 ........X.4:8 Someone must lose his **i.** that someone
T-27 ........I.1:1 attempt that would combine attack and **i.**.
T-27 ........I.2:3 to be the sign that he has lost his **i.**, and
T-27 ........I.2:7 for him. But in his **i.** you find your own.
T-27 ........I.3:3 you are beyond attack and prove his **i.**.
T-27 ........I.3:6 guilt becomes the perfect witness to his **i.**.
T-27 ........I.5:4 beyond itself to both your **i.** and his.
T-27 ........I.5:6 beyond it to the **i.** that he beholds in you.
T-27 ........I.6:1 Attest his **i.** and not his guilt. Your
T-27 ........I.8:1 and **i.** and sin will end alike within the
T-27 ........II.4:4 **i.** be justified unless his sins have no effect
T-27 ........II.5:7 can it offer him mute testimony of his **i.** It
T-27 ........II.6:3 so is he convinced his **i.** was never lost,
T-27 ........II.8:8 **i.** has been established in your sight and
T-27 .. VII.13:3 and made him think that he has lost his **i.**,
T-27 .. VII.15:1 brother, who unites with you in holy **i.**.
T-27 ... VIII.8:3 your **i.** by pushing guilt outside yourself,
T-27 . VIII.13:3 it. Its **i.** does not demand your guilt, nor
T-28 .......I.10:7 And so your **i.** has not been lost. You need
T-28 ........II.2:8 the body, and its **i.** is quite apart from it,
T-28 ....... V.7:6 and you behold the **i.** and emptiness of
T-29 ....... V.5:4 in which your hands are joined in **i.**.
T-31 .......I.10:1 be remembered when he learns his **i.**. For
T-31 ....... V.2:6 The first presents the face of **i.**, the aspect
T-31 ....... V.3:1 to provide the love and shelter **i.** deserves.
T-31 ....... V.3:4 things make small assaults upon its **i.**,
T-31 ....... V.4:1 face of **i.** the concept of the self so proudly
T-31 ....... V.4:1 the world deals harshly with defenseless **i.**
T-31 ....... V.5:1 Beneath the face of **i.** there is a lesson that
T-31 ....... V.6:5 deeper in the mists below the face of **i.**.
T-31 .... V.10:2 if he did, who gave the face of **i.** to you? Is
T-31 .... VII.2:4 You cannot give yourself your **i.**, for you
T-31 .. VII.11:3 holy eyes that look upon the **i.** within, and
T-31 .. VII.11:5 that he see his **i.** in all he looks upon, and
T-31 .. VII.13:7 to shine upon the one who asks, in **i.**, to
W-pI .... 58.1:4 can accept the **i.** that is the truth about me
W-pI .... 60.1:3 accepted their **i.** see nothing to forgive.
W-pI .... 60.1:4 the means by which I will recognize my **i.**.
W-pI .. 111.1:3 *up my mind, and let me see the* **i.** *within.*
W-pI 134.10:3 is **i.** the only thing there is. Forgiveness
W-pI .. 159.3:5 parts. The real world pictures Heaven's **i.**.
W-pI .. 164.5:4 world unfold in perfect **i.** before your eyes
W-pI .. 181.3:5 We seek for **i.** and nothing else. We seek
W-pI .. 182.4:4 eternal, with an **i.** that will endure forever.
W-pI 182.12:1 You have not lost your **i.**. It is for this you
W-pI 187.10:3 one Self Whose **i.** has joined us all as one,
W-pI .. 189.1:7 you is to see the world anew, shining in **i.**,
W-pI .. 189.4:2 and **i.** they see surrounding them; the joy
W-pI .. 189.9:8 within, and lightens up the world in **i.**.
W-pI .. 190.5:8 now becomes a source of **i.** and holiness.
W-pI 198.10:4 and see your **i.** shining upon you from the
W-pI .. 199.4:2 Declare your **i.** and you are free. The body
W-pII . 263.2:2 pure to us, that we may pass them by in **i.**,
W-pII ..... 6.1:4 nor lost the **i.** in which He was created. He
W-pII . 309.1:1 Within me is eternal **i.**, because it is
M-1 ........... 3:5 is guiltless, and in his **i.** is his salvation." It
P-2........ IV.1:7 guilt? And who could weep but for his **i.?**
S-2...........I.4:6 and in him must your **i.** now be found.
S-2........ III.1:2 It does not ask for proof of **i.**, nor pay of

## innocent 47

T-3 .............. h THE **I.** PERCEPTION
T-3 ..........I.6:1 **i.** mind has everything and strives only to
T-3 ..........I.8:4 The understanding of the **i.** is truth. That
T-3 .........II.2:3 The partly **i.** are apt to be quite foolish at
T-3 .........II.2:5 **I.** or true perception means that you
T-3 .........II.3:7 This, then, is all the **i.** can see. They do
T-3 .........II.5:7 vision can be perceived only by the truly **i.**
T-3 .........II.5:8 the **i.** defend true perception instead of
T-8 ..... VIII.4:2 appears to be **i.** and trustworthy because
T-15 ..... XI.3:4 is as **i.** as our relationship with our Father,
T-17 .... VII.8:5 Yet you are as **i.** of what you were as he is.
T19 .IV.C.10:1 What danger can assail the wholly **i.?**
T-20 ........I.2:1 white and holy sign the Son of God is **i.**.
T-20 ... III.11:5 The **i.** see safety, and the pure in heart see
T-21 ..... IV.8:3 Little child, **i.** of sin, follow in gladness
T-21 ..... VI.2:3 as sinful and still perceive the other **i.**.
T-23 ...... in.3:2 The **i.** are safe because they share their
T-23 ...... in.3:8 where it is. Where could it be but in the **i.**
T-25 ....... V.2:6 attack whatever he perceives as wholly **i.?**
T-25 ....... V.2:8 the Son of God as **i.** and wish him dead?
T-25 ... VIII.8:1 knows that they are wholly **i.** in truth. In
T-25 ... VIII.8:2 and cannot understand that they are **i.**.
T-25 ... VIII.9:6 to hold out to you the gifts the **i.** deserve.
T-25VIII.11:10 can be to warrant an attack upon the **i.?**
T-25 ..... IX.6:5 less? And is this justice to the wholly **i.?** A
T-26 ....... X.4:6 it not safer to believe that you are **i.** of this
T-26 ....... X.5:1 one must be unfair to make the other **i.**.
T-27 ....... II.3:3 but retain the proof he is not really **i.**. The
T-27 ..... II.11:4 correction, as the one more **i.** than he.
T-27 .... VII.1:5 be **i.** because he knows not what he does,
T-27 .... VII.3:3 While you attack I must be **i.**. And what I
T-27 . VIII.13:6 to learn that both of you are **i.** or guilty.
T-28 ....... II.2:4 nature of the **i.** to be forever uncontained,
T-28 ....... II.7:9 own attack, and he is **i.** of what he caused.
T-29 ......... I.8:1 The body, **i.** of goals, is your excuse for
T-31 ...... I.7:11 And you will learn God's Son is **i.**, and see
T-31 ......... I.9:4 But only if His Son is **i.** can He be Love.
T-31 ......... I.9:5 He created **i.** could be a slave to guilt.
T-31 ...... I.13:1 **i.** of judgment, unaware of any thoughts
T-31 ..... III.7:1 The **i.** release in gratitude for their release
T-31 ... VI.6:10 in heart? And what could hurt the truly **i.**
T-31 ..... VI.7:4 as a star, as pure as light, as **i.** as love itself
T-31 ..... VII.1:5 are the guilty "bad"; the "good" are **i.**.
T-31 .. VII.13:1 savior's vision is as **i.** of what your brother
W-pI .. 133.8:7 from rust, that you may see how "**i.**" it is.
W-pI 188.10:4 Now we choose that it be **i.**, devoid of sin
W-pII ... 10.5:1 "You are still My holy Son, forever **i.**,

## innumerable 1

W-pI.....76.8:2 and of the body's protection in **i.** ways.

## inroads 2

W-pI.....34.6:1 **i.** on your peace of mind take the form of
P-2........IV.6:8 circle closed against the "**i.**" of salvation.

## insane 195

T-2........VI.2:2 You would not excuse **i.** behavior on your
T-2........VI.2:3 it. Why should you condone **i.** thinking?
T-4......III.10:4 **i.** would undertake to believe what is not
T-4.........V.3:1 confuses God and the body must be **i.**.
T-5.......VII.3:1 you listen to the endless **i.** calls you think
T-6.........in.1:5 be expected from **i.** premises except an
T-6.........in.1:5 insane premises except an **i.** conclusion?
T-6.........in.1:6 The way to undo an **i.** conclusion is to
T-6......V.B.1:3 These **i.** ideas are clearly the result of
T-6......V.B.1:6 An **i.** learner learns strange lessons. What
T-6......V.B.4:1 the ego perceives the first lesson as **i.**. In
T-6......V.B.4:2 to it, would obviously be that *it* is **i.**. The
T-6......V.B.5:5 you. Its lesson is not **i.**; the conflict is.
T-6......V.B.7:1 You are not asked to make **i.** decisions,
T-6......V.B.7:2 **i.** to believe that it is up to you to decide
T-7........III.2:6 This is why the ego is **i.**; it teaches that
T-7.........V.3:7 This belief is its totally **i.** premise, and so
T-7........VI.3:4 It is perfectly logical but clearly **i.**. The
T-7........VI.3:8 Remaining logical but still **i.**, the ego
T-7........VI.3:8 ego resolves this completely **i.** dilemma in
T-7........VI.3:8 insane dilemma in a completely **i.** way. It
T-7....VI.11:11 This can only be an **i.** attempt.
T-7.......VII.9:2 Projecting its **i.** belief that you have been
T-7.....VII.11:1 of the ego's thought system as wholly **i.**,
T-7........IX.6:5 God's Will is meaningful only to the **i.**. In
T-9...........I.8:4 of these **i.** decisions will induce panic,
T-9........IV.8:4 Anyone who elects a totally **i.** guide must
T-9........IV.8:4 insane guide must be totally **i.** himself.
T-9........IV.8:5 true that you do not realize the guide is **i.**.
T-9.......VII.6:1 evaluate an **i.** belief system from within it.
T-9.......VII.6:4 this contrast can insanity be judged as **i.**.
T-9.....VIII.4:6 It will tell you that you are **i.**, and argue
T-9.....VIII.7:5 Yet it must be **i.** because it is not true.
T-10.......II.6:1 you could not make such an **i.** decision.
T-10.......V.3:7 him out of your insanity, he is an **i.** idea.
T-10.....V.10:3 be to attack Himself, and God is not **i.**.
T-10.....V.10:4 When you deny Him *you* are **i.**. Would you
T-11.......in.1:1 Either God or the ego is **i.**. If you will
T-11.......in.2:6 It sounds **i.** when it is stated with perfect
T-11.......in.2:7 Yet that is its **i.** premise, which is carefully
T-11.....V.12:7 God's Son is not **i.**, and cannot believe it.
T-11.....V.12:9 the **i.** would choose fear in place of love,
T-11.....V.12:9 and only the **i.** could believe that love can
T-11.....V.16:3 The case for insanity is strong to the **i.**.
T-12.......III.6:5 sort of **i.** "arrangement" with the world.
T-12.......III.7:2 His **i.** thoughts, too, must be in his mind,
T-12... VIII.5:3 the **i.** desire to control reality. You who
T-13.......in.1:7 you, and it is guilt that has driven you **i.**.
T-13.......in.2:9 they love, perhaps the most **i.** belief of all.
T-13...... I.10:3 to the **i.** notion that attack is salvation.
T-13.......II.3:3 murderous but **i.** idea lies hidden there,
T-13.......III.4:1 built your whole **i.** belief system because
T-13....III.12:6 He could but answer your **i.** request with
T-13....III.12:9 can look back on them and see them as **i.**.
T-13.......V.1:5 have one thing in common; they are all **i.**.
T-13.......V.3:1 that the **i.** relate to their insane world. For
T-13.......V.3:1 that the insane relate to their **i.** world. For
T-13......IX.5:3 himself and make himself guilty is **i.**. In
T-13......IX.5:6 for punishment upon yourself must be **i.**.
T-13.......X.1:2 awareness the full perception that it is **i.**.
T-13.......X.2:1 **I.** ideas have no real relationships, for
T-13.......X.2:1 relationships, for that is why they are **i.**.
T-13.......X.6:3 must learn that guilt is always totally **i.**,
T-13.......X.8:6 The moment that you realize guilt is **i.**,
T-14.......in.1:4 ego, except that His conclusions are not **i.**
T-14.........I.2:6 the truth. This *is* an **i.** world, and do not
T-14.........I.3:8 the world is totally **i.** and leads to nothing
T-14.........I.3:9 Yet in him who made this **i.** logic there is
T-14......IV.5:6 Give up this frantic and **i.** attempt that
T-14.....VII.2:7 you have erected your **i.** system of belief,
T-14......XI.2:2 a lesson so unthinkable that only the **i.**, in
T-15.....VII.4:6 of anger and dedicated to but one **i.** belief
T-15.....VII.7:1 In such **i.** relationships, the attraction of
T-15...VII.11:3 alone? It is clearly **i.** to believe that by
T-16......VI.8:8 For you are no longer wholly **i.**, and you
T-16....VI.10:3 the wholly **i.** could look on death and
T-16.....VII.3:2 It is completely savage and completely **i.**.
T-16.....VII.3:8 That this is **i.** is obvious. But what is less
T-16.....VII.6:1 Against the ego's **i.** notion of salvation
T-17.......III.2:2 into which they enter are totally **i.**.
T-17......IV.5:2 It does not realize that it is totally **i.**. And
T-17......IV.5:4 The **i.** protect their thought systems, but
T-17......IV.5:5 as **i.** as what they are supposed to protect.
T-17......IV.5:6 "reason," and no attribute that is not **i.**.
T-17......IV.5:7 "protection" is part of it, as **i.** as the whole
T-17......IV.5:8 is its chief defense, must therefore be **i.**.
T-17......IV.6:2 at least in general terms, that the ego is **i.**.
T-17.......V.6:9 now you find yourself in an **i.** relationship
T-17.......V.7:9 You are not now wholly **i.**. Can you deny
T-17...VII.10:2 You are no longer wholly **i.**, nor no longer
T-18..........I.8:4 He brings all your **i.** projections and the
T-18.......II.5:15 fixed and **i.** idea that you can change it. In
T-18......VI.6:1 It is **i.** to use the body as the scapegoat for
T-18......IX.3:1 **i.** messages seem to be returned to the
T-18......IX.4:2 all the twisted thoughts, all the **i.** attacks,
T-19.......II.1:6 that punishment *is* correction is clearly **i.**.
T-19.......II.4:1 major tenet in the ego's **i.** religion is that
T-19......III.5:8 If it does not obey, the mind is judged **i.**.
T-19......III.6:4 good and evil; partly sane and partially **i.**.
T19... IV.A.7:1 The little **i.** wish to get rid of Him Whom
T19..IV.B.13:6 is this **i.** relationship that it keeps hidden,
T19....IV.C.3:2 lie but in the sick minds of the **i.**,
T19....IV.C.5:7 has answered this **i.** idea with His Own;
T-20......III.8:4 and adjusted it according to its **i.** answer.
T-20......IV.3:1 Your **i.** laws were made to guarantee that
T-21.......II.5:2 This witness is **i.**. You trained it in its
T-21......IV.8:4 not held back by fear's **i.** insistence that
T-21.......V.7:9 Only the totally **i.** can disregard them,
T-21.......V.8:8 The partially **i.** have access to it, and only
T-21......VI.4:2 if it be the choice of the **i.** to listen to it.
T-21......VI.4:3 it. But the **i.** know not their will, for they
T-21......VI.5:1 brother, and if you think it does you are **i.**
T-21......VI.5:3 reason tells you must be joined must be **i.**.
T-23.........I.6:6 What made them is **i.**, and they remain
T-23... II.13:12 The means of madness must be **i.**. Are
T-25.....VII.4:8 *because* the Father and the Son are not **i.**.
T-25.....VII.5:1 you see to something else; a basis not **i.**,
T-25.....VII.6:3 perceives the other as **i.** and meaningless.
T-25.....VII.6:5 sin is equally **i.** within the sight of love,
T-25.....VII.7:1 the fact that God is not **i.** appears most
T-25.....VII.7:5 to those who are **i.** requires special choice.
T-25.....VII.7:6 Nor can this choice be made by the **i.**,
T-25.....VII.8:1 be madness to entrust salvation to the **i.**.
T-25...VII.11:1 the underlying tenet God must be **i.**. For
T-25...VII.11:7 it must be either God or this must be **i.**,
T-25...VII.12:5 for all **i.** beliefs can be corrected here.
T-26.....VII.7:6 For such an **i.** picture an insane defense
T-26.....VII.7:6 picture an **i.** defense can be expected, but
T-26......IX.4:6 **i.** have shed their garments of insanity to
T-27......VI.6:3 How foolish and **i.** it is to think a miracle
T-28......VI.1:1 Who punishes the body is **i.**. For here the
T-30.......I.11:6 by the **i.** belief you want it for the goal of
T-31.....IV.10:6 How foolish and **i.** it is to think that there
T-31...VII.14:1 that it is but a wish, **i.** and meaningless, to
W-pI.....12.1:2 world, or a violent world, or an **i.** world.
W-pI.....41.5:2 within, under a heavy cloud of **i.** thoughts
W-pI.....49.4:4 and sights and sounds of this **i.** world.
W-pI.....50.1:3 placed in the most trivial and **i.** symbols;
W-pI.....53.1:3 What is producing this world is **i.**, and so
W-pI.....53.1:4 Reality is not **i.**, and I have real thoughts
W-pI.....53.1:4 and I have real thoughts as well as **i.** ones.
W-pI.....53.2:2 **I.** thoughts are upsetting. They produce a
W-pI.....53.2:7 what is totally **i.** and has no meaning.
W-pI.....53.3:2 The totally **i.** engenders fear because it is
W-pI.....53.4:5 from the effects of my own **i.** thoughts,
W-pI.....53.5:4 only the representation of my **i.** thoughts,
W-pI.....56.4:4 Beyond all my **i.** wishes is my will, united
W-pI.....56.5:2 my **i.** thoughts of separation and attack, is
W-pI.....57.1:9 I would give up my **i.** wishes and walk
W-pI.....71.3:2 According to this **i.** plan, any perceived
W-pI.....71.8:4 your own **i.** attempts and mad proposals
W-pI.....73.8:3 and end forever the **i.** belief that it is hell
W-pI.....86.3:5 defeat my own best interests in this **i.** way
W-pI.....92.2:2 you could but laugh at this **i.** idea. It is as
W-pI...101.7:1 yourself with the **i.** belief that sin is real.
W-pI...135.2:3 The world is based on this **i.** belief. And
W-pI...136.2:2 it is an **i.** device for self-deception. And
W-pI...163.7:1 even the **i.** have difficulty in believing it.
W-pI...170.2:1 thoroughly **i.** is the idea that to defend
W-pI...170.6:4 enemies who are unreasonable and **i.**,
W-pI.170.10:1 totally **i.** belief in gods of vengeance come
W-pI...190.1:7 and His **i.** desire for revenge and death.
W-pI...190.4:2 time has come to laugh at such **i.** ideas.
W-pI...190.4:5 feared than the **i.** illusions which it shields
W-pI...191.1:4 wild, lacking all reason, blind, **i.** with hate
W-pI...195.2:1 It is **i.** to offer thanks because of suffering
W-pI...195.2:2 equally **i.** to fail in gratitude to One Who
W-pI...195.9:4 we substitute for these **i.** perceptions.
W-pI...196.1:3 will be free of the **i.** belief that to attack a
W-pI...199.3:2 not concerned that to the ego it is quite **i.**.
W-pII ....in.9:3 believed that our **i.** desires were the truth.
W-pII .....3.2:5 could not cause such **i.** thoughts. But eyes
W-pII .259.2:1 *Father, I would not be* **i.** *today. I would not*
W-pII .282.1:2 This the decision not to be **i.**, and to
W-pII .325.1:4 From **i.** wishes comes an insane world.
W-pII .325.1:4 From insane wishes comes an **i.** world.
W-pII ... 12.2:1 The ego is **i.**. In fear it stands beyond the
Wfl........in.5:4 in which we understand that anger is **i.**,
M-5 .........I.2:1 And what, in this **i.** conviction, does
M-5 .... III.1:10 They have no idea how **i.** this concept is.
M-8 ...........5:2 Is it harder to dispel the belief of the **i.** in
M-18 .........3:2 Reality is blotted out as this **i.** belief is
M-27 .........3:8 of life." God is **i.**, and fear alone is real.
C-3.............2:4 And it is just this **i.** perception that makes
P-2.........in.2:4 rests on the **i.** belief that this is possible.
P-2..........II.5:6 all **i.** or they would not be here. Together
P-2........IV.8:5 the **i.** believe it because they are insane.
P-2........IV.8:5 the insane believe it because they are **i.**.
P-2......IV.10:5 strongly emphasized that the **i.** believe
P-2......IV.11:2 the **i.** burden of guilt it carries so wearily,
P-2.........V.3:4 the **i.** within the bounds of the attainable.
P-2.......VII.6:1 Yet it is as **i.** not to accept a function God
P-2.......VII.7:1 The **i.**, thinking they are God, are not
S-1 ........III.4:8 be released without an **i.** fear for yourself?
S-2 ..........I.8:1 for who but the **i.** would look on sin when

## insanely 10

T-6...........I.4:7 and are therefore regarding yourself **i.**.
T-6......IV.11:5 proved to you that you have thought **i.**?
T-7........VI.9:2 except by you, when you are thinking **i.**.
T-7.......VII.2:1 When a brother acts **i.**, he is offering you
T-9........III.5:1 When a brother behaves **i.**, you can heal
T-17......IV.5:4 their thought systems, but they do so **i.**.
T-18.........I.7:6 course like feathers dancing **i.** in the wind
T-19.........I.3:6 what truth has never said and behaving **i.**,
W-pI.136.16:3 pursuits with double purposes **i.** sought,
W-pI...138.6:1 In this **i.** complicated world, Heaven

## insanity 66

T-6......V.A.5:4 The **i.** of this perception makes it a fearful
T-6......V.B.6:1 can be no conflict between sanity and **i.**.
T-7......VI.12:1 Allowing **i.** to enter your mind means
T-9.......VII.6:4 by this contrast can **i.** be judged as insane.
T-10.......V.3:7 because, having made him out of your **i.**,
T-10.....V.10:5 Would you have Him share your **i.**? God
T-10.....V.10:9 To deny it is **i.**. God gave Himself to you
T-11.....V.16:3 The case for **i.** is strong to the insane. For
T-13.......III.5:1 You can accept **i.** because you made it,
T-13....III.12:6 that would abide with you in your **i.**. And
T-13....III.12:8 who hears His answer but will give up **i.**.
T-13.......V.6:1 to you that you have withdrawn into **i.**.
T-13.......V.7:6 know not what you do can learn what **i.** is
T-13.......V.7:7 It is given you to learn how to deny **i.**, and
T-13.......V.8:7 is what denial does, for by it you accept **i.**,
T-13......IX.5:6 love. Nothing can justify **i.**, and to call for

T-13...... XI.7:4 sanity because **i.** is not the Will of God. If
T-14.........I.2:6 do not underestimate the extent of its **i.**.
T-14.... III.15:5 loves you, and would lead you out of **i.**.
T-15...VII.12:5 And despite the evident **i.** of this lesson,
T-17....... II.5:5 Son of God made in **i.** could be without a
T-18.........I.7:4 Inward is sanity; **i.** is outside you. You but
T-18.........I.7:6 touched with **i.** and swirling lightly off on
T-18.........I.8:5 the course of **i.** and restores you to reason
T-18...... III.1:5 hide from truth forever, in complete **i.**.
T-18...... IX.3:1 From the world of bodies, made by **i.**,
T-19.........I.3:6 behaving insanely, being imprisoned *by* **i.**.
T-19....... II.3:5 wild **i.** inherent in the whole idea of sin, it
T19....IV.C.8:7 but **i.** could look upon the defeat of God,
T19. IV.D.11:2 Only the sane can look on stark **i.** and
T-20...... III.7:1 to make the Son of God adjust to his **i.**.
T-20...... IV.3:3 you would see within your savior from **i.**?
T-21...... IV.4:2 much of your **i.** and recognize its madness
T-21...... IV.4:3 is moving inward, past **i.** and on to reason
T-21....... V.8:6 There is no reason in **i.**, for it depends
T-21....... V.9:1 with your Father's, to the undoing of **i.**.
T-21....... V.9:3 Reason is alien to **i.**, and those who use it
T-21...... VI.3:7 do not leave **i.** by going somewhere else.
T-21...... VI.8:7 would direct you how to leave **i.** behind.
T-21...... VI.8:8 behind **i.** in order to escape from reason.
T-22....... V.2:4 What can this be except an invitation to **i.**
T-23..... II.14:3 the function of **i.** to take the place of truth
T-23...... IV.3:3 function of the Son is murder, but it *is* **i.**.
T-25...... III.2:5 He could not enter His Son's **i.** with him,
T-25..... VII.3:5 makes no sense and has no meaning is **i.**.
T-25..... VII.8:2 of everyone who chose **i.** as his salvation.
T-25... VII.10:6 a heaven of hell, had such **i.** been possible
T-25... VII.13:1 a mad belief that God's **i.** would make you
T-25.... VIII.3:6 This is not justice, but **i.**. Yet how could
T-25.... VIII.3:7 defined without **i.** where love means hate,
T-26...... IX.4:6 insane have shed their garments of **i.** to
T-27....... II.9:8 delayed because you pause to listen to **i.**?
W-pI..... 76.4:1 It is **i.** that thinks these things. You call
W-pI..... 91.3:1 what you do not see is there sounds like **i.**.
W-pI..... 91.3:2 that it is **i.** not to see what is there, and to
W-pI... 152.6:5 die? You but accuse Him of **i.**, to think He
W-pII ..... 4.1:1 Sin is **i.**. It is the means by which the
W-pII .260.1:1 *myself, although in my* **i.** *I thought I did. Yet,*
W-pII .285.1:4 loss avail me if **i.** departs from me today,
W-pII ... 12.2:3 its **i.** it thinks it has become a victor over
M-4 ...... IV.1:7 curriculum, and its replacement by **i.**. No
M-19 ......... 5:1 not confuse His mercy with your own **i.**.
M-22 ......... 7:3 This is **i.** indeed. It is not up to God's
P-2........ IV.7:3 in truth, for to overlook reality is **i.**. Yet
P-2........ IV.8:1 is **i.** because all sickness is mental illness,
P-2........ VI.3:7 its "remedies"; its "safeguards" from **i.**.

## insatiable 1

W-pI... 161.7:5 Fear is **i.**, consuming everything its eyes

## insecurity 1

W-pI..... 39.6:2 anger, fear, worry, attack, **i.** and so on.

## inseparable 4

T-3....... V.10:5 God and His miracle are **i.**. How beautiful
T-4......... V.5:5 Learning and wanting to learn are **i.**. You
T-7...........I.5:3 forever, since joy and eternity are **i.**. God
T-15....... X.6:7 and is therefore **i.** from attack and fear.

## inside 7

T-4........ III.1:2 interprets it as if something outside is **i.**,
T-7......... II.3:1 law that prevails **i.** is adapted to "What
T-18.... VIII.9:1 the barrier you built to come **i.** and shine
T-18..VIII.10:3 locked away from love, and leaving you **i.**.
T-19...... IV.1:1 As peace extends from deep **i.** yourself to
T-26.........I.2:3 as if what is **i.** can never reach without,
C-3...........4:10 this gate it is no more than just a step **i.**. It

## insidious 1

T-15.........I.6:3 is hidden a far more **i.** threat to peace.

## insight 1

W-pI... 123.2:1 the benefit of some **i.** into the real extent

## insignificance 1

M-5 ...... II.3:12 **i.** of the body must be an acceptable idea.

## insignificant 3

T-16 ..... VI.7:3 What is little and **i.** is magnified, and
T-22 ...... V.4:2 **i.** before the quiet strength of those whom
W-pI. 183.10:3 Words are **i.**, and all requests unneeded

## insist 12

T-3 ....... VI.5:8 you will **i.** on holding on to judgment.
T-7 ..... VIII.2:3 intolerable that you will **i.** on giving it up.
T-9 ..........I.7:1 You may **i.** that the Holy Spirit does not
T-12 ..... III.2:3 you **i.** on refusing and experience a quick
T-12 ..... III.4:4 Why would you **i.** in denying him? For to
T-18 ..... IV.7:2 **i.** there must be more that you need do.
T-18 .... VII.6:5 making use of the course if you **i.** on using
T-20 ...... V.4:5 and yet **i.** that judgment still has meaning
T-28 ... IV.10:7 the result when you do not **i.** on seeing in
T-31 ..... II.11:3 you still **i.** on leading or on following, you
W-pI..... 61.2:4 It is not humility to **i.** you cannot be the
W-pI..... 79.8:1 you do not **i.** on defining the problem.

## insisted 2

T-4 ........ V.4:8 itself **i.** that it is identified with the body,
T-28 ..... IV.8:3 a little, broken bit that he **i.** was himself.

## insistence 7

T-8 ..... VIII.7:4 example of your **i.** on asking guidance of a
T-12 ..... III.2:2 His very **i.** should tell you that he believes
T-12 ..... III.2:5 **I.** means investment, and what you invest
T-12 ..... IV.1:6 For the ego pursues its goal with fanatic **i.**
T-15 ........I.6:3 For underneath its fanatical **i.** that the
T-20 ...... V.4:6 For this **i.** is of those who do not see.
T-21 ..... IV.8:4 fear's insane **i.** that sureness lies in doubt.

## insistent 1

T-8 ..... VIII.8:1 something that does not exist can be so **i.**.

## insisting 3

T-9 ....... IV.4:7 **i.** that you must accept the meaningless to
T-29 .... VII.1:7 what you want, **i.** where it must be found.
W-pI... 186.1:3 to you, without **i.** on another role. It does

## insists 4

T-12 ..... III.2:1 Suppose a brother **i.** on having you do
T-13 ....... II.1:3 for if you are to retain guilt, as the ego **i.**,
T-27 ....... I.11:2 **i.** your crippled picture is a lasting sign of
W-pI..... 72.5:6 every grievance that you hold **i.** that the

## insofar 1

T-4 ...... VII.2:2 communication, except **i.** as it is utilized

## Inspiration 3

*inspiration*

T-5 ..........I.4:6 from the Holy Spirit or the Universal **I.**,
T-5 ..........I.4:6 me first and foremost that this **I.** is for all.
T-5 ..........I.7:1 Spirit, the shared **I.** of all the Sonship,

## inspiration 3

*Inspiration*

T-4 ........ in.1:5 The result of genuine devotion is **i.**, a
T-7 ....... IV.1:2 **I.** is of the Holy Spirit, and certainty is of
T-7 ....... IV.1:3 since **i.** comes from the Voice for God and

## inspire 7

T-1 ........I.31:1 Miracles should **i.** gratitude, not awe.
T-1 ........I.32:1 I **i.** all miracles, which are really
T-1 ......... II.1:8 induces action, though it does not **i.** it.
T-4 ..... IV.11:8 you believe it is harder for me to **i.** the dis-
T-6 ..........I.8:5 church that does not **i.** love has a hidden
T-6 ......... II.9:7 can **i.** perception and lead it toward God.
T-9 ....... VI.1:4 you **i.** joy and others react to you with joy,

## inspired 8

T-1 ......... II.5:1 Revelations are indirectly **i.** by me
T-2 ....... VI.8:6 need for the remedy **i.** its establishment.
T-4 ........ in.1:6 but to be **i.** is to be in the spirit. To be
T-4 ........ in.1:7 in the right sense is to be **i.** or in spirit.
T-4 ........ in.1:8 truly **i.** are enlightened and cannot abide
T-4 ........ in.2:3 are **i.** because they reflect knowledge. If
T-7 ..........I.1:3 you share it, you are **i.** to create like God.
T-7 ......... V.6:9 be counted on because it is **i.** by His Voice

## inspires 3

T-1 ..........I.3:2 The real miracle is the love that **i.** them.
T-7 ....... IV.2:3 Spirit **i.** can have no order of difficulty,
T-7 ....... VI.1:5 ego or the Holy Spirit begets or **i.** them,

## inspiring 1

T-5 ..........I.5:2 **i.** the Atonement principle at the same

## instability 2

T-4 ......... II.2:1 to enormous variation because of its **i.**.
W-pI .. 186.9:2 Could He create such **i.** and call it Son?

## instance 3

T-22 ....... II.4:2 way, in every **i.** and without exception. To
T-31 ..... V.12:2 You might, for **i.**, be the thing you chose
W-pI .. 108.8:5 You might, for **i.**, say: *To everyone I offer*

## instances 2

T-8 ..... VIII.8:3 are many **i.** of how what you want distorts
T-27 ....... V.8:6 But healing is apparent in specific **i.**, and

## instant 390

*See also* Appendix C

T-2 ....... VI.9:7 sleeps. Every **i.** it is creating. It is hard to
T-5 ..........I.7:2 for one **i.** that sharing it involves anything
T-5 ......... V.8:7 return to full creation the **i.** it has done so.
T-7 ......... V.7:5 in one **i.** and change the world in the next.
T-10 ........I.2:4 **i.** you waken you realize that everything
T-10 ........I.4:1 everything the **i.** you desire it wholly, for
T-10 ..... III.9:6 for you the **i.** you signify your willingness
T-11 ... VIII.1:5 but an **i.** to realize that this alone is true.
T-12 ..... III.5:4 allow yourself to believe, even for an **i.**,
T-12 ... VIII.6:4 the **i.** you thought you had deserted Him.
T-13 ..... VII.7:6 He must deny the world of pain the **i.** he
T-14 ....... II.8:3 vision of Christ is given the very **i.** that it
T-14 .. VII.5:10 the **i.** it was given Him for you. Do not
T-14 ..... IX.7:1 realize for a single **i.** the power of healing
T-14 ........X.5:3 was light, darkness removes it in an **i.**,
T-14 ... XI.6:11 in your awareness the **i.** you abandon it,
T-15 ........I.8:3 no fear in the present when each **i.** stands
T-15 ........I.8:4 Each **i.** is a clean, untarnished birth, in
T-15 ........I.9:5 Take this very **i.**, now, and think of it as
T-15 ........I.9:7 From this holy **i.** wherein holiness was
T-15 ......I.10:2 Learn from this **i.** more than merely that
T-15 ......I.10:3 In this redeeming **i.** lies Heaven. And
T-15 ......I.10:7 In the holy **i.**, in which you see yourself as
T-15 ......I.11:1 ask yourself, "How long is an **i.**?" Could
T-15 ......I.11:4 tiny **i.** to offer you the whole of Heaven. In
T-15 ......I.11:5 In exchange for this **i.** He stands ready to
T-15 ......I.12:1 You will never give this holy **i.** to the
T-15 ......I.12:2 theirs. For the **i.** of holiness is shared, and
T-15 ......I.12:3 a brother, that his **i.** of release is yours.

T-15...... I.13:1 How long is an **i.**? It is as short for your
T-15...... I.13:3 Practice giving this blessed **i.** of freedom
T-15...... I.13:4 blessed **i.** to you through your giving it.
T-15...... I.14:1 How long is an **i.**? As long as it takes to re-
T-15...... I.15:5 never was an **i.** in which God's Son could
T-15...... I.15:9 For caught in the single **i.** of the eternal
T-15.... I.15:10 Give the eternal **i.**, that eternity may be
T-15.... I.15:10 you, in that shining **i.** of perfect release.
T-15.... I.15:11 of the holy **i.** through the Holy Spirit, and
T-15....... II.1:6 An **i.** offered to the Holy Spirit is offered
T-15....... II.1:6 in that **i.** you will awaken gently in Him.
T-15....... II.1:7 the blessed **i.** you will let go all your past
T-15....... II.2:1 fear not the **i.** of holiness that will remove
T-15....... II.2:2 For the **i.** of peace is eternal *because* it is
T-15....... II.3:4 blessed **i.** reaches out to encompass time,
T-15....... II.3:6 holy **i.** you will unchain all your brothers,
T-15..... II.4:10 a single **i.** completely to the Holy Spirit.
T-15....... II.5:1 The holy **i.** has not yet happened to you.
T-15....... II.5:4 can practice the mechanics of the holy **i.**,
T-15....... II.5:6 And here it is, all in this **i.**, complete,
T-15....... II.6:1 little part in separating out the holy **i.**.
T-15....... II.6:7 Use it but for one **i.**, and you will never
T-15...... IV.1:3 holy **i.** is this instant and every instant.
T-15...... IV.1:3 holy instant is this **i.** and every instant.
T-15...... IV.1:3 holy instant is this instant and every **i.**.
T-15...... IV.2:2 **i.** in which magnitude dawns upon you is
T-15...... IV.4:2 This you will recognize in the holy **i.**, in
T-15...... IV.4:4 holy **i.** any time and anywhere you want it
T-15...... IV.4:7 Use the holy **i.** only to recognize that you
T-15...... IV.5:1 I stand within the holy **i.**, as clear as you
T-15...... IV.5:2 the time in which the holy **i.** will be yours.
T-15...... IV.5:3 to you to make the holy **i.** yours at once,
T-15...... IV.6:3 could live forever in the holy **i.**, beginning
T-15...... IV.6:5 The holy **i.** is a time in which you receive
T-15...... IV.7:2 that makes the holy **i.** what it is. You
T-15...... IV.8:6 For the holy **i.** is given and received with
T-15...... IV.9:1 the holy **i.** does not require that you have
T-15...... IV.9:4 It is given you the **i.** you would have it.
T-15....... V.1:1 holy **i.** is the Holy Spirit's most useful
T-15....... V.3:7 Yet the holy **i.** teaches you it is not so.
T-15....... V.8:2 In the holy **i.** no one is special, for your
T-15....... V.8:5 In the holy **i.**, you see in each relationship
T-15....... V.9:3 holy **i.** reflects His knowing by bringing
T-15....... V.9:7 For in the holy **i.**, free of the past, you see
T-15..... V.10:1 relationships are blessed in the holy **i.**,
T-15..... V.10:2 In the holy **i.** the Sonship gains as one,
T-15..... V.10:8 in the holy **i.** you unite directly with God,
T-15..... V.11:4 In the holy **i.** there is no conflict of needs,
T-15..... V.11:5 For the holy **i.** reaches to eternity, and to
T-15...... VI.2:5 the holy **i.** we share our faith in God's Son
T-15...... VI.5:3 holy **i.** you recognize the idea of love in
T-15...... VI.5:5 The holy **i.** thus becomes a lesson in how
T-15...... VI.5:8 In the holy **i.** the laws of God prevail, and
T-15.... VI.5:11 **i.** he is as free as God would have him be.
T-15.... VI.5:12 For the **i.** he refuses to be bound, he is not
T-15...... VI.6:1 In the holy **i.** nothing happens that has
T-15...... VI.6:7 Fear not the holy **i.** will be denied you, for
T-15.... VI.6:10 For in the holy **i.** you will recognize the
T-15...... VI.8:1 In the holy **i.** God is remembered, and
T-15...... VI.8:3 in the holy **i.** because the past is gone, and
T-15... VII.14:1 It is through the holy **i.** that what seems
T-15... VII.14:2 In the holy **i.** guilt holds no attraction,
T-15... VIII.1:1 The holy **i.** does not replace the need for
T-15... VIII.1:1 the holy **i.** has extended far beyond time.
T-15... VIII.2:4 in making the holy **i.** all that there is, by
T-15... VIII.4:1 an **i.** on this: God gave the Sonship to you
T-15...... IX.1:2 vision that is accomplished in the holy **i.**.
T-15...... IX.3:1 the holy **i.**, where the Great Rays replace
T-15...... IX.7:3 In the holy **i.** there are no bodies, and you
T-15...... IX.7:4 as undivided you join Him wholly, in an **i.**
T-15....... X.2:1 The holy **i.** is truly the time of Christ. For
T-15....... X.2:2 liberating **i.** no guilt is laid upon the Son
T-15...... XI.7:1 In the holy **i.** the condition of love is met,
T-15.. XI.10:10 Accept the holy **i.** as this year is born, and
T-16...... IV.5:8 But conflict enters the **i.** the choice seems
T-16...... VI.3:2 His. The holy **i.** is His most helpful aid in
T-16.... VI.11:7 And may the holy **i.** speed you on the way
T-16.... VI.12:1 attracts you, enter with Him into a holy **i.**,
T-16..... VII.6:1 the Holy Spirit gently lays the holy **i.**. We
T-16..... VII.6:3 The holy **i.** is the opposite of the ego's
T-16..... VII.6:4 the holy **i.** it is understood that the past is
T-16..... VII.7:1 attempt to bring illusions into the holy **i.**,
T-16..... VII.7:3 holy **i.** the power of the Holy Spirit will
T-16..... VII.7:5 mind. Yet the holy **i.** is eternal, and your
T-16..... VII.8:5 He gave the holy **i.** to be given you, and it
T-16..... VII.8:7 In the holy **i.** is His reminder that His Son
T-16..... VII.9:7 In the holy **i.** this is done for you in time,
T-16... VII.11:1 Seek and *find* His message in the holy **i.**,
T-17.... IV.10:1 is why the holy **i.** is so important in the
T-17.... IV.11:1 The holy **i.** is a miniature of Heaven, sent
T-17.... IV.11:4 The holy **i.** is a miniature of eternity. It is
T-17.... IV.11:8 gifts, so the whole of Heaven lies in this **i.**,
T-17.... IV.16:8 holy **i.** shines alike on all relationships,
T-17....... V.1:1 of the holy **i.** in living in this world. Like
T-17....... V.1:2 salvation, the holy **i.** is a practical device,
T-17....... V.1:3 The holy **i.** never fails. The experience of
T-17..... V.10:2 You have joined with many in the holy **i.**,
T-17... V.11:10 yourself unable to express the holy **i.**, and
T-17..... V.12:1 experience of an **i.**, however compelling it
T-17..... V.12:3 it. The **i.** remains. But where are you? To
T-17..... V.12:5 to your brother is to appreciate the holy **i.**
T-17..... V.12:6 To attack your brother is not to lose the **i.**
T-17..... V.13:1 You *have* received the holy **i.**, but you may
T-17..... V.15:1 the effects of the holy **i.** and use them to
T-17... VIII.1:1 holy **i.** is nothing more than a special case
T-17... VIII.1:4 The holy **i.** is the shining example, the
T-17... VIII.3:1 want to make a holy **i.** of every situation?
T-18....... II.4:4 **i.** the illusion of satisfaction is invaded by
T-18...... III.2:5 Let us then join quickly in an **i.** of light,
T-18...... III.5:1 Each **i.** that we spend together will teach
T-18...... III.7:3 from the holy **i.** to which you brought it.
T-18...... IV.1:1 holy **i.** is the result of your determination
T-18...... IV.1:9 He joins with you to make the holy **i.** far
T-18...... IV.2:6 them you would not need the holy **i.**.
T-18...... IV.2:8 it. The miracle of the holy **i.** lies in your
T-18...... IV.3:3 Your difficulty with the holy **i.** arises from
T-18...... IV.4:1 The holy **i.** does not come from your little
T-18...... IV.5:4 given. In preparing for the holy **i.**, do not
T-18...... IV.6:5 preparation for the holy **i.** belongs to Him
T-18...... IV.7:1 makes the holy **i.** so easy and so natural.
T-18...... IV.8:2 If you believe the holy **i.** is difficult for you
T-18....... V.1:3 The holy **i.**, the holy relationship, the
T-18....... V.2:1 Never approach the holy **i.** after you have
T-18....... V.3:1 and blessed in every holy **i.** you do not
T-18....... V.6:1 let Him exchange this **i.** for the holy one
T-18....... V.6:6 the holy **i.** come to either of you without
T-18....... V.7:3 say: *I desire this holy* ***i.*** *for myself, that I may*
T-18....... V.7:6 *I choose this* ***i.*** *as the one to offer to the Holy*
T-18.... VI.13:6 much of what happens in the holy **i.**; the
T-18.... VI.14:2 is the irresistible appeal the holy **i.** holds.
T-18..... VII.2:3 to let this happen for more than an **i.**, yet
T-18..... VII.2:3 **i.** that the miracle of Atonement happens.
T-18..... VII.2:5 every **i.** that you spend without awareness
T-18..... VII.3:1 At no single **i.** does the body exist at all.
T-18..... VII.3:5 single **i.** the attraction of guilt would be
T-18..... VII.4:1 the holy **i.** without reservation unless, just
T-18..... VII.4:1 without reservation unless, just for an **i.**,
T-18..... VII.4:3 Release is given you the **i.** you desire it.
T-18..... VII.5:3 One **i.** spent together with your brother
T-18..... VII.6:8 Believe it for just one **i.**, and you will
T-18. VIII.11:1 The holy **i.** is your invitation to love to
T-18. VIII.11:4 In the holy **i.**, you ask of love only what it
T-18.... IX.13:3 The holy **i.** in which you and your brother
T-19........ I.10:5 just as he is perceived in the holy **i.**,
T-19........ I.14:1 In the holy **i.**, you and your brother stand
T-19...... III.9:5 and all its ravages the **i.** that you give it no
T-19.... III.10:1 In the holy **i.**, you will see the smile of
T-19.... III.10:4 was healed in the holy **i.** Heaven gave you.
T19. IV.A.16:3 a holy **i.** grace is said by everyone together
T19... IV.D.9:6 Let us join together in a holy **i.**, here in
T19... IV.D.9:6 place where the purpose, given in a holy **i.**
T-20...... III.9:1 not leap up in joy the **i.** they are made free
T-20....... V.6:1 look upon each holy **i.** as a different point
T-20...... VI.8:6 The **i.** that the mad idea of making your
T-20...... VI.8:7 In that unholy **i.** time was born, and
T-20...... VI.8:9 this mad idea against reality but for an **i.**?
T-20...... VI.9:2 unholy **i.** of their seeming power is frail as
T-20...... VI.9:3 the holy **i.** and its unlimited beneficence?
T-20...... VI.9:4 attraction your preference to the holy **i.**,
T-20.... VI.10:4 unholy **i.** is exchanged in gladness for the
T-20.... VI.11:2 given but an **i.** in which to sigh and grieve
T-20.... VI.11:3 And this unholy **i.** seems to be life; an
T-20.... VI.11:3 instant seems to be life; an **i.** of despair, a
T-20.... VI.11:7 to spend this **i.** paying tribute to the body
T-20.... VI.11:8 it. Here he can accept the holy **i.**, offered
T-20.... VI.12:2 The holy **i.** is of greater value now to you
T-20..... VII.5:2 The unholy **i.** *is* the time of bodies. But the
T-20..... VII.6:7 serving the cause of sin an **i.** before he
T-20.. VIII.11:3 after? Think but an **i.** just on this; you can
T-21........ II.4:5 In the holy **i.** is this exchange effected and
T-21........ II.8:1 Be willing, for an **i.**, to leave your altars
T-21........ II.8:2 The holy **i.** is not an instant of creation,
T-21........ II.8:2 The holy instant is not an **i.** of creation,
T-21...... II.13:3 and the **i.** of release has come to you. All
T-21...... III.9:6 The **i.** for its recognition is at hand. Join
T-21....... V.5:6 Him arose, and was fulfilled in the same **i.**
T-21...... VI.7:6 mind, which is one with you, in just an **i.**.
T-21...... VI.7:7 **i.** serves to bring complete correction of
T-21...... VI.7:8 **i.** that you choose to let yourself be healed
T-21...... VI.7:8 in that same **i.** is his whole salvation seen
T-21...... VI.9:7 Spend but an **i.** in the glad acceptance of
T-21.... VIII.5:1 What is the holy **i.** but God's appeal to
T-22........ I.10:2 perception, and yet reborn in just an **i.**.
T-22........ I.10:4 what that **i.** brought; the recognition that
T-23....... II.22:5 any **i.** it is possible to have all this undone
T-23...... III.6:4 return because the guns are stilled an **i.**,
T-24...... III.1:7 receive it wholly the **i.** that he gave it so.
T-24...... IV.4:8 just a dream of specialness that lasts an **i.**,
T-24....... V.4:2 **i.** from the fireflies of sin and then go out,
T-25...... III.5:3 is met with **i.** and complete forgiveness.
T-25...... III.5:4 Nothing remains an **i.**, to obscure the
T-25...... III.6:2 Nor need he stay more than an **i.**. For he
T-25...... III.9:8 **i.** when all time becomes a means to reach
T-25...... VI.6:6 from the very **i.** that the choice was made.
T-26.......... I.5:4 No **i.** passes here in which your brother's
T-26.......... I.7:1 Yet every **i.** can you be reborn, and given
T-26.......... I.7:7 Born again each **i.**, untouched by time,
T-26....... V.3:3 Time lasted but an **i.** in your mind, with
T-26....... V.3:6 And in that tiny **i.** time was gone, for that
T-26....... V.4:3 thing you look upon you saw but for an **i.**,
T-26....... V.5:1 tiny **i.** you would keep and make eternal,
T-26....... V.5:5 belief in sin, is that one **i.** still called back,
T-26....... V.8:4 you? And do you want that fearful **i.** kept,
T-26..... V.10:3 now. A dreadful **i.** in a distant past, now
T-26..... V.10:7 of death, a vault God's Son entered an **i.**,
T-26..... V.11:2 the **i.** that he chose to die instead of live.
T-26..... V.13:1 day, and every **i.** that each minute holds,
T-26..... V.13:1 you but relive the single **i.** when the time
T-26..... V.13:3 a repetition of an **i.** gone by long ago that
T-26... VII.10:6 And every miracle is possible the **i.** that
T-26... VII.16:5 Each **i.** is the Son of God reborn until he
T-26... VII.16:7 Yet every **i.** offers life to him because his
T-27........ II.9:7 could the Holy Spirit be deterred an **i.**,
T-27...... III.6:3 Nor delay an **i.** in deciding that it is the
T-27...... IV.2:4 Such is the holy **i.**. It is here that all your
T-27...... IV.6:1 Only within the holy **i.** can an honest
T-27...... IV.6:9 holy **i.** is the interval in which the mind is
T-27...... IV.7:5 In the holy **i.**, you can bring the question
T-27....... V.1:4 is its nature to extend itself the **i.** it is born
T-27....... V.1:5 it is born the **i.** it is offered and received.
T-27..... V.2:12 But it does mean, if only for an **i.**, you love
T-27..... V.2:13 An **i.** is sufficient. Miracles wait not on
T-27....... V.3:1 The holy **i.** is the miracle's abiding place.
T-27....... V.4:2 And nothing more than just one **i.** of your
T-27....... V.4:3 In that one **i.** you are healed, and in that
T-27....... V.4:3 and in that single **i.** is all healing done.
T-27....... V.4:4 accept the blessing that the holy **i.** brings?
T-27....... V.5:5 you rest an **i.** from attack upon yourself,
T-27....... V.6:1 Come to the holy **i.** and be healed, for
T-27..... V.11:4 occurred within the **i.** that love entered in
T-27...... VI.8:2 The holy **i.** will replace all sin if you but
T-27... VII.12:4 and of ancient hate, the **i.** of disaster, all
T-27.... VIII.4:5 The **i.** that he sees them as they are they
T-27.... VIII.9:8 And you will leave the holy **i.** with your
T-28........ I.11:1 into the mind that stops an **i.** and is still.
T-28........ I.12:1 offers thanks for every quiet **i.** given Him.
T-28........ I.12:2 For in that **i.** is God's memory allowed to

T-28.......I.12:6 **i.** does the Son of God do nothing that
T-28.......I.15:3 a bridge an **i.** will suffice to reach beyond?
T-28.....VII.4:6 this choice, and given you the **i.** it is made
T-29.........I.9:4 serve to hold you back an **i.** from His Love
T-30......III.8:7 no **i.** when its light grew dimmer or less
T-31.......I.12:1 Let us be still an **i.**, and forget all things
T-31....... II.6:4 *myself.* Then let us wait an **i.** and be still,
T-31....... II.8:1 very still an **i.**. Come without all thought
T-31..... II.10:1 An **i.** spent without your old ideas of who
T-31......VI.2:4 no one is exactly as he was an **i.** previous,
T-31......VI.2:4 he be the same as he is now an **i.** hence.
T-31...VII.10:5 they are; all those you saw an **i.** and forgot
W-pI.....33.4:1 idea the **i.** you are aware of distress. It
W-pI.....41.8:7 fail completely, and **i.** success is possible.
W-pI.....48.3:3 **i.** you are willing to do this there is indeed
W-pI.....98.9:6 exchanging every **i.** of the time you offer
W-pI...128.4:3 here is worth one **i.** of delay and pain; one
W-pI.135.19:1 increases, as this life becomes a holy **i.**, set
W-pI...136.7:3 **i.** truth arises in your own deluded mind,
W-pI.136.20:1 Give **i.** remedy, should this occur, by not
W-pI.137.11:2 time elapse between the **i.** they are healed
W-pI...153.8:3 for the Son of God; its tiny **i.** for eternity.
W-pI...156.6:5 but who would waste an **i.** in approach to
W-pI...157.2:4 It leaves us here an **i.**, and we go beyond it
W-pI...157.9:2 will be an **i.** which transcends all vision,
W-pI...157.9:4 rememberance of what you knew that **i.**,
W-pI.159.10:6 Let us an **i.** dream with Him. His dream
W-pI...164.1:3 so today, this **i.**, now, we come to look
W-pI...165.2:2 nor have you ever been apart from it an **i.**.
W-pI.167.10:5 to life abide even an **i.** where the Thought
W-pI...168.4:2 will come, with knowledge but an **i.** later.
W-pI...168.4:4 that Heaven be delayed an **i.** longer?
W-pI.169.13:3 unity he felt an **i.** back to bless the world?
W-pI.169.14:1 to return, as you were glad to go an **i.**, and
W-pI...181.3:4 And what we saw an **i.** previous has no
W-pI...181.7:3 we seek but for surcease an **i.** from the
W-pI...181.9:8 of God. This **i.** is our willing one with His.
W-pI......182.h I will be still an **i.** and go home.
W-pI...182.8:1 When you are still an **i.**, when the world
W-pI...182.8:3 In that **i.** He will take you to His home,
W-pI.182.12:9 Be still an **i.** and go home with Him, and
W-pI...185.1:3 If you could but mean them for just an **i.**,
W-pI...186.9:5 leaves that form a patterning an **i.**, break
W-pI.193.10:3 another day, another minute or another **i.**
W-pI...194.3:1 In no one **i.** is depression felt, or pain
W-pI...194.3:2 no one **i.** sorrow can be set upon a throne,
W-pI...194.3:3 In no one **i.** can one even die. And so each
W-pI...194.3:4 And so each **i.** given unto God in passing,
W-pI...194.5:2 becomes the **i.** in which time escapes the
W-pI...194.5:3 Then is each **i.** which was slave to time
W-pI...194.5:3 slave to time transformed into a holy **i.**,
W-pI...196.4:5 be done in just one **i.** by the grace of God.
W-pI.196.10:1 **i.** in which terror seems to grip your mind
W-pI.196.11:1 Now, for an **i.**, is a murderer perceived
W-pI.196.11:2 Yet in this **i.** is the time as well in which
W-pI.196.11:5 Pray that the **i.** may be soon,–today.
W-pI.196.12:1 not go with you to help you reach that **i.**,
W-pI.198.11:5 it. Only that can be perceived an **i.** longer.
W-pI.198.12:6 so brief that not an **i.** stands between this
W-pI.200.10:5 eyes but serving for an **i.** longer now.
W-pI...202.1:1 (182) I will be still an **i.** and go home.
W-pI...202.1:2 *Why would I choose to stay an* **i.** *more where*
W-pII ....227.h This is my holy **i.** of release.
W-pII .227.1:6 *This is my holy* **i.** *of release. Father, I know*
W-pII .....2.2:1 the **i.** that his mind had thought of war.
W-pII .....2.5:2 and God's Son has but an **i.** more to wait
W-pII .234.1:2 left. Merely a tiny **i.** has elapsed between
W-pII ....241.h This holy **i.** is salvation come.
W-pII .241.1:3 For today holds out the **i.** to the darkened
W-pII .270.1:4 *the one remaining* **i.** *more of time which*
W-pII .271.1:1 Each day, each hour, every **i.**, I am
W-pII .285.1:3 joyous things the **i.** I accept my holiness.
W-pII .290.1:5 belief the dream I made is real an **i.** longer
W-pII .....8.5:2 one **i.** more for God to take His final step,
W-pII .....8.5:3 That **i.** is our goal, for it contains the
W-pII ....300.h Only an **i.** does this world endure.
W-pII .300.2:4 *thanks today the world endures but for an* **i.**.
W-pII .300.2:5 *We would go beyond that tiny* **i.** *to eternity.*
W-pII ....308.h This **i.** is the only time there is.
W-pII .308.1:5 this **i.** has forgiveness come to set me free.
W-pII .308.2:1 *Thanks for this* **i.***, Father. It is now I am*
W-pII .308.2:3 *This* **i.** *is the time You have appointed for*
W-pII .324.2:2 stray except an **i.** from His loving Hand.
W-pII .355.1:6 *not wait an* **i.** *more to be at peace forever. It is*
WpII ..361-5.h This holy **i.** would I give to You. Be You
M-2 ........... 2:6 The **i.** the idea of separation entered the
M-2 ........... 2:6 in that same **i.** was God's Answer given.
M-2 ........... 4:1 goes backward to an **i.** so ancient that it is
M-2 ........... 4:2 Yet because it is an **i.** that is relived again
M-2 ........... 4:5 in that ancient **i.** which he now relives. So
M-5 .........I.1:1 Healing is accomplished the **i.** the
M-6 ........... 2:2 The **i.** it is welcome it is there. Where
M-10 ......... 6:3 down happily the **i.** he recognizes its cost.
M-14 ......... 3:4 the **i.** any one of them accepts Atonement
M-15 ......... 2:6 One **i.** of complete belief in this, and you
M-15 ......... 2:7 One **i.** out of time can bring time's end.
M-15 ......... 3:2 to occupy your holy mind an **i.** longer.
M-16 ......... 4:6 One can as easily give God only an **i.**, and
M-16 ......... 4:6 and in that **i.** join with Him completely.
M-16 ......... 8:5 the **i.** this occurs he will return to earlier
C-2 ............ 7:6 And look an **i.**, too, on what you left
C-3 ............ 8:1 that single **i.** when you see the truth about
C-4 ............ 4:2 that it can last no longer than an **i.**. It is
C-4 ............ 4:5 appears, and in that **i.** is the world forgot,
C-4 ............ 6:7 guilt and forgiveness for an **i.** lie together,
C-4 ............ 7:6 of Christ has shone away time's final **i.**,
C-ep........... 1:9 Love is but an **i.** farther on the road where
C-ep........... 4:1 and kneel down an **i.** in our gratitude to
C-ep........... 4:6 again which had been stopped only an **i.**,
C-ep........... 4:7 until the world is still an **i.** and forgets all
P-2..........II.1:3 within an **i.** and without a word. Yet he
P-2........ VI.2:1 to hear this song of death only an **i.**, and
P-3...........I.3:5 perhaps even more, at the **i.** they are sent.
P-3..........II.6:1 It is in the **i.** that the therapist forgets to
P-3..........II.8:7 laws of healing can be theirs in just an **i.**.
S-1........ III.5:1 Stand still an **i.**, now, and think what you
S-1........ IV.1:3 so has been recognized if only for an **i.**, it
S-2...........I.6:5 an **i.** only seem to hide the face of Christ,
S-2.........I.10:2 must choose between them every **i.** while
S-3........ IV.2:5 embrace of prayer rest on the earth an **i.**,
S-3........ IV.2:6 away. This **i.** is the goal of all true healers,
S-3........ IV.7:4 Be still an **i.**. Underneath the sounds of
S-3........ IV.7:6 Me. Hear this an **i.** and you will be healed.
S-3........ IV.7:7 Hear this an **i.** and you have been saved.

## instant's 6

T-27 ..... IV.3:1 no problems but within the holy **i.** surety.
T-27 ...... V.6:5 The holy **i.** radiance will light your eyes,
T-28 ......I.11:4 minds, and bringing them an **i.** stillness,
T-28 ......I.12:5 The **i.** silence that His Son accepts gives
W-pI...129.5:1 stand an **i.** space away from timelessness.
S-1...........I.4:6 advice about a problem of an **i.** duration?

## instantaneous 1

T-15 ......I.13:7 you give is your **i.** escape from guilt. You

## instantly 21

T-13 ..... III.2:2 would **i.** restore you to your proper place,
T-14 ....VII.4:9 complete incompatibility is **i.** apparent.
T-16 ........II.3:4 you **i.** that order of difficulty in miracles is
T-17 ...VIII.3:4 power **i.** transforms all situations into one
T-18 ...... V.6:1 stop **i.** and offer the Holy Spirit your
T-18 ... VI.11:8 The love that **i.** replaces it extends to what
T-18 ...VIII.3:3 you would see **i.** that it is like the smallest
T-19 ........I.13:2 that receives it looks **i.** beyond the body,
T-22 .......I.10:5 And truth came **i.**, to show you where
T-24 .......II.6:2 the memory of Him springs **i.** to mind.
T-26 .... V.10:7 **i.** restored unto his Father's perfect Love.
T-26 ....VIII.3:4 you still, and let you **i.** become as one.
T-28 .......I.13:1 How **i.** the memory of God arises in the
T-29 .........I.3:7 you approached, did he but **i.** withdraw.
W-pI.161.12:5 fear. Be sure you use it **i.**, should you be
W-pI...163.8:3 they believe, they would be **i.** released.
W-pI...165.3:2 not **i.** prepare to go where they are found,
W-pI...169.1:4 Grace becomes inevitable **i.** in those who
W-pI 198.10:1 God's Son, and Heaven is remembered **i.**;
M-18 ......... 4:2 let him **i.** realize that he has made an
P-2....... VII.4:3 healer would **i.** become a teacher of God,

## instants 9

T-15 ......I.12:4 Miracles are the **i.** of release you offer,
T-18 ... VI.13:6 **i.** of release from physical restrictions,
T-18 .... VII.4:4 have indeed achieved their **i.** of success.
T-20 .......V.5:6 many holy **i.** to let this be accomplished,
W-pI 169.13:2 returned by you from holy **i.** you receive,
W-pI .. 182.5:4 ask for more than just a few **i.** of respite;
W-pII .... in.3:2 the remaining holy **i.** which conclude the
W-pII .. in.11:4 one of the holy and blessed **i.** in the day.
P-3..........II.8:3 Many holy **i.** can be his along the way. A

## instead 208

T-2 ..........I.1:7 can fill it with your own ideas **i.** of truth.
T-2 ....... VI.4:3 should ask, **i.**, for help in the conditions
T-3 .........II.5:8 the innocent defend true perception **i.** of
T-3 .........V.6:6 In electing perception **i.** of knowledge,
T-3 ..... VI.11:8 **I.** of "Seek ye first the Kingdom of Heaven
T-4 ........ in.2:4 disclaiming knowledge **i.** of affirming it,
T-4 ..........I.9:6 ego has chosen to be afraid **i.** of meeting it
T-4 ....... VI.3:1 often to me **i.** of to your ego for guidance.
T-6 .........II.5:3 **I.** of anger this arouses love for both,
T-6 .........V.3:3 and make you unsafe; but if you do that **i.**
T-6 ..... V.C.2:5 so that you will not project, **i.** of extend.
T-8 .........V.5:8 chosen me as your companion *i.* of the ego
T-8 .... VII.13:2 learning promotes depression **i.** of joy,
T-11 ... III.4:10 But deny them **i.**, for the light is here and
T-13 ......I.10:2 plan, which it offers **i.** of dispelling it. The
T-13 ..... VI.1:5 him that you made and cherish **i.** of him.
T-13 ..... IX.5:5 other, calling for punishment **i.** of love.
T-13 ..... IX.8:3 **I.**, it bids you look upon your brothers,
T-14 ... III.11:6 **I.**, accept His answer, for He knows that
T-14 ... IV.4:11 **i.** offer to God and you His blameless Son.
T-14 ..... IV.5:5 and trying to teach him guilt **i.** of love.
T-14 ..... XI.9:5 to light, having accepted them **i.** of you,
T-15 ..... IV.2:3 you desire it not and cherish littleness **i.**,
T-17 ..... IV.2:7 and glorifies yours **i.** of His because of the
T-17 .... VII.7:3 if you would use the faithlessness **i.**.
T-17 ... VIII.3:3 the Holy Spirit's purpose is free to use **i.**.
T-18 ........I.1:1 To substitute is to accept **i.**. If you would
T-18 ......I.10:4 never accept something else **i.** of you. He
T-18 . VI.11:11 You have accepted this **i.** of the body, and
T19 .IV.A.14:1 send **i.** of those you trained through fear.
T19 .IV.A.15:6 replace the hungry dogs of fear you sent **i.**
T19 .IV.A.17:2 of your sin, and so I had to die **i.** of you.
T19 .IV.A.17:4 which the Son of God was killed **i.** of you.
T19 ... IV.B.9:2 to accept the peace He gives **i.**, without
T-20 ..... IV.2:4 See sin in him **i.**, and Heaven is lost to you
T-21 ........I.2:1 to attempt to judge what could be seen **i.**.
T-21 ..... III.3:4 hold him, and placing it in his freedom **i.**.
T-21 ..... III.4:6 have accepted them completely **i.** of yours
T-21 ..... VI.6:1 If you choose sin **i.** of healing, you would
T-21 ..... VI.7:2 neither can accept a miracle **i.** without the
T-21 . VI.11:10 free. But where he chooses to condemn **i.**,
T-21 .. VII.5:11 *I desire a world I rule* **i.** *of one that rules me?*
T-21 .. VII.5:12 *a world where I am powerful* **i.** *of helpless?*
T-22 ........I.7:1 to communicate **i.** of separate reborn. Yet
T-23 .......II.3:5 When brought to truth **i.** of to each other,
T-23 ..... IV.5:6 above, the choice is miracles **i.** of murder.
T-23 ..... IV.6:5 but quickly choose a miracle **i.** of murder.
T-24 ........I.2:6 least decision to choose attack **i.** of love,
T-24 .......II.1:5 him a tiny measure of your specialness **i.**.
T-24 .......II.3:7 chose their specialness **i.** of Heaven and
T-24 .......II.3:7 instead of Heaven and **i.** of peace, and
T-24 .......II.6:1 What would they see **i.**? The shining
T-24 ..... III.6:7 He could not give, and that you made **i.**.
T-24 .... III.8:11 Love not your specialness **i.** of Them. The
T-24 ... IV.3:12 Father asks from Him, and give it there **i.**?
T-24 ..... IV.5:4 the one whom God has given you **i.**. So
T-24 .... VII.3:1 your worth while specialness claims you **i.**
T-25 ........I.2:5 who tells you this, and seek his death **i.**?
T-25 .......II.5:7 would you rather see the frame **i.** of this?
T-25 .......II.6:5 picture, and cherishes the frame **i.** of it.
T-25 .......II.7:1 Accept God's frame **i.** of yours, and you

T-25....... II.8:8 that looks on Christ **i.** of seeing death.
T-25....... III.5:4 it must be, and light the body up **i.** of it.
T-25....... III.7:2 you to see the world He made **i.** of yours.
T-25....... V.2:5 a "something" to be feared **i.** of loved.
T-25...... VI.4:1 use of what you made, to heal **i.** of harm.
T-25.... VI.5:11 and thus become a means to save **i.** of lose
T-25...... IX.3:9 punishment becomes his due **i.** of justice.
T-26......... I.5:1 see the witnesses to truth **i.** of to illusion
T-26....... II.8:1 be remembered until justice is loved **i.** of
T-26....... II.8:5 to wish that Heaven be given you **i.** of hell
T-26....... III.2:6 denied, and everything that *is* received **i.**.
T-26..... V.11:2 the instant that he chose to die **i.** of live.
T-26... VII.16:6 death **i.** of what his Father wills for him.
T-26... VII.18:3 choose a little senseless wish **i.** of what He
T-27....... V.6:5 all suffering and see Christ's face **i.**.
T-27... VII.14:1 Accept the dream He gave **i.** of yours. It is
T-27... VII.15:3 Dream of your brother's kindnesses **i.** of
T-27... VII.15:4 about **i.** of counting up the hurts he gave.
T-27... VIII.7:4 dreams and thinks your thoughts **i.** of you
T-28......... I.7:7 see, **i.**, the new effects of cause accepted
T-28..... II.12:6 the mind is free to make another choice **i.**.
T-28...... IV.1:3 Nor do you wish that they be turned, **i.**,
T-28...... IV.5:3 in his dreams, **i.** of dreamer of your own.
T-28...... IV.8:3 whole picture represents, **i.** of just a little,
T-28..... VII.7:2 No secret promise you have made **i.** has
T-29....... II.1:2 the truth **i.** of looking on it as an enemy?
T-29....... II.1:4 it as the road to hell **i.** of looking on it as a
T-29....... V.5:7 being empty they receive, **i.**, a brother's
T-29....... V.6:8 But learn, **i.**, how blessed are you who can
T-29....... V.7:2 **i.** of dreaming evil separate dreams of
T-29...... VI.1:2 much do you desire peace **i.** of endless
T-29...... VI.1:5 asks, and gladly offers peace **i.** of this.
T-29...... IX.5:5 his thoughts and gives them to the toys **i.**.
T-30....... II.3:1 the one you chose to hate **i.** of love. For
T-30....... V.1:5 **I.**, there is a wish to understand all things
T-30...... VI.2:5 is real. **I.**, it merely asks that you respond
T-30... VIII.3:4 obscure and give to them reality **i.**. And
T-30... VIII.4:9 the willing slave of what he chose **i.**.
T-30... VIII.6:5 but will fade, if you request a miracle **i.**.
T-31.... III.3:10 to its prison house, which acts **i.** of it. A
T-31...... IV.5:2 begin with this, to seek another way **i.**?
T-31...... IV.6:1 that there is a real alternative **i.**. To fight
T-31...... VI.2:7 guilt, because they chose to let it go **i.**.
T-31..... VII.6:4 Give it **i.** to Him Who understands the
T-31..... VII.6:6 of the world, **i.** of as salvation's enemy?
T-31... VII.14:2 well upon the thing that you would be **i.**.
T-31... VIII.2:7 Him, and He has given you His strength **i.**
T-31... VIII.4:4 His strength **i.** of their own weakness,
W-pI..... 10.2:3 with "My thoughts" **i.** of "These thoughts
W-pI..... 12.2:4 markedly longer or shorter, but try, **i.**, to
W-pI..... 25.2:5 world, **i.** of attempting to reinforce them.
W-pI..... 28.6:3 **i.** of placing your own judgment upon it.
W-pI..... 30.2:3 **I.**, we are trying to see in the world what
W-pI........ 34.h I could see peace **i.** of this.
W-pI..... 34.5:4 *in this situation* **i.** *of what I now see in it.*
W-pI..... 41.6:5 Try, **i.**, to get a sense of turning inward,
W-pI..... 45.4:6 **I.**, we will try to recognize that only what
W-pI..... 57.4:1 (34) I could see peace **i.** of this. When I
W-pI..... 57.4:2 God **i.** of the rules I made up for it to obey
W-pI..... 72.7:5 Your chosen savior takes His place **i.**. It is
W-pI..... 72.8:2 We will try to welcome it **i.**. Your upside-
W-pI..... 72.9:5 plan for salvation, and to accept it **i.**. And
W-pI... 72.13:4 *Let me accept it* **i.**. *What is salvation, Father?*
W-pI... 73.11:7 **i.** of cherishing them and hiding them in
W-pI..... 76.7:4 We realize **i.** it is a truth that keeps us free
W-pI..... 78.1:4 in light, but you behold your grievances **i.**
W-pI..... 78.2:1 the grievances, to look upon the miracle **i.**
W-pI..... 89.2:3 *offer you the miracle that belongs to you* **i.**.
W-pI..... 91.3:2 is there, and to see what is not there **i.**.
W-pI... 100.5:3 **i.** of what has been assigned to you by
W-pI... 103.1:6 sin can enter, bringing pain **i.** of joy. This
W-pI... 104.1:5 that has **i.** received the gifts it made where
W-pI... 104.4:1 aside, and seek **i.** that which is truly ours,
W-pI... 106.4:7 They end the dream **i.**; and last forever,
W-pI... 108.1:4 behind it will appear **i.** to take its place.
W-pI... 110.9:3 **i.** of what he is be worshipped not today.
W-pI... 122.4:5 no more. You will not find another one **i.**.
W-pI... 125.7:1 choose **i.** a gentle listening to the Word of
W-pI... 129.3:1 find a world **i.** where losing is impossible;
W-pI... 129.6:3 but what you choose **i.** you want indeed!
W-pI... 129.7:4 *I choose to see that world* **i.** *of this, for here is*
W-pI. 131.10:1 today, and turn your mind to true ideas **i.**.
W-pI. 132.17:2 *thought it was, and choose my own reality* **i.**.
W-pI... 133.1:3 ideas, but dwell **i.** on benefits to you.
W-pI... 134.9:3 Ask **i.**, "Would I accuse myself of doing
W-pI. 135.22:2 Today we will receive **i.** of plan, that we
W-pI. 135.22:2 of plan, that we may give **i.** of organize.
W-pI... 136.4:3 effect on you, **i.** of one effected by yourself
W-pI... 138.4:7 There is no opposite to choose **i.**. There is
W-pI... 139.3:3 yourself, and what but you can be alive **i.**?
W-pI... 152.9:4 lift our hearts in true humility **i.** to Him
W-pI. 155.12:7 could be a path that you would choose **i.**?
W-pI... 161.2:4 It sees **i.** but fragments of the whole, for
W-pI... 161.9:4 Yet you will take his hand **i.**, for you are
W-pI... 186.5:2 you. Accept the plan you did not make **i.**.
W-pI. 186.12:6 Hear **i.** a certain Voice, which tells you of
W-pI... 187.9:5 and leave **i.** the perfect gift forever there,
W-pI... 188.8:2 what you are, **i.** of fantasies and shadows.
W-pI...... 190.h I choose the joy of God **i.** of pain.
W-pI. 190.11:2 as we are free to choose our joy **i.** of pain,
W-pI. 190.11:2 place of sin, the peace of God **i.** of conflict
W-pI... 192.9:2 Release **i.** of bind, for thus are you made
W-pI... 192.9:7 And so you owe him thanks **i.** of pain.
W-pI... 193.6:1 and death becomes our choice **i.** of life?
W-pI... 198.5:3 teach, **i.** of trying to dismiss His words,
W-pI... 198.7:4 Their blood, you will perceive a miracle **i.**.
WpI rVI.in.6:3 *I choose* **i.** _ And then repeat the idea for
WpI rVI.in.6:6 **I.**, we give these times of quiet to the
W-pI... 210.1:1 (190) I choose the joy of God **i.** of pain.
W-pI... 210.1:5 *And that I choose,* **i.** *of what I made.* I am not
W-pII... in.10:3 **I.** of words, we need but feel His Love.
W-pII... in.10:4 **I.** of prayers, we need but call His Name.
W-pII... in.10:5 **I.** of judging, we need but be still and let
W-pII.. 223.2:1 *let us see the face of Christ* **i.** *of our mistakes.*
W-pII.. 224.2:4 *I see. Reveal what You would have me see* **i.**.
W-pII.. 233.1:4 *Your Will* **i.** *of seeking goals which cannot be*
W-pII.. 239.1:2 Let us **i.** be thankful for the gifts our
W-pII...... 3.3:1 mechanisms of illusion have been born **i.**.
W-pII.. 250.2:2 *behold his gentleness* **i.** *of my illusions. He is*
W-pII...... 4.2:7 will seek **i.** for witnesses to what is true.
W-pII.. 258.1:3 and trinkets of the world are sought **i.**?
W-pII.. 263.1:4 **i.** *of all the loveliness with which You blessed*
W-pII.. 265.1:3 was in the world, **i.** of in my mind alone.
W-pII.. 278.2:4 *way to You* **i.** *of madness and instead of fear.*
W-pII.. 278.2:4 *way to You instead of madness and* **i.** *of fear.*
W-pII.. 285.1:4 me today, and I accept my holiness **i.**?
W-pII.. 291.2:2 *what comes from You,* **i.** *of from myself. I do*
W-pII.. 298.1:5 I accept **i.** what God establishes as mine,
W-pII.. 301.1:5 *Let me see Your world* **i.** *of mine. And all the*
W-pII..... 349.h not, but give Each one a miracle of love **i.**.
W-ep......... 3:2 retire from the world, to seek reality **i.**. He
M-4..... I.A.5:8 grief, he finds a happy lightheartedness **i.**;
M-10......... 5:9 he has chosen now to trust, **i.** of his own.
M-11....... 4:12 peace be possible in this world?" but **i.**,
C-2............ 9:2 Ask this **i.** of what the ego is, and you will
C-3............ 2:3 to be an enemy **i.** of what He really is.
C-5.......... 6:11 *me* **i.** *to share the resurrection of God's Son.*
P-2........ IV.5:4 temporary, or another illness rise **i.**, for
P-2........ VI.2:3 The sound of healing can be heard **i.**. But
P-2........ VI.2:6 are heard **i.** of loud discordant shrieks.
S-1......... II.8:1 prayer, giving it timelessness **i.** of end.
S-1......... III.3:8 it may seem to be dangerous **i.** of merciful
S-2........... I.8:1 sin when he could see the face of Christ **i.**?
S-2......... II.3:3 Now he says **i.** that here is one whose
S-2......... II.4:3 as meekness and as charity **i.** of cruelty. Is
S-2......... III.7:7 Give it to Him to use **i.** of you, and you
S-3........ IV.8:2 Let Me **i.** remind you of eternity, in which

## instill 1

W-pI..... 38.5:5 to begin to **i.** in you a sense that you have

## instincts 1

M-5....... II.1:8 Terms like "**i.**," "reflexes" and the like

## instruct 4

T-15... VII.13:2 Holy Spirit's teaching function to **i.** those
W-pI..... 91.5:2 as you **i.** yourself that you are not a body.
W-pI..... 91.5:3 want, and you **i.** your mind accordingly.
W-pI... 181.3:2 We **i.** our minds that it is this we seek,

## instructed 1

W-pI... 168.3:3 All steps but this we learn, **i.** by His Voice.

## instructing 1

W-pII. 357.1:4 *I hear Your Voice* **i.** *me to find the way to You*

## instruction 4

T-11.... VIII.3:5 **I.** in perception is your great need, for you
T-12....... V.7:4 Every legitimate teaching aid, every real **i.**
W-pI..... 99.9:5 learn today with this **i.** in the way of truth
W-pI... 108.8:1 the practice periods with the **i.** for today,

## instructions 5

T-15........ II.6:2 will receive very specific **i.** as you go along
W-pI..... 95.8:3 follow the **i.** for practicing the day's idea.
W-pI... 181.6:3 with **i.** to our minds to change their focus,
W-pII.. in.11:2 **i.** on a theme of special relevance will
W-pII.. in.11:5 the day. We give the first of these **i.** now.

## instructs 3

W-pI. 153.12:3 game **i.** in happiness because there is no
WpI rVI.in.6:6 of quiet to the Teacher Who **i.** in quiet,
W-pII. 357.1:3 *Voice* **i.** *me patiently to hear Your Word,*

## instrument 4

T-18...... VI.6:7 **i.** of vengeance and the perceived source
T-19......... I.3:6 The body thus becomes the **i.** of illusion,
W-pI... 135.8:2 serviceable **i.** through which the mind can
W-pII..... 4.2:1 body is the **i.** the mind made in its efforts

## instruments 2

T-18...... VI.5:1 **i.** of separation reinterpreted as means for
W-pI. 137.11:1 who are healed become the **i.** of healing.

## insufficiency 1

W-pI... 105.1:8 loses. This implies a limit and an **i.**.

## insufficient 2

T-3........ VI.1:1 the Last Judgment, but in **i.** detail. After
T-9....... V.8:14 works" is a sound though **i.** statement.

## insult 1

T-31....... V.3:4 irritation, and at last to open **i.** and abuse.

## insulting 2

T-18...... IV.7:4 to realize it is not personally **i.** that your
M-9........... 2:4 it is apt to be perceived as personally **i.**.

## intact 9

T-9....... VII.5:4 its methods for keeping this picture **i.**?
T-9....... VII.7:3 keep the ego's whole thought system **i.**.
T-23..... III.3:8 be different, and yet the same remain **i.**,
T-26......... I.3:2 incomplete to keep its own identity **i.**. In
T-26........ II.8:4 of His Love kept perfectly **i.** and undefiled
T-27..... II.15:6 only thus can He keep yours preserved **i.**,
T-27..... IV.6:8 thus the question is preserved **i.** because
T-29......... I.3:9 was a point you both agreed to keep **i.**.
W-pI... 137.3:4 his Self with all Its parts **i.** and unassailed.

**intangible** 1
W-pI...158.6:1 of doubt and shadows made with the **i.**.

**integral** 1
T-2.......VII.6:2 must be an **i.** part of the whole Sonship.

**integrate** 2
T-1........VI.2:4 As you **i.** you become one, and your needs
T-5.........in.2:5 the same as to **i.** and to make one. That is

**integrated** 2
T-5.........in.1:6 Joy calls forth an **i.** willingness to share it,
T-8...........I.5:5 opposed ideas, it cannot be **i.**. If it is

**integrates** 1
T-7......... II.2:3 unifies by increasing and **i.** by extending.

**integration** 6
T-3......... II.5:6 perfect **i.** and establishes the peace of God
T-5...........I.7:5 its own **i.** toward the paths of creation. It
T-5........ II.10:9 it to the perfect **i.** that can make it whole?
T-6......V.C.5:3 and goes beyond them towards real **i.**. If
T-7......... V.6:6 harmony, because it proceeds from **i.**. It is
T-12.....VII.6:8 The mind always strives for **i.**, and if it is

**integrity** 3
T-5...........I.5:4 or the restoration of the **i.** of the mind.
T-12.........I.2:5 a split or an attack on the **i.** of your mind,
T-12.....VII.7:9 This gives it an illusion of **i.**, and enables

**intellectual** 1
W-pI.....39.1:3 concerned with **i.** feats nor logical toys.

**intellectually** 1
W-pI.......9.1:2 But while you may be able to accept it **i.**,

**intelligence** 1
T-29....VIII.8:8 more of what; more beauty, more **i.**, more

**intelligent** 1
W-pI...198.5:2 it not more **i.** to thank the One Who gives

**intend** 2
T-10......IV.5:2 it. You cannot do what God did not **i.**,
T-10......IV.5:2 what He did not **i.** does not happen. Your

**intended** 21
T-2.......VII.2:3 time collapse for which the miracle was **i.**.
T-4.......in.3:10 This is not the gospel I **i.** to offer you. We
T-6...........I.4:6 The message the crucifixion was **i.** to
T-6...........I.8:5 serving the purpose for which God **i.** it. I
T-6.........I.14:1 as the call for peace for which it was **i.**.
T-14....VIII.5:5 be accepted by the Son, for whom it is **i.**.
T-20.....VII.7:5 without the end for which it was **i.**, nor is
W-pI.....51.4:7 replaced by what they were **i.** to replace.
W-pI.....55.2:6 and give me the peace God **i.** me to have.
W-pI.....58.5:4 are mine, because God **i.** them for me. I
W-pI.....70.4:1 from the sickness for which it was **i.**, and
W-pI...126.6:6 It is not what God **i.** it to be for you.
W-pI.134.10:1 of guilt and pain as God Himself **i.** it to be
WpI.rIV.in7:3 for you are using time for its **i.** purpose.
W-pI...154.5:3 it, give it to the ones for whom it is **i.**, and
W-pI...154.6:2 that they deliver are **i.** first for them. And
W-pI...166.8:5 to make for him whom God **i.** only joy?
W-pI...192.5:6 the peace that God **i.** for His holy Son.
W-pI...206.1:3 *I would give His gifts where He **i.** them to be.* I
M-1...........4:1 **i.** for teachers of a special form of the
M-29.........1:1 manual is not **i.** to answer all questions

**intends** 2
T-30.....VI.4:8 will you think that God **i.** for you a fearful
W-pI.....82.3:4 not experience the joy that God **i.** for me.

**intense** 16
T-7.......IX.6:9 is so **i.** that It creates in perfect joy, and
T-13.......II.3:3 for the ego's destructive urge is so **i.** that
T-13.....III.2:8 ever be, is your **i.** and burning love of God
T-13.....X.14:2 so **i.** that none of us alone can even think
T-14....VII.7:7 and brightness so **i.** you could not wish,
T-17.......II.8:3 to give you this is so **i.** He would not wait,
T-17......V.4:1 extremely **i.** with this shift in goals. For
T-31...VIII.8:3 yet be so **i.** and so inclusive it is but a step
W-pI.....13.2:1 arouses **i.** anxiety in all the separated ones
W-pI.....21.2:5 is nothing but a veil drawn over **i.** fury.
W-pI.....41.1:3 misery, suffering and **i.** fear of loss.
W-pI.....93.1:3 you would be struck with horror so **i.** that
M-3...........4:3 two people enter into a fairly **i.** teaching-
M-6...........1:7 healing might precipitate **i.** depression,
M-17.........4:5 Or it may also take the form of **i.** rage,
M-17.........8:5 an **i.** white light against a black horizon,

**intensely** 3
T-1.........II.2:1 Revelation is **i.** personal and cannot be
T-4......VII.7:4 it is **i.** personal to the mind that receives it
T-12.....IV.1:2 to be **i.** engaged in the search for love. Yet

**intensified** 1
Wi181-200 2:5 will be so **i.** that words become of little

**intensify** 1
W-pI...105.4:1 As Heaven's peace and joy **i.** when you

**intensity** 11
T-6..........I.3:4 the *apparent* **i.** of the assault of some of the
T-16....VII.3:1 underestimate the **i.** of the ego's drive for
T-18.....IX.4:4 Yet its **i.** is veiled by its heavy coverings,
W-pI...138.8:1 can gain unconscious hold of great **i.**, and
W-pI...153.4:3 far beyond the frenzy and **i.** of which you
W-pI...161.8:3 the **i.** of rage projected fear must spawn.
W-pII.252.1:3 with an **i.** that holds all things within it, in
M-8...........1:4 from another with less **i.** of appeal. And a
M-8...........2:4 out of its **i.** of desire to have it for itself.
M-17.........4:3 too, of the **i.** of the anger that is aroused.
P-2........IV.8:2 as real is the belief that illness varies in **i.**;

**intent** 35
T-5........V.5:8 It attributes to God a punishing **i.**, and
T-5........V.5:8 then takes this **i.** as its own prerogative. It
T-17......V.9:6 from which your true **i.** was never absent.
T-23...II.17:11 is **i.** on your destruction is not your friend
T-23.....III.1:5 Its sole **i.** is murder, and what form of
T-23.....III.1:7 will look on his **i.** in nightmares where the
T-23.....III.1:9 If the **i.** is death, what matter the form it
T-23...III.6:10 and the unnatural **i.** to murder and to die.
T-23.....IV.1:8 the form it takes conceals the same **i.**.
T-24.....IV.3:3 To minds **i.** on specialness it is impossible
T-24......V.4:2 And both will walk in danger, each **i.**, in
T-28.....II.10:3 perceived as friends with merciful **i.**.
T-31.......II.8:3 the new without your opposition or **i.**.
WpI..rII.in.4:1 Do not allow your **i.** to waver in the face
W-pI.131.13:1 open with your one **i.** to go beyond it.
W-pI...136.1:3 and without a meaningful **i.** of any kind,
W-pI...136.4:3 it, so it seems to be external to your own **i.**
W-pI...138.7:2 now transformed from the **i.** you gave it;
W-pI.153.20:1 your mind from wandering from its **i.**. Be
W-pI.155.12:3 your effort, of your love and of your full **i.**
W-pI.161.10:3 vision. If you are **i.** on reaching it, you will
W-pI...170.1:1 No one attacks without **i.** to hurt. This
Wi181-200 1:1 your scattered goals blend into one **i.**.
W-pI..181.2:4 give support to the **i.** which has replaced
W-pI..181.3:4 time wherein we practice changing our **i.**.
W-pI..181.5:7 enter in the time of practicing with one **i.**;
W-pI..185.3:1 Two minds with one **i.** become so strong
W-pI..185.3:3 In dreams, no two can share the same **i.**.
W-pI..185.4:8 lost to sleeping minds **i.** on compromise,
W-pI 185.10:4 your own **i.** with what they seek above all
W-pI 185.13:5 with all your brothers, whose **i.** is yours.
W-pI 185.14:1 It is this one **i.** we seek today, uniting our
W-pI 196.11:1 **i.** on plotting punishment for you until
W-pII.221.2:6 We wait with one **i.**; to hear our Father's
M-17.........3:2 and pupil, who have shared in one **i.**.

**intention** 2
T-20....VII.7:5 as a separate thing apart from the **i.**. The
T-21...III.10:5 The **i.** is in the mind, which tries to use

**intentional** 1
W-pI....20.1:3 approach has been **i.**, and very carefully

**intentions** 2
T-15....VII.4:4 belief that you are exempt from its evil **i.**.
T-18.....IV.2:1 Trust not your good **i.**. They are not

**interact** 1
T-31.....V.15:5 perceive that you can **i.** but with yourself.

**interaction** 7
T-4..........I.6:5 their **i.** as a means of ego preservation. I
T-4.........II.2:3 **i.** is a process that alters both, because
T-4.........II.2:4 as readily when the **i.** takes place in the
T-4.........II.2:5 relative perception as is physical **i.**. There
T-31.....V.12:3 some acknowledgment that **i.** must have
P-2..........V.5:8 This holy **i.** is the plan of God Himself, by
P-3..........II.1:3 limits be laid on an **i.** in which everyone is

**interacts** 1
T-31.....V.15:3 while you perceive a self that **i.** with evil,

**intercede** 1
T-1........I.32:2 They **i.** for your holiness and make your

**intercessions** 1
T-1........I.32:1 I inspire all miracles, which are really **i.**.

**interchanged** 2
T-24.......V.2:2 In dreams effect and cause are **i.**, for here
T-31....VII.4:2 which can be **i.** but never jointly held. The

**interest** 6
T-4.........V.1:6 by the ego in the **i.** of its self-preservation.
W-pI....20.1:2 active cooperation and **i.** have been asked
W-pI..105.2:2 return; a loan with **i.** to be paid in full; a
M-2...........5:7 the same course share one **i.** and one goal.
M-4.....VII.2:1 teacher of God is generous out of Self **i.**.
M-24.........6:3 the past and total lack of **i.** in the future.

**interests** 27
T-7.......III.3:6 *is* the belief that conflicting **i.** are possible,
T-26...VIII.2:4 a little watchful of **i.** perceived as separate
T-29........I.3:5 provided that your separate **i.** made your
W-pI.......24.h I do not perceive my own best **i.**.
W-pI....24.1:4 that you will not serve your own best **i.**.
W-pI....24.2:1 that you do not perceive your own best **i.**,
W-pI....24.7:2 *not perceive my own best **i.** in this situation,*
W-pI....25.1:5 Everything is for your own best **i.**. That is

W-pI.....25.2:2 have nothing to do with your own best **i.**,
W-pI.....25.3:1 they are all concerned with "personal" **i.**.
W-pI.....25.3:2 Since you have no personal **i.**, your goals
W-pI.....26.1:6 how it can be used for your own best **i.**,
W-pI.....55.4:1 (24) I do not perceive my own best **i.**.
W-pI.....55.4:2 own best **i.** when I do not know who I am
W-pI.....55.4:3 What I think are my best **i.** would merely
W-pI.....55.4:4 me to find out what my own best **i.** are,
W-pI.....86.3:5 defeat my own best **i.** in this insane way. I
M-1............1:2 not see his **i.** as apart from someone else's
M-2............5:6 minds, their bodies, their needs, their **i.**,
M-2............5:9 in another person the same **i.** as his own.
M-3............2:6 for two people to lose sight of separate **i.**,
M-4......I.A.5:5 sacrifice his own best **i.** on behalf of truth.
M-8............2:8 other minds, with different **i.** of its own,
M-16..........7:2 in the name of safety no longer **i.** him. For
M-28..........1:9 of all other purposes, all other **i.**, all other
P-2......... II.8:4 in so doing, lose all sense of separate **i.**.
S-1.........in.2:4 leaves separate goals and separate **i.** by,

## interfere 46

T-7........IX.3:7 can no more **i.** with their reality than your
T-7........IX.3:7 unawareness of your spirit can **i.** with its
T-8...........I.2:1 the ego may seem to **i.** with your learning,
T-8......... V.6:4 the ego the power to **i.** with the journey. It
T-8.....VII.15:3 Believe you can **i.** with His purpose, and
T-9......... V.8:8 speak to him through you if you do not **i.**.
T-10..... V.10:2 Yet He would not **i.** with you, because He
T-10..... V.10:3 To **i.** with you would be to attack Himself,
T-13......XI.8:2 and this belief does **i.** with the deep peace
T-16...... I.3:12 *is here. I need do nothing except not to **i.**.*
T-16....IV.13:2 **i.** with God must interfere with you. Only
T-16....IV.13:2 interfere with God must **i.** with you. Only
T-16....... V.5:6 nothing would remain to **i.** with the ego.
T-16....... V.5:8 is a condition in which the ego cannot **i.**,
T-16....... V.8:4 not **i.** with the ego's illusion of Heaven,
T-16....... V.8:4 which it offered him to **i.** with Heaven.
T-17.....VII.3:9 brought to faith will never **i.** with truth.
T-17.....VII.6:9 as it serves the universe. But do not **i.**.
T-17.....VII.8:6 causeless, and is not there to **i.** with truth.
T-18....IV.5:11 *only that I do not **i.** with His plan to restore to*
T-18. VIII.11:3 no barriers to **i.** with its glad coming. In
T-18....IX.10:4 for here does nothing **i.** with love, letting
T-19...... I.16:1 and learn how not to **i.** with it and make it
T19... IV.A.9:3 Can it **i.** with the effects of summer's sun
T19.IV.D.20:7 given anything in hell or Heaven to **i.** with
T-20......III.3:1 The holy do not **i.** with truth. They are
T-22......VI.7:4 nothing **i.** with those whose wills are His,
T-23....... II.3:1 Think how this seems to **i.** with the first
T-27......III.2:8 What can **i.** with the awareness of reality
T-27......III.7:5 Yet only this appears to **i.** with power
T-28.........I.3:3 memory, that is not used to **i.** with truth.
T-28...... I.10:9 Effects, and doing nothing that would **i.**.
T-30... VIII.4:2 awareness is unreal, and does not **i.** at all.
T-31......III.6:4 your sleep, nor **i.** with your awakening.
T-31... VIII.5:7 laid by, and nothing left to **i.** with truth.
W-in..........6:4 This will **i.** with transfer of training. The
W-pI.....65.5:4 each thought that arises to **i.** with it. Note
W-pI.....85.4:3 *I will not let this **i.** with my awareness of the*
W-pI.....93.9:5 Try not to **i.** with the Self which God
W-pI...105.9:3 not to **i.** today with what He wills. And if
W-pI.189.10:3 *We will not **i.**. Salvation's ways are not our*
W-pII..268.1:2 *Let me not attempt to **i.** with Your creation,*
W-pII..292.2:2 *end. Help us not **i.**, and so delay the happy*
M-4........ V.1:2 and what could come to **i.** with joy? The
P-2........III.3:6 goals alone can **i.** with perfect healing.
S-2........III.2:6 you need do is to step back and not to **i.**.

## interfered 2

T-21....... V.4:1 the idea of separation has **i.** with reason.
W-pI.184.13:3 you see, but have not **i.** with truth at all.

## interference 17

T-12......VI.6:4 Love transfers to love without any **i.**, for
T-14......III.1:4 this entails the recognition that guilt is **i.**,
T-14......VI.8:3 keep no source of **i.** from His sight, for He
T-14. VIII.2:14 you. All **i.** in the communication that God
T-15...... IX.2:1 at all the **i.** and seeing it exactly as it is.
T-15...... IX.7:1 then there will be no **i.** in communication
T-15...... XI.7:1 for minds are joined without the body's **i.**,
T-16....IV.13:3 Only in time does **i.** in God's completion
T-17.....VII.1:6 **i.** in the way of understanding would have
T-18....IX.12:4 *not.* That is the **i.**; that is what needs to be
T-20......III.2:5 studied **i.** that makes it difficult for you to
T-21....... II.7:8 only to stop your **i.** with what will happen
T-27......III.2:7 and empty space can not be **i.**. What can
T-28.........I.1:3 it cancels out the **i.** to what has been done
T-28.........I.9:4 perfectly untouched by time and **i.**. Never
W-pI.....44.7:2 letting go every kind of **i.** and intrusion by
W-pI...70.10:2 You are free from all external **i.**. You are

## interferences 2

T-20......III.2:3 relationships, in which there are no **i.**, are
W-pI.....42.5:5 If such **i.** occur, open your eyes and repeat

## interferers 1

T-23.......in.4:1 Let not the little **i.** pull you to littleness.

## interferes 14

T-7......... II.7:2 apparent that confusion **i.** with meaning,
T-8...........I.5:6 each one merely **i.** with the other. This
T-14......VI.7:7 communication. The other but **i.** with it.
T-14......VI.8:2 therefore must remove whatever **i.** with
T-14.....VII.2:1 out of everything that **i.** with truth. Truth
T-14... VIII.1:4 It is the closing of the doors that **i.** with
T-15......IV.8:3 to let everything that **i.** with it go forever?
T-15......IX.6:7 of God's Son to what **i.** with his release,
T-17......VI.4:2 what **i.** with the accomplishment of your
T-17.....VII.5:8 It **i.**, not with the goal, but with the value
T-19.......I.14:5 No error **i.** with its calm sight, which
T-22....... V.1:9 the way of truth when only weakness **i.**?
T-26..... X.1:10 size of the confusion, or how much it **i.**.
WpI. rIII.in4:2 only if it **i.** with goals you hold more dear.

## interfering 7

T-8.....VII.14:6 and one that is **i.** with his ability to accept
T-9.........I.11:7 because you are **i.** with the laws of seeing.
T-18......IV.3:6 wills to be, you must be **i.** with His Will.
T-18......IV.4:8 you are **i.** with the lesson by believing that
W-pI.....65.6:1 **i.** thoughts will become harder to find.
W-pI.140.11:2 is to let our **i.** thoughts be laid aside, not
W-pII......1.3:2 and overturning what it sees as **i.** with its

## interim 1

T-2.......VII.4:5 In the **i.**, however, the sense of conflict is

## interlaced 1

T-17......IV.8:3 **i.** with gilded threads of self-destruction.

## interlocking 1

T-1.........I.25:1 part of an **i.** chain of forgiveness which,

## intermediary 1

T-7........IV.2:2 **i.** step toward the knowledge that you are

## intermediate 1

M-16.........9:6 All **i.** lessons will but lead to this, and

## intermittent 1

T-6......V.B.9:3 At the second step progress is **i.**, but the

## intermittently 1

Wi181-200 1:3 unified commitment will bestow, if only **i.**

## internal 6

T-2...........I.2:5 Its real source is **i.**. This is as true of the
T-12......III.7:2 an **i.** conflict of this magnitude he cannot
T-18......VI.8:4 mind. But the communication is **i.**. Mind
W-pI.....34.1:2 Peace of mind is clearly an **i.** matter. It
M-12.........2:3 everything **i.** now reflects only the Love of
M-24.........5:3 the belief unless his **i.** Teacher so advised.

## internally 2

T-11.......in.1:4 system. Each is **i.** consistent, but they are
M-4..... I.A.3:5 at which he can make the shift entirely **i.**.

## interpersonal 3

T-1..........II.1:4 Miracles, however, are genuinely **i.**, and
T-1..........II.2:5 more useful now because of their **i.** nature
P-in........... 1:6 perception of **i.** relationships that enables

## interpose 8

T-10.... IV.5:10 break through the obstructions you **i.**, but
T-10...... IV.6:6 No false gods you attempt to **i.** between
T-12....VIII.7:1 to **i.** between your awareness and truth.
T-17.... III.10:5 the truth that I would **i.** between you and
T-19.........I.5:5 Faithlessness would **i.** illusions between
T19. IV.A.4:12 as those that you **i.** will be surmounted.
T19....IV.B.4:5 obstacles that you would **i.** between peace
T-28.....VII.7:6 What gap can **i.** itself between the safety

## interposed 13

T-13...... III.1:3 is one more obstacle you have **i.** between
T-14...... IX.1:9 and **i.** between what always was and now.
T-14...... XI.1:4 **i.** so much between it and your awareness
T-18..VIII.11:3 and **i.** no barriers to interfere with its glad
T-22.....II.12:1 that you **i.** between you and your brother,
T-29...... IX.3:7 which are **i.** between your judgment and
T-29...... IX.7:4 nor **i.** between the thoughts the mind
T-30....VIII.4:2 but show what you have **i.** between reality
W-pI... 125.9:4 illusions **i.** between the wholly indivisible
W-pI... 160.7:7 to Him. No stranger can be **i.** between His
W-pI... 165.7:6 **i.** between Him and your certainty of Him
W-pI... 189.8:3 that you have **i.** between the Son and God
W-pII . 329.1:1 ***i.** a second will more powerful than Yours.*

## interposing 1

T-20...... III.2:4 **i.** them between those who would meet,

## interpret 25

T-2...........I.4:6 he may initially **i.** the light itself as part of
T-3........ IV.6:3 then permits you to **i.** the body as yourself
T-3......... V.5:2 You may try to "**i.**" meaning, but this is
T-5......... V.6:1 it can **i.** them according to what it wants,
T-6.........I.14:1 If you **i.** the crucifixion in any other way,
T-8........ VII.4:8 **I.** anything apart from the Holy Spirit and
T-8.....VII.14:2 beyond it and does not **i.** it as limitation.
T-9......... V.4:2 may **i.** the ego's symbols in a nightmare,
T-11...... VI.3:9 Let the Christ in you **i.** for you, and do not
T-11....VIII.2:4 for you, and if you will let Him **i.** it, He
T-12.........I.1:8 To **i.** error is to give it power, and having
T-12....... V.6:7 If they could **i.** the aids correctly, they
T-13........II.8:2 Yet even when I **i.** it for you, you may
T-13...... IV.9:1 too, will **i.** the function of time as you
T-13...... IV.9:1 the function of time as you **i.** yours. If you
T-13...... IV.9:6 But if you **i.** your function as destruction,
T-13...... IV.9:7 And time will be as you **i.** it, for of itself it
T-14...... VI.6:7 He will **i.** it to you with perfect clarity, for
T-15..... VII.6:4 that no one could **i.** direct attack as love.
T-16........II.8:1 Do not **i.** against God's Love, for you
T-20...... IV.1:2 power as the laws of this world **i.** giving;
T-22..........I.2:7 The brain cannot **i.** what your vision sees.
T-27........II.8:2 Holy Spirit and the world **i.** differently.
T-30..... VII.7:1 Do not **i.** out of solitude, for what you see
T-31..... VII.3:5 For you will not **i.** what you see without

**interpretation** 67

T-3..........I.1:6 This particularly unfortunate **i.**, which
T-3........ III.2:3 many ways because perception involves **i.**
T-3......... V.5:1 Knowing is not open to **i.**. You may try to
T-3.......VII.3:9 but you may be sure that any **i.** that sees
T-4......... II.9:3 itself, and its **i.** of its own beginning. This
T-5........ III.8:7 because, according to its **i.** of reality, war
T-6..........I.1:5 positive **i.** of the crucifixion that is wholly
T-6..........I.5:5 I therefore offered a different **i.** of attack,
T-8.......VII.1:2 body, since this is the ego's **i.** of the body.
T-8.......VII.1:3 have to attack physically to accept this **i.**.
T-8.......VII.2:6 This **i.** of the body will change your mind
T-8.....VII.10:3 or not mind, is a fragmented or sick **i.**.
T-8......VIII.1:8 body's condition lies solely in your **i.** of its
T-8......VIII.5:7 the ego's **i.** of the body rests are true; that
T-8......VIII.9:8 when **i.** is left to the Holy Spirit, Who
T-11.........I.9:2 this **i.** it seems possible for God's Will and
T-11....... V.6:9 not be deceived by its **i.** of your conflict.
T-11...... VI.2:5 for awareness and for the **i.** of awareness.
T-11...... VI.2:6 Yet you cannot be aware without **i.**, for
T-11...... VI.2:6 for what you perceive *is* your **i.**.
T-12.........I.1:4 to anything directly, but to your **i.** of it.
T-12.........I.1:5 Your **i.** thus becomes the justification for
T-12.........I.3:1 one **i.** of motivation that makes any sense.
T-12.........I.7:1 your brother's needs are your **i.** of yours.
T-12.........I.8:1 By applying the Holy Spirit's **i.** of the
T-12.........I.8:6 Consider how well the Holy Spirit's **i.** of
T-12.......I.10:3 The Holy Spirit's **i.** of fear does dispel it,
T-13.......in.3:4 would be salvation, and this is the ego's **i.**,
T-13....... II.4:3 because, by not valuing its **i.** of salvation,
T-13....... II.6:4 this course stems ultimately from this **i.**,
T-13...... IV.8:4 **i.** of the means of salvation that you must
T-13...... IV.9:5 This **i.** ties the future to the present, and
T-13...... VI.4:1 depending on whose **i.** of it you use. Past,
T-14.....VII.7:1 **i.** of perception that leads to knowledge.
T-14...... IX.6:3 The reflection of God needs no **i.**. It is
T-14..... X.11:4 Every **i.** you would lay upon a brother is
T-15...... VI.3:5 another **i.** of relationships that transcends
T-16.........I.1:2 That is the ego's **i.** of empathy, and is
T-16.........I.4:2 will learn His **i.** of it if you let Him use
T-16....... II.7:5 to His **i.** the results have brought you joy.
T-16....... II.7:6 Would you prefer the results of your **i.**,
T-17...... III.5:1 How can the Holy Spirit bring His **i.** of
T-18.....VII.1:3 body an end and not a means in your **i.**,
T-19....... II.5:5 purpose of the special relationship in its **i.**
T19. IV.D.12:2 him, and your **i.** of him is very fearful.
T-20....... II.1:5 trying to justify your own **i.** of its value by
T-21...... VI.6:6 are joined to him is but a fact, not an **i.**.
T-22.........I.5:6 What needs **i.** must be alien. Nor will it
T-27..... II.14:1 this **i.** of correction, your own mistakes
T-30........VII.h The New **I.**
T-30.....VII.1:1 left the meaning of the world to your **i.**? If
T-30.....VII.1:6 to **i.** which is different every time you
T-30.....VII.4:1 and one **i.** given to the world and all
T-30.....VII.5:6 your agreement makes **i.** stabilize and last
T-30.....VII.6:2 things? The Holy Spirit's goal gives one **i.**,
M-4 ..VIII.1:10 Sure of the ultimate **i.** of all things in time
M-17 .........4:2 an **i.** that gives rise to negative emotions,
M-17 .........8:6 If anger comes from an **i.** and not a fact, it
M-17 .........8:9 step. The **i.** can be changed at last. Magic
M-17 .........9:8 see you have responded to your own **i.**,
M-18 .........1:1 of God has ceased to confuse **i.** with fact,
M-18 .........3:7 *You but mistake* **i.** *for the truth. And you are*
M-18 .........4:2 that he has made an **i.** that is not true.
M-19 .........2:1 Justice, like its opposite, is an **i.**. It is,
M-19 .........2:2 is, however, the one **i.** that leads to truth.
M-28 .........1:3 the Holy Spirit's **i.** of the world's purpose;
P-2...........I.2:4 at things; its **i.** of progress and growth.

**interpretations** 16

T-3.......VII.3:9 symbolism here has been given many **i.**,
T-5...........I.4:5 because symbolism is open to different **i.**.
T-5........ III.7:1 is the Mediator between the **i.** of the ego
T-5........ VI.3:5 speak for different **i.** of the same thing
T-5........ VI.3:6 Alternate **i.** were unnecessary until the
T-5........ VI.5:1 of how the ego's **i.** are misleading, but a
T-11..... V.14:1 The ego's **i.** of the laws of perception are,
T-11..VIII.13:2 are willing to let their own **i.** go in favor of
T-12 ........I.2:3 you react to your **i.** as if they were correct.
T-12 ........I.6:8 your **i.** of reality are meaningless in your
T-12 ........I.7:1 Your **i.** of your brother's needs are your
T-14 ..... IX.6:2 meaning seems to lie only in shifting **i.**,
T-30 .... VII.7:3 is but your **i.** which are lacking in stability
M-19 ......... 1:3 corrects the **i.** to which injustice gives rise,
M-19 ......... 1:7 only just **i.** and laying all injustices aside.
P-2...........I.2:5 **i.** will be wrong of necessity, because they

**interpretative** 1

T-3 ....... IV.6:3 The **i.** function of perception, a distorted

**interpreted** 12

T-5 ....... VI.4:3 Nothing the ego perceives is **i.** correctly.
T-5 ....... VI.8:1 and fourth generation," as **i.** by the ego, is
T-9 .........II.1:3 be incorrectly **i.** as "proof" that the course
T-12 ......I.10:6 only the denial of union, and correctly **i.**,
T-13 .......II.6:3 and guiltlessness must be **i.** as the final
T-13 .......II.8:1 The Atonement has always been **i.** as the
T-22 ........I.5:5 directly, without a need to be **i.** to you.
T-23 .......II.4:4 is thus **i.** as an irrevocable sentence upon
T-30 .. VII.6:12 script, which cannot be **i.** with meaning.
M-4 ..... I.A.5:2 If this is **i.** as giving up the desirable, it
M-24 ......... 6:9 All beliefs will point to this if properly **i.**.
S-1..........II.4:2 in the way in which they are usually **i.**.

**Interpreter** 4
*interpreter*

T-14 ..... VI.6:4 make it meaningful if its **I.** is not its maker
T-14 ..... VI.7:2 Yet your **I.** perceives the meaning in your
T-15 ...... V.4:5 In His function as **I.** of what you made,
T-30 .... VII.7:6 We have one **I.**. And through His use of

**interpreter** 2
*Interpreter*

T-22 ........I.5:7 made understandable by an **i.** you cannot
T-22 ........I.8:4 He will need no **i.** to you, for it was you

**interpreting** 7

T-7 .........II.6:6 while you listen to two ways of **i.** them.
T-11 ..... VI.3:2 it clearly, it is because you are **i.** against it,
T-12 ........I.3:7 to attack his reality by **i.** it as you see fit.
T-12 ........I.5:8 does not need your help in **i.** motivation,
T-12 ........I.9:7 **i.** fear correctly as a positive affirmation
T-12 ...... V.3:2 be unable to avoid **i.** this as reinforcement
T-13 ..... IV.4:5 the future by **i.** the present in past terms.

**interprets** 13

T-4 ..........I.6:5 and therefore **i.** their interaction as a
T-4 ....... III.1:2 **i.** it as if something outside is inside, and
T-5 ....... VI.4:4 it even **i.** Scripture as a witness for itself.
T-5 ....... VI.4:6 it as frightening, it **i.** it fearfully. Being
T-5 ....... VI.6:1 so shall ye reap" He **i.** to mean what you
T-6 ....... IV.4:2 It **i.** this as a justification for attacking its
T-8 ...... VII.2:1 Remember that the Holy Spirit **i.** the
T-8 ...... VII.2:2 Holy Spirit **i.** everything you have made
T-13 ..... IV.7:3 Holy Spirit **i.** time's purpose as rendering
T-13 ..... IV.8:1 the ego **i.** the goal of time as its own. The
T-20 ..... IV.2:9 is a lesson in giving, as the Holy Spirit **i.** it
T-22 ........I.2:9 The brain **i.** to the body, of which it is a
M-8 ........... 3:4 mind that **i.** the eyes' messages and gives

**interrupt** 4

T-5 .........II.8:3 God, which you can **i.** but cannot destroy.
T-17 ...VIII.2:3 it, do not attack it, do not **i.** its coming.
T-29 ...VIII.7:3 infinite, a place where time can **i.** eternity
W-pI... 107.2:3 less–when nothing came to **i.** your peace

**interrupted** 2

T-13 ...VIII.3:3 The separation has not **i.** it. Creation
T-13 ...VIII.3:4 it. Creation cannot be **i.**. The separation is

**interrupting** 1

W-pI .... 49.1:1 **i.** your regular activities in any way. The

**interruption** 2

T-4 ....... VI.1:7 Your other life has continued without **i.**,
T-13 ... XI.3:12 There is no **i.**. There is a sense of peace so

**interruptions** 2

T19 ...IV.A.7:4 no more than tiny **i.** in love's appeal.
W-pI .... 40.1:5 If there are long **i.**, try again. Whenever

**intersperse** 2

W-pI .... 39.9:1 these practice periods easier if you **i.** them
W-pII .. in.11:2 theme of special relevance will **i.** our daily

**interval** 29

T-1 ........I.47:2 time **i.** not under the usual laws of time.
T-1 .........II.6:4 This introduces an **i.** from which the giver
T-1 .........II.6:5 renders the **i.** of time it spans unnecessary
T-2 ... V.A.11:2 Since it is an out-of-pattern time **i.**, the
T-11 .... VII.1:5 implying that before, or in the **i.** between,
T-26 .......V.5:4 So very long ago, for such a tiny **i.** of time,
T-26 .....V.13:3 a seeming **i.** from birth to death and on to
T-26 ... VIII.1:1 an **i.** between the time when you forgive,
T-26 ... VIII.2:6 The **i.** you think lies in between the giving
T-26 ... VIII.3:9 And this but makes the **i.** between the
T-26 ... VIII.5:9 within the only **i.** of time that sin and fear
T-26 ... VIII.7:9 reason for an **i.** in which disaster strikes,
T-26 ... VIII.8:3 **i.** in time, when retribution is perceived
T-27 ..... III.4:1 an unused **i.** of time not seen as spent and
T-27 ..... III.5:9 learning **i.** it has a use that now you fear,
T-27 ..... IV.6:9 holy instant is the **i.** in which the mind is
T-30 ..... III.7:8 is the same within the **i.** when you forgot.
W-pI .... 12.2:3 another involves a fairly constant time **i.**.
W-pI .... 27.3:4 you set a definite time **i.** for using the idea
W-pI .... 35.8:2 to think up specific things to fill the **i.**, but
W-pI .... 67.3:1 drop away for a brief preparatory **i.**, and
W-pI .... 67.4:3 **i.** of thoughtlessness to the awareness of a
W-pI .. 156.7:5 in the little **i.** of doubt that still remains,
W-pI .. 167.9:3 **i.** in which what seems to happen never
W-pI 169.13:1 The **i.** suffices. It is here that miracles are
W-pI .. 181.3:4 within this **i.** of time wherein we practice
W-pI .. 182.5:4 respite; just an **i.** in which He can return
W-pII . 234.1:3 the **i.** there was no lapse in continuity,
W-pII . 308.1:4 The only **i.** in which I can be saved from

**intervals** 11

T-1 .........II.6:9 it, thus eliminating certain **i.** within it. It
T-2 .... VII.5:12 time itself involves **i.** that do not exist.
T-3 ...... IV.1:5 introduced degrees, aspects and **i.**. Spirit
T-29 ........I.4:6 to time, and keep apart in **i.** of separation,
T-29 ........I.6:2 in "love," with **i.** of hatred in between.
W-pI .... 12.4:1 the time **i.** between applying today's idea
W-pI .... 35.8:1 there will probably be **i.** in which nothing
W-pI .... 39.9:2 it helpful to include a few short **i.** in which
W-pI .... 74.7:1 at regular and predetermined **i.** today, say
W-pI .. 91.11:1 six times an hour, at reasonably regular **i.**,
W-pI 184.10:1 Thus what you need are **i.** each day in

**intervene** 3

T-13 ..... VI.4:8 the miracle, which could **i.** between them,
T-13 ..... IX.1:7 and the past the laws of God must **i.**, if
T-20 ........I.2:2 Let no dark sign of crucifixion **i.** between

**intervened** 1

T-2 ...... VII.1:4 If I **i.** between your thoughts and their

**intervening** 1

T-13 ..... IV.4:4 them continuous without an **i.** present.

**intervention** 1
T-11......IV.2:4 lessened without the **i.** of God against it,

**intimation** 1
W-pI...107.3:1 not more than just the faintest **i.** of the

**into** 471

**intolerable** 9
T-2........III.3:4 in the extreme, becomes altogether **i.**.
T-2........VI.5:3 **i.** to you because the part of the mind that
T-3........VI.5:6 strain of constant judgment is virtually **i.**.
T-7........VI.3:7 its own existence, a state which it finds **i.**.
T-7.....VIII.2:3 to find conflict so **i.** that you will insist on
T-12......III.7:3 opposed thoughts within itself is **i.**.
T-13.......II.1:2 the ego wants to retain guilt *you* find it **i.**,
T-17...VIII.4:6 but the **i.** strain of refusing to give faith to
P-2........VI.4:2 it is. Seen undisguised it is **i.**. Without

**intricacies** 1
W-pI...122.7:6 and that the **i.** of your dreams no longer

**introduce** 17
T-2........IV.3:5 power in itself to **i.** actual learning errors.
T-2.....VII.3:12 from those you **i.** into miscreation. The
T-5........VI.9:6 you cannot **i.** the concept of fear into it.
T-11......VI.3:8 is only the distortions you **i.** that tire you.
T-14.........I.5:2 He must **i.** the simple truth into a thought
T-18.........I.3:5 this appears to **i.** quite variable behavior,
W-pI.......2.1:6 see in a given area, or you will **i.** strain.
W-pI.......8.4:5 **I.** the practice period by saying: *I seem to*
W-pI.....10.4:1 **i.** them by repeating the idea for today
W-pI.....20.2:1 This is our first attempt to **i.** structure.
W-pI.....32.2:3 try to **i.** the thought that both are in your
W-pI.....38.5:4 *it.* **I.** whatever variations appeal to you, but
W-pI...39.10:1 you should feel free to **i.** variety into the
W-pI...101.6:8 joy these thoughts will **i.** into your mind.
W-pI.136.15:5 We **i.** it with a healing prayer, to help us
W-pI.151.13:2 We **i.** these times with but a single, slow
W-pII.....in.3:1 will use that thought to **i.** our times of rest

**introduced** 11
T-1........I.37:1 is a correction **i.** into false thinking by me.
T-1........VI.3:3 must be **i.** vertically from the bottom up.
T-3........IV.1:5 not exist until the separation **i.** degrees,
T-3........IV.2:1 split **i.** into the mind after the separation,
T-3.........V.1:1 was **i.** only after the separation. No one
T-8...........I.5:3 change to be **i.** is a change in direction.
T-17.......V.6:4 now that the rewards of faith are being **i.**.
T-21.........II.9:6 the adjustments you have **i.** to make it so.
W-pI......10.2:3 This time the idea is **i.** with "My thoughts
W-pI....92.11:3 and recognize that we are being **i.** to sight
W-pI....152.4:4 seem to be but contradictions **i.** by you.

**introduces** 6
T-1.........II.6:4 This **i.** an interval from which the giver
T-2.........V.1:6 it **i.** correction at the level of the error. It
T-5.........II.1:3 the perception of time that the miracle **i.**.
W-pI.....11.1:3 Today's idea **i.** the concept that your
W-pI.....23.5:1 The idea for today **i.** the thought that you
W-pI.....26.3:1 The idea for today **i.** the thought that you

**introducing** 2
T-17.......V.3:1 Spirit wastes no time in **i.** the practical
W-pI....103.1:7 and **i.** opposition in what has no limit and

**introduction** 35
T-in...............h Introduction
T-4..........in.h Introduction
T-5............in.h Introduction
T-6............in.h Introduction
T-6........IV.8:1 **i.** of abilities into being was the beginning
T-10..........in.h Introduction
T-11..........in.h Introduction
T-13..........in.h Introduction
T-14..........in.h Introduction
T-21..........in.h Introduction
T-22..........in.h Introduction
T-22......III.1:1 **i.** of reason into the ego's thought system
T-23..........in.h Introduction
T-24..........in.h Introduction
T-25..........in.h Introduction
T-30..........in.h Introduction
W-in..............h Introduction
W-pI.....11.3:3 The **i.** to this idea, in particular, should be
W-pI.....31.1:1 idea is the **i.** to your declaration of release
WpI......rI.in.h Introduction
WpI.....rII.in.h Introduction
WpI.....rIII.inh Introduction
WpI.....rIV.inh Introduction
WpI.....rV.inh Introduction
Wi181-200...h **I.** to Lessons 181-200.
WpI...rVI.in.h Introduction
W-pII........in.h Introduction
Wfl...........in.h Introduction
M-in.............h Introduction
C-in..............h Introduction
P-in...............h Introduction
P-2............in.h Introduction
S-1............in.h Introduction
S-2............in.h Introduction
S-3............in.h Introduction

**introductions** 1
W-pII.....in.1:4 The lessons that remain are merely **i.** to

**introductory** 3
W-pI.....15.2:1 **i.** idea to the process of image making
W-pI...74.3:10 *Son.* During this **i.** phase, be sure to deal
W-pI.....77.5:1 After this brief **i.** phase, wait quietly for

**intrude** 17
T-15.......V.8:2 personal needs **i.** on no one to make your
T-16.......I.3:10 *and I would not* **i.** *the past upon my Guest. I*
T-17...VIII.2:3 Do not **i.** upon it, do not attack it, do not
T-20......VI.2:3 body does not **i.** upon it. Any relationship
T-23.......in.5:3 Do not let time **i.** upon your sight of him.
T-27......III.1:6 be itself. No weakness can **i.** on it without
T-27....VIII.6:4 that time cannot **i.** upon eternity. It is a
T-29.......V.2:4 can **i.** upon the sacred Son of God within.
T-29....VIII.9:3 but laugh, if idols could **i.** upon his peace.
W-pI.....42.5:3 have let obviously irrelevant thoughts **i.**.
W-pI.....50.3:3 can **i.** upon the eternal calm of the Son of
W-pI...109.4:4 Appearances cannot **i.** on you. You call to
W-pI...164.4:1 is a silence into which the world can not **i.**
W-pI...181.5:6 we will believe will not **i.** upon us now.
W-pI...183.2:2 thought that would **i.** upon your holiness.
W-pII..273.1:4 and nothing can **i.** upon the peace that
W-pII..304.1:1 my holy sight, if I **i.** my world upon it.

**intruded** 2
T-2.........V.4:3 is always because fear has **i.** on your right-
W-pII..298.1:3 that **i.** on my holy sight forgiveness takes

**intruder** 1
T-23.........I.4:4 as an **i.** on your peace is here transformed

**intrudes** 1
T-8.........V.5:5 Whenever fear **i.** anywhere along the road

**intrusion** 5
T-13......XI.1:1 perceived and harsh **i.** of guilt on peace.
T-17.....VII.3:6 It is their **i.** on the relationship, an error
T-24....VI.11:3 itself, with every entry shut against **i.**, and
W-pI.....44.7:2 and **i.** by quietly sinking past them. Your
W-pI...125.3:1 today without **i.** of our petty thoughts,

**intrusions** 4
T-1.........I.34:3 The spirit's strength leaves no room for **i.**.
T-2........III.4:7 regarded as very minor **i.** of discomfort.
T-24.....II.13:3 safe from all **i.** of sanity upon illusions;
P-2...........I.3:3 Holy Spirit fight against the **i.** of the ego

**invade** 1
T-23.........I.9:5 Yet no illusion can **i.** His home and drive

**invaded** 1
T-18........II.4:4 of satisfaction is **i.** by the illusion of terror

**invader** 1
T-15........X.8:7 it is an **i.** who but seems to offer kindness,

**invariable** 1
T-13......XI.5:6 He is **i.** as the peace in which you dwell,

**invariably** 1
T-21....III.10:7 so is sacrifice **i.** a means for limitation,

**invasion** 2
W-pI.....19.2:2 may even be regarded as an "**i.** of privacy.
W-pI...170.1:5 secure from dangerous **i.** and from fear.

**invent** 4
W-pI.....98.3:2 **i.** escapes from fancied threats without
W-pI...161.2:4 thus could it **i.** the partial world you see.
W-pII .280.1:2 I can **i.** imprisonment for him, but only in
P-2.......VII.6:1 God has given you as to **i.** one He has not.

**invented** 9
T-3.........V.2:5 The ego has **i.** many ingenious thought
T-20......VI.1:4 the Son of God **i.** an unholy relationship
W-pI........32.h I have **i.** the world I see.
W-pI.....32.1:2 of the world you see because you **i.** it. You
W-pI.....32.6:3 yourself: *I have* **i.** *this situation as I see it.*
W-pI.....41.2:1 The separated ones have **i.** many "cures"
W-pI.....57.2:1 (32) I have **i.** the world I see. I made up
W-pI.....65.1:5 all the other goals you have **i.** for yourself.
W-pI...152.7:1 contradicts His Will, **i.** opposites to truth,

**invention** 2
T-3.........V.2:8 highly specific nature of **i.** is not worthy
W-pI.....70.1:5 that all guilt is solely an **i.** of your mind,

**inventive** 1
T-6........IV.2:9 most **i.** activities of the ego have never

**inventiveness** 2
T-3.........V.2:7 is creative. **I.** is wasted effort even in its
C-in...........3:6 not attempt to resort to **i.** or ingenuity.

**invert** 1
T-3...........I.2:2 concept if you have to **i.** a whole frame of

**inverts** 1

W-pII ...13.2:3 A miracle **i.** perception which was upside

**invest** 10

*See also* re-invest

T-3......... II.6:1 faith in them and **i.** it only in what is true.
T-12...... III.2:5 and what you **i.** in is always related to
T-12...... IV.7:3 Yet you must **i.** in it, not with money but
T-12...... VI.1:3 **i.** without profit is surely to impoverish
T-15..... VII.4:6 the more anger you **i.** outside yourself,
T-15...... IX.6:4 you **i.** in guilt you withdraw from God.
T-16....... II.9:7 This year **i.** in truth, and let it work in
T-18.........I.6:8 **I.** it not with guilt, for guilt implies it was
T-18...... VI.6:5 worthy of the hate that you **i.** in it. How
T19....IV.B.9:9 Would you **i.** your hope of peace and

**invested** 13

T-12...... III.1:3 are merely those who have **i.** wrongly,
T-12...... III.3:6 If you had not **i.** as they had, it would
T-13...... IX.2:5 and where it is **i.** determines its reward.
T-16..... V.12:4 and **i.** in His killer as the sign that form
T19..IV.B.14:7 the feeling with which they are **i.** is given
T-20...... VI.9:4 so **i.** in a false attraction your preference
T-20..... VII.4:6 be **i.** with attributes of Christ or of the ego
T-21....... II.6:8 seems to attack your faith, for here is it **i.**.
T-24...... IV.1:2 Faith is **i.** in yourself alone. Everything
W-pI..... 47.4:4 in your life which you have **i.** with fear,
W-pI. 138.11:4 demands obscurity for fear to be **i.** there.
W-pI... 170.9:5 and love appears to be **i.** now with cruelty
W-pII . 294.1:5 death, for thoughts of fear are not **i.** there,

**investment** 26

T-2........ III.3:8 weakening the **i.** in physical sight. The
T-2........ III.3:9 The alternating **i.** in the two levels of
T-4.........I.10:1 ego, and become totally without **i.** in fear.
T-4.........I.10:2 **i.** is great now because fear is a witness to
T-7....... VII.4:4 illusions is to withdraw all **i.** from them,
T-8......VIII.3:2 The ego has a profound **i.** in sickness. If
T-9......VIII.4:2 mind, because you will give up all **i.** in it.
T-12.........I.5:2 one with a personal **i.** is a reliable witness,
T-12......... III.h The **I.** in Reality
T-12...... III.1:2 If you have no **i.** in anything in this world,
T-12...... III.2:5 Insistence means **i.**, and what you invest
T-12.... III.10:9 must relinquish your **i.** in the world as
T-12...... IV.7:6 but you must relinquish your **i.** in death,
T-12...... VI.1:4 Not only is there no profit in the **i.**, but
T-12...... VI.1:5 For this **i.** costs you the world's reality by
T-12...... VI.4:9 Son begins with his **i.** in the real world,
T-13... VII.12:7 He has no **i.** in the things that He supplies
T-15..... VII.3:2 it clearly, and by withdrawing your **i.** in it,
T-15..... VII.3:7 This host of God can have no real **i.** here.
T-16...... VI.4:7 whole **i.** in seeing it would be withdrawn
T-16... VII.10:4 and to place all your **i.** in salvation in your
T19..IV.B.13:5 all of the ego's heavy **i.** in the body. And it
W-pI....... 8.4:3 With as little **i.** as possible, search your
W-pI..... 31.3:4 without any special **i.** on your part. As
M-25 ......... 5:2 **i.** has been withdrawn from the world's
S-1...... III.4:10 Your **i.** in this escape is heavy, and your

**investments** 1

T-7....... VII.4:1 Illusions are **i.**. They will last as long as

**invests** 1

T-13...... IV.4:2 The ego **i.** heavily in the past, and in the

**invincible** 4

T-4...... III.10:2 is desperate because it opposes literally **i.**
T-4...... IV.11:5 to join with mine, and together we are **i.**.
T-8...... IV.5:14 I can offer my strength to make yours **i.**,
T-8......... V.1:8 This Mind is **i.** because it is undivided.

**inviolate** 7

T-10 ...... in.1:6 protection and are as **i.** as your safety.
T-19 .....II.6:10 As truth it is **i.**, and everything is brought
T-24 ..... III.2:2 sin. **I.** it stands, strongly defended with all
W-pI..... 99.4:2 What plan could hold the truth **i.**, yet
W-pII . 225.1:2 *and keeping it within its kindly light,* **i.**,
W-pII ... 11.3:3 oneness is forever guaranteed **i.**; forever
M-22 ......... 3:3 the mind, and keeps the idea of attack **i.**.

**invisibility** 1

T-1 ........I.17:2 They are sudden shifts into **i.**, away from

**invisible** 21

T-12 .... VII.1:1 learning is **i.** and what has been learned
T-12 .... VII.2:2 You cannot see the **i.**. Yet if you see its
T-12 .... VII.3:1 The Holy Spirit is **i.**, but you can see the
T-12 ... VIII.3:1 is not true, what *is* true became **i.** to you.
T-12 ... VIII.3:2 Yet it cannot be **i.** in itself, for the Holy
T-12 ... VIII.3:3 It is **i.** to you because you are looking at
T-12 ... VIII.3:4 you to decide what is visible and what is **i.**
T-12 ... VIII.4:4 what you have made **i.** is the only truth,
T-12 ... VIII.6:5 is **i.** because the Holy Spirit does not see it
T-12 ... VIII.6:7 made **i.** the only truth that this world
T-12 . VIII.6:11 And Christ is **i.** to you because of what
T-12 ... VIII.7:4 What is **i.** to you is perfect in His sight,
T-12 ... VIII.8:3 Its reality will make everything else **i.**, for
T-12 ... VIII.8:5 Nothingness will become **i.**, for you will at
T-13 ........ I.2:3 By making him **i.**, the world of retribution
T-19 ..... III.9:3 it seems to be seen, and it becomes **i.**.
T19..IV.A.11:7 upon is meaningless to fear, and quite **i.**.
T-20 ...... V.3:5 it? Judge not what is **i.** to you or you will
T-20 ..... VII.6:3 In the darkness of sin he is **i.**. He can but
T-26 ........ I.4:8 He is **i.** in such a world. Nor can his song
T-30 ..... III.9:4 nor the time that keeps this star **i.** to earth

**invitation** 30

T-5 ............. I.h The **I.** to the Holy Spirit
T-5 .......... I.3:1 This is the **i.** to the Holy Spirit. I have
T-5 .......... I.3:2 I can bring Him to you only at your own **i.**
T-5 ...... VII.6:6 will respond fully to your slightest **i.**: *I*
T-7 ....... IV.7:9 Love needs only this **i.**. It comes freely to
T-11 ......... II.h The **I.** to Healing
T-11 ....... II.4:5 And yet the **i.** must come from you, for
T-11 ....... II.7:5 He cannot help you without your **i.**. And
T-12 .... VII.5:2 Your perception is the result of your **i.**,
T-15 ..... XI.4:5 that they are where your **i.** bids them be.
T-17 ...... V.3:1 This **i.** is accepted immediately, and the
T-18 . VIII.11:1 The holy instant is your **i.** to love to enter
T19..IV.B.12:4 with the body, which is the **i.** to pain. For
T-22 ...... V.2:4 What can this be except an **i.** to insanity,
T-27 ..... III.4:1 become a silent **i.** to the truth to enter,
W-pI. 136.15:4 waits for just this **i.** which we give today.
W-pI. 137.12:3 home. And can this **i.** be refused? Ask the
W-pI. 152.12:1 concluding it with this same **i.** to your Self
W-pI... 162.6:2 welcome you into his heart with loving **i.**,
W-pI... 183.7:1 we give an **i.** which can never be refused.
W-pII .... in.4:3 Him the **i.** that He seeks to make us happy
W-pII .... in.4:6 say the words of **i.** that His Voice suggests
W-pII . 285.1:2 and realize my **i.** will be answered by the
W-pII ..... 9.1:3 **i.** to God's Word to take illusion's place;
M-28 ......... 1:8 It is the **i.** to God to take His final step. It
P-2.......... II.6:1 is an **i.** to God to enter into His Kingdom,
P-2.......... II.6:1 does it make how the **i.** is written? Does
P-2.......... II.6:3 Or is it he who writes that gives the **i.**?
P-3.......... II.3:1 can use, and will use, given the slightest **i.**.
P-3........ III.8:3 refuses an **i.** to enter and abide with you.

**invitation's** 1

T-27 ..... III.4:2 that would enhance the **i.** real appeal. For

**invitations** 1

T-12 .... VII.8:2 merely the reflection of your conflicting **i.**

**invite** 15

T-11 ....... II.4:5 that whom you **i.** as your guest will abide
T-11 ....... II.6:4 **I.** this knowledge back into your mind,
T-11 ....... II.7:2 You will accept only whom you **i.**. You are
T-11 ....... II.7:6 ego is nothing, whether you **i.** it in or not.
T-12 .... VII.5:1 you expect, and you expect what you **i.**.
T-15 ..... XI.2:7 need but **i.** Him in Who is there already,
T-15 ..... XI.4:5 Through peace you **i.** them back, realizing
T-17 ..... V.11:1 to **i.** the Holy Spirit into your relationship
T-26 .. VII.13:5 their source is to **i.** illusions to be true,
W-pI .... 90.1:6 I **i.** the solution to come to me through
W-pI 137.12:2 You but **i.** your Self to be at home. And
W-pI 152.12:1 hourly **i.** Him with the words with which
W-pI .. 183.2:2 **i.** the angels to surround the ground on
WpI.rVI.in.1:4 and **i.** the memory of God to come again.
P-1............. 2:1 than to **i.** the Holy Spirit to enter into it

**invited** 16

T-12 .... VII.6:1 see me it will be because you have **i.** Him.
T-12 .... VII.8:6 will come to you because you **i.** them.
T-13 ....... V.5:7 with figures of fear you have **i.** into it, and
T-14 ... XI.13:4 will have **i.** Him to do so by abandoning
T-15 .. VII.14:7 wholeness, all are **i.** and made welcome.
T-15 ....... X.6:4 to recognize that the ego, which you **i.**, is
T-15 ....... X.8:6 it is what you **i.** in that would destroy you,
T-16 ...... I.3:11 *Guest. I have* **i.** *Him, and He is here. I need do*
T-16 ..... VI.9:3 to enter your mind, and because you **i.** it,
T19 ... IV.A.7:1 rid of Him Whom you **i.** in and push Him
T-28 ..... III.8:8 And they will meet with your **i.** Guests the
T-29 ....... II.5:2 for you to come where you **i.** Him to be.
T-31 ... VIII.5:5 *Son.* Thus is Christ's strength **i.** to prevail,
W-pII .... in.4:1 He would not fail to take when we **i.** Him.
W-pII . 313.1:1 *fear has gone, and where it was is love* **i.** *in.*
P-2.......... II.5:3 because He has been **i.** to come in. In the

**invites** 6

T-6 ......... II.5:5 This **i.** Atonement automatically, because
T-15 ..... III.5:3 this, and **i.** sorrow or joy accordingly.
T19 . IV.B.12:5 **i.** fear to enter and become your purpose.
W-pII . 271.2:2 *beholds* **i.** *Your memory to be restored to me*
M-4 ........ X.1:3 so open-mindedness **i.** Him to come in.
P-2....... VII.2:4 home, into which psychotherapy **i.** Him.

**inviting** 3

T-15 ....... X.8:5 **i.** it to take His place to protect you from
T-24 ... IV.3:15 an open door **i.** everything that would
W-pI .... 49.5:3 that you are **i.** God's Voice to speak to you

**invocation** 1

M-23 ......... 1:6 nor does an **i.** call forth any special power

**involuntary** 3

T-1 .......... I.5:1 Miracles are habits, and should be **i.**.
T-2 ....... VI.1:1 Being afraid seems to be **i.**; something
T-2 ....... VI.1:2 that only constructive acts should be **i.**.

**involve** 19

T-1 ........ I.46:2 medium. Miracles do not **i.** this type of
T-1 ......... II.6:2 Sonship appears to **i.** almost endless time.
T-1 ...... VII.3:2 they always **i.** twisting perception into
T-1 ...... VII.5:7 **i.** a more direct approach to God Himself.
T-2 ....... III.5:3 and do not **i.** any effort at all on their part
T-3 ....... IV.3:2 **i.** knowledge and cannot be perceived.
T-6 ......... II.1:1 split in mind must **i.** a rejection of part of
T-7 ......... II.5:5 God's law of creation does not **i.** the use
T-8 ...... VII.7:2 since it seems to **i.** the translation of one
T-10 ..... IV.2:3 To know reality must **i.** the willingness to
T-17 .. VII.8:11 that does not **i.** your whole relationship,
T-18 .... VII.1:2 What plans do you make that do not **i.** its
W-pI ...... 9.3:1 **i.** looking about you and applying the
W-pI .... 24.3:3 periods which the exercises **i.**.
W-pI .... 37.4:1 each to **i.** three to five minutes of practice,
M-9 ........... 1:2 may or may not **i.** changes in the external

M-13..........2:4 world's terms that does not **i.** the body.
S-1 ......... II.1:4 appeal to God, or even **i.** belief in Him. At
S-1 ......... II.2:1 **i.** feelings of weakness and inadequacy,

### involved 21

T-3........III.4:5 fact that perception is **i.** at all removes the
T-3........IV.4:2 demonstrating that knowledge is not **i.**.
T-4......... II.6:2 is obvious when you consider what is **i.**.
T-4......... V.6:4 By becoming **i.** with tangential issues, it
T-7..... VIII.3:1 are two major errors **i.** in this attempt.
T-14....... X.7:1 The only judgment **i.** is the Holy Spirit's
T-17...... VI.6:5 the fact that everyone **i.** in it will play his
T-19.........I.1:4 This faith encompasses everyone **i.**, for
T-19.........I.1:5 And everyone must be **i.** in it, or else your
T-27...... IV.2:1 Thus it must be that time is not **i.** and
W-in..........6:2 will help you to generalize the ideas **i.** to
W-pI.....19.5:1 required, shortening the length of time **i.**,
W-pI.....27.2:2 uneasy about the lack of reservation **i.**,
W-pI.....66.3:3 will not become hopelessly **i.** in defining
W-pI.....74.4:2 persons and the situation or situations **i.**,
M-1............3:3 So do the particular teaching aids **i.**. But
M-3............4:1 the sense that each person **i.** will learn the
M-3............5:3 their existence implies that those **i.** have
M-10..........3:4 and everything **i.** in them in any way. And
M-10..........4:9 on everyone and everything **i.** in any way.
C-1.............7:2 Will is not **i.** in perception at any level,

### involvement 4

T-12.........I.2:1 and never without your own ego **i.**. The
W-pI.....44.7:5 observe your passing thoughts without **i.**,
W-pI.....65.5:5 you, with as little **i.** or concern as possible
W-pI...181.4:1 been **i.** with your past and future goals.

### involves 35

T-1........IV.1:1 escape from darkness **i.** two stages: First,
T-1.......VII.4:2 learning **i.** attention and study at some
T-2...........I.1:8 This process **i.** the following steps: First,
T-2... V.A.17:4 Only the latter **i.** an awareness of time,
T-2.....VII.5:12 time itself **i.** intervals that do not exist.
T-2..... VIII.4:1 first step toward freedom **i.** a sorting out
T-3...... III.2:3 ways because perception **i.** interpretation,
T-3......III.5:11 spiritualized form perception **i.** the body.
T-3........IV.5:1 always **i.** some misuse of mind, because it
T-3........IV.6:2 perception **i.** an exchange or translation,
T-3......... V.7:6 At every level it **i.** selectivity. Perception is
T-3......... V.8:5 of it. Only perception **i.** partial awareness.
T-3........VI.2:4 Judgment always **i.** rejection. It never
T-3........VI.7:4 the ego makes **i.** a contradiction in terms,
T-4........ I.13:2 **i.** no confusion about the child's origin.
T-4......... II.2:4 the mind as when it **i.** physical proximity.
T-4..... II.11:12 Knowledge never **i.** comparisons. That is
T-5...........I.7:2 instant that sharing it **i.** anything but gain
T-6.........in.1:2 Anger always **i.** projection of separation,
T-6......... I.16:5 of punishment **i.** the projection of blame,
T-6........IV.5:2 of all, if you consider what it really **i.**. The
T-7......... V.3:6 always **i.** the belief that healing is harmful
T-8........IX.5:2 since all healing **i.** replacing fear with love
T-9..... VIII.2:5 always **i.** attack. It is a delusional attempt
T-11.......in.2:1 believed this question really **i.** conflict? If
T-11......VI.3:7 for to perceive with Him **i.** no strain at all.
T-13.....VII.2:2 each of them **i.** a different kind of seeing,
T-16....... II.3:4 **i.** a contradiction of what miracles mean.
T-16....... V.1:1 is necessary first to realize that it **i.** a great
T-18.........I.3:2 Fear **i.** substitution by definition, for it is
T-18.....VII.7:1 To do anything **i.** the body. And if you
W-pI.....12.2:3 another **i.** a fairly constant time interval.
M-3............1:2 level. Each teaching-learning situation **i.** a
M-5............1:1 Healing **i.** an understanding of what the
C-3.............4:3 Seeing the face of Christ **i.** perception. No

### involving 6

T-1......... II.1:2 **i.** the extremely personal sense of creation
W-pI.....10.5:2 each **i.** no more than a minute or so of
W-pI.....24.5:3 *In the situation* ***i.*** *–, I would like_to happen,*
W-pI.....32.2:2 one **i.** the world you see outside you, and
W-pI.....38.4:5 *In the situation* ***i.*** *– in which I see myself,*
W-pI.....38.4:6 *In the situation* ***i.*** *_in which_sees himself,*

### invulnerability 13

T-2........ IV.3:6 shares the **i.** of the Atonement to two-
T-10...... III.3:3 of love therefore brings **i.** with it. Do not
T-12....... V.2:1 recognition of your own **i.** is so important
T-12....... V.2:2 sanity. For if you accept your **i.**, you are
T-12....... V.2:6 of your **i.** has more than negative value. If
T-13............I.h Guiltlessness and **I.**
T-14...... III.7:1 lesson is merely this: Guiltlessness is **i.**.
T-14...... III.7:2 make your **i.** manifest to everyone. Teach
W-pI........26.h My attack thoughts are attacking my **i.**.
W-pI.....26.2:4 and **i.** cannot be accepted together. They
W-pI.....26.4:1 or **i.** is the result of your own thoughts.
W-pI.....56.1:1 My attack thoughts are attacking my **i.**.
W-pI.....62.3:5 will restore the **i.** and power God gave His

### invulnerable 15

T-1...... IV.2:11 place. The mind that serves spirit *is* **i.**.
T-2........ III.2:2 the separation the mind was **i.** to fear,
T-2........ III.2:4 thoughts and making you perfectly **i.**.
T-4.......VII.8:3 The truly helpful are **i.**, because they are
T-5......... V.2:4 makes it **i.** to the ego because its peace is
T-5......... V.2:5 It is **i.** to disruption because it is whole.
T-8......... V.5:7 **i.** to its retaliation because I am with you.
T-8..... VIII.3:3 to the ego's firm belief that you are not **i.**?
T-13.........I.8:1 You are **i.** because you are guiltless. You
T-13.......I.11:8 And being wholly pure, you are **i.**.
T-14..... III.10:1 Those who accept the Atonement *are* **i.**.
T-31...... VI.6:1 Are you **i.**? Then the world is harmless in
W-pI.....26.1:1 that if you can be attacked you are not **i.**.
W-pI.....26.2:2 must believe that you are not **i.**. Attack
P-2.........in.3:5 the vulnerable **i.** and the finite limitless.

### inward 15

T-12...... III.7:9 outward what is antagonistic to what is **i.**,
T-13....... X.4:1 guilt lies in the past, you are not looking **i.**
T-18.........I.6:3 For truth extends **i.**, where the idea of loss
T-18.........I.7:4 **I.** is sanity; insanity is outside you. You
T-18.........I.9:1 has set the course **i.** to the truth you share
T-18....... IX.9:6 ready for the final step in the journey **i.**.
T-18.... IX.10:5 still further **i.** but the one *you* cannot take,
T-21.......in.1:5 the outside picture of an **i.** condition. As a
T-21....... IV.2:3 Loudly the ego tells you not to look **i.**, for
T-21....... IV.4:3 Your faith is moving **i.**, past insanity and
T-29........ II.2:8 Look **i.** now, and you will not behold a
W-pI.....41.6:5 Try, instead, to get a sense of turning **i.**,
W-pI.....41.7:2 But most of all, try to sink down and **i.**,
W-pI...188.2:6 the shadow of the seen through **i.** vision.
W-pI...188.5:7 For what your **i.** vision looks upon is your

### iron 4

W-pI.134.12:3 **i.** doors he thought would make him safe.
W-pI...153.3:2 in heavy bands of steel with **i.** overlaid,
W-pI...153.5:3 who feel its **i.** grip upon your heart. You
W-pI...200.5:1 where you beheld but chains and **i.** doors.

### irrational 5

T-5......... V.7:1 **I.** thought is disordered thought. God
T-6.........in.1:4 Given these three wholly **i.** premises, the
T-6.........in.1:4 the equally **i.** conclusion that a brother is
W-pI...151.1:5 It needs **i.** defense because it is irrational.
W-pI...151.1:5 It needs irrational defense because it is **i.**.

### irreconcilable 11

T-3.........VII.6:6 knowledge and perception, are **i.**. To
T-4.........I.2:11 They are fundamentally **i.**, because spirit
T-10...... IV.1:1 magic is an attempt at reconciling the **i.**.
T-10...... IV.1:2 that the **i.** cannot be reconciled. Sickness
T-10...... IV.1:3 Sickness and perfection are **i.**. If God
T-10...... IV.2:5 illusions, because truth and illusions are **i.**
T-10...... IV.4:3 Since freedom and bondage are **i.**, their
T-11.......in.1:5 and their fundamentally **i.** natures cannot
T-23............I.h The **I.** Beliefs
W-pI... 170.3:2 into two camps which seem wholly **i.**. For
P-2..........II.2:3 **i.** that it hardly requires elaboration here.

### irrelevant 17

T-2........ IV.1:6 error to which Atonement is applied is **i.**.
T-4..........II.1:4 and examples are **i.** to its understanding.
T-4....... VII.5:6 "How," "what" and "to whom" are **i.**,
T-7........ IV.3:4 kind of learning is as **i.** as is the particular
T-21...... VII.9:2 It is **i.** to how it happens, but not to why.
T-22........II.3:2 The form in which they are accepted is **i.**.
W-pI..... 42.5:3 you have let obviously **i.** thoughts intrude
W-pI..... 42.7:2 is included that is contradictory or **i.**.
W-pI..... 43.6:2 you become preoccupied with **i.** thoughts.
W-pI... 134.2:3 false. It is **i.** to everything except illusions.
W-pI... 167.3:2 but an idea, **i.** to what is seen as physical.
W-pI... 169.9:2 is entirely **i.** to what must be a constant
M-in .......... 3:4 verbal content of your teaching is quite **i.**.
M-8 ........... 5:9 seem to make them different are really **i.**,
M-21 ......... 5:3 It may also seem to be quite **i.** to the
M-25 ......... 3:3 this, the question of how they arise is **i.**.
C-in ........... 1:4 "individual consciousness" is essentially **i.**

### irreplaceable 1

T-9....VIII.10:1 You are altogether **i.** in the Mind of God.

### irresistible 3

T-12..VIII.7:10 the attraction of love for love remains **i.**.
T-18.... VI.14:2 it is the **i.** appeal the holy instant holds. It
T-22....... V.5:5 to be immovable; this Force is **i.** in truth.

### irresistibly 2

T-5........ IV.4:3 Mind that was in me is still **i.** drawn to
T-15...... VI.6:5 himself drawn **i.** into the light behind it,

### irresponsibly 1

T-5......... V.7:7 this responsibility, they are reacting **i.**. If

### irreverent 1

W-pI..... 29.2:2 You may find it silly, **i.**, senseless, funny

### irreversible 3

T-5....... V.6:11 what God creates is **i.** and unchangeable.
T-19........II.1:3 But sin, were it possible, would be **i.**. The
W-pI... 121.5:2 it regards its judgment of the world as **i.**,

### irrevocable 1

T-23........II.4:4 interpreted as an **i.** sentence upon himself

### irrevocably 2

T-6...... V.B.6:4 undo a decision that was **i.** made for you.
S-3 ...........I.2:4 moment goes **i.** past their grasping hands,

### irritate 2

W-pI.....94.5:5 who seems to **i.** you with these words: *You*
W-pI. 121.10:1 you do not like, who seems to **i.** you, or to

### irritates 1

W-pI....... 8.6:1 during the day, unless you find it **i.** you. If

### irritating 1

W-pI..... 78.4:5 **i.** or untrue to the ideal he should accept

**irritation** 5

| | |
|---|---|
| T-31 V.3:4 | upon its innocence, provoking it to **i.**, and |
| W-pI 8.6:3 | find it helpful, however, to include your **i.** |
| W-pI 21.2:3 | any reaction ranging from mild **i.** to rage. |
| M-17 4:4 | It may be merely slight **i.**, perhaps too |
| M-18 4:2 | of **i.** in himself as he responds to anyone, |

**is** 15812

**island** 1

| | |
|---|---|
| T-20 VI.11:3 | an instant of despair, a tiny **i.** of dry sand, |

**isolated** 5

| | |
|---|---|
| T-13 V.6:4 | as **i.** from reality as if you were alone in all |
| T-14 III.9:4 | Son can be separate or **i.** in its effects. |
| T-20 VI.5:2 | The body is an **i.** speck of darkness; a |
| T-30 VII.6:15 | the senseless, **i.** scripts you write in sleep. |
| W-pI 137.1:4 | a separate self, and keeps it **i.** and alone. |

**isolation** 11

| | |
|---|---|
| T-1 I.42:1 | in releasing you from your false sense of **i.** |
| T-8 IV.2:3 | It is therefore an illusion of **i.**, maintained |
| T-10 V.5:8 | Depression is **i.**, and so it could not have |
| T-13 VI.12:6 | dream of **i.** because your eyes are closed. |
| T-14 III.18:3 | Unlearn **i.** through His loving guidance, |
| T-20 VI.8:4 | It is a state of **i.**, which seems to be what it |
| T-26 VII.11:9 | this he cannot do without a sense of **i.**, |
| T-30 I.16:5 | results *because* they are not made in **i.**. |
| WpI rI.in.4:5 | and seeking a haven of **i.** for yourself. |
| W-pI 137.2:1 | Sickness is **i.**. For it seems to keep one |
| W-pII 223.1:1 | God, a separate entity that moved in **i.**, |

**issue** 5

| | |
|---|---|
| T-3 VI.8:1 | The **i.** of authority is really a question of |
| T-4 V.6:3 | ego compromises with the **i.** of the eternal |
| T-6 V.C.1:9 | The ego's beliefs on this crucial **i.** vary, |
| T-13 II.1:3 | it. On this **i.**, then, the deepest split of all |
| M-17 1:2 | If this **i.** is mishandled, the teacher of God |

**issues** 5

| | |
|---|---|
| T-4 V.6:3 | just as it does with all **i.** touching on the |
| T-4 V.6:4 | By becoming involved with tangential **i.**, |
| M-24 4:2 | **i.** such as the validity of reincarnation |
| M-24 4:5 | teach that theoretical **i.** but waste time, |
| C-in 5:1 | on structural **i.** in the course is brief and |

**issuing** 1

| | |
|---|---|
| W-pII 4.3:1 | **i.** from thoughts that are untrue. They are |

**It** 114
*it*

| | |
|---|---|
| T-5 I.4:7 | I could not have **I.** myself without knowing |
| T-5 II.7:1 | because **I.** is incapable of arrogance. It |
| T-5 II.7:2 | **I.** does not demand, because It does not |
| T-5 II.7:2 | demand, because **I.** does not seek control. |
| T-5 II.7:3 | **I.** does not overcome, because It does not |
| T-5 II.7:3 | not overcome, because **I.** does not attack. |
| T-5 II.7:4 | **I.** merely reminds. It is compelling only |
| T-5 II.7:5 | **I.** is compelling only because of what It |
| T-5 II.7:5 | only because of what **I.** reminds you *of.* It |
| T-5 II.7:6 | *of.* **I.** brings to your mind the other way, |
| T-5 II.7:7 | is always quiet, because **I.** speaks of peace. |
| T-5 III.4:2 | That is why you must share **I.**. It must be |
| T-5 III.4:3 | It. **I.** must be increased in strength before |
| T-5 III.4:3 | in strength before you can hear **I.**. It is |
| T-5 III.4:4 | It is impossible to hear **I.** in yourself while |
| T-5 III.4:4 | yourself while **I.** is so weak in your mind. |
| T-5 III.4:5 | **I.** is not weak in Itself, but It is limited by |
| T-5 III.4:5 | but **I.** is limited by your unwillingness to |
| T-5 III.4:5 | is limited by your unwillingness to hear **I.**. |
| T-5 IV.4:2 | to share **I.** in order to hear It yourself. The |
| T-5 IV.4:2 | to share It in order to hear **I.** yourself. The |
| T-5 VI.11:7 | Voice was in me as **I.** is in you, speaking |
| T-7 IX.6:8 | **I.** extends forever and in perfect peace. Its |
| T-7 IX.6:9 | is so intense that **I.** creates in perfect joy, |
| T-7 IX.7:1 | which maintain **I.** in wholeness and peace |
| T-8 II.8:6 | **I.** is the Voice for his creations and for his |
| T-8 IV.8:9 | The Holy Trinity is holy *because* **I.** is One. |
| T-8 IV.8:11 | You must be included in **I.**, because It is |
| T-8 IV.8:11 | be included in It, because **I.** is everything. |
| T-8 IV.8:12 | your place in **I.** and fulfill your function as |
| T-8 IV.8:12 | in It and fulfill your function as part of **I.**, |
| T-8 IV.8:13 | No part of **I.** can be imprisoned if Its truth |
| T-10 IV.7:4 | he strengthens **I.** in a sick brother by |
| T-11 IV.1:2 | Self. As God's creation **I.** is yours, and |
| T-11 IV.1:2 | It is yours, and belonging to you **I.** is His. |
| T-11 VIII.10:3 | willing to accept this Help by asking for **I.**, |
| T-11 VIII.10:3 | for It, you will give **I.** because you want It. |
| T-11 VIII.10:3 | for It, you will give It because you want **I.**. |
| T-12 I.7:3 | God's Answer as you want **I.** to be, and if |
| T-12 I.7:3 | want It to be, and if you want **I.** in truth, It |
| T-12 I.7:3 | you want It in truth, **I.** will be truly yours. |
| T-13 XI.8:2 | You may believe you want **I.** broken, and |
| T-14 IX.4:7 | leaves not what **I.** created holy as Itself. |
| T-14 X.12:6 | miracle becomes the means of sharing **I.**. |
| T-14 X.12:7 | Identity wherever **I.** is not recognized, you |
| T-14 X.12:7 | It is not recognized, you will recognize **I.**. |
| T-15 II.6:9 | of the universe that witnesses to **I.**, your |
| T-15 V.11:2 | God has created **I.** beyond judgment, out |
| T-16 III.3:6 | not recognize **I.** even though It functions. |
| T-16 III.3:6 | not recognize It even though **I.** functions. |
| T-16 III.3:8 | And it is only if you deny what **I.** has done |
| T-18 VI.11:9 | of your Identity, and would not limit **I.**. |
| T19 IV.C.5:7 | which heard His Answer and accepted **I.**. |
| T-21 II.12:3 | union with **I.** is the source of his creating. |
| T-21 V.1:6 | ravings to those who want to hear **I.**. |
| T-21 VI.9:5 | **I.** would have you learn what you must be. |
| T-21 VI.9:6 | And being one with **I.**, it must be given |
| T-21 VI.9:6 | be given you to give what **I.** has given, and |
| T-25 I.7:4 | must **I.** use the language that this mind |
| T-25 I.7:5 | is. And **I.** must use all learning to transfer |
| T-28 I.7:9 | so ancient that **I.** far exceeds the span of |
| T-28 I.8:2 | **I.** is not past because He let It not be |
| T-28 I.8:2 | because He let **I.** not be unremembered. It |
| T-28 I.8:3 | **I.** has never changed, because there never |
| T-28 I.8:3 | He did not keep **I.** safely in your mind. Its |
| T-28 I.8:5 | Yet was **I.** never absent from your mind, |
| T-28 I.9:5 | Never changed from what **I.** is. And you |
| T-28 I.9:8 | **I.** is not revealed in miracles. They but |
| T-28 I.9:9 | They but remind you that **I.** has not gone. |
| T-28 I.9:10 | When you forgive **I.** for your sins, It will |
| T-28 I.9:10 | It for your sins, **I.** will no longer be denied |
| T-28 I.14:6 | There never was a cause beside **I.** that |
| T-28 II.3:4 | **I.** has but *one* Effect. And in that |
| T-28 V.3:5 | because you think that **I.** is fearful. And |
| T-29 V.4:2 | him, and let **I.** tell you what his function is |
| T-30 II.2:7 | Hear **I.** now, that you may be reminded of |
| T-31 I.6:1 | so small and still **I.** cannot rise above the |
| W-pI 49.3:5 | His Voice. He gave **I.** to you to be heard. |
| W-pI 67.3:3 | in your mind **I.** is there for you to find. |
| W-pI 71.10:6 | of your salvation, and to see **I.** where It is. |
| W-pI 71.10:6 | of your salvation, and to see It where **I.** is. |
| W-pI 72.7:4 | Voice of truth and welcome **I.** as Friend. |
| W-pI 93.9:4 | and the love from which **I.** was created. |
| W-pI 93.9:5 | and sinfulness you have made to replace **I.** |
| W-pI 93.9:6 | It. Let **I.** come into Its Own. Here you are; |
| W-pI 95.13:3 | and let **I.** shine away all your illusions and |
| W-pI 96.3:3 | and still be what **I.** is and must forever be. |
| W-pI 96.8:3 | is the Bridge between your mind and **I.**. |
| W-pI 96.8:4 | do, restored to **I.** and free to serve Its Will. |
| W-pI 96.11:4 | your Self experiences **I.** will save for you, |
| W-pI 123.6:1 | lets **I.** echo round and round the world. |
| W-pI 137.3:5 | and without the unity that gives **I.** life. But |
| W-pI 160.6:7 | **I.** asked no stranger in, and took no alien |
| W-pI 160.6:8 | And **I.** will call Its Own unto Itself in |
| W-pI 184.15:2 | *In* **I.** *we are united with all living things, and* |
| W-pI 186.12:2 | And if **I.** asks a thing of you which seems |
| W-pI 190.2:5 | leave the Son whom **I.** created out of love. |
| W-pII 224.1:1 | that Heaven looks to **I.** to give it light. It |
| W-pII 224.1:2 | **I.** lights the world as well. It is the gift my |
| W-pII 224.1:3 | **I.** is the gift my Father gave to me; the one |
| W-pII 224.1:7 | this. This is illusion's end. **I.** is the truth. |
| W-pII 224.2:2 | *I have forgotten* **I.**, *and do not know where I* |
| W-pII 229.1:1 | Identity, and find **I.** in these words: "Love, |
| W-pII 229.1:4 | So still **I.** waited for my coming home, |
| W-pII 252.2:2 | *Reveal* **I.** *now to me who am Your Son, that I* |
| W-pII 7.5:2 | Call from Love to Love, that **I.** be but Itself |
| W-pII 288.1:9 | *Name, and so remember that* **I.** *is my own.* |
| W-pII 330.2:3 | *We would return to* **I.** *today, to be made free* |
| W-pII 352.1:9 | *Identity, and find in* **I.** *the memory of You.* |
| M-1 2:5 | **I.** goes on all the time everywhere. It calls |
| M-1 2:6 | **I.** calls for teachers to speak for It and |
| M-1 2:6 | It calls for teachers to speak for **I.** and |
| M-1 2:7 | Many hear **I.**, but few will answer. Yet it is |
| M-12 5:10 | just as **I.** tells him what his function is. He |

**it** 11029
*It*

**itemizes** 1

| | |
|---|---|
| T-6 V.4:1 | The Holy Spirit never **i.** errors because |

**Its** 57
*its*

| | |
|---|---|
| T-3 II.5:5 | There is no confusion within **I.** Levels, |
| T-5 II.3:3 | that the ego always dissolves at **I.** sound. |
| T-5 III.2:10 | in him, and thus acknowledge **I.** being. |
| T-6 V.B.6:4 | Spirit's Voice, and **I.** perfect consistency, |
| T-7 IX.6:9 | **I.** radiance is so intense that It creates in |
| T-7 IX.6:9 | the whole can be born of **I.** Wholeness. |
| T-8 IV.8:13 | be imprisoned if **I.** truth is to be known. |
| T-9 IV.1:6 | is shared, and that **I.** sharing is Its reality. |
| T-9 IV.1:6 | is shared, and that Its sharing is **I.** reality. |
| T-9 VIII.11:7 | but the Source is true and so is **I.** answer. |
| T-16 III.3:8 | that you could possibly deny **I.** Presence. |
| T-17 VII.8:8 | any situation that shares **I.** purpose. The |
| T-28 I.8:4 | **I.** consequences will indeed seem new, |
| T-28 I.9:6 | And you are **I.** Effect, as changeless and as |
| T-28 I.9:7 | **I.** memory does not lie in the past, nor |
| T-28 I.10:9 | in allowing Cause to have **I.** Own Effects, |
| T-28 I.14:1 | of present Cause and **I.** benign Effects. |
| T-28 I.14:5 | His Cause *is* **I.** Effects. There never was a |
| T-28 I.14:7 | **I.** Effects are changelessly eternal, beyond |
| T-31 I.5:4 | and teach you that **I.** lessons are not true; |
| W-pI 68.2:1 | remains aware of **I.** likeness to Its Creator, |
| W-pI 68.2:1 | remains aware of Its likeness to **I.** Creator, |
| W-pI 92.9:2 | stands ready to embrace you as **I.** Own. |
| W-pI 93.9:4 | Try to appreciate **I.** Holiness and the love |
| W-pI 93.9:5 | by hiding **I.** majesty behind the tiny idols |
| W-pI 93.9:6 | It. Let It come into **I.** Own. Here you are; |
| W-pI 94.3:7 | Self that never left **I.** home in God to walk |
| W-pI 95.3:2 | one Self, which is united with **I.** Creator. |
| W-pI 95.13:4 | Son of God Himself, sinless as **I.** Creator, |
| W-pI 96.7:1 | Your Self retains **I.** Thoughts, and they |
| W-pI 96.8:4 | do, restored to It and free to serve **I.** Will. |
| W-pI 96.9:3 | **I.** *Thoughts are mine to use.* Then seek Its |
| W-pI 96.9:4 | Then seek **I.** Thoughts, and claim them as |
| W-pI 101.4:3 | he try to listen and accept **I.** offering? If |
| W-pI 106.1:1 | and completely certain in **I.** messages. |
| W-pI 137.3:4 | Self with all **I.** parts intact and unassailed. |
| W-pI 151.8:1 | that doubt is meaningless before **I.** face. |
| W-pI 156.5:5 | transforming in **I.** gentle light all things |
| W-pI 156.5:5 | all things unto **I.** likeness and Its purity. |
| W-pI 156.5:5 | all things unto Its likeness and **I.** purity. |
| W-pI 160.6:8 | will call **I.** Own unto Itself in recognition |
| W-pI 160.6:8 | Itself in recognition of what is **I.** Own. |
| W-pI 160.7:4 | as certain of **I.** Own as God is of His Son. |
| WpI rV.in4:5 | is perfectly consistent in **I.** Thoughts; |
| WpI rV.in4:5 | Thoughts; knows **I.** Creator, understands |
| WpI rV.in4:5 | is perfect in **I.** knowledge and Its Love, |
| WpI rV.in4:5 | is perfect in Its knowledge and **I.** Love, |
| WpI rV.in4:5 | and never changes from **I.** constant state |
| WpI rV.in4:5 | state of union with **I.** Father and Itself. |
| W-pI 181.9:2 | of anything without **I.** sinlessness. We |
| W-pI 184.14:3 | And through **I.** use, all foolish separations |

W-pI.186.11:3 and His Voice is certain of **I.** messages.
W-pII..222.1:3 directs my actions, offers me **I.** Thoughts,
W-pII..252.1:2 **I.** shimmering and perfect purity is far
W-pII..252.1:3 **I.** love is limitless, with an intensity that
W-pII..252.1:4 certainty. **I.** strength comes not from
W-pII..326.1:5 *Cause and* **I.** *Effect are indistinguishable. Let*

**its** 2014
*Its*

**Itself** 38
*itself*

T-3......... II.5:4 the Holy Trinity, but the Trinity **I.** is One.
T-5........ III.4:5 It is not weak in **I.**, but It is limited by
T-7...........I.7:5 that He is the First in the Holy Trinity **I.**.
T-8... VIII.9:10 what life is, being the Voice for Life **I.**.
T-14...... IX.4:7 and leaves not what It created holy as **I.**.
T19... IV.C.7:7 the victory of lifelessness on Life **I.**.
T19... IV.D.5:6 of the obstacles to love, Love **I.** has called.
T-21...... VI.9:5 Love plans is like **I.** in this: Being united,
T-25.........I.7:2 a Oneness which unites all things within **I.**
T-28.........I.9:6 Its Effect, as changeless and as perfect as **I.**
T-28...... IV.7:1 no gap that separates His Oneness from **I.**
T-31..... V.17:9 born. And What you are will tell you of **I.**.
W-pI..... 92.9:3 His Son, is waiting now to meet **I.** again,
W-pI... 96.10:3 in all things created by the Spirit as **I.**.
W-pI... 118.2:2 *the mighty Voice for Truth* **I.** *assure me that I*
W-pI. 151.12:2 for unholiness, within the Holy, holy as **I.**.
W-pI... 156.5:5 their reverence, for it is due to Holiness **I.**,
W-pI... 160.6:7 in, and took no alien thought to be **I.**. And
W-pI... 160.6:8 unto **I.** in recognition of what is Its Own.
W-pI... 169.5:7 Source. And like its Source **I.**, it merely is.
W-pI. 170.10:4 more fearful than the Heart of Love **I.**?
WpI...rV.in4:5 knows Its Creator, understands **I.**, is
WpI...rV.in4:5 state of union with Its Father and **I.**.
W-pI. 184.11:3 Source which unifies all things within **I.**.
W-pI. 186.14:1 because they come from Formlessness **I.**.
W-pI. 187.11:6 altar, making it a home for Innocence **I.**,
W-pI. 198.12:5 forgiveness to the Son of Sinlessness **I.**, so
W-pII. 240.1:8 fear in us, for we are each a part of Love **I.**.
W-pII. 253.2:2 *to Yours, that it may be extended to* **I.**.
W-pII..... 7.5:2 a Call from Love to Love, that It be but **I.**.
W-pII. 285.2:5 *part of You. And what can alter Holiness* **I.**?
W-pII. 299.2:8 *For Holiness* **I.** *created me, and I can know*
W-pII... 11.5:2 in the Name of its Creator, Holiness **I.**,
W-pII... 12.5:1 the altar to illusions to the shrine of Life **I.**
W-pII. 331.1:5 *How could I think that Love has left* **I.**?
W-pII... 14.1:6 *I am His holy Sinlessness* **I.**, *for in my purity*
M-1......... 2:14 it. To the Call **I.** time has no meaning.
M-28......... 5:2 have disappeared and Love looks on **I.**.

**itself** 466
*Itself*

# J

**jagged** 1
T-28....... V.5:7 but you, who put together every **j.** piece,

**jail** 1
W-pI... 200.4:5 to be a prison house or **j.** for anyone.

**jailer** 7
T-19...... I.16:5 to its source, which is its **j.** or its liberator,
T-31.... III.3:11 A **j.** does not follow orders, but enforces
W-pI... 191.1:3 the world the role of **j.** to the Son of God.
W-pI... 192.8:3 A **j.** is not free, for he is bound together
W-pI... 192.8:5 him become the world in which his **j.** lives
S-1........ III.4:7 make a **j.** of an enemy seems to be safety.
S-1........ III.5:8 He is no **j.**, but a messenger of Christ. Be

**jailers** 1
S-1........ III.6:1 made to set up **j.** and to hide from guilt.

**jealous** 1
T-10...... III.8:4 God is not **j.** of the gods you make, but

**jealously** 1
T-7......... X.7:1 prerogative, which the ego guards so **j.**, is

**jealousy** 1
W-pI........ 5.1:3 anger, hatred, **j.** or any number of forms,

**jeopardize** 2
T-16.........I.7:2 the needs of one you do not **j.** another,
T-24....... in.2:2 and obscure but it will **j.** your learning.

**jeopardized** 1
T-24.........I.6:6 must never reach them, or your goal is **j.**.

**jest** 2
T-27... VIII.8:4 not easy to perceive the **j.** when all around
T-27... VIII.8:7 cause that follows nothing and is but a **j.**.

**jests** 1
W-pI... 153.1:1 world, its twists of fortune and its bitter **j.**

**Jesus** 17
*See also* he, him, himself, his, I, me, mine, my, myself, one, our, ours, ourselves, us, we, who, whose
T-5...........I.3:4 mind be in you that was also in Christ **J.**,"
M-23 ............h **J.** HAVE A SPECIAL PLACE IN HEALING
M-23 ......... 1:4 Bible says, "Ask in the name of **J.** Christ."
M-23 ......... 1:7 What does it mean to call on **J.** Christ?
M-23 ......... 3:2 in remembering **J.** you are remembering
M-23 ......... 4:1 name of **J.** Christ as such is but a symbol.
M-23 ......... 4:5 Remembering the name of **J.** Christ is to
M-23 ......... 5:1 **J.** has led the way. Why would you not be
M-23 ......... 7:6 **J.** has come to answer yours. In him you
C-5................h **J.** – CHRIST
C-5............. 2:1 The name of ***J.*** is the name of one who was
C-5............. 2:5 **J.** remains a Savior because he saw the
C-5............. 3:1 Him– **J.** became what all of you must be.
C-5............. 6:4 **J.** is for you the bearer of Christ's single
C-6............. 1:1 **J.** is the manifestation of the *Holy Spirit*,
C-6............. 2:2 established **J.** as the leader in carrying out
C-6............. 2:4 Holy Spirit long before **J.** set it in motion.

**jewels** 2
T-17...... IV.7:5 The frame is very elaborate, all set with **j.**,
W-pI. 124.12:1 Add further **j.** to the golden frame that

**join** 183
T-1........ III.1:6 you must **j.** the great crusade to correct it;
T-1........ III.3:3 must **j.** in releasing their brothers, for this
T-4......... in.3:3 you are also free to **j.** my resurrection.
T-4...... IV.10:3 called you to **j.** with me in the Second. I
T-4...... IV.11:5 Your mind will elect to **j.** with mine, and
T-5....... II.11:3 that "yoke" means "**j.** together," and
T-5....... II.11:4 light" in this way; "Let us **j.** together, for
T-5........ IV.6:3 complete until you **j.** it and give it away.
T-6........ IV.5:1 part of you, they **j.** in the attack together.
T-6...... V.A.5:9 do **j.** together in temporary allegiance,
T-8........ IV.5:8 It is the power by which you separate or **j.**
T-8........ IV.7:8 **J.**, then, with me in praise of Him and you
T-8......... V.3:2 To **j.** with me is to restore His power to
T-8......... V.5:5 to **j.** the journey with us and cannot do so.
T-8..... VII.12:1 is to **j.** and to attack is to separate. How
T-11........ II.2:3 your willingness to **j.** them is your healing
T-11...... IV.2:5 and **j.** with your brothers in His peace.
T-11...... VI.2:1 **j.** in the resurrection or the crucifixion?
T-12...... VI.7:6 Redeemer and the redeemed **j.** in perfect
T-13...... VI.8:6 as I am calling you to **j.** with me. Each
T-13.. VI.11:10 will **j.** with theirs in power so compelling,
T-13.... VIII.9:1 in this world **j.** you to your brothers, so
T-14........ II.7:8 may **j.** Him in the holy task of bringing
T-14...... IV.5:6 Holiness that **j.** together as the truth in
T-14....... V.7:1 **J.** your own efforts to the power that
T-14....... V.8:6 attract all tortured minds to **j.** with you in
T-14....... V.9:8 Stand not outside, but **j.** with me within.
T-14..... V.11:3 If you leave him without, you **j.** him there.
T-14..... V.11:9 let us **j.** him in the holy place of peace
T-14... VII.6:11 it to you as you **j.** your perception to His.
T-14... VIII.3:6 You cannot **j.** with anything except reality
T-14........X.9:6 or more **j.** together in searching for truth,
T-15....... I.13:6 of Him, for you **j.** with Him in giving. In
T-15...... III.7:1 **j.** with me who decided for holiness for
T-15...... III.9:9 Let us **j.** in honoring you, who must
T-15.... III.11:3 Rather, **j.** with me in His, that we may
T-15...... IV.3:3 you must fill if you would **j.** with me, by
T-15...... IV.3:3 by your decision to **j.** in any plan but His.
T-15..... V.10:8 God, and all your brothers **j.** in Christ.
T-15.... VI.6:10 recognition you will **j.** with me in offering
T-15...... VI.7:2 **J.** me in the idea of peace, for in ideas
T-15.... VIII.2:4 Let us **j.** together in making the holy
T-15.... VIII.3:8 from loneliness, and **j.** you in your love.
T-15.... VIII.6:2 of disagreement, to **j.** them into one. He
T-15...... IX.7:4 it as undivided you **j.** Him wholly, in an
T-15...... XI.3:2 that you may **j.** with Him in healing, and
T-15...... XI.8:2 from joy. Let us **j.** in celebrating peace by
T-16.........I.1:1 does not mean to **j.** in suffering, for that is
T-16.........I.1:7 He does not **j.** in pain, understanding that

T-16 II.4:3 minds j. as one and share one idea equally
T-16 VI.5:2 seeking to j. each other in separate unions
T-16 VI.11:3 Yet as you cross to j. it, it will join with
T-16 VI.11:3 will j. with you and become one with you.
T-16 VII.11:4 To j. in close relationship with Him is to
T-17 III.4:8 j. with fantasies in uninterrupted "bliss."
T-17 III.9:1 still up to you to choose to j. with truth or
T-17 V.10:4 J. in His blessing, and withhold not yours
T-17 V.10:7 for it has come to j. you and your brother
T-18 I.10:9 Let us j. in Him in peace and gratitude,
T-18 I.12:7 j. in making whole what has been ravaged
T-18 I.13:5 purpose in which you j. with your brother
T-18 II.9:5 the truth of Heaven j. in the Will of God.
T-18 III.2:5 Let us then j. quickly in an instant of light
T-18 III.6:4 And they will j. with me in carrying their
T-18 III.7:7 for no two minds can j. in the desire for
T-18 VI.12:1 seems to be between you and what you j.;
T-18 VI.12:4 you j. it without reservation because you
T-18 VI.14:7 For peace will j. you there, simply because
T-18 VIII.2:3 into a body, nor can you j. Him there.
T19 IV.A.3:2 are still unwilling to let it j. you wholly.
T19 IV.A.4:6 across it, and j. you without hindrance.
T19. IV.A.16:3 as they j. in gentleness before the table of
T19. IV.A.16:4 I will j. you there, as long ago I promised
T19 IV.B.3:1 the mind to j. in holy communion and be
T19 IV.B.4:11 When you agreed to j. your brother, you
T19 IV.D.2:2 to meet Him, and to j. with Him at last.
T19 IV.D.4:6 the face of Christ and j. Him in His Father
T19 IV.D.9:6 Let us j. together in a holy instant, here in
T19 IV.D.9:7 And let us j. in faith that He Who brought
T19. IV.D.16:4 J. him in gladness, and remove all trace of
T-20 I.2:7 give. J. now with me and throw away the
T-20 II.10:1 in which we j. in glad awareness that the
T-20 V.1:5 the parts of God's Son gradually j. in time
T-21 III.9:7 hand. J. your awareness to what has been
T-21 III.11:4 and cannot meaningfully j. in any way. It
T-21 IV.3:5 you j. with what is part of you in truth.
T-21 IV.5:2 but to j. with him and to be free again, as
T-21 VII.2:6 They j. the army of the powerless, to wage
T-22 I.9:3 that anything not part of Him *can* j..
T-22 I.9:4 must have been restored to those who j.,
T-22 VI.9:8 He will j. to it all the power that God has
T-23 I.3:6 And yet illusions cannot j.. They are the
T-23 II.5:5 the Son meet only to conflict but not to j..
T-23 II.22:13 Ask, then, your Friend to j. with you, and
T-24 III.8:5 to you from him to j. His Will to save you
T-25 I.1:7 meet and j. and raise Him to His Father,
T-25 I.5:2 link that has been given you to j. the truth
T-25 I.5:3 One, as all your brothers j. as one in truth
T-25 II.11:3 Will is brought together as you j. in will,
T-25 V.3:4 and j. with him in innocence and peace.
T-26 I.1:8 or go a little farther off, but cannot j..
T-26 I.2:3 is out can never reach and j. with what is
T-26 IV.2:4 And what has been forgiven must j., for
T-26 IV.2:6 space that sin left vacant do they j. as one,
T-26 IV.5:1 and you will j. the lights of Heaven there,
T-26 IV.6:3 j. the mighty chorus to the Love of God!
T-26 VII.12:8 What is thus kept apart can never j..
T-26 IX.3:7 ground so holy Heaven leans to j. with it,
T-26 IX.4:6 their garments of insanity to j. Them on
T-27 I.1:2 and make a unity of what can never j.?
T-27 III.1:8 does it j. to the idea a something it is not,
T-28 I.11:3 they will j. in doing nothing to prevent its
T-28 III.h The Agreement to J.
T-28 III.2:6 Healing is the effect of minds that j., as
T-28 III.3:2 which are separated and which cannot j..
T-28 III.4:3 it is a wish to keep apart and not to j..
T-28 III.8:2 you and your brother, j. him there. And
T-28 IV.2:5 the dreamer from the dream, and j. in one
T-28 IV.4:2 To j. his dreams is thus to meet him not,
T-28 IV.5:1 do his, for he will j. you where you stand.
T-28 IV.7:7 comes to j. His Son the Holy Spirit joined.
T-28 IV.10:1 J. not your brother's dreams but join
T-28 IV.10:1 not your brother's dreams but j. with him
T-28 IV.10:1 and where you j. His Son the Father is.
T-28 VII.4:5 It will not j. a purpose not your own, and
T-29 I.4:4 and thereby signify a meeting place to j..
T-30 I.14:9 will j. with you and tell you what to do.
T-30 V.7:1 brothers j. in purpose in the world of fear,
T-30 V.8:3 hold was waiting but for you to j. Him.
T-31 I.8:2 to be your friend, and let it j. with you.
T-31 II.5:10 and you j. with him and in your answer is
T-31 VII.12:6 of whether you would j. with what you see
T-31 VIII.7:2 fear. For it is given you to j. with him, and
T-31 VIII.9:4 me, my brothers, hear and j. with me.
T-31 VIII.11:1 j. with me in reaching past temptation,
T-31 VIII.11:5 And as each one elects to j. with me, the
W-pI 30.2:4 Thus, we are trying to j. with what we see,
W-pI 52.5:7 Would I not rather j. the thinking of the
W-pI 73.10:6 J. with Them as They lead the way.
W-pI 78.7:3 *in which he stands, that I may j. with him.*
W-pI 78.9:2 The world and Heaven j. in thanking you,
W-pI 92.10:1 minutes twice today to j. this meeting. Let
W-pI 98.4:2 Those still uncertain, too, will j. with us,
W-pI 98.7:3 His words will j. with yours, and make
W-pI 99.9:1 shine through them to j. them to the rest.
W-pI 102.2:6 you free today to j. the happy Will of God
W-pI 109.4:5 You call to all to j. you in your rest, and
W-pI 124.7:1 We j. in this awareness as we say that we
W-pI 128.6:4 sureness and in joy to j. its holy purpose.
W-pI. 135.20:3 followers will j. their light with yours, and
W-pI 137.8:6 within a body free to j. with other minds,
WpI. rIV.in6:4 so will He j. with you who are complete as
W-pI. 152.11:1 Now do we j. in glad acknowledgment
W-pI 183.5:4 j. a brother as you sit with him in silence,
W-pI 185.3:2 For minds can only j. in truth. In dreams,
W-pI 185.6:1 it wants is peace must j. with other minds
W-pI. 185.10:4 and j. your own intent with what they
W-pI. 191.10:4 Then j. with me today. Your glory is the
W-pII. 264.2:1 My brothers, j. with me in this today.
W-pII. 264.2:3 Must we not j. in what will save the world
W-pII. 275.1:3 J. me in hearing. For the Voice for God
W-pII 9.5:5 God's Will, and j. together in its holy light
W-pII. 307.2:1 because we j. our holy will with God's, in
W-pII. 313.2:4 Brother, come and j. with me today. We
W-pII. 328.1:5 To j. with His is but to find our own. And
W-pII 14.4:3 that j. together as we bless the world. And
M-2 5:3 two who j. together for learning purposes.
M-4 IV.2:9 Thus did they j. their thoughts with Him
M-16 4:6 and in that instant j. with Him completely
M-29 8:7 *for you, And j. your efforts on behalf of God,*
C-4 7:6 his. And here They j., for here the face of
C-5 5:5 And when you j. your will with his, your
P-2 I.3:6 reconciled as one until they j. with His.
P-2 II.2:2 astonishing tendency to j. contradictory
P-2 II.5:3 if pupil and teacher j. in sharing one goal,
P-2 III.2:3 can do this alone, but when they j., the
P-2 VI.7:5 in which they meet and j. and are as one.
P-3 II.10:6 his patient be helped to j. with him there.
S-1 IV.1:3 instant, it becomes possible to j. in prayer
S-1 IV.2:4 those who j. in prayer is not the goal that
S-1 V.3:8 who comes to j. in prayer with you: *I*
S-1 V.4:5 At this gate eternity itself will j. with you.
S-3 IV.1:10 j. the song of prayer in which the healed

## joined 150

T-8 VI.9:4 Whom God has j. cannot be separated,
T-8 VI.9:4 and God has j. all His Sons with Himself.
T-11 II.6:1 your will and your Father's be wholly j..
T-14 V.5:1 We are all j. in the Atonement here, and
T-14 V.6:1 each in his own way, have j. together,
T-14 VIII.3:4 are j. in giving you the gift of oneness,
T-14 VIII.4:9 place are j. the Father and His creations,
T-15 III.5:6 make little whom God has j. with Him.
T-15 V.10:9 who are j. in Christ are in no way separate
T-15 VII.1:5 pure, everyone j. in it has everything. This
T-15 VII.9:6 The fury of those j. at the ego's altar far
T-15 VII.13:3 and you is j. in a real relationship so holy
T-15 VIII.4:6 all its parts are j. in God through Christ,
T-15 XI.6:6 Unless the universe were j. in you it would
T-15 XI.7:1 are j. without the body's interference, and
T-16 II.4:2 have reached another mind and j. with it.
T-16 III.6:5 gratitude has j. with yours and God's to
T-16 III.8:4 make Heaven what it is, being j. within it.
T-16 IV.8:7 and what you are j. with Him in giving.
T-16 IV.11:14 In Him are j. your willingness to love and
T-16 VII.7:3 Spirit will prevail, because you j. Him.
T-17 III.7:3 Whom God has j. as one, the ego cannot
T-17 V.10:2 You have j. with many in the holy instant,
T-17 V.10:2 the holy instant, and they have j. with you
T-17 V.14:7 You *are* j. in purpose, but remain still
T-18 I.2:2 Holy Spirit sees them j. and indivisible.
T-18 I.2:7 has j. and what the Holy Spirit sees as one
T-18 I.9:5 Here you are j. in God, as much together
T-18 I.10:3 so firmly j. in truth that only God is there.
T-18 I.10:7 You are not j. together in illusions, but in
T-18 I.11:8 Heaven looks with love on what is j. in it,
T-18 II.7:10 For we are j. as in one purpose, being of
T-18 II.9:7 reflects your will j. with the Will of God.
T-18 III.4:1 when you j. each other you were not alone
T-18 III.6:1 In your relationship you have j. with me
T-18 III.6:5 you, j. with me in the holy light of your
T-18 III.6:7 to me? For when you j. your brother, you
T-18 III.8:3 is j. with you in your advance to Heaven.
T-18 III.8:4 When such great lights have j. with you to
T-18 V.2:6 your little faith, j. with His understanding
T-18 VI.3:1 Minds are j.; bodies are not. Only by
T-18 VI.7:4 The minds *are* j., but you do not identify
T-18 VI.10:2 You whose hand is j. with your brother's
T-18 VI.14:7 and j. it where it is and where it led you,
T-18 VIII.5:2 alone and in no way j. to the Thought by
T-19 I.2:7 and j. the Mind in which all healing rests.
T-19 I.8:3 beyond the barrier to what is j. with you.
T-19 I.12:7 eyes, but in the sight of Him Who j. you,
T-19 I.16:5 For it remains j. to its source, which is its
T19 IV.B.5:6 together, when you have j. the limitless?
T19 IV.B.7:3 in which the Father and the Son are j.. O
T19 IV.B.8:5 our communion, where we are j. already,
T-21 in.2:4 you j. the Will of God to set him free.
T-21 I.8:5 it everything is j. in perfect continuity.
T-21 I.9:3 and j. to all as surely as all is joined in you
T-21 I.9:3 and joined to all as surely as all is j. in you
T-21 III.9:7 awareness to what has been already j..
T-21 III.11:5 with night and day, and so they must be j.
T-21 IV.3:4 who have j. their brothers have detached
T-21 IV.5:4 the ego that j. the Holy Spirit's purpose,
T-21 IV.8:2 What it would keep apart has met and j.,
T-21 V.5:4 j. the Will of God must be in you now,
T-21 VI.2:8 If you and your brother are j., how could
T-21 VI.2:10 *is* yours? If minds are j., this is impossible.
T-21 VI.5:3 reason tells you must be j. must be insane
T-21 VI.6:6 That you are j. to him is but a fact, not an
T-21 VI.8:1 and your brother are j. is your salvation;
T-21 VII.3:3 come together, but have not j. each other.
T-22 in.1:2 Rejoice whom God hath j. have come
T-22 in.4:6 as you extended when you and he j.. It
T-22 in.4:7 the body, to let you and your brother be j.
T-22 I.9:2 what is part of Him is worthy of being j..
T-22 I.9:5 What, then, has j. them? Reason will tell
T-22 I.10:7 that it is one with you who j. to let it enter
T-22 IV.5:8 Into your hand, j. with your brother's, is
T-22 IV.7:6 hold out your hand, j. with your brother's
T-22 V.3:5 separate whom He has j. as one with Him
T-22 V.4:2 quiet strength of those whom love has j.!
T-22 V.4:8 brother are not j. together by this mouse,
T-22 V.4:9 And can a mouse betray whom God has j.
T-22 VI.4:8 *because* your will and your brother's are j..
T-22 VI.5:2 is no longer seen, and reason, j. with love,
T-22 VI.15:2 And in Him is all creation j.. Would you
T-24 II.7:8 between you. What is one is j. in truth.
T-25 I.7:1 of a Oneness j. as One is meaningless. It is
T-25 II.6:2 Yet its frame is j. to its Creator, One with
T-25 IV.1:1 Minds that are j. and recognize they are,
T-26 I.2:5 j. each one would lose its own identity,
T-26 IV.5:5 the universe has j. with but a single voice.
T-26 VII.9:2 It is the wish that you be j. with him, and
T-26 IX.1:2 your own salvation, with his freedom j.!
T-26 X.3:1 so firmly j. that where one is perceived
T-27 VI.2:4 These witnesses are j. by many more.
T-27 VII.4:2 those within the world are j. in sharing.
T-27 VIII.9:8 laughter and your brother's j. with His.
T-28 III.3:1 does nothing just *because* the minds are j.,
T-28 III.3:5 Thus are you j. in sickness, to preserve the
T-28 III.5:4 gap between the waves when they have j.,
T-28 III.5:5 j. to close the little gap between them,
T-28 IV.3:6 Your mind and his are j. in brotherhood.

T-28......IV.3:7 a little gap, where yours have **j.** with his.
T-28......IV.7:2 not, for what is **j.** in Him is always one.
T-28......IV.7:7 comes to join His Son the Holy Spirit **j.**.
T-28......IV.9:3 are **j.** because what is in one is in them all.
T-28.....VII.2:9 not. What is unseparated must be **j.**. And
T-28...VII.2:10 joined. And what is **j.** cannot be separate.
T-29....... V.5:4 in which your hands are **j.** in innocence.
T-30...... I.17:5 two are **j.** before there can be a decision.
T-30....... II.3:5 has **j.** with God Himself in all creation's
T-30.... III.11:4 Son **j.** in creation which can have no end.
T-30....... V.3:6 Yet is he glad to wait till every hand is **j.**,
T-30....... V.7:4 **j.** their hands it was Christ's hand they
T-30..... V.11:1 forever lies in those whose hands are **j.**.
T-30..... V.11:2 Until they **j.**, they thought He was their
T-30..... V.11:3 But when they **j.** and shared a purpose,
T-30.....VII.7:7 And through His use of symbols are we **j.**,
T-31... VIII.4:5 are **j.** in all the power of the Will of God.
W-pI.....18.1:2 also emphasizes the idea that minds are **j.**
W-pI.....19.2:1 emphasizing the fact that minds are **j.**.
W-pI.....45.8:2 is your mind **j.** with the Mind of God.
W-pI...73.10:4 **j.** with the power of God and united with
W-pI.....75.7:7 It is His Will, and you have **j.** with Him.
W-pI.....85.1:5 light and vision must be **j.** for me to see.
W-pI...154.3:3 it. God has **j.** His Son in this, and thus His
W-pI...154.4:4 in which its will and that of God are **j.**.
W-pI...157.4:2 And having **j.** your will with His this day,
W-pI...158.5:5 Father's Will and His are **j.** in knowledge.
W-pI...160.8:5 Whom God has **j.** remain forever one, at
W-pI...182.4:6 wherein are earth and Heaven **j.** as one.
W-pI.187.10:3 Self Whose innocence has **j.** us all as one,
W-pI...195.4:3 can only be sincere if it be **j.** to love. We
W-pI...197.2:4 freedom and salvation are perceived as **j.**,
W-pII..221.2:5 Our minds are **j.**. We wait with one intent
W-pII......3.5:1 the world has **j.** our changed perception.
W-pII..313.2:5 We save the world when we have **j.**. For in
W-pII.....336.h lets me know that minds are **j.**.
W-pII.....14.2:3 And thus you **j.** with me, so what I am are
W-pII..353.1:2 *is mine alone, for He and I have* **j.** *in purpose.*
M-12..........1:6 his thoughts are **j.** with God's forever and
M-12..........2:6 Yet being **j.** in one purpose, and one they
M-26..........1:6 as yet, but they have **j.** with others. This is
C-1.............2:2 Nor do their minds seem to be **j.**. In this
C-4.............6:8 single remedy **j.** in one healing brightness
C-4.............8:2 His, for they are **j.** here in this holy place.
C-6.............4:3 God and also for you, being **j.** with Both.
C-6.............5:4 But **j.** with you he is the shining Savior of
P-2......... II.6:5 If any two are **j.**, He must be there. It does
P-2......... V.4:4 Where two have **j.** for healing, God is
P-2......... V.6:1 For two have **j.**. And now God's promises
P-3......... II.8:1 therapist has realized that minds are **j.**, he

## joining 50

T-5...........I.3:6 as I thought, **j.** with me in Christ thinking.
T-5........IV.1:2 **J.** the Atonement is the way out of fear.
T-6....... II.13:5 **j.** our minds in this light we proclaim the
T-8....... V.2:12 **j.** your mind with mine you are signifying
T-8.......VII.2:5 as a means of **j.** minds and uniting them
T-8........IX.3:6 Sleep is withdrawing; waking is **j.**.
T-8........IX.3:7 Dreams are illusions of **j.**, because they
T-8........IX.3:7 ego's distorted notions about what **j.** is.
T-10.......IV.7:3 his mind, a call that is strengthened by **j.**.
T-13......XI.8:1 placed within you, **j.** your mind with His,
T-14.....VII.4:6 Their **j.** thus becomes the source of fear,
T-14.....VII.7:1 **J.** with Him in seeing is the way in which
T-14....... X.9:2 **j.** them is incoherent and utterly chaotic.
T-16....... II.4:4 made this **j.** as the Holy Spirit bids you,
T-16....... V.6:1 ego device for **j.** hell and Heaven, and
T-17.....VII.3:1 is a relationship, being the **j.** of thoughts.
T-18.......III.7:7 the desire for love without love's **j.** them.
T-18....... V.6:4 The power of **j.** its blessing lies in the fact
T-18.....VI.11:4 and a **j.** of yourself and something else in
T-18... VIII.6:4 it, preventing it from **j.** with the rest, and
T-19.........I.2:5 It is this **j.** Him in a united purpose that
T19... IV.A.1:6 who calls, and bring him rest by **j.** you.
T-20.... III.10:2 there is only holiness and **j.** without limit.
T-20....... V.1:5 each **j.** is the end of time brought nearer.
T-20....... V.1:6 miracle of **j.** is a mighty herald of eternity.
T-21.... III.10:6 believes. Thus is the **j.** of mind and body
T-22.......in.3:3 he would extend it by **j.** with another,
T-23.........I.3:8 Their **j.** lies in nothingness; two are as
T-26.........I.2:2 of complete disunity and total lack of **j.**.
T-26... VIII.4:4 But present **j.** is your dread. Who can feel
T-28...... III.5:3 the gap, and as the waves in **j.** cover it.
T-28.........IV.h The Greater **J.**
W-pI.....49.3:3 so we are **j.** our will with the Will of God.
W-pI.....69.8:4 that you are at last **j.** your will to God's.
W-pI...102.5:4 be sure that you are **j.** with God's Will in
W-pI.134.14:1 that the time of **j.** be no more delayed. For
W-pI...137.1:3 from others, and a shutting off of **j.**. It
W-pI...154.4:1 It is this **j.**, through the Voice for God, of
W-pI.154.10:1 **j.** that we undertake to recognize today.
W-pI.154.10:3 **j.** in one Voice the getting and the giving
W-pI...158.6:1 the **j.** of the world of doubt and shadows
M-12..........2:8 Their minds are one; their **j.** is complete.
M-26........1:10 But in their **j.** is the power of God.
C-3.............8:4 Creator; the **j.** of the Father and the Son,
C-3.............8:4 stands behind all **j.** but beyond them all.
P-2.......VII.2:3 What is prayer except the **j.** of minds in a
P-2.......VII.3:6 capable of **j.** with the patient in a holy
P-2.......VII.8:1 what the **j.** of two brothers really means.
P-3...........I.3:9 The **j.** is in the hands of the Holy Spirit. It
S-1........ IV.3:1 Even the **j.**, then, is not enough, if those

## joins 28

T-1........ IV.2:6 miracle **j.** in the Atonement by placing
T-10...... III.2:6 Link with all His children **j.** them together
T-14. VIII.4:10 There is one link that **j.** Them all together,
T-14... VIII.5:1 The link with which the Father **j.** Himself
T-14..... X.10:5 it not unless he **j.** with you in seeking it. If
T-14.... XI.11:8 creation, and all creation **j.** in willing this.
T-15...... XI.8:5 He **j.** us in the celebration of His Son's
T-16.........I.2:2 These it selects out, and **j.** with. And it
T-16.........I.2:3 And it never **j.** except to strengthen itself.
T-18......IV.1:9 He **j.** with you to make the holy instant far
T-19.......I.10:4 It is His Love that **j.** you and your brother,
T-22.... VI.15:1 light that **j.** you and your brother shines
T-22.... VI.15:1 universe, and because it **j.** you and him,
T-23.........I.3:5 The ego **j.** with an illusion of yourself you
T-23.........I.3:9 The ego **j.** with nothing, being nothing.
T-24...VII.11:6 It is this that **j.** them to their like, and
T-25....... II.9:5 when any part of Him **j.** in His praise, to
T-26...... IV.5:4 And each one **j.** the singing at the altar
T-30....... II.1:6 He **j.** with *you*. He did not set His Kingdom
T-30....... II.2:9 He **j.** with you in willing you be free. And
W-pI...96.11:5 seeking Him Who **j.** your mind and Self,
W-pI......99.4:1 What **j.** the separated mind and thoughts
W-pI...125.9:4 Will of God the Son **j.** in his Father's Will,
W-pI.134.13:4 yet it **j.** your mind with the reality in you.
WpI. rIV.in6:4 And as His Own completion **j.** with Him,
W-pI...197.4:2 is a part that **j.** with yours in thanking you
W-pII..310.2:2 And all the world **j.** with us in our song of
S-1......... V.2:6 where it gladly **j.** with every Son of God,

## joint 19

T-3......... II.1:3 everything and nothing as **j.** possibilities.
T-5....... II.12:4 of our **j.** motivation is beyond belief, but
T-5........ IV.7:4 **j.** will of the Sonship is the only creator
T-6...........I.5:1 be demonstrated only through **j.** decision.
T-6.........I.18:2 and must be used for their **j.** salvation.
T-8...........I.6:3 **j.** curriculum presents an impossible
T-8........ III.3:2 unity together by extending Their **j.** Will.
T-8........IV.5:1 Healing reflects our **j.** will. This is
T-8......IV.5:11 are possible through our **j.** decision, but
T-8........ VI.1:1 We are the **j.** will of the Sonship, whose
T-9...........I.6:2 because that, and only that is Your **j.** Will.
T-9....... VII.2:1 then, that in this **j.** will you are all united,
T-11..... V.12:4 cannot be found apart from Your **j.** Will.
T-14...... VI.1:8 but value always lies in **j.** appreciation.
T-14.....VII.4:4 their **j.** acceptance becomes impossible.
T-22...... VI.4:6 Only in your **j.** will does healing lie. For
T-28...... III.2:2 And thus it is their **j.** decision to be sick. If
T-31..... II.11:1 is your **j.** inheritance remembered and
W-pII.....14.3:2 through our **j.** forgiveness is redeemed.

## jointly 1

T-31..... VII.4:2 can be interchanged but never **j.** held.

## joke 1

T-27....VIII.6:5 It is a **j.** to think that time can come to

## journey 94

T-4.........in.1:2 not suggest that you set him back on his **j.**
T-4.........in.3:1 **j.** to the cross should be the last "useless
T-4.........in.3:1 to the cross should be the last "useless **j.**."
T-4.........in.3:3 can accept it as your own last useless **j.**,
T-4.......in.3:11 We have another **j.** to undertake, and if
T-5........ III.4:6 an ego-alien **j.** with the ego as guide. This
T-6...........I.2:6 the last useless **j.** the Sonship need take,
T-6......V.A.6:3 way, you place yourself in charge of the **j.**,
T-8...............h THE **J.** BACK
T-8......... V.5:4 is simply the **j.** back to God Who is our
T-8......... V.5:5 ego has attempted to join the **j.** with us
T-8......... V.5:8 **j.** you have chosen me as your companion
T-8......... V.6:4 the ego the power to interfere with the **j.**.
T-8......... V.6:5 because the **j.** is the way to what is true.
T-8........ VI.1:2 begin the **j.** back by setting out together,
T-8........ VI.9:6 **j.** to God is merely the reawakening of the
T-8........ VI.9:7 It is a **j.** without distance to a goal that has
T-11.......in.4:6 You will not take this **j.** alone. I will lead
T-11........II.5:7 Whatever **j.** you choose to take, He will go
T-11...... III.4:5 But the dark **j.** is not the way of God's Son
T-11...... III.5:4 you but undertake a **j.** that is not real. The
T-12........II.5:5 the end of strife and this is the **j.** to peace.
T-12........II.7:7 that mean that peace goes with *us* on the **j.**
T-12...... IV.2:2 guidance leads you to a **j.** which must end
T-12...... IV.2:6 what the **j.** is on which the ego sets you.
T-12...... IV.4:1 the ego must set you on a **j.** which cannot
T-12...... IV.4:6 His is the **j.** to accomplishment, and the
T-12...... IV.5:1 *will* undertake a **j.** because you are not at
T-13.........I.3:7 **j.** will seem long and cruel and senseless,
T-13.........I.4:1 **j.** the Son of God has set himself is useless
T-13.........I.4:1 but the **j.** on which his Father sets him is
T-13.........I.7:1 you, you will realize that there is no **j.**, but
T-13..... VII.6:4 and learned of Him the joyful **j.** home.
T-13... VII.13:4 guidance you will travel light and **j.** lightly
T-13... VII.14:1 useless **j.** that would lead away from light,
T-13... VII.15:3 undertake a quiet **j.** to the peace of God,
T-14...... VI.1:1 The **j.** that we undertake together is the
T-14..... X.10:7 The lonely **j.** fails because it has excluded
T-16.... IV.11:2 For such the **j.** seems to be. Love calls, but
T-16.... IV.12:3 **j.** that seemed endless is almost complete,
T-16.... IV.12:6 We will take the last useless **j.** away from
T-18.........I.8:3 and retraces with you your mad **j.** outside
T-18...... III.3:3 not know because the **j.** into darkness has
T-18...... III.8:5 meaningless **j.** that you undertook apart,
T-18..VIII.13:1 You have reached the end of an ancient **j.**
T-18...... IX.9:6 ready for the final step in the **j.** inward.
T-19.... III.11:4 is the rest that waits for all, after the **j.**.
T19....IV.A.6:9 Such was the **j.**; such its ending. And in
T19. IV.D.10:5 A **j.** without a purpose is still meaningless
T19. IV.D.19:3 without which is the **j.** meaningless. Here
T19. IV.D.19:5 the reason for the **j.** from its beginning.
T19. IV.D.21:1 You came this far because the **j.** was your
T19. IV.D.21:4 world, and the long **j.** through this world,
T-20.........I.2:2 intervene between the **j.** and its purpose;
T-20.........I.3:1 whole **j.** the Son of God has undertaken.
T-22...... IV.1:8 no part of the **j.** that seems more hopeless
T-22...... IV.4:3 long and lonely **j.** where you walked alone
T-24.........I.6:2 attack him if you realized you **j.** with him,
T-24..... V.7:10 hold. There is no **j.** but to walk with Him.
T-24...... VI.8:3 both may end a **j.** that has never begun,
T-26..... V.14:4 repeat again a **j.** that was over long ago.
T-31......II.11:6 these are but appearances of what the **j.** is
T-31.... IV.9:4 to separate the **j.** from the purpose it
T-31.... IV.10:5 A **j.** from yourself does not exist. How
T-31..VIII.12:3 The **j.** closes, ending at the place where it
W-pI. 127.12:2 think of one who makes the **j.** with you,
W-pI. 155.11:4 us. This is our final **j.**, which we make for
W-pI...157.8:2 dreamed for you this **j.** which you make
W-pI...158.3:6 We but undertake a **j.** that is over. Yet it
W-pI...158.4:5 see the **j.** from the point at which it ended

W-pI...158.6:3 reconciled, for here the j. ends.
W-pI...169.8:3 before that you but make a j. that is done.
WpI...rV.in6:1 I take the j. with you. For I share your
WpI...rV.in7:1 the place at which the j. ends and is forgot
WpI...rV.in7:5 lead you back to where the j. was begun,
Wi181-200 3:1 And so we start our j. beyond words by
W-pI.182.12:8 open, and the j. has an end in sight at last.
W-pI...194.1:6 goal! How short the j. still to be pursued!
W-pII .225.2:5 steps which end a j. that was not begun.
W-pII .249.1:7 And so the j. which the Son of God began
M-19 .........2:6 that rise to meet one as the j. continues,
M-23 .......5:11 again, when he has made the j. for you?
M-24 .......5:10 all there is to learn. His j. has begun.
C-3.............6:3 Is this a j.? No, not in truth, for truth goes
C-4.............7:7 memory has come at last there is no j., no
C-ep...........1:1 not once this j. is begun the end is certain.
C-ep...........2:4 We *have* begun the j.. Long ago the end
C-ep...........3:2 We only start again an ancient j. long ago
C-ep...........3:5 has the certainty the j. lacked till now.
P-3......... II.8:4 way. A goal marks the end of a j., not the
P-3......... II.8:5 start of the beginning stage of the first j..
P-3......... II.8:8 The j. is not long except in dreams.
S-1......... V.3:7 more to learn before the j. is complete.
S-3......... II.4:4 peace, the j. over and the lessons learned.

## journey's 12

T-13...VII.13:4 lightly, for His sight is ever on the j. end,
T19... IV.A.6:1 gladness in acknowledgment of the j. end.
T19. IV.D.10:7 Here, with the j. end before you, you *see* its
T19. IV.D.19:3 This is the j. purpose, without which is
T-22.......I.3:11 of misery, waiting to tell you, at the j. end,
T-23..........I.4:2 The j. end is at the place of peace. Would
T-26...... III.3:1 This is the j. end. We have referred to it
T-31....... II.9:5 For so do you forget the j. goal, which is
W-pI. 155.10:1 Yet at the j. ending there will be no gap,
W-pI...165.6:1 all doubting past, the j. end made certain,
WpI...rV.in5:1 this that waits to meet us at the j. ending.
W-pII ....in.6:4 ahead, and fix our eyes upon the j. end.

## journeys 6

T-4.........in.2:5 Do not embark on useless j., because they
T-31....IV.11:1 forget all senseless j. and all goal-less aims
W-pI. 155.11:1 holy Son of God will make no j.. There
W-pI...200.8:3 answer to conflicting goals, to senseless j.,
W-pII .298.1:4 And I draw near the end of senseless j.,
W-pII .325.1:6 where he can rest a while before he j. on,

## joy 397

T-1..........IV.1:5 but will also understand peace and j..
T-2..........I.3:10 you for your j. in creating the perfect.
T-4.........I.10:1 The ego is afraid of the spirit's j., because
T-4........VI.3:3 that one choice brings peace and j. while
T-4........VI.5:6 misery with the ego and j. with the spirit.
T-4.......VII.5:1 who want to share it to increase their j..
T-4.......VII.5:4 Divine Abstraction takes j. in sharing.
T-4.......VII.6:4 His j. is not complete because yours is
T-4.......VII.7:1 but He cannot share His j. with you until
T-4.......VII.8:5 there is great j. throughout the Kingdom.
T-4.......VII.8:6 to this j. with its individual willingness to
T-4.......VII.8:7 we are all united in the j. of the Kingdom.
T-5.........in.1:4 light that belongs to you is the light of j..
T-5.........in.1:6 J. calls forth an integrated willingness to
T-5.........in.1:7 thus deprive others of the j. of responding
T-5.........in.2:3 There is no difference between love and j..
T-5.........in.3:4 to the Father for radiating His j. upon it.
T-5.........in.3:5 are worthy channels of His beautiful j.,
T-5...........I.1:3 revelation is an experience of pure j.. If
T-5...........I.5:7 creations and keep them in the light of j..
T-5......... II.2:1 The Holy Spirit is the spirit of j.. He is the
T-5......... II.3:2 God placed in the mind the Call to j.. This
T-5.... III.11:10 by sharing it to increase His j. in you.
T-5......... V.2:3 giving rise to guilt, and must give rise to j.
T-5......... V.4:7 This engenders j., not guilt, because it is
T-5........ VI.2:7 will simultaneously exchange guilt for j.,
T-5.......VII.1:3 for your safety and j. better than He can?
T-6......... II.6:1 How else can you find j. in a joyless place
T-6 ........ V.1:5 so that He cannot impart His j. and know
T-6 ........ V.1:6 Giving His j. is an ongoing process, not in
T-6 ........ V.3:2 but what you need to learn to have j..
T-6 ... V.C.1:10 and so the one mood He engenders is j..
T-6 ... V.C.1:11 rejecting everything that does not foster j.
T-7 ..........I.5:3 Only j. increases forever, since joy and
T-7 ..........I.5:3 since j. and eternity are inseparable. God
T-7 ..........I.5:6 The eternal are in peace and j. forever.
T-7 ..........I.6:2 that your j. may be complete because the
T-7 ...... V.9:10 The whole glory and perfect j. that *is* the
T-7 ..... VI.12:4 the Kingdom, and its extension is your j..
T-7 ..... VI.13:1 and are therefore depriving yourself of j..
T-7 ..... VI.13:7 extending the j. in which it was created,
T-7 ....... IX.3:5 It therefore blocks your j., so that you
T-7 ....... IX.4:2 You do not know your j. because you do
T-7 ....... IX.6:9 is so intense that It creates in perfect j.,
T-7 ........... X.h The Confusion of Pain and J.
T-7 .........X.3:6 you will be confused about j. and pain.
T-7 .........X.7:3 how to distinguish between pain and j.,
T-7 .........X.8:3 do not accept His Will, you are denying j..
T-7 .........X.8:4 miracle is therefore a lesson in what j. is.
T-7 .........X.8:5 in sharing it is a lesson in love, which *is* j..
T-7 .........X.8:6 the difference between pain and j..
T-7 ....... XI.1:1 guide you truly, because your j. is His.
T-7 ....... XI.1:2 speaks for the Kingdom of God, which *is* j..
T-7 ....... XI.3:5 Does it teach him that this giving is his j.,
T-8 .........II.5:1 you the difference between pain and j..
T-8 .........II.6:5 you. This is freedom and this is j.. Deny
T-8 ....... III.1:7 perfectly, because that is His j. and yours.
T-8 ....... III.2:1 only j. and peace that can be fully known,
T-8 ....... III.5:9 He will respond either with pain or with j.
T-8 ....... IV.1:1 Will for you is complete peace and j.,
T-8 ....... IV.5:8 join, and experience pain or j. accordingly
T-8 ....... V.3:7 to our j. in uniting with His Will for us.
T-8 ....... VI.3:2 can find j. in anything except the eternal;
T-8 ....... VI.3:3 eternal, and in this and this only is their j.
T-8 ....... VI.4:3 home the father welcomed him with j.,
T-8 ....... VI.5:5 of God Himself take j. in what is not real?
T-8 ....... VI.5:9 give anything else, and expect j. in return
T-8 ..... VI.5:10 And what else but j. would you want? You
T-8 ....... VI.6:3 creation from you because His j. is in it.
T-8 ....... VI.6:4 it. You cannot find j. except as God does.
T-8 ....... VI.6:5 His j. lay in creating you, and He extends
T-8 ....... VI.8:9 thus increase the j. of the Holy Trinity.
T-8 ...... VII.8:5 depressing, because it is a curriculum of j.
T-8 .... VII.13:1 The opposite of j. is depression. When
T-8 .... VII.13:2 promotes depression instead of j., you
T-8 .... VII.14:5 and to believe that j. could possibly result
T-8 .... VII.15:1 J. is unified purpose, and unified purpose
T-9 .........II.6:1 than you can find j. for yourself alone.
T-9 ....... VI.1:4 inspire j. and others react to you with joy,
T-9 ....... VI.1:4 inspire joy and others react to you with j.,
T-9 ....... VI.1:4 you are not experiencing j. yourself there
T-9 ....... VI.1:5 it. If it is in you and can produce j., and if
T-9 ....... VI.1:5 if you see that it does produce j. in others,
T-9 ....... VI.2:1 that the Holy Spirit does not produce j.
T-9 ....... VI.2:1 you do not consistently arouse j. in others
T-9 ....... VI.2:3 you will not always give rise to j., and so
T-9 ...... VII.1:7 return, but because delay of j. is needless.
T-9 ..... VIII.8:3 you lies in the j. you bring to its witnesses,
T-9 ..... VIII.8:5 behold what He created because it is His j.
T-10 ....... II.2:2 lie j. and peace and the glory of creation.
T-10 ...... V.1:2 J. is never permitted, for depression is the
T-10 ...... V.2:4 Do not attribute your denial of j. to them,
T-10 ...... V.2:4 spark in them that would bring j. to you.
T-10 ...... V.4:3 This was his alternative to j., because he
T-10 ... V.11:5 deny yourself the j. that was created for
T-11 ......in.4:8 Will you not answer the call of love with j.
T-11 ........I.6:7 because only this can bring you the j. that
T-11 ..... III.3:1 wills for you, your j. would be complete!
T-11 ..... III.3:4 your j. you will create beauty in His Name
T-11 ..... III.3:4 j. could no more be contained than His.
T-11 ..... III.3:5 filled with j. that it will leap into Heaven,
T-11 ..... VI.6:1 gladly, because it is the symbol of j.. Its
T-12 ..... IV.4:4 promise, and one that will lead to j.. For
T-13 ........I.4:1 his Father sets him is one of release and j..
T-13 .......II.9:6 great j. in Heaven on your homecoming,
T-13 .......II.9:6 homecoming, and the j. will be yours. For
T-13 ..... III.9:1 magnitude of your Father in peace and j..
T-13 ... VI.10:5 and in their j. they shine with holy thanks
T-13 ... VI.10:6 And this they offer you who gave them j..
T-13 ... VI.10:7 joy. They are your guides to j., for having
T-13 ... VI.11:8 and spreads across this world in quiet j..
T-13 .... VII.9:8 Therefore the call of j. is in it, and your
T-13 VII.10:13 it bids you get, leaving you no j. in them.
T-13 .. VII.15:1 Then follow Him in j., with faith that He
T-13 .. VII.17:5 j. cannot establish its eternal reign where
T-13 ..... IX.6:9 release from guilt great is the j. in Heaven,
T-13 ..... XI.2:5 Gladness and j. belong to God for your
T-14 ..... III.5:1 have chosen guiltlessness, freedom and j..
T-14 ..... III.6:6 j. of learning that darkness has no power
T-14 ..... III.6:7 It is His j. to teach it, as it will be yours.
T-14 ..... IV.5:6 the j. of living with your God and Father,
T-14 .......V.3:1 blessing Father, j. was created for you.
T-14 .......V.8:4 J. is its unifying attribute, with no one left
T-14 ..... IX.4:4 fear of death will be replaced with j. of life
T-15 ........I.8:7 and immortality and j. are now.
T-15 .......II.2:4 j. it is to teach God's holy Son his holiness
T-15 .......II.2:5 j. is not contained in time. His teaching is
T-15 .......II.2:6 teaching is for you because His j. is yours.
T-15 ..... III.5:3 this, and invites sorrow or j. accordingly.
T-15 ..... XI.8:1 Let no despair darken the j. of Christmas,
T-15 ..... XI.8:1 time of Christ is meaningless apart from j.
T-15 ... XI.10:8 So will the year begin in j. and freedom.
T-16 ........II.7:1 This is a year of j., in which your listening
T-16 ........II.7:5 the results have brought you j.. Would
T-16 ..... III.1:7 has disappeared to be replaced by j..
T-16 ..... III.7:3 for it, the j. of teaching will yet be yours.
T-16 ..... III.7:4 For the j. of teaching is in the learner,
T-16 ... IV.12:2 and created by His j. in union with you.
T-16 ... VI.11:5 The j. of Heaven, which has no limit, is
T-17 .......II.1:5 that made your heart sing with j. has ever
T-17 ... IV.10:5 j. of His eternal Spirit are marshalled to
T-18 .......I.12:4 loveliness and j. the other holds within it.
T-18 .......II.6:7 guilt, but as a source of j. and freedom. It
T-18 .......V.5:5 which He can spread j. to thousands on
T-18 ... VI.13:6 the sudden experience of peace and j.,
T-18 ... VIII.8:7 And realize the life and j. that love would
T19 . IV.B.10:4 peace nor turmoil; neither j. nor pain. It is
T19 . IV.B.14:9 The Holy Spirit tells you this with j.. The
T19 .. IV.D.2:2 with j. because He is in His Father's Love,
T19 IV.D.20:4 give j. because they have been healed of
T-20 ........I.4:6 The time of Easter is a time of j., and not
T-20 .......II.9:3 that looks upon the lilies and brings you j.
T-20 ..... III.8:6 meet your brother with j. to bless the Son
T-20 ..... III.9:1 leap up in j. the instant they are made free
T-20 .... VII.1:1 holy relationship can bring you only j..
T-20 ... VIII.2:3 be free of misery, and learn again of j.?
T-20 ... VIII.3:3 may rise before your vision and give you j.
T-20 . VIII.10:5 are looked on happily, and heard with j..
T-21 ......in.2:7 shows you how much j. you have allowed
T-21 ......in.2:8 the power to give it j. must lie within you.
T-21 ........I.3:5 learned will bring to you the j. it promises
T-21 .......II.1:2 your whole relationship transformed to j.;
T-21 .. VII.13:3 J. cannot be perceived except through
T-21 ... VIII.2:1 The constancy of j. is a condition quite
T-22 .......II.1:6 covered, and hidden from the j. of truth.
T-22 .......II.2:1 opposite of illusions because it offers j..
T-22 .......II.2:2 else but j. could be the opposite of misery
T-22 .......II.2:5 The search for j. in misery is senseless, for
T-22 .......II.2:5 for how could j. be found in misery? All
T-22 .......II.2:6 as different, and define the difference as j.
T-22 .......II.3:3 in reason's eyes can be confused with j..
T-22 .......II.3:4 J. is eternal. You can be sure indeed that
T-22 .......II.3:6 J. does not turn to sorrow, for the eternal
T-22 .......II.3:7 But sorrow can be turned to j., for time
T-22 .....II.6:10 lies only on one side and j. upon the other
T-22 .......II.7:7 to choose between the j. of Heaven and
T-22 .....II.10:4 You would condemn His j. to misery, and
T-22 ...II.12:10 as well? No misery is here, but only j..
T-22 ... VI.14:8 J. is unlimited, because each shining
T-24 .......II.2:6 pursuit will bring you j.. But the pursuit
T-24 .....II.14:2 fail to bring you peace and j. of any kind?
T-24 ..... III.7:2 Freedom and peace and j. stand there,
T-24 .......V.1:4 Specialness, too, takes j. in what it sees,
T-24 .......V.1:5 seek for is a source of j. as you conceive it.
T-24 .......V.4:7 it saw in you, and looks on still with j..
T-24 .......V.4:8 is it j. to look upon decay and madness,

| | |
|---|---|
| T-24.......V.7:5 | to look upon with Him and share His j.. |
| T-24.VII.10:10 | For as His Son's creation gave Him j. and |
| T-25.......II.9:5 | And so His j. is made complete when any |
| T-25.......II.9:5 | of Him joins in His praise, to share His j.. |
| T-25.......II.9:8 | shine on you who would complete His j., |
| T-25......III.6:8 | as just another chance to bring him j.. |
| T-25......IV.1:3 | Their j. is in the innocence they see. And |
| T-25......IV.1:5 | for what will bring him j. as he defines it. |
| T-25......IV.2:2 | that suffering and sin will bring you j., so |
| T-25......IV.2:5 | to be the bringers of rejoicing and of j.. |
| T-25......IV.2:7 | The Son of God creates to bring him j., |
| T-25......IV.2:7 | creation, that his j. might be increased, |
| T-25.......V.4:8 | depriving him of all the j. he would have |
| T-25.......V.5:5 | And how great will be your j., when he is |
| T-25.....VII.5:2 | would lead the Son of God to sanity and j. |
| T-25...VII.10:4 | from deepest mourning into perfect j.. |
| T-25... VIII.9:7 | you accept brings j. to Him as well as you. |
| T-26......IV.2:2 | and every bird sings of the j. of Heaven. |
| T-26......IV.3:7 | come, to be rekindled and increased in j.. |
| T-26......IV.6:3 | And how great will be the j. in Heaven |
| T-26.....VII.8:5 | serves to bring the j. this world denies to |
| T-26......IX.4:5 | Heaven's j. has been increased because |
| T-27......IV.4:6 | Which ones establish peace and offer j.? |
| T-27.....VII.9:4 | of evil or a happy wakening and j. of life. |
| T-27...VII.13:5 | God willed he waken gently and with j., |
| T-28....IV.10:6 | the belief that there is j. in separation, |
| T-28......VI.1:4 | not seek to make of pain a j. and look for |
| T-29.......II.5:4 | And nowhere else His gifts of peace and j. |
| T-29......IV.3:4 | The thin disguise of pleasure and of j. in |
| T-29......IV.5:7 | dreams of sadness thus are turned to j.. |
| T-29.......V.3:5 | to peace eternal and to endless j.. |
| T-29......IX.7:6 | has changed into a dream where all is j., |
| T-30......I.17:2 | the j. they asked for will be wholly shared. |
| T-30......IV.4:7 | Their dancing never brought you j.. But |
| T-30.......V.9:9 | J. has no cost. It is your sacred right, and |
| T-31.........I.7:8 | There is no j. that you can seek for here |
| T-31......I.11:5 | call beyond it that appeals for peace and j. |
| T-31......I.11:6 | all the world will give you j. and peace. |
| T-31... VIII.3:4 | from you whom God created altar unto j.. |
| W-pI.....20.2:6 | cannot distinguish between j. and sorrow, |
| W-pI.....41.4:2 | of all j. goes with you wherever you go. |
| W-pI.....55.3:4 | will see a world of peace and safety and j.. |
| W-pI.....58.2:3 | in its light shares in the j. it brings to me. |
| W-pI.....58.2:4 | There is nothing that is apart from this j., |
| W-pI.....59.1:5 | can I suffer when love and j. surround me |
| W-pI.....71.8:6 | will succeed. It will lead to release and j.. |
| W-pI.....74.5:4 | deep sense of j. and an increased alertness |
| W-pI.....74.6:1 | J. characterizes peace. By this experience |
| W-pI...76.10:5 | About the endless j. He offers you. About |
| W-pI.....82.3:4 | will not experience the j. that God intends |
| W-pI........93.h | Light and j. and peace abide in me. |
| W-pI.....93.4:1 | that light and j. and peace abide in you? |
| W-pI.....93.6:7 | and light and j. and peace abide in you. |
| W-pI.....93.7:7 | created. Light and j. and peace abide in |
| W-pI.....93.8:2 | *Light and j. and peace abide in me. My* |
| W-pI.....93.9:8 | And light and j. and peace abide in you |
| W-pI...93.10:4 | hour: *Light and j. and peace abide in me. My* |
| W-pI...93.11:3 | *Light and j. and peace abide in you. Your* |
| W-pI...95.12:1 | and secure in light and j. and peace. You |
| W-pI.....96.4:2 | the spirit is at peace and filled with j.. Its |
| W-pI...96.11:4 | j. your Self experiences It will save for you |
| W-pI.....97.2:2 | all your Father's Love and peace and j.. |
| W-pI.....98.6:1 | kind, and j. the world does not contain. |
| W-pI.....98.9:4 | will respond with all His faith and j. and |
| W-pI...100.2:5 | Your j. must be complete to let His plan |
| W-pI...100.3:2 | Without your j., His joy is incomplete. |
| W-pI...100.3:2 | Without your joy, His j. is incomplete. |
| W-pI...100.4:2 | so your j. on earth calls to all minds to let |
| W-pI...100.4:3 | and their j. heals sorrow and despair. |
| W-pI...100.6:1 | to understand j. is our function here. If |
| W-pI...100.6:2 | and all the world is thus deprived of j., |
| W-pI...100.6:3 | and wills no sorrow rises to abate his j.; |
| W-pI...100.8:1 | Now let us try to find that j. that proves |
| W-pI...101.6:2 | J. is just, and pain is but the sign you have |
| W-pI...101.6:8 | and then attempt again to find the j. these |
| W-pI...103.1:5 | And therefore j. is everywhere as well. Yet |
| W-pI...103.1:6 | sin can enter, bringing pain instead of j.. |
| W-pI...103.2:2 | God, forgetting being Love, He must be j.. |
| W-pI...103.2:5 | *To fear Him is to be afraid of j..* Begin your |
| W-pI...103.3:2 | and j. becomes what you expect to take |
| W-pI...104.1:1 | that j. and peace are not but idle dreams. |
| W-pI...104.3:3 | *truth, And j. and peace are my inheritance.* |
| W-pI...104.4:2 | His gifts of peace and j. are welcome, and |
| W-pI...104.5:1 | and that j. and peace belong to us as His |
| W-pI...104.5:5 | *God's gifts of j. and peace are all I want.* |
| W-pI......105.h | God's peace and j. are mine. |
| W-pI...105.1:1 | God's peace and j. are yours. Today we |
| W-pI...105.3:3 | Accept God's peace and j., and you will |
| W-pI...105.4:1 | As Heaven's peace and j. intensify when |
| W-pI...105.4:1 | so does the j. of your Creator grow when |
| W-pI...105.4:1 | when you accept His j. and peace as yours |
| W-pI...105.5:1 | Today accept God's peace and j. as yours. |
| W-pI...105.5:6 | Receive His gift of j. and peace today, and |
| W-pI...105.6:2 | by you the peace and j. that are their right |
| W-pI...105.7:2 | *My brother, peace and j. I offer you, That I* |
| W-pI...105.7:2 | *That I may have God's peace and j. as mine.* |
| W-pI...105.7:4 | gift of peace and j. that God has given you |
| W-pI...105.7:5 | the j. and peace you have denied yourself. |
| W-pI...105.7:6 | you can say, "God's peace and j. are mine, |
| W-pI...105.8:2 | let all bars to peace and j. be lifted up, |
| W-pI...105.8:3 | tell yourself, "God's peace and j. are mine |
| W-pI...105.9:6 | *My brother, peace and j. I offer you, That I* |
| W-pI...105.9:6 | *That I may have God's peace and j. as mine.* |
| W-pI...107.9:3 | To share His function is to share His j.. |
| W-pI...112.1:1 | (93) Light and j. and peace abide in me. *I* |
| W-pI...112.1:2 | me. *I am the home of light and j. and peace. I* |
| W-pI...112.3:2 | Light and j. and peace abide in me. On |
| W-pI...117.1:2 | *love is happiness, and nothing else brings j..* |
| W-pI...117.2:2 | *Love is my heritage, and with it j.. These are* |
| W-pI...118.1:1 | (105) God's peace and j. are mine. *Today* |
| W-pI...118.1:2 | *Today I will accept God's peace and j., in* |
| W-pI...118.3:2 | God's peace and j. are mine. On the half |
| W-pI...122.2:2 | gives you j. with which to meet the day. It |
| W-pI.122.11:2 | j. the lifting of the veil holds out to you. |
| W-pI.124.11:2 | a j. too deep for you to comprehend, a |
| W-pI...128.1:1 | anything at all that serves to give you j.. |
| W-pI...128.6:4 | sureness and in j. to join its holy purpose. |
| W-pI...129.1:3 | what is far more satisfying, filled with j., |
| W-pI.135.19:1 | and with j. that constantly increases, as |
| W-pI.135.20:3 | until the world is lighted up with j.. And |
| W-pI.135.24:2 | And in the light and j. of simple trust, you |
| W-pI.137.13:1 | exchanging curse for blessing, pain for j., |
| W-pI.140.12:6 | given us as we attend in silence and in j.. |
| WpI. rIV.in9:3 | from darkness to the light, from grief to j. |
| W-pI...152.2:4 | Can pain be part of peace, or grief of j.? |
| W-pI...153.8:2 | exchange for foolishness the endless j. our |
| W-pI.153.15:6 | give less at night, in gratitude and j.. |
| W-pI...157.1:6 | death. Today you learn to feel the j. of life. |
| W-pI...157.4:3 | it rest in still anticipation and in quiet j., |
| W-pI...162.5:4 | could despair when perfect j. is yours, |
| W-pI...164.7:4 | All that we see will but increase our j., |
| W-pI...164.9:4 | exchange all suffering for j. this very day. |
| W-pI...165.3:1 | would deny his safety and his peace, his j., |
| W-pI...166.8:5 | make for him whom God intended only j. |
| W-pI.166.15:7 | He has shared His j. with you. And now |
| W-pI...167.2:5 | response of any kind that is not perfect j.. |
| W-pI...189.4:2 | the j. with which they look out from the |
| W-pI...189.4:2 | out from the endless wells of j. within. |
| W-pI......190.h | I choose the j. of God instead of pain. |
| W-pI...190.6:4 | the j. of God as what you really want. |
| W-pI...190.6:5 | want. Your Self is radiant in this holy j., |
| W-pI...190.8:5 | pain that waits to end all j. in misery. |
| W-pI.190.10:2 | Here does the j. of God belong to you. |
| W-pI.190.10:4 | It is this: Pain is illusion; j., reality. Pain is |
| W-pI.190.10:5 | Pain is but sleep; j. is awakening. Pain is |
| W-pI.190.10:6 | Pain is deception; j. alone is truth. |
| W-pI.190.11:1 | illusions and the truth, or pain and j., or |
| W-pI.190.11:2 | we are free to choose our j. instead of pain |
| W-pI...193.1:2 | scope, eternally expanding in the j. of full |
| W-pI...195.3:1 | a plunderer who takes his j. from you, |
| W-pI...197.5:3 | j. while you forgive but to attack again. |
| W-pI...198.6:3 | all blessing and all j. that ever can be |
| W-pI...199.7:6 | would give you perfect freedom, perfect j. |
| W-pI...199.8:5 | of j. your practice brings even to it. And |
| W-pI...200.2:1 | hurt; of making peace of chaos, j. of pain, |
| W-pI...210.1:1 | I choose the j. of God instead of pain. *Pain* |
| W-pI...210.1:4 | *His Will is j., and only joy for His beloved* |
| W-pI...210.1:4 | *Will is joy, and only j. for His beloved Son.* |
| W-pII .241.1:1 | j. there is today! It is a time of special |
| W-pII .249.1:5 | world becomes a place of j., abundance, |
| W-pII .263.1:4 | *You blessed creation; all its purity, its j., and* |
| W-pII .282.1:3 | remains forever living in the j. of love. |
| W-pII .285.1:1 | Today I wake with j., expecting but the |
| W-pII .....8.3:2 | surrounding it but safety, love and j.? |
| W-pII .292.1:2 | And He guarantees that only j. can be the |
| W-pII .....9.4:4 | His Son, His one creation and His only j.. |
| W-pII .301.2:2 | who look on it can only add their j. to it, |
| W-pII .301.2:2 | and bless it as a cause of further j. in them |
| W-pII .310.1:3 | *j. that comes to me is not of days nor hours,* |
| W-pII .310.2:2 | and j. to Him Who gave salvation to us, |
| W-pII .314.1:5 | and peace into a quiet future filled with j. |
| W-pII .320.1:2 | no limits on his strength, his peace, his j., |
| W-pII .323.1:1 | *of pain, and giving him Your Own eternal j..* |
| W-pII .323.2:1 | truth returns to us in wholeness and in j.. |
| W-pII .329.1:9 | *am safe, untroubled and serene, in endless j.* |
| W-pII .330.1:4 | spirit, and extends its freedom and its j., |
| W-pII ...12.3:3 | of suffering, when he lives in eternal j.? |
| W-pII ...12.5:2 | as His Son, His dwelling place, His j., His |
| W-pII .339.1:4 | he can think that j. is painful, threatening |
| W-pII .339.1:9 | without confusing pain with j., or fear |
| W-pII .340.1:6 | *and what it holds in j. and freedom for Your* |
| W-pII .340.2:3 | for anything but j. and thanks today. Our |
| W-pII ...13.3:5 | in the light of perfect purity and endless j. |
| W-pII .348.1:3 | *the perfect peace and j. I share with You.* |
| W-pII ...14.1:3 | *and j. established without opposite. I am the* |
| W-pII ...14.4:4 | to share our peace and consummate our j. |
| W-pII ....355.h | There is no end to all the peace and j., |
| W-pII .355.1:1 | *I wait, my Father, for the j. You promised me* |
| W-pII ....359.h | pain Is healed; all misery replaced with j.. |
| W-ep .........5:6 | J. attends our way. For we go homeward |
| M-in ..........4:8 | as they teach His lessons of j. and hope, |
| M-4 ..........V.h | Joy |
| M-4 .......V.1:1 | J. is the inevitable result of gentleness. |
| M-4 .......V.1:2 | and what could come to interfere with j.? |
| M-4 .......V.1:8 | J. goes with gentleness as surely as grief |
| M-4 .....V.1:12 | J. is their song of thanks. And Christ looks |
| M-4 ......VI.1:4 | Their j. comes from their understanding |
| M-4 ....VI.1:14 | is safety. It is peace. It is j.. And it is God. |
| M-4 ....IX.2:11 | attends it naturally, and j. is its condition. |
| M-4 .......X.2:3 | to them in newness and in j. so glorious |
| M-14 .........5:1 | The world will end in j., because it is a |
| M-14 .........5:2 | When j. has come, the purpose of the |
| M-16 .........6:2 | day. It is a thought of pure j.; a thought of |
| M-17 .........3:4 | the case if the result is anything but j.. |
| M-20 .........5:1 | Living is j., but death can only weep. You |
| M-28 .........2:8 | earth. The j. of Heaven has come upon it. |
| M-28 .........6:1 | prepared as yet to welcome them with j.. |
| P-3......III.8:10 | of God for the restoration of j. and peace. |
| S-2...........I.5:4 | your despair or hope, your misery or j.. |
| S-3........IV.3:3 | to share with Him creation's holy j.. Do |
| S-3........IV.8:2 | your j. grows greater as your love extends |

## joyful 10

| | |
|---|---|
| T-7.........X.3:4 | what is painful than you know what is j., |
| T-7.........X.3:6 | What is j. to you is painful to the ego, and |
| T-8..........II.2:7 | is j. if it leads you along your natural path, |
| T-13.....VII.6:4 | and learned of Him the j. journey home. |
| T-16.........II.8:5 | to accept the j. tidings that disaster is not |
| T-30......VI.9:5 | j. statement that there are no forms of evil |
| W-pI.....75.9:1 | too, will be j. reminders of your release. |
| W-pI...189.8:4 | do His part in j. and immediate response. |
| W-pI...192.3:6 | behold the j. sights their offerings contain |
| S-3........IV.7:3 | his j. thanks in unison with all creation, in |

## joyfully 3

| | |
|---|---|
| T-30.......V.6:2 | what you are, forgiveness washes j. away. |
| W-pI.151.16:3 | redeemed, and j. released from guilt. Now |
| S-3..........II.2:1 | choice, made j. and with a sense of peace, |

## joyless 6

| | |
|---|---|
| T-6..........II.6:1 | else can you find joy in a j. place except by |
| T-18....VIII.8:6 | –dry and unproductive, scorched and j. |
| T-18..VIII.11:1 | to enter into your bleak and j. kingdom, |
| T-18......IX.4:3 | despair and loneliness to it and keep it j.. |

T-30..... V.9:12 free from bitter cost and j. consequence.
W-pI..... 92.3:3 the sad, the poor, the starving and the j..

## joylessness 1

T-30...... VI.6:1 sickness and of j. forgiveness cannot heal.

## joyous 47

T-4.........I.9:10 is fearful to the ego, but j. to the spirit.
T-4........ IV.2:2 and this is so whenever you are not j.,
T-5.........in.1:7 to heal without being wholly j. themselves
T-5.........in.2:4 only possible whole state is the wholly j..
T-5.........in.2:5 To heal or to make j. is therefore the same
T-5...........I.1:4 If you do not choose to be wholly j., your
T-5....... II.10:7 the j. one of waking it to the Call for God.
T-5....... VII.5:1 Whenever you are not wholly j., it is
T-5....... VII.6:2 not to be wholly j. if that is how you feel.
T-6......... V.1:5 and know that His children are wholly j..
T-6.... V.C.1:11 and so He alone can keep you wholly j..
T-8.... VII.13:2 God's j. Teacher and learning His lessons.
T-10..... V.12:3 If God knows His children to be wholly j.,
T-12...... IV.4:2 To seek and not to find is hardly j.. Is this
T-13...... III.3:3 For you could not control your j. response
T-13... VII.10:8 Yet because of Him the answer is a j. *yes!*
T-13... VII.12:8 delay to wait upon your j. homecoming.
T-14........ II.6:2 And then begin to learn the j. lessons that
T-14....... III.6:4 throws away the j. opportunity to learn
T-15...... XI.8:3 What can be more j. than to perceive we
T-16.... IV.12:6 in j. answer to His Call for His completion
T-17....... V.5:3 it grows increasingly beneficent and j..
T-17..... V.10:1 freedom heard, in j. echo of your choice.
T19. IV.A.16:1 and a softly j. whispering is ever heard.
T19.... IV.B.7:6 to all the world the j. message of the end
T-21.........I.4:3 learned it, not through j. lessons, but
T-25..VIII.14:1 life eternal, j. and complete in every way,
T-26... VII.10:2 In j. answer will creation rise within you,
T-29...... VI.6:3 j. thing it is to dwell a little while in such a
T-31...... III.5:3 and sin cannot abide the j. and the free,
T-31..VIII.11:1 In j. welcome is my hand outstretched to
W-pI..... 17.3:2 see anything that is really alive or really j..
W-pI..... 22.2:2 Is it not j. news to hear that it is not real?
W-pI... 100.4:3 God's messengers are j., and their joy
W-pI... 106.6:5 become the j. giver of what you received.
W-pI. 127.12:5 *For I would learn the j. lesson that there is no*
W-pI. 151.17:3 the j. news that truth has no illusions, and
W-pI. 153.12:2 replace their fearful toys with j. games,
W-pII . 284.2:2 *You today, accepting but the j. as Your gifts;*
W-pII . 284.2:2 *Your gifts; accepting but the j. as the truth.*
W-pII . 285.1:3 I will ask for only j. things the instant I
M-4 ...... V.1:6 Why would they not be j.? They are sure
M-4 .... V.1:15 j. it is to share the purpose of salvation!
M-4 ...... IX.2:5 Being certain, it is j.. And being confident
M-11 ......... 4:7 And peace descends on it in j. answer.
P-2........ VI.7:2 j. song salvation sings to all who hear its
S-1.........in.1:3 j. concord of the Love They give forever to

## joyously 10

T-8........ IX.4:5 Spirit. Only when you awaken j. have you
T-14....... XI.4:6 and j. laid down by hands open to receive,
T-16....... II.5:2 be in j. accepting truth for what it is, and
T-19....... III.9:6 by j. releasing him from the belief in sin.
T-20...... II.11:4 Give j. to your brother the freedom and
T-21.........I.3:2 And gentle lessons are acquired j., and
W-pI. 151.14:1 which j. proclaim the wholeness and the
W-pI. 152.10:5 from hell, are j. accepted as our own.
W-pI... 160.9:2 beholds His Own and j. unites with them.
W-pI... 192.6:4 for, met with thanks and j. accepted? We

## joys 8

T-27.........I.7:3 and not esteem the worth of passing j.?
T-27.........I.8:2 for passing j. and cherish little pleasures
T-27.... VIII.1:8 and j. are different and can be told apart.
W-pI... 76.11:3 well as of the j. of Heaven which His laws
W-pI... 131.7:1 goals, its painful pleasures and its tragic j.
W-pI... 190.8:5 where sorrow rules and little j. give way
W-pII . 300.1:1 their j. are gone before they are possessed
C-5 ............ 6:7 you will share your pains and j. with him,

## Judas 3

T-6 ........I.15:4 described my reactions to J. as they did, if
T-6 ........I.15:7 called forth upon J. was a similar mistake.
T-6 ........I.15:8 J. was my brother and a Son of God, as

## Judge 4

*judge*

T-25 ... VIII.8:1 have a J. Who knows that they are wholly
W-pI... 151.7:1 let the Voice for God alone be J. of what is
W-pI... 151.8:1 Let Him be J. of what you are, for He has
W-pI... 151.9:6 Let Him be J. as well of everything that

## judge 138

*Judge*

T-3 ....... VI.1:4 the Bible says "J. not that ye be not judged
T-3 ....... VI.1:4 it means that if you j. the reality of others
T-3 ....... VI.2:1 The choice to j. rather than to know is the
T-4 ....... IV.8:6 J. how well you have done this by your
T-4 ......... V.1:6 Sane judgment would inevitably j. against
T-4 ...... VII.6:3 and no perception with which to j. it. But
T-6 ..... V.C.1:2 teaches you to j. every thought you allow
T-6 ..... V.C.2:1 Holy Spirit does not teach you to j. others,
T-7 ....... XI.3:1 you have made and j. its worth fairly. Is it
T-8 ..... VIII.4:8 ego as a j. gives anything but an impartial
T-8 ..... VIII.6:9 premises give rise in order to j. them truly
T-9 ....... III.3:4 does not understand it, He does not j. it,
T-9 ....... IV.3:4 of the ego, or you will j. them as *it* does. All
T-9 ....... VI.4:9 you will j. it as you judge your brother's,
T-9 ....... VI.4:9 you will judge it as you j. your brother's,
T-10 ..... III.5:1 of the ego's thought system and j. whether
T-10 ..... IV.2:3 the willingness to j. unreality for what it is
T-10 ..... IV.2:4 nothingness is merely to j. it correctly,
T-10 ...... V.2:3 You may believe that you j. your brothers
T-11 ....... in.3:8 Be willing to j. it with perfect honesty.
T-11 ..... VI.7:6 God does not j. His guiltless Son. Having
T-12 .........I.5:1 you not to j. what you do not understand.
T-12 ........II.9:6 them, for to lay aside means to j. against.
T-12 ........II.9:7 If you will look, the Holy Spirit will j., and
T-12 ........II.9:7 Holy Spirit will judge, and He will j. truly.
T-12 .. VII.12:8 You will j. against yourself, but He will
T-12 .. VII.12:8 against yourself, but He will j. *for* you.
T-13 .........I.3:1 upon yourself and j. what you do honestly
T-13 .........I.5:8 Deny your world and j. him not, for his
T-13 ..... VI.2:1 point from which to j. the present. Yet
T-13 .... VII.5:5 You who would j. reality cannot see it, for
T-13 ..... XI.4:4 finally let Him j. the difference for you,
T-14 ... III.15:1 to evaluate his Father and j. against Him.
T-14 .... V.11:4 J. not except in quietness which is not of
T-14 ....... X.5:8 you. To order is to j., and to arrange by
T-14 ....... X.6:4 It does not j. the call. It merely recognizes
T-14 ....... X.9:5 For no one alone can j. the ego truly. Yet
T-14 ..... XI.4:1 hardly j. the truth and value of this course
T-15 ...... V.1:3 experience is the basis on which you j..
T-15 ...... V.1:5 You would make no attempt to j., because
T-15 ...... V.9:3 have built by which to j. your brothers.
T-15 .... V.11:1 Think you that you can j. the Self of God?
T-15 .... VII.5:3 and let the Holy Spirit j. them truly. For it
T-16 .........I.3:8 tempted you may be to j. any situation,
T-16 ..... III.2:3 you j. yourself according to your teaching.
T-16 ..... III.2:5 you are willing to j. yourself accordingly.
T-18 .........I.2:3 He does not j. between them, knowing
T-18 .........I.7:8 To j. them individually is pointless. Their
T-19 ....... I.11:4 because it looks not to the past to j. him,
T-19 ........II.6:7 can be corrected, if truth be left to j. it.
T19..IV.C.11:5 seeming uncertainty of meaning, j. it not.
T19..IV.C.11:7 Give it to Him to j. for you, and say: *Take*
T-20 ........II.2:6 what their minds j. to be worthy of them.
T-20 ...... V.3:4 the meaningless attempt to j. what lies so
T-20 ...... V.3:5 J. not what is invisible to you or you will
T-20 ...... V.4:5 glad. You will not think to j. him, for who
T-20 .... VII.9:7 No one who loves can j., and what he sees
T-21 .........I.2:1 foolish is it to attempt to j. what could be
T-21 ... VIII.2:8 to those who choose to heal and not to j..
T-22 ........II.7:3 either you are each other's savior or his j.,
T-22 ........II.8:3 with. A savior cannot be a j., nor mercy
T-24 .........I.3:6 and a need to j. that cannot be escaped.
T-25 . VIII.13:3 J. not because you cannot, not because
T-25 . VIII.13:8 He is no j. of what must be another's due,
T-26 .........I.6:4 But j. him not, for you will hear no song of
T-26 ........II.4:8 to j. whether the hurt be large or little. He
T-26 ........II.5:7 or j. that it is one that has no resolution,
T-26 ........X.6:1 this injustice does to you who j. unfairly,
T-27 ... VIII.9:4 *You* j. effects, but *He* has judged their cause
T-28 ....... V.4:7 as it can j. or understand or know. Its eyes
T-29 ..... IX.2:5 So must he j. not, and he will waken. For
T-29 ..... IX.2:7 J. not, for he who judges will have need of
T-29 ..... IX.2:9 J. not, because you make yourself a part of
T-30 .........I.2:3 are choosing not to be the j. of what to do.
T-30 .........I.2:4 But it must also mean you will not j. the
T-30 .........I.2:5 For if you j. them, you have set the rules
T-30 ..... VI.7:2 cannot be to j. which forms are real, and
T-30 .... VII.2:2 be? And thus you j. disaster and success,
T-30 .... VII.4:3 see. You do not have to j., for you have
T-31 .........I.2:8 pause in diligence to j. it hard to learn or
T-31 ..... IV.4:4 j. the lesson that is but begun with this.
T-31 .... VII.8:5 what he looks upon, to j. what he beholds.
T-31 .. VII.13:4 It cannot j. because it does not know. And
W-in.......... 8:4 You are not asked to j. them at all. You
W-pI .. 125.3:2 We will not j. ourselves today, for what
W-pI .. 126.2:4 of yourself, while you can j. their sin, and
W-pI .. 127.2:6 to j. between the righteous and the sinner,
W-pI .. 127.3:1 Love cannot j.. As it is one itself, it looks
W-pI .. 151.1:1 No one can j. on partial evidence. That is
W-pI .. 151.3:1 How can you j.? Your judgment rests
W-pI .. 151.3:4 But how else do you j. the world you see?
W-pI .. 151.4:3 You cannot j.. You merely can believe the
W-pI 151.10:3 of God, for He will j. all happenings, and
W-pI .. 154.1:3 We cannot j. ourselves, nor need we do so
W-pI .. 154.1:5 It is not our part to j. our worth, nor can
W-pI 159.10:3 J. not God's Son, but follow in the way He
W-pI .. 160.1:6 he is what he is not, and j. against himself
W-pI .. 164.7:1 We will not j. today. We will receive but
W-pI .. 186.1:4 role. It does not j. your proper role. It but
W-pI .. 186.5:3 J. not your value to it. If God's Voice
W-pII ..... 1.4:4 He who would not forgive must j., for he
W-pII .... 243.h Today I will j. nothing that occurs.
W-pII . 268.1:1 *Your critic, Lord, today, and j. against You.*
W-pII ..... 8.3:3 and what is there that it would j. against?
W-pII . 301.1:1 *Father, unless I j. I cannot weep. Nor can I*
W-pII . 301.1:3 *is my home because I j. it not, and therefore*
W-pII . 301.1:7 *is gone. Father, I will not j. Your world today.*
W-pII . 305.2:2 *us today but to accept Your gift, and j. it not.*
W-pII .... 311.h I j. all things as I would have them be.
W-pII . 311.2:2 *We do not know him, and we cannot j.. And*
W-pII . 327.2:2 *therefore to try them, and to j. them not.*
W-pII . 347.1:5 *to the One You gave to me to j. for me. He*
W-pII . 347.1:9 *Let Him j. today. I do not know my will, but*
W-pII .... 349.h upon All things for me and j. them not,
M-4 ..... I.A.7:5 had made it impossible for him to j.. He
M-4 ...... III.1:1 God's teachers do not j.. To judge is to be
M-4 ...... III.1:2 To j. is to be dishonest, for to judge is to
M-4 ...... III.1:2 j. is to assume a position you do not have.
M-4 ...... III.1:8 acceptable, for who could j. otherwise?
M-4 .... III.1:11 teacher of God can j. and hope to learn.
M-6 ........... 2:8 him to j. when his gift should be accepted.
M-10 .......... 2:1 of God to realize, not that he should not j.
M-10 .......... 3:3 In order to j. anything rightly, one would
M-10 ........ 5:12 And where he came to j., he comes to
M-14 .......... 4:7 He does not j. it either as hard or easy. His
M-15 .......... 2:8 J. not, for you but judge yourself, and thus
M-15 .......... 2:8 Judge not, for you but j. yourself, and thus
M-18 .......... 4:3 let Him j. what the response should be. So
M-19 .......... 5:7 From this one standpoint does it j., and
M-21 .......... 5:6 J. not the words that come to you, but
M-22 .......... 7:4 because it is not up to them to j. His Son.
M-22 .......... 7:5 And to j. His Son is to limit his Father.
P-3..........II.2:4 with the aim of making the therapist a j..
P-3..........II.6:1 to j. the patient that healing occurs. In
S-1..........V.1:4 j. all things as you would have them be.
S-2........ III.5:2 The form the seeking takes you need not j.
S-2........ III.6:9 Listen and learn, and do not j.. It is to
S-2........ III.7:3 in this; do not attempt to j. forgiveness,

## judged 62

| | |
|---|---|
| T-3........VI.1:4 | the Bible says "Judge not that ye be not j., |
| T-3........VI.2:5 | only the positive aspects of what is j., |
| T-3........VI.2:6 | and rejected, or j. and found wanting, |
| T-3........VI.2:7 | that what you j. against has no effect. This |
| T-3........VI.2:8 | that what you j. against does not exist. |
| T-3........VI.2:9 | this, or you would not have j. against it. |
| T-3........VI.5:1 | have j. yourself as capable of being tired. |
| T-3........VI.5:2 | it is because you have j. him as unworthy. |
| T-4......IV.8:10 | Let it be j. truly and you must withdraw |
| T-4.......VII.4:2 | is j. to be worth undertaking. Being is |
| T-6...........I.9:1 | most outrageous assault, as j. by the ego, |
| T-6......... II.2:3 | you have also j. against what you project, |
| T-7......VI.12:1 | you have not j. sanity as wholly desirable. |
| T-7....... VIII.6:2 | keep a belief he has j. to be unbelievable. |
| T-9........IV.8:6 | you have j. it by the same standard I have. |
| T-9.......VII.6:4 | this contrast can insanity be j. as insane. |
| T-10....... V.2:3 | j. them by the message you give to them. |
| T-12...VII.13:1 | you have j. yourself unworthy and have |
| T-13.......in.1:4 | itself as separate from the mind being j., |
| T-13......XI.3:3 | value of what God esteems cannot be j., |
| T-15......III.2:2 | for you will have j. yourself unworthy of it |
| T-15....... V.6:4 | them, but you have also j. against both. |
| T-15....... V.6:5 | Yet you had j. against yourself first, or |
| T-15....... V.6:6 | could not have j. them so like you in lack. |
| T-15.....VII.3:4 | it is, and have j. it completely in the dark. |
| T-15....... X.7:3 | of the two is j. as the lesser of two evils, |
| T-16....... V.3:3 | are usually j. to be acceptable and even |
| T-17.....VII.3:2 | the thoughts are j. to be in conflict. But if |
| T-18.........I.1:4 | one is j. more valuable and the other is |
| T-18.........I.7:7 | patterns that need not be j. at all. To |
| T-18....... V.1:6 | greatest advances you have j. as failures, |
| T-19.......III.5:8 | If it does not obey, the mind is j. insane. |
| T-20. VIII.10:3 | you saw at all or merely j. against. Vision |
| T-25. VIII.10:4 | His Son be j. by those who seek his death, |
| T-26......III.2:3 | the truth, where they are j. to be untrue. |
| T-26... VIII.5:4 | had been caused, and j. disastrous *now?* |
| T-26... VIII.5:6 | if its effects already have been j. as fearful. |
| T-26....... X.6:1 | judge unfairly, and who see as you have j., |
| T-27.........I.9:6 | offered that it may be j. in any way at all. |
| T-27... VIII.9:4 | *You* judge effects, but *He* has j. their cause. |
| T-28......VI.1:3 | It has not j. itself, nor made itself to be |
| T-28.....VII.5:9 | cannot be j. apart from its foundation. If |
| T-29....IX.10:5 | not fear his judgment for he has j. no one, |
| T-30.........I.5:1 | will still be times when you have j. already |
| W-pI......51.2:2 | I have j. everything I look upon, and it is |
| W-pI......51.3:2 | what I see when I have j. it amiss? What I |
| W-pI...125.2:4 | only love. He is not j., but only sanctified. |
| W-pI...125.3:2 | today, for what we are can not be j.. We |
| W-pI...136.4:1 | reduce the threat that has been j. as real? |
| W-pI...138.9:3 | be raised to understanding, to be j. again, |
| W-pI...139.4:4 | lives; has j. against it and denied its worth |
| W-pI...151.7:2 | be j. by what your eyes behold in him, nor |
| W-pI...151.8:4 | Whom He has j. can only laugh at guilt, |
| W-pII..312.1:2 | Having j., we therefore see what we would |
| W-pII..347.2:2 | you that He has j. you as the Son He loves. |
| M-4........ X.1:4 | to be j. by the Voice for God on His behalf |
| M-14..........2:8 | in it have been rightly j. by His judgment. |
| M-15.............h | IS EACH ONE TO BE J. IN THE END? |
| M-15..........3:5 | You will be j., and judged in fairness and |
| M-15..........3:5 | judged, and j. in fairness and in honesty. |
| M-19..........1:8 | If God's Son were fairly j., there would be |
| P-2....... V.6:10 | a help. Yet let the outcome not be j. by us. |

## judges 31

| | |
|---|---|
| T-4......... V.3:2 | j. only in terms of threat or non-threat to |
| T-6...........I.5:3 | that I was persecuted as the world j., and |
| T-6...........I.9:2 | As the world j. these things, but not as |
| T-9.......VII.7:6 | The Holy Spirit j. against the reality of the |
| T-9.......VII.7:8 | j. every belief you hold in terms of where |
| T-12.....VII.3:2 | every law of reality as this world j. it. |
| T-13.......in.1:4 | For the mind that j. perceives itself as |
| T-13.....VII.5:3 | who j. what is true and what is false. And |
| T-13.....VII.5:4 | And what he j. false he does not see. You |
| T-14....... X.7:6 | of his offering by which the ego j. it. |
| T-19...... I.11:2 | God, and j. him unworthy of forgiveness. |
| T-25. VIII.13:9 | and try to take away from whom he j.. He |
| T-28......VI.2:7 | takes no sides and j. not the road it travels |
| T-29......IX.2:7 | not, for he who j. will have need of idols, |
| T-29......IX.3:5 | it *is* justice that who j. him will not escape |
| T-29......IX.6:6 | Except he j. this as does a child, who does |
| W-pI.....92.6:3 | It j. and condemns, but does not love. In |
| W-pI...140.6:6 | not a thought that j. an illusion by its size, |
| W-pI...151.9:1 | And thus He j. you. Accept His Word for |
| W-pI...164.5:3 | scale of judgment left to Him Who j. true. |
| W-pI...166.2:4 | looks upon the world and j. it as certain, |
| W-pI...186.4:5 | are. It is but arrogance that j. otherwise. |
| W-pI...189.7:2 | good or bad, of every thought it j. worthy, |
| W-pII...... 1.4:3 | It merely looks, and waits, and j. not. He |
| W-pII..311.1:4 | It j. what it cannot understand, because it |
| W-pII..311.1:4 | cannot see totality and therefore j. falsely. |
| W-pII..325.1:2 | of the thing the mind desires, j. valuable, |
| W-pII..352.1:1 | *looks on sinlessness alone, and j. not.* |
| M-1 .........2:13 | a thousand years of time as the world j. it. |
| M-4 ....... X.1:4 | As condemnation j. the Son of God as evil |
| M-8 ...........3:3 | the mind that j. what the eyes behold. It is |

## judging 18

| | |
|---|---|
| T-3........ VI.1:4 | you will be unable to avoid j. your own. |
| T-3........ VI.3:2 | realize that j. them in any way is without |
| T-3........ VI.3:3 | to you precisely *because* you are j. them. |
| T-6......V.C.1:5 | of accord entirely He rejects by j. against. |
| T-8......... V.1:4 | J. truth as something they do not want, |
| T-9...........I.3:4 | that you are j. something of which you are |
| T-12...VII.12:7 | share His function only by j. as He does, |
| T-14..... V.11:1 | j. him fit for crucifixion or for redemption |
| T-16.........I.3:8 | and to determine your response *by* j. it. |
| T-16....IV.10:2 | you accept into your mind by j. it to be |
| T19..IV.C.11:8 | *this from me and look upon it, j. it for me. Let* |
| T-24.... VI.13:2 | j. against the Christ and setting forth for |
| T-24...VII.10:5 | it sinful and you hate its acts, j. it evil. Yet |
| W-pI.....24.1:2 | action, and no way of j. the result. What |
| W-pI.....72.4:4 | confusing it with him, and j. them as one. |
| W-pI...151.4:2 | have often been urged to refrain from j., |
| W-pII...in.10:5 | Instead of j., we need but be still and let |
| M-8 ...........4:3 | values, j. where each sense datum fits best |

## Judgment 41
*judgment*

| | |
|---|---|
| T-2........ VIII.h | The Meaning of the Last J. |
| T-2..... VIII.1:6 | into the real meaning of the Last J.. |
| T-2..... VIII.2:1 | The Last J. is one of the most threatening |
| T-2..... VIII.2:5 | the Last J. will extend over a similarly long |
| T-2..... VIII.3:1 | The Last J. is generally thought of as a |
| T-2..... VIII.3:4 | the aim of the Last J. is to restore right- |
| T-2..... VIII.3:5 | The Last J. might be called a process of |
| T-2..... VIII.5:1 | The term "Last J." is frightening not only |
| T-2..... VIII.5:3 | of the Last J. is objectively examined, it is |
| T-3........ VI.1:1 | We have already discussed the Last J., but |
| T-3........ VI.1:2 | After the Last J. there will be no more. |
| T-9........ IV.9:2 | Do not fear the Last J., but welcome it and |
| W-pII........ 9.3:1 | Spirit teaches, making way for the Last J., |
| W-pII.......10.h | What Is the Last J.? |
| W-pII.... 10.3:1 | who believed that God's Last J. would |
| W-pII.... 10.3:1 | God's J. is the gift of the Correction He |
| W-pII.... 10.4:1 | God's Final J. is as merciful as every step |
| W-pII.... 10.5:1 | God's Final J.: "You are still My holy Son, |
| W-pII..311.1:6 | of mind by giving us God's J. of His Son. |
| W-pII..311.2:1 | *today, to hear Your J. of the Son You love.* |
| M-11 .........3:4 | –God has sent His J. to answer yours. |
| M-11 .........3:5 | Gently His J. substitutes for yours. And |
| M-11 .........3:9 | But in the J. of God what is reflected here |
| M-11 .........4:6 | God's J. on this distorted world redeemed |
| M-12 .........1:7 | of himself is based upon God's J., not his |
| M-15 .........1:2 | No one can escape God's Final J.. Who |
| M-15 .........1:4 | But the Final J. will not come until it is no |
| M-15 .........1:6 | it free as God's Final J. on him is received. |
| M-15 .........1:7 | This is the J. in which salvation lies. This |
| M-15 .........1:8 | This is the J. that will set him free. This is |
| M-15 .........1:9 | J. in which all things are freed with him. |
| M-15 .......1:10 | may hear this J. of the Son of God: *Holy* |
| M-15 .........2:5 | hear this J. and to recognize that it is true. |
| M-15 .........2:8 | judge yourself, and thus delay this Final J.. |
| M-15 .......2:10 | aside and hear the Voice of J. in yourself? |
| M-15 .......2:13 | And His J. comes to all who stand aside in |
| M-15 .........3:3 | God's J. waits for you to set you free. |
| M-15 .........3:9 | His promises have guaranteed His J., and |
| M-19 .........4:6 | Him. God's J. is His justice. Onto this,–a |
| M-19 .........4:7 | –a J. wholly lacking in condemnation; an |
| M-28 .........6:6 | His Final J. is restored the truth about the |

## judgment 245
*Judgment*

| | |
|---|---|
| T-2....V.A.16:2 | has no element of j. at all. The statement |
| T-2......VIII.2:3 | it. J. is not an attribute of God. It was |
| T-2......VIII.5:5 | last j. cannot be directed toward yourself, |
| T-2......VIII.5:8 | solely to "give you time" to achieve this j.. |
| T-2......VIII.5:9 | is your own perfect j. of your own perfect |
| T-3........... VI.h | J. and the Authority Problem |
| T-3........ VI.1:3 | J. is symbolic because beyond perception |
| T-3........ VI.1:3 | because beyond perception there is no j.. |
| T-3........ VI.2:2 | J. is the process on which perception but |
| T-3........ VI.2:4 | J. always involves rejection. It never |
| T-3...... VI.2:10 | matter whether your j. is right or wrong. |
| T-3...... VI.2:12 | This cannot be avoided in any type of j., |
| T-3........ VI.3:1 | and your brothers totally without j.. |
| T-3........ VI.3:4 | belief that you are under the coercion of j. |
| T-3........ VI.3:5 | You do not need j. to organize your life, |
| T-3........ VI.3:6 | all j. is automatically suspended, and this |
| T-3........ VI.5:6 | strain of constant j. is virtually intolerable |
| T-3........ VI.5:8 | reality, you will insist on holding on to j.. |
| T-3........ VI.5:9 | You will also regard j. with fear, believing |
| T-3...... VI.5:10 | in the efficacy of j. as a weapon of defense |
| T-3........ VI.9:6 | without j. and merely know that it is there |
| T-3...... VI.11:4 | J. always imprisons because it separates |
| T-4....... II.10:3 | The ego cannot survive without j., and is |
| T-4........ IV.8:6 | feelings, for this is the one right use of j.. |
| T-4........ IV.8:7 | J., like any other defense, can be used to |
| T-4........ IV.8:8 | be brought to j. and found wanting there. |
| T-4...... IV.10:4 | charge of the Second Coming, and my j., |
| T-4......... V.1:2 | are no exceptions except in the ego's j.. |
| T-4......... V.1:6 | Sane j. would inevitably judge against the |
| T-4....... VII.3:9 | in application and not subject to any j., |
| T-5...... IV.8:13 | My j. is as strong as the wisdom of God, |
| T-5......... V.6:3 | moment of decision is a j. that is anything |
| T-5........ VI.4:1 | The ego speaks in j., and the Holy Spirit |
| T-5........ VI.4:5 | The Bible is a fearful thing in the ego's j.. |
| T-5........ VI.4:7 | you believe its j. would also be against you |
| T-5........ VI.6:2 | Your j. of what is worthy makes it worthy |
| T-6.........I.11:5 | the j. of the Holy Spirit can be justified. I |
| T-6..........II.2:2 | the very j. that you are different from the |
| T-6...... V.B.4:3 | *it* is insane. The ego's j., here as always, is |
| T-6...... V.C.2:3 | the mind so it can perceive without j.. |
| T-6...... V.C.2:4 | This enables the mind to teach without j., |
| T-6...... V.C.2:4 | and therefore to learn to *be* without j.. The |
| T-7......VIII.7:2 | the unbelievable cannot make this j. alone |
| T-8......VIII.4:7 | that j. is the function of the Holy Spirit, |
| T-8......VIII.4:8 | a judge gives anything but an impartial j.. |
| T-9..........II.9:5 | There is a price you will pay for j., because |
| T-9..........II.9:5 | because j. is the setting of a price. And as |
| T-9....... II.10:2 | return is in proportion to your j. of worth. |
| T-9........ IV.3:5 | All their harmfulness lies in the ego's j.. |
| T-9........ IV.3:6 | helpfulness lies in the j. of the Holy Spirit. |
| T-9....... VII.4:5 | unloving and you are going against its j.. |
| T-9......VIII.3:3 | it incapable of j. except in terms of attack. |
| T-12............I.h | The J. of the Holy Spirit |
| T-12.........I.3:2 | Holy Spirit's j. it requires no effort at all |
| T-12...... IV.1:6 | its goal with fanatic insistence, and its j., |
| T-12... VII.12:4 | without is a j. of what you beheld within. |
| T-12... VII.12:5 | within. If it is your j. it will be wrong, for |
| T-12... VII.12:5 | it will be wrong, for j. is not your function |
| T-12... VII.12:6 | it is the j. of the Holy Spirit it will be right, |
| T-12... VII.12:6 | Spirit it will be right, for j. *is* His function. |
| T-12... VII.12:7 | He does, reserving no j. at all for yourself. |
| T-13.......in.1:2 | j. of one mind by another as unworthy of |
| T-13...... VI.6:1 | J. and condemnation are behind you, and |
| T-13..... VII.5:5 | for whenever j. enters reality has slipped |
| T-13...... XI.4:5 | true. He has perfect faith in your final j., |
| T-14... VII.6:11 | His j. must prevail, and He will give it to |
| T-14....VIII.1:5 | be brought to the j. of the Holy Spirit, and |
| T-14........X.5:8 | To order is to judge, and to arrange by j.. |
| T-14........X.6:7 | you who are still bound to j. can be asked |
| T-14........X.6:7 | do that which requires no j. of your own. |

T-14....... X.7:1 The only **j.** involved is the Holy Spirit's
T-15....... V.1:2 For its purpose is to suspend **j.** entirely.
T-15....... V.1:3 **J.** always rests on the past, for past
T-15....... V.1:4 **J.** becomes impossible without the past,
T-15..... V.11:2 God has created It beyond **j.**, out of His
T-17...... VI.3:4 Not only is your **j.** in the past, but you
T-17...... VI.3:6 now the only **j.** left to make is whether or
T-18...... III.3:5 it, and terribly afraid of its **j.** upon you.
T-19...... II.6:10 and everything is brought to *it* for **j.**. As a
T19..IV.C.11:6 the One given to you to be the Source of **j.**.
T-20....... II.3:6 your **j.** on the Son of God for what he is.
T-20...... III.5:2 The world you see is but a **j.** on yourself. It
T-20...... III.5:4 Yet **j.** lays a sentence on it, justifies it and
T-20...... III.5:5 Such is the world you see; a **j.** on yourself,
T-20...... III.6:7 Take not the **j.** of the world as answer to
T-20...... III.8:1 ask **j.** of what is totally bereft of judgment
T-20...... III.8:1 ask judgment of what is totally bereft of **j.**
T-20....... V.3:4 far beyond your **j.** you cannot even see it?
T-20....... V.4:5 and yet insist that **j.** still has meaning? For
T-20....... V.4:7 Vision or **j.** is your choice, but never both
T-20..... VII.5:7 body, you have chosen **j.** and not vision.
T-20..... VII.6:1 sees a brother's body has laid a **j.** on him,
T-20..... VII.7:7 And **j.** has no value unless the goal is sin.
T-20..... VII.8:1 cannot be looked upon except through **j.**.
T-20..... VII.8:4 **J.** you taught yourself; vision is learned
T-20.... VIII.1:5 Vision would not be necessary had **j.** not
T-20.... VIII.5:5 **J.** will seem to make your savior weak. Yet
T-20.... VIII.7:1 **J.** is but a toy, a whim, the senseless
T-21....... in.2:1 Damnation is your **j.** on yourself, and this
T-21......... I.2:5 **J.** will always give you false directions, but
T-21......... I.3:7 that vision gives you more than **j.** does,
T-21....... II.1:5 that this little cost seemed, in your **j.**, to
T-21....... II.8:3 comes of vision and suspended **j.**. Then
T-21....... II.8:4 wholly independent of inference and **j.**.
T-23..... II.17:9 It is a **j.** that defeats itself, condemning
T-24......... I.4:2 But what is different calls for **j.**, and this
T-24....... I.8:10 blow, each slight, or fancied **j.** on itself?
T-24...... VI.5:5 with one **j.** made for all it looks upon. And
T-24...... VI.8:6 you see the **j.** you have laid on both of you
T-24.... VI.13:1 be sure you understand what made this **j.**.
T-24.... VI.13:3 Forget not that this **j.** must apply to what
T-24.... VI.13:5 To Him this **j.** makes no sense at all, for
T-25....... V.6:6 out to him because it is your **j.** on yourself
T-25.... VIII.8:5 For love has lost when **j.** left its side, and
T-26....... II.4:9 He makes but one **j.**; that to hurt God's
T-26...... III.4:2 be possible, the final **j.** upon this world. It
T-26...... III.4:3 It is the **j.** of the truth upon illusion, of
T-26....... V.5:5 thought, in every **j.** and in all belief in sin,
T-27.... VIII.9:5 cause. And by His **j.** are effects removed.
T-28....... I.10:1 You who have sought to lay a **j.** on your
T-28....... I.10:1 it is not He Who laid a **j.** on His Son. You
T-29...... IX.2:1 dream of **j.** came into the mind that God
T-29...... IX.2:4 It is a dream of **j.**. So must he judge not,
T-29...... IX.2:7 will hold the **j.** off from resting on himself.
T-29...... IX.2:9 from the **j.** laid in terror and in guilt upon
T-29...... IX.3:5 **J.** is an injustice to God's Son, and it *is*
T-29...... IX.3:7 dream of **j.** you attack and are condemned
T-29...... IX.3:7 between your **j.** and the penalty it brings.
T-29...... IX.6:4 The dream of **j.** is a children's game, in
T-29...... IX.7:6 And what was once a dream of **j.** now has
T-29...... IX.7:8 are now perceived as brothers, not in **j.**,
T-29...... IX.8:7 when dreams of **j.** have been put away?
T-29...... IX.9:3 must result in fear, for fear *is* **j.**, leading
T-29.... IX.10:5 not fear his **j.** for he has judged no one,
T-29.... IX.10:5 has sought to be released through **j.** from
T-29.... IX.10:5 judgment from what **j.** must impose. And
T-29.... IX.10:6 when **j.** seemed to be the way to save him
T-30....... in.1:5 you from dreams of **j.** to forgiving dreams
T-30....... I.13:3 sorry dream of **j.** has forever been undone
T-30....... I.16:4 it with a dream of **j.** or the Voice for God.
T-30....... I.17:7 Your **j.** has been lifted from the world by
T-30...... VI.4:8 fearful **j.** that your brother does not merit.
T-30..... VII.3:8 Fear is a **j.** never justified. Its presence has
T-30..... VII.4:2 In this shared purpose is one **j.** shared by
T-30..... VII.5:1 Escape from **j.** simply lies in this; all
T-31....... I.13:1 innocent of **j.**, unaware of any thoughts of
T-31..... VII.9:2 sword of **j.** is the weapon that you give to
T-31... VII.13:1 is as it is free of any **j.** made upon yourself.
W-pI....... 3.1:4 These are not exercises in **j.**. Anything is
W-pI....... 3.2:2 a perfectly open mind, unhampered by **j.**,
W-pI....... 4.6:1 kind, you may find the suspension of **j.** in
W-pI..... 10.4:4 available to you, without selection or **j.**.
W-pI..... 28.6:3 you, instead of placing your own **j.** upon it
W-pI... 72.10:5 Now we are going to try to lay **j.** aside,
W-pI..... 73.2:2 to attack you and call for "righteous" **j.**.
W-pI... 79.10:4 suspend all **j.** about what the problem is.
W-pI... 121.5:2 it regards its **j.** of the world as irreversible,
W-pI... 121.5:3 it sees bears witness that its **j.** is correct. It
W-pI... 125.3:1 and without all **j.** of His holy Word. We
W-pI. 136.19:2 thoughts, yield to **j.** or make plans against
W-pI... 138.9:4 And all mistakes in **j.** that the mind had
W-pI... 151.1:2 That is not **j.**. It is merely an opinion
W-pI... 151.3:2 Your **j.** rests upon the witness that your
W-pI... 151.4:1 Can this be **j.**? You have often been urged
W-pI... 164.5:3 the scale of **j.** left to Him Who judges true.
W-pI... 164.5:4 And in His **j.** will a world unfold in perfect
W-pI... 164.7:2 is given us from **j.** made beyond the world
W-pI. 183.10:6 God becomes his **j.** of their worthlessness.
W-pI... 190.9:4 the cruel sword of **j.** that you hold against
W-pII ..... 1.2:1 makes a **j.** that it will not raise to doubt,
W-pII . 305.2:3 *come to us to save us from our **j.** on ourselves*
W-pII ... 10.1:2 And this the **j.** is in which perception ends
W-pII ... 10.2:1 The final **j.** on the world contains no
W-pII . 311.1:1 **J.** was made to be a weapon used against
W-pII . 312.1:1 Perception follows **j.**. Having judged, we
W-pII . 325.1:5 From **j.** comes a world condemned. And
W-pII .... 347.h Anger must come from **j.**. Judgment is
W-pII .... 347.h **J.** is The weapon I would use against
W-pII . 347.1:5 *I give all **j.** to the One You gave to me to judge*
W-pII . 351.1:7 *Voice. For He alone gives **j.** in Your Name.*
W-pII .... 352.h **J.** and love are opposites. From one Come
W-pII . 352.1:3 ***J.** will bind my eyes and make me blind. Yet*
M-4 ..... I.A.7:8 He must learn to lay all **j.** aside, and ask
M-4 ...... III.1:3 **J.** without self-deception is impossible.
M-4 ...... III.1:4 **J.** implies that you have been deceived in
M-4 ...... III.1:6 **J.** implies a lack of trust, and trust
M-4 ...... III.1:8 goes. Without **j.** are all things equally
M-4 ...... III.1:9 Without **j.** are all men brothers, for who is
M-4 .... III.1:10 **J.** destroys honesty and shatters trust. No
M-4 ...... IV.1:3 Harm is the outcome of **j.**. It is the
M-4 ........ X.1:2 Open-mindedness comes with lack of **j.**.
M-4 ........ X.1:3 **j.** shuts the mind against God's Teacher,
M-8 .......... 4:7 true. On this the **j.** of all differences rests,
M-9 .......... 2:3 teacher of God learns to give up his own **j.**
M-9 .......... 2:4 judgment. The giving up of **j.**, the obvious
M-9 .......... 2:6 The world trains for reliance on one's **j.** as
M-9 .......... 2:7 **j.** as the necessary condition of salvation.
M-10 ........... h HOW IS **J.** RELINQUISHED?
M-10 ......... 1:1 **J.**, like other devices by which the world
M-10 ......... 1:3 is capable of "good" and "bad" **j.**, and his
M-10 ......... 1:5 is "good" **j.** to one is "bad" judgment to
M-10 ......... 1:5 judgment to one is "bad" **j.** to another.
M-10 ......... 1:6 as showing "good" **j.** at one time and "bad
M-10 ......... 1:6 at one time and "bad" **j.** at another time.
M-10 ......... 1:9 "Good" **j.**, in these terms, does not mean
M-10 ......... 2:2 In giving up **j.**, he is merely giving up
M-10 ......... 2:5 Recognizing that **j.** was always impossible
M-10 ......... 2:7 puts himself in a position where **j.** *through*
M-10 ......... 2:8 And this **j.** is neither "good" nor "bad." It
M-10 ......... 2:9 It is the only **j.** there is, and it is only one:
M-10 ......... 3:1 the recognition that **j.** in the usual sense is
M-10 ......... 3:5 his **j.** would be wholly fair to everyone on
M-10 ......... 4:1 you knew all the "facts" you needed for **j.**,
M-10 ......... 4:5 Wisdom is not **j.**; it is the relinquishment
M-10 ......... 4:5 judgment; it is the relinquishment of **j.**.
M-10 ......... 4:6 Make then but one more **j.**. It is this:
M-10 ......... 4:7 is Someone with you Whose **j.** is perfect.
M-10 ......... 4:9 He does know all the effects of His **j.** on
M-10 ......... 5:1 Therefore lay **j.** down, not with regret but
M-10 ......... 5:8 He has given it away, along with **j.**. He
M-10 ......... 5:9 Him Whose **j.** he has chosen now to trust,
M-10 ......... 6:1 It is not difficult to relinquish **j.**. But it is
M-11 ......... 2:1 Again we come to the question of **j.**. This
M-11 ......... 2:2 This time ask yourself whether your **j.** or
M-11 ......... 2:4 world salvation; your **j.** would condemn it
M-11 ......... 2:5 your **j.** sees but death as the inevitable end
M-11 ......... 2:6 loves the world; your **j.** says it is unlovable
M-11 ......... 3:8 In your **j.** it is not possible, and can never
M-11 ......... 4:3 easily, then, is your **j.** of the world escaped
M-14 ......... 2:8 in it have been rightly judged by His **j.**.
M-15 ......... 2:1 Is this your **j.** on yourself, teacher of God?
M-15 ......... 2:9 What is your **j.** of the world, teacher of
M-17 ....... 2:10 this gift is his **j.** upon the holy Son of God.
M-19 ......... 1:7 Except in His **j.** justice is impossible, for
M-22 ......... 7:8 he withdraws his **j.** from the Son of God,
M-28 ......... 6:5 **J.** is laid by, and given Him Whose
M-28 ......... 6:5 by, and given Him Whose function **j.** is.
P-2........ IV.1:2 It is a **j.** on the Son of God, and judgment
P-2........ IV.1:2 the Son of God, and **j.** is a mental activity.
P-2........ IV.1:3 **J.** is a decision, made again and again,
P-2....... VII.4:6 who use their **j.** in making their decisions.
P-3.......... II.2:4 world's teaching follows a curriculum in **j.**
P-3.......... II.7:1 Yet it is when **j.** ceases that healing occurs
S-3........... I.3:4 sign of **j.** made by brother upon brother,
S-3........ IV.5:2 Nor will your **j.** fail to reach to God, for

## judgmental 4

T-2 ... V.A.15:4 Without this it is essentially **j.**, rather
T-3 ......... V.1:1 and that perception, which is inherently **j.**
T-3 ....... VI.6:4 It is **j.** only because you are capable of
T-6 ..... V.C.2:3 In the mind of the thinker, then, He *is* **j.**,

## judgments 21

T-3 ......... V.7:8 because **j.** are necessary in order to select.
T-3 ......... V.8:1 are no **j.** and nothing but perfect equality?
T-7 ...... VII.4:3 are powerful because they are mental **j.**.
T-14 ....... X.9:1 is characteristic of the ego's **j.**. Separately,
T-23 ..... II.19:5 Yet both are **j.** on what is not life, equal in
T-30 .... VII.2:3 **j.** all are made according to the roles the
T-30 .... VII.2:4 which these labels change with other **j.**,
W-pI .... 51.2:4 my **j.** have been made quite apart from
W-pI .... 51.2:5 to recognize the lack of validity in my **j.**,
W-pI .... 51.2:6 My **j.** have hurt me, and I do not want to
W-pI .. 123.3:5 your meager gifts and petty **j.** of the one
W-pI .. 125.3:3 We stand apart from all the **j.** which the
W-pI .. 151.4:4 You merely can believe the ego's **j.**, all of
W-pII . 243.1:5 so I am relieved of **j.** that I cannot make.
W-pII . 311.1:6 all the **j.** we have made against ourselves,
W-pII . 312.2:1 *world, set free from all the **j.** I have made.*
M-8 .......... 4:7 it is on this that **j.** of the world depend.
M-10 ......... 3:4 all the effects of his **j.** on everyone and
M-15 ......... 3:4 out to you, regardless of your **j.** on its gifts
M-19 ......... 1:2 is the basis for all the **j.** of the world.
M-21 ......... 5:4 All these are **j.** that have no value. They

## jump 1

T-27 ....... V.9:3 for learning does not **j.** from situations to

## jumped 1

T-29 ........ I.3:7 him come close to you, and you **j.** back; as

## just 25

• fair, deserved
*other*

T-20 ..... IV.3:1 by accepting their results as your **j.** due.
T-24 ......... I.4:4 the special one is "natural" and "**j.**." The
T-25 ... VIII.4:3 It is not **j.** that one should lack for what
T-25 ... VIII.5:6 To be **j.** is to be fair, and not be vengeful.
T-25 ... VIII.5:9 Yet how could He be **j.** if He condemns a
T-25 . VIII.13:2 How can specialness be **j.**? Judge not
T-25 . VIII.14:6 For only love is **j.**, and can perceive what
T-25 ..... IX.8:6 And pardon must be **j.** to everyone.
T-26 ....... II.6:1 God is **j.**, then can there be no problems
T-26 ... VIII.9:2 has no meaning, and is not your **j.** reward.
T-26 ....... X.1:3 think that a response of anger now is **j.**.
T-26 ....... X.3:4 to be unfair and not your **j.** deserts. Yet it
T-27 ....... II.7:1 How **j.** are miracles! For they bestow an
T-30 ..... VI.4:2 alive. And recognizing God is **j.**, it seems
T-31 ..... III.1:6 yours, and therefore meriting a "**j.**" attack
W-pI .. 101.2:1 punishment is **j.** and cannot be escaped.
W-pI .. 101.3:4 is boundless, merciless, but wholly **j.**.
W-pI .. 101.6:2 Joy is **j.**, and pain is but the sign you have

W-pI...126.4:2 Unmerited, withholding it is j., nor is it
W-pI...151.4:5 how apprehensive of j. punishment, how
W-pI...170.6:4 while they are always merciful and j..
M-15..........3:1 feel your j. due is not given you, and your
M-19..........1:7 capable of making only j. interpretations
S-2.........III.4:3 for prayer is merciful and God is j.. His is
S-3...........I.1:2 that seems to have reality and to be j.,

## just 173

• other
*fair, deserved*

T-1........IV.3:7 when you were created, j. as everyone was
T-2..... VIII.2:5 J. as the separation occurred over millions
T-2..... VIII.4:3 j. as God Himself looked upon what He
T-4......IV.11:2 j. as your ego does with your lower mind,
T-4......... V.6:3 j. as it does with all issues touching on the
T-5...........I.2:1 reawakening with j. a few simple concepts
T-5....... II.10:1 can let it change you j. as it changed me.
T-5........ III.2:9 dissociated the Call for God, j. as you have
T-5...... III.8:11 with His strength j. as the ego welcomes it
T-5........ III.9:4 j. as the Holy Spirit is the symbol of peace.
T-5........ IV.1:6 you, j. as you are part of God because He
T-5......... V.1:2 ego has a purpose, j. as the Holy Spirit has
T-5......... V.6:1 according to what it wants, j. as you can.
T-5........ VI.1:2 your return, j. as you are waiting for theirs
T-6........ I.16:8 This conflict seems j. as real now, and its
T-6......V.A.5:1 j. as He ultimately translates perception
T-7......... II.3:9 depends on it, j. as their own creation did.
T-7.....VII.10:9 j. as there was only one way into it.
T-7......... X.1:1 is the result of premises, j. as this world is.
T-8.......VII.7:3 exist, j. as different orders of miracles do.
T-12.........I.6:3 comes from your attempts not to do j. this
T-13... VIII.1:7 it is everywhere, j. as it has everything,
T-15.........I.1:2 is for; to learn j. that and nothing more.
T-15.......IX.1:3 is needful for you to learn j. what this shift
T-15....... X.9:5 is the recognition of the decision, *j. as it is,*
T-16....... II.2:1 concerned about the truth of j. a little part
T-16....... II.6:6 is true, j. as you fear, that to acknowledge
T-16..... V.14:4 in perceiving the decision as j. what it is,
T-17.........I.6:5 to forgive yourself for j. this same attempt
T-17......IV.5:3 And you must realize j. what this means if
T-17....IV.14:6 fact that it is j. a picture is brought home
T-17..... V.14:4 It is j. this same discrepancy between the
T-17......VI.3:1 outset, the situation j. seems to happen,
T-17... VIII.1:3 It calls forth j. the same suspension of
T-18.......IV.7:7 Salvation is easy j. *because* it asks nothing
T-18........ V.6:6 Yet j. as this is impossible, so is it equally
T-18.....VII.3:2 anticipated, but never experienced j. *now.*
T-18.....VII.4:1 reservation unless, j. for an instant, you
T-18.....VII.5:7 anyone, it always comes with j. one happy
T-18.....VII.6:8 Believe it for j. one instant, and you will
T-18......IX.4:1 of fear lies j. below the level the body sees,
T-19...... I.10:5 Each one appears j. as he is perceived in
T-19....... II.6:9 sin is kept in place by j. this strange device
T19... IV.A.3:3 still oppose the Will of God, j. by a little.
T19. IV.A.10:9 exist. Fear looks on guilt with j. the same
T19..IV.B.14:3 And j. as certainly it has no feeling. It
T19... IV.D.5:1 across is surmounted in j. the same way;
T-20......III.6:2 j. as the world the ego looks upon is like
T-20. VIII.11:3 Think but an instant j. on this; you can
T-21.........I.6:2 with you, but j. a little wisp of melody,
T-21.........I.6:3 But you remember, from j. this little part,
T-21......VI.7:6 which is one with you, in j. an instant.
T-22.......in.3:7 J. under Heaven does he stand, but close
T-22....... I.10:2 perception, and yet reborn in j. an instant
T-23.........I.1:9 Yet j. as certain is its fixed belief it has an
T-23....... II.5:5 j. as the separate aspects of the Son meet
T-23......III.1:2 and will do so j. as much as in another
T-23......III.4:1 is easy j. because it makes no compromise
T-24....... II.7:3 certain that the truth is j. the same in both
T-24....... II.9:2 J. one step more, and every vestige of the
T-24......III.3:1 and open to attack that j. a word, a little
T-24......IV.4:8 but j. a dream of specialness that lasts an
T-24....... V.8:4 and j. as like to Him in holiness as you
T-25......III.6:8 as j. another chance to bring him joy.
T-25......VII.2:1 is j. as strong as is God's Will for life. Nor
T-25. VIII.11:2 For j. *one* witness is enough, if he sees truly
T-26.........I.1:5 in the name of saving j. a little for yourself
T-26.........I.3:5 j. as they are on everything you think is
T-26....... II.1:3 because each one is solved in j. the same
T-26....... II.7:4 than j. a tiny sigh before they disappear,
T-26...... III.2:4 is j. beyond the gate of Heaven. Here is
T-26...... III.5:1 Salvation stops j. short of Heaven, for
T-26...... VI.1:2 but j. because you have denied it is but an
T-26...VII.14:6 A tiny sacrifice is j. the same in its effects
T-27....... II.4:5 Sins are beyond forgiveness j. because
T-27......IV.2:9 Yet j. as surely it must be resolved, if it is
T-27......IV.5:4 itself. J. as the body's witnesses are but the
T-27....... V.4:2 And nothing more than j. one instant of
T-28......III.3:1 miracle does nothing j. *because* the minds
T-28......III.5:3 And covered j. as fast, as water rushes in
T-28....IV.1:10 You can be sure of j. one thing; that you
T-28......IV.8:3 picture represents, instead of j. a little,
T-28......IV.9:7 of God is j. the same as every other part.
T-29.........I.1:5 His Love could harbor j. a hint of hate,
T-29......III.3:1 no more, perhaps, than j. a tiny spark, a
T-29....IV.4:11 is not its core, but j. the flimsy covering.
T-29........ V.6:8 can release him, j. by offering him yours.
T-30.........I.1:8 which this very day can happen j. like that
T-30.........I.9:4 you go ahead with j. a few more steps you
T-30...... III.7:7 will be j. the same when you remember.
T-30....... V.2:8 share, if hope be more than j. a dream.
T-31.........I.1:9 and j. what to do if you become confused.
T-31....... V.9:1 but j. a re-translation of what seems to be
T-31..... V.11:6 asks if j. a little question might be raised.
T-31.....VII.3:1 it is thus you see him more than j. a body,
T-31.....VII.3:3 than j. a shadow circling round the good.
T-31.....VII.4:1 You live in that world j. as much as this.
T-31.....VII.5:6 whose need for it is j. the same as yours.
T-31.....VII.9:1 all are different names for j. one error;
W-pI.....28.4:5 to the table j. as much as to anything else,
W-pI.....28.5:1 in fact, gain vision from j. that table, if
W-pI.....39.9:2 which you j. relax and do not seem to be
W-pI.....44.4:3 j. as it seems to be the most unnatural and
W-pI.....45.1:2 j. as nothing that you think you see is
W-pI.....64.5:8 different from j. this one simple choice.
W-pI.....66.1:3 more than j. a connection between them;
W-pI.....68.1:5 you do not yet fully realize j. what holding
W-pI.....70.4:1 have tried to do j. the opposite, making
W-pI.....71.1:5 after we have considered j. what the ego's
W-pI.....76.5:3 The body suffers j. in order that the mind
W-pI.....79.5:4 j. as you think you have resolved the
W-pI...100.1:1 J. as God's Son completes his Father, so
W-pI...100.4:2 J. as your light increases every light that
W-pI...107.3:1 not more than j. the faintest intimation of
W-pI...110.3:3 You need no thought but j. this one, to let
WpI. rIII.in1:3 are urged to follow j. as closely as you can.
WpI. rIII.in8:2 other in the hour j. before you go to sleep.
WpIrIII.in10:4 give more than j. a moment to each one.
W-pI...128.7:3 on the world will shift by j. a little, every
W-pI...130.6:3 learn today is more than j. the lesson that
W-pI...133.5:2 It cannot give you j. a little, for there is no
W-pI.133.12:2 obtain. Choosing is easy j. because of this.
W-pI.136.15:4 It merely waits for j. this invitation which
W-pI...137.5:2 J. as forgiveness overlooks all sins that
W-pI...137.5:3 J. as the real world will arise to take the
W-pI...137.7:1 J. as forgiveness shines away all sin and
W-pI...139.9:4 more than j. our happiness alone we came
W-pI...156.7:1 many years on j. this foolish thought. The
W-pI...168.3:5 His gift of grace is more than j. an answer.
W-pI...181.3:2 we seek, and only this, for j. a little while.
W-pI...182.1:6 J. a persistent feeling, sometimes not
W-pI...182.5:4 for more than j. a few instants of respite;
W-pI...182.5:4 j. an interval in which He can return to
W-pI...182.5:7 But give Him j. a little time to be Himself,
W-pI...185.1:3 you could but mean them for j. an instant,
W-pI...185.9:6 Yet will God's peace come j. as certainly,
W-pI.193.10:1 seeming obstacles to peace in j. one day.
W-pI...194.1:2 it sets you down j. short of Heaven, with
W-pI...196.4:5 done in j. one instant by the grace of God.
W-pII..272.2:2 Heaven can be chosen j. as easily as hell,
W-pII......7.2:1 teaching sets is j. this end of dreams. For
W-pII..345.1:4 *miracles I give are given back in j. the form I*
W-pII..358.1:4 *me, in j. the form You choose that it be mine.*
W-pII..360.1:2 *I am Your Son, forever j. as You created me,*
M-4..... V.1:14 need of them is j. as great as theirs of Him
M-4...... IX.1:5 begins by resting on j. some problems,
M-7...........4:3 Usually it seems to be j. the opposite. It
M-8...........6:7 J. as reality is wholly real, apart from size
M-12.......5:10 role, j. as It tells him what his function is.
M-16.........5:2 feasible for you to take it j. before going to
M-16.........5:6 j. before going to sleep is a desirable time
M-16.......11:8 by j. one simple-minded illusion;–that it
M-17.........3:6 is easily responded to with j. one answer,
M-19.........3:3 concept of the world built up in j. this way
M-19.........5:5 points to Heaven j. because it is entirely
M-20.........2:2 peace is recognized at first by j. one thing;
M-20.........2:8 The past j. slips away, and in its place is
M-22.........1:4 j. as special areas of hell in Heaven are
C-in...........1:6 And it is j. this process of overlooking at
C-3.............2:4 j. this insane perception that makes them
C-3...........4:10 this gate it is no more than j. a step inside.
C-3.............8:1 the world become in j. that single instant
C-4.............4:2 on it as nothing more than j. a fragile veil,
C-4...........5:11 you, j. as its presence once had been your
C-5.............5:6 shared. Walking with him is j. as natural
P-2...........I.4:5 are patients who need him j. that way.
P-2.........II.9:7 except a help in j. this same direction? It
P-2........ IV.8:3 compromise by seeing j. a little bit of hell.
P-2......... V.6:5 for more than j. the smallest willingness,
P-3...........I.3:8 or perhaps j. a feeling of reaching out to
P-3.........II.8:7 of healing can be theirs in j. an instant.
S-1........ III.6:8 But j. as surely will he lose the only true
S-1........ IV.4:5 this, in j. the little space that lasts until it

## justice 99

T-3........ VI.6:3 J. is a temporary expedient, or an attempt
T-25.............h THE J. OF GOD
T-25.......VIII.h J. Returned to Love
T-25....VIII.2:9 know of Heaven and the j. of the saved?
T-25....VIII.3:1 a kind of j. in salvation of which the world
T-25....VIII.3:2 the world, j. and vengeance are the same,
T-25....VIII.3:2 for sinners see j. only as their punishment
T-25....VIII.3:6 This is not j., but insanity. Yet how could
T-25....VIII.3:7 j. be defined without insanity where love
T-25....VIII.4:1 You who know not of j. still can ask, and
T-25....VIII.4:2 J. looks on all in the same way. It is not
T-25....VIII.4:5 J. demands no sacrifice, for any sacrifice is
T-25..VIII.4:10 And j., being blind, is satisfied by being
T-25....VIII.5:1 Can this be j.? God knows not of this. But
T-25....VIII.5:3 But j. does He know, and knows it well.
T-25....VIII.5:5 to God's Mind *because* He knows of j.. To
T-25....VIII.5:8 to share the Holy Spirit's j. with a mind
T-25..VIII.5:10 And where would j. be if He demanded of
T-25....VIII.6:1 to understand the Holy Spirit's j.. They
T-25....VIII.6:2 that their own belief in j. must entail. And
T-25....VIII.6:8 the "threat" of what God knows as j. to be
T-25....VIII.8:1 Yet j. cannot punish those who ask for
T-25....VIII.8:2 In j. He is bound to set them free, and
T-25....VIII.8:3 they think that j. is split off from love,
T-25....VIII.8:7 helpless hands, bereft of j. and vitality,
T-25....VIII.9:2 Could He, in j. and in love, believe in your
T-25....VIII.9:5 Own j. does He recognize all you deserve,
T-25....VIII.9:9 what loving j. knows to be his due. For
T-25..VIII.9:10 For love and j. are not different. *Because*
T-25..VIII.10:7 No j. would be given him by you. Yet God
T-25..VIII.10:8 God ensured that j. would be done unto
T-25..VIII.11:3 Simple j. asks no more. Of each one does
T-25..VIII.11:4 one, so j. may return to love and there be
T-25..VIII.11:5 one learn that love and j. are not separate.
T-25..VIII.11:7 Without love is j. prejudiced and weak.
T-25..VIII.11:8 And love without j. is impossible. For love
T-25VIII.11:11 In j., then, does love correct mistakes, but
T-25..VIII.12:1 perfect witness to the power of love and j.
T-25..VIII.12:9 Spirit that simple j. may be given you.
T-25..VIII.13:1 Without impartiality there is no j.. How
T-25..VIII.13:4 the special really understand that j. is the
T-25..VIII.14:2 This is the only j. Heaven knows, and all
T-25..VIII.14:3 else but perfect j. can prevail for you. And
T-25..VIII.14:5 replace God's j. with a version of its own.
T-25..VIII.14:6 what j. must accord the Son of God. Let
T-25..VIII.14:7 yourself of what God's j. has allotted you.
T-25..........IX.h The J. of Heaven
T-25...... IX.1:1 errors cannot be undone by Heaven's j.?
T-25...... IX.1:2 and to be met with vengeance, not with j.

T-25...... IX.2:3 you. God's j. warrants gratitude, not fear.
T-25...... IX.2:9 Yet would His j. not be satisfied until it is
T-25...... IX.3:7 Thus is j. not accorded to the Son of God.
T-25...... IX.3:9 punishment becomes his due instead of j..
T-25...... IX.4:1 punishment impossible, and j. sure. The
T-25...... IX.4:6 for only j. can set up a state in which there
T-25...... IX.5:2 solved because it has been met with j..
T-25...... IX.5:4 principle that j. means no one can lose is
T-25...... IX.5:5 For miracles depend on j.. Not as it is
T-25...... IX.6:5 And is this j. to the wholly innocent? A
T-25...... IX.6:6 A miracle *is* j.. It is not a special gift to
T-25...... IX.6:9 Where is salvation's j. if some errors are
T-25.... IX.10:2 salvation rests; that j. must be done to all,
T-25.... IX.10:4 Each miracle is an example of what j. can
T-26.........I.8:1 God's j. rests in gentleness upon His Son,
T-26.........I.8:5 he made to keep himself from j.? Could
T-26....... II.4:1 The miracle of j. can correct all errors.
T-26....... II.5:1 to yourself, remember this: J. is total.
T-26....... II.5:2 There is no such thing as partial j.. If the
T-26....... II.5:3 he deserves no mercy from the God of j..
T-26....... II.5:8 You deny the miracle of j. *can* be fair.
T-26....... II.6:1 there be no problems that j. cannot solve.
T-26....... II.6:8 The miracle of j. you call forth will rest on
T-26....... II.8:1 until j. is loved instead of feared. He
T-26...... IV.1:1 is this world's equivalent of Heaven's j.. It
T-26...... IV.1:2 where j. can be reflected from beyond the
T-26...... IV.1:4 j. past the gate that opens into Heaven.
T-26....... V.9:6 Such is the j. your All-Loving Father has
T-26....... X.5:8 And simple j. has been thus denied to
T-26....... X.6:4 and been replaced with j. and with love. If
T-29...... IX.3:5 it *is* j. that who judges him will not escape
T-29...... IX.3:6 God knows of j., not of penalty. But in the
W-pI... 166.9:1 now, and j. has caught up with you at last.
M-19 ............h WHAT IS J.?
M-19 ......... 1:1 J. is the divine correction for injustice.
M-19 ......... 1:3 J. corrects the interpretations to which
M-19 ......... 1:4 Neither j. nor injustice exists in Heaven,
M-19 ......... 1:5 world, however, forgiveness depends on j.
M-19 ......... 1:6 J. is the Holy Spirit's verdict upon the
M-19 ......... 1:7 Except in His judgment j. is impossible,
M-19 ......... 2:1 J., like its opposite, is an interpretation. It
M-19 ......... 2:3 j. includes nothing that opposes truth.
M-19 ......... 2:4 no inherent conflict between j. and truth;
M-19 ......... 2:9 one must start. J. is the beginning.
M-19 ......... 4:1 Salvation is God's j.. It restores to your
M-19 ......... 4:6 God's Judgment is His j.. Onto this,–a
M-19 ......... 5:1 Pray for God's j., and do not confuse His
M-19 ......... 5:5 God's j. points to Heaven just because it is
S-2........ III.4:4 His is a j. He can understand, but you
S-3......... II.5:4 gate to higher prayer and kindly j. done?

## justification 14

T-6.........in.1:7 You cannot *be* attacked, attack *has* no j.,
T-6...........I.6:8 There can be no j. for the unjustifiable.
T-6........ IV.4:2 it. It interprets this as a j. for attacking its
T-12...........I.1:5 thus becomes the j. for the response. That
T-17...... III.8:1 past becomes the j. for entering into a
T-17..... V.7:12 you will see the j. for your faith emerge, to
T-17..... VII.3:6 then becomes the j. for your lack of faith.
T-19.........I.9:7 There is no j. for faithlessness, but faith is
T-19.......I.11:5 body's eyes, nor looks to bodies for its j..
T19..IV.B.11:7 your error as the j. for your faithlessness.
T-30......... VI.h The J. for Forgiveness
W-pI..... 64.1:2 and provide you with a j. for forgetting it.
W-pI..... 84.4:2 *This is no j. for denying my Self. I will not use*
M-17 ......... 4:2 of their seeming j. by what *appears* as facts

## justifications 1

T-6 ..........I.6:7 not to accept them as false j. for anger.

## justified 66

T-6 ........in.1:3 attacked, that your attack is j. in return,
T-6 ........I.11:5 the judgment of the Holy Spirit can be j.. I
T-6 ........I.16:5 and reinforces the idea that blame is j..
T-7 ..... VI.11:9 justify its existence, which cannot be j..
T-9 .........II.8:1 you will learn that my belief in you is j..
T-12 .........I.3:5 anyone be j. in responding with anger to a
T-13 ........X.6:1 as you believe that guilt is j. in any way, in
T-15 ..... XI.5:2 a victim of sacrifice, j. in sacrificing others
T-15 ..... XI.5:6 attack, being the belief that attack is j..
T-19 .........I.8:2 an attack that seems to be j. by its results.
T-19 .........I.9:6 in that one you see your faith is fully j..
T-19 .........I.9:7 for faithlessness, but faith is always j..
T-19 .......I.10:6 on what makes faith forever j. in everyone
T-19 ........II.2:3 that attack is real and guilt is j.. It
T19..IV.B.10:1 Faith in the eternal is always j., for the
T-20 ... III.11:2 this faith with me, and know that it is j..
T-22 ......in.2:3 the need for sin, not real but seen, seem j..
T-22 ...... V.2:3 Can this *be* j.? What can this be except an
T-22 ... VI.12:4 The only way it could be j. is if you and
T-23 ........II.2:5 And this is j. because the values differ,
T-23 ........II.7:4 to be at war with Him, and j. in its attack.
T-23 ......II.10:1 your j. position and attack for what has
T-23 ......II.12:2 attack is j. unless you know what it is for?
T-23 ......II.12:7 Here is what makes your vengeance j..
T-23 ..... III.5:1 and that attack is j. on its behalf, cannot
T-24 ... VI.11:4 always furious, with anger always fully j.,
T-25 ..... III.1:1 you perceive a world in which attack is j..
T-25 ..... III.1:2 extent you will perceive attack cannot *be* j..
T-25 ..... III.3:6 its perception; not one but can be fully j..
T-25 ..... III.7:3 What, then, *is* j.? What do you want? For
T-25 ... III.9:10 the world you see is chosen, and will be j..
T-25 .... VII.4:7 sane in any way, is j. in anything it thinks,
T-25 ..... IX.9:4 vengeance j. and mercy lost, condemns
T-26 ........II.2:6 possible, attack be j. and vengeance fair.
T-26 ... VIII.3:9 and given seem dangerous, with terror j..
T-26 ........X.1:2 a differential view of when attack is j., and
T-27 .........I.5:8 he laid upon his heart was ever j., and no
T-27 .........I.7:1 them paint the picture in which sin is j., is
T-27 ........II.4:4 And how could his innocence be j. unless
T-29 ..... IV.4:2 this become the "reason" your attack is j.?
T-30 ..... VI.1:1 Anger is *never* j.. Attack has *no* foundation.
T-30 ..... VI.1:6 where attack is due, and would be j.. For
T-30 ..... VI.1:9 by responding in a way which is not j.,
T-30 ..... VI.2:1 Pardon is *always* j.. It has a sure
T-30 ..... VI.3:2 Fear cannot arise unless attack is j., and if
T-30 ..... VI.3:3 of forgiveness is quite real and fully j..
T-30 .... VII.3:8 Fear is a judgment never j.. Its presence
T-31 ........II.4:2 you think that it is murder j. at last. You
W-pI..... 21.3:5 forms of attack are more j. than others.
W-pI..... 47.6:2 in your real strength is fully j. in every
W-pI..... 51.5:4 anger is j. and my attacks are warranted. I
W-pI... 126.5:3 not escape the j. repayment for his sin.
W-pI... 135.3:4 it speaks of fear made real and terror j.. Is
W-pI... 137.6:4 can be seen and j. and fully understood.
W-pI... 165.7:2 For hope indeed is j.. Your doubts are
W-pI. 166.14:4 you fear but teaches them their fears are j.
W-pI... 198.7:1 has no meaning, and attack appears as j..
W-pII .... 240.h Fear is not j. in any form.
W-pII ... 13.2:5 to the truth. Now is forgiveness seen as j..
M-17 ......... 8:6 interpretation and not a fact, it is never j..
M-19 ......... 3:4 way. "Sins" are perceived and j. by careful
M-20 ......... 3:4 Who sees anger as j. in any way or any
P-2...... IV.10:6 sin"; the belief that guilt is real and fully j.
P-2...... IV.10:7 teach that guilt, being unreal, cannot be j.
S-1........ IV.2:3 The way is open, and hope is j.. Yet it is
S-3........ IV.5:5 source of fear, for only fear can now be j..

## justifier 1

T-25 .......V.1:3 each the cause and aim and j. of the other.

## justifies 7

T-6 .........II.3:4 ego j. this on the grounds that it makes
T-13 .......II.6:3 as the final guilt that fully j. murder. You
T19 ... IV.B.2:6 you that j. your strange belief that in it
T-20 ..... III.5:4 lays a sentence on it, j. it and makes it real
T-25 ..... III.5:2 nothing is seen but j. forgiveness and the
T-25 ..... III.6:5 anger turned to an event which j. his love.
T-27 .... VII.3:2 Your presence j. my wrath, and you exist

## justify 28

T-3 ..........I.2:2 a whole frame of reference in order to j. it.
T-3 ..........I.2:4 to "j." the terrible misperception that
T-6 ..........I.4:4 destruction, therefore, does not j. anger.
T-7 ..... VI.11:9 That would j. its existence, which cannot
T-13 ..... IX.5:6 Nothing can j. insanity, and to call for
T19 . IV.B.10:8 for its accomplishment, and j. its use.
T-20 ........II.1:5 and trying to j. your own interpretation
T-21 ........II.9:4 of a fearful world to j. its purpose. What
T-21 ......II.12:5 maker, and cannot serve to j. the madness
T-22 ..... III.9:3 because he seems to j. the other's sin.
T-22 .......V.2:2 Always to j. what goes against the truth,
T-22 ... VI.11:3 and j. *is* an attack upon your Father. And
T-23 ..... III.1:6 he is a murderer and j. his savagery with
T-24 .........I.3:3 What else could j. attack? For who could
T-24 ..... IV.4:5 Your brother's sin would j. itself, and give
T-25 ..... III.6:5 before was means to j. his anger turned to
T-25 .... VII.4:1 To j. one value that the world upholds is
T-25 ..... IX.4:3 Only a loss could j. attack, and loss of any
T-26 .. VII.15:3 j. a miracle whatever form they took. In
T-27 .......II.9:3 the grounds on which they j. his pain. The
W-pI .... 47.2:2 where trust is unwarranted, and to j. fear,
W-pI .... 51.5:2 I am constantly trying to j. my thoughts. I
W-pI .... 83.2:4 *use this to j. a function God did not give me.*
W-pI .... 83.4:4 *can j. the illusion of happiness apart from*
W-pI .. 192.7:2 reason but to j. our rage and our attack.
W-pII ..... 1.4:4 judge, for he must j. his failure to forgive.
W-pII ... 13.4:3 And thus the miracle will j. your faith in it
P-2........ VI.4:1 to j. attack and thus keep unforgiveness

## justifying 5

T-6 ........I.11:4 constantly engaged in j. the unjustifiable.
T-6 .........II.3:5 projection is always a means of j. attack.
T-17 ........I.5:4 and keep them by j. your belief in them.
C-1 ............ 6:1 illusions; perceiving sin and j. anger, and
P-2.........in.1:5 that by j. attack he is protecting himself.

## justly 2

T-16 .... VII.3:5 of the vengeance it believes you so j. merit
P-2........ IV.4:1 therapists of the world, and j. so. For not

# K

## keep 316

T-2......... II.6:5 it unnecessary for you to **k.** retracing your
T-3........ III.6:7 "Fear God and **k.** His commandments"
T-3......... V.4:2 all. You **k.** asking what it is you are. This
T-4........ III.6:3 the Father in my name to **k.** you mindful
T-4........ IV.1:4 This is what you are fighting to **k.**, and
T-4......... V.6:4 the real question and **k.** it out of mind.
T-5........... I.5:7 to bless their creations and **k.** them in the
T-5......... II.1:5 can **k.** it asleep you cannot obliterate it.
T-5....... II.12:3 teaches you how to **k.** me as the model for
T-5....... IV.3:4 ego can **k.** you in exile from the Kingdom,
T-5....... VII.3:3 He wills to **k.** it in perfect peace, because
T-5....... VII.6:4 **k.** yourself fully aware that the undoing
T-6......... II.2:3 it because you continue to **k.** it separated.
T-6......... II.2:4 you try to **k.** the fact that you attacked
T-6......... II.3:2 only purpose is to **k.** the separation going.
T-6........ III.4:2 will **k.** you free as others learn it of you.
T-6........ IV.9:5 a Guide to find it and a means to **k.** it.
T-6... V.A.5:11 back, because He wants you to **k.** it.
T-6.... V.C.1:11 and so He alone can **k.** you wholly joyous.
T-6...... V.C.9:4 **k.** *only* the Kingdom of God in your mind,
T-7........ VI.7:1 will **k.** in mind what the Holy Spirit offers
T-7....... VII.5:7 **K.** His way to remember yourself, and
T-7..... VIII.1:6 you give what you value in order to **k.** it in
T-7..... VIII.3:3 Any attempt to **k.** part of it and get rid of
T-7..... VIII.3:7 Giving it is how you *k.* it. The belief that by
T-7..... VIII.5:5 the errors as yours, do not **k.** them. Give
T-7..... VIII.6:2 and no one can **k.** a belief he has judged
T-7........ XI.3:4 Does it **k.** his heart untouched by fear,
T-9........ III.7:3 If you would find your way and **k.** it, see
T-9........ VI.4:1 but not even this would He **k.** from you.
T-9....... VII.7:3 **k.** the ego's whole thought system intact.
T-10...... III.5:3 And you are willing to **k.** it hidden, to
T-10...... IV.4:1 God's laws will **k.** your mind at peace
T-10....... V.3:4 Unless you are sick you cannot **k.** the gods
T-11....... in.4:4 in order to **k.** a dark cornerstone hidden,
T-11......... I.6:2 Yet you can **k.** it only by giving it, as it
T-12....... II.4:3 hide their nightmares they will **k.** them. It
T-12....... II.9:8 He cannot shine away what you **k.** hidden
T-12...... IV.1:5 out to you, and the one promise it will **k.**.
T-12...... IV.4:3 Is this the promise you would **k.**? The
T-12..... VII.6:8 and if it is split and wants to **k.** the split, it
T-12... VIII.5:2 has obliterated it and wants to **k.** it so.
T-13....... II.1:4 guilt, and thereby **k.** it in your mind.
T-13...... III.1:8 **k.** it hidden because you are more afraid
T-13...... III.6:1 your illusions and not **k.** them hidden,
T-13...... IV.8:3 Its continuity, then, would **k.** you in time,
T-13.... VI.10:7 having received it of you they would **k.** it.
T-13... VII.15:3 yourself with what you will as surely **k.**,
T-13....... X.1:2 guilt, and **k.** from your awareness the full
T-13....... X.7:1 Holy Spirit does not **k.** illusions in your
T-13....... X.9:8 Nothing can **k.** from you what Christ
T-13...... XI.7:1 in Heaven, and nothing can **k.** you from it
T-13...... XI.7:6 will not **k.** what God would have removed
T-14.... III.19:3 *never k. from me what He would have me*
T-14....... V.4:3 steal it away and **k.** it from his sight. Bring
T-14...... VI.3:5 for fear, for what they **k.** obscure *is* fearful.
T-14...... VI.4:3 **K.** not guilt and guiltlessness apart, for
T-14...... VI.8:3 **k.** no source of interference from His
T-14..... VII.4:5 their separation seems to **k.** them both
T-14...... IX.1:5 **K.** not your making from your Father, for
T-14...... XI.1:3 tried to **k.** power for yourself have "lost"
T-14...... XI.2:5 yourself that you can possibly prefer to **k.**,
T-15...... I.4:10 to **k.** fear from you to hold your allegiance
T-15...... IV.7:1 to have private thoughts and **k.** them?
T-15...... IV.7:4 think you find a way to **k.** what you would
T-15...... IV.8:1 would **k.** hidden shuts communication off
T-15...... IV.9:2 that you have none that you would **k.**.
T-15...... IV.9:8 the thoughts you would **k.** to yourself. Let
T-15..... VII.2:2 **k.** the giver bound to itself through guilt.
T-15..... VII.2:5 that it can get and **k.** *by making guilty*. This
T-15... VII.11:6 way in which they would **k.** minds apart.
T-15... VII.12:2 to attempt to **k.** your brother in his body,
T-15...... XI.1:5 try longer to **k.** apart your thoughts and
T-15...... XI.6:5 what you prefer to **k.** that has no meaning
T-15...... XI.6:5 while all that you would **k.** away holds all
T-16......... I.3:5 nothing from the past that you would **k.**.
T-16......... I.3:8 **K.** but one thought in mind and do not
T-16......... I.7:2 because you **k.** them separate and secret
T-16....... II.2:3 still try to **k.** understanding to yourself. A
T-16...... IV.3:3 barricades against it, and **k.** within them.
T-16...... VI.4:3 body. And what you value you will **k.**. The
T-16...... VI.8:2 it will **k.** gentle pace with you in your
T-16...... VI.9:2 **k.** part of the thought system that taught
T-17......... I.3:2 because you would **k.** them from truth.
T-17......... I.5:4 **k.** them by justifying your belief in them.
T-17...... III.1:8 who **k.** them by your own selection do not
T-17...... III.2:1 you what you do to **k.** it safe is really love.
T-17.... IV.10:4 now be undertaken, to **k.** truth whole.
T-17..... VII.1:7 remove the problem elsewhere is to **k.** it,
T-17... VII.8:12 outside it and **k.** the situation holy. For it
T-17... VIII.6:7 and **k.** you separate from Him Whose Call
T-18......... I.9:9 you made for Heaven can **k.** you from it.
T-18....... I.10:1 substitute can **k.** you from your brother.
T-18...... II.5:19 is your determination to **k.** your hold on
T-18....... V.7:6 *may descend on us, and k. us both in peace.*
T-18.... VII.8:5 that will **k.** it so in your awareness of it.
T-18... VIII.2:4 shut Him out, and **k.** you apart from Him.
T-18... VIII.8:3 and **k.** complete what it would give. In
T-18. VIII.13:2 to cloud your eyes and **k.** you sightless.
T-18...... IX.4:2 that were made to **k.** the guilt in place, so
T-18...... IX.4:2 world could rise from it and **k.** it hidden.
T-18...... IX.4:3 and loneliness to it and **k.** it joyless. Yet
T-18...... IX.4:4 apart from what was made to **k.** it hidden.
T-19......... I.6:3 but it *will* **k.** the delusional thought system
T-19......... I.6:7 to **k.** both truth and illusion in the mind,
T-19......... I.7:8 for this concealment seems to **k.** your
T-19....... I.10:4 you would **k.** no one separate from yours.
T-19....... I.15:1 faithlessness will **k.** your little kingdoms
T-19....... II.4:5 away from truth, and **k.** it separate?
T-19...... III.4:9 it be but a mistake you would **k.** hidden; a
T-19...... III.4:9 would **k.** unheard and thus unanswered?
T-19.... III.11:2 For sin would **k.** you separate from him,
T19... IV.A.1:2 For it cannot extend unless you **k.** it. You
T19. IV.A.2:11 oppose the Will of God, and **k.** it limited.
T19... IV.A.3:7 and **k.** separate from your brother seems
T19... IV.A.3:8 purpose of Heaven, and **k.** it *from* Heaven.
T19... IV.A.6:6 How can a shadow **k.** you from the sun?
T19. IV.A.17:6 I teach that bodies cannot **k.** us apart?
T19.... IV.B.7:5 And **k.** you not apart from what is offered
T19.... IV.B.8:4 to **k.** away One Who is there already. And
T19 IV.B.14:10 hides it, for it would **k.** you unaware of it.
T19.... IV.C.4:2 to sin to feed upon and **k.** itself alive; a
T19.... IV.C.5:1 have another dedication that would **k.** the
T19... IV.D.3:3 ego to **k.** what lies beyond the veil forever
T19... IV.D.8:5 it has no power to **k.** you from the truth.
T19. IV.D.12:3 to **k.** what seems to be yourself unharmed
T-20...... III.2:4 **k.** them separate and prevent their union.
T-20...... IV.1:7 Thus would He **k.** you free of them. Being
T-20...... VI.2:6 nothing that it would **k.** apart and hide. It
T-20...... VI.3:6 can hide and **k.** their secrets hidden along
T-20...... VI.5:3 and seeks for crumbs to **k.** itself alive.
T-20.. VI.12:11 and **k.** remembrance of His Love apart
T-21......... I.4:5 not understand the lessons *k.* them blind.
T-21......... I.4:7 **k.** the world they learned to "see" in their
T-21......... I.5:4 believing that to **k.** the body is to save the
T-21....... II.4:2 it, and you **k.** the world as now you see it.
T-21..... II.10:2 to **k.** obscure the cause of the effect, and
T-21...... III.1:4 to **k.** the bargain in the name of "fairness,
T-21...... III.3:3 For faith can **k.** the Son of God in chains
T-21...... IV.8:2 it would **k.** apart has met and joined, and
T-22...... III.8:1 Let not the form of his mistakes **k.** you
T-22....... V.3:7 Yet it remains impossible to **k.** love out.
T-22.... VI.10:7 that seems to **k.** the fear of God in place,
T-22.... VI.15:4 to **k.** a little of the ego with this gift. For it
T-23........ II.9:7 would **k.** from you must be worth having,
T-23........ II.9:7 because they **k.** it hidden from your sight.
T-24......... I.5:6 become to **k.** your specialness *is* an illusion
T-24......... I.7:4 What you **k.** is lost to you. God gave you
T-24........ II.3:7 it carefully in sin, to **k.** it "safe" from truth
T-24...... II.10:4 not **k.** one part of what He is unto Himself
T-24.... IV.3:12 **k.** the gift your Father asks from Him, and
T-25......... I.4:6 that seems to **k.** you separate and apart.
T-25........ II.1:7 no rewards which you would want to **k.**.
T-25.... VIII.1:6 it than that you **k.** it for yourself alone,
T-25.... VIII.4:7 to "atone" for all that you would **k.**, and
T-25...... IX.7:6 **k.** it for yourself to solve without His help
T-25...... IX.9:1 you **k.** and hide become your secret sins,
T-26......... I.2:4 the other part, to **k.** itself complete. For if
T-26......... I.3:2 incomplete to **k.** its own identity intact.
T-26......... I.6:2 nor **k.** the Holy Spirit from His task of
T-26......... I.8:5 he made to **k.** himself from justice? Could
T-26........ II.5:1 to be corrected while you **k.** the others to
T-26........ II.5:7 you **k.** a problem for yourself to solve, or
T-26........ II.7:2 You will not **k.** one, for pain in any form
T-26....... IV.2:4 between to **k.** them separate and apart.
T-26....... V.5:1 instant you would **k.** and make eternal,
T-26....... V.5:6 **k.** an ancient memory before your eyes.
T-26..... V.10:7 the power to **k.** you in a place of death, a
T-26...... VI.1:8 can choose to **k.** the ones that he prefers,
T-26.... VIII.1:2 would **k.** between you and your brother,
T-26.... VIII.2:1 a distance you would **k.** apart from your
T-26.... VIII.3:8 If you would **k.** a little space between you
T-26...... IX.7:1 to **k.** away all darkened thoughts of sin,
T-26...... IX.7:1 and **k.** the light where it has entered in.
T-27..... II.15:6 only thus can He **k.** yours preserved intact
T-27...... VI.1:2 and **k.** His words from your awareness.
T-27..... VII.2:3 were made to **k.** the problem unresolved?
T-27.... VIII.8:3 the petulant device to **k.** your innocence
T-27.. VIII.12:8 They seem to **k.** it secret from you. Yet
T-28......... I.5:2 not seek to use it as a means to **k.** the past
T-28......... I.5:8 associations made to **k.** the past alive, the
T-28......... I.6:2 to **k.** concealed the truth about yourself.
T-28......... I.7:2 would **k.** a senseless lesson in his mind,
T-28......... I.8:3 which He did not **k.** It safely in your mind
T-28....... I.13:1 that has no fear to **k.** the memory away!
T-28....... I.13:3 is no past to **k.** its fearful image in the way
T-28........ II.8:1 and powerless to **k.** them since He was no
T-28...... III.4:3 it is a wish to **k.** apart and not to join.
T-28...... III.4:6 For it was made to **k.** you separated, in a
T-28...... III.5:4 to **k.** them separate for a little while?
T-28...... III.6:3 with eager hands, to **k.** them for yourself.
T-28...... III.7:1 **k.** within the storehouse of the world. The
T-28...... III.9:8 seemed to **k.** your Guests apart from you.
T-28.... VI.3:10 want your mind to have and see and **k.**.
T-28...... VI.6:2 he will **k.** the promise that you make with
T-28..... VII.5:5 to **k.** a promise to be true to faithlessness.
T-29......... I.3:9 was a point you both agreed to **k.** intact.
T-29......... I.4:6 and **k.** apart in intervals of separation,
T-29......... I.5:7 do, and **k.** your purpose limited and weak
T-29...... III.2:7 the wall the world has built to **k.** apart all
T-29...... III.4:4 saw the light that he would **k.** beside him,
T-29...... IV.1:5 choice is not between which dreams to **k.**,
T-29....... V.6:1 you would not **k.** hold on any thought,
T-29....... V.7:6 sword, to **k.** his ancient promises to die.
T-29...... VI.2:2 You make a bargain that you cannot **k.**.
T-29..... VII.6:1 to **k.** the truth within from being known

T-29......IX.3:3 an idol **k.** the dream alive and terrible, for
T-29......IX.5:7 Yet do they **k.** his thoughts alive and real,
T-29....IX.10:2 try to worship idols and to **k.** attack.
T-30.......I.17:6 be the one reminder that you **k.** in mind,
T-30.......II.4:5 **k.** your will forever and forever limitless.
T-30....III.11:8 that idols must **k.** hidden what you are,
T-30......VI.4:1 world employs to **k.** the sense of sin alive.
T-30......VI.6:2 means that you prefer to **k.** some idols,
T-30......VI.7:6 you will **k.** an image of yourself that is not
T-30......VI.8:2 And do not **k.** a part of him outside your
T-30....VIII.3:4 but **k.** their unreality obscure and give to
T-31.......II.6:9 way unless you **k.** him safely by your side.
T-31......III.5:1 to **k.** it in the prison house it chose and
T-31......III.6:6 your chosen enemies, nor **k.** in chains, to
T-31......IV.1:1 from problems that its purpose is to **k.**.
T-31......IV.6:5 this would ***k.*** the truth from being reached
T-31....IV.10:2 from them than they could **k.** Him out. In
T-31.....VII.6:3 the hope of change and **k.** it static and
T-31.....VII.9:2 that it may fight to **k.** the space that holds
T-31...VII.12:6 you see, or **k.** yourself apart and separate.
W-pI.......3.2:2 essential that you **k.** a perfectly open
W-pI.......5.6:3 this: *I cannot* ***k.*** *this form of upset and let the*
W-pI.......6.3:5 *I cannot* ***k.*** *this form of upset and let the*
W-pI.....12.2:4 shorter, but try, instead, to **k.** a measured,
W-pI.....27.4:5 try to **k.** on your schedule from then on. If
W-pI.....28.1:3 The question of whether you will **k.** them
W-pI.....37.6:4 may learn to **k.** it in your own awareness.
W-pI.....38.5:4 but **k.** the exercises focused on the theme,
W-pI.....64.8:3 **k.** your eyes open after reviewing the
W-pI.....65.8:4 sometimes **k.** them open and look about
W-pI.....69.8:5 Try to **k.** the thought clearly in mind that
W-pI.....70.4:1 it was intended, and thus **k.** the sickness.
W-pI.....72.3:1 attempt to **k.** the limitations that a body
W-pI...73.10:1 and determining to **k.** your will clearly in
W-pI.....75.6:2 **K.** a completely open mind, washed of all
W-pI...75.11:2 **K.** it in your awareness of yourself and see
W-pI...76.11:3 Heaven which His laws **k.** limitless forever
W-pI.....79.4:1 to **k.** the problem of separation unsolved.
W-pI.....84.3:3 attack love and **k.** its light obscure. If I
W-pI.....85.1:4 They **k.** me in darkness and hide the light.
W-pI.....95.7:1 **k.** to the five-minutes-an-hour practice
W-pI....95.10:2 to **k.** you unaware you are one Self, united
W-pI...100.9:5 What foolish goal can **k.** you from success
WpIrIII.in10:6 things, but try to **k.** the thought with you,
WpIrIII.in10:6 and let it serve to help you **k.** your peace
W-pI...124.7:4 For we would **k.** the gifts our Father gave.
W-pI...127.5:2 meaning, and to **k.** it dark and secret.
W-pI...129.5:3 the world sets forth to **k.** you prisoner.
W-pI...130.3:6 would you wish to **k.** in such a dream?
W-pI...132.3:4 and **k.** the world a prisoner to your beliefs
W-pI...133.8:7 for it needs to **k.** the halo which it uses to
W-pI.133.10:1 though he tries to **k.** its halo clear within
W-pI.134.10:1 and **k.** your mind as free of guilt and pain
W-pI...135.8:3 want to **k.** it when its usefulness is done?
W-pI.135.26:7 *And I would* ***k.*** *it holy. I will not defend*
W-pI...136.2:4 aim of all defenses is to **k.** the truth from
W-pI.136.16:2 and **k.** defended from the light of truth.
W-pI...137.2:2 seems to **k.** one self apart from all the rest
W-pI...137.2:3 real, and **k.** the mind in solitary prison,
W-pI...138.8:3 unaware, to **k.** them safely undisturbed;
W-pI.139.12:3 the chains that seem to **k.** the knowledge
W-pI.153.18:3 **k.** your mind away from Him a moment,
W-pI.153.20:1 to help you **k.** your mind from wandering
W-pI.154.10:2 We will not seek to **k.** our minds apart
W-pI.155.10:2 nothing left to **k.** the truth apart from
W-pI...156.7:3 **k.** you bound no longer. The approach to
W-pI...165.1:4 What could **k.** from you what you already
W-pI...166.9:6 your plan to **k.** His Son in deep oblivion,
W-pI.167.11:1 we strive to **k.** today as He established it,
WpI...rV.in5:3 if we **k.** in mind that this remains our goal
WpI.rV.in11:4 up before our minds, and **k.** it clear in our
Wi181-200 2:1 special blocks that **k.** your vision narrow,
W-pI...181.7:1 thought to **k.** us safe throughout the day.
W-pI...182.2:2 time, and **k.** their sadness from them.
W-pI...183.2:2 they spread out their wings to **k.** you safe,
W-pI...187.4:4 in time, however much you try to **k.** it safe
W-pI...190.6:6 and **k.** it as a hospital for pain; a sickly
W-pII ....in.7:5 be kept which are Your Will to **k.**. We will
W-pII .226.1:4 I want to **k.** as mine or search for as a goal
W-pII .235.1:2 I need but **k.** in mind my Father's Will for
W-pII .254.2:4 And so we do not choose to **k.** them. They
W-pII .....6.4:3 what could there be to **k.** things separate,
W-pII .273.2:2 *can rob me of what You would have me* ***k.****? I*
W-pII .287.1:4 and **k.** that can compare with my Identity
W-pII294.1:10 to **k.** its usefulness while it can serve, and
W-pII .300.1:2 lets no false perception **k.** us in its hold,
W-pII .308.1:3 Time's purpose cannot be to **k.** the past
W-pII .314.2:2 *sure that You will* ***k.*** *Your present promises,*
W-pII ....347.h myself, To **k.** the miracle away from me.
W-pII .355.1:2 *will* ***k.*** *Your Word You gave Your Son in exile*
M-4 .....I.A.6:6 you do not want, and **k.** what you do."
M-4 .....VII.1:5 God, it means giving away in order to **k.**.
M-4 .....VII.2:7 he does not seek what only he could **k.**,
M-4 ...VII.2:10 to **k.** for himself all things that are of God,
M-5 .........I.1:8 eager to **k.** all power for Himself. Only by
M-6 ..........1:2 be brought to truth and **k.** the illusions.
M-10 .........6:2 But it is difficult indeed to try to **k.** it. The
M-15 ........3:11 and offer it to all the world to **k.** it safe.
M-17 ..........5:9 and make himself a shield to **k.** him safe
M-20 .........6:7 He does not seek to **k.** it for Himself. Why
M-20 .........6:8 Why would you seek to **k.** your tiny frail
M-21 .........1:7 to **k.** them in the illusion of separation.
M-23 .........3:7 it is likely that he will fail to **k.** them. Can
C-4 ............5:7 remains to **k.** a separated world in place?
P-2........ III.4:4 and too near to God to **k.** his feet on earth
P-2........ VI.4:1 to justify attack and thus **k.** unforgiveness
S-2.........in.1:4 to hold you up and **k.** your feet secure;
S-2..........II.4:1 Son He loves, and **k.** him from his Source.
S-2..........II.5:7 to **k.** the witnesses of guilt away from love
S-3..........II.6:3 no veil of sin to **k.** it dark and comfortless.

## keeping 47

*See also* safe-keeping

T-1 .........II.5:3 **k.** the direct channel from God to you
T-7 ....... IX.6:3 it forever, He gave you the means for **k.** it.
T-8 .....VIII.4:1 it is entirely out of **k.** with what you want.
T-9 ....... IV.5:3 beginning, and thus **k.** it unreal for you.
T-9 .....VII.5:4 using its methods for **k.** this picture intact
T-9 .....VIII.5:2 illusions and **k.** yourself in the Mind of
T-13 ........II.4:4 for its existence depends on **k.** this secret.
T-14 ..... VI.4:4 All you have done by **k.** them apart is lose
T-14 ..... XI.8:5 for **k.** certain dark lessons from Him. And
T-15 ..... IV.7:3 lies in **k.** thoughts to yourself alone. For in
T-16 ..... III.5:5 **k.** one with you what you would exclude.
T-16 ...... V.2:3 chief weapon for **k.** you from Heaven. It
T-16 .... VII.7:4 you from **k.** the experience in your mind.
T-17 ... III.1:11 with **k.** separation could hear them. They
T-17 ... IV.16:3 and **k.** no illusions of where they are.
T-18 ..... VI.9:1 from others and **k.** you apart from them,
T-18 ... VIII.6:4 the rest, and **k.** it apart from its Creator.
T-18 ..... IX.1:4 The rest is fully in God's **k.**, and needs no
T-18 ..... IX.4:5 which depends on **k.** it not seen. The
T-19 ..... III.3:6 it was an error, but **k.** it uncorrectable.
T-20 ... VI.11:2 **k.** it prisoner in a tiny spot of space and
T-20 .... VII.5:4 quite in **k.** with the purpose of unholiness
T-21 .....II.13:3 **k.** you from each other and separate from
T-23 .....II.10:1 the "enemy" made strong by **k.** hidden
T-24 ......in.1:1 attainment and the **k.** of the state of peace
T-24 .......II.1:3 by searching for, and **k.** clear in sight, all
T-26 ....... V.2:5 hand and **k.** step to Heaven's song, is
T-28 ...... V.1:5 off the self from good, and **k.** evil in. God
T-29 ... III.3:10 the gap so long perceived as **k.** you apart.
T-29 ..... VI.4:5 Forgiveness does not aim at **k.** time, but
T-31 ..... VI.2:7 has released from looking at the cost of **k.**
W-pI......18.3:1 and **k.** your eyes on each one long enough
W-pI......28.1:4 you have started on the way to **k.** them.
W-pI......30.2:4 we see, rather than **k.** it apart from us.
W-pI......39.8:3 *unloving thoughts about_are* ***k.*** *me in hell.*
W-pI......41.6:6 **k.** it clear of any thoughts that might
W-pI......44.9:1 **k.** your eyes closed unless you are aware
W-pI......45.6:2 thoughts of your own, **k.** the idea in mind
W-pI......72.2:3 mind with a body, **k.** it separate and alone
W-pI......91.9:5 You will be accustomed to **k.** faith with
WpIrIV.in10:1 you who practice thus the **k.** of His Word.
W-pI... 192.8:4 so he spends his time in **k.** watch on him.
W-pII .225.1:2 *blazing in my mind and* ***k.*** *it within its kindly*
W-pII .229.2:1 *am; for* ***k.*** *my Identity untouched and sinless*
W-pII ..... 5.1:5 remains within the body, **k.** love outside?
W-pII . 358.1:6 *and care,* ***k.*** *Your promise to Your Son in my*
M-4 ...... IX.1:2 to his learning, while **k.** others apart? If so

## keeps 52

T-4 .........V.1:4 because it **k.** its primary motivation from
T-5 .........II.1:6 obliterate it. God Himself **k.** your will
T-5 ....... IV.2:1 What the ego makes it **k.** to itself, and so
T-5 ....... IV.3:8 that are of God and that He **k.** for you.
T-6 .........II.1:5 defense, or the device that **k.** it going. The
T-6 ..... V.C.1:6 This is how He **k.** the Kingdom perfectly
T-7 ....... III.5:1 and **k.** your mind lit by His light because
T-7 .....VIII.1:4 Kingdom, and **k.** it in the Mind of God.
T-9 ... VIII.10:3 Himself **k.** your extensions safe within it.
T-11 ...... I.11:4 remember that what He gives He **k.**, so
T-12 ..... VI.4:5 The Holy Spirit **k.** the vision of Christ for
T-14 ..... III.5:5 Everyone you attack **k.** it and cherishes it
T-15 ... VIII.5:5 And so He **k.** this channel open to receive
T-15 .......X.9:1 for it **k.** no bargains and would leave you
T-18 ...... VI.3:4 Its guilt, which **k.** it separate, is projected
T19 . IV.B.13:6 this insane relationship that it **k.** hidden,
T-21 ......II.13:5 of its source that **k.** you prisoner. This is
T-21 .......V.8:9 not depend on it, and madness **k.** it out.
T-22 ...... I.4:10 Here is the one emotion that **k.** you blind,
T-23 ...... I.10:3 **k.** God homeless and His Son with Him.
T-24 .....II.13:1 prison house that **k.** His Son from Him.
T-24 ..... VI.5:4 sin you see in him but **k.** you both in hell.
T-24 .... VII.5:1 The Father **k.** what He created safe. You
T-26 ........ I.8:1 **k.** him safe from all injustice the world
T-26 ..... VI.2:4 and **k.** His friendship and forgiveness
T-26 .....X.1:11 to Theirs, and **k.** Them there unknown.
T-27 .....II.16:4 that its Giver **k.** *because* it has been shared
T-27 ... VIII.7:6 It **k.** you narrowly confined within a body
T-28 ..... VI.6:3 God **k.** His promises; His Son keeps his.
T-28 ..... VI.6:3 God keeps His promises; His Son **k.** his.
T-30 ..... III.9:4 the time that **k.** this star invisible to earth.
T-30 ..... VI.2:9 It ***k.*** your rights from being sacrificed.
T-30 ... VIII.1:7 and **k.** it separate from all appearances. It
W-pI .... 57.1:8 Only my wish to stay **k.** me a prisoner. I
W-pI .... 69.2:4 the veil of darkness that **k.** it concealed.
W-pI .... 76.7:4 instead it is a truth that **k.** us free forever.
W-pI .... 92.4:2 It **k.** its steady gaze upon the light that lies
W-pI 131.14:4 Today God **k.** His ancient promise to His
W-pI .. 132.1:1 **k.** the world in chains but your beliefs?
W-pI .. 137.1:4 separate self, and **k.** it isolated and alone.
W-pI .. 182.1:3 A memory of home **k.** haunting you, as if
W-pI .. 189.2:2 and sings your praises as it **k.** you safe
W-pI .. 193.2:6 and **k.** his sinlessness forever safe.
W-pI .. 218.1:2 *My condemnation* ***k.*** *my vision dark, and*
W-pII . 235.1:3 Son and **k.** his sinlessness forever perfect,
W-pII . 264.1:4 *Your Son and* ***k.*** *him safe is Love itself. There*
W-pII ...... 6.2:1 is the link that **k.** you one with God, and
W-pII ..... 341.h And it is only that which **k.** me safe.
M-4 ......... I.1:6 It is this power that **k.** all things safe. It is
M-12 ......... 5:9 purpose from the one that **k.** it holy.
M-16 ......... 1:9 he **k.** in constant contact with the Answer
M-22 ......... 3:3 mind, and **k.** the idea of attack inviolate.

## kept 120

T-4 .........V.5:4 be formulated clearly and **k.** in mind.
T-4 ...... VII.7:1 God has **k.** your Kingdom for you, but He
T-5 ....... IV.8:4 and **k.** them for you in their own perfect
T-10 ..... IV.8:2 Yet God has **k.** the spark alive so that the
T-11 .......I.5:11 you will learn what God has **k.** for you.
T-12 ..... IV.7:2 you chose to "sell" had to be **k.** for you,
T-12 ... VIII.1:2 and **k.** him far away from your destructive
T-13 ........ I.7:2 not, has **k.** faith with his Father for you.
T-13 ...... III.7:6 you have **k.** to hurt you and cleanse it of
T-13 .. VII.13:3 hidden in your mind and **k.** to hurt you.
T-14 ..... VI.1:8 The hidden is **k.** apart, but value always
T-14 ..... VI.2:4 What is **k.** apart from love cannot share
T-14 ..... VI.2:4 has been separated off and **k.** in darkness.
T-14 .... VII.1:3 must be brought together, not **k.** apart.
T-14 .... VII.4:5 But if one is **k.** in darkness from the other,
T-15 .. VII.11:5 must be **k.** private or they will lose them,
T-16 ..... IV.3:4 from which hatred is split off and **k.** apart
T-17 ..... III.8:6 is **k.** but witnesses to the reality of dreams

T-17.....V.12:2 It must be **k.** shining and gracious in your
T-18.......II.6:9 As its unholiness **k.** it a thing apart, its
T-18.......IX.4:4 and **k.** apart from what was made to keep
T-19.........I.4:4 and **k.** you both apart from being healed.
T-19......I.16:4 incapable of being **k.** in prison or limited
T-19.......II.6:9 sin is **k.** in place by just this strange device
T-19......III.5:9 change perception is thus **k.** impotent,
T19...IV.A.6:7 No more can you be **k.** by shadows from
T19.IV.A.12:5 are **k.** cold and starving and made very
T-20.......II.8:8 freed from all the terror that **k.** it hidden.
T-20....III.11:7 God created His Son holy, and **k.** him so.
T-20......VI.4:1 are **k.** obscure and hidden from the sun.
T-20......VI.6:4 **k.** apart from those who worship them.
T-20......VI.6:7 have *not* be is here **k.** "safe" from Him. But
T-20......VI.6:8 God seem fearful to you, and **k.** unknown.
T-20.....VII.6:5 Here are illusions and reality **k.** separated
T-21.........I.7:2 Yet you have **k.** them with you, not for
T-21......IV.7:5 which the ego's rule has **k.** it out so long.
T-21......VI.5:6 enters part be **k.** away from other parts?
T-22......III.8:2 be **k.** from you by what the body's eyes
T-22......VI.7:1 error is excluded and nothing **k.** hidden,
T-23........in.5:5 yours protected and **k.** in your awareness.
T-23.........I.4:9 shall be part of you and what is **k.** apart.
T-23......III.4:8 it? It can be **k.** shining before your vision,
T-23......III.5:6 hates him still, for what he **k.** from him.
T-24.......in.2:2 Not one can be **k.** hidden and obscure but
T-24.........I.2:2 the results of conflict are **k.** unknown and
T-24.........I.2:3 decisions have been made and **k.** hidden,
T-24.....II.10:4 not given to His Son but **k.** for Him alone.
T-24.....II.10:7 and **k.** separate from what it is and must
T-24.....VII.8:5 It is essential it be **k.** in mind that all
T-25.......II.7:5 God **k.** it safe that you might look on it,
T-25......III.4:1 link that **k.** it still within the laws of God;
T-25...VIII.4:5 is made that sin may be preserved and **k.**.
T-25.VIII.10:1 can it be that anything be **k.** from him?
T-25......IX.1:7 will you hold dear that sin be **k.** in place.
T-25......IX.2:4 given to God's Son are **k.** for him, and
T-25......IX.7:2 and **k.** apart from others as less deserving,
T-26.......II.8:4 His Love **k.** perfectly intact and undefiled.
T-26......IV.2:6 them has not been **k.** apart and separate.
T-26.......V.8:4 And do you want that fearful instant **k.**,
T-26.....V.10:8 And how can he be **k.** in chains long since
T-26.....VII.2:4 a relationship **k.** hidden from awareness
T-26.....VII.3:9 **K.** apart from truth, it seems to have a
T-26...VII.12:8 What is thus **k.** apart can never join.
T-26...VII.14:1 are brought together, not **k.** separate. The
T-26...VIII.5:7 it protected and **k.** separate from healing.
T-27.VIII.12:4 is a secret you have **k.** but from yourself.
T-27.VIII.13:4 a secret **k.** from no one but yourself. And
T-27.VIII.13:5 and **k.** your brother separate from you.
T-28.........I.1:5 but being **k.** in memory appears to have
T-28......I.12:2 Son of God, for whom they have been **k.**.
T-28......III.3:5 where sickness is **k.** carefully protected,
T-28......IV.4:5 and you are **k.** in bondage to his dreams.
T-28......VI.5:4 mind and yours" has **k.** God's promise,
T-29......IV.1:4 Could it be some dreams are **k.**, and
T-29.......V.8:1 that has been **k.** apart from use by Him
T-29...VIII.4:4 has been excluded and been **k.** apart?
T-30....III.10:4 peace. Here is your one reality **k.** safe,
T-30......VI.8:4 missing parts that have been **k.** outside.
T-31....IV.10:3 in Their Oneness Both are **k.** complete.
T-31.......V.5:4 the pathways of the world are safely **k.**,
T-31.......V.6:5 **k.** still deeper in the mists below the face
T-31.......V.6:6 and yours preserved and **k.** in darkness,
T-31.....V.10:8 from whom must something be **k.** hidden
T-31.....V.11:1 this concept must be **k.** in darkness is that
T-31.....VII.7:3 The light is **k.** from everything you see. At
T-31.....VII.9:1 **k.** apart by an illusion of yourself that
W-pI.....56.1:7 But God has **k.** my inheritance safe for me
W-pI.....56.5:4 It has been **k.** for me in the Mind of God,
W-pI.....57.5:5 what my illusions about myself **k.** hidden.
W-pI.....70.3:4 so He has **k.** the Source of healing where
W-pI.....96.7:4 Thus is salvation **k.** among the Thoughts
W-pI...96.11:5 Him another treasure to be **k.** for you.
W-pI...106.4:1 Today the promise of God's Word is **k.**.
W-pI...106.4:9 to you and all your brothers to be **k.**.
W-pI.106.10:1 the holy Word of God is **k.** through your
W-pI...122.3:5 effect or transient promise, never to be **k.**,
W-pI.122.12:2 us since time began, **k.** waiting for today.
W-pI.134.11:2 They are not **k.** to swell and bluster, and
W-pI...152.5:3 and the false **k.** separate from the truth,
W-pI...159.1:5 that to possess a thing, it must be **k.**.
W-pI...159.3:2 which never dies, but has been **k.** obscure
W-pI...162.4:3 giving; **k.** complete because its sharing is
WpI...rV.in8:8 time was and **k.** unchanged by time,
W-pI...184.3:1 bodies **k.** apart and holding bits of mind
W-pI.184.14:3 separations disappear which **k.** us blind.
W-pI...189.1:5 in you to be **k.** hidden from your sight.
W-pI.193.11:4 by ourselves, and **k.** apart from healing.
W-pI...194.5:3 light that was **k.** hidden in God's Son is
W-pI...196.1:1 understood and **k.** in full awareness, you
W-pII.....in.2:4 And we are sure His promises are **k.**. We
W-pII.....in.5:2 all ancient promises upheld and fully **k.**.
W-pII.....in.7:5 be **k.** which are Your Will to keep. We
W-pII......1.2:3 to doubt, and further **k.** from reason.
W-pII..229.1:5 but which my Father has **k.** safe for me.
W-pII......2.1:2 last. It cannot but be **k.**. It guarantees that
W-pII......3.3:5 is but illusion which is **k.** apart from truth
W-pII..313.1:6 *which You have **k.** completely undefiled*
W-pII..336.2:2 *find Your promise of my sinlessness is **k.**;*
P-2.........V.6:2 And now God's promises are **k.** by Him.
S-1........IV.1:5 a goal. It is in this their enmity is **k.**. Their

## key 28

T-14.......II.7:5 This simple lesson holds the **k.** to the
T-14.......II.7:7 The **k.** is only the light that shines away
T-14.......II.7:8 Accept this **k.** to freedom from the hands
T-22......III.3:2 like a heavy gate, locked and without a **k.**,
T-24.......II.7:6 brother with the **k.** to Heaven in his hand,
T-24.....II.14:1 **k.** you threw away God gave your brother,
T-26.........I.1:1 "dynamics" of attack is sacrifice a **k.** idea.
T-26.......V.6:2 It is the **k.** to learning that the past is over
W-pI.....11.1:5 made sure. The **k.** to forgiveness lies in it.
W-pI.....45.1:1 the **k.** to what your real thoughts are.
W-pI.....65.3:3 It places the **k.** to the door of peace, which
W-pI...101.1:2 a **k.** idea in understanding what salvation
W-pI.110.11:7 is the **k.** that opens up the gate of Heaven,
W-pI......121.h Forgiveness is the **k.** to happiness.
W-pI...121.1:2 the **k.** to meaning in a world that seems to
W-pI...121.8:2 learn today to take the **k.** to happiness,
W-pI.121.13:6 *Forgiveness is the **k.** to happiness. I will*
W-pI...122.9:2 aware we hold the **k.** within our hands,
W-pI...141.1:1 (121) Forgiveness is the **k.** to happiness.
W-pI.193.13:5 you hold the **k.** that opens Heaven's gate,
W-pI...198.9:2 the **k.** to light and let the darkness end:
W-pII..342.1:4 *The **k.** is in my hand, and I have reached the*
S-1........IV.1:7 The **k.** to rising further still in prayer lies
S-2...........I.9:2 Forgiveness is the **k.**, but who can use a
S-2...........I.9:2 but who can use a **k.** when he has lost the
S-2...........I.9:2 lost the door for which the **k.** was made,
S-2........III.7:6 door to which forgiveness is the only **k.**.
S-3...........I.4:3 For he has thrown away the prison's **k.**;

## keynote 1

W-pII..325.1:1 This is salvation's **k.**: What I see reflects a

## kill 44

T-12...VII.13:4 Wanting to **k.** you as the final expression
T-12...VIII.1:1 believe that you can **k.** the Son of God?
T-13.......in.3:3 *Love does not **k.** to save.* If it did, attack
T-13.......II.5:4 to **k.** yourself by not knowing who you are
T-13.......II.5:6 For the ego does want to **k.** you, and if
T-13.......II.6:2 of God's Son it did attempt to **k.** him, and
T-13.......II.8:4 redemption and you believe it will **k.** you.
T-13......III.2:4 upon your savage wish to **k.** God's Son, if
T-14.....V.10:7 and by its condemnation it would **k.**. The
T-16.....V.11:5 people, on which each seeks to **k.** his self,
T19....IV.C.2:1 And yet a shadow cannot **k.**. What is a
T19....IV.C.4:6 of guilt you laid upon the body would **k.** it
T19....IV.C.4:8 But what obeys it not, it cannot **k.**.
T19....IV.C.8:1 created against the ego's savage wish to **k.**
T-20......III.4:5 *is* frightened, and those who **k.** fear death.
T-21...VII.13:7 thought but has the power to release or **k.**
T-21...VIII.1:3 The thoughts that seem to **k.** are those
T-23.....II.13:3 this substitute for love, and **k.** you both.
T-24........II.8:7 you, to save his specialness and **k.** his Self.
T-24........II.9:3 bound in hate to **k.** each other and deny
T-24......II.12:2 serves its purpose must be given to **k.**. No
T-24......IV.1:5 In danger of destruction it must **k.**, and
T-24......IV.1:5 kill, and you are drawn to it to **k.** it first.
T-24.......V.4:3 what can specialness delight in but to **k.**?
T-25......IV.3:7 and every wish to hurt and **k.** and die, will
T-26......IX.8:5 replace an ancient enmity that came to **k.**.
T-27.........I.4:5 in contagion do they seek to **k.**. Death
T-29......VI.5:1 and tie your hands and **k.** your body only
T-29.....VII.3:4 Yet does he seek to **k.** God's Son within,
T-31......III.5:3 for they are enemies which sin must **k.**. In
T-31...V.15:10 you see your own concealed desire to **k.**.
T-31......VI.6:6 perceived as treacherous, and out to **k.**.
W-pI.....22.2:4 that you hate and would attack and **k.**. All
W-pI...101.3:3 Salvation must be feared, for it will **k.**, but
W-pI.134.12:2 He does not have to **k.** the dragons which
W-pI.196.11:1 you until the time when it can **k.** at last.
W-pI...197.1:5 that when He strikes He will not fail to **k.**.
W-pII .....5.4:5 to heal the mind that it was made to **k.**.
M-8 ..........5:4 a whispered demand to **k.** than a shout?
M-17 ..........7:8 Except to **k.**. Here is salvation now. An
M-17 .......7:11 **K.** or be killed, for here alone is choice.
C-2............8:1 pain, the fear of dying and the urge to **k.**,
C-5............3:5 that it is impossible to **k.** God's Son; nor
S-3...........I.5:3 amiss and seeming charity forgive to **k.**,

## killed 11

T-6...........I.9:2 abandoned, beaten, torn, and finally **k.**. It
T-19.........II.7:6 then, the death of God, Whom sin has **k.**!
T19.IV.A.17:4 the Son of God was **k.** instead of you. Yet
T-21....VIII.1:3 that teach the thinker that he *can* be **k.**.
T-29......VI.2:3 keep. The Son of Life cannot be **k.**. He is
W-pI...161.7:3 and seen and heard, and ultimately **k.**.
W-pI...163.7:2 was once alive and somehow perished; **k.**,
M-5 .........I.2:6 he will be **k.** to prove to him how weak
M-17 .......7:11 son. Kill or be **k.**, for here alone is choice.
M-22 .........3:8 to the Holy Spirit unless the body is **k.**?
P-2.......IV.9:6 of danger, to be attacked and even **k.**.

## killer 1

T-16.....V.12:4 and invested in His **k.** as the sign that

## kills 2

T19....IV.C.4:7 what the ego loves, it **k.** for its obedience.
W-pI.....73.3:5 Would God create a world that **k.** Himself

## kind 172

T-1...........I.9:1 Miracles are a **k.** of exchange. Like all
T-1........IV.3:5 have everything have no needs of any **k.**.
T-1.......VII.3:2 vision. Fantasies of any **k.** are distortions,
T-2........II.1:10 of being shaken by errors of any **k.**. It
T-2..........II.2:3 This **k.** of denial is not a concealment but
T-2........IV.1:6 **k.** of error to which Atonement is applied
T-2.....VII.1:10 miracle workers need that **k.** of training.
T-3...........I.1:9 the **k.** of thinking which His Own words
T-3...........I.2:9 nothing of this **k.** remains in your mind. I
T-3.........I.2:11 with this **k.** of distortion in any form.
T-3...........I.3:9 This **k.** of error is responsible for a host of
T-4........III.4:8 and this **k.** of wanting is wholly without
T-4........III.5:1 There is a **k.** of experience so different
T-5...........I.1:9 While this **k.** of thinking is totally alien to
T-5...........I.7:1 induces a **k.** of perception in which many
T-6.........in.2:4 developed a thought system of any **k.**, you
T-6...........I.2:2 lies solely in the **k.** of learning it facilitates
T-6..........II.9:6 Although perception of any **k.** is unreal,
T-6........III.3:6 Without anxiety the mind is wholly **k.**,
T-6.......IV.10:4 This is the **k.** of "reasoning" in which the
T-7..........II.1:1 To heal is the only **k.** of thinking in this
T-7.......IV.3:4 The **k.** of learning is as irrelevant as is the
T-8.......IV.6:7 cannot be learned by tyranny of any **k.**,
T-8.......VII.5:2 Loss of any **k.** is impossible. But when you
T-9...........I.7:1 to consider the **k.** of questioner you are.
T-9........III.1:1 to the errors of other egos is not the **k.** of
T-9........III.1:2 in terms of the **k.** of "sense" they stand for

T-9........ III.1:3 They understand this **k.** of sense, because
T-9........ III.2:1 the ego it is **k.** and right and good to point
T-9......... V.7:4 no longer believes in nightmares of any **k.**
T-9....... VII.7:2 is. Lack of knowledge of any **k.** is always
T-10....... V.9:9 and wholly without suffering of any **k.**. If
T-11...... VI.3:6 I am leading you to a new **k.** of experience
T-12...... III.9:6 "laws," and without meaning of any **k.**.
T-13..... VII.2:1 of it is costing you a different **k.** of vision.
T-13..... VII.2:2 of them involves a different **k.** of seeing,
T-13...... XI.6:6 over you without a difference of any **k.**.
T-13.... XI.11:3 different **k.** of reconciliation in His Mind
T-14.... III.16:2 light, error of any **k.** becomes impossible.
T-14....... V.5:4 release from suffering of every **k.** lie in it.
T-14...... VI.4:6 other is wholly without sense of any **k.**.
T-14...... XI.1:8 and truth is beyond semblance of any **k.**.
T-14...... XI.5:2 If you are wholly free of fear of any **k.**, and
T-15....... X.2:6 of me. Learn now that sacrifice of any **k.** is
T-15...... XI.2:4 No sacrifice of any **k.**, of anyone, is asked
T-16....... II.8:6 and wholly **k.** to everyone and everything.
T-16.... IV.13:1 of any **k.** would hinder God's completion,
T-16....... V.6:4 **k.** of union from which union is excluded,
T-16..... V.12:1 love is content, and not form of any **k.**.
T-16...... VI.8:2 Time is **k.**, and if you use it on behalf of
T-16..... VII.9:4 for He is incapable of illusions of any **k.**.
T-17...... III.4:2 hands, as it is **k.** when used for gentleness
T19. IV.A.14:3 and the beautiful, the gentle and the **k.**.
T19. IV.A.14:8 of safety, for they see the world as **k.**.
T19IV.A.17:15 Communion is another **k.** of completion,
T19..IV.B.10:1 justified, for the eternal is forever **k.**,
T19. IV.D.18:2 upon him with condemnation of any **k.**.
T-20....... III.2:1 Adjustments of any **k.** are of the ego. For
T-21....... V.9:4 is far beyond attainment of any **k.**. But
T-21...... VI.1:6 For uncorrected error of any **k.** deceives
T-21.... VI.7:10 **k.** as is the purpose for which it is the
T-21.... VIII.2:3 has no exceptions; no change of any **k.**. It
T-22......... I.1:7 a plan of any **k.** except to wander off, for
T-22....... II.2:3 leave one **k.** of misery and seek another is
T-22.... VI.12:2 believe attack of any **k.** means anything. It
T-23....... in.1:3 cannot fear, for sin of any **k.** is weakness.
T-23....... in.4:7 is at variance with littleness of any **k.**.
T-23....... in.6:4 **k.** forgiveness will the world sparkle and
T-23......... I.4:5 and attack of any **k.** are all unknown. He
T-23....... II.3:4 Errors of any **k.** can be corrected *because*
T-23..... II.10:4 in a savage world the **k.** cannot survive, so
T-23...... III.3:1 Salvation is no compromise of any **k.**. To
T-23...... IV.8:3 Sorrow of any **k.** is inconceivable. Only
T-23...... IV.8:6 could ever suffer change of any **k.**.
T-24......... I.3:6 of any **k.** imposes orders of reality, and a
T-24......... I.7:7 of any **k.** between you and him? Look
T-24...... II.14:2 fail to bring you peace and joy of any **k.**?
T-24...... IV.5:2 and when you suffer pain of any **k.**, you
T-24...... VI.9:2 and without accomplishment of any **k.**, is
T-24..... VII.7:3 held to limits or uncertainties of any **k.**.
T-25...... VI.4:1 Holy Spirit's **k.** perception of specialness;
T-25.... VIII.3:1 is a **k.** of justice in salvation of which the
T-25...... IX.4:3 attack, and loss of any **k.** He cannot see.
T-25...... IX.6:3 he does not merit an attack of any **k.**.
T-26... VII.14:5 is his, unlimited by loss of any **k.**. A tiny
T-26... VII.17:2 is the answer to attack of any **k.**. So is
T-26....... X.2:6 and cannot have effects of any **k.**. Their
T-27......... I.5:7 ever done, or ever had effects of any **k.**.
T-27...... III.4:7 Yet true undoing must be **k.**. And so the
T-27...... III.4:8 picture is another picture of another **k.**.
T-27...... III.6:1 and vacant will not need defense of any **k.**
T-27...... III.7:7 no other **k.** can be at all. Give welcome to
T-29.... IX.10:3 Forgiving dreams are **k.** to everyone who
T-30......... I.1:8 But think about the **k.** of day you want,
T-30......... I.4:1 tell yourself again the **k.** of day you want;
T-30....... I.16:9 What **k.** of day will you decide to have?
T-31... V.15:10 your suffering of any **k.** you see your own
T-31...... VI.6:9 Who is unwelcome to the **k.** in heart?
T-31..... VII.5:6 may have the gift of **k.** forgiveness which
W-in .......... 7:3 conditions necessary for this **k.** of transfer
W-pI....... 3.1:1 without making distinctions of any **k.**.
W-pI....... 4.6:1 these exercises are the first of their **k.**, you
W-pI....... 7.3:4 not this **k.** of cup will break if you drop it?
W-pI..... 10.2:1 second time we have used this **k.** of idea.
W-pI..... 10.4:5 Try to avoid classification of any **k.**. In
W-pI..... 13.6:1 of a **k.** which you are very inexperienced
W-pI..... 30.2:1 are trying to use a new **k.** of "projection."
W-pI..... 31.3:2 establish any **k.** of hierarchy among them.
W-pI..... 35.3:3 We will use a somewhat different **k.** of
W-pI..... 38.1:2 time, space, distance and limits of any **k.**.
W-pI..... 38.4:1 loss or unhappiness of any **k.** as you see it.
W-pI..... 39.7:1 of any **k.** are suitable subjects for today's
W-pI..... 41.8:6 about this **k.** of practice as we go along.
W-pI..... 43.7:6 not to make distinctions of this **k.** at all.
W-pI..... 44.7:2 letting go every **k.** of interference and
W-pI..... 45.8:4 **k.** of practice only one thing is necessary;
W-pI..... 46.7:3 of any **k.** of negative reaction to anyone,
W-pI..... 49.2:3 distraught, but without reality of any **k.**.
W-pI..... 67.2:4 *holy. Kindness created me* **k.**. *Helpfulness*
W-pI... 73.11:6 are tempted to hold a grievance of any **k.**.
W-pI..... 98.6:1 you your full release from pain of every **k.**,
W-pI... 103.3:4 with this assurance, **k.** and wholly true:
W-pI... 108.5:3 law which holds for every **k.** of learning, if
WpIrIII.in1:5 and whenever you need help of any **k.**.
W-pI... 127.1:2 Perhaps you think there is a **k.** of love for
W-pI... 127.1:2 there is a kind of love for this, a **k.** for that
W-pI... 130.5:1 worlds which have no overlap of any **k.**.
W-pI... 130.9:4 **k.** of seeing that your eyes alone have ever
W-pI. 131.11:3 *a different* **k.** *of thought from those I made.*
W-pI. 132.10:2 To free the world from every **k.** of pain is
W-pI. 135.10:4 of a **k.** from which it gains no benefit at all
W-pI. 135.23:4 they are answers to another **k.** of question
W-pI... 136.1:3 and without a meaningful intent of any **k.**
W-pI... 155.5:1 road that leads away from loss of every **k.**,
W-pI... 157.1:4 a different **k.** of feeling and awareness.
W-pI... 167.2:5 response of any **k.** that is not perfect joy.
W-pI... 167.4:3 apart from it in **k.** as well as distance,
W-pI... 167.8:4 Forever unopposed by opposites of any **k.**
W-pI... 168.2:2 satisfied; despair of any **k.** unthinkable.
W-pI... 184.7:5 which another **k.** of learning can begin, a
W-pI... 190.7:7 while in your **k.** forgiveness does it live.
W-pI... 192.3:6 **k.** so close to waking that the light of day
W-pI. 196.12:3 **k.** and merciful is the idea we practice!
W-pI... 198.8:2 of any **k.** are strange and alien to the truth
W-pI. 198.10:4 as well. Be **k.** to Both, as you forgive the
W-pII . 284.1:4 suffering of any **k.** is nothing but a dream.
W-pII ..... 8.3:5 danger lurks in anything it sees, for it is **k.**
W-pII . 333.1:2 name, or hidden by deceit of any **k.**, if it
W-pII . 341.2:2 to us. And in its **k.** reflection we are saved.
M-8 ........... 6:8 one answer to sickness of any **k.** is healing
M-16 ......... 9:7 magic of any **k.**, in all its forms, simply
M-20 ......... 1:1 that there is a **k.** of peace that is not of
M-21 ......... 2:5 It always requests some **k.** of experience,
M-28 ......... 2:3 and misery of any **k.** perceived as hell.
C-3 ............ 2:1 Forgiveness might be called a **k.** of happy
P-2......... IV.6:1 Illness of any **k.** may be defined as the
P-2......... V.8:9 returns to Heaven through its **k.** embrace.
P-2........ VI.5:5 can possibly give rise to sickness of any **k.**.
P-3........... I.1:2 choose the **k.** of treatment that is suitable.
S-1........... I.5:2 be confused with supplication of any **k.**,
S-1.......... II.7:7 Now, without needs of any **k.**, and clad
S-1......... III.6:1 human love, for external "gifts" of any **k.**,
S-1......... III.6:5 lost in the quest for lesser goals of any **k.**,
S-1......... V.3:1 things, of bodies, and of gods of every **k.**,
S-2.......... II.4:4 it not **k.** to be accepting of another's spite,
S-2.......... II.8:1 and comparisons of every **k.** are death.
S-2......... III.1:2 for proof of innocence, nor pay of any **k.**.
S-3.......... II.1:8 Yet there is a **k.** of seeming death that has
S-3.......... II.4:1 a **k.** forgiveness of the ways of earth, can
S-3......... III.2:2 that is based on inequality of any **k.**.
S-3...... IV.10:4 Be **k.** to it and to yourself, and then be
S-3...... IV.10:4 to it and to yourself, and then be **k.** to Me.

## kinder 1

T-17 ...... V.5:1 not be **k.** to shift the goal more slowly, for

## kindest 1

T-6 ....... IV.9:2 **k.** solution possible for what you made. In

## kindly 16

T-6 ........ V.2:1 wake children in a more **k.** way than by a
T-20 ... VIII.7:2 gently within the **k.** sway of Heaven's laws
W-pI .... 99.8:4 Open your secrets to His **k.** light, and see
W-pI .. 133.5:1 Another **k.** and related law is that there is
W-pI .. 159.8:4 and **k.** care Christ's charity provides.
W-pI .. 192.7:2 Without its **k.** light we grope in darkness,
W-pII . 225.1:2 *in my mind and keeping it within its* **k.** *light,*
W-pII . 271.1:4 **k.** sight redeems the world from death,
W-pII . 325.1:6 to offer him a **k.** home where he can rest a
W-pII ... 14.3:4 and perceive all things as **k.** and as good.
C-2 ............ 7:4 more. Look at the **k.** world you see extend
P-3........ II.7:10 of other images, and help with **k.** dreams.
S-3.......... II.1:2 combining with forgiveness **k.** meant but
S-3.......... II.2:1 because the body has been **k.** used to help
S-3.......... II.5:4 gate to higher prayer and **k.** justice done?
S-3........ III.6:2 His **k.** remedy to those He sends to you,

## kindness 16

T-13 ..... X.14:3 into **k.** will never more be what it was.
T-15 ....... X.8:7 it is an invader who but seems to offer **k.**,
T-23 ..... II.10:3 enemy, they would respond with only **k.**.
T-23 ..... II.14:6 madness sanity, illusions true, attack a **k.**,
T-25 ..... VI.1:6 The **k.** of his sight rests on himself with all
T-27 .. VII.16:3 seen in light of charity and **k.** offered you.
T-29 ... III.3:11 set forth the gentle way of **k.** to God's Son
T-31 ... VIII.8:7 And God ordained, in loving **k.**, that it be
W-pI .... 67.2:4 **K.** *created me kind. Helpfulness created me*
W-pI .. 193.3:2 reflect His loving **k.** to the Son He loves.
W-pI .. 197.1:2 You make attempts at **k.** and forgiveness.
W-pI .. 198.5:3 **k.** to yourself to hear His Voice and learn
W-pII . 222.1:4 He covers me with **k.** and with care, and
W-pII ..... 8.3:5 it is kind, and only **k.** does it look upon.
W-pII . 306.1:4 of care; of loving **k.** and the peace of God.
S-2........... I.1:4 Forgiveness' **k.** is obscure at first, because

## kindnesses 2

T-5 ....... IV.8:3 I have saved all your **k.** and every loving
T-27 .. VII.15:3 Dream of your brother's **k.** instead of

## kinds 17

T-5 ........ in.1:7 different **k.** of responses at the same time,
T-9 ..... VIII.3:2 these two very different **k.** of threat. Its
T-13 ....... X.1:4 willing to look upon all **k.** of "sources,"
T-30 ... VIII.2:5 of lack, and safety from disaster of all **k.**.
T-31 .... VII.1:2 the **k.** of change you could not recognize.
W-pI ...... 1.3:1 the **k.** of things to which they are applied.
W-pI .... 24.5:4 so on. Try to cover as many different **k.** of
W-pI .... 35.4:1 and search your mind for the various **k.** of
W-pI .... 72.3:2 But let us consider the **k.** of things you are
W-pI .... 76.8:1 the different **k.** of "laws" we have believed
W-pI .... 79.7:3 different **k.** of problems we think we have.
W-pI .. 127.1:1 think that different **k.** of love are possible.
W-pI .. 127.1:4 parts and no degrees; no **k.** nor levels, no
W-pI .. 167.1:1 There are not different **k.** of life, for life is
M-17 ......... 2:7 be better shown than in the **k.** of help the
M-24 ....... 1:11 In between, many **k.** of folly are possible.
P-3.......... II.1:8 to certain **k.** of needs in their professional

## king 3

T-18 ... VIII.7:5 within your tiny kingdom, a sorry **k.**, a
T-20 ....... II.7:8 Son of God, and crown him **k.** of death.
W-pII . 236.1:2 At times, it does not seem I am its **k.** at all

## Kingdom 168

*kingdom*

T-3 ..... VI.11:8 Instead of "Seek ye first the **K.** of Heaven"
T-3 ..... VI.11:8 say, "*Will* ye first the **K.** of Heaven," and
T-3 ...... VII.6:9 Your **K.** is not of this world because it was
T-3 .... VII.6:11 by all those for whom the **K.** was created,
T-4 ........ I.12:5 The **K.** of Heaven is the spirit's right,
T-4 ....... III.1:1 It is hard to understand what "The **K.** of
T-4 ....... III.1:4 The **K.** of Heaven *is* you. What else *but* you
T-4 ....... III.1:5 create, and what else *but* you is His **K.**?
T-4 ....... III.1:7 too, have a **K.** that your spirit created. It
T-4 ..... III.1:12 are. *The* **K.** *is perfectly united and perfectly*
T-4 ....... III.8:5 Him. How long will you deny Him His **K.**?

T-4........III.9:7 K. of God and *being* the Kingdom of God.
T-4........III.9:7 Kingdom of God and *being* the K. of God.
T-4.......III.10:1 The calm being of God's K., which in
T-4........VI.7:7 K. of God I can lead you back to your own
T-4.......VII.5:7 itself. Remember that in the K. there is no
T-4.......VII.7:1 God has kept your K. for you, but He
T-4.......VII.8:5 and there is great joy throughout the K..
T-4.......VII.8:7 until we are all united in the joy of the K..
T-5...........I.7:1 are like those in the K. of Heaven itself:
T-5.........II.4:1 You *are* the K. of Heaven, but you have let
T-5.........II.4:3 K. of Heaven breaks through into its own.
T-5.......II.10:9 for any part of the K. than to restore it to
T-5........IV.1:9 is the guarantee of the safety of the K.,
T-5.......IV.1:10 the K. because the Sonship is united. In
T-5........IV.3:4 The ego can keep you in exile from the K.,
T-5........IV.3:4 but in the K. itself it has no power. Ideas
T-5........IV.3:9 And of such is the K. of Heaven. The rest
T-5.......IV.3:10 reinterpreted them in the light of the K.,
T-5........IV.7:3 any of God's ideas is withheld from the K.
T-5.........V.2:1 the K. is attained through the Atonement,
T-5........VI.1:1 waiting, but His K. is bereft while *you* wait.
T-5........VI.3:1 Remember the K. always, and remember
T-5........VI.3:1 you who are part of the K. cannot be lost.
T-5........VI.9:5 to the ego will merely return to the K.,
T-5........VI.9:6 You can delay the completion of the K.,
T-5.......VI.10:8 His verdict will always be "thine is the K.,
T-6...........I.7:5 our brothers in the name of the K. of God,
T-6.........II.8:5 cannot extend His K. until you know of its
T-6........II.12:5 He is united He offers the whole K. always
T-6........II.12:8 of the K. shines in your mind forever, but
T-6........II.13:3 No darkness abides anywhere in the K.,
T-6........II.13:5 we proclaim the K. of God together and as
T-6........IV.2:2 is why attack within the K. is impossible.
T-6........IV.2:4 not remain within the K. without love,
T-6........IV.2:4 without love, and since the K. *is* love, you
T-6........IV.6:1 a child of God, a priceless part of His K.,
T-6........IV.6:8 K. and all that you have created there will
T-6........IV.7:1 In the K., where you are and what you are
T-6........IV.7:4 *been. Being* alone lives in the K., where
T-6........IV.9:5 This leaves you in charge of the K., with
T-6......V.A.2:1 is destructible, and therefore not of the K.
T-6......V.A.4:4 the K. to let this crucial concept slip away.
T-6..........V.C.h Be Vigilant Only for God and His K.
T-6......V.C.1:3 He retains, to strengthen the K. in you.
T-6......V.C.1:6 He keeps the K. perfectly consistent and
T-6......V.C.2:8 is: *Be vigilant only for God and His K.*.
T-6....V.C.4:10 direct it towards creation within the K..
T-6......V.C.5:1 the Holy Spirit will lead you to the K.. You
T-6......V.C.6:3 is the condition for identifying with the K.
T-6......V.C.6:3 Kingdom, since it is the condition *of* the K.
T-6......V.C.6:4 have believed that you are without the K.,
T-6......V.C.7:4 long as belief in God and His K. is assailed
T-6......V.C.8:3 wholeness of the K. does not depend on
T-6......V.C.9:1 illusions and therefore within the K..
T-6......V.C.9:2 Everything outside the K. is illusion.
T-6......V.C.9:4 not keep *only* the K. of God in your mind,
T-7................h THE GIFTS OF THE K.
T-7...........I.2:1 the K. could not increase through its own
T-7...........I.2:7 it. You have the power to add to the K.,
T-7...........I.2:7 though not to add to the Creator of the K..
T-7...........I.2:8 become vigilant only for God and His K..
T-7...........I.4:8 gifts to the K. must be like His gifts to you
T-7...........I.5:1 gave only love to the K. because I believed
T-7...........I.5:4 His K. forever and beyond limit. Eternity
T-7...........I.6:2 complete because the K. of God is whole. I
T-7............II.h The Law of the K.
T-7.........II.1:3 absent from the K. or separated from it,
T-7.........II.1:3 thus making the K. itself obscure to both
T-7.........II.1:4 separation are not of God, but the K. is. If
T-7.........II.1:5 If you obscure the K., you are perceiving
T-7.........II.2:2 This places you both within the K., and
T-7.........II.2:5 the mind in this world as well as in the K..
T-7.........II.2:6 very different from the Thoughts in the K.
T-7.........II.3:1 Outside the K., the law that prevails
T-7.........II.3:2 outside the K. learning is essential. This
T-7.........II.3:4 In the K. there is no teaching or learning,
T-7.........II.3:9 that the increase of the K. depends on it,
T-7.........II.5:6 of truth, which *is* the law of the K., rests
T-7.........II.7:1 of the K. mean to those who are confused?
T-7.........II.7:3 There is no confusion in the K., because
T-7.........II.7:9 That is why it is the K. of God. It belongs
T-7...........III.h The Reality of the K.
T-7........III.1:3 the power of the K. of God Himself, He
T-7........III.2:1 God's meaning waits in the K., because
T-7........III.2:3 rests in the K. because it belongs there, as
T-7........III.4:1 To be in the K. is merely to focus your full
T-7........III.4:5 *are* the K. are not concerned with seeming.
T-7........III.4:7 are ultimately reconciled, not in the K.,
T-7........IV.7:1 Seek ye first the K. of Heaven, because
T-7.........V.9:9 of the increase of the K. by your creations,
T-7........V.9:10 perfect joy that *is* the K. lies in you to give.
T-7........VI.7:1 vigilant for anything *but* God and His K..
T-7........VI.9:2 identification with the K. is totally beyond
T-7......VI.12:4 mind is blocking the extension of the K.,
T-7......VI.12:5 If you do not extend the K., you are not
T-7..........VII.h The Totality of the K.
T-7.......VII.8:4 you to tear the K. of Heaven from you.
T-7.....VII.11:4 the gifts you offer to the K. are gifts to you
T-7.....VII.11:6 and glory are yours because the K. is His.
T-7.....VIII.1:4 It is the law that unifies the K., and keeps
T-7.....VIII.7:3 with the whole K. as literally part of you.
T-7...........IX.h The Extension of the K.
T-7........IX.4:1 K. is forever extending because it is in the
T-7........IX.4:3 Exclude any part of the K. from yourself
T-7........IX.4:5 it to the K. because of its acceptance of
T-7........IX.4:7 That is why there is perfect peace in the K.
T-7.........X.1:1 The K. is the result of premises, just as
T-7.........X.2:7 and you are denying His K. *and* yours.
T-7........XI.1:2 because He speaks for the K. of God,
T-7........XI.4:1 chosen you to teach the K. *to* the Kingdom
T-7........XI.4:1 chosen you to teach the Kingdom *to* the K..
T-7........XI.4:3 Every Son who returns to the K. with this
T-7.......XI.7:10 The K. of God includes all His Sons and
T-8...........I.1:3 because it is the condition of the K..
T-8...........I.3:8 This is a condition so alien to the K. that
T-8.........II.6:6 this and you are denying God His K.,
T-8.........II.7:1 and glory are yours because the K. is His,"
T-8.........II.8:1 the Holy Spirit appeal to restore God's K.
T-8.........II.8:2 appeal, then, is merely to what the K. is,
T-8.........II.8:5 runs easily and gladly through the K., in
T-8......III.5:12 his place in the K. and you will have yours
T-8........III.6:1 The K. cannot be found alone, and you
T-8........III.6:1 who are the K. cannot find yourself alone.
T-8........IV.6:6 How else can it be, if God's K. is freedom?
T-8........VI.1:5 Forget not the K. of God for anything the
T-8........VI.3:1 for over His K. the world has no power.
T-8.......VII.5:9 is to reach beyond the K. to its Creator,
T-9...VIII.10:5 them. You cannot replace the K., and you
T-10.......II.3:3 counterpart of creating in the K.. God will
T-10.......II.6:5 yourself vigilant *against* God and His K..
T-10......III.6:1 There are no idolaters in the K., but there
T-10......III.7:3 to deny illusions anywhere in the K.,
T-10.....V.11:1 to Him the K. will be restored to His Son.
T-11.......II.1:6 His K. your understanding is not perfect,
T-11......III.2:2 his own. The K. is his, and yet he wanders
T-11......VI.1:7 and ascends to the Father and His K..
T-11...VIII.8:3 The K. of Heaven *is* within you. Believe
T-12......IV.6:6 Yet you cannot sell the K. of Heaven. Your
T-12......IV.7:4 is will, and will is the "price" of the K..
T-13.....X.13:6 K. in honor of its wholeness that is of God
T-13.....X.14:3 Before the glorious radiance of the K. guilt
T-14.......II.7:1 the conditions of knowledge in the K.. All
T-14.......V.4:1 of the K. is the right of God's Son, given
T-15......III.9:7 My K. is not of this world because it is in
T-16......III.7:7 His K. has no limits and no end, and there
T-16...VII.10:4 understands how to restore the K. to you,
T-18......VI.1:2 that the K. of Heaven is restored to you.
T-18......VI.1:4 The K. of Heaven is the dwelling place of
T-18. VIII.10:4 gently transformed into the K. of Heaven,
T-26...VII.15:8 His K. is united; thus it was created, and
T-30.......II.1:7 *you.* He did not set His K. up alone. And
W-pI.....45.8:7 and an attempt to reach the K. of Heaven.
W-pI.....47.7:3 down and below them to the K. of Heaven
W-pI.....50.5:4 God. Such is the K. of Heaven. Such is the
W-pI.....77.3:3 assured that the K. of God is within you,
P-2.........II.6:1 is an invitation to God to enter into His K.
S-1...........I.3:6 You have sought first the K. of Heaven,

**kingdom** 20
*Kingdom*
T-1.......III.5:3 free to establish your k. where you see fit,
T-6.......V.C.9:4 it. By making another k. that you valued,
T-7........XI.3:1 Consider the k. you have made and judge
T-11.....V.18:2 the k. you have chosen for your vigilance.
T-18....VIII.2:6 proclaiming that within it is your k.,
T-18....VIII.3:1 Within this k. the ego rules, and cruelly.
T-18....VIII.6:3 It is not a separate k., ruled by an idea of
T-18....VIII.7:5 Would you remain within your tiny k., a
T-18....VIII.7:6 This little self is not your k.. Arched high
T-18....VIII.8:4 In your tiny k. you have so little! Should it
T-18....VIII.8:6 and joyless–that makes up your little k..
T-18....VIII.9:1 Thought of God surrounds your little k.,
T-18..VIII.11:1 love to enter into your bleak and joyless k.
T-18......IX.1:5 sole ruler of the k. it set apart to tyrannize
T-18......IX.1:9 the withered k. in which you set it off,
T-18......IX.2:3 being based on what this little k. really is.
T-24.....II.13:4 madness and in loneliness your special k.,
T-30.......I.16:8 Whose k. is the world for you today?
W-pII .236.1:1 I have a k. I must rule. At times, it does
C-4.............7:1 and wholly understandable, enters its k..

**kingdoms** 4
T-3.......VII.2:6 builds k. in which everything is in direct
T-7........VI.9:1 is dividing its allegiance between two k.,
T-18..VIII.10:3 no lonely little k. locked away from love,
T-19.......I.15:1 keep your little k. barren and separate, so

**kings** 1
T-14........II.2:7 they are k. with golden crowns because of

**kiss** 1
T-6.........I.15:5 with a k.?" unless I believed in betrayal.

**kneel** 2
T-13...VII.15:2 K. not before the altars to sacrifice, and
C-ep...........4:1 and k. down an instant in our gratitude to

**kneeling** 2
W-pI...161.9:3 you could scarce refrain from k. at his feet
W-pI...163.5:4 k. down with foreheads to the ground,

**knew** 34
T-2.......VIII.4:3 He had created and k. that it was good. At
T-3........III.2:2 again," implying that you k. before. You
T-5..........II.4:5 You k. as you will know again, but as you
T-6...........I.7:6 because I k. I could not *be* abandoned.
T-7......VI.4:11 if the mind that made it k. itself. And if it
T-11......III.3:1 my child, if you k. what God wills for you,
T-12........II.1:4 If they k. the truth about themselves they
T-12....VIII.3:8 You who k. have forgotten, and unless He
T-16......III.1:3 how alien it is to what you thought you k.,
T-18......III.3:2 k. Who walks beside you on the way that
T-18.....IX.12:5 never was a time in which you k. it not.
T-20.........II.8:6 You heard, but k. not how to look, nor
T-21.........I.7:5 you remember an ancient song you k. so
T-22.........I.8:4 him what he knows *because* you k. it. He
T-27.......I.11:1 sure you k. its purpose was to foster guilt.
T-27....VIII.5:5 was a time when he k. nothing of a body,
T-27..VIII.10:5 in a dream you k. that you were dreaming
T-29.......V.6:1 but k. the glorious goal that lies beyond
T-30......IV.1:5 And this you k. when you made idols.
T-30.......V.6:5 of God k. in creation he must know again.
T-31...VII.10:5 forgot, and those you k. a long while since
W-pI.131.13:3 you in the light reflects the truth you k.,
W-pI.135.18:1 if you but k. that everything that happens
W-pI...139.4:2 be alive at all unless he k. the answer. If
W-pI...157.9:4 rememberance of what you k. that instant
W-pI...168.2:1 If you but k. the meaning of His Love,
WpI.rV.in10:6 practice but an ancient truth we k. before
W-pI...182.7:3 He came because He k. you would not fail
WpI rVI.in.4:3 all that we thought we k. and understood.

| | |
|---|---|
| W-pII ..... 7.3:1 | k. how much your Father yearns to have |
| M-10 ......... 4:1 | k. all the "facts" you needed for judgment |
| M-16 ....... 11:2 | gladly make it, if it k. it could be made. It |
| C-4............ 8:1 | if you only k. the peace that will envelop |
| C-5............ 5:6 | brother whom you k. since you were born |

**knife** 4

| | |
|---|---|
| T-4......... II.5:2 | in rage if you take away a k. or scissors, |
| T-27..... VII.4:7 | is the avenger's k. in his own hand, and |
| T-27..... VII.4:9 | he suffers from the wounds a k. he does |
| S-2........... I.2:6 | God's mercy has become a twisted k. that |

**know** 564

| | |
|---|---|
| T-1........... I.4:3 | You will be told all you need to k.. |
| T-1........ III.8:5 | position to k. where they can be bestowed |
| T-1......... V.3:4 | you cannot k. the real power of the Son in |
| T-1........ VII.3:3 | of those who k. not what they do. Fantasy |
| T-2.... V.A.16:3 | for they k. not what they do" in no way |
| T-2......... VI.7:1 | to k. first that the conflict is an expression |
| T-2......... VI.7:5 | K. first that this is fear. Fear arises from |
| T-2........ VII.1:3 | I k. it does not exist, but you do not. If I |
| T-3........ III.1:2 | out before you can k. anything. To know |
| T-3........ III.1:3 | To k. is to be certain. Uncertainty means |
| T-3........ III.1:4 | Uncertainty means that you do not k.. |
| T-3........ III.2:2 | or God. To recognize means to "k. again," |
| T-3........ III.2:5 | but you do not question when you k.. |
| T-3...... III.2:11 | k. when you have ceased to ask questions. |
| T-3........ III.5:1 | The Bible tells you to k. yourself, or to be |
| T-3........ III.5:3 | this makes it possible for you to k. him. |
| T-3........ III.5:4 | perceive him as he is you cannot k. him. |
| T-3........ III.5:5 | clearly implying that you do not k. God. |
| T-3...... III.5:13 | perceive the truth is not the same as to k. |
| T-3........ III.6:7 | "K. God and accept His certainty." |
| T-3........ III.7:2 | k. your brother when you attack him. |
| T-3........ III.7:4 | and so you cannot k. him. It is because |
| T-3........ III.7:6 | him correctly so that you can k. him. |
| T-3........ III.7:8 | created you can create only what you k., |
| T-3........ IV.2:4 | Yet you can k. yourself only as you are, |
| T-3........ IV.5:4 | Until then it wills only to k.. Afterwards it |
| T-3........ IV.5:6 | its proper function only when it wills to k. |
| T-3........ IV.7:1 | therefore k. that no miscreation exists. |
| T-3......... V.3:2 | literally impossible for you to k. anything. |
| T-3......... V.4:3 | that the answer is not only one you k., but |
| T-3......... V.4:8 | implies that there is nothing stable to k.. |
| T-3......... V.8:4 | and knowing any part of it is to k. all of it. |
| T-3......... V.8:8 | but k. yourself and your knowledge is |
| T-3......... V.8:9 | To k. God's miracle is to know Him. |
| T-3......... V.8:9 | To know God's miracle is to k. Him. |
| T-3....... V.10:4 | prayer, is the natural state of those who k. |
| T-3....... V.10:9 | K. yourself in the One Light where the |
| T-3........ VI.2:1 | than to k. is the cause of the loss of peace. |
| T-3........ VI.9:1 | k. that their own rejection is impossible. |
| T-3........ VI.9:6 | judgment and merely k. that it is there. |
| T-3...... VI.11:8 | said, "I k. what I am and I accept my own |
| T-4......... in.2:2 | chosen to "Be still and k. that I am God." |
| T-4......... I.2:11 | cannot perceive and the ego cannot k.. |
| T-4........... I.8:6 | are afraid, be still and k. that God is real, |
| T-4........... I.8:7 | the ego cannot k. what is as far beyond its |
| T-4......... II.4:9 | longer necessary you will merely k. God. |
| T-4........ IV.2:2 | you are not joyous, then *k. this need not be.* |
| T-4........ IV.3:1 | When you are sad, *k. this need not be.* |
| T-4........ IV.4:1 | of the ego, and *k. this need not be.* You can |
| T-4........ IV.9:2 | because I k. these images are not true." |
| T-4........ VI.4:1 | ego and the spirit do not k. each other. |
| T-4........ VI.7:3 | knowing that to k. your brother *is* to know |
| T-4........ VI.7:3 | that to know your brother *is* to k. God. If |
| T-4........ VI.7:5 | gratitude you come to k. your brother, |
| T-4....... VII.6:5 | And this He does k.. He knows it in His |
| T-4....... VII.7:1 | His joy with you until you k. it with your |
| T-5......... in.3:3 | You need not k. them individually, or |
| T-5......... in.3:8 | is: *Let me k. this brother as I know myself.* |
| T-5......... in.3:8 | is: *Let me know this brother as I k. myself.* |
| T-5........... I.4:8 | The word "k." is proper in this context, |
| T-5......... II.4:5 | You knew as you will k. again, but as you |
| T-5......... II.4:5 | will know again, but as you do not k. now |
| T-5....... II.7:13 | You cannot lose it, but you can not k. it. It |
| T-5....... III.7:6 | are light, but you yourself do not k. this. |
| T-5 ....... IV.8:6 | you, and we k. what God creates is eternal |
| T-5 ........ V.7:3 | are always a sign that you do not k. this. |
| T-5 ...... VII.3:1 | you can k. the Voice for God is in you? |
| T-6 .......... I.8:2 | I k. they cannot really betray themselves |
| T-6 ........ I.12:1 | to enable the Sonship to k. its Wholeness. |
| T-6 ........ I.18:6 | as He thinks if you are to k. Him again. |
| T-6 ........ I.19:2 | will listen to His Voice you will k. that you |
| T-6 ......... II.8:5 | His Kingdom until you k. of its wholeness |
| T-6 ........ III.3:5 | bless because they k. that they are blessed |
| T-6 ........ IV.3:1 | basic fact that the ego cannot k. anything. |
| T-6 ........ IV.6:6 | because you were asleep and did not k.. |
| T-6 ......... V.1:5 | God does k. is that His communication |
| T-6 ......... V.1:5 | and k. that His children are wholly joyous |
| T-6 ..... V.A.1:1 | gone, you will k. that you will last forever. |
| T-6 ..... V.C.8:7 | you cannot k. what you are with certainty |
| T-7 ........ I.7:11 | as not increasing you do not k. what it is. |
| T-7 ........ I.7:12 | is. You also do not k. Who created it. God |
| T-7 ......... II.3:6 | of being, k. that what you extend you are. |
| T-7 ..... III.2:10 | even though the ego does not k. what it is. |
| T-7 ....... IV.1:6 | in a state of mind that does not k. Him. |
| T-7 ....... IV.1:8 | Because they are unaware, they do not k.. |
| T-7 ....... IV.6:8 | it, you do not k. what you are. Healing, |
| T-7 ......... V.8:6 | He therefore does not k. what his Self is. |
| T-7 ..... VI.3:10 | that you will not k. your own safety. |
| T-7 ....... VI.4:1 | The ego cannot afford to k. anything. |
| T-7 ..... VI.4:12 | any part of the Sonship, it *would* k. itself. |
| T-7 ....... VI.7:8 | When you believe what God does not k., |
| T-7 ..... VI.10:3 | creation truly you cannot k. the Creator, |
| T-7 ...... VII.5:4 | and *are,* and so you do not k. your being. |
| T-7 ...... VII.6:6 | You cannot k. your own perfection until |
| T-7 ...... VII.7:5 | who attack do not k. they are blessed. |
| T-7 .... VII.10:5 | you will k. that you are in Him with them. |
| T-7 .... VII.10:7 | is lonely when His Sons do not k. Him. |
| T-7 ....... IX.3:6 | but God does not k. unfulfillment and |
| T-7 ....... IX.3:7 | You may not k. your own creations, but |
| T-7 ....... IX.4:2 | You do not k. your joy because you do not |
| T-7 ....... IX.4:2 | you do not k. your own Self-fullness. |
| T-7 .......... X.3:4 | what is painful than you k. what is joyful, |
| T-7 .......... X.8:1 | Whose Will you do not k. because you are |
| T-7 ..... XI.3:10 | when they deny Him they do not k. this, |
| T-7 ....... XI.5:3 | you to recognize and appreciate and k.. |
| T-7 ....... XI.6:2 | You do not k. yourself, because you do |
| T-7 ....... XI.6:2 | because you do not k. your Creator. You |
| T-7 ....... XI.6:3 | You do not k. your creations because you |
| T-7 ....... XI.6:3 | because you do not k. your brothers, who |
| T-7 ....... XI.7:2 | You do not k. your creations because you |
| T-7 ....... XI.7:2 | because you do not k. their creator. You |
| T-7 ....... XI.7:3 | You do not k. yourself because you do not |
| T-7 ....... XI.7:3 | yourself because you do not k. yours. |
| T-7 ....... XI.7:5 | But you can *k.* both. Being is known by |
| T-7 ....... XI.7:7 | His Being with you, you can k. Him. But |
| T-7 ....... XI.7:8 | But you must also k. all He created, to |
| T-7 ....... XI.7:8 | He created, to k. what they have shared. |
| T-7 ....... XI.7:9 | Father you will not k. your fatherhood. |
| T-7 ..... XI.7:11 | K., then, the Sons of God, and you will |
| T-7 ..... XI.7:11 | Sons of God, and you will k. all creation. |
| T-8 ......... II.1:4 | ego does not k. what it is trying to teach. |
| T-8 ....... III.3:6 | can k. what it means only of God Himself. |
| T-8 ....... III.5:1 | of the teacher you choose, is "K. thyself." |
| T-8 ....... III.5:6 | because it does not k. where to look. The |
| T-8 ....... III.6:3 | The ego does not k. this, because it does |
| T-8 ....... III.6:3 | know this, because it does not k. anything |
| T-8 ....... III.6:4 | But you can k. it, and you will know it if |
| T-8 ....... III.6:4 | and you will k. it if you are willing to look |
| T-8 ....... IV.4:9 | by believing that I k. what you should do. |
| T-8 ........ V.2:6 | can you k. it without recognizing Him? |
| T-8 ........ V.5:1 | Would you k. the Will of God for you? |
| T-8 ........ V.5:2 | of me who k. it for you and you will find it |
| T-8 ....... VI.2:2 | You cannot behold the world and k. God. |
| T-8 ....... VI.8:1 | –"Do I want to k. my Father's Will for me |
| T-8 ... VIII.1:11 | to k. in part is to know entirely because of |
| T-8 ... VIII.1:11 | to know in part is to k. entirely because of |
| T-8 ..... VIII.7:3 | You do not k. how you feel because you |
| T-8 ..... VIII.7:4 | of a teacher who does not k. the answer. |
| T-8 ..... VIII.7:6 | I said that the ego does not k. anything, I |
| T-8 ....... IX.1:3 | ego does not k. what a real question is, |
| T-8 ....... IX.9:7 | He cannot lose this, but you *can* not k. it. |
| T-9 .......... I.2:5 | course is that you do not k. what you are. |
| T-9 .......... I.3:1 | If you do not k. what your reality is, why |
| T-9 .......... I.3:2 | of those who do not k. what truth is. All |
| T-9 .......... I.3:5 | a Guide Who *does* k. what your reality is. |
| T-9 ......... I.11:8 | will not k. it because your cooperation is |
| T-9 ......... I.14:3 | cannot distort reality and k. what it is. |
| T-9 ......... II.4:1 | you would k. your prayers are answered, |
| T-9 ......... II.4:3 | If you would k. God and His Answer, |
| T-9 ......... II.4:8 | way you can hear it now, and finally k. it. |
| T-9 ......... II.5:8 | it? Your brother may not k. who he is, but |
| T-9 ......... II.5:8 | there is a light in his mind that does k.. |
| T-9 ......... II.6:7 | will not k. the trust I have in you unless |
| T-9 ....... II.11:6 | have, but it is possible not to k. you have. |
| T-9 ....... II.12:6 | *Because I will to k. myself, I see you as God's* |
| T-9 ....... III.7:9 | is of God, Who does not k. of arrogance. |
| T-9 ....... IV.1:4 | your brother is, if you would k. yourself. |
| T-9 ....... IV.1:5 | he is not and you cannot k. what you are, |
| T-9 ..... IV.10:5 | only because you did not k. who you were |
| T-9 ......... V.2:3 | he does not k. where to look for truth, |
| T-9 ......... V.5:6 | healer therefore does not k. how to give, |
| T-9 ......... V.5:8 | is real, although he does not k. it himself. |
| T-9 ......... V.9:6 | *By their fruits ye shall k. them, and they shall* |
| T-9 ......... V.9:6 | *know them, and they shall k. themselves.* |
| T-9 ....... VI.3:7 | is. Would you k. what this means? If what |
| T-9 ....... VI.4:7 | k. yourself only as God knows His Son, |
| T-9 ....... VI.4:8 | When you awake in Him you will k. your |
| T-9 ....... VI.7:2 | open Arms, and finally k. His open Mind. |
| T-9 ....... VI.7:9 | You will never k. that you are co-creator |
| T-9 ...... VII.7:1 | the ego does not k. what a real question is |
| T-9 ...... VII.7:2 | always associated with unwillingness to k. |
| T-9 ... VIII.10:4 | do not k. them until you return to them. |
| T-9 ... VIII.11:9 | cease to question it and k. it for what it is. |
| T-10 ...... in.3:2 | because He does not k. it only for Himself |
| T-10 ......... I.1:1 | not k. your creations simply because you |
| T-10 ......... I.1:5 | that does not k. this has banished itself |
| T-10 ......... I.3:4 | that you will k. it can be so again. What is |
| T-10 ......... I.3:7 | will k. that what you remember is eternal, |
| T-10 ........ II.1:1 | first k. something you cannot dissociate it |
| T-10 ........ II.2:5 | Him and k. your own reality again. Let |
| T-10 ..... III.4:3 | to k. that creation shares power and never |
| T-10 ..... III.6:2 | knows no idols, but he does k. his Father. |
| T-10 ..... III.7:1 | peace, and therefore does not k. he has it. |
| T-10 ..... III.7:4 | I can heal you because I k. you. I know |
| T-10 ..... III.7:5 | I k. your value for you, and it is this value |
| T-10 ..... III.7:6 | and does not k. of conflicting laws. I will |
| T-10 ..... IV.2:3 | To k. reality must involve the willingness |
| T-10 ........ V.3:6 | not to k. yourself in order to be sick. This |
| T-10 ........ V.6:4 | love Him, and that you k. He loves you. |
| T-10 ........ V.8:2 | you will k. that He has never ceased to |
| T-10 ...... V.10:2 | would not k. His Son if he were not free. |
| T-10 ...... V.10:8 | To k. that is sanity. To deny it is insanity. |
| T-11 ......... I.4:3 | You do not k. this simply because you |
| T-11 ......... I.4:4 | How, then, could you k. your creations, |
| T-11 ......... I.7:3 | like Him if you would k. His gift to you? |
| T-11 ......... I.8:1 | Yet what you will you do not k.. This is |
| T-11 ......... I.8:2 | when you realize that to deny is to "not k. |
| T-11 ......... I.8:4 | will, and therefore do not k. what it is. |
| T-11 ......... I.8:6 | You do not k. what it is, but the Holy |
| T-11 ......... I.8:8 | be too often repeated that you do not k. it |
| T-11 ....... I.10:3 | You are afraid to k. God's Will, because |
| T-11 ....... I.10:5 | is the belief that makes you *want* not to k.. |
| T-11 ....... I.11:5 | who share His life must share it to k. it, |
| T-11 ....... I.11:6 | the Will of your Father is to k. your own. |
| T-11 ........ II.1:5 | of Him, you k. there is but one Will. Yet |
| T-11 ........ II.3:6 | yourself, and therefore k. not what you do |
| T-11 ........ II.3:7 | will, you do not k. what you really want. |
| T-11 ........ II.6:1 | until you k. your function and fulfill it, for |
| T-11 ........ II.7:8 | K., then, Who abides with you merely by |
| T-11 ..... III.1:3 | You do not k. how, for if you did you |
| T-11 ..... III.3:3 | beauty that you will k. it is not of you. Out |
| T-11 ..... III.7:4 | God, or you will not k. that you are there. |
| T-11 ..... III.7:6 | His, if you would k. what belongs to you. |
| T-11 ... III.7:10 | if he would k. the Wholeness of his Father |
| T-11 ..... IV.2:1 | to make God homeless and k. that you are |
| T-11 ..... IV.5:4 | it to yourself and you cannot k. yourself, |
| T-11 ..... IV.8:3 | he will not k. the Father or the Son. Peace |
| T-11 ..... V.12:4 | you to k. that God's function is yours, and |
| T-11 ..... VI.9:5 | you will not k. that your redeemer liveth, |
| T-11 .... VII.4:3 | you do you will not k. it is yours already. |
| T-11 .... VII.4:6 | k. the difference between what you have |
| T-11 .... VII.4:6 | k. the difference between what you have |

T-11.....VII.4:7 world is to believe that you can **k.** yourself
T-11.....VII.4:8 **k.** God because it is His Will to be known.
T-11... VIII.2:5 Yet while you think you **k.** its meaning,
T-11... VIII.3:1 **k.** the meaning of anything you perceive.
T-11... VIII.8:4 the truth is in me, for I **k.** that it is in you.
T-11. VIII.14:8 You do not **k.** what they are, and so you
T-12....... II.3:4 your Father wills you to **k.** your brother as
T-12....... II.7:6 not **k.** that I walked with Him in peace?
T-12....... II.9:2 The Lord is with you, but you **k.** it not.
T-12........ V.6:1 You do not **k.** the meaning of love, and
T-12........ V.6:6 They do not **k.**. If they could interpret the
T-12...... VI.1:7 but you will not **k.** it while you perceive
T-12...... VI.2:2 aware that you do not **k.** yourself, and
T-12..... VII.2:3 if you see its effects you **k.** it must be there
T-12..... VII.3:4 He must be, and finally **k.** what He is.
T-12... VIII.1:2 but you **k.** neither the Father nor the Son
T-12... VIII.4:6 are waiting only for Him, and do not **k.** it.
T-13.........I.1:1 by teaching their pupils all they **k.**. The
T-13.........I.6:4 you cannot **k.** that you are God's Son.
T-13....... II.3:4 not **k.** who the Son of God is because it is
T-13...... IV.3:6 it. And even though you **k.** not Heaven,
T-13....... V.7:6 You who **k.** not what you do can learn
T-13.... VI.10:1 of Light, you **k.** not that the light is in you.
T-13..... VII.5:7 is still there, although you **k.** Him not. His
T-13... VII.11:5 yourself what you need, for you do not **k.**,
T-13... VIII.1:3 therefore no one in the world can **k.**. It
T-13... VIII.5:3 you cannot **k.** this until you see that every
T-13. VIII.10:6 They witness to what you do not **k.**, and
T-13....... X.3:6 go. They cannot **k.** they love, and cannot
T-13....... X.7:8 Yet what He knows you do not **k.**, though
T-13...... XI.3:6 To value it partially is not to **k.** its value.
T-13.... XI.10:5 to **k.** that Heaven is yours to make it so. It
T-13.... XI.10:7 *is* so. Yet to **k.** it, the Will of God must be
T-14.......in.1:2 Yet in this world you do not **k.** it. But you
T-14.........I.1:1 If you are blessed and do not **k.** it, you
T-14.........I.2:2 that to deny is the decision not to **k.**. The
T-14.... III.12:5 You **k.** not of salvation, for you do not
T-14.... III.14:4 His guidance you will think you **k.** alone,
T-14.... III.16:3 frantically to anticipate all you cannot **k.**,
T-14.... III.17:8 only good to everyone? Would you **k.** this
T-14.... III.19:2 *me and knows the way, which I **k.** not. Yet He*
T-14...... IV.2:5 but cannot **k.** that you are one with Him.
T-14...... IV.5:2 want, in recognition that you do not **k.**.
T-14...... IV.7:1 Unless you are guiltless you cannot **k.**
T-14...... IV.7:1 know God, Whose Will is that you **k.** Him
T-14...... IV.8:7 Would you **k.** of One Who gives forever,
T-14...... IV.9:1 because they **k.** that they are sinless. The
T-14...... IV.9:5 that stand between you and what you **k.**.
T-14........ V.2:6 You **k.** not what you do, but He Who
T-14........ V.9:3 In guiltlessness we **k.** Him, as He knows
T-14...... VI.7:1 You **k.** not what you say, and so you
T-14...... VI.7:1 say, and so you **k.** not what is said to you.
T-14..... VII.2:8 Yet you cannot **k.** this, for by hiding truth
T-14..... VII.3:1 to convince the unknowing that they **k.**.
T-14... VIII.2:8 **k.** not God because you know not this.
T-14... VIII.2:8 know not God because you **k.** not this.
T-14... VIII.2:9 And yet you do **k.** God and also this. All
T-14...... XI.1:1 thing is learning that *you do not **k.***.
T-14...... XI.1:6 You **k.** not what it is, nor where. You have
T-14...... XI.6:2 How would you **k.**? Your part is very
T-14...... XI.6:7 *I do not **k.** what anything, including this,*
T-14...... XI.6:8 *And so I do not **k.** how to respond to it. And I*
T-14.... XI.6:10 to teach yourself what you do not **k.**, the
T-14.... XI.12:1 remember always that they **k.** nothing,
T-14.... XI.12:3 for learning by thinking they already **k.**.
T-14.... XI.13:1 those who recognize they cannot **k.** unless
T-14.... XI.13:3 Whenever you think you **k.**, peace will
T-14.... XI.13:4 Whenever you fully realize that you **k.** not
T-14.... XI.15:2 You think you **k.** Him not, only because,
T-14.... XI.15:2 because, alone, it is impossible to **k.** Him.
T-15..... III.8:5 You **k.** not what love means because you
T-15.... III.10:7 yourself, for you will **k.** you are complete,
T-15...... IV.4:7 that you alone cannot **k.** where it is, and
T-15...... VI.7:8 of communication, which you **k.** perfectly
T-15..... VII.5:5 What He can make of them you do not **k.**,
T-15... VIII.6:1 lies the awareness of what God cannot **k.**,
T-15....... X.1:6 Yet you **k.** not how to do it. Let the Holy
T-15.... XI.10:6 *I **k.** that you will be released, unless I want to*
T-16.........I.2:6 You do not **k.** what empathizing means.
T-16.........I.3:3 You do not **k.** what healing is. All you
T-16.........I.4:4 fact that you do not **k.** is to recognize and
T-16.........I.4:4 and accept the fact that He *does* **k.**. You
T-16.........I.4:6 You cannot **k.** how to respond to what
T-16....... II.6:6 Him is to deny all that you think you **k.**.
T-16....... II.6:7 But what you think you **k.** was never true.
T-16...... III.2:2 earlier, "By their fruits ye shall **k.** them,
T-16...... III.2:2 know them, and they shall **k.** themselves.
T-16...... III.3:6 Yet this Self you clearly do not **k.**, and do
T-16...... III.4:1 This is a course in how to **k.** yourself. You
T-16...... III.5:7 quite real, as part of the Self you do not **k.**
T-16...... IV.1:2 impossible not to **k.** the meaning of love,
T-16..... V.15:2 cannot **k.** yourself who share its meaning.
T-16..... V.15:3 is only the decision *not* to **k.** yourself. This
T-17.... IV.16:1 of relationship and **k.** it to be true. Let us
T-17...... VI.2:7 does not **k.** what it wants to come of the
T-18...... III.3:3 **k.** because the journey into darkness has
T-18...... VI.3:4 in the mind, and let it not **k.** its Identity.
T-18... VIII.1:5 see yourself within a body **k.** yourself as
T-18... VIII.2:1 The body cannot **k.**. And while you limit
T-18. VIII.12:4 You could no more **k.** God alone than He
T-18. VIII.12:5 of love than love could **k.** you not, or fail
T-18. VIII.13:5 of Him, for He would have you **k.** Him.
T-18.... IX.14:2 cannot **k.** until every perception has been
T19... IV.A.6:2 Heaven knows you well, as you **k.** Heaven.
T19..IV.C.2:14 We **k.** that an idea leaves not its source.
T19. IV.D.10:6 How can you **k.** that it is over unless you
T19. IV.D.12:2 a stranger. You do not **k.** him, and your
T19. IV.D.14:6 of sin, **k.** not Whom they attack.
T-20.........I.4:4 Yet for your gift of lilies you will **k.**. In
T-20....... II.8:7 And now you **k.**. In you the knowledge
T-20...... III.7:6 thing in all the universe that does not **k.**.
T-20...... III.9:6 him to Paradise, and **k.** the peace of God.
T-20.... III.11:2 faith with me, and **k.** that it is justified.
T-20..... IV.5:5 who **k.** that they are all the same need not
T-20....... V.8:4 offer it to him and **k.** it rests in safety? He
T-20... VIII.2:1 Do you not want to **k.** your own Identity?
T-21.........I.4:2 They think they **k.** their way about in it.
T-21.........I.7:4 And yet you **k.** that nothing in the world
T-21.........I.9:1 of the Son of God, whom you **k.** well.
T-21.........I.9:5 You **k.** the ancient song, and know it well.
T-21.........I.9:5 You know the ancient song, and **k.** it well.
T-21....... V.7:4 O yes, you **k.** this, and more than this
T-21..... V.10:3 come from something that you do not **k.**,
T-21...... VI.4:3 it. But the insane **k.** not their will, for they
T-21..... VII.2:7 they do not **k.** that they *are* one with him,
T-21..... VII.2:7 one with him, they **k.** not whom they hate
T-21..... VII.3:2 Yet they **k.** not their "enemy," except they
T-22....... II.6:5 *You* **k.** what your Creator wills is possible,
T-22...... VI.5:7 The means of sinlessness can **k.** no fear
T-22.... VI.11:7 of the universe, Whose power you **k.**.
T-22.... VI.12:1 oneness, you would **k.** His power is yours.
T-23.......in.5:6 For who can **k.** his glory, and perceive the
T-23.........I.7:7 You will remember what you **k.** when you
T-23..... II.12:2 is justified unless you **k.** what it is for?
T-23..... II.22:6 **k.** whether you chose the stairs to Heaven
T-23...... III.3:7 a little, love a little, and **k.** the difference.
T-23...... III.5:2 How could they **k.**? Could they accept
T-23...... IV.6:2 you do not recognize, the signs you **k.**.
T-23...... IV.6:4 This you **k.** well. When they occur leave
T-23...... IV.8:1 purpose, and who **k.** that it is theirs. They
T-23...... IV.8:6 They **k.** it is impossible their happiness
T-24.........I.1:2 the smallest gift is not to **k.** love's purpose
T-24....... II.4:2 you really are, how can you **k.** the truth?
T-24...... VI.4:3 you will not **k.** the Father nor yourself.
T-24.... VI.13:4 what you do through Christ it does not **k.**.
T-24..... VII.3:1 **k.** your worth while specialness claims
T-24..... VII.3:2 How can you fail to **k.** it in his holiness?
T-25.......in.1:8 made manifest to those who **k.** Him not,
T-25.......in.3:6 To those who **k.** Him not it carries Him in
T-25... VIII.1:6 brings loss to no one you would not **k.**.
T-25... VIII.2:9 **k.** of Heaven and the justice of the saved?
T-25... VIII.4:1 You who **k.** not of justice still can ask,
T-25... VIII.5:3 But justice does He **k.**, and knows it well.
T-25...... IX.1:9 to you, because you **k.** not what it is.
T-26....... V.4:1 still believe you live in time and **k.** not it is
T-26... VII.14:8 Nor will he **k.** himself, nor recognize his
T-26... VII.20:5 true be recognized by those who **k.** it not;
T-26...... IX.1:4 And never will you **k.** He is in you as well
T-26........X.3:6 him because you do not **k.** him *as* yourself.
T-26........X.6:7 *I would rather **k.** of Them than see injustice,*
T-27.......I.11:4 it. You do *not* **k.** its purpose. You but gave
T-27......II.10:6 and by your function do you **k.** yourself.
T-27......II.12:2 then you also **k.** the Holy Spirit's Mind
T-27...... III.7:6 do not **k.** the peace of power that opposes
T-27...... IV.5:6 that asks for something that you do not **k.**
T-27...... VI.3:3 *It does not **k.***. It tells you but the names you
T-27..VIII.12:7 they attest the thing you do not want to **k.**
T-28.......II.6:7 is not awake, but does not **k.** he sleeps. He
T-28.... IV.2:10 in yourself you do not **k.** and cannot tell
T-28....... V.3:5 you will not want to **k.** your own Identity,
T-28....... V.4:6 It does not **k.** what seeing *is*; what listening
T-28....... V.4:7 as it can judge or understand or **k.**. Its
T-28...... VI.3:1 and loathe and want, the body does not **k.**
T-29.........I.6:4 because you do not **k.** what loving means.
T-29.........I.8:3 **k.** that nothing stands between you and
T-29.........I.8:4 **k.** there is no gap behind which you can
T-29...... III.1:8 Unless he gives he will not **k.** he has, for
T-29...... III.2:7 all living things who **k.** not that they live.
T-29...... IV.6:2 You do not **k.**, because your function is
T-29... VII.1:12 But it is given you to **k.** the truth, and not
T-29..... VII.8:1 you do not **k.** the purpose of the world.
T-29.... VIII.1:2 idol? Do you think you **k.**? For idols are
T-29.... VIII.1:5 *because* you do not **k.** what they are for,
T-29...... IX.2:8 Nor can he **k.** the Self he has condemned.
T-29...... IX.6:6 does not **k.** what hurts and what will heal.
T-30.........I.1:2 not always **k.** when you are making them.
T-30...... III.8:5 those outside of Heaven **k.** not it is there.
T-30...... III.9:5 seek for idols cannot **k.** the star is there.
T-30....... V.6:5 of God knew in creation he must **k.** again.
T-30...... VI.9:2 Nor will you **k.** him, if you think he does
T-30...... VI.9:3 if you would **k.** the truth about yourself. *I*
T-31.......I.10:6 and you will **k.** in Him that God is Love.
T-31.......I.12:3 for. We do not **k.**. Let every image held of
T-31.......I.13:2 Now do you **k.** him not. But you are free
T-31........II.6:4 remembering how much we do not **k.**.
T-31....... V.9:5 does he **k.** exactly what would happen?
T-31..... V.14:7 self appear to answer what it does not **k.**.
T-31..... V.17:2 and you will see you **k.** not what you are.
T-31..... V.17:7 *I do not **k.** the thing I am, and therefore do*
T-31..... V.17:7 *I am, and therefore do not **k.** what I am doing*
T-31... VII.11:2 How would you **k.** his holiness while you
T-31... VII.13:4 It cannot judge because it does not **k.**.
W-pI....... 7.3:4 else would you **k.** whether or not this kind
W-pI....... 7.3:5 **k.** about this cup except what you learned
W-pI..... 24.2:2 conviction that you do **k.** what they are,
W-pI........ 25.h I do not **k.** what anything is for.
W-pI..... 25.1:3 You do not **k.** what it is for. Therefore, it
W-pI..... 25.3:4 thus you do not **k.** what anything is for.
W-pI..... 25.6:4 *I do not **k.** what this chair is for. I do not know*
W-pI..... 25.6:5 *for. I do not **k.** what this pencil is for. I do not*
W-pI..... 25.6:6 *for. I do not **k.** what this hand is for.* Say this
W-pI..... 29.3:3 Would you **k.** what is in them? Nothing is
W-pI..... 39.4:5 God does not **k.** unholiness. Can it be He
W-pI..... 39.4:6 Can it be He does not **k.** His Son?
W-pI..... 54.2:5 I **k.** that my state of mind can change.
W-pI..... 54.2:6 I also **k.** the world I see can change as well
W-pI..... 55.1:6 I see tells me that I do not **k.** who I am. I
W-pI..... 55.4:2 best interests when I do not **k.** who I am?
W-pI..... 55.5:1 (25) I do not **k.** what anything is for. To
W-pI..... 56.1:2 How can I **k.** who I am when I see myself
W-pI..... 68.1:1 can hold no grievances and **k.** your Self.
W-pI..... 68.6:3 *you are part of me and come to **k.** myself.*
W-pI..... 68.6:9 *my grievances go I will **k.** I am perfectly safe.*
W-pI..... 69.9:2 and that you do **k.** where to look for it.
W-pI... 72.10:7 *I do not **k.**. Tell me, that I may understand.*
W-pI... 72.12:3 *I do not **k.**. Tell me, that I may understand.*
W-pI..... 73.2:5 you do not **k.** your brothers or your Self.
W-pI..... 73.6:2 You **k.** it is not so. You cannot want this
W-pI..... 75.6:5 You do not **k.** yet what it looks like. You
W-pI..... 75.8:1 Tell Him you **k.** you cannot fail because
W-pI..... 78.5:1 You **k.** the one to choose; his name has
W-pI..... 79.1:1 cannot be solved if you do not **k.** what it is
W-pI..... 79.7:2 it. We will not assume that we already **k.**.
W-pI..... 98.3:4 their own ability because they **k.** their
W-pI..... 99.5:5 Yet does He **k.** one thing must still be true
W-pI..... 99.9:8 **k.** your Self as Love which has no opposite
W-pI... 101.2:5 For they **k.** it waits for them, and it will

W-pI...104.3:1 we choose to have them now, and **k.**, in
W-pI...110.9:5 are lost and do not **k.** yourself while He is
W-pI.121.13:7 *full of sin, and* **k.** *I am the perfect Son of God.*
W-pI...124.6:1 those who **k.** that they are one with God.
W-pI.127.12:1 us outside our love if we would **k.** our Self
W-pI...129.3:2 and **k.** they have no ending and they will
W-pI...130.9:5 will **k.** God's strength upheld you as you
W-pI.132.10:1 to **k.** your Self is the salvation of the world
W-pI.132.11:6 may **k.** the Thoughts you share with God.
W-pI.132.15:3 *world is not, and I would* **k.** *my own reality.*
W-pI.135.12:1 it cannot **k.** the outcome which is best,
W-pI...139.3:2 be alive and not to **k.** yourself is to believe
W-pI...139.4:3 If he asks as if he does not **k.**, it merely
W-pI...139.4:4 not **k.** the only certainty by which he lives
W-pI...139.5:4 into what knows and does not **k.** the truth
W-pI...139.7:2 who claim they do not **k.** themselves can
W-pI...139.8:3 you **k.** not what you cannot fail to know.
W-pI...139.8:3 you know not what you cannot fail to **k.**.
W-pI...139.9:7 that they may **k.** that they are part of you,
W-pI...151.6:2 with certainty of what they do not **k.**.
W-pI...152.6:4 What can He **k.** of the ephemeral, the
W-pI...153.5:2 You **k.** not what you do, in fear of it. You
W-pI.153.18:2 For you will **k.** that Heaven goes with you.
W-pI...154.1:5 nor can we **k.** what role is best for us;
W-pI...154.8:5 And so you do not **k.** that they are yours,
W-pI.154.12:3 but will not **k.** that God Himself has left
W-pI.155.10:4 You **k.** not where you go. But One Who
W-pI...157.9:4 knew that instant, and will surely **k.** again
W-pI...160.2:1 looks upon a world truth does not **k.**, and
W-pI...160.7:8 He does not **k.** of strangers. He is certain
W-pI...164.4:5 that you will **k.** that here your treasure is,
W-pI.166.10:4 not **k.** about a plan so alien to His Will.
W-pI...169.3:6 aware that there are things it does not **k.**,
WpI...rV.in4:2 Self we share and now prepare to **k.** again
WpI...rV.in6:4 pain, although I **k.** they have no meaning.
W-pI...182.1:2 somewhere in your mind you **k.** that this
W-pI...182.6:4 Yet does He **k.** that in you still abides His
W-pI...183.1:5 are, even within a world that does not **k.**;
W-pI.185.13:5 you will also **k.** you share one Will with all
W-pI...186.7:2 seeks to attack the threat it does not **k.**,
W-pI...188.6:5 They **k.** the way. For honest thoughts,
W-pI...189.8:2 You need not **k.** the way to Him. Your
W-pI.189.10:1 *Father, we do not* **k.** *the way to You. But we*
W-pI...193.1:1 God does not **k.** of learning. Yet His Will
W-pI...197.2:1 who **k.** not what their thoughts can do.
W-pI.198.12:5 perceive no more, and only **k.** the Father?
WpI rVI.in.4:4 all we did not **k.** and failed to understand.
W-pII .....in.7:3 We did not **k.** the way, but You did not
W-pII .....in.7:4 And we **k.** that You will not forget us now
W-pII .223.1:2 Now I **k.** my life is God's, I have no other
W-pII .224.2:2 *forgotten It, and do not* **k.** *where I am going,*
W-pII .227.1:7 *release. Father, I* **k.** *my will is one with Yours.*
W-pII ......2.2:5 Now it did not **k.** itself, and thought its
W-pII .238.1:2 *You created me, and* **k.** *me as I am. And yet*
W-pII .242.2:5 *us. You* **k.** *all our desires and our wants. And*
W-pII .243.1:2 I will not think that I already **k.** what
W-pII .244.1:3 *he fear or doubt or fail to* **k.** *he cannot suffer,*
W-pII .246.1:2 think that I can **k.** his Father or my Self.
W-pII ......4.1:8 To sense is not to **k.**. And truth can be but
W-pII .252.2:1 *Father, You* **k.** *my true Identity. Reveal It*
W-pII .252.2:2 *in You, and* **k.** *that Heaven is restored to me.*
W-pII .260.2:2 are we, because our Source can **k.** no sin.
W-pII ......6.5:3 will we **k.** we have no need of learning or
W-pII .274.1:3 *Your Son will* **k.** *he is as You created him.*
W-pII .278.1:3 way, I do not **k.** my Father nor my Self.
W-pII .288.1:3 *And to* **k.** *my Source, I first must recognize*
W-pII .288.2:2 will **k.** you have forgiven me if you behold
W-pII .291.2:3 *I do not* **k.** *the way to You. But You are wholly*
W-pII .299.1:1 my own ability to understand or **k.**. Yet
W-pII .299.2:7 *And I can* **k.** *my holiness. For Holiness Itself*
W-pII .299.2:8 *and I can* **k.** *my Source because it is Your Will*
W-pII .311.2:2 *We do not* **k.** *him, and we cannot judge. And*
W-pII ....11.4:5 **k.** their oneness and their unity with their
W-pII .326.1:6 *Let me* **k.** *that I am an Effect of God, and so I*
W-pII .326.1:8 *I* **k.** *that You will gather Your effects into the*
W-pII .330.2:2 *fail to* **k.** *our one Identity we share with You.*
W-pII ....12.3:2 he **k.** of madness and the death of God,
W-pII ....12.3:3 What can he **k.** of sorrow and of suffering
W-pII ....12.3:4 What can he **k.** of fear and punishment,
W-pII ....12.4:1 To **k.** reality is not to see the ego and its
W-pII .....336.h Forgiveness lets me **k.** that minds are
W-pII .337.1:3 What must I do to **k.** all this is mine? I
W-pII .337.1:6 Son; to **k.** I am the Son my Father loves.
W-pII .346.1:6 *You, and* **k.** *no laws except Your law of love.*
W-pII347.1:10 *I do not* **k.** *my will, but He is sure it is Your*
W-pII .355.1:8 *and* **k.** *You as his Father and Creator, and his*
W-pII .358.1:5 *Let me remember all I do not* **k.**, *and let my*
M-4 ..... I.A.7:2 that he did not really **k.** what was valuable
M-4 ..... I.A.7:6 he does not **k.** what the willingness is for.
M-10 ......... 4:3 **k.** how many times you merely thought
M-10 ......... 4:8 He does **k.** all the facts; past, present and
M-10 ......... 4:9 He does **k.** all the effects of His judgment
M-13 ......... 3:3 to **k.** not what it really wants to find. Who
M-16 ....... 11:7 His teachers **k.** that this is so, and have
M-24 ......... 4:8 told how to use it. What more need he **k.**?
C-ep........... 4:5 we **k.** that we will never lose the way again
P-2..........II.4:6 Not to **k.** God is to have no knowledge,
P-2......... III.3:8 or talk to him or even **k.** of his existence.
P-2..... VII.1:11 God does not **k.** of separation. What He
P-2....... VII.9:2 and so you will not **k.** you are His Son.
P-3...........I.1:5 assume that you **k.** what to offer everyone
S-2...........I.6:7 He does not **k.** of shadows. His the eyes
S-2......... III.4:5 and **k.** at last that condemnation is not
S-2......... III.7:1 Still does He **k.**, and that should be
S-3......... IV.1:6 because they **k.** that this is what He wills.

## knowable 2

T-8 ....... VI.7:8 to his Creator, it is forever **k.** to him.
T-24 ..... VI.1:5 that God is **k.** and will be known to you.

## knoweth 1

T-13 .. VII.10:2 Father **k.** that you have need of nothing.

## knowing 62

T-2 .........II.7:8 **k.** yourself as both a brother and a Son.
T-2 ...V.A.18:5 *He wishes,* **k.** *He goes there with me. I will be*
T-3 ..........I.8:3 **K.** His Son as he is, you realize that the
T-3 ...... III.1:10 **k.** is the affirmation of truth and beyond
T-3 ....... III.4:2 and therefore not a device for **k.**. It is,
T-3 ..... III.7:10 certainty. He created them by **k.** them. He
T-3 ....... IV.4:1 is not to be confused with the **k.** mind,
T-3 ........ V.3:1 **K.**, as we have already observed, does not
T-3 ........ V.5:1 **K.** is not open to interpretation. You may
T-3 ........ V.8:4 and **k.** any part of it is to know all of it.
T-4 ....... IV.9:3 peace, **k.** that this and only this must be.
T-4 ..... IV.11:7 restored. I raised the dead by **k.** that life is
T-4 ....... VI.7:3 **k.** that to know your brother *is* to know
T-5 ..........I.4:7 I could not have It myself without **k.** this.
T-5 ...... VII.2:7 He gave, **k.** that this giving will heal you.
T-6 .........II.5:2 **K.** this perfection is shared He recognizes
T-6 .........II.7:1 of the perfect equality of God's **k.**. The
T-6 ..... V.B.9:1 unified perception that reflects God's **k.**.
T-7 .........II.3:9 follow it gladly, **k.** that the increase of the
T-7 ....... III.5:8 this is what they share, **k.** what they are.
T-7 ..... VI.13:7 Creator and its creations, **k.** They are One
T-8 .........II.1:5 you what you are without **k.** what you are.
T-8 .........II.4:3 **k.** that the Will of the Son is the Father's.
T-8 ....... IV.6:3 like me I will help you, **k.** that we are alike
T-8 .....VIII.7:5 The ego is incapable of **k.** how you feel.
T-9 .........II.7:3 me. **K.** what you are, I cannot doubt you. I
T-9 ....... III.3:4 it, **k.** that nothing the ego makes means
T-9 ....... VI.3:5 God has but one Son, **k.** them all as One.
T-10 ........I.4:2 **K.** Them you will have no wish to sleep,
T-10 ...... IV.8:4 spark will heal, but **k.** the light will create.
T-10 ...... V.6:2 you, **k.** that you could not sin against Him
T-10 ...... V.6:3 **k.** that if you recognized your love for
T-11 ......I.11:5 must share it to know it, for sharing *is* **k.**.
T-12 ...... VI.5:7 And **k.** this, He would give you what is
T-13 .......II.5:4 wish to kill yourself by not **k.** who you are
T-13 ... III.12:3 **k.** that your peace lies in His Oneness? He
T-13 ...VIII.4:2 Mind of Both, and **k.** that Mind is One.
T-13 ...VIII.8:5 you. And **k.** that the light is in you, your
T-13 ..... XI.4:4 **k.** that you will finally let Him judge the
T-14 .......II.2:1 Spirit, seeing where you are but **k.** you are
T-14 ..... IV.7:3 the necessary conditions for **k.** Him, you
T-14 ..... IV.7:4 guiltlessness is the condition for **k.** Him.
T-15 ... III.10:2 wills, **k.** His Will is constant and at peace
T-15 .......V.9:3 holy instant reflects His **k.** by bringing all
T-18 ........I.2:3 not judge between them, **k.** they are one.
T19 .IV.A.17:5 my body, you whom I love, ***k.*** its littleness?
T19 IV.D.19:2 And **k.**, nothing in the plan God has
T-20 ........I.4:3 and you took me in, not **k.** who I was. Yet
T-20 .......II.7:4 illusions, **k.** his savior stands beside him?
T-28 ..... IV.9:1 **k.** You will come to close each little gap
T-31 .. VII.10:5 meet or look upon, not **k.** who they are;
W-pI .... 49.3:3 **k.** that in doing so we are joining our will
W-pI .... 50.1:3 prestige, being liked, **k.** the "right" people
W-pI .. 105.1:2 we will accept them, **k.** they belong to us.
W-pI .. 160.5:4 is he exiled of necessity, not **k.** who he is,
W-pI 170.13:5 *for all our brothers,* **k.** *they are one with us.*
W-pI .. 198.3:7 his Self and to his Father, **k.** They are One
W-pII . 239.1:4 constancy, **k.** he is as He created him?
M-29 ......... 8:7 *of God,* **K.** *they are on my behalf as well, And*
C-ep ........ 5:1 world, **k.** that Christ has been reborn in it
P-2....... VII.3:3 Only Christ forgives, **k.** His sinlessness.
S-1..........V.2:5 what it is, **k.** creation is the Will of God.

## knowledge 246

T-1 ........I.37:4 **k.** of the Divine Order is impossible.
T-2 ..........I.4:9 **k.** that illuminates not only sets you free,
T-3 .......... III.h Perception versus **K.**
T-3 ....... III.1:1 and have said very little about **k.** as yet.
T-3 ....... III.1:5 **K.** is power because it is certain, and
T-3 ....... III.1:9 That is why it is not **k.**. True perception is
T-3 ...... III.1:10 True perception is the basis for **k.**, but
T-3 ...... III.2:4 being a way of perceiving, is not **k.**. It is
T-3 ..... III.2:10 **K.** is timeless, because certainty is not
T-3 ....... III.4:5 the experience from the realm of **k.**. That
T-3 ....... III.5:7 you say you are acting on the basis of **k.**,
T-3 ....... III.5:7 are really confusing **k.** with perception.
T-3 ....... III.5:8 **K.** provides the strength for creative
T-3 ..... III.5:10 **K.** is the result of revelation and induces
T-3 ..... III.5:12 **K.** comes from the altar within and is
T-3 ....... III.6:2 His **k.** will bring peace without question.
T-3 ....... III.6:4 **K.** preceded both perception and time,
T-3 ....... III.6:6 can and must be stabilized, but **k.** *is* stable.
T-3 ....... IV.1:3 them, and are therefore incapable of **k.**.
T-3 ....... IV.1:4 also incapable of **k.** because you can still
T-3 ....... IV.3:2 would involve **k.** and cannot be perceived.
T-3 ....... IV.4:2 demonstrating that **k.** is not involved.
T-3 ....... IV.6:2 or translation, which **k.** does not need.
T-3 ....... IV.6:8 emphasized, **k.** does not do anything. It
T-3 ..... IV.6:10 that **k.** can always be remembered, never
T-3 ....... IV.7:3 a man who remembered spirit and its **k.**.
T-3 ....... IV.7:4 not attempt to counteract error with **k.**,
T-3 .........V.1:3 was the means for the return to **k.**, which
T-3 .........V.3:3 **K.** is always stable, and it is quite evident
T-3 .........V.4:6 perception-related, and not a part of **k.**.
T-3 .........V.5:6 Ingenuity is totally divorced from **k.**,
T-3 .........V.5:6 because **k.** does not require ingenuity.
T-3 .........V.6:6 In electing perception instead of **k.**, you
T-3 .........V.6:7 lost the **k.** that you yourself are a miracle
T-3 .........V.8:6 partial awareness. **K.** transcends the laws
T-3 .........V.8:6 because partial **k.** is impossible. It is all
T-3 .........V.8:8 but know yourself and your **k.** is complete
T-3 ....... VI.2:2 on which perception but not **k.** rests. I
T-3 ....... VI.3:6 organize yourself. In the presence of **k.** all
T-3 ...... VII.3:7 tree" was named the "tree of **k.**." Yet God
T-3 ...... VII.3:8 God created **k.** and gave it freely to His
T-3 ...... VII.4:1 Eating of the fruit of the tree of **k.** is a
T-3 ...... VII.4:5 **K.** cannot deceive, but perception can.
T-3 ...... VII.6:6 light and darkness, **k.** and perception, are
T-3 ...... VII.6:8 Only the oneness of **k.** is free of conflict.
T-4 ........ in.2:3 words are inspired because they reflect **k.**.
T-4 ........ in.2:4 are disclaiming **k.** instead of affirming it,
T-4 .........II.1:4 Abstract thought applies to **k.** because
T-4 .........II.1:4 because **k.** is completely impersonal, and
T-4 .........II.3:2 threw **k.** away it is as if you never had it.
T-4 .........II.8:6 Spirit in its **k.** is unaware of the ego. It
T-4 .......II.11:2 because misperception is a block to **k.**,
T-4 .....II.11:12 **K.** never involves comparisons. That is its
T-4 ....... III.3:6 **k.** of permanence and unshakable being.
T-4 ....... III.7:1 every idea you ever had that opposes **k.**.

T-4......IV.10:9 you are. That **k.**, and I assure you that it *is*
T-4......IV.10:9 knowledge, and I assure you that it *is* **k.**,
T-4.........V.2:7 as it would surely be in the presence of **k.**.
T-4........VI.2:4 you come as close to **k.** as perception can.
T-4........VI.2:5 The gap is then so small that **k.** can easily
T-4.......VII.7:5 attitudes the **k.** from the revelation brings
T-5...........I.4:8 Spirit is so close to **k.** that He calls it forth
T-5........ I.4:10 **K.** is always ready to flow everywhere, but
T-5...........I.5:1 of the **k.** that lies beyond perception. He
T-5...........I.6:5 Perception is not **k.**, but it can be
T-5...........I.6:5 knowledge, but it can be transferred to **k.**,
T-5...........I.7:4 that although it does not engender **k.**, it
T-5......... II.5:1 because He can share only perfect **k.**.
T-5......... II.5:6 share His **k.** with you without hindrance.
T-5........III.1:2 Bridge for the transfer of perception to **k.**,
T-5........III.7:1 of the ego and the **k.** of the spirit. His
T-5........III.7:5 is light, and light leads to **k.**. The Holy
T-5........VI.1:1 God in His **k.** is not waiting, but His
T-6........ I.12:2 to know its Wholeness. Only this is **k.**.
T-6......... II.7:2 the Bridge between perception and **k.**. By
T-6......... II.7:3 to use perception in a way that reflects **k.**,
T-6........III.1:3 because the Holy Spirit still holds **k.** safe
T-6........III.4:5 you win back the **k.** that you threw away.
T-6......V.A.5:1 ultimately translates perception into **k.**.
T-7...........I.6:3 in the reawakening of **k.** is taken by God.
T-7......... II.5:6 rests only on the **k.** of what truth is. This
T-7........IV.2:2 the **k.** that you are in God because you are
T-7........IV.6:9 is a way of approaching **k.** by thinking in
T-7........VI.4:2 **K.** is total, and the ego does not believe in
T-7........VI.5:1 recognition, all sane perception and all **k.**.
T-7........VI.9:8 to the Holy Spirit and to the **k.** of God.
T-7......VI.10:1 Spirit because your being *is* the **k.** of God.
T-7........IX.2:7 That is how it retains the **k.** of itself. Spirit
T-8...........I.1:1 **K.** is not the motivation for learning this
T-8...........I.1:3 the prerequisite for **k.** only because those
T-8...........I.1:3 and peace is the condition of **k.** because it
T-8...........I.1:4 **K.** can be restored only when you meet its
T-8...........I.1:7 **K.** *is* His Will. If you are opposing His Will,
T-8...........I.1:8 opposing His Will, how can you have **k.**? I
T-8...........I.1:9 I have told you what **k.** offers you, but
T-8......... II.1:3 to that **k.** is the purpose of the curriculum
T-8......... V.1:4 perceive their illusions which block **k.**.
T-8........VI.9:1 God the **k.** of the value He puts upon you.
T-8........VI.9:2 being born of my **k.** of myself and Him.
T-8........VI.9:6 of the **k.** of where you are always, and
T-8... VIII.1:11 difference between **k.** and perception. In
T-8... VIII.1:13 But **k.** never changes, so its constellation
T-8..... VIII.7:7 if only **k.** has being and the ego has no
T-8..... VIII.7:7 has being and the ego has no **k.**, then the
T-9......... V.7:7 perception ultimately is translated into **k.**
T-9........VI.4:7 knows His Son, for **k.** is shared with God.
T-9.......VII.3:2 of you is based on His **k.** of what you are,
T-9.......VII.7:2 Lack of **k.** of any kind is always associated
T-9.......VII.7:2 of **k.** simply because knowledge is total.
T-9.......VII.7:2 of knowledge simply because **k.** is total.
T-9.......VII.7:3 your littleness therefore is to deny all **k.**,
T-10.........I.1:5 not know this has banished itself from **k.**,
T-10....... II.1:2 it. **K.** must precede dissociation, so that
T-10....... II.1:5 have replaced your **k.** by an awareness of
T-10....... II.2:3 retains the **k.** of God and of yourself for
T-10....... II.2:6 in this remembering is the **k.** of yourself.
T-10....... II.3:4 yours is the exchange of **k.** for perception.
T-10.......III.6:1 of the calm **k.** that each one is part of Him
T-10......IV.2:5 **K.** cannot dawn on a mind full of illusions
T-11.........I.1:3 this lies the beginning of the return to **k.**;
T-11....... II.6:4 Invite this **k.** back into your mind, and let
T-11....... V.2:1 removal of all that stands in the way of **k.**?
T-11....... V.6:7 you the **k.** of your dependence on God, in
T-11.....VII.4:1 The perception of goodness is not **k.**, but
T-11.....VII.4:2 And this *is* the condition of **k.**. Without
T-11... VIII.1:5 real perception will be translated into **k.**
T-11... VIII.1:9 world is the transfer of all perception to **k.**
T-12...... I.10:6 attests to your eternal **k.** that union is
T-12..... II.10:5 otherwise His **k.** remains useless to you.
T-12......VI.6:3 Father, perception fuses into **k.** because
T-12......VI.6:7 perception and **k.** have become so similar
T-12......VI.7:1 the separation is the reinstatement of **k.**.
T-12... VIII.2:5 Father, and could not live in the **k.** of Him
T-12... VIII.8:6 perception is easily translated into **k.**, for
T-12... VIII.8:7 Being corrected it gives place to **k.**, which
T-13.......in.3:7 in that belief the **k.** of the Father was lost,
T-13.....VII.9:4 **K.** needs no correction. Yet the dreams of
T-13.....VII.9:5 Yet the dreams of love lead unto **k.**. In
T-13.....VII.9:6 this they are the welcome that you offer **k.**
T-13...... VIII.h From Perception to K.
T-13... VIII.1:3 a fact which belongs to the sphere of **k.**,
T-13... VIII.1:4 impossible to be in the world with this **k.**.
T-13... VIII.2:1 and **k.** becomes quite apparent if you
T-13... VIII.2:1 this: There is nothing partial about **k.**.
T-13... VIII.2:3 You are an aspect of **k.**, being in the Mind
T-13... VIII.2:4 you. All **k.** must be yours, for in you is all
T-13... VIII.2:4 must be yours, for in you is all **k.**.
T-13... VIII.3:1 has many elements in common with **k.**,
T-13... VIII.7:4 **K.** is far beyond your individual concern.
T-13... VIII.8:1 as yourself you will be released to **k.**,
T-13.... IX.8:12 You can deny His **k.**, but you cannot
T-14.........I.1:2 so. The **k.** is not taught, but its conditions
T-14....... II.7:1 meets the conditions of **k.** in the Kingdom
T-14.... III.16:3 when all **k.** lies behind every decision the
T-14......IV.3:2 Himself is all He knows, and so it is all **k.**.
T-14......IV.4:1 before that **k.** would be meaningful to you
T-14......IV.7:5 that **k.** is swept away from recognition in
T-14....IV.10:3 He shares the **k.** of what you are with God
T-14.....VII.1:2 or darkness, **k.** or ignorance are yours,
T-14.....VII.1:6 so ignorance fades away when **k.** dawns.
T-14.....VII.1:7 by which ignorance is brought to **k.**. Yet
T-14.....VII.7:1 of perception that leads to **k.**. You cannot
T-14... VIII.4:6 Nothing can change the **k.**, given you by
T-14......IX.1:5 it has cost you **k.** of Him and of yourself.
T-14......IX.1:6 The **k.** is safe, but where is your safety
T-14........ X.1:1 the **k.** of creation must continue forever.
T-14......XI.1:2 **K.** is power, and all power is of God. You
T-15......VI.7:6 mind. **K.** is therefore of the mind, and its
T-15......IX.1:5 is translated into **k.** by the part that God
T-16.........I.5:3 This is not **k.**, and the form of empathy
T-16....... II.5:5 the miracle into the **k.** which it represents
T-16....IV.10:1 leads to union in yourself *must* lead to **k.**,
T-16....IV.10:3 deprives you of **k.** for fantasies are the veil
T-18.........I.5:6 to shatter **k.** into meaningless bits of
T-18......III.2:3 The goal you accepted is the goal of **k.**, for
T-18....... V.1:4 from which you waken easily to **k.**. Put
T-18......VI.1:6 and the **k.** that there is nothing else;
T-18......VI.2:1 What could God give but **k.** of Himself?
T-18....IX.11:1 This course will lead to **k.**, but knowledge
T-18....IX.11:1 but **k.** itself is still beyond the scope of
T-18....IX.11:7 The readiness for **k.** still must be attained.
T-18....IX.12:6 by the **k.** of love and its one meaning.
T-19.........I.12:1 easily exchanged for **k.** as is the real world
T-20........ II.8:8 In you the **k.** lies, ready to be unveiled
T-20.......III.1:4 **K.** requires no adjustments and, in fact, is
T-21....... V.7:5 Yet any part of **k.** threatens dissociation
T-21....... V.8:9 it. **K.** does not depend on it, and madness
T-21....... V.9:4 **K.** is far beyond attainment of any kind.
T-25......III.3:1 Perception rests on choosing; **k.** does not
T-25......III.3:2 **K.** has but one law because it has but one
T-25......IX.5:6 but as God knows it and as **k.** is reflected
T-26......III.3:4 **k.** makes no attack upon perception. They
T-26......III.4:3 of **k.** on perception: "It has no meaning,
T-26....... V.5:2 the simple **k.** of the Son of God can hardly
T-26.....VII.3:4 made to take the place of changeless **k.**.
T-26.....VII.4:1 is true of **k.** is not true of anything that is
T-26....... X.1:9 all. Confused perception will block **k.**. It is
T-30........ II.1:4 And all He knows is but your **k.**, saved for
T-30........ V.7:8 And then will come the **k.** They are One.
W-pI.....15.3:5 perception, and they are not related to **k.**.
W-pI.....15.3:6 These exercises will not reveal **k.** to you.
W-pI.....43.1:2 His is the realm of **k.**. Yet He has created
W-pI.....43.1:3 the Mediator between perception and **k.**.
W-pI.....43.1:4 perception would have replaced **k.** forever
W-pI.....43.1:5 changed and purified that it will lead to **k.**
W-pI.....56.5:2 and attack, is the **k.** that all is one forever.
W-pI.....56.5:3 I have not lost the **k.** of Who I am because
W-pI...113.2:2 *Self, Whose* **k.** *still remains within my mind,*
W-pI...129.4:4 Their **k.** is direct and wholly shared and
W-pI...138.5:4 **k.** is beyond the goals we seek to teach
W-pI.139.11:4 We have not lost the **k.** that God gave to
W-pI.139.12:3 **k.** of yourself apart from your awareness,
W-pI...158.1:2 The **k.** that you are a mind, in Mind and
W-pI...158.1:4 was given you as **k.** which you cannot lose
W-pI...158.1:5 living thing, for by that **k.** only does it live
W-pI...158.2:3 It is not this **k.** which you give, for that is
W-pI...158.5:4 can give directly, for Christ's **k.** is not lost,
W-pI...158.5:5 The Father's Will and His are joined in **k.**.
W-pI.158.11:2 true **k.** is reflected in a way so accurate its
W-pI...160.7:7 between His **k.** and His Son's reality. He
W-pI...168.4:2 first will come, with **k.** but an instant later
W-pI...169.5:4 for in that **k.** words are meaningless.
WpI...rV.in4:5 Itself, is perfect in Its **k.** and Its Love, and
W-pI...198.2:4 It is not a law that **k.** understands, for
W-pI...198.2:4 understands, for freedom is a part of **k.**.
W-pII.228.1:2 Shall I deny His **k.**, and believe in what
W-pII.228.1:2 believe in what His **k.** makes impossible?
W-pII.....3.2:5 **k.** could not cause such insane thoughts.
W-pII.....4.1:9 And truth can be but filled with **k.**, and
W-pII.....7.1:2 perception leads to **k.** through the grace
W-pII.....7.1:3 truth, to be dispelled before the light of **k.**
W-pII.....7.4:1 From **k.**, where He has been placed by
W-pII.336.1:2 **K.** is restored after perception first is
W-pII...14.3:6 **K.** will return when we have done our
M-4....... X.3:2 **k.** and eternal truth do not appear in this
C-1.............7:6 demonstrates that it cannot reach **k.**.
C-3.............2:2 go directly from perception to **k.** because
C-3.............4:4 No one can look on **k.**. But the face of
C-4...............h TRUE PERCEPTION – K.
C-4.............3:1 **K.** is not the remedy for false perception
C-4.............7:1 And now God's ***k.***, changeless, certain,
P-2..........II.4:5 but **k.** of God has no true opposite. Not to
P-2..........II.4:6 Not to know God is to have no **k.**, and it is
P-2..........II.4:7 And without **k.** one can have only belief.
P-2.....VII.1:13 Son. His **k.** is reflected in the ideal patient-
P-2.......VII.5:4 a **k.** that no one here can have; a certainty

## known 43

*See also* well-known

T-3......... V.8:3 Truth can only be **k.**. All of it is equally
T-3.......VII.4:4 Images are perceived, not **k.**. Knowledge
T-3.....VII.6:11 and truth can be **k.** by all those for whom
T-7........ XI.7:6 both. Being is **k.** by sharing. Because God
T-8........ III.2:1 the only joy and peace that can be fully **k.**,
T-8......IV.8:13 It can be imprisoned if Its truth is to be **k.**
T-9......IV.10:6 Had you **k.**, you could no more have been
T-9........ VI.5:5 its Oneness it will be **k.** by its creations,
T-10.......in.3:2 And what He knows can be **k.**, because
T-10...... IV.2:6 whole, and cannot be **k.** by part of a mind
T-10...... V.6:5 that what you deny you must have once **k.**
T-10..... V.13:5 be acknowledged if the real Son is to be **k.**
T-11.....VII.4:8 know God because it is His Will to be **k.**.
T-12.........II.8:3 You do not fear the unknown but the **k.**.
T-13...... XI.8:2 God would share with you is **k.**. Yet His
T-14...... IV.7:4 He cannot be **k.** without His Son, whose
T-14....... V.1:4 Would you deny His yearning to be **k.**?
T-15...... IV.7:4 in private thoughts, **k.** only to yourself,
T-15....... V.9:2 having always **k.** you exactly as He knows
T-16........ V.3:7 Heaven, where the meaning of love is **k.**,
T-18.... IX.10:7 forgiven nor transformed. But merely **k.**,
T19. IV.D.19:1 to be lost but found; not to be seen but **k.**.
T-20...... VI.2:5 idolatry. Love wishes to be **k.**, completely
T-24...... VI.1:5 God is knowable and will be **k.** to you. For
T-25.........II.9:3 Would He not make **k.** to you His Love, if
T-26.........I.7:2 die because his sinlessness is **k.** to God;
T-26.....VII.3:6 It cannot be perceived, but only **k.**. What
T-26.....VII.9:7 they were **k.** before they were denied.
T-26.........X.1:8 are **k.** with clarity or not at all. Confused
T-26.........X.5:4 Presence of your holy Guests be **k.** to you.
T-27...... III.5:2 Reality is ultimately **k.** without a form,
T-27...... III.5:3 not yet a power **k.** as wholly free of limits.
T-29..... VII.6:1 the truth within from being **k.** to you, and
T-31.........II.1:2 It is not vanquished that the truth be **k.**,
W-pI... 138.5:3 lies, and as it is accepted it is **k.**. But
W-pI... 139.2:3 surely **k.** by any living thing is what it is.
W-pI. 169.10:2 comes, it will be **k.** and fully understood.
W-pI. 186.13:1 is calling from the **k.** to the unknowing.
W-pII.224.2:1 *My Name, O Father, still is* **k.** *to You. I have*
W-pII.299.2:8 *Source because it is Your Will that You be* **k.**.
M-26.........2:7 All needs are **k.** to them, and all mistakes
P-2..........II.4:4 concept, for God can be but **k.**. Belief

S-1......... II.4:1 in terms **k.** as "praying for one's enemies.

## knows 301

T-3...........I.5:5 mind **k.** the truth and this is its strength.
T-3...........I.8:2 In this state your mind **k.** God, for God is
T-3......... III.7:9 God **k.** His children with perfect certainty
T-3......... IV.6:4 Spirit, which **k.**, could not be reconciled
T-3...... IV.7:16 God **k.** you only in peace, and this *is* your
T-3.......... V.9:3 Spirit **k.** God completely. That is its
T-3........ VI.8:6 He **k.** that it makes them unhappy. God's
T-3....... VII.3:6 If God **k.** His children, and I assure you
T-4......... III.9:5 The Holy Spirit **k.** that you both *have*
T-4....... VII.3:1 in the same way to everything it **k.** is true,
T-4....... VII.3:3 **k.** that what is true is everything that God
T-4....... VII.6:6 **k.** it in His Own Being and its experience
T-5...........I.1:5 be. Remember that spirit **k.** no difference
T-5...... VI.12:5 in time, also **k.** that time is meaningless.
T-6...........I.9:2 these things, but not as God **k.** them, I
T-6......... II.1:3 recognition it **k.** its Creator. Exclusion
T-6......... III.1:2 in it, and from *what* it extends it **k.** itself.
T-6......... III.1:3 The word "**k.**" is correct here, because the
T-6...... IV.10:5 Who **k.** that His creations are perfect,
T-6...... IV.12:2 to imply a lack, which God **k.** is not there.
T-6.......... V.1:1 the Holy Spirit **k.** more than you do now,
T-6.......... V.1:4 when He **k.** your mind only as whole?
T-7......... IV.1:4 Who **k.** His creations as perfectly whole.
T-7......... IV.4:2 healing, because He **k.** you only as whole.
T-7..... VII.3:10 last until the Sonship **k.** itself as whole.
T-7......... IX.1:7 **k.** its fullness and cannot conceive of any
T-7......... IX.2:1 Spirit **k.** that the awareness of all its
T-7......... IX.5:1 **k.** of them and can bring them into your
T-7.......... X.2:6 Share His Will and you share what He **k.**.
T-7......... XI.2:6 Son of God is happy only when he **k.** he is
T-7......... XI.5:1 a mind has only light, it **k.** only light. Its
T-8.......... II.1:2 Only one Teacher **k.** what your reality is.
T-8.......... II.1:9 from the ego, because the ego **k.** nothing.
T-8......... III.1:4 to listen to the Teacher Who **k.** of light,
T-8......... VI.6:7 accept his function unless he **k.** what *he* is.
T-8....... VII.3:6 because He **k.** the only reality of anything
T-8.... VIII.9:10 of the one Teacher Who **k.** what life is,
T-8......... IX.1:2 He **k.** what the answer to everything is.
T-9......... IV.6:1 forgiveness is His function and He **k.** how
T-9.......... V.7:6 acknowledgment the healer **k.** it is there.
T-9......... VI.4:7 can know yourself only as God **k.** His Son,
T-9....... VII.7:6 because He **k.** its foundation is not true.
T-9....... VII.7:9 If it comes from God, He **k.** it to be true. If
T-9..... VII.7:10 If it does not, He **k.** that it is meaningless.
T-9.... VIII.10:6 God, Who **k.** your value, would not have
T-10....... in.3:2 And what He **k.** can be known, because
T-10...... III.6:2 God's Son **k.** no idols, but he does know
T-10...... V.12:1 If God **k.** His children as wholly sinless, it
T-10...... V.12:2 If God **k.** His children as wholly without
T-10...... V.12:3 If God **k.** His children to be wholly joyous
T-11...... III.1:5 **k.** no attack and His peace surrounds you
T-11...... III.2:1 of comfort, for he **k.** not what he does,
T-11...... III.4:2 the way of pain, of which God **k.** nothing.
T-11...... IV.7:2 God **k.** His Son as wholly blameless as
T-11...... VI.4:7 God, which **k.** no time and no exceptions.
T-11.. VIII.14:9 their reality is from the One Who **k.** it,
T-12..... II.10:2 want. He **k.** what to do with it. You do not
T-12..... II.10:3 do not understand how to use what He **k.**.
T-12......... V.9:2 if you follow the Teacher Who **k.** the way
T-12........ VI.2:1 He **k.** nothing but the spirit as you. He is
T-12........ VI.4:2 He **k.** that they have not lost their vision,
T-12........ VI.5:6 He **k.** of the Father's Love for Him. And
T-12........ VI.6:2 **k.** because He knows His Father's Love for
T-12........ VI.6:2 because He **k.** His Father's Love for Him.
T-12.... VII.13:2 death as God **k.** you are deserving of life.
T-12.... VIII.2:1 Son **k.** his Father's protection and cannot
T-12.... VIII.3:7 He created it, and He **k.** what it is. You
T-13......... I.4:3 he believes in it the Holy Spirit **k.** it is not
T-13....... I.11:5 Son of God, He **k.** that this is true. And
T-13..... V.10:4 And seeing what He is, He **k.** His Father.
T-13... VII.10:9 He **k.** what you have need of and what
T-13... VII.12:1 Only the Holy Spirit **k.** what you need.
T-13... VII.12:6 **k.** that everything you need is temporary,
T-13... VII.12:8 He **k.** that you are not at home there, and
T-13.... VIII.1:5 the mind that **k.** this unequivocally knows
T-13 ... VIII.1:5 unequivocally **k.** also it dwells in eternity,
T-13 ... VIII.1:7 it. It **k.** that it is everywhere, just as it has
T-13 ... VIII.2:3 being in the Mind of God, Who **k.** you.
T-13 ... VIII.7:3 Holy Spirit **k.** your part in the redemption
T-13 ... VIII.8:1 yourself through Him Who **k.** of freedom.
T-13 . VIII.10:2 God **k.** it, but you do not, and so you do
T-13 ..... IX.8:9 He **k.** Himself, and knows the truth in you
T-13 ..... IX.8:9 He knows Himself, and **k.** the truth in you
T-13 ... IX.8:10 He **k.** there is no difference, for He knows
T-13 ... IX.8:10 no difference, for He **k.** not of differences.
T-13 ... IX.8:11 where God **k.** there is perfect innocence?
T-13 ....... X.7:5 He has seen separation, but **k.** of union.
T-13 ....... X.7:6 teaches healing, but He also **k.** of creation
T-13 ....... X.7:8 Yet what He **k.** you do not know, though
T-13 ..... XI.4:5 because He **k.** that He will make it for you
T-13 ..... XI.8:8 The Holy Spirit **k.** only of His Will. There
T-14 ........ I.3:9 there is One Who **k.** it leads to nothing,
T-14 ........ I.3:9 it leads to nothing, for He **k.** everything.
T-14 ........ I.4:2 He **k.** to be true you have denied yourself,
T-14 ....... II.4:2 Like God, He **k.** it to be true. He brings
T-14 ... III.10:6 as naturally as peace that **k.** no limits.
T-14 ... III.11:2 of help, and Help that **k.** the answer.
T-14 ... III.11:6 **k.** that you are worthy of everything God
T-14 . III.11:10 you are deserving of it. God **k.** you are.
T-14 ... III.13:1 The One Who **k.** the plan of God that
T-14 ... III.13:4 Spirit **k.** that all salvation is escape from
T-14 ... III.14:2 He **k.** the way, and leads you gladly on it.
T-14 ... III.16:2 are reflections of what God **k.** about you,
T-14 ... III.19:2 *He leadeth me and **k.** the way, which I know*
T-14 ... III.19:4 *to communicate to me all that He **k.** for me.*
T-14 ..... IV.3:2 Giving Himself is all He **k.**, and so it is all
T-14 ..... IV.3:3 what He **k.** not cannot be, and therefore
T-14 ..... IV.4:7 He **k.** what you are. Remember that there
T-14 ..... IV.5:4 for God, and for your function as He **k.** it.
T-14 ..... IV.6:5 He **k.**. And He will tell you, and then do it
T-14 ..... IV.8:7 and Who **k.** of nothing except giving?
T-14 ... IV.10:4 God for you, for only He **k.** what God is.
T-14 ...... V.2:6 what you do, but He Who **k.** is with you.
T-14 ...... V.9:3 we know Him, as He **k.** us guiltless. I
T-14 ..... VI.5:4 He **k.** you are not separate from God, but
T-14 ..... VI.6:7 for He **k.** with Whom you are in perfect
T-14 .... VII.3:3 Yet it is true because God **k.** it. These are
T-14 .... VII.5:5 God **k.** it not. The Holy Spirit uses
T-14 .. VII.5:12 Leave that to Him Who **k.**. You are not
T-14 ... VIII.4:7 Everything God created **k.** its Creator. For
T-14 ..... IX.4:2 Presence **k.** they will return to purity and
T-14 ..... IX.6:7 for it, but **k.** not where to look to find it.
T-14 ...... X.10:5 but **k.** it not unless he joins with you in
T-14 ... XI.14:4 and He **k.** that faith in His Creator must
T-15 ........ I.7:5 the Holy Spirit, Who **k.** only the present,
T-15 ..... III.4:1 function is, for the Holy Spirit **k.** what it is
T-15 ...... V.3:2 unlike to God, Who **k.** no special love,
T-15 ...... V.5:1 The Holy Spirit **k.** no one is special. Yet
T-15 ...... V.8:1 the Holy Spirit **k.** how to bring a touch of
T-15 ...... V.9:1 God **k.** you *now.* He remembers nothing,
T-15 ...... V.9:2 known you exactly as He **k.** you now. The
T-15 ... VIII.1:6 perceives as clearly as He **k.** forgiveness is
T-15 ... VIII.4:7 Christ **k.** of no separation from His Father
T-15 ... VIII.5:8 Spirit **k.** that it is not understandable,
T-15 ... VIII.6:4 **k.** it must be possible because it is the
T-16 ........ I.4:1 True empathy is of Him Who **k.** what it is
T-16 ...... V.5:4 Holy Spirit **k.** that completion lies first in
T-16 ..... VI.9:2 understand the Thought that ***k.*** what you
T-17 ........ I.6:1 outside the truth to Him Who **k.** the truth
T-17 ....... II.7:2 **k.** that he has always rested there in peace
T-17 ..... III.7:6 sees, because He **k.** that only this is true.
T-17 ..... VI.5:9 The Holy Spirit **k.** that the situation is as
T-18 ..... IV.8:2 unwilling to give place to One Who **k.**.
T-18 ... VIII.8:1 Love **k.** no bodies, and reaches to
T-18 . VIII.12:4 than He **k.** you without your brother. But
T-19 ..... III.4:3 But sin He **k.** not, nor can He recognize
T19.... IV.A.6:2 end. For Heaven **k.** you well, as you know
T19.... IV.C.3:4 He **k.** of neither sin nor its results. The
T19. IV.D.18:5 of his Father, Who **k.** no sin, no death,
T-20 ... III.11:3 no fear in perfect love *because* it **k.** no sin,
T-20 ..... IV.1:4 Spirit, Who **k.** that as you give you gain.
T-20 ..... IV.6:2 **k.** the rest will see to it without your help.
T-20 ...... V.7:7 He *is* the gift, and yet he **k.** it not. No more
T-20 ...... V.8:2 sees. He **k.** the Son of God, and shares his
T-20 ....... V.8:5 upon himself not as his Father **k.** him.
T-21 ........ I.9:2 Here is the sight of him who **k.** his Father.
T-21 ..... III.9:2 Spirit **k.** that sacrifice brings nothing. He
T-21 ..... IV.4:5 by the part of your mind the ego **k.** not of.
T-21 ..... IV.4:8 It **k.** no sin. How, otherwise, could it have
T-21 ....... V.6:3 a part of you that **k.** His Will and shares it
T-21 ....... V.6:6 because its Source **k.** not of incompletion.
T-21 ... VIII.2:5 in its vision as its Creator is in what He **k.**,
T-22 ........ I.8:4 taught him what he **k.** *because* you knew it
T-22 ..... VI.2:5 He **k.** this mad decision was made by one
T-22 ... VI.9:11 be dispelled by Him Who **k.** the light, and
T-23 ..... IV.9:4 No one who **k.** that he has everything
T-24 ...... in.2:9 The truth arises from what He **k.**. And
T-24 .... in.2:10 rose in His Mind *because* of what He **k.**.
T-24 ........ I.3:4 whose Self is his, and Whom he **k.**? Only
T-24 ..... III.5:8 Who **k.** that death is not your will, must
T-24 ....... V.1:2 on what He loves, and **k.** it as Himself.
T-24 ....... V.1:3 because He **k.** that it is one with Him and
T-24 ....... V.6:2 He **k.** where you are going, and He leads
T-24 ....... V.7:1 He quiet, for He **k.** that love is in you now,
T-24 ..... VI.3:4 the world began, and as He **k.** you still.
T-25 ........ I.6:2 He **k.** the Will of God and what you really
T-25 .... VII.1:6 Yet each one **k.** the cost of sin is death.
T-25 ... VIII.3:1 in salvation of which the world **k.** nothing
T-25 ... VIII.5:2 God **k.** not of this. But justice does He
T-25 ... VIII.5:3 But justice does He know, and **k.** it well.
T-25 ... VIII.5:5 to God's Mind *because* He **k.** of justice. To
T-25 ... VIII.6:8 perceive the "threat" of what God **k.** as
T-25 ... VIII.8:1 Who **k.** that they are wholly innocent in
T-25 ... VIII.9:8 He **k.** that Heaven is richer made by each
T-25 ... VIII.9:9 what loving justice **k.** to be his due. For
T-25 . VIII.10:3 not. God **k.** of no injustice. He would not
T-25 . VIII.14:2 This is the only justice Heaven **k.**, and all
T-25 ..... IX.5:6 God **k.** it and as knowledge is reflected in
T-26 ........ I.7:8 Who **k.** His gifts can never suffer sacrifice
T-26 ....... II.8:2 **k.** that everything that is belongs to Him,
T-26 ..... III.1:2 How could it be, when all He **k.** is One?
T-26 ..... III.1:3 He **k.** of one creation, one reality, one
T-27 ....... II.8:4 Spirit **k.** your healing is the witness unto
T-27 ..... II.10:2 It belongs to One Who **k.** of fairness, not
T-27 ..... II.16:1 Correction must be left to One Who **k.**
T-27 ..... V.11:9 for He **k.** it is a gift of love unto His Son,
T-27 ..... VI.4:3 He **k.** it is not real. For nothing could
T-27 ..... VI.4:7 to your life in Him Who **k.** no death. Each
T-27 .... VII.1:5 innocent because he **k.** not what he does,
T-27 . VIII.12:1 Him Who **k.** that every one is like the rest.
T-29 ........ I.2:4 Certain it is he **k.** not what love means.
T-29 ....... II.7:4 in immortality, and Heaven **k.** it not. Yet
T-29 ..... IX.3:6 God **k.** of justice, not of penalty. But in
T-29 ..... IX.8:6 song again, he **k.** he never heard it not.
T-30 ....... II.1:4 own. And all He **k.** is but your knowledge,
T-30 ..... III.4:5 God **k.** not form. He cannot answer you
T-30 ..... III.6:1 Nothing that God **k.** not exists. And what
T-30 ..... III.6:2 not exists. And what He **k.** exists forever,
T-30 ..... III.9:1 Who **k.** the Father knows this light, for
T-30 ..... III.9:1 Who knows the Father **k.** this light, for
T-30 ... III.10:4 that worships idols, and that **k.** not God.
T-30 ... III.10:5 left the Mind of its Creator Whom it **k.**, as
T-30 ... III.10:5 it knows, as its Creator **k.** that it is there.
T-30 ... III.11:2 a world which your reality **k.** nothing of?
T-30 ....... V.4:2 one outside of Heaven **k.** how this can be,
T-30 ....... V.4:5 God **k.** everything his Father understands
T-30 ... VIII.3:7 you, but not of God Who **k.** no limits.
T-31 ........ I.9:3 the certainty with which He **k.** His Love.
T-31 . VIII.12:6 You, and **k.** You as the only Source it has.
W-pI ..... 66.2:5 He **k.** what your function is. He knows
W-pI ..... 66.2:6 is. He **k.** that it is your happiness.
W-pI ..... 78.7:1 let us ask of Him Who **k.** this Son of God
W-pI ..... 94.3:8 This is the Self that **k.** no fear, nor could
W-pI .. 96.11:1 Your Self **k.** that you cannot fail today.
W-pI .... 97.5:2 will lay them everywhere He **k.** they will
W-pI .... 98.9:5 then of Him Who **k.** the function that you
W-pI .... 99.6:2 is not created by the only Source it **k.**.
W-pI .. 107.8:3 your Father **k.** that You are both the same
W-pI .. 108.5:3 it be directed by the One Who **k.** the truth
W-pI .. 121.5:4 It does not ask, because it thinks it **k.**. It
W-pI .. 125.3:4 It **k.** him not. Today we will not listen to
W-pI .. 125.5:4 He **k.** His Son, and wills that he remain as
W-pI .. 128.6:3 It **k.** where it belongs. But free its wings,

W-pI.136.11:1 God **k.** not of your plans to change His
W-pI.136.12:5 you throw away its gifts, and yet it **k.**,
W-pI...138.2:1 Creation **k.** no opposite. But here is
W-pI...139.5:4 into what **k.** and does not know the truth.
W-pI.139.5:10 For it asks of one who **k.** the answer.
W-pI.139.10:1 by his belief he **k.** not what he is. Today
W-pI...140.6:7 it is, and **k.** that no illusion can be real.
W-pI...151.9:3 body mean to Him Who **k.** the glory of
W-pI...153.2:6 and **k.** not where to turn to find escape
W-pI.155.10:5 But One Who **k.** goes with you. Let Him
W-pI...160.8:2 **k.** to be His Son belongs where He has set
W-pI...166.1:3 He **k.** His Son. He gives without exception
W-pI...166.4:1 Here is the only home he thinks he **k.**.
W-pI.167.12:7 wakened mind is one that **k.** its Source,
WpI.. rV.in4:4 *I*. This Self alone **k.** Love. This Self alone is
WpI.. rV.in4:5 consistent in Its Thoughts; **k.** Its Creator,
WpI.. rV.in8:1 and **k.** the answer God has given Him.
W-pI...181.9:2 of the holy Self which **k.** no sin, and never
W-pI...182.2:1 No one but **k.** whereof we speak. Yet
W-pI...182.4:3 house, and **k.** that He is alien here. This
W-pI...182.5:1 in you your Father **k.** as His Own Son. It is
W-pI...182.5:2 Son. It is this Child Who **k.** His Father. He
W-pI...186.2:7 part assigned to us by One Who **k.** us well
W-pI...186.4:3 be certain only that He **k.** our strengths,
W-pI.186.11:3 It comes from One Who **k.** no error, and
W-pI.186.12:4 Who **k.** all things exactly as they are, or a
W-pI.186.13:2 comfort you, although He **k.** no sorrow.
W-pI.186.13:3 He **k.** that you have everything already.
W-pI...189.6:1 its Love which **k.** us perfect as itself, its
W-pI...189.8:1 Is it not He Who **k.** the way to you? You
W-pI...189.9:6 God **k.** His Son, and knows the way to
W-pI...189.9:6 knows His Son, and **k.** the way to him. He
W-pI.193.11:5 Let us give them all to Him Who **k.** the
W-pI.198.11:6 that God forever **k.** to be His only Son.
W-pII..222.1:5 who **k.** the truth of what He speaks today!
W-pII..228.1:1 My Father **k.** my holiness. Shall I deny
W-pII..228.1:4 One Who **k.** the true condition of His Son
W-pII..242.1:3 there is One Who **k.** all that is best for me.
W-pII..242.1:5 home, and it is He Who **k.** the way to God
W-pII......6.2:5 the Self Who, like His Father, **k.** no sin.
W-pII..277.1:6 *because he **k.** no law except the law of love.*
W-pII..299.1:4 it. And Our Will, together, **k.** that it is so.
W-pII..324.2:1 So let us follow One Who **k.** the way. We
W-pII..347.1:6 *He sees what I behold, and yet He **k.** the truth*
W-pII..349.2:1 Our Father **k.** our needs. He gives us
W-ep .........1:7 He **k.** the way to solve all problems, and
M-10 .........6:7 now he **k.** that these things need not be.
M-16 .........7:3 For he is safe, and **k.** it to be so. He has a
M-24 .........5:9 he **k.** is not necessarily all there is to learn.
M-27 .........2:5 Who loves such a god **k.** not of love,
M-29 .........4:6 The Holy Spirit **k.** the truth about you.
M-29 .........4:8 this image assumes it **k.** all things because
M-29 .......4:10 Who **k.** the truth has not forgotten it. His
M-29 .......7:10 God **k.** but His Son, and as he was created
C-3.............3:2 God **k.** what His Son needs before he asks
C-4.............7:5 God **k.** it is His Own, as it is his. And here
C-5.............1:7 God does not help because He **k.** no need.
C-6.............1:5 which God alone **k.** along with Christ, His
C-6.............3:3 **k.** because He is part of God; He perceives
P-2.....VII.1:12 What He **k.** is only that He has one Son.
P-3...........I.1:9 of God, and He **k.** nothing of sacrifice.
S-1...........I.7:7 pray with one who **k.** that this is true is to
S-1..........II.2:1 made by a Son of God who **k.** Who he is.
S-2........ III.3:2 He **k.** the way to make of every call a help
S-2........ III.5:6 well. He **k.** the need; the question and the
S-3........ III.2:4 this. Someone **k.** better, has been better
S-3........ III.3:1 Someone **k.** better; this the magic phrase
S-3........ IV.3:3 for He **k.** the Cause of healing is Himself,

---

# L

## labels 1

T-30.....VII.2:4 these **l.** change with other judgments,

## labor 1

S-3 ......... II.3:3 from **l.** gladly done and gladly ended.

## lack 122

T-1...........I.8:1 are healing because they supply a **l.**; they
T-1........ I.34:2 for **l.** they establish perfect protection.
T-1........ I.41:2 or atone for, the faulty perception of **l.**.
T-1........ I.42:1 false sense of isolation, deprivation and **l.**.
T-1........IV.3:1 Darkness is **l.** of light as sin is lack of love
T-1........IV.3:1 Darkness is lack of light as sin is **l.** of love
T-1........VI.1:3 While **l.** does not exist in the creation of
T-1........VI.1:5 **L.** implies that you would be better off in
T-1........VI.2:1 God is the only **l.** you really need correct.
T-1........VI.2:5 because this produces a **l.** of conflict.
T-2...........I.1:7 that some emptiness or **l.** exists in you,
T-2...........I.5:6 unaffected by all expressions of **l.** of love.
T-2........ I.5:12 by **l.** of love from without and capable,
T-2........ I.5:12 proceeding from **l.** of love in others.
T-2........VI.7:6 fear. Fear arises from **l.** of love. The only
T-2........VI.7:7 only remedy for **l.** of love is perfect love.
T-3......... II.3:1 you **l.** confidence in what someone will do
T-3......... V.2:2 do so out of a specific sense of **l.** or need.
T-3......... V.2:4 you make something to fill a perceived **l.**,
T-3.......V.10:2 Since perception rests on **l.**, those who
T-4........III.9:6 the idea of "getting," which implies a **l.**,
T-4......... V.2:1 its **l.** of discrimination between the body
T-5.......V.4:10 ego does not perceive sin as a **l.** of love,
T-5.......V.4:11 because, as soon as you regard sin as a **l.**,
T-5.......VII.5:1 with a **l.** of love to one of God's creations.
T-6.......IV.12:2 teach. To teach is to imply a **l.**, which God
T-6......... V.4:1 and those who **l.** wisdom *are* children. Yet
T-6.......V.B.8:7 **L.** of order of difficulty in miracles has not
T-7......... V.4:5 he thinks he has something that others **l.**.
T-7.......VII.2:6 What you deny you **l.**, not because it is
T-7........XI.4:2 because the **l.** of exceptions *is* the lesson.
T-9........ III.4:5 than merely a **l.** of correction for him. It is
T-9.......VII.7:2 is. **L.** of knowledge of any kind is always
T-9.......VII.7:2 and this produces a total **l.** of knowledge
T-10....... II.2:1 reality brings more than merely **l.** of fear.
T-11. VIII.14:5 their **l.** of understanding that frightens
T-12...... III.1:6 For poverty is **l.**, and there is but one lack
T-12...... III.1:6 is but one **l.** since there is but one need.
T-13...... X.14:8 **l.** faith in you and love Him perfectly?
T-14....... X.3:4 What is more difficult to grasp is the **l.** of
T-14....... X.4:1 of **l.** of competition among your thoughts,
T-14....... X.8:9 **l.** any consistent sense when they are put
T-14....... X.9:3 and the underlying **l.** of content makes a
T-14....... X.9:6 ego can no longer defend its **l.** of content.
T-15....... V.6:6 not have judged them so like you in **l.**.
T-16...... VI.4:5 total **l.** of value of the special relationship,
T-17.........I.3:3 your **l.** of faith in the power that heals all
T-17....... II.5:4 seemed ugly in the darkness of your **l.** of
T-17... V.11:10 And by this **l.** of thanks and gratitude you
T-17......VII.1:1 are the witnesses to your **l.** of faith. They
T-17......VII.1:3 The problem *was* the **l.** of faith, and it is
T-17......VII.3:6 the justification for your **l.** of faith. You
T-17...VII.3:11 faith. If you **l.** faith, ask that it be restored
T-17......VII.6:2 If you **l.** faith in anyone to fulfill, and
T-17......VII.8:4 **l.** faith in him because of what you were.
T-17... VIII.5:6 you to realize what your **l.** of faith in him
T-18....VI.13:6 above all, the **l.** of awareness of the body,
T-18.... VIII.8:2 itself. Its total **l.** of limit *is* its meaning. It is
T-20....... II.1:6 acknowledges the **l.** of value he places on
T-20......VII.8:2 see the body is the sign that you **l.** vision,
T-21...... III.5:1 is impossible that the Son of God **l.** faith,
T-21...... III.5:2 Faithlessness is not a **l.** of faith, but faith
T-21...... III.5:3 Faith given to illusions does not **l.** power,
T-22.......in.3:2 Each one has looked within and seen no **l.**
T-22.........I.1:6 fear of **l.** of meaning in yourself arise? It is
T-22...... VI.3:5 The **l.** of contradiction makes the soft
T-23.... II.19:5 in their inaccuracy and **l.** of meaning. Life
T-23.... II.20:7 And **l.** of faith in love, in any form, attests
T-24...... II.1:3 It is established by a **l.** seen in another,
T-24.......IV.1:1 is a **l.** of trust in anyone except yourself.
T-24....... V.1:7 for something and **l.** faith that it is so.
T-24....... V.7:6 His perfect **l.** of specialness He offers you,
T-24...... VI.2:1 Without you there would be a **l.** in God, a
T-24.... VI.13:6 Out of His **l.** of conflict comes your peace.
T-25...... VI.7:2 Think not you **l.** a special value here. You
T-25.....VIII.4:3 that one should **l.** for what another has.
T-26.........I.2:2 of complete disunity and total **l.** of joining
T-26...... IV.1:2 the gate behind which total **l.** of limits lies
T-27....... V.2:8 that is required for a healing is a **l.** of fear.
T-27...... VI.1:9 the **l.** of meaning which their purpose has
T-28..... VII.1:2 For there is no **l.** in him. An empty space,
T-28..... VII.1:3 An empty space, a little gap, would be a **l.**.
T-29.........I.8:2 weakness, but its **l.** of strength *or* weakness
T-29...... IV.1:3 Their equal **l.** of truth becomes the basis
T-29.....VII.4:2 For you believe that you can suffer **l.**, and
T-29.....VII.4:2 that you can suffer lack, and **l.** *is* death. To
T-30.......I.12:1 of **l.** of opposition to be helped. It is a
T-30...... VI.8:5 the miracle must **l.** the power to heal.
T-30....VIII.2:5 his perfect freedom from all forms of **l.**,
T-31....... V.9:1 some **l.** of ease at times and some distress,
W-pI..... 10.2:4 The emphasis is now on the **l.** of reality of
W-pI..... 19.4:3 throughout. **L.** of order in this connection
W-pI..... 19.4:3 **l.** of order in miracles meaningful to you.
W-pI..... 27.2:2 about the **l.** of reservation involved, add:
W-pI..... 51.2:5 willing to recognize the **l.** of validity in my
W-pI..... 69.5:4 be really convinced of their **l.** of substance
W-pI..... 92.5:5 It sees that **l.** in anyone would be a lack in
W-pI..... 92.5:5 that lack in anyone would be a **l.** in all.
W-pI..... 95.4:4 the extent of your **l.** of mental discipline,
W-pI..... 98.7:2 deep conviction and the certainty you **l.**.
WpI. rIV.in2:7 **L.** of forgiveness blocks this thought from
WpI. rIV.in3:1 in which the **l.** of true forgiveness may be
W-pI... 159.6:5 not already healed, no **l.** unsatisfied, no
W-pI... 163.1:2 as anger, faithlessness and **l.** of trust;
W-pI... 181.1:1 doubt and **l.** of sure conviction in yourself
W-pI... 184.4:4 them. And a **l.** of space, a sense of unity or
W-pI... 187.2:4 **l.** for proof that when you give ideas away
W-pI... 194.4:4 to understand the **l.** of sequence really
W-pI... 194.7:7 may be faulty, but will never **l.** correction.
WpI rVI.in.5:1 but one exception to this **l.** of structuring.
M-4 ..... I.A.3:3 initially that their **l.** of value is merely

M-4 ..... I.A.3:4 How can l. of value be perceived unless
M-4 ...... III.1:6 Judgment implies a l. of trust, and trust
M-4 ....... X.1:2 comes with l. of judgment. As judgment
M-7 ........... 4:1 is a mistake in the form of l. of trust. As
M-15 ......... 3:1 with l. of appreciation and even contempt
M-16 ......... 2:2 such l. of structuring on their own part.
M-24 ......... 6:3 past and total l. of interest in the future.
P-3 ......... II.4:5 need for each other implies a sense of l.. A
S-1 ......... II.1:5 wanting, out of a sense of scarcity and l..
S-1 ......... II.7:4 is no asking, for there is no l.. Identity in
S-3 ......... II.1:5 the cause remains, and will not l. effects.

## lacked 4

T-1......... V.4:4 mocked if any of His creations l. holiness.
T-17..... VII.1:5 Had you not l. faith that it could be solved
M-7 ......... 1:10 He l. the trust that makes for giving truly,
C-ep........... 3:5 has the certainty the journey l. till now.

## lacking 18

T-1........ VI.1:6 is the meaning of the "fall," nothing was l.
T-1........ VI.2:2 and had thus perceived yourself as l.. The
T-2.........I.1:10 is perfect can be rendered imperfect or l..
T-4...........I.1:3 share their lessons conviction will be l.. A
T-5........ IV.7:5 that is not through the Holy Spirit *is* l..
T-7....... VII.2:6 you deny you lack, not because it is l., but
T-7....... VII.7:8 scarcity, or you will perceive yourself as l..
T-13... VII.10:5 which you find yourself *because* you are l..
T-15.... XI.10:3 Nothing will be l., and you will make
T-17..... V.11:4 And He has not been l. in appreciation for
T-17..... VII.4:1 have not given can be l. in any situation.
T-30..... VII.7:3 interpretations which are l. in stability,
W-pI..... 42.7:2 in which nothing is l. that is needed, and
W-pI... 102.2:4 you think it offers you is l. in existence,
W-pI. 154.12:2 a hundred times, and yet belief is l. still.
W-pI... 191.1:4 shadows, punitive and wild, l. all reason,
M-19 ......... 4:7 –a Judgment wholly l. in condemnation;
P-2......... V.4:3 however limited, however l. in sincerity.

## lacks 15

T-1........ IV.2:7 its errors, which are merely l. of love.
T-5........ IV.7:4 thinking of God l. nothing. Everything
T-19....... II.2:1 an arrogance which the idea of error l.. To
T-24....... II.1:3 keeping clear in sight, all l. it can perceive
T-26..... V.11:7 but l. conviction in what he perceives.
T-28..... VII.3:5 this, because it l. foundation in the truth.
T-29..... VII.2:4 upon the body; that it seek for what he l.,
T-29.... VIII.2:4 They have the power to supply your l.,
W-pI..... 44.3:4 precisely what the untrained mind l.. Yet
W-pI... 102.1:4 but l. the roots that once secured it tightly
W-pI... 135.9:2 the limits and the l. from which you think
W-pI... 167.6:5 are, and cannot give them attributes it l.,
W-pII .250.1:2 perceive the l. in him with which I would
M-4 ....... II.1:6 and no word l. agreement with another.
P-3........ III.4:4 other; whatever one l. the other supplies.

## ladder 10

T-18....... V.2:7 build a l. planted in the solid rock of faith,
T-28..... II.12:7 the steps have been retraced, the l. gone,
T-28...... III.1:2 up the l. separation led you down. The
S-1 ........... II.h The L. of Prayer
S-1 ......... II.7:1 Prayer is a l. reaching up to Heaven. At
S-1 ......... II.8:3 is no need for a l. to reach what one has
S-1 ........ III.2:1 forms of prayer, at the bottom of the l.,
S-1 ........... V.h The L. Ends
S-1 ......... V.3:5 High has the l. risen. You have come
S-1 ......... V.4:1 The l. ends with this, for learning is no

## lag 1

P-3....... II.10:9 In time there can be a great l. between the

## laid 95

*See also* heavy-laid

T-4....... II.10:3 judgment, and is l. aside accordingly. The
T-6 ..........I.1:3 only emphasis l. upon it so far has been
T-7 ..... VIII.5:4 will have l. aside all anger and all attack,
T-10 ..... IV.7:1 Son of God who has l. aside all false gods,
T-12 ....... II.4:6 heavy blankets you have l. upon yourself.
T-13 .... in.2:10 wither and gasp and are l. in the ground,
T-13 ..... XI.5:1 guilt that His dear Son has l. upon himself
T-14 ..... IV.5:5 you have l. upon yourself by loving not
T-14 ..... XI.4:6 joyously l. down by hands open to receive
T-15 ....... X.2:2 instant no guilt is l. upon the Son of God,
T-17 ... VIII.3:2 given wherever faithlessness is l. aside,
T-18 ....... II.3:6 No limits on substitution are l. upon you.
T-18 ....... II.7:3 Holy Spirit has l. upon it will be extended.
T-18 ....... II.9:4 the Holy Spirit has gently l. the real world
T-18 ..... IX.9:4 of every evil thought you l. upon it. Here
T-18 ..... IX.9:7 the dark and heavy garments of guilt l. by
T-19 ...... I.11:3 free of all the guilt he l. upon himself.
T-19 ...... I.13:4 altar where grace was l. for both of you.
T19..IV.A.15:3 contains no fear that you l. not upon it.
T19....IV.C.4:6 of guilt you l. upon the body would kill it.
T19....IV.C.8:5 and unrelenting orders you l. upon it, and
T19. IV.D.16:5 l. upon him and he accepted as his own,
T-20 ....... II.4:5 see what you have l. upon it to offer me. If
T-20 ....... II.6:5 to be tossed about a while and l. aside.
T-20 ....... II.9:2 him where you l. the lilies of forgiveness.
T-20 .... VII.6:1 a brother's body has l. a judgment on him
T-20 ... VIII.4:4 with the shining lilies you l. upon it.
T-21 ..... III.4:2 from all illusions where your faith was l..
T-22 ...... V.2:8 peace, and l. between you and its return.
T-22 ..... VI.6:4 gift he let be l. in Heaven through himself
T-24 ..... VI.8:6 the judgment you have l. on both of you.
T-25 .... VII.1:1 that you l. upon yourself into a blessing,
T-25 ... VIII.4:7 to be l. beside your little payment, to
T-26 ..... III.2:3 all illusions are l. down beside the truth,
T-26 .. VII.17:1 crucifixion is redemption l., for healing is
T-26 ... VIII.5:1 make for safety all are l. within the future,
T-26 ....... X.5:7 have l. on it by rendering it purposeless,
T-27 ........ I.5:8 he l. upon his heart was ever justified, and
T-28 ...... I.10:1 it is not He Who l. a judgment on His Son
T-29 ....... II.4:5 He has l. them at your feet, and asks you
T-29 ....... II.4:7 stand, and where His gifts for them are l..
T-29 ..... IX.2:9 salvation from the judgment l. in terror
T-29 ..... IX.3:5 l. upon himself within the dream he made
T-31 ....... II.1:3 no plans that need be l. for bringing in
T-31 .... V.17:4 been l. by is truth revealed exactly as it is.
T-31 .... VII.8:5 Thus is the concept of himself l. by, for
T-31 ... VIII.5:7 gone, illusory alternatives l. by, and
W-pI..... 78.9:1 today in which you l. your images aside,
W-pI..... 80.2:4 You have l. deception aside, and seen the
W-pI..... 95.9:4 It is this process that must be l. aside, for
W-pI... 99.12:5 mind and let all fear be gently l. aside,
W-pI... 104.5:2 to seek for them where He has l. them.
W-pI... 125.3:3 the world has l. upon the Son of God. It
W-pI. 126.10:1 are changed and false beliefs l. by. Repeat
W-pI. 132.13:5 are a shadow briefly l. upon a dying world
W-pI. 133.13:2 state today, with self-deception l. aside,
W-pI. 134.11:1 powerful as love which l. its blessing on it,
W-pI. 134.16:4 your brother, but were l. upon yourself.
W-pI. 136.18:2 to it. As these are l. aside, the strength the
W-pI. 140.11:2 to let our interfering thoughts be l. aside,
WpI. rIV.in7:5 that He has l. in it for you to have of Him.
W-pI. 152.10:3 that all self-concepts have been l. aside,
W-pI. 153.12:5 The game of fear is gladly l. aside, when
W-pI... 159.2:5 storehouse of your mind where they are l.
W-pI... 159.6:2 All are l. here already. All can be received
W-pI... 163.4:4 and l. to rest beneath the headstone death
W-pI... 164.3:4 On this day is grief l. by, for sights and
W-pI... 169.1:4 it can be gently l. and willingly received;
W-pI. 169.13:2 is here that miracles are l.; to be returned
W-pI... 187.9:1 brother offers you are l. upon your altar,
W-pI... 191.6:5 have l. the mark of death upon its heart.
W-pI... 192.4:3 aid, to be l. by when learning is complete,
W-pI... 194.4:6 your experience that you have l. the past
W-pI... 197.8:5 In your heart the Heart of God is l.. He
W-pII ...... 2.3:4 the gifts of your forgiveness l. before it,
W-pII . 265.1:1 because I l. my sins on it and saw them
W-pII ..... 7.1:4 are sights and sounds forever l. aside.
W-pII . 294.1:7 without a purpose, it is l. aside. It is not
W-pII ... 13.3:5 And each is l. before the Word of God,
W-ep ......... 2:1 pathway of the sun l. down before it rises,
M-4 ......... I.2:3 when the gifts of God are l. before him?
M-4 .... VI.1:11 that comes when defenses are l. down. It
M-6 ........... 2:5 the storehouse of treasures l. up equally
M-12 ......... 5:6 When its usefulness is done it is l. by, and
M-23 ......... 6:5 we teach the limitations we have l. on us.
M-23 ......... 6:8 Then turn to one who l. all limits by, and
M-25 ......... 6:7 they l. upon their minds be lifted. It can
M-26 ......... 3:9 Those who have l. the body down merely
M-27 ......... 3:4 he is "l. to rest" in devastation's arms,
M-28 ......... 6:5 Judgment is l. by, and given Him Whose
C-4 ............ 6:3 all illusions brought to truth and l. upon
P-2.........V.6:3 The limits l. on both the patient and the
P-3.........II.1:3 any limits be l. on an interaction in which
S-3.........II.4:2 it dreamed about and l. upon the world.
S-3.........II.6:3 overcome until all faith in it has been l. by

## lake 1

T-18 ..... IX.7:2 A solid mountain range, a l., a city, all rise

## lamb 4

T-3 .......... I.5:1 as "the l. of God who taketh away the sins
T-3 .......... I.5:1 but those who represent the l. as blood-
T-3 .......... I.5:3 The lion and the l. lying down together
T-3 .......... I.6:4 The l. "taketh away the sins of the world"

## lament 2

T-9 ...... VII.6:5 chosen to be little and to l. your littleness.
T-9 ...... VII.6:6 dictated this choice the l. is inevitable.

## lamented 1

T19 ... IV.C.4:2 damned by its maker and l. by every

## lamenting 1

W-pI .... 23.2:2 There is no point in l. the world. There is

## laments 1

W-pI 131.15:1 from dismal thoughts and meaningless l..

## lamp 6

T-11 ...... in.4:5 I give you the l. and I will go with you.
T-11 ....... V.1:3 together we have the l. that will dispel it,
T-13 ..... IX.1:8 like a l. shining so brightly that the chain
T-20 .... II.11:6 The l. is lit in you for your brother. And
W-pI ...... 1.2:4 *That l. does not mean anything. That sign*
W-pI .... 29.5:6 *God is in this l.. God is in that body. God is in*

## lamps 3

T-10 ..... IV.7:5 all the l. of God were lit by the same spark
T-25 ..... III.5:5 l. of Heaven are not for mind to choose to
T-25 ..... III.5:6 remain in darkness where the l. are not.

## land 2

T19 ... IV.A.7:2 can l. and settle briefly upon anything, for
T-26 ..... IX.3:8 forever from the l. where They have come

## language 25

T-2 ....... IV.5:3 efficacy, must be expressed in a l. that the
T-4 ....... III.9:4 In the ego's l., "to have" and "to be" are
T-5 ....... III.7:2 to work with the ego's beliefs in its own l..
T-14 ..... VI.6:1 do not understand the l. you have made.
T-14 ..... VI.6:3 If the purpose of l. is communication,
T-14 ..... VI.7:2 perceives the meaning in your alien l.. He
T-15 ..... VI.7:8 not remember the l. of communication,
T-15 ..... VI.8:1 and the l. of communication with all your
T19IV.A.10:10 the l. in which their going forth was asked
T-22 ........ I.6:2 This is *your* l.. You do not understand it
T-22 ........ I.7:3 he will speak the l. you can understand.
T-22 ........ I.9:6 in a l. the body does not speak. Nor could

T-24....... II.5:2 a different l. and they fall on different ears
T-25.........I.7:4 It use the l. that this mind can understand
T-30......VII.7:8 us. Our common l. lets us speak to all our
T-31....... I.10:5 you give Him answer in the l. that He calls
W-pI...129.3:3 into a silence where the l. is unspoken
W-pI...129.4:3 Their l. has no words, for what They say
W-pI...160.2:1 foreign to the truth he speaks a different l.
W-pI...192.2:2 can understand a l. far beyond his simple
M-1............3:6 or soundlessly; in any l. or in no language;
M-1............3:6 or soundlessly; in any language or in no l.;
M-23..........7:1 you in a l. you can love and understand.
M-26..........4:3 those who suffer, you must speak their l..
M-29..........6:5 your prayers of the heart into His l.. He

## languages 4

T-7......... II.4:2 translated for those who speak different l.
T-7......... II.5:2 meaning in all respects and in all l..
T-14......VI.7:5 You speak two l. at once, and this must
T19. IV.A.11:3 messages of different things in different l.

## lapse 3

T-4......... II.9:5 to exist after a temporary l. into ego life.
T-4......... II.9:6 that the soul will be punished for this l..
W-pII..234.1:3 the interval there was no l. in continuity,

## lapses 2

W-pI.....95.7:3 use your l. from this schedule as an excuse
W-pI.....95.8:3 to forgive ourselves for our l. in diligence,

## large 12

T-24......III.3:7 However l. and overblown it seems to be,
T-25....IV.4:10 it is l. enough to hold the world within its
T-26....... II.4:8 to judge whether the hurt be l. or little.
T-26....... V.1:1 A little hindrance can seem l. indeed to
T-29......IX.5:4 grow l. and dangerous and fierce and wild
T-31......IV.3:3 can offer seem to be quite l. in number,
W-pI.....15.4:4 It is not necessary to include a l. number
W-pI.....24.3:2 more cursory examination of a l. number.
W-pI.....24.6:1 you are making a l. number of demands
WpIrIII.in12:3 with each of these ideas will bring such l.
P-3......... II.1:5 that a l. number of others turn for help.
S-2...........I.2:3 and mistakes loom l. and grow and swell

## largely 1

M-4........ II.2:1 is l. due to their perfect honesty. It is only

## larger 12

T-1....... II.6:10 however, within the l. temporal sequence.
T-2........VI.7:3 the l. process of accepting the Atonement
T-4...........I.6:2 perceive a teacher as merely "a l. ego" you
T-14......III.9:5 a constellation l. than anything you ever
T-14....... X.4:3 thoughts as more important, l. or better,
T-25. VIII.12:4 need comes not of you, but from a l. Self,
T-29....... II.7:2 the l. dream that change is possible. To
W-pI.....26.8:2 thoroughly than to touch on a l. number.
W-pI.....78.6:3 and all the little and the l. hurts he gave.
W-pI...154.1:5 a l. plan we cannot see in its entirety. Our
M-8............1:3 A l. object overshadows a smaller one. A
M-8............5:2 the insane in a l. hallucination as opposed

## largest 1

W-pI...127.6:5 destiny. Today we take the l. single step

## Last 15

*last*

T-2........ VIII.h The Meaning of the L. Judgment
T-2..... VIII.1:6 into the real meaning of the L. Judgment.
T-2..... VIII.2:1 The L. Judgment is one of the most
T-2..... VIII.2:5 L. Judgment will extend over a similarly
T-2..... VIII.3:1 The L. Judgment is generally thought of
T-2..... VIII.3:4 aim of the L. Judgment is to restore right-
T-2..... VIII.3:5 L. Judgment might be called a process of
T-2..... VIII.5:1 The term "L. Judgment" is frightening
T-2..... VIII.5:3 the L. Judgment is objectively examined,
T-3........ VI.1:1 have already discussed the L. Judgment,
T-3........ VI.1:2 the L. Judgment there will be no more.
T-9........ IV.9:2 Do not fear the L. Judgment, but welcome
W-pII......9.3:1 teaches, making way for the L. Judgment,
W-pII.......10.h What Is the L. Judgment?
W-pII....10.3:1 You who believed that God's L. Judgment

## last 184

*Last*

*See also* last-ditch; Appendix C

T-2........IV.4:7 This is because the l. thing that can help
T-2.....VIII.5:1 of the association of "l." with death. This
T-2..... VIII.5:5 Your own l. judgment cannot be directed
T-3........ III.4:6 is why visions, however holy, do not l..
T-4.........in.3:1 the cross should be the l. "useless journey.
T-4.........in.3:3 accept it as your own l. useless journey,
T-4......... II.5:7 This will not l.. Be patient a while and
T-4......... V.5:8 be chosen *because* their value will not l..
T-5...........I.6:4 One-mindedness that transfer to it is at l.
T-5...........I.6:6 over," since the l. step is taken by God.
T-6...........I.2:6 l. useless journey the Sonship need take,
T-6......V.A.1:1 you will know that you will l. forever.
T-6......V.B.2:1 that only fundamental change will l., but
T-6......V.B.2:3 It is also their l. and final one. Increasing
T-7.............I.h The L. Step
T-7...........I.6:3 is whole. I have said that the l. step in the
T-7...........I.6:6 tell you something about this l. step.
T-7...........I.7:3 He does nothing l., because He created
T-7...........I.7:8 "l. step" that God will take was therefore
T-7.....VII.3:10 perception will l. until the Sonship knows
T-7.....VII.3:11 made perception and it must l. as long as
T-7.......VII.4:2 They will l. as long as you value them.
T-10.........I.4:3 want only truth, and being at l. your will,
T-11.......in.4:2 l. looked at the ego's foundation without
T-11....... V.8:1 You must recognize that the l. thing the
T-11......VI.7:1 and taken the l. thorn from his forehead.
T-11. VIII.15:5 down to you and take the l. step for you,
T-12.... III.10:1 else, you will at l. have placed its source,
T-12.......VI.6:3 When the Holy Spirit has at l. led you to
T-12... VIII.8:5 invisible, for you will at l. have seen truly.
T-13...VII.12:6 and will but l. until you step aside from all
T-13... VIII.2:8 perception, however holy, will l. forever.
T-13... VIII.3:2 Yet the l. step must be taken by God,
T-13... VIII.3:2 because the l. step in your redemption,
T-14.......IX.8:4 in them, are ready at l. for Heaven. There,
T-14....... X.5:2 of Heaven l. but a moment and grow dim,
T-15..... X.5:11 Guilt cannot l. when the idea of sacrifice
T-16.......IV.2:3 through this l. undoing quite unharmed,
T-16.......IV.2:3 and will at l. emerge as yourself. This is
T-16.......IV.2:4 This is the l. step in the readiness for God.
T-16....IV.12:6 We will take the l. useless journey away
T-17....... II.4:5 For God will take the l. step swiftly, when
T-17....IV.13:6 upon the picture itself, seeing at l. that,
T-17....IV.14:4 of both pictures can at l. occur. And each
T-17....IV.14:6 it is just a picture is brought home at l..
T-18....... II.8:6 you do not see that you have made, at l.,
T-18......VII.5:7 peace comes at l. to those who wrestle
T-18......VII.5:7 at l. into the mind given to contemplation
T-19.......IV.3:8 When God has taken the l. step Himself,
T19. IV.A.17:1 which means you have at l. forgiven me.
T19... IV.D.2:2 to meet Him, and to join with Him at l..
T-21.......IV.7:5 it sees that Heaven has come to earth at l.,
T-21........VII.h The L. Unanswered Question
T-21......VII.6:1 the first three questions, but not yet the l..
T-21......VII.6:5 which is indeed the l. you need decide,
T-21......VII.6:7 to be the l. remaining hope of finding sin,
T-21......VII.8:1 Consider carefully your answer to the l.
T-21...VII.11:4 l. question adds the wish for constancy in
T-21...VII.12:3 Until the l. decision has been made, the
T-22........ II.3:5 happiness that does not l. is really fear.
T-23.......IV.8:9 your certainty? And that will l. forever?
T-24...... II.11:6 with the hope of peace at l. in sight.
T-24.......VI.7:6 set forth at l. in terms you recognized and
T-25. VIII.11:1 heeds not who looks on innocence at l.,
T-26...... III.4:2 the l. comparison that he will ever make;
T-26...... III.4:2 the l. evaluation that will be possible, the
T-26......VII.7:5 His Love at l. to vengeance's heels. For
T-26...... IX.8:3 thanks that They are welcome made at l..
T-26...... IX.8:9 They have come! For They have come at l.
T-27.........I.11:7 both be reconciled at l. and seen as one.
T-27.........II.6:7 will yet be the l. trumpet that the world
T-28.........I.6:5 cause that will endure, or else it will not l..
T-28.........I.14:1 Now is the Son of God at l. aware of
T-29...... IX.2:6 dream will seem to l. while he is part of it.
T-29...... IX.8:1 Forgiving dreams have little need to l..
T-30......VII.5:6 makes interpretation stabilize and l..
T-31........II.4:2 you think that it is murder justified at l..
T-31....... V.3:4 and at l. to open insult and abuse.
T-31..... V.16:4 happy in the confidence that it will go at l.
W-pI.......7.5:3 practice periods, each to l. a minute or so,
W-pI.....15.3:4 signs that you are opening your eyes at l..
W-pI.....22.3:4 *I see nothing that will l.. What I see is not real*
W-pI.....38.4:1 each preferably to l. a full five minutes,
W-pI.....57.1:9 wishes and walk into the sunlight at l..
W-pI.....64.3:1 review our l. few lessons, your function
W-pI.....69.8:4 that you are at l. joining your will to God's
W-pI.....70.6:1 should l. some ten to fifteen minutes. We
W-pI.....75.4:4 rises before us in gladness, to be seen at l..
W-pI.....77.6:6 We are asking a real question at l.. The
WpI..rII.in.1:2 We will begin where our l. review left off,
W-pI.....97.3:4 Salvation is a miracle, the first and l.; the
W-pI.....97.3:4 the first and last; the first that is the l., for
W-pI...102.3:5 no fear. Here is salvation. Here is rest at l..
W-pI...105.8:2 and what is yours can come to you at l..
W-pI...106.4:7 end the dream instead; and l. forever, for
WpI. rIII.in8:1 and also give the l. five minutes of your
W-pI...121.1:4 the end of all uncertainty ensured at l..
W-pI...129.3:3 will be exchanged at l. for what we cannot
W-pI...129.5:1 Now is the l. step certain; now you stand
W-pI...129.9:2 For we have seen its opposite at l., and we
W-pI...132.1:7 the hope of freedom comes to him at l..
W-pI...133.6:1 you choose a thing that will not l. forever,
W-pI. 135.23:4 until the Answer comes to you at l..
W-pI. 138.12:2 And now we give the l. five minutes of our
W-pI...151.2:4 believe them to the l. detail which they
W-pI. 151.17:3 Now has our ministry begun at l., to carry
W-pI. 153.14:4 Let this day bring the l. chapter closer to
W-pI. 153.14:6 God's Son can smile at l., on learning that
W-pI...154.3:1 aware at l. there is one Voice in you. And
W-pI. 154.11:4 who wait in misery may be at l. delivered.
W-pI...161.5:1 makes us suffer, and at l. puts out our life.
W-pI...166.9:1 and justice has caught up with you at l..
W-pI. 170.11:2 For you look for the l. time upon this bit
W-pI. 170.12:4 by your Creator, are restored to you at l..
WpI...rV.in8:8 safe, as it will be at l. when time is done.
W-pI. 182.12:8 and the journey has an end in sight at l..
W-pI...190.6:6 where living things must come at l. to die?
W-pI...190.9:1 Heaven's peace holds all things still at l..
W-pI...191.8:4 Son has come again at l. to set it free?
W-pI. 193.13:5 Love of God the Father down to earth at l.
W-pI...195.7:3 would find, the way is opening at l. to us.
W-pI...195.8:4 The fear of God is now undone at l., and
W-pI. 196.11:1 for you until the time when it can kill at l..
W-pI...198.6:6 the words in which all merge as one at l..
W-pI. 198.10:1 face of Christ appears unveiled at l. in this
W-pI...200.2:1 point to which each one must come at l.,
W-pI. 200.10:6 Peace is already recognized at l., and you
WpI rVI.in.2:1 bestowed on us in our l. twenty lessons.
WpI rVI.in.3:1 These practice sessions, like our l. review,
W-pII .....in.7:8 we undertake these l. few steps to You,
W-pII . 227.2:3 with his right mind restored to him at l..
W-pII .....2.1:1 that you would find your way to Him at l..
W-pII . 241.2:1 *now, and so we come at l. to You again.*
W-pII . 250.2:4 *that this day I may at l. identify with him.*
W-pII . 251.1:9 want. And now at l. I find myself at peace.
W-pII . 256.1:9 by which our minds return to Him at l..
W-pII . 260.2:1 and Therein we find our true Identity at l..
W-pII .....6.3:4 your holy Self, the Christ, to you at l..
W-pII .....6.5:1 of the Atonement has been reached at l.?
W-pII . 290.1:2 see. Eyes that begin to open see at l.. And I
W-pII . 293.1:5 light, and I perceive a world forgiven at l..
W-pII . 298.1:2 And thus am I restored to my reality at l..
W-pII .....9.2:4 one. And thus is oneness recognized at l..
W-pII .....9.3:1 learning ends in one l. summary that will

W-pII .302.1:1 *Father, our eyes are opening at l.. Your holy*
W-pII .321.1:7 *way to You is opening and clear to me at l..*
W-pII .327.2:4 *surety of Your abiding Love is gained at l..*
W-pII .329.2:4 Through it we find our way at l. to God.
W-pII .338.1:2 is everyone released at l. from fear. Now
W-pII .342.1:8 *I am Your Son, and opening the door at l.,*
M-4 ....... X.1:1 perhaps the l. of the attributes the teacher
M-17 ......... 8:9 The interpretation can be changed at l..
M-27 ......... 3:4 and to l. a little while by his destruction.
M-27 ......... 6:1 "And the l. to be overcome will be death.
M-28 ......... 3:8 The l. illusion spreads across the world,
M-28 ....... 3:12 And now the truth can come at l.. How
C-1............. 5:3 This is the final vision, the l. perception,
C-2............. 1:1 Illusions will not l.. Their death is sure
C-2............. 7:6 you left behind at l. and finally passed by.
C-2........... 10:4 and having met at l. the choice is clear.
C-4............. 1:4 Some things will l. in time a little while
C-4............. 2:3 For everything they see not only will not l.
C-4............. 4:2 that it can l. no longer than an instant. It
C-4............. 4:3 It is seen at l. for only what it is. And now
C-4............. 5:1 A world forgiven cannot l.. It was the
C-4............. 6:8 at l. are sickness and its single remedy
C-4............. 7:6 and now is the l. perception of the world
C-4............. 7:7 memory has come at l. there is no journey
C-5............. 5:9 set your mind at rest at l. and carry it with
C-ep........... 5:1 the holiness of this rebirth will l. forever.
C-ep........... 5:6 him enters his home and is at peace at l..
P-2...........I.2:3 we mean, but here is the ego's l. defense.
P-2...........I.4:7 give for now. Yet both will find sanity at l.
P-3......... II.4:3 His creations do not change and l. forever
P-3........ III.1:7 he must yet strive to have the l. illusion be
S-1......... V.1:3 and true humility will come at l. to grace
S-1......... V.3:1 kind, and you can rest in holiness at l.
S-2...........I.9:6 established for returning be achieved at l.,
S-2........ III.3:2 haste to go at l. unto your Father's house.
S-2........ III.4:5 and know at l. that condemnation is not
S-3......... II.6:4 At l. the gate of Heaven opens and God's
S-3........ III.6:6 stand, and fear has given way at l. to God.
S-3........ IV.2:5 Time remains only to let the l. embrace of
S-3...... IV.10:7 you until you come to Him in peace at l..

### last-ditch 1
T-5....... VII.3:4 is the ego's l. defense of its own existence.

### lasted 1
T-26....... V.3:3 Time l. but an instant in your mind, with

### lasting 14
T-3......... II.6:4 and emptiness can never find l. solace. If
T-4......... II.6:1 Only those who have a real and l. sense of
T-4......... V.5:7 you may want to learn has l. value. Indeed
T-5...........I.1:3 can experience revelation with l. effect,
T-6......... V.4:7 Nothing l. lies in dreams, and the Holy
T-25...... IX.7:6 and l. in its power of injustice and attack.
T-26..... VII.7:2 of healing, and the l. grounds for hell. If
T-27.......I.11:2 insists your crippled picture is a l. sign of
T-28...... VI.1:4 a joy and look for l. pleasure in the dust.
W-pI..... 44.4:1 today, each l. three to five minutes. A
W-pI... 129.2:5 No l. love is found, for none is here. This
W-pI... 154.4:3 created it, and of His l. union with itself.
W-pI... 197.3:3 they be a l. offering of a thankful heart,
M-18 ......... 1:1 Correction of a l. nature,–and only this

### lasts 15
T-3....... V.10:1 long as perception l. prayer has a place.
T-4.........I.7:10 is possible as long as this delusion l..
T-6......... V.4:7 Himself, speaks only for what l. forever.
T-7....... VII.3:9 image of yourself as long as perception l..
T-10..... V.14:3 time l. in your mind there will be choices.
T-16...... IV.5:4 As long as the illusion of hatred l., so long
T-18.... VI.11:9 while this l. you are not uncertain of your
T-24...... IV.4:8 a dream of specialness that l. an instant,
T-26....... II.1:5 and it will do so while the problem l.. It
T-27..... II.14:2 be a part of you while this perception l..
T-28....... II.9:4 and while it l. will wakening be feared.

T-31 ...... V.4:4 "reality" is set, to see to it the idol l..
T-31 .... VII.1:3 Concepts are needed while perception l.,
C-4 ............ 3:4 But for the time it l. it comes to heal. For
S-1........ IV.4:5 space that l. until it crumbles into dust?

### late 1
W-pI..... 43.4:1 early and one as l. as possible in the day.

### lately 1
T-27 ..... III.6:1 the space so l. left unoccupied and vacant

### later 13
T-1 ...... VII.4:3 Some of the l. parts of the course rest too
T-1 ...... VII.4:6 implications that will be amplified l. on.
T-1 ...... VII.5:7 Some of the l. steps in this course,
T-5 ....... VI.8:3 statement means that in l. generations He
T-6 ........I.16:1 there was much they would understand l.,
T-9 ..... VIII.3:4 to attack now or to withdraw to attack l..
T-16 ..... III.8:2 Sooner or l. must everyone bridge the gap
W-pI....... 4.6:3 during the day. We will return to them l..
W-pI..... 18.1:2 which will be given increasing stress l. on.
W-pI..... 41.8:5 and sooner or l. it is always successful.
WpIrIII.in10:3 hour, and the other one a half an hour l..
W-pI... 168.4:2 come, with knowledge but an instant l..
P-3..........II.3:6 or l. that something will rise and grow; a

### latter 7
T-2 ... V.A.17:4 Only the l. involves an awareness of time,
T-9 ..........I.8:3 for the atheist and the l. for the martyr,
T-9 ..........II.1:3 The l. in particular might be incorrectly
W-pI..... 35.5:2 Toward the l. part of the exercise period,
W-pI..... 47.7:1 In the l. phase of the practice period, try
WpI..rII.in.1:3 and the l. part of the day to the other. We
M-10 ......... 1:3 the former and minimizing the l.. There is

### laugh 19
T-3 ....... VI.5:2 When you l. at someone, it is because you
T-3 ....... VI.5:3 you l. at yourself you must laugh at others
T-3 ....... VI.5:3 you laugh at yourself you must l. at others
T-11 . VIII.14:3 will l. at your fears and replace them with
T19.... IV.C.2:6 to his funeral, and hear him l. at death.
T-27 ... VIII.6:2 the Son of God remembered not to l.. In
T-27 ... VIII.6:4 Together, we can l. them both away, and
T-27 ... VIII.9:3 its foolish cause and l. with Him a while.
T-29 ... VIII.9:3 In Heaven would the Son of God but l., if
T-30 ..... IV.3:6 l. at popping heads and squeaking toys,
W-pI... 41.10:1 can indeed afford to l. at fear thoughts,
W-pI..... 92.2:2 you could but l. at this insane idea. It is as
W-pI... 100.2:6 hear God calling to them in your happy l..
W-pI... 134.6:2 but collects them lightly, with a little l.,
W-pI... 151.8:4 Whom He has judged can only l. at guilt,
W-pI... 166.8:3 make you l. at this perception of yourself.
W-pI... 186.8:4 We can l. or weep, and greet the day with
W-pI... 187.6:2 means must l. at the idea of sacrifice. Nor
W-pI... 190.4:2 time has come to l. at such insane ideas.

### laughed 1
T-27 ... VIII.5:6 ridiculous for anything but to be l. away.

### laughs 5
T-11 . VIII.13:3 afraid, and l. happily at his own fear.
W-pI... 100.3:4 and no one l. because all laughter can but
W-pI... 187.6:4 He l. as well at pain and loss, at sickness
W-pI... 191.3:1 that mocks creation and that l. at God.
M-10 ....... 5:13 Where now he l., he used to come to weep

### laughter 18
T-18 . VIII.13:7 Blow on it lightly and with happy l., and
T19. IV.D.16:5 lightly and with happy l. away from him.
T-27 ........I.5:5 every tear is wiped away in l. and in love.
T-27 .......II.8:9 his. And l. will replace your sighs, because

T-27 ... VIII.5:8 would have met with l. and with disbelief.
T-27 . VIII.5:10 And we will see the grounds for l., not a
T-27 ... VIII.9:1 gentle l. does the Holy Spirit perceive the
T-27 ... VIII.9:8 your l. and your brother's joined with His
T-28 ........I.9:3 It can deserve but l., when you learn you
W-pI .... 54.5:4 love to replace fear, l. to replace tears, and
W-pI .. 100.3:4 laughs because all l. can but echo yours.
W-pI .. 156.6:4 In lightness and in l. is sin gone, because
W-pI .. 183.3:5 dried as happy l. comes to bless the world
W-pI .. 187.6:5 all, and in his gentle l. are they healed.
W-pI .. 193.9:5 has willed that l. should replace each one,
W-pI .. 195.2:2 replaced with l. and with happiness. Nor
M-14 ......... 5:5 The world will end in l., because it is a
M-14 ......... 5:6 Where there is l., who can longer weep?

### lavish 1
W-pI .. 197.1:3 you find external gratitude and l. thanks.

### lavished 1
T-24 .. VII.1:10 this child of earth on whom such love is l.

### law 81
T-1 ....... IV.4:3 I came to fulfill the l. by reinterpreting it.
T-1 ....... IV.4:4 The l. itself, if properly understood, offers
T-2 ...... VII.1:4 be tampering with a basic l. of cause and
T-2 ...... VII.1:4 effect; the most fundamental l. there is. I
T-4 .........II.6:5 to get" is an inescapable l. of the ego,
T-5 .........V.2:7 divisive because it obeys the l. of division.
T-6 ..... IV.11:3 Fidelity to premises is a l. of mind, and
T-7 ............II.h The L. of the Kingdom
T-7 .........II.2:5 This is an immutable l. of the mind in this
T-7 .........II.3:1 l. that prevails inside is adapted to "What
T-7 .........II.3:7 That form of the l. is not adapted at all,
T-7 .........II.3:7 not adapted at all, being the l. of creation.
T-7 .........II.3:8 God Himself created the l. by creating *by* it
T-7 .........II.5:5 God's l. of creation does not involve the
T-7 .........II.5:6 of truth, which *is* the l. of the Kingdom,
T-7 .......V.11:8 one. This is part of the l. of creation, and
T-7 ...... VII.2:5 it. This is the l. of God, and it has no
T-7 ..... VIII.1:2 These reflect a fundamental l. of the mind
T-7 ..... VIII.1:3 l. by which you create and were created. It
T-7 ..... VIII.1:4 It is the l. that unifies the Kingdom, and
T-7 ..... VIII.1:5 l. is perceived as a means of getting rid of
T-7 ..... VIII.1:6 Spirit, it is the fundamental l. of sharing,
T-7 ..... VIII.1:7 To the Holy Spirit it is the l. of extension.
T-7 ..... VIII.1:8 To the ego it is the l. of deprivation. It
T-7 ... VIII.1:10 whether or not you will utilize the l..
T-9 ........I.11:8 your cooperation is the l. of its being. You
T-10 ........I.1:3 The l. of creation is that you love your
T-11 ..... IV.3:7 That is the l. of God, for the protection of
T-12 .... VII.3:2 miracles violate every l. of reality as this
T-12 .... VII.3:3 Every l. of time and space, of magnitude
T-12 .... VII.7:1 do one or the other, for that is a l. of mind
T-13 VII.10:11 things for salvation, for possession is its l.
T-13 ..... IX.1:2 the future to the past as is the ego's l..
T-13 ..... IX.1:3 law. Fidelity to this l. lets no light in, for it
T-14 ... XI.12:5 for it is the l. of God they be not separate.
T-23 .......II.2:1 chaotic l. is that the truth is different for
T-23 .......II.4:1 The *second* l. of chaos, dear indeed to
T-23 .......II.9:2 This leads to the *fourth* l. of chaos, which,
T-23 .......II.9:3 This seeming l. is the belief you have what
T-23 .....II.16:5 No l. of chaos could compel belief but for
T-24 ..... VI.5:3 for not one l. of death you bind him to
T-24 .... VII.1:2 truth! His wish is l. to him, and he obeys.
T-25 ..... III.1:3 perception's fundamental l.: You see what
T-25 ..... III.1:4 Perception has no other l. than this. The
T-25 ..... III.1:6 to this world, of God's more basic l.; that
T-25 ..... III.3:2 but one l. because it has but one Creator.
T-25 ..... III.4:1 not as the l. itself upholds the universe as
T-25 ..... IV.2:1 Perception's basic l. could thus be said,
T-25 ..... IV.2:6 Even in Heaven does this l. obtain. The
T-25 ... IX.10:2 of the l. on which salvation rests; that
T-26 .. VII.13:3 Such is creation's l.; that each idea the
T-27 .......II.7:4 well. This is the l. the miracle obeys; that
T-27 ..... VI.1:6 This is the l. of purpose, which unites all
T-29 .......II.6:6 the l. on which they predicate their lives.

W-pI.....76.9:3 says there is no loss under the l. of God.
W-pI.....76.9:6 else. God's l. forever give and never take.
W-pI...76.10:1 and realize how foolish are the "l." you
W-pI...76.11:3 Heaven which His l. keep limitless forever
W-pI...76.11:4 and understood there are no l. but God's.
W-pI...76.11:6 concludes: *I am under no l. but God's.*
W-pI...76.12:1 as subject to other l. throughout the day.
W-pI.....77.2:5 creation, and guaranteed by the l. of God.
W-pI.....77.4:4 Miracles do not obey the l. of this world.
W-pI.....77.4:5 They merely follow from the l. of God.
W-pI.....88.3:1 (76) I am under no l. but God's. Here is
W-pI.....88.3:3 freedom. I am under no l. but God's. I am
W-pI.....88.3:4 up other l. and give them power over me.
W-pI.....88.3:7 free of the effects of all l. save God's. And
W-pI.....88.3:8 save God's. And His are the l. of freedom.
W-pI.....88.4:2 *this shows me I believe in l. that do not exist.*
W-pI.....88.4:3 *I see only the l. of God at work in this. Let me*
W-pI.....88.4:4 *Let me allow God's l. to work in this, and not*
W-pI.....89.1:2 because I am under no l. but God's. His
W-pI.....89.1:3 His l. release me from all grievances, and
W-pI.....89.1:5 only what the l. of God entitle me to have,
W-pI...105.6:2 are their right under the equal l. of God.
W-pI...127.6:4 mind of all the l. you think you must obey
W-pI...133.3:3 l. that govern choice you cannot make, no
W-pI...133.3:5 the l. you set in motion when you choose,
W-pI...134.2:5 Him, reflects His l. and radiates His Love.
W-pI.134.13:2 to any understanding of the l. it follows,
W-pI.136.10:2 all the universe made slave to l. which
W-pI.136.11:2 of the l. by which you thought to govern it
W-pI.136.18:3 drink, or any l. you made it serve before.
W-pI...137.3:1 world obeys the l. that sickness serves,
W-pI...137.7:2 of all the l. that hold it cannot but be real,
W-pI...137.7:3 l. can be no longer cherished nor obeyed.
W-pI...137.8:4 attribute it proves that l. unlike the ones
W-pI...137.9:2 to let His l. replace the ones you made to
W-pI...154.4:2 Voice which speaks of l. the world does
W-pI...157.3:2 to alter time sufficiently to rise above its l.
W-pI...159.1:3 Here the l. of Heaven and the world agree.
W-pI...199.2:1 all ways, beyond the l. of time and space,
W-pI...204.1:2 *by l. which rule the world of sick illusions,*
W-pII ....277.h Let me not bind Your Son with l. I made.
W-pII .277.1:2 *bound him with the l. I made to rule the body*
W-pII .277.1:3 *subject to any l. I made by which I try to make*
W-pII .277.1:5 *He is not slave to any l. of time. He is as You*
W-pII .278.1:2 the l. the world obeys must I obey; the
W-pII .329.1:1 *from Your Will, defied it, broke its l., and*
W-pII ... 12.4:1 its works, its acts, its l. and its beliefs, its
W-pII .346.1:4 *all l. of time and things perceived in time. I*
W-pII .346.1:6 *You, and know no l. except Your law of love.*
M-4 .........I.1:4 not governed by the l. the world made up.
M-18 .......3:10 *and His l. alone prevail upon you and upon*
P-3......... II.8:7 all the l. of healing can be theirs in just an
S-1......... II.4:3 have limited prayer to the l. of this world,

## lay 104

T-8........ VI.1:3 can l. aside their weakness and add their
T-8........ VI.6:5 His joy l. in creating you, and He extends
T-8......VIII.8:6 When you l. the ego aside, it will be gone.
T-11....... II.4:3 He will l. His Own complete Will and
T-11...... IV.5:4 L. it to yourself and you cannot know
T-12....... II.9:6 cannot l. aside the obstacles to real vision
T-12....... II.9:6 for to l. aside means to judge against. If
T-13..... III.7:4 L. before His eternal sanity all your hurt,
T-13.... VI.11:5 will l. aside the world and find another.
T-13.VII.10:13 altar it demands you l. all of the things it
T-13...... IX.5:1 L. not his guilt upon him, for his guilt lies
T-13....... X.3:1 which you seek to l. your guilt upon him,
T-14.... III.14:4 you decided that salvation l. in you alone.
T-14....VIII.2:2 with the one promise given unto Him to l.
T-14....VIII.5:4 you. L. no gifts other than this upon your
T-14...... IX.1:7 l. in the decision to be not as you are.
T-14....... X.1:5 holiness calls everyone to l. all guilt aside.
T-14..... X.11:4 you would l. upon a brother is senseless.
T-15.... III.12:6 L. not littleness before His holy altar,
T-16.... VII.2:9 seek to l. the blame for deprivation on it,
T-18....... II.6:8 be for you alone, for therein l. its misery.
T-19.......I.14:2 you. L. faithlessness aside, and come to it
T-19...... IV.1:6 The peace He l., deep within you and your
T-19 ..... IV.3:8 and l. them gently before His Creator in
T19....IV.C.2:7 The sentence sin would l. upon him he
T19....IV.C.8:1 world the ego would l. the Son of God,
T-20 .......II.3:5 you l. upon your brother and on yourself.
T-20 ..... VI.9:5 l. aside the body and quietly transcend it,
T-21 ... VI.7:11 will l. down the burden of denying truth.
T-23 ......in.4:5 meaningless distractions, l. Heaven aside
T-24 ..... VI.3:2 has He failed to l. before you lovingly, as
T-25 .VIII.5:10 idea of punishment that they l. it aside,
T-26 ........I.8:1 all injustice the world would l. upon him.
T-26 ..... IV.4:1 miracles to l. before the gate of Heaven.
T-26 .. VII.18:3 it is arrogant to l. aside the power that He
T-26 .......X.5:7 that the world appears to l. upon you, you
T-28 ......I.10:1 You who have sought to l. a judgment on
T-29 ...... V.6:5 would l. bloody hands on Heaven itself,
T-31 ...VIII.7:1 I l. before your feet the peace of God, and
W-pI....... 3.1:7 Try to l. such feelings aside, and merely
W-pI..... 70.6:3 be a good time to l. aside for each of them
W-pI... 72.10:5 we are going to try to l. judgment aside,
W-pI..... 78.2:3 but l. it down and gently lift our eyes in
W-pI..... 78.3:1 and as you l. them down he will appear in
W-pI..... 78.4:4 l. the grievances aside and look at him.
W-pI..... 78.5:3 you will learn that what l. hidden while
W-pI..... 85.1:6 To see, I must l. grievances aside. I want
W-pI..... 94.4:1 except to l. all idols and self-images aside;
W-pI... 96.12:1 l. another treasure in your growing store.
W-pI..... 97.4:2 promised to l. timelessness beside them.
W-pI..... 97.5:2 and He will l. them everywhere He knows
W-pI..... 98.2:2 All our doubts we l. aside today, and take
W-pI... 98.11:1 be thankful and l. down all earthly tasks,
W-pI..... 99.9:8 what you need to learn to l. all fear aside,
W-pI... 99.12:5 Thus do you l. forgiveness on your mind
W-pI... 101.7:1 to remove the heavy load you l. upon
W-pI... 104.3:4 Then l. aside the conflicts of the world
W-pI... 104.4:1 All this we l. aside, and seek instead that
W-pI... 106.1:1 you will l. aside the ego's voice, however
WpIrIII.in11:3 Do not repeat the thought and l. it down.
W-pI... 120.2:3 *Today I l. aside all sick illusions of myself,*
W-pI... 128.8:2 refuse to l. this chain upon your mind,
W-pI. 134.16:4 chains you sought to l. upon your brother
W-pI. 134.17:5 *this? I will not l. this chain upon myself.* In
W-pI. 135.20:4 And gladly will our brothers l. aside their
W-pI... 136.7:3 It is a choice you make, a plan you l.,
W-pI. 136.14:2 to any mind that would l. down its arms,
W-pI. 139.12:1 l. aside all thoughts that would distract us
W-pI. 140.10:1 So do we l. aside our amulets, our charms
W-pI. 151.16:2 l. the gift of snow-white lilies on the world
W-pI... 152.9:4 We l. aside the arrogance which says that
W-pI. 153.20:7 You l. aside but what was never real, to
W-pI... 156.4:4 l. their leaves before you on the ground
W-pI... 165.5:6 your mind has come to l. aside denial,
W-pI... 168.5:3 by giving us the means to l. them down,
W-pI... 170.2:7 *L. down your arms, and only then do you*
W-pI... 170.5:4 you l. down all defense as merely foolish.
W-pI... 170.8:4 and l. before this mindless piece of stone?
W-pI... 181.5:5 We l. these pointless limitations by a little
W-pI. 182.11:1 Take time today to l. aside your shield
W-pI. 182.11:1 l. down the spear and sword you raised
W-pI... 184.1:6 space you l. between all things to which
W-pI... 186.4:1 All false humility we l. aside today, that
W-pI. 187.11:6 in form of lilies we can l. upon our altar,
W-pI. 188.10:5 And we l. our saving blessing on it, as we
W-pI... 189.7:1 and l. aside all thoughts of what you are
W-pI... 190.9:1 L. down your arms, and come without
W-pI... 190.9:2 L. down all thoughts of danger and of fear
W-pI... 190.9:4 L. down the cruel sword of judgment that
W-pI... 195.8:2 is forgotten when we l. comparisons aside
W-pI... 198.1:4 against you, till you l. it down as valueless
W-pI... 200.2:1 to l. aside all hope of finding happiness
W-pII .227.1:5 *up, and l. them down before the feet of truth,*
W-pII ....280.h What limits can I l. upon God's Son?
W-pII .280.1:6 Can I l. limits on the Son of God, whose
W-pII .280.2:2 *I l. no limits on the Son You love and You*
M-4 .... I.A.7:8 He must learn to l. all judgment aside,
M-10 ......... 5:1 Therefore l. judgment down, not with
M-20 ......... 4:4 must you once again l. down your sword,
M-25 ......... 6:8 they l. upon themselves if they utilize
P-2......... V.8:3 And it is there that we will l. them down,
S-1.........in.3:1 L. down your dreams, you holy Son of
S-2..........II.8:3 but l. them by as worthless in their tragic
S-3........ IV.6:4 arise and l. all dreaming down forever.

## layer 1

W-pI .... 69.4:2 a vast circle, surrounded by a l. of heavy,

## laying 6

T19 .IV.A.11:2 and l. them respectfully before their lord
W-pI .... 68.7:6 *grievances. I would wake to my Self by l. all*
W-pI .. 129.9:3 by l. by whatever thoughts you have, and
W-pI .. 183.3:1 the world responds by l. down illusions.
M-19 ......... 1:7 interpretations and l. all injustices aside.
M-24 ......... 2:3 If he is l. the groundwork for a future life,

## lays 18

T-8 ....... IX.8:4 no limits because God l. none upon you.
T-13 .... VII.6:2 Yet while he still l. value on his own, he
T-16 .... VII.6:1 the Holy Spirit gently l. the holy instant.
T-20 ..... III.5:4 Yet judgment l. a sentence on it, justifies
T-22 ..... III.9:5 And thus he l. his sins upon the other,
T-22 ..... VI.5:3 error, and l. a part of Heaven in its place.
T-22 ... VI.9:11 and l. it gently in each quiet smile of faith
T-22 ... VI.14:4 think not that it l. a heavy burden on you.
T-27 ........I.5:1 Holy Spirit l. a picture of a different you.
T-28 ..... III.9:5 Here is a feast the Father l. before His Son
W-pI .... 99.6:2 because it l. no faith in what is not created
W-pI .. 134.6:2 and gently l. them at the feet of truth.
W-pI .. 194.8:5 He l. aside the sick illusions of the world
W-pII . 227.2:2 Son of God this day l. down his dreams.
W-pII . 320.1:4 and l. before it all the strength and love in
M-10 ......... 6:3 The teacher of God l. it down happily the
S-1..........V.1:5 be. All little gods it gladly l. aside, not in
S-3........II.1:11 as one l. by a garment now outworn.

## lead 147

T-1 ....... III.4:5 and under my guidance miracles l. to the
T-1 ....... III.4:7 follow. "L. us not into temptation" means
T-1 ....... VI.2:5 Unified needs l. to unified action, because
T-3 .........V.3:1 already observed, does not l. to doing.
T-3 ..... VI.11:3 Free will must l. to freedom. Judgment
T-4 ........in.1:4 It can l. only to mutual progress. The
T-4 ..........I.4:7 I will correct it very gently and l. you back
T-4 ....... VI.7:7 Kingdom of God I can l. you back to your
T-6 ..........II.9:7 inspire perception and l. it toward God.
T-6 ..... V.B.9:4 awareness that the Holy Spirit will l. you
T-6 ..... V.C.5:1 the Holy Spirit will l. you to the Kingdom.
T-7 ....... III.5:5 the questionable and thus l. to certainty.
T-7 .........X.7:3 will l. you out of the confusion you have
T-8 ...... VII.4:9 will l. you to hatred and attack and loss of
T-8 .... VII.12:6 Learning must l. beyond the body to the
T-11 .......in.4:7 I will l. you to your true Father, Who hath
T-11 ..... VI.3:4 different experiences l. to different beliefs
T-11 ..... VII.3:9 Perceiving only the real world will l. you
T-12 ..... IV.4:1 but l. to a sense of futility and depression
T-12 ..... IV.4:4 promise, and one that will l. to joy. For
T-12 .......V.6:3 and this cannot l. to successful learning.
T-12 .......V.8:4 This resignation will not l. to depression.
T-12 .......V.9:1 is limitless because it will l. you to God.
T-12 ..... VI.5:9 Spirit will l. everyone home to his Father,
T-13 . III.12:10 it, for Love is in you and will l. you there.
T-13 .... VII.9:5 Yet the dreams of love l. unto knowledge.
T-13 .. VII.14:1 journey that would l. away from light,
T-13 .. VII.15:1 faith that He will l. you safely through all
T-14 ........I.2:3 of the world must therefore l. to nothing,
T-14 ........I.4:1 direction that would l. you where the
T-14 ... III.15:5 you, and would l. you out of insanity.
T-14 ..... VI.7:5 once, and this must l. to unintelligibility.
T-14 ...VIII.3:2 brother may choose to l. yourselves astray
T-14 ...VIII.3:3 He will surely l. you to where God and His
T-14 ...VIII.4:3 gentle understanding which can l. you
T-15 ........I.6:5 belief in guilt must l. to the belief in hell,
T-16 ... IV.10:1 to union in yourself *must* l. to knowledge,
T-16 ... IV.10:1 and will l. you straight to Him where your
T-16 .....V.15:4 to l. away from truth and into fantasy. Yet
T-17 .... VII.9:3 the means you once employed to l. you to

| | |
|---|---|
| T-18.VIII.10:2 | And l. them gently to your quiet garden, |
| T-18......IX.3:9 | l. you safely through and far beyond. |
| T-18....IX.11:1 | This course will l. to knowledge, but |
| T-20....... II.9:1 | not have your holy brother l. you there? |
| T-20..... II.10:5 | to greet you, and l. you home with him. |
| T-20..... II.11:1 | and free to l. you now where he would be. |
| T-20..... II.11:4 | freedom and the strength to l. you there. |
| T-20....III.11:5 | look unto the Son to l. them to the Father. |
| T-20....III.11:7 | brother now will l. the other to the Father |
| T-21..... III.6:2 | But as He uses them they l. away from sin, |
| T-21....III.11:2 | not what it is His purpose to l. you *from.* |
| T-21..... V.10:4 | cannot fail to l. to changed perception. |
| T-22.......in.4:5 | Reason now can l. you and your brother |
| T-22.........I.3:8 | you have called upon this thing to l. you, |
| T-22...... I.3:11 | does not l. you through a world of misery, |
| T-22...... I.4:10 | l. you through the world it made for you. |
| T-22..... II.13:7 | as yourself, and let him l. you there. |
| T-22...... VI.1:6 | serve the other and l. to its predominance |
| T-23.......in.5:1 | let littleness l. God's Son into temptation. |
| T-23....... II.9:5 | Yet all the other laws must l. to this. For |
| T-24....... V.4:2 | to l. the other to a nameless precipice and |
| T-24....... V.4:5 | Where does it l. but to destruction? Yet |
| T-24....... V.5:5 | see and hear and hold and l. is given light, |
| T-24....... V.5:5 | light, that you may l. as you were led. |
| T-24....... V.6:4 | hand you hold, and whom you l. to Him. |
| T-25...... III.6:3 | ready to l. him out of darkness into light |
| T-25.....VII.5:2 | would l. the Son of God to sanity and joy. |
| T-26...... VI.2:1 | L. not your little life in solitude, with one |
| T-29....... V.6:2 | and l. God's Son unto his Father's house. |
| T-30.......in.1:5 | And together will these steps l. you from |
| T-31.........I.2:4 | that l. you gently from one to another, |
| T-31...... III.6:3 | can never l. you where you would not be. |
| T-31......IV.1:5 | which road will l. you out of conflict, and |
| T-31......IV.2:3 | All its roads but l. to disappointment, |
| T-31......IV.2:9 | end, for it is here that all its roads will l., |
| T-31....IV.2:11 | All of them will l. to death. On some you |
| T-31......IV.4:8 | will learning l. to heights of happiness, in |
| T-31......IV.9:3 | No pathway in the world can l. to Him, |
| T-31......IV.9:4 | What road in all the world will l. within, |
| T-31......IV.9:5 | All roads that l. away from what you are |
| T-31......IV.9:5 | are will l. you to confusion and despair. |
| T-31....IV.11:7 | There *is* no path that does not l. to Him. |
| T-31.....VII.7:7 | the vision and the inner Guide all l. you |
| W-pI.....14.3:3 | Some of them will l. you directly into fear. |
| W-pI.....43.1:5 | and purified that it will l. to knowledge. |
| W-pI.....54.1:3 | make a false world or l. me to the real one |
| W-pI.....60.4:3 | thoughts, guide my actions and l. my feet. |
| W-pI.....64.5:4 | one will l. to happiness or unhappiness. |
| W-pI.....71.8:6 | will succeed. It will l. to release and joy. |
| W-pI...73.10:6 | Join with Them as They l. the way. |
| W-pI.....78.7:3 | *me to ask to l. me to the holy light in which he* |
| W-pI...100.1:2 | l. separate lives and go their separate |
| W-pI...107.9:6 | Then let Him l. you gently to the truth, |
| W-pI...125.2:2 | mind and at his side to l. him surely to his |
| W-pI...131.2:4 | Where can they l.? And what could they |
| W-pI.135.20:2 | And it will l. you on in ways appointed for |
| W-pI...140.3:4 | They l. from sleep to gentle waking, so |
| W-pI......155.h | I will step back and let Him l. the way. |
| W-pI...155.2:3 | then they step back and let it l. the way. |
| W-pI...155.7:1 | All roads will l. to this one in the end. For |
| W-pI...155.7:2 | and deprivation are paths that l. nowhere |
| W-pI...155.7:3 | to l. your brothers from the ways of death |
| W-pI...155.7:5 | Yet they need a guide to l. them out of it, |
| W-pI...155.9:4 | something they understand to l. the way. |
| W-pI.155.10:3 | Step back in faith and let truth l. the way. |
| W-pI.155.10:6 | with you. Let Him l. you with the rest. |
| W-pI.155.13:2 | not to ways that seem to l. you elsewhere. |
| W-pI.155.14:3 | *I will step back and let Him l. the way, For I* |
| WpI.. rV.in2:5 | *L. our practicing as does a father lead a little* |
| WpI.. rV.in2:5 | *Lead our practicing as does a father l. a little* |
| WpI.. rV.in6:5 | him out, and now will l. you out with him |
| WpI.. rV.in7:1 | again each time I l. a brother safely to the |
| WpI.. rV.in7:5 | Help me now to l. you back to where the |
| W-pI...173.1:1 | I will step back and let Him l. the way. |
| W-pI...188.7:5 | They l. you back to peace, from where |
| W-pI...193.2:3 | give him vision that will l. him back to |
| W-pII..233.2:1 | Today we have one Guide to l. us on. And |
| W-pII......3.4:1 | As sight was made to l. away from truth, |
| W-pII..242.1:1 | I will not l. my life alone today. I do not |
| W-pII..242.1:2 | to l. my life alone must be but foolishness |
| W-pII..242.1:4 | choices for me but the ones that l. to God. |
| W-pII..304.2:1 | *You l. me from the darkness to the light;* |
| W-pII..315.2:3 | *may l. me on to my Creator and His memory.* |
| W-pII..317.2:2 | *Where it would l. me do I choose to go; what* |
| W-pII.....324.h | I merely follow, for I would not l.. |
| W-pII..324.1:6 | *brothers all can follow in the way I l. them.* |
| W-pII..338.2:4 | *Mine alone will fail, and l. me nowhere. But* |
| W-pII..338.2:5 | *the Thought You gave me promises to l. me* |
| M-16 .........9:6 | All intermediate lessons will but l. to this, |
| M-17 .........2:4 | value, and must l. to undesired outcomes. |
| M-17 .........3:2 | A lesson truly taught can l. to nothing but |
| M-17 .......8:10 | thoughts need not l. to condemnation, for |
| M-20 .........3:8 | For what except attack will l. to war? And |
| M-21 .........4:6 | "I will step back and let Him l. the way." |
| M-22 .........5:9 | L. not the way, for you have lost it. Turn |
| M-23 .........7:2 | l. the way to those who speak in different |
| M-24 .........6:8 | No teaching that does not l. to this is of |
| M-24 .......6:11 | that l. to progress should be honored. |
| C-in ...........1:5 | the error itself does not l. to correction, if |
| C-4.............2:1 | upon must l. to more illusions of reality. |
| C-4.............3:7 | to l. to oneness far beyond themselves. |
| C-5.............1:9 | God for them for they will l. you home. |
| C-5.............5:4 | you to l. you from the hell you made to |
| P-2......... II.2:6 | is truth itself, but both can l. to truth. |
| P-2.......VII.9:8 | of pathways that can ever l. to peace. O let |
| S-2...........I.4:5 | the only one that does not l. to death. |
| S-2......... II.8:1 | forgiveness takes that do not l. away from |

## leader 4

| | |
|---|---|
| T-31....... II.3:3 | The l. and the follower emerge as separate |
| T-31....... II.5:7 | the l. or the follower to you it matters not, |
| C-6.............2:2 | established Jesus as the l. in carrying out |
| P-2........ III.1:1 | psychotherapist is a l. in the sense that he |

## leader's 1

| | |
|---|---|
| T-31....... II.4:3 | hate the one you gave the l. role when you |

## leaders 3

| | |
|---|---|
| T-31....... II.7:5 | tenderness, seeing no l. and no followers, |
| W-pI...135.2:4 | its codes, its ethics and its l. and its gods, |
| Wfl........in.2:6 | And let us be the l. of our many brothers |

## leadership 1

| | |
|---|---|
| T-31....... II.4:3 | in you arise, and give away the role of l.. |

## leadeth 2

| | |
|---|---|
| T-14.... III.19:2 | *He l. me and knows the way, which I know* |
| T19.IV.D.17:9 | He l. you and me together, that we might |

## leading 14

| | |
|---|---|
| T-11...... VI.3:6 | I am l. you to a new kind of experience |
| T-18.........I.8:3 | l. you gently back to the truth and safety |
| T-23..... II.21:4 | l. still deeper into terror and away from |
| T-24....... V.9:5 | l. the way that He must go to find Himself |
| T-25.........I.7:5 | and l. you beyond them to the truth that |
| T-29....... V.8:6 | And l. finally beyond all dreams, unto the |
| T-29...... IX.9:3 | l. surely to the frantic search for idols and |
| T-31..... II.11:3 | while you still insist on l. or on following, |
| WpI...rI.in.6:4 | thought system to which they are l. you. |
| W-pI.....70.9:3 | think of me holding your hand and l. you. |
| W-pI...196.4:1 | Today's idea is one step we take in l. us |
| W-pI...200.8:2 | l. from this fresh perception to the gate of |
| M-4 ...........1:5 | set in time as a means of l. out of time. |
| S-3........IV.6:6 | l. you in prayer beyond the sorry reaches |

## leads 106

| | |
|---|---|
| T-1.........I.20:2 | that l. to the healing power of the miracle. |
| T-1.........I.22:3 | exist. This l. to a denial of spiritual sight. |
| T-2...... VIII.1:6 | This basic distinction l. directly into the |
| T-4...........I.3:2 | because it l. to the relinquishment, not |
| T-4....... II.10:2 | Right-mindedness l. to the next step |
| T-5...........I.7:5 | l. the mind beyond its own integration |
| T-5........ III.7:5 | is light, and light l. to knowledge. The |
| T-6..........II.3:8 | and l. directly to excluding you from your |
| T-6.......V.A.5:1 | Holy Spirit, Who l. to God, translates |
| T-7...........I.6:2 | To this the Holy Spirit l. you, that your |
| T-8...........I.5:7 | This l. to fluctuation, but not to change. |
| T-8..........II.2:7 | is joyful if it l. you along your natural path |
| T-8..........II.4:4 | Holy Spirit l. you steadily along the path |
| T-9......... IV.4:3 | situation, to which the ego always l. you. |
| T-9......... V.7:1 | situation" to which the ego always l.. It |
| T-11...... III.5:3 | will never lose your way, for God l. you. |
| T-11....... V.2:6 | and what l. to nothing has not happened. |
| T-11....... V.2:7 | what l. to nothing could not be real. Do |
| T-11...... VI.1:2 | of experience, and experience l. to beliefs. |
| T-12...... IV.2:2 | guidance l. you to a journey which must |
| T-12.....VII.7:7 | it. This l. directly to dissociation, for it |
| T-13.........I.3:6 | this carpet, believing that it l. to death. |
| T-13.... VI.10:4 | Love always l. to love. The sick, who ask |
| T-13..... VII.3:7 | find in it the road that l. away from it into |
| T-13..... VII.6:3 | Love l. so gladly! As you follow Him, you |
| T-13..... VII.8:4 | The real world is the way that l. you to |
| T-13... VII.14:2 | *The Holy Spirit l. me unto Christ, and where* |
| T-13....VIII.7:6 | Your role in the redemption l. you to it by |
| T-14.........I.3:8 | world is totally insane and l. to nothing. |
| T-14.........I.3:9 | there is One Who knows it l. to nothing, |
| T-14.........I.4:1 | lead you where the Holy Spirit l. you not, |
| T-14.... III.14:2 | He knows the way, and l. you gladly on it. |
| T-14.... VII.7:1 | of perception that l. to knowledge. You |
| T-15.........I.7:4 | The Holy Spirit l. as steadily to Heaven as |
| T-16.........I.7:3 | is not the way, for it l. not to life and truth |
| T-16...... IV.7:6 | you and the bridge that l. you into it. |
| T-16.... IV.10:1 | The bridge that l. to union in yourself |
| T-17........II.1:9 | teaching l. to seeing it and giving thanks |
| T-18....VIII.6:6 | It l. no separate life, because its life *is* the |
| T-18...... IX.8:3 | nature as He l. you past them, for beneath |
| T-19.........I.4:1 | that faithlessness l. straight to illusions. |
| T-19...... III.7:3 | For the belief that bodies limit mind l. to |
| T19....IV.C.8:3 | of condemnation to which the body l. you |
| T-20........II.9:5 | The holiness that l. us is within us, as is |
| T-20........II.9:6 | we were meant to find by Him Who l. us. |
| T-20......II.11:5 | the bright awareness that l. you home. |
| T-20..... VII.8:6 | sin. And thus it l. you to reality. Your holy |
| T-21.........I.2:4 | safety lies; and which way l. to darkness, |
| T-21........II.9:3 | Faith in the unreal l. to adjustments of |
| T-21...... III.4:2 | the Holy Spirit l. you to the real world, |
| T-21...... VI.1:1 | can see errors, and l. to their correction. |
| T-21.... VI.7:10 | l. steadily away from madness toward the |
| T-21..... VII.7:6 | this decision l. to its effects is not your |
| T-22.........I.4:9 | always l. to sight of differences and loss of |
| T-22...... III.2:6 | The ego's opposition to correction l. to its |
| T-22...... VI.3:3 | This is the only service that l. to freedom. |
| T-23.......I.12:2 | The meeting of illusions l. to war. Peace, |
| T-23........II.6:5 | This l. directly to the *third* preposterous |
| T-23........II.9:2 | This l. to the *fourth* law of chaos, which, if |
| T-23......II.22:4 | the twisted stairway that l. from Heaven. |
| T-24....... V.6:2 | l. you there in gentleness and blessing all |
| T-26....... V.1:8 | go along the way your chosen teacher l.. |
| T-26....... V.2:6 | that l. to nothing and that has no purpose |
| T-28...... III.3:5 | to bridge the little gap that l. to Him. |
| T-30.........I.3:4 | This l. to fear, because it contradicts what |
| T-31........II.6:5 | This brother neither l. nor follows us, but |
| T-31........II.9:5 | to walk with him, so neither l. nor follows |
| T-31...... IV.7:4 | And every road that l. the other way will |
| T-31.... IV.10:4 | There is no road that l. away from Him. A |
| W-pI......64.3:2 | is only the arrogance of the ego that l. you |
| W-pI......87.1:5 | I will follow it where it l. me, and I will |
| W-pI......91.2:5 | Denial of light l. to failure to perceive it. |
| W-pI......96.1:2 | and l. to frantic attempts to reconcile the |
| W-pI......97.6:3 | light remains and l. you out of darkness, |
| W-pI....128.3:3 | door that l. to true awareness of your Self. |
| W-pI....131.2:6 | real? Pursuit of the imagined l. to death |
| W-pI.134.13:2 | the world that l. to any understanding of |
| W-pI....155.5:1 | road that l. away from loss of every kind, |
| W-pI....155.6:4 | illusions, for the road l. past illusion now, |
| W-pI.155.12:6 | and l. us to where He has always been. |
| W-pI.155.13:1 | feet are safely set upon the road that l. the |
| W-pI....160.9:5 | And He l. them gently home again, where |
| W-pI....166.2:3 | that l. to opposite effects from those He |
| W-pI....169.1:2 | for it l. beyond the world entirely. It is |

WpI...rV.in2:6 *is safe because his father l. the way for him.*
W-pI...188.1:8 and l. you back to where it came from and
W-pI...198.4:1 is the only road that l. out of disaster, past
W-pI...220.1:3 *But let me follow Him Who l. me home, and*
W-pII .....3.1:4 another light; and one which l. to truth,
W-pII .258.2:1 *goal is but to follow in the way that l. to You.*
W-pII .....7.1:2 perception l. to knowledge through the
W-pII .287.2:3 *but that which l. to You could I desire to walk*
W-pII .288.1:1 *This is the thought that l. the way to You,*
W-pII .288.1:4 *is the hand that l. me on the way to You. His*
W-pII .291.2:5 *Your Son along the quiet path that l. to You.*
W-pII .327.1:4 and still farther on the road that l. to Him
W-pII .338.2:3 *me the only Thought that l. me to salvation.*
W-pII .352.1:7 *the memory of You, and One Who l. me to it.*
Wfl........in.1:3 Let us turn to Him Who l. the way and
M-16 .......11:5 in magic, for it is only this that l. to pain.
M-19 .........2:2 the one interpretation that l. to truth.
C-3............1:4 it l. away from error and not towards it.
C-5............3:3 He l. you back to God because he saw the
C-ep.........1:11 an ancient door that l. beyond the world?
P-1............5:8 all psychotherapy l. to God in the end.
P-2......... II.4:6 and it is to this that all unforgiveness l..

## leaf 2

T-17....... II.6:3 The smallest l. becomes a thing of wonder
T-25...... IV.5:2 Every l. that falls is given life in you. Each

## lean 7

T-11..VIII.15:5 And then your Father will l. down to you
T-23...... IV.6:6 the lights of Heaven will gently l. to you,
T-28...... III.9:7 Here can the l. years enter not, for time
W-pI.....60.3:4 I see will l. toward me to bless me. I will
WpI. rIII.in6:6 at the outset; then l. back in quiet faith,
W-pI...195.7:1 Then let our brothers l. their tired heads
P-2......... V.4:8 l. upon a strength beyond our little scope

## leans 6

T-26...... IX.3:7 ground so holy Heaven l. to join with it,
W-pI.....78.8:4 The Holy Spirit l. from him to you, seeing
W-pI...168.3:2 gift by which God l. to us and lifts us up,
M-11 .......4:10 Presence, and it l. down in answer, to
C-4............8:3 Here He l. down to lift you up to Him, out
S-3........IV.9:1 Creation l. across the bars of time to lift

## leap 6

T-11...... III.3:5 so filled with joy that it will l. into Heaven
T-13...... III.2:6 you to answer His Call and l. into Heaven.
T-15.........I.5:3 and bids him l. from hell into oblivion.
T-20...... III.9:1 l. up in joy the instant they are made free.
W-pI.....91.4:5 of weakness hides will l. into awareness as
W-pI.154.14:4 spring to our sight and l. into our hands,

## leaping 1

T-27.....VII.8:7 l. up and down according to a senseless

## learn 528

T-1.........I.15:2 you to l. how to use time constructively. It
T-1........ III.1:6 voice, l. to undo error and act to correct it
T-1........ VI.1:2 he wants to l. it and believes in some way
T-2......... II.5:4 The ability to l. has no value when change
T-2......... II.5:5 The eternally creative have nothing to l..
T-2......... II.5:6 You can l. to improve your perceptions,
T-2...... III.5:12 They must l. to look upon the world as a
T-2......... V.6:1 body does not l. any more than it creates.
T-3.........I.7:10 no need to l. from many smaller lessons.
T-4.........I.2:13 Nevertheless, the ego can l., even though
T-4.........I.13:6 Let us undertake to l. this lesson together
T-4......... V.5:5 and wanting to l. are inseparable. You
T-4......... V.5:6 You l. best when you believe what you are
T-4......... V.5:6 what you are trying to l. is of value to you.
T-4......... V.5:7 everything you may want to l. has lasting
T-4......... V.5:8 many of the things you want to l. may be
T-4......... V.6:8 that *you* must l. to ask in connection with
T-4 ....... VI.2:4 as you l. how much you are indebted to
T-4 ....... VI.5:3 and slowly bring it nearer so he can l. how
T-4 ....... VI.8:5 L. first of them and you will be ready to
T-5 .......II.3:10 It takes effort and great willingness to l..
T-5 ..... III.11:4 Correct and l., and be open to learning.
T-5 ....... IV.6:4 As you teach so shall you l.. I will never
T-5 ....... IV.6:7 You must l. to see them as they are, and
T-5 ........ V.4:5 before that you must l. to think with God.
T-5 ...... V.4:13 but you must l. to regard it as freedom.
T-5 ..... VI.12:1 Now you must l. that only infinite
T-6 ..........I.6:1 said before, "As you teach so shall you l.."
T-6 .........I.10:2 Spirit is glad when you can l. from mine,
T-6 .........I.10:5 in others you can l. from their experiences
T-6 .........I.18:3 Each one must l. to teach that all forms of
T-6 ....... III.1:7 can hear and teach and l. what is not true.
T-6 ....... III.2:2 you must l. only from the Holy Spirit and
T-6 ....... III.2:3 are something you must l. to remember. I
T-6 ....... III.2:6 Only by teaching it can you l. it. "As you
T-6 ....... III.2:7 "As you teach so will you l.." If that is true
T-6 ....... III.4:2 you will l. the truth that will set you free,
T-6 ....... III.4:2 and will keep you free as others l. it of you
T-6 ....... III.4:4 By teaching peace you must l. it yourself,
T-6 ....... III.4:9 and l. that love is yours and you are love.
T-6 ........ V.3:2 harm, but what you need to l. to have joy.
T-6 ........ V.B.h To Have Peace, Teach Peace to L. It
T-6 ..... V.B.1:2 that is what they perceive and teach and l.
T-6 ..... V.B.3:9 the first lesson is the hardest to l.. Still
T-6 ..... V.B.7:5 lesson is: *To have peace, teach peace to l. it.*
T-6 ..... V.C.2:1 want you to teach error and l. it yourself.
T-6 ..... V.C.2:2 to strengthen what you must l. to avoid.
T-6 ..... V.C.2:4 and therefore to l. to *be* without judgment.
T-6 ..... V.C.5:2 what you are you must l. to remember.
T-6 ..... V.C.6:1 You l. first that *having* rests on giving, and
T-6 ..... V.C.6:2 Next you l. that you learn what you teach,
T-6 ..... V.C.6:2 Next you learn that you l. what you teach,
T-6 ..... V.C.6:2 you teach, and that you want to l. peace.
T-6 ... V.C.10:4 until you l. that effort itself is unnecessary
T-7 .........II.3:3 form implies that you will l. what you are
T-7 .........II.6:8 This is the only way you can l. consistency
T-7 ....... III.2:8 It is therefore a lesson you cannot really l.
T-7 ....... IV.3:2 Therefore it does not really l. at all. The
T-7 ....... IV.3:5 All you need do is make the effort to l., for
T-7 ....... IV.4:3 By healing you l. of wholeness, and by
T-7 ....... IV.4:3 learning of wholeness you l. to remember
T-7 ........ V.7:7 it as long as you l. through the ego. This
T-7 ........ V.7:8 to l. a lesson that seems contradictory;–
T-7 ........ V.7:8 must l. to change your mind about your
T-7 ........ V.7:9 Only by this can you l. that it *is* changeless.
T-7 ...... V.11:1 unto me, and l. of the truth in you. The
T-7 ...... VII.6:5 or you cannot l. of His peace and accept
T-7 .....VIII.6:3 The more you l. about the ego, the more
T-8 ..........I.6:2 l. simultaneously from two teachers who
T-8 .........II.1:3 of the curriculum, you must l. it of Him.
T-8 .........II.1:9 you could still l. nothing from the ego,
T-8 .........II.4:2 to l. it is a violation of your own freedom,
T-8 ....... III.1:3 Ask for light and l. that you *are* light. If
T-8 ....... III.1:4 and enlightenment you will l. it, because
T-8 ....... III.1:4 decision to l. it is the decision to listen to
T-8 ....... VI.4:1 and l. what God's treasure is and yours:
T-8 ..... VI.10:5 L. this of me, and free the holy will of all
T-8 ..... VII.8:1 to a learner as a curriculum he cannot l..
T-8 ....... IX.1:4 l. this as you learn to question the value of
T-8 ....... IX.1:4 learn this as you l. to question the value of
T-9 ..........I.2:3 impossible to l. anything consistently in a
T-9 ..........I.2:4 must follow that you will not l. this course
T-9 ..........I.7:5 Of him you can never l. what it is, and
T-9 .........II.8:1 you will l. that my belief in you is justified
T-9 .........II.8:3 you if you l. to ask only truth of them. Do
T-9 .........II.8:4 in this way can you l. how blessed you are
T-9 ....... III.5:5 telling you that what you teach you l.?
T-9 ....... III.8:5 You do not need to l. that, but you do
T-9 ....... III.8:5 learn that, but you do need to l. to want it
T-9 ....... IV.6:4 unless you accept this you cannot l. what
T-9 ........ V.5:4 and he must l. from his own teaching. His
T-9 ........ V.9:5 you will l. the simplest of all lessons: *By*
T-9 ....... VI.4:6 but you cannot l. of your wholeness until
T-9 ....... VI.5:1 yet awake, but you can l. how to awaken.
T-9 ....... VI.5:3 see them waken you will l. what waking
T-9 ....... VI.7:9 l. that your brother is co-creator with you.
T-10 ......in.1:4 must l. that time is solely at your disposal,
T-10 ..... III.8:1 and you will l. this as you learn that you
T-10 ..... III.8:1 and you will learn this as you l. that you
T-10 ..... IV.8:3 little spark you will l. of the greater light,
T-10 .......V.7:5 and you will l. of Him if you hear aright.
T-10 .....V.11:7 you will l. how to remember what you are
T-10 .....V.12:5 must l. to see him to learn of his reality.
T-10 .....V.12:5 must learn to see him to l. of his reality.
T-10 .....V.12:6 is how you must see yourself to l. of yours
T-11 ......I.5:11 and you will l. what God has kept for you.
T-11 ........I.7:4 end, to l. how much He has given you.
T-11 ......I.11:6 Blessed are you who l. that to hear the
T-11 ..... IV.1:3 your mind needs to l. what salvation is.
T-11 ..... IV.4:3 you must l. to recognize and to oppose
T-11 .......V.2:3 you are beginning to l. that fear is not real
T-11 .....V.11:2 learning what fear is can you finally l. to
T-11 ..... VI.5:8 only have you l. your will and follow it,
T-11 ... VI.10:3 part must be like mine if you l. it of me. If
T-11 ... VIII.3:8 Yet your willingness to l. of Him depends
T-11 ... VIII.5:8 Yet only by asking will you l. that nothing
T-11 ... VIII.6:4 question you must ask to l. His answer?
T-11 ... VIII.7:7 only thus can you l. that His answer is the
T-11 . VIII.10:6 then, to l. of the reality of your brother,
T-11 . VIII.11:6 and you will l. of the Father's Love for you
T-11 . VIII.14:5 they l. to perceive truly they are not afraid
T-11 . VIII.15:3 l. the truth about yourself from the Holy
T-12 ........I.9:2 it in others you l. to supply the loss, the
T-12 .......I.10:2 And how could you better l. of its reality
T-12 .......I.10:5 thus will you l. of Him how to replace
T-12 .......II.5:5 L. to be quiet in the midst of turmoil, for
T-12 ... III.10:7 changed, and there you will l. to see truly.
T-12 ..... IV.6:1 that you might l. you have eternal life. For
T-12 .......V.4:3 cannot l. of perfect love with a split mind,
T-12 .......V.5:3 because of yourself you cannot l.. The
T-12 .......V.6:3 Your learning goal has been *not* to l., and
T-12 .......V.6:5 have failed to l. what learning aids are for
T-12 .......V.7:2 this means, "Try to l. but do not succeed.
T-12 .......V.7:5 If you are trying to l. how not to learn,
T-12 .......V.7:5 If you are trying to learn how not to l.,
T-12 .....V.7:11 yet, that there is something you want to l.
T-12 .....V.7:11 can l. it because it *is* your choice to do so.
T-12 .......V.8:1 to l. what you do not want should take
T-12 .......V.9:2 You can teach the way to Him and l. it, if
T-12 .......V.9:6 you. For you really want to l. aright, and
T-12 ..... VI.4:9 by this he will l. to re-invest in himself.
T-12 ..... VI.5:2 Yet you must l. the cost of sleeping, and
T-12 ..... VI.6:6 Gradually you l. to apply it to everyone
T-12 .... VII.2:5 And by what it does, you l. what it is. You
T-12 .... VII.3:1 through them you will l. that He is there.
T-12 .. VII.11:5 you, you will l. that you do want only that
T-12 .. VII.15:5 When you l. to make me manifest, you
T-13 ......in.2:6 l. of sorrow and separation and death.
T-13 ......in.4:6 Atonement is the final lesson he need l.,
T-13 ........I.5:1 see me as you l. the Son of God is guiltless
T-13 ........I.7:6 his purity as yours, l. of him that it *is* yours
T-13 ........I.9:1 you l. that the past has never been, and so
T-13 ..... IV.6:5 Unless you l. that past pain is an illusion,
T-13 ..... IV.8:4 of salvation that you must l. to accept, if
T-13 .......V.7:6 not what you do can l. what insanity is,
T-13 .......V.7:7 It is given you to l. how to deny insanity,
T-13 ..... VI.2:3 will be able to l. from what you see *now*.
T-13 ..... VI.5:6 L., then, to seek it where it is, and it will
T-13 .... VII.4:4 willingness to l. the one you made is false.
T-13 ..... IX.6:4 so you l. that it is true for you. Remember
T-13 ... IX.8:13 and l. that what you feared was there has
T-13 .......X.6:3 must l. that guilt is always totally insane,
T-13 ..... XI.6:3 you l. what to avoid and what to seek.
T-13 ..... XI.8:6 and by extending it, to l. that it is in you.
T-13 ..... XI.9:1 You will l. salvation because you will
T-13 ..... XI.9:1 salvation because you will l. how to save.
T-13 ..... XI.9:5 L. that even the darkest nightmare that
T-13 ..... XI.9:6 him. He will l. the lesson of awaking. God
T-14 ........I.1:1 not know it, you need to l. it must be so.
T-14 ........I.1:3 You can l. to bless, and cannot give what
T-14 ........I.1:8 could you l. what has been done for you,
T-14 ........I.4:7 while you think it possible to l. to do this,
T-14 ........I.4:7 not believe all that *is* possible to l. to do.
T-14 ........I.5:1 by showing you what you can never l.. His
T-14 .......II.1:4 undertaken to l. to do what you can never

T-14....... II.1:4 that unless you l. it you will not be happy.
T-14..... II.1:11 you *can* l. how to make the untrue true.
T-14....... II.2:2 This is the hardest lesson you will ever l.,
T-14....... II.3:5 *for you that you cannot make, but need to l..*
T-14....... II.5:1 that truth is true, you l. it with him. And
T-14....... II.5:2 And so you l. that what seemed hardest
T-14....... II.5:3 L. to be a happy learner. You will never
T-14....... II.5:4 never l. how to make nothing everything.
T-14....... II.6:2 And then begin to l. the joyous lessons
T-14....... II.8:1 and l. of them how to be free of darkness.
T-14...... III.3:3 will not l. how to be happy. Say therefore,
T-14...... III.6:4 to l. that nothing has no power. And by
T-14...... III.8:6 will l. communication with this oneness
T-14...... III.8:6 only when you l. to deny the causeless,
T-14.... III.14:3 will not fail to l. that what God wills for
T-14.... III.16:4 L. of His wisdom and His Love, and teach
T-14.... III.18:3 and l. of all the happy communication
T-14.... III.19:3 *keep from me what He would have me l..*
T-14...... IV.3:5 Ask, rather, to l. how to forgive, and to
T-14...... IV.3:7 you must l. that it is all you want to learn.
T-14...... IV.3:7 you must learn that it is all you want to l..
T-14...... IV.3:8 You will feel guilty till you l. this. For in
T-14...... IV.7:6 but listen, and l. how impossible this is!
T-14....... V.5:7 those who have failed to l. need teaching,
T-14....... V.5:8 need of teaching is to fail to l. from them.
T-14....... V.7:5 guilt you will inevitably l. your innocence.
T-14...... VI.5:7 made it to crucify yourself must l. of Him
T-14..... VII.7:1 the way in which you l. to share with Him
T-14....... X.6:1 It will seem difficult for you to l. that you
T-14...... XI.2:3 Can God l. how not to be God? And can
T-14...... XI.2:4 given all power by Him, l. to be powerless
T-14...... XI.4:5 L. of His happiness, which is yours. But to
T-14...... XI.6:1 concerned about how you can l. a lesson
T-14.... XI.11:2 as one in God, so do we l. as one in Him.
T-14.... XI.12:1 who have become willing to l. everything,
T-14.... XI.12:1 willing to learn everything, will l. it. But
T-14.... XI.12:2 they trust themselves, they will not l..
T-14.... XI.13:1 are with them, can really l. at all. For this
T-15......... I.1:2 is for; to l. just that and nothing more.
T-15......... I.1:4 consistent learner that you l. only of Him.
T-15......... I.1:5 need a teacher or time in which to l..
T-15...... I.10:2 L. from this instant more than merely
T-15....... II.5:4 instant, and will l. much from doing so.
T-15....... II.6:3 To l. to separate out this single second,
T-15...... III.3:1 one you must l. to remember all the time.
T-15...... III.3:2 but you will l. to love it when you realize
T-15...... III.8:4 L. that you must be worthy of the Prince
T-15...... III.9:1 will you l. that only holiness can content
T-15...... III.9:2 that you l. not for yourself alone, no more
T-15...... III.9:3 I learned for you that you can l. of me. I
T-15...... IV.4:1 l. how perfect and immaculate is the holy
T-15...... IV.5:2 And the extent to which you l. to accept
T-15...... VI.7:3 Self, you will l. to understand Selfhood.
T-15...... VI.8:7 to do this you will l. what you must be, for
T-15..... VII.3:2 your investment in it, to l. to let it go. No
T-15... VII.10:2 who will l. that love brings no guilt at all,
T-15... VIII.1:3 to l. of Him what the truth must be. He is
T-15... VIII.2:1 l. of Him that you have need of no special
T-15... VIII.2:3 never l. the value of what you have cast
T-15...... IX.1:3 for you to l. just what this shift entails, so
T-15...... IX.7:2 will l. you have no need of a body at all. In
T-15....... X.2:6 of me. L. now that sacrifice of any kind is
T-15...... XI.4:1 that sacrifice is love must l. that sacrifice
T-16......... I.4:2 You will l. His interpretation of it if you
T-16...... III.6:4 your teaching have gathered to help you l.
T-16...... III.6:8 you must l. that you but taught yourself,
T-16...... III.7:1 This year you will begin to l., and make
T-16...... III.7:5 him. As you l., your gratitude to your Self,
T-16...... III.7:6 will l. His power and strength and purity,
T-16....... V.3:5 and those who l. that it is not natural at
T-16.... VI.10:7 l. how much awaits you for the simple
T-16..... VII.9:6 will you l. that you have been forgiven, for
T-17......... I.4:3 l. to deal with part of the truth in one way
T-17......... I.5:1 l. what truth means from the perspective
T-17....... II.3:4 real world, in its loveliness, you l. to reach
T-17.... III.6:11 And you will l. to seek for and establish
T-17.... VII.8:1 l. the cause of faithlessness: You think
T-18...... IV.6:8 that you may l. how little is your part, and
T-18...... VI.1:2 That is what you must ultimately l., for it
T-18.... IX.11:6 There is too much to l.. The readiness for
T-19....... I.16:1 l. how not to interfere with it and make it
T19.... IV.B.8:2 So will you l. the freedom that I taught by
T19.... IV.C.1:3 you must l. still more about this strange
T19... IV.D.8:5 and l. it has no power to keep you from
T-20....... II.1:5 L. you but offer him a crown of thorns,
T-20...... IV.6:1 the part that has been given you to l.. For
T-20...... IV.6:6 l. its special function in the Holy Spirit's
T-20....... V.8:3 Let us consider now what he must l., to
T-20.... VI.11:9 can he l. relationships are his salvation,
T-20..... VII.2:7 yet I do not want to l. the means to get it?
T-20... VIII.2:3 be free of misery, and l. again of joy? Your
T-21....... in.2:6 and l. from this to recognize which one
T-21......... I.3:1 There is no need to l. through pain. And
T-21......... I.3:3 happiness you want to l. and not forget. It
T-21....... II.1:1 how little is asked of you to l. this course.
T-21...... VI.6:3 you will l. of him exactly what you taught.
T-21...... VI.9:5 It would have you l. what you must be.
T-21...... VI.9:7 and l. with him what has been given both
T-22..... II.10:6 Are you not glad to l. it is not true? Is it
T-22...... III.2:1 on its belief you cannot l. this course.
T-22...... IV.6:2 And so they l. that it is theirs forever. All
T-22...... IV.7:6 and you will l. how easily your fingers slip
T-24....... in.2:1 To l. this course requires willingness to
T-24.... VII.6:9 any way to l. what this condition means.
T-25......... I.1:2 And in the doing of it will you l. the body
T-25......... I.3:6 you l. what seems to have a life apart has
T-25....... II.1:7 is that you l. it gave you no rewards which
T-25..... II.10:5 it, you l. to understand His gift to you.
T-25... VIII.1:4 would not l. it *is* your will to be without it.
T-25... VIII.4:1 of justice still can ask, and l. the answer.
T-25. VIII.11:5 each one l. that love and justice are not
T-26....... V.1:3 purpose, for only that is all there is to l..
T-26....... V.1:4 And you can l. it in many different ways.
T-26... VII.13:2 God wills you l. what always has been
T-27....... II.6:9 you l. when you but wish to show your
T-27..... V.11:2 And you will l. that peace is given you
T-27. VIII.12:9 you need but l. you chose but not to listen
T-27. VIII.13:6 Now need you but to l. that both of you
T-27. VIII.13:8 This is the only secret yet to l.. And it will
T-28......... I.7:2 he can l. and can preserve a better one?
T-28......... I.9:3 l. you have remembered consequences
T-28..... II.10:1 lesson that the Holy Spirit requests you l.,
T-28..... II.10:2 demonstrates what He would have you l.,
T-28..... II.11:6 The miracle is useless if you l. but that the
T-29......... I.8:5 who l. their savior is their enemy no more
T-29....... II.1:1 from suffering to l. that you are free? Why
T-29...... III.1:3 But he must l. he is a savior first, before
T-29....... V.6:8 But l., instead, how blessed are you who
T-29..... VII.9:3 Save time, my brother; l. what time is for.
T-30....... II.2:7 be reminded of His Love and l. your will.
T-30....... II.5:2 that he l. death has no power over him,
T-30...... IV.2:5 Now must he l. the boxes and the bears
T-30..... V.11:3 they were free to l. their will is one. And
T-30...... VI.5:3 how you l. that you must be forgiven too.
T-31......... I.1:5 be hard to l. by anyone who wants it to be
T-31......... I.1:6 Only unwillingness to l. it could make
T-31......... I.2:2 in the simple things salvation asks you l..
T-31......... I.2:6 confused is easier to l. and understand.
T-31......... I.2:8 judge it hard to l. or too complex to grasp
T-31......... I.3:5 Say not you cannot l. them. For your
T-31......... I.3:6 For your power to l. is strong enough to
T-31......... I.4:6 say not that you cannot l. the simple
T-31......... I.5:4 that Its lessons are not true; too hard to l.,
T-31......... I.5:5 Yet you will l. them, for their learning is
T-31......... I.6:4 Which lesson will you l.? What outcome
T-31........ I.7:11 And you will l. God's Son is innocent, and
T-31........ I.11:1 the wrong decision on what you would l.,
T-31........ I.13:3 But you are free to l. of him, and learn of
T-31........ I.13:3 free to learn of him, and l. of him anew.
T-31....... II.6:3 *what I l. of him is what I learn about myself.*
T-31....... II.6:3 *what I learn of him is what I l. about myself.*
T-31....... II.8:6 to listen silently and l. the truth of what
T-31....... II.8:7 No more than this will you be asked to l..
T-31..... II.10:5 that you l. you love your brother with a
T-31...... III.1:4 L. this, and learn it well, for it is here
T-31...... III.1:4 Learn this, and l. it well, for it is here
T-31...... III.4:3 has no power to l., to pardon, nor enslave
T-31.... III.4:10 For mind can l., and there is all change
T-31...... IV.3:2 all, before you really l. they are but one.
T-31...... IV.4:3 L. now, without despair, there is no hope
T-31...... IV.4:7 what you have learned to what is yet to l..
T-31...... IV.6:3 You did not come to l. to find a road the
T-31...... IV.7:3 to find this course to be too difficult to l.,
T-31...... IV.7:5 then is this course impossible to l.. But
T-31..... V.14:6 can l. that everything it thinks reflects the
T-31..... V.17:1 images of you unless you want to l. them.
T-31...... VI.5:4 change the world for eyes that l. to see,
T-31... VII.15:5 l. that it is you for whom He asks release?
T-31... VII.15:7 And what but this is there for you to l.?
T-31.... VIII.3:1 that you failed to l. presented once again,
T-31.... VIII.5:1 L., then, the happy habit of response to
W-pI....... 5.1:5 until you l. that form does not matter,
W-pI..... 13.3:1 that you l. to recognize the meaningless,
W-pI..... 17.1:4 you must l. that it is the way you think. If
W-pI..... 23.2:1 you must l. that it is these thoughts which
W-pI..... 23.7:5 finally l. that thoughts of attack and of
W-pI..... 24.2:2 you do know what they are, you cannot l..
W-pI..... 26.1:6 You must therefore l. how it can be used
W-pI..... 29.3:1 to l. how to look on all things with love,
W-pI..... 37.6:4 may l. to keep it in your own awareness.
W-pI..... 44.5:2 to l. the form of exercise we will use today
WpI... rI.in.4:2 that you l. to require no special settings in
WpI... rI.in.5:1 You will yet l. that peace is part of you,
WpI... rI.in.5:2 finally you will l. that there is no limit to
W-pI..... 51.1:3 that I recognize this, that I may l. to see.
W-pI..... 52.3:6 Let me l. to give the past away, realizing
W-pI..... 63.1:2 blessed are you who can l. to recognize
W-pI..... 64.2:3 the world is a place where you l. to forgive
W-pI... 72.11:1 Now we would see and hear and l..
W-pI..... 78.5:3 you will l. that what lay hidden while you
W-pI..... 81.4:2 *Let this help me l. what forgiveness means.*
W-pI..... 83.3:5 And I must l. to recognize what makes me
W-pI..... 99.9:5 and start the lesson that we l. today with
W-pI..... 99.9:8 what you need to l. to lay all fear aside,
W-pI... 102.4:4 fail to find it when you l. it is your choice,
W-pI... 105.3:3 will l. a different way of looking at a gift.
W-pI... 106.6:3 And you will l. your function from the
W-pI... 108.6:1 l. that giving and receiving are the same
W-pI... 110.2:4 for all the world to l. escape from time,
WpI. rIII.in3:4 control. L. to distinguish situations that
WpIrIII.in11:2 what you l. each day to everything you do.
WpIrIII.in13:2 Do not forget how much you can l. now.
W-pI... 119.2:2 *that I may l. how to accept the truth in me,*
W-pI... 121.6:4 Through Him you l. how to forgive the
W-pI... 121.7:5 The unforgiving mind must l. through
W-pI... 121.7:6 And as you teach salvation, you will l..
W-pI... 121.8:2 can l. today to take the key to happiness,
W-pI... 121.9:2 Yet we will try to l. today that they are
W-pI... 121.9:3 And as you l. to see them both as one, we
W-pI. 126.11:4 *I need to l. that this is true is with me now.*
W-pI. 127.10:1 before the timelessness of what you l.. Let
W-pI. 127.11:2 its blessing upon all who come to l. to cast
W-pI. 127.12:2 and who came to l. what you must learn.
W-pI. 127.12:2 and who came to learn what you must l..
W-pI. 127.12:5 *For I would l. the joyous lesson that there is*
W-pI... 130.6:3 What we would l. today is more than just
W-pI... 131.4:2 Be glad as well to l. you search for Heaven
W-pI... 132.7:1 who are prepared to l. there is no world,
W-pI... 133.3:5 wise to l. the laws you set in motion when
W-pI... 133.5:4 l. the tests by which you can distinguish
W-pI. 135.22:5 *strong, and I will l. what my defenses hide.*
W-pI. 135.25:5 l. the part for you within the plan of God.
W-pI. 135.26:3 L. today. And all the world will take this
W-pI... 139.7:3 they l. it is impossible to doubt yourself,
W-pI. 139.12:3 And l. the fragile nature of the chains that
W-pI. 140.12:5 This will we l. today. And we will say our
WpI. rIV.in5:1 preparation of your mind to l. what each
W-pI... 151.7:1 Yet you must l. to doubt their evidence
W-pI. 153.11:4 Nor will you l. that light has come to you,
W-pI. 153.14:4 that everyone may l. the tale he reads of
W-pI. 153.17:2 and l. what He would have us do the hour
W-pI. 154.12:1 Let us but l. this lesson for today: We will
W-pI... 155.3:3 They cannot l. directly from the truth,
W-pI... 157.1:6 death. Today you l. to feel the joy of life.
W-pI... 157.2:2 and prepares us for what we have yet to l..
W-pI... 157.3:3 This you will l. to do increasingly, as
W-pI...... 158.h Today I l. to give as I receive.

W-pI...158.2:5 What, then, are you to l. to give today?
W-pI...158.5:1 give experience, because he did not l. it. It
W-pI.158.10:1 Thus do you l. to give as you receive. And
W-pI.158.10:3 This lesson is not difficult to l., if you
W-pI...161.4:8 We need to see a little, that we l. a lot.
W-pI...162.4:4 thus you l. to think with God. Christ's
W-pI.166.12:4 come to offer you, you now must l. to give
W-pI...168.3:3 All steps but this we l., instructed by His
W-pI...170.2:4 Today we l. a lesson which can save you
W-pI...174.2:1 (158) Today I l. to give as I receive. God
W-pI...182.9:2 that you might l. of Him how strong is he
W-pI.182.10:2 For he must l. that what he would protect
W-pI...189.5:3 But l. and do not let your mind forget this
W-pI...189.6:2 We l. the way today. It is as sure as Love
W-pI...191.6:2 holy thought you l. as well that you have
W-pI......193.h things are lessons God would have me l..
W-pI...193.3:1 are the lessons God would have you l..
W-pI...193.6:1 l. to say these words when we are tempted
W-pI...193.6:2 we not l. to say these words when we have
W-pI...193.7:1 failing to perceive the lesson he should l.?
W-pI...193.8:6 you fail to l. the simple lessons Heaven's
W-pI...193.9:1 things are lessons God would have you l..
W-pI.193.11:7 His are the lessons God would have us l..
W-pI.193.13:1 This is the lesson God would have you l.:
W-pI...194.6:3 And as you l. to see salvation in all things,
W-pI...195.1:1 Gratitude is a lesson hard to l. for those
W-pI...195.9:1 Today we l. to think of gratitude in place
W-pI...196.2:4 you can l. to see these foolish applications
W-pI...197.6:2 But l. to let forgiveness take away the sins
W-pI...198.5:3 and l. the simple lessons He would teach,
W-pI...200.7:6 Yet can he l. to look on it another way,
WpI rVI.in.2:5 one, as each contributes to the whole we l.
W-pI...213.1:1 things are lessons God would have me l..
W-pI...213.1:3 *I l. of Him becomes the way I am set free. And*
W-pI...213.1:4 *I choose to l. His lessons and forget my own.* I
W-pII .....1.4:5 forgive himself must l. to welcome truth
W-pII .273.1:2 to l. how such a day can be achieved. If we
W-pII .273.1:3 us l. how to dismiss it and return to peace
W-pII .275.1:2 will seek and hear and l. and understand.
W-pII .275.1:4 we cannot understand alone, nor l. apart.
W-pII .296.2:1 We teach today what we would l., and
W-pII .319.1:6 of God I l. that what one gains is given
W-pII .321.2:3 l. our freedom can be found in God alone.
W-pII .327.1:3 but l. from my experience that this is true,
W-pII .337.1:6 And I must l. I need do nothing of myself,
W-pII .338.2:3 *me, until I l. that You have given me the only*
W-pII .343.2:4 And it is this that we would l. today.
W-pII ....344.h Today I l. the law of love; that what I give
W-pII .346.2:2 For we will l. today what peace is ours,
W-pII .349.1:6 *I l. Your healing miracles belong to me.*
W-pII ...14.5:1 to us, we l. that it is written on our hearts.
W-pII .359.1:6 *we rejoice to l. that we have made mistakes*
Wfl........in.6:1 and ask Him to help us to l. His lessons,
M-in..........1:5 hand, emphasizes that to teach *is* to l., so
M-in..........2:3 From your demonstration others l., and
M-in..........2:5 teach on the basis of what you want to l..
M-in..........2:6 yourself, and this you l. through teaching.
M-in..........3:3 you really teach, and therefore really l..
M-2...........1:7 When he is ready to l., the opportunities
M-2...........3:6 or even the form in which you will l. it.
M-2...........3:7 however, to decide when you want to l. it.
M-2...........5:7 Those who would l. the same course share
M-3...........1:3 from whom a teacher of God cannot l., so
M-3...........4:1 that each person involved will l. the most
M-3...........5:6 Yet should they decide to l. it, the perfect
M-3...........5:7 And if they decide to l. that lesson, they
M-4.....I.A.5:7 He can l. this only as he actually does give
M-4.....I.A.7:8 He must l. to lay all judgment aside, and
M-4....III.1:11 teacher of God can judge and hope to l..
M-4......IV.1:8 No teacher of God but must l., –and
M-4....IV.1:10 the Holy Spirit's lessons impossible to l..
M-13.........1:4 illusion, for in reality there is nothing to l.
M-13.........8:5 Remember only what you would l.. For it
M-13.......8:10 not. But l. this course and it is yours. God
M-14.........3:6 God must l. to pass by and leave behind.
M-14.........4:5 He need merely l. how to approach it; to
M-14.........4:6 Voice tells him it is a lesson he can l., he
M-14.........4:6 him it is a lesson he can learn, he can l. it.
M-14.........4:8 trusts that He will show him how to l. it.
M-14.......5:11 say you cannot l. His Own curriculum.
M-15.......2:12 L. to be quiet, for His Voice is heard in
M-16.........1:6 they can l. the lessons for the day together
M-16.........2:3 must they do to l. to give the day to God?
M-16.......11:9 must God's teachers l. to recognize the
M-17.........1:8 because it is not this that he would l..
M-18.........2:1 God's teachers' major lesson is to l. how
M-20.........4:5 But you will l., as you remember even
M-21.........4:4 however, l. to use words in a new way.
M-23.......5:10 Would you not l. the lesson of salvation
M-23.........6:4 whose learning far exceeds what we can l..
M-24.........4:4 has much to teach and l. apart from them
M-24.........4:5 both l. and teach that theoretical issues
M-24.........5:9 knows is not necessarily all there is to l..
C-5............6:8 most of all that he would have you l., and
C-ep...........1:7 but l. how not to be deceived by them.
P-1.............1:3 causes and l. to evaluate them correctly.
P-1.............2:2 l. to call upon God and hear His Answer?
P-1.............3:3 not realize and needs to l. is that this "self
P-2.........in.3:3 patient hopes to l. how to get the changes
P-2.........in.4:3 both will l. to give up their original goals,
P-2..........II.8:6 I, accept Atonement and l. to give it as it
P-2......... V.4:8 for what to teach as well as what to l..
P-2.......VII.1:9 And every therapist must l. to heal from
P-3..........I.4:3 Meanwhile he must l., and his patients
S-1......... IV.2:2 but there are still many lessons to l.. The
S-1......... V.3:7 more to l. before the journey is complete.
S-2..........I.3:2 Then l. that God has given you the means
S-2..........I.6:4 look through His and l. to see like Him.
S-2..........I.7:1 how to l. forgiveness as His vision lets it
S-2..........I.9:1 But to achieve this end you first must l.,
S-2.........I.10:3 Yet you must l. alternatives for choice, or
S-2.........I.10:4 and l. what it should be to set you free.
S-2........ III.1:6 asks for trust and willingness to l. how to
S-2........ III.1:9 Yet He has willed you l. the way to Him,
S-2........ III.4:5 will He give the means to you to l. of Him,
S-2........ III.6:9 Listen and l., and do not judge. It is to

## learned 188

T-1....... IV.4:8 abundance they have l. belongs to them.
T-2.........II.3:6 it? Once you have l. to consider these
T-2........ V.6:6 has l. to look beyond it toward the light.
T-4..........I.3:4 like yours, and because I l. it I can teach it
T-4..........I.7:4 and repeat their lessons until they are l.. I
T-5......II.3:11 It is the final lesson that I l., and God's
T-5....... IV.5:3 forget my need to teach what I have l.,
T-5....... IV.5:3 learned, which arose in me *because* I l. it. I
T-5....... IV.5:4 I call upon you to teach what you have l.,
T-5....... IV.5:6 What I l. I give you freely, and the Mind
T-5..... VI.11:6 from Whom I l. of infinite patience. His
T-5......VII.2:5 He has not l. that every mind God created
T-6........I.11:5 one lesson, which I must teach as I l. it, is
T-6........I.16:8 its lessons must be l. now as well as then.
T-6........I.19:3 you will have l. of me and will be as eager
T-6.........II.4:1 l., however, that there *is* an alternative to
T-6......... III.1:9 You cannot teach what you have not l.,
T-6......... III.3:9 attack in any form and you have l. it, and
T-6..... V.B.3:6 since it is being l. by a conflicted mind.
T-6..... V.B.3:7 the lesson cannot be l. consistently as yet.
T-6..... V.C.8:1 its wholeness, and have l. that it is one.
T-7..........I.2:9 you have l. to remember what you are.
T-7....... IV.3:1 not want to teach everyone all it has l.,
T-7....... IV.3:3 teach the opposite of what the ego has "l..
T-7........ V.2:4 l. that behavior is not the level for either
T-7........ V.2:6 lesson will be poorly taught and poorly l..
T-7....... XI.4:4 because he has l. it of the Holy Spirit.
T-8.........II.4:2 This unnatural lesson cannot be l., and
T-8.........II.6:4 When you have l. that your will is God's,
T-8........ IV.6:7 cannot be l. by tyranny of any kind, and
T-8....... VI.8:3 Him, and l. of what He had already given.
T-9....... IV.5:1 is l. of me does not use fear to undo fear.
T-9....... VI.6:5 When you have l. they are the same, the
T-11........I.1:1 You have l. your need of healing. Would
T-11.......II.4:5 surely l. that whom you invite as your
T-11..... VI.3:5 For perceptions are l. *with* beliefs, and
T-11...VIII.3:7 Perceptions are l., and you are not
T-11...VIII.3:8 to question everything you l. of yourself,
T-11...VIII.3:8 l. amiss should not be your own teacher.
T-12.......I.8:11 We have already l. that fear and attack are
T-12..... III.1:5 how perfectly your lesson would be l. if
T-12.......V.6:4 You cannot transfer what you have not l.,
T-12.......V.6:7 correctly, they would have l. from them.
T-12.... VII.1:1 learning is invisible and what has been l.
T-12.... VII.1:3 You will recognize that you have l. there
T-13..... VI.2:3 l. to look on everyone with no reference at
T-13..... VII.6:4 and l. of Him the joyful journey home.
T-13... VIII.8:1 having l. to free yourself through Him
T-13..... XI.6:4 When you have l. this, you will find the
T-13..... XI.6:6 When you have l. that you belong to truth
T-13... XI.11:1 undo for you everything you have l. that
T-14.......II.6:1 everything you have l. to the Holy Spirit,
T-14..... IV.6:1 you have l. how to decide with God, all
T-14.......V.5:6 not yet have l. how to exchange guilt for
T-14..... IX.8:4 it. Those who have l. to offer only healing,
T-14.....X.12:5 have already l. that this Identity is shared.
T-14..... XI.3:5 all. Nothing you have ever l. can help you
T-14..... XI.4:3 already l. for every child of light by Him
T-14..... XI.4:8 one for the bright lesson He has l. for you.
T-14..... XI.4:9 have l. apart from Him means anything.
T-14..... XI.5:1 by which to recognize if what you l. is true
T-14..... XI.5:2 can be sure that you have l. God's lesson,
T-14..... XI.6:4 that everything you l. you do not want.
T-14..... XI.6:5 experiences to confirm what you have l..
T-15..... III.9:3 I l. for you that you can learn of me. I
T-15... III.10:4 remembering that everything I l. is yours.
T-15... III.10:7 When you have l. to accept what you are,
T-15.......V.2:1 past that you l. to define your own needs
T-15.. VII.12:5 insanity of this lesson, many have l. it.
T-16........I.3:4 you have l. of empathy is from the past.
T-16..... III.1:1 We have already l. that everyone teaches,
T-16..... III.1:2 and yet you may not have l. how to accept
T-16..... III.2:1 but you have not l. how to be free. I said
T-16..... III.3:1 fact that you have not l. what you have
T-16..... III.4:5 What can it be that has not l. it? It must
T-16..... III.6:8 and l. from the conviction you shared
T-17.......II.1:8 for you, until you l. to see it for yourself.
T-17.......II.3:2 All else is l., but this is given, complete
T-17.......II.3:7 born of the new perspective he has l., has
T-17.......V.2:1 the perception of the real world, is l.. It is
T-17.......V.15:2 have also l. how to release all the Sonship,
T-18.... VII.4:5 attempt to teach more than they l. in time
T-18... IX.12:1 Love is not l.. Its meaning lies within
T-18... IX.12:5 Love is not l., because there never was a
T-18... IX.12:6 that everything you l. is meaningless,
T-19.......I.15:4 longer needed when the lesson has been l.
T19.. IV.D.9:1 Atonement and l. illusions are not real.
T-20..... IV.4:6 It is of them who l. of freedom that you
T-20.... VI.12:2 and you have l. you really want but one.
T-20.... VII.8:4 vision is l. from Him Who would undo
T-21........I.3:5 is l. will bring to you the joy it promises. If
T-21........I.3:7 and you have l. that both you cannot have
T-21........I.4:3 They l. it, not through joyous lessons, but
T-21........I.4:7 world they l. to "see" in their imagination
T-21........I.4:8 They hate the world they l. through pain.
T-21........I.7:3 you would lose the world you l. since then
T-21........I.7:4 in the world you l. is half so dear as this.
T-21..... IV.5:6 perfectly from what you have already l..
T-21... VIII.1:4 And so he "dies" because of what he l.. He
T-22..... IV.7:3 it, he l. it was not given him alone. Such is
T-23........I.7:7 when you have l. you cannot be in conflict
T-24.... VII.8:1 attempt to teach what cannot easily be l..
T-27..... IV.5:5 add nothing new and nothing has been l..
T-27.......V.7:2 needs one lesson that has perfectly been l.
T-27 .VIII.11:1 lesson l. will set you free from suffering,
T-27 .VIII.11:2 lesson of deliverance until it has been l.,
T-27 .VIII.12:3 undone by but a single lesson truly l..
T-30.......V.5:2 which the mind has l. how easily do idols
T-30..... VI.4:7 l. forgiveness is your right as much as his.
T-30.... VII.4:3 l. one meaning has been given everything,
T-31........I.3:1 No one who understands what you have l.
T-31........I.3:1 you have learned, how carefully you l. it,
T-31........I.4:2 Yet you have l. more than this. You have
T-31........I.5:3 and you have l. what it was made to teach
T-31........I.7:1 The lessons to be l. are only two. Each
T-31.......I.11:9 Your answer is the proof of what you l..
T-31.......I.12:1 an instant, and forget all things we ever l.,
T-31.......II.4:4 for, and l. to think that this his purpose is

| | |
|---|---|
| T-31 II.7:4 | Forget the dismal lessons that you l. |
| T-31 II.8:2 | all thought of what you ever l. before, and |
| T-31 IV.3:6 | they could have l. their greatest lesson. |
| T-31 IV.4:1 | when you have l. the way the lesson starts |
| T-31 IV.4:7 | what you have l. to what is yet to learn. |
| T-31 V.7:1 | Concepts are l.. They are not natural. |
| T-31 V.9:1 | there is no shattering of what was l., but |
| T-31 V.9:3 | surely l. by now that you behave as if it |
| T-31 VII.10:3 | Who has l. to see his brother not as this |
| W-pI 7.3:5 | this cup except what you l. in the past? |
| WpI rI.in.4:2 | in which to apply what you have l.. You |
| W-pI 64.2:2 | l. that the Holy Spirit has another use for |
| W-pI 98.4:1 | all that they l. and every gain they made. |
| W-pI 106.7:2 | And the lesson has been l.. Today we |
| WpI. rIII.in9:2 | without applying what you l. to them. As |
| WpIrIII.in13:1 | Do not forget how little you have l.. Do |
| W-pI 121.6:3 | forgiveness must be l. by you as well, but |
| W-pI.121.12:2 | a friend. Try to transfer the light you l. to |
| W-pI 133.1:1 | far from what the student has already l., |
| W-pI.135.16:2 | What it has l. before becomes the basis |
| W-pI 138.3:5 | for nothing is accomplished; nothing l.. |
| W-pI 138.5:2 | truth cannot be l., but only recognized. In |
| W-pI 151.2:3 | even though you l. a long while since your |
| W-pI.153.11:3 | while you fail to teach what you have l., |
| W-pI 157.2:2 | sheds a light on all that we have l. already, |
| W-pI 158.2:4 | All this cannot be l.. What, then, are you |
| W-pI.166.13:4 | For you have l. of Christ there is another |
| W-pI.167.2:3 | l. that the idea of death takes many forms. |
| W-pI 169.3:1 | Grace is not l.. The final step must go |
| W-pI 169.7:2 | Yet forgiveness, taught and l., brings with |
| W-pI 185.5:6 | has l. their only difference is one of form, |
| W-pI 185.6:4 | will meet with acceptance and be truly l.. |
| W-pI 187.2:3 | Yet we have l. that things but represent |
| W-pI 189.7:1 | all concepts you have l. about the world; |
| W-pI 189.7:4 | belief you ever l. before from anything. |
| W-pI 193.7:3 | If it does, be sure the lesson is not l.. And |
| WpI rVI.in.1:3 | sufficient for salvation, if it were l. truly. |
| W-pII..300.2:3 | *L. exactly what to do to be restored to Heaven* |
| W-pII..301.2:4 | But we have l. the world we saw was false, |
| W-pII..315.1:5 | that what he l. is surely mine as well. |
| W-pII..338.1:3 | Now has he l. that no one frightens him, |
| WfI in.5:5 | wrath because we l. we were mistaken. |
| M-in 5:6 | in many, many ways, until they have l. it. |
| M-2 3:4 | l. and understood and long ago passed by |
| M-2 3:8 | it. And as you accept it, it is already l.. |
| M-3 4:5 | each has l. the most he can at the time. |
| M-3 5:6 | perfect lesson is before them and can be l. |
| M-4 I.1:4 | because they have l. it is not governed by |
| M-4 I.A.3:8 | When the teacher of God has l. that much |
| M-4 I.A.4:2 | having l. that the changes in his life are |
| M-4 I.A.4:3 | he has l. to new situations as they arise. |
| M-4 I.A.6:4 | to see the transfer value of what he has l.. |
| M-4 I.A.7:3 | All that he really l. so far was that he did |
| M-4 I.A.7:6 | He thought he l. willingness, but now he |
| M-4 VI.1:1 | God's teachers have l. how to be simple. |
| M-4 VII.1:2 | that must be l. and learned very carefully. |
| M-4 VII.1:2 | that must be learned and l. very carefully. |
| M-12 6:4 | l. that all choices are made consciously, |
| M-15 2:10 | yet l. to stand aside and hear the Voice of |
| M-16 1:7 | set, and one which can be l. that very day. |
| M-16 11:4 | function to make sure that they have l. it. |
| M-16 11:7 | have l. that everything but this is magic. |
| M-17 8:4 | It can be l. and taught, but it requires |
| M-22 2:3 | l. all that his acceptance holds out to him. |
| C-5 5:3 | the mighty lesson that he l. for all of you. |
| P-2 II.1:4 | has l. all things does not need a teacher, |
| P-2 II.3:2 | be taught, because it is all that need be l.. |
| P-3 II.7:3 | He has l. that it is no harder to wake a |
| S-3 II.2:4 | light that we have l. to look upon again. |
| S-3 II.4:4 | peace, the journey over and the lessons l.. |

## learner 36

| | |
|---|---|
| T-2 II.5:6 | and can become a better and better l.. |
| T-2 V.5:6 | the mind to its true position as the l.. |
| T-2 V.6:2 | a learning device it merely follows the l., |
| T-2 V.6:5 | body by recognizing that it is not the l., |
| T-5 III.10:3 | Spirit can deal with a reluctant l. without |
| T-6 V.B.1:6 | An insane l. learns strange lessons. What |
| T-6 V.B.2:4 | for change in the l. is all that a teacher |
| T-6 V.B.3:8 | the mind of the l. projects its own conflict |
| T-6 V.B.4:5 | makes it impossible for the l. not to listen. |
| T-7 II.5:7 | yourself you became a l. of necessity. |
| T-7 II.7:2 | prevents the l. from appreciating it. There |
| T-7 V.2:5 | weaken you as a teacher and a l. because, |
| T-7 V.2:7 | you are both a poor teacher and a poor l.. |
| T-7 VIII.3:4 | teacher is a poor teacher and a poor l.. |
| T-8 VII.8:1 | There is nothing so frustrating to a l. as a |
| T-8 VII.14:5 | result, is a clear-cut indication of a poor l.. |
| T-11 II.2:1 | it the better teacher and l. you become. If |
| T-12 V.4:3 | a split mind has made itself a poor l.. You |
| T-12 V.8:6 | an excellent l. and an excellent teacher. |
| T-14 II.h | The Happy L. |
| T-14 II.1:1 | Holy Spirit needs a happy l., in whom His |
| T-14 II.5:3 | Learn to be a happy l.. You will never |
| T-14 II.6:1 | If you would be a happy l., you must give |
| T-14 II.7:1 | happy l. meets the conditions of learning |
| T-14 III.1:1 | happy l. cannot feel guilty about learning. |
| T-14 III.1:3 | The guiltless l. learns easily because his |
| T-15 I.1:4 | a consistent l. that you learn only of Him. |
| T-16 I.5:6 | You are the l.; He the Teacher. Do not |
| T-16 III.7:4 | For the joy of teaching is in the l., who |
| T-18 IV.4:8 | that you must make the l. different. You |
| T-18 IV.4:9 | You did not make the l., nor can you |
| T-21 I.3:7 | not a happy l. yet because you still remain |
| M-in 1:3 | as if the teacher and the l. are separated, |
| M-in 1:3 | something to the l. rather than to himself. |
| M-in 1:5 | learn, so that teacher and l. are the same. |
| M-2 5:8 | goal. And thus he who was the l. becomes |

## learners 8

| | |
|---|---|
| T-5 II.3:11 | Sons are as equal as l. as they are as Sons. |
| T-6 I.8:1 | it weakens them as teachers and as l.. Yet |
| T-6 I.10:1 | We are still equal as l., although we do |
| T-12 V.4:5 | you, and poor l. do need special teaching. |
| T-12 V.5:5 | Poor l. are not good choices as teachers, |
| T-14 II.3:2 | unhappy l. who would teach themselves |
| T-14 II.4:5 | will be happy l. of the lesson this light |
| T-14 V.3:7 | The happy l. of the Atonement become |

## learning 340

*See also* teaching-learning

| | |
|---|---|
| T-1 I.15:4 | when it is no longer useful in facilitating l. |
| T-1 I.47:1 | is a l. device that lessens the need for time |
| T-1 II.2:6 | In this phase of l., working miracles is |
| T-1 II.6:7 | The miracle substitutes for l. that might |
| T-1 V.1:1 | that both are l. aids for facilitating a state |
| T-1 VI.1:2 | No l. is acquired by anyone unless he |
| T-1 VII.2:5 | incapable. L. to do this is the body's only |
| T-1 VII.4:2 | All l. involves attention and study at some |
| T-2 II.5:1 | itself, and ultimately to make l. complete. |
| T-2 II.5:3 | L. itself, like the classrooms in which it |
| T-2 II.5:8 | is a belief in differences is l. meaningful. |
| T-2 IV.3:1 | and the body is a l. device for the mind. |
| T-2 IV.3:2 | L. devices are not lessons in themselves. |
| T-2 IV.3:3 | Their purpose is merely to facilitate l.. |
| T-2 IV.3:4 | The worst a faulty use of a l. device can do |
| T-2 IV.3:4 | device can do is to fail to facilitate l.. It |
| T-2 IV.3:5 | in itself to introduce actual l. errors. The |
| T-2 V.1:9 | not exist except as a l. device for the mind |
| T-2 V.1:10 | l. device is not subject to errors of its own, |
| T-2 V.5:6 | from overevaluating its own l. device, and |
| T-2 V.6:2 | As a l. device it merely follows the learner, |
| T-2 V.6:2 | to the very l. it should facilitate. Only the |
| T-2 V.6:5 | learner, and is therefore unamenable to l.. |
| T-2 V.7:1 | Corrective l. always begins with the |
| T-2 VIII.2:4 | it became one of the many l. devices to be |
| T-3 I.4:7 | the teacher offers. The result is l. failure. |
| T-4 I.h | Right Teaching and Right L. |
| T-4 I.1:2 | and pupil are alike in the l. process. They |
| T-4 I.1:3 | They are in the same order of l., and |
| T-4 I.2:1 | systems as they are, and l. means change. |
| T-4 I.3:2 | L. is ultimately perceived as frightening |
| T-4 I.4:1 | and l. are your greatest strengths now, |
| T-4 I.5:1 | his own l. that they will one day no longer |
| T-4 I.7:1 | worth is not established by teaching or l.. |
| T-4 I.7:5 | I have no right to set your l. limits for you. |
| T-4 V.5:5 | L. and wanting to learn are inseparable. |
| T-4 V.6:6 | ego devices for impeding l. progress. In |
| T-4 VI.2:1 | In l. to escape from illusions, your debt |
| T-4 VI.3:4 | L. through rewards is more effective than |
| T-4 VI.3:4 | is more effective than l. through pain, |
| T-5 III.11:4 | Correct and learn, and be open to l.. You |
| T-5 VI.12:4 | said that time is a l. device to be abolished |
| T-6 in.2:1 | been asked to take me as your model for l. |
| T-6 in.2:1 | example is a particularly helpful l. device. |
| T-6 I.1:1 | l. purposes, let us consider the crucifixion |
| T-6 I.2:2 | lies solely in the kind of l. it facilitates. It |
| T-6 I.3:6 | Otherwise, I cannot serve as a model for l. |
| T-6 I.19:3 | will be as eager to share your l. as I am. |
| T-6 III.1:10 | it. Every lesson you teach you are l.. |
| T-6 III.3:10 | Yet this l. is not immortal, and you can |
| T-6 III.4:8 | it. Everything you teach you are l.. Teach |
| T-6 IV.5:3 | *is* real, that the mind is the ego's l. device; |
| T-6 V.A.2:4 | made and translates it into a l. device. |
| T-6 V.B.5:3 | both, you are teaching conflict and l. it. |
| T-7 II.3:2 | outside the Kingdom l. is essential. This |
| T-7 II.3:4 | In the Kingdom there is no teaching or l., |
| T-7 II.5:7 | your inheritance and requires no l. at all, |
| T-7 II.6:1 | one questions the connection of l. and |
| T-7 II.6:2 | L. is impossible without memory since it |
| T-7 IV.3:4 | The kind of l. is as irrelevant as is the |
| T-7 IV.3:4 | particular ability that was applied to the l. |
| T-7 IV.4:3 | by l. of wholeness you learn to remember |
| T-7 V.2:4 | is not the level for either teaching or l., |
| T-7 V.7:3 | teaching is limited because he is l. so little |
| T-7 V.7:5 | True l. is constant, and so vital in its |
| T-7 V.8:1 | you heal, that is exactly what you *are* l.. |
| T-7 X.8:6 | are l. the difference between pain and joy. |
| T-8 I.1:1 | is not the motivation for l. this course. |
| T-8 I.2:1 | the ego may seem to interfere with your l. |
| T-8 I.4:1 | past l. must have taught you the wrong |
| T-8 I.4:3 | If l. aims at change, and that is always its |
| T-8 I.4:3 | with the changes your l. has brought you? |
| T-8 I.4:4 | Dissatisfaction with l. outcomes is a sign |
| T-8 I.4:4 | learning outcomes is a sign of l. failure, |
| T-8 I.6:3 | curriculum presents an impossible l. task. |
| T-8 II.1:3 | is. If l. to remove the obstacles to that |
| T-8 II.2:6 | done more harm to your l. than this alone |
| T-8 II.2:7 | alone. L. is joyful if it leads you along your |
| T-8 II.2:8 | lose by your l. because your learning will |
| T-8 II.2:8 | learning because your l. will imprison you |
| T-8 III.1:5 | is no limit on your l. because there is no |
| T-8 III.5:8 | you are l. what you are because you are |
| T-8 VII.8:3 | faced with an impossible l. situation is the |
| T-8 VII.8:6 | Whenever the reaction to l. is depression, |
| T-8 VII.12:5 | To confuse a l. device with a curriculum |
| T-8 VII.12:6 | L. must lead beyond the body to the re- |
| T-8 VII.13:2 | your l. promotes depression instead of joy |
| T-8 VII.13:2 | to God's joyous Teacher and l. His lessons |
| T-8 VII.14:4 | for l. should be to escape from limitations |
| T-8 VII.14:6 | poor learner. He has accepted a l. goal in |
| T-8 VIII.7:1 | A l. device is not a teacher. It cannot tell |
| T-8 VIII.7:3 | believe that a l. device *can* tell you how you |
| T-9 III.8:6 | For that all l. was made. This is the Holy |
| T-9 III.8:10 | by l. how to look on everything without it. |
| T-9 V.9:1 | a very direct and a very simple l. situation |
| T-9 VI.3:2 | l. is the result of what you taught them. |
| T-11 V.2:4 | are also l. that its effects can be dispelled |
| T-11 V.11:2 | Only by l. what fear is can you finally |
| T-11 VI.3:7 | L. of Christ is easy, for to perceive with |
| T-12 I.8:10 | ultimate value in l. to perceive attack as a |
| T-12 II.10:1 | aimed at l. how to offer to the Holy Spirit |
| T-12 V.5:1 | have l. handicaps in a very literal sense. |
| T-12 V.5:2 | There are areas in your l. skills that are so |
| T-12 V.5:4 | l. situation in which you placed yourself is |
| T-12 V.6:3 | Your l. goal has been *not* to learn, and this |
| T-12 V.6:3 | learn, and this cannot lead to successful l. |
| T-12 V.6:4 | ability to generalize is a crucial l. failure. |
| T-12 V.6:5 | have failed to learn what l. aids are for? |
| T-12 V.7:4 | sensible guide to l. will be misinterpreted, |
| T-12 V.7:4 | the l. this strange curriculum is against. If |
| T-12 V.7:7 | This attempt at "l." has so weakened your |
| T-12 V.7:8 | this curriculum is l. how *not* to overcome |
| T-12 V.7:9 | for all your l. will be on its behalf. Yet |

T-12..... V.7:10 Yet your mind speaks against your l. as
T-12..... V.7:10 as your l. speaks against your mind, and
T-12..... V.7:10 and so you fight against all l. and succeed,
T-12....... V.8:5 and of the l. outcomes that have resulted.
T-12....... V.8:6 Under the proper l. conditions, which you
T-12....... V.8:7 will not be so until the whole l. situation
T-12....... V.9:1 Your l. potential, properly understood, is
T-12....... V.9:2 and understands His curriculum for l. it.
T-12....... V.9:7 God's Son. His l. is as unlimited as he is.
T-12..... VII.1:1 demonstrate that l. has occurred under
T-12..... VII.1:1 l. is invisible and what has been learned
T-13....... II.7:5 must believe that by not l. the course you
T-14....... in.1:3 means for l. it and seeing it quite clearly.
T-14............ I.h The Conditions of L.
T-14......... I.1:7 for yourself and l. you are guiltless. How
T-14....... II.1:5 l. goal depends means absolutely nothing
T-14....... II.6:4 The universe of l. will open up before you
T-14....... II.7:1 learner meets the conditions of l. here, as
T-14...... III.1:1 happy learner cannot feel guilty about l..
T-14...... III.1:2 to l. that it should never be forgotten. The
T-14...... III.3:2 L. is living here, as creating is being in
T-14...... III.6:6 The joy of l. that darkness has no power
T-14...... IV.2:7 L. applies only to the condition in which
T-14....... V.6:2 is no unity of l. goals apart from this.
T-14...... XI.1:1 essential thing is l. that *you do not know.*
T-14...... XI.1:9 of God in you is but your l. of the false,
T-14...... XI.3:2 *now.* L. has been accomplished before its
T-14...... XI.3:3 L. is therefore in the past, but its
T-14...... XI.3:4 *Your* l. gives the present no meaning at all.
T-14...... XI.6:9 *my own past l. as the light to guide me now.*
T-14.... XI.12:3 for l. by thinking they already know.
T-15......... I.1:3 His teaching until it constitutes all your l..
T-15....... II.1:7 instant you will let go all your past l., and
T-15....... II.1:8 the obstacles to l. it have been removed?
T-15....... IV.1:1 This course is not beyond immediate l.,
T-15....... V.1:1 l. device for teaching you love's meaning.
T-15....... V.2:1 The past is the ego's chief l. device, for it
T-15....... V.4:5 ego, as l. experiences that point to truth.
T-15.... VIII.1:1 instant does not replace the need for l.,
T-16...... III.2:6 because all your l. has been directed
T-16...... III.7:1 and make l. commensurate with teaching.
T-16..... V.15:4 is a carefully contrived l. experience,
T-16..... V.15:5 Yet for every l. that would hurt you, God
T-17....... II.4:2 has been used for l. will have no function.
T-17..... V.15:2 And l. this, you will have also learned
T-18...... IV.4:8 you maintain you are unworthy of l. this,
T-18.... IX.11:3 the real world, beyond which l. cannot go
T-18.... IX.11:4 way. Where l. ends there God begins, for
T-18.... IX.11:4 for l. ends before Him Who is complete
T-18.... IX.12:3 And l. ends when you have recognized all
T-18.... IX.12:6 it not. L. is useless in the Presence of your
T-18.... IX.12:6 so far transcend all l. that everything you
T-18.... IX.14:1 else, and memory will be as useless as l.,
T-19....... I.15:4 For faith is still a l. goal, no longer needed
T-20.... VI.12:1 You who are l. this may still be fearful,
T-21......... I.3:6 it would, the l. of it would be no problem.
T-22.... VI.10:1 your l. depends the welfare of the world.
T-24....... in.2:2 and obscure but it will jeopardize your l..
T-24... VII.6:10 Not till you go past l. to the Given; not till
T-25......... I.7:5 use all l. to transfer illusions to the truth,
T-26...... III.5:4 difference is the l. goal this course has set.
T-26....... V.1:5 All l. is a help or hindrance to the gate of
T-26....... V.2:3 to reach a goal as high as l. can achieve?
T-26....... V.6:2 It is the key to l. that the past is over.
T-27...... III.5:6 when aids are meaningless and l. done.
T-27...... III.5:7 No l. aid has use that can extend beyond
T-27...... III.5:7 use that can extend beyond the goal of l..
T-27...... III.5:9 l. interval it has a use that now you fear,
T-27...... III.6:8 this you need no pictures and no l. aids.
T-27...... III.6:9 the place of every l. aid will merely *be.*
T-27...... IV.5:6 An honest question is a l. tool that asks
T-27....... V.8:8 All l. aims at transfer, which becomes
T-27....... V.8:10 total transfer of your l. is not made by you
T-27....... V.9:3 l. does not jump from situations to their
T-27..... V.10:1 transfer of your l. to the One Who really
T-27..... V.10:3 And it is thus the power of your l. will be
T-29......... I.8:6 is a wariness that is aroused by l. that the
T-30......... I.3:7 occur at first, while you are l. how to hear.
T-31....... I.1:10 do you persist in l. not such simple things
T-31 ........ I.2:7 such a giant l. feat it is indeed incredible.
T-31 ........ I.3:1 could ever doubt the power of your l. skill
T-31 ........ I.4:4 arises from the first accomplishment of l.;
T-31 ........ I.5:1 L. is an ability you made and gave
T-31 ........ I.5:3 it. And this has l. sought to demonstrate,
T-31 ........ I.5:5 for their l. is the only purpose for your
T-31 ........ I.5:5 learning is the only purpose for your l.
T-31 ........ I.6:6 Can it be your little l., strange in outcome
T-31 ........ I.6:6 since time began and l. had been made?
T-31 ........ I.7:9 only outcome which your l. can produce.
T-31 ...... I.13:5 free, because an ancient l. passed away,
T-31 ..... III.4:8 L. is all that causes change. And so the
T-31 ..... III.4:9 And so the body, where no l. can occur,
T-31 ..... IV.3:5 And l. they led nowhere, lost their hope.
T-31 ..... IV.4:7 Make fast your l. now, and understand
T-31 ..... IV.4:8 point will l. lead to heights of happiness,
T-31 ..... IV.4:8 clear, and perfectly within your l. grasp.
T-31 ..... IV.5:4 begin with l. where it really has a use.
T-31 ..... IV.6:1 l. that the world can offer but one choice,
T-31 ...... V.1:1 l. of the world is built upon a concept of
T-31 ...... V.1:5 of the self is what the l. of the world is for.
T-31 ...... V.4:4 is here the l. of the world has set its sights,
T-31 ...... V.7:3 Apart from l. they do not exist. They are
T-31 ...... V.8:2 is all l. that the world directs begun and
T-31 .... V.13:3 have done the l. which gave rise to them.
T-31 .... V.15:6 sign your l. has been guided by the world,
T-31 .... V.16:1 many concepts of the self as l. goes along.
T-31 .... V.16:3 be you thankful that the l. of the world is
T-31 .... V.17:8 Yet in this l. is salvation born. And What
T-31 .... VII.1:1 L. is change. Salvation does not seek to
W-pI....... 4.3:3 of l. to see the meaningless as outside you,
W-pI....... 7.2:1 on your not l. these new ideas about it.
W-pI....... 7.3:6 what this cup is, except for your past l..
W-pI..... 12.2:7 beginning step in l. to give them all equal
W-pI..... 14.3:1 idea for today is another step in l. to let go
W-pI..... 18.1:1 idea for today is another step in l. that the
W-pI..... 20.2:7 You are now l. how to tell them apart.
W-pI..... 24.2:3 opening your mind so that l. can begin.
W-pI..... 25.5:1 It is crucial to your l. to be willing to give
WpI... rI.in.4:1 for practice periods at your stage of l.. It
WpI... rI.in.4:3 You will need your l. most in situations
WpI... rI.in.4:4 The purpose of your l. is to enable you to
W-pI..... 55.5:7 I have given it, and l. the truth about it.
W-pI..... 62.2:4 you are l. how to remember the truth. For
W-pI..... 69.3:4 L. salvation is our only goal. Let us end
W-pI..... 94.5:9 and a milestone in l. the thought system
W-pI..... 95.4:1 the stage of l. in which you are at present.
W-pI..... 95.6:3 who remain heavily defended against l..
W-pI..... 95.8:4 it, rather than give it power to delay our l.
W-pI... 105.3:1 A major l. goal this course has set is to
W-pI. 106.10:1 giving means by listening and l. it of Him.
W-pI... 108.5:3 of one law which holds for every kind of l.
W-pI. 108.10:3 for today as quick advances in your l.,
WpI..rIII.in2:2 L. will not be hampered when you miss a
WpI..rIII.in3:1 But l. will be hampered when you skip a
WpI..rIII.in9:3 and have not given your l. a fair chance to
WpIrIII.in10:1 we stress the need to let your l. not lie idly
WpIrIII.in12:3 these reviews with l. gains so great we will
W-pI... 121.7:7 all your teaching and your l. will be not of
W-pI... 121.8:1 Today we practice l. to forgive. If you are
W-pI... 121.8:3 to l. how to give forgiveness and receive
W-pI. 133.12:4 What is the gain to you in l. this? It is far
W-pI. 135.15:3 controlled by l. and experience obtained
W-pI. 135.26:5 remind yourself this is a special day for l.,
W-pI... 138.5:1 Choosing depends on l.. And the truth
W-pI... 138.5:5 be attained through l. how to reach them,
W-pI... 138.5:6 Decisions are the outcome of your l., for
WpI. rIV.in1:1 part of l. how the truth can be applied.
WpIrIV.in10:2 l. now to claim again as your inheritance.
W-pI. 153.14:6 can smile at last, on l. that it is not true.
W-pI... 157.2:3 It brings us to the door where l. ceases,
W-pI... 157.3:1 though you will return to paths of l.. Yet
W-pI... 157.9:3 teach, for you attained it not through l..
W-pI... 162.1:2 repeat it, as we reach another stage in l.. It
W-pI... 169.1:3 It is past l., yet the goal of learning, for
W-pI... 169.1:3 It is past learning, yet the goal of l., for
W-pI... 169.3:2 final step must go beyond all l.. Grace is
W-pI... 169.8:1 All l. was already in His Mind,
W-pI. 169.15:1 l. goal today does not exceed this prayer.
W-pI .. 184.5:3 Yet you believe this is what l. means; its
W-pI .. 184.7:2 a phase of l. everyone who comes must go
W-pI .. 184.7:4 L. that stops with what the world would
W-pI .. 184.7:5 from which another kind of l. can begin, a
W-pI 184.10:1 l. of the world becomes a transitory phase
W-pI 184.12:2 are one, and at this lesson does all l. end.
W-pI .. 192.4:3 aid, to be laid by when l. is complete, but
W-pI .. 193.1:1 God does not know of l.. Yet His Will
W-pI .. 193.4:3 It is this sameness which makes l. sure,
W-pI .. 194.6:2 you extend your l. to the world. And as
W-pI 195.10:1 and shorten our l. time by more than you
W-pII ..... 6.5:1 the symbol that the time for l. now is over
W-pII ..... 6.5:3 have no need of l. or perception or of time
W-pII ..... 7.2:3 l. has achieved the only goal it has in
W-pII ..... 7.2:4 For l., as the Holy Spirit guides it to the
W-pII . 296.2:2 our l. goal becomes an unconflicted one,
W-pII ..... 9.3:1 in which l. ends in one last summary that
W-pII . 353.1:3 *Thus has l. come almost to its appointed end*
M-in .......... 1:1 role of teaching and l. is actually reversed
M-in .......... 4:7 Into this hopeless and closed l. situation,
M-in .......... 4:8 hope, their l. finally becomes complete.
M-2 ........... 5:3 any two who join together for l. purposes.
M-3 ........... 5:2 in which each person is given a chosen l.
M-3 ........... 5:2 him with unlimited opportunities for l..
M-4 ........... 1:6 of God who have advanced in their own l.
M-4 ......... I.1:2 rests. Perception is the result of l.. In fact,
M-4 ......... I.1:3 In fact, perception *is* l., because cause and
M-4 ..... I.A.4:5 takes great l. to understand that all things
M-4 ..... I.A.6:3 Now he consolidates his l.. Now he begins
M-4 ..... I.A.8:2 It is here that l. is consolidated. Now what
M-4 ..... I.A.8:4 is their result; the outcome of honest l.,
M-4 ...... III.1:7 this be lost, and all his l. goes. Without
M-4 ...... IV.1:6 It is the end of peace and the denial of l..
M-4 ...... IX.1:2 some aspects of his life to bring to his l.,
M-4 ...... X.2:10 the way for what goes far beyond all l..
M-4 ...... X.2:12 aim, at which all l. ultimately converges.
M-4 ........ X.3:4 that l. but disappears in its presence. Yet
M-4 ........ X.3:6 teachers to bring true l. to the world.
M-4 ........ X.3:7 bring, for that is "true l." in the world. It
M-5 ........ II.4:4 l. will generalize and transform the world.
M-10 ......... 3:1 unlike the goal of the world's l., is the
M-12 ......... 1:2 perfect teacher, whose l. is complete,
M-13 ......... 2:1 takes great l. both to realize and to accept
M-13 ......... 8:8 Your l. claims it and your learning gives it
M-13 ......... 8:8 Your learning claims it and your l. gives it
M-16 ......... 1:7 one is sent without a l. goal already set,
M-16 ......... 3:3 important throughout the l. process,
M-16 ......... 3:7 are l. within the framework of our course.
M-21 ......... 5:1 this aspect of his l. is the teacher of God's
M-23 ......... 3:4 completed l. guarantees your own success
M-23 ....... 5:10 learn the lesson of salvation through his l.
M-23 ......... 6:4 whose l. far exceeds what we can learn.
M-23 ......... 6:8 and went beyond the farthest reach of l..
M-25 ......... 1:6 Let all his l. and all his efforts be directed
M-28 ......... 1:7 It is the lesson in which l. ends, for it is
P-2.......... II.8:1 What must the teacher do to ensure l.?
P-3.......... I.4:3 are the means sent to him for his l.. What
S-1.......... II.1:3 with l. until it reaches its formless state,
S-1.......... II.3:1 and so it must entail levels of l.. Here, the
S-1.......... II.8:5 Prayer is tied up with l. until the goal of
S-1.......... II.8:5 until the goal of l. has been reached. And
S-1.......... II.8:7 God. Being beyond l., this state cannot be
S-1........ III.3:1 l. goal must be to recognize that prayer
S-1.......... V.4:1 ends with this, for l. is no longer needed.
S-2.......... I.7:2 and your salvation rests on l. this of Him.
S-2.......... I.9:1 learn, before you reach where l. cannot go
S-2.......... I.9:6 be achieved at last, and l. be complete.
S-3........ III.2:8 to find a wiser one who, by his arts and l.,
S-3........ III.3:2 goes to profit by his l. and his skill; to find

## learning's 1

T-31 ....... II.9:7 And in this choice is l. outcome changed,

## learns 29

T-4 ....... VI.3:3 No one who l. from experience that one
T-4 ...... VII.8:1 whenever any mind l. to be wholly helpful
T-6 ..... V.B.1:6 An insane learner l. strange lessons. What

| | |
|---|---|
| T-7........XI.4:4 | Everyone who l. this lesson has become |
| T-14......III.1:3 | learner l. easily because his thoughts are |
| T-14.......V.2:2 | message differently, and l. it differently. |
| T-14.......V.2:3 | Yet until he teaches it and l. it, he will |
| T-25......VI.5:2 | himself, he l. the gift was given to himself, |
| T-26......IV.1:6 | which he l. he has done nothing to forgive |
| T-27.....II.10:4 | No one can forgive until he l. correction is |
| T-29......III.1:7 | Thus he l. it must be his to give. Unless he |
| T-30......IV.3:6 | the child who l. they are no threat to him. |
| T-31......I.10:1 | be remembered when he l. his innocence. |
| T-31.....VII.8:4 | l. when first he looks upon one brother as |
| WpI.. rV.in7:2 | I am renewed each time a brother l. there |
| W-pI...184.6:2 | And everyone who l. to think that it is so |
| W-pI...192.4:3 | but hardly changing him who l. at all. |
| M-2............5:5 | one l. that giving and receiving are the |
| M-3............3:3 | and then l. more and more about the new |
| M-4......I.A.5:8 | this, he l. that where he anticipated grief, |
| M-4.....VI.1:10 | But he l. faster as his trust increases. It is |
| M-9............2:1 | training, he l. one lesson with increasing |
| M-9............2:3 | as the teacher of God l. to give up his own |
| M-21..........4:5 | l. how to let his words be chosen for him |
| M-23..........6:7 | offer them is limited by what he l. himself |
| P-2...........I.1:3 | for no one l. beyond his own readiness. |
| P-2...........I.4:4 | He l. through teaching, and the more |
| P-2...........I.4:4 | is the more he teaches and the more he l.. |
| P-2.........II.3:1 | one who l. to forgive can fail to remember |

## least 47

| | |
|---|---|
| T-4.........V.3:3 | sense the ego's fear of God is at l. logical, |
| T-17......IV.6:2 | You recognize, at l. in general terms, that |
| T-24.........I.2:6 | l. decision to choose attack instead of love |
| T-24.....VII.1:6 | to save his specialness from the l. slight, |
| T-25......IX.3:6 | error is a perception in which one, at l., is |
| T-28.......II.5:2 | you perceive this much at l.: that you have |
| T-29.........I.1:4 | compromise the l. and littlest gap would |
| T-30.........I.8:2 | *At l. I can decide I do not like what I feel now.* |
| T-31.....V.12:3 | and at l. makes way for active choice, and |
| T-31.....VII.7:5 | At l., you merely look on darkness, and |
| W-pI.....19.5:1 | at l. three practice periods are required, |
| W-pI.....20.5:1 | and positively at l. twice an hour today, |
| W-pI.....22.3:1 | the world about you at l. five times today, |
| W-pI.....22.3:1 | times today, for at l. a minute each time. |
| W-pI.....27.3:2 | It should be used at l. every half hour, and |
| W-pI.....28.1:4 | If you are willing at l. to make them now, |
| W-pI....29.5:10 | the idea for today at l. once an hour, |
| W-pI....29.5:11 | At l. once or twice, you should experience |
| W-pI.....44.4:1 | Have at l. three practice periods today, |
| W-pI.....46.3:1 | at l. three full five-minute practice periods |
| W-pI.....49.3:1 | at l. four five-minute practice periods |
| WpI...rI.in.2:2 | each one should be practiced at l. once. |
| W-pI.....64.6:5 | At l. once devote ten or fifteen minutes |
| W-pI.....65.8:1 | should be undertaken at l. once an hour, |
| W-pI...76.12:1 | today; at l. four or five times an hour, as |
| W-pI...93.10:3 | At l. remember to repeat these thoughts |
| W-pI...93.10:6 | try to devote at l. a minute or so to closing |
| W-pI.....94.5:1 | of every hour, at l. remind yourself hourly |
| W-pI.....97.3:2 | awareness is brought a little nearer at l.; |
| W-pI.....98.5:4 | made a thousand losing bargains at the l.. |
| W-pI...102.1:3 | now, at l. enough to let you question it, |
| W-pI...105.9:2 | At l. remember hourly to say the words |
| WpI. rIII.in8:2 | l. try to divide them so you undertake one |
| W-pI.122.14:1 | attempts to think of them at l. a minute as |
| W-pI.127.12:2 | At l. three times an hour think of one who |
| W-pI...135.8:2 | valueless and hardly worth the l. defense, |
| W-pI.153.15:3 | Five minutes now becomes the l. we give |
| W-pI...159.6:4 | no one is denied his l. request or his most |
| W-pI...196.6:3 | Until you see that this, at l., must be |
| W-pI...196.7:1 | form must first be changed at l. as much |
| W-pI...196.7:2 | From there you can at l. consider if you |
| M-16..........5:8 | at l. be sure that you do not forget a brief |
| M-21..........1:8 | the exclusion, or at l. the control, of |
| M-24..........1:9 | At l., such misuse offers preoccupation |
| P-1.............4:4 | Until this is at l. in part accepted, the |
| P-2.........V.6:5 | the smallest willingness, the l. advance, |
| S-1........IV.1:1 | Until the second level at l. begins, one |

## leave 166

*See also* Appendix C

| | |
|---|---|
| T-2.......VII.2:1 | I cannot let you l. your mind unguarded, |
| T-4.........I.10:3 | L. it behind! Do not listen to it and do not |
| T-4.........I.11:4 | to l. it empty by their own dispossession. |
| T-4.........I.13:2 | A father can safely l. a child with an elder |
| T-4........IV.5:2 | not. L. the "sins" of the ego to me. That is |
| T-5.........II.5:6 | When you chose to l. Him He gave you a |
| T-5.........II.6:8 | God did not l. His children comfortless, |
| T-5.........II.6:8 | even though they chose to l. Him. The |
| T-5........IV.3:5 | spirit do not l. the mind that thinks them, |
| T-5........IV.6:5 | I will never l. you or forsake you, because |
| T-8........III.4:7 | Do not l. anyone without giving salvation |
| T-8.........V.6:6 | L. all illusions behind, and reach beyond |
| T-8........VI.5:4 | l. you any more than you left your Creator |
| T-9... VIII.10:2 | while you l. your part of it empty your |
| T-11.........I.4:2 | You who made delay can l. time behind |
| T-11.......II.5:8 | patience, for He cannot l. a part of God. |
| T-11......VI.6:3 | The freedom to l. behind everything that |
| T-11... VIII.1:5 | translated into knowledge will l. you but |
| T-12.......II.5:4 | of hatred will not l. you without help, and |
| T-13......III.2:2 | it is this place that you have sought to l.. |
| T-13......III.7:5 | l. any spot of pain hidden from His light, |
| T-13....VI.13:8 | he slept, Christ's vision did not l. him. |
| T-13.....VII.5:9 | and waits for you to l. the past behind |
| T-13...VII.13:1 | L., then, your needs to Him. He will |
| T-13... VIII.8:2 | will l. no one untouched and no one left |
| T-13. VIII.10:7 | He l. His Own beloved Son outside them, |
| T-14.......II.8:2 | them, and they will not l. you asleep. The |
| T-14.....III.12:6 | and l. all decisions to His gentle counsel. |
| T-14......IV.5:4 | L. all decisions to the One Who speaks for |
| T-14.......V.1:8 | L. the world of death behind, and return |
| T-14.....V.11:1 | the holy circle of Atonement or l. outside, |
| T-14.....V.11:3 | If you l. him without, you join him there. |
| T-14......VI.6:6 | L. what you would communicate to Him. |
| T-14...VII.5:12 | L. that to Him Who knows. You are not |
| T-14......IX.5:5 | You need but l. the mirror clean and clear |
| T-14.......X.1:7 | enter into it they l. all reflections behind. |
| T-14....XI.15:5 | of you. L. room for Him, and you will find |
| T-15.......I.15:1 | friend, if you l. it to the Holy Spirit to use. |
| T-15......I.15:11 | Spirit, and l. His giving it to you to Him. |
| T-15......III.8:1 | Is it a sacrifice to l. littleness behind, and |
| T-15....III.11:1 | If you are wholly willing to l. salvation to |
| T-15......IV.3:3 | For you l. empty your place in His plan, |
| T-15... VIII.1:1 | for the Holy Spirit must not l. you as your |
| T-15... VIII.3:1 | Relate only with what will never l. you, |
| T-15... VIII.3:1 | never leave you, and what you can never l. |
| T-15... VIII.6:4 | L., then, what seems to you to be |
| T-15......IX.1:4 | Given this willingness it will not l. you, |
| T-15.......X.9:1 | no bargains and would l. you nothing. |
| T-15......XI.3:3 | L. nothing behind, for release is total, and |
| T-16.........I.7:4 | if you l. them all to Him Whose function |
| T-16.........I.7:9 | L. Him His function, for He will fulfill it if |
| T-16......VI.8:4 | This will not l. you homeless and without |
| T-17.....V.10:3 | not your choice will l. you comfortless, for |
| T-17...VII.8:12 | You can l. nothing of yourself outside it |
| T-18......III.4:2 | believe that I would l. you in the darkness |
| T-18......III.4:2 | the darkness that you agreed to l. with me |
| T-18......VI.1:3 | not depart from it nor l. it separate from |
| T-18......IX.3:7 | Him not to abandon you and l. you there. |
| T19....IV.B.2:2 | it would dispossess, and l. you homeless. |
| T19...IV.D.7:2 | will occur is you will l. the world forever. |
| T-20.....II.11:2 | He will not l. you, nor forsake the savior |
| T-20......IV.7:6 | You could no more l. one of them outside |
| T-20......IV.7:6 | one of them outside than I could l. you, |
| T-20......VI.9:1 | and l. no trace behind their going. The |
| T-20......VII.2:2 | are refusing to l. the means to Him Who |
| T-21.......II.6:6 | l. himself without what God has willed for |
| T-21.......II.8:1 | l. your altars free of what you placed upon |
| T-21......VI.3:6 | easy to l. the home of madness if you see |
| T-21......VI.3:7 | not l. insanity by going somewhere else. |
| T-21......VI.3:8 | l. it simply by accepting reason where |
| T-21......VI.8:7 | direct you how to l. insanity behind. Hide |
| T-21...VII.13:8 | And none can l. the thinker's mind, or |
| T-21...VII.13:8 | the thinker's mind, or l. him unaffected. |
| T-22.......II.2:3 | To l. one kind of misery and seek another |
| T-22.......II.9:3 | meaningless idea that thoughts can l. the |
| T-22.......II.9:6 | the Son of God could l. his Father's Mind, |
| T-22......VI.9:3 | L. this to Him. Let your concern be only |
| T-23.......in.5:4 | L. him not frightened and alone in his |
| T-23......IV.6:5 | When they occur l. not your place on high |
| T-24.........I.2:5 | their mercy while you decide to l. it there. |
| T-24........II.9:6 | L. all illusions of yourself outside this |
| T-24......III.3:3 | frail. Illusions l. it perfectly unmoved and |
| T-24......VI.1:6 | For He could never l. His Own creation. |
| T-25......IV.4:8 | can never fall away and l. you homeless. |
| T-25......IX.9:2 | that you perceive and l. you fair to no one |
| T-26.....VII.4:7 | Ideas l. not their source, and their effects |
| T-26...VII.12:3 | the firm conviction that ideas can l. their |
| T-26...VII.13:2 | this must still be true because ideas l. not |
| T-26...VII.13:5 | And to believe ideas can l. their source is |
| T-26......IX.5:3 | that light may shine on it and l. no space |
| T-27......II.15:3 | It cannot l. mistakes in one unhealed and |
| T-27......II.16:3 | L., then, correction to the Mind that is |
| T-27......III.4:3 | For what you l. as vacant God will fill, and |
| T-27......IV.7:4 | though they l. the first unanswered. In |
| T-27.....V.10:1 | L., then, the transfer of your learning to |
| T-27....VIII.9:8 | And you will l. the holy instant with your |
| T-28......III.8:5 | miracle would l. no proof of guilt to bring |
| T-29.........I.1:9 | and l. a gap between you and His Love, |
| T-29.........I.7:5 | away, and l. you quietly alone in "peace." |
| T-29......IV.1:6 | dreams to l. untouched by its beneficence |
| T-29....VIII.3:3 | and cannot l. the mind that is its source. |
| T-30........II.2:5 | And would God l. His Son without what |
| T-31.........I.9:1 | and that you do not l. its call unheard. |
| T-31.....V.16:4 | it will go at last, and l. your mind at peace |
| T-31....VIII.3:3 | would not l. one source of pain unhealed, |
| T-31....VIII.3:5 | He would not l. you comfortless, alone in |
| W-pI.....41.7:4 | are trying to l. appearances and approach |
| W-pI.....44.5:4 | l. behind everything that you now believe, |
| W-pI.....45.2:5 | think with the Mind of God l. your mind, |
| W-pI.....45.2:5 | because thoughts do not l. their source. |
| W-pI.....45.4:2 | will attempt to l. the unreal and seek for |
| W-pI.....57.1:6 | I can l. simply by walking out. Nothing |
| W-pI.....63.2:4 | your function and l. the Son of God in |
| WpI..rII.in.5:4 | day not to l. your function unfulfilled. |
| W-pI.....91.5:1 | which you try to l. your weakness behind. |
| W-pI.....92.8:2 | its abode can l. without a miracle before |
| W-pI...92.10:4 | L., then, the dark a little while today, and |
| W-pI...125.4:3 | holiness that He created and will never l.. |
| W-pI.127.10:3 | the past. Today we l. the past behind us, |
| W-pI.127.12:1 | because we cannot l. a part of us outside |
| W-pI...128.1:3 | if he would l. the world behind and soar |
| W-pI...128.5:2 | l. it free of purposes we gave its aspects |
| W-pI.131.10:1 | L. foolish thoughts like these behind |
| W-pI...132.5:3 | Ideas l. not their source. This central |
| W-pI.132.10:3 | ideas because ideas l. not their source, |
| W-pI...156.1:3 | in the text; ideas l. not their source. If this |
| W-pI...157.4:3 | wherein you quickly l. the world behind. |
| W-pI...159.9:2 | His lilies do not l. their home when they |
| W-pI...159.9:4 | They do not l. their source, but carry its |
| W-pI...160.2:4 | will not l. because a madman says I must. |
| W-pI...160.5:3 | And so I l. my home to one more like me |
| W-pI...163.3:1 | l. the taste of dust and ashes in their wake |
| W-pI...164.8:2 | and l. a clean and open space within your |
| W-pI...167.3:6 | Ideas l. not their source. The emphasis |
| W-pI...167.4:3 | is the fixed belief ideas can l. their source, |
| W-pI.167.11:3 | l. the Source of life from where it came. |
| W-pI...170.4:2 | it is obvious ideas must l. their source, for |
| W-pI.170.11:5 | This time you l. it there. And you return |
| W-pI.182.10:1 | each time a wanderer would l. his home. |
| W-pI...184.6:4 | l. no doubt that what is named is there. It |
| W-pI.186.10:1 | and l. your mind unclouded and serene, |
| W-pI...187.9:5 | and l. instead the perfect gift forever there |
| W-pI...190.2:5 | not l. the Son whom It created out of love. |
| W-pI...193.9:2 | He would not l. an unforgiving thought |
| W-pI...197.2:4 | Nor will you l. the prison house, or claim |
| W-pI...200.8:1 | will cross, to l. this world behind. But |
| W-pI.200.11:5 | happy way to l. the world of ambiguity, |
| W-pII ....in.1:4 | the times in which we l. the world of pain, |
| W-pII ....in.6:2 | Him Who taught us how to l. the world of |
| W-pII .225.2:4 | your hand to me, and I will never l. you. |
| W-pII .243.2:1 | *Father, today I l. creation free to be itself. I* |
| W-pII .275.2:1 | *all things today, and so I l. all things to You. I* |
| W-pII .314.2:2 | *free. Now do we l. the future in Your Hands,* |
| W-pII .316.1:2 | l. no shadow on the holy mind my Father |
| W-pII .331.1:4 | *You could never l. me desolate, to die within* |
| Wfl........in.1:4 | To Him we l. these lessons, as to Him we |

W-ep ......... 6:8 sure; that I will never l. you comfortless.
M-14 ......... 3:6 God must learn to pass by and l. behind.
M-14 ......... 4:3 those not yet prepared to l. the world and
M-21 ......... 5:5 self-perception which he would l. behind.
M-23 ......... 7:4 God l. anyone without a very present help
M-26 ......... 1:8 enables others to l. the world with them.
C-3........... 4:12 It is the final step. And this we l. to God.
C-5............. 6:7 and l. them both to find the peace of God.
S-1 ......... V.1:3 Let it but l. the ground where it begins to
S-2 ........ III.7:5 He will not l. you comfortless, nor fail to

## leaves 30

T-1.........I.34:3 spirit's strength l. no room for intrusions.
T-1....... II.3:13 l. me in a state which is only potential in
T-3........ VI.8:9 This l. you in a position where it sounds
T-6........ IV.9:5 This l. you in charge of the Kingdom,
T-12... VII.13:3 The death penalty never l. the ego's mind,
T-13....... VI.1:2 sight, for reality l. no room for any error.
T-13... VII.11:2 again and again to get, it l. you nothing,
T-14..... III.17:2 He l. you no one outside you. And so He
T-14...... IX.4:7 and l. not what It created holy as Itself.
T-15.........I.4:6 which it craves for you, l. it unsatisfied.
T19..IV.C.2:14 We know that an idea l. not its source.
T-25...... IX.4:2 Holy Spirit's perception l. no ground for
T-26.... III.1:12 is everything l. room for nothing else. Yet
T-27.......I.11:3 This l. no space in which a different view,
T-27.... IV.4:17 It l. no room to question its beliefs, except
T-27....... V.4:5 l. nothing within the world that could be
W-pI... 105.2:4 and l. you nothing in the ones you take.
W-pI... 136.1:5 and merely l. them there to disappear.
W-pI. 153.19:4 never l. our weakness unsupported by His
W-pI... 156.4:4 and lay their l. before you on the ground
W-pI... 157.2:4 It l. us here an instant, and we go beyond
W-pI... 157.3:3 more swiftly to this holy place and l. you,
W-pI... 157.6:3 Yet it l. a vision in our eyes which we can
W-pI... 186.9:5 blow across his mind like wind-swept l.
W-pI... 188.3:2 l. a blessing with it that remains forever
W-pI... 192.4:1 and l. the world a clean and unmarked
W-pI... 194.9:5 choice for us that l. temptation far behind
W-pI... 195.3:1 and l. you nothing but a black despair so
W-pI. 200.10:3 the road is carpeted with l. of false desires
S-1 .........in.2:4 l. separate goals and separate interests by,

## leaving 25

T-1........ III.4:6 but he does direct, l. it up to you to follow
T-7....... VII.3:4 escape from this image by l. it behind.
T-13...... IV.1:5 l. you no inheritance except the dust out
T-13.VII.10:13 it bids you get, l. you no joy in them.
T-15....... III.7:5 to His Son's creations, but without l. you.
T-16....... V.2:2 guilty, l. the Sonship open to attack and
T-16..... V.11:3 truth, triumphing over it and l. it helpless
T-18...... VI.7:7 would not escape from it, l. it unharmed,
T-18..VIII.10:3 l. no lonely little kingdoms locked away
T-18..VIII.10:3 locked away from love, and l. you inside.
T19... IV.A.1:4 it gently reaches out, but never l. you. If
T-20...... IV.8:5 and l. in your way no stones to trip on,
T-20.... VI.10:5 l. the body thankfully behind and resting
T-22...... IV.3:8 He will return with you, not l. it nor you.
T-24...... III.2:7 to it, l. him alone and unforgiven, and
T-26...... III.5:6 l. room to make the only choice that can
T-27......... V.4:6 withheld its peace and comfort, l. it to die
T-29...... III.4:3 will not forget his savior, l. him unsaved.
T-31...... IV.1:7 you escape from them by l. them behind?
W-pI..... 92.7:1 it sees, l. its dreams as fearful as itself. No
W-pI... 107.1:4 l. not a trace by which to be remembered.
W-pI... 191.3:3 of hope, l. you nothing but the wish to die
W-pII ..... 8.5:2 as it goes, and l. but the truth to be itself.
W-pII . 314.2:2 *in Your Hands, l. behind our past mistakes,*
S-3 ......... II.6:1 cure, l. the cause of illness still unchanged

## led 36

T-1......... V.6:1 chosen to be l. by me in Christ's service.
T-3............I.1:6 l. many people to be bitterly afraid of God
T-5........ IV.6:2 you are l. back to God where you belong,
T-6............I.2:7 and how it actually l. to the resurrection
T-6.........I.10:6 is inevitably l. to demonstrate His way for
T-7 ....... VI.7:4 within it that have l. to a state of war, and
T-12 ..... VI.6:3 Holy Spirit has at last l. you to Christ at
T-13 ..... VII.3:3 The roads you made have l. you nowhere,
T-14 ...... III.9:2 of the concept of decision that l. to it. It is
T-14 ... III.17:4 In everything be l. by Him, and do not
T-14 ...... IV.6:2 and you will be l. as gently as if you were
T-14 ... VIII.4:3 And there you must be l., through gentle
T-16 ...... V.6:2 worlds has merely l. to fantasies of both,
T-18 ...... III.1:3 Each dream has l. to other dreams, and
T-18 ...... III.8:5 you undertook apart, and that l. nowhere.
T-18 ... VI.14:7 joined it where it is and where it l. you, in
T-18 ... IX.10:4 Here you are l., that God Himself can take
T19... IV.D.8:2 it was surely not the ego that l. you here.
T19... IV.D.9:6 given in a holy instant, has l. you. And let
T-20 ......II.11:7 it to him shall you be l. past fear to love.
T-21 ..... III.8:6 sin are given vision, and are l. to holiness.
T-24 ...... V.5:5 light, that you may lead as you were l..
T-28 ...... III.1:2 up the ladder separation l. you down. The
T-31 ...... IV.3:5 And learning they l. nowhere, lost their
W-pI..... 55.5:6 world has l. to a frightening picture of it.
W-pI..... 71.8:5 They have l. to depression and anger; but
W-pI... 92.11:3 l. away from darkness to the light where
W-pI... 125.2:3 He is not l. by force, but only love. He is
W-pI... 131.4:6 off, he is l. back to his appointed task.
W-pI... 132.6:4 let himself be l. along the road to truth.
W-pI. 135.18:4 for death, He l. you gently to eternal life.
WpI...rV.in6:5 in his mind the way that l. him out, and
W-pII . 225.1:3 *the way Your loving Son is l. along to You!*
W-pII . 253.1:6 am I l. past this world to my creations,
M-23 ......... 5:1 Jesus has l. the way. Why would you not
C-5 ............ 3:2 He l. the way for you to follow him. He

## left 151

T-3 ........ V.9:6 anyone has everything, there is nothing l..
T-3 ..... VI.8:10 The dispute over authorship has l. such
T-3 .... VII.6:11 The world is not l. by death but by truth,
T-4 ....... IV.2:5 you have done and l. undone accordingly,
T-5 ....... IV.8:2 is gone, and nothing is l. but a blessing. I
T-6 .......II.10:5 mind to God, because it has never l. Him.
T-6 .......II.10:6 Him. If it has never l. Him, you need only
T-6 ....... IV.6:4 will be nothing l. of your dream when you
T-7 ...VIII.3:12 the projections have not l. their minds,
T-7 .........X.7:2 of God, Who has not l. you comfortless.
T-8 ....... VI.4:1 This son of a loving father l. his home and
T-8 ....... VI.5:4 you any more than you l. your Creator,
T-8 .....VIII.9:8 when interpretation is l. to the Holy Spirit
T-11 .... V.15:2 it and is l. with a series of fragmented
T-12 ........I.8:4 If you were l. with the fear, once you had
T-13 VII.10:10 is a dangerous concept if it is l. to you.
T-13 ...VIII.8:2 no one untouched and no one l. alone.
T-14 ....... V.8:4 with no one l. outside to suffer guilt alone
T-14 ..... IX.3:8 you. God has not l. His altar, though His
T-15 ..... III.5:5 He has not l. you, and you have not left
T-15 ..... III.5:5 has not left you, and you have not l. Him.
T-15 . XI.10:10 and take your place, so long l. unfulfilled,
T-16 .........I.7:4 No needs will long be l. unmet if you
T-16 ..... III.5:2 God, He l. neither God nor His creation.
T-16 ... III.5:10 For nothing real has ever l. the mind of its
T-16 ..... VI.5:5 more is l. outside than would be taken in,
T-16 ..... VI.5:5 for God is l. without and *nothing* taken in.
T-17 ..... III.7:5 has l. no part of it without Himself. This
T-17 ..... VI.3:6 And now the only judgment l. to make is
T-17 ...VIII.1:3 of faithlessness, withheld and l. unused,
T-18 .........I.7:3 It has not l. you, to go out into the mad
T-18 .........I.8:2 stillness dwells the living God you never l.
T-18 .........I.8:2 God you never left, and Who never l. you.
T-18 ..... VI.1:4 who l. not his Father and dwells not apart
T-19 .......II.6:7 can be corrected, if truth be l. to judge it.
T19....IV.C.5:7 His Own; an Answer which l. Him not,
T19. IV.D.19:2 established for salvation will be l. undone
T-20 ..... VI.9:7 transcended them, and l. them far behind
T-21 .......II.7:2 But you have not l. open and unoccupied
T-21 .....II.13:6 which you were created, and have never l.
T-21 .... VII.8:1 last question you have l. unanswered still.
T-22 .......in.2:7 they think that there is nothing l. to steal,
T-22 ..... III.6:2 the idea they represent l. not its maker,
T-23 ..... III.6:3 door is open; you have l. the battleground
T-23 ..... III.6:8 one tree l. still standing will shelter you.
T-24 ..... III.4:2 Would God have l. His Son in such a state
T-24 ..... III.5:6 to be brought to Them, and l. behind.
T-24 ... IV.3:15 given specialness has l. you bankrupt and
T-25 .... VII.9:5 Nor is he l. without escape from madness,
T-25 .... VII.9:6 He can no more be l. outside, without a
T-25 ... VIII.8:5 For love has lost when judgment l. its side
T-25 ..... IX.4:6 no one l. unfairly treated and deprived,
T-26 ........ IV.h Where Sin Has L.
T-26 ..... IV.2:6 space that sin l. vacant do they join as one
T-26 ..... IV.3:1 you stand is but the space that sin has l..
T-26 ..... IV.3:4 stand upon the ground where sin has l. a
T-26 ..... VI.3:2 realized its emptiness has l. yours empty
T-26 .... VII.4:9 of what is in, and has not l. its source.
T-26 ..... IX.2:1 l. without a single one you cherish still?
T-26 ........X.6:3 unfairly l. without a purpose in a futile
T-27 .....II.14:5 And only what is l. without his presence
T-27 .....II.16:1 Correction must be l. to One Who knows
T-27 ..... III.6:1 so lately l. unoccupied and vacant will not
T-27 ..... III.6:7 is God l. free to take the final step Himself
T-27 ..... IV.2:5 your problems should be brought and l..
T-27 .......V.6:1 that is there received is l. behind on your
T-28 ........I.2:3 went its consequences, l. without a cause.
T-28 ......I.15:5 l. a stranded Son forever on a shore where
T-28 ..... III.6:1 space l. clean and vacant by the miracle.
T-28 ..... III.7:3 have nothing l. behind the open door.
T-28 ..... III.9:2 the more is l. for all the rest to share. The
T-28 ..... IV.7:6 has l. the space between them vacant.
T-28 ..... IV.8:5 l. clean of all the seeds of sickness and of
T-28 .......V.6:5 has l. no room for them in any place or
T-29 .......V.1:2 There is a place in you which time has l.,
T-29 .......V.5:6 for they have l. their hold on every vain
T-29 ... VIII.7:5 l. no room for anything to be except His
T-29 ..... IX.8:5 holiness that never l. the altar that abides
T-30 ... III.10:5 Thought God holds of you has never l. the
T-30 ..... IV.2:7 made him safe, and thought that it had l..
T-30 .......V.3:7 step in which is all forgiveness l. behind.
T-30 .... VII.1:1 Would God have l. the meaning of the
T-31 ........I.8:3 nor l. unanswered in the selfsame tongue
T-31 ........I.9:2 Without your answer is it l. to die, as it is
T-31 ......I.13:5 away, and l. a place for truth to be reborn.
T-31 ..... IV.9:1 has not l. His Thoughts! But you forgot
T-31 ..... IV.9:6 Yet has He never l. His Thoughts to die,
T-31 ... IV.10:1 He has not l. His Thoughts! He could no
T-31 .....V.17:5 is the truth l. free to enter in its sanctuary,
T-31 ... VIII.3:3 nor any image l. to veil the truth. He
T-31 ... VIII.5:7 by, and nothing l. to interfere with truth.
W-pI .... 14.3:4 You will not be l. there. You will go far
W-pI .... 45.3:4 because they cannot have l. their source.
W-pI .... 56.5:4 of God, Who has not l. His Thoughts.
W-pI .... 68.5:5 This has l. you alone in all the universe in
W-pI .... 75.2:6 one has l. no trace upon it in its passing.
WpI.. rII.in.1:2 We will begin where our last review l. off,
W-pI .... 85.3:4 It has not l. its Source, and so it cannot
W-pI .... 85.3:4 Source, and so it cannot have l. my mind.
W-pI .... 94.3:7 Self that never l. Its home in God to walk
W-pI .. 123.2:2 your Father has not l. you to yourself, nor
W-pI .. 125.8:4 let Him tell you God has never l. His Son,
W-pI .. 125.8:4 His Son, and you have never l. your Self.
W-pI .. 133.7:1 someone else, you will have nothing l..
W-pI 134.12:5 his foot to stride ahead a star is l. behind,
W-pI .. 140.4:7 with nothing l. to which it can return.
W-pI 152.11:6 never l. will come again to our awareness,
W-pI .. 153.9:2 for we have l. all fearful thoughts behind.
W-pI 153.13:1 l. alone in terror in a fearful world made
W-pI .. 154.9:3 you need, nor has it been l. unaccepted.
W-pI 154.12:3 that God Himself has l. no gift beyond
W-pI .. 155.5:1 deprivation both are quickly l. behind.
W-pI 155.10:2 with nothing l. to keep the truth apart
W-pI .. 158.1:3 Nor have you l. your Source, remaining as
W-pI .. 164.5:3 of judgment l. to Him Who judges true.
W-pI .. 165.2:2 It l. you not, nor have you ever been apart
W-pI .. 165.2:5 is one with you because it l. you not. The
W-pI .. 165.2:7 the Thought of God has l. you not, and
W-pI .. 195.3:3 as little l. within his grasping fingers as in
W-pI .. 196.8:5 back within the holy mind He never l..
W-pI .. 197.9:3 And from this Self is no one l. outside.
W-pII .... in.4:2 He has not l. His Son in all his madness,
W-pII . 227.2:1 return to Heaven, which we never really l.
W-pII . 228.2:2 *not l. that Source to enter in a body and to die*

W-pII..234.1:1 have reached the holy peace we never l..
W-pII......3.1:2 is born of error, and it has not l. its source
W-pII..241.2:2 *Father, Your Son, who never l., returns to*
W-pII..260.1:2 *as Your Thought, I have not l. my Source,*
W-pII......6.1:4 He has not l. His holy home, nor lost the
W-pII..280.1:3 Thought of God has l. its Father's Mind.
W-pII..289.2:2 *present world the past has l. untouched and*
W-pII..319.1:3 up the space the ego l. unoccupied by lies.
W-pII..326.1:1 *Mind, a holy Thought that never l. its home.*
W-pII..331.1:2 *and be l. without a certain way to his release?*
W-pII..331.1:5 *How could I think that Love has l. Itself?*
W-pII..352.1:6 *way. You have not l. me comfortless. I have*
W-pII.....358.h to God can be unheard nor l. Unanswered
Wfl ........in.1:1 will be l. as free of words as possible. We
M-21..........3:7 Son of God has but this power l. to him. It
M-22..........3:6 What, then, is l. to heal? The body has
M-28........3:10 is l. to contradict the Word of God. There
C-2.............7:6 you l. behind at last and finally passed by.
C-5.............1:1 help to enter Heaven for you have never l.
S-1 ...........I.5:6 to ask because there is nothing l. to want.
S-1 ......... II.7:3 you. The things of earth are l. behind, all
S-1 ......... II.8:3 for a ladder to reach what one has never l.
S-1 ....... V.3:12 For you have understood he never l., and
S-3 ...........I.2:2 It has not l. its source, and in its pain and
S-3 ........IV.4:5 and understood that you have never l..
S-3 ........IV.6:5 your Father loves, who never l. his home,
S-3 ........IV.8:5 Return to Me Who never l. My Son.

**legal** 1

W-pI...135.2:4 armaments, its l. definitions and its codes

**legion** 4

T-6....... II.13:2 The ego is l., but the Holy Spirit is One.
T-14....... X.3:2 They can be simultaneous and l.. This is
W-pI.127.10:1 Today the l. of the future years of waiting
C-5.............1:6 Their names are l., but we will not go

**legions** 4

T-27.....VII.6:6 mighty l. of its witnesses for its undoing.
W-pI.137.10:4 And l. upon legions will receive the gift
W-pI.137.10:4 And legions upon l. will receive the gift
W-pI...191.3:2 tiny particle of dust against the l. of your

**legitimate** 2

T-12....... V.7:4 obvious. Every l. teaching aid, every real
M-4...... X.2:11 curriculum makes no effort to exceed its l.

**leisure** 1

W-pI.......1.4:3 A comfortable sense of l. is essential.

**leisurely** 1

W-pI.....11.3:2 be used in an unhurried, even l. fashion.

**lend** 3

T-4........ VI.6:7 because I will l. them my strength as long
T-24......... V.5:2 Be glad that only Christ can l. you His,
T-27.........I.6:6 and l. conviction to the system they speak

**lending** 1

W-pI...105.2:2 interest to be paid in full; a temporary l.,

**lends** 4

T-2... V.A.14:5 content, it l. itself to projection.
T-4...........I.7:3 particularly any situation that l. itself to
W-pI...153.1:1 the "gifts" it merely l. to take away again;
C-4.............2:3 but l. itself to thoughts of sin and guilt.

**length** 5

T-2..... VIII.2:6 Its l. can, however, be greatly shortened
T-31..... VII.3:3 and will at l. be seen as little more than
W-pI.....16.6:3 The l. of the exercise period should also
W-pI.....17.4:2 l. of the practice period may be reduced
W-pI.....19.5:1 shortening the l. of time involved, if

**lens** 3

M-19 .........3:2 is the l. which, held before the body's eyes
M-19 .........3:2 that made the l. and holds it very dear.
M-19 .........4:7 giving God the l. of warped perception

**lent** 2

T-13..... VII.8:5 For all else you have l. yourself in time,
W-pI...197.6:2 never think the gifts of God are l. but for a

**leper's** 1

T19... IV.D.2:3 make the face of Christ Himself like to a l.

**less** 111

T-1...........I.8:1 more for those who temporarily have l..
T-1......... V.6:6 nothing is l. stable than an upside-down
T-3......... V.7:5 without a belief in "more" and "l.." At
T-4......... II.6:8 and is therefore temporarily l. predatory.
T-4........ IV.8:4 do. Do not settle for anything l. than this,
T-6...........I.6:7 l. extreme temptations to misperceive,
T-6......V.A.4:8 Nothing more and nothing l.. Without a
T-6...... V.B.4:2 which would be much l. acceptable to it,
T-9........ VI.3:6 than they but they are not l. than He is.
T-9...... VI.3:11 cannot, then, be l. glorious than He is.
T-11...... VI.3:6 you will become l. and less willing to deny
T-11...... VI.3:6 you will become less and l. willing to deny
T-13....... X.1:3 onto what you believed to be l. fearful.
T-13....... X.5:3 A minute, even l., will be enough to free
T-14....... II.2:5 and nothing are you l. inclined to listen to
T-14..... VII.2:8 the more you look at fear the l. you see it,
T-15.... III.4:10 Son be content with l. than everything.
T-15.... III.4:11 cannot be content with l. than his Father
T-15...... III.8:3 is sacrifice to accept anything l. than glory
T-15.... III.10:4 His Will. Accept no l., remembering that
T-15....... V.6:3 placed l. value on one and more on the
T-15..... V.10:5 as He loves you; neither l. nor more. He
T-15....... X.7:3 ego seems to demand l. of you than God,
T-16..... VII.3:9 But what is l. obvious is that the present
T-17...... III.4:6 And the l. the other really brings to the
T-17.... IV.13:4 darkness and of death grows l. convincing
T-18...... IV.3:2 require that you be not content with l.
T-18. VIII.11:4 it offers everyone, neither l. nor more.
T-19.........I.5:2 in how they operate is l. apparent, though
T-21........in.1:3 though it is no more than that, it is not l..
T-21...... VI.9:9 blessed than to receive. But neither is it l..
T-23.........I.9:2 vanquisher of the illusion that was l. real,
T-23..... II.20:5 attack are no l. certain in their witnessing,
T-23...... IV.9:7 And what is there that offers l., yet could
T-24...... IV.3:7 as one. Nothing could make l. sense to
T-24.... VI.12:1 pursue another goal with far l. vigilance;
T-25...... VI.2:4 l. painful to the eyes than what is wholly
T-25..... VII.9:3 sees within the world, offer him l. and less
T-25..... VII.9:3 sees within the world, offer him less and l.
T-25... VIII.4:9 total cost, the greater his the l. is yours.
T-25. VIII.13:7 or l. is not aware that he has everything.
T-25...... IX.2:5 Nor is the treasure l. as it is given out.
T-25...... IX.6:4 deserves to suffer more and others l.?
T-25...... IX.6:7 to be withheld from others as l. worthy,
T-25...... IX.7:2 and kept apart from others as l. deserving
T-26....... II.4:4 injustices as great or small, or more or l..
T-26....... II.8:6 you should offer or receive l. than He gave
T-26..... VII.6:1 be l. amenable to truth than are the rest.
T-26..... VII.6:2 l. willingly offered to truth for healing
T-26... VII.14:4 God's Son could never be content with l.
T-26....... IX.7:4 Son give l. in gratitude for so much more?
T-27....... II.6:1 miracle can offer nothing l. to him than it
T-27....... II.9:7 Holy Spirit be deterred an instant, even l.,
T-27....... V.11:7 will be far l. than all there really are.
T-28..... VII.7:7 and neither l. nor more in worth than the
T-29.........I.9:2 Nothing more than that, and nothing l..
T-29........II.8:4 it asks that God be l. than all He really is.
T-29......II.10:7 cannot be more or l. than what is his.
T-29...... IV.4:6 Dreams are not wanted more or l.. They
T-29.... VIII.9:2 Who can have more, and who be given l.?
T-29.... VIII.9:6 for idols that would make of Heaven l., to
T-29..VIII.9:11 you will never be content with being l..
T-30...... III.8:7 light grew dimmer or l. perfect ever was.
T-30...... VI.4:9 you can merit neither more nor l. than he.
W-pI....... 5.6:1 You may also find yourself l. willing to
W-pI..... 10.5:3 minute or l. if you experience discomfort.
W-pI..... 15.5:2 L. than a minute will do for the practice
W-pI..... 17.4:1 and no l. than three are required for
W-pI..... 17.4:2 reduced to l. than the minute or so that is
W-pI..... 18.3:5 minute or so, or even l., will be sufficient
W-pI..... 26.8:3 you toward the end, l. acceptable to you.
W-pI..... 28.4:5 as to anything else, neither more nor l..
W-pI..... 32.4:1 with not l. than three required. More
W-pI..... 39.9:4 mind becomes more disciplined and l.
W-pI..... 43.5:8 or l. directly to today's idea is suitable.
W-pI... 66.11:3 take more than a minute, and probably l.,
W-pI... 71.10:6 or l. than to remember the Source of your
W-pI..... 77.3:5 that we will not content ourselves with l..
W-pI..... 77.8:1 satisfied with l. than the perfect answer.
W-pI... 102.5:2 You have no need to be l. loving to God's
W-pI... 105.4:4 more, for that implies that it was l. before
W-pI... 105.9:1 but do not think that l. is worthless when
W-pI... 107.2:3 a time,–perhaps a minute, maybe even l.
W-pI... 122.4:2 l. than halfway diligence and partial trust.
W-pI... 124.9:1 be l. if you believe that nothing happens.
W-pI... 136.3:4 that second, even l., in which the choice is
W-pI. 153.15:6 Nor will we willingly give l. at night, in
W-pI. 153.16:2 At times, perhaps, a minute, even l., will
W-pI. 155.12:4 or offer l. and still content the holy Son of
W-pI... 187.2:7 Nor can the form it takes be l. acceptable.
W-pI... 187.5:8 to lose is always something he will value l.
W-pI. 193.10:6 time be l. than meets your deepest need.
W-pI... 195.1:5 for thanks while others have l. cause? And
W-pI... 195.1:6 suffer l. because he sees another suffer
WpI rVI.in.1:2 should not be l. than fifteen minutes, and
W-pII ..... 1.2:3 more obscure; l. easily accessible to doubt
W-pII . 272.1:6 *I will accept no l. than You have given me. I*
W-pII . 288.2:3 He cannot be l. holy than can I, and you
W-pII . 318.1:3 one of more or l. importance than the rest
W-pII . 334.2:2 *Son can be content with nothing l. than this.*
M-in ........ 2:11 you. No more than that, but also never l..
M-5 ........II.3:7 to see. No more and no l.. The world does
M-6 ......... 4:12 exchange can receive l. than everything?
M-8 ........... 1:4 from another with l. intensity of appeal.
M-13 ......... 2:3 cannot mean that you have l. because of it
M-16 ......... 3:3 process, becomes l. and less emphasized.
M-16 ......... 3:3 process, becomes less and l. emphasized.
M-27 ....... 7:10 not let yourself forget it is not l. than this.
P-2......... V.3:6 no l. than all he has to give is worthy of
S-1........ IV.3:6 that it is pitiful to be content with l..
S-3........ IV.1:9 bestow unequal gifts on those l. fortunate

**lessen** 3

T-5.........I.1:11 share an idea, however, you do not l. it.
T-11........II.5:5 ask the ego to enter, you l. His welcome.
W-pI... 105.3:4 gift. God's gifts will never l. when they are

**lessened** 4

T-11.........I.6:4 God's Mind cannot be l.. It can only be
T-11...... IV.2:4 will cannot be l. without the intervention
T-29.........II.8:7 made more and He is l. by the loss of you.
T-29...... III.1:9 Only those who think that God is l. by

**lessens** 2

T-1.........I.47:1 The miracle is a learning device that l. the
T-4........ VI.5:3 how his misery l. as he approaches it. This

**lesser** 4

T-1..........II.3:2 one of a l. order stands before his Creator.
T-15........X.7:3 of the two is judged as the l. of two evils,

| | |
|---|---|
| T-18 III.2:1 | sometimes retreating to the l. forms of |
| S-1 III.6:5 | is lost in the quest for l. goals of any kind, |

**lesson** 192

| | |
|---|---|
| T-2 II.5:2 | The Atonement is the final l.. Learning |
| T-2 VI.6:5 | your own. The l. here is quite simple, but |
| T-3 I.2:11 | wholly benign l. the Atonement teaches is |
| T-3 I.7:8 | The Atonement is therefore the perfect l.. |
| T-3 II.5:9 | it. Understanding the l. of the Atonement |
| T-4 I.3:4 | My l. was like yours, and because I |
| T-4 I.12:2 | Humility is a l. for the ego, not for the |
| T-4 I.13:6 | Let us undertake to learn this l. together |
| T-5 II.3:11 | It is the final l. that I learned, and God's |
| T-6 I.6:3 | This is not a l. a Son of God should want |
| T-6 I.11:5 | My one l., which I must teach as I learned |
| T-6 I.16:6 | The result is a l. in blame, for all behavior |
| T-6 III.1:10 | it. Every l. you teach you are learning. |
| T-6 III.2:1 | That is why you must teach only one l.. If |
| T-6 III.2:5 | This is the one l. that is perfectly unified, |
| T-6 III.2:5 | unified, because it is the only l. that is one |
| T-6 V.A.5:12 | Therefore, His teaching begins with the l.: |
| T-6 V.B.3:2 | the Holy Spirit's first l. was "To have, give |
| T-6 V.B.3:6 | first l. seems to contain a contradiction, |
| T-6 V.B.3:7 | l. cannot be learned consistently as yet. |
| T-6 V.B.3:9 | respects, the first l. is the hardest to learn. |
| T-6 V.B.4:1 | the ego perceives the first l. as insane. In |
| T-6 V.B.5:5 | you. Its l. is not insane; the conflict is. |
| T-6 V.B.7:4 | Therefore, His second l. is: *To have peace,* |
| T-6 V.C.2:7 | Therefore, the Holy Spirit's third l. is: *Be* |
| T-6 V.C.3:3 | It has advanced far from the first l., which |
| T-6 V.C.4:3 | This l. teaches not only that you can be, |
| T-6 V.C.4:5 | This l. is unequivocal in that it teaches |
| T-7 II.6:3 | Spirit's teaching is a l. in remembering. I |
| T-7 III.1:1 | Holy Spirit teaches one l., and applies it |
| T-7 III.2:8 | It is therefore a l. you cannot really learn, |
| T-7 V.2:6 | An inconsistent l. will be poorly taught |
| T-7 V.7:4 | little. His healing l. is limited by his own |
| T-7 V.7:4 | own ingratitude, which is a l. in sickness. |
| T-7 V.7:8 | to learn a l. that seems contradictory;– |
| T-7 VII.7:2 | all minds and He teaches the same l. to all |
| T-7 IX.7:4 | The miracle is a l. in total perception. By |
| T-7 IX.7:5 | By including any part of totality in the l., |
| T-7 X.8:4 | The miracle is therefore a l. in what joy is. |
| T-7 X.8:5 | Being a l. in sharing it is a lesson in love, |
| T-7 X.8:5 | Being a lesson in sharing it is a l. in love, |
| T-7 X.8:6 | Every miracle is thus a l. in truth, and by |
| T-7 XI.4:2 | There are no exceptions to this l., because |
| T-7 XI.4:2 | because the lack of exceptions *is* the l.. |
| T-7 XI.4:3 | the Kingdom with this l. in his heart has |
| T-7 XI.4:4 | Everyone who learns this l. has become |
| T-8 II.3:5 | Spirit's l. because that is what you *are.* The |
| T-8 II.3:6 | The l. is that your will and God's cannot |
| T-8 II.4:2 | This unnatural l. cannot be learned, and |
| T-8 IV.6:9 | Father. This is the only l. I came to teach. |
| T-8 VII.3:4 | it becomes a beautiful l. in communion, |
| T-9 IV.3:1 | The Atonement is a l. in sharing, which is |
| T-11 II.2:1 | thus becomes a l. in understanding, and |
| T-11 V.1:5 | of the ego will be our l. for a while, for we |
| T-11 V.3:1 | Let us begin this l. in "ego dynamics" by |
| T-12 III.1:5 | Consider how perfectly your l. would be |
| T-13 in.4:6 | Atonement is the final l. he need learn, |
| T-13 XI.9:6 | him. He will learn the l. of awaking. God |
| T-14 II.2:1 | elsewhere, begins His l. in simplicity with |
| T-14 II.2:2 | This is the hardest l. you will ever learn, |
| T-14 II.4:5 | learners of the l. this light brings to them, |
| T-14 II.7:5 | This simple l. holds the key to the dark |
| T-14 III.6:6 | is the happy l. the Holy Spirit teaches, |
| T-14 III.7:1 | The way to teach this simple l. is merely |
| T-14 V.7:4 | from the effects of this most holy l., which |
| T-14 X.6:2 | This l. the Holy Spirit teaches by giving |
| T-14 XI.2:2 | a l. so unthinkable that only the insane, in |
| T-14 XI.4:3 | And so you have another l. sent from Him |
| T-14 XI.4:4 | it. This l. shines with God's glory, for in it |
| T-14 XI.4:7 | Every dark l. that you bring to Him Who |
| T-14 XI.4:8 | for the bright l. He has learned for you. |
| T-14 XI.4:9 | Never believe that any l. you have learned |
| T-14 XI.5:2 | can be sure that you have learned God's l. |
| T-14 XI.5:5 | Every dark l. teaches this, in one form or |
| T-14 XI.5:6 | And each bright l. with which the Holy |
| T-14 XI.6:1 | concerned about how you can learn a l. so |
| T-14 XI.10:7 | that no dark l. of guilt can abide in what |
| T-14 XI.11:5 | and before His l. division disappears. |
| T-15 I.9:1 | This l. takes no time. For what is time |
| T-15 II.1:7 | will quickly offer you the whole l. of peace |
| T-15 II.2:3 | It will come, being the l. God gives you, |
| T-15 II.6:5 | and His l. will support your strength. It is |
| T-15 III.3:2 | The l. may seem hard at first, but you will |
| T-15 V.4:6 | every relationship becomes a l. in love. |
| T-15 VI.5:5 | The holy instant thus becomes a l. in how |
| T-15 VII.12:5 | And despite the evident insanity of this l., |
| T-15 XI.7:3 | And if you understand this l., you will |
| T-15 XI.7:5 | The l. I was born to teach, and still would |
| T-18 IV.4:8 | you are interfering with the l. by believing |
| T-19 I.15:4 | needed when the l. has been learned. Yet |
| T-20 IV.2:9 | Salvation is a l. in giving, as the Holy |
| T-24 VII.7:5 | retains one unlearned l. in his memory, |
| T-27 V.7:2 | one l. that has perfectly been learned. |
| T-27 VIII.3:4 | This single l. does it try to teach again, |
| T-27 VIII.11:1 | single l. learned will set you free from |
| T-27 VIII.11:2 | this one inclusive l. of deliverance until it |
| T-27 VIII.12:3 | undone by but a single l. truly learned. |
| T-28 I.7:2 | who would keep a senseless l. in his mind, |
| T-28 I.10:9 | see in the miracle a l. in allowing Cause to |
| T-28 II.10:1 | every l. that the Holy Spirit requests you |
| T-28 II.11:5 | Yet half the l. will not teach the whole. |
| T-28 II.11:6 | for this is not the l. it was sent to teach. |
| T-28 II.11:7 | The l. is the *mind* was sick that thought |
| T-31 I.1:6 | it could make such an easy l. difficult. |
| T-31 I.2:4 | goes from one apparent l. to the next, in |
| T-31 I.4:4 | every l. that makes up the world arises |
| T-31 I.4:5 | The world began with one strange l., |
| T-31 I.6:4 | Which l. will you learn? What outcome is |
| T-31 I.7:4 | certain outcome of the l. that God's Son is |
| T-31 I.7:10 | l. that reflects the Love of God is stronger |
| T-31 I.8:1 | The outcome of the l. that God's Son is |
| T-31 I.8:8 | heard throughout the world this second l. |
| T-31 I.10:1 | as surely from the l. that His Son is guilty |
| T-31 II.1:1 | An ancient l. is not overcome by the |
| T-31 IV.3:6 | they could have learned their greatest l.. |
| T-31 IV.3:9 | But this is not the l. in itself. The lesson |
| T-31 IV.3:10 | The l. has a purpose, and in this you come |
| T-31 IV.4:1 | you have learned the way the l. starts, but |
| T-31 IV.4:4 | not judge the l. that is but begun with this |
| T-31 IV.4:8 | you see the purpose of the l. shining clear, |
| T-31 V.5:1 | there is a l. that the concept of the self was |
| T-31 V.5:2 | It is a l. in a terrible displacement, and a |
| T-31 V.5:3 | l. teaches this: "I am the thing you made |
| T-31 V.6:1 | the central l. that ensures your brother is |
| T-31 V.9:1 | are the Holy Spirit's l. plans arranged in |
| T-31 VIII.1:1 | Temptation has one l. it would teach, in |
| W-pI 6.3:1 | the two cautions stated in the previous l.: |
| W-pI 90.1:4 | the l. that there is one problem and one |
| W-pI 99.9:5 | and start the l. that we learn today with |
| W-pI 106.7:2 | And the l. has been learned. Today we |
| W-pI 108.7:2 | We will use this simple l. in the obvious |
| W-pI 108.10:1 | simple l. for today will teach you much. |
| W-pI 121.9:3 | as one, we will extend the l. to yourself, |
| W-pI 127.9:6 | And He will bless the l. with His Love. |
| W-pI 127.12:5 | *For I would learn the joyous l. that there is no* |
| W-pI 130.6:3 | just the l. that you cannot see two worlds. |
| W-pI 132.5:4 | if you would understand the l. for today. |
| W-pI 132.7:1 | is no world, and can accept the l. now. |
| W-pI 132.7:2 | readiness will bring the l. to them in some |
| W-pI 132.9:1 | A l. earlier repeated once must now be |
| W-pI 132.10:1 | l. for today except another way of saying |
| W-pI 151.10:3 | teach the single l. that they all contain. |
| W-pI 151.15:3 | the Son of God the holy l. of his sanctity. |
| W-pI 153.1:1 | to take away again; attend this l. well. The |
| W-pI 154.12:1 | Let us but learn this l. for today: We will |
| W-pI 154.13:1 | Our l. for today is stated thus: *I am among* |
| W-pI 157.3:3 | will learn to do increasingly, as every l., |
| W-pI 158.2:6 | l. yesterday evoked a theme found early in |
| W-pI 158.10:3 | well. This l. is not difficult to learn, if you |
| W-pI 166.12:5 | This is the l. that His giving holds, for He |
| W-pI 170.2:4 | Today we learn a l. which can save you |
| W-pI 184.12:2 | becomes the final l. that all things are one |
| W-pI 184.12:2 | one, and at this l. does all learning end. |
| W-pI 185.6:3 | Whatever form the l. takes is planned for |
| W-pI 185.6:4 | there is no form in which the l. will meet |
| W-pI 190.10:3 | day when it is given you to realize the l. |
| W-pI 193.3:3 | Each l. has a central thought, the same in |
| W-pI 193.4:3 | l. is so simple that it cannot be rejected in |
| W-pI 193.4:4 | if one but wants to see the simple l. there. |
| W-pI 193.7:1 | is failing to perceive the l. he should learn |
| W-pI 193.7:3 | If it does, be sure the l. is not learned. |
| W-pI 193.12:1 | practicing the l. in forgiveness in the form |
| W-pI 193.13:1 | This is the l. God would have you learn: |
| W-pI 194.6:1 | the l. for today as the deliverance it really |
| W-pI 195.1:1 | Gratitude is a l. hard to learn for those |
| WpI.rVI.in.3:1 | theme with which we start and end each l. |
| W-pI 213.1:2 | *A l. is a miracle which God offers to me, in* |
| W-pII 275.1:1 | Voice for God, which speaks an ancient l., |
| W-pII 286.1:3 | *the l. that there is no need that I do anything.* |
| M-3 5:6 | it, the perfect l. is before them and can be |
| M-3 5:7 | And if they decide to learn that l., they |
| M-4 I.A.4:4 | he will not generalize the l. for fear of loss |
| M-5 II.4:6 | or limit. The final outcome of this l. is the |
| M-9 2:1 | one l. with increasing thoroughness. He |
| M-12 4:5 | l. is enough to let the thought of unity |
| M-12 5:1 | The central l. is always this; that what |
| M-13 1:3 | for it. Now its real meaning is a l.. Like all |
| M-14 3:10 | it is the final l. in which unity is restored. |
| M-14 4:3 | The final l., which brings the ending of |
| M-14 4:4 | of the teacher of God in this concluding l. |
| M-14 4:6 | God's Voice tells him it is a l. he can learn |
| M-17 1:4 | a major l. for the teacher of God to master |
| M-17 3:2 | A l. truly taught can lead to nothing but |
| M-18 2:1 | God's teachers' major l. is to learn how to |
| M-21 4:6 | case of the l. in the workbook that says, "I |
| M-22 2:2 | of the l. of the Atonement to all situations |
| M-23 5:10 | the l. of salvation through his learning? |
| M-28 1:7 | It is the l. in which learning ends, for it is |
| C-5 5:3 | the mighty l. that he learned for all of you |
| C-5 6:8 | still it is his l. most of all that he would |
| P-2 IV.10:4 | teaching, if his l. is to be that sanity is safe |
| P-2 V.2:6 | the l. of defenselessness above all else, to |

**lesson's** 2

| | |
|---|---|
| T-31 IV.8:5 | when all the l. purpose is to teach that |
| M-17 8:5 | the l. manifest simplicity stands out like |

**lessons** 76

| | |
|---|---|
| T-2 IV.3:2 | Learning devices are not l. in themselves. |
| T-3 I.7:9 | that all the other l. I taught are true. If |
| T-3 I.7:10 | be no need to learn from many smaller l.. |
| T-4 in.3:11 | and if you will read these l. carefully they |
| T-4 I.1:3 | share their l. conviction will be lacking. A |
| T-4 I.7:4 | and repeat their l. until they are learned. I |
| T-6 h | THE L. OF LOVE |
| T-6 I.16:8 | its l. must be learned now as well as then. |
| T-6 V.h | The L. of the Holy Spirit |
| T-6 V.B.1:6 | An insane learner learns strange l.. What |
| T-6 V.C.5:3 | together the l. implied in the others, and |
| T-7 VIII.3:5 | His l. are confused, and their transfer |
| T-8 VII.13:2 | God's joyous Teacher and learning His l.. |
| T-9 V.9:5 | Guide, you will learn the simplest of all l.: |
| T-14 II.6:2 | And then begin to learn the joyous l. that |
| T-14 XI.4:6 | dark l. must be brought willingly to truth, |
| T-14 XI.5:3 | dark l. in your mind that hurt and hinder |
| T-14 XI.8:5 | for keeping certain dark l. from Him. And |
| T-14 XI.9:6 | dark l. He has not already lightened for |
| T-14 XI.9:7 | The l. you would teach yourself He has |
| T-21 I.3:2 | And gentle l. are acquired joyously, and |
| T-21 I.4:3 | They learned it, not through joyous l., but |
| T-21 I.4:4 | still believing this, they hold those l. dear, |
| T-21 I.4:5 | do not understand the l. *keep* them blind. |
| T-31 I.3:1 | to practice and repeat the l. endlessly, in |
| T-31 I.3:4 | The l. you have taught yourself have been |
| T-31 I.4:1 | maintain that l. such as these are easy? |
| T-31 I.5:4 | truth, and teach you that Its l. are not true |
| T-31 I.5:6 | His simple l. in forgiveness have a power |
| T-31 I.6:6 | the simple l. being taught to you in every |
| T-31 I.7:1 | The l. to be learned are only two. Each |
| T-31 II.7:4 | Forget the dismal l. that you learned |

| | |
|---|---|
| T-31 II.9:1 | ancient l. you have taught yourself about |
| T-31 V.8:4 | unlearned except by l. aimed to teach that |
| T-31 VIII.3:1 | Trials are but l. that you failed to learn |
| W-in 4:2 | are planned to help you generalize the l., |
| W-pI 1.4:1 | Each of the first three l. should not be |
| W-pI 64.3:1 | To review our last few l., your function |
| W-pI 66.1:1 | our recent l. on the connection between |
| W-pI 70.6:3 | will follow this practice for a number of l., |
| WpI.rIII.in1:2 | We will review two recent l. every day for |
| W-pI 137.9:2 | gentle l. teach how easily salvation can be |
| WpI.rIV.in1:3 | for this review, and for the l. following. |
| WpI.rIV.in1:4 | we review the recent l. and their central |
| WpI.rIV.in4:4 | minds to understand the l. that we read, |
| W-pI 151.9:7 | His l. will enable you to bridge the gap |
| Wi181-200 h | Introduction to L. 181-200. |
| Wi181-200 1:1 | next few l. make a special point of firming |
| Wi181-200 2:1 | l. now are geared specifically to widening |
| W-pI 193.h | All things are l. God would have me learn |
| W-pI 193.3:1 | are the l. God would have you learn. His |
| W-pI 193.8:6 | you fail to learn the simple l. Heaven's |
| W-pI 193.9:1 | things are l. God would have you learn. |
| W-pI.193.11:7 | is. His are the l. God would have us learn. |
| W-pI 198.5:3 | and learn the simple l. He would teach, |
| WpI rVI.in.2:1 | has bestowed on us in our last twenty l.. |
| W-pI 213.1:1 | All things are l. God would have me learn. |
| W-pI 213.1:4 | *so I choose to learn His l. and forget my own.* I |
| W-pII in.1:4 | l. that remain are merely introductions to |
| W-pII.. in.11:2 | our daily l. and the periods of wordless, |
| W-pII..269.1:3 | *l. to surpass perception and return to truth. I* |
| W-pII 9.3:1 | Second Coming ends the l. that the Holy |
| Wfl h | FINAL L.. |
| Wfl in.1:1 | Our final l. will be left as free of words as |
| Wfl in.1:4 | To Him we leave these l., as to Him we |
| Wfl in.6:1 | and ask Him to help us to learn His l., |
| W-ep 3:1 | No more specific l. are assigned, for there |
| M-in 4:8 | And as they teach His l. of joy and hope, |
| M-4 IV.1:10 | It will make the Holy Spirit's l. impossible |
| M-13 1:4 | Like all l. it is an illusion, for in reality |
| M-14 5:9 | teach are l. in which Heaven is reflected. |
| M-16 1:2 | is no program, for the l. change each day. |
| M-16 1:6 | they can learn the l. for the day together. |
| M-16 9:6 | All intermediate l. will but lead to this, |
| S-1 IV.2:2 | ascent, but there are still many l. to learn. |
| S-3 II.4:4 | peace, the journey over and the l. learned. |

## lest 11

| | |
|---|---|
| T-7 VII.5:7 | and teach His way l. you forget yourself. |
| T-7 VIII.2:4 | l. you give the ego up and free yourself. |
| T-25 III.5:6 | error, l. you remain in darkness where the |
| T-27 I.4:3 | you send l. he forget the injuries he gave, |
| T-27 II.13:4 | l. your errors and his own be seen as one. |
| T-28 III.3:5 | l. God should come to bridge the little |
| T-29 I.3:6 | and him, l. he turn again into an enemy. |
| T-31 V.5:2 | away, l. it perceive the treachery it hides. |
| W-pI 166.7:4 | cast down l. you might catch a glimpse of |
| W-pI 166.8:1 | cower fearfully l. you should feel Christ's |
| W-pI 197.1:4 | received with honor, l. they be withdrawn |

## let 1007

| | |
|---|---|
| T-2 V.A.18:6 | *I will be healed as I l. Him teach me to heal.* |
| T-2 VII.2:1 | cannot l. you leave your mind unguarded, |
| T-2 VII.7:9 | but l. me remind you that time and space |
| T-3 II.6:3 | you perceive, you l. it be true for you. |
| T-3 V.5:7 | to engage in it when you are willing to l. it |
| T-4 I.8:7 | Do not l. your ego dispute this, because |
| T-4 I.13:6 | them myself. L. us undertake to learn this |
| T-4 III.6:3 | L. us ask the Father in my name to keep |
| T-4 IV.7:1 | actively refuse to l. your mind slip away. |
| T-4 IV.8:10 | exist. L. it be judged truly and you must |
| T-4 IV.9:3 | l. the Holy One shine on you in peace, |
| T-4 VI.1:5 | We cannot safely l. it go at that, however, |
| T-5 in.3:8 | is: *L. me know this brother as I know myself.* |
| T-5 I.2:1 | L. us start our process of reawakening |
| T-5 II.4:1 | l. the belief in darkness enter your mind |
| T-5 II.4:2 | you must l. banish the idea of darkness. |
| T-5 II.10:1 | can l. it change you just as it changed me. |
| T-5 II.11:4 | L. us restate "My yoke is easy and my |
| T-5 II.11:4 | light" in this way; "L. us join together, for |
| T-5 III.9:6 | You may l. your mind misperceive, but |
| T-5 VI.3:3 | L. the Holy Spirit remind you always of |
| T-5 VI.3:3 | and l. me teach you how to share it with |
| T-5 VII.6:10 | *of my wrong decision if I will l. Him. I choose* |
| T-5 VII.6:11 | *I choose to l. Him, by allowing Him to decide* |
| T-6 I.1:1 | l. us consider the crucifixion again. I did |
| T-6 V.A.4:4 | to l. this crucial concept slip away. It is a |
| T-6 V.C.8:2 | your mind because, if you l. doubt enter, |
| T-7 V.11:3 | L. your mind shine with mine upon their |
| T-7 IX.5:1 | your awareness whenever you will l. Him. |
| T-8 III.3:6 | it. L. the Holy Spirit teach you how to do |
| T-8 III.8:5 | Fulfilling it perfectly will l. you remember |
| T-8 IV.7:2 | and have not l. it be free. Of yourself you |
| T-8 V.2:10 | L. the Love of God shine upon you by |
| T-8 V.6:3 | yours. L. us not lose sight of His direction |
| T-8 VI.3:1 | L. us glorify Him Whom the world denies |
| T-8 VII.6:5 | L. no Son of God remain hidden for His |
| T-8 VIII.9:6 | l. it be an image of your own perception |
| T-8 VIII.9:7 | Do not l. it reflect your decision to attack. |
| T-8 IX.2:10 | your little part, and l. the whole be yours. |
| T-8 IX.3:8 | on behalf of waking if you will l. Him. |
| T-9 II.2:1 | L. us suppose, then, that what you ask of |
| T-9 II.5:11 | faith in him strong enough to l. you hear? |
| T-9 IV.1:3 | and do not l. your perception rest upon it, |
| T-9 IV.5:4 | not l. any belief in its realness enter your |
| T-9 IV.8:3 | L. me repeat that the ego's qualifications |
| T-9 V.1:3 | L. us consider the unhealed healer more |
| T-9 V.6:2 | When God said, "L. there be light," there |
| T-9 V.8:6 | You can only l. Him fulfill His function. |
| T-10 II.2:6 | again. L. nothing in this world delay your |
| T-10 IV.2:4 | your ability to evaluate it truly, to l. it go. |
| T-10 IV.5:10 | you completely when you l. them go. |
| T-11 II.6:4 | and l. nothing that obscures it enter. The |
| T-11 II.6:5 | the little spark and are willing to l. it grow |
| T-11 II.6:7 | that you will gladly l. it be increased. And |
| T-11 III.2:4 | Would God l. this be real, when He did |
| T-11 III.6:2 | never l. them enter the mind of God's Son |
| T-11 V.1:4 | L. us be very calm in doing this, for we are |
| T-11 V.3:1 | L. us begin this lesson in "ego dynamics" |
| T-11 V.12:8 | it. L. him but recognize it and he will not |
| T-11 VI.3:9 | L. the Christ in you interpret for you, and |
| T-11 VIII.2:4 | for you, and if you will l. Him interpret it, |
| T-11. VIII.12:4 | L. the Holy Spirit remove all offenses of |
| T-11. VIII.13:2 | willing to l. their own interpretations go |
| T-12 II.5:1 | L. us not save nightmares, for they are |
| T-12 II.5:4 | L. us not delay this, for your dream of |
| T-12 II.6:5 | not l. your hatred stand in the way of love |
| T-12 VI.2:4 | He cannot l. you forget your worth. For |
| T-13 I.7:6 | L. the holiness of God's Son shine away |
| T-13 II.3:5 | Yet l. it perceive guiltlessness anywhere, |
| T-13 II.4:3 | they are in an excellent position to l. it go. |
| T-13 II.5:1 | l. us recognize that you believe you have |
| T-13 III.7:4 | sanity all your hurt, and l. Him heal you. |
| T-13 IV.5:6 | you are forbidding yourself to l. it go. You |
| T-13 V.4:2 | die, yet they will not l. condemnation go. |
| T-13 V.8:5 | But l. the darkness go and all you made |
| T-13 VI.3:5 | To be born again is to l. the past go, and |
| T-13 VI.5:4 | L. no dark cloud out of your past obscure |
| T-13 VII.13:7 | to l. the rays extend in quiet to infinity. |
| T-13 VIII.5:6 | and l. Him gather them into His quiet |
| T-13 X.3:5 | they will not look within and l. it go. They |
| T-13 X.4:4 | Yet you l. them stand between you and |
| T-13 X.12:3 | L. us look upon him together and love |
| T-13 X.13:6 | and for the many gifts that you will l. me |
| T-13 XI.4:4 | finally l. Him judge the difference for you, |
| T-14 in.1:8 | seen. L. us now turn away from them, and |
| T-14 I.1:7 | forgiveness you must have l. guilt go, |
| T-14 II.3:5 | *L. Me make the one distinction for you that* |
| T-14 III.3:9 | *it. L. me bring peace to God's Son from his* |
| T-14 III.14:1 | L. Him, therefore, be the only Guide that |
| T-14 III.15:8 | quite impossible that He could ever l. His |
| T-14 III.19:5 | l. Him teach you quietly how to perceive |
| T-14 IV.3:1 | l. all that obscured the truth in your most |
| T-14 V.11:9 | l. us join him in the holy place of peace |
| T-14 VI.3:6 | But l. them go, and what was fearful will |
| T-14 VI.8:4 | Him and l. His gentleness teach you that, |
| T-14 VI.8:5 | must open all doors and l. the light come |
| T-14 VII.5:1 | believes in darkness, and will not l. it go. |
| T-14 VIII.1:5 | but l. all that would hide your glory be |
| T-14 VIII.3:1 | L. your mind wander not through |
| T-14 IX.6:8 | it. L. him, then, see it in you and share it |
| T-14 X.8:4 | ego, l. me assure you that you understand |
| T-14 X.10:4 | l. the Holy Spirit order your thoughts and |
| T-14 X.11:5 | L. the Holy Spirit show him to you, and |
| T-14 XI.3:7 | *L. it all go.* Do not attempt to understand |
| T-14.. XI.10:10 | with every one you l. Him do through you |
| T-15 II.1:7 | instant you will l. go all your past learning |
| T-15 III.5:2 | L. this question be asked you by the Holy |
| T-15 III.9:9 | L. us join in honoring you, who must |
| T-15 III.11:4 | Thus will we l. no one forget what you |
| T-15 IV.2:1 | upon your willingness to l. all littleness go |
| T-15 IV.6:4 | not to recognize it and not to l. it go. The |
| T-15 IV.8:3 | and am I wholly willing to l. everything |
| T-15 IV.9:9 | L. the Holy Spirit's purity shine them |
| T-15 V.5:2 | He would purify and not l. you destroy. |
| T-15 V.5:3 | removing as much fear as you will l. Him. |
| T-15 V.5:7 | be afraid to l. go your imagined needs, |
| T-15 V.10:7 | and l. the Holy Spirit bring to you those |
| T-15 VI.6:9 | it. L. no need you perceive obscure your |
| T-15 VII.3:2 | your investment in it, to learn to l. it go. |
| T-15 VII.3:3 | choose to l. go what he believes has value. |
| T-15 VII.5:3 | l. us look more closely at the relationships |
| T-15 VII.5:3 | and l. the Holy Spirit judge them truly. |
| T-15 VIII.2:4 | L. us join together in making the holy |
| T-15 VIII.6:5 | And l. Him Whose teaching is only of |
| T-15 IX.1:1 | Holy Spirit release your vision and l. you |
| T-15 IX.5:1 | If you would but l. the Holy Spirit tell you |
| T-15 IX.7:2 | As you l. the Holy Spirit teach you how to |
| T-15 X.1:7 | it. L. the Holy Spirit teach you, and let me |
| T-15 X.1:7 | l. me celebrate *your* birth through Him. |
| T-15 X.6:5 | The ego will never l. you perceive this, |
| T-15 XI.3:2 | L. yourself be healed completely that you |
| T-15 XI.3:2 | and l. us celebrate our release together by |
| T-15 XI.8:1 | L. no despair darken the joy of Christmas |
| T-15 XI.8:2 | joy. L. us join in celebrating peace by |
| T-15.. XI.10:12 | And l. all your relationships be made holy |
| T-16 I.1:3 | provided you l. Him use it in His way. His |
| T-16 I.2:7 | and l. the Holy Spirit relate through you, |
| T-16 I.3:7 | aside, and l. healing be done for you. |
| T-16 I.4:2 | you l. Him use your capacity for strength, |
| T-16 I.5:9 | And l. Him offer you His strength and His |
| T-16 I.6:3 | L. this be, and do not try to substitute |
| T-16 II.5:6 | L. His understanding of the miracle be |
| T-16 II.8:5 | l. us resolve together to accept the joyful |
| T-16 II.9:7 | invest in truth, and l. it work in peace. |
| T-16 III.4:2 | but have not l. what you are teach you. |
| T-16 IV.1:3 | solely to offset the hate, but not to l. it go. |
| T-16 IV.12:5 | and l. nothing stand in the way of truth. |
| T-16 V.10:2 | L. us not think of its fearful nature, nor of |
| T-16 V.12:8 | He merely could not l. this happen. You |
| T-16 VI.7:5 | you have been willing to l. go your hold |
| T-16 VI.11:7 | it will surely do if you but l. it come to you |
| T-16 VI.12:1 | holy instant, and there l. Him release you. |
| T-16 VI.12:7 | Call. And l. Him call on Heaven for you. |
| T-16 VII.1:1 | It is impossible to l. the past go without |
| T-16 VII.2:10 | really *not* l. go what has already gone. It |
| T-16 VII.4:3 | Would you act out the dream, or l. it go? |
| T-16 VII.12:5 | *L. us not wander into temptation, for the* |
| T-16 VII.12:6 | *And l. us receive only what You have given,* |
| T-17 III.6:7 | undone. L. Him uncover the hidden spark |
| T-17 III.6:9 | And you will l. this spark transform the |
| T-17 III.6:10 | unwilling to l. it be hidden from you. And |
| T-17 III.7:1 | you but l. Him hold the spark before you, |
| T-17 III.8:4 | alliance are retained, and all the rest l. go. |
| T-17 III.8:5 | And what is thus l. go is all the truth the |
| T-17 III.9:2 | that to choose one is to l. the other go. |
| T-17 III.10:2 | L. my relationship to you be real to you, |
| T-17 III.10:2 | and l. me bring reality to your perception |
| T-17 III.10:6 | and l. not the holy purpose of Atonement |
| T-17 III.10:8 | L. me enter in the Name of God and bring |
| T-17 IV.6:4 | that you have been more willing to l. go. |
| T-17 IV.6:5 | one remains, you will not l. the others go. |
| T-17 IV.9:2 | Do not l. the frame distract you. This gift |
| T-17 IV.9:10 | L. not your gaze dwell on the hypnotic |
| T-17 IV.16:2 | true. L. us ascend in peace together to the |
| T-17 V.6:2 | You l. this goal be set for you. That was |
| T-17 V.8:1 | l. it be explained to you as you perceive its |

| | |
|---|---|
| T-17.....VII.5:4 | L. it enter and look upon it calmly, but do |
| T-17....VIII.1:6 | simply because you have l. it be what it is. |
| T-17....VIII.2:2 | you. L. truth be what it is. Do not intrude |
| T-17....VIII.2:4 | L. it encompass every situation and bring |
| T-17....VIII.2:6 | L. it enter, and it will call forth and secure |
| T-17....VIII.5:3 | Think carefully before you l. yourself use |
| T-18.........I.8:1 | L. them all go, dancing in the wind, |
| T-18.........I.9:8 | L. Him bring it here, where *you* would |
| T-18........I.10:9 | L. us join in Him in peace and gratitude, |
| T-18........I.11:5 | rejoices that you have l. it come to you. |
| T-18..... II.5:20 | than in waking, you will not l. go of it. |
| T-18....... II.8:1 | L. not the dream take hold to close your |
| T-18....... II.9:3 | because you have been willing to l. your |
| T-18...... III.2:5 | L. us then join quickly in an instant of |
| T-18...... III.7:5 | L. not time worry you, for all the fear that |
| T-18...... IV.1:3 | and the willingness to l. it come precede |
| T-18...... IV.2:8 | lies in your willingness to l. it be what it is |
| T-18....... V.2:5 | to l. Him remove all fear and hatred, and |
| T-18....... V.5:6 | L. Him fulfill the function that He gave to |
| T-18....... V.6:1 | l. Him exchange this instant for the holy |
| T-18....... V.7:2 | L. him remember this, and say: *I desire* |
| T-18...... VI.3:4 | in the mind, and l. it not know its Identity |
| T-18..VI.11:11 | l. yourself be one with something beyond |
| T-18.... VI.14:7 | simply because you have been willing to l. |
| T-18..... VII.2:3 | to l. this happen for more than an instant, |
| T-18..VIII.12:2 | because you have not yet l. go of all the |
| T-18...... IX.1:9 | L. the Holy Spirit remove it from the |
| T-18...... IX.8:3 | through. L. your Guide teach you their |
| T-19.......I.16:1 | L., then, your dedication be to the eternal |
| T-19...... III.1:4 | will suffer, and not l. go of the idea of sin. |
| T-19...... III.2:7 | think is real you want, and will not l. it go |
| T-19...... III.3:5 | repeat it; you will merely stop and l. it go, |
| T-19.... III.11:1 | l. not sin arise again to blind your eyes. |
| T19... IV.A.2:6 | are not asked to l. it go for yourself alone. |
| T19... IV.A.2:9 | Would you l. a little bank of sand, a wall |
| T19... IV.A.3:2 | are still unwilling to l. it join you wholly. |
| T19. IV.A.5:11 | But l. Him quietly extend the miracle of |
| T19. IV.A.14:4 | be as careful to l. no little act of charity, |
| T19....IV.B.5:5 | l. peace through to bless the tired world! |
| T19....IV.B.6:1 | L. me be to you the symbol of the end of |
| T19..IV.C.11:9 | *L. me not see it as a sign of sin and death, nor* |
| T19IV.C.11:10 | *it an obstacle to peace, but l. You use it for me* |
| T19... IV.D.4:6 | agreed never to l. the fear of God be lifted, |
| T19... IV.D.6:4 | if you look on this and l. the veil be lifted, |
| T19... IV.D.9:6 | L. us join together in a holy instant, here |
| T19... IV.D.9:7 | l. us join in faith that He Who brought us |
| T19. IV.D.13:8 | one. L. him be what he is, and seek not to |
| T19. IV.D.15:6 | L. him withhold it not, for by receiving it |
| T19. IV.D.17:5 | L. us give redemption to each other and |
| T19. IV.D.18:5 | l. him rise again to glad remembrance of |
| T-20.........I.1:2 | L. us not spend this holy week brooding |
| T-20.........I.2:2 | L. no dark sign of crucifixion intervene |
| T-20.........I.3:3 | L. him not wander into the temptation of |
| T-20.........I.3:6 | But l. the whiteness of your shining gift of |
| T-20..... II.8:11 | L. us lift up our eyes together, not in fear |
| T-20....... II.9:3 | L. him be to you the savior from illusions, |
| T-20...... III.9:3 | uncertain whether to l. it go or to take |
| T-20....... V.2:3 | hearts of everyone, to l. them beat as one. |
| T-20....... V.5:6 | holy instants to l. this be accomplished, |
| T-20....... V.8:3 | L. us consider now what he must learn, to |
| T-20...... VI.7:2 | L. love draw near them and overlook the |
| T-20.... VI.11:7 | or l. himself be given freedom from it. |
| T-20..... VII.2:5 | not, l. us admit that *you* are inconsistent. |
| T-21..... II.4:10 | strong enough to make a world can l. it go |
| T-21....... II.7:8 | All you are asked to do is *l. it in;* only to |
| T-21...... III.8:2 | choosing to l. all limitations be removed. |
| T-21.... III.12:7 | body. L. them now be given back to what |
| T-21...... IV.1:6 | It has no fear to l. you feel ashamed. It |
| T-21...... VI.4:3 | and l. their madness tell them it is real. |
| T-21...... VI.7:8 | that you choose to l. yourself be healed, in |
| T-21...... VI.8:7 | willing to l. reason be the means by which |
| T-21..... VII.5:9 | and l. sin tell him that his enemy must be |
| T-21... VII.5:10 | l. him only ask himself these questions, |
| T-21..... VII.7:5 | l. him be revealed to you through vision? |
| T-21..... VII.8:2 | And l. your reason tell you that it must be |
| T-21... VII.10:8 | l. an "enemy" tempt you to use the body's |
| T-22.......in.4:7 | body, to l. you and your brother be joined |
| T-22.........I.1:1 | L. reason take another step. If you attack |
| T-22.........I.4:6 | L. not your fear of sin protect it from |
| T-22 ........I.8:7 | the holiness of your relationship to l. Him |
| T-22 ........I.10:7 | it is one with you who joined to l. it enter. |
| T-22 ........II.6:2 | For if you have the means to l. the Holy |
| T-22 ........II.9:1 | L. us look closer at the whole illusion that |
| T-22 ......II.13:7 | as yourself, and l. him lead you there. |
| T-22 ..... III.8:1 | L. not the form of his mistakes keep you |
| T-22 ..... III.8:2 | L. not the vision of his holiness, the sight |
| T-22 ..... III.8:3 | L. your awareness of your brother not be |
| T-22 ..... IV.3:2 | L. it be lifted! Raise it together with your |
| T-22 ..... IV.5:5 | For you are here to l. it be received. God's |
| T-22 ..... IV.6:5 | l. illusions be lifted from their minds are |
| T-22 ..... VI.5:4 | blessed are you who l. this gift be given! |
| T-22 ..... VI.6:4 | he l. be laid in Heaven through himself? |
| T-22 ..... VI.7:4 | God would l. nothing interfere with those |
| T-22 ..... VI.9:4 | L. your concern be only that you give to |
| T-22 ... VI.9:11 | And l. the darkness be dispelled by Him |
| T-22 ... VI.10:7 | L. us look straight at how this error came |
| T-22 ... VI.15:7 | L. truth decide if you and your brother be |
| T-23 .......in.4:1 | L. not the little interferers pull you to |
| T-23 .......in.5:1 | L. us not let littleness lead God's Son into |
| T-23 .......in.5:1 | Let us not l. littleness lead God's Son into |
| T-23 .......in.5:3 | not l. time intrude upon your sight of him |
| T-23 .........I.8:9 | L. all this madness be undone for you, |
| T-23 ........I.10:3 | and l. forgiveness sweep away all trace of |
| T-23 ........II.1:4 | L. us, then, look upon them calmly, that |
| T-23 ......II.14:8 | to hold love captive, and l. sin go free. |
| T-23 ......II.17:5 | salvation? L. not the form of the attack on |
| T-23 ..... III.3:5 | L. the idea of compromise but enter, and |
| T-24 .......in.1:9 | wait upon illusions to l. Him be Himself. |
| T-24 .........I.7:8 | l. you think that you are better off apart. |
| T-24 ........II.7:7 | L. not the dream of specialness remain |
| T-24 ........II.8:5 | it. L. him forgive you all your specialness, |
| T-24 ...... V.4:1 | Yet l. your specialness direct his way, and |
| T-24 ..... VI.5:3 | L. not his specialness obscure the truth in |
| T-24 ..... VI.6:5 | L. not your eyes be blinded by the veil of |
| T-24 ..... VI.6:6 | And l. the fear of God no longer hold the |
| T-24 .... VII.5:3 | L. not your foolish fancies frighten you. |
| T-25 .........I.4:6 | to l. Him draw aside the veil that seems to |
| T-25 ..... III.2:4 | His Son's belief He could not l. Himself be |
| T-25 ..... III.7:2 | sin? L. all your brother's errors be to you |
| T-25 ...... V.5:2 | l. his function be fulfilled is but the means |
| T-25 ...... V.5:2 | be fulfilled is but the means to l. yours be. |
| T-25 ...... V.5:8 | until you see him differently and l. him be |
| T-25 ...... V.6:2 | is God made free to l. His Will be done. In |
| T-25 ..... VI.3:6 | L. him no more be lonely, for the lonely |
| T-25 ... VI.5:11 | form, to l. it serve his brother and himself |
| T-25 ..... VI.7:7 | and l. him understand that he is safe, as |
| T-25 ..... VI.7:9 | l. salvation be perfectly fulfilled in you. |
| T-25 .... VII.3:1 | L. us go back to what we said before, and |
| T-25 .VIII.14:7 | L. love decide, and never fear that you, in |
| T-25 ..... IX.9:1 | not choose to l. them be removed for you. |
| T-26 .........I.6:3 | sings to you, and l. the world recede, and |
| T-26 .... V.10:4 | value. L. the dead and gone be peacefully |
| T-26 .... V.14:1 | Forgive the past and l. it go, for it *is* gone. |
| T-26 .... VII.1:3 | L. us review the principles that we have |
| T-26 .. VII.12:1 | L. us consider what the error is, so it can |
| T-26 .. VII.19:3 | L. us unite in bringing blessing to the |
| T-26 .. VII.20:5 | by this little gift of truth but l. to be itself, |
| T-26 ... VIII.3:4 | still, and l. you instantly become as one. |
| T-26 ... VIII.9:8 | And do not l. it be disguised as time, and |
| T-26 ..... IX.3:1 | fades to l. the grass grow green again, and |
| T-26 ..... IX.3:1 | l. the flowers be all white and sparkling in |
| T-26 ........X.5:4 | Holy Spirit's purpose is to l. the Presence |
| T-27 .......I.10:4 | L. it have healing as its purpose. Then will |
| T-27 .......I.10:6 | L. it receive the power to represent an |
| T-27 .......I.10:7 | And to your brother l. its message be, |
| T-27 .......I.11:1 | way to l. this be achieved is merely this; to |
| T-27 .......I.11:1 | l. the body have no purpose from the past |
| T-27 .......I.11:7 | L., then, its purpose and your function |
| T-27 ........II.4:7 | L. yourself be healed that you may be |
| T-27 ...... III.3:8 | L., then, the empty space it occupies be |
| T-27 ...... V.1:7 | But he can l. *himself* be healed, and thus |
| T-27 ...... V.7:4 | who l. yourself be healed that it might live |
| T-27 .... V.11:3 | by you to l. you understand that you have |
| T-27 ..... VI.3:2 | to hear, and l. it tell you what it is it feels. |
| T-27 ..... VI.8:6 | to l. love's symbols take the place of sin. |
| T-27 .... VII.2:6 | to l. a simple problem be resolved if it is |
| T-27 .. VII.16:3 | L. all your brother's gifts be seen in light |
| T-27 .. VII.16:4 | l. no pain disturb your dream of deep |
| T-27 ... VIII.5:2 | Is it your wish to l. no dream appear to be |
| T-27 ... VIII.5:3 | Then l. us merely look upon the dream's |
| T-27 ... VIII.6:1 | L. us return the dream he gave away unto |
| T-27 .VIII.10:6 | L. them be as hateful and as vicious as |
| T-28 .........I.4:4 | as those you l. the world impose on you. |
| T-28 .........I.5:2 | the past, but rather as a way to l. it go. |
| T-28 .........I.7:5 | L. not the cause that you would give them |
| T-28 .........I.8:2 | because He l. It not be unremembered. It |
| T-28 ..... III.6:3 | L. its effects be gone and clutch them not |
| T-28 ..... III.8:1 | but l. your world be gently lit by miracles. |
| T-28 ..... IV.1:2 | and l. him turn illusions on himself. Nor |
| T-28 ..... IV.1:5 | of dreams of pain because you l. him be. |
| T-28 ..... IV.2:5 | dream, and join in one, but l. the other go |
| T-28 ..... IV.4:4 | L. him acknowledge who he is, by not |
| T-28 ..... IV.6:3 | dreams are yours because you l. them be. |
| T-28 ... IV.10:8 | Your willingness to l. illusions go is all the |
| T-28 .......V.5:3 | be? L. not your eyes behold a dream; your |
| T-28 .......V.5:8 | L. not the body's ears and eyes perceive |
| T-28 .......V.5:8 | and l. them persuade their maker his |
| T-28 ..... VI.6:1 | L. this be your agreement with each one; |
| T-29 .........I.1:9 | Be wary, then; l. Him not come too close, |
| T-29 .........I.3:7 | enemy. L. him come close to you, and you |
| T-29 ..... III.3:3 | Yet you can l. yourself be wakened. You |
| T-29 .......V.4:2 | him, and l. It tell you what his function is. |
| T-29 .......V.8:4 | L. us be glad indeed that this is so, and |
| T-29 ..... VI.5:2 | you need not l. it stand for this to you. Let |
| T-29 ..... VI.5:3 | you. L. *this* be changed, and nothing in the |
| T-29 .... VII.7:1 | L. us forget the purpose of the world the |
| T-29 .. VII.10:5 | L. Him remind you of His Love for you, |
| T-29 ... VIII.2:1 | L. not their form deceive you. Idols are |
| T-29 ..... IX.1:2 | willing he must be to l. himself bow down |
| T-29 ..... IX.1:3 | l. himself fall lower than the stones upon |
| T-30 .........I.1:4 | wise to l. yourself become preoccupied |
| T-30 .........I.4:3 | serve to l. you be directed without fear, |
| T-30 .........I.8:1 | you cannot even l. your question go, you |
| T-30 .........I.9:4 | This tiny opening will be enough to l. you |
| T-30 .........I.9:4 | steps you need to l. yourself be helped. |
| T-30 .......I.13:5 | L. us, then, consider once again the very |
| T-30 .......I.15:4 | L. this be understood, and you can see |
| T-30 .......I.17:6 | L. this be the one reminder that you keep |
| T-30 ..... IV.5:4 | what you have made to l. you be deceived, |
| T-30 ..... IV.7:4 | You are but asked to l. your will be done, |
| T-30 ..... IV.7:5 | And you are asked to l. yourself be free of |
| T-30 .......V.5:3 | willingly the mind can l. them go when it |
| T-30 .....V.9:11 | and l. not your experiences here deceive |
| T-30 ..... VI.6:2 | are not prepared, as yet, to l. all idols go. |
| T-30 .... VII.4:5 | all events, and l. them offer you stability. |
| T-30 ... VIII.5:7 | l. there be no dreams about him that you |
| T-30 ... VIII.5:8 | in him because you l. Him come to you. |
| T-30 ... VIII.6:2 | L. no temptation to prefer a dream allow |
| T-31 .........I.8:2 | to be your friend, and l. it join with you. |
| T-31 .......I.12:1 | L. us be still an instant, and forget all |
| T-31 .......I.12:2 | is. L. us remember not our own ideas of |
| T-31 .......I.12:4 | know. L. every image held of everyone be |
| T-31 ........II.2:1 | L. us review again what seems to stand |
| T-31 ........II.4:3 | you want to l. the follower in you arise, |
| T-31 ........II.6:4 | Then l. us wait an instant and be still, |
| T-31 ........II.6:6 | from what we want as we will l. him be. |
| T-31 ......II.10:1 | for, will be enough to l. this happen. And |
| T-31 ...... III.6:1 | L. us be glad that you will see what you |
| T-31 ..... IV.7:3 | l. me repeat that to achieve a goal you |
| T-31 ... IV.11:4 | and did not l. His Son abandon Him. For |
| T-31 ........V.9:2 | L. us consider, then, what proof there is |
| T-31 ......V.10:6 | L. us forget the concept's foolishness, |
| T-31 ......V.12:7 | on the one to choose, and l. the other go. |
| T-31 ..... VI.2:7 | guilt, because they chose to l. it go instead |
| T-31 ..... VI.3:4 | l. you see another world your eyes could |
| T-31 .... VII.2:6 | his, because you l. them all affect you not. |
| T-31 .... VII.5:7 | l. the cruel concept of yourself be changed |
| T-31 .... VII.6:4 | it needs to l. it serve the function given |
| T-31 .. VII.15:1 | L. not the world's light, given unto you, |
| T-31 ... VIII.4:2 | and l. Christ's strength prevail in every |
| T-31 ... VIII.7:2 | and l. him look upon the Christ in him. |
| T-31 ... VIII.9:1 | L. us be glad that we can walk the world, |
| W-pI ...... 5.6:3 | *keep this form of upset and l. the others go.* |
| W-pI ...... 6.3:5 | *keep this form of upset and l. the others go.* |
| W-pI .... 12.5:3 | and l. the truth be written upon it for you, |
| W-pI .... 14.3:1 | to l. go the thoughts that you have written |
| W-pI .... 21.3:1 | l. the "little" thoughts of anger escape you |

W-pI.....23.5:2 that the cause be identified and then l. go,
W-pI.....23.7:5 you will be ready to l. the cause go.
W-pI.....28.6:3 them to l. its purpose be revealed to you,
W-pI.....31.3:1 merely l. whatever thoughts cross your
W-pI.....31.3:4 try to l. the stream move on evenly and
W-pI.....34.3:3 arise in your mind, and l. each one go, to
W-pI.....42.5:3 L. them come without censoring unless
W-pI.....42.5:3 l. obviously irrelevant thoughts intrude.
W-pI.....42.6:2 to step back and l. the thoughts come. If
W-pI.....43.5:2 and then l. whatever relevant thoughts
W-pI.....45.4:4 not l. the thoughts of the world hold us
W-pI.....45.4:5 We will not l. the beliefs of the world tell
W-pI.....47.7:3 L. go all the trivial things that churn and
W-pI.....48.3:2 and l. His strength take the place of your
W-pI.....50.5:1 l. the idea for today sink deep into your
W-pI.....50.5:2 it, l. related thoughts come to help you
W-pI.....50.5:3 L. no idle and foolish thoughts enter to
W-pI.....51.1:5 vision. I must l. it go by realizing it has no
W-pI.....51.3:6 it. But there is every reason to l. it go, and
W-pI.....51.4:6 do not mean anything, and to l. them go.
W-pI.....51.5:7 I no longer want. I am willing to l. it go.
W-pI.....52.3:4 L. me remember that I look on the past to
W-pI.....52.3:5 L. me understand that I am trying to use
W-pI.....52.3:6 God. L. me learn to give the past away,
W-pI.....53.4:6 home? L. me remember the power of my
W-pI.....54.1:5 my eyes as I l. my errors be corrected. My
W-pI.....54.2:4 thought. L. me look on the world I see as
W-pI.....54.5:5 l. it teach me that my will and the Will of
W-pI.....55.5:7 it. L. me open my mind to the world's real
W-pI.....56.2:4 is essential that I l. this image of myself go
W-pI.....56.3:4 I would l. the door behind this world be
W-pI........57.h Today l. us review these ideas:
W-pI.....59.1:6 L. me not cherish illusions about myself. I
W-pI.....59.2:3 gift. L. me not look to my own eyes to see
W-pI.....59.2:4 L. me be willing to exchange my pitiful
W-pI.....59.2:6 L. me call upon this gift today, so that this
W-pI.....59.4:7 I see. L. me welcome vision and the happy
W-pI.....61.5:7 L. a few related thoughts come to you,
W-pI.....62.4:1 L. us be glad to begin and end this day by
W-pI.....62.5:5 L. related thoughts come freely, for your
W-pI.....63.4:1 will probably find it easier to l. the related
W-pI........64.h L. me not forget my function.
W-pI.....64.1:1 "L. me not wander into temptation." The
W-pI.....64.5:1 L. us remember this today. Let us remind
W-pI.....64.5:2 today. L. us remind ourselves of it in the
W-pI.....64.5:6 L. not the form of the decision deceive
W-pI.....64.6:1 then, l. us practice with these thoughts:
W-pI.....64.6:2 *L. me not forget my function. Let me not try*
W-pI.....64.6:3 *L. me not try to substitute mine for God's.*
W-pI.....64.6:4 *L. me forgive and be happy.* At least once
W-pI.....64.7:3 You may need to repeat "L. me not forget
W-pI.....65.6:4 *clean slate l. my true function be written for*
W-pI.....66.5:7 L. us, then, think about the premises for a
W-pI...66.10:8 L. us try today to realize that only the
W-pI.....67.3:1 try to l. all thoughts drop away for a brief
W-pI.....68.1:4 hold a grievance is to l. the ego rule your
W-pI.....68.4:2 do not think you can l. your grievances go
W-pI.....68.6:9 *When I l. all my grievances go I will know I*
W-pI.....68.7:3 *L. me not betray my Self.* In addition, repeat
W-pI.....69.2:1 Today l. us make another real attempt to
W-pI.....69.2:2 l. us devote several minutes to thinking
W-pI.....69.2:5 We are trying to l. the veil be lifted, and
W-pI.....69.3:1 L. us begin our longer practice period
W-pI.....69.3:5 L. us end the ancient search today by
W-pI.....69.4:1 try to l. go of all the content that generally
W-pI.....69.8:6 Then l. the power of God work in you and
W-pI.....69.9:6 *Yet I want to l. it be revealed to me, for my*
W-pI.....70.6:2 still l. you decide when to undertake them
W-pI.....71.7:1 L. us practice recognizing this certainty
W-pI.....71.7:2 And l. us rejoice that there is an answer to
W-pI.....71.9:1 this, l. us devote the remainder of the
W-pI.....71.9:6 and l. Him tell you what needs to be done
W-pI.....72.3:2 But l. us consider the kinds of things you
W-pI.....72.6:4 L. us accept this and be glad. As a body,
W-pI.....72.6:5 do not l. yourself be deprived of what the
W-pI...72.13:4 *L. me accept it instead. What is salvation,*
W-pI.....73.8:3 Today l. your will be done, and end
W-pI...73.10:3 *L. me behold the light that reflects God's*
W-pI...73.10:4 Then l. your will assert itself, joined with
W-pI...73.11:7 This will help you l. your grievances go,
W-pI.....74.2:5 L. us try to recognize this today, and
W-pI...76.11:1 L. us today open God's channels to Him,
W-pI...76.11:1 and l. His Will extend through us to Him.
W-pI........78.h L. miracles replace all grievances.
W-pI.....78.4:2 We will not l. ourselves be blind to him;
W-pI.....78.5:5 L. him be savior unto you today. Such is
W-pI.....78.7:1 Then l. us ask of Him Who knows this
W-pI.....78.7:3 *L. me behold my savior in this one You have*
W-pI.....78.7:4 l. your mind be shown the light in him
W-pI...78.10:5 we pray: *L. miracles replace all grievances.*
W-pI........79.h L. me recognize the problem so it can be
W-pI.....79.6:1 and therefore not to l. it be resolved. If
W-pI...79.10:3 *L. me recognize this problem so it can be*
W-pI........80.h L. me recognize my problems have been
W-pI.....80.5:1 Now l. the peace that your acceptance
W-pI.....80.6:5 *L. me recognize this problem has been*
W-pI.....80.7:1 L. us be determined not to collect
W-pI.....80.7:2 today. L. us be determined to be free of
W-pI.....81.1:3 L. me be still before my holiness. In its
W-pI.....81.1:4 its calm light l. all my conflicts disappear.
W-pI.....81.1:5 In its peace l. me remember Who I am.
W-pI.....81.2:2 *L. me not obscure the light of the world in me*
W-pI.....81.2:3 *L. the light of the world shine through this*
W-pI.....81.4:2 might include: *L. this help me learn what*
W-pI.....81.4:3 *L. me not separate my function from my will*
W-pI.....82.1:5 L. me, then, forgive the world, that it may
W-pI.....82.2:2 are: *L. peace extend from my mind to yours,*
W-pI.....82.3:1 (64) L. me not forget my function. I
W-pI.....82.4:2 *L. me not use this to hide my function from*
W-pI........83.h Today l. us review these ideas:
W-pI.....83.2:4 *L. me not use this to justify a function God*
W-pI.....84.2:2 *L. me not see an illusion of myself in this. As*
W-pI.....84.2:3 *As I look on this, l. me remember my Creator*
W-pI.....84.4:4 *love. L. this not tempt me to attack myself.*
W-pI.....85.2:2 *L. me not use this as a block to sight. The*
W-pI.....85.4:2 *L. this not tempt me to look away from me*
W-pI.....85.4:3 *I will not l. this interfere with my awareness*
W-pI.....86.2:4 *L. me perceive this only in the light of God's*
W-pI.....87.4:2 *L. me perceive this in accordance with the*
W-pI.....88.4:4 *L. me allow God's laws to work in this, and*
W-pI.....89.2:3 *L. me not hold a grievance against you,*
W-pI.....89.3:1 (78) L. miracles replace all grievances. By
W-pI.....89.4:3 *L. our grievances be replaced by miracles,*
W-pI.....90.1:1 (79) L. me recognize the problem so it
W-pI.....90.1:2 L. me realize today that the problem is
W-pI.....90.1:3 L. me also understand that the solution is
W-pI.....90.1:3 with which I l. the grievance be replaced.
W-pI.....90.3:1 (80) L. me recognize my problems have
W-pI.....90.3:6 Spirit will teach me this, if I will l. Him.
W-pI.....91.4:3 to the attempt to l. you feel this strength.
W-pI...91.11:5 *light. L. me not close my eyes because of this.*
W-pI.....92.2:3 hand, securely bound until you l. it go.
W-pI...92.10:1 L. us give twenty minutes twice today to
W-pI...92.10:2 L. yourself be brought unto your Self. Its
W-pI...92.11:3 L. us repeat as often as we can the idea for
W-pI.....93.9:6 It. L. It come into Its Own. Here you are;
W-pI.....95.7:5 a refusal to l. your mistake be corrected,
W-pI.....95.8:2 only by your unwillingness to l. them go.
W-pI.....95.8:3 them go. L. us therefore be determined,
W-pI...95.10:1 L. all these errors go by recognizing them
W-pI...95.12:3 l. the light in you come through to teach
W-pI...95.13:3 and l. It shine away all your illusions and
W-pI.....96.8:4 and l. Him speak to you about your Self,
W-pI.....96.9:5 and l. your mind go wandering in a world
W-pI.....97.7:1 l. them echo round the world through
W-pI.....97.8:3 l. Him tell your mind that they are true.
W-pI.....98.1:3 We side with truth and l. illusions go. We
W-pI...98.10:1 the hour, l. your time be spent in happy
W-pI...98.10:3 you have l. your mind be readied for the
W-pI.....99.7:6 Then l. the Thought with which He has
W-pI.....99.8:3 L. in the light, and you will look upon no
W-pI.....99.9:1 and l. His light seek out and lighten up all
W-pI.....99.9:8 and l. Him teach you what you need to
W-pI...99.12:5 mind and l. all fear be gently laid aside,
W-pI...100.2:5 Your joy must be complete to l. His plan
W-pI...100.4:2 joy on earth calls to all minds to l. their
W-pI...100.5:1 We will not l. ourselves be sad today. For
W-pI...100.8:1 Now l. us try to find that joy that proves
W-pI...100.8:4 L. this one be the day that you succeed!
W-pI...102.1:3 now, at least enough to l. you question it,
W-pI...104.5:2 We will not l. ourselves lose sight of them
W-pI...105.5:2 L. Him complete Himself as He defines
W-pI...105.7:3 and l. your mind be free of all that would
W-pI...105.8:2 l. all bars to peace and joy be lifted up,
W-pI...105.8:3 and l. His Voice assure you that the words
W-pI...105.9:4 see it as but another chance to l. yourself
W-pI......106.h L. me be still and listen to the truth.
W-pI.106.10:3 *L. me be still and listen to the truth. I am*
W-pI...107.2:5 Then l. the sense of quiet that you felt be
W-pI...107.6:9 dreams be gone. L. truth correct them all.
W-pI...107.9:2 to l. His function be fulfilled through you.
W-pI...107.9:6 Then l. Him lead you gently to the truth,
W-pI.107.10:3 as you l. them be corrected in your mind.
W-pI...109.4:6 rest in Him and l. Him speak through you
W-pI...109.5:5 into stillness. L. these periods of rest and
W-pI...109.5:6 L. it be still and thankfully accept its
W-pI...109.8:3 Open the temple doors and l. them come
W-pI...110.2:1 to l. complete correction heal your mind,
W-pI...110.2:3 to l. the present be accepted as it is. It is
W-pI...110.2:4 It is enough to l. time be the means for all
W-pI...110.3:3 l. redemption come to light the world and
W-pI...110.9:3 L. graven images you made to be the Son
W-pI.110.11:5 L. us declare this truth as often as we can.
WpI. rIII.in6:1 your mind, and l. it use them as it chooses
WpI. rIII.in6:6 and l. the mind employ the thoughts you
WpIrIII.in10:1 we stress the need to l. your learning not
WpIrIII.in10:6 and l. it serve to help you keep your peace
W-pI...111.1:3 *L. the light of holiness and truth light up my*
W-pI...111.1:3 *mind, and l. me see the innocence within.*
W-pI...117.1:2 *L. me remember love is happiness, and*
W-pI...118.2:1 (106) L. me be still and listen to the truth
W-pI...118.2:2 *L. my own feeble voice be still, and let me*
W-pI...118.2:2 *and l. me hear the mighty Voice for Truth*
W-pI...118.3:4 hour: L. me be still and listen to the truth.
W-pI...120.1:2 *and l. Him work in me and through me,*
W-pI...120.2:3 *and l. my Father tell me Who I really am.*
W-pI...121.6:4 you think you made, and l. it disappear.
W-pI.121.11:4 to l. this light extend until it covers him,
W-pI.121.13:1 l. him offer you the light you see in him,
W-pI.121.13:1 and l. your "enemy" and friend unite in
W-pI...122.6:6 L. us today rejoice that this is so, for here
W-pI.122.13:3 L. not your gifts recede throughout the
W-pI.122.14:1 Be tempted not to l. your gifts slip by and
W-pI...123.1:1 Today l. us be thankful. We have come to
W-pI...123.2:2 nor l. you wander in the dark alone. Be
W-pI......124.h L. me remember I am one with God.
W-pI.124.12:2 *L. me remember I am one with God, at one*
W-pI...125.1:1 L. this day be a day of stillness and of
W-pI...125.8:4 l. Him tell you God has never left His Son,
W-pI...125.9:2 to l. your practicing today lift you above
W-pI...126.2:1 L. us consider what you do believe, in
W-pI...126.5:3 Yet it remains your right to l. the sinner
W-pI...126.9:3 means, and l. you realize its worth to you.
W-pI.126.11:2 not l. your mind forget this goal for long,
W-pI...127.7:2 L. us together, then, be glad to give some
W-pI...127.8:4 and l. the gift of God replace them all.
W-pI.127.10:2 L. us give thanks today that we are spared
W-pI...128.4:1 L. nothing that relates to body thoughts
W-pI...128.6:1 release your mind from chains and l. it
W-pI...128.6:5 L. it rest in its Creator, there to be
W-pI...128.7:3 time you l. your mind escape its chains.
W-pI...129.6:4 L. it be given you today. It waits but for
W-pI...130.8:6 *L. me accept the strength God offers me and*
W-pI...131.8:5 L. us not try longer to impose an alien
W-pI.131.11:7 Then l. them go, and sink below them to
W-pI...132.3:3 For as you l. the past be lifted and release
W-pI...132.6:4 as far as he can l. himself be led along the
W-pI...132.8:4 healed as you l. go all thoughts of sickness
W-pI...132.8:4 the dead arise when you l. thoughts of life
W-pI.132.15:4 and l. your mind in quietness be changed
W-pI...133.2:2 l. your mind be drawn to bodily concerns,
W-pI...133.4:3 most ungenerous to you to l. alternatives
W-pI.133.14:2 begin to l. yourself collect some needless
W-pI......134.h L. me perceive forgiveness as it is.
W-pI...134.1:1 L. us review the meaning of "forgive," for
W-pI.134.14:4 l. us give a quarter of an hour twice today,
W-pI.134.14:5 teach it. L. us ask of Him: *Let me perceive*

W-pI.134.14:6 of Him: *L. me perceive forgiveness as it is.*
W-pI.134.16:1 L. him be freed from all the thoughts you
W-pI.134.17:3 *L. me perceive forgiveness as it is. Would I*
W-pI...135.4:1 L. us consider first what you defend. It
W-pI.135.15:4 to l. the mind direct its future course.
W-pI.135.18:3 your defenses did not l. you see His loving
W-pI.135.19:2 L. no defenses but your present trust
W-pI.136.15:5 and l. truth be as it has always been:
W-pI.136.15:7 *I am, and l. my mind be wholly healed today.*
W-pI.136.19:2 you l. your mind harbor attack thoughts,
W-pI...137.9:2 little practice you need undertake to l. His
W-pI.137.10:1 And as you l. yourself be healed, you see
W-pI.137.10:2 world, when you l. healing come to you.
W-pI.137.13:1 our function is to l. our minds be healed,
W-pI.137.15:1 L. healing be through you this very day.
W-pI.137.15:4 Nor will we l. this function be forgot as
W-pI...139.8:5 L. us not allow our holy minds to occupy
W-pI...139.9:3 L. us not forget the goal that we accepted.
W-pI.139.12:2 several minutes l. your mind be cleared of
W-pI...140.7:1 L. us not try today to seek to cure what
W-pI.140.11:1 and l. Him speak to us five minutes as the
W-pI.140.11:2 to l. our interfering thoughts be laid aside
WpI. rIV.in3:1 L. us begin our preparation with some
WpI. rIV.in5:2 and l. this thought alone engage it fully,
WpI. rIV.in7:4 L. each word shine with the meaning God
WpI. rIV.in7:5 L. each idea which you review that day
WpI. rIV.in8:2 and l. them be received where they were
WpI. rIV.in9:1 but l. these be the messages they are. We
W-pI...142.2:1 (124) L. me remember I am one with
W-pI...147.2:1 (134) L. me perceive forgiveness as it is.
W-pI...151.7:1 and l. the Voice for God alone be Judge of
W-pI...151.8:1 L. Him be Judge of what you are, for He
W-pI...151.9:6 L. Him be Judge as well of everything that
W-pI.151.13:4 L. Him evaluate each thought that comes
W-pI...152.8:1 L. us today be truly humble, and accept
W-pI...153.8:3 not l. our happiness slip by because a
W-pI.153.14:4 L. this day bring the last chapter closer to
W-pI.153.19:3 in Christ, and l. our weakness disappear,
W-pI...154.1:1 L. us today be neither arrogant nor
W-pI.154.12:1 L. us but learn this lesson for today: We
W-pI......155.h I will step back and l. Him lead the way.
W-pI...155.2:3 then they step back and l. it lead the way.
W-pI...155.2:5 l. illusions walk ahead of truth is madness
W-pI...155.2:6 to l. illusion sink behind the truth and let
W-pI...155.2:6 and l. the truth stand forth as what it is, is
W-pI...155.8:2 accept the truth, and l. it go before you,
W-pI...155.9:2 of truth, and l. illusions be your guide.
W-pI.155.10:3 back in faith and l. truth lead the way.
W-pI.155.10:6 with you. L. Him lead you with the rest.
W-pI.155.14:3 *I will step back and l. Him lead the way, For I*
W-pI...156.8:3 Today l. doubting cease. God speaks for
W-pI...157.4:3 and l. it rest in still anticipation and in
W-pI.158.10:5 chance to l. Christ's vision shine on you,
W-pI.159.10:6 L. us an instant dream with Him. His
W-pI...160.3:2 place, and l. you be a stranger to yourself?
W-pI...160.3:3 one would l. himself be dispossessed so
W-pI...164.9:1 L. not today slip by without the gifts it
W-pI......165.h L. not my mind deny the Thought of God
W-pI...165.5:5 to l. it fade away from your ecstatic vision
W-pI...165.6:5 Would God consent to l. His Son remain
W-pI.166.13:6 L. sorrow not tempt you to be unfaithful
W-pI.167.10:1 L. us today be children of the truth, and
W-pI.167.10:5 will we l. imagined opposites to life abide
W-pI...170.9:2 L. us remember what the text has stressed
WpI...rV.in2:2 *L. our doubts be quiet and our holy minds be*
WpI...rV.in5:4 L. us raise our hearts from dust to life, as
WpI...rV.in9:1 L. this review be then your gift to me. For
WpI.rV.in10:1 L. this review become a time in which we
W-pI...173.1:1 I will step back and l. Him lead the way.
W-pI...178.1:1 (165) L. not my mind deny the Thought
Wi181-200 2:1 limited to l. you see the value of our goal.
W-pI...181.3:1 we first l. all such little focuses give way to
W-pI...181.3:1 to l. our sinlessness become apparent. We
W-pI...182.5:3 voice cries unto you to l. Him rest a while.
W-pI...182.7:7 you, calling you to l. Him go in peace,
W-pI...183.4:5 although before you l. the Name of God
W-pI...183.6:4 L. all your thoughts become anchored on
W-pI...183.8:3 l. His Name become the all-encompassing
W-pI...183.8:4 L. all thoughts be still except this one.
W-pI.183.10:6 He calls on Him to l. all things he thought
W-pI.184.12:6 our purpose is to l. our minds accept
W-pI...185.7:1 L. us today devote our practicing to
W-pI...185.8:6 L. not some dreams be more acceptable,
W-pI...186.2:1 L. us not fight our function. We did not
W-pI...186.7:3 L. it go. Salvation of the world depends
W-pI.186.12:5 L. not its voice direct you. Hear instead a
W-pI...188.6:4 l. your thoughts fly to the peace within.
W-pI...188.9:3 We will not l. them stray. We let the light
W-pI...188.9:4 l. the light within our minds direct them
W-pI.188.10:7 *L. all things shine upon me in that peace,*
W-pI.188.10:7 *And l. me bless them with the light in me.*
W-pI...189.5:3 But learn and do not l. your mind forget
W-pI...189.8:7 way to reach Him is merely to l. Him be.
W-pI...189.9:2 But we do choose to l. Him come. And
W-pI...190.9:3 L. no attack enter with you. Lay down the
W-pI.190.11:2 L. our gratitude unto our Teacher fill our
W-pI...191.5:1 But l. today's idea find a place among
W-pI.191.10:1 l. the Son of God awaken from his sleep,
W-pI...192.2:6 you need the means to l. illusions go.
W-pI...193.2:5 to l. the light of Heaven shine upon it. It is
W-pI.193.10:2 L. mercy come to you more quickly. Do
W-pI.193.10:6 and do not l. the time be less than meets
W-pI.193.11:4 l. us think about all things we saved to
W-pI.193.11:5 L. us give them all to Him Who knows the
W-pI.193.12:4 L. no one hour cast its shadow on the one
W-pI.193.12:4 l. everything that happened in its course
W-pI...194.4:5 You are but asked to l. the future go, and
W-pI...195.5:2 And l. your gratitude make room for all
W-pI...195.5:4 L. us not compare ourselves with them,
W-pI...195.7:1 Then l. our brothers lean their tired
W-pI...196.4:2 L. us take this step today, that we may
W-pI...197.6:2 But learn to l. forgiveness take away the
W-pI...198.9:2 the key to light and l. the darkness end:
W-pI.198.10:3 L. today be celebrated both on earth and
W-pI...199.7:4 L. love replace their fears through you.
W-pI...200.9:1 L. us not lose our way again today. We go
W-pI...200.9:5 nor l. him stray forever from his home.
WpI rVI.in.2:5 to use them all and l. them blend as one,
WpI rVI.in.5:4 gently l. the thought which you denied be
WpI rVI.in.6:4 l. it take the place of what you thought.
WpI rVI.in.7:2 and l. Him teach you what to do and say
WpI rVI.in.7:4 L. us offer Him the whole review we now
WpI rVI.in.7:4 and l. us also not forget to Whom it has
W-pI...208.1:2 *be still, and l. the earth be still along with me.*
W-pI...220.1:2 *L. me not wander from the way of peace, for I*
W-pI...220.1:3 *But l. me follow Him Who leads me home,*
W-pII ....in.2:1 to l. the exercise be merely a beginning.
W-pII ..in.10:5 need but be still and l. all things be healed
W-pII ..... 1.5:1 and l. forgiveness show you what to do,
W-pII .....221.h to my mind. L. all my thoughts be still.
W-pII . 221.2:6 l. our thoughts be still and find His peace,
W-pII . 223.2:1 *l. us see the face of Christ instead of our*
W-pII . 228.2:5 *I l. them go today. And I stand ready to*
W-pII ..... 2.4:1 L. us come daily to this holy place, and
W-pII . 231.1:5 *find. L. me remember You. What else could I*
W-pII . 232.1:2 *L. every minute be a time in which I dwell*
W-pII . 232.1:3 *And l. me not forget my hourly thanksgiving*
W-pII . 232.1:4 *l. all my thoughts be still of You and of Your*
W-pII . 232.1:5 *And l. me sleep sure of my safety, certain of*
W-pII . 232.2:5 L. Him reveal all things to you, and be
W-pII . 238.1:3 *in my hands, and l. it rest on my decision. I*
W-pII . 239.1:1 L. not the truth about ourselves today be
W-pII . 239.1:2 L. us instead be thankful for the gifts our
W-pII . 240.1:6 L. us not be deceived today. We are the
W-pII . 240.2:4 *L. us forgive him in Your Name, that we may*
W-pII ..... 3.4:5 And l. Him give you peace and certainty,
W-pII ..... 3.5:1 L. us not rest content until the world has
W-pII ..... 3.5:2 L. us not be satisfied until forgiveness has
W-pII ..... 3.5:3 l. us not attempt to change our function.
W-pII . 245.1:7 *L. me bring Your peace with me. For I would*
W-pII . 246.1:1 L. me not think that I can find the way to
W-pII . 246.1:2 L. me not try to hurt God's Son, and
W-pII . 246.1:3 L. me not fail to recognize myself, and
W-pII . 247.1:4 L. me accept what His sight shows me as
W-pII . 247.1:5 Brother, come and l. me look on you.
W-pII . 248.1:2 Now l. me be as faithful in disowning
W-pII .....250.h L. me not see myself as limited.
W-pII . 250.1:1 L. me behold the Son of God today, and
W-pII . 250.1:2 L. me not try to obscure the holy light in
W-pII ..... 4.1:2 seeks to l. illusions take the place of truth.
W-pII .....254.h L. every voice but God's be still in me.
W-pII . 254.2:1 Today we l. no ego thoughts direct our
W-pII . 254.2:2 and look at them, and then we l. them go.
W-pII . 255.1:3 L. me this day have faith in Him Who
W-pII . 255.1:4 And l. the peace I choose be mine today
W-pII .....257.h L. me remember what my purpose is.
W-pII . 257.1:4 depression. L. us therefore be determined
W-pII . 257.2:2 *L. us not forget today that we can have no*
W-pII .....258.h L. me remember that my goal is God.
W-pII .....259.h L. me remember that there is no sin.
W-pII .....260.h L. me remember God created me.
W-pII . 260.1:4 *L. me remember You created me. Let me*
W-pII . 260.1:5 *L. me remember my Identity. And let my*
W-pII . 260.1:6 *l. my sinlessness arise again before Christ's*
W-pII . 261.1:3 L. me today seek not security in danger,
W-pII . 261.2:1 *L. me not seek for idols. I would come, my*
W-pII .....262.h L. me perceive no differences today.
W-pII . 262.1:7 *L. me not see him as a stranger to his Father,*
W-pII . 263.2:1 of Heaven, l. us look on all we see through
W-pII . 263.2:2 L. all appearances seem pure to us, that
W-pII . 265.1:6 L. no appearance of my sins obscure the
W-pII . 265.2:2 *L. me remember that they are the same, and*
W-pII . 266.1:3 *L. not Your Son forget Your holy Name. Let*
W-pII . 266.1:4 *L. not Your Son forget his holy Source. Let*
W-pII . 266.1:5 *L. not Your Son forget his Name is Yours.*
W-pII . 267.2:1 *L. me attend Your Answer, not my own.*
W-pII .....268.h L. all things be exactly as they are.
W-pII . 268.1:1 *L. me not be Your critic, Lord, today, and*
W-pII . 268.1:2 *L. me not attempt to interfere with Your*
W-pII . 268.1:3 *L. me be willing to withdraw my wishes from*
W-pII . 268.1:3 *its unity, and thus to l. it be as You created it.*
W-pII . 268.1:6 *me, when I l. all things be exactly as they are?*
W-pII . 268.2:1 L. not our sight be blasphemous today,
W-pII . 268.2:1 nor l. our ears attend to lying tongues.
W-pII ..... 6.5:2 So therefore l. us seek to find Christ's face
W-pII . 273.1:3 l. us learn how to dismiss it and return to
W-pII .....274.h Today belongs to love. L. me not fear.
W-pII . 274.1:1 *I would l. all things be as You created them,*
W-pII . 275.1:1 L. us today attend the Voice for God,
W-pII . 276.1:5 L. us accept His Fatherhood, and all is
W-pII .....277.h L. me not bind Your Son with laws I
W-pII . 277.1:2 *L. me not imagine I have bound him with the*
W-pII . 277.2:1 L. us not worship idols, nor believe in
W-pII . 280.2:1 *Today l. me give honor to Your Son, for thus*
W-pII ..... 7.3:1 you would not l. His Voice appeal in vain,
W-pII ..... 7.4:1 to l. forgiveness rest upon your dreams,
W-pII . 282.2:5 *a mistake. L. me not be afraid of truth today.*
W-pII . 283.1:3 *L. me not worship idols. I am he my Father*
W-pII . 284.2:2 *L. me not fail to trust in You today, accepting*
W-pII . 285.2:2 *L. me rejoice in it, and through forgiveness*
W-pII .....288.h L. me forget my brother's past today.
W-pII . 288.1:6 *L. me not cherish it within my heart, or I will*
W-pII . 288.1:8 *L. me not attack the savior You have given*
W-pII . 288.1:9 *But l. me honor him who bears Your Name,*
W-pII . 289.2:1 *l. me not look upon a past that is not there.*
W-pII . 291.2:6 *L. my forgiveness be complete, and let the*
W-pII . 291.2:6 *and l. the memory of You return to me.*
W-pII . 292.1:3 we l. an alien will appear to be opposing
W-pII . 293.2:1 *l. not Your holy world escape my sight today*
W-pII . 293.2:2 *Nor l. my ears be deaf to all the hymns of*
W-pII294.1:10 L. me not see it more than this today; of
W-pII . 294.2:3 *L. me, then, use this dream to help Your plan*
W-pII . 296.1:2 *I am resolved to l. You speak through me, for*
W-pII ..... 9.1:3 the willingness to l. forgiveness rest upon
W-pII ..... 9.5:5 L. us rejoice that we can do God's Will,
W-pII . 301.1:4 *will. L. me today behold it uncondemned,*
W-pII . 301.1:5 *L. me see Your world instead of mine. And*
W-pII . 302.1:7 *L. me forgive Your holy world today, that I*
W-pII . 303.1:2 L. all God's holy Thoughts surround me,
W-pII . 303.1:3 L. earthly sounds be quiet, and the sights
W-pII . 303.1:4 L. Christ be welcomed where He is at
W-pII . 303.1:5 l. Him hear the sounds He understands,
W-pII . 303.1:6 L. Him no longer be a stranger here, for
W-pII . 303.2:8 *Safe in Your Arms l. me receive Your Son.*
W-pII .....304.h L. not my world obscure the sight of
W-pII . 304.2:2 *L. me forgive, and thus receive salvation for*
W-pII . 307.1:3 *L. me not try to make another will, for it is*

W-pII..311.1:5 L. us not use it today, but make a gift of it
W-pII..311.2:3 *so we l. Your Love decide what he whom You*
W-pII.....313.h Now l. a new perception come to me.
W-pII..313.1:6 *Now l. His true perception come to me, that I*
W-pII..313.2:1 L. us today behold each other in the sight
W-pII..316.1:5 L. me come to where my treasures are,
W-pII..318.2:1 *L. me today, my Father, take the role You*
W-pII....11.4:6 L. our function be only to let this memory
W-pII....11.4:6 function be only to l. this memory return,
W-pII....11.4:6 only to l. God's Will be done on earth,
W-pII..323.1:1 *and freely l. Your Love come streaming in to*
W-pII..324.2:1 So l. us follow One Who knows the way.
W-pII..325.2:2 *L. me behold what only Yours reflect, for*
W-pII..326.1:6 *L. me know that I am an Effect of God, and so*
W-pII..326.2:1 L. us today behold earth disappear, at
W-pII..327.1:3 L. me but learn from my experience that
W-pII..327.2:2 *L. me attempt therefore to try them, and to*
W-pII..330.1:1 L. us this day accept forgiveness as our
W-pII..330.1:6 L. us choose today that He be our Identity
W-pII..331.2:2 share it. L. us look upon the holy sights
W-pII..334.1:3 L. me not accept such meager gifts again
W-pII..336.2:2 *sin. Then l. me, Father, look within, and find*
W-pII..338.1:1 this to l. salvation come to all the world.
W-pII..339.1:9 L. us resolve today to ask for what we
W-pII..341.2:1 L. us not, then, attack our sinlessness, for
W-pII.....342.h I l. forgiveness rest upon all things, For
W-pII..342.1:6 *L. me not wait again today. Let me forgive all*
W-pII..342.1:7 *L. me forgive all things, and let creation be as*
W-pII..342.1:7 *l. creation be as You would have it be and as*
W-pII..342.1:8 *is. L. me remember that I am Your Son, and*
W-pII..344.1:7 *L. my forgiven brothers fill my store with*
W-pII..345.1:7 *Then l. me give this gift alone today, which,*
W-pII..347.1:9 *L. Him judge today. I do not know my will,*
W-pII..348.1:1 *Father, l. me remember You are here, and I*
W-pII.....349.h Today I l. Christ's vision look upon All
W-pII..350.1:8 *teaches me to l. Your memory return to me,*
W-pII..358.1:5 *L. me remember all I do not know, and let*
W-pII..358.1:5 *all I do not know, and l. my voice be still,*
W-pII..358.1:6 *But l. me not forget Your Love and care,*
W-pII..358.1:7 *L. me not forget myself is nothing, but my*
W-pII..359.1:1 *Your world, and l. creation be Your Own.*
W-pII.....360.h me. L. all the world be blessed with peace
Wfl ........in.1:3 L. us turn to Him Who leads the way and
Wfl ........in.2:5 L. us together follow in the way that truth
Wfl ........in.2:6 l. us be the leaders of our many brothers
Wfl ........in.3:1 to this purpose l. us dedicate our minds,
Wfl ........in.4:2 So l. us not forget our goal is shared, for it
W-ep .........4:3 good. L. Him prepare you further. He has
M-4....... III.1:7 L. this be lost, and all his learning goes.
M-4........ X.2:2 have l. go all things that would prevent
M-4........ X.2:3 l. it be restored to them in newness and in
M-6............1:2 It is impossible to l. illusions be brought
M-6............2:9 L. him be certain it has been received,
M-7............3:7 l. him remember Who gave the gift and
M-7..........3:11 what it is, and l. it be corrected for him.
M-8............6:2 But the mind that has l. itself be healed
M-12..........4:2 that the body's function is but to l. God's
M-12..........4:5 enough to l. the thought of unity come in,
M-16..........4:3 l. him but remember that he chooses to
M-16..........4:3 God as soon as possible, and l. him do so.
M-16..........7:6 and as he will be when he has l. them go.
M-17..........1:8 L. him remember, then, it is not this that
M-17..........3:1 It is easiest to l. error be corrected where
M-17..........7:2 which you have hidden but have not l. go.
M-17..........9:9 L. this grim sword be taken from you now
M-18..........4:1 to l. all his own mistakes be corrected. If
M-18..........4:2 l. him instantly realize that he has made
M-18..........4:3 l. him turn within to his eternal Guide,
M-18..........4:3 l. Him judge what the response should be.
M-20..........1:5 L. us consider each of these questions
M-21..........1:9 L. us not forget, however, that words are
M-21..........4:5 he learns how to l. his words be chosen
M-21..........4:6 "I will step back and l. Him lead the way."
M-22..........2:6 If the way seems long, l. him be content.
M-22........5:10 to your Teacher, and l. yourself be healed.
M-25..........1:6 is. L. all his learning and all his efforts be
M-25..........6:7 "psychic" powers have simply l. some of
M-26..........4:9 L. us not, then, be too concerned with
M-27..........7:2 nor l. attack conceal the truth from you.
M-27 .........7:4 it becomes your task to l. the illusion be
M-27 .......7:10 not l. yourself forget it is not less than this
M-28 .........6:8 he l. God's Voice proclaim the truth. And
M-29 .........3:3 is to l. yourself be absolved of guilt. It is
M-29 .........6:8 cruel if He l. your words replace His Own.
M-29 .........6:9 father does not l. his child harm himself,
C-in ...........4:5 only this, and do not l. theology delay you
C-ep...........4:1 L. us wait here in silence, and kneel down
C-ep...........4:2 And then l. us arise and go in faith along
C-ep...........5:1 L. us go out and meet the newborn world
C-ep...........5:3 us. L. us go and bid Him welcome Who
P-2......... II.9:4 L. him be still and recognize his brother's
P-2......... II.9:5 And l. him then meet his brother's need
P-2......... V.2:1 L. us remember that the ones who come
P-2......... V.4:8 L. us not forget that we are helpless of
P-2....... V.6:10 Yet l. the outcome not be judged by us.
P-2......... V.7:6 L. us help him to forgive himself for all
P-2......... V.8:1 L. us stand silently before God's Will,
P-2........ VI.6:6 of his sins, enabling him to l. them go. Let
P-2........ VI.6:7 L. him retain one spot of sin in what he
P-2....... VII.9:9 O l. your patient in, for he has come to
P-3...........I.4:6 on the savior of the world to l. in a ghost?
P-3...........I.4:7 L. him not betray the Son of God. Who
P-3......... II.7:5 to stay and l. their understanding remain
P-3........ III.8:7 L. the Christ in you bid him welcome, for
S-1 ...........I.4:3 them, and l. them go into God's Hands.
S-1 ......... II.6:1 L. it never be forgotten that prayer at any
S-1 ........ III.5:2 who did it, and who can therefore l. it go.
S-1 ........ IV.3:5 l. it be a freely chosen remedy from every
S-1 ......... V.1:3 L. it but leave the ground where it begins
S-2 ...........I.9:5 and then l. go forever and forever. There
S-2 .........I.10:4 L. it then be clear to you exactly what
S-2 ........ III.2:3 but l. it be a way to draw you up to where
S-2 ........ III.3:4 L. Him take charge of how you would
S-2 ........ III.5:3 l. it not be you who sets the form in which
S-2 ........ III.7:4 L. it arise to Christ, Who welcomes it as
S-3 ........ III.6:2 He sends to you, to l. Him heal them, and
S-3 ........ IV.2:5 Time remains only to l. the last embrace
S-3 ........ IV.6:6 and l. Him be your Guide to healing,
S-3 ........ IV.8:2 L. Me instead remind you of eternity, in
S-3 ........ IV.9:8 Arise and l. My thanks be given you. And

## lets 49

T-1........ IV.4:6 that I will witness for anyone who l. me,
T-4.........I.13:4 and l. me teach you their unimportance. I
T-5.........I.1:2 and l. God go out into them and through
T-5........ III.9:6 Holy Spirit l. your mind reinterpret its
T-5...... IV.3:11 purified He l. you give them away. The
T-6....... II.11:6 God, and l. your mind converge with His.
T-9......... V.8:1 A therapist does not heal; *he l. healing be.*
T-12...VII.13:4 for you, it l. you live but to await death. It
T-13...... IX.1:3 law. Fidelity to this law l. no light in, for it
T-14....... II.4:3 into the darkness, and l. it shine on you.
T-14...... VI.5:4 in your mind that l. you think you are. All
T-15...... XI.9:1 l. Him enter and abide where He would
T-17........ II.6:2 l. you see the real world reaching quietly
T-27....... III.5:6 It l. the Holy Spirit make exchange of
T-28.......I.12:5 l. Them enter where They would abide.
T-28...... VI.6:7 sick, but l. his mind be healed and unified
T-29... VIII.2:7 from the world, and l. you stand apart, in
T-29... VIII.5:6 veil, and l. the truth shine unencumbered
T-30.........I.6:6 l. the answer show you what the question
T-30...... VI.3:1 that l. the real world rise to take the place
T-30.....VII.7:8 language l. us speak to all our brothers,
W-pI.....37.3:2 It l. you teach the world that it is one with
W-pI.....62.1:2 forgiveness that l. you recognize the light
W-pI.....73.5:4 will, and l. you look upon a world of light.
W-pI.110.11:7 and that l. you enter in the peace of God
W-pI...122.3:1 Forgiveness l. the veil be lifted up that
W-pI...122.3:2 It l. you recognize the Son of God, and
W-pI...123.6:1 and l. It echo round and round the world.
W-pI.135.12:3 true, then is it healed, and l. the body go.
W-pI.136.13:2 For time l. you think what God has given
W-pI...138.3:2 as opposites. Decision l. one of conflicting
W-pI...140.3:2 dreams forgiveness l. the mind perceive
W-pI...192.4:3 Forgiveness l. the body be perceived as
W-pI.193.13:1 to look on everything that l. it be to you
W-pII......1.1:6 sees its falsity, and therefore l. it go. What
W-pII .....2.3:2 Thus it l. illusions go. By not supporting
W-pII .....2.3:3 it merely l. them quietly go down to dust.
W-pII .248.2:1 *and l. me love Your Son again as well. Father,*
W-pII .270.1:4 *his Father, l. his dreams be brought to truth,*
W-pII .300.1:2 is also the idea that l. no false perception
W-pII ....336.h Forgiveness l. me know that minds are
M-4 ...... VI.1:9 Slowly at first he l. himself be undeceived.
M-4 ....... X.1:5 so open-mindedness l. Christ's image be
M-29 .........3:9 that l. the memory of love return to you.
C-4.............6:1 and there forgiveness l. it disappear. For
P-2..........II.7:3 and l. him formulate his own curriculum;
S-2 ...........I.7:1 to learn forgiveness as His vision l. it be.
S-2 ..........II.7:8 all. It is His face forgiveness l. you see. It is
S-3 ........ III.4:4 l. forgiveness be what it is meant to be.

## letting 29

T-4........ IV.9:6 prevent you from l. Him shine through
T-5..........II.1:4 decision to heal the separation by l. it go.
T-12......II.10:7 at the cause of fear and l. it go forever?
T-15.........II.4:2 seem to provide reasons for not l. it go.
T-18.. VI.11:11 simply by not l. your mind be limited by
T-18.... VI.12:5 rush to meet it, l. your limits melt away,
T-18.... IX.10:4 nothing interfere with love, l. it be itself.
T-20..... VII.4:3 the result of l. the effects of sin be lifted,
T-22....... V.1:3 way. Merely by l. reason tell you that they
T-27....VIII.8:3 guilt outside yourself, but never l. go! It is
T-28...... III.2:3 your aid in l. it perceive itself as separate
W-pI..... 15.4:1 name and l. your eyes rest on it as you say
W-pI..... 25.6:2 followed by looking about you and l. your
W-pI..... 44.7:2 mind, l. go every kind of interference and
W-pI..... 63.1:2 the means for l. this be done through you!
W-pI..... 79.8:2 in l. all your preconceived notions go, but
W-pI..... 97.1:5 madness, l. go illusions of a split identity.
W-pI... 105.4:5 adds by l. what cannot contain itself fulfill
W-pI. 110.10:4 a great advance to truth by l. idols go, and
WpI. rIII.in5:3 while l. your mind relate them to your
W-pI... 128.5:1 Today we practice l. go all thought of
W-pI... 129.2:2 is no loss in l. go all thought of value here.
W-pI. 133.12:5 far more than merely l. you make choices
W-pI... 164.8:1 merely l. go all things you think you want.
W-pI. 182.11:3 to ask your help in l. Him go home today,
W-pI... 198.9:1 Today we practice l. freedom come to
W-pII .323.2:1 –a debt that merely is the l. go of self-
S-1 ...........I.5:1 Prayer is a stepping aside; a l. go, a quiet
S-1 ..... III.4:10 is heavy, and your fear of l. it go is strong.

## level 68

*See also* level-adjustment

T-1.........I.12:2 the lower or bodily l. of experience, or the
T-1.........I.12:2 or the higher or spiritual l. of experience.
T-1.........I.17:2 into invisibility, away from the bodily l..
T-1........ VI.3:1 requires correction at its own l. before the
T-1........ VI.5:1 because they do not exist at the creative l.,
T-1....... VII.4:2 involves attention and study at some l..
T-2........ IV.2:2 is the result of l. confusion, because it
T-2........ IV.2:2 on one l. can adversely affect another. We
T-2........ IV.2:3 as the means of correcting l. confusion,
T-2........ IV.2:3 be corrected at the l. on which they occur.
T-2...... IV.2:10 that the mind, the only l. of creation,
T-2........ IV.5:4 this is the highest l. of communication of
T-2........ IV.5:5 that it is the highest l. of communication
T-2........ IV.5:6 miracle is to raise the l. of communication
T-2......... V.1:6 device than any form of l. confusion,
T-2......... V.1:6 introduces correction at the l. of the error
T-2......... V.1:7 that correction belongs at the thought l..
T-2......... V.5:2 recognize that mind is the only creative l.,
T-2......... V.5:4 to undo the l. confusion of others. The
T-2....V.A.12:2 fundamental correction in l. perception.
T-2........ VI.1:6 raised body thoughts to the l. of the mind
T-2........ VI.2:1 I do not foster l. confusion, but you must
T-2........ VI.2:6 only at this l. that you can exercise choice.
T-2........ VI.3:5 not need guidance except at the mind l..
T-2........ VI.3:6 Correction belongs only at the l. where
T-2........ VI.3:7 not mean anything at the symptom l.,
T-2........ VI.4:5 At that l. you *can* help it. You are much too
T-2...... VI.5:10 Correcting at the behavioral l. can shift
T-2...... VI.9:14 All thinking produces form at some l..

|  |  |
|---|---|
| T-3........IV.2:1 | Consciousness, the l. of perception, was |
| T-3.........V.7:6 | "less." At every l. it involves selectivity. |
| T-3........VI.7:1 | at that l. there is almost endless variation. |
| T-5........III.5:6 | it at the same l. on which the ego operates |
| T-5........III.6:1 | emphasized that one l. of the mind is not |
| T-5........IV.3:6 | include opposite thoughts at the same l.. |
| T-6......V.B.2:1 | will last, but they do not begin at that l.. |
| T-7.........V.2:4 | is not the l. for either teaching or learning |
| T-7........VI.9:4 | at any l. are not problems of fact. They |
| T-8....VIII.1:14 | has meaning only at the l. of perception, |
| T-8........IX.9:2 | only l. at which healing means anything. |
| T-9........III.2:8 | He needs correction at another l., because |
| T-9........III.2:8 | level, because his error is at another l.. He |
| T-9......VIII.6:5 | untrue and are therefore on the same l.. |
| T-9......VIII.6:6 | Being the l. of shift, it is experienced as |
| T-12.........I.2:5 | pitting one l. within it against another. |
| T-18......IX.4:1 | of fear lies just below the l. the body sees, |
| W-pI...128.6:1 | it seek the l. where it finds itself at home. |
| M-2 ...........1:2 | them in view of their l. of understanding. |
| M-3 ...........1:1 | teachers of God have no set teaching l.. |
| M-3 ...........2:1 | The simplest l. of teaching appears to be |
| M-3 ...........2:6 | at the l. of the most casual encounter, it is |
| M-3 ...........3:5 | to say that any l. of the teaching-learning |
| M-3 ...........4:3 | second l. of teaching is a more sustained |
| M-3 ...........4:4 | As with the first l., these meetings are not |
| M-3 ...........5:1 | third l. of teaching occurs in relationships |
| M-4 ....... II.1:8 | no l. are they in conflict with themselves. |
| M-22 .........4:4 | Nor is it at this l. that the teacher of God |
| M-29 .........1:7 | to start at the more abstract l. of the text. |
| C-1.............7:2 | Will is not involved in perception at any l. |
| C-4.............3:1 | for false perception since, being another l. |
| S-1...........I.2:5 | the l. of need that you can recognize. |
| S-1...........I.6:1 | l. of prayer that everyone can attain as yet |
| S-1......... II.3:4 | It is possible at this l. to continue to ask |
| S-1......... II.4:1 | l. also comes that curious contradiction in |
| S-1......... II.6:1 | that prayer at any l. is always for yourself. |
| S-1........IV.1:1 | Until the second l. at least begins, one |
| S-2.........I.10:5 | The l. of your prayer depends on this, for |
| S-3........IV.4:6 | This l. cannot be attained until there is no |

## level-adjustment 1

|  |  |
|---|---|
| T-2....V.A.15:1 | (5) The l. power of the miracle induces |

## Levels 2

*levels*

|  |  |
|---|---|
| T-3......... II.5:5 | One. There is no confusion within Its L., |
| T-3........IV.1:7 | the L. of the Trinity are capable of unity. |

## levels 37

*Levels*

|  |  |
|---|---|
| T-1.........I.23:1 | and place all l. in true perspective. This is |
| T-1.........I.23:2 | sickness comes from confusing the l.. |
| T-1.........I.30:1 | miracles adjust the l. of perception and |
| T-1........VI.2:3 | yourself into l. with different needs. As |
| T-1........VI.3:1 | of perceiving l. at all can be corrected. |
| T-1........VI.3:2 | while you function on different l.. |
| T-2........III.3:9 | The alternating investment in the two l. of |
| T-2........IV.2:1 | Atonement plan is to undo error at all l.. |
| T-2........VI.1:8 | them. This is an obvious confusion of l.. |
| T-3........IV.1:6 | Spirit has no l., and all conflict arises from |
| T-3........IV.1:6 | all conflict arises from the concept of l.. |
| T-3........IV.1:8 | The l. created by the separation cannot |
| T-3........IV.5:8 | itself when it chooses to make its own l.. |
| T-5........IV.3:6 | because they occur at different l. and also |
| W-pI.....24.4:3 | also that these goals are on different l. and |
| W-pI.....25.4:2 | the most superficial l., you do recognize |
| W-pI.....25.4:3 | purpose cannot be understood at these l.. |
| W-pI.....79.5:2 | They seem to be on so many l., in such |
| W-pI...105.2:3 | means pervades all l. of the world you see. |
| W-pI...127.1:4 | parts and no degrees; no kinds nor l., no |
| W-pI.133.11:1 | is overlaid with many l. of obscurity. If |
| M-3 .............h | WHAT ARE THE L. OF TEACHING? |
| M-3 ...........3:1 | difficult to understand that l. of teaching |
| M-3 ...........3:4 | but the illusion of l. of teaching seems to |
| M-3 ...........3:5 | to demonstrate that these l. cannot exist |
| M-3 ...........3:5 | Atonement, and His plan can have no l., |
| M-3 ...........3:7 | God's teachers work at different l., but the |
| M-3 ...........4:2 | sense only, we can speak of l. of teaching. |
| M-4 .....VII.1:8 | way possible, and at the simplest of l., the |
| C-1 ............7:4 | Consciousness has l. and awareness can |
| C-1 ............7:6 | Yet the very fact that it has l. and can be |
| P-2...........I.1:4 | Yet l. of readiness change, and when |
| P-2..........II.2:5 | At the highest l. they become one. Neither |
| S-1..........II.1:5 | At these l. prayer is merely wanting, out |
| S-1..........II.3:1 | and so it must entail l. of learning. Here, |
| S-1........ III.3:1 | At these l., then, the learning goal must |
| S-1........ III.3:3 | here it will be an easy step to the next l.. |

## liability 1

|  |  |
|---|---|
| T-18 ..... VI.6:4 | but make it a l. where it could be an asset. |

## liar 1

|  |  |
|---|---|
| W-pI.....72.5:3 | and not of death, He is a l. and a deceiver, |

## liberate 3

|  |  |
|---|---|
| T-6 ... V.C.4:10 | This will finally l. your mind from choice, |
| T-28 .... VII.7:7 | can be used to l. God's Son unto his home |
| W-pII . 349.1:1 | *So would I l. all things I see, and give to them* |

## liberated 1

|  |  |
|---|---|
| W-pII . 312.2:1 | *for today except to look upon a l. world, set* |

## liberates 1

|  |  |
|---|---|
| T-29 ...VIII.2:7 | and quiet calm that l. you from the world, |

## liberating 2

|  |  |
|---|---|
| T-15 .......X.2:2 | For in this l. instant no guilt is laid upon |
| W-pI...107.3:4 | l. you from all beliefs in the ephemeral. |

## liberation 6

|  |  |
|---|---|
| T-18 ... VI.11:2 | This feeling of l. far exceeds the dream of |
| T-21 ..... IV.4:1 | Your l. still is only partial; still limited |
| T-26 ........I.6:4 | for you will hear no song of l. for yourself, |
| T-26 ...VIII.7:8 | punishment until the time of l. is at hand. |
| Wi181-200 2:3 | the sense of l. which their lifting brings. |
| W-pI...196.3:4 | and of death, to thoughts of l. and of life. |

## liberator 1

|  |  |
|---|---|
| T-19 ......I.16:5 | to its source, which is its jailer or its l., |

## liberty 2

|  |  |
|---|---|
| W-pI...192.8:6 | his freedom that the way to l. depends for |
| S-3..........II.3:1 | We call it death, but it is l.. It does not |

## lie 52

|  |  |
|---|---|
| T-2 ....... IV.5:1 | the Atonement does not l. in the manner |
| T-3 ...... VII.5:4 | of truth, because its foundation is a l.. |
| T-6 ... V.B.1:11 | it. But if a l. is at its center, only deception |
| T-8 ..........II.7:1 | limit, and all power and glory l. within it. |
| T-10 ........II.2:2 | decision l. joy and peace and the glory of |
| T-11 .... V.13:4 | understanding and truth l. in separation, |
| T-11 .... V.17:3 | for nothing can prove that a l. is true. |
| T-13 .... VII.9:3 | In these l. your true perceptions, for the |
| T-14 ....... V.5:4 | release from suffering of every kind l. in it |
| T-14 ..... IX.6:2 | seems to l. only in shifting interpretations |
| T-15 ..... III.6:5 | and the glory that l. in you from God are |
| T-16 . IV.11:12 | In your completion l. the memory of His |
| T-16 . IV.11:13 | In His link with you l. both His inability |
| T-18 ..... IX.8:4 | shadows l. upon the world beyond them, |
| T-18 ... IX.11:2 | of what must forever l. beyond words. We |
| T19....IV.C.3:2 | opposition l. but in the sick minds of the |
| T19....IV.C.7:6 | For in it l. hidden all the ego's secrets, all |
| T19..IV.C.11:3 | Their meaning cannot l. in them, but |
| T-21 ......in.2:8 | the power to give it joy must l. within you |
| T-21 .... VI.11:3 | Where could his freedom l. but in himself |
| T-22 ..... VI.4:6 | Only in your joint will does healing l.. For |
| T-23 ........II.7:4 | can salvation l. within the Son, whose |
| T-24 .... VII.4:5 | in that choice l. both its health and harm. |
| T-24 .. VII.11:4 | difference does not l. in how they look, |
| T-25 .... VII.4:4 | sanity must l. apart from both the Father |
| T-26 .. VII.17:6 | And in your hands does all salvation l., to |
| T-26 .. VII.19:8 | wishes l. between a brother and his own. |
| T-26 ... VIII.3:5 | And it is here you fear the loss would l.. |
| T-27 .... VII.5:7 | here the cause of suffering and sin must l.. |
| T-27 .. VII.11:8 | could you doubt it while you l. asleep, |
| T-28 ........I.9:7 | Its memory does not l. in the past, nor |
| T-29 .......II.9:5 | unmindful that the failure does not l. in |
| T-29 ..... IX.9:2 | that it will save you l. the guilt and pain of |
| T-30 ..... VI.2:4 | Salvation does not l. in being asked to |
| T-31 ..... IV.8:3 | of decision cannot l. in choosing different |
| W-pI .... 59.3:5 | else. Beyond His Will l. only illusions. It is |
| W-pI .... 75.5:2 | see Heaven's reflection l. across the world |
| W-pI .... 77.2:1 | does not l. in your illusions about yourself |
| WpIrIII.in10:1 | to let your learning not l. idly by between |
| W-pI .. 134.4:2 | as true and not believe forgiveness is a l.. |
| W-pI 135.10:5 | see where hope must l. if it be meaningful |
| W-pI .. 195.3:3 | to bring him down to l. in death with you, |
| W-pII . 277.2:5 | cannot be bound unless God's truth can l. |
| M-16 ......... 5:3 | It is not wise to l. down for it. It is better |
| M-21 ......... 3:6 | Herein l. hell and Heaven. The sleeping |
| M-25 ......... 3:6 | does their value l. in proving anything; |
| C-2 ........... 3:1 | for a l. that serves to make it true. Nor can |
| C-2 .......... 10:4 | Problem and answer l. together here, and |
| C-4 ........... 6:4 | is seen outside must l. beyond forgiveness |
| C-4 ........... 6:7 | and forgiveness for an instant l. together, |
| P-2........ IV.1:5 | decision that truth can l. and must be lies. |
| S-1........ III.4:5 | His real escape from guilt can l. only in |

## lies 299

|  |  |
|---|---|
| T-in .......... 2:4 | ***unreal exists.*** Herein l. the peace of God. |
| T-2 ..........I.3:2 | Adam listened to the "l. of the serpent," |
| T-2 ..........I.5:1 | Whatever l. you may believe are of no |
| T-2 ....... III.1:8 | true holiness l. at the inner altar around |
| T-2 .......V.10:4 | still l. within the limitations of this world. |
| T-3 ...... VII.1:3 | Their resemblance l. in their power as |
| T-3 ...... VII.1:4 | difference l. in what rests upon them. |
| T-3 ...... VII.1:6 | that a thought system based on l. is weak. |
| T-3 ...... VII.2:6 | devil deceives by l., and builds kingdoms |
| T-4 .......II.11:3 | The whole value of right perception l. in |
| T-5 ..........I.5:1 | the knowledge that l. beyond perception. |
| T-6 ..........I.2:2 | device, l. solely in the kind of learning it |
| T-6 ..........I.3:4 | The real meaning of the crucifixion l. in |
| T-6 .......II.6:10 | Its truth l. only in its perfect inclusion in |
| T-6 .......II.12:7 | The peace of God l. in that message, and |
| T-6 .......II.12:7 | message, and so the peace of God l. in you |
| T-6 ....... III.3:1 | only safety l. in extending the Holy Spirit, |
| T-6 ....... III.4:1 | salvation l. in teaching the exact opposite |
| T-6 ....... IV.1:7 | of you. Herein l. its primary error, the |
| T-6 .........V.4:7 | Nothing lasting l. in dreams, and the |
| T-7 .........V.9:10 | joy that *is* the Kingdom l. in you to give. |
| T-7 ....... IX.1:5 | that l. between the ego and the spirit, |
| T-7 .........X.6:7 | The whole separation l. in this error. The |
| T-8 ....... IV.7:5 | of you l. your remembrance of yourself. |
| T-8 ....... IV.7:6 | of each other l. our remembrance of God. |
| T-8 ....... IV.7:7 | And in this remembrance l. your freedom |
| T-8 .........V.3:3 | of His power in you, but in that l. all truth |
| T-8 .........V.3:6 | glory l. in Them *because* They are united. |
| T-8 ..... VI.5:14 | value l. in God's sharing Himself with it |
| T-8 ..... VI.8:5 | whole power of God's Son l. in all of us, |
| T-8 ..... VI.10:3 | is. Your heart l. where your treasure is, as |
| T-8 .... VII.16:3 | impossibility l. your only hope for release. |
| T-8 .... VII.16:5 | illusions l. only in not believing them. |
| T-8 ..... VIII.1:8 | The body's condition l. solely in your |
| T-9 .........II.7:6 | The answer to all prayers l. in them. You |
| T-9 ....... III.2:3 | errors l. in the relinquishment of the ego. |
| T-9 ....... IV.3:5 | their harmfulness l. in the ego's judgment |
| T-9 ....... IV.3:6 | All their helpfulness l. in the judgment of |
| T-9 ....... IV.5:3 | Holy Spirit l. simply in looking beyond |
| T-9 ..... VIII.8:3 | you l. in the joy you bring to its witnesses, |
| T-10 ........I.1:7 | for in this recognition l. the realization |
| T-10 .......V.8:2 | His acknowledgment of you l. your being. |
| T-11 ........I.1:3 | For in this l. the beginning of the return |

T-11....... II.2:6 l. the denial of God's Fatherhood and of
T-11......IV.3:1 Your peace l. in its limitlessness. Limit
T-11....... V.3:3 the whole separation fallacy l. in the belief
T-11....... V.6:2 Your whole creative function l. in your
T-11....... V.6:7 on God, in which your freedom l.. The
T-11......VI.6:2 whole compelling power l. in the fact that
T-11......VI.8:4 dream of crucifixion still l. heavy on your
T-11. VIII.14:4 For fear l. not in reality, but in the minds
T-12......III.2:2 tell you that he believes salvation l. in it. If
T-12......III.2:3 that your salvation l. in *not* doing it. You,
T-12....III.10:2 For in this same place also l. salvation.
T-12.....VII.1:6 In every child of God His blessing l., and
T-13.......in.1:3 But herein l. the split. For the mind that
T-13....... II.3:3 but insane idea l. hidden there, for the
T-13....... II.9:5 this understanding l. your remembering,
T-13......III.4:2 you believe that magnitude l. in defiance,
T-13....III.12:3 knowing that your peace l. in His Oneness
T-13.....IV.7:6 of the appreciation of eternity l.. For only
T-13......VI.3:2 and in His changelessness l. your release.
T-13......VI.5:4 from you, for truth l. only in the present,
T-13......VI.6:3 healing l. within it because its continuity
T-13...VII.16:7 Salvation from the world l. only here. My
T-13... VIII.4:6 glimpses of the Heaven that l. beyond
T-13......IX.5:1 for his guilt l. in his secret thought that he
T-13......IX.6:2 of God l. the conviction of your own guilt.
T-13....... X.4:1 but the source of your guilt l. in the past,
T-13....XI.11:8 truth, in which the peace of Heaven l..
T-14.........I.5:4 of its dullness that l. upon your mind,
T-14........ II.7:2 All this l. in the Holy Spirit's plan to free
T-14....III.12:6 no decisions about what it is or where it l.
T-14....III.16:3 all knowledge l. behind every decision the
T-14.....V.11:6 therein l. everything that makes it holy.
T-14......VI.1:8 but value always l. in joint appreciation.
T-14.....VII.2:7 system of belief, the truth l. hidden. Yet
T-14... VIII.1:2 All this l. hidden in every darkened place,
T-14... VIII.1:3 the dark doors you have closed l. nothing,
T-14. VIII.2:13 His Son l. in the Holy Spirit and in you.
T-14......XI.4:4 with God's glory, for in it l. His power,
T-14....XI.14:5 this consistency l. His Holiness which He
T-15...... I.10:3 In this redeeming instant l. Heaven. And
T-15...... I.15:4 Holiness l. not in time, but in eternity.
T-15......IV.4:3 For there l. peace, perfectly clear because
T-15......IV.7:3 that salvation l. in keeping thoughts to
T-15....... V.3:4 of the Atonement in which salvation l..
T-15....... V.9:6 The Holy Spirit's timelessness l. only here
T-15......VI.4:7 Herein l. peace, for here there *is* no conflict
T-15...VII.13:1 Forgiveness l. in communication as
T-15...VII.13:1 as surely as damnation l. in guilt. It is the
T-15... VIII.6:1 Holy Spirit alone l. the awareness of what
T-15......XI.6:4 of love l. in what you have cast outside
T-16.........I.2:1 the ego uses it is destructive l. in the fact
T-16.........I.6:2 l. in the strength of God that hovers over
T-16......IV.1:1 for freedom l. in looking at it. It would be
T-16......IV.1:9 extent of the split that l. in this you do not
T-16....IV.11:5 your completion l. in truth, and nowhere
T-16....... V.5:4 Holy Spirit knows that completion l. first
T-16....... V.5:5 To the ego completion l. in triumph, and
T-16....... V.9:1 of hell l. only in the terrible attraction of
T-16....... V.9:2 of littleness l. in every special relationship
T-16.....V.14:1 Salvation l. in the simple fact that
T-16.....V.15:1 core of the separation illusion l. simply in
T-16......VI.3:3 ego has taught you that freedom l. in it.
T-16...VII.11:6 The truth l. there and nowhere else. You
T-17.........I.1:1 of the Son of God l. only in illusions, and
T-17......IV.9:9 Death l. in this glittering gift. Let not your
T-17....IV.11:8 thought system of the ego l. in its gifts, so
T-17....IV.11:8 so the whole of Heaven l. in this instant,
T-17....IV.15:1 into what l. beyond the picture. As you
T-17....IV.16:7 Him l. in our relationship to one another.
T-17.....VII.7:3 and to the universe that l. beyond them,
T-18.........I.3:5 behavior, a far more serious effect l. in the
T-18...... I.11:1 your relationship, for in it l. the Sonship,
T-18......III.5:2 And in your desire l. its accomplishment.
T-18......IV.2:8 The miracle of the holy instant l. in your
T-18......IV.2:9 willingness for this l. also your acceptance
T-18....... V.6:4 The power of joining its blessing l. in the
T-18......IX.3:5 that speak of what l. underneath, for it is
T-18......IX.4:1 of fear l. just below the level the body sees
T-18....IX.12:2 Its meaning l. within itself. And learning

T-18....IX.13:3 to remind you of all that l. beyond it. Yet
T-19....... II.5:4 For here l. its "best" defense, which all the
T-19......IV.2:2 already l. deeply within must first expand
T19....IV.B.2:6 your strange belief that in it l. salvation?
T19..IV.B.11:3 But all that l. in it will come with it, and
T19..IV.B.11:5 In it l. disillusionment and the seeds of
T19....IV.C.9:6 deathless, and within it l. the end of death
T19....IV.D.1:4 and of everything that l. even beyond
T19....IV.D.3:3 what l. beyond the veil forever blotted out
T19....IV.D.5:7 power of the attraction of what l. beyond.
T19. IV.D.21:4 this world, whatever meaning l. in them.
T-20.........I.4:5 l. his release and your redemption with
T-20....... II.8:8 you the knowledge l., ready to be unveiled
T-20......III.9:4 in whom the meaning of your freedom l..
T-20......IV.2:2 therein l. your need to see your brother
T-20......IV.2:7 It l. in him to overlook all your mistakes,
T-20......IV.2:7 mistakes, and therein l. his own salvation.
T-20......IV.6:4 For in your part l. all of it, without which
T-20....... V.3:4 the meaningless attempt to judge what l.
T-20......VI.1:1 meaning of the Son of God l. solely in his
T-20......VI.7:8 purpose l. safe in your relationship, and
T-20.....VII.7:2 The difference l. not in them, but in their
T-21.......in.2:5 choice that l. between these two decisions
T-21.........I.2:4 are open, and you can see where safety l.;
T-21.......I.10:5 who is there in whom this memory l. not?
T-21....... II.2:2 for here the power of salvation l.: *I am*
T-21....... II.7:7 or do what l. beyond your understanding.
T-21......III.6:2 His purpose l. in the opposite direction.
T-21......IV.3:4 their belief that their identity l. in the ego.
T-21......IV.8:4 insane insistence that sureness l. in doubt
T-21....... V.3:1 another Voice in which your freedom l.,
T-21....... V.4:2 Reason l. in the other self you have cut off
T-21....... V.9:1 of mind where reason l. was dedicated, by
T-22.......in.4:8 that the sameness that l. beneath them all
T-22..... II.6:10 reason tells you misery l. only on one side
T-22..... II.12:3 How great the power that l. in it. Time
T-22......VI.2:1 as means whose value l. in its ability to
T-22....VI.10:7 for here l. buried the heavy anchor that
T-22....VI.12:7 Yet wherein l. its value, except in the
T-23.........I.3:8 Their joining l. in nothingness; two are as
T-23.... II.21:6 whole descent from Heaven l. in each one.
T-23......III.5:1 behalf, cannot perceive it l. within them.
T-24......VI.1:7 the sign that this is so l. in your brother,
T-24......VI.9:3 haunt you while your brother l. asleep, till
T-25.........I.3:2 It chooses where you think your safety l.,
T-25.........I.6:1 can be corrected where the error l..
T-25....... II.2:5 where no hope l. must make you hopeless
T-26......III.4:8 And herein l. the difference between the
T-26......III.6:5 Yet within this one l. the undoing of every
T-26......III.7:3 recognition this is so l. the ability to give
T-26......IV.1:2 gate behind which total lack of limits l..
T-26.....V.14:2 on the ground that l. between the worlds.
T-26.....V.14:3 reached the world that l. at Heaven's gate.
T-26.....VII.5:1 answer l. where the belief in sin must be,
T-26.....VII.5:4 corrected where the illusion of reversal l..
T-26...VII.12:6 Its failure l. in that you still feel guilty,
T-26...VII.15:4 In every miracle all healing l., for God
T-26... VIII.2:6 interval you think l. in between the giving
T-26... VIII.8:3 aspect of the little space that l. between
T-27..... II.3:11 in his healing l. the proof that he has truly
T-27....... II.4:6 undoing l. the proof that they are merely
T-27..... II.16:5 In His acceptance of this function l. the
T-27......VI.3:9 And otherwise he l., if you should call
T-27...VII.11:4 The gap between reality and dreams l. not
T-27... VIII.5:3 the second part, whose cause l. in the first
T-28......III.8:4 The dream of healing in forgiveness l.,
T-28......IV.9:1 to close each little gap that l. between the
T-28......IV.9:2 and perfect, l. in every one of them. And
T-28....... V.4:1 to be the place where all your safety l.,
T-28.....VII.6:2 and heavy anchors, when its weakness l.,
T-28.....VII.7:4 for its strength l. not within itself alone. It
T-29.........I.5:2 it with a power that l. not within itself.
T-29.........I.5:3 And herein l. its power over you. For now
T-29....... II.8:3 it be more than this l. the idea of sickness.
T-29....... V.5:3 and where it l. in him behold your peace.
T-29....... V.5:7 a brother's hand in which completion l..
T-29....... V.6:1 glorious goal that l. beyond forgiveness,
T-29......VI.1:4 for herein l. the end of separation and the
T-29.....VII.6:3 within, and your completion l. in Him.

T-30........II.3:5 l. in you has joined with God Himself in
T-30....... III.3:1 every idol l. the yearning for completion.
T-30.....IV.1:10 What l. beyond them cannot be attacked.
T-30....... V.8:5 blessing l. on you as surely as His Father's
T-30....... V.9:3 for what l. ahead is all you ever wanted in
T-30..... V.11:1 forever l. in those whose hands are joined.
T-30.....VII.5:1 Escape from judgment simply l. in this;
T-31.....VII.7:4 you glimpse a shadow of what l. beyond.
W-pI........4.2:4 ones are but shadows of what l. beyond,
W-pI......11.1:5 made sure. The key to forgiveness l. in it.
W-pI......12.1:1 importance of this idea l. in the fact that it
W-pI......31.4:3 your freedom l. the freedom of the world.
W-pI......38.5:3 *cannot do because the power of God l. in it.*
W-pI......51.4:8 all creation l. in the thoughts I think with
W-pI......55.3:2 Herein l. salvation, and nowhere else.
W-pI......58.5:2 Herein l. my claim to all good and only
W-pI......62.1:5 in your forgiveness l. your salvation.
W-pI......70.3:4 of healing where the need for healing l..
W-pI......76.1:4 must first realize salvation l. not there.
W-pI......80.5:6 is in this that the simplicity of salvation l..
W-pI......91.3:5 Your faith l. in the darkness, not the light.
W-pI......92.4:2 gaze upon the light that l. beyond them.
W-pI......99.7:2 these are words in which your freedom l..
W-pI....106.5:1 which lifts the veil that l. upon the earth,
W-pI....126.8:5 that l. in the idea we practice for today,
W-pI....127.3:3 Its meaning l. in oneness. And it must
W-pI....131.3:4 to choose a goal that l. beyond the world
W-pI. 131.11:8 completely lock to hide what l. beyond.
W-pI. 131.12:4 want, and only what l. past it do you seek.
W-pI....132.5:1 wish, and herein l. your ultimate release.
W-pI....134.7:3 It looks on l., but it is not deceived. It
W-pI....134.8:2 it becomes the undeceiver in the face of l.;
W-pI. 134.10:2 It is but l. that would condemn. In truth
W-pI. 134.10:4 world you see and that which l. beyond;
W-pI....135.1:2 And herein l. the folly of defense; it gives
W-pI. 136.10:2 by your illusions, truth turned into l., and
W-pI....137.4:1 would prove that l. must be the truth. But
W-pI....138.5:3 In recognition its acceptance l., and as it
W-pI. 152.11:1 in glad acknowledgment that l. are false,
W-pI.......153.h In my defenselessness my safety l..
W-pI....153.4:2 In them l. madness in a form so grim that
W-pI....157.2:3 and we catch a glimpse of what l. past the
W-pI....158.9:3 vision of the holiness that l. beyond them
W-pI....163.5:3 but this: "Here l. a witness God is dead."
W-pI....164.5:1 a curtain, to reveal what l. beyond them.
W-pI....165.1:1 own denial of the truth that l. beyond?
W-pI....165.4:5 Conviction l. within it. Till you welcome
W-pI....165.6:4 Your destiny l. there and nowhere else.
W-pI....165.8:3 His sureness l. beyond our every doubt.
W-pI....168.2:3 for in it l. remembrance of His Love.
W-pI....168.5:2 us. Our faith l. in the Giver, not our own
W-pI....169.6:4 It l. beyond salvation; past all thought of
WpI.rV.in12:3 recognize that it is only here conviction l..
W-pI....172.1:1 (153) In my defenselessness my safety l..
W-pI....181.1:4 the Self that l. beyond your own mistakes,
W-pI....181.2:8 and see the sinlessness that l. beyond.
W-pI. 185.14:1 mind, the hope that l. beyond despair,
W-pI....187.7:3 Your blessing l. on everyone who suffers,
W-pI....196.2:2 is quick to cite the truth to save its l.. Yet
W-pI....196.9:8 and freedom. Yet salvation l. in them.
W-pI....200.3:6 eyes to find that Heaven l. before you,
W-pI....200.8:4 where freedom l. within the peace of God.
W-pII ......3.3:4 where truth exists, upheld apart from l..
W-pII . 248.1:7 deceits and l. about the holy Son of God.
W-pII ......4.2:6 Truth can be its aim as well as l.. The
W-pII ......5.5:3 Your safety l. in truth, and not in lies.
W-pII ......5.5:3 Your safety lies in truth, and not in l..
W-pII ......6.2:3 He is the part in which God's Answer l.;
W-pII . 319.1:3 up the space the ego left unoccupied by l..
W-pII . 336.1:3 recall the memory that l. beyond them all.
W-pII . 342.1:4 *the door beyond which l. the end of dreams.*
M-4 ...... IV.2:8 of God's teachers l. in their gentleness, for
M-4 .....VII.1:7 Its greater strangeness l. merely in the
M-8 ........... 2:5 of creation; attempts to bring truth to l..
M-15 ......... 1:7 This is the Judgment in which salvation l..
M-15 ....... 1:10 silence l. across the world that everyone
M-16 ......... 6:6 Your safety l. not there. What you give up
M-17 ......... 5:7 And herein l. the birthplace of guilt. Who
M-18 ......... 1:9 the form alone in which the difference l..

M-19 .........5:4 this. In this l. either Heaven or hell, as you
M-20 .........5:4 it is not life in which the problem l.. Life
M-22 .......6:13 It is in the receiving, then, that healing l..
M-23 .........3:3 of the Son to the Father l. in him. His part
M-24 .......6:10 said that their truth l. in their usefulness.
C-in ...........3:3 cannot express what l. beyond symbols. It
C-2.............3:2 there be a truth that l. conceal effectively.
P-2......... II.3:5 for in it l. the ending of the world and all
P-2........IV.1:5 a decision that truth can lie and must be l.
P-2........IV.5:2 error l. in the belief that it can cure itself.
P-2........IV.8:3 Herein l. the basis of all errors, for all of
S-1...........I.7:4 are. Herein l. the power of prayer. It asks
S-1......... II.4:2 contradiction l. not in the actual words,
S-1......... II.6:7 enemies, for herein l. your own salvation.
S-1........IV.1:7 still in prayer l. in this simple thought;
S-2...........I.6:1 way in which your only hope of freedom l.
S-2........ III.1:8 His readiness to give l. far beyond your
S-3........ III.1:2 not removed the curse of sin that l. on it.
S-3........IV.3:5 creation, for it l. in you as His eternal gift.

**Life** 5
*life*

T-8....VIII.9:10 what life is, being the Voice for L. Itself.
T19....IV.C.7:7 the victory of lifelessness on L. Itself.
T-23.......IV.2:6 what is lifeless cannot be the Son of L..
T-29...... VI.2:3 keep. The Son of L. cannot be killed. He is
W-pII ...12.5:1 altar to illusions to the shrine of L. Itself.

**life** 315
*Life*
*See also* life-given, life-giving

T-1...........I.4:1 All miracles mean l., and God is the Giver
T-1...........I.4:1 mean life, and God is the Giver of l.. His
T-1........ III.2:2 word, which is the resurrection and the l.,
T-1........ III.2:2 shall not pass away because l. is eternal.
T-2.....VII.5:14 but have everlasting l." needs only one
T-2.....VIII.5:3 apparent that it is really the doorway to l..
T-3........VI.3:5 do not need judgment to organize your l.,
T-3.......VII.5:3 at your l. and see what the devil has made.
T-3.......VII.6:3 will shine from the true Foundation of l.,
T-3.......VII.6:6 death. L. and death, light and darkness,
T-4.........in.3:4 Until you do so your l. is indeed wasted. It
T-4......... II.9:5 to exist after a temporary lapse into ego l..
T-4........ III.3:5 you this l. is your existence because it is its
T-4......IV.11:7 I raised the dead by knowing that l. is an
T-4........VI.1:7 l. has continued without interruption,
T-5........ III.8:3 This is your l., your eternity and your Self.
T-6.........in.2:3 his l. without some thought system. Once
T-6...........I.2:8 contribution to make to your own l., and
T-6.........I.10:3 perceived as the way, the truth and the l..
T-6......V.A.1:3 Everything is accomplished through l.,
T-6......V.A.1:3 life, and l. is of the mind and in the mind.
T-6......V.A.1:4 because it cannot contain you who are l..
T-7........ III.1:9 you, *you* are the way, the truth and the l..
T-7.......VII.4:4 and they will have no l. for you because
T-7.......VII.4:5 in it, you are giving l. to them. Except
T-7.......VII.5:1 The gift of l. is yours to give, because it
T-7.......VII.5:5 All confusion comes from not extending l.
T-7....VIII.1:11 that is how it lives, and every mind is l..
T-8........VI.9:5 be separated from your l. and your being?
T-8....VIII.9:10 of the one Teacher Who knows what l. is,
T-8....VIII.9:10 beginning of the proper perspective on l.
T-10....... V.1:6 literal; denial of l. perceives its opposite,
T-11.......in.1:6 alive is fatherless, for l. is creation.
T-11.........I.9:5 Your will is His l., which He has given to
T-11.......I.9:10 death for himself because his Father is l.,
T-11.......I.11:5 who share His l. must share it to know it,
T-11......IV.6:7 God is my l. and yours, and nothing is
T-11......VI.4:1 I am *your* resurrection and *your* l.. You live
T-11......VI.8:3 to death whom God has given eternal l..
T-12......IV.6:1 that you might learn you have eternal l..
T-12......IV.6:3 pay no price for l. for that was given you,
T-12......IV.7:6 The Holy Spirit guides you into l. eternal,
T-12......IV.7:6 will not see l. though it is all around you.
T-12...VII.13:2 as God knows you are deserving of l.. The
T-12...VII.15:4 eternal l. have been given me of the Father
T-13.........I.2:5 Without guilt the ego has no l., and God's
T-13 .......II.4:4 it guards this one secret with its l., for its
T-13 ..... IV.3:2 be argued that death suggests there *was* l.,
T-13 ..... IV.3:2 no one would claim that it proves there *is* l.
T-13 ..... IV.3:3 Even the past l. that death might indicate,
T-14 .... IV.10:6 Communication with God is l.. Nothing
T-14 ..... VI.4:1 yields to l. simply because destruction is
T-14 ..... IX.4:4 fear of death will be replaced with joy of l.
T-14 ..... IX.4:5 For God is l., and they abide in life. Life is
T-14 ..... IX.4:5 For God is life, and they abide in l.. Life is
T-14 ..... IX.4:6 L. is as holy as the Holiness by which it
T-14 ..... IX.4:7 that lives, for Holiness created l., and
T-14 ..... XI.8:4 deal with certain aspects of your l. alone,
T-15 ........I.2:9 But to the Holy Spirit the goal is l., which
T-15 ........I.3:2 For it is as mistrustful of death as it is of l.,
T-15 ........I.5:2 to take the l. of someone who thinks its is
T-16 ........I.7:3 not the way, for it leads not to l. and truth
T-16 .... V.11:8 complete, for l. arises not from death, nor
T-17 ..... III.5:7 is given to Him Who gives it l. and beauty
T-17 ...... V.8:4 and do not breathe l. into your failing ego
T-18 ........I.4:4 to illusion, infinity to time, and l. to death
T-18 .... III.1:1 spent your l. in bringing truth to illusion,
T-18 ...VIII.5:4 Nor has it any l. apart and by itself.
T-18 ...VIII.6:6 It leads no separate l., because its life *is* the
T-18 ...VIII.6:6 its l. *is* the oneness in which its being was
T-18 ...VIII.8:7 And realize the l. and joy that love would
T-18 ...VIII.9:2 See how l. springs up everywhere! The
T-19 ..... IV.1:6 quietly extend to every aspect of your l.,
T19IV.A.17:12 meager store and make your l. complete.
T19....IV.C.1:9 because the ego is the "enemy" of l..
T19....IV.C.2:4 chorus, plodding so heavily away from l.,
T19..IV.C.2:13 you renounced death, exchanging it for l..
T19..IV.C.2:15 as l. is the result of the Thought of God.
T19....IV.C.3:1 death, in opposition to l. and innocence,
T19....IV.C.8:1 unable to protect the l. that He created
T19....IV.C.8:6 it to die, for only death could conquer l..
T19..IV.C.10:6 The miracle of l. is ageless, born in time
T19..IV.C.10:9 cross, but to the resurrection and the l..
T19... IV.D.1:4 The Creator of l., the Source of everything
T19... IV.D.4:2 this were gone, what could you fear but l.?
T19... IV.D.4:3 attraction of death that makes l. seem to
T19. IV.D.18:5 knows no sin, no death, but only l. eternal
T-20 ........I.2:3 This week we celebrate l., not death. And
T-20 .... III.9:3 it go or to take hold on l. so long forgotten
T-20 ... VI.11:3 And this unholy instant seems to be l.; an
T-21 ...........I.5:1 they define their l. and where they live,
T-21 ...VIII.1:5 He goes from l. to death, the final proof
T-22 .......II.7:3 Either you give each other l. or death;
T-23 ........I.5:3 It *is* forgotten in the body's l., and if you
T-23 .....II.12:9 that would give meaning to your l.. The
T-23 .....II.19:1 There is no l. outside of Heaven. Where
T-23 .....II.19:2 Where God created l., there life must be.
T-23 .....II.19:2 Where God created life, there l. must be.
T-23 .....II.19:3 any state apart from Heaven l. is illusion.
T-23 .....II.19:4 At best it seems like l.; at worst, like death
T-23 .....II.19:5 Yet both are judgments on what is not l.,
T-23 .....II.19:6 L. not in Heaven is impossible, and what
T-23 ..... IV.1:2 The fear of God is fear of l., and not of
T-23 ..... IV.3:7 is. L. makes not death, creating like itself.
T-24 .....II.14:4 death, but your awaking into l. eternal.
T-24 ..... III.6:1 Creator of the universe, the Source of l., of
T-24 ...... V.7:6 receiving from each one the gift of l. that
T-25 ......in.1:5 from what is at the very center of your l..
T-25 ......in.1:6 gives you l. cannot be housed in death. No
T-25 ........I.3:6 what seems to have a l. apart has none.
T-25 ........I.4:1 not separate, nor with a l. apart from His.
T-25 ........I.4:2 His l. is manifest in you who are His Son.
T-25 ..... IV.5:2 Every leaf that falls is given l. in you. Each
T-25 .... VII.2:1 is just as strong as is God's Will for l.. Nor
T-25 .. VII.13:2 Death demands l., but life is not
T-25 .. VII.13:2 life, but l. is not maintained at any cost.
T-25 ... VIII.3:7 over eternity and timelessness and l.?
T-25 .VIII.10:6 to plead for him, and not against his l.?
T-25 .VIII.14:1 from all effects of sin, and to the l. eternal,
T-26 ........I.7:1 can you be reborn, and given l. again. His
T-26 ........I.7:2 His holiness gives l. to you, who cannot
T-26 ........I.7:3 You who would make a sacrifice of l., and
T-26 ........I.7:7 the reach of any sacrifice of l. or death.
T-26 .... V.13:3 Such is each l.; a seeming interval from
T-26 .... V.13:3 from birth to death and on to l. again, a
T-26 ..... VI.2:1 Lead not your little l. in solitude, with
T-26 .. VII.16:7 Yet every instant offers l. to him because
T-27 ........I.6:3 not will for l. but wish for death that is the
T-27 ......I.6:10 how frail and vulnerable is your l.; how
T-27 ........I.7:3 For who could live a l. so soon cut short
T-27 ........I.7:7 The end of l. must come, whatever way
T-27 ........I.7:7 must come, whatever way that l. be spent.
T-27 ........I.9:7 It has no l., but neither is it dead. It stands
T-27 ......I.10:3 death. The body can become a sign of l., a
T-27 ......I.10:6 the power to represent an endless l.,
T-27 .......II.6:5 before the ancient clarion call of l.. This
T-27 .......V.6:3 L. is given you to give the dying world.
T-27 ..... VI.4:7 to your l. in Him Who knows no death.
T-27 ..... VI.5:7 death, so is the miracle the witness unto l.
T-27 ..... VI.5:8 can deny, for it is the effects of l. it brings.
T-27 .... VII.9:4 of evil or a happy wakening and joy of l..
T-27 .. VII.10:1 could you choose between but l. or death,
T-27 .. VII.10:4 to peace, because it is the opposite of l..
T-27 .. VII.10:5 life. And l. is peace. Awaken and forget all
T-27 .. VII.15:7 see as offering both l. and death to you.
T-27 .. VII.16:1 Brother, He gives but l.. Yet what you see
T-29 .......II.6:1 Son have l. and every living thing be part
T-29 .......II.6:1 be part of him, and nothing else have l..
T-29 .......II.6:2 What you have given "l." is not alive, and
T-29 .......II.6:2 but your wish to be alive apart from l.,
T-29 .......II.6:2 alive in death, with death perceived as l.,
T-29 .... IV.6:4 what you dream your l. was meant to be.
T-29 .......V.8:6 all dreams, unto the peace of everlasting l.
T-29 .... VII.4:4 And by this giving up is l. renounced.
T-29 .... VII.5:1 Idols must fall *because* they have no l.,
T-29 .... VII.5:3 found that represents a parody of l. which
T-29 .... VII.5:4 because a form of death cannot be l., and
T-29 .. VII.9:10 thus appears to threaten l. and offer death
T-29 .. VII.10:2 prove there is no death, and only l. exists.
T-29 ... VIII.5:3 be believed before it seems to come to l.,
T-29 ... VIII.5:4 Its l. and power are its believer's gift, and
T-29 ... VIII.5:4 miracle restores to what *has* l. and power
T-29 ..... IX.1:2 bow down in worship to what has no l.,
T-30 .......II.1:9 spark of l. but was created with your glad
T-30 .......II.3:3 to death, a little creature with a little l..
T-30 ..... III.6:6 nor have they a separate l. apart from his.
T-31 ........I.9:2 heard its calling as the ancient call to l.,
T-31 .......II.5:4 Herein is l. as easily as death, for what you
T-31 .......II.5:8 But if he calls for death or calls for l., for
T-31 .... VII.8:2 Lord of Love and l. entrusted all salvation
W-pI .... 20.3:6 Son, and he is the resurrection and the l..
W-pI .... 41.4:3 of all l. goes with you wherever you go.
W-pI .... 44.1:3 then think you see in it, but light reflects l.
W-pI .... 44.1:4 coexist, but light and l. must go together,
W-pI .... 47.4:4 your l. which you have invested with fear,
W-pI .... 54.2:3 I would not exist, because l. is thought.
W-pI .... 62.2:5 thoughts of l. may replace thoughts of
W-pI .... 72.5:3 as the Author of l. and not of death, He is
WpI..rII.in.5:1 to the way, the truth and the l.. Refuse to
W-pI .... 93.4:3 You think that this is death, but it is l..
W-pI .. 106.2:3 of l. and offer it to you for your belief.
W-pI .. 107.1:5 because, without belief, they have no l..
W-pI .. 107.8:2 which gave the gift of l. to Him as well. He
W-pI .. 110.3:1 sickness, nor can death be substitute for l.
W-pI .. 121.4:2 rising to attack its miserable parody of l..
W-pI .. 124.2:3 and death give place to everlasting l.. Our
W-pI .. 124.5:3 and the dead as well, restoring them to l..
W-pI .. 131.2:6 and while you seek for l. you ask for death
W-pI .. 132.8:4 you let thoughts of l. replace all thoughts
W-pI .. 133.2:1 You do not ask too much of l., but far too
W-pI .. 135.4:4 concern are needful to protect its little l.?
W-pI .. 135.5:4 all. Defend its l., or give it gifts to make it
W-pI .. 135.5:4 it must be guarded with your very l..
W-pI 135.18:4 for death, He led you gently to eternal l..
W-pI 135.19:1 increases, as this l. becomes a holy instant
W-pI 135.19:2 l. becomes a meaningful encounter with
W-pI .. 136.9:2 body is more powerful than everlasting l.,
W-pI 136.11:3 has not bowed to hell, nor l. to death. You
W-pI .. 137.3:5 and without the unity that gives It l.. But
W-pI .. 137.9:3 His l. becomes your own, as you extend
W-pI .. 138.7:2 and l. itself must in the end be overcome
W-pI .. 138.7:4 be seen as death, for l. is seen as conflict.
W-pI .. 138.7:5 resolve the conflict is to end your l. as well
W-pI .. 139.3:3 For what is l. except to be yourself, and

W-pI...139.5:1 Thus he becomes uncertain of his l., for
W-pI.151.12:1 for your l. is not a part of anything you see
W-pI...152.7:1 truth, and suffers death to triumph over l.
W-pI...156.2:5 He is what your l. is. Where you are He is.
W-pI...156.2:7 is. There is one l.. That life you share with
W-pI...156.2:8 That l. you share with Him. Nothing can
W-pI...156.3:1 He is, there must be holiness as well as l..
W-pI...156.3:3 what shares His l. is part of Holiness, and
W-pI...157.1:6 death. Today you learn to feel the joy of l..
W-pI...157.8:2 One, the Giver of the happy dreams of l.,
W-pI.159.10:5 transition can be made from death to l.;
W-pI...161.5:1 makes us suffer, and at last puts out our l..
W-pI...163.3:4 never fail to take all l. as hostage to itself.
W-pI...163.4:3 creation, stronger than God's Will for l.,
W-pI...163.7:3 His, and so eternal l. gave way to death.
W-pI...163.8:9 to look past death, and see the l. beyond.
W-pI...163.9:4 *We are not separate from Your eternal l..*
W-pI...163.9:6 *in the l. we share with You and with all living*
W-pI...165.1:2 and the eternal l. your Father wills for you
W-pI...165.2:5 It is your Source of l., holding you one
W-pI...165.2:7 Eternity and everlasting l. shine in your
W-pI......167.h There is one l., and that I share with God.
W-pI...167.1:1 There are not different kinds of l., for life
W-pI...167.1:1 kinds of life, for l. is like the truth. It does
W-pI...167.1:5 because what God created shares His l..
W-pI...167.5:1 Death cannot come from l.. Ideas remain
W-pI...167.7:1 opposite of l. can only be another form of
W-pI...167.7:1 of life can only be another form of l.. As
W-pI...167.8:3 death is not the opposite to thoughts of l..
W-pI...167.9:1 to be the opposite of l. is merely sleeping.
W-pI.167.10:2 l. is not as we imagine it. Who changes life
W-pI.167.10:3 Who changes l. because he shuts his eyes,
W-pI.167.10:5 will we let imagined opposites to l. abide
W-pI.167.10:5 of l. eternal has been set by God Himself.
W-pI.167.11:3 no opposite, we understand there is one l.
W-pI.167.11:3 He created in a unity of l. that cannot
W-pI.167.11:3 leave the Source of l. from where it came.
W-pI.167.12:1 share one l. because we have one Source, a
W-pI.167.12:3 the Lord of l. so perfectly it fades into
WpI.. rV.in5:4 Let us raise our hearts from dust to l., as
W-pI...179.1:1 (167) There is one l., and that I share
W-pI...184.2:3 think that you have given l. in separation.
W-pI.188.10:1 us to all living things that share our l.. We
W-pI...190.3:6 has shown that death is victor over l.. The
W-pI.191.11:5 die till you accept your own eternal l.. You
W-pI...193.6:1 death becomes our choice instead of l.?
W-pI...196.3:4 death, to thoughts of liberation and of l..
W-pI...196.5:5 and waiting to destroy his l. and blot him
W-pI...200.3:1 for eternal l. in peace that has no ending.
W-pI...205.1:3 *seek, my purpose and my function and my l.,*
W-pII..222.1:2 He is my Source of l., the life within, the
W-pII..222.1:2 He is my Source of life, the l. within, the
W-pII.....223.h God is my l.. I have no life but His.
W-pII.....223.h God is my life. I have no l. but His.
W-pII..223.1:2 Now I know my l. is God's, I have no
W-pII.....233.h I give my l. to God to guide today.
W-pII......3.5:5 to die can be restored to everlasting l..
W-pII..242.1:1 I will not lead my l. alone today. I do not
W-pII..242.1:2 lead my l. alone must be but foolishness.
W-pII......4.3:3 must have an end; eternal l. must die.
W-pII......4.4:3 guilt, with but a little l. that ends in death.
W-pII..263.1:1 *Spirit entered into it, Your Love gave l. to it.*
W-pII..267.1:1 is all the l. that God created in His Love. It
W-pII..314.1:4 claim the future now, for l. is now its goal,
W-pII....12.1:1 doomed to suffer and to end its l. in death
W-pII....12.1:3 weak and love is fearful, l. is really death,
W-pII..331.1:9 *Death is illusion; l., eternal truth. There is no*
W-pII....13.5:4 And everywhere the signs of l. spring up,
W-pII....13.5:4 never die, for what has l. has immortality.
W-pII....14.1:2 *sanctified and guaranteed eternal l.. In me is*
Wfl ........in.4:4 the truth and l. that shows the way to us.
M-3............5:5 other for some time, and perhaps for l..
M-4......I.A.4:2 the changes in his l. are always helpful, he
M-4.......IX.1:2 still select some aspects of his l. to bring
M-5..........I.2:4 would hide from himself to protect his "l..
M-5.....III.2:11 you Son of God, what l. can offer you.
M-6............1:6 if the patient uses sickness as a way of l.,
M-9...............h ARE CHANGES REQUIRED IN THE L.
M-9............1:6 are called upon to change their l. situation
M-11 .........2:5 sees but death as the inevitable end of l..
M-20 .........5:4 it is not l. in which the problem lies. Life
M-20 .........5:5 L. has no opposite, for it is God. Life and
M-20 .........5:6 is God. L. and death seem to be opposites
M-20 .........5:6 because you have decided death ends l..
M-23 .........2:5 death because he has accepted l.. He has
M-24 .........1:6 the recognition of the eternal nature of l.,
M-24 .........2:3 he is laying the groundwork for a future l.,
M-24 .........2:8 idea that l. and the body are not the same.
M-27 .........1:2 it not madness to think of l. as being born
M-27 .........1:5 to be accepted as the "natural" law of l..
M-27 .........2:3 He holds your little l. in his hand but by a
M-27 .........2:5 love, because he has denied that l. is real.
M-27 .........3:7 Devouring is nature's "law of l.." God is
M-27 .........4:2 If death is real for anything, there is no l..
M-27 .........4:3 Death denies l.. But if there is reality in
M-27 .........4:4 But if there is reality in l., death is denied.
M-27 .........6:7 can be born of death and still have l.? But
M-28 .........2:1 denial of death, being the assertion of l..
M-28 .........2:3 L. is now recognized as salvation, and
C-5.............3:5 l. in any way be changed by sin and evil,
C-5.............5:3 little l. on earth was not enough to teach
C-5.............6:6 them without accepting him into your l..
C-ep...........4:7 will grow in l. and strength and hope,
P-1.............2:3 than to recall the way, the truth and the l.,
P-1.............3:4 willing to "sacrifice" his "l." on its behalf.
P-2.......VII.4:3 God, devoting his l. to the function of true
S-1 ......... II.1:2 It is a part of l.. But it does change in form
S-1 ......... II.2:4 And prayer is as continual as l.. Everyone
S-2 ...........I.1:6 appears to be a terrible alternative to l..
S-3 ...........I.2:3 be to those who think their l. is tied to its
S-3 ........IV.8:1 of retribution and a little l. beset with fear

## life's 4

T-29....VI.4:10 L. function cannot be to die. It must be
T-29....VI.4:11 It must be l. extension, that it be as one
W-pI...167.2:1 appears to be a state that is l. opposite.
M-27 .........2:6 Death has become l. symbol. His world is

## life-given 1

T-4.........I.2:14 make the totally lifeless out of the l..

## life-giving 1

T-20. VIII.11:1 l. water running happily beside them in

## lifeless 6

T-4.........I.2:14 make the totally l. out of the life-given.
T-17....IV.13:5 is exposed to light, it becomes dull and l.,
T-23......IV.2:6 And what is l. cannot be the Son of Life.
T-29.....VII.5:1 no life, and what is l. is a sign of death.
M-4 ....... X.2:5 now which seemed so dull and l. before.
C-ep.........1:11 Who stands before a l. image when a step

## lifelessness 3

T-18......IX.2:4 The barren sands, the darkness and the l.,
T19....IV.C.7:7 creation, the victory of l. on Life Itself.
T-29.....VII.5:3 represents a parody of life which, in its l.,

## lifelong 1

M-3 ...........5:1 which, once they are formed, are l.. These

## lifetime 2

T-18.....VII.4:4 Many have spent a l. in preparation, and
T-18.....VII.4:9 a l. of contemplation and long periods of

## lift 26

T-16....IV.10:4 l. the veil that seems so dark and heavy, it
T-16....IV.13:9 the Love of God in us together cannot l..
T-18. VIII.11:6 shining Self will l. the tiny aspect that you
T19...IV.D.3:2 in secret to the ego never to l. this veil,
T19...IV.D.8:7 l. up your eyes and look on your brother
T19. IV.D.16:5 Help him to l. the heavy burden of sin you
T19. IV.D.21:3 that it would l. you far beyond the veil,
T-20......II.8:11 Let us l. up our eyes together, not in fear
T-22...... IV.6:4 This veil you and your brother l. together
T-31....VIII.9:3 to l. us high above the thorny roads we
W-pI.....50.3:2 It will l. you out of every trial, and raise
W-pI.....78.2:3 but lay it down and gently l. our eyes in
W-pI.....91.7:3 your faith in, as you l. it from the body.
W-pI...95.12:3 to l. the veil of darkness from the world,
W-pI...123.4:1 gratitude we l. our hearts above despair,
W-pI...125.9:2 let your practicing today l. you above the
W-pI...128.5:4 Thus do we l. the chains that bar the door
W-pI.151.16:4 Now do we l. our resurrected minds in
W-pI...152.9:4 and l. our hearts in true humility instead
W-pI.161.11:5 and l. the crown of thorns which you have
Wi181-200 2:2 We are attempting now to l. these blocks,
C-4.............8:3 Here He leans down to l. you up to Him,
S-1.........in.3:2 and bless you as you l. your heart to Him
S-2..........II.8:8 prayer will l. you up and bring you home
S-3........ IV.9:1 to l. the heavy burden from the world.
S-3........ IV.9:2 L. up your hearts to greet its advent. See

## lifted 38

T-13...VII.17:2 until I have l. every voice with mine. And
T-13..VIII.10:5 The miracles you do on earth are l. up to
T-13...... IX.4:6 and l. from his mind the cloud of guilt
T-15...... VI.6:2 veil that has been drawn across reality is l.
T-16...... VI.8:1 be abruptly l. up and hurled into reality.
T-17........II.7:1 forgiven world the Son of God is l. easily
T-18.... VI.13:4 You are not really "l. out" of it; it cannot
T-18.... VI.14:4 There are the laws of limit l. for you, to
T-18.... IX.13:2 l. high above the darkness and gently
T19....IV.A.9:4 this little wisp is l. up and carried away,
T19... IV.D.4:6 agreed never to let the fear of God be l., so
T19... IV.D.6:4 if you look on this and let the veil be l.,
T-20..... VII.4:3 the result of letting the effects of sin be l.,
T-22...... IV.3:2 Let it be l.! Raise it together with your
T-22...... IV.6:5 let illusions be l. from their minds are this
T-23......II.15:6 to look upon, is l. to the throne of love, its
T-23...... IV.5:1 Be l. up, and from a higher place look
T-25.........I.4:5 The veil is l. through its gentleness, and
T-26...... IX.3:4 It is Their Presence which has l. holiness
T-27....... V.3:4 dead, are gently l. up and comforted.
T-28.......I.15:6 that he be l. up and gently carried over.
T-29...... III.4:2 the darkness may be l. from your mind.
T-30.......I.17:7 Your judgment has been l. from the world
T-30...... III.9:1 it safe, forever l. up and anchored sure. Its
T-31..... VII.8:7 and now the veil is l. from his sight.
W-pI.....69.1:3 But as the veil of your grievances is l., you
W-pI.....69.2:5 We are trying to let the veil be l., and to
W-pI.....69.7:1 will begin to feel a sense of being l. up and
W-pI...105.8:2 have let all bars to peace and joy be l. up,
W-pI...122.3:1 Forgiveness lets the veil be l. up that
W-pI...132.3:3 For as you let the past be l. and release the
W-pI.140.12:1 with l. hearts and listening minds we pray
W-pI...192.6:1 pain was l. from a sick and tortured mind.
W-pII .333.1:4 For only then are its defenses l., and the
M-25 .........6:7 they laid upon their minds be l.. It can be
M-28 .........4:8 world, as it is l. up and brought to truth.
S-1........ III.5:5 how your heart is l. and your fear released
S-1......... V.3:1 Now prayer is l. from the world of things,

## lifting 8

T-15...... VI.6:5 has not yet experienced the l. of the veil,
T-18.... VI.13:6 the l. of the barriers of time and space,
T-18.... IX.14:3 the untrue, l. the shadows from the world
T19....IV.D.i.h The L. of the Veil
W-pI.122.11:2 the joy the l. of the veil holds out to you.
W-pI.134.16:3 honesty, you will begin to sense a l. up, a
Wi181-200 2:3 sense of liberation which their l. brings.
S-1........ III.1:4 becomes a means for l. your projections

## lifts 10

T-5........ IV.6:1 and thus l. the burden you have placed in
T-11...... IV.5:7 His Son l. his voice in praise of his Creator
T-16.... IV.13:4 you across l. you from time into eternity.

| | |
|---|---|
| T-26 IX.4:4 | up every living thing and l. it into Heaven, |
| T-29 VIII.5:6 | out. It merely l. the veil, and lets the truth |
| W-pI 73.5:4 | Forgiveness l. the darkness, reasserts your |
| W-pI 78.3:2 | and as it l. you see the Son of God where |
| W-pI 106.5:1 | which l. the veil that lies upon the earth, |
| W-pI 134.12:5 | and as he l. his foot to stride ahead a star |
| W-pI 168.3:2 | gift by which God leans to us and l. us up, |

## Light 5

*light*

| | |
|---|---|
| T-3 V.10:9 | Know yourself in the One L. where the |
| T-8 VII.12:4 | and gives it over entirely to the One L. in |
| T-10 IV.8:6 | the spark is still as pure as the Great L., |
| T-11 III.4:7 | Great L. always surrounds you and shines |
| T-13 VI.10:1 | Child of L., you know not that the light is |

## light 752

*Light*

| | |
|---|---|
| T-1 I.24:4 | not exist. Only the creations of l. are real. |
| T-1 I.33:2 | about yourself and perceive the l. in you. |
| T-1 I.39:2 | is the same as saying that by perceiving l., |
| T-1 IV.3:1 | Darkness is lack of l. as sin is lack of love. |
| T-2 I.4:6 | l. is suddenly turned on while someone is |
| T-2 I.4:6 | may initially interpret the l. itself as part |
| T-2 I.4:7 | l. is correctly perceived as the release from |
| T-2 II.1:14 | It brings all error into the l., and since |
| T-2 III.1:1 | within you by releasing the inner l.. Since |
| T-2 V.6:6 | learned to look beyond it toward the l.. |
| T-2 VII.5:4 | Whenever l. enters darkness, the |
| T-3 I.6:6 | It is perfectly clear because it exists in l.. |
| T-3 I.7:7 | of evil, as l. abolishes forms of darkness. |
| T-3 II.1:3 | impossible to conceive of l. and darkness |
| T-3 II.1:7 | has not experienced *some* l. and *some* thing |
| T-3 IV.6:6 | because l. abolishes darkness merely by |
| T-3 V.10:6 | are the Thoughts of God who live in His l. |
| T-3 VII.4:9 | to attack ideas that might bring it to l.. |
| T-3 VII.5:4 | this making will surely dissolve in the l. of |
| T-3 VII.5:5 | cannot be shaken, because the l. is in it. |
| T-3 VII.6:3 | The l. will shine from the true Foundation |
| T-3 VII.6:6 | and death, l. and darkness, knowledge |
| T-4 I.3:2 | destruction, of the ego to the l. of spirit. |
| T-4 I.12:3 | and gladly sheds its l. everywhere. The |
| T-4 III.5:2 | and hiding is why the l. cannot enter. The |
| T-4 III.7:3 | L. cannot penetrate through the walls you |
| T-4 IV.9:1 | in which God Himself shines in perfect l.. |
| T-5 in.1:4 | l. that belongs to you is the light of joy. |
| T-5 in.1:4 | light that belongs to you is the l. of joy. |
| T-5 in.3:4 | l. is so strong that it radiates throughout |
| T-5 I.5:7 | creations and keep them in the l. of joy. |
| T-5 II.4:1 | enter your mind and so you need a new l.. |
| T-5 II.10:3 | You are the l. of the world with me. Rest |
| T-5 II.11:4 | yoke is easy and my burden l." in this way |
| T-5 II.11:4 | "Let us join together, for my message is l.. |
| T-5 III.7:5 | Understanding is l., and light leads to |
| T-5 III.7:5 | is light, and l. leads to knowledge. The |
| T-5 III.7:6 | is in l. because He is in you who are light, |
| T-5 III.7:6 | is in light because He is in you who are l., |
| T-5 IV.3:10 | them in the l. of the Kingdom, making |
| T-5 IV.8:4 | them of the errors that hid their l., and |
| T-5 VI.5:1 | Spirit can reinterpret them in His Own l.. |
| T-5 VI.11:1 | I said "I am come as a l. into the world," I |
| T-5 VI.11:1 | meant that I came to share the l. with you. |
| T-6 II.13:4 | mind. This alignment with l. is unlimited, |
| T-6 II.13:4 | it is in alignment with the l. of the world. |
| T-6 II.13:5 | Each of us is the l. of the world, and by |
| T-6 II.13:5 | joining our minds in this l. we proclaim |
| T-6 V.2:1 | that the night is over and the l. has come? |
| T-6 V.2:5 | they will themselves call on the l. to dispel |
| T-6 V.4:6 | away. His l. is always the Call to awaken, |
| T-6 V.4:7 | shining with the l. from God Himself, |
| T-6 V.C.1:2 | to enter it in the l. of what God put there. |
| T-6 V.C.1:3 | is in accord with this l. He retains, to |
| T-7 I.7:14 | His l. was never obscured, because it is |
| T-7 III.4:10 | brothers, because it sees only in its own l.. |
| T-7 III.5:1 | keeps your mind lit by His l. because His |
| T-7 III.5:1 | light because His l. is what your mind is. |
| T-7 V.10:6 | Your mind is so powerful a l. that you can |
| T-7 V.11:3 | them make them aware of the l. in them. |
| T-7 V.11:4 | This l. will shine back upon you and on |
| T-7 VI.8:5 | the l. of your understanding would dispel |
| T-7 XI.5:1 | When a mind has only l., it knows only |
| T-7 XI.5:1 | a mind has only light, it knows only l.. Its |
| T-8 III.1:3 | Ask for l. and learn that you *are* light. If |
| T-8 III.1:3 | Ask for light and learn that you *are* l.. If |
| T-8 III.1:4 | to listen to the Teacher Who knows of l., |
| T-8 IV.2:1 | I am come as a l. into a world that does |
| T-8 IV.2:5 | That is why I am the l. of the world. If I |
| T-8 IV.2:9 | my l. must dispel it because of what it is. |
| T-8 IV.2:10 | is. L. does not attack darkness, but it does |
| T-8 IV.2:11 | If my l. goes with you everywhere, you |
| T-8 IV.2:12 | me. The l. becomes ours, and you cannot |
| T-8 VII.2:2 | you have made in the l. of what He is. The |
| T-9 II.5:8 | there is a l. in his mind that does know. |
| T-9 II.5:9 | This l. can shine into yours, giving truth |
| T-9 V.6:2 | When God said, "Let there be l.," there |
| T-9 V.6:2 | God said, "Let there be light," there *was* l.. |
| T-9 V.6:3 | Can you find l. by analyzing darkness, as |
| T-9 V.6:3 | and looking for a distant l. to remove it, |
| T-9 V.6:5 | it is understood, since l. *is* understanding. |
| T-9 V.7:5 | The l. in his mind will therefore answer |
| T-9 V.7:5 | with God that there is l. *because* he sees it. |
| T-9 V.7:8 | miracle worker begins by perceiving l., |
| T-9 V.8:2 | darkness but he cannot bring l. of himself |
| T-9 V.8:2 | bring light of himself, for l. is not of him. |
| T-9 VI.4:3 | this. Neither God's l. nor yours is dimmed |
| T-10 IV.8:3 | little spark you will learn of the greater l., |
| T-10 IV.8:4 | will heal, but knowing the l. will create. |
| T-10 IV.8:5 | the little l. must be acknowledged first, |
| T-11 in.3:2 | for His thought system is l.. Remember |
| T-11 in.3:4 | thought system, the clearer the l. becomes |
| T-11 in.3:7 | it. Bring this l. fearlessly with you, and |
| T-11 in.3:9 | which it rests, and bring it out into the l.. |
| T-11 I.10:6 | in darkness, denying that the l. is in you. |
| T-11 II.5:4 | little spark becomes a blazing l. that fills |
| T-11 III.h | From Darkness to L. |
| T-11 III.3:3 | When the l. comes and you have said, |
| T-11 III.4:6 | in l. and do not see the dark companions, |
| T-11 III.4:6 | of God, who was created *of* l. and *in* light. |
| T-11 III.4:6 | of God, who was created *of* light and *in* l.. |
| T-11 III.4:8 | the dark companions in a l. such as this? |
| T-11 III.4:9 | it is only because you are denying the l.. |
| T-11 III.4:10 | for the l. is here and the way is clear. |
| T-11 III.5:2 | and gave him the l. that shines in him. |
| T-11 III.5:6 | Turn toward the l., for the little spark in |
| T-11 III.5:6 | for the little spark in you is part of a l. so |
| T-11 III.6:1 | children of l. cannot abide in darkness, |
| T-11 III.8:1 | and bless it with the l. your Father gave it. |
| T-11 IV.3:3 | because the l. He created is one with Him. |
| T-11 IV.3:4 | cut off a brother from the l. that is yours? |
| T-11 IV.4:2 | it is truly the beginning of the dawn of l.. |
| T-11 V.2:9 | upon darkness through l. must dispel it. |
| T-11 V.17:6 | in His l. and behold what He created. |
| T-12 II.1:7 | l. in another mind must shine into theirs |
| T-12 II.1:7 | shine into theirs because that l. *is* theirs. |
| T-12 II.2:1 | l. in them shines as brightly regardless of |
| T-12 II.2:2 | give no power to the fog to obscure the l., |
| T-12 VI.5:8 | in the quiet l. of the Holy Spirit's blessing. |
| T-12 VI.7:2 | so enlightened that l. streams into it, and |
| T-13 II.5:1 | In the calm l. of truth, let us recognize |
| T-13 II.9:2 | and if you will but bring it to the l., the |
| T-13 II.9:2 | but bring it to the light, the l. will dispel it |
| T-13 III.7:5 | leave any spot of pain hidden from His l., |
| T-13 III.11:5 | For a darkened mind cannot live in the l., |
| T-13 V.8:1 | Vision depends on l.. You cannot see in |
| T-13 V.8:8 | Yet for this, l. must be excluded. Dreams |
| T-13 V.8:9 | disappear when l. has come and you can |
| T-13 V.9:2 | the vision of Christ, Who looks on all in l.. |
| T-13 V.11:1 | Holy Spirit is the l. in which Christ stands |
| T-13 V.11:2 | can see Him, for they have asked for l.. |
| T-13 VI.2:4 | the present, *unless you are afraid of l.* And |
| T-13 VI.7:1 | in the l. that would unite you with them, |
| T-13 VI.7:3 | refusing to accept the l. that is offered you |
| T-13 VI.7:4 | For the l. of perfect vision is freely given |
| T-13 VI.8:4 | God's guiltless Son is only l.. There is no |
| T-13 VI.8:7 | for the l. to the Creator of light. The holy |
| T-13 VI.8:7 | for the light to the Creator of l.. The holy |
| T-13 VI.8:8 | holy l. that shines forth from God's Son is |
| T-13 VI.8:8 | is the witness that his l. is of his Father. |
| T-13 VI.10:1 | of Light, you know not that the l. is in you |
| T-13 VI.10:2 | having given l. to them they will return it. |
| T-13 VI.10:3 | it. Each one you see in l. brings your light |
| T-13 VI.10:3 | brings your l. closer to your awareness. |
| T-13 VI.11:1 | There is a l. that this world cannot give. |
| T-13 VI.11:4 | l. will attract you as nothing in this world |
| T-13 VI.11:8 | L. is unlimited, and spreads across this |
| T-13 VI.11:10 | Your l. will join with theirs in power so |
| T-13 VI.12:2 | attraction of l. must draw you willingly, |
| T-13 VI.12:7 | cannot look upon the l. you gave to them. |
| T-13 VII.1:4 | It is not lit with artificial l., and night |
| T-13 VII.11:6 | to tighten up your world against the l., |
| T-13 VII.12:2 | all things that do not block the way to l.. |
| T-13 VII.13:4 | Under His guidance you will travel l. and |
| T-13 VII.13:7 | for l. needs nothing but to shine in peace, |
| T-13 VII.14:1 | journey that would lead away from l., |
| T-13 VII.16:10 | like a veil of l. across the world's sad face, |
| T-13 VIII.2:7 | vision of Christ beholds everything in l.. |
| T-13 VIII.4:6 | that spring to l. under His loving gaze are |
| T-13 VIII.5:3 | perceived in the same l. and therefore one |
| T-13 VIII.5:5 | For l. must come into the darkened world |
| T-13 VIII.5:6 | Help Him to give His gift of l. to all who |
| T-13 VIII.8:4 | The holy l. you saw outside yourself, in |
| T-13 VIII.8:5 | And knowing that the l. is in you, your |
| T-13 IX.1:3 | law. Fidelity to this law lets no l. in, for it |
| T-13 IX.7:1 | of guilt within you, you will not see the l.. |
| T-13 IX.8:5 | are too afraid to look upon the l. within. |
| T-13 IX.8:13 | then, upon the l. He placed within you, |
| T-13 X.9:6 | to the holy place where you will see the l.. |
| T-13 X.10:2 | way to look within and see the l. of love, |
| T-13 XI.9:7 | watches over him and l. surrounds him. |
| T-14 II.4:3 | He brings the l. of truth into the darkness, |
| T-14 II.4:4 | realizing that this l. is not what you have |
| T-14 II.4:5 | learners of the lesson this l. brings to |
| T-14 II.4:6 | as nothing, until you bring the l. to them. |
| T-14 II.7:7 | The key is only the l. that shines away the |
| T-14 II.7:8 | join Him in the holy task of bringing l.. |
| T-14 II.7:9 | realize the l. has come and freed you from |
| T-14 II.8:2 | The l. in you will waken them, and they |
| T-14 III.6:2 | replace darkness with l. and fear with love |
| T-14 III.6:3 | to free his brother and enter l. with him. |
| T-14 III.6:5 | he became afraid of darkness and of l.. |
| T-14 III.16:2 | what God knows about you, and in this l., |
| T-14 IV.9:1 | live in the l. of the blessing of their Father, |
| T-14 V.4:4 | Bring innocence to l., in answer to the call |
| T-14 VI.h | The L. of Communication |
| T-14 VI.1:1 | together is the exchange of dark for l., of |
| T-14 VI.2:1 | quiet l. in which the Holy Spirit dwells |
| T-14 VI.2:3 | darkness that the l. of love will not dispel, |
| T-14 VI.3:7 | of obscurity only the l. of love remains, |
| T-14 VI.3:7 | for only this has meaning and can live in l. |
| T-14 VI.4:2 | The l. of guiltlessness shines guilt away |
| T-14 VI.8:4 | let His gentleness teach you that, in the l., |
| T-14 VI.8:5 | must open all doors and let the l. come |
| T-14 VII.1:2 | L. or darkness, knowledge or ignorance |
| T-14 VII.1:6 | As darkness disappears in l., so ignorance |
| T-14 VII.5:1 | L. cannot enter darkness when a mind |
| T-14 VII.6:4 | He brings the l. to darkness if you make |
| T-14 VII.6:9 | He holds the l., and you the darkness. |
| T-14 IX.2:4 | What disappears in l. is not attacked. It |
| T-14 IX.6:1 | Reflections are seen in l.. In darkness |
| T-14 IX.7:4 | their different problems to its healing l., |
| T-14 X.5:3 | Where there was l., darkness removes it |
| T-14 X.5:3 | alternating patterns of l. and darkness |
| T-14 X.10:6 | you bring with you a l. so powerful that |
| T-14 XI.3:8 | any event or anything or anyone in its "l., |
| T-14 XI.3:9 | for if you do you contradict the l., and |
| T-14 XI.4:1 | you have taught yourself into the l. in you, |
| T-14 XI.4:3 | child of l. by Him to Whom God gave it. |
| T-14 XI.4:7 | Who teaches l. He will accept from you, |
| T-14 XI.6:9 | *own past learning as the l. to guide me now.* |
| T-14 XI.9:5 | He has brought all of them to l., having |
| T-15 VI.6:5 | drawn irresistibly into the l. behind it, can |
| T-15 VII.3:5 | As we bring it to l., your only question |
| T-15 XI.2:1 | sign of Christmas is a star, a l. in darkness |
| T-16 VI.11:5 | increased with each l. that returns to take |
| T-17 II.4:1 | The stars will disappear in l., and the sun |

| | |
|---|---|
| T-17....... II.5:3 | In the l. of the real reason that He brings, |
| T-17...... III.7:1 | to l. your way and make it clear to you. |
| T-17...... IV.8:4 | in the dim l. in which the offering is made |
| T-17.. IV.12:11 | The other is lightly framed and hung in l., |
| T-17.... IV.13:5 | the frame in darkness is exposed to l., it |
| T-17.... IV.14:6 | The dark picture, brought to l., is not |
| T-17.... IV.15:1 | l., in clear-cut and unmistakable contrast, |
| T-17....... V.6:9 | recognized as such in the l. of its goal. |
| T-17..... V.11:8 | what seemed to be the l. of the mistakes? |
| T-17..... VII.8:9 | The l. of truth shines from the center of |
| T-18...... I.13:6 | holy l. that brought you and him together |
| T-18......... III.h | L. in the Dream |
| T-18...... III.1:3 | that seemed to bring a l. into the darkness |
| T-18...... III.1:4 | darkness, in which no ray of l. could enter |
| T-18...... III.1:7 | The l. is *in* you. Darkness can cover it, but |
| T-18...... III.2:1 | l. comes nearer you will rush to darkness, |
| T-18...... III.2:5 | Let us then join quickly in an instant of l., |
| T-18...... III.2:5 | enough to remind you that your goal is l.. |
| T-18...... III.4:3 | In your relationship is this world's l.. And |
| T-18...... III.6:2 | been willing to bring the darkness to l., |
| T-18...... III.6:4 | me in carrying their l. into the darkness, |
| T-18...... III.6:4 | the darkness in them is offered to the l., |
| T-18...... III.6:5 | with me in the holy l. of your relationship, |
| T-18...... III.7:1 | the function of bringing l. to darkness. |
| T-18...... III.7:2 | darkness in you has been brought to l.. |
| T-18...... III.8:1 | Not one l. in Heaven but goes with you. |
| T-18...... III.8:6 | brother, and you will l. each other's way. |
| T-18...... III.8:7 | this l. will the Great Rays extend back into |
| T-18...... III.8:7 | in which everything is radiant in the l.. |
| T-18..... VII.5:7 | the l. comes at last into the mind given to |
| T-18...... IX.1:1 | been told to bring the darkness to the l., |
| T-18...... IX.2:1 | little offering of darkness to the eternal l.. |
| T-18...... IX.5:3 | not apparent until you see the l. behind it. |
| T-18...... IX.5:4 | then you see it as a fragile veil before the l. |
| T-18...... IX.8:3 | world of l. whereon they cast no shadows. |
| T-18...... IX.8:4 | beyond them, still further from the l.. Yet |
| T-18...... IX.8:5 | them to the l. their shadows cannot fall. |
| T-18...... IX.9:1 | This world of l., this circle of brightness is |
| T-18.... IX.10:6 | Here is the Source of l.; nothing perceived |
| T-18.... IX.13:1 | and firmly rooted in the world of l.. From |
| T-19...... IV.3:5 | And the l. in them will show you all that |
| T19... IV.A.6:7 | shadows from the l. in which illusions end |
| T19.... IV.B.6:3 | And in the l. of your forgiveness he will |
| T19.... IV.B.8:5 | new perception that will bring l. to all the |
| T19... IV.C.7:2 | the great dark savior from the l. of truth, |
| T19... IV.D.2:3 | bright Rays of His Father's Love that l. His |
| T19... IV.D.2:3 | fades in the blazing l. beyond it when the |
| T-20......... I.3:4 | l. of his own innocence lighting his way to |
| T-20....... II.3:4 | And each has set a l. upon his altar, that |
| T-20....... II.4:6 | points gleam sharply in a blood-red l., the |
| T-20....... II.9:2 | His innocence will l. your way, offering |
| T-20....... II.9:2 | you its guiding l. and sure protection, and |
| T-20...... III.7:3 | the shining l. the Holy Spirit offered, and |
| T-20...... III.9:1 | in darkness they remember not the l., do |
| T-20.... III.11:8 | In your brother is the l. of God's eternal |
| T-20....... V.5:8 | through time like golden l. is all the same; |
| T-20... VIII.3:1 | sinlessness is given you in shining l., to |
| T-21......... I.2:4 | which way leads to darkness, which to l.. |
| T-21......... I.8:1 | is an arc of golden l. that stretches as you |
| T-21......... I.8:2 | all the circle fills with l. before your eyes. |
| T-21......... I.8:4 | all. The l. expands and covers everything, |
| T-21......... I.8:6 | for there is nowhere that this l. is not. |
| T-21...... I.10:6 | The l. in one awakens it in all. And when |
| T-21.... III.11:7 | Nor is it possible that what gives l. be one |
| T-21.... III.12:2 | in the l. of vision it is looked upon quite |
| T-21...... IV.2:3 | for if you do your eyes will l. on sin, and |
| T-22..... II.12:1 | and shining in the golden l. that reaches it |
| T-22..... II.12:8 | to l. His home with vision that overlooks |
| T-22...... IV.3:7 | The Love of Christ will l. your face, and |
| T-22...... IV.3:7 | it into a darkened world that needs the l.. |
| T-22...... IV.4:6 | which you will bring to l. the tired eyes of |
| T-22......... VI.h | The L. of the Holy Relationship |
| T-22...... VI.4:1 | and blazing with a l. far brighter than the |
| T-22...... VI.5:6 | you fill again with the eternal l. you bring, |
| T-22...... VI.6:1 | Child of peace, the l. *has* come to you. The |
| T-22...... VI.6:2 | The l. you bring you do not recognize, |
| T-22.... VI.9:11 | be dispelled by Him Who knows the l., |
| T-22.... VI.15:1 | l. that joins you and your brother shines |
| T-23....... in.5:4 | it and perceive the l. of which he is a part. |
| T-23....... in.5:5 | Your innocence will l. the way to his, and |
| T-23....... in.6:2 | it lovingly, and see the l. of Heaven in it. |
| T-23....... I.11:3 | The altar disappears, the l. grows dim, the |
| T-23....... II.1:1 | The "laws" of chaos can be brought to l., |
| T-23...... IV.4:1 | The lovely l. of your relationship is like |
| T-23...... IV.8:4 | Only the l. they love is in awareness, and |
| T-24....... V.5:5 | see and hear and hold and lead is given l., |
| T-24.... VI.11:3 | and every window barred against the l.. |
| T-24..... VII.5:7 | holiness, and rests in l. as safely as itself. |
| T-24..... VII.5:8 | Nor will that l. go out when it is gone. Its |
| T-24..... VII.5:9 | immortality, setting another l. in Heaven, |
| T-24..... VII.9:2 | body in a different l. and it looks different |
| T-24..... VII.9:3 | And without a l. it seems that it is gone. |
| T-25....... in.3:4 | His purpose folds the body in His l., and |
| T-25......... I.4:4 | into l. merely by looking past it *to* the light |
| T-25......... I.4:4 | into light merely by looking past it *to* the l. |
| T-25...... II.7:3 | and casts a veil of l. across the picture's |
| T-25...... II.7:3 | the l. that shines from it to its Creator. |
| T-25..... II.11:5 | from darkness into l. be yours to share; |
| T-25..... III.5:4 | it must be, and l. the body up instead of it |
| T-25..... III.6:3 | him out of darkness into l. at any time. |
| T-25..... III.7:9 | descend on them, and offer them the l.. |
| T-25......... IV.h | The L. You Bring |
| T-25..... IV.3:5 | and covers them in gentleness and l.. And |
| T-25..... IV.3:6 | this widening world of l. the darkness that |
| T-25..... IV.4:5 | they may be pushed away before the l.. |
| T-25.... IV.5:12 | to bring the l. of Heaven with you, as you |
| T-25.... IV.5:12 | walk beyond the world of darkness into l. |
| T-25...... VI.2:1 | and the l. of brilliant day seems painful to |
| T-25...... VI.3:1 | and brings the gift of l. that makes sight |
| T-25...... VI.7:7 | In l., you see it as your special function in |
| T-25..... VII.7:6 | and made with reason in the l. of sense. |
| T-26......... I.7:2 | can the l. in you be blotted out because he |
| T-26..... IV.2:2 | Each flower shines in l., and every bird |
| T-26..... IV.3:7 | And here does every l. of Heaven come, to |
| T-26..... V.11:9 | but still a present l. is dimly recognized. |
| T-26... V.11:10 | it is seen, this l. can never be forgotten. It |
| T-26..... VII.2:4 | be carefully preserved from reason's l.. |
| T-26... VII.18:5 | which is not resolved within its gracious l. |
| T-26...... IX.3:2 | become a living temple in a world of l.. |
| T-26...... IX.5:3 | what was held apart from l. is given up, |
| T-26...... IX.5:3 | that l. may shine on it and leave no space |
| T-26...... IX.5:3 | between the l. of Heaven and the world. |
| T-26...... IX.6:5 | the brightest l. in Heaven's radiance. And |
| T-26...... IX.7:1 | sin, and keep the l. where it has entered in |
| T-26....... X.6:3 | And so you see yourself deprived of l., |
| T-26....... X.6:4 | has brought injustice to the l. within, and |
| T-27...... IV.1:4 | of view is not an answer in another l.. You |
| T-27....... V.6:5 | holy instant's radiance will l. your eyes, |
| T-27... VII.16:3 | in l. of charity and kindness offered you. |
| T-29......... I.3:3 | make the way to l. seem dark and fearful, |
| T-29...... III.3:1 | tiny spark, a space of l. created in the dark |
| T-29...... III.3:6 | see him shining in the space of l. where |
| T-29...... III.3:7 | is. Before this l. the body disappears, as |
| T-29...... III.3:7 | as heavy shadows must give way to l.. The |
| T-29...... III.3:9 | The coming of the l. means it is gone. In |
| T-29...... III.4:3 | When l. has come to him through your |
| T-29...... III.4:4 | your face he saw the l. that he would keep |
| T-29...... III.4:4 | through darkness to the everlasting l.. |
| T-29...... III.5:4 | l. in him is brighter still because you gave |
| T-29...... III.5:4 | still because you gave your l. to him, to |
| T-29...... III.5:5 | And now the l. in you must be as bright as |
| T-29....... V.6:1 | l. the touch of evil on it may appear to be. |
| T-29..... VII.9:8 | you must protect against the l. of truth. |
| T-29... VIII.3:7 | Yet the l. is there. A cloud does not put |
| T-29... VIII.3:9 | nor darken by one whit the l. itself. |
| T-29... VIII.5:5 | the l. the veil between has not put out. It |
| T-29... VIII.7:4 | A place of darkness set where all is l., a |
| T-29...... IX.4:2 | you sinful and put out the l. within you. |
| T-29...... IX.4:3 | child, the l. is there. You do but dream, |
| T-30....... II.3:8 | No l. of Heaven shines except for you, for |
| T-30...... III.8:7 | its l. grew dimmer or less perfect ever was. |
| T-30...... III.9:1 | Who knows the Father knows this l., for |
| T-30....... V.8:1 | l. and easy is the step across the narrow |
| T-30..... VII.2:7 | a meaning in the l. of goals that change, |
| T-30..... VII.6:7 | For there is no l. by which they can be |
| T-31..... II.11:4 | l. cannot be given while you walk alone, |
| T-31..... II.11:7 | to you is One Who holds the l. before you, |
| T-31..... II.11:9 | And He Who travels with you *has* the l.. |
| T-31....... V.6:6 | as errors, which the l. would surely show. |
| T-31..... V.11:1 | must be kept in darkness is that, in the l., |
| T-31..... V.17:5 | on no assumptions that would stand the l. |
| T-31...... VI.7:4 | remains as radiant as a star, as pure as l., |
| T-31..... VII.7:3 | The l. is kept from everything you see. At |
| T-31..... VII.8:7 | For there is l. where darkness was before, |
| T-31... VII.11:7 | He brings the l. to what he looks upon, |
| T-31... VII.15:1 | Let not the world's l., given unto you, be |
| T-31... VII.15:2 | It needs the l., for it is dark indeed, and |
| T-31.... VIII.2:6 | And the l. of Christ in you is given charge |
| T-31.. VIII.11:1 | l. that shines beyond in perfect constancy. |
| T-31.. VIII.12:7 | Clear in Your likeness does the l. shine |
| W-pI..... 15.2:2 | you have seen little edges of l. around the |
| W-pI..... 15.3:1 | go along, you may have many "l. episodes |
| W-pI..... 23.4:5 | now. Loveliness can l. your images, and so |
| W-pI..... 28.2:8 | The l. you will see in any one of them is |
| W-pI..... 28.2:8 | them is the same l. you will see in them all |
| W-pI..... 28.8:1 | of the subject your eyes happen to l. on, |
| W-pI..... 41.5:3 | and to go through it to the l. beyond. |
| W-pI........ 44.h | God is the l. in which I see. |
| W-pI..... 44.1:2 | see in darkness, and you cannot make l.. |
| W-pI..... 44.1:3 | then think you see in it, but l. reflects life, |
| W-pI..... 44.1:4 | coexist, but l. and life must go together, |
| W-pI..... 44.2:1 | to see, you must recognize that l. is within |
| W-pI..... 44.2:3 | is the l. that makes seeing possible. It is |
| W-pI..... 44.3:1 | we are going to attempt to reach that l.. |
| W-pI..... 44.6:2 | that to reach l. is to escape from darkness, |
| W-pI..... 44.6:3 | God is the l. in which you see. You are |
| W-pI... 44.10:1 | if not actually entering into l.. Try to |
| W-pI... 44.10:2 | Try to think of l., formless and without |
| W-pI..... 53.5:4 | to cast their beneficent l. on what I see. |
| W-pI..... 56.4:3 | the face of love, its l. remains undimmed. |
| W-pI..... 57.5:4 | upon has taken on the l. of my forgiveness |
| W-pI..... 57.5:5 | In this l. I begin to see what my illusions |
| W-pI..... 58.2:3 | see in its l. shares in the joy it brings to me |
| W-pI..... 59.4:1 | (44) God is the l. in which I see. I cannot |
| W-pI..... 59.4:3 | God is the only l.. Therefore, if I am to see |
| W-pI..... 59.4:6 | that God is the l. in which I see. Let me |
| W-pI........ 61.h | I am the l. of the world. |
| W-pI..... 61.1:1 | is the l. of the world except God's Son? |
| W-pI..... 61.2:4 | humility to insist you cannot be the l. of |
| W-pI..... 61.5:3 | *I am the l. of the world. That is my only* |
| W-pI..... 61.7:5 | You are the l. of the world. God has built |
| W-pI........ 62.h | Forgiveness is my function as the l. of the |
| W-pI..... 62.1:1 | will bring the world of darkness to the l.. |
| W-pI..... 62.1:2 | lets you recognize the l. in which you see. |
| W-pI..... 62.1:3 | that you are the l. of the world. Through |
| W-pI..... 62.5:2 | *is my function as the l. of the world. I would* |
| W-pI........ 63.h | The l. of the world brings peace to every |
| W-pI..... 63.2:1 | the l. of the world with such a function. |
| W-pI..... 63.3:4 | *l. of the world brings peace to every mind* |
| W-pI..... 64.3:1 | function here is to be the l. of the world, a |
| W-pI..... 67.1:2 | are. This is why you are the l. of the world. |
| W-pI..... 67.4:3 | the awareness of a blazing l. in which you |
| W-pI........ 69.h | grievances hide the l. of the world in me. |
| W-pI..... 69.1:2 | grievances are hiding the l. of the world in |
| W-pI..... 69.1:5 | in the l. of the world that saves you both. |
| W-pI..... 69.2:1 | another real attempt to reach the l. in you |
| W-pI..... 69.3:5 | search today by finding the l. in us, and |
| W-pI..... 69.5:1 | there is a brilliant l. hidden by the clouds. |
| W-pI..... 69.6:1 | you want to reach the l. in you today,– |
| W-pI..... 69.7:2 | will raise you from darkness into l.. You |
| W-pI..... 69.8:3 | attempt to go through the clouds to the l., |
| W-pI..... 69.9:1 | the l. of the world from your awareness. |
| W-pI..... 69.9:4 | *My grievances hide the l. of the world in me. I* |
| W-pI..... 69.9:8 | *I hold this grievance the l. of the world will be* |
| W-pI..... 70.8:1 | we will try again to reach the l. in you, |
| W-pI..... 70.8:2 | find it in the clouds that surround the l., |
| W-pI..... 70.8:4 | It is past the clouds and in the l. beyond. |
| W-pI..... 70.8:5 | the clouds before you can reach the l.. But |
| W-pI..... 70.9:1 | easily walk on into the l. of real salvation. |
| W-pI..... 72.9:1 | l. of truth is in us, where it was placed by |
| W-pI..... 72.9:4 | To recognize the l. of truth in us is to |
| W-pI........ 73.h | I will there be l.. |
| W-pI..... 73.4:2 | The l. is in it because it does not oppose |
| W-pI..... 73.4:3 | Heaven, but the l. of Heaven shines on it. |
| W-pI..... 73.4:6 | l. that shines upon this world reflects your |
| W-pI..... 73.5:2 | of neither l. nor darkness can be found |
| W-pI..... 73.5:4 | will, and lets you look upon a world of l.. |

W-pI.....73.9:6 to look upon the l. in him and be saved.
W-pI...73.10:2 *I will there be l.. Let me behold the light that*
W-pI...73.10:3 *the l. that reflects God's Will and mine.* Then
W-pI...73.11:3 *I will there be l.. Darkness is not my will.* This
W-pI........75.h The l. has come.
W-pI.....75.1:1 The l. has come. You are healed and you
W-pI.....75.1:3 The l. has come. You are saved and you
W-pI.....75.1:7 death have disappeared. The l. has come.
W-pI.....75.2:3 The l. has come. Today the time of light
W-pI.....75.2:4 the time of l. begins for you and everyone.
W-pI.....75.2:7 a different world, because the l. has come.
W-pI.....75.3:5 We will to see the l.; the light has come.
W-pI.....75.3:5 We will to see the light; the l. has come.
W-pI.....75.4:5 Sight is given us, now that the l. has come.
W-pI.....75.5:2 We see the l., and in it we see Heaven's
W-pI.....75.5:4 *The l. has come. I have forgiven the world.*
W-pI.....75.6:8 *The l. has come. I have forgiven the world.*
W-pI...75.7:10 The l. has come. You have forgiven the
W-pI.....75.8:4 Today the l. has come. And you will see
W-pI...75.10:2 *The l. has come. I have forgiven the world.*
W-pI...75.10:5 *The l. has come. I have forgiven you.*
W-pI.....76.7:6 The l. has come because there are no laws
W-pI.....78.1:4 Yet all the while it waits for you in l., but
W-pI.....78.3:1 in shining l. where each one stood before.
W-pI.....78.3:3 He stands in l., but you were in the dark.
W-pI.....78.7:1 savior shining in the l. of true forgiveness,
W-pI.....78.7:3 *to lead me to the holy l. in which he stands,*
W-pI.....78.7:4 the l. in him beyond your grievances.
W-pI...78.10:2 refuse to hide his l. behind our grievances.
W-pI.....80.2:4 deception aside, and seen the l. of truth.
W-pI.....81.1:1 (61) I am the l. of the world. How holy
W-pI.....81.1:4 In its calm l. let all my conflicts disappear.
W-pI.....81.2:2 *Let me not obscure the l. of the world in me.*
W-pI.....81.2:3 *me. Let the l. of the world shine through this*
W-pI.....81.2:4 *This shadow will vanish before the l..*
W-pI.....81.3:1 is my function as the l. of the world. It is
W-pI.....81.3:2 my function that I will see the l. in me.
W-pI.....81.3:3 And in this l. will my function stand clear
W-pI.....81.3:5 Yet I will trust that, in the l., I will see it as
W-pI.....82.1:1 l. of the world brings peace to every mind
W-pI.....82.1:2 is the means by which the l. of the world
W-pI.....82.1:3 become aware of the l. of the world in me.
W-pI.....82.2:3 *I share the l. of the world with you, [name].*
W-pI.....84.3:3 attack love and keep its l. obscure. If I
W-pI.....85.1:1 grievances hide the l. of the world in me.
W-pI.....85.1:4 They keep me in darkness and hide the l..
W-pI.....85.1:5 Grievances and l. cannot go together, but
W-pI.....85.1:5 l. and vision must be joined for me to see.
W-pI.....85.2:3 *The l. of the world will shine all this away. I*
W-pI.....85.3:7 reflect the l. that shines in me and in itself
W-pI.....86.2:4 *this only in the l. of God's plan for salvation.*
W-pI.....87.1:1 (73) I will there be l.. I will use the power
W-pI.....87.1:4 L. shall be my guide today. I will follow it
W-pI.....87.2:2 *This cannot hide the l. I will to see. You stand*
W-pI.....87.2:3 *You stand with me in l., [name]. In the light*
W-pI.....87.2:4 *[name]. In the l. this will look different.*
W-pI.....88.1:1 The l. has come. In choosing salvation
W-pI.....88.1:6 The l. has come. I can but choose the light
W-pI.....88.1:7 come. I can but choose the l., for it has no
W-pI.....88.2:2 *show me darkness, for the l. has come. The*
W-pI.....88.2:3 *The l. in you is all that I would see, [name]. I*
W-pI........91.h Miracles are seen in l..
W-pI.....91.1:7 You will see them in the l.; you will not
W-pI.....91.2:1 To you, then, l. is crucial. While you
W-pI.....91.2:5 Denial of l. leads to failure to perceive it.
W-pI.....91.2:6 to perceive l. is to perceive darkness. The
W-pI.....91.2:7 The l. is useless to you then, even though
W-pI.....91.2:9 darkness makes the idea of l. meaningless
W-pI.....91.3:5 Your faith lies in the darkness, not the l..
W-pI.....91.6:2 *Miracles are seen in l.. The body's eyes do*
W-pI.....91.6:3 *The body's eyes do not perceive the l.. But I*
W-pI.....91.8:9 *a reality. I cannot see in darkness, but in l..*
W-pI...91.10:5 is the l. in which you will see miracles,
W-pI...91.11:1 yourself that miracles are seen in l.. Also,
W-pI...91.11:4 *Miracles are seen in l.. Let me not close my*
W-pI........92.h Miracles are seen in l., and light and
W-pI........92.h seen in light, and l. and strength are one.
W-pI.....92.1:2 You do not think of l. in terms of strength
W-pI.....92.3:1 in you that is the l. in which you see, as it
W-pI.....92.4:2 gaze upon the l. that lies beyond them. It
W-pI.....92.4:3 It unites with l., of which it is a part. It
W-pI.....92.4:5 It brings the l. in which your Self appears.
W-pI.....92.4:7 God appointed that there should be l..
W-pI.....92.5:1 and shines with l. its Source has given it;
W-pI.....92.5:6 it gives its l. that all may see and benefit as
W-pI.....92.7:3 while l. and strength perceive themselves
W-pI.....92.7:4 The l. of strength is not the light you see.
W-pI.....92.7:4 The light of strength is not the l. you see.
W-pI.....92.8:1 The l. of strength is constant, sure as love
W-pI.....92.8:2 and strength and l. abiding in his heart.
W-pI.....92.9:1 The strength in you will offer you the l.,
W-pI.....92.9:2 Strength and l. unite in you, and where
W-pI...92.10:3 the l. in which the gift of sight is given you
W-pI...92.10:4 today, and we will practice seeing in the l.,
W-pI...92.10:4 self and Self, where l. and strength are one
W-pI...92.11:3 led away from darkness to the l. where
W-pI........93.h L. and joy and peace abide in me.
W-pI.....93.4:1 and that l. and joy and peace abide in you
W-pI.....93.6:7 and l. and joy and peace abide in you.
W-pI.....93.7:7 L. and joy and peace abide in you because
W-pI.....93.8:2 *L. and joy and peace abide in me. My*
W-pI.....93.9:8 l. and joy and peace abide in you because
W-pI...93.10:4 hour: *L. and joy and peace abide in me. My*
W-pI...93.11:3 *L. and joy and peace abide in you. Your*
W-pI.....94.2:1 True l. is strength, and strength is
W-pI.....94.2:2 you must be strong and l. must be in you.
W-pI.....94.2:3 be the guarantee of strength and l. as well.
W-pI.....94.2:6 You stand in l., strong in the sinlessness
W-pI...95.12:1 united and secure in l. and joy and peace.
W-pI...95.12:3 let the l. in you come through to teach the
W-pI.....97.6:3 steady brilliance of this l. remains and
W-pI.....98.7:4 will bring the l. to all the words you say,
W-pI.....98.8:1 will l. the world with hope and gladness.
W-pI.....99.8:3 Let in the l., and you will look upon no
W-pI.....99.8:4 Open your secrets to His kindly l., and see
W-pI.....99.8:4 see how bright this l. still shines in you.
W-pI.....99.9:1 and let His l. seek out and lighten up all
W-pI...100.3:4 the l. that God Himself appointed as the
W-pI...100.4:2 Just as your l. increases every light that
W-pI...100.4:2 increases every l. that shines in Heaven,
W-pI...107.6:3 not hide. It stands in open l., in obvious
W-pI...108.1:2 The l. is in it, for it reconciles all seeming
W-pI...108.1:3 And what is l. except the resolution, born
W-pI...108.2:1 True l. that makes true vision possible is
W-pI...108.2:1 is not the l. the body's eyes behold. It is a
W-pI...108.3:1 This is the l. that shows no opposites,
W-pI...108.3:2 l. that brings your peace of mind to other
W-pI...108.3:3 This is the l. that heals because it brings
W-pI...108.7:5 to us. L. is tranquility, and in that peace is
W-pI...110.3:3 to l. the world and free it from the past.
W-pI...111.1:1 (91) Miracles are seen in l.. *I cannot see in*
W-pI...111.1:3 *the l. of holiness and truth light up my mind,*
W-pI...111.1:3 *the light of holiness and truth l. up my mind,*
W-pI...111.2:1 (92) Miracles are seen in l., and light and
W-pI...111.2:1 seen in light, and l. and strength are one. *I*
W-pI...111.3:2 Miracles are seen in l.. On the half hour:
W-pI...111.3:4 hour: Miracles are seen in l., and light and
W-pI...111.3:4 seen in light, and l. and strength are one.
W-pI...112.1:1 (93) L. and joy and peace abide in me. *I*
W-pI...112.1:2 me. *I am the home of l. and joy and peace. I*
W-pI...112.3:2 L. and joy and peace abide in me. On the
W-pI...121.3:1 yet more terrified at the approach of l..
W-pI.121.11:2 Try to perceive some l. in him somewhere
W-pI.121.11:4 till you see a l. somewhere within it, and
W-pI.121.11:4 try to let this l. extend until it covers him,
W-pI.121.12:2 Try to transfer the l. you learned to see
W-pI.121.12:3 that l. his holiness shows you your savior,
W-pI.121.13:1 let him offer you the l. you see in him, and
W-pI.122.12:1 Before the l. you will receive today the
W-pI.122.12:2 Now we walk directly into l., and we
W-pI.122.13:4 change; the l. of truth behind appearances
W-pI...124.1:4 on a shining l. that blesses and that heals.
W-pI...124.2:5 way because the l. we carry stays behind,
W-pI.124.11:1 the sinless l. you see belongs to you; the
W-pI...129.7:5 that are not of this world l. one by one,
W-pI...129.8:2 Here is l. your eyes can not behold. And
W-pI.131.13:2 it. Angels l. the way, so that all darkness
W-pI.131.13:2 and you are standing in a l. so bright and
W-pI 131.13:3 you in the l. reflects the truth you knew,
W-pI 131.14:2 His aid slip effortlessly past it, to the l..
W-pI 134.12:5 His step is l., and as he lifts his foot to
W-pI 135.20:1 you become a l. which Heaven gratefully
W-pI 135.20:3 Your followers will join their l. with yours
W-pI 135.24:2 And in the l. and joy of simple trust, you
W-pI 135.25:5 Now is the l. of hope reborn in you, for
W-pI 136.16:2 and keep defended from the l. of truth.
W-pI 138.10:1 shield of unawareness, and is brought to l.
W-pI 138.11:3 is real, is flimsy and transparent in the l..
W-pI .. 140.2:4 He has not seen the l. that would awaken
WpI..rIV.in9:3 restored the world from darkness to the l.
W-pI .. 151.7:4 the holy l. of what He sees do all the ego's
W-pI 153.10:1 secure you rest, untouchable within its l..
W-pI 153.11:4 Nor will you learn that l. has come to you,
W-pI 153.11:5 For you will not see the l., until you offer
W-pI 154.14:1 The world recedes as we l. up our minds,
W-pI .. 156.4:1 There is a l. in you which cannot die;
W-pI .. 156.5:1 The l. in you is what the universe longs to
W-pI .. 156.5:3 The l. you carry is their own. And thus
W-pI .. 156.5:5 you, transforming in Its gentle l. all things
W-pI .. 156.6:2 l. in you steps forward and encompasses
W-pI .. 156.8:6 *I l. the world, I light my mind and all the*
W-pI .. 156.8:6 *I l. my mind and all the minds which God*
W-pI .. 157.1:3 upon, and cast a timeless l. upon this day,
W-pI .. 157.2:2 that sheds a l. on all that we have learned
W-pI .. 157.4:3 is needed but today's idea to l. your mind,
W-pI .. 157.6:1 you experience this day to l. the world.
W-pI .. 157.7:2 it l. will come to see the light more sure;
W-pI .. 157.7:2 it light will come to see the l. more sure;
W-pI .. 158.7:3 It beholds a l. beyond the body; an idea
W-pI .. 158.7:5 without the slightest fading of the l. it sees
W-pI 158.10:4 in sin, so must you be; if you see l. in him,
W-pI .. 159.5:3 to obscure the l. that shines beyond them.
W-pI .. 159.7:2 made new again, but in a different l..
W-pI .. 159.8:4 They need the l. and warmth and kindly
W-pI .. 162.6:5 The l. is come today to bless the world.
W-pI .. 164.6:2 the world, looks back on them in a new l..
W-pI .. 164.7:6 it in the l. in which our Savior looks on us,
W-pI 167.12:5 and the l. which makes reflection possible
W-pI .. 168.4:3 grace you see a l. that covers all the world
W-pI .. 168.4:3 as hearts rise up and claim the l. as theirs.
W-pI 169.13:2 all who see the l. that lingers in your face.
WpI...rV.in5:4 was sent to open up the path of l. to us,
WpI...rV.in7:3 turns to the l. in him and looks for me. I
W-pI .. 182.4:6 to earth the pure reflection of the l. above,
W-pI .. 188.1:2 seek the l. are merely covering their eyes.
W-pI .. 188.1:3 The l. is in them now. Enlightenment is
W-pI .. 188.1:5 L. is not of the world, yet you who bear
W-pI .. 188.1:5 bear the l. in you are alien here as well.
W-pI .. 188.1:6 l. came with you from your native home,
W-pI .. 188.2:1 This l. can not be lost. Why wait to find it
W-pI .. 188.4:4 blessing does the l. in you shine brighter,
W-pI .. 188.6:2 The l. within you is sufficient. It alone has
W-pI .. 188.9:1 coming nearer to the l. in us today. We
W-pI .. 188.9:4 We let the l. within our minds direct them
W-pI 188.10:7 *And let me bless them with the l. in me.*
W-pI .. 189.1:1 is a l. in you the world can not perceive.
W-pI .. 189.1:2 And with its eyes you will not see this l.,
W-pI .. 189.1:6 l. is a reflection of the thought we practice
W-pI .. 189.2:5 salvation in you, and protects the l. in you
W-pI .. 189.3:5 and peace offers its gentle l. to everyone,
W-pI 190.11:2 l. of Heaven for the darkness of the world.
W-pI 191.10:5 Your glory is the l. that saves the world.
W-pI .. 192.3:6 that the l. of day already shines in them,
W-pI .. 192.7:2 Without its kindly l. we grope in darkness
W-pI .. 192.7:4 thoughts, our eyes shut tight against the l.
W-pI .. 193.2:5 to let the l. of Heaven shine upon it. It is
W-pI .. 194.5:3 when the l. that was kept hidden in God's
W-pI .. 196.3:4 within today's idea the l. of resurrection,
W-pI .. 197.8:4 Nor can you dim the l. of your perfection.
W-pI .. 198.9:2 find the key to l. and let the darkness end:
W-pI 198.11:3 is there tranquil l. across the face of earth,
W-pII . 224.1:1 guilt, that Heaven looks to It to give it l.. It
W-pII . 225.1:2 *my mind and keeping it within its kindly l.,*
W-pII ..... 2.4:6 gone, and we have come together in the l..
W-pII . 237.1:2 allow the l. in me to shine upon the world
W-pII . 239.2:1 *Father, for the l. that shines forever in us.*
W-pII . 239.2:3 *are one, united in this l. and one with You, at*

T-11.......I.9:10 his Father is life, and His Son is l. Him.
T-11.......I.11:7 For it is your will to be l. Him, Whose
T-11....... II.5:4 Think l. Him ever so slightly, and the
T-11....... II.6:2 To have Him is to be l. Him, and He has
T-11...... III.3:6 I cannot tell you what this will be l., for
T-11...... III.5:7 Father *is* your Creator, and you *are* l. Him.
T-11.... VI.10:3 part must be l. mine if you learn it of me.
T-11.... VI.10:9 And to Christ it is given to be l. the Father
T-11..... VII.2:5 And being loving they are l. the Father,
T-11..... VII.3:8 Yet everything true *is* l. Him. Perceiving
T-12...... IV.6:8 is whole and all His extensions are l. Him.
T-13.........I.3:5 reach its end it will roll up l. a long carpet
T-13...... III.1:6 You do not l. it, but it is not your desire to
T-13...... III.8:4 l. you they long for the grandeur that is in
T-13...... IV.4:3 by making the future l. the past, and thus
T-13...... IV.8:1 in place of eternity, for l. the Holy Spirit,
T-13..... VII.1:1 tell yourself: "The real world is not l. this.
T-13. VII.16:10 we will spread it l. a veil of light across the
T-13...... IX.1:8 l. a lamp shining so brightly that the
T-13...... IX.3:3 faith in the past, the future will be l. it.
T-13....... X.9:9 His Will is l. His Father's, and He offers
T-13..... X.11:6 true, you will have no idea what love is l..
T-13..... X.13:1 L. you, my faith and my belief are
T-14....... II.4:1 L. you, the Holy Spirit did not make
T-14....... II.4:2 L. God, He knows it to be true. He brings
T-14....... II.7:9 For, l. your brothers, you do not realize
T-14...... IV.2:1 by Him l. unto Himself and part of Him,
T-14.... IV.10:2 Each perceives the other as l. himself,
T-14..... VII.5:8 Defenses, l. everything you made, must
T-14.... XI.11:3 God's Teacher is as l. to His Creator as is
T-14.... XI.11:6 Teach l. Him here, and you will
T-14.... XI.11:6 you have always created l. your Father.
T-15.........I.2:7 The ego, l. the Holy Spirit, uses time to
T-15...... III.6:5 lie in you from God are for all who, l. you,
T-15....... V.6:6 not have judged them so l. you in lack.
T-15....... V.8:3 see them all the same and l. yourself. Nor
T-15...... VI.4:5 to accept is the fact that, l. your Father,
T-15...... VI.4:6 an idea. And l. Him, you can give yourself
T-15.... VIII.4:6 where they become l. to their Father.
T-15....... X.4:3 It seems l. many, but it is all the same. For
T-16.........I.2:4 increase itself by sharing what is l. itself.
T-16..... II.9:10 Can you be alone with witnesses l. these?
T-16..... IV.9:1 special, but only to be wholly l. to Him,
T-17....... II.1:4 And nothing will you value l. unto this,
T-17.... III.2:10 gathering to itself what it perceives as l.
T-17...... III.5:4 transformed past is made l. the present.
T-17...... IV.8:4 The glitter of blood shines l. rubies, and
T-17...... IV.8:4 and the tears are faceted l. diamonds and
T-17....... V.1:2 L. everything about salvation, the holy
T-18.........I.7:6 l. feathers dancing insanely in the wind,
T-18...... VI.9:8 love. Yet love must be forever l. itself,
T-18.... VIII.3:3 instantly that it is l. the smallest sunbeam
T-18.... VIII.3:3 or l. the faintest ripple on the surface of
T-18.... VIII.6:1 L. to the sun and ocean your Self
T-18.... VIII.8:1 and reaches to everything created l. itself.
T-18...... IX.6:1 this artificial floor that looks l. rock, is
T-18...... IX.6:1 is l. a bank of low dark clouds that seem
T-19.......I.10:3 most loving Father, loved by Him l. you,
T-19....... II.8:1 is l. walking through a mist into the sun?
T19..IV.B.14:5 L. any communication medium the body
T19..IV.B.17:4 Son. L. the ego, the Holy Spirit is both the
T19... IV.D.2:1 to be surmounted hangs l. a heavy veil
T19... IV.D.2:3 the face of Christ Himself l. to a leper's,
T19. IV.D.16:6 Press it not l. thorns against his brow, nor
T-20...... III.4:2 Do you l. what you have made?–a world
T-20...... III.5:1 not wondered what the world is really l.;
T-20...... III.6:2 as the world the ego looks upon is l. itself.
T-20....... V.5:8 runs through time l. golden light is all the
T-20....... V.7:1 Can you evaluate the giver of a gift l. this?
T-20.... VI.12:6 l. your real relationship with God as equal
T-20.... VI.12:6 God as equal things are l. unto each other
T-20..... VII.5:8 For vision, l. relationships, has no order.
T-21.........I.1:1 what it really looks l. is unknown to them.
T-21.........I.2:2 to imagine what the world must look l.. It
T-21.........I.6:1 l. a song whose name is long forgotten,
T-21..... II.12:1 The Son's creations are l. his Father's. Yet
T-21.... III.11:5 is l. saying that the moon and sun are one
T-21....... V.4:6 it. L. all that stems from reason, the basic
T-21...... VI.2:9 but seems l. yours alone have no effect at

T-21 ..... VI.7:3 Reason, l. love, would reassure you, and
T-21 ..... VI.9:5 Love plans is l. Itself in this: Being united,
T-21 .. VII.3:11 a giant and a mouse roars l. a lion. And
T-21 ... VIII.2:6 for it desires everything be l. itself, and
T-22 ........in.3:9 home can a relationship so l. to Heaven
T-22 ........I.6:3 your whole communication is l. a baby's.
T-22 ........I.7:2 replaced, is l. a baby now in its rebirth.
T-22 .......I.11:1 Christ comes to what is l. Himself; the
T-22 .......I.11:3 What is as l. Him as a holy relationship?
T-22 .......II.5:5 This must be so, if the idea is l. its source.
T-22 ..... III.3:2 Sin is a block, set l. a heavy gate, locked
T-22 ...... V.5:3 eyes it looks l. an enormous solid body,
T-22 ... VI.14:9 in it, for every thought is l. itself.
T-23 ........II.2:2 L. all these principles, this one maintains
T-23 ......II.16:1 can it be that laws l. these can be believed
T-23 .....II.19:4 At best it seems l. life; at worst, like death.
T-23 .....II.19:4 At best it seems like life; at worst, l. death.
T-23 ..... IV.2:5 is not the body that is l. the Son's Creator.
T-23 ..... IV.3:7 is. Life makes not death, creating l. itself.
T-23 ..... IV.4:1 of your relationship is l. the Love of God.
T-24 ........I.4:2 incapable of being l. what he condemns,
T-24 ........I.6:1 to hate your brother if you were l. him?
T-24 ........I.7:1 because his Father created him l. you.
T-24 ........II.3:4 His Son l. to itself and not like unto Him.
T-24 ........II.3:4 His Son like to itself and not l. unto Him.
T-24 ........II.6:2 so l. his Father that the memory of Him
T-24 ........II.6:3 as l. to him as he is to his Father. And all
T-24 ......II.10:5 then He willed His Son to be l. Him, and
T-24 ......II.10:5 to be like Him, and your brother *is* l. you.
T-24 ...... III.3:1 a word, a little whisper that you do not l.,
T-24 ...... III.4:7 while specialness stands l. a flaming
T-24 ...... III.5:2 would have no separation, l. an alien will,
T-24 ...... V.4:8 and sightless holes for eyes, is l. yourself?
T-24 ...... V.6:5 And what you see is l. yourself. For what
T-24 ...... V.8:4 as l. to Him in holiness as you must be?
T-24 .... VII.7:2 this Son have been created l. Himself. A
T-24 .. VII.10:8 identical, not even l., but still a means to
T-24 .. VII.11:6 It is this that joins them to their l., and
T-25 ...... V.2:2 you not be afraid with "enemies" l. these?
T-25 ... VIII.7:4 to hell that seems to look l. Heaven's gate
T-26 ..... III.7:1 Is not this l. your special function, where
T-26 .... V.11:7 You are l. to one who still hallucinates,
T-26 ... VIII.5:5 Belief in sin arouses fear, and l. its cause,
T-26 ..... IX.3:7 leans to join with it, and make it l. itself.
T-27 ..... VI.3:5 real, for any one you choose is l. the rest.
T-27 .... VII.1:3 L. to a dream of punishment, in which the
T-27 ... VIII.1:3 the dust with other bodies dying l. itself.
T-27 . VIII.12:1 Who knows that every one is l. the rest.
T-28 ........I.2:7 Memory, l. perception, is a skill made up
T-28 ........I.2:8 And l. all the things you made, it can be
T-28 ........I.5:5 L. to the body, it is purposeless within
T-28 .......II.3:7 And as their "father," you must be l. them
T-28 .......II.4:5 A dream is l. a memory in that it pictures
T-28 .......II.5:3 dreamed the dreaming that you do not l..
T-28 .....II.10:1 L. every lesson that the Holy Spirit
T-28 ..... III.7:2 stored a heap of snow that shone l. silver.
T-28 ..... IV.3:1 L. you, your brother thinks he is a dream.
T-28 ..... VI.2:1 and blame it for the sounds you do not l.,
T-28 .... VII.1:1 asks for nothing, and His Son, l. Him,
T-28 .... VII.3:5 The body can be made a home l. this,
T-28 .... VII.5:7 It is l. the house set upon straw. It seems
T-29 ..... IV.2:1 The dreams you think you l. would hold
T-29 ..... IV.4:3 The dreams you think you l. are those in
T-29 ..... IV.4:9 If it succeeds you think you l. the dream.
T-29 ...... V.4:1 This sacred Son of God is l. yourself; the
T-29 .... VII.7:2 otherwise, the future will be l. the past,
T-29 ... VIII.3:6 And fall before His face l. a dark veil that
T-30 ........I.1:8 this very day can happen just l. that. Then
T-30 ........I.8:2 *least I can decide I do not l. what I feel now.*
T-30 ........I.9:1 that you do not l. the way you feel, what
T-30 ........I.9:3 because you do not l. the way you feel.
T-30 ..... III.3:4 will achieve completion in a form you l..
T-30 ..... III.8:4 The Thought God holds of you is l. a star,
T-30 ..... IV.5:8 illusion, making things appear l. to itself?
T-30 ... VIII.3:5 you to heal appearances you do not l..
T-30 ... VIII.5:9 to you, you will be certain you are l. Him,
T-31 ........I.3:4 so overlearned and fixed they rise l. heavy
T-31 .......II.6:6 He is l. us, as near or far away from what
T-31 .....II.10:6 same as yours, as he is l. yourself in truth.

T-31 ..... III.5:2 rules, and orders that the world be l. itself
T-31 ..... IV.3:3 to see how l. they are to one another. Men
T-31 .... VII.7:1 The concept of the self stands l. a shield,
T-31 ... VIII.4:4 The saviors of the world, who see l. Him,
T-31 ... VIII.9:3 appear l. lawns of Heaven to our sight, to
W-pI ...... 1.3:7 excluded. One thing is l. another as far as
W-pI ...... 3.2:3 For this purpose one thing is l. another;
W-pI ......... 4.h are l. the things I see in this room [on this
W-pI ...... 4.4:3 *l. the things I see in this room [on this street,*
W-pI ...... 5.1:1 This idea, l. the preceding one, can be
W-pI ...... 7.1:6 and why they are l. the things you see. It
W-pI .... 24.5:1 you would l. to be met in its resolution.
W-pI .... 24.5:3 *–, I would l. _to happen, and_to happen,*
W-pI .... 30.2:2 of what we do not l. by seeing it outside.
W-pI .... 32.2:1 The idea for today, l. the preceding ones,
W-pI .... 38.5:2 You might l., for example, to include
W-pI .... 39.1:2 L. the text for which this workbook was
W-pI .... 43.5:7 *I see my own thoughts, which are l. God's.*
W-pI .... 45.6:5 *I would l. to find them.* Then try to go past
W-pI .... 46.4:2 is a safe rule that anyone you do not l. is a
W-pI .... 50.5:2 you l. a blanket of protection and surety.
W-pI .... 60.3:3 look anything l. what I imagine I see now.
W-pI ....... 67.h Love created me l. itself.
W-pI .... 67.3:2 If love created you l. itself, this Self must
W-pI .... 67.5:3 yourself that love created you l. itself.
W-pI .... 67.6:4 of God. You were created by love l. itself.
W-pI .... 68.1:1 You who were created by love l. itself can
W-pI .... 68.1:7 He is l. what you think you have become,
W-pI .... 68.3:1 certain that God created them l. Himself,
W-pI .... 68.5:3 those you l. and even think you love. It
W-pI .... 72.3:4 A person says something you do not l..
W-pI .. 72.12:1 of infinity, Who created you l. Himself:
W-pI .... 75.6:5 You do not know yet what it looks l.. You
W-pI .... 78.1:2 Each grievance stands l. a dark shield of
W-pI .... 84.1:1 (67) Love created me l. itself. I am in the
W-pI .... 84.1:8 of my Creator. Love created me l. itself.
W-pI .... 91.3:1 you do not see is there sounds l. insanity.
W-pI .. 91.10:4 which you share a purpose l. Their Own.
W-pI .... 92.5:2 and looks on sickness, which is l. itself.
W-pI .... 96.5:4 Now must it reconcile unlike with l., for
W-pI .. 102.2:4 it offers you is lacking in existence, l. itself
W-pI .. 105.1:4 are not l. to the gifts the world can give, in
W-pI .. 107.2:4 Then try to picture what it would be l. to
W-pI .. 107.8:3 and so l. to you your Father knows that
W-pI .. 112.2:2 *as I was, created by the Changeless l. Himself*
W-pI 121.10:1 by thinking of someone you do not l.,
W-pI .. 122.5:3 it stands before you l. an open door, with
W-pI .. 124.9:4 every minute l. a diamond set around the
W-pI .. 127.1:5 It is l. itself, unchanged throughout. It
W-pI 127.10:2 that we are spared a future l. the past.
W-pI 131.10:1 foolish thoughts l. these behind today,
W-pI 132.11:3 Does it create l. Him? Unless it does, it is
W-pI .. 134.4:3 is forgiveness really but a sin, l. all the rest
W-pI .. 136.2:2 L. all defenses, it is an insane device for
W-pI .. 136.2:3 And l. all the rest, its purpose is to hide
W-pI 137.13:2 worth the giving to receive a gift l. this? Is
W-pI 138.10:4 Who hesitates to make a choice l. this?
W-pI 139.11:4 God gave to us when He created us l. Him
W-pI .. 152.6:7 Yet only madness makes a world l. this.
W-pI .. 152.9:4 l. to Himself in power and in love.
W-pI .. 154.6:4 L. earthly messengers, they did not write
W-pI .. 155.1:5 you also, and believe that you are l. them,
W-pI .. 157.6:2 We cannot give experience l. this directly.
W-pI .. 157.7:1 of time; a little more l. Heaven in its ways;
W-pI .. 159.3:3 it sees a world so l. to Heaven that what
W-pI .. 159.9:4 into a garden l. the one they came from,
W-pI .. 160.5:3 my home to one more l. me than myself,
W-pI .. 161.9:4 are l. him in the sight that sees him thus.
W-pI .. 162.5:3 could cherish sin when holiness l. this has
W-pI .. 162.6:2 eager to unite with one l. him in holiness?
W-pI .. 163.8:2 And yet, can thoughts l. these be fearful?
W-pI .. 163.9:6 *things, to be l. You and part of You forever.*
W-pI .. 164.5:1 when vain imaginings part l. a curtain, to
W-pI 166.12:2 His touch on you has made you l. Himself
W-pI .. 167.1:1 different kinds of life, for life is l. the truth
W-pI .. 167.1:4 L. all His Thoughts, it has no opposite.
W-pI .. 169.1:1 l. the state prevailing in the unity of truth.
W-pI .. 169.5:7 And l. its Source Itself, it merely is.
W-pI 170.13:1 *Father, we are l. You. No cruelty abides in us*

W-pI.185.14:2 it. With Help l. this beside us, can we fail
W-pI...186.9:5 They blow across his mind l. wind-swept
W-pI...186.9:6 Or l. mirages seen above a desert, rising
W-pI.186.10:3 concentrated drive toward goals l. these?
W-pI.186.10:5 What hope of gain can rest on goals l. this
W-pI...191.6:1 One holy thought l. this and you are free:
W-pI...198.8:1 unmoved, untouched by thoughts l. these
W-pI.198.12:5 Itself, so l. to Him Whose Son he is, that
WpI rVI.in.3:1 These practice sessions, l. our last review,
W-pII..249.1:6 It is now so l. to Heaven that it quickly is
W-pII..253.2:1 *Son, creating l. Yourself and One with You.*
W-pII..255.1:2 God assures me that His Son is l. Himself.
W-pII..260.2:3 And we who are His Sons are l. each other
W-pII......5.3:2 L. other dreams it sometimes seems to
W-pII..264.1:6 *Father, Your Son is l. Yourself. We come to*
W-pII......6.2:5 He remain the Self Who, l. His Father,
W-pII..280.1:6 and l. Himself in freedom and in love?
W-pII......8.1:1 l. the rest of what perception offers. Yet it
W-pII..306.1:1 which I see a world so l. to Heaven that an
W-pII....11.1:2 Only love creates, and only l. itself. There
W-pII..326.1:5 *to have a Son so l. his Cause that Cause and*
W-pII..326.1:6 *God, and so I have the power to create l. You.*
W-pII..335.2:2 *he was created one with me, and l. myself. In*
W-pII....13.5:1 Miracles fall l. drops of healing rain from
W-pII..343.1:5 *And You created me to be l. You, so sacrifice*
W-pII..354.1:4 *And He is l. His Father. Thus must I be one*
W-pII..360.1:6 *Your Son is l. to You in perfect sinlessness.*
M-4......VII.1:3 very carefully. L. all the other attributes of
M-4........X.3:2 Terms l. love, sinlessness, perfection,
M-5........II.1:8 Terms l. "instincts," "reflexes" and the
M-5........II.1:8 "reflexes" and the l. represent attempts to
M-10..........1:1 l. other devices by which the world of
M-13..........1:2 L. all things in the world, its meaning is
M-13..........1:4 L. all lessons it is an illusion, for in reality
M-17..........8:5 simplicity stands out l. an intense white
M-17..........9:3 L. the magic which becomes its servant, it
M-18........3:12 *there is. Fear is illusion, for you are l. Him.*
M-19..........2:1 Justice, l. its opposite, is an
M-19..........4:5 remains forever and forever l. its Creator,
M-24..........1:8 L. many other beliefs, it can be bitterly
M-25..........1:1 this question is much l. the preceding one
M-27..........3:2 holds it from awareness l. a shield held up
C-1.............1:3 of God which He created l. Himself. The
C-2...........1:11 of this except a dream which, l. all dreams
C-2.............2:2 but in a form that seems l. something. In
C-2.............8:3 Is not a song l. this what you would hear?
C-3.............7:5 And what He gives is always l. Himself.
C-4.............4:1 stands l. a block before Christ's face. But
C-5.............3:1 forever l. Himself and One with Him–
C-5.............6:9 *death because the Son of God is l. his Father.*
C-ep...........1:6 could despair when hope l. this is his?
P-2........III.3:2 for the result to look l. retrogression. But
P-3.........II.5:4 therapeutic relationship must become l.
S-1.........II.7:2 is a transformation much l. your own, for
S-1........III.2:7 could never make a prayer l. that.
S-2...........I.6:4 look through His and learn to see l. Him.
S-2...........I.7:6 Who sees no evil in it sees l. Him. For
S-2.........II.1:2 concealed beneath what seems l. charity.
S-2.........II.3:1 still very l. the first if it is understood,
S-2.........II.5:1 will often hide behind a cloak l. this. It
S-2.........II.6:8 There is no giving but to give l. Him. All
S-3........III.1:4 understands the other is exactly l. himself
S-3........III.4:4 It is l. the role that helps in prayer, and
S-3........IV.2:6 to see His likeness and to teach l. Him.
S-3........IV.9:5 How l. to Me! How lovingly I hold you in

## liked 1

W-pI.....50.1:3 clothing, influence, prestige, being l.,

## likely 22

T-2......IV.4:10 l. to occur when upside-down perception
T-2.........V.2:4 You are therefore l. to misunderstand any
T-2........VI.5:7 rage, and projection is l. to follow.
T-2......VI.9:12 of it, but you are hardly l. to respect it.
T-3...........I.1:9 Is it l. that God Himself would be capable
T-3...........I.3:7 it l. that He would hold them against me?
T-4.........II.5:4 l. to decide that you need precisely what
T-6.........I.15:9 Was it l. that I would condemn him when
T-9........IV.7:4 the ego l. to attack anyone and anything
T-9.........V.1:6 he is more l. to start with the equally
T-9.........V.3:4 they are l. to condemn themselves, teach
T-9.......VII.4:5 particularly l. to attack you when you
T-21.......V.1:5 you are far more l. to discover than what
T-21.....VII.2:8 each one as l. to attack his brother or turn
T-22.......V.4:4 How l. is it that it will succeed? Can it be
W-pI.....13.1:5 particularly l. to think you do perceive it.
W-pI.....17.1:6 its highly variable nature, this is hardly l..
W-pI.186.12:3 consider this; which is more l. to be right?
M-11.........2:2 or the Word of God is more l. to be true.
M-23.........3:7 it is l. that he will fail to keep them. Can
M-24.........4:3 they are l. to be merely controversial. The
S-1........IV.2:4 is l. at first that what is asked for even by

## likeness 22

T-1.........I.24:2 of creating in the l. of your Creator.
T-2...........I.1:5 of your l. to your Creator you are creative.
T-3.........II.4:1 which He created in the l. of His Own, to
T-3.........V.7:1 own image and l." needs reinterpretation.
T-3.........V.7:2 as "thought," and "l." as "of a like quality.
T-8.........V.2:1 creator, being wholly in the l. of God,
T-8.........V.2:5 this l. is to recognize the Father. If your
T-15.......V.7:2 seeking a picture whose l. does not exist.
T-31.......V.2:2 It bears no l. to yourself at all. It is an idol,
T-31...VII.12:4 will behold your brother in the l. of the
T-31. VIII.12:7 Clear in Your l. does the light shine forth
W-pI.....16.1:6 Those that are true create their own l..
W-pI.....68.2:1 remains aware of Its l. to Its Creator, your
W-pI.....84.1:2 I am in the l. of my Creator. I cannot
W-pI.....84.1:7 I am in the l. of my Creator. Love created
W-pI.....92.3:3 about in darkness to behold the l. of itself
W-pI...156.5:5 light all things unto Its l. and Its purity.
W-pI.158.11:2 its l. shines with its immortal love. We
W-pI...160.4:3 Is fear His Own, created in His l.? Is it fear
W-pII..322.1:4 which is God's only Son, the l. of Himself,
C-6.............1:2 creating with Him and in His l. or spirit,
S-3........IV.2:6 Christ has taught to see His l. and to teach

## likes 4

T-17......VI.3:6 left to make is whether or not the ego l. it;
T-30......IV.3:7 Yet while he l. to play with them, he still
W-pI...133.6:5 by nothing in a form he thinks he l..
W-pII......1.4:2 nor seeks to twist it to appearances it l.. It

## likewise 1

T-10......IV.7:1 gods, and calls on his brothers to do l.. It

## liking 2

T-15.......V.7:2 it assemble reality to its own capricious l.,
T-17.......V.5:1 each slow step according to its l.. Only a

## lilies 22

T-20.........I.2:1 week begins with palms and ends with l.,
T-20.........I.2:5 Offer your brother the gift of l., not the
T-20.........I.2:6 thorns in one hand and l. in the other,
T-20.........I.2:7 the thorns, offering the l. to replace them.
T-20.........I.3:6 of l. speed him on his way to resurrection.
T-20.........I.4:2 l. you have received and given as your gift
T-20.........I.4:4 Yet for your gift of l. you will know. In
T-20..........II.h The Gift of L.
T-20.......II.3:9 Offer him l. and it is yourself you free.
T-20.......II.4:1 I have great need for l., for the Son of
T-20.......II.5:6 He sees no thorns but only l., gleaming in
T-20.......II.6:3 use your gift of l. while you see them not.
T-20.......II.9:2 him where you laid the l. of forgiveness.
T-20.......II.9:3 that looks upon the l. and brings you joy.
T-20.....II.10:3 the l. of his innocence untouched by guilt,
T-20... VIII.4:4 with the shining l. you laid upon it. What
W-pI.151.16:2 lay the gift of snow-white l. on the world,
W-pI...159.8:1 which the l. of forgiveness set their roots.
W-pI...159.9:2 His l. do not leave their home when they
W-pI...187.9:1 The l. that your brother offers you are
W-pI.187.11:6 us in form of l. we can lay upon our altar,
W-pII .336.1:5 Its l. shine into the mind, and call it to

## lily 2

W-pII ... 12.5:1 Yet will one l. of forgiveness change the
W-pII ... 13.3:4 Each l. of forgiveness offers all the world

## limbs 2

T-27.......V.3:4 the broken bodies and the shattered l.,
W-pI...136.8:5 suffer, twist your l. and stop your heart,

## limit 95

T-1.........V.5:3 only l. put on its choice is that it cannot
T-2..........II.5:1 to set a l. on the need for the belief itself,
T-2........III.3:5 pain may be high, but it is not without l..
T-4........IV.8:2 is no l. to the power of a Son of God, but
T-4........IV.8:2 but he can l. the expression of his power
T-6.........I.18:2 Their influence on each other is without l.
T-6..V.C.10:10 inclusion is total and creation is without l.
T-7...........I.4:4 To bargain is to l. giving, and this is not
T-7...........I.4:6 God does not l. His gifts in any way. You
T-7...........I.5:4 His Kingdom forever and beyond l..
T-7.......VII.1:5 of your mind, whose power is without l..
T-7........IX.1:1 Only you can l. your creative power, but
T-8..........II.7:1 I meant: The Will of God is without l.,
T-8........III.1:5 no l. on your learning because there is no
T-8........III.1:5 because there is no l. on your mind. There
T-8........III.1:6 There is no l. on His teaching because He
T-8.....VII.13:3 is to l. your mind and to hurt yourself.
T-8.....VII.14:3 body, you are imposing this l. on yourself.
T-8........IX.8:5 you l. yourself we are not of one mind,
T-10.....III.1:10 He will not l. your power to help them,
T-10......IV.3:4 and you will not be able to l. the split,
T-11.........I.4:3 you have tried to l. what He created, and
T-11.........I.6:6 Love does not l., and what it creates is not
T-11.........I.6:7 To give without l. is God's Will for you,
T-11.........I.7:4 Give, then, without l. and without end, to
T-11......IV.3:2 L. the peace you share, and your Self must
T-11......VI.3:9 not try to l. what you see by narrow little
T-13......VI.7:4 and can be accepted only without l.. In
T-13......X.13:5 My trust in you is without l., and without
T-15.......V.2:2 We have said that to l. love to part of the
T-15......IX.1:1 the ego would l. your perception of your
T-15......IX.2:4 more than attempts to l. communication,
T-15......IX.3:3 the ego would l. everyone to a body for its
T-15......IX.4:4 L. your sight of a brother to his body,
T-15......IX.5:3 relationships that any l. is impossible.
T-15......IX.6:5 from the Son, and l. their communication
T-15......IX.6:7 And l. not your vision of God's Son to
T-16......IV.1:5 this. You cannot l. hate. The special love
T-16......IV.3:1 is an attempt to l. the destructive effects
T-16......VI.11:5 The joy of Heaven, which has no l., is
T-16...VII.10:2 power of God and all His Love, without l.,
T-18......VI.8:3 The body is a l. imposed on the universal
T-18....VI.11:9 of your Identity, and would not l. It. You
T-18....VI.13:3 It does not l. you, merely because you
T-18....VI.14:4 There are the laws of l. lifted for you, to
T-18....VIII.1:2 For the body *is* a l. on love. The belief in
T-18....VIII.1:3 origin, and it was made to l. the unlimited
T-18....VIII.1:4 allegorical, for it was made to l. *you.* Can
T-18....VIII.2:2 you l. your awareness to its tiny senses,
T-18....VIII.8:2 itself. Its total lack of l. *is* its meaning. It is
T-18......IX.2:5 to l. your awareness are little and limited,
T-19.........I.5:3 Faithlessness would always l. and attack;
T-19......III.7:3 For the belief that bodies l. mind leads to
T19....IV.A.3:4 that little is a l. you would place upon the
T19IV.A.17:12 l. the happiness that you would have calls
T19....IV.B.4:4 want neither to get rid of peace nor l. it.
T19....IV.B.9:2 back, and so would l. your awareness of it
T19....IV.B.9:4 be rid of, and having it you cannot l. it. If
T-20.....III.10:2 is only holiness and joining without l..
T-21.........I.8:4 shining and with no break or l. anywhere.
T-21......III.1:3 Forget not this; to bargain is to set a l.,
T-21......III.7:2 to l. to the body you hate because you fear
T-21......III.9:4 And if you seek to l. Him, you will hate
T-22......VI.9:7 no blessing from it, nor l. it in any way.

T-25.....VII.7:3 time, and all that you believe must l. you.
T-26.........I.1:4 for it is always an attempt to l. loss. The
T-26....... II.3:5 on what you see can l. God in any way.
T-26....... VII.8:8 They l. you to time and place, and give a
T-27...... III.1:3 power used to weaken is employed to l..
T-27...... III.1:7 it is not. To weaken is to l., and impose an
T-29..... II.10:1 He is with littleness and l. and despair. It
W-pI.....42.7:1 is no l. on the number of short practice
W-pI...44.10:2 to think of light, formless and without l.,
WpI...rI.in.5:2 learn that there is no l. to where you are,
W-pI.....72.2:4 The l. on communication cannot be the
W-pI.....97.4:1 a time that has no l. and that has no end.
W-pI...103.1:7 This strange belief would l. happiness by
W-pI...103.1:7 introducing opposition in what has no l.
W-pI...105.1:8 This implies a l. and an insufficiency.
W-pI...127.4:5 There is no l. placed upon Himself, and so
W-pI...128.3:3 value greater in your sight l. you further,
W-pI...192.8:5 The bars that l. him become the world in
W-pI...199.1:2 The body is a l.. Who would seek for
W-pII .320.2:2 *There is no l. on Your Will. And so all power*
W-pII ...11.1:1 infinite, and everywhere without all l..
M-5 ....... II.4:5 value of one true idea has no end or l..
M-7 ........... 1:5 the result of healing is to l. the healing. It
M-22 ......... 7:1 Who can l. the power of God Himself?
M-22 ......... 7:5 And to judge His Son is to l. his Father.
M-23 ......... 2:7 There is now no l. on his power, because
M-23 ......... 5:7 because in you he sees no l. and no stain
M-24 ......... 3:3 of him, it would merely l. his usefulness,
M-29 ......... 5:3 And His gifts have no l.. To ask the Holy
P-2...........I.3:2 it sets a l. on psychotherapy because it
P-3....... II.10:7 hear does not l. the Holy Spirit in any way

### limitation 14

T-8.....VII.14:2 beyond it and does not interpret it as l..
T-9........IV.2:6 This sense of l. is where all errors arise.
T-11......IV.2:4 l. on your power is not the Will of God.
T-15....... X.2:6 kind is nothing but a l. imposed on giving
T-15....... X.2:7 l. you have limited acceptance of the gift I
T-21...... III.7:2 For what you think is sin is l., and whom
T-21.... III.10:7 so is sacrifice invariably a means for l.,
T-23......IV.9:4 that he has everything could seek for l.,
T-28....... II.2:4 uncontained, without a barrier or l.. Thus
T-28....... II.2:6 Nor can it be found where l. is. The body
T-28....... V.1:1 is a sense of sickness but a sense of l.? Of a
W-pI...114.1:3 *nor impose on me a l. God created not.*
M-6 ........... 3:5 That is a l. on the giving itself, and neither
M-23 ....... 3:10 transcends the body has transcended l..

### limitations 22

T-2....... V.10:4 charity still lies within the l. of this world.
T-8.....VII.14:4 for learning should be to escape from l.?
T-12....... V.5:6 by which they can escape from their l.. If
T-18.... VI.11:3 It is a sense of actual escape from l.. If you
T-19.........I.5:3 faith would remove all l. and make whole.
T-21...... III.8:2 for sin by choosing to let all l. be removed
T-27...... III.7:8 beyond the world of symbols and of l.. He
T-28.........I.4:4 The l. on remembering the world imposes
T-28...... VI.3:9 your hatred for the l. that it brings to you.
T-28.... VI.3:10 for the l. that you want your mind to have
T-29.........I.5:7 set up the l. on what you would do, and
W-pI.....72.3:1 Although the attempt to keep the l. that a
W-pI.....72.4:3 to help in freeing him from the body's l..
W-pI.....72.8:4 from your awareness by the body's l..
W-pI.....92.6:4 a victor over l. that but grow in darkness
W-pI...181.5:5 We lay these pointless l. by a little while.
M-23 ......... 6:5 would we teach the l. we have laid on us.
M-25 ......... 6:7 the l. they laid upon their minds be lifted.
M-25 ......... 6:8 further l. they lay upon themselves if they
M-26 ......... 4:1 Do not despair, then, because of l.. It is
P-2........ III.2:1 is limited by the l. of the psychotherapist,
P-2........ III.2:3 the potentiality for transcending all l. has

### limited 88

T-2......... V.1:3 the belief that harm can be l. to the body.
T-2......... V.9:7 l. sense in which it can now be attained.
T-3......... II.4:4 It is therefore l., and the will is not free to
T-5 ....... III.4:5 but It is l. by your unwillingness to hear It
T-5 ..... IV.2:13 you cannot be l. to the self the ego sees.
T-7 ..........I.2:2 Creation would therefore be l., and you
T-7 ......... V.7:3 His teaching is l. because he is learning so
T-7 ......... V.7:4 healing lesson is l. by his own ingratitude,
T-7 .....VIII.3:5 their transfer value is l. by his confusion.
T-8 ......VII.3:5 way of making unlimited what you have l.
T-8 ....VII.14:1 You are not l. by the body, and thought
T-8 ....VII.14:3 you see another as l. to or by the body,
T-9 ....... IV.2:5 of your l. ideas about what you are. This
T-9 ....... VI.2:5 simply because you have l. your receiving.
T-11 ........I.4:3 and so you believe that all creation is l..
T-11 ........I.6:6 does not limit, and what it creates is not l.
T-11 ... VI.10:4 me. If you believe that yours is l., you are
T-12 ....... V.5:2 Who can transcend your l. resources. He
T-14 ..... XI.8:4 that the guidance of the Holy Spirit is l..
T-15 .... V.10:1 holy instant, because the blessing is not l..
T-15 ..... VI.2:4 it is in you, or it would be a l. gift to you.
T-15 ... VI.5:10 that he be bound, or l. in any way. In that
T-15 ..... IX.5:5 For the body *is* little and l., and only those
T-15 ..... IX.6:5 your sight grows weak and dim and l., for
T-15 .......X.2:7 have l. acceptance of the gift I offer you.
T-16 ..... VI.6:3 this spark cannot be l. long to littleness.
T-17 ..... III.3:2 already a severely l. perception of him, is
T-17 .... VII.4:3 faith in your brother was so l. and little.
T-18 ... VI.11:7 given up the illusion of a l. awareness,
T-18 . VI.11:11 simply by not letting your mind be l. by it
T-18 ...VIII.1:1 of the body that makes love seem l.. For
T-18 ...VIII.1:3 The belief in l. love was its origin, and it
T-18 ..... IX.2:5 it to limit your awareness are little and l.,
T-19 ........I.1:5 faith is l. and your dedication incomplete.
T-19 ........I.6:2 possible only if the mind is l. to the body
T-19 ......I.16:4 incapable of being kept in prison or l. in
T19..IV.A.2:11 still oppose the Will of God, and keep it l.
T19....IV.A.8:6 induces merely indicates its l. results.
T-21 ..... III.1:3 with whom you have a l. relationship, you
T-21 ..... III.8:4 had l. their understanding of the world,
T-21 ..... IV.4:1 still is only partial; still l. and incomplete,
T-24 ........I.7:9 your specialness is l. by your relationship
T-24 ..... IV.3:6 it is. Nor is the mind l.; so must it be that
T-26 ........I.3:4 bodies becomes the sign that sacrifice is l.
T-26 ..... III.3:3 here, in that the words imply a l. reality, a
T-26 .......X.1:5 Confusion is not l.. If it occurs at all it will
T-26 .......X.2:9 And what is l. cannot be Heaven. So it
T-27 ..... III.1:4 And therefore it must be l. and weak,
T-27 ..... IV.1:6 at all, for conflict has no l. effects. Yet if
T-29 ........I.3:8 and l. in scope and carefully restricted in
T-29 ........I.5:7 do, and keep your purpose l. and weak.
T-29 ........I.6:2 It will allow but l. indulgences in "love,"
T-29 ........I.7:5 not see how l. and weak is your allegiance,
T-30 ..... III.2:5 And can the limitless be l.? You do not
T-30 ..... III.5:5 to any form and l. to what is not in him,
T-30 ..... VI.6:5 means you think forgiveness must be l..
T-30 ..... VI.6:6 pardon and a l. escape from guilt for you.
T-30 ...VIII.3:8 knows no limits. You have l. yourself.
W-pI.....21.5:2 believing that the anger is l. to this aspect.
W-pI.....30.4:1 not l. to concepts such as "near" and "far.
W-pI.....91.8:6 *I am not l., but unlimited. I am not doubtful,*
W-pI.....96.5:2 and sees itself as helpless, l. and weak.
W-pI...98.11:1 tasks, all little thoughts and l. ideas, and
W-pI...103.1:7 limit happiness by redefining love as l.,
W-pI...134.2:2 is true. It must be l. to what is false. It is
W-pI...135.9:4 conception of the mind as l. and fragile,
W-pI. 136.18:3 guaranteed, because it is not l. by time, by
Wi181-200 2:1 too l. to let you see the value of our goal.
W-pI...181.1:2 he is l. by what you have perceived in him
W-pI. 185.12:3 how could your request be l. to you alone
W-pI...192.7:3 Our understanding is so l. that what we
W-pII ....250.h Let me not see myself as l..
W-pII . 280.1:4 Mind. No Thought of God is l. at all. No
W-pII . 319.1:4 Only the ego can be l., and therefore it
W-pII ... 12.1:1 is idolatry; the sign of l. and separated self
M-1 ........ 2:12 at its center it is a light that cannot be l..
M-4 ...... IX.1:3 If so, his advancement is l., and his trust
M-4 ...... IX.1:5 remaining carefully l. for a time. To give
M-23 ......... 6:7 offer them is l. by what he learns himself.
M-25 ......... 2:2 Communication is not l. to the small
P-2........ III.2:1 Healing is l. by the limitations of the
P-2........ III.2:1 as it is l. by those of the patient. The aim
P-2..........V.4:3 close to God in this attempt, however l.,
P-3...........I.3:2 gifts to you l. to the few you actually see.
P-3...........I.3:3 well, for seeing is not l. to the body's eyes.
S-1..........II.4:3 have l. prayer to the laws of this world,
S-1..........II.4:3 and have also l. your ability to receive and
S-3........ III.2:3 body, and indeed are generally l. to this.

### limiting 9

*See also* self-limiting

T-4 ...... VII.4:5 you are l. your sense of your own reality,
T-11 ... VI.10:4 that yours is limited, you are l. mine.
T-14 ..... XI.8:6 so l. the guidance that you would accept,
T-15 ..... III.3:4 and by l. yourself you will not be satisfied.
T-16 ..... VI.4:4 special relationship is a device for l. your
T-16 ..... VI.4:4 for l. your perception of others to theirs.
T-30 ..... III.1:5 that will bring happiness, and that, by l.,
W-pI .... 28.3:4 nor are you l. its purpose to your little
W-pII . 319.1:4 seek for aims which are curtailed and l..

### limitless 53

T-7 ..........I.1:1 power of God and His creations is l., but
T-7 ..........I.3:5 Being l. it does not stop. It creates forever,
T-7 ..... VI.10:4 wholeness, your sanity and your l. power.
T-7 ..... VI.10:5 This l. power is God's gift to you, because
T-11 ........I.2:2 No one can be beyond the l., because
T-12 .......V.9:1 is l. because it will lead you to God. You
T-14 .......V.6:7 this teaching, and guarantees its l. results.
T-14 .......X.3:1 the number of them that you can do is l..
T-14 .....X.6:12 The power of God is l.. And being always
T-15 ...VIII.1:5 His concern and care for you are l.. In the
T19 ... IV.B.5:6 together, when you have joined the l.?
T19 ... IV.B.9:3 be extended if you would have its l. power
T-20 .......V.6:7 and here the l. forgiveness you will give
T-23 ......I.10:7 You dwell in peace as l. as its Creator, and
T-26 ........I.5:3 house as rich and l. as Heaven itself. No
T-26 ........I.5:4 add a l. supply to every meager scrap and
T-26 .. VII.18:4 The gift of God to you is l.. There is no
T-27 ..... III.7:2 power wholly l. has come, not to destroy,
T-28 .......II.2:7 by its effects, which are as l. as is itself.
T-30 .......II.4:5 but keep your will forever and forever l..
T-30 ..... III.1:2 But your will is universal, being l.. And so
T-30 ..... III.2:5 And can the l. be limited? You do not
W-pI .. 76.11:3 of Heaven which His laws keep l. forever.
W-pI .... 92.5:4 to everyone who asks, in l. supply. It sees
W-pI .. 95.10:2 of creation, and l. in power and in peace.
W-pI .. 95.11:2 *of creation, and l. in power and in peace.*
W-pI .... 98.6:5 lose. And what you gain is l. indeed!
W-pI .. 105.4:3 It extends the l. to the unlimited, eternity
W-pI .. 110.5:1 The healing power of today's idea is l.. It
WpIrIII.in11:4 Its usefulness is l. to you. And it is meant
W-pI .. 123.8:1 Mind, how deep and l. His care for you,
W-pI .. 133.4:3 ungenerous to you to let alternatives be l.,
W-pI 155.14:1 you how great His trust; how l. His Love.
W-pI .. 166.1:2 God's trust in you is l.. He knows His Son.
W-pI .. 193.1:2 and eternally open and wholly l. in Him.
W-pI .. 196.2:1 mercy, l. and with all things held in its
W-pI .. 197.5:3 His gifts are sure, eternal, changeless, l.,
W-pII . 252.1:3 Its love is l., with an intensity that holds
W-pII . 280.1:1 Whom God created l. is free. I can invent
W-pII . 280.1:6 of God, whose Father willed that he be l.,
W-pII . 280.2:2 *limits on the Son You love and You created l.*
W-pII ..... 9.2:2 brings, as God's creation must be l..
W-pII . 309.1:2 I, His Son, whose will is l. as is His Own,
W-pII ... 10.2:6 fade away, because the Son of God is l..
W-pII ... 10.5:1 and forever loved, as l. as your Creator,
W-pII . 320.1:1 The Son of God is l.. There are no limits
M-4 ...... IV.2:7 and l. strength of gentleness? The might
M-12 ......... 1:5 Therefore he is l.. And being limitless, his
M-12 ......... 1:6 And being l., his thoughts are joined with
M-14 ......... 1:4 excluding no one, l. in gentleness, will
M-16 ......... 6:2 a thought of peace, a thought of l. release,
M-16 ......... 6:2 l. because all things are freed within it.
P-2......... in.3:5 vulnerable invulnerable and the finite l..

### limitlessness 3

T-9 ....... VI.4:8 magnitude by accepting His l. as yours.

| | |
|---|---|
| T-11......IV.3:1 | Your peace lies in its l.. Limit the peace |
| T-14....... X.2:4 | You on earth have no conception of l., for |

## limits 80

| | |
|---|---|
| T-2........III.3:3 | Who set the l. on your ability to miscreate |
| T-4...........I.7:5 | no right to set your learning l. for you. |
| T-5....... II.12:5 | we can accomplish together has no l., |
| T-7...........I.5:4 | outward beyond l. and beyond time, and |
| T-7..... VIII.7:5 | Your wholeness has no l. because being is |
| T-8........III.3:5 | His Fatherhood by placing no l. upon it. |
| T-8........IX.8:4 | you no l. because God lays none upon you |
| T-9...........I.3:8 | effort, within the l. you impose on Him, |
| T-9........VI.2:5 | This is not because He l. His giving, but |
| T-11.........I.2:2 | what has no l. must be everywhere. There |
| T-11.........I.4:2 | Who placed no l. on His creation or upon |
| T-11......VI.9:4 | Do not set l. on what you believe I can do |
| T-14....III.10:6 | as naturally as peace that knows no l.. |
| T-14....... X.2:4 | world you seem to live in is a world of l.. |
| T-14....... X.5:7 | you impose upon your mind l. the ego, it |
| T-14....... X.5:7 | your mind limits the ego, it also l. you. To |
| T-15......IX.2:6 | real relationships, which have no l., |
| T-15......IX.3:1 | of relationships without l. is given you. |
| T-15......IX.4:3 | increase. L. are demanded by the ego, and |
| T-15......IX.5:5 | the l. the ego would impose on them can |
| T-15......IX.6:1 | the l. you have placed on your perception, |
| T-15......IX.6:8 | For his belief in l. *has* imprisoned him. |
| T-15......IX.7:4 | would place no l. on your union with Him |
| T-16....... II.1:5 | extension, far beyond the l. you perceive, |
| T-16......III.7:7 | His Kingdom has no l. and no end, and |
| T-18...... I.13:2 | is the only one that has no l., and reaches |
| T-18....... II.3:6 | No l. on substitution are laid upon you. |
| T-18.......VI.8:8 | out. Within itself it has no l., and there is |
| T-18....VI.10:7 | What l. can there be on you whom He |
| T-18....VI.12:5 | rush to meet it, letting your l. melt away, |
| T-18....VI.14:7 | to let go the l. you have placed upon love, |
| T-18... VIII.2:4 | L. on love will always seem to shut Him |
| T19....IV.B.9:2 | the l. that would hold its extension back, |
| T-21.........I.4:3 | necessity of l. they believed they could not |
| T-23......IV.4:3 | l. the healing and the miracles you have |
| T-23......IV.7:7 | l. it exerts on those in battle still are gone, |
| T-24....... II.2:4 | gauge of littleness, and be released from l. |
| T-24......VII.7:3 | nor held to l. or uncertainties of any kind. |
| T-26.........I.3:5 | to you are l. placed on everything outside, |
| T-26.........I.3:7 | And to accept the l. of a body is to impose |
| T-26.........I.3:7 | these l. on each brother whom you see. |
| T-26........ II.3:5 | Think not the l. you impose on what you |
| T-26......IV.1:2 | the gate behind which total lack of l. lies. |
| T-26....... X.2:8 | God l. not. And what is limited cannot be |
| T-27......III.5:3 | not yet a power known as wholly free of l.. |
| T-27......III.5:4 | Yet it sets no l. you have chosen to impose |
| T-29.........I.5:4 | and l. your ability to make communion |
| T-30......III.1:4 | Idols are l.. They are the belief that there |
| T-30......III.3:8 | beyond the boundaries of l. on yourself. |
| T-30... VIII.3:6 | You have established l.. What you ask *is* |
| T-30... VIII.3:7 | you, but not of God Who knows no l.. |
| T-31... VIII.1:3 | It sets the l. on what he can do; its power |
| W-in..........6:5 | of true perception is that it has no l.. It is |
| W-pI......38.1:2 | of time, space, distance and l. of any kind. |
| W-pI......97.7:2 | *Spirit am I, a holy Son of God, free of all l.,* |
| W-pI...103.1:4 | Love has no l., being everywhere. And |
| W-pI...127.6:4 | obey; of all the l. under which you live, |
| W-pI.130.10:1 | by remembering the l. of your choice. The |
| W-pI...135.9:2 | the l. and the lacks from which you think |
| W-pI.136.18:1 | this removes the l. you had placed upon |
| W-pI...161.5:1 | to be the body that we feel l. our freedom, |
| W-pI...182.7:6 | His patience has no l.. He will wait until |
| W-pII.....280.h | What l. can I lay upon God's Son? |
| W-pII..280.1:6 | Can I lay l. on the Son of God, whose |
| W-pII..280.2:2 | *Father, I lay no l. on the Son You love and* |
| W-pII..320.1:2 | There are no l. on his strength, his peace, |
| W-pII....13.1:5 | Thus it stays within time's l.. Yet it paves |
| M-22..........7:4 | up to God's teachers to set l. upon Him, |
| M-23..........6:8 | Then turn to one who laid all l. by, and |
| M-25..........2:5 | l. the world places on communication are |
| M-25..........2:6 | These l. are placed out of fear, for without |
| M-25..........2:7 | transcends these l. in any way is merely |
| M-26..........2:1 | of worldly l. and remembering their own |
| P-2............ I.h | The L. on Psychotherapy |
| P-2........ III.2:2 | process, therefore, is to transcend these l.. |
| P-2........ IV.6:4 | must overcome all l. perceived in the self, |
| P-2......... V.6:3 | The l. laid on both the patient and the |
| P-3......... II.1:3 | any l. be laid on an interaction in which |
| S-2 ...........I.8:6 | beyond all l. into timelessness, with |
| S-3 ......... II.2:3 | the need is done to walk the world of l., |

## line 20

| | |
|---|---|
| T-1......... V.5:4 | creates along the l. of its own creation. If |
| T-2...........I.2:8 | is freely given in one continuous l., in |
| T-6....... II.11:5 | into the one l. the Holy Spirit sees. This |
| T-6....... II.11:6 | This l. is the direct line of communication |
| T-6....... II.11:6 | the direct l. of communication with God, |
| T-9......... II.1:2 | that are strictly in l. with this course. The |
| T-17....... V.3:5 | relationship as it *is* is out of l. with its own |
| T-17...... VI.3:5 | set with which to bring the means in l.. |
| T-19...... IV.1:5 | which He will bring means and goal in l.. |
| T-20........ V.5:5 | and end have not been brought in l.. Why |
| T-20.....VII.1:1 | must be brought in l. before your holy |
| T-20.....VII.3:7 | goal, and they are perfectly in l. with it. |
| T-21...... VI.8:6 | and brings your reason into l. with His. |
| T-22.... VI.13:9 | and more in l. with your experience. And |
| T-22.. VI.13:10 | other experiences, more in l. with truth, |
| T-26.....VII.9:4 | Yet is this wish in l. with Heaven's state, |
| T-30.....VII.7:3 | they are not in l. with what you really are. |
| W-pI...188.9:2 | l. with all the thoughts we share with God |
| M-25 .........2:1 | that are clearly in l. with this course. |
| C-2...........10:3 | sure, or more in l. with what salvation is? |

## lines 3

| | |
|---|---|
| T-1........ VI.5:3 | true, the miracle proceeds along these l.: |
| W-in..........1:4 | to think along the l. the text sets forth. |
| WpI. rIV.in5:4 | the day along the l. which God appointed, |

## linger 10

| | |
|---|---|
| T-15...... IX.5:2 | of this and long remain willing to l. here. |
| T-25......IV.4:6 | light. They l. for a while, a little while, in |
| T-28.........I.4:7 | part of time where guilt appears to l. still. |
| W-pI.......7.5:1 | Do not l. over any one thing in particular |
| W-pI.....11.3:1 | should not l. on anything in particular. |
| W-pI...107.3:3 | and dead ideas to l. in your mind. Truth |
| W-pI...109.2:5 | came and yet will come to l. for a while. |
| W-pI.193.11:3 | too long, and we would l. here no more. |
| W-pII..226.2:3 | *to l. in a place of vain desires and of shattered* |
| W-pII..272.2:2 | call to us to stay and l. in a dream, we |

## lingered 1

| | |
|---|---|
| T-23...... III.6:4 | You have not l. there in cowering hope |

## lingering 7

| | |
|---|---|
| T-13...VII.12:7 | will not use them on behalf of l. in time. |
| T-26.......IX.5:3 | space nor distance l. between the light of |
| T-27...VII.12:1 | your death, yet plans that it be l. and slow |
| T-29.....VII.2:1 | but must still have hope, some l. illusion, |
| T-29.....VII.3:1 | The l. illusion will impel him to seek out |
| W-pI...101.5:3 | which cherishes no l. belief that you have |
| W-pI...185.8:5 | But be you not dismayed by l. illusions, |

## lingers 2

| | |
|---|---|
| T-29....... V.1:1 | no memory of sin and of illusion l. still. |
| W-pI.169.13:2 | to all who see the light that l. in your face. |

## link 20

| | |
|---|---|
| T-6.........I.19:1 | the Communication L. between God the |
| T-8.......VII.2:2 | Being the Communication L. between |
| T-10.......III.2:6 | God's remaining Communication L. with |
| T-13.........XI.8:1 | The Communication L. that God Himself |
| T-14. VIII.4:10 | is one l. that joins Them all together, |
| T-14... VIII.5:1 | l. with which the Father joins Himself to |
| T-16......... II.4:3 | the first l. in the awareness of the Sonship |
| T-16..IV.11:13 | In His l. with you lie both His inability to |
| T-25...........I.h | The L. to Truth |
| T-25.........I.5:2 | l. that has been given you to join the truth |
| T-25...... III.4:1 | l. that kept it still within the laws of God; |
| T-28.........I.4:5 | There is no l. of memory to the past. If |
| T-28.........I.4:7 | But only your desire made the l., and only |
| W-pI..... 10.2:3 | and no l. is made overtly with the things |
| W-pI.....43.1:4 | Without this l. with God, perception |
| W-pI.....43.1:5 | With this l. with God, perception will |
| W-pI.....49.4:3 | and obscure your eternal l. with God. |
| W-pI... 127.3:8 | l. between the Father and the Son which |
| W-pII ..... 6.2:1 | is the l. that keeps you one with God, and |
| C-6............ 3:1 | L. between God and His separated Sons. |

## linked 1

| | |
|---|---|
| S-3 ...........I.2:3 | tied to its command and l. to its unstable, |

## linking 1

| | |
|---|---|
| T-13...... IX.1:2 | l. the future to the past as is the ego's law. |

## links 2

| | |
|---|---|
| T-14....... V.1:1 | reality is the part that l. you still with God |
| T-25.........I.5:5 | The Holy Spirit l. the other part–the tiny |

## lion 2

| | |
|---|---|
| T-3...........I.5:3 | The l. and the lamb lying down together |
| T-21... VII.3:11 | a giant and a mouse roars like a l.. And |

## Lips 1

*lips*

| | |
|---|---|
| W-pI. 170.10:5 | The blood appears to be upon His L.; the |

## lips 9

*Lips*

| | |
|---|---|
| T-19....... III.9:1 | you look with Heaven's smile upon your l. |
| T-23........II.15:6 | And fear, with ashen l. and sightless eyes, |
| T-23........II.18:8 | Can you paint rosy l. upon a skeleton, |
| W-pI.......7.3:2 | feeling the rim of a cup against your l., |
| W-pI... 169.5:5 | There are no l. to speak them, and no part |
| W-pI... 170.7:2 | that though his l. are smeared with blood, |
| WpI.rV.in11:3 | again with these same words upon our l., |
| W-pI. 187.10:4 | The Name of God is on our l.. And as we |
| W-pII . 222.2:1 | *Your Name upon our l. and in our minds, as* |

## list 11

| | |
|---|---|
| T-13..... VII.1:3 | an endless l. of things they do not need. It |
| W-pI..... 24.7:1 | After covering the l. of as many hoped- |
| W-pI..... 26.8:3 | As the l. of anticipated outcomes for each |
| W-pI..... 29.5:1 | Your l. of subjects should therefore be as |
| W-pI..... 29.5:2 | For example, a suitable l. might include: |
| W-pI..... 35.6:1 | A suitable unselected l. for applying the |
| W-pI..... 50.1:3 | and an endless l. of forms of nothingness |
| W-pI..... 94.4:1 | aside; go past the l. of attributes, both |
| W-pI..... 96.2:2 | you will attempt an endless l. of goals you |
| W-pI... 133.3:1 | Today we l. the real criteria by which to |
| M-4 ....... X.3:1 | may have noticed that the l. of attributes |

## listen 108

| | |
|---|---|
| T-1........ III.1:6 | great crusade to correct it; l. to my voice, |
| T-2........ VI.6:6 | I will therefore repeat it, urging you to l.. |
| T-3...... IV.7:12 | be, "All are called but few choose to l.." |
| T-4.........I.10:4 | Do not l. to it and do not preserve it. |
| T-4.........I.10:5 | it. L. only to God, Who is as incapable of |
| T-4........ IV.1:1 | God, it is because you do not choose to l.. |
| T-4........ IV.1:2 | That you *do* l. to the voice of your ego is |
| T-5..........II.3:6 | you by God, Who asks you only to l. to it. |
| T-5....... II.7:12 | l. to the wrong voice you *have* lost sight of |
| T-5..... II.10:10 | your brothers to l. as I am teaching you. |
| T-5...... IV.2:12 | even in this world to l. to one Voice. If |
| T-5.......VII.3:1 | Why should you l. to the endless insane |
| T-6.........I.19:2 | will l. to His Voice you will know that you |
| T-6...... V.B.4:5 | it impossible for the learner not to l.. For |
| T-7..........II.6:6 | you l. to two ways of interpreting them. |

T-7......... X.3:3 whether you want to l. to what He says.
T-8...........I.6:5 is unaffected by both, but if you l. to both,
T-8......... II.3:1 will is free, because you will not l. to it. It
T-8........ III.1:4 to l. to the Teacher Who knows of light,
T-8........ III.6:2 curriculum, then, you cannot l. to the ego
T-8........ IV.6:5 only you can choose to l. to my teaching.
T-8........ VI.4:1 L. to the story of the prodigal son, and
T-8......VIII.8:5 anyone doubt your willingness to l. until
T-8......VIII.8:7 Voice is as loud as your willingness to l..
T-9......... II.7:8 Do not l. to anything else or you will not
T-9....VIII.11:8 L. and do not question what you hear, for
T-10...... III.9:3 You will hear the god you l. to. You made
T-10.... III.10:4 not realize how much you l. to your gods,
T-10..... V.11:7 L., and you will learn how to remember
T-11....... V.8:4 this belief you would not l. to it at all.
T-11....... V.9:3 and would you l. to it if you recognized
T-11..... V.16:1 demonstrations to those who would l..
T-13..... XI.5:4 may be, whatever voice you choose to l. to
T-14....... II.2:5 and nothing are you less inclined to l. to.
T-14...... IV.7:6 it. If you would but l., and learn how
T-14..... V.1:10 L. to the Holy Spirit, and to God through
T-14.... XI.11:4 L. in silence, and do not raise your voice
T-16..... II.6:12 again will you be wholly willing not to l..
T-16..... V.16:1 The decision whether or not to l. to this
T-20....... II.6:6 L. and hear this carefully, nor think it but
T-21.........I.5:5 L., and try to think if you remember what
T-21.........I.6:1 L., –perhaps you catch a hint of an
T-21.........I.7:5 L., and see if you remember an ancient
T-21....... V.2:3 L. to what the ego says, and see what it
T-21...... VI.4:2 if it be the choice of the insane to l. to it.
T-21...... VI.8:6 L. to Him Who speaks with reason, and
T-22.........I.3:8 world it sees, you have no reason not to l.,
T-24....... II.4:3 when it is your specialness to which you l.
T-24....... II.4:4 praise of what you are, is all you l. to. And
T-24....... V.5:1 no eyes with which to see; no ears to l.,
T-24.....VII.9:7 with which you l. to the sounds it makes.
T-27....... II.9:8 be delayed because you pause to l. to
T-27..VIII.12:9 you need but learn you chose but not to l.
T-31........I.11:5 But l., rather, to the deeper call beyond it
T-31..... II.5:13 for? And l. well! For he is asking what will
T-31....... II.7:2 Be still and l.. Think not ancient thoughts
T-31....... II.8:6 to which you come to l. silently and learn
T-31...VII.15:5 "Release My Son!" be tempted not to l.,
T-31....VIII.8:1 fail to hear my voice and l. to my words. I
W-pI.....49.1:1 It is quite possible to l. to God's Voice all
W-pI.....49.2:4 Try today not to l. to it. Try to identify
W-pI.....49.4:1 L. in deep silence. Be very still and open
W-pI.....60.5:2 As I l. to God's Voice, I am sustained by
W-pI...66.10:1 You will l. to madness or hear the truth.
W-pI.....71.9:9 that you have some willingness to l.. This
W-pI...72.13:6 your eyes closed, and l. for His answer.
W-pI...76.10:2 Then l. further. He will tell you more.
WpI..rII.in.2:2 you wish, and then close your eyes and l..
W-pI.....97.8:3 L. for His assurance every time you speak
W-pI...101.4:3 would he try to l. and accept Its offering?
W-pI...106.h Let me be still and l. to the truth.
W-pI...106.1:1 want; if you will l. with an open mind,
W-pI...106.2:1 L., and hear your Father speak to you
W-pI...106.2:2 Be still today and l. to the truth. Be not
W-pI...106.2:4 Attend them not, but l. to the truth.
W-pI...106.3:4 Be still today and l. to the truth. Go past
W-pI...106.5:1 and l. to the Word which lifts the veil that
W-pI...106.6:4 L. today, and you will hear a Voice which
W-pI...106.7:5 *I will be still and l. to the truth. What does it*
W-pI...106.9:1 Be still and l. to the truth today. For each
W-pI.106.10:3 *Let me be still and l. to the truth. I am the*
W-pI...118.2:1 (106) Let me be still and l. to the truth.
W-pI...118.3:4 hour: Let me be still and l. to the truth.
W-pI...125.3:5 Today we will not l. to the world, but wait
W-pI...125.8:1 voice to which you l. as He speaks to you.
W-pI...125.8:4 In quiet l. to your Self today, and let Him
W-pI...125.9:3 eyes. Only be still and l.. You will hear the
W-pI.140.10:2 will be still and l. for the Voice of healing,
W-pI.151.15:4 No one can fail to l., when you hear the
W-pI.153.17:2 sit by and wait on Him and l. to His Voice
W-pI.169.10:3 l. to words which explain what is to come
WpI...rV.in2:4 *We would but l. to Your Word, and make it*
W-pI...186.4:1 that we may l. to God's Voice reveal to us
W-pI...188.8:1 your Father's Voice when you refuse to l..
W-pII .221.1:3 *of my mind, I wait and l. for Your Voice. My*
W-pII .237.2:1 *He the ears that l. to the Voice for God today.*
W-pII .271.1:2 would have me see, to l. to God's Voice,
W-pII .296.1:1 *today, that all the world may l. to Your Voice*
W-pII .328.1:1 down until we l. to the Voice for God. It
W-pII .347.2:1 L. today. Be very still, and hear the gentle
M-12......... 3:6 can see. A voice they understand and l. to,
P-3...........I.2:3 in him that will tell you, if you l.. And that
P-3...........I.2:4 And that is the answer; l.. Do not demand
P-3...........I.2:6 L.. What you hear is true. Would God
S-2........ III.6:5 Do you but l.. For He will be heard by
S-2........ III.6:9 L. and learn, and do not judge. It is to
S-3........ III.6:2 L., and you will never fail to bring His
S-3........ IV.8:6 L., My child, your Father calls to you. Do

## listened 10

T-2..........I.3:2 When Adam l. to the "lies of the serpent,"
T-16........II.7:5 that whenever you l. to His interpretation
T-21.........I.6:3 those who were there and l. with you.
T-21........II.5:3 you l. and convinced yourself that what it
T-21...... V.5:7 Such would your reason tell you, if you l..
T-22.......I.2:11 Yet you have l. to it. And long and hard
T-22.........I.3:3 l. to what can never communicate at all.
W-pI. 72.10:11 so loudly that we have not l. to His Voice.
W-pI...76.11:4 until we have l. and understood there are
W-pII .300.2:3 *But we have l. to Your Voice, and learned*

## listening 28

T-5....... IV.4:2 L. to one Voice implies the decision to
T-5...... V.3:10 for it. L. to the ego's voice means that you
T-8 .... VII.13:2 you cannot be l. to God's joyous Teacher
T-9.........II.4:8 L. to truth is the only way you can hear it
T-9.........II.5:7 But are you l. to it? Your brother may not
T-9....... III.4:1 to errors, you are not l. to the Holy Spirit.
T-9....... III.4:3 you are l. to your ego and making as little
T-12 .. VII.14:4 feel guilty you are l. to the voice of the ego
T-16........II.7:1 in which your l. will increase and peace
T-27 .... V.1:12 Yet by your l. His Voice extends, because
T-28...... V.4:6 does not know what seeing *is*; what l. is *for*.
W-pI.....49.2:1 part that is l. to the Voice for God is calm,
W-pI.....66.3:4 will not indulge the ego by l. to its attacks
W-pI.....76.9:3 You will be l. to One Who says there is no
WpI..rII.in.3:1 part of the time l. quietly but attentively.
W-pI...106.9:2 today. For each five minutes spent in l., a
W-pI. 106.10:1 giving means by l. and learning it of Him.
W-pI...123.5:3 to us. And thanks to you for l. to Him. His
W-pI...125.1:1 this day be a day of stillness and of quiet l.
W-pI...125.1:5 the world; until your mind, in quiet l.,
W-pI...125.7:1 ten minutes set apart from l. to the world,
W-pI...125.7:1 instead a gentle l. to the Word of God. He
W-pI. 135.11:2 through l. to wisdom that is not its own.
W-pI. 140.11:1 and end the day by l. again five minutes
W-pI. 140.12:1 with lifted hearts and l. minds we pray:
M-15........2:13 comes to all who stand aside in quiet l.,
M-18......... 2:5 He can speak the Word of God to l. ears,
S-1...........I.5:1 a letting go, a quiet time of l. and loving.

## listens 7

T-6........I.10:6 and anyone who l. is inevitably led to
W-pI...154.2:4 you are, and l. only to His Voice in you.
M-21......... 4:9 his speaking. He l. and hears and speaks.
C-1............ 5:1 depending on the voice to which it l..
C-1............ 5:2 *Right-mindedness* l. to the Holy Spirit,
C-1............ 6:1 *Wrong-mindedness* l. to the ego and
P-2..........II.7:3 the contrary, he l. patiently to each one,

## lit 9

*See also* half-lit

T-7....... III.5:1 God has l. your mind Himself, and keeps
T-7....... III.5:1 keeps your mind l. by His light because
T-10..... IV.7:5 lamps of God were l. by the same spark. It
T-13 ... VII.1:4 It is not l. with artificial light, and night
T-20.....II.11:6 The lamp is l. in you for your brother.
T-25..... III.5:6 they l. a place where they could never be,
T-28..... III.8:1 but let your world be gently l. by miracles
T-31........I.8:1 everything is l. with hope and sparkles
W-pII....in.8:4 His Thoughts have l. the darkness of our

## litanies 1

WpI..rIII.in4:3 to be replacements for your l. to them.

## litany 1

T-16.....V.10:4 The central theme in its l. to sacrifice is

## literal 6

T-5..........I.6:6 l. meaning of transferred or "carried over,
T-5.........II.3:7 The Holy Spirit is in you in a very l. sense.
T-5.........II.5:5 God is not in you in a l. sense; you are
T-7....... IV.7:4 else. God is All in all in a very l. sense. All
T-10.......V.1:6 The sense is very l.; denial of life perceives
T-12.......V.5:1 have learning handicaps in a very l. sense.

## literally 35

T-1.........II.2:7 Revelation is l. unspeakable because it is
T-1...... VII.3:3 stem from distortions are l. the reactions
T-2..........I.3:4 All that can l. disappear in the twinkling
T-2.........II.7:5 They will l. take it over because of their
T-2....... III.4:1 Spiritual vision l. cannot see error, and
T-2....... VI.9:8 a power surge that can l. move mountains
T-3.........V.3:2 l. impossible for you to know anything.
T-3....... VI.8:3 are l. fighting you for your authorship.
T-3 .... VII.4:11 the one thing that is l. inconceivable.
T-3...... VII.5:2 God, because it l. denies His Fatherhood.
T-4..........I.9:7 understand this, because it is l. incredible
T-4.........II.7:1 The ego l. lives by comparisons. Equality
T-4..... III.10:2 desperate because it opposes l. invincible
T-4....... IV.2:8 ego together, but has l. split your mind.
T-5.........V.3:7 ego is quite l. a fearful thought. However
T-6..........I.8:6 accept me as a model are l. my disciples.
T-7....... III.1:7 I said "I am with you always," I meant it l.
T-7.........V.9:8 It l. believes that every time it deprives
T-7.....VIII.7:3 with the whole Kingdom as l. part of you.
T-7..... XI.3:11 are l. denying Heaven to yourself.
T-8....... IX.8:3 this, and given this quite l., nothing can
T-9....... IV.9:1 The ego l. lives on borrowed time, and its
T-9.....VIII.4:2 reality l. drives the ego from your mind,
T-11 .... VII.1:4 and a new earth, yet this cannot be l. true,
T-13.......V.3:8 attacking others you are l. attacking what
T-15.......II.5:5 will l. blind you to this world by its own
T-16..... III.8:5 would cross over is l. transported there.
T-17.......II.6:2 For forgiveness l. transforms vision, and
T-18.......II.4:1 temper tantrums, in which you l. scream,
T-21.......V.1:2 It l. picks it out as the mind directs. The
T-22..... III.1:6 Vision is sense, quite l.. If it is not the
WpI... rI.in.3:1 l. or thoroughly in the practice periods.
W-pI .... 69.2:3 We are l. attempting to get in touch with
M-4..... I.A.6:5 Its potential is l. staggering, and the
P-2........ VI.2:2 given us l. "to change our tune." The

## little 475

*See also* Appendix C

T-1.........V.3:4 "Except ye become as l. children" means
T-1...... VII.2:3 The Love of God, for a l. while, must still
T-2.........II.3:6 have l. difficulty in clarifying the means.
T-2....... VI.9:2 very l. right thinking to realize why fear
T-3....... III.1:1 have said very l. about knowledge as yet.
T-4....... III.7:2 You retain thousands of l. scraps of fear
T-4 .... III.10:3 ego, and how l. to protect your right mind
T-4...... VI.3:1 You have very l. trust in me as yet, but it
T-4...... VI.7:1 my perception He can bridge the l. gap.
T-5..........I.4:9 God Himself can flow across the l. gap.
T-6..........I.4:2 is l. doubt that one body can assault
T-7.........V.7:3 is limited because he is learning so l.. His
T-8...... VII.9:2 with l. or no relationship to each other, so
T-8....... IX.2:9 You need do so l. because your little part
T-8....... IX.2:9 You need do so little because your l. part
T-8...... IX.2:10 then, your l. part, and let the whole be
T-9.......II.10:6 Valuing it l., you will not appreciate it
T-9.......II.11:2 to get much for l. is to believe that you

T-9........III.4:3 to your ego and making as l. sense as the
T-9.......VII.6:5 have chosen to be l. and to lament your
T-10......IV.8:3 the l. spark you will learn of the greater
T-10......IV.8:5 the l. light must be acknowledged first,
T-11.......in.3:6 l. spark in your mind is enough to lighten
T-11....... II.5:4 and the l. spark becomes a blazing light
T-11....... II.6:5 the l. spark and are willing to let it grow.
T-11....... II.6:7 If you will merely offer Him a l. place, He
T-11...... III.3:5 His. The bleak l. world will vanish into
T-11...... III.5:6 for the l. spark in you is part of a light so
T-11...... VI.3:9 not try to limit what you see by narrow l.
T-11... VIII.2:1 Bible tells you to become as l. children.
T-11... VIII.2:2 L. children recognize that they do not
T-11... VIII.7:1 L. child of God, you do not understand
T-12....... II.4:1 the frightening perceptions of l. children,
T-12....... II.4:6 L. child, you are hiding your head under
T-12....... II.7:1 A l. while and you will see me, for I am
T-12....... II.8:5 Give me but a l. trust in the name of the
T-13....... II.9:1 L. child, this is not so. Your "guilty secret
T-13...... III.4:2 you away from yourself and make you l.,
T-13...... III.7:6 For He will heal every l. thought you have
T-13....... V.7:1 L. child, would you offer this to your
T-14..... II.1:10 A l. piece of glass, a speck of dust, a body
T-14.... III.11:3 Would you be content with l., which is all
T-14...... IV.8:3 throw yourself away and valued God so l.,
T-14... VII.5:14 merely asked to do the l. He suggests you
T-14... VIII.2:2 great or small, however much or l. valued,
T-14... VIII.5:5 l. offerings are brought together with the
T-14... VIII.5:7 l. gifts will vanish on the altar, where He
T-14....... X.4:2 used to this that it causes you l. surprise.
T-14....... X.5:4 l. sanity that still remains is held together
T-14...... XI.7:3 not meet, if he but turn to Him ever so l..
T-14...... XI.8:4 you think that you can run some l. part,
T-15...... I.15:2 needs but very l. to restore God's whole
T-15....... II.6:1 now to practice your l. part in separating
T-15...... III.1:5 Everything in this world is l. because it is
T-15...... III.3:4 Believe the l. can content you, and by
T-15...... III.3:5 For your function is not l., and it is only
T-15...... III.4:5 littleness is a task the l. cannot undertake.
T-15...... III.4:9 Search for the l., and you deny yourself
T-15...... III.5:6 make l. whom God has joined with Him.
T-15...... III.6:1 untouched by every l. gift the world of
T-15...... III.6:5 all who, like you, perceive themselves as l.
T-15...... III.7:6 Far beyond your l. world but still in you,
T-15...... III.8:5 have sought to purchase it with l. gifts,
T-15...... III.8:5 it too l. to understand its magnitude.
T-15...... III.8:6 Love is not l. and love dwells in you, for
T-15...... III.8:7 of yourself and all the l. offerings you give
T-15...... VI.2:1 have so l. faith in yourself because you are
T-15..... VII.9:5 and wounding him, perhaps in l. ways,
T-15...... IX.4:3 its demands to make l. and ineffectual.
T-15...... IX.5:4 not exchange your l. relationships for this
T-15...... IX.5:5 For the body *is* l. and limited, and only
T-15....... X.7:3 the lesser of two evils, one to be feared a l.
T-16....... II.2:1 concerned about the truth of just a l. part
T-16..... II.6:10 You can delay this now, but only a l. while
T-16....... II.8:4 yet you have so l. faith in what you heard,
T-16...... III.8:3 some l. effort on behalf of bridging it. His
T-16...... III.8:4 l. efforts are powerfully supplemented by
T-16..... V.10:8 it you have made it l. and unworthy,
T-16..... V.11:2 become to you that unless it is weak and l.
T-16..... V.11:3 You think it safer to endow the l. self you
T-16...... VI.6:3 l. spark that holds the Great Rays within
T-16...... VI.7:3 What is l. and insignificant is magnified,
T-16.... VI.12:1 The Holy Spirit asks only this l. help of
T-17....... II.1:5 even a l. part of the happiness this sight
T-17....... II.2:4 world and this is so l. and so easy to cross,
T-17....... II.2:5 Yet this l. bridge is the strongest thing
T-17....... II.2:6 This l. step, so small it has escaped your
T-17...... IV.6:1 You have but l. difficulty now in realizing
T-17.... IV.15:5 of creation in exchange for your l. picture,
T-17..... V.7:11 Now He asks for faith a l. longer, even in
T-17..... VII.4:3 faith in your brother was so limited and l.
T-17..... VII.7:1 is so far beyond your l. conception of the
T-17..... VII.7:3 your l. faithlessness can make it useless, if
T-18........ I.7:6 Your l., senseless substitutions, touched
T-18........ I.9:9 Give Him but a l. faith in your brother, to
T-18...... III.3:4 A l. flicker of your eyelids, closed so long,
T-18...... III.3:8 for there is l. doubt that what you think it
T-18...... III.5:4 No l., faltering footsteps that you may
T-18...... III.8:4 you to give the l. spark of your desire the
T-18........ IV.h The L. Willingness
T-18...... IV.1:7 two. He asks but l.. It is He Who adds the
T-18.... IV.1:10 do so l. that enables Him to give so much.
T-18...... IV.4:1 not come from your l. willingness alone.
T-18...... IV.6:2 will merely take away the l. that is asked.
T-18...... IV.6:8 that you may learn how l. is your part,
T-18...... IV.7:3 to accept the idea that you need give so l.,
T-18....... V.2:5 part is only to offer Him a l. willingness to
T-18....... V.2:6 forgiven. On your l. faith, joined with His
T-18....... V.4:6 l. faith it needed to change the purpose is
T-18...... VIII.h The L. Garden
T-18... VIII.2:5 body is a tiny fence around a l. part of a
T-18... VIII.2:6 small, around a very l. segment of Heaven
T-18... VIII.3:2 And to defend this l. speck of dust it bids
T-18... VIII.3:5 alone and frightened is this l. thought,
T-18... VIII.3:6 ocean terrifies the l. ripple and wants to
T-18... VIII.6:5 l. aspect is no different from the whole,
T-18... VIII.7:1 Do not accept this l., fenced-off aspect as
T-18... VIII.7:6 This l. self is not your kingdom. Arched
T-18... VIII.7:8 The l. aspect that you think you set apart
T-18... VIII.8:4 give. In your tiny kingdom you have so l.!
T-18... VIII.8:6 joyless–that makes up your l. kingdom.
T-18... VIII.9:1 The Thought of God surrounds your l.
T-18... VIII.9:8 its beneficence your l. garden will expand,
T-18. VIII.10:3 lonely l. kingdoms locked away from love,
T-18. VIII.10:4 and see your l. garden gently transformed
T-18. VIII.13:6 Only a l. wall of dust still stands between
T-18...... IX.1:3 the l. thought that seems split off and
T-18...... IX.1:6 l. part you think you stole from Heaven.
T-18...... IX.2:1 your l. offering of darkness to the eternal
T-18...... IX.2:3 based on what this l. kingdom really is.
T-18...... IX.2:5 to limit your awareness are l. and limited,
T-19........ I.6:2 divided into l. parts of seeming wholeness
T-19....... I.15:1 your l. kingdoms barren and separate, so
T-19...... III.8:7 cherished but a l. while before it vanishes.
T19... IV.A.2:4 The l. barrier of sand still stands between
T19... IV.A.2:9 Would you let a l. bank of sand, a wall of
T19. IV.A.2:10 this l. remnant of attack you cherish still
T19. IV.A.2:11 This l. wall of hatred would still oppose
T19... IV.A.3:3 still oppose the Will of God, just by a l..
T19... IV.A.3:4 that l. is a limit you would place upon the
T19... IV.A.3:7 still contain behind your l. barrier and
T19... IV.A.3:8 l. wall would hide the purpose of Heaven,
T19... IV.A.4:4 Fear not this l. obstacle. It cannot contain
T19. IV.A.4:11 l. wall will fall away so quietly beneath the
T19... IV.A.5:1 difficult than to surmount your l. wall.
T19... IV.A.6:1 a l. pause of gladness in acknowledgment
T19... IV.A.6:4 Look not upon the l. wall of shadows. The
T19... IV.A.7:1 l. insane wish to get rid of Him Whom
T19... IV.A.7:2 As you look upon the world, this l. wish,
T19... IV.A.8:6 variability the l. remnant induces merely
T19... IV.A.9:1 How mighty can a l. feather be before the
T19... IV.A.9:4 but how easily this l. wisp is lifted up and
T19. IV.A.12:6 No l. shred of guilt escapes their hungry
T19. IV.A.14:4 will be as careful to let no l. act of charity,
T19. IV.A.14:4 no l. breath of love escape their notice.
T19IV.A.17:12 and happy with so l. is to hurt yourself,
T19.... IV.B.4:8 want your Father, not a l. mound of clay,
T19.... IV.B.9:1 Your l. part is but to give the Holy Spirit
T-20...... III.4:2 that death will wait a l. longer before it
T-20...... IV.4:7 for those with l. wings have not accepted
T-20....... V.3:2 for itself, and therefore values him too l..
T-20....... V.5:1 brother's body is as l. use to you as it is to
T-20....... V.5:8 l. breath of eternity that runs through
T-20..... VI.8:8 that held together for a l. while in time,
T-20.... VI.12:8 Perhaps you fear your brother a l. yet;
T-20..... VII.1:8 impossible to imagine one that asks so l.,
T-20..... VII.3:1 the goal the Holy Spirit indeed asks l.. He
T-20..... VII.3:8 with it. Before we look at them a l. closer,
T-20... VIII.5:4 Is the pitifully l. the perfect choice to call
T-21........ I.5:1 must, afraid to lose the l. that they have.
T-21........ I.5:4 the body is to save the l. that they have.
T-21........ I.6:2 with you, but just a l. wisp of melody,
T-21........ I.6:3 But you remember, from just this l. part,
T-21....... II.1:1 how l. is asked of you to learn this course.
T-21....... II.1:2 the l. gift you offer to the Holy Spirit for
T-21....... II.1:2 the very l. on which salvation rests; the
T-21........ II.1:5 but rather that this l. cost seemed, in your
T-21........ II.3:7 is the l. gift you offer to the Holy Spirit,
T-21........ II.4:1 Begrudge not then this l. offering.
T-21........ II.4:4 Never was so much given for so l.. In the
T-21........ II.6:1 see the need for you to give this l. offering
T-21...... III.3:2 This is indeed a l. feat for such a power.
T-21...... IV.8:3 L. child, innocent of sin, follow in
T-21..... VII.1:5 it. Enormity has no appeal save to the l..
T-21..... VII.1:6 that they are l. could see attraction there.
T-21... VII.10:7 and lose this same desire as a l. glint of sin
T-22....... V.4:1 weak is fear; how l. and how meaningless.
T-22....... V.5:1 but recognized how l. stands between you
T-22.... VI.8:10 will one l. smile or willingness to overlook
T-22...... VI.9:8 to make each l. gift of love a source of
T-22...... VI.9:9 Each l. gift you offer to your brother lights
T-22.... VI.15:4 to keep a l. of the ego with this gift. For it
T-23....... in.4:1 not the l. interferers pull you to littleness.
T-23....... in.4:4 of freedom for a l. sigh of seeming sin, nor
T-23....... in.5:6 perceive the l. and the weak about him?
T-23........ I.7:6 indivisible, and far beyond their l. reach.
T-23...... III.3:2 you want; to take a l. and give up the rest.
T-23...... III.3:7 It would maintain you can attack a l., love
T-23...... III.3:7 maintain you can attack a little, love a l.,
T-23...... III.3:8 teach a l. of the same can still be different,
T-23...... III.4:5 Forgiveness cannot be withheld a l.. Nor
T-23...... IV.4:4 your l. gifts and make them mighty. Also
T-24...... III.3:1 a word, a l. whisper that you do not like, a
T-24...... III.7:7 Open your eyes a l.; see the savior God
T-24..... VI.12:1 vigilance; with l. effort and with little time
T-24..... VI.12:1 vigilance; with little effort and with l. time
T-24..... VII.4:2 The body, yes, a l.; not from time, but
T-25...... IV.4:6 linger for a while, a l. while, in twisted
T-25.... IV.5:11 entered it and were mistaken for a l. while
T-25... VII.11:5 For every l. gain must someone lose, and
T-25.... VIII.2:6 Have l. faith that wisdom could be found
T-25.... VIII.2:7 thankful that only l. faith is asked of you.
T-25.... VIII.2:8 a l. faith remains to those who still believe
T-25.... VIII.3:4 Who it may be makes l. difference. But
T-25.... VIII.4:7 another, to be laid beside your l. payment
T-25.. VIII.12:9 How l. need you give the Holy Spirit that
T-25...... IX.1:1 arrogance to think your l. errors cannot
T-25...... IX.9:1 The l. problems that you keep and hide
T-26........ I.1:5 in the name of saving just a l. for yourself.
T-26........ I.1:6 to see a l. part of him and sacrifice the rest
T-26........ I.1:8 All seeming entities can come a l. nearer,
T-26........ I.1:8 come a little nearer, or go a l. farther off,
T-26........ I.3:1 The l. that the body fences off becomes
T-26........ I.3:2 rest. And all the rest must lose this l. part,
T-26........ I.3:5 And for this l. to belong to you are limits
T-26........ II.4:8 to judge whether the hurt be large or l..
T-26........ II.7:3 will see each l. hurt resolved before the
T-26........ II.7:4 For all of them *are* l. in His sight, and
T-26...... IV.4:1 Forgiveness brings no l. miracles to lay
T-26...... IV.6:2 How l. is the hindrance that withholds
T-26.......... V.h The L. Hindrance
T-26....... V.1:1 A l. hindrance can seem large indeed to
T-26....... V.2:2 For it is but a l. hindrance to eternity,
T-26...... VI.2:1 Lead not your l. life in solitude, with one
T-26..... VII.8:8 time and place, and give a l. space to you,
T-26..... VII.8:8 little space to you, another l. space to him
T-26... VII.10:1 asks but a l. wish that what is true be true;
T-26... VII.10:1 a l. willingness to overlook what is not
T-26... VII.10:1 there; a l. sigh that speaks for Heaven as a
T-26... VII.11:7 of God ask not too much, but far too l..
T-26... VII.11:8 everything, to find a l. treasure of his own
T-26... VII.18:3 a l. senseless wish instead of what He wills
T-26... VII.20:5 by this l. gift of truth but let to be itself,
T-26.... VIII.1:2 but reflects the l. you would keep between
T-26.... VIII.1:2 that you and he might be a l. separate.
T-26.... VIII.2:4 do you think it safer to remain a l. careful
T-26.... VIII.2:4 to remain a little careful and a l. watchful
T-26.... VIII.3:8 If you would keep a l. space between you
T-26.... VIII.3:8 you then would want a l. time in which
T-26.... VIII.3:8 in which forgiveness is withheld a l. while.
T-26.... VIII.8:3 aspect of the l. space that lies between you
T-26.... VIII.9:7 time, but to the l. space between you still,
T-26...... IX.2:1 to ask a l. trust for him who carries Christ
T-27........ I.4:8 sins. Sickness is but a "l." death; a form of
T-27........ I.7:5 is their righteous payment for their l. lives

T-27.........I.8:2 and cherish l. pleasures where you can.
T-27......VI.6:6 a tiny stab of pain, a l. worldly pleasure,
T-27.....VII.7:1 to sin all stand within one l. space. And it
T-27.....VII.8:7 So l. is his worth that he is but a dancing
T-27...VII.12:3 between your l. dreams and your reality.
T-27...VII.12:4 reality. The l. gap you do not even see, the
T-27....VIII.1:3 outside the body, lives a l. while and dies,
T-27....VIII.2:2 itself that it has bought with l. metal discs
T-28.........I.1:7 of them and loved them for a l. while. The
T-28.......I.15:3 better way to close the l. gap between
T-28......III.3:5 sickness, to preserve the l. gap unhealed,
T-28......III.3:5 to bridge the l. gap that leads to Him.
T-28......III.4:2 gap *is* l.. Yet it holds the seeds of pestilence
T-28......III.5:4 to keep them separate for a l. while?
T-28......III.5:5 joined to close the l. gap between them,
T-28......III.7:4 the world except a l. gap perceived to tear
T-28......III.8:2 l. gap was seen to stand between you and
T-28......IV.3:7 and his dreams but seem to make a l. gap,
T-28......IV.4:6 And dreams of fear will haunt the l. gap,
T-28......IV.8:3 picture represents, instead of just a l.,
T-28......IV.8:5 the miracle will place within the l. gap,
T-28......IV.9:1 You will come to close each l. gap that lies
T-28.......V.4:1 conceived a l. gap between illusions and
T-28.......V.4:7 It is as l. able to perceive as it can judge or
T-28.......V.6:2 It is not made of l. bits of glass, a piece of
T-28.......V.7:1 is a l. gap between you and your brother,
T-28.......V.7:6 Look at the l. gap, and you behold the
T-28......VI.1:2 For here the l. gap is seen, and yet it is not
T-28......VI.3:8 And it is frail and l. by your wish. It seems
T-28......VI.4:1 body represents the gap between the l. bit
T-28.....VII.1:3 An empty space, a l. gap, would be a lack.
T-28.....VII.6:2 in the frailty of the l. gap of nothingness
T-28.....VII.7:8 is it made a home of holiness a l. while,
T-29.........I.2:6 the l. gap must bring to those who cherish
T-29.........I.3:5 made your friendship possible a l. while.
T-29......VI.6:3 is to dwell a l. while in such a happy place
T-29......VI.6:4 *is* a l. while till timelessness comes quietly
T-29....VIII.2:3 you believe they will complete your l. self,
T-29....VIII.2:6 loss. And thus must seek beyond his l. self
T-29....VIII.6:6 as his Father, come to hate a l. while; to
T-29......IX.4:3 L. child, the light is there. You do but
T-29......IX.6:4 but with the l. wisdom of a child. What
T-29......IX.8:1 Forgiving dreams have l. need to last.
T-30.......in.1:4 Each one will help a l., every time it is
T-30.........I.1:3 a l. practice with the ones you recognize,
T-30.......II.3:3 to death, a l. creature with a little life.
T-30.......II.3:3 to death, a little creature with a l. life.
T-30......III.1:7 l. thing I want, and it will be as everything
T-30....III.2:11 be content with small ideas and l. things.
T-30......IV.4:4 They seem to dance a l. while, according
T-30......IV.8:4 Be glad indeed salvation asks so l., not so
T-30.......V.3:5 he can barely stay and wait a l. longer,
T-31.........I.6:1 this a l. Voice, so small and still It cannot
T-31.........I.6:6 Can it be your l. learning, strange in
T-31......IV.1:5 a l. time is given you to use for you alone;
T-31.......V.3:4 every day a hundred l. things make small
T-31......V.11:6 asks if just a l. question might be raised.
T-31.....VII.3:3 and will at length be seen as l. more than
T-31....VIII.7:1 Deny me not the l. gift I ask, when in
W-pI.......3.2:1 how l. you really understand about them.
W-pI.......5.5:1 much or how l. you think it is doing so.
W-pI.......8.4:3 With as l. investment as possible, search
W-pI.......9.2:5 step will clear a l. of the darkness away,
W-pI.....10.4:6 has l. if any personal meaning to you. As
W-pI.....11.4:2 is l. or no uneasiness and an inclination to
W-pI.....15.2:2 you have seen l. edges of light around the
W-pI.....16.1:4 Thoughts are not big or l.; powerful or
W-pI.....16.4:1 and actively seek not to overlook any "l."
W-pI.....20.3:3 Do not mistake the l. effort that is asked
W-pI.....20.3:3 an indication that our goal is of l. worth.
W-pI.....21.3:1 let the "l." thoughts of anger escape you
W-pI.....27.1:5 the idea will be wholly true a l. nearer.
W-pI.....28.3:4 its purpose to your l. personal thoughts.
W-pI.....29.3:5 holy purpose stands beyond your l. range.
W-pI.....36.1:5 You cannot be without sin a l.. You are
W-pI.....38.4:2 it. Try to make as l. distinction as possible
W-pI.....40.3:1 Today's exercises take l. time and no
W-pI.....44.4:2 slipping by with l. or no sense of strain.
W-pI.....44.6:1 can stand aside from the ego by ever so l.,
W-pI.....45.8:7 l. understanding you have already gained,
W-pI.....65.5:5 as l. involvement or concern as possible,
W-pI...66.11:3 about them a l. while as you say them.
W-pI.....68.4:5 If you succeed even by ever so l., there will
W-pI.....69.7:2 l. effort and small determination call on
W-pI.....72.6:6 Take the l. you can get. God gave you
W-pI.....78.6:3 and all the l. and the larger hurts he gave.
W-pI.....91.4:1 Your efforts, however l. they may be,
W-pI.....92.1:4 by putting l. bits of glass before your eyes.
W-pI...92.10:4 Leave, then, the dark a l. while today, and
W-pI...95.14:2 your l. part in bringing happiness to all
W-pI...96.11:2 mind remains uncertain yet a l. while. Be
W-pI.....97.3:2 awareness is brought a l. nearer at least;
W-pI.....97.4:3 strength to every l. effort that you make.
W-pI.....97.6:2 it will surpass in might the l. gift you gave
W-pI.....98.6:2 can exchange a l. of your time for peace of
W-pI...98.11:1 once more to spend a l. time with you, be
W-pI...98.11:1 tasks, all l. thoughts and limited ideas,
W-pI...100.8:5 undismayed by all the l. thoughts and
W-pI...100.9:4 l. thought has power to hold you back?
W-pI...101.3:3 victims who are l. more than bones before
W-pI...102.1:2 believe a l. that it buys you what you want
W-pI...105.6:1 practice periods will start a l. differently.
W-pI...105.7:1 Think of your "enemies" a l. while, and
WpI..rIII.in9:3 a result, you have gained l. reinforcement,
WpIrIII.in10:5 your mind to rest a l. time in silence and
WpIrIII.in13:1 Do not forget how l. you have learned.
W-pI. 121.11:2 a l. gleam which you had never noticed.
W-pI. 121.11:3 Try to find some l. spark of brightness
W-pI...123.1:4 some small objections and a l. hesitance,
W-pI...124.2:4 as we walk the world a l. while. And those
W-pI...125.5:2 have wandered off a l. while from Him.
W-pI...128.1:3 soar beyond its petty scope and l. ways.
W-pI...128.5:4 beyond all l. values and diminished goals.
W-pI...128.6:1 Pause and be still a l. while, and see how
W-pI...128.7:3 on the world will shift by just a l., every
W-pI...129.2:1 It might be worth a l. time to think once
W-pI...129.5:3 as you unbind your mind from l. things
W-pI...130.7:2 to bring with us a l. part of unreality, as
W-pI. 130.11:1 Accept a l. part of hell as real, and you
W-pI...131.2:7 and protection for the l. dream you made.
W-pI...133.2:1 do not ask too much of life, but far too l..
W-pI...133.2:3 to take from you the l. that you have. It
W-pI...133.5:2 It cannot give you just a l., for there is no
W-pI...134.6:2 but collects them lightly, with a l. laugh,
W-pI...135.4:4 concern are needful to protect its l. life?
W-pI...135.6:4 set its value far beyond a l. pile of dust
W-pI. 135.13:2 and which needs its service for a l. while.
W-pI. 135.25:6 What l. plans or magical beliefs can still
W-pI. 135.26:5 the day, as foolish l. things appear to raise
W-pI...136.2:3 reduce it to a l. pile of unassembled parts.
W-pI...136.8:4 this l. pile of dust silenced and stilled. For
W-pI. 136.12:5 it sighs a l. when you throw away its gifts,
W-pI...137.9:2 how l. practice you need undertake to let
W-pI...137.9:3 extend the l. help He asks in freeing you
W-pI. 137.13:3 Is not a l. time a small expense to offer for
W-pI. 153.16:4 we will be unable to withdraw a l. while,
W-pI...156.7:5 the l. interval of doubt that still remains,
W-pI...157.7:1 and all goals but this become of l. worth,
W-pI...157.7:1 becomes a l. closer to the end of time; a
W-pI...157.7:1 of time; a l. more like Heaven in its ways;
W-pI...157.7:1 in its ways; a l. nearer its deliverance. And
W-pI...161.4:8 We need to see a l., that we learn a lot.
W-pI...164.9:8 Can you withhold so l., when His Hand
W-pI...166.5:4 perceiving how his l. lot but dwindles, as
W-pI...166.6:1 feet that bleed a l. from the rocky road he
W-pI...167.2:6 and pain, even a l. sigh of weariness, a
W-pI. 169.11:5 salvation comes a l. nearer each uncertain
W-pI. 169.12:3 the thought of time but for a l. while.
WpI...rV.in2:5 *a l. child along a way he does not understand*
WpI...rV.in5:2 Every step we take brings us a l. nearer.
WpI...rV.in6:2 I share your doubts and fears a l. while,
Wi181-200 2:5 that words become of l. consequence.
Wi181-200 3:4 go past all defenses for a l. while each day.
W-pI...181.3:1 we first let all such l. focuses give way to
W-pI...181.3:2 we seek, and only this, for just a l. while.
W-pI...181.5:5 these pointless limitations by a l. while.
W-pI...181.6:3 So, for a l. while, without regard to past
W-pI...182.5:7 But give Him just a l. time to be Himself,
W-pI .. 182.6:3 He is so l. that He seems so easily shut out
W-pI .. 182.9:2 For He was willing to become a l. Child
W-pI 182.10:1 Christ is reborn as but a l. Child each
W-pI 182.11:4 He has come as does a l. child, who must
W-pI .. 183.4:1 and l. names have lost their meaning. No
W-pI .. 183.4:5 the Name of God replace their l. names,
W-pI .. 183.7:3 Think not He hears the l. prayers of those
W-pI .. 183.8:5 the thousand l. names you gave your
W-pI 183.11:1 All l. things are silent. Little sounds are
W-pI 183.11:2 L. sounds are soundless now. The little
W-pI 183.11:3 The l. things of earth have disappeared.
W-pI .. 184.4:3 of l. things and looks upon them. And a
W-pI 184.11:1 Use all the l. names and symbols which
W-pI .. 186.7:4 on you, and not upon this l. pile of dust.
W-pI .. 190.6:6 you deny a l. corner of your mind its own
W-pI .. 190.8:5 where sorrow rules and l. joys give way
W-pI 193.11:1 Give all you can, and give a l. more. For
W-pI 193.12:1 Each hour, spend a l. time today, and in
W-pI 193.13:7 deny the l. steps He asks you take to Him.
W-pI .. 195.3:3 as l. left within his grasping fingers as in
W-pI .. 197.6:2 the gifts of God are lent but for a l. while,
W-pII .... in.1:1 Words will mean l. now. We use them
W-pII .... in.6:5 Accept these l. gifts of thanks from us, as
W-pII .. in.11:4 slowly read and thought about a l. while,
W-pII ..... 4.4:3 guilt, with but a l. life that ends in death.
W-pII . 258.1:1 our minds to overlook all l. senseless aims
W-pII . 258.1:2 our pointless l. goals which offer nothing,
W-pII . 281.1:4 *put my l. meaningless ideas in place of where*
M-in .......... 5:1 there would be l. hope of salvation, for
M-13 ......... 7:4 You cannot be a l. bit in hell. The Word
M-17 ......... 2:4 wish that makes the help of l. value, and
M-18 ......... 3:4 Its l. space and tiny breath become the
M-20 ......... 4:8 A tranquil mind is not a l. gift. Would you
M-21 ......... 2:3 the word has l. or no practical meaning,
M-23 ......... 4:4 that the l. space between the two is lost,
M-25 ......... 1:6 the l. ones that may come to teach him on the
M-25 ......... 2:3 be l. point in trying to teach salvation. It
M-27 ......... 2:3 He holds your l. life in his hand but by a
M-27 ......... 3:4 and to last a l. while by his destruction.
M-29 ....... 2:11 about which you understand so l.? Be
C-2 .......... 10:6 And who would not go on a l. while when
C-4 ............ 1:4 last in time a l. while longer than others.
C-5 ............ 5:3 l. life on earth was not enough to teach
C-5 ............ 6:7 Yet he would help you yet a l. more if you
C-6 ............ 5:7 place the hymn to God is heard a l. while.
C-ep .......... 3:3 on before and lost our way a l. while. And
P-2......... in.2:2 contrary, such concepts mean l. to them,
P-2........ III.1:6 the l. light that can be then accepted is all
P-2........ IV.7:6 of health is substituted for a l. while, but
P-2........ IV.8:3 compromise by seeing just a l. bit of hell.
P-2..........V.4:8 lean upon a strength beyond our l. scope
P-2....... VII.7:5 except to some extent and for a l. while.
P-2....... VII.8:2 all its l. triumphs and its dreams of death.
P-3..........II.2:2 taught him l. or nothing about the real
P-3..........II.6:5 But only l. time is saved. The new dreams
S-1......... in.2:1 To you who are in time a l. while, prayer
S-1...........I.4:8 still all l. answers are contained in this.
S-1......... IV.4:5 just the l. space that lasts until it crumbles
S-1..........V.1:5 be. All l. gods it gladly lays aside, not in
S-1..........V.3:7 is l. more to learn before the journey is
S-3..........II.6:2 It can be held at bay a l. while, and there
S-3........ IV.8:1 of retribution and a l. life beset with fear,

**littleness** 68

T-8 ...... VII.5:6 but give him freedom from his belief in l.,
T-8 ..... VIII.9:6 be an image of your own perception of l..
T-9 ...... VII.6:5 chosen to be little and to lament your l..
T-9 ...... VII.6:7 Your l. is taken for granted there and you
T-9 ...... VII.7:3 your l. therefore is to deny all knowledge,
T-9 ..... VIII.2:3 real. It is an attempt to counteract your l.,
T-9 ..... VIII.2:3 based on the belief that the l. is real.
T-9 ..... VIII.4:6 you because of the l. in which it believes.
T-9 ..... VIII.6:4 L. and grandeur cannot coexist, nor is it
T-9 ..... VIII.6:5 L. and grandiosity can and must alternate
T-9 ..... VIII.7:1 Truth and l. are denials of each other
T-9 ..... VIII.7:4 Perhaps it is the belief in l.; perhaps it is
T-9 ... VIII.10:9 To accept your l. *is* arrogant, because it
T-9 ... VIII.11:9 replace the ego's belief in l. with His Own

T-10......IV.8:5 was a descent from magnitude to l.. But
T-13......III.7:6 kept to hurt you and cleanse it of its l.,
T-14... VIII.1:7 you would be released from l. to glory. To
T-15.........III.h L. versus Magnitude
T-15......III.1:1 Be not content with l.. But be sure you
T-15......III.1:2 But be sure you understand what l. is, and
T-15......III.1:3 it. L. is the offering you give yourself. You
T-15......III.1:5 is little because it is a world made out of l.
T-15......III.1:5 the strange belief that l. can content you.
T-15......III.1:7 L. and glory are the choices open to your
T-15......III.2:2 Choose l. and you will not have peace, for
T-15......III.2:4 is no form of l. that can ever content you.
T-15......III.3:3 who have sought and found l., remember
T-15......III.3:5 fulfilling it that you can escape from l..
T-15......III.4:4 your striving must be directed against l.,
T-15......III.4:5 of l. is a task the little cannot undertake.
T-15......III.4:6 tribute to your magnitude and not your l..
T-15......III.6:1 can hold your magnitude, clean of all l.,
T-15......III.6:1 little gift the world of l. would offer you.
T-15......III.6:4 Him. For l., and the belief that you can be
T-15......III.6:4 the belief that you can be content with l.,
T-15......III.6:5 and believe that l. can be blown up into a
T-15......III.6:6 Neither give l., nor accept it. All honor is
T-15......III.6:8 Your l. deceives you, but your magnitude
T-15......III.6:9 one, then, with l. in the Name of Christ,
T-15......III.7:3 is beyond all your l. to give the gift of God
T-15......III.8:1 Is it a sacrifice to leave l. behind, and
T-15......III.9:4 together we can replace the shabby l. that
T-15......III.9:9 you, who must remain forever beyond l..
T-15....III.12:3 are. Hear not his appeal to hell and l., but
T-15....III.12:6 Lay not l. before His holy altar, which
T-15......IV.1:9 it, for it holds the whole release from l..
T-15......IV.2:1 rest upon your willingness to let all l. go.
T-15......IV.2:3 as you desire it not and cherish l. instead,
T-15......IV.3:4 given to the world for its release from l..
T-15......IV.4:5 have accepted for finding magnitude in l..
T-15......IV.5:3 for the release from l. in the mind of the
T-15......XI.3:4 and sacrifice and l. will disappear in our
T-16....... V.9:1 out to those who place their faith in l..
T-16....... V.9:2 of l. lies in every special relationship, for
T-16......VI.6:3 and this spark cannot be limited long to l.
T-16......VI.7:3 is strong and powerful cut down to l.. In
T-18......IV.3:1 never ask that you remain content with l..
T19.IV.A.17:5 my body, you whom I love, *knowing* its l.?
T-23.......in.4:1 Let not the little interferers pull you to l.
T-23.......in.4:6 in the clean place where l. does not exist.
T-23.......in.4:7 purpose is at variance with l. of any kind.
T-23.......in.5:1 not let l. lead God's Son into temptation.
T-24....... II.1:6 Against the l. you see in him you stand as
T-24....... II.2:4 And who can use him as the gauge of l.,
T-28......VI.3:4 what it hears, and hate its frailty and l..
T-29....... II.9:5 And you will hate it for its l., unmindful
T-29..... II.10:1 replacing what He is with l. and limit and
T-29... VIII.2:5 has not enslaved himself to l. and loss.

## littlest 1

T-29.........I.1:4 compromise the least and l. gap would

## live 104

T-1........VI.3:4 This is because you think you l. in space,
T-3...........I.5:3 not in conflict, but naturally l. in peace.
T-3......... II.6:4 and those who l. in error and emptiness
T-3....... V.10:6 the Thoughts of God who l. in His light!
T-4...........I.6:3 you and l. with you if you will think with
T-4.........VI.6:3 You are asked to l. so as to demonstrate
T-6.........in.2:4 of any kind, you l. by it and teach it. Your
T-7.......VII.5:3 give it. You cannot make nothing l., since
T-11.........I.9:6 in time you cannot l. apart from Him.
T-11......IV.6:6 for you, for while I l. it cannot be shut,
T-11......IV.6:6 I live it cannot be shut, and I l. forever.
T-11......VI.4:2 You l. in me because you live in God. And
T-11......VI.4:2 You live in me because you l. in God. And
T-11......VI.4:3 lives in you, as you l. in everyone. Can you
T-11......VI.7:4 not die by demonstrating that I l. in you.
T-11......VI.9:2 If I l. in you, you are awake. Yet you must
T-11. VIII.11:4 as we l. together and love together. Be not
T-12...VII.13:4 for you, it lets you l. but to await death. It
T-12...VII.13:5 It will torment you while you l., but its
T-12... VIII.1:7 remain hidden, for it can l. only in peace.
T-12... VIII.2:5 and could not l. in the knowledge of Him.
T-13....III.11:5 For a darkened mind cannot l. in the light
T-14.........I.4:5 but indirect expressions of the will to l.,
T-14......IV.9:1 The children of Heaven l. in the light of
T-14......VI.3:7 only this has meaning and can l. in light.
T-14....... X.2:4 world you seem to l. in is a world of limits
T-14....... X.4:4 the mind of those who think they l. apart.
T-15......IV.6:3 You could l. forever in the holy instant,
T-15......XI.4:7 loathsome, and l. within himself in peace
T-16......IV.4:5 trying to l. with guilt rather than die of it.
T-16..... V.10:4 sacrifice is that God must die so you can l.
T-18......III.2:4 Fear seems to l. in darkness, and when
T19.IV.A.17:9 But you can l. to show it is not real. The
T19....IV.C.2:4 what of those whose dedication is not to l.
T19....IV.C.3:5 of their Creator, Whose Will it is they l..
T-20..... II.8:12 and where we l. in gentleness and peace,
T-20......VI.3:6 They l. in secrecy, hating the sunlight and
T-21.........I.5:1 they define their life and where they l.,
T-22.........I.8:7 holiness of your relationship to let Him l..
T-23..... II.11:8 demands his death, that you may l.. And
T-23..... II.18:8 pet it and pamper it, and make it l.? And
T-24.........I.5:7 that your specialness can l. on his defeat.
T-24.........I.5:9 How can he l., with all your sins upon
T-25.........I.3:1 yourself to be; the world you want to l. in,
T-26....... V.4:1 you l. in time and know not it is gone, the
T-26....... V.4:2 You think you l. in what is past. Each
T-26..... V.11:2 instant that he chose to die instead of l..
T-26..... V.13:2 And so you die each day to l. again, until
T-26...VII.16:7 because his Father wills that he should l..
T-27.........I.7:3 For who could l. a life so soon cut short
T-27.......I.10:7 be, "Behold me, brother, at your hand I l..
T-27....... V.7:4 who let yourself be healed that it might l..
T-27......VI.5:9 The dying l., the dead arise, and pain has
T-27... VIII.1:4 In the brief time allotted it to l., it seeks
T-28......III.7:5 And what are you who l. within the world
T-29......III.2:7 all living things who know not that they l.
T-29......IV.1:5 but only if you want to l. in dreams or to
T-29....IX.10:1 Forgiving dreams remind you that you l.
T-30.......in.1:7 until they are the rules by which you l..
T-30.......I.15:2 It is set by what you choose to l. it with,
T-31.......I.13:5 him. Now is he free to l. as you are free,
T-31.....VII.4:1 You l. in that world just as much as this.
W-pI.....49.4:5 You do not l. here. We are trying to reach
W-pI.....53.2:5 I cannot l. in peace in such a world. I am
W-pI...107.7:5 we l. and hope and breathe and think. We
W-pI...121.4:3 It wants to l., yet wishes it were dead. It
W-pI...127.6:4 obey; of all the limits under which you l.,
W-pI...136.9:1 stronger than the truth, which asks you l.,
W-pI...156.2:9 Nothing can be apart from Him and l..
W-pI...156.4:2 All things that l. bring gifts to you, and
W-pI...158.1:5 for by that knowledge only does it l..
W-pI...162.2:6 And those who l. and hear this sound will
W-pI...163.6:3 things die, or else they l. and cannot die.
W-pI...163.9:3 *We l. and move in You alone. We are not*
W-pI...165.2:4 you. By it you l.. It is your Source of life,
W-pI...165.6:5 denial of the nourishment he needs to l.?
W-pI.166.11:1 Now do we l., for now we cannot die. The
W-pI...167.2:7 acknowledge death. And thus deny you l..
W-pI......169.h By grace I l.. By grace I am released.
W-pI.169.15:3 *By grace I l.. By grace I am released. By grace I*
W-pI...180.1:1 (169) By grace I l.. By grace I am released.
W-pI...182.1:1 world you seem to l. in is not home to you
W-pI...184.1:1 You l. by symbols. You have made up
W-pI...188.8:3 you are the co-creator of all things that l..
W-pI...190.7:7 while in your kind forgiveness does it l..
W-pI...197.7:3 for everyone must l. and move in Him.
W-pI...199.8:2 In immortality you l. forever. Would you
W-pI...200.2:2 to win through losing, nor to die to l..
W-pII......222.h God is with me. I l. and move in Him.
W-pII..222.1:3 He is my home, wherein I l. and move;
W-pII......2.4:4 have come to l. within their branches.
W-pII..261.1:2 and think I l. within the citadel where I
W-pII..261.1:4 I l. in God. In Him I find my refuge and
W-pII..271.1:4 for nothing that He looks on but must l.,
W-pII..278.1:1 all things that seem to l. appear to die,
W-pII..287.1:5 And would I rather l. with fear than love?
W-pII..297.1:4 I l. within a world that needs salvation,
W-pII.357.1:1 *escape the prison house in which I think I l..*
M-6...........1:8 Having nothing to l. for, he may ask for
M-20.........4:9 you not rather l. than choose to die?
M-27.........3:6 And so do all things l. because of death.
P-3.......III.1:7 But no one here can l. with no illusions,
P-3.......III.4:1 to l. is something no one need fight for. It
S-3......IV.10:5 comforted and l. no more in terror and in

## lived 3

T-3.........II.1:7 is impossible. No one has ever l. who has
T-28.........I.5:8 that they be brought to you, and l. again.
W-pII.223.1:1 I was mistaken when I thought I l. apart

## lives 44

T-2......VIII.5:4 No one who l. in fear is really alive. Your
T-3.......VII.1:5 for systems of belief by which one l.. It is a
T-4..........II.7:1 ego literally l. by comparisons. Equality is
T-6........IV.7:4 *been. Being* alone l. in the Kingdom, where
T-6........IV.7:4 everything l. in God without question.
T-6......V.A.1:4 The body neither l. nor dies, because it
T-7....VIII.1:11 project or extend, because that is how it l.
T-9.........IV.9:1 The ego literally l. on borrowed time, and
T-11.......IV.7:4 l. in His Creator and shines with His glory
T-11......VI.4:3 God. And everyone l. in you, as you live in
T-13......VII.5:9 He l. within you in the quiet present, and
T-14.......IX.4:7 of Holiness l. in everything that lives, for
T-14.......IX.4:7 of Holiness lives in everything that l., for
T-14....... X.11:3 Nothing l. in secret, and what you would
T-15......III.8:7 Before the greatness that l. in you, your
T19...IV.D.1:4 of life, the Source of everything that l., the
T-24......III.4:4 creeps or crawls, or even l. at all. Nothing
T-24......VI.5:6 in everything that l. and shares His Being.
T-24......VI.6:4 memory of Him in Whom your brother l.,
T-25......VII.8:4 and recognizes as the world in which he l.
T-26....... V.5:7 l. in memories alone is unaware of where
T-27.........I.7:5 their righteous payment for their little l.?
T-27....VIII.1:3 outside the body, l. a little while and dies,
T-29........II.6:6 the law on which they predicate their l..
T-29......II.10:5 He l. in God, and it is this that makes him
T-29......VI.2:9 the tides, the seasons and the l. of men;
T-31..VIII.12:7 from everything that l. and moves in You.
W-pI...100.1:2 lead separate l. and go their separate ways
W-pI...139.4:4 he is. He has accepted it because he l.; has
W-pI...139.4:4 not know the only certainty by which he l.
W-pI...152.6:4 mind that l. within a body that must die?
W-pI...156.3:2 remains unshared by everything that l..
W-pI...156.3:3 What l. is holy as Himself, because what
WpI...rV.in9:9 l. but must not then be one with you?
W-pI...182.7:5 l. an outcast in a world of alien thoughts.
W-pI...187.4:6 the form of things that l. unchangeable.
W-pI...192.8:5 become the world in which his jailer l.,
W-pI...197.7:3 To everyone who l. will Christ yet come,
W-pI...199.2:4 who can be afraid who l. in Innocence,
W-pI...199.3:3 l. united with the home that it has made.
W-pII......5.1:2 It is within this fence he thinks he l., to
W-pII ...12.3:3 and of suffering, when he l. in eternal joy?
Wfl........in.1:4 as to Him we give our l. henceforth. For
S-1..........II.8:8 who l. now with the illusion of death and

## liveth 2

T-11......VI.9:5 you will not know that your redeemer l.,
T-12........II.9:3 Yet your Redeemer l., and abideth in you

## living 76

T-4....... II.11:5 as long as you appear to be l. in this world
T-4....... II.11:8 Who is the "you" who are l. in this world?
T-4......IV.11:7 of everything that the l. God created.
T-7.......VII.5:8 Give only honor to the Sons of the l. God,
T-8.........IX.3:5 "Rest in peace" is a blessing for the l., not
T-10....... V.14:6 with the temporal, you are l. in time. As
T-13......III.5:3 seems more valuable than your l. oneness
T-13.....VII.3:6 not the power to touch the l. world at all.
T-14......III.3:2 Learning is l. here, as creating is being in
T-14......IV.5:6 of the joy of l. with your God and Father,
T-16......IV.4:5 certain ones as partners in any aspect of l.

T-17....... V.1:1 of the holy instant in l. in this world. Like
T-18.........I.8:2 stillness dwells the l. God you never left,
T-18....VIII.5:2 thought, l. alone and in no way joined to
T-18....VIII.9:8 out to everyone who thirsts for l. water,
T19. IV.A.12:7 sin they pounce on any l. thing they see,
T19....IV.C.1:9 its dark shadow falls across all l. things,
T19....IV.C.2:2 What is a shadow to the l.? They but walk
T19. IV.D.15:3 as God created every l. thing and loves it.
T-20.... VI.11:5 And here he is more dead than l.. Yet it is
T-22.......in.2:8 themselves, l. with their bodies perhaps
T-22....... II.4:7 excludes one l. thing and holds it out,
T-23.... II.18:9 be content with an illusion that you are l.?
T-24....... V.6:8 in each l. thing that He beholds and loves.
T-24....... V.7:4 hand, that everyone may bless all l. things
T-24....... V.7:6 that you may save all l. things from death,
T-26...... IX.3:2 now become a l. temple in a world of light
T-26...... IX.4:4 freedom lights up every l. thing and lifts it
T-26...... IX.6:2 And They come quickly to the l. temple,
T-26...... IX.8:1 Now is the temple of the l. God rebuilt as
T-26....... X.2:7 belongs to every l. thing along with you.
T-26....... X.5:8 denied to every l. thing upon the earth.
T-27.........I.2:6 Wish not to make yourself a l. symbol of
T-27..... II.3:11 would hold against himself or any l. thing
T-27...... III.2:1 power," and above all, a "l. death." And
T-29....... II.6:1 Such is the promise of the l. God; His Son
T-29....... II.6:1 have life and every l. thing be part of him,
T-29....... II.6:2 death, with death perceived as life, and l.,
T-29...... III.2:7 all l. things who know not that they live.
T-29...... VI.4:9 There is no death because the l. share the
T-29..... VII.5:3 death, conceived as real and given l. form.
T-29....VIII.4:2 grass from something l. to a sign of death.
T-29....VIII.6:5 peace of God, forever given to all l. things,
T-29....VIII.9:8 also give the same to every l. thing as well.
T-29....VIII.9:9 And thus is every l. thing a part of you, as
T-31.........I.9:1 There is no l. thing that does not share
T-31....VIII.6:1 you, and so is every l. thing you look upon
W-pI.....57.5:6 to understand the holiness of all l. things,
W-pI.....93.1:3 l. on after seeing this being impossible.
W-pI.....97.4:4 calls through His Voice to every l. thing;
W-pI. 132.14:1 it, and about all l. things we see upon it.
W-pI...139.2:3 surely known by any l. thing is what it is.
W-pI...155.1:1 is a way of l. in the world that is not here,
W-pI...156.5:2 All l. things are still before you, for they
W-pI...158.1:5 It was given as well to every l. thing, for
W-pI...163.2:2 hold all l. things within its withered hand;
W-pI...163.9:6 *life we share with You and with all l. things,*
W-pI. 166.15:2 Become the l. proof of what Christ's touch
W-pI. 184.15:2 *In It we are united with all l. things, and You*
W-pI...188.3:2 It pauses to caress each l. thing, and
W-pI...188.5:5 is shining in you now, and in all l. things.
W-pI. 188.10:1 from us to all l. things that share our life.
W-pI...190.6:6 sickly place where l. things must come at
W-pI...194.8:3 every l. creature not respond with healed
W-pI...195.6:1 that we are separate from no l. thing, and
W-pI...195.6:3 We give thanks for every l. thing, for
W-pI...205.1:3 *God is my one goal; the aim of all my l. here,*
W-pII .248.1:6 What dies was never l. in reality, and did
W-pII .282.1:3 truth remains forever l. in the joy of love.
W-pII .....9.2:1 which encompasses all l. things with you.
W-pII .341.1:3 *Love bestowed upon us, l. one with You, in*
M-20 .........5:1 L. is joy, but death can only weep. You
M-23 .........2:6 has recognized all l. things as part of him.
M-28 .........2:6 Christ's face is seen in every l. thing, and
M-28 .........4:1 All l. hearts are tranquil with a stir of
S-3........IV.2:3 wing and all the l. things upon the earth.

## load 1

W-pI...101.7:1 remove the heavy l. you lay upon yourself

## loan 1

W-pI...105.2:2 return; a l. with interest to be paid in full;

## loans 1

W-pI...197.1:5 And so you think God's gifts are l. at best;

## loathe 1

T-28 ...... VI.3:1 thing you hate and fear and l. and want,

## loathsome 2

T-15 ..... XI.4:7 Who can perceive part of himself as l.,
W-pI...134.4:6 right the plainly wrong; the l. as the good.

## lock 4

T-28 ..VII.5:10 to bar the door and l. the windows and
T-31 ... III.3:10 are sin you l. the mind within the body,
W-pI. 131.11:8 not completely l. to hide what lies beyond
W-pI. 153.13:3 and l. our quaint and childish thoughts of

## locked 12

T-14 .......II.7:5 the dark door that you believe is l. forever
T-14 .... VII.6:1 to Him every secret you have l. away from
T-18 ..... VI.7:5 You see yourself l. in a separate prison,
T-18 .VIII.10:3 leaving no lonely little kingdoms l. away
T-22 ..... III.3:2 set like a heavy gate, l. and without a key,
T-26 ........I.2:3 join with what is l. away within the wall.
T-26 .......II.8:5 and l. will merely fall away and disappear.
T-26 ..... IX.5:3 What has been l. is opened; what was
W-pI..... 72.8:4 you, l. away from your awareness by the
W-pI... 159.6:4 Here the door is never l., and no one is
W-pI... 194.2:2 chains that l. the door to freedom on it.
W-pI... 195.8:5 some other things still l. away as "sins."

## locks 2

T-28 .... VII.6:2 Why burden it with further l. and chains
W-pI... 135.3:5 your armor thicker and your l. more tight

## loftier 1

T-2 ........ V.9:5 Most of the l. concepts of which you are

## loftiest 2

T-4 .......II.4:10 l. idea of which ego thinking is capable.
T-13 ... VIII.2:5 Perception, at its l., is never complete.

## lofty 6

T-4 ..........I.9:5 a very l. function that you are not meeting
T-9 ...... VII.4:2 because you do not understand how l. the
T-9 ...... VII.8:4 The truth about you is so l. that nothing
W-pI... 133.1:3 do today. We will not speak of l., world-
W-pI... 169.1:2 It is the world's most l. aspiration, for it
W-pII . 224.1:1 My true Identity is so secure, so l., sinless

## logic 8

T-5 ........ V.1:4 The ego's l. is as impeccable as that of the
T-14 ......in.1:4 uses l. as easily and as well as does the ego
T-14 ......in.1:6 We have followed much of the ego's l.,
T-14 ......in.1:8 and follow the simple l. by which the
T-14 ........I.2:3 The l. of the world must therefore lead to
T-14 ........I.3:8 to teach him that the l. of the world is
T-14 ........I.3:9 Yet in him who made this insane l. there
W-pI..... 66.5:5 Try to see the l. in this sequence, even if

## logical 15

T-4 ........ V.3:3 sense the ego's fear of God is at least l.,
T-7 ....... VI.3:4 It is perfectly l. but clearly insane. The ego
T-7 ....... VI.3:8 Remaining l. but still insane, the ego
T-7 .........X.1:2 the ego's reasoning to its l. conclusion,
T-7 .........X.1:5 ego's premises, but not at their l. outcome
T-7 .........X.1:7 are the l. outcome of His premises. His
T-7 .........X.2:3 It is the l. outcome of what you are. The
T-7 .........X.2:4 The ability to see a l. outcome depends on
T-10 .......II.6:4 l. outcome of your decision is perfectly
T-10 ..... III.5:1 Look calmly at the l. conclusion of the
T-14 ......in.1:6 logic, and have seen its l. conclusions.
T-22 ......in.4:5 brother to the l. conclusion of your union.
T-22 ... VI.13:5 Either position is a l. conclusion. Either
T-23 .....II.21:2 follows that it seems to be a l. conclusion;
W-pI .... 39.1:3 with intellectual feats nor l. toys. We are

## logically 1

T-7 ....... VI.8:2 ego proceeds perfectly l. to the belief that

## loneliness 24

T-8 ....... IV.2:3 maintained by fear of the same l. that *is* its
T-8 ....... IV.2:6 If I am with you in the l. of the world, the
T-8 ....... IV.2:6 the loneliness of the world, the l. is gone.
T-8 ....... IV.2:7 the illusion of l. if you are not alone. My
T-15 .... VII.9:3 born of the fear of l. and yet dedicated to
T-15 .... VII.9:3 and yet dedicated to the continuance of l.,
T-15 .. VII.12:1 the body and its ability to overcome l. is
T-15 .. VII.12:4 will always teach that l. is solved by guilt,
T-15 .. VII.12:4 and that communication is the cause of l..
T-15 .. VII.14:5 to it, and overcomes l. completely. There
T-15 ... VIII.3:2 The l. of God's Son is the loneliness of his
T-15 ... VIII.3:2 of God's Son is the l. of his Father. Refuse
T-15 ... VIII.3:8 that it calls to everyone to escape from l.,
T-15 ..... IX.4:7 be accepted and the l. in Heaven is gone.
T-16 .....V.10:2 must entail, nor of the sadness and the l..
T-17 .. VII.10:3 For l. in God must be a dream. You whose
T-17 .. VII.10:4 apart from l. because the truth has come.
T-18 ..... IX.4:3 despair and l. to it and keep it joyless. Yet
T-21 .........I.5:4 And they adjust to l., believing that to
T-24 .....II.13:4 madness and in l. your special kingdom,
T-26 ..... VI.3:1 alone indeed, and l. is not the Will of God
T-26 .. VII.11:9 do without a sense of isolation, loss and l.
W-pI .... 41.1:1 the sense of l. and abandonment all the
M-10 ......... 6:6 All of the l. and sense of loss; of passing

## lonely 26

T-2 ..... III.5:11 God is l. without His Sons, and they are
T-2 ..... III.5:11 His Sons, and they are l. without Him.
T-4 ...... VII.6:7 He is l. when the minds He created do not
T-7 .... VII.10:7 You are as l. without understanding this
T-7 .... VII.10:7 is l. when His Sons do not know Him. The
T-8 ....... IV.1:8 only if you do, you will feel l. and helpless
T-11 ...... III.2:3 At home in God he is l., and amid all his
T-11 ...... III.4:3 That way is hard indeed, and very l.. Fear
T-13 ... III.12:1 out" is to "make alone," and thus make l..
T-14 ...........V.1:2 with all the l. ones who have denied Him?
T-14 .....X.10:7 l. journey fails because it has excluded
T-15 ..... XI.4:8 experiencing himself as incomplete and l.
T-15 ..... XI.5:1 you perceive yourself as l. and deprived.
T-18 . VIII.10:3 leaving no l. little kingdoms locked away
T-22 ......in.2:2 sin? Only the l. and alone, who see their
T-22 ..... IV.4:3 after such a long and l. journey where you
T-25 ..... VI.3:6 Let him no more be l., for the lonely ones
T-25 ..... VI.3:6 l. ones are those who see no function in
T-31 ... VIII.7:1 who wanders in the world uncertain, l.,
W-pI .. 124.5:2 sad and the distressed, the l. and afraid,
W-pI .. 152.6:4 the guilty, the afraid, the suffering and l.,
W-pI .. 166.5:1 Yet in his l., senseless wanderings, God's
W-pI 166.11:4 you perceive yourself as l. and afraid.
W-pI 166.13:1 all who chose the l. road you have escaped
W-pII . 223.2:5 *We are l. here, and long for Heaven, where*
W-pII . 245.1:4 *I bring it to the desolate and l. and afraid. I*

## long 225

*See also* long-held, long-range

T-1 .... VII.3:13 As l. as a single "slave" remains to walk
T-2 ..........I.3:8 rebirth is impossible as l. as you continue
T-2 .........II.4:2 in effect l. before the Atonement began.
T-2 .........II.6:7 As l. as there is need for Atonement, there
T-2 .........V.2:6 l. as your sense of vulnerability persists,
T-2 .........V.4:2 perfectly safe as l. as you are completely
T-2 .........V.8:3 As l. as you believe in what your physical
T-2 .........V.9:3 However, as l. as time persists, healing is
T-2 ....... VI.8:7 As l. as you recognize only the need for
T-2 ...... VII.6:4 obscured as l. as any of its parts is missing
T-2 ..... VIII.2:5 will extend over a similarly l. period, and
T-3 .......V.10:1 l. as perception lasts prayer has a place.

T-4 I.6:6 be a devoted teacher as l. as you believe it.
T-4 I.7:3 As l. as you dispute this everything you
T-4 I.7:10 is possible as l. as this delusion lasts.
T-4 I.8:2 will remain doubtful as l. as you believe in
T-4 II.4:8 and as l. as your origin is open to belief
T-4 II.11:5 may ask how this is possible as l. as you
T-4 III.7:8 wait as l. as you choose to forsake yourself
T-4 III.8:5 How l. will you deny Him His Kingdom?
T-4 VI.1:5 necessarily conflicted as l. as you are here,
T-4 VI.1:5 or as l. as you believe that you are here.
T-4 VI.6:7 I will lend them my strength as l. as theirs
T-5 II.1:6 His Mind to yours as l. as there is time.
T-5 IV.7:3 of creation cannot be expressed as l. as
T-6 I.18:5 As l. as you teach this you will believe it.
T-6 V.A.6:6 Some remain at this step for a l. time,
T-6 V.B.5:3 you will surely do as l. as you accept both,
T-6 V.C.4:7 and consistency cannot coexist for l.,
T-6 V.C.4:8 l. as you must be vigilant against anything
T-6 V.C.7:4 As l. as belief in God and His Kingdom is
T-7 III.4:2 l. as you believe you can attend to what is
T-7 IV.3:6 abilities are applied l. enough to one goal,
T-7 V.7:7 it as l. as you learn through the ego. This
T-7 VI.8:10 requires vigilance only as l. as you do not
T-7 VII.3:9 image of yourself as l. as perception lasts.
T-7 VII.3:11 perception and it must last as l. as you
T-7 VII.4:2 They will last as l. as you value them.
T-7 X.3:6 l. as you are in doubt about what you are,
T-7 X.5:2 As l. as you avoid His guidance in any way
T-8 II.3:1 teach you anything as l. as your will is free
T-9 I.6:7 Yet as l. as you are afraid of your will, that
T-9 I.13:5 As l. as you believe that fear is possible,
T-9 VIII.2:8 suspicious as l. as you despair of yourself.
T-10 in.1:3 l. as you believe that anything happening
T-10 I.1:1 against them as l. as your mind is split,
T-10 V.14:2 As l. as both appear to you to be desirable
T-11 II.7:3 and how l. he shall remain with you. Yet
T-11 VI.8:6 l. as you believe that you can crucify him,
T-11 VIII.5:5 l. as you believe that problems are specific
T-11 VIII.5:6 as l. as you believe that the one is many.
T-12 VII.4:9 l. as you believe you have other functions,
T-12 VII.4:9 functions, so l. will you need correction.
T-12 VII.7:10 Yet as l. as you perceive the world as split,
T-12 VII.14:4 For as l. as you feel guilty you are listening
T-13 I.3:5 reach its end it will roll up like a l. carpet
T-13 I.3:6 l. as you believe the Son of God is guilty
T-13 I.3:7 will seem l. and cruel and senseless, for so
T-13 III.6:4 and concealed as l. as they are hidden, is
T-13 III.8:4 like you they l. for the grandeur that is in
T-13 IV.1:6 As l. as it is reasonably satisfied with you,
T-13 VII.12:4 renew them as l. as you have need of them
T-13 VII.12:5 from you as l. as you have any need of it.
T-13 X.6:1 As l. as you believe that guilt is justified
T-13 X.6:2 as l. as you believe there is a reason for it.
T-14 IX.2:3 How l. can contradiction stand when its
T-15 I.11:1 how l. it would take to change your mind
T-15 I.11:1 ask yourself, "How l. is an instant?"
T-15 I.13:1 How l. is an instant? It is as short for
T-15 I.14:1 How l. is an instant? As long as it takes to
T-15 I.14:2 l. as it takes to re-establish perfect sanity,
T-15 I.14:3 As l. as it takes to remember immortality,
T-15 I.14:4 l. as it takes to exchange hell for Heaven.
T-15 I.14:5 L. enough to transcend all of the ego's
T-15 II.3:1 How l. can it take to be where God would
T-15 IV.2:3 for it. As l. as you desire it not and cherish
T-15 IV.9:6 as l. as you would hide it from yourself.
T-15 VI.1:6 be guilt as l. as you accept the possibility,
T-15 VI.7:8 as l. as you prefer to be something else, or
T-15 VII.8:4 As l. as the body is there to receive its
T-15 VII.10:2 but it cannot l. deceive those who will
T-15 VII.10:4 ego has, and as l. as you identify with it,
T-15 VII.12:2 As l. as you believe that to be with a body
T-15 IX.4:4 as l. as you would not release him from it,
T-15 IX.5:2 of this and l. remain willing to linger here.
T-15 X.5:2 as l. as you would retain the principle that
T-15 XI.5:1 l. as you perceive the body as your reality,
T-15 XI.5:1 l. will you perceive yourself as lonely and
T-15 XI.5:2 And so l. will you also perceive yourself as
T-15 XI.5:7 as l. as you would retain the deprivation,
T-15 XI.10:9 much to do, and we have been l. delayed.
T-15 XI.10:10 and take your place, so l. left unfulfilled,
T-16 I.7:4 No needs will l. be left unmet if you leave
T-16 IV.3:5 is acceptable only as l. as he serves this
T-16 IV.5:4 As l. as the illusion of hatred lasts, so long
T-16 IV.5:4 lasts, so l. will love be an illusion to you.
T-16 VI.6:3 this spark cannot be limited l. to littleness
T-16 VI.8:7 You could not l. find even the illusion of
T-16 VII.7:2 Yet you will not attempt this l.. In the
T-17 I.4:1 As l. as you would have it so, so long will
T-17 I.4:1 l. will the illusion of an order of difficulty
T-18 III.3:3 into darkness has been l. and cruel, and
T-18 III.3:4 A little flicker of your eyelids, closed so l.,
T-18 III.3:4 you confidence in yourself, so l. despised.
T-18 III.8:5 after a l. and meaningless journey that
T-18 VII.4:6 very l. road to the goal you have accepted.
T-18 VII.4:9 and l. periods of meditation aimed at
T-18. VIII.13:4 He has waited l. to give you this. Receive
T-18 IX.5:1 directs as l. as you believe that guilt is real
T-18 IX.7:4 go, as l. as you would play the game of
T-18 IX.7:5 Yet however l. you play it, and regardless
T-19 III.9:2 You will not see sin l.. For in the new
T19. IV.A.16:4 as l. ago I promised and promise still. For
T19 IV.C.5:1 as l. as it is useful for your holy purpose.
T19. IV.D.21:4 and the l. journey through this world,
T-20 III.5:7 you adjust as l. as you believe this picture
T-20 III.6:1 a holy relationship can l. remain unholy?
T-20 III.9:1 and with eyes so l. cast down in darkness
T-20 III.9:3 it go or to take hold on life so l. forgotten.
T-20 VI.12:10 Can they be l. held back from looking on
T-20 VI.12:11 And can they l. withhold the memory of
T-21 I.6:1 like a song whose name is l. forgotten,
T-21 I.7:5 you knew so l. ago and held more dear
T-21 III.3:3 in chains as l. as he believes he is in chains
T-21 IV.7:5 which the ego's rule has kept it out so l..
T-22 in.1:1 Take pity on yourself, so l. enslaved.
T-22 I.2:12 And l. and hard you tried to understand
T-22 IV.4:3 after such a l. and lonely journey where
T-22 V.5:7 illusion of immovability be l. defended
T-22 VI.6:8 No trace of anything in time can l. remain
T-22 VI.7:6 could remembrance of what they are be l.
T-23 I.9:2 For it seems real only as l. as it is seen as
T-23 III.2:4 the receiver nor the giver is l. deceived.
T-24 VI.9:1 he is, that your deliverance may not be l..
T-25 in.2:3 And as l. as he believes he is in a body,
T-25 II.2:3 l. is needed for you to realize the chance
T-25 II.2:4 is sure; the way you see, and l. have seen,
T-25 IV.2:2 joy, so l. will they be there for you to see.
T-25 IV.3:6 not l. to be remembered as the sun shines
T-25 VI.2:1 the eyes grown l. accustomed to the dim
T-26 V.4:1 in time, though it has l. since gone. You
T-26 V.4:3 upon you saw but for an instant, l. ago,
T-26 V.4:5 to certainty so l. ago that it is hard indeed
T-26 V.5:4 So very l. ago, for such a tiny interval of
T-26 V.6:6 a place and time that have l. since gone by
T-26 V.9:1 has been so l. ago corrected and undone.
T-26 V.10:1 a road l. since a memory of time gone by?
T-26 V.10:8 And how can he be kept in chains l. since
T-26 V.13:3 repetition of an instant gone by l. ago that
T-26 V.14:4 repeat again a journey that was over l. ago
T-26 IX.5:1 this gift of what has been withheld so l..
T-27 II.8:5 As l. as he consents to suffer, you will be
T-27 V.2:2 As l. as it is unattested, it remains without
T-28 I.1:5 And what it takes away is l. since gone,
T-28 I.1:6 This world was over l. ago. The thoughts
T-28 I.4:3 You are so l. accustomed to believe that
T-29 III.3:10 gap so l. perceived as keeping you apart.
T-30 III.6:3 thoughts endure as l. as does the mind
T-30 V.11:5 they forget for l. that it is but their own.
T-31 VII.2:1 thoughts as l. as you see value in attack.
T-31 VII.10:5 and those you knew a l. while since, and
T-31 VII.13:7 and ancient concepts held so l. and dear
W-pI 12.6:3 You may find even this too l.. Terminate
W-pI 17.2:3 on each thing you note l. enough to say: *I*
W-pI 18.3:1 your eyes on each one l. enough to say: *I*
W-pI 40.1:2 No l. practice periods are required today,
W-pI 40.1:5 If there are l. interruptions, try again.
W-pI 41.6:1 will be only one l. practice period today.
W-pI 43.9:2 Try today not to allow any l. periods of
W-pI 44.9:1 pause l. enough to repeat today's idea,
W-pI 72.10:3 l. as we attack it, we cannot understand
W-pI 75.2:1 happy ending to your l. dream of disaster.
W-pI 76.4:2 different names in a l. catalogue of rituals
W-pI 78.8:2 Your savior has been waiting l. for this.
W-pI 79.3:3 A l. series of different problems seems to
W-pI 95.5:2 to forget about it for l. periods of time.
W-pI 106.8:2 has been waiting l. to be received by you.
W-pI 109.6:1 sing, a stream l. dry begins to flow again.
W-pI. 126.11:2 Do not let your mind forget this goal for l.
W-pI 151.2:3 though you learned a l. while since your
W-pI. 153.15:2 to the daily thought as l. as possible. Five
W-pI 157.1:5 spent l. days and nights in celebrating
W-pI 166.4:4 wandering so far from home, so l. away,
W-pI 169.9:3 We merely take the part assigned l. since,
W-pI 187.8:6 and suffering can l. endure before the face
W-pI. 193.11:3 We have been gone too l., and we would
W-pI 195.7:4 a l. forgotten Word re-echoes in our
W-pI 199.1:1 as l. as you perceive a body as yourself.
W-pII in.2:6 and at night, as l. as makes us happy. We
W-pII. 223.2:5 *We are lonely here, and l. for Heaven, where*
W-pII 4.5:1 How l., O Son of God, will you maintain
W-pII 4.5:8 How l., O holy Son of God, how long?
W-pII 4.5:8 How long, O holy Son of God, how l.?
W-pII 6.5:1 And how l. will this holy face be seen,
W-pII. 292.1:3 how l. we let an alien will appear to be
M-1 2:9 answer in the end, but the end can be a l.,
M-1 2:9 end, but the end can be a long, l. way off.
M-2 2:7 In time this happened very l. ago. In
M-2 3:2 happened l. ago seems to be happening
M-2 3:3 Choices made l. since appear to be open;
M-2 3:4 learned and understood and l. ago passed
M-4 I.A.7:7 may remain impossible to reach for a l.,
M-4 I.A.7:7 impossible to reach for a long, l. time. He
M-14 3:1 Certainly this seems to be a l., long while
M-14 3:1 this seems to be a long, l. while away.
M-22 2:3 the function God has given him l. before
M-22 2:6 If the way seems l., let him be content. He
M-26 3:8 the body would not be l. maintained.
M-26 4:7 Nor will its coming be l. delayed. All the
M-28 6:2 As l. as any mind remains possessed of
C-6 2:4 Holy Spirit l. before Jesus set it in motion.
C-ep 2:5 L. ago the end was written in the stars
C-ep 3:2 journey l. ago begun that but seems new.
P-2 IV.7:6 substituted for a little while, but not for l..
P-2 IV.7:7 Fear cannot l. be hidden by illusions, for
P-2 IV.11:9 is no need for l. analyses and wearying
P-2 V.3:3 the perfect teacher could not l. remain;
P-3 II.8:8 The journey is not l. except in dreams.
P-3 III.4:8 release from l. imprisonment and doubt.
P-3 III.7:7 while, l. enough to think of this: You have
S-1 II.8:4 is part of forgiveness as l. as forgiveness,
S-1 III.3:8 This may be l. delayed, because it may
S-1 III.4:6 recognized as l. as he hides it in another,
S-1 V.4:3 you should come has waited l. for you.
S-2 I.6:2 as l. as this illusion of a world appears to

## long-held 1

M-24 3:6 because it advocates a l. belief of his own.

## long-range 4

W-pI 4.3:3 first attempt in the l. purpose of learning
W-pI 65.4:4 of the l. disciplinary training your mind
W-pI 181.7:2 day. We do not seek for l. goals. As each
M-14 3:2 remains" appears to be a l. goal indeed.

## longed 1

T-21 IV.7:2 song it l. to hear since first the ego came

## longer 198

T-1 I.15:4 Time will cease when it is no l. useful in
T-1 V.2:1 to wait on time any l. than is necessary.
T-1 V.2:6 to the Sonship will no l. be necessary.
T-2 I.4:7 which is then no l. accorded reality. This
T-2 II.5:4 no value when change is no l. necessary.
T-2 VIII.2:5 long period, and perhaps an even l. one.

T-2......VIII.4:5 which, without belief, will no l. exist.
T-4...........I.5:1 that they will one day no l. need him. This
T-4......... II.4:9 no l. necessary you will merely know God.
T-4......... II.8:11 it makes is then no l. creative. Myths are
T-5......... II.5:6 for Him because He could no l. share His
T-5......VI.12:4 to be abolished when it is no l. useful. The
T-6........IV.1:5 home and you no l. need His guidance.
T-6........IV.6:7 will no l. believe in dreams because they
T-6......V.A.6:9 complete alone, they are no l. alone.
T-9......... II.2:2 of it would no l. *be* what you want. This is
T-9......... V.7:4 no l. believes in nightmares of any kind.
T-11..VIII.13:3 "dragon" into a dream he is no l. afraid,
T-12....... V.1:5 weakened. No l. perceiving yourself and
T-12....... V.2:5 Once you realize this you will no l. see any
T-13....... II.2:6 Believing you are no l. you, you do not
T-13.... III.10:5 for he no l. understood his Father. He
T-13....... V.8:5 go and all you made you will no l. see, for
T-14...... VI.1:6 clear and you would be no l. in the dark.
T-14...... VI.3:6 go, and what was fearful will be so no l..
T-14...... IX.2:2 because the contradiction can no l. stand.
T-14....... X.2:3 and he can no l. be satisfied with anything
T-14....... X.9:6 the ego can no l. defend its lack of content
T-15.........I.1:5 will no l. need a teacher or time in which
T-15.......I.11:4 It takes far l. to teach you to be willing to
T-15.......I.15:8 And so it is no l. time at all. For caught in
T-15.....VII.8:9 no l. believe that bodies communicate,
T-15...... XI.1:5 Do not try l. to keep apart your thoughts
T-16...... VI.2:3 of God, no l. seek for union in separation,
T-16...... VI.8:8 For you are no l. wholly insane, and you
T-16.... VI.11:6 it. Wait no l., for the Love of God and *you.*
T-17...... III.5:5 No l. does the past conflict with *now.* This
T-17....... V.5:8 their perception no l. serves the purpose
T-17..... V.7:11 Now He asks for faith a little l., even in
T-17...VII.10:2 You are no l. wholly insane, nor no longer
T-17...VII.10:2 no longer wholly insane, nor no l. alone.
T-17....VIII.3:6 from which faith can no l. be withheld.
T-19.......I.15:4 no l. needed when the lesson has been
T19... IV.A.8:2 It is no l. an unrelenting barrier to peace.
T-20...... II.4:8 you will see your altar is no l. what it was.
T-20...... III.4:2 that death will wait a little l. before it
T-20...... VI.7:7 are an idolater no l.. The Holy Spirit's
T-20....VIII.8:6 that purpose is no l. held they disappear.
T-21.........I.8:3 and what is in it is no l. contained at all.
T-21....... II.2:6 *asked.* Deceive yourself no l. that you are
T-21...... III.2:3 is not your purpose and you no l. want it.
T-21...... III.3:4 simply because he no l. believes in them,
T-21...... III.4:6 of yours, you will have need of them no l..
T-21...... IV.7:7 earth can hold no l. what has been given
T-21..... VII.5:5 him seek no l. what is not there to find.
T-22.......in.1:2 together and need no l. look on sin apart.
T-22...... IV.1:5 The way you came no l. matters. It can no
T-22...... IV.1:6 It can no l. serve. No one who reaches this
T-22...... VI.5:2 The form of error is no l. seen, and reason
T-24....... II.6:5 of truth: You will no l. see what never was
T-24...... VI.6:6 let the fear of God no l. hold the vision
T-26....... V.6:5 For what has been undone no l. is. And
T-26..... V.14:2 You stand no l. on the ground that lies
T-27....... V.6:4 And suffering eyes no l. will accuse, but
T-27...... VI.5:5 It is no l. there. The One Who brings the
T-28.........I.1:7 The thoughts that made it are no l. in the
T-28.......I.9:10 It for your sins, It will no l. be denied.
T-28....... II.8:1 them since He was no l. their Creator. In
T-28...... III.8:7 those may come who would no l. starve,
T-29....... II.8:6 told that part of Him belongs to Him no l.
T-29...VII.1:10 abides, and seek no l. elsewhere. You will
T-30.......I.11:6 Its purpose has no l. been obscured by the
T-30...... IV.7:4 seek no l. for the things you do not want.
T-30....... V.1:3 the place of idols, which are sought no l.,
T-30....... V.3:5 he can barely stay and wait a little l., with
T-30....... V.9:3 Look back no l., for what lies ahead is all
T-31.........I.1:8 no l. say that you perceive no differences
T-31...... IV.4:6 No l. look for hope where there is none.
T-31....... V.6:4 No l. does it matter what he does, for
T-31..... VII.2:7 No l. do you choose that you should be
T-31...VII.12:3 the wish that fathered it no l. is held dear.
W-pI..... 12.2:4 the shift to become markedly l. or shorter
W-pI..... 19.4:1 now, and will no l. be repeated each day,
W-pI..... 26.3:4 in them, you can no l. believe in yourself.
W-pI..... 26.6:4 a l. time than usual should be spent with
W-pI..... 31.2:1 Two l. periods of practice with the idea
W-pI..... 32.1:5 it you will see it; when you no l. want it, it
W-pI..... 32.4:1 For the two l. practice periods three to
W-pI..... 34.2:1 Three l. practice periods are required for
W-pI..... 34.3:1 required for each of the l. practice periods
W-pI..... 35.8:1 During the l. exercise periods, there will
W-pI..... 36.2:3 l. practice periods should take this form:
W-pI..... 37.4:1 Today's four l. exercise periods, each to
W-pI..... 38.4:1 four l. practice periods, each preferably to
W-pI..... 39.5:1 for the four l. practice periods for today,
W-pI..... 39.5:1 l. and more frequent practice sessions are
W-pI..... 39.5:2 rather than l. sessions are recommended,
W-pI..... 43.5:2 For the second and l. phase, close your
W-pI..... 44.4:2 A l. time is highly recommended, but
W-pI..... 44.5:1 Your mind is no l. wholly untrained. You
W-pI..... 46.3:2 Begin the l. practice periods by repeating
W-pI..... 47.4:2 and l. and more frequent ones are urged.
W-pI..... 51.5:6 that has hurt me, and that I no l. want. I
W-pI..... 57.2:5 mistaken in this belief, which I no l. want.
W-pI..... 58.1:3 forgiven, I no l. see myself as guilty. I can
W-pI..... 61.6:3 practice periods may be l. than the rest, if
W-pI..... 65.5:1 the l. practice period, begin by reviewing
W-pI..... 65.6:2 however, to continue a minute or so l.,
W-pI..... 66.4:1 l. practice period today has as its purpose
W-pI..... 66.9:1 this during the l. practice period today.
W-pI..... 67.2:1 In the l. practice period, we will think
W-pI..... 69.3:1 Let us begin our l. practice period today
W-pI..... 70.6:1 are ready for two l. practice periods today
W-pI..... 71.8:1 Begin the two l. practice periods for
W-pI... 72.10:1 Our goal in the l. practice periods today
W-pI... 72.11:5 We are no l. asking the ego what salvation
W-pI... 72.13:1 since they will be somewhat l. than usual.
W-pI..... 73.9:1 We will begin our l. practice periods with
W-pI..... 74.3:1 Begin the l. practice periods by repeating
W-pI..... 75.4:1 Our l. practice periods will be devoted to
W-pI..... 75.5:3 Begin the l. practice periods by telling
W-pI..... 76.7:3 It is no l. a truth that we would hide. We
W-pI..... 76.8:1 will begin the l. practice periods today
W-pI..... 77.4:1 Begin the l. practice periods by telling
W-pI..... 78.6:1 Our l. practice periods today will see him
W-pI..... 79.7:1 l. practice periods today we will ask what
W-pI..... 80.4:1 In our l. practice periods today, we will
WpI..rII.in.1:4 We will have one l. exercise period, and
WpI..rII.in.2:1 l. practice periods will follow this general
W-pI..... 86.3:5 I would no l. defeat my own best interests
W-pI..... 91.6:1 Begin the l. practice periods with this
W-pI..... 93.8:1 In our l. exercise periods today, which
W-pI... 104.3:2 Our l. practice periods today, the hourly
W-pI... 106.3:6 today, and do not wait to reach Him l..
WpI..rIII.in5:1 twice a day, or l. if you would prefer it, to
WpIrIII.in10:1 idly by between your l. practice periods.
W-pI. 121.10:1 Begin the l. practice periods by thinking
W-pI... 122.7:6 intricacies of your dreams no l. hide their
W-pI... 123.4:1 eyes, no l. looking downward to the dust.
W-pI... 131.8:5 Let us not try l. to impose an alien will
W-pI. 136.20:1 allowing your defensiveness to hurt you l.
W-pI... 137.7:3 laws can be no l. cherished nor obeyed.
W-pI. 151.10:3 You will no l. doubt that only good can
W-pI... 152.3:4 without the second, is the first no l. true.
W-pI... 153.3:1 until escape no l. can be hoped for nor
W-pI... 156.7:3 They keep you bound no l.. The approach
W-pI... 161.4:7 itself to think specifically can no l. grasp
W-pI... 168.4:4 that Heaven be delayed an instant l.?
W-pI. 170.11:2 stone you made, and call it god no l.. You
W-pI... 182.8:2 calls to you that you will not resist Him l..
W-pI. 185.11:2 that he deceive himself no l. by denying to
W-pI. 191.10:6 Do not withhold salvation l.. Look about
W-pI... 194.9:6 No l. is the world our enemy, for we have
W-pI... 196.3:2 distort the truth will not deceive you l..
W-pI. 198.11:5 Only that can be perceived an instant l..
W-pI... 199.1:4 free when it no l. sees itself as in a body,
W-pI... 200.3:5 and seek no l. what you cannot find. For
W-pI... 200.4:5 the world no l. seems to be a prison house
W-pI. 200.10:5 eyes but serving for an instant l. now.
W-pII .... in.9:4 undone, and we no l. think illusions true.
W-pII . 223.2:4 *Son. And we would not forget You l.. We are*
W-pII . 229.1:4 I will turn away no l. from the holy face of
W-pII ..... 3.1:3 It will remain no l. than the thought that
W-pII . 289.2:5 *Shall I demand that You wait l. for Your Son*
W-pII . 290.1:5 the dream I made is real an instant l..
W-pII ..... 8.4:1 guilt is over, and God's Son no l. sleeps.
W-pII . 303.1:6 Let Him no l. be a stranger here, for He is
W-pII . 323.2:2 joy. We are deceived no l.. Love has now
M-5 .........I.1:1 the sufferer no l. sees any value in pain.
M-8 ........... 6:2 let itself be healed will no l. acknowledge
M-10 ......... 2:5 impossible for him, he no l. attempts it.
M-11 ....... 4:12 It is no l., "Can peace be possible in this
M-12 ......... 1:4 spirit now no l. sees himself as a body, or
M-12 ......... 2:4 God can no l. be feared, for the mind sees
M-14 ......... 1:7 as purposeless, they are no l. seen. Their
M-14 ......... 5:6 Where there is laughter, who can l. weep?
M-15 ......... 1:4 come until it is no l. associated with fear.
M-15 ......... 3:2 to occupy your holy mind an instant l..
M-16 ......... 7:2 in the name of safety no l. interests him.
M-18 ......... 4:8 him, and he no l. condemns himself. How
M-22 ......... 7:9 him. No l. does he stand apart from God,
M-23 ......... 2:8 he no l. sees himself as separate from Him
M-25 ......... 5:1 who no l. value the material things of the
M-25 ......... 5:6 Now the "power" is no l. a genuine ability
M-26 ......... 2:2 because, although they are no l. visible,
M-28 ......... 2:4 Love is no l. feared, but gladly welcomed.
C-3 ............ 4:8 looks on this no l. sees the world. He is as
C-4 ............ 1:4 will last in time a little while l. than others
C-4 ............ 4:2 easily dispelled that it can last no l. than
C-5 ............ 2:2 became identified with *Christ*, a man no l.,
C-6 ............ 5:8 no l. to take form but to return to the
P-2........ VI.6:4 sins as gone into a past that is no l. here.
P-3........ III.5:9 they will recognize him as a brother no l..
S-1..........II.5:4 Now it is no l. a contradiction in terms. It
S-1..........II.7:6 The light no l. flickers, and will never go
S-1..........V.2:3 idols, and defense no l. serves a purpose.
S-1..........V.4:1 ends with this, for learning is no l. needed
S-3........ IV.5:3 He is then no l. Cause but only an effect.

## longing 3

T-11 .......V.6:8 and has twisted even your l. for God into
T-16 ... VI.10:1 and look not back with l. on the travesty
M-13 ......... 4:4 look back with l. on a slaughter house?

## longings 1

M-28 ......... 3:7 hell. All l. are satisfied, for what remains

## longitudinal 1

T-1 .........II.6:2 l. or horizontal plane the recognition of

## longs 2

T-12 ..... VI.4:6 and He l. to share His vision with you. He
W-pI .. 156.5:1 in you is what the universe l. to behold.

## look 666

T-1 ....... III.6:7 You should l. out from the perception of
T-2 ..... III.5:12 They must learn to l. upon the world as a
T-2 .........V.6:6 learned to l. beyond it toward the light.
T-2 .........V.7:5 to l. upon the defilement of the altar, He
T-2 ....... VI.2:4 here that you would do well to l. at clearly
T-2 .....VIII.4:3 Everyone will ultimately l. upon his own
T-2 .....VIII.4:4 the mind can begin to l. with love on its
T-3 ....... VI.9:6 possible to l. on reality without judgment
T-3 ...... VII.5:3 L. at your life and see what the devil has
T-4 ....... IV.1:8 where you l. to find yourself is up to you.
T-4 ....... IV.2:9 as you l. at yourself and at your brother,
T-4 ....... IV.9:2 "I will not l. there because I know these
T-5 ....... III.7:3 ability to l. beyond symbols into eternity
T-5 ....... III.11:6 you free. L. as the Holy Spirit looks, and
T-5 ..... VI.11:2 also that I said, "Do not l. there." It is still
T-5 ..... VI.11:3 still true that where you l. to find yourself
T-7 ....... III.3:2 war must l. for brothers and recognize all
T-7 .......V.10:6 you can l. into theirs and enlighten them,
T-7 .........X.1:5 You are willing to l. at the ego's premises,
T-8 .........II.4:4 how to disregard or l. beyond everything
T-8 ....... III.5:6 because it does not know where to l.. The
T-8 ....... III.5:7 that if you l. only at yourself you cannot
T-8 ....... III.6:4 you are willing to l. at what the ego would

T-8.......VII.5:3 you l. upon a brother as a physical entity,
T-9..........I.4:2 I meant that He has the power to l. into
T-9.........I.14:5 do not try to l. beyond yourself for truth,
T-9.......III.8:10 learning how to l. on everything without
T-9........IV.1:3 L., then, beyond error and do not let your
T-9........IV.3:4 you cannot l. on your abilities through
T-9.......IV.11:4 But do not l. for meaning in them. They
T-9.........V.2:3 he does not know where to l. for truth,
T-9.......VII.5:3 you l. to the ego to help you escape from a
T-9.......VII.6:3 it, l. back from a point where sanity exists
T-9.....VIII.6:2 are willing to l. upon your grandeur you
T-10.......II.6:4 is perfectly clear, if you will only l. at it. By
T-10......III.5:1 L. calmly at the logical conclusion of the
T-10......IV.5:9 your vision will automatically l. beyond it
T-10.......V.7:7 L. with peace upon your brothers, and
T-10.......V.8:1 l. to the god of sickness for healing but
T-10.....V.14:5 eternity, you must l. only on the eternal.
T-11......I.5:11 L. upon the glory of His creation, and you
T-11......IV.2:5 l. only to the power that God gave to save
T-11.......V.1:3 We are ready to l. more closely at the
T-11.......V.1:5 for we must l. first at this to see beyond it,
T-11.......V.1:6 together, and then l. beyond it to truth.
T-11.......V.2:8 Do not be afraid, then, to l. upon fear, for
T-11.......V.2:9 and to l. upon darkness through light
T-11.......V.4:1 When we l. at the ego, then, we are not
T-12......I.10:1 If you would l. upon love, which *is* the
T-12.......II.4:7 refusing to open your eyes and l. at them.
T-12.......II.5:2 the covers and l. at what you are afraid of.
T-12.......II.5:6 L. straight at every image that rises to
T-12.......II.9:7 If you will l., the Holy Spirit will judge,
T-12.....II.10:5 must l. at it yourself in perfect willingness
T-12....III.10:8 will l. out in peace and behold the world
T-12......IV.5:4 You do not remember how to l. within for
T-12.......V.8:1 indeed, it is merely ridiculous if you l. at it
T-12......VI.3:2 is whatever part of it you l. upon with love
T-12......VI.4:4 and He will l. upon whatever you see with
T-12.....VII.5:5 and as you l. out so will you see in. Two
T-12.....VII.6:2 His witnesses if you will but l. upon them.
T-12.....VII.7:1 and you must l. in before you look out. As
T-12.....VII.7:1 and you must look in before you l. out. As
T-12.....VII.7:2 out. As you l. in, you choose the guide for
T-12.....VII.7:3 then you l. out and behold his witnesses.
T-12...VII.11:3 but you will not l. upon me nor hear the
T-12...VII.11:6 And you will see me as you l. within, and
T-12...VII.11:6 we will l. upon the real world together.
T-12...VII.12:1 When you l. within and see me, it will be
T-12...VII.13:1 that whenever you l. without and react
T-12...VII.15:2 this is true when you l. within and *see* me.
T-12...VII.15:6 the eternal as you l. out upon a world that
T-12...VIII.5:5 But l. upon what you have made of it, and
T-12...VIII.8:2 it from the hand of Christ and l. upon it.
T-12...VIII.8:4 And as you l. upon it you will remember
T-13.......in.2:3 L. carefully at this world, and you will
T-13.........I.3:1 As you l. upon yourself and judge what
T-13.........I.6:2 And only as you l. upon him as guiltless
T-13.......II.4:5 So it is this secret that we must l. upon,
T-13.......II.8:3 yet l. upon the alternative with gladness.
T-13......III.1:1 is so crucial that you l. upon your hatred
T-13......III.1:9 You could l. even upon the ego's darkest
T-13......III.2:4 You would be willing to l. even upon your
T-13......III.6:1 You must l. upon your illusions and not
T-13....III.12:9 l. back on them and see them as insane.
T-13.......V.6:1 As you l. with open eyes upon your world
T-13.......V.6:5 your own split mind everywhere you l..
T-13.......V.6:7 your sight, for you l. upon yourself alone.
T-13.......V.7:6 learn what insanity is, and l. beyond it. It
T-13.....V.10:6 And this *you* will see as you l. with Him,
T-13......VI.1:7 the past as you l. upon your brother, you
T-13......VI.2:3 When you have learned to l. on everyone
T-13......VI.3:5 and l. without condemnation upon the
T-13......VI.6:2 L. lovingly upon the present, for it holds
T-13......VI.7:5 l. at Christ and call His witnesses to shine
T-13..VI.11:10 others out of darkness as you l. on them.
T-13....VI.12:7 cannot l. upon the light you gave to them.
T-13.....VII.1:1 Sit quietly and l. upon the world you see,
T-13......IX.7:3 cannot see it because you cannot l. within
T-13......IX.7:6 If you would l. within you would see only
T-13......IX.8:1 Do not be afraid to l. within. The ego
T-13......IX.8:2 guilt within you, and bids you not to l..
T-13......IX.8:3 Instead, it bids you l. upon your brothers,
T-13......IX.8:5 are too afraid to l. upon the light within.
T-13.....IX.8:13 L., then, upon the light He placed within
T-13.......X.1:4 willing to l. upon all kinds of "sources,"
T-13.......X.3:5 suffer, they will not l. within and let it go.
T-13.......X.5:5 of guilt, and would not l. within and see it
T-13.......X.6:1 whatever he may do, you will not l. within
T-13.......X.8:6 will not fear to l. upon the Atonement
T-13.......X.9:5 Fear not to l. upon the lovely truth in you.
T-13.......X.9:6 L. through the cloud of guilt that dims
T-13.......X.9:6 l. past darkness to the holy place where
T-13.....X.10:2 no other way to l. within and see the light
T-13.....X.10:5 reason, to l. within and see your holiness.
T-13...X.11:10 *Son of God, and l. upon his purity and be still*
T-13...X.11:11 *still. In quiet l. upon his holiness, and offer*
T-13.....X.12:3 Let us l. upon him together and love him.
T-13.....X.12:5 But l. upon yourself, and gladness and
T-13......XI.1:4 could l. upon himself and see his freedom
T-14.......II.5:6 for when you l. at it in simple honesty, it *is*
T-14.......II.6:5 truth before you, you will not l. back.
T-14......III.2:1 do not l. upon it as having value in itself.
T-14......III.8:7 or choose to l. upon without imposing on
T-14.....V.11:7 and l. out in peace on all who think they
T-14......VI.3:5 and of ignorance l. to them only for fear,
T-14.....VII.2:8 the more you l. at fear the less you see it,
T-14.....VII.6:5 But what you hide He cannot l. upon. He
T-14.....VII.6:6 and unless you l. with Him He cannot see.
T-14.....VII.6:8 to Him, and l. upon them with Him. He
T-14...VII.6:10 when both of You together l. on them.
T-14......IX.6:7 for it, but knows not where to l. to find it.
T-14......IX.7:3 to those who l. upon it is not obscure, for
T-15.........I.5:4 to l. upon with equanimity is the past.
T-15.......V.2:3 l. to them to meet your imagined needs,
T-15.......V.9:7 and you have no need to l. without and
T-15.....VII.3:2 real to you, it is essential to l. at it clearly,
T-15.....VII.5:3 let us l. more closely at the relationships
T-15.....VII.5:4 For it is certain that if you will l. at them,
T-15.......X.5:9 it is this that you must l. upon; sacrifice is
T-15.......X.8:3 have given God away rather than l. at it.
T-16.......II.7:8 l. with greater charity on whom God loves
T-16......III.1:4 Therefore He could l. upon it fairly, and
T-16......IV.1:1 to l. upon the special hate relationship,
T-16......IV.1:4 before your open eyes as you l. on this.
T-16......IV.7:5 essential that we l. very closely at exactly
T-16......IV.8:5 enables you to l. on all your brothers with
T-16.....V.11:2 of value, you would not dare to l. upon it.
T-16......VI.2:2 To l. for it by placing yourself in bondage
T-16......VI.3:4 the closer you l. at the special relationship
T-16....VI.10:1 l. not back with longing on the travesty it
T-16....VI.10:3 Only the wholly insane could l. on death
T-16.....VII.5:5 you l. not for glory in yourself. You have
T-17.......II.1:1 beautiful those you forgive will l. to you?
T-17.......II.1:7 the beauty the Holy Spirit loves to l. upon
T-17.......II.6:1 you l. upon the world with forgiving eyes.
T-17......IV.9:1 L. at the *picture.* Do not let the frame
T-17....IV.9:11 L. at the picture, and realize that death is
T-17....IV.12:8 L. at the pictures. Both of them. One is a
T-17..IV.12:11 in light, lovely to l. upon for what it is.
T-17....IV.13:6 And finally you l. upon the picture itself,
T-17....IV.14:3 grows more convincing as you l. at it. And
T-17....IV.15:2 As you l. on this, you realize that it is not
T-17......VI.1:7 can more safely l. beyond each situation,
T-17......VI.3:2 Then you l. back at it, and try to piece
T-17.....VII.5:4 Let it enter and l. upon it calmly, but do
T-17.....VII.5:9 but l. upon its offering and recognize it *is*
T-18.........I.5:5 fearful enough, as you begin to l. at them.
T-18.......I.12:6 Is it here that you would l. for happiness?
T-18...VII.4:11 all of them l. to the future for release from
T-18...VIII.8:6 L. at the desert–dry and unproductive,
T-18......IX.4:6 The body's eyes will never l. on it. Yet
T-19.........I.8:3 and cannot l. beyond the barrier to what
T-19.......I.10:6 healed because you l. on what makes faith
T-19......III.5:5 to l. on time differently and see beyond it,
T-19......III.9:1 you l. with Heaven's smile upon your lips,
T-19....III.10:7 L. not for what has been removed, but for
T-19....III.11:1 L. upon your Redeemer, and behold
T-19....III.11:2 have you l. upon your brother as yourself.
T-19......IV.3:2 And when you l. with gentle graciousness
T19...IV.A.6:4 L. not upon the little wall of shadows. The
T19....IV.A.7:2 As you l. upon the world, this little wish,
T19. IV.A.10:1 love, for love would never l. on guilt at all.
T19. IV.A.10:2 nature of love to l. upon only the truth,
T19. IV.A.10:3 As love must l. past fear, so must fear see
T19. IV.A.11:7 love would l. upon is meaningless to fear,
T19. IV.A.12:2 on to send its messengers to l. upon it,
T19....IV.B.3:3 the body, for they l. for what can suffer. Is
T19....IV.B.5:8 stop now to l. for guilt in your brother?
T19....IV.B.6:1 and l. upon your brother as you would
T19....IV.B.6:1 upon your brother as you would l. on me.
T19....IV.C.6:4 As you l. on it, so will it seem to be. Death
T19....IV.C.8:7 insanity could l. upon the defeat of God,
T19..IV.C.11:8 *Take this from me and l. upon it, judging it*
T19...IV.D.4:6 so you could l. upon the face of Christ and
T19...IV.D.6:1 before what you swore never to l. upon.
T19...IV.D.6:2 Your eyes l. down, remembering your
T19...IV.D.6:4 realize that if you l. on this and let the veil
T19...IV.D.7:4 will. L. upon it, open-eyed, and you will
T19...IV.D.7:5 It *is* your will to l. on this. No mad desire,
T19...IV.D.8:4 bid you l. on them and go beyond them.
T19...IV.D.8:6 be ready to l. on terror with no fear at all.
T19...IV.D.8:7 lift up your eyes and l. on your brother in
T19...IV.D.9:1 can l. upon the fear of God unterrified,
T19...IV.D.9:3 And no one would dare to l. on it without
T19. IV.D.10:1 Nor is it possible to l. on this too soon.
T19. IV.D.10:8 choose whether to l. upon it or wander on
T19. IV.D.11:1 l. upon the fear of God does need some
T19. IV.D.11:2 Only the sane can l. on stark insanity and
T19. IV.D.11:3 share in it until you l. upon your brother
T19. IV.D.17:3 L. on your brother, and see in him the gift
T19. IV.D.18:2 nor l. upon him with condemnation of
T19. IV.D.18:3 See him as guiltless as I l. on you, and
T19. IV.D.20:1 you would l. upon the giver of this gift,
T19. IV.D.20:1 l. on him so will the gift itself appear to be
T-20.........I.4:7 L. on your risen Friend, and celebrate his
T-20........II.1:1 L. upon all the trinkets made to hang
T-20........II.4:4 you may l. upon the Son of God as whole.
T-20........II.4:5 l. you first upon the altar in your chosen
T-20........II.4:8 L. you still closer at them now, and you
T-20........II.5:1 You l. still with the body's eyes, and they
T-20........II.6:1 l. with different eyes upon your brother.
T-20........II.7:1 have the vision now to l. past all illusions.
T-20........II.7:4 now. Who is afraid to l. upon illusions,
T-20........II.7:8 the strength to l. upon this final obstacle,
T-20........II.8:6 You heard, but knew not how to l., nor
T-20........II.9:3 and l. on him with the new vision that
T-20......III.3:3 They l. on it directly, without attempting
T-20......III.4:7 l. out in sorrow from what is sad within,
T-20......III.5:1 like; how it would l. through happy eyes?
T-20......III.5:9 if mercilessness seems to l. back at you, it
T-20....III.7:10 ask, "How shall I l. upon the Son of God?
T-20......III.8:3 world you l. on is the answer that it gave
T-20....III.11:3 no sin, and it must l. on others as on itself
T-20....III.11:5 l. unto the Son to lead them to the Father.
T-20......IV.5:6 he is ready to l. upon the face of Christ,
T-20........V.5:5 And while you l. upon your brother thus,
T-20........V.6:1 l. upon each holy instant as a different
T-20........V.6:7 of Christ you yet will l. upon already seen.
T-20......VI.9:6 temple, l. you not back on what you have
T-20.....VII.3:8 with it. Before we l. at them a little closer,
T-20.....VII.4:1 as sinless and yet to l. upon him as a body
T-20.....VII.8:5 see the body because it cannot l. on sin.
T-20.....VII.9:6 For what the seeing l. upon *is* sinless. No
T-20....VIII.3:1 to l. on with the Holy Spirit's vision and
T-20....VIII.4:4 And as you l. upon your brother, you will
T-20....VIII.4:7 would you rather l. on it than on the truth
T-20....VIII.6:7 L. through its eyes, and everything will
T-21.........I.2:2 to imagine what the world must l. like. It
T-21.........I.8:1 as you l. into a great and shining circle.
T-21.......I.10:3 will l. upon the vision of the Son of God,
T-21........II.5:9 And as you l. upon the change in him, it
T-21........II.6:2 L. closer, then, at what it is. And, very
T-21........II.8:4 to l. within and see what must be there,
T-21......III.8:3 desire to l. upon their brothers in holiness
T-21......III.8:6 choose to l. away from sin are given vision
T-21....III.12:4 But in their seeing they l. past it, as do
T-21..........IV.h The Fear to L. Within
T-21......IV.1:3 indeed afraid to l. within and see the sin
T-21......IV.2:3 Loudly the ego tells you not to l. inward,

| | |
|---|---|
| T-21 IV.2:4 | This you believe, and so you do not l.. Yet |
| T-21 IV.2:8 | Beneath your fear to l. within because of |
| T-21 IV.3:6 | now entirely unwilling to l. within and see |
| T-21 IV.4:2 | willing to l. on much of your insanity and |
| T-21 IV.4:7 | now identify, is not afraid to l. upon itself. |
| T-21 IV.6:6 | at your "presumptuous" wish to l. within, |
| T-21 IV.8:1 | L. gently on your brother, and remember |
| T-21 V.1:5 | For what you l. for you are far more likely |
| T-21 VI.2:5 | can see a sinful world and l. upon himself |
| T-21 VI.3:9 | certain that they l. upon them differently. |
| T-21 VI.8:9 | out for everyone to l. upon with gladness. |
| T-21 VII.8:3 | as you l. on the effects of sin in any form, |
| T-21 VII.11:3 | l. on sin are seeing the denial of the real |
| T-21 VII.13:6 | want, and you will l. on it and think it real |
| T-22 in.1:2 | and need no longer l. on sin apart. No |
| T-22 in.1:3 | No two can l. on sin together, for they |
| T-22 I.2:5 | of the eyes that l. upon the world. If this is |
| T-22 II.9:1 | Let us l. closer at the whole illusion that |
| T-22 II.10:1 | but l. on it with the decision that it must |
| T-22 II.11:3 | *is* impossible to l. upon your savior as your |
| T-22 II.11:7 | l. upon the savior that has been given you |
| T-22 II.13:7 | for you. L. on your holy brother, sinless as |
| T-22 III.5:5 | made to l. on error and not see past it. |
| T-22 III.5:6 | to l. beyond the granite block of sin, and |
| T-22 IV.4:2 | will you and your brother l. to the other! |
| T-22 V.6:8 | brother that makes it l. impenetrable, and |
| T-22 VI.9:1 | but universal blessing to l. on what your |
| T-22 VI.9:10 | l. away from it and toward your brother. |
| T-22 VI.10:7 | us l. straight at how this error came about |
| T-22 VI.14:4 | L. not with fear upon this happy fact, and |
| T-23 in.6:2 | you. L. on it lovingly, and see the light of |
| T-23 I.8:5 | occurs whenever you l. on anything that |
| T-23 II.1:4 | Let us, then, l. upon them calmly, that we |
| T-23 II.1:4 | them calmly, that we may l. beyond them, |
| T-23 II.11:5 | hidden where you would not think to l.. |
| T-23 II.13:6 | And it *is* here you l. for meaning. These are |
| T-23 II.15:6 | eyes, blinded and terrible to l. upon, is |
| T-23 II.18:2 | And when you l. at what they say, they |
| T-23 III.1:7 | will l. on his intent in nightmares where |
| T-23 III.6:6 | l. down on it in safety from above and not |
| T-23 IV.5:1 | and from a higher place l. down upon it. |
| T-23 IV.7:1 | for there you l. on him from nowhere. |
| T-23 IV.7:2 | have no reference point from where to l., |
| T-24 I.7:8 | L. fairly at whatever makes you give your |
| T-24 II.5:6 | for it sees not what they would l. upon, |
| T-24 III.7:7 | God gave to you that you might l. on him, |
| T-24 III.8:6 | L. on the print of nails upon his hands |
| T-24 V.4:7 | in him and love to l. upon it saw in you, |
| T-24 V.4:8 | Yet is it joy to l. upon decay and madness, |
| T-24 V.7:5 | to l. upon with Him and share His joy. |
| T-24 VI.3:4 | you, and l. upon yourself as lovingly as He |
| T-24 VI.5:1 | L. on your brother, and behold in him |
| T-24 VI.6:1 | sinlessness that eyes that see can l. upon. |
| T-24 VI.6:3 | And it is He they l. for everywhere, and |
| T-24 VI.7:1 | and which you choose is yours to l. upon. |
| T-24 VII.9:1 | L. at yourself, and you will see a body. |
| T-24 VII.9:2 | L. at this body in a different light and it |
| T-24 VII.9:7 | It gives the eyes with which you l. on it, |
| T-24 VII.11:4 | Their difference does not lie in how they l. |
| T-25 I.2:1 | except to l. on holiness and see Him there |
| T-25 I.2:4 | that you l. upon reminds you of yourself; |
| T-25 II.7:2 | L. at its loveliness, and understand the |
| T-25 II.7:5 | God kept it safe that you might l. on it, |
| T-25 II.8:2 | step forth from darkness as you l. on him, |
| T-25 II.8:3 | who brought him forth for you to l. upon. |
| T-25 II.8:5 | strength, and both will gladly l. within, |
| T-25 IV.3:2 | that l. on sin and beat its sad refrain. |
| T-25 IV.3:4 | rise a world they will rejoice to l. upon, |
| T-25 V.2:9 | you, each time you l. upon your brother. |
| T-25 V.3:2 | confused with Christ, you l. upon. And |
| T-25 V.6:5 | hell. L. once again upon your brother, not |
| T-25 VI.1:1 | they l. on speaks of Him to the beholder. |
| T-25 VI.2:2 | the clarity it brings to what they l. upon. |
| T-25 VI.2:4 | and more obscure seems easier to l. upon; |
| T-25 VI.3:3 | God is glad to have you l. on him. He does |
| T-25 VII.6:5 | gentle eyes would l. beyond the madness |
| T-25 VII.11:7 | believe that God is mad, l. carefully at this |
| T-25 VIII.7:4 | to hell that seems to l. like Heaven's gate? |
| T-25 VIII.12:3 | you l. to your experience within the world |
| T-26 I.1:7 | L. at the world, and you will see nothing |
| T-26 II.5:6 | you will not l. at what is there to see? Each |
| T-26 V.4:3 | Each thing you l. upon you saw but for an |
| T-26 V.14:5 | L. gently on your brother, and behold the |
| T-26 VIII.9:7 | one. L. not to time, but to the little space |
| T-26 IX.1:6 | L. with loving eyes on him who carries |
| T-27 I.2:3 | and need but l. on you to realize that he |
| T-27 I.5:6 | And he will l. on his forgiveness there, |
| T-27 I.5:6 | and with healed eyes will l. beyond it to |
| T-27 V.7:6 | which all eyes l. lovingly upon the Friend |
| T-27 VII.2:2 | needed is you l. upon the problem as it is, |
| T-27 VII.5:6 | L., then, beyond effects. It is not here the |
| T-27 VII.6:6 | nor l. among the mighty legions of its |
| T-27 VII.6:8 | is not where you should l. to *find* the truth. |
| T-27 VIII.1:7 | It tries to l. for pleasure, and avoid the |
| T-27 VIII.5:3 | us merely l. upon the dream's beginning, |
| T-27 VIII.5:9 | this, if we but l. directly at their cause. |
| T-27 VIII.9:3 | you may l. together on its foolish cause |
| T-28 V.5:4 | made to l. upon a world that is not there; |
| T-28 V.7:6 | L. at the little gap, and you behold the |
| T-28 VI.1:4 | a joy and l. for lasting pleasure in the dust |
| T-29 II.2:8 | L. inward now, and you will not behold a |
| T-29 II.4:5 | asks you now that you will l. on them and |
| T-29 II.5:7 | And when you l. on them, you will believe |
| T-29 II.10:2 | you love, or l. upon it as a thing you hate. |
| T-29 VII.4:6 | and fear to l. upon your devastation, but |
| T-29 VII.6:5 | place. L. not to idols. Do not seek outside |
| T-29 IX.1:3 | and l. to idols that they raise him up? |
| T-30 I.11:4 | *I want another way to l. at this.* Now you |
| T-30 I.12:3 | *Perhaps there is another way to l. at this.* |
| T-30 II.3:1 | L. once again upon your enemy, the one |
| T-30 II.5:4 | chose to l. upon your brother as a friend. |
| T-30 III.3:5 | of an idol; that you will not l. beyond it, |
| T-30 IV.5:9 | L. calmly at its toys, and understand that |
| T-30 IV.7:3 | and not to l. upon the unreal as reality. |
| T-30 V.7:2 | Perhaps they still l. back, and think they |
| T-30 V.7:4 | they will l. on Him Whose hand they hold |
| T-30 V.9:3 | L. back no longer, for what lies ahead is |
| T-30 V.10:1 | Do not l. back except in honesty. And |
| T-30 V.10:7 | For he will be delayed when you l. back, |
| T-30 V.10:8 | L. forward, then; in confidence walk with |
| T-30 VI.6:4 | are harder to l. past than others are. It |
| T-30 VI.7:6 | and will remain afraid to l. within and |
| T-30 VI.8:1 | L. on your brother with the willingness |
| T-30 VI.10:1 | L. on your brother with this hope in you, |
| T-30 VII.6:16 | L. not to separate dreams for meaning. |
| T-30 VIII.5:2 | be given you to l. upon your brother thus. |
| T-30 VIII.5:6 | Is it this that you would l. upon? Then let |
| T-30 VIII.6:1 | will you l. upon when you decide there is |
| T-31 I.10:2 | father fear, and l. upon its father as itself. |
| T-31 I.11:10 | Its outcome is the world you l. upon. |
| T-31 II.2:9 | before you can l. past them to the one |
| T-31 IV.4:6 | No longer l. for hope where there is none. |
| T-31 V.5:2 | that smiles above it must forever l. away, |
| T-31 V.5:3 | you made of me, and as you l. on me, you |
| T-31 V.15:7 | of the self embraces all you l. upon, and |
| T-31 V.17:7 | *am, or how to l. upon the world or on myself.* |
| T-31 VI.4:6 | It makes no difference what you l. upon, |
| T-31 VII.5:2 | And l. upon the good in him, that you |
| T-31 VII.6:6 | Would you not rather l. upon yourself as |
| T-31 VII.7:2 | l. on them as through a barrier that dims |
| T-31 VII.7:5 | At least, you merely l. on darkness, and |
| T-31 VII.10:5 | save are but everyone you meet or l. upon |
| T-31 VII.11:3 | eyes that l. upon the innocence within, |
| T-31 VII.11:4 | they call it forth in everyone they l. upon, |
| T-31 VII.12:6 | Yet it can l. with love or look with hate, |
| T-31 VII.12:6 | Yet it can look with love or l. with hate, |
| T-31 VII.13:3 | to l. on only what the present holds. It |
| T-31 VIII.6:1 | and so is every living thing you l. upon, |
| T-31 VIII.7:2 | eyes, and let him l. upon the Christ in him |
| W-pI 1.1:1 | Now l. slowly around you, and practice |
| W-pI 1.2:1 | l. farther away from your immediate area, |
| W-pI 4.1:6 | if you train yourself to l. at your thoughts, |
| W-pI 7.3:1 | L. at a cup, for example. Do you see a cup |
| W-pI 7.4:1 | L. about you. This is equally true of |
| W-pI 7.4:2 | This is equally true of whatever you l. at. |
| W-pI 11.2:3 | Then open your eyes and l. about, near |
| W-pI 12.2:2 | L. around you, this time quite slowly. Try |
| W-pI 12.3:1 | As you l. about you, say to yourself: *I* |
| W-pI 13.4:3 | open your eyes, and l. about you slowly, |
| W-pI 13.4:5 | this statement to yourself as you l. about. |
| W-pI 15.4:5 | to continue to l. at each subject while you |
| W-pI 17.2:3 | Then l. about you, resting your glance on |
| W-pI 18.3:1 | L. about you, selecting subjects for the |
| W-pI 22.3:1 | L. at the world about you at least five |
| W-pI 23.6:2 | As you l. about you, repeat the idea slowly |
| W-pI 28.5:1 | l. upon it with a completely open mind. It |
| W-pI 29.3:1 | to learn how to l. on all things with love, |
| W-pI 30.1:2 | and you will l. upon it and see in it what |
| W-pI 31.2:3 | l. about you slowly while repeating the |
| W-pI 32.3:2 | your eyes and l. around your inner world. |
| W-pI 35.4:3 | not l. upon yourself through the eyes of |
| W-pI 36.3:2 | your eyes and l. quite slowly about you, |
| W-pI 36.4:1 | idea; l. about you as you repeat it again; |
| W-pI 42.5:5 | continue to l. for related thoughts in your |
| W-pI 45.3:3 | We will have to l. for them in your mind, |
| W-pI 51.2:2 | I have judged everything I l. upon, and it |
| W-pI 52.2:2 | As I l. about, I condemn the world I look |
| W-pI 52.2:2 | look about, I condemn the world I l. upon |
| W-pI 52.2:7 | And I will l. with love on all that I failed to |
| W-pI 52.3:4 | Let me remember that I l. on the past to |
| W-pI 53.1:5 | if I l. to my real thoughts as my guide for |
| W-pI 54.2:4 | is thought. Let me l. on the world I see as |
| W-pI 54.5:3 | I would l. upon the witnesses that show |
| W-pI 54.5:5 | I would l. upon the real world, and let it |
| W-pI 55.3:5 | choose to see, in place of what I l. on now. |
| W-pI 56.2:6 | I will l. upon the world and on myself |
| W-pI 56.3:4 | I may l. past it to the world that reflects |
| W-pI 56.4:6 | part of Him will yet l. past all appearances |
| W-pI 57.3:6 | I would l. upon the world as it is, and see |
| W-pI 57.5:4 | The world I l. upon has taken on the light |
| W-pI 59.2:3 | Let me not l. to my own eyes to see today. |
| W-pI 60.3:2 | the world will l. to me when I can see it! It |
| W-pI 60.3:3 | It will not l. anything like what I imagine I |
| W-pI 60.5:5 | And as I l. upon the world with the vision |
| W-pI 64.1:4 | It is this the body's eyes l. upon. |
| W-pI 64.8:3 | l. slowly and unselectively around you, |
| W-pI 65.8:4 | keep them open and l. about you. It is |
| W-pI 69.1:1 | can l. upon what your grievances conceal. |
| W-pI 69.3:5 | searches with us to l. upon and rejoice. |
| W-pI 69.9:2 | and that you do know where to l. for it. |
| W-pI 73.4:6 | so it must be in you that we will l. for it. |
| W-pI 73.5:3 | mind, and you l. out on a darkened world |
| W-pI 73.5:4 | will, and lets you l. upon a world of light. |
| W-pI 73.9:6 | this very day to l. upon the light in him |
| W-pI 75.6:4 | l. upon it now as if you never saw it before |
| W-pI 75.8:2 | to l. upon the world He promised you. |
| W-pI 76.2:4 | L. for it where it waits for you, and there |
| W-pI 76.2:5 | L. nowhere else, for it is nowhere else. |
| W-pI 78.2:1 | grievances, to l. upon the miracle instead. |
| W-pI 78.4:2 | to him; we will not l. upon our grievances. |
| W-pI 78.4:3 | world reversed, as we l. out toward truth, |
| W-pI 78.4:4 | and lay the grievances aside and l. at him. |
| W-pI 78.7:1 | that we may l. on him a different way, |
| W-pI 78.8:6 | now, and l. upon your shining savior. No |
| W-pI 84.2:3 | *As I l. on this, let me remember my Creator.* |
| W-pI 85.3:5 | I will not l. for it outside myself. It is not |
| W-pI 85.4:2 | *me to l. away from me for my salvation. I will* |
| W-pI 86.4:2 | *misperception and salvation as I l. on this. If* |
| W-pI 87.1:5 | me, and I will l. only on what it shows me. |
| W-pI 87.2:4 | *[name]. In the light this will l. different.* |
| W-pI 99.5:4 | does the Holy Spirit l. on what you see; on |
| W-pI 99.8:3 | and you will l. upon no obstacle to what |
| W-pI 100.6:5 | bring His happiness to all you l. upon; His |
| W-pI 100.8:5 | L. deep within you, undismayed by all the |
| W-pI 100.9:3 | What could you rather l. upon in place of |
| W-pI 100.9:3 | of Him Who waits that you may l. on Him |
| W-pI 107.10:1 | will be glad to l. again upon this world. |
| W-pI 109.1:3 | we seem to l. on danger and on sorrow. |
| W-pI 121.11:1 | him in your mind, and l. at him a while. |
| W-pI 121.11:4 | of him. L. at this picture till you see a light |
| W-pI 121.12:1 | L. at this changed perception for a while, |
| W-pI 122.3:1 | l. with unforgiving eyes upon the world. |
| W-pI 122.8:1 | Open your eyes today and l. upon a |
| W-pI 124.4:5 | behold His loveliness in all we l. upon. |
| W-pI 124.10:1 | will hold out to you, to l. upon yourself. |
| W-pI 124.11:1 | tomorrow, you will l. into this glass, and |
| W-pI 124.11:1 | you; the loveliness you l. on is your own. |

W-pI...129.5:2 Here can you but l. forward, never back
W-pI...130.1:6 no one can fail to l. upon what he believes
W-pI...130.9:4 You will not doubt what you will l. upon,
W-pI...131.1:2 l. for permanence in the impermanent,
W-pI...131.2:7 You l. for safety and security, while in
W-pI...132.4:3 so you can l. on them and think them real
W-pI.132.13:6 and you will l. upon a world released.
W-pI...133.9:2 to anyone who cares to l. for them. Here
W-pI...134.3:2 as a vain attempt to l. past what is there;
W-pI...134.4:1 are real, you l. on pardon as deception.
W-pI.135.10:3 Yet is this where you l. for its defense?
W-pI...137.4:5 be shown that what they l. upon is false.
W-pI...139.9:7 L. lovingly on them, that they may know
W-pI.151.10:2 gives you vision which can l. beyond these
W-pI...153.9:1 We l. past dreams today, and recognize
W-pI.153.20:7 real, to l. on Christ and see His sinlessness
W-pI...155.3:2 for those to l. upon who chose to come,
W-pI...155.3:4 but Who still can l. beyond illusion to the
W-pI...155.6:3 eyes to l. on and their minds to grasp.
W-pI.155.13:2 God. L. not to ways that seem to lead you
W-pI...157.5:1 you touch, and blesses those you l. upon.
W-pI...158.7:2 It does not l. upon a body, and mistake it
W-pI...160.6:3 can find no home wherever he may l., for
W-pI.160.10:4 Him until you l. on all as He does. Who
W-pI...161.2:3 It does not l. on everything as one. It sees
W-pI...161.6:4 times been urged to l. beyond the body,
W-pI...162.2:6 and hear this sound will never l. on death.
W-pI...163.8:9 And it is given us to l. past death, and see
W-pI...163.9:2 *and we would l. upon the glorious reflection*
W-pI...164.1:3 we come to l. upon what is forever there;
W-pI...166.5:3 But he will not l. at what is given him. He
W-pI...166.8:1 hand directing you to l. upon your gifts.
W-pI.166.14:1 of those who l. to you for their release.
W-pI.169.14:8 We do not l. beyond what grace can give.
W-pI...170.7:1 we l. upon this cruel god dispassionately.
W-pI.170.11:2 For you l. for the last time upon this bit of
W-pI...181.1:3 You do not l. beyond his errors. Rather,
W-pI...181.5:6 We do not l. to past beliefs, and what we
W-pI...181.5:7 intent; to l. upon the sinlessness within.
W-pI...181.6:4 *It is not this that I would l. upon. I trust my*
W-pI...181.8:2 For what we seek to l. upon is really there.
W-pI...181.9:2 love for everyone we l. upon attests to our
W-pI...181.9:4 We l. neither ahead nor backwards. We
W-pI...181.9:5 We l. straight into the present. And we
W-pI...185.2:8 You have but to l. upon the world you see
W-pI.185.10:5 of what you wanted, where to l. for it, and
W-pI...187.3:3 miracles it brings to everyone you l. upon.
W-pI...187.9:2 could fear to l. upon such lovely holiness?
W-pI...187.9:3 before the purity that you will l. on here.
W-pI...187.9:4 Be not afraid to l.. The blessedness you
W-pI.187.10:5 And as we l. within, we see the purity of
W-pI.187.11:4 it be withheld from anything we l. upon.
W-pI...188.2:5 It is not difficult to l. within, for there all
W-pI...189.1:4 it. It is there for you to l. upon. It was not
W-pI...189.4:2 the joy with which they l. out from the
W-pI...189.4:3 What they have felt in them they l. upon,
W-pI...189.5:3 will l. upon that which you feel within. If
W-pI...189.5:5 will l. out on a world of mercy and of love.
W-pI.189.10:5 *And it is unto You we l. for them. Our hands*
W-pI...191.2:4 You l. on chaos and proclaim it is yourself
W-pI...191.3:3 Deny your own Identity, and l. on evil, sin
W-pI...191.7:5 is everything you l. on wholly changed.
W-pI.191.10:7 L. about the world, and see the suffering
W-pI...192.5:7 the Son to l. again upon his holiness.
W-pI.193.11:5 l. upon them so that they will disappear.
W-pI.193.13:1 There is a way to l. on everything that lets
W-pI...195.1:1 for those who l. upon the world amiss.
W-pI...198.7:4 you will l. again upon the place where you
W-pI...200.3:6 when you have but to l. with open eyes to
W-pI...200.7:6 Yet can he learn to l. on it another way,
W-pI.200.10:5 And you l. up and on toward Heaven,
W-pII.....in.6:3 We l. not backward now. We look ahead,
W-pII.....in.6:4 We l. ahead, and fix our eyes upon the
W-pII..223.2:3 *We would l. upon our sinlessness, for guilt*
W-pII..229.1:5 And what I l. upon attests the truth of the
W-pII..235.1:1 I need but l. upon all things that seem to
W-pII..240.1:2 l. upon a world which is impossible. Not
W-pII..243.1:6 Thus do I free myself and what I l. upon,
W-pII..247.1:5 Brother, come and let me l. on you. Your
W-pII..247.2:1 *would I l. on everyone today. My brothers*
W-pII..254.2:2 occur, we quietly step back and l. at them,
W-pII..260.1:6 *would l. upon my brothers and myself today*
W-pII..262.1:2 *And it is he that I would l. upon today. He is*
W-pII..263.1:2 *And would I l. upon what You created as if it*
W-pII..263.2:1 let us l. on all we see through holy vision
W-pII..264.1:2 *You are in all the things I l. upon, the sounds*
W-pII..265.2:1 *In quiet would I l. upon the world, which*
W-pII..266.1:2 *does Christ l. back upon me from my Self.*
W-pII..266.2:3 Him, and given us the sight to l. on them?
W-pII.....269.h sight goes forth to l. upon Christ's face.
W-pII..269.1:2 *show me my mistakes, and l. beyond them.*
W-pII..269.1:5 *teaches me that what I l. upon belongs to me;*
W-pII..269.2:2 l. upon the face of Him Whose Self is ours
W-pII......6.5:2 to find Christ's face and l. on nothing else
W-pII..271.1:1 I am choosing what I want to l. upon, the
W-pII..271.1:2 to l. upon what Christ would have me see,
W-pII..271.2:3 *I choose, to be what I would l. upon today.*
W-pII..289.2:1 *let me not l. upon a past that is not there. For*
W-pII..290.1:1 Unless I l. upon what is not there, my
W-pII..290.1:6 l. on nothing else except the thing I seek.
W-pII......8.3:5 is kind, and only kindness does it l. upon.
W-pII......8.5:4 And as we l. upon a world forgiven, it is
W-pII..291.1:4 What loveliness we l. upon today! What
W-pII..295.2:2 *Love to bless all things which I may l. upon,*
W-pII..301.2:2 who l. on it can only add their joy to it,
W-pII..301.2:4 and we will l. upon God's world today.
W-pII.....302.h Where darkness was I l. upon the light.
W-pII..302.1:5 *imagining, and light is there for us to l. upon.*
W-pII..302.1:7 *I may l. upon its holiness and understand it*
W-pII..304.1:4 fact. And what I l. on is my state of mind,
W-pII..304.1:6 And I will l. upon the certain signs that all
W-pII.....309.h I will not fear to l. within today.
W-pII..309.1:4 To l. within is but to find my will as God
W-pII..309.1:5 I fear to l. within because I think I made
W-pII..312.1:2 we therefore see what we would l. upon.
W-pII..312.1:6 to l. upon what Christ would have him
W-pII..312.2:1 *for today except to l. upon a liberated world,*
W-pII..313.1:4 *The eyes of Christ l. on a world forgiven. In*
W-pII..313.1:6 *of sin and l. within upon my sinlessness,*
W-pII..321.1:1 *what my freedom is, nor where to l. to find it.*
W-pII..331.2:2 Let us l. upon the holy sights forgiveness
W-pII..335.1:5 I choose to see what I would l. upon, and
W-pII..335.1:6 shows me that I would l. upon my own.
W-pII..336.1:5 mind, and call it to return and l. within,
W-pII..336.2:2 *Then let me, Father, l. within, and find Your*
W-pII.....13.3:2 to all they l. upon in mercy and in love.
W-pII..346.1:3 *things of time, and so I will not l. upon them.*
W-pII.....349.h Today I let Christ's vision l. upon All
W-pII.....14.3:4 us. We l. on everyone as brother, and
W-pII..357.1:4 *And as I l. upon Your Son today, I hear Your*
M-2 ...........1:1 and they will begin to l. for him as soon as
M-3 ...........1:2 both can l. upon the Son of God as sinless
M-4 ...........1:2 They do not l. alike to the body's eyes,
M-4 .........I.1:7 the teachers of God l. on a forgiven world.
M-4 .......VI.1:8 of God finally agrees to l. past them, he
M-8 ...........1:7 only conflict. L. not to them for peace and
M-11 .........4:1 is impossible to those who l. on war.
M-12 .........6:2 teachers choose to l. on dreams a while. It
M-13 .........4:4 l. back with longing on a slaughter house?
M-17 .......4:11 is unaware of truth must l. upon illusions.
M-17 .........9:4 its thought system is to l. on nothing. Can
M-19 .........4:7 warped perception through which you l..
M-26 .........2:9 teachers of God who l. to them for help,
M-27 .......5:10 His image. To l. on His creations is to die.
M-28 .........4:7 dust and l. upon our perfect sinlessness.
C-2.............4:4 L. at its opposite and you can see the only
C-2.............5:3 and here alone we l. on what the ego was,
C-2.............7:3 But l. at all the aspects of *this* dream and
C-2.............7:4 L. at the kindly world you see extend
C-2.............7:5 L. at the helpers all along the way you
C-2.............7:6 And l. an instant, too, on what you left
C-3.............4:4 No one can l. on knowledge. But the face
C-3.............7:8 But l. on this and you have been forgiven.
C-4.............2:1 for the illusions that they l. upon must
C-ep...........3:6 L. up and see His Word among the stars,
C-ep...........3:7 L. up and find your certain destiny the
P-2.........III.3:2 for the result to l. like retrogression. But
P-2........VI.3:6 its slaves to change the forms they l. upon
P-2........VI.6:3 and is thus given another chance to l. at it
P-2........VI.7:4 that still believe that sin is there to l. upon
P-3......III.5:11 himself, he can l. only upon darkness. He
P-3........III.7:7 salvation without recognizing where to l..
S-1...........I.4:2 the same as to l. on sin and then forgive it
S-1.........V.3:4 you. Now can you l. upon His sinlessness.
S-2...........I.6:4 l. through His and learn to see like Him.
S-2...........I.6:8 eyes that l. past error to the Christ in you.
S-2...........I.8:1 insane would l. on sin when he could see
S-2........III.5:5 be His eyes through which you l. on him,
S-3..........II.2:4 light that we have learned to l. upon again

## looked 61

T-2......VIII.4:3 just as God Himself l. upon what He had
T-8........III.6:5 once you have really l. at it you *will* accept
T-11........in.4:2 at last l. at the ego's foundation without
T-11........in.4:2 shrinking you will also have l. upon ours.
T-12.....VII.8:3 You have l. upon your mind and accepted
T-12.....VII.9:5 l. within and thought you saw the power
T-12...VII.10:1 afraid of me because you l. within and are
T-12...VII.10:3 only bring you peace *if you really l. upon it.*
T-12...VII.10:5 have l. upon me and all your brothers, in
T-12...VII.15:6 will have l. upon the deathless in yourself,
T-12....VIII.7:6 You l. upon the unreal and found despair.
T-13..... V.11:5 l. within and saw beyond the darkness the
T-13..... V.11:6 vision they l. upon themselves with love,
T-13...... VI.5:5 You have l. for it where it is not, and
T-13...... VI.7:6 you l. for it in them and found it there.
T-13........X.8:4 has l. within and seen the radiance there,
T-13........X.8:5 him not, and l. upon him as condemned.
T-13........ X.11:8 is delusional, and has not l. upon himself.
T-15..... VII.3:4 only because you have not l. at what it is,
T-17...... IV.6:4 Yet we have l. at it far closer than we have
T19. IV.A.17:4 Salvation is l. upon as a way by which the
T-20..... VII.8:1 be l. upon except through judgment. To
T-20....VIII.5:8 All is redeemed when l. upon with vision.
T-20....VIII.6:1 Everything l. upon with vision falls gently
T-20..VIII.10:5 gentle sights and sounds are l. on happily,
T-20..VIII.11:1 you have l. on what seemed terrifying,
T-20..VIII.11:1 have l. on scenes of violence and death,
T-21.....in.1:10 Everything l. upon with vision is healed
T-21..... III.12:2 Yet in the light of vision it is l. upon quite
T-21...... IV.3:1 What if you l. within and saw no sin?
T-22........in.3:2 Each one has l. within and seen no lack.
T-22...... VI.7:1 have l. upon your brother with complete
T-23........in.3:5 of love *because* they l. on innocence. And
T-23........II.1:7 broken; merely l. upon and gone beyond.
T-24........II.8:1 when you have l. on him as on a friend.
T-24........ V.4:6 think not that it l. upon your brother first
T-24........ V.6:7 He l. upon you first, but recognized that
T-25........II.8:5 there because of what you l. upon in him.
T-25...VII.2:10 believe, if you but l. at what it really is.
T-26....VIII.6:4 They can be l. at *now.* Why wait till they
T-27........I.4:10 sent your brother *you* have l. upon in grief.
T-27........ V.5:1 not a world so bitterly bereft be l. on as a
T-27..... VII.5:2 And l. at thus, the world provides the
T-30..... IV.4:9 merely l. upon as children's toys without
T-30........ V.7:5 face of Christ is l. upon before the Father
T-30..... VII.6:6 And l. at separately they have no meaning
W-pI.....70.7:5 where you have l. for salvation in the past
W-pI.....78.9:1 l. upon the miracle of love the Holy Spirit
W-pI...128.7:2 see as much as when you l. at it before.
W-pI...132.4:5 exactly what you l. for when you came.
W-pI.166.11:2 and the sight that l. upon it now has been
W-pI...185.5:3 has l. on them, and found them wanting.
W-pI.187.11:2 What we have l. upon we would extend,
W-pI...188.2:3 It can so easily be l. upon that arguments
W-pII .252.1:2 than is any light that I have ever l. upon.
W-pII .289.1:4 this the world that can be l. on only now.
W-pII .325.1:3 are then projected outward, l. upon,
W-pII .344.1:3 *as I l. upon the treasure that I thought I had, I*
M-2 ...........3:4 ago passed by is l. upon as a new thought,
M-11 .........1:8 that the world must be l. at differently, if
P-3..........II.4:1 God is said to have l. on all He created

## looking 81

T-2........ III.4:4 over all others, l. past error to truth.

## looks 149



## loom 1

### loose 7

W-pI...102.2:1 we try to l. its weakened hold still further,
W-pI......132.h I l. the world from all I thought it was.
W-pI......132.8:3 then you can l. it from all things you ever
W-pI.132.14:5 as He created us would l. the world this
W-pI.132.15:2 *would l. the world from all I thought it was.*
W-pI.132.17:2 *I l. the world from all I thought it was, and*
W-pI...146.2:1 I l. the world from all I thought it was.

### loosed 1

W-pI...195.4:5 be that some are l. while others still are

### loosen 2

T-20......VI.7:2 of their temple begin to shake and l..
W-pI...128.5:3 minds, and l. it from all we wish it were.

### loosened 3

T-24.......V.4:8 with flesh already l. from the bone and
T-31.......I.12:4 be l. from our minds and swept away.
W-pI.....57.1:3 My chains are l.. I can drop them off

### loosening 2

T-31.....V.16:3 of the world is l. its grasp upon your mind
W-pI...194.2:2 the world from all imprisonment by l. the

### Lord 14

*lord*

T-3...........I.3:1 sayeth the L." is a misperception by which
T-5........VI.7:1 sayeth the L." is easily reinterpreted if you
T-12.......II.9:2 The L. is with you, but you know it not.
T-24.......V.8:1 holy L. of Heaven has Himself come down
T-25.......II.9:1 How could the L. of Heaven not be glad if
T-26......IX.7:4 And shall the L. of Heaven and His Son
T-27...VII.15:2 And from this dream the L. of Heaven will
T-31.....VII.8:2 To every part of true creation has the L. of
W-pI...126.5:4 Think you the L. of Heaven would allow
WpI.rIV.in6:3 communion with the L. of Hosts be yours,
W-pI.167.11:2 He is L. of what we think today. And in
W-pI.167.12:3 sees its own perfection mirroring the L. of
W-pII..268.1:1 *Let me not be Your critic, L., today, and*
W-pII..341.1:3 *the L. of Sinlessness conceives us as His Son,*

### lord 8

*Lord*

T-19......I.16:3 His Son is slave to nothing, being l. of all,
T19.IV.A.11:2 respectfully before their l. and master.
T19...IV.C.2:4 that honors their grim master, l. of death?
T-29.......V.7:6 serve the l. of death have come to worship
W-pI...151.6:3 their l. can not completely vanquish. You
W-pI...163.2:1 god of the guilty and the l. of all illusions
W-pI...163.4:3 of God proclaimed as l. of all creation,
M-22..........3:7 The body has become l. of the mind. How

### lordliness 1

S-2.........II.2:2 attitude of gracious l. so far from love that

### lose 131

T-2...........I.1:6 No child of God can l. this ability because
T-3........VI.9:3 to l. something does not mean that it has
T-4.....VII.3:12 totally l. the ability to communicate, even
T-5........I.4:11 obstruct it, although you can never l. it.
T-5.......II.7:11 gain the whole world and l. his own soul?
T-5.......II.7:13 You cannot l. it, but you can not know it.
T-5......IV.8:12 We cannot l.. My judgment is as strong as
T-6......IV.11:6 Can God l. His Own certainty? I have
T-6......V.A.5:2 You do not l. what you communicate. The
T-6......V.C.8:2 you will l. awareness of its wholeness and
T-7.......VII.8:2 l. anything unless you do not value it, and
T-8.........II.2:8 you will l. by your learning because your
T-8........III.4:5 in him you will find yourself or l. yourself.
T-8.........V.5:9 in different directions and will l. the way.
T-8.........V.6:3 Let us not l. sight of His direction through
T-8.......VII.7:7 is to l. sight of the Holy Spirit's purpose,
T-8.......VIII.5:4 is to l. sight of the function of everything.
T-8........IX.9:7 He cannot l. this, but you *can* not know it.
T-9...........I.4:5 this process is what you think you will l..
T-9.......II.10:5 The price for getting is to l. sight of value,
T-9........III.6:8 guide and will therefore l. your way.
T-9......VII.1:7 Do not l. these chances, not because they
T-10......III.3:6 denial of God and thus l. sight of yourself
T-10......III.5:2 your brothers, and thus l. sight of yours.
T-11......III.5:3 You will never l. your way, for God leads
T-11.......V.7:3 reality, but it does not l. sight of its goal.
T-12......III.5:4 Never l. sight of this, and never allow
T-12......VI.1:1 gain the whole world and l. your own soul
T-12......VI.1:2 that you cannot l. your soul and there is
T-12...VIII.4:2 You can deny it, but you cannot l. it. A
T-13.......in.2:9 They appear to l. what they love, perhaps
T-13......IV.9:6 you will l. sight of the present and hold
T-13...VII.11:4 l. whatever you have gotten in its name.
T-13...VII.15:2 seek not what you will surely l.. Content
T-13...VIII.7:1 and your Father's gift you cannot l.. Offer
T-13...XI.10:1 God's Son l. himself in dreams, when
T-14......III.2:6 will l. appreciation of the value of your
T-14...III.18:3 you have thrown away but could not l..
T-14......VI.4:4 you have done by keeping them apart is l.
T-14......XI.7:5 It is impossible that God l. His Identity,
T-14......XI.7:5 Identity, for if He did, you would l. yours.
T-15.......I.15:5 in which God's Son could l. his purity.
T-15......VI.3:4 always l. if you perceive yourself as weak.
T-15.....VII.3:6 have nothing to l. by looking open-eyed,
T-15.....VII.7:7 that to forgive another is to l. him. It is
T-15...VII.11:5 must be kept private or they will l. them,
T-16.........I.3:8 thought in mind and do not l. sight of it,
T-17.........I.6:5 When you become disturbed and l. your
T-17......III.6:8 be unwilling ever to l. the sight of it again.
T-17...V.11:10 the holy instant, and thus l. sight of it.
T-17.....V.12:6 attack your brother is not to l. the instant,
T-17......VI.7:5 Thus do you l. the understanding of the
T-18......VI.4:5 but it will not l. it through projection.
T-20......IV.1:2 world interpret giving; as you give you l..
T-21.........I.5:1 must, afraid to l. the little that they have.
T-21.........I.7:3 would l. the world you learned since then.
T-21...VII.10:7 and l. this same desire as a little glint of
T-22.......II.1:4 the way to l. the misery the other brings.
T-23......III.4:7 it become impossible that you l. sight of it
T-25....VI.5:11 thus become a means to save instead of l..
T-25...VII.11:5 For every little gain must someone l., and
T-25...VII.12:1 the idea no one can l. for anyone to gain.
T-25...VII.13:1 that either God or you must l. to madness
T-25...VII.13:6 He cannot l., for if he could the loss would
T-25...VIII.1:7 to the idea no one can l. for you to gain.
T-25......IX.4:5 is decided who shall win and who shall l.;
T-25......IX.5:4 no one can l. is crucial to this course. For
T-25......IX.6:1 No one deserves to l.. And what would be
T-25...IX.10:3 No one can l., and everyone must benefit.
T-26.........I.1:3 the central theme that *somebody must l.*.
T-26.........I.2:5 joined each one would l. its own identity,
T-26.........I.3:2 And all the rest must l. this little part,
T-26.........I.6:1 You can l. sight of oneness, but can not
T-26.........I.6:2 Nor can you l. what you would sacrifice,
T-26.......V.9:8 You cannot l. your way because there is
T-26.....V.10:1 Would God allow His Son to l. his way
T-26.......X.4:8 loss. Someone must l. his innocence that
T-27.....II.10:3 role, you l. the function of forgiveness. No
T-27.....II.10:9 for you must l. what you would take away
T-27......III.7:4 The choice you fear to l. you never had.
T-28......IV.2:2 they take, for you will l. identity in them.
T-29.......II.1:3 marked it is impossible to l. the way,
T-29....III.1:10 and who could l. by giving what must be
T-29.......V.8:2 dreams are shared they l. the function of
T-29...VIII.9:8 And to be sure you could not l. it, did He
T-30........I.12:4 *What can I l. by asking?* Thus you now can
T-30.......II.2:6 that you would never l. your will when He
T-30......III.2:9 you l. the understanding of its purpose.
T-31.......II.1:2 nor fought against to l. to truth's appeal.
T-31.......II.3:3 advantages you would not want to l.. So
T-31......IV.8:4 and you will gain as much as he will l.,
T-31......IV.8:4 lose, and what you l. is what is given him.
W-pI.....37.2:3 As a result, the perceiver will l.. Nor will
W-pI...96.10:1 has found the function that it sought to l..
W-pI.....98.6:4 Here is a bargain that you cannot l.. And
W-pI.....98.8:2 l. one chance to be the glad receiver of His
W-pI...99.10:2 You cannot l. the gifts your Father gave.
W-pI...100.7:7 God's plan, and never l. or sacrifice or die
W-pI...104.5:2 We will not let ourselves l. sight of them
W-pI...106.8:3 world from thinking giving is a way to l..
W-pI...129.8:5 that what you feared to l. was only loss.
W-pI...131.8:4 l. what the Eternal Will has given him to
W-pI...140.8:4 thoughts; so close it is impossible to l..
W-pI.155.11:5 We must not l. our way. For as truth goes
W-pI...156.7:5 may perhaps l. sight of your Companion,
W-pI...158.1:4 you as knowledge which you cannot l.. It
W-pI...166.5:2 He cannot l. them. But he will not look at
W-pI.166.10:3 imprisoned in your plan to l. your Self.
W-pI...181.4:3 you will inevitably l. your way again.
W-pI.185.13:1 No one can l. and everyone must gain
W-pI...187.4:1 you are sure that you will never l. them.
W-pI...187.5:8 What he seems to l. is always something
W-pI...200.9:1 Let us not l. our way again today. We go
W-pII.229.1:5 the truth of the Identity I sought to l., but
W-pII.234.2:1 *l. the memory of You and of Your Love. We*
W-pII.266.2:3 How can we l. the way to Him, when He
W-pII.273.2:3 *I cannot l. Your gifts to me. And so the peace*
W-pII.288.1:6 *my heart, or I will l. the way to walk to You.*
W-pII.319.1:5 that what one gains, totality must l.. And
W-pII.324.1:3 *path. I cannot l. the way. I can but choose to*
W-pII343.1:11 *I cannot l., for I can only give, and everything*
W-pII.353.1:5 *purpose. Then I l. myself in my Identity, and*
M-3...........2:6 two people to l. sight of separate interests
M-4.....VII.2:5 He could only l. because of it. He could
M-6...........3:6 part that guarantees the giver will not l.,
C-ep..........4:5 know that we will never l. the way again.
P-2..........II.8:4 so doing, l. all sense of separate interests.
P-3..........II.6:6 new dreams will l. their temporary appeal
P-3.......III.5:8 But they will l. this understanding unless
S-1..........II.4:6 l. the recognition of your own Identity. Be
S-1.......III.6:8 he l. the only true goal that is given him.

### loser 4

T-25......IX.4:5 take, and how much can the l. still defend
T-25......IX.4:6 can set up a state in which there is no l.;
W-pI.153.12:3 in happiness because there is no l..
W-pI...185.3:5 both. L. and gainer merely shift about in

### loses 19

T-2........VI.9:5 powerful, and never l. its creative force. It
T-7........VI.2:4 This l. the awareness of being, induces
T-8.....VII.11:5 true. A medium of communication l. its
T-9...........I.6:4 This l. the ability to communicate simply
T-15......VI.3:3 from another, and what you gain he l..
T-15......XI.2:5 the whole idea of sacrifice l. all meaning.
T-16......IV.4:9 relationship l. the illusion that it is what it
T-18......VII.7:4 in which sin l. all attraction *right now*. For
T-25.....VII.5:4 one, and no one l. that each one may gain
T-25...VII.11:1 whole belief that someone l. but reflects
T-25......IX.3:1 will always be one in which no one l.. And
T-26........II.2:3 situation is worked out so no one l. is the
T-30.....VII.5:3 for the one who gains and him who l..
T-31......IV.8:5 that what your brother l. *you* have lost,
W-pI.....37.1:4 No one l.; nothing is taken away from
W-pI...105.1:4 in which the giver l. as he gives the gift;
W-pI...105.1:7 that one can gain because another l.. This
W-pI...129.7:5 ends l. all meaning as they blend in one.
P-3.......III.2:9 who would do this l. the name of healer,

### losing 20

T-5.........I.1:14 ego makes between giving and l. is gone.
T-5...........I.2:5 *How, then, can giving and l. be associated?*
T-8.........IV.8:5 imprison yourself you are l. sight of your
T-10...III.4:10 to save? Are you really afraid of l. this?
T-13......IV.6:5 choosing a future of illusions and l. the
T-16...........I.6:8 you how to meet both without l. either.
T-16......VI.5:2 separate unions and to become one by l..
T-18....VI.13:5 go where you would be, gaining, not l., a

| | |
|---|---|
| T-19....... II.2:4 | and has thus succeeded in l. his innocence |
| T19. IV.A.11:2 | can find, l. none of them on pain of death, |
| T-21...... III.5:5 | as means for l. certainty and finding sin. |
| T-25...... IX.3:8 | When anyone is seen as l., he has been |
| T-28...... VI.4:5 | not see himself attacked, and l. by attack. |
| W-pI..... 35.6:8 | *I see myself as l. out. I see myself as charitable* |
| W-pI..... 37.2:4 | Nor will he have any idea why he is l.. Yet |
| W-pI..... 98.5:4 | made a thousand l. bargains at the least. |
| W-pI... 129.3:1 | find a world instead where l. is impossible |
| W-pI... 200.2:2 | Attempt no more to win through l., nor |
| M-13 ......... 2:9 | its Identity and l. sight of what it really is. |
| M-27 ......... 1:2 | of life as being born, aging, l. vitality, and |

## loss 150

| | |
|---|---|
| T-2......... II.7:2 | may still think this is associated with l., a |
| T-3........ IV.6:4 | not be reconciled with this l. of power, |
| T-3........ VI.2:1 | than to know is the cause of the l. of peace |
| T-4.........in.3:5 | re-enacts the separation, the l. of power, |
| T-6...... IV.12:5 | The separation was not a l. of perfection, |
| T-7........ IX.2:5 | Creating is the opposite of l., as blessing |
| T-7........ XI.3:4 | him to give always, without any sense of l. |
| T-8...........I.2:6 | not want them on the basis of l. of peace, |
| T-8....... VII.4:9 | you to hatred and attack and l. of peace. |
| T-8....... VII.5:1 | Yet all l. comes only from your own |
| T-8....... VII.5:2 | L. of any kind is impossible. But when |
| T-9....... II.10:3 | with giving it cannot be perceived as l., |
| T-12.........I.9:1 | is a symptom of your own deep sense of l. |
| T-12.........I.9:2 | it in others you learn to supply the l., the |
| T-13.... VII.1:6 | There is no l.. Nothing is there but shines, |
| T-14...... IX.4:3 | cover all their sense of pain and l. with |
| T-15...... VI.3:5 | the concept of l. of power completely. |
| T-15...... VI.4:6 | wholly without l. and only with gain. |
| T-15...... VI.5:2 | For gain and l. are both accepted, and so |
| T-15...... VI.5:4 | holding it within itself, there *is* no l.. The |
| T-15...... VI.5:5 | mind, experiencing not l. but completion. |
| T-15.... VIII.1:6 | you to remember that forgiveness is not l. |
| T-15...... XI.5:3 | aside without a sense of sacrifice and l.? |
| T-15...... XI.5:4 | suffer sacrifice and l. without attempting |
| T-16....... V.4:4 | you see that separation could only be l., |
| T-16..... VII.5:7 | escape from vengeance becomes your l.. |
| T-17....... V.9:2 | *Your* way *is* lost, but think not this is l.. In |
| T-18.........I.6:3 | idea of l. is meaningless and only increase |
| T-19...... III.3:3 | results, but without the l. of its appeal. |
| T-20.... VIII.5:1 | of weakness, vulnerability and l. of power |
| T-22.........I.4:9 | to sight of differences and l. of sameness. |
| T-23....... II.9:4 | By this, another's l. becomes your gain, |
| T-23..... II.10:1 | inevitable l. the enemy must suffer to save |
| T-23...... IV.2:9 | creations all that it is and never suffer l.? |
| T-23...... IV.6:3 | twinge of guilt, and above all, a l. of peace |
| T-23...... IV.9:2 | could they gain but l. of their perfection? |
| T-25... VII.13:6 | for if he could the l. would be his Father's, |
| T-25... VII.13:6 | his Father's, and in Him no l. is possible. |
| T-25.... VIII.1:6 | brings l. to no one you would not know. |
| T-25.... VIII.7:1 | So do they think the l. of sin a curse. And |
| T-25...... IX.3:3 | answer which demands the slightest l. to |
| T-25...... IX.4:3 | Only a l. could justify attack, and loss of |
| T-25...... IX.4:3 | attack, and l. of any kind He cannot see. |
| T-26.........I.1:4 | for it is always an attempt to limit l.. The |
| T-26.........I.3:3 | the body's l. would be a sacrifice indeed. |
| T-26.........I.4:1 | body *is* a l., and *can* be made to sacrifice. |
| T-26.........I.7:8 | His gifts can never suffer sacrifice and l.. |
| T-26....... II.2:2 | demand that someone suffer l. and make |
| T-26....... II.2:5 | mistake; the whole idea that l. is possible, |
| T-26....... II.3:2 | is no l.; to think there is, is a mistake. You |
| T-26....... II.6:4 | For there are those you want to suffer l., |
| T-26....... II.6:7 | him because you could not will he suffer l. |
| T-26....... II.7:7 | shine away all memory of sacrifice and l.. |
| T-26... VII.11:9 | a sense of isolation, l. and loneliness. This |
| T-26... VII.14:5 | is his, unlimited by l. of any kind. A tiny |
| T-26... VII.14:7 | If l. in any form is possible, then is God's |
| T-26.... VIII.2:6 | be one in which you sacrifice and suffer l.. |
| T-26.... VIII.3:2 | of it, believing that the risk of l. is great |
| T-26.... VIII.3:5 | And it is here you fear the l. would lie. Do |
| T-26.... VIII.4:3 | Future l. is not your fear. But present |
| T-26....... X.4:7 | game of guilt is played, there must be l.. |
| T-28.......I.15:2 | of God has come to take the place of l.? |
| T-28.... IV.10:4 | What God has given cannot be a l., and |
| T-28.. IV.10:10 | And there will be no l., but only gain. |
| T-28 ...... V.2:1 | death, of sin and suffering and pain and l. |
| T-29 ........I.9:5 | afraid to find a l. of self in finding God? |
| T-29 .......II.1:4 | a simple way, without a sacrifice or any l., |
| T-29 .......II.1:5 | until you understand there is no l., you |
| T-29 .......II.3:6 | free of pain and sickness, misery and l., |
| T-29 .......II.8:7 | more and He is lessened by the l. of you. |
| T-29 .....II.10:2 | It is His l. you celebrate when you behold |
| T-29 ..... VI.1:4 | of madness and of murder, grief and l.. |
| T-29 .... VII.4:3 | thus to be without and to have suffered l.. |
| T-29 .... VII.9:6 | fear of God is but the fear of l. of idols. It |
| T-29 .... VII.9:7 | It is not the fear of l. of your reality. But |
| T-29 ... VIII.2:5 | not enslaved himself to littleness and l.. |
| T-29 ... VIII.6:4 | to die, the all-encompassing to suffer l., |
| T-30 .... III.1:9 | Decide for idols and you ask for l.. Decide |
| T-30 .... VII.2:2 | success, advance, retreat, and gain and l.. |
| T-30 .... VII.6:5 | All sacrifice entails the l. of your ability to |
| T-30 .. VII.6:10 | In any thought of l. there is no meaning. |
| T-30 ... VIII.2:6 | is not bound by l. or suffering in any form |
| T-31 ...... V.8:5 | of what you now believe for total l. of self, |
| T-31 .... V.13:6 | But this gain is paid in almost equal l., for |
| T-31 ..... VI.2:3 | that one is doomed to suffering and l.. |
| T-31 ... VIII.6:2 | pain, as weakness and as suffering and l., |
| W-pI..... 27.2:4 | If fear of l. still persists, add further: *It can* |
| W-pI..... 38.4:1 | search your mind for any sense of l. or |
| W-pI..... 41.1:3 | misery, suffering and intense fear of l.. |
| W-pI..... 41.3:2 | and pain and fear and l. because it will |
| W-pI..... 44.5:6 | it is l. of identity and a descent into hell. |
| W-pI..... 53.5:4 | which there is suffering and l. and death |
| W-pI..... 54.5:4 | replace tears, and abundance to replace l.. |
| W-pI..... 56.1:3 | Pain, illness, l., age and death seem to |
| W-pI..... 58.5:5 | I cannot suffer any l. or deprivation or |
| W-pI..... 76.9:3 | says there is no l. under the laws of God. |
| W-pI..... 84.1:3 | I cannot experience l. and I cannot die. I |
| W-pI..... 94.3:8 | could conceive of l. or suffering or death. |
| W-pI..... 99.5:4 | death, on grief and separation and on l.. |
| W-pI... 105.1:4 | the gift; the taker is the richer by his l.. |
| W-pI... 105.1:6 | guilt. The truly given gift entails no l.. It is |
| W-pI... 105.5:4 | He cannot give through l.. No more can |
| W-pI... 109.3:2 | past misery and pain, past l. and death, |
| W-pI... 129.2:2 | no l. in letting go all thought of value here |
| W-pI... 129.3:1 | a l. to find a world instead where losing is |
| W-pI... 129.3:2 | Is it l. to find all things you really want, |
| W-pI... 129.6:2 | What l. can be for you in choosing not to |
| W-pI... 129.8:5 | that what you feared to lose was only l.. |
| W-pI... 129.9:1 | Now do we understand there is no l.. For |
| W-pI... 133.7:4 | deceived by the illusion l. can offer gain. |
| W-pI... 133.7:5 | Yet l. must offer loss, and nothing more. |
| W-pI... 133.7:5 | Yet loss must offer l., and nothing more. |
| W-pI. 151.10:1 | placed in pain, disaster, suffering and l.. |
| W-pI... 152.1:1 | can suffer l. unless it be his own decision. |
| W-pI... 152.2:3 | have the gift of everything, can l. be real? |
| W-pI... 155.4:3 | And they have suffered from a sense of l., |
| W-pI... 155.4:4 | suffered from a sense of l. still deeper, |
| W-pI... 155.5:1 | road that leads away from l. of every kind, |
| W-pI... 162.5:4 | remedy for grief and misery, all sense of l. |
| W-pI... 167.2:6 | All sorrow, l., anxiety and suffering and |
| W-pI... 185.3:5 | ratio of gain to l. and loss to gain takes on |
| W-pI... 185.3:5 | ratio of gain to loss and l. to gain takes on |
| W-pI... 185.4:8 | each to his gain and to another's l.. |
| W-pI... 187.6:4 | take. He laughs as well at pain and l., at |
| W-pI... 191.7:4 | *suffer, cannot be in pain; I cannot suffer l.,* |
| W-pI... 194.3:1 | felt, or pain experienced or l. perceived. |
| W-pI... 194.5:2 | bequest of grief and misery, of pain and l. |
| W-pI... 194.7:3 | him pain, or bring experience of l. to him |
| W-pI... 195.5:2 | mourn a seeming l. or feel apparent pain, |
| W-pII . 245.1:5 | *to those who suffer pain, or grieve for l., or* |
| W-pII .... 249.h | Forgiveness ends all suffering and l.. |
| W-pII . 249.1:1 | l. becomes impossible and anger makes |
| W-pII . 249.1:4 | What l. can be sustained? The world |
| W-pII . 268.2:3 | Only reality is free of l.. Only reality is |
| W-pII . 284.1:1 | L. is not loss when properly perceived. |
| W-pII . 284.1:1 | Loss is not l. when properly perceived. |
| W-pII . 285.1:4 | and how would grief and l. avail me if |
| W-pII ... 11.1:4 | anything that it created suffers any l.. |
| W-pII . 322.2:5 | *What l. can I anticipate except the loss of fear* |
| W-pII . 322.2:5 | *What loss can I anticipate except the l. of fear* |
| W-pII . 323.1:1 | *up all suffering, all sense of l. and sadness, all* |
| W-pII . 328.1:3 | find is sickness, suffering and l. and death |
| W-pII . 337.1:1 | freedom forever from all thought of l.; |
| W-pII . 343.1:1 | *The end of suffering can not be l.. The gift of* |
| M-4 ..... I.A.4:4 | the lesson for fear of l. and sacrifice. It |
| M-4 ..... VII.2:7 | keep, because that is a guarantee of l.. He |
| M-6 ........... 1:7 | a sense of l. so deep that the patient might |
| M-10 ......... 6:6 | All of the loneliness and sense of l.; of |
| P-2........ VI.1:4 | they mourn their l. and yet rejoice in it. |
| S-3........ IV.5:8 | suffering and grievous l. become the lot of |

## lost 166

| | |
|---|---|
| T-1 ........I.31:3 | holiness, which can be hidden but never l. |
| T-1 ........I.45:1 | A miracle is never l.. It may touch many |
| T-1 ....... III.8:3 | asked to perform have not l. their value. |
| T-1 .... VII.3:12 | Reality is "l." through usurpation, which |
| T-3 ........I.2:11 | the Atonement teaches is l. if it is tainted |
| T-3 .........V.6:7 | l. the knowledge that you yourself are a |
| T-3 ....... VI.3:3 | meaning is l. to you precisely *because* you |
| T-3 ....... VI.4:2 | to accept it, you have l. control over it. |
| T-3 ....... VI.9:2 | of God, but you *have* l. it. Fortunately, to |
| T-5 .......II.7:12 | wrong voice you *have* l. sight of your soul. |
| T-5 .......II.7:14 | "l." to you until you choose right. |
| T-5 ....... IV.1:7 | Nothing that is good can be l. because it |
| T-5 ....... VI.3:1 | who are part of the Kingdom cannot be l.. |
| T-5 ...... VII.4:5 | children who believe they are l. to Him. |
| T-7 ...... VII.1:8 | you have l. the awareness of all of it. Yet |
| T-7 ....... IX.7:1 | Be confident that you have never l. your |
| T-7 ....... XI.6:6 | He cannot have l. what you recognize, |
| T-8 ....... III.5:3 | for the power and glory he thinks he has l. |
| T-8 ...... VII.5:3 | and glory are "l." to you and so are yours. |
| T-8 ...... VII.8:6 | goal of the curriculum has been l. sight of. |
| T-9 .........II.3:5 | It is impossible, however, that it will be l.. |
| T-9 .........V.7:2 | but the point is l. unless he is also helped |
| T-10 .......II.5:4 | the way in which your identification is l., |
| T-11 ........I.2:6 | part of God can be missing or l. to Him? |
| T-11 .......I.5:10 | have your closed eyes l. the ability to see. |
| T-11 ........II.1:6 | what you really want is therefore l. to you. |
| T-11 ..... IV.1:6 | of your Self all your understanding is l., |
| T-11 ... VIII.2:3 | you perceive, for its meaning is l. to you. |
| T-11 ... VIII.7:3 | you have l. sight of the real world. You are |
| T-12 ..... VI.4:2 | knows that they have not l. their vision, |
| T-12 ..... VI.5:5 | to be seen, for He has never l. sight of you |
| T-12 ... VIII.8:8 | is but the way back to what was never l.. |
| T-13 .... in.3:7 | belief the knowledge of the Father was l., |
| T-13 .... VII.9:8 | is your awakening to what you have not l.. |
| T-13 .......X.8:3 | Son of God believes that he is l. in guilt, |
| T-14 .... VII.2:3 | It can neither be l. nor sought nor found. |
| T-14 .... VII.4:8 | Apart, this fact is l. from sight, for each in |
| T-14 ..... XI.1:3 | to keep power for yourself have "l." it. |
| T-15 ..... IV.1:5 | one you would not have it be is l. to you. |
| T-16 ........I.6:1 | meaning of love is l. in any relationship |
| T-16 .....V.12:4 | over content, and love has l. its meaning. |
| T-16 ..... VI.4:6 | disappear, because its value would be l.. |
| T-17 ... III.10:6 | of Atonement be l. to you in dreams of |
| T-17 .......V.9:1 | salvation, and think you have l. your way. |
| T-17 .......V.9:2 | *Your* way *is* l., but think not this is loss. In |
| T-17 .... VII.2:3 | the meaning of the problem must be l., |
| T-17 .. VII.3:11 | ask that it be restored where it was l., and |
| T-18 ... VI.11:7 | awareness, and l. your fear of union. The |
| T-18 ... VIII.4:3 | Even that segment is not l. to them, for it |
| T-18 ... VIII.9:3 | those who l. their way and wander in the |
| T-18 ..... IX.1:8 | Heaven has not l. it, but *you* have lost sight |
| T-18 ..... IX.1:8 | not lost it, but *you* have l. sight of Heaven. |
| T19 . IV.B.4:10 | He has not l. communion with Him, nor |
| T19 .. IV.D.5:5 | And the appeal of death is l. forever as |
| T19 IV.D.19:1 | beyond the veil, not to be l. but found; |
| T-20 ..... III.1:4 | is l. if any shift or change is undertaken. |
| T-20 ..... III.1:5 | certainty is l. and doubt has entered. To |
| T-20 ..... IV.2:4 | sin in him instead, and Heaven is l. to you |
| T-20 .......V.1:3 | outside them, and finding what was l.. |
| T-20 .......V.1:4 | Only in time can anything be l., and never |
| T-20 .......V.1:4 | can anything be lost, and never l. forever. |
| T-20 ..... VI.3:4 | in which they enter has l. its meaning. |
| T-20 ... VIII.1:2 | as it was l. to you through your desire for |
| T-20 ... VIII.1:3 | and what was never l. will quietly return. |
| T-21 .... VII.6:5 | to hold a threat the rest have l. for you. |
| T-21 ... VIII.4:1 | His, a power that is not l. in your illusions |
| T-22 ... VI.8:10 | to overlook the tiniest mistake be l. to |
| T-23 ..... III.3:5 | purpose is l. because it is not recognized. |
| T-24 ........I.7:4 | What you keep is l. to you. God gave you |

T-24....... II.7:1 He has not l. the power to forgive you all
T-24..... II.11:2 be that you have l. because he is complete
T-24...... III.7:4 They are l. in dreams of specialness. They
T-24...... VI.3:1 Nothing is l. to you in all the universe.
T-24..... VII.3:3 truth, for if it were you would be l. indeed
T-25...... III.2:5 be l. forever in the madness of his wish.
T-25....... V.4:9 But think not Heaven is l. to him alone.
T-25... VII.11:2 that one must gain *because* another l.. If
T-25... VIII.8:5 For love has l. when judgment left its side,
T-25...... IX.2:4 Nothing you give is l. to you or anyone,
T-25...... IX.9:4 with vengeance justified and mercy l.,
T-26.........I.6:2 task of showing you that it has not been l.
T-26...... III.5:2 Heaven was never l., and so cannot be
T-26...... IV.3:8 For here is what was l. restored to them,
T-26...... IV.4:3 Not one is l., and none is cherished more
T-26....... V.2:1 Nothing is ever l. but time, which in the
T-26..... VII.7:5 Thus has He l. His Mind, proclaiming sin
T-26... VII.11:4 It is impossible that anything be l., if what
T-27.........I.2:3 to be the sign that he has l. his innocence,
T-27....... II.6:3 is he convinced his innocence was never l.
T-27..... II.15:7 divided function, you were l. indeed. His
T-27... VII.13:3 him think that he has l. his innocence,
T-28...... I.10:7 And so your innocence has not been l..
T-28...... I.15:1 What has been l., to see the causeless not
T-28.... IV.10:2 when he perceives he has l. nothing? Who
T-28....... V.7:6 you have l. the fear of recognizing love.
T-28...... VI.4:2 and that, without it, would your self be l..
T-29.........I.9:6 Yet can your self be l. by being found?
T-29...... III.2:1 the Father l. Himself when He created you
T-29...... III.5:4 Father l. not part of him in your creation,
T-29... VII.10:3 The sacrifice of death is nothing l.. An
T-30....... V.2:2 is clear that by attack is understanding l..
T-31.........I.8:7 and had l. a friend who always wanted to
T-31....... II.5:9 and you are separate from him and are l..
T-31...... IV.3:5 learning they led nowhere, l. their hope.
T-31...... IV.8:5 that what your brother loses *you* have l.,
W-pI.....20.1:4 l. sight of the crucial importance of the
W-pI.....46.6:1 the central idea should not be l. sight of.
W-pI.....56.5:3 I have not l. the knowledge of Who I am
W-pI.....63.4:3 should be l. for reinforcing today's idea.
W-pI.....73.3:1 will is l. to you in this strange bartering,
W-pI.....77.3:3 of God is within you, and can never be l..
W-pI.....95.7:4 to regard the day as l. because you have
W-pI...110.9:5 And you are l. and do not know yourself
WpI. rIII.in4:1 practice periods that you have l. because
W-pI.139.11:4 We have not l. the knowledge that God
W-pI...152.3:8 And truth has l. its meaning. Nothing but
W-pI.153.13:1 who have played that you are l. to hope,
W-pI...158.5:4 directly, for Christ's knowledge is not l.,
W-pI.158.10:4 If he be l. in sin, so must you be; if you see
W-pI...159.7:1 remember what was l. when it was made.
W-pI...160.6:4 His way is l., except a miracle will search
W-pI...163.3:1 quickly l. however hard to gain, uncertain
W-pI...164.4:2 you carry in your heart and have not l..
WpI.. rV.in5:4 return to the eternal Self we thought we l.
W-pI...181.6:1 recognize that we have l. this goal if anger
W-pI.182.12:1 You have not l. your innocence. It is for
W-pI...183.4:1 and little names have l. their meaning. No
W-pI...183.4:4 have l. the name of god you gave them.
W-pI...185.4:8 He means is l. to sleeping minds intent on
W-pI...187.1:7 that you have l. what you possessed. The
W-pI...187.5:4 as they are shared, for they can not be l..
W-pI...188.2:1 This light can not be l.. Why wait to find
W-pI...188.2:2 the future, or believe it has been l. already
W-pI...191.8:2 For time has l. its hold upon the world.
W-pI...191.8:3 of God has come in glory to redeem the l.,
W-pI...192.5:4 those who have l. the source of all attack,
W-pI...192.7:4 We are l. in mists of shifting dreams and
W-pI...197.4:3 matter if your gifts seem l. and ineffectual
W-pI...220.1:2 *of peace, for I am l. on other roads than this.*
W-pII.......2.2:5 itself, and thought its own Identity was l..
W-pII.......4.3:4 And God Himself has l. the Son He loves,
W-pII.......6.1:4 l. the innocence in which He was created.
W-pII..278.1:4 And I am l. to all reality. For truth is free,
W-pII..300.2:2 *we, Your loving Sons, have l. our way a while*
W-pII.......9.1:2 of the condition that restores the never l.,
W-pII..314.1:3 so that fear has l. its idols and its images,
W-pII..316.1:4 watch its open doors that not one gift is l.,
W-pII..321.1:6 *freedom as Your holy Son will not be l. to me.*

M-4 ...... III.1:7 Let this be l., and all his learning goes.
M-6 ...........2:6 Not one is l., for they can but increase. No
M-6 ...........4:5 to him. How can it be l. ? How can it be
M-19 .........3:4 which all thought of wholeness must be l..
M-19 .........5:11 What had been l. has now been found.
M-22 .........5:9 Lead not the way, for you have l. it. Turn
M-23 .........4:4 that the little space between the two is l.,
M-28 .........5:9 Illusions of another will are l., for unity of
C-ep...........3:3 on before and l. our way a little while.
C-ep...........5:2 had l. our way but He has found it for us.
P-2......... V.1:1 to those who have already l. their way in
P-2....... VII.9:5 You l. the way. And can you now expect
P-3....... II.10:2 has l. sight of the Source of his salvation.
P-3........ III.7:4 How much is l. by throwing God away?
P-3...... III.8:12 *You were l. in the darkness of the world until*
S-1........ III.6:5 The goal of God is l. in the quest for lesser
S-2...........I.9:2 can use a key when he has l. the door for
S-3........ III.1:8 the meaning of true healing has been l.,

## lot 5

W-pI.....28.2:5 You see a l. of separate things about you,
W-pI...161.4:8 We need to see a little, that we learn a l..
W-pI...166.5:4 perceiving how his little l. but dwindles,
W-pII..300.1:1 are the certain l. of all who come here, for
S-3........ IV.5:8 loss become the l. of everyone on earth,

## loud 4

T-8..... VIII.8:7 Voice is as l. as your willingness to listen.
T-21..... VII.3:1 and l. and strong the dark ones seem to
T-27...... VI.1:2 It is a l., obscuring voice whose shrieks
P-2........ VI.2:6 are heard instead of l. discordant shrieks.

## louder 3

T-8..... VIII.8:8 be l. without violating your freedom of
T-14....... X.6:6 consider which call is l. or greater or more
M-8 ...........5:3 the unreality of a l. voice he hears than to

## loudly 7

T19....IV.C.7:1 see not how often and how l. they call to it
T-21...... IV.2:3 L. the ego tells you not to look inward, for
T-21...... IV.2:6 L. indeed the ego claims it is; too loudly
T-21...... IV.2:6 the ego claims it is; too l. and too often.
T-21...... IV.8:6 matters it to you how l. it is proclaimed?
W-pI.72.10:11 shouted our grievances so l. that we have
W-pI...106.1:1 ego's voice, however l. it may seem to call,

## lovable 4

T-1.........I.33:1 Miracles honor you because you are l..
T-1........ III.2:3 His work is wholly l. and wholly loving.
T-2.... VIII.5:10 When everything you retain is l., there is
W-pI...124.4:6 Today we see only the loving and the l..

## Love 383

*love*

T-1......... V.3:3 All His children have His total L., and all
T-1....... VII.2:3 The L. of God, for a little while, must still
T-4.........I.12:5 mark of the L. of God for His creations,
T-4........ III.6:3 of His L. for you and yours for Him. He
T-4....... VII.6:7 constant going out of His L. is blocked
T-7...........I.6:1 to share the perfect L. He shares with you.
T-7....... VII.6:4 in His L. and protect your rest by loving.
T-7....... VII.7:3 born of the infinite L. for which He speaks
T-7..... VII.10:4 But see the L. of God in you, and you will
T-7....... XI.3:11 give the L. of God to everything you see
T-8....... V.2:10 Let the L. of God shine upon you by your
T-9...........I.9:7 God is L. and you do want Him. This *is*
T-9.........I.11:5 fact that God is L. does not require belief,
T-9..... VIII.4:8 is of God, Who created it out of His L..
T-10.......in.3:5 Can anything exceed the L. of God? Can
T-10.........I.1:4 the laws of God protect it by His L.. Any
T-10...... III.3:4 the L. of God he has forgotten. Your
T-10....... V.7:4 the Sonship, because of His L. for His Son
T-10....... V.7:6 The L. of God is in everything He created,

T-10..... V.10:1 yourself, and how much God, in His L.,
T-11.........I.7:1 Could any part of God be without His L.,
T-11.........I.7:1 and could any part of His L. be contained
T-11...... IV.6:4 But love yourself with the L. of Christ, for
T-11...... IV.7:5 the L. and the loveliness of God, as perfect
T-11...... IV.8:3 Sharing the perfect L. of the Father the
T-11... V.12:10 the L. of God completely protects them.
T-11...... VI.7:2 The L. of God surrounds His Son whom
T-11..VIII.11:6 you will learn of the Father's L. for you.
T-12........II.3:6 Healing is the L. of Christ for His Father
T-12........II.6:5 nothing can withstand the L. of Christ for
T-12........II.6:5 for His Father, or His Father's L. for Him.
T-12...... IV.4:7 whom He loves with the L. of the Father.
T-12....... V.4:1 The Holy Spirit's L. is your strength, for
T-12...... VI.5:6 He knows of the Father's L. for Him. And
T-12...... VI.5:8 holding out the Father's L. to you in the
T-12...... VI.6:2 God. Christ's L. for you is His Love for His
T-12...... VI.6:2 Love for you is His L. for His Father,
T-12...... VI.6:2 because He knows His Father's L. for Him
T-12.... VIII.2:2 His Father's L. holds him in perfect peace,
T-12.... VIII.4:1 your Father's L. you can never forget Him,
T-13.........I.1:2 for sharing the Father's L. for His Son, He
T-13.........I.6:7 has always extended the L. of his Father.
T-13...... III.4:1 His L. because you think it would crush
T-13...... III.4:4 you come to the L. that is hidden there.
T-13.. III.12:10 it, for L. is in you and will lead you there.
T-13..... VII.6:3 L. leads so gladly! As you follow Him, you
T-13..... VII.8:3 and His Son returns his Father's L. forever
T-13........X.9:1 do not remember your Father's L.. And
T-14...... III.3:4 conviction born of the L. of God and of
T-14..... III.15:7 Never forget the L. of God, Who has
T-14..... III.16:4 you? Learn of His wisdom and His L., and
T-14..... III.17:1 Whose equal L. is given equally to all alike
T-14..... III.17:5 L. for everyone who will be touched in
T-14...... IV.4:9 nor anyone unworthy of His perfect L..
T-14..... IV.4:12 this small gift of appreciation for His L.,
T-14...... IV.5:6 waking gladly to His L. and Holiness that
T-14....... V.1:2 into a radiant message of God's L., to
T-14..... VII.7:8 accepting it as His, with all His L. as yours
T-14....... IX.4:3 immortal assurance of their Father's L..
T-14..... X.12:8 of His Son with all the L. He holds for him
T-14..... X.12:9 Nor will the power of all His L. be absent
T-15..... V.11:2 out of His need to extend His L.. With
T-15.... VIII.3:4 redemption over to your Redeemer's L..
T-15...... IX.5:1 let the Holy Spirit tell you of the L. of God
T-15........X.7:1 a sacrifice do you believe His L. demands!
T-15........X.7:6 total L. would completely destroy you.
T-16........II.7:8 on whom God loves with perfect L.?
T-16........II.8:1 Do not interpret against God's L., for you
T-16.. IV.11:14 willingness to love and all the L. of God,
T-16.... IV.13:9 no veil the L. of God in us together cannot
T-16....... V.4:2 is the renunciation of the L. of God, and
T-16...... VI.2:3 it. For the L. of God, no longer seek for
T-16...... VI.2:5 L. will be unable to find you and comfort
T-16.... VI.11:6 Wait no longer, for the L. of God and *you.*
T-16... VII.10:2 The power of God and all His L., without
T-16... VII.10:2 the plan of Atonement arising from His L.
T-16... VII.12:4 *to remember Your forgiveness and Your L..*
T-17..... IV.10:5 The power of Heaven, the L. of God, the
T-18.........I.7:1 you, say only, "God is not fear, but L.,"
T-18.. VIII.10:4 all the L. of its Creator shining upon it.
T-19.......I.10:4 It is His L. that joins you and your brother
T-19.......I.10:4 L. you would keep no one separate from
T19... IV.D.2:2 with joy because He is in His Father's L.,
T19... IV.D.2:3 bright Rays of His Father's L. that light
T19... IV.D.5:6 of the obstacles to love, L. Itself has called.
T19... IV.D.5:9 you heard the Voice of L. beyond them,
T-20.. VI.12:11 keep remembrance of His L. apart from
T-21...... VI.9:4 This gracious plan was given love by L..
T-21...... VI.9:5 L. plans is like Itself in this: Being united,
T-21.... VIII.2:4 as is the L. of God for His creation. Sure in
T-22...... IV.3:7 The L. of Christ will light your face, and
T-22...... IV.6:1 To all who share the L. of God the grace
T-22...... VI.2:4 outcome as He is sure of His Creator's L..
T-23...... IV.4:1 of your relationship is like the L. of God.
T-23...... IV.9:8 Who with the L. of God upholding him
T-24........II.6:6 and to receive the L. of God forever?
T-24......II.11:4 God's L. gave you to him and him to you
T-24....... V.6:3 His L. for God replaces all the fear you

T-24....... V.6:9 that each might offer you the **L.** of God.
T-24....... VI.3:4 It is His Will you share His **L.** for you, and
T-24.... VI.10:5 how great the **L.** of God for you must be,
T-24. VII.10:10 witness to His **L.** and shared His purpose,
T-25.........I.1:7 and pure and worthy of His everlasting **L.**.
T-25....... II.9:3 Would He not make known to you His **L.**,
T-25....... II.11:5 apart from all God's **L.** as given equally.
T-25....... IV.4:1 Would you not do this for the **L.** of God?
T-25....... V.6:4 forgiveness will you understand His **L.** for
T-25... VII.10:1 What is dependable except God's **L.**?
T-25.... VIII.9:1 What can **L.** ask of you who think that all
T-26....... II.7:7 its place the **L.** of God can be remembered
T-26....... II.8:4 His **L.** kept perfectly intact and undefiled.
T-26...... IV.4:4 him of his Father's **L.** as surely as the rest.
T-26...... IV.6:3 join the mighty chorus to the **L.** of God!
T-26...... V.10:7 restored unto his Father's perfect **L.**. And
T-26..... VII.7:5 brought His **L.** at last to vengeance's heels
T-26....... X.3:7 to sacrifice his Father's **L.** and yours as
T-29.........I.1:4 in His eternal **L.** is quite impossible. For it
T-29.........I.1:5 His **L.** could harbor just a hint of hate, His
T-29.........I.1:8 For He must be deceptive in His **L.**. Be
T-29.........I.1:9 and leave a gap between you and His **L.**,
T-29.........I.8:7 around the happy message, "God is **L.**."
T-29.........I.9:4 to hold you back an instant from His **L.**?
T-29...... III.2:2 He made weak because He shared His **L.**?
T-29...... IV.6:7 For at its center is His **L.** for you, which
T-29....... V.4:1 the mirror of his Father's **L.** for you, the
T-29....... V.4:1 soft reminder of his Father's **L.** by which
T-29... VII.10:5 Let Him remind you of His **L.** for you, and
T-30....... II.2:7 be reminded of His **L.** and learn your will.
T-30....... III.2:2 can be a substitute for God the Father's **L.**
T-30....... V.7:6 beyond forgiveness to the **L.** of God. Yet is
T-30....... V.7:7 Yet is the **L.** of Christ accepted first. And
T-30....... V.8:5 as surely as His Father's **L.** rests upon Him
T-31.......I.7:10 that reflects the **L.** of God is stronger still.
T-31.........I.9:3 the certainty with which He knows His **L.**.
T-31.........I.9:4 only if His Son is innocent can He be **L.**.
T-31.......I.10:1 as God's **L.** must be remembered when he
T-31.......I.10:6 and you will know in Him that God is **L.**.
T-31....... II.7:1 Because he is your equal in God's **L.**, you
T-31...... IV.9:2 His Presence and remembered not His **L.**.
T-31..... VII.8:2 of true creation has the Lord of **L.** and life
W-pI........46.h God is the **L.** in which I forgive.
W-pI.....46.2:1 **L.** is nevertheless the basis of forgiveness.
W-pI.....46.4:4 *God is the* **L.** *in which I forgive you, [name].*
W-pI.....46.5:3 *God is the* **L.** *in which I forgive myself.* Then
W-pI.....46.5:5 *God is the* **L.** *with which I love myself. God is*
W-pI.....46.5:6 *myself. God is the* **L.** *in which I am blessed.*
W-pI.....46.7:5 silently: *God is the* **L.** *in which I forgive you.*
W-pI........50.h I am sustained by the **L.** of God.
W-pI.....50.2:1 are your replacements for the **L.** of God.
W-pI.....50.3:1 Only the **L.** of God will protect you in all
W-pI.....50.4:3 all your faith in the **L.** of God within you;
W-pI.....50.4:5 Through the **L.** of God within you, you
W-pI.....55.2:4 anything but a reflection of the **L.** of God
W-pI.....55.2:4 of the Love of God and the **L.** of His Son. It
W-pI.....56.3:4 it to the world that reflects the **L.** of God.
W-pI.....60.1:1 (46) God is the **L.** in which I forgive. God
W-pI.....60.1:5 It is the reflection of God's **L.** on earth. It
W-pI.....60.1:6 that the **L.** of God can reach down to me
W-pI.....60.2:6 begin to remember the **L.** I chose to forget
W-pI.....60.5:1 (50) I am sustained by the **L.** of God. As I
W-pI.....60.5:2 to God's Voice, I am sustained by His **L.**.
W-pI.....60.5:3 His **L.** lights up the world for me to see.
W-pI.....60.5:4 His **L.** reminds me that His Son is sinless.
W-pI.....66.6:3 is not. **L.** cannot give evil, and what is not
W-pI.....75.9:3 Give thanks for mercy and the **L.** of God.
W-pI...76.10:4 About the **L.** your Father has for you.
W-pI...95.13:4 His strength within you and His **L.** forever
W-pI.....97.2:2 with all your Father's **L.** and peace and joy
W-pI.....99.5:5 one thing must still be true; God is still **L.**,
W-pI.....99.6:8 *here. God still is* **L.**, *and this is not His Will.*
W-pI.....99.9:8 Self as **L.** which has no opposite in you.
W-pI...99.11:4 *here. God still is* **L.**, *and this is not His Will.*
W-pI...102.5:2 He Whose **L.** created him as loving as
W-pI......103.h God, being **L.**, is also happiness.
W-pI...103.2:2 to the fear of God, forgetting being **L.**, He
W-pI...103.2:4 *God, being* **L.**, *is also happiness. To fear Him*
W-pI...103.3:3 God, being **L.**, it will be given you. Bolster
W-pI...103.3:5 *God, being* **L.**, *is also happiness. And it is*
W-pI...117.1:1 (103) God, being **L.**, is also happiness. *Let*
W-pI...117.3:2 God, being **L.**, is also happiness. On the
W-pI...123.3:1 His **L.** forever will remain shining on you,
W-pI...124.4:1 Today we will not doubt His **L.** for us, nor
W-pI...125.7:4 His **L.** is everything you are and that He is;
W-pI. 126.11:6 your mind to His correction and His **L.**.
W-pI...127.9:6 And He will bless the lesson with His **L.**.
W-pI. 127.11:4 Now are they all our brothers in God's **L.**.
W-pI. 127.12:4 *bless you, brother, with the* **L.** *of God, which*
W-pI...131.5:1 His perfect, timeless and unchanging **L.**.
W-pI. 132.11:1 does not share His timelessness and **L.**.
W-pI...134.2:5 Him, reflects His laws and radiates His **L.**.
W-pI. 139.10:2 way rejoicing in the endless **L.** of God. It is
W-pI. 139.11:6 and how our Father's **L.** contains them all.
WpI. rIV.in6:2 one will bring the message of His **L.** to you
W-pI. 151.14:1 wills His Son, as proof of His eternal **L.**.
W-pI. 152.10:5 his perfect sinlessness, his Father's **L.**, his
W-pI. 153.17:1 remembrance of our mission and His **L.**.
W-pI. 155.14:1 He may speak to you and tell you of His **L.**
W-pI. 155.14:1 how great His trust; how limitless His **L.**.
W-pI...157.9:1 except His shining face and perfect **L.**.
W-pI...162.2:1 happiness, His **L.** and His completion.
W-pI...162.4:3 God places all His gifts and all His **L.**, to
W-pI...163.9:2 *of Your* **L.** *which shines in everything. We*
W-pI...165.6:6 God's sustaining **L.** and from his home.
W-pI...165.8:4 His **L.** remains beyond our every fear. The
W-pI. 168.1:11 He loves him with a never-changing **L.**.
W-pI...168.2:1 If you but knew the meaning of His **L.**,
W-pI...168.2:3 in it lies remembrance of His **L.**. Would
W-pI...168.6:4 through His Own Voice, His Word, His **L.**
W-pI...169.1:1 Grace is an aspect of the **L.** of God which
W-pI...169.2:1 Grace is acceptance of the **L.** of God
W-pI. 170.10:4 more fearful than the Heart of **L.** Itself?
WpI...rV.in4:3 *God is but* **L.**, *and therefore so am I.* This Self
WpI...rV.in4:4 This Self alone knows **L.**. This Self alone is
WpI...rV.in4:5 Itself, is perfect in Its knowledge and Its **L.**
WpI.rV.in10:8 we say: *God is but* **L.**, *and therefore so am I.*
W-pI......171.h God is but **L.**, and therefore so am I.
W-pI...171.1:2 God. God is but **L.**, and therefore so am I.
W-pI...171.2:2 own. God is but **L.**, and therefore so am I.
W-pI......172.h God is but **L.**, and therefore so am I.
W-pI...172.1:2 lies. God is but **L.**, and therefore so am I.
W-pI...172.2:2 God. God is but **L.**, and therefore so am I.
W-pI......173.h God is but **L.**, and therefore so am I.
W-pI...173.1:2 way. God is but **L.**, and therefore so am I.
W-pI...173.2:2 God is but **L.**, and therefore so am I.
W-pI......174.h God is but **L.**, and therefore so am I.
W-pI...174.1:2 now. God is but **L.**, and therefore so am I.
W-pI...174.2:2 God is but **L.**, and therefore so am I.
W-pI......175.h God is but **L.**, and therefore so am I.
W-pI...175.1:2 God is but **L.**, and therefore so am I.
W-pI...175.2:3 here. God is but **L.**, and therefore so am I.
W-pI......176.h God is but **L.**, and therefore so am I.
W-pI...176.1:2 God. God is but **L.**, and therefore so am I.
W-pI...176.2:2 me. God is but **L.**, and therefore so am I.
W-pI......177.h God is but **L.**, and therefore so am I.
W-pI...177.1:3 free. God is but **L.**, and therefore so am I.
W-pI...177.2:2 God is but **L.**, and therefore so am I.
W-pI......178.h God is but **L.**, and therefore so am I.
W-pI...178.1:2 God. God is but **L.**, and therefore so am I.
W-pI...178.2:2 God. God is but **L.**, and therefore so am I.
W-pI......179.h God is but **L.**, and therefore so am I.
W-pI...179.1:2 God. God is but **L.**, and therefore so am I.
W-pI...179.2:3 now. God is but **L.**, and therefore so am I.
W-pI......180.h God is but **L.**, and therefore so am I.
W-pI...180.1:3 God is but **L.**, and therefore so am I.
W-pI...180.2:2 me. God is but **L.**, and therefore so am I.
W-pI...181.8:5 **L.** He feels for us becomes our own as well
W-pI. 186.13:5 For **L.** must give, and what is given in His
W-pI. 187.10:5 shine in our reflection of our Father's **L.**.
W-pI......189.h I feel the **L.** of God within me now.
W-pI...189.1:7 To feel the **L.** of God within you is to see
W-pI...189.3:1 This is the world the **L.** of God reveals. It
W-pI...189.4:1 to those who feel God's **L.** in them. Their
W-pI...189.5:5 If you feel the **L.** of God within you, you
W-pI...189.6:1 its **L.** which knows us perfect as itself, its
W-pI...189.6:1 sight which is the gift its **L.** bestows on us.
W-pI...189.6:3 It is as sure as **L.** itself, to which it carries
W-pI .. 189.9:4 His **L.** will blaze its pathway of itself.
W-pI .. 189.9:8 every opened door His **L.** shines outward
W-pI .. 190.2:5 of abandonment by an Eternal **L.**, which
W-pI 192.10:5 His Father's **L.** for him belongs to you.
W-pI .. 193.8:4 God would have him not forget His **L.**,
W-pI .. 193.8:4 Love, and all the gifts His **L.** brings with it
W-pI 193.13:5 the **L.** of God the Father down to earth at
W-pI 195.10:3 the **L.** which is the Source of all creation.
W-pI 196.11:4 Him to save you from illusions by His **L.**,
W-pI .. 199.8:6 His **L.** and happiness each time you say: *I*
W-pI .. 207.1:3 *away, as I accept His boundless* **L.** *for me.* I
W-pI .. 209.1:1 (189) I feel the **L.** of God within me now.
W-pI .. 209.1:2 *The* **L.** *of God is what created me. The Love*
W-pI .. 209.1:3 *The* **L.** *of God is everything I am. The Love of*
W-pI .. 209.1:4 *The* **L.** *of God proclaimed me as His Son. The*
W-pI .. 209.1:5 *The* **L.** *of God within me sets me free.* I am
W-pI .. 220.1:3 *home, and peace is certain as the* **L.** *of God.* I
W-pII .... in.7:8 You, and rest in confidence upon Your **L.**,
W-pII .... in.8:5 His **L.** has called to us unceasingly since
W-pII .. in.10:3 Instead of words, we need but feel His **L.**.
W-pII . 225.1:1 *Father, I must return Your* **L.** *for me, for*
W-pII . 225.1:1 *same, and You have given all Your* **L.** *to me. I*
W-pII . 231.1:1 *What can I seek for, Father, but Your* **L.**?
W-pII . 231.1:3 *Yet is Your* **L.** *the only thing I seek, or ever*
W-pII . 232.1:4 *all my thoughts be still of You and of Your* **L.**
W-pII . 233.1:7 **L.** *whose tenderness I cannot comprehend,*
W-pII . 234.2:1 *lose the memory of You and of Your* **L.**. *We*
W-pII . 235.1:3 but remember that God's **L.** surrounds
W-pII . 235.2:2 *is mine. Your* **L.** *created me, and made my*
W-pII . 238.2:2 And how dear His Son, created by His **L.**,
W-pII . 238.2:2 Him Whose **L.** is made complete in him.
W-pII . 240.1:8 fear in us, for we are each a part of **L.** Itself
W-pII . 244.1:2 *and he will recollect his safety and Your* **L.**,
W-pII . 245.2:3 Whose **L.** we recognize because we share
W-pII . 248.2:3 *Now is Your* **L.** *remembered, and my own.*
W-pII ..... 4.4:4 loves him with an everlasting **L.** which his
W-pII . 252.1:4 but from the boundless **L.** of God Himself
W-pII . 254.2:6 And in the stillness, hallowed by His **L.**,
W-pII . 258.1:4 God is our only goal, our only **L.**. We have
W-pII . 262.1:8 *are our Source, eternally united in Your* **L.**;
W-pII . 263.1:1 *Spirit entered into it, Your* **L.** *gave life to it.*
W-pII .... 264.h I am surrounded by the **L.** of God.
W-pII . 264.1:4 *Your Son and keeps him safe is* **L.** *itself.*
W-pII . 264.1:5 *without the* **L.** *which holds all things within*
W-pII . 264.1:7 *to be at peace within Your everlasting* **L.**.
W-pII . 266.2:1 in each of us; united in the holy **L.** of God.
W-pII . 267.1:1 me is all the life that God created in His **L.**
W-pII . 267.2:2 *is beating in the peace the Heart of* **L.** *created*
W-pII . 272.1:7 *I am surrounded by Your* **L.**, *forever still,*
W-pII . 276.1:6 us. Deny we were created in His **L.** and we
W-pII . 279.1:1 God's Son is not abandoned by His **L.**.
W-pII ..... 7.4:3 the memory of all your Father's **L.** will not
W-pII ..... 7.5:2 It is a Call from **L.** to Love, that It be but
W-pII ..... 7.5:2 It is a Call from Love to **L.**, that It be but
W-pII . 282.2:1 *Father, Your Name is* **L.** *and so is mine. Such*
W-pII . 283.1:5 *the light of Heaven and the* **L.** *of God. Is not*
W-pII . 286.1:9 *Your* **L.** *is Heaven, and Your Love is mine.*
W-pII . 286.1:9 *Your Love is Heaven, and Your* **L.** *is mine.*
W-pII ..... 8.4:2 the sure reflection of his Father's **L.**; the
W-pII . 295.2:2 *and thus allow the Holy Spirit's* **L.** *to bless all*
W-pII . 295.2:2 *upon, that His forgiving* **L.** *may rest on me.*
W-pII . 298.1:5 sure that I go through fear to meet my **L.**.
W-pII ..... 9.5:6 we can reach our Father's **L.** through Him.
W-pII . 302.2:1 Our **L.** awaits us as we go to Him, and
W-pII . 303.1:5 see but sights that show His Father's **L.**.
W-pII . 306.2:4 *Son. But in Your* **L.** *the gift of Christ is his.*
W-pII . 311.2:3 *And so we let Your* **L.** *decide what he whom*
W-pII . 312.1:6 share Christ's **L.** for what he looks upon.
W-pII . 318.1:7 I am God's Son, His one eternal **L.**. I am
W-pII . 323.1:1 *Your* **L.** *come streaming in to his awareness,*
W-pII . 326.1:8 *effects into the tranquil Heaven of Your* **L.**,
W-pII . 327.2:4 *surety of Your abiding* **L.** *is gained at last.*
W-pII . 330.1:3 when God holds out His power and His **L.**
W-pII . 331.1:5 *How could I think that* **L.** *has left Itself?*
W-pII . 331.1:6 *There is no will except the Will of* **L.**. *Fear is a*
W-pII . 332.2:3 *Your* **L.** *has given us the means to set it free.*
W-pII . 336.2:2 *my mind, Your* **L.** *is still abiding in my heart.*
W-pII . 337.1:6 to feel God's **L.** protecting me from harm,
W-pII . 340.2:6 awake in Heaven in the Heart of **L.**.

W-pII..341.1:3 *Smile, with all Your L. bestowed upon us,*
W-pII.....346.h me, And I forget all things except His L..
W-pII..346.1:5 *I would forget all things except Your L.. I*
W-pII..346.2:2 when we forget all things except God's L..
W-pII..348.1:2 *Surrounding me is everlasting L.. I have no*
W-pII.....350.h Miracles mirror God's eternal L.. To offer
W-pII..350.2:2 will be restored to us in the reality of L..
W-pII....14.1:1 *and whole, shining in the reflection of His L.*
W-pII....14.1:5 *I am the Heaven where His L. resides. I am*
W-pII..355.1:8 *You as his Father and Creator, and his L..*
W-pII..356.1:4 *him. The miracle reflects Your L., and thus it*
W-pII..358.1:6 *let me not forget Your L. and care, keeping*
W-ep .........6:8 His L. surrounds you, and of this be sure;
M-12..........2:3 internal now reflects only the L. of God.
M-13..........4:9 and remembrance of his Father's L.. Who
M-17........9:13 L. is Cause of everything beyond all fear,
M-18........3:11 *His L. remains the only thing there is. Fear is*
M-27..........3:2 His L. is blotted out in the idea, which
M-27..........4:6 There is either a god of fear or One of L..
M-27..........5:5 is indeed the death of God, if He is L..
M-28..........5:2 have disappeared and L. looks on Itself.
M-28..........5:5 His sinlessness, His L. behind all forms,
M-29..........7:1 you are His completion and His L..
C-5............6:4 of Christ's single message of the L. of God.
C-5...........6:10 *Nothing you can do can change Eternal L..*
C-6.............3:9 And He brings the L. of your Father to
C-ep...........1:9 His L. is but an instant farther on the road
P-2.......VII.6:5 Whose L. is in him and Who cannot fail.
P-3......... II.5:3 a gift from their Creator as a sign of His L.
S-1 .........in.1:3 joyous concord of the L. They give forever
S-1 .........in.1:7 The L. They share is what all prayer will
S-1 ...........I.2:9 is always a song of thanksgiving and of L..
S-1 ...........I.4:4 have no gods before Him; no L. but His.
S-1 ...........I.5:3 fully entitled to everything L. has to offer?
S-1 ...........I.5:4 And it is to L. you go in prayer. Prayer is
S-1 ...........I.5:5 a giving up of yourself to be at one with L.
S-2 ...........I.8:3 from death by offering Christ's L. to him.
S-2 ......... II.8:6 redeemed from sin and in the L. of God.
S-2 ........III.6:8 to come from His eternal vigilance and L..
S-3 ...........I.4:3 and the remembrance of his Father's L..
S-3 ...........I.5:3 the world or to the everlasting L. of God.
S-3 ........IV.3:3 the Cause of healing is Himself, His L.,
S-3 ........IV.3:4 L. has never changed and never will. You
S-3 ........IV.5:5 He Who is L. becomes the source of fear,
S-3 ........IV.7:2 of everlasting L. and perfect peace. My
S-3 ........IV.7:3 with all creation, in the holiness of L.. Be
S-3 ........IV.8:7 Do not refuse to hear the Call for L.. Do
S-3 ......IV.10:6 pain. Do not abandon L.. Remember this;

## love 1069

*Love*

*See also* love-encompassment, Self-love; Appendix C

T-in............1:6 *does not aim at teaching the meaning of l.,*
T-in............1:8 *The opposite of l. is fear, but what is all-*
T-1...........I.1:4 same. All expressions of l. are maximal.
T-1...........I.3:1 occur naturally as expressions of l.. The
T-1...........I.3:2 real miracle is the l. that inspires them. In
T-1...........I.3:3 everything that comes from l. is a miracle.
T-1...........I.9:2 Like all expressions of l., which are always
T-1...........I.9:3 more l. both to the giver *and* the receiver.
T-1........ I.11:3 prayer l. is received, and through miracles
T-1........ I.11:3 and through miracles l. is expressed.
T-1........ I.35:1 Miracles are expressions of l., but they
T-1......... II.2:7 it is an experience of unspeakable l..
T-1......... II.3:4 is therefore a sign of l. among equals.
T-1......... II.3:8 is also entitled to l. because he is a brother
T-1........IV.2:7 its errors, which are merely lacks of l..
T-1........IV.2:9 If a mind perceives without l., it perceives
T-1........IV.3:1 Darkness is lack of light as sin is lack of l..
T-1........VI.5:4 *Perfect l. casts out fear. If fear exists, Then*
T-1........VI.5:5 *If fear exists, Then there is not perfect l..* But:
T-1........VI.5:7 But: *Only perfect l. exists. If there is fear, It*
T-2...........I.5:6 unaffected by all expressions of lack of l..
T-2........ I.5:12 by lack of l. from without and capable,
T-2........ I.5:12 conditions proceeding from lack of l. in
T-2......... II.4:3 was l. and the Atonement was an *act* of
T-2......... II.4:3 love and the Atonement was an *act* of l..
T-2........VI.7:2 you must somehow have chosen not to l.,
T-2........ VI.7:6 is fear. Fear arises from lack of l.. The only
T-2........ VI.7:7 only remedy for lack of l. is perfect love.
T-2........ VI.7:7 only remedy for lack of love is perfect l..
T-2........ VI.7:8 is perfect love. Perfect l. is the Atonement.
T-2........ VI.8:4 loveless, having chosen without l.. This is
T-2.....VII.3:14 in the second, and all l. in the first. The
T-2.....VII.3:15 conflict is therefore one between l. and
T-2.......VII.4:4 rests entirely on mastery through l.. In the
T-2.......VII.5:3 Fear is really nothing and l. is everything.
T-2.......VII.7:7 that the only real mastery is through l..
T-2..... VIII.4:4 the mind can begin to look with l. on its
T-3........ III.1:7 and time, it is subject to either fear or l..
T-3........ III.1:8 produce fear and true perceptions foster l.
T-3........ III.5:3 When you l. someone you have perceived
T-4......... II.4:1 of the l. of animals for their offspring, and
T-4......... II.4:4 as God does to His creations,–with l.,
T-4...........III.h L. without Conflict
T-4........ III.4:2 You do not l. what you made, and what
T-4........ III.4:2 made, and what you made does not l. you.
T-4........ III.4:5 with the l. you feel for the ego because you
T-4........ III.4:6 made it. No l. in this world is without this
T-4........ III.4:6 since no ego has experienced l. without
T-4........ III.4:7 L. will enter immediately into any mind
T-4........ III.7:7 I will l. you and honor you and maintain
T-4........ III.7:9 Because I wait in l. and not in impatience,
T-4........IV.8:9 your own allegiance, protection and l., the
T-4......IV.8:10 allegiance, protection and l. from it.
T-4.....IV.11:11 natural, because they are expressions of l..
T-4........ VI.7:6 L. does not conquer all things, but it does
T-4........ VI.8:6 That is because the function of l. is one.
T-5.........in.2:2 If fear and l. cannot coexist, and if it is
T-5.........in.2:2 the only possible whole state is that of l..
T-5.........in.2:3 There is no difference between l. and joy.
T-5.........in.3:6 of God to l. his neighbor except as himself
T-5....... V.4:10 ego does not perceive sin as a lack of l.,
T-5........ VI.2:7 exchange guilt for joy, viciousness for l.,
T-5...... VI.12:3 Infinite patience calls upon infinite l., and
T-5.......VII.5:1 with a lack of l. to one of God's creations.
T-6...............h THE LESSONS OF L.
T-6.........in.1:4 of attack rather than of l. must follow.
T-6..........I.8:5 A church that does not inspire l. has a
T-6.........I.13:2 clear: *Teach only l., for that is what you are.*
T-6.........I.14:3 own imperfect l. made them vulnerable to
T-6.........I.15:1 its gospel is really only the message of l.. If
T-6.........I.17:3 You cannot l. what you do not appreciate,
T-6......... II.5:3 Instead of anger this arouses l. for both,
T-6........ III.2:3 You are only l., but when you deny this,
T-6........ III.2:4 of the crucifixion was, "Teach only l., for
T-6........ III.4:9 Teach only l., and learn that love is yours
T-6........ III.4:9 and learn that l. is yours and you are love.
T-6........ III.4:9 and learn that love is yours and you are l..
T-6........ IV.2:3 You made the ego without l., and so it
T-6........ IV.2:3 ego without love, and so it does not l. you.
T-6........ IV.2:4 not remain within the Kingdom without l.
T-6........ IV.2:4 without love, and since the Kingdom *is* l.,
T-6......V.A.5:6 fear as well as l. can be communicated;
T-7...........I.3:3 To create is to l.. Love extends outward
T-7...........I.3:4 love. L. extends outward simply because it
T-7...........I.5:1 I gave only l. to the Kingdom because I
T-7........ IV.7:9 L. needs only this invitation. It comes
T-7......... V.5:7 L. is incapable of any exceptions. Only if
T-7......... V.9:2 may worship out of fear, but will never l..
T-7......... V.9:3 you will l. because you will understand it.
T-7......... V.9:4 it part of you, you have accepted it with l..
T-7......... V.9:5 understanding, in appreciation and in l..
T-7......... V.9:6 does not appreciate it and does not l. it. It
T-7....... V.11:6 calls upon you to l. God and His creation.
T-7........ VI.1:1 you can l. the Sonship only as one, you
T-7........ VI.1:5 Fear and l. make or create, depending on
T-7........ VI.1:8 all of Them if he regards Them with l..
T-7........ VI.2:1 The mind that accepts attack cannot l..
T-7........ VI.2:2 That is because it believes it can destroy l.,
T-7........ VI.2:2 therefore does not understand what l. is.
T-7........ VI.2:3 is. If it does not understand what l. is, it
T-7........ VI.4:3 while the ego does not l. you it *is* faithful to
T-7........ VI.4:6 makes it treacherous to l. because you *are*
T-7........ VI.4:6 it treacherous to love because you *are* l..
T-7........ VI.4:7 L. is your power, which the ego must deny
T-7........ VI.6:6 appreciation and appreciation brings l..
T-7....... VII.1:1 deprived, because denial is as total as l.. It
T-7....... VII.1:2 part of the Sonship as it is to l. it in part.
T-7....... VII.1:3 Nor is it possible to l. it totally at times.
T-7....... VII.3:3 You cannot l. this. Yet you can very easily
T-7....... VII.6:5 But l. everything He created, of which you
T-7......VIII.1:1 that without extension there can be no l..
T-7......... X.8:5 Being a lesson in sharing it is a lesson in l.,
T-7........ XI.3:3 it protect his peace and shine l. upon him
T-8..........II.7:2 in strength and in l. and in peace. It has
T-8........ IV.3:7 the world *is* the belief that l. is impossible.
T-8........ IV.8:2 is creation, because it is l.. Whom you
T-8........ IV.8:3 Whom you seek to imprison you do not l..
T-8........ IV.8:4 l. him and you cannot identify with him.
T-8........ VI.5:7 Your creations l. you as you love your
T-8........ VI.5:7 you l. your Father for the gift of creation.
T-8........ VI.8:9 Through our creations we extend our l.,
T-8........ IX.5:2 to wake is the reflection of the will to l.,
T-8........ IX.5:2 all healing involves replacing fear with l..
T-8........ IX.7:3 works of l. because we share this Oneness.
T-9..........I.11:8 seeing. If you deny l., you will not know it
T-9..........II.7:1 I l. you for the truth in you, as God does.
T-9........ III.7:6 Atonement is no more separate than l..
T-9........ III.7:7 be separate because it comes from l.. Any
T-9....... VII.3:1 Spirit looks with l. on all He perceives, He
T-9....... VII.3:1 all He perceives, He looks with l. on you.
T-9....... VII.3:5 Spirit's, because the ego does not l. you. It
T-9......VIII.8:1 because l. is returned and pride is not.
T-10..........I.1:3 *God.* The law of creation is that you l. your
T-10...... III.1:1 have not attacked God and you do l. Him.
T-10...... III.3:2 L. cannot suffer, because it cannot attack.
T-10...... III.3:3 of l. therefore brings invulnerability with
T-10...... III.4:2 God created l., not idolatry. All forms of
T-10...... III.6:4 merit that I contribute to you but my l.,
T-10.. III.10:11 fear l. because of its perfect harmlessness,
T-10....... V.6:3 that if you recognized your l. for Him, you
T-10....... V.6:4 of Him therefore means that you l. Him,
T-10....... V.8:1 for healing but only to the God of l., for
T-10....... V.8:5 without l. on God and His creation, from
T-10....... V.9:1 eternal can be loved, for l. does not die.
T-10..... V.10:6 God will never cease to l. His Son, and His
T-10..... V.10:6 and His Son will never cease to l. Him.
T-10..... V.14:1 Arrogance is the denial of l., because love
T-10..... V.14:1 because l. shares and arrogance withholds
T-11........in.4:8 Will you not answer the call of l. with joy?
T-11........I.5:10 of l. does not stop because you do not see
T-11..........I.6:6 L. does not limit, and what it creates is
T-11..........I.6:8 l. is as boundless as His because it *is* His.
T-11.........II.3:1 And denial is as total as l.. You cannot
T-11....... IV.1:6 what God created as yourself without l..
T-11....... IV.6:4 But l. yourself with the Love of Christ, for
T-11....... IV.6:4 of Christ, for so does your Father l. you.
T-11...... V.10:5 overlook l. you are overlooking yourself,
T-11...... V.12:9 the insane would choose fear in place of l.,
T-11...... V.12:9 believe that l. can be gained by attack. But
T-11..VIII.11:3 To l. yourself is to heal yourself, and you
T-11..VIII.11:4 as we live together and l. together. Be not
T-11..VIII.11:6 L. him who is beloved of his Father, and
T-12..........I.6:2 both are capable of bringing l. into your
T-12........I.8:10 learning to perceive attack as a call for l..
T-12........I.8:13 you. For fear *is* a call for l., in unconscious
T-12..........I.9:5 Fear and l. are the only emotions of which
T-12........I.9:10 You have denied its power to conceal l.,
T-12........I.9:11 across the face of l. has disappeared.
T-12........I.10:1 If you would look upon l., which *is* the
T-12........I.10:4 fear with l. and translate error into truth.
T-12.........II.1:2 If to l. oneself is to heal oneself, those who
T-12.........II.1:2 those who are sick do not l. themselves.
T-12.........II.1:3 are asking for the l. that would heal them,
T-12.........II.3:1 Perceive in sickness but another call for l.
T-12.........II.3:3 is to recognize in hatred the call for l..
T-12.........II.3:5 Answer his call for l., and yours is
T-12.........II.5:7 The goal of l. is but your right, and it
T-12.........II.6:5 not let your hatred stand in the way of l.,
T-12.........II.8:1 There is no fear in perfect l.. We will but
T-12.........II.9:1 have tried to banish l. have not succeeded
T-12....... III.5:3 Any response other than l. arises from a
T-12....... III.8:2 God does l. the real world, and those who
T-12....... IV.1:1 The ego is certain that l. is dangerous,
T-12....... IV.1:2 to be intensely engaged in the search for l.

T-12......IV.1:3 encouraging the search for l. very actively,
T-12......IV.2:3 For the ego cannot l., and in its frantic
T-12......IV.2:3 for l. it is seeking what it is afraid to find.
T-12......IV.3:2 him. Being unable to l., the ego would be
T-12......IV.3:4 The ego will therefore distort l., and teach
T-12......IV.3:4 and teach you that l. really calls forth the
T-12......IV.3:5 teaching, then, and you will search for l.,
T-12....... V.1:1 Only l. is strong because it is undivided.
T-12....... V.4:2 trust your own l. when you attack it. You
T-12....... V.4:3 cannot learn of perfect l. with a split mind
T-12....... V.6:1 You do not know the meaning of l., and
T-12....... V.7:7 so weakened your mind that you cannot l.
T-12....... V.7:7 curriculum you have chosen is against l.,
T-12...... VI.3:2 whatever part of it you look upon with l..
T-12...... VI.4:4 see with l. if you accept His vision as yours
T-12...... VI.6:4 extension. L. transfers to love without any
T-12...... VI.6:4 extension. Love transfers to l. without any
T-12...... VI.7:6 join in perfect l. of God and of each other.
T-12..... VII.6:5 It does not find l., for that is not what it is
T-12..... VII.8:1 you want only l. you will see nothing else.
T-12..... VII.8:5 L., too, is recognized by its messengers. If
T-12..... VII.8:6 If you make l. manifest, its messengers
T-12..... VII.9:4 give anything but l. to anyone or anything
T-12..... VII.9:4 really receive anything but l. from them.
T-12...... VIII.h The Attraction of L. for Love
T-12...... VIII.h The Attraction of Love for L.
T-12....VIII.1:4 If you seek l. in order to attack it, you will
T-12....VIII.1:5 it. For if l. is sharing, how can you find it
T-12....VIII.1:7 But offer attack and l. will remain hidden,
T-12..VIII.7:10 attraction of l. for love remains irresistible
T-12..VIII.7:10 attraction of love for l. remains irresistible
T-12..VIII.7:11 function of l. to unite all things unto itself,
T-12....VIII.8:9 Your Father could not cease to l. His Son.
T-13.......in.1:2 of l. and deserving of punishment. But
T-13.......in.2:8 They seem to l., yet they desert and are
T-13.......in.2:9 They appear to lose what they l., perhaps
T-13.......in.3:3 *L. does not kill to save.* If it did, attack would
T-13.......in.4:4 only l. because he has given only love. He
T-13.......in.4:4 only love because he has given only l.. He
T-13.........I.1:4 L. and guilt cannot coexist, and to accept
T-13.........I.6:6 Out of l. he was created, and in love he
T-13.........I.6:6 of love he was created, and in l. he abides.
T-13....... II.9:5 for it is the recognition of l. without fear.
T-13...... III.2:3 is nothing compared to your fear of l..
T-13...... III.2:4 did not believe that it saves you from l..
T-13...... III.2:6 your l. for your Father would impel you to
T-13...... III.2:8 be, is your intense and burning l. of God,
T-13...... III.3:1 harder for you to say "I l." than "I hate"?
T-13...... III.3:2 You associate l. with weakness and hatred
T-13...... III.3:3 response to the call of l. if you heard it,
T-13...... III.4:4 you have used the world to cover your l.,
T-13...... III.5:1 you cannot accept l. because you did not.
T-13...... III.5:4 l. cannot enter where it is not welcome.
T-13...... III.8:2 For you call for l. to your Father as your
T-13...... III.8:7 Only his l. is real, and he will be content
T-13...... III.9:2 But exempt no one from your l., or you
T-13...... III.9:3 total l. you will not be healed completely.
T-13...... III.9:4 for l. cannot enter where there is one spot
T-13.... III.11:3 gentleness of l. respond to his demands,
T-13...... IV.1:2 For this is a course on l., because it is
T-13....... V.1:1 you have but two emotions, l. and fear.
T-13....... V.5:2 l. cannot abide in a world apart, where
T-13....... V.5:5 And you react with fear to l., and draw
T-13....... V.5:6 Yet fear attracts you, and believing it is l.,
T-13....... V.5:7 it, and all the l. your brothers offer you,
T-13....... V.7:9 For you will l. them, and by drawing nigh
T-13....... V.9:3 "vision" comes from fear, as His from l..
T-13..... V.10:6 Him, for His vision is His gift of l. to you,
T-13..... V.11:6 they looked upon themselves with l.,
T-13.... VI.10:4 L. always leads to love. The sick, who ask
T-13.... VI.10:4 Love always leads to l.. The sick, who ask
T-13.... VI.10:5 The sick, who ask for l., are grateful for it,
T-13.... VI.11:6 is bright with l. which you have given it.
T-13.... VI.12:1 is following the laws of l. of your free will,
T-13.... VI.12:3 Those who accept l. of you become your
T-13.... VI.12:3 willing witnesses to the l. you gave them,
T-13.... VI.13:1 of l. are not suspended because you sleep.
T-13..... VII.4:1 to touch you even here, because you l. it.
T-13..... VII.4:2 And what you call with l. will come to you

T-13 .... VII.4:3 L. always answers, being unable to deny a
T-13 .... VII.5:9 into the world He holds out to you in l..
T-13 .... VII.6:2 following not the road that l. points out.
T-13 .... VII.7:3 world about him shines with l. because
T-13 .... VII.7:3 and l. surrounds him without end or flaw.
T-13 .... VII.7:5 In perfect sanity he looks on l., for it is all
T-13 .... VII.7:6 he perceives the arms of l. around him.
T-13 .... VII.9:2 of nightmares for the happy dreams of l..
T-13 .... VII.9:5 Yet the dreams of l. lead unto knowledge.
T-13 .... VII.9:7 L. waits on welcome, not on time, and the
T-13 ... VIII.4:4 Christ's vision looks on everything with l..
T-13 .... IX.5:5 other, calling for punishment instead of l.
T-13 ... IX.8:13 feared was there has been replaced with l..
T-13 ........X.3:6 go. They cannot know they l., and cannot
T-13 ........X.9:2 do not remember how much you l. Him.
T-13 .....X.10:2 way to look within and see the light of l.,
T-13 .....X.10:4 There is no fear in l., for love is guiltless.
T-13 .....X.10:4 There is no fear in love, for l. is guiltless.
T-13 .....X.11:1 Sons unless you l. them all and equally.
T-13 .....X.11:2 L. is not special. If you single out part of
T-13 .....X.11:3 single out part of the Sonship for your l.,
T-13 .....X.11:4 You can l. only as God loves. Seek not to
T-13 .....X.11:5 Seek not to l. unlike Him, for there is no
T-13 .....X.11:5 Him, for there is no l. apart from His.
T-13 .....X.11:6 is true, you will have no idea what l. is like
T-13 .....X.12:3 Let us look upon him together and l. him.
T-13 .....X.12:4 For in l. of him is your guiltlessness. But
T-13 .....X.13:2 is that I l. *only* what God loves with me,
T-13 .....X.13:3 I l. all that He created, and all my faith
T-13 .....X.13:4 is as strong as all the l. I give my Father.
T-13 .....X.14:8 then, lack faith in you and l. Him perfectly
T-14 ........I.3:5 truth, that he has chosen to defend and l..
T-14 ........II.3:9 *you will l. it because you will understand it.*
T-14 ..... III.6:2 darkness with light and fear with l.. If he
T-14 ..... IV.5:5 and trying to teach him guilt instead of l..
T-14 ...... V.2:7 and all the l. you share with God He holds
T-14 ...... V.8:5 to its safe embrace of l. and union. Stand
T-14 .... V.10:8 from fear and re-establish the reign of l..
T-14 .... V.10:9 The power of l. is in His gentleness, which
T-14 ..... VI.2:2 fearful. Attack will always yield to l. if it is
T-14 ..... VI.2:2 always yield to love if it is brought to l.,
T-14 ..... VI.2:3 darkness that the light of l. will not dispel,
T-14 ..... VI.2:4 kept apart from l. cannot share its healing
T-14 ..... VI.3:7 of obscurity only the light of l. remains,
T-14 ..... VI.6:4 enough of l. to make it meaningful if its
T-14 .... VII.5:2 ignorance, and l. does not attack fear.
T-14 . VIII.2:15 Unbroken and uninterrupted l. flows
T-14 ..... IX.4:1 quietly for the return of them that l. it.
T-14 ........X.7:1 one division into two categories; one of l.,
T-14 ........X.7:1 one of love, and the other the call for l..
T-14 ........X.7:2 much too confused either to recognize l.,
T-14 ........X.7:2 everything else is nothing but a call for l..
T-14 .....X.10:5 Everyone seeks for l. as you do, but knows
T-14 .....X.11:5 teach you both his l. and his call for love.
T-14 .....X.11:5 teach you both his love and his call for l..
T-14 .....X.12:2 Where there is l., your brother must give
T-14 .....X.12:3 is. But where there is a call for l., you must
T-15 .......I.14:2 perfect peace and perfect l. for everyone,
T-15 ..... III.3:2 but you will learn to l. it when you realize
T-15 ..... III.8:5 You know not what l. means because you
T-15 ..... III.8:6 L. is not little and love dwells in you, for
T-15 ..... III.8:6 Love is not little and l. dwells in you, for
T-15 ... III.10:5 What my Father loves I l. as He does, and
T-15 ...... V.1:7 you that without the ego, all would be l..
T-15 ...... V.2:2 We have said that to limit l. to part of the
T-15 ...... V.3:1 l. parts of reality and understand what
T-15 ...... V.3:1 of reality and understand what l. means.
T-15 ...... V.3:2 If you would l. unlike to God, Who knows
T-15 ...... V.3:2 unlike to God, Who knows no special l.,
T-15 ...... V.3:3 that *special* relationships, with *special* l.,
T-15 ...... V.4:3 They are not based on changeless l. alone.
T-15 ...... V.4:4 And l., where fear has entered, cannot be
T-15 ...... V.4:6 every relationship becomes a lesson in l..
T-15 ...... V.5:6 All the l. from His. Do not, then, be afraid
T-15 ...... V.6:2 There *is* no substitute for l.. If you would
T-15 ...... V.6:3 to substitute one aspect of l. for another,
T-15 ...... V.6:6 Unless you had seen yourself as without l.,
T-15 ...... V.9:7 free of the past, you see that l. is in you,
T-15 ...... V.9:7 no need to look without and snatch l.

T-15 .....V.10:3 of l. is the meaning God gave to it. Give to
T-15 .....V.11:3 With l. in you, you have no need except to
T-15 .....V.11:6 And it is only there l. has meaning, and
T-15 ..... VI.2:1 to accept the fact that perfect l. is in you.
T-15 ..... VI.2:6 doubt his holiness. And so we l. him.
T-15 ..... VI.4:1 that when another calls on God for l.,
T-15 ..... VI.5:1 l. has no meaning and peace is impossible
T-15 ..... VI.5:2 so no one is aware that perfect l. is in him.
T-15 ..... VI.5:3 instant you recognize the idea of l. in you,
T-15 ..... VI.5:7 give. And this *is* l., for this alone is natural
T-15 ..... VI.6:5 behind it, can have faith in l. without fear.
T-15 .... VII.1:1 attraction of the special l. relationship,
T-15 .... VII.1:2 There is no other l. that can satisfy you,
T-15 .... VII.1:2 can satisfy you, because there *is* no other l..
T-15 .... VII.1:3 is the only l. that is fully given and fully
T-15 .... VII.2:7 the ego always seems to attract through l.,
T-15 .... VII.6:4 no one could interpret direct attack as l..
T-15 .... VII.7:4 He is not in l. with the other at all. He
T-15 .... VII.7:5 He merely believes he is in l. with sacrifice
T-15 .. VII.10:2 who will learn that l. brings no guilt at all,
T-15 .. VII.10:2 brings guilt cannot be l. and *must* be anger
T-15 ... VIII.3:8 from loneliness, and join you in your l..
T-15 ..... IX.4:2 L. would *always* give increase. Limits are
T-15 ..... IX.6:3 as great as His, you can turn away from l..
T-15 ........X.4:5 What is not l. is always fear, and nothing
T-15 ........X.5:8 Your confusion of sacrifice and l. is so
T-15 ........X.5:8 you cannot conceive of l. without sacrifice
T-15 ........X.5:9 must look upon; sacrifice is attack, not l..
T-15 .....X.5:10 this one idea, your fear of l. would vanish.
T-15 ........X.6:7 behind them all; that l. demands sacrifice,
T-15 ........X.6:8 fear. And that guilt is the price of l., which
T-15 ........X.7:2 For total l. would demand total sacrifice.
T-15 ........X.7:4 For you see l. as destructive, and your
T-15 ..... XI.2:8 L. must be total to give Him welcome, for
T-15 ..... XI.3:6 And without sacrifice there l. *must* be.
T-15 ..... XI.4:1 You who believe that sacrifice is l. must
T-15 ..... XI.4:1 learn that sacrifice is separation from l..
T-15 ..... XI.4:2 brings guilt as surely as l. brings peace.
T-15 ..... XI.5:7 salvation and sacrifice becomes l..
T-15 ..... XI.6:1 So is it that, in all your seeking for l., you
T-15 ..... XI.6:2 it. Yet you find not l.. It is impossible to
T-15 ..... XI.6:3 It is impossible to deny what l. is and still
T-15 ..... XI.6:4 meaning of l. lies in what you have cast
T-15 ..... XI.7:1 the holy instant the condition of l. is met,
T-15 ..... XI.7:2 re-establish the condition of l. by teaching
T-15 ..... XI.7:5 sacrifice is nowhere and l. is everywhere.
T-15 ..... XI.7:6 peace it re-establishes, l. comes of itself.
T-15 ..... XI.8:2 for so you offer me the l. I offer you. What
T-16 .........I.6:1 meaning of l. is lost in any relationship
T-16 .........I.6:1 to weakness, and hopes to find l. there.
T-16 .........I.6:2 The power of l., which *is* its meaning, lies
T-16 ........II.8:7 greater l. than to accept this and be glad.
T-16 ........II.8:8 For l. asks only that you be happy, and
T-16 ..... III.7:6 and purity, and l. Him as His Father does.
T-16 ........ IV.h The Illusion and the Reality of L.
T-16 ..... IV.1:2 impossible not to know the meaning of l.,
T-16 ..... IV.1:3 For the special l. relationship, in which
T-16 ..... IV.1:3 in which the meaning of l. is hidden, is
T-16 ..... IV.1:6 The special l. relationship will not offset it
T-16 ..... IV.1:8 attempt to balance hate with l. that makes
T-16 ..... IV.1:8 love that makes l. meaningless to you.
T-16 ..... IV.2:1 of l. play out a conflict that does not exist.
T-16 ..... IV.2:2 symbol of l. is without meaning if love is
T-16 ..... IV.2:2 love is without meaning if l. is everything.
T-16 ..... IV.2:6 For the illusion of l. will never satisfy, but
T-16 ..... IV.3:1 The special l. relationship is an attempt
T-16 ..... IV.3:4 The special l. relationship is not perceived
T-16 ..... IV.3:5 The special l. partner is acceptable only as
T-16 ..... IV.3:6 it is still held together by the illusion of l..
T-16 ..... IV.4:1 L. is not an illusion. It is a fact. Where
T-16 ..... IV.4:3 is possible, there was not l. but hate. For
T-16 ..... IV.4:4 illusion, and what can change was never l.
T-16 ..... IV.4:7 And l., to them, is only an escape from
T-16 ..... IV.4:9 the l. relationship loses the illusion that it
T-16 ..... IV.5:1 There are no triumphs of l.. Only hate is
T-16 ..... IV.5:2 is at all concerned with the "triumph of l..
T-16 ..... IV.5:3 of l. can triumph over the illusion of hate,
T-16 ..... IV.5:4 lasts, so long will l. be an illusion to you.
T-16 ..... IV.6:1 Your task is not to seek for l., but merely

T-16......IV.6:5 If you seek l. outside yourself you can be
T-16......IV.6:6 will never come from the illusion of l., but
T-16......IV.7:1 The special l. relationship is an attempt to
T-16......IV.7:1 is an attempt to bring l. into separation.
T-16......IV.7:2 more than an attempt to bring l. into fear,
T-16......IV.7:3 special l. relationship would accomplish
T-16......IV.8:4 The special l. relationship is but a shabby
T-16....IV.10:3 Every fantasy, be it of l. or hate, deprives
T-16....IV.11:1 Would you not go through fear to l.? For
T-16....IV.11:3 be. L. calls, but hate would have you stay.
T-16....IV.11:8 wholly without illusion, as you must l..
T-16....IV.11:9 love. For l. *is* wholly without illusion, and
T-16..IV.11:14 willingness to l. and all the Love of God,
T-16....... V.2:3 special l. relationship is the ego's chief
T-16....... V.3:1 The special l. relationship is the ego's
T-16....... V.3:4 considers it bizarre to l. and hate together
T-16....... V.3:7 Heaven, where the meaning of l. is known
T-16....... V.3:7 of love is known, l. is the same as union.
T-16....... V.3:8 the illusion of l. is accepted in love's place,
T-16....... V.3:8 l. is perceived as separation and exclusion
T-16....... V.4:1 of the hidden wish for special l. from God,
T-16....... V.8:5 is buried deep and rises in the form of "l..
T-16....... V.9:3 of the giving of specialness as an act of l.,
T-16....... V.9:3 as an act of love, would make l. hateful.
T-16..... V.12:1 relationship tempts you to seek for l. in
T-16..... V.12:1 for love in ritual, remember l. is content,
T-16..... V.12:4 over content, and l. has lost its meaning.
T-16...... VI.1:3 meaning, for it perceives all l. as special.
T-16...... VI.1:5 For God created l. as He would have it be,
T-16...... VI.1:6 is. L. has no meaning except as its Creator
T-16...... VI.2:1 L. is freedom. To look for it by placing
T-16...... VI.8:7 of l. in any special relationship here. For
T-16...... VI.9:4 Your l. for it will not allow you to betray
T-16..... VII.5:2 the illusion of l. is not profoundly shaken.
T-16... VII.12:6 *minds which You created and which You l.*
T-17...... III.2:1 you what you do to keep it safe is really l..
T-17...... III.2:5 you, and seems to go by the name of l., no
T-17...... IV.8:3 of fanciful and fragmented illusions of l.,
T-17.... IV.10:6 must save you, for They l. Themselves.
T-18......... I.3:1 in which substitution is impossible is l..
T-18......... I.9:3 Within yourself you l. your brother with a
T-18......... I.9:3 you love your brother with a perfect l..
T-18...... I.11:1 whole and beautiful, safe in your l..
T-18...... I.11:2 truth in you, and l. has shined upon you,
T-18...... I.11:8 looks with l. on what is joined in it, along
T-18...... III.3:5 go toward l. still hating it, and terribly
T-18...... III.3:6 do not realize that you are not afraid of l.,
T-18...... III.7:7 desire for l. without love's joining them.
T-18...... IV.6:4 you will add, if you prepare yourself for l..
T-18....... V.5:1 is no dream to l. your brother as yourself.
T-18....... V.5:5 on thousands who believe that l. is fear,
T-18....... V.7:3 *I may share it with my brother, whom I l.. It is*
T-18...... VI.4:7 be. The body was not made by l.. Yet love
T-18...... VI.4:8 Yet l. does not condemn it and can use it
T-18...... VI.5:1 for salvation, and used for purposes of l.?
T-18...... VI.9:7 of reality, only some of which were l.. Yet
T-18...... VI.9:8 were love. Yet l. must be forever like itself,
T-18.... VI.11:8 The l. that instantly replaces it extends to
T-18.... VI.12:4 it without reservation because you l. it,
T-18.... VI.14:7 to let go the limits you have placed upon l.
T-18... VIII.1:1 of the body that makes l. seem limited.
T-18... VIII.1:2 For the body *is* a limit on l.. The belief in
T-18... VIII.1:3 The belief in limited l. was its origin, and
T-18... VIII.2:4 Limits on l. will always seem to shut Him
T-18... VIII.7:7 it with l. is the glorious whole, which
T-18... VIII.8:1 L. knows no bodies, and reaches to
T-18... VIII.8:5 be there that you would call on l. to enter?
T-18... VIII.8:7 realize the life and joy that l. would bring
T-18... VIII.9:4 by l. for them where once a desert was.
T-18... VIII.9:5 bring l. with him from Heaven for you.
T-18... VIII.9:7 The l. they brought with them will stay
T-18. VIII.10:3 lonely little kingdoms locked away from l.
T-18. VIII.11:1 The holy instant is your invitation to l. to
T-18. VIII.11:4 you ask of l. only what it offers everyone,
T-18. VIII.11:7 No part of l. calls on the whole in vain. No
T-18. VIII.12:1 l. has entered your special relationship,
T-18. VIII.12:2 You do not recognize that l. has come,
T-18. VIII.12:3 not be able to give l. welcome separately.
T-18. VIII.12:5 of l. than love could know you not, or fail
T-18. VIII.12:5 of love than l. could know you not, or fail
T-18. VIII.13:8 the garden l. has prepared for both of you
T-18...... IX.9:7 by, and gently replaced by purity and l..
T-18.... IX.10:3 it is the messenger of l. and not its Source.
T-18.... IX.10:4 for here does nothing interfere with l.,
T-18.... IX.12:1 L. is not learned. Its meaning lies within
T-18.... IX.12:5 L. is not learned, because there never was
T-18.... IX.12:6 the knowledge of l. and its one meaning.
T-18.... IX.13:3 were united is but the messenger of l.,
T-19....... I.10:1 as much a part of l. as fear is of attack.
T-19....... I.14:6 the messengers of l. are sent to do they do
T-19...... III.2:1 The ego does not think it possible that l.,
T-19...... III.4:7 Every mistake *must* be a call for l.. What,
T-19...... III.8:5 in sin has been uprooted in its smile of l..
T-19...... IV.1:7 will carry its message of l. and safety and
T19... IV.A.5:4 from the appeal of guilt to the appeal of l..
T19. IV.A.10:1 The attraction of guilt produces fear of l.,
T19. IV.A.10:1 love, for l. would never look on guilt at all.
T19. IV.A.10:2 nature of l. to look upon only the truth,
T19. IV.A.10:3 As l. must look past fear, so must fear see
T19. IV.A.10:3 must look past fear, so must fear see l. not
T19. IV.A.10:4 For l. contains the end of guilt, as surely
T19. IV.A.10:5 it. L. is attracted only to love. Overlooking
T19. IV.A.10:5 it. Love is attracted only to l.. Overlooking
T19. IV.A.10:8 Fear is attracted to what l. sees not, and
T19. IV.A.10:9 the same devotion that l. looks on itself.
T19. IV.A.11:1 return with messages of l. and gentleness.
T19. IV.A.11:4 What fear would feed upon, l. overlooks.
T19. IV.A.11:5 What fear demands, l. cannot even see.
T19. IV.A.11:7 l. would look upon is meaningless to fear,
T19. IV.A.14:4 no little breath of l. escape their notice.
T19. IV.A.15:5 and return to you with what l. sees. They
T19. IV.A.16:1 L., too, would set a feast before you, on a
T19. IV.A.17:5 would I offer you my body, you whom I l.,
T19.... IV.B.2:9 Here is the source of the idea that l. is fear
T19.... IV.B.7:1 proclaims the truth, and l. looks on itself.
T19.... IV.C.7:5 The obstacle of your seeming l. for death
T19.... IV.C.9:3 of salvation is carefully guarded by l.,
T19... IV.D.5:1 fear that raised it yields to the l. beyond,
T19... IV.D.5:3 of the quiet recognition that you l. Him.
T19... IV.D.5:4 you l. as you could never love the body.
T19... IV.D.5:4 you love as you could never l. the body.
T19... IV.D.5:6 From beyond each of the obstacles to l.,
T19... IV.D.9:7 that you will accept it for my l. and His.
T19. IV.D.11:3 with perfect faith and l. and tenderness.
T19. IV.D.11:7 no one reaches l. with fear beside him.
T19. IV.D.13:8 he is, and seek not to make of l. an enemy.
T-20......... I.2:5 the gift of l. and not the "gift" of fear. You
T-20....... II.8:9 There *is* no fear in l.. The song of Easter is
T-20..... II.11:7 it to him shall you be led past fear to l..
T-20.... III.11:3 no fear in perfect l. *because* it knows no sin
T-20...... IV.2:6 Your savior gives you only l., but what
T-20....... V.2:4 unity of l. proclaimed and given welcome.
T-20....... V.4:4 that you will merely l. him and be glad.
T-20..... V.7:10 His understanding recognize it and l. it as
T-20....... V.8:1 feel the Holy Spirit watching over you in l.
T-20...... VI.2:2 The first is based on l., and rests on it
T-20...... VI.2:4 in which the body enters is based not on l.
T-20...... VI.2:5 L. wishes to be known, completely
T-20...... VI.3:3 They can be loved, but cannot l.. They do
T-20...... VI.3:5 The l. of them has made love meaningless.
T-20...... VI.3:5 The love of them has made l. meaningless.
T-20...... VI.4:1 L. has no darkened temples where
T-20...... VI.5:5 Here it is "safe," for here l. cannot enter.
T-20...... VI.5:6 build His temples where l. can never be.
T-20...... VI.6:1 temple, and it will never be the seat of l..
T-20...... VI.6:3 is l. made fearful and hope abandoned.
T-20...... VI.7:1 Idolaters will always be afraid of l., for
T-20...... VI.7:2 Let l. draw near them and overlook the
T-20.... VI.10:3 and l. shines on it with the gentle smile
T-20.... VI.11:6 his choice again between idolatry and l..
T-21......... I.9:6 l. the Son of God sings to his Father still.
T-21...... III.2:7 it is always recognized if it is placed in l..
T-21...... VI.7:3 Reason, like l., would reassure you, and
T-21...... VI.9:4 This gracious plan was given l. by Love.
T-21..... VII.1:8 him; either you l. him or attack him,
T-21... VII.3:12 And l. is turned to hate as easily. This is
T-22......... I.4:9 This is the one emotion that opposes l.,
T-22....... I.10:7 fear is powerless l. enters thankfully,
T-22....... V.3:7 Yet it remains impossible to keep l. out.
T-22..... V.3:10 L. rests in certainty. Only uncertainty can
T-22....... V.4:2 quiet strength of those whom l. has joined
T-22...... VI.2:5 one as dear to His Creator as l. is to itself.
T-22...... VI.5:2 no longer seen, and reason, joined with l.,
T-22...... VI.5:7 fear because they carry only l. with them.
T-22...... VI.6:6 now His means must l. all that He loves.
T-22...... VI.9:8 gift of l. a source of healing for everyone.
T-22.. VI.12:12 And thus it seems as if l. could attack and
T-22.... VI.14:8 because each shining thought of l. extends
T-22.... VI.15:3 can also teach the power of l. is there,
T-23....... in.2:4 you will l. what you perceive as sinless. He
T-23....... in.2:5 sinlessly along the way l. shows him. For
T-23....... in.2:6 For l. walks with him there, protecting
T-23....... in.3:4 sin and fear and happily returned to l..
T-23....... in.3:5 share the strength of l. *because* they looked
T-23......... I.1:3 the warlike would remember is not l..
T-23....... I.2:10 and will seem to have replaced l. there.
T-23......... I.8:5 that God created with anything but l..
T-23....... I.10:6 Illusions have no place where l. abides,
T-23....... I.12:5 Peace is the state where l. abides, and
T-23...... II.12:4 It holds there is a substitute for l.. This is
T-23... II.12:10 The substitute for l., born of your enmity
T-23...... II.13:3 He must have this substitute for l., and
T-23...... II.14:6 illusions true, attack a kindness, hatred l.,
T-23...... II.14:8 do the laws of sin appear to hold l. captive
T-23...... II.15:6 to look upon, is lifted to the throne of l.,
T-23...... II.17:2 Can an attack in any form be l.? What
T-23...... II.20:7 And lack of faith in l., in any form, attests
T-23...... III.3:7 maintain you can attack a little, l. a little,
T-23...... III.4:6 and l. for that and understand forgiveness
T-23.... IV.1:10 What is not l. is murder. What is not
T-23.... IV.1:12 of l. because it seems to be of equal truth.
T-23...... IV.2:2 Murder and l. are incompatible. Yet if
T-23...... IV.8:4 Only the light they l. is in awareness, and
T-23...... IV.8:4 and only l. shines upon them forever. It is
T-23...... IV.8:8 and a sense of l. so deep and quiet that no
T-24............ I.h Specialness as a Substitute for L.
T-24......... I.1:1 L. is extension. To withhold the smallest
T-24......... I.1:3 L. offers everything forever. Hold back
T-24......... I.1:4 but one belief, one offering, and l. is gone,
T-24......... I.1:5 one alternative that you can choose for l..
T-24......... I.2:6 decision to choose attack instead of l.,
T-24......... I.6:7 l. have meaning where the goal is triumph
T-24......... I.7:3 to your brother that l. might be extended,
T-24......... I.9:3 You l. your brother not while it is this you
T-24........ II.1:1 must be an ego device, for l. makes none.
T-24........ II.3:6 Nor do they l. the Oneness which created
T-24........ II.4:5 And that vast song of honor and of l. for
T-24........ II.5:5 each in his special sins and "safe" from l.,
T-24........ II.9:2 of the fear of God will melt away in l..
T-24...... II.10:7 to you and your brother in equal l., that
T-24...... II.10:7 Who chose that l. could never be divided,
T-24...... II.11:1 brother's; part of l. was not denied to him
T-24...... II.12:1 is the seal of treachery upon the gift of l..
T-24...... II.12:6 of all illusions from the "threat" of l..
T-24...... III.5:4 How could They will the death of l. itself?
T-24...... III.6:1 the Source of life, of l. and holiness, the
T-24...... III.6:5 The way is barred to l. and to salvation.
T-24.... III.8:10 seek your l. that you may love yourself.
T-24.... III.8:10 seek your love that you may l. yourself.
T-24.... III.8:11 L. not your specialness instead of Them.
T-24....... V.1:9 illusions as strongly as does l. extend itself
T-24....... V.4:7 in him and l. to look upon it saw in you,
T-24....... V.6:6 Christ is there to see and hear and l. and
T-24....... V.7:1 quiet, for He knows that l. is in you now,
T-24....... V.8:1 seek salvation in a war with l., consider
T-24.... VI.10:6 each part of Him with equal l. and care.
T-24... VII.1:10 child of earth on whom such l. is lavished
T-24..... VII.2:7 to you. All of the l. and care, the strong
T-25....... in.3:6 not it carries Him in gentleness and l., to
T-25......... I.4:3 l. celestial and so complete it wishes only
T-25........ II.9:2 thanks to you who l. His Son as He does?
T-25...... III.1:6 God's more basic law; that l. creates itself,
T-25...... III.6:5 turned to an event which justifies his l..
T-25....... V.6:2 l. he shows himself is God made free to let
T-25...... VI.1:3 looks upon himself with l. and gentleness.
T-25...... VI.6:8 His special hate became his special l..
T-25..... VII.1:8 to make this world's foundation sure as l.,

T-25..... VII.1:9 is safe from l. to everyone who thinks sin
T-25..... VII.6:3 else. What is not l. is sin, and either one
T-25..... VII.6:4 L. is the basis for a world perceived as
T-25..... VII.6:5 sin is equally insane within the sight of l.,
T-25...... VIII.h Justice Returned to L.
T-25.... VIII.3:7 without insanity where l. means hate, and
T-25.... VIII.6:5 that Heaven is hell, and *are* afraid of l..
T-25.... VIII.6:8 vengeance, which they understand and l..
T-25.... VIII.8:3 are innocent. L. is not understandable to
T-25.... VIII.8:3 they think that justice is split off from l.,
T-25.... VIII.8:4 else. And thus is l. perceived as weak, and
T-25.... VIII.8:5 For l. has lost when judgment left its side,
T-25.... VIII.8:6 But vengeance without l. has gained in
T-25.... VIII.8:6 by being separate and apart from l.. And
T-25.... VIII.8:7 while l. stands feebly by with helpless
T-25.... VIII.9:2 Could He, in justice and in l., believe in
T-25.. VIII.9:10 For l. and justice are not different. *Because*
T-25.. VIII.11:4 may return to l. and there be satisfied.
T-25.. VIII.11:5 learn that l. and justice are not separate.
T-25.. VIII.11:7 Without l. is justice prejudiced and weak.
T-25.. VIII.11:8 And l. without justice is impossible. For
T-25.. VIII.11:9 For l. is fair, and cannot chasten without
T-25VIII.11:11 In justice, then, does l. correct mistakes,
T-25.. VIII.12:1 witness to the power of l. and justice, if
T-25.. VIII.14:6 For only l. is just, and can perceive what
T-25.. VIII.14:7 Let l. decide, and never fear that you, in
T-26......... I.4:9 his song of union and of l. be heard at all.
T-26........ II.8:6 He gave, when He created you in perfect l.
T-26....... IV.1:3 in boundless l. could need forgiveness.
T-26....... IV.3:4 is? Who could fear l., and stand upon the
T-26....... IV.3:5 Heaven but a song of gratitude and l. and
T-26....... IV.4:6 he understands that l. cannot be feared?
T-26..... V.13:1 when the time of terror took the place of l.
T-26..... V.14:5 has been transformed into a world of l..
T-26... VII.17:3 and hate is answered in the name of l.. To
T-26...... IX.4:4 What hatred claimed is given up to l., and
T-26...... IX.6:1 an ancient hatred has become a present l..
T-26...... IX.6:5 What hatred has released to l. becomes
T-26....... X.6:4 and been replaced with justice and with l..
T-27......... I.5:5 tear is wiped away in laughter and in l..
T-27........ I.6:10 life; how easily destroyed is what you l..
T-27......... I.9:8 apart from all experience of l. or fear. For
T-27........ II.1:3 For accusation is a bar to l., and damaged
T-27........ II.1:5 brother, and could l. and trust him still?
T-27........ II.7:5 all. It does not come from pity but from l..
T-27........ II.7:6 And l. would prove all suffering is but a
T-27...... III.1:9 such as "weakened power" or "hateful l."?
T-27...... III.2:1 your brother is a symbol for a "hateful l.,"
T-27...... III.3:2 nothing to attack or to deny; to l. or hate,
T-27...... III.5:9 has a use that now you fear, but yet will l..
T-27..... V.2:12 if only for an instant, you l. without attack
T-27....... V.4:2 just one instant of your l. without attack is
T-27..... V.11:4 occurred within the instant that l. entered
T-27..... V.11:9 for He knows it is a gift of l. unto His Son,
T-27...... VI.4:6 is. Yet must He l. whatever you hold dear.
T-27...... VI.6:1 L., too, has symbols in a world of sin. The
T-27... VII.13:4 the Voice that calls with l. to waken him; a
T-28....... I.13:6 of l. the Son of God remembers from
T-28....... II.2:2 L. must be extended. Purity is not
T-28...... III.4:1 and l. was never in the world of dreams.
T-28...... III.9:8 l. has set its table in the space that seemed
T-28....... V.2:4 Where fear has gone there l. must come,
T-28....... V.7:6 you have lost the fear of recognizing l..
T-29......... I.2:2 For l. *is* treacherous to those who fear,
T-29......... I.2:3 No one who hates but is afraid of l., and
T-29......... I.2:4 Certain it is he knows not what l. means.
T-29......... I.2:5 He fears to l. and loves to hate, and so he
T-29......... I.2:5 to hate, and so he thinks that l. is fearful;
T-29......... I.2:5 so he thinks that love is fearful; hate is l..
T-29......... I.4:6 do protect you from the "sacrifice" of l..
T-29......... I.6:2 It will allow but limited indulgences in "l.,
T-29......... I.6:3 And it will take command of when to "l.,"
T-29......... I.7:1 It is not l. that asks a sacrifice. But fear
T-29......... I.7:2 But fear demands the sacrifice of l., for in
T-29......... I.7:3 hate to be maintained, l. must be feared;
T-29......... I.7:4 Thus is l. seen as treacherous, because it
T-29......... I.7:5 you have demanded that l. go away, and
T-29....... II.3:4 and l. must come wherever they are not.
T-29....... II.3:7 and you should welcome the effects of l..

T-29 ....... II.5:8 without the l. and grace His Presence
T-29 ..... II.10:2 you behold the body as a thing you l., or
T-29 ..... III.4:1 Make way for l., which you did not create
T-29 ..... III.5:2 him, and shines on you in gratitude and l.
T-29 ..... IV.6:6 each dream becomes an offering of l.. For
T-29 ..... IV.6:7 which lights whatever form it takes with l.
T-29 ...... V.3:5 And every thought of l. you offer him but
T-29 ..... IX.7:8 as brothers, not in judgment, but in l..
T-30 ...... II.3:1 the one you chose to hate instead of l.. For
T-30 ..... III.2:3 of all the l. in the Divinity of God the Son?
T-31 ...... I.10:3 and pleads that l. restore the dying world.
T-31 ....... II.4:1 Perhaps you call it l.. Perhaps you think
T-31 ....... II.6:8 Take not his hand in anger but in l., for in
T-31 ..... II.10:5 you l. your brother with a brother's love.
T-31 ..... II.10:5 you love your brother with a brother's l..
T-31 ..... III.6:6 in chains, to the illusion of a changing l.,
T-31 ...... V.2:7 smiles and charms and even seems to l.. It
T-31 ...... V.3:1 the l. and shelter innocence deserves. And
T-31 ...... VI.7:4 as pure as light, as innocent as l. itself.
T-31 .... VII.4:3 for you will l. this concept of yourself,
T-31 .... VII.7:7 out of hell with those you l. beside you,
T-31 .... VII.9:1 of salvation, and the l. of guilt and death,
T-31 .... VII.9:2 holds your brother off unoccupied by l..
T-31 .. VII.12:6 Yet it can look with l. or look with hate,
W-pI..... 16.3:1 brings either peace or war; either l. or fear
W-pI..... 20.2:6 and sorrow, pleasure and pain, l. and fear.
W-pI..... 23.4:5 so transform them that you will l. them,
W-pI..... 29.3:1 to learn how to look on all things with l.,
W-pI..... 46.2:2 Fear condemns and l. forgives.
W-pI..... 46.5:5 *God is the Love with which I l. myself. God is*
W-pI..... 46.6:6 *no need to attack because l. has forgiven me.*
W-pI..... 52.2:7 I will look with l. on all that I failed to see
W-pI..... 54.5:4 through me has enabled l. to replace fear,
W-pI..... 55.3:4 allows l. to return to my awareness, I will
W-pI..... 56.2:6 world and on myself with charity and l..
W-pI..... 56.4:3 every veil I have drawn across the face of l.
W-pI..... 59.1:5 can I suffer when l. and joy surround me
W-pI..... 66.7:5 the l. that the Holy Spirit always offers to
W-pI........ 67.h L. created me like itself.
W-pI..... 67.3:2 If l. created you like itself, this Self must
W-pI..... 67.4:3 you recognize yourself as l. created you.
W-pI..... 67.5:3 yourself that l. created you like itself. Hear
W-pI..... 67.6:4 of God. You were created by l. like itself.
W-pI........ 68.h L. holds no grievances.
W-pI..... 68.1:1 You who were created by l. like itself can
W-pI..... 68.2:4 grievances denies he was created by l.,
W-pI..... 68.5:3 those you like and even think you l.. It will
W-pI..... 68.6:4 and loves you, and that you l. in return.
W-pI..... 68.6:8 *L. holds no grievances. When I let all my*
W-pI..... 68.7:2 *L. holds no grievances. Let me not betray my*
W-pI..... 68.7:5 *L. holds no grievances. I would wake to my*
W-pI..... 72.7:3 Others l. the body, and try to glorify and
W-pI..... 78.4:5 someone you think you l. who angered
W-pI..... 78.9:1 and looked upon the miracle of l. the Holy
W-pI..... 84.1:1 (67) L. created me like itself. I am in the
W-pI..... 84.1:8 of my Creator. L. created me like itself.
W-pI..... 84.3:1 (68) L. holds no grievances. Grievances
W-pI..... 84.3:2 Grievances are completely alien to l..
W-pI..... 84.3:3 attack l. and keep its light obscure. If I
W-pI..... 84.3:4 If I hold grievances I am attacking l., and
W-pI..... 84.4:3 *Self. I will not use this to attack l.. Let this not*
W-pI..... 92.5:7 unite in purpose and forgiveness and in l..
W-pI..... 92.6:1 see a purpose in forgiveness and in l.. It
W-pI..... 92.6:3 It judges and condemns, but does not l..
W-pI..... 92.8:1 The light of strength is constant, sure as l.
W-pI..... 93.5:8 eternal sinlessness to sin, and l. to hate.
W-pI..... 93.9:4 and the l. from which It was created. Try
W-pI... 99.12:5 that l. may find its rightful place in you
W-pI... 103.1:1 Happiness is an attribute of l.. It cannot
W-pI... 103.1:3 Nor can it be experienced where l. is not.
W-pI... 103.1:4 L. has no limits, being everywhere. And
W-pI... 103.1:6 believing there are gaps in l. where sin can
W-pI... 103.1:7 limit happiness by redefining l. as limited,
W-pI... 103.2:1 Fear is associated then with l., and its
W-pI... 105.4:3 eternity to timelessness, and l. unto itself.
W-pI... 106.3:5 held out to you in welcome and in l.. Hear
W-pI... 107.5:1 l. which does not falter in the face of pain,
W-pI... 110.3:1 death be substitute for life, or fear for l..
W-pI... 117.1:2 *Let me remember l. is happiness, and*

W-pI .. 117.1:3 *so I choose to entertain no substitutes for l..*
W-pI .. 117.2:2 *L. is my heritage, and with it joy. These are*
W-pI .. 121.2:1 of fear, and offers l. no room to be itself;
W-pI .. 124.3:2 with the equal l. in which we were created
W-pI 124.11:2 be a sense of l. you cannot understand, a
W-pI .. 125.2:3 He is not led by force, but only l.. He is
W-pI ..... 127.h There is no l. but God's.
W-pI .. 127.1:1 think that different kinds of l. are possible
W-pI .. 127.1:2 you think there is a kind of l. for this, a
W-pI .. 127.1:3 L. is one. It has no separate parts and no
W-pI .. 127.2:1 to anyone who thinks that l. can change.
W-pI .. 127.2:2 see that changing l. must be impossible.
W-pI .. 127.2:3 And thus he thinks that he can l. at times,
W-pI .. 127.2:4 also thinks that l. can be bestowed on one
W-pI .. 127.2:5 these things of l. is not to understand it. If
W-pI .. 127.3:1 L. cannot judge. As it is one itself, it looks
W-pI .. 127.3:5 There is no l. but God's, and all of love is
W-pI .. 127.3:5 is no love but God's, and all of l. is His.
W-pI .. 127.3:6 other principle that rules where l. is not.
W-pI .. 127.3:7 is not. L. is a law without an opposite. Its
W-pI .. 127.4:1 in what you really are and what l. is.
W-pI .. 127.4:4 There is no l. but His, and what He is, is
W-pI .. 127.5:3 upholds but violates the truth of what l. is
W-pI .. 127.6:2 L. is not found in darkness and in death.
W-pI .. 127.7:1 glimmering of what l. means today, you
W-pI .. 127.9:3 of your own reality and what l. means. He
W-pI .. 127.9:4 and help you understand the truth of l.. In
W-pI 127.12:1 outside our l. if we would know our Self.
W-pI 127.12:5 *learn the joyous lesson that there is no l. but*
W-pI .. 128.6:5 be restored to sanity, to freedom and to l..
W-pI .. 129.2:5 No lasting l. is found, for none is here.
W-pI .. 129.3:1 is impossible; where l. endures forever,
W-pI .. 130.2:1 Yet who can really hate and l. at once?
W-pI .. 130.2:5 L. and perception thus go hand in hand,
W-pI .. 130.4:5 up. Yet l. can have no enemy, and so they
W-pI .. 131.1:2 impermanent, for l. where there is none,
W-pI 134.11:1 powerful as l. which laid its blessing on it,
W-pI .. 137.6:4 mind. And l. becomes a dream, while fear
W-pI .. 144.1:1 (127) There is no l. but God's.
W-pI 151.11:3 And you will see the l. beyond the hate,
W-pI .. 152.2:5 a mind where l. and perfect holiness abide
W-pI .. 152.9:4 like to Himself in power and in l..
W-pI 153.20:1 will now begin to take the earnestness of l.
W-pI 153.20:4 because the l. and strength and peace that
W-pI 155.12:3 effort, of your l. and of your full intent?
W-pI .. 158.1:2 because you were created out of l.. Nor
W-pI .. 158.6:2 world made holy by forgiveness and by l..
W-pI 158.11:2 its likeness shines with its immortal l.. We
W-pI .. 159.3:2 it reflects eternal l. and the rebirth of love
W-pI .. 159.3:2 love and the rebirth of l. which never dies,
W-pI .. 159.8:5 need the l. with which He looks on them.
W-pI .. 160.1:1 Fear is a stranger to the ways of l..
W-pI .. 160.4:4 likeness? Is it fear that l. completes, and is
W-pI .. 160.4:5 There is no home can shelter l. and fear.
W-pI .. 161.1:1 fears may disappear and offer room to l..
W-pI .. 161.5:4 L. needs no symbols, being true. But fear
W-pI .. 161.9:1 the angels l. and God created perfect. This
W-pI .. 161.9:8 Would you request that l. destroy itself?
W-pI .. 163.4:3 the endlessness of l. and Heaven's perfect,
W-pI .. 164.6:5 is worthy of your l. receives your love,
W-pI .. 164.6:5 is worthy of your love receives your l.,
W-pI .. 165.2:6 lighting your mind with happiness and l..
W-pI .. 168.1:9 He will l. His Son forever. When his mind
W-pI .. 168.4:3 see a light that covers all the world in l.,
W-pI .. 168.5:3 down, and rise to Him in gratitude and l..
W-pI .. 168.6:9 *will come to me who ask. I am the Son You l..*
W-pI .. 170.3:3 For l. now has an "enemy," an opposite;
W-pI .. 170.5:1 attributes of l. bestowed upon its "enemy.
W-pI .. 170.5:3 And as l. is shorn of what belongs to it
W-pI .. 170.5:3 alone, l. is endowed with attributes of fear
W-pI .. 170.5:4 For l. would ask you lay down all defense
W-pI .. 170.6:1 With l. as enemy, must cruelty become a
W-pI .. 170.8:4 he is. Will you restore to l. what you have
W-pI .. 170.9:5 l. appears to be invested now with cruelty.
W-pI 170.10:2 L. has not confused its attributes with
W-pI 170.10:3 "enemy"; its cruelty as now a part of l..
W-pI 170.12:6 Now has fear made way for l., as God
W-pI .. 181.9:2 l. for everyone we look upon attests to our
W-pI .. 182.5:7 resting in silence and in peace and l..

W-pI.182.11:4 beseech his father for protection and for l.
W-pI.185.14:1 beyond despair, the l. attack would hide,
W-pI...186.8:3 mourner to ecstatic bliss of l. and loving.
W-pI.186.14:2 Forgiveness is an earthly form of l., which
W-pI.186.14:4 l. will mean to you when formlessness has
W-pI...189.1:7 and blessed with perfect charity and l..
W-pI...189.5:5 will look out on a world of mercy and of l..
W-pI...190.2:5 leave the Son whom It created out of l..
W-pI...190.3:5 For vengeance is not part of l.. And fear,
W-pI...190.3:6 denying l. and using pain to prove that
W-pI...190.8:4 pain does fear appear to triumph over l.,
W-pI...192.1:1 as He, of l. created and in love preserved,
W-pI...192.1:1 as He, of love created and in l. preserved,
W-pI...192.1:1 in love preserved, extending l., creating in
W-pI...194.7:5 And what can he regard except with l.?
W-pI...194.8:2 thoughts of sin and evil with the truth of l.
W-pI......195.h L. is the way I walk in gratitude.
W-pI...195.4:2 L. makes no comparisons. And gratitude
W-pI...195.4:3 can only be sincere if it be joined to l.. We
W-pI...195.4:6 For who can bargain in the name of l.?
W-pI...195.8:1 Walk, then, in gratitude the way of l.. For
W-pI...195.8:6 has earned the right to l. by being loving,
W-pI.195.10:2 Gratitude goes hand in hand with l., and
W-pI.195.10:4 His Own completion and the Source of l.,
W-pI.195.10:6 For l. can walk no road except the way of
W-pI.196.11:6 back from fear, and make advance to l..
W-pI...197.5:3 out, extending l. and adding to your never-
W-pI...197.7:5 no end, for gratitude remains a part of l..
W-pI...198.6:4 come to you with Heaven's l. upon them.
W-pI...199.2:2 it has been given to the Source of l., and
W-pI...199.2:2 in a mind that has attached itself to l.. It
W-pI...199.7:4 Let l. replace their fears through you.
W-pI...200.3:1 you can ask as easily for l., for happiness,
W-pI...200.6:6 between success and failure; l. and fear?
W-pI.200.10:6 heart and mind with comfort and with l..
W-pI...215.1:1 (195) L. is the way I walk in gratitude.
W-pI...215.1:3 *He walks with me in l.. And I give thanks to*
W-pII..221.1:5 *Your Voice in silence and in certainty and l.,*
W-pII..222.1:4 and holds in l. the Son He shines upon,
W-pII.....229.h L., which created me, is what I am.
W-pII..229.1:1 Identity, and find It in these words: "L.,
W-pII..229.1:3 L. has prevailed. So still It waited for my
W-pII..240.2:4 *feel the l. for him which is Your Own as well.*
W-pII.....246.h To l. my Father is to love His Son.
W-pII.....246.h To love my Father is to l. His Son.
W-pII..246.1:3 conceive of all the l. my Father has for me,
W-pII..246.1:3 me, and all the l. which I return to Him.
W-pII..246.2:4 *that. And so I choose to l. Your Son. Amen.*
W-pII..248.2:1 *Father, my ancient l. for You returns, and*
W-pII..248.2:1 *returns, and lets me l. Your Son again as well*
W-pII......4.3:4 forever overcome by death, l. slain by hate
W-pII..252.1:3 Its l. is limitless, with an intensity that
W-pII..259.1:5 l. the attributes of fear and of attack?
W-pII..259.2:2 *I would not be afraid of l., nor seek for refuge*
W-pII..259.2:3 *For l. can have no opposite. You are the*
W-pII......5.1:3 this fence he thinks that he is safe from l..
W-pII......5.1:5 within the body, keeping l. outside?
W-pII......5.3:3 For only l. creates in truth, and truth can
W-pII......5.5:4 lies. L. is your safety. Fear does not exist.
W-pII......5.5:6 Identify with l., and you are safe. Identify
W-pII......5.5:7 safe. Identify with l., and you are home.
W-pII......5.5:8 home. Identify with l., and find your Self.
W-pII..267.1:6 by His Voice, sustained by Him in l., and
W-pII..268.1:5 *In l. was I created, and in love will I remain*
W-pII..268.1:5 *was I created, and in l. will I remain forever.*
W-pII..272.2:2 as hell, and l. will happily replace all fear.
W-pII..273.2:4 *quietness and in my own eternal l. for You.*
W-pII.....274.h Today belongs to l.. Let me not fear.
W-pII..274.1:1 *the l. of brother to his brother and his Friend*
W-pII..274.2:2 fear today, because the day is given unto l.
W-pII..277.1:6 *because he knows no law except the law of l..*
W-pII..278.2:5 *of fear. For truth is safe, and only l. is sure.*
W-pII..280.1:6 and like Himself in freedom and in l.?
W-pII..280.2:2 *on the Son You l. and You created limitless.*
W-pII......7.2:2 from the witnesses of fear to those of l..
W-pII..281.2:4 loves, for what He loves is also mine to l..
W-pII.....282.h I will not be afraid of l. today.
W-pII..282.1:3 truth remains forever living in the joy of l.
W-pII..287.1:5 And would I rather live with fear than l.?
W-pII......8.3:2 surrounding it but safety, l. and joy?
W-pII.....293.h All fear is past and only l. is here.
W-pII..293.1:2 L. remains the only present state, whose
W-pII..293.1:4 Yet in the present l. is obvious, and its
W-pII..294.1:5 nor is a mockery of l. bestowed upon it.
W-pII..295.1:7 in many different forms, but l. is one.
W-pII.....298.h I l. You, Father, and I love Your Son.
W-pII.....298.h I love You, Father, and I l. Your Son.
W-pII..298.1:1 permits my l. to be accepted without fear.
W-pII..298.2:4 *my l. for God my Father and His holy Son.*
W-pII..302.1:6 *for fear must disappear when l. has come.*
W-pII..303.2:5 *He is the Son You l. above all things. He is my*
W-pII..305.1:4 For l. has come, and healed the world by
W-pII..306.1:3 be restored to l. and holiness and peace.
W-pII..308.1:7 world, restoring it to timelessness and l..
W-pII..308.1:8 love. And l. is ever-present, here and now.
W-pII.....310.h In fearlessness and l. I spend today.
W-pII..310.2:4 for we have welcomed l. into our hearts.
W-pII....10.4:2 Be not afraid of l.. For it alone can heal all
W-pII..311.2:1 *to hear Your Judgment of the Son You l.. We*
W-pII..313.1:1 *fear has gone, and where it was is l. invited in*
W-pII..313.1:2 *in. And l. will come wherever it is asked. This*
W-pII..320.1:4 all the strength and l. in earth and Heaven
W-pII....11.1:2 Only l. creates, and only like itself. There
W-pII....11.2:2 For He would add to l. by its extension.
W-pII....11.4:4 For l. remains with all its Thoughts, its
W-pII..322.2:5 *of fear, and the return of l. into my mind?*
W-pII..323.2:3 L. has now returned to our awareness.
W-pII..323.2:4 for fear has gone and only l. remains.
W-pII....12.1:3 that strength is weak and l. is fearful, life
W-pII....12.5:2 His Son, His dwelling place, His joy, His l.
W-pII..331.1:3 *You l. me, Father. You could never leave me*
W-pII..337.1:1 perfect peace, eternal safety, everlasting l.,
W-pII..338.1:5 fear thought for a happy thought of l.. He
W-pII..339.1:9 confusing pain with joy, or fear with l..
W-pII....13.3:2 to all they look upon in mercy and in l..
W-pII....13.3:4 offers all the world the silent miracle of l..
W-pII..341.1:2 *is holy. I am he on whom You smile in l. and*
W-pII.....344.h Today I learn the law of l.; that what I
W-pII..344.1:8 *Thus is the law of l. fulfilled. And thus Your*
W-pII..345.1:2 *to me, reminding me the law of l. is universal*
W-pII..346.1:6 *You, and know no laws except Your law of l..*
W-pII.....349.h but give Each one a miracle of l. instead.
W-pII..349.1:2 *For thus do I obey the law of l., and give what*
W-pII....14.1:3 *In me is l. perfected, fear impossible, and joy*
W-pII.....352.h Judgment and l. are opposites. From one
W-pII..352.1:4 *Yet l., reflected in forgiveness here, reminds*
W-pII..352.1:9 *For I would l. my own Identity, and find in It*
W-ep .........6:4 He loves God's Son as we would l. him.
W-ep .........6:5 through His eyes, and l. him as He does.
M-4 ....... X.3:2 Terms like l., sinlessness, perfection,
M-7 ...........2:5 that his own uncertainty is not l. but fear,
M-7 ...........2:6 offering hate to one to whom he offered l..
M-7 ...........2:8 Having offered l., only love can be
M-7 ...........2:8 offered love, only l. can be received.
M-7 ...........4:5 It has all the appearances of l.. Yet love
M-7 ...........4:6 Yet l. without trust is impossible, and
M-7 ...........4:7 hate must be the opposite of l., regardless
M-19 .........4:7 an evaluation based entirely on l., –you
M-23 .........4:2 But it stands for l. that is not of this world
M-23 .........4:6 for l. cannot be far behind a grateful heart
M-23 .........5:3 He has asked for l., but only that he might
M-23 .........5:4 You do not l. yourself. But in his eyes your
M-23 .........7:1 in a language you can l. and understand.
M-25 .........4:9 what is withheld from l. is given to fear,
M-27 .........2:5 Who loves such a god knows not of l.,
M-27 .........6:9 and yet to think l. real are mindless magic
M-27 .......6:11 an opposite, and fear would be as real as l.
M-28 .........2:4 as hell. L. is no longer feared, but gladly
M-29 .........3:9 that lets the memory of l. return to you.
M-29 .......6:11 more than this does your Father l. His Son
C-4.............8:3 eternity; out of all fear and given back to l.
P-2.........IV.4:8 How could l. be there? And how could
P-2.........IV.5:4 until the meaning of l. is understood. And
P-2.........IV.6:7 L. becomes feared because reality is love.
P-2.........IV.6:7 Love becomes feared because reality is l..
S-1 ........ III.2:2 They call for vengeance, not for l.. Nor do
S-1 ........ III.6:1 prayers for things, for status, for human l.
S-1 ........ IV.3:4 what was another's and he seemed to l., –
S-1 ......... V.1:2 and grows in strength and l. and holiness.
S-2 ...........I.2:2 no guilt that it can seek and find and "l.."
S-2 ..........II.2:2 l. that arrogance could never be dislodged
S-2 ..........II.3:5 l. for God's creation and the holiness that
S-2 ..........II.5:5 Is this l.? Or is it rather treachery to one
S-2 ..........II.5:7 to keep the witnesses of guilt away from l.
S-3 ...........I.3:2 is the gift of holiness and l.. Forgiveness
S-3 ........ III.5:7 separation must be healed by l. and union
S-3 ........ III.5:9 Him there is no healing, for there is no l..
S-3 ........ III.6:6 for l. has entered now where idols used to
S-3 ........ IV.1:2 brothers share their healing and their l..
S-3 ........ IV.2:4 here, for l. has come in all its holy oneness
S-3 ........ IV.6:5 hard against the l. that is the truth in you.
S-3 ........ IV.7:3 My Arms are open to the Son I l., who
S-3 ........ IV.8:2 greater as your l. extends along with Mine
S-3 ........ IV.8:3 song is part of the eternal harmony of l..

## Love's 3

*love's*

T-20.... VI.10:6 L. Arms are open to receive you, and give
T-28........II.3:2 he does not believe that he is L. Effect,
W-pI... 168.3:6 forgot; all certainty of what L. meaning is.

## love's 40

*Love's*

T-in ........... 1:7 *the blocks to the awareness of l. presence,*
T-12...... IV.3:2 would be totally inadequate in l. presence,
T-14...... VI.2:3 unless it is concealed from l. beneficence.
T-15....... V.1:1 device for teaching you l. meaning. For its
T-15....... VI.7:4 And therein is l. meaning understood. But
T-16...... IV.7:3 fundamental violation of l. one condition,
T-16........ V.3:8 the illusion of love is accepted in l. place,
T-16..... V.15:1 in the fantasy of destruction of l. meaning
T-16..... V.15:2 And unless l. meaning is restored to you,
T-18.........I.3:2 by definition, for it is l. replacement. Fear
T-18...... III.3:7 it. You are advancing to l. meaning, and
T-18...... III.7:7 the desire for love without l. joining them.
T-18..VIII.11:2 L. answer is inevitable. It will come
T19....IV.A.7:4 more than tiny interruptions in l. appeal.
T19. IV.A.11:1 L. messengers are gently sent, and return
T19. IV.A.11:6 is wholly absent from l. gentle perception.
T19. IV.A.14:1 Holy Spirit has given you l. messengers to
T19. IV.A.15:4 you cannot ask l. messengers to remove
T19....IV.C.9:1 as its appeal is yielded to l. real attraction.
T19.... IV.D.5:5 as l. attraction stirs and calls to you. From
T-20...... VI.6:2 of the idolater, and of l. condemnation.
T-20...... VI.7:1 so severely threatens them as l. approach.
T-23........II.15:8 Give thanks unto the hero on l. throne,
T-24.........I.1:2 the smallest gift is not to know l. purpose.
T-24......II.12:5 that would establish sin l. substitute, and
T-27....... VI.8:6 chose to let l. symbols take the place of sin
T-29.........I.7:2 love, for in l. presence fear cannot abide.
W-pI... 127.2:1 L. meaning is obscure to anyone who
W-pI... 127.4:2 is. L. meaning is your own, and shared by
W-pI... 127.5:1 obeys can help you grasp l. meaning.
W-pI... 127.5:2 believes was made to hide l. meaning, and
W-pI... 127.6:3 eyes that see and ears that hear l. Voice.
W-pI... 127.9:5 you allow His Voice to teach l. meaning to
W-pI. 127.11:2 thought was made in hate to be l. enemy.
W-pI... 130.4:4 L. enemy has made them up. Yet love can
W-pI... 161.6:4 symbol of l. "enemy" Christ's vision does
W-pI... 182.9:2 offering only l. messages to those who
W-pI... 194.9:4 it will be soon replaced by l. reflection.
W-pII ..... 3.2:3 And what is fear except l. absence? Thus
W-pII ... 13.1:6 return of timelessness and l. awakening,

## love-encompassment 1

T-2......... V.9:6 of a much more powerful l. that is far

## loved 30

T-2..... VII.5:14 The statement "For God so l. the world
T-3...........I.6:3 of the truly l. to others who are like them.
T-5........ IV.8:7 because I have l. you as I loved myself.
T-5........ IV.8:7 because I have loved you as I l. myself.
T-7...... VI.11:8 capable of being appreciated and l.. That

T-10....... V.6:3 You denied Him because you l. Him,
T-10....... V.9:1 Only the eternal can be l., for love does
T-12...... III.8:1 I said before that God so l. the world that
T-13.... III.10:3 ask this of a Father Who truly l. His Son.
T-13....... X.8:5 that he ever thought his Father l. him not,
T-13..... X.10:2 as God Himself has always l. His Son. *And*
T-13..... X.10:5 always l. your Father can have no fear, for
T-14...... VI.1:9 What is concealed cannot be l., and so it
T-16....... V.8:2 self is "l." for what can be taken from him
T-19.......I.10:3 most loving Father, l. by Him like you,
T-19.......I.10:3 you, and therefore l. by you as yourself. It
T-20....... II.5:5 only dearly l. and loving friends. He sees
T-20...... VI.3:3 They can be l., but cannot love. They do
T-21.........I.6:3 and how you l. those who were there and
T-25....... V.2:5 a "something" to be feared instead of l..
T-26....... II.8:1 until justice is l. instead of feared. He
T-27.......I.4:11 guilt in him which you perceived and l..
T-28.........I.1:7 of them and l. them for a little while. The
T-31...... VI.6:8 where nothing need be feared, but only l..
W-pI.....51.3:6 what can be seen and understood and l.. I
W-pI...107.2:3 you were certain you were l. and safe.
W-pI...170.9:5 For fear is l. by those who worship it, and
W-pI...198.6:7 for it will be remembered then and l..
W-pII .276.2:2 *own, as I am l. and blessed and saved by You.*
W-pII ...10.5:1 innocent, forever loving and forever l., as

## loveless 4

T-1......... V.1:3 between l. and miraculous channels of
T-2........ VI.8:4 You have done something l., having
T-5........ VI.9:2 Every l. thought must be undone, a word
T-14.... IV.4:10 your function of loving in a l. place made

## lovelessly 2

T-3........ IV.1:4 because you can still perceive l..
T-8......VIII.9:9 all attempts to use the body l.. Health is

## loveliest 1

T-12...VII.10:2 of your mind is the l. of God's creations.

## loveliness 38

T-11...... IV.7:5 extension of the Love and the l. of God, as
T-13..... X.13:6 I thank the Father for your l., and for the
T-15...... IX.6:1 and no idea of all the l. that you could see.
T-17....... II.1:3 sleeping or waking, comes near to such l..
T-17....... II.2:1 This l. is not a fantasy. It is the real world
T-17....... II.3:4 The real world, in its l., you learn to reach
T-17....... II.5:4 lack of reason is suddenly released to l..
T-17...... III.6:8 Its l. will so attract you that you will be
T-18.......I.12:4 to the l. and joy the other holds within it.
T-18...... IX.7:3 appear and shift from l. to the grotesque.
T-19.......I.15:2 what has already been prepared for l..
T19... IV.D.6:3 The "l." of sin, the delicate appeal of guilt,
T19. IV.D.14:3 cast the veil of sin upon Him to hide His l.
T-20....... V.6:6 Here is the l. of your relationship, with
T-20...... VI.9:2 is frail as is a snowflake, but without its l..
T-20..VIII.11:1 seen it change to sights of l. and peace;
T-22...... IV.4:1 Think of the l. that you will see, who walk
T-22...... IV.5:2 For in his sight your l. is his salvation,
T-23..... II.18:8 rosy lips upon a skeleton, dress it in l., pet
T-24....... II.8:1 of the l. that you will see within yourself,
T-24...... III.7:1 by a world of l. they do not see. Freedom
T-24...... VI.6:2 It is His l. they see in everything. And it is
T-24..... VII.4:6 or weave a frame of l. around your hate,
T-25....... II.7:2 Look at its l., and understand the Mind
T-25...... IV.5:4 has saved its perfume and its l. for you.
T-27.......I.10:5 and by its health and l. proclaim the truth
T-28.........I.7:8 They will surprise you with their l.. The
T-31....VIII.8:3 for hell within a world whose l. can yet be
T-31....VIII.9:3 all the l. which they concealed appear like
W-pI.....23.4:5 see now. L. can light your images, and so
W-pI...124.4:5 our eyes behold His l. in all we look upon.
W-pI. 124.11:1 to you; the l. you look on is your own.
W-pI...161.9:3 And in Christ's vision is his l. reflected in
W-pII .247.1:6 Your l. reflects my own. Your sinlessness
W-pII .263.1:4 *of all the l. with which You blessed creation;*
W-pII . 289.2:5 *wait longer for Your Son to find the l. You*
W-pII . 291.1:4 well. What l. we look upon today! What
M-23 ......... 5:5 his eyes your l. is so complete and flawless

## lovely 29

T-13 .......X.9:5 Fear not to look upon the l. truth in you.
T-17 .......II.1:2 fantasy have you ever seen anything so l..
T-17 . IV.12:11 hung in light, l. to look upon for what it is
T-18 ......I.11:4 How l. and how holy is your relationship,
T-18 ... IX.10:2 Forgiveness does make l., but it does not
T-19 ......I.15:2 it calls on truth to enter and make l. what
T-19 ......I.15:3 the process of making l. that they begin.
T-19 .......II.5:3 the ego's system; l. and powerful, wholly
T-20 .......II.1:3 were made to make seem l. what you hate
T-21 ........I.6:3 just this little part, how l. was the song,
T-22 ..... VI.4:1 This holy relationship, l. in its innocence,
T-23 .....II.15:7 l. do the laws of fear make death appear.
T-23 ...II.17:10 when madness takes a form you think is l.
T-23 ..... III.2:1 l. and charitable it may seem to be, a
T-23 ..... IV.4:1 The l. light of your relationship is like the
T-24 ..... III.1:4 for he holds one error to himself as l. still.
T-24 ...... V.2:1 the form, however l. it may seem to be,
T-25 .......II.7:2 and bones, but in a frame as l. as itself. Its
T-27 ........I.6:9 to show how l. are the witnesses for guilt.
T-29 ..... VI.6:1 How l. is the world whose purpose is
T-30 ... III.5:11 completely l. Thought God holds of you.
T-30 ..... III.8:6 still and white and l. will it shine through
T-30 ..... IV.1:3 truth behind them is so l. and so still in
W-pI. 186.11:1 In l. contrast, certain as the sun's return
W-pI... 187.9:2 could fear to look upon such l. holiness?
C-3 ............ 8:1 How l. does the world become in just
C-4 ............ 8:1 safe and pure and l. in the Mind of God,
S-3..........II.2:3 and clearly seen at most in l. flashes. Now
S-3........ IV.9:4 How l. are you, child of Holiness! How

## loves 103

T-4 ....... III.4:1 with your ego cannot believe God l. you.
T-5 ...... VII.1:5 You are His care because He l. you. His
T-10 ...... V.6:4 love Him, and that you know He l. you.
T-12 ..... IV.4:7 whom He l. with the Love of the Father.
T-12 ..... VI.2:3 Because He l. you, He will gladly teach
T-12 ..... VI.2:3 you, He will gladly teach you what He l.,
T-13 ...... V.5:4 Everyone draws nigh unto what he l., and
T-13 ...... V.9:6 He l. what He sees within you, and He
T-13 ... VII.6:2 maintaining that he l. what he loves not,
T-13 ... VII.6:2 maintaining that he loves what he l. not,
T-13 ... VII.8:3 it *now.* God l. His Son forever, and His Son
T-13 .......X.8:4 remember how much his Father l. him.
T-13 .....X.10:3 *And as His Son l. Him.* There is no fear in
T-13 .....X.11:4 You can love only as God l.. Seek not to
T-13 .....X.13:2 is that I love *only* what God l. with me, and
T-13 .....X.14:7 God l. you. Could I, then, lack faith in you
T-14 ... III.15:5 Be quiet in your faith in Him Who l. you,
T-14 ..... IV.8:4 understand how much your Father l. you,
T-15 ... III.10:5 What my Father l. I love as He does, and I
T-15 .... V.10:5 it. God l. every brother as He loves you;
T-15 .... V.10:5 it. God loves every brother as He l. you;
T-16 .......II.7:8 charity on whom God l. with perfect Love
T-16 ... IV.11:8 He l. you, wholly without illusion, as you
T-17 .......II.1:7 the beauty the Holy Spirit l. to look upon,
T-18 ......I.10:5 He l. you both, equally and as one. And as
T-18 ......I.10:6 And as He l. you, so you are. You are not
T19....IV.C.4:7 kill it. For what the ego l., it kills for its
T19. IV.D.15:3 as God created every living thing and l. it.
T-20 .......II.5:6 shines on everything He looks upon and l.
T-20 ..... III.5:6 the ego, whose image it is and which it l.,
T-20 .... VII.9:7 No one who l. can judge, and what he sees
T-21 ..... III.9:9 He Who l. the world is seeing it for you,
T-22 ........I.1:2 God would heal and hate the one He l.,
T-22 ..... VI.3:1 of means and end so easily in what God l.,
T-22 ..... VI.6:6 are now His means must love all that He l.
T-22 ..... VI.9:1 look on what your Father l. with charity?
T-23 ........I.4:6 l. you perfectly, completely and eternally.
T-23 ........I.9:5 and drive Him out of what He l. forever.
T-23 ........I.9:6 And what He l. must be forever quiet and
T-24 ..... IV.5:1 in which God is bereft of what He l., and
T-24 ...... V.1:2 He looks on what He l., and knows it as
T-24 .......V.6:8 in each living thing that He beholds and l.
T-24 ... VI.10:6 Who l. each part of Him with equal love
T-24 .... VII.1:4 it needs does he deny to what he l.. And
T-25 .......II.9:3 if you but share His praise of what He l.?
T-25 ..... VI.1:3 as he l. them, so he looks upon himself
T-25 . VIII.10:8 justice would be done unto the Son He l.,
T-26 .......II.8:3 it. Nothing He l. but must be sinless and
T-26 ..... IV.4:5 him that what he feared he l. the most.
T-27 .......V.4:5 the One Who blesses you l. all the world,
T-27 .... VII.8:6 It l. him not, but casts him as it will in any
T-29 ........I.2:5 He fears to love and l. to hate, and so he
T-29 ...... IV.6:6 Because He l. the dreamer, not the dream,
T-30 .......II.4:3 whom God so l. is done to God Himself.
W-pI .... 68.6:4 in a world that protects you and l. you,
W-pI .. 95.15:4 *I am, and What He is, Who l. us both as One.*
W-pI .... 99.7:3 Your Father l. you. All the world of pain is
W-pI .. 100.6:3 the world can see how much He l. His Son
W-pI .. 123.3:2 for the Son He l. is changeless as Himself.
W-pI .. 124.3:2 Who l. us with the equal love in which we
W-pI .. 151.7:4 He recognizes only what God l., and in
W-pI 153.12:2 was designed by One Who l. His children,
W-pI .. 168.1:7 He l. His Son. There is no certainty but
W-pI 168.1:10 his mind remains asleep, He l. him still.
W-pI 168.1:11 He l. him with a never-changing Love.
W-pI .. 168.4:1 God l. His Son. Request Him now to give
W-pI .. 168.6:3 Such is His Will, because He l. His Son.
W-pI 184.12:6 made as fitting tribute to the Son He l..
W-pI .. 190.8:3 In pain is God denied the Son He l.. In
W-pI .. 193.3:2 His loving kindness to the Son He l.. Each
W-pI .. 199.2:4 afraid who lives in Innocence, and only l.?
W-pI .. 219.1:5 *as to what my Father l. forever as His Son.* I
W-pII .... 224.h God is my Father, and He l. His Son.
W-pII .... 225.h God is my Father, and His Son l. Him.
W-pII . 235.1:4 Arms. I am the Son He l.. And I am saved
W-pII . 238.2:1 pause to think how much our Father l. us.
W-pII . 239.1:4 when He l. His Son forever and with
W-pII ..... 4.3:4 And God Himself has lost the Son He l.,
W-pII ..... 4.4:4 and l. him with an everlasting Love which
W-pII . 276.1:3 God become the Father of the Son He l.,
W-pII . 279.2:2 *Father l. the Son Whom He created as His*
W-pII . 281.2:4 And I would not attack the Son He l., for
W-pII . 281.2:4 loves, for what He l. is also mine to love.
W-pII . 282.1:4 Self Whom God created as the Son He l.,
W-pII . 283.1:4 *I am he my Father l.. My holiness remains*
W-pII . 316.1:2 no shadow on the holy mind my Father l..
W-pII . 327.1:5 He has not abandoned me and l. me still,
W-pII . 337.1:6 harm, to understand my Father l. His Son
W-pII . 337.1:6 Son; to know I am the Son my Father l..
W-pII . 347.2:2 that He has judged you as the Son He l..
W-ep ......... 6:4 do. He l. God's Son as we would love him.
M-11 ......... 1:6 world you see cannot be the world God l.,
M-11 ......... 1:6 His Word assures us that He l. the world.
M-11 ......... 2:6 Word assures you that He l. the world;
M-27 ......... 2:5 Who l. such a god knows not of love,
M-29 ......... 8:4 *You are the Son He l., And it is given you to be*
C-ep .......... 2:2 you belong to Him Who l. you as He loves
C-ep .......... 2:2 to Him Who loves you as He l. Himself.
S-2..........I.2:6 that would destroy the holy Son He l..
S-2...........I.3:7 He l. His Son. Can you remember Him
S-2...........I.3:9 hate his Father if you hate the Son He l..
S-2..........II.4:1 goal is to separate from God the Son He l.
S-3........ IV.6:5 You are he your Father l., who never left

## Loving

*See* All-Loving

## loving 104

T-1 ........I.18:3 It is a way of l. your neighbor as yourself.
T-1 ....... III.2:3 His work is wholly lovable and wholly l..
T-2 ..........I.1:2 them with the same l. Will to create. You
T-2 ..........I.2:8 because all l. creation is freely given in
T-4 ....... IV.2:9 a l. brother I am deeply concerned with
T-5 ....... IV.1:3 and teach you that only what is l. is true.
T-5 ....... IV.3:1 Every l. thought held in any part of the
T-5 ....... IV.3:2 It is shared *because* it is l.. Sharing is God's
T-5 ....... IV.8:3 and every l. thought you ever had. I have
T-7 ..........I.4:1 because it is competitive rather than l.. It

| | |
|---|---|
| T-7........VI.2:3 | what love is, it cannot perceive itself as l.. |
| T-7.......VII.6:4 | in His Love and protect your rest by l.. |
| T-8........VI.4:1 | This son of a l. father left his home and |
| T-10.......in.1:1 | beyond yourself can make you fearful or l. |
| T-10.........I.3:3 | because l. then seems possible to you, but |
| T-11.....VII.2:1 | Every l. thought that the Son of God ever |
| T-11.....VII.2:2 | The l. thoughts his mind perceives in this |
| T-11.....VII.2:4 | Yet they are eternal because they are l.. |
| T-11.....VII.2:5 | And being l. they are like the Father, and |
| T-11... VIII.9:2 | and see only his l. thoughts as his reality, |
| T-11... VIII.9:4 | every thought is as l. as the Thought of |
| T-11. VIII.10:2 | Only l. thoughts are recognized, and |
| T-12.........I.3:3 | Every l. thought is true. Everything else is |
| T-12.........I.6:2 | both his l. thoughts and his appeals for |
| T-12.........I.8:7 | to accept only l. thoughts in others and to |
| T-12......III.7:1 | only the l. thoughts of God's Son are the |
| T-12......VI.3:5 | from the extension of l. thoughts outward |
| T-12......VI.7:3 | l. the extension of Himself that is His Son. |
| T-12... VIII.8:1 | you by God in l. exchange for the world |
| T-13.......in.3:2 | to this as the price of salvation and *be* l.. |
| T-13......III.4:3 | world God would destroy; and by l. Him, |
| T-13......III.6:4 | is the l. mind that thought it made them |
| T-13......III.8:3 | the Father, in l. remembrance of Him. |
| T-13....VI.13:5 | gave. God's Son is still as l. as his Father. |
| T-13... VIII.4:6 | that spring to light under His l. gaze are |
| T-13....... X.3:6 | love, and cannot understand what l. is. |
| T-13..... X.12:2 | wholly untouched by guilt and wholly l., |
| T-14....III.15:8 | from the l. Mind wherein he was created, |
| T-14....III.18:3 | Unlearn isolation through His l. guidance |
| T-14....IV.4:10 | Fail not in your function of l. in a loveless |
| T-14......IV.5:5 | upon yourself by l. not the Son of God, |
| T-15......IX.5:3 | in such sure and l. relationships that any |
| T-17......III.1:1 | only the l. thoughts you gave in the past, |
| T-17......III.5:3 | If all but l. thoughts have been forgotten, |
| T-17......III.5:7 | In these l. thoughts is the spark of beauty |
| T-18....... V.4:2 | And so they must be l.. Their message is, |
| T-19...... I.10:3 | everyone as a Son of your most l. Father, |
| T19..IV.B.10:1 | kind, infinite in its patience and wholly l.. |
| T-20....... II.5:5 | strangers; only dearly loved and l. friends. |
| T-20......VI.1:3 | And this is wholly l. and forever. Yet has |
| T-21..... II.13:1 | brother were both created by a l. Father, |
| T-22....VI.14:6 | From l. minds there *is* no separation. And |
| T-23....IV.1:11 | What is not l. must be an attack. Every |
| T-24....... II.4:4 | you eternally in l. praise of what you are, |
| T-25... VIII.9:9 | what l. justice knows to be his due. For |
| T-26......IX.1:6 | Look with l. eyes on him who carries |
| T-29.........I.6:4 | because you do not know what l. means. |
| T-29... VIII.6:6 | as perfect, sinless and as l. as his Father, |
| T-30......IV.1:3 | is so lovely and so still in l. gentleness, |
| T-30..... V.10:7 | will not perceive Whose l. hand you hold. |
| T-31... VIII.8:7 | And God ordained, in l. kindness, that it |
| W-pI.....40.3:5 | *happy, peaceful, l. and contented.* Another |
| W-pI.....55.2:2 | is hardly the representation of l. thoughts |
| W-pI.....55.2:6 | My l. thoughts will save me from this |
| W-pI.....96.1:1 | two; as both good and evil, l. and hating, |
| W-pI...102.5:2 | no need to be less l. to God's Son than He |
| W-pI...102.5:2 | Whose Love created him as l. as Himself. |
| W-pI.110.11:1 | l. thoughts for all who meet with us today |
| W-pI...123.2:2 | Be glad today, in l. thankfulness, your |
| W-pI...123.5:6 | speaks, however l. may the message be. |
| W-pI...123.6:3 | since He receives your gifts in l. gratitude, |
| W-pI...124.4:6 | Today we see only the l. and the lovable. |
| W-pI...127.1:2 | for this, a kind for that; a way of l. one, |
| W-pI...127.1:2 | loving one, another way of l. still another. |
| W-pI...127.9:5 | In l. gentleness He will abide with you, as |
| W-pI.135.18:3 | defenses did not let you see His l. blessing |
| W-pI.153.18:1 | hear His l. Voice guiding your footsteps |
| W-pI...162.6:2 | you into his heart with l. invitation, eager |
| W-pI...186.8:3 | mourner to ecstatic bliss of love and l.. |
| W-pI...193.3:2 | reflect His l. kindness to the Son He loves. |
| W-pI...194.7:1 | gives his future to the l. Hands of God? |
| W-pI...195.8:6 | has earned the right to love by being l., |
| WpI rVI.in.7:4 | become a l. gift of freedom to the world. |
| W-pII..225.1:3 | *still the way Your l. Son is led along to You!* |
| W-pII..234.2:2 | *on us, for all the l. help we have received, for* |
| W-pII..244.1:3 | *when he belongs to You, beloved and l., in* |
| W-pII..267.1:6 | quiet and at peace within His l. Arms. |
| W-pII..300.2:2 | *For we, Your l. Sons, have lost our way a* |
| W-pII..306.1:4 | care; of l. kindness and the peace of God. |
| W-pII.... 10.5:1 | innocent, forever l. and forever loved, as |
| W-pII..313.2:3 | How holy and how l.! Brother, come and |
| W-pII..317.2:5 | *from the sure protection of Your l. Arms.* |
| W-pII..324.1:5 | *Your l. Voice will always call me back, and* |
| W-pII..324.2:2 | stray except an instant from His l. Hand. |
| M-27 .........2:1 | would be impossible to think of Him as l.. |
| M-27 .........4:1 | not proclaim a l. God nor re-establish any |
| M-27 .........5:3 | real. But God would not be l.. There is no |
| M-29 .........6:9 | A l. father does not let his child harm |
| C-2.............8:2 | as a l. mother sings her child to rest. Is |
| P-2........VI.1:3 | its l. protection and alert defense, -- all |
| S-1...........I.5:1 | letting go, a quiet time of listening and l.. |
| S-2...........I.2:4 | things, and overlooks the l. as a plague; a |
| S-2...........I.3:5 | it real. Select the l. and forgive the sin by |
| S-3......... II.4:2 | to bless the mind with l. pardon for the |

## lovingly 19

| | |
|---|---|
| T-9.......VII.4:5 | likely to attack you when you react l., |
| T-13......VI.6:2 | Look l. upon the present, for it holds the |
| T-18......VI.4:8 | love does not condemn it and can use it l., |
| T19. IV.A.14:5 | they found, to share them l. with you. Be |
| T-23.......in.6:2 | Look on it l., and see the light of Heaven |
| T-24....... V.3:7 | brother's, and how l. He walks beside him |
| T-24......VI.3:2 | created has He failed to lay before you l., |
| T-24......VI.3:4 | look upon yourself as l. as He conceived |
| T-26......IX.1:1 | Voice for God calls l. unto your brother, |
| T-26......IX.7:1 | Around you angels hover l., to keep away |
| T-27.....IV.4:15 | you want, and it will serve you l. and well. |
| T-27.....IV.7:2 | only place that holds the answer l. for you |
| T-27....... V.7:6 | which all eyes look l. upon the Friend who |
| W-pI.....49.2:6 | Try to hear God's Voice call to you l., |
| W-pI.....97.2:2 | You are the spirit l. endowed with all your |
| W-pI...123.8:1 | will understand how l. He holds you in |
| W-pI...139.9:7 | Look l. on them, that they may know that |
| W-pII..283.2:2 | to all things, uniting l. with all the world, |
| S-3........IV.9:6 | l. I hold you in My Heart and in My Arms |

## low 3

| | |
|---|---|
| T-9....... II.10:1 | set the price l. but demand a high return. |
| T-18......IX.6:1 | is like a bank of l. dark clouds that seem |
| S-1.........in.3:2 | until both high and l. have disappeared. |

## lower 9

*See also* lower-order

| | |
|---|---|
| T-1.........I.12:2 | the l. or bodily level of experience, or the |
| T-1..........II.5:3 | mediates higher to l. communication, |
| T-2......... IV.5:6 | not to l. it by increasing fear. |
| T-4...... IV.11:2 | just as your ego does with your l. mind, |
| T-5...........I.1:9 | the l. mind it is quite comprehensible in |
| T-5........ III.6:4 | Time is a belief of the ego, so the l. mind, |
| T-5........ VI.4:1 | reverse a l. court's decisions in this world. |
| T-29...... IX.1:3 | let himself fall l. than the stones upon the |
| S-3..........II.1:2 | can occur at l. forms of prayer, combining |

## lower-order 1

| | |
|---|---|
| T-2....V.A.11:1 | miracle abolishes the need for l. concerns. |

## lowered 1

| | |
|---|---|
| W-pI... 126.3:3 | have l. him beneath a true equality with |

## lowest 1

| | |
|---|---|
| T-31...... IV.4:8 | For from this l. point will learning lead to |

## lowly 1

| | |
|---|---|
| T-13..... X.14:2 | Alone we are all l., but together we shine |

## loyalty 2

| | |
|---|---|
| T-1........ III.5:8 | are defending misplaced or misdirected l. |
| T-18..... VII.6:7 | of allegiance, a truly undivided l.. Believe |

## lump 1

| | |
|---|---|
| T-29...... IV.3:4 | veils the heavy l. of fear that is their core. |

## lure 1

| | |
|---|---|
| T-16...... VI.3:2 | guilt, the real l. in the special relationship. |

## lurk 1

| | |
|---|---|
| T-31..... VII.1:7 | believing that the "bad" must l. behind. |

## lurking 1

| | |
|---|---|
| W-pI... 121.2:3 | not, yet certain of the danger l. there. |

## lurks 1

| | |
|---|---|
| W-pII ..... 8.3:5 | No danger l. in anything it sees, for it is |

## lusterless 1

| | |
|---|---|
| W-pI... 100.3:4 | the means to save the world is dim and l., |

## lying 2

| | |
|---|---|
| T-3...........I.5:3 | The lion and the lamb l. down together |
| W-pII . 268.2:1 | today, nor let our ears attend to l. tongues |

# M

**mad** 51

T-13.......in.2:2 system of those made **m.** by guilt. Look
T-18.........I.6:6 and take no part in all the **m.** projection
T-18.........I.7:3 into the **m.** world and so depart from you.
T-18.........I.7:6 and swirling lightly off on a **m.** course like
T-18.........I.8:3 with you your **m.** journey outside yourself
T-18.........I.9:2 In the **m.** world outside you nothing can
T19....IV.C.5:6 a tiny, **m.** idea of corruption that can be
T19... IV.D.7:6 No **m.** desire, no trivial impulse to forget
T-20...... VI.8:6 The instant that the **m.** idea of making
T-20...... VI.8:7 bodies made to house the **m.** idea and
T-20...... VI.8:9 house this **m.** idea against reality but for
T-21....... II.6:5 a **m.** revolt against what must forever be.
T-21....... II.6:7 This is the **m.** idea you have enshrined
T-21...... III.5:6 This **m.** direction was your choice, and by
T-21...... IV.4:2 Not wholly **m.**, you have been willing to
T-22...... VI.2:5 He knows this **m.** decision was made by
T-23.........I.2:8 only the **m.** belief the Will of God can be
T-25.........I.5:5 part–the tiny, **m.** desire to be separate,
T-25...... III.4:1 simultaneous Corrector of the **m.** belief
T-25..... VII.3:2 It must be so that either God is **m.**, or is
T-25..... VII.4:4 not his Father's Son because the Son is **m.**
T-25..... VII.6:4 a world perceived as wholly **m.** to sinners,
T-25..... VII.8:2 Because He is not **m.** has God appointed
T-25..... VII.8:3 into it in quietness and show him he is **m.**
T-25... VII.11:3 If this were true, then God is **m.** indeed!
T-25... VII.11:7 all. You who believe that God is **m.**, look
T-25... VII.13:1 **m.** belief that God's insanity would make
T-26...... V.13:4 all of time is but the **m.** belief that what is
T-27.....VIII.6:2 all is one, there crept a tiny, **m.** idea, at
W-pI..... 45.7:1 the senseless thoughts and **m.** ideas with
W-pI..... 54.3:3 the **m.** idea of separation had to be shared
W-pI..... 71.8:4 and **m.** proposals to free yourself. They
W-pI... 100.1:2 Salvation must reverse the **m.** belief in
W-pI... 134.7:4 shrieks of sinners **m.** with guilt. It looks
W-pI... 135.7:4 for the many **m.** attacks you make upon it
W-pI. 136.10:2 quails before such **m.** attacks as these,
W-pI... 138.8:1 These **m.** beliefs can gain unconscious
W-pI... 139.6:4 does this mean except the world is **m.**?
W-pI... 152.6:6 He is not **m.**. Yet only madness makes a
W-pI. 153.13:1 a fearful world made **m.** by sin and guilt;
W-pI... 155.3:2 **m.** illusion will remain awhile in evidence
W-pI... 187.7:5 idea so **m.** that sanity dismisses it at once.
W-pI... 190.3:2 confused with fear, perceived as **m.**, and
W-pI... 190.4:5 Their witness, pain, is **m.** as they, and no
W-pI... 198.7:7 **m.** to think that you could be condemned
W-pII ..... 4.1:2 the means by which the mind is driven **m.**
W-pII ..... 4.1:3 And being **m.**, it sees illusions where the
W-pII . 298.1:4 journeys, **m.** careers and artificial values.
Wfl ........in.5:4 that anger is insane, attack is **m.**, and
M-4 ...... VI.1:6 are but foolish guardians of **m.** illusions.
P-2....... VII.5:7 That many therapists are **m.** is obvious.

**made** 1023
*See also* self-made

T-1.........I.24:1 you **m.** sickness and death yourself, and
T-1.........I.50:1 compares what you have **m.** with creation
T-1........ III.5:9 you reinforce errors they have already **m.**.
T-1......... V.6:4 can be deepened, and thus **m.** to hold, is
T-1........ VI.1:3 it is very apparent in what you have **m.**. It
T-1........ VI.2:3 having **m.** this fundamental error, you
T-1........ VI.4:2 of fear yourself, because you **m.** fear, and
T-1........ VI.4:2 fear, and you believe in what you **m.**. In
T-1........ VI.4:6 It is true for you because it was **m.** by you.
T-1....... VII.5:1 already referred, and which is often **m.**. I
T-2......... II.1:2 have **m.** it clear that miracles are natural,
T-2......... II.4:1 because it is not a device you **m.**. The
T-2........ IV.2:8 The whole distortion that **m.** magic rests
T-2 ... V.A.12:1 what is created and what is **m.** is essential
T-2 ....... VI.5:8 is because you have not **m.** up your mind.
T-2 ...... VII.3:6 Us, and believe in what you have **m.**. You
T-2 ...... VII.4:1 control fear because you yourself **m.** it,
T-2 .... VII.5:13 exist. Miscreation **m.** this necessary as a
T-2 ..... VIII.3:8 Until this distinction is **m.**, however, the
T-2 ..... VIII.5:6 and at any time to everything you have **m.**
T-3 ........I.3:11 I have **m.** every effort to use words that
T-3 .........I.6:7 it in darkness have **m.** it inaccessible to
T-3 .........II.1:5 commitment to one or the other is **m.**. A
T-3 ....... III.7:3 Attack is always **m.** upon a stranger. You
T-3 ....... III.7:5 It is because you have **m.** him a stranger
T-3 ....... IV.3:1 self, which was **m.** rather than created. It
T-3 ....... IV.6:1 ability to perceive **m.** the body possible,
T-3 ........ V.1:3 anything since. I have also **m.** it clear that
T-3 ........ V.2:3 Anything **m.** for a specific purpose has no
T-3 ........ V.3:2 and what you have **m.** of yourself is so
T-3 ....... VI.4:5 but you have **m.** it seem dangerous to you
T-3 ...... VII.1:7 Nothing **m.** by a child of God is without
T-3 ...... VII.1:8 to escape from the prison you have **m.**.
T-3 ...... VII.5:3 at your life and see what the devil has **m.**.
T-4 ..........I.5:5 to try to protect itself once you have **m.** it,
T-4 ..........I.8:3 You who **m.** it cannot trust it, because in
T-4 ..........I.9:3 and have therefore **m.** fear for yourself.
T-4 .........II.1:1 how the mind could ever have **m.** the ego.
T-4 .........II.2:3 were not **m.** by or with the Unalterable. It
T-4 .........II.3:1 is a good example of how the ego was **m.**.
T-4 .........II.4:5 to the self you **m.** are not surprising. In
T-4 .........II.7:3 because it was **m.** as a substitute for it.
T-4 ....... III.4:2 You do not love what you **m.**, and what
T-4 ....... III.4:2 made, and what you **m.** does not love you
T-4 ....... III.4:3 Being **m.** out of the denial of the Father,
T-4 ....... III.4:4 because of your hatred for the self you **m.**.
T-4 ....... III.4:5 love you feel for the ego because you **m.** it.
T-4 ....... III.7:3 unwilling to destroy what you have **m.**.
T-4 ....... III.7:7 complete respect for what you have **m.**,
T-4 ....... IV.7:1 God and His creations is easily **m.** if you
T-4 ...... V.6:11 **m.** a decision about your future effort;
T-4 ....... VI.3:6 recognition is **m.** by you and not the ego,
T-5 ..........I.6:1 of His children because they had **m.** them
T-5 .........II.3:2 When the ego was **m.**, God placed in the
T-5 .........II.3:5 One you **m.** yourself, and that one is not
T-5 .........II.5:7 broken because you had **m.** another voice
T-5 .......II.8:12 It is **m.** on the basis of which call is worth
T-5 .........II.9:5 It is **m.** by giving, and is therefore the one
T-5 .........II.9:7 I showed you that this decision can be **m.**,
T-5 ....... III.5:5 the task of undoing what the ego has **m.**.
T-5 ..... III.11:1 The ego **m.** the world as it perceives it,
T-5 ..... III.11:1 the reinterpreter of what the ego **m.**, sees
T-5 ..... III.11:5 You have not **m.** truth, but truth can still
T-5 ....... IV.2:8 but having **m.** them you did not realize
T-5 ........ V.2:2 you have **m.** is undone by the Holy Spirit,
T-5 ...... V.6:10 it. You **m.** the other, and so you can. Only
T-5 ...... V.6:12 you **m.** can always be changed because,
T-5 ....... VI.3:6 unnecessary until the first one was **m.**.
T-5 ....... VI.4:2 on the error they were **m.** to uphold.
T-5 ...... VII.3:1 insane calls you think are **m.** upon you,
T-5 ...... VII.4:3 **m.** that is not in accord with His holy Will
T-5 ...... VII.6:5 to the point at which the error was **m.**,
T-5 ...... VII.6:8 *I* **m.** *the decision myself, but I can also decide*
T-6 ..........I.4:1 Assault can ultimately be **m.** only on the
T-6 ..........I.5:1 I have **m.** it perfectly clear that I am like
T-6 ........I.14:3 own imperfect love **m.** them vulnerable to
T-6 ........I.14:4 their sense of guilt had **m.** them angry.
T-6 .........II.2:4 imagine that you have **m.** yourself safe.
T-6 .........II.9:6 **m.** it and the Holy Spirit can therefore use
T-6 ....... IV.2:1 God created you He **m.** you part of Him.
T-6 ....... IV.2:3 You **m.** the ego without love, and so it
T-6 ....... IV.4:1 part of the mind that **m.** it is against it. It
T-6 ....... IV.9:2 kindest solution possible for what you **m.**.
T-6 ..... IV.11:4 laws are true, but because you **m.** them.
T-6 ..... IV.11:9 you **m.** with the truth He created for you,
T-6 .........V.1:4 teach you that you had **m.** a split mind,
T-6 ..... V.A.2:4 takes what you have **m.** and translates it
T-6 ..... V.B.6:4 a decision that was irrevocably **m.** for you
T-6 ..... V.C.9:5 it. What you **m.** has imprisoned your will,
T-6 ... V.C.10:5 what you **m.** because it was not true.
T-7 ....... IV.3:3 teaches you to use what the ego has **m.**, to
T-7 ..... IV.6:10 you have **m.** the laws meaningless to you.
T-7 .........V.5:9 are fearful because they are **m.** by fear.
T-7 .........V.8:8 the change his ego thinks it has **m.** in him
T-7 ..... VI.4:11 if the mind that **m.** it knew itself. And if it
T-7 ....... VI.5:5 in them, because that is how it **m.** them.
T-7 ....... VI.7:7 something, you have **m.** it true for you.
T-7 ...... VII.3:7 together as they were **m.** together. Teach
T-7 .... VII.3:11 **m.** perception and it must last as long as
T-7 ..... VIII.5:2 mind, and as you **m.** it by believing in it,
T-7 ..... VIII.6:5 beyond belief, because it is **m.** *by* belief.
T-7 ..... VIII.7:2 **m.** the ego by believing the unbelievable
T-7 .........X.7:3 lead you out of the confusion you have **m.**
T-7 ....... XI.2:3 for the environment that he has **m.**. He
T-7 ....... XI.3:1 you have **m.** and judge its worth fairly. Is
T-8 ..........I.1:5 This is not a bargain **m.** by God, Who
T-8 ..........I.4:1 simply because it has not **m.** you happy.
T-8 ..........I.5:2 the outcome of yours has **m.** you unhappy
T-8 .........II.7:4 all things, it **m.** them part of itself. You
T-8 ....... III.6:7 you make? Having **m.** this choice you will
T-8 ..... VI.5:11 You **m.** neither yourself nor your function
T-8 ..... VI.5:12 You **m.** only the decision to be unworthy
T-8 ...... VII.2:2 you have **m.** in the light of what He is.
T-8 ...... VII.7:1 "The Word (or thought) was **m.** flesh."
T-8 ...... VII.7:4 cannot be **m.** into flesh except by belief,
T-8 .... VII.10:4 Mind cannot be **m.** physical, but it can be
T-8 .... VII.10:4 **m.** manifest *through* the physical if it uses
T-8 .... VII.14:1 the body, and thought cannot be **m.** flesh.
T-8 ..... VIII.4:9 it has already **m.** the witness an ally.
T-9 ..........I.1:1 beliefs the human mind has ever **m.**. It
T-9 ........I.12:2 can be **m.** into a very persistent goal even
T-9 ....... III.8:6 it. For that all learning was **m.**. This is the
T-9 ....... III.8:7 that you do not need, but that you **m.**.
T-9 ....... IV.3:3 what you have **m.** into what God created.
T-9 ....... IV.4:5 can you overlook what you have **m.** real?
T-9 ....... IV.4:6 you have **m.** it real and *cannot* overlook it.
T-9 ....... IV.5:4 what you have **m.** in order to be forgiven.
T-9 ....... IV.9:3 Coming that was **m.** for you as the First
T-9 .........V.4:3 Having **m.** it real, he then attempts to
T-9 ...... VII.1:3 it, He must have **m.** it possible and easy to
T-9 ..... VIII.4:8 **m.** grandiosity and are afraid of it because
T-9 ..... VIII.7:3 replaced it with something you have **m.**.
T-10 ........II.6:5 you have **m.** yourself vigilant *against* God
T-10 ..... III.4:6 **m.** in the image of what its maker thinks
T-10 ..... III.8:5 because you believe that they **m.** you. You
T-10 ..... III.8:6 fact that you **m.** them to replace God. Yet
T-10 ..... III.9:4 to. You **m.** the god of sickness, and by
T-10 ..... III.9:4 him you **m.** yourself able to hear him. Yet
T-10 ... III.10:8 and the father you **m.** did not make you.
T-10 ... III.11:6 because he was **m.** as God's replacement.
T-10 ..... IV.1:6 not at war with the god of sickness you **m.**
T-10 ..... IV.1:9 the nothingness out of which he was **m.**.
T-10 ... IV.4:10 "given" your peace to the gods you **m.**,
T-10 ..... IV.5:7 What you have **m.** is so unworthy of you
T-10 ....... V.3:4 are sick you cannot keep the gods you **m.**,
T-10 ....... V.3:7 having **m.** him out of your insanity, he is
T-10 ....... V.4:2 God" **m.** His Son think he was Fatherless,
T-10 ....... V.4:2 and out of his depression he **m.** the god of
T-10 ....... V.5:2 were, what you have **m.** would be true,
T-10 ..... V.11:5 for the misery you have **m.** for yourself.
T-10 ..... V.11:6 the means for undoing what you have **m.**.

T-10..... V.13:6 things you have **m.** are your real creations
T-11.......in.2:2 If you **m.** the ego, how can the ego have
T-11.......in.2:2 the ego, how can the ego have **m.** you?
T-11.......in.2:3 because the ego was **m.** out of the wish of
T-11.......in.2:4 system in which you **m.** your own father.
T-11.......in.2:8 And either the ego, which you **m.**, *is* your
T-11.........I.4:2 You who **m.** delay can leave time behind
T-11....... V.1:5 to see beyond it, since you have **m.** it real.
T-11..... V.14:6 mind, and protecting what it has **m.** real,
T-11......VI.5:2 god he **m.** or the God Who created him.
T-11.....VII.3:7 what you **m.** is capable of being unlike
T-11.....VII.4:4 have **m.** many ideas that you have placed
T-11.....VII.4:6 what you have **m.** and what God created,
T-11.....VII.4:6 you have **m.** and what *you* have created.
T-11.....VII.4:9 has saved for you out of what you have **m.**
T-11... VIII.1:6 then everything you **m.** will be forgotten;
T-11... VIII.4:4 You **m.** the problem God has answered.
T-11. VIII.15:4 in place of the false one you have **m.**. And
T-12.........I.1:7 done so, having **m.** his error real to you.
T-12.........I.9:6 One is false, for it was **m.** out of denial;
T-12....... II.3:3 You will be **m.** whole as you make whole,
T-12......III.4:3 who have **m.** the request outrageous, and
T-12......III.4:8 No "outrageous" requests can be **m.** of
T-12......III.8:4 for the one you **m.** out of your split mind,
T-12......III.9:4 have no control over the world you **m.**. It
T-12......III.9:6 world you **m.** is therefore totally chaotic,
T-12......III.9:7 For it is **m.** out of what you do not want,
T-12....... V.1:5 to "equalize" the situation you **m.**. You
T-12....... V.4:3 a split mind has **m.** itself a poor learner.
T-12.....VII.1:5 this holy perception you will be **m.** whole,
T-12.....VII.7:7 each other because you **m.** them different.
T-12.....VII.9:3 What you **m.** of it is not its reality, for its
T-12... VIII.3:1 When you **m.** visible what is not true,
T-12... VIII.4:4 you have **m.** invisible is the only truth,
T-12... VIII.5:5 But look upon what you have **m.** of it, and
T-12... VIII.6:5 Everything you **m.** has never been, and is
T-12... VIII.6:7 You have **m.** invisible the only truth that
T-12. VIII.6:11 of what you have **m.** visible to yourself.
T-12... VIII.8:1 the world you **m.** and the world you see.
T-13.......in.2:2 system of those **m.** mad by guilt. Look
T-13.........I.2:1 you have **m.** the Son of God *has* sinned.
T-13.........I.5:3 to escape from the prison he has **m.**, and
T-13......III.3:3 world you thought you **m.** would vanish.
T-13......III.4:3 you have **m.** a world God would destroy;
T-13......III.5:1 You can accept insanity because you **m.** it
T-13......III.5:3 is given you is not so dear as what you **m.**.
T-13......III.6:4 mind that thought it **m.** them in anger.
T-13....III.10:4 **m.** of Him an unloving father, demanding
T-13....III.10:6 He feared what he had **m.**, but still more
T-13......IV.1:5 dust out of which it thinks you were **m.**.
T-13......IV.2:3 hell and oblivion are ideas that you **m.** up
T-13....... V.1:6 They are **m.** of sights that are not seen,
T-13....... V.2:2 **m.** up only of his reactions to his brothers
T-13....... V.2:3 Therefore, he does not see he **m.** them,
T-13....... V.8:4 And it is here that what you see you **m.**.
T-13....... V.8:5 let the darkness go and all you **m.** you will
T-13....... V.9:1 **m.** your way of seeing that you might see
T-13..... V.10:1 and one you **m.** and one was given you.
T-13......VI.1:5 that you **m.** and cherish instead of him. In
T-13......VI.5:7 Your past was **m.** in anger, and if you use
T-13....VI.10:8 peace, for you have **m.** it manifest in them
T-13.....VII.3:3 The roads you **m.** have led you nowhere,
T-13.....VII.3:4 you **m.** but has the mark of death upon it.
T-13.....VII.3:5 ready to return to dust even as you **m.** it.
T-13.....VII.4:3 strange world you **m.** but do not want. All
T-13.....VII.4:4 willingness to learn the one you **m.** is false
T-13.....VII.9:2 first exchange of what you **m.** for what
T-13....... X.2:4 strange relationships you have **m.** for this
T-13......XI.2:5 for your release, because you **m.** it not.
T-13......XI.2:6 Yet as you **m.** not freedom, so you made
T-13......XI.2:6 so you **m.** not a war that could endanger
T-13....XI.11:6 will not remember anything you **m.** that
T-14.........I.2:1 world **m.** of denial and without direction.
T-14.........I.3:2 system you **m.** would be forever dark. The
T-14.........I.3:4 his belief, but those he **m.** *are* his beliefs.
T-14.........I.3:9 Yet in him who **m.** this insane logic there
T-14.........I.5:4 you who cannot undo what you have **m.**,
T-14....... II.1:11 For if you value one thing **m.** of nothing,
T-14....... II.2:4 all the distortions you have **m.** of nothing;
T-14....... II.4:4 that this light is not what you have **m.**,
T-14....... II.7:6 You **m.** this door of nothing, and behind
T-14......III.9:5 effects. Every decision is **m.** for the whole
T-14....IV.4:10 place **m.** out of darkness and deceit, for
T-14......IV.7:8 You **m.** Him not, and anything you
T-14......IV.9:7 If you remember what you have **m.**, you
T-14....... V.6:4 Each effort **m.** on its behalf is offered for
T-14......VI.2:5 who **m.** these guardians of illusion out of
T-14......VI.5:2 was not broken, but *has* been **m.** obscure.
T-14......VI.5:3 All things you **m.** have use to Him, for His
T-14......VI.5:6 you **m.** in place of the power of creation,
T-14......VI.5:7 **m.** it to crucify yourself must learn of Him
T-14......VI.6:1 not understand the language you have **m.**
T-14......VI.6:5 You who **m.** it are but expressing conflict,
T-14.....VII.5:6 truth only because you **m.** them against it
T-14.....VII.5:8 Defenses, like everything you **m.**, must be
T-14......IX.1:3 holiness; or what you **m.** to what you are.
T-14......IX.1:8 Thus truth was **m.** past, and the present
T-14......XI.1:5 you have taught yourself has **m.** your
T-14......XI.1:7 You have **m.** a semblance of power and a
T-14......XI.7:1 for it is you who **m.** them necessary. And
T-14....XI.10:4 He has **m.** you free of what you made.
T-14....XI.10:4 He has made you free of what you **m.**.
T-15.........I.7:2 is only what the ego has **m.** of the present.
T-15......III.1:5 because it is a world **m.** out of littleness,
T-15......IV.2:6 Give over every plan you have **m.** for your
T-15....... V.4:5 function as Interpreter of what you **m.**,
T-15....... V.5:2 He also perceives that you have **m.** special
T-15....... V.5:3 unholy the reason you **m.** them may be,
T-15.....VII.3:2 it is. For having been **m.** real to you, it is
T-15.....VII.5:5 first to perceive what you have **m.** of them
T-15...VII.14:7 all are invited and **m.** welcome. And you
T-15... VIII.5:8 yet He understands it because you **m.** it.
T-15....... X.4:2 is necessary, for you **m.** but one mistake.
T-15..XI.10:12 all your relationships be **m.** holy for you.
T-16....... II.3:1 to hurt your mind has **m.** it so unnatural
T-16....... II.4:3 of the Sonship as One has been **m.**. When
T-16....... II.4:4 **m.** this joining as the Holy Spirit bids you
T-16....... II.8:4 greater faith in the disaster you have **m.**.
T-16....... II.9:3 these facts together and **m.** sense of them
T-16....IV.12:2 **m.** from your willingness to unite with
T-16....... V.3:6 of Heaven, being **m.** to be its opposite,
T-16....... V.8:3 other, the ego sees "a union **m.** in Heaven.
T-16..... V.10:8 it you have **m.** it little and unworthy,
T-16..... V.11:3 **m.** with power you wrested from truth,
T-16..... V.12:6 you would have **m.** yourself helpless. God
T-16......VI.5:6 If one such union were **m.** in perfect faith,
T-16....VI.10:1 on the travesty it **m.** of your relationships.
T-16.....VII.1:5 past? Every such choice is **m.** because of
T-17....... II.1:5 Nothing that you remember that **m.** your
T-17....... II.3:6 see. Yet what you see is only what you **m.**,
T-17....... II.4:3 that **m.** perception possible will still occur
T-17....... II.4:5 the real world and have been **m.** ready for
T-17....... II.5:2 searching of the mind that **m.** this world,
T-17....... II.5:5 the Son of God **m.** in insanity could be
T-17......III.5:4 transformed past is **m.** like the present.
T-17......III.5:9 must be corrected where it was **m.**.
T-17......III.6:1 their source, but where they were not **m.**.
T-17......III.7:7 You have **m.** the relationship unreal, and
T-17......III.7:9 what you have **m.** the past to represent,
T-17......IV.2:7 Every special relationship you have **m.** is a
T-17......IV.3:1 You have **m.** very real relationships even
T-17......IV.3:3 special relationship you have **m.** has, as
T-17......IV.8:4 the dim light in which the offering is **m.**.
T-17....IV.11:6 frame that **m.** you think it *was* a picture.
T-17..... V.11:3 may have **m.** many mistakes since then,
T-17..... V.11:3 you have also **m.** enormous efforts to help
T-17....... VI.4:6 because the goal has **m.** it meaningful.
T-17...VII.3:11 seek not to have it **m.** up to you elsewhere
T-17.....VII.9:6 situation was thus **m.** free of the past,
T-17.....VII.9:6 past, which would have **m.** it purposeless.
T-18.........I.4:1 that God is fear **m.** but one substitution.
T-18.........I.4:4 time, and life to death, was all you ever **m.**
T-18.........I.4:6 relationship that you have ever **m.** is part
T-18.........I.6:6 projection by which this world was **m.**.
T-'8.........I.9:9 you **m.** for Heaven can keep you from it.
T-18....... II.4:8 would do to it. And thus is guilt **m.** real.
T-18....... II.5:4 do not respond to it as though you **m.** it,
T-18....... II.8:6 dreams you do not see that you have **m.**,
T-18...... III.1:3 the darkness but **m.** the darkness deeper.
T-18...... III.3:6 of love, but only of what you have **m.** of it.
T-18...... III.7:4 are **m.** whole in our desire to make whole.
T-18.... IV.4:10 and then expect one to be **m.** *for* you?
T-18...... IV.6:3 Remember you **m.** guilt, and that your
T-18...... VI.4:7 be. The body was not **m.** by love. Yet love
T-18...... VI.4:8 respecting what the Son of God has **m.**
T-18...... VI.6:5 fantasies have **m.** your body your "enemy
T-18...... VI.7:1 This is the host of God that *you* have **m.**.
T-18...... VI.7:3 thing you **m.** to serve your guilt stands
T-18...... VI.7:6 You hate this prison you have **m.**, and
T-18...... VI.8:6 It is *not* **m.** up of different parts, which
T-18..... VII.6:5 well, neglecting what was **m.** for *you*. Save
T-18.... VIII.1:3 and it was **m.** to limit the unlimited.
T-18.... VIII.1:4 allegorical, for it was **m.** to limit *you*. Can
T-18...... IX.2:5 messages it transmits to you who **m.** it to
T-18...... IX.3:1 From the world of bodies, **m.** by insanity,
T-18...... IX.3:1 seem to be returned to the mind that **m.** it
T-18...... IX.4:2 that were **m.** to keep the guilt in place, so
T-18...... IX.4:4 apart from what was **m.** to keep it hidden.
T-19.........I.4:6 **m.** of it an "enemy" of healing and the
T-19.......I.14:3 as it was **m.** again through faith. And
T-19........II.1:2 can be corrected, and the wrong **m.** right.
T-19........II.6:1 indeed be said the ego **m.** its world on sin.
T-19........II.6:5 wants; a world it rules, **m.** up of bodies,
T-19........II.7:1 what the Son of God has **m.** himself to be,
T19. IV.A.12:5 and **m.** very vicious by their master, who
T19. IV.A.16:5 your new relationship am I **m.** welcome.
T19. IV.A.16:6 And where I am **m.** welcome, there I am.
T19. IV.A.17:1 I am **m.** welcome in the state of grace,
T19....IV.B.1:4 attraction of guilt **m.** manifest in the body
T19..IV.B.14:2 Certainly what it is **m.** of is not precious.
T19....IV.C.1:9 **M.** by the ego, its dark shadow falls across
T19....IV.C.9:3 and quietly **m.** ready to fulfill the mighty
T19... IV.D.3:2 the promise **m.** in secret to the ego never
T19... IV.D.3:3 This is the secret bargain **m.** with the ego
T-20........II.1:1 all the trinkets **m.** to hang upon the body,
T-20........II.1:2 all the useless things **m.** for its eyes to see.
T-20........II.1:3 on the many offerings **m.** for its pleasure,
T-20........II.1:3 remember all these were **m.** to make seem
T-20........II.2:1 Gifts are not **m.** through bodies, if they
T-20...... III.1:2 what was so before has been **m.** different.
T-20...... III.3:7 in your perception, which **m.** them both.
T-20...... III.4:2 Do you like what you have **m.**? –a world
T-20...... III.4:3 *You **m.** this up.* It is a picture of what you
T-20...... III.4:6 to a world **m.** fearful by their adjustments
T-20...... III.5:5 a judgment on yourself, and **m.** by you.
T-20...... III.5:9 Yet it was you who **m.** it merciless, and
T-20...... III.6:8 that **m.** it as you see it is not outside you.
T-20...... III.7:4 is **m.** homeless and *you* are welcome. Ask
T-20...... III.9:1 leap up in joy the instant they are **m.** free.
T-20.... III.10:6 in separation are now **m.** free in Paradise.
T-20...... IV.3:1 insane laws were **m.** to guarantee that you
T-20....... V.2:6 and in your gift is everyone **m.** glad.
T-20...... VI.1:6 The one he **m.** is partial, self-centered,
T-20...... VI.1:8 The one he **m.** is wholly self-destructive
T-20...... VI.3:5 The love of them has **m.** love meaningless
T-20...... VI.6:3 is love **m.** fearful and hope abandoned.
T-20...... VI.8:6 your relationships were **m.** meaningless.
T-20...... VI.8:7 and bodies **m.** to house the mad idea and
T-20.... VI.11:1 sin **m.** flesh and then projected outward.
T-20..... VII.9:8 was the vision that **m.** his seeing possible.
T-20.... VIII.1:5 be necessary had judgment not been **m.**.
T-20.... VIII.2:6 as its holy purpose was not **m.** by you, the
T-20.... VIII.3:6 nor see in him what you have **m.** of him.
T-20.... VIII.7:4 if you really understood you **m.** it up?
T-20.... VIII.9:8 Yet upon nothing are all projections **m.**.
T-20..VIII.10:7 the errors which you **m.** can be corrected.
T-21.......in.2:6 will see the witness to the choice you **m.**,
T-21.......I.10:2 blindness that they **m.** will not withstand
T-21......II.11:1 as needful that you recognize you **m.** the
T-21......II.11:4 have **m.** can tell you what you see and feel
T-21......II.11:4 and believing that you **m.** yourself. For if
T-21......II.11:5 you think the world you **m.** has power to
T-21......II.12:6 brother thinks he **m.** the world with you.
T-21......II.12:8 With you, he thinks the world he **m.**,
T-21......II.12:8 you, he thinks the world he made, **m.** him
T-21......II.12:9 made, made him. Thus he denies he **m.** it.
T-21......II.13:3 from your Father, you **m.** in secret, and

T-21 III.5:5 For faith, perception and belief you **m.**, as
T-21 III.5:6 what you chose, you **m.** what you desired.
T-21 III.6:3 not the purpose for which you **m.** them.
T-21 III.6:5 You **m.** perception that you might choose
T-21 III.12:1 The body was **m.** to be a sacrifice to sin,
T-21 III.12:7 them still to save itself from what it **m.**.
T-21 IV.6:3 and not been **m.** afraid because you did
T-21 IV.8:7 The senseless is not **m.** meaningful by
T-21 V.2:6 the world you **m.** directs your destiny. For
T-21 V.10:5 in this change is room **m.** way for vision.
T-21 VII.5:4 he admit that no one **m.** him powerless?
T-21 VII.10:4 The others are decisions that can be **m.**,
T-21 VII.10:4 be made, and then unmade and **m.** again.
T-21 VII.11:5 you have already **m.** to all the rest. For
T-21 VII.12:3 Until the last decision has been **m.**, the
T-21 VIII.3:6 **m.** by one whom God Himself will never
T-21 VIII.4:2 answer to the others has **m.** it possible to
T-22 in.1:6 Brother, it is the same, **m.** by the same,
T-22 I.3:5 have **m.** to be yourself becomes your sight
T-22 I.4:7 fear. Here is the one emotion that you **m.**,
T-22 I.4:10 dependent on the self you think you **m.** to
T-22 I.4:10 lead you through the world it **m.** for you.
T-22 I.5:7 Nor will it ever be **m.** understandable by
T-22 II.6:1 of you and the ego must be **m.** complete.
T-22 II.6:5 but what you **m.** believes it is not so. Now
T-22 II.6:9 It must be **m.**. Faith and belief can fall to
T-22 II.8:7 choice. For time you **m.**, and time you can
T-22 II.8:8 a slave to time than to the world you **m.**.
T-22 II.9:1 you **m.** has power to enslave its maker.
T-22 II.9:6 would it be possible that the self he **m.**,
T-22 II.9:6 that the self he made, and all it **m.**, should
T-22 II.10:2 Nothing you **m.** has any power over you
T-22 II.10:3 it seem possible that what you **m.** is yours
T-22 II.10:5 all the misery you **m.** has been your own.
T-22 II.10:7 illusions that you **m.** replaced the truth?
T-22 III.4:7 heavy anchor in the shifting world it **m.**;
T-22 III.5:4 see beyond what they were **m.** to see. And
T-22 III.5:5 **m.** to look on error and not see past it.
T-22 III.5:9 having been **m.** to guarantee that nothing
T-22 III.6:1 These eyes, **m.** not to see, will never see.
T-22 IV.2:3 A choice **m.** with the power of Heaven to
T-22 VI.2:5 knows this mad decision was **m.** by one as
T-23 I.6:6 What **m.** them is insane, and they remain
T-23 I.6:6 and they remain part of what **m.** them.
T-23 I.9:2 that was less real, **m.** an illusion by defeat.
T-23 II.1:6 are the laws that rule the world you **m.**.
T-23 II.5:7 **m.** real by what the Son of God has done
T-23 II.7:5 And now is conflict **m.** inevitable, beyond
T-23 II.10:1 the "enemy" **m.** strong by keeping hidden
T-23 II.13:1 Never is your possession **m.** complete.
T-23 II.13:7 are the laws you **m.** for your salvation.
T-23 II.13:9 is their purpose; they were **m.** for this.
T-24 I.2:3 decisions have been **m.** and kept hidden,
T-24 I.6:8 can be **m.** for this that will not hurt you?
T-24 I.8:8 has been **m.** clean of special goals. And
T-24 II.3:1 Specialness is the idea of sin **m.** real. Sin
T-24 II.3:4 **m.** His Son like to itself and not like unto
T-24 II.6:4 all the world he **m.**, and all his specialness
T-24 II.8:3 Not one attack you thought you **m.** on
T-24 II.13:1 it seem possible God **m.** the body as the
T-24 III.2:1 specialness you cherish, you have **m.** sin.
T-24 III.6:7 could not give, and that you **m.** instead.
T-24 III.7:6 die, but not by Him Who **m.** not death;
T-24 V.2:2 that what he **m.** is happening to him. He
T-24 VI.5:5 one judgment **m.** for all it looks upon.
T-24 VI.5:6 And that is **m.**, not of itself, but through
T-24 VI.13:1 you understand what **m.** this judgment.
T-24 VII.1:9 son that you have **m.** to be your strength?
T-24 VII.5:2 touch it with the false ideas you **m.**,
T-24 VII.8:3 because they were so **m.** and so perceived.
T-24 VII.10:1 Thus is the body **m.** a theory of yourself,
T-24 VII.10:1 provisions **m.** for evidence beyond itself,
T-24 VII.10:10 does the body testify to the idea that **m.** it
T-24 VII.11:1 thus are two sons **m.**, and both appear to
T-25 in.1:8 **m.** manifest to those who know Him not,
T-25 II.9:5 And so His joy is **m.** complete when any
T-25 II.11:3 be **m.** complete by offering completion to
T-25 III.3:3 But this world has two who **m.** it, and
T-25 III.5:1 purpose in the world that error **m.**,
T-25 III.7:2 to see the world He **m.** instead of yours.
T-25 III.7:6 see them as the same, your choice is **m.**.
T-25 III.8:7 And thus is change **m.** possible. The Holy
T-25 V.2:4 yourself, and **m.** your Self your "enemy."
T-25 V.3:4 in content in whatever form the call is **m.**,
T-25 V.6:2 he shows himself is God **m.** free to let His
T-25 VI.4:1 of specialness; His use of what you **m.**, to
T-25 VI.5:10 and choosing it, he **m.** it for himself. His
T-25 VI.6:6 the very instant that the choice was **m.**.
T-25 VI.6:7 His special sin was **m.** his special grace.
T-25 VI.7:4 you **m.** can serve salvation easily and well.
T-25 VII.7:6 Nor can this choice be **m.** by the insane,
T-25 VII.7:6 and **m.** with reason in the light of sense.
T-25 VII.10:6 **m.** a hell of Heaven and a heaven of hell,
T-25 VII.12:8 For here your special function is **m.** whole
T-25 VIII.4:5 is **m.** that sin may be preserved and kept.
T-25 VIII.9:8 is richer **m.** by each one you accept. And
T-25 IX.3:3 but has added to it and **m.** it greater,
T-26 I.4:1 body *is* a loss, and *can* be **m.** to sacrifice.
T-26 I.8:5 he **m.** to keep himself from justice? Could
T-26 II.5:7 has no resolution, you have **m.** it great,
T-26 III.2:5 every thought **m.** pure and wholly simple.
T-26 III.3:3 truth, a segment of the universe **m.** true.
T-26 III.3:6 and every choice has been already **m.**.
T-26 III.4:9 In this one, choice is **m.** impossible. In the
T-26 III.5:6 to make the only choice that can be **m.**.
T-26 III.6:3 real world is the area of choice **m.** real,
T-26 IV.3:8 and all their radiance **m.** whole again.
T-26 V.1:10 road be **m.** except the way to Heaven. You
T-26 V.3:1 His Teacher to replace the one you **m.**,
T-26 V.3:4 was before the way to nothingness was **m.**
T-26 V.3:5 of time in which the first mistake was **m.**,
T-26 V.5:5 back, as if it could be **m.** again in time.
T-26 V.8:2 be **m.** real again and seen as here and now
T-26 V.8:4 was feared and **m.** a symbol of your hate?
T-26 V.11:3 because he **m.** an error in the past that
T-26 VI.1:2 denied it is but an illusion, and **m.** it real.
T-26 VII.3:4 **m.** to take the place of changeless
T-26 VII.7:2 the belief that it is real has **m.** some errors
T-26 VII.12:3 leave their source **m.** real and meaningful.
T-26 VII.14:7 God's Son **m.** incomplete and not himself
T-26 VII.14:9 and **m.** Them both his enemies in hate.
T-26 VII.15:1 serve the purpose they were **m.** to serve.
T-26 VII.15:3 gave to all illusions that were **m.** another
T-26 VIII.3:2 is **m.** yours and its effects will come to you
T-26 IX.4:5 The incomplete is **m.** complete again, and
T-26 IX.8:3 thanks that They are welcome **m.** at last.
T-27 I.2:1 release from sacrifice is his **m.** manifest,
T-27 I.2:6 will not escape the death you **m.** for him.
T-27 I.5:1 Now in the hands **m.** gentle by His touch,
T-27 I.9:9 mind **m.** free again to choose what it is for
T-27 I.11:5 **m.** to hide your function from yourself.
T-27 II.7:7 his heart **m.** heavy with the proof of sin.
T-27 III.4:2 No preparation can be **m.** that would
T-27 IV.4:7 from all the pain of which this world is **m.**
T-27 IV.7:5 receive the answer that was **m.** for you.
T-27 V.8:10 transfer of your learning is not **m.** by you.
T-27 V.8:11 **m.** in spite of all the differences you see,
T-27 V.9:3 be their differences which **m.** this possible
T-27 VI.7:3 and sorrow of the world have **m.** it deaf to
T-27 VII.2:3 were **m.** to keep the problem unresolved?
T-27 VII.3:1 The "reasoning" by which the world is **m.**
T-27 VII.4:9 he does not hold has **m.** upon himself.
T-27 VII.11:1 choices can be **m.** between two states, but
T-27 VII.13:3 Son, and **m.** him think that he has lost his
T-27 VII.13:3 his Father, and **m.** war upon himself. So
T-27 VIII.1:3 the story of how it was **m.** by other bodies
T-27 VIII.7:1 A timelessness in which is time **m.** real; a
T-28 I.1:7 The thoughts that **m.** it are no longer in
T-28 I.2:7 is a skill **m.** up by you to take the place of
T-28 I.2:8 And like all the things you **m.**, it can be
T-28 I.3:4 the purposes for which they have been **m.**
T-28 I.4:7 But only your desire **m.** the link, and only
T-28 I.5:8 associations **m.** to keep the past alive, the
T-28 I.6:4 be **m.** possible because its cause has gone.
T-28 I.6:6 can be **m.** in the present if its cause is past
T-28 I.7:5 what it was that **m.** them what they were,
T-28 I.13:5 is the Cause that fear was **m.** to render
T-28 I.14:2 he understand what he has **m.** is causeless
T-28 II.1:2 The cause a cause is ***m.*** by its effects; the
T-28 II.5:8 only that you see you **m.** the one you
T-28 II.7:3 of them when he perceives he **m.** them up
T-28 II.8:2 In the dream, the dreamer **m.** himself.
T-28 II.8:3 But what he **m.** has turned against him,
T-28 II.11:1 returns the cause of fear to you who **m.** it.
T-28 II.11:4 because they show the mind **m.** sickness,
T-28 II.11:4 body to be victim, or effect, of what it **m.**.
T-28 III.1:5 will the way be **m.** serene and simple in
T-28 III.4:6 For it was **m.** to keep you separated, in a
T-28 III.5:2 ripples that a ship has **m.** in passing by.
T-28 IV.3:4 He is not brother **m.** by what he dreams,
T-28 IV.6:6 he will understand what **m.** the dream.
T-28 V.3:1 perceive that he is not the dream he **m.**.
T-28 V.4:1 Self is safely hidden by what you have **m.**.
T-28 V.4:3 the voices that its ears were **m.** to hear.
T-28 V.5:4 **m.** to look upon a world that is not there;
T-28 V.6:2 It is not **m.** of little bits of glass, a piece of
T-28 VI.1:3 itself, nor **m.** itself to be what it is not. It
T-28 VI.2:9 hate, but it cannot be hateful **m.** thereby.
T-28 VI.3:3 it is, but for the uses you have **m.** of it.
T-28 VI.3:10 **m.** of it a symbol for the limitations that
T-28 VI.4:3 that you have **m.** with every brother who
T-28 VI.5:2 the obvious effect of what was **m.** in secret
T-28 VI.6:2 it is the one that he has **m.** to God, as God
T-28 VI.6:2 has made to God, as God has **m.** to him.
T-28 VI.6:9 who has **m.** promise of himself to God.
T-28 VII.3:5 The body can be **m.** a home like this,
T-28 VII.4:6 choice, and given you the instant it is **m.**.
T-28 VII.4:7 the choice cannot be **m.** in terms of form.
T-28 VII.6:1 in what was **m.** for danger and for fear?
T-28 VII.7:2 No secret promise you have **m.** instead
T-28 VII.7:8 holy purpose is it **m.** a home of holiness a
T-29 I.3:5 provided that your separate interests **m.**
T-29 I.3:8 the treaty that you had **m.** with him. Thus
T-29 I.4:3 of a promise **m.** to meet when you prefer,
T-29 II.3:2 pain of what was **m.** to serve the function
T-29 II.7:5 For it can be **m.** to teach opposing things.
T-29 II.8:7 and in His sacrifice are you **m.** more and
T-29 III.2:2 He **m.** weak because He shared His Love?
T-29 III.2:3 Was He **m.** incomplete by your perfection
T-29 III.2:6 He must be savior from the dream he **m.**,
T-29 IV.2:5 of dreams, from which they all are **m.**.
T-29 IV.2:6 but they cannot be **m.** of something else.
T-29 IV.3:3 of every dream, for they are **m.** of fear.
T-29 V.7:4 the dream its function, it was **m.** for hate,
T-29 V.8:2 it was for this that every dream was **m.**.
T-29 VI.2:11 can never change by what men **m.** of him.
T-29 VI.3:3 only thing that can be **m.** a blessing here,
T-29 VI.5:1 think that it was **m.** to crucify God's Son.
T-29 VII.6:1 All idols of this world were **m.** to keep
T-29 VII.9:4 the end of idols in a world **m.** sad and sick
T-29 VII.9:8 But you have **m.** of your reality an idol,
T-29 VIII.1:5 they are for, and why they have been **m.**.
T-29 VIII.1:7 Idols are **m.** that he may be replaced, no
T-29 VIII.3:2 idol is a wish, **m.** tangible and given form,
T-29 VIII.6:4 the timeless to be **m.** the slaves of time.
T-29 IX.1:4 then, your story in the dream you **m.**, and
T-29 IX.2:2 to hell, and God **m.** enemy unto His Son.
T-29 IX.3:1 are idols, **m.** to save you from the dream.
T-29 IX.3:2 are part of what they have been **m.** to save
T-29 IX.3:5 laid upon himself within the dream he **m.**
T-29 IX.4:8 that they **m.** up the dream in which their
T-29 IX.5:2 the child who thought he **m.** them real.
T-29 IX.6:7 he thinks is governed by the laws he **m.**.
T-29 IX.8:2 not **m.** to separate the mind from what it
T-29 IX.9:1 goes with you,–be sure you **m.** an idol,
T-29 IX.10:2 a sign that you have **m.** a new beginning,
T-30 I.14:8 For they are **m.** with idols or with God.
T-30 I.16:5 results *because* they are not **m.** in isolation
T-30 I.16:6 They are **m.** by you and your adviser, for
T-30 II.2:8 Son **m.** prisoner to what he does not want
T-30 II.4:4 **m.** you co-creator of the universe along
T-30 III.3:8 the search for wholeness to be **m.** beyond
T-30 III.4:7 forms, **m.** but to fill a gap that is not there
T-30 IV.1:1 and thus you will not see you **m.** it up.
T-30 IV.1:5 And this you knew when you **m.** idols.
T-30 IV.1:6 They were **m.** that this might be forgotten
T-30 IV.1:8 All idols are the false ideas you **m.** to fill

T-30......IV.2:1 gods you **m.** are blown-up children's toys.
T-30......IV.2:3 he **m.** for boxes and for bears have failed
T-30......IV.2:5 mean his world is **m.** chaotic and unsafe.
T-30......IV.2:7 He misunderstood what **m.** him safe, and
T-30......IV.3:7 as obeying rules he **m.** for his enjoyment.
T-30......IV.5:4 what you have **m.** to let you be deceived,
T-30......IV.5:7 Who could be **m.** fearful by a power that
T-30......IV.8:2 without the toys of terror that you **m.**. No
T-30.......V.1:4 no demands are **m.** of anyone or anything
T-30.......V.3:2 remains until it is **m.** perfect in himself.
T-30.......V.3:6 heart **m.** ready to arise and go with him.
T-30.......V.3:7 thus is he **m.** ready for the step in which is
T-30......VI.1:3 from fear begins, and will be **m.** complete
T-30......VI.1:9 the answer to attack that has been **m.**.
T-30.....VII.2:3 These judgments all are **m.** according to
T-30.....VII.2:4 **m.** on different aspects of experience.
T-30... VIII.6:3 Be not **m.** guilty and afraid when you are
T-30... VIII.6:9 As he is healed are you **m.** free of guilt, for
T-31.........I.3:3 The world was **m.** by it, and even now
T-31.........I.5:1 is an ability you **m.** and gave yourself. It
T-31.........I.5:2 It was not **m.** to do the Will of God, but to
T-31.........I.5:3 you have learned what it was **m.** to teach.
T-31.........I.6:6 time began and learning had been **m.**?
T-31.........I.8:3 selfsame tongue in which the call was **m.**.
T-31.........I.8:4 within the world has always **m.**, but you
T-31....... II.2:6 by your wish you set two choices to be **m.**,
T-31..... II.2:10 But not in dreams you **m.**, that this might
T-31....... II.4:4 And this is what you **m.** your brother for,
T-31....... II.8:2 before, and put aside all images you **m.**.
T-31....... II.8:5 wish to hear a call that never has been **m.**.
T-31..... II.11:6 the journey is, and how it must be **m.**. For
T-31..... II.11:7 is **m.** in certainty and sureness of the road
T-31....III.4:10 mind can learn, and there is all change **m.**
T-31......III.5:3 For here are you **m.** sin, and sin cannot
T-31......III.7:4 asked; there *is* no sacrifice that can be **m.**.
T-31......IV.2:6 world was **m.** that problems could not *be*
T-31......IV.9:4 every road was **m.** to separate the journey
T-31....IV.10:8 And how could you be **m.** to travel on it,
T-31....... V.2:1 A concept of the self is **m.** by you. It bears
T-31....... V.2:3 **m.** to take the place of your reality as Son
T-31....... V.2:5 For it is **m.** to serve two purposes, but one
T-31....... V.5:1 the concept of the self was **m.** to teach. It
T-31....... V.5:3 teaches this: "I am the thing you **m.** of me
T-31....... V.7:4 They are not given, so they must be **m.**.
T-31....... V.7:9 For all of them are **m.** within the world,
T-31....... V.9:2 that you are what your brother **m.** of you.
T-31....... V.9:7 He must have **m.** the world as well as you
T-31..... V.10:1 brother **m.** of you seems most unlikely.
T-31..... V.10:4 Who is, then, the "you" who **m.** it? And
T-31..... V.10:9 is still no need to hide what you are **m.** of.
T-31..... V.14:6 it feels about how it was **m.** and what it is.
T-31..... V.17:5 recognized as **m.** on no assumptions that
T-31......VI.4:2 the world that will replace the one you **m.**
T-31.....VII.4:3 because it was not **m.** for you alone. Born
T-31...VII.13:1 is free of any judgment **m.** upon yourself.
T-31... VIII.3:1 you **m.** a faulty choice before you now can
T-31... VIII.5:6 be before the choice for holiness was **m.**.
T-31... VIII.9:7 And in this choice is everyone **m.** free.
W-pI.....10.1:3 We have **m.** this distinction before, and
W-pI.....10.2:3 is **m.** overtly with the things around you.
W-pI.....11.1:4 for in this idea is your release **m.** sure.
W-pI........15.h My thoughts are images that I have **m.**.
W-pI.....15.1:3 This is how your "seeing" was **m.**. This is
W-pI.....15.4:2 *This_is an image that I have* **m.**. *That_is an*
W-pI.....15.4:3 *That_is an image that I have* **m.**. It is not
W-pI.....22.2:4 escape? You **m.** what you would destroy;
W-pI.....23.4:1 You see the world that you have **m.**, but
W-pI.....23.4:5 them, even though they were **m.** of hate.
W-pI.....28.8:3 application should be **m.** quite slowly,
W-pI.....32.1:3 You can give it up as easily as you **m.** it up
W-pI.....33.3:2 idea should also be **m.** immediately, when
W-pI.....34.2:4 applications of today's idea should be **m.**.
W-pI.....34.5:1 **m.** whenever you feel your peace of mind
W-pI.....35.2:3 the image of yourself that you have **m.**.
W-pI.....36.4:2 should, of course, be **m.** quite slowly, as
W-pI.....38.2:1 holiness the power of God is **m.** manifest.
W-pI.....38.2:2 holiness the power of God is **m.** available.
W-pI...39.11:1 **m.** some three or four times an hour and
W-pI.....43.2:4 purpose. **M.** by the Son of God for an
W-pI.....44.5:4 and all the thoughts that you have **m.** up.
W-pI.....51.2:4 my judgments have been **m.** quite apart
W-pI.....51.3:8 a better choice than the one I **m.** before?
W-pI.....51.4:5 I have **m.** my thoughts to take their place.
W-pI.....52.1:5 replaced reality with illusions I **m.** up.
W-pI.....53.5:1 My thoughts are images that I have **m.**.
W-pI.....53.5:6 images I have **m.** cannot prevail against
W-pI.....56.2:3 fearful nature of the self-image I have **m.**.
W-pI.....56.4:2 Behind every image I have **m.**, the truth
W-pI.....57.2:2 I **m.** up the prison in which I see myself.
W-pI.....57.4:2 instead of the rules I **m.** up for it to obey. I
W-pI.....61.1:4 not describe the self-concept you have **m.**.
W-pI.....61.4:3 you have **m.** about yourself to the truth,
W-pI.....64.2:2 use for all the illusions you have **m.**, and
W-pI.....66.7:3 ruled by the ego, and is **m.** up of illusions.
W-pI.....66.8:1 or is **m.** by the ego which you have made
W-pI.....66.8:1 the ego which you have **m.** to replace Him
W-pI.....72.2:3 the body that was **m.** to imprison it. The
W-pI.....72.6:2 you. God **m.** you a body. Very well. Let us
W-pI.....75.6:2 and clean of every concept you have **m.**.
W-pI.....76.6:2 you have **m.** in opposition to God's Will.
W-pI.....76.9:5 Exchange cannot be **m.**; there are no
W-pI.....77.3:2 full release from the world you **m.**. You
W-pI.....78.3:4 Each grievance **m.** the darkness deeper,
W-pI.....85.2:1 for this idea might be **m.** in these forms:
W-pI.....88.1:3 Salvation is a decision **m.** already. Attack
W-pI.....93.2:2 That you have **m.** mistakes is obvious.
W-pI.....93.2:3 and have bowed down to idols **m.** of dust,
W-pI.....93.5:1 The self you **m.** is not the Son of God.
W-pI.....93.5:9 What power can this self you **m.** possess,
W-pI.....93.6:6 The self you **m.**, evil and full of sin, is
W-pI.....93.7:1 created you, not what you **m.** of yourself.
W-pI.....93.7:3 you. Whatever mistakes you **m.**, the truth
W-pI.....93.9:1 You are what God created or what you **m.**
W-pI.....93.9:5 and sinfulness you have **m.** to replace It.
W-pI.....94.3:6 sinned, nor **m.** an image to replace reality
W-pI.....95.9:1 this course, you have merely **m.** a mistake
W-pI.....96.3:3 The self you **m.** can never be your Self,
W-pI.....98.4:1 that they learned and every gain they **m.**.
W-pI.....98.5:4 **m.** a thousand losing bargains at the least
W-pI.....98.7:3 **m.** in faith as perfect and as sure as His in
W-pI...98.11:2 He has **m.** with you and you with Him.
W-pI...99.10:5 Forgive yourself the one you think you **m.**
W-pI...99.10:7 Forgive what you have **m.** and you are
W-pI...101.5:3 that you have **m.** a devil of God's Son.
W-pI...103.2:1 that think what they have **m.** is real.
W-pI...104.1:4 must there be a place **m.** ready to receive
W-pI...104.1:5 received the gifts it **m.** where His belong,
W-pI...104.3:1 in choosing them in place of what we **m.**,
W-pI...104.3:4 other gifts and other goals **m.** of illusions,
W-pI...105.1:5 are not gifts, but bargains **m.** with guilt.
W-pI...107.8:2 are not **m.** of flesh and blood and bone,
W-pI.108.10:3 **m.** still faster and more sure each time
W-pI...109.6:1 today, a tired mind is suddenly **m.** glad, a
W-pI...109.9:3 here, for thus our rest is **m.** complete, and
W-pI...110.1:3 Its truth would mean that you have **m.** no
W-pI...110.2:1 that any mind has **m.** at any time or place
W-pI...110.9:3 Let graven images you **m.** to be the Son of
W-pI.110.10:2 be your Savior from all idols you have **m.**.
W-pI...115.1:2 *forgive the world for all the errors I have* **m.**.
W-pI...118.1:2 *that I have* **m.** *for happiness and peace.*
W-pI...121.6:4 how to forgive the self you think you **m.**,
W-pI...122.9:2 Heaven's answer to the hell we **m.**, but
W-pI...123.2:1 extent of all the gains which you have **m.**;
W-pI...123.2:3 the self you thought you **m.** to take the
W-pI...127.5:2 believes was **m.** to hide love's meaning,
W-pI.127.11:2 thought was **m.** in hate to be love's enemy
W-pI.127.11:3 Now are they all **m.** free, along with us.
W-pI...129.9:2 and we are grateful that the choice is **m.**.
W-pI...130.4:1 Fear has **m.** everything you think you see.
W-pI...130.4:4 Love's enemy has **m.** them up. Yet love
W-pI...130.6:2 proof you have already **m.** a choice as all-
W-pI...130.9:5 strength upheld you as you **m.** this choice
W-pI...131.2:7 and protection for the little dream you **m.**
W-pI...131.7:1 this strange world you **m.** and all its ways;
W-pI...131.7:2 God **m.** no contradictions. What denies
W-pI...131.9:4 He thinks he **m.** a hell opposing Heaven,
W-pI.131.11:3 *a different kind of thought from those I* **m.**.
W-pI...132.4:4 came unwillingly to what was **m.** already,
W-pI...132.5:5 not pride which tells you that you **m.** the
W-pI.132.11:6 thoughts which **m.** it and must set it free,
W-pI.132.13:1 and **m.** to separate the Father and the Son
W-pI...133.4:3 there is but one choice that must be **m.**.
W-pI.134.12:4 **m.** to chain his mind to fear and misery.
W-pI...135.3:2 fear, increasing fear as each defense is **m.**.
W-pI...135.3:4 speaks of fear **m.** real and terror justified.
W-pI...135.4:3 must be something **m.** easy prey, unable
W-pI.135.12:1 the problem that the plan is **m.** to solve. It
W-pI.135.14:1 the purpose all of them were **m.** to realize.
W-pI.135.18:4 While you **m.** plans for death, He led you
W-pI...136.3:1 nor are they **m.** without awareness. They
W-pI...136.3:4 even less, in which the choice is **m.**, you
W-pI...136.4:3 requires that you must forget you **m.** it, so
W-pI...136.8:3 and in this pain are you **m.** one with it.
W-pI.136.10:2 these, with God **m.** blind by your illusions
W-pI.136.10:2 all the universe **m.** slave to laws which
W-pI.136.10:3 illusions but the one who **m.** them up?
W-pI.136.13:4 defense you **m.** against the truth. Yet
W-pI.136.18:3 drink, or any laws you **m.** it serve before.
W-pI.136.19:2 and **m.** a bodily identity which will attack
W-pI...137.7:1 will occupy the place of what you **m.**, so
W-pI...137.9:2 **m.** to hold yourself a prisoner to death.
W-pI...138.4:5 one. And when that one is **m.**, you will
W-pI...138.7:1 choice that time was **m.** to help us make.
W-pI...138.8:3 And these decisions are **m.** unaware, to
W-pI...138.9:2 The choice cannot be **m.** until alternatives
W-pI...138.9:4 had **m.** before are open to correction, as
W-pI.138.11:1 we have **m.** the one decision that is sane.
W-pI.138.11:4 no terror now, for what was **m.** enormous
W-pI.138.12:1 reaffirm the choice that we have **m.** each
W-pI...139.5:3 Your denial **m.** no change in what you are
W-pI...140.9:3 can never be a meaningful distinction **m.**
WpI. rIV.in3:3 off through self-deceptions **m.** to take its
WpI. rIV.in9:3 repeating first the thought that **m.** the
W-pI.151.17:2 which Heaven has corrected and **m.** pure.
W-pI...152.6:1 you **m.** the world you see is arrogance?
W-pI...152.6:2 God **m.** it not. Of this you can be sure.
W-pI...152.6:5 to think He **m.** a world where such things
W-pI...152.7:1 To think that God **m.** chaos, contradicts
W-pI...152.8:1 and accept what we have **m.** as what it is.
W-pI...152.8:3 and all you think you **m.** will disappear.
W-pI...152.8:5 take the place of self-deceptions **m.** but to
W-pI...153.5:3 how much you have been **m.** to sacrifice,
W-pI...153.5:5 by dreams, and by illusions he has **m.**; yet
W-pI...153.6:3 that choice is always **m.** between Christ's
W-pI.153.13:1 in a fearful world **m.** mad by sin and guilt;
W-pI.155.13:6 His trust has **m.** your pathway certain and
W-pI...158.6:1 and shadows **m.** with the intangible. Here
W-pI...158.6:2 world **m.** holy by forgiveness and by love.
W-pI...159.5:2 this world into one **m.** holy by forgiveness
W-pI...159.7:1 remember what was lost when it was **m.**.
W-pI...159.7:2 For here it is repaired, **m.** new again, but
W-pI.159.10:5 transition can be **m.** from death to life;
W-pI...160.6:3 may look, for he has **m.** return impossible
W-pI...160.8:4 nor is your Creator stranger **m.** to you.
W-pI...161.1:4 Here is Atonement **m.** complete, the
W-pI...161.3:1 Thus were specifics **m.**. And now it is
W-pI...161.3:4 Yet He can use but what we **m.**, to teach
W-pI...162.1:4 God gave in answer to the world you **m.**.
W-pI...163.4:2 perceived within an idol **m.** of dust. Here
W-pI...163.8:6 God **m.** not death. Whatever form it takes
W-pI...164.5:2 Now is what is really there **m.** visible,
W-pI...164.7:2 us from judgment **m.** beyond the world.
W-pI...165.6:1 past, the journey's end **m.** certain, and
W-pI...166.3:3 and suffer to preserve the world he **m.**.
W-pI...166.4:3 Without the world he **m.** is he an outcast;
W-pI...166.7:1 one you **m.** as a replacement for reality.
W-pI.166.12:2 His touch on you has **m.** you like Himself.
W-pI...167.5:6 As they are **m.**, so will their making be. As
W-pI...170.4:3 with perfect faith the split you **m.** is real.
W-pI...170.7:2 to flame from him, he is but **m.** of stone.
W-pI.170.11:2 time upon this bit of carven stone you **m.**,
W-pI.170.12:6 Now has fear **m.** way for love, as God
WpI...rV.in1:5 and doubts have **m.** us walk uncertainly
WpI...rV.in8:8 And as I am **m.** whole we go together to
W-pI...182.3:5 The home he seeks can not be **m.** by him.
W-pI...182.3:7 for Heaven. All he ever **m.** was hell.
W-pI.182.12:7 for all the toys of battle you have **m.**. And

| | |
|---|---|
| W-pI.183.10:6 | things he thought he **m.** be nameless now |
| W-pI...184.1:2 | have **m.** up names for everything you see. |
| W-pI...184.4:1 | is the way reality is **m.** by partial vision, |
| W-pI...184.8:1 | Think not you **m.** the world. Illusions, |
| W-pI.184.12:6 | **m.** as fitting tribute to the Son He loves. |
| W-pI.184.15:3 | ***m.*** *and call by many different names is but a* |
| W-pI.184.15:7 | *is our salvation and escape from what we* ***m.***. |
| W-pI...187.1:3 | We have **m.** this point before. What |
| W-pI...187.8:3 | has arisen and correction must be **m.**. |
| W-pI.190.11:1 | make the only choice that ever can be **m.**; |
| W-pI.191.10:1 | return again to bless the world he **m.**. In |
| W-pI...192.9:2 | instead of bind, for thus are you **m.** free. |
| W-pI...193.2:5 | which perception is **m.** true and beautiful |
| W-pI.193.10:4 | Time was **m.** for this. Use it today for |
| W-pI...194.5:4 | shines upon a world **m.** free with him, to |
| W-pI...194.7:8 | change his mind when he has **m.** mistakes |
| W-pI...195.1:7 | gratitude is due to Him alone Who **m.** all |
| W-pI...195.6:2 | be **m.** which would reduce our wholeness, |
| W-pI...198.2:1 | Condemn and you are **m.** a prisoner. |
| W-pI.198.11:2 | frantic rush of thoughts that **m.** no sense. |
| W-pI.198.11:3 | of earth, **m.** quiet in a dreamless sleep. |
| W-pI.198.11:6 | you **m.** completely vanished from the |
| W-pI...199.1:4 | mind can be **m.** free when it no longer |
| W-pI...199.3:3 | lives united with the home that it has **m.**. |
| W-pI...200.5:3 | and everyone **m.** free of your mistakes |
| W-pI...200.5:4 | You **m.** him not; no more yourself. And |
| WpI rVI.in.2:4 | that one, there must be no exceptions **m.**. |
| W-pI...210.1:5 | *And that I choose, instead of what I* ***m.***. I am |
| W-pI...213.1:2 | *to me, in place of thoughts I* ***m.*** *that hurt me.* |
| W-pII ....in.6:5 | we behold a world beyond the one we **m.**, |
| W-pII ....in.8:2 | and **m.** the choice to follow it as He would |
| W-pII .229.2:1 | *all the thoughts of sin my foolish mind* ***m.*** *up* |
| W-pII .....2.1:1 | Salvation is a promise, **m.** by God, that |
| W-pII .235.2:2 | *and* ***m.*** *my sinlessness forever part of You. I* |
| W-pII .238.2:2 | Him Whose Love is **m.** complete in him. |
| W-pII .....3.2:1 | The world was **m.** as an attack on God. It |
| W-pII .....3.3:3 | world was **m.** to witness and make real. |
| W-pII .....3.4:1 | As sight was **m.** to lead away from truth, |
| W-pII .....3.5:2 | until forgiveness has been **m.** complete. |
| W-pII .....3.5:5 | For we who **m.** it must behold it through |
| W-pII .....3.5:5 | that what was **m.** to die can be restored to |
| W-pII .....4.2:1 | the mind **m.** in its efforts to deceive itself. |
| W-pII .....5.3:4 | **M.** to be fearful, must the body serve the |
| W-pII .....5.4:2 | it was **m.** to fence him into hell without |
| W-pII .....5.4:5 | to heal the mind that it was **m.** to kill. |
| W-pII .263.1:2 | *what You created as if it could be* ***m.*** *sinful? I* |
| W-pII .269.1:4 | *the illusion which transcends all those I* ***m.***. |
| W-pII .....6.2:3 | lies; where all decisions are already **m.**, |
| W-pII ....277.h | Let me not bind Your Son with laws I **m.**. |
| W-pII .277.1:2 | *him with the laws I* ***m.*** *to rule the body. He is* |
| W-pII .277.1:3 | *is not subject to any laws I* ***m.*** *by which I try to* |
| W-pII .....7.1:5 | has **m.** possible perception's tranquil end. |
| W-pII .....7.3:1 | for the fearful images and dreams you **m.**. |
| W-pII .....7.3:2 | Spirit understands the means you **m.**, by |
| W-pII .....7.3:3 | He will employ the means you **m.** for exile |
| W-pII .283.1:1 | *Father, I* ***m.*** *an image of myself, and it is this* |
| W-pII .283.2:2 | which our forgiveness has **m.** one with us. |
| W-pII .286.1:4 | *In You is every choice already* ***m.***. *In You has* |
| W-pII .289.1:4 | This the past was **m.** to hide, for this the |
| W-pII .289.2:4 | *And here am I* ***m.*** *ready for Your final step.* |
| W-pII .290.1:4 | I **m.** is frightening and painful to behold. |
| W-pII .290.1:5 | the dream I **m.** is real an instant longer. |
| W-pII .....8.1:2 | for what is opposite to what you **m.**. Your |
| W-pII .294.2:3 | *plan that we awaken from all dreams we* ***m.***. |
| W-pII .296.1:3 | *true. I would be savior to the world I* ***m.***. *For* |
| W-pII .....9.4:2 | now, is equally released from what he **m.**. |
| W-pII .303.2:2 | *He has come to save me from the evil self I* ***m.*** |
| W-pII .306.1:2 | Today I can forget the world I **m.**. Today I |
| W-pII .309.1:5 | I think I **m.** another will that is not true, |
| W-pII .309.1:5 | another will that is not true, and **m.** it real |
| W-pII .311.1:1 | was **m.** to be a weapon used against the |
| W-pII .311.1:6 | judgments we have **m.** against ourselves, |
| W-pII .312.2:1 | *set free from all the judgments I have* ***m.***. |
| W-pII .321.1:1 | *I did not understand what* ***m.*** *me free, nor* |
| W-pII .321.1:4 | *I have neither* ***m.*** *nor understood the way to* |
| W-pII .329.1:6 | *That choice was* ***m.*** *for all eternity. It cannot* |
| W-pII .330.1:4 | mind that is **m.** willing to accept God's |
| W-pII .330.2:3 | *to be* ***m.*** *free forever from all our mistakes,* |
| W-pII .340.1:6 | *for Your holy Son and for the world he* ***m.***, |
| W-pII ... 13.4:1 | the mind has been **m.** ready to conceive of |
| W-pII .342.1:1 | *for Your plan to save me from the hell I* ***m.***. *It* |
| W-pII .346.1:7 | *all the foolish toys I* ***m.*** *as I behold Your glory* |
| W-pII .359.1:3 | *have not* ***m.*** *sinners of the holy Sons of God.* |
| W-pII .359.1:6 | *we rejoice to learn that we have* ***m.*** *mistakes* |
| Wfl........in.1:5 | that **m.** the world seem ugly and unsafe, |
| M-1 ........... 1:2 | somewhere he has **m.** a deliberate choice |
| M-2 ........... 3:3 | Choices **m.** long since appear to be open; |
| M-2 ........... 3:3 | long since appear to be open; yet to be **m.** |
| M-2 ........... 4:5 | **m.** the right choice in that ancient instant |
| M-2 ........... 4:6 | **m.** an inevitable choice out of an ancient |
| M-2 ........... 5:8 | for he has **m.** the one decision that gave |
| M-3 ........... 1:5 | contacts to be **m.** for each teacher of God. |
| M-4 .........I.1:4 | not governed by the laws the world **m.** up |
| M-4 ..... I.A.7:5 | had **m.** it impossible for him to judge. He |
| M-7 ........... 1:9 | He has **m.** a mistake, and must be willing |
| M-8 ........... 4:2 | And it is here correction must be **m.**. The |
| M-9 ........... 1:4 | in the newly **m.** teacher of God's training. |
| M-11 ......... 3:1 | is the Answer to all problems you have **m.** |
| M-11 ......... 3:3 | And everyone believes in what he **m.**, for |
| M-11 ......... 3:3 | he made, for it was **m.** by his believing it. |
| M-11 ......... 3:6 | un-understandable **m.** understandable. |
| M-11 ......... 4:6 | it and **m.** it fit to welcome peace. And |
| M-12 ......... 6:4 | learned that all choices are **m.** consciously |
| M-14 ......... 1:5 | So ends the world that guilt had **m.**, for |
| M-14 ......... 2:4 | where sin was **m.** and guilt seemed real. |
| M-16 ......... 4:7 | one generalization that can be **m.** is this; |
| M-16 ......... 6:3 | think you **m.** a place of safety for yourself. |
| M-16 ......... 6:4 | You think you **m.** a power that can save |
| M-16 ....... 11:2 | gladly make it, if it knew it could be **m.**. It |
| M-18 ............ h | HOW IS CORRECTION **M.?** |
| M-18 ......... 1:1 | cannot be **m.** until the teacher of God has |
| M-18 ......... 4:2 | has **m.** an interpretation that is not true. |
| M-19 ......... 3:2 | that **m.** the lens and holds it very dear. |
| M-20 ......... 5:2 | You see in death escape from what you **m.** |
| M-20 ......... 5:3 | But this you do not see; that you **m.** death |
| M-21 ......... 1:7 | for they were **m.** by separated minds to |
| M-22 ......... 6:7 | sense of separation that has **m.** him sick. |
| M-23 ....... 5:11 | again, when he has **m.** the journey for you |
| M-25 ......... 5:5 | wish to be deceived, deception is **m.** easy. |
| M-29 ......... 4:5 | The image you **m.** of yourself has none. |
| M-29 ......... 4:7 | The image you **m.** does not. Yet, despite |
| M-29 ......... 4:9 | of the world that was **m.** to uphold it. But |
| M-29 ......... 5:8 | If you have **m.** it a habit to ask for help |
| C-2 .......... 1:10 | thought that what is **m.** has immortality. |
| C-2 ............ 9:1 | no answer, being **m.** to still God's Voice, |
| C-2 ............ 9:2 | brightness cover up the world the ego **m.**. |
| C-4 ............ 4:4 | now there is an empty place **m.** clean and |
| C-5 ............ 3:4 | He **m.** a clear distinction, still obscure to |
| C-5 ............ 5:4 | to lead you from the hell you **m.** to God. |
| C-5 ............ 5:7 | is. Some bitter idols have been **m.** of him |
| C-6 ............ 5:4 | in its redemption you have **m.** complete. |
| C-ep........... 4:7 | all that the dream of sin had **m.** of it. |
| C-ep........... 5:3 | and the end of all we thought we **m.**. The |
| P-1............. 3:3 | be attacked as well, is a concept he **m.** up. |
| P-1............. 4:2 | were **m.** by his projections on the world. |
| P-2...........I.2:8 | is **m.** of nothingness cannot be called new |
| P-2..........II.1:5 | will be **m.** perfect in time and restored to |
| P-2........ IV.1:3 | is a decision, **m.** again and again, against |
| P-2........ IV.2:4 | are only shadows of a decision already **m.**. |
| P-2........ IV.3:1 | the decision that guilt is real has been **m.**. |
| P-2......... V.7:2 | In time no effort can be **m.** in vain. It is |
| P-3........ III.4:5 | Herein is the relationship **m.** holy, for |
| S-1...........I.2:4 | be **m.** whether they be illusions or not. |
| S-1...........II.2:1 | be **m.** by a Son of God who knows Who |
| S-1........ III.2:3 | **m.** out of fear by those who cherish guilt. |
| S-1........ III.3:1 | in the form in which the prayer was **m.**. |
| S-1........ III.3:6 | *have. Thus have I* ***m.*** *of him my enemy. It is* |
| S-1........ III.4:9 | **m.** of him your salvation and your escape |
| S-1........ III.6:1 | are always **m.** to set up jailers and to hide |
| S-2............I.7:8 | Salvation's plan is **m.** complete, and |
| S-2............I.9:2 | has lost the door for which the key was **m.** |
| S-2...........II.5:4 | But having been **m.** enemy, he must |
| S-2........ III.6:8 | Hand, **m.** free to save as true forgiveness |
| S-3............I.3:4 | of judgment **m.** by brother upon brother, |
| S-3............I.5:1 | must be **m.** between true healing and its |
| S-3...........II.2:1 | **m.** joyfully and with a sense of peace, |
| S-3........ III.1:4 | Nor is it **m.** by one who understands the |
| S-3........ III.2:7 | and change are what the dream is **m.** of. |
| S-3........ III.4:7 | dispelled, and it is this that **m.** him sick. |
| S-3........ IV.6:5 | heavy heart **m.** hard against the love that |
| S-3........ IV.9:7 | dear is every gift to Me that you have **m.**, |

## madhouse 1

| | |
|---|---|
| T-21 .. VII.3:13 | This is no army, but a **m.**. What seems to |

## madman 5

| | |
|---|---|
| W-pI .. 132.1:5 | A **m.** thinks the world he sees is real, and |
| W-pI .. 160.1:6 | but a **m.** could believe he is what he is not |
| W-pI .. 160.2:4 | will not leave because a **m.** says I must." |
| W-pI .. 190.4:4 | Who but a **m.** could conceive of them as |
| P-2........ IV.9:1 | **m.** will defend his own illusions because |

## madman's 2

| | |
|---|---|
| W-pII ..... 4.4:1 | A **m.** dreams are frightening, and sin |
| W-pII .263.1:4 | *A* ***m.*** *dream is hardly fit to be my choice,* |

## madness 99

| | |
|---|---|
| T-13 .......V.6:5 | your **m.** you overlook reality completely, |
| T-14 ... III.15:6 | **M.** may be your choice, but not your |
| T-17 ... III.10:5 | between you and your goal of **m.**. Be not |
| T-18 ........I.6:7 | Call it not sin but **m.**, for such it was and |
| T-18 ...... IX.1:5 | by **m.** into obedience and slavery. This is |
| T-19 ........II.7:7 | in its **m.** it believes it has accomplished. |
| T-19 ..... III.7:7 | to its conqueror. Is this humility or **m.?** |
| T19 . IV.B.16:1 | Hear not its **m.**, and believe not the |
| T19 ... IV.C.3:2 | to **m.** and set against the peace of Heaven |
| T19 IV.D.11:2 | and raving **m.** with pity and compassion, |
| T19 IV.D.12:5 | You see his **m.**, which you hate because |
| T19 IV.D.12:7 | you will share in **m.** or in Heaven together |
| T-20 ..... III.8:4 | You asked this puff of **m.** for the meaning |
| T-20 ..... IV.3:2 | What could this be but **m.?** And is it this |
| T-20 ... VIII.9:5 | serve to meet the goal of **m.**. They are the |
| T-21 .......II.9:3 | of reality to make it fit the goal of **m.**. The |
| T-21 .....II.12:5 | depends entirely upon the **m.** of its maker |
| T-21 .....II.12:5 | maker, and cannot serve to justify the **m.**. |
| T-21 ..... IV.4:2 | of your insanity and recognize its **m.**. |
| T-21 ..... IV.5:5 | Think not that this is **m.**. For this your |
| T-21 ..... IV.6:3 | You have perceived the ego's **m.**, and not |
| T-21 .......V.8:2 | But reason has no place at all in **m.**, nor |
| T-21 .......V.8:3 | Faith and belief are strong in **m.**, guiding |
| T-21 .......V.8:9 | does not depend on it, and **m.** keeps it out |
| T-21 ........ VI.h | Reason versus **M.** |
| T-21 ..... VI.3:5 | home of **m.** cannot be the home of reason |
| T-21 ..... VI.3:6 | to leave the home of **m.** if you see reason. |
| T-21 ..... VI.3:8 | simply by accepting reason where **m.** was. |
| T-21 ..... VI.3:9 | **M.** and reason see the same things, but it |
| T-21 ..... VI.4:1 | **M.** is an attack on reason that drives it |
| T-21 ..... VI.4:2 | attack, but takes the place of **m.** quietly, |
| T-21 ..... VI.4:2 | replacing **m.** if it be the choice of the |
| T-21 ..... VI.4:3 | body, and let their **m.** tell them it is real. |
| T-21 ..... VI.5:2 | But **m.** has a purpose, and believes it also |
| T-21 ... VI.7:10 | leads steadily away from **m.** toward the |
| T-21 ..... VI.8:3 | In **m.**, yes. And yet what madness sees |
| T-21 ..... VI.8:4 | what **m.** sees must be dispelled by reason. |
| T-21 ..... VI.8:9 | What **m.** would conceal, the Holy Spirit |
| T-22 ..... III.3:4 | thick it would be **m.** to attempt to pass it. |
| T-23 ........I.2:9 | belief, but never will it be more than **m.**. |
| T-23 .......I.2:10 | And fear will reign in **m.**, and will seem to |
| T-23 ........I.6:7 | **M.** holds out no menace to reality, and |
| T-23 ........I.8:9 | Let all this **m.** be undone for you, and |
| T-23 .....II.10:1 | All of the mechanisms of **m.** are seen |
| T-23 .....II.12:5 | factor in your **m.** that makes it "sane." |
| T-23 .....II.13:3 | **m.** He must have this substitute for love, |
| T-23 ...II.13:12 | The means of **m.** must be insane. Are you |
| T-23 ...II.13:13 | as certain that you realize the goal is **m.?** |
| T-23 .....II.14:1 | No one wants **m.**, nor does anyone cling |
| T-23 .....II.14:1 | anyone cling to his **m.** if he sees that this |
| T-23 .....II.14:2 | protects **m.** is the belief that it is true. It is |
| T-23 .....II.14:5 | which was the truth before, be **m.** now. |
| T-23 .....II.14:6 | completely turned around, with **m.** sanity |
| T-23 .....II.15:5 | Their goal of **m.** must be seen as sanity. |
| T-23 .....II.17:8 | can it matter what the form this **m.** takes? |
| T-23 ...II.17:10 | when **m.** takes a form you think is lovely. |

T-24 II.13:4 rule in **m.** and in loneliness your special
T-24 V.4:8 Yet is it joy to look upon decay and **m.**,
T-25 III.2:5 not be lost forever in the **m.** of his wish.
T-25 VII.3:2 God is mad, or is this world a place of **m.**.
T-25 VII.3:6 And what is **m.** cannot be the truth. If one
T-25 VII.6:5 the **m.** and rest peacefully on truth. Each
T-25 VII.7:5 Yet if His Will is seen as **m.**, then the form
T-25 VII.8:1 be **m.** to entrust salvation to the insane.
T-25 VII.9:5 Nor is he left without escape from **m.**, for
T-25 VII.13:1 either God or you must lose to **m.** because
T-26 V.6:3 over. **M.** speaks no more. There *is* no other
T-26 V.6:10 mere imagining into belief and into **m.**,
T-27 I.5:7 nothing which his **m.** bid him do was ever
T-29 VI.1:4 sin and death; of **m.** and of murder, grief
T-31 IV.11:1 Forgive yourself your **m.**, and forget all
T-31 IV.11:5 is your escape from **m.** and from death.
T-31 VII.14:3 It is a thing of **m.**, pain and death; a thing
W-pI 53.3:3 Nothing in **m.** is dependable. It holds out
W-pI 66.10:1 You will listen to **m.** or hear the truth.
W-pI 76.5:1 These are not laws, but **m.**. The body is
W-pI 97.1:5 for your mind has been absolved from **m.**,
W-pI 101.7:2 Today escape from **m.**. You are set on
W-pI 125.5:4 regardless of his **m.** that his will is not his
W-pI 139.6:2 are. This is the depth of **m.**. Yet it is the
W-pI 139.6:5 Why share its **m.** in the sad belief that
W-pI 139.9:2 not come to reinforce the **m.** that we once
W-pI 152.6:7 mad. Yet only **m.** makes a world like this.
W-pI 153.4:2 In them lies **m.** in a form so grim that
W-pI 155.2:5 To let illusions walk ahead of truth is **m.**.
W-pI 155.3:4 need a Teacher Who perceives their **m.**,
W-pI 184.6:7 To question it is **m.**; to accept its presence
W-pI 191.3:1 escape the **m.** which induced this weird,
W-pI 196.6:1 Such is the form of **m.** you believe, if you
W-pII in.4:2 He has not left His Son in all his **m.**, nor
W-pII 249.1:2 Attack is gone, and **m.** has an end. What
W-pII 278.2:4 *way to You instead of* **m.** *and instead of fear.*
W-pII 12.3:2 can he know of **m.** and the death of God,
M-5 I.1:7 Sickness is a method, conceived in **m.**, for
M-17 7:6 raised **m.** to the throne of God Himself.
M-17 9:1 **M.** but seems terrible. In truth it has no
M-27 1:2 Is it not **m.** to think of life as being born,
C-2 1:7 not. It is a thing of **m.**, not reality at all. A
P-2 VII.5:6 assume he has such wisdom except in **m.**.

## magazine 1

W-pI 29.5:4 *God is in this* **m.**. *God is in this finger. God is*

## magic 62

*See also* magic-miracle

T-1 I.14:3 conviction they deteriorate into **m.**,
T-2 IV.2:7 Physical illness represents a belief in **m.**.
T-2 IV.2:8 The whole distortion that made **m.** rests
T-2 IV.4:1 ills are restatements of **m.** principles. This
T-2 V.2:1 **M.** is the mindless or the miscreative use
T-2 VIII.1:2 where a belief in **m.** is virtually inevitable.
T-4 II.9:1 Myths and **m.** are closely associated,
T-4 II.9:1 **m.** to the powers the ego ascribes to itself.
T-4 II.9:2 this with its particular form of **m.**. The so-
T-5 V.5:4 I said before that illness is a form of **m.**. It
T-6 V.2:2 not real, because children believe in **m.**.
T-7 V.3:6 can be used either for healing or for **m.**,
T-7 V.3:6 but you must remember that **m.** always
T-7 V.4:2 **M.** always tries to weaken. Healing
T-7 V.4:4 **M.** always sees something "special" in the
T-9 V.6:6 sinner" cannot be healed without **m.**, nor
T-9 V.6:6 mind" esteem itself without **m.**.
T-10 IV.1:1 All **m.** is an attempt at reconciling the
T-23 II.12:5 is the **m.** that will cure all of your pain;
T-25 VII.1:5 The **m.** of the world can seem to hide the
W-pI 76.6:3 Will. Your **m.** has no meaning. What it is
W-pI 76.7:5 **M.** imprisons, but the laws of God make
W-pI 98.3:2 They do not appeal to **m.**, nor invent
W-pI 136.3:2 **m.** wands you wave when truth appears
W-pI 140.2:2 he found a **m.** formula to make him well.
W-pI 140.6:4 is. This is no **m.**. It is merely an appeal to
W-pI 140.10:1 and bits of **m.** in whatever form they take.
W-pI 158.4:1 in which figures come and go as if by **m.**.
M-16 8:6 Forget not this is **m.**, and magic is a sorry
M-16 8:6 **m.** is a sorry substitute for true assistance.
M-16 9:1 of **m.** is the avoidance of temptation. For
M-16 9:5 all **m.** is recognized as merely nothing,
M-16 9:7 For **m.** of any kind, in all its forms, simply
M-16 10:8 each temptation to accept **m.** as true must
M-16 11:5 the day except to put your trust in **m.**, for
M-16 11:7 learned that everything but this is **m.**. All
M-16 11:8 All belief in **m.** is maintained by just one
M-16 11:9 of **m.** and perceive their meaninglessness.
M-17 h DO GOD'S TEACHERS DEAL WITH **M.**
M-17 1:3 the **m.** seem quite real to both of them.
M-17 1:4 deal with **m.** thus becomes a major lesson
M-17 1:6 If a **m.** thought arouses anger in any form
M-17 2:1 temptation to respond to **m.** in a way that
M-17 5:1 Anger in response to perceived **m.**
M-17 5:3 A **m.** thought, by its mere presence,
M-17 6:4 **M.** again must help. Forget the battle.
M-17 7:1 now be your reaction to all **m.** thoughts?
M-17 8:10 at last. **M.** thoughts need not lead to
M-17 9:3 Like the **m.** which becomes its servant, it
M-18 1:2 argues with his pupil about a **m.** thought,
M-18 1:6 **M.** thoughts are but illusions. Otherwise
M-18 2:1 to **m.** thoughts wholly without anger.
M-23 1:5 Is this merely an appeal to **m.**? A name
M-25 1:2 obviously merely an appeal to **m.** to make
M-25 2:8 there is no **m.** in his accomplishments.
M-25 3:8 of **m.** are special powers "demonstrated."
M-25 4:3 What is used for **m.** is useless to Him. But
M-25 4:4 But what He uses cannot be used for **m.**. 
M-27 6:9 and yet to think love real are mindless **m.**,
P-2 in.2:5 so clearly impossible, what they seek is **m.**
P-2 IV.4:3 seek for **m.** by which to heal the ills with
S-3 III.3:1 **m.** phrase by which the body seems to be

## magic's 1

P-2 IV.7:4 Yet that is **m.** purpose; to make illusions

## magic-miracle 1

T-2 VIII.1:1 which you can correct the **m.** confusion is

## magical 9

T-5 V.5:5 to say that it is a form of **m.** solution. The
W-pI 50.1:3 of nothingness that you endow with **m.**
W-pI 76.9:2 Dismiss all foolish **m.** beliefs today, and
W-pI 77.2:2 on any **m.** powers you have ascribed to
W-pI 92.1:5 This is among the many **m.** beliefs that
W-pI 135.25:6 plans or **m.** beliefs can still have value,
P-2 in.3:4 the **m.** powers he seeks in psychotherapy.
P-2 in.4:4 goals not completely free of **m.** overtones.
P-2 IV.6:3 the defenses sought for must be **m.**. They

## magically 1

W-pI 138.8:2 to be safe, and **m.** armored against truth.

## magnificence 1

M-19 2:6 Nor could all the **m.**, the grandeur of the

## magnified 2

T-16 VI.7:3 What is little and insignificant is **m.**, and
W-pI 181.1:4 Rather, they are **m.**, becoming blocks to

## magnify 2

T-16 VI.6:4 that you will see no need at all to **m.** it.
W-pI 181.6:2 which we will **m.** and call our "sins." So,

## Magnitude 1

*magnitude*

T-15 III.4:2 for it reaches you through Him *from* **M.**.

## magnitude 31

*Magnitude*

T-1 III.9:3 no account of the **m.** of the miracle itself,
T-2 I.5:4 may seem to be of greater **m.** than others.
T-9 VI.4:8 awake in Him you will know your **m.** by
T-10 IV.8:5 was a descent from **m.** to littleness. But
T-12 III.7:2 conflict of this **m.** he cannot tolerate. A
T-12 VII.3:3 and space, of **m.** and mass is transcended,
T-13 III.4:2 you believe that **m.** lies in defiance, and
T-13 III.7:6 its littleness, restoring it to the **m.** of God.
T-13 III.9:1 the **m.** of your Father in peace and joy.
T-15 III.h Littleness versus **M.**
T-15 III.1:4 You offer this in place of **m.**, and you
T-15 III.2:6 For you will be content only in **m.**, which
T-15 III.4:2 it is. There is no doubt about its **m.**, for it
T-15 III.4:4 vigilance to protect your **m.** in this world.
T-15 III.4:5 To hold your **m.** in perfect awareness in a
T-15 III.4:6 tribute to your **m.** and not your littleness.
T-15 III.5:6 All your attempts to deny His **m.**, and
T-15 III.6:1 The Holy Spirit can hold your **m.**, clean
T-15 III.6:5 into a sense of **m.** that can content them.
T-15 III.6:8 but your **m.** is of Him Who dwells in you,
T-15 III.7:2 to restore the awareness of **m.** to the host
T-15 III.8:5 valuing it too little to understand its **m.**.
T-15 IV.2:2 The instant in which **m.** dawns upon you
T-15 IV.4:5 have accepted for finding **m.** in littleness.
T-16 VI.5:3 one, they are trying to decrease their **m.**.
T-18 I.5:2 do not realize the **m.** of that one error. It
T-26 III.1:13 **m.** beyond the scope of this curriculum.
T-26 IV.5:5 tiny then has soared into a **m.** of song in
T-31 I.4:4 Voice seems small and still before its **m.**.
W-pI 139.3:1 so vast, its **m.** can hardly be conceived. To
W-pI 166.5:5 world contains is valueless before its **m.**.

## main 7

T-4 II.11:13 That is its **m.** difference from everything
T-6 II.1:5 occurs projection becomes its **m.** defense,
T-7 X.3:5 The Holy Spirit's **m.** function is to teach
T-13 X.3:7 Their **m.** concern is to perceive the source
T-27 VIII.1:5 Its safety is its **m.** concern. Its comfort is
T-31 V.13:5 **m.** advantage of the shifting to the second
W-in 3:1 workbook is divided into two **m.** sections,

## maintain 41

T-2 III.1:2 Atonement, and thus **m.** the separation.
T-2 V.4:2 but **m.** a consistent trust in mine. If your
T-3 I.3:3 He did not create it and He does not **m.** it.
T-4 I.2:5 if you **m.** that the same thought system
T-4 II.9:4 hard to **m.** that the ego existed before that
T-4 III.7:7 you and **m.** complete respect for what you
T-4 IV.1:7 it **m.** the trick of its existence except with
T-4 VI.4:2 mind cannot **m.** the separation except by
T-7 II.2:7 to circumstances if they are to **m.** order.
T-7 IX.7:1 which **m.** It in wholeness and peace.
T-8 IV.2:7 You cannot **m.** the illusion of loneliness if
T-9 III.1:1 the Holy Spirit would have you **m.**. Egos
T-9 VII.5:3 produced, and must **m.** for its existence?
T-11 V.12:5 and it becomes difficult to **m.** that fear is
T-12 I.5:5 Would you **m.** that you do not need it?
T-12 III.7:5 attempt to **m.** your ego identification, for
T-13 X.4:1 When you **m.** that you are guilty but the
T-15 I.4:11 it must engender fear in order to **m.** itself.
T-15 VII.4:1 the ego attempts to **m.** and increase guilt,
T-17 I.3:1 you **m.** that there must be an order of
T-18 IV.4:8 you **m.** you are unworthy of learning this,
T-21 VI.2:2 Sin would **m.** it can. Yet reason tells you
T-21 VI.2:6 Sin would **m.** you and your brother must
T-23 II.1:4 what they are, not what they would **m.**. It
T-23 II.18:1 You would **m.**, and think it true, that you
T-23 III.3:7 It would **m.** you can attack a little, love a
T-25 V.2:7 to think he must be guilty to **m.** the wish,
T-25 VI.2:5 the darkness and **m.** he wants to see?
T-26 VI.1:9 same, and still **m.** that even one is best?
T-26 VIII.9:6 and the "reasoning" that would **m.** effects
T-29 I.8:1 goals you hold, and force the body to **m.**.
T-29 VII.6:1 **m.** allegiance to the dream that you must
T-31 I.4:1 **m.** that lessons such as these are easy? Yet

|  |  |
|---|---|
| T-31....... V.7:7 | Concepts **m.** the world. But they can not |
| W-pI..... 33.2:2 | and to **m.** this detachment as you repeat |
| W-pI..... 73.2:2 | grievances, which are necessary to **m.** it, |
| W-pI. 132.10:3 | and you **m.** the world within your mind |
| W-pI. 153.15:1 | in a form we will **m.** for quite a while. We |
| W-pI... 182.2:4 | Still others will **m.** that what we speak of |
| W-pII ..... 4.5:1 | O Son of God, will you **m.** the game of sin |
| W-pII . 278.1:2 | I **m.** the laws the world obeys must I obey; |

## maintained 20

*See also* self-maintained

|  |  |
|---|---|
| T-5......... V.7:5 | and **m.** by guilt in its continuance. Guilt is |
| T-7........ IX.7:3 | that your identification is **m.** by extension |
| T-8........ IV.2:3 | **m.** by fear of the same loneliness that *is* its |
| T-13....... X.1:3 | Displacement always is **m.** by the illusion |
| T-14..... VII.4:3 | of belief which cannot coexist are both **m.** |
| T-20...... IV.4:4 | thus their freedom is established and **m.**. |
| T-21....... II.4:5 | instant is this exchange effected and **m.**. |
| T-22.... VI.13:6 | Either could be **m.**, but never both. The |
| T-24....... II.1:3 | seen in another, and **m.** by searching for, |
| T-25...... III.4:1 | that anything could be established and **m.** |
| T-25..... VII.4:7 | it thinks, or is **m.** by any form of reason, |
| T-25... VII.13:2 | demands life, but life is not **m.** at any cost |
| T-26.......... I.2:5 | and by their separation are their selves **m.** |
| T-27..... VII.3:1 | made, on which it rests, by which it is **m.**, |
| T-27.. VIII.13:5 | that has **m.** you separate from the world, |
| T-29.......... I.7:3 | For hate to be **m.**, love must be feared; |
| M-10 ........... 1:1 | by which the world of illusions is **m.**, is |
| M-16 ......... 11:8 | All belief in magic is **m.** by just one simple- |
| M-26 ........... 3:3 | then be **m.** for much of the time on earth. |
| M-26 ........... 3:8 | the body would not be long **m.**. Those |

## maintaining 10

|  |  |
|---|---|
| T-4........ III.3:3 | you some sort of reward for **m.** this belief. |
| T-4........ VI.4:4 | The ego is a device for **m.** this belief, but it |
| T-12.......... I.5:6 | you are **m.** when you refuse to recognize a |
| T-13..... VII.6:2 | other, **m.** that he loves what he loves not, |
| T-16....... II.5:2 | And are you really safer in **m.** the reality |
| T-16... VII.2:11 | that you are **m.** the illusion that it has not |
| T-17...... III.3:4 | the **m.** and the breaking off of the unholy |
| T-21...... VI.1:5 | so you will not give it, thus **m.** the belief. |
| T-24.... VI.12:1 | time, and with the power of God **m.** it, |
| W-pI. 138.12:3 | in a brief quiet time devoted to **m.** sanity. |

## maintains 8

|  |  |
|---|---|
| T-18...... VI.4:2 | It cannot attack, but it **m.** it can, and uses |
| T19..IV.B.13:2 | guilt **m.** the whole illusion of its existence. |
| T-23....... II.2:2 | this one **m.** that each is separate and has a |
| T-27....... II.3:2 | **m.** what has been done to you deserves no |
| W-pI..... 71.2:2 | It **m.** that, if someone else spoke or acted |
| W-pI... 153.6:3 | Perhaps you will recall the text **m.** that |
| W-pI... 160.2:2 | and yet **m.** his home belongs to him, |
| W-pI... 187.1:8 | The truth **m.** that giving will increase |

## Majesty 3

*majesty*

|  |  |
|---|---|
| T-7........ XI.5:3 | **M.** of God is there, for you to recognize |
| T-7........ XI.5:4 | know. Recognizing the **M.** of God as your |
| T-16... VII.11:3 | will not give place to Him and to His **M.**. |

## majesty 5

*Majesty*

|  |  |
|---|---|
| T-7........ XI.5:2 | other minds, transforming them into **m.**. |
| T-26...... VI.2:4 | obscures His grace and **m.** from you, and |
| T-31.... VIII.4:3 | face of Christ is powerless before His **m.**, |
| W-pI..... 93.9:5 | by hiding Its **m.** behind the tiny idols of |
| W-pI... 122.6:7 | power and the **m.** of this extremely simple |

## major 30

|  |  |
|---|---|
| T-1......... I.42:1 | A **m.** contribution of miracles is their |
| T-1....... VII.1:2 | impulses is a **m.** perceptual distortion. |
| T-2........ IV.2:1 | **m.** step in the Atonement plan is to undo |
| T-4......... V.2:1 | **m.** source of the ego's off-balanced state is |
| T-6 ..... V.C.3:1 | is a **m.** step toward fundamental change. |
| T-7 ..... VIII.3:1 | are two **m.** errors involved in this attempt |
| T-17 ...... V.2:1 | **m.** step toward the perception of the real |
| T-17 ...... V.7:4 | exclude **m.** areas of fantasy from your |
| T-19 ........ II.4:1 | A **m.** tenet in the ego's insane religion is |
| T-23 ...... II.16:4 | where only shadows play the **m.** roles, it |
| T-29 .... VII.4:1 | betterment is cast as **m.** beneficiary, you |
| T-30 ......... I.3:1 | This is your **m.** problem now. You still |
| W-pI........ 4.3:1 | This is a **m.** exercise, and will be repeated |
| W-pI...... 11.1:1 | to a **m.** phase of the correction process; |
| W-pI...... 12.1:1 | correction for a **m.** perceptual distortion. |
| W-pI...... 42.1:1 | thoughts, both of **m.** importance. It also |
| W-pI...... 44.3:3 | and represents a **m.** goal of mind training |
| W-pI...... 68.5:1 | hold what you regard as **m.** grievances. |
| WpI..rII.in.3:1 | but try to spend the **m.** part of the time |
| W-pI... 105.3:1 | A **m.** learning goal this course has set is |
| W-pI... 134.3:1 | The **m.** difficulty that you find in genuine |
| W-pI... 154.6:1 | There is one **m.** difference in the role of |
| W-pI... 181.4:1 | A **m.** hazard to success has been |
| M-8 ............ 2:3 | real that is regarded as of **m.** importance, |
| M-16 .......... 4:4 | Duration is not the **m.** concern. One can |
| M-17 .......... 1:4 | deal with magic thus becomes a **m.** lesson |
| M-18 .......... 2:1 | God's teachers' **m.** lesson is to learn how |
| M-21 .......... 5:1 | **m.** hindrance in this aspect of his learning |
| M-29 .......... 1:2 | the **m.** concepts in the text and workbook |
| P-3........... II.3:3 | be uninterested in healing as his **m.** goal. |

## majority 1

|  |  |
|---|---|
| M-9 ........... 1:7 | By far the **m.** are given a slowly evolving |

## make 889

*See also* make-believe

|  |  |
|---|---|
| T-1 ......... I.19:1 | Miracles **m.** minds one in God. They |
| T-1 ......... I.32:2 | holiness and **m.** your perceptions holy. By |
| T-1 ......... V.1:4 | can **m.** an empty shell, but you cannot |
| T-1 ....... VII.3:7 | can never **m.** them real except to yourself. |
| T-1 ....... VII.3:8 | You believe in what you **m.**. If you offer |
| T-1 ....... VII.4:5 | is to come to **m.** constructive use of it. |
| T-2 ......... II.5:1 | and ultimately to **m.** learning complete. |
| T-2 ......... II.7:2 | Sons of God **m.** in one way or another. It |
| T-2 ....... III.5:2 | to **m.** themselves more comfortable by |
| T-2 ...... VIII.1:5 | you alone **m.** is real in your own sight, |
| T-3 ........... I.1:4 | in scarcity could possibly **m.** this mistake. |
| T-3 ......... II.6:2 | You cannot **m.** untruth true. If you are |
| T-3 ..... IV.3:10 | can never **m.** your misperceptions true, |
| T-3 ....... IV.5:8 | itself when it chooses to **m.** its own levels. |
| T-3 ....... IV.5:9 | it derives its whole power to **m.** or create. |
| T-3 ..... IV.7:11 | I can help you **m.** your own right choice. |
| T-3 ......... V.2:1 | "create" and "**m.**" have become confused. |
| T-3 ......... V.2:2 | When you **m.** something, you do so out of |
| T-3 ......... V.2:4 | you **m.** something to fill a perceived lack, |
| T-3 ......... V.5:4 | It is impossible to **m.** so fundamental a |
| T-3 ....... VII.4:3 | of the self to **m.** an image of itself. Images |
| T-3 ....... VII.4:7 | it. You cannot **m.** it true. And, as I said |
| T-3 .... VII.4:12 | and are filled with fear about what you **m.** |
| T-3 ....... VII.5:1 | The mind can **m.** the belief in separation |
| T-4 ......... in.3:7 | Do not **m.** the pathetic error of "clinging |
| T-4 ......... I.2:14 | **m.** the totally lifeless out of the life-given. |
| T-4 ........... I.5:6 | The ego cannot **m.** this choice because of |
| T-4 ........... I.7:6 | or **m.** is necessary to establish your worth. |
| T-4 ......... I.11:2 | try to **m.** this impoverished house stand. |
| T-4 ......... I.11:4 | Only God could **m.** a home that is worthy |
| T-4 ....... III.7:3 | through the walls you **m.** to block it, and |
| T-4 ....... III.8:4 | to help me **m.** other minds ready for Him. |
| T-4 ....... III.9:7 | That is why we **m.** no distinction between |
| T-4 ......... V.2:4 | It cannot, however, **m.** them cease to be. |
| T-4 ....... V.6:11 | When you **m.** a decision of purpose, then, |
| T-4 ....... VI.3:2 | choice is the only sane one you can **m.**. |
| T-4 ....... VII.3:2 | it **m.** any attempt to establish what is true |
| T-5 ......... in.1:1 | To heal is to **m.** happy. I have told you to |
| T-5 ......... in.2:5 | heal or to **m.** joyous is therefore the same |
| T-5 ......... in.2:5 | the same as to integrate and to **m.** one. |
| T-5 ......... II.6:3 | As a result, there are choices you must **m.**. |
| T-5 ......... II.7:6 | in the midst of the turmoil you may **m.**. |
| T-5 ......... II.9:3 | to you is to help you **m.** the same decision |
| T-5 ......... II.9:7 | can be made, and that you can **m.** it. |
| T-5 ....... II.10:9 | perfect integration that can **m.** it whole? |
| T-5 ....... III.4:6 | **m.** the mistake of looking for the Holy |
| T-5 ....... IV.2:7 | your own thoughts can **m.** you really free. |
| T-5 ....... IV.5:5 | **M.** it dependable in my name because my |
| T-5 ......... V.8:6 | Your mind *does* **m.** your future, and it will |
| T-5 ....... VI.2:7 | When you choose to **m.** this exchange, |
| T-5 ...... VII.1:1 | can **m.** a voice that can drown out God's? |
| T-6 ........... I.2:5 | my decision, and thus **m.** it stronger. I |
| T-6 ........... I.2:8 | contribution to **m.** to your own life, and if |
| T-6 ......... II.3:3 | is solely a device of the ego to **m.** you feel |
| T-6 ....... II.11:1 | it can so easily **m.** the idea seem difficult. |
| T-6 ....... II.11:3 | ***m.*** the idea of return both necessary and |
| T-6 ....... II.12:8 | must shine outward to **m.** you aware of it. |
| T-6 ....... III.2:3 | you **m.** what you are something you must |
| T-6 ......... V.1:1 | He teaches only to **m.** you equal with Him |
| T-6 ......... V.3:3 | it will hurt you and **m.** you unsafe; but if |
| T-6 ..... V.A.2:1 | God did not **m.** the body, because it is |
| T-6 ..... V.B.7:1 | You are not asked to **m.** insane decisions, |
| T-6 ..... V.C.4:5 | that the temptation to **m.** exceptions will |
| T-7 ......... II.6:4 | is only to **m.** the remembering consistent. |
| T-7 ....... III.1:10 | You did not **m.** this power, any more than |
| T-7 ....... IV.3:5 | All you need do is **m.** the effort to learn, |
| T-7 ....... V.11:3 | them **m.** them aware of the light in them. |
| T-7 ....... VI.1:5 | Fear and love **m.** or create, depending on |
| T-7 ....... VI.5:5 | The mind can, however, **m.** up illusions, |
| T-7 ..... VI.11:3 | Therefore they **m.** up images, perceive |
| T-7 ... VI.11:10 | cannot **m.** the meaningless meaningful. |
| T-7 ..... VI.12:2 | something else you will **m.** something else |
| T-7 ...... VII.2:7 | Every response you **m.** is determined by |
| T-7 ...... VII.2:8 | must determine every response you **m.**. |
| T-7 ...... VII.5:3 | You cannot **m.** nothing live, since nothing |
| T-7 ..... VIII.7:2 | the unbelievable cannot **m.** this judgment |
| T-7 ....... XI.2:8 | own worth is beyond anything he can **m.**. |
| T-7 ....... XI.3:7 | You cannot **m.** it, any more than you can |
| T-7 ....... XI.3:7 | it, any more than you can **m.** yourself. It |
| T-8 ........... I.3:3 | reality that you must **m.** to secure peace, |
| T-8 ........... I.3:3 | peace, and the only one you need ever **m.**. |
| T-8 ......... II.2:2 | anything it teaches **m.** anything but sense |
| T-8 ......... II.5:3 | You cannot **m.** this distinction without |
| T-8 ....... III.6:4 | to look at what the ego would **m.** of you. |
| T-8 ....... III.6:6 | What other choice could you **m.**? Having |
| T-8 ..... IV.5:14 | offer my strength to **m.** yours invincible, |
| T-8 ......... V.2:4 | Yet to heal is still to **m.** whole. Therefore, |
| T-8 ....... VI.2:4 | choice of which is true is not yours to **m.**. |
| T-8 ..... VI.5:13 | **m.** yourself unworthy because you are the |
| T-8 ....... VI.7:7 | does **m.** the Son's function unknown to |
| T-8 ..... VI.9:10 | I can **m.** you aware of the conditions of |
| T-8 ..... VIII.5:5 | A sick body does not **m.** any sense. It |
| T-8 ..... VIII.5:6 | It could not **m.** sense because sickness is |
| T-8 ....... IX.6:3 | and that to **m.** mindless is to heal. But to |
| T-8 ....... IX.6:4 | But to **m.** mindless is impossible, since it |
| T-8 ....... IX.6:4 | it would mean to **m.** nothing out of what |
| T-9 ........... I.4:3 | His recognition of this Will can **m.** it real |
| T-9 ......... I.11:9 | You cannot change laws you did not **m.**, |
| T-9 ......... I.13:4 | You cannot **m.** the unreal because the |
| T-9 ......... I.13:6 | orders of reality **m.** reality meaningless, |
| T-9 ......... I.14:4 | you are trying to **m.** yourself unreal. |
| T-9 ....... III.6:7 | if they were real, is to **m.** them real to you. |
| T-9 ....... III.7:8 | Any attempt you **m.** to correct a brother |
| T-9 ....... IV.2:2 | errors, or you would not **m.** them. It |
| T-9 ....... IV.2:3 | to believe either that you do not **m.** them, |
| T-9 ....... IV.4:8 | forgetting that my words **m.** perfect sense |
| T-9 ....... IV.5:2 | it **m.** real the unreal and then destroy it. |
| T-9 ......... V.2:2 | can "uncovering" them **m.** them real? |
| T-9 ......... V.3:5 | onto God, they **m.** Him appear retaliative, |
| T-9 ......... V.7:4 | the healer can **m.** is to present an example |
| T-9 ..... VIII.1:5 | Self-inflation is the only offering it can **m.** |
| T-9 ..... VIII.4:5 | ego will **m.** every effort to recover and |
| T-9 ..... VIII.4:7 | not delusional because you did not **m.** it. |
| T-10 ...... in.1:1 | yourself can **m.** you fearful or loving, |
| T-10 ...... in.2:7 | you **m.** to everything you perceive is up to |
| T-10 ....... II.3:2 | You do not **m.** what you remember; you |
| T-10 ....... II.6:1 | you could not **m.** such an insane decision. |
| T-10 ....... II.6:2 | You **m.** it only because you still believe it |
| T-10 ..... III.1:7 | those who **m.** idols do worship them. The |
| T-10 ..... III.7:8 | faith in it will **m.** you whole when you |
| T-10 ..... III.8:4 | God is not jealous of the gods you **m.**, but |
| T-10 ... III.10:8 | cannot **m.** your Father, and the father you |
| T-10 ... III.10:8 | and the father you made did not **m.** you. |
| T-10 ..... IV.1:8 | attack him, you will **m.** him real to you. |

T-10....... V.5:3 It is because you did not **m.** yourself that
T-10....... V.5:5 **m.** creators who are unlike your Creator,
T-10....... V.14:9 to understand eternity and **m.** it yours.
T-11.......in.2:5 **M.** no mistake about this. It sounds
T-11.......in.3:1 You **m.** by projection, but God creates by
T-11....... II.4:1 is a sign that you want to **m.** whole. And
T-11....... II.4:3 beside your small willingness to **m.** whole
T-11....... II.4:3 Own complete Will and **m.** yours whole.
T-11......IV.2:1 Could you try to **m.** God homeless and
T-11..... V.15:1 does **m.** every attempt to demonstrate it,
T-11......VI.4:8 But **m.** no exceptions yourself, or you will
T-11.....VII.3:9 it will **m.** you capable of understanding it.
T-11... VIII.2:3 Do not **m.** the mistake of believing that
T-11... VIII.4:3 what is yours, but which you did not **m.**,
T-12.........I.1:1 You have been told not to **m.** error real,
T-12.........I.1:2 have to **m.** it real because it is not true.
T-12........ II.3:3 You will be made whole as you **m.** whole,
T-12...... III.6:1 is to attack yourself and **m.** yourself poor.
T-12....... V.4:4 You tried to **m.** the separation eternal,
T-12....... V.7:6 Such a curriculum does not **m.** sense.
T-12......VI.3:6 **M.** the world real unto yourself, for the
T-12.....VII.7:5 you want in yourself you will **m.** manifest,
T-12.....VII.8:6 If you **m.** love manifest, its messengers
T-12...VII.15:5 When you learn to **m.** me manifest, you
T-12... VIII.8:3 Its reality will **m.** everything else invisible,
T-13.........I.1:1 whose ultimate aim is to **m.** themselves
T-13....... II.8:5 **M.** no mistake about the depth of this
T-13...... III.4:2 you away from yourself and **m.** you little,
T-13....III.12:1 To "single out" is to "**m.** alone," and thus
T-13....III.12:1 is to "make alone," and thus **m.** lonely.
T-13....... V.1:7 They **m.** up a private world that cannot
T-13....... V.8:7 believing you can **m.** a private world and
T-13......VI.4:3 as continuous, and **m.** them so for you.
T-13.....VII.4:4 for what you did not **m.** is willingness to
T-13...VII.12:7 except to **m.** certain that you will not use
T-13... VIII.5:5 to **m.** Christ's vision possible even here.
T-13......IX.2:2 ***M.** no one fearful,* for his guilt is yours, and
T-13......IX.3:5 The power of your valuing will **m.** it so.
T-13......IX.5:3 himself and **m.** himself guilty is insane. In
T-13......IX.6:3 have the Holy Spirit **m.** you free of it,
T-13....... X.8:1 to heal and teach, to **m.** what will be *now.*
T-13..... X.14:1 who **m.** the Father One with His Own Son
T-13......XI.4:5 He knows that He will **m.** it for you. To
T-13....XI.10:5 to know that Heaven is yours to **m.** it so.
T-14....... II.1:6 Yet it may still **m.** sense to you. Have faith
T-14..... II.1:11 you *can* learn how to **m.** the untrue true.
T-14....... II.2:7 **m.** palaces and royal robes of nothing,
T-14....... II.3:5 *Let Me **m.** the one distinction for you that*
T-14....... II.3:5 *one distinction for you that you cannot **m.**,*
T-14....... II.4:1 Like you, the Holy Spirit did not **m.** truth
T-14....... II.5:4 never learn how to **m.** nothing everything
T-14...... III.3:1 no compromise that you can **m.** with guilt
T-14...... III.3:5 *What I experience I will **m.** manifest. If I am*
T-14...... III.5:6 this or does it not will **m.** no difference;
T-14...... III.7:2 **m.** your invulnerability manifest to
T-14...... III.9:1 Whenever you choose to **m.** decisions for
T-14...... III.9:3 It is not true that you can **m.** decisions by
T-14....III.11:1 that you must **m.** decisions for yourself.
T-14....III.11:4 done to **m.** you worthy of the gift of God.
T-14....III.12:6 **M.** no decisions about what it is or where
T-14....III.14:7 not and He will **m.** every decision for you,
T-14......IV.1:2 by proclaiming it in him you **m.** it yours,
T-14......IV.4:2 no barriers; neither did He **m.** them.
T-14......IV.5:1 Before you **m.** any decisions for yourself,
T-14......IV.5:1 whether you want to **m.** decisions here.
T-14......IV.6:3 own volition seems to **m.** deciding hard.
T-14......IV.8:1 Your task is not to **m.** reality. It is here
T-14......VI.4:2 the truth of one must **m.** the falsity of its
T-14......VI.6:4 to **m.** it meaningful if its Interpreter is not
T-14.....VII.6:4 if you **m.** the darkness open to Him. But
T-14... VIII.4:2 And truth will **m.** this plain to you as you
T-14......IX.1:1 The Atonement does not **m.** holy. You
T-14......IX.7:1 wait to **m.** the mirror of your mind clean
T-14....... X.7:2 You cannot safely **m.** this division, for
T-14......XI.7:3 God's Son can **m.** no needs his Father will
T-14......XI.7:7 was, and not as he would **m.** himself. The
T-14......XI.8:5 Thus would you **m.** Him undependable,
T-14....XI.14:7 it. **M.** way for peace, and it will come. For
T-15.........I.7:5 the ego would **m.** the present useless.
T-15.......I.13:3 and thus **m.** time their friend for them.
T-15...... III.3:3 Every decision you **m.** stems from what
T-15...... III.4:8 effort you **m.** on behalf of His dear Son.
T-15...... III.5:2 Holy Spirit every time you **m.** a decision.
T-15...... III.5:3 every decision you **m.** does answer this,
T-15...... III.5:6 **m.** His Son hostage to the ego, cannot
T-15...... III.5:6 **m.** little whom God has joined with Him.
T-15...... III.5:7 Every decision you **m.** is for Heaven or for
T-15...... III.6:4 are decisions you **m.** about yourself. The
T-15.... III.10:7 will **m.** no more gifts to offer to yourself,
T-15...... IV.5:3 you to **m.** the holy instant yours at once,
T-15...... IV.8:4 give it to you is not enough to **m.** it yours,
T-15.... IV.9:10 offers you. Thus will He **m.** you ready to
T-15....... V.1:5 would **m.** no attempt to judge, because it
T-15....... V.2:2 relationships, and thus **m.** them unreal. If
T-15....... V.8:2 no one to **m.** your brothers seem different
T-15...... VI.1:6 you can **m.** a brother into what he is not,
T-15..... VII.5:2 who cannot **m.** himself host to the ego. In
T-15..... VII.5:5 What He can **m.** of them you do not know
T-15..... VII.6:5 Yet to **m.** guilty *is* direct attack, although it
T-15... VII.10:3 than an attempt to **m.** someone feel guilty
T-15... VII.11:2 to communicate is to **m.** yourself alone? It
T-15...... IX.1:3 will become willing to **m.** it permanent.
T-15...... IX.2:4 and thereby to **m.** it impossible. For
T-15...... IX.4:3 and represent its demands to **m.** little and
T-15....... X.4:1 It is in your power to **m.** this season holy,
T-15....... X.4:1 power to **m.** the time of Christ be now. It
T-15....... X.5:5 the decision you believe that you must **m.**
T-15....... X.6:5 this recognition would **m.** it homeless.
T-15....... X.8:7 but always to **m.** the sacrifice complete.
T-15....... X.9:4 recognizing the one decision you must **m.**
T-15.... XI.10:3 and you will **m.** complete and not destroy
T-15.. XI.10:11 **M.** this year different by making it all the
T-16.........I.2:5 **M.** no mistake about this maneuver; the
T-16.........I.3:6 Do not use empathy to **m.** the past real,
T-16...... III.7:1 **m.** learning commensurate with teaching.
T-16...... III.8:4 united will of all who **m.** Heaven what it is
T-16...... IV.1:7 into sight, and to **m.** no attempt to hide it
T-16...... IV.7:2 bring love into fear, and **m.** it real in fear.
T-16....... V.1:4 an attack on the self to **m.** the other guilty
T-16....... V.2:1 the attempt to **m.** guilty is always directed
T-16....... V.7:2 the relationship to **m.** itself complete. Yet
T-16....... V.9:3 as an act of love, would **m.** love hateful.
T-16..... V.14:3 and so are failing to **m.** the simple choice
T-16..... V.16:4 only fantasies **m.** confusion in choosing
T-16..... V.17:1 year is thus the time to **m.** the easiest
T-16..... V.17:3 impossible not to **m.** the natural decision
T-16..... VII.2:4 of the past envelop it, and **m.** it what it is.
T-17.........I.5:4 you are trying to **m.** illusions real, and
T-17...... III.1:4 shadow figures you would **m.** immortal
T-17.... III.1:12 and **m.** your relationships the witness to
T-17...... III.2:1 that would **m.** the ego holy in your sight,
T-17...... III.2:4 and **m.** of both the slaves of vengeance.
T-17...... III.2:9 that go to **m.** the relationship unholy. For
T-17...... III.6:3 The Holy Spirit wants only to **m.** His
T-17...... III.7:1 to light your way and **m.** it clear to you.
T-17...... IV.1:1 relationship with you to **m.** you happy,
T-17...... IV.1:3 of relationships became forever "to **m.**
T-17...... IV.2:2 Yet it *is* possible to **m.** happy. I have said
T-17...... IV.2:5 given them is clearly not to **m.** happy. But
T-17...... IV.2:6 than aiming to **m.** a substitute for it.
T-17...... IV.7:8 Defenses operate to **m.** you think you can.
T-17....... V.3:7 Now it seems to **m.** no sense. Many
T-17....... V.4:2 as yet been changed sufficiently to **m.** its
T-17....... V.8:1 its purpose work in it to **m.** it holy. You
T-17... V.11:10 and gratitude you **m.** yourself unable to
T-17..... V.12:6 but to **m.** it powerless in its effects.
T-17..... V.14:4 stand now which seems to **m.** you suffer,
T-17...... VI.1:5 He will work with you to **m.** it specific, for
T-17...... VI.3:6 left to **m.** is whether or not the ego likes it
T-17...... VI.4:1 the situation as a means to ***m.*** it happen.
T-17...... VI.4:2 will therefore **m.** every effort to overlook
T-17..... VII.1:7 yourself from it and **m.** it unsolvable.
T-17..... VII.2:2 problem but will **m.** solution impossible.
T-17..... VII.3:7 You will **m.** this error, but be not at all
T-17..... VII.7:3 your little faithlessness can **m.** it useless,
T-17... VIII.3:1 you not want to **m.** a holy instant of every
T-18.........I.5:6 to force you to **m.** further substitutions.
T-18.......I.7:12 else is necessary to **m.** them all the same?
T-18........II.1:5 to **m.** over whatever seemed to attack you
T-18........II.3:7 were given you, to **m.** it what you wish.
T-18........II.3:8 trying to triumph over it and **m.** it serve
T-18........II.5:1 to **m.** a world as you would have it be, and
T-18........II.5:5 what they do that seem to **m.** the dream.
T-18......II.5:10 Your wish to **m.** another world that is not
T-18......II.5:17 try to **m.** your sleeping dreams come true.
T-18........II.6:6 as a help to **m.** His purpose real to you.
T-18........II.8:2 that dreams can **m.** a world that is unreal.
T-18........II.8:3 It is the *wish* to **m.** it that is incredible.
T-18...... III.7:4 are made whole in our desire to **m.** whole.
T-18...... III.8:7 and so **m.** room for His eternal Presence,
T-18...... IV.1:9 He joins with you to **m.** the holy instant
T-18...... IV.3:4 to be as you would **m.** yourself? God did
T-18...... IV.4:4 to **m.** arrogant preparations for holiness,
T-18...... IV.4:7 Your willingness is needed only to **m.** it
T-18...... IV.4:8 that you must **m.** the learner different.
T-18...... IV.4:9 You did not **m.** the learner, nor can you
T-18...... IV.4:9 the learner, nor can you **m.** him different.
T-18.... IV.4:10 Would you first **m.** a miracle yourself,
T-18...... IV.5:4 to **m.** yourself holy to be ready to receive
T-18...... IV.5:6 than simple willingness to **m.** way for it.
T-18.... IV.5:11 *be. It is not needful that I **m.** it ready for Him,*
T-18...... IV.6:3 Atonement to it, and **m.** salvation fearful.
T-18...... IV.7:2 You **m.** it difficult, because you insist
T-18...... IV.8:1 it has been your decision to **m.** everything
T-18....... V.2:6 and **m.** sure that you fulfill it easily. And
T-18....... V.5:6 would **m.** of it what He would have it be.
T-18...... VI.3:5 **m.** fantasies and direct the body to act
T-18...... VI.5:4 your wish to **m.** destructive what cannot
T-18...... VI.5:6 You cannot **m.** His Will destructive. You
T-18...... VI.5:7 You can **m.** fantasies in which your will
T-18...... VI.6:4 **m.** it a liability where it could be an asset.
T-18...... VI.9:6 Himself from His Son to **m.** this possible.
T-18..... VII.1:2 What plans do you **m.** that do not involve
T-18..... VII.3:3 Only its past and future **m.** it seem real.
T-18..... VII.4:8 to **m.** holy what is hated and despised.
T-18..... VII.7:7 **m.** a place within you where the activity
T-18...... IX.5:2 that seems to **m.** it heavy and opaque,
T-18...... IX.7:5 the world below, nor seek to **m.** it real.
T-18...... IX.9:6 and **m.** you ready for the final step in the
T-18.... IX.10:2 Forgiveness does **m.** lovely, but it does
T-19.........I.2:2 every demand your ego would **m.** of him.
T-19.........I.2:5 this purpose real, because you **m.** it whole
T-19.........I.3:1 heal, because it cannot **m.** itself sick. It
T-19.........I.5:3 remove all limitations and **m.** whole.
T-19.......I.15:1 most holy garden that He would **m.** of it.
T-19.......I.15:2 calls on truth to enter and **m.** lovely what
T-19.......I.16:1 to interfere with it and **m.** it slave to time.
T-19........II.3:3 in any way, nor **m.** him really guilty. That
T-19........II.8:4 you allow yourself to **m.** this choice.
T-19...... III.5:1 sees the Son of God can **m.** mistakes. On
T19....IV.A.1:5 If you would **m.** it homeless, how can it
T19IV.A.17:12 meager store and **m.** your life complete.
T19.....IV.B.2:4 "sacrifice" you feel to be too great to **m.**,
T19IV.B.14:12 accuse, **m.** guilty and condemn himself?
T19IV.C.11:10 *me how not to **m.** of it an obstacle to peace,*
T19... IV.D.2:3 seems to **m.** the face of Christ Himself like
T19. IV.D.10:5 when it is over it seems to **m.** no sense.
T19. IV.D.10:8 on, only to return and **m.** the choice again
T19. IV.D.13:8 he is, and seek not to **m.** of love an enemy
T19. IV.D.17:9 this holy place, and **m.** the same decision.
T-20........II.1:3 made to **m.** seem lovely what you hate.
T-20...... III.2:2 to **m.** of them what it would have them be
T-20...... III.3:6 You **m.** the world and then adjust to it,
T-20...... III.6:4 did not **m.** adjustments to fit their orders.
T-20...... III.7:1 Seek not to **m.** the Son of God adjust to
T-20...... III.8:3 to adjust the world to **m.** its answer true.
T-20...... III.8:5 How happy did it **m.** you? Did you meet
T-20...... IV.3:1 to guarantee that you would **m.** mistakes,
T-20...... VI.3:2 Idols accept, but never **m.** return. They
T-20...... VI.6:1 **m.** the body the Holy Spirit's temple, and
T-20..... VII.3:5 this, for otherwise you will **m.** the error of
T-20..... VII.5:1 to **m.** the unholy relationship seem real.
T-20..... VII.9:8 And what he sees he did not **m.**, for it was
T-20.... VIII.2:7 not that you need **m.** either means or end.
T-20.... VIII.5:5 will seem to **m.** your savior weak. Yet it is
T-21.........I.7:2 soft reminder of what would **m.** you weep
T-21......II.4:10 strong enough to **m.** a world can let it go,

T-21....... II.6:6 the power to **m.** God powerless and so to
T-21....... II.7:6 All that is asked of you is to **m.** room for
T-21....... II.7:7 You are not asked to **m.** or do what lies
T-21....... II.9:1 ego deals with what it wants, to **m.** it so.
T-21....... II.9:2 to **m.** its goals seem real and possible.
T-21....... II.9:3 of reality to **m.** it fit the goal of madness.
T-21....... II.9:6 adjustments you have introduced to **m.** it
T-21..... II.10:2 effect, and **m.** effect appear to be a cause.
T-21..... II.11:5 made has power to **m.** you what it wills,
T-21...... III.1:6 **m.** it useful to Him and harmless to you.
T-21...... VI.1:6 the power that is in you to **m.** correction.
T-21.... VI.1:10 reason would not **m.** way for correction in
T-21...... VI.5:2 also has the means to **m.** its purpose real.
T-21...... VI.7:7 correction of his errors and **m.** him whole
T-21..... VII.2:4 by their envy **m.** themselves afraid of it?
T-21..... VII.2:6 spite on him, to **m.** him one with them.
T-22....... in.1:5 each one seems to **m.** a different error,
T-22......... I.2:3 are not yours must **m.** no sense to you. To
T-22......... I.8:2 you do not understand, and **m.** it plain.
T-22....... I.10:1 the first direct perception that you can **m.**
T-22....... I.10:2 You **m.** it through awareness older than
T-22....... II.2:4 To change illusions is to **m.** no change.
T-22....... II.2:7 exists will surely fail to **m.** a difference.
T-22....... II.5:1 this, but what they **m.** of it is not the same
T-22....... II.5:4 idea as what will **m.** it either true or false.
T-22....... II.9:6 **m.** himself different and oppose His Will,
T-22..... II.10:4 His joy to misery, and **m.** Him different.
T-22...... III.1:3 reason's goal is to **m.** plain, and therefore
T-22...... III.2:2 errors and **m.** way for their correction.
T-22...... III.4:6 preserve all errors and **m.** them sins. For
T-22...... IV.1:7 reaches this far can **m.** the wrong decision
T-22...... IV.2:1 you can go back and **m.** the other choice.
T-22...... IV.5:1 Every mistake you and your brother **m.**,
T-22.... VI.1:10 and he will **m.** the other serve his choice
T-22...... VI.9:6 and **m.** of it a potent force for peace. He
T-22...... VI.9:8 to **m.** each little gift of love a source of
T-23......... I.3:2 and **m.** your strange alliances on grounds
T-23......... I.4:8 possibly establish this, and **m.** it true?
T-23......... I.6:1 struggling to **m.** them different from each
T-23......... I.8:4 And *by* attacking it you **m.** two illusions of
T-23....... II.1:5 it is their purpose to **m.** meaningless, and
T-23....... II.4:5 the Son of God can **m.** mistakes for which
T-23....... II.6:5 belief that seems to **m.** chaos eternal. For
T-23..... II.13:5 *are* the principles which **m.** the ground
T-23..... II.15:7 lovely do the laws of fear **m.** death appear
T-23..... II.18:8 pet it and pamper it, and **m.** it live? And
T-23...... III.2:2 wrapping does not **m.** the gift you give.
T-23...... III.3:9 Does this **m.** sense? Can it be understood
T-23...... IV.4:4 your little gifts and **m.** them mighty. Also
T-23...... IV.6:1 the temptation to attack rises to **m.** your
T-23...... IV.9:8 choice of miracles or murder hard to **m.**?
T-24....... in.2:4 the power to dictate each decision you **m.**.
T-24......... I.4:5 what would **m.** them special *is* their enemy
T-24......... I.5:3 is what must **m.** the body dear and worth
T-24....... II.1:5 had you not chosen to **m.** of him a tiny
T-24....... II.8:5 **m.** you whole in mind and one with him.
T-24....... II.9:4 which seems to **m.** God and His Heaven
T-24..... II.11:6 And only specialness could **m.** the truth
T-24...... III.2:4 **m.** you separate from Him as its defender.
T-24...... III.5:5 are powerless to **m.** attack upon illusions.
T-24...... III.7:5 because He did not **m.** their dream reality
T-24...... IV.2:3 was conceived to **m.** *you* frail and helpless.
T-24...... IV.3:7 as one. Nothing could **m.** less sense to
T-24...... IV.3:8 Nothing could **m.** more sense to miracles.
T-24..... VII.3:3 Seek not to **m.** your specialness the truth,
T-24... VII.6:10 not till you **m.** again a holy home for your
T-24..... VII.9:6 It is the means to **m.** your wish come true.
T-24. VII.11:12 it is given you to **m.** a different choice,
T-25....... in.2:4 and does not **m.** Him manifest. And thus
T-25......... I.5:5 **m.** the oneness clear to what is really one.
T-25....... II.2:5 where no hope lies must **m.** you hopeless.
T-25....... II.3:3 **m.** sense to hold the fixed belief that there
T-25....... II.6:3 **m.** the frame into the picture when you
T-25....... II.9:3 Would He not **m.** known to you His Love,
T-25..... II.9:10 to **m.** their Father's happiness complete,
T-25...... III.3:5 for illusions which it would **m.** real. Not
T-25...... III.9:7 he is to you will **m.** this choice your future
T-25...... III.9:8 For you **m.** it *now,* the instant when all
T-25...... III.9:9 **M.**, then, your choice. But recognize that
T-25..... VI.4:3 to **m.** himself complete within a world
T-25..... VI.5:1 *one* perfect thing and **m.** *one* perfect choice
T-25..... VI.7:5 Son of God can **m.** no choice the Holy
T-25.... VII.1:8 to **m.** this world's foundation sure as love,
T-25.... VII.2:2 the basis of a world He did not **m.** be firm
T-25.... VII.3:8 to are false, and **m.** no sense at all. This is
T-25.... VII.3:9 This is the choice you **m.**. Do not attempt
T-25.. VII.3:11 For only this decision can you **m.**. The
T-25.... VII.6:7 to **m.** that viewpoint meaningful and sane
T-25.. VII.13:1 that God's insanity would **m.** you sane
T-25.. IX.10:7 Because it does not **m.** the same unlike, it
T-26...... I.4:10 it given him to **m.** the world recede before
T-26........ I.6:1 but can not **m.** sacrifice of its reality. Nor
T-26........ I.6:5 **M.** not his holiness a sacrifice to your
T-26........ I.7:3 You who would **m.** a sacrifice of life, and
T-26........ I.7:3 and **m.** your eyes and ears bear witness to
T-26........ I.7:3 think not that you have power to **m.** of
T-26........ I.7:8 For neither did he **m.**, and only one was
T-26........ I.8:2 it be that you could **m.** his sins reality,
T-26....... II.2:2 loss and **m.** a sacrifice that you might gain
T-26...... III.4:2 to the last comparison that he will ever **m.**
T-26...... III.4:7 one essential thing to **m.** a choice at all is
T-26...... III.5:3 Yet who can **m.** a choice between the wish
T-26...... III.5:6 leaving room to **m.** the only choice that
T-26...... III.7:3 between them, and to **m.** them different.
T-26...... IV.4:8 be to **m.** the space between you disappear
T-26....... V.5:1 instant you would keep and **m.** eternal,
T-26....... V.5:3 short to **m.** a world in answer to creation,
T-26...... VI.1:7 For no one can **m.** one illusion real, and
T-26...... VI.3:3 **M.** no illusion friend, for if you do, it can
T-26...... VI.3:5 given can **m.** sure that you receive them.
T-26...... VI.3:6 when you **m.** room for Him on His.
T-26..... VII.8:2 And truth needs no defense to **m.** it true.
T-26.. VII.13:4 but cannot **m.** it be what it is not. And to
T-26.. VII.14:5 demands that he must **m.** some sacrifice,
T-26.. VII.18:2 nor to **m.** use of what He gave to answer
T-26.. VII.20:4 A miracle can **m.** no change at all. But it
T-26.. VII.20:5 But it can **m.** what always has been true
T-26... VIII.5:1 plans you **m.** for safety all are laid within
T-26..... IX.3:7 leans to join with it, and **m.** it like itself.
T-26........ X.5:1 must be unfair to **m.** the other innocent.
T-27........ I.1:2 and **m.** a unity of what can never join?
T-27........ I.2:3 Thus would you **m.** yourself to be the sign
T-27........ I.2:6 Wish not to **m.** yourself a living symbol of
T-27..... II.2:10 One denies the other and must **m.** it false.
T-27...... III.1:8 it is not, and **m.** it unintelligible. Who can
T-27...... III.4:1 truth to enter, and to **m.** itself at home.
T-27...... III.5:6 Spirit **m.** exchange of pictures possible,
T-27...... IV.1:2 its purpose is to **m.** no resolution possible
T-27....... V.8:1 and these specific shapes **m.** up the world
T-27...... VI.1:4 they both are means to **m.** the body real.
T-27...... VI.3:7 You do not **m.** a witness true because you
T-27..... VII.8:3 to waken from a dream he did not **m.**.
T-27..... VII.9:4 choice is yours to **m.** between a sleeping
T-27... VIII.7:7 have no power to **m.** the body stop its evil
T-27... VIII.7:7 its evil deeds because you did not **m.** it,
T-27. VIII.11:3 will **m.** answer with this very simple truth
T-28........ I.4:1 Holy Spirit can indeed **m.** use of memory,
T-28........ I.6:4 And yet you **m.** strange use of it, as if the
T-28........ I.6:7 past is held in memory as you **m.** use of it,
T-28....... I.12:6 do nothing that would **m.** himself afraid.
T-28..... II.2:11 to causelessness, and **m.** it be a cause.
T-28....... II.3:1 of God attempt to **m.** himself his cause,
T-28....... II.5:8 It does not ask you **m.** another; only that
T-28..... II.7:11 the consequences that would **m.** it cause.
T-28..... II.10:4 causeless now, because they did not **m.** it.
T-28..... II.12:6 mind is free to **m.** another choice instead.
T-28...... III.6:4 thus **m.** room for Him Who wills to come
T-28...... III.8:6 And in your storehouse it will **m.** a place
T-28...... IV.3:7 and his dreams but seem to **m.** a little gap
T-28....... V.3:6 ground which your Creator did not **m.**,
T-28....... V.3:7 You will **m.** war upon your Self, which
T-28....... V.5:4 to hear the voices that can **m.** no sound.
T-28....... V.5:7 and **m.** a witness to the world you want.
T-28...... VI.1:4 It does not seek to **m.** of pain a joy and
T-28...... VI.6:2 keep the promise that you **m.** with him,
T-28.. VII.5:10 lock the windows and **m.** fast the bolts.
T-29........ I.3:3 **m.** the way to light seem dark and fearful,
T-29........ I.5:4 limits your ability to **m.** communion with
T-29........ I.5:6 and what will tire it and **m.** it sick. And its
T-29...... III.4:1 **M.** way for love, which you did not create
T-29...... VI.2:2 You **m.** a bargain that you cannot keep.
T-29...... VI.4:1 God gave to all that you would **m.** eternal,
T-29..... VII.2:4 give him what would **m.** himself complete
T-29..... VII.8:3 with power to **m.** complete what is within
T-29... VIII.4:6 voice could **m.** demand He enter not? The
T-29... VIII.4:7 to **m.** you tremble and to quail in fear.
T-29... VIII.9:6 for idols that would **m.** of Heaven less, to
T-29...... IX.2:9 you **m.** yourself a part of evil dreams,
T-29...... IX.4:2 **m.** you sinful and put out the light within
T-29...... IX.5:9 to **m.** his world remain outside himself,
T-30...... in.1:8 We seek to **m.** them habits now, so you
T-30........ I.2:2 *Today I will* **m.** *no decisions by myself.* This
T-30........ I.2:4 you will be called upon to **m.** response.
T-30........ I.3:2 You still **m.** up your mind, and *then* decide
T-30........ I.4:2 *If I* **m.** *no decisions by myself, this is the day*
T-30...... I.12:5 and so the answer will **m.** sense as well.
T-30...... I.14:1 not to **m.** decisions by yourself. This
T-30...... I.14:3 yet, you *cannot* **m.** decisions by yourself.
T-30...... I.14:4 really is with what you choose to **m.** them
T-30...... I.14:7 will not **m.** decisions by yourself whatever
T-30..... II.2:10 Him is to **m.** a choice against yourself,
T-30...... III.2:4 What idol can **m.** two of what is one? And
T-30...... III.3:3 to add to you to **m.** yourself complete,
T-30...... III.5:8 What is not whole cannot **m.** whole. But
T-30...... IV.4:8 nor **m.** you safe if they obeyed your rules.
T-30...... IV.5:5 Attack has power to **m.** illusions real. Yet
T-30...... IV.6:2 And you can **m.** a simple choice that will
T-30...... VI.2:4 to **m.** unnatural responses which are
T-30...... VI.5:7 and to **m.** a world that could replace it
T-30...... VI.8:3 To heal is to **m.** whole. And what is whole
T-30...... VI.9:5 by your wish to **m.** illusions real. And
T-30... VI.10:1 understand he could not **m.** an error that
T-30... VI.10:3 as having power to **m.** an idol of the Son
T-30..... VII.3:7 and **m.** allowance for stability of meaning
T-30... VIII.3:1 temptation but a wish to **m.** illusions real
T-31........ I.1:6 it could **m.** such an easy lesson difficult.
T-31........ I.7:7 is no plan for safety you can **m.** that ever
T-31...... I.11:1 What is temptation but a wish to **m.** the
T-31....... II.2:3 The first is a decision that you **m.**. But
T-31....... II.5:5 Two calls you **m.** to him, as he to you.
T-31....... II.6:7 We **m.** no gains he does not make with us
T-31....... II.6:7 We make no gains he does not **m.** with us
T-31....... II.9:4 you **m.** progress if you think the same,
T-31..... II.11:8 but cannot **m.** the way itself grow dark.
T-31...... III.1:2 As you prepare to **m.** a choice that will
T-31...... IV.4:7 is none. **M.** fast your learning now, and
T-31...... IV.8:1 *is* a choice that you have power to **m.** when
T-31....... V.1:6 without a self, and **m.** one as you go along
T-31....... V.3:4 a hundred little things **m.** small assaults
T-31..... V.7:10 **m.** a single picture representing truth.
T-31....... V.8:5 be asked to **m.** exchange of what you now
T-31..... V.10:7 brother, who was there to **m.** the other?
T-31..... V.16:1 You will **m.** many concepts of the self as
T-31...... VI.2:2 and happenings that **m.** no sense at all.
T-31...... VI.4:1 that you must **m.** the way to Heaven plain
T-31..... VII.1:2 nor to **m.** the kinds of change you could
T-31.. VII.14:1 to **m.** yourself a thing that you are not.
T-31... VIII.2:1 How do you **m.** the choice? How easily is
T-31... VIII.3:1 before you now can **m.** a better one, and
T-31... VIII.4:1 The images you **m.** cannot prevail against
T-31... VIII.6:5 that every choice you **m.** establishes your
T-31... VIII.8:6 To give this gift is how to **m.** it yours. And
T-31. VIII.10:7 the world with every choice they **m.**. For
W-in.......... 1:1 as a framework to **m.** the exercises in this
W-in.......... 1:2 that will **m.** the goal of the course possible
W-in.......... 9:4 do not allow yourself to **m.** exceptions in
W-pI...... 1.3:1 and **m.** no allowance for differences in the
W-pI...... 2.2:5 on it. **M.** no attempt to include anything
W-pI...... 4.2:4 beyond, and shadows **m.** sight difficult.
W-pI...... 4.2:5 blocks to sight, and **m.** seeing impossible.
W-pI.... 12.5:3 you, it would **m.** you indescribably happy
W-pI.... 15.5:1 to **m.** the selection as random as possible.
W-pI.... 16.1:7 likeness. Those that are false **m.** theirs.
W-pI.... 16.4:3 for you not to **m.** artificial distinctions.
W-pI.... 17.3:1 is essential to **m.** no distinctions between
W-pI.... 19.4:3 in this connection will ultimately **m.** the
W-pI.... 20.5:2 to do so, but **m.** a real effort to remember.

| | |
|---|---|
| W-pI.....24.1:1 | the outcome that would **m.** you happy. |
| W-pI.....25.4:1 | Before you can **m.** any sense out of the |
| W-pI.....26.2:3 | therefore **m.** you vulnerable in your own |
| W-pI.....26.4:3 | can **m.** you think you are vulnerable. And |
| W-pI.....28.1:4 | If you are willing at least to **m.** them now, |
| W-pI.....34.4:2 | however, not to **m.** any specific exclusions |
| W-pI.....36.2:2 | **m.** the shorter applications frequently, to |
| W-pI.....37.2:7 | see themselves as whole **m.** no demands. |
| W-pI.....38.3:5 | We will **m.** no distinctions because there |
| W-pI.....38.4:2 | Try to **m.** as little distinction as possible |
| W-pI.....41.5:3 | Today we will **m.** our first real attempt to |
| W-pI.....41.6:4 | Then **m.** no effort to think of anything. |
| W-pI.....43.7:6 | not to **m.** distinctions of this kind at all. |
| W-pI.....44.1:2 | see in darkness, and you cannot **m.** light. |
| W-pI.....44.1:3 | **m.** darkness and then think you see in it, |
| W-pI.....45.2:4 | To share is to **m.** alike, or to make one. |
| W-pI.....45.2:4 | To share is to make alike, or to **m.** one. |
| W-pI.....46.7:2 | to **m.** more specific applications if they |
| W-pI.....51.3:6 | go, and **m.** room for what can be seen and |
| W-pI.....51.5:3 | I am constantly trying to **m.** them true. I |
| W-pI.....51.5:4 | I **m.** all things my enemies, so that my |
| W-pI.....54.1:3 | either **m.** a false world or lead me to the |
| W-pI.....57.2:7 | him, and not what I would **m.** of him. He |
| W-pI.....58.4:4 | my holiness, nothing can **m.** me afraid. |
| W-pI.....62.4:2 | It will help to **m.** the day as happy for you |
| W-pI.....64.5:3 | for all the decisions you will **m.** today by |
| W-pI.....64.5:5 | a simple decision really be difficult to **m.**? |
| W-pI.....65.5:3 | **m.** no attempt to concentrate only on |
| W-pI.....65.6:2 | not strain or **m.** undue effort in doing this |
| W-pI...66.10:2 | Try to **m.** this choice as you think about |
| W-pI.....67.1:6 | We will **m.** every effort today to reach this |
| W-pI.....68.1:6 | from your Source and **m.** you unlike Him. |
| W-pI.....69.2:1 | Today let us **m.** another real attempt to |
| W-pI.....69.5:5 | substance. We will **m.** this attempt today. |
| W-pI.....70.7:5 | in self-concepts that you sought to **m.** real |
| W-pI.....73.1:5 | they can **m.** a world of illusions in which |
| W-pI.....73.1:7 | of creation. They **m.** nothing that is real. |
| W-pI...73.11:1 | again **m.** a declaration of what you really |
| W-pI.....76.1:5 | you bind yourself to laws that **m.** no sense |
| W-pI.....76.7:5 | imprisons, but the laws of God **m.** free. |
| W-pI.....76.8:7 | you hold must be obeyed to **m.** you safe. |
| W-pI.....77.3:5 | will also **m.** sure that we will not content |
| W-pI.....78.1:1 | you that each decision that you **m.** is one |
| W-pI.....78.8:3 | would be free, and **m.** his freedom yours. |
| W-pI.....88.3:4 | I am constantly tempted to **m.** up other |
| W-pI.....89.3:5 | **m.** no exceptions and no substitutes. I |
| W-pI.....94.5:8 | **M.** every effort to do the hourly exercises |
| W-pI.....95.9:3 | to continue is to **m.** additional mistakes, |
| W-pI.....96.3:5 | **M.** no attempt to reconcile the two, for |
| W-pI.....96.6:6 | Salvation cannot **m.** illusions real, nor |
| W-pI.....97.4:3 | strength to every little effort that you **m.**. |
| W-pI.....98.4:2 | our certainty, will **m.** it stronger still. |
| W-pI.....98.4:3 | they have come to **m.** their choice again. |
| W-pI.....98.5:3 | five minutes but a small request to **m.** in |
| W-pI.....98.7:3 | and **m.** each repetition of today's idea a |
| W-pI...98.11:2 | He will **m.** you sure you want this choice, |
| W-pI.....99.8:2 | **m.** them real by hiding them from Him. |
| W-pI...107.9:2 | and **m.** your pledge to let His function be |
| W-pI.108.10:2 | and we will **m.** much faster progress now. |
| W-pI...110.2:2 | to heal the past and **m.** the future free. It |
| W-pI.110.10:4 | Today we **m.** a great advance to truth by |
| WpI . rIII.in2:3 | Nor is it necessary that you **m.** excessive |
| WpIrIII.in11:6 | in the business of the day and **m.** it holy, |
| W-pI...121.1:2 | in a world that seems to **m.** no sense. |
| W-pI...122.5:3 | bidding you to enter in and **m.** yourself at |
| W-pI...125.6:4 | to help **m.** ready your most holy mind to |
| W-pI...126.8:2 | You will need help to **m.** this meaningful, |
| W-pI...127.2:6 | If it could **m.** such distinctions, it would |
| W-pI...128.3:2 | value you **m.** part of you as you perceive |
| W-pI...128.3:3 | yourself. All things you seek to **m.** your |
| W-pI...129.7:1 | Practice your willingness to **m.** this |
| W-pI...130.2:4 | Fear must **m.** blind, for this its weapon is: |
| W-pI...130.4:2 | of differences you believe **m.** up the world |
| W-pI...130.7:2 | We will not **m.** a thousand meaningless |
| W-pI...131.7:4 | He did not **m.** two minds, with Heaven as |
| W-pI...131.9:2 | God **m.** time to take away the Will of God |
| W-pI.131.11:4 | *The world I seek I did not* **m.** *alone, the* |
| W-pI.131.12:3 | truth. And it is this request you **m.** today. |
| W-pI.131.13:3 | will **m.** you pause before you realize the |
| W-pI...132.4:4 | you think you did not **m.** the world, but |
| W-pI.132.11:1 | **m.** what does not share His timelessness |
| W-pI...133.3:3 | laws that govern choice you cannot **m.**, |
| W-pI...133.3:3 | can **m.** alternatives from which to choose. |
| W-pI...133.5:3 | choice you **m.** brings everything to you or |
| W-pI...133.5:4 | nothing, you will **m.** the better choice. |
| W-pI...133.8:2 | Why is the choice you **m.** of value to you? |
| W-pI.133.12:5 | you **m.** choices easily and without pain. |
| W-pI.134.12:3 | iron doors he thought would **m.** him safe. |
| W-pI...135.2:2 | to call on you to **m.** appropriate defense. |
| W-pI...135.3:5 | as you elaborate your plans and **m.** your |
| W-pI...135.5:4 | it gifts to **m.** it beautiful or walls to make |
| W-pI...135.5:4 | to make it beautiful or walls to **m.** it safe, |
| W-pI...135.6:5 | Who would **m.** defense of something that |
| W-pI...135.7:4 | for the many mad attacks you **m.** upon it. |
| W-pI.135.13:1 | up to save itself must **m.** the body sick. It |
| W-pI.135.17:1 | you undertake to **m.** against the truth. |
| W-pI.135.21:3 | We **m.** no plans for how it will be done, |
| W-pI.135.23:2 | If there are plans to **m.**, you will be told of |
| W-pI...136.5:5 | Defenses must **m.** facts unrecognizable. |
| W-pI...136.7:3 | It is a choice you **m.**, a plan you lay, when |
| W-pI...136.8:5 | For see, this dust can **m.** you suffer, twist |
| W-pI.136.12:2 | does not **m.** appeal to might nor triumph. |
| W-pI.136.18:4 | You need do nothing now to **m.** it well, |
| W-pI.136.19:2 | or **m.** plans against uncertainties to come, |
| W-pI...137.2:3 | body final power to **m.** the separation real |
| W-pI.137.15:3 | come together to **m.** well all that was sick, |
| W-pI......138.h | Heaven is the decision I must **m.**. |
| W-pI...138.1:3 | is the way we **m.** what we perceive, and |
| W-pI...138.4:1 | you, when there is really only one to **m.**. |
| W-pI...138.4:4 | You **m.** but one. And when that one is |
| W-pI...138.6:2 | all the choices you have tried to **m.** this is |
| W-pI...138.7:1 | choice that time was made to help us **m.**. |
| W-pI.138.10:3 | Yet who can fail to **m.** a choice between |
| W-pI.138.10:4 | Who hesitates to **m.** a choice like this? |
| W-pI.138.11:1 | We **m.** the choice for Heaven as we wake, |
| W-pI.138.11:2 | We recognize we **m.** a conscious choice |
| W-pI.138.12:5 | *Heaven is the decision I must* **m.**. *I make it* |
| W-pI.138.12:6 | *I* **m.** *it now, and will not change my mind,* |
| W-pI...139.2:2 | could **m.** the question seem to be sincere. |
| W-pI...140.1:2 | is but what will **m.** the body "better." |
| W-pI...140.2:2 | he found a magic formula to **m.** him well. |
| W-pI...140.2:5 | does the content of a dream **m.** in reality? |
| W-pI...140.6:2 | not **m.** distinctions among unrealities. |
| WpI.140.11:4 | We have no need to **m.** them different, |
| WpI...149.2:1 | (138) Heaven is the decision I must **m.**. |
| W-pI.153.18:4 | Think you He will not **m.** this possible, |
| W-pI...155.2:4 | What other choice is really theirs to **m.**? |
| W-pI...155.3:1 | This is the simple choice we **m.** today. |
| W-pI.155.11:1 | the holy Son of God will **m.** no journeys. |
| W-pI.155.11:4 | final journey, which we **m.** for everyone. |
| W-pI...157.8:2 | this journey which you **m.** and start today |
| W-pI...158.4:5 | back on it, imagining we **m.** it once again; |
| W-pI...161.4:4 | thoughts **m.** clear the meaning of creation |
| W-pI...165.3:3 | would he not **m.** sure they stay with him, |
| W-pI...166.1:6 | But what would **m.** you think there is |
| W-pI...166.8:3 | He would **m.** you laugh at this perception |
| W-pI...166.8:5 | **m.** for him whom God intended only joy? |
| W-pI.166.12:5 | sought to **m.** in which to hide from God. |
| W-pI...167.4:2 | causes you cannot control, you did not **m.** |
| W-pI...167.6:3 | It cannot **m.** a body, nor abide within a |
| W-pI...167.6:6 | It cannot **m.** the physical. What seems to |
| W-pI...167.7:5 | it seems to **m.** when it believes it sleeps. |
| W-pI...167.8:2 | **m.** conditions which He does not share |
| W-pI...169.8:3 | that you but **m.** a journey that is done. |
| W-pI...170.2:2 | blood, to **m.** it grow and swell and rage. |
| W-pI...170.2:6 | *You* **m.** *what you defend against, and by* |
| W-pI...170.4:2 | their source, for it is you who **m.** attack, |
| W-pI...170.8:3 | You **m.** a choice, standing before this idol |
| W-pI...170.8:5 | Or will you **m.** another idol to replace it? |
| W-pI.170.11:1 | The choice you **m.** today is certain. For |
| W-pI.170.13:5 | *again, and* **m.** *our choice for all our brothers,* |
| WpI...rV.in2:4 | *but listen to Your Word, and* **m.** *it ours. Lead* |
| WpI...rV.in7:5 | was begun, to **m.** another choice with me. |
| Wi181-200 1:1 | Our next few lessons **m.** a special point of |
| Wi181-200 1:1 | to **m.** your weak commitment strong; |
| W-pI...184.8:4 | it is to his body that you **m.** appeal. His |
| W-pI...185.2:3 | He cannot **m.** a hell and think it real. He |
| W-pI...185.7:5 | nor try to **m.** another bargain in the hope |
| W-pI...185.9:1 | This is the choice you **m.**. Be not deceived |
| W-pI.185.10:3 | this when you **m.** this request with deep |
| W-pI...186.5:2 | Accept the plan you did not **m.** instead. |
| W-pI...186.8:2 | that we can **m.** another for ourselves. Our |
| W-pI...186.9:4 | appears to **m.** have no effect on what he is |
| W-pI.186.10:2 | you **m.** give rise to but conflicting goals, |
| W-pI.186.12:2 | it is that asks, and who would **m.** denial. |
| W-pI.186.13:3 | He would **m.** a restitution, though He is |
| W-pI...187.1:4 | seems to **m.** it hard to credit is not this. |
| W-pI...187.2:3 | but represent the thoughts that **m.** them. |
| W-pI.188.10:3 | we who **m.** the world as we would have it. |
| W-pI...189.8:6 | But do not **m.** demands, nor point the |
| W-pI...190.5:5 | that has the power to **m.** you ill or sad, or |
| W-pI...190.7:3 | As an effect, it cannot **m.** effects. As an |
| W-pI.190.11:1 | again we **m.** the only choice that ever can |
| W-pI...192.5:1 | without the body cannot **m.** mistakes. It |
| W-pI...194.6:1 | effort as you can, to **m.** it be a part of you. |
| W-pI...194.9:5 | Who guards our rest to **m.** the choice for |
| W-pI...195.5:2 | let your gratitude **m.** room for all who |
| W-pI...196.1:1 | nor **m.** your body slave to vengeance. You |
| W-pI...196.5:1 | hopeless thought that you can **m.** attacks |
| W-pI.196.11:6 | back from fear, and **m.** advance to love. |
| W-pI...197.1:2 | **m.** attempts at kindness and forgiveness. |
| W-pI...198.9:1 | freedom come to **m.** its home with you. |
| W-pI...199.5:2 | **M.** it a part of every practice period you |
| W-pI...199.7:3 | can **m.** use of your escape from bondage, |
| W-pI...199.7:5 | Who calls to you to **m.** this gift to Him. |
| W-pI...200.4:2 | you sought to **m.** them meaningful. This |
| W-pI...200.6:6 | a choice to **m.** between success and failure |
| W-pI...200.7:1 | because He has one Son who cannot **m.** a |
| WpI rVI.in.1:2 | hourly remembrances you **m.** throughout |
| W-pII ....in.4:3 | invitation that He seeks to **m.** us happy? |
| W-pII ....in.9:2 | and be what we would **m.** of Him. And we |
| W-pII ..... 1.1:2 | It does not pardon sins and **m.** them real. |
| W-pII .227.1:2 | *I thought to* **m.** *another will. Yet nothing* |
| W-pII ..... 3.3:3 | world was made to witness and **m.** real. |
| W-pII .242.1:4 | glad to **m.** no choices for me but the ones |
| W-pII .243.1:5 | am relieved of judgments that I cannot **m.** |
| W-pII .244.2:4 | or **m.** afraid what will forever be a part of |
| W-pII .259.1:2 | and **m.** the strange and the distorted |
| W-pII .260.1:1 | *Father, I did not* **m.** *myself, although in my* |
| W-pII ..... 5.5:1 | with what you think will **m.** you safe. |
| W-pII .277.1:3 | *by which I try to* **m.** *the body more secure. He* |
| W-pII .277.2:1 | believe in any law idolatry would **m.** to |
| W-pII .292.1:1 | God's promises **m.** no exceptions. And |
| W-pII .297.1:4 | I, who would be saved, would **m.** it mine, |
| W-pII .306.2:3 | **m.** *an offering sufficient for Your Son. But in* |
| W-pII .307.1:3 | *Let me not try to* **m.** *another will, for it is* |
| W-pII .311.1:5 | **m.** a gift of it to Him Who has a different |
| W-pII .317.1:3 | do. Until I **m.** this choice, I am the slave of |
| W-pII ....323.h | I gladly **m.** the "sacrifice" of fear. |
| W-pII .323.1:2 | sacrifice" *You ask of me, and one I gladly* **m.** |
| W-pII .325.2:1 | *mine apart from Yours but* **m.** *up dreams.* |
| W-pII .331.1:2 | *Could he* **m.** *a plan for his damnation, and be* |
| W-pII ....343.h | I am not asked to **m.** a sacrifice To find |
| W-pII .343.1:9 | *Your Son can* **m.** *no sacrifice, for he must be* |
| W-pII .349.1:2 | *and give what I would find and* **m.** *my own. It* |
| W-pII .351.1:3 | *Yet this perception is a choice I* **m.**, *and can* |
| W-pII .352.1:3 | *Judgment will bind my eyes and* **m.** *me blind* |
| W-pII .356.1:1 | *to answer any call Your Son might* **m.** *to You* |
| W-pII ....357.h | Truth answers every call we **m.** to God, |
| W-ep ......... 5:3 | for you each time there is a choice to **m.**. |
| W-ep ......... 5:4 | each choice you **m.** brings Heaven nearer |
| M-3 ........... 1:2 | **m.** of the relationship a holy relationship, |
| M-4 .........I.2:4 | is it that induces them to **m.** the shift? |
| M-4 ..... I.A.3:5 | point at which he can **m.** the shift entirely |
| M-4 ...... IV.1:9 | It will **m.** him confused, fearful, angry |
| M-4 .... IV.1:10 | and suspicious. It will **m.** the Holy Spirit's |
| M-4 ...... VI.1:3 | They do not try to **m.** themselves. Their |
| M-5 ...... III.3:4 | remind him that he did not **m.** himself, |
| M-8 ........... 2:3 | an illusion is an attempt to **m.** something |
| M-8 ........... 2:4 | The mind therefore seeks to **m.** it true out |
| M-8 ........... 5:9 | to **m.** them different are really irrelevant, |
| M-9 ........... 2:2 | He does not **m.** his own decisions; he asks |
| M-10 ......... 4:6 | **M.** then but one more judgment. It is this: |
| M-12 ......... 5:8 | of God does not **m.** this decision alone. |
| M-13 ......... 8:1 | decision you **m.** must mean in terms of |
| M-14 ......... 3:7 | teacher of God can **m.** salvation complete |
| M-15 ....... 3:10 | It is your function to **m.** that end be soon. |

| | |
|---|---|
| M-16 ......... 7:5 | He need **m.** no distinctions among the |
| M-16 ........ 11:2 | The world would gladly **m.** it, if it knew it |
| M-16 ........ 11:4 | function to **m.** sure that they have learned |
| M-17 ......... 5:9 | and **m.** himself a shield to keep him safe |
| M-17 ......... 9:2 | In truth it has no power to **m.** anything. |
| M-19 ......... 5:2 | Perception can **m.** whatever picture the |
| M-22 ......... 1:7 | and what remains to **m.** sickness possible |
| M-22 ......... 3:1 | if the teacher of God is to **m.** progress. |
| M-25 ......... 1:2 | to **m.** up a power that does not exist. It is |
| M-27 ......... 2:7 | reigns and opposites **m.** endless war. |
| M-27 ......... 4:9 | **m.** death because He did not make fear. |
| M-27 ......... 4:9 | make death because He did not **m.** fear. |
| M-29 ......... 2:12 | have a Teacher Who cannot **m.** a mistake. |
| C-in ........... 5:2 | away to **m.** way for the central teaching. |
| C-2............. 2:5 | behind the words that seem to **m.** it so. |
| C-2............. 3:1 | definition for a lie that serves to **m.** it true |
| C-2............. 4:1 | really **m.** a definition for what the ego is, |
| C-2............. 8:4 | and even **m.** the question meaningless? |
| C-6........... 4:10 | It is from these that He would **m.** you safe |
| P-1............. 4:1 | the ability to **m.** his own decisions. He |
| P-1............. 5:1 | God in order to **m.** progress in salvation. |
| P-2......... in.1:4 | If it can **m.** way for reality, it has achieved |
| P-2......... in.3:5 | wants to **m.** the vulnerable invulnerable |
| P-2........... I.2:6 | the ego seeks to **m.** are not really changes. |
| P-2......... II.6:1 | difference does it **m.** how the invitation is |
| P-2........ IV.4:3 | but **m.** the body real in their own minds, |
| P-2........ IV.7:4 | **m.** illusions true through false perception |
| P-2........ VI.2:5 | **m.** this ugly sound seem truly beautiful. |
| P-2........ VI.3:3 | is to **m.** agreeable whatever is called on, |
| P-2....... VI.4:10 | cure what cannot be sick and **m.** it well? |
| P-2....... VII.4:2 | with God. All "unhealed healers" **m.** this |
| P-2....... VII.6:7 | who call upon his sanctity to **m.** it theirs. |
| P-3........... I.1:7 | to **m.** sacrifices of yourself for those who |
| P-3........... I.4:1 | he did not **m.** the curriculum of salvation, |
| P-3......... II.2:3 | taught him how to **m.** healing impossible. |
| P-3........ III.3:2 | They **m.** demands, and so they cannot |
| S-1........... I.2:4 | There are decisions to **m.** here, and they |
| S-1......... II.1:4 | not, and often does not, **m.** appeal to God |
| S-1......... II.6:2 | anyone in prayer, you **m.** him part of you. |
| S-1........ III.2:7 | could never **m.** a prayer like that. |
| S-1........ III.4:7 | **m.** a jailer of an enemy seems to be safety. |
| S-2......... in.1:1 | to **m.** its rising easy and its progress swift. |
| S-2........... I.3:4 | Do not **m.** it real. Select the loving and |
| S-2........... I.6:2 | Others will **m.** mistakes and so will you, |
| S-2........... I.8:2 | This is the choice you **m.**; the simplest |
| S-2........... I.8:2 | one, and yet the only one that you *can* **m.**. |
| S-2........... I.9:3 | fits? Therefore we **m.** distinctions, so that |
| S-2......... II.1:3 | separate and **m.** what God created equal, |
| S-2......... II.7:4 | How pitiful it is to **m.** of it the means for |
| S-2........ III.3:2 | knows the way to **m.** of every call a help to |
| S-2........ III.3:3 | Now can He **m.** your footsteps sure, your |
| S-2........ III.6:7 | and to **m.** the means for separation, sin |
| S-3......... in.1:1 | and witnesses which **m.** the steep ascent |
| S-3........ III.4:5 | You do not **m.** yourself the bearer of the |

## make-believe 1

| | |
|---|---|
| T-18...... IX.7:4 | you would play the game of children's **m.**. |

## Maker 4

*maker*

| | |
|---|---|
| T-25...... III.4:1 | There is another **M.** of the world, the |
| T-25...... III.5:1 | has another **M.** Who can reconcile its goal |
| T-25...... III.5:6 | the **M.** of the world correct your error, |
| T-25...... III.8:1 | **M.** of the world of gentleness has perfect |

## maker 33

*Maker*

| | |
|---|---|
| T-4......... I.2:13 | even though its **m.** can be misguided. He |
| T-4........ III.4:3 | Father, the ego has no allegiance to its **m.**. |
| T-5...... VI.2:10 | And as its **m.**, you recognize what it can |
| T-6........ IV.1:3 | capricious and does not mean its **m.** well. |
| T-6........ IV.1:4 | **m.** may withdraw his support from it at |
| T-6........ IV.2:5 | regard itself as separate and outside its **m.** |
| T-6........ IV.4:2 | this as a justification for attacking its **m.**. |
| T-7...... VI.4:10 | ego. Its own **m.**, then, does not want it. |
| T-10...... III.4:6 | in the image of what its **m.** thinks he is. |
| T-12 ...... III.9:8 | Yet this world is only in the mind of its **m.** |
| T-13 ...... V.1:8 | For they are meaningful only to their **m.**, |
| T-13 ...... V.1:9 | all. In this world their **m.** moves alone, for |
| T-14 ..... VI.6:4 | it meaningful if its Interpreter is not its **m.** |
| T-17 ...... V.1:7 | hymn of hate in praise of its **m.**, so is the |
| T19.... IV.C.4:2 | damned by its **m.** and lamented by every |
| T-21 ..... II.10:3 | events and feelings its **m.** thinks it causes. |
| T-21 ..... II.12:5 | entirely upon the madness of its **m.**, and |
| T-22 ...... in.1:6 | and forgiven for its **m.** in the same way. |
| T-22 ....... II.9:1 | you made has power to enslave its **m.**. |
| T-22 ..... III.6:2 | For the idea they represent left not its **m.**, |
| T-22 ..... III.6:2 | and it is their **m.** that sees through them. |
| T-22 . VI.12:11 | to attack to see it separated from its **m.**. |
| T-24 ...... V.2:2 | for here the **m.** of the dream believes that |
| T-25 ..... IV.3:1 | You **m.** of a world that is not so, take rest |
| T-28 ....... II.8:7 | dreamer could not be the **m.** of the dream |
| T-28 ..... II.10:5 | you can accept the role of **m.** of their hate, |
| T-28 ...... V.5:8 | persuade their **m.** his imaginings are real. |
| T-31 ...... V.7:6 | to which its **m.** gives a meaning of his own |
| W-pI..... 23.4:1 | you do not see yourself as the image **m.**. |
| W-pI..... 92.5:1 | it; weakness reflects the darkness of its **m.** |
| W-pI..... 95.2:2 | together by its erratic and capricious **m.**, |
| W-pI... 161.8:4 | it can reach to its **m.** and devour him. |
| M-5 ........ II.1:7 | on the body being the decision **m.**. Terms |

## maker's 1

| | |
|---|---|
| T-22 ..... III.6:3 | What was its **m.** goal but not to see? For |

## makers

*See* co-makers

## makes 319

| | |
|---|---|
| T-1 ........ I.12:3 | One **m.** the physical, and the other |
| T-1 ........ I.49:1 | miracle **m.** no distinction among degrees |
| T-1 ...... III.5:10 | **m.** them vulnerable to the distortions of |
| T-1 ....... III.9:2 | Since this **m.** it inevitable that they will |
| T-1 ....... IV.2:2 | deception **m.** you fearful because you |
| T-2 .......... I.5:2 | **m.** no distinctions among misperceptions |
| T-2 ....... III.4:6 | **m.** it increasingly unable to tolerate delay, |
| T-2 ....... IV.4:2 | believing that the body **m.** its own illness. |
| T-2 ........ V.2:3 | you are afraid **m.** your mind vulnerable to |
| T-2 ....... VI.1:7 | and **m.** you feel personally responsible for |
| T-3 ....... III.5:3 | this **m.** it possible for you to know him. |
| T-3 ....... IV.3:7 | This **m.** its aspects strangers to each other |
| T-3 ....... IV.6:5 | This **m.** spirit almost inaccessible to the |
| T-3 ....... VI.5:4 | are. All this **m.** you feel tired because it is |
| T-3 ....... VI.7:4 | ego **m.** involves a contradiction in terms, |
| T-3 ....... VI.7:4 | ego **m.** is incomplete and contradictory. |
| T-3 ....... VI.8:6 | He knows that it **m.** them unhappy. God's |
| T-3 ...... VII.2:8 | real worth. This **m.** absolutely no sense. |
| T-4 ......... II.2:1 | Everyone **m.** an ego or a self for himself, |
| T-4 ......... II.2:2 | He also **m.** an ego for everyone else he |
| T-4 ....... II.8:11 | what it **m.** is then no longer creative. |
| T-4 ....... III.9:3 | not exist, and this **m.** it profoundly afraid. |
| T-4 ....... IV.2:3 | images your ego **m.** in a darkened glass. |
| T-4 ........ V.3:4 | ego identifies so closely, **m.** no sense at all |
| T-4 ....... VI.7:5 | of real recognition **m.** everyone your |
| T-5 ........ in.2:6 | why it **m.** no difference to what part or by |
| T-5 ........ I.1:14 | ego **m.** between giving and losing is gone. |
| T-5 .......... I.4:5 | His symbolic function **m.** the Holy Spirit |
| T-5 ....... III.7:4 | of reinterpreting what the ego **m.**, not by |
| T-5 ....... IV.2:1 | What the ego **m.** it keeps to itself, and so |
| T-5 ........ V.2:4 | This **m.** it invulnerable to the ego because |
| T-5 ........ V.4:2 | It is your acceptance of it that **m.** it real. If |
| T-5 ........ V.4:3 | your allowing it to enter **m.** it your reality. |
| T-5 ........ V.7:7 | **m.** them feel responsible for their errors |
| T-5 ....... VI.6:2 | judgment of what is worthy **m.** it worthy |
| T-6 .......... I.8:4 | of the altar is what **m.** the church holy. A |
| T-6 ........ I.11:2 | Whom we share, **m.** this unnecessary. To |
| T-6 ........ I.17:3 | for fear **m.** appreciation impossible. |
| T-6 ......... II.3:4 | that it **m.** you seem "better" than they are |
| T-6 ....... IV.4:6 | This **m.** the body the ego's friend. It is an |
| T-6 ........ V.4:2 | His dependability **m.** them more certain. |
| T-6 ........ V.4:4 | Spirit **m.** no distinction among dreams. |
| T-6 ..... V.A.5:4 | this perception **m.** it a fearful one indeed. |
| T-6 ..... V.B.4:5 | of the Holy Spirit's Voice **m.** it impossible |
| T-6 ..... V.C.3:5 | **m.** the ultimate choice inevitable. |
| T-7 ..... III.1:12 | Such a perception **m.** it meaningless by |
| T-7 ......... V.6:3 | Fear always **m.** exceptions. Healing never |
| T-7 ......... V.9:6 | because it does not understand what it **m.** |
| T-7 ....... VI.4:6 | and this allegiance **m.** it treacherous to |
| T-7 ....... VI.5:2 | all commitments the mind **m.** are total. |
| T-7 ....... VI.7:8 | **m.** it appear as if you are attacking Him. |
| T-7 ...... VII.8:3 | it. This **m.** you feel deprived of it, and by |
| T-7 ..... VIII.4:4 | that it can, an error the ego always **m.**, |
| T-7 ....... IX.4:6 | of the mind's Self-fullness **m.** selfishness |
| T-8 .......... I.1:5 | made by God, Who **m.** no bargains. It is |
| T-8 ...... IV.4:11 | decision for you **m.** healing impossible. |
| T-8 ..... VIII.2:3 | ego **m.** a fundamental confusion between |
| T-8 ....... IX.6:5 | even though it **m.** every effort to induce it. |
| T-9 .......... I.6:5 | be communicated unless it **m.** sense. How |
| T-9 ....... III.1:4 | To the Holy Spirit it **m.** no sense at all. |
| T-9 ....... III.2:2 | This **m.** perfect sense to the ego, which is |
| T-9 ....... III.3:3 | The ego **m.** no sense, and the Holy Spirit |
| T-9 ....... III.3:4 | that nothing the ego **m.** means anything. |
| T-9 ....... IV.4:2 | of course, **m.** no sense and will not work. |
| T-9 ....... IV.7:4 | and confusion that **m.** the ego likely to |
| T-9 ......... V.8:5 | **m.** healing clear in any situation in which |
| T-9 ..... VIII.3:2 | but **m.** no distinctions between these two |
| T-10 ....... II.6:1 | the complete havoc this **m.** of your peace |
| T-10 ....... II.6:6 | vigilance that **m.** you afraid to remember |
| T-10 ..... III.1:6 | image **m.** you do can be very destructive. |
| T-10 ..... III.7:5 | you, and it is this value that **m.** you whole |
| T-11 ......... I.9:1 | The projection of the ego **m.** it appear as |
| T-11 ....... I.10:5 | is the belief that **m.** you *want* not to know. |
| T-11 ....... V.3:2 | the very contradiction in terms that **m.** it |
| T-11 ..... V.14:3 | It **m.** real every mistake it perceives, and |
| T-11 ..... V.15:1 | ego **m.** no attempt to understand this, |
| T-12 ........ I.3:1 | of motivation that **m.** any sense. And |
| T-12 ........ I.4:2 | only this that **m.** you willing to engage in |
| T-12 ..... III.6:7 | He does not realize that he **m.** this world, |
| T-12 ..... IV.1:3 | for love very actively, **m.** one proviso; do |
| T-12 ....... V.7:8 | split that **m.** its primary aim believable. |
| T-13 ...... I.11:3 | For attack **m.** guilt real, and if it is real |
| T-13 ..... IV.6:8 | of salvation, which **m.** the encounter holy |
| T-13 ....... V.3:5 | Projection **m.** perception, and you cannot |
| T-13 ....... V.6:2 | not there, and you hear what **m.** no sound |
| T-13 ... VIII.5:6 | into His quiet sight that **m.** them one. |
| T-13 ..... IX.2:5 | Faith **m.** the power of belief, and where it |
| T-13 ..... IX.7:1 | Guilt **m.** you blind, for while you see one |
| T-13 ....... X.2:6 | Spirit, and it is that which **m.** them pure. |
| T-13 ..... XI.6:4 | will find the answer that **m.** the need for |
| T-14 ... III.16:3 | every decision the Holy Spirit **m.** for you? |
| T-14 ....... V.1:3 | *God **m.** this possible.* Would you deny His |
| T-14 ..... V.11:6 | for therein lies everything that **m.** it holy. |
| T-14 ..... IX.2:8 | Its changelessness is what **m.** it real. This |
| T-14 ....... X.9:3 | content **m.** a cohesive system impossible. |
| T-14 ... XI.9:11 | corrects your use of time, and **m.** it His. |
| T-14 ... XI.13:6 | fill every mind that so **m.** room for Him. |
| T-15 .... IV.7:2 | that **m.** the holy instant what it is. You |
| T-15 .... VII.2:3 | for the ego believes that anger **m.** friends. |
| T-15 .... VII.6:1 | every relationship the ego **m.** is based on |
| T-15 .... VII.8:8 | **m.** another guilty and holds him through |
| T-15 .. VII.14:9 | completion **m.** you His in your awareness. |
| T-15 ....... X.9:5 | *just as it is,* that **m.** the decision so easy. |
| T-16 ....... II.8:8 | give you everything that **m.** for happiness. |
| T-16 ..... IV.1:8 | with love that **m.** love meaningless to you. |
| T-16 ..... IV.3:2 | It **m.** no attempt to rise above the storm, |
| T-16 ..... IV.8:4 | substitute for what **m.** you whole in truth, |
| T-16 . IV.11:11 | has never forgotten what **m.** Him whole. |
| T-17 ........ I.2:3 | devoting it to "evil," it also **m.** it unreal. |
| T-17 ....... V.3:3 | but it **m.** the relationship seem disturbed, |
| T-17 ..... V.14:4 | you suffer, but which **m.** Heaven glad. If |
| T-17 ..... VI.3:1 | **m.** no sense until it has already happened |
| T-17 ..... VI.3:7 | advance, **m.** understanding doubtful and |
| T-17 .... VII.9:4 | calls for faith, and faith **m.** room for truth |
| T-18 ..... IV.7:1 | **m.** the holy instant so easy and so natural. |
| T-18 ..... IV.7:5 | to the truth, and **m.** it what it is. Yet we |
| T-18 .... VII.1:3 | This **m.** the body an end and not a means |
| T-18 ... VIII.1:1 | of the body that **m.** love seem limited. For |
| T-18 ... VIII.8:6 | joyless–that **m.** up your little kingdom. |
| T-19 ........ I.2:5 | united purpose that **m.** this purpose real, |
| T-19 ...... I.10:6 | what **m.** faith forever justified in everyone |
| T-19 ....... II.1:1 | this distinction that **m.** salvation possible. |
| T-19 ....... II.6:3 | strange illusion that **m.** the clouds of guilt |

T19...IV.A.8:3 pointless wandering m. its results appear
T19.IV.C.11:1 you with terror and m. your body tremble
T19...IV.D.4:3 of death that m. life seem to be ugly, cruel
T-20......III.2:5 studied interference that m. it difficult for
T-20......III.5:4 a sentence on it, justifies it and m. it real.
T-20......VI.6:8 him, is what m. God seem fearful to you,
T-20....VI.11:6 Yet it is also here he m. his choice again
T-20...VIII.4:2 vision that m. it yours is ready to be given
T-21.......in.1:1 Projection m. perception. The world you
T-21.....II.12:4 to create, and what he m. is meaningless.
T-21......III.9:3 He m. no bargains. And if you seek to
T-21......III.9:9 in the innocence that m. the sight of it as
T-21......IV.1:2 He will correct, but this m. no one fearful.
T-21......IV.2:8 fear, and one which m. the ego tremble.
T-21.......V.1:1 selects, and m. the world you see. It
T-21.......V.2:8 believe because it is your faith it m. reality
T-21.......V.3:5 calls for help, the only one it m.. Miracles
T-22.......in.2:3 seen but not real, that m. the need for sin,
T-22.........I.6:4 The sounds a baby m. and what he hears
T-22.......II.4:4 against the truth m. all truth meaningless
T-22......III.3:1 but it m. way for peace and brings you to
T-22......III.5:1 form of error is not what m. it a mistake.
T-22.......V.2:2 flies in the face of reason and m. no sense.
T-22.......V.6:8 your brother that m. it look impenetrable
T-22......VI.3:5 The lack of contradiction m. the soft
T-22....VI.15:1 it m. you and him one with your Creator.
T-22....VI.15:3 love is there, which m. all fear impossible
T-23.......II.2:4 m. it true by his attack on what another
T-23.......II.4:3 For the destruction of the one who m. the
T-23.....II.12:5 factor in your madness that m. it "sane."
T-23.....II.12:7 Here is what m. your vengeance justified.
T-23.....II.16:2 is a strange device that m. it possible. Nor
T-23.....II.17:4 Who m. his savior powerless and finds
T-23......III.4:1 is easy just because it m. no compromise.
T-23......IV.3:7 is. Life m. not death, creating like itself.
T-24.........I.7:8 Look fairly at whatever m. you give your
T-24......I.7:10 And is not this the "enemy" that m. you
T-24.......II.1:1 must be an ego device, for love m. none.
T-24.......II.1:2 Specialness always m. comparisons. It is
T-24.......II.6:5 never was, nor hear what m. no sound. Is
T-24.....II.11:3 has been given him m. you complete, as it
T-24.....II.13:1 hope of specialness m. it seem possible
T-24......III.1:5 so he calls it "unforgivable," and m. it sin.
T-24......III.4:7 between them, and m. them enemies.
T-24......IV.2:2 m. it frail and helpless in its own defense.
T-24.......V.1:8 so. Wishing m. real, as surely as does will
T-24....VI.13:5 To Him this judgment m. no sense at all,
T-24.....VII.6:2 The answer m. it what it is for you. It has
T-24.....VII.8:1 This course m. no attempt to teach what
T-24.....VII.8:7 And it is this that m. it hard to grasp the
T-24.....VII.9:7 with which you listen to the sounds it m..
T-25.......in.3:5 body says or does but m. Him manifest.
T-25......IV.1:7 that m. the choice of means inevitable,
T-25......IV.2:4 that m. it what it is in its effects on you.
T-25.......V.2:1 Attack m. Christ your enemy, and God
T-25......VI.3:1 the gift of light that m. sight possible.
T-25.....VII.3:3 His m. any sense at all within this world.
T-25.....VII.3:5 What m. no sense and has no meaning is
T-25.....VII.4:3 agreement of their thought that m. the
T-25.....VII.7:5 then the form of sanity which m. it most
T-25...VIII.3:4 Who it may be m. little difference. But
T-25......IX.4:1 of innocence m. punishment impossible,
T-26.........I.5:1 that gives it sense and m. it meaningful.
T-26.......II.3:4 which you perceive that m. each one seem
T-26.......II.4:9 He m. but one judgment; that to hurt
T-26......III.1:7 For it is conflict that m. choice possible.
T-26....III.1:10 is? The truth m. no decisions, for there is
T-26......III.3:4 knowledge m. no attack upon perception.
T-26......IV.5:3 power to the song, and m. it sweeter still.
T-26.....VII.6:4 although this clearly m. no sense at all.
T-26...VIII.2:2 This m. trust impossible. And you cannot
T-26...VIII.3:9 And this but m. the interval between the
T-27.......V.2:6 Your single purpose m. this possible. But
T-27....VI.2:10 Yet which is foremost m. no difference.
T-27......VI.5:1 miracle m. no distinctions in the names
T-27.....VII.3:5 see it does not follow and it m. no sense.
T-27.....VII.7:7 one who m. them does not see himself as
T-28.......V.2:1 and pain and loss, that m. them real.
T-28.......V.6:6 time, and m. them wholly indivisible.
T-28......VI.2:3 in ways you want, but never m. the choice
T-29.....II.10:5 and it is this that m. him savior unto you,
T-29......IX.5:9 And so he m. of anything a toy, to make
T-30.......I.12:5 you now can ask a question that m. sense,
T-30.......I.17:3 understood the basic law that m. decision
T-30......IV.5:6 Yet what it m. is nothing. Who could be
T-30.....VII.5:5 idea of different goals that m. perception
T-30.....VII.5:6 agreement m. interpretation stabilize and
T-30...VIII.1:7 this that m. it real, and keeps it separate
T-30...VIII.3:3 that m. them harder to resist than those
T-31.........I.4:4 And every lesson that m. up the world
T-31......IV.7:2 This m. no sense, and cannot be the way.
T-31.......V.3:3 This aspect never m. the first attack. But
T-31.......V.4:2 one who m. a picture of himself omits this
T-31.......V.6:7 can you change the things it m. you do.
T-31.....V.12:3 and at least m. way for active choice, and
T-31......VI.4:6 It m. no difference what you look upon,
W-in..........5:3 held apart from true perception m. its
W-pI.....23.1:4 fail. Every thought you have m. up some
W-pI.....25.2:3 This false identification m. you incapable
W-pI.....25.4:6 And it is this that m. your contact with
W-pI.....44.2:3 is the light that m. seeing possible. It is
W-pI.....68.1:7 It m. you believe that He is like what you
W-pI.....70.5:2 want to be sick, because it m. us unhappy
W-pI.....72.5:4 apparent reality m. this view of God quite
W-pI.....75.4:3 Our single purpose m. our goal inevitable
W-pI.....83.3:5 learn to recognize what m. me happy, if I
W-pI.....91.2:9 darkness m. the idea of light meaningless.
W-pI.....91.4:4 m. all miracles within your easy reach,
W-pI.....94.1:1 the one statement which m. all forms of
W-pI.....95.1:4 perfect unity m. change in you impossible
W-pI.....95.3:1 hear and see, and what m. perfect sense.
W-pI.....96.4:1 Spirit m. use of mind as means to find its
W-pI.....97.3:3 and over, for the miracle m. use of time,
W-pI.....97.6:2 m. an uncertain moment and goes out.
W-pI...102.1:3 it, and to suspect it really m. no sense. It
W-pI...108.2:1 True light that m. true vision possible is
W-pI.121.11:4 and m. the picture beautiful and good.
W-pI.126.11:1 an aim which m. this day of special value
W-pI.127.12:2 think of one who m. the journey with you,
W-pI.132.12:3 m. no distinctions in what is Himself and
W-pI...133.6:4 and m. no offering to him who chooses it.
W-pI.133.10:3 and serve them as his own m. no mistakes
W-pI...134.6:1 sin's unreality that m. forgiveness natural
W-pI.135.15:2 for, unless it m. its own provisions. Time
WpI.135.24:4 that m. extravagant demands for sacrifice
W-pI...136.5:1 your "reality" that m. defenses seem to be
W-pI...136.7:2 m. you weak and brings you suffering. It
W-pI...138.2:3 perception of the truth that m. the choice
W-pI...138.2:8 Opposition m. the truth unwelcome, and
W-pI...140.4:5 It takes away the guilt that m. the sickness
W-pI...152.6:7 Yet only madness m. a world like this.
W-pI...153.2:2 anger, anger m. attack seem reasonable,
W-pI...156.1:1 that m. the thought of sin impossible. It
W-pI...161.5:1 we feel limits our freedom, m. us suffer,
W-pI.161.11:4 gestures which he m. so frequently. Then
W-pI...162.3:1 indeed is he who m. these words his own;
W-pI...165.1:1 m. this world seem real except your own
W-pI...165.2:6 m. soft your resting place and smooth
W-pI.167.10:3 or m. himself what he is not because he
W-pI.167.12:5 and the light which m. reflection possible.
W-pI...168.1:4 He m. no attempt to hide from us. We try
Wi181-200 1:4 It is experiencing this that m. it sure that
W-pI...182.3:3 seeks. A thousand homes he m., yet none
W-pI.183.10:5 He m. his claim to all his Father gave, is
W-pI...184.8:6 body m. response to what you call him,
W-pI...186.6:1 Arrogance m. an image of yourself that is
W-pI...192.3:6 What He m. are dreams, but of a kind so
W-pI...193.4:3 It is this sameness which m. learning sure
W-pI...195.4:2 Love m. no comparisons. And gratitude
W-pI...197.9:2 to anyone who m. your Self complete.
W-pI...198.1:2 And yet illusion m. illusion. If you can
W-pI...198.2:8 they had. Illusion m. illusion. Except one.
WpI rVI.in.3:8 up the mind, and m. it deaf to reason,
W-pII.....in.2:6 and at night, as long as m. us happy. We
W-pII......1.2:1 which m. a judgment that it will not raise
W-pII..226.1:2 It is not death which m. this possible, but
W-pII..228.1:2 in what His knowledge m. impossible?
W-pII..249.1:1 impossible and anger m. no sense. Attack
W-pII.259.1:1 Sin is the only thought that m. the goal of
W-pII.....8.4:3 for its perception m. time purposeless.
W-pII.311.1:3 then it m. of it what you would have it be.
W-pII.324.2:4 And it is He Who m. the ending sure, and
W-pII.325.1:2 the mind m. up an image of the thing the
W-pII.332.1:1 The ego m. illusions. Truth undoes its
W-pII.332.1:3 Truth never m. attack. It merely is. And
Wfl........in.1:3 leads the way and m. our footsteps sure.
M-4........II.2:2 is only the wish to deceive that m. for war
M-4........II.2:6 teachers rest secure m. doubt impossible.
M-4.......X.2:11 The curriculum m. no effort to exceed its
M-5.......II.1:6 it is the mind and not the body that m. it.
M-6..........3:6 fact, it is the part that m. sharing possible
M-6..........4:1 about the gift that m. it truly given. And it
M-6..........4:2 And it is trust that m. true giving possible
M-7.........1:10 lacked the trust that m. for giving truly,
M-10.......5:10 Now he m. no mistakes. His Guide is sure
M-11.........4:4 the world that m. peace seem impossible.
M-12.........4:1 m. God's teachers is their recognition of
M-12.........5:7 The mind m. this decision, as it makes all
M-12.........5:7 as it m. all decisions that are responsible
M-13.........5:5 It is the idea of sacrifice that m. him blind
M-13.........7:6 this that m. it holy and beyond the world.
M-13.........7:8 It is its holiness that m. you safe. It is
M-17.........1:3 and m. the magic seem quite real to both
M-17.........2:4 wish that m. the help of little value, and
C-1............4:1 is entirely illusory and m. only illusions.
C-1............6:1 listens to the ego and m. illusions;
C-3............2:3 m. God appear to be an enemy instead of
C-3............2:4 just this insane perception that m. them
C-4............5:9 Only the body m. the world seem real, for
P-2.........II.9:8 the goal that m. these processes the same,
P-3........III.2:5 be the therapist who m. these decisions.
S-1........III.4:7 escape m. it difficult to welcome freedom,
S-2..........II.2:5 Who m. a slave to teach what freedom is?
S-2........III.4:5 is not real and m. illusions in its evil name
S-3..........II.1:1 False healing merely m. a poor exchange
S-3........III.1:5 For it is this that m. true healing possible.

**making** 147
*See also* decision-making

T-1.......VII.1:1 m. it hard for them to reach your own
T-1.......VII.3:6 of m. false associations and attempting to
T-2..........II.6:5 thus m. it unnecessary for you to keep
T-2........III.2:4 separation thoughts and m. you perfectly
T-2.......V.10:4 m. it apparent that charity still lies within
T-2.......VII.1:1 nevertheless persist in m. yourself fearful.
T-3........III.7:4 m. him a stranger by misperceiving him,
T-3........IV.2:1 m. the mind a perceiver rather than a
T-3.......VII.1:2 It begins with either a m. or a creating, a
T-3.....VII.4:10 believe you are an image of your own m..
T-3.......VII.5:4 realize that this m. will surely dissolve in
T-4.........I.11:7 perishable as the ego is of m. the eternal.
T-5.......II.11:1 by sharing my decision and m. it stronger
T-5......IV.2:10 the Atonement, a remedy not of your m..
T-5......IV.3:10 in the light of the Kingdom, m. them, too,
T-5.........V.4:4 capable of creating reality or m. illusions.
T-5.......VII.4:2 the remedy could not be of your m.. God
T-5.......VII.4:4 I am m. His plan perfectly explicit to you,
T-6......V.A.5:8 breaks communication, m. it impossible.
T-6......V.B.3:8 m. him suspicious of their motivation.
T-6......V.C.9:4 By m. another kingdom that you valued,
T-7..........II.1:3 it, thus m. the Kingdom itself obscure to
T-7.........V.9:4 can identify with, and by m. it part of you
T-7........VI.2:5 this because its power is not of your m..
T-8..........II.4:2 m. you afraid of your will *because* it is free.
T-8.......VII.3:5 God's way of m. unlimited what you have
T-8.....VII.10:2 Since this is natural it heals by m. whole,
T-8......VIII.2:2 other, m. the concepts of both health and
T-9...........I.1:2 m. it possible for it to be afraid of what it
T-9...........I.3:8 you. He is merely m. every possible effort,
T-9..........II.5:9 giving truth to his words and m. you able
T-9.......II.10:5 m. it inevitable that you will not value
T-9........III.2:5 He may be m. no sense at the time, and it
T-9........III.2:5 from the ego, he will not be m. sense. But
T-9........III.4:3 listening to your ego and m. as little sense
T-10......III.9:4 and by m. him you made yourself able to
T-10......IV.6:1 the m. of idols becomes inconceivable.

T-11 ..... VII.2:8 true and **m.** no distinction between them.
T-12 ......... I.4:2 of the need for healing by **m.** it unreal.
T-12 ....... II.8:2 We will but be **m.** perfect to you what is
T-12 ...... III.2:4 You, then, are **m.** the same mistake he is,
T-12 ...... III.2:4 is, and are **m.** his error real to both of you
T-12 ...... III.6:3 for self-hate, **m.** him afraid of himself. He
T-12 ...... III.6:5 always tries to handle it by **m.** some sort
T-12 ..... VII.6:8 it has one goal by **m.** it seem to be one.
T-12 ... VII.11:1 peace, for by **m.** it manifest you will see it.
T-12 .... VIII.6:9 By **m.** nothing real to you, you have seen
T-13 ......... I.2:3 then? By **m.** him invisible, the world of
T-13 ....... I.10:1 You cannot dispel guilt by **m.** it real, and
T-13 ...... IV.4:3 continuity by **m.** the future like the past,
T-13 ...... IV.4:4 future, **m.** them continuous without an
T-13 ...... IV.5:6 past because, by **m.** it real in the present,
T-13 .... VIII.3:1 with knowledge, **m.** transfer to it possible
T-13 ..... X.11:3 all your relationships and **m.** them unreal
T-14 ...... III.3:8 *guiltlessness by* **m.** *it manifest and sharing it*
T-14 ...... IV.5:6 as the truth in you, **m.** you one with Him.
T-14 ...... IV.8:2 reality. It is here without your **m.**, but not
T-14 .... IV.10:2 himself, **m.** both unable to communicate,
T-14 ..... VII.5:4 Defense is of your **m.**. God knows it not.
T-14 ...... IX.1:5 Keep not your **m.** from your Father, for
T-14 ...... IX.1:7 it? The **m.** of time to take the place of
T-15 ....... I.14:5 enough to transcend all of the ego's **m.**,
T-15 ...... IV.9:3 Innocence is not of your **m.**. It is given
T-15 ..... VII.2:5 that it can get and keep *by* **m.** *guilty*. This is
T-15 ... VII.14:1 **m.** it evident that it is not impossible. In
T-15 .... VIII.2:4 Let us join together in **m.** the holy instant
T-15 ....... XI.1:1 whole idea of sacrifice as solely of your **m.**
T-15 .. XI.10:11 this year different by **m.** it all the same.
T-16 ....... II.5:1 yours while you are bent on **m.** it unreal?
T-16 ...... IV.5:3 always at the price of **m.** both illusions.
T-16 ....... V.6:1 Heaven, and **m.** them indistinguishable.
T-17 ....... II.5:2 to you the seeming reasons for your **m.** it.
T-17 ...... III.3:4 of value. Every step taken in the **m.**, the
T-18 ....... I.12:7 join in **m.** whole what has been ravaged
T-18 ....... II.5:6 that you are **m.** them act out for you, for if
T-18 ..... VII.6:5 **m.** use of the course if you insist on using
T-19 ......... I.7:7 to it, **m.** it sick because of the mind's
T-19 ....... I.15:3 the process of **m.** lovely that they begin.
T-19 ....... II.2:4 and **m.** himself what God created not.
T-19 ...... III.1:5 **m.** itself a willing captive to its sick appeal
T-19 ...... III.8:2 capable of **m.** another will that could
T19 .... IV.C.7:7 the triumph of the ego's **m.** over creation,
T-20 ....... II.2:5 **m.** it ready to receive the gifts it wants by
T-20 ....... II.3:3 upon it, **m.** it worthy of their devotion.
T-20 ...... III.2:4 relationships, **m.** whatever adjustments it
T-20 ...... IV.8:5 will go before you **m.** straight your path,
T-20 ...... VI.8:6 The instant that the mad idea of **m.** your
T-21 ...... III.2:1 accepted the idea of **m.** room for truth.
T-22 ...... III.8:8 saved by **m.** sinful the one whose holiness
T-23 ....... II.3:2 **m.** it seem that some of them are harder
T-23 ..... II.11:6 it in his body, **m.** it the cover for his guilt,
T-23 ... II.12:12 purpose of seizing it and **m.** it your own.
T-23 ..... II.20:2 **m.** it seem quite possible to value some
T-25 ...... VI.6:4 his part in its undoing, as he did in **m.** it.
T-26 ....... X.4:8 else can take it from him, **m.** it his own.
T-27 ..... VII.2:6 No one has difficulty **m.** up his mind to
T-27 ..... VII.7:7 them does not see himself as **m.** them,
T-27 ..... VII.7:9 the part he plays in **m.** them and making
T-27 ..... VII.7:9 in making them and **m.** them seem real.
T-27 .... VIII.4:5 by causing them and **m.** them seem real.
T-28 ....... I.15:3 it, **m.** it a bridge an instant will suffice to
T-28 ..... II.12:3 deny the active role in **m.** up the dream.
T-28 ...... III.2:3 the part you play in **m.** sickness real, the
T-29 ..... VII.9:2 And can a dream succeed in **m.** real the
T-30 ......... I.1:2 not always know when you are **m.** them.
T-30 ...... IV.5:8 an illusion, **m.** things appear like to itself?
W-pI ....... 3.1:1 ones, without **m.** distinctions of any kind.
W-pI ....... 9.5:2 honest with yourself in **m.** this distinction
W-pI ..... 14.1:5 It is of your own **m.**, and it does not exist.
W-pI ..... 15.1:6 It is image **m.**. It takes the place of seeing,
W-pI ..... 15.2:1 process of image **m.** that you call seeing
W-pI ..... 23.4:6 hate. For you will not be **m.** them alone.
W-pI ..... 24.6:1 you are **m.** a large number of demands of
W-pI ..... 28.1:2 periods, you will be **m.** a series of definite
W-pI ..... 28.3:1 you are **m.** a commitment to withdraw
W-pI ..... 28.6:2 You will be **m.** this same request of each
W-pI ..... 28.6:3 And you are **m.** a commitment to each of
W-pI ..... 31.4:2 day. Remind yourself that you are **m.** a
W-pI ..... 44.2:4 **m.** vision possible in every circumstance.
W-pI ..... 52.2:4 and everything, **m.** them my enemies.
W-pI ..... 70.4:1 to do just the opposite, **m.** every attempt,
W-pI ..... 71.8:1 each **m.** equal contribution to the whole.
W-pI ... 127.6:4 Today we practice **m.** free your mind of
W-pI ... 134.3:2 to deceive yourself by **m.** an illusion true.
W-pI ... 135.1:3 thus **m.** correction doubly difficult. And it
W-pI ... 136.5:1 forgetting of the part you play in **m.** your
W-pI. 138.11:1 and spend five minutes **m.** sure that we
W-pI ... 166.2:1 that underlies the **m.** of the world. This
W-pI ... 167.5:6 As they are made, so will their **m.** be. As
W-pI ... 185.8:3 the words you use in **m.** your requests.
W-pI. 187.11:6 altar, **m.** it a home for Innocence Itself,
W-pI ... 200.2:1 what can only hurt; of **m.** peace of chaos,
W-pII ..... 9.3:1 teaches, **m.** way for the Last Judgment, in
W-pII ... 11.3:2 **m.** every part container of the whole. Its
W-ep ......... 5:4 thus **m.** sure that hell will claim you not,
M-4 ..... V.1:10 them, **m.** sure no harm can come to them.
M-10 ......... 4:4 such an arbitrary basis for decision **m.**?
M-17 ......... 3:7 into his pupil's mind, **m.** it one with his.
M-19 ......... 1:7 one in the world is capable of **m.** only just
M-24 ......... 3:3 usefulness, as well as his own decision **m.**.
M-29 ......... 3:7 that you have done so, **m.** fear inevitable.
P-1 ............ 4:4 himself as really capable of **m.** decisions.
P-2 ......... in.2:6 but only at the cost of **m.** illusions true.
P-2 ........... I.1:5 in the same relationship, **m.** it holier. Or
P-2 ........ IV.6:4 the same time **m.** a new self-concept into
P-2 ....... VII.4:6 use their judgment in **m.** their decisions.
P-3 .......... II.2:4 with the aim of **m.** the therapist a judge.

### malady 1

S-3 ........ III.5:5 every **m.** has been revealed exactly as it is.

### malevolence 1

T-20 ..... VI.9:4 Is the **m.** of the unholy relationship, so

### malice 11

T-23 ..... II.12:8 hidden there in **m.** and in hatred for the
T-24 ......... I.8:4 Every twinge of **m.**, or stab of hate or wish
T-24 ..... III.6:6 without the heat and **m.** of one thought of
T-28 ...... V.2:1 sharing of the evil dreams of hate and **m.**,
W-pI ... 122.2:3 no dreams of fear and evil, **m.** and attack.
W-pI ... 189.3:2 through darkened eyes of **m.** and of fear,
W-pI ... 195.9:1 in place of anger, **m.** and revenge. We
W-pII ..... 2.3:1 to support the world of dreams and **m.**.
C-5 ............ 3:5 in any way be changed by sin and evil, **m.**,
S-1 ........ III.2:1 ladder, will not be free from envy and **m.**.
S-3 ........ IV.7:2 Son to Me from dreams of **m.** to the sweet

### man 18

T-1 ......... II.4:1 "No **m.** cometh unto the Father but by
T-1 ......... II.4:4 the distance between God and **m.** would
T-1 ........ III.2:4 a **m.** must think of himself in his heart,
T-3 ........ IV.7:3 I was a **m.** who remembered spirit and its
T-3 ........ IV.7:4 a **m.** I did not attempt to counteract error
T-3 ......... V.7:1 The statement "God created **m.** in his
T-4 ....... VI.6:6 because I completed my part in it as a **m.**,
T-5 .......... I.4:6 As a **m.** and also one of God's creations,
T-5 ....... II.7:11 What profiteth it a **m.** if he gain the whole
T-6 ........ I.15:5 "Betrayest thou the Son of **m.** with a kiss?
T-13 ........ II.9:7 son of **m.** is the guiltless Son of God, and
T-21 ...... in.1:6 As a **m.** thinketh, so does he perceive.
T-24 .. VII.11:8 The son of **m.** perceives an alien will and
T-25 ...... in.2:6 The son of **m.** is not the risen Christ. Yet
M-12 ......... 2:1 does the son of **m.** become the Son of God
C-5 ............ 2:1 the name of one who was a **m.** but saw the
C-5 ............ 2:2 identified with *Christ*, a **m.** no longer, but
C-5 ............ 2:3 The **m.** was an illusion, for he seemed to

### man's 1

M-11 ......... 1:5 occur, and that rebirth is **m.** inheritance.

### managed 1

T-19 ....... II.7:5 he has somehow **m.** to corrupt his Father,

### maneuver 2

T-16 ........ I.2:5 Make no mistake about this **m.**; the ego
C-in .......... 2:3 against truth in the form of a delaying **m.**.

### manger 1

T-15 ..... III.9:6 Welcome me not into a **m.**, but into the

### manifest 26

T-8 .... VII.10:4 but it can be made **m.** *through* the physical
T-12 .... VII.4:5 as its presence becomes **m.** through you.
T-12 .... VII.5:5 For you will believe in what you **m.**, and
T-12 .... VII.7:5 you want in yourself you will make **m.**,
T-12 .... VII.8:6 If you make love **m.**, its messengers will
T-12 .. VII.11:1 peace, for by making it **m.** you will see it.
T-12 .. VII.12:1 be because you have decided to **m.** truth.
T-12 .. VII.12:2 you **m.** it you will see it both without and
T-12 .. VII.15:5 When you learn to make me **m.**, you will
T-13 ... VI.10:8 to peace, for you have made it **m.** in them.
T-14 ..... III.3:5 *What I experience I will make* **m.**. *If I am*
T-14 ..... III.3:8 *guiltlessness by making it* **m.** *and sharing it.*
T-14 ..... III.7:2 make your invulnerability **m.** to everyone.
T-14 ..... XI.3:2 accomplished before its effects are **m.**.
T19 ... IV.B.1:4 attraction of guilt made **m.** in the body,
T-25 ...... in.1:8 be made **m.** to those who know Him not,
T-25 ...... in.2:4 unknowingly, and does not make Him **m.**
T-25 ...... in.3:5 the body says or does but makes Him **m.**.
T-25 ........ I.1:6 And you are **m.** unto your holy brother,
T-25 ........ I.2:1 How can you **m.** the Christ in you except
T-25 ........ I.2:2 Perception tells you *you* are **m.** in what
T-25 ........ I.4:2 His life is **m.** in you who are His Son. Each
T-27 ........ I.2:1 your release from sacrifice is his made **m.**,
W-pI .... 38.2:1 holiness the power of God is made **m.**.
W-pII ... 13.2:3 ends the strange distortions that were **m.**.
M-17 ......... 8:5 the lesson's **m.** simplicity stands out like

### manifestation 4

T-12 .... VII.6:1 I am the **m.** of the Holy Spirit, and when
T-13 ....... V.9:5 He is the Holy Spirit's **m.**, looking always
C-6 ............ 1:1 Jesus is the **m.** of the *Holy Spirit*, Whom
C-6 ............ 5:1 are His **m.** in this world. Your brother

### manifestations 6

T-12 .... VII.4:1 see the Holy Spirit, but you can see His **m.**
T-12 .... VII.5:3 for it. Whose **m.** would you see? Of whose
T-13 ....... V.6:3 Your **m.** of emotions are the opposite of
T-15 ....... X.5:3 but as different **m.** of the same idea, and
T-18 ..... IX.4:3 to hold its most external **m.** in darkness,
P-in ........... 1:4 for the **m.** of this world seem real indeed.

### manifested 1

T-8 .... VII.14:2 Yet mind can be **m.** through the body if it

### manifestly 1

T-12 ....... V.2:5 **m.** does not work and cannot protect you.

### mankind 1

M-4 ...... II.2:10 They choose for all **m.**; for all the world

### manner 5

T-2 ....... IV.5:1 not lie in the **m.** in which it is expressed.
T-10 ..... IV.5:6 and the **m.** of your creation established
T-27 ....... V.9:4 All healing must proceed in lawful **m.**, in
W-pI .... 34.4:1 the idea to yourself in an unhurried **m.**,
M-1 ........... 3:6 in no language; in any place or time or **m.**

## manual 6

| | |
|---|---|
| M-in ..........5:4 | This is a **m.** for the teachers of God. They |
| M-in ........5:12 | **m.** attempts to answer these questions. |
| M-1.............4:1 | This is a **m.** for a special curriculum, |
| M-29..........1:1 | **m.** is not intended to answer all questions |
| M-29..........1:4 | While it is called a **m.** for teachers, it must |
| M-29..........1:5 | helpful for the pupil to read the **m.** first. |

## many 210

*See also* many-faceted

| | |
|---|---|
| T-1........ I.45:2 | It may touch **m.** people you have not even |
| T-2........ III.1:4 | **m.** body fantasies in which minds engage |
| T-2..... VIII.2:4 | became one of the **m.** learning devices to |
| T-3...........I.1:3 | resurrection did. **M.** sincere Christians |
| T-3...........I.1:6 | led **m.** people to be bitterly afraid of God. |
| T-3...........I.1:7 | concepts enter into **m.** religions. Yet the |
| T-3...........I.2:6 | **m.** have been unwilling to give it up in |
| T-3...........I.4:4 | hard for **m.** Christians to realize that this |
| T-3........ I.7:10 | no need to learn from **m.** smaller lessons. |
| T-3........ III.2:3 | can see in **m.** ways because perception |
| T-3......IV.7:12 | "**M.** are called but few are chosen" should |
| T-3......... V.2:5 | ego has invented **m.** ingenious thought |
| T-3.......VII.3:9 | here has been given **m.** interpretations, |
| T-4...........I.2:1 | **M.** stand guard over their ideas because |
| T-4......... II.4:6 | resemble in **m.** ways how you will one day |
| T-4.........III.5:3 | enter. The Bible gives **m.** references to the |
| T-4.........IV.2:1 | but I have also said, and **m.** times, that |
| T-4.........IV.8:1 | really considered how **m.** opportunities |
| T-4.........IV.8:1 | and how **m.** of them you have refused? |
| T-4......... V.5:8 | **m.** of the things you want to learn may be |
| T-5.........in.1:2 | you to think how **m.** opportunities you |
| T-5.........in.1:2 | yourself, and how **m.** you have refused. |
| T-5...........I.7:1 | kind of perception in which **m.** elements |
| T-5........IV.5:1 | Teaching is done in **m.** ways, above all by |
| T-5........VI.5:1 | There are **m.** examples of how the ego's |
| T-5.......VII.2:1 | **m.** healers who did not heal themselves. |
| T-6...........I.9:3 | not harmed anyone and had healed **m.**. |
| T-6........ I.19:2 | **m.** need your blessing to help them hear |
| T-6........IV.2:8 | since, although it has raised a great **m.**. |
| T-6........IV.6:5 | dreams contain **m.** of the ego's symbols |
| T-6......V.B.1:5 | **M.** thought I was attacking them, even |
| T-6......V.B.3:9 | This is the real reason why, in **m.** respects |
| T-8.......VII.9:2 | as fragmented into **m.** functions with |
| T-8.....VII.12:4 | temptation to see the body in **m.** lights, |
| T-8..... VIII.8:3 | There are **m.** instances of how what you |
| T-9...........I.5:1 | I have emphasized **m.** times that the Holy |
| T-9...........I.8:5 | even though **m.** may seek both. Can you |
| T-9......... II.3:6 | **m.** answers you have already received but |
| T-9.........IV.4:8 | **M.** have tried to do this in my name, |
| T-9......IV.11:3 | of the ego, and of these you will find **m.**. |
| T-10......IV.8:1 | In **m.** only the spark remains, for the |
| T-10....... V.1:4 | **M.** are afraid of blasphemy, but they do |
| T-10....... V.3:8 | He has **m.** forms, but although he may |
| T-10....... V.3:8 | be **m.** different things he is but one idea; |
| T-10..... V.12:4 | **m.** other forms that blasphemy may take, |
| T-11......IV.4:3 | denial of this simple fact takes **m.** forms, |
| T-11......VII.4:4 | have made **m.** ideas that you have placed |
| T-11... VIII.5:6 | His answer is both **m.** and one, as long as |
| T-11... VIII.5:6 | as long as you believe that the one is **m.**. |
| T-13.......IV.6:5 | and losing the **m.** opportunities you could |
| T-13....... V.1:4 | The other has **m.** forms, for the content of |
| T-13... VIII.3:1 | **m.** elements in common with knowledge, |
| T-13..... X.13:6 | and for the **m.** gifts that you will let me |
| T-15......III.2:5 | You are free to try as **m.** as you wish, but |
| T-15...VII.10:2 | Anger takes **m.** forms, but it cannot long |
| T-15...VII.11:4 | And yet **m.** do believe it. For they think |
| T-15...VII.12:5 | insanity of this lesson, **m.** have learned it. |
| T-15....... X.4:3 | It seems like **m.**, but it is all the same. For |
| T-15....... X.4:4 | For though the ego takes **m.** forms, it is |
| T-15....... X.9:4 | You have tried **m.** compromises in the |
| T-16....... II.8:1 | for you have **m.** witnesses that speak of it |
| T-17......IV.6:4 | than we have at **m.** other aspects of the |
| T-17....... V.3:8 | **M.** relationships have been broken off at |
| T-17....... V.8:2 | You will find **m.** opportunities to blame |
| T-17..... V.10:2 | have joined with **m.** in the holy instant, |
| T-17..... V.11:3 | may have made **m.** mistakes since then, |
| T-18.........I.3:4 | It seems to take **m.** forms, and each one |
| T-18.........I.4:2 | It has taken **m.** forms, because it was the |
| T-18.....VII.4:4 | **M.** have spent a lifetime in preparation, |
| T-19......IV.1:1 | give it rest, it will encounter **m.** obstacles. |
| T19... IV.A.3:5 | God's Will is One, not **m.**. It has no |
| T-20....... II.1:3 | on the **m.** offerings made for its pleasure, |
| T-20....... V.5:6 | Why should it take so **m.** holy instants to |
| T-20...... VI.4:7 | the ego seeks as **m.** bodies as it can collect |
| T-20... VIII.8:8 | This world seems to hold out **m.** purposes |
| T-22....... II.9:5 | illusion we have seen **m.** times before. |
| T-23.... II.16:3 | it appears to function **m.** times before. In |
| T-24.........I.2:3 | **m.** senseless outcomes have been reached |
| T-24.........I.3:2 | This takes **m.** forms, but always clashes |
| T-24....... II.3:5 | His "special" sons are **m.**, never one, each |
| T-25...... III.7:8 | peace, and **m.** chances to extend your |
| T-26.......... II.h | **M.** Forms; One Correction |
| T-26....... II.1:5 | A problem can appear in **m.** forms, and it |
| T-26....... V.1:4 | And you can learn it in **m.** different ways. |
| T-26.......VII.3:7 | What is perceived takes **m.** forms, but |
| T-27.........I.6:7 | And each has **m.** voices, speaking to your |
| T-27....... II.1:2 | To **m.**, yes. For accusation is a bar to love, |
| T-27....... IV.3:6 | with **m.** answers can have no answers. |
| T-27....... V.7:7 | the **m.** friends he thought were enemies. |
| T-27....... V.9:2 | your **m.** different problems will be solved |
| T-27..... V.10:3 | by all the **m.** different witnesses it finds. |
| T-27...... VI.2:4 | These witnesses are joined by **m.** more. |
| T-27..... VII.7:4 | sure: Of all the **m.** causes you perceived as |
| T-27... VII.15:6 | brush aside his **m.** gifts because he is not |
| T-27... VIII.2:1 | dreaming of the world takes **m.** forms, |
| T-27... VIII.2:1 | the body seeks in **m.** ways to prove it is |
| T-27... VIII.3:3 | Though the dream itself takes **m.** forms, |
| T-27... VIII.3:3 | has but one purpose, taught in **m.** ways. |
| T-29....... II.1:6 | the **m.** gains your choice has offered you. |
| T-29... VIII.8:3 | is the only question that has **m.** answers, |
| T-29... VIII.9:1 | God has not **m.** Sons, but only One. Who |
| T-31....... V.7:5 | and **m.** come from feverish imaginations, |
| T-31..... V.16:1 | You will make **m.** concepts of the self as |
| T-31..... V.16:5 | appear in **m.** places and in many forms. |
| T-31..... V.16:5 | appear in many places and in **m.** forms. |
| T-31... VII.14:8 | deceived by what appears as **m.** choices. |
| T-31.... VIII.9:1 | find so **m.** chances to perceive another |
| W-pI..... 11.4:2 | do more, as **m.** as five may be undertaken |
| W-pI..... 15.3:1 | go along, you may have **m.** "light episodes |
| W-pI..... 15.3:2 | They may take **m.** different forms, some |
| W-pI..... 15.5:1 | to apply the idea to very **m.** things during |
| W-pI..... 16.3:4 | will practice this idea in **m.** forms before |
| W-pI..... 23.6:2 | for as **m.** attack thoughts as occur to you. |
| W-pI..... 24.5:1 | and then enumerate carefully as **m.** goals |
| W-pI..... 24.5:4 | on. Try to cover as **m.** different kinds of |
| W-pI..... 24.6:2 | will also recognize that **m.** of your goals |
| W-pI..... 24.7:1 | list of as **m.** hoped-for goals as possible, |
| W-pI..... 26.6:4 | to use very **m.** for any one practice period, |
| W-pI..... 27.3:1 | today needs **m.** repetitions for maximum |
| W-pI..... 27.4:6 | sure that you have saved yourself **m.** years |
| W-pI..... 41.2:1 | separated ones have invented **m.** "cures" |
| W-pI..... 46.3:1 | and as **m.** shorter ones as possible. Begin |
| W-pI..... 61.5:1 | As **m.** practice periods as possible should |
| W-pI..... 66.9:2 | today. Think also about the **m.** forms the |
| W-pI..... 66.9:2 | and the **m.** ways in which you tried to |
| W-pI..... 76.1:1 | observed before how **m.** senseless things |
| W-pI..... 76.8:5 | **M.** "religions" have been based on this. |
| W-pI..... 79.4:1 | problems as **m.** is the temptation to keep |
| W-pI..... 79.5:2 | They seem to be on so **m.** levels, in such |
| W-pI..... 79.7:3 | our minds of all the **m.** different kinds of |
| W-pI..... 79.9:2 | You will see **m.** problems today, each one |
| W-pI..... 80.3:4 | Their **m.** forms will not deceive you while |
| W-pI..... 86.1:3 | seen it in **m.** people and in many things, |
| W-pI..... 86.1:3 | seen it in many people and in **m.** things, |
| W-pI..... 92.1:5 | This is among the **m.** magical beliefs that |
| W-pI..... 95.2:2 | divided into **m.** warring parts, separate |
| W-pI..... 96.1:3 | You have sought **m.** such solutions, and |
| W-pI. 132.16:1 | comes to **m.** brothers far across the world |
| W-pI... 133.4:1 | but two, however **m.** there appear to be. |
| W-pI. 133.11:1 | is overlaid with **m.** levels of obscurity. If |
| W-pI. 134.17:1 | for there will still be **m.** times when you |
| W-pI... 135.7:4 | for the **m.** mad attacks you make upon it. |
| WpI. rIV.in3:1 | some understanding of the **m.** forms in |
| W-pI. 154.14:4 | our **m.** gifts from our Creator will spring |
| W-pI... 155.4:2 | **M.** have chosen to renounce the world |
| W-pI... 156.7:1 | Yet you have wasted **m.**, many years on |
| W-pI... 156.7:1 | **m.** years on just this foolish thought. The |
| W-pI... 161.6:4 | **m.** times been urged to look beyond the |
| W-pI... 163.1:1 | is a thought that takes on **m.** forms, often |
| W-pI... 167.2:3 | that the idea of death takes **m.** forms. It is |
| W-pI... 170.8:6 | it? For the god of cruelty takes **m.** forms. |
| W-pI. 184.13:3 | realize the **m.** names you gave its aspects |
| W-pI. 184.15:3 | *made and call by* **m.** *different names is but a* |
| W-pI... 185.2:6 | **M.** have said these words. But few indeed |
| W-pI... 187.6:3 | the **m.** forms which sacrifice may take. He |
| W-pI... 198.7:1 | world has **m.** seeming separate haunts |
| W-pI... 199.7:3 | to set free the **m.** who perceive themselves |
| W-pII ..... 1.3:1 | An unforgiving thought does **m.** things. |
| W-pII . 231.1:2 | *else; a something I have called by* **m.** *names.* |
| W-pII . 251.1:1 | I sought for **m.** things, and found despair |
| W-pII . 266.2:2 | How **m.** saviors God has given us! How |
| W-pII . 278.2:2 | *I have had* **m.** *foolish thoughts about myself* |
| W-pII . 284.1:5 | to be but said and then repeated **m.** times |
| W-pII . 284.1:5 | as but partly true, with **m.** reservations. |
| W-pII . 295.1:7 | Fear appears in **m.** different forms, but |
| W-pII . 315.2:1 | **m.** *gifts that come to me today and every day* |
| Wfl........in.2:6 | let us be the leaders of our **m.** brothers |
| M-in .......... 5:6 | they teach perfection over and over, in **m.** |
| M-in .......... 5:6 | over and over, in many, **m.** ways, until |
| M-1 ........... 2:7 | **M.** hear It, but few will answer. Yet it is all |
| M-1 ........... 4:2 | There are **m.** thousands of other forms, |
| M-4 ..... I.A.4:3 | it. He will find that **m.**, if not most of the |
| M-4 ..... VII.1:6 | than **m.** other ideas in our curriculum. Its |
| M-6 ........... 2:5 | We have referred **m.** times in the text to |
| M-7 ........... 5:3 | This illusion can take **m.** forms. Perhaps |
| M-9 ........... 1:7 | as **m.** previous mistakes as possible are |
| M-10 ......... 4:1 | Remember how **m.** times you thought |
| M-10 ......... 4:3 | know how **m.** times you merely thought |
| M-12 ............h | **M.** TEACHERS OF GOD ARE NEEDED |
| M-12 ......... 2:5 | God's teachers appear to be **m.**, for that is |
| M-12 ......... 2:7 | it matter if they then appear in **m.** forms? |
| M-12 ......... 3:1 | Why is the illusion of **m.** necessary? Only |
| M-17 ......... 2:6 | **m.** times has it been emphasized that you |
| M-21 ......... 4:3 | **m.** who must be reached through words, |
| M-23 ......... 4:3 | as a replacement for the **m.** names of all |
| M-24 ......... 1:2 | has no meaning either once or **m.** times. |
| M-24 ......... 1:8 | Like **m.** other beliefs, it can be bitterly |
| M-24 ....... 1:11 | In between, **m.** kinds of folly are possible. |
| M-25 ......... 1:3 | each individual has **m.** abilities of which |
| M-25 ......... 2:1 | Certainly there are **m.** "psychic" powers |
| M-25 ......... 5:4 | guile. **M.** have not seen through the ego's |
| M-26 ......... 1:4 | In how **m.** is this the case? Here, then, is |
| C-in ........... 4:1 | ego will demand **m.** answers that this |
| C-in ........... 4:3 | happen?", and may ask this in **m.** forms. |
| C-4............. 3:5 | perception is a remedy with **m.** names. |
| C-5............. 1:3 | reality. Helpers are given you in **m.** forms, |
| C-5............. 6:3 | For Christ takes **m.** forms with different |
| P-2..........II.7:2 | But both have **m.** forms, because no good |
| P-2..........II.7:6 | They can succeed where **m.** who believe |
| P-2........ VI.2:2 | the **m.** opportunities given us literally "to |
| P-2........ VI.5:1 | Sickness takes **m.** forms, and so does |
| P-2....... VII.5:7 | That **m.** therapists are mad is obvious. No |
| P-3..........II.5:6 | and **m.** of their patients would not be able |
| P-3..........II.8:3 | **M.** holy instants can be his along the way. |
| P-3..........II.9:3 | by **m.** obstacles to peace quite quickly, if |
| P-3..........II.9:9 | **M.** patients, too, consider this strange |
| P-3......... III.8:2 | **M.** will come to you carrying the gift of |
| S-1 ..........II.3:4 | for forgiveness for the **m.** sources of guilt |
| S-1 ........ IV.2:2 | but there are still **m.** lessons to learn. The |
| S-2 ..........II.1:1 | Forgiveness-to-destroy has **m.** forms, |

## many-faceted 1

| | |
|---|---|
| M-23 ......... 7:5 | Yet do we need a **m.** curriculum, not |

## mar 5

| | |
|---|---|
| T-13...... III.9:4 | there is one spot of fear to **m.** its welcome. |
| T-13........X.2:2 | or even hold one spot of it to **m.** its purity |
| T-23...... IV.8:8 | touch of doubt can ever **m.** your certainty |
| T-24...... III.6:6 | one thought of specialness to **m.** your rest |
| M-23 ......... 5:7 | no stain to **m.** your beautiful perfection. |

| | |
|---|---|
| T-31 V.15:3 | **m.** it which concept you accept while you |
| T-31 VI.4:5 | It **m.** not where you believe you are, nor |
| W-pI 158.9:4 | It **m.** not what form they took, nor how |
| W-pI 158.11:1 | It **m.** not when revelation comes, for that |
| W-pI 185.8:5 | for their form is not what **m.** now. Let not |
| S-1 I.2:6 | it is not the form of the question that **m.**, |
| S-2 III.4:6 | **m.** not the form that dreams may seem to |

## maturing 1

| | |
|---|---|
| T-31 V.7:9 | in its ways and finally "**m.**" in its thought. |

## maturity 2

| | |
|---|---|
| T-31 V.1:7 | time you reach "**m.**" you have perfected it |
| M-9 2:6 | as the criterion for **m.** and strength. Our |

## maxim 1

| | |
|---|---|
| T-16 V.6:5 | example could there be of the ego's **m.**, |

## maximal 7

| | |
|---|---|
| T-1 I.1:4 | the same. All expressions of love are **m.**. |
| T-1 I.18:2 | the **m.** service you can render to another. |
| T-4 V.1:3 | The ego exerts **m.** vigilance about what it |
| T-7 III.1:5 | It is always **m.**. Your vigilance does not |
| T-14 X.6:13 | And being always **m.**, it offers everything |
| M-3 4:1 | Each teaching-learning situation is **m.** in |
| M-7 2:3 | That was already **m.**, because the Holy |

## maximizes 1

| | |
|---|---|
| T-7 III.1:2 | **m.** all efforts and all results. By teaching |

## maximum 3

| | |
|---|---|
| W-pI 11.3:1 | To do these exercises for **m.** benefit, the |
| W-pI 17.4:1 | less than three are required for **m.** benefit |
| W-pI 27.3:1 | needs many repetitions for **m.** benefit. It |

## may 579

## maybe 1

| | |
|---|---|
| W-pI 107.2:3 | a time,–perhaps a minute, **m.** even less– |

## maze 1

| | |
|---|---|
| T-26 V.4:1 | and senseless **m.** you still perceive in time |

## mazes 1

| | |
|---|---|
| P-2 V.1:1 | lost their way in endless **m.** of complexity. |

## Me 14

- God
  *Holy Spirit*
  *me*

| | |
|---|---|
| T-28 VI.6:4 | are beloved of **M.** and I of you forever. Be |
| T-28 VI.6:5 | for you can never be apart from **M.**." His |
| W-pII 10.5:2 | Therefore awaken and return to **M.**. I am |
| S-3 IV.6:1 | Come unto **M.**, My children, once again, |
| S-3 IV.7:1 | comes for **M.** and speaks My Word to you |
| S-3 IV.7:2 | I would recall My weary Son to **M.** from |
| S-3 IV.7:5 | there is a Voice that speaks to you of **M.**. |
| S-3 IV.8:1 | Help **M.** to wake My children from the |
| S-3 IV.8:2 | Let **M.** instead remind you of eternity, in |
| S-3 IV.8:5 | Return to **M.** Who never left My Son. |
| S-3 IV.9:5 | How like to **M.**! How lovingly I hold you |
| S-3 IV.9:7 | How dear is every gift to **M.** that you have |
| S-3 IV.10:1 | So now return your holy voice to **M.**. The |
| S-3 IV.10:4 | it and to yourself, and then be kind to **M.**. |

## Me 3

- Holy Spirit
  *God*
  *me*

| | |
|---|---|
| T-14 II.3:5 | *Let **M.** make the one distinction for you that* |
| T-14 II.3:7 | *you. Offer your faith to **M.**, and I will place it* |
| C-2 9:1 | you ready yet to help **M.** save the world?" |

## me 264

- Jesus
  *noise word*
  *Me*

| | |
|---|---|
| T-1 I.27:1 | from God through **m.** to all my brothers. |
| T-1 I.37:1 | introduced into false thinking by **m.**. It |
| T-1 II.3:6 | therefore an inappropriate reaction to **m.**. |
| T-1 II.3:9 | only my devotion that entitles **m.** to yours |
| T-1 II.3:10 | nothing about **m.** that you cannot attain. |
| T-1 II.3:13 | leaves **m.** in a state which is only potential |
| T-1 II.4:1 | the Father but by **m.**" does not mean that |
| T-1 II.4:3 | stand below **m.** and I stand below God. In |
| T-1 II.4:4 | up," I am higher because without **m.** the |
| T-1 II.4:6 | has placed **m.** in charge of the Sonship, |
| T-1 II.5:1 | Revelations are indirectly inspired by **m.** |
| T-1 III.1:2 | my brothers, you do it to *yourself* and **m.**. |
| T-1 III.1:3 | reason you come before **m.** is that I do not |
| T-1 III.3:4 | serve the Holy Spirit unite with **m.** for the |
| T-1 III.4:3 | to you. Ask **m.** which miracles you should |
| T-1 III.4:5 | it enables **m.** to direct its application, and |
| T-1 III.8:4 | of the miracle should be controlled by **m.** |
| T-1 IV.4:6 | that I will witness for anyone who lets **m.**, |
| T-1 IV.4:8 | Those who witness for **m.** are expressing, |
| T-1 V.6:1 | chosen to be led by **m.** in Christ's service. |
| T-1 VII.5:6 | to **m.** because of our inherent equality. |
| T-2 V.A.17:2 | this in remembrance of **m.**" is the appeal |
| T-2 VI.1:4 | Fear cannot be controlled by **m.**, but it |
| T-2 VI.1:5 | prevents **m.** from giving you my control. |
| T-2 VI.2:9 | This is controlled by **m.** automatically as |
| T-2 VI.2:10 | to miscreate and have not allowed **m.** to |
| T-2 VI.4:9 | ask **m.** if your choice is in accord with |
| T-2 VII.1:2 | cannot ask **m.** to release you from fear. I |
| T-2 VII.2:1 | or you will not be able to help **m.**. Miracle |
| T-2 VII.3:5 | are afraid of God, of **m.** and of yourself. |
| T-2 VII.7:9 | but let **m.** remind you that time and space |
| T-3 I.3:7 | likely that He would hold them against **m.** |
| T-4 I.4:7 | of your thought system and open it to **m.**, |
| T-4 I.6:3 | and live with you if you will think with **m.**, |
| T-4 I.13:4 | and lets **m.** teach you their unimportance. |
| T-4 III.7:5 | or you will be unable to ask **m.** to do so. I |
| T-4 III.7:9 | in impatience, you will surely ask **m.** truly |
| T-4 III.8:4 | to help **m.** make other minds ready for |
| T-4 IV.5:2 | Leave the "sins" of the ego to **m.**. That is |
| T-4 IV.7:3 | Side with **m.** consistently against this |
| T-4 IV.7:4 | are useless to themselves and to **m.**, but |
| T-4 IV.10:3 | called you to join with **m.** in the Second. I |
| T-4 IV.11:8 | Why do you believe it is harder for **m.** to |
| T-4 VI.2:2 | It is the same debt that you owe to **m.**. |
| T-4 VI.2:4 | to the whole Sonship, which includes **m.**, |
| T-4 VI.3:1 | You have very little trust in **m.** as yet, but |
| T-4 VI.3:1 | to **m.** instead of to your ego for guidance. |
| T-4 VI.6:1 | is greater than yours in **m.** at the moment, |
| T-4 VI.8:1 | come closer to a brother you approach **m.** |
| T-4 VI.8:3 | they are disengaging themselves from **m.**. |
| T-5 I.3:6 | joining with **m.** in Christ thinking. |
| T-5 I.4:6 | taught **m.** first and foremost that this |
| T-5 II.9:2 | only my decision that gave **m.** all power in |
| T-5 II.10:1 | Mind that decided for **m.** is also in you, |
| T-5 II.10:1 | can let it change you just as it changed **m.**. |
| T-5 II.10:3 | You are the light of the world with **m.**. |
| T-5 II.11:1 | call on **m.** to remind you how to heal by |
| T-5 II.12:3 | to keep **m.** as the model for your thought, |
| T-5 II.12:3 | thought, and to behave like **m.** as a result. |
| T-5 III.11:7 | looks back to God in remembrance of **m.**. |
| T-5 IV.4:3 | Mind that was in **m.** is still irresistibly |
| T-5 IV.5:3 | which arose in **m.** *because* I learned it. I |
| T-5 IV.5:6 | was in **m.** rejoices as you choose to hear it. |
| T-5 IV.6:5 | forsake myself and God Who created **m.**. |
| T-5 VI.3:2 | The Mind that was in **m.** *is* in you, for God |
| T-5 VI.3:3 | and let **m.** teach you how to share it with |
| T-5 VI.11:7 | Voice was in **m.** as It is in you, speaking |
| T-6 in.2:1 | been asked to take **m.** as your model for |
| T-6 I.2:5 | can always call on **m.** to share my decision |
| T-6 I.5:1 | that I am like you and you are like **m.**, but |
| T-6 I.5:6 | will believe it, you will help **m.** teach it. |
| T-6 I.6:11 | Believe with **m.**, and we will become equal |
| T-6 I.7:4 | it, and therefore accepted it as true for **m.**. |
| T-6 I.7:5 | Help **m.** to teach it to our brothers in the |
| T-6 I.8:2 | cannot really betray themselves or **m.**, |
| T-6 I.8:6 | who accept **m.** as a model are literally my |
| T-6 I.9:3 | of the projection of others onto **m.**, since I |
| T-6 I.15:2 | they never could have quoted **m.** as saying |
| T-6 I.15:4 | they did, if they had really understood **m.**. |
| T-6 I.16:1 | not wholly ready to follow **m.** at the time. |
| T-6 I.19:3 | you will have learned of **m.** and will be as |
| T-6 V.C.9:8 | you as a teacher who teaches like **m.**. |
| T-6 V.C.9:9 | was required of **m.** as much as of you, and |
| T-7 V.10:2 | To forget **m.** is to forget yourself and Him |
| T-7 V.10:4 | remembrance of **m.** and of Him Who |
| T-7 V.10:4 | of me and of Him Who created **m.**. |
| T-7 V.11:1 | Come therefore unto **m.**, and learn of the |
| T-7 X.6:6 | are. Sharing His Will with **m.** is not really |
| T-8 IV.2:11 | everywhere, you shine it away with **m.**. |
| T-8 IV.2:13 | of **m.** is the remembrance of yourself, and |
| T-8 IV.2:13 | yourself, and of Him Who sent **m.** to you. |
| T-8 IV.3:7 | must therefore despise and reject **m.**, |
| T-8 IV.3:9 | decision to hear **m.** is the decision to hear |
| T-8 IV.3:10 | sent **m.** to you so will I send you to others. |
| T-8 IV.4:4 | If you want to have it of **m.**, you must give |
| T-8 IV.4:10 | then will your mind choose to follow **m.**. |
| T-8 IV.6:3 | If you want to be like **m.** I will help you, |
| T-8 IV.7:4 | Father and you are nothing without **m.**, |
| T-8 IV.7:8 | with **m.** in praise of Him and you whom |
| T-8 IV.8:5 | identification with **m.** and with the Father |
| T-8 V.2:10 | shine upon you by your acceptance of **m.**. |
| T-8 V.3:2 | To join with **m.** is to restore His power to |
| T-8 V.4:1 | with **m.** you are uniting without the ego, |
| T-8 V.5:2 | Ask it of **m.** who know it for you and you |
| T-8 V.5:3 | you nothing, as God denies **m.** nothing. |
| T-8 V.5:8 | this journey you have chosen **m.** as your |
| T-8 V.6:2 | minds, and the one He taught **m.** is yours. |
| T-8 V.6:10 | I need you as much as you need **m.**. |
| T-8 VI.8:3 | revealed it to **m.** because I asked it of Him |
| T-8 VI.10:5 | Learn this of **m.**, and free the holy will of |
| T-8 VII.5:8 | As part of **m.**, you are. To communicate |
| T-8 IX.7:5 | you are sick you are withdrawing from **m.** |
| T-8 IX.7:6 | Yet you cannot withdraw from **m.** alone. |
| T-8 IX.7:7 | can only withdraw from yourself *and* **m.**. |
| T-9 II.4:3 | in **m.** whose faith in you cannot be shaken |
| T-9 II.4:7 | *be* true. As you hear him you will hear **m.**. |
| T-9 II.6:12 | what you would have **m.** hear of you, for |
| T-9 II.6:12 | for you would not want **m.** to be deceived. |
| T-9 II.7:2 | deceive you, but they cannot deceive **m.**. |
| T-9 II.7:4 | in you, Who speaks to **m.** through you. If |
| T-9 II.7:5 | If you would hear **m.**, hear my brothers in |
| T-9 II.8:2 | Believe in **m.** *by* believing in them, for the |
| T-9 IV.5:1 | is learned of **m.** does not use fear to undo |
| T-9 IV.8:3 | Let **m.** repeat that the ego's qualifications |
| T-9 IV.12:2 | It belongs to you and **m.** and God, and is |
| T-9 VI.3:8 | If what you do to my brother you do to **m.** |
| T-10 III.6:7 | Peace comes from God through **m.** to you |
| T-10 III.7:8 | you whole when you have faith in **m.**. |
| T-11 in.4:1 | you are part of God and part of **m.**. When |
| T-11 IV.6:6 | Come unto **m.** who hold it open for you, |
| T-11 VI.4:2 | You live in **m.** because you live in God. |
| T-11 VI.10:3 | part must be like mine if you learn it of **m.** |
| T-11 VIII.8:4 | Believe that the truth is in **m.**, for I know |
| T-11 VIII.8:6 | Son of God, and you have asked it of **m.**. |
| T-12 II.7:1 | A little while and you will see **m.**, for I am |
| T-12 II.7:5 | with you as our Father walked with **m.**. |
| T-12 II.8:5 | Give **m.** but a little trust in the name of |
| T-12 III.1:1 | have and give to the poor and follow **m.**. |
| T-12 VII.6:1 | see **m.** it will be because you have invited |
| T-12 VII.10:1 | You are afraid of **m.** because you looked |
| T-12 VII.10:5 | looked upon **m.** and all your brothers, in |
| T-12 VII.11:3 | will not look upon **m.** nor hear the answer |
| T-12 VII.11:6 | And you will see **m.** as you look within, |
| T-12 VII.12:1 | When you look within and see **m.**, it will |
| T-12 VII.15:2 | is true when you look within and *see* **m.**. |

| | |
|---|---|
| T-12...VII.15:4 | And would eternal life have been given **m.** |
| T-12...VII.15:5 | When you learn to make **m.** manifest, you |
| T-13.........I.5:1 | will see **m.** as you learn the Son of God is |
| T-13...... VI.8:6 | as I am calling you to join with **m.**. Each |
| T-13...VII.16:1 | In **m.** you have already overcome every |
| T-13...VII.16:3 | God. Hold **m.** dear, for what except your |
| T-13...VII.16:9 | Take it of **m.** in glad exchange for all the |
| T-13...VII.17:3 | gift to you, so was it the Father's gift to **m.** |
| T-13...VII.17:3 | gift to me, given **m.** through His Spirit. |
| T-13....VIII.8:2 | Unite with **m.** under the holy banner of |
| T-13...... X.13:2 | is that I love *only* what God loves with **m.**, |
| T-13...... X.13:5 | without the fear that you will hear **m.** not. |
| T-13...... X.13:6 | that you will let **m.** offer to the Kingdom |
| T-14...... IV.8:3 | hear **m.** speak for Him and for yourself. |
| T-14....... V.8:7 | Abide with **m.** within it, as a teacher of |
| T-14....... V.9:1 | Blessed are you who teach with **m.**. Our |
| T-14....... V.9:5 | Teach peace with **m.**, and stand with me |
| T-14....... V.9:5 | me, and stand with **m.** on holy ground. |
| T-14....... V.9:8 | Stand not outside, but join with **m.** within |
| T-14....... X.8:4 | let **m.** assure you that you understand |
| T-15...... III.7:1 | with **m.** who decided for holiness for you. |
| T-15...... III.9:3 | I learned for you that you can learn of **m.**. |
| T-15...... III.9:6 | Welcome **m.** not into a manger, but into |
| T-15.... III.10:1 | Decide with **m.**, who has decided to abide |
| T-15.... III.11:3 | Rather, join with **m.** in His, that we may |
| T-15.... III.12:4 | his call is yours, and answer him with **m.**. |
| T-15...... IV.3:3 | you must fill if you would join with **m.**, by |
| T-15...... IV.5:1 | instant, as clear as you would have **m.**. |
| T-15...... IV.5:2 | extent to which you learn to accept **m.** is |
| T-15...... VI.6:6 | He offered it to **m.** and I accepted it. Fear |
| T-15...... VI.6:8 | **m.** the Holy Spirit gives it unto you, as |
| T-15.... VI.6:10 | join with **m.** in offering what is needed. |
| T-15..... VI.7:2 | Join **m.** in the idea of peace, for in ideas |
| T-15....... X.1:7 | let **m.** celebrate *your* birth through Him. |
| T-15....... X.1:9 | Release **m.** as I choose your own release. |
| T-15....... X.2:3 | What other gift can you offer **m.**, when |
| T-15....... X.2:4 | And to see **m.** is to see me in everyone, |
| T-15....... X.2:4 | And to see me is to see **m.** in everyone, |
| T-15....... X.2:4 | and offer everyone the gift you offer **m.**. I |
| T-15....... X.2:5 | sacrifice you ask of yourself you ask of **m.**. |
| T-15....... X.3:5 | Give it to **m.**, that you may have it. The |
| T-15...... XI.3:3 | accepted it with **m.** you will give it with |
| T-15...... XI.3:3 | it with me you will give it with **m.**. All |
| T-15...... XI.8:2 | for so you offer **m.** the love I offer you. |
| T-15...... XI.8:4 | return it to the Father, Who gave it to **m.**. |
| T-16.... IV.12:5 | with **m.** firmly away from all illusions |
| T-16.. IV.13:11 | way to truth is open. Follow it with **m.**. |
| T-17.... III.10:2 | and let **m.** bring reality to your perception |
| T-17.... III.10:6 | Be not separate from **m.**, and let not the |
| T-17.... III.10:7 | dreams are cherished have excluded **m.**. |
| T-17.... III.10:8 | me. Let **m.** enter in the Name of God and |
| T-17.... III.10:8 | you peace, that you may offer peace to **m.**. |
| T-18.......I.12:4 | Return with **m.** to Heaven, walking |
| T-18...... III.4:2 | darkness that you agreed to leave with **m.** |
| T-18...... III.6:1 | relationship you have joined with **m.** in |
| T-18...... III.6:4 | will join with **m.** in carrying their light |
| T-18...... III.6:5 | joined with **m.** in the holy light of your |
| T-18...... III.6:6 | Would I not give you what you gave to **m.** |
| T-18...... III.6:7 | you joined your brother, you answered **m.** |
| T-18..... VII.6:6 | time for **m.** by only this one preparation, |
| T19. IV.A.17:1 | which means you have at last forgiven **m.**. |
| T19....IV.B.6:1 | Let **m.** be to you the symbol of the end of |
| T19....IV.B.6:1 | your brother as you would look on **m.**. |
| T19....IV.B.6:2 | Forgive **m.** all the sins you think the Son |
| T19....IV.B.6:5 | overcame the world, you were with **m.**. |
| T19....IV.B.6:6 | Would you see in **m.** the symbol of guilt |
| T19....IV.B.7:2 | home you offered to my Father and to **m.**. |
| T19....IV.B.8:1 | Forgive **m.** your illusions, and release me |
| T19....IV.B.8:1 | and release **m.** from punishment for what |
| T19....IV.B.8:2 | to your brother, and so releasing **m.**. I am |
| T19....IV.B.8:3 | yet you would imprison **m.** behind the |
| T19. IV.D.17:9 | He leadeth you and **m.** together, that we |
| T-20.........I.2:7 | now with **m.** and throw away the thorns, |
| T-20.........I.2:8 | of your forgiveness offered by you to **m.**, |
| T-20.........I.2:8 | by you to me, and returned by **m.** to you. |
| T-20.........I.4:3 | it. I was a stranger and you took **m.** in, not |
| T-20.........I.4:7 | and celebrate his holiness along with **m.**. |
| T-20....... II.4:1 | for the Son of God has not forgiven **m.**. |
| T-20....... II.4:2 | forgiveness when he offers thorns to **m.**? |
| T-20 .......II.4:3 | offers thorns to anyone is against **m.** still, |
| T-20 .......II.4:4 | Be you his friend for **m.**, that I may be |
| T-20 .......II.4:5 | see what you have laid upon it to offer **m.**. |
| T-20 .......II.4:6 | and it is separation that you offer **m.**. And |
| T-20 .......II.6:2 | You *have* forgiven **m.**. And yet I cannot use |
| T-20 ... III.11:1 | gift unto your brother has given **m.** the |
| T-20 ... III.11:2 | Share, then, this faith with **m.**, and know |
| T-22 ..... IV.5:4 | both. So shall you walk the world with **m.**, |
| T-31 ..... IV.7:3 | let **m.** repeat that to achieve a goal you |
| T-31 ...VIII.7:1 | Deny **m.** not the little gift I ask, when in |
| T-31 ...VIII.9:4 | Hear **m.**, my brothers, hear and join with |
| T-31 ...VIII.9:4 | me, my brothers, hear and join with **m.**. |
| T-31 .VIII.10:3 | to **m.** as You are sure of what they are, |
| T-31 .VIII.10:4 | because You gave it **m.** on their behalf. |
| T-31 .VIII.11:1 | join with **m.** in reaching past temptation, |
| T-31 .VIII.11:2 | Give **m.** my own, for they belong to You. |
| T-31 .VIII.11:5 | And as each one elects to join with **m.**, the |
| W-pI..... 70.9:3 | of **m.** holding your hand and leading you. |
| WpI...rV.in6:2 | that you may come to **m.** who recognize |
| WpI...rV.in6:6 | until you walk along the road with **m.**. |
| WpI...rV.in7:3 | turns to the light in him and looks for **m.**. |
| WpI...rV.in7:5 | Help **m.** now to lead you back to where |
| WpI...rV.in7:5 | begun, to make another choice with **m.**. |
| WpI...rV.in8:1 | Release **m.** as you practice once again the |
| WpI...rV.in8:7 | I am incomplete without your part in **m.**. |
| WpI...rV.in9:1 | Let this review be then your gift to **m.**. |
| WpI...rV.in9:7 | In him I walk with you, and you with **m.**. |
| W-pI. 191.10:4 | Then join with **m.** today. Your glory is the |
| W-pII . 225.2:4 | You have reached your hand to **m.**, and I |
| W-pII . 231.2:2 | And you share this will with **m.**, and with |
| W-pII . 264.2:1 | My brothers, join with **m.** in this today. |
| W-pII . 275.1:3 | Join **m.** in hearing. For the Voice for God |
| W-pII . 288.2:1 | Forgive **m.**, then, today. And you will |
| W-pII . 288.2:2 | And you will know you have forgiven **m.** if |
| W-pII . 313.2:4 | Brother, come and join with **m.** today. We |
| W-pII . 342.2:1 | Brother, forgive **m.** now. I come to you to |
| W-pII . 342.2:2 | I come to you to take you home with **m.**. |
| W-pII ... 14.2:3 | And thus you joined with **m.**, so what I |
| M-29 ......... 8:7 | *And for all those who walk to God with **m.**.* |
| C-5 .......... 6:11 | *guilt, and come with **m.** instead to share the* |

**me** 844

- noise word
  *Jesus*
  *Me*

**meager** 7

| | |
|---|---|
| T-4 ....... III.3:8 | its **m.** offering to you prevail against the |
| T19IV.A.17:12 | **m.** store and make your life complete. |
| T-26 ........I.5:4 | to add a limitless supply to every **m.** scrap |
| W-pI... 91.10:1 | confident that your efforts, however **m.**, |
| W-pI... 123.3:5 | your **m.** gifts and petty judgments of the |
| W-pI... 127.8:4 | upon its **m.** offerings and senseless gifts, |
| W-pII . 334.1:3 | me not accept such **m.** gifts again today. |

**mean** 137

| | |
|---|---|
| T-in ........... 1:4 | *not **m.** that you can establish the curriculum* |
| T-1 ..........I.4:1 | All miracles **m.** life, and God is the Giver |
| T-1 .........II.4:1 | the Father but by me" does not **m.** that I |
| T-2 ....... IV.5:4 | necessarily **m.** that this is the highest level |
| T-2 ....... IV.5:5 | It does **m.**, however, that it is the highest |
| T-2 ....... VI.3:7 | not **m.** anything at the symptom level, |
| T-3 ....... VI.9:3 | something does not **m.** that it has gone. It |
| T-4 ....... III.1:2 | is inside, and this does not **m.** anything. |
| T-4 ........ V.5:2 | "Seek and ye shall find" does not **m.** that |
| T-5 ....... VI.6:1 | so shall ye reap" He interprets to **m.** what |
| T-6 ....... IV.1:3 | capricious and does not **m.** its maker well |
| T-7 .........II.7:1 | Kingdom **m.** to those who are confused? |
| T-7 .....VIII.3:3 | another part does not really **m.** anything. |
| T-7 .........X.4:9 | His. The ego's wishes do not **m.** anything, |
| T-7 .........X.5:4 | decision **m.** except that you want to be |
| T-7 .........X.5:8 | not **m.** that the guide is untrustworthy. In |
| T-8 ....... IV.7:2 | would **m.** you have imprisoned yours, |
| T-8 ....... VI.7:1 | An "unwilling will" does not **m.** anything |
| T-8 ....... IX.6:4 | since it would **m.** to make nothing out of |
| T-9 ..........I.3:3 | All this could **m.** is that you are arbitrarily |
| T-9 ..........I.6:4 | communication does not **m.** anything. A |
| T-9 .........II.1:3 | that the course does not **m.** what it says. |
| T-9 ....... VI.7:2 | This cannot **m.** anything to you until you |
| T-9 ...... VII.4:9 | **m.** except that you are agreeing with the |
| T-11 .......V.3:1 | that the term itself does not **m.** anything. |
| T-12 .......II.4:4 | not understand what his perceptions **m.**. |
| T-12 .......II.7:7 | **m.** that peace goes with *us* on the journey? |
| T-13 ... VIII.1:6 | concept "where" does not **m.** anything to |
| T-13 ..... XI.7:2 | your blackest nightmares all **m.** nothing. |
| T-14 ..... VI.6:3 | how can this tongue **m.** anything? Yet |
| T-15 .... VII.8:2 | the ego, **m.** only that bodies are together. |
| T-16 ........I.1:2 | empathize does not **m.** to join in suffering |
| T-16 ........I.6:5 | But be certain that this does not **m.** to do |
| T-16 ........II.3:4 | a contradiction of what miracles **m.**. And |
| T-17 ........I.3:1 | all you **m.** is that there are some things |
| T-17 ... VIII.5:6 | your lack of faith in him must **m.** to you. |
| T-18 ... VIII.5:3 | meaning, for by itself it does **m.** nothing. |
| T19 .IV.C.11:4 | they may thus **m.** everything or nothing, |
| T-21 .......II.2:2 | only this, but **m.** it with no reservations, |
| T-21 .. VII.12:4 | perceiving that "yes" must **m.** "not no." |
| T-22 ... VI.14:3 | What can this **m.** except your mind and |
| T-23 ....II.13:10 | There is no point in asking what they **m.**. |
| T-23 .....II.17:1 | can some forms of murder not **m.** death? |
| T-24 ..... IV.1:7 | salvation can only **m.** destruction of the |
| T-25 ..... IX.1:2 | And what could this **m.** except that they |
| T-25 ..... IX.1:8 | You **m.** that truth has greater value now |
| T-26 .......X.2:1 | What does it **m.** if you perceive attack in |
| T-27 .......II.2:8 | it. Who can say and **m.**, "My brother, you |
| T-27 .....II.11:6 | a single function that would **m.** a shared |
| T-27 .....V.2:10 | **m.** the conflict must be gone forever from |
| T-27 .....V.2:12 | But it does **m.**, if only for an instant, you |
| T-28 ........I.3:2 | which **m.** that something must be done. It |
| T-28 ..... IV.9:5 | broken pieces seem to take **m.** nothing. |
| T-28 .... VII.5:3 | To be alone must **m.** you are apart, and if |
| T-29 ........I.1:5 | For it would **m.** His Love could harbor |
| T-29 ..... IV.5:4 | but what they **m.** has changed because |
| T-30 ........I.2:4 | But it must also **m.** you will not judge the |
| T-30 ..... III.3:3 | can only **m.** that you believe some form is |
| T-30 ..... IV.2:5 | **m.** his world is made chaotic and unsafe. |
| T-30 ..... VI.1:7 | For that would **m.** that you forgive a sin |
| T-30 .... VII.6:1 | symbols that are used **m.** different things |
| T-30 .. VII.6:18 | shared. They **m.** the same to both of you. |
| T-30 .... VII.7:7 | so that they **m.** the same to all of us. Our |
| T-31 ......I.12:1 | what things **m.** and what their purpose is. |
| W-pI ...... 1.1:2 | *This table does not **m.** anything. This chair* |
| W-pI ...... 1.1:3 | *This chair does not **m.** anything. This hand* |
| W-pI ...... 1.1:4 | *This hand does not **m.** anything. This foot* |
| W-pI ...... 1.1:5 | *This foot does not **m.** anything. This pen* |
| W-pI ...... 1.1:6 | *anything. This pen does not **m.** anything.* |
| W-pI ...... 1.2:2 | *That door does not **m.** anything. That body* |
| W-pI ...... 1.2:3 | *That body does not **m.** anything. That lamp* |
| W-pI ...... 1.2:4 | *That lamp does not **m.** anything. That sign* |
| W-pI ...... 1.2:5 | *sign does not **m.** anything. That shadow* |
| W-pI ...... 1.2:6 | *That shadow does not **m.** anything.* |
| W-pI ......... 4.h | These thoughts do not **m.** anything. They |
| W-pI ...... 4.1:7 | This is why they do not **m.** anything. |
| W-pI ...... 4.4:2 | *This thought about_does not **m.** anything.* |
| W-pI ...... 7.1:6 | why your thoughts do not **m.** anything, |
| W-pI ...... 9.1:2 | unlikely that it will **m.** anything to you as |
| W-pI ....... 10.h | My thoughts do not **m.** anything. |
| W-pI .... 10.1:5 | were your thoughts did not **m.** anything. |
| W-pI .... 10.4:8 | *My thought about_does not **m.** anything.* |
| W-pI .... 10.4:9 | *My thought about_does not **m.** anything.* |
| W-pI .... 27.1:3 | that you are not sure you really **m.** it. This |
| W-pI .... 28.2:4 | And what does "in itself" **m.**? You see a |
| W-pI .... 41.9:2 | what you are saying; what the words **m.**. |
| W-pI .... 51.4:1 | (4) These thoughts do not **m.** anything. |
| W-pI .... 51.4:2 | thoughts of which I am aware do not **m.** |
| W-pI .... 51.4:6 | that my thoughts do not **m.** anything, |
| W-pI .... 52.5:1 | (10) My thoughts do not **m.** anything. I |
| W-pI .... 52.5:4 | What can these thoughts **m.**? They do not |
| W-pI .... 52.5:5 | They do not exist, and so they **m.** nothing |
| W-pI .... 53.1:2 | of which I am aware do not **m.** anything, |
| W-pI .... 65.2:2 | the only way in which you can say and **m.**, |
| W-pI .... 74.3:1 | to understand what they **m.**, and to hold |
| W-pI .... 96.6:3 | What could the resolution **m.** in truth? |
| W-pI .... 98.7:4 | beyond their sound to what they really **m.** |
| W-pI .. 106.7:6 | *truth. What does it **m.** to give and to receive?* |
| W-pI .. 110.1:3 | Its truth would **m.** that you have made no |

W-pI...139.6:4 does this **m.** except the world is mad?
W-pI...151.9:3 body **m.** to Him Who knows the glory of
W-pI.154.12:4 What can this **m.** to you, until you have
W-pI...162.1:3 It will **m.** far more to you as you advance.
W-pI...170.1:3 you **m.** that to be cruel is protection; you
W-pI...170.1:4 **m.** that you believe to hurt another brings
W-pI...170.1:5 And you **m.** that to attack is to exchange
W-pI...185.1:2 But to **m.** these words is everything. If you
W-pI...185.1:3 you could but **m.** them for just an instant,
W-pI...185.2:1 one can **m.** these words and not be healed
W-pI...185.5:1 To **m.** you want the peace of God is to
W-pI...185.7:1 that we really **m.** the words we say. We
W-pI...185.7:6 To **m.** these words acknowledges illusions
W-pI.186.14:4 love will **m.** to you when formlessness has
W-pI...192.1:2 such a function **m.** within a world of envy,
W-pII.....in.1:1 Words will **m.** little now. We use them
M-in ..........3:9 **m.** that the self you are trying to protect is
M-in ........3:10 But it does **m.** that the self you think is
M-3............5:4 not **m.** that they necessarily recognize this
M-5........ II.4:7 pain, disaster and all suffering **m.** now?
M-10..........1:4 confusion about what these categories **m.**.
M-10..........1:9 in these terms, does not **m.** anything. No
M-13..........2:2 What can the sacrifice of nothing **m.**? It
M-13..........2:3 cannot **m.** that you have less because of it.
M-13..........2:7 Could they **m.** anything except to a body?
M-13..........8:1 decision you make must **m.** in terms of
M-23..........1:7 What does it **m.** to call on Jesus Christ?
M-23..........3:1 What does this **m.** for you? It means that
M-24..........5:1 this **m.** that the teacher of God should not
M-29..........5:5 **m.** that you cannot say anything without
M-29..........6:3 Does this **m.** that, while attack remains
P-2.........in.2:2 contrary, such concepts **m.** little to them,
P-2...........I.2:3 "the final dream," this is not what we **m.**,
P-3...........I.1:2 This does not **m.** that you select him, nor
P-3...........I.1:3 **m.** that no one comes to you by mistake.
S-1...........I.6:3 Help in prayer does not **m.** that another
S-1...........I.6:4 But it does **m.** that another stands beside
S-1......... II.4:5 What does the phrase really **m.**? Pray for

## meaning 359

T-in............1:6 *does not aim at teaching the **m.** of love, for*
T-1................h THE **M.** OF MIRACLES
T-1........VI.1:6 "separation," which is the **m.** of the "fall,"
T-2.......VII.6:6 Only then can the **m.** of wholeness in the
T-2........ VIII.h The **M.** of the Last Judgment
T-2..... VIII.1:6 into the real **m.** of the Last Judgment.
T-2..... VIII.4:2 and reflects the true **m.** of the Apocalypse
T-2..... VIII.5:3 the **m.** of the Last Judgment is objectively
T-3...........I.5:1 do not understand the **m.** of the symbol.
T-3...........I.6:4 one in which the **m.** of the Atonement is
T-3........III.6:5 That is the real **m.** of "Alpha and Omega,
T-3.........V.5:2 You may try to "interpret" **m.**, but this is
T-3.........V.5:2 because it refers to the *perception* of **m.**.
T-3........VI.3:2 judging them in any way is without **m.**. In
T-3........VI.3:3 **m.** is lost to you precisely *because* you are
T-3........VI.6:3 an attempt to teach you the **m.** of mercy.
T-3.......VII.3:1 but its **m.** must be clearly understood.
T-5...........I.6:6 literal **m.** of transferred or "carried over,"
T-5........III.8:2 no **m.** apart from your rightful place in
T-5........III.9:1 Perception derives **m.** from relationships
T-5........IV.4:6 This is the **m.** of "turning the other cheek.
T-6...........I.3:4 The real **m.** of the crucifixion lies in the
T-7......... II.4:3 what he translates, never changes the **m.**.
T-7......... II.4:4 form so that the original **m.** is retained.
T-7......... II.4:6 mind cannot be faithful to one **m.**, and
T-7......... II.4:6 therefore change the **m.** to preserve the
T-7......... II.5:2 to preserve the original **m.** in all respects
T-7......... II.5:4 The **m.** of His message is always the same;
T-7......... II.5:4 is always the same; only the **m.** matters.
T-7......... II.7:2 that confusion interferes with **m.**, and
T-7......... II.7:3 Kingdom, because there is only one **m.**.
T-7......... II.7:4 This **m.** comes from God and *is* God.
T-7......III.1:12 or overlooking its real and only **m.**.
T-7........III.2:1 God's **m.** waits in the Kingdom, because
T-7........III.2:4 God's **m.** perceive yourself as absent from
T-7........III.2:5 your **m.** only by experiencing yourself as
T-7......IV.6:11 all **m.** is contained by them and in them.
T-7....... V.6:12 Since that is His **m.**, it is also yours. Your
T-7....... V.6:13 Your **m.** cannot be out of accord with His,
T-7....... V.6:13 whole **m.** and your only meaning comes
T-7....... V.6:13 only **m.** comes from His and is like His.
T-7........ VI.6:7 is real and therefore nothing else has **m.**.
T-7...... VI.10:1 You can be perceived with **m.** only by the
T-7...... VI.11:6 It has no **m.**. It does not exist. Do not try
T-7...... VI.13:3 God's, you would be willing without **m.**.
T-8... VIII.1:14 has **m.** only at the level of perception,
T-8......... IX.9:3 re-establishing of **m.** in a chaotic thought
T-8......... IX.9:4 task is only to meet the conditions for **m.**,
T-8......... IX.9:4 for meaning, since **m.** itself is of God. Yet
T-8......... IX.9:5 Yet your return to **m.** is essential to His,
T-8......... IX.9:5 to His, because your **m.** is part of His.
T-9.........I.10:4 with form, being aware only of **m.**. The
T-9.........I.13:6 make reality meaningless, and reality *is* **m.**
T-9...... IV.11:4 But do not look for **m.** in them. They have
T-9...... IV.11:5 They have no more **m.** than the fantasies
T-9....... VI.7:7 God's **m.** is incomplete without you, and
T-10...... IV.4:9 chaotic is without **m.** because it is without
T-11.........I.4:1 possible only in time, but time has no **m.**.
T-11........ II.3:2 to be separate and therefore without **m.**.
T-11........ II.3:3 And being without **m.** to you, you will not
T-11........ II.3:4 To deny **m.** is to fail to understand. You
T-11...... V.13:5 relationships and therefore without **m.**.
T-11...... V.13:6 ego will always substitute chaos for **m.**,
T-11...... V.15:2 Analyzing to attack **m.**, the ego succeeds
T-11...... V.16:5 without **m.** cannot demonstrate anything
T-11... VIII.2:3 what you perceive, for its **m.** is lost to you.
T-11... VIII.2:4 the Holy Spirit has saved its **m.** for you,
T-11... VIII.2:5 Yet while you think you know its **m.**, you
T-11... VIII.3:1 not know the **m.** of anything you perceive
T-11. VIII.13:2 they trust for the **m.** of what they perceive
T-12...... III.9:6 "laws," and without **m.** of any kind. For it
T-12....... V.6:1 You do not know the **m.** of love, and that
T-13...... IV.5:1 "Now" has no **m.** to the ego. The present
T-13.... IV.6:10 cannot be, and the present is without **m.**.
T-13....... V.1:8 their maker, and so they have no **m.** at all.
T-13... VIII.2:6 be, is without **m.** in Heaven. Perception
T-13...... IX.3:1 it has no **m.** apart from what you found in
T-13....... X.4:3 to it have no **m.** in the present. Yet you let
T-13...... XI.1:5 perceives them as wholly without **m.**.
T-14...... VI.1:5 because you do not understand its **m.**. If
T-14...... VI.3:7 for only this has **m.** and can live in light.
T-14...... VI.4:4 **m.** by confusing them with each other.
T-14...... VI.6:2 made. It has no **m.**, for its purpose is not
T-14...... VI.7:2 perceives the **m.** in your alien language.
T-14...... VI.7:4 But He will separate out all that has **m.**,
T-14..... VII.7:5 Seeing with Him will show you that all **m.**
T-14..... VII.7:5 the gentle fusing of everything into *one* **m.**,
T-14...... IX.6:2 and their **m.** seems to lie only in shifting
T-14...... IX.7:3 Its **m.** to those who look upon it is not
T-14...... X.9:3 For form is not enough for **m.**, and the
T-14..... X.10:6 so powerful that what you see is given **m.**.
T-14...... XI.3:3 by giving it whatever **m.** it holds for you.
T-14...... XI.3:4 *Your* learning gives the present no **m.** at all
T-15....... V.1:1 learning device for teaching you love's **m.**.
T-15..... V.10:3 **m.** of love is the meaning God gave to it.
T-15..... V.10:3 meaning of love is the **m.** God gave to it.
T-15..... V.10:4 Give to it any **m.** apart from His, and it is
T-15..... V.11:6 And it is only there love has **m.**, and only
T-15...... VI.5:1 love has no **m.** and peace is impossible.
T-15...... VI.5:8 of God prevail, and only they have **m.**.
T-15...... VI.5:9 of this world cease to hold any **m.** at all.
T-15...... VI.7:4 And therein is love's **m.** understood. But
T-15... VIII.6:5 teach you the only **m.** of relationships.
T-15... VIII.6:6 created the only relationship that has **m.**,
T-15...... IX.2:5 must be unlimited in order to have **m.**,
T-15...... IX.2:5 to have meaning, and deprived of **m.**, it
T-15..... X.1:10 together, for it has no **m.** if we are apart.
T-15...... XI.2:5 the whole idea of sacrifice loses all **m.**. For
T-15...... XI.6:4 The **m.** of love lies in what you have cast
T-15...... XI.6:4 yourself, and it has no **m.** apart from you.
T-15...... XI.6:5 is what you prefer to keep that has no **m.**,
T-15...... XI.6:5 keep away holds all the **m.** of the universe
T-15...... XI.6:5 and holds the universe together in its **m.**.
T-15...... XI.6:6 and to be without Him *is* to be without **m.**.
T-16.........I.6:1 The **m.** of love is lost in any relationship
T-16.........I.6:2 The power of love, which *is* its **m.**, lies in
T-16....... II.3:5 And if you could understand their **m.**,
T-16...... IV.1:2 be impossible not to know the **m.** of love,
T-16...... IV.1:3 the **m.** of love is hidden, is undertaken
T-16...... IV.2:2 of love is without **m.** if love is everything.
T-16....... V.3:7 In Heaven, where the **m.** of love is known,
T-16..... V.12:3 There is no **m.** in the form, and there will
T-16..... V.12:4 over content, and love has lost its **m.**.
T-16..... V.15:1 in the fantasy of destruction of love's **m.**.
T-16..... V.15:2 And unless love's **m.** is restored to you,
T-16..... V.15:2 cannot know yourself who share its **m.**.
T-16...... VI.1:3 relationship has special value it has no **m.**
T-16...... VI.1:6 it is. Love has no **m.** except as its Creator
T-16...... VI.7:7 could be no **m.** you would still seek here.
T-16..... VII.2:5 it is. It has no **m.** in the present, and if it
T-16..... VII.2:5 now, it cannot have any real **m.** at all.
T-17.........I.5:2 Truth *has* no **m.** in illusion. The frame of
T-17.........I.5:3 frame of reference for its **m.** must be itself
T-17........II.7:4 the closing of the dream will have no **m.**.
T-17...... III.8:4 is referred for **m.** is an *illusion* of the past,
T-17.... IV.12:5 or the comparison is wholly without **m.**.
T-17.... IV.13:6 unprotected by the frame, it has no **m.**.
T-17.... IV.15:5 without value and entirely deprived of **m.**.
T-17.... IV.16:1 again the **m.** of relationship and know it
T-17....... V.3:6 *your* goal was all that seemed to give it **m.**.
T-17...... VI.4:6 view. The situation now has **m.**, but only
T-17..... VII.2:3 the **m.** of the problem must be lost, and
T-17..... VII.2:3 to the problem is inherent in its **m.**. Is it
T-17... VII.8:13 relationship, and derives its **m.** from it.
T-17.... VIII.1:2 The **m.** that the Holy Spirit's purpose has
T-17.... VIII.1:4 unequivocal demonstration of the **m.** of
T-18...... III.3:7 You are advancing to love's **m.**, and away
T-18....... V.1:2 the Atonement would have no **m.**. The
T-18...... VI.6:8 have done this to a thing that has no **m.**,
T-18.... VIII.5:3 needing the whole to give it any **m.**, for by
T-18.... VIII.8:2 itself. Its total lack of limit *is* its **m.**. It is
T-18.... IX.12:2 Its **m.** lies within itself. And learning ends
T-18.... IX.12:6 by the knowledge of love and its one **m.**.
T19..IV.C.11:3 Their **m.** cannot lie in them, but must be
T19..IV.C.11:5 with such seeming uncertainty of **m.**,
T19. IV.D.21:4 this world, whatever **m.** lies in them.
T-20.........I.1:4 pain. A slain Christ has no **m.**. But a risen
T-20...... III.7:9 it you turn to ask the **m.** of the universe.
T-20...... III.8:4 for the **m.** of your unholy relationship,
T-20...... III.9:4 in whom the **m.** of your freedom lies. He
T-20....... V.4:5 and yet insist that judgment still has **m.**?
T-20...... VI.1:1 The **m.** of the Son of God lies solely in his
T-20...... VI.3:4 in which they enter has lost its **m.**. The
T-20.... VI.12:5 You have a *real* relationship, and it has **m.**.
T-20... VII.8:10 and while this purpose seems to have a **m.**
T-20.... VIII.6:9 of your salvation, will be deprived of **m.**,
T-20.... VIII.9:9 gives the "nothing" all the **m.** that it holds
T-20.. VIII.10:1 What has no **m.** cannot be perceived.
T-20.. VIII.10:2 And **m.** always looks within to find itself,
T-20.. VIII.10:3 All **m.** that you give the world outside
T-21.....in.1:12 And where there is no **m.**, there is chaos.
T-21.......in.2:8 And, if this *is* its **m.**, then the power to give
T-21...... IV.8:5 This has no **m.**. What matters it to you
T-21... VII.13:1 and place, is an illusion that has no **m.**.
T-22.........I.1:6 fear of lack of **m.** in yourself arise? It is as
T-22.........I.6:4 **m.** different things to him at different
T-22...... III.1:5 is the beginning of a vision that has **m.**.
T-22...... III.4:2 **M.** it does not recognize, and does not see
T-22...... III.4:3 without the **m.** that the whole would give.
T-22...... III.6:6 unable to go beyond the form to **m.**.
T-22...... VI.2:2 Yet freedom of the body has no **m.**, and
T-22... VI.12:3 in any form, because it has no **m.**. The
T-23.........I.3:2 alliances on grounds that have no **m.**. For
T-23......II.12:9 ingredient that would give **m.** to your life.
T-23......II.13:4 through a world where **m.** can be found,
T-23......II.13:6 And it *is* here you look for **m.**. These are
T-23......II.16:7 Some forms it takes seem to have **m.**, and
T-23......II.19:5 equal in their inaccuracy and lack of **m.**.
T-23...... IV.7:2 look, where **m.** can be given what you see.
T-24.........I.6:7 love have **m.** where the goal is triumph?
T-24........II.5:3 message, and one with different **m.**, is the
T-24........II.7:4 no different messages, and has one **m.**.
T-24...... III.4:2 in such a state, where safety has no **m.**?
T-24...... IV.4:5 itself, and give it **m.** that the truth denies.
T-24...... IV.5:2 that has no **m.** in reality: When peace is
T-24....... V.2:4 nothing to the parts to give them **m.**.

T-24...... VI.3:5 has no **m.** in eternity where He abides,
T-24..... VII.5:5 Only the purpose that you see in it has **m.**
T-24..... VII.6:3 you. It has no **m.** of itself, yet you can give
T-24..... VII.7:5 has no **m.** to anyone who still retains one
T-25....... II.4:7 the picture is the frame without its **m.**. Its
T-25...... III.2:1 the Mind to which perception has no **m.**.
T-25....... V.1:4 but seems to draw a **m.** from the other.
T-25..... VII.3:4 as true has any **m.** in His Mind at all.
T-25..... VII.3:5 makes no sense and has no **m.** is insanity.
T-25..... VII.3:8 beliefs the world gives any **m.** to are false,
T-25... VII.12:7 the Holy Spirit gives **m.** and direction to
T-26......... I.5:2 function has this world no **m.** for you. Yet
T-26...... III.3:6 place and time and choice have **m.** still,
T-26...... III.4:3 knowledge on perception: "It has no **m.**,
T-26..... VII.3:7 takes many forms, but none has **m.**.
T-26..... VII.3:9 truth, it seems to have a **m.** and be real.
T-26..... VII.8:1 Nothing gives **m.** where no meaning is.
T-26..... VII.8:1 Nothing gives meaning where no **m.** is.
T-26... VII.11:6 and therefore has no **m.** in this world.
T-26... VII.15:2 derive whatever **m.** that they seem to have
T-26.... VIII.7:7 And then its **m.** will be clear. This is not
T-26.... VIII.9:2 It has no **m.**, and is not your just reward.
T-26....... X.2:4 are given **m.** and perceived as sensible.
T-27...... III.2:2 And so he has no **m.** to you, for he stands
T-27...... IV.6:2 And from the **m.** of the question does the
T-27...... VI.1:8 nothing, for they have a goal without a **m.**
T-27...... VI.1:9 the lack of **m.** which their purpose has.
T-30...... III.4:6 answer you in terms that have no **m.**. And
T-30...... IV.4:9 toys without a single **m.** of their own. See
T-30...... VI.6:4 not deceived about the **m.** of a fixed belief
T-30..... VII.1:1 the **m.** of the world to your interpretation
T-30..... VII.1:2 If He had, it *has* no **m.**. For it cannot be
T-30..... VII.1:3 it cannot be that **m.** changes constantly,
T-30..... VII.1:8 element, and every **m.** shifts accordingly.
T-30..... VII.2:4 The fact they have no **m.** in themselves is
T-30..... VII.2:5 you see another **m.** in what went before.
T-30..... VII.2:6 except to show there was no **m.** there? But
T-30..... VII.2:7 a **m.** in the light of goals that change, with
T-30..... VII.2:7 with every **m.** shifting as they change.
T-30..... VII.3:1 purpose can endow events with stable **m.**.
T-30..... VII.3:2 But it must accord *one* **m.** to them all. If
T-30..... VII.3:4 And this is all the **m.** that they have. Can
T-30..... VII.3:5 Can this be **m.**? Can confusion be what
T-30..... VII.3:6 confusion be what **m.** means? Perception
T-30..... VII.3:7 allowance for stability of **m.** anywhere.
T-30..... VII.3:9 has no **m.** but to show you wrote a fearful
T-30... VII.3:10 the thing you fear has fearful **m.** in itself.
T-30..... VII.4:3 learned one **m.** has been given everything,
T-30..... VII.5:5 makes perception shift and **m.** change. In
T-30..... VII.6:4 understand the sacrifice of **m.** is undone.
T-30..... VII.6:6 And looked at separately they have no **m.**.
T-30... VII.6:10 In any thought of loss there is no **m.**. No
T-30... VII.6:12 which cannot be interpreted with **m.**. It
T-30... VII.6:16 Look not to separate dreams for **m.**. Only
T-31......... I.6:1 senseless noise of sounds that have no **m.**
T-31.... IV.11:2 They have no **m.**. You can not escape
T-31....... V.7:6 to which its maker gives a **m.** of his own?
T-31..... V.12:4 represents has **m.** that was given it by you
T-31... VII.13:5 asks, "What is the **m.** of what I behold?"
W-in.......... 8:6 It is their use that will give them **m.** to you
W-pI.......... 2.h in this place] all the **m.** that it has for me.
W-pI........ 3.1:6 may have emotionally charged **m.** for you
W-pI........ 7.1:4 you see all the **m.** that it has for you. It is
W-pI...... 10.4:6 which has little if any personal **m.** to you.
W-pI...... 13.1:3 Nothing without **m.** exists. However, it
W-pI...... 13.1:4 you perceive something that has no **m.**.
W-pI...... 13.2:2 to whose **m.** is to be written in the empty
W-pI...... 14.6:6 Therefore, it has no **m.**. In recognition of
W-pI...... 15.2:1 call seeing will not have much **m.** for you.
W-pI...... 25.1:1 Purpose is **m.**. Today's idea explains why
W-pI...... 25.1:8 this that what you see is given **m.**.
W-pI...... 28.3:4 its **m.** to your tiny experience of tables,
W-pI.... 39.10:3 the idea should be stated so that its **m.** is
W-pI...... 43.2:5 Perception has no **m.**. Yet does the Holy
W-pI...... 43.2:6 Holy Spirit give it a **m.** very close to God's
W-pI...... 44.8:3 It is also the only one that has any **m.**,
W-pI...... 51.1:2 that I see nothing, and nothing has no **m.**.
W-pI...... 51.1:5 I must let it go by realizing it has no **m.**,
W-pI...... 51.2:1 (2) I have given what I see all the **m.** it has
W-pI...... 53.1:2 world that pictures them can have no **m.**.
W-pI...... 53.2:7 value what is totally insane and has no **m.**
W-pI...... 53.4:3 He is the Source of all **m.**, and everything
W-pI...... 76.1:5 would seek for it in things that have no **m.**
W-pI...... 76.6:3 Your magic has no **m.**. What it is meant
WpI..rII.in.4:2 may take, they have no **m.** and no power.
W-pI... 95.11:3 attempting to allow the **m.** of the words
W-pI... 95.11:5 then attempt to feel the **m.** that the words
W-pI...... 96.3:1 Problems that have no **m.** cannot be
W-pI...... 98.6:3 And since time has no **m.**, you are being
W-pI... 105.2:4 It strips all **m.** from the gifts you give, and
W-pI... 108.3:3 of reference, from which one **m.** comes.
W-pI... 110.1:4 remain as God created you fear has no **m.**
W-pI... 121.1:2 key to **m.** in a world that seems to make
W-pI... 127.2:1 Love's **m.** is obscure to anyone who
W-pI... 127.3:3 Its **m.** lies in oneness. And it must elude
W-pI... 127.4:2 Love's **m.** is your own, and shared by God
W-pI... 127.5:1 world obeys can help you grasp love's **m.**.
W-pI... 127.5:2 world believes was made to hide love's **m.**
W-pI... 127.9:5 His Voice to teach love's **m.** to your clean
W-pI... 129.3:1 cannot exist and vengeance has no **m.**? Is
W-pI... 129.7:5 ends loses all **m.** as they blend in one.
W-pI. 131.10:3 in the place of thoughts that have no **m.**,
W-pI. 131.12:4 Nothing but this has any **m.** now; no
W-pI... 132.4:2 Your mind must give it **m.**. And what you
W-pI... 132.4:4 waiting for your thoughts to give it **m.**.
W-pI... 134.1:1 Let us review the **m.** of "forgive," for it is
W-pI. 134.13:1 for the world cannot perceive its **m.**, nor
W-pI. 134.14:4 Who understands the **m.** of forgiveness,
W-pI. 134.17:1 when you forget its **m.** and attack yourself
W-pI... 136.1:2 understands as well its purpose has no **m.**
WpI. rIV.in4:4 we read, and see the **m.** that they offer us.
WpI. rIV.in7:4 word shine with the **m.** God has given it,
W-pI... 152.3:3 Without the first, the second has no **m.**.
W-pI... 152.3:8 And truth has lost its **m.**. Nothing but the
W-pI... 153.9:1 wish or dream in which attack has any **m.**
W-pI... 161.4:4 thoughts make clear the **m.** of creation?
W-pI... 168.2:1 If you but knew the **m.** of His Love, hope
W-pI... 168.3:6 forgot; all certainty of what Love's **m.** is.
W-pI. 169.10:4 Yet what **m.** can the words convey to
WpI...rV.in6:4 pain, although I know they have no **m.**.
WpI.rV.in12:4 try again to go beyond them to their **m.**,
WpI.rV.in12:5 as we approach the Source of **m.**. It is
W-pI... 183.4:1 of God, and little names have lost their **m.**
W-pI... 183.6:6 wish we have, the only sound with any **m.**
W-pI... 184.3:4 is named is given **m.** and will then be seen
W-pI... 184.7:4 the world would teach stops short of **m.**.
W-pI. 184.10:3 have **m.** in the world that darkness rules.
W-pI. 184.11:3 not forget creation has one Name, one **m.**
W-pI. 184.13:1 fail who seeks the **m.** of the Name of God.
W-pI... 185.4:3 form. The **m.** must escape the dream, for
W-pI... 186.3:1 seem quite sobering, until you see its **m.**.
W-pI... 187.3:4 is the idea of giving clarified and given **m.**
W-pI... 192.3:2 has no **m.** here. Forgiveness is the closest
W-pI... 196.2:4 and deny the **m.** they appear to have.
W-pI... 197.6:3 For death will have no **m.** for you then.
W-pI... 198.7:1 separate haunts where mercy has no **m.**,
W-pI... 200.4:2 and in alien forms that have no **m.** to you,
WpI rVI.in.6:6 our thoughts whatever **m.** they may have.
M-1......... 2:14 judges it. To the Call Itself time has no **m.**.
M-4...... IV.2:4 To those to whom harm has no **m.**, it is
M-4...... IV.2:5 What choice but this has **m.** to the sane?
M-4..... VII.1:1 The term generosity has special **m.** to the
M-4..... VII.1:2 It is not the usual **m.** of the word; in fact,
M-4..... VII.1:2 **m.** that must be learned and learned very
M-8........... 3:4 the eyes' messages and gives them "**m.**."
M-8........... 3:5 And this **m.** does not exist in the world
M-11......... 3:4 one without **m.** and devoid of sense, yet
M-13............ h WHAT IS THE REAL **M.** OF SACRIFICE?
M-13......... 1:1 meaningless, it does have **m.** in the world.
M-13......... 1:2 **m.** is temporary and will ultimately fade
M-13......... 1:3 Now its real **m.** is a lesson. Like all lessons
M-13......... 5:1 What is the real **m.** of sacrifice? It is the
M-13......... 8:1 of God, do not forget the **m.** of sacrifice,
M-21......... 2:3 the word has little or no practical **m.**, and
M-21........ 3:10 Only the Word of God has any **m.**,
M-24......... 1:2 body has no **m.** either once or many times
M-28......... 1:2 change of mind about the **m.** of the world
M-28......... 6:7 heard God's Word and understood its **m.**.
C-1............ 4:4 and therefore has no **m.** in this world. It
C-2............ 3:3 is its **m.** clear because its nature seems to
P-2........ IV.5:4 until the **m.** of love is understood. And
S-3........ III.1:8 here the **m.** of true healing has been lost,
S-3........ IV.8:2 where time and distance have no **m.**.

## meaningful 70

T-1......... II.4:2 The statement is more **m.** in terms of a
T-1........ VI.3:4 concepts such as "up" and "down" are **m.**
T-2......... II.5:8 is a belief in differences is learning **m.**.
T-2......... V.1:5 None of these errors is **m.**, because the
T-2........ V.1:11 of creative ability that is truly **m.**.
T-2..... VII.5:14 slight correction to be **m.** in this context;
T-3........ IV.3:2 but not of perceiving **m.** answers, because
T-3......... V.6:3 But the only **m.** prayer is for forgiveness,
T-3....... VI.8:9 **m.** to believe that you created yourself.
T-3.... VII.6:10 is the idea of an authority problem **m.**.
T-4....... III.9:6 distinction in this respect is **m.** only when
T-4......... V.5:3 **M.** seeking is consciously undertaken,
T-5......... V.1:1 **m.** if the ego's use of guilt is clarified. The
T-6..... V.A.3:4 To be of one mind is **m.**, but to be one
T-7.......... I.6:5 the useful, the meaningless into the **m.**,
T-7......... II.5:3 the idea that differences in form are **m.**,
T-7......... V.5:8 does the idea of exceptions seem to be **m.**.
T-7....... V.5:10 mind could possibly perceive as **m.**.
T-7... VI.11:10 You cannot make the meaningless **m.**.
T-7....... IX.6:5 so. Disobeying God's Will is **m.** only to the
T-8.......... I.5:4 A **m.** curriculum cannot be inconsistent.
T-8..... VIII.2:2 concepts of both health and sickness **m.**.
T-8..... VIII.5:7 is for. Sickness is **m.** only if the two basic
T-9......... V.7:4 only **m.** contribution the healer can make
T-11....... V.6:6 that autonomy is **m.** apart from Him?
T-11..... V.13:5 without **m.** relationships and therefore
T-13..... IV.4:2 past is the only aspect of time that is **m.**.
T-13....... V.1:8 For they are **m.** only to their maker, and
T-14..... IV.4:1 that knowledge would be **m.** to you. God
T-14..... VI.6:4 it **m.** if its Interpreter is not its maker.
T-17..... VI.4:6 but only because the goal has made it **m.**.
T-17.... VII.1:6 the situation would have been **m.** to you,
T-19........ I.1:4 is perceived as **m.** and as a whole. And
T-21..... III.4:7 For faith and vision and belief are **m.** only
T-21..... IV.8:7 not made **m.** by repetition and by clamor.
T-21....... V.6:4 it. It is not **m.** to ask if what must be is so.
T-21....... V.6:5 But it is **m.** to ask why you are unaware of
T-23....... II.1:2 Chaotic laws are hardly **m.**, and therefore
T-25..... VI.5:3 is the only function **m.** in time. It is the
T-25.... VII.6:7 be, to make that viewpoint **m.** and sane.
T-25.... VII.7:1 appears most sensible and **m.** to you. The
T-25... VIII.6:1 **m.** to understand the Holy Spirit's justice.
T-26........ I.5:1 world that gives it sense and makes it **m.**.
T-26....... V.1:9 take, while time remains and choice is **m.**.
T-26.. VII.12:3 can leave their source made real and **m.**.
T-27..... IV.6:7 asking not if sacrifice is **m.** at all. And so,
T-30.... VII.6:2 **m.** to you and to your brother. Thus can
W-in.......... 1:1 to make the exercises in this workbook **m.**
W-pI....... 4.3:2 separating the meaningless from the **m.**.
W-pI....... 4.3:3 as outside you, and the **m.** within. It is
W-pI..... 19.4:3 of lack of order in miracles **m.** to you.
W-pI..... 25.2:1 in it as **m.** in terms of ego goals. These
W-pI..... 25.4:6 makes your contact with him **m.** or not.
W-pI.. 126.8:2 same. You will need help to make this **m.**,
W-pI 134.10:1 choice in terms that render choosing **m.**,
W-pI 135.10:5 fail to see where hope must lie if it be **m.**.
W-pI 135.19:2 and this life becomes a **m.** encounter with
W-pI.. 136.1:3 Being causeless and without a **m.** intent of
W-pI.. 140.9:3 that there can never be a **m.** distinction
W-pI.. 164.1:6 the Voice for God more clear, more **m.**,
W-pI 169.12:1 holding all its parts in **m.** relationships,
WpI...rV.in4:2 of this thought, or helps it be more **m.**,
W-pI.. 184.3:4 meaning and will then be seen as **m.**; a
W-pI.. 200.4:2 you, though you sought to make them **m.**.
M-8........... 6:5 only two categories are **m.** in sorting out
C-1........... 2:3 of an "individual mind" seems to be **m.**. It
C-2........... 4:4 and you can see the only answer that is **m.**
P-2......... II.4:4 Nor is belief in God a really **m.** concept,
P-2......... II.6:7 His eyes is too fragmented to be **m.**.
P-2........ IV.5:3 where "degrees of error" is a **m.** concept.

## meaningfully 7

| | |
|---|---|
| T-1 II.2:1 | personal and cannot be m. translated. |
| T-2 VIII.5:6 | apply it m. and at any time to everything |
| T-7 III.1:11 | be m. perceived as belonging to anyone at |
| T-20 VII.4:6 | it is, the body cannot m. be invested with |
| T-21 III.11:4 | opposites, and cannot m. join in any way. |
| W-pI 184.5:3 | achieved, and concepts can be m. shared. |
| W-pII 257.1:4 | may unify our thoughts and actions m., |

## meaningfulness 1

| | |
|---|---|
| T-27 IV.6:2 | question does the m. of the answer come. |

## meaningless 198

| | |
|---|---|
| T-1 VI.3:5 | Ultimately, space is as m. as time. Both |
| T-3 I.2:5 | words are m.. It has been particularly |
| T-3 IV.1:9 | This is because they are m. to each other. |
| T-3 V.6:4 | in the usual sense becomes utterly m.. |
| T-5 I.1:7 | To spirit getting is m. and giving is all. |
| T-5 II.6:4 | power is unlimited and choice is m.. |
| T-5 III.5:2 | Both time and delay are m. in eternity. I |
| T-5 V.2:11 | is a totally m. concept except to the ego, |
| T-5 VI.12:5 | God in time, also knows that time is m.. |
| T-6 I.18:3 | to teach that all forms of rejection are m.. |
| T-6 IV.8:4 | When they are perfect, abilities are m.. It |
| T-6 V.A.3:4 | is meaningful, but to be one body is m.. |
| T-6 V.A.3:5 | By the laws of mind, then, the body is m.. |
| T-6 V.A.4:9 | Without a range, order of difficulty is m., |
| T-7 I.6:5 | the useful, the m. into the meaningful, |
| T-7 III.1:12 | perception makes it m. by eliminating or |
| T-7 IV.6:10 | you have made the laws m. to you. Yet the |
| T-7 IV.6:11 | Yet the laws are not m., since all meaning |
| T-7 VI.6:3 | engender by perceiving conflict as m.. I |
| T-7 VI.6:4 | the conflict exactly as it is, and it *is* m.. The |
| T-7 VI.6:5 | you to realize that, because conflict is m., |
| T-7 VI.11:10 | You cannot make the m. meaningful. |
| T-8 IV.4:7 | be what you want, or it will be m. to you. |
| T-8 VIII.6:6 | are m. there is no point in analyzing them |
| T-9 I.9:4 | In the security of reality, fear is totally m.. |
| T-9 I.13:6 | orders of reality make reality m., and |
| T-9 IV.4:7 | you must accept the m. to save yourself. |
| T-9 V.3:1 | real, and that anything they contain is m.. |
| T-9 VI.7:6 | offer. Everything else would be totally m.. |
| T-9 VII.6:8 | is m. within the ego's thought system, |
| T-9 VII.7:10 | true. If it does not, He knows that it is m.. |
| T-9 VIII.2:4 | Without this belief grandiosity is m., and |
| T-10 IV.4:8 | "Laws of chaos" is a m. term. Creation is |
| T-10 V.13:3 | Your gifts to yourself are m., but your |
| T-11 I.5:4 | Infinity is m. without you, and you are |
| T-11 I.5:4 | without you, and you are m. without God |
| T-11 V.3:2 | contradiction in terms that makes it m.. |
| T-11 V.14:3 | the mistake consistent truth must be m.. |
| T-11 V.14:5 | If consistent truth is m., inconsistency |
| T-12 I.6:8 | of reality are m. in your divided state, His |
| T-12 I.9:9 | predominance, fear becomes m.. You |
| T-14 VI.4:3 | belief that you can have them both is m.. |
| T-14 VI.7:3 | will not attempt to communicate the m.. |
| T-14 IX.2:6 | Different realities are m., for reality must |
| T-14 X.8:8 | Yet they but study form with m. content. |
| T-15 XI.8:1 | for the time of Christ is m. apart from joy. |
| T-16 IV.1:8 | hate with love that makes love m. to you. |
| T-16 V.13:1 | than a m. attempt to raise other gods |
| T-16 VI.4:1 | relationship is totally m. without a body. |
| T-17 I.4:4 | truth is to destroy it by rendering it m.. |
| T-17 II.4:2 | will be m. when it has been perfected, for |
| T-18 I.5:6 | into m. bits of disunited perceptions, and |
| T-18 I.6:3 | loss is m. and only increase is conceivable |
| T-18 I.7:7 | and totally m. patterns that need not be |
| T-18 III.8:5 | and m. journey that you undertook apart, |
| T-18 VIII.4:1 | aware of all this strange and m. activity. |
| T-18 IX.2:5 | limited, and so fragmented they are m.. |
| T-18 IX.12:6 | learning that everything you learned is m. |
| T-19 III.4:4 | that cannot be corrected is m. to Him. |
| T19 IV.A.11:7 | What love would look upon is m. to fear, |
| T19 IV.D.10:5 | A journey without a purpose is still m., |
| T19 IV.D.19:3 | purpose, without which is the journey m.. |
| T19 IV.D.21:2 | undertakes to do what he believes is m.. |
| T19 IV.D.21:5 | Beyond this, they are m.. You and your |
| T-20 III.7:8 | tiny and so m. it slips unnoticed through |
| T-20 V.3:4 | the fear that rises from the m. attempt to |
| T-20 VI.3:5 | The love of them has made love m.. They |
| T-20 VI.5:2 | a m. enclosure carefully protected, yet |
| T-20 VI.8:6 | all your relationships were made m.. In |
| T-20 VI.12:7 | Idolatry is past and m.. Perhaps you fear |
| T-20 VII.7:5 | Either is m. without the end for which it |
| T-21 in.1:9 | is why order of difficulty in miracles is m.. |
| T-21 II.12:4 | power to create, and what he makes is m.. |
| T-22 I.10:6 | illusions is to recognize that fear is m.. |
| T-22 II.1:2 | Only to the ego, to which truth is m., do |
| T-22 II.4:4 | against the truth makes all truth m., and |
| T-22 II.9:3 | is the m. idea that thoughts can leave the |
| T-22 V.4:1 | How weak is fear; how little and how m.. |
| T-23 in.4:5 | Would you, for all these m. distractions, |
| T-23 I.3:8 | two are as m. as one or as a thousand. |
| T-23 I.3:10 | The victory it seeks is m. as is itself. |
| T-23 II.1:5 | for, because it is their purpose to make m. |
| T-23 IV.5:8 | may battle, but the clash of forms is m.. |
| T-24 I.2:3 | and m. decisions have been made and |
| T-25 I.7:1 | concept of a Oneness joined as One is m.. |
| T-25 III.1:2 | to which you recognize that guilt is m., to |
| T-25 V.1:2 | purpose, and is m. without the goal of sin |
| T-25 V.1:4 | Each is m. alone, but seems to draw a |
| T-25 VII.4:9 | This world is m. *because* it rests on sin. |
| T-25 VII.6:3 | one perceives the other as insane and m.. |
| T-26 V.2:1 | ever lost but time, which in the end is m.. |
| T-26 V.2:2 | quite m. to the real Teacher of the world. |
| T-26 X.2:5 | And only some are seen as m.. And this |
| T-27 III.1:3 | Weak strength is m., and power used to |
| T-27 III.2:2 | to you, for he stands for what is m.. He |
| T-27 III.5:6 | time when aids are m. and learning done. |
| T-28 II.2:11 | sickness is a m. attempt to give effects to |
| T-28 IV.5:4 | own. Identity in dreams is m. because the |
| T-28 V.2:2 | Unshared, they are perceived as m.. The |
| T-28 V.4:4 | and sounds the body can perceive are m.. |
| T-29 II.6:6 | Stability to those who are confused is m., |
| T-30 III.5:4 | For more than whole is m.. If there were |
| T-30 V.5:4 | sin be seen without a purpose, and as m.. |
| T-31 V.8:1 | A concept of the self is m., for no one |
| T-31 V.15:4 | of yourself will still remain quite m.. And |
| T-31 VII.2:2 | sometimes, but will not see them as m.. |
| T-31 VII.14:1 | that it is but a wish, insane and m., to |
| W-pI 4.3:2 | of separating the m. from the meaningful. |
| W-pI 4.3:3 | of learning to see the m. as outside you, |
| W-pI 10.3:1 | thoughts of which you are aware are m., |
| W-pI 11.h | My m. thoughts are showing me a |
| W-pI 11.h | thoughts are showing me a m. world. |
| W-pI 12.h | I am upset because I see a m. world. |
| W-pI 12.1:4 | given it by you. The world is m. in itself. |
| W-pI 12.4:4 | add: *But I am upset because I see a m. world.* |
| W-pI 12.5:1 | What is m. is neither good nor bad. Why |
| W-pI 12.5:2 | Why, then, should a m. world upset you? |
| W-pI 12.5:3 | If you could accept the world as m. and |
| W-pI 12.5:4 | But because it is m., you are impelled to |
| W-pI 12.5:6 | It is this that is m. in truth. Beneath your |
| W-pI 13.h | A m. world engenders fear. |
| W-pI 13.1:2 | Actually, a m. world is impossible. |
| W-pI 13.3:1 | that you learn to recognize the m., and |
| W-pI 13.4:4 | *I am looking at a m. world.* Repeat this |
| W-pI 13.4:7 | *m. world engenders fear because I think I am* |
| W-pI 14.h | God did not create a m. world. |
| W-pI 14.1:1 | the reason why a m. world is impossible. |
| W-pI 14.6:8 | today's idea: *God did not create a m. world.* |
| W-pI 14.7:4 | *God did not create a m. world. He did not* |
| W-pI 23.1:2 | else will work; everything else is m.. But |
| W-pI 25.1:4 | Therefore, it is m. to you. Everything is |
| W-pI 25.5:2 | The recognition that they are m., rather |
| W-pI 44.6:1 | that its opposition and its fears are m.. |
| W-pI 51.4:8 | My thoughts are m., but all creation lies |
| W-pI 52.5:7 | with my pitiful and m. "private" thoughts |
| W-pI 53.1:1 | (11) My m. thoughts are showing me a |
| W-pI 53.1:1 | thoughts are showing me a m. world. |
| W-pI 53.2:1 | (12) I am upset because I see a m. world. |
| W-pI 53.3:1 | (13) A m. world engenders fear. The |
| W-pI 53.4:1 | (14) God did not create a m. world. How |
| W-pI 53.4:2 | a m. world exist if God did not create it? |
| W-pI 63.2:4 | no trivial purpose or m. desire in its place |
| W-pI 66.3:1 | to go past this wholly m. battle and arrive |
| W-pI 74.3:13 | *but God's. These conflict thoughts are m..* |
| W-pI 91.2:9 | of the darkness makes the idea of light m. |
| W-pI 93.3:1 | from which such idle thoughts are m.. |
| W-pI 93.6:6 | self you made, evil and full of sin, is m.. |
| W-pI 96.3:7 | then the body must be m. to your reality. |
| W-pI 104.2:1 | Today we would remove all m. and self- |
| W-pI 106.2:1 | which silences the thunder of the m., and |
| W-pI 106.3:2 | Walk lightly past their m. persuasion. |
| W-pI 122.4:2 | given to imperfect questions, m. requests, |
| W-pI 124.4:2 | No m. anxieties can come between our |
| W-pI 125.6:2 | a while, and m. desires have been stilled. |
| W-pI 130.7:2 | will not make a thousand m. distinctions, |
| W-pI 131.2:1 | Goals that are m. are not attained. There |
| W-pI 131.2:2 | you strive for them are m. as they are. |
| W-pI 131.15:1 | from dismal thoughts and m. laments. |
| W-pI 134.2:4 | God's creation, and to pardon that is m.. |
| W-pI 135.17:3 | Yet what remains is m. indeed. For it is |
| W-pI 136.1:5 | It dispels this m. illusion by the same |
| W-pI 136.13:4 | time is but another m. defense you made |
| W-pI 136.16:3 | nor their obscure and m. pursuits with |
| W-pI 151.8:1 | so great that doubt is m. before Its face. |
| W-pI 153.14:2 | where truth abides and games are m.. So |
| W-pI 161.5:3 | for symbols can stand for the m.. Love |
| W-pI 165.7:3 | Your doubts are m., for God is certain. |
| W-pI 169.5:4 | speak, for in that knowledge words are m. |
| W-pI 185.13:3 | To take away is m. to Him. And when it is |
| W-pI 185.13:4 | And when it is as m. to you, you can be |
| W-pI 189.3:4 | all. The other one is wholly m.. A world in |
| W-pI 194.4:6 | no more, and future dread will now be m. |
| W-pI 200.8:3 | frantic, vain pursuits, and m. endeavors. |
| W-pII 264.1:3 | *disappears, and place becomes a m. belief.* |
| W-pII 281.1:4 | *and put my little m. ideas in place of where* |
| M-3 3:1 | is a concept as m. in reality as is time. The |
| M-4 I.A.7:4 | out was m. in teaching him the difference. |
| M-11 3:2 | that is m. to those who believe in them. |
| M-13 1:1 | in truth the term sacrifice is altogether m. |
| M-14 1:11 | them not. It merely overlooked the m.. |
| M-14 3:9 | No; it is m. to anyone here. Yet it is the |
| M-15 3:2 | They are too small and m. to occupy your |
| M-16 1:1 | teacher of God this question is m.. There |
| M-16 10:8 | it is dangerous, but merely that it is m.. |
| M-18 3:5 | And truth becomes diminutive and m.. |
| M-19 1:4 | for error is impossible and correction m.. |
| M-19 5:8 | becomes m. and indefensible. Perception |
| M-20 3:4 | circumstance proclaims that peace is m., |
| M-20 3:11 | Yet when peace is found, the war is m.. |
| M-21 5:9 | raising them from m. symbols to the Call |
| M-22 1:4 | Partial Atonement is a m. idea, just as |
| M-22 7:6 | Both are equally m.. Yet this will not be |
| M-24 4:2 | the validity of reincarnation become m.. |
| M-27 4:10 | make fear. Both are equally m. to Him. |
| M-27 6:9 | are mindless magic, ineffectual and m.. |
| M-28 3:4 | Attack is m. and peace has come. The |
| C-2 8:4 | to ask, and even make the question m.? |
| P-3 II.8:1 | that order of difficulty in healing is m.. |

## meaninglessly 1

| | |
|---|---|
| T-7 III.5:3 | that to question reality is to question m.. |

## meaninglessness 6

| | |
|---|---|
| T-7 VIII.6:5 | unbelievable. The m. of perception based |
| T-9 VIII.1:3 | presence of the grandeur of God the m. of |
| T-11 in.3:10 | There you will see that it rested on m., |
| W-pI 13.2:1 | Recognition of m. arouses intense |
| W-pI 13.2:2 | in the empty space that m. provides. The |
| M-16 11:9 | the forms of magic and perceive their m.. |

## meanings 1

| | |
|---|---|
| T-30 VII.3:3 | If they are given different m., it must be |

## Means 2

*means*

| | |
|---|---|
| T-24 VII.6:5 | it. God is a M. as well as End. In Heaven, |
| W-pII 302.2:3 | and He the M. by which we go to Him. |

**means** 340
- noun
- *verb*
- *Means*

T-1 I.11:2 It is a **m.** of communication of the created
T-1 I.15:3 thus a teaching device and a **m.** to an end.
T-1 I.28:3 Miracles are thus a **m.** and revelation is an
T-1 III.3:1 The forgiven are the **m.** of the Atonement
T-1 VII.3:6 Fantasies are a **m.** of making false
T-1 VII.5:10 **m.** are being carefully explained to you.
T-1 VII.5:11 to you, but to reach it the **m.** are needed.
T-2 II.3:2 The **m.** are easier to understand after the
T-2 II.3:6 have little difficulty in clarifying the **m.**.
T-2 II.3:7 The **m.** are available whenever you ask.
T-2 III.1:4 be used as a **m.** for attaining "atonement."
T-2 III.5:2 more comfortable by inappropriate **m.**.
T-2 III.5:3 But the real **m.** are already provided, and
T-2 III.5:12 world as a **m.** of healing the separation.
T-2 IV.1:2 The miracle is the **m.**, the Atonement is
T-2 IV.2:3 as the **m.** of correcting level confusion, for
T-2 IV.4:1 All material **m.** that you accept as
T-2 V.9:3 healing is needed as a **m.** of protection.
T-2 VII.7:4 but it is by no **m.** necessarily undivided.
T-3 III.4:3 It is, however, a **m.** of right perception,
T-3 V.1:3 was the **m.** for the return to knowledge,
T-4 I.6:5 interaction as a **m.** of ego preservation. I
T-4 VI.3:7 but you are by no **m.** convinced as yet.
T-5 II.2:5 **m.** by which the Atonement heals until
T-5 V.1:4 mind has the **m.** at its disposal to side
T-6 II.3:5 is always a **m.** of justifying attack. Anger
T-6 IV.9:5 both a Guide to find it and a **m.** to keep it.
T-6 V.A.5:5 the body only as a **m.** of communication,
T-7 VII.8:1 you perceived it as a **m.** of depriving you
T-7 VIII.1:5 the law is perceived as a **m.** of getting rid
T-7 IX.6:3 forever, He gave you the **m.** for keeping it.
T-8 III.7:7 why He has given you the **m.** for undoing
T-8 IV.5:7 mind is the **m.** by which you determine
T-8 VII.h The Body as a **M.** of Communication
T-8 VII.2:1 the body only as a **m.** of communication.
T-8 VII.2:5 not regard bodies solely as a **m.** of joining
T-8 VII.4:5 If the body becomes a **m.** you give to the
T-8 VII.9:5 It becomes a **m.** by which the part of the
T-8 VII.13:3 To see a body as anything except a **m.** of
T-8 VII.14:5 To conceive of the body as a **m.** of attack
T-8 VIII.h The Body as **M.** or End
T-8 VIII.2:3 between **m.** and end as it always does.
T-9 VII.1:2 He not have given you the **m.** to find it? If
T-10 in.1:2 time solely as a **m.** to regain eternity. You
T-10 V.11:6 the **m.** for undoing what you have made.
T-11 V.6:8 for God into a **m.** of establishing itself.
T-12 I.9:4 The **m.** for removing it is in yourself, and
T-12 V.9:3 the **m.** and the end are in complete accord
T-13 IV.8:4 interpretation of the **m.** of salvation that
T-13 IX.4:1 **m.** by which the Holy Spirit can separate
T-13 X.4:5 your brothers as a **m.** to "solve" the past,
T-14 in.1:3 the **m.** for learning it and seeing it quite
T-14 IV.9:2 the **m.** of restoring guiltlessness to minds
T-14 VI.5:1 as a **m.** for breaking your communication
T-14 VI.5:2 Holy Spirit reinterprets it as a **m.** of re-
T-14 VII.5:8 translated by the Holy Spirit from **m.** of
T-14 VII.5:8 to **m.** of preservation and release. His task
T-14 X.12:6 The miracle becomes the **m.** of sharing It.
T-14 XI.7:2 **m.** on which you can depend for miracles
T-15 IX.2:6 Yet it remains the only **m.** by which you
T-15 IX.3:3 you will choose to utilize the **m.** by which
T-15 IX.7:1 no value on it as a **m.** of getting anything,
T-15 XI.7:2 as the necessary **m.** of communication.
T-17 III.2:6 bodies can be seen as **m.** for vengeance.
T-17 III.5:1 the body as a **m.** of communication into
T-17 V.14:3 arrange the **m.** for its accomplishment? It
T-17 V.14:4 and the **m.** as they stand now which
T-17 V.14:7 still separate and divided on the **m.**. Yet
T-17 V.14:8 and the **m.** will surely fall in place because
T-17 VI.3:5 was set with which to bring the **m.** in line.
T-17 VI.4:1 the situation as a **m.** to *make* it happen.
T-17 VII.5:1 you find yourself is but a **m.** to meet the
T-17 VII.9:3 will see the **m.** you once employed to lead
T-17 VII.9:3 to illusions transformed to **m.** for truth.
T-17 VIII.3:4 **m.** for establishing His purpose, and
T-17 VIII.5:8 and it will be a **m.** for bringing only this.
T-18 II.5:17 It is the **m.** by which you try to make your
T-18 II.6:1 dreams and uses them as **m.** for waking.
T-18 II.7:1 Your special relationship will be a **m.** for
T-18 II.7:6 Him as **m.** for the salvation of everyone.
T-18 V.1:3 the **m.** by which salvation is accomplished
T-18 V.3:6 The **m.** and purpose both belong to Him.
T-18 V.3:8 A purpose such as this, without the **m.**, is
T-18 V.3:9 the **m.** to anyone who shares His purpose.
T-18 V.4:4 The alignment of **m.** and purpose is an
T-18 V.4:5 bring unholy **m.** to its accomplishment.
T-18 V.4:6 is required to receive the **m.** and use them
T-18 VI.5:1 reinterpreted as **m.** for salvation, and
T-18 VII.1:3 end and not a **m.** in your interpretation,
T-18 VII.4:11 **m.** are tedious and very time consuming,
T-18 VII.5:1 will be different, not in purpose but in **m.**.
T-18 VII.5:2 A holy relationship is a **m.** of saving time.
T-18 VII.6:4 special **m.** this course is using to save you
T-18 VII.6:5 on using **m.** which have served others well
T-18 VIII.5:3 but by no **m.** totally dependent on its one
T-19 I.5:10 a **m.** for seeking out reality through attack
T-19 IV.1:5 in which He will bring **m.** and goal in line.
T19 IV.A.17:7 better **m.** for communication of salvation,
T19 IV.B.10:5 pain. It is a **m.**, and not an end. It has no
T19 IV.B.10:7 to be whatever is the **m.** for reaching the
T19 IV.B.10:8 can see the **m.** for its accomplishment,
T-20 III.8:10 Ask not the **m.** of its attainment of the
T-20 III.8:11 Give it no power to adjust the **m.** and end.
T-20 V.5:5 **m.** and end have not been brought in line.
T-20 V.6:6 **m.** and end in perfect harmony already.
T-20 VII.h The Consistency of **M.** and End
T-20 VII.1:1 much about discrepancies of **m.** and end,
T-20 VII.1:2 But we have also said the **m.** to meet the
T-20 VII.1:4 where **m.** and end are still discrepant.
T-20 VII.2:2 the **m.** to Him Who changed the purpose.
T-20 VII.2:4 Are you not also willing to accept the **m.**?
T-20 VII.2:6 A purpose is attained by **m.**, and if you
T-20 VII.2:6 you must be willing to want the **m.** as well
T-20 VII.2:7 yet I do not want to learn the **m.** to get it?
T-20 VII.3:2 He asks no more to give the **m.** as well.
T-20 VII.3:3 The **m.** are second to the goal. And when
T-20 VII.3:4 the purpose frightens you, and not the **m.**
T-20 VII.3:5 the error of believing the **m.** are difficult.
T-20 VII.3:9 the **m.** to do so must be possible as well.
T-20 VII.5:1 The body *is* the **m.** by which the ego tries
T-20 VII.5:5 **m.** remain unquestioned while the end is
T-20 VII.7:3 Both are but **m.**, each one appropriate to
T-20 VII.7:6 **m.** seem real because the goal is valued.
T-20 VII.8:2 denied the **m.** the Holy Spirit offers you to
T-20 VII.8:3 achieve its purpose through the **m.** of sin?
T-20 VII.8:10 the **m.** for its attainment will be evaluated
T-20 VII.9:5 The **m.** is vision. For what the seeing look
T-20 VIII.2:6 the **m.** by which its happy end is yours is
T-20 VIII.2:7 not that you need make either **m.** or end.
T-20 VIII.6:9 its most holy purpose bereft of **m.** for its
T-20 VIII.7:1 senseless **m.** to play the idle game of death
T-20 VIII.9:6 are the **m.** by which the outside world,
T-20 VIII.10:4 Vision is the **m.** by which the Holy Spirit
T-21 I.3:5 Your question is whether the **m.** by which
T-21 III.4:1 Faith and belief and vision are the **m.** by
T-21 III.5:5 as **m.** for losing certainty and finding sin.
T-21 III.6:1 Holy Spirit has a use for all the **m.** for sin
T-21 III.6:3 sees the **m.** you use, but not the purpose
T-21 III.6:4 sees their value as a **m.** for what He wills
T-21 III.6:6 The Holy Spirit sees perception as a **m.** to
T-21 III.7:1 as all the **m.** that once served sin are
T-21 III.7:3 because the **m.** for sin are dear to you.
T-21 III.8:2 They have renounced the **m.** for sin by
T-21 III.10:5 the **m.** for sin in which the mind believes.
T-21 III.10:7 is sacrifice invariably a **m.** for limitation,
T-21 III.12:3 to serve as **m.** to help the blind to see. But
T-21 V.7:10 this. Reason is a **m.** that serves the Holy
T-21 V.7:12 For reason is beyond the ego's range of **m.**
T-21 V.9:3 use it have gained a **m.** which cannot be
T-21 V.10:6 and all the **m.** for its accomplishment.
T-21 VI.5:2 it also has the **m.** to make its purpose real.
T-21 VI.7:10 as is the purpose for which it is the **m.**,
T-21 VI.8:7 Be willing to let reason be the **m.** by which
T-21 VII.9:4 helpless, the **m.** to see it will be given you.
T-22 II.5:3 And if this seeing is the only **m.** by which
T-22 II.5:6 the **m.** for its attainment are more than
T-22 II.6:2 the **m.** to let the Holy Spirit's purpose be
T-22 III.6:4 For this the body's eyes are perfect **m.**,
T-22 V.3:3 it. See how the **m.** and the material of evil
T-22 VI.1:5 For one you see as **m.**; the other, end. And
T-22 VI.1:7 own. **M.** serve the end, and as the end is
T-22 VI.1:7 is reached the value of the **m.** decreases,
T-22 VI.1:10 the other serve his choice as **m.** to find it.
T-22 VI.2:1 the mind is used as **m.** whose value lies in
T-22 VI.3:1 of **m.** and end so easily in what God loves,
T-22 VI.3:2 that you can be the **m.** to serve His end.
T-22 VI.3:5 the soft transition from **m.** to end as easy
T-22 VI.4:1 chosen of your Father as a **m.** for His Own
T-22 VI.5:7 The **m.** of sinlessness can know no fear
T-22 VI.6:6 are now His **m.** must love all that He loves
T-22 VI.6:9 a relationship that has become the **m.** of
T-23 I.1:3 The **m.** of war are not the means of peace,
T-23 I.1:3 The means of war are not the **m.** of peace,
T-23 I.2:12 think that it is possible, the **m.** seem real.
T-23 II.13:12 The **m.** of madness must be insane. Are
T-23 II.14:7 These are the **m.** by which the laws of God
T-23 IV.3:5 Creation is the **m.** for God's extension,
T-24 I.4:3 specialness become a **m.** and end at once.
T-24 IV.2:11 See it as **m.** to hurt, and it is hurt. See it as
T-24 IV.2:12 hurt. See it as **m.** to heal, and it is healed.
T-24 IV.4:1 not the **m.** by which salvation is attained,
T-24 VI.12:5 of truth itself is given to provide the **m.**,
T-24 VI.13:7 the **m.** for effortless accomplishment and
T-24 VII.5:6 it has no purpose, and is **m.** for nothing.
T-24 VII.5:7 as **m.** for truth shares in its holiness, and
T-24 VII.6:4 Here you are but **m.**, along with it. God is
T-24 VII.6:6 In Heaven, **m.** and end are one, and one
T-24 VII.7:4 Here do the **m.** and end unite as one, nor
T-24 VII.8:3 Here are the **m.** and the purpose separate
T-24 VII.8:6 Perception does not seem to be a **m.**. And
T-24 VII.9:6 It is the **m.** to make your wish come true.
T-24 VII.10:7 the **m.** to serve his "father's" purpose. Not
T-24 VII.10:8 a **m.** to offer to the "father" what he wants
T-25 I.1:2 body merely seems to be the **m.** to do it.
T-25 I.3:5 behold, for **m.** and end are never separate
T-25 I.4:1 *You* are the **m.** for God; not separate, nor
T-25 II.4:3 for the form is but a **m.** for content. And
T-25 II.4:4 frame is but a **m.** to hold the picture up,
T-25 III.3:4 and to each it is a perfect **m.** to serve the
T-25 III.6:5 before was **m.** to justify his anger turned
T-25 III.9:8 all time becomes a **m.** to reach a goal.
T-25 IV.1:7 that makes the choice of **m.** inevitable,
T-25 IV.1:8 And then the **m.** are chosen once again, as
T-25 IV.2:5 chose it as a **m.** to gain these same effects,
T-25 V.5:2 be fulfilled is but the **m.** to let yours be.
T-25 VI.5:4 is the **m.** the Holy Spirit uses to translate
T-25 VI.5:11 thus become a **m.** to save instead of lose.
T-25 VI.6:5 He has the **m.** for either, as he always did.
T-25 VI.6:6 God appoint to be the **m.** for his salvation
T-26 II.5:5 God offers you the **m.** to see his innocence
T-26 IV.1:6 Forgiveness thus becomes the **m.** by
T-26 VII.19:2 **m.** whereby your brother finds the peace
T-27 II.5:6 Your body can be **m.** to teach that it has
T-27 II.16:5 lies the **m.** whereby your mind is unified.
T-27 III.5:5 Forgiveness is the **m.** by which the truth is
T-27 VI.1:4 for they both are **m.** to make the body real
T-27 VI.1:8 Thus are they **m.** for nothing, for they
T-27 VII.5:2 the world provides the **m.** by which this
T-27 VII.5:3 The **m.** attest the purpose, but are not
T-27 VII.13:5 and gave him **m.** to waken without fear.
T-28 I.2:8 and to be the **m.** for something else. It can
T-28 I.5:2 not seek to use it as a **m.** to keep the past,
T-29 IV.6:5 as **m.** to serve the function given Him.
T-29 V.8:5 Forgiving dreams are **m.** to step aside
T-29 VII.9:9 the **m.** by which this idol can be saved.
T-29 VIII.8:12 An idol is a **m.** for getting more. And it is
T-30 IV.8:13 be, except a **m.** to give him to Himself?
T-30 V.2:6 and the **m.** by which it can be gained can
T-30 VII.4:1 is the only **m.** whereby perception can be
T-30 VIII.2:1 The miracle is **m.** to demonstrate that all
T-31 I.11:2 the **m.** whereby the choice is reassessed;
T-31 II.3:6 or enemy becomes a **m.** to help you save
T-31 IV.2:9 And each is but the **m.** to gain that end,

T-31......VI.4:2 The **m.** are given you by which to see the
T-31.....VII.1:2 Salvation does not seek to use a **m.** as yet
W-pI.....43.2:4 it must become the **m.** for the restoration
W-pI.....43.2:7 Healed perception becomes the **m.** by
W-pI.....46.2:5 It is the **m.** by which illusions disappear.
W-pI.....60.1:4 Yet forgiveness is the **m.** by which I will
W-pI.....63.1:2 **m.** for letting this be done through you!
W-pI.....63.3:5 *I am the **m.** God has appointed for the*
W-pI.....64.4:2 function is to be happy by using the **m.** by
W-pI.....66.3:3 and determining the **m.** for achieving it.
W-pI.....70.9:2 the clouds by whatever **m.** appeals to you.
W-pI.....72.2:4 be the best **m.** to expand communication.
W-pI.....77.5:3 the **m.** by which this is accomplished. You
W-pI.....79.6:3 understand that you have the **m.** to solve
W-pI.....79.6:4 And you would use the **m.**, because you
W-pI.....80.7:3 The **m.** is simple honesty. Do not deceive
W-pI.....82.1:2 My forgiveness is the **m.** by which the
W-pI.....82.1:3 me. My forgiveness is the **m.** by which I
W-pI.....82.1:4 me. My forgiveness is the **m.** by which the
W-pI.....85.1:7 this will be the **m.** by which I will succeed.
W-pI.....96.2:1 what **m.** you use and where you see the
W-pI.....96.4:1 of mind as **m.** to find its Self expression.
W-pI.....99.2:4 the **m.** by which you can escape illusions.
W-pI.....99.4:2 and offer **m.** by which they are undone
W-pI...100.3:4 **m.** to save the world is dim and lusterless,
W-pI...105.3:2 would avoid the only **m.** by which you can
W-pI...110.2:4 is enough to let time be the **m.** for all the
WpI . rIII.in6:4 the **m.** the Holy Spirit uses will not fail.
WpI . rIII.in7:4 Holy Spirit's chosen **m.** for your salvation.
WpI . rIII.in7:5 His **m.** must surely merit yours as well.
W-pI...122.8:2 Forgiveness is the **m.** by which it comes to
W-pI...125.2:2 No other **m.** can save it, for God's plan is
W-pI...126.1:3 the **m.** by which salvation comes to you,
W-pI...126.6:4 a **m.** for your release from what you see in
W-pI...126.7:5 as the **m.** by which it is attained, must
W-pI...131.2:2 for the **m.** by which you strive for them
W-pI...131.2:3 Who can use such senseless **m.**, and hope
W-pI.135.12:1 is best, the **m.** by which it is achieved, nor
W-pI.135.13:2 is not free to be the **m.** of helping in a plan
W-pI.135.14:2 the **m.** by which a frightened mind would
W-pI...137.9:1 are the **m.** by which the Holy Spirit urges
W-pI...138.7:2 it be a **m.** for demonstrating hell is real,
W-pI.154.13:2 *that I have the **m.** by which to recognize that*
W-pI.159.10:8 His vision gives the **m.** for a return to our
W-pI...168.2:4 the **m.** by which His Will is recognized?
W-pI...168.2:6 the **m.** of Him whereby its sleep is done.
W-pI...168.4:2 the **m.** by which this world will disappear,
W-pI...168.5:3 by giving us the **m.** to lay them down, and
W-pI...170.4:1 If you consider carefully the **m.** by which
WpI rV.in12:2 comes from practice, not the **m.** we use.
W-pI...184.2:1 the **m.** by which the world's perception is
W-pI...184.9:5 They become but **m.** by which you can
W-pI...185.5:2 seeks the **m.** which bring illusions. He has
W-pI...185.6:2 is genuine, the **m.** for finding it is given, in
W-pI...186.2:4 The **m.** are given us by which it will be
W-pI...188.5:3 **m.** for giving it are in his understanding.
W-pI...192.2:4 is the **m.** by which untruth can be undone
W-pI...192.2:6 earth, you need the **m.** to let illusions go.
W-pI...192.4:2 Forgiveness is the **m.** by which the fear of
W-pI...193.1:4 provides the **m.** to guarantee that it is
W-pI...193.2:5 gives the **m.** by which perception is made
W-pI...195.2:2 the certain **m.** whereby all pain is healed,
W-pI...200.4:5 But it is given you to find the **m.** whereby
W-pII......1.3:3 **m.** by which it would accomplish it as well
W-pII..247.1:3 For forgiveness is the only **m.** whereby
W-pII......4.1:2 is the **m.** by which the mind is driven mad
W-pII..256.1:9 forgiveness is the **m.** by which our minds
W-pII..257.2:1 *is Your chosen **m.** for our salvation. Let us*
W-pII......5.4:1 is the **m.** by which God's Son returns to
W-pII..269.1:2 *the **m.** which You have chosen to become the*
W-pII......6.2:5 Father placed the **m.** for your salvation,
W-pII......7.2:4 for it, becomes the **m.** to go beyond itself,
W-pII......7.3:2 Holy Spirit understands the **m.** you made,
W-pII......7.3:3 He will employ the **m.** you made for exile
W-pII..314.1:4 all the needed **m.** are happily provided.
W-pII..316.2:3 *provide the **m.** by which I can behold them,*
W-pII.....318.h In me salvation's **m.** and end are one.
W-pII..318.1:4 I am the **m.** by which God's Son is saved,
W-pII..318.1:8 Love. I am salvation's **m.** and end as well.
W-pII..327.2:4 *You give the **m.** whereby conviction comes,*
W-pII..332.1:8 and giving it the **m.** to realize the freedom
W-pII..332.2:3 *yet Your Love has given us the **m.** to set it free*
W-pII..336.1:1 the **m.** appointed for perception's ending.
W-pII..342.1:3 *given me the **m.** to prove its unreality to me.*
W-ep .........5:1 The end is certain, and the **m.** as well. To
M-in ..........2:5 to provide you with a **m.** of choosing what
M-4 ...........1:5 set in time as a **m.** of leading out of time.
M-16 .........3:2 This is by no **m.** the ultimate criterion,
M-29 .........7:5 He has given you the **m.** to prove it so.
M-29 .........8:4 *is given you to be the **m.** Through which His*
C-in ...........1:3 The **m.** of the Atonement is forgiveness.
C-4.............2:1 body's eyes are therefore not the **m.** by
C-4.............3:8 True perception is the **m.** by which the
P-1.............1:5 becomes the **m.** through which He offers
P-1.............5:6 is one of the **m.** He uses to save time, and
P-2......... II.9:8 in purpose and must thus be one in **m.**.
P-3...........I.4:3 his patients are the **m.** sent to him for his
P-3......... II.4:7 Yet it is the **m.** of return; the way God
S-1 .........in.2:4 God. Prayer now must be the **m.** by which
S-1 ........ III.1:4 becomes a **m.** for lifting your projections
S-1 ........ III.1:6 For this the **m.** is prayer, of rising power
S-2 ...........I.2:1 honest **m.** by which this goal is reached.
S-2 ...........I.3:2 that God has given you the **m.** by which
S-2 ......... II.7:3 Forgiveness is the **m.** for your escape.
S-2 ......... II.7:4 it is to make of it the **m.** for further slavery
S-2 ........ III.4:5 will He give the **m.** to you to learn of Him,
S-2 ........ III.6:7 and to make the **m.** for separation, sin

## means 194

• verb
*noun*
*Means*

T-in ...........1:5 *It **m.** only that you can elect what you want to*
T-1.........I.26:2 "Atoning" **m.** "undoing." The undoing of
T-1........ III.2:1 and earth shall pass away" **m.** that they
T-1........ III.4:7 "Lead us not into temptation" **m.**
T-1........ III.6:3 This **m.** that the perception of both must
T-1........ IV.4:2 is what the Bible **m.** by "There is no death
T-1......... V.3:4 as little children" **m.** that unless you fully
T-1......... V.5:7 To change your mind **m.** to place it at the
T-2......... IV.5:3 This **m.** that a miracle, to attain its full
T-2......... V.3:1 miracle-mindedness **m.** right-mindedness
T-2......... V.5:2 This **m.** you recognize that mind is the
T-2..... VIII.3:6 simply **m.** that everyone will finally come
T-3......... II.2:5 Innocent or true perception **m.** that you
T-3......... II.2:6 **m.** that you never see what does not exist,
T-3........ II.5:10 This is what the Bible **m.** when it says,
T-3........ III.1:4 Uncertainty **m.** that you do not know.
T-3........ III.2:2 or God. To recognize **m.** to "know again,"
T-3........ III.2:3 this **m.** that it is not whole or consistent.
T-3........ VI.1:4 it **m.** that if you judge the reality of others
T-3........ VI.9:4 It merely **m.** that you do not remember
T-4...........I.2:1 as they are, and learning **m.** change.
T-4......... II.6:8 "Self-esteem" in ego terms **m.** nothing
T-4........ III.1:1 of Heaven is within you" really **m.**. This is
T-4........ III.4:8 **m.** that it wants it without ambivalence,
T-4........ III.9:3 This one fact **m.** the ego does not exist,
T-4......IV.10:2 The Second Coming of Christ **m.** nothing
T-4......IV.10:9 **m.** that Christ has come into your mind
T-4........VII.5:5 That is what creation **m.**. "How," "what"
T-4........VII.6:2 This hardly **m.** that you should tell Him
T-5...........I.7:4 **m.** that although it does not engender
T-5........ II.11:3 Remember that "yoke" **m.** "join together,
T-5........ II.11:3 together," and "burden" **m.** "message."
T-5........ V.3:10 it. Listening to the ego's voice **m.** that you
T-5........ VI.8:3 the statement **m.** that in later generations
T-5........ VI.9:3 the ego, to be undone **m.** to be destroyed.
T-5........VII.3:6 willingness **m.** that you do not want to be
T-6...........I.3:3 Projection **m.** anger, anger fosters assault,
T-6........ II.11:7 because it **m.** that all perception is guided
T-6........ IV.3:4 **m.** that everyone has the answer *now.*
T-6......V.B.3:7 This **m.** conflicting motivation, and so the
T-6......V.B.8:4 since it **m.** that alternatives have been
T-7...........I.4:2 another **m.** that no bargains are possible.
T-7......... II.7:6 need extension because it ***m.*** extension.
T-7....... V.6:11 Understanding **m.** consistency because
T-7....... V.6:11 consistency because God **m.** consistency.
T-7........ VI.3:2 **m.** that the ego attacks what is preserving
T-7...... VI.12:1 to enter your mind **m.** that you have not
T-7...... VI.13:6 that opposes this **m.** anything at all. Being
T-7....... VII.1:8 is why denying any part of it **m.** you have
T-7......... X.5:9 this case, it always **m.** that the follower is.
T-7......... X.8:2 **m.** that you are confused about what you
T-8...........I.4:4 since it **m.** that you did not get what you
T-8........ III.3:6 can know what it **m.** only of God Himself.
T-8........ VI.7:1 in terms that actually **m.** nothing. When
T-8........ IX.8:1 and one that **m.** exactly what it says. I
T-8........ IX.9:2 only level at which healing **m.** anything.
T-9........ III.3:4 that nothing the ego makes **m.** anything.
T-9........ III.7:8 you make to correct a brother **m.** that you
T-9........ VI.3:7 is. Would you know what this **m.**? If what
T-9........ VI.5:3 waken you will learn what waking **m.**, and
T-9....... VII.7:7 nothing that arises from it **m.** anything.
T-9....VIII.10:9 it **m.** that you believe your evaluation of
T-10...... IV.3:5 This **m.** it is out of control. To be out of
T-10....... V.1:3 Depression **m.** that you have forsworn
T-10....... V.1:4 but they do not understand what it **m.**.
T-10....... V.3:3 But consider what this **m.** to you. Unless
T-10....... V.3:6 It **m.** that you are willing not to know
T-10....... V.6:4 of Him therefore **m.** that you love Him,
T-10....... V.8:5 for it **m.** that you are looking without love
T-11..... V.13:2 analyze **m.** to break down or to separate
T-11...... VI.2:5 confusion about what perception **m.**,
T-11...... VI.3:3 what it **m.** and therefore do not accept it.
T-11....VIII.2:2 they perceive, and so they ask what it **m.**.
T-12.........I.8:8 This is what recognizing fear really **m.**. If
T-12........II.9:6 them, for to lay aside **m.** to judge against.
T-12...... III.2:5 Insistence **m.** investment, and what you
T-12....... V.7:2 Translated into curricular terms this **m.**,
T-13.........I.8:4 this can understand what "always" **m.**,
T-13...... VI.1:3 **m.** that you perceive a brother only as you
T-14.........I.5:2 complex you cannot see that it **m.** nothing
T-14........II.1:5 goal depends **m.** absolutely nothing. Yet
T-14...... IV.1:7 The first in time **m.** nothing, but the First
T-14...... VI.4:5 do not realize that only one **m.** anything.
T-14...... VI.7:6 one **m.** nothing and the other everything,
T-14.....VII.7:4 that nothing you see **m.** anything alone.
T-14...... X.10:2 remembering Him **m.** you are not alone,
T-14...... XI.4:9 have learned apart from Him **m.** anything
T-14...... XI.5:4 absence of perfect peace **m.** but one thing:
T-14...... XI.6:7 *not know what anything, including this, **m.**.*
T-15.........I.1:1 you imagine what it **m.** to have no cares,
T-15...... III.8:5 You know not what love **m.** because you
T-15...... IV.1:2 And this **m.** only that you would rather
T-15...... IV.6:6 This **m.**, however, that it is a time in
T-15....... V.1:5 you do not understand what anything **m.**.
T-15....... V.3:1 of reality and understand what love **m.**. If
T-15........X.1:3 time nor season **m.** anything in eternity.
T-15........X.5:7 apart from sacrifice **m.** nothing to you.
T-16.........I.2:6 You do not know what empathizing **m.**.
T-16...... III.2:5 this acceptance **m.** that you are willing to
T-16...... VI.7:5 it **m.** only that you have been willing to let
T-16.....VII.2:5 in the present, and if it **m.** nothing now, it
T-17.........I.5:1 truth **m.** from the perspective of illusions?
T-17...... IV.5:3 this **m.** if you would be restored to sanity.
T-18........II.9:3 Its coming **m.** that you have chosen truth,
T-18...... III.3:8 doubt that what you think it **m.** *is* fearful.
T-18.....VII.1:3 this always **m.** you still find sin attractive.
T19. IV.A.17:1 which **m.** you have at last forgiven me.
T19. IV.A.17:3 of you. To the ego sin **m.** death, and so
T-20........ V.3:2 all it **m.** is that it wants the other for itself,
T-21......in.1:11 Nothing perceived without it **m.** anything
T-22...... III.6:8 sight of form **m.** understanding has been
T-22.... VI.12:2 believe attack of any kind **m.** anything. It
T-23...... III.6:2 be released from conflict **m.** that it is over.
T-24..... VII.6:9 any way to learn what this condition **m.**.
T-25....VIII.3:7 without insanity where love **m.** hate, and
T-25...... IX.1:5 you answer "yes" it **m.** you will forego all
T-25...... IX.5:4 principle that justice **m.** no one can lose is
T-25...... IX.7:5 to solve for you **m.** that you *want* it solved.
T-26........X.2:2 It **m.** that there must be some forms in
T-27...... III.3:1 of your brother that you see **m.** nothing.
T-27....VIII.6:5 eternity, which ***m.*** there is no time.
T-28...... IV.1:1 the Atonement for yourself **m.** not to give
T-28...... IV.1:2 **m.** that you share not his wish to separate,
T-28..... VII.5:5 all it **m.** is that you tried to keep a promise

T-29.........I.2:4 Certain it is he knows not what love **m.**.
T-29.........I.6:4 because you do not know what loving **m.**.
T-29....... II.6:5 is that except the state confusion really **m.**
T-29....... II.7:8 but **m.** the mind remains unchanged in its
T-29....... III.3:9 The coming of the light **m.** it is gone. In
T-29....... III.4:2 On earth this **m.** forgive your brother,
T-29...... IV.1:3 which **m.** that you have understood that
T-30.........I.2:3 This **m.** that you are choosing not to be
T-30.........I.5:4 This **m.** you have decided by yourself, and
T-30...... III.7:2 Yet all this **m.** is that you are sometimes
T-30...... VI.6:2 This **m.** that you prefer to keep some idols
T-30...... VI.6:5 always **m.** you think forgiveness must be
T-30..... VII.1:7 all that happens now **m.** something else.
T-30..... VII.3:6 Can confusion be what meaning **m.**?
T-30... VII.6:11 No one has agreed with you on what it **m.**.
T-30..... VII.7:1 of solitude, for what you see **m.** nothing.
T-30.... VIII.5:4 For this but **m.** you would not have him
W-pI.......... 1.h this window, in this place] **m.** anything.
W-pI....... 7.1:3 why nothing that you see **m.** anything. It
W-pI..... 10.3:2 "thoughts" **m.** that you are not thinking.
W-pI..... 21.3:2 believe in this connection **m.** anything.
W-pI..... 23.4:3 This is what salvation **m.**, for where is the
W-pI..... 25.1:2 explains why nothing you see **m.** anything
W-pI..... 25.1:6 is for; that is its purpose; that is what it **m.**
W-pI..... 28.2:5 which really **m.** you are not seeing at all.
W-pI..... 29.1:3 explains why nothing you see **m.** anything
W-pI..... 36.1:4 "Sinless" **m.** without sin. You cannot be
W-pI..... 39.4:2 Your holiness **m.** the end of guilt, and
W-pI..... 42.2:2 This **m.** that you can receive it any time
W-pI..... 51.1:1 (1) Nothing I see **m.** anything. The
W-pI..... 65.3:1 accept what the idea for the day really **m.**.
W-pI..... 70.2:1 **m.** that nothing outside yourself can save
W-pI..... 70.2:2 also **m.** that nothing outside yourself can
W-pI..... 81.4:2 *Let this help me learn what forgiveness* ***m.***.
W-pI..... 83.1:3 it **m.** I cannot have conflicting goals. With
W-pI..... 92.1:3 idea of what seeing **m.** is tied up with the
W-pI..... 93.5:3 it seems to do and think **m.** nothing. It is
W-pI... 100.7:5 Think what this **m.**. You have indeed
W-pI... 101.1:2 idea in understanding what salvation **m.**.
W-pI... 105.2:3 This strange distortion of what giving **m.**
W-pI. 106.10:1 the world what giving **m.** by listening and
W-pI... 126.9:3 from every bar to what forgiveness **m.**,
W-pI. 126.10:2 help in understanding what it really **m.**.
W-pI... 127.7:1 faintest glimmering of what love **m.** today
W-pI... 127.9:3 of your own reality and what love **m.**. He
W-pI... 132.2:2 change your mind **m.** you have changed
W-pI... 134.2:1 of what forgiveness **m.** is easily corrected,
W-pI... 169.7:3 Him Who teaches what forgiveness **m.**.
W-pI... 184.5:3 Yet you believe this is what learning **m.**;
W-pI... 185.4:8 And what He **m.** is lost to sleeping minds
W-pI... 185.5:2 one **m.** these words who wants illusions,
W-pI... 185.6:1 mind which **m.** that all it wants is peace
W-pI... 187.6:2 understands what giving **m.** must laugh at
W-pII . 344.1:2 *I have not understood what giving* ***m.***, *and*
M-4 ....... II.1:5 The term actually **m.** consistency. There is
M-4 ....... V.1:2 Gentleness **m.** that fear is now impossible
M-4 ..... VII.1:4 generosity **m.** "giving away" in the sense
M-4 ..... VII.1:5 of God, it **m.** giving away in order to keep.
M-4 ..... VII.1:8 the word **m.** the exact opposite to the
M-13 ......... 6:3 not be mistaken about what sacrifice **m.**.
M-13 ......... 6:4 always **m.** the giving up of what you want.
M-17 ......... 5:2 Consider what this reaction **m.**, and its
M-18 ......... 4:6 Atonement **m.** correction, or the undoing
M-23 ......... 3:2 It **m.** that in remembering Jesus you are
M-23 ......... 6:1 is, or what its one Creator really **m.**. Yet
M-25 ......... 6:5 which merely **m.** to strengthen the ego.
P-2....... VII.6:6 fail. Think what this **m.**; he has the gifts of
P-2....... VII.8:1 what the joining of two brothers really **m.**.
S-2.........I.10:4 to you exactly what forgiveness **m.** to you,
S-3........ IV.3:1 what it **m.** to help the Christ to heal! Can

## meant 38

T-2......... II.7:4 is **m.** by "the meek shall inherit the earth.
T-5...... IV.2:12 That is what I **m.** when I said it is possible
T-5...... VI.11:1 I **m.** that I came to share the light with
T-6........ IV.1:5 If it **m.** you well it would be glad, as the
T-7......... III.1:7 "I am with you always," I **m.** it literally. I
T-8......... II.7:1 I **m.**: The Will of God is without limit,
T-9 ..........I.4:2 I **m.** that He has the power to look into
T-9 ........ IV.6:2 I **m.** when I said that miracles are natural,
T-10 ..... III.6:6 I said, "My peace I give unto you," I **m.** it.
T-11 ..... VI.1:5 That is what I **m.** when I said, "Blessed
T-12 ..... III.1:2 is what I **m.**: If you have no investment in
T-17 ..... IV.2:4 all that is **m.** by that is that He will restore
T-17 ..... VI.3:2 try to piece together what it must have **m.**
T-17 ... VIII.1:1 of what every situation is **m.** to be. The
T-18 ..... IV.2:9 acceptance of yourself as you were **m.** to
T-20 .......II.9:6 we were **m.** to find by Him Who leads us.
T-24 ..... VI.6:6 the vision you were **m.** to see from you.
T-29 ..... IV.6:4 in what you dream your life was **m.** to be.
W-pI..... 76.6:4 What it is **m.** to save does not exist. Only
W-pI..... 76.6:5 Only what it is **m.** to hide will save you.
W-pI... 105.2:2 **m.** to be a pledge of debt to be repaid
W-pI... 107.6:7 You were not **m.** to suffer and to die.
WpIrIII.in11:5 And it is **m.** to serve you in all ways, all
WpI. rIV.in8:2 be received where they were **m.** to be.
W-pI. 152.11:6 His home to God, as it was **m.** to be.
W-pI... 154.6:3 them everywhere that they were **m.** to be.
W-pI... 185.2:7 But few indeed have **m.** them. You have
W-pII ..... 3.2:4 absence? Thus the world was **m.** to be a
W-pII ... 13.3:3 what was **m.** to curse has come to bless.
M-7 ........... 3:2 This is what is really **m.** by the statement
S-1 ..........II.7:7 can again become what it was **m.** to be.
S-1 ..........II.7:9 So it extends, as it was **m.** to do. And for
S-1 ......... V.4:6 Prayer has become what it was **m.** to be,
S-2 ...........I.1:2 a scourge; a curse where it was **m.** to bless
S-2 ...........I.1:5 was **m.** to heal is used to hurt because
S-2 ..........II.1:4 cannot be missed, nor is it really **m.** to be.
S-3 ..........II.1:2 combining with forgiveness kindly **m.** but
S-3 ........ III.4:4 and lets forgiveness be what it is **m.** to be.

## meanwhile 7

T-6 ..... V.B.4:5 **M.**, the increasing clarity of the Holy
T-9 ..... IV.11:9 gone. Reality has not gone in the **m.**. The
T-9 ....... VI.4:9 But **m.** you will judge it as you judge your
T-30 ......I.13:4 But **m.**, you have need for practicing the
W-pI... 39.10:1 **M.**, you should feel free to introduce
M-26 ......... 2:9 And **m.**, they give all their gifts to the
P-3...........I.4:3 **M.** he must learn, and his patients are the

## measure 10

T-9 .......II.11:8 the exact **m.** of the value you put upon it.
T-9 .......II.11:9 in turn, is the **m.** of how much you want it
T-11 ... VI.10:7 What does not exist has no size and no **m.**
T-15 .... IV.5:2 learn to accept me is the **m.** of the time in
T-24 .......II.1:5 him a tiny **m.** of your specialness instead.
W-pI..... 98.5:3 of gaining a reward so great it has no **m.**?
W-pI... 127.7:1 you have advanced in distance without **m.**
W-pI... 188.4:2 salvation radiates with gifts beyond all **m.**
M-4 ...... IX.1:1 **m.** of his advancement in the curriculum.
M-18 ......... 3:4 and tiny breath become the **m.** of reality.

## measured 1

W-pI..... 12.2:4 or shorter, but try, instead, to keep a **m.**,

## measureless 1

T-23 ......in.5:2 is beyond it, **m.** and timeless as eternity.

## mechanics 1

T-15 .......II.5:4 can practice the **m.** of the holy instant,

## mechanism 4

T-1 .........I.38:1 The Holy Spirit is the **m.** of miracles. He
T-8 ....... IV.5:7 because mind is the **m.** of decision. It is
T-12 ... III.9:10 mind, since the mind is the **m.** of decision
C-1 ............ 7:3 choice. *Consciousness* is the receptive **m.**,

## mechanisms 3

T-4 .........II.7:5 Appetites are "getting" **m.**, representing
T-23 .....II.10:1 All of the **m.** of madness are seen
W-pII ..... 3.3:1 The **m.** of illusion have been born instead

## mediates 3

T-1 .........II.5:3 Spirit **m.** higher to lower communication,
W-pII ..... 7.1:1 Spirit **m.** between illusions and the truth.
S-1...........I.6:3 that another **m.** between you and God.

## mediating 1

T-7 ....... IX.1:5 **m.** between them always in favor of the

## Mediator 3

*mediator*

T-5 ....... III.7:1 The Holy Spirit is the **M.** between the
T-13 .. VII.10:9 As **M.** between the two worlds, He knows
W-pI .... 43.1:3 created the Holy Spirit as the **M.** between

## mediator 1

*Mediator*

T-20 ..... III.2:4 the self-appointed **m.** of all relationships,

## medication 1

W-pI .... 76.8:2 of nutrition, of immunization, of **m.**, and

## medications 1

T-2 .........V.2:2 Physical **m.** are forms of "spells," but if

## medicine 2

W-pI .... 76.4:3 You think you must obey the "laws" of **m.**
W-pI .. 135.5:3 of defense, no health-inducing **m.**, no care

## medicines 1

W-pI 140.10:1 lay aside our amulets, our charms and **m.**,

## meditation 2

T-18 .... VII.4:9 long periods of **m.** aimed at detachment
W-pI .. 124.8:4 rules nor special words to guide your **m.**.

## medium 12

T-1 ........I.11:1 Prayer is the **m.** of miracles. It is a means
T-1 ........I.46:1 Spirit is the highest communication **m.**.
T-1 .........V.1:7 can destroy your **m.** of communication,
T-1 .........V.5:4 mind can become the **m.** by which spirit
T-3 .........V.6:2 **m.** of miracles. But the only meaningful
T-8 .... VII.11:5 **m.** of communication loses its usefulness
T-8 .... VII.11:6 use a **m.** of communication as a medium
T-8 .... VII.11:6 a medium of communication as a **m.** of
T-14 .... VII.1:7 Perception is the **m.** by which ignorance
T19 . IV.B.14:5 Like any communication **m.** the body
T19 . IV.B.17:3 Holy Spirit, too, is a communication **m.**,
M-12......... 3:4 need a **m.** through which communication

## meek 2

T-2 .........II.7:4 is meant by "the **m.** shall inherit the earth
T-4 ........I.12:4 The **m.** shall inherit the earth because

## meekness 1

S-2..........II.4:3 as **m.** and as charity instead of cruelty. Is

## meet 112

T-4 ..........I.1:4 but he must **m.** another condition; he
T-8 ..........I.1:4 restored only when you **m.** its conditions.
T-8 ....... III.4:1 When you **m.** anyone, remember it is a
T-8 ....... III.4:6 Whenever two Sons of God **m.**, they are
T-8 ..... VI.9:11 Together we can **m.** its conditions, but
T-8 ....... IX.2:5 and find you when you **m.** its conditions.

| | |
|---|---|
| T-8........IX.9:4 | is only to **m.** the conditions for meaning, |
| T-11......V.18:1 | Every brother you **m.** becomes a witness |
| T-13......IV.5:4 | to those you **m.** in the present from a past |
| T-13......IV.6:9 | Spirit teaches that you always **m.** yourself, |
| T-13......VI.1:2 | this no illusions can rise to **m.** your sight, |
| T-13......VI.3:4 | He stands revealed in everyone you **m.** |
| T-14.....VII.4:6 | becomes the source of fear, for if they **m.**, |
| T-14... VIII.4:2 | the place where you must **m.** with truth. |
| T-14......XI.5:2 | and if all those who **m.** or even think of |
| T-14......XI.7:3 | can make no needs his Father will not **m.**, |
| T-15......IV.4:3 | you have been willing to **m.** its conditions |
| T-15.......V.2:3 | look to them to **m.** your imagined needs, |
| T-15... VIII.2:6 | His Son share, and will to **m.** together. |
| T-16.........I.6:8 | you how to **m.** both without losing either. |
| T-16.........I.7:4 | all to Him Whose function is to **m.** them. |
| T-16.........I.7:6 | will not **m.** them secretly, for He would |
| T-16....VI.10:7 | Go on to **m.** them gladly, and learn how |
| T-17....... II.8:4 | **M.** His patience with your impatience at |
| T-17....... II.8:5 | out in gladness to **m.** with your Redeemer |
| T-17....... V.5:8 | serves the purpose they have agreed to **m.** |
| T-17......VI.4:2 | on everything that helps you **m.** it. It is |
| T-17......VI.4:4 | becomes what can be used to **m.** the goal. |
| T-17.....VII.4:4 | grow to **m.** the goal that has been set. The |
| T-17.....VII.5:1 | **m.** the purpose set for your relationship. |
| T-18....... II.9:3 | special relationship **m.** its conditions. In |
| T-18......III.3:1 | rushed to **m.** you since you called upon it. |
| T-18....VI.12:5 | it. And so you rush to **m.** it, letting your |
| T19...IV.D.2:2 | brush the veil aside and run to **m.** Him, |
| T19.IV.D.17:9 | that we might **m.** here in this holy place, |
| T-20......III.2:4 | them between those who would **m.**, to |
| T-20......III.8:6 | Did you **m.** your brother with joy to bless |
| T-20.....VII.1:2 | But we have also said the means to **m.** the |
| T-20... VIII.6:3 | sure. For it will **m.** His purpose, seen in |
| T-20... VIII.6:3 | form and suited perfectly to **m.** it. |
| T-20... VIII.9:4 | is merely how you elect to **m.** your goal. |
| T-20... VIII.9:5 | serve to **m.** the goal of madness. They are |
| T-23.........I.3:1 | the ego, or yourself and it, will ever **m.**. |
| T-23.........I.3:2 | You seem to **m.**, and make your strange |
| T-23.........I.3:4 | You **m.** at a mistake; an error in your self- |
| T-23....... II.5:5 | the Son **m.** only to conflict but not to join. |
| T-23.......III.1:7 | and where the purpose rises to **m.** his |
| T-25.........I.1:7 | **m.** and join and raise Him to His Father, |
| T-25.....VII.8:2 | sane as He to raise a saner world to **m.** the |
| T-26......III.2:3 | conflicting values **m.** and all illusions are |
| T-28......III.8:8 | And they will **m.** with your invited Guests |
| T-28......IV.4:2 | To join his dreams is thus to **m.** him not, |
| T-28......IV.5:2 | to him to **m.** you in the gap between you, |
| T-29.........I.4:3 | of a promise made to **m.** when you prefer, |
| T-29.........I.4:3 | separate till you and he elect to **m.** again. |
| T-29.........I.4:6 | you and he agree to **m.** from time to time, |
| T-29.........I.4:7 | diminishes as you and your brother **m.**. |
| T-29.........I.5:4 | when your brother and you **m.**, and limits |
| T-29.........I.6:5 | each circumstance and everyone you **m.**, |
| T-29........ II.5:3 | host, nor where His host can **m.** with Him |
| T-31....... V.1:7 | it, to **m.** the world on equal terms, at one |
| T-31......VI.3:6 | how what you see arose to **m.** your sight. |
| T-31...VII.10:5 | are but everyone you **m.** or look upon, |
| T-31...VII.10:5 | while since, and those you will yet **m.**; the |
| W-in..........7:3 | exercises themselves **m.** the conditions |
| W-pI.......9.2:2 | and may **m.** with active resistance in any |
| W-pI.....37.6:2 | to apply it silently to anyone you **m.**, |
| W-pI...78.10:2 | when we allow each one we **m.** to save us, |
| W-pI...78.10:3 | To everyone you **m.**, and to the ones you |
| W-pI...91.11:2 | sure to **m.** temptation with today's idea. |
| W-pI.....92.9:2 | and light unite in you, and where they **m.**, |
| W-pI.....92.9:3 | His Son, is waiting now to **m.** Itself again, |
| W-pI...92.11:2 | at night when we will **m.** again in trust. |
| W-pI.....94.5:1 | **m.** the requirement of practicing for the |
| W-pI...95.15:2 | To everyone you **m.** today, be sure to give |
| W-pI...100.8:5 | pass as you ascend to **m.** the Christ in you |
| W-pI.110.11:1 | thoughts for all who **m.** with us today. For |
| W-pI.121.10:1 | cause regret in you if you should **m.** him; |
| W-pI...122.2:2 | gives you joy with which to **m.** the day. It |
| W-pI.122.13:3 | you return again to **m.** a world of shifting |
| W-pI...133.3:2 | Unless they **m.** these sound requirements, |
| W-pI.134.14:2 | **m.** with our reality in freedom and in |
| W-pI.153.19:2 | in it, as we prepare to **m.** the day. We rise |
| W-pI...157.5:2 | A vision reaches everyone you **m.**, and |
| W-pI.158.10:5 | you **m.** today provides another chance to |
| W-pI...168.6:1 | And He descends to **m.** us, as we come to |
| WpI...rV.in5:1 | that waits to **m.** us at the journey's ending |
| W-pI...185.6:4 | no form in which the lesson will **m.** with |
| W-pII..245.1:3 | *It sheds its light on everyone I **m.**. I bring it to* |
| W-pII..271.1:3 | sight, the world and God's creation **m.**, |
| W-pII..292.1:4 | we see, and every situation that we **m.**. |
| W-pII..292.2:2 | *for every trial we think we still must **m.**.* |
| W-pII..298.1:5 | sure that I go through fear to **m.** my Love. |
| W-pII..349.2:2 | He gives us grace to **m.** them all. And so |
| M-3 ...........1:4 | point of view he cannot **m.** everyone, nor |
| M-3 ...........1:7 | Those who are to **m.** will meet, because |
| M-3 ...........1:7 | Those who are to meet will **m.**, because |
| M-3 ...........4:6 | Yet all who **m.** will someday meet again, |
| M-3 ...........4:6 | Yet all who meet will someday **m.** again, |
| M-15 ..........3:1 | best efforts **m.** with lack of appreciation |
| M-17 .......7:13 | this stain on him must **m.** with death. |
| M-19 ..........2:6 | rise to **m.** one as the journey continues, |
| M-28 ..........6:9 | as he prepares with them to **m.** his God. |
| C-4.............3:1 | being another level, they can never **m.**. |
| C-4.............8:1 | but rush to **m.** Him where His altar is. |
| C-ep...........5:1 | Let us go out and **m.** the newborn world, |
| P-2...........I.4:1 | which brothers **m.** to bless each other and |
| P-2......... II.9:5 | And let him then **m.** his brother's need as |
| P-2......IV.10:2 | He must **m.** attack without attack, and |
| P-2........ VI.7:5 | in which they **m.** and join and are as one. |
| S-1 ......... V.2:1 | share a dwelling place where they can **m.**. |
| S-2 ......... II.6:2 | "I will forgive you if you **m.** my needs, for |

## meeting 30

| | |
|---|---|
| T-3........ VI.3:1 | that comes from **m.** yourself and your |
| T-4...........I.9:5 | a very lofty function that you are not **m.**. |
| T-4...........I.9:6 | has chosen to be afraid instead of **m.** it. |
| T-13...... IV.6:7 | perceiving it as a **m.** with your own past? |
| T-13...... IV.6:8 | For you would be **m.** no one, and the |
| T-14...... VIII.h | The Holy **M.** Place |
| T-14. VIII.2:11 | in division, but in the **m.** place where God |
| T-14. VIII.2:13 | holy **m.** place of the unseparated Father |
| T-14... VIII.4:9 | In the holy **m.** place are joined the Father |
| T-15....... V.2:1 | methods for **m.** them on your own terms. |
| T-16.........I.7:2 | And you will think that by **m.** the needs of |
| T-17....... II.2:4 | not believe it is the **m.** place of worlds so |
| T-17....... II.8:4 | with your impatience at delay in **m.** Him. |
| T-17....... V.4:2 | inappropriateness for **m.** its new purpose. |
| T-23.......I.12:2 | The **m.** of illusions leads to war. Peace, |
| T-24........VII.h | The **M.** Place |
| T-24...VII.11:1 | without a **m.** place and no encounter. |
| T-25.........I.1:7 | is the **m.** of the holy Christ unto Himself; |
| T-26...... III.2:3 | Here is the **m.** place where thoughts are |
| T-29.........I.4:4 | and thereby signify a **m.** place to join. But |
| W-pI.....92.9:3 | **m.** place we try today to find and rest in, |
| W-pI...92.10:1 | minutes twice today to join this **m.**. Let |
| W-pI...92.10:4 | us how to find the **m.** place of self and Self |
| W-pI...92.11:2 | After the morning **m.**, we will use the day |
| W-pI.....96.3:2 | and good and evil have no **m.** place. The |
| W-pI.....99.3:1 | a **m.** place at all where earth and Heaven |
| M-3 ...........2:2 | a "chance" **m.** of two apparent strangers |
| P-3......... II.5:1 | from every **m.** of patient and therapist. |
| P-3....... II.9:10 | Yet at each **m.** there is One Who says, |
| S-1 ......... V.2:6 | is Self, and this it sees in every **m.**, where |

## meetings 1

| | |
|---|---|
| M-3 ...........4:4 | the first level, these **m.** are not accidental, |

## meets 10

| | |
|---|---|
| T-6........... II.7:6 | Everything **m.** in God, because everything |
| T-14.......... II.7:1 | learner **m.** the conditions of learning here |
| T-14.......... II.7:1 | as he **m.** the conditions of knowledge in |
| T-14...... IX.2:1 | because it is the opposite of what it **m.**. It |
| T-18...... IX.9:1 | world, where guilt **m.** with forgiveness. |
| T-23.......I.12:1 | Illusion **m.** illusion; truth, itself. The |
| T-25.....VII.6:1 | that everything that **m.** this one demand |
| W-pI.193.10:6 | time be less than **m.** your deepest need. |
| C-6.............4:7 | whatever **m.** the needs you think you have |
| P-2...........I.1:4 | out to them that **m.** the changing need. |

## melodies 1

| | |
|---|---|
| W-pI.161.10:5 | will see will sing to you of ancient **m.** you |

## melody 8

| | |
|---|---|
| T-21.........I.6:2 | with you, but just a little wisp of **m.**, |
| T-21.........I.7:5 | **m.** you taught yourself to cherish since. |
| T-24........II.4:4 | soundless in the **m.** that pours from God |
| T-29...... IX.8:4 | a **m.** is heard that everyone remembers, |
| T-31..VIII.11:5 | of **m.** to one inclusive chorus from a |
| W-pI...164.2:3 | dim. A **m.** from far beyond the world |
| C-6.............5:6 | in which you dance to death's thin **m.**. |
| S-3........ IV.8:3 | wait in sorrow Heaven's **m.** is incomplete, |

## melt 5

| | |
|---|---|
| T-18.... VI.12:5 | to meet it, letting your limits **m.** away, |
| T-20...... IV.8:7 | but will **m.** away before you reach it. You |
| T-24........II.9:2 | vestige of the fear of God will **m.** away in |
| T-25.......in.1:9 | Then will their bodies **m.** away, that they |
| T-29.... IX.10:2 | So do your childish terrors **m.** away, and |

## melting 1

| | |
|---|---|
| T-18.... VI.14:6 | breaking out, but merely by a quiet **m.** in. |

## melts 2

| | |
|---|---|
| T-13..... X.14:3 | radiance of the Kingdom guilt **m.** away. |
| W-pI...207.1:3 | *but turn to Him, and every sorrow **m.** away,* |

## member 1

| | |
|---|---|
| T-1......... V.4:1 | every **m.** of the family of God must return |

## members 2

| | |
|---|---|
| T-1..........II.6:2 | recognition of the equality of the **m.** of |
| T-1........ III.6:6 | your neighbor are equal **m.** of one family, |

## memories 5

| | |
|---|---|
| T-26....... V.5:7 | lives in **m.** alone is unaware of where he is |
| T-27...... VI.3:1 | itself, holds all your **m.** and all your hopes |
| T-28.........I.7:3 | one? When ancient **m.** of hate appear, |
| T-28........II.5:1 | holds all your shreds of **m.** and dreams. |
| W-pI...168.3:6 | It restores all **m.** the sleeping mind forgot; |

## memory 116

| | |
|---|---|
| T-2......VIII.5:6 | in your **m.** only what is creative and good. |
| T-6..........II.7:4 | prefer to believe that this **m.** is impossible |
| T-7..........II.6:1 | the connection of learning and **m.**. |
| T-7..........II.6:2 | Learning is impossible without **m.** since it |
| T-10........II.2:4 | your remembering, for God is in your **m.**. |
| T-12...... VI.2:6 | God is in your **m.** because of Him. You |
| T-12....VIII.4:1 | forget what God Himself placed in his **m.**. |
| T-12....VIII.4:7 | His **m.** shines in your mind and cannot be |
| T-12....VIII.5:1 | You have but to ask for this **m.**, and you |
| T-12....VIII.5:2 | Yet the **m.** of God cannot shine in a mind |
| T-12....VIII.5:3 | **m.** of God can dawn only in a mind that |
| T-13...... III.2:1 | ego's dark foundation is the **m.** of God, |
| T-13...... III.2:2 | For this **m.** would instantly restore you to |
| T-14...... IV.9:6 | His **m.** is yours. If you remember what |
| T-16.. IV.11:12 | completion lie the **m.** of His Wholeness |
| T-18.... VI.12:3 | a sound, a sight, a thought, a **m.**, and |
| T-18.... IX.14:1 | And when the **m.** of God has come to you |
| T-18.... IX.14:1 | else, and **m.** will be as useless as learning, |
| T19... IV.D.1:5 | And as this **m.** rises in your mind, peace |
| T19... IV.D.3:4 | the **m.** of God seems quite forgotten; the |
| T-20.. VI.12:11 | long withhold the **m.** of their relationship |
| T-21.........I.9:3 | Here is the **m.** of what you are; a part of |
| T-21.........I.10:2 | will not withstand the **m.** of this song. |
| T-21.........I.10:5 | And who is there in whom this **m.** lies not |
| T-23.........I.1:1 | The **m.** of God comes to the quiet mind. |
| T-23.........I.5:2 | the **m.** of his Father must be forgotten. It |
| T-23.......I.12:8 | So is the **m.** of God obscured in minds |
| T-24........II.6:2 | like his Father that the **m.** of Him springs |

T-24...... II.6:3 And with this **m.**, the Son remembers his
T-24...... VI.6:4 shining **m.** of Him in Whom your brother
T-24.... VII.2:1 The **m.** of God shines not alone. What is
T-24.... VII.7:5 retains one unlearned lesson in his **m.**,
T-26........ I.4:6 **m.** of God must be denied if any sacrifice
T-26...... II.7:7 will shine away all **m.** of sacrifice and loss.
T-26...... II.8:4 which is the **m.** of His Love kept perfectly
T-26...... V.5:6 You keep an ancient **m.** before your eyes.
T-26..... V.10:1 a road long since a **m.** of time gone by?
T-26... VII.16:1 recognize because the truth is in your **m.**.
T-26...... IX.2:2 obscures the face of Christ and **m.** of God.
T-28........... I.h The Present **M.**
T-28........ I.1:5 in **m.** appears to have immediate effects.
T-28........ I.2:4 Why would you cling to it in **m.** if you did
T-28........ I.2:7 **M.**, like perception, is a skill made up by
T-28........ I.3:3 It is an unselective **m.**, that is not used to
T-28........ I.4:1 Holy Spirit can indeed make use of **m.**,
T-28........ I.4:2 Yet this is not a **m.** of past events, but
T-28........ I.4:3 to believe that **m.** holds only what is past,
T-28........ I.4:5 There is no link of **m.** to the past. If you
T-28........ I.5:1 Spirit's use of **m.** is quite apart from time.
T-28........ I.5:3 go. **M.** holds the message it receives, and
T-28........ I.6:7 the past is held in **m.** as you make use of it
T-28........ I.7:9 the span of **m.** which your perception sees
T-28........ I.9:7 Its **m.** does not lie in the past, nor waits
T-28....... I.11:4 when the **m.** of God returns to them.
T-28....... I.12:2 For in that instant is God's **m.** allowed to
T-28....... I.13:1 How instantly the **m.** of God arises in the
T-28....... I.13:1 mind that has no fear to keep the **m.** away
T-28....... I.15:2 **m.** of God has come to take the place of
T-28....... I.15:3 to allow the **m.** of God to flow across it,
T-28....... I.15:5 **m.** has not gone by, and left a stranded
T-28....... II.4:5 dream is like a **m.** in that it pictures what
T-29....... V.1:1 no **m.** of sin and of illusion lingers still.
W-pI..... 62.1:4 the truth about yourself return to your **m.**
W-pI... 122.3:2 and clears your **m.** of all dead thoughts so
W-pI. 139.11:6 And in our **m.** is the recall how dear our
W-pI. 153.14:5 bewildered **m.** of this distorted tale.
W-pI... 168.2:6 And **m.** of Him awakens in the mind that
W-pI... 182.1:3 A **m.** of home keeps haunting you, as if
W-pI... 182.4:2 are a **m.** now so distorted that you merely
W-pI... 185.1:4 awareness, **m.** of God entirely restored,
W-pI... 188.4:1 the world restores the **m.** to you as well.
W-pI... 194.8:2 thus you call the **m.** of Him to come again
W-pI... 195.7:4 long forgotten Word re-echoes in our **m.**,
WpI rVI.in.1:4 and invite the **m.** of God to come again.
W-pII .... in.9:5 The **m.** of God is shimmering across the
W-pII ..... 2.3:4 it, and the **m.** of God not far behind.
W-pII . 234.2:1 *cannot lose the* **m.** *of You and of Your Love.*
W-pII . 243.2:3 *are one because each part contains Your* **m.**,
W-pII . 258.1:2 His **m.** is hidden in our minds, obscured
W-pII . 270.1:4 *ends forever, as Your* **m.** *returns to him. And*
W-pII . 271.2:2 *beholds invites Your* **m.** *to be restored to me*
W-pII . 272.1:5 *What but Your* **m.** *can satisfy Your Son? I*
W-pII ..... 7.4:3 And the **m.** of all your Father's Love will
W-pII . 287.2:4 *And what except the* **m.** *of You could signify*
W-pII ..... 8.5:3 is our goal, for it contains the **m.** of God.
W-pII . 291.2:6 *complete, and let the* **m.** *of You return to me.*
W-pII . 304.2:3 *Son, that he may find again the* **m.** *of You,*
W-pII . 306.1:1 Heaven that an ancient **m.** returns to me?
W-pII . 309.1:8 of God. Within me is the **m.** of Him.
W-pII . 315.2:3 *may lead me on to my Creator and His* **m.**.
W-pII . 317.2:4 *The* **m.** *of You awaits me there. And all my*
W-pII ... 11.4:5 God's **m.** is in our holy minds, which
W-pII ... 11.4:6 our function be only to let this **m.** return,
W-pII . 322.1:3 His **m.** abides in every gift that I receive of
W-pII . 323.1:2 *only "cost" of restoration of Your* **m.** *to me,*
W-pII . 335.2:1 *What could restore Your* **m.** *to me, except*
W-pII . 335.2:3 *and in Your Son I find the* **m.** *of You as well.*
W-pII . 336.1:3 serve but to recall the **m.** that lies beyond
W-pII . 342.1:8 *light of truth, as* **m.** *of You returns to me.*
W-pII .... 350.h And through His **m.** to save the world.
W-pII . 350.1:3 *Your* **m.** *depends on his forgiveness. What*
W-pII . 350.1:7 *Only Your* **m.** *will set me free. And only my*
W-pII . 350.1:8 *teaches me to let Your* **m.** *return to me, and*
W-pII . 352.1:7 *I have within me both the* **m.** *of You, and*
W-pII . 352.1:9 *my own Identity, and find in It the* **m.** *of You.*
Wfl........ in.3:6 And thus His **m.** is given back, completely
Wfl........ in.4:2 which contains the **m.** of God, and points
M-2 .......... 4:1 instant so ancient that it is beyond all **m.**,
M-17 ....... 6:10 but do not retain the slightest **m.** of Who
M-26 ......... 1:2 His awareness is in everyone's **m.**, and
M-26 ......... 1:3 awareness and this **m.** can arise across the
M-29 ......... 3:9 this that lets the **m.** of love return to you.
C-3 ............ 4:1 be seen before the **m.** of God can return.
C-4 ............ 7:7 God's **m.** has come at last there is no
P-2.......... II.5:4 and then through the **m.** of God Himself.
P-2..... VII.9:10 holiness enough to wake your **m.** of Him?

## men 8

T-3 ...... VII.2:7 Yet he attracts **m.** rather than repels them
T-29 ..... VI.2:9 the tides, the seasons and the lives of **m.**;
T-29 ... VI.2:11 Son can never change by what **m.** made of
T-29 ... VIII.8:6 will give him more than other **m.** possess.
T-31 ..... IV.3:4 **M.** have died on seeing this, because they
T-31 .. VII.15:2 and **m.** despair because the savior's vision
M-4 ...... III.1:9 Without judgment are all **m.** brothers, for
C-5 ............ 2:6 form that He might appear to **m.** and save

## menace 1

T-23 ........ I.6:7 Madness holds out no **m.** to reality, and

## mental 6

*See also* non-mental
T-7 ...... VII.4:3 powerful because they are **m.** judgments.
W-pI..... 95.4:4 the extent of your lack of **m.** discipline,
M-8 ........... 1:5 completely upsets the **m.** balance. What
P-2......... IV.1:1 psychotherapy, so all illness is **m.** illness.
P-2......... IV.1:2 Son of God, and judgment is a **m.** activity.
P-2......... IV.8:1 insanity because all sickness is **m.** illness,

## mentally 1

W-pI... 158.4:5 again; reviewing **m.** what has gone by.

## mention 1

W-pI..... 46.4:3 **M.** each one by name, and say: *God is the*

## mentioned 1

W-pI... 156.1:3 the basic thought so often **m.** in the text;

## mercies 1

W-pII . 233.2:4 is a day of countless gifts and **m.** unto us.

## merciful 17

T-3 .......... I.4:3 that you should be **m.** even as your Father
T-3 .......... I.4:3 even as your Father in Heaven is **m.**. It
T-13 ..... III.7:2 Holy Spirit's vision is **m.** and His remedy
T-21 ... VI.11:9 And where he chooses to be **m.**, there is
T-28 ..... II.10:3 perceived as friends with **m.** intent. Their
T-30 .... V.10:5 Be **m.** unto your brother, then. And do
T-31 ... IV.11:4 For God is **m.**, and did not let His Son
W-pI. 166.11:3 all your fears with this one **m.** reply, "It is
W-pI... 170.6:4 insane, while they are always **m.** and just.
W-pI. 192.10:1 Be **m.** today. The Son of God deserves
W-pI. 196.12:3 How kind and **m.** is the idea we practice!
W-pII . 230.1:4 How **m.** is God my Father, that when He
W-pII ... 10.4:1 God's Final Judgment is as **m.** as every
S-1........ III.3:8 may seem to be dangerous instead of **m.**.
S-1........ III.4:2 and a glimpse of the **m.** nature of this step
S-2........ III.4:3 undone, for prayer is **m.** and God is just.
S-3........ IV.2:3 Forgiveness shines its **m.** reprieve upon

## merciless 10

T19..IV.A.12:4 him. For fear is **m.** even to its friends. Its
T19.... IV.C.8:5 free it from the **m.** and unrelenting orders
T-20 ..... III.5:8 This world *is* **m.**, and were it outside you,
T-20 ..... III.5:9 Yet it was you who made it **m.**, and now if
T-25 ..... IV.3:7 their dreams of guilt and **m.** revenge, and
T-27 ........ I.4:5 him. The sick are **m.** to everyone, and in
W-pI .. 101.3:4 Its wrath is boundless, **m.**, but wholly just
W-pI .. 129.2:3 The world you see is **m.** indeed, unstable,
W-pI .. 192.5:2 it will die, nor be the prey of **m.** attack.
W-pI .. 195.9:3 which regards us in a place of **m.** pursuit,

## mercilessness 1

T-20 ..... III.5:9 and now if **m.** seems to look back at you,

## mercy 51

T-3 ...... VI.6:1 God offers only **m.**. Your words should
T-3 ...... VI.6:2 words should reflect only **m.**, because
T-3 ...... VI.6:3 attempt to teach you the meaning of **m.**.
T-13 ........ I.6:7 and **m.** have always followed him, for he
T-13 ....... X.9:2 looking without **m.** upon your brothers,
T-13 ....... X.9:9 and He offers **m.** to every child of God, as
T19 .. IV.D.7:4 you are at the **m.** of things beyond you,
T19 IV.D.17:1 faith and hope and **m.** are yours to give.
T-20 ..... III.5:7 picture is outside, and has you at its **m.**.
T-21 ... VI.11:8 is at his own **m.**. And where he chooses to
T-22 ....... II.8:3 cannot be a judge, nor **m.** condemnation.
T-22 ... VI.10:6 and at the **m.** of countless attackers more
T-24 ........ I.2:5 their **m.** while you decide to leave it there.
T-24 ..... III.8:7 asks your **m.** on His Son and on Himself.
T-25 . VIII.9:11 are the same does **m.** stand at God's right
T-25 ..... IX.9:4 with vengeance justified and **m.** lost,
T-25 ..... IX.9:5 have no **m.** to bestow upon another. That
T-26 ....... II.5:3 he deserves no **m.** from the God of justice.
T-27 ....... II.3:3 you grant your brother **m.** but retain the
T-30 ..... IV.3:9 Yet *is* he at the **m.** of his toys? And *can*
T-31 ....... II.9:2 Hear but his call for **m.** and release from
T-31 ..... III.5:2 itself; a place where nothing can find **m.**,
W-pI .... 56.1:4 to be at the **m.** of a world I cannot control
W-pI .... 72.6:1 animals seek for prey and **m.** cannot enter
W-pI .... 75.9:3 Give thanks for **m.** and the Love of God.
W-pI .. 159.7:3 of redemption and the hearth of **m.**,
W-pI .. 189.5:5 will look out on a world of **m.** and of love.
W-pI .. 191.9:3 in a world which shows no **m.** to you. Yet
W-pI .. 191.9:4 Yet when you accord it **m.**, will its mercy
W-pI .. 191.9:4 accord it mercy, will its **m.** shine on you.
W-pI 191.11:3 They cannot see the **m.** of the world until
W-pI 192.10:2 The Son of God deserves your **m.**. It is he
W-pI 193.10:2 Let **m.** come to you more quickly. Do not
W-pI .. 196.2:1 at first you will not understand how **m.**,
W-pI .. 198.7:1 haunts where **m.** has no meaning, and
W-pI 198.12:3 He needs no thoughts of **m.**. Who could
W-pII .... 235.h God in His **m.** wills that I be saved.
W-pII . 235.1:5 I am saved because God in His **m.** wills it
W-pII . 306.1:4 born anew into a world of **m.** and of care;
W-pII . 315.1:4 speaks a word of gratitude or **m.**, and my
W-pII . 325.1:6 forth, with **m.** for the holy Son of God, to
W-pII ... 13.3:2 to all they look upon in **m.** and in love.
W-pII .... 343.h To find the **m.** and the peace of God.
W-pII . 343.2:1 The **m.** and the peace of God are free.
M-14 ......... 1:3 Yet will its ending be an illusion of **m.**.
M-19 ......... 5:1 confuse His **m.** with your own insanity.
S-2........... I.2:6 God's **m.** has become a twisted knife that
S-2........... I.7:4 God's **m.** would remove this withering
S-2.......... II.2:7 grief. This is not really **m.**. This is death.
S-2.......... II.6:6 Have **m.** on yourself who bargains thus.
S-3......... IV.2:1 to prayer, and the effect of **m.** truly taught

## mere 8

T-9 ....... IV.7:3 are. This is more than **m.** confusion. It is a
T-20 ..... III.1:5 this reduces it at once to **m.** perception; a
T-26 ..... V.6:10 and pass from **m.** imagining into belief
W-pI .... 27.1:1 stronger than **m.** determination. It gives
W-pI .. 134.1:2 forgiveness must be seen as **m.** eccentric
W-pI 167.12:4 And now it is no more a **m.** reflection. It
M-17 ......... 5:3 A magic thought, by its **m.** presence,
C-in .......... 4:2 as questions the **m.** form of a question to

## merely 385

T-1 ....... IV.2:7 its errors, which are **m.** lacks of love. Your
T-1 ....... VI.3:6 meaningless as time. Both are **m.** beliefs.
T-2 .......... I.3:4 of an eye because it is **m.** a misperception.

T-2........III.4:1 see error, and **m.** looks for Atonement.
T-2........IV.3:3 Their purpose is **m.** to facilitate learning.
T-2........IV.3:8 The body is **m.** part of your experience in
T-2.........V.6:2 a learning device it **m.** follows the learner,
T-2.........V.7:7 is **m.** channelized toward correction.
T-2........VII.5:6 deny it is **m.** to use denial inappropriately
T-3.....IV.5:10 its Source, or it would **m.** cease to be. This
T-3........IV.6:6 light abolishes darkness **m.** by showing
T-3......IV.7:14 "chosen ones" are **m.** those who choose
T-3........VI.9:4 It **m.** means that you do not remember
T-3........VI.9:6 judgment and **m.** know that it is there.
T-4..........in.3:5 It **m.** re-enacts the separation, the loss of
T-4...........I.6:2 as **m.** "a larger ego" you will be afraid,
T-4...........I.9:9 is **m.** to postpone the inevitable. The
T-4.........II.4:9 longer necessary you will **m.** know God.
T-4.........II.8:1 which is **m.** another way of describing
T-4.........II.8:7 attack it; it **m.** cannot conceive of it at all.
T-4.......II.11:1 perception is **m.** a temporary expedient.
T-4......IV.10:1 Christ is **m.** another name for the creation
T-4.......VII.2:7 It **m.** responds in certain specific ways to
T-5.........II.7:4 **m.** reminds. It is compelling only because
T-5........III.9:3 is **m.** another term for a split mind. The
T-5........IV.2:3 It does not die; it was **m.** never born.
T-5.........V.2:9 Guilt is more than **m.** not of God. It is the
T-5........VI.8:2 becomes **m.** an attempt to guarantee the
T-5........VI.9:5 to the ego will **m.** return to the Kingdom,
T-5......VI.10:2 It will **m.** dismiss the case against you.
T-5.......VII.1:4 you need **m.** cast your cares upon Him
T-5.......VII.2:6 **m.** asked to return to God the mind as He
T-5.......VII.6:5 Your part is **m.** to return your thinking to
T-6...........I.6:7 You are **m.** asked to follow my example in
T-6...........I.7:2 but rebirth itself is **m.** the dawning on
T-6.........I.11:6 case, **m.** because it would serve as a good
T-6........IV.5:1 **m.** by recognizing they are not part of you
T-6....IV.12:10 He **m.** gave the Answer. His Answer is
T-6.........V.2:1 but will **m.** remind them that the night is
T-6.........V.2:3 **m.** reassure them that they are safe *now.*
T-6.........V.4:5 He **m.** shines them away. His light is
T-6......V.C.3:3 **m.** the beginning of the thought reversal,
T-7........III.2:3 It **m.** rests in the Kingdom because it
T-7........III.4:1 is **m.** to focus your full attention on it. As
T-7........III.5:3 The Answer **m.** undoes the question by
T-7........IV.2:7 I said before that forgetting is **m.** a way of
T-7......IV.7:11 it, you are **m.** forgetting what you are not.
T-7.......X.5:10 this, too, is **m.** a matter of his own belief.
T-8...........I.1:6 is **m.** the result of your misuse of His laws
T-8...........I.2:5 are **m.** asked to evaluate them in terms of
T-8...........I.5:6 each one **m.** interferes with the other.
T-8.........II.8:2 then, is **m.** to what the Kingdom is, and
T-8........VI.9:6 The journey to God is **m.** the reawakening
T-8.......VII.7:3 orders of reality **m.** appear to exist, just as
T-8.....VIII.7:4 Sickness is **m.** another example of your
T-8........IX.1:5 for this would **m.** be to accept the ego's
T-9...........I.3:6 purpose of this Guide is **m.** to remind you
T-9...........I.3:8 He is **m.** making every possible effort,
T-9.........I.10:3 It is **m.** a denial in the form of a request.
T-9........III.4:2 He has **m.** disregarded them, and if you
T-9........III.4:5 more than **m.** a lack of correction for him.
T-9........III.6:4 brother, but **m.** to accept him as he is. His
T-9........IV.2:3 **m.** be further error to believe either that
T-9........IV.3:2 Holy Spirit **m.** reminds you of the natural
T-9........IV.4:3 By following its plan you will **m.** place
T-9........IV.6:3 wrong. Miracles are **m.** the sign of your
T-9........IV.9:4 Second Coming is **m.** the return of sense.
T-9.........V.3:6 have done is **m.** to identify with the ego,
T-9........VII.7:6 the ego's thought system **m.** because He
T-9...VIII.10:2 eternal place **m.** waits for your return.
T-9...VIII.11:5 It **m.** *is.* Ask the Holy Spirit what it is and
T-10.........I.2:6 not possible that you **m.** shifted from one
T-10.......II.2:1 of reality brings more than **m.** lack of fear
T-10.......II.3:1 remember is **m.** to restore to your mind
T-10.......II.3:2 you **m.** accept again what is already there,
T-10.......III.7:3 in the Kingdom, **m.** by denying them
T-10.......III.7:7 you **m.** because I have only one message,
T-10.......IV.2:4 To overlook nothingness is **m.** to judge it
T-10.......IV.4:5 else is **m.** lawless and therefore chaotic.
T-10.......V.9:8 It is **m.** because your acknowledgment of
T-11.......II.6:7 If you will **m.** offer Him a little place, He
T-11.......II.7:8 with you **m.** by recognizing what is there
T-11.......V.1:4 for we are **m.** looking honestly for truth.
T-11.......V.2:4 be dispelled **m.** by denying their reality.
T-11.......V.5:2 way to undo its results is **m.** to recognize
T-11.....V.12:5 so diligently, has **m.** brought you fear,
T-11.....VII.1:5 To perceive anew is **m.** to perceive again,
T-11. VIII.14:2 But you are **m.** deceived in them. Ask
T-12.......II.1:1 are **m.** the translation of denial into truth.
T-12......III.1:3 are **m.** those who have invested wrongly,
T-12......III.7:5 as the outside world is **m.** your attempt to
T-12.......V.8:1 indeed, it is **m.** ridiculous if you look at it.
T-12.......V.8:5 It is **m.** the result of an honest appraisal of
T-12......VI.4:2 have not lost their vision, but **m.** sleep.
T-12......VI.6:3 to holiness is **m.** its natural extension.
T-12.....VII.8:2 you perceive is **m.** the reflection of your
T-13.......II.2:2 of it, but you are actually **m.** concealing it.
T-13......IV.5:2 The present **m.** reminds it of past hurts,
T-13......IV.6:7 you are **m.** perceiving it as a meeting with
T-13...VII.11:6 For what you think you need will **m.** serve
T-13...VIII.3:5 is **m.** a faulty formulation of reality, with
T-13......XI.3:5 It can **m.** be appreciated or not. To value
T-13......XI.4:2 Perfect perception can **m.** show you what
T-14.........I.5:3 **m.** looks at its foundation and dismisses
T-14.........I.5:6 deceived will **m.** attack direct approaches,
T-14......III.2:1 guiltlessness **m.** to offset the pain of guilt,
T-14......III.7:1 is **m.** this: Guiltlessness is invulnerability.
T-14......IV.2:1 part of Him, are more than **m.** guiltless.
T-14......IV.9:5 **m.** teaches you how to remove the blocks
T-14......VI.2:1 dwells within you is **m.** perfect openness,
T-14.....VII.3:6 but **m.** a belief in something that does not
T-14.....VII.5:7 **m.** changes them into a call for what you
T-14...VII.5:14 **m.** asked to do the little He suggests you
T-14......IX.1:3 It **m.** brings unholiness to holiness; or
T-14......IX.2:5 It **m.** vanishes because it is not true.
T-14......IX.3:1 **M.** by being what it is, does truth release
T-14......IX.8:7 They do not **m.** reflect truth, for they *are*
T-14.......X.6:5 It **m.** recognizes what it is, and answers
T-14.......X.7:5 It is **m.** form, and nothing else. For you
T-15.........I.1:1 but **m.** to be perfectly calm and quiet all
T-15.........I.4:8 if death were thought of **m.** as an end to
T-15.......I.10:2 more than **m.** that hell does not exist. In
T-15......IV.6:8 nothing, but **m.** to accept everything.
T-15.....VII.7:5 He **m.** believes he is in love with sacrifice.
T-16.........I.2:7 you will **m.** sit quietly by and let the Holy
T-16.........I.6:6 are foolish **m.** because they conflict, since
T-16......IV.1:6 will **m.** drive it underground and out of
T-16......IV.6:1 but **m.** to seek and find all of the barriers
T-16.......V.3:4 who believe that hate is sin **m.** feel guilty,
T-16.......V.6:2 worlds has **m.** led to fantasies of both,
T-16.....V.12:8 He **m.** could not let this happen. You
T-17......III.1:1 forgive is **m.** to remember only the loving
T-17......VI.1:3 simple is **m.** what is easily understood,
T-18....III.4:12 necessary was **m.** the *wish* to understand.
T-18......IV.5:1 You **m.** ask the question. The answer is
T-18......IV.5:3 but **m.** to receive the answer as it is given.
T-18......IV.6:2 will **m.** take away the little that is asked.
T-18.......V.4:5 and you would **m.** bring unholy means to
T-18......VI.1:6 It is **m.** an awareness of perfect Oneness,
T-18..VI.11:10 questions of reality, but **m.** accepting it.
T-18....VI.13:3 you, **m.** because you would not have it so.
T-18....VI.14:6 breaking out, but **m.** by a quiet melting in
T-18.....VII.5:6 It would be far more profitable now **m.** to
T-18...VIII.1:4 Think not that this is **m.** allegorical, for it
T-18...VIII.4:2 They **m.** continue, unaware that they are
T-18....IX.10:7 forgiven nor transformed. But **m.** known.
T-19......III.3:5 not repeat it; you will **m.** stop and let it go
T19...IV.A.8:6 induces **m.** indicates its limited results.
T19.IV.D.10:4 Yet **m.** to reach the place is not enough. A
T-20......III.3:5 Their looking **m.** asks a question, and it is
T-20......IV.1:8 Holy Spirit **m.** gives everything to God,
T-20.......V.4:4 that you will **m.** love him and be glad.
T-20.......V.7:4 And **m.** by remembering them, the laws
T-20......VI.4:6 The rest it **m.** throws away, for all that it
T-20.....VII.1:4 are **m.** indications of areas where means
T-20.....VII.3:6 they be difficult if they are **m.** given you?
T-20.....VII.4:3 For holiness is **m.** the result of letting the
T-20.....VII.4:4 is positive and the body is **m.** neutral. It is
T-20...VIII.9:4 see is **m.** how you elect to meet your goal.
T-20. VIII.10:3 if you saw at all or **m.** judged against.
T-21.......II.3:1 be **m.** driven by events outside of him. It
T-21......II.10:8 two is **m.** to fail to understand them both.
T-21....IV.1:10 This **m.** seems to be the source of fear.
T-22.......V.1:3 **M.** by letting reason tell you that they
T-22.......V.1:7 What **m.** is needs no defense, and offers
T-22......VI.5:2 quietly on all confusion, observing **m.**,
T-23........II.1:7 broken; **m.** looked upon and gone beyond
T-23........II.3:5 of to each other, they **m.** disappear. No
T-24......IV.3:9 miracles are **m.** change of purpose from
T-24....VI.12:1 Now you are **m.** asked that you pursue
T-25.........I.1:2 will you learn the body **m.** seems to be the
T-25.........I.4:4 into light **m.** by looking past it *to* the light.
T-25.......V.1:1 state of sinlessness is **m.** this: The whole
T-26.........I.5:1 of to illusion **m.** ask that they might see a
T-26........II.8:5 locked will **m.** fall away and disappear.
T-26...VII.14:2 cause can **m.** shift effects to other forms.
T-26....VIII.9:h is **m.** a denial of the fact that consequence
T-27.......I.11:1 way to let this be achieved is **m.** this; to let
T-27........II.4:6 lies the proof that they are **m.** errors. Let
T-27......III.6:9 the place of every learning aid will **m.** *be.*
T-27......III.7:9 He would **m.** be, and so He merely is.
T-27......III.7:9 He would merely be, and so He **m.** is.
T-27......IV.5:7 but **m.** asks what the response should be.
T-27......IV.7:4 *is.* Within the world the answers **m.** raise
T-27.....V.10:2 part is **m.** to apply what He has taught
T-27.....V.11:8 by **m.** counting up its separate parts. God
T-27......VI.5:2 It **m.** proves that what they represent has
T-27....VIII.5:3 do? Then let us **m.** look upon the dream's
T-28.........I.1:4 It does not add, but **m.** takes away. And
T-28........II.4:2 but **m.** shows you who the dreamer is. It
T-28......IV.4:3 him, **m.** by your claim on brotherhood,
T-28.....VII.3:3 to both, and **m.** sets you spinning round,
T-28.....VII.3:6 **m.** as an aid to help you reach the home
T-29......IV.4:4 matter if they be fulfilled or **m.** wanted. It
T-29....VIII.5:6 It **m.** lifts the veil, and lets the truth shine
T-30.......I.11:2 but **m.** hope to get a thing you want. And
T-30........II.4:1 that **m.** waits your blessing to be free? If
T-30......IV.4:9 **m.** looked upon as children's toys without
T-30......VI.2:5 it **m.** asks that you respond appropriately
T-30......VI.2:7 But you are **m.** asked to see forgiveness as
T-31.........I.2:4 **m.** goes from one apparent lesson to the
T-31.....V.10:6 concept's foolishness, and **m.** think of this
T-31.....V.11:6 **m.** asks if just a little question might be
T-31......VI.3:2 It **m.** asks that this should be your choice.
T-31.....VII.7:5 At least, you **m.** look on darkness, and
T-31...VII.13:5 And recognizing this, it **m.** asks, "What is
T-31....VIII.4:4 **m.** those who choose His strength instead
W-in..........8:3 are **m.** asked to apply the ideas as you are
W-pI.......1.3:3 should **m.** be applied to anything you see.
W-pI.......2.2:1 **M.** glance easily and fairly quickly
W-pI.......2.2:4 is **m.** that your eyes have lighted on it.
W-pI.......3.1:7 **m.** use these things exactly as you would
W-pI.......7.3:2 you **m.** reviewing your past experiences of
W-pI.......8.3:3 that your mind has been **m.** blank, rather
W-pI.......8.4:3 so, **m.** noting the thoughts you find there.
W-pI.....10.3:3 is **m.** another way of repeating our earlier
W-pI.....11.2:4 in using the idea **m.** repeat it to yourself,
W-pI.....15.3:5 they **m.** symbolize true perception, and
W-pI.....16.1:5 They are **m.** true or false. Those that are
W-pI.....21.3:5 It is **m.** an example of the belief that some
W-pI.....23.2:4 of change because it is **m.** an effect. But
W-pI.....31.3:1 **m.** let whatever thoughts cross your mind
W-pI.....33.2:1 **M.** glance casually around the world you
W-pI.....35.5:5 direction in reality. They are **m.** not true.
W-pI.....35.8:2 **m.** relax and repeat today's idea slowly
W-pI.....35.9:2 to you, **m.** repeat the idea to yourself,
W-pI.....37.3:2 but **m.** by your quiet recognition that in
W-pI.....39.9:1 you **m.** repeat today's idea to yourself
W-pI.....40.3:9 **m.** telling yourself that you are blessed as
W-pI.....42.5:3 you find your mind is **m.** wandering, and
W-pI.....42.6:2 Try **m.** to step back and let the thoughts
W-pI.....43.9:1 **m.** repeat the idea in its original form. Try
W-pI.....44.7:4 it. It is **m.** taking its natural course. Try to
W-pI.....48.2:2 **M.** repeat the idea as often as possible.
W-pI.....51.2:4 It is **m.** an illusion of reality, because my
W-pI.....51.3:7 now for this **m.** by being willing to do so.
W-pI.....52.4:4 the choice is **m.** whether to see or not.
W-pI.....55.4:3 are my best interests would **m.** bind me
W-pI.....57.1:4 can drop them off **m.** by desiring to do so.
W-pI.....61.1:2 **m.** a statement of the truth about yourself

W-pI.....64.1:1 Today's idea is **m.** another way of saying
W-pI.....66.3:5 We will **m.** be glad that we can find out
W-pI.....75.6:6 like. You **m.** wait to have it shown to you.
W-pI.....77.1:5 It is **m.** a statement of your true Identity.
W-pI.....77.4:5 They **m.** follow from the laws of God.
WpI..rII.in.6:3 These, however, are **m.** suggestions. It is
W-pI.....88.1:2 I **m.** choose to recognize what is already
W-pI.....95.7:5 however, **m.** be recognized as what it is; a
W-pI.....95.9:1 this course, you have **m.** made a mistake.
W-pI...107.1:4 They **m.** vanish, leaving not a trace by
W-pI...107.4:4 They will **m.** blow away, when truth
W-pI...107.7:2 We **m.** ask for what belongs to us, that we
W-pI.121.10:1 you actively despise, or **m.** try to overlook
W-pI...126.3:2 **m.** to point out that you are better, on a
W-pI.130.10:1 **m.** by remembering the limits of your
W-pI...132.8:3 you ever thought it was by **m.** changing
W-pI.132.15:4 Then **m.** rest, alert but with no strain, and
W-pI...133.9:3 not perceive that he has **m.** failed to gain.
W-pI.133.12:5 It is far more than **m.** letting you make
W-pI...134.5:2 a view. It **m.** is a further sign that sin is
W-pI...134.7:5 them with quiet eyes, and **m.** says to them
W-pI...135.8:2 need **m.** be perceived as quite apart from
W-pI.135.10:4 all, but **m.** adds to your distress of mind.
W-pI.135.10:5 but **m.** take away the hope of healing, for
W-pI...136.1:5 and **m.** leaves them there to disappear.
W-pI.136.12:4 Truth **m.** wants to give you happiness, for
W-pI.136.15:4 It **m.** waits for just this invitation which
W-pI...137.4:4 To be healed is **m.** to accept what always
W-pI...138.6:1 of choice, rather than **m.** being what it is.
W-pI...139.4:1 He **m.** states that he is not himself, and
W-pI...139.4:3 it **m.** shows he does not want to be the
W-pI.139.10:2 but **m.** to accept the truth about yourself,
W-pI...140.2:2 He **m.** had a dream that he was sick, and
W-pI...140.3:1 where one can **m.** dream he is awake. The
W-pI...140.6:5 It is **m.** an appeal to truth, which cannot
W-pI...140.6:7 It **m.** focuses on what it is, and knows that
WpI. rIV.in7:1 **m.** read each of the two ideas assigned to
W-pI...151.1:3 is **m.** an opinion based on ignorance and
W-pI...151.4:4 You **m.** can believe the ego's judgments,
W-pI...151.7:3 which **m.** bear false witness to God's Son.
W-pI...152.7:4 To think you can is **m.** to believe you can
W-pI...153.1:1 the "gifts" it **m.** lends to take away again;
W-pI...155.2:6 truth stand forth as what it is, is **m.** sanity
W-pI...158.6:4 unlearned, untaught, unseen–is **m.** there
W-pI...158.8:2 set up a goal that does not **m.** disappear
W-pI...158.9:3 gone. Unseen by One they **m.** disappear,
W-pI...159.5:3 quite solid here are **m.** shadows there;
W-pI.161.12:3 whom you have seen as **m.** flesh and bone
W-pI...164.5:2 which appeared to hide it **m.** sink away.
W-pI...164.8:1 your practicing by **m.** letting go all things
W-pI.166.10:2 oppose. It **m.** is. It is not God you have
W-pI...167.9:1 to be the opposite of life is **m.** sleeping.
W-pI...167.9:2 Source, it **m.** seems to go to sleep a while.
W-pI...169.5:7 Source. And like its Source Itself, it **m.** is.
W-pI...169.6:5 of God has **m.** disappeared into his Father
W-pI...169.9:3 We **m.** take the part assigned long since,
W-pI...170.5:4 ask you lay down all defense as **m.** foolish.
W-pI...182.4:2 so distorted that you **m.** hold a picture of
W-pI...185.3:5 both. Loser and gainer **m.** shift about in
W-pI...185.4:5 They **m.** bargain. And what bargain can
W-pI.185.11:2 For he **m.** asks that he deceive himself no
W-pI...188.1:2 seek the light are **m.** covering their eyes.
W-pI...189.8:7 The way to reach Him is **m.** to let Him be.
W-pI...190.5:6 you see by **m.** recognizing what you are.
W-pI...190.6:3 all. It **m.** represents your thoughts. And it
W-pI...192.2:7 Creation **m.** waits for your return to be
W-pI...196.5:3 it **m.** stood for the belief the fear of God is
WpI rVI.in.4:3 We **m.** close our eyes, and then forget all
W-pII ....in.1:4 lessons that remain are **m.** introductions
W-pII ....in.2:1 to let the exercise be **m.** a beginning. For
W-pII .....1.1:6 Son? Forgiveness **m.** sees its falsity, and
W-pII .....1.4:3 It **m.** looks, and waits, and judges not. He
W-pII .....2.2:2 was given without opposite, and **m.** was.
W-pII .....2.3:3 it **m.** lets them quietly go down to dust.
W-pII .233.1:6 *I will step back and* **m.** *follow You. Be You*
W-pII .234.1:2 left. **M.** a tiny instant has elapsed between
W-pII .235.1:1 from this," and **m.** watch them disappear.
W-pII .282.2:3 *the truth be changed by* **m.** *giving it another*
W-pII .....9.1:1 as God, is **m.** the correction of mistakes,
W-pII ... 10.2:3 sight, it **m.** slips away to nothingness.
W-pII . 312.1:3 For sight can **m.** serve to offer us what we
W-pII . 323.2:1 a debt that **m.** is the letting go of self-
W-pII .... 324.h I **m.** follow, for I would not lead.
W-pII . 324.1:7 *Yet I* **m.** *follow in the way to You, as You*
W-pII . 332.1:4 It **m.** is. And by its presence is the mind
W-pII . 335.1:3 What I see in him is **m.** what I wish to see,
W-pII ... 13.1:3 It **m.** looks on devastation, and reminds
W-pII .... 359.h And all sin Is understood as **m.** a mistake.
Wfl........in.5:4 is mad, and vengeance **m.** foolish fantasy.
M-1 .......... 4:3 They **m.** save time. Yet it is time alone
M-4 ..... I.A.3:3 their lack of value is **m.** being recognized.
M-4 ..... I.A.4:3 the things he valued before will **m.** hinder
M-4 ..... I.A.8:3 as **m.** shadows before become solid gains,
M-4 ...... IV.2:4 harm has no meaning, it is **m.** natural.
M-4 ..... VII.1:7 Its greater strangeness lies **m.** in the
M-5 ........II.1:9 terms **m.** state or describe the problem.
M-5 ......II.2:12 could **m.** rise up without their aid and say
M-5 .... III.2:10 They **m.** give what has been given them.
M-6 .......... 3:2 It is **m.** their function to give them. Once
M-8 .......... 5:1 healing **m.** because all sickness is illusion.
M-10 ......... 2:2 he is **m.** giving up what he did not have.
M-10 ......... 2:4 He has actually **m.** become more honest.
M-10 ......... 4:3 you **m.** thought you were right, without
M-10 ......... 5:2 could **m.** stagger and fall down beneath it
M-11 ......... 4:9 hell to Heaven **m.** by being what it is? The
M-14 ....... 1:11 not. It **m.** overlooked the meaningless.
M-14 ....... 2:12 touched. It will **m.** cease to seem to be.
M-14 ......... 4:5 He need **m.** learn how to approach it; to
M-14 ......... 4:6 He need **m.** trust that, if God's Voice tells
M-16 ......... 6:7 you give up is **m.** the illusion of protecting
M-16 ......... 9:3 seem frightening, but they are **m.** pathetic
M-16 ......... 9:5 all magic is recognized as **m.** nothing, the
M-16 ....... 10:8 dangerous, but **m.** that it is meaningless.
M-16 ....... 10:9 he **m.** chooses to give up all that he never
M-17 ......... 4:4 It may be **m.** slight irritation, perhaps too
M-20 ....... 2:10 The contrast first perceived has **m.** gone.
M-21 ......... 4:6 process is **m.** a special case of the lesson
M-22 ......... 3:5 to do as it sees fit could **m.** take the place
M-23 ......... 1:5 Is this **m.** an appeal to magic? A name
M-24 ......... 3:3 of him, it would **m.** limit his usefulness,
M-24 ......... 3:6 the course **m.** because it advocates a long-
M-24 ......... 4:3 they are likely to be **m.** controversial. The
M-24 ......... 5:9 He need **m.** accept the idea that what he
M-25 ......... 1:2 and it is obviously **m.** an appeal to magic
M-25 ......... 2:7 in any way is **m.** becoming more natural.
M-25 ......... 6:5 which **m.** means to strengthen the ego.
M-26 ......... 3:9 Those who have laid the body down **m.** to
M-29 ......... 1:3 substitute for either, but **m.** a supplement
M-29 ....... 3:10 **m.** because of your own inadequacies. It
C-in .......... 3:4 It is **m.** the ego that questions because it is
C-in .......... 3:5 The course **m.** gives another answer, once
C-1 ........... 6:2 because right-mindedness **m.** overlooks,
C-3 ........... 2:4 that makes them unwilling **m.** to rise up
P-2........ III.1:3 will **m.** stumble blindly on to nowhere. It
P-2........ III.3:7 world without a word, **m.** by being there.
P-2....... IV.11:4 It is **m.** recognized as what it is. Seen
P-3..........II.9:8 Some utilize the relationship **m.** to collect
P-3......... III.3:7 if it does, it **m.** crucifies God's Son again.
S-1...........I.1:2 It is not **m.** a question or an entreaty. It
S-1...........I.2:8 is **m.** an echo of the reply of His Voice.
S-1...........I.3:5 All the rest is **m.** added. You have sought
S-1..........II.1:5 At these levels prayer is **m.** wanting, out
S-3..........II.1:1 False healing **m.** makes a poor exchange
S-3........II.1:10 universe. It **m.** signifies the end has come
S-3..........II.5:4 such a view of what is **m.** opening the gate

## merest 1

W-pI... 167.2:6 discomfort or the **m.** frown, acknowledge

## merge 2

T-18 ........I.7:7 They fuse and **m.** and separate, in shifting
W-pI... 198.6:6 the words in which all **m.** as one at last.

## merit 11

T-10 ..... III.6:4 not my **m.** that I contribute to you but my
T-16 ..... VII.3:5 the vengeance it believes you so justly **m.**.
T-25 . VIII.12:1 the Son of God could **m.** vengeance. You
T-25 ..... IX.6:3 he does not **m.** an attack of any kind.
T-27 .....II.13:6 yours. His **m.** punishment, while yours, in
T-30 ..... VI.3:8 do not **m.** the forgiveness that it gives.
T-30 ..... VI.4:8 judgment that your brother does not **m.**.
T-30 ..... VI.4:9 you can **m.** neither more nor less than he.
T-30 ..... VI.9:2 you think he does not **m.** the escape from
WpI..rIII.in7:5 His means must surely **m.** yours as well.
P-2........ IV.5:3 has some **m.** in a world where "degrees of

## merited 1

T-30 ..... VI.5:1 Forgiveness recognized as **m.** will heal. It

## meriting 1

T-31 ..... III.1:6 be yours, and therefore **m.** a "just" attack.

## merits 3

T-25 . VIII.10:1 To him who **m.** everything, how can it be
T-30 ..... VI.4:7 If you can see your brother **m.** pardon,
T-31 .......II.4:6 And thus he **m.** death, because he has no

## message 73

T-2 .........V.5:5 The **m.** you then give to them is the truth
T-4 ........in.3:8 The only **m.** of the crucifixion is that you
T-4 ....... III.1:6 This is the whole **m.** of the Atonement; a
T-4 ....... III.1:6 a **m.** which in its totality transcends the
T-5 .......II.11:3 "join together," and "burden" means "**m.**
T-5 .......II.11:4 "Let us join together, for my **m.** is light."
T-5 .......II.12:6 Child of God, my **m.** is for you, to hear
T-6 .............I.h The **M.** of the Crucifixion
T-6 ..........I.4:6 The **m.** the crucifixion was intended to
T-6 ........I.13:1 The **m.** of the crucifixion is perfectly clear
T-6 ........I.15:1 its gospel is really only the **m.** of love. If
T-6 ........I.15:6 whole **m.** of the crucifixion was simply
T-6 .......II.12:6 This is the one **m.** God gave to Him and
T-6 .......II.12:7 The peace of God lies in that **m.**, and so
T-6 ....... III.2:4 before that the **m.** of the crucifixion was,
T-7 .........II.5:4 The meaning of His **m.** is always the same
T-8 .....VIII.9:1 so He can teach His **m.** through you. This
T-9 ..........I.6:5 A **m.** cannot be communicated unless it
T-9 .........II.5:1 **m.** your brother gives you is up to you.
T-9 .........II.5:4 about him determines the **m.** you receive.
T-10 ..... III.7:7 you merely because I have only one **m.**,
T-10 ..... III.8:1 I do not bring God's **m.** with deception,
T-10 .......V.2:2 You must receive the **m.** you give because
T-10 .......V.2:2 you give because it is the **m.** you want.
T-10 .......V.2:3 judged them by the **m.** you give to them.
T-10 .......V.7:5 If you hear His **m.** He has answered you,
T-11 .......II.4:2 of the Holy Spirit, Whose **m.** is wholeness
T-13 ..... IV.5:7 You thus deny yourself the **m.** of release
T-13 .. VIII.4:4 His **m.** speaks of timelessness in time, and
T-14 .........I.5:2 learn. His **m.** is not indirect, but He must
T-14 .......V.1:2 into a radiant **m.** of God's Love, to share
T-14 .......V.2:1 **m.** given to each one is always the same;
T-14 .......V.2:2 Each one teaches the **m.** differently, and
T-14 ..... IX.6:5 **m.** that shines forth from what the mirror
T-14 ..... IX.6:6 It is the **m.** that the Holy Spirit is holding
T-15 ..... XI.8:4 Such is the **m.** of the time of Christ, which
T-16 .. VII.11:1 Seek and *find* His **m.** in the holy instant,
T-18 .......V.4:3 Their **m.** is, "Thy Will be done," and not,
T-19 ..... IV.1:7 you will carry its **m.** of love and safety and
T19 ... IV.B.3:2 Such is the **m.** that I gave them for you. It
T19 ... IV.B.7:6 the world the joyous **m.** of the end of guilt
T19 . IV.B.15:1 in the belief that for your **m.** of attack and
T-22 ...........I.h The **M.** of the Holy Relationship
T-22 ..... IV.5:4 whose **m.** has not yet been given everyone
T-22 ..... IV.6:5 and carrying His **m.** of hope and freedom
T-24 .......II.5:3 To every special one a different **m.**, and
T-25 ........I.2:6 The **m.** and the messenger are one. And
T-25 ... IX.10:9 is universal, and it teaches but one **m.**:
T-27 ........I.6:8 to both the **m.** is the same. Adornment of
T-27 ......I.10:5 Then will it send forth the **m.** it received,

## messages 55



## Messenger 1

*messenger*



## messenger 19

*Messenger*



## messengers 29



## met 18



## metal 2



## meted 2



## method 4



## methods 4



## meting 1



## microscopic 1



## middle 3



## middlemen 1



## midst 11



## might 124

T-9........IV.8:2 You **m.** ask yourself, regardless of how
T-11......IV.1:5 you by your Creator that you **m.** extend it.
T-12......IV.6:1 that you **m.** learn you have eternal life.
T-13....... II.8:6 **m.** turn on yourself and destroy yourself.
T-13......IV.3:3 Even the past life that death **m.** indicate,
T-13......IV.3:6 **m.** it not be more desirable than death?
T-13......IV.4:1 that your questioning **m.** well begin. The
T-13....... V.9:1 way of seeing that you **m.** see in darkness,
T-15...... IX.3:5 will strive for them with all its **m.**, and
T-16....... II.2:2 think you **m.** be better able to understand
T-17....VII.7:3 Yet for all its **m.**, so great it reaches past
T-17....VIII.1:3 that faith **m.** answer to the call of truth.
T-18......IV.1:8 is He Who adds the greatness and the **m.**.
T19....IV.C.8:1 Himself is powerless before the ego's **m.**,
T19. IV.D.17:9 that we **m.** meet here in this holy place,
T-21...... III.6:5 that you **m.** choose among your brothers,
T-24.........I.7:3 to your brother that love **m.** be extended,
T-24...... II.10:7 that both **m.** share the universe with Him
T-24...... III.2:2 all your puny **m.** against the Will of God.
T-24...... III.7:7 God gave to you that you **m.** look on him,
T-24......IV.4:2 wish that you **m.** see your brother sinless.
T-24....... V.6:9 that each **m.** offer you the Love of God.
T-24...... VI.7:6 that you **m.** see the truth about yourself,
T-24.... VI.12:5 and all the power of Heaven and the **m.** of
T-24.....VII.1:8 that you **m.** share the Fatherhood of God,
T-25....... II.2:3 change that **m.** result in better outcome?
T-25....... II.7:5 God kept it safe that you **m.** look on it,
T-25......IV.2:7 own creation, that his joy **m.** be increased
T-25....... V.3:5 that you **m.** hear in him His Call to you,
T-25..VIII.10:8 protect from all unfairness you **m.** seek to
T-26.........I.5:1 that they **m.** see a purpose in the world
T-26....... II.2:2 loss and make a sacrifice that you **m.** gain.
T-26....VIII.1:2 that you and he **m.** be a little separate.
T-27....... V.7:4 who let yourself be healed that it **m.** live.
T-28..... V.1:11 Will with you, that His creation **m.** create.
T-29....... II.5:5 them with Him, that they **m.** be yours.
T-29....... V.2:4 and quiet, tranquil in the **m.** of its Creator
T-29....... V.4:3 He was created that you **m.** be whole, for
T-29...... VI.4:4 and change that time **m.** be preserved,
T-29....VIII.8:5 to seek for one that yet **m.** offer him a gift
T-30......IV.1:6 They were made that this **m.** be forgotten.
T-31..... II.2:10 you made, that this **m.** be obscured to you
T-31..... V.11:6 asks if just a little question **m.** be raised.
T-31..... V.12:2 be. You **m.**, for instance, be the thing you
W-pI.......5.4:2 **m.** help to precede the exercises with the
W-pI.......8.6:3 **m.** find it helpful, however, to include
W-pI.....10.4:6 you **m.** imagine that you are watching an
W-pI.....12.3:4 example, you **m.** think of "a good world,"
W-pI.....14.5:1 anything you are afraid **m.** happen to you
W-pI.....17.2:5 For example, you **m.** say: *I do not see a*
W-pI.....27.3:3 **m.** try for every fifteen or twenty minutes.
W-pI.....29.5:2 For example, a suitable list **m.** include:
W-pI.....35.6:1 the idea for today **m.** be as follows: *I see*
W-pI.....38.5:2 own. You **m.** like, for example, to include
W-pI.....40.3:3 One practice period **m.**, for example,
W-pI.....40.3:6 Another **m.** take this form: *I am blessed as*
W-pI.....41.6:6 thoughts that **m.** divert your attention.
W-pI.....41.8:3 **m.** even say it is the only natural thing in
W-pI.....42.4:4 You **m.** think, for example: *Vision must be*
W-pI.....43.4:6 You **m.** say, for example: *God is my Source*
W-pI.....44.6:2 You **m.** find it helpful to remind yourself,
W-pI.....46.6:2 You **m.** say, for example: *I cannot be guilty*
W-pI.....70.4:1 however distorted and fantastic it **m.** be,
W-pI.....70.7:2 you. You **m.** put it this way: *My salvation*
W-pI.....78.8:8 role God gave Him that you **m.** be saved.
W-pI.....81.2:1 special difficulties seem to arise **m.** be: *Let*
W-pI.....81.4:1 forms for using this idea **m.** include: *Let*
W-pI.....83.2:1 applications of this idea **m.** take these
W-pI.....84.2:1 You **m.** find these specific forms helpful
W-pI.....85.2:1 for this idea **m.** be made in these forms:
W-pI.....86.4:1 for this idea **m.** be in these forms: *I am*
W-pI.....89.2:1 You **m.** use these suggestions for specific
W-pI.....90.2:1 Specific applications of this idea **m.** be in
W-pI.....97.6:2 it will surpass in **m.** the little gift you gave
W-pI...100.2:3 that you **m.** be restored to what He wills.
W-pI...108.8:5 You **m.**, for instance, say: *To everyone I*
W-pI...108.9:4 It **m.** be helpful, too, to think of one to
W-pI...109.6:2 that it **m.** take its rest along with you.
W-pI...115.2:3 *He gave me His plan that I* **m.** *save the world.*
W-pI...123.8:2 His Son, that he **m.** rise above the world,
W-pI...129.2:1 It **m.** be worth a little time to think once
W-pI. 131.14:2 that you **m.** approach this door some day,
W-pI...136.8:4 strange, haunting thought that you **m.** be
W-pI. 136.12:2 does not make appeal to **m.** nor triumph.
W-pI...137.5:1 Healing **m.** thus be called a counter-
W-pI...153.6:4 folly, or a silly game a tired child **m.** play,
W-pI...162.2:3 that will not fade away before their **m.**.
W-pI...163.4:2 strength and **m.** of God Himself perceived
W-pI...166.7:4 down lest you **m.** catch a glimpse of truth,
W-pI...169.8:2 it to all minds that each one **m.** determine
W-pI...182.7:5 back with Him, that He Himself **m.** stay,
W-pI...182.9:2 that you **m.** learn of Him how strong is he
W-pI...182.9:3 He holds the **m.** of Heaven in His hand
W-pI...186.5:5 experience which **m.** affront their stance.
W-pII . 356.1:1 *to answer any call Your Son* **m.** *make to You.*
M-in..........2:5 The purpose of the course **m.** be said to
M-4.....I.A.3:1 what **m.** be called "a period of undoing."
M-4......IV.2:8 The **m.** of God's teachers lies in their
M-6...........1:7 healing **m.** precipitate intense depression,
M-6...........1:7 the patient **m.** even try to destroy himself.
M-23.........5:3 for love, but only that he **m.** give it to you.
M-24.........5:5 He **m.** be advised that he is misusing the
M-24.........6:3 Atonement **m.** be equated with total
M-26.........2:2 **m.** be called the Teachers of teachers
M-29.........1:6 Others **m.** do better to begin with the
C-3............2:1 Forgiveness **m.** be called a kind of happy
C-5............2:6 Christ needed his form that He **m.** appear
C-5............4:3 your dreams that they **m.** be dispelled.
S-3........IV.8:1 ends so soon it **m.** as well have never been

## mightier 3

T-19..... III.7:6 Sin is perceived as **m.** than God, before
T19....IV.A.3:7 your brother seems **m.** than the universe,
T-31........I.5:6 in forgiveness have a power **m.** than yours

## mightily 1

W-pI. 153.10:5 And who could be more **m.** protected?

## mightiness 2

T-24.......II.4:5 seems silent and unheard before its "**m.**."
W-pI...152.9:3 truth is humble in acknowledging its **m.**,

## mighty 30

T-14....VII.5:9 His task is **m.**, but the power of God is
T-14..VII.5:13 You are not asked to do **m.** tasks yourself.
T-14... XI.15:3 the **m.** works that He will do through you,
T-16.......II.9:5 For the ideas are **m.** forces, to be used and
T19....IV.A.7:3 with you it seemed to have a **m.** purpose;
T19....IV.A.9:1 How **m.** can a little feather be before the
T19....IV.C.9:2 grow into a **m.** force for God is very near.
T19....IV.C.9:3 the **m.** task for which it was given you.
T-20...... V.1:6 of joining is a **m.** herald of eternity. No
T-22..... VI.4:1 lovely in its innocence, **m.** in strength,
T-23.....IV.4:4 your little gifts and make them **m.**. Also
T-26.....IV.6:3 you join the **m.** chorus to the Love of God
T-27.....VII.6:6 look among the **m.** legions of its witnesses
T-30.....IV.6:4 But you will understand that **m.** changes
W-pI.....43.2:3 never was, perception has a **m.** purpose.
W-pI.....98.2:3 We have a **m.** purpose to fulfill, and have
W-pI...99.11:2 not withstand the truth these **m.** words
W-pI...106.1:1 then you will hear the **m.** Voice of truth,
W-pI...118.2:2 *and let me hear the* **m.** *Voice for Truth Itself*
W-pI...123.5:6 however **m.** be the Voice that speaks,
W-pI...132.1:4 thoughts you hold are **m.**, and illusions
W-pI...162.4:2 For the words we use are **m.**, and they
W-pI...163.2:1 does the thought of death seem **m.**. For it
W-pI...170.7:6 and no **m.** warrior to fight for them.
W-pI...200.6:4 and where it must serve a **m.** function. Is
M-4.........I.2:2 **m.** power of an eagle has been given him?
M-4...I.A.6:11 he goes with **m.** companions beside him.
M-20.........6:6 the **m.** Will of God Himself His gift to you
C-5............5:3 the **m.** lesson that he learned for all of you
P-3........III.1:8 He has a **m.** part in this one purpose, for

## mild 2

W-pI ....21.2:3 ranging from **m.** irritation to rage. The
M-17.........4:4 too **m.** to be even clearly recognized. Or it

## milder 1

T-3..........I.2:7 In **m.** forms a parent says, "This hurts me

## milestone 1

W-pI ....94.5:9 and a **m.** in learning the thought system

## millions 2

T-2.....VIII.2:5 the separation occurred over **m.** of years,
W-pII . 241.1:6 This is the time of hope for countless **m.**.

## mimics 1

P-2........IV.2:6 grotesque and ugly since it **m.** deformity.

## Mind 143

*mind*

T-2.....VIII.1:5 own sight, though not in the **M.** of God.
T-3..........I.3:5 His **M.** does not create that way. He does
T-3..........II.5:5 because They are of one **M.** and one Will.
T-4.......IV.9:4 His **M.** shone on you in your creation and
T-4.......IV.9:5 His **M.** still shines on you and must shine
T-4......VII.3:7 for the reception of His **M.** and Will.
T-4......VII.3:7 mind by communicating His **M.** to it,
T-5..........I.5:1 Holy Spirit is the Christ **M.** which is aware
T-5..........I.6:3 Holy Spirit is the **M.** of the Atonement.
T-5.........II.1:6 His **M.** to yours as long as there is time.
T-5.......II.10:1 you that the **M.** that decided for me is also
T-5.......II.10:2 This **M.** is unequivocal, because it hears
T-5.......II.12:1 must respond to the same **M.** to do this.
T-5.......II.12:2 This **M.** is the Holy Spirit, Whose Will is
T-5.......III.1:2 were related, because in His **M.** they are.
T-5.......III.1:3 relationship must be in His **M.** because,
T-5.......III.1:4 **M.** is partly yours and also partly God's.
T-5.......IV.4:3 The **M.** that was in me is still irresistibly
T-5.......IV.5:6 and the **M.** that was in me rejoices as you
T-5.......VI.3:2 The **M.** that was in me *is* in you, for God
T-6.........II.8:1 the extensions of His Thought in His **M.**.
T-6.......II.11:7 the Holy Spirit, Whose **M.** is fixed on God
T-6.......IV.2:5 *you* are separate and outside the **M.** of God
T-7.........V.8:4 Spirit in him that never changes His **M.**.
T-7.......V.10:9 mind with you because we are of one **M.**,
T-7.......V.10:9 we are of one Mind, and that **M.** is ours.
T-7.....V.10:10 See only this **M.** everywhere, because only
T-7......VIII.1:4 Kingdom, and keeps it in the **M.** of God.
T-7.......IX.4:1 extending because it is in the **M.** of God.
T-8.........V.1:7 the **M.** of God is established in ours and
T-8.........V.1:8 **M.** is invincible because it is undivided.
T-9.......VI.7:2 open Arms, and finally know His open **M.**
T-9.......VI.7:3 in His **M.** and with a mind like His. In
T-9.....VIII.5:2 and keeping yourself in the **M.** of God.
T-9.....VIII.5:3 be anywhere except in the **M.** of God.
T-9...VIII.10:1 altogether irreplaceable in the **M.** of God.
T-9...VIII.10:7 Your value is in God's **M.**, and therefore
T-10......in.3:1 God does not change His **M.** about you,
T-10......in.3:9 "Has God changed His **M.** about me?"
T-10.....III.1:9 their sickness and returned to His **M.**. He
T-10.....IV.6:2 are no strange images in the **M.** of God,
T-10.....IV.6:2 what is not in His **M.** cannot be in yours,
T-10.....V.10:7 creation, fixed forever in the **M.** of God.
T-11........I.1:6 dwell in the **M.** of God with your brother,
T-11........I.3:3 Can part of His **M.** contain nothing? If
T-11........I.3:4 His **M.** cannot be filled by anyone except
T-11........I.3:4 would be an empty place in God's **M.**.
T-11........I.6:1 you a place in His **M.** that is yours forever.
T-11........I.6:4 God's **M.** cannot be lessened. It can only
T-11.....III.7:5 what is unlike God cannot enter His **M.**,
T-12........I.6:7 He does not change His **M.** about reality
T-12.....III.8:5 separate yourself from the **M.** of God you
T-12.....VI.7:2 spirit of God's Son shines in the **M.** of the
T-12..VII.10:5 perfect safety of the **M.** which created us.
T-13........I.5:6 shines untouched forever in God's **M.**.

T-13.........I.5:8 guiltlessness is in the **M.** of his Father,
T-13... VIII.2:3 of knowledge, being in the **M.** of God,
T-13... VIII.4:2 from Either, being in the **M.** of Both, and
T-13... VIII.4:2 of Both, and knowing that **M.** is One. He
T-13..... X.10:7 reason because it is not in the **M.** of God,
T-13...... XI.5:5 you, because He does not change His **M.**.
T-13.... XI.11:3 kind of reconciliation in His **M.** for you,
T-14.... III.15:8 the loving **M.** wherein he was created, and
T-14...... IV.3:9 function in God's **M.** with all of yours.
T-14.... IV.10:5 in communication with the **M.** of God has
T-14....... V.3:3 is nothing in the **M.** of God that does not
T-14...... XI.9:8 They do not exist in His **M.** at all. For the
T-15..... V.11:5 reaches to eternity, and to the **M.** of God.
T-15...... VI.5:3 unite this idea with the **M.** that thought it,
T-16..... V.12:9 You cannot change His **M.**. No rituals
T-18...... III.8:2 forever in the **M.** of God but shines on
T-18....... V.3:5 Nor will He change His **M.** about it. The
T-19.........I.2:7 joined the **M.** in which all healing rests.
T-19....... II.7:5 his Father, and change His **M.** completely.
T-22....... II.9:6 the Son of God could leave his Father's **M.**
T-24.... in.2:10 rose in His **M.** *because* of what He knows.
T-24...... III.5:6 as one **M.** They wait for all illusions to be
T-24...... VI.3:3 within His **M.** is absent from your own. It
T-24...... VI.3:5 God changes not His **M.** about His Son
T-25.........I.1:3 For the **M.** is His. And so it must be yours.
T-25....... II.7:2 and understand the **M.** that thought it,
T-25....... II.8:1 as his Father's **M.** shows him to you. He
T-25...... III.2:1 **M.** to which perception has no meaning.
T-25..... VII.3:4 as true has any meaning in His **M.** at all.
T-25..... VII.4:3 with the **M.** Whose Thought created him.
T-25... VIII.5:5 Vengeance is alien to God's **M.** *because* He
T-26..... VII.7:5 Thus has He lost His **M.**, proclaiming sin
T-27..... II.12:2 also know the Holy Spirit's **M.** and yours
T-27..... II.16:3 then, correction to the **M.** that is united,
T-28....... I.11:3 into the **M.** which caused all minds to be.
T-30...... III.6:4 And in the **M.** of God there is no ending,
T-30...... III.6:7 as you are in the **M.** which thought of you.
T-30...... III.6:8 parts in what exists within God's **M.**. It is
T-30.... III.10:5 left the **M.** of its Creator Whom it knows,
T-30.... III.11:4 **M.** of Father and of Son joined in creation
T-30.... III.11:8 what you are, not from the **M.** of God, but
W-pI.....36.1:7 sinless, or a part of His **M.** would be sinful
W-pI.....38.1:3 of God, at one with the **M.** of his Creator.
W-pI.....43.3:2 you think, you think with His **M.**. If vision
W-pI........45.h God is the **M.** with which I think.
W-pI.....45.2:1 You think with the **M.** of God. Therefore
W-pI.....45.2:3 because they are thought by the same **M.**.
W-pI.....45.2:5 think with the **M.** of God leave your mind
W-pI.....45.2:6 your thoughts are in the **M.** of God, as
W-pI.....45.2:8 is. As you are part of His **M.**, so are your
W-pI.....45.2:8 Mind, so are your thoughts part of His **M.**
W-pI.....45.3:5 is thought by the **M.** of God is eternal,
W-pI.....45.8:2 is your mind joined with the **M.** of God.
W-pI.....53.4:3 and everything that is real is in His **M.**. It
W-pI.....56.5:4 It has been kept for me in the **M.** of God,
W-pI.....59.5:1 (45) God is the **M.** with which I think. I
W-pI.....59.5:4 As part of His **M.**, my thoughts are His
W-pI.....92.3:1 see, as it is His **M.** with which you think.
W-pI...95.13:5 illusions out of the one **M.** that is this Self,
W-pI.....96.7:1 within your mind and in the **M.** of God.
W-pI.....99.4:1 **M.** and Thought which are forever One?
W-pI.....99.5:1 within the **M.** of God and in your own. It
W-pI...109.9:5 and to the **M.** in which these Thoughts
W-pI...119.1:3 *Son, whose Self rests safely in the* **M.** *of God.*
W-pI...123.8:1 how lovingly He holds you in His **M.**, how
W-pI...125.8:3 in the single **M.** of Father and of Son. In
W-pI...139.8:2 It is set forever in the holy **M.** of God, and
WpI.rIV.in5:4 place His **M.** in charge of all the thoughts
W-pI...151.9:2 **M.** Whose Thought created your reality.
W-pI.151.14:2 from the **M.** which saw the truth in it, and
W-pI...158.1:2 you are a mind, in **M.** and purely mind,
W-pI...158.5:6 because the **M.** of Christ beholds it too.
W-pI...169.8:1 All learning was already in His **M.**,
W-pII..230.2:3 *into Your* **M.** *is shining there unchanged. I*
W-pII..263.1:1 *Father, Your* **M.** *created all that is, Your*
W-pII..265.1:7 What is reflected there is in God's **M.**.
W-pII......6.1:3 which still abides within the **M.** that is His
W-pII......6.1:5 unchanged forever in the **M.** of God.
W-pII..280.1:3 Thought of God has left its Father's **M.**.
W-pII..326.1:1 *Father, I was created in Your* **M.**, *a holy*
C-1.............1:2 (i.e., the **M.** of God or the Mind of Christ).
C-1.............1:2 (i.e., the Mind of God or the **M.** of Christ).
C-1.............6:3 not the *One-mindedness* of the Christ **M.**,
C-4.............8:1 safe and pure and lovely in the **M.** of God,
C-6.............4:1 of your mind that is part of the Christ **M.**.
P-2........ III.4:6 as he receives them from the **M.** of Christ.
S-1.........in.2:3 to separate is one forever in the **M.** of God
S-1......... II.8:6 returned unblemished into the **M.** of God

## mind 1607

*Mind*

*See also* mind-searching

T-1.........I.14:3 or rather, the uncreative use of **m.**.
T-1.........I.33:4 releasing your **m.** from the imprisonment
T-1.........I.34:1 Miracles restore the **m.** to its fullness. By
T-1.........I.43:1 arise from a miraculous state of **m.**, or a
T-1........ III.7:1 arise from a **m.** that is ready for them. By
T-1........ III.7:2 being united this **m.** goes out to everyone,
T-1........ III.7:4 miracle places the **m.** in a state of grace.
T-1........ III.7:5 The **m.** then naturally welcomes the Host
T-1........ IV.2:6 the **m.** in the service of the Holy Spirit.
T-1........ IV.2:7 function of the **m.** and corrects its errors,
T-1........ IV.2:8 Your **m.** can be possessed by illusions, but
T-1........ IV.2:9 If a **m.** perceives without love, it perceives
T-1...... IV.2:11 The **m.** that serves spirit *is* invulnerable.
T-1......... V.5:2 the **m.** can elect what it chooses to serve.
T-1......... V.5:4 the **m.** can become the medium by which
T-1......... V.5:7 To change your **m.** means to place it at
T-1......... V.6:1 miracle is a sign that the **m.** has chosen to
T-1....... VII.4:1 is a course in **m.** training. All learning
T-2...........I.1:9 created can be changed by your own **m.**.
T-2...........I.2:7 the Son's creations when his **m.** is healed.
T-2...........I.3:1 a state of **m.** in which nothing was needed
T-2......... II.2:4 Your right **m.** depends on it. Denial of
T-2......... II.2:6 right **m.** the denial of error frees the mind
T-2......... II.2:6 right mind the denial of error frees the **m.**
T-2......... III.2:1 and restores the wholeness of the **m.**.
T-2......... III.2:2 separation the **m.** was invulnerable to fear
T-2......... III.4:5 its vision, it brings the **m.** into its service.
T-2......... III.4:6 power of the **m.** and makes it increasingly
T-2......... III.4:7 **m.** becomes increasingly sensitive to what
T-2......... III.5:9 and your **m.** cannot serve the Holy Spirit.
T-2......... IV.2:4 Only the **m.** is capable of error. The body
T-2......... IV.2:8 in matter which the **m.** cannot control.
T-2......... IV.2:9 that the **m.** can miscreate in the body, or
T-2......... IV.2:9 or that the body can miscreate in the **m.**.
T-2....... IV.2:10 When it is understood that the **m.**, the
T-2......... IV.3:1 Only the **m.** can create because spirit has
T-2......... IV.3:1 the body is a learning device for the **m.**.
T-2....... IV.3:12 protect the **m.** by denying the unmindful.
T-2......... IV.4:5 the **m.** to render a person temporarily
T-2......... IV.4:6 a compromise approach to **m.** and body,
T-2......... V.1:4 underlying fear that the **m.** can hurt itself.
T-2......... V.1:5 miscreations of the **m.** do not really exist.
T-2......... V.1:7 to remember that only the **m.** can create,
T-2......... V.1:9 exist except as a learning device for the **m.**
T-2....... V.1:11 then, that inducing the **m.** to give up its
T-2......... V.2:1 the mindless or the miscreative use of **m.**.
T-2......... V.2:2 but if you are afraid to use the **m.** to heal,
T-2......... V.2:3 makes your **m.** vulnerable to miscreation.
T-2......... V.3:2 exalt nor depreciate the **m.** of the miracle
T-2......... V.3:4 its purpose is to restore him *to* his right **m.**
T-2......... V.3:5 that the miracle worker be in his right **m.**,
T-2......... V.5:2 recognize that **m.** is the only creative level
T-2......... V.5:3 you accept this, your **m.** can only heal. By
T-2......... V.5:4 denying your **m.** any destructive potential
T-2......... V.5:6 By affirming this you release the **m.** from
T-2......... V.5:6 the **m.** to its true position as the learner.
T-2......... V.6:3 Only the **m.** is capable of illumination.
T-2......... V.6:5 too dense. The **m.**, however, can bring its
T-2......... V.6:6 alignment with a **m.** that has learned to
T-2....V.A.17:1 injunction "Be of one **m.**" is the statement
T-2......... VI.1:6 raised body thoughts to the level of the **m.**
T-2....... VI.2:10 sure sign that you have allowed your **m.** to
T-2......... VI.3:4 for it. You must change your **m.**, not your
T-2......... VI.3:5 not need guidance except at the **m.** level.
T-2......... VI.4:6 are much too tolerant of **m.** wandering,
T-2......... VI.5:3 part of the **m.** that wants to do something
T-2......... VI.5:6 the **m.** and the behavior are out of accord,
T-2......... VI.5:8 is because you have not made up your **m.**.
T-2......... VI.5:9 mind. Your **m.** is therefore split, and your
T-2......... VI.6:1 bring your **m.** under my guidance without
T-2......... VI.6:7 Only your **m.** can produce fear. It does so
T-2......... VI.9:3 Few appreciate the real power of the **m.**,
T-2......... VI.9:5 The **m.** is very powerful, and never loses
T-2....... VI.9:11 the cost of perceiving the **m.** as impotent.
T-2........ VII.2:1 I cannot let you leave your **m.** unguarded,
T-2........ VII.2:3 be necessary to set the **m.** itself straight, a
T-2........ VII.5:9 This establishes a state of **m.** in which the
T-2........ VII.7:5 more than a potential for a change of **m.**.
T-2....... VIII.1:4 Since creative ability rests in the **m.**,
T-2....... VIII.4:4 the **m.** can begin to look with love on its
T-2....... VIII.4:5 At the same time the **m.** will inevitably
T-3...........I.2:9 nothing of this kind remains in your **m.**. I
T-3...........I.5:5 A pure **m.** knows the truth and this is its
T-3...........I.6:1 because the innocent **m.** has everything
T-3...........I.8:1 God is the true state of the **m.** of His Son.
T-3...........I.8:2 In this state your **m.** knows God, for God
T-3.......... II.3:1 to your belief that he is not in his right **m.**.
T-3.......... II.4:1 Will because you have used your own **m.**,
T-3.......... II.4:2 **m.** can miscreate only when it believes it
T-3.......... II.4:3 "imprisoned" **m.** is not free because it is
T-3.......... II.4:5 To be one is to be of one **m.** or will. When
T-3.......... II.5:2 **m.** awakens from its sleep and remembers
T-3......... III.3:1 questioning **m.** perceives itself in time,
T-3......... III.3:2 The closed **m.** believes the future and the
T-3......... IV.2:1 into the **m.** after the separation, making
T-3......... IV.2:1 the **m.** a perceiver rather than a creator.
T-3......... IV.3:3 The **m.** is therefore confused, because
T-3......... IV.3:4 separated or divided **m.** *must* be confused.
T-3......... IV.4:1 is not to be confused with the knowing **m.**
T-3......... IV.4:3 and applies to the state of **m.** that induces
T-3......... IV.5:1 always involves some misuse of **m.**,
T-3......... IV.5:1 it brings the **m.** into areas of uncertainty.
T-3......... IV.5:2 The **m.** is very active. When it chooses to
T-3......... IV.5:6 The **m.** returns to its proper function only
T-3......... IV.5:8 **m.** chooses to divide itself when it chooses
T-3....... IV.5:10 miscreation the **m.** is affirming its Source,
T-3....... IV.5:11 because the **m.** belongs to spirit which
T-3......... IV.6:5 to the **m.** and entirely inaccessible to the
T-3......... IV.7:5 of the body and the power of the **m.**. By
T-3......... IV.7:7 **m.** if you will bring it under my guidance.
T-3......... V.3:6 want to do it if you were in your right **m.**.
T-3......... V.5:5 Your **m.** may have become very ingenious
T-3......... VI.2:6 in your **m.** because it has been perceived.
T-3......... VI.7:4 because the **m.** is split between the ego
T-3....... VI.8:10 your **m.** that it may even doubt whether
T-3....... VI.11:7 no one in his right **m.** believes that what is
T-3........ VII.2:1 by depreciating the power of your **m.**. To
T-3........ VII.2:2 really understand the strength of the **m.**.
T-3...... VII.4:11 Your **m.** is split with the Holy Spirit on
T-3........ VII.5:1 The **m.** can make the belief in separation
T-3........ VII.5:8 peace, even though your **m.** is in conflict.
T-4...........I.4:1 your **m.** and help others to change theirs.
T-4...........I.4:2 Refusing to change your **m.** will not prove
T-4...........I.4:3 dreaming is not really healing his split **m.**.
T-4...........I.4:6 undo it by not changing your **m.** about it.
T-4...........I.8:3 in your right **m.** you realize it is not real.
T-4.........I.13:7 who share my aim of healing the **m.**.
T-4.......... II.1:1 how the **m.** could ever have made the ego.
T-4.......... II.2:4 **m.** as when it involves physical proximity.
T-4.......... II.3:1 Your own state of **m.** is a good example of
T-4.......... II.3:6 forget that the **m.** need not work that way,
T-4.......... II.7:9 that this is possible is a decision of the **m.**,
T-4........ II.10:4 **m.** then has only one direction in which it
T-4..... II.11:13 from everything else the **m.** can grasp.
T-4......... III.2:5 ego has set up and can shine into your **m.**.
T-4......... III.4:7 into any **m.** that truly wants it, but it must
T-4......... III.7:1 It has never really entered your **m.** to give
T-4......... III.7:5 it. Watch your **m.** for the scraps of fear, or
T-4......... III.8:3 your **m.** for the Holy One to enter. We
T-4......... III.9:1 In your own **m.**, though denied by the
T-4....... III.10:1 in your sane **m.** is perfectly conscious, is
T-4....... III.10:1 from the part of the **m.** the ego rules. The
T-4....... III.10:3 and how little to protect your right **m.**.
T-4......... IV.1:5 Your **m.** is filled with schemes to save the

| | |
|---|---|
| T-4 IV.2:1 | your **m.** by changing your behavior, but I |
| T-4 IV.2:1 | many times, that you *can* change your **m.**. |
| T-4 IV.2:5 | then change your **m.** to think with God's. |
| T-4 IV.2:7 | Your **m.** is one with God's. Denying this |
| T-4 IV.2:8 | together, but has literally split your **m.**. |
| T-4 IV.2:9 | I am deeply concerned with your **m.**, and |
| T-4 IV.5:4 | But until you change your **m.** about those |
| T-4 IV.6:1 | Watch your **m.** for the temptations of the |
| T-4 IV.6:3 | you will see how your **m.** can focus and |
| T-4 IV.7:1 | you actively refuse to let your **m.** slip away |
| T-4 IV.8:3 | **m.** and mine can unite in shining your ego |
| T-4 IV.8:5 | Watch your **m.** carefully for any beliefs |
| T-4 IV.9:4 | creation and brought your **m.** into being. |
| T-4 IV.10:2 | of the ego's rule and the healing of the **m.**. |
| T-4 IV.10:9 | has come into your **m.** and healed it. |
| T-4 IV.11:2 | I do work with your higher **m.**, the home |
| T-4 IV.11:2 | just as your ego does with your lower **m.**, |
| T-4 IV.11:5 | Your **m.** will elect to join with mine, and |
| T-4 V.1:3 | not the way a balanced **m.** holds together. |
| T-4 V.4:5 | is where the **m.** becomes actually dazed. |
| T-4 V.4:6 | the **m.** is also told that the body cannot |
| T-4 V.4:7 | **m.** asks, "Where can I go for protection?" |
| T-4 V.4:8 | The **m.**, and not without cause, reminds |
| T-4 V.5:4 | must be formulated clearly and kept in **m.** |
| T-4 V.6:4 | the real question and keep it out of **m.**. |
| T-4 V.6:11 | in effect unless you change your **m.**. |
| T-4 VI.4:2 | The separated **m.** cannot maintain the |
| T-4 VI.5:5 | as he changes his **m.** about its worth. I am |
| T-4 VII.1:2 | although the **m.** is naturally abstract. Part |
| T-4 VII.1:3 | Part of the **m.** becomes concrete, however |
| T-4 VII.1:5 | The ego is the part of the **m.** that believes |
| T-4 VII.3:7 | God created every **m.** by communicating |
| T-4 VII.3:11 | this. The **m.** can distort its function, but it |
| T-4 VII.3:12 | That is why the **m.** cannot totally lose the |
| T-4 VII.4:4 | state in which the **m.** is in communication |
| T-4 VII.5:8 | of being the **m.** gives everything always. |
| T-4 VII.7:1 | you until you know it with your whole **m.**. |
| T-4 VII.7:4 | personal to the **m.** that receives it. It can, |
| T-4 VII.7:5 | be returned by that **m.** to other minds, |
| T-4 VII.8:1 | any **m.** learns to be wholly helpful. This is |
| T-4 VII.8:6 | Every **m.** that is changed adds to this joy |
| T-5 I.1:3 | them. Only the healed **m.** can experience |
| T-5 I.1:4 | **m.** cannot have what it does not choose to |
| T-5 I.1:6 | The higher **m.** thinks according to the |
| T-5 I.1:9 | the lower **m.** it is quite comprehensible in |
| T-5 I.1:13 | reinforces it in your **m.** and thus increases |
| T-5 I.3:3 | The Holy Spirit is in your right **m.**, as He |
| T-5 I.3:4 | the **m.** be in you that was also in Christ |
| T-5 I.5:4 | the restoration of the integrity of the **m.**. |
| T-5 I.6:4 | He represents a state of **m.** close enough |
| T-5 I.7:5 | leads the **m.** beyond its own integration |
| T-5 II.1:5 | in you because God placed it in your **m.**, |
| T-5 II.2:3 | This is the vocation of the **m.**. The mind |
| T-5 II.2:4 | The **m.** had no calling until the separation |
| T-5 II.2:5 | until the whole **m.** returns to creating. |
| T-5 II.3:2 | made, God placed in the **m.** the Call to joy |
| T-5 II.4:1 | enter your **m.** and so you need a new light |
| T-5 II.6:6 | Choosing depends on a split **m.**. The Holy |
| T-5 II.7:6 | you *of*. It brings to your **m.** the other way, |
| T-5 II.8:2 | of your **m.** that always speaks for the right |
| T-5 II.8:5 | you, because the call of both is in your **m.**. |
| T-5 II.9:1 | My **m.** will always be like yours, because |
| T-5 III.3:2 | They must both be in your **m.**, because |
| T-5 III.3:4 | See him through the Holy Spirit in his **m.**, |
| T-5 III.4:4 | It in yourself while It is so weak in your **m.** |
| T-5 III.5:6 | or the **m.** would be unable to understand |
| T-5 III.6:1 | the **m.** is not understandable to another. |
| T-5 III.6:4 | Time is a belief of the ego, so the lower **m.** |
| T-5 III.8:9 | the idea of danger has entered your **m.**. |
| T-5 III.9:3 | is merely another term for a split **m.**. The |
| T-5 III.9:6 | You may let your **m.** misperceive, but the |
| T-5 III.9:6 | the Holy Spirit lets your **m.** reinterpret its |
| T-5 III.10:2 | He uses only what your **m.** already |
| T-5 III.10:3 | learner without going counter to his **m.**, |
| T-5 III.10:5 | the place in the **m.** where He is at home. |
| T-5 III.11:3 | He must work with and for a **m.** that is in |
| T-5 III.11:10 | He holds this gladness gently in your **m.**, |
| T-5 IV.2:6 | the unhealed part of your **m.** to the higher |
| T-5 IV.2:10 | will not disappear from your **m.** without |
| T-5 IV.3:5 | spirit do not leave the **m.** that thinks them |
| T-5 IV.4:3 | irresistibly drawn to every **m.** created by |
| T-5 IV.6:1 | the burden you have placed in your **m.**. By |
| T-5 IV.7:1 | gives you the power of a healed **m.**, but |
| T-5 V.1:4 | **m.** has the means at its disposal to side |
| T-5 V.3:1 | the part of the **m.** that believes in division. |
| T-5 V.3:8 | of attacking God may be to the sane **m.**, |
| T-5 V.4:1 | you accept into your **m.** has reality for you |
| T-5 V.4:3 | If you enthrone the ego in your **m.**, your |
| T-5 V.4:4 | **m.** is capable of creating reality or making |
| T-5 V.5:1 | The guiltless **m.** cannot suffer. Being sane |
| T-5 V.5:2 | the **m.** heals the body because *it* has been |
| T-5 V.5:3 | sane **m.** cannot conceive of illness because |
| T-5 V.6:7 | alternatives the **m.** can accept and obey. |
| T-5 V.8:3 | Any decision of the **m.** will affect both |
| T-5 V.8:6 | Your **m.** *does* make your future, and it will |
| T-5 VI.7:3 | you because it does not belong in your **m.**, |
| T-5 VI.9:5 | The part of your **m.** that you have given to |
| T-5 VI.9:5 | Kingdom, where your whole **m.** belongs. |
| T-5 VII.2:5 | not learned that every **m.** God created is |
| T-5 VII.2:6 | to return to God the **m.** as He created it. |
| T-5 VII.3:3 | you are of one **m.** and spirit with Him. |
| T-6 I.7:2 | on your **m.** of what is already in it. God |
| T-6 II.1:1 | in **m.** must involve a rejection of part of it, |
| T-6 II.1:2 | be appreciated except by a whole **m.** that |
| T-6 II.3:2 | reinforces your belief in your own split **m.** |
| T-6 II.4:2 | because its abilities are directed by the **m.** |
| T-6 II.9:1 | Thoughts begin in the **m.** of the thinker, |
| T-6 II.9:3 | Because your **m.** is split, you can perceive |
| T-6 II.9:4 | cannot escape the basic laws of **m.**. You |
| T-6 II.9:5 | perceive from your **m.** and project your |
| T-6 II.9:8 | in the future only because your **m.** is not |
| T-6 II.10:3 | Since the Holy Spirit is in your **m.**, your |
| T-6 II.10:3 | your **m.** can also believe only what is true. |
| T-6 II.10:5 | tells you to return your whole **m.** to God, |
| T-6 II.11:6 | God, and lets your **m.** converge with His. |
| T-6 II.11:9 | He perceives only what is true in your **m.**, |
| T-6 II.12:3 | by recognizing Himself in every **m.**, and |
| T-6 II.12:8 | of the Kingdom shines in your **m.** forever, |
| T-6 II.13:3 | no darkness to abide in your own **m.**. This |
| T-6 III.1:1 | every idea begins in the **m.** of the thinker. |
| T-6 III.1:2 | what extends from the **m.** is still in it, and |
| T-6 III.1:3 | your **m.** through His impartial perception |
| T-6 III.1:6 | Your Godlike **m.** can never be defiled. The |
| T-6 III.3:1 | own **m.** perceives itself as totally harmless |
| T-6 III.3:6 | Without anxiety the **m.** is wholly kind, |
| T-6 III.4:7 | have. It awakens in your **m.** through the |
| T-6 IV.2:5 | thus speaking for the part of your **m.** that |
| T-6 IV.4:1 | part of the **m.** that made it is against it. It |
| T-6 IV.4:5 | something alien to itself in your **m.**, the |
| T-6 IV.5:1 | uses the body to conspire against your **m.**, |
| T-6 IV.5:3 | is not real, attempts to persuade the **m.**, |
| T-6 IV.5:3 | that the **m.** is the ego's learning device; |
| T-6 IV.5:3 | that the body is more real than the **m.** is. |
| T-6 IV.5:4 | in his right **m.** could possibly believe this, |
| T-6 IV.5:4 | and no one in his right **m.** does believe it. |
| T-6 IV.7:6 | but what was once certain in your **m.** has |
| T-6 IV.11:3 | Fidelity to premises is a law of **m.**, and |
| T-6 IV.11:10 | You would doubt your right **m.**, which is |
| T-6 V.1:4 | teach you that you had made a split **m.**, |
| T-6 V.1:4 | when He knows your **m.** only as whole? |
| T-6 V.A.1:3 | life, and life is of the **m.** and in the mind. |
| T-6 V.A.1:3 | life, and life is of the mind and in the **m.**. |
| T-6 V.A.1:5 | are life. If we share the same **m.**, you can |
| T-6 V.A.2:6 | If the **m.** can heal the body, but the body |
| T-6 V.A.2:6 | the body, but the body cannot heal the **m.** |
| T-6 V.A.2:6 | the **m.** must be stronger than the body. |
| T-6 V.A.3:2 | He always tells you that only the **m.** is real |
| T-6 V.A.3:2 | real, because only the **m.** can be shared. |
| T-6 V.A.3:4 | To be of one **m.** is meaningful, but to be |
| T-6 V.A.3:5 | laws of **m.**, then, the body is meaningless. |
| T-6 V.B.2:5 | Change in motivation is a change of **m.**, |
| T-6 V.B.2:5 | change because the **m.** *is* fundamental. |
| T-6 V.B.3:6 | since it is being learned by a conflicted **m.** |
| T-6 V.B.3:8 | **m.** of the learner projects its own conflict, |
| T-6 V.B.4:4 | occur with the change of **m.** in the thinker |
| T-6 V.B.5:2 | disagreement, peace of **m.** is impossible. |
| T-6 V.B.6:4 | must dawn on your **m.** that you are trying |
| T-6 V.C.1:2 | out the true from the false in your **m.**, and |
| T-6 V.C.2:3 | avoid. In the **m.** of the thinker, then, He *is* |
| T-6 V.C.2:3 | but only in order to unify the **m.** so it can |
| T-6 V.C.2:4 | enables the **m.** to teach without judgment |
| T-6 V.C.2:5 | The undoing is necessary only in your **m.**, |
| T-6 V.C.4:10 | will finally liberate your **m.** from choice, |
| T-6 V.C.5:4 | have in your **m.** only what God put there, |
| T-6 V.C.5:4 | acknowledging your **m.** as God created it. |
| T-6 V.C.7:1 | step is thus one of protection for your **m.**, |
| T-6 V.C.7:4 | is assailed by any doubts in your **m.**, His |
| T-6 V.C.8:2 | to hold its oneness in your **m.** because, if |
| T-6 V.C.8:7 | about being must not enter your **m.**, or |
| T-6 V.C.9:4 | keep *only* the Kingdom of God in your **m.**, |
| T-6 V.C.9:4 | and thus placed part of your **m.** outside it. |
| T-6 V.C.9:5 | given you a sick **m.** that must be healed. |
| T-6 V.C.9:7 | Once your **m.** is healed it radiates health, |
| T-7 II.2:2 | and restores its wholeness in your **m.**. |
| T-7 II.2:5 | law of the **m.** in this world as well as in the |
| T-7 II.2:8 | laws of **m.** as they operate in this world is |
| T-7 II.4:6 | a conflicted **m.** cannot be faithful to one |
| T-7 III.2:12 | Your **m.** cannot be unified in allegiance to |
| T-7 III.2:12 | ego, because the **m.** does not belong to it. |
| T-7 III.4:7 | not in the Kingdom, but in your **m.**. The |
| T-7 III.4:10 | Your right **m.** sees only brothers, because |
| T-7 III.5:1 | God has lit your **m.** Himself, and keeps |
| T-7 III.5:1 | and keeps your **m.** lit by His light because |
| T-7 III.5:1 | light because His light is what your **m.** is. |
| T-7 IV.1:6 | in a state of **m.** that does not know Him. |
| T-7 IV.5:6 | a state of **m.** that is out of accord with His. |
| T-7 IV.5:7 | that it brings the **m.** into accord with His, |
| T-7 V.h | Healing and the Changelessness of **M.** |
| T-7 V.2:2 | create, and therefore does not need the **m.** |
| T-7 V.2:3 | teach you that the body can act like the **m.** |
| T-7 V.3:3 | accept the ego's confusion of **m.** and body |
| T-7 V.3:5 | has already been confused with the **m.**. |
| T-7 V.5:10 | a concept that only a conflicted **m.** could |
| T-7 V.7:6 | That is because, by changing his **m.**, he |
| T-7 V.7:7 | the changelessness of **m.** as God created it |
| T-7 V.7:8 | learn to change your **m.** about your mind. |
| T-7 V.7:8 | learn to change your mind about your **m.**. |
| T-7 V.8:2 | You are recognizing the changeless **m.** in |
| T-7 V.8:2 | that he could not have changed his **m.**. |
| T-7 V.8:8 | By changing your **m.** about his *for* him, |
| T-7 V.10:6 | **m.** is so powerful a light that you can look |
| T-7 V.10:9 | Yet I do want to share my **m.** with you |
| T-7 V.11:2 | **m.** we share is shared by all our brothers, |
| T-7 V.11:3 | Let your **m.** shine with mine upon their |
| T-7 VI.1:5 | but they *will* return to the **m.** of the thinker |
| T-7 VI.2:1 | The **m.** that accepts attack cannot love. |
| T-7 VI.3:1 | it stems from the very power of the **m.** the |
| T-7 VI.4:4 | **M.** always reproduces as it was produced. |
| T-7 VI.4:11 | if the **m.** that made it knew itself. And if it |
| T-7 VI.5:2 | all commitments the **m.** makes are total. |
| T-7 VI.5:5 | The **m.** can, however, make up illusions, |
| T-7 VI.7:1 | keep in **m.** what the Holy Spirit offers you |
| T-7 VI.8:2 | If the **m.** cannot attack, the ego proceeds |
| T-7 VI.8:5 | your **m.** in its own delusional system, |
| T-7 VI.8:8 | coexist in your **m.** without splitting it. If |
| T-7 VI.9:1 | Your **m.** is dividing its allegiance between |
| T-7 VI.10:6 | If you dissociate your **m.** from it you are |
| T-7 VI.12:1 | Allowing insanity to enter your **m.** means |
| T-7 VI.12:4 | Your divided **m.** is blocking the extension |
| T-7 VI.13:3 | your **m.** could be out of accord with God's |
| T-7 VII.1:5 | but you can give it the power of your **m.**, |
| T-7 VII.1:12 | all of it. **M.** is too powerful to be subject to |
| T-7 VII.4:4 | you will have put them out of your **m.**. |
| T-7 VII.9:1 | Being the part of your **m.** that does not |
| T-7 VIII.1:2 | These reflect a fundamental law of the **m.**, |
| T-7 VIII.1:6 | you value in order to keep it in your **m.**. |
| T-7 VIII.1:11 | Every **m.** must project or extend, because |
| T-7 VIII.1:11 | that is how it lives, and every **m.** is life. |
| T-7 VIII.2:5 | ego utilizes the power of the **m.** only to |
| T-7 VIII.2:6 | conflict from your **m.** to other minds, in |
| T-7 VIII.4:2 | it is impossible to fragment the **m.**. To |
| T-7 VIII.4:3 | and **m.** cannot attack or be attacked. The |
| T-7 VIII.4:5 | It does not understand what **m.** is, and |
| T-7 VIII.4:6 | Yet its existence is dependent on your **m.**, |
| T-7 VIII.5:2 | It depends on your **m.**, and as you made it |
| T-7 VIII.5:6 | your **m.** and from the Sonship as a whole. |
| T-7 IX.1:5 | Holy Spirit is in the part of the **m.** that lies |

| | |
|---|---|
| T-7........IX.4:4 | A split **m.** cannot perceive its fullness, and |
| T-7........IX.5:1 | the Holy Spirit, Who is in your **m.**, knows |
| T-7........X.1:10 | They belong in your **m.** as part of your |
| T-7........X.1:10 | but your state of **m.** and your recognition |
| T-7........X.1:10 | on what you believe about your **m.**. |
| T-7........X.1:11 | determine what you accept into your **m.**. |
| T-7........X.2:1 | both accept into your **m.** what is not there |
| T-7........X.2:2 | gave your **m.** through His you may deny, |
| T-7........X.7:4 | is no confusion in the **m.** of a Son of God, |
| T-7........XI.5:1 | When a **m.** has only light, it knows only |
| T-8..........I.2:6 | will be removed from your **m.** for you. |
| T-8..........I.6:5 | **m.** will be split about what your reality is. |
| T-8........II.5:5 | ask the part of your **m.** that taught you to |
| T-8........III.1:5 | because there is no limit on your **m.**. |
| T-8......IV.4:10 | Only then will your **m.** choose to follow |
| T-8........IV.5:6 | or the **m.** itself is divided and not whole. |
| T-8........IV.5:7 | **m.** is the means by which you determine |
| T-8........IV.5:7 | because **m.** is the mechanism of decision. |
| T-8........IV.6:4 | I will wait until you change your **m.**. I can |
| T-8........IV.6:7 | the dominion of one **m.** over another. |
| T-8........V.1:5 | them your unified **m.** on their behalf, as I |
| T-8........V.2:12 | His. By joining your **m.** with mine you are |
| T-8........VI.7:6 | can even imprison the **m.** of God's Son, if |
| T-8.......VII.1:2 | attack in any form enters your **m.** you are |
| T-8.......VII.2:6 | change your **m.** entirely about its value. |
| T-8.......VII.3:2 | will understand the power of the **m.** that |
| T-8.......VII.5:6 | allow him to belittle himself in your **m.**, |
| T-8.......VII.9:5 | part of the **m.** you tried to separate *from* |
| T-8.....VII.10:3 | All **m.** is whole, and the belief that part of |
| T-8.....VII.10:3 | belief that part of it is physical, or not **m.**, |
| T-8.....VII.10:4 | **M.** cannot be made physical, but it can be |
| T-8.....VII.10:5 | By reaching out, the **m.** extends itself. It |
| T-8.....VII.10:7 | A **m.** that has been blocked has allowed |
| T-8.....VII.11:2 | of a **m.** that is working through the body, |
| T-8.....VII.11:3 | If the **m.** believes the body is its goal it will |
| T-8.....VII.12:4 | This releases the **m.** from the temptation |
| T-8.....VII.12:6 | of the power of the **m.** in it. This can be |
| T-8.....VII.12:7 | only if the **m.** extends to other minds, and |
| T-8.....VII.13:3 | is to limit your **m.** and to hurt yourself. |
| T-8.....VII.13:5 | is brought under the purpose of the **m.**, it |
| T-8.....VII.13:6 | from the **m.** the body has no purpose at |
| T-8.....VII.14:2 | **m.** can be manifested through the body if |
| T-8.....VII.16:2 | Free your **m.** from the belief that this is |
| T-8.....VII.16:8 | you will open your **m.** to creation in God. |
| T-8.....VIII.9:5 | allow the body to be a mirror of a split **m.**. |
| T-8........IX.3:1 | Wholeness heals because it is of the **m.**. |
| T-8........IX.6:1 | ego, which always wants to weaken the **m.** |
| T-8........IX.6:3 | the ego believes that **m.** is dangerous, and |
| T-8........IX.8:5 | you limit yourself we are not of one **m.**, |
| T-8........IX.8:6 | sickness is not of the body, but of the **m.**. |
| T-8........IX.8:7 | of sickness are signs that the **m.** is split, |
| T-9..........I.1:1 | beliefs the human **m.** has ever made. It |
| T-9..........I.1:2 | the **m.** were already profoundly split, |
| T-9..........I.4:2 | sort out the true from the false in your **m.**, |
| T-9..........I.4:3 | it real to you because He is in your **m.**, |
| T-9..........I.4:4 | perception of your **m.** brings its reality to |
| T-9..........I.5:4 | If you did not have a split **m.**, you would |
| T-9..........I.6:3 | Will. A divided **m.** cannot communicate, |
| T-9..........I.6:3 | speaks for different things to the same **m.**. |
| T-9..........I.8:1 | No right **m.** can believe that its will is |
| T-9..........I.8:2 | a **m.** believes that its will is different from |
| T-9........I.10:6 | to Him are real, being of your right **m.**. |
| T-9........I.12:4 | devoting your **m.** to what you do not want |
| T-9........II.5:8 | there is a light in his **m.** that does know. |
| T-9........II.6:4 | Holy Spirit extends from your **m.** to his, |
| T-9........IV.5:4 | let any belief in its realness enter your **m.**, |
| T-9......IV.10:2 | hope is to change your **m.** about reality. |
| T-9........V.4:5 | Yet if the dreamer is equated with the **m.**, |
| T-9........V.5:1 | fear is to reduce the importance of the **m.**, |
| T-9........V.6:6 | "unimportant **m.**" esteem itself without |
| T-9........V.7:5 | light in his **m.** will therefore answer the |
| T-9........VI.7:3 | in His Mind and with a **m.** like His. In |
| T-9........VI.7:4 | In your open **m.** are your creations, in |
| T-9.......VII.3:3 | And this evaluation must be in your **m.**, |
| T-9.......VII.3:4 | is. The ego is also in your **m.**, because you |
| T-9.......VII.4:1 | evaluations of yourself in your **m.**, and |
| T-9.....VIII.4:2 | literally drives the ego from your **m.**, |
| T-9.....VIII.5:2 | blessing you hold it in your **m.**, protecting |
| T-10.......in.1:2 | Time and eternity are both in your **m.**, |
| T-10.......in.2:6 | Your holy **m.** establishes everything that |
| T-10.......in.2:7 | your **m.** determines your perception of it. |
| T-10.......in.3:4 | That is why your **m.** is holy. Can anything |
| T-10.......in.3:9 | anything threatens your peace of **m.**, ask |
| T-10.....in.3:10 | refuse to change your **m.** about yourself. |
| T-10.........I.1:1 | against them as long as your **m.** is split, |
| T-10.........I.1:5 | Any part of your **m.** that does not know |
| T-10.........I.4:1 | returning your **m.** simultaneously to your |
| T-10.......II.3:1 | to restore to your **m.** *what is already there.* |
| T-10.......II.6:1 | your peace of **m.** you could not make such |
| T-10.......II.6:3 | want something other than peace of **m.**, |
| T-10......III.2:3 | **m.** receives Him the remembrance of Him |
| T-10......III.7:6 | A whole **m.** is not idolatrous, and does |
| T-10......IV.2:1 | can dawn only on an unclouded **m.**. It is |
| T-10......IV.2:5 | Knowledge cannot dawn on a **m.** full of |
| T-10......IV.2:6 | and cannot be known by part of a **m.**. |
| T-10......IV.3:4 | If you perceive other gods your **m.** is split, |
| T-10......IV.3:4 | removed part of your **m.** from God's Will. |
| T-10......IV.3:6 | then the **m.** does become unreasonable. |
| T-10......IV.3:7 | By defining the **m.** wrongly, you perceive |
| T-10......IV.4:1 | your **m.** at peace because peace is His Will |
| T-10......IV.6:2 | of one **m.** and that mind belongs to Him. |
| T-10......IV.6:2 | of one mind and that **m.** belongs to Him. |
| T-10......IV.7:3 | it. It is a call to the Holy Spirit in his **m.**, a |
| T-10......IV.7:5 | power of one **m.** can shine into another, |
| T-10.......V.4:1 | enter the **m.** of God's Son against His Will |
| T-10......V.9:10 | own **m.** because of the power He gave it. |
| T-10......V.9:11 | Your **m.** is capable of creating worlds, but |
| T-10......V.14:3 | time lasts in your **m.** there will be choices. |
| T-11.......in.3:6 | little spark in your **m.** is enough to lighten |
| T-11.........I.1:5 | whatever part of the **m.** of God's Son you |
| T-11.......II.2:5 | from your brother or in your own **m.**, |
| T-11.......II.5:4 | **m.** so that He becomes your only Guest. |
| T-11.......II.6:4 | Invite this knowledge back into your **m.**, |
| T-11......III.6:2 | never let them enter the **m.** of God's Son, |
| T-11......III.7:6 | And your **m.** must be as pure as His, if |
| T-11......III.8:1 | **m.** you can accept the whole Sonship and |
| T-11......IV.1:3 | your **m.** needs to learn what salvation is. |
| T-11......IV.3:5 | that you can darken only your own **m.**. As |
| T-11......V.14:6 | be true. Holding error clearly in **m.**, and |
| T-11.....VII.2:2 | The loving thoughts his **m.** perceives in |
| T-11...VIII.9:2 | denying that his **m.** is split you will heal |
| T-11. VIII.11:1 | of himself for his split **m.** is yours, and |
| T-11. VIII.12:1 | a brother pluck the offense from your **m.**, |
| T-12.........I.2:5 | or an attack on the integrity of your **m.**, |
| T-12.........I.3:8 | to your own **m.** is not yet fully apparent. If |
| T-12.......II.1:7 | light in another **m.** must shine into theirs |
| T-12......III.5:1 | Salvation is for the **m.**, and it is attained |
| T-12......III.7:1 | reality, the real world must be in his **m.**. |
| T-12......III.7:2 | insane thoughts, too, must be in his **m.**, |
| T-12......III.7:3 | tolerate. A split **m.** is endangered, and the |
| T-12......III.7:4 | Therefore the **m.** projects the split, not |
| T-12....III.7:10 | your hatred is in your **m.** and not outside |
| T-12......III.8:4 | for the one you made out of your split **m.**, |
| T-12......III.9:7 | from your **m.** because you are afraid of it. |
| T-12......III.9:8 | this world is only in the **m.** of its maker, |
| T-12....III.9:10 | it. For you do have control over your **m.**, |
| T-12....III.9:10 | since the **m.** is the mechanism of decision. |
| T-12....III.10:1 | is in your own **m.** and nowhere else, you |
| T-12......IV.2:4 | because the ego is part of your **m.**, and |
| T-12......IV.2:5 | **m.** that believes in it and gives existence |
| T-12......IV.2:6 | Yet it is also your **m.** that has the power to |
| T-12.......V.1:3 | the idea of attack can enter your **m.**, you |
| T-12.......V.4:3 | cannot learn of perfect love with a split **m.** |
| T-12.......V.4:3 | a split **m.** has made itself a poor learner. |
| T-12.......V.7:7 | so weakened your **m.** that you cannot love |
| T-12.....V.7:10 | Yet your **m.** speaks against your learning |
| T-12.....V.7:10 | as your learning speaks against your **m.**, |
| T-12.....VII.5:6 | of looking at the world are in your **m.**, |
| T-12.....VII.6:8 | The **m.** always strives for integration, and |
| T-12.....VII.7:1 | do one or the other, for that is a law of **m.**, |
| T-12.....VII.7:8 | **m.** then sees a divided world outside itself |
| T-12.....VII.8:3 | have looked upon your **m.** and accepted |
| T-12...VII.10:2 | your **m.** is the loveliest of God's creations. |
| T-12...VII.13:3 | death penalty never leaves the ego's **m.**, |
| T-12... VIII.2:5 | split **m.** and all its works were not created |
| T-12... VIII.4:7 | in your **m.** and cannot be obliterated. It is |
| T-12... VIII.5:2 | memory of God cannot shine in a **m.** that |
| T-12... VIII.5:3 | only in a **m.** that chooses to remember, |
| T-13.......in.1:2 | It is the judgment of one **m.** by another as |
| T-13.......in.1:4 | For the **m.** that judges perceives itself as |
| T-13.......in.1:4 | as separate from the **m.** being judged, |
| T-13.......in.1:5 | delusional attempt of the **m.** to deny itself |
| T-13.......in.2:1 | acceptance of guilt into the **m.** of God's |
| T-13.........I.1:2 | his **m.** that he may remember his Father |
| T-13.........I.7:6 | the cloud of guilt that darkens your **m.**, |
| T-13.........I.8:6 | in your **m.** to ensure the ego's continuity. |
| T-13........II.1:4 | guilt, and thereby keep it in your **m.**. |
| T-13......III.1:5 | state of **m.** you are not afraid of fear. You |
| T-13......III.6:4 | loving **m.** that thought it made them in |
| T-13......III.6:5 | And the pain in this **m.** is so apparent, |
| T-13......III.7:5 | search your **m.** carefully for any thoughts |
| T-13......III.9:2 | in your **m.** where the Holy Spirit is not |
| T-13....III.10:1 | to sanity cannot obtain it in your right **m.**. |
| T-13....III.11:5 | For a darkened **m.** cannot live in the light, |
| T-13......IV.3:8 | An open **m.** is more honest than this. |
| T-13......IV.6:3 | They carry the spots of pain in your **m.**, |
| T-13.......V.2:4 | being perceived in one separate **m.** only. |
| T-13.......V.3:8 | Its only reality is in your own **m.**, and by |
| T-13.......V.6:5 | your own split **m.** everywhere you look. |
| T-13......VI.2:5 | with you, and by holding it in your **m.**, see |
| T-13.....VII.5:6 | The out of **m.** *is* out of sight, because what |
| T-13...VII.13:3 | hidden in your **m.** and kept to hurt you. |
| T-13...VII.15:1 | peace of **m.** this world may set before you. |
| T-13...VII.16:4 | the peace of **m.** that we must find together |
| T-13...VII.17:4 | from the **m.** of God's most holy Son, |
| T-13....VIII.1:5 | For the **m.** that knows this unequivocally |
| T-13....VIII.7:6 | it by re-establishing its oneness in your **m.** |
| T-13......IX.4:1 | accepted into your **m.** without distinction |
| T-13......IX.4:6 | lifted from his **m.** the cloud of guilt that |
| T-13......IX.6:7 | Guilt is always in your **m.**, which has |
| T-13........X.1:1 | accustomed to the notion that the **m.** can |
| T-13........X.5:3 | past, and give your **m.** in peace over to the |
| T-13........X.7:1 | keep illusions in your **m.** to frighten you, |
| T-13......XI.1:3 | a war would surely end his peace of **m.**, |
| T-13......XI.5:1 | whose **m.** is darkened by doubt and guilt, |
| T-13......XI.8:1 | within you, joining your **m.** with His, |
| T-13......XI.9:5 | that disturbs the **m.** of God's sleeping Son |
| T-14.........I.3:3 | The thoughts the **m.** of God's Son projects |
| T-14.........I.5:4 | of its dullness that lies upon your **m.**, |
| T-14........II.1:8 | burden to your already burdened **m.**. You |
| T-14......III.8:4 | it, and do not foster belief in it in any **m.**. |
| T-14......III.8:5 | Remember always that **m.** is one, and |
| T-14....III.12:4 | true. Peace abides in every **m.** that quietly |
| T-14....III.13:7 | your innocence from your unclouded **m.**. |
| T-14......IV.2:2 | the disordered **m.** that thought it was. |
| T-14......IV.3:1 | in your most holy **m.** be undone for you, |
| T-14......IV.3:5 | what always was to your unforgiving **m.**. |
| T-14......IV.7:5 | very **m.** where God Himself has placed it. |
| T-14....IV.10:3 | only to the Holy Spirit in your **m.**, |
| T-14....IV.10:5 | have placed within your **m.** cannot exist, |
| T-14.......V.1:1 | The only part of your **m.** that has reality |
| T-14......VI.5:4 | in your **m.** that lets you think you are. All |
| T-14.....VII.1:4 | For their separation is only in your **m.**, |
| T-14.....VII.5:1 | darkness when a **m.** believes in darkness, |
| T-14.....VII.7:7 | to your **m.** with clarity and brightness so |
| T-14....VIII.1:5 | Banish not power from your **m.**, but let all |
| T-14....VIII.3:1 | Let your **m.** wander not through |
| T-14......IX.7:1 | wait to make the mirror of your **m.** clean |
| T-14......IX.7:2 | that shines in your **m.** is not obscure, and |
| T-14........X.1:2 | your **m.** in time but bring eternity nearer |
| T-14........X.4:4 | the **m.** of those who think they live apart. |
| T-14........X.5:2 | unceasingly across the mirror of your **m.**, |
| T-14........X.5:3 | darkness sweep constantly across your **m.** |
| T-14........X.5:7 | you impose upon your **m.** limits the ego, |
| T-14........X.8:6 | study of the ego is not the study of the **m.**. |
| T-14.....X.11:6 | Neither his **m.** nor yours holds more than |
| T-14......XI.5:3 | are dark lessons in your **m.** that hurt and |
| T-14....XI.10:7 | His bright teaching so firmly in your **m.**, |
| T-14....XI.13:6 | fill every **m.** that so makes room for Him. |
| T-15........I.11:1 | take to change your **m.** so completely, ask |
| T-15......III.6:1 | clearly and in perfect safety in your **m.**, |
| T-15......IV.3:6 | value of His Will for you in your own **m.**. |
| T-15......IV.3:7 | yet it is your **m.** that is the host to Him. |
| T-15......IV.5:3 | for the release from littleness in the **m.** of |
| T-15......IV.6:6 | that it is a time in which your **m.** is open, |
| T-15......IV.8:5 | come into a **m.** that has decided to oppose |
| T-15......VI.5:5 | to hold all of your brothers in your **m.**, |

| | |
|---|---|
| T-15 VI.7:5 | remember that understanding is of the **m.** |
| T-15 VI.7:5 | the mind, and only of the **m.**. Knowledge |
| T-15 VI.7:6 | Knowledge is therefore of the **m.**, and its |
| T-15 VI.7:6 | and its conditions are in the **m.** with it. If |
| T-15 VII.3:6 | such as this belongs not in your holy **m.**. |
| T-15 VII.5:1 | Spirit would remove from his holy **m.**. For |
| T-15 VII.8:3 | object where the **m.** goes or what it thinks |
| T-15 VII.8:5 | To the ego the **m.** is private, and only the |
| T-15 VII.11:8 | forgive. They can only do as the **m.** directs |
| T-15 XI.7:3 | communication, which must be of the **m.**, |
| T-16 I.3:8 | thought in **m.** and do not lose sight of it, |
| T-16 I.3:9 | Focus your **m.** only on this: *I am not alone,* |
| T-16 II.3:1 | to hurt your **m.** has made it so unnatural |
| T-16 II.4:2 | reached another **m.** and joined with it. |
| T-16 II.7:3 | accomplished in a **m.** firmly convinced |
| T-16 III.4:8 | accept into your **m.** does not really change |
| T-16 III.5:10 | real has ever left the **m.** of its creator. And |
| T-16 IV.10:2 | Every illusion you accept into your **m.** by |
| T-16 VI.8:3 | your **m.** from its fixed position here. This |
| T-16 VI.8:5 | it took to fix your **m.** so firmly on illusions |
| T-16 VI.9:3 | Thought of your reality to enter your **m.**, |
| T-16 VII.7:4 | from keeping the experience in your **m.**. |
| T-17 I.1:10 | the **m.** that would have reality be different |
| T-17 I.6:5 | and lose your peace of **m.** because another |
| T-17 II.5:2 | searching of the **m.** that made this world, |
| T-17 II.7:3 | become a dream, and vanish from his **m.**. |
| T-17 III.1:8 | understand how they came into your **m.**, |
| T-17 III.7:8 | Who can change your **m.** about it for you. |
| T-17 IV.3:3 | aim of occupying your **m.** so completely |
| T-17 IV.5:1 | and the part of your **m.** into which the ego |
| T-17 V.5:2 | of **m.** about what the whole relationship is |
| T-18 II.5:3 | Yet here is a world, clearly within your **m.** |
| T-18 II.7:10 | in one purpose, being of one **m.** with Him |
| T-18 II.9:5 | represent the same wishes in your **m.**, so |
| T-18 IV.1:4 | prepare your **m.** for it only to the extent of |
| T-18 IV.8:7 | Only in your **m.**, which thought it did, is |
| T-18 V.2:1 | remove all fear and hatred from your **m.**. |
| T-18 VI.2:5 | your guilt to your body from your **m.**. Yet |
| T-18 VI.2:8 | You hate your **m.**, for guilt has entered |
| T-18 VI.3:2 | Only by assigning to the **m.** the properties |
| T-18 VI.3:3 | And it is **m.** that seems to be fragmented |
| T-18 VI.3:4 | attacked to hold the separation in the **m.**, |
| T-18 VI.3:5 | **M.** cannot attack, but it can make |
| T-18 VI.3:7 | Unless the **m.** believes the body is actually |
| T-18 VI.4:1 | In this, the **m.** is clearly delusional. It |
| T-18 VI.4:3 | The **m.** cannot attack, but it can deceive |
| T-18 VI.8:3 | that is an eternal property of **m.**. But the |
| T-18 VI.8:5 | **M.** reaches to itself. It is *not* made up of |
| T-18 VI.11:4 | in which your **m.** enlarges to encompass it |
| T-18 VI.11:11 | simply by not letting your **m.** be limited |
| T-18 VI.14:4 | to welcome you to openness of **m.** and |
| T-18 VII.5:7 | at last into the **m.** given to contemplation; |
| T-18 VII.7:2 | withdrawn the body's value from your **m.**. |
| T-18 VII.7:9 | return to occupy your conscious **m.**. |
| T-18 VIII.3:3 | fragment of your **m.** is such a tiny part of |
| T-18 VIII.5:2 | Each body seems to house a separate **m.**, a |
| T-18 IX.3:1 | seem to be returned to the **m.** that made it |
| T-19 I.3:3 | entirely on how the **m.** perceives it, and |
| T-19 I.3:3 | the purpose that the **m.** would use it for. |
| T-19 I.3:4 | It is obvious that a segment of the **m.** can |
| T-19 I.5:11 | calls upon the **m.** and not the body. |
| T-19 I.6:1 | the body must be healed, and not the **m.**. |
| T-19 I.6:2 | which could be possible only if the **m.** is |
| T-19 I.6:3 | the delusional thought system in the **m.**. |
| T-19 I.6:7 | to keep both truth and illusion in the **m.**, |
| T-19 I.8:1 | strange concealment has hurt your **m.**, |
| T-19 I.13:1 | Grace is not given to a body, but to a **m.**. |
| T-19 I.13:2 | And the **m.** that receives it looks instantly |
| T-19 I.16:4 | any way except by the **m.** that thought it. |
| T-19 II.1:5 | And thus the **m.** is guilty, and will forever |
| T-19 II.1:5 | so remain unless a **m.** not part of it can |
| T-19 II.3:1 | turn the power of his **m.** against himself. |
| T-19 III.1:4 | guilt remains attractive the **m.** will suffer, |
| T-19 III.1:5 | to it, and the **m.** hears it and yearns for it, |
| T-19 III.1:8 | an avenger, with a **m.** unlike your own, |
| T-19 III.5:6 | yes, for this can be corrected by the **m.**. |
| T-19 III.5:7 | and that the **m.** must accept as true what |
| T-19 III.5:8 | If it does not obey, the **m.** is judged insane |
| T-19 III.7:3 | For the belief that bodies limit **m.** leads to |
| T-19 III.9:3 | the **m.** corrects it when it seems to be seen |
| T19 IV.B.3:1 | calling the **m.** to join in holy communion |
| T19 IV.B.10:8 | it. Only the **m.** can set a purpose, and only |
| T19 IV.B.10:8 | and only the **m.** can see the means for its |
| T19 IV.B.10:9 | and guilt are both conditions of the **m.**, to |
| T19 IV.C.5:7 | to the awareness of every **m.** which heard |
| T19 IV.D.1:5 | And as this memory rises in your **m.**, |
| T19 IV.D.16:4 | guilt from his disturbed and tortured **m.**. |
| T-20 II.2:3 | Only the **m.** can value, and only the mind |
| T-20 II.2:3 | and only the **m.** decides on what it would |
| T-20 VI.9:7 | attract the **m.** that has transcended them, |
| T-20 VI.11:2 | seems to be a wall of flesh around the **m.**, |
| T-21 in.1:5 | It is the witness to your state of **m.**, the |
| T-21 in.1:7 | choose to change your **m.** about the world |
| T-21 II.1:2 | tiny change of **m.** by which the crucifixion |
| T-21 III.2:4 | and protected as is a goal the **m.** accepts. |
| T-21 III.10:3 | The **m.** could neither ask it nor receive it |
| T-21 III.10:5 | The intention is in the **m.**, which tries to |
| T-21 III.10:5 | the means for sin in which the **m.** believes |
| T-21 III.10:6 | Thus is the joining of **m.** and body an |
| T-21 III.12:6 | and belief and faith from **m.** to body. Let |
| T-21 IV.4:5 | the part of your **m.** the ego knows not of. |
| T-21 IV.7:2 | hear since first the ego came into your **m.**. |
| T-21 V.1:2 | It literally picks it out as the **m.** directs. |
| T-21 V.3:10 | that miracles do not affect another's **m.**, |
| T-21 V.3:11 | They always change *your* **m.**. There *is* no |
| T-21 V.4:4 | How can the segment of the **m.** devoid of |
| T-21 V.8:3 | perception toward what the **m.** has valued |
| T-21 V.9:1 | of **m.** where reason lies was dedicated, by |
| T-21 VI.3:3 | one **m.** think only for itself unless the |
| T-21 VI.3:3 | only for itself unless the body *were* the **m.**. |
| T-21 VI.4:1 | attack on reason that drives it out of **m.**, |
| T-21 VI.7:6 | you it is given you to change his whole **m.**, |
| T-21 VII.10:6 | that rules you not, and change your **m.**. |
| T-21 VII.11:6 | renounced the option to change your **m.** |
| T-21 VII.13:8 | And none can leave the thinker's **m.**, or |
| T-22 II.9:3 | that thoughts can leave the thinker's **m.**, |
| T-22 III.3:1 | of **m.** in which salvation can be given you. |
| T-22 III.9:7 | as what it is; a common state of **m.**, where |
| T-22 VI.1:1 | you want freedom of the body or of the **m.** |
| T-22 VI.1:10 | He will believe it possible of **m.** or body, |
| T-22 VI.2:1 | **m.** is used as means whose value lies in its |
| T-22 VI.2:2 | so the **m.** is dedicated to serve illusions. |
| T-22 VI.6:8 | remain in a **m.** that serves the timeless. |
| T-22 VI.14:3 | except your **m.** and your brother's are one |
| T-23 I.1:1 | memory of God comes to the quiet **m.**. It |
| T-23 I.1:2 | for a **m.** at war against itself remembers |
| T-23 I.8:9 | of God, still shining in your quiet **m.**. |
| T-23 IV.6:1 | make your **m.** darkened and murderous, |
| T-23 IV.7:4 | who share a purpose have a **m.** as one. |
| T-24 in.1:2 | Given this state the **m.** is quiet, and the |
| T-24 II.6:2 | memory of Him springs instantly to **m.**. |
| T-24 II.6:4 | as his **m.** accepts the truth about himself, |
| T-24 II.8:5 | make you whole in **m.** and one with him. |
| T-24 IV.2:6 | goal. Purpose is of the **m.**. And minds can |
| T-24 IV.3:5 | The purpose of attack is in the **m.**, and its |
| T-24 IV.3:6 | is. Nor is the **m.** limited; so must it be that |
| T-24 IV.3:6 | that harmful purpose hurts the **m.** as one. |
| T-24 VII.4:1 | Ask yourself this: Can *you* protect the **m.**? |
| T-24 VII.8:5 | were. It is essential it be kept in **m.** that all |
| T-25 in.3:2 | **m.** that thinks it is a body is sick indeed! |
| T-25 I.1:5 | the body through the **m.** at one with Him. |
| T-25 I.3:1 | which you think your **m.** will be content |
| T-25 I.3:4 | the purpose in your **m.** upholdeth not. |
| T-25 I.6:1 | Spirit serves Christ's purpose in your **m.**, |
| T-25 I.6:3 | this is understood by **m.** perceived as one, |
| T-25 I.7:2 | apparent that a **m.** so split could never be |
| T-25 I.7:3 | And so What is within this **m.**, and does |
| T-25 I.7:4 | the language that this **m.** can understand, |
| T-25 II.4:2 | Be glad that it is gone within your **m.**, to |
| T-25 III.5:4 | attempts of specialness to put it out of **m.**, |
| T-25 III.5:5 | for **m.** to choose to see them where it will. |
| T-25 VIII.2:6 | could be found in such a state of **m.**. But |
| T-25 VIII.5:8 | the Holy Spirit's justice with a **m.** that can |
| T-26 IV.4:6 | What but a miracle could change his **m.**, |
| T-26 V.3:3 | Time lasted but an instant in your **m.**, |
| T-26 V.4:4 | still remains unanswered in your **m.**. |
| T-26 V.10:8 | removed and gone forever from his **m.**? |
| T-26 VII.4:8 | Ideas are of the **m.**. What is projected out, |
| T-26 VII.4:9 | out, and seems to be external to the **m.**, is |
| T-26 VII.12:2 | outside the **m.** where the belief arose. |
| T-26 VII.13:3 | each idea the **m.** conceives but adds to its |
| T-26 VII.13:4 | because the **m.** can wish to be deceived, |
| T-26 VIII.1:4 | projected beyond your **m.** you think of it |
| T-26 VIII.8:1 | untrue, must be already in your **m.**. And |
| T-27 I.9:9 | **m.** made free again to choose what it is for |
| T-27 II.5:1 | body shows the **m.** has not been healed. A |
| T-27 II.6:2 | does your healing show your **m.** is healed, |
| T-27 II.11:1 | In a split **m.**, identity must seem to be |
| T-27 II.11:3 | Correction, to a **m.** so split, must be a way |
| T-27 II.12:4 | and you allow Him only half your **m.**. And |
| T-27 II.16:2 | With half a **m.** this is not understood. |
| T-27 II.16:5 | lies the means whereby your **m.** is unified. |
| T-27 IV.2:2 | it must also be that, in your state of **m.**, |
| T-27 IV.2:3 | of **m.** in which the answer is already there. |
| T-27 IV.6:9 | the interval in which the **m.** is still enough |
| T-27 V.2:10 | must be gone forever from your **m.** to heal |
| T-27 V.3:2 | a state of **m.** that has transcended conflict |
| T-27 VII.2:6 | No one has difficulty making up his **m.** to |
| T-27 VII.7:8 | and what he sees is separate from his **m.**. |
| T-27 VII.8:4 | conceived and cherished by a separate **m.**. |
| T-27 VII.8:5 | Careless indeed of him this **m.** must be, as |
| T-27 VII.9:2 | deny the cause of suffering is in your **m.**. |
| T-27 VII.13:4 | and allowed his calmer **m.** to welcome, |
| T-27 VIII.7:1 | enemy; a **m.** within a body all are forms of |
| T-28 I.1:7 | in the **m.** that thought of them and loved |
| T-28 I.7:2 | would keep a senseless lesson in his **m.**, |
| T-28 I.8:3 | which He did not keep It safely in your **m.** |
| T-28 I.8:5 | Yet was It never absent from your **m.**, for |
| T-28 I.11:1 | the **m.** that stops an instant and is still. It |
| T-28 I.11:2 | and from the **m.** it healed in quiet then, to |
| T-28 I.13:1 | memory of God arises in the **m.** that has |
| T-28 II.2:8 | **m.** is recognized as not within the body, |
| T-28 II.3:6 | A **m.** within a body and a world of other |
| T-28 II.3:6 | are your "creations," you the "other" **m.**, |
| T-28 II.11:4 | because they show the **m.** made sickness, |
| T-28 II.11:7 | The lesson is the ***m.*** was sick that thought |
| T-28 II.12:5 | is released because the **m.** acknowledges |
| T-28 II.12:6 | thus the **m.** is free to make another choice |
| T-28 III.2:1 | No **m.** is sick until another mind agrees |
| T-28 III.2:1 | another **m.** agrees that they are separate. |
| T-28 III.2:3 | other **m.** cannot project its guilt without |
| T-28 III.2:5 | Uniting with a brother's **m.** prevents the |
| T-28 IV.2:6 | The dream is but illusion in the **m.**. And |
| T-28 IV.2:7 | And with the **m.** you would unite, but |
| T-28 IV.2:8 | It is the dream you fear, and not the **m.**. |
| T-28 IV.3:3 | him as a **m.** in which illusions still persist, |
| T-28 IV.3:3 | but as a **m.** which brother is to you. He is |
| T-28 IV.3:6 | **m.** and his are joined in brotherhood. His |
| T-28 IV.4:6 | you have supported in your brother's **m.**. |
| T-28 IV.7:4 | and separated **m.** can not remain without |
| T-28 V.1:8 | his **m.** from sharing them *is* sharing Him. |
| T-28 VI.3:10 | want your **m.** to have and see and keep. |
| T-28 VI.4:1 | bit of **m.** you call your own and all the rest |
| T-28 VI.5:4 | my **m.** and yours" has kept God's promise |
| T-28 VI.6:7 | sick, but lets his **m.** be healed and unified. |
| T-29 I.5:1 | your **m.** from your brother's unless you |
| T-29 I.5:4 | make communion with your brother's **m.**. |
| T-29 II.7:8 | means the **m.** remains unchanged in its |
| T-29 III.4:2 | the darkness may be lifted from your **m.**. |
| T-29 VI.3:6 | not remove the power to change your **m.**, |
| T-29 VII.9:1 | Yet where are dreams but in a **m.** asleep? |
| T-29 VII.9:5 | Your holy **m.** is altar unto God, and where |
| T-29 VIII.2:3 | against your confidence and peace of **m.**. |
| T-29 VIII.3:2 | perceived as real and seen outside the **m.**. |
| T-29 VIII.3:3 | and cannot leave the **m.** that is its source. |
| T-29 VIII.4:3 | source abides within your **m.** where God |
| T-29 IX.2:1 | dream of judgment came into the **m.** that |
| T-29 IX.7:4 | the **m.** conceives and what it sees. No one |
| T-29 IX.8:2 | not made to separate the **m.** from what it |
| T-30 I.3:2 | You still make up your **m.**, and *then* decide |
| T-30 I.5:2 | your **m.** to want an answer that will work. |
| T-30 I.8:1 | you can begin to change your **m.** with this |
| T-30 I.11:5 | you have changed your **m.** about the day, |
| T-30 I.12:2 | is a statement of an open **m.**, not certain |
| T-30 I.17:6 | be the one reminder that you keep in **m.**, |
| T-30 III.6:3 | long as does the **m.** that thought of them. |
| T-30 III.6:7 | The thoughts you think are in your **m.**, as |

T-30....III.11:4 The **m.** of Heaven's Son in Heaven is, for
T-30....IV.6:1 deceive the **m.** that wants to be deceived.
T-30.......V.1:1 The real world is the state of **m.** in which
T-30.......V.5:2 is a state in which the **m.** has learned how
T-30.......V.5:3 willingly the **m.** can let them go when it
T-30......VI.4:6 The **m.** must think of its Creator as it
T-31...... I.11:2 it is a state of **m.** unwanted that becomes
T-31...... I.13:1 good that ever crossed your **m.** of anyone.
T-31......III.3:7 are sin you *are* a body, for the **m.** acts not.
T-31......III.3:8 purpose must be in the body, not the **m.**.
T-31....III.3:10 are sin you lock the **m.** within the body,
T-31......III.4:1 Yet is the *body* prisoner, and not the **m.**.
T-31......III.4:4 It gives no orders that the **m.** need serve,
T-31......III.4:5 but the willing **m.** that would abide in it.
T-31......III.4:6 of the **m.** that would become its prisoner.
T-31......III.4:7 dies, because that **m.** is sick within itself.
T-31......III.4:9 never change unless the **m.** preferred the
T-31......III.4:9 to suit the purpose given by the **m.**. For
T-31....III.4:10 For **m.** can learn, and there is all change
T-31......III.5:1 The **m.** that thinks it is a sin has but one
T-31......III.7:3 Open your **m.** to change, and there will be
T-31.......V.2:5 but one of which the **m.** can recognize.
T-31.......V.8:3 if any peace of **m.** is to be given you. Nor
T-31.....V.12:5 see reflects the state of the perceiver's **m.**.
T-31.....V.14:4 not concern itself with content of the **m.**,
T-31.....V.16:3 world is loosening its grasp upon your **m.**.
T-31.....V.16:4 will go at last, and leave your **m.** at peace.
T-31.....V.17:3 unsealed and open **m.** that truth returns,
T-31.....VII.6:3 it static and concealed within your **m.**.
T-31.....VII.6:5 Alternatives are in your **m.** to use, and
T-31...VII.13:3 at all. And thus it serves a wholly open **m.**,
T-31... VIII.3:5 release your **m.** from everything that
W-in..........1:3 An untrained **m.** can accomplish nothing.
W-in..........1:4 of this workbook to train your **m.** to think
W-in..........4:1 is to train your **m.** in a systematic way to a
W-pI.......3.2:1 you clear your **m.** of all past associations,
W-pI.......3.2:2 that you keep a perfectly open **m.**,
W-pI.......4.1:2 are crossing your **m.** for about a minute.
W-pI.......4.3:4 also the beginning of training your **m.** to
W-pI.......4.5:3 examine your **m.** for more than a minute
W-pI.......5.3:1 you first search your **m.** for "sources" of
W-pI.......5.4:4 *are all equally disturbing to my peace of* **m.**.
W-pI.......5.5:1 your **m.** for whatever is distressing you,
W-pI.......5.7:1 your **m.** for no more than a minute or so,
W-pI.......6.2:2 by a minute or so of **m.** searching, as
W-pI.......6.3:3 *are all equally disturbing to my peace of* **m.**.
W-pI..........8.h My **m.** is preoccupied with past thoughts.
W-pI.......8.1:5 Your **m.** cannot grasp the present, which
W-pI.......8.2:4 The **m.** is actually blank when it does this,
W-pI.......8.3:1 is to begin to train your **m.** to recognize
W-pI.......8.3:2 thoughtless ideas preoccupy your **m.**, the
W-pI.......8.3:3 Recognizing that your **m.** has been merely
W-pI.......8.4:3 search your **m.** for the usual minute or so,
W-pI.......8.5:3 *my* **m.** *is preoccupied with past thoughts.*
W-pI.......8.6:3 may induce, in the **m.** searching itself.
W-pI.......9.2:1 is difficult for the untrained **m.** to believe
W-pI.......9.2:5 the **m.** that has been cleared of the debris
W-pI.....10.3:3 statement that your **m.** is really a blank.
W-pI.....10.4:4 in searching your **m.** for all the thoughts
W-pI.....10.4:7 you. As each one crosses your **m.**, say: *My*
W-pI.....10.5:2 more than a minute or so of **m.** searching.
W-pI.....12.3:7 All terms which cross your **m.** are suitable
W-pI.....14.4:1 horrors in the world that cross your **m.**.
W-pI.....14.6:5 only be in your own **m.** apart from His.
W-pI.....16.4:1 search your **m.** for a minute or so with
W-pI.....16.5:1 and then as each one crosses your **m.** hold
W-pI.....19.3:1 The minute or so of **m.** searching which
W-pI.....19.3:2 **m.** should be carefully searched for the
W-pI.....19.3:3 and holding it in your **m.** as you do so, say
W-pI.....20.2:6 because your **m.** is totally undisciplined,
W-pI.....21.2:2 your **m.** carefully for situations past,
W-pI.....21.4:1 As you search your **m.** for all the forms in
W-pI.....21.4:1 hold each one in **m.** while you tell yourself
W-pI.....22.1:1 thoughts in his **m.** must see the world.
W-pI.....22.1:6 What peace of **m.** is possible to him then?
W-pI.....23.6:2 to searching your **m.** for as many attack
W-pI.....23.6:3 you. As each one crosses your **m.** say: *I can*
W-pI.....23.6:5 Hold each attack thought in **m.** as you say
W-pI.....24.2:3 opening your **m.** so that learning can
W-pI.....24.4:1 today's idea, followed by searching the **m.**
W-pI.....24.4:3 goals in **m.** as part of the desired outcome
W-pI.....24.6:2 that you have no unified outcome in **m.**,
W-pI.....24.7:1 that crosses your **m.** say to yourself: *I do*
W-pI.....26.2:3 make you vulnerable in your own **m.**,
W-pI.....28.3:1 the table, and open your **m.** to what it is,
W-pI.....28.5:1 look upon it with a completely open **m.**. It
W-pI........30.h everything I see because God is in my **m.**.
W-pI.....30.5:2 at all. The **m.** is its only source. To aid in
W-pI.....30.5:3 using whatever subjects come to **m.**, and
W-pI.....31.3:1 cross your **m.** come into your awareness,
W-pI.....32.2:2 the other the world you see in your **m.**. In
W-pI.....34.1:2 Peace of **m.** is clearly an internal matter. It
W-pI.....34.1:4 It is from your peace of **m.** that a peaceful
W-pI.....34.3:1 Some five minutes of **m.** searching are
W-pI.....34.3:2 Search your **m.** for fear thoughts, anxiety-
W-pI.....34.3:3 slowly as you watch them arise in your **m.**
W-pI.....34.5:1 your peace of **m.** is threatened in any way.
W-pI.....34.6:1 inroads on your peace of **m.** take the form
W-pI.....34.6:2 change your **m.** in any specific context, try
W-pI........35.h My **m.** is part of God's. I am very holy.
W-pI.....35.4:1 close your eyes and search your **m.** for the
W-pI.....35.5:2 descriptive terms may well cross your **m.**.
W-pI.....35.7:2 events in which you figure cross your **m.**.
W-pI.....35.7:5 *But my* **m.** *is part of God's. I am very holy.*
W-pI.....36.1:2 are holy because your **m.** is part of God's.
W-pI.....36.1:7 **m.** is part of God's you must be sinless, or
W-pI.....38.4:1 and then search your **m.** for any sense of
W-pI.....38.6:1 or someone else arises, or comes to **m.**. In
W-pI.....39.8:1 search your **m.** for every thought that
W-pI.....39.9:4 as your **m.** becomes more disciplined and
W-pI.....41.3:2 the **m.** that thought these things were real
W-pI.....41.4:4 your peace of **m.** because God goes with
W-pI.....41.6:6 Try to enter very deeply into your own **m.**
W-pI.....42.5:3 you find your **m.** is merely wandering,
W-pI.....42.5:4 no thoughts at all seem to come to **m.**. If
W-pI.....42.5:5 to look for related thoughts in your **m.**.
W-pI.....43.1:4 replaced knowledge forever in your **m.**.
W-pI.....43.6:1 If you find your **m.** wandering; if you
W-pI.....44.3:3 difficult form for the undisciplined **m.**,
W-pI.....44.3:3 and represents a major goal of **m.** training
W-pI.....44.3:4 precisely what the untrained **m.** lacks. Yet
W-pI.....44.4:3 easy one in the world for the trained **m.**,
W-pI.....44.4:3 and difficult for the untrained **m.**.
W-pI.....44.5:1 Your **m.** is no longer wholly untrained.
W-pI.....44.7:2 Then try to sink into your **m.**, letting go
W-pI.....44.7:3 Your **m.** cannot be stopped in this unless
W-pI.....45.2:5 think with the Mind of God leave your **m.**
W-pI.....45.2:7 They are in your **m.** as well, where He is.
W-pI.....45.3:3 We will have to look for them in your **m.**,
W-pI.....45.6:2 of your own, keeping the idea in **m.**. After
W-pI.....45.6:4 *My real thoughts are in my* **m.**. *I would like*
W-pI.....45.6:6 thoughts that cover the truth in your **m.**,
W-pI.....45.7:1 your **m.** are the thoughts that you thought
W-pI.....45.7:2 beginning. They are there in your **m.** now,
W-pI.....45.7:3 They will always be in your **m.**, exactly as
W-pI.....45.8:2 is your **m.** joined with the Mind of God.
W-pI.....45.9:1 holiness of the **m.** that thinks with God.
W-pI.....46.2:3 returning the **m.** to the awareness of God.
W-pI.....46.3:3 **m.** for those whom you have not forgiven.
W-pI.....46.5:2 the idea to all those who have come to **m.**,
W-pI.....46.6:5 *No fear is possible in a* **m.** *beloved of God.*
W-pI.....47.7:1 down into your **m.** to a place of real safety
W-pI.....47.7:3 and bubble on the surface of your **m.**, and
W-pI.....48.2:5 should anything disturb your peace of **m.**
W-pI.....48.3:2 to fear shows that somewhere in your **m.**,
W-pI.....49.1:2 The part of your **m.** in which truth abides
W-pI.....49.1:3 other part of your **m.** that functions in the
W-pI.....49.2:5 it. Try to identify with the part of your **m.**
W-pI.....49.4:2 Be very still and open your **m.**. Go past all
W-pI.....50.3:3 It will transport you into a state of **m.** that
W-pI.....50.5:3 to disturb the holy **m.** of the Son of God.
W-pI.....52.3:1 My **m.** is preoccupied with past thoughts.
W-pI.....52.3:2 and my **m.** is preoccupied with the past.
W-pI.....52.3:4 the present from dawning on my **m.**. Let
W-pI.....52.5:6 Yet my **m.** is part of creation and part of
W-pI.....53.4:4 It is in my **m.** too, because He created it
W-pI.....54.2:4 the representation of my own state of **m.**.
W-pI.....54.2:5 I know that my state of **m.** can change.
W-pI.....54.4:6 to change every **m.** along with mine, for
W-pI.....55.5:7 it. Let me open my **m.** to the world's real
W-pI.....56.5:1 everything I see because God is in my **m.**.
W-pI.....56.5:2 own **m.**, behind all my insane thoughts of
W-pI.....57.5:1 (35) My **m.** is part of God's. I am very
W-pI.....59.5:3 Him, because I have no **m.** apart from His
W-pI.....61.5:7 to yourself if your **m.** wanders away from
W-pI.....62.3:3 weakness, strain and fatigue from your **m.**
W-pI.....62.5:5 in your **m.** is the awareness they are true.
W-pI........63.h peace to every **m.** through my forgiveness.
W-pI.....63.1:1 have the power to bring peace to every **m.**
W-pI.....63.3:4 *peace to every* **m.** *through my forgiveness. I*
W-pI.....64.7:2 in the **m.** discipline that it requires. You
W-pI.....65.2:3 way in which you can find peace of **m.**.
W-pI.....65.4:4 disciplinary training your **m.** needs, so
W-pI.....65.5:2 watch your **m.** carefully to catch whatever
W-pI.....66.7:2 that there are only two parts of your **m.**.
W-pI.....66.9:2 of your function has taken in your **m.**, and
W-pI.....67.3:3 somewhere in your **m.** It is there for you
W-pI.....67.5:2 **m.** is so preoccupied with false self-images
W-pI.....68.1:4 **m.** and to condemn the body to death.
W-pI.....68.1:5 what holding grievances does to your **m.**.
W-pI.....68.2:1 while the part of your **m.** that weaves
W-pI.....68.5:1 your **m.** for those against whom you hold
W-pI.....69.4:2 Think of your **m.** as a vast circle,
W-pI.....69.6:3 Reach out and touch them in your **m.**.
W-pI.....69.8:3 light, to hold this confidence in your **m.**.
W-pI.....69.8:5 Try to keep the thought clearly in **m.** that
W-pI.....70.1:4 as in your own **m.** and nowhere else.
W-pI.....70.1:5 all guilt is solely an invention of your **m.**,
W-pI.....70.3:1 in your own **m.** entails the realization that
W-pI.....70.3:3 That is the way your **m.** has worked, but
W-pI.....71.2:5 The change of **m.** necessary for salvation
W-pI.....71.3:1 role assigned to your own **m.** in this plan,
W-pI.....72.2:3 seems to surround the **m.** with a body,
W-pI.....72.8:3 has been ruinous to your peace of **m.**. You
W-pI.....73.5:3 Grievances darken your **m.**, and you look
W-pI...73.10:1 to keep your will clearly in **m.**, tell
W-pI.....74.3:1 what they mean, and to hold them in **m.**:
W-pI...74.3:10 conflict thoughts that may cross your **m.**.
W-pI.....74.5:1 you have cleared your **m.** in this way,
W-pI.....75.6:2 Keep a completely open **m.**, washed of all
W-pI.....76.5:2 is endangered by the **m.** that hurts itself.
W-pI.....76.5:3 that the **m.** will fail to see it is the victim
W-pI.....76.5:4 the **m.** holds up to hide what really suffers
W-pI.....76.9:2 and hold your **m.** in silent readiness to
W-pI.....78.5:1 his name has crossed your **m.** already. He
W-pI.....78.6:2 You will attempt to hold him in your **m.**,
W-pI.....78.7:4 you, let your **m.** be shown the light in him
WpI..rII.in.3:1 period if you find your **m.** wandering, but
W-pI.....82.1:1 peace to every **m.** through my forgiveness.
W-pI.....82.2:2 are: *Let peace extend from my* **m.** *to yours,*
W-pI.....85.3:4 Source, and so it cannot have left my **m.**. I
W-pI.....91.5:3 and you instruct your **m.** accordingly.
W-pI.....91.7:2 to replace the image of a body in your **m.**.
W-pI...93.11:7 **m.** that the idea for the day is true indeed.
W-pI.....95.4:2 this point not to allow your **m.** to wander,
W-pI.....95.4:4 and of your need for **m.** training. It is
W-pI...95.11:1 offered to your **m.** with all the certainty
W-pI...95.11:3 meaning of the words to sink into your **m.**
W-pI...95.14:8 the stirring of the truth within his **m.**, the
W-pI.....96.1:1 and evil, loving and hating, **m.** and body.
W-pI.....96.3:4 A **m.** and body cannot both exist. Make
W-pI.....96.3:6 your **m.** is gone from your self-concept,
W-pI.....96.4:1 of **m.** as means to find its Self expression.
W-pI.....96.4:2 **m.** which serves the spirit is at peace and
W-pI.....96.4:4 **m.** can also see itself divorced from spirit,
W-pI.....96.5:1 Yet **m.** apart from spirit cannot think. It
W-pI.....96.7:1 remain within your **m.** and in the Mind of
W-pI.....96.7:2 The Holy Spirit holds salvation in your **m.**
W-pI.....96.8:1 whose presence in your **m.** is guaranteed
W-pI.....96.8:2 will be a search for Him within your **m.**.
W-pI.....96.8:3 Who is the Bridge between your **m.** and It
W-pI.....96.8:4 about your Self, and what your **m.** can do,
W-pI.....96.9:5 let your **m.** go wandering in a world of
W-pI...96.10:1 and that your **m.** has found the function
W-pI...96.10:4 Your **m.** will bless all things. Confusion
W-pI...96.11:2 Perhaps your **m.** remains uncertain yet a
W-pI...96.11:5 seeking Him Who joins your **m.** and Self,

W-pI...96.12:1 your frantic **m.** salvation comes from your
W-pI.....97.1:4 for it will bring your **m.** from conflict to
W-pI.....97.1:5 your **m.** has been absolved from madness,
W-pI.....97.2:1 you, whose **m.** has been restored to sanity
W-pI.....97.3:1 try to bring reality still closer to your **m.**.
W-pI.....97.4:1 You are the spirit in whose **m.** abides the
W-pI.....97.5:2 He will not overlook one open **m.** that will
W-pI.....97.8:3 and let Him tell your **m.** that they are true
W-pI.....98.6:2 for peace of **m.** and certainty of purpose,
W-pI...98.10:3 your **m.** be readied for the happy time to
W-pI.....99.3:1 within a **m.** where both of them exist? The
W-pI.....99.3:2 The **m.** that sees illusions thinks them real
W-pI.....99.3:4 because the **m.** that thinks these thoughts
W-pI.....99.4:1 joins the separated **m.** and thoughts with
W-pI.....99.7:6 of your **m.** that thought the thoughts that
W-pI.....99.9:2 It is God's Will your **m.** be one with His. It
W-pI...99.11:1 of doubt and fear forever from your **m.**. If
W-pI...99.12:5 your **m.** and let all fear be gently laid aside
W-pI...101.5:3 Accept Atonement with an open **m.**,
W-pI...101.6:8 these thoughts will introduce into your **m.**
W-pI...102.1:4 dark and hidden secret places of your **m.**.
W-pI...102.4:3 seek this function deep within your **m.**,
W-pI...103.1:6 as well. Yet can the **m.** deny that this is so,
W-pI...103.3:1 within your **m.** each waking hour today.
W-pI...104.1:5 welcomed gladly by a **m.** that has instead
W-pI...104.5:3 will we bring to **m.** as often as we can: *I*
W-pI...105.7:3 and let your **m.** be free of all that would
W-pI...105.8:1 if you prepare your **m.** as we suggest. For
W-pI...106.1:1 want; if you will listen with an open **m.**,
W-pI......107.h Truth will correct all errors in my **m.**.
W-pI...107.2:1 what a state of **m.** without illusions is?
W-pI...107.3:1 **m.** will rest in when the truth has come.
W-pI...107.3:3 and dead ideas to linger in your **m.**. Truth
W-pI...107.3:4 mind. Truth occupies your **m.** completely,
W-pI...107.4:4 when truth corrects the errors in your **m.**.
W-pI...107.9:1 your **m.** which tell you you could be apart
W-pI...107.9:5 *Truth will correct all errors in my* **m.**, *And I*
W-pI.107.10:3 as you let them be corrected in your **m.**.
W-pI.107.11:2 "Truth will correct all errors in my **m.**,"
W-pI...108.2:2 is a state of **m.** that has become so unified
W-pI...108.3:2 brings your peace of **m.** to other minds, to
W-pI...108.8:7 *To everyone I offer peace of* **m.**. *To everyone*
W-pI...109.5:5 your **m.** that all its frantic fantasies were
W-pI...109.6:1 today, a tired **m.** is suddenly made glad, a
W-pI...110.2:1 to let complete correction heal your **m.**,
W-pI...110.2:1 that any **m.** has made at any time or place
W-pI...110.4:2 been no separation of your **m.** from His,
W-pI...110.4:2 no split between your **m.** and other minds
W-pI...110.7:1 with this statement firmly in your **m.**, try
W-pI...110.7:1 try to discover in your **m.** the Self Who is
W-pI...110.9:4 Deep in your **m.** the holy Christ in you is
WpI. rIII.in4:1 soon as you have changed your **m.** about
WpI. rIII.in5:3 letting your **m.** relate them to your needs,
WpI. rIII.in6:1 Place the ideas within your **m.**, and let it
WpI. rIII.in6:3 What can you trust but what is in your **m.**
WpI. rIII.in6:5 The wisdom of your **m.** will come to your
WpI. rIII.in6:6 and let the **m.** employ the thoughts you
WpI. rIII.in7:2 Offer them to your **m.** in that same trust
WpIrIII.in10:5 it, and allow your **m.** to rest a little time in
W-pI...111.1:3 *the light of holiness and truth light up my* **m.**
W-pI...113.2:2 *knowledge still remains within my* **m.**, *I see*
W-pI...119.1:1 Truth will correct all errors in my **m.**. *I am*
W-pI...119.3:2 Truth will correct all errors in my **m.**. On
W-pI...121.2:1 The unforgiving **m.** is full of fear, and
W-pI...121.2:2 The unforgiving **m.** is sad, without the
W-pI...121.3:1 The unforgiving **m.** is torn with doubt,
W-pI...121.3:2 can the unforgiving **m.** perceive but its
W-pI...121.4:1 The unforgiving **m.** sees no mistakes, but
W-pI...121.5:1 The unforgiving **m.** is in despair, without
W-pI...121.6:2 It is not inherent in the **m.**, which cannot
W-pI...121.6:5 your **m.** as one to Him Who is your Self,
W-pI...121.7:1 Each unforgiving **m.** presents you with an
W-pI...121.7:5 The unforgiving **m.** must learn through
W-pI...121.9:1 The unforgiving **m.** does not believe that
W-pI.121.11:1 close your eyes and see him in your **m.**,
W-pI.121.12:1 and turn your **m.** to one you call a friend.
W-pI.121.13:4 happiness to every unforgiving **m.**, with
W-pI...122.1:4 want happiness, a quiet **m.**, a certainty of
W-pI...122.3:2 can arise across the threshold of your **m.**.
W-pI...122.7:5 gifts of any value to a **m.** that has received
W-pI.122.14:1 but hold them firmly in your **m.** by your
W-pI...124.2:2 the **m.** at one with God and with itself.
W-pI...124.5:2 peace of **m.** in which they were created.
W-pI...124.9:3 it dawns with certainty upon your **m.**.
W-pI.124.10:2 within your **m.** and waiting to be found.
W-pI...125.1:3 deep within your **m.** where He abides.
W-pI...125.1:5 is heard around the world; until your **m.**,
W-pI...125.2:2 **m.** and at his side to lead him surely to his
W-pI...125.4:3 within the **m.** where He abides forever, in
W-pI...125.5:1 your **m.** to Him to give His Word to you.
W-pI...125.6:2 be heard until your **m.** is quiet for a while,
W-pI...125.6:4 to help make ready your most holy **m.** to
W-pI...126.6:2 without requiring correction in your **m.**.
W-pI...126.7:5 it is attained, must heal the **m.** that gives,
W-pI...126.9:3 that will release your **m.** from every bar to
W-pI.126.11:2 not let your **m.** forget this goal for long,
W-pI.126.11:6 your **m.** to His correction and His Love.
W-pI...127.3:4 the **m.** that thinks of it as partial or in part
W-pI...127.6:4 Today we practice making free your **m.** of
W-pI...127.8:2 Open your **m.** and rest. The world that
W-pI...127.9:3 a spark of truth within your **m.** wherever
W-pI...127.9:5 love's meaning to your clean and open **m.**.
W-pI.127.12:3 And as he comes to **m.**, give him this
W-pI...128.2:3 The only purpose worthy of your **m.** this
W-pI...128.3:1 your **m.** when you perceive salvation here.
W-pI...128.6:1 release your **m.** from chains and let it seek
W-pI...128.7:3 little, every time you let your **m.** escape its
W-pI...128.7:7 Open your **m.** to Him. Be still and rest.
W-pI...128.8:1 your **m.** throughout the day as well. And
W-pI...128.8:2 refuse to lay this chain upon your **m.**, but
W-pI...129.5:3 as you unbind your **m.** from little things
W-pI...129.8:3 And yet your **m.** can see it plainly, and
W-pI...130.1:5 see a world his **m.** has not accorded value.
W-pI.131.10:1 and turn your **m.** to true ideas instead. No
W-pI.131.11:5 several minutes watch your **m.** and see,
W-pI.131.11:8 There is a door beneath them in your **m.**,
W-pI...132.2:1 for anyone is free to change his **m.**, and all
W-pI...132.2:2 change your **m.** means you have changed
W-pI...132.3:5 bitter thoughts of death within your **m.**.
W-pI...132.4:2 Your **m.** must give it meaning. And what
W-pI...132.5:2 but your **m.** on what you want to see, and
W-pI...132.5:4 and must be borne in **m.** if you would
W-pI...132.5:5 and that it changes as you change your **m.**
W-pI.132.10:2 is but to change your **m.** about yourself.
W-pI.132.10:3 the world within your **m.** in thought.
W-pI.132.13:6 Release your **m.**, and you will look upon a
W-pI.132.15:4 and let your **m.** in quietness be changed
W-pI.132.17:1 the power of your simple change of **m.**: *I*
W-pI...133.2:2 let your **m.** be drawn to bodily concerns,
W-pI...133.8:3 to you? What attracts your **m.** to it? What
W-pI...134.3:3 the idea of sin retains as yet upon your **m.**
W-pI...134.9:2 your **m.** to dwell on what you think he did
W-pI.134.10:1 and keep your **m.** as free of guilt and pain
W-pI.134.12:4 made to chain his **m.** to fear and misery.
W-pI.134.13:4 yet it joins your **m.** with the reality in you.
W-pI.134.15:1 "sins," as one by one they cross your **m.**.
W-pI.134.17:2 allow your **m.** to see through this illusion
W-pI...135.6:4 It is your **m.** which gave the body all the
W-pI...135.7:3 It will be strong and healthy if the **m.** does
W-pI...135.8:2 **m.** can operate until its usefulness is over.
W-pI...135.9:1 the body and you have attacked your **m.**.
W-pI...135.9:3 the **m.** as separate from bodily conditions
W-pI...135.9:4 conception of the **m.** as limited and fragile
W-pI.135.10:4 all, but merely adds to your distress of **m.**.
W-pI.135.11:1 A healed **m.** does not plan. It carries out
W-pI.135.12:1 A healed **m.** is relieved of the belief that it
W-pI.135.13:1 the body to the plans the unhealed **m.** sets
W-pI.135.13:4 For everything the **m.** employs for this
W-pI.135.14:2 means by which a frightened **m.** would
W-pI.135.15:1 The **m.** engaged in planning for itself is
W-pI.135.15:4 enough to let the **m.** direct its future
W-pI.135.16:1 **m.** that plans is thus refusing to allow for
W-pI...136.4:3 a happening beyond your state of **m.**, an
W-pI...136.7:3 truth arises in your own deluded **m.**, and
W-pI.136.14:2 it comes to any **m.** that would lay down its
W-pI.136.15:7 *I am, and let my* **m.** *be wholly healed today.*
W-pI.136.16:1 Healing will flash across your open **m.**, as
W-pI.136.16:3 insanely sought, remaining in your **m.**. It
W-pI 136.17:4 No response at all is in the **m.** to what the
W-pI 136.19:2 If you let your **m.** harbor attack thoughts,
W-pI 136.19:2 will attack the body, for the **m.** is sick.
W-pI 136.20:6 *And my* **m.** *cannot attack. So I can not be sick*
W-pI .. 137.2:3 real, and keep the **m.** in solitary prison,
W-pI .. 137.6:3 more solid and more stable than the **m.**.
W-pI 137.10:1 those around you, or who cross your **m.**,
W-pI 137.11:3 accepts it not within his **m.** becomes a
W-pI 137.14:4 *be banished from the* **m.** *of God's one Son,*
W-pI .. 138.8:1 and grip the **m.** with terror and anxiety so
W-pI .. 138.9:4 that the **m.** had made before are open to
W-pI 138.12:6 *I make it now, and will not change my* **m.**,
W-pI .. 139.5:4 split your **m.** into what knows and does
W-pI 139.11:6 truth, how much a part of us is every **m.**,
W-pI 139.12:2 For several minutes let your **m.** be cleared
W-pI .. 140.1:3 When it tries to heal the **m.**, it sees no
W-pI .. 140.1:3 the body, where it thinks the **m.** exists. Its
W-pI .. 140.2:3 so his **m.** remains exactly as it was before.
W-pI .. 140.3:2 dreams forgiveness lets the **m.** perceive do
W-pI .. 140.3:3 heralds of the dawn of truth upon the **m.**.
W-pI .. 140.4:2 **m.** which understands that sickness can
W-pI .. 140.7:4 The **m.** that brings illusions to the truth is
WpI..rIV.in2:2 *My* **m.** *holds only what I think with God.*
WpI..rIV.in2:6 his **m.** no thoughts can dwell but those his
WpI..rIV.in4:1 **m.** holds only what you think with God.
WpI..rIV.in5:1 preparation of your **m.** to learn what each
WpI..rIV.in5:2 Open your **m.**, and clear it of all thoughts
WpI..rIV.in5:3 *My* **m.** *holds only what I think with God.* Five
WpI..rIV.in8:1 bring to your **m.** the thought with which
WpIrIV.in10:2 give your **m.** to the ideas for the day again
W-pI ..... 141.h My **m.** holds only what I think with God
W-pI ..... 142.h My **m.** holds only what I think with God.
W-pI ..... 143.h My **m.** holds only what I think with God.
W-pI ..... 144.h My **m.** holds only what I think with God.
W-pI ..... 145.h My **m.** holds only what I think with God.
W-pI ..... 146.h My **m.** holds only what I think with God.
W-pI ..... 147.h My **m.** holds only what I think with God.
W-pI ..... 148.h My **m.** holds only what I think with God.
W-pI ..... 149.h My **m.** holds only what I think with God.
W-pI ..... 150.h My **m.** holds only what I think with God.
W-pI 151.13:4 evaluate each thought that comes to **m.**,
W-pI 151.15:5 you which He has retranslated in your **m.**.
W-pI .. 152.2:5 fear and sickness enter in a **m.** where love
W-pI .. 152.5:2 in conditions of the body and the **m.**; in
W-pI .. 152.6:4 **m.** that lives within a body that must die?
W-pI .. 153.1:5 No peace of **m.** is possible where danger
W-pI .. 153.2:6 The **m.** is now confused, and knows not
W-pI .. 153.3:2 the hours and the days that bind the **m.** in
W-pI .. 153.3:3 grip of the imprisonment upon the **m.**.
W-pI 153.18:3 keep your **m.** away from Him a moment,
W-pI 153.20:1 you keep your **m.** from wandering from
W-pI .. 154.4:2 guilt abolished in the **m.** that God created
W-pI .. 154.4:3 Now this **m.** becomes aware again of Who
W-pI .. 156.8:6 *I light my* **m.** *and all the minds which God*
W-pI .. 157.4:3 is needed but today's idea to light your **m.**
W-pI .. 157.5:3 so transform your **m.** that it becomes the
W-pI .. 158.1:2 The knowledge that you are a **m.**, in Mind
W-pI .. 158.1:2 you are a mind, in Mind and purely **m.**,
W-pI .. 158.2:8 Son are one will come in time to every **m.**.
W-pI .. 158.2:9 is that time determined by the **m.** itself,
W-pI .. 159.2:5 storehouse of your **m.** where they are laid,
W-pI .. 161.2:1 is the natural condition of the **m.**. But
W-pI .. 161.2:6 to your **m.** the sounds it wants to hear.
W-pI .. 161.4:2 Every **m.** contains all minds, for every
W-pI .. 161.4:2 contains all minds, for every **m.** is one.
W-pI .. 161.4:7 **m.** that taught itself to think specifically
W-pI .. 161.6:5 for attack, for no one thinks he hates a **m.**.
W-pI .. 161.6:6 Yet what but **m.** directs the body to attack
W-pI .. 162.1:1 This single thought, held firmly in the **m.**,
W-pI .. 162.3:1 his own; arising with them in his **m.**,
W-pI .. 162.4:2 to change the **m.** of him who uses them.
W-pI .. 162.4:5 restored your sight by salvaging your **m.**.
W-pI .. 164.8:2 within your **m.** where Christ can come,
W-pI .. 164.8:3 of your most holy **m.** to save the world. Is
W-pI ..... 165.h Let not my **m.** deny the Thought of God.
W-pI .. 165.2:6 lighting your **m.** with happiness and love.
W-pI .. 165.2:7 and everlasting life shine in your **m.**,
W-pI .. 165.3:1 his joy, his healing and his peace of **m.**,
W-pI .. 165.4:3 changed your **m.** will be before it comes

W-pI...165.5:6 your **m.** has come to lay aside denial, and
W-pI...165.6:2 Now is Christ's power in your **m.**, to heal
W-pI...166.2:4 but every **m.** that looks upon the world
W-pI.166.14:5 your change of **m.** becomes the proof that
W-pI.166.15:4 how transformed the **m.** becomes which
W-pI...167.3:3 A thought is in the **m.**. It can be then
W-pI...167.3:4 It can be then applied as **m.** directs it. But
W-pI...167.3:7 to change your **m.** about yourself. It is the
W-pI...167.6:1 The **m.** can think it sleeps, but that is all.
W-pI...167.6:4 What is alien to the **m.** does not exist,
W-pI...167.6:5 For **m.** creates all things that are, and
W-pI...167.6:7 seems to die is but the sign of **m.** asleep.
W-pI...167.7:4 Yet **m.** is mind, awake or sleeping. It is
W-pI...167.7:4 Yet mind is **m.**, awake or sleeping. It is
W-pI...167.8:1 God creates only **m.** awake. He does not
W-pI...167.9:2 When the **m.** elects to be what it is not,
W-pI...167.9:4 When the **m.** awakes, it but continues as
W-pI.167.12:3 A sleeping **m.** must waken, as it sees its
W-pI.167.12:7 wakened **m.** is one that knows its Source,
W-pI.168.1:10 When his **m.** remains asleep, He loves
W-pI.168.1:11 And when his **m.** awakes, He loves him
W-pI...168.2:6 memory of Him awakens in the **m.** that
W-pI...168.3:6 all memories the sleeping **m.** forgot; all
W-pI...169.1:3 the **m.** prepares itself for true acceptance.
W-pI...169.3:4 an open **m.** can hear the Call to waken. It
W-pI...169.4:2 the **m.** determines when that time will be,
W-pI...169.4:3 and speed its advent into every **m.** that
W-pI...169.5:3 No **m.** holds anything but Him. We say
W-pI...169.5:5 and no part of **m.** sufficiently distinct to
W-pI...169.6:2 comes to every **m.** when total recognition
W-pI...169.6:3 It returns the **m.** into the endless present,
W-pI...169.7:2 that the time the **m.** itself determined to
W-pI...169.9:2 be here. Whatever time the **m.** has set for
W-pI...170.3:2 splitting your **m.** into two camps which
W-pI...170.4:3 your **m.** from him who is to be attacked,
WpI.. rV.in5:3 if we keep in **m.** that this remains our goal
WpI.. rV.in6:5 still retaining in his **m.** the way that led
WpI.. rV.in7:3 reborn each time a brother's **m.** turns to
WpI rV.in12:1 of practice periods, but to recall the **m.**, as
W-pI...178.1:1 Let not my **m.** deny the Thought of God.
W-pI...182.1:2 somewhere in your **m.** you know that this
W-pI...182.1:6 but surely to return to **m.** again.
W-pI...182.3:3 makes, yet none contents his restless **m.**.
W-pI...182.8:1 cease to have value in your restless **m.**,
W-pI...183.2:1 echo in the **m.** that calls you to remember.
W-pI...183.5:4 along with him within your quiet **m.**, you
W-pI...183.8:3 idea that holds your **m.** completely. Let all
W-pI...184.3:1 holding bits of **m.** as separate awarenesses
W-pI...184.5:1 for the **m.** to channel its perception. It is
W-pI...184.5:2 It is hard to teach the **m.** a thousand alien
W-pI...184.8:6 for his **m.** consents to take the name you
W-pI...185.6:1 **m.** which means that all it wants is peace
W-pI...185.6:2 a form each **m.** that seeks for it in honesty
W-pI...185.8:1 periods to careful searching of your **m.**, to
W-pI.185.14:1 need of every heart, the call of every **m.**,
W-pI...186.1:1 day take all arrogance away from every **m.**
W-pI...186.9:5 They blow across his **m.** like wind-swept
W-pI.186.10:1 and leave your **m.** unclouded and serene,
W-pI...187.2:4 you strengthen them in your own **m.**.
W-pI...188.4:1 shining in your **m.** reminds the world of
W-pI...188.7:4 as well, for they were born within your **m.**
W-pI...189.5:3 But learn and do not let your **m.** forget
W-pI...189.7:2 Empty your **m.** of everything it thinks is
W-pI...190.5:2 your **m.** can hurt or injure you in any way.
W-pI...190.6:4 entirely as you elect to change your **m.**,
W-pI...190.6:6 corner of your **m.** its own inheritance, and
W-pI...190.8:1 form, and working havoc in your holy **m.**.
W-pI...192.5:1 The **m.** without the body cannot make
W-pI...192.5:5 Only forgiveness can relieve the **m.** of
W-pI...192.6:1 was lifted from a sick and tortured **m.**. Is
W-pI...193.5:4 the dream of sin, and rid the **m.** of fear.
W-pI...193.7:4 in the **m.** that sees the pain through eyes
W-pI...193.7:4 sees the pain through eyes the **m.** directs.
W-pI...194.6:2 it becomes a thought that rules your **m.**, a
W-pI...194.7:8 change his **m.** when he has made mistakes
W-pI...196.3:1 also teach your **m.** that you are not an ego
W-pI...196.4:2 **m.** relinquishes its burdens one by one. It
W-pI...196.8:5 back within the holy **m.** He never left.
W-pI.196.10:1 your **m.** so wholly that escape appears
W-pI.196.10:2 you fear, the **m.** perceives itself as split.
W-pI.196.12:5 indeed but you your **m.** can try to crucify.
W-pI...197.1:1 second step we take to free your **m.** from
W-pI...197.4:2 **m.** there is a part that joins with yours in
W-pI...198.9:2 truth bestows these words upon your **m.**,
W-pI.198.11:6 the **m.** that God forever knows to be His
W-pI...199.1:4 **m.** can be made free when it no longer
W-pI...199.1:5 the truth, the **m.** were vulnerable indeed!
W-pI...199.2:1 **m.** that serves the Holy Spirit is unlimited
W-pI...199.2:2 Attack thoughts cannot enter such a **m.**,
W-pI...199.2:2 and fear can never enter in a **m.** that has
W-pI...199.4:4 as useful form for what the **m.** must do. It
W-pI...199.6:5 to **m.** with but the thought of freedom as
W-pI...199.6:6 which the **m.** within the Holy Spirit seeks.
W-pI...199.7:5 and give your **m.** to Him Who calls to you
W-pI...199.8:3 Would you not return your **m.** to this?
W-pI...199.8:9 *has given me, and it is only this my* **m.** *obeys.*
W-pI...200.5:2 your **m.** about the purpose of the world, if
W-pI.200.10:6 heart and **m.** with comfort and with love.
WpI rVI.in.2:1 With this in **m.** we start our practicing, in
WpI rVI.in.3:8 of everything that clutters up the **m.**, and
WpI rVI.in.5:3 **m.** that this is not what it would have.
W-pI...219.1:4 *Be still, my* **m.**, *and think a moment upon*
W-pII...... 1.2:2 The **m.** is closed, and will not be released.
W-pII.....221.h Peace to my **m.**. Let all my thoughts be
W-pII..221.1:3 *quiet of my heart, the deep recesses of my* **m.**
W-pII..225.1:2 *my* **m.** *and keeping it within its kindly light,*
W-pII..226.1:2 of **m.** about the purpose of the world. If I
W-pII..227.1:5 *of truth, to be removed forever from my* **m.**.
W-pII..227.2:3 with his right **m.** restored to him at last.
W-pII..229.2:1 *all the thoughts of sin my foolish* **m.** *made up*
W-pII...... 2.1:4 well. God's Word is given every **m.** which
W-pII...... 2.2:1 the instant that his **m.** had thought of war
W-pII...... 2.2:3 the **m.** is split there is a need of healing.
W-pII...... 2.2:4 every fragment of the **m.** that still was one
W-pII.....232.h Be in my **m.**, my Father, through the day.
W-pII..232.1:1 *Be in my* **m.**, *my Father, when I wake, and*
W-pII..235.1:2 I need but keep in **m.** my Father's Will for
W-pII.....236.h I rule my **m.**, which I alone must rule.
W-pII..236.1:5 it. My **m.** can only serve. Today I give its
W-pII..236.1:7 I thus direct my **m.**, which I alone can rule
W-pII..236.2:1 *Father, my* **m.** *is open to Your Thoughts,*
W-pII..236.2:2 *I rule my* **m.**, *and offer it to You. Accept my*
W-pII..246.1:3 my **m.** conceive of all the love my Father
W-pII..248.1:5 What is in pain is but illusion in my **m.**.
W-pII...... 4.1:2 the means by which the **m.** is driven mad,
W-pII...... 4.2:1 the **m.** made in its efforts to deceive itself.
W-pII...... 4.2:5 the aim the **m.** has taken as replacement
W-pII..255.2:3 *The peace You gave him still is in his* **m.**, *and*
W-pII..256.1:3 If sin had not been cherished by the **m.**,
W-pII...... 5.2:3 and do the task his **m.** assigns to them.
W-pII...... 5.4:5 Now it serves to heal the **m.** that it was
W-pII..265.1:3 in the world, instead of in my **m.** alone.
W-pII..265.1:9 Yet is my **m.** at one with God's. And so I
W-pII..267.1:4 Now my **m.** is healed, and all I need to
W-pII...... 6.2:2 Your **m.** is part of His, and His of yours.
W-pII...... 6.3:1 peace within the Heaven of your holy **m.**.
W-pII..278.2:2 *and have brought a dream of fear into my* **m.**
W-pII...... 7.3:3 to restore your **m.** to where it truly is at
W-pII...... 7.4:1 and be restored to sanity and peace of **m.**.
W-pII..286.1:8 *My heart is quiet, and my* **m.** *at rest. Your*
W-pII..289.1:1 Unless the past is over in my **m.**, the real
W-pII..290.1:5 I would not allow my **m.** to be deceived by
W-pII...... 8.1:3 brings the witnesses of terror to your **m.**.
W-pII...... 8.2:2 through quiet eyes and with a **m.** at peace.
W-pII...... 8.2:6 can reach the **m.** that has forgiven itself.
W-pII...... 8.3:1 need has such a **m.** for thoughts of death,
W-pII...... 8.3:4 The world it sees arises from a **m.** at peace
W-pII..291.2:1 *day my* **m.** *is quiet, to receive the Thoughts*
W-pII..295.1:2 gift that He may offer peace of **m.** to me,
W-pII..304.1:4 fact. And what I look on is my state of **m.**,
W-pII.... 10.1:3 true, projected from a now corrected **m.**.
W-pII..311.1:6 and re-establish peace of **m.** by giving us
W-pII..311.2:1 *Father, we wait with open* **m.** *today, to hear*
W-pII..315.1:4 my **m.** receives this gift and takes it as its
W-pII..316.1:2 no shadow on the holy **m.** my Father loves
W-pII..320.1:4 because his Father shines upon his **m.**,
W-pII..322.2:5 *of fear, and the return of love into my* **m.***?*
W-pII..325.1:1 What I see reflects a process in my **m.**,
W-pII .325.1:2 the **m.** makes up an image of the thing the
W-pII .325.1:2 up an image of the thing the **m.** desires,
W-pII .330.1:4 **m.** that is made willing to accept God's
W-pII .332.1:5 presence is the **m.** recalled from fantasies,
W-pII .332.1:6 and take its rightful place within the **m.**.
W-pII .332.1:7 Without forgiveness is the **m.** in chains,
W-pII .333.1:3 with the purpose that the **m.** accorded it.
W-pII .334.2:3 *offering to his bewildered* **m.** *and frightened*
W-pII .336.1:5 Its lilies shine into the **m.**, and call it to
W-pII .336.1:6 and only here, is peace of **m.** restored, for
W-pII .336.2:2 *Word remains unchanged within my* **m.**,
W-pII ... 13.1:3 reminds the **m.** that what it sees is false. It
W-pII ... 13.4:1 to ask for it implies the **m.** has been made
W-pII .347.1:2 *Straighten my* **m.**, *my Father. It is sick. But*
WpII361-5.1:3 need but stillness and a tranquil, open **m.**,
W-ep ......... 3:3 exactly what to do, how to direct your **m.**,
M-in .......... 4:4 here does follow it until he changes his **m.**
M-2 ........... 2:6 of separation entered the **m.** of God's Son,
M-3 ........... 3:3 **m.** about the world with a single decision,
M-4 ..... I.A.8:8 if peace of **m.** is already complete? And
M-4 ........II.2:1 peace of **m.** which the advanced teachers
M-4 ....... X.1:3 shuts the **m.** against God's Teacher, so
M-5 ........II.1:4 it is obvious that decisions are of the **m.**,
M-5 ........II.1:6 it is the **m.** and not the body that makes it
M-5 ........II.2:1 of sickness as a decision of the **m.**, for a
M-5 ........II.2:6 Only the **m.** of the patient himself. The
M-5 ........II.3:2 the recognition that sickness is of the **m.**,
M-5 ........II.3:4 will never again appear to rule the **m.**. For
M-5 ...... III.1:1 must change his **m.** in order to be healed,
M-5 ...... III.1:2 Can he change the patient's **m.** for him?
M-6 ........... 1:4 of his errors in the **m.** of the patient,
M-6 ........... 4:3 Healing is the change of **m.** that the Holy
M-6 ........... 4:3 in the patient's **m.** is seeking for him. And
M-6 ........... 4:4 the Holy Spirit in the **m.** of the giver Who
M-7 ........... 1:6 God himself whose **m.** needs to be healed.
M-7 ........... 1:9 must be willing to change his **m.** about it.
M-7 ........... 6:3 about what you are has entered your **m.**,
M-8 ........... 2:4 The **m.** therefore seeks to make it true out
M-8 ........... 2:6 **m.** revolts against truth and gives itself an
M-8 ........... 2:8 And in these dreams the **m.** is separate,
M-8 ........... 3:3 the **m.** that judges what the eyes behold.
M-8 ........... 3:4 **m.** that interprets the eyes' messages and
M-8 ........... 3:6 as "reality" is simply what the **m.** prefers.
M-8 ......... 3:10 Only the **m.** evaluates their messages, and
M-8 ......... 3:10 so only the **m.** is responsible for seeing. It
M-8 ........... 4:1 of the **m.** that errors in perception enter.
M-8 ........... 4:3 **m.** classifies what the body's eyes bring to
M-8 ........... 5:6 His **m.** has categorized them all as real,
M-8 ........... 6:2 But the **m.** that has let itself be healed will
M-8 ........... 6:4 But the healed **m.** will put them all in one
M-8 ........... 6:5 the messages the **m.** receives from what
M-12 ......... 2:2 is not really a change; it is a change of **m.**.
M-12 ......... 2:4 for the **m.** sees no cause for punishment.
M-12 ......... 4:3 And these ears will carry to the **m.** of the
M-12 ......... 4:3 and the **m.** will understand because of
M-12 ......... 5:7 The **m.** makes this decision, as it makes
M-13 ......... 2:9 after such things the **m.** associates itself
M-13 ......... 3:1 it becomes impossible for the **m.** to
M-13 ......... 3:3 Now has the **m.** condemned itself to seek
M-13 ....... 4:10 Who in his sane **m.** chooses nothing as a
M-15 ......... 3:2 to occupy your holy **m.** an instant longer.
M-16 ......... 5:7 It sets your **m.** into a pattern of rest, and
M-16 ......... 7:6 before illusions were accepted into his **m.**,
M-16 ......... 8:2 his **m.** is occupied with external things?
M-16 ..... 11:11 light can shine again on an untroubled **m.**
M-17 ......... 3:6 will enter the teacher's **m.** unfailingly.
M-17 ......... 3:7 From there it shines into his pupil's **m.**,
M-17 ......... 5:4 the **m.** which believes it has a separate will
M-17 ......... 7:3 one says clearly to your frightened **m.**,
M-19 ......... 3:2 to the **m.** that made the lens and holds it
M-19 ......... 5:2 whatever picture the **m.** desires to see.
M-19 ......... 5:9 Perception rests, the **m.** is still, and light
M-20 ......... 2:3 It calls to **m.** nothing that went before. It
M-20 ......... 4:8 A tranquil **m.** is not a little gift. Would
M-21 ......... 2:2 that comes to **m.** is apt to be very concrete
M-21 ......... 2:3 to the **m.** in conjunction with the word,
M-22 ......... 3:3 body autonomy, separates it from the **m.**,
M-22 ......... 3:5 A body that can order a **m.** to do as it sees
M-22 ......... 3:7 The body has become lord of the **m.**. How

M-22 .........3:8 How could the **m.** be returned to the Holy
M-22 .........4:5 He overlooks the **m.** *and* body, seeing only
M-23 .........4:4 the moment that the name is called to **m.**.
M-23 .........4:6 behind a grateful heart and thankful **m.**.
M-25 .........5:7 changes his **m.** about its purpose, he will
M-28 .........1:2 of **m.** about the meaning of the world. It is
M-28 .........6:2 any **m.** remains possessed of evil dreams,
C-1................h **M.** – SPIRIT
C-1............1:1 term ***m.*** is used to represent the activating
C-1............2:1 In this world, because the **m.** is split, the
C-1............2:3 "individual **m.**" seems to be meaningful.
C-1............4:1 other part of the **m.** is entirely illusory
C-1............4:2 be imprisoned while the **m.** is not unified.
C-1............5:1 The **m.** can be right or wrong, depending
C-3............8:4 And now the **m.** returns to its Creator; the
C-4............6:7 expect? But seen within your **m.**, guilt and
C-5............5:9 For he will set your **m.** at rest at last and
C-6............4:1 of your **m.** that is part of the Christ Mind.
P-in...........1:2 is. Since only the **m.** can be sick, only the
P-in...........1:2 can be sick, only the **m.** can be healed.
P-in...........1:3 Only the **m.** is in need of healing. This
P-in...........1:6 start to open his **m.** without formal help,
P-in...........1:8 his **m.** about the "reality" of illusions.
P-1............3:1 peace of **m.** is suffering in consequence.
P-2.........in.2:1 relationship with this goal in **m.**. On the
P-2.........in.2:5 to the sane **m.** it is so clearly impossible,
P-2...........I.1:2 the realization that healing is of the **m.**,
P-2........IV.2:4 nothing that a change of **m.** cannot effect,
P-2........IV.5:1 recognize the **m.** as the source of illness.
P-2......IV.11:2 Relieve the **m.** of the insane burden of
P-2........VI.3:4 be. They answer the decisions of the **m.**,
P-2........VI.3:5 and the **m.** grows fearful and begins to
P-2........VI.7:5 offer the **m.** of both a covenant in which
P-3.........II.7:4 this understanding consistently in his **m.**,
S-1........IV.1:7 in this simple thought; this change of **m.**:
S-1.........V.1:3 grace the **m.** that thought it was alone and
S-2...........I.7:4 and poisoned thinking from your holy **m.**.
S-3.........in.1:3 of a change of **m.** about the goal of prayer.
S-3...........I.3:3 Forgiveness must be given by a **m.** which
S-3.........II.4:2 to bless the **m.** with loving pardon for the
S-3........III.3:4 **m.** that suffers from the agony of doubt.

## mind's 14

T-2......IV.3:13 this unfortunate aspect of the **m.** power,
T-2........VI.4:6 condoning your **m.** miscreations. The
T-4.........II.8:4 is the **m.** belief that it is completely on its
T-4.......V.4:10 the question from the **m.** awareness.
T-5.........in.1:6 the **m.** natural impulse to respond as one.
T-7......VIII.2:5 mind only to defeat the **m.** real purpose.
T-7........IX.4:6 full appreciation of the **m.** Self-fullness
T-8.....VII.12:8 because only extension is the **m.** function.
T-8.....VII.13:5 becomes whole because the **m.** purpose is
T-9.........V.4:5 the **m.** corrective power through the Holy
T-19.........I.7:7 because of the **m.** identification with it.
T-22.......II.9:4 thoughts would not be the **m.** extensions,
W-pI........8.1:4 The **m.** preoccupation with the past is the
W-pI.....45.9:2 the day, to appreciate your **m.** holiness.

## mind-searching 5

W-pI.......8.5:2 at the end of the **m.** period with: *But my*
W-pI.....14.2:2 The **m.** period should be short, a minute
W-pI.....21.1:2 specific **m.** periods are necessary, in
W-pI.....24.3:3 the **m.** periods which the exercises involve
W-pI.....35.5:1 In the earlier part of the **m.** period, you

## mindful 2

T-4........III.6:3 **m.** of His Love for you and yours for Him.
W-pI...167.6:5 lacks, nor change its own eternal, **m.** state

## mindless 7

T-1.........I.14:3 which is **m.** and therefore destructive; or
T-2.........V.2:1 is the **m.** or the miscreative use of mind.
T-8........IX.6:3 dangerous, and that to make **m.** is to heal.
T-8........IX.6:4 But to make **m.** is impossible, since it
T-19.......II.6:5 **m.** and capable of complete corruption
W-pI...170.8:4 it and lay before this **m.** piece of stone?
M-27.........6:9 and yet to think love real are **m.** magic,

## minds 206

T-1........I.19:1 Miracles make **m.** one in God. They
T-1.......III.3:4 Miracles are the way in which **m.** that
T-1.......IV.4:5 changed their **m.** who brought the "hell-
T-2.......III.1:4 many body fantasies in which **m.** engage
T-2........V.5:5 that their **m.** are similarly constructive,
T-2...V.A.16:4 do. It is an appeal to God to heal their **m.**.
T-2.....VIII.2:8 if you are to bring peace to other **m.**.
T-3..........I.6:3 can only honor other **m.**, because honor
T-3.....IV.7:15 Right **m.** can do this now, and they will
T-3........V.9:2 because **m.** have chosen to see themselves
T-4.......III.8:4 to help me make other **m.** ready for Him.
T-4......VII.6:7 and He is lonely when the **m.** He created
T-4......VII.7:5 be returned by that mind to other **m.**,
T-5..........I.1:1 which two **m.** perceive their oneness and
T-5.........II.2:2 God blessed the **m.** of His separated Sons.
T-5.........II.6:9 in their **m.** was not the Voice for His Will,
T-6.......II.11:9 outward only to what is true in other **m.**.
T-6.......II.13:5 joining our **m.** in this light we proclaim
T-6.....V.B.3:8 perceive consistency in the **m.** of others,
T-7.......III.3:4 idea of competition has entered their **m.**.
T-7.......III.5:7 nothing questionable enters their **m.**.
T-7........V.2:1 Only **m.** communicate. Since the ego
T-7........V.3:4 **M.** can communicate, but they cannot
T-7......V.10:5 you can change their **m.** about themselves
T-7......V.11:3 your mind shine with mine upon their **m.**
T-7......VII.7:2 One Teacher is in all **m.** and He teaches
T-7.....VIII.2:6 conflict from your mind to other **m.**, in an
T-7...VIII.3:11 their projections from their own **m.**, they
T-7...VIII.3:12 the projections have not left their **m.**, they
T-7.....VIII.4:9 by distorted **m.** that are misusing their
T-7.......XI.5:2 extends out into the darkness of other **m.**,
T-8........V.1:6 but together our **m.** fuse into something
T-8........V.6:2 Holy Spirit has one direction for all **m.**,
T-8......VII.2:5 **m.** and uniting them with yours and mine
T-8......VII.3:2 use it only to reach the **m.** of those who
T-8....VII.12:7 only if the mind extends to other **m.**, and
T-8.......IX.7:4 Our **m.** are whole because they are one. If
T-9..........I.3:2 is particularly inappropriate in the **m.** of
T-9......V.8:12 other **m.** to the Holy Spirit through Him,
T-10.....III.2:5 Your **m.** are not separate, and God has
T-10.....III.4:3 taught by sick **m.** too divided to know
T-11 .VIII.14:4 the **m.** of children who do not understand
T-13.......in.2:7 **m.** seem to be trapped in their brain, and
T-14.......II.2:3 Simplicity is very difficult for twisted **m.**.
T-14.....IV.9:2 guiltlessness to **m.** that have denied it,
T-14......V.8:6 attract all tortured **m.** to join with you in
T-15.....IV.6:7 give. It is the recognition that all **m.** are in
T-15.....VI.7:2 of peace, for in ideas **m.** can communicate
T-15..VII.11:5 think their **m.** must be kept private or
T-15..VII.11:5 bodies are together their **m.** remain their
T-15..VII.11:6 way in which they would keep **m.** apart.
T-15.....IX.4:7 Yet your **m.** are already continuous, and
T-15.....XI.7:1 met, for **m.** are joined without the body's
T-16.......II.4:3 two **m.** join as one and share one idea
T-16..VII.12:6 *and accept but this into the* ***m.*** *which You*
T-17...IV.16:2 by giving Him ascendance in our **m.**. We
T-17....VII.3:4 must have entered, for **m.** cannot attack.
T-18.....III.7:7 for no two **m.** can join in the desire for
T-18.....VI.3:1 **M.** are joined; bodies are not. Only by
T-18.....VI.7:3 guilt stands between you and other **m.**.
T-18.....VI.7:4 The **m.** *are* joined, but you do not identify
T-19.......II.1:4 based on the firm conviction that **m.**, not
T19....IV.C.3:2 opposition lie but in the sick **m.** of the
T-20.......II.2:6 offering and receiving what their **m.** judge
T-20...IV.2:10 in **m.** that have established other laws,
T-20......V.5:3 **m.** need not the body to communicate.
T-21......V.3:6 how separate **m.** can influence each other.
T-21......V.3:8 But **m.** cannot be separate. This other self
T-21...VI.2:10 yours? If **m.** are joined, this is impossible.
T-22.....IV.6:5 from their **m.** are this world's saviors,
T-22...VI.14:6 From loving **m.** there *is* no separation.
T-23.......I.12:8 of God obscured in **m.** that have become
T-24.....IV.2:7 And **m.** can change as they desire. What
T-24.....IV.3:3 **m.** intent on specialness it is impossible.
T-25......in.3:6 in gentleness and love, to heal their **m.**.
T-25.....IV.1:1 **M.** that are joined and recognize they are
T-28......I.11:2 then, to other **m.** to share its quietness.
T-28......I.11:3 into the Mind which caused all **m.** to be.
T-28......I.11:4 delay in hastening to all unquiet **m.**, and
T-28.......II.3:6 of other bodies, each with separate **m.**,
T-28.....III.2:4 your **m.** from separate points of view.
T-28.....III.2:6 Healing is the effect of **m.** that join, as
T-28.....III.2:6 as sickness comes from **m.** that separate.
T-28.....III.3:1 nothing just *because* the **m.** are joined, and
T-28.....III.3:2 and separate **m.** are seen as bodies, which
T-28.....III.5:5 grounds for sickness when the **m.** have
T-28.....IV.4:1 And yet, between your **m.** there is no gap
T-28.....IV.7:1 The Holy Spirit is in both your **m.**, and
T-29.......I.4:2 seems to be dividing off your separate **m.**.
T-29.......V.6:2 in **m.** that can direct the hand to bless,
T-29.....IX.4:7 is in the **m.** of those who play with them.
T-31......I.12:4 be loosened from our **m.** and swept away.
T-31.....III.3:2 They are not perceived in **m.**. They are
T-31.....III.3:4 Bodies act, and **m.** do not. And therefore
W-pI....18.1:2 emphasizes the idea that **m.** are joined,
W-pI....19.2:1 emphasizing the fact that **m.** are joined.
W-pI....30.2:3 to see in the world what is in our **m.**, and
W-pI....72.2:3 unable to reach other **m.** except through
W-pI....79.7:3 We will try to free our **m.** of all the many
W-pI..95.12:2 bring awareness of this oneness to all **m.**,
W-pI..100.1:3 separate **m.** unites them in one purpose,
W-pI..100.4:2 earth calls to all **m.** to let their sorrows go,
W-pI..103.2:1 its results become the heritage of **m.** that
W-pI..104.4:2 holy place within our **m.** before His altar,
W-pI..106.9:2 thousand **m.** are opened to the truth and
W-pI..108.3:2 brings your peace of mind to other **m.**, to
W-pI..108.5:2 is enough to bring salvation to all **m.**. For
W-pI..109.7:2 is comes closer to all worn and tired **m.**,
W-pI..110.4:2 no split between your mind and other **m.**,
W-pI 110.10:4 hands and hearts and **m.** to God today.
W-pI..124.2:1 How holy are our **m.**! And everything we
W-pI..124.4:5 Our **m.** contain His Thoughts; our eyes
W-pI..128.5:3 We hold it purposeless within our **m.**,
W-pI..130.7:2 devote our **m.** to finding only what is real.
W-pI..131.7:4 He did not make two **m.**, with Heaven as
W-pI 133.13:1 is reached with empty hands and open **m.**
W-pI..135.9:4 apart from other **m.** and separate from its
W-pI 135.21:3 truth to dawn upon our **m.** with certainty.
W-pI 135.22:1 blocks the truth from entering our **m.**.
W-pI..137.8:6 and **m.** that were walled off within a body
W-pI..137.8:6 within a body free to join with other **m.**,
W-pI 137.12:6 we ask that only truth will occupy our **m.**;
W-pI 137.13:1 our function is to let our **m.** be healed,
W-pI..139.8:5 Let us not allow our holy **m.** to occupy
W-pI 139.11:1 our **m.** to our assignment for today. We
W-pI 139.11:5 everyone, for in creation are all **m.** as one.
W-pI..140.8:1 our **m.** about the source of sickness, for
W-pI..140.8:2 **m.** because our Father placed it there for
W-pI 140.12:1 lifted hearts and listening **m.** we pray:
W-pI 140.12:4 deep that no illusion can disturb our **m.**,
WpI..rIV.in4:4 **m.** to understand the lessons that we read
W-pI 151.16:4 guilt. Now do we lift our resurrected **m.** in
W-pI 152.11:2 encouraging our frightened **m.** with this:
W-pI..153.8:3 dream happened to cross our **m.**, and we
W-pI 153.13:3 the pure and holy **m.** of Heaven's children
W-pI 154.10:2 our **m.** apart from Him Who speaks for us
W-pI 154.14:1 The world recedes as we light up our **m.**,
W-pI 154.14:3 they have changed our **m.** about ourselves
W-pI..155.6:3 their eyes to look on and their **m.** to grasp
W-pI..156.8:6 *all the* ***m.*** *which God created one with me.*
W-pI..161.4:2 Every mind contains all **m.**, for every
W-pI..161.6:1 Bodies attack, but **m.** do not. This
W-pI..165.8:5 is still beyond all dreams and in our **m.**,
W-pI 167.12:1 remaining always in the holy **m.** which He
W-pI..169.2:2 that those whose **m.** are lighted by the gift
W-pI..169.8:2 it to all **m.** that each one might determine
WpI...rV.in2:2 *our doubts be quiet and our holy* ***m.*** *be still,*
WpI.rV.in11:4 the thoughts to hold it up before our **m.**,
W-pI..181.3:2 We instruct our **m.** that it is this we seek,
W-pI..181.6:3 to our **m.** to change their focus, as we say:
W-pI..181.9:3 as we turn our **m.** to practicing today. We
W-pI..183.6:6 word, the only thing that occupies our **m.**
W-pI 184.12:6 our purpose is to let our **m.** accept what

W-pI...185.3:1 Two **m.** with one intent become so
W-pI...185.3:2 For **m.** can only join in truth. In dreams,
W-pI...185.4:4 **M.** cannot unite in dreams. They merely
W-pI...185.4:8 lost to sleeping **m.** intent on compromise,
W-pI...185.6:1 it wants is peace must join with other **m.**,
W-pI...186.2:7 **m.** are suited perfectly to take the part
W-pI...188.9:4 within our **m.** direct them to come home.
W-pI.188.10:1 Thus are our **m.** restored with them, and
W-pI...189.9:4 And in our quiet hearts and open **m.**, His
W-pI...192.7:4 our **m.** engaged in worshipping what is
W-pI...193.6:2 power to release all **m.** from bondage?
W-pI...199.6:1 Holy Spirit is the home of **m.** that seek for
W-pII.....in.3:1 our times of rest, and calm our **m.** at need
W-pII.....in.4:1 but His Word upon our **m.** and hearts,
W-pII.....in.8:4 Thoughts have lit the darkness of our **m.**.
W-pII.....in.9:5 across the wide horizons of our **m.**. A
W-pII..221.2:5 Our **m.** are joined. We wait with one
W-pII..222.2:1 *Your Name upon our lips and in our* ***m.****, as*
W-pII..242.2:2 *We come with wholly open* ***m.****. We do not*
W-pII..249.2:1 *Father, we would return our* ***m.*** *to You. We*
W-pII..256.1:9 by which our **m.** return to Him at last.
W-pII..258.1:1 our **m.** to overlook all little senseless aims
W-pII..258.1:2 is God. His memory is hidden in our **m.**,
W-pII..273.1:4 We need but tell our **m.**, with certainty,
W-pII......9.3:2 all **m.** are given to the hands of Christ, to
W-pII..306.2:2 *with empty hands and open hearts and* ***m.****,*
W-pII....11.4:5 God's memory is in our holy **m.**, which
W-pII..330.1:2 Why should we attack our **m.**, and give
W-pII....12.5:2 the holy **m.** which God created as His Son
W-pII.......336.h Forgiveness lets me know that **m.** are
W-pII..349.2:3 and heal our **m.** as we return to Him.
W-pII....14.4:3 Ours the **m.** that join together as we bless
W-pII....14.5:2 And thus our **m.** are changed about the
Wfl ........in.3:1 And to this purpose let us dedicate our **m.**
M-2............5:6 have drawn between their roles, their **m.**,
M-5.......III.1:4 already willing to change their **m.** he has
M-5.......III.2:7 in their **m.** they come in benediction, not
M-5.......III.3:6 The truth in their **m.** reaches out to the
M-5.......III.3:6 out to the truth in the **m.** of their brothers
M-8............2:8 mind is separate, different from other **m.**,
M-9............1:1 are required in the ***m.*** of God's teachers.
M-12...........1:8 bring His Thoughts to still deluded **m.**.
M-12...........2:8 forms? Their **m.** are one; their joining is
M-18...........2:6 is He free to teach all **m.** the truth of what
M-21...........1:7 made by separated **m.** to keep them in the
M-25...........6:7 they laid upon their **m.** be lifted. It can be
M-28...........6:3 goal of wakening the **m.** of those asleep,
C-1.............2:2 Nor do their **m.** seem to be joined. In this
P-2..........in.4:5 They are finally given up in the **m.** of both
P-2.........IV.4:3 but make the body real in their own **m.**,
P-2.........IV.4:3 heal the ills with which their **m.** endow it.
P-2.......VII.2:3 What is prayer except the joining of **m.** in
P-3.........II.8:1 therapist has realized that **m.** are joined,

### Mine 3

• God
*mine*

T-3...........I.3:1 The statement "Vengeance is **m.**, sayeth
T-5........VI.7:1 "Vengeance is **m.**, sayeth the Lord" is
S-3........IV.8:2 extends along with **M.** beyond infinity,

### mine 31

• Jesus
*noise word*
*Mine*

T-1........I.40:1 everyone as your brother and **m.**. It is a
T-2.........V.4:2 but maintain a consistent trust in **m.**. If
T-2........VI.4:9 ask me if your choice is in accord with **m.**.
T-4........I.13:8 beyond the need of your protection or **m.**.
T-4.......IV.8:3 and **m.** can unite in shining your ego away
T-4......IV.11:5 Your mind will elect to join with **m.**, and
T-5...........I.3:3 is in your right mind, as He was in **m.**.
T-6...........I.9:1 I elected, for your sake and **m.**, to
T-6........I.10:2 Spirit is glad when you can learn from **m.**,
T-7.......V.11:3 mind shine with **m.** upon their minds,
T-8........IV.5:9 yours, because yours is as powerful as **m.**.
T-8......IV.5:11 decision, but **m.** alone cannot help you.
T-8......IV.5:12 you. Your will is as free as **m.**, and God
T-8.......IV.7:1 were not **m.** it would not be our Father's.
T-8.........V.1:5 as I am offering you **m.** on behalf of yours.
T-8.........V.2:3 belief that your will is separate from **m.**,
T-8.........V.2:9 is no separation between your will and **m.**
T-8.......V.2:12 His. By joining your mind with **m.** you are
T-8.........V.6:1 The ego's way is not **m.**, but it is also not
T-8.......VII.2:5 and uniting them with yours and **m.**. This
T-11....VI.10:2 a part in the redemption as valuable as **m.**
T-11....VI.10:3 part must be like **m.** if you learn it of me.
T-11....VI.10:4 that yours is limited, you are limiting **m.**.
T-12.......II.8:4 your mission because I did not fail in **m.**.
T-13...VII.17:2 until I have lifted every voice with **m.**.
T-13...VII.17:3 And yet it is not **m.**, for as it is my gift to
T-18.......II.7:9 Or **m.** through His! For we are joined as in
T-18.......III.4:1 hold your brother's hand also hold **m.**, for
T19. IV.A.17:7 **M.** was of no greater value than yours; no
T-20.......I.2:10 forgiveness rests on Christ, along with **m.**.
T-20.........I.4:8 the time of your salvation, along with **m.**.

### mine 64

• noise word
*Jesus*
*God*

### miniature 3

T-17......IV.7:4 and the gift is always a **m.** of the thought
T-17....IV.11:1 The holy instant is a **m.** of Heaven, sent
T-17....IV.11:4 The holy instant is a **m.** of eternity. It is a

### minimal 1

W-pI.....20.1:2 them, **m.** effort has been required, and

### minimize 1

T-11.....V.10:4 this is the cost, and the ego cannot **m.** it.

### minimizes 1

T-1.........II.6:1 The miracle **m.** the need for time. In the

### minimizing 3

T-11.......V.9:2 **M.** fear, but not its undoing, is the ego's
T-12.......II.9:5 fear–not by hiding it, not by **m.** it, and
M-10.........1:3 the former and **m.** the latter. There is,

### minimum 1

W-pI.....39.5:2 you want to exceed the **m.** requirements,

### ministering 1

M-5.......II.2:8 Special agents seem to be **m.** to him, yet

### ministers 8

W-pI.153.10:2 God's **m.** have chosen that the truth be
W-pI.153.11:1 It is the function of God's **m.** to help their
W-pI.153.14:5 God's **m.** have come to waken him from
W-pI.153.17:1 we will observe our trust as **m.** of God, in
W-pI.153.20:4 The **m.** of God can never fail, because the
W-pI......154.h I am among the **m.** of God.
W-pI.154.13:2 *I am among the* ***m.*** *of God, and I am grateful*
W-pI...172.2:1 (154) I am among the **m.** of God. God is

### ministry 5

W-pI...106.8:3 It will begin the **m.** for which you came,
W-pI.151.15:2 Your **m.** begins as all your thoughts are
W-pI.151.17:3 Now has our **m.** begun at last, to carry
W-pI...153.9:3 **m.** extends its holy blessing through the
W-pI...157.5:1 your **m.** takes on a genuine devotion, and

### minor 3

T-2........III.4:7 have regarded as very **m.** intrusions of
T-3...........I.2:3 procedure is painful in its **m.** applications
W-pI.....68.5:3 think of the seemingly **m.** grievances you

### minute 58

*See also* fifteen-minute, five-minute, ten-to-fifteen-minute, three-to-five-minute, two-minute

T-5.........V.6:3 answering it every **m.** and every second,
T-5.........V.8:6 at any **m.** if it accepts the Atonement first.
T-9.......VII.1:6 Every **m.** and every second gives you a
T-12....VIII.1:3 every day and every hour and every **m.**,
T-13........X.5:3 A **m.**, even less, will be enough to free you
T-14.....III.4:1 Each day, each hour and **m.**, even each
T-26.....V.13:1 Each day, and every **m.** in each day, and
T-26.....V.13:1 day, and every instant that each **m.** holds,
T-30.....VII.1:7 script you write for every **m.** in the day,
W-pI.......1.4:2 be attempted for more than a **m.** or so,
W-pI.......4.1:2 are crossing your mind for about a **m.**.
W-pI.......4.5:3 your mind for more than a **m.** or so. You
W-pI.......5.7:1 your mind for no more than a **m.** or so,
W-pI.......6.2:2 preceded by a **m.** or so of mind searching,
W-pI.......7.5:3 practice periods, each to last a **m.** or so,
W-pI.......8.4:3 search your mind for the usual **m.** or so,
W-pI.....10.5:2 more than a **m.** or so of mind searching.
W-pI.....10.5:3 a **m.** or less if you experience discomfort.
W-pI.....11.2:4 During the **m.** or so to be spent in using
W-pI.....12.6:2 should the practice periods exceed a **m.**.
W-pI.....13.4:1 more than a **m.** or so at most each time,
W-pI.....14.2:2 period should be short, a **m.** at most. Do
W-pI.....15.5:1 **m.** or so of practice that is recommended,
W-pI.....15.5:2 than a **m.** will do for the practice periods,
W-pI.....16.4:1 your mind for a **m.** or so with eyes closed,
W-pI.....17.4:2 **m.** or so that is otherwise recommended.
W-pI.....18.3:5 A **m.** or so, or even less, will be sufficient
W-pI.....19.3:1 **m.** or so of mind searching which today's
W-pI.....21.1:3 are urged, allowing a full **m.** for each.
W-pI.....22.3:1 times today, for at least a **m.** each time.
W-pI.....23.6:2 close your eyes and devote about a **m.** to
W-pI.....26.5:2 to a **m.** if the discomfort is too great. Do
W-pI.....33.4:2 It may be necessary to take a **m.** or so to
W-pI.....37.4:1 followed by a **m.** or so of looking about
W-pI.....45.9:2 Take a **m.** or two, as you repeat the idea
W-pI.....46.3:3 spend a **m.** or two in searching your mind
W-pI.....47.4:4 Then spend a **m.** or two in searching for
W-pI.....48.2:4 take a **m.** or so whenever possible to close
W-pI.....61.5:1 each one need not exceed a **m.** or two.
W-pI.....62.5:4 Then devote a **m.** or two to considering
W-pI.....63.4:1 in the **m.** or two that you should devote to
W-pI.....65.6:2 however, to continue a **m.** or so longer,
W-pI...66.11:3 *both.* It will not take more than a **m.**, and
W-pI...71.10:6 be no better way to spend a half **m.** or less
W-pI...72.13:6 Then wait a **m.** or so in silence, preferably
W-pI.....74.7:5 A **m.** or two every half an hour, with eyes
W-pI...93.10:6 try to devote at least a **m.** or so to closing
W-pI.....97.4:1 miracle in which a **m.** spent in using these
W-pI...107.2:3 when there was a time,–perhaps a **m.**,
W-pI.122.14:1 a **m.** as each quarter of an hour passes by.
W-pI...124.9:4 with every **m.** like a diamond set around
W-pI.137.13:2 Is not a **m.** of the hour worth the giving to
W-pI.140.12:6 hourly, and take a **m.** as the hour strikes,
W-pI.153.16:2 At times, perhaps, a **m.**, even less, will be
W-pI.193.10:3 day, another **m.** or another instant. Time
W-pII .232.1:2 *every* ***m.*** *be a time in which I dwell with You.*
M-16.........4:7 continuing a **m.** or two after you begin to
M-16.......11:9 every hour, and even every **m.** and second

### minutes 82

*See also* five-minutes-an-hour, two-minutes

W-pI.....24.3:3 Two **m.** are suggested for each of the
W-pI.....26.5:2 two **m.** should be attempted for each of
W-pI.....27.3:3 might try for every fifteen or twenty **m.**. It
W-pI.....31.2:2 Three to five **m.** for each of these are
W-pI.....32.4:1 periods three to five **m.** are recommended
W-pI.....33.1:2 A full five **m.** should be devoted to the
W-pI.....34.3:1 Some five **m.** of mind searching are

W-pI.....34.6:2 try to take several **m.** and devote them to
W-pI.....37.4:1 each to involve three to five **m.** of practice
W-pI.....38.4:1 each preferably to last a full five **m.**,
W-pI.....39.5:1 full five **m.** are urged for the four longer
W-pI.....40.1:3 every ten **m.** would be highly desirable,
W-pI.....41.6:2 sit quietly for some three to five **m.**, with
W-pI.....44.4:1 today, each lasting three to five **m.**. A
W-pI.....50.5:1 For ten **m.**, twice today, morning and
WpI...rI.in.2:3 two **m.** or more to each practice period,
W-pI.....64.6:5 least once devote ten or fifteen **m.** today
W-pI.....64.7:1 day, devote several **m.** to reviewing these
W-pI.....65.3:1 set aside ten to fifteen **m.** for a more
W-pI.....67.2:2 a few **m.** adding some relevant thoughts,
W-pI.....69.2:2 let us devote several **m.** to thinking about
W-pI.....70.6:1 which should last some ten to fifteen **m.**.
W-pI.....70.7:5 *else.* Then devote a few **m.**, with your eyes
W-pI.....74.3:4 spend several **m.** in adding some related
WpI..rII.in.2:1 Take about fifteen **m.** for each of them,
WpI..rII.in.2:2 or four **m.** to reading them over slowly,
W-pI.....91.5:1 set aside about ten **m.** for a quiet time in
W-pI.....91.8:2 and then devote several **m.** to allowing
W-pI...92.10:1 us give twenty **m.** twice today to join this
W-pI.....93.8:1 for the first five **m.** of every waking hour,
W-pI...93.10:1 five **m.** of each hour for these exercises.
W-pI.....94.3:1 will again devote the first five **m.** of each
W-pI.....94.5:1 for the first five **m.** of every hour, at least
W-pI.....95.4:1 use of the first five **m.** of every waking
W-pI.....95.7:2 Using the first five **m.** of the hour will be
W-pI...96.11:5 Every time you spend five **m.** of the hour
W-pI.....97.3:3 The **m.** which you give are multiplied
W-pI.....97.4:2 Give, then, these **m.** willingly, and count
W-pI.....97.4:4 Give Him the **m.** which He needs today,
W-pI.....97.5:1 take five **m.** of each hour from your hands
W-pI.....98.5:1 Is it not worth five **m.** of your time each
W-pI.....98.5:2 Is it not worth five **m.** hourly to recognize
W-pI.....98.5:3 Is not five **m.** but a small request to make
W-pI.....98.7:1 give Him your tiny gift of but five **m.**. He
W-pI.....98.8:1 In each five **m.** that you spend with Him,
W-pI...98.10:1 five **m.** you will spend again with Him.
W-pI...99.12:2 this between the times you give five **m.** to
W-pI...101.7:1 Give these five **m.** gladly, to remove the
W-pI...104.3:2 five **m.** given truth for your salvation,
W-pI...105.9:1 Spend your five **m.** thus with Him each
W-pI...106.9:2 For each five **m.** spent in listening, a
W-pI.107.10:3 with every gift you give of five small **m.**,
W-pI...108.8:4 and for five **m.** think of what you would
W-pI...109.7:1 With each five **m.** that you rest today, the
WpI. rIII.in5:1 reviews is this: Devote five **m.** twice a day,
WpI. rIII.in8:1 the first five **m.** of the day to your reviews,
WpI. rIII.in8:1 last five **m.** of your waking day to them. If
W-pI...121.8:3 We will devote ten **m.** in the morning,
W-pI...123.7:1 yours to Him for fifteen **m.** twice today.
W-pI...125.7:1 give ten **m.** set apart from listening to the
W-pI...126.9:1 Give fifteen **m.** twice today to the
W-pI...127.8:1 fifteen **m.** twice today escape from every
W-pI...128.7:1 Give it ten **m.** rest three times today. And
W-pI...129.7:1 ten **m.** in the morning and at night, and
W-pI...130.7:1 we gladly give five **m.** to the thought that
W-pI...130.8:3 And you come to these five **m.** emptying
W-pI.131.10:3 ten **m.** to this goal three times today, and
W-pI.131.11:5 For several **m.** watch your mind and see,
W-pI.133.13:3 periods of fifteen **m.** each begin with this:
W-pI.135.22:1 For fifteen **m.** twice today we rest from
W-pI.137.14:2 give ten **m.** to these thoughts with which
W-pI.138.11:1 and spend five **m.** making sure that we
W-pI.138.12:2 now we give the last five **m.** of our waking
W-pI.139.11:1 Five **m.** in the morning and at night we
W-pI.139.12:2 For several **m.** let your mind be cleared of
W-pI.140.11:1 Him speak to us five **m.** as the day begins,
W-pI.140.11:1 again five **m.** more before we go to sleep.
WpI. rIV.in5:4 Five **m.** with this thought will be enough
W-pI.151.15:1 Spend fifteen **m.** thus when you awake,
W-pI.152.11:2 and spend five **m.** practicing its ways,
W-pI.153.15:3 Five **m.** now becomes the least we give to
WpI rVI.in.1:2 which should not be less than fifteen **m.**,

**miracle** 310

*See also* magic-miracle, miracle-based, miracle-minded, miracle-mindedness, miracle-readiness; Appendix C

T-1 ..........I.3:2 The real **m.** is the love that inspires them.
T-1 ..........I.3:3 everything that comes from love is a **m.**.
T-1 ........I.18:1 A **m.** is a service. It is the maximal service
T-1 ........I.20:2 that leads to the healing power of the **m.**.
T-1 ........I.24:2 *You* are a **m.**, capable of creating in the
T-1 ........I.27:1 A **m.** is a universal blessing from God
T-1 ........I.31:3 are holy and the **m.** honors their holiness,
T-1 ........I.37:1 A **m.** is a correction introduced into false
T-1 ........I.39:1 **m.** dissolves error because the Holy Spirit
T-1 ........I.40:1 The **m.** acknowledges everyone as your
T-1 ........I.44:1 **m.** is an expression of an inner awareness
T-1 ........I.45:1 A **m.** is never lost. It may touch many
T-1 ........I.47:1 The **m.** is a learning device that lessens
T-1 ........I.48:1 **m.** is the only device at your immediate
T-1 ........I.49:1 **m.** makes no distinction among degrees
T-1 ........I.50:1 The **m.** compares what you have made
T-1 .........II.3:4 The **m.** is therefore a sign of love among
T-1 .........II.6:1 The **m.** minimizes the need for time. In
T-1 .........II.6:3 **m.** entails a sudden shift from horizontal
T-1 .........II.6:5 The **m.** thus has the unique property of
T-1 .........II.6:6 the time a **m.** takes and the time it covers.
T-1 .........II.6:7 **m.** substitutes for learning that might
T-1 .........II.6:8 giver and receiver on which the **m.** rests.
T-1 .........II.6:9 The **m.** shortens time by collapsing it,
T-1 ....... III.1:2 you offer a **m.** to any of my brothers, you
T-1 ....... III.4:5 nature of the **m.** is an essential ingredient,
T-1 ..... III.5:11 The **m.** worker can only bless them, and
T-1 ....... III.7:2 the awareness of the **m.** worker himself.
T-1 ....... III.7:4 the **m.** places the mind in a state of grace.
T-1 ....... III.8:1 **m.** may have effects on your brothers that
T-1 ....... III.8:2 The **m.** will always bless *you.* Miracles you
T-1 ....... III.8:4 but the action aspect of the **m.** should be
T-1 ....... III.9:3 account of the magnitude of the **m.** itself,
T-1 ....... III.9:4 unreal. Since the **m.** aims at restoring the
T-1 ....... IV.2:3 The **m.** sets reality where it belongs.
T-1 ....... IV.2:4 and the **m.** acknowledges only truth. It
T-1 ....... IV.2:6 The **m.** joins in the Atonement by placing
T-1 ........ V.1:1 The **m.** is much like the body in that both
T-1 ........ V.1:2 the body nor the **m.** serves any purpose.
T-1 ........ V.2:3 The **m.** worker, therefore, accepts the
T-1 ........ V.4:2 **m.** calls him to return because it blesses
T-1 ........ V.6:1 The **m.** is a sign that the mind has chosen
T-1 ....... VI.5:3 the true, the **m.** proceeds along these lines
T-1 .........VII.h Distortions of **M.** Impulses
T-1 ......VII.1:1 produce a dense cover over **m.** impulses,
T-1 ......VII.1:2 confusion of **m.** impulses with physical
T-1 ......VII.1:3 impulses are misdirected **m.** impulses. All
T-1 ....VII.3:10 then sustain the belief of the **m.** receiver.
T-2 ..........I.5:1 may believe are of no concern to the **m.**,
T-2 .........II.6:6 saves time, but like the **m.** it serves, does
T-2 .........II.7:8 The **m.** turns the defense of Atonement to
T-2 ....... IV.1:2 The **m.** is the means, the Atonement is
T-2 ....... IV.1:3 speak of "a **m.** of healing" is to combine
T-2 ....... IV.1:4 Healing is not a **m.**. The Atonement, or
T-2 ....... IV.1:5 Atonement, or the final **m.**, is a remedy
T-2 ....... IV.3:7 This is not because the body is a **m.**, but
T-2 ....... IV.4:9 If they are prematurely exposed to a **m.**,
T-2 ....... IV.5:3 This means that a **m.**, to attain its full
T-2 ....... IV.5:6 whole aim of the **m.** is to raise the level of
T-2 ........... V.h The Function of the **M.** Worker
T-2 ........ V.1:1 Before **m.** workers are ready to undertake
T-2 ........ V.3:2 of the **m.** worker or the miracle receiver.
T-2 ........ V.3:2 of the miracle worker or the **m.** receiver.
T-2 ........ V.3:3 **m.** need not await the right-mindedness
T-2 ........ V.3:5 that the **m.** worker be in his right mind,
T-2 ........ V.4:3 If your **m.** working inclinations are not
T-2 ........ V.5:1 *The sole responsibility of the* **m.** *worker is to*
T-2 ...... V.10:6 The **m.**, as an expression of charity, can
T-2 ...... V.10:7 that whenever you offer a **m.** to another,
T-2 ........V.A.h Special Principles of **M.** Workers
T-2 ...V.A.11:1 The **m.** abolishes the need for lower-order
T-2 ...V.A.11:3 When you perform a **m.**, I will arrange
T-2 ...V.A.14:1 (4) The **m.** is always a denial of this error
T-2 ...V.A.15:1 level-adjustment power of the **m.** induces
T-2 ...V.A.17:2 appeal for cooperation from **m.** workers.

T-2 ....... VI.8:1 I have emphasized that the **m.**, or the
T-2 ...... VII.1:8 it would take a **m.** to enable you to do this
T-2 .... VII.1:10 All **m.** workers need that kind of training.
T-2 ...... VII.2:2 **M.** working entails a full realization of the
T-2 ...... VII.2:3 Otherwise a **m.** will be necessary to set
T-2 ...... VII.2:3 collapse for which the **m.** was intended.
T-2 ...... VII.2:4 The **m.** worker must have genuine respect
T-2 ...... VII.2:4 a necessary condition for the **m.** to occur.
T-2 ...... VII.3:3 By choosing the **m.** you *have* rejected fear,
T-3 .........II.3:3 effect of denying the power of the **m.**. The
T-3 .........II.3:4 The **m.** perceives everything as it is. If
T-3 .........II.6:7 This is the healing that the **m.** induces.
T-3 ....... III.2:4 The **m.**, being a way of perceiving, is not
T-3 ....... III.2:7 The **m.**, or the right answer, corrects
T-3 ....... III.4:3 brings it into the proper domain of the **m.**
T-3 ....... III.4:4 A "vision of God" would be a **m.** rather
T-3 ....... IV.4:4 a **m.** in view of how you perceive yourself.
T-3 .........V.6:7 knowledge that you yourself are a **m.** of
T-3 .........V.8:9 To know God's **m.** is to know Him.
T-3 .......V.10:5 God and His **m.** are inseparable. How
T-3 .......V.10:9 where the **m.** that is you is perfectly clear.
T-4 ...... VII.8:7 it. The truly helpful are God's **m.** workers,
T-5 .........II.1:3 perception of time that the **m.** introduces.
T-5 .........II.1:7 The **m.** itself is a reflection of this union
T-5 ....... III.2:8 in himself or in you for this **m.** to occur.
T-5 .........V.7:8 If the sole responsibility of the **m.** worker
T-6 ......V.A.2:7 the body. Every **m.** demonstrates this.
T-7 ....... IX.4:4 needs the **m.** of its wholeness to dawn
T-7 ....... IX.7:4 The **m.** is a lesson in total perception. By
T-7 .........X.8:4 The **m.** is therefore a lesson in what joy is.
T-7 .........X.8:6 Every **m.** is thus a lesson in truth, and by
T-9 .........V.7:8 The **m.** worker begins by perceiving light,
T-9 ....... VI.6:3 You cannot perform a **m.** for yourself,
T-9 .....VIII.3:1 it sees no difference between **m.** impulses
T-10 ..... IV.7:1 The **m.** is the act of a Son of God who has
T-10 ..... IV.7:4 the **m.** worker has heard God's Voice, he
T-11 .......II.2:4 Every **m.** that you accomplish speaks to
T-12 .......II.1:5 The task of the **m.** worker thus becomes
T-13 ..... VI.4:8 past and future, and not allowing the **m.**,
T-13 ..... VI.5:1 The **m.** enables you to see your brother
T-13 ...VIII.3:6 The **m.**, without a function in Heaven, is
T-13 ...VIII.5:1 This is the **m.** of creation; *that it is one*
T-13 ...VIII.5:2 Every **m.** you offer to the Son of God is
T-13 ...VIII.6:3 There is one **m.**, as there is one reality.
T-13 ...VIII.6:4 And every **m.** you do contains them all, as
T-13 ...VIII.6:5 only **m.** that ever was is God's most holy
T-13 ...VIII.8:4 in every **m.** you offered to your brothers,
T-13 ...VIII.9:4 The **m.** that God created is perfect, as are
T-14 ..... III.5:1 The **m.** teaches you that you have chosen
T-14 .......V.5:3 The **m.** acknowledges the guiltlessness
T-14 .......X.2:6 The **m.**, therefore, has a unique function,
T-14 .......X.2:7 The **m.** is the one thing you can do that
T-14 .......X.3:4 that stamps the **m.** as something that
T-14 .......X.6:3 The **m.** offers exactly the same response
T-14 ......X.6:10 The **m.** itself is but the witness that you
T-14 ......X.6:11 That is the reason why the **m.** gives equal
T-14 ......X.12:1 The **m.** is the recognition that this is true.
T-14 ......X.12:6 The **m.** becomes the means of sharing It.
T-14 ......X.12:9 absent from any **m.** you offer to His Son.
T-14 ..... XI.7:7 The **m.** acknowledges His changelessness
T-14 ..... XI.7:8 himself. The **m.** brings the effects that
T-14 ..... XI.9:2 that He cannot solve by offering you a **m.**.
T-14 ... XI.9:11 each **m.** He offers you corrects your use of
T-14 . XI.10:10 He offers you a **m.** with every one you let
T-14 ... XI.11:5 For He teaches the **m.** of oneness, and
T-14 ... XI.11:7 The **m.** of creation has never ceased,
T-15 ....I.15:11 Offer the **m.** of the holy instant through
T-16 ........I.6:3 do not try to substitute your "**m.**" for this.
T-16 .......II.1:6 you worry how the **m.** extends to all the
T-16 .......II.1:6 when you do not understand the **m.** itself
T-16 .......II.3:1 you the **m.** cannot seem natural, because
T-16 .......II.5:5 For His task is to translate the **m.** into the
T-16 .......II.5:6 of the **m.** be enough for you, and do not
T-16 .......II.7:4 Should not this be a sufficient **m.** to teach
T-16 .. VII.11:2 the **m.** extends to bless everyone and to
T-17 .... VII.6:6 and accomplish every **m.** needed for its
T-18 ..... IV.2:8 it. The **m.** of the holy instant lies in your
T-18 ... IV.4:10 Would you first make a **m.** yourself, and
T-18 .... VII.2:3 is in this instant that the **m.** of Atonement

T-19...... I.14:3 will you see the **m.** of your relationship as
T-19...... I.14:5 which brings the **m.** of healing with equal
T19... IV.A.5:2 For in the **m.** of your holy relationship,
T19... IV.A.5:2 this barrier, is every **m.** contained. There
T19. IV.A.5:11 But let Him quietly extend the **m.** of your
T19... IV.A.6:8 end. Every **m.** is but the end of an illusion.
T19. IV.C.10:5 perfect safety, every **m.** you will perform,
T19. IV.C.10:6 The **m.** of life is ageless, born in time but
T-20....... V.1:6 Each **m.** of joining is a mighty herald of
T-21...... I.10:4 What is a **m.** but this remembering? And
T-21...... VI.7:2 neither can accept a **m.** instead without
T-22...... IV.6:5 to everyone who needs a **m.** to save him.
T-22...... IV.7:1 How easy is it to offer this **m.** to everyone
T-23...... IV.6:5 quickly choose a **m.** instead of murder.
T-25...... IX.6:6 A **m.** *is* justice. It is not a special gift to
T-25...... IX.8:4 **m.** can never be received because another
T-25.... IX.10:1 The **m.** that you receive, you give. Each
T-25.... IX.10:4 Each **m.** is an example of what justice can
T-26....... II.4:1 The **m.** of justice can correct all errors.
T-26....... II.5:8 You deny the **m.** of justice *can* be fair.
T-26....... II.6:8 The **m.** of justice you call forth will rest on
T-26...... IV.4:6 What but a **m.** could change his mind, so
T-26...... IV.4:7 What other **m.** is there but this? And
T-26... VII.10:6 And every **m.** is possible the instant that
T-26... VII.11:5 This is the **m.** by which creation became
T-26... VII.14:1 The **m.** is possible when cause and
T-26... VII.15:3 justify a **m.** whatever form they took. In
T-26... VII.15:4 In every **m.** all healing lies, for God gave
T-26... VII.16:1 The **m.** but calls your ancient Name,
T-26... VII.20:4 A **m.** can make no change at all. But it can
T-26... VIII.5:8 For a **m.** is *now*. It stands already here, in
T-26...... IX.8:5 An ancient **m.** has come to bless and to
T-27....... II.5:2 A **m.** of healing proves that separation is
T-27....... II.6:1 A **m.** can offer nothing less to him than it
T-27....... II.6:4 you. Thus does the **m.** undo all things the
T-27....... II.7:4 This is the law the **m.** obeys; that healing
T-27....... V.1:2 The **m.** extends without your help, but
T-27....... V.1:3 Accept the **m.** of healing, and it will go
T-27....... V.4:1 is no sadness where a **m.** has come to heal
T-27...... VI.4:8 Each **m.** He brings is witness that the
T-27...... VI.5:1 **m.** makes no distinctions in the names by
T-27...... VI.5:6 brings the **m.** perceives them all as one,
T-27...... VI.5:7 death, so is the **m.** the witness unto life. It
T-27.... VI.5:10 Yet a **m.** speaks not but for itself, but
T-27...... VI.6:2 The **m.** forgives because it stands for what
T-27...... VI.6:3 it is to think a **m.** is bound by laws that it
T-27...... VI.6:7 It is their sameness that the **m.** attests. It
T-27.... VI.6:10 The purpose of a **m.** is to accomplish this.
T-27...... VI.7:1 Be you then witness to the **m.**, and not
T-28......... I.1:1 The **m.** does nothing. All it does is to
T-28......... I.1:8 The **m.** but shows the past is gone, and
T-28......... I.9:4 The **m.** reminds you of a Cause forever
T-28...... I.10:9 see in the **m.** a lesson in allowing Cause to
T-28...... I.11:1 The **m.** comes quietly into the mind that
T-28...... I.11:4 no pause in time to cause the **m.** delay in
T-28....... II.4:2 The **m.** does not awaken you, but merely
T-28....... II.5:7 dreams the **m.** exchanges for your own. It
T-28....... II.7:1 The **m.** establishes you dream a dream,
T-28..... II.7:10 **m.** does nothing but to show him that he
T-28....... II.9:3 **m.** is the first step in giving back to cause
T-28..... II.10:1 Spirit requests you learn, the **m.** is clear.
T-28..... II.11:1 The **m.** returns the cause of fear to you
T-28..... II.11:6 The **m.** is useless if you learn but that the
T-28...... III.1:3 The **m.** alone is your concern at present.
T-28...... III.1:6 When you accept a **m.**, you do not add
T-28...... III.3:1 **m.** does nothing just *because* the minds
T-28...... III.6:1 the space left clean and vacant by the **m.**.
T-28...... III.6:4 The **m.** will brush them all aside, and thus
T-28...... III.8:5 **m.** would leave no proof of guilt to bring
T-28...... III.8:8 Guests the **m.** has asked to come to you.
T-28...... IV.8:5 that the **m.** will place within the little gap,
T-28.... IV.10:9 He will place the **m.** of healing where the
T-29....... II.2:3 **m.** is not a separate thing that happens
T-29...... IV.1:3 lack of truth becomes the basis for the **m.**,
T-29...... IV.1:6 Thus it is the **m.** does not select some
T-29...... IV.2:7 **m.** were treacherous indeed if it allowed
T-29...... IV.2:8 awake, for which the **m.** prepares the way.
T-29...... IV.3:5 And it is this the **m.** perceives, and not
T-29... VIII.5:4 and this is what the **m.** restores to what
T-29... VIII.5:5 The **m.** does not restore the truth, the
T-30...... VI.5:2 the **m.** its strength to overlook illusions.
T-30...... VI.5:8 appearances that could withstand the **m.**,
T-30...... VI.7:1 true the **m.** can heal all forms of sickness,
T-30...... VI.8:5 which the **m.** must lack the power to heal.
T-30... VIII.2:1 The **m.** is means to demonstrate that all
T-30... VIII.2:2 **m.** attests salvation from appearances by
T-30... VIII.2:6 The **m.** is proof he is not bound by loss or
T-30... VIII.3:4 a prayer the **m.** touch not some dreams,
T-30... VIII.3:5 a **m.** be given you to heal appearances you
T-30... VIII.4:3 the hope of change is that the **m.** cannot
T-30... VIII.4:5 There is no **m.** you cannot have when you
T-30... VIII.4:6 But there is no **m.** that can be given you
T-30... VIII.5:1 is a **m.** already there to heal all things that
T-30... VIII.6:5 but will fade, if you request a **m.** instead.
T-31... VIII.6:4 A **m.** has come to heal God's Son, and
W-pI..... 77.7:6 are not relying on yourself to find the **m.**,
W-pI..... 78.1:1 make is one between a grievance and a **m.**
W-pI..... 78.1:2 of hate before the **m.** it would conceal.
W-pI..... 78.1:3 your eyes, you will not see the **m.** beyond.
W-pI..... 78.2:1 grievances, to look upon the **m.** instead.
W-pI..... 78.9:1 looked upon the **m.** of love the Holy Spirit
W-pI..... 89.2:2 *Behind this is a **m.** to which I am entitled. Let*
W-pI..... 89.2:3 *offer you the **m.** that belongs to you instead.*
W-pI..... 89.2:4 *you instead. Seen truly, this offers me a **m.**.*
W-pI..... 89.4:4 *this is the **m.** by which all my grievances are*
W-pI..... 90.1:3 the solution is always a **m.** with which I
W-pI..... 90.1:5 is a grievance; the solution is a **m.**. And I
W-pI..... 90.1:6 my welcome of the **m.** that takes its place.
W-pI..... 90.2:3 *The **m.** behind this grievance will resolve it*
W-pI..... 90.2:4 *The answer to this problem is the **m.** that it*
W-pI..... 91.1:4 The **m.** is always there. Its presence is not
W-pI..... 91.2:2 in darkness, the **m.** remains unseen. Thus
W-pI..... 92.5:7 may bring to all the **m.** in which they will
W-pI..... 92.8:2 can leave without a **m.** before his eyes,
W-pI..... 97.3:3 and over, for the **m.** makes use of time,
W-pI..... 97.3:4 it. Salvation is a **m.**, the first and last; the
W-pI..... 97.4:1 abides the **m.** in which all time stands still
W-pI..... 97.4:1 **m.** in which a minute spent in using these
W-pI... 124.6:1 No **m.** can ever be denied to those who
W-pI... 159.2:4 There is no **m.** you cannot give, for all are
W-pI... 159.3:1 Christ's vision is a **m.**. It comes from far
W-pI... 159.4:1 is the **m.** in which all miracles are born. It
W-pI... 159.4:2 source, remaining with each **m.** you give,
W-pI... 160.6:4 except a **m.** will search him out and show
W-pI... 160.6:5 The **m.** will come. For in his home his Self
W-pI... 183.3:2 to stand you find a star; a **m.** of grace. The
W-pI... 191.8:1 A **m.** has lighted up all dark and ancient
W-pI... 198.7:4 blood, you will perceive a **m.** instead.
W-pI... 213.1:2 *A lesson is a **m.** which God offers to me, in*
W-pII....... 13.h What Is a **M.**?
W-pII.... 13.1:1 A **m.** is a correction. It does not create,
W-pII.... 13.2:1 A **m.** contains the gift of grace, for it is
W-pII.... 13.2:3 A **m.** inverts perception which was upside
W-pII.... 13.3:4 offers all the world the silent **m.** of love.
W-pII.... 13.4:1 The **m.** is taken first on faith, because to
W-pII.... 13.4:3 And thus the **m.** will justify your faith in it
W-pII.. 345.1:1 *Father, a **m.** reflects Your gifts to me, Your*
W-pII.. 345.1:6 *the **m.** is closer to Your gifts than any other*
W-pII..... 347.h myself, To keep the **m.** away from me.
W-pII..... 349.h not, but give Each one a **m.** of love instead
W-pII.. 349.1:5 *Each one that I accept gives me a **m.** to give.*
W-pII..... 356.h for God. The **m.** is thus a call to Him.
W-pII.. 356.1:4 *him. The **m.** reflects Your Love, and thus it*
M-7 ........... 3:2 the **m.** worker is to accept the Atonement
M-7 ........... 3:3 teacher of God is a **m.** worker because he
M-7 ........... 4:9 teachers the power to be **m.** workers, for
M-18 ......... 4:7 God becomes a **m.** worker by definition.
M-22 ......... 1:8 and every **m.** has been accomplished. To
M-22 ....... 1:12 What **m.** can be withheld from him?
M-22 ......... 4:4 of God calls forth the **m.** of healing. He
C-2................h THE EGO – THE **M.**
C-2............. 5:1 effect and consequence–we call a **m.**.
C-2............. 7:1 What is a *m.*? A dream as well. But look at
C-2............. 8:2 **m.** corrects as gently as a loving mother
C-2............. 9:3 No **m.** is now withheld from anyone. The
C-2........... 10:1 The **m.** forgives; the ego damns. Neither

## miracle's 1

T-27....... V.3:1 The holy instant is the **m.** abiding place.

## miracle-based 1

T-3.......... II.3:2 This is hardly a **m.** frame of reference. It

## miracle-minded 6

T-1......... V.2:1 The basic decision of the **m.** is not to wait
T-1..... VII.3:14 of the Sonship is the only goal of the **m.**.
T-2.... V.A.16:1 (6) **M.** forgiveness is *only* correction. It
T-2....... VII.1:9 You are not used to **m.** thinking, but you
T-2...... VIII.2:7 If a sufficient number become truly **m.**,
T-3........ IV.4:4 It is **m.** because it heals misperception,

## miracle-mindedness 5

T-1........ III.8:5 nature of **m.** ensures your grace, but only
T-2......... V.3:1 said that miracles are expressions of **m.**,
T-2......... V.3:1 and **m.** means right-mindedness. The
T-5........... I.3:5 It is the blessing of **m.**. It asks that you
T-5.......... II.1:4 The Holy Spirit is the motivation for **m.**;

## miracle-readiness 1

T-1......... I.43:1 miraculous state of mind, or a state of **m.**.

## miracles 246

T-in ........... 1:1 *This is a course in **m.**. It is a required course.*
T-1................h THE MEANING OF **M.**
T-1.............. I.h Principles of **M.**
T-1........... I.1:1 There is no order of difficulty in **m.**. One
T-1........... I.2:1 **M.** as such do not matter. The only thing
T-1........... I.3:1 **M.** occur naturally as expressions of love.
T-1........... I.4:1 All **m.** mean life, and God is the Giver of
T-1........... I.5:1 **M.** are habits, and should be involuntary.
T-1........... I.5:3 Consciously selected **m.** can be misguided
T-1........... I.6:1 **M.** are natural. When they do not occur
T-1........... I.7:1 **M.** are everyone's right, but purification
T-1........... I.8:1 **M.** are healing because they supply a lack
T-1........... I.9:1 **M.** are a kind of exchange. Like all
T-1......... I.10:1 use of **m.** as spectacles to induce belief is a
T-1......... I.11:1 Prayer is the medium of **m.**. It is a means
T-1......... I.11:3 and through **m.** love is expressed.
T-1......... I.12:1 **M.** are thoughts. Thoughts can represent
T-1......... I.13:1 **M.** are both beginnings and endings, and
T-1......... I.14:1 **M.** bear witness to truth. They are
T-1......... I.15:1 Each day should be devoted to **m.**. The
T-1......... I.16:1 **M.** are teaching devices for
T-1......... I.17:1 **M.** transcend the body. They are sudden
T-1......... I.19:1 **M.** make minds one in God. They
T-1......... I.19:3 **M.** therefore reflect the laws of eternity,
T-1......... I.20:1 **M.** reawaken the awareness that the
T-1......... I.21:1 **M.** are natural signs of forgiveness.
T-1......... I.21:2 Through **m.** you accept God's forgiveness
T-1......... I.22:1 **M.** are associated with fear only because
T-1......... I.23:1 **M.** rearrange perception and place all
T-1......... I.24:1 **M.** enable you to heal the sick and raise
T-1......... I.25:1 **M.** are part of an interlocking chain of
T-1......... I.26:1 **M.** represent freedom from fear.
T-1......... I.26:3 part of the Atonement value of **m.**.
T-1......... I.28:1 **M.** are a way of earning release from fear.
T-1......... I.28:3 **M.** are thus a means and revelation is an
T-1......... I.29:1 **M.** praise God through you. They praise
T-1......... I.30:1 **m.** adjust the levels of perception and
T-1......... I.31:1 **M.** should inspire gratitude, not awe.
T-1......... I.32:1 I inspire all **m.**, which are really
T-1......... I.33:1 **M.** honor you because you are lovable.
T-1......... I.34:1 **M.** restore the mind to its fullness. By
T-1......... I.35:1 **M.** are expressions of love, but they may
T-1......... I.36:1 **M.** are examples of right thinking,
T-1......... I.38:1 The Holy Spirit is the mechanism of **m.**.
T-1......... I.41:1 is the perceptual content of **m.**. They thus
T-1......... I.42:1 major contribution of **m.** is their strength
T-1......... I.43:1 **M.** arise from a miraculous state of mind,
T-1......... I.46:2 medium. **M.** do not involve this type of
T-1......... I.46:3 direct revelation, the need for **m.** is over.

| | |
|---|---|
| T-1 ............ II.h | Revelation, Time and **M.** |
| T-1 ......... II.1:4 | **M.**, however, are genuinely interpersonal, |
| T-1 ......... II.1:6 | **M.** unite you directly with your brother. |
| T-1 ......... II.2:4 | **M.**, on the other hand, induce action. |
| T-1 ......... II.2:6 | working **m.** is important because freedom |
| T-1 ......... II.3:2 | for **m.** because a state of awe is worshipful |
| T-1 ........... III.h | Atonement and **M.** |
| T-1 ........ III.1:3 | I do not need **m.** for my own Atonement, |
| T-1 ........ III.1:7 | it. The power to work **m.** belongs to you. I |
| T-1 ........ III.3:4 | **M.** are the way in which minds that serve |
| T-1 ........ III.4:1 | one who can perform **m.** indiscriminately |
| T-1 ........ III.4:3 | Ask me which **m.** you should perform. |
| T-1 ........ III.4:5 | under my guidance **m.** lead to the highly |
| T-1 ........ III.7:1 | **M.** arise from a mind that is ready for |
| T-1 ........ III.7:3 | impersonal nature of **m.** is because the |
| T-1 ........ III.8:3 | **M.** you are not asked to perform have not |
| T-1 ........ III.9:1 | **M.** are selective only in the sense that |
| T-1 ........ IV.4:8 | for me are expressing, through their **m.**, |
| T-1 ......... V.4:6 | **M.** are affirmations of Sonship, which is a |
| T-1 ........ VII.3:9 | If you offer **m.**, you will be equally strong |
| T-2 ........... I.5:4 | other. Some **m.** may seem to be of greater |
| T-2 ........... I.5:5 | there is no order of difficulty in **m.**. In |
| T-2 ......... I.5:12 | capable, through your acceptance of **m.**, |
| T-2 ......... II.1:2 | I have asked you to perform **m.**, and have |
| T-2 ......... II.1:2 | and have made it clear that **m.** are natural |
| T-2 ......... II.7:7 | cannot be controlled except by **m.**. The |
| T-2 ......... IV.2:3 | referred to **m.** as the means of correcting |
| T-2 ...... IV.4:10 | induced the belief that **m.** are frightening. |
| T-2 ......... V.2:6 | you should not attempt to perform **m.**. |
| T-2 ......... V.3:1 | have already said that **m.** are expressions |
| T-2 ....... VII.3:1 | Both **m.** and fear come from thoughts. If |
| T-2 ...... VIII.2:6 | can, however, be greatly shortened by **m.**, |
| T-3 ........... I.1:1 | fear still associated with **m.** can disappear |
| T-3 ............ II.h | **M.** as True Perception |
| T-3 ........ III.5:9 | **m.** and doing are closely related. |
| T-3 ......... V.6:2 | medium of **m.**. But the only meaningful |
| T-3 ......... V.9:7 | But God's **m.** are as total as His Thoughts |
| T-4 ...... IV.11:9 | that there is an order of difficulty in **m.**; |
| T-4 .... IV.11:11 | I understand that **m.** are natural, because |
| T-5 ....... VII.2:4 | that there is no order of difficulty in **m.**. |
| T-6 ...... V.A.3:1 | the Holy Spirit is the motivation for **m.**. |
| T-6 ...... V.A.4:1 | Spirit, there is no order of difficulty in **m.**. |
| T-6 ...... V.A.4:6 | cannot perform **m.** without believing it, |
| T-6 ...... V.B.8:7 | difficulty in **m.** has not yet been accepted, |
| T-7 ........ IV.2:3 | The **m.** the Holy Spirit inspires can have |
| T-7 ........ IX.7:2 | **M.** are an expression of this confidence. |
| T-7 ......... X.8:1 | **M.** are in accord with the Will of God, |
| T-7 ........ XI.1:8 | there is no order of difficulty in **m.**, you |
| T-8 ......... V.3:7 | The **m.** we do bear witness to the Will of |
| T-8 ....... VII.7:3 | to exist, just as different orders of **m.** do. |
| T-9 ........ IV.6:2 | I meant when I said that **m.** are natural, |
| T-9 ........ IV.6:3 | **M.** are merely the sign of your willingness |
| T-9 ........ VI.6:1 | **M.** have no place in eternity, because |
| T-9 ........ VI.6:2 | **m.** are the only witnesses to your reality |
| T-9 ........ VI.6:3 | because **m.** are a way of giving acceptance |
| T-9 ....... VIII.8:2 | is not. Pride will not produce **m.**, and will |
| T-11 .... VI.10:5 | no order of difficulty in **m.** because all of |
| T-12 ....... II.1:1 | **M.** are merely the translation of denial |
| T-12 ..... VII.1:1 | **M.** demonstrate that learning has |
| T-12 ..... VII.1:3 | **m.** when you apply them to all situations. |
| T-12 ..... VII.1:4 | is no situation to which **m.** do not apply, |
| T-12 ..... VII.3:2 | for **m.** violate every law of reality as this |
| T-12 ..... VII.4:3 | **M.** are His witnesses, and speak for His |
| T-13 .... VIII.7:2 | gift to everyone and everywhere, for **m.**, |
| T-13 .... VIII.9:1 | **m.** in this world join you to your brothers |
| T-13 .... VIII.9:4 | the **m.** that you established in His Name. |
| T-13 .. VIII.10:5 | The **m.** you do on earth are lifted up to |
| T-14 ......... I.1:6 | is why **m.** offer *you* the testimony that you |
| T-14 .......... X.h | The Equality of **M.** |
| T-14 ....... X.3:1 | **M.** are not in competition, and the |
| T-14 ....... X.6:2 | the shining examples of **m.** to show you |
| T-14 ....... X.6:9 | of God, and not of you, engenders **m.**. |
| T-14 ...... XI.7:1 | You cannot be your guide to **m.**, for it is |
| T-14 ...... XI.7:2 | depend for **m.** has been provided for you. |
| T-14 ...... XI.8:6 | on **m.** to answer all your problems for you |
| T-14 ...... XI.9:3 | **M.** are for you. And every fear or pain or |
| T-15 ....... I.12:4 | **M.** are the instants of release you offer, |
| T-15 ..... V.10:7 | you have been told to offer **m.** as I direct, |
| T-16 ....... II.1:3 | the nature of **m.** you do not understand. |
| T-16 ....... II.1:8 | If **m.** *are* at all, their attributes would have |
| T-16 ....... II.2:4 | of **m.** is this: You do not understand them |
| T-16 ....... II.3:4 | of difficulty in **m.** is quite impossible, for |
| T-16 ....... II.3:4 | involves a contradiction of what **m.** mean. |
| T-16 ....... II.4:1 | have done **m.**, but it is quite apparent |
| T-16 ....... II.5:4 | **M.** are natural to the One Who speaks for |
| T-17 ........ I.3:1 | there must be an order of difficulty in **m.**, |
| T-17 ........ I.4:1 | order of difficulty in **m.** remain with you. |
| T-18 ..... IV.8:3 | in orders of difficulty in **m.** is centered on |
| T19 .... IV.A.5:3 | There is no order of difficulty in **m.**, for |
| T19 .... IV.C.6:2 | principle in a course on **m.** than by |
| T-21 ...... in.1:9 | order of difficulty in **m.** is meaningless. |
| T-21 ...... III.8:5 | The **m.** that follow this decision are also |
| T-21 ...... V.3:3 | This other self sees **m.** as natural. They |
| T-21 ...... V.3:6 | **M.** seem unnatural to the ego because it |
| T-21 .... V.3:10 | that **m.** do not affect another's mind, only |
| T-23 ....... II.3:1 | to interfere with the first principle of **m.**. |
| T-23 ....... II.3:3 | to understand that **m.** apply to all of them |
| T-23 ..... IV.4:3 | limits the healing and the **m.** you have the |
| T-23 ..... IV.5:6 | above, the choice is **m.** instead of murder. |
| T-23 ... IV.5:11 | the truth of **m.** be recognized if murder is |
| T-23 ..... IV.9:8 | the choice of **m.** or murder hard to make? |
| T-24 ..... IV.3:8 | Nothing could make more sense to **m.**. |
| T-24 ..... IV.3:9 | **m.** are merely change of purpose from |
| T-25 ..... IX.5:5 | For **m.** depend on justice. Not as it is seen |
| T-25 ..... IX.6:4 | What order can there be in **m.**, unless |
| T-25 ..... IX.7:2 | be. If **m.**, the Holy Spirit's gift, were given |
| T-25 ..... IX.8:1 | have an equal right to **m.** with you, you |
| T-25 ..... IX.8:5 | Only forgiveness offers **m.**. And pardon |
| T-26 ..... IV.4:1 | little **m.** to lay before the gate of Heaven. |
| T-26 ...... V.1:1 | not understand that **m.** are all the same. |
| T-26 ..... VII.1:1 | This is a course in **m.**. As such, the laws |
| T-26 ..... IX.3:5 | **m.** sprung up as grass and flowers on the |
| T-27 ....... II.7:1 | How just are **m.**! For they bestow an |
| T-27 .... V.2:14 | instant is sufficient. **M.** wait not on time. |
| T-27 ..... VI.6:6 | Who sends forth **m.** to bless the world, a |
| T-27 ... VI.6:11 | strength of **m.** for what they witness to. |
| T-27 . VIII.11:6 | will understand that **m.** reflect the simple |
| T-28 ........ I.9:8 | It is not revealed in **m.**. They but remind |
| T-28 ..... II.11:4 | Thus is the body healed by **m.** because |
| T-28 ..... II.12:1 | This world is full of **m.**. They stand in |
| T-28 ..... III.7:1 | silver **m.** and golden dreams of happiness |
| T-28 ..... III.8:1 | but let your world be gently lit by **m.**. And |
| T-28 ... IV.10:7 | **m.** are the result when you do not insist |
| T-28 .... VII.4:6 | All **m.** are based upon this choice, and |
| T-30 ... VIII.4:2 | **M.** but show what you have interposed |
| T-30 ... VIII.4:7 | gives all **m.** has not been given freedom to |
| T-31 ... VIII.5:6 | thus are **m.** as natural as fear and agony |
| W-pI ..... 19.4:3 | of lack of order in **m.** meaningful to you. |
| W-pI ........ 77.h | I am entitled to **m.**. |
| W-pI ..... 77.1:1 | are entitled to **m.** because of what you are |
| W-pI ..... 77.1:2 | will receive **m.** because of what God is. |
| W-pI ..... 77.1:3 | you will offer **m.** because you are one with |
| W-pI ..... 77.2:1 | claim to **m.** does not lie in your illusions |
| W-pI ..... 77.3:1 | we will claim the **m.** which are your right, |
| W-pI ..... 77.4:1 | confidently that you are entitled to **m.**. |
| W-pI ..... 77.4:3 | Remind yourself also that **m.** are never |
| W-pI ..... 77.4:4 | **M.** do not obey the laws of this world. |
| W-pI ..... 77.7:3 | *I am entitled to* **m.**. Ask for them whenever |
| W-pI ..... 77.8:3 | *I will not trade* **m.** *for grievances. I want only* |
| W-pI ..... 77.8:5 | *to me. God has established* **m.** *as my right.* |
| W-pI ........ 78.h | Let **m.** replace all grievances. |
| W-pI ... 78.10:5 | well, we pray: *Let* **m.** *replace all grievances.* |
| W-pI ..... 89.1:1 | (77) I am entitled to **m.**. I am entitled to |
| W-pI ..... 89.1:2 | I am entitled to **m.** because I am under no |
| W-pI ..... 89.1:3 | all grievances, and replace them with **m.**. |
| W-pI ..... 89.1:4 | accept the **m.** in place of the grievances, |
| W-pI ..... 89.1:4 | are but illusions that hide the **m.** beyond. |
| W-pI ..... 89.3:1 | (78) Let **m.** replace all grievances. By this |
| W-pI ..... 89.4:3 | *Let our grievances be replaced by* **m.**, *[name* |
| W-pI ........ 91.h | **M.** are seen in light. |
| W-pI ..... 91.1:1 | that **m.** and vision necessarily go together |
| W-pI ..... 91.1:6 | only your awareness of **m.** that is affected. |
| W-pI ..... 91.4:4 | makes all **m.** within your easy reach, you |
| W-pI ..... 91.4:5 | The **m.** your sense of weakness hides will |
| W-pI ..... 91.6:2 | **M.** *are seen in light. The body's eyes do not* |
| W-pI ... 91.10:5 | Theirs is the light in which you will see **m.** |
| W-pI ... 91.11:1 | remind yourself that **m.** are seen in light. |
| W-pI ... 91.11:4 | **M.** *are seen in light. Let me not close my eyes* |
| W-pI ....... 92.h | **M.** are seen in light, and light and |
| W-pI .... 92.7:2 | No **m.** are here, but only hate. It separates |
| W-pI .. 92.11:3 | the light where only **m.** can be perceived. |
| W-pI .... 99.7:1 | You who will yet work **m.**, be sure you |
| W-pI .. 106.4:4 | comes with **m.** a thousand times as happy |
| W-pI .. 106.4:5 | His **m.** are true. They will not fade when |
| W-pI .. 106.4:8 | you. Prepare yourself for **m.** today. Today |
| W-pI .. 106.6:5 | bringer of all **m.** has need that you receive |
| W-pI .. 110.5:2 | It is the birthplace of all **m.**, the great |
| W-pI .. 111.1:1 | (91) **M.** are seen in light. *I cannot see in* |
| W-pI .. 111.2:1 | (92) **M.** are seen in light, and light and |
| W-pI .. 111.3:2 | **M.** are seen in light. On the half hour: |
| W-pI .. 111.3:4 | hour: **M.** are seen in light, and light and |
| W-pI 151.14:1 | and He will give them back as **m.** which |
| W-pI 154.12:3 | you will receive a thousand **m.** and then |
| W-pI 155.11:1 | things that pass and **m.** are purposeless, |
| W-pI ..... 159.h | I give the **m.** I have received. |
| W-pI .. 159.4:1 | is the miracle in which all **m.** are born. It |
| W-pI 159.10:1 | the store of **m.** set out for you to give. Are |
| W-pI 169.13:2 | It is here that **m.** are laid; to be returned |
| W-pI .. 175.1:1 | (159) I give the **m.** I have received. God is |
| W-pI .. 187.3:3 | **m.** it brings to everyone you look upon. |
| W-pII ... 13.3:1 | Forgiveness is the home of **m.**. The eyes |
| W-pII ... 13.5:1 | **M.** fall like drops of healing rain from |
| W-pII .... 345.h | I offer only **m.** today, For I would have |
| W-pII . 345.1:4 | **m.** *I give are given back in just the form I need* |
| W-pII . 345.2:2 | The light has come to offer **m.** to bless the |
| W-pII . 346.1:1 | *Father, I wake today with* **m.** *correcting my* |
| W-pII . 347.1:8 | *He gives the* **m.** *my dreams would hide from* |
| W-pII347.1:11 | *for me, and call Your* **m.** *to come to me.* |
| W-pII . 349.1:6 | *I learn Your healing* **m.** *belong to me.* |
| W-pII . 349.2:3 | we trust in Him to send us **m.** to bless the |
| W-pII .... 350.h | **M.** mirror God's eternal Love. To offer |
| W-pII . 350.2:1 | And as we gather **m.** from Him, we will |
| W-pII .... 353.h | Christ To use to bless the world with **m.**. |
| W-pII .... 355.h | and joy, And all the **m.** that I will give, |
| W-pII .... 357.h | make to God, Responding first with **m.**, |
| W-pII . 357.1:1 | *truth's reflection, tells me how to offer* **m.**, |
| M-22 ......... 1:2 | no order of difficulty in **m.** because there |

## miraculous 5

| | |
|---|---|
| T-1 .......... I.9:2 | which are always **m.** in the true sense, the |
| T-1 ........ I.43:1 | Miracles arise from a **m.** state of mind, or |
| T-1 ......... V.1:3 | choose between loveless and **m.** channels |
| T-3 ......... V.9:4 | That is its **m.** power. The fact that each |
| T-16 ....... II.1:8 | at all, their attributes would have to be **m.** |

## miraculously 1

| | |
|---|---|
| T-3 ......... V.6:6 | your Father only by perceiving **m.**. You |

## mirages 1

| | |
|---|---|
| W-pI .. 186.9:6 | off. Or like **m.** seen above a desert, rising |

## mirror 22

| | |
|---|---|
| T-4 ....... IV.9:1 | are a **m.** of truth, in which God Himself |
| T-7 ...... VII.3:9 | Your brother is the **m.** in which you see |
| T-8 ..... VIII.9:5 | allow the body to be a **m.** of a split mind. |
| T-14 ..... IX.5:1 | this world you can become a spotless **m.**, |
| T-14 ..... IX.5:3 | **m.** that would hold God's reflection in it. |
| T-14 ..... IX.5:5 | You need but leave the **m.** clean and clear |
| T-14 ..... IX.6:5 | Clean but the **m.**, and the message that |
| T-14 ..... IX.6:5 | what the **m.** holds out for everyone to see, |
| T-14 ..... IX.6:6 | Spirit is holding to the **m.** that is in him. |
| T-14 ..... IX.7:1 | you could not wait to make the **m.** of your |
| T-14 ....... X.1:2 | The reflections you accept into the **m.** of |
| T-14 ....... X.5:2 | unceasingly across the **m.** of your mind, |
| T-24 ..... VI.8:6 | He is the **m.** of yourself, wherein you see |
| T-29 ....... V.4:1 | the **m.** of his Father's Love for you, the |
| T-31 .... VII.8:4 | himself, and sees the **m.** of himself in him |
| T-31 .... VII.9:3 | holds the **m.** to another view of what he is |
| W-pI .... 73.5:1 | of the world can only **m.** what is within. |
| W-pI .. 124.9:4 | the **m.** that this exercise will offer you. |
| W-pI 124.12:1 | frame that holds the **m.** offered you today |
| W-pI .. 197.3:2 | as well, for its release can only **m.** yours. |
| W-pII . 304.1:3 | Perception is a **m.**, not a fact. And what I |

W-pII.....350.h Miracles **m.** God's eternal Love. To offer

**mirrored** 1

W-pI...159.3:3 what God created perfect can be **m.** there.

**mirroring** 1

W-pI.167.12:3 as it sees its own perfection **m.** the Lord of

**mirrors** 1

T-4........IV.1:7 the trick of its existence except with **m.**?

**misapplication** 1

T-7..... VIII.4:9 It is the product of the **m.** of the laws of

**misconception** 1

W-pI.......8.1:4 cause of the **m.** about time from which

**misconstrue** 1

W-pI.....20.2:2 **m.** it as an effort to exert force or pressure

**miscreate** 10

T-2...........I.3:8 as long as you continue to project or **m.**.
T-2......... II.2:7 When the will is really free it cannot **m.**,
T-2........ III.3:3 Who set the limits on your ability to **m.**.
T-2........IV.2:9 believed that the mind can **m.** in the body
T-2........IV.2:9 body, or that the body can **m.** in the mind
T-2......VI.2:10 to **m.** and have not allowed me to guide it.
T-2.......VII.3:8 fearful *must* **m.**, because they misperceive
T-2.......VII.3:9 When you **m.** you are in pain. The cause
T-3......... II.4:1 created in the likeness of His Own, to **m.**.
T-3......... II.4:2 can **m.** only when it believes it is not free.

**miscreated** 1

T-2.......VII.3:6 You have misperceived or **m.** Us, and

**miscreation** 8

T-2......... II.2:5 of truth, but denial of truth results in **m.**,
T-2......... V.2:3 afraid makes your mind vulnerable to **m.**.
T-2.......VII.2:2 the power of thought in order to avoid **m.**
T-2.....VII.3:12 from those you introduce into **m.**. The
T-2.....VII.3:13 world, then, is between creation and **m.**.
T-2.....VII.5:13 **M.** made this necessary as a corrective
T-3......IV.5:10 in **m.** the mind is affirming its Source, or
T-3........IV.7:1 and therefore know that no **m.** exists.

**miscreations** 7

T-2........III.2:3 and the fear are **m.** that must be undone
T-2......... V.1:5 the **m.** of the mind do not really exist.
T-2.......V.1:11 that inducing the mind to give up its **m.** is
T-2......... V.5:5 their **m.** cannot hurt them. By affirming
T-2........VI.4:6 are passively condoning your mind's **m.**.
T-2..... VIII.4:5 mind will inevitably disown its **m.** which,
T-5...........I.6:1 God honored even the **m.** of His children

**miscreative** 1

T-2......... V.2:1 is the mindless or the **m.** use of mind.

**misdirected** 3

T-1........III.5:8 you are defending misplaced or **m.** loyalty
T-1.......VII.1:3 impulses are **m.** miracle impulses. All real
T-2......... V.8:3 your attempts at correction will be **m.**.

**misdirecting** 1

T-3........ I.3:10 from time to time that I am **m.** you. I have

**miserable** 12

T-4........ VI.5:3 only show him how **m.** he is without it,
T-9......... V.1:5 begin with the premise, "I am a **m.** sinner,
T-9......... V.6:6 A "**m.** sinner" cannot be healed without
T-14....... II.1:2 recognize that you are **m.** and not happy.
T-25. VIII.13:3 not because you are a **m.** sinner too. How
T-26....... V.2:6 hard indeed to wander off, alone and **m.**,
T-27....... II.6:6 the weak and **m.** cry of death and guilt.
T-31...VII.10:2 to but an image of yourself that can be **m.**
T-31... VIII.5:1 yourself as weak and **m.** with these words:
W-pI.....95.2:1 ugly and sinful, **m.** and beset with pain.
W-pI...121.4:2 rising to attack its **m.** parody of life. It
W-pI...166.9:3 You even think the **m.** self you thought

**miseries** 1

W-pI...132.3:4 with all your fears, your doubts and **m.**,

**misery** 69

T-4........ VI.5:3 how his **m.** lessens as he approaches it.
T-4........ VI.5:4 him to associate his **m.** with its absence,
T-4........ VI.5:4 and the opposite of **m.** with its presence.
T-4........ VI.5:6 I am teaching you to associate **m.** with the
T-10..... V.11:5 you for the **m.** you have made for yourself
T-14....... II.1:2 to **m.** must first recognize that you are
T-14....... II.1:3 for you believe that **m.** *is* happiness. This
T-17....... V.8:4 Forget not now the **m.** you really found,
T-18....... II.6:8 not be for you alone, for therein lay its **m.**
T-20...... IV.1:5 sickness and death and **m.** and pain.
T-20... VIII.2:3 Would you not willingly be free of **m.**,
T-21.....VII.1:1 Do you not see that all your **m.** comes
T-22.......I.3:11 does not lead you through a world of **m.**,
T-22....... II.1:4 same. Both bring the same amount of **m.**,
T-22....... II.1:4 be the way to lose the **m.** the other brings.
T-22....... II.2:2 else but joy could be the opposite of **m.**?
T-22....... II.2:3 leave one kind of **m.** and seek another is
T-22....... II.2:5 The search for joy in **m.** is senseless, for
T-22....... II.2:5 for how could joy be found in **m.**? All that
T-22....... II.2:6 of **m.** is to select some aspects out of it,
T-22....... II.3:3 No form of **m.** in reason's eyes can be
T-22....... II.4:1 **m.** is to recognize it *and go the other way*.
T-22....... II.4:2 Truth is the same and **m.** the same, but
T-22..... II.6:10 but reason tells you **m.** lies only on one
T-22....... II.7:6 either escape from **m.** entirely or not at all
T-22....... II.7:7 the joy of Heaven and the **m.** of hell. Until
T-22....... II.7:8 you choose Heaven, you *are* in hell and **m.**.
T-22..... II.10:4 You would condemn His joy to **m.**, and
T-22..... II.10:5 all the **m.** you made has been your own.
T-22... II.12:10 yours as well? No **m.** is here, but only joy.
T-22..... II.13:5 single sin still tempts you to remain in **m.**
T-23....... II.7:2 impossible to turn to Him for help in **m.**.
T-24..... II.14:2 save through the sight of all your **m.**, and
T-24...... III.2:7 and yourself in sin beside him, both in **m.**
T-27...... VI.6:6 plaintive cry for help within a world of **m.**
T-29....... II.3:6 are free of pain and sickness, **m.** and loss,
T-29...... VI.1:2 instead of endless strife and **m.** and pain?
T-29... VIII.2:6 and stand apart from all the **m.** the world
T-31.....VII.8:2 entrusted all salvation from the **m.** of hell.
T-31...VII.10:1 but the wish to stay in hell and **m.**? And
T-31... VIII.3:4 He would remove all **m.** from you whom
W-pI.....41.1:3 worry, a deep sense of helplessness, **m.**,
W-pI.....71.5:4 **m.** and a deep sense of failure and despair
W-pI.....97.5:1 world where pain and **m.** appear to rule.
W-pI...109.3:2 storms and strife, past **m.** and pain, past
W-pI...110.1:3 replaced by fear and evil, **m.** and death. If
W-pI...110.1:4 is not real, and **m.** and death do not exist.
W-pI...121.2:3 It suffers and abides in **m.**, peering about
W-pI...128.1:2 and you are saved from years of **m.**, from
W-pI.134.12:4 made to chain his mind to fear and **m.**.
W-pI.154.11:4 who wait in **m.** may be at last delivered.
W-pI...162.5:4 available to all as remedy for grief and **m.**,
W-pI...164.7:3 our release from blindness and from **m.**.
W-pI...165.1:2 What but your thoughts of **m.** and death
W-pI...166.5:5 Still he wanders on in **m.** and poverty,
W-pI...170.2:4 **m.** than you can possibly imagine. It is
WpI...rV.in7:2 learns there is a way from **m.** and pain. I
W-pI...181.7:3 from the **m.** the focus upon sin will bring,
W-pI...185.5:6 the same despair and **m.** as do the rest.
W-pI...186.6:5 and **m.** can come not near the holy home
W-pI...190.8:5 savage pain that waits to end all joy in **m.**.
W-pI...194.5:2 freed from its bequest of grief and **m.**, of
W-pI...200.1:5 of God, unless you seek for **m.** and pain.
W-pII ....359.h All pain Is healed; all **m.** replaced with joy
M-28 ......... 1:4 It is the end of dreams of **m.**, and the glad
M-28 ......... 2:3 pain and **m.** of any kind perceived as hell.
P-2........ IV.3:2 Sickness and death and **m.** now stalk the
S-2...........I.5:4 your despair or hope, your **m.** or joy. You
S-2..........II.6:4 no hope, but only greater pain and **m.**.

**misguide** 1

T-15.........I.9:3 It has taken time to **m.** you so completely,

**misguided** 4

T-1...........I.5:3 Consciously selected miracles can be **m.**.
T-4.........I.2:13 learn, even though its maker can be **m.**.
T-11....VIII.3:4 You are not **m.**; you have accepted no
P-3..........II.3:4 **m.** the direction he may have chosen.

**mishandled** 1

M-17 ......... 1:2 If this issue is **m.**, the teacher of God has

**misinterpretation** 1

T-2........ IV.3:7 because it is not inherently open to **m.**.

**misinterpreted** 1

T-12....... V.7:4 every sensible guide to learning will be **m.**

**misinterpreting** 1

T-11....VIII.6:4 be capable of **m.** the question you must

**misjudged** 1

T-13..... VII.5:1 the world because you have **m.** yourself.

**misleading** 1

T-5........ VI.5:1 of how the ego's interpretations are **m.**,

**misled** 1

W-pI...140.9:1 be **m.** today by what appears to us as sick.

**misperceive** 6

T-2......... V.2:5 cannot **m.** them as your own creations. As
T-2.......VII.3:8 *must* miscreate, because they **m.** creation.
T-3..........II.2:5 that you never **m.** and always see truly.
T-5........ III.9:6 You may let your mind **m.**, but the Holy
T-6...........I.6:7 of much less extreme temptations to **m.**,
T-18...... VI.4:6 it clearly can **m.** the function of the body,

**misperceived** 2

T-2.......VII.3:6 have **m.** or miscreated Us, and believe in
M-27 ......... 7:3 seems to die has but been **m.** and carried

**misperceiving** 1

T-3........ III.7:4 You are making him a stranger by **m.** him

**misperception** 11

T-1.........I.49:1 no distinction among degrees of **m.**. It is a
T-2...........I.3:4 of an eye because it is merely a **m.**. What
T-2...........I.4:1 to the basic **m.** that you have the ability to
T-2.......... V.1:3 This **m.** arises in turn from the belief that
T-3...........I.2:4 "justify" the terrible **m.** that God Himself
T-3...........I.3:1 sayeth the Lord" is a **m.** by which one
T-3........ IV.4:4 It is miracle-minded because it heals **m.**,
T-4....... II.11:2 only because **m.** is a block to knowledge,

| | |
|---|---|
| T-25...... III.7:1 | can a **m.** be a sin? Let all your brother's |
| T-25...... III.9:3 | What could this be except a **m.** of himself |
| W-pI..... 86.4:2 | *between* **m.** *and salvation as I look on this. If* |

## misperceptions 9

| | |
|---|---|
| T-2.......... I.5:2 | It makes no distinctions among **m.**. Its |
| T-3......... II.6:5 | perceive truly you are cancelling out **m.** in |
| T-3........ III.1:8 | **M.** produce fear and true perceptions |
| T-3...... IV.3:10 | You can never make your **m.** true, and |
| T-3........ IV.7:7 | but I can erase all **m.** from your mind if |
| T-3........ IV.7:8 | Only your **m.** stand in your way. Without |
| T-5........ III.9:6 | lets your mind reinterpret its own **m.**. |
| T-13...... XI.7:2 | Your wildest **m.**, your weird imaginings, |
| M-28 ......... 4:5 | dreams of fear and **m.** of the universe. All |

## misplaced 5

| | |
|---|---|
| T-1........ III.5:8 | are defending **m.** or misdirected loyalty. |
| T-6......... in.2:5 | allegiance to a thought system may be **m.**, |
| T-20....... V.8:6 | the confidence of God should be **m.**. |
| T-21....... V.8:1 | Faith and perception and belief can be **m.** |
| W-pI. 136.19:2 | to come, you have again **m.** yourself, and |

## miss 4

| | |
|---|---|
| W-pI..... 27.4:4 | You will probably **m.** several applications |
| W-pI..... 40.2:3 | not **m.** a practice period because of this. |
| W-pI... 108.7:2 | because it has results we cannot **m.**. To |
| WpI. rIII.in2:2 | not be hampered when you **m.** a practice |

## missed 2

| | |
|---|---|
| T-26....... V.5:4 | not one note in Heaven's song was **m.**. |
| S-2......... II.1:4 | the designed comparison cannot be **m.**, |

## missing 8

| | |
|---|---|
| T-2....... VII.6:4 | obscured as long as any of its parts is **m.**. |
| T-9...... VIII.9:8 | is total, and you cannot be **m.** from it. |
| T-11......... I.2:6 | that part of God can be **m.** or lost to Him? |
| T-18.... VIII.6:2 | It is not **m.**; it could not exist if it were |
| T-23..... II.12:5 | the **m.** factor in your madness that makes |
| T-30...... III.3:3 | mean that you believe some form is **m.**. |
| T-30...... VI.8:4 | no **m.** parts that have been kept outside. |
| M-6 ........... 4:9 | And if one gift is **m.**, it would not be full. |

## mission 25

| | |
|---|---|
| T-4........ VI.6:2 | Your **m.** is very simple. You are asked to |
| T-8........ IV.3:4 | My **m.** was simply to unite the will of the |
| T-12....... II.7:4 | Our **m.** is to escape from crucifixion, not |
| T-12....... II.8:4 | in your **m.** because I did not fail in mine. |
| T-12...... IV.5:5 | you to your home because that is His **m.**. |
| T-12...... IV.5:6 | He fulfills His **m.** He will teach you yours, |
| T-12...... IV.5:6 | you yours, for your **m.** is the same as His. |
| T-12...... VI.4:2 | eyes of the blind is the Holy Spirit's **m.**, |
| T-12... VII.11:1 | accepted your **m.** to extend peace you will |
| T-13......... I.4:5 | of the Son of God, for such was His **m.**, |
| T-13...... XI.4:6 | this would be to doubt that His **m.** will be |
| T-13...... XI.4:7 | is this possible, when His **m.** is of God? |
| T-13...... XI.5:1 | and gave Him the **m.** to remove all doubt |
| T-13...... XI.5:2 | It is impossible that this **m.** fail. Nothing |
| T-13.... XI.10:4 | The **m.** of redemption will be fulfilled as |
| T-14....... II.1:1 | His **m.** can be happily accomplished. You |
| T-25....... in.3:7 | is the **m.** that your brother has for you. |
| T-25....... in.3:8 | such it must be that your **m.** is for him. |
| T-26....... V.9:5 | you on a **m.** whose accomplishment can |
| W-pI... 139.9:1 | We have a **m.** here. We did not come to |
| W-pI. 139.11:2 | start with this review of what our **m.** is: *I* |
| W-pI. 153.17:1 | in hourly remembrance of our **m.** and His |
| W-pI. 166.15:5 | Such is your **m.** now. For God entrusts |
| W-pII ... 10.1:4 | its goal accomplished and its **m.** done. |
| M-in .......... 5:6 | Yet it is their **m.** to become perfect here, |

## misstep 1

| | |
|---|---|
| T-2........ IV.4:3 | a second **m.** to attempt to heal it through |

## missteps 1

| | |
|---|---|
| T-2 ......... II.6:2 | You correct your previous **m.** by stepping |

## mist 1

| | |
|---|---|
| T-19 ....... II.8:1 | is like walking through a **m.** into the sun? |

## mistake 95

| | |
|---|---|
| T-2 ......... II.7:2 | a **m.** all the separated Sons of God make |
| T-3 .......... I.1:4 | in scarcity could possibly make this **m.**. If |
| T-3 ...... VII.1:6 | It is a **m.** to believe that a thought system |
| T-4 ..... IV.10:6 | I assure you this is a **m.** of your ego. Do |
| T-4 ..... IV.10:7 | ego. Do not **m.** it for humility. Your ego is |
| T-5 ....... III.4:6 | If you make the **m.** of looking for the Holy |
| T-6 ........ I.15:7 | called forth upon Judas was a similar **m.**. |
| T-11 ...... in.2:5 | Make no **m.** about this. It sounds insane |
| T-11 .... V.14:3 | It makes real every **m.** it perceives, and |
| T-11 .... V.14:3 | **m.** consistent truth must be meaningless. |
| T-11 ... VIII.2:3 | Do not make the **m.** of believing that you |
| T-12 ..... III.2:4 | You, then, are making the same **m.** he is, |
| T-13 ....... II.8:5 | Make no **m.** about the depth of this fear. |
| T-15 ... VIII.3:6 | as nothing more than a **m.** in who you are |
| T-15 ....... X.4:2 | is necessary, for you made but one **m.**. It |
| T-16 ........ I.2:5 | Make no **m.** about this maneuver; the ego |
| T-19 ....... II.6:6 | If this is a **m.**, it can be undone easily by |
| T-19 ....... II.6:7 | Any **m.** can be corrected, if truth be left to |
| T-19 ....... II.6:8 | But if the **m.** is given the status of truth, |
| T-19 ..... II.6:11 | As a **m.**, *it* must be brought to truth. It is |
| T-19 ..... II.6:13 | to have faith that a **m.** can be corrected. |
| T-19 ....... II.7:2 | the ego, this is no **m.**. For this is its reality |
| T-19 ....... II.8:1 | that all this be nothing more than a **m.**, |
| T-19 ..... III.3:2 | you see clearly as a **m.** you want corrected |
| T-19 ..... III.3:4 | you change its status from a sin to a **m.**. |
| T-19 ..... III.4:4 | be corrected. For a **m.** that cannot be |
| T-19 ..... III.4:7 | Every **m.** *must* be a call for love. What, |
| T-19 ..... III.4:9 | it be but a **m.** you would keep hidden; a |
| T19.. IV.B.11:6 | **m.** be reasonable grounds for depression |
| T19.. IV.B.11:9 | of your **m.** will give you grounds for faith. |
| T-21 ..... II.11:2 | *They are the same* **m.**. Nothing created not |
| T-21 ..... II.13:6 | same **m.** as thinking you are independent |
| T-22 ......... I.4:5 | But a **m.** indeed! Let not your fear of sin |
| T-22 ..... III.4:3 | Everything the body's eyes can see is a **m.**, |
| T-22 ..... III.5:1 | form of error is not what makes it a **m.**. If |
| T-22 ..... III.5:2 | If what the form conceals is a **m.**, the |
| T-22 ..... IV.5:1 | Every **m.** you and your brother make, the |
| T-22 ..... VI.5:2 | observing merely, "This was a **m.**." And |
| T-22 ..... VI.7:1 | **m.** can there be anywhere you cannot |
| T-22 ..... VI.7:3 | there be you will not recognize as a **m.**; a |
| T-22 ... VI.8:10 | overlook the tiniest **m.** be lost to anyone. |
| T-23 ......... I.3:4 | You meet at a **m.**; an error in your self- |
| T-23 ..... III.6:1 | **M.** not truce for peace, nor compromise |
| T-24 ......... I.2:4 | **M.** you not the power of these hidden |
| T-25 ..... III.9:4 | Is this a sin or a **m.**, forgivable or not? |
| T-26 ....... II.2:4 | One **m.** is not more difficult for Him to |
| T-26 ....... II.2:5 | For there *is* but one **m.**; the whole idea that |
| T-26 ....... II.3:1 | one **m.**, in any form, has one correction. |
| T-26 ....... II.3:2 | There is no loss; to think there is, is a **m.**. |
| T-26 ....... II.7:5 | a special problem, a **m.** without a remedy, |
| T-26 ...... V.3:5 | of time in which the first **m.** was made, |
| T-26 ...... V.3:5 | made, and all of them within that one **m.** |
| T-26 VII.11:14 | Or is it a **m.** about your will, and what |
| T-26 ....... X.3:1 | Unfairness and attack are one **m.**, so |
| T-30 ... IV.5:14 | all. His one **m.** is that he thinks them real. |
| T-30 ..... VI.5:6 | would be an error that is more than a **m.**; |
| T-30 ..... VI.5:7 | be one **m.** that had the power to undo |
| T-31 ..... IV.8:3 | is still the same illusion and the same **m.**. |
| W-pI..... 20.3:3 | Do not **m.** the little effort that is asked of |
| W-pI..... 74.5:3 | to **m.** these attempts for withdrawal, but |
| W-pI..... 91.6:9 | are a body calls for correction, being a **m.**. |
| W-pI... 91.6:10 | to your awareness what the **m.** conceals. |
| W-pI..... 95.7:5 | it is; a refusal to let your **m.** be corrected, |
| W-pI..... 95.9:1 | of this course, you have merely made a **m.** |
| W-pI..... 95.9:3 | else. To allow a **m.** to continue is to make |
| W-pI..... 98.2:4 | Not one **m.** stands in our way. For we |
| W-pI... 136.5:4 | **M.** not this for fact. Defenses must make |
| W-pI. 138.11:5 | it is recognized as but a foolish, trivial **m.**. |
| W-pI... 155.7:5 | out of it, for they **m.** illusion for the truth. |
| W-pI... 156.7:5 | Companion, and **m.** Him for the senseless |
| W-pI .. 158.7:2 | and **m.** it for the Son whom God created. |
| W-pI .. 161.8:3 | **M.** not the intensity of rage projected fear |
| W-pI .. 183.5:3 | can not **m.** the nameless for the Name, |
| W-pI .. 185.6:3 | for him in such a way that he can not **m.** it |
| W-pII . 282.2:4 | *The name of fear is simply a* **m.**. *Let me not be* |
| W-pII . 316.1:2 | Each one allows a past **m.** to go, and leave |
| W-pII .... 359.h | And all sin Is understood as merely a **m.**. |
| M-7 ........... 1:9 | He has made a **m.**, and must be willing to |
| M-7 ......... 3:10 | That was a **m.**, but hardly one to stay with |
| M-7 ........... 4:1 | is a **m.** in the form of lack of trust. As such |
| M-7 ........... 5:7 | The form of the **m.** is not important. |
| M-7 ........... 5:8 | only the recognition of a **m.** as a mistake. |
| M-7 ........... 5:8 | only the recognition of a mistake as a **m.**. |
| M-7 ........... 6:1 | The **m.** is always some form of concern |
| M-18 ......... 3:7 | *You but* **m.** *interpretation for the truth. And* |
| M-18 ......... 3:9 | *But a* **m.** *is not a sin, nor has reality been* |
| M-22 ......... 7:7 | recognizes that they are the same **m.**. |
| M-24 ......... 5:3 | it would be a **m.** for him to renounce the |
| M-29 ....... 2:12 | have a Teacher Who cannot make a **m.**. |
| C-2 ............ 8:2 | terrible **m.** about yourself the miracle |
| P-2........ IV.7:1 | is therefore a **m.** and needs correction. |
| P-2........ IV.7:2 | establishing the "rightness" of the **m.** and |
| P-3........... I.1:3 | mean that no one comes to you by **m.**. |
| S-1........ IV.3:5 | from every choice that stood for a **m.**. |
| S-3........... I.1:1 | Do not **m.** effect for cause, nor think that |

## mistaken 34

| | |
|---|---|
| T-4 ..... IV.10:5 | that you believe I was **m.** in choosing you. |
| T-4 ..... IV.11:4 | I am not **m.**. Your mind will elect to join |
| T-10 ....... V.6:1 | not sinned, but you have been much **m.**. |
| T-19 ....... II.3:1 | The Son of God can be **m.**; he can deceive |
| T-19 ....... II.8:3 | that it is far better to be sinful than **m.**. |
| T-19 ..... III.6:6 | you have been **m.** than to believe in this? |
| T19 . IV.B.11:8 | but you have been **m.** in what is faithful. |
| T-21 ....... II.2:7 | Acknowledge but that you have been **m.**, |
| T-22 ..... III.7:5 | And if you see it you must be **m.**, for you |
| T-23 ....... II.6:4 | whether to take his word for it or be **m.**. |
| T-23 ....... II.6:6 | For if God cannot be **m.**, He must accept |
| T-25 ... IV.5:11 | entered it and were **m.** for a little while. |
| T-30 ..... IV.2:6 | He was **m.**. He misunderstood what made |
| T-31 ........ I.8:5 | And now you see you were **m.**. You had |
| W-pI .... 57.2:5 | I was bitterly **m.** in this belief, which I no |
| W-pI .... 86.1:4 | I was **m.** about where it is. I was mistaken |
| W-pI .... 86.1:5 | I was **m.** about what it is. I will undertake |
| W-pI .... 91.8:2 | your **m.** thoughts about your attributes to |
| W-pI .... 91.9:3 | a belief that is **m.** and deserves no faith. |
| W-pI .. 108.1:3 | of all your conflicts and **m.** thoughts into |
| W-pI .. 119.1:2 | *am* **m.** *when I think I can be hurt in any way.* |
| W-pI .. 155.3:2 | to find they were **m.** in their choice. They |
| W-pII . 223.1:1 | was **m.** when I thought I lived apart from |
| W-pII . 227.1:4 | *And I am free because I was* **m.**, *and did not* |
| W-pII . 228.2:1 | *Father, I was* **m.** *in myself, because I failed to* |
| W-pII . 314.2:1 | *Father, we were* **m.** *in the past, and choose* |
| W-pII . 337.2:1 | *me in sinlessness are not* **m.** *about what I am* |
| W-pII . 337.2:2 | *I was* **m.** *when I thought I sinned, but I accept* |
| Wfl........ in.5:5 | wrath because we learned we were **m.**. |
| M-3 ........... 4:7 | to become holy. God is not **m.** in His Son. |
| M-5 ......... I.1:5 | in the **m.** conviction that it is strength. |
| M-5 ...... II.3:10 | world, because he was **m.** about what it is. |
| M-10 .......... 6:9 | never were but the effects of his **m.** choice |
| M-13 .......... 6:3 | do not be **m.** about what sacrifice means. |

## mistakenly 1

| | |
|---|---|
| W-pII . 317.2:5 | *who thought* **m.** *that he had wandered from* |

## mistakes 82

| | |
|---|---|
| T-2 ....... IV.2:3 | for all **m.** must be corrected at the level on |
| T-17 ..... V.11:3 | you may have made many **m.** since then, |
| T-17 ..... V.11:5 | Nor does He see the **m.** at all. Have you |
| T-17 ..... V.11:7 | the good efforts, and overlooked **m.**? Or |
| T-17 ..... V.11:8 | in what seemed to be the light of the **m.**? |
| T-17 ..... V.15:1 | all your **m.** and free you from their results |
| T-19 ..... III.4:2 | sin. **M.** He recognizes, and would correct |
| T-19 ..... III.4:3 | He recognize **m.** that cannot be corrected. |
| T-19 ..... III.4:5 | **M.** are *for* correction, and they call for |
| T-19 ..... III.5:1 | clearly sees the Son of God can make **m.**. |

T-19......III.9:6 And you will help him overcome **m.** by
T-20......IV.2:7 It lies in him to overlook all your **m.**, and
T-20......IV.3:1 to guarantee that you would make **m.**,
T-21....... II.2:7 and all effects of your **m.** will disappear.
T-22...... III.2:4 can see the difference between sin and **m.**,
T-22...... III.4:4 And yet **m.**, regardless of their form, can
T-22...... III.7:1 Only **m.** have different forms, and so
T-22...... III.8:1 Let not the form of his **m.** keep you from
T-23....... II.4:5 the Son of God can make **m.** for which his
T-24...... VI.8:3 His **m.** can cause delay, which it is given
T-25....IV.5:12 better could your own **m.** be brought to
T-25...... VI.1:4 no more condemn himself for his **m.** than
T-25VIII.11:11 In justice, then, does love correct **m.**, but
T-25...... IX.1:2 mean except that they are sins and not **m.**
T-26....... II.4:6 **m.** from which the Son of God is suffering
T-26....... II.5:1 believe it safe to give but some **m.** to be
T-26...VII.18:2 answer all His Son's **m.** and set him free.
T-27..... II.13:5 Yours are **m.**, but his are sins and not the
T-27..... II.14:1 your own **m.** you will not even see. The
T-27..... II.15:2 shared, it must correct **m.** in you and him
T-27..... II.15:3 leave **m.** in one unhealed and set the
T-27...VII.15:3 of dwelling in your dreams on his **m.**.
T-30.... VI.10:2 to overlook **m.** that have been given no
W-pI.....78.6:4 will think of his **m.** and even of his "sins."
W-pI.....93.2:2 That you have made **m.** is obvious. That
W-pI.....93.7:3 Whatever **m.** you made, the truth about
W-pI.....95.8:1 is not delayed in His teaching by your **m.**.
W-pI.....95.9:3 to continue is to make additional **m.**,
W-pI.....98.2:6 away by realizing they were but **m.**.
W-pI.....99.7:6 your **m.** enter the darkened places of your
W-pI...110.2:1 that will heal all the **m.** that any mind has
W-pI...121.4:1 The unforgiving mind sees no **m.**, but
W-pI.133.10:2 His ineffectual **m.** appear as sins to him,
W-pI.133.10:3 and serve them as his own makes no **m.**,
W-pI.133.10:4 it is error to believe that sins are but **m.**,
W-pI...138.9:4 And all **m.** in judgment that the mind had
W-pI...158.7:3 a purity undimmed by errors, pitiful **m.**,
W-pI...168.5:3 acknowledge our **m.**, but He to Whom all
W-pI...168.5:3 the One Who answers our **m.** by giving us
W-pI...181.1:4 of the Self that lies beyond your own **m.**,
W-pI...181.2:7 For their **m.**, if focused on, are witnesses
W-pI...181.6:2 sight, and turn our eyes upon our own **m.**
W-pI...181.8:3 And as our focus goes beyond **m.**, we will
W-pI.184.15:5 *All our* **m.** *we give to You, that we may be*
W-pI...190.2:3 to the Son's **m.** in what he thinks he is. It
W-pI...192.5:1 mind without the body cannot make **m.**.
W-pI...194.7:8 to change his mind when he has made **m.**.
W-pI...200.5:3 made free of your **m.** and honored as he is
W-pII..223.2:1 *let us see the face of Christ instead of our* **m.**.
W-pII..228.2:4 *And my* **m.** *about myself are dreams. I let*
W-pII.......3.2:7 Now **m.** become quite possible, for
W-pII..269.1:2 *to become the way to show me my* **m.**, *and*
W-pII..293.1:3 with all my past **m.** oppressing it, and
W-pII..293.2:3 *the present holds safe from all past* **m.**. *And I*
W-pII......9.1:1 as God, is merely the correction of **m.**,
W-pII..314.1:3 Past **m.** can cast no shadows on it, so that
W-pII..314.2:2 *in Your Hands, leaving behind our past* **m.**,
W-pII..330.2:3 *to be made free forever from all our* **m.**, *and*
W-pII..359.1:6 *made* **m.** *which have no real effects on us. Sin*
M-4.... VIII.1:6 The past as well held no **m.**; nothing that
M-9............1:7 previous **m.** as possible are corrected.
M-10........5:10 Now he makes no **m.**. His Guide is sure.
M-18..........3:9 *been taken from its throne by your* **m.**. *God*
M-18..........4:1 of God to let all his own **m.** be corrected.
M-22..........4:5 all **m.** and healing all perception. Healing
M-22..........5:6 **M.** do not correct mistakes, and distorted
M-22..........5:6 Mistakes do not correct **m.**, and distorted
M-26..........2:7 and all **m.** are recognized and overlooked
M-28..........3:3 is wholly corrected and all **m.** undone.
S-2 ...........I.2:3 **m.** loom large and grow and swell within
S-2 ...........I.6:2 Others will make **m.** and so will you, as
S-2 ...........I.6:5 **M.** are tiny shadows, quickly gone, that

## mistaking 1
W-pI.....61.2:2 humility, **m.** it for self-debasement.

## misthought 2
T-2........ IV.2:5 wrongly only when it is responding to **m.**.
T-2........ VI.3:1 the outcome of **m.** can result in healing.

## mistook 4
T-24...... VI.9:5 glory in His Son, whom you **m.** as flesh,
T-28...... III.7:2 who **m.** for gold the shining of a pebble,
W-pI.136.20:3 *what I really am, for I* **m.** *my body for myself.*
W-pI...153.8:3 we **m.** the figures in it for the Son of God;

## mistrust 1
T-8....... VII.4:8 from the Holy Spirit and you will **m.** it.

## mistrustful 2
T-9....... VII.3:6 and wholly **m.** of everything it perceives
T-15.........I.3:2 For it is as **m.** of death as it is of life, and

## mists 4
T-26..... VII.8:6 and all beliefs that rise from **m.** of guilt.
T-31........ V.6:5 kept still deeper in the **m.** below the face
T-31... VIII.6:3 but disappear as **m.** before the sun. A
W-pI...192.7:4 We are lost in **m.** of shifting dreams and

## misty 2
T-28....... V.7:3 and **m.** pictures rise to cover it with vague
W-pI...162.1:5 and all things seen within its **m.** clouds

## misunderstand 2
T-2......... V.2:4 likely to **m.** any healing that might occur,
T-8....... VII.4:7 Misuse it and you will **m.** it, because you

## misunderstanding 2
T-1.........I.10:1 to induce belief is a **m.** of their purpose.
T-8....... VII.5:1 Yet all loss comes only from your own **m.**

## misunderstands 1
T-6.........I.14:2 and for the same reason that anyone **m.** it

## misunderstood 15
T-3...........I.1:3 Many sincere Christians have **m.** this. No
T-5........ VI.8:3 what former generations had **m.**, and
T-6.........I.2:3 It can be, and has been, **m.**. This is only
T-6.........I.14:2 The Apostles often **m.** it, and for the same
T-11... VIII.6:5 the answer, but you have **m.** the question.
T-20...... VI.2:7 so simple and so obvious it cannot be **m.**.
T-20...... VI.9:4 seeming powerful and so bitterly **m.** and
T-30...... IV.2:7 He **m.** what made him safe, and thought
T-31.........I.8:3 And never does a call remain unheard, **m.**
W-pI...101.6:2 pain is but the sign you have **m.** yourself.
W-pI.135.18:2 Perhaps you have **m.** His plan, for He
W-pII..265.1:1 I have indeed **m.** the world, because I laid
W-pII..359.1:2 *We have* **m.** *all things. But we have not made*
M-10 .........1:1 is maintained, is totally **m.** by the world.
S-2 ...........I.1:1 has been more **m.** than has forgiveness. It

## misuse 8
T-3........ IV.5:1 always involves some **m.** of mind, because
T-8...........I.1:6 is merely the result of your **m.** of His laws
T-8....... VII.4:7 truly. **M.** it and you will misunderstand it,
T-29.........I.6:5 must **m.** each circumstance and everyone
W-pI.....25.2:4 As a result, you are bound to **m.** it. When
W-pI.135.12:2 It must **m.** the body in its plans until it
M-24 .........1:9 **m.** offers preoccupation and perhaps
P-3......... II.9:2 there is great temptation to **m.** his role.

## misused 6
T-2......... II.4:6 was needed that it could not be **m.**,
T-8........ IX.4:6 if you have **m.** it on behalf of sickness.
T-15........II.4:1 you have **m.** your brothers by seeing them
T-22....... VI.4:3 all. Nothing entrusted to it can be **m.**, and
W-pI.....51.5:5 how much I have **m.** everything I see by
M-24 .........1:8 many other beliefs, it can be bitterly **m.**.

## misusing 5
T-7......VIII.4:9 distorted minds that are **m.** their power.
T-8....... VII.4:7 because you have already done so *by* **m.** it.
W-pI.....26.1:5 ultimately save you, but you are **m.** it now
W-pI.....90.3:2 have problems only because I am **m.** time
M-24 .........5:5 might be advised that he is **m.** the belief

## mitigate 1
T-5......... V.5:6 itself it will **m.** the punishment of God.

## mixture 1
W-pI.......4.1:6 that they represent such a **m.** that, in a

## mobilize 1
T-9......VIII.4:5 and **m.** its energies against your release. It

## mock 1
W-pII .248.1:6 and did but **m.** the truth about myself.

## mocked 4
T-1......... V.4:3 "God is not **m.**" is not a warning but a
T-1......... V.4:4 *would* be **m.** if any of His creations lacked
T-21.... VI.11:5 God is not **m.**; no more His Son can be
W-pI...134.5:5 real are pitifully **m.** and twice condemned

## mockery 5
T-16.... VI.10:1 you have escaped the **m.** of salvation the
W-pII .294.1:5 there, nor is a **m.** of love bestowed upon it
P-2........ IV.8:4 **m.** so alien to God that it must be forever
S-2 ...........I.1:2 it was meant to bless, a cruel **m.** of grace,
S-2 ..........II.6:9 All else is **m.**. For who would try to strike

## mocks 1
W-pI...191.3:1 that **m.** creation and that laughs at God.

## model 9
T-5..........II.9:6 I am your **m.** for decision. By deciding for
T-5....... II.12:3 teaches you how to keep me as the **m.** for
T-6.........in.2:1 asked to take me as your **m.** for learning,
T-6...........I.3:6 I cannot serve as a **m.** for learning.
T-6...........I.7:2 I am the **m.** for rebirth, but rebirth itself
T-6...........I.8:6 who accept me as a **m.** are literally my
T-6...........I.8:7 and if the **m.** they follow has chosen to
T-6........ IV.9:6 a **m.** to follow who will strengthen your
T-7......VIII.4:8 Never having had a consistent **m.**, it never

## modesty 1
W-pI...186.3:6 the specious grounds that **m.** is outraged.

## moment 49
T-4........ VI.6:1 you is greater than yours in me at the **m.**,
T-4........ VI.7:5 and one **m.** of real recognition makes
T-5......... V.6:3 each **m.** of decision is a judgment that is
T-5........ VI.2:9 possible **m.** and in every possible way.
T-5....... VI.12:6 you of this in every passing **m.** of time,
T-6.........in.2:3 the **m.** you accept any premise at all, and
T-6........ IV.1:4 withdraw his support from it at any **m.**. If
T-13.......X.8:6 The **m.** that you realize guilt is insane,
T-14.......X.5:2 of Heaven last but a **m.** and grow dim, as
T-30.........I.4:1 of it and have a quiet **m.** for reflection, tell
T-30....... V.9:8 What **m.** of content has not been bought

| | |
|---|---|
| T-31 I.6:6 | taught to you in every **m.** of each day, |
| W-pI 30.3:2 | Whenever you have a **m.** or so, repeat it |
| W-pI 31.3:1 | awareness, each to be considered for a **m.**, |
| W-pI 60.4:2 | **m.** in which God's Voice ceases to call on |
| W-pI 60.4:3 | There is not a **m.** in which His Voice fails |
| W-pI 67.1:6 | you, and to realize fully, if only for a **m.**, |
| W-pI 79.10:5 | close your eyes for a **m.** and ask what it is. |
| W-pI 91.9:4 | remove your faith from it, if only for a **m.**. |
| W-pI 97.6:2 | makes an uncertain **m.** and goes out. The |
| W-pI 107.2:4 | to have that **m.** be extended to the end of |
| WpIrIII.in10:4 | not give more than just a **m.** to each one. |
| W-pI 125.9:5 | be still a **m.** and remind yourself you have |
| W-pI.126.11:6 | *Him.* Then spend a quiet **m.**, opening your |
| W-pI 128.4:3 | pain; one **m.** of uncertainty and doubt. |
| W-pI 129.9:3 | take a **m.** to confirm your choice by laying |
| W-pI.131.13:3 | A tiny **m.** of surprise, perhaps, will make |
| WpI. rIV.in8:1 | day began, and spend a quiet **m.** with it. |
| W-pI.153.10:1 | Be still a **m.**, and in silence think how |
| W-pI.153.14:1 | We pause but for a **m.** more, to play our |
| W-pI.153.18:3 | you keep your mind away from Him a **m.**, |
| W-pI.153.19:6 | We will pause a **m.**, as He tells us, "I am |
| W-pI 157.3:3 | to this holy place and leaves you, for a **m.**, |
| W-pI.169.13:3 | but his who went a **m.** into timelessness, |
| W-pI 170.8:1 | This **m.** can be terrible. But it can also be |
| W-pI 219.1:4 | *Be still, my mind, and think a* **m.** *upon this.* |
| W-pII in.9:6 | **m.** more, and it will rise again. A moment |
| W-pII in.9:7 | A **m.** more, and we who are God's Sons |
| W-pII .315.1:1 | come to me with every passing **m.**. I am |
| M-in 1:6 | process; it goes on every **m.** of the day, |
| M-3 2:6 | sight of separate interests, if only for a **m.**. |
| M-3 2:7 | That **m.** will be enough. Salvation has |
| M-16 5:8 | brief period,–not more than a **m.** will do |
| M-20 4:6 | Stop for a **m.** now and think of this: Is |
| M-23 4:4 | the **m.** that the name is called to mind. |
| M-24 6:1 | **m.** that complete salvation is offered you, |
| M-24 6:1 | and it is at this **m.** that you can accept it. |
| P-3 II.5:3 | At that **m.** the good is returned to them, |
| S-3 I.2:4 | Death stares at them as every **m.** goes |

### moments 2

| | |
|---|---|
| T-4 III.2:1 | because it is useful in **m.** of temptation. It |
| T-21 IV.6:5 | Yet in your saner **m.**, its ranting strikes no |

### momentum 1

| | |
|---|---|
| T-30 I.7:3 | version of the question asks will gain **m.**, |

### money 9

| | |
|---|---|
| T-12 IV.7:3 | invest in it, not with **m.** but with spirit. |
| W-pI 50.1:3 | most trivial and insane symbols; pills, **m.**, |
| M-13 2:6 | Power, fame, **m.**, physical pleasure; who |
| P-3 III.1:4 | Should he need **m.** it will be given him, |
| P-3 III.1:5 | **M.** is not evil. It is nothing. But no one |
| P-3 III.2:1 | unhealed healer would try to heal for **m.**, |
| P-3 III.2:7 | give **m.** where God's plan allots it has no |
| P-3 III.6:6 | sent to give his brother the **m.** he needed. |
| P-3 III.6:8 | and how valueless is **m.** in comparison. |

### monster 1

| | |
|---|---|
| T-11 VIII.13:3 | into a curtain, his "**m.**" into a shadow, |

### monsters 2

| | |
|---|---|
| T-11 VIII.13:1 | frightening ghosts and **m.** and dragons, |
| T-11 VIII.14:8 | them as ghosts and **m.** and dragons. Ask |

### months 1

| | |
|---|---|
| T-28 III.7:4 | and break it into days and **m.** and years? |

### mood 4

| | |
|---|---|
| T-4 IV.2:2 | **m.** tells you that you have chosen wrongly |
| T-6 V.C.1:10 | and so the one **m.** He engenders is joy. He |
| T-14 IX.2:7 | cannot change with time or **m.** or chance. |
| W-pI 186.8:5 | as we experience a thousand shifts in **m.**, |

### moods 1

| | |
|---|---|
| T-6 V.C.1:9 | and that is why it promotes different **m.**. |

### moon 2

| | |
|---|---|
| T-21 III.11:5 | is like saying that the **m.** and sun are one |
| WpI. rIV.in4:3 | the sun, the silver of the **m.** on it by night. |

### more 752

*See also* more-than-everything

| | |
|---|---|
| T-1 I.8:1 | **m.** for those who temporarily have less. |
| T-1 I.9:3 | bring **m.** love both to the giver *and* the |
| T-1 II.2:5 | They are **m.** useful now because of their |
| T-1 II.4:2 | The statement is **m.** meaningful in terms |
| T-1 II.5:2 | I can thus bring down to them **m.** than |
| T-1 VII.5:7 | a **m.** direct approach to God Himself. It |
| T-1 VII.5:8 | the experience will be **m.** traumatic than |
| T-2 II.7:8 | and as you become **m.** and more secure |
| T-2 II.7:8 | and as you become more and **m.** secure |
| T-2 III.3:7 | As this recognition becomes **m.** firmly |
| T-2 III.5:2 | **m.** comfortable by inappropriate means. |
| T-2 V.6:1 | body does not learn any **m.** than it creates |
| T-2 V.9:6 | reflection of a much **m.** powerful love- |
| T-2 VI.6:2 | cannot ask **m.** than you are willing to do. |
| T-2 VI.7:3 | of correction becomes nothing **m.** than a |
| T-2 VII.1:7 | It is much **m.** helpful to remind you that |
| T-2 VII.7:5 | state does not imply **m.** than a potential |
| T-3 I.2:7 | says, "This hurts me **m.** than it hurts you, |
| T-3 II.2:6 | **M.** simply, it means that you never see |
| T-3 V.6:5 | prayer for forgiveness is nothing **m.** than |
| T-3 V.7:5 | without a belief in "**m.**" and "less." At |
| T-3 VI.1:2 | the Last Judgment there will be no **m.**. |
| T-3 VI.5:3 | idea of being **m.** unworthy than they are. |
| T-3 VII.2:3 | it, any **m.** than you can weaken God. The |
| T-3 VII.4:6 | but you cannot do **m.** than believe it. You |
| T-4 I.9:11 | avoid Him any **m.** than He can avoid you. |
| T-4 II.6:8 | nothing **m.** than that the ego has deluded |
| T-4 II.9:5 | **m.** "religiously" ego-oriented may believe |
| T-4 II.10:1 | is nothing **m.** than "right-mindedness," |
| T-4 III.1:9 | are no **m.** fatherless than you are. Your |
| T-4 III.7:8 | never forsake you any **m.** than God will, |
| T-4 IV.10:2 | of Christ means nothing **m.** than the end |
| T-4 IV.10:8 | if I am real, I am no **m.** real than you are. |
| T-4 VI.1:6 | The ego is nothing **m.** than a part of your |
| T-4 VI.3:1 | it will increase as you turn **m.** and more |
| T-4 VI.3:1 | you turn more and **m.** often to me instead |
| T-4 VI.3:4 | is **m.** effective than learning through pain, |
| T-4 VI.3:4 | never induce **m.** than a temporary effect. |
| T-4 VII.1:1 | is **m.** helpful in a specific context. Ego |
| T-5 I.2:3 | *The* **m.** *who believe in them the stronger* |
| T-5 I.6:6 | might even be **m.** helpful here to use the |
| T-5 II.8:12 | the basis of which call is worth **m.** to you. |
| T-5 V.1:1 | and **m.** personally meaningful if the ego's |
| T-5 V.2:9 | Guilt is **m.** than merely not of God. It is |
| T-5 V.6:1 | the laws of God any **m.** than you can, but |
| T-6 I.2:1 | crucifixion is nothing **m.** than an extreme |
| T-6 IV.2:9 | never done **m.** than obscure the question, |
| T-6 IV.5:3 | that the body is **m.** real than the mind is. |
| T-6 V.1:1 | Holy Spirit knows **m.** than you do now, |
| T-6 V.2:1 | wake children in a **m.** kindly way than by |
| T-6 V.4:2 | His dependability makes them **m.** certain. |
| T-6 V.A.4:8 | Nothing **m.** and nothing less. Without a |
| T-6 V.B.8:2 | however, **m.** advanced than the first step, |
| T-6 V.B.8:4 | and one has been chosen as **m.** desirable. |
| T-6 V.B.8:5 | the term "**m.** desirable" still implies that |
| T-6 V.C.3:3 | the identification of what is **m.** desirable. |
| T-7 III.1:10 | not make this power, any **m.** than I did. It |
| T-7 V.1:1 | body is nothing **m.** than a framework for |
| T-7 VIII.6:3 | The **m.** you learn about the ego, the more |
| T-7 VIII.6:3 | **m.** you realize that it cannot be believed. |
| T-7 IX.1:2 | He no **m.** wills you to deprive yourself of |
| T-7 IX.3:2 | any **m.** than can the fullness of its Creator |
| T-7 IX.3:7 | can no **m.** interfere with their reality than |
| T-7 X.3:4 | You no **m.** recognize what is painful than |
| T-7 XI.3:7 | it, any **m.** than you can make yourself. It |
| T-7 XI.7:4 | any **m.** than you can establish God's. But |
| T-8 II.2:6 | ego has done **m.** harm to your learning |
| T-8 II.6:4 | you could no **m.** will to be without Him |
| T-8 III.7:10 | to produce is no **m.** true than they are. |
| T-8 IV.2:12 | you cannot abide in darkness any **m.** than |
| T-8 VI.5:4 | do not leave you any **m.** than you left your |
| T-8 VII.13:4 | therefore nothing **m.** than united purpose |
| T-8 VII.15:6 | true. No **m.** are any of its seeming results. |
| T-8 VIII.4:4 | **m.** honest statement would be that those |
| T-8 VIII.6:9 | The **m.** complicated the results become |
| T-8 IX.4:7 | Sleep is no **m.** a form of death than death |
| T-8 IX.5:3 | of sickness is **m.** serious than another, He |
| T-8 IX.5:3 | that one error can be **m.** real than another |
| T-9 I.7:9 | separation is nothing **m.** than the belief |
| T-9 II.2:5 | thought system might be considerably **m.** |
| T-9 II.6:1 | You can no **m.** pray for yourself alone |
| T-9 III.4:5 | is **m.** than merely a lack of correction for |
| T-9 III.7:1 | not of him, any **m.** than yours are of you. |
| T-9 III.7:6 | Atonement is no **m.** separate than love. |
| T-9 IV.7:3 | are. This is **m.** than mere confusion. It is a |
| T-9 IV.10:6 | no **m.** have been wrong than God can. |
| T-9 IV.11:5 | no **m.** meaning than the fantasies into |
| T-9 V.1:1 | is far **m.** widely used than God's. This is |
| T-9 V.1:3 | the unhealed healer **m.** carefully now. By |
| T-9 V.1:6 | he is **m.** likely to start with the equally |
| T-9 V.9:3 | results are **m.** convincing than its words. |
| T-9 VI.3:6 | Only God Himself is **m.** than they but |
| T-9 VI.4:1 | is **m.** than you only because He created |
| T-10 II.1:2 | dissociation is nothing **m.** than a decision |
| T-10 II.2:1 | reality brings **m.** than merely lack of fear. |
| T-10 III.1:7 | destruction is no **m.** real than the image, |
| T-10 V.5:5 | any **m.** than He could have created a Son |
| T-11 in.2:4 | is nothing **m.** than a delusional system in |
| T-11 in.3:4 | The **m.** you approach the center of His |
| T-11 in.3:5 | darker and **m.** obscure becomes the way. |
| T-11 II.2:1 | **m.** you practice it the better teacher and |
| T-11 II.5:9 | God. Yet you need far **m.** than patience. |
| T-11 III.3:4 | joy could no **m.** be contained than His. |
| T-11 V.1:3 | We are ready to look **m.** closely at the |
| T-11 V.4:3 | Fear becomes **m.** obviously inappropriate |
| T-11 V.7:4 | goal. It is much **m.** vigilant than you are, |
| T-11 VIII.5:4 | Nothing could be **m.** specific than to be |
| T-12 I.8:1 | of others **m.** and more consistently, you |
| T-12 I.8:1 | of others more and **m.** consistently, you |
| T-12 V.2:6 | invulnerability has **m.** than negative value |
| T-12 VI.1:7 | perceive something else as **m.** valuable. |
| T-12 VI.6:5 | perceive **m.** and more common elements |
| T-12 VI.6:5 | and **m.** common elements in all situations |
| T-12 VII.1:2 | as you use it in **m.** and more situations. |
| T-12 VII.1:2 | as you use it in more and **m.** situations. |
| T-12 VII.11:5 | Yet as I become **m.** real to you, you will |
| T-12 VIII.3:4 | Yet it is no **m.** up to you to decide what is |
| T-12 VIII.4:8 | It is no **m.** past than future, being forever |
| T-13 in.2:10 | and are laid in the ground, and are no **m.**. |
| T-13 II.7:4 | You often dismiss it **m.** readily than you |
| T-13 III.1:3 | is one **m.** obstacle you have interposed |
| T-13 III.1:8 | you are **m.** afraid of what it covers. You |
| T-13 III.1:9 | yourself something you fear even **m.**. You |
| T-13 III.5:3 | death seems **m.** valuable than your living |
| T-13 III.5:4 | You are **m.** afraid of God than of the ego, |
| T-13 III.10:6 | but still **m.** did he fear his real Father, |
| T-13 IV.3:1 | it not be **m.** desirable to have been wrong, |
| T-13 IV.3:6 | might it not be **m.** desirable than death? |
| T-13 IV.3:8 | An open mind is **m.** honest than this. |
| T-13 IV.6:3 | in retaliation for a past that is no **m.**. And |
| T-13 V.9:8 | And there perception is no **m.**, for He has |
| T-13 V.11:3 | alone, for He is no **m.** alone than they are. |
| T-13 VI.6:5 | time was, and will be when time is no **m.**. |
| T-13 X.14:3 | into kindness will never **m.** be what it was |
| T-14 II.4:4 | made, they see in you **m.** than you see. |
| T-14 IV.2:1 | part of Him, are **m.** than merely guiltless. |
| T-14 IV.6:7 | tired will find this is **m.** restful than sleep. |
| T-14 VII.2:8 | the **m.** you look at fear the less you see it, |
| T-14 X.3:4 | What is **m.** difficult to grasp is the lack of |
| T-14 X.4:3 | some of your thoughts as **m.** important, |
| T-14 X.4:3 | **m.** productive and valuable than others. |
| T-14 X.5:5 | and that **m.** than an ego must be in you. |
| T-14 X.6:6 | call is louder or greater or **m.** important. |
| T-14 X.9:6 | or **m.** join together in searching for truth, |
| T-14 X.11:6 | love. Neither his mind nor yours holds **m.** |
| T-14 XI.1:5 | your power **m.** and more obscure to you. |
| T-14 XI.1:5 | your power more and **m.** obscure to you. |

T-14....XI.3:10 it is nothing **m.** than a condition in which
T-15.........I.1:2 is for; to learn just that and nothing **m.**.
T-15.........I.5:5 even there, its only value is that it is no **m.**
T-15.........I.6:3 hidden a far **m.** insidious threat to peace.
T-15...... I.10:2 Learn from this instant **m.** than merely
T-15...... I.11:3 He asks no **m.**, for He has no need of
T-15...... I.11:3 asks no more, for He has no need of **m.**. It
T-15........ II.1:4 No **m.** are you. For unless God is bound,
T-15........ II.4:3 are far stronger and much **m.** compelling
T-15..... II.4:14 Spirit. And then you will doubt no **m.**.
T-15...... III.9:2 not for yourself alone, no **m.** than I did. It
T-15.... III.10:5 and I can no **m.** accept it as what it is not,
T-15.... III.10:6 can. And no **m.** can you. When you have
T-15.... III.10:7 will make no **m.** gifts to offer to yourself,
T-15...... IV.6:2 and is nothing **m.** than the ego's attempt
T-15....... V.3:5 the Sonship can give you **m.** than others?
T-15....... V.6:3 less value on one and **m.** on the other.
T-15..... V.10:5 as He loves you; neither less nor **m.**. He
T-15...... VI.4:3 you are **m.** inclined to regard his success
T-15..... VII.4:6 the **m.** anger you invest outside yourself,
T-15..... VII.5:3 let us look **m.** closely at the relationships
T-15... VII.10:3 All anger is nothing **m.** than an attempt
T-15... VIII.3:6 nothing **m.** than a mistake in who you are
T-15...... IX.2:4 are nothing **m.** than attempts to limit
T-15...... XI.1:6 choice between them is nothing **m.** than a
T-15...... XI.1:6 to daylight when you have no **m.** need of
T-15...... XI.8:3 What can be **m.** joyous than to perceive
T-16....... II.1:7 itself? One attribute is no **m.** difficult to
T-16....... II.2:4 A better and far **m.** helpful way to think
T-16...... III.5:4 the separation added **m.** to you than you
T-16...... IV.7:2 nothing **m.** than an attempt to bring love
T-16.... IV.12:1 Your Father can no **m.** forget the truth in
T-16....... V.8:1 ego seeks is always one that is **m.** special.
T-16....... V.8:5 illusion of Heaven is nothing **m.** than an
T-16..... V.13:1 the special relationship nothing **m.** than a
T-16..... V.14:4 decision as just what it is, and nothing **m.**
T-16...... VI.3:4 the **m.** apparent it becomes that it must
T-16...... VI.5:5 Far **m.** is left outside than would be taken
T-16...... VI.7:1 The bridge itself is nothing **m.** than a
T-16...... VI.8:6 Delay will hurt you now **m.** than before,
T-17...... III.3:5 The shadow figures enter **m.** and more,
T-17...... III.3:5 The shadow figures enter more and **m.**,
T-17...... III.6:4 is the separation **m.** and more undone,
T-17...... III.6:4 is the separation more and **m.** undone,
T-17...... III.6:9 so you can see it **m.** and more. For you
T-17...... III.6:9 so you can see it more and **m.**. For you
T-17.... III.6:10 For you will want it **m.** and more, and
T-17.... III.6:10 For you will want it more and **m.**, and
T-17...... III.9:3 choice depends on which you value **m.**.
T-17...... IV.6:4 that you have been **m.** willing to let go.
T-17.... IV.14:3 grows **m.** convincing as you look at it.
T-17.... IV.14:7 you thought was real, and nothing **m.**.
T-17....... V.5:1 not be kinder to shift the goal **m.** slowly,
T-17....... V.9:4 road far **m.** familiar than you now believe.
T-17...... VI.1:7 can **m.** safely look beyond each situation,
T-17... VIII.1:1 instant is nothing **m.** than a special case,
T-18.........I.1:4 one is judged **m.** valuable and the other is
T-18.........I.3:5 far **m.** serious effect lies in the fragmented
T-18..... II.5:20 while you see **m.** value in sleeping than in
T-18...... IV.1:5 It is not necessary that you do **m.**; indeed,
T-18...... IV.1:5 that you realize that you cannot do **m.**.
T-18...... IV.5:6 only to those who offer it nothing **m.** than
T-18...... IV.6:2 Add **m.**, and you will merely take away
T-18...... IV.7:2 insist there must be **m.** that you need do.
T-18..... VII.2:3 to let this happen for **m.** than an instant,
T-18..... VII.4:5 to teach **m.** than they learned in time, but
T-18..... VII.5:6 It would be far **m.** profitable now merely
T-18..... VII.6:8 and you will accomplish **m.** than is given
T-18..... VII.8:2 will be **m.** aware of this quiet center of the
T-18. VIII.11:4 it offers everyone, neither less nor **m.**.
T-18. VIII.12:4 You could no **m.** know God alone than
T-18. VIII.12:5 But together you could no **m.** be unaware
T-18...... IX.8:1 of guilt, no **m.** impenetrable and no more
T-18...... IX.8:1 more impenetrable and no **m.** substantial
T-19....... II.7:1 that is **m.** heavily defended than the idea
T-19....... II.8:1 that all this be nothing **m.** than a mistake,
T19... IV.A.4:3 Peace could no **m.** depart from you than
T19... IV.A.5:1 overcome the world is no **m.** difficult than
T19... IV.A.6:7 No **m.** can you be kept by shadows from
T19... IV.A.7:4 causing no **m.** than tiny interruptions in
T19... IV.A.8:3 **m.** erratic and unpredictable than before.
T19... IV.A.8:4 be **m.** unstable than a tightly organized
T19. IV.A.15:1 but theirs, you will see fear no **m.**. The
T19.... IV.B.4:3 obstacle is no **m.** solid than the first. For
T19.... IV.B.7:9 when its great advocate is heard no **m.**?
T19.. IV.B.15:2 you suffer, yet someone else will suffer **m.**
T19.... IV.C.1:3 learn still **m.** about this strange devotion,
T19.... IV.C.5:2 The body no **m.** dies than it can feel. It
T19... IV.D.4:4 are no **m.** afraid of death than of the ego.
T-20..... IV.2:1 and can no **m.** enter than can their source
T-20..... IV.7:6 no **m.** leave one of them outside than I
T-20..... IV.8:12 what can be **m.** certain than a Son of God
T-20....... V.6:4 from it, and the future will add no **m.**.
T-20....... V.7:8 No **m.** do you. And yet, have faith that He
T-20...... VI.8:5 not. No **m.** than that. The instant that the
T-20.... VI.11:5 And here he is **m.** dead than living. Yet it
T-20..... VII.1:4 or parts you find **m.** difficult than others,
T-20..... VII.1:8 one that asks so little, or could offer **m.**.
T-20..... VII.3:2 He asks no **m.** to give the means as well.
T-20... VIII.4:5 What can you value **m.** than this? Why do
T-21........in.1:2 is what you gave it, nothing **m.** than that.
T-21........in.1:3 But though it is no **m.** than that, it is not
T-21.........I.3:7 vision gives you **m.** than judgment does,
T-21.........I.7:5 you knew so long ago and held **m.** dear
T-21...... III.1:4 of yourself, perhaps **m.** often of the other.
T-21...... III.9:5 The gift that He has given you is **m.** than
T-21.... III.10:4 And no **m.** could the body. The intention
T-21...... IV.4:6 of. No **m.** did you. And yet this part, with
T-21....... V.1:5 For what you look for you are far **m.** likely
T-21....... V.1:8 far **m.** than you may realize as yet. For on
T-21....... V.2:5 control, and far **m.** powerful than you.
T-21....... V.7:4 yes, you know this, and **m.** than this alone
T-21...... VI.6:7 with what you hold **m.** dear than truth?
T-21...... VI.9:8 To give is no **m.** blessed than to receive.
T-21.... VI.11:5 no **m.** His Son can be imprisoned save by
T-21... VIII.1:5 valued the inconstant **m.** than constancy.
T-22.........I.7:2 and yet **m.** ancient than the old illusion it
T-22....... II.5:6 for its attainment are **m.** than possible.
T-22....... II.8:8 You are no **m.** a slave to time than to the
T-22...... IV.1:8 of the journey that seems **m.** hopeless and
T-22...... IV.6:4 opens the way to truth to **m.** than you.
T-22.... VI.10:6 countless attackers **m.** powerful than you.
T-22.... VI.13:9 this seems **m.** natural and more in line
T-22.... VI.13:9 and **m.** in line with your experience. And
T-22.. VI.13:10 other experiences, **m.** in line with truth,
T-22.... VI.14:8 extends its being and creates **m.** of itself.
T-23.......in.6:6 it! What can you value **m.** than this? For
T-23.........I.2:9 but never will it be **m.** than madness. And
T-23.........I.4:7 proclaiming it is part of itself no **m.**.
T-23.........I.9:2 the conqueror to be the truer, the **m.** real,
T-23....... II.2:3 some are **m.** valuable and therefore true.
T-23....... II.3:6 No part of nothing can be **m.** resistant to
T-23....... II.6:1 not be **m.** apparent than emerges here.
T-23...... IV.4:5 raised above the battleground, in it no **m.**
T-23...... IV.9:7 that offers less, yet could be wanted **m.**?
T-24.....in.1:10 No **m.** His Son. They *are.* And what
T-24.........I.2:6 to violence far **m.** inclusive than you think
T-24.........I.4:7 for nothing in the world they value **m.**.
T-24....... II.7:2 any **m.** than you can change the truth in
T-24....... II.9:2 Just one step **m.**, and every vestige of the
T-24...... IV.3:8 Nothing could make **m.** sense to miracles.
T-24....... V.7:3 ears may hear no **m.** the sound of battle
T-24...... VI.7:3 by still one **m.** denial of Christ in him.
T-24.... VI.12:2 the two, it is this one you find **m.** difficult.
T-25.......in.1:7 No **m.** can you. Christ is within a frame of
T-25....... II.8:2 on him, and you will see the dark no **m.**.
T-25...... III.1:6 to this world, of God's **m.** basic law; that
T-25...... III.6:2 Nor need he stay **m.** than an instant. For
T-25...... III.6:7 can, with equal ease and far **m.** happiness
T-25...... VI.1:4 He would no **m.** condemn himself for his
T-25...... VI.2:4 and **m.** obscure seems easier to look upon
T-25...... VI.3:6 Let him no **m.** be lonely, for the lonely
T-25...... VI.5:7 it. Then is time no **m.**. Yet while in time,
T-25...... VI.6:1 Salvation is no **m.** than a reminder this
T-25..... VII.3:1 said before, and think of it **m.** carefully. It
T-25..... VII.9:2 as possible, and **m.** and more desired, as
T-25..... VII.9:2 as possible, and more and **m.** desired, as
T-25..... VII.9:6 He can no **m.** be left outside, without a
T-25... VII.11:4 belief except a form of the **m.** basic tenet,
T-25.... VIII.1:8 can lose for you to gain. And nothing **m.**.
T-25.... VIII.6:8 to be **m.** destructive to themselves and to
T-25.... VIII.9:4 No **m.** than what you see He offers you,
T-25.. VIII.11:3 Simple justice asks no **m.**. Of each one
T-25.. VIII.13:7 Who would have **m.** or less is not aware
T-25...... IX.3:3 it greater, harder to resolve and **m.** unfair.
T-25...... IX.6:4 deserves to suffer **m.** and others less? And
T-25...... IX.6:7 others as less worthy, **m.** condemned,
T-25...... IX.7:1 Son be **m.** unfair than he has sought to be
T-26.........I.7:2 and can no **m.** be sacrificed by you than
T-26........II.2:4 One mistake is not **m.** difficult for Him to
T-26........II.4:4 injustices as great or small, or **m.** or less.
T-26........II.7:4 worth no **m.** than just a tiny sigh before
T-26...... IV.1:7 until he sees himself as needing it no **m.**.
T-26...... IV.4:3 and none is cherished **m.** than any other.
T-26....... V.6:3 Madness speaks no **m.**. There *is* no other
T-26...... V.12:5 it was no **m.** to be experienced as there.
T-26..... VII.6:4 it appears some are **m.** true than others,
T-26.... VIII.1:5 is, the **m.** you think of it in terms of space.
T-26.... VIII.4:2 No **m.** can it be overlooked except within
T-26...... IX.7:4 Son give less in gratitude for so much **m.**?
T-26........X.3:7 What could be **m.** unjust than that he be
T-27........II.8:7 and he will consent no **m.** to suffer. For
T-27......II.11:4 different from you in that he is **m.** guilty,
T-27......II.11:4 as the one **m.** innocent than he. This
T-27...... III.4:6 for what can stand for **m.** than everything
T-27....... V.4:2 And nothing **m.** than just one instant of
T-27....... V.8:3 did, it would be there no **m.** for him to see
T-27...... V.10:4 each one of them there are a thousand **m.**.
T-27...... VI.2:4 These witnesses are joined by many **m.**.
T-27...... VI.2:8 behind the pleasure will be felt no **m.**.
T-27...... VI.3:6 This name or that, but nothing **m.**, you
T-27...... VI.7:2 sin. There is no need to suffer any **m.**. But
T-27...... VI.8:3 And no one will elect to suffer **m.**. What
T-27... VII.13:3 Nothing **m.** fearful than an idle dream
T-27.... VIII.2:4 may protect it and collect **m.** senseless
T-27.... VIII.3:4 again, and still again, and yet once **m.**;
T-27.... VIII.4:5 as they are they have no **m.** effects on him
T-28.........I.2:1 All the effects of guilt are here no **m.**. For
T-28.......I.10:6 No **m.** have you. And so your innocence
T-28....... III.9:2 For here, the **m.** that anyone receives, the
T-28....... III.9:2 the **m.** is left for all the rest to share. The
T-28..... VII.7:7 and neither less nor **m.** in worth than the
T-29.........I.6:3 and when to shrink **m.** safely into fear. It
T-29.........I.8:5 learn their savior is their enemy no **m.**.
T-29.........I.9:2 Nothing **m.** than that, and nothing less.
T-29........II.3:7 No **m.** is pain your friend and guilt your
T-29........II.8:3 it be **m.** than this lies the idea of sickness.
T-29........II.8:7 in His sacrifice are you made **m.** and He is
T-29........II.9:5 lie in that it is not **m.** than it should be,
T-29......II.10:7 cannot be **m.** or less than what is his.
T-29...... III.3:1 of death is yet one theme of truth; no **m.**,
T-29...... IV.4:6 Dreams are not wanted **m.** or less. They
T-29...... VI.2:8 night and day will be no **m.**. All things
T-29..... VII.2:3 seeks for something **m.** than everything,
T-29..... VII.3:1 to seek beyond them for a thousand **m.**.
T-29.... VIII.1:6 that you would value **m.** than what he is.
T-29.... VIII.3:9 No **m.** a veil can banish what it seems to
T-29.... VIII.8:6 will give him **m.** than other men possess.
T-29.... VIII.8:7 It must be **m.**. It does not really matter
T-29.... VIII.8:8 It does not really matter **m.** of what; more
T-29.... VIII.8:8 not really matter more of what; **m.** beauty
T-29.... VIII.8:8 of what; more beauty, **m.** intelligence,
T-29.... VIII.8:8 beauty, more intelligence, **m.** wealth, or
T-29.... VIII.8:8 or even **m.** affliction and more pain. But
T-29.... VIII.8:8 or even more affliction and **m.** pain. But
T-29.... VIII.8:9 But **m.** of something is an idol for. And
T-29.. VIII.8:10 with hope of finding **m.** of something else
T-29.. VIII.8:12 An idol is a means for getting **m.**. And it
T-29.... VIII.9:2 Who can have **m.**, and who be given less?
T-29.... VIII.9:5 For **m.** than Heaven can you never have.
T-29.... VIII.9:6 to give you **m.** than God bestowed upon
T-29.. VIII.9:10 No idol can establish you as **m.** than God.
T-29...... IX.6:3 all away, for you have need of them no **m.**
T-30.......in.1:6 **m.** ideas than rules of thought to you as
T-30.........I.9:4 you go ahead with just a few **m.** steps you
T-30.....II.1:12 asks no **m.** than that He hear you call Him
T-30...... III.5:4 For **m.** than whole is meaningless. If there

T-30.... III.11:6 Nor can you be aware of **m.** than one. An
T-30...... IV.7:5 and seek no **m.** to substitute the strength
T-30...... IV.8:3 No **m.** than this is asked. Be glad indeed
T-30....... V.2:8 share, if hope be **m.** than just a dream.
T-30...... VI.4:9 you can merit neither **m.** nor less than he.
T-30...... VI.5:6 be an error that is **m.** than a mistake; a
T-30....VIII.3:4 Temptation, then, is nothing **m.** than this
T-31.........I.4:2 Yet you have learned **m.** than this. You
T-31.........I.5:2 a will apart from it was yet **m.** real than it.
T-31....... II.8:7 No **m.** than this will you be asked to learn
T-31...... IV.8:3 This course attempts to teach no **m.** than
T-31.... IV.10:2 He could no **m.** depart from them than
T-31..... V.14:3 Salvation can be seen as nothing **m.** than
T-31..... V.15:9 Nothing **m.** than this. And in your
T-31..... V.17:6 the world is **m.** afraid to hear than this: *I*
T-31...... VI.1:8 see the world of flesh no **m.** except to heal
T-31..... VII.3:1 it is thus you see him **m.** than just a body,
T-31..... VII.3:3 and will at length be seen as little **m.** than
T-31..... VII.5:4 No **m.** than this is asked. On its behalf,
T-31... VII.14:4 *This* is temptation; nothing **m.** than this.
W-in.......... 2:6 Do not undertake to do **m.** than one set of
W-in.......... 9:5 them. Nothing **m.** than that is required.
W-pI....... 1.4:1 not be done **m.** than twice a day each,
W-pI....... 1.4:2 be attempted for **m.** than a minute or so,
W-pI....... 4.5:2 but is not a substitute for the **m.** random
W-pI....... 4.5:3 examine your mind for **m.** than a minute
W-pI....... 4.6:2 Do not repeat these exercises **m.** than
W-pI....... 5.4:1 exercises, **m.** than in the preceding ones,
W-pI....... 5.7:1 your mind for no **m.** than a minute or so,
W-pI....... 6.3:1 upsetting thoughts **m.** than to others,
W-pI....... 9.2:4 it. No **m.** than that is required for these or
W-pI..... 10.5:2 each involving no **m.** than a minute or so
W-pI..... 11.3:5 repeat the idea once **m.** slowly to yourself.
W-pI..... 11.4:2 no uneasiness and an inclination to do **m.**
W-pI..... 11.4:3 **M.** than this is not recommended.
W-pI..... 13.1:1 it is **m.** specific as to the emotion aroused.
W-pI..... 13.4:1 about three or four times for not **m.** than
W-pI..... 14.2:3 have **m.** than three practice periods with
W-pI..... 15.5:3 Do not have **m.** than three application
W-pI..... 16.2:1 There is no **m.** self-contradictory concept
W-pI..... 18.3:3 by repeating the **m.** general statement: *I*
W-pI..... 19.5:2 if necessary. Do not attempt **m.** than four.
W-pI..... 21.3:3 to dwell **m.** on some situations or persons
W-pI..... 21.3:3 grounds that they are **m.** "obvious." This
W-pI..... 21.3:5 of attack are **m.** justified than others.
W-pI..... 23.3:4 hallucination a **m.** appropriate term for
W-pI..... 24.3:1 for today require much **m.** honesty than
W-pI..... 24.3:2 will be **m.** helpful than a more cursory
W-pI..... 24.3:2 will be more helpful than a **m.** cursory
W-pI..... 25.4:1 for today, one **m.** thought is necessary. At
W-pI..... 26.8:1 situation you use, and quite possibly **m.**.
W-pI..... 26.8:2 much **m.** helpful to cover a few situations
W-pI..... 26.9:3 repeating today's idea to yourself once **m.**
W-pI..... 27.3:2 at least every half hour, and **m.** if possible
W-pI..... 28.4:5 as to anything else, neither **m.** nor less.
W-pI..... 30.5:3 in helping you to become **m.** accustomed
W-pI..... 31.1:3 practice which will be used **m.** and more,
W-pI..... 31.1:3 practice which will be used more and **m.**,
W-pI..... 31.1:4 you apply the idea on a **m.** sustained basis
W-pI..... 32.4:2 **M.** than five can be utilized, if you find
W-pI..... 34.6:1 form of **m.** generalized adverse emotions,
W-pI..... 34.6:2 find you need **m.** than one application of
W-pI..... 35.5:1 you consider to be the **m.** negative aspects
W-pI..... 35.5:2 **m.** self-inflating descriptive terms may
W-pI..... 36.4:1 and conclude with one **m.** repetition with
W-pI..... 38.6:2 the **m.** specific form in applying the idea
W-pI..... 39.5:1 longer and **m.** frequent practice sessions
W-pI..... 39.5:2 requirements, **m.** rather than longer
W-pI..... 39.9:4 mind becomes **m.** disciplined and less
W-pI... 39.10:4 the idea in its original form once **m.**, and
W-pI... 39.11:1 or four times an hour and **m.** if possible,
W-pI..... 40.2:1 will probably find it **m.** helpful if you do.
W-pI..... 41.8:6 We will go into **m.** detail about this kind
W-pI..... 42.5:5 once **m.** while looking slowly about; close
W-pI..... 42.5:5 close your eyes, repeat the idea once **m.**,
W-pI..... 42.8:1 The **m.** often you repeat the idea during
W-pI..... 42.8:1 **m.** often you will be reminding yourself
W-pI..... 43.5:8 Any thought related **m.** or less directly to
W-pI..... 44.7:1 repeating the idea several times **m.**. Then
W-pI..... 44.9:2 it **m.** reassuring to open your eyes briefly.
W-pI..... 46.7:2 make **m.** specific applications if they are
W-pI..... 47.4:2 longer and **m.** frequent ones are urged.
W-pI..... 49.3:1 practice periods today, and **m.** if possible.
WpI... rI.in.2:3 two minutes or **m.** to each practice period
WpI... rI.in.2:5 ideas appeals to you **m.** than the others,
WpI... rI.in.2:6 be sure to review all of them once **m.**.
W-pI..... 65.3:1 for a **m.** sustained practice period, in
W-pI..... 65.7:1 Finally, repeat the idea for today once **m.**,
W-pI..... 66.1:3 **m.** than just a connection between them;
W-pI... 66.11:3 It will not take **m.** than a minute, and
W-pI..... 67.5:3 five times an hour, and perhaps even **m.**,
W-pI..... 69.2:2 this in our **m.** extended practice period,
W-pI..... 70.1:1 All temptation is nothing **m.** than some
W-pI..... 71.4:3 For what could **m.** surely guarantee that
W-pI..... 72.4:3 You are doing **m.** than failing to help in
W-pI..... 73.4:1 Today we will try once **m.** to reach the
W-pI..... 76.8:7 no **m.** strange than other "laws" you hold
W-pI... 76.10:3 He will tell you **m.**. About the Love your
W-pI..... 77.3:4 no **m.** than what belongs to us in truth.
W-pI..... 78.5:4 enemy is **m.** than friend when he is freed
WpI..rII.in.6:1 and **m.** specific forms when needed. Some
W-pI..... 83.2:1 **M.** specific applications of this idea
W-pI..... 85.4:1 are suitable for **m.** specific applications:
W-pI..... 86.1:6 I will undertake no **m.** idle seeking. Only
W-pI..... 91.7:4 else, something **m.** solid and more sure;
W-pI..... 91.7:4 else, something more solid and **m.** sure;
W-pI..... 91.7:4 and more sure; **m.** worthy of your faith,
W-pI..... 91.9:5 with the **m.** worthy in you as we go along.
W-pI..... 92.2:4 is no **m.** foolish than to believe the body's
W-pI..... 93.5:5 It is unreal, and nothing **m.** than that. It
W-pI..... 96.6:1 Waste no **m.** time on this. Who can
W-pI..... 97.3:2 a thousand years or **m.** are saved. The
W-pI..... 97.6:1 a thousandfold and tens of thousands **m.**.
W-pI... 98.11:1 once **m.** to spend a little time with you, be
W-pI... 98.11:2 Tell Him once **m.** that you accept the part
W-pI... 101.3:3 of death to victims who are little **m.** than
W-pI... 105.2:2 are but a bid for a **m.** valuable return; a
W-pI... 105.2:2 a pledge of debt to be repaid with **m.** than
W-pI... 105.4:4 already, not in simple terms of adding **m.**,
W-pI... 105.5:5 No **m.** can you. Receive His gift of joy and
W-pI... 105.9:1 worthless when you cannot give Him **m.**.
W-pI... 106.9:3 you will again release a thousand **m.** who
W-pI... 107.2:5 then be multiplied another hundred **m.**.
W-pI... 107.3:1 not **m.** than just the faintest intimation of
W-pI. 108.10:3 still faster and **m.** sure each time you say,
W-pI... 109.5:7 No **m.** fearful dreams will come, now that
WpI..rIII.in4:2 if it interferes with goals you hold **m.** dear
WpIrIII.in10:4 give **m.** than just a moment to each one.
WpIrIII.in12:3 great we will continue on **m.** solid ground
W-pI... 121.3:1 of every sound, yet **m.** afraid of stillness;
W-pI... 121.3:1 yet **m.** terrified at the approach of light.
W-pI... 121.5:1 which can offer anything but **m.** despair.
W-pI. 121.12:3 him now as **m.** than friend to you, for in
W-pI... 122.2:1 All this forgiveness offers you, and **m.**. It
W-pI... 122.2:5 All this forgiveness offers you, and **m.**.
W-pI... 122.3:5 can hold **m.** hope than what forgiveness
W-pI... 122.4:4 Seek for it no **m.**. You will not find
W-pI... 122.9:2 made, but where we would remain no **m.**.
W-pI... 123.6:3 thousand **m.** than they were given. He
W-pI... 123.7:3 to save the world eons **m.** quickly for your
W-pI... 126.4:5 the gift is no **m.** yours than was his sin.
W-pI... 128.2:4 Be you deceived no **m.**. The world you see
W-pI... 129.1:3 exchanging it for what is far **m.** satisfying,
W-pI... 129.2:1 once **m.** about the value of this world.
W-pI... 129.7:1 and at night, and once **m.** in between.
W-pI... 130.5:5 between, and nothing **m.** than these.
W-pI... 130.6:3 learn today is **m.** than just the lesson that
W-pI. 132.14:3 No **m.** can we. For we are in the home our
W-pI... 133.3:2 all, for they can but replace what offers **m.**
W-pI... 133.3:3 no **m.** than you can make alternatives
W-pI... 133.7:5 Yet loss must offer loss, and nothing **m.**.
W-pI. 133.12:5 It is far **m.** than merely letting you make
W-pI. 134.14:1 that the time of joining be no **m.** delayed.
W-pI... 135.3:5 armor thicker and your locks **m.** tight,
W-pI... 136.7:4 and threaten your establishments no **m.**.
W-pI... 136.9:2 body is **m.** powerful than everlasting life,
W-pI... 136.9:2 everlasting life, Heaven **m.** frail than hell,
W-pI. 136.17:5 Its usefulness remains and nothing **m.**.
W-pI .. 137.6:2 For anti-Christ becomes **m.** powerful than
W-pI .. 137.6:3 The body seems to be **m.** solid and more
W-pI .. 137.6:3 more solid and **m.** stable than the mind.
W-pI .. 137,8:4 are **m.** potent than their sickly opposites.
W-pI .. 139.9:4 **m.** than just our happiness alone we came
W-pI 140.11:1 five minutes **m.** before we go to sleep. Our
WpI..rIV.in4:3 No **m.** than can a child who throws a stick
WpI..rIV.in9:2 no **m.** than this to give us happiness and
W-pI .. 151.3:7 and think **m.** real than what is witnessed
W-pI 151.15:1 another fifteen **m.** before you go to sleep.
W-pI .. 152.7:5 And what could be **m.** arrogant than this?
W-pI .. 153.5:5 only of defense by still **m.** fantasies, and
W-pI 153.10:5 And who could be **m.** mightily protected?
W-pI 153.14:1 We pause but for a moment **m.**, to play
W-pI 154.12:3 miracles and then receive a thousand **m.**,
W-pI .. 155.1:2 though you smile **m.** frequently. Your
W-pI .. 155.8:1 Such is salvation's call, and nothing **m.**.
W-pI 155.12:3 be holier, or **m.** deserving of your effort,
W-pI 155.12:4 way could give you **m.** than everything, or
W-pI .. 156.3:3 no **m.** be sinful than the sun could choose
W-pI .. 157.3:3 brings you **m.** swiftly to this holy place
W-pI .. 157.7:1 of time; a little **m.** like Heaven in its ways;
W-pI .. 157.7:2 it light will come to see the light **m.** sure;
W-pI .. 157.7:2 the light more sure; the vision **m.** distinct.
W-pI .. 158.9:5 them. They are no **m.**. And all effects they
W-pI .. 160.3:3 were another home **m.** suited to his tastes
W-pI .. 160.5:3 so I leave my home to one **m.** like me than
W-pI .. 162.1:3 It will mean far **m.** to you as you advance.
W-pI .. 162.6:4 dispel the night, and darkness is no **m.**.
W-pI .. 164.1:6 of Heaven, and the Voice for God **m.** clear
W-pI .. 164.1:6 Voice for God more clear, **m.** meaningful,
W-pI .. 164.1:6 more clear, more meaningful, **m.** near.
W-pI .. 164.2:3 increasingly is **m.** and more distinct; an
W-pI .. 164.2:3 increasingly is more and **m.** distinct; an
W-pI 166.10:7 you have need no **m.** of anything but this.
W-pI 166.12:1 reminds you still of one thing **m.** you had
W-pI 167.12:4 And now it is no **m.** a mere reflection. It
W-pI .. 168.3:5 His gift of grace is **m.** than just an answer.
W-pI 169.15:2 **m.** than what we ask this day of Him Who
W-pI .. 170.1:5 **m.** secure from dangerous invasion and
W-pI .. 170.2:4 which can save you **m.** delay and needless
W-pI 170.10:4 becomes **m.** fearful than the Heart of Love
WpI...rV.in1:2 This time we are ready to give **m.** effort
WpI...rV.in1:2 effort and **m.** time to what we undertake.
WpI...rV.in1:4 that we may go on again **m.** certain, more
WpI...rV.in1:4 may go on again more certain, **m.** sincere,
WpI...rV.in1:4 more sincere, with faith upheld **m.** surely.
WpI...rV.in3:5 *may walk* **m.** *certainly and quickly unto You*
WpI...rV.in4:2 this thought, or helps it be **m.** meaningful
WpI...rV.in4:2 more meaningful, **m.** personal and true,
WpI...rV.in4:2 **m.** descriptive of the holy Self we share
Wi181-200 3:5 day. No **m.** than this is asked, because no
Wi181-200 3:5 asked, because no **m.** than this is needed.
W-pI .. 181.5:4 Nothing **m.**. We lay these pointless
W-pI .. 182.1:6 sometimes not **m.** than a tiny throb, at
W-pI .. 182.2:4 not to be considered **m.** than but a dream
W-pI .. 182.5:4 for **m.** than just a few instants of respite;
W-pI 182.11:5 and take illusions as your gods no **m.**.
W-pI .. 184.5:2 thousand alien names, and thousands **m.**.
W-pI .. 185.5:4 would offer nothing **m.** than all the others
W-pI .. 185.8:6 Let not some dreams be **m.** acceptable,
W-pI 186.12:3 this; which is **m.** likely to be right? The
W-pI .. 187.2:8 it takes be less acceptable. It must be **m.**.
W-pI .. 190.4:5 and no **m.** to be feared than the insane
W-pI 191.10:3 he will sleep no **m.** and dream of death.
W-pI .. 193.5:3 and guilt, abandoned, is revered no **m.**.
W-pI 193.10:2 Let mercy come to you **m.** quickly. Do not
W-pI 193.11:1 Give all you can, and give a little **m.**. For
W-pI 193.11:3 too long, and we would linger here no **m.**.
W-pI .. 194.4:6 because the past will punish you no **m.**,
W-pI .. 195.1:3 another seems to suffer **m.** than they.
W-pI .. 195.1:6 less because he sees another suffer **m.**?
W-pI .. 195.4:1 because your brother is **m.** slave than you
W-pI .. 195.8:3 What **m.** remains as obstacles to peace?
W-pI .. 195.9:6 calls us Son. Can there be **m.** than this?
W-pI 195.10:1 our learning time by **m.** than you could
W-pI .. 198.5:2 **m.** intelligent to thank the One Who gives
W-pI 198.12:5 to behold the Son is to perceive no **m.**,
W-pI .. 199.8:5 with you, God's Son will weep no **m.**, and

W-pI ...200.1:3 agony of yet **m.** bitter disappointments,
W-pI ...200.2:2 Attempt no **m.** to win through losing, nor
W-pI ...200.3:6 For what could be **m.** foolish than to seek
W-pI ...200.5:4 You made him not; no **m.** yourself. And
W-pI ...200.6:6 could hope for **m.**, while there appears to
W-pI ...202.1:2 *to stay an instant* **m.** *where I do not belong,*
W-pII.....in.9:6 A moment **m.**, and it will rise again. A
W-pII.....in.9:7 A moment **m.**, and we who are God's
W-pII......1.2:3 so that distortions are **m.** veiled and more
W-pII......1.2:3 are more veiled and **m.** obscure; less
W-pII.....228.h God has condemned me not. No **m.** do I.
W-pII..229.1:2 I am." Now need I seek no **m.**. Love has
W-pII......2.5:2 God's Son has but an instant **m.** to wait
W-pII......4.3:4 love slain by hate, and peace to be no **m.**.
W-pII..252.1:2 and perfect purity is far **m.** brilliant than
W-pII..259.1:2 strange and the distorted seem **m.** clear?
W-pII..270.1:3 *much* **m.** *will I perceive in it than sight can*
W-pII..270.1:4 *instant* **m.** *of time which ends forever, as*
W-pII......6.2:1 is no **m.** than an illusion of despair, for
W-pII..273.1:2 we are content and even **m.** than satisfied
W-pII..275.1:1 no **m.** true today than any other day. Yet
W-pII..277.1:3 *by which I try to make the body* **m.** *secure.*
W-pII..284.1:6 to be considered seriously **m.** and more,
W-pII..284.1:6 to be considered seriously more and **m.**,
W-pII......8.5:2 instant **m.** for God to take His final step,
W-pII294.1:10 Let me not see it **m.** than this today; of
W-pII..300.1:2 represent **m.** than a passing cloud upon a
W-pII..305.1:3 it to truth, no **m.** to be the home of fear.
W-pII..316.1:4 not one gift is lost, and only **m.** are added.
W-pII..318.1:3 one of **m.** or less importance than the rest
W-pII..321.1:3 *Now I would guide myself no* **m.**. *For I have*
W-pII..322.1:1 I sacrifice illusions; nothing **m.**. And as
W-pII..329.1:1 *a second will* **m.** *powerful than Yours. Yet*
W-pII..337.1:4 Atonement for myself, and nothing **m.**.
W-pII....13.4:3 a world **m.** real than what you saw before;
W-pII..355.1:6 *not wait an instant* **m.** *to be at peace forever.*
W-pII..359.1:7 *base* **m.** *solid than the shadow world we see.*
Wfl ........in.5:6 Nothing **m.** than that. And is a father
Wfl ........in.6:5 And **m.** than that can no one ever have,
W-ep .........2:2 Indeed, your pathway is **m.** certain still.
W-ep .........3:1 No **m.** specific lessons are assigned, for
W-ep .........3:1 assigned, for there is no **m.** need of them.
M-in ........2:11 you. No **m.** than that, but also never less.
M-in ..........5:7 And then they are seen no **m.**, although
M-3............3:3 and then learns **m.** and more about the
M-3............3:3 and then learns more and **m.** about the
M-3............4:3 of teaching is a **m.** sustained relationship,
M-4......I.A.8:9 tranquility for something **m.** desirable?
M-4....I.A.8:10 What could be **m.** desirable than this?
M-4.......VI.1:7 The **m.** grotesque the dream, the fiercer
M-4.......VI.1:7 and **m.** powerful its defenses seem to be.
M-4......VII.1:6 but it is perhaps **m.** alien to the thinking
M-5........II.3:7 to see. No **m.** and no less. The world does
M-5.......III.1:5 **m.** specific function for those who do not
M-7............3:5 He need do no **m.**, nor is there more that
M-7............3:5 no more, nor is there **m.** that he could do.
M-8............1:5 appeal. And a **m.** threatening idea, or one
M-8............1:5 as **m.** desirable by the world's standards,
M-8............5:3 Will he agree **m.** quickly to the unreality
M-8............5:4 Will he dismiss **m.** easily a whispered
M-10........1:10 not mean anything. No **m.** does "bad."
M-10..........2:4 He has actually merely become **m.** honest
M-10..........4:6 Make then but one **m.** judgment. It is this
M-10..........5:4 Nothing **m.**. Now can the teacher of God
M-11..........2:2 or the Word of God is **m.** likely to be true.
M-12..........4:2 they become **m.** and more certain that the
M-12..........4:2 they become more and **m.** certain that the
M-12..........6:9 as sick and separate is no **m.** real than to
M-13..........1:2 it came when there is no **m.** use for it.
M-13..........1:7 this world itself is nothing **m.** than that?
M-14..........2:2 becomes stronger and **m.** all-embracing.
M-16..........3:8 After completion of the **m.** structured
M-16..........5:8 period,–not **m.** than a moment will do,–
M-16..........7:9 And he has no need for **m.** than this.
M-16..........9:2 For all temptation is nothing **m.** than the
M-16........10:9 two aspects of one error and no **m.**, he
M-20..........3:7 **M.** than this, given forgiveness there *must*
M-20..........4:7 Which gives you **m.**? A tranquil mind is
M-20..........6:2 peace of God? No **m.** than this; the simple
M-22 .........2:8 What **m.** was asked of him? And having
M-24 .........4:8 how to use it. What **m.** need he know?
M-24 .......6:13 requires. No **m.** than this is necessary.
M-25 .........2:7 in any way is merely becoming **m.** natural
M-25 .........6:3 the **m.** unusual and unexpected the power
M-26 .......4:11 What **m.** could you desire, when this is all
M-27 .........1:3 now we need to consider it **m.** carefully. It
M-27 .........4:7 and will attempt a thousand **m.**. Not one
M-27 .........5:4 of illusions becomes **m.** sharply evident.
M-29 .........1:2 it covers only a few of the **m.** obvious ones
M-29 .........1:7 to start at the **m.** abstract level of the text.
M-29 .........2:2 Who would profit **m.** from prayers alone?
M-29 .........2:3 but a smile, being as yet unready for **m.**?
M-29 .......6:11 much **m.** than this does your Father love
C-2............7:3 dream and you will never question any **m.**
C-2..........10:3 Yet could a definition be **m.** sure, or more
C-2..........10:3 sure, or **m.** in line with what salvation is?
C-3..........4:10 this gate it is no **m.** than just a step inside.
C-4............2:1 upon must lead to **m.** illusions of reality.
C-4............4:2 on it as nothing **m.** than just a fragile veil,
C-4............5:7 once all guilt is gone what **m.** remains to
C-5............6:7 Yet he would help you yet a little **m.** if you
P-in............1:7 so. Sometimes he needs a **m.** structured,
P-1 .............2:3 And what **m.** transcendent aim can there
P-2.........in.1:2 "new" self is a **m.** beneficent self-concept,
P-2...........I.4:3 a somewhat **m.** specialized teacher of God
P-2...........I.4:4 the **m.** advanced he is the more he teaches
P-2...........I.4:4 the **m.** he teaches and the more he learns.
P-2...........I.4:4 the more he teaches and the **m.** he learns.
P-2...........I.4:6 cannot take **m.** than he can give for now.
P-2........IV.4:1 **m.** "respectable" therapists of the world,
P-2......... V.3:6 be helped. No **m.** than that is asked of
P-2......... V.6:5 for **m.** than just the smallest willingness,
P-2........VI.2:6 all these and **m.** are heard instead of loud
P-2.......VII.2:7 There is no need for **m.** than this, for it is
P-3...........I.3:5 need you as much, and perhaps even **m.**,
P-3......... II.1:8 be far **m.** able teachers outside of them.
P-3......... II.6:7 no patient can accept **m.** than he is ready
P-3......... II.6:7 no therapist can offer **m.** than he believes
P-3......III.6:10 Only in terms of cost could one have **m.**.
S-1 ........IV.4:5 thing can give you **m.** than this, in just the
S-1 ......... V.3:7 is little **m.** to learn before the journey is
S-2 ...........I.1:1 of Heaven has been **m.** misunderstood
S-2 ...........I.7:7 has not sinned, and guilt can be no **m.**.
S-3 .........in.1:1 the steep ascent **m.** gentle and more sure,
S-3 .........in.1:1 the steep ascent more gentle and **m.** sure,
S-3 ......... II.3:5 clearer now; His vision **m.** sustained in us;
S-3 ......... II.3:5 the Word of God, **m.** certainly our own.
S-3 ........ III.2:4 perhaps **m.** talented and wise. Therefore,
S-3 ........ III.6:5 Nor will death any **m.** be feared because it
S-3 ........ IV.5:8 care, swearing He will deliver it no **m.**.
S-3 ......IV.10:5 comforted and live no **m.** in terror and in

## more-than-everything 1

T-29... VIII.4:7 "**m.**" is not a thing to make you tremble

## morning 33

W-pI.......1.4:1 a day each, preferably **m.** and evening.
W-pI.....31.2:1 needed, one in the **m.** and one at night.
W-pI.....32.3:1 begin the practice periods for the **m.** and
W-pI.....33.1:2 to the **m.** and evening applications. In
W-pI.....34.2:2 the **m.** and one in the evening are advised
W-pI.....41.6:2 In the **m.**, as soon as you get up if possible
W-pI.....50.5:1 ten minutes, twice today, **m.** and evening,
W-pI.....64.5:2 ourselves of it in the **m.** and again at night
W-pI.....92.7:6 back to darkness till the **m.** comes again.
W-pI...92.11:1 **M.** and evening we will practice thus.
W-pI...92.11:2 After the **m.** meeting, we will use the day
WpI. rIII.in8:2 them so you undertake one in the **m.**, and
W-pI......111.h For **m.** and evening review:
W-pI......112.h For **m.** and evening review:
W-pI......113.h For **m.** and evening review:
W-pI......114.h For **m.** and evening review:
W-pI......115.h For **m.** and evening review:
W-pI......116.h For **m.** and evening review:
W-pI......117.h For **m.** and evening review:
W-pI......118.h For **m.** and evening review:
W-pI......119.h For **m.** and evening review:
W-pI......120.h For **m.** and evening review:
W-pI...121.8:3 We will devote ten minutes in the **m.**, and
W-pI. 122.10:1 **M.** and evening do we gladly give a
W-pI...129.7:1 change ten minutes in the **m.** and at night
W-pI. 139.11:1 Five minutes in the **m.** and at night we
W-pI. 186.11:1 sun's return each **m.** to dispel the night,
W-pI. 193.10:6 **M.** and night, devote what time you can
WpI rVI.in.1:2 Besides the time you give **m.** and evening,
W-pII ....in.2:6 time with Him each **m.** and at night, as
M-29 .........5:9 Prepare for this each **m.**, remember God
C-ep...........5:4 The **m.** star of this new day looks on a
S-2...... III.6:11 His answer will be clear as **m.**, nor is His

## mortal 5

T-27...VII.13:4 sweat of terror and a scream of **m.** fear,
W-pI. 121.13:7 *I will awaken from the dream that I am* **m.**,
W-pI...190.3:7 in death, as **m.** as the Father he has slain.
W-pI. 196.10:5 outside yourself became your **m.** enemy;
W-pII . 294.1:3 Did God create the **m.** and corruptible?

## most 117

T-2........ IV.5:2 whatever way is **m.** helpful to the receiver.
T-2......... V.9:5 **M.** of the loftier concepts of which you
T-2.......VII.1:4 effect; the **m.** fundamental law there is. I
T-2......VIII.2:1 the **m.** threatening ideas in your thinking.
T-3...... III.5:11 **m.** spiritualized form perception involves
T-3......... V.2:7 effort even in its **m.** ingenious form. The
T-4..........II.5:4 need precisely what would hurt you **m.**.
T-4....... II.8:12 the **m.** benevolent of them is not without
T-6...........I.9:1 that the **m.** outrageous assault, as judged
T-6........ IV.2:9 The **m.** inventive activities of the ego have
T-7......... V.7:6 changed the **m.** powerful device that was
T-7....... V.10:8 the **m.** holy children of a most holy Father
T-7....... V.10:8 the most holy children of a **m.** holy Father
T-7...... VI.10:6 you are perceiving the **m.** powerful force
T-8....... VII.8:3 is the **m.** depressing thing in the world. In
T-9...........I.3:2 which would be highly artificial at **m.**, is
T-13.......in.2:9 love, perhaps the **m.** insane belief of all.
T-13...VII.10:1 for the perfect sanity of His **m.** holy Son.
T-13...VII.17:4 from the mind of God's **m.** holy Son,
T-13....VIII.6:5 miracle that ever was is God's **m.** holy
T-13..... X.12:6 Father, for the purity of Your **m.** holy Son
T-14........II.1:5 the foundation on which this **m.** peculiar
T-14..... III.18:1 taught yourself the **m.** unnatural habit of
T-14....... IV.3:1 in your **m.** holy mind be undone for you,
T-14....... V.7:4 from the effects of this **m.** holy lesson,
T-14....... VI.5:3 have use to Him, for His **m.** holy purpose.
T-15....... V.1:1 holy instant is the Holy Spirit's **m.** useful
T-16...... III.8:1 To your **m.** holy Self all praise is due for
T-16....... V.3:1 relationship is the ego's **m.** boasted gift,
T-16....... V.3:1 and one which has the **m.** appeal to those
T-16....... V.7:1 **M.** curious of all is the concept of the self
T-16....... VI.3:2 The holy instant is His **m.** helpful aid in
T-17...... III.3:3 **m.** readily associated with those on whom
T-17...... IV.8:1 special relationship has the **m.** imposing
T-17...... IV.9:8 deceived by the **m.** superficial aspects of
T-17..... V.7:10 He has given you a **m.** explicit statement?
T-18........I.10:9 His gift as our **m.** holy and perfect reality,
T-18........I.13:1 the **m.** holy function this world contains.
T-18...... VI.7:2 And neither God nor His **m.** holy Son can
T-18...... IX.4:3 its **m.** external manifestations in darkness
T-19........I.10:3 as a Son of your **m.** loving Father, loved
T-19........I.15:1 **m.** holy garden that He would make of it.
T-19.........II.5:3 the **m.** "holy" concept in the ego's system;
T-19....... IV.3:8 Creator in the Name of His **m.** holy Son.
T19. IV.D.15:5 and receive from your **m.** holy Friend. Let
T-20.........II.2:5 It will adorn its chosen home **m.** carefully,
T-20....... III.4:2 hoping at **m.** that death will wait a little
T-20....VIII.6:9 its **m.** holy purpose bereft of means for its
T-23........I.10:3 Open the door of His **m.** holy home, and
T-23......II.11:2 this **m.** treacherous and cunning enemy?
T-23......II.16:4 play the major roles, it seems **m.** powerful
T-25..... VII.7:1 **m.** sensible and meaningful to you. The
T-25..... VII.7:5 of sanity which makes it **m.** acceptable to
T-25..... VII.8:3 the choice of form **m.** suitable to him; one
T-26...... IV.4:5 him that what he feared he loves the **m.**.

T-27....IV.4:13 get that you would want the **m.** of all? It is
T-29.........I.2:1 Here is the fear of God **m.** plainly seen.
T-31.....V.10:1 brother made of you seems **m.** unlikely.
T-31.....VII.7:4 At **m.**, you glimpse a shadow of what lies
W-pI.....13.4:1 more than a minute or so at **m.** each time,
W-pI.....14.2:2 period should be short, a minute at **m.**.
W-pI.....25.4:2 the **m.** superficial levels, you do recognize
W-pI.....34.2:2 that seems **m.** conducive to readiness. All
W-pI.....41.7:2 But **m.** of all, try to sink down and inward
W-pI.....41.8:2 it is the **m.** natural thing in the world.
W-pI.....43.4:2 the **m.** convenient and suitable time that
W-pI.....44.4:3 the **m.** natural and easy one in the world
W-pI.....44.4:3 just as it seems to be the **m.** unnatural
W-pI.....50.1:3 in the **m.** trivial and insane symbols; pills,
WpI...rI.in.4:3 will need your learning **m.** in situations
W-pI...66.11:1 **m.** helpful today if undertaken twice an
W-pI.....67.5:3 **m.** beneficial to remind yourself that love
W-pI...73.11:6 It is **m.** important, however, to apply
W-pI.....93.8:1 which would be **m.** profitable if done for
W-pI.....95.6:2 **m.** beneficial form of practice in salvation
WpI. rIII.in3:3 in this. Unwillingness can be **m.** carefully
W-pI...125.6:4 to help make ready your **m.** holy mind to
W-pI...125.7:1 today, at times **m.** suitable for silence,
W-pI...133.4:3 It would be **m.** ungenerous to you to let
W-pI.135.26:1 day as you believe would benefit you **m.**.
W-pI...138.6:2 **m.** definitive and prototype of all the rest,
W-pI...152.4:1 of distinctions, yet the **m.** obscure. But
W-pI.153.16:2 less, will be the **m.** that we can offer as the
W-pI...159.6:4 his least request or his **m.** urgent need.
W-pI...164.8:3 of your **m.** holy mind to save the world. Is
W-pI...168.3:1 Today we ask of God the gift He has **m.**
W-pI...169.1:1 the Love of God which is **m.** like the state
W-pI...169.1:2 It is the world's **m.** lofty aspiration, for it
W-pI.186.10:4 ten times an hour at their **m.** secure.
W-pI.186.13:5 on the form **m.** useful in a world of form.
W-pI...187.5:7 the thought in form **m.** helpful to him.
W-pI...195.1:2 The **m.** that they can do is see themselves
W-pI...196.9:4 thing you dread the **m.** is your salvation.
W-pII .....9.5:4 And **m.** of all it needs your willingness.
M-3...........2:6 at the level of the **m.** casual encounter, it
M-3...........4:1 the **m.** that he can from the other person
M-3...........4:5 each has learned the **m.** he can at the time
M-4.....I.A.4:3 not **m.** of the things he valued before will
M-4....... X.3:3 They would be **m.** inappropriate here.
M-7...........4:1 One of the **m.** difficult temptations to
M-9...........1:4 It is **m.** unlikely that changes in attitudes
M-16.........9:5 of God has reached the **m.** advanced state
M-17.........2:8 Here is his gift **m.** clearly given him. For
M-17.........3:1 error be corrected where it is **m.** apparent
M-17.........7:5 the fear of God **m.** starkly represented.
M-21.........2:2 Even when they seem **m.** abstract, the
M-23.........1:2 Even the **m.** advanced of God's teachers
M-24.........5:4 And this is **m.** unlikely. He might be
M-29.........5:7 with which this course is **m.** concerned. If
C-5............6:8 still it is his lesson **m.** of all that he would
P-2........IV.9:3 of attack-defense is one of the **m.** difficult
P-2........IV.9:5 the patient's **m.** cherished possession; his
P-3...........I.3:6 way can be **m.** helpful to both of you. It
P-3...........I.3:8 will be sent in whatever form is **m.** helpful
P-3......... II.2:4 impossible. **M.** of the world's teaching
P-3......... II.8:5 **M.** professional therapists are still at the
S-3......... II.2:3 and clearly seen at **m.** in lovely flashes.

## mother 1

C-2............8:2 as a loving **m.** sings her child to rest. Is

## motion 2

W-pI...133.3:5 wise to learn the laws you set in **m.** when
C-6............2:4 Holy Spirit long before Jesus set it in **m.**.

## motivate 2

T-6.........I.16:6 all behavior teaches the beliefs that **m.** it.
T-31...... III.3:9 body must act on its own, and **m.** itself. If

## motivated 2

T-14 .......X.2:6 is **m.** by a unique Teacher Who brings the
T-14 .......X.4:5 of Heaven, while others are **m.** by the ego,

## motivating 1

M-21 .........1:2 The **m.** factor is prayer, or asking. What

## motivation 23

T-4 ........ V.1:4 keeps its primary **m.** from your awareness
T-5 .........II.1:4 Spirit is the **m.** for miracle-mindedness;
T-5 .......II.12:4 The power of our joint **m.** is beyond belief
T-6 .....V.A.3:1 that the Holy Spirit is the **m.** for miracles.
T-6 ..... V.B.2:2 Strengthening **m.** for change is their first
T-6 ..... V.B.2:4 Increasing **m.** for change in the learner is
T-6 ..... V.B.2:5 Change in **m.** is a change of mind, and
T-6 ..... V.B.3:7 This means conflicting **m.**, and so the
T-6 ..... V.B.3:8 others, making him suspicious of their **m.**
T-7 .........X.5:6 are confused about this distinction in **m.**,
T-7 .........X.5:7 Projection is a confusion in **m.**, and given
T-8 ..........I.1:1 Knowledge is not the **m.** for learning this
T-12 ........I.2:1 analysis of ego **m.** is very complicated,
T-12 ........I.3:1 interpretation of **m.** that makes any sense
T-12 ........I.5:8 not need your help in interpreting **m.**, but
T-14 ... XI.12:3 They have destroyed their **m.** for learning
T-24 ......in.1:1 Forget not that the **m.** for this course is
T-27 ........I.6:3 for death that is the **m.** for this world. Its
T-27 ........I.6:5 act or feeling has a **m.** other than this one.
W-pI..... 68.4:3 That, however, is simply a matter of **m.**.
W-pI..... 68.4:5 will never be a problem in **m.** ever again.
W-pI..... 95.6:3 for those whose **m.** is inconsistent, and
Wi181-200 2:5 Your **m.** will be so intensified that words

## motivators 1

M-5 ........II.1:8 to endow the body with non-mental **m.**.

## motives 5

T-7 ..... III.2:11 being undone, and does suspect your **m.**.
T-9 ...... VII.4:6 The ego will attack your **m.** as soon as
T-12 ........I.1:6 That is why analyzing the **m.** of others is
T-12 ........I.8:6 of the **m.** of others will serve you then.
T-28 .......II.8:5 abuse because the **m.** he has given it have

## mound 1

T19....IV.B.4:8 want your Father, not a little **m.** of clay, to

## mountain 3

T-18 ..... IX.6:3 way softly to the **m.** tops that rise above it
T-18 ..... IX.7:2 A solid **m.** range, a lake, a city, all rise in
T-22 ...... V.5:3 solid body, immovable as is a **m.**. Yet

## mountains 3

T-2 ....... VI.9:8 a power surge that can literally move **m.**.
T-5 ...... VII.2:2 not moved **m.** by their faith because their
T-21 ..... III.3:1 is it strange to you that faith can move **m.**

## mourn 3

T-19 .......II.7:6 **M.**, then, the death of God, Whom sin
W-pI...195.5:2 **m.** a seeming loss or feel apparent pain,
P-2........ VI.1:4 while they **m.** their loss and yet rejoice in

## mourner 2

T19....IV.C.4:2 by every **m.** who looks upon it as himself.
W-pI...186.8:3 seem to change from **m.** to ecstatic bliss

## mournful 1

T19....IV.C.2:4 "sinners," the ego's **m.** chorus, plodding

## mourning 3

T-20 ........ I.4:6 of Easter is a time of joy, and not of **m.**.
T-25 .. VII.10:4 emerge from deepest **m.** into perfect joy.
W-pI .. 183.3:5 The sorrowful cast off their **m.**, and the

## mouse 5

T-21 .. VII.3:11 becomes a giant and a **m.** roars like a lion.
T-22 .......V.4:3 a frightened **m.** that would attack the
T-22 .......V.4:7 tiny **m.** or everything that God created?
T-22 .......V.4:8 brother are not joined together by this **m.**
T-22 .......V.4:9 can a **m.** betray whom God has joined?

## mouth 1

W-pI .. 151.7:2 nor what his body's **m.** says to your ears,

## move 22

T-2 ....... VI.9:8 surge that can literally **m.** mountains. It
T-4 ..........I.2:2 it as a **m.** towards healing the separation.
T-4 ..........I.2:3 always perceive it as a **m.** toward further
T-4 .......II.10:4 has only one direction in which it can **m.**.
T-13 ... VIII.8:2 the power of God's Son will **m.** in us, and
T-17 ..... III.3:4 of the unholy relationship is a **m.** toward
T-18 ..... IX.7:3 Figures stand out and **m.** about, actions
T-21 ..... III.3:1 to you that faith can **m.** mountains? This
T-22 ......in.2:7 is nothing left to steal, and then **m.** on.
T-24 ... VII.9:4 can feel it with your hands and hear it **m.**.
T-28 .....II.10:6 and the bodies that still seem to **m.** about
T-29 ..... IX.4:6 and give their toys the power to **m.** about,
W-pI ...... 7.5:2 each subject, and then **m.** on to the next.
W-pI .... 11.3:1 eyes should **m.** from one thing to another
W-pI .... 22.3:2 eyes **m.** slowly from one object to another
W-pI .... 25.6:8 Then **m.** on to the next subject, and apply
W-pI .... 31.3:4 to let the stream **m.** on evenly and calmly,
W-pI .. 163.9:3 *We live and m. in You alone. We are not*
W-pI .. 197.7:3 for everyone must live and **m.** in Him. His
W-pII .... 222.h God is with me. I live and **m.** in Him.
W-pII . 222.1:3 He is my home, wherein I live and **m.**; the
W-pII . 252.1:4 burning impulses which **m.** the world,

## moved 2

T-5 ...... VII.2:2 **m.** mountains by their faith because their
W-pII . 223.1:1 God, a separate entity that **m.** in isolation

## moves 3

T-13 .......V.1:9 all. In this world their maker **m.** alone, for
T-31 . VIII.12:7 from everything that lives and **m.** in You.
M-27 ......... 7:6 Truth neither **m.** nor wavers nor sinks

## moving 1

T-21 ..... IV.4:3 Your faith is **m.** inward, past insanity and

## much 183

T-1 .........V.1:1 The miracle is **m.** like the body in that
T-1 ..... VII.4:5 you may become **m.** too fearful of what is
T-2 .........II.3:5 treasure, and how **m.** do you treasure it?
T-2 .........V.9:6 reflection of a **m.** more powerful love-
T-2 ... V.A.18:1 **m.** on behalf of your own healing and that
T-2 ....... VI.4:6 are **m.** too tolerant of mind wandering,
T-2 ...... VII.1:7 is **m.** more helpful to remind you that you
T-2 ..... VIII.3:3 **m.** you may think that punishment is
T-3 ...... VII.5:7 **M.** has been seen since then, but nothing
T-4 ..........I.5:1 so **m.** of his own learning that they will
T-4 .........II.4:4 your ego **m.** as God does to His creations,
T-4 ..... III.10:3 Consider how **m.** vigilance you have been
T-4 ....... IV.2:6 is **m.** easier than trying to think against it.
T-4 ....... IV.8:2 of his power as **m.** as he chooses. Your
T-4 ....... VI.1:4 how **m.** of your thinking is ego-directed.
T-4 ....... VI.2:4 you learn how **m.** you are indebted to the
T-5 ..... III.10:4 part, it is still **m.** stronger than the ego,
T-5 ....... VI.4:1 **m.** as a higher court has the power to
T-6 ..........I.6:7 in the face of **m.** less extreme temptations

T-6........ I.15:8 God, as **m.** a part of the Sonship as myself
T-6........ I.16:1 there was **m.** they would understand later
T-6......V.A.4:4 We have too **m.** to accomplish on behalf
T-6......V.B.4:2 which would be **m.** less acceptable to it,
T-6......V.C.9:9 was required of me as **m.** as of you, and
T-7......... X.6:3 question, however **m.** you may question it
T-8........IV.4:1 the world needs peace as **m.** as you do?
T-8........IV.4:2 the world as **m.** as you want to receive it?
T-8....... V.6:10 because I need you as **m.** as you need me.
T-9....... II.11:2 To believe that it is possible to get **m.** for
T-9....... II.11:9 is the measure of how **m.** you want it.
T-9....... II.12:2 how **m.** you will be asking of Him, and
T-9....... II.12:2 of Him, and how **m.** you will receive. He
T-10.......in.3:8 and you will realize how **m.** is up to you.
T-10.......III.8:1 you always receive as **m.** as you accept.
T-10....III.10:4 not realize how **m.** you listen to your gods
T-10....... V.6:1 sinned, but you have been **m.** mistaken.
T-10..... V.10:1 realize how **m.** you have denied yourself,
T-10..... V.10:1 have denied yourself, and how **m.** God, in
T-11.........I.3:6 continues forever, however **m.** it is denied
T-11.........I.3:8 and why so **m.** is waiting for your return.
T-11.........I.7:4 end, to learn how **m.** He has given you.
T-11....... II.6:7 will lighten it so **m.** that you will gladly let
T-11......IV.5:5 as **m.** an ego defense as blaming others.
T-11....... V.7:4 goal. It is **m.** more vigilant than you are,
T-11......VI.2:5 There has been **m.** confusion about what
T-12... VIII.7:1 matter how **m.** distance you have tried to
T-13....... II.1:2 for **m.** as the ego wants to retain guilt *you*
T-13....... II.4:1 **M.** of the ego's strange behavior is
T-13......III.2:8 and **m.** stronger than it will ever be, is
T-13....... X.8:4 he will remember how **m.** his Father loves
T-13....... X.9:2 do not remember how **m.** you love Him.
T-14.......in.1:6 We have followed **m.** of the ego's logic,
T-14.......IV.8:4 understand how **m.** your Father loves you
T-14.......VI.5:4 but He perceives **m.** in your mind that
T-14... VIII.2:2 great or small, however **m.** or little valued
T-14....... X.7:2 **m.** too confused either to recognize love,
T-14......XI.1:4 but you have interposed so **m.** between it
T-15....... II.4:1 not realize how **m.** you have misused your
T-15....... II.4:3 are far stronger and **m.** more compelling
T-15....... II.5:4 instant, and will learn **m.** from doing so.
T-15......III.2:3 is **m.** too poor a gift to satisfy you. It is
T-15......IV.2:3 instead, by so **m.** is it far from you. By so
T-15......IV.2:4 **m.** as you want it will you bring it nearer.
T-15....... V.5:3 by removing as **m.** fear as you will let Him
T-15....... V.7:3 and so, however **m.** you seek for its reality
T-15.....VII.7:1 you do not want seems to be **m.** stronger
T-15..... X.5:13 that remains is how **m.** is the price, and
T-15....XI.10:9 There is **m.** to do, and we have been long
T-16......III.2:8 remember how **m.** care you have exerted
T-16....... V.7:7 **m.** value can he place upon a self that he
T-16....VI.10:7 learn how **m.** awaits you for the simple
T-17....... II.8:1 How **m.** do you want salvation? It will
T-18.........I.1:2 perceive at once how **m.** at variance this is
T-18.........I.9:5 God, as **m.** together as you are with Him.
T-18....IV.1:10 do so little that enables Him to give so **m.**.
T-18......IV.7:3 you need give so little, to receive so **m.**.
T-18....... V.7:1 other and how **m.** gratitude is due him,
T-18....VI.13:6 you experience **m.** of what happens in the
T-18.....VII.1:1 You still have too **m.** faith in the body as
T-18......IX.7:5 of how **m.** imagination you bring to it,
T-18....IX.11:6 There is too **m.** to learn. The readiness for
T-19.........I.7:2 however **m.** you seek to connect them.
T-19.........I.8:1 you but understood how **m.** this strange
T-19........ I.10:1 as **m.** a part of love as fear is of attack.
T19....IV.B.2:4 be too great to make, too **m.** to ask of you.
T-20......IV.8:1 so **m.** that must be done before the way to
T-20.....VII.1:1 said **m.** about discrepancies of means and
T-21......in.2:7 you how **m.** joy you have allowed yourself
T-21....... II.1:5 judgment, to be too **m.** to pay for peace.
T-21....... II.4:4 Never was so **m.** given for so little. In the
T-21......III.8:4 they chose to recognize how **m.** their faith
T-21......IV.4:2 willing to look on **m.** of your insanity and
T-21....... V.7:3 as **m.** a true Effect of this same Source as
T-21....... V.7:5 threatens dissociation as **m.** as all of it.
T-22.........I.1:5 in this and see **m.** evidence on its behalf.
T-23.......III.1:2 and will do so just as **m.** as in another
T-24....... V.2:1 however **m.** it delicately offers the hope of
T-24....... V.5:3 They are illusions, too, as **m.** as yours.
T-24.....VII.1:6 No effort is too great, no cost too **m.**, no
T-24.....VII.4:3 And **m.** you think you save, you hurt.
T-25...... II.8:7 However **m.** he overlooks the masterpiece
T-25......III.7:8 This world has **m.** to offer to your peace,
T-25......VI.5:8 Yet while in time, there is still **m.** to do.
T-25... VIII.1:7 This **m.** is necessary to add to the idea no
T-25... VIII.9:2 in your confusion you have **m.** to give?
T-25. VIII.10:2 is in him, however **m.** he recognize it not.
T-25......IX.4:5 who shall lose; how **m.** the one shall take,
T-25......IX.4:5 and how **m.** can the loser still defend. Yet
T-26.........I.4:7 bodies, however **m.** he witnesses to truth?
T-26......IV.1:5 still believes that he has **m.** to be forgiven.
T-26....... V.7:3 And how **m.** can his own illusions about
T-26...VII.11:7 Here does the Son of God ask not too **m.**,
T-26......IX.1:3 However **m.** you wish he be condemned,
T-26......IX.2:1 **m.** to ask a little trust for him who carries
T-26......IX.7:4 Son give less in gratitude for so **m.** more?
T-26..... X.1:10 of the confusion, or how **m.** it interferes.
T-28....... II.5:2 you perceive this **m.** at least: that you
T-28..... II.10:6 are you freed from this **m.** of the dream;
T-29....... II.5:1 You do not see how **m.** you now can give,
T-29......IV.2:1 as **m.** as those in which the fear is seen.
T-29......VI.1:2 **m.** do you desire peace instead of endless
T-30.........I.8:3 This **m.** is obvious, and paves the way for
T-30.......I.10:3 But this **m.** reason have you now attained;
T-30......IV.8:4 indeed salvation asks so little, not so **m.**.
T-30......VI.4:7 forgiveness is your right as **m.** as his. Nor
T-31.......I.7:10 However **m.** you may have overlearned
T-31....... II.6:4 remembering how **m.** we do not know.
T-31......IV.8:4 and you will gain as **m.** as he will lose, and
T-31......VI.2:5 have trust where so **m.** change is seen, for
T-31.....VII.4:1 You live in that world just as **m.** as this.
W-pI.......5.5:1 regardless of how **m.** or how little you
W-pI.....15.2:1 seeing will not have **m.** meaning for you.
W-pI.....18.2:1 to what you see as **m.** as to how you see it.
W-pI.....19.4:1 requirement of as **m.** indiscriminateness
W-pI.....24.3:1 The exercises for today require **m.** more
W-pI.....26.8:2 **m.** more helpful to cover a few situations
W-pI.....27.4:2 **m.** do you want today's idea to be true?
W-pI.....28.4:5 to the table just as **m.** as to anything else,
W-pI.....39.9:4 It will become **m.** easier as your mind
W-pI.....46.3:4 "how **m.**" you have not forgiven them.
W-pI.....51.5:5 I have not realized how **m.** I have misused
W-pI.....67.4:4 Be confident that you will do **m.** today to
W-pI.....69.6:1 remembering only how **m.** you want to
W-pI...93.11:5 can do **m.** for the world's salvation today.
W-pI...93.11:6 **m.** today to bring you closer to the part in
W-pI...93.11:7 **m.** today to bring the conviction to your
W-pI...96.12:3 how **m.** is given unto you to give this day,
W-pI.....97.6:2 you gave as **m.** as does the radiance of the
W-pI...100.6:3 world can see how **m.** He loves His Son,
W-pI.108.10:1 simple lesson for today will teach you **m.**.
W-pI.108.10:2 and we will make **m.** faster progress now.
WpIrIII.in13:2 Do not forget how **m.** you can learn now.
W-pI...128.7:2 see as **m.** as when you looked at it before.
W-pI...133.2:1 You do not ask too **m.** of life, but far too
W-pI.139.11:6 in truth, how **m.** a part of us is every mind
W-pI...153.4:3 the world encourages is so **m.** deeper, and
W-pI...153.5:3 how **m.** you have been made to sacrifice,
W-pI.182.10:4 today. You are as **m.** an alien here as He.
W-pI...187.4:4 in time, however **m.** you try to keep it safe
W-pI...194.6:1 to give as **m.** consistent effort as you can,
W-pI...196.7:1 as **m.** as will permit fear of retaliation to
W-pII.....in.2:8 We use as **m.** as we will need for the result
W-pII..238.2:1 pause to think how **m.** our Father loves us
W-pII..270.1:3 *Yet how* **m.** *more will I perceive in it than*
W-pII......7.3:1 knew how **m.** your Father yearns to have
W-pII..335.1:4 however **m.** I seem to be impelled by
M-4 .....I.A.3:8 the teacher of God has learned that **m.**, he
M-16 .........3:5 How **m.** time should be so spent? This
M-24 .........4:4 **m.** to teach and learn apart from them.
M-24 .........5:8 this **m.** is not required of the beginner. He
M-25 .........1:1 this question is **m.** like the preceding one.
M-26 .........3:3 be won after **m.** devotion and dedication,
M-26 .........3:3 be maintained for **m.** of the time on earth
M-29 .......6:11 **m.** more than this does your Father love
P-2...........I.1:3 It may be they will not get **m.** further, for
P-2........III.2:4 their success depends on how **m.** of this
P-3...........I.3:5 They need you as **m.**, and perhaps even
P-3.........II.6:8 will bring as **m.** good as each can accept
P-3....... III.6:8 the therapist how **m.** he needs forgiveness
P-3....... III.7:3 How **m.** is gained by striving for illusions?
P-3....... III.7:4 How **m.** is lost by throwing God away?
S-1...........I.4:2 To ask for the specific is **m.** the same as to
S-1.........II.7:2 is a transformation **m.** like your own, for

## multiplied 5

T-27..... V.11:6 you go, will you behold its **m.** effects. Yet
W-pI.....97.3:3 which you give are **m.** over and over, for
W-pI.....97.6:1 Thus will each gift to Him be **m.** a
W-pI...107.2:5 quiet that you felt be **m.** a hundred times,
W-pI...107.2:5 and then be **m.** another hundred more.

## multiplies 1

W-pI.....16.2:3 it extends the truth or it **m.** illusions. You

## multiply 2

W-pI.....16.2:4 You can indeed **m.** nothing, but you will
W-pI...198.3:2 save this one must **m.** a thousandfold. But

## multitude 2

W-pI...106.5:4 to speak to all the **m.** who wait to hear the
W-pI...130.4:2 **m.** of differences you believe make up the

## murder 39

T-13........II.6:3 as the final guilt that fully justifies **m.**.
T-14.........I.4:5 of death and **m.** that your Father does not
T19. IV.A.17:3 and so atonement is achieved through **m.**.
T19....IV.B.2:8 of the perception of Atonement as **m.**.
T-20...... III.4:2 have made?–a world of **m.** and attack,
T-20....VIII.7:5 die, attack and **m.** and destroy themselves
T-23.....II.14:6 hatred love, and **m.** benediction, is the
T-23.....II.17:1 can some forms of **m.** not mean death?
T-23...... III.1:5 Its sole intent is **m.**, and what form of
T-23...... III.1:5 and what form of **m.** serves to cover the
T-23...... III.1:8 For no one thinks of **m.** and escapes the
T-23...... III.5:3 that **m.** takes some forms by which their
T-23...... III.6:9 protection stands against the faith in **m.**.
T-23.... III.6:10 and the unnatural intent to **m.** and to die.
T-23.... III.6:11 the form that **m.** takes can offer safety?
T-23...... IV.1:7 not asked to fight against your wish to **m.**.
T-23.... IV.1:10 What is not love is **m.**. What is not loving
T-23...... IV.2:2 **M.** and love are incompatible. Yet if they
T-23...... IV.3:3 to believe the function of the Son is **m.**,
T-23...... IV.4:3 Each form of **m.** and attack that still
T-23...... IV.4:6 realize that **m.** in any form is not your will
T-23...... IV.5:5 it. Here **m.** is your choice. Yet from above,
T-23...... IV.5:6 above, the choice is miracles instead of **m.**
T-23.... IV.5:11 of miracles be recognized if **m.** is your
T-23...... IV.6:5 but quickly choose a miracle instead of **m.**
T-23...... IV.7:3 For only bodies could attack and **m.**, and
T-23...... IV.9:8 the choice of miracles or **m.** hard to make
T-24.......II.12:6 dear but clings to **m.** as safety's weapon,
T-25...... IX.4:7 to the first, in which the **m.** is not obvious
T-27...VII.14:5 there is no **m.** and there is no death. The
T-28........II.5:5 In dreams of **m.** and attack are you the
T-29...... VI.1:4 sin and death; of madness and of **m.**, grief
T-31........II.4:2 you think that it is **m.** justified at last. You
T-31..... III.2:11 And how could **m.** bring you benefit?
T-31...... III.5:2 ravages of fear except in **m.** and in death.
W-pI...189.3:5 poised to avenge, to **m.** and destroy.
W-pII .....8.3:1 mind for thoughts of death, attack and **m.**
W-pII ...12.2:5 who seek to **m.** it before it can ensure its
M-28 .........6:4 thought of **m.** is replaced with blessing.

## murderer 8

T-20....... III.4:5 A **m.** *is* frightened, and those who kill fear
T-23....... III.1:5 fear of punishment the **m.** must feel? He
T-23....... III.1:6 He may deny he is a **m.** and justify his
T-27...VII.12:1 a **m.** who stalks you in the night and plots
T-27...VII.12:2 yet another, in which you become the **m.**,
T-27...VII.14:4 who is the **m.** and who shall be the victim.

W-pI.196.11:1 an instant, is a **m.** perceived within you,
W-pII 5.2:8 Who the **m.**? And if he did not die, what

### murderers 1

T-23 IV.3:6 Either the Father and the Son are **m.**, or

### murderous 6

T-13 II.3:3 this **m.** but insane idea lies hidden there,
T-21 VII.4:6 **m.** attack by turning into something else.
T-23 II.12:2 Can you be sure your **m.** attack is justified
T-23 IV.6:1 rises to make your mind darkened and **m.**
T-31 I.10:3 sings behind each **m.** attack and pleads
W-pII .261.1:3 nor attempt to find my peace in **m.** attack

### music 1

T-21 IV.7:2 the other part hears as the sweetest **m.**;

### musings 1

W-pI 139.8:5 themselves with senseless **m.** such as this.

### must 1561

T-1 III.1:6 you **m.** join the great crusade to correct it;
T-1 III.1:8 do them, but you **m.** be ready and willing.
T-1 III.2:4 a man **m.** think of himself in his heart,
T-1 III.3:3 who are released **m.** join in releasing their
T-1 III.6:3 the perception of both **m.** be accurate.
T-1 IV.4:1 by fear **m.** be replaced by forgiveness.
T-1 V.4:1 member of the family of God **m.** return.
T-1 V.6:3 All shallow roots **m.** be uprooted, because
T-1 VI.3:3 do, correction **m.** be introduced vertically
T-1 VII.2:3 **m.** still be expressed through one body to
T-2 III.2:3 that **m.** be undone for the restoration of
T-2 III.3:6 dimly, that there ***m.*** be a better way. As
T-2 III.5:12 They **m.** learn to look upon the world as a
T-2 IV.2:3 all mistakes **m.** be corrected at the level
T-2 IV.5:3 **m.** be expressed in a language that the
T-2 V.10:7 it. It **m.** be understood, however, that
T-2 VI.2:1 confusion, but you **m.** choose to correct it
T-2 VI.3:4 for it. You **m.** change your mind, not your
T-2 VI.7:2 that you **m.** somehow have chosen not to
T-2 VI.9:4 fear there are some things you **m.** realize,
T-2 VII.2:4 miracle worker **m.** have genuine respect
T-2 VII.3:8 The fearful ***m.*** miscreate, because they
T-2 VII.6:2 every one **m.** be an integral part of the
T-2 VIII.2:8 because you **m.** emerge from the conflict
T-3 I.1:1 further point **m.** be perfectly clear before
T-3 I.2:9 that we **m.** be sure that nothing of this
T-3 III.1:2 perception **m.** be straightened out before
T-3 III.2:9 what you do, and actions **m.** occur in time
T-3 III.6:6 Perception can and **m.** be stabilized, but
T-3 IV.3:4 separated or divided mind ***m.*** be confused.
T-3 IV.3:11 That is why you **m.** eventually choose to
T-3 IV.6:1 **m.** perceive *something* and *with* something.
T-3 VI.5:3 laugh at yourself you **m.** laugh at others, if
T-3 VI.10:3 is. The problem everyone **m.** decide is the
T-3 VI.11:2 result of his own free will he **m.** regard his
T-3 VI.11:3 Free will **m.** lead to freedom. Judgment
T-3 VII.1:1 of thought **m.** have a starting point. It
T-3 VII.3:1 but its meaning **m.** be clearly understood.
T-3 VII.5:6 and you **m.** return to your Beginning.
T-4 I.1:4 teacher **m.** believe in the ideas he teaches,
T-4 I.1:4 but he **m.** meet another condition; he
T-4 I.1:4 he **m.** believe in the students to whom he
T-4 I.3:1 need not be taught, but the ego **m.** be.
T-4 I.3:3 spirit. This is the change the ego **m.** fear,
T-4 I.7:4 Teachers **m.** be patient and repeat their
T-4 II.5:1 system **m.** be perceived as painful, even
T-4 II.5:5 helpful, attributes that **m.** go together.
T-4 II.8:9 self-esteem in ego terms **m.** be delusional.
T-4 II.10:1 **m.** be achieved before One-mindedness is
T-4 II.11:7 You **m.** be careful, however, that you
T-4 III.3:3 The ego **m.** offer you some sort of reward
T-4 III.4:7 that truly wants it, but it **m.** want it truly.
T-4 III.5:3 are for you, but for which you **m.** ask.
T-4 III.6:2 as free as God, and **m.** remain so forever.
T-4 III.7:8 I **m.** wait as long as you choose to forsake
T-4 III.8:2 for we **m.** hide nothing from each other. If
T-4 IV.8:10 truly and you **m.** withdraw allegiance,
T-4 IV.9:3 knowing that this and only this **m.** be. His
T-4 IV.9:5 His Mind still shines on you and **m.** shine
T-4 V.1:6 and **m.** be obliterated by the ego in the
T-4 V.3:1 confuses God and the body **m.** be insane.
T-4 V.5:1 question that ***m.*** be asked: "Where can I
T-4 V.5:4 goal **m.** be formulated clearly and kept in
T-4 V.6:1 because the eternal **m.** come from God.
T-4 V.6:8 This is the question that *you* **m.** learn to
T-4 VI.1:4 and **m.** realize how much of your thinking
T-4 VI.2:1 brother is something you **m.** never forget.
T-4 VI.3:8 that you believe you **m.** escape from the
T-4 VI.5:2 He **m.** have thrown it away because he did
T-4 VII.8:2 because the two beliefs **m.** coexist. The
T-5 in.2:1 To be wholehearted you **m.** be happy. If
T-5 II.3:4 That is why you **m.** choose to hear one of
T-5 II.4:2 you **m.** let banish the idea of darkness.
T-5 II.6:3 As a result, there are choices you **m.** make
T-5 II.8:9 you **m.** choose at which altar you want to
T-5 II.12:1 **m.** respond to the same Mind to do this.
T-5 III.1:3 relationship **m.** be in His Mind because,
T-5 III.3:2 They **m.** both be in your mind, because
T-5 III.3:3 They **m.** also be in his, because you are
T-5 III.4:2 That is why you **m.** share It. It must be
T-5 III.4:3 It **m.** be increased in strength before you
T-5 III.11:2 The Holy Spirit **m.** perceive time, and
T-5 III.11:3 He **m.** work through opposites, because
T-5 III.11:3 because He **m.** work with and for a mind
T-5 IV.2:11 Atonement **m.** be understood as a pure
T-5 IV.6:7 You **m.** learn to see them as they are, and
T-5 IV.7:2 those who have been forgiven **m.** devote
T-5 IV.7:2 idea of healing, they **m.** give it to hold it.
T-5 V.2:3 giving rise to guilt, and **m.** give rise to joy.
T-5 V.3:5 the ego, you **m.** perceive yourself as guilty
T-5 V.3:11 the guilt is so acute that it **m.** be projected
T-5 V.4:5 that you **m.** learn to think with God. To
T-5 V.4:13 but you **m.** learn to regard it as freedom.
T-5 V.6:2 "What do you want?" **m.** be answered.
T-5 V.7:6 and **m.** therefore obey their dictates. This
T-5 VI.2:5 it. But you can and **m.**. God offers you the
T-5 VI.9:2 Every loveless thought **m.** be undone, a
T-5 VI.12:1 Now you **m.** learn that only infinite
T-5 VI.12:8 you **m.** give Him as you received Him.
T-5 VII.6:2 realize that you **m.** already have decided
T-5 VII.6:7 *I* ***m.*** *have decided wrongly, because I am not*
T-6 in.1:2 which **m.** ultimately be accepted as one's
T-6 in.1:4 of attack rather than of love **m.** follow.
T-6 I.3:5 and **m.** be fully understood *as* impossible.
T-6 I.4:7 you **m.** be equating yourself with the
T-6 I.8:2 is still on them that I **m.** build my church.
T-6 I.8:6 it. I **m.** found His church on you, because
T-6 I.11:3 you **m.** still follow my example in how to
T-6 I.11:5 one lesson, which I **m.** teach as I learned it
T-6 I.16:8 lessons **m.** be learned now as well as then.
T-6 I.18:2 and **m.** be used for their joint salvation.
T-6 I.18:3 Each one **m.** learn to teach that all forms
T-6 I.18:6 and you **m.** think as He thinks if you are
T-6 II.1:1 in mind **m.** involve a rejection of part of it
T-6 II.11:5 in which you **m.** perceive God's creations,
T-6 II.12:6 gave to Him and for which He **m.** speak,
T-6 II.12:8 **m.** shine outward to make you aware of it.
T-6 III.2:1 That is why you **m.** teach only one lesson.
T-6 III.2:2 you **m.** learn only from the Holy Spirit
T-6 III.2:3 are something you **m.** learn to remember.
T-6 III.4:4 By teaching peace you **m.** learn it yourself
T-6 III.4:6 An idea that you share you **m.** have. It
T-6 IV.8:5 that the perfect **m.** now be perfected. In
T-6 IV.9:1 Abilities **m.** be developed before you can
T-6 V.1:8 "My children sleep and **m.** be awakened."
T-6 V.3:2 what you **m.** avoid to escape from harm,
T-6 V.A.2:6 the mind **m.** be stronger than the body.
T-6 V.A.4:9 **m.** be no range in what you offer to your
T-6 V.A.6:1 and the only one you **m.** take for yourself.
T-6 V.A.6:3 where you and only you **m.** remain. This
T-6 V.B.1:7 What you **m.** recognize is that when you
T-6 V.B.6:4 it **m.** dawn on your mind that you are
T-6 V.B.7:2 It **m.**, however, be insane to believe that it
T-6 V.B.9:4 it follows. Realizing that it ***m.*** follow is a
T-6 V.C.1:1 the Holy Spirit is evaluative, and **m.** be.
T-6 V.C.2:2 to strengthen what you **m.** learn to avoid.
T-6 V.C.3:2 is something you **m.** be vigilant *against.* It
T-6 V.C.4:3 only that you can be, but that you **m.** be. It
T-6 V.C.4:5 that it teaches there **m.** be no exceptions,
T-6 V.C.4:8 as you **m.** be vigilant against anything,
T-6 V.C.5:2 what you are you **m.** learn to remember.
T-6 V.C.5:8 nature of the steps you **m.** take with Him.
T-6 V.C.6:5 to teach you that you **m.** be included, and
T-6 V.C.6:5 not is the only thing that you **m.** exclude.
T-6 V.C.7:5 is why you **m.** be vigilant on God's behalf.
T-6 V.C.8:2 is one. Now you **m.** be vigilant to hold its
T-6 V.C.8:7 about being **m.** not enter your mind, or
T-6 V.C.9:5 given you a sick mind that **m.** be healed.
T-6 V.C.9:9 choose to teach the same thing **m.** be in
T-6 V.C.10:6 you **m.** now turn your effort against it.
T-7 I.2:3 so **m.** your creative thought proceed from
T-7 I.4:3 To gain you **m.** give, not bargain. To
T-7 I.4:7 His gifts, and so your gifts **m.** be like His.
T-7 I.4:8 to the Kingdom **m.** be like His gifts to you
T-7 I.7:4 It **m.** be understood that the word "first"
T-7 II.2:7 Laws **m.** be adapted to circumstances if
T-7 II.2:8 and I assure you that you **m.** obey them,
T-7 II.4:1 Laws **m.** be communicated if they are to
T-7 II.4:2 they **m.** be translated for those who speak
T-7 II.4:3 he **m.** alter the form of what he translates,
T-7 II.6:2 it **m.** be consistent to be remembered.
T-7 II.6:7 Therefore you **m.** forget or relinquish one
T-7 III.2:10 You **m.**, therefore, be teaching something
T-7 III.3:2 war **m.** look for brothers and recognize all
T-7 IV.2:1 The Holy Spirit **m.** work *through* you to
T-7 IV.4:4 that your forgetting **m.** be translated into
T-7 V.3:1 can develop and **m.** develop if he is to be
T-7 V.3:6 but you **m.** remember that magic always
T-7 V.7:8 you **m.** learn to change your mind about
T-7 VI.1:3 and why it **m.** be relinquished entirely. If
T-7 VI.3:2 it, which **m.** result in extreme anxiety.
T-7 VI.4:7 is your power, which the ego **m.** deny. It
T-7 VI.4:8 **m.** also deny everything this power gives
T-7 VI.8:2 to the belief that you **m.** be a body. By not
T-7 VI.8:8 Commitment to either **m.** be total; they
T-7 VI.8:9 you **m.** give up the idea of conflict entirely
T-7 VI.11:2 The attack **m.** be blind, however, because
T-7 VI.12:3 **m.** be vigilant against this divided state
T-7 VII.2:8 **m.** determine every response you make.
T-7 VII.3:11 made perception and it **m.** last as long as
T-7 VII.8:4 You **m.** be fearful if you believe that your
T-7 VIII.1:11 Every mind **m.** project or extend, because
T-7 VIII.2:1 The ego's use of projection **m.** be fully
T-7 IX.2:3 God, and any totality ***m.*** include God.
T-7 IX.2:6 Being ***m.*** be extended. That is how it
T-7 IX.3:6 unfulfillment and therefore you **m.** create
T-7 X.7:4 whose will **m.** be the Will of the Father,
T-7 XI.6:6 and you **m.** have the glory you see in him.
T-7 XI.7:8 But you **m.** also know all He created, to
T-8 I.3:3 reality that you **m.** make to secure peace,
T-8 I.4:1 learning **m.** have taught you the wrong
T-8 I.6:1 such a curriculum **m.** be fully recognized
T-8 II.1:3 of the curriculum, you **m.** learn it of Him.
T-8 II.3:8 of the curriculum that **m.** be unconflicted,
T-8 III.3:4 The Father **m.** give fatherhood to His Son,
T-8 III.3:4 Own Fatherhood **m.** be extended outward
T-8 IV.1:1 experience only this you **m.** be refusing to
T-8 IV.1:5 is complete, and you **m.** be included in it.
T-8 IV.2:9 my light **m.** dispel it because of what it is.
T-8 IV.3:7 world **m.** therefore despise and reject me,
T-8 IV.4:4 If you want to have it of me, you **m.** give it
T-8 IV.4:6 You **m.** accept guidance from within. The
T-8 IV.4:7 The guidance **m.** be what you want, or it
T-8 IV.4:9 but you **m.** collaborate by believing that I
T-8 IV.5:6 The decision to unite **m.** be unequivocal,
T-8 IV.8:8 part of One you **m.** be part of the Other,
T-8 IV.8:11 You **m.** be included in It, because It is
T-8 VI.6:10 from His, and so you **m.** will as He wills.
T-8 VII.5:4 but you **m.** have attacked yourself first.
T-8 VII.5:5 own salvation, which **m.** bring him his.
T-8 VII.8:2 suffers, and he **m.** become depressed.

| | |
|---|---|
| T-8.....VII.12:6 | Learning **m.** lead beyond the body to the |
| T-8.....VII.15:8 | it **m.** be unreal since it is a form of attack, |
| T-8..... VIII.2:5 | end. You **m.** have noticed an outstanding |
| T-8.......IX.9:8 | His Will **m.** stand forever and in all things |
| T-9...........I.2:4 | then it **m.** follow that you will not learn |
| T-9...........I.5:2 | the Holy Spirit **m.** remind you that this is |
| T-9...........I.9:1 | everyone **m.** remember the Will of God, |
| T-9...........I.9:1 | ultimately everyone **m.** recognize himself. |
| T-9........ I.11:3 | belief that you **m.** have the impossible in |
| T-9........ I.12:1 | Any attempt to deny what *is* **m.** be fearful, |
| T-9........ I.14:7 | *Christ is in me, and where He is God* **m.** *be,* |
| T-9......... II.1:4 | You **m.** remember, however, that the |
| T-9......... II.6:9 | **m.** be for your brother *because* it is for you |
| T-9........ III.3:1 | ego you **m.** be seeing through yours, |
| T-9........ III.3:2 | errors. This ***m.*** be true, since there is no |
| T-9........ III.5:3 | to the Holy Spirit, you **m.** do this with his. |
| T-9........ IV.4:7 | "mysteries," insisting that you **m.** accept |
| T-9........ IV.5:4 | or you will also believe that you **m.** undo |
| T-9........ IV.8:4 | insane guide **m.** be totally insane himself. |
| T-9......... V.2:3 | who searches fantasies for truth **m.** be |
| T-9......... V.5:4 | and he **m.** learn from his own teaching. |
| T-9......... V.7:1 | approach, then, **m.** arrive at an impasse; |
| T-9......... V.7:5 | who **m.** decide with God that there is |
| T-9......... V.8:3 | being *for* him, it **m.** also be for his patient. |
| T-9........ VI.1:4 | not experiencing joy yourself there **m.** be |
| T-9........ VI.1:5 | you **m.** be dissociating it in yourself. |
| T-9........ VI.4:4 | Because the Sonship **m.** create as one, you |
| T-9....... VII.1:3 | He **m.** have made it possible and easy to |
| T-9....... VII.3:3 | And this evaluation **m.** be in your mind, |
| T-9....... VII.5:2 | yourself and **m.** therefore regard yourself |
| T-9....... VII.5:3 | and **m.** maintain for its existence? Can |
| T-9....... VII.7:5 | And this **m.** be questioned from beyond it |
| T-9..... VIII.6:5 | and grandiosity can and **m.** alternate, |
| T-9..... VIII.7:5 | Yet it **m.** be insane because it is not true. |
| T-9... VIII.11:1 | your evaluation of yourself **m.** *be* God's. |
| T-10.......in.1:4 | You **m.** learn that time is solely at your |
| T-10....... II.1:2 | it. Knowledge **m.** precede dissociation, so |
| T-10....... II.5:4 | you **m.** have forgotten what you are. And |
| T-10....... II.6:3 | but you have not considered what it **m.** be |
| T-10...... III.4:6 | A sick god **m.** be an idol, made in the |
| T-10...... IV.2:3 | know reality **m.** involve the willingness to |
| T-10...... IV.8:5 | the little light **m.** be acknowledged first, |
| T-10....... V.2:2 | **m.** receive the message you give because it |
| T-10....... V.6:5 | what you deny you **m.** have once known. |
| T-10....... V.9:6 | you **m.** acknowledge Him as your Creator |
| T-10..... V.12:5 | **m.** learn to see him to learn of his reality. |
| T-10..... V.12:6 | how you **m.** see yourself to learn of yours. |
| T-10..... V.13:5 | real Fatherhood **m.** be acknowledged if |
| T-10..... V.14:5 | eternity, you **m.** look only on the eternal. |
| T-11.......in.1:2 | sides fairly, you will realize this **m.** be true |
| T-11.........I.2:2 | what has no limits **m.** be everywhere. |
| T-11.........I.7:9 | of His Will, yours **m.** be the same. |
| T-11.........I.8:5 | **m.** ask what God's Will is in everything, |
| T-11...... I.11:5 | who share His life **m.** share it to know it, |
| T-11....... II.4:5 | And yet the invitation **m.** come from you, |
| T-11....... II.6:3 | You who have God **m.** be as God, for His |
| T-11...... III.7:6 | And your mind **m.** be as pure as His, if |
| T-11...... III.7:9 | All your brothers **m.** enter with you, for |
| T-11...... IV.3:2 | and your Self **m.** be unknown to you. |
| T-11...... IV.4:3 | and these you **m.** learn to recognize and |
| T-11...... IV.5:3 | That is why blame **m.** be undone, not |
| T-11...... IV.8:3 | the Son **m.** share what belongs to Him, |
| T-11....... V.1:3 | you do not want it, you **m.** be ready. Let |
| T-11....... V.1:5 | for we **m.** look first at this to see beyond it |
| T-11....... V.2:9 | upon darkness through light **m.** dispel it. |
| T-11....... V.8:1 | You **m.** recognize that the last thing the |
| T-11..... V.10:5 | **m.** fear unreality *because* you have denied |
| T-11..... V.13:4 | and to establish this belief it **m.** attack. |
| T-11..... V.14:3 | consistent truth **m.** be meaningless. The |
| T-11..... V.14:5 | is meaningless, inconsistency **m.** be true. |
| T-11..... V.16:5 | who are convinced by it **m.** be deluded. |
| T-11..... V.17:4 | yet where the Son is the Father **m.** be. |
| T-11...... VI.6:1 | Resurrection **m.** compel your allegiance |
| T-11...... VI.9:3 | you **m.** see the works I do through you, or |
| T-11.... VI.10:3 | part **m.** be like mine if you learn it of me. |
| T-11..... VII.1:3 | **m.** be another world that you do not see. |
| T-11... VIII.6:4 | question you **m.** ask to learn His answer? |
| T-11... VIII.9:5 | for thereby you **m.** be deceived in yourself |
| T-12.........I.8:3 | Spirit **m.** still translate the fear into truth. |
| T-12.........I.8:12 | it is, the unreality of fear **m.** dawn on you. |
| T-12....... II.1:6 | The sick **m.** heal themselves, for the truth |
| T-12....... II.1:7 | light in another mind **m.** shine into theirs |
| T-12....... II.2:4 | to it. He **m.** himself withdraw that power, |
| T-12....... II.6:2 | **m.** accomplish it because it is His Will. |
| T-12....... II.6:4 | been accomplished for you **m.** be yours. |
| T-12....... II.9:1 | you who choose to banish fear **m.** succeed |
| T-12..... II.10:5 | Yet you **m.** look at it yourself in perfect |
| T-12...... III.7:1 | reality, the real world **m.** be in his mind. |
| T-12...... III.7:2 | insane thoughts, too, **m.** be in his mind, |
| T-12.... III.7:10 | why you **m.** realize that your hatred is in |
| T-12.... III.7:10 | why you **m.** get rid of it before you can |
| T-12.... III.10:1 | its source, and where it begins it **m.** end. |
| T-12.... III.10:9 | you **m.** relinquish your investment in the |
| T-12...... IV.2:2 | which **m.** end in perceived self-defeat. For |
| T-12...... IV.4:1 | Do you realize that the ego **m.** set you on |
| T-12...... IV.7:3 | Yet you **m.** invest in it, not with money |
| T-12...... IV.7:6 | **m.** relinquish your investment in death, |
| T-12....... V.1:3 | you **m.** have perceived yourself as weak. |
| T-12...... VI.5:2 | Yet you **m.** learn the cost of sleeping, and |
| T-12...... VI.7:7 | and being in God it **m.** also be in you. |
| T-12..... VII.2:1 | world **m.** play his part in its redemption, |
| T-12..... VII.2:3 | you see its effects you know it **m.** be there. |
| T-12..... VII.3:4 | you will understand where He **m.** be, and |
| T-12..... VII.7:1 | up to you, but you **m.** do one or the other, |
| T-12..... VII.7:1 | and you **m.** look in before you look out. |
| T-13.........I.4:4 | where you **m.** be because He is with you. |
| T-13.........I.8:4 | and therefore guilt **m.** deprive you of the |
| T-13.........I.8:5 | you are eternal, and "always" **m.** be now. |
| T-13....... I.10:4 | you who cherish guilt **m.** also believe it, |
| T-13....... I.11:1 | are guilty, and this **m.** increase the guilt, |
| T-13....... II.4:5 | So it is this secret that we **m.** look upon, |
| T-13....... II.5:6 | identify with it you **m.** believe its goal is |
| T-13....... II.6:3 | and guiltlessness **m.** be interpreted as the |
| T-13....... II.7:5 | **m.** believe that by not learning the course |
| T-13...... III.6:1 | You **m.** look upon your illusions and not |
| T-13...... III.9:4 | Healing **m.** be as complete as fear, for love |
| T-13.... III.11:5 | and it **m.** seek a place of darkness where it |
| T-13...... IV.3:3 | only have been futile if it **m.** come to this, |
| T-13...... IV.6:1 | the past are precisely what you **m.** escape. |
| T-13...... IV.8:4 | of salvation that you **m.** learn to accept, if |
| T-13...... IV.9:4 | It **m.** be accomplished in the present to |
| T-13....... V.3:7 | And thus it is you **m.** attack yourself first, |
| T-13....... V.6:1 | **m.** occur to you that you have withdrawn |
| T-13..... V.7:13 | And it is God Whom you **m.** offer them, |
| T-13....... V.8:8 | Yet for this, light **m.** be excluded. Dreams |
| T-13...... VI.3:6 | it past and gone, you **m.** not see it now. If |
| T-13.... VI.12:2 | attraction of light **m.** draw you willingly, |
| T-13..... VII.2:1 | The world you see **m.** be denied, for sight |
| T-13..... VII.7:6 | He **m.** deny the world of pain the instant |
| T-13... VII.16:4 | peace of mind that we **m.** find together. |
| T-13... VIII.2:4 | All knowledge **m.** be yours, for in you is |
| T-13... VIII.3:2 | Yet the last step **m.** be taken by God, |
| T-13... VIII.5:5 | light **m.** come into the darkened world to |
| T-13...... IX.1:6 | they are guilty, and so they **m.** condemn. |
| T-13...... IX.1:7 | and the past the laws of God **m.** intervene |
| T-13...... IX.5:6 | punishment upon yourself **m.** be insane. |
| T-13....... X.1:3 | which attention is diverted, **m.** be true; |
| T-13....... X.1:3 | diverted, must be true; and **m.** be fearful, |
| T-13....... X.6:3 | **m.** learn that guilt is always totally insane |
| T-13...... XI.1:3 | Believing this he **m.** escape, for such a war |
| T-13...... XI.4:4 | Him to demonstrate which **m.** be true. He |
| T-13.... XI.10:7 | Will of God **m.** be accepted as your will. |
| T-13.... XI.11:1 | is not true **m.** be reconciled with truth. |
| T-14.........I.1:1 | not know it, you need to learn it **m.** be so. |
| T-14.........I.1:2 | but its conditions **m.** be acquired for it is |
| T-14.........I.1:4 | blessing, it **m.** have come first to yourself. |
| T-14.........I.1:5 | And you **m.** also have accepted it as yours |
| T-14.........I.1:7 | complete forgiveness you **m.** have let guilt |
| T-14.........I.2:3 | of the world **m.** therefore lead to nothing, |
| T-14.........I.2:4 | **m.** direct your thoughts unto oblivion. |
| T-14.........I.4:2 | He **m.** therefore teach you not to deny it. |
| T-14.........I.5:1 | **m.** begin His teaching by showing you |
| T-14.........I.5:2 | but He **m.** introduce the simple truth into |
| T-14....... II.1:2 | are steadfastly devoted to misery **m.** first |
| T-14....... II.4:7 | and so they ***m.*** have been nothing. And |
| T-14....... II.6:1 | you **m.** give everything you have learned |
| T-14.... III.10:4 | that what they do not want **m.** hurt them. |
| T-14.... III.11:1 | that you **m.** make decisions for yourself. |
| T-14.... III.12:3 | against it, for being of Him it **m.** be true. |
| T-14...... IV.2:3 | This state, and only this, **m.** you attain, |
| T-14...... IV.3:7 | **m.** learn that it is all you want to learn. |
| T-14...... IV.4:1 | what **m.** be done before that knowledge |
| T-14...... IV.7:2 | Therefore, you ***m.*** be guiltless. Yet if you |
| T-14....... V.5:3 | the guiltlessness that **m.** have been denied |
| T-14....... V.7:1 | that cannot fail and **m.** result in peace. No |
| T-14... V.10:12 | Thus He creates, and thus **m.** you restore. |
| T-14...... V.11:6 | Holiness **m.** be shared, for therein lies |
| T-14...... VI.1:9 | cannot be loved, and so it **m.** be feared. |
| T-14...... VI.3:8 | live in light. Everything else **m.** disappear. |
| T-14...... VI.4:2 | the truth of one **m.** make the falsity of its |
| T-14...... VI.5:7 | it to crucify yourself **m.** learn of Him how |
| T-14...... VI.7:5 | once, and this **m.** lead to unintelligibility. |
| T-14...... VI.8:2 | therefore **m.** remove whatever interferes |
| T-14...... VI.8:5 | **m.** open all doors and let the light come |
| T-14..... VII.1:3 | Opposites **m.** be brought together, not |
| T-14..... VII.1:5 | everything that is not real **m.** disappear, |
| T-14..... VII.1:8 | Yet the perception **m.** be without deceit, |
| T-14..... VII.4:2 | that salvation **m.** come to you this way, if |
| T-14..... VII.4:6 | acceptance **m.** be withdrawn from one of |
| T-14..... VII.5:8 | **m.** be gently turned to your own good, |
| T-14... VII.6:11 | His judgment **m.** prevail, and He will give |
| T-14.... VIII.4:2 | the place where you **m.** meet with truth. |
| T-14.... VIII.4:3 | And there you **m.** be led, through gentle |
| T-14...... IX.2:6 | are meaningless, for reality **m.** be one. It |
| T-14...... IX.5:3 | images of other gods **m.** dim the mirror |
| T-14........X.1:1 | the knowledge of creation **m.** continue |
| T-14........X.3:4 | something that **m.** come from elsewhere, |
| T-14........X.5:5 | and that more than an ego **m.** be in you. |
| T-14........X.8:2 | if the form is acceptable the content **m.** be |
| T-14..... X.12:2 | brother **m.** give it to you because of what |
| T-14..... X.12:3 | you **m.** give it because of what you are. |
| T-14..... XI.1:7 | of strength so pitiful that it **m.** fail you. |
| T-14..... XI.4:6 | your dark lessons **m.** be brought willingly |
| T-14..... XI.7:8 | establishes the fact that guiltlessness **m.** |
| T-14.... XI.13:2 | all. For this it **m.** be peace they want, and |
| T-14.... XI.14:1 | want peace you **m.** abandon the teacher |
| T-14.... XI.14:4 | in His Creator **m.** encompass faith in His |
| T-14.... XI.14:8 | is in you, and from it peace **m.** come. |
| T-14.... XI.15:3 | and you **m.** be convinced you did them |
| T-15.........I.3:4 | of its strange religion **m.** therefore be the |
| T-15....... I.4:10 | For the ego **m.** seem to keep fear from you |
| T-15....... I.4:11 | it **m.** engender fear in order to maintain |
| T-15.........I.6:5 | belief in guilt **m.** lead to the belief in hell, |
| T-15....... I.13:8 | guilt. You **m.** be holy if you offer holiness. |
| T-15........ II.6:9 | witnesses to It, your doubts **m.** disappear. |
| T-15...... III.3:1 | and one you **m.** learn to remember all the |
| T-15...... III.4:4 | striving **m.** be directed against littleness, |
| T-15...... III.8:4 | Learn that you **m.** be worthy of the Prince |
| T-15...... III.9:9 | who **m.** remain forever beyond littleness. |
| T-15...... IV.1:6 | You **m.** decide when it is. Delay it not. For |
| T-15...... IV.2:1 | Your practice **m.** therefore rest upon |
| T-15...... IV.3:3 | you **m.** fill if you would join with me, by |
| T-15...... VI.2:4 | forget not that my faith **m.** be as perfect |
| T-15...... VI.3:3 | you **m.** believe that strength comes from |
| T-15...... VI.3:4 | Someone **m.** always lose if you perceive |
| T-15...... VI.8:7 | to do this you will learn what you **m.** be, |
| T-15..... VII.3:1 | sick attraction of guilt **m.** be recognized |
| T-15... VII.10:2 | guilt cannot be love and ***m.*** be anger. All |
| T-15... VII.11:5 | think their minds **m.** be kept private or |
| T-15.... VIII.1:1 | the Holy Spirit **m.** not leave you as your |
| T-15.... VIII.1:2 | **m.** use everything in this world for your |
| T-15.... VIII.1:3 | **m.** side with every sign or token of your |
| T-15.... VIII.1:3 | to learn of Him what the truth **m.** be. He |
| T-15.... VIII.3:9 | And where you are **m.** everyone seek, and |
| T-15.... VIII.6:4 | knows it **m.** be possible because it is the |
| T-15...... IX.2:5 | communication **m.** be unlimited in order |
| T-15...... IX.6:2 | But this you **m.** remember; the attraction |
| T-15...... IX.6:7 | the Holy Spirit **m.** undo to set him free. |
| T-15........X.5:5 | the decision you believe that you **m.** make |
| T-15........X.5:9 | And it is this that you **m.** look upon; |
| T-15..... X.5:12 | someone **m.** pay and someone must get. |
| T-15..... X.5:12 | someone must pay and someone **m.** get. |
| T-15........X.6:8 | the price of love, which **m.** be paid by fear |
| T-15........X.9:3 | **m.** choose between total freedom and |
| T-15........X.9:4 | recognizing the one decision you **m.** make |
| T-15...... XI.2:8 | Love **m.** be total to give Him welcome, for |
| T-15...... XI.3:6 | And without sacrifice there love ***m.*** be. |

T-15...... XI.4:1 that sacrifice is love **m.** learn that sacrifice
T-15...... XI.7:3 communication, which **m.** be of the mind
T-16.........I.1:1 that is what you **m.** *refuse* to understand.
T-16....... II.1:2 told that it **m.** include everyone to *be* holy.
T-16....... II.2:8 And so there **m.** be Something in you that
T-16....... II.4:5 you **m.** understand it or else it is not real.
T-16...... III.1:5 He **m.** have done so from the basis of a
T-16...... III.3:5 And it **m.** be that what you taught came
T-16...... III.3:7 What functions **m.** be there. And it is
T-16...... III.4:6 it? It **m.** be this part that is really outside
T-16...... III.6:3 are the universe, all else **m.** be outside,
T-16...... III.6:8 you **m.** learn that you but taught yourself,
T-16...... III.8:2 Sooner or later **m.** everyone bridge the
T-16...... IV.5:9 other, the decision **m.** be one of despair.
T-16...... IV.6:4 from one illusion into another **m.** fail. If
T-16...... IV.7:1 and truth **m.** be recognized if it is to be
T-16.... IV.10:1 to union in yourself ***m.*** lead to knowledge,
T-16.... IV.11:8 wholly without illusion, as you **m.** love.
T-16.. IV.11:10 Whom God remembers **m.** be whole.
T-16.... IV.13:2 interfere with God **m.** interfere with you.
T-16....... V.1:3 these **m.** be understood for what they are.
T-16....... V.2:4 it and why, you will realize what it **m.** be.
T-16....... V.5:8 which the ego cannot interfere, **m.** be hell
T-16..... V.10:2 fearful nature, nor of the guilt it **m.** entail,
T-16..... V.10:4 sacrifice is that God **m.** die so you can live
T-16..... V.12:4 relationship **m.** be recognized for what it
T-16...... VI.1:4 that are unlike this one ***m.*** be unnatural.
T-16...... VI.3:4 that it **m.** foster guilt and therefore must
T-16...... VI.3:4 foster guilt and therefore **m.** imprison.
T-16...... VI.4:2 If you value it, you **m.** also value the body.
T-16..... VII.1:5 and for which **m.** someone else atone.
T-16... VII.2:11 gone. It **m.** be, therefore, that you are
T-16... VII.2:12 And it **m.** also be that this purpose could
T-16..... VII.4:1 you **m.** return to the past to find salvation
T-16..... VII.6:2 Spirit **m.** teach through comparisons, and
T-16..... VII.9:2 All that **m.** be forgiven are the illusions
T-17.........I.3:1 you maintain that there **m.** be an order of
T-17.........I.3:4 If you but realized what this **m.** do to your
T-17.........I.5:3 of reference for its meaning **m.** be itself.
T-17.........I.5:6 orders of reality that **m.** imprison you.
T-17...... III.1:2 All the rest **m.** be forgotten. Forgiveness
T-17...... III.4:4 Once it is formed, doubt **m.** enter in,
T-17...... III.5:8 of separation, and where it **m.** be undone.
T-17...... III.5:9 separation **m.** be corrected where it was
T-17...... III.6:6 in separation is that it **m.** be undone. Let
T-17...... III.7:4 The spark of holiness **m.** be safe, however
T-17...... IV.5:3 And you **m.** realize just what this means if
T-17...... IV.5:8 is its chief defense, **m.** therefore be insane
T-17.... IV.10:4 And your defense **m.** now be undertaken,
T-17.... IV.10:6 part of Them, and They **m.** save you, for
T-17.... IV.12:5 **m.** be the pictures only that you compare,
T-17....... V.7:4 But you **m.** exclude major areas of fantasy
T-17..... V.12:2 It **m.** be kept shining and gracious in your
T-17..... V.13:4 for the attack **m.** blind you to yourself.
T-17...... VI.1:2 in order to be simple it ***m.*** be unequivocal.
T-17...... VI.1:3 for this it is apparent that it **m.** be clear.
T-17...... VI.3:2 to piece together what it **m.** have meant.
T-17...... VI.5:2 truth and sanity, its outcome **m.** be peace.
T-17...... VI.5:4 without them, where peace is they **m.** be.
T-17...... VI.6:3 the goal of truth is set, there faith **m.** be.
T-17...... VI.7:2 unity, and **m.** obscure the goal of truth.
T-17..... VII.2:3 the meaning of the problem **m.** be lost,
T-17..... VII.2:5 Yet faith **m.** be where something has been
T-17..... VII.3:4 Some idea of bodies **m.** have entered, for
T-17..... VII.4:4 Your faith **m.** grow to meet the goal that
T-17..... VII.6:5 hand, so **m.** its faith go everywhere with it
T-17... VII.10:3 For loneliness in God **m.** be a dream. You
T-17.... VIII.5:6 your lack of faith in him **m.** mean to you.
T-18....... I.13:6 brought you and him together **m.** extend,
T-18....... II.5:4 the dream produces **m.** come from you. It
T-18...... III.4:4 And fear **m.** disappear before you now. Be
T-18...... IV.2:7 assuming that you **m.** achieve the state its
T-18...... IV.3:6 to be, you **m.** be interfering with His Will.
T-18...... IV.4:8 that you **m.** make the learner different.
T-18...... IV.5:6 those who think that they **m.** first atone,
T-18.... IV.5:13 *it, I* ***m.*** *be willing not to substitute my own in*
T-18...... IV.7:2 insist there **m.** be more that you need do.
T-18....... V.4:2 And so they **m.** be loving. Their message
T-18....... V.6:3 it **m.** be that whatever threatens the peace
T-18 ..... VI.1:2 That is what you **m.** ultimately learn, for
T-18 ..... VI.9:8 love. Yet love **m.** be forever like itself,
T-18 .... VII.3:7 and therefore **m.** be thought of in the past
T-18 ..... IX.1:2 also been told that error **m.** be corrected
T-18 ... IX.11:2 of what **m.** forever lie beyond words. We
T-18 ... IX.11:7 The readiness for knowledge still **m.** be
T-19 ........I.1:5 And everyone **m.** be involved in it, or else
T-19 ........I.5:1 be difficult to realize that faith **m.** be the
T-19 ........I.6:1 is the belief that the body **m.** be healed,
T-19 ........I.6:7 illusion in the mind, where both **m.** be,
T-19 ........I.7:5 separation is, and where it **m.** be healed.
T-19 .....II.6:11 As a mistake, *it* **m.** be brought to truth. It
T-19 ..... III.2:3 punishment **m.** have been really done.
T-19 ..... III.2:5 What **m.** be punished, must be true. And
T-19 ..... III.2:5 What must be punished, **m.** be true. And
T-19 ..... III.2:6 And what is true **m.** be eternal, and will
T-19 ..... III.4:6 calls for punishment **m.** call for nothing.
T-19 ..... III.4:7 Every mistake ***m.*** be a call for love. What,
T-19 ..... III.5:7 the mind **m.** accept as true what it is told
T-19 ..... III.6:2 the Creator **m.** have extended Himself,
T-19 ..... III.6:3 sin is real, God **m.** be at war with Himself.
T-19 ..... III.6:4 He **m.** be split, and torn between good
T-19 ..... III.6:5 He **m.** have created what wills to destroy
T-19 ..... III.7:6 God, before which God Himself **m.** bow,
T-19 ..... III.8:1 **m.** forever be beyond the hope of healing.
T-19 ..... IV.2:2 already lies deeply within **m.** first expand,
T19....IV.A.1:1 first obstacle that peace **m.** flow across is
T19....IV.A.1:6 the whole creation, it **m.** begin with you,
T19....IV.A.2:2 that it **m.** dispossess to dwell with you?
T19....IV.A.5:7 your brother **m.** fall away because of the
T19..IV.A.6:10 which you accepted **m.** all illusions end.
T19....IV.A.7:1 in and push Him out ***m.*** produce conflict.
T19..IV.A.10:3 As love **m.** look past fear, so must fear see
T19..IV.A.10:3 look past fear, so **m.** fear see love not. For
T19....IV.B.1:1 We said that peace **m.** first surmount the
T19....IV.B.1:3 second obstacle that peace **m.** flow across,
T19....IV.B.6:4 for if you are guilty, so **m.** I be. But if I
T19....IV.B.9:3 gives **m.** be extended if you would have its
T19....IV.B.9:9 of peace and happiness in what **m.** fail?
T19..IV.B.12:6 The attraction of guilt ***m.*** enter with it, and
T19..IV.B.16:4 Not one but **m.** believe that yielding to
T19..IV.B.16:5 one but **m.** regard the body as himself,
T19..IV.B.17:2 it, and what is offered **m.** also be received,
T19....IV.C.1:3 you **m.** learn still more about this strange
T19....IV.C.1:3 third obstacle that peace **m.** flow across.
T19....IV.C.7:5 **m.** flow across seems to be very great. For
T19..IV.C.11:2 they **m.** stand for something other than
T19..IV.C.11:3 but **m.** be sought in what they represent.
T19... IV.D.1:5 peace **m.** still surmount a final obstacle,
T19... IV.D.5:1 Every obstacle that peace **m.** flow across
T19. IV.D.10:2 place to which everyone **m.** come when he
T19. IV.D.20:5 **m.** choose what it will *be* that he receives.
T-20 ....... III.5:7 And to this world **m.** you adjust as long as
T-20 ... III.11:3 sin, and it **m.** look on others as on itself.
T-20 ..... IV.6:6 Each holy relationship **m.** enter here, to
T-20 ..... IV.8:1 there is so much that **m.** be done before
T-20 ...... V.7:4 to pain and death **m.** be forgotten. This is
T-20 ...... V.8:3 Let us consider now what he **m.** learn, to
T-20 ..... VI.4:4 And its relationships **m.** be unholy, for
T-20 ..... VI.9:1 Idols **m.** disappear, and leave no trace
T-20 .... VII.1:1 **m.** be brought in line before your holy
T-20 .... VII.2:6 want a purpose you **m.** be willing to want
T-20 .... VII.3:9 the means to do so **m.** be possible as well.
T-20 .... VII.4:7 ego. Either **m.** be an error, for both would
T-20 .... VII.4:8 both **m.** be undone for purposes of truth.
T-20 .VIII.10:3 **m.** thus reflect the sight you saw within;
T-20 .VIII.11:2 who could refuse what **m.** come after?
T-21 ......in.2:8 the power to give it joy **m.** lie within you.
T-21 ........I.1:1 world the sightless "see" **m.** be imagined,
T-21 ........I.1:2 They **m.** infer what could be seen from
T-21 ........I.2:2 to imagine what the world **m.** look like. It
T-21 ........I.2:3 It **m.** be seen before you recognize it for
T-21 ........I.5:1 live, adjusting to it as they think they **m.**,
T-21 .......II.3:6 to Him Who **m.** decide for God for you.
T-21 .......II.4:8 of your wanting **m.** first be recognized.
T-21 .......II.4:9 You **m.** accept its strength, and not its
T-21 .....II.4:10 **m.** perceive that what is strong enough to
T-21 .......II.6:5 a mad revolt against what **m.** forever be.
T-21 .......II.7:4 which seems to tell you what **m.** happen,
T-21 .......II.7:5 you otherwise **m.** therefore seem unreal.
T-21 .......II.8:4 to look within and see what **m.** be there,
T-21 ..... III.1:6 And that is why the Holy Spirit **m.** change
T-21 ..... III.9:1 in sin **m.** think the Holy Spirit asks for
T-21 ... III.10:2 For sacrifice **m.** be exacted of a body, and
T-21 ... III.11:5 night and day, and so they **m.** be joined.
T-21 ..... IV.5:4 and so there **m.** be something else. Think
T-21 ..... IV.8:9 happily, and question not what **m.** be so.
T-21 .......V.5:2 **m.** have been accepted by the Son of God,
T-21 .......V.5:2 for what God wills for him he **m.** receive.
T-21 .......V.5:4 joined the Will of God **m.** be in you now,
T-21 .......V.5:5 You **m.** have set aside a place in which the
T-21 .......V.5:6 He **m.** have been there since the need for
T-21 .....V.5:10 Yet if it **m.** be so, it must exist. And if it
T-21 .....V.5:10 Yet if it must be so, it **m.** exist. And if it
T-21 .....V.5:11 purpose given it, you **m.** be free to find it.
T-21 .......V.6:2 and in this your will **m.** be included. Thus
T-21 .......V.6:3 there **m.** be a part of you that knows His
T-21 .......V.6:4 not meaningful to ask if what **m.** be is so.
T-21 .......V.6:5 for this **m.** have an answer if the plan of
T-21 .......V.6:6 And it **m.** be complete, because its Source
T-21 .......V.7:3 **m.** therefore be together and the same. O
T-21 .....V.10:3 reason tell you now the question **m.** have
T-21 .....V.10:3 you do not know, but **m.** belong to you?
T-21 ..... VI.2:6 you and your brother **m.** be separate. But
T-21 ..... VI.2:7 But reason tells you that this **m.** be wrong
T-21 ..... VI.5:3 tells you **m.** be joined must be insane.
T-21 ..... VI.5:3 tells you must be joined **m.** be insane.
T-21 ..... VI.5:8 But think what you **m.** recognize, if it be
T-21 ..... VI.7:4 given you because he **m.** be one with you.
T-21 ..... VI.8:4 madness sees **m.** be dispelled by reason.
T-21 ..... VI.9:5 It would have you learn what you **m.** be.
T-21 ..... VI.9:6 **m.** be given you to give what It has given,
T-21 ... VI.10:4 that you can understand what you **m.** be.
T-21 .... VII.2:2 see themselves as helpless **m.** believe that
T-21 .... VII.3:5 army of the powerless **m.** be disbanded in
T-21 .... VII.5:1 Yet hate **m.** have a target. There can be
T-21 .... VII.5:6 first he **m.** be willing to perceive a world
T-21 .... VII.5:9 sin tell him that his enemy **m.** be himself.
T-21 .. VII.5:10 these questions, which he **m.** decide, to
T-21 .... VII.7:4 And whom you would have healed **m.** be
T-21 .... VII.7:7 what you want to see **m.** be your choice.
T-21 .... VII.8:2 reason tell you that it **m.** be answered,
T-21 .. VII.12:4 perceiving that "yes" **m.** mean "not no."
T-21 .. VII.13:2 Happiness **m.** be constant, because it is
T-21 .. VIII.1:7 the truth, and therefore **m.** be constant.
T-21 ... VIII.2:2 if you could even imagine what it **m.** be,
T-21 ... VIII.2:8 as peace **m.** come to those who choose to
T-21 ... VIII.3:9 God's giving **m.** be incomplete unless it is
T-22 ......in.4:6 It **m.** extend, as you extended when you
T-22 ......in.4:7 **m.** reach out beyond itself, as you reached
T-22 ........I.1:3 what you **m.** then believe is that you are
T-22 ........I.2:3 are not yours **m.** make no sense to you.
T-22 ........I.3:6 Yet it **m.** be the "something else" that sees
T-22 ........I.5:6 What needs interpretation **m.** be alien.
T-22 ........I.8:7 **m.** He be reborn into His ancient home,
T-22 ........I.9:4 Communication **m.** have been restored to
T-22 ........I.9:6 Reason will tell you that they **m.** have
T-22 ......I.10:5 to show you where your Self **m.** be. It is
T-22 .......II.3:8 Only the timeless **m.** remain unchanged,
T-22 .......II.3:9 imagined, illusions **m.** give way to truth,
T-22 .......II.5:3 then the belief in sin **m.** be eternal. Yet
T-22 .......II.5:5 This **m.** be so, if the idea is like its source.
T-22 .......II.5:7 They **m.** be there, and you must have
T-22 .......II.5:7 must be there, and you **m.** have them.
T-22 .......II.6:1 of you and the ego **m.** be made complete.
T-22 .......II.6:4 Yet to the ego this **m.** be impossible, and
T-22 .......II.6:6 Now **m.** you choose between yourself and
T-22 .......II.6:9 It **m.** be made. Faith and belief can fall to
T-22 .......II.8:6 but *when* **m.** be your choice. For time you
T-22 .....II.10:1 it with the decision that it **m.** be healed,
T-22 ..... III.1:7 is not the body's sight, it ***m.*** be understood
T-22 ..... III.2:5 and thus it **m.** have been an error. The
T-22 ..... III.7:4 if form is not reality it **m.** be an illusion,
T-22 ..... III.7:5 And if you see it you **m.** be mistaken, for
T-22 ..... III.7:6 is not there **m.** be distorted perception,
T-22 ..... III.7:6 and **m.** perceive illusions as the truth.
T-22 ..... III.9:1 born, **m.** value holiness above all else.
T-22 ..... III.9:6 And so it **m.** become impossible for each

T-22......IV.1:2 You **m.** go either one way or the other.
T-22.......V.1:4 They go against what **m.** be true. The
T-22.......V.2:7 that the Holy Spirit offers **m.** be defended
T-22.......V.5:6 **m.** happen when they come together?
T-22.......V.6:6 and so easily that you **m.** be convinced, in
T-22.......V.6:7 If you forgive your brother, this ***m.*** happen
T-22......VI.1:6 And one **m.** serve the other and lead to its
T-22......VI.3:4 serve this end the body **m.** be perceived as
T-22......VI.6:6 now His means **m.** love all that He loves.
T-22....VI.11:6 And you **m.** think that They are separate,
T-22....VI.13:2 you and your brother **m.** be different. Yet
T-22....VI.13:7 to decide which **m.** be true is whether you
T-23.......in.6:8 **m.** be complete if you would recognize it.
T-23.........I.1:5 Conflict within you **m.** imply that you
T-23.........I.1:9 that it **m.** overcome and will succeed.
T-23.........I.5:2 the memory of his Father **m.** be forgotten.
T-23.........I.7:2 For you **m.** be as God created you. Truth
T-23.........I.8:1 Conflict **m.** be between two forces. It
T-23.........I.9:6 He loves **m.** be forever quiet and at peace
T-23.......II.4:1 worshipper of sin, is that each one ***m.*** sin,
T-23.......II.5:3 For One **m.** always be condemned, and by
T-23.......II.6:2 define what the Creator of reality **m.** be;
T-23.......II.6:2 He **m.** think and what He must believe;
T-23.......II.6:2 He must think and what He **m.** believe;
T-23.......II.6:2 He must believe; and how He **m.** respond,
T-23.......II.6:6 He **m.** accept His Son's belief in what he is
T-23.......II.7:6 For now salvation **m.** remain impossible,
T-23.......II.9:2 if the others are accepted, **m.** be true. This
T-23.......II.9:5 Yet all the other laws **m.** lead to this. For
T-23.......II.9:7 would keep from you **m.** be worth having,
T-23.....II.10:1 loss the enemy **m.** suffer to save yourself.
T-23.....II.10:4 so they **m.** take or else be taken from.
T-23.....II.11:3 It **m.** be what you want but never found.
T-23.....II.11:7 you. Now **m.** his body be destroyed and
T-23.....II.12:6 This is the reason why you **m.** attack.
T-23...II.12:10 enmity to your brother, **m.** be salvation.
T-23.....II.13:3 He **m.** have this substitute for love, and
T-23...II.13:12 The means of madness **m.** be insane. Are
T-23.....II.14:4 It **m.** be seen as truth to be believed. And
T-23.....II.14:5 And if it is the truth, then **m.** its opposite,
T-23.....II.15:4 its seeming laws **m.** be perceived as real.
T-23.....II.15:5 goal of madness **m.** be seen as sanity. And
T-23.....II.19:2 Where God created life, there life **m.** be.
T-23.....II.21:1 belief in sin, the faith in chaos **m.** follow.
T-23.....II.21:7 your thinking starts, there **m.** it end.
T-23......III.1:2 then it **m.** follow that you do not always
T-23......III.1:5 fear of punishment the murderer **m.** feel?
T-23....IV.1:11 What is not loving **m.** be an attack. Every
T-23......IV.2:3 both are true, then **m.** they be the same,
T-23......IV.3:5 and what is His **m.** be His Son's as well.
T-23......IV.7:3 purpose, then you **m.** be one with them.
T-23......IV.7:5 no purpose of itself, and **m.** be solitary.
T-24.........I.1:5 And now **m.** war, the substitute for peace,
T-24.........I.4:2 and this **m.** come from someone "better,"
T-24.........I.5:3 And here is what **m.** make the body dear
T-24.........I.5:4 Specialness **m.** be defended. Illusions can
T-24.........I.5:6 For what your brother **m.** become to keep
T-24.........I.5:7 who is "worse" than you **m.** be attacked,
T-24......I.5:10 And who **m.** be his conqueror but you?
T-24.........I.6:6 And he **m.** never reach them, or your goal
T-24.........I.8:3 Himself **m.** honor it or suffer vengeance.
T-24.........I.9:1 are special **m.** defend illusions against the
T-24.........I.9:6 **m.** he be your enemy and not your friend.
T-24........II.1:1 Comparison **m.** be an ego device, for love
T-24........II.2:7 pursuit of specialness **m.** bring you pain.
T-24.....II.10:7 separate from what it is and **m.** forever be
T-24.....II.12:2 serves its purpose **m.** be given to kill. No
T-24......III.3:7 it still **m.** rock and turn and whirl about
T-24......III.5:8 knows that death is not your will, **m.** say,
T-24......IV.1:5 In danger of destruction it **m.** kill, and
T-24......IV.2:9 and body states **m.** shift accordingly. Of
T-24......IV.3:6 so **m.** it be that harmful purpose hurts the
T-24......IV.4:3 To specialness the answer **m.** be "no." A
T-24.......V.8:4 as like to Him in holiness as you **m.** be?
T-24.......V.9:1 **m.** be doubt before there can be conflict.
T-24.......V.9:2 And every doubt **m.** be about yourself.
T-24.......V.9:5 that He **m.** go to find Himself complete.
T-24....VI.10:5 how great the Love of God for you **m.** be,
T-24....VI.13:3 Forget not that this judgment **m.** apply to
T-24.....VII.3:5 what is true in him **m.** be as true in you.
T-24.....VII.7:1 co-creator with the Father **m.** have a Son.
T-24.....VII.7:2 Yet **m.** this Son have been created like
T-24.....VII.8:7 which it **m.** depend on what you see it for.
T-25.......in.1:3 it **m.** be that you are not within a body.
T-25.......in.3:8 such it **m.** be that your mission is for him.
T-25.........I.1:4 is His. And so it **m.** be yours. His Holiness
T-25.........I.2:7 And you **m.** see your brother as yourself.
T-25.........I.6:4 what you **m.** do that it can be experienced
T-25.........I.7:3 all things together, **m.** be its Teacher. Yet
T-25.........I.7:4 Yet **m.** It use the language that this mind
T-25.........I.7:5 **m.** use all learning to transfer illusions to
T-25.......II.1:4 Yet it **m.** be evident the outcome does not
T-25.......II.2:5 where no hope lies **m.** make you hopeless.
T-25.......II.8:5 see the holiness that **m.** be there because
T-25.......II.8:6 and what God gave him **m.** be given you.
T-25.....II.11:2 And you **m.** have one purpose, since He
T-25......III.5:4 to put it out of mind, where it **m.** be, and
T-25......III.5:6 then **m.** the Maker of the world correct
T-25......III.8:6 sin's perception **m.** have been wrong.
T-25....III.8:10 And thus it **m.** have been an error, not a
T-25.......V.1:6 truth, for each attests the other **m.** be true
T-25.......V.2:2 **M.** you not be afraid with "enemies" like
T-25.......V.2:3 And **m.** you not be fearful of yourself? For
T-25.......V.2:5 And now you **m.** believe you are not you,
T-25.......V.2:7 think he **m.** be guilty to maintain the wish
T-25.......V.4:3 So **m.** it remain useless to both. Together,
T-25.......V.6:3 in what the Will of God **m.** be for you. In
T-25.......V.6:4 He hates you, thinking Heaven **m.** be hell.
T-25......VI.5:2 given to himself, and so they **m.** be one.
T-25......VI.5:9 And each **m.** do what is allotted him, for
T-25.....VII.3:2 It **m.** be so that either God is mad, or is
T-25.....VII.4:4 sanity **m.** lie apart from both the Father
T-25.....VII.6:7 view of what the Father and the Son **m.** be
T-25.....VII.7:3 time, and all that you believe **m.** limit you
T-25.....VII.9:1 Now **m.** he question this, because the
T-25...VII.11:1 the underlying tenet God **m.** be insane.
T-25...VII.11:2 that one **m.** gain *because* another lost. If
T-25...VII.11:5 For every little gain **m.** someone lose, and
T-25...VII.11:7 it **m.** be either God or this must be insane
T-25...VII.11:7 it must be either God or this **m.** be insane
T-25...VII.12:2 And everyone ***m.*** gain, if anyone would be
T-25...VII.12:6 And sin **m.** be impossible, if this is true.
T-25...VII.13:1 that either God or you **m.** lose to madness
T-25... VIII.3:5 death **m.** be the cost and must be paid.
T-25... VIII.3:5 death must be the cost and **m.** be paid.
T-25... VIII.6:2 **m.** believe He shares their own confusion,
T-25... VIII.6:2 that their own belief in justice **m.** entail.
T-25. VIII.13:5 another **m.** be an injustice to them both,
T-25. VIII.13:8 is no judge of what **m.** be another's due,
T-25. VIII.13:9 And so **m.** he be envious, and try to take
T-25. VIII.14:6 perceive what justice **m.** accord the Son of
T-25......IX.1:4 until you see all that the answer **m.** entail.
T-25......IX.1:9 recognize that truth **m.** be revealed to you
T-25......IX.3:2 And this **m.** be true, because He asks no
T-25......IX.3:5 unfair **m.** be corrected *because* it is unfair.
T-25......IX.6:3 Healing **m.** be for everyone, because he
T-25......IX.7:8 then **m.** problems rise to block your way,
T-25......IX.8:6 And pardon **m.** be just to everyone.
T-25......IX.9:6 why your sole responsibility **m.** be to take
T-25....IX.10:2 rests; that justice **m.** be done to all, if
T-25....IX.10:3 No one can lose, and everyone **m.** benefit.
T-26.........I.1:3 the central theme that *somebody m. lose.*
T-26.........I.2:4 Each part **m.** sacrifice the other part, to
T-26.........I.3:2 And all the rest **m.** lose this little part,
T-26.........I.3:8 For you **m.** see him as you see yourself.
T-26.........I.4:6 The memory of God **m.** be denied if any
T-26.........I.7:5 so **m.** he be eternally and everywhere. He
T-26.......II.4:9 Son **m.** be unfair and therefore is not so.
T-26.......II.8:3 loves but **m.** be sinless and beyond attack.
T-26......III.4:2 But what is truth to him **m.** be brought to
T-26......III.7:7 to give it up, and choose what ***m.*** be true?
T-26......IV.2:4 And what has been forgiven **m.** join, for
T-26......IV.2:5 The sinless **m.** perceive that they are one,
T-26.......V.9:6 Father has ensured **m.** come to you. And
T-26...V.11:11 It **m.** draw you from the past into the
T-26.....VII.1:2 laws of healing **m.** be understood before
T-26.....VII.1:3 all that **m.** occur for healing to be possible
T-26.....VII.1:4 For when it once is possible it **m.** occur.
T-26.....VII.4:6 is real, and dwells where all reality **m.** be.
T-26.....VII.5:1 answer lies where the belief in sin **m.** be,
T-26.....VII.5:2 Perception's laws **m.** be reversed, because
T-26.....VII.5:4 this **m.** be corrected where the illusion of
T-26.....VII.6:9 and all **m.** yield with equal ease to what
T-26.....VII.7:6 not establish that the picture **m.** be true.
T-26...VII.13:2 and this **m.** still be true because ideas
T-26...VII.14:5 demands that he **m.** make some sacrifice,
T-26...VII.15:5 And what is one to Him **m.** be the same. If
T-26....VIII.4:7 And therefore **m.** it be that if you fear,
T-26....VIII.5:6 Yet only here and now its cause **m.** be, if
T-26....VIII.8:1 untrue, **m.** be already in your mind. And
T-26....VIII.9:6 cause **m.** be delayed until a future time, is
T-26....VIII.9:6 consequence and cause **m.** come as one.
T-26......IX.1:1 Think but how holy you **m.** be from
T-26......IX.1:2 And think how holy he **m.** be when in
T-26........X.2:2 It means that there **m.** be some forms in
T-26.....X.2:10 cannot be Heaven. So it **m.** be hell.
T-26........X.3:1 one is perceived the other **m.** be seen. You
T-26........X.4:7 game of guilt is played, there **m.** be loss.
T-26........X.4:8 loss. Someone **m.** lose his innocence that
T-26........X.5:1 **m.** be unfair to make the other innocent.
T-27.........I.1:6 he **m.** suffer the unfairness that you see.
T-27.........I.4:7 death would prove his errors **m.** be sins.
T-27.........I.7:7 The end of life **m.** come, whatever way
T-27.........I.9:2 futile **m.** it be to see yourself a picture of
T-27........II.1:7 shows that *you* **m.** be protected from him.
T-27........II.2:5 And what has consequences **m.** be real,
T-27......II.2:10 One denies the other and **m.** make it false
T-27........II.3:8 And thus he **m.** have overlooked it and
T-27........II.4:2 **m.** attest his sins have no effect on you to
T-27........II.6:5 hopelessness and death **m.** disappear
T-27......II.10:7 you **m.** be confused about yourself and
T-27......II.10:9 for you **m.** lose what you would take away
T-27......II.11:1 split mind, identity **m.** seem to be divided
T-27......II.11:3 **m.** be a way to punish sins you think are
T-27......II.12:1 Correction *you* would do **m.** separate,
T-27......II.12:4 Yet **m.** He work with what is given Him,
T-27......II.13:1 how this self-perception **m.** extend, and
T-27......II.14:6 the Holy Spirit **m.** represent the other
T-27......II.15:2 it **m.** correct mistakes in you and him. It
T-27......II.16:1 Correction **m.** be left to One Who knows
T-27......III.1:4 And therefore it **m.** be limited and weak,
T-27......III.2:6 that cannot be **m.** stand for empty space
T-27......III.4:3 and where He is there **m.** the truth abide.
T-27......III.4:7 Yet true undoing **m.** be kind. And so the
T-27......IV.1:6 Thus it **m.** be clear you cannot answer
T-27......IV.1:7 Yet if God gave an answer there **m.** be a
T-27......IV.2:1 Thus it **m.** be that time is not involved
T-27......IV.2:2 *now.* Yet it **m.** also be that, in your state of
T-27......IV.2:3 God **m.** have given you a way of reaching
T-27......IV.2:7 is, a problem **m.** be simple and be easily
T-27......IV.2:8 It **m.** be pointless to attempt to solve a
T-27......IV.2:9 Yet just as surely it **m.** be resolved, if it is
T-27.......V.2:3 **m.** provide a witness that compels belief.
T-27.....V.2:10 not mean the conflict **m.** be gone forever
T-27.......V.9:4 All healing **m.** proceed in lawful manner,
T-27......VI.1:1 Pain demonstrates the body **m.** be real. It
T-27......VI.4:6 Yet **m.** He love whatever you hold dear.
T-27.....VII.1:5 He **m.** be innocent because he knows not
T-27.....VII.3:3 While you attack I **m.** be innocent. And
T-27.....VII.4:6 Vengeance **m.** have a focus. Otherwise is
T-27.....VII.4:8 And he **m.** see it in another's hand, if he
T-27.....VII.5:7 here the cause of suffering and sin **m.** lie.
T-27.....VII.7:3 you, uninvited and unasked, **m.** really be.
T-27.....VII.8:5 Careless indeed of him this mind **m.** be,
T-27...VII.10:7 **m.** see the causes of the things you choose
T-28.........I.3:2 which mean that something **m.** be done.
T-28.........I.6:5 change **m.** have a cause that will endure,
T-28........II.1:5 he is God's Son that he **m.** also be a father
T-28........II.2:2 Love **m.** be extended. Purity is not
T-28........II.2:8 Yet **m.** all healing come about because the
T-28........II.3:2 and **m.** be cause because of what he is.
T-28........II.3:7 And as their "father," you **m.** be like them
T-28........II.5:3 **m.** be realized that it is you who dreamed
T-28......III.1:4 Here is where we **m.** begin. And having
T-28......IV.5:2 or you **m.** believe that it is your reality as
T-28......IV.5:5 shares a dream **m.** be the dream he shares
T-28.......V.2:4 Where fear has gone there love **m.** come,

T-28..... V.3:11 **m.** be a dream and cannot be the truth.
T-28..... VII.1:8 will can come between what **m.** be One,
T-28..... VII.2:9 What is unseparated **m.** be joined. And
T-28..... VII.5:3 To be alone **m.** mean you are apart, and if
T-28..... VII.5:4 This seems to prove that you **m.** be apart.
T-29......... I.1:8 For He **m.** be deceptive in His Love. Be
T-29......... I.2:3 love, and therefore **m.** he be afraid of God
T-29......... I.2:6 little gap **m.** bring to those who cherish it,
T-29......... I.3:2 that peace **m.** flow across has not yet gone
T-29......... I.6:5 And so you **m.** misuse each circumstance
T-29......... I.7:3 hate to be maintained, love **m.** be feared;
T-29....... II.1:8 and they **m.** be present where their cause
T-29....... II.2:1 cause, and so it **m.** be you are healed. And
T-29....... II.2:2 the power to heal **m.** also now be yours.
T-29....... II.2:5 But where its cause is **m.** it be. Now is it
T-29....... II.3:4 and love **m.** come wherever they are not.
T-29....... II.5:7 you will believe His Presence **m.** be there.
T-29....... II.8:7 **m.** sacrifice your self, and in His sacrifice
T-29...... III.1:3 But he **m.** learn he is a savior first, before
T-29...... III.1:4 And he **m.** save who would be saved. On
T-29...... III.1:7 Thus he learns it **m.** be his to give. Unless
T-29...... III.1:9 could fail to understand this **m.** be so. For
T-29.... III.1:10 by giving what **m.** be increased thereby?
T-29...... III.2:6 He **m.** be savior from the dream he made,
T-29...... III.2:7 it. He **m.** see someone else as not a body,
T-29...... III.3:7 as heavy shadows **m.** give way to light.
T-29...... III.5:5 in you **m.** be as bright as shines in him.
T-29...... IV.3:3 or assault **m.** be the theme of every dream
T-29....... V.2:2 and where They are, forever **m.** you be.
T-29...... VI.2:6 thing in all the universe that **m.** be one.
T-29...... VI.3:2 then die it **m.** unless it does not take this
T-29.... VI.4:11 It **m.** be life's extension, that it be as one
T-29...... VI.5:3 in the world but **m.** be changed as well.
T-29..... VII.1:7 you want, insisting where it **m.** be found.
T-29..... VII.2:1 No one who comes here but **m.** still have
T-29..... VII.5:1 Idols **m.** fall *because* they have no life, and
T-29..... VII.5:4 Yet each **m.** fail and crumble and decay,
T-29..... VII.6:1 that you **m.** find what is outside yourself
T-29..... VII.9:8 you **m.** protect against the light of truth.
T-29.... VIII.2:6 And thus **m.** seek beyond his little self for
T-29.... VIII.5:3 It **m.** be believed before it seems to come
T-29.... VIII.7:6 Will. Nothing and nowhere **m.** an idol be,
T-29.... VIII.8:7 It **m.** be more. It does not really matter
T-29...... IX.1:2 willing he **m.** be to let himself bow down
T-29...... IX.2:5 So **m.** he judge not, and he will waken.
T-29...... IX.4:2 For idols **m.** be part of it, to save you from
T-29...... IX.9:3 Your self-betrayal **m.** result in fear, for
T-29.... IX.10:5 judgment from what judgment **m.** impose
T-30......... I.2:4 But it **m.** also mean you will not judge the
T-30......... I.6:2 and **m.** have set an answer in your terms.
T-30......... I.6:6 what the question **m.** have really been.
T-30....... I.13:1 It **m.** be clear that it is easier to have a
T-30....... I.15:5 There is no freedom from what **m.** occur.
T-30....... I.15:6 if you think there is, you **m.** be wrong.
T-30....... I.16:2 adviser **m.** agree on what you want before
T-30....... I.17:8 And as you have received, so **m.** you give.
T-30....... II.5:2 the earth but **m.** depend on your decision
T-30...... III.1:8 And this **m.** fail to satisfy, because it is
T-30.... III.11:8 that idols **m.** keep hidden what you are,
T-30...... IV.2:5 Now **m.** he learn the boxes and the bears
T-30...... IV.3:4 It **m.** appear to break your rules for safety
T-30...... IV.4:9 **m.** be neither cherished nor attacked, but
T-30....... V.1:6 it is recognized that all things **m.** be first
T-30....... V.2:8 of the world is one which all **m.** share, if
T-30....... V.6:5 God knew in creation he **m.** know again.
T-30....... V.7:6 For He **m.** be unremembered till His Son
T-30....... V.8:4 you the way that He **m.** walk with you?
T-30...... V.11:4 Will of God **m.** reach to their awareness.
T-30...... VI.3:4 it **m.** uphold the guilt you would "forgive.
T-30...... VI.4:6 The mind **m.** think of its Creator as it
T-30...... VI.5:3 how you learn that you **m.** be forgiven too
T-30...... VI.6:5 you think forgiveness **m.** be limited. And
T-30...... VI.7:1 **m.** be true the miracle can heal all forms
T-30...... VI.7:3 appearance **m.** remain apart from healing
T-30...... VI.7:3 healing, one illusion **m.** be part of truth.
T-30...... VI.7:5 You **m.** forgive God's Son entirely. Or you
T-30...... VI.8:5 the miracle **m.** lack the power to heal.
T-30..... VII.1:5 affect its aim, but **m.** be in accord with it.
T-30..... VII.3:2 But it **m.** accord *one* meaning to them all.
T-30 ..... VII.3:3 it **m.** be that they reflect but different
T-30 ..... VII.5:3 which **m.** assume a different purpose for
T-30 .. VII.6:13 It **m.** be forever unintelligible. This is not
T-30 ..... VII.7:4 state so seemingly unsafe that fear **m.** rise
T-30 ... VIII.1:8 It **m.** transcend all form to be itself. It
T-30 ... VIII.4:3 all. The cost of the belief there **m.** be some
T-31 ...... I.10:1 that His Son is guilty as God's Love **m.** be
T-31 ...... I.10:2 For hate **m.** father fear, and look upon its
T-31 ....... II.1:3 There is no battle that **m.** be prepared; no
T-31 ....... II.2:6 time you think you **m.** decide on anything
T-31 ....... II.2:9 Yet **m.** we see them both, before you can
T-31 ....... II.9:2 holds of what he is and of what you **m.** be.
T-31 ..... II.10:6 **m.** his Father be the same as yours, as he
T-31 ..... II.11:6 the journey is, and how it **m.** be made.
T-31 ..... III.1:2 is first one thing that **m.** be overlearned.
T-31 ..... III.1:3 **m.** become a habit of response so typical
T-31 ..... III.2:5 you are guilty, and **m.** give as you deserve.
T-31 ..... III.3:5 **m.** the body be at fault for what it does. It
T-31 ..... III.3:8 And purpose **m.** be in the body, not the
T-31 ..... III.3:9 The body **m.** act on its own, and motivate
T-31 ..... III.4:4 serve, nor sets conditions that it **m.** obey.
T-31 ..... III.5:3 for they are enemies which sin **m.** kill. In
T-31 ..... III.5:4 are sin **m.** die for what they think they are
T-31 ..... IV.1:8 What **m.** go with you, you will take with
T-31 ..... IV.3:3 time **m.** come when everyone begins to
T-31 ..... IV.3:7 All **m.** reach this point, and go beyond it.
T-31 ..... IV.4:2 the search that all **m.** undertake who still
T-31 ..... IV.5:4 The great release of power **m.** begin with
T-31 ..... IV.7:3 a goal you **m.** proceed in its direction, not
T-31 ..... IV.9:4 **m.** have unless it be but futile wandering?
T-31 ...... V.5:2 that smiles above it **m.** forever look away,
T-31 ...... V.7:4 They are not given, so they **m.** be made.
T-31 ...... V.8:3 Now **m.** the Holy Spirit find a way to help
T-31 ...... V.8:3 see this concept of the self **m.** be undone,
T-31 ...... V.9:7 He **m.** have made the world as well as you
T-31 .... V.10:8 from whom **m.** something be kept hidden
T-31 .... V.11:1 concept **m.** be kept in darkness is that, in
T-31 .... V.12:1 alternatives about the thing that you **m.**
T-31 .... V.12:3 that interaction **m.** have entered in. There
T-31 .... V.12:7 someone **m.** have first decided on the one
T-31 .... V.13:2 Something **m.** have gone before these
T-31 .... V.13:3 something **m.** have done the learning
T-31 .... V.13:7 And you **m.** share his guilt, because you
T-31 .... V.13:8 now **m.** you be condemned along with
T-31 .... V.14:2 And everyone believes that he **m.** find the
T-31 ..... VI.1:3 two. If one is real the other **m.** be false, for
T-31 ..... VI.3:8 **m.** be passed that both may disappear, so
T-31 ... VI.3:11 that God created that **m.** still be done?
T-31 ..... VI.4:1 you **m.** make the way to Heaven plain.
T-31 ..... VI.4:5 think the truth about yourself **m.** really be
T-31 .... VII.1:4 For it **m.** deal in contrasts, not in truth,
T-31 .... VII.1:7 believing that the "bad" **m.** lurk behind.
T-31 .... VII.9:3 you **m.** perceive the body as yourself, for
T-31 .... VII.9:3 of what he is, and thus what you **m.** be.
T-31 ... VIII.1:2 of God he is a body, born in what **m.** die,
T-31 ... VIII.8:5 which you **m.** share with everyone you see
W-pI....... 9.5:1 specific exclusion **m.** be avoided. Be sure
W-pI..... 13.3:3 as they **m.** also be to you who equate
W-pI..... 17.1:4 you **m.** learn that it is the way you think.
W-pI..... 19.2:4 it **m.** be true if salvation is possible at all.
W-pI..... 19.2:5 And salvation **m.** be possible because it is
W-pI..... 22.1:1 thoughts in his mind **m.** see the world.
W-pI..... 23.1:5 your thoughts, then, that we **m.** work, if
W-pI..... 23.2:1 **m.** learn that it is these thoughts which
W-pI..... 24.6:2 that you **m.** experience disappointment in
W-pI..... 26.1:4 through you **m.** also have effects on you.
W-pI..... 26.1:6 You **m.** therefore learn how it can be used
W-pI..... 26.2:2 **m.** believe that you are not invulnerable.
W-pI..... 26.3:2 If attack thoughts **m.** entail the belief that
W-pI..... 34.1:3 It **m.** begin with your own thoughts, and
W-pI..... 35.3:2 describes you as you **m.** really be in truth.
W-pI..... 36.1:3 you are holy, your sight **m.** be holy as well
W-pI..... 36.1:7 mind is part of God's you **m.** be sinless, or
W-pI..... 39.3:4 A savior **m.** be saved. How else can he
W-pI..... 42.4:5 *Vision* **m.** *be possible. God gives truly,* or:
W-pI..... 42.4:7 or: *God's gifts to me* **m.** *be mine, because He*
W-pI..... 43.2:4 **m.** become the means for the restoration
W-pI..... 44.1:4 coexist, but light and life **m.** go together,
W-pI..... 44.2:1 see, you **m.** recognize that light is within,
W-pI .... 44.3:5 training **m.** be accomplished if you are to
W-pI .... 45.3:4 are. They **m.** still be there, because they
W-pI .... 46.1:2 **m.** be condemnation before forgiveness is
W-pI .... 47.6:2 **m.** also gain an awareness that confidence
W-pI .... 51.1:5 vision. I **m.** let it go by realizing it has no
W-pI .... 54.1:7 They **m.** be one or the other. What I see
W-pI .... 57.2:6 The Son of God **m.** be forever free. He is
W-pI .... 57.3:2 it, there **m.** be another way of looking at it
W-pI .... 57.3:5 It **m.** be, then, that the world is really a
W-pI .... 58.4:5 everyone **m.** share in my understanding,
W-pI .... 59.4:4 if I am to see, it **m.** be through Him. I
W-pI .... 62.2:5 this attack **m.** be replaced by forgiveness,
W-pI .... 63.4:5 And Who but your Self **m.** be His Son?
W-pI .... 66.4:3 the function He gave you **m.** be happiness
W-pI .... 66.5:4 *Therefore my function* **m.** *be happiness.* Try
W-pI .... 66.6:5 gives you only happiness, He **m.** be evil.
W-pI .... 66.8:1 it **m.** be that your function is established
W-pI .... 66.8:3 function to you, it **m.** be the gift of the ego
W-pI .... 67.3:2 you like itself, this Self **m.** be in you. And
W-pI .... 69.8:5 what you undertake with God **m.** succeed
W-pI .... 70.1:5 and salvation **m.** be in the same place. In
W-pI .... 70.2:5 **m.** surely begin to see that accepting it is
W-pI .... 71.3:1 itself, **m.** change if you are to be saved.
W-pI .... 71.5:2 will, you **m.** be willing to seek there only.
W-pI .... 71.6:7 His is the only plan that **m.** succeed.
W-pI .... 71.7:4 Salvation **m.** be yours because of His plan
W-pI .... 72.4:5 Son is only a body, so **m.** He be as well. A
W-pI .... 72.5:1 a body, what **m.** His plan for salvation be?
W-pI .... 72.5:9 it asserts that his salvation **m.** be death,
W-pI .. 72.10:2 we **m.** replace attack with acceptance. As
W-pI .... 73.4:6 so it **m.** be in you that we will look for it.
W-pI .... 76.1:4 you **m.** first realize salvation lies not there
W-pI .... 76.4:3 think you **m.** obey the "laws" of medicine,
W-pI .... 76.8:1 of "laws" we have believed we **m.** obey.
W-pI .... 76.8:7 you hold **m.** be obeyed to make you safe.
W-pI .... 77.6:4 The fact that you accepted **m.** be so.
W-pI .... 78.9:2 one Thought of God but **m.** rejoice as you
W-pI .... 79.2:2 and **m.** be recognized as one if the one
W-pI .... 79.4:3 your problem solving **m.** be inadequate,
W-pI .... 80.1:3 Therefore, you **m.** be at peace. Salvation
W-pI .... 80.4:1 will claim the peace that **m.** be ours when
W-pI .... 80.4:2 The problem **m.** be gone, because God's
W-pI .... 80.7:4 and you **m.** recognize it has been solved.
W-pI .... 83.1:5 All doubt **m.** disappear as I acknowledge
W-pI .... 83.3:3 from Oneness, and **m.** be received as one.
W-pI .... 83.3:5 And I **m.** learn to recognize what makes
W-pI .... 85.1:5 light and vision **m.** be joined for me to see
W-pI .... 85.1:6 To see, I **m.** lay grievances aside. I want to
W-pI .... 90.3:3 time **m.** elapse before it can be worked
W-pI .... 91.6:8 what you really are **m.** be revealed to you.
W-pI .... 93.6:2 Over and over this **m.** be repeated, until it
W-pI .... 94.2:2 you **m.** be strong and light must be in you
W-pI .... 94.2:2 you must be strong and light **m.** be in you
W-pI .... 94.2:3 He Who ensured your sinlessness **m.** be
W-pI .... 95.1:5 this, and you fail to realize it **m.** be so,
W-pI .... 95.5:2 attention, you **m.** also have noticed that,
W-pI .... 95.9:4 It is this process that **m.** be laid aside, for
W-pI .... 96.2:1 **m.** be accepted if you would be saved.
W-pI .... 96.3:3 and still be what It is and **m.** forever be. A
W-pI .... 96.3:7 body **m.** be meaningless to your reality.
W-pI .... 96.5:4 Now **m.** it reconcile unlike with like, for
W-pI .... 99.5:5 does He know one thing **m.** still be true;
W-pI .. 100.1:2 Salvation **m.** reverse the mad belief in
W-pI .. 100.2:5 Your joy **m.** be complete to let His plan be
W-pI 100.10:4 you **m.** find what He would have you give.
W-pI .. 101.1:5 **m.** think it so while you believe that sin is
W-pI .. 101.2:3 If sin is real, then happiness **m.** be illusion
W-pI .. 101.3:1 If sin is real, salvation **m.** be pain. Pain is
W-pI .. 101.3:3 Salvation **m.** be feared, for it will kill, but
W-pI .. 101.5:2 you believe **m.** come from sin will never
W-pI .. 103.2:2 God, forgetting being Love, He **m.** be joy.
W-pI .. 104.1:4 **m.** there be a place made ready to receive
W-pI .. 105.5:3 Him **m.** complete His Son as well. He
W-pI .. 105.6:4 you **m.** return to claim them as your own.
W-pI .. 105.8:1 You **m.** succeed today, if you prepare
WpI..rIII.in7:5 His means **m.** surely merit yours as well.
W-pI .. 121.6:3 forgiveness **m.** be learned by you as well,
W-pI .. 121.7:5 The unforgiving mind **m.** learn through
W-pI .. 125.1:5 the world **m.** hear to usher in the quiet

| | |
|---|---|
| W-pI...126.7:5 | it is attained, **m.** heal the mind that gives, |
| W-pI...126.7:6 | has been given **m.** have been received. |
| W-pI...127.2:2 | see that changing love **m.** be impossible. |
| W-pI...127.3:4 | And it **m.** elude the mind that thinks of it |
| W-pI...127.6:4 | of all the laws you think you **m.** obey; of |
| W-pI.127.12:2 | and who came to learn what you **m.** learn. |
| W-pI...128.1:3 | No one but **m.** accept this thought as true |
| W-pI...128.2:2 | everything **m.** serve the purpose you have |
| W-pI...130.1:4 | for what you value you **m.** want to see, |
| W-pI...130.2:4 | Fear **m.** make blind, for this its weapon is: |
| W-pI...131.4:1 | Be glad that search you **m.**. Be glad as |
| W-pI...131.4:2 | and **m.** find the goal you really want. No |
| W-pI...132.4:2 | Your mind **m.** give it meaning. And what |
| W-pI...132.5:2 | and all the world **m.** change accordingly. |
| W-pI...132.5:4 | and **m.** be borne in mind if you would |
| W-pI...132.6:4 | each one **m.** go as far as he can let himself |
| W-pI...132.7:4 | because what they behold **m.** be the truth, |
| W-pI...132.9:1 | A lesson earlier repeated once **m.** now be |
| W-pI.132.11:6 | thoughts which made it and **m.** set it free, |
| W-pI...133.3:4 | The choosing you can do; indeed, you **m.**. |
| W-pI...133.4:3 | there is but one choice that **m.** be made. |
| W-pI...133.5:1 | compromise in what your choice **m.** bring |
| W-pI...133.7:5 | Yet loss **m.** offer loss, and nothing more. |
| W-pI.133.10:1 | still **m.** he perceive its tarnished edges |
| W-pI...134.1:2 | forgiveness **m.** be seen as mere eccentric |
| W-pI...134.2:2 | true. It **m.** be limited to what is false. It is |
| W-pI...134.3:1 | you still believe you **m.** forgive the truth, |
| W-pI.134.13:1 | Forgiveness **m.** be practiced, for the |
| W-pI...135.2:1 | operate from the belief you **m.** protect |
| W-pI...135.2:1 | because it **m.** contain what threatens you. |
| W-pI...135.2:5 | but **m.** have terror striking at his heart. |
| W-pI...135.4:2 | It **m.** be something that is very weak and |
| W-pI...135.4:3 | **m.** be something made easy prey, unable |
| W-pI...135.4:5 | body falters and **m.** fail to serve the Son of |
| W-pI...135.5:4 | so unsafe it **m.** be guarded with your very |
| W-pI...135.9:2 | which you think the body **m.** be saved. |
| W-pI.135.10:5 | see where hope **m.** lie if it be meaningful. |
| W-pI.135.12:1 | is relieved of the belief that it **m.** plan, |
| W-pI.135.12:2 | It **m.** misuse the body in its plans until it |
| W-pI.135.13:1 | up to save itself **m.** make the body sick. It |
| W-pI.135.24:2 | that you **m.** be defended from release. |
| W-pI...136.4:3 | requires that you **m.** forget you made it, |
| W-pI...136.5:5 | Defenses **m.** make facts unrecognizable. |
| W-pI...136.8:2 | and so you **m.** be separate from the truth. |
| W-pI.136.12:5 | what God wills for you **m.** be received. |
| W-pI.136.13:2 | you is not the truth right now, as it **m.** be. |
| W-pI.136.20:2 | not be confused about what **m.** be healed, |
| W-pI...137.3:3 | In sickness **m.** he be apart and separate. |
| W-pI...137.4:1 | would prove that lies **m.** be the truth. But |
| W-pI...137.4:5 | eyes accustomed to illusions **m.** be shown |
| W-pI...137.4:6 | **m.** demonstrate that sickness is not real. |
| W-pI...137.7:1 | so healing **m.** replace the fantasies of |
| W-pI.137.12:6 | what is healed to what **m.** yet be healed, |
| W-pI.137.14:1 | Yet **m.** we be prepared for such a gift. |
| W-pI......138.h | Heaven is the decision I **m.** make. |
| W-pI...138.1:3 | If Heaven exists there **m.** be hell as well, |
| W-pI...138.5:6 | what you are, and what your needs **m.** be. |
| W-pI...138.7:2 | itself **m.** in the end be overcome by death. |
| W-pI...138.7:4 | And thus salvation **m.** be seen as death, |
| W-pI...138.8:2 | It **m.** be saved from salvation, threatened |
| W-pI...138.9:3 | in shadows **m.** be raised to understanding |
| W-pI.138.12:5 | *Heaven is the decision I* **m.** *make. I make it* |
| W-pI...139.3:1 | Uncertainty about what you **m.** be is self- |
| W-pI...139.8:3 | what it **m.** be is all the proof you need to |
| W-pI...139.9:5 | we are proclaims what everyone **m.** be, |
| W-pI...140.1:4 | thus **m.** substitute illusion for illusion. |
| W-pI...140.5:2 | For cure **m.** come from holiness, and |
| W-pI...140.7:2 | Healing **m.** be sought but where it is, and |
| W-pI...140.8:5 | We need but seek it and it **m.** be found. |
| W-pI...149.2:1 | (138) Heaven is the decision I **m.** make. |
| W-pI...151.7:1 | Yet you **m.** learn to doubt their evidence |
| W-pI...152.2:6 | Truth **m.** be all-inclusive, if it be the truth |
| W-pI...152.5:1 | created you, you **m.** remain unchangeable |
| W-pI...152.6:4 | mind that lives within a body that **m.** die? |
| W-pI.153.12:4 | Everyone who plays **m.** win, and in his |
| W-pI.155.11:5 | We **m.** not lose our way. For as truth goes |
| W-pI...156.2:2 | Truth **m.** be true throughout, if it be true. |
| W-pI...156.3:1 | He is, there **m.** be holiness as well as life. |
| W-pI...157.4:2 | day, what you are asking **m.** be given you. |
| W-pI...158.8:1 | **m.** be taught by all who would achieve it. |
| W-pI.158.10:4 | If he be lost in sin, so **m.** you be; if you see |
| W-pI...159.1:5 | that to possess a thing, it **m.** be kept. |
| W-pI...160.2:4 | will not leave because a madman says I **m.** |
| W-pI...160.4:7 | If you are real, then fear **m.** be illusion. |
| W-pI...161.3:2 | now it is specifics we **m.** use in practicing. |
| W-pI...161.7:2 | There **m.** be a thing to be attacked. An |
| W-pI...161.7:3 | An enemy **m.** be perceived in such a form |
| W-pI...161.8:3 | intensity of rage projected fear **m.** spawn. |
| W-pI...163.6:5 | which we **m.** accept if we be sane; what |
| W-pI...163.8:7 | Whatever form it takes **m.** therefore be |
| W-pI...165.7:5 | Sureness **m.** abide within you who are |
| W-pI...166.2:3 | it real **m.** still believe there is another will, |
| W-pI...166.3:2 | He **m.** believe that to accept God's gifts, |
| W-pI...166.3:3 | He **m.** deny their presence, contradict the |
| W-pI.166.12:4 | to offer you, you now **m.** learn to give. |
| W-pI...167.3:5 | But its origin is where it **m.** be changed, if |
| W-pI.167.12:3 | A sleeping mind **m.** waken, as it sees its |
| W-pI...169.3:2 | The final step **m.** go beyond all learning. |
| W-pI...169.9:1 | For oneness **m.** be here. Whatever time |
| W-pI...169.9:2 | irrelevant to what **m.** be a constant state, |
| W-pI.169.11:2 | The ending **m.** remain obscure to you |
| W-pI...170.4:2 | it is obvious ideas **m.** leave their source, |
| W-pI...170.4:2 | attack, and **m.** have first conceived of it. |
| W-pI...170.6:1 | love as enemy, **m.** cruelty become a god. |
| W-pI.170.10:3 | Yet **m.** the worshippers of fear perceive |
| WpI...rV.in6:4 | I **m.** understand uncertainty and pain, |
| WpI...rV.in6:5 | a savior **m.** remain with those he teaches, |
| WpI...rV.in9:9 | lives but **m.** not then be one with you? |
| W-pI.182.10:2 | he **m.** learn that what he would protect is |
| W-pI.182.11:4 | who **m.** beseech his father for protection |
| W-pI...184.4:4 | become the threats which it **m.** overcome, |
| W-pI...184.7:2 | everyone who comes **m.** go through. But |
| W-pI.184.13:2 | Experience **m.** come to supplement the |
| W-pI.184.13:3 | first you **m.** accept the Name for all reality |
| W-pI...185.4:3 | The meaning **m.** escape the dream, for |
| W-pI...185.6:1 | it wants is peace **m.** join with other minds |
| W-pI.185.13:1 | No one can lose and everyone **m.** gain |
| W-pI...186.5:5 | The arrogant **m.** cling to words, afraid to |
| W-pI.186.13:5 | For Love **m.** give, and what is given in His |
| W-pI...187.1:5 | you **m.** first possess what you would give. |
| W-pI...187.2:6 | Yet it **m.** return to him who gives. Nor |
| W-pI...187.2:8 | it takes be less acceptable. It **m.** be more. |
| W-pI...187.3:1 | Ideas **m.** first belong to you, before you |
| W-pI...187.5:7 | And both **m.** gain in this exchange, for |
| W-pI...187.6:2 | understands what giving means **m.** laugh |
| W-pI...187.7:1 | Illusion recognized **m.** disappear. Accept |
| W-pI...187.8:3 | has arisen and correction **m.** be made. |
| W-pI...188.3:3 | What it gives **m.** be eternal. It removes all |
| W-pI...188.5:2 | recognizes it within himself **m.** give it. |
| W-pI...188.7:4 | but they **m.** remain with you as well, for |
| W-pI...188.7:5 | but to remind you how you **m.** return. |
| W-pI...188.8:4 | God is shining in you, it **m.** shine on them |
| W-pI...190.4:5 | and tries to demonstrate **m.** still be true. |
| W-pI...190.6:6 | where living things **m.** come at last to die? |
| W-pI.191.11:1 | They **m.** await your own release. They |
| W-pI...192.8:4 | He **m.** be sure that he does not escape, |
| W-pI...195.5:4 | share with them, as they **m.** share with us. |
| W-pI.195.10:2 | and where one is the other **m.** be found. |
| W-pI...196.2:3 | Yet **m.** it fail to understand the truth it |
| W-pI...196.6:3 | this, at least, **m.** be entirely impossible, |
| W-pI...196.7:1 | form **m.** first be changed at least as much |
| W-pI...196.8:3 | thoughts, the fear of God **m.** disappear. |
| W-pI...197.1:4 | Your gifts **m.** be received with honor, lest |
| W-pI...197.2:2 | and weakness **m.** become salvation to you |
| W-pI...197.3:1 | The world **m.** thank you when you offer |
| W-pI...197.5:2 | And what belongs to God **m.** be His Own. |
| W-pI...197.7:3 | for everyone **m.** live and move in Him. |
| W-pI...198.2:7 | **m.** we deal with them a while as if they |
| W-pI...198.3:2 | save this one **m.** multiply a thousandfold. |
| W-pI...198.3:6 | Yet does it point to where the truth **m.** be, |
| W-pI...198.4:3 | a thousand ways in which it **m.** be wrong; |
| W-pI...199.1:1 | Freedom **m.** be impossible as long as you |
| W-pI...199.4:4 | as useful form for what the mind **m.** do. It |
| W-pI...199.4:5 | to the all-inclusive goal that it **m.** reach, |
| W-pI...200.2:1 | point to which each one **m.** come at last, |
| W-pI...200.3:3 | ask for what you have already **m.** succeed. |
| W-pI...200.5:2 | But you **m.** change your mind about the |
| W-pI...200.6:4 | and where it **m.** serve a mighty function. |
| W-pI...200.7:5 | Or **m.** he see that, as he looks on it, the |
| WpI rVI.in.2:4 | that one, there **m.** be no exceptions made. |
| W-pII .....1.4:4 | He who would not forgive **m.** judge, for |
| W-pII .....1.4:4 | for he **m.** justify his failure to forgive. But |
| W-pII .....1.4:5 | himself **m.** learn to welcome truth exactly |
| W-pII .....1.5:3 | God. Now **m.** you share His function, and |
| W-pII .225.1:1 | *Father, I* **m.** *return Your Love for me, for* |
| W-pII .225.1:2 | *to me. I* **m.** *return it, for I want it mine in full* |
| W-pII .230.2:2 | *What was given then* **m.** *be here now, for my* |
| W-pII ....236.h | I rule my mind, which I alone **m.** rule. |
| W-pII .236.1:1 | I have a kingdom I **m.** rule. At times, it |
| W-pII .238.1:1 | *trust in me has been so great, I* **m.** *be worthy.* |
| W-pII .238.1:4 | *I* **m.** *be beloved of You indeed. And I must be* |
| W-pII .238.1:5 | *And I* **m.** *be steadfast in holiness as well, that* |
| W-pII .....3.1:4 | the world **m.** disappear and all its errors |
| W-pII .....3.5:4 | We **m.** save the world. For we who made |
| W-pII .....3.5:5 | it **m.** behold it through the eyes of Christ, |
| W-pII .242.1:2 | to lead my life alone **m.** be but foolishness |
| W-pII .243.1:2 | what **m.** remain beyond my present grasp |
| W-pII .243.2:3 | *and truth* **m.** *shine in all of us as one.* |
| W-pII .....4.3:3 | Son is evil; timelessness **m.** have an end; |
| W-pII .....4.3:3 | must have an end; eternal life **m.** die. And |
| W-pII .252.1:5 | How far beyond this world my Self **m.** be, |
| W-pII .253.1:5 | This **m.** I accept. For thus am I led past |
| W-pII .255.1:5 | **m.** remain forever in the peace of Heaven. |
| W-pII .257.2:3 | *And thus our purpose* **m.** *be Yours as well, if* |
| W-pII .....5.3:4 | **m.** the body serve the purpose given it. |
| W-pII .262.1:6 | *For Your Son* **m.** *bear Your Name, for You* |
| W-pII .264.2:3 | **M.** we not join in what will save the world |
| W-pII .271.1:4 | for nothing that He looks on but **m.** live, |
| W-pII .272.1:8 | *safe. God's Son* **m.** *be as You created him.* |
| W-pII .278.1:2 | the laws the world obeys **m.** I obey; the |
| W-pII .....7.1:2 | Since He **m.** bridge the gap between |
| W-pII .....7.2:2 | sights and sounds **m.** be translated from |
| W-pII .284.2:1 | *hurt, so grief and pain* **m.** *be impossible. Let* |
| W-pII .288.1:3 | *I first* **m.** *recognize what You created one* |
| W-pII .289.1:1 | mind, the real world **m.** escape my sight. |
| W-pII .292.2:2 | *for every trial we think we still* **m.** *meet.* |
| W-pII .294.1:4 | has God's beloved Son for what **m.** die? |
| W-pII .295.1:4 | Redemption **m.** be one. As I am saved, |
| W-pII .295.1:6 | For all of us **m.** be redeemed together. |
| W-pII .....9.2:2 | brings, as God's creation **m.** be limitless. |
| W-pII .302.1:6 | *for fear* **m.** *disappear when love has come.* |
| W-pII .307.1:5 | *You can give, I* **m.** *accept Your Will for me,* |
| W-pII .308.1:2 | I **m.** change my perception of what time is |
| W-pII .311.2:3 | *he whom You created as Your Son* **m.** *be.* |
| W-pII .312.1:5 | **m.** the real world come to greet the holy |
| W-pII .312.2:2 | *today, and therefore it* **m.** *be my goal as well.* |
| W-pII .319.1:4 | and therefore it **m.** seek for aims which |
| W-pII .319.1:5 | that what one gains, totality **m.** lose. And |
| W-pII .320.1:3 | his Creator and Redeemer **m.** be done. |
| W-pII ...11.2:3 | and **m.** therefore share in power to create. |
| W-pII .327.1:3 | and faith in Him **m.** surely come to me. |
| W-pII .328.1:6 | Him that we **m.** go to recognize our will. |
| W-pII ...12.4:2 | and blood **m.** flow before the altar where |
| W-pII .333.1:1 | Conflict **m.** be resolved. It cannot be |
| W-pII .333.1:3 | It **m.** be seen exactly as it is, where it is |
| W-pII .337.1:3 | What **m.** I do to know all this is mine? I |
| W-pII .337.1:4 | I **m.** accept Atonement for myself, and |
| W-pII .337.1:6 | I **m.** learn I need do nothing of myself, for |
| W-pII ...13.1:6 | fear **m.** slip away under the gentle remedy |
| W-pII .343.1:6 | *I, too,* **m.** *give. And so all things are given* |
| W-pII .343.1:9 | *can make no sacrifice, for he* **m.** *be complete,* |
| W-pII .343.2:3 | a gift that **m.** be freely given and received. |
| W-pII .345.1:7 | *lights the way that I* **m.** *travel to remember* |
| W-pII ....347.h | Anger **m.** come from judgment. |
| W-pII .354.1:5 | *Thus* **m.** *I be one with You as well as Him. For* |
| Wfl........in.2:2 | way that everyone **m.** travel in the end, |
| M-in ........2:10 | Any situation **m.** be to you a chance to |
| M-in ..........5:2 | The self-deceiving **m.** deceive, for they |
| M-in ..........5:2 | must deceive, for they **m.** teach deception |
| M-4 ..... I.A.3:1 | they **m.** go through what might be called |
| M-4 ..... I.A.3:4 | where he **m.** see things in a different light |
| M-4 ..... I.A.4:1 | of God **m.** go through "a period of sorting |
| M-4 ..... I.A.4:2 | he **m.** now decide all things on the basis |
| M-4 ..... I.A.5:1 | the teacher of God **m.** go can be called "a |
| M-4 ..... I.A.7:2 | Now **m.** the teacher of God understand |
| M-4 ..... I.A.7:7 | now he **m.** attain a state that may remain |
| M-4 ..... I.A.7:8 | He **m.** learn to lay all judgment aside, and |

M-4 ...... IV.1:8 No teacher of God but **m.** learn,–and
M-4 ....... IV.2:7 choose the weakness that **m.** come from
M-4 ....... V.1:7 are sure they are beloved and **m.** be safe.
M-4 ..... VII.1:2 a meaning that **m.** be learned and learned
M-5 ......... I.1:3 He **m.** think it is a small price to pay for
M-5 ....... II.1:1 Healing **m.** occur in exact proportion to
M-5 ....... II.1:3 this, one first **m.** recognize certain facts.
M-5 ..... II.3:12 of the body **m.** be an acceptable idea.
M-5 ...... III.1:1 patient **m.** change his mind in order to be
M-5 ...... III.3:4 and **m.** remain as God created him. They
M-6 ........... 1:9 death. Healing **m.** wait, for his protection.
M-7 ........... 1:7 And it is this he **m.** facilitate. He is now
M-7 ........... 1:8 the patient, and he **m.** so regard himself.
M-7 ........... 1:9 **m.** be willing to change his mind about it.
M-7 ........... 2:5 He **m.** use his reason to tell himself that
M-7 ........... 2:5 **m.** recognize that his own uncertainty is
M-7 ........... 3:1 is in this that the teacher of God **m.** trust.
M-7 ........... 3:4 Yet he **m.** first accept them. He need do
M-7 ........... 4:7 And hate **m.** be the opposite of love,
M-8 ........... 4:2 And it is here correction **m.** be made. The
M-8 ........... 4:6 it concludes that the categories **m.** be true
M-9 ........... 1:8 in particular **m.** be properly perceived,
M-11 ......... 1:1 is a question everyone **m.** ask. Certainly
M-11 ......... 1:5 is no death, that resurrection **m.** occur,
M-11 ......... 1:8 that the world **m.** be looked at differently,
M-11 ....... 1:12 would see it. Indeed, you ***m.*** choose this.
M-11 ......... 2:9 For one of you is wrong. It **m.** be so.
M-13 ......... 1:5 illusion **m.** be replaced by a corrective
M-13 ......... 1:6 **m.** be displaced before another thought
M-13 ......... 4:6 **m.** rejoice that he is free of all the sacrifice
M-13 ......... 4:9 And to possess them **m.** he sacrifice his
M-13 ......... 5:3 the price that **m.** be paid for the denial of
M-13 ......... 8:1 decision you make **m.** mean in terms of
M-14 ......... 3:6 God **m.** learn to pass by and leave behind.
M-16 ......... 2:3 **m.** they do to learn to give the day to God
M-16 ......... 2:4 one **m.** use them as best he can in his own
M-16 ......... 3:6 **m.** depend on the teacher of God himself.
M-16 ......... 5:5 you **m.** have come to some conclusions in
M-16 ......... 8:4 He **m.** be sure success is not of him, but
M-16 ....... 10:8 **m.** be abandoned through his recognition
M-16 ....... 11:3 God's teachers who **m.** teach it that it can.
M-16 ....... 11:9 **m.** God's teachers learn to recognize the
M-17 ......... 2:4 value, and **m.** lead to undesired outcomes
M-17 ......... 3:4 And this **m.** indeed have been the case if
M-17 ....... 4:11 is unaware of truth **m.** look upon illusions
M-17 ......... 5:9 And he **m.** stand alone in his protection,
M-17 ......... 6:2 is inevitable, for its outcome **m.** be death.
M-17 ......... 6:4 Magic again **m.** help. Forget the battle.
M-17 ....... 7:13 who bears this stain on him **m.** meet with
M-19 ......... 2:8 But somewhere one **m.** start. Justice is the
M-19 ......... 3:4 which all thought of wholeness **m.** be lost.
M-19 ......... 4:4 For separate fragments **m.** decay and die,
M-20 ......... 3:3 is, for anger **m.** deny that peace exists.
M-20 ......... 3:4 and **m.** believe that it cannot exist. In this
M-20 ......... 3:7 this, given forgiveness there ***m.*** be peace.
M-20 ......... 4:4 Now **m.** you once again lay down your
M-20 ......... 4:5 **m.** have taken it again as your defense.
M-21 ......... 4:3 many who **m.** be reached through words,
M-21 ......... 4:4 The teacher of God **m.**, however, learn to
M-22 ......... 6:9 is your forgiveness that **m.** show him this.
M-22 ....... 6:12 Having been received, it **m.** be accepted.
M-22 ....... 6:14 All else **m.** follow from this single purpose
M-22 ......... 7:2 **m.** remain beyond God's power to forgive
M-23 ......... 7:5 symbols **m.** shift and change to suit the
M-24 ......... 5:7 All that **m.** be recognized, however, is
M-25 ......... 4:9 to the Holy Spirit **m.** be given to weakness
M-26 ......... 3:7 All worldly states **m.** be illusory. If God
M-26 ......... 4:3 who suffer, you **m.** speak their language.
M-26 ......... 4:4 **m.** understand what needs to be escaped.
M-27 ......... 5:6 His Own creation **m.** stand in fear of Him.
M-27 ....... 6:10 in Him all created things **m.** be eternal.
M-29 ......... 1:4 **m.** be remembered that only time divides
C-in ........... 2:3 They **m.**, however, be willing to overlook
C-2............ 5:3 and cause and its effects **m.** still be one.
C-3............ 7:3 That **m.** be so because the ego cannot be
C-4............ 1:2 what He creates **m.** be eternal as Himself.
C-4............ 2:1 upon **m.** lead to more illusions of reality.
C-4............ 3:2 for false perception **m.** be *true perception.*
C-4............ 6:4 is seen outside **m.** lie beyond forgiveness,
C-5 ............ 3:1 Him–Jesus became what all of you **m.** be
P-in ........... 1:8 patient **m.** be helped to change his mind
P-1............ 4:1 **m.** restore to his awareness the ability to
P-1............ 4:2 **m.** become willing to reverse his thinking,
P-1............ 5:2 **m.** begin to separate truth from illusion,
P-2......... in.3:2 of "improvement" still **m.** differ. The
P-2......... in.4:1 be, he **m.** want to change the patient's self-
P-2......... II.4:2 where there is forgiveness truth **m.** come.
P-2......... II.6:5 If any two are joined, He **m.** be there. It
P-2......... II.6:6 is, but they **m.** share it wholly to succeed.
P-2......... II.7:1 so **m.** true psychotherapy be religious.
P-2......... II.8:1 **m.** the teacher do to ensure learning?
P-2......... II.8:2 **m.** the therapist do to bring healing about
P-2......... II.8:4 one **m.** share one goal with someone else,
P-2......... II.9:8 in purpose and **m.** thus be one in means.
P-2........ III.3:3 But in the end there **m.** be some success.
P-2........ III.3:5 is the formula for salvation, and **m.** heal.
P-2........ IV.1:5 a decision that truth can lie and **m.** be lies
P-2........ IV.4:6 Yet having started, it **m.** finish thus. It is
P-2........ IV.4:7 if God were the devil and **m.** be found in
P-2........ IV.5:4 Yet **m.** their cures remain temporary, or
P-2........ IV.6:3 the defenses sought for **m.** be magical.
P-2........ IV.6:4 They **m.** overcome all limits perceived in
P-2........ IV.8:4 to God that it **m.** be forever inconceivable
P-2........ IV.9:3 with which the psychotherapist **m.** deal.
P-2...... IV.10:2 He **m.** meet attack without attack, and
P-2...... IV.10:4 This **m.** be his teaching, if his lesson is to
P-2...... IV.10:9 it **m.** remain unwanted as well as unreal.
P-2......... V.1:1 it **m.** still be taught to those who have
P-2......... V.1:3 to be safe, one **m.** control the unknown.
P-2......... V.2:5 Yet it **m.** be taught to those who think it
P-2......... V.2:6 It **m.** be taught to those who will attack
P-2......... V.3:5 they are sick, they can and **m.** be helped.
P-2......... V.6:4 they **m.** start their Father will complete.
P-2......... V.7:1 all gifts of God **m.** be received. In time no
P-2........ VI.1:8 To question it **m.** then become his choice.
P-2........ VI.2:4 of the song of condemnation **m.** arise.
P-2........ VI.6:5 he **m.** think of evil as besetting him here
P-2....... VII.1:3 He who needs healing **m.** heal. Physician,
P-2....... VII.1:9 And every therapist **m.** learn to heal from
P-2....... VII.4:2 because they **m.** regard themselves as self-
P-2....... VII.7:7 without the god who **m.** be given him?
P-3.......... I.4:3 Meanwhile he **m.** learn, and his patients
P-3.......... II.4:5 Both **m.** have denied their perfection, for
P-3.......... II.4:8 dream a strange correction **m.** enter, for
P-3.......... II.5:1 Something good **m.** come from every
P-3.......... II.5:4 therapeutic relationship **m.** become like
P-3.......... II.8:6 begun to understand what they **m.** do
P-3.......... II.9:4 **m.** also recognize the equality of himself
P-3........ II.10:1 any form of specialness **m.** be defended,
P-3........ III.1:7 he **m.** yet strive to have the last illusion be
P-3........ III.3:4 This, indeed, **m.** demand payment, and
P-3........ III.3:6 Holy Spirit's only dream, **m.** have no cost.
P-3...... III.6:11 everyone **m.** gain a blessing without cost.
S-1.......... in.2:3 God created one **m.** recognize its oneness,
S-1.......... in.2:4 Prayer now **m.** be the means by which
S-1........... I.1:6 True prayer **m.** avoid the pitfall of asking
S-1........... I.2:4 **m.** be made whether they be illusions or
S-1.......... II.3:1 and so it **m.** entail levels of learning. Here,
S-1......... III.1:5 **m.** be relinquished before *you* can be
S-1......... III.3:1 the learning goal **m.** be to recognize that
S-1......... III.3:9 enemies, and this imagined gain **m.** go, if
S-1......... III.4:1 Guilt **m.** be given up, and not concealed.
S-1......... IV.1:2 point, each one **m.** ask for different things
S-1.......... V.1:4 not claim that you **m.** rule the universe,
S-2.......... in.1:4 Both **m.** come to hold you up and keep
S-2........... I.4:6 in him **m.** your innocence now be found.
S-2........... I.8:5 As He would give, so **m.** you give as well.
S-2........... I.9:1 But to achieve this end you first **m.** learn,
S-2........... I.9:4 Forgiveness' role **m.** be reversed, and
S-2........... I.9:5 Forgiveness-to-destroy **m.** be unveiled in
S-2.......... I.10:2 And you **m.** choose between them every
S-2.......... I.10:3 Yet you **m.** learn alternatives for choice,
S-2.......... II.4:3 Here **m.** the aim be clearly seen, for this
S-2.......... II.5:4 he **m.** accept the guilt and heavy-laid
S-3........... I.1:1 and separate from what its cause **m.** be. It
S-3........... I.1:5 The body yet **m.** die, and so its healing
S-3........... I.3:3 Forgiveness **m.** be given by a mind which
S-3........... I.3:3 which understands that it **m.** overlook all
S-3........... I.4:1 he has done now **m.** God's Son undo. But
S-3........... I.5:1 Distinctions therefore **m.** be made
S-3.......... II.4:2 first true healing **m.** have come to bless
S-3.......... II.5:3 could it be welcome when it **m.** be feared?
S-3.......... II.5:6 a viewpoint **m.** be fostered by the healing
S-3........ III.4:2 In arrogance the answer **m.** be "no." But
S-3........ III.5:7 and separation **m.** be healed by love and

## mute 1

T-27 ....... II.5:7 it offer him **m.** testimony of his innocence

## mutual 2

T-4 ........ in.1:4 It can lead only to **m.** progress. The result
T-6 ..... V.C.4:8 are not recognizing this **m.** exclusiveness,

## mutually 1

T-6 ..... V.C.4:7 for long, since they are **m.** exclusive. As

## My 18

• God
*Christ*
*Holy Spirit*
*my*

T-6 ......... V.1:8 "**M.** children sleep and must be awakened
T-31 .. VII.15:5 says, "Release **M.** Son!" be tempted not to
W-pII . 276.1:2 "**M.** Son is pure and holy as Myself." And
W-pII ... 10.5:1 Judgment: "You are still **M.** holy Son,
W-pII ... 10.5:3 I am your Father and you are **M.** Son."
Wfl........ in.6:3 to answer him, and say, "This is **M.** Son,
S-3........ IV.6:1 Come unto Me, **M.** children, once again,
S-3........ IV.7:1 comes for Me and speaks **M.** Word to you
S-3........ IV.7:2 I would recall **M.** weary Son to Me from
S-3........ IV.7:3 **M.** Arms are open to the Son I love, who
S-3........ IV.8:1 Help Me to wake **M.** children from the
S-3........ IV.8:5 Return to Me Who never left **M.** Son.
S-3........ IV.8:6 Listen, **M.** child, your Father calls to you.
S-3........ IV.9:6 lovingly I hold you in **M.** Heart and in My
S-3........ IV.9:6 I hold you in My Heart and in **M.** Arms.
S-3........ IV.9:7 healed **M.** Son and took him from the
S-3........ IV.9:8 Arise and let **M.** thanks be given you. And
S-3........ IV.9:9 And with **M.** gratitude will come the gift

## My 1

• Christ
*God*
*Holy Spirit*
*my*

T-31 ... VIII.3:2 calls to you and gently says, "**M.** brother,

## My 2

• Holy Spirit
*God*
*Christ*
*my*

T-27 ... VIII.9:7 But hear Him say, "**M.** brother, holy Son
P-3........ II.9:10 there is One Who says, "**M.** brother,

## my 185

• Jesus
*noise word*
*My*

T-1 ........ I.27:1 from God through me to all **m.** brothers.
T-1 ......... II.3:9 only **m.** devotion that entitles me to yours
T-1 ......... II.4:6 **M.** devotion to my brothers has placed
T-1 ......... II.4:6 My devotion to **m.** brothers has placed
T-1 ......... II.4:7 the statement "I and **m.** Father are one,"
T-1 ......... II.5:1 to the revelation-readiness of **m.** brothers.
T-1 ....... III.1:2 you offer a miracle to any of **m.** brothers,
T-1 ....... III.1:3 not need miracles for **m.** own Atonement,
T-1 ....... III.1:4 temporarily. **M.** part in the Atonement is
T-1 ....... III.1:6 As you share **m.** unwillingness to accept
T-1 ....... III.1:6 crusade to correct it; listen to **m.** voice,

T-1 III.2:2 **M.** word, which is the resurrection and
T-1 III.4:5 and under **m.** guidance miracles lead to
T-1 III.4:7 abandon them by following **m.** guidance.
T-1 III.8:4 **m.** complete awareness of the whole plan.
T-1 V.3:6 All **m.** brothers are special. If they believe
T-1 VII.5:4 I have been careful to clarify **m.** role in the
T-2 V.A.17:2 **M.** request "Do this in remembrance of
T-2 V.A.17:5 present. Time is under **m.** direction, but
T-2 VI.1:3 **M.** control can take over everything that
T-2 VI.1:3 while **m.** guidance can direct everything
T-2 VI.1:5 prevents me from giving you **m.** control.
T-2 VI.1:7 This removes them from **m.** control, and
T-2 VI.2:9 place what you think under **m.** guidance.
T-2 VI.6:1 **m.** guidance without conscious effort, but
T-2 VII.7:9 that time and space are under **m.** control.
T-2 VIII.3:2 undertaken by **m.** brothers with my help.
T-2 VIII.3:2 undertaken by my brothers with **m.** help.
T-3 I.4:3 is a violation of **m.** injunction that you
T-3 I.5:2 symbol that speaks of **m.** innocence. The
T-3 IV.7:6 By uniting **m.** will with that of my Creator
T-3 IV.7:6 By uniting my will with that of **m.** Creator
T-3 IV.7:7 if you will bring it under **m.** guidance.
T-3 V.1:3 by the union of **m.** will with the Father's.
T-4 in.3:3 you are also free to join **m.** resurrection.
T-4 I.3:3 fear, because it does not share **m.** charity.
T-4 I.3:4 **M.** lesson was like yours, and because I
T-4 I.6:3 but **m.** goal will always be to absolve you
T-4 I.13:7 who share **m.** aim of healing the mind.
T-4 III.2:4 The reason you need **m.** help is because
T-4 III.2:5 **M.** role is to separate the true from the
T-4 III.6:3 Let us ask the Father in **m.** name to keep
T-4 IV.2:9 and urge you to follow **m.** example as you
T-4 IV.10:4 of the Second Coming, and **m.** judgment,
T-4 IV.11:6 brother will yet come together in **m.** name
T-4 IV.11:12 love. **M.** calling you is as natural as your
T-4 VI.6:1 **M.** trust in you is greater than yours in
T-4 VI.6:4 Holy One shares **m.** trust, and accepts my
T-4 VI.6:4 accepts **m.** Atonement decisions because
T-4 VI.6:4 **m.** will is never out of accord with His. I
T-4 VI.6:6 because I completed **m.** part in it as a man
T-4 VI.6:7 **M.** chosen channels cannot fail, because I
T-4 VI.6:7 lend them **m.** strength as long as theirs is
T-4 VI.7:1 **m.** perception He can bridge the little gap
T-4 VII.8:8 whoever can follow **m.** guidance through
T-5 I.4:6 one of God's creations, **m.** right thinking,
T-5 II.9:1 **M.** mind will always be like yours,
T-5 II.9:2 only **m.** decision that gave me all power in
T-5 II.9:3 **M.** only gift to you is to help you make the
T-5 II.11:1 **m.** decision and making it stronger. As we
T-5 II.11:4 Let us restate "**M.** yoke is easy and my
T-5 II.11:4 is easy and **m.** burden light" in this way;
T-5 II.11:4 us join together, for **m.** message is light."
T-5 II.12:6 Child of God, **m.** message is for you, to
T-5 IV.5:3 I cannot forget **m.** need to teach what I
T-5 IV.5:5 Make it dependable in **m.** name because
T-5 IV.5:5 **m.** name is the Name of God's Son. What
T-5 IV.6:3 **M.** part in the Atonement is not complete
T-5 IV.8:8 go with **m.** blessing and for my blessing.
T-5 IV.8:8 go with my blessing and for **m.** blessing.
T-5 IV.8:13 **M.** judgment is as strong as the wisdom of
T-5 VI.2:8 **M.** role is only to unchain your will and
T-5 VI.11:2 Remember **m.** reference to the ego's dark
T-5 VI.11:6 because **m.** will is that of our Father, from
T-6 I.2:5 can always call on me to share **m.** decision
T-6 I.6:6 was part of **m.** own teaching contribution.
T-6 I.6:7 merely asked to follow **m.** example in the
T-6 I.7:6 **M.** brothers slept during the so-called
T-6 I.8:1 I am sorry when **m.** brothers do not share
T-6 I.8:1 share **m.** decision to hear only one Voice,
T-6 I.8:2 still on them that I must build **m.** church.
T-6 I.8:6 me as a model are literally **m.** disciples.
T-6 I.11:2 to repeat **m.** experiences because the Holy
T-6 I.11:3 To use **m.** experiences constructively,
T-6 I.11:3 still follow **m.** example in how to perceive
T-6 I.11:4 **M.** brothers and yours are constantly
T-6 I.11:5 **M.** one lesson, which I must teach as I
T-6 I.15:4 described **m.** reactions to Judas as they
T-6 I.15:8 Judas was **m.** brother and a Son of God, as
T-7 V.10:7 yours. I do not want to share **m.** body in
T-7 V.10:9 Yet I do want to share **m.** mind with you
T-8 IV.2:8 **M.** purpose, then, is still to overcome the
T-8 IV.2:9 **m.** light must dispel it because of what it
T-8 IV.2:11 If **m.** light goes with you everywhere, you
T-8 IV.3:4 **M.** mission was simply to unite the will of
T-8 IV.3:9 **M.** will is His, and your decision to hear
T-8 IV.4:11 and this rejection of **m.** decision for you
T-8 IV.5:9 **M.** decision cannot overcome yours,
T-8 IV.5:14 offer **m.** strength to make yours invincible
T-8 IV.6:5 you can choose to listen to **m.** teaching.
T-8 IV.7:5 and in **m.** remembrance of you lies your
T-8 V.2:11 me. **M.** reality is yours and His. By joining
T-8 V.6:8 **m.** hand because you want to transcend
T-8 V.6:9 **M.** strength will never be wanting, and if
T-8 VI.9:2 **M.** devotion to you is of Him, being born
T-8 VI.9:2 born of **m.** knowledge of myself and Him.
T-8 IX.7:1 and to accomplish all things in **m.** name.
T-8 IX.7:2 This is not **m.** name alone, for ours is a
T-9 II.7:5 hear **m.** brothers in whom God's Voice
T-9 II.8:1 will learn that **m.** belief in you is justified.
T-9 IV.4:8 Many have tried to do this in **m.** name,
T-9 IV.4:8 forgetting that **m.** words make perfect
T-9 IV.12:1 Behold, **m.** child, reality is here. It
T-9 VI.3:8 If what you do to **m.** brother you do to me
T-10 III.6:4 It is not **m.** merit that I contribute to you
T-10 III.6:4 merit that I contribute to you but **m.** love,
T-10 III.6:5 sick, but **m.** value of you can heal you,
T-10 III.6:6 When I said, "**M.** peace I give unto you," I
T-11 in.4:1 **M.** brother, you are part of God and part
T-11 I.2:5 I and **m.** Father are one with you, for you
T-11 III.3:1 O **m.** child, if you knew what God wills
T-11 IV.6:7 God is **m.** life and yours, and nothing is
T-11 VIII.14:1 You, **m.** child, are afraid of your brothers
T-12 II.7:3 In **m.** resurrection is your release. Our
T-12 II.7:5 Trust in **m.** help, for I did not walk alone,
T-12 VI.2:8 As it was **m.** decision, so is it yours.
T-13 VII.16:8 **M.** peace I give you. Take it of me in glad
T-13 VII.17:2 **M.** task is not completed until I have
T-13 VII.17:3 yet it is not mine, for as it is **m.** gift to you,
T-13 X.13:1 **m.** faith and my belief are centered on
T-13 X.13:1 faith and **m.** belief are centered on what I
T-13 X.13:3 all **m.** faith and my belief I offer unto it.
T-13 X.13:3 all my faith and **m.** belief I offer unto it.
T-13 X.13:4 **M.** faith in you is as strong as all the love I
T-13 X.13:4 is as strong as all the love I give **m.** Father.
T-13 X.13:5 **M.** trust in you is without limit, and
T-14 V.9:9 purpose to which **m.** teaching calls you.
T-14 V.10:2 Only the resurrection became **m.** part in it
T-15 III.9:5 him. **M.** birth in you is your awakening to
T-15 III.9:7 **M.** Kingdom is not of this world because
T-15 III.10:2 I will as **m.** Father wills, knowing His Will
T-15 III.10:5 What **m.** Father loves I love as He does,
T-15 VI.2:3 I offer you **m.** perfect faith in you, in place
T-15 VI.2:4 forget not that **m.** faith must be as perfect
T-15 X.1:5 would celebrate **m.** birth into the world.
T-15 XI.7:5 and still would teach to all **m.** brothers, is
T-17 III.10:1 **M.** holy brother, I would enter into all
T-17 III.10:2 Let **m.** relationship to you be real to you,
T-18 I.10:8 God is with you, **m.** brother. Let us join in
T-18 III.6:5 **M.** need for you, joined with me in the
T19 IV.A.17:5 Yet would I offer you **m.** body, you whom
T19 IV.B.7:2 home you offered to **m.** Father and to me.
T19 IV.B.8:3 raise to freedom, and bar **m.** way to you.
T19 IV.C.8:2 **M.** brother, child of our Father, this is a
T19 IV.D.9:7 that you will accept it for **m.** love and His.
T-20 III.10:1 Such is **m.** will for you and your brother,
T-20 III.10:7 here would I unite with you, **m.** friend,
T-20 III.10:7 you, my friend, **m.** brother and my Self.
T-20 III.10:7 you, my friend, my brother and **m.** Self.
T-22 I.8:1 Think what is given you, **m.** holy brother.
T-28 III.8:1 Be not afraid, **m.** child, but let your world
T-29 VII.9:3 Save time, **m.** brother; learn what time is
T-30 IV.4:6 They are but toys, **m.** child, so do not
T-30 VII.7:5 Do not continue thus, **m.** brother. We
T-31 VIII.8:1 **M.** brothers in salvation, do not fail to
T-31 VIII.8:1 to hear **m.** voice and listen to my words. I
T-31 VIII.8:1 to hear my voice and listen to **m.** words. I
T-31 VIII.9:4 Hear me, **m.** brothers, hear and join with
T-31 VIII.10:1 are **m.** brothers as they are Your Sons. My
T-31 VIII.10:2 **M.** faith in them is Yours. I am as sure
T-31 VIII.11:1 joyous welcome is **m.** hand outstretched
T-31 VIII.11:2 Give me **m.** own, for they belong to You.
T-31 VIII.11:4 give You thanks for what **m.** brothers are.
WpI rV.in7:1 **M.** resurrection comes again each time I
WpI rV.in9:3 You are **m.** voice, my eyes, my feet, my
WpI rV.in9:3 You are my voice, **m.** eyes, my feet, my
WpI rV.in9:3 You are my voice, my eyes, **m.** feet, my
WpI rV.in9:3 **m.** hands through which I save the world.
W-pI 190.6:1 **M.** holy brother, think of this awhile: The
W-pII 221.2:4 Accept **m.** confidence, for it is yours. Our
W-pII 231.2:1 This is your will, **m.** brother. And you
W-pII 264.2:1 **M.** brothers, join with me in this today.
M-29 8:7 *God, Knowing they are on* ***m.*** *behalf as well,*
C-4 8:1 O **m.** brothers, if you only knew the peace
C-ep 2:3 Ask but **m.** help to roll the stone away,

## my 847

• noise word
*Jesus*
*My*

## myriad 2

T-30 III.10:2 the **m.** of forms that fear can take; quite
W-pI 138.4:3 doubts that **m.** decisions would induce.

## Myself 2

• God
*myself*

T-28 VI.6:5 Be you perfect as **M.**, for you can never be
W-pII 276.1:2 "My Son is pure and holy as **M.**." And

## myself 17

• Jesus
*noise word*
*Myself*

T-4 I.6:6 to devote **m.** to teaching if I believed this,
T-4 I.6:7 I do not accept either perception for **m.**.
T-4 I.13:5 once been tempted to believe in them **m.**.
T-5 I.4:4 I **m.** said, "If I go I will send you another
T-5 I.4:7 could not have It **m.** without knowing this
T-5 IV.4:1 I understood that I could not atone for **m.**
T-5 IV.6:5 to forsake **m.** and God Who created me.
T-5 IV.8:7 because I have loved you as I loved **m.**.
T-6 I.5:3 and did not share this evaluation for **m.**.
T-6 I.15:8 God, as much a part of the Sonship as **m.**.
T-6 I.16:1 remember that I told them **m.** that there
T-8 IV.3:4 by being aware of the Father's Will **m.**.
T-8 V.4:1 renounced the ego in **m.** and therefore
T-8 VI.9:2 born of my knowledge of **m.** and Him. We
T-12 II.7:2 awaken you as surely as I awakened **m.**,
T-12 VII.15:3 I have overcome death for **m.** alone? And
T-20 IV.7:6 I could leave you, and forget part of **m.**.

## myself 113

• noise word
*Jesus*
*Myself*

## mysteries 2

T-9 IV.4:7 is where the ego is forced to appeal to "**m.**
T-20 VI.4:1 where **m.** are kept obscure and hidden

## mysterious 1

T-9 V.6:4 Healing is not **m.**. Nothing will change

## mystery 3

T-20 VI.5:2 secret room, a tiny spot of senseless **m.**, a
T-20 VI.6:4 are worshipped here are shrouded in **m.**,
T-20 VI.6:6 Here is the "**m.**" of separation perceived

**myth** 1
T-23....... II.8:2 Atonement thus becomes a **m.**, and

**mythological** 1
T-4......... II.9:2 itself. **M.** systems generally include some

**mythology** 1
T-4 .......II.8:10 creative effort can be turned to **m.**. It can

**myths** 4
T-4 .......II.8:10 The creations of God do not create **m.**,
T-4 .......II.8:12 **M.** are entirely perceptual, and so
T-4 .........II.9:1 **M.** and magic are closely associated,
T-4 .........II.9:1 since **m.** are usually related to ego origins,

# N

**nail** 2
T19. IV.D.16:6 thorns against his brow, nor **n.** him to it,
W-pI... 193.9:2 or **n.** to hurt His holy Son in any way. He

**nailed** 2
T-11...... VI.8:1 have **n.** yourself to a cross, and placed a
W-pI... 196.5:1 escape yourself has **n.** you to the cross.

**nails** 8
T-11...... VI.7:1 the **n.** from the hands of God's Son, and
T-20.........I.3:5 and **n.** when his redemption is so near.
T-20....... II.7:8 no thorns nor **n.** to crucify the Son of God
T-20....... II.10:4 gift has saved him from the thorns and **n.**,
T-24..... III.8:6 Look on the print of **n.** upon his hands
T-24.... III.8:12 The print of **n.** is on your hands as well.
T-26........ II.4:7 And so He takes the thorns and **n.** away.
W-pI. 161.11:5 take away the **n.** which pierce your own,

**Name** 114
*name*
T-5.... III.11:10 asking only that you increase it in His **N.**
T-5........ IV.5:5 because my name is the **N.** of God's Son.
T-5...... VI.11:7 the Sonship in the **N.** of its Creator.
T-8....... VII.6:5 His Name's sake, because His **N.** is yours.
T-8........ IX.7:3 The **N.** of God's Son is One, and you are
T-10..... V.11:2 he had created in the **N.** of his Father.
T-10..... V.13:3 like His, because they are given in His **N.**.
T-11...... III.3:4 your joy you will create beauty in His **N.**,
T-12.........I.7:4 Every appeal you answer in the **N.** of
T-12.... VI.4:10 Spirit blesses the real world in Their **N.**.
T-13....VIII.9:4 miracles that you established in His **N.**.
T-15...... III.6:9 then, with littleness in the **N.** of Christ,
T-15..... VII.5:3 in the **N.** of Him Who would release him,
T-16...... IV.9:5 In the **N.** of God, be wholly willing to
T-17.... III.10:8 in the **N.** of God and bring you peace, that
T-19...... IV.3:8 His Creator in the **N.** of His most holy Son
T-19...... IV.3:9 And the Father will accept them in His **N.**.
T-26... VII.16:1 The miracle but calls your ancient **N.**,
T-26... VII.16:2 And to this **N.** your brother calls for his
T-26... VII.20:1 Your ancient **N.** belongs to everyone, as
T-26... VII.20:5 freed to call upon the **N.** of God as One.
T-27...... VI.3:9 call him by the holy **N.** of God Himself.
W-pI...... 78.7:2 Him in the holy **N.** of God and of His Son,
W-pI... 106.6:3 Who chose it in your Father's **N.** for you.
W-pI. 139.12:1 **N.** of its Creator and His Oneness with all
W-pI. 155.14:2 In your **N.** and His Own, which are the
W-pI... 165.8:2 **N.** we practice as His Word directs we do.
W-pI... 169.9:3 salvation's script in His Creator's **N.**, and
W-pI... 169.9:3 Name, and in the **N.** of His Creator's Son.
WpI.rV.in10:2 Hallowed your **N.**. Your glory undefiled
W-pI...... 183.h I call upon God's **N.** and on my own.
W-pI... 183.1:1 God's **N.** is holy, but no holier than yours
W-pI... 183.1:2 upon His **N.** is but to call upon your own.
W-pI... 183.1:5 Father's **N.** reminds you who you are,
W-pI... 183.2:1 **N.** can not be heard without response,
W-pI... 183.2:2 Say His **N.**, and you invite the angels to
W-pI... 183.3:1 Repeat God's **N.**, and all the world
W-pI... 183.4:1 Repeat the **N.** of God, and little names
W-pI... 183.4:2 and unwanted thing before God's **N.**.
W-pI... 183.4:3 Repeat His **N.**, and see how easily you will
W-pI... 183.4:5 let the **N.** of God replace their little names
W-pI... 183.5:1 Repeat the **N.** of God, and call upon your
W-pI... 183.5:1 and call upon your Self, Whose **N.** is His.
W-pI... 183.5:2 Repeat His **N.**, and all the tiny, nameless
W-pI... 183.5:3 Those who call upon the **N.** of God can
W-pI... 183.5:3 can not mistake the nameless for the **N.**,
W-pI... 183.5:4 repeat God's **N.** along with him within
W-pI... 183.6:1 God's **N.** slowly again and still again.
W-pI... 183.6:6 then God's **N.** becomes our only thought,
W-pI... 183.6:6 only **N.** of everything that we desire to see
W-pI... 183.8:1 Repeat God's **N.**, and you acknowledge
W-pI... 183.8:2 His Son is part of Him, creating in His **N.**.
W-pI... 183.8:3 let His **N.** become the all-encompassing
W-pI... 183.8:5 and see God's **N.** replace the thousand
W-pI... 183.8:5 that there is one **N.** for all there is, and all
W-pI. 183.10:1 Turn to the **N.** of God for your release,
W-pI. 183.10:3 when God's Son calls on his Father's **N.**.
W-pI. 183.10:6 place the holy **N.** of God becomes his
W-pI. 183.11:5 Voice gives answer in his Father's holy **N.**.
W-pI. 183.11:7 In our Father's **N.**, we would experience
W-pI. 183.11:8 today. And in His **N.**, it shall be given us.
W-pI...... 184.h The **N.** of God is my inheritance.
W-pI. 184.10:2 Word, the **N.** which God has given you;
W-pI. 184.11:3 He does not forget creation has one **N.**,
W-pI. 184.11:4 forget they share the **N.** of God along with
W-pI. 184.12:2 **N.** becomes the final lesson that all things
W-pI. 184.12:5 The **N.** of God is the inheritance He gave
W-pI. 184.13:1 who seeks the meaning of the **N.** of God.
W-pI. 184.13:3 first you must accept the **N.** for all reality,
W-pI. 184.13:4 One **N.** we bring into our practicing. One
W-pI. 184.13:5 One **N.** we use to unify our sight.
W-pI. 184.14:1 we understand that they have but one **N.**,
W-pI. 184.14:2 It is this **N.** we use in practicing. And
W-pI. 184.15:1 *Father, our **N.** is Yours. In It we are united*
W-pI. 184.15:7 ***N.** is our salvation and escape from what we*
W-pI. 184.15:8 *Your **N.** unites us in the oneness which is our*
W-pI. 186.13:5 and what is given in His **N.** takes on the
W-pI. 187.10:4 The **N.** of God is on our lips. And as we
W-pI... 203.1:1 I call upon God's **N.** and on my own. *The*
W-pI... 203.1:2 *The **N.** of God is my deliverance from every*
W-pI... 204.1:1 (184) The **N.** of God is my inheritance.
W-pI... 204.1:2 *God's **N.** reminds me that I am His Son, not*
W-pII ...in.3:4 remain unanswered when he calls His **N.**.
W-pII ..in.10:4 Instead of prayers, we need but call His **N.**
W-pII . 222.2:1 *Your **N.** upon our lips and in our minds, as*
W-pII . 223.2:7 *Our **N.** is Yours, and we acknowledge that*
W-pII . 224.2:1 *My **N.**, O Father, still is known to You. I have*
W-pII ..... 2.3:4 altar to the holy **N.** of God whereon His
W-pII . 240.2:4 *Let us forgive him in Your **N.**, that we may*
W-pII . 244.1:2 *He need but call upon Your **N.**, and he will*
W-pII . 255.1:6 In His **N.**, I give today to finding what my
W-pII . 262.1:6 *For Your Son must bear Your **N.**, for You*
W-pII . 264.1:7 *We come to You in Your Own **N.** today, to be*
W-pII . 266.1:3 *Let not Your Son forget Your holy **N.**. Let not*
W-pII . 266.1:5 *Let not Your Son forget his **N.** is Yours.*
W-pII . 266.2:1 calling upon God's **N.** and on our own,
W-pII . 267.1:7 Each heartbeat calls His **N.**, and every one
W-pII . 282.2:1 *Father, Your **N.** is Love and so is mine. Such*
W-pII . 288.1:9 *But let me honor him who bears Your **N.**,*
W-pII ... 11.5:2 we forgive creation in the **N.** of its Creator
W-pII . 351.1:7 *For He alone gives judgment in Your **N.**.*
W-pII . 356.1:5 *Your **N.** replaces every thought of sin, and*
W-pII . 356.1:6 *Your **N.** gives answer to Your Son, because*
W-pII . 356.1:6 *because to call Your **N.** is but to call his own.*
M-5 ...... III.2:5 forgiveness for God's Son in his own **N.**.
M-22 ......... 5:4 hardly offer it to his brother in Christ's **N.**
M-23 ......... 2:8 So has his name become the **N.** of God,
C-4 ............ 8:2 is. Hallowed your **N.** and His, for they are
C-ep .......... 3:6 where He has set your **N.** along with His.
P-2...........V.6:5 advance, the tiniest of whispers of His **N.**.
P-3...........I.3:1 for you to serve them in the **N.** of God.
S-1.........in.1:6 the song of his creating in his Father's **N.**.
S-2........ III.6:6 be heard by anyone who calls upon His **N.**
S-2........ III.7:5 angels down to answer you in His Own **N.**

**name** 110
*Name*
T-4 ....... III.6:3 Let us ask the Father in my **n.** to keep you
T-4 ..... IV.10:1 is merely another **n.** for the creation, for
T-4 ..... IV.11:6 brother will yet come together in my **n.**,
T-5 ....... IV.5:5 Make it dependable in my **n.** because my
T-5 ....... IV.5:5 because my **n.** is the Name of God's Son.
T-6 ...........I.7:5 brothers in the **n.** of the Kingdom of God,
T-8 ....... IX.7:1 and to accomplish all things in my **n.**.
T-8 ....... IX.7:2 is not my **n.** alone, for ours is a shared
T-9 ....... IV.4:8 Many have tried to do this in my **n.**,
T-11 ..... VI.5:5 obey. In his **n.** they crucify themselves,
T-12 ........II.8:5 the **n.** of the complete trust I have in you,
T-13 ... VI.13:4 In your **n.** He has given for you, and given
T-13 .. VII.11:4 lose whatever you have gotten in its **n.**.
T-15 .... VII.5:3 In the **n.** of his release, and in the Name of
T-15 ... XI.10:7 *In the **n.** of my freedom I choose your release*
T-16 .....V.13:2 In the **n.** of your completion you do not
T-17 ..... III.2:5 you, and seems to go by the **n.** of love, no
T-21 ........I.6:1 like a song whose **n.** is long forgotten, and
T-21 ..... III.1:4 to keep the bargain in the **n.** of "fairness,"
T-26 .........I.1:5 in the **n.** of saving just a little for yourself.
T-26 .. VII.17:3 and hate is answered in the **n.** of love. To
T-26 .. VII.20:2 on your brother's **n.** and God will answer,
T-27 ..... VI.2:5 different because it has a different **n.**, and
T-27 ..... VI.2:9 Sin's witnesses but shift from **n.** to name,

| | |
|---|---|
| T-27......VI.2:9 | Sin's witnesses but shift from name to n., |
| T-27......VI.3:6 | This n. or that, but nothing more, you |
| T-27......VI.3:7 | true because you called him by truth's n.. |
| T-27......VI.5:4 | the n. by which you called your suffering. |
| T-27......VI.5:6 | them all as one, and called by n. of fear. |
| T-30.......II.2:3 | that ever should be called by freedom's n.. |
| W-pI.......5.2:1 | use both the n. of the form in which you |
| W-pI.......5.7:2 | using the n. of both the source of the |
| W-pI.......6.1:2 | it is necessary to n. both the form of upset |
| W-pI.......8.4:4 | N. each one by the central figure or theme |
| W-pI.......8.5:1 | Then n. each of your thoughts specifically |
| W-pI.......8.5:2 | *I seem to be thinking about [n. of a person],* |
| W-pI.......8.5:2 | *[name of a person], about [n. of an object],* |
| W-pI.......8.5:2 | *of an object], about [n. of an emotion],* and |
| W-pI.....14.4:2 | N. each one as it occurs to you, and then |
| W-pI.....14.5:2 | case, n. the "disaster" quite specifically. |
| W-pI.....15.4:1 | using its n. and letting your eyes rest on it |
| W-pI.....19.3:3 | one, n. it in terms of the central person or |
| W-pI.....21.4:2 | *determined to see_[n. of person] differently* |
| W-pI.....21.5:4 | *see_[specify the attribute] in_[n. of person]* |
| W-pI.....24.5:1 | today, n. each situation that occurs to you |
| W-pI.....26.7:1 | First, n. the situation: *I am concerned* |
| W-pI.....28.8:1 | the applications should include the n. of |
| W-pI.....31.4:2 | in the n. of your own freedom. And in |
| W-pI.....37.4:5 | who occurs to you, using his n. and saying |
| W-pI.....37.4:6 | and saying: *My holiness blesses you, [n.].* |
| W-pI.....37.6:2 | you meet, using his n. as you do so. It is |
| W-pI.....38.4:3 | and also the n. of the person concerned. |
| W-pI.....46.4:3 | Mention each one by n., and say: *God is* |
| W-pI.....46.4:4 | *God is the Love in which I forgive you, [n.].* |
| W-pI.....76.8:6 | would not save but damn in Heaven's n.. |
| W-pI.....78.5:1 | his n. has crossed your mind already. He |
| W-pI.....82.2:2 | *peace extend from my mind to yours, [n.]. I* |
| W-pI.....82.2:3 | *I share the light of the world with you, [n.].* |
| W-pI.....87.2:3 | *You stand with me in light, [n.]. In the light* |
| W-pI.....87.4:3 | *It is God's Will you are His Son, [n.], and* |
| W-pI.....88.2:3 | *The light in you is all that I would see, [n.]. I* |
| W-pI.....89.2:3 | *Let me not hold a grievance against you, [n.],* |
| W-pI.....89.4:3 | *our grievances be replaced by miracles, [n.].* |
| W-pI.....96.7:3 | and answered in your n. that it was done. |
| W-pI...106.4:7 | to His dear Son, whose other n. is you. |
| W-pI...134.5:2 | be concealed, denied or called another n., |
| W-pI...137.5:1 | the dream of sickness in the n. of truth, |
| W-pI...153.2:2 | and righteous in the n. of self-defense. Yet |
| W-pI...163.5:2 | death itself has written, gives no n. to him |
| W-pI...164.3:1 | and answers in your n. the Call He hears! |
| W-pI...181.8:4 | all we seek for in the n. of true perception, |
| W-pI...183.1:3 | A father gives his son his n., and thus |
| W-pI...183.1:4 | His brothers share his n., and thus are |
| W-pI...183.4:4 | have lost the n. of god you gave them. |
| W-pI...183.6:2 | Become oblivious to every n. but His. |
| W-pI...183.7:5 | that His Son receive another n. than His. |
| W-pI...184.1:3 | a separate entity, identified by its own n.. |
| W-pI...184.1:6 | all things to which you give a different n.; |
| W-pI...184.1:6 | time; all bodies which are greeted by a n.. |
| W-pI...184.8:6 | mind consents to take the n. you give him |
| W-pI...184.8:7 | you, and he accepts this separate n. as his. |
| W-pI.184.12:1 | God has no n.. And yet His Name |
| W-pI.184.14:1 | And though we use a different n. for each |
| W-pI...192.1:1 | extending love, creating in its n., forever |
| W-pI...195.4:6 | For who can bargain in the n. of love? |
| W-pII..282.2:3 | *be changed by merely giving it another n.?* |
| W-pII..282.2:4 | *The n. of fear is simply a mistake. Let me not* |
| W-pII..291.1:3 | And I accept this vision in its n., both for |
| W-pII......9.3:2 | the n. of true creation and the Will of God |
| W-pII..333.1:2 | seen somewhere else, called by another n. |
| W-pII.....356.h | Sickness is but another n. for sin. Healing |
| W-pII.....356.h | Healing is but another n. for God. The |
| M-4.......IX.1:8 | Nothing but that really deserves the n.. |
| M-16..........7:2 | All that he did before in the n. of safety no |
| M-23..........1:4 | Bible says, "Ask in the n. of Jesus Christ." |
| M-23..........1:6 | A n. does not heal, nor does an invocation |
| M-23..........1:8 | What does calling on his n. confer? Why |
| M-23..........2:8 | So has his n. become the Name of God, |
| M-23..........4:1 | n. of Jesus Christ as such is but a symbol. |
| M-23..........4:4 | the moment that the n. is called to mind. |
| M-23..........4:5 | Remembering the n. of Jesus Christ is to |
| M-26..........2:9 | all things in their n. and in no other. |
| C-2............1:8 | A n. for namelessness is all it is. A symbol |
| C-2...........1:10 | We n. it but to help us understand that it |
| C-5............2:1 | The n. of *Jesus* is the name of one who was |
| C-5............2:1 | The name of *Jesus* is the n. of one who was |
| P-3...........I.3:8 | sent in whatever form is most helpful; a n. |
| P-3........III.2:9 | who would do this loses the n. of healer, |
| S-2........III.4:5 | is not real and makes illusions in its evil n. |
| S-3........III.6:2 | those who serve with Him in healing's n.. |

## Name's 1

| | |
|---|---|
| T-8.......VII.6:5 | Son of God remain hidden for His N. sake |

## named 5

| | |
|---|---|
| T-3.......VII.3:7 | tree" was n. the "tree of knowledge." Yet |
| W-pI.....26.9:1 | After you have n. each outcome of which |
| W-pI.....35.7:4 | After you have n. each one, add: *But my* |
| W-pI...184.3:4 | For what is n. is given meaning and will |
| W-pI...184.6:4 | leave no doubt that what is n. is there. It |

## nameless 6

| | |
|---|---|
| T-24....... V.4:2 | to a n. precipice and hurl him over it. For |
| W-pI...183.4:2 | No temptation but becomes a n. and |
| W-pI...183.5:2 | the tiny, n. things on earth slip into right |
| W-pI...183.5:3 | God can not mistake the n. for the Name, |
| W-pI.183.10:6 | all things he thought he made be n. now, |
| W-pI...184.3:3 | The n. things were given names, and thus |

## namelessness 1

| | |
|---|---|
| C-2............1:8 | all. A name for n. is all it is. A symbol of |

## names 30

| | |
|---|---|
| T-27......VI.3:4 | It tells you but the n. you gave to it to use, |
| T-27......VI.4:2 | n. that speak in other ways for its reality. |
| T-27......VI.5:1 | the n. by which sin's witnesses are called. |
| T-31......IV.2:7 | by all the different n. its roads are given. |
| T-31.....VII.9:1 | they all are different n. for just one error; |
| W-pI.....76.4:2 | and put them under different n. in a long |
| W-pI...183.4:1 | God, and little n. have lost their meaning. |
| W-pI...183.4:3 | forget the n. of all the gods you valued. |
| W-pI...183.4:5 | let the Name of God replace their little n., |
| W-pI...183.7:3 | with n. of idols cherished by the world. |
| W-pI...183.8:5 | thousand little n. you gave your thoughts, |
| W-pI...184.1:2 | have made up n. for everything you see. |
| W-pI...184.3:1 | n. by which the world becomes a series of |
| W-pI...184.3:2 | You gave these n. to them, establishing |
| W-pI...184.3:3 | The nameless things were given n., and |
| W-pI...184.5:2 | to teach the mind a thousand alien n., |
| W-pI...184.7:5 | and all the arbitrary n. the world bestows |
| W-pI.184.11:1 | Use all the little n. and symbols which |
| W-pI.184.11:4 | Use all the n. the world bestows on them |
| W-pI.184.12:3 | All n. are unified; all space is filled with |
| W-pI.184.13:3 | realize the many n. you gave its aspects |
| W-pI.184.15:3 | *made and call by many different n. is but a* |
| W-pII..231.1:2 | *else; a something I have called by many n..* |
| W-pII..262.1:5 | *Why should I give this one a thousand n.,* |
| M-23 .........4:3 | many n. of all the gods to which you pray. |
| C-4.............3:5 | true perception is a remedy with many n.. |
| C-5.............1:5 | But they have n. which differ for a time, |
| C-5.............1:6 | Their n. are legion, but we will not go |
| C-5.............1:6 | go beyond the n. the course itself employs |
| C-5.............6:3 | Christ takes many forms with different n. |

## naming 3

| | |
|---|---|
| W-pI.....29.4:1 | about you, n. each one specifically. Try to |
| W-pI...183.4:5 | them worshipfully, n. them as gods. |
| W-pI...184.8:3 | in earth and Heaven is beyond your n.. |

## narrow 6

| | |
|---|---|
| T-11......VI.3:9 | try to limit what you see by n. little beliefs |
| T-30....... V.8:1 | is the step across the n. boundaries of the |
| T-31.......IV.1:5 | within the n. band from birth to death, a |
| Wi181-200 2:1 | the special blocks that keep your vision n. |
| P-2.........II.8:5 | it possible to transcend the n. boundaries |
| S-1.........II.4:3 | and to accept to the same n. margins. |

## narrowed 2

| | |
|---|---|
| T-13.... VI.12:4 | and your awareness is n. to yourself. And |
| W-pI... 181.6:2 | to us, our n. focus will restrict our sight, |

## narrowly 1

| | |
|---|---|
| T-27....VIII.7:6 | It keeps you n. confined within a body, |

## native 2

| | |
|---|---|
| T-22.........I.6:6 | does not understand will be his n. tongue, |
| W-pI... 188.1:6 | light came with you from your n. home, |

## natural 85

| | |
|---|---|
| T-in ........... 1:7 | *love's presence, which is your n. inheritance* |
| T-1...........I.6:1 | Miracles are n.. When they do not occur |
| T-1.........I.21:1 | Miracles are n. signs of forgiveness. |
| T-1...... III.1:10 | is the n. profession of the children of God |
| T-1......... V.6:2 | The abundance of Christ is the n. result of |
| T-2..........II.1:2 | have made it clear that miracles are n., |
| T-2..........II.7:8 | assume your n. talent of protecting others |
| T-3...........I.6:3 | honor is the n. greeting of the truly loved |
| T-3........ III.4:1 | is the n. perception of spiritual sight, but |
| T-3...... V.10:4 | prayer, is the n. state of those who know. |
| T-3...... VI.10:1 | Peace is a n. heritage of spirit. Everyone |
| T-4...........I.5:5 | It is n. for the ego to try to protect itself |
| T-4...........I.5:5 | but it is not n. for you to want to obey its |
| T-4.... IV.11:11 | I understand that miracles are n., because |
| T-4.... IV.11:12 | My calling you is as n. as your answer, |
| T-4........ VI.4:3 | done this, it denies all truly n. impulses, |
| T-5.........in.1:6 | the mind's n. impulse to respond as one. |
| T-5......... V.4:7 | engenders joy, not guilt, because it is n.. |
| T-7........ XI.1:4 | It is therefore n.. The world goes against |
| T-7........ XI.1:8 | convince yourself that, in your n. state, |
| T-7........ XI.2:1 | Grace is the n. state of every Son of God. |
| T-7........ XI.2:2 | he is out of his n. environment and does |
| T-7........ XI.5:8 | that is immediate, clear and n.. You have |
| T-7........ XI.6:1 | of your n. environment you may well ask, |
| T-8..........II.2:7 | is joyful if it leads you along your n. path, |
| T-8..........II.8:6 | the n. response of every Son of God to the |
| T-8.........III.2:7 | this is the n. outcome of their being. |
| T-8.......VII.7:6 | is the only n. use to which it can be put. |
| T-8.....VII.10:2 | Since this is n. it heals by making whole, |
| T-8.....VII.10:2 | it heals by making whole, which is also n.. |
| T-8......VIII.9:8 | Health is seen as the n. state of everything |
| T-9........ IV.3:2 | reminds you of the n. use of your abilities. |
| T-9........ IV.6:2 | I meant when I said that miracles are n., |
| T-11....... V.5:1 | purpose is always the n. outcome of what |
| T-11....... V.5:2 | ego is the n. outcome of its central belief, |
| T-11....... V.5:2 | to recognize that their source is not n., |
| T-11...... VI.3:8 | His perceptions are your n. awareness, |
| T-12...... VI.6:3 | to holiness is merely its n. extension. Love |
| T-13...... VI.2:1 | You consider it "n." to use your past |
| T-14...... III.5:3 | effect. It is the n. result of choosing right, |
| T-14....... V.3:4 | is the n. extension of perfect purity. Your |
| T-15...... VI.5:7 | for this alone is n. under the laws of God. |
| T-16........II.3:1 | you the miracle cannot seem n., because |
| T-16........II.3:1 | that it does not remember what is n. to it. |
| T-16........II.3:2 | it. And when you are told what is n., you |
| T-16........II.3:3 | of the whole in every part is perfectly n., |
| T-16........II.3:3 | and what is n. to Him is natural to you. |
| T-16........II.3:3 | and what is natural to Him is n. to you. |
| T-16........II.3:4 | Wholly n. perception would show you |
| T-16........II.4:4 | His n. perception of your gift enables Him |
| T-16........II.5:4 | it. Miracles are n. to the One Who speaks |
| T-16....... V.3:3 | judged to be acceptable and even n.. No |
| T-16....... V.3:5 | is the "n." condition of the separation, |
| T-16....... V.3:5 | not n. at all seem to be the unnatural ones |
| T-16...... V.17:3 | to make the n. decision as this is realized. |
| T-16...... VI.1:4 | Yet this cannot be n., for it is unlike the |
| T-18........II.9:4 | from which awaking is so easy and so n.. |
| T-18...... IV.7:1 | makes the holy instant so easy and so n.. |
| T-18...... IV.8:1 | that is n. and easy for you impossible. If |
| T-19........II.7:1 | the n. expression of what the Son of God |
| T-21....... V.3:3 | This other self sees miracles as n.. They |

T-21....... V.3:4 and as **n.** to it as breathing to the body.
T-22..... VI.13:9 seems more **n.** and more in line with your
T-22.. VI.13:10 with truth, to teach you what *is* **n.** and true
T-23.... III.6:10 the body, torn between the **n.** desire to
T-24.........I.4:4 the special one is "**n.**" and "just." The
T-26... VII.18:1 given you as He would have it used is **n.**.
T-30...... VI.1:5 it is on this forgiveness rests, and is but **n.**
T-30...... VI.2:7 merely asked to see forgiveness as the **n.**
T-31....... V.7:2 They are not **n.**. Apart from learning they
T-31.... VIII.5:6 thus are miracles as **n.** as fear and agony
W-pI..... 41.8:2 it is the most **n.** thing in the world. You
W-pI..... 41.8:3 might even say it is the only **n.** thing in
W-pI..... 44.4:3 the most **n.** and easy one in the world for
W-pI..... 44.7:4 it. It is merely taking its **n.** course. Try to
W-pI..... 72.9:3 be without a body is to be in our **n.** state.
W-pI... 134.6:1 that makes forgiveness **n.** and wholly sane
W-pI... 161.2:1 Complete abstraction is the **n.** condition
W-pI... 184.5:1 still remain a **n.** direction for the mind to
M-4 ..... IV.2:4 harm has no meaning, it is merely **n.**.
M-4 .... VIII.1:2 Patience is **n.** to the teacher of God. All he
M-4 .... VIII.1:9 Patience is **n.** to those who trust. Sure of
M-25 ......... 2:7 in any way is merely becoming more **n.**.
M-27 ......... 1:5 but to be accepted as the "**n.**" law of life.
C-5............. 5:6 Walking with him is just as **n.** as walking

### naturally 9

T-1........... I.3:1 Miracles occur **n.** as expressions of love.
T-1........ III.1:5 **n.** become part of the Atonement yourself
T-1........ III.7:5 mind then **n.** welcomes the Host within
T-3........... I.5:3 are not in conflict, but **n.** live in peace.
T-3........ IV.7:6 **n.** remembered spirit and its real purpose
T-4....... VII.1:2 specific, although the mind is **n.** abstract.
T-4....... VII.3:8 creations **n.** communicate with Him and
T-14.... III.10:6 as **n.** as peace that knows no limits. There
M-4 .... IX.2:11 Defenselessness attends it **n.**, and joy is

### nature 46

T-1......... II.2:5 now because of their interpersonal **n.**. In
T-1........ III.4:5 The impersonal **n.** of the miracle is an
T-1........ III.7:3 The impersonal **n.** of miracles is because
T-1........ III.8:5 The impersonal **n.** of miracle-mindedness
T-1..... VII.3:11 the wholly satisfying **n.** of reality becomes
T-3.......... V.2:8 The highly specific **n.** of invention is not
T-4........... I.5:6 this choice because of the **n.** of its origin.
T-4........... I.5:7 You can, because of the **n.** of yours.
T-4....... II.8:12 and characteristically good-and-evil in **n.**
T-6...... V.C.5:8 **n.** of the steps you must take with Him.
T-7........ XI.1:5 The world goes against your **n.**, being out
T-8......... II.2:8 When you are taught against your **n.**,
T-8......... II.2:9 you. Your will is *in* your **n.**, and therefore
T-11....... V.5:2 being out of accord with your true **n.**. I
T-11..... VI.4:9 **n.** of God's Son as his Father created him.
T-12..... VII.8:2 The contradictory **n.** of the witnesses you
T-14...... IX.2:3 when its impossible **n.** is clearly revealed?
T-16....... II.1:3 the **n.** of miracles you do not understand.
T-16...... V.10:2 Let us not think of its fearful **n.**, nor of the
T-18...... IX.8:3 **n.** as He leads you past them, for beneath
T19. IV.A.10:2 the **n.** of love to look upon only the truth,
T-21....... V.5:9 Your reason's alien **n.** to the ego is proof
T-23......... I.4:7 as ridiculous as **n.** roaring at the wind in
T-23......... I.4:8 Could **n.** possibly establish this, and
T-27....... V.1:4 its **n.** to extend itself the instant it is born.
T-27....... V.8:2 no one understands the **n.** of his problem.
T-27....... V.8:4 Its very **n.** is that it is *not*. And thus, while
T-28....... II.2:4 It is the **n.** of the innocent to be forever
W-in.......... 6:5 very **n.** of true perception is that it has no
W-pI..... 17.1:6 In view of its highly variable **n.**, this is
W-pI..... 29.4:2 today's idea because of its wholly alien **n.**.
W-pI..... 54.5:2 Recognizing the shared **n.** of my thoughts
W-pI..... 56.2:3 fearful **n.** of the self-image I have made. If
W-pI..... 67.2:1 wholly unchanged and unchangeable **n.**.
W-pI..... 92.2:2 If you but understood the **n.** of thought,
W-pI. 139.12:3 And learn the fragile **n.** of the chains that
W-pII ..... 9.2:1 It is the all-inclusive **n.** of Christ's Second
M-18 ......... 1:1 Correction of a lasting **n.**, –and only this
M-24 ......... 1:6 the recognition of the eternal **n.** of life, it
M-27 ......... 1:5 This is regarded as "the way of **n.**," not to
C-1 ............ 3:2 because of its highly controversial **n.**. It
C-2 ............ 2:5 that its illusive **n.** is concealed behind the
C-2 ............ 3:3 clear because its **n.** seems to have a form.
S-1......... III.4:2 glimpse of the merciful **n.** of this step may
S-2......... in.1:7 Unlike the timeless **n.** of its sister, prayer,
S-3........... I.1:4 this is shown by the brief **n.** of the " cure."

### nature's 1

M-27 ......... 3:7 Devouring is **n.** "law of life." God is

### natures 1

T-11 ...... in.1:5 irreconcilable **n.** cannot be reconciled by

### near 30

T-5 .......... I.4:9 is so **n.** to truth that God Himself can flow
T-16 ........ II.6:9 come too **n.** to truth to renounce it now,
T-16 ...... IV.2:5 Be not unwilling now; you are too **n.**, and
T-16 ... IV.12:3 complete, for what *is* endless is very **n.**.
T-17 ........ II.1:3 or waking, comes **n.** to such loveliness.
T19.... IV.C.9:2 into a mighty force for God is very **n.**. The
T-20 ......... I.3:5 and nails when his redemption is so **n.**.
T-20 ...... VI.7:2 love draw **n.** them and overlook the body,
T-30 ... III.10:3 no sound of battle comes remotely **n.**, it
T-31 ........ II.6:6 as **n.** or far away from what we want as we
T-31 . VIII.10:8 one in purpose, and the end of hell is **n.**.
W-pI....... 2.1:2 Begin with the things that are **n.** you, and
W-pI..... 11.2:3 open your eyes and look about, **n.** and far
W-pI..... 25.6:2 happens to catch your eye, **n.** or far,
W-pI..... 30.4:1 limited to concepts such as "**n.**" and "far.
W-pI..... 60.1:6 It will bring me **n.** enough to Heaven that
W-pI... 109.8:3 from far across the world, and **n.** as well;
W-pI... 129.4:6 world. And yet how **n.** are you, when you
W-pI... 140.8:4 It is as **n.** to us as our own thoughts; so
W-pI... 156.7:4 The approach to God is **n.**. And in the
W-pI... 164.1:6 more clear, more meaningful, more **n.**.
W-pI... 186.6:5 misery can come not **n.** the holy home of
W-pII . 252.1:5 be, and yet how **n.** to me and close to God
W-pII . 298.1:4 I draw **n.** the end of senseless journeys,
W-pII . 344.2:1 How **n.** we are to one another, as we go to
W-pII . 344.2:2 How **n.** is He to us. How close the ending
W-ep ......... 6:7 God's angels hover **n.** and all about. His
M-15 ........ 1:10 Time pauses as eternity comes **n.**, and
C-3 ............ 4:9 as **n.** to Heaven as is possible outside the
P-2........ III.4:4 too **n.** to God to keep his feet on earth.

### nearby 1

W-pI. 132.16:1 the world, as well as to the ones you see **n.**

### nearer 29

T-4 ....... VI.5:3 and slowly bring it **n.** so he can learn how
T-13 ... VIII.5:4 the past thus brings you **n.** to the end of
T-14 ........ X.1:2 in time but bring eternity **n.** or farther.
T-15 ..... IV.2:4 so much as you want it will you bring it **n.**
T-18 ..... III.2:1 light comes **n.** you will rush to darkness,
T-19 ... III.11:5 it is brought **n.** to all by your relationship.
T-20 ...... V.1:5 each joining is the end of time brought **n.**.
T-21 ... VI.10:6 that could be **n.** you than is your Self?
T-25 ..... IV.5:8 Nothing beyond nor **n.**. Nothing else. In
T-26 ........ I.1:8 All seeming entities can come a little **n.**,
T-26 ..... IV.4:2 each gift that brings him **n.** to his home.
T-26 ... VIII.1:5 The **n.** it is brought to where it is, the
T-29 ...... V.3:5 you offer him but brings you **n.** to your
W-pI..... 27.1:5 the idea will be wholly true a little **n.**.
W-pI..... 67.4:4 do much today to bring that awareness **n.**
W-pI..... 97.3:2 awareness is brought a little **n.** at least;
W-pI... 109.7:1 that you rest today, the world is **n.** waking
W-pI... 125.7:2 He speaks from **n.** than your heart to you.
W-pI... 157.7:1 in its ways; a little **n.** its deliverance. And
W-pI. 161.10:2 and you will come today **n.** Christ's vision
W-pI... 164.3:4 sights and sounds that come from **n.** than
W-pI. 169.11:5 salvation comes a little **n.** each uncertain
WpI...rV.in5:2 Every step we take brings us a little **n.**.
W-pI... 188.9:1 practice coming **n.** to the light in us today
W-pI... 191.2:6 that does not seem to bring you **n.** death;
W-pI 198.13:1 Today we come still **n.** to the end of
W-pI 200.11:8 home, and draw still **n.** every time we say:
W-ep......... 5:4 you make brings Heaven **n.** to your reach.
M-16 ......... 9:6 this, and bring this goal **n.** to recognition.

### nearest 1

W-pI ...... 9.4:1 Begin with things that are **n.** you, and

### neatly 1

T-23 ..... II.21:3 The steps to chaos do follow **n.** from their

### necessarily 16

T-2 ....... IV.5:4 **n.** mean that this is the highest level of
T-2 ...... VII.7:4 but it is by no means **n.** undivided. The
T-2 ..... VIII.1:4 everything you create is **n.** a matter of will
T-3 ....... IV.3:5 It is **n.** uncertain about what it is. It has to
T-4 ......... II.5:6 Your attitudes even toward this are **n.**
T-4 ....... VI.1:5 as **n.** conflicted as long as you are here, or
T-11 ....... V.4:3 on its behalf is **n.** expended on nothing.
T-19 ....... II.1:4 The belief in sin is **n.** based on the firm
T-19 ....... II.5:3 and **n.** protected with every defense at its
W-pI .... 48.3:2 not **n.** in a place you recognize as yet, you
W-pI .... 65.1:5 your only function **n.** entails two phases;
W-pI .... 91.1:1 that miracles and vision **n.** go together.
M-3 ........... 5:4 does not mean that they **n.** recognize this;
M-7 ........... 5:2 **n.** implies that trust has been placed in an
M-24 ......... 5:9 he knows is not **n.** all there is to learn. His
C-in ........... 2:4 as such are **n.** controversial, since they

### necessary 134

T-1 .......... I.7:1 right, but purification is **n.** first.
T-1 ......... V.2:1 not to wait on time any longer than is **n.**.
T-1 ......... V.2:6 to the Sonship will no longer be **n.**.
T-1 ...... VII.5:1 A solid foundation is **n.** because of the
T-2 ......... II.4:4 Acts were not **n.** before the separation,
T-2 ......... II.4:5 **n.** for its fulfillment were planned. Then a
T-2 ......... II.5:4 has no value when change is no longer **n.**.
T-2 ..... IV.3:12 it is not **n.** to protect the mind by denying
T-2 ......... V.8:1 to accept unequivocally that healing is **n.**.
T-2 ...... VII.2:3 will be **n.** to set the mind itself straight, a
T-2 ...... VII.2:4 as a **n.** condition for the miracle to occur.
T-2 .... VII.5:13 made this **n.** as a corrective device. The
T-2 ...... VII.7:9 time is **n.** between readiness and mastery,
T-3 ....... III.6:1 Right perception is **n.** before God can
T-3 ......... V.7:8 judgments are **n.** in order to select.
T-3 ......... V.9:2 Correct perception of your brother is **n.**,
T-4 .......... I.7:6 wish or make is **n.** to establish your worth
T-4 ......... II.4:9 is no longer **n.** you will merely know God.
T-4 ....... II.11:2 **n.** only because misperception is a block
T-4 ....... III.5:2 is **n.** to repeat that your belief in darkness
T-4 ....... VI.1:4 was **n.** to persuade you that you cannot
T-5 ....... V.4:11 This is **n.** to the ego's survival because, as
T-6 .......... I.4:6 it is not **n.** to perceive any form of assault
T-6 ........ I.12:1 reawakening of every Son of God is **n.** to
T-6 ....... II.11:1 the idea that return is **n.** because it can so
T-6 ....... II.11:3 the idea of return both **n.** and difficult.
T-6 ..... V.A.6:2 **n.** that you complete the step yourself,
T-6 ..... V.A.6:2 but it is **n.** that you turn in that direction.
T-6 ..... V.A.6:5 in direction would not have been **n.**.
T-6 ..... V.C.2:5 The undoing is **n.** only in your mind, so
T-6 ..... V.C.8:9 you. Vigilance is not **n.** for truth, but it is
T-6 ..... V.C.8:9 for truth, but it is **n.** against illusions.
T-7 ....... VI.7:6 It is **n.** against beliefs that are not true,
T-8 .......... I.5:2 a change in the curriculum is obviously **n.**
T-8 ..... VIII.6:9 but it is not **n.** to examine all possible
T-11 .... VII.2:7 is **n.** is a willingness to perceive nothing
T-12 ........ I.8:2 is **n.** to demonstrate the need for escape.
T-12 ..... III.7:8 a **n.** consequence of what you have done.
T-13 ..... XI.6:3 and differences are **n.** teaching aids, for
T-14 ..... IV.7:3 accept the **n.** conditions for knowing Him
T-14 ..... XI.7:1 miracles, for it is you who made them **n.**.
T-15 ..... IV.9:1 **n.** condition for the holy instant does not
T-15 ..... IX.2:1 the **n.** process of looking straight at all the
T-15 ..... IX.3:2 it is **n.** to give up every use the ego has for
T-15 ....... X.4:2 is but one shift in perception that is **n.**,

T-15 X.5:1 **n.** to follow fear through all the circuitous
T-15 X.5:2 Yet it *is* **n.** to examine each one as long as
T-15 XI.7:2 body as the **n.** means of communication.
T-16 II.2:6 your understanding cannot be **n.**. Yet it is
T-16 IV.6:2 It is not **n.** to seek for what is true, but it *is*
T-16 IV.6:2 is true, but it *is* **n.** to seek for what is false.
T-16 V.1:1 is **n.** first to realize that it involves a great
T-18 I.7:12 what else is **n.** to make them all the same?
T-18 III.4:11 that your understanding is not **n.**. All that
T-18 III.4:12 was **n.** was merely the *wish* to understand.
T-18 IV.1:5 It is not **n.** that you do more; indeed, it is
T-18 IV.1:5 it is **n.** that you realize that you cannot do
T-18 V.6:5 Never believe that this is **n.**, or even
T-18 VII.4:9 aimed at detachment from the body **n.**.
T-20 III.1:6 this impaired condition *are* adjustments **n.**
T-20 III.2:4 whatever adjustments it deems **n.** and
T-20 VIII.1:5 Vision would not be **n.** had judgment not
T-21 I.2:2 **n.** to imagine what the world must look
T-21 VII.5:7 **n.** that he understand how he can see it.
T-21 VII.12:2 Could it be **n.** they be asked so often, if
T-21 VIII.2:8 who see the final question is **n.** to the rest,
T-22 VI.13:10 it is **n.** that you have other experiences,
T-23 II.6:3 seen as even **n.** that He be asked about the
T-24 in.1:3 It is not **n.** to tell Him what to do. He will
T-25 VIII.1:7 This much is **n.** to add to the idea no one
T-25 VIII.2:2 Nor is it **n.** that your faith in it be strong,
T-26 II.6:2 fair and good, and **n.** to preserve yourself.
T-26 III.1:11 if there were could choosing be a **n.** step
T-26 III.1:14 it **n.** we dwell on anything that cannot be
T-27 II.13:2 comes a **n.** view of function split between
T-27 V.4:2 love without attack is **n.** that all this occur
T-30 III.3:8 And thus it would be **n.** for the search for
T-30 VI.5:5 it would be **n.** first there be some sin that
W-in 1:1 as the text provides is **n.** as a framework
W-in 7:3 the conditions **n.** for this kind of transfer.
W-pI 6.1:2 **n.** to name both the form of upset (anger,
W-pI 9.1:3 understanding is not **n.** at this point. In
W-pI 15.4:4 It is not **n.** to include a large number of
W-pI 15.4:5 It is **n.**, however, to continue to look at
W-pI 19.5:1 the length of time involved, if **n.**. Do not
W-pI 21.1:2 specific mind-searching periods are **n.**, in
W-pI 25.4:1 for today, one more thought is **n.**. At the
W-pI 33.4:2 It may be **n.** to take a minute or so to sit
W-pI 40.1:2 today, but very frequent short ones are **n.**.
W-pI 43.6:3 the exercises as often as **n.** to prevent this.
W-pI 45.8:4 this kind of practice only one thing is **n.**;
W-pI 46.1:2 be condemnation before forgiveness is **n.**.
W-pI 47.4:2 five-minute practice periods are **n.** today,
W-pI 47.6:1 is a **n.** step in the correction of your errors
W-pI 49.5:2 Do so with your eyes open when **n.**, but
WpI rI.in.2:2 it is not **n.** to follow any particular order
WpI rI.in.3:1 **n.** to cover the comments that follow each
WpI rI.in.4:2 It will be **n.**, however, that you learn to
WpI rI.in.6:3 not **n.** to return to the original statements
W-pI 51.1:3 It is **n.** that I recognize this, that I may
W-pI 61.7:2 a bringer of salvation, this is obviously **n.**.
W-pI 65.1:3 Both these thoughts are obviously **n.** for a
W-pI 66.6:2 is **n.** to define God as something He is not
W-pI 67.4:1 may find it **n.** to repeat the idea for today
W-pI 71.2:5 The change of mind **n.** for salvation is
W-pI 73.2:2 for grievances, which are **n.** to maintain it
W-pI 74.6:4 Do this as often as **n.**. There is definite
W-pI 79.8:2 notions go, but that is not **n.**. All that is
W-pI 79.8:3 All that is **n.** is to entertain some doubt
W-pI 95.4:5 It is **n.** that you be aware of this, for it is
W-pI 95.6:1 Structure, then, is **n.** for you at this time,
WpI. rIII.in2:3 it **n.** that you make excessive efforts to be
W-pI 136.4:1 evaluates a threat, decides escape is **n.**,
W-pI.183.10:2 No prayer but this is **n.**, for it holds them
M-2 2:1 is **n.** to grasp the concept of time that the
M-9 2:7 judgment as the **n.** condition of salvation.
M-10 2:1 It is **n.** for the teacher of God to realize,
M-12 3:1 Why is the illusion of many **n.**? Only
M-20 3:6 is the **n.** condition for finding the peace of
M-22 2:5 **n.** realization of inclusiveness may reach
M-24 5:6 then be recommended, because it is **n.**.
M-24 6:13 course requires. No more than this is **n.**.
M-26 1:6 not attained the **n.** understanding as yet,
M-29 3:10 the Holy Spirit's guidance is **n.** merely
C-in 2:5 experience is not only possible but **n.**. It is
P-in 1:5 Psychotherapy is **n.** so that an individual
P-2 II.1:1 not **n.** to be religious or even to believe in
P-2 II.1:2 It is **n.**, however, to teach forgiveness
P-2 II.2:7 truth. What can be **n.** to find truth, which
P-2 II.4:3 God were **n.** to psychotherapeutic success
P-2 IV.10:3 to demonstrate that defenses are not **n.**,
P-3 I.4:2 that his part is **n.** to the whole, and that
P-3 II.7:2 a **n.** understanding for the healed healer.
S-1 II.8:8 The stages **n.** to its attainment, however,

## necessity 5

T-7 II.5:7 yourself you became a learner of **n.**.
T-21 I.4:3 stern **n.** of limits they believed they could
W-pI 160.5:4 Now is he exiled of **n.**, not knowing who
M-5 II.4:3 Does not this follow of **n.**? Place cause
P-2 I.2:5 These interpretations will be wrong of **n.**,

## need 657

*See also* asking-out-of-need

T-1 I.4:3 You will be told all you **n.** to know.
T-1 I.46:3 revelation, the **n.** for miracles is over.
T-1 I.47:1 device that lessens the **n.** for time. It
T-1 II.6:1 The miracle minimizes the **n.** for time. In
T-1 III.1:3 do not **n.** miracles for my own Atonement
T-1 VI.2:1 God is the only lack you really **n.** correct.
T-1 VI.3:1 The idea of orders of **n.**, which follows
T-1 VII.4:4 You will also **n.** them for preparation.
T-2 II.5:1 to set a limit on the **n.** for the belief itself,
T-2 II.6:7 it. As long as there is **n.** for Atonement,
T-2 II.6:7 is need for Atonement, there is **n.** for time
T-2 III.1:3 generally seen as a **n.** to protect the body.
T-2 IV.2:10 itself, neither type of confusion **n.** occur.
T-2 V.3:3 miracle **n.** not await the right-mindedness
T-2 V.4:5 to recognize that those who **n.** healing are
T-2 V.7:8 bring the **n.** for correction into awareness
T-2 V.10:2 himself, or he would have no **n.** of charity
T-2 V.A.11:1 abolishes the **n.** for lower-order concerns.
T-2 VI.3:5 not **n.** guidance except at the mind level.
T-2 VI.8:3 in a position where you **n.** Atonement.
T-2 VI.8:6 offered. The **n.** for the remedy inspired its
T-2 VI.8:7 you recognize only the **n.** for the remedy,
T-2 VII.1:10 miracle workers **n.** that kind of training.
T-2 VII.4:3 very assumption that it **n.** be mastered.
T-3 I.7:10 no **n.** to learn from many smaller lessons.
T-3 IV.6:2 translation, which knowledge does not **n.**.
T-3 V.2:2 do so out of a specific sense of lack or **n.**.
T-3 V.5:7 free of the **n.** to engage in it when you are
T-3 V.8:8 are really one with it **n.** but know yourself
T-3 VI.3:5 do not **n.** judgment to organize your life,
T-3 VI.3:5 certainly do not **n.** it to organize yourself.
T-4 I.3:1 Spirit **n.** not be taught, but the ego must
T-4 I.5:1 that they will one day no longer **n.** him.
T-4 I.6:3 you finally from the **n.** for a teacher. This
T-4 I.13:7 I **n.** devoted teachers who share my aim of
T-4 I.13:8 beyond the **n.** of your protection or mine.
T-4 I.13:10 *world you* ***n.*** *not have tribulation because I*
T-4 II.3:3 apparent that one **n.** only recognize it to
T-4 II.3:6 forget that the mind **n.** not work that way
T-4 II.4:1 and the **n.** they feel to protect them. That
T-4 II.5:4 likely to decide that you **n.** precisely what
T-4 II.7:5 representing the ego's **n.** to confirm itself.
T-4 II.9:7 in danger and does not **n.** to be salvaged.
T-4 III.2:4 The reason you **n.** my help is because you
T-4 III.2:4 own Guide and therefore **n.** guidance. My
T-4 IV.h This **N.** Not Be
T-4 IV.2:2 are not joyous, then *know this* ***n.*** *not be.* In
T-4 IV.3:1 When you are sad, *know this* ***n.*** *not be.*
T-4 IV.4:1 of the ego, and *know this* ***n.*** *not be.* You can
T-4 IV.5:6 the ego can experience guilt. *This* ***n.*** *not be.*
T-4 IV.6:5 ego to disengage yourself. *This* ***n.*** *not be.*
T-4 IV.9:2 To the ego's dark glass you **n.** but say, "I
T-4 VII.2:4 is controlled by its **n.** to protect itself, and
T-4 VII.7:3 does not **n.** revelation returned to Him,
T-5 in.3:3 You **n.** not know them individually, or
T-5 I.5:3 Before that there was no **n.** for healing,
T-5 II.4:1 enter your mind and so you **n.** a new light
T-5 II.4:4 the separation you did not **n.** guidance.
T-5 IV.5:3 forget my **n.** to teach what I have learned,
T-5 VI.10:1 You **n.** not fear the Higher Court will
T-5 VII.1:4 You **n.** be neither careful nor careless; you
T-5 VII.1:4 you **n.** merely cast your cares upon Him
T-5 VII.3:5 It reflects both the ego's **n.** to separate,
T-6 I.2:6 last useless journey the Sonship **n.** take,
T-6 I.10:1 we do not **n.** to have equal experiences.
T-6 I.17:1 I do not **n.** gratitude, but you need to
T-6 I.17:1 **n.** to develop your weakened ability to be
T-6 I.17:2 He does not **n.** your appreciation, but *you*
T-6 I.19:2 many **n.** your blessing to help them hear
T-6 I.19:3 When you perceive only this **n.** in them,
T-6 II.5:5 is the one **n.** in this world that is universal
T-6 II.10:6 **n.** only perceive it as it is to be returned.
T-6 II.11:4 is surely clear that the perfect **n.** nothing,
T-6 III.3:2 this fully, it sees no **n.** to protect itself.
T-6 IV.1:5 home and you no longer **n.** His guidance.
T-6 IV.4:4 it, and the ego feels badly in **n.** of allies,
T-6 IV.10:3 **n.** help and are therefore helpless. This is
T-6 V.2:4 they **n.** not be afraid of dreams. And so
T-6 V.3:2 harm, but what you **n.** to learn to have joy
T-6 V.B.2:4 that a teacher **n.** do to guarantee change.
T-6 V.C.4:9 teach you that you **n.** not choose at all.
T-6 V.C.10:7 Only this can cancel out the **n.** for effort,
T-7 I.6:4 and nothing that is true **n.** be explained.
T-7 II.1:2 himself as not whole, and therefore in **n.**.
T-7 II.7:6 **n.** extension because it *means* extension.
T-7 III.3:1 itself at war and therefore in **n.** of allies.
T-7 III.3:5 not underestimate your **n.** to be vigilant
T-7 IV.1:1 *be* recognized and ***n.*** only be recognized.
T-7 IV.3:5 All you **n.** do is make the effort to learn,
T-7 V.1:3 so apparent that they **n.** no elaboration,
T-7 V.1:3 with healing that it does **n.** clarification.
T-7 V.2:2 and therefore does not **n.** the mind. The
T-7 V.10:4 That is why they **n.** your remembrance of
T-7 VI.8:11 truth, your **n.** for vigilance is apparent.
T-7 VII.2:2 His **n.** is yours. You need the blessing you
T-7 VII.2:3 You **n.** the blessing you can offer him.
T-7 VII.3:1 **n.** God's blessing because that you have
T-7 VII.3:1 that you have forever, but you do **n.** yours
T-7 X.4:1 why you **n.** to demonstrate the obvious to
T-8 I.3:3 peace, and the only one you **n.** ever make.
T-8 III.2:5 That is why you **n.** Him, and why God
T-8 V.6:10 because I **n.** you as much as you need me.
T-8 V.6:10 because I need you as much as you **n.** me.
T-8 VII.15:3 with His purpose, and you **n.** salvation.
T-8 VIII.6:2 your extreme **n.** to depend on external
T-8 VIII.6:3 best argument for your **n.** for *its* guidance.
T-8 IX.2:9 You **n.** do so little because your little part
T-9 III.8:5 You do not **n.** to learn that, but you do
T-9 III.8:5 that, but you do **n.** to learn to want it. For
T-9 III.8:7 Spirit's use of an ability that you do not **n.**
T-9 VI.6:2 while you still **n.** healing, your miracles
T-9 VI.6:5 they are the same, the **n.** for time is over.
T-10 V.5:3 not make yourself that you **n.** be troubled
T-11 in.4:7 to your true Father, Who hath **n.** of you,
T-11 I.1:1 You have learned your **n.** of healing.
T-11 I.1:2 recognizing your **n.** of healing for yourself
T-11 II.3:6 You **n.** it because you do not understand
T-11 II.5:9 God. Yet you **n.** far more than patience.
T-11 II.6:6 grow. Your willingness **n.** not be perfect,
T-11 III.2:1 God's Son is indeed in **n.** of comfort, for
T-11 IV.1:3 Your Self does not **n.** salvation, but your
T-11 V.1:2 There is no **n.** to shrink from illusions, for
T-11 V.17:7 of Christ they **n.** demonstrate nothing, for
T-11 VIII.1:2 you do not feel you **n.** a course which, in
T-11 VIII.2:5 you will see no **n.** to ask it of Him.
T-11 VIII.3:5 Instruction in perception is your great **n.**,
T-11VIII.14:10 what you see you **n.** reality to dispel your
T-12 I.4:1 are except your own imagined **n.** to attack
T-12 I.4:2 of the **n.** for healing by making it unreal.
T-12 I.5:5 Would you maintain that you do not **n.** it
T-12 I.5:8 The Holy Spirit does not **n.** your help in
T-12 I.5:8 motivation, but you do **n.** His.
T-12 I.6:11 will recognize your own **n.** for the Father.
T-12 I.7:2 but one **n.** in yourself you will be healed.
T-12 I.7:5 For the sake of your **n.**, then, hear every
T-12 I.8:2 to demonstrate the **n.** for escape. The

| | |
|---|---|
| T-12 I.8:5 | emphasized the **n.** to recognize fear and |
| T-12 III.1:4 | they are in **n.** it is given you to help them, |
| T-12 III.1:6 | is but one lack since there is but one **n.**. |
| T-12 III.3:6 | never occur to you to overlook their **n.**. |
| T-12 IV.3:3 | it had not taught you the response you **n.**. |
| T-12 V.1:2 | not attack because they see no **n.** to do so. |
| T-12 V.2:8 | You therefore have no **n.** to "equalize" the |
| T-12 V.4:5 | and poor learners do **n.** special teaching. |
| T-12 V.9:4 | You **n.** offer only undivided attention. |
| T-12 VII.4:9 | functions, so long will you **n.** correction. |
| T-13 in.4:6 | Atonement is the final lesson he **n.** learn, |
| T-13 in.4:6 | having sinned, he has no **n.** of salvation. |
| T-13 I.9:2 | could induce a sense of a **n.** for expiation. |
| T-13 III.1:2 | dispel it without the **n.** for you to raise it |
| T-13 III.6:5 | that its **n.** of healing cannot be denied. |
| T-13 IV.7:3 | as rendering the **n.** for time unnecessary. |
| T-13 VII.1:3 | an endless list of things they do not **n.**. It |
| T-13 VII.4:4 | All that you **n.** to give this world away in |
| T-13 VII.10:2 | knoweth that you have **n.** of nothing. In |
| T-13 VII.10:3 | this is so, for what could you **n.** in eternity |
| T-13 VII.10:4 | In your world you do **n.** things. It is a |
| T-13 VII.10:9 | you have **n.** of and what will not hurt you. |
| T-13 VII.11:1 | the ego tells you that you **n.** will hurt you. |
| T-13 VII.11:5 | Therefore ask not of yourself what you **n.**, |
| T-13 VII.11:6 | think you **n.** will merely serve to tighten |
| T-13 VII.12:1 | Only the Holy Spirit knows what you **n.**. |
| T-13 VII.12:3 | And what else could you **n.**? In time, He |
| T-13 VII.12:4 | gives you all the things that you **n.** have, |
| T-13 VII.12:4 | them as long as you have **n.** of them. He |
| T-13 VII.12:5 | from you as long as you have any **n.** of it. |
| T-13 VII.12:6 | that everything you **n.** is temporary, and |
| T-13 VII.14:3 | *I go? What* ***n.*** *have I but to awake in Him?* |
| T-13 VII.16:3 | for what except your brothers can you **n.**? |
| T-13 VII.16:6 | is the only real **n.** to be fulfilled in time. |
| T-13 VIII.7:5 | part of it and all of it **n.** only realize that it |
| T-13 VIII.9:5 | They **n.** no healing, nor do you, when you |
| T-13 XI.6:2 | have **n.** of contrast only here. Contrast |
| T-13 XI.6:4 | the **n.** for any differences disappear. |
| T-13 XI.6:7 | will **n.** no contrast to help you realize that |
| T-14 I.1:1 | not know it, you **n.** to learn it must be so. |
| T-14 I.2:2 | will perceive the **n.** for this if you realize |
| T-14 II.3:5 | *for you that you cannot make, but* ***n.*** *to learn* |
| T-14 III.10:6 | and will bring to them all that they **n.**, |
| T-14 III.10:8 | of deciding what they want and **n.** alone. |
| T-14 III.11:9 | You **n.** not decide whether or not you are |
| T-14 IV.4:1 | You **n.** not understand creation to do |
| T-14 V.5:3 | been denied to produce the **n.** of healing. |
| T-14 V.5:7 | those who have failed to learn **n.** teaching |
| T-14 V.5:8 | attack those who have **n.** of teaching is to |
| T-14 IX.3:2 | is so gentle you **n.** but whisper to it, and |
| T-14 IX.5:5 | **n.** but leave the mirror clean and clear of |
| T-14 IX.6:7 | it because he has been taught his **n.** for it, |
| T-14 XI.6:4 | You **n.** only recognize that everything you |
| T-14 XI.13:5 | for anything; it is only this that you **n.** do. |
| T-14 XI.14:6 | everyone who perceives the **n.** for peace, |
| T-15 I.1:5 | no longer **n.** a teacher or time in which to |
| T-15 I.11:3 | He asks no more, for He has no **n.** of more |
| T-15 III.10:7 | know you are complete, in **n.** of nothing, |
| T-15 IV.9:5 | would not be if there were no **n.** for it. |
| T-15 V.5:4 | willingness to have it serve no **n.** but His. |
| T-15 V.5:8 | the relationship. Your only **n.** is His. |
| T-15 V.9:7 | and you have no **n.** to look without and |
| T-15 V.11:2 | out of His **n.** to extend His Love. With |
| T-15 V.11:3 | in you, you have no **n.** except to extend it. |
| T-15 VI.6:9 | no **n.** you perceive obscure your need of |
| T-15 VI.6:9 | need you perceive obscure your **n.** of this. |
| T-15 VI.6:10 | the only **n.** the Sons of God share equally, |
| T-15 VII.10:4 | Guilt is the only **n.** the ego has, and as |
| T-15 VII.10:6 | in His Voice your own **n.** to communicate |
| T-15 VII.14:8 | Whose only **n.** is to have you be complete. |
| T-15 VIII.1:1 | does not replace the **n.** for learning, for |
| T-15 VIII.2:1 | have **n.** of no special relationships at all. |
| T-15 VIII.2:5 | is. God's Son has such great **n.** of your |
| T-15 VIII.2:5 | that you cannot conceive of **n.** so great. |
| T-15 VIII.2:6 | Behold the only **n.** that God and His Son |
| T-15 VIII.5:4 | God would respond to every **n.**, whatever |
| T-15 IX.4:7 | and their union **n.** only be accepted and |
| T-15 IX.5:1 | and the **n.** your creations have to be with |
| T-15 IX.7:2 | will learn you have no **n.** of a body at all. |
| T-15 XI.1:6 | to daylight when you have no more **n.** of |
| T-15 XI.2:7 | **n.** but invite Him in Who is there already, |
| T-16 I.3:12 | *here. I* ***n.*** *do nothing except not to interfere.* |
| T-16 VI.6:4 | that you will see no **n.** at all to magnify it. |
| T-16 VI.10:2 | Now no one **n.** suffer, for you have come |
| T-16 VI.12:3 | willingness **n.** not be complete because |
| T-17 I.1:3 | He **n.** not be forgiven but awakened. In |
| T-17 II.7:5 | that there could ever be **n.** of salvation? |
| T-17 IV.10:2 | **n.** defense against your acceptance of the |
| T-17 V.7:3 | You **n.** not part entirely if you choose not |
| T-17 VIII.2:6 | secure for you the faith you **n.** for peace. |
| T-18 I.7:7 | patterns that **n.** not be judged at all. To |
| T-18 III.6:5 | My **n.** for you, joined with me in the holy |
| T-18 III.6:5 | your relationship, is your **n.** for salvation. |
| T-18 IV.1:10 | It is your realization that you **n.** do so |
| T-18 IV.2:6 | come without them you would not **n.** the |
| T-18 IV.3:7 | You do not **n.** the strength of willingness |
| T-18 IV.5:12 | *I* ***n.*** *add nothing to His plan. But to receive it,* |
| T-18 IV.7:2 | insist there must be more that you **n.** do. |
| T-18 IV.7:3 | to accept the idea that you **n.** give so little, |
| T-18 IV.7:6 | have emphasized that you **n.** understand |
| T-18 VII.h | I **N.** Do Nothing |
| T-18 VII.5:5 | Now you **n.** but to remember you need do |
| T-18 VII.5:5 | need but to remember you **n.** do nothing. |
| T-18 VII.5:7 | one happy realization; "*I* ***n.*** *do nothing.*" |
| T-18 VII.6:2 | You do not **n.** this time. Time has been |
| T-18 VII.6:7 | else. "I **n.** do nothing" is a statement of |
| T-18 VII.7:2 | And if you recognize you **n.** do nothing, |
| T-18 VII.7:6 | Who needs do nothing has no **n.** for time. |
| T-18 IX.11:2 | Nor is there any **n.** for us to try to speak |
| T-18 IX.11:3 | **n.** remember only that whoever attains |
| T-19 IV.3:5 | them will show you all that you **n.** to see. |
| T-19 IV.3:7 | What **n.** is there for seeing, then? When |
| T-19 IV.3:10 | What **n.** is there of seeing, in the presence |
| T19 IV.D.9:7 | will offer you the innocence you **n.**, and |
| T19. IV.D.11:1 | the fear of God does **n.** some preparation. |
| T19. IV.D.12:7 | you **n.** forgiveness of your brother, for |
| T-20 II.4:1 | I have great **n.** for lilies, for the Son of |
| T-20 II.8:4 | Yet all you **n.** you have. Your home has |
| T-20 III.1:7 | Who **n.** adjust to truth, which calls on |
| T-20 IV.2:2 | lies your **n.** to see your brother sinless. In |
| T-20 IV.5:5 | that they are all the same **n.** not salvation. |
| T-20 IV.6:1 | **n.** you be concerned with anything except |
| T-20 IV.6:3 | that He does not **n.** your part to help Him |
| T-20 IV.8:6 | Nothing you **n.** will be denied you. Not |
| T-20 IV.8:8 | You **n.** take thought for nothing, careless |
| T-20 V.5:3 | minds **n.** not the body to communicate. |
| T-20 VII.1:6 | **n.** not be. This course requires almost |
| T-20 VIII.2:7 | not that you **n.** make either means or end. |
| T-20 VIII.5:3 | distress and **n.** for help unto the helpless? |
| T-20 VIII.5:6 | Yet it is *you* who **n.** his strength. There is |
| T-20 VIII.8:4 | you **n.** to do is recognize that *you* did this. |
| T-20 VIII.11:1 | who **n.** persuade you to accept the gift of |
| T-20 VIII.11:4 | never **n.** you think that there is something |
| T-21 I.3:1 | There is no **n.** to learn through pain. And |
| T-21 II.1:2 | It is the same small willingness you **n.** to |
| T-21 II.2:1 | is the only thing that you **n.** do for vision, |
| T-21 II.6:1 | see the **n.** for you to give this little offering |
| T-21 III.4:6 | yours, you will have **n.** of them no longer. |
| T-21 V.5:6 | have been there since the **n.** for Him arose |
| T-21 V.8:8 | access to it, and only they have **n.** of it. |
| T-21 VII.3:6 | no **n.** to dream of power and to act out |
| T-21 VII.6:5 | which is indeed the last you **n.** decide, still |
| T-21 VII.8:3 | form, all you **n.** do is simply ask yourself: |
| T-21 VIII.3:2 | you **n.** ask for it but once to have it always |
| T-22 in.1:2 | and **n.** no longer look on sin apart. No |
| T-22 in.1:8 | going is the **n.** for sin gone with them. |
| T-22 in.2:1 | Who has **n.** for sin? Only the lonely and |
| T-22 in.2:3 | seen but not real, that makes the **n.** for sin |
| T-22 I.4:4 | this is no secret that **n.** be hidden as a sin. |
| T-22 I.5:5 | without a **n.** to be interpreted to you. |
| T-22 I.8:4 | He will **n.** no interpreter to you, for it was |
| T-22 II.13:1 | All you **n.** do to dwell in quiet here with |
| T-22 V.1:8 | none. Only illusions **n.** defense because of |
| T-22 V.1:11 | And you **n.** no defense. Everything that |
| T-22 V.6:1 | you feel the **n.** arise to be defensive about |
| T-23 in.6:5 | a world in bitter **n.** of the redemption that |
| T-23 II.1:7 | govern nothing, and **n.** not be broken; |
| T-24 I.3:6 | and a **n.** to judge that cannot be escaped. |
| T-24 II.8:4 | **n.** to give it is as great as yours to have it. |
| T-24 II.10:2 | **n.** of your acceptance of himself as part of |
| T-24 V.3:2 | condemnation that could **n.** forgiveness. |
| T-24 V.5:2 | lend you His, while you have **n.** of them. |
| T-24 VI.11:2 | self-maintained, in **n.** of nothing, and |
| T-25 II.10:2 | You **n.** no forgiveness, for the wholly pure |
| T-25 III.4:1 | to the **n.** the Son of God believes he has. |
| T-25 III.6:2 | Nor **n.** he stay more than an instant. For |
| T-25 III.8:3 | And therefore it **n.** not be there in yours. |
| T-25 III.9:5 | Does he **n.** help or condemnation? Is it |
| T-25 V.1:2 | The **n.** for guilt is gone because it has no |
| T-25 V.5:6 | He has no **n.** but this; that you allow him |
| T-25 VIII.1:5 | You **n.** not give it to Him wholly willingly, |
| T-25 VIII.1:5 | for if you could you had no **n.** of Him. But |
| T-25 VIII.12:2 | vengeance. You **n.** not perceive, in every |
| T-25 VIII.12:3 | Nor **n.** you look to your experience within |
| T-25 VIII.12:4 | that you **n.** comes not of you, but from a |
| T-25 VIII.12:9 | How little **n.** you give the Holy Spirit that |
| T-26 II.1:4 | The aspects that **n.** solving do not change, |
| T-26 II.8:5 | all you **n.** to do is but to wish that Heaven |
| T-26 IV.1:3 | in boundless love could **n.** forgiveness. |
| T-26 IV.4:8 | And what else **n.** there be to make the |
| T-26 V.14:4 | nor any **n.** that you repeat again a journey |
| T-26 X.6:5 | injustice anywhere, you **n.** but say: *By this* |
| T-27 I.2:3 | and **n.** but look on you to realize that he |
| T-27 I.3:1 | unfairly treated or in **n.** of anything, you |
| T-27 II.9:8 | And **n.** your healing be delayed because |
| T-27 II.11:4 | more guilty, thus in **n.** of your correction, |
| T-27 III.6:1 | and vacant will not **n.** defense of any kind |
| T-27 III.6:8 | you **n.** no pictures and no learning aids. |
| T-27 V.2:11 | it were, there were no **n.** for healing then. |
| T-27 V.11:3 | Its total value **n.** not be appraised by you |
| T-27 VI.7:2 | sin. There is no **n.** to suffer any more. But |
| T-27 VI.7:3 | But there *is* **n.** that you be healed, because |
| T-27 VII.3:7 | seems as if there is no **n.** to go beyond the |
| T-27 VII.4:1 | There is indeed a **n.**. The world's escape |
| T-27 VII.4:2 | is a **n.** which those within the world are |
| T-27 VII.4:3 | they do not recognize their common **n.**. |
| T-27 VII.6:2 | for what has seen a **n.** for evil in the world |
| T-27 VIII.2:3 | it does not **n.** and does not even want. It |
| T-27 VIII.12:9 | **n.** but learn you chose but not to listen, |
| T-27 VIII.13:6 | Now **n.** you but to learn that both of you |
| T-28 I.10:8 | lost. You **n.** no healing to be healed. In |
| T-28 I.14:4 | he never had a **n.** for doing anything, and |
| T-28 II.10:6 | about as separate things **n.** not be feared. |
| T-28 VI.1:8 | And so it has no **n.** to be competitive. It |
| T-28 VII.1:1 | and His Son, like Him, **n.** ask for nothing. |
| T-28 VII.5:10 | there is no **n.** to bar the door and lock the |
| T-29 I.1:9 | can escape if there be **n.** for you to flee. |
| T-29 VI.5:2 | you **n.** not let it stand for this to you. Let |
| T-29 VII.8:1 | you **n.** but to decide you do not know the |
| T-29 VIII.5:7 | It does not **n.** belief to be itself, for it has |
| T-29 IX.2:7 | not, for he who judges will have **n.** of idols |
| T-29 IX.4:5 | Who has **n.** of toys but children? They |
| T-29 IX.6:3 | all away, for you have **n.** of them no more. |
| T-29 IX.8:1 | Forgiving dreams have little **n.** to last. |
| T-30 in.1:2 | now you **n.** specific methods for attaining |
| T-30 in.1:7 | yet. So now we **n.** to practice them awhile, |
| T-30 in.1:8 | you will have them ready for whatever **n.**. |
| T-30 I.5:5 | you **n.** a quick restorative before you ask |
| T-30 I.9:3 | something that you want and that you **n.**, |
| T-30 I.9:4 | steps you **n.** to let yourself be helped. |
| T-30 I.13:4 | **n.** for practicing the rules for its undoing. |
| T-30 III.1:6 | as if you said, "I have no **n.** of everything. |
| T-30 III.5:2 | He has no **n.** to seek for it at all. Beyond |
| T-30 III.5:6 | What idol can he **n.** to be himself? For |
| T-30 IV.6:3 | You **n.** not concern yourself with how this |
| T-30 IV.8:10 | the Son of God can have no **n.** of them. |
| T-30 V.6:3 | Yet God **n.** not create His Son again, that |
| T-30 V.8:2 | Within your hand is everything you **n.** to |
| T-31 II.1:3 | no plans that **n.** be laid for bringing in the |
| T-31 II.8:4 | thought were precious and in **n.** of care. |
| T-31 II.8:8 | will understand you **n.** but come away |
| T-31 III.4:4 | It gives no orders that the mind **n.** serve, |
| T-31 V.4:2 | himself omits this face, for he has **n.** of it. |
| T-31 V.10:9 | is still no **n.** to hide what you are made of. |
| T-31 V.10:11 | And what but is attacked could **n.** defense |
| T-31 VI.6:8 | in for a while, where nothing **n.** be feared, |
| T-31 VII.5:6 | whose **n.** for it is just the same as yours. |

| | |
|---|---|
| T-31.....VII.6:3 | Yet it **n.** not be fixed, unless you choose to |
| W-in..........2:3 | They **n.** no preparation. The training |
| W-in..........9:1 | only this; you **n.** not believe the ideas, you |
| W-in..........9:1 | believe the ideas, you **n.** not accept them, |
| W-in..........9:1 | them, and you **n.** not even welcome them. |
| W-pI.......7.2:2 | why you **n.** new ideas about time. This |
| W-pI.......9.1:6 | do not **n.** to practice what you already |
| W-pI.......9.3:1 | remembering the **n.** for its indiscriminate |
| W-pI.....23.6:1 | it throughout the day as the **n.** arises, five |
| W-pI.....34.6:2 | find you **n.** more than one application of |
| W-pI.....39.2:5 | is, and you would not **n.** a workbook at all |
| W-pI.....39.6:4 | so it is from them that you **n.** to be saved. |
| W-pI.....40.2:1 | **n.** not close your eyes for the exercise |
| W-pI.....43.5:9 | The thoughts **n.** not bear any obvious |
| W-pI.....46.1:3 | Forgiveness is the great **n.** of this world, |
| W-pI.....46.6:6 | *no* ***n.*** *to attack because love has forgiven me.* |
| W-pI.....47.6:1 | in giving you the confidence which you **n.** |
| W-pI.....49.3:1 | will **n.** at least four five-minute practice |
| WpI...rI.in.4:3 | will **n.** your learning most in situations |
| W-pI.....53.2:6 | that I **n.** not see it at all unless I choose to |
| W-pI.....56.2:2 | I am, I realize that vision is my greatest **n.** |
| W-pI.....57.2:3 | All I **n.** do is recognize this and I am free. I |
| W-pI.....61.5:1 | each one **n.** not exceed a minute or two. |
| W-pI.....64.7:3 | You may **n.** to repeat "Let me not forget |
| W-pI.....65.6:5 | You **n.** not use these exact words, but try |
| W-pI.....66.9:6 | We **n.** great honesty today. Remember |
| W-pI.....67.4:2 | and that you **n.** to continue adding other |
| W-pI.....67.5:2 | You **n.** to hear the truth about yourself as |
| W-pI.....69.3:2 | Salvation is our only **n.**. There is no other |
| W-pI.....70.3:4 | of healing where the **n.** for healing lies. |
| W-pI.....73.2:2 | rise to it, and the ego's **n.** for grievances, |
| W-pI.....79.9:1 | for today will not be set by time, but by **n.** |
| W-pI.....85.2:4 | *this away. I have no* ***n.*** *for this. I want to see.* |
| W-pI.....90.4:2 | *I* ***n.*** *not wait for this to be resolved. The* |
| W-pI.....91.7:2 | You **n.** to be aware of what the Holy Spirit |
| W-pI.....91.7:3 | **n.** to feel something to put your faith in, |
| W-pI.....91.7:4 | You **n.** a real experience of something else |
| W-pI.....92.3:3 | weak, the sickly and the dying, those in **n.** |
| W-pI.....95.4:4 | and of your **n.** for mind training. It is |
| W-pI...95.14:2 | today. We **n.** your help; your little part in |
| W-pI.....98.2:3 | been given everything we **n.** with which to |
| W-pI.....99.2:2 | becomes the thing you **n.** forgiveness for, |
| W-pI.....99.4:2 | yet recognize the **n.** illusions bring, and |
| W-pI.....99.9:8 | what you **n.** to learn to lay all fear aside, |
| W-pI...101.5:1 | You **n.** the practice periods today. The |
| W-pI...102.5:2 | You have no **n.** to be less loving to God's |
| W-pI...104.2:5 | And we **n.** not wait to have them. They |
| W-pI...106.6:5 | miracles has **n.** that you receive them first |
| W-pI...107.4:3 | always was, to be depended on in every **n.** |
| W-pI...110.2:1 | Today's idea is therefore all you **n.** to let |
| W-pI...110.3:3 | You **n.** no thought but just this one, to let |
| WpIrIII.in10:1 | we stress the **n.** to let your learning not lie |
| WpIrIII.in10:4 | You **n.** not give more than just a moment |
| WpIrIII.in11:5 | and whenever you **n.** help of any kind. |
| WpIrIII.in13:3 | Do not forget your Father's **n.** of you, As |
| W-pI...125.9:2 | You will **n.** no rule but this, to let your |
| W-pI...126.8:2 | You will **n.** help to make this meaningful, |
| W-pI...126.8:3 | But the Help you **n.** is there. Give Him |
| W-pI.126.11:4 | *I* ***n.*** *to learn that this is true is with me now.* |
| W-pI...128.1:1 | see holds nothing that you **n.** to offer you; |
| W-pI.130.11:3 | All you **n.** say to any part of hell, whatever |
| W-pI.132.16:1 | **n.** not realize that healing comes to many |
| W-pI...134.2:6 | Does this **n.** pardon? How can you forgive |
| W-pI.134.12:3 | Nor **n.** he erect the heavy walls of stone |
| W-pI...135.7:1 | The body is in **n.** of no defense. This |
| W-pI...135.8:2 | **n.** merely be perceived as quite apart |
| W-pI.135.10:1 | These are the thoughts in **n.** of healing, |
| W-pI.135.21:2 | will be sure that everything we **n.** is given |
| W-pI.135.23:4 | which remains unanswered yet in **n.** of |
| W-pI.136.18:4 | You **n.** do nothing now to make it well, |
| W-pI...137.9:2 | how little practice you **n.** undertake to let |
| W-pI...138.4:1 | You **n.** to be reminded that you think a |
| W-pI...139.5:2 | It is for this denial that you **n.** Atonement |
| W-pI...139.8:3 | it must be is all the proof you **n.** to show |
| W-pI...140.6:3 | unmindful where the **n.** for healing is. |
| W-pI...140.8:5 | We **n.** but seek it and it must be found. |
| W-pI.140.11:4 | We have no **n.** to make them different, |
| WpI.rIV.in9:2 | **n.** no more than this to give us happiness |
| W-pI...153.9:1 | recognize that we **n.** no defense because |
| W-pI.153.20:6 | is all you **n.** to give Him in return. You lay |
| W-pI...154.1:3 | cannot judge ourselves, nor **n.** we do so. |
| W-pI...154.9:3 | God has not failed to offer what you **n.**, |
| W-pI...155.3:4 | And so they **n.** a Teacher Who perceives |
| W-pI...155.7:5 | Yet they **n.** a guide to lead them out of it, |
| W-pI...157.7:3 | now appear, for you will have no **n.** of it. |
| W-pI...159.6:4 | his least request or his most urgent **n.**. |
| W-pI...159.6:5 | no **n.** unmet within this golden treasury |
| W-pI...159.8:4 | They **n.** the light and warmth and kindly |
| W-pI...159.8:5 | **n.** the love with which He looks on them. |
| W-pI...161.4:8 | We **n.** to see a little, that we learn a lot. |
| W-pI...162.4:2 | they **n.** no thoughts beyond themselves to |
| W-pI...164.8:3 | He has **n.** of your most holy mind to save |
| W-pI...165.4:3 | Nor **n.** you perceive how great the gift, |
| W-pI...165.5:2 | You **n.** not be sure that you request the |
| W-pI...166.6:3 | and **n.** but realize Who walks with him |
| W-pI.166.10:5 | There was a **n.** He did not understand, to |
| W-pI.166.10:7 | you have **n.** no more of anything but this. |
| W-pI.169.10:1 | no **n.** to further clarify what no one in the |
| W-pI.169.13:4 | and in **n.** of you as witness to the truth? |
| W-pI...170.7:4 | We **n.** not defy his power. He has none. |
| WpI...rV.in8:1 | to you from Him Who sees your bitter **n.**, |
| WpI...rV.in9:2 | For this alone I **n.**; that you will hear the |
| W-pI...181.3:1 | **n.** to let our sinlessness become apparent. |
| W-pI...184.9:2 | **n.** to use the symbols of the world a while. |
| W-pI.184.10:1 | Thus what you **n.** are intervals each day |
| W-pI.185.14:1 | our desires with the **n.** of every heart, the |
| W-pI...186.7:6 | Why **n.** he be concerned with it at all? |
| W-pI.186.13:4 | which answer every **n.** His Son perceives, |
| W-pI...189.8:2 | You **n.** not know the way to Him. Your |
| W-pI...189.9:7 | He does not **n.** His Son to show Him how |
| W-pI...190.4:3 | is no **n.** to think of them as savage crimes, |
| W-pI...191.6:3 | You have no **n.** to use it cruelly, and then |
| W-pI...191.6:3 | and then perceive this savage **n.** in it. You |
| W-pI...191.7:2 | You **n.** but tell yourself: *I am the holy Son of* |
| W-pI...192.2:6 | earth, you **n.** the means to let illusions go. |
| W-pI...192.7:1 | **n.** forgiveness to perceive that this is so. |
| W-pI...193.2:3 | Thus he has a **n.** for One Who can correct |
| W-pI.193.10:6 | time be less than meets your deepest **n.**. |
| W-pI...196.4:3 | one. It is not time we **n.** for this. It is but |
| W-pI...196.4:5 | seem to **n.** a thousand years can easily be |
| W-pI...196.9:2 | and **n.** not fear its vengeance and pursuit. |
| W-pI...196.9:3 | Nor **n.** you hide in terror from the deadly |
| W-pI...198.8:1 | condemnation which could **n.** forgiveness |
| W-pI...199.4:3 | no **n.** of it except the need the Holy Spirit |
| W-pI...199.4:3 | of it except the **n.** the Holy Spirit sees. For |
| W-pI...200.9:5 | He will not desert His Son in **n.**, nor let |
| WpI rVI.in.2:5 | And so we **n.** to use them all and let them |
| W-pI...207.1:3 | *I* ***n.*** *but turn to Him, and every sorrow melts* |
| W-pII.....in.2:8 | as we will **n.** for the result that we desire. |
| W-pII.....in.2:9 | calling to God when we have **n.** of Him as |
| W-pII.....in.3:1 | times of rest, and calm our minds at **n.**. |
| W-pII...in.10:1 | Now is the **n.** for practice almost done. |
| W-pII...in.10:2 | to understand that we **n.** only call to God, |
| W-pII...in.10:3 | Instead of words, we **n.** but feel His Love. |
| W-pII...in.10:4 | prayers, we **n.** but call His Name. Instead |
| W-pII...in.10:5 | **n.** but be still and let all things be healed. |
| W-pII..226.2:3 | *What* ***n.*** *have I to linger in a place of vain* |
| W-pII..229.1:2 | I am." Now **n.** I seek no more. Love has |
| W-pII..230.2:5 | *I* ***n.*** *but call on You to find the peace You gave* |
| W-pII......2.2:2 | was no **n.** for such a Thought before, for |
| W-pII......2.2:3 | the mind is split there is a **n.** of healing. |
| W-pII..235.1:1 | I **n.** but look upon all things that seem to |
| W-pII..235.1:2 | I **n.** but keep in mind my Father's Will for |
| W-pII..235.1:3 | And I **n.** but remember that God's Love |
| W-pII..242.2:6 | *we* ***n.*** *in helping us to find the way to You.* |
| W-pII..244.1:2 | *He* ***n.*** *but call upon Your Name, and he will* |
| W-pII......4.1:5 | **n.** have they of sights or sounds or touch? |
| W-pII.....251.h | I am in **n.** of nothing but the truth. |
| W-pII..251.1:2 | do I seek but one, for in that one is all I **n.**, |
| W-pII..251.1:2 | in that one is all I need, and only what I **n.** |
| W-pII..251.1:4 | My only **n.** I did not recognize. But now I |
| W-pII..251.1:5 | But now I see that I **n.** only truth. In that |
| W-pII..251.1:7 | Now have I everything that I could **n.**. |
| W-pII..256.1:3 | what **n.** would there have been to find the |
| W-pII..267.1:4 | and all I **n.** to save the world is given me. |
| W-pII......6.5:3 | no **n.** of learning or perception or of time, |
| W-pII..273.1:4 | We **n.** but tell our minds, with certainty, |
| W-pII..273.2:2 | *What* ***n.*** *have I to fear that anything can rob* |
| W-pII .275.2:2 | *I* ***n.*** *be anxious over nothing. For Your Voice* |
| W-pII .276.1:7 | we **n.** but to acknowledge Him Who gave |
| W-pII .286.1:3 | *lesson that there is no* ***n.*** *that I do anything.* |
| W-pII .....8.3:1 | **n.** has such a mind for thoughts of death, |
| W-pII .....8.5:1 | Holy Spirit has no **n.** of time when it has |
| W-pII .324.2:2 | way. We **n.** not tarry, and we cannot stray |
| W-pII ....327.h | I **n.** but call and You will answer me. |
| W-pII .327.1:5 | to give me all the help I **n.** to come to Him |
| W-pII .337.1:5 | already done all things that **n.** be done. |
| W-pII .337.1:6 | And I must learn I **n.** do nothing of myself |
| W-pII .337.1:6 | of myself, for I **n.** but accept my Self, my |
| W-pII .345.1:4 | *I* ***n.*** *to help me with the problems I perceive.* |
| W-pII ....348.h | me. And in every **n.** That I perceive, Your |
| W-pII .348.1:4 | *You. What* ***n.*** *have I for anger or for fear?* |
| W-pII .355.1:3 | *me, and I* ***n.*** *but reach out my hand to find it.* |
| W-pII .355.1:6 | *I* ***n.*** *not wait an instant more to be at peace* |
| WpII361-5.1:1 | And if I **n.** a word to help me, He will give |
| WpII361-5.1:2 | If I **n.** a thought, that will He also give. |
| WpII361-5.1:3 | And if I **n.** but stillness and a tranquil, |
| W-ep.........1:6 | will not withhold all answers that you **n.** |
| W-ep.........1:9 | You **n.** but ask it of Him, and it will be |
| W-ep.........2:4 | of what you really want and really **n.**. His |
| W-ep.........3:1 | assigned, for there is no more **n.** of them. |
| M-4 .....I.A.3:2 | This **n.** not be painful, but it usually is so |
| M-4 ......IV.2:2 | They **n.** the strength of gentleness, for it is |
| M-4 ..... V.1:14 | **n.** of them is just as great as theirs of Him. |
| M-4 ...... VI.1:2 | dreams that **n.** defense against the truth. |
| M-4 ...... VI.1:5 | And does what God created **n.** defense? |
| M-5 ........II.1:2 | One **n.** but say, "There is no gain at all to |
| M-7 ...........3:5 | He **n.** do no more, nor is there more that |
| M-10 .........6:7 | now he knows that these things **n.** not be. |
| M-12 .........2:5 | be many, for that is what is the world's **n.**. |
| M-12 .........3:4 | them. They **n.** a medium through which |
| M-12 .........3:8 | So do God's teachers **n.** a body, for their |
| M-13 .......8:11 | His Word to you, for He has **n.** of teachers |
| M-14 .........1:6 | that they serve a **n.** or gratify a want. |
| M-14 .........2:5 | home, for here there is **n.** of Him indeed. |
| M-14 .........4:5 | He **n.** merely learn how to approach it; to |
| M-14 .........4:6 | He **n.** merely trust that, if God's Voice |
| M-16 .........3:8 | contains, individual **n.** becomes the chief |
| M-16 .......6:12 | You have no **n.** of them. Recognize this, |
| M-16 .........7:5 | He **n.** make no distinctions among the |
| M-16 .........7:9 | And he has no **n.** for more than this. |
| M-16 .........8:1 | **n.** of reminding himself throughout the |
| M-17 .........2:7 | of God gives to those who **n.** his aid? Here |
| M-17 .......8:10 | thoughts **n.** not lead to condemnation, |
| M-19 .........1:8 | judged, there would be no **n.** for salvation |
| M-22 .........4:6 | teacher, of who it is that is in **n.** of healing |
| M-23 .......7:5 | Yet do we **n.** a many-faceted curriculum, |
| M-23 .........7:5 | must shift and change to suit the **n.**. Jesus |
| M-24 .........4:8 | how to use it. What more **n.** he know? |
| M-24 .........5:9 | He **n.** merely accept the idea that what he |
| M-25 .........6:4 | Salvation has **n.** of all abilities, for what |
| M-26 .......3:10 | **n.** helpers who are still in bondage and |
| M-26 .........4:8 | and not one **n.** you have will not be met. |
| M-26 .......4:11 | could you desire, when this is all you **n.**? |
| M-27 .........1:3 | now we **n.** to consider it more carefully. It |
| M-29 .........1:7 | Still others may **n.** to start at the more |
| M-29 .........5:8 | wisdom will be given you when you **n.** it. |
| C-2...........6:16 | Who has **n.** to ask? Where is the ego? |
| C-2...........6:18 | **n.** to seek for an illusion now that dreams |
| C-2.............8:1 | the **n.** for vengeance and the cries of pain, |
| C-2...........10:2 | Neither **n.** be defined except by this. Yet |
| C-3.............1:2 | He created that could **n.** forgiveness. |
| C-3.............3:1 | And so they **n.** an illusion of help because |
| C-3.............3:5 | The form adapts itself to **n.**; the content is |
| C-5.............1:1 | There is no **n.** for help to enter Heaven |
| C-5.............1:2 | But there is **n.** for help beyond yourself as |
| C-5.............1:7 | does not help because He knows no **n.**. |
| C-5.............6:5 | You **n.** no other. It is possible to read his |
| C-6.............4:6 | a far country, for you **n.** that form of help. |
| P-in............1:3 | Only the mind is in **n.** of healing. This |
| P-1.............5:1 | The patient **n.** not think of truth as God |
| P-2.........in.2:2 | little to them, or they would not **n.** help. |
| P-2...........I.1:4 | out to them that meets the changing **n.**. |
| P-2...........I.4:5 | are patients who **n.** him just that way. |
| P-2..........II.1:4 | learned all things does not **n.** a teacher, |
| P-2..........II.1:4 | and the healed have no **n.** for a therapist. |
| P-2..........II.3:2 | Forgiveness, then, is all that **n.** be taught, |

P-2 II.3:2 taught, because it is all that **n.** be learned.
P-2 II.9:4 and recognize his brother's **n.** is his own.
P-2 II.9:5 let him then meet his brother's **n.** as his
P-2 III.3:8 No one **n.** see him or talk to him or even
P-2 III.4:5 he can help through those in **n.** of help,
P-2 IV.6:1 and thus in **n.** of constant defense. Yet if
P-2 IV.11:6 What is the **n.** for sickness then? Given
P-2 IV.11:8 There is no **n.** for complicated change.
P-2 IV.11:9 is no **n.** for long analyses and wearying
P-2 V.2:6 **n.** the lesson of defenselessness above all
P-2 V.7:4 already, if we think there is a **n.** of healing
P-2 VII.1:6 And who else is in **n.** of healing? Each
P-2 VII.2:1 you pray, and who is in **n.** of healing. For
P-2 VII.2:7 There is no **n.** for more than this, for it is
P-3 I.3:1 patients **n.** not be physically present for
P-3 I.3:4 Some do not **n.** your physical presence.
P-3 I.3:5 They **n.** you as much, and perhaps even
P-3 II.1:9 These people **n.** no special rules, of course
P-3 II.4:5 very **n.** for each other implies a sense of
P-3 III.1:4 Should he **n.** money it will be given him,
P-3 III.4:1 to live is something no one **n.** fight for. It
P-3 III.5:7 it. All that they **n.** will thus be given them.
P-3 III.5:9 believe they **n.** anything from a brother,
S-1 in.2:1 takes the form that best will suit your **n.**.
S-1 I.2:1 receive a specific answer if such is your **n.**.
S-1 I.2:5 the level of **n.** that you can recognize.
S-1 I.2:7 by God, will suit your **n.** as you see it.
S-1 I.4:1 is to forget the things you think you **n.**. To
S-1 I.6:2 not reached it still **n.** your help in prayer
S-1 II.1:4 In its asking form it **n.** not, and often does
S-1 II.3:4 that inevitably underlie any prayer of **n.**.
S-1 II.4:4 if you have enemies you have **n.** of prayer,
S-1 II.4:4 you have need of prayer, and great **n.**, too
S-1 II.8:3 is no **n.** for a ladder to reach what one has
S-1 II.8:8 attainment, however, **n.** to be understood
S-1 III.6:4 One **n.** not ask explicitly. The goal of God
S-1 IV.1:3 once the **n.** to hold the other as an enemy
S-1 V.2:3 no goal but God because they **n.** no idols,
S-2 in.1:9 you cannot go, nor have you **n.** to go.
S-2 I.4:7 Who but the sinful **n.** to be forgiven? And
S-2 I.7:2 You are in **n.** of what He gives, and your
S-2 I.8:4 This is your **n.**, and God holds out this
S-2 III.2:6 that you **n.** do is to step back and not to
S-2 III.5:2 form the seeking takes you **n.** not judge.
S-2 III.5:6 He knows the **n.**; the question and the
S-3 II.2:3 the **n.** is done to walk the world of limits,
S-3 IV.3:6 **n.** have you for shifting dreams within a

## needed 56

T-1 VII.5:11 to you, but to reach it the means are **n.**.
T-2 I.3:1 a state of mind in which nothing was **n.**.
T-2 II.4:6 a defense so splendid was **n.** that it could
T-2 V.9:3 healing is **n.** as a means of protection.
T-2 VII.5:8 indication that immediate correction is **n.**
T-5 II.1:2 of God were before healing was **n.**, and
T-13 III.11:1 he **n.** nothing and asked for nothing. In
T-13 VII.17:5 abide. Healing in time is **n.**, for joy cannot
T-14 I.2:1 Indirect proof of truth is **n.** in a world
T-15 V.6:5 that you **n.** your brothers as they were not
T-15 VI.6:10 will join with me in offering what is **n.**.
T-17 VII.6:6 and accomplish every miracle **n.** for its
T-18 IV.4:7 willingness is **n.** only to make it possible
T-18 V.4:6 The little faith it **n.** to change the purpose
T-19 I.6:4 Here, then, is healing **n.**. And it is here
T-19 I.15:4 no longer **n.** when the lesson has been
T-25 II.2:3 long is **n.** for you to realize the chance of
T-25 VI.3:6 for them to fill; no place where they are **n.**
T-25 VIII.2:4 remember salvation is not **n.** by the saved
T-26 VII.4:3 though it works in time, where it is **n.**. Yet
T-26 VII.17:1 not **n.** where there is no pain or suffering.
T-27 V.1:2 your help, but you are **n.** that it can begin.
T-27 VII.2:2 is **n.** is you look upon the problem as it is,
T-31 VII.1:3 Concepts are **n.** while perception lasts,
T-31 VII.6:6 yourself as **n.** for salvation of the world,
W-pI 15.5:4 can be applied as **n.** throughout the day.
W-pI 19.5:1 the "as **n.**" application of today's idea, at
W-pI 31.2:1 of practice with the idea for today are **n.**,
W-pI 42.7:2 in which nothing is lacking that is **n.**, and
W-pI 46.7:2 more specific applications if they are **n.**.
W-pI 46.7:3 They will be **n.** at any time during the day
WpI..rII.in.6:1 and more specific forms when **n.**. Some
W-pI 91.6:6 ends is **n.** for our exercises today. What
W-pI. 135.23:3 may not be the plans you thought were **n.**
W-pI 137.4:6 So healing, never **n.** by the truth, must
W-pI. 153.10:6 What defense could possibly be **n.** by the
W-pI 157.4:3 is **n.** but today's idea to light your mind,
W-pI. 167.12:6 No vision now is **n.**. For the wakened
WpI.rV.in12:1 periods, but to recall the mind, as **n.**, to
Wi181-200 3:5 is asked, because no more than this is **n.**.
W-pI. 186.14:3 what is **n.** here is given here as it is needed
W-pI. 186.14:3 what is needed here is given here as it is **n.**
W-pI 200.6:4 It is only hell where it is **n.**, and where it
W-pII .251.1:3 All that I sought before I **n.** not, and did
W-pII .314.1:4 and all the **n.** means are happily provided
M-5 II.2:11 They are not actually **n.** at all. The patient
M-10 4:1 knew all the "facts" you **n.** for judgment,
M-12 h OF GOD ARE **N.** TO SAVE THE WORLD
M-14 2:3 Here is it nourished, for here it is **n.**. A
M-28 3:2 From here on, no directions are **n.**. Vision
M-28 5:3 What further sight is **n.**? What remains
C-in 3:1 within the ego framework, where it is **n.**.
C-5 2:6 Christ **n.** his form that He might appear
P-3 III.6:6 sent to give his brother the money he **n.**.
S-1 V.4:1 ends with this, for learning is no longer **n.**
S-2 III.5:1 when help is **n.** and forgiveness sought.

## needful 12

T-13 VIII.3:6 without a function in Heaven, is **n.** here.
T-15 IX.1:3 Yet it is **n.** for you to learn just what this
T-16 IV.10:4 is only **n.** to value truth beyond all fantasy
T-18 IV.4:3 that it is **n.** to prepare yourself for Him. It
T-18 IV.5:11 *It is not **n.** that I make it ready for Him, but*
T-18 IV.8:7 which thought it did, is its undoing **n.**.
T-21 II.11:1 **n.** that you recognize you made the world
T-31 IV.5:2 Is it not **n.** that he should begin with this,
W-pI 44.8:1 what is **n.** is a sense of the importance of
W-pI 135.4:4 deep concern are **n.** to protect its little life
W-pI 153.5:5 **n.** only of defense by still more fantasies,
W-pII .258.1:1 All that is **n.** is to train our minds to

## needing 6

T-7 V.7:8 This places you in a position of **n.** to learn
T-12 VIII.2:2 him in perfect peace, and **n.** nothing, he
T-18 VIII.5:3 self-contained, **n.** another for some things
T-18 VIII.5:3 **n.** the whole to give it any meaning, for by
T-26 IV.1:7 it, until he sees himself as **n.** it no more.
W-pI 135.4:3 to protect itself and **n.** your defense.

## needle 1

W-pI 76.3:3 **n.** will ward off disease and death. You

## needless 7

T-1 III.4:4 This spares you **n.** effort, because you will
T-9 VII.1:7 not return, but because delay of joy is **n.**.
T-13 I.9:1 and so the future is **n.** and will not be.
T-15 VII.h The **N.** Sacrifice
W-pI. 133.14:2 to let yourself collect some **n.** burdens, or
W-pI 170.2:4 **n.** misery than you can possibly imagine.
W-pI 200.9:3 and **n.** wasted time on thorny byways.

## needlessly 2

T-26 II.4:6 which the Son of God is suffering, but **n.**.
W-pI 160.3:3 would let himself be dispossessed so **n.**,

## needs 187

T-1 IV.3:5 have everything have no **n.** of any kind.
T-1 VI.h The Illusion of **N.**
T-1 VI.1:2 it and believes in some way that he **n.** it.
T-1 VI.1:7 There were no **n.** at all. Needs arise only
T-1 VI.1:8 **N.** arise only when you deprive yourself.
T-1 VI.1:9 to the particular order of **n.** you establish.
T-1 VI.2:3 The idea of order of **n.** arose because,
T-1 VI.2:3 yourself into levels with different **n.**. As
T-1 VI.2:4 one, and your **n.** become one accordingly.
T-1 VI.2:5 Unified **n.** lead to unified action, because
T-1 VII.3:4 to control reality according to false **n.**.
T-2 III.4:3 and **n.** to be repaired and protected.
T-2 V.10:3 both an acknowledgment that he **n.** help,
T-2 VII.5:14 perish but have everlasting life" **n.** only
T-3 V.7:1 image and likeness" **n.** reinterpretation.
T-3 V.10:3 anyone who perceives at all **n.** healing.
T-4 II.7:6 as it is of the so-called "higher ego **n.**."
T-4 VI.3:3 and disaster **n.** additional convincing.
T-5 III.1:5 This **n.** clarification, not in statement but
T-6 II.5:4 the Holy Spirit perceives equal **n.**. This
T-6 V.C.8:4 is only your awareness that **n.** protection,
T-6 V.C.10:8 it is already true and **n.** no protection. It
T-7 II.7:6 **n.** no translation because it is perfectly
T-7 IV.7:9 fear. Love **n.** only this invitation. It comes
T-7 IX.4:4 **n.** the miracle of its wholeness to dawn
T-8 IV.4:1 the world **n.** peace as much as you do? Do
T-9 III.2:8 He **n.** correction at another level, because
T-9 V.8:7 He **n.** no help for this. He will tell you
T-9 VIII.11:2 establish your value and it **n.** no defense.
T-11 II.3:5 yourself, for only God's Son **n.** healing.
T-11 II.5:3 He **n.** your protection, only because your
T-11 IV.1:3 your mind **n.** to learn what salvation is.
T-12 I.7:1 your brother's **n.** are your interpretation
T-13 IV.3:3 this, and **n.** this to prove that it was at all.
T-13 VII.9:4 is. Knowledge **n.** no correction. Yet the
T-13 VII.12:6 you step aside from all your **n.** and realize
T-13 VII.13:1 Leave, then, your **n.** to Him. He will
T-13 VII.13:7 Within himself he has no **n.**, for light
T-13 VII.13:7 for light **n.** nothing but to shine in peace,
T-14 II.1:1 The Holy Spirit **n.** a happy learner, in
T-14 VII.5:3 **n.** no protection does not defend itself.
T-14 IX.6:3 The reflection of God **n.** no interpretation
T-14 XI.7:3 can make no **n.** his Father will not meet, if
T-15 I.15:2 **n.** but very little to restore God's whole
T-15 III.10:9 host of God **n.** not seek to find anything.
T-15 V.2:1 your own **n.** and acquired methods for
T-15 V.2:3 look to them to meet your imagined **n.**,
T-15 V.5:7 then, be afraid to let go your imagined **n.**,
T-15 V.8:2 for your personal **n.** intrude on no one to
T-15 V.10:6 He **n.** them all equally, and so do you. In
T-15 V.11:4 the holy instant there is no conflict of **n.**,
T-15 VI.3:3 in gratifying your **n.** as you perceive them
T-16 I.6:7 recognizes foolish **n.** as well as real ones.
T-16 I.7:2 will think that by meeting the **n.** of one
T-16 I.7:4 No **n.** will long be left unmet if you leave
T-16 VI.12:2 He **n.** only your willingness to share His
T-16 VII.12:3 *us that **n.** forgiveness when Yours is perfect?*
T-17 IV.10:2 The truth itself **n.** no defense, but you do
T-17 V.10:5 For all it **n.** now is your blessing, that you
T-17 VIII.6:4 nothing that it **n.** to be forever changeless
T-18 VII.7:6 Who **n.** do nothing has no need for time.
T-18 IX.1:3 split off and separate, the Holy Spirit **n.**.
T-18 IX.1:4 is fully in God's keeping, and **n.** no guide.
T-18 IX.1:5 and delusional thought **n.** help because,
T-18 IX.12:4 interference; that is what **n.** to be undone.
T-19 I.3:2 sick. It *n.* no healing. Its health or sickness
T19 IV.C.9:5 It **n.** not your protection; it is *yours.* For it
T-20 III.4:1 question yet remains, and **n.** an answer.
T-21 V.2:1 Reality **n.** no cooperation from you to be
T-21 V.2:2 But your awareness of it **n.** your help,
T-21 V.8:1 the great deceiver's **n.** as well as truth. But
T-22 I.5:6 What **n.** interpretation must be alien.
T-22 IV.3:7 it into a darkened world that **n.** the light.
T-22 IV.6:5 to everyone who **n.** a miracle to save him.
T-22 V.1:7 What merely is **n.** no defense, and offers
T-22 V.1:12 Everything that **n.** defense you do not
T-22 V.1:12 anything that **n.** defense will weaken you.
T-22 V.2:6 fear? Belief in sin **n.** great defense, and at
T-23 II.12:1 But what is it you want that **n.** his death?
T-24 VI.8:3 that has never begun, and **n.** no end.
T-24 VII.1:4 it **n.** does he deny to what he loves. And
T-25 in.3:1 The body **n.** no healing. But the mind
T-25 II.5:5 Yet what God has created **n.** no frame, for
T-25 VI.7:1 The Holy Spirit **n.** your special function,
T-25 VII.7:3 The form is suited to your special **n.**, and

T-25... VIII.1:6 But this He **n.**; that you prefer He take it
T-25... VIII.2:1 Here is the only principle salvation **n.**.
T-26...... III.5:1 Heaven, for only perception **n.** salvation.
T-26..... VII.8:2 And truth **n.** no defense to make it true.
T-26... VIII.4:8 And it is *this* that **n.** correction, not a
T-27.........I.7:2 of their unnatural desires and strange **n.**.
T-27....... V.7:2 It **n.** one lesson that has perfectly been
T-28.........I.3:2 is a recognition that you have no **n.** which
T-29....... II.4:6 He **n.** your help in giving them to all who
T-29...... IV.4:3 the **n.** which you ascribe to you are met. It
T-29...... IX.5:8 thinks he **n.** them that he may escape his
T-30...... I.17:1 It **n.** but two who would have happiness
T-30...... I.17:2 **n.** but two to understand that they cannot
T-30...... I.17:4 It **n.** but two. These two are joined before
T-30.... IV.5:12 Son **n.** no defense against his dreams. His
T-31..... II.10:3 for what you want, and **n.** the same as you
T-31..... VII.6:4 that it **n.** to let it serve the function given
T-31... VII.15:2 It **n.** the light, for it is dark indeed, and
W-pI..... 27.3:1 today **n.** many repetitions for maximum
W-pI..... 39.2:6 one **n.** practice to gain what is already his.
W-pI..... 65.4:4 disciplinary training your mind **n.**, so
W-pI..... 71.9:6 and let Him tell you what **n.** to be done by
W-pI..... 76.6:2 This **n.** repeating, over and over, until you
W-pI..... 91.1:2 This **n.** repeating, and frequent repeating.
W-pI..... 97.4:4 Give Him the minutes which He **n.** today,
W-pI..... 99.1:2 for; something amiss that **n.** corrective
W-pI... 106.5:3 He **n.** your voice to speak to them, for
W-pI... 107.5:2 gift of healing, for the truth **n.** no defense,
WpI. rIII.in5:3 letting your mind relate them to your **n.**,
W-pI... 133.8:7 for it **n.** to keep the halo which it uses to
W-pI... 135.5:2 has no **n.** but those which you assign to it.
W-pI... 135.5:3 It **n.** no complicated structures of defense,
W-pI... 135.7:5 it seems to fail your hopes, your **n.**, your
W-pI... 135.8:1 The "self" that **n.** protection is not real.
W-pI. 135.13:2 and which **n.** its service for a little while.
W-pI. 135.16:4 and now is everything it **n.** to guarantee a
W-pI. 135.26:8 *of God* **n.** *no defense against the truth of his*
W-pI. 136.19:1 protection **n.** to be preserved by careful
W-pI... 138.5:6 what you are, and what your **n.** must be.
W-pI... 151.1:5 conceal. It **n.** irrational defense because it
W-pI. 154.11:2 **n.** our voice that He may speak through
W-pI. 154.11:3 us. He **n.** our hands to hold His messages,
W-pI. 154.11:4 He **n.** our feet to bring us where He wills,
W-pI. 154.11:5 And He **n.** our will united with His Own,
W-pI... 158.6:5 it transcends what **n.** to be accomplished.
W-pI... 161.5:4 Love **n.** no symbols, being true. But fear
W-pI... 165.6:5 his denial of the nourishment he **n.** to live
W-pI... 170.3:3 now **n.** your defense against the threat of
W-pI... 182.6:1 This Child **n.** your protection. He is far
W-pI... 186.5:4 assures you that salvation **n.** your part,
W-pI. 198.12:3 He **n.** no thoughts of mercy. Who could
W-pII.. 251.1:6 In that all **n.** are satisfied, all cravings end
W-pII.. 296.1:1 *The Holy Spirit* **n.** *my voice today, that all*
W-pII.. 297.1:4 way I live within a world that **n.** salvation,
W-pII...... 9.5:2 **n.** your eyes and ears and hands and feet.
W-pII...... 9.5:3 It **n.** your voice. And most of all it needs
W-pII...... 9.5:4 And most of all it **n.** your willingness. Let
W-pII.. 338.1:1 **n.** but this to let salvation come to all the
W-pII.. 345.1:5 *it is different, for there, there are no* **n.**. *But*
W-pII.. 349.2:1 Our Father knows our **n.**. He gives us
M-2............ 5:6 roles, their minds, their bodies, their **n.**,
M-3............ 5:8 of God can fail to find the Help he **n.**.
M-4...... I.A.6:9 teacher of God **n.** this period of respite.
M-7............ 1:6 God himself whose mind **n.** to be healed.
M-8............ 2:8 and able to gratify its **n.** at the expense of
M-16.......... 1:7 Not one is absent whom he **n.**; not one is
M-16........ 10:5 Perhaps he **n.** to remember, "God is with
M-22.......... 3:1 forgiveness is healing **n.** to be understood
M-25.......... 4:6 which the Holy Spirit wants and **n.**. Yet
M-25.......... 6:9 The Holy Spirit **n.** these gifts, and those
M-26.......... 2:7 All **n.** are known to them, and all
M-26.......... 4:4 must understand what **n.** to be escaped.
M-29.......... 2:3 Who **n.** but a smile, being as yet unready
C-3............ 3:2 knows what His Son **n.** before he asks. He
C-5............ 1:5 differ for a time, for time **n.** symbols,
C-6............ 4:7 He seems to be whatever meets the **n.** you
C-6............ 4:8 your self entrapped in **n.** you do not have.
P-in........... 1:7 so. Sometimes he **n.** a more structured,
P-1............ 3:1 Everyone who **n.** help, regardless of the
P-1............ 3:3 not realize and **n.** to learn is that this "self
P-2........ IV.7:1 is therefore a mistake and **n.** correction.
P-2......... V.5:6 Yet He **n.** a voice through which to speak
P-2......... V.6:7 best can serve His Son in all his present **n.**
P-2........ VI.4:8 sick, and **n.** no remedy. To concentrate
P-2....... VII.1:3 He who **n.** healing must heal. Physician,
P-2....... VII.3:6 **n.** the help of a very advanced therapist,
P-2....... VII.8:5 is done, for what is perfect **n.** no healing,
P-3........... I.2:1 Who, then, decides what each brother **n.**
P-3........... I.2:8 you and not be sure you recognize his **n.**?
P-3........... I.2:9 you; He **n.** your voice to speak for Him.
P-3......... II.1:8 kinds of **n.** in their professional activities,
P-3......... II.2:2 For this, however, he **n.** special training,
P-3........ III.1:3 therapist has some earthly **n.** while he is
P-3...... III.1:10 he stays he will be given what he **n.** to stay
P-3........ III.4:4 whatever one **n.** is given by the other;
P-3........ III.6:8 the therapist how much he **n.** forgiveness,
S-1........... I.4:3 overlook your specific **n.** as you see them,
S-1......... II.3:6 there is no scarcity. The sinless have no **n.**
S-1......... II.7:7 Now, without **n.** of any kind, and clad
S-2......... II.5:6 who **n.** salvation from the pain of guilt?
S-2......... II.6:2 "I will forgive you if you meet my **n.**, for
S-3...... IV.10:7 your Father **n.** you and will call to you

## needy 1

W-pI... 195.5:2 you; the sick, the weak, the **n.** and afraid,

## negative 7

T-6........... I.1:4 can be explained in **n.** terms only. There
T-12....... V.2:6 invulnerability has more than **n.** value. If
W-pI..... 12.3:3 seem positive rather than **n.** occur to you,
W-pI..... 35.4:2 you ascribe to yourself, positive or **n.**,
W-pI..... 35.5:1 **n.** aspects of your perception of yourself.
W-pI..... 46.7:3 aware of any kind of **n.** reaction to anyone
M-17......... 4:2 that gives rise to **n.** emotions, regardless

## negatively 2

T-7....... VII.1:9 of being used positively as well as **n.**. Used
T-7..... VII.1:10 Used **n.** it will be destructive, because it

## neglect 1

W-pI..... 78.6:3 with him, the pain he caused you, his **n.**,

## neglecting 1

T-18..... VII.6:5 others well, **n.** what was made for *you.*

## neighbor 3

T-1......... I.18:3 It is a way of loving your **n.** as yourself.
T-1........ III.6:6 Since you and your **n.** are equal members
T-5......... in.3:6 of God to love his **n.** except as himself.

## neighbor's 1

T-1......... I.18:4 own and your **n.** worth simultaneously.

## neither 108

T-1......... II.1:7 **N.** emanates from consciousness, but
T-1......... V.1:2 **n.** the body nor the miracle serves any
T-2........... I.4:2 you **n.** can nor have been able to do this.
T-2...... IV.2:10 itself, **n.** type of confusion need occur.
T-2......... V.3:2 The right-minded **n.** exalt nor depreciate
T-3........ III.1:8 **n.** brings certainty because all perception
T-4........... I.2:7 spirit. Spirit can **n.** strengthen the ego nor
T-5....... VII.1:4 You need be **n.** careful nor careless; you
T-6...... V.A.1:4 The body **n.** lives nor dies, because it
T-7........... I.7:7 applies **n.** to Him nor to what He created.
T-7........ VI.9:1 and you are totally committed to **n.**. Your
T-8...... VI.5:11 You made **n.** yourself nor your function.
T-9........ VI.4:3 this. **N.** God's light nor yours is dimmed
T-10......... I.3:1 discovered that reality is in accord with **n.**
T-11....... in.1:3 **N.** God nor the ego proposes a partial
T-11......... I.4:2 that **n.** beginnings nor endings were
T-12...... IV.6:7 inheritance can **n.** be bought nor sold.
T-12....... V.8:6 which you can **n.** provide nor understand,
T-12.... VII.6:6 will find them, but you will recognize **n.**.
T-12.... VIII.1:2 know **n.** the Father nor the Son because of
T-13...... IV.2:1 **n.** oblivion nor hell is as unacceptable to
T-14......... I.4:4 created only to create, **n.** to see nor do.
T-14...... IV.4:2 breaks no barriers; **n.** did He make them.
T-14...... VI.3:2 They are **n.** safe nor unsafe. They do not
T-14...... VI.3:3 They do not protect; **n.** do they attack.
T-14.... VII.2:3 *is.* It can **n.** be lost nor sought nor found. It
T-14...... X.11:6 **N.** his mind nor yours holds more than
T-15...... III.6:6 **N.** give littleness, nor accept it. All honor
T-15...... V.10:5 brother as He loves you; **n.** less nor more.
T-15........ X.1:3 **N.** time nor season means anything in
T-15........ X.7:5 in part, but able to be **n.** completely. And
T-16......... I.3:2 choose **n.** to hurt it nor to heal it in your
T-16...... III.5:2 by God, He left **n.** God nor His creation.
T-16....... V.8:4 **n.** one will recognize that he has asked for
T-18...... VI.7:2 And **n.** God nor His most holy Son can
T-18.... VI.11:6 whole, as **n.** is perceived as separate.
T-18.... VIII.4:1 Yet **n.** sun nor ocean is even aware of all
T-18.... VIII.7:4 Yet in **n.** sun nor ocean is the power that
T-18.. VIII.11:4 what it offers everyone, **n.** less nor more.
T19.... IV.B.3:6 But **n.** can it bring you fear of pain. Pain is
T19.... IV.B.4:4 you want **n.** to get rid of peace nor limit it
T19.. IV.B.10:4 body can bring you **n.** peace nor turmoil;
T19.. IV.B.10:4 neither peace nor turmoil; **n.** joy nor pain
T19.... IV.C.3:3 sure; God, Who created **n.** sin nor death,
T19.... IV.C.3:4 He knows of **n.** sin nor its results. The
T19.... IV.C.5:4 itself it is **n.** corruptible nor incorruptible.
T19.. IV.C.11:2 **n.** sign nor symbol should be confused
T19. IV.D.13:6 **N.** can give it to himself alone. And yet
T-20........ II.2:2 For bodies can **n.** offer nor accept; hold
T-20...... IV.1:9 The untrue He has **n.** received nor given.
T-20..... VII.4:5 It is not sinful, but **n.** is it sinless. As
T-20..... VII.7:4 **N.** can serve the purpose of the other, for
T-21.... III.10:3 mind could **n.** ask it nor receive it of itself.
T-21.... III.11:8 **N.** demands the sacrifice of the other. Yet
T-21...... VI.7:1 **N.** your brother nor yourself can be
T-21...... VI.7:2 **n.** can accept a miracle instead without
T-21...... VI.9:9 blessed than to receive. But **n.** is it less.
T-22....... in.2:8 under a common roof that shelters **n.**; in
T-22......... I.6:5 **N.** the sounds he hears nor sights he sees
T-22...... VI.4:5 **N.** you nor your brother alone can serve
T-22.... VI.12:8 Attack is **n.** safe nor dangerous. It is
T-23...... III.2:4 And **n.** the receiver nor the giver is long
T-23...... IV.3:6 Father and the Son are murderers, or **n.** is
T-24...... III.5:3 *are* the same, for **n.** One wills specialness.
T-25..... II.9:13 His Will to be alone. And **n.** is it yours.
T-25....... V.4:2 Alone does **n.** have it. So must it remain
T-26......... I.7:8 For **n.** did he make, and only one was
T-27......... I.9:5 a purpose, it is seen as **n.** sick nor well,
T-27......... I.9:7 It has no life, but **n.** is it dead. It stands
T-27..... II.15:1 the function given both, but **n.** one alone.
T-27...... VI.4:2 **N.** does He harken to the witnesses by
T-28......... I.6:3 Time **n.** takes away nor can restore. And
T-28..... VII.7:7 **n.** less nor more in worth than the extent
T-30...... IV.4:8 But **n.** were they things to frighten you,
T-30...... IV.4:9 They must be **n.** cherished nor attacked,
T-30...... VI.4:9 truth that you can merit **n.** more nor less
T-31........ II.2:7 **N.** is true. Nor are they different. Yet
T-31........ II.6:5 This brother **n.** leads nor follows us, but
T-31........ II.9:5 to walk with him, so **n.** leads nor follows.
T-31....... V.6:7 You can be **n.** blamed for what you are,
W-pI..... 12.5:1 What is meaningless is **n.** good nor bad.
W-pI..... 28.4:5 much as to anything else, **n.** more nor less
W-pI..... 35.8:4 **N.** force nor discrimination should be
W-pI..... 54.1:6 My thoughts cannot be **n.** true nor false.
W-pI..... 70.1:4 You see **n.** guilt nor salvation as in your
W-pI..... 70.5:5 **N.** do we. He wants us to be healed. So do
W-pI..... 73.5:2 The source of **n.** light nor darkness can be
W-pI..... 76.9:4 of God. Payment is **n.** given nor received.
W-pI..... 93.5:4 It is **n.** bad nor good. It is unreal, and
W-pI. 131.10:3 and **n.** source nor substance in the truth.
W-pI... 154.1:1 today be **n.** arrogant nor falsely humble.
W-pI... 181.9:4 We look **n.** ahead nor backwards. We
W-pII. 294.2:2 *cannot be sinful nor sinless;* **n.** *good nor bad*
W-pII. 321.1:4 *For I have* **n.** *made nor understood the way*
M-4...... IV.1:2 They can **n.** harm nor be harmed. Harm

M-4 ...... IV.2:8 came **n.** from God's Son nor his Creator.
M-6 ........... 3:5 and **n.** the giver nor the receiver would
M-10 ......... 2:8 And this judgment is **n.** "good" nor "bad.
M-16 ......... 9:4 They can have no effects; **n.** good nor bad
M-16 ......... 9:4 **n.** rewarding nor demanding sacrifice,
M-17 ......... 9:3 its servant, it **n.** attacks nor protects. To
M-19 ......... 1:4 **N.** justice nor injustice exists in Heaven,
M-27 ......... 7:6 Truth **n.** moves nor wavers nor sinks
C-2........... 10:2 **N.** need be defined except by this. Yet
P-2......... II.2:6 one. **N.** is truth itself, but both can lead to
P-2......... III.2:3 **N.** can do this alone, but when they join,
P-2...... IV.10:8 But **n.** is it safe. And thus it must remain
P-3......... II.4:4 **n.** a perfect therapist nor a perfect patient

## nemesis 1

S-1 ........ III.1:5 enemy, your evil counterpart, your **n.**,

## nestles 1

T19....IV.C.9:2 sin, which **n.** quietly in the safety of your

## neutral 29

T-20..... VII.4:4 is positive and the body is merely **n.**. It is
T-24.......in.2:3 No belief is **n.**. Every one has the power to
T-26.... VIII.3:7 Time is as **n.** as the body is, except in
T-27.........I.8:3 as **n.** and without a goal inherent in itself.
T-28..... II.10:6 this much of the dream; the world is **n.**,
W-pI........16.h I have no **n.** thoughts.
W-pI.....16.3:2 A **n.** result is impossible because a neutral
W-pI.....16.3:2 because a **n.** thought is impossible. There
W-pI.....16.5:2 *This thought about_is not a* **n.** *thought.*
W-pI.....16.5:3 *That thought about_is not a* **n.** *thought.* As
W-pI.....16.5:6 *This thought about_is not a* **n.** *thought,*
W-pI.....16.5:6 *thought, because I have no* **n.** *thoughts.*
W-pI........17.h I see no **n.** things.
W-pI.....17.1:2 You see no **n.** things because you have no
W-pI.....17.1:2 things because you have no **n.** thoughts.
W-pI.....17.2:2 *I see no* **n.** *things because I have no neutral*
W-pI.....17.2:2 *neutral things because I have no* **n.** *thoughts*
W-pI.....17.2:4 say: *I do not see a* **n.** *–, because my thoughts*
W-pI.....17.2:4 *because my thoughts about_are not* **n.**.
W-pI.....17.2:6 *I do not see a* **n.** *wall, because my thoughts*
W-pI.....17.2:6 *because my thoughts about walls are not* **n.**.
W-pI.....17.2:7 *I do not see a* **n.** *body, because my thoughts*
W-pI.....17.2:7 *my thoughts about bodies are not* **n.**.
W-pI.....18.1:1 what you see are never **n.** or unimportant.
W-pI.....54.1:1 (16) I have no **n.** thoughts. Neutral
W-pI.....54.1:2 **N.** thoughts are impossible because all
W-pI.....54.2:1 (17) I see no **n.** things. What I see
W-pII ....294.h My body is a wholly **n.** thing.
W-pII .294.1:5 And yet a **n.** thing does not see death, for

## neutrality 1

W-pII .294.1:6 it. Its **n.** protects it while it has a use. And

## never 652

*See also* never-changing, never-ending

T-1.........I.31:3 holiness, which can be hidden but **n.** lost.
T-1.........I.45:1 A miracle is **n.** lost. It may touch many
T-1........ IV.2:1 can **n.** be really hidden in darkness, but
T-1........ VI.2:2 sense of separation would **n.** have arisen
T-1........ VI.4:2 can **n.** control the effects of fear yourself,
T-1....... VII.3:7 can **n.** make them real except to yourself.
T-2...........I.4:4 realize that your errors **n.** really occurred.
T-2.... V.A.13:1 **N.** confuse right- and wrong-mindedness.
T-2........ VI.9:5 powerful, and **n.** loses its creative force. It
T-2........ VI.9:6 It **n.** sleeps. Every instant it is creating. It
T-3...........I.4:5 Good teachers **n.** terrorize their students.
T-3......... II.2:5 you **n.** misperceive and always see truly.
T-3......... II.2:6 means that you **n.** see what does not exist,
T-3......... II.6:4 and emptiness can **n.** find lasting solace.
T-3...... IV.3:10 can **n.** make your misperceptions true,
T-3...... IV.6:10 remembered, **n.** having been destroyed.
T-3...... VI.2:5 It **n.** emphasizes only the positive aspects
T-3...... VI.10:5 The offense is **n.** to God, but only to those
T-4 ........I.2:12 not in communication and can **n.** be in
T-4 ..........I.3:5 I will **n.** attack your ego, but I am trying
T-4 ..........I.7:8 is **n.** at stake because God did not create it
T-4 ..........I.7:9 Your spirit is **n.** at stake because He did.
T-4 ........I.13:1 your ego if you wish, but **n.** for your spirit
T-4 .........II.3:2 knowledge away it is as if you **n.** had it.
T-4 .........II.7:3 ego **n.** gives out of abundance, because it
T-4 .....II.11:12 Knowledge **n.** involves comparisons. That
T-4 ..... III.1:10 ego and your spirit will **n.** be co-creators,
T-4 ....... III.5:1 you will **n.** want to cover or hide it again.
T-4 ....... III.6:4 He has **n.** failed to answer this request,
T-4 ....... III.7:1 It has **n.** really entered your mind to give
T-4 ....... III.7:8 I will **n.** forsake you any more than God
T-4 ..... IV.10:4 cannot be wrong because it **n.** attacks.
T-4 ........ V.6:7 that is **n.** asked by those who pursue them
T-4 ....... VI.2:1 brother is something you must **n.** forget.
T-4 ....... VI.3:4 **n.** induce more than a temporary effect.
T-4 ....... VI.6:4 my will is **n.** out of accord with His. I have
T-5 ........I.4:11 can obstruct it, although you can **n.** lose it
T-5 ....... IV.2:3 It does not die; it was merely **n.** born.
T-5 ....... IV.6:5 I will **n.** leave you or forsake you, because
T-5 ........ V.3:8 mind, **n.** forget that the ego is not sane. It
T-6 ........I.10:4 one Voice you are **n.** called on to sacrifice.
T-6 ........I.15:2 they **n.** could have quoted me as saying, "I
T-6 .......II.10:5 mind to God, because it has **n.** left Him. If
T-6 .......II.10:6 Him. If it has **n.** left Him, you need only
T-6 .......II.10:7 recognition that *the separation* **n.** *occurred*
T-6 .......II.10:8 it is an explicit statement that the ego **n.**
T-6 .......II.11:2 what **n.** happened cannot be difficult.
T-6 ....... III.1:5 Therefore, being is **n.** threatened. Your
T-6 ....... III.1:6 Your Godlike mind can **n.** be defiled. The
T-6 ....... III.1:7 The ego **n.** was and never will be part of it
T-6 ....... III.1:7 The ego never was and **n.** will be part of it
T-6 ....... IV.2:6 was ever asked, but one it can **n.** answer.
T-6 ....... IV.2:8 ego has **n.** answered any questions since,
T-6 ....... IV.2:9 **n.** done more than obscure the question,
T-6 ....... IV.7:2 because the first question was **n.** asked.
T-6 ....... IV.7:3 been wholly answered, *it has* **n.** *been. Being*
T-6 ....... IV.9:6 and **n.** detract from it in any way. You
T-6 ..... IV.11:1 That is why the Holy Spirit **n.** commands
T-6 ........ V.4:1 Holy Spirit **n.** itemizes errors because He
T-6 ... V.A.5:11 all. He **n.** takes anything back, because He
T-6 ... V.C.1:10 The Holy Spirit **n.** varies on this point,
T-7 ........I.7:13 reveal this to you because it was **n.** hidden
T-7 ........I.7:14 His light was **n.** obscured, because it is
T-7 .........II.4:3 he translates, **n.** changes the meaning. In
T-7 ....... III.5:4 That is why the Holy Spirit **n.** questions.
T-7 ....... IV.5:1 goals can **n.** be reconciled in any way or
T-7 ........ V.6:4 Healing **n.** does. Fear produces
T-7 ........ V.8:4 the Holy Spirit in him that **n.** changes His
T-7 ........ V.9:2 may worship out of fear, but will **n.** love.
T-7 ....... VI.1:3 That is why attack is **n.** discrete, and why
T-7 ....... VI.3:3 why the ego **n.** recognizes what it is doing
T-7 ....... VI.7:6 and would **n.** have been called upon by
T-7 .... VII.1:13 You will **n.** be able to exclude yourself
T-7 ...... VII.8:1 Attack could **n.** promote attack unless
T-7 ..... VIII.4:8 **N.** having had a consistent model, it
T-7 ..... VIII.4:8 model, it **n.** developed consistently. It is
T-7 ....... IX.7:1 Be confident that you have **n.** lost your
T-7 .........X.5:5 The Holy Spirit **n.** asks for sacrifice, but
T-8 .........II.2:4 ego has **n.** given you a sensible answer to
T-8 .........II.3:4 It is **n.** God Who coerces you, because He
T-8 ....... III.4:5 **N.** forget this, for in him you will find
T-8 ..... III.5:11 you. **N.** forget your responsibility to him,
T-8 ........ V.6:4 **N.** accord the ego the power to interfere
T-8 ........ V.6:9 My strength will **n.** be wanting, and if you
T-8 ....... VI.7:7 unknown to him, but **n.** to his Creator.
T-8 ....... VI.9:7 distance to a goal that has **n.** changed.
T-8 ...... VII.8:5 Holy Spirit's curriculum is **n.** depressing,
T-8 ... VIII.1:13 knowledge **n.** changes, so its constellation
T-8 ..... VIII.8:8 Spirit seeks to restore, **n.** to undermine.
T-9 ..........I.5:1 will **n.** call upon you to sacrifice anything.
T-9 ..........I.7:5 Of him you can **n.** learn what it is, and
T-9 ..........I.8:8 cannot be given because it was **n.** created.
T-9 ..........I.8:9 It was **n.** created, because it was never
T-9 ..........I.8:9 because it was **n.** your will for *you.*
T-9 ........I.11:4 depended on what you could **n.** have. The
T-9 ........I.12:6 If you do not want it, it was **n.** created. If
T-9 ........I.12:7 If it were **n.** created, it is nothing. Can you
T-9 .........II.4:1 are answered, **n.** doubt a Son of God. Do
T-9 .......II.11:1 **N.** forget, then, that you set the value on
T-9 ..... IV.10:2 that you will **n.** find satisfaction in fantasy
T-9 ...... VI.7:9 You will **n.** know that you are co-creator
T-9 .... VII.3:10 And it can **n.** go beyond it because it can
T-9 .... VII.3:10 go beyond it because it can **n.** *be* certain.
T-9 ...... VII.4:3 do, because He **n.** forgets what you are.
T-9 ..... VIII.7:6 Your grandeur will **n.** deceive you, but
T-10 .... in.3:11 God will **n.** decide against you, or He
T-10 ..... III.4:3 creation shares power and **n.** usurps it.
T-10 ..... IV.5:4 All this has **n.** been. Nothing but the laws
T-10 ..... IV.8:2 the Rays can **n.** be completely forgotten.
T-10 .......V.1:2 Joy is **n.** permitted, for depression is the
T-10 .......V.5:2 would be true, and you could **n.** escape. It
T-10 .......V.8:2 that He has **n.** ceased to acknowledge you
T-10 .....V.10:6 God will **n.** cease to love His Son, and His
T-10 .....V.10:6 Son, and His Son will **n.** cease to love Him
T-11 ...... in.2:6 but the ego **n.** looks on what it does with
T-11 ...... I.11:2 **n.** forget that God did not will to be alone
T-11 .......II.6:1 will **n.** rest until you know your function
T-11 ..... III.1:3 if you did you could **n.** have grown weary.
T-11 ..... III.1:4 yourself you could **n.** suffer in any way,
T-11 ..... III.5:3 You will **n.** lose your way, for God leads
T-11 ..... III.6:2 **n.** let them enter the mind of God's Son,
T-11 ..... IV.1:1 **N.** forget that the Sonship is your
T-11 ..... IV.2:3 your protection, and they **n.** hold in vain.
T-11 .... VII.3:1 ego may see some good, but **n.** only good.
T-12 ........ I.2:1 and **n.** without your own ego involvement
T-12 ..... III.3:6 **n.** occur to you to overlook their need.
T-12 ..... III.4:7 Poverty is of the ego, and **n.** of God. No
T-12 ..... III.5:4 **N.** lose sight of this, and never allow
T-12 ..... III.5:4 of this, and **n.** allow yourself to believe,
T-12 ..... IV.1:2 It **n.** puts it this way; on the contrary,
T-12 ..... IV.4:7 will **n.** deceive God's Son whom He loves
T-12 .......V.3:1 You will **n.** realize the utter uselessness of
T-12 .......V.3:4 of your attack, and if this has **n.** been, it
T-12 ..... VI.2:5 the Father **n.** ceases to remind Him of His
T-12 ..... VI.2:5 **n.** ceases to remind His Son of the Father.
T-12 ..... VI.5:4 to your sight, for Christ has **n.** slept. He is
T-12 ..... VI.5:5 to be seen, for He has **n.** lost sight of you.
T-12 .. VII.13:3 death penalty **n.** leaves the ego's mind, for
T-12 .. VII.15:5 make me manifest, you will **n.** see death.
T-12 ... VIII.1:4 in order to attack it, you will **n.** find it. For
T-12 ... VIII.4:1 your Father's Love you can **n.** forget Him,
T-12 ... VIII.6:5 Everything you made has **n.** been, and is
T-12 ... VIII.7:8 world *is* a thing of despair, for it can **n.** be.
T-12 ... VIII.7:9 Him could **n.** be content without reality.
T-12 ... VIII.8:6 of error and perception has **n.** been.
T-12 ... VIII.8:8 is but the way back to what was **n.** lost.
T-13 ...... in.4:5 cannot be condemned because he has **n.**
T-13 ...... in.4:6 for it teaches him that, **n.** having sinned,
T-13 ........I.2:4 of Christ is the proof that the ego **n.** was,
T-13 ........I.2:4 that the ego never was, and can **n.** be.
T-13 ........I.4:3 he fears and that he sees will **n.** touch him
T-13 ........I.9:1 you learn that the past has **n.** been, and so
T-13 ........I.9:4 For God has **n.** condemned His Son, and
T-13 ......I.11:4 the calm recognition that it has **n.** been.
T-13 .......II.9:4 and have **n.** been separated from him. In
T-13 .......V.2:2 Yet the figures that he sees were **n.** real,
T-13 .......V.7:5 but His offering to you has **n.** changed.
T-13 ..... VI.9:4 For it can **n.** be that His Son called upon
T-13 ... VI.13:7 **n.** ceased to be his Father's witness and
T-13 ... VI.13:9 witnesses that teach him that he **n.** slept.
T-13 .... VII.3:2 homes you built have **n.** sheltered you.
T-13 .... VII.7:4 Disturbance of his peace can **n.** be. In
T-13 .. VII.13:3 will ensure it **n.** can become a dark spot,
T-13 ... VIII.2:5 Perception, at its loftiest, is **n.** complete.
T-13 . VIII.10:7 For **n.** would He leave His Own beloved
T-13 .......X.6:2 The end of guilt will **n.** come as long as
T-13 .....X.14:3 into kindness will **n.** more be what it was.
T-13 .....X.14:5 for He will **n.** cease His praise of you.
T-13 ... XI.11:7 how can you remember what was **n.** true,
T-14 ........I.5:1 by showing you what you can **n.** learn.
T-14 .......II.1:4 undertaken to learn to do what you can **n.**
T-14 .......II.5:4 You will **n.** learn how to make nothing
T-14 ..... III.1:2 to learning that it should **n.** be forgotten.
T-14 .... III.11:1 It will **n.** happen that you must make
T-14 .... III.11:4 will **n.** ask what you have done to make
T-14 .... III.15:7 **N.** forget the Love of God, Who has

T-14....III.19:3 *Yet He will* **n.** *keep from me what He would*
T-14....IV.10:5 with the Mind of God has **n.** been.
T-14.......V.4:5 **N.** allow purity to remain hidden, but
T-14... VIII.5:1 the power to create can **n.** be dissolved.
T-14....IX.1:10 The past that you remember **n.** was, and
T-14.......X.5:1 pattern that **n.** rests and is never still. It
T-14.......X.5:1 pattern that never rests and is **n.** still. It
T-14......XI.4:9 you. **N.** believe that any lesson you have
T-14......XI.9:5 of you, and recognized they **n.** were.
T-14....XI.11:7 The miracle of creation has **n.** ceased,
T-14....XI.12:4 go together and **n.** can be found alone.
T-14....XI.14:2 The Teacher of peace will **n.** abandon you
T-14....XI.14:3 can desert Him but He will **n.** reciprocate,
T-15.........I.4:9 system before, but **n.** so clearly as here.
T-15.......I.12:1 You will **n.** give this holy instant to the
T-15.......I.15:5 There **n.** was an instant in which God's
T-15.......II.6:7 one instant, and you will **n.** deny it again.
T-15......III.1:2 and why you could **n.** be content with it.
T-15.......V.6:5 or you would **n.** have imagined that you
T-15.....VII.9:5 yet **n.** without demand of sacrifice. The
T-15... VIII.2:3 And through them you will **n.** learn the
T-15... VIII.3:1 Relate only with what will **n.** leave you,
T-15... VIII.3:1 leave you, and what you can **n.** leave. The
T-15......IX.3:4 This will **n.** be accomplished. Yet you
T-15.......X.6:3 it **n.** seems to be demanding it of you.
T-15.......X.6:5 The ego will **n.** let you perceive this, since
T-16.........I.2:3 And it **n.** joins except to strengthen itself.
T-16.........I.4:5 you have **n.** yet done yours completely.
T-16.........I.5:7 His, for this will **n.** bring peace to anyone.
T-16........II.6:7 But what you think you know was **n.** true.
T-16.....II.6:12 **N.** again will you be wholly willing not to
T-16.......II.9:1 **n.** given any problem to the Holy Spirit
T-16.......II.9:2 **n.** tried to solve anything yourself and
T-16......III.3:4 You could **n.** have taught freedom unless
T-16....III.5:11 creator. And what is not real was **n.** there.
T-16......IV.2:6 For the illusion of love will **n.** satisfy, but
T-16......IV.4:4 illusion, and what can change was **n.** love.
T-16......IV.6:6 will **n.** come from the illusion of love, but
T-16......IV.8:6 without which you could **n.** be complete.
T-16..IV.11:11 has **n.** forgotten what makes Him whole.
T-16........V.4:4 ego would **n.** have you see that separation
T-16.....V.11:7 And it is **n.** completed, nor ever will be
T-16.....V.12:3 meaning in the form, and there will **n.** be.
T-16.....VII.5:3 the one thing the ego **n.** allows to reach
T-17.......II.2:6 will **n.** cease to cause you wonderment at
T-17......III.9:5 For you can **n.** choose except between
T-17......IV.4:6 relationship with Him has **n.** been broken
T-17.......V.1:3 The holy instant **n.** fails. The experience
T-17.......V.3:9 of holiness, it can **n.** again be what it was.
T-17.......V.9:6 from which your true intent was **n.** absent
T-17.....VII.3:9 to faith will **n.** interfere with truth. But
T-17.....VII.8:6 What **n.** was is causeless, and is not there
T-17... VIII.4:4 This was **n.** true. For what the "something
T-17... VIII.6:3 for you accepted what can **n.** change. And
T-18.........I.2:1 Holy Spirit **n.** uses substitutes. Where the
T-18.........I.8:2 stillness dwells the living God you **n.** left,
T-18.........I.8:2 God you never left, and Who **n.** left you.
T-18.......I.10:4 **n.** accept something else instead of you.
T-18.......II.9:8 Will would have accomplished has **n.** *not*
T-18......IV.3:1 Humility will **n.** ask that you remain
T-18......IV.8:6 It **n.** happened in reality. Only in your
T-18........V.1:1 you *now* for the undoing of what **n.** was. If
T-18........V.2:1 **N.** approach the holy instant after you
T-18........V.2:3 **N.** attempt to overlook your guilt before
T-18........V.6:2 He will **n.** fail in this. But forget not that
T-18........V.6:5 **N.** believe that this is necessary, or even
T-18......VI.3:6 Yet it is **n.** what the body does that seems
T-18.....VII.2:1 There is one thing that you have **n.** done;
T-18.....VII.2:4 see the body again, but **n.** quite the same.
T-18.....VII.3:2 anticipated, but **n.** experienced just *now.*
T-18.....VII.3:4 entirely, for sin is **n.** wholly in the present
T-18......IX.4:6 The body's eyes will **n.** look on it. Yet they
T-18....IX.12:5 **n.** was a time in which you knew it not.
T-19.........I.1:3 peace without faith will **n.** be attained, for
T-19.........I.3:6 there, hearing what truth has **n.** said and
T-19.........I.7:6 of an idea is **n.** separate from its source.
T19...IV.A.1:4 it gently reaches out, but **n.** leaving you. If
T19...IV.A.9:4 is lifted up and carried away, **n.** to return,
T19.IV.A.10:1 love, for love would **n.** look on guilt at all.
T19....IV.B.6:3 who he is, and forget what **n.** was. I ask
T19..IV.B.11:3 you think you are can **n.** be apart from it.
T19...IV.D.3:2 made in secret to the ego **n.** to lift this veil
T19...IV.D.3:4 Here is your promise **n.** to allow union to
T19...IV.D.4:6 agreed **n.** to let the fear of God be lifted,
T19...IV.D.5:4 you love as you could **n.** love the body.
T19...IV.D.6:1 before what you swore **n.** to look upon.
T-20......II.8:10 refrain the Son of God was **n.** crucified.
T-20.......V.1:4 can anything be lost, and **n.** lost forever.
T-20.......V.3:5 is invisible to you or you will **n.** see it, but
T-20.......V.4:7 is your choice, but **n.** both of these.
T-20.......V.6:2 It **n.** changes. All that it ever held or will
T-20......VI.3:2 Idols accept, but **n.** make return. They
T-20......VI.5:6 build His temples where love can **n.** be.
T-20......VI.6:1 temple, and it will **n.** be the seat of love. It
T-20.....VII.6:6 Here are illusions **n.** brought to truth, and
T-20... VIII.1:3 and what was **n.** lost will quietly return. It
T-20... VIII.6:8 All that could save you, you will **n.** see.
T-20... VIII.8:7 the question **n.** is whether you want them
T-20. VIII.11:1 in dancing brooks that **n.** waste away;
T-20. VIII.11:4 **n.** need you think that there is something
T-21.........I.1:1 **N.** forget the world the sightless "see"
T-21.......II.4:4 **N.** was so much given for so little. In the
T-21......II.13:6 which you were created, and have **n.** left.
T-21......III.2:6 faith is **n.** recognized if it is placed in sin.
T-21......IV.1:1 Spirit will **n.** teach you that you are sinful.
T-21......IV.3:2 "fearful" question is one the ego **n.** asks.
T-21......V.1:10 is a witness but to this, and **n.** to reality.
T-21......V.1:11 is possible, or those where it could **n.** be.
T-21.......V.2:8 **n.** believe because it is your faith it makes
T-21.......V.6:1 **n.** circular and never self-defeating. He
T-21.......V.6:1 never circular and **n.** self-defeating. He
T-21.......V.8:7 The ego **n.** uses it, because it does not
T-21.....V.10:2 asked the question the ego will **n.** ask.
T-21......VI.6:1 Son of God to what can **n.** be corrected.
T-21.....VII.3:6 Those who are strong are **n.** treacherous,
T-21.....VII.4:4 But it can **n.** find what is not there. Yes, it
T-21.....VII.4:5 another, and **n.** comes to rest in victory.
T-21... VIII.3:6 whom God Himself will **n.** fail to answer.
T-21... VIII.5:6 of your desire for what will **n.** change. For
T-22.......in.1:3 could **n.** see it in the same place and time.
T-22.....in.4:10 is born into a holy relationship can **n.** end
T-22.........I.3:3 to what can **n.** communicate at all. Think,
T-22.........I.8:5 to anyone but you, **n.** to "something else.
T-22.........I.8:6 **n.** could He find a home in separate ones.
T-22......III.6:1 These eyes, made not to see, will **n.** see.
T-22....VI.13:6 Either could be maintained, but **n.** both.
T-23.........I.2:9 but **n.** will it be more than madness. And
T-23.........I.5:4 Yet truth can **n.** be forgotten by itself, and
T-23.........I.9:4 Here will the Father **n.** be remembered.
T-23.......I.10:8 sure that its peace can **n.** be disturbed.
T-23.......II.1:1 be brought to light, though **n.** understood
T-23.......II.5:2 it appears that They can **n.** be One again.
T-23.......II.9:4 you can **n.** take away save from yourself.
T-23......II.11:3 It must be what you want but **n.** found.
T-23......II.13:1 **N.** is your possession made complete.
T-23......II.13:2 And **n.** will your brother cease his attack
T-23......II.18:7 It **n.** changes. Can you paint rosy lips
T-23......II.19:9 are but forms. Their content is **n.** true.
T-23......III.4:8 vision, forever clear and **n.** out of sight, if
T-23......IV.2:9 its creations all that it is and **n.** suffer loss
T-23......IV.5:9 it is over when you realize it **n.** was begun.
T-23......IV.9:1 in their awareness could **n.** think of battle
T-24.........I.2:1 Beliefs will **n.** openly attack each other
T-24.........I.2:2 kept unknown and **n.** brought to reason,
T-24.........I.6:5 Specialness can **n.** share, for it depends
T-24.........I.6:6 And he must **n.** reach them, or your goal
T-24.........I.9:7 **N.** can there be peace among the different
T-24.......II.3:5 His "special" sons are many, **n.** one, each
T-24.......II.5:1 **n.** will you hear the Voice for God beside
T-24.......II.6:5 truth: You will no longer see what **n.** was,
T-24.....II.10:7 Who chose that love could **n.** be divided,
T-24......III.3:6 What rests on nothing **n.** can be stable.
T-24......III.4:6 that what God wants for you will **n.** be,
T-24.......V.8:3 Son could **n.** will that you be brotherless.
T-24......VI.1:6 For He could **n.** leave His Own creation.
T-24......VI.8:3 both may end a journey that has **n.** begun
T-24......VI.8:4 What **n.** was is not a part of you. Yet you
T-24....VI.10:6 And **n.** doubt but that your specialness
T-24....VI.11:4 goal with vigilance you **n.** thought to yield
T-24....VI.11:4 and effort that you **n.** thought to cease.
T-25.........I.3:4 your purpose, from which it **n.** separates,
T-25.........I.3:5 behold, for means and end are **n.** separate
T-25.........I.5:4 and His Father **n.** have been separate, and
T-25.........I.7:2 mind so split could **n.** be the Teacher of a
T-25........II.3:3 and bring what it has **n.** brought before?
T-25.....II.10:2 for the wholly pure have **n.** sinned. Give,
T-25.....II.11:5 may see as one what **n.** has been separate,
T-25......III.5:6 as if they lit a place where they could **n.** be
T-25.... III.8:11 For what it claimed could **n.** be, has been.
T-25......III.9:1 The Son of God could **n.** sin, but he can
T-25......IV.4:8 can **n.** fall away and leave you homeless.
T-25....VIII.6:6 they are told that they have **n.** sinned.
T-25..VIII.14:7 Let love decide, and **n.** fear that you, in
T-25......IX.8:4 A miracle can **n.** be received because
T-26.........I.2:3 as if what is inside can **n.** reach without,
T-26.........I.2:3 and what is out can **n.** reach and join with
T-26.........I.7:8 His gifts can **n.** suffer sacrifice and loss.
T-26......III.5:2 Heaven was **n.** lost, and so cannot be
T-26......III.7:7 been withdrawn from what was **n.** true,
T-26.....V.1:10 For **n.** will another road be made except
T-26...V.11:10 it is seen, this light can **n.** be forgotten. It
T-26...VII.12:8 What is thus kept apart can **n.** join.
T-26...VII.13:3 but adds to its abundance, **n.** takes away.
T-26...VII.13:6 For **n.** will success be possible in trying to
T-26...VII.14:4 God's Son could **n.** be content with less
T-26......IX.1:4 And **n.** will you know He is in you as well
T-26......IX.4:3 What **n.** was passes to nothingness when
T-26......IX.8:2 His Son dwells with Him, **n.** separate.
T-27.........I.1:2 and make a unity of what can **n.** join?
T-27.........I.4:3 from which you swear he **n.** will escape.
T-27.........I.5:3 and therefore **n.** suffered pain at all. It
T-27.........I.5:7 Here is the proof that he has **n.** sinned;
T-27.........I.8:4 to see, so that the cause can **n.** be denied.
T-27.........I.9:2 proof that what your function is can **n.** be
T-27........II.5:6 that it has **n.** suffered pain because of him
T-27........II.6:3 is he convinced his innocence was **n.** lost,
T-27........II.6:4 things the world attests can **n.** be undone.
T-27.....II.10:4 is but to forgive, and **n.** to accuse. Alone,
T-27.....II.14:3 can **n.** be returned to its accuser, who had
T-27......III.3:7 you see is wholly absent and has **n.** been.
T-27......III.7:4 The choice you fear to lose you **n.** had.
T-27.......V.9:4 been properly perceived but **n.** violated.
T-27...VII.10:3 Yet a thing can **n.** be its opposite. And
T-27...VII.11:3 An honest choice could **n.** be perceived as
T-27....VIII.3:2 The "hero" of this dream will **n.** change,
T-27....VIII.5:5 could **n.** have conceived this world as real.
T-27....VIII.8:3 guilt outside yourself, but **n.** letting go! It
T-28.........I.8:3 It has **n.** changed, because there never
T-28.........I.8:3 because there **n.** was a time in which He
T-28.........I.8:5 Yet was It **n.** absent from your mind, for
T-28.........I.9:1 What *you* remember **n.** was. It came from
T-28.........I.9:3 that were causeless and could **n.** be effects
T-28.........I.9:5 **N.** changed from what It is. And you are
T-28.......I.10:2 His Effects, yet have They **n.** been denied.
T-28.......I.14:4 he **n.** had a need for doing anything, and
T-28.......I.14:4 had a need for doing anything, and **n.** did
T-28.......I.14:6 There **n.** was a cause beside It that could
T-28.......I.15:5 another shore that he can **n.** reach. His
T-28........II.6:5 a dream, but **n.** will you give it real effects
T-28......II.7:12 that would make it cause. And so it **n.** was
T-28......III.4:1 and love was **n.** in the world of dreams.
T-28......III.8:4 and gently shows you that you **n.** sinned.
T-28......III.8:5 guilt to bring you witness to what **n.** was.
T-28......IV.2:7 you would unite, but **n.** with the dream. It
T-28.......V.1:7 Who shares in them can **n.** share in Him.
T-28......VI.2:3 in ways you want, but **n.** makes the choice
T-28......VI.6:5 Myself, for you can **n.** be apart from Me."
T-28.....VII.5:1 But **n.** you alone. This world is but the
T-29.........I.2:2 fear, since fear and hate can **n.** be apart.
T-29......IV.2:5 But **n.** is it absent from the dream, for
T-29......IV.5:3 the Holy Spirit gives is **n.** one of fear. The
T-29....VI.2:11 can **n.** change by what men made of him.
T-29.....VII.1:4 when God calls will **n.** answer in His place
T-29....VIII.1:3 such, and **n.** seen for what they really are.
T-29....VIII.1:8 is this that **n.** is perceived and recognized.
T-29....VIII.9:5 For more than Heaven can you **n.** have. If
T-29..VIII.9:11 But you will **n.** be content with being less.

T-29...... IX.8:5 but with the holiness that **n.** left the altar
T-29...... IX.8:6 song again, he knows he **n.** heard it not.
T-30....... II.2:6 God but ensured that you would **n.** lose
T-30.... III.2:11 Yet this could **n.** be your will, because
T-30...... III.4:1 It **n.** is the idol that you want. But what
T-30.... III.10:5 the Thought God holds of you has **n.** left
T-30.... III.11:9 star shines still; the sky has **n.** changed.
T-30...... IV.1:4 The truth could **n.** be attacked. And this
T-30...... IV.1:7 attack but false ideas, and **n.** truthful ones
T-30...... IV.3:3 it. It **n.** was the thing you thought. It must
T-30...... IV.4:7 Their dancing **n.** brought you joy. But
T-30...... IV.7:5 free of all the dreams of what you **n.** were,
T-30....... V.6:4 your brother and yourself was **n.** there.
T-30....... V.9:6 You **n.** wanted it. What happiness have
T-30..... V.10:3 ***n.** was a time an idol brought you anything*
T-30...... VI.1:1 Anger is ***n.*** justified. Attack has *no*
T-30..... VII.3:8 Fear is a judgment **n.** justified. Its
T-30.... VIII.2:7 This demonstrates that it was **n.** real, and
T-31......... I.1:2 it says is what was **n.** true is not true now,
T-31......... I.1:2 never true is not true now, and **n.** will be.
T-31......... I.8:3 you. And **n.** does a call remain unheard,
T-31....... II.8:5 wish to hear a call that **n.** has been made.
T-31....... II.8:8 you did not want, and that were **n.** true.
T-31...... III.1:5 You **n.** hate your brother for his sins, but
T-31...... III.2:7 it **n.** would occur to you to give attack to
T-31...... III.4:9 **n.** change unless the mind preferred the
T-31...... III.6:3 It can **n.** lead you where you would not be
T-31...... IV.9:6 Yet has He **n.** left His Thoughts to die,
T-31....... V.3:3 This aspect **n.** makes the first attack. But
T-31....... V.8:2 **n.** seek to go beyond its roads nor realize
T-31...... VI.1:7 you **n.** will escape the body as your own
T-31...... VI.3:4 see another world your eyes could **n.** find.
T-31...... VI.7:3 your Father wills of you can **n.** change.
T-31..... VII.3:1 the good is **n.** what the body seems to be.
T-31..... VII.4:2 can be interchanged but **n.** jointly held.
T-31.... VIII.2:5 Simply by **n.** using weakness to direct
T-31.... VIII.4:2 Be **n.** fearful of temptation, then, but see
T-31.... VIII.5:5 that comes from God and that can **n.** fail.
W-pI.......... 5.h I am **n.** upset for the reason I think.
W-pI....... 7.1:7 you are **n.** upset for the reason you think.
W-pI..... 16.3:1 your recognizing that thoughts are **n.** idle
W-pI..... 18.1:1 you see are **n.** neutral or unimportant. It
W-pI..... 19.1:4 for cause and effect are **n.** separate.
W-pI..... 30.1:2 and see in it what you have **n.** seen before.
W-pI..... 41.4:1 You can **n.** be deprived of your perfect
W-pI..... 41.4:2 You can **n.** suffer because the Source of all
W-pI..... 41.4:3 You can **n.** be alone because the Source of
W-pI..... 41.8:7 But it will **n.** fail completely, and instant
W-pI..... 43.2:3 which is the undoing of what **n.** was,
W-pI..... 46.1:1 not forgive because He has **n.** condemned
W-pI..... 51.5:1 (5) I am **n.** upset for the reason I think. I
W-pI..... 51.5:2 think. I am **n.** upset for the reason I think
W-pI..... 52.1:2 Reality is **n.** frightening. It is impossible
W-pI..... 60.1:2 not forgive because He has **n.** condemned
W-pI..... 68.4:5 will **n.** be a problem in motivation ever
W-pI..... 70.8:6 remember also that you have **n.** found
W-pI..... 75.6:4 look upon it now as if you **n.** saw it before
W-pI..... 75.7:2 Understand that the Holy Spirit **n.** fails to
W-pI..... 76.2:2 salvation where it is not, and **n.** find it.
W-pI..... 76.7:1 The laws of God can **n.** be replaced. We
W-pI..... 76.9:6 else. God's laws forever give and **n.** take.
W-pI..... 77.3:3 of God is within you, and can **n.** be lost.
W-pI..... 77.4:3 also that miracles are **n.** taken from one
W-pI..... 86.1:8 I will rejoice because His plan can **n.** fail.
W-pI..... 93.4:1 evil that you think you did was **n.** done,
W-pI..... 94.3:6 This is the Self that **n.** sinned, nor made
W-pI..... 94.3:7 Self that **n.** left Its home in God to walk
W-pI..... 96.1:4 you see in you will **n.** be compatible. But
W-pI..... 96.3:3 The self you made can **n.** be your Self, nor
W-pI..... 99.1:3 between what is and what could **n.** be.
W-pI..... 99.2:5 truth because it undoes what was **n.** done.
W-pI..... 99.4:3 plan, by which the **n.** done is overlooked,
W-pI..... 99.4:3 and sins forgotten which were **n.** real?
W-pI..... 99.7:6 thought the thoughts that **n.** were His
W-pI... 100.7:7 God's plan, and **n.** lose or sacrifice or die.
W-pI... 101.3:2 of sin, and suffering can **n.** be escaped, if
W-pI... 101.5:2 must come from sin will **n.** happen, for it
W-pI... 105.3:4 will **n.** lessen when they are given away.
W-pI... 109.5:2 your rest can **n.** change in any way at all.
W-pI... 121.6:5 Who is your Self, and Who can **n.** sin.
W-pI. 121.11:2 a little gleam which you had **n.** noticed.
W-pI... 122.1:6 a gentleness that **n.** can be hurt, a deep,
W-pI... 122.1:6 and a rest so perfect it can **n.** be upset?
W-pI... 122.3:5 effect or transient promise, **n.** to be kept,
W-pI... 122.8:4 will remember then can **n.** be described.
W-pI... 125.4:3 holiness that He created and will **n.** leave.
W-pI... 125.8:4 let Him tell you God has **n.** left His Son,
W-pI... 125.8:4 left His Son, and you have **n.** left your Self
W-pI... 127.1:6 **n.** alters with a person or a circumstance.
W-pI... 127.4:1 that there can **n.** be a difference in what
W-pI... 129.5:2 **n.** back to see again the world you do not
W-pI. 132.16:2 as yet that you could **n.** be released alone.
W-pI... 133.6:3 Time can **n.** take away a value that is real.
W-pI... 133.6:4 What fades and dies was **n.** there, and
W-pI. 134.11:3 what he thought he saw was **n.** there. And
W-pI. 135.18:2 plan, for He would **n.** offer pain to you.
W-pI... 136.6:3 in effect, and **n.** to be seen as whole again.
W-pI. 136.15:3 will come, for it has **n.** been apart from us
W-pI... 137.4:3 would impose has **n.** really happened. To
W-pI... 137.4:6 So healing, **n.** needed by the truth, must
W-pI... 137.5:2 forgiveness overlooks all sins that **n.** were
W-pI... 137.5:3 to take the place of what has **n.** been at all
W-pI. 137.10:3 But you are **n.** healed alone. And legions
W-pI. 137.12:4 the inevitable to occur, and you will **n.** fail
W-pI... 139.4:2 could **n.** be alive at all unless he knew the
W-pI... 140.9:3 realize that there can **n.** be a meaningful
W-pI... 151.3:3 Yet witness **n.** falser was than this. But
W-pI. 152.11:6 **n.** left will come again to our awareness,
W-pI... 153.6:4 Him. Defenselessness can **n.** be attacked,
W-pI. 153.18:1 practice, you will **n.** cease to think of Him,
W-pI. 153.19:4 and **n.** leaves our weakness unsupported
W-pI. 153.20:4 The ministers of God can **n.** fail, because
W-pI. 153.20:7 You lay aside but what was **n.** real, to look
W-pI... 157.9:3 This you will **n.** teach, for you attained it
W-pI... 158.9:6 with them, undone and **n.** to be done.
W-pI... 159.3:2 love and the rebirth of love which **n.** dies,
W-pI... 159.5:3 **n.** able to obscure the light that shines
W-pI... 159.6:4 Here the door is **n.** locked, and no one is
W-pI... 159.8:3 but they can **n.** grow in its unnourishing
W-pI... 161.1:3 answer to temptation which can **n.** fail to
W-pI... 162.2:6 and hear this sound will **n.** look on death.
W-pI... 163.3:4 It will **n.** fail to take all life as hostage to
W-pI... 164.4:3 in you the thought of sin has **n.** touched.
W-pI... 165.7:4 And the Thought of Him is **n.** absent.
W-pI... 166.2:5 in one, himself alone. But **n.** in one God.
W-pI. 166.14:5 accepts God's gifts can **n.** suffer anything.
W-pI... 167.4:2 you did not make, and you can **n.** change.
W-pI... 167.5:5 not give birth to what was **n.** given them.
W-pI... 167.9:3 what seems to happen **n.** has occurred,
W-pI... 169.6:6 him. The world has **n.** been at all. Eternity
WpI...rV.in4:5 and **n.** changes from Its constant state of
W-pI... 181.9:2 **n.** could conceive of anything without Its
W-pI... 182.4:2 hold a picture of a past that **n.** happened.
W-pI... 183.7:1 give an invitation which can **n.** be refused
W-pI. 186.11:6 God's can **n.** fail because He is its Source.
W-pI. 186.14:1 These are the forms which **n.** can deceive,
W-pI... 187.4:1 you are sure that you will **n.** lose them.
W-pI... 187.6:1 **N.** forget you give but to yourself. Who
W-pI... 187.8:1 **N.** believe that you can sacrifice. There is
W-pI... 188.2:2 it has been lost already, or was **n.** there? It
W-pI... 188.5:1 The peace of God can **n.** be contained.
W-pI... 194.7:6 certainty of care the world can **n.** threaten
W-pI... 194.7:7 may be faulty, but will **n.** lack correction.
W-pI... 195.4:5 It will **n.** be that some are loosed while
W-pI... 196.2:2 can **n.** be escaped because the ego, under
W-pI... 196.8:5 back within the holy mind He **n.** left.
W-pI... 197.5:3 Yet you will **n.** realize His gifts are sure,
W-pI... 197.6:2 and you can **n.** think the gifts of God are
W-pI... 197.9:8 But **n.** think that He has ever ceased to
W-pI... 199.2:2 and fear can **n.** enter in a mind that has
W-pI... 200.7:3 have reality, because it **n.** was created. Is
W-pII .... in.5:7 have **n.** come this far unless you saw,
W-pII . 225.2:4 your hand to me, and I will **n.** leave you.
W-pII . 227.2:1 return to Heaven, which we **n.** really left.
W-pII . 234.1:1 we have reached the holy peace we **n.** left.
W-pII . 240.1:2 you have seen yourself as you could **n.** be,
W-pII . 241.2:2 *Father, Your Son, who **n.** left, returns to*
W-pII . 248.1:6 What dies was **n.** living in reality, and did
W-pII ..... 5.3:3 love creates in truth, and truth can **n.** fear
W-pII ..... 9.1:2 of the condition that restores the **n.** lost,
W-pII . 306.2:1 *to You, remembering we **n.** went away;*
W-pII ... 10.1:1 is false, and what is true has **n.** changed.
W-pII . 320.1:4 His holy will can **n.** be denied, because his
W-pII .... 322.h I can give up but what was **n.** real.
W-pII . 326.1:1 *Mind, a holy Thought that **n.** left its home. I*
W-pII . 327.2:1 *I thank You that Your promises will **n.** fail in*
W-pII . 329.1:3 *This am I, and this will **n.** change. As You are*
W-pII . 331.1:4 *You could **n.** leave me desolate, to die within*
W-pII . 332.1:3 Truth **n.** makes attack. It merely is. And
W-pII . 333.2:4 *For this alone will **n.** fail in anything, being*
W-pII . 335.1:2 I **n.** see my brother as he is, for that is far
W-pII ... 13.5:4 up, to show that what is born can **n.** die,
W-pII . 343.1:4 *You **n.** take away. And You created me to be*
W-pII . 356.1:1 *You promised You would **n.** fail to answer*
W-ep......... 6:8 sure; that I will **n.** leave you comfortless.
M-in........ 2:11 you. No more than that, but also **n.** less.
M-1........... 3:4 But the content of the course **n.** changes.
M-1........... 4:6 There was **n.** a question of outcome, for
M-2........... 2:3 it corrects what **n.** was. Further, the plan
M-2........... 2:8 long ago. In reality it **n.** happened at all.
M-4......... I.1:3 because cause and effect are **n.** separated.
M-4........ II.2:9 because they **n.** do their will alone. They
M-4........ X.2:3 could **n.** have conceived of such a change.
M-5........ II.3:4 will **n.** again appear to rule the mind. For
M-6........... 4:8 God's treasure house can **n.** be empty.
M-8........... 3:8 eyes will **n.** see except through differences
M-10......... 6:9 **n.** were but the effects of his mistaken
M-11......... 3:8 it is not possible, and can **n.** be possible.
M-13......... 3:7 he is. He can doubt all things, but **n.** this.
M-16....... 10:9 chooses to give up all that he **n.** had. And
M-17......... 4:8 and this can **n.** be a matter of degree.
M-17......... 5:9 him safe from fury that can **n.** be abated,
M-17......... 5:9 and vengeance that can **n.** be satisfied.
M-17....... 7:13 The stain of blood can **n.** be removed,
M-17......... 8:6 and not a fact, it is **n.** justified. Once this
M-20......... 3:3 God's peace can **n.** come where anger is,
M-23......... 2:3 may recur to others, but **n.** to this One.
M-29......... 6:1 **N.** forget that the Holy Spirit does not
C-1............ 3:3 being of God, it is eternal and was **n.** born
C-1............ 6:2 overlooks, or forgives, what **n.** happened.
C-2............ 7:3 dream and you will **n.** question any more.
C-4............ 3:1 being another level, they can **n.** meet. The
C-5............ 1:1 help to enter Heaven for you have **n.** left.
C-5............ 1:4 a Thought of God, and this will **n.** change.
C-6............ 1:2 or spirit, is eternal and has **n.** changed.
C-6............ 3:6 He **n.** forgets the Creator or His creation.
C-6............ 3:7 He **n.** forgets the Son of God. He never
C-6............ 3:8 He **n.** forgets you. And He brings the Love
C-6............ 3:9 to you in an eternal shining that will **n.** be
C-ep.......... 4:5 Now we know that we will **n.** lose the way
P-1............ 5:5 as He thinks best, and He is **n.** wrong.
P-2.......... II.3:4 This is **n.** apparent to the patient, and
P-2.......... V.1:4 steps which **n.** reach to consciousness.
P-2.......... V.6:5 For He has **n.** asked for more than just the
P-3.......... I.4:1 teacher of God, **n.** forgets one thing; he
P-3.......... II.6:2 relationships this point is **n.** reached,
P-3........ III.2:9 he could **n.** understand what healing is.
P-3........ III.8:3 The Holy Spirit **n.** refuses an invitation to
S-1.......... II.2:1 and could **n.** be made by a Son of God
S-1.......... II.6:1 Let it **n.** be forgotten that prayer at any
S-1.......... II.7:6 light no longer flickers, and will **n.** go out.
S-1.......... II.8:2 because the goal has **n.** changed. Prayer
S-1.......... II.8:3 for a ladder to reach what one has **n.** left.
S-1........ III.2:7 could **n.** make a prayer like that.
S-1........ V.3:12 For you have understood he **n.** left, and
S-2.......... II.2:2 love that arrogance could **n.** be dislodged.
S-3.......... I.4:5 home, but it will **n.** be his home in truth.
S-3........ III.1:1 heals the body in a part, but **n.** as a whole.
S-3........ III.4:8 is, for **n.** thus can it be truly healed.
S-3........ III.6:2 will **n.** fail to bring His kindly remedy to
S-3........ IV.1:4 but speak for Him and **n.** for themselves.
S-3........ IV.3:4 Love has **n.** changed and never will. You
S-3........ IV.3:4 Love has never changed and **n.** will. You
S-3........ IV.4:5 and understood that you have **n.** left. This
S-3........ IV.5:1 **N.** forget this; it is you who are God's Son
S-3........ IV.6:5 he your Father loves, who **n.** left his home
S-3........ IV.7:3 and that his prayers have **n.** ceased to sing

## nightmare 6

| | |
|---|---|
| T-1.........I.24:3 | Everything else is your own **n.**, and does |
| T-9......... V.4:2 | may interpret the ego's symbols in a **n.**, |
| T-9......... V.4:2 | then use them to prove that the **n.** is real. |
| T-12........ II.6:1 | and no **n.** can defeat a child of God in his |
| T-13...... XI.9:5 | even the darkest **n.** that disturbs the mind |
| W-pI... 190.2:5 | a **n.** of abandonment by an Eternal Love, |

## nightmares 19

| | |
|---|---|
| T-1.........I.33:3 | your errors by freeing you from your **n.**. |
| T-2...........I.4:5 | fell upon Adam could he experience **n.**. If |
| T-3......... VI.4:3 | This is why you see it in **n.**, or in pleasant |
| T-6......... V.2:2 | You do not inform them that the **n.** that |
| T-9......... V.3:1 | advantage to bringing **n.** into awareness, |
| T-9......... V.7:4 | who no longer believes in **n.** of any kind. |
| T-11...... VI.8:6 | can crucify him, you are only having **n.**. |
| T-12........ II.4:3 | if they hide their **n.** they will keep them. It |
| T-12........ II.4:7 | You are hiding your **n.** in the darkness of |
| T-12........ II.5:1 | Let us not save **n.**, for they are not fitting |
| T-13...... IV.6:6 | The ego would preserve your **n.**, and |
| T-13.... VI.12:5 | And that is why the **n.** come. You dream |
| T-13.... VI.13:2 | have followed them through all your **n.**, |
| T-13.... VII.9:2 | of **n.** for the happy dreams of love. In |
| T-13...... XI.7:2 | your blackest **n.** all mean nothing. They |
| T-15.........I.4:2 | **n.** and their fears are all associated with it |
| T-20..VIII.10:4 | translates your **n.** into happy dreams; |
| T-23...... III.1:7 | his intent in **n.** where the smiles are gone, |
| T-29...... IX.5:1 | **N.** are childish dreams. The toys have |

## nights 1

| | |
|---|---|
| W-pI... 157.1:5 | have spent long days and **n.** in celebrating |

## no 2735

| | |
|---|---|
| T-in ........... 1:8 | *is all-encompassing can have **n.** opposite.* |
| T-1...........I.1:1 | There is **n.** order of difficulty in miracles. |
| T-1.........I.15:4 | when it is **n.** longer useful in facilitating |
| T-1.........I.34:3 | strength leaves **n.** room for intrusions. |
| T-1.........I.49:1 | The miracle makes **n.** distinction among |
| T-1......... II.4:1 | "**N.** man cometh unto the Father but by |
| T-1......... II.6:6 | There is **n.** relationship between the time |
| T-1........ III.9:3 | this selectivity takes **n.** account of the |
| T-1........ IV.3:2 | It has **n.** unique properties of its own. It is |
| T-1........ IV.3:5 | have everything have **n.** needs of any kind |
| T-1........ IV.4:2 | the Bible means by "There is **n.** death," |
| T-1......... V.2:6 | to the Sonship will **n.** longer be necessary. |
| T-1........ VI.1:2 | **N.** learning is acquired by anyone unless |
| T-1........ VI.1:7 | There were **n.** needs at all. Needs arise |
| T-1........ VI.4:5 | can believe what **n.** one else thinks is true. |
| T-2...........I.1:4 | There is **n.** emptiness in you. Because of |
| T-2...........I.1:6 | are creative. **N.** child of God can lose this |
| T-2...........I.4:7 | which is then **n.** longer accorded reality. |
| T-2...........I.5:1 | believe are of **n.** concern to the miracle, |
| T-2...........I.5:2 | ease. It makes **n.** distinctions among |
| T-2...........I.5:5 | there is **n.** order of difficulty in miracles. |
| T-2......... II.5:4 | ability to learn has **n.** value when change |
| T-2......... II.5:4 | value when change is **n.** longer necessary. |
| T-2........ IV.3:5 | has **n.** power in itself to introduce actual |
| T-2......... V.7:4 | There is **n.** doubt that this may produce |
| T-2....... V.10:2 | or he would have **n.** need of charity. The |
| T-2....V.A.14:3 | has **n.** real effect has no real existence. Its |
| T-2....V.A.14:3 | has no real effect has **n.** real existence. Its |
| T-2....V.A.16:2 | It has **n.** element of judgment at all. The |
| T-2....V.A.16:3 | they do" in **n.** way evaluates *what* they do. |
| T-2....V.A.16:5 | is **n.** reference to the outcome of the error |
| T-2...... VI.4:10 | you are sure that it is, there will be **n.** fear. |
| T-2........ VI.6:4 | is **n.** strain in doing God's Will as soon as |
| T-2........ VI.9:3 | and **n.** one remains fully aware of it all the |
| T-2...... VI.9:13 | it. There *are* **n.** idle thoughts. All thinking |
| T-2..... VII.5:10 | that ultimately **n.** compromise is possible |
| T-2....... VII.7:4 | it is by **n.** means necessarily undivided. |
| T-2..... VIII.4:5 | which, without belief, will **n.** longer exist. |
| T-2..... VIII.5:4 | life. **N.** one who lives in fear is really alive. |
| T-2.... VIII.5:10 | is **n.** reason for fear to remain with you. |
| T-3...........I.1:4 | **N.** one who is free of the belief in scarcity |
| T-3...........I.2:6 | error itself is **n.** harder to correct than any |
| T-3.........I.7:10 | there will be **n.** need to learn from many |
| T-3 .........II.1:7 | impossible. **N.** one has ever lived who has |
| T-3 .........II.1:8 | **N.** one, therefore, is able to deny truth |
| T-3 .........II.5:5 | There is **n.** confusion within Its Levels, |
| T-3 ........ III.7:7 | There are **n.** strangers in God's creation. |
| T-3 ........ IV.1:6 | Spirit has **n.** levels, and all conflict arises |
| T-3 ........ IV.7:1 | therefore know that **n.** miscreation exists. |
| T-3 ......... V.1:2 | **N.** one has been sure of anything since. I |
| T-3 ......... V.2:3 | purpose has **n.** true generalizability. |
| T-3 ......... V.4:5 | You have **n.** image to be perceived. The |
| T-3 ......... V.8:1 | if there are **n.** judgments and nothing but |
| T-3 ......... V.8:7 | It is all one and has **n.** separate parts. You |
| T-3 ........ VI.1:2 | the Last Judgment there will be **n.** more. |
| T-3 ........ VI.1:3 | beyond perception there is **n.** judgment. |
| T-3 ........ VI.2:7 | that what you judged against has **n.** effect. |
| T-3 ........ VI.3:1 | **n.** idea of the tremendous release and |
| T-3 ...... VI.11:1 | There is **n.** one who does not feel that he |
| T-3 ...... VI.11:7 | Yet **n.** one in his right mind believes that |
| T-3 ........ VII.2:7 | souls in return for gifts of **n.** real worth. |
| T-3 ........ VII.2:8 | worth. This makes absolutely **n.** sense. |
| T-3 ..... VII.4:11 | is **n.** resolution while you believe the one |
| T-3 ..... VII.5:11 | There is **n.** death, but there *is* a belief in |
| T-3 ........ VII.6:1 | The branch that bears **n.** fruit will be cut |
| T-4 ...........I.2:4 | You believe that if you allow **n.** change to |
| T-4 ...........I.5:1 | that they will one day **n.** longer need him. |
| T-4 ...........I.7:5 | I have **n.** right to set your learning limits |
| T-4 .........I.7:10 | **n.** form of devotion is possible as long as |
| T-4 .........I.13:2 | involves **n.** confusion about the child's |
| T-4 ..........II.1:3 | **n.** point in giving an answer in terms of |
| T-4 ..........II.2:6 | There could be **n.** better example that the |
| T-4 ..........II.4:3 | **N.** one dismisses something he considers |
| T-4 ..........II.4:9 | When teaching is **n.** longer necessary you |
| T-4 ..........II.5:4 | You have **n.** sense of real self-preservation |
| T-4 ........II.8:11 | what it makes is then **n.** longer creative. |
| T-4 ......II.11:10 | will be, because it implies **n.** change at all. |
| T-4 ........ III.1:9 | are **n.** more fatherless than you are. Your |
| T-4 ........ III.3:7 | being. **N.** one who has experienced the |
| T-4 ........ III.4:3 | the ego has **n.** allegiance to its maker. You |
| T-4 ........ III.4:6 | it. **N.** love in this world is without this |
| T-4 ........ III.4:6 | since **n.** ego has experienced love without |
| T-4 ........ III.6:1 | **N.** force except your own will is strong |
| T-4 ........ III.6:6 | Thou shalt have **n.** other gods before Him |
| T-4 ........ III.7:4 | **n.** one can see through a wall, but I can |
| T-4 ........ III.9:7 | is why we make **n.** distinction between |
| T-4 ........ IV.7:2 | concentration; it is the belief that **n.** one, |
| T-4 ........ IV.8:2 | is **n.** limit to the power of a Son of God, |
| T-4 ...... IV.10:8 | if I am real, I am **n.** more real than you are |
| T-4 ......... V.1:2 | There are **n.** exceptions except in the |
| T-4 ......... V.3:4 | identifies so closely, makes **n.** sense at all. |
| T-4 ......... V.4:8 | is **n.** point in turning to *it* for protection. |
| T-4 ......... V.4:9 | The ego has **n.** real answer to this because |
| T-4 ........ VI.3:3 | **N.** one who learns from experience that |
| T-4 ........ VI.3:7 | but you are by **n.** means convinced as yet. |
| T-4 ....... VII.5:7 | is **n.** difference between *having* and *being,* |
| T-4 ....... VII.6:3 | **n.** ego with which to accept such praise, |
| T-4 ....... VII.6:3 | and **n.** perception with which to judge it. |
| T-5 .........in.2:3 | is **n.** difference between love and joy. |
| T-5 .........in.2:6 | That is why it makes **n.** difference to what |
| T-5 ...........I.1:5 | Remember that spirit knows **n.** difference |
| T-5 ...........I.5:3 | Before that there was **n.** need for healing, |
| T-5 ...........I.5:3 | for healing, for **n.** one was comfortless. |
| T-5 ...........I.5:5 | is healed there will be **n.** Call to return. |
| T-5 ...........I.7:2 | and **n.** one who attains it could believe for |
| T-5 ..........II.2:4 | mind had **n.** calling until the separation, |
| T-5 ..........II.3:9 | world to hear only that Voice and **n.** other |
| T-5 ..........II.5:6 | for Him because He could **n.** longer share |
| T-5 ........II.7:10 | **N.** one gains from strife. What profiteth it |
| T-5 ........II.12:5 | we can accomplish together has **n.** limits, |
| T-5 ........ III.8:2 | **n.** meaning apart from your rightful place |
| T-5 ........ IV.3:4 | but in the Kingdom itself it has **n.** power. |
| T-5 ......... V.2:1 | In Heaven there is **n.** guilt, because the |
| T-5 ...... VI.10:3 | can be **n.** case against a child of God, and |
| T-5 ...... VI.12:4 | to be abolished when it is **n.** longer useful. |
| T-5 ....... VII.2:4 | there is **n.** order of difficulty in miracles. |
| T-6 .........in.1:3 | that you are in **n.** way responsible for it. |
| T-6 .........in.1:7 | *be* attacked, attack *has* **n.** justification, and |
| T-6 .........in.2:3 | and **n.** one can organize his life without |
| T-6 ...........I.6:8 | can be **n.** justification for the unjustifiable |
| T-6 ...........I.8:3 | There is **n.** choice in this, because only |
| T-6 .........I.11:5 | is that **n.** perception that is out of accord |
| T-6 .........I.16:4 | **N.** one is punished for sins, and the Sons |
| T-6 ..........II.7:2 | perception has **n.** counterpart in God, but |
| T-6 ........II.11:7 | is **n.** conflict anywhere in this perception, |
| T-6 ........II.13:3 | One. **N.** darkness abides anywhere in the |
| T-6 ........II.13:3 | part is only to allow **n.** darkness to abide |
| T-6 ........ III.1:4 | presents **n.** barrier to the communication |
| T-6 ........ III.3:2 | this fully, it sees **n.** need to protect itself. |
| T-6 ........ III.3:8 | **N.** compromise is possible in this. Teach |
| T-6 ........ IV.1:5 | and you **n.** longer need His guidance. The |
| T-6 ........ IV.5:4 | is. **N.** one in his right mind could possibly |
| T-6 ........ IV.5:4 | **n.** one in his right mind does believe it. |
| T-6 ........ IV.6:7 | and you will **n.** longer believe in dreams |
| T-6 ........ IV.6:7 | because they will have **n.** reality for you. |
| T-6 ........ IV.7:2 | is **n.** doubt, because the first question was |
| T-6 ........ IV.9:4 | you have **n.** commander except yourself. |
| T-6 ..........V.4:4 | makes **n.** distinction among dreams. He |
| T-6 ......V.A.4:1 | there is **n.** order of difficulty in miracles. |
| T-6 ......V.A.4:9 | must be **n.** range in what you offer to your |
| T-6 ......V.A.6:9 | complete alone, they are **n.** longer alone. |
| T-6 ...... V.B.6:1 | be **n.** conflict between sanity and insanity |
| T-6 ...... V.C.4:5 | it teaches there must be **n.** exceptions, |
| T-6 ... V.C.10:8 | it is already true and needs **n.** protection. |
| T-7 ...........I.4:2 | means that **n.** bargains are possible. To |
| T-7 ..........II.3:4 | Kingdom there is **n.** teaching or learning, |
| T-7 ..........II.3:4 | or learning, because there is **n.** belief. |
| T-7 ..........II.5:7 | inheritance and requires **n.** learning at all, |
| T-7 ..........II.6:1 | **N.** one questions the connection of |
| T-7 ..........II.7:3 | it. There is **n.** confusion in the Kingdom, |
| T-7 ..........II.7:6 | needs **n.** translation because it is perfectly |
| T-7 ........ IV.2:3 | inspires can have **n.** order of difficulty, |
| T-7 ........ IV.5:4 | Spirit sees **n.** order of difficulty in healing. |
| T-7 ..........V.1:3 | so apparent that they need **n.** elaboration, |
| T-7 ..........V.3:3 | He recognizes **n.** other, because He does |
| T-7 ..........V.7:7 | **n.** way contradicts the changelessness of |
| T-7 ........ VI.4:9 | **N.** one who has everything wants the ego. |
| T-7 ........ VI.7:5 | Vigilance has **n.** place in peace. It is |
| T-7 ........ VI.8:6 | It wants **n.** part of truth, because the ego |
| T-7 ...... VI.11:6 | It has **n.** meaning. It does not exist. Do |
| T-7 ...... VI.13:4 | **n.** conflict of will is possible. This is the |
| T-7 ....... VII.1:5 | Denial has **n.** power in itself, but you can |
| T-7 ....... VII.2:4 | There is **n.** way for you to have it except |
| T-7 ....... VII.2:5 | is the law of God, and it has **n.** exceptions. |
| T-7 ....... VII.3:8 | Teach **n.** one that he is what you would |
| T-7 ....... VII.4:4 | and they will have **n.** life for you because |
| T-7 ......VIII.1:1 | without projection there can be **n.** anger, |
| T-7 ......VIII.1:1 | without extension there can be **n.** love. |
| T-7 ......VIII.4:2 | There is **n.** way out of this, because it is |
| T-7 ......VIII.6:2 | and **n.** one can keep a belief he has judged |
| T-7 ......VIII.7:5 | wholeness has **n.** limits because being is |
| T-7 ........ IX.1:2 | He **n.** more wills you to deprive yourself |
| T-7 ........ IX.3:7 | but this can **n.** more interfere with their |
| T-7 ..........X.3:2 | Surely **n.** one would object to this goal if |
| T-7 ..........X.3:4 | You **n.** more recognize what is painful |
| T-7 ........X.3:11 | believed this, there would be **n.** conflict. |
| T-7 ..........X.5:8 | **N.** one gladly obeys a guide he does not |
| T-7 ..........X.7:4 | **n.** confusion in the mind of a Son of God, |
| T-7 ........ XI.1:8 | there is **n.** order of difficulty in miracles, |
| T-7 ........ XI.1:8 | is **n.** difficulty at all *because* it is a state of |
| T-7 ........ XI.2:5 | There is **n.** point in trying. A Son of God |
| T-7 ........ XI.4:2 | There are **n.** exceptions to this lesson, |
| T-8 ...........I.1:5 | made by God, Who makes **n.** bargains. It |
| T-8 ...........I.2:1 | but the ego has **n.** power to distract you |
| T-8 ...........I.3:2 | Yet in this war there is **n.** opponent. This |
| T-8 ...........I.5:8 | volatile have **n.** direction. They cannot |
| T-8 .........I.5:10 | and gives them **n.** rationale for choice. |
| T-8 ..........II.6:4 | you could **n.** more will to be without Him |
| T-8 ..........II.7:3 | It has **n.** boundaries because its extension |
| T-8 ........ III.1:5 | There is **n.** limit on your learning because |
| T-8 ........ III.1:5 | because there is **n.** limit on your mind. |
| T-8 ........ III.1:6 | There is **n.** limit on His teaching because |
| T-8 ........ III.2:2 | then, there is **n.** other experience. Yet the |
| T-8 ........ III.3:5 | Fatherhood by placing **n.** limits upon it. |
| T-8 ........ III.7:5 | God wills **n.** one suffer. He does not will |
| T-8 ........ III.7:9 | Wrong decisions have **n.** power, because |
| T-8 ...... III.7:10 | to produce is **n.** more true than they are. |
| T-8 ...... IV.8:13 | **N.** part of It can be imprisoned if Its truth |
| T-8 ..........V.2:8 | is **n.** separation of God and His creation. |
| T-8 ..........V.2:9 | **n.** separation between your will and mine |
| T-8 ........ VI.3:1 | over His Kingdom the world has **n.** power |

T-8 VI.3:2 **N.** one created by God can find joy in
T-8 VI.5:8 There is **n.** other gift that is eternal, and
T-8 VI.5:8 therefore there is **n.** other gift that is true.
T-8 VI.5:14 There can be **n.** question of its worth,
T-8 VI.6:7 **N.** one who does not accept his function
T-8 VI.6:7 and **n.** one can accept his function unless
T-8 VI.8:1 is **n.** question but one you should ever ask
T-8 VII.1:5 of attack would have **n.** appeal for you.
T-8 VII.6:5 Let **n.** Son of God remain hidden for His
T-8 VII.9:2 with little or **n.** relationship to each other,
T-8 VII.13:6 from the mind the body has **n.** purpose at
T-8 VII.15:6 **N.** more are any of its seeming results.
T-8 VII.15:8 a form of attack, then it can *have* **n.** results
T-8 VII.16:6 There is **n.** attack, but there *is* unlimited
T-8 VIII.1:15 **n.** difference between the part and whole.
T-8 VIII.2:4 ego has **n.** real use for it because it is *not* an
T-8 VIII.5:1 true that the body has **n.** function of itself
T-8 VIII.6:6 If data are meaningless there is **n.** point in
T-8 VIII.7:7 has being and the ego has **n.** knowledge,
T-8 VIII.7:7 no knowledge, then the ego has **n.** being.
T-8 VIII.8:4 perception. **N.** one can doubt the ego's
T-8 VIII.9:8 Who perceives **n.** attack on anything.
T-8 IX.4:7 Sleep is **n.** more a form of death than
T-8 IX.7:1 to take **n.** thought of the body as separate
T-8 IX.8:4 you **n.** limits because God lays none upon
T-9 I.5:3 **n.** difference between your will and God's
T-9 I.8:1 **N.** right mind can believe that its will is
T-9 I.8:2 is **n.** God or that God's Will is fearful. The
T-9 I.8:5 **n.** one really wants either abandonment
T-9 I.9:3 there are **n.** unbelievers and no sacrifices.
T-9 I.9:3 there are no unbelievers and **n.** sacrifices.
T-9 II.2:2 of it would **n.** longer *be* what you want.
T-9 II.3:3 Yet it is equally certain that **n.** response
T-9 II.6:1 You can **n.** more pray for yourself alone
T-9 III.1:4 To the Holy Spirit it makes **n.** sense at all.
T-9 III.2:5 He may be making **n.** sense at the time,
T-9 III.2:10 wrong, **n.** matter what it says or does.
T-9 III.3:2 since there is **n.** communication between
T-9 III.3:3 The ego makes **n.** sense, and the Holy
T-9 III.6:6 can have **n.** effect at all on the truth in you
T-9 III.7:6 Atonement is **n.** more separate than love.
T-9 IV.4:2 course, makes **n.** sense and will not work.
T-9 IV.5:5 What has **n.** effect does not exist, and to
T-9 IV.7:2 even though it has **n.** idea what they are.
T-9 IV.7:4 anyone and anything for **n.** reason at all.
T-9 IV.7:6 because it has **n.** idea of what it perceives.
T-9 IV.8:1 If you have **n.** idea what is happening,
T-9 IV.10:6 **n.** more have been wrong than God can.
T-9 IV.11:5 **n.** more meaning than the fantasies into
T-9 IV.11:6 or fearful, but **n.** one calls them true.
T-9 V.5:2 for why **n.** one has really explained what
T-9 V.7:4 and who **n.** longer believes in nightmares
T-9 V.8:7 He needs **n.** help for this. He will tell you
T-9 VI.6:1 Miracles have **n.** place in eternity,
T-9 VIII.3:1 because it sees **n.** difference between
T-9 VIII.3:2 but makes **n.** distinctions between these
T-9 VIII.9:2 what can be real that has **n.** witnesses?
T-9 VIII.9:4 if **n.** good can come of it the Holy Spirit
T-9 VIII.10:2 **N.** one else can fill your part in it, and
T-9 VIII.11:2 not establish your value and it needs **n.**
T-10 I.4:2 Them you will have **n.** wish to sleep, but
T-10 III.1:3 **N.** one can will to destroy himself. When
T-10 III.1:7 destruction is **n.** more real than the image
T-10 III.2:7 it is the awareness that **n.** one is separate,
T-10 III.2:7 no one is separate, and so **n.** one is sick.
T-10 III.6:1 There are **n.** idolaters in the Kingdom,
T-10 III.6:2 God's Son knows **n.** idols, but he does
T-10 III.8:3 But have **n.** other gods before Him or you
T-10 III.11:3 when you place **n.** other gods before Him.
T-10 IV.4:4 and there are **n.** other laws beside His.
T-10 IV.6:2 are **n.** strange images in the Mind of God,
T-10 IV.6:6 is. **N.** false gods you attempt to interpose
T-10 V.1:7 **N.** one can really do this, but that you can
T-11 in.2:5 Make **n.** mistake about this. It sounds
T-11 I.2:1 but how can this be if infinity has **n.** end?
T-11 I.2:2 end? **N.** one can be beyond the limitless,
T-11 I.2:2 what has **n.** limits must be everywhere.
T-11 I.2:3 are **n.** beginnings and no endings in God,
T-11 I.2:3 are no beginnings and **n.** endings in God,
T-11 I.3:5 cannot be blocked, and it has **n.** voids. It
T-11 I.4:1 only in time, but time has **n.** meaning.
T-11 I.4:2 Who placed **n.** limits on His creation or
T-11 I.5:5 There is **n.** end to God and His Son, for
T-11 III.1:5 knows **n.** attack and His peace surrounds
T-11 III.1:6 very quiet, for there is **n.** conflict in Him.
T-11 III.3:4 joy could **n.** more be contained than His.
T-11 III.6:2 Son, for they have **n.** place in His temple.
T-11 III.6:3 there *are* **n.** other gods to place before Him
T-11 III.7:10 and **n.** part of the Son can be excluded if
T-11 IV.4:6 for there is **n.** distinction between within
T-11 IV.8:2 There is **n.** condemnation in the Son, for
T-11 IV.8:2 for there is **n.** condemnation in the Father
T-11 V.1:1 **N.** one can escape from illusions unless
T-11 V.1:2 There is **n.** need to shrink from illusions,
T-11 V.2:5 that what has **n.** effects does not exist.
T-11 V.3:7 *is not of Him has* **n.** *power to do anything.*
T-11 V.10:8 And **n.** one wants to find what he believes
T-11 V.15:1 ego makes **n.** attempt to understand this,
T-11 V.16:4 **n.** thought system transcends its source.
T-11 VI.3:7 perceive with Him involves **n.** strain at all.
T-11 VI.4:7 which knows **n.** time and no exceptions.
T-11 VI.4:7 which knows no time and **n.** exceptions.
T-11 VI.4:8 But make **n.** exceptions yourself, or you
T-11 VI.10:5 There is **n.** order of difficulty in miracles
T-11 VI.10:7 does not exist has **n.** size and no measure.
T-11 VI.10:7 does not exist has no size and **n.** measure.
T-11 VII.2:8 and making **n.** distinction between them.
T-11 VIII.2:5 you will see **n.** need to ask it of Him.
T-11 VIII.3:4 have accepted **n.** guide at all. Instruction
T-11 VIII.4:1 **N.** one can withhold truth except from
T-11 VIII.9:4 is in **n.** way separate from His Father,
T-11 VIII.9:6 Father, in Whom **n.** deceit is possible.
T-11 VIII.10:1 In the real world there is **n.** sickness, for
T-11 VIII.10:1 for there is **n.** separation and no division.
T-11 VIII.10:1 for there is no separation and **n.** division.
T-11 VIII.10:2 and because **n.** one is without your help,
T-11 VIII.12:2 by Him, for there is **n.** offense in Him. If
T-11 VIII.12:4 perceive **n.** one but through His guidance,
T-11 VIII.13:3 into a dream he is **n.** longer afraid, and
T-12 I.3:2 it requires **n.** effort at all on your part.
T-12 I.3:6 **N.** response can be appropriate except
T-12 I.5:2 **N.** one with a personal investment is a
T-12 I.6:5 reality, for reality evokes **n.** conflict at all.
T-12 II.2:2 give **n.** power to the fog to obscure the
T-12 II.6:1 **n.** nightmare can defeat a child of God in
T-12 II.8:1 There is **n.** fear in perfect love. We will
T-12 III.1:2 **n.** investment in anything in this world,
T-12 III.4:8 **N.** "outrageous" requests can be made of
T-12 III.6:7 world, for there is **n.** world outside of him
T-12 III.9:4 is why you have **n.** control over the world
T-12 IV.3:1 is surely obvious that **n.** one wants to find
T-12 IV.6:3 pay **n.** price for life for that was given you,
T-12 IV.6:8 be **n.** disinherited parts of the Sonship,
T-12 V.1:2 attack because they see **n.** need to do so.
T-12 V.1:5 **N.** longer perceiving yourself and your
T-12 V.2:2 are recognizing that attack has **n.** effect.
T-12 V.2:5 you will **n.** longer see any sense in attack,
T-12 V.2:8 You therefore have **n.** need to "equalize"
T-12 V.3:1 that your attack on yourself has **n.** effects.
T-12 V.3:4 has never been, it has **n.** consequences.
T-12 VI.1:2 your soul and there is **n.** gain in the world
T-12 VI.1:4 only is there **n.** profit in the investment,
T-12 VI.7:4 The world has **n.** purpose as it blends into
T-12 VII.1:3 that you have learned there is **n.** order of
T-12 VII.1:4 There is **n.** situation to which miracles do
T-12 VII.12:7 reserving **n.** judgment at all for yourself.
T-12 VIII.3:4 Yet it is **n.** more up to you to decide what
T-12 VIII.4:1 for **n.** one can forget what God Himself
T-12 VIII.4:8 is **n.** more past than future, being forever
T-12 VIII.6:2 is not real cannot be seen and has **n.** value
T-12 VIII.6:3 could not offer His Son what has **n.** value,
T-12 VIII.7:10 did not give you has **n.** power over you,
T-13 in.2:10 are laid in the ground, and are **n.** more.
T-13 in.3:2 For **n.** Father could subject His children
T-13 in.3:6 Adam's "sin" could have touched **n.** one,
T-13 in.4:6 having sinned, he has **n.** need of salvation
T-13 I.2:5 be. Without guilt the ego has **n.** life, and
T-13 I.3:3 "sinned" in the past, but there is **n.** past.
T-13 I.3:4 Always has **n.** direction. Time seems to go
T-13 I.6:1 will realize there is **n.** guilt in God's Son.
T-13 I.7:1 you will realize that there is **n.** journey,
T-13 I.7:3 There is **n.** road to travel on, and no time
T-13 I.7:3 to travel on, and **n.** time to travel through
T-13 I.8:4 **N.** one who believes this can understand
T-13 I.11:2 then, there is **n.** escape from guilt. For
T-13 I.11:3 if it is real there *is* **n.** way to overcome it.
T-13 II.2:3 the guilt, but you have **n.** idea why. On
T-13 II.2:5 **n.** idea that you are failing the Son of God
T-13 II.2:6 Believing you are **n.** longer you, you do
T-13 II.8:5 Make **n.** mistake about the depth of this
T-13 II.9:3 **n.** dark cloud will remain between you
T-13 III.1:4 said that **n.** one will countenance fear if
T-13 III.8:6 and **n.** illusions can satisfy him or save
T-13 III.9:2 But exempt **n.** one from your love, or you
T-13 III.10:5 for he **n.** longer understood his Father. He
T-13 III.12:8 **N.** one who hears His answer but will give
T-13 IV.1:4 and you have **n.** function at all in Heaven.
T-13 IV.1:5 leaving you **n.** inheritance except the dust
T-13 IV.3:2 **n.** one would claim that it proves there *is*
T-13 IV.5:1 "Now" has **n.** meaning to the ego. The
T-13 IV.6:2 **n.** hold over you unless you bring them
T-13 IV.6:3 in retaliation for a past that is **n.** more.
T-13 IV.6:8 For you would be meeting **n.** one, and the
T-13 IV.8:2 it closes over the present so that **n.** gap in
T-13 V.1:8 maker, and so they have **n.** meaning at all
T-13 V.2:4 For these figures have **n.** witnesses, being
T-13 V.3:4 And **n.** one hears their answer save him
T-13 V.6:2 there, and you hear what makes **n.** sound.
T-13 V.6:4 You communicate with **n.** one, and you
T-13 V.8:5 go and all you made you will **n.** longer see
T-13 V.9:8 And there perception is **n.** more, for He
T-13 V.11:3 for He is **n.** more alone than they are.
T-13 VI.1:2 **n.** illusions can rise to meet your sight, for
T-13 VI.1:2 for reality leaves **n.** room for any error.
T-13 VI.1:4 His past has **n.** reality in the present, so
T-13 VI.2:3 with **n.** reference at all to the past, either
T-13 VI.2:4 can cast **n.** shadow to darken the present,
T-13 VI.3:2 Christ as revealed to you now has **n.** past,
T-13 VI.3:3 as He was created, there is **n.** guilt in Him.
T-13 VI.3:4 **N.** cloud of guilt has risen to obscure Him
T-13 VI.5:4 Let **n.** dark cloud out of your past obscure
T-13 VI.6:5 was, and will be when time is **n.** more. In
T-13 VI.7:5 where there is **n.** sight of what you were,
T-13 VI.8:5 There is **n.** darkness in him anywhere, for
T-13 VI.13:6 his Father, he has **n.** past apart from Him.
T-13 VII.1:2 It has **n.** buildings and there are no streets
T-13 VII.1:2 It has no buildings and there are **n.** streets
T-13 VII.1:3 There are **n.** stores where people buy an
T-13 VII.1:5 is **n.** day that brightens and grows dim.
T-13 VII.1:6 dim. There is **n.** loss. Nothing is there but
T-13 VII.3:3 and **n.** city that you built has withstood
T-13 VII.6:1 **N.** one in this distracted world but has
T-13 VII.9:4 is. Knowledge needs **n.** correction. Yet the
T-13 VII.10:7 the Holy Spirit the answer would be **n.**.
T-13 VII.10:13 it bids you get, leaving you **n.** joy in them.
T-13 VII.12:7 Therefore He has **n.** investment in the
T-13 VII.12:8 He wills **n.** delay to wait upon your joyous
T-13 VII.13:2 them with **n.** emphasis at all upon them.
T-13 VII.13:6 become, **n.** world outside himself holds
T-13 VII.13:7 Within himself he has **n.** needs, for light
T-13 VIII.1:3 therefore **n.** one in the world can know. It
T-13 VIII.1:5 eternity, and utilizes **n.** perception at all.
T-13 VIII.2:2 whole, and therefore **n.** aspect is separate.
T-13 VIII.2:8 Yet **n.** perception, however holy, will last
T-13 VIII.3:5 formulation of reality, with **n.** effect at all.
T-13 VIII.4:1 the Son, the Holy Spirit has **n.** function.
T-13 VIII.4:3 He has **n.** Thoughts He does not share.
T-13 VIII.8:2 leave **n.** one untouched and no one left
T-13 VIII.8:2 no one untouched and **n.** one left alone.
T-13 VIII.9:5 They need **n.** healing, nor do you, when
T-13 IX.1:3 Fidelity to this law lets **n.** light in, for it
T-13 IX.1:5 Therefore give **n.** obedience to its laws,
T-13 IX.2:2 *Make* **n.** *one fearful,* for his guilt is yours,
T-13 IX.3:1 **n.** meaning apart from what you found in
T-13 IX.6:1 See **n.** one, then, as guilty, and you will
T-13 IX.8:10 He knows there is **n.** difference, for He
T-13 X.1:4 which they bear **n.** real relationship at all.

T-13 X.2:1 Insane ideas have **n.** real relationships,
T-13 X.2:2 **N.** real relationship can rest on guilt, or
T-13 X.2:9 **N.** one who would unite in any way with
T-13 X.4:3 weird associations to it have **n.** meaning
T-13 X.4:4 whom you find **n.** real relationships at all.
T-13 X.5:2 Use **n.** relationship to hold you to the past
T-13 X.5:4 to your Father, you will see **n.** guilt in you.
T-13 X.6:3 is always totally insane, and has **n.** reason
T-13 X.7:3 Give **n.** reality to guilt, and see no reason
T-13 X.7:3 no reality to guilt, and see **n.** reason for it.
T-13 X.10:2 There is **n.** other way to look within and
T-13 X.10:4 There is **n.** fear in love, for love is guiltless
T-13 X.10:5 always loved your Father can have **n.** fear,
T-13 X.11:5 Him, for there is **n.** love apart from His.
T-13 X.11:6 true, you will have **n.** idea what love is like
T-13 X.11:7 **N.** one who condemns a brother can see
T-13 X.11:11 *his Father that* ***n.*** *guilt has ever touched him.*
T-13 X.12:1 **N.** illusion that you have ever held
T-13 XI.1:2 Yet **n.** one sees himself in conflict and
T-13 XI.1:5 **N.** one finds himself ravaged and torn in
T-13 XI.3:10 is **n.** darkness and there is no contrast.
T-13 XI.3:10 is no darkness and there is **n.** contrast.
T-13 XI.3:11 contrast. There is **n.** variation. There is no
T-13 XI.3:12 There is **n.** interruption. There is a sense
T-13 XI.3:13 deep that **n.** dream in this world has ever
T-13 XI.6:7 For you will need **n.** contrast to help you
T-13 XI.8:9 is **n.** chance that Heaven will not be yours
T-13 XI.9:5 sleeping Son holds **n.** power over him. He
T-13 XI.11:5 **n.** possibility that the plan the Holy Spirit
T-14 I.2:7 There is **n.** area of your perception that it
T-14 II.3:8 *You will find* ***n.*** *deception there, but only the*
T-14 III.1:4 and serves **n.** useful function at all.
T-14 III.2:5 There is **n.** conflict here. To wish for guilt
T-14 III.3:1 is **n.** compromise that you can make with
T-14 III.4:4 **n.** alternatives except truth and illusion.
T-14 III.4:5 And there is **n.** overlap between them,
T-14 III.5:6 this or does it not will make **n.** difference;
T-14 III.6:1 **N.** penalty is ever asked of God's Son
T-14 III.6:4 to learn that nothing has **n.** power. And
T-14 III.6:6 joy of learning that darkness has **n.** power
T-14 III.7:6 **N.** one can hurt the Son of God. His guilt
T-14 III.8:2 Teach **n.** one he has hurt you, for if you
T-14 III.9:4 **N.** thought of God's Son can be separate
T-14 III.10:6 as naturally as peace that knows **n.** limits.
T-14 III.12:6 it. Make **n.** decisions about what it is or
T-14 III.13:5 You have **n.** other "enemy," and against
T-14 III.15:2 which **n.** one in this world or Heaven
T-14 III.15:4 cannot happen can have **n.** effects to fear.
T-14 III.17:2 He leaves you **n.** one outside you. And so
T-14 IV.1:8 Beyond the First there is **n.** other, for
T-14 IV.1:8 First there is no other, for there is **n.** order
T-14 IV.1:8 for there is no order, **n.** second or third,
T-14 IV.4:2 God breaks **n.** barriers; neither did He
T-14 IV.4:8 Remember that there is **n.** second to Him.
T-14 IV.6:2 There is **n.** effort, and you will be led as
T-14 IV.8:4 for there is **n.** parallel in your experience
T-14 V.1:12 There is **n.** guilt in you, for God is blessed
T-14 V.6:2 **n.** unity of learning goals apart from this.
T-14 V.6:3 There is **n.** conflict in this curriculum,
T-14 V.6:6 There is **n.** pain, no trial, no fear that
T-14 V.6:6 There is no pain, **n.** trial, no fear that
T-14 V.6:6 trial, **n.** fear that teaching this can fail to
T-14 V.7:2 **N.** one can be untouched by teaching
T-14 V.7:6 The circle of Atonement has **n.** end. And
T-14 V.8:2 purity, from which **n.** one is excluded.
T-14 V.8:4 **n.** one left outside to suffer guilt alone.
T-14 V.10:1 crucifixion had **n.** part in the Atonement.
T-14 V.11:8 Cast **n.** one out, for here is what he seeks
T-14 VI.1:6 be clear and you would be **n.** longer in the
T-14 VI.2:3 There is **n.** darkness that the light of love
T-14 VI.3:6 and what was fearful will be so **n.** longer.
T-14 VI.6:2 It has **n.** meaning, for its purpose is not
T-14 VI.8:3 keep **n.** source of interference from His
T-14 VI.8:6 are **n.** hidden chambers in God's temple.
T-14 VI.8:8 **N.** one can fail to come where God has
T-14 VII.2:8 you see **n.** reason to believe that the more
T-14 VII.5:3 needs **n.** protection does not defend itself.
T-14 VIII.2:3 **N.** altar stands to God without His Son.
T-14 VIII.3:8 They have **n.** opposite, and nothing else

T-14 VIII.4:1 There is **n.** substitute for truth. And truth
T-14 VIII.5:4 Lay **n.** gifts other than this upon your
T-14 IX.2:2 the contradiction can **n.** longer stand.
T-14 IX.5:3 Yet **n.** reflections of the images of other
T-14 IX.6:3 reflection of God needs **n.** interpretation.
T-14 IX.6:5 to see, **n.** one can fail to understand. It is
T-14 IX.8:2 There is **n.** contradiction in what holiness
T-14 IX.8:6 God is **n.** image, and His creations, as
T-14 X.1:1 When **n.** perception stands between God
T-14 X.2:3 **n.** longer be satisfied with anything but
T-14 X.2:4 earth have **n.** conception of limitlessness,
T-14 X.5:6 of you, **n.** order at all would be possible.
T-14 X.6:1 **n.** basis at all for ordering your thoughts.
T-14 X.6:7 which requires **n.** judgment of your own.
T-14 X.6:14 There is **n.** order of difficulty here. A call
T-14 X.9:5 For **n.** one alone can judge the ego truly.
T-14 X.9:6 can **n.** longer defend its lack of content.
T-14 X.10:3 it. Take **n.** thought for yourself, for no
T-14 X.10:3 for **n.** thought you hold *is* for yourself. If
T-14 X.11:2 God has **n.** secret communications, for
T-14 XI.3:4 learning gives the present **n.** meaning at
T-14 XI.3:9 Put **n.** confidence at all in darkness to
T-14 XI.7:3 make **n.** needs his Father will not meet, if
T-14 XI.9:2 have **n.** problems that He cannot solve by
T-14 XI.9:6 There are **n.** dark lessons He has not
T-14 XI.10:7 that **n.** dark lesson of guilt can abide in
T-15 I.1:1 imagine what it means to have **n.** cares,
T-15 I.1:1 what it means to have no cares, **n.** worries
T-15 I.1:1 to have no cares, no worries, **n.** anxieties,
T-15 I.1:5 you will **n.** longer need a teacher or time
T-15 I.2:9 Spirit the goal is life, which *has* **n.** end.
T-15 I.4:7 **N.** one who follows the ego's teaching is
T-15 I.5:5 there, its only value is that it is **n.** more.
T-15 I.6:7 **n.** one who considers himself as deserving
T-15 I.7:1 Holy Spirit teaches thus: There is **n.** hell.
T-15 I.7:6 There is **n.** escape from fear in the ego's
T-15 I.8:3 There is **n.** fear in the present when each
T-15 I.8:7 is there. **N.** darkness is remembered, and
T-15 I.9:1 This lesson takes **n.** time. For what is
T-15 I.9:3 it takes **n.** time at all to be what you are.
T-15 I.9:7 and with **n.** sense of change with time.
T-15 I.10:6 is **n.** change in Heaven because there is no
T-15 I.10:6 Heaven because there is **n.** change in God
T-15 I.11:3 He asks **n.** more, for He has no need of
T-15 I.11:3 asks no more, for He has **n.** need of more.
T-15 I.15:8 not. And so it is **n.** longer time at all. For
T-15 II.1:4 **N.** more are you. For unless God is bound
T-15 II.4:14 Spirit. And then you will doubt **n.** more.
T-15 II.5:3 **N.** gift of God is recognized in any other
T-15 III.2:4 that there is **n.** form of littleness that can
T-15 III.4:1 is **n.** doubt about what your function is,
T-15 III.4:2 There is **n.** doubt about its magnitude, for
T-15 III.6:9 Touch **n.** one, then, with littleness in the
T-15 III.9:2 not for yourself alone, **n.** more than I did.
T-15 III.10:4 Will. Accept **n.** less, remembering that
T-15 III.10:5 I can **n.** more accept it as what it is not,
T-15 III.10:6 And **n.** more can you. When you have
T-15 III.10:7 will make **n.** more gifts to offer to yourself
T-15 III.11:4 will we let **n.** one forget what you would
T-15 IV.2:8 peace is of God, and **n.** one beside Him.
T-15 IV.3:2 value **n.** plan of the ego before the plan of
T-15 IV.8:4 If the answer is **n.**, then the Holy Spirit's
T-15 IV.9:1 you have **n.** thoughts that are not pure.
T-15 IV.9:5 would not be if there were **n.** need for it.
T-15 IV.9:10 and hostage to **n.** one and to nothing.
T-15 V.1:5 You would make **n.** attempt to judge,
T-15 V.3:2 unlike to God, Who knows **n.** special love
T-15 V.5:1 The Holy Spirit knows **n.** one is special.
T-15 V.5:4 to have it serve **n.** need but His. All the
T-15 V.6:2 There *is* **n.** substitute for love. If you would
T-15 V.8:2 In the holy instant **n.** one is special, for
T-15 V.8:2 for your personal needs intrude on **n.** one
T-15 V.9:7 and you have **n.** need to look without and
T-15 V.10:9 are joined in Christ are in **n.** way separate.
T-15 V.11:3 you, you have **n.** need except to extend it.
T-15 V.11:4 holy instant there is **n.** conflict of needs,
T-15 VI.4:7 lies peace, for here there *is* **n.** conflict.
T-15 VI.5:1 scarcity, love has **n.** meaning and peace is
T-15 VI.5:2 **n.** one is aware that perfect love is in him.

T-15 VI.5:4 By holding it within itself, there *is* **n.** loss.
T-15 VI.6:5 **N.** one who has not yet experienced the
T-15 VI.6:9 it. Let **n.** need you perceive obscure your
T-15 VI.8:3 is **n.** exclusion in the holy instant because
T-15 VII.1:2 There is **n.** other love that can satisfy you,
T-15 VII.1:2 satisfy you, because there *is* **n.** other love.
T-15 VII.2:6 so weak that it would have **n.** hold at all,
T-15 VII.2:6 at all, except that **n.** one recognizes it. For
T-15 VII.2:7 and has **n.** attraction at all to anyone who
T-15 VII.3:3 go. **N.** one would choose to let go what he
T-15 VII.3:7 of God can have **n.** real investment here.
T-15 VII.4:3 ego wishes **n.** one well. Yet its survival
T-15 VII.6:4 and recognizes that **n.** one could interpret
T-15 VII.8:6 Ideas are basically of **n.** concern, except as
T-15 VII.8:9 because he would **n.** longer believe that
T-15 VII.10:2 will learn that love brings **n.** guilt at all,
T-15 VII.14:2 the holy instant guilt holds **n.** attraction,
T-15 VII.14:3 communication, has **n.** function here.
T-15 VII.14:4 Here there is **n.** concealment, and no
T-15 VII.14:4 no concealment, and **n.** private thoughts.
T-15 VII.14:6 for there is **n.** desire to exclude anyone
T-15 VIII.2:1 have need of **n.** special relationships at all
T-15 VIII.4:7 knows of **n.** separation from His Father,
T-15 IX.1:6 will be **n.** delay when you are ready for it.
T-15 IX.2:6 real relationships, which have **n.** limits,
T-15 IX.3:2 the ego has **n.** purpose you would share
T-15 IX.5:2 **N.** one can hear Him speak of this and
T-15 IX.6:1 You have **n.** conception of the limits you
T-15 IX.6:1 **n.** idea of all the loveliness that you could
T-15 IX.7:1 place **n.** value on it as a means of getting
T-15 IX.7:1 will be **n.** interference in communication
T-15 IX.7:2 will learn you have **n.** need of a body at all
T-15 IX.7:3 all. In the holy instant there are **n.** bodies,
T-15 IX.7:4 place **n.** limits on your union with Him.
T-15 X.1:10 for it has **n.** meaning if we are apart.
T-15 X.2:2 liberating instant **n.** guilt is laid upon the
T-15 X.3:2 real, guilt will hold **n.** attraction for you.
T-15 X.5:6 You see **n.** other alternatives, for you
T-15 X.8:7 you. **N.** partial sacrifice will appease this
T-15 X.9:1 it keeps **n.** bargains and would leave you
T-15 X.9:3 for there are **n.** alternatives but these. You
T-15 XI.1:6 when you have **n.** more need of sleep.
T-15 XI.2:4 **N.** sacrifice of any kind, of anyone, is
T-15 XI.2:7 **n.** thought alien to His Oneness can abide
T-15 XI.2:9 it. **N.** fear can touch the Host Who cradles
T-15 XI.3:5 and without pain there can be **n.** sacrifice.
T-15 XI.6:4 and it has **n.** meaning apart from you. It
T-15 XI.6:5 you prefer to keep that has **n.** meaning,
T-15 XI.8:1 **n.** despair darken the joy of Christmas,
T-15 XI.8:2 by demanding **n.** sacrifice of anyone, for
T-16 I.2:5 Make **n.** mistake about this maneuver;
T-16 I.5:2 And yet you recognize **n.** triumph but this
T-16 I.7:4 **N.** needs will long be left unmet if you
T-16 II.1:7 itself? One attribute is **n.** more difficult to
T-16 II.6:1 **N.** evidence will convince you of the truth
T-16 II.8:7 There is **n.** greater love than to accept this
T-16 III.7:7 His Kingdom has **n.** limits and no end,
T-16 III.7:7 His Kingdom has no limits and **n.** end,
T-16 III.9:2 **n.** fear that the attraction of those who
T-16 IV.1:7 sight, and to make **n.** attempt to hide it.
T-16 IV.3:2 makes **n.** attempt to rise above the storm,
T-16 IV.5:1 There are **n.** triumphs of love. Only hate
T-16 IV.5:6 There *is* **n.** conflict in the choice between
T-16 IV.5:7 Seen in these terms, **n.** one would hesitate
T-16 IV.8:7 **N.** specialness can offer you what God has
T-16 IV.11:4 not the call of hate, and see **n.** fantasies.
T-16 IV.12:1 Your Father can **n.** more forget the truth
T-16 IV.13:9 is **n.** veil the Love of God in us together
T-16 V.3:4 **N.** one considers it bizarre to love and
T-16 V.5:2 There can be **n.** disagreement on this,
T-16 V.7:4 for there is **n.** increase and no extension.
T-16 V.7:4 for there is no increase and **n.** extension.
T-16 V.12:3 There is **n.** meaning in the form, and
T-16 V.12:10 **N.** rituals that you have set up in which
T-16 V.14:4 will have **n.** difficulty in perceiving the
T-16 VI.1:3 has special value it has **n.** meaning, for it
T-16 VI.1:6 Love has **n.** meaning except as its Creator
T-16 VI.2:3 **n.** longer seek for union in separation,
T-16 VI.6:4 you will see **n.** need at all to magnify it.

T-16......VI.7:7 be **n.** meaning you would still seek here.
T-16......VI.8:8 For you are **n.** longer wholly insane, and
T-16....VI.10:2 Now **n.** one need suffer, for you have
T-16....VI.10:5 See **n.** illusion of truth and beauty there.
T-16....VI.11:5 The joy of Heaven, which has **n.** limit, is
T-16....VI.11:6 it. Wait **n.** longer, for the Love of God and
T-16.....VII.2:3 **N.** special relationship is experienced in
T-16.....VII.2:5 It has **n.** meaning in the present, and if it
T-16.....VII.4:2 There is **n.** fantasy that does not contain
T-16.....VII.8:2 God's gifts have **n.** reality apart from your
T-16.....VII.9:3 reality has **n.** past, and only illusions can
T-16...VII.11:5 relationship with Him and to **n.** other.
T-16...VII.12:1 *with You, in which there are* **n.** *illusions, and*
T-17.........I.1:7 that they had **n.** effect upon reality at all,
T-17.........I.5:2 Truth *has* **n.** meaning in illusion. The
T-17.........I.5:7 you. There is **n.** order in reality, because
T-17....... II.1:2 In **n.** fantasy have you ever seen anything
T-17....... II.2:3 and there are **n.** fantasies to hide the truth
T-17....... II.3:3 **N.** one but Him Who planned salvation
T-17....... II.3:5 **n.** one and nothing remain still bound by
T-17....... II.4:2 used for learning will have **n.** function.
T-17....... II.4:3 will ever change; **n.** shifts nor shadings,
T-17....... II.4:3 no shifts nor shadings, **n.** differences, no
T-17....... II.4:3 no differences, **n.** variations that made
T-17....... II.5:3 show you that there is **n.** reason here at all
T-17....... II.7:4 closing of the dream will have **n.** meaning
T-17....III.1:11 clearly for the separation that **n.** one not
T-17......III.2:5 **n.** matter how distorted the associations
T-17......III.5:5 **N.** longer does the past conflict with *now.*
T-17......III.6:2 to guarantee there will be **n.** solution. The
T-17......III.7:5 has left **n.** part of it without Himself. This
T-17......IV.5:6 The separation has nothing in it, **n.** part,
T-17......IV.5:6 has nothing in it, no part, **n.** "reason,"
T-17......IV.5:6 and **n.** attribute that is not insane. And its
T-17......IV.9:5 is the frame, for there you see **n.** conflict.
T-17....IV.10:2 The truth itself needs **n.** defense, but you
T-17....IV.13:6 by the frame, it has **n.** meaning.
T-17....IV.14:2 There is **n.** distraction here. The picture
T-17....IV.15:3 is **n.** figured representation of a thought
T-17....IV.16:3 and keeping **n.** illusions of where they are
T-17....... V.3:1 Holy Spirit wastes **n.** time in introducing
T-17....... V.3:7 Now it seems to make **n.** sense. Many
T-17....... V.4:5 there is **n.** course except to change the
T-17....... V.5:8 organization of their perception **n.** longer
T-17....... V.8:2 it will seem at times to have **n.** purpose. A
T-17......VI.2:9 but only that. It has **n.** positive goal at all.
T-17......VI.3:1 and makes **n.** sense until it has already
T-17......VI.3:4 but you have **n.** idea what should happen.
T-17......VI.3:5 **N.** goal was set with which to bring the
T-17......VI.6:7 **N.** one will fail in anything. This seems to
T-17.....VII.2:1 There is **n.** problem in any situation that
T-17.....VII.2:2 **n.** shift in any aspect of the problem but
T-17.....VII.6:4 **N.** relationship is holy unless its holiness
T-17.....VII.7:1 you have **n.** idea how great the strength
T-17.....VII.8:7 There is **n.** cause for faithlessness, but
T-17...VII.8:11 There is **n.** situation that does not involve
T-17...VII.10:2 You are **n.** longer wholly insane, nor no
T-17...VII.10:2 longer wholly insane, nor **n.** longer alone.
T-17... VIII.3:6 which faith can **n.** longer be withheld.
T-17... VIII.3:8 answer truth with faith entails **n.** strain at
T-17... VIII.6:2 and you had faith in it for **n.** one accepts
T-18.........I.3:6 **N.** one is seen complete. The body is
T-18.........I.6:6 and take **n.** part in all the mad projection
T-18.........I.7:6 insanely in the wind, have **n.** substance.
T-18.........I.7:9 in form are **n.** real differences at all. None
T-18.........I.9:4 in which **n.** substitution can enter, and
T-18.........I.9:9 help Him show you that **n.** substitute you
T-18...... I.10:1 In you there is **n.** separation, and no
T-18...... I.10:1 and **n.** substitute can keep you from your
T-18...... I.10:2 was God's creation, and has **n.** substitute.
T-18...... I.12:1 God has called should hear **n.** substitutes.
T-18...... I.13:2 It is the only one that has **n.** limits, and
T-18....... II.2:1 they have **n.** concern with what is true.
T-18....... II.3:6 **N.** limits on substitution are laid upon
T-18....... II.9:2 This is **n.** dream. Its coming means that
T-18......III.1:4 in which **n.** ray of light could enter. And
T-18......III.5:4 **N.** little, faltering footsteps that you may
T-18......III.7:7 for **n.** two minds can join in the desire for
T-18....... V.1:2 the Atonement would have **n.** meaning.
T-18....... V.1:3 is accomplished, would have **n.** purpose.
T-18....... V.5:1 **n.** dream to love your brother as yourself.
T-18...... VI.5:4 destroy can have **n.** real effect at all. What
T-18...... VI.6:8 done this to a thing that has **n.** meaning,
T-18...... VI.8:8 Within itself it has **n.** limits, and there is
T-18...... VI.9:3 is **n.** barrier between God and His Son,
T-18..VI.11:10 to peace, asking **n.** questions of reality,
T-18.... VI.13:1 There is **n.** violence at all in this escape.
T-18.....VII.1:4 **N.** one accepts Atonement for himself
T-18.....VII.3:1 **n.** single instant does the body exist at all.
T-18.....VII.3:6 avoided. It has **n.** attraction *now.* Its whole
T-18.....VII.4:1 you are willing to see **n.** past or future.
T-18.....VII.7:6 needs do nothing has **n.** need for time. To
T-18... VIII.4:4 And what it thinks it is in **n.** way changes
T-18... VIII.5:2 living alone and in **n.** way joined to the
T-18... VIII.5:3 but by **n.** means totally dependent on its
T-18... VIII.6:5 little aspect is **n.** different from the whole,
T-18... VIII.6:6 It leads **n.** separate life, because its life *is*
T-18... VIII.7:8 you think you set apart is **n.** exception.
T-18... VIII.8:1 Love knows **n.** bodies, and reaches to
T-18. VIII.10:3 leaving **n.** lonely little kingdoms locked
T-18. VIII.11:3 interposed **n.** barriers to interfere with its
T-18. VIII.11:7 **N.** part of love calls on the whole in vain.
T-18. VIII.11:8 vain. **N.** Son of God remains outside His
T-18. VIII.12:4 You could **n.** more know God alone than
T-18. VIII.12:5 together you could **n.** more be unaware of
T-18...... IX.1:4 fully in God's keeping, and needs **n.** guide
T-18...... IX.3:5 There are **n.** messages that speak of what
T-18...... IX.6:3 has **n.** power at all to hold back anyone
T-18...... IX.8:1 guilt, **n.** more impenetrable and no more
T-18...... IX.8:1 impenetrable and **n.** more substantial.
T-18...... IX.8:3 of light whereon they cast **n.** shadows.
T-18...... IX.9:5 there is **n.** attack upon the Son of God,
T-18.... IX.11:4 where He begins, and where there *is* **n.** end
T-19.........I.3:2 It *needs* **n.** healing. Its health or sickness
T-19.........I.7:1 Truth and illusion have **n.** connection.
T-19.........I.9:7 There is **n.** justification for faithlessness,
T-19.......I.10:4 His Love you would keep **n.** one separate
T-19.......I.14:5 **N.** error interferes with its calm sight,
T-19.......I.15:4 **n.** longer needed when the lesson has
T-19....... II.7:1 **n.** stone in all the ego's embattled citadel
T-19....... II.7:2 To the ego, this is **n.** mistake. For this is
T-19...... III.9:5 you give it **n.** power over your brother.
T19... IV.A.3:6 It has **n.** opposition, for there is none
T19... IV.A.4:3 could **n.** more depart from you than from
T19. IV.A.4:10 have **n.** purpose apart from your brother,
T19... IV.A.5:1 overcome the world is **n.** more difficult
T19... IV.A.5:3 There is **n.** order of difficulty in miracles,
T19... IV.A.5:6 Guilt can raise **n.** real barriers against it.
T19... IV.A.6:3 **N.** illusions stand between you and your
T19... IV.A.6:7 sun? **N.** more can you be kept by shadows
T19... IV.A.7:2 upon anything, for it has **n.** purpose now.
T19... IV.A.7:4 causing **n.** more than tiny interruptions
T19... IV.A.8:2 **n.** longer an unrelenting barrier to peace.
T19. IV.A.10:6 guilt completely, it sees **n.** fear. Being
T19. IV.A.12:6 him. **N.** little shred of guilt escapes their
T19. IV.A.14:4 be as careful to let **n.** little act of charity,
T19. IV.A.14:4 charity, **n.** tiny expression of forgiveness,
T19. IV.A.14:4 **n.** little breath of love escape their notice.
T19. IV.A.15:1 gives you, wanting **n.** messages but theirs,
T19. IV.A.15:1 but theirs, you will see fear **n.** more. The
T19. IV.A.15:3 contains **n.** fear that you laid not upon it.
T19. IV.A.16:1 set in a quiet garden where **n.** sound but
T19. IV.A.17:7 Mine was of **n.** greater value than yours;
T19. IV.A.17:7 **n.** better means for communication of
T19. IV.A.17:8 **N.** one can die for anyone, and death does
T19....IV.B.3:5 body's pleasure; it *has* **n.** hope of pleasure.
T19....IV.B.4:3 second obstacle is **n.** more solid than the
T19..IV.B.4:12 This has **n.** cost, but it has release from
T19....IV.B.5:3 **n.** obstacle that you can place before our
T19....IV.B.7:9 when its great advocate is heard **n.** more?
T19..IV.B.10:6 It has **n.** purpose of itself, but only what is
T19..IV.B.14:3 And just as certainly it has **n.** feeling. It
T19..IV.B.14:6 given. It has **n.** feeling for them. All of the
T19....IV.C.1:4 **N.** one can die unless he chooses death.
T19....IV.C.1:7 Yet it could have **n.** hold at all except on
T19....IV.C.2:8 This is **n.** arrogance. It is the Will of God.
T19....IV.C.5:2 The body **n.** more dies than it can feel. It
T19....IV.C.8:3 There is **n.** funeral, no dark altars, no
T19....IV.C.8:3 There is no funeral, **n.** dark altars, no
T19....IV.C.8:3 **n.** grim commandments nor twisted
T19... IV.D.1:2 think if death held **n.** attraction for you?
T19... IV.D.4:4 **n.** more afraid of death than of the ego.
T19... IV.D.7:6 **N.** mad desire, no trivial impulse to forget
T19... IV.D.7:6 desire, **n.** trivial impulse to forget again,
T19... IV.D.7:6 again, **n.** stab of fear nor the cold sweat of
T19... IV.D.8:3 **N.** obstacle to peace can be surmounted
T19... IV.D.8:5 it has **n.** power to keep you from the truth
T19... IV.D.8:6 ready to look on terror with **n.** fear at all.
T19... IV.D.9:1 **N.** one can look upon the fear of God
T19... IV.D.9:2 real. **N.** one can stand before this obstacle
T19... IV.D.9:3 **n.** one would dare to look on it without
T19. IV.D.10:5 when it is over it seems to make **n.** sense.
T19. IV.D.11:7 **n.** one reaches love with fear beside him.
T19. IV.D.15:5 **n.** grace of Heaven that you cannot offer
T19. IV.D.18:5 of his Father, Who knows **n.** sin, no death
T19. IV.D.18:5 of his Father, Who knows no sin, **n.** death
T19. IV.D.21:2 **n.** one undertakes to do what he believes
T-20.........I.1:4 A slain Christ has **n.** meaning. But a risen
T-20.........I.2:2 Let **n.** dark sign of crucifixion intervene
T-20........II.3:2 **N.** one but sees his chosen home as an
T-20........II.3:3 himself. **N.** one but seeks to draw to it the
T-20........II.4:8 will see your altar is **n.** longer what it was.
T-20........II.5:5 He sees **n.** strangers; only dearly loved
T-20........II.5:6 He sees **n.** thorns but only lilies, gleaming
T-20........II.6:5 The Holy Spirit's vision is **n.** idle gift, no
T-20........II.6:5 **n.** plaything to be tossed about a while
T-20........II.7:2 It has been given you to see **n.** thorns, no
T-20........II.7:2 **n.** strangers and no obstacles to peace.
T-20........II.7:2 no strangers and **n.** obstacles to peace.
T-20........II.7:8 and see **n.** thorns nor nails to crucify the
T-20........II.8:9 There *is* **n.** fear in love. The song of Easter
T-20......II.8:12 And there will be **n.** fear in us, for in our
T-20......II.8:12 in us, for in our vision will be **n.** illusions;
T-20...... III.1:4 Knowledge requires **n.** adjustments and,
T-20...... III.2:3 in which there are **n.** interferences, are
T-20.... III.8:11 it **n.** power to adjust the means and end.
T-20.... III.11:3 **n.** fear in perfect love *because* it knows no
T-20.... III.11:3 fear in perfect love *because* it knows **n.** sin,
T-20.... III.11:9 as sinless, and there can *be* **n.** fear in you.
T-20...... IV.1:5 He gives **n.** power to sin, and therefore it
T-20...... IV.1:6 gives **n.** power to their seeming source.
T-20...... IV.2:1 Sin has **n.** place in Heaven, where its
T-20...... IV.2:1 alien and can **n.** more enter than can their
T-20...... IV.6:4 all of it, without which is **n.** part complete
T-20...... IV.7:6 **n.** more leave one of them outside than I
T-20...... IV.8:5 leaving in your way **n.** stones to trip on,
T-20...... IV.8:5 trip on, and **n.** obstacles to bar your way.
T-20....... V.1:7 **N.** one who has a single purpose, unified
T-20....... V.1:8 **N.** one who shares his purpose with him
T-20....... V.5:2 the Holy Spirit teaches, it has **n.** function.
T-20....... V.5:4 sight that sees the body has **n.** use which
T-20....... V.6:4 from it, and the future will add **n.** more.
T-20....... V.7:5 is **n.** gift your brother's body offers you.
T-20....... V.7:8 **N.** more do you. And yet, have faith that
T-20...... VI.2:6 It has **n.** secrets; nothing that it would
T-20...... VI.3:7 And they have **n.** relationships, for no one
T-20...... VI.3:7 for **n.** one else is welcome there. They
T-20...... VI.3:8 They smile on **n.** one, and those who
T-20...... VI.4:1 Love has **n.** darkened temples where
T-20...... VI.6:5 to **n.** relationships and no return. Here is
T-20...... VI.6:5 to no relationships and **n.** return. Here is
T-20...... VI.7:7 You are an idolater **n.** longer. The Holy
T-20...... VI.8:1 There is **n.** order in relationships. They
T-20...... VI.8:3 An unholy relationship is **n.** relationship.
T-20...... VI.8:5 **N.** more than that. The instant that the
T-20...... VI.9:1 and leave **n.** trace behind their going. The
T-20...... VI.9:7 For **n.** illusions can attract the mind that
T-20.... VI.12:3 one. This is **n.** time for sadness. Perhaps
T-20..... VII.3:2 He asks **n.** more to give the means as well.
T-20..... VII.5:8 For vision, like relationships, has **n.** order
T-20..... VII.7:7 judgment has **n.** value unless the goal is
T-20..... VII.8:7 of whom is your release, is **n.** illusion.
T-20..... VII.9:7 **N.** one who loves can judge, and what he
T-20....VIII.3:4 place **n.** value on your brother's body,
T-20....VIII.5:7 There is **n.** problem, no event or situation
T-20....VIII.5:7 There is no problem, **n.** event or situation
T-20....VIII.5:7 **n.** perplexity that vision will not solve. All

T-20....VIII.8:6 purpose is **n.** longer held they disappear.
T-20..VIII.8:10 Again there is **n.** order; only a seeming
T-20..VIII.10:1 has **n.** meaning cannot be perceived. And
T-21.......in.1:3 But though it is **n.** more than that, it is
T-21.....in.1:12 And where there is **n.** meaning, there is
T-21.......in.2:5 There is **n.** choice that lies between these
T-21.........I.3:1 There is **n.** need to learn through pain.
T-21.........I.3:6 the learning of it would be **n.** problem.
T-21.........I.8:3 what is in it is **n.** longer contained at all.
T-21.........I.8:4 and with **n.** break or limit anywhere.
T-21....... II.2:2 only this, but mean it with **n.** reservations
T-21....... II.2:6 Deceive yourself **n.** longer that you are
T-21....... II.3:4 **N.** accident nor chance is possible within
T-21....... II.9:2 is **n.** better demonstration of the power of
T-21..... II.12:4 Apart from this he has **n.** power to create,
T-21...... III.2:3 your purpose and you **n.** longer want it.
T-21...... III.2:4 it. **N.** one allows a purpose to be replaced
T-21...... III.3:4 because he **n.** longer believes in them,
T-21...... III.4:6 you will have need of them **n.** longer. For
T-21...... III.8:1 brothers from the body can have **n.** fear.
T-21...... III.9:3 He makes **n.** bargains. And if you seek to
T-21.... III.10:4 of itself. And **n.** more could the body. The
T-21...... IV.1:2 will correct, but this makes **n.** one fearful.
T-21...... IV.1:6 It has **n.** fear to let you feel ashamed. It
T-21...... IV.3:1 What if you looked within and saw **n.** sin
T-21...... IV.4:6 **N.** more did you. And yet this part, with
T-21...... IV.4:8 It knows **n.** sin. How, otherwise, could it
T-21...... IV.6:1 is **n.** inconsistency in what the Holy Spirit
T-21...... IV.6:5 its ranting strikes **n.** terror in your heart.
T-21...... IV.7:7 And earth can hold **n.** longer what has
T-21...... IV.8:5 This has **n.** meaning. What matters it to
T-21....... V.2:1 needs **n.** cooperation from you to be itself
T-21..... V.3:12 change *your* mind. There *is* **n.** other.
T-21....... V.6:2 has **n.** Thoughts except the Self-extending
T-21....... V.8:2 But reason has **n.** place at all in madness,
T-21....... V.8:6 is **n.** reason in insanity, for it depends
T-21...... VI.2:9 alone have **n.** effect at all on what *is* yours?
T-21...... VI.3:1 **N.** one can think but for himself, as God
T-21...... VI.9:8 To give is **n.** more blessed than to receive.
T-21.... VI.11:5 **n.** more His Son can be imprisoned save
T-21..... VII.1:5 Enormity has **n.** appeal save to the little.
T-21..... VII.2:1 **N.** one believes the Son of God is
T-21..... VII.3:6 **n.** need to dream of power and to act out
T-21... VII.3:10 Dreams have **n.** reason in them. A flower
T-21... VII.3:13 This is **n.** army, but a madhouse. What
T-21..... VII.4:2 It has **n.** weapons and it has no enemy.
T-21..... VII.4:2 It has no weapons and it has **n.** enemy.
T-21..... VII.5:2 can be **n.** faith in sin without an enemy.
T-21..... VII.5:3 in sin would dare believe he has **n.** enemy
T-21..... VII.5:4 he admit that **n.** one made him powerless
T-21..... VII.5:5 seek **n.** longer what is not there to find.
T-21... VII.5:13 *in which I have **n.** enemies and cannot sin?*
T-21... VII.12:3 made, the answer is both "yes" and "**n.**."
T-21... VII.12:4 perceiving that "yes" must mean "not **n.**."
T-21... VII.12:5 **N.** one decides against his happiness, but
T-21... VII.13:1 place, is an illusion that has **n.** meaning.
T-21... VII.13:7 **N.** thought but has the power to release
T-21.... VIII.2:3 constancy of happiness has **n.** exceptions;
T-21.... VIII.2:3 has no exceptions; **n.** change of any kind.
T-21.... VIII.3:4 it. For **n.** one fails to ask for his desire of
T-22.......in.1:2 and need **n.** longer look on sin apart. No
T-22.......in.1:3 **N.** two can look on sin together, for they
T-22.......in.3:2 one has looked within and seen **n.** lack.
T-22.......in.3:4 He sees **n.** difference between these selves
T-22.........I.2:3 are not yours must make **n.** sense to you.
T-22.........I.3:2 You have received **n.** messages at all you
T-22.........I.3:8 it sees, you have **n.** reason not to listen,
T-22.......I.3:10 God has **n.** secrets. He does not lead you
T-22.........I.4:4 is **n.** secret that need be hidden as a sin.
T-22.........I.5:2 understand. You will perceive **n.** difficulty
T-22.........I.7:6 **n.** two brothers can unite except through
T-22.........I.8:3 For his will be **n.** alien tongue. He will
T-22.........I.8:4 He will need **n.** interpreter to you, for it
T-22.........I.8:6 Where Christ has entered **n.** one is alone,
T-22....... II.2:4 To change illusions is to make **n.** change.
T-22....... II.3:3 **N.** form of misery in reason's eyes can be
T-22..... II.3:10 but equally unreal. This is **n.** difference.
T-22....... II.5:2 for you to see **n.** guilt in anyone. And if
T-22....... II.6:4 and **n.** one undertakes to do what holds

T-22 .......II.6:4 do what holds **n.** hope of ever being done.
T-22 .......II.6:8 There is **n.** point in trying to avoid this
T-22 .......II.7:7 you that there is **n.** middle ground where
T-22 .......II.8:1 **n.** part of Heaven you can take and weave
T-22 .......II.8:8 **n.** more a slave to time than to the world
T-22 .....II.12:5 be. Here is **n.** separate will, nor the desire
T-22 .....II.12:6 Its will has **n.** exceptions, and what it wills
T-22 ...II.12:10 as well? **N.** misery is here, but only joy.
T-22 .....II.13:3 **n.** one can remain beyond this willingness
T-22 ..... III.3:3 **N.** one who looks on it without the help
T-22 ..... IV.1:5 The way you came **n.** longer matters. It
T-22 ..... IV.1:6 can **n.** longer serve. No one who reaches
T-22 ..... IV.1:7 **N.** one who reaches this far can make the
T-22 ..... IV.1:8 is **n.** part of the journey that seems more
T-22 ..... IV.7:2 **N.** one who has received it for himself
T-22 ..... IV.7:7 It is **n.** solid wall. And only an illusion
T-22 ...... V.1:7 What merely is needs **n.** defense, and
T-22 .... V.1:11 And you need **n.** defense. Everything that
T-22 ...... V.2:2 in the face of reason and makes **n.** sense.
T-22 ...... V.3:9 Here can **n.** weakness enter, for here is no
T-22 ...... V.3:9 here is **n.** attack and therefore no illusions
T-22 ...... V.3:9 here is no attack and therefore **n.** illusions
T-22 ...... V.5:4 you is a Force that **n.** illusions can resist.
T-22 ..... VI.1:8 **N.** one but yearns for freedom and tries to
T-22 ..... VI.2:2 Yet freedom of the body has **n.** meaning,
T-22 ..... VI.2:3 this has **n.** idea of what is valuable. Yet
T-22 ..... VI.5:1 Before a holy relationship there is **n.** sin.
T-22 ..... VI.5:2 The form of error is **n.** longer seen, and
T-22 ..... VI.5:7 The means of sinlessness can know **n.** fear
T-22 ..... VI.6:8 **N.** trace of anything in time can long
T-22 ..... VI.6:9 And **n.** illusion can disturb the peace of a
T-22 ..... VI.7:1 from which **n.** error is excluded and
T-22 ..... VI.9:5 Save **n.** dark secrets that He cannot use,
T-22 ..... VI.9:7 He will withhold **n.** blessing from it, nor
T-22 ... VI.12:3 in any form, because it has **n.** meaning.
T-22 ... VI.14:6 From loving minds there *is* **n.** separation.
T-22 ... VI.14:9 There is **n.** difference anywhere in it, for
T-23 ......in.1:5 **N.** one is strong who has an enemy, and
T-23 ......in.1:5 **n.** one can attack unless he thinks he has.
T-23 ......in.3:1 with your head held high, and fear **n.** evil.
T-23 ......in.4:2 can be **n.** attraction of guilt in innocence.
T-23 ........I.1:8 Certain it is it has **n.** enemy. Yet just as
T-23 ........I.2:8 This is **n.** war; only the mad belief the
T-23 ........I.3:2 on grounds that have **n.** meaning. For
T-23 ........I.4:7 proclaiming it is part of itself **n.** more.
T-23 ........I.6:2 *is* **n.** conflict between them and the truth.
T-23 ........I.6:7 Madness holds out **n.** menace to reality,
T-23 ........I.6:7 to reality, and has **n.** influence upon it.
T-23 ........I.7:9 There is **n.** victor and there is no victory.
T-23 ........I.7:9 There is no victor and there is **n.** victory.
T-23 ........I.9:5 **n.** illusion can invade His home and drive
T-23 ......I.10:1 who are beloved of Him are **n.** illusion,
T-23 ......I.10:6 Illusions have **n.** place where love abides,
T-23 .......II.3:6 **N.** part of nothing can be more resistant
T-23 .......II.8:1 There can be **n.** release and no escape.
T-23 .......II.8:1 There can be no release and **n.** escape.
T-23 .......II.8:3 there is **n.** sight of help that can succeed.
T-23 ...II.12:11 It has **n.** substitute, and there is only one.
T-23 ...II.13:10 is **n.** point in asking what they mean.
T-23 .....II.14:1 **N.** one wants madness, nor does anyone
T-23 .....II.15:3 Chaos is lawlessness, and has **n.** laws. To
T-23 .....II.16:5 **N.** law of chaos could compel belief but
T-23 .....II.16:6 **N.** one who thinks that one of these laws
T-23 .....II.19:1 There is **n.** life outside of Heaven. Where
T-23 .....II.20:5 are **n.** less certain in their witnessing, or
T-23 ..... III.1:8 For **n.** one thinks of murder and escapes
T-23 ..... III.3:1 Salvation is **n.** compromise of any kind.
T-23 ..... III.4:1 easy just because it makes **n.** compromise
T-23 ..... III.5:5 **N.** one unites with enemies, nor is at one
T-23 ..... III.5:6 And **n.** one compromises with an enemy
T-23 ..... III.6:5 There *is* **n.** safety in a battleground. You
T-23 ..... III.6:7 But from within it you can find **n.** safety.
T-23 ..... IV.1:1 conflict, for there *is* **n.** war without attack.
T-23 ..... IV.1:3 In Him is **n.** attack, and no illusion in any
T-23 ..... IV.1:4 and **n.** illusion in any form stalks Heaven.
T-23 ..... IV.1:6 **N.** difference enters, and what is all the
T-23 ..... IV.3:4 is the same can have **n.** different function.
T-23 ..... IV.4:5 above the battleground, in it **n.** more.
T-23 ..... IV.6:7 and **n.** illusion can attack the peace of

T-23 ..... IV.7:1 See **n.** one from the battleground, for
T-23 ..... IV.7:2 **n.** reference point from where to look,
T-23 ..... IV.7:5 The body has **n.** purpose of itself, and
T-23 ..... IV.7:8 for His Son *because* it has **n.** purpose.
T-23 ..... IV.8:8 so deep and quiet that **n.** touch of doubt
T-23 ..... IV.9:4 **N.** one who knows that he has everything
T-24 .... in.1:10 **N.** more His Son. They *are*. And what
T-24 ...... in.2:3 **N.** belief is neutral. Every one has the
T-24 ...... in.2:7 There is **n.** substitute for peace. What
T-24 ...... in.2:8 What God creates has **n.** alternative. The
T-24 ........I.7:2 you. There is **n.** difference. You have been
T-24 ........I.7:7 to see **n.** specialness of any kind between
T-24 ........I.8:7 You have **n.** purpose that is not the same,
T-24 .......II.3:3 an evil flower with **n.** roots at all. Here is
T-24 .......II.6:5 You will **n.** longer see what never was, nor
T-24 .......II.6:5 never was, nor hear what makes **n.** sound.
T-24 .......II.7:4 It gives **n.** different messages, and has one
T-24 .....II.12:3 to kill. **N.** gift that bears its seal but offers
T-24 .....II.12:6 And **n.** relationship that holds its purpose
T-24 ..... III.1:4 **N.** one who clings to one illusion can see
T-24 ..... III.4:2 such a state, where safety has **n.** meaning?
T-24 ..... III.4:3 **N.**, His Son is safe, resting on Him. It is
T-24 ..... III.5:2 He would have **n.** separation, like an alien
T-24 ..... IV.2:5 Yet bodies have **n.** goal. Purpose is of the
T-24 ... IV.3:14 Offered to them, **n.** gifts can be returned.
T-24 ..... IV.4:3 To specialness the answer must be "**n.**." A
T-24 ..... IV.5:2 this shifting world that has **n.** meaning in
T-24 .......V.2:1 There is **n.** dream of specialness, however
T-24 .......V.3:2 and sees **n.** condemnation that could
T-24 .......V.3:3 is at peace *because* He sees **n.** sin. Identify
T-24 .......V.3:7 see nothing and there is **n.** sound to hear.
T-24 .......V.5:1 you have **n.** eyes with which to see; no
T-24 .......V.5:1 no eyes with which to see; **n.** ears to listen
T-24 .......V.5:1 and **n.** hands to hold nor feet to guide. Be
T-24 .......V.7:3 ears may hear **n.** more the sound of battle
T-24 .....V.7:10 There is **n.** journey but to walk with Him.
T-24 .......V.9:3 Christ has **n.** doubt, and from His
T-24 ..... VI.2:2 There could be **n.** universe and no reality.
T-24 ..... VI.2:2 There could be no universe and **n.** reality.
T-24 ..... VI.3:3 **n.** Thought within His Mind is absent
T-24 ..... VI.3:5 **n.** meaning in eternity where He abides,
T-24 ..... VI.6:3 find **n.** sight nor place nor time where He
T-24 ..... VI.6:6 And let the fear of God **n.** longer hold the
T-24 ..... VI.7:2 through time that seems to have **n.** end,
T-24 ..... VI.8:3 that has never begun, and needs **n.** end.
T-24 ..... VI.9:5 to laws that have **n.** power over him at all.
T-24 ... VI.12:5 as God established it **n.** sacrifice is asked,
T-24 ... VI.12:5 no sacrifice is asked, **n.** strain called forth,
T-24 ... VI.13:5 Him this judgment makes **n.** sense at all,
T-24 ... VI.13:5 and there is **n.** alternative for Him to see.
T-24 .... VII.1:5 it calls to him he hears **n.** other Voice. No
T-24 .... VII.1:6 **N.** effort is too great, no cost too much,
T-24 .... VII.1:6 No effort is too great, **n.** cost too much,
T-24 .... VII.1:6 **n.** price too dear to save his specialness
T-24 .... VII.5:4 what is but temporal has **n.** effect. Only
T-24 .... VII.5:6 If not, it has **n.** purpose, and is means for
T-24 .... VII.6:3 It has **n.** meaning of itself, yet you can
T-24 .... VII.6:8 To **n.** one here is this describable. Nor is
T-24 .... VII.7:5 and yet it has **n.** meaning to anyone who
T-24 .... VII.8:1 This course makes **n.** attempt to teach
T-24 .. VII.10:1 **n.** provisions made for evidence beyond
T-24 .. VII.10:1 itself, and **n.** escape within its sight. Its
T-24 .. VII.11:1 without a meeting place and **n.** encounter
T-25 ......in.1:7 **N.** more can you. Christ is within a frame
T-25 ......in.2:1 **N.** one who carries Christ in him can fail
T-25 ......in.3:1 The body needs **n.** healing. But the mind
T-25 .......II.1:6 And there is **n.** exception, nor will there
T-25 .......II.1:7 **n.** rewards which you would want to keep
T-25 .......II.2:2 In **n.** respect, at any time or place, has
T-25 .......II.2:4 gives **n.** support to base your future hopes
T-25 .......II.2:4 hopes, and **n.** suggestions of success at all.
T-25 .......II.2:5 place your hopes where **n.** hope lies must
T-25 .......II.4:5 that hides the picture has **n.** purpose. It
T-25 .......II.5:5 Yet what God has created needs **n.** frame,
T-25 .......II.8:2 on him, and you will see the dark **n.** more
T-25 .....II.10:2 You need **n.** forgiveness, for the wholly
T-25 ..... III.1:4 Perception has **n.** other law than this. The
T-25 ..... III.2:1 Mind to which perception has **n.** meaning
T-25 ..... III.6:1 darkness, yet **n.** one has entered it alone.

T-25......IV.1:1 and recognize they are, can feel **n.** guilt.
T-25......IV.5:7 it. **N.** other place; no other state nor time.
T-25......IV.5:7 place; **n.** other state nor time. Nothing
T-25.......V.1:1 is **n.** reason to perceive the Son of God as
T-25.......V.1:2 for guilt is gone because it has **n.** purpose,
T-25.......V.1:6 And **n.** one could believe in one unless the
T-25.......V.3:3 hate because there is **n.** sin in him for you
T-25.......V.5:1 It is **n.** sacrifice that he be saved, for by
T-25.......V.5:6 He has **n.** need but this; that you allow
T-25......VI.1:2 He can see **n.** evil; nothing in the world to
T-25......VI.1:2 and **n.** one who is different from himself.
T-25......VI.1:4 He would **n.** more condemn himself for
T-25......VI.3:6 Let him **n.** more be lonely, for the lonely
T-25......VI.3:6 lonely ones are those who see **n.** function
T-25......VI.3:6 to fill; **n.** place where they are needed,
T-25......VI.3:6 **n.** aim which only they can perfectly fulfill
T-25......VI.5:7 Then is time **n.** more. Yet while in time,
T-25......VI.6:1 Salvation is **n.** more than a reminder this
T-25......VI.7:5 The Son of God can make **n.** choice the
T-25.....VII.3:5 makes **n.** sense and has no meaning is
T-25.....VII.3:5 no sense and has **n.** meaning is insanity.
T-25.....VII.3:8 to are false, and make **n.** sense at all. This
T-25.....VII.5:4 and **n.** one loses that each one may gain.
T-25.....VII.9:6 He can **n.** more be left outside, without a
T-25...VII.12:1 the idea **n.** one can suffer for anyone to gain
T-25...VII.13:3 **N.** one can suffer for the Will of God to be
T-25...VII.13:6 his Father's, and in Him **n.** loss is possible
T-25... VIII.1:5 for if you could you had **n.** need of Him.
T-25... VIII.1:6 brings loss to **n.** one you would not know.
T-25... VIII.1:7 to the idea **n.** one can lose for you to gain.
T-25... VIII.2:3 to it. You have **n.** fixed allegiance. But
T-25... VIII.4:5 Justice demands **n.** sacrifice, for any
T-25... VIII.9:4 **N.** more than what you see He offers you,
T-25. VIII.10:3 God knows of **n.** injustice. He would not
T-25. VIII.10:7 **N.** justice would be given him by you. Yet
T-25. VIII.11:3 Simple justice asks **n.** more. Of each one
T-25. VIII.13:1 Without impartiality there is **n.** justice.
T-25. VIII.13:8 is **n.** judge of what must be another's due,
T-25......IX.3:1 will always be one in which **n.** one loses.
T-25......IX.3:2 because He asks **n.** sacrifice of anyone. An
T-25......IX.4:2 perception leaves **n.** ground for an attack.
T-25......IX.4:6 can set up a state in which there is **n.** loser
T-25......IX.4:6 **n.** one left unfairly treated and deprived,
T-25......IX.5:4 principle that justice means **n.** one can
T-25......IX.6:1 **N.** one deserves to lose. And what would
T-25......IX.7:3 He cannot perceive He bears **n.** witness to
T-25......IX.7:7 **N.** one can be unjust to you, unless you
T-25......IX.9:2 you perceive and leave you fair to **n.** one.
T-25......IX.9:5 unforgiven have **n.** mercy to bestow upon
T-25....IX.10:3 **N.** one can lose, and everyone must
T-25....IX.10:7 it sees **n.** differences where none exists.
T-25....IX.10:8 because it sees **n.** differences in them. Its
T-26.........I.5:2 has this world **n.** meaning for you. Yet it
T-26.........I.5:4 **N.** instant passes here in which your
T-26.........I.6:4 will hear **n.** song of liberation for yourself,
T-26.........I.7:2 and can **n.** more be sacrificed by you than
T-26.......II.1:6 It serves **n.** purpose to attempt to solve it
T-26.......II.2:3 out so **n.** one loses is the problem gone,
T-26.......II.3:2 There is **n.** loss; to think there is, is a
T-26.......II.3:3 You have **n.** problems, though you think
T-26.......II.4:5 They have **n.** properties to Him. They are
T-26.......II.5:2 There is **n.** such thing as partial justice. If
T-26.......II.5:3 deserves **n.** mercy from the God of justice.
T-26.......II.5:7 judge that it is one that has **n.** resolution,
T-26.......II.6:1 be **n.** problems that justice cannot solve.
T-26.......II.6:4 **n.** one whom you wish to be preserved
T-26.......II.6:7 will ask **n.** sacrifice of him because you
T-26.......II.7:4 worth **n.** more than just a tiny sigh before
T-26....III.1:10 The truth makes **n.** decisions, for there is
T-26......III.3:4 because knowledge makes **n.** attack upon
T-26......III.4:3 on perception: "It has **n.** meaning, and
T-26......III.4:6 But in this world there are **n.** simple facts,
T-26......III.6:1 is **n.** basis for a choice in this complex and
T-26......III.6:2 For **n.** one understands what is the same,
T-26......III.6:2 seems to choose where **n.** choice really is.
T-26......III.7:5 There is **n.** conflict here. No sacrifice is
T-26......III.7:6 conflict here. **N.** sacrifice is possible in the
T-26......IV.1:5 **N.** one forgives unless he has believed in
T-26......IV.1:7 until he sees himself as needing it **n.** more
T-26......IV.2:3 is **n.** sadness and there is no parting here,
T-26......IV.2:3 is no sadness and there is **n.** parting here,
T-26......IV.4:1 Forgiveness brings **n.** little miracles to lay
T-26......IV.5:3 For **n.** one hears the song of Heaven and
T-26.......V.2:6 leads to nothing and that has **n.** purpose.
T-26.......V.3:3 in your mind, with **n.** effect upon eternity
T-26.......V.6:3 Madness speaks **n.** more. There *is* no other
T-26.......V.6:4 There *is* **n.** other teacher and no other way.
T-26.......V.6:4 There *is* no other teacher and **n.** other way.
T-26.......V.6:5 For what has been undone **n.** longer is.
T-26.......V.9:8 your way because there is **n.** way but His,
T-26.....V.10:3 corrected, is of **n.** concern nor value. Let
T-26.....V.10:7 **N.** past illusions have the power to keep
T-26.....V.12:5 it was **n.** more to be experienced as there.
T-26.....V.14:2 You stand **n.** longer on the ground that
T-26.....V.14:4 There is **n.** hindrance to the Will of God,
T-26......VI.1:7 For **n.** one can make one illusion real, and
T-26......VI.2:2 This is **n.** friendship worthy of God's Son,
T-26......VI.2:7 place. There *is* **n.** other friend. What God
T-26......VI.2:8 What God appointed has **n.** substitute,
T-26......VI.3:3 Make **n.** illusion friend, for if you do, it
T-26.....VII.6:3 help. **N.** illusion has any truth in it. Yet it
T-26.....VII.6:4 although this clearly makes **n.** sense at all.
T-26.....VII.6:8 Your preference gives them **n.** reality. Not
T-26...VII.6:11 His Will has **n.** foundation in the truth.
T-26.....VII.8:1 gives meaning where **n.** meaning is. And
T-26.....VII.8:2 truth needs **n.** defense to make it true.
T-26.....VII.8:3 Illusions have **n.** witnesses and no effects.
T-26.....VII.8:3 Illusions have no witnesses and **n.** effects.
T-26...VII.10:5 itself? There is **n.** sin. And every miracle is
T-26...VII.11:6 therefore has **n.** meaning in this world.
T-26...VII.17:1 needed where there is **n.** pain or suffering
T-26...VII.18:5 There is **n.** circumstance it cannot answer
T-26...VII.18:5 **n.** problem which is not resolved within
T-26...VII.19:5 is **n.** difference among the Sons of God.
T-26...VII.19:6 all, for what is one can have **n.** specialness
T-26...VII.19:8 **N.** wishes lie between a brother and his
T-26...VII.20:4 A miracle can make **n.** change at all. But it
T-26... VIII.4:2 time. **N.** more can it be overlooked except
T-26... VIII.4:6 A future cause as yet has **n.** effects. And
T-26... VIII.5:2 **N.** purpose has been given it as yet, and
T-26... VIII.5:2 and what will happen has as yet **n.** cause.
T-26... VIII.6:1 out of all correction takes **n.** time at all.
T-26... VIII.7:9 there is **n.** reason for an interval in which
T-26... VIII.9:2 It has **n.** meaning, and is not your just
T-26......IX.5:3 light may shine on it and leave **n.** space
T-26......IX.6:3 There is **n.** place in Heaven holier. And
T-26......IX.7:3 **N.** one on earth but offers thanks to one
T-26.......X.3:6 You have **n.** enemy except yourself, and
T-27.........I.1:3 you will fear **n.** evil and no shadows in the
T-27.........I.1:3 you will fear no evil and **n.** shadows in the
T-27.........I.1:4 But place **n.** terror symbols on your path,
T-27.........I.3:5 there is **n.** pain and no reproach at all.
T-27.........I.3:5 there is no pain and **n.** reproach at all.
T-27.........I.5:8 That **n.** reproach he laid upon his heart
T-27.........I.5:8 and **n.** attack can ever touch him with the
T-27.........I.6:5 **N.** worldly thought or act or feeling has a
T-27.........I.9:1 show your brother sin can have **n.** cause.
T-27.........I.9:6 **N.** grounds are offered that it may be
T-27.........I.9:7 all. It has **n.** life, but neither is it dead. It
T-27.......I.11:1 the body have **n.** purpose from the past,
T-27.......I.11:3 leaves **n.** space in which a different view,
T-27.......II.1:4 the frail can have **n.** trust and that the
T-27.......II.1:4 the damaged have **n.** grounds for peace.
T-27.......II.2:4 **n.** one can forgive a sin that he believes is
T-27.......II.3:2 has been done to you deserves **n.** pardon.
T-27.......II.3:6 For **n.** one in whom true forgiveness rests
T-27.....II.3:11 and retains **n.** trace of condemnation that
T-27.......II.4:2 You must attest his sins have **n.** effect on
T-27.......II.4:4 his sins have **n.** effect to warrant guilt?
T-27.......II.6:8 Brother, there is **n.** death. And this you
T-27.......II.6:9 your brother that you had **n.** hurt of him.
T-27.......II.7:4 that healing sees **n.** specialness at all. It
T-27.......II.7:6 imagining, a foolish wish with **n.** effects.
T-27.......II.7:7 brother with **n.** blood upon his hands,
T-27.......II.8:7 and he will consent **n.** more to suffer. For
T-27.....II.10:4 of forgiveness. **N.** one can forgive until he
T-27......III.1:6 **N.** weakness can intrude on it without
T-27......III.2:2 And so he has **n.** meaning to you, for he
T-27......III.3:4 And thus the picture has **n.** cause at all.
T-27......III.4:2 **N.** preparation can be made that would
T-27......III.4:4 Unweakened power, with **n.** opposite, is
T-27......III.4:5 is. For this there are **n.** symbols. Nothing
T-27......III.5:1 pictured, so there is **n.** symbol for totality.
T-27......III.5:4 it sets **n.** limits you have chosen to impose
T-27......III.5:7 **N.** learning aid has use that can extend
T-27......III.6:8 you need **n.** pictures and no learning aids.
T-27......III.6:8 you need no pictures and **n.** learning aids.
T-27......III.7:3 There is **n.** choice of function anywhere.
T-27......III.7:7 **n.** other kind can be at all. Give welcome
T-27......IV.1:2 there can be **n.** answer and no resolution,
T-27......IV.1:2 there can be no answer and **n.** resolution,
T-27......IV.1:2 purpose is to make **n.** resolution possible,
T-27......IV.1:2 and to ensure **n.** answer will be plain. A
T-27......IV.1:3 A problem set in conflict has **n.** answer,
T-27......IV.1:6 at all, for conflict has **n.** limited effects.
T-27......IV.3:1 Attempt to solve **n.** problems but within
T-27......IV.3:3 Outside there will be **n.** solution, for there
T-27......IV.3:3 is **n.** answer there that could be found.
T-27......IV.3:6 with many answers can have **n.** answers.
T-27....IV.4:17 it. It leaves **n.** room to question its beliefs,
T-27......IV.5:1 A pseudo-question has **n.** answer. It
T-27......IV.5:8 But **n.** one in a conflict state is free to ask
T-27......IV.6:6 honest answer asks **n.** sacrifice because it
T-27......IV.7:1 attempt to solve **n.** problems in a world
T-27.......V.1:6 **N.** one can ask another to be healed. But
T-27.......V.2:4 **N.** one is healed through double messages
T-27.....V.2:11 were, there were **n.** need for healing then.
T-27.......V.3:3 and demonstrates that war has **n.** effects.
T-27.......V.4:1 is **n.** sadness where a miracle has come to
T-27.......V.6:4 And suffering eyes **n.** longer will accuse,
T-27.......V.7:4 **N.** reinforcement will its thanks withhold
T-27.......V.8:2 And **n.** one understands the nature of his
T-27.......V.8:3 it would be there **n.** more for him to see.
T-27......VI.2:8 behind the pleasure will be felt **n.** more.
T-27....VI.2:10 Yet which is foremost makes **n.** difference
T-27......VI.4:1 God's Witness sees **n.** witnesses against
T-27......VI.4:7 to your life in Him Who knows **n.** death.
T-27......VI.5:1 The miracle makes **n.** distinctions in the
T-27......VI.5:2 that what they represent has **n.** effects.
T-27......VI.5:5 It is **n.** longer there. The One Who brings
T-27......VI.5:8 It is a witness **n.** one can deny, for it is the
T-27......VI.7:2 There is **n.** need to suffer any more. But
T-27......VI.8:3 And **n.** one will elect to suffer more. What
T-27.....VII.1:4 he has **n.** reason to be held responsible.
T-27.....VII.2:6 **N.** one has difficulty making up his mind
T-27.....VII.3:5 **N.** one who looks upon this "reasoning"
T-27.....VII.3:5 it does not follow and it makes **n.** sense.
T-27.....VII.3:7 And so it seems as if there is **n.** need to go
T-27.....VII.8:1 **N.** one can waken from a dream the
T-27...VII.13:2 **N.** other cause it has, nor ever will.
T-27...VII.14:5 He brings there is **n.** murder and there is
T-27...VII.14:5 there is no murder and there is **n.** death.
T-27...VII.16:4 And let **n.** pain disturb your dream of
T-27....VIII.1:2 There is **n.** dream without it, nor does it
T-27....VIII.4:5 they are they have **n.** more effects on him,
T-27....VIII.5:2 your wish to let **n.** dream appear to be the
T-27....VIII.5:4 **N.** one asleep and dreaming in the world
T-27....VIII.5:5 **N.** one believes there really was a time
T-27....VIII.5:8 **n.** one can remember when they would
T-27....VIII.6:5 eternity, which *means* there is **n.** time.
T-27....VIII.7:7 You have **n.** power to make the body stop
T-27..VIII.10:2 **N.** matter what the form of the attack,
T-27..VIII.10:6 have **n.** effect on you unless you failed to
T-27..VIII.11:5 of all of them, **n.** matter what their form.
T-27..VIII.12:2 He sees **n.** differences where none exists.
T-27..VIII.12:6 Yet to its witnesses you pay **n.** heed at all.
T-27..VIII.13:4 a secret kept from **n.** one but yourself.
T-27..VIII.13:9 And it will be **n.** secret you are healed.
T-28.........I.1:7 The thoughts that made it are **n.** longer in
T-28.........I.1:8 and what has truly gone has **n.** effects.
T-28.........I.2:1 All the effects of guilt are here **n.** more.
T-28.........I.3:2 It is a recognition that you have **n.** needs
T-28.........I.3:7 use. They have **n.** dedication and no aim.
T-28.........I.3:7 use. They have no dedication and **n.** aim.
T-28.........I.4:5 There is **n.** link of memory to the past. If
T-28.........I.6:4 a consequence in which **n.** change can be
T-28.........I.6:6 **N.** change can be made in the present if

T-28 I.9:10 It for your sins, It will **n.** longer be denied.
T-28 I.10:3 There was **n.** time in which His Son could
T-28 I.10:6 **N.** more have you. And so your innocence
T-28 I.10:8 lost. You need **n.** healing to be healed. In
T-28 I.11:4 there can be **n.** pause in time to cause the
T-28 I.13:1 that has **n.** fear to keep the memory away!
T-28 I.13:3 **n.** past to keep its fearful image in the way
T-28 I.14:2 made is causeless, having **n.** effects at all.
T-28 I.15:8 **n.** fear that He will fail in what He wills.
T-28 II.1:1 Without a cause there can be **n.** effects,
T-28 II.1:1 and yet without effects there is **n.** cause.
T-28 II.1:6 him. The circle of creation has **n.** end. Its
T-28 II.3:5 causelessness is given **n.** effects and none
T-28 II.5:6 But in forgiving dreams is **n.** one asked to
T-28 II.6:2 **N.** plans are possible, and no design
T-28 II.6:2 and **n.** design exists that could be found
T-28 II.6:3 be expected from a thing that has **n.** cause
T-28 II.6:4 Yet if it has **n.** cause, it has no purpose.
T-28 II.6:4 Yet if it has no cause, it has **n.** purpose.
T-28 II.7:3 illusions. **N.** one is afraid of them when
T-28 II.8:1 them since He was **n.** longer their Creator
T-28 II.10:5 hate, because you see that it has **n.** effects.
T-28 II.11:2 But it also shows that, having **n.** effects, it
T-28 II.11:3 where effects are gone, there is **n.** cause.
T-28 II.11:7 guilt caused nothing, and had **n.** effects.
T-28 III.2:1 **N.** mind is sick until another mind agrees
T-28 III.8:5 The miracle would leave **n.** proof of guilt
T-28 III.8:7 may come who would **n.** longer starve,
T-28 III.9:4 And **n.** one is deprived or can deprive.
T-28 III.9:6 And in Their sharing there can be **n.** gap
T-28 III.9:7 not upon this feast, which has **n.** end. For
T-28 IV.1:4 Thus have they **n.** effects. And you are
T-28 IV.4:1 yet, between your minds there is **n.** gap.
T-28 IV.6:1 for in the gap **n.** stable self exists. What is
T-28 IV.6:6 Yet if you see there is **n.** truth in yours, his
T-28 IV.7:1 and He is One because there is **n.** gap that
T-28 IV.7:3 **N.** one is sick if someone else accepts his
T-28 IV.10:4 loss, and what is not of Him has **n.** effects.
T-28 IV.10:10 And there will be **n.** loss, but only gain.
T-28 V.1:9 There is **n.** other choice. Except you share
T-28 V.3:1 share **n.** evil dreams if you forgive the
T-28 V.3:8 There is **n.** compromise. You are your Self
T-28 V.5:4 to hear the voices that can make **n.** sound.
T-28 V.6:4 There is **n.** gap that separates the truth
T-28 V.6:5 left **n.** room for them in any place or time.
T-28 V.7:5 And there are **n.** awesome secrets and no
T-28 V.7:5 and **n.** darkened tombs where terror rises
T-28 VI.1:6 It does not victimize, because it has **n.** will
T-28 VI.1:6 has no will, **n.** preferences and no doubts.
T-28 VI.1:6 has no will, no preferences and **n.** doubts.
T-28 VI.1:8 And so it has **n.** need to be competitive. It
T-28 VI.1:10 It accepts **n.** role, but does what it is told,
T-28 VI.2:2 the punishment you give because it has **n.**
T-28 VI.2:7 It takes **n.** sides and judges not the road it
T-28 VI.2:8 It perceives **n.** gap, because it does not
T-28 VI.4:5 attacked. **N.** one can suffer if he does not
T-28 VI.5:3 that is your wish, it can have **n.** effects.
T-28 VI.5:4 "There is **n.** gap between my mind and
T-28 VII.1:2 For there is **n.** lack in him. An empty
T-28 VII.1:6 and there is **n.** one who could be untrue
T-28 VII.1:7 The promise that there is **n.** gap between
T-28 VII.1:8 in Whose Wholeness there can be **n.** gap?
T-28 VII.2:7 There is **n.** middle ground in any aspect
T-28 VII.3:2 There is **n.** in between, no other choice,
T-28 VII.3:2 There is no in between, **n.** other choice,
T-28 VII.3:2 **n.** allegiance to be split between the two.
T-28 VII.4:7 **N.** forms of sickness are immune, because
T-28 VII.5:10 there is **n.** need to bar the door and lock
T-28 VII.7:2 **N.** secret promise you have made instead
T-28 VII.7:3 rain will beat against it, but with **n.** effect.
T-29 I.1:1 There is **n.** time, no place, no state where
T-29 I.1:1 There is no time, **n.** place, no state where
T-29 I.1:1 no place, **n.** state where God is absent.
T-29 I.1:3 There is **n.** way in which a gap could be
T-29 I.2:3 **N.** one who hates but is afraid of love, and
T-29 I.7:4 uncertainly, and offer **n.** stability to you.
T-29 I.8:4 there is **n.** gap behind which you can hide
T-29 I.8:5 learn their savior is their enemy **n.** more.
T-29 I.9:5 the body to say "**n.**" to Heaven's calling,
T-29 II.1:5 until you understand there is **n.** loss, you
T-29 II.3:7 **N.** more is pain your friend and guilt your
T-29 II.5:3 **n.** other place where He can find His host,
T-29 II.7:4 There is **n.** change in immortality, and
T-29 II.8:6 that part of Him belongs to Him **n.** longer
T-29 III.3:1 death is yet one theme of truth; **n.** more,
T-29 IV.2:2 **n.** matter what the form it seems to take.
T-29 IV.5:2 **N.** one can fail but your idea of him, and
T-29 IV.5:2 of him, and there is **n.** betrayal but of this.
T-29 V.1:1 where **n.** memory of sin and of illusion
T-29 V.1:3 is a resting place so still **n.** sound except a
T-29 V.5:1 There is **n.** gift the Father asks of you but
T-29 V.5:6 They hold **n.** sword, for they have left
T-29 VI.2:8 and night and day will be **n.** more. All
T-29 VI.2:14 may disappear because they have **n.** use.
T-29 VI.4:5 time, but at its ending, when it has **n.** use.
T-29 VI.4:8 Time can set **n.** end to its fulfillment nor
T-29 VI.4:9 There is **n.** death because the living share
T-29 VII.1:3 and there can be **n.** peace excepting there.
T-29 VII.1:5 is **n.** other answer you can substitute, and
T-29 VII.1:10 abides, and seek **n.** longer elsewhere. You
T-29 VII.2:1 **N.** one who comes here but must still
T-29 VII.5:1 Idols must fall *because* they have **n.** life,
T-29 VII.5:3 **N.** sadness and no suffering proclaim a
T-29 VII.5:3 No sadness and **n.** suffering proclaim a
T-29 VII.6:4 **N.** idol takes His place. Look not to idols.
T-29 VII.9:5 God, and where He is **n.** idols can abide.
T-29 VII.10:2 Salvation seeks to prove there is **n.** death,
T-29 VIII.1:7 be replaced, **n.** matter what their form.
T-29 VIII.2:5 have. **N.** one believes in idols who has not
T-29 VIII.3:9 **N.** more a veil can banish what it seems to
T-29 VIII.4:9 take **n.** form in which he ever will be real.
T-29 VIII.7:4 off from what is endless, *has* **n.** place to be.
T-29 VIII.7:5 left **n.** room for anything to be except His
T-29 VIII.8:5 **N.** one comes unless he worshipped them
T-29 VIII.9:4 and tells you idols have **n.** purpose here.
T-29 VIII.9:10 **N.** idol can establish you as more than
T-29 IX.1:2 bow down in worship to what has **n.** life,
T-29 IX.4:1 There can be **n.** salvation in the dream as
T-29 IX.6:3 away, for you have need of them **n.** more.
T-29 IX.7:4 It is a dream in which **n.** one is used to
T-29 IX.7:5 **N.** one is used for something he is not, for
T-29 IX.10:5 fear his judgment for he has judged **n.** one
T-30 I.2:2 *Today I will make* **n.** *decisions by myself.*
T-30 I.4:2 *If I make* **n.** *decisions by myself, this is the*
T-30 I.6:4 *I have* **n.** *question. I forgot what to decide.*
T-30 I.11:6 Its purpose has **n.** longer been obscured
T-30 I.15:5 is **n.** freedom from what must occur. And
T-30 II.1:9 **N.** spark of life but was created with your
T-30 II.1:11 God is **n.** enemy to you. He asks no more
T-30 II.1:12 He asks **n.** more than that He hear you
T-30 II.3:8 **N.** light of Heaven shines except for you,
T-30 II.5:2 And **n.** one walks upon the earth but
T-30 II.5:2 that he learn death has **n.** power over him
T-30 III.1:3 And so it has **n.** form, nor is content for
T-30 III.1:6 if you said, "I have **n.** need of everything.
T-30 III.3:2 has **n.** form because it is unlimited. To
T-30 III.4:6 answer you in terms that have **n.** meaning
T-30 III.4:9 Creation gives **n.** separate person and no
T-30 III.4:9 person and **n.** separate thing the power to
T-30 III.5:2 He has **n.** need to seek for it at all. Beyond
T-30 III.6:4 And in the Mind of God there is **n.** ending
T-30 III.6:8 And so there are **n.** separate parts in what
T-30 III.8:7 There was **n.** time it was not there; no
T-30 III.8:7 **n.** instant when its light grew dimmer or
T-30 III.10:3 Surrounded by a stillness so complete **n.**
T-30 III.11:3 of? Outside you there is **n.** eternal sky, no
T-30 III.11:3 sky, **n.** changeless star and no reality. The
T-30 III.11:3 sky, no changeless star and **n.** reality. The
T-30 III.11:4 joined in creation which can have **n.** end.
T-30 IV.2:5 bears did not deceive him, broke **n.** rules,
T-30 IV.3:6 child who learns they are **n.** threat to him.
T-30 IV.4:3 you believe about yourself obey **n.** laws.
T-30 IV.5:7 a power that can have **n.** real effects at all?
T-30 IV.5:12 Son needs **n.** defense against his dreams.
T-30 IV.7:3 you forgive all things that **n.** one ever did;
T-30 IV.7:4 seek **n.** longer for the things you do not
T-30 IV.7:5 seek **n.** more to substitute the strength of
T-30 IV.8:3 **N.** more than this is asked. Be glad indeed
T-30 IV.8:10 the Son of God can have **n.** need of them.
T-30 IV.8:11 him **n.** single thing that he could ever
T-30 V.1:3 place of idols, which are sought **n.** longer,
T-30 V.1:4 **N.** rules are idly set, and no demands are
T-30 V.1:4 and **n.** demands are made of anyone or
T-30 V.2:5 **N.** one is tempted by its vain appeal, for
T-30 V.2:8 And **n.** one stands outside this hope,
T-30 V.3:3 He has **n.** wish for anything but this. And
T-30 V.4:2 **N.** one outside of Heaven knows how this
T-30 V.9:3 Look back **n.** longer, for what lies ahead is
T-30 V.9:9 Joy has **n.** cost. It is your sacred right, and
T-30 VI.1:2 Attack has ***n.*** foundation. It is here escape
T-30 VI.4:4 **N.** one who sees himself as guilty can
T-30 VI.5:4 **n.** appearance that can not be overlooked.
T-30 VI.6:1 is **n.** surer proof idolatry is what you wish
T-30 VI.8:4 whole can have **n.** missing parts that have
T-30 VI.9:3 There is **n.** way to think of him but this, if
T-30 VI.9:5 joyful statement that there are **n.** forms of
T-30 VI.10:2 mistakes that have been given **n.** effects.
T-30 VII.1:2 If He had, it *has* **n.** meaning. For it cannot
T-30 VII.1:5 And **n.** situation can affect its aim, but
T-30 VII.2:4 fact they have **n.** meaning in themselves is
T-30 VII.2:6 to show there was **n.** meaning there? But
T-30 VII.3:9 Its presence has **n.** meaning but to show
T-30 VII.5:4 be **n.** thought of sacrifice apart from this
T-30 VII.6:6 looked at separately they have **n.** meaning
T-30 VII.6:7 For there is **n.** light by which they can be
T-30 VII.6:8 They have **n.** purpose. And what they are
T-30 VII.6:10 In any thought of loss there is **n.** meaning
T-30 VII.6:11 **N.** one has agreed with you on what it
T-30 VIII.2:8 and has **n.** effects that anything in Heaven
T-30 VIII.3:2 seem to be the wish that **n.** reality be so.
T-30 VIII.3:5 And Heaven gives **n.** answer to the prayer
T-30 VIII.3:7 you, but not of God Who knows **n.** limits.
T-30 VIII.4:5 There is **n.** miracle you cannot have when
T-30 VIII.4:6 But there is **n.** miracle that can be given
T-30 VIII.5:7 let there be **n.** dreams about him that you
T-30 VIII.6:2 Let **n.** temptation to prefer a dream allow
T-30 VIII.6:5 There is **n.** false appearance but will fade,
T-30 VIII.6:6 There is **n.** pain from which he is not free,
T-31 I.1:3 has not occurred, and can have **n.** effects.
T-31 I.1:8 You can **n.** longer say that you perceive
T-31 I.1:8 perceive **n.** differences in false and true.
T-31 I.2:4 from one to another, with **n.** strain at all.
T-31 I.3:1 **N.** one who understands what you have
T-31 I.3:2 There is **n.** greater power in the world.
T-31 I.6:1 noise of sounds that have **n.** meaning?
T-31 I.7:7 There is **n.** plan for safety you can make
T-31 I.7:8 There is **n.** joy that you can seek for here
T-31 I.8:1 is a world in which there is **n.** fear, and
T-31 I.9:1 is **n.** living thing that does not share the
T-31 II.1:3 There is **n.** battle that must be prepared;
T-31 II.1:3 must be prepared; **n.** time to be expended
T-31 II.1:3 **n.** plans that need be laid for bringing in
T-31 II.1:6 He has **n.** enemy in truth. And can he be
T-31 II.4:6 has **n.** purpose and no usefulness to you.
T-31 II.4:6 has no purpose and **n.** usefulness to you.
T-31 II.6:7 make **n.** gains he does not make with us,
T-31 II.7:5 seeing **n.** leaders and no followers, and
T-31 II.7:5 seeing no leaders and **n.** followers, and
T-31 II.8:4 There will be **n.** attack upon the things
T-31 II.8:5 There will be **n.** assault upon your wish to
T-31 II.8:7 **N.** more than this will you be asked to
T-31 II.11:3 you walk alone, with **n.** one by your side?
T-31 III.4:2 The body thinks **n.** thoughts. It has no
T-31 III.4:3 It has **n.** power to learn, to pardon, nor
T-31 III.4:4 It gives **n.** orders that the mind need serve
T-31 III.4:9 so the body, where **n.** learning can occur,
T-31 III.6:5 and you will see **n.** one as prisoner to
T-31 III.7:3 will be **n.** ancient penalty exacted from
T-31 III.7:4 said there *is* **n.** sacrifice that can be asked;
T-31 III.7:4 there *is* **n.** sacrifice that can be made.
T-31 IV.2:1 Real choice is **n.** illusion. But the world
T-31 IV.2:4 There is **n.** choice in its alternatives. Seek
T-31 IV.2:10 certain, for there is **n.** choice among them
T-31 IV.3:1 There is **n.** choice where every end is sure
T-31 IV.3:4 saw **n.** way except the pathways offered
T-31 IV.3:8 true indeed there is **n.** choice at all within
T-31 IV.4:3 there is **n.** hope of answer in the world.

T-31......IV.4:6 **N.** longer look for hope where there is
T-31......IV.6:1 choice, **n.** matter what its form may be, is
T-31......IV.7:2 it. This makes **n.** sense, and cannot be the
T-31......IV.8:2 that point is reached you have **n.** choice,
T-31......IV.8:3 This course attempts to teach **n.** more
T-31......IV.9:3 **N.** pathway in the world can lead to Him,
T-31....IV.10:2 He could **n.** more depart from them than
T-31....IV.10:4 is **n.** road that leads away from Him. A
T-31....IV.11:2 aims. They have **n.** meaning. You can not
T-31....IV.11:7 There *is* **n.** path that does not lead to Him.
T-31.......V.2:2 It bears **n.** likeness to yourself at all. It is
T-31.......V.4:2 **N.** one who makes a picture of himself
T-31.......V.6:3 sin. For this is **n.** forgiveness possible. No
T-31.......V.6:4 **N.** longer does it matter what he does, for
T-31.......V.8:1 for **n.** one here can see what it is for, and
T-31.......V.9:1 there is **n.** shattering of what was learned,
T-31.....V.10:9 still **n.** need to hide what you are made of.
T-31.....V.15:2 **n.** concept that can stand for what you are
T-31.....V.16:7 Yet have **n.** fear it will not be undone.
T-31.....V.17:1 world can teach **n.** images of you unless
T-31.....V.17:5 recognized as made on **n.** assumptions
T-31.....V.17:6 **n.** statement that the world is more afraid
T-31......VI.1:2 There is **n.** compromise between the two.
T-31......VI.1:4 There is **n.** choice in vision but this one.
T-31......VI.1:8 may see the world of flesh **n.** more except
T-31......VI.2:2 and happenings that make **n.** sense at all.
T-31......VI.2:4 And **n.** one is exactly as he was an instant
T-31......VI.3:8 so that perception finds **n.** hiding place.
T-31......VI.4:6 It makes **n.** difference what you look upon
T-31......VI.5:1 forget not that **n.** concept of yourself will
T-31.....VII.1:4 which has **n.** opposite and cannot change.
T-31.....VII.1:6 **n.** one here but holds a concept of himself
T-31.....VII.2:7 **N.** longer do you choose that you should
T-31.....VII.5:4 **N.** more than this is asked. On its behalf,
T-31...VII.11:6 He holds **n.** concept of himself between
T-31...VII.12:3 wish that fathered it **n.** longer is held dear
T-31...VII.12:5 a wish, because it has **n.** power to create.
T-31...VII.13:2 It sees **n.** past in anyone at all. And thus it
T-31...VII.14:3 and **n.** remaining hope except to die, and
T-31... VIII.2:5 your actions, you have given it **n.** power.
T-31... VIII.8:3 There is **n.** place for hell within a world
T-31. VIII.12:4 **N.** trace of it remains. Not one illusion is
W-in..........2:3 They need **n.** preparation. The training
W-in..........6:5 of true perception is that it has **n.** limits.
W-in..........7:2 This will require **n.** effort on your part.
W-pI.......1.3:1 and make **n.** allowance for differences in
W-pI.......2.2:5 it. Make **n.** attempt to include anything
W-pI.......5.4:3 *are* **n.** *small upsets. They are all equally*
W-pI.......5.7:1 mind for **n.** more than a minute or so,
W-pI.......6.3:2 *are* **n.** *small upsets. They are all equally*
W-pI.......7.3:6 You would have **n.** idea what this cup is,
W-pI.......8.1:2 **N.** one really sees anything. He sees only
W-pI.......8.4:2 and it is easier to recognize that **n.** matter
W-pI.......9.2:4 **N.** more than that is required for these or
W-pI.....10.1:4 You have **n.** basis for comparison as yet.
W-pI.....10.1:5 you will have **n.** doubt that what you once
W-pI.....10.2:3 **n.** link is made overtly with the things
W-pI.....10.5:2 each involving **n.** more than a minute or
W-pI.....11.2:4 and with **n.** sense of urgency or effort.
W-pI.....11.4:2 little or **n.** uneasiness and an inclination
W-pI.....12.4:2 there is **n.** difference between them. At
W-pI.....13.1:4 perceive something that has **n.** meaning.
W-pI.....14.6:6 it has **n.** meaning. In recognition of this
W-pI........16.h I have **n.** neutral thoughts.
W-pI.....16.1:1 belief that your thoughts have **n.** effect.
W-pI.....16.1:3 is **n.** exception to this fact. Thoughts are
W-pI.....16.2:1 is **n.** more self-contradictory concept than
W-pI.....16.5:6 *thought, because I have* **n.** *neutral thoughts.*
W-pI........17.h I see **n.** neutral things.
W-pI.....17.1:2 see **n.** neutral things because you have no
W-pI.....17.1:2 because you have **n.** neutral thoughts. It is
W-pI.....17.1:5 not so, perception would have **n.** cause,
W-pI.....17.2:2 *I see* **n.** *neutral things because I have no*
W-pI.....17.2:2 *things because I have* **n.** *neutral thoughts.*
W-pI.....17.3:1 essential to make **n.** distinctions between
W-pI.....17.4:1 and **n.** less than three are required for
W-pI.....19.2:3 is a fact that there are **n.** private thoughts.
W-pI.....19.4:1 and will **n.** longer be repeated each day,
W-pI.....20.1:2 virtually **n.** attempt to direct the time for
W-pI.....23.2:2 There is **n.** point in lamenting the world.
W-pI.....23.2:3 is **n.** point in trying to change the world.
W-pI.....24.1:1 In **n.** situation that arises do you realize
W-pI.....24.1:2 you have **n.** guide to appropriate action,
W-pI.....24.1:2 action, and **n.** way of judging the result.
W-pI.....24.6:2 that you have **n.** unified outcome in mind
W-pI.....25.3:2 Since you have **n.** personal interests, your
W-pI.....25.3:3 them, therefore, you have **n.** goals at all.
W-pI.....26.3:4 you can **n.** longer believe in yourself. A
W-pI.....27.2:3 *Vision has* **n.** *cost to anyone.* If fear of loss
W-pI.....28.8:4 as possible. There is **n.** hurry.
W-pI.....31.3:5 as you care to, but with **n.** sense of hurry.
W-pI.....32.1:5 you will see it; when you **n.** longer want it,
W-pI.....35.5:4 Illusions have **n.** direction in reality. They
W-pI.....37.1:4 **N.** one loses; nothing is taken away from
W-pI.....37.2:1 There is **n.** other way in which the idea of
W-pI.....37.2:7 themselves as whole make **n.** demands.
W-pI.....38.3:5 will make **n.** distinctions because there
W-pI.....38.3:5 make no distinctions because there are **n.**
W-pI.....39.2:6 all. **N.** one needs practice to gain what is
W-pI.....40.1:2 are. **N.** long practice periods are required
W-pI.....40.3:1 exercises take little time and **n.** effort.
W-pI.....41.6:4 Then make **n.** effort to think of anything.
W-pI.....42.5:4 may also reach a point where **n.** thoughts
W-pI.....42.7:1 is **n.** limit on the number of short practice
W-pI.....43.2:2 Perception has **n.** function in God, and
W-pI.....43.2:5 Perception has **n.** meaning. Yet does the
W-pI.....43.9:1 If **n.** particular subject presents itself to
W-pI.....44.4:2 slipping by with little or **n.** sense of strain.
W-pI.....44.5:1 Your mind is **n.** longer wholly untrained.
W-pI.....44.6:1 you will have **n.** difficulty in recognizing
W-pI.....44.8:1 **n.** particular approach is advocated for
W-pI.....45.1:3 There is **n.** relationship between what is
W-pI.....45.8:7 remind yourself that this is **n.** idle game,
W-pI.....46.4:1 you should have **n.** difficulty in finding a
W-pI.....46.6:5 *N. fear is possible in a mind beloved of God.*
W-pI.....46.6:6 *is* **n.** *need to attack because love has forgiven*
W-pI.....47.3:3 There are **n.** exceptions because God has
W-pI.....47.3:3 exceptions because God has **n.** exceptions
W-pI.....50.5:3 Let **n.** idle and foolish thoughts enter to
WpI...rI.in.4:2 you learn to require **n.** special settings in
WpI...rI.in.5:2 that there is **n.** limit to where you are, so
W-pI.....51.1:2 see nothing, and nothing has **n.** meaning.
W-pI.....51.1:5 let it go by realizing it has **n.** meaning, so
W-pI.....51.3:5 is **n.** sense in trying to understand it. But
W-pI.....51.5:6 has hurt me, and that I **n.** longer want. I
W-pI.....52.2:6 There will be **n.** past, and therefore no
W-pI.....52.2:6 will be no past, and therefore **n.** enemies.
W-pI.....52.5:2 I have **n.** private thoughts. Yet it is only
W-pI.....53.1:2 that pictures them can have **n.** meaning.
W-pI.....53.2:3 world in which there is **n.** order anywhere
W-pI.....53.2:4 chaotic thinking, and chaos has **n.** laws. I
W-pI.....53.2:7 what is totally insane and has **n.** meaning.
W-pI.....53.3:2 and offers **n.** grounds for trust. Nothing
W-pI.....53.3:4 It holds out **n.** safety and no hope. But
W-pI.....53.3:4 It holds out no safety and **n.** hope. But
W-pI.....53.5:7 and I will place **n.** other gods before Him.
W-pI.....54.1:1 (16) I have **n.** neutral thoughts. Neutral
W-pI.....54.2:1 (17) I see **n.** neutral things. What I see
W-pI.....54.3:2 If I have **n.** private thoughts, I cannot see
W-pI.....57.2:5 in this belief, which I **n.** longer want. The
W-pI.....58.1:3 forgiven, I **n.** longer see myself as guilty. I
W-pI.....59.5:2 have **n.** thoughts I do not share with God.
W-pI.....59.5:3 God. I have **n.** thoughts apart from Him,
W-pI.....59.5:3 because I have **n.** mind apart from His. As
W-pI.....61.2:3 role in salvation and in taking **n.** other. It
W-pI.....63.2:4 Accept **n.** trivial purpose or meaningless
W-pI.....63.2:5 **n.** idle request that is being asked of you.
W-pI.....63.4:3 **N.** chance should be lost for reinforcing
W-pI.....64.4:3 There is **n.** other way. Therefore, every
W-pI.....65.1:2 that you have **n.** function other than that.
W-pI.....65.5:3 make **n.** attempt to concentrate only on
W-pI.....65.8:3 *gave me. I want* **n.** *other and I have no other.*
W-pI.....65.8:3 *gave me. I want no other and I have* **n.** *other.*
W-pI.....66.7:5 There are **n.** other guides but these to
W-pI.....66.7:5 and **n.** other outcomes possible as a result
W-pI...66.10:3 share in this conclusion, but in **n.** other.
W-pI........68.h Love holds **n.** grievances.
W-pI.....68.1:1 can hold **n.** grievances and know your Self
W-pI.....68.1:7 for **n.** one can conceive of his Creator as
W-pI.....68.5:4 that there is **n.** one against whom you do
W-pI.....68.6:8 *Love holds* **n.** *grievances. When I let all my*
W-pI.....68.7:2 *Love holds* **n.** *grievances. Let me not betray*
W-pI.....68.7:5 *Love holds* **n.** *grievances. I would wake to*
W-pI.....69.1:1 **N.** one can look upon what your
W-pI.....69.3:3 There is **n.** other purpose here, and no
W-pI.....69.3:3 here, and **n.** other function to fulfill.
W-pI.....69.5:1 you can see **n.** reason to believe there is a
W-pI.....70.9:4 I assure you this will be **n.** idle fantasy.
W-pI.....71.6:5 There can be **n.** real conflict about this,
W-pI.....71.6:5 because there is **n.** possible alternative to
W-pI.....71.7:2 to be a conflict with **n.** resolution possible
W-pI...71.10:6 be **n.** better way to spend a half minute or
W-pI...72.11:5 **n.** longer asking the ego what salvation is
W-pI.....73.1:4 and therefore have **n.** power at all. Its
W-pI.....73.7:3 You have **n.** will that can really oppose it,
W-pI.....73.8:2 **N.** idle wishes can detain us, nor deceive
W-pI........74.h There is **n.** will but God's.
W-pI.....74.1:6 the Will of God, you have **n.** goal but His.
W-pI.....74.3:2 *There is* **n.** *will but God's. I cannot be in*
W-pI...74.3:12 *There is* **n.** *will but God's. These conflict*
W-pI.....74.4:3 *There is* **n.** *will but God's. I share it with Him.*
W-pI.....74.7:2 *There is* **n.** *will but God's. I seek His peace*
W-pI.....75.2:2 There are **n.** dark dreams now. The light
W-pI.....75.2:6 one has left **n.** trace upon it in its passing.
W-pI.....75.3:2 new. **N.** shadows from the past remain to
W-pI........76.h I am under **n.** laws but God's.
W-pI.....76.1:5 seek for it in things that have **n.** meaning,
W-pI.....76.1:5 bind yourself to laws that make **n.** sense.
W-pI.....76.4:2 that have **n.** use and serve no purpose.
W-pI.....76.4:2 that have no use and serve **n.** purpose.
W-pI.....76.6:1 There are **n.** laws except the laws of God.
W-pI.....76.6:3 Your magic has **n.** meaning. What it is
W-pI.....76.7:3 It is **n.** longer a truth that we would hide.
W-pI.....76.7:6 light has come because there are **n.** laws
W-pI.....76.8:7 are **n.** more strange than other "laws" you
W-pI.....76.9:1 There are **n.** laws but God's. Dismiss all
W-pI.....76.9:3 says there is **n.** loss under the laws of God
W-pI.....76.9:5 cannot be made; there are **n.** substitutes;
W-pI...76.11:4 understood there are **n.** laws but God's.
W-pI...76.11:6 concludes: *I am under* **n.** *laws but God's.*
W-pI.....77.3:4 ask **n.** more than what belongs to us in
W-pI.....77.6:5 **n.** room for doubt and uncertainty today.
W-pI.....78.8:4 to you, seeing **n.** separation in God's Son.
W-pI.....78.8:7 **N.** dark grievances obscure the sight of
W-pI.....79.3:4 There seems to be **n.** end to them. There
W-pI.....79.3:5 **n.** time in which you feel completely free
W-pI.....79.5:1 **N.** one could solve all the problems the
W-pI.....79.6:2 is separation, **n.** matter what form it takes
W-pI.....80.1:1 will recognize that you have **n.** problems.
W-pI.....80.1:2 has been answered, and you have **n.** other
WpI..rII.in.4:2 take, they have **n.** meaning and no power.
WpI..rII.in.4:2 take, they have no meaning and **n.** power.
W-pI.....83.1:2 have **n.** function but the one God gave me
W-pI.....84.1:6 I will worship **n.** idols, nor raise my own
W-pI.....84.3:1 (68) Love holds **n.** grievances. Grievances
W-pI.....84.4:2 *This is* **n.** *justification for denying my Self. I*
W-pI.....85.2:4 *away. I have* **n.** *need for this. I want to see.*
W-pI.....85.4:4 *has* **n.** *power to remove salvation from me.*
W-pI.....86.1:6 it is. I will undertake **n.** more idle seeking.
W-pI.....86.2:3 **n.** *exception in God's plan for my salvation.*
W-pI.....86.3:5 I would **n.** longer defeat my own best
W-pI.....87.3:1 (74) There is **n.** will but God's. I am safe
W-pI.....87.3:2 today because there is **n.** will but God's. I
W-pI.....87.3:6 am safe because there is **n.** will but God's.
W-pI.....88.1:7 choose the light, for it has **n.** alternative.
W-pI.....88.3:1 (76) I am under **n.** laws but God's. Here
W-pI.....88.3:3 I am under **n.** laws but God's. I am
W-pI.....88.3:6 They have **n.** real effect on me at all. I am
W-pI.....89.1:2 because I am under **n.** laws but God's. His
W-pI.....89.3:5 make **n.** exceptions and no substitutes. I
W-pI.....89.3:5 make no exceptions and **n.** substitutes. I
W-pI.....91.9:3 that is mistaken and deserves **n.** faith. Try
W-pI.....92.2:4 Yet this is **n.** more foolish than to believe
W-pI.....92.7:2 **N.** miracles are here, but only hate. It
W-pI.....92.8:2 **N.** one can ask in vain to share its sight,
W-pI.....94.3:8 This is the Self that knows **n.** fear, nor
W-pI...95.10:4 there is **n.** doubt that only this is true.

W-pI.....96.2:1 be reconciled, **n.** matter how you try,
W-pI.....96.3:1 Problems that have **n.** meaning cannot
W-pI.....96.3:2 and good and evil have **n.** meeting place.
W-pI.....96.3:5 Make **n.** attempt to reconcile the two, for
W-pI.....96.3:6 **n.** place in which it could be really part of
W-pI.....96.4:5 Without its function then it has **n.** peace,
W-pI.....96.6:1 Waste **n.** more time on this. Who can
W-pI.....97.1:2 It accepts **n.** split identity, nor tries to
W-pI.....97.1:5 **N.** chill of fear can enter, for your mind
W-pI.....97.4:1 time that has **n.** limit and that has no end.
W-pI.....97.4:1 time that has no limit and that has **n.** end.
W-pI.....98.3:1 The guiltless have **n.** fear, for they are
W-pI.....98.5:3 a reward so great it has **n.** measure? You
W-pI.....98.6:3 And since time has **n.** meaning, you are
W-pI.....99.4:2 without attack and with **n.** touch of pain?
W-pI.....99.6:2 lays **n.** faith in what is not created by the
W-pI.....99.8:3 upon **n.** obstacle to what He wills for you.
W-pI.....99.9:8 Self as Love which has **n.** opposite in you.
W-pI...99.10:4 You have **n.** function that is not of God.
W-pI...100.3:4 and **n.** one laughs because all laughter can
W-pI...100.6:3 and wills **n.** sorrow rises to abate his joy;
W-pI...100.6:3 joy; **n.** fear besets him to disturb his peace
W-pI...101.5:2 sin will never happen, for it has **n.** cause.
W-pI...101.5:3 cherishes **n.** lingering belief that you have
W-pI...101.5:4 Son. There is **n.** sin. We practice with this
W-pI...101.6:1 perfect happiness because there is **n.** sin,
W-pI...101.6:7 *There is **n.** sin; it has no consequence.* So
W-pI...101.6:7 *There is no sin; it has **n.** consequence.* So
W-pI...101.7:4 There is **n.** sin. Remember this today, and
W-pI...101.7:7 *This is the truth, because there is **n.** sin.*
W-pI...102.1:3 it, and to suspect it really makes **n.** sense.
W-pI...102.2:1 with **n.** power to accomplish anything. It
W-pI...102.3:3 is your peace, and here there is **n.** fear.
W-pI...102.5:2 You have **n.** need to be less loving to
W-pI...103.1:4 Love has **n.** limits, being everywhere. And
W-pI...103.1:7 opposition in what has **n.** limit and no
W-pI...103.1:7 in what has no limit and **n.** opposite.
W-pI...103.2:2 These images, with **n.** reality in truth,
W-pI...105.1:6 The truly given gift entails **n.** loss. It is
W-pI...105.2:1 **N.** gift is given thus. Such "gifts" are but
W-pI...105.5:5 **N.** more can you. Receive His gift of joy
W-pI...107.1:5 because, without belief, they have **n.** life.
W-pI...107.3:2 Without illusions there could be **n.** fear,
W-pI...107.3:2 could be no fear, **n.** doubt and no attack.
W-pI...107.3:2 could be no fear, no doubt and **n.** attack.
W-pI...107.3:3 **n.** room for transitory thoughts and dead
W-pI...107.3:5 have **n.** place because the truth has come,
W-pI...107.5:2 of healing, for the truth needs **n.** defense,
W-pI...107.5:2 therefore **n.** attack is possible. Illusions
W-pI...108.3:1 This is the light that shows **n.** opposites,
W-pI...109.3:3 There is **n.** suffering it cannot heal. There
W-pI...109.3:4 There is **n.** problem but it cannot solve.
W-pI...109.3:5 And **n.** appearance but will turn to truth
W-pI...109.5:1 Him you have **n.** cares and no concerns,
W-pI...109.5:1 and **n.** concerns, no burdens, no anxiety,
W-pI...109.5:1 no cares and no concerns, **n.** burdens, no
W-pI...109.5:1 and no concerns, no burdens, **n.** anxiety,
W-pI...109.5:1 concerns, no burdens, no anxiety, **n.** pain
W-pI...109.5:1 pain, **n.** fear of future and no past regrets.
W-pI...109.5:1 pain, no fear of future and **n.** past regrets.
W-pI...109.5:7 **N.** more fearful dreams will come, now
W-pI...109.8:2 to your trust today, forgetting **n.** one,
W-pI...110.1:3 that you have made **n.** changes in yourself
W-pI...110.1:4 as God created you fear has **n.** meaning,
W-pI...110.3:3 You need **n.** thought but just this one, to
W-pI...110.4:2 been **n.** separation of your mind from His
W-pI...110.4:2 His, **n.** split between your mind and other
W-pI...114.1:3 ***N.** body can contain my spirit, nor impose*
W-pI...117.1:3 *I choose to entertain **n.** substitutes for love.*
W-pI...121.1:2 in a world that seems to make **n.** sense.
W-pI...121.2:1 of fear, and offers love **n.** room to be itself
W-pI...121.2:1 **n.** place where it can spread its wings in
W-pI...121.4:1 The unforgiving mind sees **n.** mistakes,
W-pI...121.4:4 It wants forgiveness, yet it sees **n.** hope. It
W-pI...121.7:3 It has **n.** hope, but you become its hope.
W-pI...122.2:3 so you see **n.** dreams of fear and evil,
W-pI...122.4:4 Seek for it **n.** more. You will not find
W-pI...122.6:5 There is **n.** plan but this for the salvation
W-pI...122.7:5 The world can give **n.** gifts of any value to
W-pI...122.7:6 intricacies of your dreams **n.** longer hide
W-pI...122.9:2 but where we would remain **n.** more.
W-pI.122.12:1 world arise you have **n.** words to picture.
W-pI...123.1:3 There is **n.** thought of turning back, and
W-pI...123.1:3 and **n.** implacable resistance to the truth.
W-pI...123.4:1 **n.** longer looking downward to the dust.
W-pI...124.4:2 care. **N.** meaningless anxieties can come
W-pI...124.6:1 **N.** miracle can ever be denied to those
W-pI...124.6:2 **N.** thought of theirs but has the power to
W-pI...124.8:4 which we give **n.** rules nor special words
W-pI.124.10:3 thankfully aware **n.** time was ever better
W-pI...125.1:5 **N.** peace is possible until His Word is
W-pI...125.2:2 **N.** other means can save it, for God's plan
W-pI...125.8:3 with **n.** separation nor division in the
W-pI...125.9:2 You will need **n.** rule but this, to let your
W-pI...125.9:4 with **n.** illusions interposed between the
W-pI...126.1:2 be **n.** problem in complete forgiveness,
W-pI...126.2:2 which have **n.** bearing on your thoughts,
W-pI...126.2:3 your attitudes have **n.** effect on them, and
W-pI...126.3:1 a sin, there is **n.** gain to you directly. You
W-pI...126.3:4 He has **n.** claim on your forgiveness. It
W-pI...126.4:5 the gift is **n.** more yours than was his sin.
W-pI...126.5:1 forgiveness has **n.** grounds on which to
W-pI...126.6:5 It has **n.** power to restore your unity with
W-pI......127.h There is **n.** love but God's.
W-pI...127.1:4 It has **n.** separate parts and no degrees;
W-pI...127.1:4 It has no separate parts and **n.** degrees;
W-pI...127.1:4 parts and no degrees; **n.** kinds nor levels,
W-pI...127.1:4 levels, **n.** divergencies and no distinctions
W-pI...127.1:4 levels, no divergencies and **n.** distinctions
W-pI...127.3:5 There is **n.** love but God's, and all of love
W-pI...127.3:6 **n.** other principle that rules where love is
W-pI...127.4:1 **N.** course whose purpose is to teach you
W-pI...127.4:4 There is **n.** love but His, and what He is, is
W-pI...127.4:5 is. There is **n.** limit placed upon Himself,
W-pI...127.5:1 **N.** law the world obeys can help you
W-pI...127.7:2 understand there is **n.** better use for time
W-pI.127.12:5 *that there is **n.** love but God's and yours and*
W-pI...128.1:3 **N.** one but must accept this thought as
W-pI...128.2:1 and it will serve **n.** other end but this. For
W-pI...128.2:4 Be you deceived **n.** more. The world you
W-pI...129.2:2 Perhaps you will concede there is **n.** loss
W-pI...129.2:5 **N.** lasting love is found, for none is here.
W-pI...129.3:1 exist and vengeance has **n.** meaning? Is it
W-pI...129.3:2 and know they have **n.** ending and they
W-pI...129.4:3 Their language has **n.** words, for what
W-pI...129.9:1 Now do we understand there is **n.** loss.
W-pI...130.1:5 **N.** one can see a world his mind has not
W-pI...130.1:6 And **n.** one can fail to look upon what he
W-pI...130.4:5 Yet love can have **n.** enemy, and so they
W-pI...130.4:5 have no enemy, and so they have **n.** cause,
W-pI...130.4:5 no cause, **n.** being and no consequence.
W-pI...130.4:5 no cause, no being and **n.** consequence.
W-pI...130.5:1 worlds which have **n.** overlap of any kind.
W-pI...130.6:1 Today we will attempt **n.** compromise
W-pI...130.8:6 *God offers me and see **n.** value in this world,*
W-pI......131.h **N.** one can fail who seeks to reach the
W-pI...131.2:2 There is **n.** way to reach them, for the
W-pI...131.4:3 **N.** one can fail to want this goal and reach
W-pI...131.5:1 **N.** one remains in hell, for no one can
W-pI...131.5:1 hell, for **n.** one can abandon his Creator,
W-pI...131.7:2 God made **n.** contradictions. What denies
W-pI...131.9:3 and contradicts what has **n.** opposite. He
W-pI.131.10:2 **N.** one can fail who seeks to reach the
W-pI.131.10:3 place of thoughts that have **n.** meaning,
W-pI.131.10:3 thoughts that have no meaning, **n.** effect,
W-pI.131.12:2 remind yourself **n.** one can fail who seeks
W-pI.131.12:4 **n.** other goal is valued now nor sought,
W-pI.131.15:7 ***N.** one can fail who seeks to reach the truth.*
W-pI...132.5:1 is **n.** world apart from what you wish, and
W-pI...132.6:2 it is. There is **n.** world! This is the central
W-pI...132.7:1 are prepared to learn there is **n.** world,
W-pI...132.9:3 There is **n.** place where you can suffer,
W-pI...132.9:3 and **n.** time that can bring change to your
W-pI.132.10:3 is **n.** world apart from your ideas because
W-pI.132.12:3 makes **n.** distinctions in what is Himself
W-pI.132.13:1 There is **n.** world because it is a thought
W-pI.132.14:3 **N.** more can we. For we are in the home
W-pI.132.15:4 Then merely rest, alert but with **n.** strain,
W-pI .. 133.2:5 There are **n.** satisfactions in the world.
W-pI .. 133.3:3 **n.** more than you can make alternatives
W-pI .. 133.5:1 that there is **n.** compromise in what your
W-pI .. 133.5:2 you just a little, for there is **n.** in between.
W-pI .. 133.6:4 makes **n.** offering to him who chooses it.
W-pI 133.10:3 serve them as his own makes **n.** mistakes,
W-pI 133.12:3 fact that **n.** decision can be difficult. What
W-pI .. 134.5:1 Pardon is **n.** escape in such a view. It
W-pI 134.13:2 is **n.** thought in all the world that leads to
W-pI 134.14:1 the time of joining be **n.** more delayed.
W-pI 134.17:7 ***N.** one is crucified alone, and yet no one can*
W-pI 134.17:7 *and yet **n.** one can enter Heaven by himself.*
W-pI .. 135.2:5 For **n.** one walks the world in armature
W-pI .. 135.5:2 **n.** needs but those which you assign to it.
W-pI .. 135.5:3 to it. It needs **n.** complicated structures of
W-pI .. 135.5:3 of defense, **n.** health-inducing medicine,
W-pI .. 135.5:3 medicine, **n.** care and no concern at all.
W-pI .. 135.5:3 medicine, no care and **n.** concern at all.
W-pI .. 135.7:1 The body is in need of **n.** defense. This
W-pI 135.10:4 a kind from which it gains **n.** benefit at all
W-pI 135.16:5 Anticipation plays **n.** part at all, for
W-pI 135.19:2 Let **n.** defenses but your present trust
W-pI 135.21:3 We make **n.** plans for how it will be done,
W-pI 135.26:8 *the Son of God needs **n.** defense against the*
W-pI .. 136.1:1 **N.** one can heal unless he understands
W-pI .. 136.1:2 as well its purpose has **n.** meaning. Being
W-pI .. 136.7:4 threaten your establishments **n.** more.
W-pI 136.14:1 for **n.** illusions can remain where truth
W-pI 136.16:2 There will be **n.** dark corners sickness can
W-pI 136.16:3 will be **n.** dim figures from your dreams,
W-pI 136.17:3 will be **n.** sense of feeling ill or feeling well
W-pI 136.17:4 **N.** response at all is in the mind to what
W-pI .. 137.3:6 as he sees the body has **n.** power to attack
W-pI .. 137.7:3 can be **n.** longer cherished nor obeyed.
W-pI 137.10:1 of those who seem to have **n.** contact with
W-pI .. 138.2:1 Creation knows **n.** opposite. But here is
W-pI .. 138.3:5 There is **n.** sense of gain, for nothing is
W-pI .. 138.4:5 you will perceive it was **n.** choice at all.
W-pI .. 138.4:7 There is **n.** opposite to choose instead.
W-pI .. 138.4:8 There is **n.** contradiction to the truth.
W-pI 138.11:4 It holds **n.** terror now, for what was made
W-pI .. 139.1:4 There is **n.** doubt that is not rooted here.
W-pI .. 139.1:5 There is **n.** question but reflects this one.
W-pI .. 139.1:6 **n.** conflict that does not entail the single,
W-pI .. 139.5:3 denial made **n.** change in what you are.
W-pI .. 139.5:6 There is **n.** doubt of this. And yet you
W-pI .. 140.1:3 mind, it sees **n.** separation from the body,
W-pI .. 140.5:5 Yet there is **n.** place where He is not. And
W-pI .. 140.5:6 And therefore sin can have **n.** home in
W-pI .. 140.5:7 There is **n.** place where holiness is not,
W-pI .. 140.6:4 This is **n.** magic. It is merely an appeal to
W-pI .. 140.6:7 it is, and knows that **n.** illusion can be real
W-pI .. 140.7:3 is **n.** remedy the world provides that can
W-pI .. 140.7:5 There is **n.** change but this. For how can
W-pI .. 140.7:6 but in attributes that have **n.** substance,
W-pI .. 140.7:6 that have no substance, **n.** reality, no core
W-pI .. 140.7:6 that have no substance, no reality, **n.** core
W-pI .. 140.9:4 Here there are **n.** degrees, and no beliefs
W-pI .. 140.9:4 and **n.** beliefs that what does not exist is
W-pI 140.10:3 **N.** voice but this can cure. Today we hear
W-pI 140.11:4 We have **n.** need to make them different,
W-pI 140.12:4 peace so deep that **n.** illusion can disturb
WpI..rIV.in2:6 For in his mind **n.** thoughts can dwell but
WpI..rIV.in4:3 **N.** more than can a child who throws a
WpI..rIV.in7:3 There is **n.** hurry now, for you are using
WpI..rIV.in7:6 use **n.** format for our practicing but this:
WpI..rIV.in9:1 We add **n.** other thoughts, but let these
WpI..rIV.in9:2 are. We need **n.** more than this to give us
W-pI .. 144.1:1 (127) There is **n.** love but God's.
W-pI .. 146.1:1 (131) **N.** one can fail who seeks to reach
W-pI .. 151.1:1 **N.** one can judge on partial evidence.
W-pI .. 151.8:1 has certainty in which there is **n.** doubt,
W-pI 151.10:3 You will **n.** longer doubt that only good
W-pI 151.12:4 in everything **n.** sound except the echo of
W-pI 151.15:4 **N.** one can fail to listen, when you hear
W-pI 151.17:3 the joyous news that truth has **n.** illusions
W-pI .. 152.1:1 **N.** one can suffer loss unless it be his own
W-pI .. 152.1:2 **N.** one suffers pain except his choice
W-pI .. 152.1:3 **N.** one can grieve nor fear nor think him

W-pII .242.1:4 And He is glad to make **n.** choices for me
W-pII .244.2:2 **N.** storms can come into the hallowed
W-pII .249.1:1 impossible and anger makes **n.** sense.
W-pII .....4.3:2 the "proof" that what has **n.** reality is real.
W-pII .....4.3:4 slain by hate, and peace to be **n.** more.
W-pII .....4.5:5 There is **n.** sin. Creation is unchanged.
W-pII .254.1:3 *I have* **n.** *prayer but this: I come to You to ask*
W-pII .254.2:1 Today we let **n.** ego thoughts direct our
W-pII .255.1:5 God's Son can have **n.** cares, and must
W-pII .256.1:2 There is **n.** other way. If sin had not been
W-pII .256.2:2 *We have* **n.** *goal except to hear Your Voice,*
W-pII .257.1:2 **N.** one can serve contradicting goals and
W-pII .257.2:2 *today that we can have* **n.** *will but Yours.*
W-pII .258.1:5 We have **n.** aim but to remember Him.
W-pII .258.2:2 *We have* **n.** *goal but this. What could we*
W-pII ....259.h Let me remember that there is **n.** sin.
W-pII .259.2:3 *For love can have* **n.** *opposite. You are the*
W-pII .260.2:2 we, because our Source can know **n.** sin.
W-pII ....262.h Let me perceive **n.** differences today.
W-pII .264.1:5 *There is* **n.** *source but this, and nothing is*
W-pII .265.1:5 There is **n.** fear in it. Let no appearance of
W-pII .265.1:6 Let **n.** appearance of my sins obscure the
W-pII .....6.2:1 is **n.** more than an illusion of despair, for
W-pII .....6.2:5 Self Who, like His Father, knows **n.** sin.
W-pII .....6.5:3 will we know we have **n.** need of learning
W-pII .272.1:6 *I will accept* **n.** *less than You have given me. I*
W-pII .274.2:2 to Him, and there will be **n.** fear today,
W-pII .275.1:1 **n.** more true today than any other day.
W-pII .277.1:6 *he knows* **n.** *law except the law of love.*
W-pII .280.1:3 **N.** Thought of God has left its Father's
W-pII .280.1:4 **N.** Thought of God is limited at all. No
W-pII .280.1:5 **N.** Thought of God but is forever pure.
W-pII .280.2:2 *I lay* **n.** *limits on the Son You love and You*
W-pII .284.1:3 There is **n.** grief with any cause at all. And
W-pII .286.1:3 *lesson that there is* **n.** *need that I do anything*
W-pII .289.1:5 It has **n.** past. For what can be forgiven
W-pII .....8.2:4 are **n.** cries of pain and sorrow heard, for
W-pII .....8.3:5 **N.** danger lurks in anything it sees, for it
W-pII .....8.4:1 is over, and God's Son **n.** longer sleeps.
W-pII .....8.5:1 The Holy Spirit has **n.** need of time when
W-pII .292.1:1 God's promises make **n.** exceptions. And
W-pII .296.1:2 *me, for I would use* **n.** *words but Yours, and*
W-pII .296.1:2 **n.** *thoughts which are apart from Yours, for*
W-pII .300.1:2 lets **n.** false perception keep us in its hold,
W-pII .....9.2:2 There is **n.** end to the release the Second
W-pII .303.1:6 Let Him **n.** longer be a stranger here, for
W-pII .305.1:1 that the world contains **n.** counterpart.
W-pII .305.1:3 it to truth, **n.** more to be the home of fear.
W-pII .307.1:2 *There is* **n.** *other will for me to have. Let me*
W-pII .309.1:2 as is His Own, can will **n.** change in this.
W-pII .309.1:6 real. Yet it has **n.** effects. Within me is the
W-pII .310.2:4 There is **n.** room in us for fear today, for
W-pII ...10.2:1 on the world contains **n.** condemnation.
W-pII .312.2:1 *I have* **n.** *purpose for today except to look*
W-pII .313.1:5 *for He sees* **n.** *sin in anything He looks upon.*
W-pII .314.1:3 Past mistakes can cast **n.** shadows on it,
W-pII .314.1:3 being formless, it has **n.** effects. Death
W-pII .316.1:2 and leave **n.** shadow on the holy mind my
W-pII .319.1:3 But when there is **n.** arrogance the truth
W-pII .320.1:2 There are **n.** limits on his strength, his
W-pII .320.2:2 *me. There is* **n.** *limit on Your Will. And so all*
W-pII ...11.1:3 There was **n.** time when all that it created
W-pII .321.1:3 *me. Now I would guide myself* **n.** *more. For I*
W-pII .322.2:4 *What You did not give has* **n.** *reality. What*
W-pII .323.2:2 We are deceived **n.** longer. Love has now
W-pII .328.2:1 *There is* **n.** *will but Yours. And I am glad that*
W-pII .329.2:2 We have **n.** will apart from His, and all of
W-pII ....331.h There is **n.** conflict, for my will is Yours.
W-pII .331.1:6 *There is* **n.** *will except the Will of Love. Fear*
W-pII .331.1:7 *and has* **n.** *will that can conflict with Yours.*
W-pII331.1:10 *There is* **n.** *opposition to Your Will. There is*
W-pII331.1:11 *Will. There is* **n.** *conflict, for my will is Yours.*
W-pII .333.2:2 *N. light but this can end our evil dream. No*
W-pII .333.2:3 *N. light but this can save the world. For this*
W-pII .338.1:3 has he learned that **n.** one frightens him,
W-pII .338.1:4 He has **n.** enemies, and he is safe from all
W-pII .339.1:1 **N.** one desires pain. But he can think that
W-pII .339.1:3 **N.** one would avoid his happiness. But he
W-pII .340.2:3 There is **n.** room for anything but joy and
W-pII .343.1:9 *Your Son can make* **n.** *sacrifice, for he must*
W-pII .343.2:2 Salvation has **n.** cost. It is a gift that must
W-pII .345.1:5 *it is different, for there, there are* **n.** *needs.*
W-pII .346.1:6 *and know* **n.** *laws except Your law of love.*
W-pII ....348.h I have **n.** cause for anger or for fear, For
W-pII .348.1:3 *Love. I have* **n.** *cause for anything except the*
W-pII .354.1:2 *I have* **n.** *self except the Christ in me. I have*
W-pII .354.1:3 *I have* **n.** *purpose but His Own. And He is like*
W-pII ....355.h There is **n.** end to all the peace and joy,
W-pII ....358.h **N.** call to God can be unheard nor left
W-pII .359.1:6 *mistakes which have* **n.** *real effects on us. Sin*
Wfl........in.6:5 And more than that can **n.** one ever have,
W-ep ......... 1:4 **N.** one who calls on Him can call in vain.
W-ep ......... 3:1 **N.** more specific lessons are assigned, for
W-ep ......... 3:1 there is **n.** more need of them. Henceforth
M-in .......... 2:4 will teach, for in that there is **n.** choice.
M-in ........ 2:11 **N.** more than that, but also never less.
M-in .......... 4:2 There is **n.** escape from it. How could it
M-in .......... 5:7 And then they are seen **n.** more, although
M-1 ........... 2:2 from all religions and from **n.** religion.
M-1 ......... 2:14 it. To the Call Itself time has **n.** meaning.
M-1 ........... 3:6 in any language or in **n.** language; in any
M-3 ........... 1:1 teachers of God have **n.** set teaching level.
M-3 ........... 1:3 There is **n.** one from whom a teacher of
M-3 ........... 1:3 so there is **n.** one whom he cannot teach.
M-3 ........... 1:6 There are **n.** accidents in salvation. Those
M-3 ........... 3:5 and His plan can have **n.** levels, being a
M-3 ........... 5:8 **N.** teacher of God can fail to find the Help
M-4 ..... I.A.5:4 **n.** point in sorting out the valuable from
M-4 ........II.1:6 do; **n.** thought opposes any other thought
M-4 ........II.1:6 any other thought; **n.** act belies your word
M-4 ........II.1:6 **n.** word lacks agreement with another.
M-4 ........II.1:8 honest. At **n.** level are they in conflict
M-4 ........II.2:3 war. **N.** one at one with himself can even
M-4 ........II.2:5 There is **n.** challenge to a teacher of God.
M-4 .... III.1:11 **N.** teacher of God can judge and hope to
M-4 ...... IV.1:8 **N.** teacher of God but must learn,–and
M-4 .... IV.1:12 achieve nothing. **N.** gain can come of it.
M-4 ...... IV.2:4 To those to whom harm has **n.** meaning,
M-4 ....... V.1:4 The gentle have **n.** pain. They cannot
M-4 ..... V.1:10 making sure **n.** harm can come to them.
M-4 ...... VI.1:2 They have **n.** dreams that need defense
M-4 ...... VI.1:6 **N.** one can become an advanced teacher
M-4 ..... VII.1:3 trust **n.** one can be generous in the true
M-4 .... VIII.1:6 The past as well held **n.** mistakes; nothing
M-4 .. VIII.1:10 **n.** outcome already seen or yet to come
M-4 ........X.2:7 gone. **N.** clouds remain to hide the face of
M-4 ......X.2:11 makes **n.** effort to exceed its legitimate
M-5 .........I.1:1 sufferer **n.** longer sees any value in pain.
M-5 ........II.1:2 "There is **n.** gain at all to me in this" and
M-5 .....II.2:12 their aid and say, "I have **n.** use for this."
M-5 .....II.2:13 There is **n.** form of sickness that would
M-5 ........II.3:7 see. **N.** more and no less. The world does
M-5 ........II.3:7 see. No more and **n.** less. The world does
M-5 ........II.4:5 value of one true idea has **n.** end or limit.
M-5 ........II.4:8 Having **n.** purpose, they are gone. And
M-5 ...... III.1:4 **n.** function except to rejoice with them,
M-5 .... III.1:10 have **n.** idea how insane this concept is. If
M-5 ...... III.3:5 They recognize illusions can have **n.** effect
M-5 ...... III.3:9 to see **n.** will as separate from their own,
M-6 ........... 1:3 demonstrates illusions have **n.** value. The
M-6 ........... 2:7 increase. **N.** teacher of God should feel
M-6 ........... 3:4 **N.** one can give if he is concerned with the
M-7 ........... 3:5 He need do **n.** more, nor is there more
M-8 ........... 5:1 be **n.** order of difficulty in healing merely
M-8 ........... 6:2 healed will **n.** longer acknowledge them.
M-9 ........... 1:3 that **n.** one is where he is by accident, and
M-9 ........... 1:3 and chance plays **n.** part in God's plan. It
M-9 ........... 1:5 There is, however, **n.** set pattern, since
M-10 ....... 1:10 not mean anything. **N.** more does "bad."
M-10 ......... 2:5 for him, he **n.** longer attempts it. This is
M-10 ......... 2:6 it. This is **n.** sacrifice. On the contrary, he
M-10 ......... 3:5 there is **n.** distortion in his perception, so
M-10 ....... 4:10 for there is **n.** distortion in His perception
M-10 ....... 5:10 Now he makes **n.** mistakes. His Guide is
M-11 ......... 1:5 It has also promised that there is **n.** death,
M-11 ......... 2:5 God says there is **n.** death; your judgment
M-11 ......... 3:4 yet out of which **n.** way seems possible,–
M-11 ....... 4:12 It is **n.** longer, "Can peace be possible in
M-12 ......... 1:4 now **n.** longer sees himself as a body, or
M-12 ......... 2:4 God can **n.** longer be feared, for the mind
M-12 ......... 2:4 for the mind sees **n.** cause for punishment
M-12 ......... 6:9 as sick and separate is **n.** more real than
M-13 ......... 1:2 it came when there is **n.** more use for it.
M-13 ......... 2:4 There is **n.** sacrifice in the world's terms
M-13 ......... 3:6 and **n.** one doubts what he believes he is.
M-13 ......... 4:1 God's teachers can have **n.** regret on
M-13 ......... 4:5 **N.** one who has escaped the world and all
M-13 ......... 5:4 There is **n.** pleasure of the world that does
M-13 ......... 5:4 and **n.** one asks for pain if he recognizes it
M-13 ......... 5:8 and **n.** one who pursues the world's goals
M-13 ......... 6:9 is **n.** other hope in all the world that they
M-13 ....... 6:10 **n.** other voice in all the world that echoes
M-13 ......... 7:2 There are **n.** half sacrifices. You cannot
M-13 ......... 7:5 The Word of God has **n.** exceptions. It is
M-13 ......... 8:2 everything is given you at **n.** cost at all.
M-14 ......... 1:1 Can what has **n.** beginning really end?
M-14 ......... 1:4 of forgiveness, complete, excluding **n.** one
M-14 ......... 1:5 for now it has **n.** purpose and is gone. The
M-14 ......... 1:7 as purposeless, they are **n.** longer seen.
M-14 ......... 3:9 **N.**; it is meaningless to anyone here. Yet it
M-15 ......... 1:2 **N.** one can escape God's Final Judgment.
M-15 ......... 1:4 until it is **n.** longer associated with fear.
M-15 ......... 2:3 **N.**; not yet, not yet. But this is still your
M-15 ......... 3:6 There is **n.** deceit in God. His promises
M-16 ......... 1:2 is **n.** program, for the lessons change each
M-16 ......... 3:2 This is by **n.** means the ultimate criterion,
M-16 ....... 6:12 You have **n.** need of them. Recognize this,
M-16 ......... 7:2 the name of safety **n.** longer interests him.
M-16 ......... 7:5 He need make **n.** distinctions among the
M-16 ......... 7:5 of them recognizes **n.** order of difficulty
M-16 ......... 7:7 **n.** difference in his state at different times
M-16 ......... 7:9 And he has **n.** need for more than this.
M-16 ......... 9:4 They can have **n.** effects; neither good nor
M-16 ......... 9:9 What has **n.** effects can hardly terrify.
M-16 ....... 10:1 There is **n.** substitute for the Will of God.
M-16 ....... 10:9 two aspects of one error and **n.** more, he
M-16 ....... 11:5 it. **N.** risk is possible throughout the day
M-16 ....... 11:6 "There is **n.** will but God's." His teachers
M-17 ......... 4:1 that **n.** one can be angry at a fact. It is
M-17 ......... 7:7 And now there is **n.** hope. Except to kill.
M-17 ......... 9:2 In truth it has **n.** power to make anything.
M-17 ....... 9:10 There is **n.** death. This sword does not
M-18 ......... 4:8 him, and he **n.** longer condemns himself.
M-19 ......... 1:7 **n.** one in the world is capable of making
M-19 ......... 1:8 there would be **n.** need for salvation. The
M-19 ......... 2:4 is **n.** inherent conflict between justice and
M-19 ......... 3:5 Forgiveness has **n.** place in such a scheme,
M-20 ......... 2:4 It brings with it **n.** past associations. It is a
M-20 ......... 3:2 **N.** one can fail to find it who but seeks
M-20 ......... 5:5 Life has **n.** opposite, for it is God. Life and
M-20 ......... 6:2 of God? **N.** more than this; the simple
M-20 ......... 6:3 is **n.** thought that contradicts His Will,
M-20 ......... 6:5 In truth there was **n.** conflict, for His Will
M-21 ......... 1:1 words play **n.** part at all in healing. The
M-21 ......... 2:3 the word has little or **n.** practical meaning
M-21 ....... 3:10 that which has **n.** human symbols at all.
M-21 ......... 4:2 **N.**, indeed! There are many who must be
M-21 ......... 5:4 All these are judgments that have **n.** value
M-22 ......... 1:2 There is **n.** order of difficulty in miracles
M-22 ......... 1:2 there are **n.** degrees of Atonement. It is
M-22 ......... 4:7 This recognition has **n.** special reference.
M-22 ......... 7:9 **N.** longer does he stand apart from God,
M-23 ......... 2:7 him. There is now **n.** limit on his power,
M-23 ......... 2:8 he **n.** longer sees himself as separate from
M-23 ......... 5:7 he sees **n.** limit and no stain to mar your
M-23 ......... 5:7 limit and **n.** stain to mar your beautiful
M-23 ......... 6:1 **N.** one on earth can grasp what Heaven is
M-23 ......... 6:6 on us. **N.** one who has become a true and
M-24 ......... 1:2 There is **n.** past or future, and the idea of
M-24 ......... 1:2 has **n.** meaning either once or many times
M-24 ......... 6:7 There is **n.** other time. No teaching that
M-24 ......... 6:8 **N.** teaching that does not lead to this is of
M-24 ....... 6:13 requires. **N.** more than this is necessary.
M-25 ......... 1:2 are, of course, **n.** "unnatural" powers, and
M-25 ......... 2:8 there is **n.** magic in his accomplishments.
M-25 ......... 3:5 in themselves, **n.** matter how this is done,
M-25 ......... 3:7 God gives **n.** special favors, and no one

| | |
|---|---|
| M-25..........3:7 | and **n.** one has any powers that are not |
| M-25..........5:1 | **n.** longer value the material things of the |
| M-25..........5:6 | the "power" is **n.** longer a genuine ability, |
| M-25..........6:2 | To this there is **n.** exception. And the |
| M-26..........1:1 | is **n.** distance between Him and His Son. |
| M-26..........2:1 | retaining **n.** trace of worldly limits and |
| M-26..........2:2 | although they are **n.** longer visible, their |
| M-26..........2:5 | **N.** one can call on them in vain. Nor is |
| M-26..........2:9 | all things in their name and in **n.** other. |
| M-27..........1:7 | And **n.** one asks if a benign Creator could |
| M-27..........4:2 | If death is real for anything, there is **n.** life |
| M-27..........4:5 | **N.** compromise in this is possible. There |
| M-27..........5:4 | is **n.** point at which the contrast between |
| M-27..........6:3 | the idea of death there is **n.** world. All |
| M-27..........7:1 | Accept **n.** compromise in which death |
| M-28..........1:6 | having **n.** function except communication |
| M-28..........2:4 | as hell. Love is **n.** longer feared, but gladly |
| M-28..........2:7 | There is **n.** sorrow still upon the earth. |
| M-28..........3:2 | From here on, **n.** directions are needed. |
| M-28........3:11 | There is **n.** opposition to the truth. And |
| M-28..........4:2 | There is **n.** death. The Son of God is free. |
| M-28..........4:5 | **N.** hidden places now remain on earth to |
| M-28..........5:1 | Now there are **n.** distinctions. |
| M-29..........2:4 | **N.** one should attempt to answer these |
| M-29..........2:5 | Surely **n.** teacher of God has come this far |
| M-29..........5:3 | And His gifts have **n.** limit. To ask the |
| M-29..........5:6 | Him? **N.**, indeed! That would hardly be |
| C-in............4:4 | Yet there is **n.** answer; only an experience. |
| C-1.............4:4 | therefore has **n.** meaning in this world. It |
| C-1.............4:5 | world. It has **n.** opposite and no degrees. |
| C-1.............4:5 | world. It has no opposite and **n.** degrees. |
| C-2.............3:1 | There is **n.** definition for a lie that serves |
| C-2.............9:1 | Your questions have **n.** answer, being |
| C-2.............9:3 | **N.** miracle is now withheld from anyone. |
| C-3.............4:4 | **N.** one can look on knowledge. But the |
| C-3.............4:8 | looks on this **n.** longer sees the world. He |
| C-3...........4:10 | gate it is **n.** more than just a step inside. It |
| C-3.............6:4 | **N.**, not in truth, for truth goes nowhere. |
| C-3.............7:1 | are **n.** wishes now for wishes change. Even |
| C-4.............4:2 | that it can last **n.** longer than an instant. |
| C-4.............7:7 | has come at last there is **n.** journey, no |
| C-4.............7:7 | at last there is no journey, **n.** belief in sin, |
| C-4.............7:7 | is no journey, no belief in sin, **n.** walls, no |
| C-4.............7:7 | no belief in sin, no walls, **n.** bodies, and |
| C-5.............1:1 | There is **n.** need for help to enter Heaven |
| C-5.............1:7 | does not help because He knows **n.** need. |
| C-5.............2:2 | identified with *Christ*, a man **n.** longer, but |
| C-5.............4:1 | because they carried **n.** effects at all. And |
| C-5.............6:2 | **N.**, indeed. For Christ takes many forms |
| C-5.............6:5 | You need **n.** other. It is possible to read |
| C-5.............6:9 | *There is* **n.** *death because the Son of God is* |
| C-6.............5:6 | when time is over and **n.** trace remains of |
| C-6.............5:8 | **n.** longer to take form but to return to the |
| C-ep...........1:4 | **N.** one can fail to do what God appointed |
| P-1.............1:3 | **N.** one in this world escapes fear, but |
| P-1.............5:7 | There is **n.** end to the help that He begins |
| P-2...........I.1:3 | **n.** one learns beyond his own readiness. |
| P-2.........II.1:4 | the healed have **n.** need for a therapist. |
| P-2.........II.2:1 | religion has **n.** place in psychotherapy, |
| P-2.........II.2:1 | but it also has **n.** real place in religion. In |
| P-2.........II.3:1 | **N.** one who learns to forgive can fail to |
| P-2.........II.4:5 | knowledge of God has **n.** true opposite. |
| P-2.........II.4:6 | Not to know God is to have **n.** knowledge, |
| P-2.........II.5:7 | out, for **n.** one will find sanity alone. |
| P-2.........II.7:2 | **n.** good teacher uses one approach to |
| P-2.........II.9:2 | **N.** one who stands apart can receive |
| P-2........III.2:6 | go **n.** further than a step or two from hell. |
| P-2........III.3:8 | **N.** one need see him or talk to him or |
| P-2........IV.8:1 | illness, and in it there are **n.** degrees. One |
| P-2......IV.11:8 | There is **n.** need for complicated change. |
| P-2......IV.11:9 | is **n.** need for long analyses and wearying |
| P-2.........V.3:6 | be helped. **N.** more than that is asked of |
| P-2.........V.3:6 | **n.** less than all he has to give is worthy of |
| P-2.........V.7:2 | In time **n.** effort can be made in vain. It is |
| P-2.........V.8:6 | There is **n.** other way to hear His Voice. |
| P-2.........V.8:7 | There is **n.** other way to seek His Son. |
| P-2.........V.8:8 | There is **n.** other way to find your Self. |
| P-2........VI.1:1 | for **n.** healing can be anything else. The |
| P-2........VI.4:8 | It is not sick, and needs **n.** remedy. To |
| P-2........VI.6:4 | as gone into a past that is **n.** longer here. |
| P-2........VI.7:1 | **N.** one is healed alone. This is the joyous |
| P-2.......VII.2:7 | There is **n.** need for more than this, for it |
| P-2.......VII.4:1 | in **n.** way confuses himself with God. All |
| P-2.......VII.5:4 | presupposes a knowledge that **n.** one here |
| P-2.......VII.5:6 | Yet **n.** perception is omniscient, nor is the |
| P-2.......VII.5:8 | **N.** unhealed healer can be wholly sane. |
| P-2.......VII.6:2 | The advanced therapist in **n.** way can ever |
| P-2.......VII.8:5 | done, for what is perfect needs **n.** healing, |
| P-2.......VII.8:5 | remains to be forgiven where there is **n.** |
| P-2.......VII.9:8 | There is **n.** other choice of pathways that |
| P-3...........I.1:3 | it does mean that **n.** one comes to you by |
| P-3...........I.1:4 | are **n.** errors in God's plan. It would be an |
| P-3.........II.1:1 | Strictly speaking the answer is **n.**. How |
| P-3.........II.1:9 | These people need **n.** special rules, of |
| P-3.........II.2:1 | there is **n.** order of difficulty in healing. |
| P-3.........II.4:2 | **N.**, He declared it perfect, and so it was. |
| P-3.........II.5:5 | There is **n.** other, for there is nothing else. |
| P-3.........II.5:7 | Yet **n.** therapist really sets the goal for the |
| P-3.........II.6:7 | Yet **n.** patient can accept more than he is |
| P-3.........II.6:7 | and **n.** therapist can offer more than he |
| P-3.........II.7:1 | there is **n.** order of difficulty in healing. |
| P-3.........II.7:3 | He has learned that it is **n.** harder to wake |
| P-3.........II.7:4 | **N.** professional therapist can hold this |
| P-3.........II.9:4 | there is **n.** order of difficulty in healing, he |
| P-3.........II.9:5 | There is **n.** halfway point in this. Either |
| P-3........III.1:1 | **N.** one can pay for therapy, for healing is |
| P-3........III.1:7 | But **n.** one here can live with no illusions, |
| P-3........III.1:7 | But no one here can live with **n.** illusions, |
| P-3........III.2:7 | where God's plan allots it has **n.** cost. To |
| P-3........III.3:6 | Spirit's only dream, must have **n.** cost. |
| P-3........III.4:1 | to live is something **n.** one need fight for. |
| P-3........III.4:7 | There is **n.** cost to either. But thanks are |
| P-3........III.5:9 | will recognize him as a brother **n.** longer. |
| P-3........III.6:1 | **N.** one should be turned away because he |
| P-3........III.6:2 | pay. **N.** one is sent by accident to anyone. |
| S-1...........I.4:4 | they tell Him that you would have **n.** gods |
| S-1...........I.4:4 | have no gods before Him; **n.** Love but His. |
| S-1.........II.1:1 | Prayer has **n.** beginning and no end. It is |
| S-1.........II.1:1 | Prayer has no beginning and **n.** end. It is |
| S-1.........II.2:2 | is. **N.** one, then, who is sure of his Identity |
| S-1.........II.2:3 | is also true that **n.** one who is uncertain of |
| S-1.........II.3:5 | Without guilt there is **n.** scarcity. The |
| S-1.........II.3:6 | is no scarcity. The sinless have **n.** needs. |
| S-1.........II.4:7 | to **n.** one, or you will be treacherous to |
| S-1.........II.5:4 | it is **n.** longer a contradiction in terms. It |
| S-1.........II.7:4 | There is **n.** asking, for there is no lack. |
| S-1.........II.7:4 | There is no asking, for there is **n.** lack. |
| S-1.........II.7:6 | The light **n.** longer flickers, and will never |
| S-1.........II.8:3 | **n.** need for a ladder to reach what one has |
| S-1........III.3:7 | who sees **n.** value or advantage to himself |
| S-1........III.5:8 | He is **n.** jailer, but a messenger of Christ. |
| S-1........III.6:7 | **N.** one who wants an enemy will fail to |
| S-1........IV.2:8 | have. For **n.** one can receive effects alone, |
| S-1.........V.2:3 | The truly humble have **n.** goal but God |
| S-1.........V.2:3 | goal but God because they need **n.** idols, |
| S-1.........V.2:3 | and defense **n.** longer serves a purpose. |
| S-1.........V.4:1 | with this, for learning is **n.** longer needed. |
| S-2...........I.1:1 | **N.** gift of Heaven has been more |
| S-2...........I.2:2 | will overlook **n.** sin, no crime, no guilt |
| S-2...........I.2:2 | will overlook no sin, **n.** crime, no guilt |
| S-2...........I.2:2 | **n.** guilt that it can seek and find and "love |
| S-2...........I.5:5 | have **n.** freedom unless he gives it to you. |
| S-2...........I.7:6 | Who sees **n.** evil in it sees like Him. For |
| S-2...........I.7:7 | has not sinned, and guilt can be **n.** more. |
| S-2...........I.9:6 | There can be **n.** trace of it remaining, if |
| S-2.........II.2:6 | is? There is **n.** union here, but only grief. |
| S-2.........II.6:4 | further bargains which can give **n.** hope, |
| S-2.........II.6:8 | There is **n.** giving but to give like Him. All |
| S-3.........II.5:7 | There is **n.** partial healing. What but |
| S-3.........II.6:3 | a world in which there is **n.** veil of sin to |
| S-3........III.4:2 | In arrogance the answer must be "**n.**." |
| S-3........III.4:8 | There is **n.** point in giving remedy apart |
| S-3........III.5:4 | It heals **n.** part, but wholly and forever. |
| S-3........III.5:9 | Without Him there is **n.** healing, for there |
| S-3........III.5:9 | there is no healing, for there is **n.** love. |
| S-3........III.6:6 | is **n.** fear in one who has been truly healed |
| S-3........IV.1:5 | **n.** gifts but those they have from God. |
| S-3........IV.2:4 | Fear has **n.** haven here, for love has come |
| S-3........IV.4:6 | until there is **n.** hatred in your heart, and |
| S-3........IV.4:6 | and **n.** desire to attack the Son of God. |
| S-3........IV.5:3 | is then **n.** longer Cause but only an effect. |
| S-3........IV.5:8 | care, swearing He will deliver it **n.** more. |
| S-3........IV.8:2 | where time and distance have **n.** meaning |
| S-3......IV.10:5 | and live **n.** more in terror and in pain. Do |

## nod 1

| | |
|---|---|
| T-24....VI.12:4 | But a tiny willingness, a **n.** to God, a |

## noise 1

| | |
|---|---|
| T-31.........I.6:1 | **n.** of sounds that have no meaning? God |

## noises 1

| | |
|---|---|
| W-pI...182.6:3 | and harsh and rasping **n.** of the world. |

## non-creative 1

| | |
|---|---|
| T-2........IV.4:3 | to attempt to heal it through **n.** agents. It |

## non-mental 1

| | |
|---|---|
| M-5........II.1:8 | to endow the body with **n.** motivators. |

## non-right-minded 1

| | |
|---|---|
| T-2........IV.4:7 | because the last thing that can help the **n.**, |

## non-threat 1

| | |
|---|---|
| T-4.........V.3:2 | only in terms of threat or **n.** to itself. In |

## none 68

| | |
|---|---|
| T-2...........I.2:2 | **N.** of this existed before the separation, |
| T-2.........V.1:5 | **N.** of these errors is meaningful, because |
| T-3.........V.2:6 | **N.** of them is creative. Inventiveness is |
| T-4........III.6:6 | other gods before Him because there *are* **n.** |
| T-4.........V.4:9 | no real answer to this because there is **n.**, |
| T-6.........I.11:7 | with God that **n.** of His Sons should suffer |
| T-8.........V.6:5 | It has **n.**, because the journey is the way to |
| T-8........VII.2:7 | entirely about its value. Of itself it has **n.**. |
| T-8........IX.8:4 | no limits because God lays **n.** upon you. |
| T-12........II.2:2 | to the fog to obscure the light, it has **n.**. |
| T-13.....X.14:2 | that **n.** of us alone can even think of it. |
| T-15......IV.9:2 | require that you have **n.** that you would |
| T-16...VII.12:1 | *are no illusions, and where* **n.** *can ever enter.* |
| T-18.......I.7:10 | all. **N.** of them matters. *That* they have in |
| T-18....VI.9:10 | God placed **n.** between Himself and you. |
| T19....IV.A.3:6 | has no opposition, for there is **n.** beside it. |
| T19. IV.A.11:2 | find, losing **n.** of them on pain of death, |
| T19. IV.A.15:4 | And **n.** you cannot ask love's messengers |
| T-20......IV.1:5 | no power to sin, and therefore it has **n.**; |
| T-21...VII.13:8 | And **n.** can leave the thinker's mind, or |
| T-22........II.2:7 | perceive a difference where **n.** exists will |
| T-22......IV.4:5 | And **n.** who looks upon the Christ in you |
| T-22.......V.1:7 | merely is needs no defense, and offers **n.**. |
| T-24.........I.8:7 | **n.** your Father does not share with you. |
| T-24........II.1:1 | must be an ego device, for love makes **n.**. |
| T-24......II.13:2 | a hiding place where **n.** is welcome but |
| T-25.........I.3:6 | what seems to have a life apart has **n.**. |
| T-25........II.2:6 | you would seek for hope where **n.** is ever |
| T-25.....IX.10:7 | it sees no differences where **n.** exists. And |
| T-26......IV.4:3 | and **n.** is cherished more than any other. |
| T-26.....VII.3:7 | takes many forms, but **n.** has meaning. |
| T-27......IV.3:7 | **N.** of them will do. It does not ask a |
| T-27..VIII.12:2 | He sees no differences where **n.** exists, |
| T-27..VIII.12:3 | **N.** has a different cause from all the rest, |
| T-28........II.3:5 | is given no effects and **n.** is seen. A mind |
| T-30.....IV.4:11 | all. See **n.** in them and they will touch you |
| T-30......VI.3:2 | a real foundation pardon would have **n.**. |
| T-31......IV.2:2 | But the world has **n.** to offer. All its roads |
| T-31......IV.4:6 | No longer look for hope where there is **n.**. |
| T-31......IV.5:3 | while he sees a choice where there is **n.**, |
| W-in..........9:3 | **N.** of this will matter, or decrease their |
| W-pI.......4.1:6 | **n.** of them can be called "good" or "bad." |

| | |
|---|---|
| W-pI.......4.2:3 | **N.** of them represents your real thoughts, |
| W-pI.....47.2:1 | Of yourself you can do **n.** of these things. |
| W-pI.....92.8:2 | **n.** who enters its abode can leave without |
| W-pI.....96.1:3 | solutions, and **n.** of them has worked. |
| W-pI...121.4:5 | of **n.** because it sees the sinful everywhere. |
| W-pI...128.2:3 | to perceive some hope where there is **n.**. |
| W-pI...129.2:5 | No lasting love is found, for **n.** is here. |
| W-pI...130.6:1 | no compromise where **n.** is possible. The |
| W-pI...131.1:2 | impermanent, for love where there is **n.**, |
| W-pI......170.h | There is no cruelty in God and **n.** in me. |
| W-pI...170.7:5 | He has **n.**. And those who see in him their |
| W-pI.170.13:2 | *No cruelty abides in us, for there is* **n.** *in You.* |
| W-pI...180.2:1 | There is no cruelty in God and **n.** in me. |
| W-pI...182.3:3 | makes, yet **n.** contents his restless mind. |
| W-pI...193.9:4 | away, with **n.** remaining yet unshed, and |
| W-pI...193.9:4 | **n.** but waiting their appointed time to fall |
| W-pI...199.5:3 | and **n.** which will not gain in added gifts |
| W-pI...200.2:1 | of finding happiness where there is **n.**; of |
| W-pII .223.1:3 | and I have **n.** but those which are of Him. |
| W-pII .233.1:2 | *I would have* **n.** *of mine. In place of them,* |
| W-pII .235.2:3 | *no guilt nor sin in me, for there is* **n.** *in You.* |
| W-pII .340.2:6 | **n.** the Father will not gather to Himself, |
| M-10 .........5:7 | His sense of care is gone, for he has **n.**. He |
| M-16 .......10:7 | other words, or only one, or **n.** at all. Yet |
| M-17 .......7:12 | Beyond this there is **n.**, for what was done |
| M-29 .........4:5 | The image you made of yourself has **n.**. |

## nonessentials 1

| | |
|---|---|
| T-4......... V.6:5 | ego's characteristic busyness with **n.** is for |

## nonexistence 1

| | |
|---|---|
| T-4......... V.2:2 | they clearly point to the **n.** of the ego itself |

## nonexistent 3

| | |
|---|---|
| T-7........ VI.3:9 | onto *you,* and perceiving your being as **n.**. |
| T-9........ IV.5:5 | the Holy Spirit the effects of error are **n.**. |
| M-20 .......3:12 | now that is perceived as **n.** and unreal. |

## nonhuman 1

| | |
|---|---|
| W-pI.....25.6:2 | or "unimportant," "human" or "**n.**." |

## nor 603

## normal 1

| | |
|---|---|
| T-8.....VII.11:2 | Help and healing are the **n.** expressions of |

## not 6735

## not-right-mindedness 2

| | |
|---|---|
| T-2........ IV.2:2 | or "**n.**" is the result of level confusion, |
| T-2......... V.4:4 | All forms of **n.** are the result of refusal to |

## note 10

| | |
|---|---|
| T-25.........I.7:1 | All this takes **n.** of time and place as if |
| T-26....... V.5:4 | not one **n.** in Heaven's song was missed. |
| W-pI.....13.5:4 | **N.** carefully, however, any signs of overt |
| W-pI.....17.2:3 | on each thing you **n.** long enough to say: |
| W-pI.....34.3:3 | **N.** them all casually, repeating the idea |
| W-pI.....36.3:2 | to whatever you **n.** in your casual survey. |
| WpI...rI.in.6:1 | You will **n.** that, for review purposes, |
| W-pI.....65.5:5 | it. **N.** each one as it comes to you, with as |
| W-pI...107.7:3 | Today we practice on the happy **n.** of |
| W-pI...170.7:2 | **n.** that though his lips are smeared with |

## noted 1

| | |
|---|---|
| T-2.......VII.6:1 | especially be **n.** that God has only *one* Son. |

## notes 3

| | |
|---|---|
| T-9 ........ V.4:6 | which it usually **n.** even in its confusion. |
| T-21 ........I.7:1 | The **n.** are nothing. Yet you have kept |
| M-4 .... IX.1:10 | Readiness, as the text **n.**, is not mastery. |

## nothing 1003

| | |
|---|---|
| T-in ........... 2:2 | ***N. real can be threatened. Nothing unreal*** |
| T-in ........... 2:3 | ***N. unreal exists.*** Herein lies the peace of |
| T-1 ........I.48:2 | it, having **n.** to do with time at all. |
| T-1 ........II.3:10 | is **n.** about me that you cannot attain. I |
| T-1 ........II.3:11 | I have **n.** that does not come from God. |
| T-1 ........II.3:12 | between us now is that I have **n.** else. This |
| T-1 ....... IV.1:3 | is **n.** you want to hide even if you could. |
| T-1 ....... IV.1:5 | When you have become willing to hide **n.**, |
| T-1 ........ V.1:4 | shell, but you cannot express **n.** at all. |
| T-1 ........ V.1:5 | or reduce your creativity almost to **n.**. But |
| T-1 ........ V.6:6 | **n.** is less stable than an upside-down |
| T-1 ....... VI.1:6 | is the meaning of the "fall," **n.** was lacking |
| T-2 ..........I.3:1 | a state of mind in which **n.** was needed. |
| T-2 .........II.1:3 | is **n.** they cannot do, but they cannot be |
| T-2 .........II.5:5 | The eternally creative have **n.** to learn. |
| T-2 ........ V.7:6 | **N.** He perceives can induce fear. |
| T-2 ....... VI.7:3 | of correction becomes **n.** more than a |
| T-2 ...... VII.5:1 | **N.** and everything cannot coexist. To |
| T-2 ...... VII.5:3 | Fear is really **n.** and love is everything. |
| T-2 .... VII.5:10 | is possible between everything and **n.**. |
| T-3 ..........I.2:9 | that **n.** of this kind remains in your mind. |
| T-3 ..........I.3:2 | The "evil" past has **n.** to do with God. He |
| T-3 ..........I.7:1 | Atonement itself radiates **n.** but truth. It |
| T-3 ..........I.7:6 | demonstrated that **n.** can destroy truth. |
| T-3 ..........I.8:3 | altar, where **n.** except perfection belongs. |
| T-3 .........II.1:3 | or everything and **n.** as joint possibilities. |
| T-3 .........II.3:5 | is. If **n.** but the truth exists, right-minded |
| T-3 .........II.5:1 | **N.** can prevail against a Son of God who |
| T-3 ........ V.4:8 | also implies that there is **n.** stable to know |
| T-3 ........ V.6:5 | The prayer for forgiveness is **n.** more than |
| T-3 ........ V.7:4 | There *is* **n.** else. Perception, on the other |
| T-3 ........ V.8:1 | no judgments and **n.** but perfect equality? |
| T-3 ........ V.9:6 | if anyone has everything, there is **n.** left. |
| T-3 ....... VI.4:4 | **N.** that you have refused to accept can be |
| T-3 ...... VII.1:7 | **N.** made by a child of God is without |
| T-3 ...... VII.5:7 | since then, but **n.** has really happened. |
| T-4 ..........I.2:6 | **N.** can reach spirit from the ego, and |
| T-4 ..........I.2:6 | ego, and **n.** can reach the ego from spirit. |
| T-4 ..........I.7:6 | **n.** you do or think or wish or make is |
| T-4 ........I.12:1 | your ego you can do **n.** to save yourself or |
| T-4 ........I.12:6 | **N.** else is sufficiently worthy to be a gift |
| T-4 .........II.6:8 | "Self-esteem" in ego terms means **n.** more |
| T-4 .......II.10:1 | is **n.** more than "right-mindedness," |
| T-4 ....... III.8:2 | this, for we must hide **n.** from each other. |
| T-4 ....... IV.3:3 | of **n.** except by your own decisions, and |
| T-4 ....... IV.6:2 | It offers you **n.**. When you have given up |
| T-4 ..... IV.10:2 | of Christ means **n.** more than the end of |
| T-4 ....... VI.1:6 | ego is **n.** more than a part of your belief |
| T-4 ...... VII.5:2 | **N.** real can be increased except by sharing |
| T-4 ...... VII.8:3 | their egos and so **n.** can hurt them. Their |
| T-5 ....... IV.1:7 | you. **N.** that is good can be lost because it |
| T-5 ....... IV.1:8 | **N.** that is not good was ever created, and |
| T-5 ....... IV.4:5 | cannot hurt you and hold **n.** against him, |
| T-5 ....... IV.7:4 | the thinking of God lacks **n.**. Everything |
| T-5 ....... IV.8:2 | beauty is gone, and **n.** is left but a blessing |
| T-5 ....... VI.4:3 | made to uphold. **N.** the ego perceives is |
| T-6 ..........I.1:4 | **N.**, however, can be explained in negative |
| T-6 ..........I.2:1 | is **n.** more than an extreme example. Its |
| T-6 ........II.11:4 | it is surely clear that the perfect need **n.**, |
| T-6 ........II.12:4 | **N.** conflicts in this perception, because |
| T-6 ........ III.1:4 | By attacking **n.**, He presents no barrier to |
| T-6 ........ IV.6:2 | **N.** else exists and only this is real. You |
| T-6 ........ IV.6:4 | be **n.** left of your dream when you hear |
| T-6 ......... V.4:7 | **N.** lasting lies in dreams, and the Holy |
| T-6 ...... V.A.1:2 | but **n.** is accomplished through death, |
| T-6 ...... V.A.1:2 | death, because death is **n.**. Everything is |
| T-6 ...... V.A.4:8 | **N.** more and nothing less. Without a |
| T-6 ...... V.A.4:8 | Nothing more and **n.** less. Without a |
| T-6 ...... V.B.8:7 | because **n.** is difficult that is *wholly* desired |
| T-7 ..........I.6:4 | and **n.** that is true need be explained. |
| T-7 ..........I.7:3 | He does **n.** last, because He created first |
| T-7 .........II.7:8 | free, because **n.** discordant ever enters. |
| T-7 .......II.7:11 | That is its reality, and **n.** can assail it. |
| T-7 ....... III.5:7 | **n.** questionable enters their minds. This |
| T-7 ....... IV.6:5 | It is **n.** at all. God has given you a gift that |
| T-7 ....... IV.7:2 | this only, because you can find **n.** else. |
| T-7 ....... IV.7:3 | There *is* **n.** else. God is All in all in a very |
| T-7 .........V.1:1 | The body is **n.** more than a framework |
| T-7 .........V.4:3 | Healing perceives **n.** in the healer that |
| T-7 ........V.10:7 | in communion because this is to share **n.**. |
| T-7 ....... VI.5:4 | But there *is* **n.** else. The mind can, however |
| T-7 ....... VI.6:7 | love. **N.** else can be understood, because |
| T-7 ....... VI.6:7 | **n.** else is real and therefore nothing else |
| T-7 ....... VI.6:7 | is real and therefore **n.** else has meaning. |
| T-7 ..... VI.11:2 | however, because there is **n.** to attack. |
| T-7 ..... VI.11:5 | is. **N.**. It has no meaning. It does not exist. |
| T-7 ..... VI.13:6 | **n.** that opposes this means anything at all |
| T-7 ...... VII.4:6 | Except there is **n.** there to receive your gift |
| T-7 ...... VII.5:3 | it. You cannot make **n.** live, since nothing |
| T-7 ...... VII.5:3 | nothing live, since **n.** cannot be enlivened |
| T-7 ...... VII.5:6 | You can do **n.** apart from Him, and you |
| T-7 ...... VII.5:6 | Him, and you *do* do **n.** apart from Him. |
| T-7 .........X.2:4 | truth has **n.** to do with your willingness. |
| T-7 .........X.3:9 | ego. But you will be sacrificing **n.**. On the |
| T-7 ....... XI.1:7 | the ego perceives **n.** as wholly desirable. |
| T-7 ....... XI.3:9 | over His children and denies them **n.**. Yet |
| T-7 ....... XI.5:7 | **N.** is so easy to recognize as truth. This is |
| T-8 .........II.1:9 | you could still learn **n.** from the ego, |
| T-8 .........II.1:9 | from the ego, because the ego knows **n.**. |
| T-8 ....... III.5:2 | is **n.** else to seek. Everyone is looking for |
| T-8 ....... IV.6:1 | **N.** God created can oppose your decision |
| T-8 ....... IV.6:1 | as **n.** God created can oppose His Will. |
| T-8 ....... IV.7:3 | free. Of yourself you can do **n.**, because of |
| T-8 ....... IV.7:3 | do nothing, because of yourself you *are* **n.**. |
| T-8 ....... IV.7:4 | I am **n.** without the Father and you are |
| T-8 ....... IV.7:4 | the Father and you are **n.** without me, |
| T-8 .........V.1:6 | Alone we can do **n.**, but together our |
| T-8 .........V.4:6 | all. **N.** can prevail against our united wills |
| T-8 .........V.4:6 | wills because **n.** can prevail against God's. |
| T-8 .........V.5:3 | it. I will deny you **n.**, as God denies me |
| T-8 .........V.5:3 | deny you nothing, as God denies me **n.**. |
| T-8 ....... VI.2:1 | The world can add **n.** to the power and |
| T-8 ....... VI.3:2 | else, but because **n.** else is worthy of him. |
| T-8 ....... VI.4:1 | squandered everything for **n.** of any value |
| T-8 ....... VI.4:4 | *was* his father's treasure. He wanted **n.** else |
| T-8 ....... VI.7:1 | in terms that actually means **n.**. When |
| T-8 ...... VII.6:1 | then, that of yourself you can do **n.**. You |
| T-8 ...... VII.8:1 | There is **n.** so frustrating to a learner as a |
| T-8 ... VII.13:4 | is therefore **n.** more than united purpose. |
| T-8 ..... VIII.6:8 | *Any* way you handle error results in **n.**. |
| T-8 ....... IX.6:4 | mean to make **n.** out of what God created |
| T-8 ....... IX.8:3 | **n.** can prevent you from doing exactly |
| T-9 ..........I.7:9 | separation is **n.** more than the belief that |
| T-9 ........I.10:1 | cannot answer because **n.** can hurt you, |
| T-9 ........I.10:1 | can hurt you, and so you are asking for **n.**. |
| T-9 ........I.10:2 | that stems from the ego is a wish for **n.**, |
| T-9 ........I.12:7 | If it were never created, it is **n.**. Can you |
| T-9 ........I.12:8 | Can you really devote yourself to **n.**? |
| T-9 ........I.14:1 | is already possible, and **n.** else will ever be |
| T-9 .......II.12:3 | deny you **n.** because you have denied Him |
| T-9 .......II.12:3 | nothing because you have denied Him **n.**, |
| T-9 ....... III.3:4 | it, knowing that **n.** the ego makes means |
| T-9 .........V.5:3 | **N.** really does. Nothing real has happened |
| T-9 .........V.5:4 | **N.** real has happened to the unhealed |
| T-9 .........V.6:5 | **N.** will change unless it is understood, |
| T-9 ........V.8:16 | the good *can* work. **N.** else works at all. |
| T-9 ....... VI.7:8 | brother in this world and accept **n.** else, |
| T-9 ...... VII.7:7 | **n.** that arises from it means anything. He |
| T-9 ...... VII.8:4 | that **n.** unworthy of God is worthy of you. |
| T-9 ...... VII.8:5 | and accept **n.** that you would not offer to |
| T-9 ...VIII.11:3 | **N.** can attack it nor prevail over it. It does |
| T-10 ......in.1:1 | **N.** beyond yourself can make you fearful |
| T-10 ......in.1:1 | fearful or loving, because **n.** *is* beyond you. |
| T-10 ......in.1:4 | and that **n.** in the world can take this |
| T-10 ......in.2:1 | God created **n.** beside you and nothing |
| T-10 ......in.2:1 | beside you and **n.** beside you exists, for |
| T-10 ......in.2:3 | **N.** beyond Him can happen, because |
| T-10 ......in.2:3 | can happen, because **n.** except Him is real |
| T-10 ......in.2:4 | but **n.** is added that is different because |
| T-10 ......in.3:7 | **N.** can reach you from beyond it because, |
| T-10 .......II.1:2 | is **n.** more than a decision to forget. What |

T-10....... II.2:6 again. Let **n.** in this world delay your
T-10....... II.3:5 **N.** is beyond His Will for you. But signify
T-10...... III.1:8 The idols are **n.**, but their worshippers
T-10...... III.8:7 to you, remember that **n.** can replace God
T-10...... III.8:7 replacements you have attempted are **n.**.
T-10...... III.9:1 but you are really afraid of **n.**. And in that
T-10.... III.10:9 illusions, for to honor them is to honor **n.**
T-10.. III.10:10 due them either, for **n.** cannot be fearful.
T-10.... III.11:8 it is clear this has **n.** to do with reality, it is
T-10...... IV.5:5 **N.** but the laws of God has ever been, and
T-10...... IV.5:5 ever been, and **n.** but His Will will ever be
T-10...... IV.5:8 You will see **n.** at all. And your vision will
T-10...... IV.6:8 God created you. And He created **n.** else.
T-10....... V.5:1 I said before that of yourself you can do **n.**
T-10....... V.5:3 yourself that you need be troubled over **n.**
T-10....... V.5:4 Your gods are **n.**, because your Father did
T-11....... in.1:6 **N.** alive is Fatherless, for life is creation.
T-11....... in.2:4 is **n.** more than a delusional system in
T-11.... in.3:10 you have been afraid was based on **n.**.
T-11......... I.3:3 Can part of His Mind contain **n.**? If your
T-11....... I.11:4 so that **n.** He gives can contradict Him.
T-11....... II.6:4 mind, and let **n.** that obscures it enter.
T-11....... II.7:6 And the ego is **n.**, whether you invite it in
T-11...... III.4:2 is the way of pain, of which God knows **n.**
T-11...... III.5:1 God hides **n.** from His Son, even though
T-11...... IV.6:7 yours, and **n.** is denied by God to His Son.
T-11....... V.2:6 and what leads to **n.** has not happened. If
T-11....... V.2:7 what leads to **n.** could not be real. Do not
T-11....... V.4:3 on its behalf is necessarily expended on **n.**
T-11....... V.7:2 it has the power to do this it does **n.** else,
T-11....... V.7:2 else, because its goal of autonomy *is* **n.** else
T-11..... V.17:3 Him. **N.** can demonstrate that His Son is
T-11..... V.17:3 for **n.** can prove that a lie is true. What
T-11..... V.17:7 of Christ they need demonstrate **n.**, for
T-11...... VI.5:6 The God of resurrection demands **n.**, for
T-11.... VI.10:6 and **n.** contradictory to His Will is either
T-11..... VII.2:7 is a willingness to perceive **n.** else. For if
T-11... VIII.3:5 is your great need, for you understand **n.**.
T-11... VIII.5:4 **N.** could be more specific than to be told
T-11... VIII.5:8 that **n.** of God demands anything of you.
T-11... VIII.6:1 what is yours, and will take **n.** in return.
T-11... VIII.7:6 **N.** of God will enslave His Son whom He
T-11... VIII.8:5 God's Sons have **n.** they do not share. Ask
T-11. VIII.10:4 It. **N.** will be beyond your healing power,
T-11. VIII.10:4 **n.** will be denied your simple request.
T-12......... I.4:1 is **n.** to prevent you from recognizing all
T-12....... II.6:5 for **n.** can withstand the Love of Christ for
T-12...... III.4:8 is valuable and wants to accept **n.** else.
T-12....... V.2:3 be demonstrating that **n.** really happened
T-12....... V.9:6 **n.** can oppose the decision of God's Son.
T-12...... VI.1:2 gain in the world, for of itself it profits **n.**.
T-12...... VI.1:5 denying yours, and gives you **n.** in return.
T-12...... VI.2:1 because He knows **n.** but the spirit as you.
T-12..... VII.8:1 you want only love you will see **n.** else.
T-12... VIII.2:2 him in perfect peace, and needing **n.**, he
T-12... VIII.2:2 peace, and needing nothing, he asks for **n.**
T-12... VIII.6:1 Son of God, be not content with **n.**! What
T-12... VIII.6:8 Valuing **n.**, you have sought nothing. By
T-12... VIII.6:8 Valuing nothing, you have sought **n.**. By
T-12... VIII.6:9 By making **n.** real to you, you have seen it.
T-12... VIII.7:3 looks upon him, and sees **n.** else in you.
T-13....... II.3:3 so intense that **n.** short of the crucifixion
T-13....... II.9:2 Your "guilty secret" is **n.**, and if you will
T-13...... III.2:3 attack is **n.** compared to your fear of love.
T-13.... III.11:1 peace he needed **n.** and asked for nothing
T-13.... III.11:1 peace he needed nothing and asked for **n.**
T-13.... III.11:2 he demanded everything and found **n.**.
T-13...... IV.9:7 be as you interpret it, for of itself it is **n.**.
T-13.... VI.11:4 will attract you as **n.** in this world can do.
T-13..... VII.1:7 **N.** is there but shines, and shines forever.
T-13..... VII.3:4 **N.** you made but has the mark of death
T-13..... VII.7:1 Will that **n.** touch His Son except Himself
T-13..... VII.7:1 Himself, and **n.** else comes nigh unto him
T-13..... VII.9:6 In them you see **n.** fearful, and because of
T-13... VII.10:2 Father knoweth that you have need of **n.**.
T-13... VII.11:2 again and again to get, it leaves you **n.**, for
T-13... VII.12:5 will take **n.** from you as long as you have
T-13... VII.13:7 for light needs **n.** but to shine in peace,
T-13... VIII.2:1 this: There is **n.** partial about knowledge.
T-13...... IX.3:1 it, for being **n.** but your own projection, it
T-13...... IX.5:6 **N.** can justify insanity, and to call for
T-13....... X.9:8 **N.** can keep from you what Christ would
T-13...... XI.2:7 **N.** destructive ever was or will be. The
T-13...... XI.3:1 you will value **n.** that you value here. For
T-13...... XI.3:2 **n.** that you value here do you value wholly
T-13...... XI.3:7 is everything God values, and **n.** else.
T-13...... XI.4:1 **N.** in this world can give this peace, for
T-13...... XI.4:1 for **n.** in this world is wholly shared.
T-13...... XI.5:3 fail. **N.** can prevent what God would have
T-13...... XI.6:9 Him to do. The Will of God can fail in **n.**.
T-13...... XI.7:1 be in Heaven, and **n.** can keep you from it
T-13...... XI.7:2 your blackest nightmares all mean **n.**.
T-13...... XI.8:7 Heaven, and will always will you **n.** else.
T-14......... I.2:3 of the world must therefore lead to **n.**, for
T-14......... I.2:3 therefore lead to nothing, for its goal is **n.**.
T-14......... I.2:4 to have and give and be **n.** except a dream
T-14......... I.3:8 There is **n.** in the world to teach him that
T-14......... I.3:8 the world is totally insane and leads to **n.**.
T-14......... I.3:9 there is One Who knows it leads to **n.**, for
T-14......... I.5:2 complex you cannot see that it means **n.**.
T-14....... II.1:5 goal depends means absolutely **n.**. Yet it
T-14....... II.1:7 faith in **n.** and you will find the "treasure"
T-14....... II.1:9 You will believe that **n.** is of value, and
T-14..... II.1:11 For if you value one thing made of **n.**, you
T-14..... II.1:11 you have believed that **n.** can be precious,
T-14....... II.2:4 all the distortions you have made of **n.**; all
T-14....... II.2:5 it. **N.** is so alien to you as the simple truth,
T-14....... II.2:5 and **n.** are you less inclined to listen to.
T-14....... II.2:7 would make palaces and royal robes of **n.**,
T-14....... II.3:2 learners who would teach themselves **n.**,
T-14....... II.3:2 themselves into believing that it is not **n.**,
T-14....... II.3:4 *N. else matters, nothing else is real, and*
T-14....... II.3:4 *Nothing else matters,* ***n.*** *else is real, and*
T-14....... II.3:6 *Your faith in* ***n.*** *is deceiving you. Offer your*
T-14....... II.4:5 from **n.** and from all the works of nothing
T-14....... II.4:5 from nothing and from all the works of **n.**
T-14....... II.4:6 bind them to despair they do not see as **n.**
T-14....... II.4:7 and so they *must* have been **n.**. And you
T-14....... II.5:4 never learn how to make **n.** everything.
T-14....... II.5:7 I said before, "Be not content with **n.**," for
T-14....... II.5:7 have believed that **n.** could content you. *It*
T-14....... II.7:6 You made this door of **n.**, and behind it *is*
T-14....... II.7:6 this door of nothing, and behind it *is* **n.**.
T-14....... II.7:7 away the shapes and forms and fears of **n.**
T-14....... II.8:6 For there is **n.** else. God is everywhere,
T-14...... III.3:6 *If I am guiltless, I have* ***n.*** *to fear. I choose to*
T-14...... III.6:4 By giving power to **n.**, he throws away the
T-14...... III.6:4 opportunity to learn that **n.** has no power
T-14...... III.7:4 He can do **n.** that can hurt you, and by
T-14...... III.7:5 There is **n.** to forgive. No one can hurt the
T-14...... III.8:7 and **n.** else can His Son see or choose to
T-14.... III.10:7 There is **n.** their will fails to provide that
T-14.... III.12:2 Son? **N.** can shake God's conviction of the
T-14...... IV.1:7 The first in time means **n.**, but the First in
T-14...... IV.1:8 no second or third, and **n.** but the First.
T-14...... IV.8:5 is **n.** on earth with which it can compare,
T-14...... IV.8:5 and **n.** you have ever felt apart from Him
T-14...... IV.8:7 and Who knows of **n.** except giving?
T-14...... IV.9:7 you have made, you are remembering **n.**.
T-14.... IV.10:7 with God is life. **N.** without it is at all.
T-14....... V.1:9 There is **n.** of value here, and everything
T-14....... V.2:8 teach you **n.** except how to be happy.
T-14....... V.3:3 There is **n.** in the Mind of God that does
T-14....... V.5:1 here, and **n.** else can unite us in this world
T-14...... VI.1:2 **N.** you understand is fearful. It is only in
T-14...... VI.1:7 **N.** has hidden value, for what is hidden
T-14...... VI.2:1 openness, in which **n.** is hidden and
T-14...... VI.2:1 nothing is hidden and therefore **n.** is
T-14...... VI.2:5 illusion out of **n.** are now afraid of them.
T-14...... VI.3:4 They do **n.** at all, being nothing at all. As
T-14...... VI.3:4 They do nothing at all, being **n.** at all. As
T-14...... VI.5:5 are. All this and **n.** else would He separate
T-14...... VI.7:6 if one means **n.** and the other everything,
T-14...... VI.8:4 which **n.** at all is carefully concealed. We
T-14..... VII.7:4 It is the recognition that **n.** you see means
T-14... VIII.1:3 the dark doors you have closed lies **n.**,
T-14... VIII.1:3 because **n.** can obscure the gift of God. It
T-14... VIII.2:4 And **n.** brought there that is not equally
T-14.... VIII.3:8 and **n.** else can you bestow upon yourself.
T-14.... VIII.4:6 **N.** can change the knowledge, given you
T-14.... VIII.5:4 upon your altars, for **n.** can coexist with it
T-14..... IX.3:4 you. Yet without Him you are **n.**. The
T-14........ X.7:2 that everything else is **n.** but a call for love
T-14........ X.7:5 It is merely form, and **n.** else. For you do
T-14........ X.8:4 assure you that you understand **n.** of it.
T-14...... X.11:3 all. **N.** lives in secret, and what you would
T-14...... X.11:3 you would hide from the Holy Spirit is **n.**.
T-14...... XI.3:5 all. **N.** you have ever learned can help you
T-14.... XI.3:10 for it is **n.** more than a condition in which
T-14.... XI.12:1 who remember always that they know **n.**,
T-14.... XI.13:2 it must be peace they want, and **n.** else.
T-14.... XI.15:5 that **n.** will prevail against your peace.
T-15......... I.1:2 time is for; to learn just that and **n.** more.
T-15......... I.7:7 **n.** but a teaching device for compounding
T-15......... I.8:6 free of guilt that **n.** but happiness is there.
T-15......... I.9:6 **N.** can reach you here out of the past, and
T-15.... III.10:3 You will be content with **n.** but His Will.
T-15.... III.10:7 will know you are complete, in need of **n.**,
T-15...... IV.2:7 you, and **n.** else can bring you peace. For
T-15...... IV.6:2 **n.** more than the ego's attempt to obscure
T-15...... IV.6:8 It therefore seeks to change **n.**, but merely
T-15.... IV.9:10 to God, and hostage to no one and to **n.**.
T-15....... V.7:3 is **n.** in Heaven or earth that it resembles,
T-15....... V.9:2 He remembers **n.**, having always known
T-15...... VI.6:1 instant **n.** happens that has not always
T-15...... VI.6:3 **N.** has changed. Yet the awareness of
T-15...... VI.7:7 If you were not an idea, and **n.** but an idea
T-15...... VI.7:8 to be **n.** else and something else together,
T-15..... VII.1:4 Being complete, it asks **n.**. Being wholly
T-15..... VII.3:6 You have **n.** to lose by looking open-eyed,
T-15... VII.10:3 All anger is **n.** more than an attempt to
T-15.... VIII.1:7 you recognize that there is **n.** to forgive,
T-15.... VIII.3:6 as **n.** more than a mistake in who you are.
T-15.... VIII.3:7 failure, and **n.** that he wills can be denied.
T-15.... VIII.4:3 **N.** that ever was created but is yours.
T-15...... IX.2:4 And both are **n.** more than attempts to
T-15........ X.2:6 is **n.** but a limitation imposed on giving.
T-15........ X.4:5 What is not love is always fear, and **n.** else
T-15........ X.5:6 accept the fact that sacrifice gets **n.**.
T-15........ X.5:7 apart from sacrifice means **n.** to you.
T-15........ X.9:1 keeps no bargains and would leave you **n.**
T-15...... XI.1:6 them is **n.** more than a gentle awakening,
T-15...... XI.2:3 He comes demanding **n.**. No sacrifice of
T-15...... XI.3:3 Leave **n.** behind, for release is total, and
T-15...... XI.7:3 that to sacrifice the body is to sacrifice **n.**,
T-15...... XI.8:3 than to perceive we are deprived of **n.**?
T-15.... XI.10:3 **N.** will be lacking, and you will make
T-16......... I.3:5 is **n.** from the past that you would share,
T-16......... I.3:5 is **n.** from the past that you would keep.
T-16....... I.3:12 *is here. I need do* ***n.*** *except not to interfere.*
T-16...... III.1:5 and one with **n.** in common with yours.
T-16...... III.1:6 have **n.** in common with what you taught
T-16.... III.5:10 **n.** real has ever left the mind of its creator
T-16...... III.6:3 all else must be outside, where **n.** is. You
T-16...... III.7:7 is **n.** in Him that is not perfect and eternal
T-16...... III.7:8 All this is *you,* and **n.** outside of this *is* you.
T-16...... IV.7:2 it is **n.** more than an attempt to bring love
T-16...... IV.9:1 be wholly in God, willing for **n.** special,
T-16...... IV.9:4 where **n.** is certain and where everything
T-16.... IV.12:5 now, and let **n.** stand in the way of truth.
T-16.... IV.13:6 bridge to timelessness you understand **n.**.
T-16....... V.5:6 **n.** would remain to interfere with the ego.
T-16....... V.7:6 taking, and of giving **n.** of value in return.
T-16....... V.8:5 are of fear, and they can be of **n.** else, the
T-16....... V.8:5 the illusion of Heaven is **n.** more than an
T-16..... V.13:1 See in the special relationship **n.** more
T-16..... V.14:4 the decision as just what it is, and **n.** more
T-16..... V.17:2 is on the other side, and **n.** at all is here. It
T-16...... VI.5:5 in, for God is left without and ***n.*** taken in.
T-16...... VI.5:8 of him, and sees only this part and **n.** else.
T-16...... VI.7:1 bridge itself is **n.** more than a transition
T-16...... VI.9:1 **N.** you seek to strengthen in the special
T-16.... VI.10:7 simple willingness to give up **n.** *because* it
T-16.... VI.10:7 to give up nothing *because* it is **n.**.
T-16.... VI.11:4 that for all this you gave up ***n.!*** The joy of
T-16..... VII.2:5 in the present, and if it means **n.** now, it
T-16..... VII.2:8 of? The past is **n.**. Do not seek to lay the

T-16.....VII.9:1 There is **n.** you can hold against reality.
T-16.....VII.9:4 God holds **n.** against anyone, for He is
T-16...VII.11:3 There is **n.** that will not give place to Him
T-16...VII.11:7 and nowhere else. You choose this or **n.**.
T-17....... II.1:3 **N.** you see here, sleeping or waking,
T-17....... II.1:4 And **n.** will you value like unto this, nor
T-17....... II.1:5 **N.** that you remember that made your
T-17....... II.2:3 **N.** is hidden here, for everything has been
T-17....... II.3:5 no one and **n.** remain still bound by them
T-17....... II.4:3 **N.** will ever change; no shifts nor
T-17......IV.1:1 **n.** you do that does not share His purpose
T-17......IV.1:4 *And n. else.* To fulfill this function you
T-17......IV.1:6 **n.** God created is apart from happiness,
T-17......IV.1:6 and **n.** God created but would extend
T-17......IV.5:6 The separation has **n.** in it, no part, no
T-17....IV.14:7 what you thought was real, and **n.** more.
T-17....IV.14:8 For beyond this picture you will see **n.**.
T-17.....VII.6:7 **N.** too small or too enormous, too weak
T-17...VII.8:12 You can leave **n.** of yourself outside it and
T-17....VIII.1:1 holy instant is **n.** more than a special case,
T-17....VIII.2:5 even faith is asked of you, for truth asks **n.**
T-17....VIII.4:6 And it was **n.** but the intolerable strain of
T-17....VIII.6:4 **n.** that it needs to be forever changeless
T-18.........I.2:7 separate. **N.** can come between what God
T-18.........I.5:6 But **n.** you have seen begins to show you
T-18.........I.7:11 *That* they have in common and **n.** else. Yet
T-18.........I.9:2 you **n.** can be shared but only substituted,
T-18.........I.9:2 substituting have **n.** in common in reality.
T-18......IV.5:6 but only to those who offer it **n.** more
T-18....IV.5:12 *I need add n. to His plan. But to receive it, I*
T-18......IV.7:6 emphasized that you need understand **n.**.
T-18......IV.7:7 it asks **n.** you cannot give right now.
T-18....... V.5:6 and **n.** will be wanting that would make
T-18......VI.1:1 There is **n.** outside you. That is what you
T-18......VI.1:6 and the knowledge that there is **n.** else;
T-18......VI.1:6 is nothing else; **n.** outside this Oneness,
T-18......VI.1:6 outside this Oneness, and **n.** else within.
T-18......VI.2:6 cannot be guilty, for it can do **n.** of itself.
T-18......VI.6:3 have **n.** to do with what the body does. It
T-18......VI.8:8 it has no limits, and there is **n.** outside it.
T-18....VI.8:11 you. There is **n.** else, anywhere or ever.
T-18........VII.h I Need Do N.
T-18.....VII.3:5 would be experienced as pain and **n.** else,
T-18.....VII.5:5 you need but to remember you need do **n.**
T-18.....VII.5:7 just one happy realization; "*I need do n..*"
T-18.....VII.6:6 preparation, and practice doing **n.** else. "I
T-18.....VII.6:7 "I need do **n.**" is a statement of allegiance,
T-18.....VII.7:2 And if you recognize you need do **n.**, you
T-18.....VII.7:6 Who needs do **n.** has no need for time. To
T-18.....VII.7:7 time. To do **n.** is to rest, and make a place
T-18.....VII.8:3 This quiet center, in which you do **n.**, will
T-18....VIII.5:3 any meaning, for by itself it does mean **n.**.
T-18....VIII.7:2 and ocean are as **n.** beside what you are.
T-18....VIII.7:5 on **n.** yet who would still die to defend it?
T-18......IX.6:5 **N.** can rest upon it, for it is but an illusion
T-18......IX.6:6 to grasp it and your hands hold **n.**.
T-18....IX.10:4 for here does **n.** interfere with love, letting
T-18....IX.10:6 Here is the Source of light; **n.** perceived,
T-18....IX.14:1 of forgiveness you will remember **n.** else,
T-19.......I.14:4 realize that there is **n.** faith cannot forgive
T-19.......I.16:3 God created as His Son is slave to **n.**,
T-19....... II.3:3 **n.** he can do that would really change his
T-19....... II.8:1 that all this be **n.** more than a mistake,
T-19......III.4:5 are *for* correction, and they call for **n.** else.
T-19......III.4:6 calls for punishment must call for **n.**.
T-19......IV.2:3 do, for **n.** undertaken with the Holy Spirit
T-19......IV.2:4 indeed be sure of **n.** you see outside you,
T19... IV.A.9:5 For it is **n.** in itself, and stood for nothing
T19... IV.A.9:5 stood for **n.** when you had greater faith in
T19....IV.B.5:1 **n.** you have paid for brought you peace.
T19....IV.C.5:3 It does **n.**. Of itself it is neither corruptible
T19....IV.C.5:5 It *is* **n.**. It is the result of a tiny, mad idea of
T19..IV.C.11:4 And they may thus mean everything or **n.**
T19... IV.D.6:6 vanish. **N.** that you remember now will
T19. IV.D.19:2 **n.** in the plan God has established for
T-20....... II.7:3 The fear of God is **n.** to you now. Who is
T-20......IV.1:1 **N.** can hurt you unless you give it the
T-20......IV.4:3 **N.** but this can touch them, for they see
T-20......IV.8:4 there will be **n.** else the Holy Spirit will
T-20 ..... IV.8:6 **N.** you need will be denied you. Not one
T-20 ..... IV.8:8 You need take thought for **n.**, careless of
T-20 ...... V.5:8 golden light is all the same; **n.** before it,
T-20 ...... V.5:8 the same; nothing before it, **n.** afterwards.
T-20 ...... V.6:4 The past takes **n.** from it, and the future
T-20 ..... VI.1:2 rest on contingency, but there *is* **n.** else.
T-20 ..... VI.2:1 **N.** can show the contrast better than the
T-20 ..... VI.2:6 **n.** that it would keep apart and hide. It
T-20 ..... VI.5:2 carefully protected, yet hiding **n.**. Here
T-20 ..... VI.7:1 for **n.** so severely threatens them as love's
T-20 .... VII.1:3 course has **n.** in it that is not consistent.
T-20 .... VII.1:7 This course requires almost **n.** of you. It is
T-20 .... VII.4:6 sinless. As **n.**, which it is, the body cannot
T-20 ...VIII.9:3 **N.** is in between, and which you choose
T-20 ...VIII.9:7 It still is true that **n.** is without. Yet upon
T-20 ...VIII.9:8 Yet upon **n.** are all projections made. For
T-20 ...VIII.9:9 is the projection that gives the "**n.**" all the
T-21 ......in.1:2 see is what you gave it, **n.** more than that.
T-21 ....in.1:11 **N.** perceived without it means anything.
T-21 ........I.4:7 believing that their choice is that or **n.**.
T-21 ........I.7:1 The notes are **n.**. Yet you have kept them
T-21 ........I.7:4 know that **n.** in the world you learned is
T-21 ........I.9:6 **N.** will ever be as dear to you as is this
T-21 .......II.3:4 as God created it, outside of which is **n.**.
T-21 .....II.10:8 **N.** can have effects without a cause, and
T-21 .....II.11:3 **N.** created not by your Creator has any
T-21 .....II.12:5 It changes **n.** in creation, depends entirely
T-21 ..... III.2:4 for **n.** is so cherished and protected as is a
T-21 ..... III.5:2 is not a lack of faith, but faith in **n.**. Faith
T-21 ..... III.9:2 Holy Spirit knows that sacrifice brings **n.**.
T-21 ..... IV.5:2 And it desired **n.** but to join with him and
T-21 ...... V.4:3 And **n.** you have allowed to stay in your
T-21 ..... VI.5:6 And if there is **n.** in between, how can
T-21 .. VII.12:6 and now an elusive shadow attached to **n.**
T-21 ... VIII.2:7 **N.** has power to confound its constancy,
T-21 ... VIII.5:7 For you have asked that **n.** stand between
T-22 ......in.2:7 they think that there is **n.** left to steal, and
T-22 ......in.3:5 Therefore, he looks on **n.** he would take.
T-22 ........I.9:2 **N.** but what is part of Him is worthy of
T-22 .......II.5:6 to Whom **n.** He wills can be impossible,
T-22 .....II.10:2 fear. **N.** you made has any power over you
T-22 ..... III.2:7 It looks on **n.** that can be corrected. Thus
T-22 ..... III.5:6 sin, and stopping at the outside form of **n.**
T-22 ..... III.5:9 that **n.** else but form will be perceived.
T-22 ..... III.6:7 **N.** so blinding as perception of form. For
T-22 ..... IV.2:5 There will be **n.** you will not be told, if
T-22 ...... V.1:6 Reality opposes **n.**. What merely is needs
T-22 ...... V.3:2 still whole, and **n.** has been taken from it.
T-22 ...... V.3:3 and the material of evil dreams are **n.**. In
T-22 ...... V.3:4 stand together, with **n.** in between. God
T-22 ...... V.6:6 of what you thought it was, that it is **n.**. If
T-22 ..... VI.4:3 all. **N.** entrusted to it can be misused, and
T-22 ..... VI.4:3 misused, and **n.** given it but will be used.
T-22 ..... VI.7:1 no error is excluded and **n.** kept hidden,
T-22 ..... VI.7:4 God would let **n.** interfere with those
T-23 ......in.1:2 is strength, and **n.** else is strong. The
T-23 ......in.3:3 **N.** they see is harmful, for their awareness
T-23 ......in.6:1 **N.** around you but is part of you. Look on
T-23 ........I.3:7 They are the same, and they are **n.**. Their
T-23 ........I.3:9 The ego joins with **n.**, being nothing. The
T-23 ........I.3:9 The ego joins with nothing, being **n.**. The
T-23 ........I.7:8 two illusions is a state where **n.** happens.
T-23 ........I.8:3 **n.** you could attack that is not part of you.
T-23 ........I.8:7 of **n.** cannot win reality through battle.
T-23 .......I.11:4 And **n.** is remembered except illusions.
T-23 .......II.1:7 And yet they govern **n.**, and need not be
T-23 .......II.3:6 No part of **n.** can be more resistant to the
T-23 ..... III.2:3 and gently given, still contains **n.**. And
T-23 ..... III.2:6 You give him **n.**, and receive of him but
T-23 ..... III.3:3 Salvation gives up **n.**. It is complete for
T-23 ..... IV.8:2 They want for **n.**. Sorrow of any kind is
T-24 ........I.4:1 for there is **n.** in the universe unlike itself.
T-24 ........I.4:7 for **n.** in the world they value more.
T-24 .......II.6:6 Is it a sacrifice to give up **n.**, and to receive
T-24 .......II.9:5 so encompassing that **n.** stands outside.
T-24 .....II.13:3 **N.** is sacred here but unto you, and you
T-24 ..... III.3:6 What rests on **n.** never can be stable.
T-24 ..... III.4:1 Without foundation **n.** is secure. Would
T-24 ..... III.4:5 all. **N.** is safe from its attack, and it is safe
T-24 ..... III.4:5 safe from its attack, and it is safe from **n.**.
T-24 ..... III.7:3 Yet they hear **n.**. They are lost in dreams
T-24 ... IV.2:10 Of itself the body can do **n.**. See it as
T-24 ..... IV.3:7 **N.** could make less sense to specialness.
T-24 ..... IV.3:8 **N.** could make more sense to miracles.
T-24 .......V.2:3 from there, and wove a picture out of **n.**.
T-24 .......V.2:4 contributes **n.** to the parts to give them
T-24 .......V.3:7 will see **n.** and there is no sound to hear.
T-24 ..... VI.2:4 One. **N.** alive that is not part of Him, and
T-24 ..... VI.2:4 part of Him, and **n.** is but is alive in Him.
T-24 ..... VI.3:1 **N.** is lost to you in all the universe.
T-24 ..... VI.3:2 **N.** that God created has He failed to lay
T-24 ... VI.11:2 self-created, self-maintained, in need of **n.**
T-24 .... VII.1:3 obeys. **N.** his specialness demands does
T-24 .... VII.1:4 **N.** it needs does he deny to what he loves.
T-24 .... VII.2:8 **N.** you gave to specialness but is his due.
T-24 .... VII.2:9 his due. And **n.** due him is not due to you.
T-24 .... VII.5:6 not, it has no purpose, and is means for **n.**
T-24 .... VII.7:3 **n.** to add and nothing taken from; not
T-24 .... VII.7:3 nothing to add and **n.** taken from; not
T-25 ......in.3:5 **n.** that the body says or does but makes
T-25 ........I.4:5 and **n.** hides the face of Christ from its
T-25 .....II.10:7 **N.** has power over you except His Will
T-25 ..... III.1:6 that love creates itself, and **n.** but itself.
T-25 ..... III.5:2 **n.** is seen but justifies forgiveness and the
T-25 ..... III.5:3 **N.** arises but is met with instant and
T-25 ..... III.5:4 **N.** remains an instant, to obscure the
T-25 ..... III.7:2 your brother's errors be to you **n.** except a
T-25 ..... IV.2:3 **N.** is harmful or beneficent apart from
T-25 ..... IV.5:6 **N.** before and nothing after it. No other
T-25 ..... IV.5:6 Nothing before and **n.** after it. No other
T-25 ..... IV.5:8 **N.** beyond nor nearer. Nothing else. In
T-25 ..... IV.5:9 **N.** else. In any form. This can you bring
T-25 ..... VI.1:2 He can see no evil; **n.** in the world to fear,
T-25 ..... VI.6:3 And **n.** that you think you see in it is
T-25 .... VII.2:8 realize **n.** is changeless but the Will of
T-25 .. VII.2:10 Yet there is **n.** else you could believe, if
T-25 .... VII.3:4 And **n.** that the world believes as true has
T-25 .... VII.5:2 And one in which **n.** is contradicted that
T-25 .... VII.5:3 and joy. **N.** attests to death and cruelty; to
T-25 .... VII.6:2 But **n.** else. What is not love is sin, and
T-25 ... VIII.1:8 one can lose for you to gain. And **n.** more.
T-25 ... VIII.3:1 in salvation of which the world knows **n.**.
T-25 . VIII.14:3 Your special function shows you **n.** else
T-25 ..... IX.2:4 **N.** you give is lost to you or anyone, but
T-26 ........I.1:7 see **n.** attached to anything beyond itself.
T-26 .......II.8:3 it. **N.** He loves but must be sinless and
T-26 ..... III.1:4 **N.** conflicts with oneness. How, then,
T-26 ... III.1:10 for there is **n.** to decide *between.* And only
T-26 ... III.1:12 What is everything leaves room for **n.** else
T-26 ..... III.4:1 **N.** the Son of God believes can be
T-26 ..... IV.1:3 lies. **N.** in boundless love could need
T-26 ..... IV.1:6 which he learns he has done **n.** to forgive.
T-26 ..... IV.2:4 **n.** stands between to keep them separate
T-26 ..... IV.2:5 **n.** stands between to push the other off.
T-26 .......V.1:6 **N.** in between is possible. There are two
T-26 .....V.1:12 to nowhere. There is **n.** else to choose.
T-26 .......V.2:1 **N.** is ever lost but time, which in the end
T-26 .......V.2:5 **N.** you undertake with certain purpose
T-26 .......V.2:6 down a road that leads to **n.** and that has
T-26 ..... VI.1:4 It is not **n.**. And through its perceived
T-26 .... VII.8:1 **N.** gives meaning where no meaning is.
T-26 .......X.5:5 And to this purpose **n.** can be added, for
T-27 ........I.5:7 that **n.** which his madness bid him do was
T-27 ........I.9:9 For now it witnesses to **n.** yet, its purpose
T-27 .......II.6:1 miracle can offer **n.** less to him than it has
T-27 ..... III.2:5 And now he stands for **n.**. Symbols which
T-27 ..... III.3:1 of your brother that you see means **n.**.
T-27 ..... III.3:2 There is **n.** to attack or to deny; to love or
T-27 ..... III.4:6 **N.** points beyond the truth, for what can
T-27 ..... III.7:1 and **n.** that the eyes have ever seen or ears
T-27 ..... III.7:6 know the peace of power that opposes **n.**.
T-27 ..... IV.5:5 add **n.** new and nothing has been learned.
T-27 ..... IV.5:5 add nothing new and **n.** has been learned.
T-27 .......V.4:2 And **n.** more than just one instant of your
T-27 .......V.4:5 leaves **n.** within the world that could be
T-27 .......V.6:1 for **n.** that is there received is left behind
T-27 ..... VI.1:8 Thus are they means for **n.**, for they have
T-27 ..... VI.3:6 name or that, but **n.** more, you choose.

T-27......VI.4:4 **n.** could contain what you believe it holds
T-27...VII.13:3 **N.** more fearful than an idle dream has
T-27... VIII.5:5 was a time when he knew **n.** of a body,
T-27... VIII.8:7 their cause that follows **n.** and is but a jest
T-28.........I.1:1 The miracle does **n.**. All it does is to undo
T-28.........I.3:1 **N.** employed for healing represents an
T-28.........I.6:1 time is but another phase of what does **n.**.
T-28.........I.7:1 Remember **n.** that you taught yourself,
T-28...... I.10:9 Effects, and doing **n.** that would interfere.
T-28...... I.11:3 And they will join in doing **n.** to prevent
T-28...... I.12:6 God do **n.** that would make himself afraid
T-28...... I.14:3 all. He has done **n.**. And in seeing this, he
T-28...... II.4:1 **N.** at all has happened but that you have
T-28..... II.7:10 The miracle does **n.** but to show him that
T-28..... II.7:10 but to show him that he has done **n.**.
T-28..... II.11:7 be sick; projecting out its guilt caused **n.**,
T-28...... III.3:1 does **n.** just *because* the minds are joined,
T-28...... III.5:2 is but empty space, enclosing **n.**, doing
T-28...... III.5:2 empty space, enclosing nothing, doing **n.**,
T-28...... III.7:3 They have **n.** left behind the open door.
T-28...... IV.9:5 the broken pieces seem to take mean **n.**.
T-28.... IV.10:2 when he perceives he has lost **n.**? Who
T-28...... V.1:10 Except you share it, **n.** can exist. And you
T-28....... V.7:4 Yet in the gap is **n.**. And there are no
T-28..... VII.1:1 God asks for **n.**, and His Son, like Him,
T-28..... VII.1:1 and His Son, like Him, need ask for **n.**.
T-29.........I.1:2 There is **n.** to be feared. There is no way
T-29.........I.8:3 you know that **n.** stands between you and
T-29.........I.9:2 **N.** more than that, and nothing less.
T-29.........I.9:2 Nothing more than that, and **n.** less.
T-29....... II.1:5 Until you realize you give up **n.**, until you
T-29....... II.6:1 thing be part of him, and **n.** else have life.
T-29....... II.6:3 based, and there is **n.** else it rests upon.
T-29....... II.9:5 only in your failure to perceive that it is **n.**
T-29....... V.2:3 within that **n.** in this world but passes by,
T-29....... V.2:4 **n.** can intrude upon the sacred Son of
T-29....... V.3:3 him. **N.** is asked of you but to accept the
T-29....... V.8:3 Yet **n.** in the world of dreams remains
T-29...... VI.3:1 **N.** survives its purpose. If it be conceived
T-29...... VI.5:3 and **n.** in the world but must be changed
T-29...... VI.5:4 For **n.** here but is defined as what you see
T-29... VII.10:3 The sacrifice of death is **n.** lost. An idol
T-29... VIII.5:2 What is an idol? **N.**! It must be
T-29... VIII.7:6 **N.** and nowhere must an idol be, while
T-30...... I.16:4 **N.** can be caused without some form of
T-30....... II.2:3 There is **n.** else that ever should be called
T-30...... III.6:1 **N.** that God knows not exists. And what
T-30.... III.11:2 in a world which your reality knows **n.** of?
T-30...... IV.5:6 Yet what it makes is **n.**. Who could be
T-30...... IV.8:5 much. It asks for **n.** in reality. And even in
T-30...... IV.8:9 Dreams are for **n.**. And the Son of God
T-30....... V.5:3 understood that idols are **n.** and nowhere
T-30..... VII.5:2 And **n.** in the world can be opposed to it,
T-30..... VII.7:1 out of solitude, for what you see means **n.**
T-30... VIII.3:4 Temptation, then, is **n.** more than this; a
T-31.........I.3:3 by it, and even now depends on **n.** else.
T-31.........I.8:2 **N.** but calls to you in soft appeal to be
T-31....... II.8:6 **N.** will hurt you in this holy place, to
T-31...... III.3:6 commands, and doing **n.** of itself at all. If
T-31...... III.5:2 like itself; a place where **n.** can find mercy
T-31..... V.14:3 as **n.** more than the escape from concepts.
T-31..... V.15:7 upon, and **n.** is outside of this perception.
T-31..... V.15:9 **N.** more than this. And in your suffering
T-31...... VI.6:8 in for a while, where **n.** need be feared,
T-31..... VII.7:2 vision, so that you behold **n.** with clarity.
T-31..... VII.8:5 for **n.** stands between his sight and what
T-31... VII.14:4 *This* is temptation; **n.** more than this. Can
T-31... VIII.5:3 *His Son can suffer **n.**. And I am His Son.*
T-31... VIII.5:7 laid by, and **n.** left to interfere with truth.
T-31... VIII.8:2 I ask for **n.** but your own release. There is
W-in..........1:3 An untrained mind can accomplish **n.**. It
W-in..........9:5 use them. **N.** more than that is required.
W-pI..........1.h **N.** I see in this room [on this street, from
W-pI.......1.3:6 Only be sure that **n.** you see is specifically
W-pI.......2.2:5 but be sure that **n.** is specifically excluded
W-pI.......7.1:3 why **n.** that you see means anything. It is
W-pI.......7.5:1 but remember to omit **n.** specifically.
W-pI..........9.h I see **n.** as it is now.
W-pI.......9.3:1 and the essential rule of excluding **n.**. For
W-pI.....13.1:3 **N.** without meaning exists. However, it
W-pI.....14.1:4 world you see has **n.** to do with reality. It
W-pI.....15.1:1 that you do not recognize them as **n.**. You
W-pI.....16.2:4 You can indeed multiply **n.**, but you will
W-pI.....21.2:5 is **n.** but a veil drawn over intense fury.
W-pI.....21.3:2 and **n.** that you believe in this connection
W-pI.....22.3:4 *I see **n.** that will last. What I see is not real.*
W-pI.....23.1:2 **N.** else will work; everything else is
W-pI.....24.6:1 the situation which have **n.** to do with it.
W-pI.....25.1:2 explains why **n.** you see means anything.
W-pI.....25.2:2 have **n.** to do with your own best interests
W-pI.....25.3:2 your goals are really concerned with **n.**. In
W-pI.....26.4:2 **N.** except your thoughts can attack you.
W-pI.....26.4:3 **N.** except your thoughts can make you
W-pI.....26.4:4 And **n.** except your thoughts can prove to
W-pI.....29.1:2 It explains why **n.** is separate, by itself or
W-pI.....29.1:3 it explains why **n.** you see means anything
W-pI.....29.3:4 **N.** is as it appears to you. Its holy purpose
W-pI.....35.8:1 in which **n.** specific occurs to you. Do not
W-pI.....35.8:3 Although **n.** that does occur should be
W-pI.....35.8:3 **n.** should be "dug out" with effort.
W-pI.....35.9:2 If **n.** particular occurs to you, merely
W-pI.....37.1:4 one loses; **n.** is taken away from anyone;
W-pI.....37.2:6 holiness blesses him by asking **n.** of him.
W-pI........38.h There is **n.** my holiness cannot do.
W-pI.....38.2:3 there is **n.** the power of God cannot do.
W-pI.....38.4:5 *there is **n.** that my holiness cannot do. In the*
W-pI.....38.4:6 *himself, there is **n.** my holiness cannot do.*
W-pI.....38.5:3 ***n.** my holiness cannot do because the power*
W-pI.....38.5:4 "There is **n.** my holiness cannot do." The
W-pI.....41.4:4 go. **N.** can destroy your peace of mind
W-pI.....42.4:3 try to think of **n.** except thoughts that
W-pI.....42.7:2 in which **n.** is lacking that is needed, and
W-pI.....42.7:2 and **n.** is included that is contradictory or
W-pI.....45.1:2 They are **n.** that you think you think, just
W-pI.....45.1:2 just as **n.** that you think you see is related
W-pI.....45.1:4 **N.** that you think are your real thoughts
W-pI.....45.1:5 respect. **N.** that you think you see bears
W-pI.....47.7:5 is a place in you where **n.** is impossible.
W-pI........48.h There is **n.** to fear.
W-pI.....48.1:3 In truth there is **n.** to fear. It is very easy
W-pI.....48.3:2 awareness that there is **n.** to fear shows
W-pI.....48.3:3 willing to do this there is indeed **n.** to fear
W-pI.....50.3:3 into a state of mind that **n.** can threaten,
W-pI.....50.3:3 that nothing can threaten, **n.** can disturb,
W-pI.....50.3:3 **n.** can intrude upon the eternal calm of
W-pI.....51.1:1 (1) **N.** I see means anything. The reason
W-pI.....51.1:2 The reason this is so is that I see **n.**, and
W-pI.....51.1:2 that I see nothing, and **n.** has no meaning
W-pI.....52.1:7 **N.** in God's creation is affected in any way
W-pI.....52.1:8 of mine. I am always upset by **n.**.
W-pI.....52.3:6 that in so doing I am giving up **n.**.
W-pI.....52.4:1 (9) I see **n.** as it is now. If I see nothing as
W-pI.....52.4:2 If I see **n.** as it is now, it can truly be said
W-pI.....52.4:2 it is now, it can truly be said that I see **n.**. I
W-pI.....52.5:5 They do not exist, and so they mean **n.**.
W-pI.....53.3:3 **N.** in madness is dependable. It holds out
W-pI.....54.3:4 Yet that sharing was a sharing of **n.**. I can
W-pI.....54.4:2 I am alone in **n.**. Everything I think or say
W-pI.....57.1:7 **N.** holds me in this world. Only my wish
W-pI.....58.2:4 me. There is **n.** that is apart from this joy,
W-pI.....58.2:4 there is **n.** that does not share my holiness
W-pI.....58.3:1 (38) There is **n.** my holiness cannot do.
W-pI.....58.4:4 my holiness, **n.** can make me afraid. And
W-pI.....60.1:3 accepted their innocence see **n.** to forgive.
W-pI.....60.3:1 (48) There is **n.** to fear. How safe the
W-pI.....64.2:1 **N.** the body's eyes seem to see can be
W-pI.....64.7:1 thinking about them and about **n.** else.
W-pI.....68.6:6 briefly, that **n.** can harm you in any way.
W-pI.....70.1:1 All temptation is **n.** more than some
W-pI.....70.2:1 It means that **n.** outside yourself can save
W-pI.....70.2:1 **n.** outside yourself can give you peace.
W-pI.....70.2:2 it also means that **n.** outside yourself can
W-pI.....70.7:1 salvation comes from **n.** outside of you.
W-pI...70.10:1 **n.** but your own thoughts can hamper
W-pI...70.10:7 *N. outside of me can hold me back. Within*
W-pI.....72.6:7 God gave you **n.**. The body is your only
W-pI.....73.1:7 of creation. They make **n.** that is real.
W-pI.....73.7:7 will is free, and **n.** can prevail against it.
W-pI.....74.3:6 *N. can disturb me. My will is God's. My will*
W-pI.....76.9:5 and **n.** is replaced by something else.
W-pI.....83.4:4 *N., including this, can justify the illusion of*
W-pI.....92.6:2 and **n.** in the world that it would share. It
W-pI.....93.2:1 to help you see that they are based on **n.**.
W-pI.....93.4:1 was never done, that all your sins are **n.**,
W-pI.....93.5:3 it seems to do and think means **n.**. It is
W-pI.....93.5:5 It is unreal, and **n.** more than that. It does
W-pI.....93.6:5 God. **N.** can touch it, or change what God
W-pI.....94.4:1 **N.** is required of you to reach this goal
W-pI.....95.2:5 for it is senseless and understands **n.**.
W-pI.....95.9:2 This calls for correction, and for **n.** else.
W-pI...95.10:3 This is the truth, and **n.** else is true. Today
W-pI.....98.6:3 being asked for **n.** in return for everything
W-pI...102.2:3 at all. It offers **n.**, and does not exist. And
W-pI...102.2:5 You have been slave to **n.**. Be you free
W-pI...104.4:4 gives. And we would wish for **n.** else, for
W-pI...104.4:4 else, for **n.** else belongs to us in truth.
W-pI...105.2:4 and leaves you **n.** in the ones you take.
W-pI...106.1:1 gifts that give you **n.** that you really want;
W-pI...107.2:3 when **n.** came to interrupt your peace;
W-pI...110.6:3 *me. His Son can suffer **n.**. And I am His Son.*
WpI. rIII.in4:4 They gave you **n.**. But your practicing can
W-pI...117.1:2 *love is happiness, and **n.** else brings joy. And*
W-pI...124.1:3 We can fail in **n.**. Everything we touch
W-pI...124.9:1 not be less if you believe that **n.** happens.
W-pI......128.h The world I see holds **n.** that I want.
W-pI...128.1:1 world you see holds **n.** that you need to
W-pI...128.1:1 offer you; **n.** that you can use in any way,
W-pI...128.2:5 The world you see holds **n.** that you want.
W-pI...128.4:1 Let **n.** that relates to body thoughts delay
W-pI...128.4:2 **N.** is here to cherish. Nothing here is
W-pI...128.4:3 **N.** here is worth one instant of delay and
W-pI...128.4:4 The worthless offer **n.**. Certainty of worth
W-pI...128.8:4 *myself. The world I see holds **n.** that I want.*
W-pI...129.6:3 This world holds **n.** that you really want,
W-pI...129.7:4 *of this, for here is **n.** that I really want.* Then
W-pI...129.9:4 *The world I see holds **n.** that I want. Beyond*
W-pI...130.5:5 choose between, and **n.** more than these.
W-pI.131.12:4 **N.** but this has any meaning now; no
W-pI.131.12:4 **n.** before this door you really want, and
W-pI...132.4:1 The world is **n.** in itself. Your mind must
W-pI...133.5:3 you make brings everything to you or **n.**.
W-pI...133.5:4 you can distinguish everything from **n.**,
W-pI...133.6:5 deceived by **n.** in a form he thinks he likes
W-pI...133.7:1 from someone else, you will have **n.** left.
W-pI...133.7:5 Yet loss must offer loss, and **n.** more.
W-pI.133.12:3 Complexity is **n.** but a screen of smoke,
W-pI.133.13:1 come with **n.** to find everything and claim
W-pI.135.20:4 availed them **n.** and could only terrify.
W-pI.135.23:1 **N.** but that. If there are plans to make,
W-pI.135.24:3 Heaven asks **n.**. It is hell that makes
W-pI.135.24:5 You give up **n.** in these times today when,
W-pI.136.17:5 does. Its usefulness remains and **n.** more.
W-pI.136.18:4 You need do **n.** now to make it well, for
W-pI...138.3:4 It is spent for **n.** in return, and time goes
W-pI...138.3:5 is no sense of gain, for **n.** is accomplished;
W-pI...138.3:5 for nothing is accomplished; **n.** learned.
W-pI...138.4:6 For truth is true, and **n.** else is true. There
W-pI.138.11:2 has **n.** but an appearance of the truth. Its
W-pI...139.7:1 **N.** the world believes is true. It is a place
W-pI...140.2:7 sleeps or wakens. There is **n.** in between.
W-pI...140.4:2 that sickness can be **n.** but a dream is not
W-pI...140.4:7 is gone, with **n.** left to which it can return.
W-pI...140.7:6 no core, and **n.** that is truly different?
W-pI...140.9:2 of healing, from which **n.** is exempt. We
W-pI.140.12:1 With **n.** in our hands to which we cling,
W-pI...144.2:1 (128) The world I see holds **n.** that I want
W-pI.151.12:3 you of **n.** but your Self and your Creator,
W-pI...152.1:5 **N.** occurs but represents your wish, and
W-pI...152.1:5 wish, and **n.** is omitted that you choose.
W-pI...152.3:1 that the truth is true, and **n.** else is true.
W-pI...152.3:9 **N.** but the truth is true, and what is false
W-pI...155.4:4 Others have chosen **n.** but the world, and
W-pI...155.8:1 Such is salvation's call, and **n.** more. It
W-pI.155.10:2 with **n.** left to keep the truth apart from
W-pI...156.2:9 Him. **N.** can be apart from Him and live.
W-pI...157.4:3 **N.** is needed but today's idea to light your
W-pI...164.6:5 your love, while **n.** to be feared remains.

| | |
|---|---|
| W-pI...166.1:4 | holding **n.** back that can contribute to |
| W-pI...170.7:3 | He can do **n.**. We need not defy his power |
| W-pI...170.9:3 | The final one, the hardest to believe is **n.**, |
| W-pI...181.3:5 | We seek for innocence and **n.** else. We |
| W-pI...181.5:4 | **N.** more. We lay these pointless |
| W-pI...182.1:5 | **N.** so definite that you could say with |
| W-pI.182.11:1 | to lay aside your shield which profits **n.**, |
| W-pI...183.6:3 | Hear **n.** else. Let all your thoughts become |
| W-pI.183.11:4 | universe consists of **n.** but the Son of God |
| W-pI...184.2:2 | You see something where **n.** is, and see as |
| W-pI...184.2:2 | is, and see as well **n.** where there is unity; |
| W-pI...185.1:1 | To say these words is **n.**. But to mean |
| W-pI...185.5:4 | would offer **n.** more than all the others. |
| W-pI...189.7:3 | Hold onto **n.**. Do not bring with you one |
| W-pI...190.5:2 | **N.** external to your mind can hurt or |
| W-pI...190.5:5 | is **n.** in the world that has the power to |
| W-pI...190.6:1 | of this awhile: The world you see does **n.**. |
| W-pI...191.3:3 | of hope, leaving you **n.** but the wish to die |
| W-pI...191.9:2 | There is **n.** that you cannot do. You play |
| W-pI...192.6:5 | We are one, and therefore give up **n.**. But |
| W-pI...195.3:1 | leaves you **n.** but a black despair so bitter |
| W-pI...195.6:3 | thing, for otherwise we offer thanks for **n.** |
| W-pI...200.1:5 | There is **n.** else for you to find except the |
| W-pI...200.6:2 | In truth it has no function, and does **n.**. |
| W-pII ....in.7:7 | holy Will created all that is, can fail in **n.**. |
| W-pII .....1.4:1 | the other hand, is still, and quietly does **n.** |
| W-pII .....1.5:1 | Do **n.**, then, and let forgiveness show you |
| W-pII .226.1:4 | it, **n.** that I want to keep as mine or search |
| W-pII .227.1:3 | *Yet **n.** that I thought apart from You exists.* |
| W-pII .....2.3:1 | is undoing in the sense that it does **n.**, |
| W-pII .231.1:4 | *is **n.** else that I could ever really want to find.* |
| W-pII .234.1:4 | **N.** has ever happened to disturb the peace |
| W-pII ....243.h | Today I will judge **n.** that occurs. |
| W-pII .....4.1:9 | filled with knowledge, and with **n.** else. |
| W-pII ....251.h | I am in need of **n.** but the truth. |
| W-pII .258.1:2 | by our pointless little goals which offer **n.**, |
| W-pII .264.1:5 | *this, and **n.** is that does not share its holiness* |
| W-pII .269.1:5 | *what I look upon belongs to me; that **n.** is,* |
| W-pII .....6.5:2 | to find Christ's face and look on **n.** else. |
| W-pII .271.1:4 | for **n.** that He looks on but must live, |
| W-pII .273.1:4 | and **n.** can intrude upon the peace that |
| W-pII .275.2:2 | *I need be anxious over **n.**. For Your Voice will* |
| W-pII .278.2:1 | *Father, I ask for **n.** but the truth. I have had* |
| W-pII ....281.h | I can be hurt by **n.** but my thoughts. |
| W-pII .281.1:5 | *are. I can be hurt by **n.** but my thoughts. The* |
| W-pII .284.1:4 | suffering of any kind is **n.** but a dream. |
| W-pII .290.1:6 | and look on **n.** else except the thing I seek |
| W-pII .....8.2:3 | **N.** but rest is there. There are no cries of |
| W-pII .....8.2:4 | for **n.** there remains outside forgiveness. |
| W-pII .302.2:2 | He fails in **n.**. He the End we seek, and He |
| W-pII .307.1:5 | ***n.** contradicts the holy truth that I remain as* |
| W-pII .322.1:1 | I sacrifice illusions; **n.** more. And as |
| W-pII .322.2:3 | *You created me, I can give up **n.** You gave me* |
| W-pII .328.2:2 | *And I am glad that **n.** I imagine contradicts* |
| W-pII .334.2:2 | *Son can be content with **n.** less than this.* |
| W-pII .337.1:4 | Atonement for myself, and **n.** more. God |
| W-pII .337.1:6 | And I must learn I need do **n.** of myself, |
| W-pII .338.1:3 | frightens him, and **n.** can endanger him. |
| W-pII .339.2:2 | *It is a day in which I would do **n.** by myself,* |
| W-pII .344.1:3 | *empty place where **n.** ever was or is or will be.* |
| W-pII .346.2:1 | we will remember **n.** but the peace of God |
| W-pII .353.1:2 | ***N.** is mine alone, for He and I have joined in* |
| W-pII .358.1:7 | *Let me not forget myself is **n.**, but my Self is* |
| Wfl........in.5:6 | **N.** more than that. And is a father angry |
| M-in ..........4:7 | which teaches **n.** but despair and death, |
| M-4 .....I.A.4:7 | The word "value" can apply to **n.** else. |
| M-4 .......II.1:6 | There is **n.** you say that contradicts what |
| M-4 ....IV.1:11 | realize that harm can actually achieve **n.**. |
| M-4 ......VI.1:8 | look past them, he finds that **n.** was there. |
| M-4 ....VIII.1:6 | **n.** that did not serve to benefit the world, |
| M-4 ......IX.1:8 | **N.** but that really deserves the name. Yet |
| M-4 .......X.2:4 | **N.** is now as it was formerly. Nothing but |
| M-4 .......X.2:5 | **N.** but sparkles now which seemed so dull |
| M-5 ....II.2:10 | And it is this they do, and **n.** else. They |
| M-5 .......II.3:2 | the mind, and has **n.** to do with the body. |
| M-5 .......II.3:8 | no less. The world does **n.** to him. He only |
| M-5 ....III.1:12 | healed. Yet they suspect **n.**. To them the |
| M-6 ...........1:8 | Having **n.** to live for, he may ask for death |
| M-10 .........5:4 | **N.** more. Now can the teacher of God rise |
| M-12 .........2:3 | **N.** external alters, but everything internal |
| M-13 .........1:4 | illusion, for in reality there is **n.** to learn. |
| M-13 .........1:7 | since this world itself is **n.** more than that |
| M-13 .........2:1 | the fact that the world has **n.** to give. |
| M-13 .........2:2 | give. What can the sacrifice of **n.** mean? It |
| M-13 .........3:1 | that all the "pleasures" of the world are **n.** |
| M-13 .......4:10 | chooses **n.** as a substitute for everything? |
| M-13 .........8:3 | Decide against Him, and you choose **n.**, at |
| M-16 .........4:5 | hour with closed eyes and accomplish **n.**. |
| M-16 .........6:9 | How foolish to be so afraid of **n.**! Nothing |
| M-16 .......6:10 | **N.** at all! Your defenses will not work, but |
| M-16 .........9:2 | For all temptation is **n.** more than the |
| M-16 .........9:5 | When all magic is recognized as merely **n.** |
| M-16 .........9:7 | any kind, in all its forms, simply does **n.**. |
| M-17 .........3:2 | to **n.** but release for teacher and pupil, |
| M-17 .........9:4 | its thought system is to look on **n.**. Can |
| M-17 .........9:5 | Can **n.** give rise to anger? Hardly so. |
| M-19 .........2:3 | justice includes **n.** that opposes truth. |
| M-19 .........5:6 | it, omitting **n.** and assessing nothing as |
| M-19 .........5:6 | it, omitting nothing and assessing **n.** as |
| M-20 .........2:3 | It calls to mind **n.** that went before. It |
| M-20 .........5:7 | an end, and **n.** He did not create is real. In |
| M-25 .........1:5 | Yet **n.** he can do can compare even in the |
| M-25 .........2:8 | He is doing **n.** special, and there is no |
| M-25 .........4:1 | **N.** that is genuine is used to deceive. The |
| M-26 .........1:9 | Alone they are **n.**. But in their joining is |
| M-27 .........7:8 | **N.** but this; the realization that the Son of |
| M-27 .........7:9 | **N.** but this. But do not let yourself forget |
| M-28 .........2:6 | living thing, and **n.** is held in darkness, |
| M-28 .......3:10 | **N.** is left to contradict the Word of God. |
| M-28 .........5:8 | we wish for **n.** but His Will to be our own. |
| M-29 .........4:2 | myself I can do **n.**" is to gain all power. |
| C-1 ............7:2 | at any level, and has **n.** to do with choice. |
| C-2 ..........1:10 | to help us understand that it is **n.** but an |
| C-2 ............6:7 | **N.** and nowhere. Now the light has come: |
| C-4 ............1:3 | is **n.** in the world you see that will endure |
| C-4 ............4:2 | on it as **n.** more than just a fragile veil, so |
| C-5 ..........6:10 | ***N.** you can do can change Eternal Love.* |
| P-2..........II.3:3 | are forms of unforgiveness, and **n.** else. |
| P-2..........II.5:2 | forms of religion have **n.** to do with God, |
| P-2..........II.5:2 | psychotherapy have **n.** to do with healing. |
| P-2........IV.2:4 | be **n.** that a change of mind cannot effect, |
| P-2.........V.4:2 | **N.** in the world is holier than helping one |
| P-2.........V.6:3 | patient and the therapist will count as **n.**, |
| P-2.......VII.8:3 | **n.** now can be remembered of the world |
| P-3...........I.1:9 | of God, and He knows **n.** of sacrifice. |
| P-3..........II.2:2 | or **n.** about the real principles of healing. |
| P-3..........II.5:5 | There is no other, for there is **n.** else. The |
| P-3........III.1:1 | for healing is of God and He asks for **n.**. It |
| P-3........III.1:6 | It is **n.**. But no one here can live with no |
| P-3........III.7:6 | Surely it is impractical to strive for **n.**, and |
| S-1...........I.1:3 | succeed until you realize that it asks for **n.** |
| S-1...........I.5:6 | There is **n.** to ask because there is nothing |
| S-1...........I.5:6 | is nothing to ask because there is **n.** left to |
| S-1...........I.7:5 | It asks **n.** and receives everything. This |
| S-2...........I.8:6 | with **n.** of the past to hold it back from |
| S-2..........II.7:6 | you. Take **n.** else, or you have sought your |
| S-2........III.2:4 | Give up all else, for there *is* **n.** else. When |
| S-2........III.7:2 | has a Teacher Who will fail in **n.**. Rest a |
| S-3...........I.3:4 | **N.** but that; the sign of judgment made by |
| S-3..........II.5:8 | What but shifts illusions has done **n.**. |
| S-3........III.5:8 | union. **N.** else can heal as God established |

## nothingness 52

| | |
|---|---|
| T-2 ......VII.6:8 | so, he is believing in the existence of **n.**. |
| T-3 .........II.1:6 | A firm commitment to darkness or **n.**, |
| T-8 .....VIII.6:9 | the harder it may be to recognize their **n.**, |
| T-10 .....III.9:1 | then, you may believe you are afraid of **n.**, |
| T-10 .....IV.1:9 | will disappear into the **n.** out of which he |
| T-10 .....IV.2:4 | overlook **n.** is merely to judge it correctly, |
| T-11 .....III.3:5 | The bleak little world will vanish into **n.**, |
| T-12 .......II.5:3 | for the reality of **n.** cannot be frightening. |
| T-12 ...VIII.8:5 | **N.** will become invisible, for you will at |
| T-13 .....III.4:1 | you think it would crush you into **n.**. You |
| T-15 .....III.8:7 | all the little offerings you give slip into **n.**. |
| T-22 .......II.1:5 | the heavy garments in which it hides its **n.** |
| T-22 .....III.5:8 | Yet how can sight that stops at **n.**, as if it |
| T-22 .....III.6:6 | Watch how they stop at **n.**, unable to go |
| T-22 .....IV.7:6 | how easily your fingers slip through its **n.**. |
| T-23 ........I.3:8 | joining lies in **n.**; two are as meaningless |
| T-23 ........I.8:2 | It cannot exist between one power and **n.**. |
| T-23 ...IV.5:10 | be perceived as **n.** when you engage in it? |
| T-24 .......II.3:3 | For sin arose from it, out of **n.**; an evil |
| T-25 .....IV.3:6 | remembered as the sun shines them to **n.**. |
| T-26 .......V.3:4 | as it was before the way to **n.** was made. |
| T-26 .....IX.4:3 | was passes to **n.** when They have come. |
| T-27 .....III.2:6 | be must stand for empty space and **n.**. Yet |
| T-27 .....III.2:7 | nothingness. Yet **n.** and empty space can |
| T-27 .....III.3:6 | What can the causeless be but **n.**? The |
| T-27 .....III.5:1 | As **n.** cannot be pictured, so there is no |
| T-28 ...VII.6:2 | the frailty of the little gap of **n.** whereon it |
| T-29 .......II.8:2 | Its **n.** is guarantee that it can *not* be sick. In |
| T-29 .......II.9:1 | because its **n.** has not been recognized. |
| T-29 .......II.9:6 | Yet its **n.** is your salvation, from which |
| T-29 ....II.10:3 | not exist, and His completion is its **n.**. |
| T-29 ....II.10:6 | His body's **n.** releases yours from sickness |
| T-31 .....IV.2:3 | but lead to disappointment, **n.** and death. |
| W-pI ....10.3:4 | this is to recognize **n.** when you think you |
| W-pI ....50.1:3 | of **n.** that you endow with magical powers |
| W-pI ....73.1:2 | wishes, out of which darkness and **n.** arise |
| W-pI ..107.1:6 | And so they disappear to **n.**, returning |
| W-pI ..122.7:6 | dreams no longer hide their **n.** from you. |
| W-pI ..129.6:2 | can be for you in choosing not to value **n.** |
| W-pI ..131.2:6 | to death because it is the search for **n.**, |
| W-pI 133.11:3 | too dangerous to be the **n.** it actually is. |
| W-pI ..134.7:2 | It sees their **n.**, and looks straight through |
| W-pI ..138.9:6 | concealed, because their **n.** is recognized. |
| W-pI ..185.7:6 | in what they offer, but are one in **n.**. |
| W-pI ..187.9:3 | of God diminishes to **n.** before the purity |
| W-pII ...10.2:3 | in Christ's sight, it merely slips away to **n.** |
| M-13 .........1:2 | the **n.** from which it came when there is |
| C-2 ............2:2 | the ego? **N.**, but in a form that seems like |
| C-3 ............6:2 | is. We can but go from **n.** to everything; |
| C-4 ............4:5 | world spins into **n.** from where it came. |
| P-2...........I.2:8 | of **n.** cannot be called new or different. |
| S-1...........I.5:7 | want. That **n.** becomes the altar of God. It |

## notice 7

| | |
|---|---|
| T-17 .......II.2:6 | little step, so small it has escaped your **n.**, |
| T19 .IV.A.14:4 | no little breath of love escape their **n.**. |
| T-26 .......V.5:1 | too soon for anything to **n.** it had come. |
| W-pI ......1.3:1 | **N.** that these statements are not |
| W-pI ....19.1:2 | You will **n.** that at times the ideas related |
| WpI.rVI.in.5:3 | If you **n.** one, deny its hold and hasten to |
| C-in ...........5:1 | will **n.** that the emphasis on structural |

## noticeable 1

| | |
|---|---|
| T-17 .....VI.4:3 | is quite **n.** that this approach has brought |

## noticed 5

| | |
|---|---|
| T-8 .....VIII.2:5 | an end. You must have **n.** an outstanding |
| W-pI ....66.1:1 | surely **n.** an emphasis throughout our |
| W-pI ....95.5:2 | attention, you must also have **n.** that, |
| W-pI 121.11:2 | a little gleam which you had never **n.**. Try |
| M-4 ........X.3:1 | You may have **n.** that the list of attributes |

## noting 2

| | |
|---|---|
| W-pI ......4.1:2 | periods, begin with **n.** the thoughts that |
| W-pI ......8.4:3 | so, merely **n.** the thoughts you find there. |

## notion 10

| | |
|---|---|
| T-3 ..........I.4:1 | Sacrifice is a **n.** totally unknown to God. |
| T-6 ........I.18:4 | The separation is the **n.** of rejection. As |
| T-6 .....IV.10:6 | as the ego's **n.** that it has affronted Him. |
| T-12 .....III.2:5 | in is always related to your **n.** of salvation. |
| T-13 ......I.10:3 | to the insane **n.** that attack is salvation. |
| T-13 .....IV.4:1 | The ego has a strange **n.** of time, and it is |
| T-13 .....IV.4:1 | **n.** that your questioning might well begin |
| T-13 .....IV.4:4 | the **n.** of paying for the past in the future, |
| T-13 .......X.1:1 | accustomed to the **n.** that the mind can |
| T-16 ....VII.6:1 | Against the ego's insane **n.** of salvation |

T-23....... II.5:7 and of each other **n.** appears as sensible,
T-23....... II.7:2 **N.** it becomes impossible to turn to Him
T-23....... II.7:3 For **n.** He has become the "enemy" Who
T-23....... II.7:5 attack. And **n.** is conflict made inevitable,
T-23....... II.7:6 For **n.** salvation must remain impossible,
T-23..... II.11:1 **n.** there is a vague unanswered question,
T-23..... II.11:4 And **n.** you "understand" the reason why
T-23..... II.11:7 you. **N.** must his body be destroyed and
T-23..... II.14:5 was the truth before, be madness **n.**. Such
T-23...... IV.4:7 of the battleground is **n.** your purpose.
T-24.........I.1:5 And **n.** must war, the substitute for peace,
T-24.........I.2:3 to become beliefs **n.** given power to direct
T-24.........I.7:5 this is **n.** the only purpose that you share.
T-24.........I.8:9 **n.** defeat the goal of holiness that Heaven
T-24....... II.9:1 along the way of truth; too far to falter **n.**.
T-24..... II.14:3 Through this despair you travel **n.**, yet it
T-24...... IV.1:7 as savior; crucifixion is **n.** redemption,
T-24....... V.7:1 quiet, for He knows that love is in you **n.**,
T-24...... VI.1:4 assurance God is here, and with you **n.**.
T-24.... VI.12:1 **N.** you are merely asked that you pursue
T-24...VII.1:12 **n.** that the host of God has found another
T-25.........I.4:6 and your brother stand before Him **n.**, to
T-25...... III.9:8 For you make it ***n.***, the instant when all
T-25...... IV.4:4 that haunt you **n.** will seem increasingly
T-25....... V.2:5 And **n.** you must believe you are not you,
T-25..... VII.9:1 **N.** must he question this, because the
T-25.... VIII.8:7 what but vengeance **n.** can help and save,
T-25...... IX.1:8 has greater value **n.** than all illusions. And
T-26....... II.2:3 in perception that **n.** has been corrected.
T-26...... III.7:1 once was specialness, and **n.** is union? All
T-26....... V.7:2 fact in what is there to hear where he is **n.**
T-26....... V.8:2 made real again and seen as here and **n.**,
T-26....... V.8:2 now, in place of what is *really* **n.** and here.
T-26..... V.10:2 This course will teach you only what is **n.**.
T-26..... V.10:3 in a distant past, **n.** perfectly corrected, is
T-26..... V.10:6 And **n.** you are a part of resurrection, not
T-26..... V.11:3 And will you not forgive him **n.**, because
T-26..... V.11:4 there? **N.** you are shifting back and forth
T-26..... V.12:2 not the true existence of the here and **n.**.
T-26..... V.13:4 belief that what is over is still here and **n.**.
T-26.... VIII.2:3 that trust would settle every problem **n.**.
T-26.... VIII.2:5 of gaining what forgiveness offers ***n.***. The
T-26.... VIII.4:1 brother is apparent only in the present, ***n.***
T-26.... VIII.4:5 Who can feel desolation except **n.**? A
T-26.... VIII.5:4 been caused, and judged disastrous ***n.?***
T-26.... VIII.5:5 back, but overlooking what is here and **n.**.
T-26.... VIII.5:6 Yet only here and **n.** its cause must be, if
T-26.... VIII.5:8 For a miracle is ***n.***. It stands already here,
T-26.... VIII.6:4 see. They can be looked at ***n.***. Why wait till
T-26.... VIII.7:6 "reasoning" you do not understand it **n.**,
T-26.... VIII.7:9 as "good" some day but **n.** in form of pain
T-26.. VIII.7:10 This is a sacrifice of ***n.***, which could not be
T-26.... VIII.9:3 For you have cause for freedom ***n.***. What
T-26.... VIII.9:9 The Holy Spirit's purpose **n.** is yours.
T-26...... IX.3:2 What was a place of death has **n.** become
T-26...... IX.3:7 **n.** you stand on ground so holy Heaven
T-26...... IX.8:1 **N.** is the temple of the living God rebuilt
T-26...... IX.8:4 stood a cross stands **n.** the risen Christ,
T-26...... IX.8:7 **N.** is the Holy Spirit's purpose done. For
T-26....... X.1:3 think that a response of anger **n.** is just.
T-27.........I.2:5 that you suffer **n.** belongs to him, and
T-27.........I.5:1 **N.** in the hands made gentle by His touch
T-27.........I.9:9 fear. For **n.** it witnesses to nothing yet, its
T-27........I.9:10 **N.** is it not condemned, but waiting for a
T-27....... III.2:5 And **n.** he stands for nothing. Symbols
T-27....... III.5:9 interval it has a use that **n.** you fear, but
T-27...... IV.2:1 and every problem can be answered ***n.***. Yet
T-27..... VII.2:1 **N.** you are being shown you *can* escape.
T-27.... VII.14:8 face. The sleep is peaceful **n.**, for these are
T-27.... VIII.5:7 How serious they **n.** appear to be! And no
T-27.... VIII.7:3 Except that **n.** you think that what you
T-27.. VIII.13:6 **N.** need you but to learn that both of you
T-28.........I.2:6 of the past as if it were occurring **n.**, and
T-28.........I.4:3 realize it is a skill that can remember ***n.***.
T-28.........I.6:7 it is a way to hold the past against the **n.**.
T-28.........I.7:5 the cause that you would give them **n.** be
T-28.........I.7:7 the new effects of cause accepted ***n.***, with
T-28........I.11:5 Their own remembering is quiet **n.**, and
T-28........I.13:5 And what is **n.** remembered is not fear,
T-28 ......I.14:1 **N.** is the Son of God at last aware of
T-28 ......I.14:2 **N.** does he understand what he has made
T-28 .....II.10:4 enmity is seen as causeless **n.**, because
T-28 .....II.10:6 **N.** are you freed from this much of the
T-28 ...... III.8:3 so sickness will **n.** be seen without a cause
T-28 ...... IV.2:1 way of finding certainty right here and **n.**.
T-28 ...... V.1:3 brother, and what is **n.** seen as health?
T-29 ........I.5:4 For **n.** you think that it determines when
T-29 ........I.5:5 And **n.** it tells you where to go and how to
T-29 ........II.2:2 the power to heal must also **n.** be yours.
T-29 ........II.2:6 it be. **N.** is it caused, though not as yet
T-29 ........II.2:8 Look inward **n.**, and you will not behold a
T-29 ........II.4:5 asks you **n.** that you will look on them
T-29 ........II.5:1 You do not see how much you **n.** can give
T-29 ........II.5:8 For what you **n.** can do could not be done
T-29 ...... III.5:5 And **n.** the light in you must be as bright
T-29 ...... VI.4:7 once held seeming sway is **n.** restored the
T-29 ...... IX.7:6 once a dream of judgment **n.** has changed
T-29 ...... IX.7:8 in the dream are **n.** perceived as brothers,
T-30 ......in.1:1 beginning **n.** becomes the focus of the
T-30 ......in.1:2 **n.** you need specific methods for attaining
T-30 ......in.1:7 So **n.** we need to practice them awhile,
T-30 ......in.1:8 We seek to make them habits **n.**, so you
T-30 ........I.3:1 This is your major problem **n.**. You still
T-30 ........I.5:2 **N.** the answer will provoke attack, unless
T-30 ........I.5:5 **N.** you need a quick restorative before
T-30 ........I.8:2 *least I can decide I do not like what I feel* ***n.***.
T-30 ......I.10:1 **N.** you have reached the turning point,
T-30 ......I.10:3 this much reason have you **n.** attained;
T-30 ......I.11:5 **N.** you have changed your mind about
T-30 ......I.12:5 you **n.** can ask a question that makes
T-30 ......II.2:7 Hear It **n.**, that you may be reminded of
T-30 ......II.3:3 **N.** hear God speak to you, through Him
T-30 ......II.5:4 And **n.** is God forgiven, for you chose to
T-30 ...... IV.2:5 **N.** must he learn the boxes and the bears
T-30 ...... V.2:6 it can be gained can **n.** be understood.
T-30 ...... V.8:4 **N.** that you have come, would He delay in
T-30 .... VII.1:7 all that happens **n.** means something else.
T-30 ...VIII.1:4 real before, and **n.** you think it real again.
T-31 ........I.1:2 it says is what was never true is not true **n.**
T-31 ........I.3:3 by it, and even **n.** depends on nothing else
T-31 ........I.5:4 **N.** does your ancient overlearning stand
T-31 ........I.8:5 And **n.** you see you were mistaken. You
T-31 ......I.13:2 **N.** do you know him not. But you are free
T-31 ......I.13:4 **N.** is he born again to you, and you are
T-31 ......I.13:5 him. **N.** is he free to live as you are free,
T-31 ...... IV.4:3 Learn **n.**, without despair, there is no
T-31 ...... IV.4:7 is none. Make fast your learning **n.**, and
T-31 ...... V.6:2 For what you are has **n.** become his sin.
T-31 ...... V.8:3 **N.** must the Holy Spirit find a way to help
T-31 ...... V.8:5 of what you **n.** believe for total loss of self,
T-31 ...... V.9:3 learned by **n.** that you behave as if it were.
T-31 .... V.13:6 for **n.** you stand accused of guilt for what
T-31 .... V.13:8 **n.** must you be condemned along with
T-31 ..... VI.2:4 he be the same as he is **n.** an instant hence
T-31 .... VII.4:5 him, has been accepted **n.** for both of you.
T-31 .... VII.5:5 **n.** you hold has brought you in its wake,
T-31 .... VII.6:1 The concept of yourself that **n.** you hold
T-31 .... VII.8:7 and **n.** the veil is lifted from his sight.
T-31 ...VIII.3:1 before you **n.** can make a better one, and
T-31 .VIII.12:1 And **n.** we say "Amen." For Christ has
W-in.......... 3:1 with the undoing of the way you see **n.**,
W-in.......... 6:6 It is the opposite of the way you see **n.**.
W-pI....... 1.1:1 **N.** look slowly around you, and practice
W-pI....... 3.2:1 see things exactly as they appear to you **n.**
W-pI.......... 9.h I see nothing as it is **n.**.
W-pI....... 9.3:3 *I do not see this typewriter as it is* ***n.***. *I do not*
W-pI....... 9.3:4 *I do not see this telephone as it is* ***n.***. *I do not*
W-pI....... 9.3:5 *it is now. I do not see this arm as it is* ***n.***.
W-pI....... 9.4:2 *I do not see that coat rack as it is* ***n.***. *I do not*
W-pI....... 9.4:3 *I do not see that door as it is* ***n.***. *I do not see*
W-pI....... 9.4:4 *is now. I do not see that face as it is* ***n.***.
W-pI..... 10.2:4 The emphasis is **n.** on the lack of reality of
W-pI..... 10.3:2 **N.** we are emphasizing that the presence
W-pI..... 10.4:3 *help to release me from all that I* ***n.*** *believe.*
W-pI..... 10.5:5 *help to release me from all that I* ***n.*** *believe.*
W-pI..... 12.5:8 The truth upsets you **n.**, but when your
W-pI..... 15.2:2 the same familiar objects which you see **n.**
W-pI..... 19.4:1 should be quite familiar to you by **n.**, and
W-pI .... 20.2:6 You do not have them **n.**, because your
W-pI .... 20.2:7 You are **n.** learning how to tell them apart
W-pI .... 20.4:2 the recognition that you do not see **n.**.
W-pI .... 23.4:4 for everything you think you see **n.**.
W-pI .... 25.3:1 of describing the goals you **n.** perceive is
W-pI .... 26.1:5 save you, but you are misusing it **n.**. You
W-pI .... 28.1:4 If you are willing at least to make them **n.**,
W-pI .... 29.3:2 You do not see them **n.**. Would you know
W-pI .... 29.4:1 for today should follow a **n.** familiar
W-pI .... 30.3:2 idea applies to everything you do see **n.**,
W-pI .... 30.3:2 see **n.** if it were within the range of your
W-pI .... 34.5:4 *in this situation instead of what I* ***n.*** *see in it.*
W-pI .... 35.1:1 not describe the way you see yourself **n.**.
W-pI .... 39.4:1 that was ever asked, is being asked **n.**, or
W-pI .... 44.5:4 behind everything that you **n.** believe,
W-pI .... 45.7:2 are there in your mind **n.**, completely
W-pI .... 47.5:1 **N.** try to slip past all concerns related to
WpI... rI.in.6:4 We are **n.** emphasizing the relationships
W-pI .... 51.1:4 I think I see **n.** is taking the place of vision
W-pI .... 51.3:7 loved. I can exchange what I see **n.** for this
W-pI .... 52.4:1 (9) I see nothing as it is **n.**. If I see
W-pI .... 52.4:2 If I see nothing as it is **n.**, it can truly be
W-pI .... 52.4:3 I can see only what is **n.**. The choice is not
W-pI .... 52.4:6 **N.** I would choose again, that I may see.
W-pI .... 53.3:7 it. **N.** I choose to withdraw this belief, and
W-pI .... 55.1:2 What I see **n.** are but signs of disease,
W-pI .... 55.3:5 choose to see, in place of what I look on **n.**
W-pI .... 56.3:3 While I see the world as I see it **n.**, truth
W-pI .... 59.4:6 **N.** it is given me to understand that God
W-pI .... 60.3:3 look anything like what I imagine I see **n.**.
W-pI .... 62.2:4 **N.** you are learning how to remember the
W-pI .... 65.8:5 It is what you see **n.** that will be totally
W-pI .... 68.6:1 Determine **n.** to see all these people as
W-pI .... 69.1:4 Share your salvation **n.** with him who
W-pI .... 69.4:1 Very quietly **n.**, with your eyes closed, try
W-pI .... 69.6:1 want to reach the light in you today,– **n.**!
W-pI .... 70.8:1 **N.** we will try again to reach the light in
W-pI .... 72.8:5 limitations. **N.** we are going to try to see
W-pI .. 72.10:5 **N.** we are going to try to lay judgment
W-pI .. 72.11:1 **N.** we would see and hear and learn.
W-pI .... 73.9:5 His will is **n.** restored to his awareness. He
W-pI .... 75.2:2 There are no dark dreams **n.**. The light
W-pI .... 75.4:5 is given us, **n.** that the light has come.
W-pI .... 75.6:4 upon it **n.** as if you never saw it before.
W-pI .... 75.7:3 Believe He will not fail you **n.**. You have
W-pI .... 78.6:2 in your mind, first as you **n.** consider him.
W-pI .... 78.8:6 Be very quiet **n.**, and look upon your
W-pI .... 79.3:1 the position in which you find yourself **n.**.
W-pI .... 80.5:1 **N.** let the peace that your acceptance
WpI.. rII.in.1:1 We are **n.** ready for another review. We
W-pI .... 89.1:5 **N.** I would accept only what the laws of
W-pI .... 92.9:3 His Son, is waiting **n.** to meet Itself again,
W-pI .... 93.2:3 all this is true by what you **n.** believe.
W-pI .... 94.3:5 **N.** try to reach the Son of God in you.
W-pI .... 94.4:3 for it. You are asking **n.**. You cannot fail
W-pI .... 95.4:3 You have surely realized this by **n.**. You
W-pI .... 96.5:3 Dissociated from its function **n.**, it thinks
W-pI .... 96.5:4 **N.** must it reconcile unlike with like, for
W-pI .... 99.2:1 Truth and illusions both are equal **n.**, for
W-pI .... 99.2:3 Salvation **n.** becomes the borderland
W-pI .... 99.6:5 **N.** are you entrusted with this plan, along
W-pI .. 100.8:1 **N.** let us try to find that joy that proves to
W-pI .. 100.8:2 you find it here, and that you find it **n.**.
W-pI .. 100.9:2 And you can reach Him **n.**. What could
W-pI .. 101.7:3 and **n.** today's idea brings wings to speed
W-pI .. 102.1:3 Yet this belief is surely shaken **n.**, at least
W-pI .. 102.4:2 *for me, and I accept it as my function* ***n.***.
W-pI .. 102.5:3 to tell yourself that you have **n.** accepted
W-pI .. 104.2:4 His are the gifts that are within us **n.**, for
W-pI .. 104.3:1 Therefore, we choose to have them **n.**,
W-pI .. 105.7:4 **N.** are you ready to accept the gift of
W-pI .. 105.7:5 **N.** are you ready to experience the joy and
W-pI .. 105.7:6 **N.** you can say, "God's peace and joy are
W-pI .. 106.7:3 giving, not the way you understand it **n.**,
W-pI .. 107.3:1 And **n.** you have a hint, not more than
W-pI .. 107.3:6 found, for truth is everywhere forever, **n.**.
W-pI .. 107.6:1 in this appearance **n.** and then in that,
W-pI .. 108.1:5 And **n.** you are at peace forever, for the
W-pI .. 108.8:3 *I will receive what I am giving* ***n.***. Then close

| | |
|---|---|
| W-pI.108.10:2 | and we will make much faster progress **n.**. |
| W-pI...109.4:6 | and **n.** you rest in Him and let Him speak |
| W-pI...109.5:7 | dreams will come, **n.** that you rest in God. |
| W-pI...109.7:2 | minds, too weary **n.** to go their way alone. |
| WpIrIII.in13:2 | Do not forget how much you can learn **n.**. |
| W-pI...121.7:2 | to you imploringly for Heaven here and **n.** |
| W-pI.121.11:1 | **N.** close your eyes and see him in your |
| W-pI.121.12:3 | him **n.** as more than friend to you, for in |
| W-pI.121.13:2 | **N.** are you one with them, and they with |
| W-pI.121.13:3 | **N.** have you been forgiven by yourself. Do |
| W-pI...122.7:3 | Accept salvation **n.**. It is the gift of God, |
| W-pI.122.10:3 | And **n.** the way is short that yet we travel. |
| W-pI.122.12:2 | **N.** we walk directly into light, and we |
| W-pI...123.2:1 | A day devoted **n.** to gratitude will add the |
| W-pI...124.6:2 | as in the ones who walk beside them **n.**. |
| W-pI...124.7:3 | We have accepted, and we **n.** would give. |
| W-pI...126.1:3 | to you, and would not hesitate to use it **n.**. |
| W-pI.126.11:4 | *I need to learn that this is true is with me* **n.**. |
| W-pI...127.8:1 | from every law in which you **n.** believe. |
| W-pI.127.11:3 | **N.** are they all made free, along with us. |
| W-pI.127.11:4 | **N.** are they all our brothers in God's Love. |
| W-pI...129.5:1 | **N.** is the last step certain; now you stand |
| W-pI...129.5:1 | **n.** you stand an instant's space away from |
| W-pI...129.9:1 | **N.** do we understand there is no loss. For |
| W-pI...131.6:6 | What He wills is **n.**, without a past and |
| W-pI...131.8:6 | wills to be, and what He wills is present **n.** |
| W-pI.131.12:4 | Nothing but this has any meaning **n.**; no |
| W-pI.131.12:4 | now; no other goal is valued **n.** nor sought |
| W-pI...132.2:2 | **N.** the source of thought has shifted, for |
| W-pI...132.3:1 | The present **n.** remains the only time. |
| W-pI...132.7:1 | is no world, and can accept the lesson **n.**. |
| W-pI...132.9:1 | repeated once must **n.** be stressed again, |
| W-pI...134.8:4 | **N.** are you free to follow in the way your |
| W-pI.134.11:4 | And **n.** he cannot feel that all escape has |
| W-pI.134.16:2 | And **n.** you are prepared for freedom. If |
| W-pI.135.16:4 | see that here and **n.** is everything it needs |
| W-pI.135.25:5 | **N.** is the light of hope reborn in you, for |
| W-pI.135.25:5 | in you, for **n.** you come without defense, |
| W-pI...136.7:4 | **N.** are you sick, that truth may go away |
| W-pI.136.13:2 | God has given you is not the truth right **n.** |
| W-pI.136.17:1 | **N.** is the body healed, because the source |
| W-pI.136.18:4 | You need do nothing **n.** to make it well, |
| W-pI.137.15:3 | **N.** we come together to make well all that |
| W-pI...138.7:2 | **n.** transformed from the intent you gave |
| W-pI...138.9:5 | **N.** are they without effects. They cannot |
| W-pI.138.11:4 | It holds no terror **n.**, for what was made |
| W-pI.138.11:5 | **N.** it is recognized as but a foolish, trivial |
| W-pI.138.12:2 | And **n.** we give the last five minutes of our |
| W-pI.138.12:6 | *I make it* **n.***, and will not change my mind,* |
| W-pI...140.1:5 | so the patient **n.** perceives himself as well. |
| W-pI...140.4:7 | For sickness **n.** is gone, with nothing left |
| W-pI.140.11:5 | We hear Him **n.**. We come to Him today. |
| WpI.rIV.in1:1 | **N.** we review again, this time aware we |
| WpI.rIV.in1:4 | the readiness that we would **n.** achieve. |
| WpI.rIV.in7:3 | There is no hurry **n.**, for you are using |
| WpIrIV.in10:2 | and are learning **n.** to claim again as your |
| W-pI...151.8:4 | guilt, unwilling **n.** to play with toys of sin; |
| W-pI.151.16:4 | **N.** do we lift our resurrected minds in |
| W-pI.151.17:3 | **N.** has our ministry begun at last, to carry |
| W-pI...152.8:4 | all that there ever was, eternally as it is **n.**. |
| W-pI.152.11:1 | **N.** do we join in glad acknowledgment |
| W-pI...153.2:5 | **N.** are the weak still further undermined, |
| W-pI...153.2:6 | The mind is **n.** confused, and knows not |
| W-pI...153.7:3 | can save you **n.** from your delusion of an |
| W-pI...153.7:4 | What but illusions could defend you **n.**, |
| W-pI...153.9:2 | **N.** we cannot fear, for we have left all |
| W-pI...153.9:3 | secure, serenely certain of our safety **n.**, |
| W-pI.153.13:1 | made mad by sin and guilt; be happy **n.**. |
| W-pI.153.13:3 | **N.** a quiet time has come, in which we put |
| W-pI.153.15:3 | Five minutes **n.** becomes the least we give |
| W-pI.153.20:1 | will **n.** begin to take the earnestness of |
| W-pI...154.4:3 | **N.** this mind becomes aware again of |
| W-pI...154.8:3 | You are appointed **n.**. And yet you wait to |
| W-pI...154.9:1 | You who are **n.** the messenger of God, |
| W-pI.154.14:3 | our Creator. **N.** we demonstrate how they |
| W-pI...155.5:2 | This is the way appointed for you **n.**. You |
| W-pI...155.6:4 | for the road leads past illusion **n.**, while |
| W-pI...155.9:1 | Walk safely **n.**, yet carefully, because this |
| W-pI...155.9:4 | It goes before you **n.**, that they may see |
| W-pI.155.12:6 | that walks before us **n.** is one with Him, |
| W-pI.155.14:1 | And **n.** He asks but that you think of Him |
| W-pI...156.7:5 | senseless, ancient dream that **n.** is past. |
| W-pI......157.h | Into His Presence would I enter **n.**. |
| W-pI...157.2:2 | a new dimension **n.**; a fresh experience |
| W-pI...157.4:1 | for what you ask for **n.** is what He wills. |
| W-pI...157.6:1 | only purpose being **n.** to bring the vision |
| W-pI...157.7:3 | in the same form in which you **n.** appear, |
| W-pI...157.7:4 | it. Yet **n.** it has a purpose, and will serve it |
| W-pI...157.9:1 | Into Christ's Presence will we enter **n.**, |
| W-pI...159.2:5 | you. Receive them **n.** by opening the |
| W-pI...159.9:5 | **N.** are they twice blessed. The messages |
| W-pI...160.2:2 | to him, while he is alien **n.** who is at home |
| W-pI...160.5:4 | **N.** is he exiled of necessity, not knowing |
| W-pI...160.6:1 | What does he search for **n.**? What can he |
| W-pI...160.6:4 | and show him that he is no stranger **n.**. |
| W-pI...160.7:3 | are unable **n.** to recognize this stranger in |
| W-pI...161.1:4 | passed safely by and Heaven **n.** restored. |
| W-pI...161.2:2 | But part of it is **n.** unnatural. It does not |
| W-pI...161.3:2 | **n.** it is specifics we must use in practicing. |
| W-pI.161.10:2 | Your readiness is closer **n.**, and you will |
| W-pI.161.11:5 | What you are seeing **n.** conceals from you |
| W-pI.161.12:3 | Behold him **n.**, whom you have seen as |
| W-pI...162.4:3 | So wholly is it changed that it is **n.** the |
| W-pI...162.5:2 | the right to perfect holiness you **n.** accept. |
| W-pI...162.6:1 | And who would not be brother to you **n.**; |
| W-pI...163.8:5 | and we renounce it **n.** in every form, for |
| W-pI......164.h | **N.** are we one with Him Who is our |
| W-pI...164.1:1 | What time but **n.** can truth be recognized |
| W-pI...164.1:3 | And so today, this instant, **n.**, we come to |
| W-pI...164.5:2 | **N.** is what is really there made visible, |
| W-pI...164.5:3 | **N.** is the balance righted, and the scale of |
| W-pI...164.5:5 | **N.** will you see it with the eyes of Christ. |
| W-pI...164.5:6 | **N.** is its transformation clear to you. |
| W-pI...165.5:5 | induce you **n.** to let it fade away from |
| W-pI...165.6:1 | **N.** is all doubting past, the journey's end |
| W-pI...165.6:2 | **N.** is Christ's power in your mind, to heal |
| W-pI...165.6:3 | **n.** you are among the saviors of the world. |
| W-pI...166.9:1 | Your ancient fear has come upon you **n.**, |
| W-pI.166.11:1 | **N.** do we live, for now we cannot die. The |
| W-pI.166.11:1 | Now do we live, for **n.** we cannot die. The |
| W-pI.166.11:2 | and the sight that looked upon it **n.** has |
| W-pI.166.12:4 | to offer you, you **n.** must learn to give. |
| W-pI.166.13:3 | It is you who teach them **n.**. For you have |
| W-pI.166.14:1 | Your sighs will **n.** betray the hopes of |
| W-pI.166.15:5 | Such is your mission **n.**. For God entrusts |
| W-pI.166.15:8 | And **n.** you go to share it with the world. |
| W-pI.167.12:2 | we were, so are we **n.** and will forever be. |
| W-pI.167.12:4 | And **n.** it is no more a mere reflection. It |
| W-pI.167.12:6 | No vision **n.** is needed. For the wakened |
| W-pI......168.h | Your grace is given me. I claim it **n.**. |
| W-pI...168.4:2 | Son. Request Him **n.** to give the means by |
| W-pI...168.4:4 | What **n.** remains that Heaven be delayed |
| W-pI...168.6:6 | *I claim it* **n.***. Father, I come to You. And You* |
| W-pI...169.5:5 | that it is **n.** aware of something not itself. |
| W-pI...169.7:2 | to abandon all but this is **n.** at hand. We |
| W-pI...169.9:2 | it always was; forever to remain as it is **n.**. |
| W-pI.169.10:3 | **N.** we have work to do, for those in time |
| W-pI.169.12:2 | sure. And **n.** we ask for grace, the final gift |
| W-pI...170.3:3 | For love **n.** has an "enemy," an opposite; |
| W-pI...170.3:3 | **n.** needs your defense against the threat |
| W-pI...170.9:5 | love appears to be invested **n.** with cruelty |
| W-pI.170.10:3 | "enemy"; its cruelty as **n.** a part of love. |
| W-pI.170.12:1 | **N.** do your eyes belong to Christ, and He |
| W-pI.170.12:2 | **N.** your voice belongs to God and echoes |
| W-pI.170.12:3 | **n.** your heart remains at peace forever. |
| W-pI.170.12:6 | **N.** has fear made way for love, as God |
| W-pI.170.13:6 | *Your salvation as we have received it* **n.***. And* |
| WpI...rV.in1:1 | We **n.** review again. This time we are |
| WpI...rV.in1:6 | But **n.** we hasten on, for we approach a |
| WpI...rV.in3:5 | *Quicken our footsteps* **n.***, that we may walk* |
| WpI...rV.in4:2 | we share and **n.** prepare to know again: |
| WpI...rV.in6:5 | out, and **n.** will lead you out with him. |
| WpI...rV.in7:5 | Help me **n.** to lead you back to where the |
| WpI rV.in10:4 | And your wholeness **n.** complete, as God |
| W-pI...174.1:1 | (157) Into His Presence would I enter **n.**. |
| W-pI...177.2:1 | (164) **N.** are we one with Him Who is our |
| W-pI...179.2:2 | me. I claim it **n.**. God is but Love, and |
| Wi181-200 1:3 | But you are asked to practice **n.** in order |
| Wi181-200 2:1 | Our lessons **n.** are geared specifically to |
| Wi181-200 2:2 | We are attempting **n.** to lift these blocks, |
| Wi181-200 3:4 | we **n.** attempt to go past all defenses for a |
| W-pI...181.2:4 | Your vision **n.** will shift, to give support |
| W-pI...181.3:6 | else. We seek for it with no concern but **n.** |
| W-pI...181.5:6 | we will believe will not intrude upon us **n.** |
| W-pI...181.9:6 | our trust to the experience we ask for **n.**. |
| W-pI...182.4:2 | a memory **n.** so distorted that you merely |
| W-pI.182.12:8 | And **n.** the way is open, and the journey |
| W-pI.183.10:6 | things he thought he made be nameless **n.** |
| W-pI.183.11:2 | Little sounds are soundless **n.**. The little |
| W-pI.184.14:5 | **N.** our sight is blessed with blessings we |
| W-pI...185.5:4 | wanting. **N.** he seeks to go beyond them, |
| W-pI...185.8:5 | for their form is not what matters **n.**. Let |
| W-pI.186.12:6 | and urges that you **n.** remember Him. |
| W-pI...187.3:5 | **N.** you can perceive that by your giving is |
| W-pI...187.8:5 | first to you, it **n.** is yours to give as well. |
| W-pI.187.10:1 | **N.** are we one in thought, for fear has |
| W-pI.187.11:1 | **N.** are we blessed, and now we bless the |
| W-pI.187.11:1 | are we blessed, and **n.** we bless the world. |
| W-pI......188.h | The peace of God is shining in me **n.**. |
| W-pI...188.1:3 | The light is in them **n.**. Enlightenment is |
| W-pI...188.3:1 | The peace of God is shining in you **n.**, |
| W-pI...188.5:5 | The peace of God is shining in you **n.**, and |
| W-pI...188.9:6 | But **n.** we call them back, and wash them |
| W-pI.188.10:4 | **N.** we choose that it be innocent, devoid |
| W-pI.188.10:6 | *The peace of God is shining in me* **n.***. Let all* |
| W-pI......189.h | I feel the Love of God within me **n.**. |
| W-pI...189.1:6 | a reflection of the thought we practice **n.**. |
| W-pI.189.10:9 | *the world, that it become a part of Heaven* **n.**. |
| W-pI...190.5:8 | And what was seen as fearful **n.** becomes |
| W-pI...192.4:1 | which the Word of God can **n.** replace the |
| W-pI...192.4:2 | it holds no fierce attraction **n.** and guilt is |
| W-pI.192.10:3 | that you accept the way to freedom **n.**. |
| W-pI.192.10:9 | Forgive him **n.** his sins, and you will see |
| W-pI...193.8:5 | you **n.** renounce your own salvation? |
| W-pI.193.11:2 | For **n.** we would arise in haste and go |
| W-pI...194.1:4 | How far are we progressing **n.** from earth! |
| W-pI...194.4:6 | and future dread will **n.** be meaningless. |
| W-pI...194.5:4 | **N.** is he free, and all his glory shines upon |
| W-pI...194.9:1 | **N.** are we saved indeed. For in God's |
| W-pI...195.2:3 | door to the deliverance they **n.** perceive. |
| W-pI...195.3:2 | **N.** is vengeance all there is to wish for. |
| W-pI...195.3:3 | **N.** can you but try to bring him down to |
| W-pI...195.8:4 | The fear of God is **n.** undone at last, and |
| W-pI.196.11:1 | **N.**, for an instant, is a murderer |
| W-pI...197.9:7 | Earn **n.** the gratitude you have denied |
| W-pI...198.1:4 | for yourself can be **n.** used against you, till |
| W-pI...198.1:6 | and you can **n.** receive the gift you gave. |
| W-pI.198.11:1 | **N.** is there silence all around the world. |
| W-pI.198.11:2 | **N.** is there stillness where before there |
| W-pI.198.11:3 | **N.** is there tranquil light across the face of |
| W-pI.198.11:4 | And **n.** the Word of God alone remains |
| W-pI.198.13:2 | brought us here will not forsake us **n.**. For |
| W-pI.198.13:4 | **N.** is the time for your deliverance. The |
| W-pI...199.6:3 | The body's purpose **n.** is unambiguous. |
| W-pI...199.7:5 | Accept salvation **n.**, and give your mind |
| W-pI...200.8:4 | **N.** the way is easy, sloping gently toward |
| W-pI.200.10:1 | **N.** is there silence. Seek no further. You |
| W-pI.200.10:4 | **N.** are they underfoot. And you look up |
| W-pI.200.10:5 | eyes but serving for an instant longer **n.**. |
| WpI rVI.in.7:4 | us offer Him the whole review we **n.** begin |
| W-pI...208.1:1 | The peace of God is shining in me **n.**. *I will* |
| W-pI...209.1:1 | (189) I feel the Love of God within me **n.**. |
| W-pI...214.1:3 | *N. am I freed from both. For what God gives* |
| W-pII ....in.1:1 | Words will mean little **n.**. We use them |
| W-pII ....in.1:2 | as guides on which we do not **n.** depend. |
| W-pII ....in.1:3 | **n.** we seek direct experience of truth alone |
| W-pII ....in.1:5 | **N.** we begin to reach the goal this course |
| W-pII ....in.2:1 | **N.** we attempt to let the exercise be |
| W-pII ....in.2:5 | far along the road, and **n.** we wait for Him |
| W-pII ....in.2:7 | not consider time a matter of duration **n.**. |
| W-pII ....in.4:1 | **N.** do we come to Him with but His |
| W-pII ....in.4:5 | So our times with Him will **n.** be spent. |
| W-pII ....in.5:1 | **N.** is the time of prophecy fulfilled. Now |
| W-pII ....in.5:2 | **N.** are all ancient promises upheld and |
| W-pII ....in.5:4 | For **n.** we cannot fail. Sit silently and wait |
| W-pII ....in.6:3 | We look not backward **n.**. We look ahead, |
| W-pII ....in.7:1 | And **n.** we wait in silence, unafraid and |

W-pII ....in.7:4 we know that You will not forget us **n.**.
W-pII ....in.9:4 **N.** we are glad that this is all undone, and
W-pII ..in.10:1 **N.** is the need for practice almost done.
W-pII ..in.10:7 **N.** it is complete. This year has brought
W-pII ..in.11:5 We give the first of these instructions **n.**.
W-pII ..... 1.1:7 free to take its place is **n.** the Will of God.
W-pII ..... 1.5:3 God. **N.** must you share His function, and
W-pII .221.2:1 **N.** do we wait in quiet. God is here,
W-pII .222.2:1 *as we come quietly into Your Presence* ***n.***,
W-pII .223.1:2 **N.** I know my life is God's, I have no other
W-pII .224.2:3 *Remind me, Father,* ***n.***, *for I am weary of the*
W-pII .225.2:1 Brother, we find that stillness **n.**. The way
W-pII .225.2:3 **N.** we follow it in peace together. You
W-pII .226.1:3 If I believe it has a value as I see it **n.**, so
W-pII .227.1:5 ***N.*** *I give them up, and lay them down before*
W-pII .229.1:2 I am." **N.** need I seek no more. Love has
W-pII ....230.h **N.** will I seek and find the peace of God.
W-pII .230.1:5 **N.** I ask but to be what I am. And can this
W-pII .230.2:2 *What was given then must be here* ***n.***, *for my*
W-pII ..... 2.2:5 **N.** it did not know itself, and thought its
W-pII ..... 2.3:4 And what they hid is **n.** revealed; an altar
W-pII ..... 2.4:4 through the soil, the trees are budding **n.**,
W-pII ..... 2.5:2 the world, and only Heaven **n.** exists at all
W-pII ....237.h **N.** would I be as God created me.
W-pII ..... 3.1:5 **N.** its source has gone, and its effects are
W-pII ..... 3.2:7 **N.** mistakes become quite possible, for
W-pII ..... 3.3:2 And **n.** they go to find what has been
W-pII .241.1:7 They will be united **n.**, as you forgive
W-pII .241.2:1 *We have forgiven one another* ***n.***, *and so we*
W-pII .248.1:2 **N.** let me be as faithful in disowning
W-pII .248.1:7 **N.** I disown self-concepts and deceits and
W-pII .248.1:8 **N.** am I ready to accept him back as God
W-pII .248.2:3 ***N.*** *is Your Love remembered, and my own.*
W-pII .248.2:4 *own.* ***N.*** *do I understand that they are one.*
W-pII .249.1:3 What suffering is **n.** conceivable? What
W-pII .249.1:6 It is **n.** so like to Heaven that it quickly is
W-pII .249.2:3 *death.* ***N.*** *would we rest again in You, as You*
W-pII ..... 4.2:4 And **n.** the body serves a different aim for
W-pII ..... 4.2:5 What it seeks for **n.** is chosen by the aim
W-pII .251.1:2 **N.** do I seek but one, for in that one is all I
W-pII .251.1:5 But **n.** I see that I need only truth. In that
W-pII .251.1:7 **N.** have I everything that I could need.
W-pII .251.1:8 **N.** have I everything that I could want.
W-pII .251.1:9 want. And **n.** at last I find myself at peace.
W-pII .252.1:1 of holiness of which I **n.** conceive. Its
W-pII .252.2:2 *Reveal It* ***n.*** *to me who am Your Son, that I*
W-pII .254.2:5 They are silent **n.**. And in the stillness,
W-pII .260.2:1 **N.** is our Source remembered, and
W-pII ..... 5.4:4 **N.** is the body holy. Now it serves to heal
W-pII ..... 5.4:5 **N.** it serves to heal the mind that it was
W-pII .267.1:4 **N.** my mind is healed, and all I need to
W-pII .270.1:5 *to him. And* ***n.*** *his will is one with Yours. His*
W-pII .270.1:6 *His function* ***n.*** *is but Your Own, and every*
W-pII ..... 6.5:1 that the time for learning **n.** is over,
W-pII .273.1:1 Perhaps we are **n.** ready for a day of
W-pII .279.1:4 And **n.** is freedom his already. Should I
W-pII .279.1:5 when God is offering me freedom **n.**?
W-pII .283.2:1 **N.** are we One in shared Identity, with
W-pII .289.1:4 the world that can be looked on only **n.**. It
W-pII ..... 8.5:2 **N.** He waits but that one instant more for
W-pII ..... 9.4:2 die, or yet will come or who is present **n.**,
W-pII .302.1:5 *created.* ***N.*** *we see that darkness is our own*
W-pII .308.1:4 in which I can be saved from time is **n.**.
W-pII .308.1:6 The birth of Christ is **n.**, without a past or
W-pII .308.1:8 love. And love is ever-present, here and **n.**
W-pII .308.2:2 *It is* ***n.*** *I am redeemed. This instant is the*
W-pII ... 10.1:3 true, projected from a **n.** corrected mind.
W-pII ... 10.2:3 and **n.** without a function in Christ's sight
W-pII ... 10.2:6 it. Bodies **n.** are useless, and will therefore
W-pII ....313.h **N.** let a new perception come to me.
W-pII .313.1:6 ***N.*** *let His true perception come to me, that I*
W-pII .314.1:2 future **n.** is recognized as but extension of
W-pII .314.1:4 Death will not claim the future **n.**, for life
W-pII .314.1:4 claim the future now, for life is **n.** its goal,
W-pII .314.2:2 ***N.*** *do we leave the future in Your Hands,*
W-pII .315.2:3 ***N.*** *may I offer them my thankfulness, that*
W-pII .321.1:3 ***N.*** *I would guide myself no more. For I have*
W-pII .323.2:3 Love has **n.** returned to our awareness.
W-pII .332.2:4 *Father, we would release it* ***n.***. *For as we offer*
W-pII .337.1:6 created for me, **n.** already mine, to feel
W-pII .337.2:3 *Father, my dream is ended* ***n.***. *Amen.*
W-pII .338.1:3 **N.** has he learned that no one frightens
W-pII ... 13.2:4 **N.** is perception open to the truth. Now is
W-pII ... 13.2:5 truth. **N.** is forgiveness seen as justified.
W-pII ... 13.5:2 die. **N.** they have water. Now the world is
W-pII ... 13.5:3 **N.** the world is green. And everywhere
W-pII .342.2:1 Brother, forgive me **n.**. I come to you to
W-pII ... 14.2:1 Our use for words is almost over **n.**. Yet
W-pII ... 14.5:4 **N.** is he redeemed. And as he sees the gate
W-pII .355.1:4 *Even* ***n.*** *my fingers touch it. It is very close. I*
Wfl ........in.5:2 We are forgiven **n.**. And we are saved
W-ep ......... 4:1 And **n.** I place you in His hands, to be His
W-ep ......... 4:6 **N.** you walk with Him, as certain as is He
M-1 ........... 4:4 on wearily, and the world is very tired **n.**.
M-2 ........... 3:2 long ago seems to be happening **n.**.
M-2 ........... 4:2 and again and still again, it seems to be **n.**
M-2 ........... 4:5 in that ancient instant which he **n.** relives.
M-4 ..... I.A.4:2 he must **n.** decide all things on the basis
M-4 ..... I.A.6:1 **N.** comes "a period of settling down."
M-4 ..... I.A.6:3 **N.** he consolidates his learning. Now he
M-4 ..... I.A.6:4 **N.** he begins to see the transfer value of
M-4 ..... I.A.6:5 the teacher of God is **n.** at the point in his
M-4 ... I.A.6:12 **N.** he rests a while, and gathers them
M-4 ..... I.A.7:2 **N.** must the teacher of God understand
M-4 ..... I.A.7:6 but **n.** he sees that he does not know what
M-4 ..... I.A.7:7 **n.** he must attain a state that may remain
M-4 ..... I.A.8:3 **N.** what was seen as merely shadows
M-4 ....... V.1:2 means that fear is **n.** impossible, and
M-4 .... VIII.1:5 that happens **n.** or in the future. The past
M-4 ........X.2:4 Nothing is **n.** as it was formerly. Nothing
M-4 ........X.2:5 Nothing but sparkles **n.** which seemed so
M-4 ........X.2:8 **N.** is the goal achieved. Forgiveness is the
M-5 .........I.2:8 **N.** has he given himself what God would
M-5 ........II.4:7 pain, disaster and all suffering mean **n.**?
M-7 ........... 1:6 **n.** the teacher of God himself whose mind
M-7 ........... 1:8 is **n.** the patient, and he must so regard
M-7 ........... 2:4 **N.** the teacher of God has only one course
M-10 ......... 3:5 on whom it rests **n.** and in the future.
M-10 ......... 5:2 **N.** are you free of a burden so great that
M-10 ......... 5:5 more. **N.** can the teacher of God rise up
M-10 ......... 5:9 Him Whose judgment he has chosen **n.** to
M-10 ....... 5:10 **N.** he makes no mistakes. His Guide is
M-10 ....... 5:13 Where **n.** he laughs, he used to come to
M-10 ......... 6:7 **n.** he knows that these things need not be.
M-11 ......... 4:8 Peace **n.** belongs here, because a Thought
M-11 ....... 4:11 **N.** is the question different. It is no longer
M-12 ......... 1:4 was always wholly spirit **n.** no longer sees
M-12 ......... 2:3 internal **n.** reflects only the Love of God.
M-12 ......... 2:9 And God works through them **n.** as one,
M-12 ....... 5:12 Sickness is **n.** impossible to him.
M-13 ......... 1:3 it. **N.** its real meaning is a lesson. Like all
M-13 ......... 3:3 **N.** has the mind condemned itself to seek
M-13 ......... 6:7 Would you **n.** sacrifice that Call? Few
M-14 ......... 1:5 made, for **n.** it has no purpose and is gone
M-14 ....... 5:10 And **n.** sit down in true humility, and
M-15 ....... 1:12 *Where is the world, and where is sorrow* ***n.***?
M-17 ......... 5:8 it for himself **n.** has a deadly "enemy."
M-17 ......... 7:1 what will **n.** be your reaction to all magic
M-17 ......... 7:7 And **n.** there is no hope. Except to kill.
M-17 ......... 7:9 kill. Here is salvation **n.**. An angry father
M-17 ......... 8:8 **N.** it is possible to take the next step. The
M-17 ......... 9:8 **N.** is escape impossible, until you see you
M-17 ......... 9:9 Let this grim sword be taken from you **n.**.
M-18 ......... 2:3 Holy Spirit can **n.** speak of the reality of
M-18 ......... 2:4 **N.** He can remind the world of sinlessness
M-18 ......... 2:5 **N.** He can speak the Word of God to
M-18 ......... 2:6 **N.** is He free to teach all minds the truth
M-18 ......... 2:7 Him. And **n.** is guilt forgiven, overlooked
M-18 ......... 3:3 The body's eyes **n.** "see"; its ears alone
M-19 ......... 4:8 **N.** it belongs to Him and not to you. You
M-19 ....... 5:10 Vision is **n.** restored. What had been lost
M-19 ....... 5:11 What had been lost has **n.** been found.
M-20 ....... 3:12 conflict **n.** that is perceived as nonexistent
M-20 ......... 4:4 **N.** must you once again lay down your
M-20 ......... 4:5 even faintly **n.** what happiness was yours
M-20 ......... 4:6 Stop for a moment **n.** and think of this: Is
M-20 ......... 6:6 **N.** is the mighty Will of God Himself His
M-22 ......... 5:7 Step back **n.**, teacher of God. You have
M-22 ....... 7:10 **N.** can he say with God, "This is my
M-23 ......... 2:7 There is **n.** no limit on his power, because
M-23 ....... 6:10 you were with him then, as you are **n.**.
M-24 ......... 2:1 be the problem to be dealt with ***n.***. If it
M-24 ......... 2:2 of the difficulties the individual faces **n.**,
M-24 ......... 2:2 would still be only to escape from them **n.**
M-24 ......... 2:3 he can still work out his salvation only **n.**.
M-24 ......... 6:6 Heaven is **n.**. There is no other time. No
M-25 ......... 5:6 **N.** the "power" is no longer a genuine
M-27 ......... 1:3 **n.** we need to consider it more carefully.
M-27 ......... 2:7 His world is **n.** a battleground, where
M-27 ......... 5:6 **n.** His Own creation must stand in fear of
M-27 ......... 7:4 **N.** it becomes your task to let the illusion
M-27 ......... 7:8 the Son of God is guiltless **n.** and forever.
M-28 ......... 2:3 Life is **n.** recognized as salvation, and
M-28 ....... 3:12 And **n.** the truth can come at last. How
M-28 ......... 4:1 the time of everlasting things is **n.** at hand
M-28 ......... 4:5 places **n.** remain on earth to shelter sick
M-28 ......... 5:1 **N.** there are no distinctions. Differences
M-29 ......... 7:7 Not in the future but immediately; **n.**.
M-29 ......... 8:1 *And* ***n.*** *in all your doings be you blessed.*
C-2 ............ 6:1 there was darkness **n.** we see the light.
C-2 ............ 6:6 What is it **n.** and where can it be found?
C-2 ............ 6:8 **N.** the light has come: Its opposite has
C-2 ............ 6:9 Where evil was there **n.** is holiness. What
C-2 .......... 6:18 need to seek for an illusion **n.** that dreams
C-2 ............ 9:3 No miracle is **n.** withheld from anyone.
C-3 ............ 7:1 There are no wishes **n.** for wishes change.
C-3 ............ 8:2 there. **N.** you are sinless and behold your
C-3 ............ 8:3 **N.** you are holy and perceive it so. And
C-3 ............ 8:4 And **n.** the mind returns to its Creator;
C-4 ............ 4:4 And **n.** it cannot fail to disappear, for now
C-4 ............ 4:4 for **n.** there is an empty place made clean
C-4 ............ 7:1 And **n.** God's *knowledge*, changeless,
C-4 ............ 7:6 and **n.** is the last perception of the world
C-6 ............ 1:3 the sense that it was **n.** possible to accept
C-ep .......... 3:4 And **n.** we try again. Our new beginning
C-ep .......... 3:5 has the certainty the journey lacked till **n.**.
C-ep .......... 4:3 **N.** we are sure we do not walk alone. For
C-ep .......... 4:5 **N.** we know that we will never lose the
P-2......... in.2:8 this price. **N.** he wants a "better" illusion.
P-2........... I.4:6 cannot take more than he can give for **n.**.
P-2......... III.2:4 **N.** the extent of their success depends on
P-2......... III.4:5 **N.** he can help through those in need of
P-2......... IV.2:3 all who ask for illness have **n.** condemned
P-2......... IV.3:2 Sickness and death and misery **n.** stalk
P-2......... IV.6:6 illusions, reality **n.** becomes a threat and
P-2..........V.6:2 And **n.** God's promises are kept by Him.
P-2........ VI.4:6 **n.** it is the "something else" that seems to
P-2........ VI.6:5 think of evil as besetting him here and **n.**.
P-2....... VII.8:3 and nothing **n.** can be remembered of the
P-2....... VII.9:3 Who is your brother **n.**? What saint can
P-2....... VII.9:6 **n.** expect to see in him an answer that you
P-3..........II.4:3 do not change and last forever, so it is **n.**.
S-1......... in.2:4 Prayer **n.** must be the means by which
S-1......... in.3:2 Prayer will sustain you **n.**, and bless you
S-1..........II.5:4 **N.** it is no longer a contradiction in terms.
S-1..........II.5:6 **n.** it has become holy, for it acknowledges
S-1..........II.7:7 **N.**, without needs of any kind, and clad
S-1..........II.7:8 For **n.** it rises as a song of thanks to your
S-1..........II.7:8 desires, unneedful **n.** of anything at all. So
S-1..........II.8:8 who lives **n.** with the illusion of death and
S-1........ III.5:1 Stand still an instant, **n.**, and think what
S-1........ IV.2:1 **N.** it is possible to help in prayer, and so
S-1........ IV.3:6 What prayer can offer **n.** so far exceeds all
S-1..........V.2:4 Enemies are useless **n.**, because humility
S-1..........V.3:1 **N.** prayer is lifted from the world of
S-1..........V.3:4 **N.** can you look upon His sinlessness.
S-1..........V.3:8 **N.** can you say to everyone who comes to
S-1........V.3:11 **N.** can you pray only for what you truly
S-1..........V.4:2 **N.** you stand before the gate of Heaven,
S-2......... in.1:9 Yet **n.** it has a purpose beyond which you
S-2........... I.4:6 in him must your innocence **n.** be found.
S-2..........II.3:3 **N.** he says instead that here is one whose
S-2..........II.6:5 How fearful has forgiveness **n.** become,
S-2........ III.3:3 **N.** can He make your footsteps sure, your
S-3........... I.4:1 he has done **n.** must God's Son undo. But
S-3........... I.4:5 The power to heal is **n.** his Father's gift,
S-3........II.1:11 as one lays by a garment **n.** outworn.

S-3 ......... II.2:4 **N.** we can behold Him without blinders,
S-3 ......... II.3:4 **N.** we go in peace to freer air and gentler
S-3 ......... II.3:5 For Christ is clearer **n.**; His vision more
S-3 ......... II.4:3 **N.** are its dreams dispelled in quiet rest.
S-3 ......... II.4:4 **N.** its forgiveness comes to heal the world
S-3 ........ III.5:5 **N.** the cause of every malady has been
S-3 ........ III.5:6 place is written **n.** the holy Word of God.
S-3 ........ III.6:4 And **n.** without a cause, it cannot come
S-3 ........ III.6:6 has entered **n.** where idols used to stand,
S-3 ........ IV.5:4 **N.** healing is impossible, for He is blamed
S-3 ........ IV.5:5 of fear, for only fear can **n.** be justified.
S-3 ........ IV.6:3 Dream **n.** of healing. Then arise and lay
S-3 ...... IV.10:1 So **n.** return your holy voice to Me. The

### nowhere 47

T-2 ........... I.3:6 and **n.** is there reference to his waking up.
T-12 .... III.10:1 perceive is in your own mind and **n.** else,
T-13 ...... VI.6:8 Only the past can separate, and it is **n.**.
T-13 ..... VII.3:3 The roads you made have led you **n.**, and
T-14 ......... I.4:1 the Holy Spirit leads you not, goes **n.**.
T-14 ... VIII.4:3 understanding which can lead you **n.** else.
T-15 ...... XI.7:5 that sacrifice is **n.** and love is everywhere.
T-16 .... IV.11:5 your completion lies in truth, and **n.** else.
T-16 ... VII.11:6 truth lies there and **n.** else. You choose
T-18 ...... III.8:5 that you undertook apart, and that led **n.**.
T-21 ......... I.8:6 outside, for there is **n.** that this light is not
T-22 ...... IV.1:3 you reached the branch, you will go **n.**.
T-23 ...... IV.7:1 for there you look on him from **n.**. You
T-26 ...... V.1:11 to go toward Heaven, or away to **n.**. There
T-26 ....... V.2:3 in it, why should you waste it going **n.**,
T-26 ....... V.9:8 but His, and **n.** can you go except to Him.
T-27 ...... IV.3:4 **N.** outside a single, simple question is
T-29 ....... II.5:4 And **n.** else His gifts of peace and joy, and
T-29 ... VIII.4:3 Its form is **n.**, for its source abides within
T-29 ... VIII.4:8 Christ's enemy is **n.**. He can take no form
T-29 ... VIII.7:2 **N.!** Can there be a gap in what is infinite,
T-29 ... VIII.7:6 Nothing and **n.** must an idol be, while
T-30 ....... V.5:3 understood that idols are nothing and **n.**,
T-31 ...... II.11:4 This is the road to **n.**, for the light cannot
T-31 ...... IV.3:5 And learning they led **n.**, lost their hope.
T-31 .... IV.11:6 **N.** but where He is can you be found.
W-pI ..... 55.3:2 Herein lies salvation, and **n.** else. Without
W-pI ..... 60.4:5 There is **n.** else I can go, because God's
W-pI ..... 70.1:4 salvation as in your own mind and **n.** else.
W-pI ..... 76.2:5 found. Look **n.** else, for it is nowhere else.
W-pI ..... 76.2:5 found. Look nowhere else, for it is **n.** else.
W-pI ... 107.3:5 the truth has come, and they are **n.**. They
W-pI. 132.12:4 from Him, and **n.** does the Father end,
W-pI ... 140.5:7 is not, and **n.** sin and sickness can abide.
W-pI ... 155.7:2 and deprivation are paths that lead **n.**,
W-pI ... 165.6:4 Your destiny lies there and **n.** else. Would
W-pI ... 166.5:4 lot but dwindles, as he goes ahead to **n.**.
W-pI ... 167.9:3 are substanceless, and all events are **n.**.
W-pII ..... 244.h I am in danger **n.** in the world.
W-pII .. 262.2:3 and **n.** else can peace be sought and found
W-pII .. 289.1:2 For I am really looking **n.**; seeing but
W-pII .. 338.2:4 *Mine alone will fail, and lead me* **n.**. *But the*
W-pII .. 360.1:3 *certainty, for* **n.** *else can certainty be found.*
M-24 ......... 6:5 There is **n.** else. Heaven is now. There is
C-2 ............ 6:7 Nothing and **n.**. Now the light has come:
C-3 ............ 6:4 No, not in truth, for truth goes **n.**. But
P-2 ........ III.1:3 both will merely stumble blindly on to **n.**.

### number 23

T-2 ..... VIII.2:7 If a sufficient **n.** become truly miracle-
T-8 ........ IX.1:3 question is, although it asks an endless **n.**.
T-14 ....... X.3:1 the **n.** of them that you can do is limitless.
T-31 ...... IV.3:3 can offer seem to be quite large in **n.**, but
W-pI ....... 5.1:3 anger, hatred, jealousy or any **n.** of forms,
W-pI ....... 5.7:1 and try to identify a **n.** of different forms
W-pI ....... 9.2:2 with active resistance in any **n.** of forms.
W-pI ..... 15.4:4 It is not necessary to include a large **n.** of
W-pI ..... 24.3:2 a more cursory examination of a large **n.**.
W-pI ..... 24.4:3 that you have a **n.** of goals in mind as part
W-pI ..... 24.6:1 that you are making a large **n.** of demands
W-pI ..... 26.8:2 thoroughly than to touch on a larger **n.**.
W-pI ..... 27.4:4 applications, and perhaps quite a **n.**. Do
W-pI ..... 40.2:2 may be in a **n.** of situations during the day
W-pI ..... 42.7:1 is no limit on the **n.** of short practice
W-pI ..... 46.4:1 a **n.** of people you have not forgiven. It is
W-pI ..... 61.7:3 This is the first of a **n.** of giant steps we
W-pI ..... 65.3:1 Today, and for a **n.** of days to follow, set
W-pI ..... 70.6:3 will follow this practice for a **n.** of lessons,
W-pI ..... 79.4:2 to present you with a vast **n.** of problems,
W-pII ... 11.1:1 sum of all God's Thoughts, in **n.** infinite,
M-8 ........... 5:5 **n.** of pitchforks the devils he sees carrying
P-3 .......... II.1:5 that a large **n.** of others turn for help.

### numbered 2

T-9 ........ IV.9:1 on borrowed time, and its days are **n.**. Do
W-in .......... 2:5 The exercises are **n.** from 1 to 365. Do not

### numbers 2

T-14 ........ X.4:1 can occur together and in great **n.**. You
WpI. rIII.in2:3 to be sure that you catch up in terms of **n.**

### nursed 1

T19 .... IV.C.9:4 Your newborn purpose is **n.** by angels,

### nurtured 1

T-22 ......... I.7:4 He is not **n.** by the "something else" you

### nutrition 1

W-pI ..... 76.8:2 include, for example, the "laws" of **n.**, of

### O 10

T-11 ...... III.3:1 **O.** my child, if you knew what God wills
T19 .... IV.B.7:4 **O.** come ye faithful to the holy union of
T-21 ....... V.7:4 **O.** yes, you know this, and more than this
W-pII .. 224.2:1 *My Name,* **O.** *Father, still is known to You. I*
W-pII ...... 4.5:1 long, **O.** Son of God, will you maintain
W-pII ...... 4.5:8 How long, **O.** holy Son of God, how long?
M-13 .......... 6:5 And what, **O.** teacher of God, is it that
C-4 ............. 8:1 **O.** my brothers, if you only knew the
C-5 ............. 5:2 **O.** yes, along with you. His little life on
P-2 ....... VII.9:9 **O.** let your patient in, for he has come to

### oath 2

T-28 ...... VI.4:4 apart. This is the secret **o.** you take again,
T-28 ...... VI.5:4 tiny **o.** to be forever faithful unto death.

### obedience 7

T-1 ......... II.3:7 experience, and **o.** for his greater wisdom.
T-11 ...... VI.5:7 He does not require **o.**, for obedience
T-11 ...... VI.5:7 obedience, for **o.** implies submission. He
T-13 ...... IX.1:5 Therefore give no **o.** to its laws, for they
T-18 ...... IX.1:5 tyrannize by madness into **o.** and slavery.
T19 ... IV.C.4:7 what the ego loves, it kills for its **o.**. But
W-pI. 136.12:3 It does not command **o.**, nor seek to

### obey 26

T-4 ........... I.5:5 want to **o.** its laws unless *you* believe them.
T-5 ......... V.6:7 alternatives the mind can accept and **o.**.
T-5 ......... V.7:6 and must therefore **o.** their dictates. This
T-7 ......... II.2:8 and I assure you that you must **o.** them,
T-7 ......... X.3:8 **O.** the Holy Spirit, and you will be giving
T-11 ...... VI.5:3 for he will **o.** only the god he accepts. The
T-11 ...... VI.5:4 that he crucify, and his worshippers **o.**. In
T-13 ...... IX.2:2 the punishment it offers those who **o.** it.
T-19 ...... III.5:8 If it does not **o.**, the mind is judged insane
T19. IV.A.11:3 Perception cannot **o.** two masters, each
T-30 ...... IV.4:3 that you believe about yourself **o.** no laws.
T-31 ...... III.4:4 serve, nor sets conditions that it must **o.**.
W-pI ..... 57.4:2 instead of the rules I made up for it to **o.**. I
W-pI ..... 76.4:3 think you must **o.** the "laws" of medicine,
W-pI ..... 76.8:1 of "laws" we have believed we must **o.**.
W-pI ..... 77.4:4 Miracles do not **o.** the laws of this world.
W-pI ... 127.6:4 mind of all the laws you think you must **o.**
W-pI. 136.16:4 that it tried to authorize the body to **o.**.
W-pI ... 154.4:2 speaks of laws the world does not **o.**;
W-pI ... 170.6:2 those who worship them **o.** their dictates,
W-pII ...... 5.3:5 change the purpose that the body will **o.**
W-pII . 278.1:2 the laws the world obeys must I **o.**; the
W-pII ... 13.2:2 the law of truth the world does not **o.**,
W-pII . 349.1:2 *For thus do I* **o.** *the law of love, and give what*
W-ep ......... 2:4 Therefore **o.** your will, and follow Him
M-5 ...... III.1:9 body tells them what to do and they **o.**.

### obeyed 3

T-30 ...... IV.4:8 nor make you safe if they **o.** your rules.
W-pI ..... 76.8:7 you hold must be **o.** to make you safe.
W-pI ... 137.7:3 the laws can be no longer cherished nor **o.**

### obeying 7

T-7 .......... II.2:8 operate in this world is that by **o.** them,
T-9 ....... V.8:12 that you are not **o.** the laws of this world.
T-9 ....... V.8:13 But the laws you are **o.** work. "The good is
T-13 ...... IX.2:2 and by **o.** the ego's harsh commandments
T19 .. IV.B.13:4 and **o.** the idea that pain is pleasure. It is
T-30 ...... IV.3:7 he still perceives them as **o.** rules he made
T-31 ...... III.3:6 to be a passive thing, **o.** your commands,

### obeys 12

T-5 ........... I.1:6 thinks according to the laws spirit **o.**, and

T-5 V.2:7 is divisive because it **o.** the law of division.
T-7 X.5:8 No one gladly **o.** a guide he does not trust,
T-18 VI.12:5 body **o.** and gently setting them aside.
T19 IV.C.4:8 But what **o.** it not, it cannot kill.
T-24 VII.1:2 His wish is law to him, and he **o.**. Nothing
T-27 II.7:4 This is the law the miracle **o.**; that healing
W-pI 49.1:3 in the world and **o.** the world's laws. It is
W-pI 127.5:1 law the world **o.** can help you grasp love's
W-pI 137.3:1 The world **o.** the laws that sickness serves
W-pI 199.8:9 *has given me, and it is only this my mind* **o.**.
W-pII 278.1:2 the laws the world **o.** must I obey; the

## object 7

T-7 X.3:2 Surely no one would **o.** to this goal if he
T-8 VIII.3:3 **o.** to the ego's firm belief that you are not
T-15 VII.8:3 **o.** where the mind goes or what it thinks,
T-29 VIII.1:9 or a circumstance, an **o.** owned or wanted
W-pI 8.5:2 *[name of a person], about [name of an* **o.***]*,
W-pI 22.3:2 eyes move slowly from one **o.** to another,
M-8 1:3 A larger **o.** overshadows a smaller one. A

## objectionable 1

W-pI 29.2:2 irreverent, senseless, funny and even **o.**.

## objections 1

W-pI 123.1:4 some small **o.** and a little hesitance, but

## objective 2

T-17 VI.4:2 with the accomplishment of your **o.**, and
S-2 I.2:1 of the world far better than its true **o.**,

## objectively 1

T-2 VIII.5:3 of the Last Judgment is **o.** examined, it is

## objects 1

W-pI 15.2:2 the same familiar **o.** which you see now.

## obliterate 4

T-2 VI.5:10 to the second type, but will not **o.** the fear
T-4 VI.2:5 can easily flow across it and **o.** it forever.
T-5 II.1:5 you can keep it asleep you cannot **o.** it.
T-7 V.2:2 Since the ego cannot **o.** the impulse to

## obliterated 6

T-4 II.10:2 and therefore wrong-mindedness is **o.**.
T-4 V.1:6 and must be **o.** by the ego in the interest
T-12 VIII.4:7 shines in your mind and cannot be **o.**. It is
T-12 VIII.5:2 mind that has **o.** it and wants to keep it so
T-17 IV.8:2 is almost **o.** by its imposing structure.
C-6 3:9 never be **o.** because God has put it there.

## obliterates 2

T-4 V.4:10 It **o.** the question from the mind's
M-4 IV.1:8 harmfulness completely **o.** his function

## oblivion 11

T-12 VIII.3:8 you would have condemned yourself to **o.**
T-13 IV.1:6 you, as its reasoning goes, it offers you **o.**.
T-13 IV.2:1 Yet neither **o.** nor hell is as unacceptable
T-13 IV.2:2 Your definition of Heaven *is* hell and **o.**,
T-13 IV.2:3 For hell and **o.** are ideas that you made up
T-14 I.2:4 you must direct your thoughts unto **o.**.
T-15 I.5:3 well, and bids him leap from hell into **o.**.
T-20 VI.11:3 of water and set uncertainly upon **o.**.
T-28 VII.5:11 it, and rain will come and carry it into **o.**.
W-pI 136.5:2 decision which is doubly shielded by **o.**.
W-pI 166.9:6 by your plan to keep His Son in deep **o.**,

## oblivious 1

W-pI 183.6:2 Become **o.** to every name but His. Hear

## obscure 69

T-6 IV.2:9 never done more than **o.** the question,
T-7 II.1:3 thus making the Kingdom itself **o.** to both
T-7 II.1:5 If you **o.** the Kingdom, you are perceiving
T-7 VI.10:2 apart from this will **o.** God's Voice in you,
T-7 VI.10:2 in you, and will therefore **o.** God to you.
T-8 V.6:3 illusions of another direction can **o.** the
T-9 VIII.8:3 reality. Truth is not **o.** nor hidden, but its
T-11 in.3:5 the darker and more **o.** becomes the way.
T-11 VII.4:5 Truth is not absent here, but it is **o.**. You
T-12 II.2:2 give no power to the fog to **o.** the light, it
T-13 VI.3:4 No cloud of guilt has risen to **o.** Him, and
T-13 VI.5:4 Let no dark cloud out of your past **o.** him
T-14 III.13:7 that would **o.** your innocence from your
T-14 VI.1:5 The **o.** is frightening because you do not
T-14 VI.3:5 for fear, for what they keep **o.** *is* fearful.
T-14 VI.5:2 was not broken, but *has* been made **o.**. All
T-14 VIII.1:3 because nothing can **o.** the gift of God. It
T-14 IX.6:2 in light. In darkness they are **o.**, and their
T-14 IX.7:2 holiness that shines in your mind is not **o.**
T-14 IX.7:3 to those who look upon it is not **o.**, for
T-14 XI.1:5 your power more and more **o.** to you. You
T-14 XI.3:8 in which you try to see can only **o.**. Put no
T-15 IV.6:2 than the ego's attempt to **o.** the obvious.
T-15 IV.6:4 Do not **o.** the simplicity of this reason, for
T-15 VI.6:9 no need you perceive **o.** your need of this.
T-16 V.13:1 to **o.** their tininess and His greatness. In
T-17 VI.7:2 with unity, and must **o.** the goal of truth.
T-18 II.5:7 In dreams these features are not **o.**. You
T-20 VI.4:1 are kept **o.** and hidden from the sun. It
T-21 II.1:5 against it now it will not be because it is **o.**
T-21 II.10:2 becomes to keep **o.** the cause of the effect,
T-24 in.2:2 and **o.** but it will jeopardize your learning
T-24 VI.5:3 Let not his specialness **o.** the truth in him,
T-25 III.5:4 **o.** the sinlessness that shines unchanged,
T-25 VI.2:4 and more **o.** seems easier to look upon;
T-29 IV.6:2 know, because your function is **o.** to you.
T-29 VIII.1:5 Their purpose is **o.**, and they are feared
T-30 IV.5:3 They but **o.** reality, and they bring fear
T-30 VIII.3:4 their unreality **o.** and give to them reality
T-31 I.3:4 curtains to **o.** the simple and the obvious.
T-31 II.11:8 A blindfold can indeed **o.** your sight, but
W-pI 9.5:3 distinction. You may be tempted to **o.** it.
W-pI 49.4:3 and **o.** your eternal link with God. Sink
W-pI 52.5:7 thinking of the universe than to **o.** all that
W-pI 64.1:2 see is to **o.** your function of forgiveness,
W-pI 78.8:7 No dark grievances **o.** the sight of him.
W-pI 81.2:2 *Let me not* **o.** *the light of the world in me. Let*
W-pI 84.3:3 attack love and keep its light **o.**. If I hold
W-pI 94.2:5 cannot **o.** the glory of God's Son. You
W-pI 127.2:1 Love's meaning is **o.** to anyone who
W-pI. 135.17:4 which your defenses would attack, **o.**, and
W-pI. 136.16:3 **o.** and meaningless pursuits with double
W-pI 152.4:1 simplest of distinctions, yet the most **o.**.
W-pI 159.3:2 which never dies, but has been kept **o.**.
W-pI 159.5:3 and never able to **o.** the light that shines
W-pI 165.1:2 your thoughts of misery and death **o.** the
W-pI. 169.11:2 ending must remain **o.** to you until your
W-pII 1.2:3 distortions are more veiled and more **o.**;
W-pII 250.1:2 Let me not try to **o.** the holy light in him,
W-pII 265.1:6 Let no appearance of my sins **o.** the light
W-pII 298.2:4 *that would* **o.** *my love for God my Father and*
W-pII 299.2:4 *Illusions can* **o.** *it, but can not put out its*
W-pII 304.h Let not my world **o.** the sight of Christ.
W-pII 304.1:1 I can **o.** my holy sight, if I intrude my
M-17 4:8 They **o.** the truth, and this can never be a
M-27 3:2 like a shield held up to **o.** the sun. The
C-5 3:4 He made a clear distinction, still **o.** to you
S-2 I.1:4 it thus. Forgiveness' kindness is **o.** at first,
S-3 III.1:8 to **o.** the unity that is the Son of God.

## obscured 25

T-2 V.8:4 The real vision is **o.**, because you cannot
T-2 VII.6:4 is **o.** as long as any of its parts is missing.
T-7 I.7:14 His light was never **o.**, because it is His
T-8 VIII.5:2 because, as such, its true function is **o.**.
T-10 IV.8:1 spark remains, for the Great Rays are **o.**.
T-12 II.1:7 Yet having **o.** it, the light in another mind
T-13 in.1:7 For it is guilt that has **o.** the Father to you,
T-14 IV.3:1 When you have let all that **o.** the truth in
T-14 VIII.1:1 you have **o.** the glory God gave you, and
T-15 VII.1:1 love relationship, and always **o.** by it, is
T-17 V.5:1 more slowly, for the contrast would be **o.**,
T-22 III.6:8 of form means understanding has been **o.**
T-22 VI.15:5 For it was given you to be used, and not **o.**
T-23 I.12:8 So is the memory of God **o.** in minds that
T-24 I.8:5 share becomes **o.** from both of you. You
T-25VIII.13:10 because his own have been **o.** to him.
T-26 VIII.3:3 form is the error still **o.** that is the source
T-26 X.2:7 Presence is **o.** by any veil that stands
T-27 VII.2:3 been **o.** by heavy clouds of complication,
T-30 I.11:6 Its purpose has no longer been **o.** by the
T-30 VIII.2:4 It is **o.** by changing views of him that you
T-31 II.2:10 you made, that this might be **o.** to you.
W-pI 182.6:3 easily shut out, His tiny voice so readily **o.**
W-pII 258.1:2 **o.** but by our pointless little goals which
M-4 X.3:5 Yet while its presence is **o.**, the focus

## obscures 10

T-8 VIII.3:4 it **o.** the obvious attack that underlies the
T-11 II.6:4 your mind, and let nothing that **o.** it enter
T-12 II.2:1 of the density of the fog that **o.** it. If you
T-13 III.2:6 that, by removing the dark cloud that **o.** it
T-13 VI.3:6 cloud that **o.** God's Son to you *is* the past,
T-25 II.6:5 your separate purpose that **o.** the picture,
T-26 VI.2:4 friend **o.** His grace and majesty from you,
T-26 IX.2:2 **o.** the face of Christ and memory of God.
T-31 III.1:6 it but **o.** the fact that you believe them to
W-pI 130.2:5 hand, but fear **o.** in darkness what is there

## obscuring 8

T-6 II.3:4 are, thus **o.** your equality with them still
T-12 I.2:1 motivation is very complicated, very **o.**,
T-13 IV.5:4 reference point, **o.** their present reality. In
T-25 II.5:4 it for a while, without **o.** it in any way. Yet
T-27 VI.1:2 **o.** voice whose shrieks would silence what
W-pI 41.5:2 cloud of insane thoughts, dense and **o.**,
W-pII 259.1:5 be the source of fear, **o.** God's creation;
M-13 2:9 **o.** its Identity and losing sight of what it

## obscurity 3

T-14 VI.3:7 Without protection of **o.** only the light of
W-pI 133.11:1 is overlaid with many levels of **o.**. If you
W-pI 138.11:4 demands **o.** for fear to be invested there.

## observable 1

T-1 I.35:1 but they may not always have **o.** effects.

## observe 5

T-30 I.7:1 Try to **o.** this rule without delay, despite
W-pI 44.7:5 Try to **o.** your passing thoughts without
WpI..rIII.in1:3 will **o.** a special format for these practice
W-pI 153.17:1 we will **o.** our trust as ministers of God, in
M-16 3:2 the outset it is probably the simplest to **o.**

## observed 4

T-3 V.3:1 Knowing, as we have already **o.**, does not
W-in 6:1 only general rules to be **o.** throughout,
W-pI 76.1:1 **o.** before how many senseless things have
P-3 III.6:1 One rule should always be **o.**: No one

## observes 1

T-30 IV.4:1 Reality **o.** the laws of God, and not the

### observing 1

T-22......VI.5:2 looks quietly on all confusion, **o.** merely,

### obsessed 3

T-11.....V.13:5 and **o.** with the conviction that separation
T-17....III.1:11 for the separation that no one not **o.** with
T-25. VIII.5:10 He demanded of the ones **o.** with the idea

### obstacle 28

T-13......III.1:3 one more **o.** you have interposed between
T19......IV.A.h The First **O.**: The Desire to Get Rid of It
T19...IV.A.1:1 The first **o.** that peace must flow across is
T19. IV.A.2:10 your brother *is* the first **o.** the peace in you
T19...IV.A.4:4 Fear not this little **o.**. It cannot contain
T19......IV.B.h The Second **O.**: The Belief the Body is
T19....IV.B.1:1 the **o.** of your desire to get rid of it. Where
T19....IV.B.1:3 The second **o.** that peace must flow across
T19....IV.B.4:3 second **o.** is no more solid than the first.
T19....IV.B.5:3 no **o.** that you can place before our union,
T19......IV.C.h The Third **O.**: The Attraction of Death
T19...IV.C.1:3 contains the third **o.** that peace must flow
T19...IV.C.7:5 The **o.** of your seeming love for death that
T19IV.C.11:10 *Teach me how **not** to make of it an **o.** to peace*
T19......IV.D.h The Fourth **O.**: The Fear of God
T19...IV.D.1:5 mind, peace must still surmount a final **o.**
T19...IV.D.2:1 The fourth **o.** to be surmounted hangs
T19...IV.D.5:1 Every **o.** that peace must flow across is
T19...IV.D.8:3 here. No **o.** to peace can be surmounted
T19...IV.D.9:2 No one can stand before this **o.** alone, for
T-20.......II.7:8 the strength to look upon this final **o.**,
T-22.....IV.6:3 as every **o.** was finally surmounted that
T-23.......II.1:3 appear to be an **o.** to reason and to truth.
T-24.......II.9:4 this final **o.** which seems to make God
T-29.........I.3:2 greatest **o.** that peace must flow across
W-pI.....99.8:3 look upon no **o.** to what He wills for you.
W-pI...170.9:3 seeming **o.** with the appearance of a solid
M-14..........3:6 illusion of orders of difficulty is an **o.** the

### obstacles 24

T-8.........II.1:3 is. If learning to remove the **o.** to that
T-12........II.9:6 You cannot lay aside the **o.** to real vision
T-15........II.1:8 all the **o.** to learning it have been removed
T-19.........I.5:5 faith would remove all **o.** that seem to rise
T-19.........IV.h The **O.** to Peace
T-19......IV.1:1 and give it rest, it will encounter many **o.**.
T-19......IV.2:2 and flow across the **o.** you placed before it
T19....IV.B.4:5 **o.** that you would interpose between
T19....IV.B.5:4 We will surmount all **o.** together, for we
T19....IV.B.8:3 me behind the **o.** you raise to freedom,
T19...IV.D.5:6 From beyond each of the **o.** to love, Love
T-20.........II.7:2 thorns, no strangers and no **o.** to peace.
T-20......IV.8:5 to trip on, and no **o.** to bar your way.
T-20.....IV.8:10 God's guarantee will hold against all **o.**,
T-26.....VII.9:5 it does remove the **o.** that you have placed
W-pI.135.11:5 secure in certainty that **o.** can not impede
W-pI...170.9:2 the text has stressed about the **o.** to peace.
W-pI...189.8:3 Your part is simply to allow all **o.** that you
W-pI.193.10:1 seeming **o.** to peace in just one day. Let
W-pI...194.1:2 with the goal in sight and **o.** behind. Your
W-pI...195.8:3 What more remains as **o.** to peace? The
W-pI.196.12:2 there are no **o.** that still remain between
P-2.........II.2:7 remove the seeming **o.** to true awareness?
P-3.........II.9:3 to pass by many **o.** to peace quite quickly,

### obstruct 2

T-5........I.4:11 Therefore you can **o.** it, although you can
T-5...........I.7:4 knowledge, it does not **o.** it in any way.

### obstructing 1

T-21......III.8:3 the body, supporting vision, not **o.** it. But

### obstruction 2

T-2.........V.6:2 a serious **o.** to the very learning it should
W-pI...181.7:3 As each **o.** seems to block the vision of

### obstructions 1

T-10....IV.5:10 break through the **o.** you interpose, but it

### obtain 8

T-1.......VII.3:6 and attempting to **o.** pleasure from them.
T-9.......VII.1:3 have made it possible and easy to **o.** it.
T-10......III.5:2 To **o.** this you are willing to attack the
T-13....III.10:1 prefer separation to sanity cannot **o.** it in
T-20.....VII.3:1 To **o.** the goal the Holy Spirit indeed asks
T-25......III.2:1 not **o.** directly to a world perception rules
T-25......IV.2:6 Even in Heaven does this law **o.**. The Son
W-pI.133.12:1 or not worth the slightest effort to **o.**.

### obtained 6

T-29.......II.5:4 happiness His Presence brings, can be **o.**.
W-pI.135.15:3 and experience **o.** from past events and
W-pI...153.3:1 escape no longer can be hoped for nor **o.**.
W-pI...185.6:1 other minds, for that is how peace is **o.**.
W-pII..233.1:4 *instead of seeking goals which cannot be **o.**,*
W-pII..328.1:2 creation is the way in which salvation is **o.**

### obvious 78

T-2.......V.1:11 It is **o.**, then, that inducing the mind to
T-2........VI.1:8 for them. This is an **o.** confusion of levels.
T-2........VI.8:3 It is **o.**, then, that when you are afraid,
T-3........III.2:8 change, their dependence on time is **o.**.
T-3........VI.2:3 out that evaluation is its **o.** prerequisite.
T-4.........II.6:2 is **o.** when you consider what is involved.
T-5.......VII.6:2 This is **o.**, if you realize that you must
T-6.........in.1:1 The relationship of anger to attack is **o.**,
T-6.........II.1:6 however, may not be so **o.** as you think.
T-7.........X.4:1 need to demonstrate the **o.** to yourself. It
T-7.........X.4:2 It is not **o.** to you. You believe that doing
T-8........IV.5:2 **o.** when you consider what healing is for.
T-8.....VII.11:6 of attack is an **o.** confusion in purpose.
T-8.....VII.14:6 He has accepted a learning goal in **o.**
T-8.....VIII.3:4 the **o.** attack that underlies the sickness. If
T-9.......VII.2:6 and so **o.** that it is often overlooked. The
T-9.......VII.2:7 ego is afraid of the **o.**, since obviousness is
T-9.......VII.3:1 is perfectly **o.** that if the Holy Spirit looks
T-11.......V.14:4 The next step, then, is **o.**. If consistent
T-12........IV.3:1 is surely **o.** that no one wants to find what
T-12........V.7:3 The result of this curriculum goal is **o.**.
T-14.......II.2:7 The simple and the **o.** are not apparent to
T-15......IV.6:2 than the ego's attempt to obscure the **o.**.
T-15.......X.6:3 While it is **o.** that the ego does demand
T-16.......III.4:3 You have been very careful to avoid the **o.**
T-16......VII.3:8 That this is insane is **o.**. But what is less
T-16......VII.3:9 less **o.** is that the present is useless to you
T-19.........I.3:4 It is **o.** that a segment of the mind can see
T-20.......VI.2:7 and so **o.** it cannot be misunderstood.
T-21.......V.3:5 They are the **o.** response to calls for help,
T-21.......V.4:6 from reason, the basic question is **o.**,
T-22......III.1:3 goal is to make plain, and therefore **o.**.
T-22......III.1:8 is plain, and what is **o.** is not ambiguous.
T-24......IV.3:4 wish to heal and not attack, it is quite **o.**.
T-25......IX.4:7 to the first, in which the murder is not **o.**.
T-27.....VII.3:7 need to go beyond the **o.** in terms of cause
T-27. VIII.13:4 This is the **o.**; a secret kept from no one
T-28.....VI.5:2 is the **o.** effect of what was made in secret,
T-30.........I.8:3 This much is **o.**, and paves the way for the
T-31.........I.2:3 It teaches but the very **o.**. It merely goes
T-31.........I.3:4 curtains to obscure the simple and the **o.**.
T-31......IV.7:7 otherwise, it is a simple teaching in the **o.**.
W-pI.....21.3:3 fallacious grounds that they are more "**o.**.
W-pI.....22.3:9 *I really want to see?* The answer is surely **o.**.
W-pI.....26.1:1 is surely **o.** that if you can be attacked you
W-pI.....39.1:4 We are dealing only in the very **o.**, which
W-pI.....43.5:9 not bear any **o.** relationship to the idea,
W-pI.....47.5:2 It is **o.** that any situation that causes you
W-pI.....72.3:1 that a body would impose is **o.** here, it is
W-pI.....93.2:2 That you have made mistakes is **o.**. That
W-pI...107.6:3 It stands in open light, in **o.** accessibility.
W-pI...108.7:2 We will use this simple lesson in the **o.**
W-pI...133.9:2 goals are **o.** to anyone who cares to look
W-pI.135.14:3 take, where the denial of reality is very **o.**.
W-pI...138.3:1 is the **o.** escape from what appears as
W-pI...163.6:5 For here again we see an **o.** position,
W-pI...170.4:2 First, it is **o.** ideas must leave their source,
W-pI...193.4:4 very **o.** that it appears in countless forms,
W-pII .259.1:2 What else could blind us to the **o.**, and
W-pII .293.1:4 Yet in the present love is **o.**, and its effects
W-pII .300.1:3 serenity we seek, unclouded, **o.** and sure,
M-4 .....I.A.5:4 valueless unless the next **o.** step is taken.
M-4 .....I.A.6:7 How simple is the **o.**! And how easy to do!
M-5 ........II.1:4 First, it is **o.** that decisions are of the mind
M-9 ...........2:4 **o.** prerequisite for hearing God's Voice, is
M-16 .........2:8 are **o.** advantages in terms of saving time.
M-17 .........2:2 it. Nor is this always **o.**. It can, in fact, be
M-17 .........5:5 That this can hardly be a fact is **o.**. Yet
M-17 .........5:6 that it can be believed as fact is equally **o.**.
M-25 .........1:3 exist. It is equally **o.**, however, that each
M-29 .........1:2 it covers only a few of the more **o.** ones, in
M-29 .........3:2 of this aspect, but its centrality is **o.**. To
M-29 .........4:8 Yet, despite its **o.** and complete ignorance
C-3.............4:2 The reason is **o.**. Seeing the face of Christ
P-2..........II.2:7 to find truth, which remains perfectly **o.**,
P-2.......VII.5:1 of therapy and the **o.** aim of forgiveness.
P-2.......VII.5:7 That many therapists are mad is **o.**. No
S-2..........II.1:2 form. Not all of them are **o.**, and some are

### obviously 19

T-6.......V.B.4:2 to it, would **o.** be that *it* is insane. The
T-7.........V.1:4 healer **o.** does not understand his own
T-7.........V.5:4 the healer is **o.** accepting inconsistency.
T-8...........I.5:2 a change in the curriculum is **o.** necessary
T-10.......V.3:2 sickness **o.** demands the denial of health,
T-11.......V.2:5 The next step is **o.** to recognize that what
T-11.......V.4:3 Fear becomes more **o.** inappropriate if
T-12.........I.2:5 This would **o.** be a split or an attack on
T-19......III.3:3 over and over, with **o.** distressing results,
W-pI.......9.1:1 idea **o.** follows from the two preceding
W-pI.....10.5:1 Today's thought can **o.** serve for any
W-pI.....15.5:1 Although you will **o.** not be able to apply
W-pI.....19.1:1 The idea for today is **o.** the reason why
W-pI.....21.1:1 The idea for today is **o.** a continuation
W-pI.....42.5:3 have let **o.** irrelevant thoughts intrude.
W-pI.....61.7:2 a bringer of salvation, this is **o.** necessary.
W-pI.....65.1:3 Both these thoughts are **o.** necessary for a
M-25 .........1:2 and it is **o.** merely an appeal to magic to
P-2..........II.2:3 is so **o.** an ego attempt to reconcile the

### obviousness 4

T-9.......VII.2:7 since **o.** is the essential characteristic of
T-9......VIII.8:3 its **o.** to you lies in the joy you bring to its
W-pI.133.11:1 because its **o.** is overlaid with many levels
M-4 .....VII.1:7 in the **o.** of its reversal of the world's

### occasion 1

S-2........III.3:4 each **o.** then will be to you another step to

### occasionally 2

T-1.....VII.5:11 Revelation may **o.** reveal the end to you,
W-pI.....19.4:1 it will **o.** be included as a reminder. Do

### occupied 4

T-27......III.4:1 of time not seen as spent and fully **o.**,
W-pI.....27.3:5 conversation, or otherwise **o.** at the time.
W-pI.135.15:1 itself is **o.** in setting up control of future
M-16 .........8:2 when his mind is **o.** with external things?

### occupies 4

T-27......III.3:8 empty space it **o.** be recognized as vacant,
W-pI.....69.4:1 that generally **o.** your consciousness.
W-pI...107.3:4 Truth **o.** your mind completely, liberating
W-pI...183.6:6 word, the only thing that **o.** our minds,

## occupy 7

T-18.....VII.7:9 activities return to **o.** your conscious
T-27......III.6:1 picture of your brother given you to **o.** the
W-pI...137.7:1 world will **o.** the place of what you made,
W-pI.137.12:6 we ask that only truth will **o.** our minds;
W-pI...139.8:5 to **o.** themselves with senseless musings
W-pI...182.2:2 in games they play to **o.** their time, and
M-15.........3:2 too small and meaningless to **o.** your holy

## occupying 1

T-17......IV.3:3 the aim of **o.** your mind so completely

## occur 75

T-1...........I.3:1 Miracles **o.** naturally as expressions of
T-1...........I.6:2 they do not **o.** something has gone wrong.
T-2.........IV.2:3 be corrected at the level on which they **o.**.
T-2......IV.2:10 itself, neither type of confusion need **o.**.
T-2......IV.4:10 likely to **o.** when upside-down perception
T-2.........V.2:4 misunderstand any healing that might **o.**,
T-2.........V.2:4 egocentricity and fear usually **o.** together,
T-2........VII.2:4 a necessary condition for the miracle to **o.**
T-3........III.2:9 what you do, and actions must **o.** in time.
T-4.........II.2:4 this alteration can and does **o.** as readily
T-5........III.2:8 in himself or in you for this miracle to **o.**.
T-5........IV.3:6 because they **o.** at different levels and also
T-6.........in.1:3 Anger cannot **o.** unless you believe that
T-6......V.B.4:4 fundamental change will still **o.** with the
T-6......V.B.9:2 where the fundamental change will **o.**. At
T-6......V.C.4:5 the temptation to make exceptions will **o.**
T-7.........V.3:5 but this cannot **o.** unless the body has
T-9........IV.6:2 they do not **o.** something has gone wrong.
T-12......III.3:6 never **o.** to you to overlook their need.
T-13......IV.8:2 so that no gap in its own continuity can **o.**
T-13......IV.9:2 the aspect of time in which healing can **o.**.
T-13.......V.6:1 it must **o.** to you that you have withdrawn
T-13.....XI.5:4 whatever strange thoughts may **o.** to you,
T-14.......X.2:5 anything without order of difficulty can **o.**
T-14.......X.4:1 can **o.** together and in great numbers.
T-16.....V.10:3 total context in which it is thought to **o.**.
T-16......VI.7:4 a sense of actual disorientation may **o.**.
T-17.......II.4:3 that made perception possible will still **o.**.
T-17....IV.14:4 of both pictures can at last **o.**. And each is
T-18....VI.12:1 **o.** regardless of the physical distance that
T-18....VI.12:2 relevant; it can **o.** with something past,
T19....IV.D.7:2 will **o.** is you will leave the world forever.
T-23......IV.6:5 they **o.** leave not your place on high, but
T-25......IX.6:2 what would be unjust to him cannot **o.**.
T-26.....VII.1:3 all that must **o.** for healing to be possible.
T-26.....VII.1:4 For when it once is possible it must **o.**.
T-27.........I.1:9 **o.** at all it would entail the whole of God's
T-27.......V.4:2 without attack is necessary that all this **o.**.
T-27....VIII.9:7 your idle dream, in which this could **o.**."
T-30.........I.3:7 it does **o.** at first, while you are learning
T-30.......I.15:5 There is no freedom from what must **o.**.
T-30.......I.16:2 agree on what you want before it can **o.**. It
T-31......III.2:7 would **o.** to you to give attack to anyone
T-31......III.4:9 so the body, where no learning can **o.**,
T-31.....VII.5:3 you be willing that this happy change **o.**.
W-pI.....12.3:2 descriptive terms happen to **o.** to you. If
W-pI.....12.3:3 positive rather than negative **o.** to you,
W-pI.....12.3:5 If such terms **o.** to you, use them along
W-pI.....23.6:2 for as many attack thoughts as **o.** to you.
W-pI.....24.5:4 of outcomes as may honestly **o.** to you,
W-pI.....26.8:3 especially those that **o.** to you toward the
W-pI.....35.7:2 They will **o.** to you as various situations,
W-pI.....35.8:3 that does **o.** should be omitted from the
W-pI.....42.4:3 **o.** to you in relation to the idea for the day
W-pI.....42.5:5 If such interferences **o.**, open your eyes
W-pI.....43.5:2 let whatever relevant thoughts **o.** to you
W-pI.....43.6:2 allow any protracted period to **o.** in which
W-pI.....43.8:1 various situations and events that may **o.**,
W-pI.....70.4:2 was to ensure that healing did not **o.**.
W-pI...108.4:2 it is understood that both **o.** together,
W-pI.136.20:1 Give instant remedy, should this **o.**, by
W-pI.137.12:4 Ask the inevitable to **o.**, and you will
W-pI.137.12:6 healed, aware that they will both **o.** as one
W-pI...181.6:2 form. And if a brother's sins **o.** to us, our
W-pII.253.1:4 not **o.** is what I do not want to happen.
W-pII.254.2:2 When such thoughts **o.**, we quietly step
M-5........II.1:1 Healing must **o.** in exact proportion to
M-10.........2:7 *through* him rather than *by* him can **o.**.
M-11.........1:5 is no death, that resurrection must **o.**,
M-21.........2:3 Unless a specific referent does **o.** to the
C-in...........4:3 ego may ask, "How did the impossible **o.**?
P-2.......VII.5:4 and of all the effects that may **o.** in them.
S-1...........I.7:8 a specific problem will **o.** to either of you;
S-3..........II.1:2 This can **o.** at lower forms of prayer,
S-3........III.6:3 healing will **o.** because its cause has gone.

## occurred 31

T-1........I.37:4 Until this has **o.**, knowledge of the Divine
T-2..........I.2:1 of what actually **o.** in the separation, or
T-2..........I.4:4 to realize that your errors never really **o.**.
T-2...V.A.15:2 this has **o.** healing cannot be understood.
T-2......VII.5:6 In this sense the separation *has* **o.**, and to
T-2.....VIII.2:5 as the separation **o.** over millions of years,
T-4..........I.4:2 not prove that the separation has not **o.**.
T-4.........II.3:4 why is it surprising that it **o.** in the past?
T-6........II.10:7 recognition that *the separation never* **o.**.
T-6........II.10:8 an explicit statement that the ego never **o.**
T-9..........I.1:2 not possibly have **o.** unless the mind were
T-12....VII.1:1 learning has **o.** under the right guidance,
T-18.........I.1:5 the substitution **o.** is thus fragmented,
T-19.........I.3:5 the "fact" that separation has **o.**. The
T-20.....IV.1:6 things have not **o.** because the Holy Spirit
T-27....V.11:4 **o.** within the instant that love entered in
T-30.........I.6:1 that something has **o.** that is not part of it
T-30.......I.10:1 because it has **o.** to you that you will gain
T-30.....VI.2:5 not real by not perceiving what has not **o.**
T-31.........I.1:3 The impossible has not **o.**, and can have
W-pI.....15.2:4 vision will come quickly when this has **o.**.
W-pI.....26.7:3 that has **o.** to you in that connection and
W-pI.....87.3:5 I will recognize that all this has not **o.**. I
W-pI.....99.1:3 a thing impossible but yet which has **o.**,
W-pI...110.3:2 All this has not **o.**, if you remain as God
W-pI...137.5:2 but removes illusions that have not **o.**.
W-pI...167.9:3 which what seems to happen never has **o.**,
W-pI...198.2:6 influence and its effects have not **o.** at all.
W-pII.....1.1:1 your brother did to you has not **o.**. It does
M-13.........3:1 Once this confusion has **o.**, it becomes
S-3..........II.5:4 What healing has **o.** in such a view of

## occurrence 1

W-pI.....90.3:4 the answer as simultaneous in their **o.**.

## occurrences 1

W-pI.151.11:2 He will reinterpret all you see, and all **o.**,

## occurring 1

T-28.........I.2:6 perception of the past as if it were **o.** now,

## occurs 42

T-1.........V.3:8 When this **o.** the whole family of God, or
T-2..........I.1:7 **o.** when you believe that some emptiness
T-2.........II.5:3 itself, like the classrooms in which it **o.**, is
T-2.......VI.8:9 the fear. This is how true healing **o.**.
T-2.......VI.9:2 little right thinking to realize why fear **o.**.
T-2......VII.7:4 As soon as a state of readiness **o.**, there is
T-4.........II.3:4 happen. If this **o.** in the present, why is it
T-4.........II.3:5 something that **o.** with such persistence.
T-5..........I.7:6 **o.** to produce a real qualitative shift.
T-6.........II.1:5 it **o.** projection becomes its main defense,
T-9.....VIII.1:4 When this **o.**, even though it does not
T-13........II.1:3 this issue, then, the deepest split of all **o.**,
T-19.........I.3:5 this **o.** the body becomes its weapon, used
T-21....VII.9:1 decision; this the condition for what **o.**. It
T-23.........I.8:5 **o.** whenever you look on anything that
T-26........X.1:6 it **o.** at all it will be total. And its presence,
T-31.....III.1:3 temptation, and to every situation that **o.**.
T-31...VIII.1:1 teach, in all its forms, wherever it **o.**. It
T-31...VIII.6:3 see all pain, in every form, wherever it **o.**,
W-pI......5.6:2 If this **o.**, think first of this: *I cannot keep*
W-pI.....14.4:2 Name each one as it **o.** to you, and then
W-pI.....16.4:4 Every thought that **o.** to you, regardless of
W-pI.....24.5:1 today, name each situation that **o.** to you,
W-pI.....35.7:3 up any specific situation that **o.** to you,
W-pI.....35.8:1 in which nothing specific **o.** to you. Do
W-pI.....35.8:2 idea slowly until something **o.** to you.
W-pI.....35.9:2 If nothing particular **o.** to you, merely
W-pI.....37.4:5 the idea to any person who **o.** to you,
W-pI..105.7:1 while, and tell each one, as he **o.** to you:
W-pI 134.17:2 When this **o.**, allow your mind to see
W-pI..152.1:5 Nothing **o.** but represents your wish, and
W-pI..167.3:5 is where it must be changed, if change **o.**.
W-pI..187.8:3 If the thought **o.**, its very presence proves
W-pII.....243.h Today I will judge nothing that **o.**.
M-3...........5:1 level of teaching **o.** in relationships which,
M-5.........I.1:6 When this **o.**, real strength is seen as
M-13.......7:10 For it is here the split with God **o.**. A split
M-16.........8:5 the instant this **o.** he will return to earlier
P-2........VI.1:5 Healing **o.** as a patient begins to hear the
P-2........VI.6:4 When this **o.**, he sees his sins as gone into
P-3..........II.6:1 forgets to judge the patient that healing **o.**
P-3..........II.7:1 it is when judgment ceases that healing **o.**

## ocean 11

T-18...VIII.3:3 the faintest ripple on the surface of the **o.**.
T-18...VIII.3:4 imperceptible ripple hails itself as the **o.**.
T-18...VIII.3:6 **o.** terrifies the little ripple and wants to
T-18...VIII.4:1 Yet neither sun nor **o.** is even aware of all
T-18...VIII.4:6 the ripple without the **o.** is inconceivable.
T-18...VIII.6:1 Like to the sun and **o.** your Self continues
T-18...VIII.7:2 and **o.** are as nothing beside what you are.
T-18...VIII.7:3 the ripple dances as it rests upon the **o.**.
T-18...VIII.7:4 sun nor **o.** is the power that rests in you.
T-26.......V.6:6 shore, and dream himself across an **o.**, to
WpI..rIV.in4:3 the **o.** change the coming and the going of

## oddly 1

W-pI.....10.4:6 an **o.** assorted procession going by, which

## odds 3

T-4.....III.10:2 because it opposes literally invincible **o.**,
T-12.....III.7:7 have become at **o.** with the world as you
M-17.........6:7 remember the impossible **o.** against you.

## of 12735

## off 83

*See also* fenced-off, off-balanced

T-1.......VI.1:5 you would be better **o.** in a state somehow
T-3......VII.6:1 no fruit will be cut **o.** and will wither away
T-4.........V.1:4 ego is thrown further **o.** balance because
T-8.....VII.1:8 them, he has cut himself **o.** from salvation
T-11......IV.3:4 you cut **o.** a brother from the light that is
T-12........II.5:2 Take **o.** the covers and look at what you
T-12......IV.2:4 of its source the ego is not wholly split **o.**,
T-14.........I.2:5 thought system is closed **o.** and wholly
T-14......VI.2:4 been separated **o.** and kept in darkness.
T-14......VI.7:4 dropping **o.** the rest and offering your
T-15......IV.8:1 keep hidden shuts communication **o.**,
T-16......III.6:4 this, and from far **o.** in the universe, yet
T-16......IV.3:4 which hatred is split **o.** and kept apart.
T-17......III.3:3 centered on and separated **o.** as being the
T-17......III.3:4 the maintaining and the breaking **o.** of
T-17........V.3:8 have been broken **o.** at this point, and the
T-17......V.13:3 by cutting yourself **o.** from its expression,
T-17...VI.6:10 seeks to split **o.** segments of the situation
T-18.........I.7:6 and swirling lightly **o.** on a mad course
T-18......VI.9:1 shutting you **o.** from others and keeping
T-18......IX.1:3 thought that seems split **o.** and separate,
T-18......IX.1:9 withered kingdom in which you set it **o.**,
T-20......III.7:2 the home of truth and who will wander **o.**
T-20...VIII.1:3 closed **o.** by valuing the "something else,"
T-21.......V.4:2 self you have cut **o.** from your awareness.

T-22.........I.1:7 a plan of any kind except to wander **o.**,
T-23....... II.2:2 of thoughts that set him **o.** from others.
T-24.........I.7:3 might be extended, not cut **o.** from him.
T-24.........I.7:8 let you think that you are better **o.** apart.
T-24...... III.2:4 So does it seem to split you **o.** from God,
T-24...... III.3:5 *It* can be thrown **o.** balance by anything.
T-25....... II.4:8 Its purpose is to set the picture **o.**, and
T-25...... III.3:5 it is the perfect frame to set it **o.**; the
T-25...... IV.4:5 you. And they go farther and farther **o.**,
T-25... VIII.8:3 they think that justice is split **o.** from love
T-26.........I.1:8 a little nearer, or go a little farther **o.**, but
T-26.........I.3:1 that the body fences **o.** becomes the self,
T-26...... IV.2:5 stands between to push the other **o.**. And
T-26....... V.2:6 But it is hard indeed to wander **o.**, alone
T-26..... VII.8:9 This separating **o.** is symbolized, in your
T-27.........I.3:2 closing **o.** the gate and damning him to
T-27..... II.11:5 This splits his function **o.** from yours, and
T-28....... II.8:8 Effect and cause are first split **o.**, and then
T-28....... V.1:2 Of a splitting ***o.*** and separating *from*?
T-28....... V.1:5 sickness separating **o.** the self from good,
T-29.........I.4:2 to be dividing **o.** your separate minds. It
T-29..... VII.2:3 if a part of it were separated **o.** and found
T-29... VIII.3:6 veil that seems to shut you **o.** from Him,
T-29... VIII.7:4 alcove separated **o.** from what is endless,
T-29...... IX.2:7 the judgment **o.** from resting on himself.
T-30...... I.10:3 you would be better **o.** if you were wrong.
T-30...... III.3:7 and separated **o.** from what is whole. And
T-31..... VII.9:1 of yourself that holds him **o.** from you,
T-31..... VII.9:2 holds your brother **o.** unoccupied by love.
W-pI..... 57.1:4 drop them **o.** merely by desiring to do so.
W-pI..... 68.1:6 It seems to split you **o.** from your Source
W-pI..... 68.2:1 Shut **o.** from your Self, which remains
W-pI..... 74.6:3 feel yourself slipping **o.** into withdrawal,
W-pI..... 76.3:3 needle will ward **o.** disease and death.
WpI. rII.in.1:2 We will begin where our last review left **o.**
W-pI... 125.5:2 have wandered **o.** a little while from Him.
W-pI... 131.4:6 When he wanders **o.**, he is led back to his
W-pI... 137.1:3 from others, and a shutting **o.** of joining.
W-pI... 137.8:6 and minds that were walled **o.** within a
WpI. rIV.in3:3 else, and hold correction **o.** through self-
W-pI... 154.1:4 These are but attempts to hold decision **o.**
W-pI... 154.6:1 them **o.** from those the world appoints.
W-pI... 165.6:6 deprivation cannot cut him **o.** from God's
WpI.. rV.in3:4 *We wander* ***o.****, but You will not forget to call*
W-pI... 183.3:5 The sorrowful cast **o.** their mourning, and
W-pI... 184.1:5 set it **o.** from other things by emphasizing
W-pI... 184.2:1 This space you see as setting **o.** all things
W-pI... 186.9:5 apart to group again, and scamper **o.**. Or
W-pI.193.10:3 not try to hold it **o.** another day, another
W-pI... 195.1:2 is see themselves as better **o.** than others.
W-pI... 195.5:4 thus we split them **o.** from our awareness
W-pII.. 294.1:9 is but functionless, unneeded and cast **o.**.
W-pII.. 311.1:2 and sets it **o.** as if it were a thing apart.
W-pII.. 324.1:4 *I can but choose to wander* ***o.*** *a while, and*
Wfl ........in.2:3 In the dream of time it seems to be far **o.**.
M-1............2:9 but the end can be a long, long way **o.**. It
M-19..........4:2 you perceive as broken **o.** and separate.
M-27..........2:3 ready to break it **o.** without regret or care,

## off-balanced 1

T-4......... V.2:1 A major source of the ego's **o.** state is its

## offended 4

T-11. VIII.12:1 are **o.** by Christ and are deceived in Him.
T-11. VIII.12:2 Heal in Christ and be not **o.** by Him, for
T-11. VIII.12:3 **o.** in yourself and are condemning God's
T-16..... VII.3:3 everything you have done that has **o.** it,

## offending 1

W-pI..... 34.3:2 situations, "**o.**" personalities or events, or

## offends 2

T-11. VIII.12:3 Him. If what you perceive **o.** you, you are
W-pII...... 1.4:2 It **o.** no aspect of reality, nor seeks to twist

## offense 4

T-3..... VI.10:5 The **o.** is never to God, but only to those
T-11. VIII.12:1 If you perceive **o.** in a brother pluck the
T-11. VIII.12:1 in a brother pluck the **o.** from your mind,
T-11. VIII.12:2 offended by Him, for there is no **o.** in Him

## offenses 2

T-11. VIII.12:4 Let the Holy Spirit remove all **o.** of God's
W-pI.134.15:2 but realize that you are using his "**o.**" but

## offer 320

T-1........ III.1:2 you **o.** a miracle to any of my brothers,
T-1....... VII.3:9 If you **o.** miracles, you will be equally
T-2....... V.10:7 that whenever you **o.** a miracle to another
T-3......... II.6:6 **o.** them your acceptance of their truth so
T-4....... in.3:10 This is not the gospel I intended to **o.** you.
T-4........ III.3:3 The ego must **o.** you some sort of reward
T-4........ III.3:4 it can **o.** is a sense of temporary existence,
T-4........ III.5:1 the ego can **o.** that you will never want to
T-6...... V.A.4:9 no range in what you **o.** to your brother.
T-7........ IV.6:2 that it can **o.** you its own "will" as a gift.
T-7......... V.4:4 he believes he can **o.** as a gift to someone
T-7....... VII.2:3 You need the blessing you can **o.** him.
T-7..... VII.11:4 this. The gifts you **o.** to the ego are always
T-7..... VII.11:4 you **o.** to the Kingdom are gifts to you.
T-8..... IV.5:14 will. I can **o.** my strength to make yours
T-8........ IV.8:1 is the only gift you can **o.** to God's Sons,
T-8......... V.3:3 I **o.** you only the recognition of His power
T-8........ VI.1:5 of God for anything the world has to **o.**.
T-8..... VIII.2:7 you will continue to hope it can yet **o.** you
T-9........ VI.2:4 you **o.** to your brother you offer to Him,
T-9........ VI.2:4 you offer to your brother you **o.** to Him,
T-9........ VI.7:5 not want anything the world has to **o.**.
T-9....... VII.8:5 not **o.** to God as wholly fitting for Him.
T-9..... VIII.1:4 and attempts to **o.** gifts to induce you to
T-9..... VIII.3:5 If you accept its **o.** of grandiosity it will
T-10....... II.2:3 **O.** the Holy Spirit only your willingness
T-10...... III.8:2 **o.** them perfect freedom from all illusions
T-10....... V.9:4 And would He **o.** His Son anything that is
T-11....... in.4:3 our Father to **o.** you everything again. Do
T-11....... II.6:7 If you will merely **o.** Him a little place, He
T-12.........I.3:7 for. **O.** him anything else, and you are
T-12....... II.3:1 and **o.** your brother what he believes he
T-12....... II.3:1 what he believes he cannot **o.** himself.
T-12....... II.3:4 he really wants is to **o.** it unto yourself, for
T-12...... II.10:1 to **o.** to the Holy Spirit everything you do
T-12....... V.9:4 You need **o.** only undivided attention.
T-12... VIII.1:6 **O.** it and it will come to you, because it is
T-12... VIII.1:7 But **o.** attack and love will remain hidden,
T-12... VIII.6:3 could not **o.** His Son what has no value,
T-13...... III.6:6 the tricks and games you **o.** it can heal it,
T-13....... V.5:7 it, and all the love your brothers **o.** you,
T-13....... V.7:1 child, would you **o.** this to your Father?
T-13....... V.7:2 For if you **o.** it to yourself, you *are* offering
T-13..... V.7:11 and gladness is what we should **o.** Him.
T-13..... V.7:13 And it is God Whom you must **o.** them,
T-13.... VI.10:6 And this they **o.** you who gave them joy.
T-13..... VII.6:7 Christ will always **o.** you the Will of God,
T-13..... VII.9:6 are the welcome that you **o.** knowledge.
T-13... VIII.5:2 Every miracle you **o.** to the Son of God is
T-13... VIII.6:2 will **o.** them unto His Father as they were
T-13... VIII.7:2 lose. **O.** Christ's gift to everyone and
T-13...... IX.6:2 every condemnation that you **o.** the Son
T-13...... IX.6:3 His **o.** of Atonement for all your brothers.
T-13... X.11:11 *and* ***o.*** *thanks unto his Father that no guilt*
T-13..... X.13:3 and all my faith and my belief I **o.** unto it.
T-13..... X.13:6 many gifts that you will let me **o.** to the
T-14.........I.1:4 then, you **o.** blessing, it must have come
T-14.........I.1:6 miracles **o.** *you* the testimony that you are
T-14.........I.1:7 If what you **o.** is complete forgiveness you
T-14....... II.3:7 ***O.*** *your faith to Me, and I will place it gently*
T-14...... III.2:2 from what the other does not **o.** you. You
T-14...... III.5:4 Everyone you **o.** healing to returns it.
T-14...... III.5:7 is impossible to **o.** what you do not want
T-14...... III.8:7 the Holy Spirit would gladly **o.** him.
T-14.... III.11:3 which is all that you alone can **o.** yourself,
T-14.... III.11:3 you everything will simply **o.** it to you? He
T-14.... IV.4:11 instead **o.** to God and you His blameless
T-14.... VIII.2:5 Son. Can you **o.** guilt to God? You cannot,
T-14.... VIII.2:6 You cannot, then, **o.** it to His Son. For
T-14...... IX.8:4 who have learned to **o.** only healing,
T-14..... X.12:9 absent from any miracle you **o.** to His Son
T-14.... XI.6:11 instant you abandon it, and **o.** it to Him.
T-15.........I.6:4 still believe that it can **o.** them escape. But
T-15....... I.11:4 tiny instant to **o.** you the whole of Heaven
T-15....... I.12:4 Miracles are the instants of release you **o.**,
T-15....... I.12:5 **o.** time to the Holy Spirit for His use of it.
T-15....... I.13:8 guilt. You must be holy if you **o.** holiness.
T-15..... I.15:11 **O.** the miracle of the holy instant through
T-15........ II.1:7 quickly **o.** you the whole lesson of peace.
T-15...... III.1:4 You **o.** this in place of magnitude, and
T-15...... III.2:3 whatever you **o.** as a substitute is much
T-15...... III.6:1 gift the world of littleness would **o.** you.
T-15... III.10:7 will make no more gifts to **o.** to yourself,
T-15....... V.3:3 love, can **o.** you salvation is the belief that
T-15....... V.5:4 if you **o.** Him your willingness to have it
T-15..... V.10:7 have been told to **o.** miracles as I direct,
T-15...... VI.2:3 I **o.** you my perfect faith in you, in place of
T-15..... VII.5:4 at them, you will **o.** them gladly to Him.
T-15.... VIII.1:4 whatever you **o.** Him on behalf of this.
T-15...... IX.5:5 on them can **o.** you the gift of freedom.
T-15........X.2:3 What other gift can you **o.** me, when only
T-15........X.2:3 me, when only this I choose to **o.** you?
T-15........X.2:4 and **o.** everyone the gift you offer me. I
T-15........X.2:4 and offer everyone the gift you **o.** me. I
T-15........X.2:7 have limited acceptance of the gift I **o.** you
T-15........X.3:7 acceptance of it, you **o.** it to everyone.
T-15........X.8:7 an invader who but seems to **o.** kindness,
T-15..... XI.8:2 for so you **o.** me the love I offer you. What
T-15..... XI.8:2 for so you offer me the love I **o.** you. What
T-16.........I.5:1 is not what you would **o.** to a brother.
T-16.........I.5:8 anyone. **O.** your empathy to Him for it is
T-16.........I.5:9 And let Him **o.** you His strength and His
T-16...... III.5:8 they **o.** gladly to your teaching of yourself,
T-16...... IV.8:7 can **o.** you what God has given, and what
T-17.... III.1:12 **o.** you the "reasons" why you should
T-17...... III.8:5 all the truth the past could ever **o.** to the
T-17.... III.10:8 you peace, that you may **o.** peace to me.
T-17...... IV.7:2 is that they **o.** what they defend. What
T-17..... V.15:2 and **o.** it in gladness and thanksgiving to
T-18...... IV.5:6 but only to those who **o.** it nothing more
T-18....... V.2:5 part is only to **o.** Him a little willingness
T-18....... V.6:1 and **o.** the Holy Spirit your willingness, in
T-18....... V.7:6 *this instant as the one to* ***o.*** *to the Holy Spirit,*
T-19.........I.9:3 you **o.** the gift of freedom from the past,
T-19....... I.12:3 gift you **o.** to the Son of God through Him
T-19....... I.13:4 **o.** grace and blessing to your brother, for
T-19...... III.7:6 bow, and **o.** His creation to its conqueror.
T-19...... IV.2:4 Holy Spirit asks that you **o.** Him a resting
T19. IV.A.14:7 They **o.** you salvation. Theirs are the
T19. IV.A.17:5 Yet would I **o.** you my body, you whom I
T19... IV.D.9:7 will **o.** you the innocence you need, and
T19. IV.D.15:2 Would you not **o.** him forgiveness, when
T19. IV.D.15:2 forgiveness, when only he can **o.** it to you
T19. IV.D.15:5 that you cannot **o.** to your brother, and
T19. IV.D.15:6 it not, for by receiving it you **o.** it to him.
T19. IV.D.16:3 And **o.** thanks to God that he is holy, and
T19. IV.D.17:7 as you **o.** to the Holy Spirit this same gift.
T19. IV.D.18:4 **O.** your brother freedom and complete
T19. IV.D.19:6 the debt of gratitude you **o.** to the Son of
T-20.........I.2:5 **O.** your brother the gift of lilies, not the
T-20........ II.1:5 Learn you but **o.** him a crown of thorns,
T-20........ II.2:8 For bodies can neither **o.** nor accept; hold
T-20........ II.3:8 **O.** him thorns and *you* are crucified. Offer
T-20........ II.3:9 **O.** him lilies and it is yourself you free.
T-20........ II.4:2 I **o.** him forgiveness when he offers thorns
T-20........ II.4:5 see what you have laid upon it to **o.** me. If
T-20........ II.4:6 home and it is separation that you **o.** me.
T-20..... II.11:5 **o.** and receive the bright awareness that
T-20....... V.6:7 day **o.** to your brother already offered you
T-20....... V.7:9 brother will **o.** and receive it for you both.
T-20....... V.8:4 Creator of the universe should **o.** it to him
T-20...... VI.4:6 for all that it could **o.** is seen as valueless.
T-20.... VI.11:4 **o.** his devotion to death's idols and then
T-20..... VII.1:8 one that asks so little, or could **o.** more.
T-21........ II.1:2 the little gift you **o.** to the Holy Spirit for

| | |
|---|---|
| T-21 II.3:7 | is the little gift you **o.** to the Holy Spirit, |
| T-21 III.3:7 | **o.** holiness has been removed from sin. |
| T-22 IV.5:6 | received. God's **o.** still is open, yet it waits |
| T-22 IV.7:1 | easy is it to **o.** this miracle to everyone! |
| T-22 VI.9:5 | but **o.** Him the tiny gifts He can extend |
| T-22 VI.9:9 | you **o.** to your brother lights up the world |
| T-23 III.6:11 | the form that murder takes can **o.** safety? |
| T-23 IV.2:9 | And can it **o.** its creations all that it is and |
| T-23 IV.8:7 | can **o.** something you can win. Can it be |
| T-23 IV.9:3 | body; something it seems to **o.** or to own. |
| T-24 II.14:1 | whose holy hands would **o.** it to you when |
| T-24 V.6:9 | that each might **o.** you the Love of God. |
| T-24 V.8:1 | to you, to **o.** you your own completion. |
| T-24 VI.9:2 | any kind, is all the other choice can **o.** you |
| T-24 VII.10:8 | means to **o.** to the "father" what he wants |
| T-25 II.9:2 | What could He do but **o.** thanks to you |
| T-25 III.1:5 | from this, to hold it up and **o.** it support. |
| T-25 III.7:8 | This world has much to **o.** to your peace, |
| T-25 III.7:9 | descend on them, and **o.** them the light. |
| T-25 IV.4:9 | **o.** peace to everyone have found a home |
| T-25 V.5:5 | when he is free to **o.** you the gift of sight |
| T-25 VII.9:3 | sees within the world, **o.** him less and less |
| T-25 VIII.10:8 | from all unfairness you might seek to **o.**, |
| T-26 II.8:6 | that you should **o.** or receive less than He |
| T-27 I.3:4 | of yourself you **o.** him you show yourself, |
| T-27 II.5:7 | it **o.** him mute testimony of his innocence |
| T-27 II.6:1 | A miracle can **o.** nothing less to him than |
| T-27 IV.4:6 | Which ones establish peace and **o.** joy? |
| T-27 V.1:7 | thus **o.** the other what he has received. |
| T-28 I.12:2 | to **o.** all its treasures to the Son of God, |
| T-28 I.12:3 | How gladly does He **o.** them unto the one |
| T-28 II.8:6 | hate it for the vengeance it would **o.** them. |
| T-29 I.7:4 | go uncertainly, and **o.** no stability to you. |
| T-29 V.3:5 | And every thought of love you **o.** him but |
| T-29 VII.9:10 | thus appears to threaten life and **o.** death. |
| T-29 VIII.8:5 | **o.** him a gift reality does not contain. |
| T-30 I.16:7 | The day you want you **o.** to the world, for |
| T-30 IV.8:11 | They **o.** him no single thing that he could |
| T-30 VI.1:6 | asked to **o.** pardon where attack is due, |
| T-30 VII.4:5 | And so you **o.** it to all events, and let them |
| T-30 VII.4:5 | to all events, and let them **o.** you stability. |
| T-30 VIII.5:1 | and **o.** them to you to see in happy form, |
| T-31 IV.1:1 | to think the world can **o.** consolation and |
| T-31 IV.2:2 | But the world has none to **o.**. All its roads |
| T-31 IV.3:3 | can **o.** seem to be quite large in number, |
| T-31 IV.6:1 | that the world can **o.** but one choice, no |
| T-31 VII.3:4 | the sight your eyes alone can **o.** you to see |
| T-31 VII.5:6 | which you **o.** one whose need for it is just |
| T-31 VII.6:4 | that you may **o.** peace to have it yours. |
| T-31 VIII.10:4 | be. They will accept the gift I **o.** them, |
| W-pI 37.6:4 | you. **O.** him the blessing of your holiness |
| W-pI 71.3:4 | another situation will yet **o.** success. |
| W-pI 75.3:1 | in which we **o.** thanks for the passing of |
| W-pI 77.1:3 | will **o.** miracles because you are one with |
| W-pI 89.2:3 | *but* **o.** *you the miracle that belongs to you* |
| W-pI 92.9:1 | The strength in you will **o.** you the light, |
| W-pI 96.11:5 | you **o.** Him another treasure to be kept |
| W-pI 97.4:3 | will **o.** all His strength to every little effort |
| W-pI 97.8:1 | **O.** each practice period today gladly to |
| W-pI 97.8:6 | Receive His words, and **o.** them to Him. |
| W-pI 98.4:1 | the stand we take today will gladly **o.** us |
| W-pI 98.6:1 | **o.** guaranteeing you your full release from |
| W-pI 98.9:6 | you **o.** Him for timelessness and peace. |
| W-pI 99.4:2 | and **o.** means by which they are undone |
| W-pI 104.3:4 | conflicts of the world that **o.** other gifts |
| W-pI 105.7:2 | *My brother, peace and joy I* **o.** *you, That I* |
| W-pI 105.9:6 | *My brother, peace and joy I* **o.** *you, That I* |
| W-pI 106.2:3 | of life and **o.** it to you for your belief. |
| W-pI 106.5:4 | and **o.** Him your voice to speak to all the |
| W-pI 108.7:4 | we will attempt to **o.** peace to everyone, |
| W-pI 108.8:6 | *To everyone I* **o.** *quietness. To everyone I* |
| W-pI 108.8:7 | *To everyone I* **o.** *peace of mind. To everyone* |
| W-pI 108.8:8 | *peace of mind. To everyone I* **o.** *gentleness.* |
| W-pI 109.9:2 | comes to take his rest, and **o.** it to you. |
| WpI. rIII.in4:5 | your practicing can **o.** everything to you. |
| WpI. rIII.in7:2 | **O.** them to your mind in that same trust |
| W-pI 121.5:1 | which can **o.** anything but more despair. |
| W-pI 121.13:1 | let him **o.** you the light you see in him, |
| W-pI 123.6:3 | For He would **o.** you the thanks you give, |
| W-pI 123.7:1 | Receive His thanks and **o.** yours to Him |
| W-pI 123.7:2 | you will realize to Whom you **o.** thanks, |
| W-pI 124.9:4 | the mirror that this exercise will **o.** you. |
| W-pI 128.1:1 | see holds nothing that you need to **o.** you; |
| W-pI 128.4:4 | The worthless **o.** nothing. Certainty of |
| W-pI 129.1:4 | Think you this world can **o.** that to you? |
| W-pI 133.7:4 | deceived by the illusion loss can **o.** gain. |
| W-pI 133.7:5 | Yet loss must **o.** loss, and nothing more. |
| W-pI 134.6:1 | sane, a deep relief to those who **o.** it; a |
| W-pI 135.10:4 | You **o.** it protection of a kind from which |
| W-pI 135.18:2 | plan, for He would never **o.** pain to you. |
| W-pI 137.12:1 | Would you not **o.** shelter to God's Will? |
| W-pI 137.13:3 | little time a small expense to **o.** for the gift |
| W-pI 137.15:3 | and **o.** blessing where there was attack. |
| W-pI 138.5:5 | them, what they are, and what they **o.** you |
| W-pI 140.12:4 | our minds, nor **o.** proof to us that it is real |
| WpI. rIV.in4:4 | read, and see the meaning that they **o.** us. |
| WpI. rIV.in5:1 | day can **o.** you in freedom and in peace. |
| W-pI 151.3:2 | upon the witness that your senses **o.** you. |
| W-pI 153.11:5 | light, until you **o.** it to all your brothers. |
| W-pI 153.16:2 | the most that we can **o.** as the hour strikes |
| W-pI 154.9:3 | God has not failed to **o.** what you need, |
| W-pI 155.12:4 | or **o.** less and still content the holy Son of |
| W-pI 156.4:2 | and **o.** them in gratitude and gladness at |
| W-pI 157.6:3 | in our eyes which we can **o.** everyone, that |
| W-pI 158.10:5 | shine on you, and **o.** you the peace of God |
| W-pI 160.9:1 | Today we **o.** thanks that Christ has come |
| W-pI 161.1:1 | fears may disappear and **o.** room to love. |
| W-pI 164.7:6 | **o.** it the freedom given us through His |
| W-pI 164.8:2 | come, and **o.** you the treasure of salvation |
| W-pI 166.12:4 | What He has come to **o.** you, you now |
| W-pI 166.15:2 | of what Christ's touch can **o.** everyone. |
| W-pI 169.7:3 | you will **o.** was concealed from Him Who |
| WpI...rV.in3:6 | *the Word You* **o.** *us to unify our practicing,* |
| W-pI 183.9:3 | forgot, and **o.** it your own remembering. |
| W-pI 185.5:4 | would **o.** nothing more than all the others |
| W-pI 185.7:6 | which seem to change in what they **o.**, but |
| W-pI 186.4:2 | adequacy for the function He will **o.** us. |
| W-pI 187.9:1 | with the ones you **o.** him beside them. |
| W-pI 187.11:5 | sight is ours, we **o.** it to everything we see. |
| W-pI 188.4:4 | to the gifts you have to **o.** to the world. |
| W-pI 195.2:1 | is insane to **o.** thanks because of suffering. |
| W-pI 195.4:1 | not **o.** God your gratitude because your |
| W-pI 195.4:4 | We **o.** thanks to God our Father that in us |
| W-pI 195.6:3 | for otherwise we **o.** thanks for nothing, |
| W-pI 195.7:2 | We **o.** thanks for them. For if we can |
| W-pI 197.3:1 | when you **o.** it release from your illusions. |
| W-pI 197.9:8 | He has ever ceased to **o.** thanks to you. |
| WpI rVI.in.7:1 | To Him I **o.** this review for you. I place |
| WpI rVI.in.7:4 | us **o.** Him the whole review we now begin, |
| W-pI 212.1:3 | *function God has given me can* **o.** *freedom.* |
| W-pII in.4:4 | We will **o.** it, and it will be accepted. So |
| W-pII 236.2:2 | *I rule my mind, and* **o.** *it to You. Accept my* |
| W-pII 253.2:2 | *own, which can but* **o.** *glad assent to Yours,* |
| W-pII 258.1:2 | our pointless little goals which **o.** nothing |
| W-pII 270.2:3 | we **o.** healing to the world through Him, |
| W-pII 7.3:3 | if you **o.** them to Him, He will employ the |
| W-pII 283.2:2 | of us. And so we **o.** blessing to all things, |
| W-pII 291.2:1 | *is quiet, to receive the Thoughts You* **o.** *me.* |
| W-pII 295.1:2 | gift that He may **o.** peace of mind to me, |
| W-pII 304.2:3 | *my Father, given me to* **o.** *to Your holy Son,* |
| W-pII 306.1:1 | when it can **o.** me a day in which I see a |
| W-pII 312.1:3 | merely serve to **o.** us what we would have. |
| W-pII 315.2:3 | *Now may I* **o.** *them my thankfulness, that* |
| W-pII 318.2:1 | *take the role You* **o.** *me in Your request that I* |
| W-pII 325.1:6 | to **o.** him a kindly home where he can rest |
| W-pII 330.1:6 | things the dream of fear appears to **o.** us. |
| W-pII 332.2:5 | *For as we* **o.** *freedom, it is given us. And we* |
| W-pII 339.2:2 | *I do; requesting only what You* **o.** *me,* |
| W-pII 344.1:5 | *And what can an illusion* **o.** *me? Yet he* |
| W-pII 345.h | I **o.** only miracles today, For I would have |
| W-pII 345.2:2 | light has come to **o.** miracles to bless the |
| W-pII 345.2:3 | for we will **o.** what we have received. |
| W-pII 350.h | To **o.** them is to remember Him, And |
| W-pII 357.1:1 | *truth's reflection, tells me how to* **o.** *miracles* |
| W-pII 358.1:4 | *as well, and all I want is what You* **o.** *me,* |
| Wfl in.4:3 | forgive our brother, who can **o.** this to us? |
| M-5 III.2:11 | you Son of God, what life can **o.** you. |
| M-11 4:2 | Peace is inevitable to those who **o.** peace. |
| M-15 3:11 | and **o.** it to all the world to keep it safe. |
| M-21 5:6 | come to you, but **o.** them in confidence. |
| M-22 5:4 | can hardly **o.** it to his brother in Christ's |
| M-22 6:1 | The **o.** of Atonement is universal. It is |
| M-23 6:7 | can **o.** them is limited by what he learns |
| M-25 6:9 | and those who **o.** them to Him and Him |
| C-ep 5:5 | We who complete Him **o.** thanks to Him, |
| P-2 VI.7:5 | **o.** the mind of both a covenant in which |
| P-2 VII.7:1 | are not afraid to **o.** weakness to God's Son |
| P-3 I.1:5 | you know what to **o.** everyone who comes |
| P-3 II.6:7 | no therapist can **o.** more than he believes |
| P-3 III.3:5 | "bought" relationship cannot **o.** the only |
| S-1 I.5:3 | fully entitled to everything Love has to **o.**? |
| S-1 IV.2:8 | which they do not come to **o.** them to him |
| S-1 IV.3:6 | What prayer can **o.** now so far exceeds all |
| S-2 III.1:4 | does not **o.** gifts in treachery, nor promise |
| S-3 III.4:1 | one can use to **o.** help for someone else? |

## offered 88

| | |
|---|---|
| T-2 III.5:4 | is worthy of being **o.** at the altar of God, |
| T-2 VI.8:5 | situation for which the Atonement was **o.**. |
| T-5 in.2:6 | what part of the Sonship the healing is **o.**. |
| T-6 I.5:5 | I therefore **o.** a different interpretation of |
| T-6 V.A.4:7 | Only one equal gift can be **o.** to the equal |
| T-8 VI.1:3 | Every gain in our strength is **o.** for all, so |
| T-11 VI.6:3 | it can be **o.** you through the grace of God. |
| T-12 II.9:8 | **o.** it to Him and He cannot take it from |
| T-13 V.1:2 | being **o.** by the eternal to the eternal. In |
| T-13 V.7:5 | you what you have **o.** yourself is not true, |
| T-13 VI.7:3 | refusing to accept the light that is **o.** you. |
| T-13 VII.16:9 | for all the world has **o.** but to take away. |
| T-13 VIII.6:2 | unto His Father as they were **o.** unto Him. |
| T-13 VIII.7:2 | **o.** the Son of God through the Holy Spirit |
| T-13 VIII.8:4 | in every miracle you **o.** to your brothers, |
| T-14 IV.1:6 | Yet truth is **o.** first to be received, even as |
| T-14 V.6:4 | Each effort made on its behalf is **o.** for the |
| T-14 VIII.2:7 | apart, and gifts to One are **o.** to the Other. |
| T-14 X.6:2 | is wrong, but that a better way is **o.** you. |
| T-15 II.1:6 | An instant **o.** to the Holy Spirit is offered |
| T-15 II.1:6 | the Holy Spirit is **o.** to God on your behalf |
| T-15 V.6:1 | not been **o.** to the Holy Spirit for His use. |
| T-15 VI.6:6 | because He **o.** it to me and I accepted it. |
| T-15 X.3:6 | for the gift of freedom, **o.** to everyone. |
| T-16 II.4:4 | and have **o.** it to Him to use as He sees fit, |
| T-16 V.8:4 | which it **o.** him to interfere with Heaven. |
| T-16 VI.10:1 | the mockery of salvation the ego **o.** you, |
| T-16 VII.9:6 | for it is you who **o.** them illusions. In the |
| T-17 IV.8:2 | Its thought system is **o.** here, surrounded |
| T-17 IV.9:11 | picture, and realize that death is **o.** you. |
| T-17 IV.12:1 | Two gifts are **o.** you. Each is complete, |
| T-18 I.13:3 | This is **o.** you, in your holy relationship. |
| T-18 II.7:7 | you who **o.** your relationship to Him. If |
| T-18 III.4:5 | the gift of faith you **o.** to your brother. |
| T-18 III.6:4 | the darkness in them is **o.** to the light, and |
| T-19 I.2:2 | he is healed *because* you **o.** faith to him, |
| T-19 I.12:4 | to Him. And therefore **o.** you. Your holy |
| T-19 IV.2:7 | **o.** your relationship the gift of holiness, |
| T-19 IV.3:8 | and gratitude that you have **o.** Him, and |
| T19 IV.B.7:2 | the home you **o.** to my Father and to me. |
| T19 IV.B.7:5 | keep you not apart from what is **o.** you in |
| T19 IV.B.17:2 | is **o.** them but they have not accepted it, |
| T19 IV.B.17:2 | it, and what is **o.** must also be received, to |
| T19 IV.C.1:2 | For it was **o.** you, and you accepted. Yet |
| T19 IV.C.4:2 | **o.** to sin to feed upon and keep itself alive; |
| T19 IV.D.15:4 | it truly, for it will be both **o.** and received. |
| T-20 I.2:8 | gift of your forgiveness **o.** by you to me, |
| T-20 II.3:7 | that it is your savior to whom the gift is **o.** |
| T-20 III.7:3 | before the shining light the Holy Spirit **o.**, |
| T-20 IV.5:2 | power of the release from sin you **o.** him. |
| T-20 V.6:7 | day offer to your brother already **o.** you; |
| T-20 VI.3:4 | They do not understand what they are **o.**, |
| T-20 VI.11:8 | **o.** him to replace the unholy one he chose |
| T-23 I.4:3 | you not now accept the peace **o.** you here? |
| T-24 IV.3:14 | **O.** to them, no gifts can be returned. |
| T-24 VI.1:7 | **o.** you that all your doubts about yourself |

W-pI...102.2:3 all. It o. nothing, and does not exist. And
W-pI...102.2:4 you think it o. you is lacking in existence,
W-pI...121.2:1 of fear, and o. love no room to be itself;
W-pI......122.h Forgiveness o. everything I want.
W-pI...122.1:3 Forgiveness o. it. Do you want happiness,
W-pI...122.2:1 All this forgiveness o. you, and more. It
W-pI...122.2:4 it o. you another day of happiness and
W-pI...122.2:5 All this forgiveness o. you, and more.
W-pI...122.8:5 Yet your forgiveness o. it to you.
W-pI.122.11:2 given you to feel the peace forgiveness o.,
W-pI.122.13:1 Forgiveness o. everything you want.
W-pI.122.14:3 *Forgiveness o. everything I want. Today I*
W-pI...124.3:2 smiles on us and o. us the happiness we
W-pI...130.8:6 *the strength God o. me and see no value in*
W-pI...131.2:5 they achieve that o. any hope of being real
W-pI.131.15:6 *My single purpose o. it to me. No one can fail*
W-pI...133.3:2 all, for they can but replace what o. more.
W-pI...135.3:3 You think it o. safety. Yet it speaks of fear
W-pI...137.5:3 all, healing but o. restitution for imagined
WpIrIV.in10:1 God o. thanks to you who practice thus
W-pI...141.2:1 (122) Forgiveness o. everything I want.
W-pI.151.14:4 Thought that o. its perfection everywhere
W-pI...153.8:2 the endless joy our function o. us. We
W-pI.169.14:6 We welcome the release it o. everyone.
W-pI...186.1:3 It o. your acceptance of a part assigned to
W-pI...186.3:2 and o. you the perfect trust He holds in
W-pI...187.9:1 brother o. you are laid upon your altar,
W-pI.187.11:6 dwells in us and o. us His Holiness as ours
W-pI...189.2:3 o. you a warm and gentle home in which
W-pI...189.2:6 own. It o. you its flowers and its snow, in
W-pI...189.3:5 and peace o. its gentle light to everyone,
W-pI...194.8:5 world along with his, and o. peace to both
W-pI...195.2:2 to fail in gratitude to One Who o. you the
W-pI...199.8:5 and Heaven o. thanks for the increase of
W-pI...213.1:2 *A lesson is a miracle which God o. to me, in*
W-pII .222.1:3 directs my actions, o. me Its Thoughts,
W-pII .289.1:3 I then perceive the world forgiveness o.?
W-pII .....8.1:1 symbol, like the rest of what perception o.
W-pII .291.1:2 and o. this same vision to the world. And
W-pII .334.1:1 to find the treasures that my Father o. me
W-pII ...13.3:4 Each lily of forgiveness o. all the world the
M-11 .........2:4 them. God o. the world salvation; your
M-21 .........3:5 of his decision o. it to him as he requests.
M-24 .........1:9 misuse o. preoccupation and perhaps
M-29 .........8:3 *Teacher of God, His thanks He o. you, And*
C-6.............5:5 He o. thanks to you as well as him for you
P-1.............1:5 which He o. His greater gifts to both.
P-2......... V.5:2 He o. us salvation, for he comes to us as
P-2.......VII.1:7 therapist o. him a chance to heal himself.
S-1.........in.1:2 returns the thanks it o. Him unto the Son.
S-2.........in.1:1 Forgiveness o. wings to prayer, to make
S-2......... II.5:3 witness that it o. one who could be savior,
S-2......... II.7:5 goal of God, and find the peace He o. you.

## official 1

P-in............1:7 relationship with an "o." therapist. Either

## officially 1

P-3......... II.1:7 These are therefore "o." helpers. They are

## offset 4

T-14...... III.2:1 guiltlessness merely to o. the pain of guilt,
T-16......IV.1:3 hidden, is undertaken solely to o. the hate
T-16......IV.1:6 The special love relationship will not o. it,
T-25...... III.8:1 of gentleness has perfect power to o. the

## offspring 1

T-4......... II.4:1 Think of the love of animals for their o.,

## oft 1

T-24......IV.3:2 This has been o. repeated, but is difficult

## often 77

T-1 ......VII.5:1 already referred, and which is o. made. I
T-2 ........ V.7:2 This o. entails fear, because you are afraid
T-4 ........in.3:9 free to crucify yourself as o. as you choose
T-4 .......II.11:1 It cannot be emphasized too o. that
T-4 ....... VI.3:1 you turn more and more o. to me instead
T-6 ........I.14:2 The Apostles o. misunderstood it, and for
T-7 ........ V.9:9 I have spoken o. of the increase of the
T-9 ......VII.2:6 and so obvious that it is o. overlooked.
T-11 ........I.8:8 be too o. repeated that you do not know it
T-11 ..... III.3:7 Yet I can tell you, and remind you o., that
T-11 ..... IV.4:5 phases of this reversal are o. quite painful
T-13 .......II.7:4 You o. dismiss it more readily than you
T-16 ...... V.3:2 that center around it are o. quite overt.
T19....IV.C.7:1 how o. and how loudly they call to it, and
T-21 ..... III.1:4 of yourself, perhaps more o. of the other.
T-21 ..... IV.2:6 the ego claims it is; too loudly and too o..
T-21 .. VII.12:2 Could it be necessary they be asked so o.,
T-31 ...... V.3:2 And so this face is o. wet with tears at the
W-pI.....24.4:3 are on different levels and o. conflict.
W-pI.....27.4:1 question is, how o. will you remember?
W-pI.....30.3:1 as o. as possible throughout the day.
W-pI.....31.3:5 repeat today's idea to yourself as o. as you
W-pI.....31.4:1 for today as o. as possible during the day.
W-pI.....32.3:4 for today unhurriedly as o. as you wish, as
W-pI.....32.5:1 during the day, as o. as possible. The
W-pI.....33.1:3 be repeated as o. as you find comfortable,
W-pI.....35.9:1 As o. as possible during the day, pick up
W-pI.....37.6:1 of repeating the idea as o. as you can. It is
W-pI.....41.9:1 Throughout the day use today's idea o.,
W-pI.....42.8:1 more o. you repeat the idea during the
W-pI.....42.8:1 more o. you will be reminding yourself
W-pI.....43.6:3 exercises as o. as necessary to prevent this
W-pI...44.11:1 Throughout the day repeat the idea o.,
W-pI.....47.8:1 During the day, repeat the idea o.. Use it
W-pI.....48.2:2 Merely repeat the idea as o. as possible.
W-pI.....50.4:6 Tell yourself this o. today. It is a
WpI...rI.in.2:4 Do this as o. as possible during the day. If
W-pI.....61.4:1 about this idea as o. as possible today. It
W-pI.....62.5:1 As o. as you can, closing your eyes if
W-pI.....63.3:1 be happy to remember it very o. today.
W-pI.....63.3:3 the day we will repeat this as o. as we can:
W-pI.....64.7:3 function" quite o. to help you concentrate
W-pI.....67.5:1 the idea for the day as o. as you can. You
W-pI.....69.9:1 will want to do as o. as possible in view of
W-pI...71.10:1 yourself o. that God's plan for salvation,
W-pI.....74.6:4 again. Do this as o. as necessary. There is
W-pI...76.12:1 this dedication as o. as possible today; at
W-pI.....77.7:2 fact. Tell yourself o. today: *I am entitled to*
W-pI.....80.6:1 Assure yourself o. today that your
W-pI...92.11:3 repeat as o. as we can the idea for today,
W-pI.....95.5:3 o. fail to remember the short applications
W-pI.....97.1:4 Practice this truth today as o. as you can,
W-pI...98.10:3 Repeat it o., and do not forget each time
W-pI...101.5:5 practice with this thought as o. as we can
W-pI...101.7:5 today, and tell yourself as o. as you can:
W-pI...104.5:3 will we bring to mind as o. as we can: *I*
W-pI.106.10:2 given to yourself as o. as is possible today:
W-pI.110.11:5 Let us declare this truth as o. as we can.
W-pI.126.11:1 As o. as you can, remind yourself you
W-pI.131.15:1 Remember o. that today should be a time
W-pI...132.5:4 This central theme is o. stated in the text,
W-pI...135.7:2 This cannot be too o. emphasized. It will
W-pI.135.14:4 planning is not o. recognized as a defense
W-pI...151.4:2 o. been urged to refrain from judging, not
W-pI...152.3:6 can not be too o. said and thought about.
W-pI...154.1:7 believe to be our strength is o. arrogance.
W-pI...156.1:3 basic thought so o. mentioned in the text;
W-pI...161.6:2 of our text, where it is o. emphasized.
W-pI...163.1:1 takes on many forms, o. unrecognized. It
WpI rVI.in.1:1 day, and practice it as o. as is possible.
WpI rVI.in.1:2 day, use the idea as o. as you can between
M-29 .........4:1 is the paradox o. referred to in the course.
P-1.............3:2 are o. described as "self-destructive," and
P-1.............3:2 the patient o. regards them in that way
P-2........VI.7:3 statement cannot be too o. remembered
S-1..........II.1:4 asking form it need not, and o. does not,
S-2..........II.5:1 will o. hide behind a cloak like this. It

## oh 1

W-pI .... 68.2:3 O., yes! For he who holds grievances

## old 23

*See also* age-old

T-4 ........in.3:7 error of "clinging to the o. rugged cross."
T-13 .... VII.3:5 for it is o. and tired and ready to return to
T-17 .......II.5:1 by the complete forgiveness of the o., the
T-17 .......V.2:2 learned. It is the o., unholy relationship,
T-17 .......V.3:8 the pursuit of the o. goal re-established in
T-22 ........I.7:2 ancient than the o. illusion it has replaced
T-22 ........I.8:7 home, so seeming new and yet as o. as He
T-31 .......II.1:1 by the opposing of the new and o.. It is
T-31 .......II.8:3 o. will fall away before the new without
T-31 .....II.10:1 An instant spent without your o. ideas of
T-31 ..... III.4:7 And it grows o. and dies, because that
T-31 .. VII.13:3 open mind, unclouded by o. concepts,
T-31 .. VII.13:7 see beyond the veil of o. ideas and ancient
W-pI ...... 7.2:1 O. ideas about time are very difficult to
W-pI .... 75.2:6 The o. one has left no trace upon it in its
W-pI .... 75.3:1 of the o. and the beginning of the new.
W-pI .. 131.3:4 relinquished yet remembered, o. yet new;
W-pI 135.16:4 continuity of any o. ideas and sick beliefs.
WpI.rV.in10:1 you, yet one as o. as time and older still.
W-pII . 294.1:8 It is not sick nor o. nor hurt. It is but
M-1 ........... 4:5 It is o. and worn and without hope. There
M-9 ........... 1:9 Otherwise the o. thought system still has
P-2........ IV.6:4 into which the o. one cannot return. In a

## older 3

T-9 .........V.4:1 ego's plan are as unhelpful as the o. ones,
T-22 ......I.10:2 it through awareness o. than perception,
WpI.rV.in10:1 for you, yet one as old as time and o. still.

## Omega 1

T-3 ....... III.6:5 That is the real meaning of "Alpha and O.

## omit 2

W-pI ...... 7.5:1 but remember to o. nothing specifically.
W-pI .... 95.7:1 and urge you to o. as few as possible.

## omits 1

T-31 .......V.4:2 makes a picture of himself o. this face, for

## omitted 2

W-pI .... 35.8:3 occur should be o. from the exercises,
W-pI .. 152.1:5 wish, and nothing is o. that you choose.

## omitting 1

M-19 ......... 5:6 it, o. nothing and assessing nothing as

## omnipotence 3

T-22 .......V.4:5 its feeble squeaks that tell of its o., and
T-24 .......II.2:3 Who can detract from his o., yet share his
T-29 ...VIII.6:2 the strange idea there is a power past o., a

## omnipotent 1

T-18 ..... IX.1:5 it thinks it is the Son of God, whole and o.

## omniscient 2

P-2....... VII.5:5 Only from this o. point of view would
P-2....... VII.5:6 Yet no perception is o., nor is the tiny self

## on 1454

**once** 153

T-2......... II.3:6 it? O. you have learned to consider these
T-2........ III.4:7 to what it would o. have regarded as very
T-2......... V.5:3 O. you accept this, your mind can only
T-3......... V.6:4 O. forgiveness has been accepted, prayer
T-4........... I.5:5 to try to protect itself o. you have made it,
T-4........ I.10:1 because o. you have experienced it you
T-4........ I.13:5 o. been tempted to believe in them myself
T-4........ III.8:4 for this together, for o. He has come, you
T-4....... V.4:11 O. out of awareness the question can and
T-5......... V.2:2 o. what you have made is undone by the
T-6.........in.2:4 O. you have developed a thought system
T-6......... II.1:5 and that o. it occurs projection becomes
T-6........ III.3:2 O. it can accept this fully, it sees no need
T-6........ IV.7:6 but what was o. certain in your mind has
T-6......V.A.6:9 O. they have chosen what they cannot
T-6......V.C.9:7 O. your mind is healed it radiates health,
T-8........ III.6:5 because o. you have really looked at it you
T-8........ III.6:7 will understand why you o. believed that,
T-10.......... I.3:3 you do not remember yet that it o. was so.
T-10.......... I.3:6 Yet what has o. been is so now, if it is
T-10....... V.6:5 what you deny you must have o. known.
T-12.......... I.8:4 left with the fear, o. you had recognized it
T-12....... III.1:1 I o. asked you to sell all you have and give
T-12....... V.2:5 O. you realize this you will no longer see
T-14...... VI.7:5 You speak two languages at o., and this
T-14....... X.3:3 o. you conceive of them as possible at all.
T-15....... II.1:9 far beyond time that all of it happens at o.
T-15...... IV.5:3 you to make the holy instant yours at o.,
T-15....... V.9:4 O. this is gone, the Holy Spirit substitutes
T-15...... IX.1:5 permanent. O. you have accepted it as the
T-15....... X.4:2 It is possible to do this all at o. because
T-16...... VI.6:4 O. you have crossed the bridge, the value
T-17...... III.4:3 to fade and to be questioned almost at o..
T-17...... III.4:4 O. it is formed, doubt must enter in,
T-17....... V.3:2 At o. His goal replaces yours. This is
T-17....... V.3:9 o. the unholy relationship has accepted
T-17....... V.8:3 all the ways you o. sought for satisfaction
T-17..... VII.9:3 you will see the means you o. employed to
T-18.......... I.1:2 perceive at o. how much at variance this
T-18.......... I.4:3 impossible to perceive it o. was one, and
T-18... VIII.9:4 by love for them where o. a desert was.
T19... IV.A.8:1 is all that remains of what o. seemed to be
T19. IV.D.10:3 O. he has found his brother he *is* ready.
T-20...... III.1:5 this reduces it at o. to mere perception; a
T-20...... IV.8:4 work. O. you accept His plan as the one
T-20... VIII.8:5 O. you accept this simple fact and take
T-21...... III.7:1 as all the means that o. served sin are
T-21...... IV.5:2 with him and to be free again, as o. it was.
T-21....... V.8:5 For the perception would fall away at o.,
T-21....... V.9:2 accepted and accomplished, both at o..
T-21..... VII.4:5 so that it runs at o. to find another, and
T-21... VIII.3:2 you need ask for it but o. to have it always
T-22...... IV.4:6 eyes of those as weary now as o. you were.
T-23.......in.6:4 and everything you o. thought sinful now
T-24.......... I.4:3 specialness become a means and end at o.
T-25...... IV.1:8 And then the means are chosen o. again,
T-25....... V.6:5 Look o. again upon your brother, not
T-26....... II.6:5 Consider o. again your special function.
T-26....... II.7:5 What seemed o. to be a special problem,
T-26...... III.7:1 of purpose in what o. was specialness,
T-26...... IV.3:6 is set where o. sin was believed to be. And
T-26...... IV.5:1 sin o. was perceived will rise a world that
T-26... V.11:10 O. it is seen, this light can never be
T-26..... VII.1:4 For when it o. is possible it must occur.
T-27..... VII.7:3 O. you were unaware of what the cause of
T-27... VII.14:2 when o. the dreamer has been recognized
T-27... VIII.3:4 again, and still again, and yet o. more;
T-27... VIII.5:6 seen at o. that these ideas are one illusion,
T-27... VIII.8:2 But o. deluded into blaming them you
T-29...... VI.4:7 And where it o. held seeming sway is now
T-29...... IX.7:6 o. a dream of judgment now has changed
T-29...... IX.8:5 o. complete, brings timelessness so close
T-30.......... I.6:1 (3) Remember o. again the day you want,
T-30.......... I.7:5 when o. you have decided by yourself the
T-30...... I.13:5 consider o. again the very first of the
T-30....... II.3:1 Look o. again upon your enemy, the one
T-31.... IV.2:13 And on some the thorns are felt at o.. The
T-31...... VIII.h Choose O. Again
T-31... VIII.1:5 *Choose o. again if you would take your place*
T-31... VIII.3:1 that you failed to learn presented o. again
T-31... VIII.6:5 Choose o. again what you would have
T-31... VIII.9:1 gift can o. again be recognized as ours!
W-pI..... 10.1:5 what you o. believed were your thoughts
W-pI..... 11.3:5 repeat the idea o. more slowly to yourself.
W-pI..... 26.9:3 repeating today's idea to yourself o. more.
W-pI..... 27.4:6 If only o. during the day you feel that you
W-pI... 29.5:10 the idea for today at least o. an hour,
W-pI... 29.5:11 At least o. or twice, you should experience
W-pI..... 39.2:5 see at o. how direct and simple the text is,
W-pI... 39.10:4 the idea in its original form o. more, and
W-pI..... 40.1:3 O. every ten minutes would be highly
W-pI..... 42.5:5 open your eyes and repeat the thought o.
W-pI..... 42.5:5 close your eyes, repeat the idea o. more,
WpI... rI.in.2:2 each one should be practiced at least o..
WpI... rI.in.2:6 be sure to review all of them o. more.
W-pI..... 58.4:4 O. I have accepted my holiness, nothing
W-pI..... 64.6:5 At least o. devote ten or fifteen minutes
W-pI..... 65.5:2 eyes, repeat the idea to yourself o. again,
W-pI..... 65.7:1 Finally, repeat the idea for today o. more,
W-pI..... 65.7:1 by resolving your conflicts o. and for all,
W-pI..... 65.8:1 should be undertaken at least o. an hour,
W-pI..... 73.4:1 Today we will try o. more to reach the
W-pI..... 76.2:3 tells you o. again how simple is salvation.
W-pI... 98.11:1 the hour goes and He is there o. more to
W-pI... 98.11:2 Tell Him o. more that you accept the part
W-pI... 102.1:4 lacks the roots that o. secured it tightly to
W-pI... 129.2:1 to think o. more about the value of this
W-pI... 129.7:1 and at night, and o. more in between.
W-pI... 130.2:1 Yet who can really hate and love at o.?
W-pI... 132.9:1 A lesson earlier repeated o. must now be
W-pI... 134.5:5 and o. again by those who pardon them.
W-pI... 139.9:2 the madness that we o. believed in. Let us
W-pI... 152.7:2 see at o. these things are not of Him. And
W-pI... 158.4:5 back on it, imagining we make it o. again;
W-pI. 161.10:4 And o. you have succeeded, you will not
W-pI... 163.3:1 apt to fail the hopes they o. engendered,
W-pI... 163.7:2 God was o. alive and somehow perished;
WpI... rV.in8:1 Release me as you practice o. again the
WpI rV.in11:3 to waken o. again with these same words
W-pI... 181.9:1 The world which o. proclaimed our sins
W-pI... 183.6:5 when we say today's idea but o.. And then
W-pI... 187.7:5 idea so mad that sanity dismisses it at o..
W-pI... 195.7:4 clarity as we are willing o. again to hear.
W-pI... 196.8:3 For o. you understand it is impossible
W-pI. 196.10:2 When you realize, o. and for all, that it is
M-1 ........... 1:3 else's. O. he has done that, his road is
M-2 ........... 1:5 O. he has chosen to fulfill his role, they
M-3 ........... 5:1 in relationships which, o. they are formed
M-4 ......... I.2:1 this power has o. been experienced, it is
M-4 ....... II.1:2 O. that has been achieved, the others
M-5 ..... II.2:13 of sickness that would not be cured at o..
M-5 ...... III.3:1 Not o. do the advanced teachers of God
M-6 ........... 3:3 O. they have done that they have also
M-12 ......... 6:5 would put his faith in dreams o. they are
M-13 ......... 3:1 O. this confusion has occurred, it
M-17 ......... 8:7 O. this is even dimly grasped, the way is
M-20 ......... 4:1 is the peace of God retained, o. it is found
M-20 ......... 4:2 form, will drop the heavy curtain o. again,
M-20 ......... 4:4 must you o. again lay down your sword,
M-24 ......... 1:2 has no meaning either o. or many times.
C-in ........... 3:5 answer, o. a question has been raised.
C-4............. 5:7 o. all guilt is gone what more remains to
C-4........... 5:11 as its presence o. had been your certainty.
C-ep........... 1:1 not o. this journey is begun the end is
P-2........ IV.2:1 O. God's Son is seen as guilty, illness
P-2........ IV.3:1 o. the decision that guilt is real has been
P-2........ IV.3:4 could have faith in them o. this is realized
P-2....... VII.2:6 But o. Christ enters in, what choice is
P-2....... VII.3:5 again, o. its cause has been removed. This
P-3......... II.8:1 O. the professional therapist has realized
S-1........ IV.1:3 o. the need to hold the other as an enemy
S-1........ IV.4:2 to free yourself from all of them at o.? Do
S-3........ IV.6:1 Come unto Me, My children, o. again,

**One** 28

• God
*God and Christ*
*Christ*
*Holy Spirit*
*Unity*
*one*
*See also* One-mindedness; Appendix C

T-4........ III.7:2 that prevent the Holy O. from entering.
T-4........ III.8:3 your mind for the Holy O. to enter. We
T-4........ IV.9:3 let the Holy O. shine on you in peace,
T-4........ VI.6:4 The Holy O. shares my trust, and accepts
T-4........ VI.7:1 I will go with you to the Holy O., and
T-8........ IV.8:7 It cannot be with O. and not the Other. If
T-14...... IV.8:7 Would you know of O. Who gives forever,
T-15.... VIII.3:5 for He comes from O. Who cannot fail.
T-22......... II.5:6 and by O. to Whom nothing He wills can
T-23....... I.11:1 seek to overcome the O. Who dwells there
T-23....... I.11:3 temple of the Holy O. becomes a house of
T-23......... II.5:3 For O. must always be condemned, and
T-24...... III.5:3 the same, for neither O. wills specialness.
T-24...... III.6:7 Holy O. the specialness He could not give,
T-26.......... I.7:8 only one was given him by O. Who knows
W-pI..... 98.1:4 two, but take a firm position with the O..
W-pI. 153.12:2 designed by O. Who loves His children,
W-pI. 155.10:5 go. But O. Who knows goes with you. Let
W-pI... 168.5:3 all error is unknown is yet the O. Who
W-pI. 186.11:3 It comes from O. Who knows no error,
W-pI... 195.2:2 to fail in gratitude to O. Who offers you
W-pI... 195.6:2 the O. Who is Himself completion. We
W-pII . 228.1:4 and the O. Who knows the true condition
W-pII . 231.2:2 and with the O. as well Who is our Father.
W-pII . 322.1:4 Holy O. Who still abides in Him forever,
W-pII . 324.1:1 *O. Who gave the plan for my salvation to me.*
W-pII . 324.2:1 So let us follow O. Who knows the way.
M-27 ......... 4:6 There is either a god of fear or O. of Love.

**One** 2

• God and Christ
*God*
*Christ*
*Holy Spirit*
*Unity*
*one*

T-8........ IV.8:8 part of O. you must be part of the Other,
T-14.... VIII.2:7 and gifts to O. are offered to the Other.

**One** 6

• Christ
*God*
*God and Christ*
*Holy Spirit*
*Unity*
*one*

T-31...... II.11:7 you is O. Who holds the light before you,
W-pI... 158.9:3 Unseen by O. they merely disappear,
W-pI. 166.11:3 O. walks with you Who gently answers all
M-23 ......... 2:3 may recur to others, but never to this O..
P-3....... II.9:10 Yet at each meeting there is O. Who says,
S-2........ III.2:5 any form, He is the O. to answer for you.

**One** 42

• Holy Spirit
*God*
*God and Christ*
*Christ*
*Unity*
*one*

T-11.. VIII.14:9 their reality is from the O. Who knows it,
T-14.......... I.3:9 there is O. Who knows it leads to nothing,
T-14.... III.13:1 The O. Who knows the plan of God that
T-14..... IV.5:4 Leave all decisions to the O. Who speaks
T-16......... II.5:4 are natural to the O. Who speaks for God.
T-16......... II.6:4 The O. you called upon *is* with you. Bid
T-18...... IV.8:2 unwilling to give place to O. Who knows.
T-18...... IX.2:1 the O. Who does surround it has brought

T19....IV.B.8:4 not possible to keep away O. Who is there
T19..IV.C.11:6 the holy Presence of the O. given to you to
T-25.....VII.8:2 mad has God appointed O. as sane as He
T-25.....VII.8:3 To this O. is given the choice of form most
T-25.....VII.8:4 mad. This O. but points to an alternative,
T-25...VII.10:3 O. Who speaks for Him can show you this
T-27..... II.10:2 It belongs to O. Who knows of fairness,
T-27..... II.16:1 Correction must be left to O. Who knows
T-27....... V.4:5 the O. Who blesses you loves all the world
T-27....... V.8:9 Yet this can only be attained by O. Who
T-27....... V.9:6 but there is O. within you Who is right.
T-27..... V.10:1 to the O. Who really understands its laws,
T-27...... VI.5:6 The O. Who brings the miracle perceives
T-27...... VI.6:6 the O. Who sends forth miracles to bless
W-pI.....76.9:3 You will be listening to O. Who says there
W-pI.....99.6:4 with the O. to Whom the plan was given.
W-pI...106.6:3 will learn your function from the O. Who
W-pI...108.5:3 directed by the O. Who knows the truth.
WpI. rIII.in6:2 by the O. Who gave the thoughts to you.
W-pI.135.18:1 gently planned by O. Whose only purpose
W-pI...157.8:2 of. But the Holy O., the Giver of the happy
W-pI...186.2:7 assigned to us by O. Who knows us well.
W-pI...192.3:5 Yet God created O. Who has the power to
W-pI...193.2:3 he has a need for O. Who can correct his
W-pI...198.5:2 not more intelligent to thank the O. Who
W-pII .....3.4:2 by the O. Whom God appointed Savior to
W-pII .242.1:3 is O. Who knows all that is best for me.
W-pII .347.1:5 *to the O. You gave to me to judge for me. He*
W-pII .352.1:7 *memory of You, and O. Who leads me to it.*
M-7 ...........2:5 given the problem to O. Who cannot fail,
M-29 .........3:8 To return the function to the O. to Whom
P-2........ III.1:2 for O. should walk ahead of him to give
P-2........ III.1:3 Without this O., both will merely stumble
P-2........ III.1:4 that this O. be wholly absent if the goal is

**One** 72
• Unity
*God*
*God and Christ*
*Christ*
*Holy Spirit*
*one*

T-1......... V.2:4 in which the Son and the Father are O..
T-3......... II.4:6 Will of the Sonship and the Father are O.,
T-3......... II.5:4 Holy Trinity, but the Trinity Itself is O..
T-3....... V.10:9 Know yourself in the O. Light where the
T-5....... II.10:8 Spirit, or the Sonship cannot be as O..
T-5...... IV.2:13 you are part of God and the Sonship is O.,
T-6.........I.10:6 That is because the Holy Spirit is O., and
T-6....... II.13:2 The ego is legion, but the Holy Spirit is O.
T-7...... VI.13:7 and its creations, knowing They are O..
T-8........ III.3:1 Will of the Father and of the Son are O.,
T-8........ IV.8:8 be part of the Other, because They are O..
T-8........ IV.8:9 The Holy Trinity is holy *because* It is O.. If
T-8........ V.2:12 your awareness that the Will of God is O..
T-8.....VII.12:4 and gives it over entirely to the O. Light in
T-8........ IX.7:3 The Name of God's Son is O., and you are
T-9........ VI.3:5 has but one Son, knowing them all as O..
T-10...... IV.3:2 it at all. If the Sonship is O., it is One in all
T-10...... IV.3:2 the Sonship is One, it is O. in all respects.
T-11..........I.7:6 Your fatherhood and your Father are O..
T-11.......I.11:8 so. God's Will is that His Son be O., and
T-11....... V.5:4 His Will is O. *because* the extension of His
T-13....VIII.4:2 of Both, and knowing that Mind is O.. He
T-13..... X.14:1 make the Father O. with His Own Son.
T-14...... IV.1:7 God the Father, Who is both First and O..
T-15...... XI.2:7 by recognizing that His Host is O., and no
T-16....... II.4:3 of the Sonship as O. has been made.
T-17...... III.7:2 God's Son is O.. Whom God has joined as
T19... IV.A.3:5 God's Will is O., not many. It has no
T-23.......I.10:2 of You, Who dwell as O. and not apart.
T-23....... II.5:2 it appears that They can never be O. again
T-24....... V.9:4 doubts, if you agree that He is O. with you
T-24...... VI.2:3 and part of Him because His Will is O..
T-24...... VI.2:5 you that God is O. with him and you; that
T-25.........I.5:3 Father and Son and Holy Spirit are as O.,
T-25.........I.7:1 of a Oneness joined as O. is meaningless.
T-25....... II.6:2 O. with Him and with His masterpiece.
T-25 .....II.11:1 brother are the same, as God Himself is O.
T-26 ..... III.1:2 How could it be, when all He knows is O.?
T-26 ..VII.6:10 God's Will is O.. And any wish that seems
T-26 ..VII.15:7 What God calls O. will be forever One,
T-26 ..VII.15:7 What God calls One will be forever O.,
T-26 ..VII.20:5 freed to call upon the Name of God as O..
T-27 .....II.12:2 the Holy Spirit's Mind and yours are O..
T-28 ..... IV.7:1 and He is O. because there is no gap that
T-28 .... VII.1:5 of Either, Who have promised to be O..
T-28 .... VII.1:8 will can come between what must be O.,
T-29 ...VIII.9:1 God has not many Sons, but only O..
T-30 ..... III.6:9 It is forever O., eternally united and at
T-30 ...... V.7:8 then will come the knowledge They are O.
W-pI.....92.9:3 now to meet Itself again, and be as O..
W-pI...95.15:4 *am, and What He is, Who loves us both as O..*
W-pI.....99.4:1 Mind and Thought which are forever O.?
W-pI. 151.12:3 and your Creator, Who is O. with Him. So
W-pI... 167.1:7 because the Father and the Son are O..
W-pI... 169.4:1 and the Son as O. has been already set.
W-pI... 188.7:3 Where God the Father and the Son are O..
W-pI... 197.7:4 Father is secure, because Their Will is O..
W-pI... 198.3:7 and to his Father, knowing They are O..
W-pI...201.1:3 *the whole that is my Self, forever O. with me.*
W-pII .253.2:1 *Son, creating like Yourself and O. with You.*
W-pII .270.2:3 the holy Son whom God created O..
W-pII .283.2:1 Now are we O. in shared Identity, with
W-pII .286.2:3 and in our Self, Who still is O. with Him.
W-pII ... 11.2:4 God has willed to be forever O. will still
W-pII ... 11.2:4 One will still be O. when time is over; and
W-pII .329.1:4 *As You are O., so am I one with You. And this*
W-pII .331.2:1 shows us that God's Will is O., and that
M-20 ......... 6:9 The Will of God is O. and all there is. This
C-1 ............ 6:3 Christ Mind, Whose Will is O. with God's
C-5 ............ 3:1 forever like Himself and O. with Him–
C-6 ............ 4:2 your Self and your Creator, Who are O..
C-6 ............ 4:4 therefore it is He Who proves Them O..

**one** 5
• Jesus
*other*
*One*

T-1 ....... III.4:1 I am the only o. who can perform
T-5 ...........I.4:6 As a man and also o. of God's creations,
M-23 ......... 3:9 can o. who is one with God be unlike Him
M-23 ......... 6:8 Then turn to o. who laid all limits by, and
C-5 ............ 2:1 name of *Jesus* is the name of o. who was a

**one** 2216
• other
*Jesus*
*One*
*See also* one-dimensional

T-1 ...........I.1:2 in miracles. O. is not "harder" or "bigger"
T-1 .........I.12:3 O. makes the physical, and the other
T-1 .........I.19:1 Miracles make minds o. in God. They
T-1 .........II.3:2 implying that o. of a lesser order stands
T-1 .........II.3:5 Equals should not be in awe of o. another
T-1 .........II.4:5 as an elder brother to you on the o. hand,
T-1 .........II.4:7 the statement "I and my Father are o.,"
T-1 ....... III.6:6 neighbor are equal members of o. family,
T-1 ....... III.7:3 is because the Atonement itself is o.,
T-1 ........ V.6:4 o. of the distortions on which the reverse
T-1 ....... VI.1:5 somehow different from the o. you are in.
T-1 ....... VI.2:4 As you integrate you become o., and your
T-1 ....... VI.2:4 and your needs become o. accordingly.
T-1 ....... VI.3:1 error that o. can be separated from God,
T-1 ....... VI.4:5 why you can believe what no o. else thinks
T-1 ...... VII.2:3 be expressed through o. body to another,
T-2 ...........I.2:8 is freely given in o. continuous line, in
T-2 ...........I.5:3 distinguish between truth on the o. hand,
T-2 .........II.6:1 to proceed from o. degree to the next. You
T-2 .........II.7:2 Sons of God make in o. way or another. It
T-2 ....... III.2:4 you the o. effective defense against all
T-2 ....... IV.2:2 on o. level can adversely affect another.
T-2 ..... IV.3:13 If o. denies this unfortunate aspect of the
T-2 ..... IV.3:13 power, o. is also denying the power itself.
T-2 ...V.A.17:1 (7) The injunction "Be of o. mind" is the
T-2 ....... VI.9:3 no o. remains fully aware of it all the time.
T-2 ...... VII.3:2 If you are not free to choose o., you would
T-2 .... VII.3:15 conflict is therefore o. between love and
T-2 ...... VII.5:2 To believe in o. is to deny the other. Fear
T-2 .... VII.5:14 only o. slight correction to be meaningful
T-2 ...... VII.6:1 be noted that God has only *o.* Son. If all
T-2 ...... VII.6:2 every o. must be an integral part of the
T-2 ..... VIII.1:1 O. of the ways in which you can correct
T-2 ..... VIII.2:1 The Last Judgment is o. of the most
T-2 ..... VIII.2:4 became o. of the many learning devices to
T-2 ..... VIII.2:5 period, and perhaps an even longer o.. Its
T-2 ..... VIII.5:4 No o. who lives in fear is really alive. Your
T-3 ...........I.1:4 No o. who is free of the belief in scarcity
T-3 ...........I.1:5 even encouraged o. of His Sons to suffer
T-3 ...........I.3:1 o. assigns his own "evil" past to God. The
T-3 ...........I.6:4 or grace, is o. in which the meaning of the
T-3 .........I.7:10 you can accept this o. generalization now,
T-3 .........II.1:5 commitment to o. or the other is made. A
T-3 .........II.1:7 impossible. No o. has ever lived who has
T-3 .........II.1:8 No o., therefore, is able to deny truth
T-3 .........II.4:5 itself. To be o. is to be of one mind or will.
T-3 .........II.4:5 itself. To be one is to be of o. mind or will.
T-3 .........II.5:5 because They are of o. Mind and one Will
T-3 .........II.5:5 because They are of one Mind and o. Will
T-3 .........V.1:2 No o. has been sure of anything since. I
T-3 .........V.4:3 that the answer is not only o. you know,
T-3 .........V.4:3 but is also o. that is up to you to supply.
T-3 .........V.8:7 It is all o. and has no separate parts. You
T-3 .........V.8:8 really o. with it need but know yourself
T-3 .........V.9:5 power. The fact that each o. has this
T-3 ....... VI.2:7 O. of the illusions from which you suffer
T-3 ....... VI.7:2 only o. cause for all of them: the authority
T-3 ....... VI.7:5 accepts the o. inconceivable thought as its
T-3 ....... VI.8:3 then perceive the situation as o. in which
T-3 ..... VI.11:1 There is no o. who does not feel that he is
T-3 ..... VI.11:7 no o. in his right mind believes that what
T-3 ...... VII.1:5 for systems of belief by which o. lives. It is
T-3 ...... VII.3:4 fruit of only o. tree was "forbidden" in the
T-3 .... VII.4:11 the o. thing that is literally inconceivable.
T-4 ...........I.5:1 that they will o. day no longer need him.
T-4 ...........I.5:2 This is the o. true goal of the teacher. It is
T-4 .........II.3:3 apparent that o. need only recognize it to
T-4 .........II.4:3 No o. dismisses something he considers
T-4 .........II.4:6 you will o. day react to your real creations
T-4 .......II.8:11 do so, however, only under o. condition;
T-4 .......II.10:4 has only o. direction in which it can move
T-4 ....... III.3:7 No o. who has experienced the revelation
T-4 ....... III.7:4 No o. can see through a wall, but I can
T-4 ....... III.9:3 This o. fact means the ego does not exist,
T-4 ....... IV.2:7 Your mind is o. with God's. Denying this
T-4 ....... IV.7:2 The problem is not o. of concentration; it
T-4 ....... IV.7:2 of concentration; it is the belief that no o.,
T-4 ....... IV.8:6 for this is the o. right use of judgment.
T-4 .........V.3:3 In o. sense the ego's fear of God is at least
T-4 .........V.6:2 Eternalness is the o. function the ego has
T-4 .........V.6:7 o. question that is never asked by those
T-4 ....... VI.3:2 choice is the only sane o. you can make.
T-4 ....... VI.3:3 No o. who learns from experience that
T-4 ....... VI.3:3 who learns from experience that o. choice
T-4 ....... VI.7:5 and o. moment of real recognition makes
T-4 ....... VI.8:6 That is because the function of love is o..
T-5 ........ in.1:6 mind's natural impulse to respond as o..
T-5 ........ in.2:5 the same as to integrate and to make o..
T-5 ........I.1:13 the o. to whom you give it accepts it as his
T-5 ........I.1:14 the concept that the world is o. of ideas,
T-5 ...........I.5:3 for healing, for no o. was comfortless. The
T-5 ...........I.7:2 and no o. who attains it could believe for
T-5 ...........I.7:2 it could believe for o. instant that sharing
T-5 .........II.3:4 choose to hear o. of two voices within you
T-5 .........II.3:5 O. you made yourself, and that one is not
T-5 .........II.3:5 made yourself, and that o. is not of God.
T-5 .........II.5:2 way, o. to be chosen and the other to be
T-5 .........II.5:3 By choosing o. you give up the other. The
T-5 .........II.6:7 The Holy Spirit is o. way of choosing. God
T-5 .......II.7:10 No o. gains from strife. What profiteth it
T-5 .........II.9:5 the o. choice that resembles true creation.
T-5 .......II.10:2 only o. Voice and answers in only one way
T-5 .......II.10:2 only one Voice and answers in only o. way
T-5 .......II.10:7 joyous o. of waking it to the Call for God.

T-5 III.6:1 I have repeatedly emphasized that **o.** level
T-5 IV.1:11 who hear the Holy Spirit's Call to be as **o.**,
T-5 IV.2:12 even in this world to listen to **o.** Voice. If
T-5 IV.4:1 I heard **o.** Voice because I understood
T-5 IV.4:2 Listening to **o.** Voice implies the decision
T-5 V.6:9 to you. God created **o.**, and so you cannot
T-5 VI.3:6 unnecessary until the first **o.** was made.
T-5 VII.3:3 you are of **o.** mind and spirit with Him.
T-5 VII.5:1 with a lack of love to **o.** of God's creations.
T-6 in.2:3 no **o.** can organize his life without some
T-6 I.4:2 doubt that **o.** body can assault another,
T-6 I.5:5 and **o.** which I want to share with you. If
T-6 I.8:1 share my decision to hear only **o.** Voice,
T-6 I.10:4 hear only **o.** Voice you are never called on
T-6 I.11:5 My **o.** lesson, which I must teach as I
T-6 I.16:4 No **o.** is punished for sins, and the Sons of
T-6 I.18:3 Each **o.** must learn to teach that all forms
T-6 II.2:2 different from the **o.** on whom you project
T-6 II.5:5 the **o.** need in this world that is universal.
T-6 II.6:11 impossible to accept **o.** without the other.
T-6 II.11:5 into the **o.** line the Holy Spirit sees. This
T-6 II.12:3 every mind, and thus perceives them as **o.**
T-6 II.12:6 is the **o.** message God gave to Him and for
T-6 II.13:5 the Kingdom of God together and as **o.**.
T-6 III.2:1 That is why you must teach only **o.** lesson
T-6 III.2:5 is the **o.** lesson that is perfectly unified,
T-6 III.2:5 because it is the only lesson that is **o.**.
T-6 IV.2:6 was ever asked, but **o.** it can never answer.
T-6 IV.3:3 for help at **o.** time or another and in one
T-6 IV.3:3 time or another and in **o.** way or another,
T-6 IV.5:4 is. No **o.** in his right mind could possibly
T-6 IV.5:4 and no **o.** in his right mind does believe it.
T-6 IV.6:1 the **o.** answer of the Holy Spirit to all the
T-6 IV.10:1 because you think it is possible to be in **o.**.
T-6 V.1:7 does not communicate with Him as **o.**. So
T-6 V.A.3:4 To be of **o.** mind is meaningful, but to be
T-6 V.A.3:4 but to be **o.** body is meaningless. By the
T-6 V.A.4:7 Only **o.** equal gift can be offered to the
T-6 V.A.5:4 perception makes it a fearful **o.** indeed.
T-6 V.A.5:9 always for what each **o.** can get *separately.*
T-6 V.A.5:10 only what each **o.** can give to all. He never
T-6 V.A.6:1 and the only **o.** you must take for yourself.
T-6 V.B.2:3 It is also their last and final **o.**. Increasing
T-6 V.B.5:1 to choose **o.** and relinquish the other. If
T-6 V.B.6:2 Only **o.** is true, and therefore only one is
T-6 V.B.6:2 one is true, and therefore only **o.** is real.
T-6 V.B.8:4 and **o.** has been chosen as more desirable.
T-6 V.B.8:6 decision, it is clearly not the final **o.**. Lack
T-6 V.C.1:10 and so the **o.** mood He engenders is joy.
T-6 V.C.4:8 still believe that you can choose either **o.**.
T-6 V.C.7:1 step is thus **o.** of protection for your mind
T-6 V.C.8:1 wholeness, and have learned that it is **o.**.
T-7 II.4:6 mind cannot be faithful to **o.** meaning,
T-7 II.6:1 No **o.** questions the connection of
T-7 II.6:7 or relinquish **o.** to understand the other.
T-7 II.7:3 because there is only **o.** meaning. This
T-7 III.1:1 The Holy Spirit teaches **o.** lesson, and
T-7 IV.2:3 every part of creation is of **o.** order. This is
T-7 IV.3:6 are applied long enough to **o.** goal, the
T-7 IV.3:7 they are channelized in **o.** direction, or in
T-7 IV.3:7 channelized in one direction, or in **o.** way.
T-7 IV.3:8 then, they all contribute to **o.** result, and
T-7 IV.5:5 only way of perceiving the Sonship as **o.**.
T-7 V.3:1 Healing is the **o.** ability everyone can
T-7 V.3:2 in this world, and the only **o.** He accepts.
T-7 V.7:5 Son of God can recognize his power in **o.**
T-7 V.9:2 **O.** way shows you an image, or an idol
T-7 V.10:9 mind with you because we are of **o.** Mind,
T-7 V.11:7 You can appreciate the Sonship only as **o.**.
T-7 VI.1:1 you can love the Sonship only as **o.**, you
T-7 VI.3:5 The ego draws upon the **o.** source that is
T-7 VI.4:9 No **o.** who has everything wants the ego.
T-7 VII.3:8 Teach no **o.** that he is what you would not
T-7 VII.7:1 **O.** child of God is the only teacher
T-7 VII.7:2 **O.** Teacher is in all minds and He teaches
T-7 VII.10:9 is only **o.** way out of the world's thinking,
T-7 VII.10:9 just as there was only **o.** way into it.
T-7 VIII.1:2 and therefore **o.** that always operates. It is
T-7 VIII.6:2 and no **o.** can keep a belief he has judged
T-7 X.3:2 Surely no **o.** would object to this goal if he
T-7 X.4:5 and **o.** which is both fearful and desirable.
T-7 X.5:8 No **o.** gladly obeys a guide he does not
T-8 I.3:3 peace, and the only **o.** you need ever make
T-8 I.5:2 unhappy, and if you want a different **o.**, a
T-8 I.5:6 each **o.** merely interferes with the other.
T-8 I.5:9 choose **o.** because they cannot relinquish
T-8 II.1:2 Only **o.** Teacher knows what your reality
T-8 II.3:6 be out of accord because they are **o.**. This
T-8 II.6:1 only ***o.*** direction and has only *one* goal. His
T-8 II.6:1 only *one* direction and has only ***o.*** goal. His
T-8 III.7:5 God wills no **o.** suffer. He does not will
T-8 IV.6:7 the dominion of **o.** mind over another.
T-8 V.6:2 Holy Spirit has **o.** direction for all minds,
T-8 V.6:2 minds, and the **o.** He taught me is yours.
T-8 V.6:3 the **o.** for which God's Voice speaks in all
T-8 VI.2:3 Only **o.** is true. I am come to tell you that
T-8 VI.3:2 No **o.** created by God can find joy in
T-8 VI.6:7 No **o.** who does not accept his function
T-8 VI.6:7 and no **o.** can accept his function unless
T-8 VI.8:1 but **o.** you should ever ask of yourself;–
T-8 VII.7:2 the translation of **o.** order of reality into
T-8 VII.12:3 body can be unified only by **o.** purpose.
T-8 VII.13:5 whole because the mind's purpose is **o.**.
T-8 VII.14:6 and **o.** that is interfering with his ability
T-8 VIII.2:2 shifting its allegiance from **o.** to the other,
T-8 VIII.2:7 to shift ceaselessly from **o.** goal to another
T-8 VIII.4:7 and **o.** He is perfectly equipped to fulfill.
T-8 VIII.7:6 the **o.** thing about the ego that is wholly
T-8 VIII.8:4 No **o.** can doubt the ego's skill in building
T-8 VIII.9:10 of the **o.** Teacher Who knows what life is,
T-8 IX.5:3 for if He taught that **o.** form of sickness is
T-8 IX.5:3 be teaching that **o.** error can be more real
T-8 IX.7:4 Our minds are whole because they are **o.**.
T-8 IX.8:1 and **o.** that means exactly what it says. I
T-8 IX.8:5 you limit yourself we are not of **o.** mind,
T-9 I.1:1 Fear of the Will of God is **o.** of the
T-9 I.8:5 no **o.** really wants either abandonment or
T-9 I.9:2 recognition that his will and God's are **o.**.
T-9 II.3:3 will ever be **o.** that would increase fear. It
T-9 III.5:4 the **o.** way in which you handle all errors,
T-9 IV.4:1 forgiveness because you are asking for **o.**,
T-9 IV.11:6 fearful, but no **o.** calls them true. Children
T-9 V.3:3 plan for forgiveness in **o.** form or another.
T-9 V.4:2 In **o.** of the newer forms, for example, a
T-9 V.4:6 and **o.** which it usually notes even in its
T-9 V.5:2 for why no **o.** has really explained what
T-9 V.7:4 an example of **o.** whose direction has been
T-9 V.8:10 But remember also that the right **o.** will.
T-9 VI.3:5 God has but **o.** Son, knowing them all as
T-9 VI.4:4 Because the Sonship must create as **o.**,
T-9 VI.7:1 Eternity is **o.** time, its only dimension
T-9 VI.7:5 but accept **o.** of them you would not want
T-9 VIII.10:2 God. No **o.** else can fill your part in it, and
T-10 I.2:6 merely shifted from **o.** dream to another,
T-10 III.1:3 No **o.** can will to destroy himself. When
T-10 III.2:5 and God has only **o.** channel for healing
T-10 III.2:5 for healing because He has but **o.** Son.
T-10 III.2:7 it is the awareness that no **o.** is separate,
T-10 III.2:7 no one is separate, and so no **o.** is sick.
T-10 III.6:1 the calm knowledge that each **o.** is part of
T-10 III.6:5 you, because the value of God's Son is **o.**.
T-10 III.7:7 merely because I have only **o.** message,
T-10 III.10:1 If God has but **o.** Son, there is but one
T-10 III.10:1 God has but one Son, there is but **o.** God.
T-10 IV.6:2 of **o.** mind and that mind belongs to Him.
T-10 IV.7:5 power of **o.** mind can shine into another,
T-10 V.1:7 No **o.** can really do this, but that you can
T-10 V.3:8 be many different things he is but **o.** idea;
T-11 I.1:4 Not **o.** stone you place upon it but will be
T-11 I.2:2 end? No **o.** can be beyond the limitless,
T-11 I.2:5 I and my Father are **o.** with you, for you
T-11 I.7:2 heritage, because His **o.** gift is Himself.
T-11 II.1:5 of Him, you know there is but **o.** Will. Yet
T-11 IV.3:3 light He created is **o.** with Him. Would
T-11 V.1:1 No **o.** can escape from illusions unless he
T-11 V.2:2 how else can **o.** dispel illusions except by
T-11 V.8:3 Yet its **o.** claim to your allegiance is that it
T-11 V.10:8 And no **o.** wants to find what he believes
T-11 VIII.1:7 For as Heaven and earth become **o.**, even
T-11 VIII.3:2 Not **o.** thought you hold is wholly true.
T-11 VIII.4:1 No **o.** can withhold truth except from
T-11 VIII.4:5 yourself, therefore, but **o.** simple question
T-11 VIII.5:6 His answer is both many and **o.**, as long
T-11 VIII.5:6 as long as you believe that the **o.** is many.
T-11 VIII.8:7 Not **o.** of us but has the answer in him, to
T-11 VIII.10:2 and because no **o.** is without your help,
T-11 VIII.11:5 is **o.** with himself and one with his Father.
T-11 VIII.11:5 is one with himself and **o.** with his Father.
T-11 VIII.12:4 perceive no **o.** but through His guidance,
T-11 VIII.15:4 in place of the false **o.** you have made.
T-12 I.2:5 pitting **o.** level within it against another.
T-12 I.3:1 is but **o.** interpretation of motivation that
T-12 I.5:2 No **o.** with a personal investment is a
T-12 I.6:5 There is but **o.** response to reality, for
T-12 I.6:6 all. There is but **o.** Teacher of reality, Who
T-12 I.7:2 but **o.** need in yourself you will be healed.
T-12 I.9:6 **O.** is false, for it was made out of denial;
T-12 II.3:2 the sickness, there is but **o.** remedy. You
T-12 III.1:6 is but **o.** lack since there is but one need.
T-12 III.1:6 is but one lack since there is but **o.** need.
T-12 III.4:8 of **o.** who recognizes what is valuable and
T-12 III.8:4 for the **o.** you made out of your split mind
T-12 IV.1:3 for love very actively, makes **o.** proviso;
T-12 IV.1:5 is the **o.** promise the ego holds out to you,
T-12 IV.1:5 out to you, and the **o.** promise it will keep.
T-12 IV.3:1 is surely obvious that no **o.** wants to find
T-12 IV.4:4 promise, and **o.** that will lead to joy. For
T-12 IV.6:3 pay a price for death, and a very heavy **o.**.
T-12 VI.4:10 reality is **o.** with the Father and the Son,
T-12 VI.6:1 Every child of God is **o.** in Christ, for his
T-12 VI.6:4 any interference, for the two are **o.**. As
T-12 VI.7:1 is **o.** cannot be perceived as separate, and
T-12 VI.7:2 Mind of the Father and becomes **o.** with it
T-12 VII.6:8 it has **o.** goal by making it seem to be one.
T-12 VII.6:8 it has one goal by making it seem to be **o.**.
T-12 VII.7:1 up to you, but you must do **o.** or the other
T-12 VII.7:9 it to believe that it is pursuing **o.** goal. Yet
T-12 VII.7:11 For to be healed is to pursue **o.** goal,
T-12 VII.7:11 have accepted only **o.** and want but one.
T-12 VII.7:11 have accepted only one and want but **o.**.
T-12 VII.9:1 power of decision is your **o.** remaining
T-12 VII.13:6 is the **o.** end toward which it works, and
T-12 VIII.4:1 no **o.** can forget what God Himself placed
T-13 in.1:2 It is the judgment of **o.** mind by another
T-13 in.2:11 Not **o.** of them but has thought that God
T-13 in.3:6 it. Adam's "sin" could have touched no **o.**,
T-13 I.1:4 and to accept **o.** is to deny the other. Guilt
T-13 I.3:5 Time seems to go in **o.** direction, but
T-13 I.4:1 his Father sets him is **o.** of release and joy.
T-13 I.6:3 a belief in condemnation of **o.** by another,
T-13 I.8:4 No **o.** who believes this can understand
T-13 II.4:4 it guards this **o.** secret with its life, for its
T-13 III.1:3 is **o.** more obstacle you have interposed
T-13 III.1:4 said that no **o.** will countenance fear if he
T-13 III.9:2 But exempt no **o.** from your love, or you
T-13 III.9:4 where there is **o.** spot of fear to mar its
T-13 III.12:8 No **o.** who hears His answer but will give
T-13 IV.3:2 no **o.** would claim that it proves there *is* life
T-13 IV.6:4 And this decision is **o.** of future pain.
T-13 IV.6:8 For you would be meeting no **o.**, and the
T-13 IV.8:1 as **o.** of extending itself in place of eternity
T-13 IV.9:2 in the world of time as **o.** of healing, you
T-13 V.1:2 and fear. **O.** is changeless but continually
T-13 V.1:5 Yet they have **o.** thing in common; they
T-13 V.2:1 Each **o.** peoples his world with figures
T-13 V.2:4 being perceived in **o.** separate mind only.
T-13 V.3:4 And no **o.** hears their answer save him
T-13 V.6:4 You communicate with no **o.**, and you are
T-13 V.10:1 and **o.** you made and one was given you.
T-13 V.10:1 and one you made and **o.** was given you.
T-13 VI.6:6 all things that are eternal, and they are **o.**.
T-13 VI.7:5 In this **o.**, still dimension of time that
T-13 VI.10:3 Each **o.** you see in light brings your light
T-13 VII.2:3 The sight of **o.** is possible because you
T-13 VII.2:4 yet either **o.** will seem as real to you as the
T-13 VII.4:4 is willingness to learn the **o.** you made is
T-13 VII.6:1 No **o.** in this distracted world but has

T-13.....VII.7:7 recognizes that the world is **o.** with him.
T-13.....VII.8:4 you to remembrance of the **o.** thing that is
T-13.....VII.8:6 But this **o.** thing is always yours, being the
T-13.....VII.8:7 Your **o.** reality was given you, and by it
T-13.....VII.8:7 and by it God created you as **o.** with Him.
T-13....VIII.1:3 therefore no **o.** in the world can know. It
T-13....VIII.3:9 them as **o.** with the final gift of eternity.
T-13....VIII.5:1 the miracle of creation; *that it is **o.** forever.*
T-13....VIII.5:2 true perception of **o.** aspect of the whole.
T-13....VIII.5:3 in the same light and therefore **o.**.
T-13....VIII.5:6 into His quiet sight that makes them **o.**.
T-13....VIII.6:3 There is **o.** miracle, as there is one reality.
T-13....VIII.6:3 There is one miracle, as there is **o.** reality.
T-13....VIII.6:4 blends quietly into the **o.** reality of God.
T-13....VIII.6:5 created in the **o.** reality that is his Father.
T-13....VIII.8:2 will leave no **o.** untouched and no one left
T-13....VIII.8:2 no one untouched and no **o.** left alone.
T-13..VIII.10:3 unto Him, for reality is witnessed to as **o.**.
T-13......IX.2:2 *Make no **o.** fearful,* for his guilt is yours,
T-13......IX.4:2 you cannot value **o.** without the other,
T-13......IX.5:5 and the belief in **o.** is faith in the other,
T-13......IX.6:1 See no **o.**, then, as guilty, and you will
T-13......IX.7:1 while you see **o.** spot of guilt within you,
T-13.......X.2:2 or even hold **o.** spot of it to mar its purity.
T-13.......X.2:9 No **o.** who would unite in any way with
T-13.......X.5:2 but with each **o.** each day be born again.
T-13.....X.11:7 No **o.** who condemns a brother can see
T-13......XI.1:2 no **o.** sees himself in conflict and ravaged
T-13......XI.1:5 No **o.** finds himself ravaged and torn in
T-13......XI.2:8 past are gone as **o.** into the unreality from
T-13......XI.3:9 and bright, and calls forth **o.** response.
T-13......XI.7:1 Have faith in only this **o.** thing, and it will
T-13.....XI.11:3 and **o.** He will effect as surely as the ego
T-14.....II.1:10 of dust, a body or a war are **o.** to you. For
T-14.....II.1:11 For if you value **o.** thing made of nothing,
T-14.......II.2:2 will ever learn, and in the end the only **o.**.
T-14.......II.3:5 *Let Me make the **o.** distinction for you that*
T-14......III.7:6 No **o.** can hurt the Son of God. His guilt is
T-14......III.8:2 Teach no **o.** he has hurt you, for if you do,
T-14......III.8:5 Remember always that mind is **o.**, and
T-14......III.8:5 always that mind is one, and cause is **o.**.
T-14....III.15:2 which no **o.** in this world or Heaven could
T-14....III.17:2 He leaves you no **o.** outside you. And so
T-14......IV.2:5 but cannot know that you are **o.** with Him
T-14......IV.5:6 the truth in you, making you **o.** with Him.
T-14.....IV.10:1 incapable of understanding **o.** another.
T-14.......V.2:1 given to each **o.** is always the same; *God's*
T-14.......V.2:2 Each **o.** teaches the message differently,
T-14.......V.6:3 which has **o.** aim however it is taught.
T-14.......V.7:2 No **o.** can be untouched by teaching such
T-14.......V.8:2 purity, from which no **o.** is excluded.
T-14.......V.8:4 with no **o.** left outside to suffer guilt alone
T-14.....V.11:1 Each **o.** you see you place within the holy
T-14.....V.11:8 Cast no **o.** out, for here is what he seeks
T-14.....V.11:9 us, united as **o.** within the Cause of peace.
T-14......VI.4:2 the truth of **o.** must make the falsity of its
T-14......VI.4:5 do not realize that only **o.** means anything
T-14......VI.7:6 Yet if **o.** means nothing and the other
T-14......VI.7:6 only that **o.** is possible for purposes of
T-14......VI.8:8 No **o.** can fail to come where God has
T-14.....VII.4:5 But if **o.** is kept in darkness from the other
T-14.....VII.4:6 must be withdrawn from **o.** of them. You
T-14...VII.4:10 **O.** will go, because the other is seen in the
T-14.....VII.7:5 gentle fusing of everything into ***o.*** meaning
T-14.....VII.7:5 *one* meaning, ***o.*** emotion and *one* purpose.
T-14.....VII.7:5 *one* meaning, *one* emotion and ***o.*** purpose.
T-14.....VII.7:6 has **o.** purpose which He shares with you.
T-14....VIII.2:2 He will replace with the **o.** promise given
T-14..VIII.4:10 is **o.** link that joins Them all together,
T-14....VIII.5:2 all of creation, and with its **o.** Creator.
T-14......IX.2:6 are meaningless, for reality must be **o.**. It
T-14......IX.6:5 to see, no **o.** can fail to understand. It is
T-14......IX.8:3 Its **o.** response is healing, without regard
T-14.......X.2:6 brings the laws of another world to this **o.**
T-14.......X.2:7 is the **o.** thing you can do that transcends
T-14.......X.7:1 Spirit's **o.** division into two categories;
T-14.......X.7:1 one division into two categories; **o.** of love
T-14.......X.9:5 For no **o.** alone can judge the ego truly.
T-14......XI.4:8 will gladly exchange each **o.** for the bright
T-14 ..... XI.5:1 You have **o.** test, as sure as God, by which
T-14 ..... XI.5:4 of perfect peace means but **o.** thing: You
T-14 ..... XI.5:5 lesson teaches this, in **o.** form or another.
T-14 . XI.10:10 with every **o.** you let Him do through you.
T-14 ... XI.11:2 As we are held as **o.** in God, so do we
T-14 ... XI.11:2 as one in God, so do we learn as **o.** in Him
T-14 ... XI.12:6 so where **o.** is absent the other cannot be.
T-15 ........I.2:1 **O.** source of perceived discouragement
T-15 ........I.4:7 No **o.** who follows the ego's teaching is
T-15 ........I.6:7 no **o.** who considers himself as deserving
T-15 .....II.1:10 For as it was created **o.**, so its oneness
T-15 .....II.4:13 will doubt until you hear **o.** witness whom
T-15 .......II.6:7 you. Use it but for **o.** instant, and you will
T-15 ..... III.1:8 will always choose **o.** at the expense of the
T-15 ..... III.3:1 and **o.** you must learn to remember all the
T-15 ..... III.6:9 Touch no **o.**, then, with littleness in the
T-15 ... III.11:4 let no **o.** forget what you would remember
T-15 ..... IV.1:4 The **o.** you want it to be it is. The one you
T-15 ..... IV.1:5 **o.** you would not have it be is lost to you.
T-15 ..... IV.2:8 For peace is of God, and no **o.** beside Him
T-15 ... IV.9:10 God, and hostage to no **o.** and to nothing.
T-15 ...... V.5:1 The Holy Spirit knows no **o.** is special.
T-15 ...... V.6:3 to substitute **o.** aspect of love for another,
T-15 ...... V.6:3 less value on **o.** and more on the other.
T-15 ...... V.7:1 **o.** part of one aspect suits its purposes,
T-15 ...... V.7:1 one part of **o.** aspect suits its purposes,
T-15 ...... V.8:2 In the holy instant no **o.** is special, for
T-15 ...... V.8:2 personal needs intrude on no **o.** to make
T-15 .... V.10:2 In the holy instant the Sonship gains as **o.**
T-15 .... V.10:2 in your blessing it becomes **o.** to you. The
T-15 .... V.11:4 is no conflict of needs, for there is only **o.**.
T-15 ..... VI.1:1 is impossible to use **o.** relationship at the
T-15 ..... VI.1:3 do not conflict with **o.** another in any way
T-15 ..... VI.1:4 Perfect faith in each **o.**, for its ability to
T-15 ..... VI.5:2 no **o.** is aware that perfect love is in him.
T-15 ..... VI.6:5 No **o.** who has not yet experienced the
T-15 .... VII.2:6 This is its **o.** attraction; an attraction so
T-15 .... VII.2:6 hold at all, except that no **o.** recognizes it.
T-15 .... VII.3:3 go. No **o.** would choose to let go what he
T-15 .... VII.4:3 The ego wishes no **o.** well. Yet its survival
T-15 .... VII.4:6 and dedicated to but **o.** insane belief; that
T-15 .... VII.6:1 In **o.** way or another, every relationship
T-15 .... VII.6:4 no **o.** could interpret direct attack as love.
T-15 .... VII.7:2 For each **o.** thinks that he has sacrificed
T-15 ... VIII.4:7 His Father, Who is His **o.** relationship, in
T-15 ... VIII.6:2 of disagreement, to join them into **o.**. He
T-15 ...... IX.5:2 No **o.** can hear Him speak of this and long
T-15 .......X.3:1 We who are **o.** cannot give separately.
T-15 .......X.4:2 but **o.** shift in perception that is necessary
T-15 .......X.4:2 is necessary, for you made but **o.** mistake.
T-15 .......X.5:2 it *is* necessary to examine each **o.** as long
T-15 .......X.5:3 of the same idea, and **o.** you do not want,
T-15 .....X.5:10 If you would accept but this **o.** idea, your
T-15 .......X.6:7 for the **o.** idea that hides behind them all;
T-15 .......X.7:3 lesser of two evils, **o.** to be feared a little,
T-15 .......X.9:4 the **o.** decision you must make. And yet it
T-15 ..... XI.9:4 who receive the Father are **o.** with Him,
T-16 ........I.3:8 Keep but **o.** thought in mind and do not
T-16 ........I.6:5 for what would hurt **o.** will hurt the other.
T-16 ........I.7:2 needs of **o.** you do not jeopardize another,
T-16 .......II.1:7 itself? **O.** attribute is no more difficult to
T-16 .......II.4:3 join as **o.** and share one idea equally, the
T-16 .......II.4:3 join as one and share **o.** idea equally, the
T-16 ..... III.1:5 **o.** with nothing in common with yours.
T-16 ..... III.3:1 that you do not perceive the Sonship as **o.**
T-16 ..... III.3:2 you that you do not regard *yourself* as **o.**?
T-16 ..... III.5:5 keeping **o.** with you what you would
T-16 ..... III.8:3 Each **o.** builds this bridge, which carries
T-16 ..... III.8:5 so the **o.** who would cross over is literally
T-16 ..... IV.5:7 Seen in these terms, no **o.** would hesitate.
T-16 ..... IV.5:8 choice seems to be **o.** between illusions,
T-16 ..... IV.5:9 **o.** choice is as dangerous as the other, the
T-16 ..... IV.5:9 other, the decision must be **o.** of despair.
T-16 ..... IV.6:3 Every illusion is **o.** of fear, whatever form
T-16 ..... IV.6:4 to escape from **o.** illusion into another
T-16 ..... IV.7:3 violation of love's **o.** condition, the special
T-16 ...... V.3:1 and **o.** which has the most appeal to those
T-16 ...... V.3:4 No **o.** considers it bizarre to love and hate
T-16 ...... V.4:4 being the **o.** condition in which Heaven
T-16 .......V.7:5 not want for **o.** he thinks he would prefer.
T-16 .......V.7:7 he would give away to get a "better" **o.**?
T-16 .......V.8:1 "better" self the ego seeks is always **o.** that
T-16 .......V.8:4 neither **o.** will recognize that he has asked
T-16 .....V.17:1 ever confronted you, and also the only **o.**.
T-16 ..... VI.1:4 that are unlike this **o.** *must* be unnatural.
T-16 ..... VI.5:2 unions and to become **o.** by losing. When
T-16 ..... VI.5:3 When two individuals seek to become **o.**,
T-16 ..... VI.5:6 If **o.** such union were made in perfect faith
T-16 ..... VI.5:7 does not include even **o.** whole individual.
T-16 ... VI.10:2 Now no **o.** need suffer, for you have come
T-16 ... VI.11:3 will join with you and become **o.** with you
T-16 .... VII.5:3 the **o.** thing the ego never allows to reach
T-17 ........I.4:2 in reality by giving some of it to **o.** teacher
T-17 ........I.4:3 to deal with part of the truth in **o.** way,
T-17 ........I.5:6 Reserve not **o.** idea aside from truth, or
T-17 .......II.3:3 No **o.** but Him Who planned salvation
T-17 .......II.3:5 and no **o.** and nothing remain still bound
T-17 ... III.1:11 for the separation that no **o.** not obsessed
T-17 ..... III.3:5 **o.** in whom they seem to be decreases in
T-17 ..... III.4:5 thus becomes **o.** in which the reality of the
T-17 ..... III.4:7 the **o.** with whom the union was sought.
T-17 ..... III.7:3 One. Whom God has joined as **o.**, the ego
T-17 ..... III.7:5 For the Creator of the **o.** relationship has
T-17 ..... III.9:2 that to choose **o.** is to let the other go.
T-17 ..... III.9:3 Which **o.** you choose you will endow with
T-17 ..... IV.6:5 While this **o.** remains, you will not let the
T-17 ..... IV.6:6 For this **o.** is not different. Retain this one
T-17 ..... IV.6:7 Retain this **o.**, and you have retained the
T-17 . IV.12:10 **O.** is a tiny picture, hard to see at all
T-17 ... IV.13:2 **O.** is framed to be out of focus and not
T-17 ... IV.16:7 Him lies in our relationship to **o.** another.
T-17 ... IV.16:8 on all relationships, for in it they *are* **o.**.
T-17 ..... VI.6:7 No **o.** will fail in anything. This seems to
T-17 ... VIII.3:4 transforms all situations into **o.** sure and
T-17 ... VIII.6:2 had faith in it for no **o.** accepts what he
T-18 ........I.1:3 renouncing **o.** aspect of the Sonship in
T-18 ........I.1:4 **o.** is judged more valuable and the other
T-18 ........I.2:2 perceives **o.** person as a replacement for
T-18 ........I.2:3 judge between them, knowing they are **o.**.
T-18 ........I.2:4 they are **o.** because they are the same.
T-18 ........I.2:6 **O.** would unite; the other separate.
T-18 ........I.2:7 joined and what the Holy Spirit sees as **o.**.
T-18 ........I.3:1 The **o.** emotion in which substitution is
T-18 ........I.3:4 and each **o.** seems to require a different
T-18 ........I.3:6 stems. No **o.** is seen complete. The body is
T-18 ........I.4:1 that God is fear made but **o.** substitution.
T-18 ........I.4:3 impossible to perceive it once was **o.**, and
T-18 ........I.4:4 was. That **o.** error, which brought truth to
T-18 ........I.5:2 not realize the magnitude of that **o.** error.
T-18 ......I.10:5 He loves you both, equally and as **o.**. And
T-18 ......I.13:2 It is the only **o.** that has no limits, and
T-18 .......II.1:6 unless you saw yourself as **o.** with the ego,
T-18 .......II.7:2 **o.** which you will share with all who come
T-18 .....II.7:10 For we are joined as in **o.** purpose, being
T-18 .....II.7:10 one purpose, being of **o.** mind with Him.
T-18 .......II.8:4 **o.** in which the wish has been removed,
T-18 .......II.8:4 changed from **o.** of dreams to one of truth
T-18 .......II.8:4 changed from one of dreams to **o.** of truth
T-18 ...... III.8:1 Not **o.** light in Heaven but goes with you.
T-18 ...... III.8:2 Not **o.** Ray that shines forever in the Mind
T-18 ... IV.4:10 and then expect **o.** to be made *for* you?
T-18 .......V.3:7 You have accepted **o.**; the other will be
T-18 .......V.6:1 for the holy **o.** that you would rather have.
T-18 .......V.6:3 But forget not that your relationship is **o.**,
T-18 .......V.6:3 peace of **o.** is an equal threat to the other.
T-18 .......V.7:6 *so I choose this instant as the **o.** to offer to the*
T-18 . VI.11:11 yourself be **o.** with something beyond it,
T-18 .... VII.1:4 No **o.** accepts Atonement for himself who
T-18 .... VII.1:5 have thus not met your ***o.*** responsibility.
T-18 .... VII.2:1 is **o.** thing that you have never done; you
T-18 .... VII.5:3 time. **O.** instant spent together with your
T-18 .... VII.5:7 comes with just **o.** happy realization; "*I*
T-18 .... VII.6:1 everyone will **o.** day find in his own way,
T-18 .... VII.6:6 time for me by only this **o.** preparation,
T-18 .... VII.6:8 Believe it for just **o.** instant, and you will
T-18 ... VIII.5:3 dependent on its **o.** Creator for everything
T-18 ... VIII.6:5 being continuous with it and at **o.** with it.
T-18 ... VIII.9:6 They enter **o.** by one into this holy place,

T-18... VIII.9:6 They enter one by **o.** into this holy place,

T-18.... IX.10:5 further inward but the **o.** *you* cannot take,

T-18.... IX.12:6 the knowledge of love and its **o.** meaning.

T-19.........I.9:5 yourself and him, and seeing them as **o.**.

T-19.........I.9:6 that **o.** you see your faith is fully justified.

T-19...... I.10:4 you would keep no **o.** separate from yours

T-19...... I.10:5 Each **o.** appears just as he is perceived in

T-19...... III.5:9 which its Teacher, Who is **o.** with it,

T19. IV.A.4:10 nor apart from the **o.** you asked the Holy

T19. IV.A.17:8 No **o.** can die for anyone, and death does

T19..IV.B.12:2 for it is **o.** the ego sees as proof of sin. It is

T19..IV.B.16:4 Not **o.** but must believe that yielding to

T19..IV.B.16:5 **o.** but must regard the body as himself,

T19... IV.C.1:4 No **o.** can die unless he chooses death.

T19... IV.C.2:5 Touch any **o.** of them with the gentle

T19... IV.C.3:3 **O.** thing is sure; God, Who created

T19... IV.C.6:2 than by showing you the **o.** that seems to

T19. IV.C.11:1 over it, remember it is always for *o.* reason;

T19... IV.D.7:7 unseparated from it and completely **o.**.

T19... IV.D.9:1 No **o.** can look upon the fear of God

T19... IV.D.9:2 No **o.** can stand before this obstacle alone

T19... IV.D.9:3 no **o.** would dare to look on it without

T19. IV.D.11:7 no **o.** reaches love with fear beside him.

T19. IV.D.13:1 Beside you is **o.** who offers you the chalice

T19. IV.D.13:7 And yet your savior stands beside each **o.**.

T19. IV.D.17:5 in it, that we may rise as **o.** in resurrection

T19. IV.D.21:2 no **o.** undertakes to do what he believes is

T-20.........I.2:6 thorns in **o.** hand and lilies in the other,

T-20....... II.3:2 No **o.** but sees his chosen home as an altar

T-20....... II.3:3 himself. No **o.** but seeks to draw to it the

T-20..... II.8:12 live in gentleness and peace, as **o.** together

T-20...... III.6:2 The world the holy see is **o.** with them,

T-20...... III.7:8 adjust. This **o.** wild thought, fierce in its

T-20.... III.7:10 And of the **o.** blind thing in all the seeing

T-20..... III.8:1 **o.** ask judgment of what is totally bereft of

T-20.... III.8:10 **o.** thing that still would have it be unholy.

T-20.... III.10:1 each of you for **o.** another and for himself.

T-20.... III.10:4 it? Here are we **o.**, looking with perfect

T-20...... IV.5:6 And each **o.** finds his savior when he is

T-20...... IV.7:6 no more leave **o.** of them outside than I

T-20...... IV.8:4 as the **o.** function that you would fulfill,

T-20...... IV.8:7 Not **o.** seeming difficulty but will melt

T-20....... V.1:7 No **o.** who has a single purpose, unified

T-20....... V.1:8 No **o.** who shares his purpose with him

T-20....... V.1:8 purpose with him can *not* be **o.** with him.

T-20....... V.2:3 hearts of everyone, to let them beat as **o.**.

T-20....... V.5:6 this be accomplished, when **o.** would do?

T-20....... V.5:7 There *is* but **o.**. The little breath of eternity

T-20....... V.6:7 that you will **o.** day offer to your brother

T-20...... VI.1:5 His real relationship is **o.** of perfect union

T-20...... VI.1:6 The **o.** he made is partial, self-centered,

T-20...... VI.1:7 The **o.** created by his Father is wholly Self-

T-20...... VI.1:8 The **o.** he made is wholly self-destructive

T-20...... VI.3:7 for no **o.** else is welcome there. They smile

T-20...... VI.3:8 They smile on no **o.**, and those who smile

T-20.... VI.10:4 in gladness for the holy **o.** of safe return.

T-20.... VI.11:8 to replace the unholy **o.** he chose before.

T-20.... VI.12:2 you have learned you really want but **o.**.

T-20.... VI.12:9 given **o.** true relationship beyond the

T-20..... VII.1:8 impossible to imagine **o.** that asks so little

T-20..... VII.2:7 How can **o.** be sincere and say, "I want

T-20..... VII.7:3 each **o.** appropriate to the end for which it

T-20..... VII.7:4 the other, for each **o.** is a *choice* of purpose

T-20..... VII.9:7 No **o.** who loves can judge, and what he

T-20... VIII.3:2 and at **o.** with Him on what salvation is.

T-20... VIII.8:6 **O.** thing is sure; hallucinations serve a

T-20... VIII.9:2 And **o.** is sin, the other holiness. Nothing

T-21.......in.2:6 from this to recognize which **o.** you chose.

T-21...... I.10:6 The light in **o.** awakens it in all. And when

T-21....... II.4:6 you do not want brought to the **o.** you do.

T-21....... II.4:7 **o.** you do is given you because you want it

T-21..... II.13:1 Who created you together and as **o.**. See

T-21...... III.2:4 it. No **o.** allows a purpose to be replaced

T-21...... III.4:3 is His direction; the only **o.** He ever sees.

T-21...... III.4:4 wander, He reminds you there is but **o.**.

T-21...... III.9:9 it for you, without **o.** spot of sin upon it,

T-21.... III.11:5 that the moon and sun are **o.** because they

T-21.... III.11:6 Yet sight of **o.** is but the sign the other has

T-21.... III.11:7 it possible that what gives light be **o.** with

T-21...... IV.1:2 will correct, but this makes no **o.** fearful.

T-21...... IV.2:8 fear, and **o.** which makes the ego tremble.

T-21...... IV.3:2 "fearful" question is **o.** the ego never asks.

T-21...... IV.3:5 A holy relationship is **o.** in which you join

T-21....... V.3:5 to calls for help, the only **o.** it makes.

T-21...... VI.3:1 No **o.** can think but for himself, as God

T-21...... VI.3:3 **o.** mind think only for itself unless the

T-21...... VI.7:4 given you because he must be **o.** with you.

T-21...... VI.7:6 his whole mind, which is **o.** with you, in

T-21...... VI.9:6 And being **o.** with It, it must be given you

T-21.... VI.10:1 The Son of God is always blessed as **o.**.

T-21..... VII.1:3 the **o.** requirement that it demands to be

T-21..... VII.2:1 **o.** believes the Son of God is powerless.

T-21..... VII.2:6 spite on him, to make him **o.** with them.

T-21..... VII.2:7 they do not know that they *are* **o.** with him

T-21..... VII.2:8 each **o.** as likely to attack his brother or

T-21..... VII.5:4 he admit that no **o.** made him powerless?

T-21... VII.5:11 *a world I rule instead of o. that rules me? Do I*

T-21..... VII.6:2 For this **o.** still seems fearful, and unlike

T-21..... VII.7:4 healed must be the **o.** you chose to be

T-21..... VII.9:1 is your **o.** decision; this the condition for

T-21... VII.11:2 each **o.** asks if you are willing to exchange

T-21... VII.11:4 the desire becomes the only **o.** you have.

T-21... VII.12:5 No **o.** decides against his happiness, but

T-21... VIII.3:4 for it. For no **o.** fails to ask for his desire of

T-21... VIII.3:6 made by **o.** whom God Himself will never

T-21... VIII.4:3 final **o.** that really asks if you are willing to

T-22.......in.1:5 each **o.** seems to make a different error,

T-22.......in.1:5 error, and **o.** the other cannot understand

T-22.......in.2:5 each **o.** thinks the other has what he has

T-22.......in.3:2 Each **o.** has looked within and seen no

T-22.........I.1:2 God would heal and hate the **o.** He loves,

T-22.........I.4:7 Here is the **o.** emotion that you made,

T-22.........I.4:9 This is the **o.** emotion that opposes love,

T-22.......I.4:10 is the **o.** emotion that keeps you blind,

T-22.........I.7:6 Christ, Whose vision sees them **o.**.

T-22.........I.8:6 Where Christ has entered no **o.** is alone,

T-22.........I.9:7 or sound that drew them gently into **o.**.

T-22.......I.10:7 it is **o.** with you who joined to let it enter.

T-22....... II.1:4 though each **o.** seems to be the way to lose

T-22....... II.2:3 leave **o.** kind of misery and seek another is

T-22....... II.4:3 To believe that **o.** exception can exist is to

T-22....... II.4:4 is different. **O.** illusion cherished and

T-22....... II.4:7 excludes **o.** living thing and holds it out,

T-22....... II.6:4 and no **o.** undertakes to do what holds no

T-22....... II.6:7 Not both, but **o.**. There is no point in

T-22....... II.6:8 no point in trying to avoid this **o.** decision

T-22..... II.6:10 lies only on **o.** side and joy upon the other

T-22....... II.8:2 **o.** illusion you can enter Heaven with. A

T-22..... II.10:7 Is it not welcome news to hear not **o.** of

T-22..... II.11:8 you gave him for the **o.** he has in truth?

T-22..... II.13:3 no **o.** can remain beyond this willingness,

T-22...... III.3:3 No **o.** who looks on it without the help of

T-22...... III.8:8 the **o.** whose holiness is your salvation?

T-22...... III.9:3 each **o.** is valued because he seems to

T-22...... III.9:7 that both may happily be healed as **o.**.

T-22...... IV.1:2 You must go either **o.** way or the other.

T-22...... IV.1:7 No **o.** who reaches this far can make the

T-22...... IV.7:2 No **o.** who has received it for himself

T-22....... V.1:1 How does **o.** overcome illusions? Surely

T-22..... V.1:10 are the strong **o.** in this seeming conflict.

T-22....... V.3:5 whom He has joined as **o.** with Him? It is

T-22....... V.4:5 the universe forever sings as **o.**? Which is

T-22....... V.6:4 Not **o.** but rests on the belief that you are

T-22....... V.6:5 Not **o.** that does not seem to stand, heavy

T-22....... V.6:6 not **o.** that truth cannot pass over lightly,

T-22...... VI.1:5 For **o.** you see as means; the other, end.

T-22...... VI.1:6 And **o.** must serve the other and lead to

T-22...... VI.1:8 No **o.** but yearns for freedom and tries to

T-22...... VI.2:5 knows this mad decision was made by **o.**

T-22...... VI.8:1 each **o.** is released as he beholds his savior

T-22...... VI.8:6 goal. This **o.** was given you, and only this.

T-22...... VI.8:7 Accept this **o.** and serve it willingly, for

T-22...... VI.8:9 He will use every **o.** of them for peace. Nor

T-22.... VI.8:10 Nor will **o.** little smile or willingness to

T-22...... VI.9:6 will take each **o.** and make of it a potent

T-22.... VI.12:1 **o.** with God and recognized this oneness,

T-22.. VI.12:10 And this is so because the universe is **o.**.

T-22.... VI.14:2 what **o.** thinks, the other will experience

T-22.... VI.14:3 your mind and your brother's are **o.**?

T-22.... VI.14:7 And every thought in **o.** brings gladness

T-22.... VI.15:1 makes you and him **o.** with your Creator.

T-23.......in.1:5 No **o.** is strong who has an enemy, and no

T-23.......in.1:5 no **o.** can attack unless he thinks he has.

T-23.........I.3:8 are as meaningless as **o.** or as a thousand.

T-23.........I.6:1 the belief the **o.** that conquers will be true.

T-23.........I.7:8 **O.** illusion about yourself can battle with

T-23.........I.8:2 exist between **o.** power and nothingness.

T-23.........I.9:3 between illusions, **o.** to be crowned as real

T-23.......I.12:7 Where **o.** abides the other cannot be;

T-23........II.2:2 this **o.** maintains that each is separate and

T-23........II.2:4 Each **o.** establishes this for himself, and

T-23........II.4:1 worshipper of sin, is that each **o.** *must* sin,

T-23........II.4:3 destruction of the **o.** who makes the error

T-23........II.5:5 And Their relationship is **o.** of opposition,

T-23........II.5:6 **O.** becomes weak, the other strong by his

T-23........II.9:6 do not give willingly to **o.** another, nor

T-23......II.12:8 hatred for the **o.** to whom the gift belongs

T-23... II.12:11 It has no substitute, and there is only **o.**.

T-23......II.14:1 No **o.** wants madness, nor does anyone

T-23......II.16:6 No **o.** who thinks that one of these laws is

T-23......II.16:6 No one who thinks that **o.** of these laws is

T-23......II.20:3 Yet each **o.** rests as surely on the belief the

T-23......II.20:4 Each **o.** upholds these laws completely,

T-23......II.21:5 Think not **o.** step is smaller than another,

T-23......II.21:5 another, nor that return from **o.** is easier.

T-23......II.21:6 whole descent from Heaven lies in each **o.**

T-23......II.22:1 take not **o.** step in the descent to hell. For

T-23......II.22:2 to hell. For having taken **o.**, you will not

T-23...... III.1:8 For no **o.** thinks of murder and escapes

T-23...... III.3:8 and yet the same remain intact, as **o.**.

T-23...... III.5:5 No **o.** unites with enemies, nor is at one

T-23...... III.5:5 enemies, nor is at **o.** with them in purpose

T-23...... III.5:6 And no **o.** compromises with an enemy

T-23...... III.6:8 Not **o.** tree left still standing will shelter

T-23...... III.6:9 **o.** illusion of protection stands against the

T-23.... IV.1:12 and every **o.** does violence to the idea of

T-23...... IV.2:3 and indistinguishable from **o.** another. So

T-23...... IV.7:1 See no **o.** from the battleground, for there

T-23...... IV.7:3 purpose, then you must be **o.** with them.

T-23...... IV.7:4 who share a purpose have a mind as **o.**.

T-23...... IV.9:4 No **o.** who knows that he has everything

T-24.......in.2:2 **o.** can be kept hidden and obscure but it

T-24.......in.2:4 Every **o.** has the power to dictate each

T-24.........I.1:4 Hold back but **o.** belief, one offering, and

T-24.........I.1:4 Hold back but one belief, **o.** offering, and

T-24.........I.1:5 the **o.** alternative that you can choose for

T-24.........I.4:4 the special **o.** is "natural" and "just." The

T-24.........I.7:6 And so it is the only **o.** you have. Could

T-24........II.3:5 His "special" sons are many, never **o.**,

T-24........II.3:5 never one, each **o.** in exile from himself,

T-24........II.3:6 which created them as **o.** with Him. They

T-24........II.5:3 To every special **o.** a different message,

T-24........II.5:3 message, and **o.** with different meaning, is

T-24........II.5:4 Yet how can truth be different to each **o.**?

T-24........II.7:4 different messages, and has **o.** meaning.

T-24........II.7:5 And it is **o.** you and your brother both can

T-24........II.7:5 and **o.** that brings release to both of you.

T-24........II.7:8 between you. What is **o.** is joined in truth.

T-24........II.8:3 Not **o.** attack you thought you made on

T-24........II.8:5 make you whole in mind and **o.** with him.

T-24........II.9:2 Just **o.** step more, and every vestige of the

T-24......II.10:4 keep **o.** part of what He is unto Himself,

T-24......II.11:5 What is the same as God is **o.** with Him.

T-24......II.11:6 and you as **o.** seem anything but Heaven,

T-24......II.12:4 Not **o.** glance from eyes it veils but looks

T-24......II.12:5 Not **o.** believer in its potency but seeks for

T-24...... III.1:4 No **o.** who clings to one illusion can see

T-24...... III.1:4 to **o.** illusion can see himself as sinless, for

T-24...... III.1:4 he holds **o.** error to himself as lovely still.

T-24...... III.5:6 as **o.** Mind They wait for all illusions to be

T-24...... III.6:6 without the heat and malice of **o.** thought

T-24...... IV.3:6 that harmful purpose hurts the mind as **o.**

T-24...... IV.5:4 the **o.** whom God has given you instead.

T-24...... IV.5:5 So are you bound with him, for you are **o.**.

T-24....... V.1:3 that it is **o.** with Him and with His Father.

T-24..... V.1:10 Except that **o.** deludes; the other heals.

T-24....... V.7:6 receiving from each **o.** the gift of life that

T-24......VI.1:1 that not **o.** trace of conflict still remains to
T-24......VI.4:2 Spirit sees in it, and thus the only **o.** it has
T-24......VI.5:3 for not **o.** law of death you bind him to
T-24......VI.5:4 And not **o.** sin you see in him but keeps
T-24......VI.5:5 **o.** judgment made for all it looks upon.
T-24......VI.7:3 by still **o.** more denial of Christ in him.
T-24....VI.12:2 the two, it is this **o.** you find more difficult
T-24.....VII.6:6 In Heaven, means and end are **o.**, and one
T-24.....VII.6:6 means and end are one, and **o.** with Him.
T-24.....VII.6:8 To no **o.** here is this describable. Nor is
T-24.....VII.7:4 Here do the means and end unite as **o.**,
T-24.....VII.7:4 as one, nor does this **o.** have any end at all
T-24.....VII.7:5 retains **o.** unlearned lesson in his memory
T-24.....VII.7:5 **o.** thought with purpose still uncertain, or
T-24.....VII.7:5 uncertain, or **o.** wish with a divided aim.
T-24...VII.11:2 **O.** do you perceive outside yourself, your
T-25.......in.2:1 No **o.** who carries Christ in him can fail to
T-25.........I.1:5 the body through the mind at **o.** with Him
T-25.........I.2:5 you not despise the **o.** who tells you this,
T-25.........I.2:6 The message and the messenger are **o.**.
T-25.........I.5:3 as all your brothers join as **o.** in truth.
T-25.........I.5:5 make the oneness clear to what is really **o.**
T-25.........I.6:2 still is **o.** with Both the Father and the Son
T-25.........I.6:3 this is understood by mind perceived as **o.**
T-25.........I.6:3 mind perceived as one, aware that it is **o.**,
T-25.........I.7:7 *and what is **o.** can not have separate parts.*
T-25....... II.2:4 For **o.** thing is sure; the way you see, and
T-25..... II.9:10 **o.** ray of darkness can be seen by those
T-25..... II.10:3 given you, that you may see His Son as **o.**,
T-25..... II.10:8 your brother with you and at **o.** with you.
T-25..... II.11:2 And you must have **o.** purpose, since He
T-25..... II.11:5 see as **o.** what never has been separate,
T-25...... III.3:2 but **o.** law because it has but one Creator.
T-25...... III.3:2 but one law because it has but **o.** Creator.
T-25...... III.3:6 Not **o.** but it upholds in its perception;
T-25...... III.3:6 not **o.** but can be fully justified.
T-25...... III.6:1 darkness, yet no **o.** has entered it alone.
T-25...... III.7:7 seeing them as **o.** that brings release from
T-25....... V.1:3 Attack and sin are bound as **o.** illusion,
T-25....... V.1:6 And no **o.** could believe in one unless the
T-25....... V.1:6 no one could believe in **o.** unless the other
T-25....... V.4:8 function, the only **o.** he has in truth, you
T-25...... VI.1:2 and no **o.** who is different from himself.
T-25...... VI.5:1 can he yet do ***o.*** perfect thing and make *one*
T-25...... VI.5:1 perfect thing and make ***o.*** perfect choice
T-25...... VI.5:2 act of special faithfulness to **o.** perceived
T-25...... VI.5:2 given to himself, and so they must be **o.**.
T-25...... VI.6:4 as each **o.** takes his part in its undoing, as
T-25.... VI.7:10 Do this ***o.*** thing, that everything be given
T-25..... VII.1:6 Yet each **o.** knows the cost of sin is death.
T-25..... VII.3:3 Not **o.** Thought of His makes any sense at
T-25..... VII.3:7 If **o.** belief so deeply valued here were true
T-25..... VII.3:8 And if but **o.** Thought of His is true, then
T-25..... VII.4:1 To justify **o.** value that the world upholds
T-25..... VII.4:4 to believe **o.** thought opposed to truth, he
T-25..... VII.5:2 And **o.** in which nothing is contradicted
T-25..... VII.5:4 For here is everything perceived as **o.**, and
T-25..... VII.5:4 and no **o.** loses that each one may gain.
T-25..... VII.5:4 and no one loses that each **o.** may gain.
T-25..... VII.6:1 you believe against this **o.** requirement,
T-25..... VII.6:1 this **o.** demand is worthy of your faith.
T-25..... VII.6:3 and either **o.** perceives the other as insane
T-25..... VII.8:3 **o.** which will not attack the world he sees,
T-25..... VII.9:1 the alternative is **o.** which he cannot deny,
T-25...VII.11:2 that **o.** must gain *because* another lost. If
T-25...VII.12:1 the idea no **o.** can lose for anyone to gain.
T-25...VII.13:3 No **o.** can suffer for the Will of God to be
T-25....VIII.1:6 brings loss to no **o.** you would not know.
T-25....VIII.1:7 to the idea no **o.** can lose for you to gain.
T-25....VIII.2:5 not called upon to do what **o.** divided still
T-25....VIII.4:3 that **o.** should lack for what another has.
T-25....VIII.5:7 each **o.** contradicts the other and denies
T-25....VIII.9:7 And every **o.** that you accept brings joy to
T-25....VIII.9:8 is richer made by each **o.** you accept. And
T-25..VIII.11:2 For just ***o.*** witness is enough, if he sees
T-25..VIII.11:4 Of each **o.** does the Holy Spirit ask if he
T-25..VIII.11:4 the Holy Spirit ask if he will be that **o.**, so
T-25..VIII.11:5 that each **o.** learn that love and justice are
T-25..VIII.13:5 To take from **o.** to give another must be

T-25 ..... IX.1:6 Not **o.** sin would you retain. And not one
T-25 ..... IX.1:7 And not **o.** doubt that this is possible will
T-25 ..... IX.3:1 will always be **o.** in which no one loses.
T-25 ..... IX.3:1 will always be one in which no **o.** loses.
T-25 ..... IX.3:6 every error is a perception in which **o.**, at
T-25 ..... IX.4:5 who shall lose; how much the **o.** shall take
T-25 ..... IX.4:6 no **o.** left unfairly treated and deprived,
T-25 ..... IX.5:4 that justice means no **o.** can lose is crucial
T-25 ..... IX.6:1 No **o.** deserves to lose. And what would
T-25 ..... IX.7:7 No **o.** can be unjust to you, unless you
T-25 ..... IX.8:1 you were unjust to **o.** with equal rights.
T-25 ..... IX.9:2 you perceive and leave you fair to no **o.**.
T-25 ..... IX.9:3 Not **o.** right do you believe you have. And
T-25 ... IX.10:2 Each **o.** becomes an illustration of the law
T-25 ... IX.10:3 No **o.** can lose, and everyone must benefit
T-25 ... IX.10:9 is universal, and it teaches but **o.** message:
T-26 ........I.2:5 joined each **o.** would lose its own identity,
T-26 ........I.7:8 only **o.** was given him by One Who knows
T-26 ......... II.h Many Forms; **O.** Correction
T-26 .......II.1:3 because each **o.** is solved in just the same
T-26 .......II.2:2 They are the same to Him because each **o.**
T-26 .......II.2:3 out so no **o.** loses is the problem gone,
T-26 .......II.2:4 **O.** mistake is not more difficult for Him to
T-26 .......II.2:5 For there *is* but **o.** mistake; the whole idea
T-26 .......II.3:1 This **o.** mistake, in any form, has one
T-26 .......II.3:1 mistake, in any form, has **o.** correction.
T-26 .......II.3:4 think so if you saw them vanish **o.** by one,
T-26 .......II.3:4 think so if you saw them vanish one by **o.**,
T-26 .......II.3:4 each **o.** seem different from the rest.
T-26 .......II.4:9 He makes but **o.** judgment; that to hurt
T-26 .......II.5:7 or judge that it is **o.** that has no resolution
T-26 .......II.6:4 and no **o.** whom you wish to be preserved
T-26 .......II.6:6 **O.** is given you to see in him his perfect
T-26 .......II.7:2 You will not keep **o.**, for pain in any form
T-26 ..... III.1:3 He knows of **o.** creation, one reality, one
T-26 ..... III.1:3 He knows of one creation, **o.** reality, one
T-26 ..... III.1:3 one reality, **o.** truth and but one Son.
T-26 ..... III.1:3 one reality, one truth and but **o.** Son.
T-26 ..... III.1:8 The truth is simple; it is **o.**, without an
T-26 ..... III.3:5 and only **o.** continues past the gate where
T-26 ..... III.4:7 The **o.** essential thing to make a choice at
T-26 ..... III.4:9 In this **o.**, choice is made impossible. In
T-26 ..... III.6:2 For no **o.** understands what is the same,
T-26 ..... III.6:5 Yet within this **o.** lies the undoing of every
T-26 ..... III.7:2 union? All illusions are but **o.**. And in the
T-26 ..... IV.1:5 No **o.** forgives unless he has believed in
T-26 ..... IV.1:7 always rests upon the **o.** who offers it,
T-26 ..... IV.2:5 The sinless must perceive that they are **o.**,
T-26 ..... IV.2:6 space that sin left vacant do they join as **o.**
T-26 ..... IV.4:3 Not **o.** is lost, and none is cherished more
T-26 ..... IV.4:5 each **o.** teaches him that what he feared he
T-26 ..... IV.5:3 For no **o.** hears the song of Heaven and
T-26 ..... IV.5:4 And each **o.** joins the singing at the altar
T-26 ...... V.3:1 His Teacher to replace the **o.** you made,
T-26 ...... V.3:5 and all of them within that **o.** mistake,
T-26 ...... V.3:5 held also the Correction for that **o.**, and
T-26 ...... V.4:4 Not **o.** illusion still remains unanswered
T-26 ...... V.5:4 not **o.** note in Heaven's song was missed.
T-26 ...... V.5:5 in sin, is that **o.** instant still called back, as
T-26 .... V.11:7 You are like to **o.** who still hallucinates,
T-26 ..... VI.1:7 For no **o.** can make one illusion real, and
T-26 ..... VI.1:7 For no one can make **o.** illusion real, and
T-26 ..... VI.1:9 and still maintain that even **o.** is best?
T-26 ..... VI.2:1 with **o.** illusion as your only friend. This is
T-26 ..... VI.2:2 **o.** with which he could remain content.
T-26 ..... VI.2:4 The **o.** illusion that you think is friend
T-26 ..... VI.3:2 Would you allow **o.** shadow to usurp the
T-26 .... VII.6:1 It is impossible that **o.** illusion be less
T-26 .... VII.6:9 Not **o.** is true in any way, and all must
T-26 .. VII.10:6 his wishes and the Will of God are **o.**.
T-26 .. VII.13:1 Cause and effect are **o.**, not separate. God
T-26 .. VII.15:4 lies, for God gave answer to them all as **o.**.
T-26 .. VII.15:5 And what is **o.** to Him must be the same.
T-26 .. VII.17:6 lie, to be both offered and received as **o.**.
T-26 .. VII.19:4 what can save each **o.** of us can save us all.
T-26 .. VII.19:6 all, for what is **o.** can have no specialness.
T-26 .. VII.19:9 To get from **o.** is to deprive them all. And
T-26 VII.19:10 to bless but **o.** gives blessing to them all as
T-26 VII.19:10 but one gives blessing to them all as **o.**.

T-26 ...VIII.1:1 The **o.** remaining problem that you have
T-26 ...VIII.1:3 For time and space are **o.** illusion, which
T-26 ...VIII.2:6 be **o.** in which you sacrifice and suffer loss
T-26 ...VIII.3:4 still, and let you instantly become as **o.**.
T-26 ...VIII.8:2 illusion is but **o.** effect that it engenders,
T-26 ...VIII.8:2 **o.** form in which its outcome is perceived.
T-26 ...VIII.8:3 is but **o.** aspect of the little space that lies
T-26 ...VIII.9:6 consequence and cause must come as **o.**.
T-26 ..... IX.2:1 left without a single **o.** you cherish still?
T-26 ..... IX.4:4 grow ever brighter as each **o.** comes home
T-26 ..... IX.7:3 No **o.** on earth but offers thanks to one
T-26 ..... IX.7:3 thanks to **o.** who has restored his home,
T-26 .......X.3:1 Unfairness and attack are **o.** mistake, so
T-26 .......X.3:1 so firmly joined that where **o.** is perceived
T-26 .......X.5:1 because you think that **o.** must be unfair
T-26 .......X.5:2 do you perceive **o.** purpose for your whole
T-26 .......X.5:6 To add or take away from this **o.** goal is
T-27 ........I.5:3 **o.** has not been used for purpose of attack
T-27 ........I.6:5 feeling has a motivation other than this **o.**
T-27 ........I.7:2 The sick have reason for each **o.** of their
T-27 ......I.11:7 both be reconciled at last and seen as **o.**.
T-27 .......II.2:4 no **o.** can forgive a sin that he believes is
T-27 .....II.2:10 **O.** denies the other and must make it false
T-27 .......II.3:6 For no **o.** in whom true forgiveness rests
T-27 .......II.3:9 cannot be for **o.** and not the other. Who
T-27 .....II.10:4 of forgiveness. No **o.** can forgive until he
T-27 .....II.11:4 as the **o.** more innocent than he. This
T-27 .....II.11:6 And so you cannot be perceived as **o.**, and
T-27 .....II.11:6 mean a shared identity with but **o.** end.
T-27 .....II.12:5 different purpose from the **o.** you cherish,
T-27 .....II.13:4 lest your errors and his own be seen as **o.**.
T-27 .....II.14:2 on **o.** who cannot be a part of you while
T-27 .....II.14:7 by giving you and him a function that is **o.**
T-27 .....II.15:1 function given both, but neither **o.** alone.
T-27 .....II.15:3 in **o.** unhealed and set the other free. That
T-27 .....II.16:3 as **o.** because it is not split in purpose, and
T-27 .....II.16:3 conceives a single function as its only **o.**.
T-27 ..... III.6:3 in deciding that it is the only **o.** you want.
T-27 ..... IV.1:4 an answer from **o.** point of view is not an
T-27 ..... IV.3:6 question. **O.** with many answers can have
T-27 ..... IV.4:4 The world asks but **o.** question. It is this:
T-27 ... IV.4:11 That is the **o.** that you should choose. The
T-27 ..... IV.5:8 But no **o.** in a conflict state is free to ask
T-27 .......V.1:6 No **o.** can ask another to be healed. But he
T-27 .......V.2:4 No **o.** is healed through double messages.
T-27 .......V.3:2 each **o.** is born into this world as witness
T-27 .......V.4:2 And nothing more than just **o.** instant of
T-27 .......V.4:3 In that **o.** instant you are healed, and in
T-27 .......V.5:1 by the **o.** who could have saved it, but
T-27 .......V.6:7 looks on **o.** cannot perceive the other, for
T-27 .......V.7:2 It needs **o.** lesson that has perfectly been
T-27 .......V.7:6 of accusation is replaced by **o.** in which all
T-27 .......V.8:2 And no **o.** understands the nature of his
T-27 .......V.8:8 within two situations that are seen as **o.**,
T-27 .......V.9:2 solved as any **o.** of them has been escaped
T-27 .....V.10:4 each **o.** of them there are a thousand more
T-27 .....V.10:5 Each **o.** may seem to have a problem that
T-27 .....V.11:5 Your healing will be **o.** of its effects, as will
T-27 ..... VI.2:2 and carries but **o.** message: "You are here,
T-27 ..... VI.2:5 Each **o.** seems different because it has a
T-27 ..... VI.2:9 as **o.** steps forward and another back. Yet
T-27 ..... VI.3:5 real, for any **o.** you choose is like the rest.
T-27 ..... VI.5:6 brings the miracle perceives them all as **o.**
T-27 ..... VI.5:8 It is a witness no **o.** can deny, for it is the
T-27 ..... VII.8:3 And no **o.** will elect to suffer more. What
T-27 .... VII.2:6 No **o.** has difficulty making up his mind
T-27 .... VII.3:5 No **o.** who looks upon this "reasoning"
T-27 .... VII.4:4 For each **o.** thinks that if he does his part,
T-27 .... VII.7:1 to sin all stand within **o.** little space. And
T-27 .... VII.7:4 Of **o.** thing you were sure: Of all the many
T-27 .... VII.7:7 **o.** who makes them does not see himself
T-27 .... VII.8:1 No **o.** can waken from a dream the world
T-27 .... VII.9:1 see; the **o.** alternative that you can choose,
T-27 .... VII.9:3 thus are you the **o.** decider of your destiny
T-27 .. VII.11:1 but **o.** of which is clearly recognized?
T-27 .. VII.11:2 effects, when only **o.** is seen as up to him?
T-27 .. VII.11:3 as **o.** in which the choice is split between a
T-27 .. VII.11:5 They are **o.**. The dreaming of the world is
T-27 ... VIII.3:3 finds itself, the dream has but **o.** purpose,

T-27... VIII.5:4 No o. asleep and dreaming in the world
T-27... VIII.5:5 No o. believes there really was a time
T-27... VIII.5:6 at once that these ideas are o. illusion, too
T-27... VIII.5:8 no o. can remember when they would
T-27... VIII.6:2 Into eternity, where all is o., there crept a
T-27. VIII.11:2 Holy Spirit will repeat this o. inclusive
T-27. VIII.11:4 For this o. answer takes away the cause of
T-27. VIII.12:1 Who knows that every o. is like the rest.
T-27. VIII.12:2 He will teach you how each o. is caused.
T-27. VIII.13:4 a secret kept from no o. but yourself. And
T-27. VIII.13:7 The o. thing that is impossible is that you
T-28.........I.7:2 he can learn and can preserve a better o.?
T-28....... I.12:3 the o. for whom He has been given them!
T-28....... II.3:4 It has but *o.* Effect. And in that recognition
T-28....... II.5:6 forgiving dreams is no o. asked to be the
T-28....... II.5:8 made the o. you would exchange for this.
T-28....... II.7:3 No o. is afraid of them when he perceives
T-28...... III.1:6 of fear to o. that is already being dreamed.
T-28...... III.9:4 And no o. is deprived or can deprive.
T-28......IV.1:10 You can be sure of just o. thing; that you
T-28......IV.2:5 dreamer from the dream, and join in o.,
T-28......IV.5:4 because the dreamer and the dream are o.
T-28......IV.7:2 not, for what is joined in Him is always o..
T-28......IV.7:3 No o. is sick if someone else accepts his
T-28......IV.9:2 and perfect, lies in every o. of them. And
T-28......IV.9:3 joined because what is in o. is in them all.
T-28......IV.9:6 For the whole is in each o.. And every
T-28....... V.2:5 Where o. appears, the other disappears.
T-28....... V.2:6 you share becomes the only o. you have.
T-28....... V.2:7 You have the o. that you accept, because
T-28....... V.2:7 because it is the only o. you wish to have.
T-28......VI.4:5 No o. can suffer if he does not see himself
T-28......VI.6:1 Let this be your agreement with each o.;
T-28......VI.6:1 that you be o. with him and not apart.
T-28......VI.6:2 it is the o. that he has made to God, as
T-28.....VII.1:6 and there is no o. who could be untrue to
T-28.....VII.2:5 it. For healing will be o. or not at all, its
T-28.....VII.3:1 you and your brother, or you are as o..
T-28.....VII.4:8 of sickness seems to be of form, yet it is o.,
T-29.........I.2:3 No o. who hates but is afraid of love, and
T-29.........I.3:3 but this o. still remains to block your path
T-29.........I.4:1 o. of space between two separate bodies.
T-29....... II.3:3 For pain and sin are o. illusion, as are hate
T-29....... II.3:3 are hate and fear, attack and guilt but o..
T-29....... II.7:3 the o. in which you found yourself before.
T-29...... III.1:6 is savior but the o. who gives salvation?
T-29...... III.2:7 o. with him without the wall the world
T-29...... III.3:1 and of death is yet o. theme of truth; no
T-29......IV.1:8 And dreaming goes with only o. of these.
T-29......IV.4:8 each o. represents some function that you
T-29......IV.5:1 you were not the o. who gave the "proper
T-29......IV.5:2 No o. can fail but your idea of him, and
T-29......IV.5:3 the Holy Spirit gives is never o. of fear.
T-29......VI.2:6 thing in all the universe that must be o..
T-29......VI.4:4 time might be preserved, excepting o..
T-29....VI.4:11 it be as o. forever and forever, without
T-29.....VII.2:1 No o. who comes here but must still have
T-29.....VII.3:2 And each will fail him, all excepting o.; for
T-29.....VII.7:2 in which all idols fail you, o. by one, and
T-29.....VII.7:2 in which all idols fail you, one by o., and
T-29... VIII.2:5 have. No o. believes in idols who has not
T-29... VIII.3:9 nor darken by o. whit the light itself.
T-29... VIII.4:2 power to change o. blade of grass from
T-29... VIII.8:3 on the o. of whom the question has been
T-29... VIII.8:5 No o. comes unless he worshipped them,
T-29... VIII.8:5 still attempts to seek for o. that yet might
T-29. VIII.8:10 And when o. fails another takes its place,
T-29... VIII.9:6 your brother and on you, as o. with Him?
T-29......IX.3:3 for o. unless he were in terror and despair
T-29......IX.7:4 dream in which no o. is used to substitute
T-29......IX.7:5 No o. is used for something he is not, for
T-29....IX.10:5 fear his judgment for he has judged no o.,
T-30.......in.1:3 be reached depends on this o. thing alone;
T-30.......in.1:4 Each o. will help a little, every time it is
T-30.........I.7:3 until you believe the day you want is o. in
T-30...... I.17:6 be the o. reminder that you keep in mind,
T-30..... II.1:10 not o. Thought that God has ever had but
T-30....... II.3:1 the o. you chose to hate instead of love.
T-30....... II.3:7 Not o. created thing but gives you thanks,
T-30....... II.5:2 And no o. walks upon the earth but must
T-30...... III.2:4 What idol can make two of what is o.?
T-30...... III.2:7 It is not your will to have o.. It will not
T-30.... III.10:4 peace. Here is your o. reality kept safe,
T-30.... III.11:5 You have not two realities, but o.. Nor can
T-30.... III.11:6 Nor can you be aware of more than o.. An
T-30......IV.3:2 each o. seems to break the rules you set
T-30....IV.4:10 See o. in them and you will see them all.
T-30....IV.5:14 His o. mistake is that he thinks them real.
T-30......IV.6:4 when you decide o. very simple thing; you
T-30......IV.7:3 you forgive all things that no o. ever did;
T-30....... V.2:5 No o. is tempted by its vain appeal, for
T-30....... V.2:8 no o. stands outside this hope, because
T-30....... V.2:8 of the world is o. which all must share, if
T-30....... V.4:2 No o. outside of Heaven knows how this
T-30..... V.10:4 *Not o. was bought except at cost of pain, nor*
T-30..... V.11:3 they were free to learn their will is o.. And
T-30......VI.4:4 No o. who sees himself as guilty can avoid
T-30......VI.5:7 be o. mistake that had the power to undo
T-30......VI.7:3 If o. appearance must remain apart from
T-30......VI.7:3 healing, o. illusion must be part of truth.
T-30.....VII.1:4 looks upon the world as with o. purpose,
T-30.....VII.1:6 could each o. be open to interpretation
T-30.....VII.3:2 But it must accord *o.* meaning to them all.
T-30.....VII.4:1 and o. interpretation given to the world
T-30.....VII.4:2 shared purpose is o. judgment shared by
T-30.....VII.4:3 have learned o. meaning has been given
T-30.....VII.5:1 lies in this; all things have but o. purpose,
T-30.....VII.5:3 for the o. who gains and him who loses.
T-30.....VII.5:6 In o. united goal does this become
T-30.....VII.6:2 Holy Spirit's goal gives o. interpretation,
T-30...VII.6:11 No o. has agreed with you on what it
T-30.....VII.7:6 We have o. Interpreter. And through His
T-30... VIII.6:1 you decide there is not o. appearance you
T-31.........I.1:9 told exactly how to tell o. from the other,
T-31.........I.2:4 goes from o. apparent lesson to the next,
T-31.........I.2:4 that lead you gently from o. to another,
T-31.........I.3:1 No o. who understands what you have
T-31.........I.4:5 The world began with o. strange lesson,
T-31....... II.2:9 the o. alternative that *is* a different choice.
T-31....... II.3:1 free, for it will have o. outcome either way
T-31....... II.4:3 You hate the o. you gave the leader's role
T-31....... II.5:9 Hear the o., and you are separate from
T-31....... II.7:5 and hearing but o. answer to them all.
T-31....... II.7:6 all. Because He hears o. Voice, He cannot
T-31....... II.7:6 hear a different answer from the o. He
T-31..... II.10:5 for you have come with but o. purpose;
T-31..... II.11:3 you walk alone, with no o. by your side?
T-31...... III.1:2 is first o. thing that must be overlearned.
T-31...... III.5:1 that thinks it is a sin has but o. purpose;
T-31...... III.6:5 will see no o. as prisoner to what you have
T-31......IV.2:8 They have but o. end. And each is but the
T-31......IV.3:2 all, before you really learn they are but o..
T-31......IV.3:3 to see how like they are to o. another.
T-31......IV.6:1 that the world can offer but o. choice, no
T-31......IV.9:3 Him, nor any worldly goal be o. with His.
T-31....IV.10:8 without your own reality at o. with you?
T-31....... V.1:4 at home, where what it sees is o. with it.
T-31....... V.1:6 a self, and make o. as you go along. And
T-31....... V.1:7 on equal terms, at o. with its demands.
T-31....... V.2:5 but o. of which the mind can recognize.
T-31....... V.4:2 No o. who makes a picture of himself
T-31....... V.7:5 Not o. of them is true, and many come
T-31....... V.8:1 for no o. here can see what it is for, and
T-31..... V.10:7 If o. were generated by your brother, who
T-31..... V.11:1 the o. who would not think it true is you.
T-31..... V.11:4 go, if either o. were ever raised to doubt.
T-31..... V.12:7 have first decided on the o. to choose, and
T-31..... V.16:2 Each o. will show the changes in your own
T-31......VI.1:3 If o. is real the other must be false, for
T-31......VI.1:4 There is no choice in vision but this o..
T-31......VI.1:6 this o. choice does all your world depend,
T-31......VI.2:3 This o. appears and disappears in death;
T-31......VI.2:3 that o. is doomed to suffering and loss.
T-31......VI.2:4 And no o. is exactly as he was an instant
T-31......VI.4:2 world that will replace the o. you made.
T-31......VI.5:4 O. vision, clearly seen, that does not fit
T-31.....VII.1:6 no o. here but holds a concept of himself
T-31.....VII.2:5 *o.* brother dawn upon your sight as wholly
T-31.....VII.5:6 which you offer o. whose need for it is just
T-31.....VII.5:7 be changed to o. that brings the peace of
T-31.....VII.8:3 to each o. has He allowed the grace to be a
T-31.....VII.8:4 he looks upon o. brother as he looks upon
T-31.....VII.8:6 he looks on everyone as he beholds this o.
T-31.....VII.9:1 all are different names for just o. error;
T-31...VII.10:4 savior would be o. who is but partly saved
T-31...VII.13:7 of Christ to shine upon the o. who asks, in
T-31...VII.14:9 or Heaven, and of these you choose but o.
T-31....VIII.1:1 Temptation has o. lesson it would teach,
T-31....VIII.3:1 before you now can make a better o., and
T-31....VIII.3:3 not leave o. source of pain unhealed, nor
T-31..VIII.10:8 For we are o. in purpose, and the end of
T-31..VIII.11:5 And as each o. elects to join with me, the
T-31..VIII.11:5 of melody to o. inclusive chorus from a
T-31..VIII.12:5 Not o. illusion is accorded faith, and not
T-31..VIII.12:5 and not o. spot of darkness still remains
T-31..VIII.12:8 For we have reached where all of us are o.,
W-in..........2:4 training period is o. year. The exercises
W-in..........2:6 to do more than o. set of exercises a day.
W-in..........3:2 are planned around o. central idea, which
W-in..........5:3 hand, o. exception held apart from true
W-pI....... 1.3:7 excluded. O. thing is like another as far as
W-pI.......2.1:1 idea are the same as those for the first o..
W-pI.......3.2:3 For this purpose o. thing is like another;
W-pI.......5.1:1 This idea, like the preceding o., can be
W-pI.......7.5:1 not linger over any o. thing in particular,
W-pI.......8.1:2 No o. really sees anything. He sees only
W-pI.......8.2:1 o. wholly true thought one can hold about
W-pI.......8.2:1 one wholly true thought o. can hold about
W-pI.......8.4:4 Name each o. by the central figure or
W-pI.....10.4:7 As each o. crosses your mind, say: *My*
W-pI.....11.3:1 from o. thing to another fairly rapidly,
W-pI.....12.2:3 slow shifting of your glance from o. thing
W-pI.....12.3:6 that a "good world" implies a "bad" o.,
W-pI.....12.3:6 world" implies an "unsatisfying" o.. All
W-pI.....13.1:1 is really another form of the preceding o.,
W-pI.....13.5:1 to avoid resistance, in o. form or another,
W-pI.....14.4:2 Name each o. as it occurs to you, and then
W-pI.....16.5:1 and then as each o. crosses your mind
W-pI.....18.3:1 your eyes on each o. long enough to say: *I*
W-pI.....19.3:3 As you consider each o., name it in terms
W-pI.....20.3:6 God has o. Son, and he is the resurrection
W-pI.....20.4:3 change your present state for a better o.,
W-pI.....20.4:3 for a better one, and o. you really want.
W-pI.....21.1:1 and extension of the preceding o.. This
W-pI.....21.4:1 each o. in mind while you tell yourself: *I*
W-pI.....22.3:2 move slowly from o. object to another,
W-pI.....22.3:2 to another, from o. body to another, say
W-pI.....23.3:3 O. can well ask if this can be called seeing.
W-pI.....23.5:4 The final o. does not. Your images have
W-pI.....23.6:3 As each o. crosses your mind say: *I can*
W-pI.....24.7:2 *in this situation,* and go on to the next o..
W-pI.....25.4:1 for today, o. more thought is necessary.
W-pI.....26.6:4 use very many for any o. practice period,
W-pI.....26.6:4 than usual should be spent with each o..
W-pI.....26.7:3 referring to each o. quite specifically,
W-pI.....27.3:6 You can still repeat o. short sentence to
W-pI.....27.4:3 Answer o. of these questions, and you
W-pI.....28.2:7 When you have seen o. thing differently,
W-pI.....28.2:8 The light you will see in any o. of them is
W-pI.....28.7:2 each o. should be accorded equal sincerity
W-pI.....29.4:1 about you, naming each o. specifically.
W-pI.....31.1:4 o. in which you apply the idea on a more
W-pI.....31.2:1 o. in the morning and one at night. Three
W-pI.....31.2:1 one in the morning and o. at night. Three
W-pI.....31.3:4 Do not dwell on any o. in particular, but
W-pI.....31.5:1 for today is also a particularly useful o. to
W-pI.....32.2:2 o. involving the world you see outside you
W-pI.....34.2:2 O. in the morning and one in the evening
W-pI.....34.2:2 morning and o. in the evening are advised
W-pI.....34.2:2 with an additional o. to be undertaken at
W-pI.....34.3:3 arise in your mind, and let each o. go, to
W-pI.....34.6:2 find you need more than o. application of
W-pI.....35.7:4 After you have named each o., add: *But*
W-pI.....36.4:1 with o. more repetition with your eyes
W-pI.....37.1:4 No o. loses; nothing is taken away from
W-pI.....37.3:2 you teach the world that it is o. with you,
W-pI.....38.1:3 of God, at o. with the Mind of his Creator.

W-pI.....38.4:2 and **o.** that is difficult for someone else.
W-pI.....39.2:6 at all. No **o.** needs practice to gain what is
W-pI.....39.8:1 undue emphasis on any **o.** in particular,
W-pI.....40.3:3 **O.** practice period might, for example,
W-pI.....41.2:2 **o.** thing they do not do is to question the
W-pI.....41.6:1 will be only **o.** long practice period today.
W-pI.....42.3:1 **o.** as soon as possible after you wake, and
W-pI.....43.4:1 **o.** as early and one as late as possible in
W-pI.....43.4:1 early and **o.** as late as possible in the day.
W-pI.....44.4:3 easy **o.** in the world for the trained mind,
W-pI.....44.8:3 It is also the only **o.** that has any meaning,
W-pI.....44.8:3 only **o.** that has any real use to you at all.
W-pI.....45.2:4 To share is to make alike, or to make **o.**.
W-pI.....45.8:3 Here are your thoughts **o.** with His. For
W-pI.....45.8:4 kind of practice only **o.** thing is necessary;
W-pI.....46.4:3 Mention each **o.** by name, and say: *God is*
W-pI.....47.4:4 fear, dismissing each **o.** by telling yourself
W-pI.....47.6:1 but it is hardly a sufficient **o.** in giving you
WpI...rI.in.2:2 each **o.** should be practiced at least once.
WpI...rI.in.2:5 If any **o.** of the five ideas appeals to you
WpI...rI.in.2:5 than the others, concentrate on that **o.**. At
W-pI.....51.3:8 a better choice than the **o.** I made before?
W-pI.....54.1:3 a false world or lead me to the real **o.**. But
W-pI.....54.1:7 They must be **o.** or the other. What I see
W-pI.....54.5:5 me that my will and the Will of God are **o.**
W-pI.....55.5:7 by withdrawing the **o.** I have given it, and
W-pI.....56.5:2 is the knowledge that all is **o.** forever. I
W-pI.....56.5:5 them, am **o.** with them and one with Him.
W-pI.....56.5:5 them, am one with them and **o.** with Him.
W-pI.....57.3:2 of the world is not the **o.** I ascribed to it,
W-pI.....61.5:1 each **o.** need not exceed a minute or two.
W-pI.....62.2:1 about yourself and the world are **o.**. That
W-pI.....64.5:4 simple. Each **o.** will lead to happiness or
W-pI.....64.5:8 different from just this **o.** simple choice.
W-pI........65.h My only function is the **o.** God gave me.
W-pI.....65.2:2 "My only function is the **o.** God gave me."
W-pI.....65.5:5 it. Note each **o.** as it comes to you, with as
W-pI.....65.5:5 dismissing each **o.** by telling yourself: *This*
W-pI.....65.8:2 *My only function is the* **o.** *God gave me. I*
W-pI........66.h My happiness and my function are **o.**.
W-pI.....66.1:4 but their content is completely **o.**.
W-pI.....66.7:3 **O.** is ruled by the ego, and is made up of
W-pI...66.10:6 On **o.** side stand all illusions. All truth
W-pI...66.11:2 *My happiness and function are* **o.**, *because*
W-pI.....68.1:7 no **o.** can conceive of his Creator as unlike
W-pI.....68.5:4 that there is no **o.** against whom you do
W-pI.....68.6:2 thinking of each **o.** in turn as you do so: *I*
W-pI.....69.1:1 **o.** can look upon what your grievances
W-pI.....72.4:4 with him, and judging them as **o.**. Herein
W-pI...72.13:1 **O.** or perhaps two shorter practice
W-pI.....73.9:3 It is the **o.** purpose here on which you and
W-pI.....74.3:8 *My will and God's are* **o.**. *God wills peace for*
W-pI.....74.4:1 is **o.** conflict area that seems particularly
W-pI.....75.2:6 The old **o.** has left no trace upon it in its
W-pI.....77.1:3 miracles because you are **o.** with God.
W-pI.....77.4:3 never taken from **o.** and given to another,
W-pI.....78.1:1 is **o.** between a grievance and a miracle.
W-pI.....78.3:1 shining light where each **o.** stood before.
W-pI.....78.4:4 We will select **o.** person you have used as
W-pI.....78.5:1 You know the **o.** to choose; his name has
W-pI.....78.5:2 He will be the **o.** of whom we ask God's
W-pI.....78.7:3 *Let me behold my savior in this* **o.** *You have*
W-pI.....78.7:3 **o.** *for me to ask to lead me to the holy light in*
W-pI.....78.9:2 **o.** Thought of God but must rejoice as you
W-pI...78.10:2 when we allow each **o.** we meet to save us,
W-pI.....79.2:2 and must be recognized as **o.** if the one
W-pI.....79.2:2 as one if the **o.** solution that solves them
W-pI.....79.3:3 and as **o.** is settled the next one and the
W-pI.....79.3:3 is settled the next **o.** and the next arise.
W-pI.....79.5:1 No **o.** could solve all the problems the
W-pI.....79.7:4 try to realize that we have only **o.** problem
W-pI.....79.9:2 today, each **o.** calling for an answer. Our
W-pI.....79.9:3 there is only **o.** problem and one answer.
W-pI.....79.9:3 there is only one problem and **o.** answer.
W-pI.....80.1:2 **o.** central problem has been answered,
W-pI.....80.1:4 depends on recognizing this **o.** problem,
W-pI.....80.1:5 **O.** problem, one solution. Salvation is
W-pI.....80.1:5 One problem, **o.** solution. Salvation is
W-pI.....80.3:5 this. **O.** problem, one solution. Accept the
W-pI.....80.3:5 problem, **o.** solution. Accept the peace
W-pI.....80.4:3 fail. Having recognized **o.**, you have
W-pI.....80.5:5 all, remember that you have **o.** problem,
W-pI.....80.5:5 and that the problem has **o.** solution. It is
WpI..rII.in.1:3 day will be devoted to **o.** of these ideas,
WpI..rII.in.1:4 We will have **o.** longer exercise period,
W-pI.....83.1:1 My only function is the **o.** God gave me. I
W-pI.....83.1:2 I have no function but the **o.** God gave me
W-pI.....83.1:4 With **o.** purpose only, I am always certain
W-pI.....83.1:5 my only function is the **o.** God gave me.
W-pI.....83.2:3 *me a function other than the* **o.** *God gave me.*
W-pI.....83.3:1 (66) My happiness and my function are **o.**
W-pI.....83.3:2 one. All things that come from God are **o.**.
W-pI.....83.3:3 from Oneness, and must be received as **o.**.
W-pI.....89.3:2 the Holy Spirit's, and perceive them as **o.**.
W-pI.....90.1:4 that there is **o.** problem and one solution.
W-pI.....90.1:4 that there is one problem and **o.** solution.
W-pI........92.h seen in light, and light and strength are **o.**
W-pI.....92.1:1 today is an extension of the previous **o.**.
W-pI.....92.5:6 its light that all may see and benefit as **o.**.
W-pI.....92.7:3 and strength perceive themselves as **o.**.
W-pI.....92.8:2 No **o.** can ask in vain to share its sight,
W-pI...92.10:4 and Self, where light and strength are **o.**.
W-pI.....93.7:1 requires the acceptance of but **o.** thought;
W-pI.....93.9:2 **O.** Self is true; the other is not there. Try
W-pI.....93.9:3 Try to experience the unity of your **o.** Self.
W-pI.....94.1:1 Today we continue with the **o.** idea which
W-pI.....94.1:1 the **o.** statement which makes all forms of
W-pI.....94.1:1 **o.** thought which renders the ego silent
W-pI.....94.1:3 are wiped away forever by this **o.** idea.
W-pI.....94.5:9 today. Each **o.** you do will be a giant stride
W-pI........95.h I am **o.** Self, united with my Creator.
W-pI.....95.1:2 You are **o.** within yourself, and one with
W-pI.....95.1:2 are one within yourself, and **o.** with Him.
W-pI.....95.3:2 exercises towards reaching your **o.** Self,
W-pI...95.10:2 attempts to keep you unaware you are **o.**
W-pI...95.10:2 Creator, at **o.** with every aspect of creation
W-pI...95.11:2 *I am* **o.** *Self, united with my Creator, at one*
W-pI...95.11:2 *Creator, at* **o.** *with every aspect of creation,*
W-pI...95.11:4 *I am* **o.** *Self.* Repeat this several times, and
W-pI...95.12:1 You are **o.** Self, united and secure in light
W-pI...95.12:2 are God's Son, **o.** Self, with one Creator
W-pI...95.12:2 one Self, with **o.** Creator and one goal; to
W-pI...95.12:2 one Self, with one Creator and **o.** goal; to
W-pI...95.12:3 You are **o.** Self, complete and healed and
W-pI...95.13:1 You are **o.** Self, in perfect harmony with
W-pI...95.13:2 be. You are **o.** Self, the holy Son of God,
W-pI...95.13:3 Feel this **o.** Self in you, and let It shine
W-pI...95.13:5 You are **o.** Self, and it is given you to feel
W-pI...95.13:5 out of the **o.** Mind that is this Self, the
W-pI...95.15:1 own acknowledgment you are **o.** Self,
W-pI...95.15:1 a call to all the world to be at **o.** with you.
W-pI...95.15:3 this: *You are* **o.** *Self with me, united with our*
W-pI........96.h Salvation comes from my **o.** Self.
W-pI.....96.1:1 Although you are **o.** Self, you experience
W-pI.....96.1:5 will never be compatible. But **o.** exists.
W-pI.....96.2:2 doubt, each **o.** as futile as the one before,
W-pI.....96.2:2 doubt, each one as futile as the **o.** before,
W-pI.....96.2:2 and failing as the next **o.** surely will.
W-pI.....96.3:5 the two, for **o.** denies the other can be real
W-pI.....96.8:1 Him Who speaks to you from your **o.** Self.
W-pI.....96.8:3 Salvation comes from this **o.** Self through
W-pI.....96.9:2 this: *Salvation comes from my* **o.** *Self. Its*
W-pI...96.12:1 mind salvation comes from your **o.** Self,
W-pI.....97.1:1 idea identifies you with your **o.** Self. It
W-pI.....97.3:4 and last; the first that is the last, for it is **o.**
W-pI.....97.5:2 He will not overlook **o.** open mind that
W-pI.....97.8:2 that you are spirit, **o.** with Him and God,
W-pI.....98.1:2 We take a stand on but **o.** side today. We
W-pI.....98.2:4 Not **o.** mistake stands in our way. For we
W-pI.....98.8:2 lose **o.** chance to be the glad receiver of
W-pI.....99.5:5 does He know **o.** thing must still be true;
W-pI.....99.6:6 Him. He has **o.** answer to appearances;
W-pI.....99.9:2 It is God's Will your mind be **o.** with His.
W-pI.....99.9:3 It is God's Will that He has but **o.** Son. It
W-pI.....99.9:4 It is God's Will that His **o.** Son is you.
W-pI...99.10:5 God. Forgive yourself the **o.** you think you
W-pI...99.12:1 Your only function tells you you are **o.**.
W-pI...100.1:3 **O.** function shared by separate minds
W-pI .. 100.1:3 separate minds unites them in **o.** purpose,
W-pI .. 100.1:3 for each **o.** of them is equally essential to
W-pI .. 100.3:4 and no **o.** laughs because all laughter can
W-pI .. 100.8:4 Let this **o.** be the day that you succeed!
W-pI .. 102.5:3 accepted happiness as your **o.** function.
W-pI .. 103.3:1 Allow this **o.** correction to be placed
W-pI .. 104.3:1 wills, and recognize the same as being **o.**.
W-pI .. 105.1:7 that **o.** can gain because another loses.
W-pI .. 105.7:1 "enemies" a little while, and tell each **o.**,
W-pI .. 106.3:7 to reach Him longer. Hear **o.** Voice today.
W-pI .. 106.8:2 Your request is **o.** whose answer has been
W-pI ..... 108.h To give and to receive are **o.** in truth.
W-pI .. 108.1:3 into **o.** concept which is wholly true? Even
W-pI .. 108.1:4 Even that **o.** will disappear, because the
W-pI .. 108.2:3 And thus what is the same is seen as **o.**,
W-pI .. 108.3:2 they are **o.** with you and with themselves.
W-pI .. 108.3:3 based upon **o.** frame of reference, from
W-pI .. 108.3:3 reference, from which **o.** meaning comes.
W-pI .. 108.4:1 as different aspects of **o.** Thought whose
W-pI .. 108.5:1 **O.** thought, completely unified, will serve
W-pI .. 108.5:2 as saying **o.** correction will suffice for all
W-pI .. 108.5:2 to forgive **o.** brother wholly is enough to
W-pI .. 108.5:3 of **o.** law which holds for every kind of
W-pI .. 108.6:3 the **o.** Thought which underlies them all.
W-pI .. 108.8:2 *To give and to receive are* **o.** *in truth. I will*
W-pI .. 108.9:1 Say each **o.** slowly and then pause a while
W-pI .. 108.9:4 to think of **o.** to whom to give your gifts.
W-pI 108.10:3 say, "To give and to receive are **o.** in truth.
W-pI .. 109.8:2 to your trust today, forgetting no **o.**,
W-pI .. 110.1:2 For this **o.** thought would be enough to
W-pI .. 110.3:3 You need no thought but just this **o.**, to
W-pI .. 110.4:1 In this **o.** thought is all the past undone;
WpI..rIII.in8:2 them so you undertake **o.** in the morning,
WpIrIII.in10:3 Use **o.** on the hour, and the other one a
WpIrIII.in10:3 hour, and the other **o.** a half an hour later.
WpIrIII.in10:4 give more than just a moment to each **o.**.
WpIrIII.in12:1 **o.** to be applied on each half hour as well.
W-pI .. 111.2:1 seen in light, and light and strength are **o.**
W-pI .. 111.3:4 in light, and light and strength are **o.**.
W-pI .. 112.2:3 *And I am* **o.** *with Him, and He with me.*
W-pI .. 113.1:1 (95) I am **o.** Self, united with my Creator.
W-pI .. 113.1:2 *perfect peace are mine, because I am* **o.** *Self,*
W-pI .. 113.1:2 *whole, at* **o.** *with all creation and with God.*
W-pI .. 113.2:1 (96) Salvation comes from my **o.** Self.
W-pI .. 113.2:2 *From my* **o.** *Self, Whose knowledge still*
W-pI .. 113.3:2 I am **o.** Self, united with my Creator. On
W-pI .. 113.3:4 hour: Salvation comes from my **o.** Self.
W-pI .. 119.2:1 To give and to receive are **o.** in truth. *I will*
W-pI .. 119.3:4 To give and to receive are **o.** in truth.
W-pI .. 121.6:5 your mind as **o.** to Him Who is your Self,
W-pI .. 121.7:2 Each **o.** awaits release from hell through
W-pI .. 121.9:2 today that they are **o.** through practicing
W-pI .. 121.9:2 toward **o.** whom you think of as an enemy
W-pI .. 121.9:2 and **o.** whom you consider as a friend.
W-pI .. 121.9:3 And as you learn to see them both as **o.**,
W-pI 121.10:1 should meet him; **o.** you actively despise,
W-pI 121.12:1 and turn your mind to **o.** you call a friend.
W-pI 121.13:2 Now are you **o.** with them, and they with
W-pI .. 122.4:5 You will not find another **o.** instead.
W-pI .. 123.3:5 the **o.** whom God established as His Son.
W-pI ..... 124.h Let me remember I am **o.** with God.
W-pI .. 124.1:5 At **o.** with God and with the universe we
W-pI .. 124.2:2 the mind at **o.** with God and with itself.
W-pI .. 124.4:3 We are **o.** with Him today in recognition
W-pI .. 124.6:1 those who know that they are **o.** with God
W-pI .. 124.7:1 as we say that we are **o.** with God. For in
W-pI .. 124.7:5 experience ourselves at **o.** with Him, so
W-pI .. 124.8:2 awareness you are **o.** with your Creator, as
W-pI .. 124.8:3 to the thought that you are **o.** with God.
W-pI 124.12:2 *Let me remember I am* **o.** *with God, at one*
W-pI 124.12:2 *God, at* **o.** *with all my brothers and my Self,*
W-pI .. 125.9:4 Son joins in his Father's Will, at **o.** with it,
W-pI .. 126.3:2 You give charity to **o.** unworthy, merely
W-pI .. 126.3:3 you bestow on **o.** unworthy of the gift,
W-pI .. 127.1:2 for this, a kind for that; a way of loving **o.**,
W-pI .. 127.1:3 Love is **o.**. It has no separate parts and no
W-pI .. 127.2:4 thinks that love can be bestowed on **o.**,
W-pI .. 127.3:2 As it is **o.** itself, it looks on all as one. Its
W-pI .. 127.3:2 As it is one itself, it looks on all as **o.**. Its

W-pI.192.10:9 and you will see that you are **o.** with him.
W-pI...193.4:4 No **o.** can hide forever from a truth so
W-pI...193.4:4 **o.** but wants to see the simple lesson there
W-pI...193.9:2 nor **o.** thorn or nail to hurt His holy Son
W-pI...193.9:5 that laughter should replace each **o.**, and
W-pI.193.10:1 seeming obstacles to peace in just **o.** day.
W-pI.193.12:2 so that the next **o.** is free of the one before
W-pI.193.12:2 so that the next one is free of the **o.** before
W-pI.193.12:4 Let no **o.** hour cast its shadow on the one
W-pI.193.12:4 hour cast its shadow on the **o.** that follows
W-pI.193.12:4 one that follows, and when that **o.** goes,
W-pI...194.3:1 In no **o.** instant is depression felt, or pain
W-pI...194.3:2 In no **o.** instant sorrow can be set upon a
W-pI...194.3:3 In no **o.** instant can one even die. And so
W-pI...194.3:3 In no one instant can **o.** even die. And so
W-pI...194.3:4 with the next **o.** given Him already, is a
W-pI...194.4:2 They are **o.** to Him, and so they should be
W-pI...194.4:2 to Him, and so they should be **o.** to you.
W-pI...194.7:1 What worry can beset the **o.** who gives
W-pI...195.6:1 We thank our Father for **o.** thing alone;
W-pI...195.6:1 no living thing, and therefore **o.** with Him
W-pI.195.10:2 and where **o.** is the other must be found.
W-pI.195.10:5 gratitude to Him is **o.** with His to you. For
W-pI...196.4:1 Today's idea is **o.** step we take in leading
W-pI...196.4:2 mind relinquishes its burdens **o.** by one.
W-pI...196.4:2 mind relinquishes its burdens one by **o.**.
W-pI...196.4:5 done in just **o.** instant by the grace of God
W-pI...196.8:1 steps will be easy, if you take this **o.** today.
W-pI...197.2:4 until guilt and salvation are not seen as **o.**,
W-pI...197.9:3 And from this Self is no **o.** left outside.
W-pI...198.2:9 Except **o.**. Forgiveness is illusion that is
W-pI...198.3:2 save this **o.** must multiply a thousandfold.
W-pI...198.4:2 when this **o.** is the plan of God Himself?
W-pI...198.6:6 the words in which all merge as **o.** at last.
W-pI...198.6:7 And as this **o.** will fade away, the Word of
W-pI...198.7:2 all are **o.**; a place where death is offered to
W-pI.198.10:1 Accept the **o.** illusion which proclaims
W-pI.198.10:1 appears unveiled at last in this **o.** dream.
W-pI...200.2:1 point to which each **o.** must come at last,
W-pI...200.5:5 as you free the **o.**, the other is accepted as
W-pI...200.7:1 because He has **o.** Son who cannot make a
WpI rVI.in.1:1 this review we take but **o.** idea each day,
WpI rVI.in.2:3 **O.** is enough. But from that one, there
WpI rVI.in.2:4 from that **o.**, there must be no exceptions
WpI rVI.in.2:5 to use them all and let them blend as **o.**,
WpI rVI.in.5:1 but **o.** exception to this lack of structuring
WpI rVI.in.5:3 If you notice **o.**, deny its hold and hasten
W-pI...201.1:1 I trust my brothers, who are **o.** with me.
W-pI...201.1:2 *No* **o.** *but is my brother. I am blessed with*
W-pI...201.1:3 *Father,* **o.** *Creator of the whole that is my Self*
W-pI...204.1:2 *free in God, forever and forever* **o.** *with Him.*
W-pI...205.1:3 *The peace of God is my* **o.** *goal; the aim of all*
W-pI...210.1:3 *but* **o.** *I thought apart from Him and from*
W-pII ....in.6:5 we behold a world beyond the **o.** we made
W-pII ....in.8:1 upon the final part of this **o.** holy year,
W-pII ....in.8:1 for truth and God, Who is its **o.** Creator.
W-pII ..in.11:1 **O.** further use for words we still retain.
W-pII ..in.11:3 each **o.** of them to be continued till the
W-pII ..in.11:4 a little while, preceding **o.** of the holy and
W-pII .....1.2:1 unforgiving thought is **o.** which makes a
W-pII .221.2:6 joined. We wait with **o.** intent; to hear our
W-pII .224.1:3 gave to me; the **o.** as well I give the world.
W-pII .225.2:5 We are **o.**, and it is but this oneness that
W-pII .227.1:7 *Father, I know my will is* **o.** *with Yours.*
W-pII .....2.2:4 fragment of the mind that still was **o.**, but
W-pII .233.2:1 Today we have **o.** Guide to lead us on.
W-pII .234.1:3 in thoughts which are forever unified as **o.**
W-pII .239.2:3 *We are* **o.**, *united in this light and one with*
W-pII .239.2:3 *are one, united in this light and* **o.** *with You,*
W-pII .240.1:3 Not **o.** thing in this world is true. It does
W-pII .....3.1:4 has been changed to **o.** of true forgiveness
W-pII .....3.1:4 another light; and **o.** which leads to truth,
W-pII .241.2:1 *We have forgiven* **o.** *another now, and so we*
W-pII .241.2:3 *to us, and to remember that we all are* **o.**.
W-pII .243.2:3 **o.** *because each part contains Your memory,*
W-pII .243.2:3 *and truth must shine in all of us as* **o.**.
W-pII .244.1:2 *his safety and Your Love, for they are* **o.**.
W-pII .248.2:4 *own. Now do I understand that they are* **o.**.
W-pII .251.1:2 Now do I seek but **o.**, for in that one is all I
W-pII .251.1:2 I seek but one, for in that **o.** is all I need,
W-pII .257.1:2 No **o.** can serve contradicting goals and
W-pII .....5.5:2 be, you will believe that it is **o.** with you.
W-pII .262.1:1 *Father, You have* **o.** *Son. And it is he that I*
W-pII .262.1:3 *today. He is Your* **o.** *creation. Why should I*
W-pII .262.1:4 *a thousand forms in what remains as* **o.**?
W-pII .262.1:5 *Why should I give this* **o.** *a thousand names,*
W-pII .262.1:5 *one a thousand names, when only* **o.** *suffices*
W-pII .262.2:1 We who are **o.** would recognize this day
W-pII .264.1:5 *that stands beyond Your* **o.** *creation, or*
W-pII .265.1:9 Yet is my mind at **o.** with God's. And so I
W-pII .267.1:7 and every **o.** is answered by His Voice,
W-pII .269.2:2 We share **o.** vision, as we look upon the
W-pII .269.2:3 **o.** because of Him Who is the Son of God;
W-pII .270.1:4 *waits expectantly the* **o.** *remaining instant*
W-pII .270.1:5 *to him. And now his will is* **o.** *with Yours. His*
W-pII .....6.1:2 Self we share, uniting us with **o.** another,
W-pII .....6.2:1 is the link that keeps you **o.** with God, and
W-pII .282.1:4 loves, and Who remains my **o.** Identity.
W-pII .283.2:2 which our forgiveness has made **o.** with us
W-pII .287.2:7 *my Self, and be at* **o.** *with my Identity?*
W-pII .288.1:3 *must recognize what You created* **o.** *with me*
W-pII .....8.5:2 Now He waits but that **o.** instant more for
W-pII .295.1:4 Redemption must be **o.**. As I am saved,
W-pII .295.1:7 in many different forms, but love is **o.**.
W-pII .295.2:1 *a gift of me, and* **o.** *I give that it be given me.*
W-pII .296.2:2 learning goal becomes an unconflicted **o.**,
W-pII .....9.2:3 way, because it shines on everything as **o.**.
W-pII .....9.3:1 in which learning ends in **o.** last summary
W-pII .....9.4:1 The Second Coming is the **o.** event in
W-pII .....9.4:2 For every **o.** who ever came to die, or yet
W-pII .....9.4:3 equality is Christ restored as **o.** Identity,
W-pII .....9.4:3 of God acknowledge that they all are **o.**.
W-pII .....9.4:4 His Son, His **o.** creation and His only joy.
W-pII .....9.5:6 Behold, the Son of God is **o.** in us, and we
W-pII .307.1:5 *Your Son is* **o.** *with You in being and in will,*
W-pII .308.1:3 cannot be to keep the past and future **o.**.
W-pII .316.1:2 Each **o.** allows a past mistake to go, and
W-pII .316.1:4 watch its open doors that not **o.** gift is lost
W-pII ....318.h In me salvation's means and end are **o.**.
W-pII .318.1:2 the parts have but **o.** purpose and one aim
W-pII .318.1:2 the parts have but one purpose and **o.** aim
W-pII .318.1:3 or **o.** of more or less importance than the
W-pII .318.1:7 I am God's Son, His **o.** eternal Love. I am
W-pII .319.1:5 The ego thinks that what **o.** gains, totality
W-pII .319.1:6 I learn that what **o.** gains is given unto all.
W-pII .323.1:2 *You ask of me, and* **o.** *I gladly make; the only*
W-pII .327.2:3 *not. Your Word is* **o.** *with You. You give the*
W-pII .329.1:4 *As You are One, so am I* **o.** *with You. And this*
W-pII .329.1:5 *where my will became forever* **o.** *with Yours.*
W-pII .329.2:2 all of us are **o.** because His Will is shared
W-pII .329.2:3 Through it we recognize that we are **o.**.
W-pII .330.2:2 *but fail to know our* **o.** *Identity we share with*
W-pII ... 12.5:1 Yet will **o.** lily of forgiveness change the
W-pII ... 12.5:2 completely His, completely **o.** with Him.
W-pII .335.2:2 *reminds me that he was created* **o.** *with me,*
W-pII .338.1:3 has he learned that no **o.** frightens him,
W-pII .339.1:1 No **o.** desires pain. But he can think that
W-pII .339.1:3 No **o.** would avoid his happiness. But he
W-pII .340.2:5 Not **o.** of us but will be saved today. Not
W-pII .340.2:6 Not **o.** who will remain in fear, and none
W-pII ... 13.2:1 of grace, for it is given and received as **o.**.
W-pII .341.1:3 *Love bestowed upon us, living* **o.** *with You,*
W-pII .344.2:1 How near we are to **o.** another, as we go
W-pII .345.1:2 *And every* **o.** *I give returns to me, reminding*
W-pII ....349.h but give Each **o.** a miracle of love instead.
W-pII .349.1:5 *Each* **o.** *that I accept gives me a miracle to*
W-pII ... 14.2:2 of this **o.** year we gave to God together,
W-pII ....352.h From **o.** Come all the sorrows of the world
W-pII ....353.h hands, my feet today Have but **o.** purpose
W-pII .354.1:5 *Thus must I be* **o.** *with You as well as Him.*
W-pII ....358.h be sure; His answer is the **o.** I really want.
W-pII ....360.h Peace to my brother, who is **o.** with me.
Wfl........in.6:5 And more than that can no **o.** ever have,
W-ep ......... 1:4 No **o.** who calls on Him can call in vain.
M-in ......... 1:4 in which **o.** engages only a relatively small
M-in ......... 2:2 believe **o.** or the other is true all the time.
M-1 .......... 1:1 of God is anyone who chooses to be **o.**.
M-1 ......... 2:12 Each **o.** begins as a single light, but with
M-1 ......... 2:13 each **o.** saves a thousand years of time as
M-2 .......... 5:2 is not really the **o.** who does the teaching.
M-2 .......... 5:5 each **o.** learns that giving and receiving
M-2 .......... 5:6 thought separated them from **o.** another,
M-2 .......... 5:7 same course share **o.** interest and one goal
M-2 .......... 5:7 same course share one interest and **o.** goal
M-2 .......... 5:8 made the **o.** decision that gave his teacher
M-3 .......... 1:3 no **o.** from whom a teacher of God cannot
M-3 .......... 1:3 so there is no **o.** whom he cannot teach.
M-3 .......... 2:5 in the elevator will smile to **o.** another,
M-3 .......... 3:2 of **o.** permits the illusion of the other. In
M-4 ..... I.A.5:5 period of overlap is apt to be **o.** in which
M-4 ........II.2:3 war. No **o.** at one with himself can even
M-4 ........II.2:3 war. No one at **o.** with himself can even
M-4 ...... VI.1:6 No **o.** can become an advanced teacher of
M-4 ..... VII.1:3 teachers this **o.** rests ultimately on trust,
M-4 ..... VII.1:3 without trust no **o.** can be generous in the
M-4 ...... IX.1:6 To give up all problems to **o.** Answer is to
M-5 ........II.1:2 **O.** need but say, "There is no gain at all to
M-5 ........II.1:3 this, **o.** first must recognize certain facts.
M-5 ......II.3:11 guilt and sickness both, for they are **o.**.
M-5 ........II.4:4 effect in their true sequence in **o.** respect,
M-5 ........II.4:5 transfer value of **o.** true idea has no end or
M-5 ...... III.3:8 but by the union of the **o.** Will with itself.
M-6 .......... 2:6 Not **o.** is lost, for they can but increase.
M-6 .......... 3:4 No **o.** can give if he is concerned with the
M-6 .......... 4:9 And if **o.** gift is missing, it would not be
M-7 .......... 2:4 Now the teacher of God has only **o.** course
M-7 .......... 2:6 hate to **o.** to whom he offered love. This is
M-7 .......... 3:2 the **o.** responsibility of the miracle worker
M-7 ......... 3:10 was a mistake, but hardly **o.** to stay with.
M-7 .......... 4:1 **O.** of the most difficult temptations to
M-8 .......... 1:3 A larger object overshadows a smaller **o.**.
M-8 .......... 1:5 or **o.** conceived of as more desirable by
M-8 .......... 5:2 hallucination as opposed to a smaller **o.**?
M-8 .......... 5:3 voice he hears than to that of a softer **o.**?
M-8 .......... 6:4 mind will put them all in **o.** category; they
M-8 .......... 6:6 And of these two, but **o.** is real. Just as
M-8 .......... 6:8 The **o.** answer to sickness of any kind is
M-8 .......... 6:9 The **o.** answer to all illusions is truth.
M-9 .......... 1:3 that no **o.** is where he is by accident, and
M-9 .......... 2:1 **o.** lesson with increasing thoroughness.
M-10 ......... 1:5 "good" judgment to **o.** is "bad" judgment
M-10 ......... 1:6 as showing "good" judgment at **o.** time
M-10 ......... 2:9 is, and it is only **o.**: "God's Son is guiltless,
M-10 ......... 3:3 **o.** would have to be fully aware of an
M-10 ......... 3:4 **O.** would have to recognize in advance all
M-10 ......... 3:5 And **o.** would have to be certain there is
M-10 ......... 4:6 Make then but **o.** more judgment. It is
M-10 ......... 6:8 Not **o.** is true. For he has given up their
M-11 ......... 2:8 For **o.** of you is wrong. It must be so.
M-11 ......... 3:4 – **o.** without meaning and devoid of sense
M-12 ......... 1:1 The answer to this question is– **o.**. One
M-12 ......... 1:2 **O.** wholly perfect teacher, whose learning
M-12 ......... 1:3 suffices. This **o.**, sanctified and redeemed,
M-12 ......... 1:9 He is forever **o.**, because he is as God
M-12 ......... 2:6 Yet being joined in **o.** purpose, and one
M-12 ......... 2:6 one purpose, and **o.** they share with God,
M-12 ......... 2:8 forms? Their minds are **o.**; their joining is
M-12 ......... 2:9 And God works through them now as **o.**,
M-12 ......... 4:5 in, and what is **o.** is recognized as one.
M-12 ......... 4:5 in, and what is one is recognized as **o.**.
M-12 ......... 5:9 purpose from the **o.** that keeps it holy.
M-13 ......... 3:6 and no **o.** doubts what he believes he is.
M-13 ......... 4:4 **o.** whose vision has already glimpsed the
M-13 ......... 4:5 No **o.** who has escaped the world and all
M-13 ......... 5:4 and no **o.** asks for pain if he recognizes it.
M-13 ......... 5:8 and no **o.** who pursues the world's goals
M-13 ......... 6:2 In **o.** sense this is true, for you hold dear
M-14 ......... 1:4 of forgiveness, complete, excluding no **o.**,
M-14 ....... 2:10 When not **o.** thought of sin remains, the
M-14 ......... 3:2 **o.** thought of sin remains" appears to be a
M-14 ......... 3:4 **o.** thought of sin will remain the instant
M-14 ......... 3:4 **o.** of them accepts Atonement for himself.
M-14 ......... 3:5 to forgive **o.** sin than to forgive all of them
M-14 ......... 3:7 **O.** sin perfectly forgiven by one teacher of
M-14 ......... 3:7 One sin perfectly forgiven by **o.** teacher of
M-15 ............ h EACH **O.** TO BE JUDGED IN THE END?
M-15 ......... 1:2 No **o.** can escape God's Final Judgment.

| | |
|---|---|
| M-15..........1:5 | **O.** day each one will welcome it, and on |
| M-15..........1:5 | One day each **o.** will welcome it, and on |
| M-15..........2:6 | **O.** instant of complete belief in this, and |
| M-15..........2:7 | **O.** instant out of time can bring time's |
| M-16..........1:3 | the teacher of God is sure of but **o.** thing; |
| M-16..........1:7 | Not **o.** is absent whom he needs; not one |
| M-16..........1:7 | **o.** is sent without a learning goal already |
| M-16..........1:7 | and **o.** which can be learned that very day. |
| M-16..........2:4 | although each **o.** must use them as best he |
| M-16..........4:5 | **O.** can easily sit still an hour with closed |
| M-16..........4:6 | **O.** can as easily give God only an instant, |
| M-16..........4:7 | the **o.** generalization that can be made is |
| M-16..........6:1 | is **o.** thought in particular that should be |
| M-16..........7:7 | places, because they are all **o.** to God. This |
| M-16........10:7 | Perhaps he prefers other words, or only **o.** |
| M-16........10:9 | two aspects of **o.** error and no more, he |
| M-16........11:8 | by just **o.** simple-minded illusion;–that it |
| M-17..........3:2 | and pupil, who have shared in **o.** intent. |
| M-17..........3:5 | divided goal of the pupil into **o.** direction, |
| M-17..........3:5 | the call for help becoming his **o.** appeal. |
| M-17..........3:6 | is easily responded to with just **o.** answer, |
| M-17..........3:7 | his pupil's mind, making it **o.** with his. |
| M-17..........4:1 | remember that no **o.** can be angry at a fact |
| M-17..........6:3 | then, can **o.** believe in one's defenses? |
| M-17..........7:3 | go. Each **o.** says clearly to your frightened |
| M-18..........2:4 | the world of sinlessness, the **o.** unchanged |
| M-18..........3:6 | Correction has **o.** answer to all this, and |
| M-19..........1:7 | for no **o.** in the world is capable of making |
| M-19..........2:2 | the **o.** interpretation that leads to truth. |
| M-19..........2:4 | truth; **o.** is but the first small step in the |
| M-19..........2:5 | becomes quite different as **o.** goes along. |
| M-19..........2:6 | rise to meet **o.** as the journey continues, |
| M-19..........2:7 | indescribable heights as **o.** proceeds, fall |
| M-19..........2:8 | it. But somewhere **o.** must start. Justice is |
| M-19..........3:5 | for not **o.** "sin" but seems forever true. |
| M-19..........4:5 | forever like its Creator, being **o.** with Him. |
| M-19..........5:7 | From this **o.** standpoint does it judge, and |
| M-20..........2:2 | peace is recognized at first by just **o.** thing |
| M-20..........3:2 | No **o.** can fail to find it who but seeks out |
| M-20..........4:3 | War is again accepted as the **o.** reality. |
| M-20..........5:8 | In this **o.** sentence is our course explained |
| M-20..........5:9 | In this **o.** sentence is our practicing given |
| M-20..........5:9 | is our practicing given its **o.** direction. |
| M-20........5:10 | And in this **o.** sentence is the Holy Spirit's |
| M-21..........3:3 | in the perception of the **o.** who asks. If he |
| M-22..........1:3 | **o.** complete concept possible in this world |
| M-22..........7:2 | can say which **o.** can be healed of what, |
| M-23..........2:1 | We have repeatedly said that **o.** who has |
| M-23..........3:9 | can one who is **o.** with God be unlike Him |
| M-23..........6:1 | No **o.** on earth can grasp what Heaven is, |
| M-23..........6:1 | is, or what its **o.** Creator really means. Yet |
| M-23..........6:6 | on us. No **o.** who has become a true and |
| M-24..........6:2 | it. This is still your **o.** responsibility. |
| M-25..........1:1 | this question is much like the preceding **o.** |
| M-25..........1:6 | directed toward this **o.** great final surprise |
| M-25..........3:7 | and no **o.** has any powers that are not |
| M-26..........2:5 | No **o.** can call on them in vain. Nor is |
| M-26..........4:8 | and not **o.** need you have will not be met. |
| M-27..........1:4 | It is the **o.** fixed, unchangeable belief of |
| M-27..........1:7 | no **o.** asks if a benign Creator could will |
| M-27..........4:8 | **o.** can be acceptable to God's teachers, |
| M-27..........4:8 | because not **o.** could be acceptable to God |
| M-27..........6:4 | All dreams will end with this **o.**. This is |
| M-27..........7:1 | your **o.** assignment could be stated thus: |
| M-29..........2:4 | No **o.** should attempt to answer these |
| M-29..........3:1 | advantage,–and a very important **o.,–in** |
| C-in............3:9 | It has **o.** function and one goal. Only in |
| C-in............3:9 | It has one function and **o.** goal. Only in |
| C-1.............1:4 | The unified spirit is God's **o.** Son, or |
| C-2.............5:3 | and cause and its effects must still be **o.**. |
| C-2.............9:1 | which asks of everyone **o.** question only: |
| C-3.............1:3 | is the Holy Spirit's, it has **o.** difference. |
| C-3.............4:4 | No **o.** can look on knowledge. But the face |
| C-4.............3:2 | **o.** correction possible for false perception |
| C-4.............3:6 | Atonement, true perception, all are **o.**. |
| C-4.............3:7 | They are the **o.** beginning, with the end to |
| C-4.............6:7 | lie together, side by side, upon **o.** altar. |
| C-4.............6:8 | remedy joined in **o.** healing brightness. |
| C-5.............1:3 | forms, although upon the altar they are **o.** |
| C-5.............1:4 | Beyond each **o.** there is a Thought of God, |
| C-5.............2:2 | *Christ*, a man no longer, but at **o.** with God |
| C-5.............3:1 | of God, His **o.** creation and His happiness |
| C-5.............4:4 | And shares them still, to be at **o.** with you. |
| C-6.............1:2 | Spirit, being a creation of the **o.** Creator, |
| C-ep...........1:4 | No **o.** can fail to do what God appointed |
| C-ep...........1:8 | Behind each **o.** there is reality and there is |
| P-1.............1:3 | rests. No **o.** in this world escapes fear, but |
| P-1.............5:6 | is **o.** of the means He uses to save time, |
| P-2.........in.1:5 | the patient deal with **o.** fundamental error |
| P-2.........in.4:2 | task of therapy is **o.** of reconciling these |
| P-2...........I.1:3 | for no **o.** learns beyond his own readiness. |
| P-2...........I.1:4 | or patient has reached the next **o.**, there |
| P-2...........I.1:9 | overall direction is **o.** of progress toward |
| P-2...........I.2:2 | is **o.** of the errors which the ego fosters; |
| P-2...........I.3:6 | become completely reconciled as **o.** until |
| P-2...........I.4:2 | And this will **o.** day come to pass for every |
| P-2.........II.1:3 | for **o.** who had achieved that point could |
| P-2.........II.2:2 | to join contradictory words into **o.** term |
| P-2.........II.2:5 | At the highest levels they become **o.**. |
| P-2.........II.3:1 | No **o.** who learns to forgive can fail to |
| P-2.........II.3:5 | all its forces against this **o.** awareness, for |
| P-2.........II.4:7 | without knowledge **o.** can have only belief |
| P-2.........II.5:3 | if pupil and teacher join in sharing **o.** goal |
| P-2.........II.5:7 | out, for no **o.** will find sanity alone. |
| P-2.........II.7:2 | no good teacher uses **o.** approach to every |
| P-2.........II.7:3 | contrary, he listens patiently to each **o.**, |
| P-2.........II.8:3 | Only **o.** thing; the same requirement |
| P-2.........II.8:4 | **o.** must share one goal with someone else, |
| P-2.........II.8:4 | one must share **o.** goal with someone else, |
| P-2.........II.9:2 | alone. No **o.** who stands apart can receive |
| P-2.........II.9:5 | need as his and see that they are met as **o.**, |
| P-2.........II.9:8 | for they are **o.** in purpose and must thus |
| P-2.........II.9:8 | in purpose and must thus be **o.** in means. |
| P-2........III.2:5 | may come from either **o.** at the beginning, |
| P-2........III.3:4 | **O.** asks for help; another hears and tries |
| P-2........III.3:7 | **O.** wholly egoless therapist could heal the |
| P-2........III.3:8 | No **o.** need see him or talk to him or even |
| P-2........III.4:1 | The ideal therapist is **o.** with Christ. But |
| P-2........IV.4:2 | For not **o.** of them can cure, and not one |
| P-2........IV.4:2 | and not **o.** of them understands healing. |
| P-2......IV.4:10 | cure? Are not these both **o.** question? |
| P-2........IV.6:4 | into which the old **o.** cannot return. In a |
| P-2........IV.8:2 | **O.** of the illusions by which sickness is |
| P-2........IV.9:2 | he will attack the **o.** who tries to save him |
| P-2........IV.9:3 | of attack-defense is **o.** of the most difficult |
| P-2........IV.9:5 | therapist is seen as **o.** who is attacking the |
| P-2....IV.11:10 | The truth is simple, being **o.** for all. |
| P-2.........V.1:3 | to be safe, **o.** must control the unknown. |
| P-2.........V.4:2 | is holier than helping **o.** who asks for help |
| P-2.........V.7:5 | truth will come to us only through **o.** who |
| P-2.........V.8:2 | There is **o.** way alone by which we come |
| P-2........VI.4:1 | the senses bring have but **o.** purpose; to |
| P-2........VI.5:2 | of **o.** but reproduce the forms of the other, |
| P-2........VI.5:3 | So closely is **o.** translated into the other, |
| P-2........VI.5:5 | That is achieved by only **o.** recognition; |
| P-2........VI.6:7 | go. Let him retain **o.** spot of sin in what he |
| P-2........VI.7:1 | No **o.** is healed alone. This is the joyous |
| P-2........VI.7:5 | in which they meet and join and are as **o.**. |
| P-2.....VII.1:12 | What He knows is only that He has **o.** Son |
| P-2.......VII.3:1 | in this relationship is actually **o.** in which |
| P-2.......VII.4:1 | **o.** thing and one thing only is required: |
| P-2.......VII.4:1 | one thing and **o.** thing only is required: |
| P-2.......VII.4:2 | confusion in **o.** form or another, because |
| P-2.......VII.5:4 | a knowledge that no **o.** here can have; a |
| P-2.......VII.5:6 | nor is the tiny self of **o.** alone against the |
| P-2.......VII.6:1 | has given you as to invent **o.** He has not. |
| P-2.......VII.7:7 | he give to **o.** who seems to be a stranger; |
| P-2.......VII.8:3 | The same are **o.**, and nothing now can be |
| P-3...........I.1:3 | mean that no **o.** comes to you by mistake. |
| P-3...........I.4:1 | teacher of God, never forgets **o.** thing; he |
| P-3.........II.1:2 | could a separate profession be **o.** in which |
| P-3.........II.1:4 | **o.** sort or another as their chief function. |
| P-3.........II.4:6 | relationship is not **o.** Relationship. Yet it |
| P-3.........II.7:3 | brother from **o.** dream than from another |
| P-3.........II.9:1 | professional therapist has **o.** advantage |
| P-3........III.1:1 | No **o.** can pay for therapy, for healing is |
| P-3........III.1:7 | But no **o.** here can live with no illusions, |
| P-3........III.1:8 | He has a mighty part in this **o.** purpose, |
| P-3........III.4:1 | to live is something no **o.** need fight for. It |
| P-3........III.4:4 | whatever **o.** needs is given by the other; |
| P-3........III.4:4 | other; whatever **o.** lacks the other supplies |
| P-3........III.6:1 | **O.** rule should always be observed: No |
| P-3........III.6:1 | No **o.** should be turned away because he |
| P-3........III.6:2 | pay. No **o.** is sent by accident to anyone. |
| P-3......III.6:10 | Only in terms of cost could **o.** have more. |
| P-3........III.7:2 | not **o.** worldly thought is really practical. |
| S-1.........in.2:2 | You have but **o.**. What God created one |
| S-1.........in.2:3 | God created **o.** must recognize its oneness |
| S-1.........in.2:3 | separate is **o.** forever in the Mind of God. |
| S-1...........I.2:2 | there is only **o.** problem and one answer. |
| S-1...........I.2:2 | there is only one problem and **o.** answer. |
| S-1...........I.5:5 | giving up of yourself to be at **o.** with Love. |
| S-1...........I.6:5 | **O.** who has realized the goodness of God |
| S-1...........I.6:6 | And **o.** who prays without fear cannot but |
| S-1...........I.7:7 | pray with **o.** who knows that this is true is |
| S-1...........I.7:9 | if you are genuinely attuned to **o.** another. |
| S-1..........II.2:2 | is. No **o.**, then, who is sure of his Identity |
| S-1..........II.2:3 | also true that no **o.** who is uncertain of his |
| S-1..........II.4:7 | Identity. Be traitor to no **o.**, or you will be |
| S-1..........II.8:3 | for a ladder to reach what **o.** has never left |
| S-1........III.2:3 | come from **o.** who understands that they |
| S-1........III.6:4 | **O.** need not ask explicitly. The goal of |
| S-1........III.6:7 | No **o.** who wants an enemy will fail to find |
| S-1........III.6:7 | who wants an enemy will fail to find **o.**. |
| S-1........IV.1:1 | at least begins, **o.** cannot share in prayer. |
| S-1........IV.1:2 | each **o.** must ask for different things. But |
| S-1........IV.2:8 | For no **o.** can receive effects alone, asking |
| S-1........IV.3:2 | satisfied; all separate wishes unified in **o.**. |
| S-1.........V.2:2 | Where **o.** has come the other disappears. |
| S-1.......V.3:12 | you, who seemed alone, are **o.** with him. |
| S-2...........I.4:5 | the only **o.** that does not lead to death. |
| S-2...........I.5:2 | is evil, and in his sin you are the injured **o.** |
| S-2...........I.8:2 | is the choice you make; the simplest **o.**, |
| S-2...........I.8:2 | one, and yet the only **o.** that you *can* make. |
| S-2..........II.2:1 | to save a "baser" **o.** from what he truly is. |
| S-2..........II.3:2 | The **o.** who would forgive the other does |
| S-2..........II.3:3 | that here is **o.** whose sinfulness he shares, |
| S-2..........II.5:3 | that it offers **o.** who could be savior, not |
| S-2..........II.5:6 | Or is it rather treachery to **o.** who needs |
| S-2........III.1:1 | Forgiveness-for-salvation has **o.** form, |
| S-2........III.1:1 | has one form, and only **o.**. It does not ask |
| S-2........III.4:8 | you are **o.** with Him in Will and purpose. |
| S-2......III.5:10 | He is the Answer. You the **o.** who hears. |
| S-3...........I.3:3 | which sickness should be seen as **o.**. |
| S-3..........II.1:1 | exchange of **o.** illusion for a "nicer" one; a |
| S-3..........II.1:1 | exchange of one illusion for a "nicer" **o.**; a |
| S-3........II.1:11 | as **o.** lays by a garment now outworn. |
| S-3........III.1:4 | Nor is it made by **o.** who understands the |
| S-3........III.1:6 | has, not equally bestowed on both as **o.**. |
| S-3........III.2:5 | give healing to the **o.** who stands beneath |
| S-3........III.2:8 | appears to be to find a wiser **o.** who, by |
| S-3........III.3:2 | And to this wiser **o.** another goes to profit |
| S-3........III.4:1 | **o.** can use to offer help for someone else? |
| S-3........III.4:6 | oneness with the **o.** who calls for help. For |
| S-3........III.5:1 | all their Source creates is **o.** with them. |
| S-3........III.6:6 | is no fear in **o.** who has been truly healed, |

## one's 7

| | |
|---|---|
| T-6.........in.1:2 | be accepted as **o.** own responsibility, |
| W-pII .325.1:3 | esteemed as real and guarded as **o.** own. |
| M-in..........1:4 | a relatively small proportion of **o.** time. |
| M-4.........I.2:1 | to trust **o.** own petty strength again. Who |
| M-9...........2:6 | world trains for reliance on **o.** judgment |
| M-17.........6:3 | How, then, can one believe in **o.** defenses? |
| S-1..........II.4:1 | terms known as "praying for **o.** enemies." |

## one-dimensional 1

| | |
|---|---|
| T-13.........I.8:3 | have done, and thus depends on **o.** time, |

## One-mindedness 5

| | |
|---|---|
| T-3.........IV.3:3 | because only **O.** can be without confusion |
| T-4.......II.10:1 | which is not the **O.** of the Holy Spirit, but |
| T-4.......II.10:1 | must be achieved before **O.** is restored. |
| T-5...........I.6:4 | to **O.** that transfer to it is at last possible. |

C-1 ... 6:3 it is not the *O.* of the Christ Mind, Whose

## one-to-one 1

P-3 ... II.4:6 A o. relationship is not one Relationship.

## Oneness 25

*oneness*

T-2 ... VII.6:3 Sonship in its O. transcends the sum of its
T-7 ... VI.10:4 The O. of the Creator and the creation is
T-8 ... III.3:2 Their extension is the result of Their O.,
T-8 ... V.3:1 God's O. and ours are not separate,
T-8 ... V.3:1 because His O. encompasses ours. To join
T-8 ... IX.7:3 the works of love because we share this O.
T-9 ... VI.5:5 its O. it will be known by its creations,
T-11 ... I.11:8 be One, and united with Him in His O..
T-13 ... III.12:3 knowing that your peace lies in His O.?
T-14 ... XI.11:3 does God proclaim His O. and His Son's.
T-15 ... V.2:7 to deny the O. of the Father and His Son,
T-15 ... XI.2:7 alien to His O. can abide with Him there.
T-16 ... IV.8:6 is the acceptance of the O. of creation,
T-18 ... VI.1:6 It is merely an awareness of perfect O.,
T-18 ... VI.1:6 is nothing else; nothing outside this O.,
T-24 ... II.3:6 the O. which created them as one with
T-24 ... V.9:4 One with you, and that this O. is endless,
T-25 ... I.7:1 of a O. joined as One is meaningless. It is
T-25 ... I.7:2 of a O. which unites all things within Itself
T-28 ... IV.7:1 is no gap that separates His O. from Itself.
T-31 ... IV.10:3 and in Their O. Both are kept complete.
W-pI ... 83.3:3 They come from O., and must be received
W-pI ... 137.3:6 to attack the universal O. of God's Son.
W-pI. 139.10:1 and demonstrates the O. of God's Son is
W-pI. 139.12:1 and His O. with all aspects of creation, we

## oneness 53

*Oneness*

T-3 ... VII.6:8 Only the o. of knowledge is free of conflict
T-5 ... I.1:1 minds perceive their o. and become glad.
T-5 ... II.11:2 it back into the o. in which it was created.
T-6 ... V.C.8:2 to hold its o. in your mind because, if you
T-10 ... IV.3:3 O. cannot be divided. If you perceive
T-11 ... VI.10:5 equal value, and their equality is their o..
T-13 ... I.6:2 him as guiltless can you understand his o.
T-13 ... III.5:3 seems more valuable than your living o.,
T-13 ... VIII.7:6 to it by re-establishing its o. in your mind.
T-14 ... III.8:6 this o. only when you learn to deny the
T-14 ... VII.7:7 you will bring this o. to your mind with
T-14 ... VIII.3:4 They are joined in giving you the gift of o.,
T-14 ... VIII.4:10 in the o. out of which creation happens.
T-14 ... XI.11:5 Him. For He teaches the miracle of o., and
T-15 ... II.1:10 one, so its o. depends not on time at all.
T-18 ... VIII.6:6 life *is* the o. in which its being was created.
T-22 ... VI.12:1 were one with God and recognized this o.,
T-25 ... I.5:5 to make the o. clear to what is really one.
T-25 ... I.6:4 to teach you how this o. is experienced,
T-26 ... I.h The "Sacrifice" of O.
T-26 ... I.2:1 world you see is based on "sacrifice" of o..
T-26 ... I.6:1 You can lose sight of o., but can not make
T-26 ... III.1:4 Son. Nothing conflicts with o.. How, then,
T-26 ... III.1:9 and bring complexity where o. is? The
T-26 ... III.1:11 a necessary step in the advance toward o..
T-26 ... III.3:5 one continues past the gate where o. is.
T-28 ... VII.2:5 not at all, its o. being where the healing is.
W-pI ... 57.5:6 including myself, and their o. with me.
W-pI ... 83.4:3 *o. of my happiness and my function remains*
W-pI ... 95.2:4 It does not see the o. in you, for it is blind.
W-pI ... 95.12:2 to bring awareness of this o. to all minds,
W-pI ... 127.3:3 Its meaning lies in o.. And it must elude
W-pI ... 169.5:1 O. is simply the idea God is. And in His
W-pI ... 169.9:1 For o. must be here. Whatever time the
W-pI. 169.10:2 When revelation of your o. comes, it will
W-pI. 184.15:8 *in the o. which is our inheritance and peace.*
W-pI ... 201.1:3 *blessed with o. with the universe and God,*
W-pII. 225.2:5 are one, and it is but this o. that we seek,
W-pII ... 2.2:4 still was one, but failed to recognize its o..
W-pII ... 5.2:4 For if his o. still remained untouched,
W-pII ... 9.2:4 as one. And thus is o. recognized at last.
W-pII ... 11.3:3 Its o. is forever guaranteed inviolate;
W-pII ... 11.4:5 their o. and their unity with their Creator.
W-pII ... 14.4:4 And from the o. that we have attained we
W-pII. 354.1:1 *My o. with the Christ establishes me as Your*
M-12 ... 6:1 O. and sickness cannot coexist. God's
C-4 ... 3:7 end to lead to o. far beyond themselves.
C-5 ... 6:3 names until their o. can be recognized.
P-2 ... VII.5:2 In this their o. can be clearly seen. Yet
S-1 ... in.2:3 God created one must recognize its o.,
S-3 ... III.4:6 your o. with the one who calls for help.
S-3 ... III.4:7 in this o. is his separate sense dispelled,
S-3 ... IV.2:4 here, for love has come in all its holy o..

## ones 65

T-3 ... IV.7:14 "chosen o." are merely those who choose
T-9 ... V.4:1 ego's plan are as unhelpful as the older o.,
T-14 ... V.1:2 to share with all the lonely o. who have
T-14 ... XI.5:6 will replace the dark o. you do not accept,
T-16 ... I.6:7 recognizes foolish needs as well as real o..
T-16 ... IV.4:5 is sure that those who select certain o. as
T-16 ... V.3:5 natural at all seem to be the unnatural o..
T-19 ... III.11:3 where all the weary o. can come and rest.
T-21 ... VII.2:5 it? These are the dark o., silent and afraid,
T-21 ... VII.3:1 loud and strong the dark o. seem to be.
T-22 ... I.6:7 shifting o. he sees about him will become
T-22 ... I.8:6 never could He find a home in separate o.
T-23 ... II.10:2 do the guilty o. protest their "innocence."
T-24 ... I.4:5 The special o. feel weak and frail because
T-24 ... III.7:1 The special o. are all asleep, surrounded
T-25 ... VI.3:6 lonely o. are those who see no function in
T-25 . VIII.5:10 He demanded of the o. obsessed with the
T-26 ... VI.1:8 can choose to keep the o. that he prefers,
T-27 ... IV.4:6 Which o. establish peace and offer joy?
T-30 ... I.1:3 a little practice with the o. you recognize,
T-30 ... IV.1:7 but false ideas, and never truthful o.. All
T-31 ... III.6:6 changing love, the o. you think are friends
T-31 ... VII.8:3 the holy o. especially entrusted to his care
T-31 .. VII.10:5 The holy o. whom God has given you to
T-31 . VIII.10:1 for these holy o. who are my brothers as
W-pI ... 3.1:1 idea in the same way as the previous o.,
W-pI ... 4.1:1 Unlike the preceding o., these exercises
W-pI ... 4.2:4 "good" o. are but shadows of what lies
W-pI ... 4.2:5 The "bad" o. are blocks to sight, and
W-pI ... 5.4:1 exercises, more than in the preceding o.,
W-pI ... 6.1:1 idea are very similar to the preceding o..
W-pI ... 7.1:2 is the rationale for all of the preceding o..
W-pI ... 9.1:1 follows from the two preceding o.. But
W-pI ... 11.2:1 differently from the previous o.. Begin
W-pI ... 13.2:1 intense anxiety in all the separated o.. It
W-pI ... 13.4:1 different way from the preceding o.. With
W-pI ... 29.1:4 thus far, and all subsequent o. as well.
W-pI ... 32.2:1 The idea for today, like the preceding o.,
W-pI ... 40.1:2 but very frequent short o. are necessary.
W-pI ... 41.1:1 and abandonment all the separated o.
W-pI ... 41.2:1 separated o. have invented many "cures"
W-pI ... 46.3:1 and as many shorter o. as possible. Begin
W-pI ... 47.4:2 longer and more frequent o. are urged.
W-pI ... 53.1:4 I have real thoughts as well as insane o.. I
W-pI ... 75.3:1 Our exercises for today will be happy o.,
W-pI ... 78.10:3 the o. you think of or remember from the
W-pI ... 78.10:4 you both, and all the sightless o. as well,
W-pI ... 79.5:4 think you have resolved the previous o..
WpI..rII.in.1:4 frequent shorter o. in which we practice
W-pI ... 96.9:6 are your thoughts, the only o. you have.
W-pI ... 105.2:4 and leaves you nothing in the o. you take.
W-pI ... 124.6:2 as in the o. who walk beside them now.
W-pI. 132.16:1 world, as well as to the o. you see nearby,
W-pI ... 137.8:4 unlike the o. which hold that sickness is
W-pI ... 137.9:2 replace the o. you made to hold yourself a
W-pI. 153.10:6 o. who are among the chosen ones of God
W-pI. 153.10:6 ones who are among the chosen o. of God
W-pI ... 154.5:3 it, give it to the o. for whom it is intended,
W-pI ... 155.1:4 And the o. who walk the world as you do
W-pI ... 187.9:1 with the o. you offer him beside them.
W-pII. 242.1:4 choices for me but the o. that lead to God.
M-1 ... 2:3 They are the o. who have answered. The
M-25 ... 1:6 little o. that may come to him on the way.
M-29 ... 1:2 it covers only a few of the more obvious o.
P-2 ... V.2:1 Let us remember that the o. who come to

## oneself 4

T-12 ... II.1:2 If to love o. is to heal oneself, those who
T-12 ... II.1:2 If to love oneself is to heal o., those who
M-4 ... IV.1:5 guilt upon a brother, and therefore on o..
M-28 ... 1:3 the acceptance of the Atonement for o.. It

## ongoing 2

T-6 ... V.1:6 Giving His joy is an o. process, not in
T-7 ... I.1:3 This is an o. process in which you share,

## only 1853

## onslaught 1

W-pI .. 190.8:5 and little joys give way before the o. of the

## onto 16

T-2 ... VIII.5:1 only because it has been projected o. God
T-3 ... VI.8:2 and project your delusion o. others. You
T-4 ... III.4:5 project o. the ego the decision to separate,
T-6 ... I.9:3 because of the projection of others o. me,
T-7 ... II.3:3 from what you have projected o. others,
T-7 ... VI.3:9 threatened by projecting the threat o. *you,*
T-7 ... VIII.5:3 for your belief in it o. anyone else, or you
T-9 ... V.3:5 Projecting condemnation o. God, they
T-10 ... III.8:6 are projecting o. them the fearful fact that
T-13 ... X.1:3 displaced the guilt o. what you believed to
W-pI ... 22.1:2 Having projected his anger o. the world,
W-pI ... 72.5:9 be death, projecting this attack o. God,
W-pI .. 189.7:3 Hold o. nothing. Do not bring with you
M-17 ... 6:11 is. Projecting your "forgetting" o. Him, it
M-19 ... 4:7 O. this,–a Judgment wholly lacking in
S-1 ... III.5:6 Do not hold on to it, nor o. him. He is a

## onward 1

W-pI .. 109.3:2 and death, and o. to the certainty of God.

## opaque 1

T-18 ... IX.5:2 that seems to make it heavy and o.,

## open 172

*See also* open-eyed, open-minded, open-mindedness

T-1 ... II.5:3 channel from God to you o. for revelation
T-2 ... IV.3:7 it is not inherently o. to misinterpretation
T-3 ... IV.1:2 are divided and o. to question and doubt.
T-3 ... IV.2:5 sure of. Everything else *is* o. to question.
T-3 ... V.5:1 Knowing is not o. to interpretation. You
T-3 ... V.5:2 always o. to error because it refers to the
T-4 ... I.4:7 of your thought system and o. it to me, I
T-4 ... II.4:8 and as long as your origin is o. to belief
T-4 ... II.8:3 however, to o. the premise to question,
T-5 ... I.4:5 is o. to different interpretations. As a man
T-5 ... I.7:3 of attack and is therefore truly o.. This
T-5 ... III.1:3 of thinking would not be o. to healing. He
T-5 ... III.11:4 Correct and learn, and be o. to learning.
T-5 ... V.6:8 and the ego are the only choices o. to you.
T-6 ... V.1:5 channels are not o. to Him, so that He
T-7 ... X.4:5 that an impossible choice is o. to you, and
T-7 ... X.6:6 His Will with me is not really o. to choice,
T-8 ... VII.16:8 you will o. your mind to creation in God.
T-9 ... VI.7:2 to you until you remember God's o. Arms
T-9 ... VI.7:2 open Arms, and finally know His o. Mind
T-9 ... VI.7:4 His. In your o. mind are your creations, in
T-9 ... VII.6:8 o. the whole thought system to question.
T-11 ... in.3:9 O. the dark cornerstone of terror on
T-11 ... IV.6:5 cannot bar the door that Christ holds o..
T-11 ... IV.6:6 Come unto me who hold it o. for you, for
T-12 ... II.4:7 refusing to o. your eyes and look at them.
T-12 ... VI.4:2 o. the eyes of the blind is the Holy Spirit's
T-12 ... VI.4:4 Christ's eyes are o., and He will look upon

T-13......IV.3:8 An **o.** mind is more honest than this.
T-13.......V.6:1 As you look with **o.** eyes upon your world
T-13. VIII.10:6 the gates of Heaven, God will **o.** them. For
T-14....... II.6:4 The universe of learning will **o.** up before
T-14....... II.7:2 and **o.** up the way to freedom for you. For
T-14......VI.8:5 must **o.** all doors and let the light come
T-14......VI.8:7 Its gates are **o.** wide to greet His Son. No
T-14.....VII.6:2 **O.** every door to Him, and bid Him enter
T-14.....VII.6:4 if you make the darkness **o.** to Him. But
T-14..... X.11:2 is perfectly **o.** and freely accessible to all,
T-14......XI.4:6 joyously laid down by hands **o.** to receive,
T-15......III.1:7 Littleness and glory are the choices **o.** to
T-15......IV.6:6 that it is a time in which your mind is **o.**,
T-15... VIII.5:5 channel **o.** to receive His communication
T-16......IV.1:4 before your **o.** eyes as you look on this.
T-16..IV.13:10 The way to truth is **o.**. Follow it with me.
T-16....... V.2:2 the Sonship **o.** to attack and unprotected
T-17....... II.2:2 everything sparkling under the **o.** sun.
T-18.....VII.7:3 quick and **o.** door through which you slip
T-19....... II.2:5 Will of God **o.** to opposition and defeat.
T19...IV.D.8:4 It does not **o.** up its secrets, and bid you
T-20..... II.8:12 only a pathway to the **o.** door of Heaven,
T-20..... II.11:3 as you behold the **o.** door of Heaven and
T-20......IV.8:1 must be done before the way to peace is **o.**
T-20....VI.10:5 way to true relationships held gently **o.**,
T-20....VI.10:6 Love's Arms are **o.** to receive you, and
T-20... VIII.1:3 **O.** the holy place that you closed off by
T-20. VIII.11:1 to quiet views of gardens under **o.** skies,
T-21.........I.1:2 walk unharmed through **o.** doorways that
T-21.........I.1:5 but which stand **o.** before unseeing eyes,
T-21.........I.2:4 is. You can be shown which doors are **o.**,
T-21....... II.7:2 left **o.** and unoccupied the altar where the
T-21......IV.8:8 The quiet way is **o.**. Follow it happily, and
T-21....... V.9:5 can serve to **o.** doors you closed against it.
T-22.........I.6:1 course alone is **o.** to your understanding
T-22......IV.4:4 The gates of Heaven, **o.** now for you, will
T-22......IV.4:4 for you, will you now **o.** to the sorrowful.
T-22......IV.5:6 received. God's offer still is **o.**, yet it waits
T-23...... I.10:3 **O.** the door of His most holy home, and
T-23......III.6:3 it is over. The door is **o.**; you have left the
T-24......III.3:1 *you* who are so vulnerable and **o.** to attack
T-24......III.7:7 **O.** your eyes a little; see the savior God
T-24....IV.3:15 an **o.** door inviting everything that would
T-27.........I.9:9 to nothing yet, its purpose being **o.**, and
T-28....... II.5:1 An empty storehouse, with an **o.** door,
T-28......III.7:2 The door is **o.**, not to thieves, but to your
T-28......III.7:3 They have nothing left behind the **o.** door
T-28......III.8:7 The door is **o.**, that all those may come
T-29.....VII.8:1 and **o.** up a road of hope and of release in
T-30...... I.12:2 It is a statement of an **o.** mind, not certain
T-30.....VII.1:6 each one be **o.** to interpretation which is
T-31......III.7:3 **O.** your mind to change, and there will be
T-31....... V.3:4 and at last to **o.** insult and abuse.
T-31..... V.17:3 unsealed and **o.** mind that truth returns,
T-31...VII.11:6 his calm and **o.** eyes and what he sees. He
T-31...VII.13:3 at all. And thus it serves a wholly **o.** mind,
T-31...VII.13:7 And the door held **o.** for the face of Christ
W-pI.......3.2:2 essential that you keep a perfectly **o.** mind
W-pI.....11.2:3 Then **o.** your eyes and look about, near
W-pI.....12.2:1 These exercises are done with eyes **o.**.
W-pI.....13.4:3 Then **o.** your eyes, and look about you
W-pI.....17.2:1 today's idea, say to yourself, with eyes **o.**: *I*
W-pI.....28.3:1 the table, and **o.** your mind to what it is,
W-pI.....28.5:1 look upon it with a completely **o.** mind. It
W-pI.....30.1:2 this idea will the world **o.** up before you,
W-pI.....36.3:2 Then **o.** your eyes and look quite slowly
W-pI...36.3:11 Then **o.** your eyes, and continue as before
W-pI.....37.5:1 you may **o.** your eyes again and apply the
W-pI.....37.5:2 following immediately, with your eyes **o.**.
W-pI.....41.8:4 The way will **o.**, if you believe that it is
W-pI.....42.4:1 idea for today slowly, with your eyes **o.**,
W-pI.....42.5:5 **o.** your eyes and repeat the thought once
W-pI.....42.6:3 slow repetitions of the idea with eyes **o.**,
W-pI.....43.4:3 the idea for today to yourself with eyes **o.**.
W-pI.....43.6:1 unable to think of anything, **o.** your eyes,
W-pI.....44.7:1 repeating today's idea with your eyes **o.**,
W-pI.....44.9:2 it more reassuring to **o.** your eyes briefly.
W-pI...44.11:1 eyes **o.** or closed as seems better to you at
W-pI.....48.2:3 eyes **o.** at any time and in any situation. It
W-pI.....49.4:2 Be very still and **o.** your mind. Go past all
W-pI.....49.5:2 Do so with your eyes **o.** when necessary,
W-pI.....55.5:7 it. Let me **o.** my mind to the world's real
W-pI.....57.1:5 The prison door is **o.**. I can leave simply
W-pI.....60.5:3 As I **o.** my eyes, His Love lights up the
W-pI.....64.8:3 your eyes **o.** after reviewing the thoughts,
W-pI.....65.8:4 sometimes keep them **o.** and look about
W-pI.....75.6:2 Keep a completely **o.** mind, washed of all
W-pI...76.11:1 Let us today **o.** God's channels to Him,
W-pI.....97.5:2 He will not overlook one **o.** mind that will
W-pI.....98.9:3 He will **o.** up the way to happiness, and
W-pI.....99.8:4 **O.** your secrets to His kindly light, and
W-pI...101.5:3 Accept Atonement with an **o.** mind,
W-pI...106.1:1 want; if you will listen with an **o.** mind,
W-pI...107.6:3 not hide. It stands in **o.** light, in obvious
W-pI...109.8:3 **O.** the temple doors and let them come
W-pI...122.5:3 it stands before you like an **o.** door, with
W-pI...122.8:1 **O.** your eyes today and look upon a
W-pI...122.8:3 quietness it rises up to greet your **o.** eyes,
W-pI...127.8:2 **O.** your mind and rest. The world that
W-pI...127.9:5 love's meaning to your clean and **o.** mind.
W-pI...128.7:7 **O.** your mind to Him. Be still and rest.
W-pI.131.12:2 find it. But before you try to **o.** it, remind
W-pI.131.13:1 see how easily the door swings **o.** with
W-pI.133.13:1 reached with empty hands and **o.** minds,
W-pI.133.14:1 of Heaven, which swings **o.** as he comes.
W-pI...134.8:5 this gift of you, the door is **o.** to yourself.
W-pI...134.9:1 and perceive it **o.** wide in welcome. When
W-pI...135.5:4 say your home is **o.** to the thief of time,
W-pI.136.16:1 Healing will flash across your **o.** mind, as
W-pI...138.9:4 had made before are **o.** to correction, as
WpI. rIV.in5:2 **O.** your mind, and clear it of all thoughts
W-pI...164.8:1 **O.** the curtain in your practicing by
W-pI...164.8:2 and leave a clean and **o.** space within your
W-pI...166.6:3 with him and **o.** up his treasures to be free
W-pI...169.3:4 an **o.** mind can hear the Call to waken. It
WpI...rV.in5:4 was sent to **o.** up the path of light to us,
W-pI.182.12:8 And now the way is **o.**, and the journey
W-pI.188.10:4 innocent, devoid of sin and **o.** to salvation
W-pI...189.9:4 And in our quiet hearts and **o.** minds, His
W-pI.189.10:6 *Our hands are* **o.** *to receive Your gifts. We*
W-pI...193.1:2 eternally **o.** and wholly limitless in Him.
W-pI...200.3:6 look with **o.** eyes to find that Heaven lies
W-pII..225.2:2 The way is **o.**. Now we follow it in peace
W-pII..226.2:2 *Your Arms are* **o.** *and I hear Your Voice.*
W-pII..236.2:1 *Father, my mind is* **o.** *to Your Thoughts,*
W-pII..242.2:2 *We come with wholly* **o.** *minds. We do not*
W-pII..290.1:2 see. Eyes that begin to **o.** see at last. And I
W-pII..306.2:2 *with empty hands and* **o.** *hearts and minds,*
W-pII..311.2:1 *Father, we wait with* **o.** *mind today, to hear*
W-pII..316.1:4 watch its **o.** doors that not one gift is lost,
W-pII....13.2:4 Now is perception **o.** to the truth. Now is
W-pII....14.5:5 the gate of Heaven stand **o.** before him,
WpII361-5.1:3 need but stillness and a tranquil, **o.** mind,
W-ep.........5:7 For we go homeward to an **o.** door which
M-2...........3:3 Choices made long since appear to be **o.**;
M-4.....I.A.8:6 here, the way to Heaven is **o.** and easy. In
M-4....... V.1:3 **o.** hands of gentleness are always filled.
M-17.........8:7 this is even dimly grasped, the way is **o.**.
P-in............1:6 start to **o.** his mind without formal help,
P-2........VI.6:3 at it, **o.** it to re-evaluation and forgive it.
P-3........III.8:4 to **o.** the door to your salvation, for such
S-1........IV.2:3 The way is **o.**, and hope is justified. Yet it
S-2........III.7:7 silently **o.** upon the shining face of Christ.
S-3........IV.7:3 My Arms are **o.** to the Son I love, who

## open-eyed 3

T-15.....VII.3:6 it. You have nothing to lose by looking **o.**,
T19...IV.D.7:4 Look upon it, **o.**, and you will nevermore
T-20......VI.2:7 walks in sunlight, **o.** and calm, in smiling

## open-minded 3

M-4....... X.1:6 Only the **o.** can be at peace, for they alone
M-4....... X.2:1 How do the **o.** forgive? They have let go
M-5......III.1:8 Nor are they **o.** on this point. The body

## open-mindedness 7

W-pI.....29.3:1 all things with love, appreciation and **o.**.
M-4.......... X.h Open-mindedness
M-4....... X.1:1 The centrality of **o.**, perhaps the last of
M-4....... X.1:2 **O.** comes with lack of judgment. As
M-4....... X.1:3 Teacher, so **o.** invites Him to come in. As
M-4....... X.1:4 **o.** permits him to be judged by the Voice
M-4....... X.1:5 **o.** lets Christ's image be extended to him.

## opened 12

T-17........II.4:1 that **o.** up the world to beauty will vanish.
T19....IV.B.5:5 How easily the gates are **o.** from within,
T-26.........I.8:4 special function to ensure the door be **o.**,
T-26...... IX.5:3 What has been locked is **o.**; what was held
T-30...... IV.2:2 springs up as a closed box is **o.** suddenly,
W-pI.....56.3:4 the door behind this world be **o.** for me,
W-pI...106.9:2 a thousand minds are **o.** to the truth and
W-pI...128.7:2 And when your eyes are **o.** afterwards,
W-pI.136.17:1 the source of sickness has been **o.** to relief
W-pI...155.5:4 on the way that God has **o.** up to you, and
W-pI...189.9:8 Through every **o.** door His Love shines
W-pII ....359.h joy. All prison doors are **o.**. And all sin Is

## opening 20

T-2........ III.2:3 **o.** of the altar to receive the Atonement.
T-15...... XI.1:6 as simple as **o.** your eyes to daylight when
T-26...... IV.6:1 back the happy **o.** of Heaven's gate. How
T-30.........I.9:4 tiny **o.** will be enough to let you go ahead
T-31....VIII.6:4 **o.** the way to his salvation and release.
W-pI.......8.3:3 is the first step to **o.** the way to vision.
W-pI.....15.3:4 are signs that you are **o.** your eyes at last.
W-pI.....24.2:3 for today is a step toward **o.** your mind so
W-pI.....80.2:3 **o.** the way for the Holy Spirit to give you
W-pI.110.10:4 and **o.** our hands and hearts and minds to
W-pI.126.11:6 **o.** your mind to His correction and His
W-pI...159.2:5 Receive them now by **o.** the storehouse of
W-pI.191.10:1 his sleep, and **o.** his holy eyes, return
W-pI...192.3:6 eyes already **o.** behold the joyful sights
W-pI...195.7:3 we would find, the way is **o.** at last to us.
W-pII .302.1:1 *Father, our eyes are* **o.** *at last. Your holy*
W-pII .321.1:7 *the way to You is* **o.** *and clear to me at last*
W-pII .342.1:8 *that I am Your Son, and* **o.** *the door at last,*
M-19.........2:6 the scene and the enormous **o.** vistas that
S-3..........II.5:4 such a view of what is merely **o.** the gate

## openly 1

T-24.........I.2:1 Beliefs will never **o.** attack each other

## openness 2

T-14...... VI.2:1 dwells within you is merely perfect **o.**, in
T-18.... VI.14:4 welcome you to **o.** of mind and freedom.

## opens 12

T-11........II.4:2 willingness **o.** your ears to the Voice of
T-22...... IV.6:4 and your brother lift together **o.** the way
T-26........II.8:4 special function **o.** wide the door beyond
T-26........ IV.1:4 justice past the gate that **o.** into Heaven.
W-pI.110.11:7 is the key that **o.** up the gate of Heaven,
W-pI...134.8:3 what is not there, it **o.** up the way to truth
W-pI...134.8:4 the way your true forgiveness **o.** up to you
W-pI.193.13:5 you hold the key that **o.** Heaven's gate,
W-pI...200.3:6 a door that **o.** easily to welcome you?
W-pII .336.1:4 and **o.** the hidden altar to the truth. Its
C-ep......... 1:11 Holy of the Holies **o.** up an ancient door
S-3..........II.6:4 At last the gate of Heaven **o.** and God's

## operate 9

T-7..........II.2:8 **o.** in this world is that by obeying them,
T-7......... IV.7:1 that is where the laws of God **o.** truly, and
T-7......... IV.7:1 **o.** only truly because they are the laws of
T-11....... V.2:6 Laws do not **o.** in a vacuum, and what
T-17....... IV.7:3 and as they **o.** they bring it to you. Every
T-17...... IV.7:8 Defenses **o.** to make you think you can.

T-19.........I.5:2 difference in how they **o.** is less apparent,
W-pI...135.2:1 You **o.** from the belief you must protect
W-pI...135.8:2 the mind can **o.** until its usefulness is over

**operates** 7

T-5........III.5:6 it at the same level on which the ego **o.**, or
T-7......VIII.1:2 mind, and therefore one that always **o.**. It
T-17......IV.7:4 Every defense **o.** by giving gifts, and the
W-pI.....17.1:1 cause and effect as it really **o.** in the world
W-pI.....20.5:6 law of cause and effect as it **o.** in the world
W-pI.....99.5:3 Yet it **o.** in time, because of your belief
W-pI...137.3:1 serves, but healing **o.** apart from them. It

**opinion** 3

W-pI...151.1:3 an **o.** based on ignorance and doubt. Its
M-10.........3:2 This is not an **o.** but a fact. In order to
M-21.........2:5 desired experience in the **o.** of the asker.

**opponent** 2

T-8...........I.3:2 Yet in this war there is no **o.**. This is the
M-17.......6:10 memory of Who your great "**o.**" really is.

**opponents** 2

T-8...........I.3:4 you perceive as **o.** are part of your peace,
T-13......XI.1:2 he believes that both **o.** in the war are real

**opportunities** 10

T-1........III.1:8 I will provide the **o.** to do them, but you
T-4........IV.8:1 many **o.** you have had to gladden yourself
T-5..........in.1:2 many **o.** you have had to gladden yourself
T-13......IV.6:5 **o.** you could find for release in the present
T-13......IV.7:7 and only "now" presents the **o.** for the
T-17....... V.8:2 will find many **o.** to blame your brother
M-2...........1:7 the **o.** to teach will be provided for him.
M-3...........5:2 him with unlimited **o.** for learning. These
P-2........VI.2:2 **o.** given us literally "to change our tune."
P-3........III.8:4 will give you endless **o.** to open the door

**opportunity** 9

T-7.......VII.2:1 he is offering you an **o.** to bless him. His
T-8.......III.5:4 anyone, you have another **o.** to find them.
T-14......III.6:2 to heal is another **o.** to replace darkness
T-14......III.6:4 he throws away the joyous **o.** to learn that
T-19.........I.2:1 becomes an **o.** to heal the Son of God.
W-pI.....63.4:2 Do not, however, wait for such an **o.**. No
W-pI.....82.4:3 *I would use this as an **o.** to fulfill my function.*
W-pI...121.7:1 **o.** to teach your own how to forgive itself.
M-25.........4:7 these same strengths an **o.** to glorify itself.

**oppose** 30

T-5.........I.4:10 ready to flow everywhere, but it cannot **o.**
T-5......... V.6:1 cannot **o.** the laws of God any more than
T-5........VI.2:9 will **o.** it at every possible moment and in
T-7........IV.6:1 can **o.** the Will of God is a real delusion.
T-8......... II.4:1 to teach that you want to **o.** God's Will.
T-8......IV.5:14 but I cannot **o.** your decision without
T-8........IV.6:1 God created can **o.** your decision, as
T-8........IV.6:1 as nothing God created can **o.** His Will.
T-11......IV.4:2 Do not **o.** this realization, for it is truly
T-11......IV.4:3 learn to recognize and to **o.** steadfastly,
T-12....... V.9:6 nothing can **o.** the decision of God's Son.
T-15......IV.8:5 come into a mind that has decided to **o.** it
T19. IV.A.2:11 little wall of hatred would still **o.** the Will
T19... IV.A.3:3 You still **o.** the Will of God, just by a little.
T19... IV.A.9:2 Can it **o.** an eagle's flight, or hinder the
T-22....... II.9:6 make himself different and **o.** His Will,
T-24.........I.8:6 **o.** this course because it teaches you you
T-24......III.4:6 be, and that you will **o.** His Will forever.
T-27......III.1:1 Power cannot **o.**. For opposition would
T-29....VIII.3:5 All forms of anti-Christ **o.** the Christ. And
T-30....... II.1:1 to **o.** the Holy Spirit is to fight *yourself?* He
T-30..... II.2:10 And to **o.** Him is to make a choice against

W-pI.....73.4:2 in it because it does not **o.** the Will of God
W-pI.....73.7:3 You have no will that can really **o.** it, and
W-pI...99.10:1 would **o.** the truth of your completion,
W-pI.166.10:1 God's Will does not **o.**. It merely is. It is
W-pI...198.4:3 And why would you **o.** it, quarrel with it,
M-17.........5:4 a separate will that can **o.** the Will of God,
P-3.........II.8:6 they must do may still **o.** the setting-out.
S-1......... V.2:4 useless now, because humility does not **o.**

**opposed** 27

T-2.....VIII.3:4 is a concept totally **o.** to right-mindedness
T-4.........I.2:10 They are **o.** in source, in direction and in
T-5....... III.3:1 two diametrically **o.** ways of seeing your
T-5....... III.5:4 and false perceptions are themselves **o.**.
T-6........I.16:7 the result of clearly **o.** thought systems;
T-6.........II.4:4 As their goals are **o.**, so is the result.
T-7.........II.2:8 you can arrive at diametrically **o.** results.
T-7.........II.2:9 in which diametrically **o.** outcomes seem
T-8..........I.5:5 each believing in diametrically **o.** ideas, it
T-11......in.1:4 are diametrically **o.** in all respects so that
T-12..... III.7:3 **o.** thoughts within itself is intolerable.
T-13..... IV.7:2 the goal of time as diametrically **o.**. The
T-19........I.4:5 has thus **o.** the Holy Spirit's purpose, and
T-19...... III.8:3 would have a different will, **o.** to His, and
T-22.....II.10:2 your Creator, and with a will **o.** to His.
T-23......in.1:7 Being **o.** to it, it is God's "enemy." And
T-25....VII.4:4 chooses to believe one thought **o.** to truth
T-25...VIII.2:2 and without attack from all beliefs **o.** to it.
T-26....VII.7:3 would Heaven be **o.** by its own opposite,
T-30....VII.5:2 And nothing in the world can be **o.** to it,
T-31........I.5:2 but to uphold a wish that it could be **o.**,
T-31........I.5:4 to see, and too **o.** to what is really true.
T-31..... IV.8:5 How utterly **o.** to truth is this, when all
W-pI.....71.5:3 that are diametrically **o.** in all ways. The
W-pI...136.9:2 **o.** by a decision stronger than His Will.
W-pI.137.11:3 What is **o.** to God does not exist, and who
M-8..........5:2 larger hallucination as **o.** to a smaller one

**opposes** 16

T-4....... III.7:1 every idea you ever had that **o.** knowledge
T-4.....III.10:2 The ego is desperate because it **o.** literally
T-7.........II.5:3 He **o.** the idea that differences in form are
T-7....... VI.5:1 The ego therefore **o.** all appreciation, all
T-7.....VI.13:6 nothing that **o.** this means anything at all.
T-8.........II.4:3 The Holy Spirit **o.** any imprisoning of the
T-15..... IX.6:2 attraction of guilt **o.** the attraction of God
T-22........I.4:9 This is the one emotion that **o.** love, and
T-22...... V.1:6 Reality **o.** nothing. What merely is needs
T-25..VII.1:11 of His creation, when it **o.** it in every way?
T-27..... III.7:6 know the peace of power that **o.** nothing.
W-pII.319.1:2 For arrogance **o.** truth. But when there is
W-pII...12.1:3 death, and what **o.** God alone is true.
M-4........II.1:6 or do; no thought **o.** any other thought;
M-19.........2:3 justice includes nothing that **o.** truth.
P-2........IV.7:5 This cannot heal, for it **o.** truth. Perhaps

**opposing** 14

T-5.....III.8:11 **o.** it with His strength just as the ego
T-5.......IV.3:7 *It is impossible to share **o.** thoughts.* You can
T-6.....V.B.5:1 out of conflict between two **o.** thought
T-8..........I.1:8 If you are **o.** His Will, how can you have
T-9........I.13:6 create. **O.** orders of reality make reality
T19....IV.C.3:6 are not following His Will; they are **o.** it.
T-22...... V.1:2 force or anger, nor by **o.** them in any way.
T-23......in.1:8 "enemy." And God is feared as an **o.** will.
T-26....VII.7:4 be subjected to the laws of two **o.** powers,
T-29.......II.7:5 for it can be made to teach **o.** things. And
T-31.......II.1:1 not overcome by the **o.** of the new and old
W-pI.....97.1:2 nor tries to weave **o.** factors into unity. It
W-pI...131.9:4 He thinks he made a hell **o.** Heaven, and
W-pII.292.1:3 we let an alien will appear to be **o.** His.

**opposite** 119

T-in..........1:8 *The **o.** of love is fear, but what is all-*
T-in..........1:8 *but what is all-encompassing can have no **o.**.*

T-4........in.1:5 properly understood is the **o.** of fatigue.
T-4..........I.6:4 is the **o.** of the ego-oriented teacher's goal.
T-4.....II.11:11 it understood by being compared to an **o.**.
T-4....... VI.5:4 and the **o.** of misery with its presence. It
T-4....... VI.5:7 You have taught yourself the **o.**. You are
T-5....... IV.3:6 also include **o.** thoughts at the same level.
T-6........I.15:3 This is clearly the **o.** of everything I taught
T-6....... III.4:1 the exact **o.** of everything the ego believes.
T-6..... V.B.3:5 it is, *having* appears to be the **o.** of *giving.*
T-7.........II.5:1 purpose in translating is exactly the **o.**.
T-7....... IV.2:8 It is therefore not the **o.** of remembering
T-7....... IV.3:3 teach the **o.** of what the ego has "learned.
T-7....... IX.2:5 Creating is the **o.** of loss, as blessing is the
T-7....... IX.2:5 of loss, as blessing is the **o.** of sacrifice.
T-7.........X.4:3 the **o.** of God's Will can be better for you.
T-7.........X.4:4 that it is possible to *do* the **o.** of God's Will
T-8..........I.5:1 curriculum of the Atonement is the **o.** of
T-8.... VII.13:1 The **o.** of joy is depression. When your
T-9...... VII.3:5 is the exact **o.** of the Holy Spirit's, because
T-10.......V.1:6 is very literal; denial of life perceives its **o.**
T-11.....V.14:1 have to be, the exact **o.** of the Holy Spirit's
T-11.... VII.4:1 denial of the **o.** of goodness enables you
T-13........I.8:9 And immortality is the **o.** of time, for
T-13...... IV.7:1 of time is the exact **o.** of the ego's. The
T-13.......V.6:3 are the **o.** of what the emotions are. You
T-14......in.1:5 They take a direction exactly **o.**, pointing
T-14..... VI.4:2 make the falsity of its **o.** perfectly clear.
T-14.... VII.3:4 are clearly **o.** viewpoints on what the
T-14...VIII.3:8 They have no **o.**, and nothing else can you
T-14..... IX.2:1 because it is the **o.** of what it meets. It is
T-16.......V.3:6 For this world *is* the **o.** of Heaven, being
T-16.......V.3:6 of Heaven, being made to be its **o.**, and
T-16.......V.3:6 takes a direction exactly **o.** of what is true.
T-16.... VII.6:3 The holy instant is the **o.** of the ego's fixed
T-17.......V.2:6 shifted to the exact **o.** of what it was. This
T-17...... VI.5:8 you see the **o.** of the ego's way of looking,
T-19........I.4:6 an "enemy" of healing and the **o.** of truth.
T-19........I.5:1 that faith must be the **o.** of faithlessness.
T-19......I.10:1 Faith is the **o.** of fear, as much a part of
T-21..... III.3:5 to place equal faith in **o.** directions. What
T-21..... III.6:2 His purpose lies in the **o.** direction. He
T-22.......II.1:1 The **o.** of illusions is not disillusionment
T-22.......II.2:1 is the **o.** of illusions because it offers joy.
T-22.......II.2:2 else but joy could be the **o.** of misery? To
T-23......in.1:1 not see the **o.** of frailty and weakness is
T-23.....II.14:5 And if it is the truth, then must its **o.**,
T-26..... III.1:8 truth is simple; it is one, without an **o.**.
T-26.... VII.4:1 Perception's laws are **o.** to truth, and
T-26.... VII.7:3 would Heaven be opposed by its own **o.**,
T-27..... III.1:7 impose an **o.** that contradicts the concept
T-27..... III.4:4 Unweakened power, with no **o.**, is what
T-27..... III.7:5 complete and happy, without **o.**. You do
T-27.. VII.10:3 Yet a thing can never be its **o.**. And death
T-27.. VII.10:4 And death is **o.** to peace, because it is the
T-27.. VII.10:4 to peace, because it is the **o.** of life. And
T-28.... VII.2:6 could correct for separation but its **o.**?
T-28.... VII.4:8 to be of form, yet it is one, as is its **o.**. And
T-31..... VI.1:3 must be false, for what is real denies its **o.**.
T-31.... VII.1:4 truth, which has no **o.** and cannot change
W-in..........6:6 limits. It is the **o.** of the way you see now.
W-pI.... 39.1:1 If guilt is hell, what is its **o.**? Like the text
W-pI.... 39.2:1 If guilt is hell, what is its **o.**? This is not
W-pI.. 39.10:5 and adding: *If guilt is hell, what is its **o.**?*
W-pI.... 57.3:3 down, and my thoughts are the **o.** of truth
W-pI.... 61.1:3 It is the **o.** of a statement of pride, of
W-pI.... 70.4:1 You have tried to do just the **o.**, making
W-pI.... 71.1:3 Since it is the **o.** of God's, you also believe
W-pI.. 71.10:3 *is the **o.** of God's plan for salvation. And only*
W-pI.... 72.1:1 ego's plan for salvation is the **o.** of God's,
W-pI.... 99.9:8 your Self as Love which has no **o.** in you.
W-pI.. 103.1:7 opposition in what has no limit and no **o.**.
W-pI.. 127.3:7 Love is a law without an **o.**. Its wholeness
W-pI.. 129.9:2 For we have seen its **o.** at last, and we are
W-pI.. 130.6:2 made a choice as all-embracing as its **o.**.
W-pI.. 131.7:4 outcome which is Heaven's **o.** in every
W-pI.. 131.9:3 himself, and contradicts what has no **o.**.
W-pI.. 137.1:2 healing is the **o.** of all the world's ideas
W-pI.. 138.1:2 We think that all things have an **o.**, and
W-pI.. 138.2:1 Creation knows no **o.**. But here is

W-pI...138.4:7 There is no **o.** to choose instead. There is
W-pI...152.3:5 Truth cannot have an **o.**. This can not be
W-pI...163.4:3 Here is the **o.** of God proclaimed as lord
W-pI...163.6:5 not be true, unless its **o.** is proven false.
W-pI...166.2:3 that leads to **o.** effects from those He wills
W-pI...167.1:4 Like all His Thoughts, it has no **o.**. There
W-pI...167.1:6 death because an **o.** to God does not exist.
W-pI...167.2:1 there appears to be a state that is life's **o.**.
W-pI...167.7:1 **o.** of life can only be another form of life.
W-pI...167.7:2 created it, because it is not **o.** in truth. Its
W-pI...167.7:5 It is not its **o.** in anything created, nor in
W-pI...167.8:3 thought of death is not the **o.** to thoughts
W-pI...167.9:1 What seems to be the **o.** of life is merely
W-pI.167.10:3 and sees in dreams an **o.** to what he is?
W-pI.167.11:3 And in His Thoughts, which have no **o.**,
W-pI...169.2:2 so **o.** to everything the world contains,
W-pI...170.3:3 For love now has an "enemy," an **o.**; and
W-pII......2.2:2 before, for peace was given without **o.**,
W-pII..259.2:2 *be afraid of love, nor seek for refuge in its* **o.**.
W-pII..259.2:3 *For love can have no* **o.**. *You are the Source of*
W-pII......8.1:2 it stands for what is **o.** to what you made.
W-pII.....11.3:1 Creation is the **o.** of all illusions, for
W-pII.....14.1:3 *impossible, and joy established without* **o.**. *I*
M-4......VII.1:8 word means the exact **o.** to the teachers of
M-7............4:3 Usually it seems to be just the **o.**. It does
M-7............4:7 coexist. And hate must be the **o.** of love,
M-11..........2:3 and things so **o.** that it is pointless to try
M-19..........2:1 Justice, like its **o.**, is an interpretation. It
M-20..........3:9 And what but peace is **o.** to war? Here the
M-20..........5:5 Life has no **o.**, for it is God. Life and death
M-20..........6:2 that His Will is wholly without **o.**. There
M-27........6:11 you not see that otherwise He has an **o.**,
C-1.............4:5 in this world. It has no **o.** and no degrees.
C-2.............4:4 is. Look at its **o.** and you can see the only
C-2.............5:1 The ego's **o.** in every way,–in origin,
C-2.............5:3 ego's **o.** and here alone we look on what
C-2.............6:8 has come: Its **o.** has gone without a trace.
P-2.........II.4:5 but knowledge of God has no true **o.**. Not

**opposites** 29

T-3.........II.1:2 cannot be understood in terms of **o.**. It is
T-5.........II.6:2 of opposition in which **o.** are possible. As
T-5......III.11:3 He must work through **o.**, because He
T-11.....VII.4:1 a condition in which **o.** do not exist. And
T-14......III.4:5 **o.** which cannot be reconciled and cannot
T-14.....VII.1:3 **O.** must be brought together, not kept
T-16.....VII.6:2 comparisons, and uses **o.** to point to truth
T-21....III.11:4 But "good" and "deprivation" are **o.**, and
T-23........I.12:6 Conflict and peace are **o.**. Where one
T-27.......V.9:3 to their **o.** and bring the same results. All
W-pI.....91.8:2 corrected, and their **o.** to take their place.
W-pI.....96.1:2 This sense of being split into **o.** induces
W-pI.....96.1:4 **o.** you see in you will never be compatible
W-pI...108.1:2 is in it, for it reconciles all seeming **o.**.
W-pI...108.3:1 This is the light that shows no **o.**, and
W-pI...108.4:3 is the base on which all **o.** are reconciled,
W-pI...137.8:4 are more potent than their sickly **o.**.
W-pI...138.3:1 obvious escape from what appears as **o.**.
W-pI...138.7:3 In death alone are **o.** resolved, for ending
W-pI...152.2:7 Accept no **o.** and no exceptions, for to do
W-pI...152.7:1 contradicts His Will, invented **o.** to truth,
W-pI...167.8:4 Forever unopposed by **o.** of any kind, the
W-pI.167.10:5 Nor will we let imagined **o.** to life abide
W-pII.....352.h Judgment and love are **o.**. From one
M-20..........5:6 Life and death seem to be **o.** because you
M-27..........2:7 contradiction reigns and **o.** make endless
S-2........I.10:1 This is the world of **o.**. And you must
S-2.........II.7:5 Within the world of **o.** there is a way to
S-3...........I.5:2 The world of **o.** is healing's place, for

**opposition** 46

T-2.......VII.1:6 in direct **o.** to the purpose of this course.
T-3.......VII.2:6 in which everything is in direct **o.** to God.
T-3.......VII.5:2 active, destructive and clearly in **o.** to God
T-4...........I.2:9 Your self and God's Self *are* in **o.**. They are
T-5.........II.6:2 state of **o.** in which opposites are possible.
T-5........III.5:4 you is in direct **o.** to the ego's notions,
T-5......III.11:3 work with and for a mind that is in **o.**.
T-10.......V.3:2 health is in direct **o.** to its own survival.
T-12......III.2:3 and experience a quick response of **o.**,
T-12......III.4:2 **o.** establishes that it does matter to you. It
T-12...VII.4:10 in direct **o.** to the Holy Spirit's purpose.
T-12.....VII.8:3 upon your mind and accepted **o.** there,
T-12.....VII.8:4 believe that the witnesses for **o.** are true,
T-17....VIII.2:7 it, for against your **o.** it cannot come.
T-19.......II.2:5 and the Will of God open to **o.** and defeat
T-19......III.8:3 and in eternal **o.** to Him and to each other
T19...IV.A.3:6 It has no **o.**, for there is none beside it.
T19....IV.C.3:1 and death, in **o.** to life and innocence, and
T19....IV.C.3:2 **o.** lie but in the sick minds of the insane,
T-22.......II.9:3 mind, be different from it and in **o.** to it.
T-22......III.2:6 The ego's **o.** to correction leads to its fixed
T-22.......V.1:5 The **o.** comes from them, and not reality.
T-23.......II.5:5 And Their relationship is one of **o.**, just as
T-26.....VII.9:4 state, and not in **o.** to God's Will.
T-27......II.12:6 seem divided, with a half in **o.** to a half.
T-27......III.1:2 For **o.** would weaken it, and weakened
T-30.........I.4:3 for **o.** will not first arise and then become
T-30.........I.7:1 this rule without delay, despite your **o.**.
T-30.........I.9:3 This works against the sense of **o.**, and
T-30.......I.12:1 of lack of **o.** to be helped. It is a statement
T-30.......I.15:4 nor grounds for **o.** that you may be free.
T-31.......II.8:3 before the new without your **o.** or intent.
W-pI.....20.1:6 and if you give in to resentment and **o.**.
W-pI.....43.5:9 the idea, but they should not be in **o.** to it.
W-pI.....44.6:1 that its **o.** and its fears are meaningless.
W-pI.....71.1:1 set up a plan for salvation in **o.** to God's.
W-pI.....76.6:2 that you have made in **o.** to God's Will.
W-pI...103.1:7 introducing **o.** in what has no limit and
W-pI...138.2:2 But here is **o.** part of being "real." It is this
W-pI...138.2:8 **O.** makes the truth unwelcome, and it
W-pI...138.7:3 opposites resolved, for ending **o.** is to die.
W-pI...200.7:1 a world in **o.** to God's Will and to his own
W-pII..329.1:7 *It cannot change, and be in* **o.** *to itself. Father*
W-pII331.1:10 *truth. There is no* **o.** *to Your Will. There is no*
M-9...........2:5 goal in direct **o.** to that of our curriculum.
M-28.......3:11 There is no **o.** to the truth. And now the

**oppresses** 1

W-pI.166.11:4 each time the thought of poverty **o.** you,

**oppressing** 1

W-pII..293.1:3 welcoming, with all my past mistakes **o.** it

**oppression** 1

W-pI...190.5:3 yourself that can reach down and bring **o.**

**optimal** 1

WpI. rIII.in2:1 as **o.** each day and every hour of the day.

**option** 1

T-21...VII.11:6 the **o.** to change your mind again. When

**optional** 1

T-7.........X.6:5 your identification with His Will is not **o.**,

**options** 1

C-2.............1:9 a choice for **o.** that do not exist. We name

**or** 1159

**ordain** 1

T-31.......V.9:6 Can he see your future and **o.**, before it

**ordained** 3

T-31...VIII.8:7 And God **o.**, in loving kindness, that it be
T-31....VIII.9:5 God has **o.** I cannot call in vain, and in
S-2.........in.1:5 that God **o.** to be with you until you reach

**Order** 1
*order*

T-1.........I.37:4 knowledge of the Divine **O.** is impossible.

**order** 108
*Order*
*See also* lower-order; Appendix C

T-1...........I.1:1 There is no **o.** of difficulty in miracles.
T-1.........I.13:1 endings, and so they alter the temporal **o.**.
T-1.........I.32:3 raise you into the sphere of celestial **o.**. In
T-1.........I.32:4 of celestial order. In this **o.** you *are* perfect.
T-1..........II.3:2 one of a lesser **o.** stands before his Creator
T-1........VI.1:9 to the particular **o.** of needs you establish.
T-1........VI.2:3 The idea of **o.** of needs arose because,
T-2...........I.2:8 in which all aspects are of the same **o.**.
T-2...........I.5:5 there is no **o.** of difficulty in miracles. In
T-2....V.A.17:3 are not in the same **o.** of reality. Only the
T-2.......VII.2:2 of thought in **o.** to avoid miscreation.
T-3...........I.2:2 whole frame of reference in **o.** to justify it.
T-3.........V.7:8 judgments are necessary in **o.** to select.
T-4...........I.1:3 They are in the same **o.** of learning, and
T-4...........I.8:1 for itself in **o.** to overcome its doubts. It
T-4........IV.11:9 that there is an **o.** of difficulty in miracles;
T-4.......VII.3:8 beings of a like **o.** can truly communicate,
T-5........IV.4:2 decision to share It in **o.** to hear It yourself
T-5.........V.7:6 who believe they **o.** their own thoughts,
T-5.......VII.2:4 that there is no **o.** of difficulty in miracles.
T-6......V.A.4:1 there is no **o.** of difficulty in miracles. This
T-6......V.A.4:9 a range, **o.** of difficulty is meaningless,
T-6......V.B.8:7 Lack of **o.** of difficulty in miracles has not
T-6......V.C.2:3 but only in **o.** to unify the mind so it can
T-6......V.C.4:4 does not concern itself with **o.** of difficulty
T-7..........II.2:7 to circumstances if they are to maintain **o.**
T-7..........II.6:5 You forget in **o.** to remember better. You
T-7........IV.2:3 Spirit inspires can have no **o.** of difficulty,
T-7........IV.2:3 because every part of creation is of one **o.**.
T-7........IV.5:4 Spirit sees no **o.** of difficulty in healing.
T-7......VIII.1:6 you value in **o.** to keep it in your mind. To
T-7....VIII.3:12 in constant activity in **o.** not to recognize
T-7........XI.1:8 there is no **o.** of difficulty in miracles, you
T-8.......VII.7:2 of one **o.** of reality into another. Different
T-8......VIII.6:9 premises give rise in **o.** to judge them
T-9.........I.11:3 the impossible in **o.** to be happy is totally
T-9........IV.5:4 what you have made in **o.** to be forgiven.
T-10.......V.3:6 not to know yourself in **o.** to be sick. This
T-11.......in.4:4 it in **o.** to keep a dark cornerstone hidden,
T-11.....VI.10:5 is no **o.** of difficulty in miracles because all
T-12.....VII.1:3 that you have learned there is no **o.** of
T-12.....VII.2:1 in **o.** to recognize that the world has been
T-12....VIII.1:4 If you seek love in **o.** to attack it, you will
T-14......IV.1:8 First there is no other, for there is no **o.**,
T-14......VI.8:2 with communication in **o.** to restore it.
T-14........X.2:5 anything without **o.** of difficulty can occur
T-14........X.2:7 one thing you can do that transcends **o.**,
T-14........X.3:4 more difficult to grasp is the lack of **o.** of
T-14........X.5:4 together by a sense of **o.** that you establish
T-14........X.5:5 and bring any **o.** into chaos shows you
T-14........X.5:6 all of you, no **o.** at all would be possible.
T-14........X.5:7 Yet though the **o.** you impose upon your
T-14........X.5:8 you. To **o.** is to judge, and to arrange by
T-14.....X.6:14 There is no **o.** of difficulty here. A call for
T-14.....X.10:4 let the Holy Spirit **o.** your thoughts and
T-14...X.12:10 there be any **o.** of difficulty among them?
T-15........I.4:11 must engender fear in **o.** to maintain itself
T-15......IX.2:5 must be unlimited in **o.** to have meaning,
T-15......IX.3:2 But in **o.** to see this, it is necessary to give
T-16........II.3:4 show you instantly that **o.** of difficulty in
T-17.........I.3:1 must be an **o.** of difficulty in miracles, all
T-17.........I.4:1 long will the illusion of an **o.** of difficulty
T-17.........I.4:2 For you have established this **o.** in reality
T-17.........I.5:7 you. There is no **o.** in reality, because
T-17.......VI.1:2 in **o.** to be simple it *must* be unequivocal.
T-18........II.3:5 have them be, and what they do you **o.**.
T19....IV.A.5:3 There is no **o.** of difficulty in miracles, for

T-20...... VI.8:1 There is no o. in relationships. They
T-20..... VII.5:8 For vision, like relationships, has no o..
T-20.. VIII.8:10 same. Again there is no o.; only a seeming
T-21....... in.1:9 that is why o. of difficulty in miracles is
T-21...... VI.8:8 Hide not behind insanity in o. to escape
T-22.... VI.13:7 The only question to be answered in o. to
T-23..... II.15:1 reversal they appear to be the laws of o..
T-23..... II.20:3 of chaos are the laws of o. as do the others
T-25...... IX.6:4 What o. can there be in miracles, unless
W-pI....... 1.3:1 statements are not arranged in any o.,
W-pI..... 19.1:2 while at other times the o. is reversed. The
W-pI..... 19.1:3 The reason is that the o. does not matter.
W-pI..... 19.4:3 throughout. Lack of o. in this connection
W-pI..... 19.4:3 of lack of o. in miracles meaningful to you
W-pI..... 29.4:3 that any o. you impose is equally alien to
W-pI..... 44.2:1 In o. to see, you must recognize that light
WpI... rI.in.2:2 to follow any particular o. in considering
W-pI..... 53.2:3 a world in which there is no o. anywhere.
W-pI..... 66.6:2 o. to be false it is necessary to define God
W-pI..... 76.5:3 The body suffers just in o. that the mind
Wi181-200 1:3 But you are asked to practice now in o. to
M-2 ........... 2:1 In o. to understand the teaching-learning
M-4 ..... VII.1:5 of God, it means giving away in o. to keep
M-5 ....... II.2:9 chooses them in o. to bring tangible form
M-5 ...... III.1:1 must change his mind in o. to be healed,
M-8 .............. h OF O. OF DIFFICULTIES BE AVOIDED?
M-8 ........... 1:1 The belief in o. of difficulties is the basis
M-8 ........... 1:2 with every other in o. to be recognized. A
M-8 ........... 5:1 There can be no o. of difficulty in healing
M-10 ......... 3:3 In o. to judge anything rightly, one would
M-16 ......... 7:5 no o. of difficulty in resolving them. He is
M-18 ......... 4:1 In o. to heal, it thus becomes essential for
M-22 ......... 1:2 is no o. of difficulty in miracles because
M-22 ......... 3:5 A body that can o. a mind to do as it sees
C-6............. 3:2 o. to fulfill this special function the Holy
P-1............. 5:1 as God in o. to make progress in salvation
P-3......... II.2:1 that there is no o. of difficulty in healing.
P-3......... II.7:1 that there is no o. of difficulty in healing.
P-3......... II.7:5 accepted the gift entirely in o. to stay and
P-3......... II.8:1 recognize that o. of difficulty in healing is
P-3......... II.9:4 there is no o. of difficulty in healing, he

## ordered 3

T19. IV.A.11:2 of fear are harshly o. to seek out guilt, and
T19.... IV.C.8:5 upon it, and forgive it what you o. it to do
T-23..... II.21:2 conclusion; a valid step in o. thought. The

## ordering 4

T-5......... V.8:8 the proper o. of thought becomes quite
T-14....... X.6:1 have no basis at all for o. your thoughts.
T-14....... X.6:2 to show you that your way of o. is wrong,
W-pI... 188.9:5 them, o. that they depart from us. But

## orders 23

T-1........ VI.3:1 The idea of o. of need, which follows
T-2........ IV.1:3 combine two o. of reality inappropriately.
T-5......... V.7:2 God Himself o. your thought because
T-7........ XI.1:6 perceives o. of difficulty in everything.
T-8....... VII.7:3 Different o. of reality merely appear to
T-8....... VII.7:3 to exist, just as different o. of miracles do.
T-9......... I.13:6 create. Opposing o. of reality make reality
T-14..... X.11:6 holds more than these two o. of thought.
T-17......... I.4:5 O. of reality is a perspective without
T-17......... I.5:6 establish o. of reality that must imprison
T-18...... IV.8:3 whole belief in o. of difficulty in miracles
T-18...... VI.9:7 and to establish different o. of reality,
T19.. IV.B.13:2 Under fear's o. the body will pursue guilt,
T19.... IV.C.8:1 would lay the Son of God, slain by its o.,
T19.... IV.C.8:5 and unrelenting o. you laid upon it, and
T-20...... III.6:4 did not make adjustments to fit their o..
T-24......... I.3:6 of any kind imposes o. of reality, and a
T-31.... III.3:11 it. A jailer does not follow o., but enforces
T-31.... III.3:11 orders, but enforces o. on the prisoner.
T-31...... III.4:4 It gives no o. that the mind need serve,
T-31...... III.5:2 rules, and o. that the world be like itself; a
T-31.... VIII.1:2 and bound by what it o. him to feel. It

M-14 ......... 3:6 illusion of o. of difficulty is an obstacle

## ordinary 1

T-2 ... V.A.11:2 the o. considerations of time and space

## organization 1

T-17 ...... V.5:8 former o. of their perception no longer

## organize 5

T-3 ....... VI.3:5 You do not need judgment to o. your life,
T-3 ....... VI.3:5 you certainly do not need it to o. yourself.
T-6 ........ in.2:3 one can o. his life without some thought
W-pI... 135.1:4 the past, or o. the present as you wish.
W-pI. 135.22:2 of plan, that we may give instead of o..

## organized 3

T-4 ........ V.5:3 consciously o. and consciously directed.
T-12 ..... II.10:1 We are therefore embarking on an o.,
T19.... IV.A.8:4 more unstable than a tightly o. delusional

## organizing 1

T-3 ........ V.7:7 rejecting, o. and reorganizing, shifting

## orientation 1

T-1 ........ V.6:6 is less stable than an upside-down o.. Nor

## oriented

*See* ego-oriented

## orients 1

M-16 ......... 5:7 pattern of rest, and o. you away from fear.

## origin 10

T-4 .......... I.5:6 this choice because of the nature of its o..
T-4 ........ I.13:2 involves no confusion about the child's o.
T-4 ......... II.4:8 as long as your o. is open to belief you are
T-4 ......... II.7:7 Body appetites are not physical in o.. The
T-7 ....... VI.4:3 This unbelief is its o., and while the ego
T-18 ....... II.4:3 And yet the dream cannot escape its o..
T-18 ... VIII.1:3 The belief in limited love was its o., and it
W-pI... 167.3:5 But its o. is where it must be changed, if
W-pI... 167.4:3 becoming different from their own o.,
C-2 ............ 5:1 The ego's opposite in every way,–in o.,

## original 23

T-1 ........ I.46:3 return to your o. form of communication
T-1 ......... II.1:2 It reflects the o. form of communication
T-1 ....... III.1:5 to the recognition of your o. state, you
T-1 ........ V.1:2 spirit's o. state of direct communication
T-1 ....... VI.3:1 which follows from the o. error that one
T-7 ......... II.4:4 form so that the o. meaning is retained.
T-7 ......... II.5:2 translates only to preserve the o. meaning
T-18 ........ I.5:6 to show you the enormity of the o. error,
T-18 ........ I.7:1 form of the o. error rising to frighten you,
T-18 ........ I.9:6 The o. error has not entered here, nor
T-18 ....... I.12:2 echo of the o. error that shattered Heaven
W-pI..... 34.6:1 or worry, use the idea in its o. form. If you
W-pI..... 38.6:1 apply the idea in its o. form unless a
W-pI... 39.10:4 the idea in its o. form once more, and
W-pI..... 43.9:1 time, merely repeat the idea in its o. form.
W-pI..... 46.7:1 for today in the o. or in a related form, as
WpI... rI.in.6:1 ideas are not given in quite their o. form.
WpI... rI.in.6:3 necessary to return to the o. statements,
WpI.. rII.in.6:1 using the o. form of the idea for general
C-in ........... 1:4 the "o. error" or the "original sin." To
C-in ........... 1:4 the "original error" or the "o. sin." To
P-2......... in.4:3 both will learn to give up their o. goals,
P-2...... IV.10:6 This is the corollary of the "o. sin"; the

## originally 1

W-pI .... 46.6:7 a repetition of today's idea as o. stated.

## originated 1

T-4 ......... II.8:1 way of describing how it thinks it o.. This

## origins 2

T-2 ............. I.h The O. of Separation
T-4 ......... II.9:1 since myths are usually related to ego o.,

## Other 6

*other*

T-2 ....... III.5:6 are completely dependent on Each O.. He
T-8 ....... IV.8:7 It cannot be with One and not the O.. If
T-8 ....... IV.8:8 are part of One you must be part of the O.
T-14 ... VIII.2:7 apart, and gifts to One are offered to the O.
T-23 ....... II.5:3 always be condemned, and by the O..
S-1......... in.1:3 of the Love They give forever to Each O..

## other 496

*Other*

T-1 ........ I.12:3 physical, and the o. creates the spiritual.
T-1 ......... II.2:4 Miracles, on the o. hand, induce action.
T-1 ......... II.4:5 one hand, and as a Son of God on the o..
T-2 .......... I.5:3 truth on the one hand, and error on the o.
T-2 ......... II.4:7 the inherent characteristic of o. defenses.
T-2 ...... III.1:11 Spiritual sight, on the o. hand, cannot see
T-2 ... V.A.17:6 In time we exist for and with each o.. In
T-2 ....... VII.3:2 would also not be free to choose the o.. By
T-2 ....... VII.5:2 To believe in one is to deny the o.. Fear is
T-2 ..... VIII.2:8 if you are to bring peace to o. minds.
T-3 .......... I.2:6 itself is no harder to correct than any o.,
T-3 .......... I.6:3 can only honor o. minds, because honor
T-3 .......... I.7:9 final demonstration that all the o. lessons
T-3 ......... II.1:5 firm commitment to one or the o. is made
T-3 ....... III.6:3 and His Sons are not strangers to each o..
T-3 ..... III.7:12 When they do not recognize each o., they
T-3 ....... IV.1:9 is because they are meaningless to each o..
T-3 ....... IV.3:7 This makes its aspects strangers to each o.
T-3 ......... V.7:5 Perception, on the o. hand, is impossible
T-4 .......... I.6:5 with the effect of his ego on o. egos, and
T-4 ......... II.6:5 evaluates itself in relation to o. egos. It is
T-4 ......... II.6:7 whole perception of o. egos as real is only
T-4 ......... II.8:2 it can only turn to o. egos and try to unite
T-4 ....... III.6:6 Thou shalt have no o. gods before Him
T-4 ....... III.8:2 for we must hide nothing from each o.. If
T-4 ....... III.8:4 to help me make o. minds ready for Him.
T-4 ....... IV.8:7 Judgment, like any o. defense, can be used
T-4 ....... VI.1:7 o. life has continued without interruption
T-4 ....... VI.4:1 ego and the spirit do not know each o..
T-4 ..... VII.7:5 be returned by that mind to o. minds,
T-5 ......... II.3:6 But the o. is given you by God, Who asks
T-5 ......... II.3:9 world to hear only that Voice and no o.. It
T-5 ......... II.5:2 one to be chosen and the o. to be avoided.
T-5 ......... II.5:3 By choosing one you give up the o.. The
T-5 ......... II.7:6 you *of.* It brings to your mind the o. way,
T-5 ......... II.8:8 Yet you have o. devotions now. Your
T-5 ....... III.2:5 the property of o. ideas because it follows
T-5 ....... IV.3:5 them, nor can they conflict with each o..
T-5 ....... IV.4:6 is the meaning of "turning the o. cheek."
T-5 ....... V.6:10 it. You made the o., and so you can. Only
T-6 ........ I.14:1 you interpret the crucifixion in any o. way
T-6 ........ I.18:2 Their influence on each o. is without limit
T-6 ........ I.19:3 in them, and do not respond to any o.,
T-6 ....... II.6:11 is impossible to accept one without the o..
T-6 ......... II.8:2 united within themselves and with each o.
T-6 ....... II.11:9 outward only to what is true in o. minds.
T-6 ..... IV.11:4 laws. Fidelity to o. laws is also possible,
T-6 ..... V.A.1:7 Like any o. impossible solution the ego
T-6 ..... V.B.4:2 its only alternative since the o. possibility,
T-6 ..... V.B.5:1 clearly to choose one and relinquish the o.
T-7 .......... I.4:1 The ego, on the o. hand, always demands
T-7 ......... II.6:7 or relinquish one to understand the o..
T-7 ........ III.3:4 as anything o. than their perfect equals,
T-7 ......... V.3:3 He recognizes no o., because He does not

T-7 V.3:5 in the service of the ego can hurt **o.** bodies
T-7 V.9:3 The **o.** shows you only truth, which you
T-7 VIII.2:6 conflict from your mind to **o.** minds, in an
T-7 XI.5:2 extends out into the darkness of **o.** minds,
T-8 I.5:6 each one merely interferes with the **o.**.
T-8 I.5:9 one because they cannot relinquish the **o.**,
T-8 III.2:2 then, there is no **o.** experience. Yet the
T-8 III.2:3 Yet the wish for **o.** experience will block
T-8 III.6:6 What **o.** choice could you make? Having
T-8 IV.7:6 of each **o.** lies our remembrance of God.
T-8 VI.5:8 There is no **o.** gift that is eternal, and
T-8 VI.5:8 therefore there is no **o.** gift that is true.
T-8 VI.8:4 apart from each **o.** we cannot function at
T-8 VII.9:2 with little or no relationship to each **o.**, so
T-8 VII.12:7 only if the mind extends to **o.** minds, and
T-8 VII.16:4 what **o.** hope would you want? Freedom
T-8 VIII.2:2 of shifting its allegiance from one to the **o.**
T-9 III.1:1 alertness of the ego to the errors of **o.** egos
T-9 V.8:12 As you awaken **o.** minds to the Holy Spirit
T-9 VIII.7:1 of each **o.** because grandeur is truth.
T-10 II.6:3 want something **o.** than peace of mind,
T-10 III.8:3 no **o.** gods before Him or you will not
T-10 III.10:3 To accept **o.** gods before Him is to place
T-10 III.10:3 Him is to place **o.** images before yourself.
T-10 III.11:3 will be heard when you place no **o.** gods
T-10 IV.1:5 sick, you have placed **o.** gods before Him.
T-10 IV.3:4 If you perceive **o.** gods your mind is split,
T-10 IV.4:4 good, and there are no **o.** laws beside His.
T-10 V.11:4 anywhere else, or in any **o.** condition. Do
T-10 V.12:4 many **o.** forms that blasphemy may take,
T-10 V.14:8 be real, because they contradict each **o.**. If
T-11 III.6:3 there *are* no **o.** gods to place before Him,
T-12 III.5:3 it. Any response **o.** than love arises from a
T-12 VI.7:6 join in perfect love of God and of each **o.**.
T-12 VII.4:9 long as you believe you have **o.** functions,
T-12 VII.7:1 up to you, but you must do one or the **o.**,
T-12 VII.7:7 separated from each **o.** because you made
T-13 I.1:4 coexist, and to accept one is to deny the **o.**
T-13 IV.8:1 The ego, on the **o.** hand, regards the
T-13 V.1:4 The **o.** has many forms, for the content of
T-13 V.5:1 to each of them as though it were the **o.**.
T-13 VI.6:4 and thus enables them to reach each **o.**.
T-13 VI.11:6 This **o.** world is bright with love which
T-13 VII.2:3 is possible because you have denied the **o.**
T-13 VII.6:1 some glimpses of the **o.** world about him.
T-13 VII.6:2 his own, he will deny the vision of the **o.**,
T-13 IX.4:2 you cannot value one without the **o.**, and
T-13 IX.5:5 and the belief in one is faith in the **o.**,
T-13 X.10:2 There is no **o.** way to look within and see
T-14 III.2:2 from what the **o.** does not offer you. You
T-14 III.13:5 You have no **o.** "enemy," and against this
T-14 IV.1:8 Beyond the First there is no **o.**, for there is
T-14 IV.10:2 Each perceives the **o.** as like himself,
T-14 IV.10:2 sees the **o.** unlike the way he sees himself.
T-14 VI.4:4 meaning by confusing them with each **o.**.
T-14 VI.4:6 The **o.** is wholly without sense of any kind
T-14 VI.7:6 one means nothing and the **o.** everything,
T-14 VI.7:7 The **o.** but interferes with it.
T-14 VII.4:5 But if one is kept in darkness from the **o.**,
T-14 VII.4:7 have them both, for each denies the **o.**.
T-14 VII.4:10 because the **o.** is seen in the same place.
T-14 VIII.5:4 Lay no gifts **o.** than this upon your altars,
T-14 IX.3:8 His worshippers placed **o.** gods upon it.
T-14 IX.5:3 Yet no reflections of the images of **o.** gods
T-14 X.7:1 one of love, and the **o.** the call for love.
T-14 XI.12:5 Each brings the **o.** with it, for it is the law
T-14 XI.12:6 They are cause and effect, each to the **o.**,
T-14 XI.12:6 so where one is absent the **o.** cannot be.
T-15 II.5:3 No gift of God is recognized in any **o.** way.
T-15 III.1:8 always choose one at the expense of the **o.**
T-15 V.6:3 less value on one and more on the **o.**. You
T-15 VII.1:2 There is no **o.** love that can satisfy you,
T-15 VII.1:2 can satisfy you, because there *is* no **o.** love.
T-15 VII.7:2 that he has sacrificed something to the **o.**,
T-15 VII.7:4 He is not in love with the **o.** at all. He
T-15 VII.7:6 he demands that the **o.** accept the guilt
T-15 VII.9:3 relief from guilt by increasing it in the **o.**.
T-15 VII.9:5 The **o.** seems always to be attacking and
T-15 X.2:3 What **o.** gift can you offer me, when only
T-15 X.5:6 You see no **o.** alternatives, for you cannot
T-15 X.7:3 little, perhaps, but the **o.** to be destroyed.
T-16 I.6:5 for what would hurt one will hurt the **o.**.
T-16 I.7:2 them separate and secret from each **o.**.
T-16 III.9:2 who stand on the **o.** side and wait for you
T-16 IV.2:6 its reality, which awaits you on the **o.** side,
T-16 IV.5:9 one choice is as dangerous as the **o.**, the
T-16 V.1:4 an attack on the self to make the **o.** guilty.
T-16 V.8:3 partners see this special self in each **o.**, the
T-16 V.10:6 the **o.** to replace the self that you despise.
T-16 V.13:1 attempt to raise **o.** gods before Him, and
T-16 V.17:2 will recognize that God is on the **o.** side,
T-16 VI.5:2 seeking to join each **o.** in separate unions
T-16 VII.11:5 your relationship with Him and to no **o.**.
T-17 I.4:3 in one way, and in another way the **o.** part
T-17 III.2:3 the exclusion of the truth about the **o.**,
T-17 III.3:1 not the body of the **o.** with which union is
T-17 III.3:2 For even the body of the **o.**, already a
T-17 III.4:5 the reality of the **o.** does not enter at all to
T-17 III.4:6 less the **o.** really brings to the relationship
T-17 III.9:2 that to choose one is to let the **o.** go.
T-17 IV.6:4 than we have at many **o.** aspects of the
T-17 IV.12:11 The **o.** is lightly framed and hung in light,
T-17 IV.13:3 The **o.** is framed for perfect clarity. The
T-17 IV.14:1 The **o.** picture is lightly framed, for time
T-17 IV.14:5 when both are seen in relation to each **o.**.
T-18 I.1:3 aspect of the Sonship in favor of the **o.**.
T-18 I.1:4 valuable and the **o.** is replaced by him.
T-18 I.2:6 One would unite; the **o.** separate. Nothing
T-18 I.7:5 You but believe it is the **o.** way; that truth
T-18 I.12:4 loveliness and joy the **o.** holds within it.
T-18 III.1:3 Each dream has led to **o.** dreams, and
T-18 III.4:1 you joined each **o.** you were not alone. Do
T-18 V.3:7 have accepted one; the **o.** will be provided
T-18 V.6:3 peace of one is an equal threat to the **o.**.
T-18 V.6:6 come to either of you without the **o.**. And
T-18 V.7:1 the **o.** and how much gratitude is due him
T-18 VI.7:3 guilt stands between you and **o.** minds.
T-18 VI.8:6 up of different parts, which reach each **o.**.
T-19 I.5:11 The **o.** part would heal, and therefore calls
T-19 I.7:4 but totally disconnected to each **o.**. And
T-19 III.3:1 An error, on the **o.** hand, is not attractive.
T-19 III.8:3 eternal opposition to Him and to each **o.**.
T19. IV.A.10:8 that what the **o.** looks upon does not exist
T19..IV.B.15:1 guilt will someone **o.** than yourself suffer.
T19..IV.C.11:2 stand for something **o.** than themselves.
T19. IV.D.17:5 give redemption to each **o.** and share in it,
T-20 I.2:6 thorns in one hand and lilies in the **o.**,
T-20 II.8:1 chosen home is on the **o.** side, beyond the
T-20 III.8:8 both you and your brother, to bless the **o.**.
T-20 III.10:4 gentleness upon each **o.** and on ourselves.
T-20 III.11:7 lead the **o.** to the Father as surely as God
T-20 IV.2:10 in minds that have established **o.** laws,
T-20 IV.3:7 them to suffer the results of any **o.** source.
T-20 V.3:2 all it means is that it wants the **o.** for itself
T-20 V.7:2 Would you exchange this gift for any **o.**?
T-20 VI.12:6 God as equal things are like unto each **o.**.
T-20 VII.6:7 in unholy relationships with **o.** bodies,
T-20 VII.7:4 Neither can serve the purpose of the **o.**,
T-20 VIII.9:2 And one is sin, the **o.** holiness. Nothing is
T-21 I.5:3 They try to reach each **o.**, and they fail,
T-21 II.7:4 This **o.** "will," which seems to tell you
T-21 II.13:3 each **o.** and separate from your Father,
T-21 III.1:4 of yourself, perhaps more often of the **o.**.
T-21 III.11:6 the sign the **o.** has disappeared from sight
T-21 III.11:8 Neither demands the sacrifice of the **o.**.
T-21 III.11:9 on the absence of the **o.** does each depend
T-21 IV.7:2 the **o.** part hears as the sweetest music;
T-21 V.1:3 hold, perhaps, if **o.** things were equal.
T-21 V.3:3 This **o.** self sees miracles as natural. They
T-21 V.3:6 how separate minds can influence each **o.**.
T-21 V.3:9 This **o.** self is perfectly aware of this. And
T-21 V.3:12 always change *your* mind. There *is* no **o.**.
T-21 V.4:2 Reason lies in the **o.** self you have cut off
T-21 VI.2:3 as sinful and still perceive the **o.** innocent.
T-21 VI.5:6 enters part be kept away from **o.** parts?
T-21 VI.7:2 instead without the **o.** being blessed by it,
T-21 VII.3:3 together, but have not joined each **o.**. For
T-21 VII.8:2 answered, and is answered in the **o.** three.
T-21 VII.10:3 It is the same as are the **o.** three, except in
T-22 in.1:4 seen in the **o.** yet believed by each to be
T-22 in.1:5 error, and one the **o.** cannot understand.
T-22 in.2:5 each one thinks the **o.** has what he has not
T-22 in.2:6 each to complete himself and rob the **o.**.
T-22 I.9:6 each **o.** through a vision not of the body,
T-22 I.9:8 in each the **o.** saw a perfect shelter where
T-22 II.1:2 alternatives, and different from each **o.**. In
T-22 II.1:4 be the way to lose the misery the **o.** brings
T-22 II.3:9 to **o.** dreams that are but equally unreal.
T-22 II.4:1 misery is to recognize it *and go the o. way*.
T-22 II.4:2 are different from each **o.** in every way, in
T-22 II.6:10 lies only on one side and joy upon the **o.**.
T-22 II.7:3 Either you give each **o.** life or death; either
T-22 III.9:4 Each sees within the **o.** what impels him
T-22 III.9:5 And thus he lays his sins upon the **o.**, and
T-22 IV.1:2 You must go either one way or the **o.**. For
T-22 IV.2:1 you can go back and make the **o.** choice.
T-22 IV.4:2 will you and your brother look to the **o.**!
T-22 IV.5:1 the **o.** will gently have corrected for you.
T-22 VI.1:5 For one you see as means; the **o.**, end.
T-22 VI.1:6 serve the **o.** and lead to its predominance,
T-22 VI.1:10 will make the **o.** serve his choice as means
T-22 VI.12:4 your brother were separate from the **o.**,
T-22 VI.12:5 hurt yourself without the **o.** feeling pain.
T-22 VI.13:10 is necessary that you have **o.** experiences,
T-22 VI.14:2 thinks, the **o.** will experience with him.
T-22 VI.14:7 to the **o.** because they are the same. Joy is
T-23 I.6:1 to make them different from each **o.**, in
T-23 I.6:3 Nor are they different from each **o.**. Both
T-23 I.8:4 of yourself, in conflict with each **o.**. And
T-23 I.9:3 as real, the **o.** vanquished and despised.
T-23 I.12:7 Where one abides the **o.** cannot be; where
T-23 I.12:7 be; where either goes the **o.** disappears.
T-23 II.3:5 brought to truth instead of to each **o.**,
T-23 II.5:6 becomes weak, the **o.** strong by his defeat.
T-23 II.5:7 fear of God and of each **o.** now appears as
T-23 II.9:5 Yet all the **o.** laws must lead to this. For
T-24 I.2:1 Beliefs will never openly attack each **o.**.
T-24 I.7:10 you and your brother illusions to each **o.**?
T-24 II.9:3 to kill each **o.** and deny they are the same.
T-24 V.1:10 Except that one deludes; the **o.** heals.
T-24 V.4:2 to lead the **o.** to a nameless precipice and
T-24 VI.9:2 any kind, is all the **o.** choice can offer you.
T-24 VII.1:5 while it calls to him he hears no **o.** Voice.
T-24 VII.11:3 son. The **o.** rests within, his Father's Son,
T-25 I.5:5 The Holy Spirit links the **o.** part–the tiny
T-25 III.1:4 Perception has no **o.** law than this. The
T-25 IV.5:7 it. No **o.** place; no other state nor time.
T-25 IV.5:7 other place; no **o.** state nor time. Nothing
T-25 V.1:1 to perceive the Son of God as **o.** than he is
T-25 V.1:3 the cause and aim and justifier of the **o.**.
T-25 V.1:4 but seems to draw a meaning from the **o.**.
T-25 V.1:5 the **o.** for whatever sense it seems to have.
T-25 V.1:6 believe in one unless the **o.** were the truth,
T-25 V.1:6 truth, for each attests the **o.** must be true.
T-25 V.4:4 to each an equal strength to save the **o.**,
T-25 VI.5:2 to one perceived as **o.** than himself, he
T-25 VII.6:3 the **o.** as insane and meaningless. Love is
T-25 VIII.5:7 contradicts the **o.** and denies that it is real
T-25 VIII.11:6 strengthened by their union with each **o.**.
T-26 I.2:4 Each part must sacrifice the **o.** part, to
T-26 I.4:5 that they be separate and without the **o.**.
T-26 IV.2:5 nothing stands between to push the **o.** off.
T-26 IV.4:3 and none is cherished more than any **o.**.
T-26 IV.4:7 What **o.** miracle is there but this? And
T-26 V.6:4 There *is* no **o.** teacher and no other way.
T-26 V.6:4 There *is* no other teacher and no **o.** way.
T-26 VI.2:7 There *is* no **o.** friend. What God appointed
T-26 VII.9:3 because it still conceives of **o.** choices, and
T-26 VII.14:2 cause can merely shift effects to **o.** forms.
T-26 X.3:1 one is perceived the **o.** must be seen. You
T-26 X.5:1 must be unfair to make the **o.** innocent.
T-27 I.6:5 feeling has a motivation **o.** than this one.
T-27 II.2:10 One denies the **o.** and must make it false.
T-27 II.3:9 cannot be for one and not the **o.**. Who
T-27 II.12:5 And thus He represents the **o.** half, and
T-27 II.14:4 you and thus outside yourself; the **o.** half,
T-27 II.14:6 the Holy Spirit must represent the **o.** half

T-27..... II.14:6 half until you recognize it *is* the o. half.
T-27..... II.15:3 in one unhealed and set the o. free. That is
T-27..... II.16:7 And each forgives the o., that he may
T-27..... II.16:7 he may accept his o. half as part of him.
T-27..... III.6:6 The o. half of what it represents remains
T-27..... III.7:7 Yet no o. kind can be at all. Give welcome
T-27....... V.1:7 and thus offer the o. what he has received.
T-27....... V.6:7 Who looks on one cannot perceive the o.,
T-27...... VI.4:2 to the witnesses by o. names that speak in
T-27...... VI.4:2 names that speak in o. ways for its reality.
T-27..... VII.9:1 you can choose, the o. possibility of cause,
T-27... VII.13:2 No o. cause it has, nor ever will. Nothing
T-27.... VIII.1:3 the story of how it was made by o. bodies,
T-27.... VIII.1:3 in the dust with o. bodies dying like itself.
T-27.... VIII.1:4 for o. bodies as its friends and enemies.
T-27.... VIII.2:4 It hires o. bodies, that they may protect it
T-27.. VIII.13:7 is impossible is that you be unlike each o.;
T-28......... I.6:2 all the o. attributes with which you seek to
T-28....... I.11:2 then, to o. minds to share its quietness.
T-28....... II.3:6 within a body and a world of o. bodies,
T-28....... II.3:6 are your "creations," you the "o." mind,
T-28....... II.9:1 salvation, which proceeds to go the o. way
T-28...... III.2:3 o. mind cannot project its guilt without
T-28...... IV.2:5 dream, and join in one, but let the o. go.
T-28...... IV.9:7 of God is just the same as every o. part.
T-28....... V.1:9 There is no o. choice. Except you share it,
T-28....... V.2:5 Where one appears, the o. disappears.
T-28....... V.5:5 o. sounds and other sights that *can* be seen
T-28....... V.5:5 other sounds and o. sights that *can* be seen
T-28..... VII.3:2 There is no in between, no o. choice, and
T-29....... II.5:3 is no o. place where He can find His host,
T-29...... VI.4:4 All o. goals are set in time and change
T-29..... VII.1:5 There is no o. answer you can substitute,
T-29..... VII.5:3 and no suffering proclaim a message o.
T-29.... VIII.8:6 will give him more than o. men possess. It
T-30..... VII.2:4 these labels change with o. judgments,
T-31......... I.1:9 told exactly how to tell one from the o.,
T-31..... II.5:10 But hear the o., and you join with him
T-31...... IV.7:4 And every road that leads the o. way will
T-31....... V.4:3 The o. side he does not want to see. Yet it
T-31..... V.10:7 brother, who was there to make the o.?
T-31..... V.12:7 on the one to choose, and let the o. go.
T-31...... VI.1:3 If one is real the o. must be false, for what
W-in.......... 5:3 On the o. hand, one exception held apart
W-pI....... 9.2:4 is required for these or any o. exercises.
W-pI..... 13.2:2 God and the ego "challenge" each o. as to
W-pI..... 17.1:3 to believe that it is the o. way around.
W-pI..... 19.1:2 while at o. times the order is reversed.
W-pI..... 26.2:5 together. They contradict each o..
W-pI..... 27.4:3 questions, and you have answered the o..
W-pI..... 31.1:4 o. consisting of frequent applications of
W-pI..... 32.2:2 and the o. the world you see in your mind.
W-pI..... 34.1:1 that prevail in the o. way of seeing. Peace
W-pI..... 37.2:1 is no o. way in which the idea of sacrifice
W-pI..... 37.2:2 o. way of seeing will inevitably demand
W-pI..... 49.1:3 o. part of your mind that functions in the
W-pI..... 49.2:3 The o. part is a wild illusion, frantic and
W-pI..... 53.5:7 and I will place no o. gods before Him.
W-pI..... 54.1:7 They must be one or the o.. What I see
W-pI..... 61.2:3 your role in salvation and in taking no o..
W-pI..... 64.4:3 There is no o. way. Therefore, every time
W-pI..... 64.8:3 At o. times, keep your eyes open after
W-pI..... 65.1:2 you that you have no function o. than that
W-pI..... 65.1:5 the o. goals you have invented for yourself
W-pI..... 65.8:3 *I want no o. and I have no other.* Sometimes
W-pI..... 65.8:3 *I want no other and I have no o..* Sometimes
W-pI..... 66.7:4 The o. is the home of the Holy Spirit,
W-pI..... 66.7:5 no o. guides but these to choose between,
W-pI..... 66.7:5 and no o. outcomes possible as a result of
W-pI... 66.10:3 can share in this conclusion, but in no o..
W-pI... 66.10:7 All truth stands on the o.. Let us try today
W-pI..... 67.4:2 to continue adding o. thoughts related to
W-pI..... 69.3:3 There is no o. purpose here, and no other
W-pI..... 69.3:3 purpose here, and no o. function to fulfill.
W-pI..... 70.7:5 for salvation in the past;–in o. people, in
W-pI..... 71.3:1 is simply to determine what, o. than itself,
W-pI..... 71.3:3 is still grounds for hope in o. places and in
W-pI..... 71.3:3 for hope in other places and in o. things.
W-pI..... 71.8:2 salvation will work, and o. plans will not.
W-pI..... 72.2:3 unable to reach o. minds except through
W-pI..... 76.8:7 no more strange than o. "laws" you hold
W-pI... 76.12:1 as subject to o. laws throughout the day.
W-pI..... 80.1:2 has been answered, and you have no o..
W-pI..... 80.4:3 one, you have recognized the o.. The
WpI..rII.in.1:3 and the latter part of the day to the o.. We
W-pI..... 83.2:3 *me a function o. than the one God gave me.*
W-pI..... 88.3:4 up o. laws and give them power over me. I
W-pI..... 93.9:2 One Self is true; the o. is not there. Try to
W-pI..... 95.5:1 have o. advantages for you at this time. In
W-pI..... 96.3:5 the two, for one denies the o. can be real.
W-pI... 104.3:4 o. gifts and other goals made of illusions,
W-pI... 104.3:4 other gifts and o. goals made of illusions,
W-pI... 106.4:7 to His dear Son, whose o. name is you.
W-pI... 108.3:2 brings your peace of mind to o. minds, to
W-pI... 108.6:2 to o. areas of doubt and double vision.
W-pI... 110.4:2 no split between your mind and o. minds,
WpI..rIII.in8:2 o. in the hour just before you go to sleep.
WpI..rIII.in9:2 and then go on your way to o. things,
WpIrIII.in10:3 hour, and the o. one a half an hour later.
WpIrIII.in10:6 Then turn to o. things, but try to keep the
W-pI... 121.6:3 well, but from a Teacher o. than yourself,
W-pI... 121.6:3 represents the o. Self in you. Through
W-pI... 122.4:1 Why would you seek an answer o. than
W-pI... 125.2:2 No o. means can save it, for God's plan is
W-pI... 126.2:2 seems to you that o. people are apart from
W-pI... 126.4:1 bestowed at times, at o. times withheld.
W-pI... 126.6:4 what you see in someone o. than yourself.
W-pI... 127.2:3 he can love at times, and hate at o. times.
W-pI... 127.3:6 no o. principle that rules where love is not
W-pI... 128.2:1 world, and it will serve no o. end but this.
W-pI... 130.5:2 Seek for the one; the o. disappears. But
W-pI... 130.8:1 Begin your searching for the o. world by
W-pI. 131.12:4 now; no o. goal is valued now nor sought,
W-pI... 135.9:4 apart from o. minds and separate from its
W-pI... 137.8:6 within a body free to join with o. minds,
W-pI. 137.12:5 The o. choice is but to ask what cannot be
W-pI. 138.10:3 the o. as a wholly worthless thing, a but
W-pI... 139.2:4 it looks on o. things as certain as itself.
WpI. rIV.in9:1 We add no o. thoughts, but let these be
W-pI. 153.16:4 At o. times the business of the world will
W-pI... 155.2:4 What o. choice is really theirs to make?
W-pI... 182.1:6 tiny throb, at o. times hardly remembered
W-pI... 183.6:5 on this. No o. word we use except at the
W-pI... 183.8:5 And to all o. thoughts respond with this,
W-pI... 184.1:5 set it off from o. things by emphasizing
W-pI... 184.5:1 o. vision still remain a natural direction
W-pI... 185.6:1 it wants is peace must join with o. minds,
W-pI... 189.3:2 of malice and of fear, that one belies the o.
W-pI... 189.3:4 The o. one is wholly meaningless. A world
W-pI... 195.8:5 some o. things still locked away as "sins."
W-pI. 195.10:2 and where one is the o. must be found.
W-pI... 198.3:1 Forgiveness sweeps all o. dreams away,
W-pI... 198.4:3 must be wrong; a thousand o. possibilities
W-pI... 198.8:3 to it that brings illusions to the o. side?
W-pI... 200.5:5 you free the one, the o. is accepted as he is
W-pI... 220.1:2 *of peace, for I am lost on o. roads than this.*
W-pII ..... 1.4:1 Forgiveness, on the o. hand, is still, and
W-pII . 223.1:2 I know my life is God's, I have no o. home
W-pII . 256.1:2 There is no o. way. If sin had not been
W-pII . 260.2:3 And we who are His Sons are like each o.,
W-pII ..... 5.1:1 to separate parts of his Self from o. parts.
W-pII ..... 5.3:2 Like o. dreams it sometimes seems to
W-pII . 275.1:1 no more true today than any o. day. Yet
W-pII . 307.1:2 *There is no o. will for me to have. Let me not*
W-pII . 313.2:1 today behold each o. in the sight of Christ
W-pII . 329.2:1 our union with each o. and our Source.
W-pII . 338.2:2 *All o. plans will fail. And I will have thoughts*
W-pII . 345.1:6 *to Your gifts than any o. gift that I can give.*
W-pII ..... 352.h The o. comes the peace of God Himself.
M-in.......... 1:5 The course, on the o. hand, emphasizes
M-in.......... 2:2 believe one or the o. is true all the time.
M-1 ........... 4:2 There are many thousands of o. forms, all
M-2 ........... 4:3 each o. as if they had not met before. The
M-3 ........... 1:8 relationship. They are ready for each o..
M-3 ........... 3:2 of one permits the illusion of the o.. In
M-3 ........... 4:1 he can from the o. person at that time. In
M-3 ........... 5:5 be quite hostile to each o. for some time,
M-4 ........ II.1:1 All o. traits of God's teachers rest on trust
M-4 ........ II.1:6 or do; no thought opposes any o. thought;
M-4 ..... VII.1:3 Like all the o. attributes of God's teachers
M-4 ..... VII.1:6 than many o. ideas in our curriculum. Its
M-4 ...... IX.2:7 in itself the o. attributes of God's teachers
M-8 ........... 1:2 with every o. in order to be recognized. A
M-8 ........... 2:8 mind is separate, different from o. minds,
M-10 ......... 1:1 like o. devices by which the world of
M-11 ......... 1:3 promises o. things that seem impossible,
M-12 ......... 2:6 how could they be separate from each o.?
M-13 ......... 6:9 is no o. hope in all the world that they can
M-13 ....... 6:10 is no o. voice in all the world that echoes
M-13 ....... 8:12 What o. way is there to save His Son?
M-16 ....... 10:7 Perhaps he prefers o. words, or only one,
M-19 ......... 2:4 first small step in the direction of the o..
M-23 ......... 7:2 Are o. teachers possible, to lead the way
M-24 ......... 1:7 Is any o. question about it really useful in
M-24 ......... 1:8 Like many o. beliefs, it can be bitterly
M-24 ......... 6:7 There is no o. time. No teaching that does
M-26 ......... 2:9 all things in their name and in no o..
M-28 ......... 1:9 It is the relinquishment of all o. purposes,
M-28 ......... 1:9 of all other purposes, all o. interests, all
M-28 ......... 1:9 all o. wishes and all other concerns. It is
M-28 ......... 1:9 all other wishes and all o. concerns. It is
C-1 ............ 3:1 abides in this part but sees the o. part as
C-1 ............ 4:1 The o. part of the mind is entirely illusory
C-3 ............ 1:4 Unlike all o. illusions it leads away from
C-5 ............ 6:5 You need no o.. It is possible to read his
P-2........... I.4:1 each o. and to receive the peace of God.
P-2........ III.2:5 at the beginning, and as the o. shares it, it
P-2........ III.4:6 working through o. patients to express his
P-2.......... V.8:6 Him. There is no o. way to hear His Voice.
P-2.......... V.8:7 There is no o. way to seek His Son. There
P-2.......... V.8:8 There is no o. way to find your Self. Holy
P-2........ VI.5:2 of one but reproduce the forms of the o.,
P-2........ VI.5:3 So closely is one translated into the o.,
P-2....... VII.9:8 There is no o. choice of pathways that can
P-3.......... II.4:5 need for each o. implies a sense of lack. A
P-3........ II.4:11 that any two should ever give each o..
P-3.......... II.5:5 There is no o., for there is nothing else.
P-3........ II.7:10 They take the place of o. images, and help
P-3........ III.4:4 whatever one needs is given by the o.;
P-3........ III.4:4 other; whatever one lacks the o. supplies.
S-1....... III.6:10 it well. All o. goals are at the cost of God.
S-1........ IV.1:3 need to hold the o. as an enemy has been
S-1.......... V.2:2 Where one has come the o. disappears.
S-2.......... II.3:2 who would forgive the o. does not claim
S-3........ III.1:4 understands the o. is exactly like himself.

## other's 5

T-18 ..... III.8:6 brother, and you will light each o. way.
T-20 ....... II.9:4 the veil of fear, lighting each o. way. The
T-22 ....... II.7:3 either you are each o. savior or his judge,
T-22 ..... III.9:3 because he seems to justify the o. sin.
W-pI .. 131.7:4 and earth the o. sorry outcome which is

## others 169

T-1 ........ I.21:2 God's forgiveness by extending it to o..
T-1 ......... II.1:4 result in true closeness to o.. Revelation
T-1 ....... III.1:6 to accept error in yourself and o., you
T-1 ....... III.5:9 you project this to o. you imprison them,
T-1 ..... III.5:10 them vulnerable to the distortions of o.,
T-1 ....... III.6:2 you to do unto o. as you would have them
T-1 ....... III.6:7 of your own holiness to the holiness of o..
T-1 ....... III.9:2 inevitable that they will extend them to o.
T-2 .......... I.5:4 seem to be of greater magnitude than o..
T-2 .......... I.5:7 These can be from yourself and o., from
T-2 .......... I.5:7 yourself and others, from yourself to o.,
T-2 .......... I.5:7 from yourself to others, or from o. to you.
T-2 ........ I.5:12 proceeding from lack of love in o..
T-2 ......... II.7:8 your natural talent of protecting o.,
T-2 ....... III.4:4 of the right defense it passes over all o.,
T-2 ......... V.5:4 position to undo the level confusion of o..
T-2 ... V.A.18:1 of your own healing and that of o. if, in a
T-3 .......... I.6:3 of the truly loved to o. who are like them.
T-3 ......... II.6:5 in yourself and in o. simultaneously.
T-3 ....... VI.1:4 that if you judge the reality of o. you will
T-3 ....... VI.2:5 of what is judged, whether in you or in o..

T-3 VI.5:3 you laugh at yourself you must laugh at o.
T-3 VI.8:2 yourself and project your delusion onto o.
T-3 VI.8:3 which o. are literally fighting you for your
T-4 I.4:1 your mind and help o. to change theirs.
T-4 I.10:6 Release yourself and release o.. Do not
T-4 I.10:7 and unworthy picture of yourself to o.,
T-4 I.12:1 you can do nothing to save yourself or o.,
T-4 VI.6:6 man, and can now complete it through o..
T-4 VII.7:3 but He does want it brought to o.. This
T-5 in.1:7 thus deprive o. of the joy of responding
T-5 III.9:5 in o. you are strengthening in yourself.
T-6 in.1:2 rather than being blamed on o.. Anger
T-6 I.4:5 false premises and teaching them to o..
T-6 I.9:3 because of the projection of o. onto me,
T-6 I.10:5 in o. you can learn from their experiences
T-6 II.5:2 perfection is shared He recognizes it in o.,
T-6 III.3:1 see His gentleness in o. your own mind
T-6 III.4:2 and will keep you free as o. learn it of you.
T-6 V.B.3:8 perceive consistency in the minds of o.,
T-6 V.B.3:10 and responding primarily to the ego in o.,
T-6 V.C.2:1 Holy Spirit does not teach you to judge o.,
T-6 V.C.5:3 together the lessons implied in the o., and
T-7 II.3:3 are from what you have projected onto o.,
T-7 V.4:5 if he thinks he has something that o. lack.
T-7 VII.8:3 then believe that o. are taking it from you.
T-7 VII.9:4 Projection always sees your wishes in o..
T-7 VII.9:5 is what you will think o. are doing to you.
T-8 IV.3:10 sent me to you so will I send you to o..
T-8 VII.2:4 The Holy Spirit reaches through it to o..
T-9 II.6:8 that it is for you unless you hear it in o.. It
T-9 VI.1:4 inspire joy and o. react to you with joy,
T-9 VI.1:5 if you see that it does produce joy in o.,
T-9 VI.2:1 you do not consistently arouse joy in o..
T-9 VI.5:2 the Holy Spirit teaches you to awaken o..
T-9 VIII.7:9 your exalted state you seek o. like you and
T-10 V.2:1 will believe that o. and not yourself have
T-11 IV.5:5 and as much an ego defense as blaming o.
T-11 VI.8:8 awakening of o. to share your redemption
T-12 I.1:6 the motives of o. is hazardous to you. If
T-12 I.8:1 of o. more and more consistently, you will
T-12 I.8:6 of the motives of o. will serve you then.
T-12 I.8:7 only loving thoughts in o. and to regard
T-12 I.9:2 it in o. you learn to supply the loss, the
T-12 V.3:2 For o. do react to attack if they perceive it,
T-13 III.6:3 fundamental illusion on which the o. rest.
T-13 V.3:7 first, for what you attack is not in o.. Its
T-13 V.3:8 by attacking o. you are literally attacking
T-13 VI.11:10 it will draw the o. out of darkness as you
T-14 X.4:3 or more productive and valuable than o..
T-14 X.4:5 Heaven, while o. are motivated by the ego
T-15 V.3:5 of the Sonship can give you more than o.?
T-15 VII.4:2 that what you do to o. you have escaped.
T-15 XI.5:2 of sacrifice, justified in sacrificing o.. For
T-16 IV.4:5 which they would not share with o., are
T-16 VI.4:4 for limiting your perception of o. to theirs
T-17 IV.6:5 this one remains, you will not let the o. go
T-17 VII.9:2 faith will call the o. to share your purpose,
T-18 VI.9:1 from o. and keeping you apart from them
T-18 VII.6:5 on using means which have served o. well
T-19 II.5:4 its "best" defense, which all the o. serve.
T-19 IV.1:3 O. will seem to arise from elsewhere; from
T-19 IV.1:5 purpose from your relationship to o., to
T19 IV.A.1:3 which it radiates outward, to call the o. in
T19 IV.A.14:2 to you what they hold dear as are the o.. If
T-20 III.11:3 no sin, and it must look on o. as on itself.
T-20 VII.1:4 or parts you find more difficult than o.,
T-21 V.7:11 from the goal of sin, as are the o.. For
T-21 VII.6:2 one still seems fearful, and unlike the o..
T-21 VII.10:4 The o. are decisions that can be made,
T-21 VII.12:1 you are unsure the o. have been answered
T-21 VIII.4:2 answer to the o. has made it possible to
T-22 VI.6:3 himself the vision that he brings to o.?
T-23 II.2:2 set of thoughts that set him off from o..
T-23 II.3:2 of them are harder to overcome than o.. If
T-23 II.9:2 law of chaos, which, if the o. are accepted,
T-23 II.20:2 quite possible to value some above the o..
T-23 II.20:3 of chaos are the laws of order as do the o..
T-25 VI.1:6 himself with all the tenderness it offers o..
T-25 IX.6:4 deserves to suffer more and o. less? And
T-25 IX.6:7 to be withheld from o. as less worthy,
T-25 IX.7:2 and kept apart from o. as less deserving,
T-26 II.1:2 difficulty in resolving some than o.. Every
T-26 II.5:1 to be corrected while you keep the o. to
T-26 VII.6:4 Yet it appears some are more true than o.,
T-27 IV.4:12 The o. are not true. What can the body
T-27 VIII.8:1 you will believe that o. do to you exactly
T-29 IV.1:4 dreams are kept, and o. wakened from?
T-30 VI.6:4 are harder to look past than o. are. It
W-in 8:1 and o. may seem to be quite startling.
W-pI 5.4:1 greater weight to some subjects than to o.
W-pI 5.6:1 perceived sources of upset than to o.. If
W-pI 5.6:3 *keep this form of upset and let the o. go. For*
W-pI 6.3:1 some upsetting thoughts more than to o.,
W-pI 6.3:5 *keep this form of upset and let the o. go. For*
W-pI 14.6:3 and o. are part of your personal hell. It
W-pI 21.3:3 on some situations or persons than on o.,
W-pI 21.3:5 forms of attack are more justified than o..
WpI rI.in.2:5 five ideas appeals to you more than the o.,
W-pI 54.3:6 call to the separation thoughts of o., so
W-pI 61.3:4 of the power that is given you to save o..
W-pI 65.1:4 you hold while you still cherish o.. The
W-pI 72.7:3 it. O. love the body, and try to glorify and
W-pI 79.5:5 O. remain unsolved under a cloud of
W-pI 92.6:2 love. It sees all o. different from itself, and
W-pI 108.9:5 He represents the o., and through him
W-pI 127.2:4 itself although it is withheld from o.. To
W-pI 132.7:4 O. find it in experience that is not of this
W-pI 133.8:1 is the one on which the o. rest. Why is the
W-pI 137.1:3 states. Sickness is a retreat from o., and a
W-pI 137.2:2 the rest, to suffer what the o. do not feel.
W-pI 138.6:4 solve this one, the o. are resolved with it,
W-pI 140.9:4 not exist is truer in some forms than o..
W-pI 155.4:4 O. have chosen nothing but the world,
W-pI 155.5:3 You walk this path as o. walk, nor do you
W-pI 156.2:3 nor be in parts uncertain and in o. sure.
W-pI 181.2:6 from what you see in o. past their sins.
W-pI 182.2:3 O. will deny that they are sad, and do not
W-pI 182.2:4 Still o. will maintain that what we speak
W-pI 185.5:4 would offer nothing more than all the o..
W-pI 185.8:6 reserving shame and secrecy for o.. They
W-pI 195.1:2 do is see themselves as better off than o..
W-pI 195.1:5 cause for thanks while o. have less cause?
W-pI 195.4:5 some are loosed while o. still are bound.
W-pI 196.5:1 you can make attacks on o. and escape
W-pI 198.3:1 though it is itself a dream, it breeds no o..
M-in 2:3 From your demonstration o. learn, and so
M-in 2:10 to you a chance to teach o. what you are,
M-in 3:1 you believe the relationship of o. is to you
M-4 II.1:2 been achieved, the o. cannot fail to follow
M-4 IX.1:2 to his learning, while keeping o. apart? If
M-8 2:8 to gratify its needs at the expense of o..
M-8 6:3 be those who seem to be "sicker" than o.,
M-22 4:3 perception of himself and of all o. as well.
M-23 2:3 Temptation may recur to o., but never to
M-24 5:1 himself, or discuss it with o. who do? The
M-26 1:6 as yet, but they have joined with o.. This
M-26 1:8 enables o. to leave the world with them.
M-29 1:6 first. O. might do better to begin with the
M-29 1:7 Still o. may need to start at the more
C-4 1:4 last in time a little while longer than o..
P-3 I.3:3 You can see o. as well, for seeing is not
P-3 II.1:5 that a large number of o. turn for help.
S-1 III.h Praying for O.
S-1 III.1:2 Why, then, should you pray for o. at all?
S-1 III.1:4 it? Praying for o., if rightly understood,
S-1 III.3:7 or advantage to himself in setting o. free.
S-1 IV.h Praying with O.
S-2 I.6:2 O. will make mistakes and so will you, as

## otherwise 71

T-1 II.6:4 in time than they would o. have been. The
T-1 III.1:4 of all errors that you could not o. correct.
T-2 V.1:2 O. they may unwittingly foster the belief
T-2 VII.2:3 O. a miracle will be necessary to set the
T-3 VII.1:8 because o. you will be unable to escape
T-3 VII.6:4 It cannot stand o.. You who fear salvation
T-4 I.11:1 home for you, because it cannot build o..
T-4 IV.2:8 thinking o. has held your ego together,
T-4 IV.3:3 by your own decisions, and then decide o.
T-5 VII.6:3 wrongly, but can as actively decide o.. Be
T-5 VII.6:8 *the decision myself, but I can also decide o.. I*
T-5 VII.6:9 *I want to decide o., because I want to be at*
T-6 I.3:6 O., I cannot serve as a model for learning.
T-7 VI.8:5 o. the light of your understanding would
T-8 VIII.1:15 O., there is no difference between the part
T-8 VIII.9:4 Everything used o. is. Do not allow the
T-9 I.13:2 *to.* O. you would not have been created
T-10 V.9:7 is not because you will be punished o.. It
T-11 I.10:2 for o. His Will would not be extended.
T-11 III.6:4 you in peace. For you cannot accept it o..
T-11 IV.6:2 o. you will believe that the door is barred
T-11 IV.8:3 o. he will not know the Father or the Son.
T-11 VI.6:7 for o. you will not awake in God, safely
T-11 VI.7:7 given Himself to him, how could it be o.?
T-12 II.10:5 o. His knowledge remains useless to you.
T-12 VI.2:7 to do so, and therefore you can decide o..
T-14 VII.1:8 o. it becomes the messenger of ignorance
T-14 VIII.2:2 you. Everything that promises o., great or
T-14 X.8:3 O. it will attack the form. If you believe
T-16 VI.1:7 impossible to define it o. and understand
T-17 V.11:2 He could not have entered o.. Although
T-18 V.4:3 "Thy Will be done," and not, "I want it o..
T-20 VII.3:5 for o. you will make the error of believing
T-21 II.7:5 show you o. must therefore seem unreal.
T-21 II.13:2 See what "proves" o., and you deny your
T-21 IV.4:9 How, o., could it have been willing to see
T-23 I.2:7 And God thinks o.. This is no war; only
T-25 VII.11:6 suffering. For o. would evil triumph, and
T-26 VII.14:5 For o. he still demands that he must make
T-26 X.2:3 For o., how could some be evaluated as
T-27 VI.3:9 And o. he lies, if you should call him by
T-27 VII.4:7 O. is the avenger's knife in his own hand,
T-29 VII.7:2 For o., the future will be like the past, and
T-30 VIII.5:3 you would have it o. in some respects. For
T-31 IV.7:7 then. For o., it is a simple teaching in the
T-31 V.8:5 else. For o., you would be asked to make
T-31 VIII.8:5 you see, for o. you will behold it not. To
W-pI 13.2:3 fearful that the void may o. be used to
W-pI 17.4:2 the minute or so that is o. recommended.
W-pI 22.1:5 O., thoughts of attack and counter-attack
W-pI 24.1:6 O., you will not recognize what they are.
W-pI 27.3:5 conversation, or o. occupied at the time.
W-pI 47.5:2 for o. you would believe that you could
W-pI 71.5:3 O., your purpose is divided and you will
W-pI 131.3:4 O., you still are free to choose a goal that
W-pI 159.1:6 Salvation teaches o.. To give is how to
W-pI 185.9:2 you make. Be not deceived that it is o.. No
W-pI 186.4:5 we are. It is but arrogance that judges o..
W-pI 195.6:3 thing, for o. we offer thanks for nothing,
M-in 4:3 How could it be o.? Everyone who follows
M-4 III.1:8 equally acceptable, for who could judge o.
M-8 2:2 How could it be o.? By definition, an
M-9 1:9 O. the old thought system still has a basis
M-12 6:5 The dream says o., but who would put his
M-13 5:4 for o. the pleasure would be seen as pain,
M-13 5:8 who pursues the world's goals can do o..
M-14 5:12 His Word says o.. His Will be done. It
M-14 5:14 It cannot be o.. And be you thankful it is
M-18 1:7 O. salvation would be only the same age-
M-27 6:11 Do you not see that o. He has an opposite
S-2 I.3:6 How o. can prayer return to God? He

## Our 2

• God and Jesus
*our*

W-pII 299.1:3 O. Will, together, understands it. And
W-pII 299.1:4 And O. Will, together, knows that it is so.

## our 644

• Jesus
*noise word*
*Our*

T-1 VII.5:6 to me because of o. inherent equality.
T-2 IV.1:1 O. emphasis is now on healing. The

T-3 I.2:8 believe o. Father really thinks this way? It
T-3 V.1:4 clarify some of o. subsequent statements.
T-4 III.2:6 Against o. united strength the ego cannot
T-4 III.7:6 I can help you only as o. Father created us
T-5 I.2:1 Let us start o. process of reawakening
T-5 II.10:7 O. task is the joyous one of waking it to
T-5 II.12:4 of o. joint motivation is beyond belief, but
T-5 IV.8:13 Whose Heart and Hands we have o. being
T-5 V.1:1 Perhaps some of o. concepts will become
T-5 VI.11:6 because my will is that of o. Father, from
T-6 I.5:1 me, but o. fundamental equality can be
T-6 I.7:5 Help me to teach it to o. brothers in the
T-6 II.13:5 joining o. minds in this light we proclaim
T-7 V.10:3 O. brothers are forgetful. That is why they
T-7 V.11:2 mind we share is shared by all o. brothers,
T-7 V.11:3 o. gratitude to them make them aware of
T-8 IV.5:1 Healing reflects o. joint will. This is
T-8 IV.5:11 are possible through o. joint decision, but
T-8 IV.7:1 were not mine it would not be o. Father's.
T-8 IV.7:6 In o. remembrance of each other lies our
T-8 IV.7:6 of each other lies o. remembrance of God.
T-8 IV.7:9 This is o. gift of gratitude to Him, which
T-8 V.1:6 but together o. minds fuse into something
T-8 V.3:7 to o. joy in uniting with His Will for us.
T-8 V.4:2 O. union is therefore the way to renounce
T-8 V.4:4 ego. O. success in transcending the ego is
T-8 V.4:6 all. Nothing can prevail against o. united
T-8 V.5:4 the journey back to God Who is o. home.
T-8 VI.1:2 and gather in o. brothers as we continue
T-8 VI.1:3 Every gain in o. strength is offered for all,
T-8 VI.8:4 O. function is to work together, because
T-8 VI.8:8 O. creations are as holy as we are, and we
T-8 VI.8:9 Through o. creations we extend our love,
T-8 VI.8:9 Through our creations we extend o. love,
T-8 IX.7:4 O. minds are whole because they are one.
T-11 in.4:3 you from o. Father to offer you everything
T-11 V.1:5 of the ego will be o. lesson for a while, for
T-12 II.7:4 O. mission is to escape from crucifixion,
T-12 II.7:5 with you as o. Father walked with me. Do
T-13 VII.16:10 which we hide o. brothers from the world,
T-13 X.14:6 we will surely enter in o. sinlessness. God
T-14 V.9:2 me. O. power comes not of us, but of our
T-14 V.9:2 power comes not of us, but of o. Father.
T-14 VII.4:1 O. emphasis has been on bringing what is
T-15 III.7:2 o. task together to restore the awareness
T-15 VI.2:5 holy instant we share o. faith in God's Son
T-15 VI.2:5 in o. appreciation of his worth we cannot
T-15 IX.2:1 O. task is but to continue, as fast as
T-15 X.3:2 are willing to accept o. relationship as real
T-15 X.3:3 For in o. union you will accept all of our
T-15 X.3:3 union you will accept all of o. brothers.
T-15 XI.3:2 and let us celebrate o. release together by
T-15 XI.3:4 littleness will disappear in o. relationship,
T-15 XI.3:4 as o. relationship with our Father, and as
T-15 XI.3:4 as our relationship with o. Father, and as
T-15 XI.3:5 to us and disappear in o. presence, and
T-15 XI.10:13 made holy for you. This is o. will. Amen.
T-16 VII.12:1 *Forgive us o. illusions, Father, and help us*
T-16 VII.12:1 *us to accept o. true relationship with You, in*
T-16 VII.12:2 *O. holiness is Yours. What can there be in us*
T-17 IV.16:2 by giving Him ascendance in o. minds.
T-17 IV.16:7 Him lies in o. relationship to one another.
T-18 I.10:9 His gift as o. most holy and perfect reality,
T-18 III.7:4 made whole in o. desire to make whole.
T-18 IX.11:1 is still beyond the scope of o. curriculum.
T-19 I.4:1 Do not overlook o. earlier statement that
T19 IV.B.5:3 that you can place before o. union, for in
T19 IV.B.8:5 in Him it *is* possible that o. communion,
T19 IV.B.9:6 He Who is o. home is homeless with us. Is
T19 IV.C.8:2 My brother, child of o. Father, this is a
T-20 II.8:11 Let us lift up o. eyes together, not in fear
T-20 II.8:12 in us, for in o. vision will be no illusions;
T-20 II.9:5 that leads us is within us, as is o. home. So
T-20 III.11:1 me the certainty o. union will be soon.
T-28 III.1:1 beyond salvation is not o. concern. For
T-30 VII.7:8 O. common language lets us speak to all
T-30 VII.7:8 language lets us speak to all o. brothers,
T-31 I.12:2 Let us remember not o. own ideas of what
T-31 I.12:4 loosened from o. minds and swept away.
T-31 VIII.9:3 appear like lawns of Heaven to o. sight, to
W-pI 10.3:3 of repeating o. earlier statement that your
W-pI 13.6:1 o. first attempt at stating an explicit cause
W-pI 14.3:6 O. direction is toward perfect safety and
W-pI 20.1:1 casual about o. practice periods thus far.
W-pI 20.2:1 is o. first attempt to introduce structure.
W-pI 20.3:3 an indication that o. goal is of little worth.
W-pI 28.1:3 them in the future is not o. concern here.
W-pI 29.4:1 O. six two-minute practice periods for
W-pI 30.2:3 to see in the world what is in o. minds,
W-pI 41.5:3 Today we will make o. first real attempt
W-pI 45.4:1 O. three five-minute practice periods for
W-pI 49.3:3 we are joining o. will with the Will of God
W-pI 56.h O. review for today covers the following:
W-pI 63.3:2 day with the thought of it in o. awareness.
W-pI 64.3:1 review o. last few lessons, your function
W-pI 66.1:1 an emphasis throughout o. recent lessons
W-pI 66.4:1 O. longer practice period today has as its
W-pI 66.10:2 the premises on which o. conclusion rests.
W-pI 69.2:2 this in o. more extended practice period,
W-pI 69.3:1 Let us begin o. longer practice period
W-pI 69.3:2 else. Salvation is o. only need. There is no
W-pI 69.3:4 Learning salvation is o. only goal. Let us
W-pI 72.9:2 that is outside us, and is not o. concern.
W-pI 72.9:3 without a body is to be in o. natural state.
W-pI 72.9:5 To see o. Self as separate from the body is
W-pI 72.10:1 O. goal in the longer practice periods
W-pI 72.10:11 We have shouted o. grievances so loudly
W-pI 72.10:12 We have used o. grievances to close our
W-pI 72.10:12 used our grievances to close o. eyes and
W-pI 72.10:12 grievances to close our eyes and stop o.
W-pI 73.9:1 We will begin o. longer practice periods
W-pI 74.1:1 toward which all o. exercises are directed.
W-pI 75.3:1 O. exercises for today will be happy ones,
W-pI 75.3:2 the past remain to darken o. sight and
W-pI 75.4:1 O. longer practice periods will be devoted
W-pI 75.4:1 at the world that o. forgiveness shows us.
W-pI 75.4:3 this. O. single purpose makes our goal
W-pI 75.4:3 single purpose makes o. goal inevitable.
W-pI 76.12:2 is o. statement of freedom from all danger
W-pI 76.12:3 It is o. acknowledgment that God is our
W-pI 76.12:3 acknowledgment that God is o. Father,
W-pI 77.7:1 O. shorter practice periods will be
W-pI 78.2:3 but lay it down and gently lift o. eyes in
W-pI 78.4:2 him; we will not look upon o. grievances.
W-pI 78.6:1 O. longer practice periods today will see
W-pI 78.7:1 and see o. savior shining in the light of
W-pI 78.10:1 of God's salvation plan, and not o. own.
W-pI 78.10:2 to hide his light behind o. grievances. To
W-pI 79.7:1 In o. longer practice periods today we
W-pI 79.7:3 will try to free o. minds of all the many
W-pI 79.9:3 answer. O. efforts will be directed toward
W-pI 80.4:1 In o. longer practice periods today, we
WpI rII.in.1:2 We will begin where o. last review left off,
W-pI 81.h O. ideas for review today are:
W-pI 87.h O. review today will cover these ideas:
W-pI 89.h These are o. review ideas for today:
W-pI 91.6:6 ends is needed for o. exercises today.
W-pI 93.8:1 In o. longer exercise periods today, which
W-pI 95.3:2 We will again direct o. exercises towards
W-pI 95.8:3 forgive ourselves for o. lapses in diligence,
W-pI 95.8:3 and o. failures to follow the instructions
W-pI 95.8:4 than give it power to delay o. learning. If
W-pI 96.8:2 O. hourly five-minute practicing will be a
W-pI 98.2:2 All o. doubts we lay aside today, and take
W-pI 98.2:2 take o. stand with certainty of purpose,
W-pI 98.2:4 Not one mistake stands in o. way. For we
W-pI 98.2:6 All o. sins are washed away by realizing
W-pI 98.4:2 join with us, and, borrowing o. certainty,
W-pI 100.5:2 to God's plan, as well as to o. vision.
W-pI 100.6:1 to understand joy is o. function here. If
W-pI 100.7:1 today, in o. five-minute practice periods,
W-pI 100.7:1 us according to o. Father's Will and ours.
W-pI 102.3:1 we will continue to devote o. periods of
W-pI 104.2:2 His are the gifts that are o. own in truth.
W-pI 104.3:1 we but unite o. will with what God wills,
W-pI 104.3:2 one. O. longer practice periods today, the
W-pI 104.4:2 clear a holy place within o. minds before
W-pI 105.6:1 Today o. practice periods will start a little
W-pI 107.7:2 to us, that we may recognize it as o. own.
W-pI 107.7:4 of illusion are not o. approach today. We
W-pI 108.10:1 O. very simple lesson for today will teach
W-pI 109.1:4 answer o. asking with what we request.
W-pI 109.9:3 here, for thus o. rest is made complete,
W-pI 110.10:4 opening o. hands and hearts and minds
W-pI 110.11:3 may be reminded of His Son, o. holy Self,
WpI rIII.in1:1 O. next review begins today. We will
WpI rIII.in2:4 Rituals are not o. aim, and would defeat
WpI rIII.in2:4 are not our aim, and would defeat o. goal.
W-pI 122.9:1 undertake o. practicing today with hope
W-pI 122.9:2 aware we hold the key within o. hands,
W-pI 123.4:1 in gratitude we lift o. hearts above despair
W-pI 123.4:1 above despair, and raise o. thankful eyes,
W-pI 123.4:2 has willed to be o. true Identity in Him.
W-pI 123.5:2 give thanks that in o. solitude a Friend has
W-pI 124.1:1 we will again give thanks for o. Identity in
W-pI 124.1:2 O. home is safe, protection guaranteed in
W-pI 124.1:2 available to us in all o. undertakings. We
W-pI 124.1:5 with the universe we go o. way rejoicing,
W-pI 124.2:1 How holy are o. minds! And everything
W-pI 124.2:4 life. O. shining footprints point the way to
W-pI 124.2:4 for God is o. Companion as we walk the
W-pI 124.3:1 is o. eternal gift to those who follow after,
W-pI 124.4:2 o. faith and our awareness of His Presence
W-pI 124.4:2 our faith and o. awareness of His Presence
W-pI 124.4:4 We feel Him in o. hearts. Our minds
W-pI 124.4:5 O. minds contain His Thoughts; our eyes
W-pI 124.4:5 o. eyes behold His loveliness in all we look
W-pI 124.7:4 For we would keep the gifts o. Father gave
W-pI 124.7:5 world may share o. recognition of reality.
W-pI 124.7:6 In o. experience the world is freed. As we
W-pI 124.7:7 As we deny o. separation from our Father,
W-pI 124.7:7 As we deny our separation from o. Father,
W-pI 124.8:4 o. first attempt at an extended period for
W-pI 125.3:1 without intrusion of o. petty thoughts,
W-pI 125.3:1 thoughts, without o. personal desires, and
W-pI 127.10:4 we raise o. eyes upon a different present,
W-pI 127.11:4 Now are they all o. brothers in God's Love
W-pI 127.12:1 outside o. love if we would know our Self.
W-pI 127.12:1 outside our love if we would know o. Self.
W-pI 128.5:3 We hold it purposeless within o. minds,
W-pI 129.1:3 O. emphasis is not on giving up the world
W-pI 130.7:2 devote o. minds to finding only what is
W-pI 131.11:1 as we start upon o. practice periods. Begin
W-pI 132.14:1 Today o. purpose is to free the world
W-pI 132.14:4 For we are in the home o. Father set for us
W-pI 132.14:5 this day from every one of o. illusions,
W-pI 133.13:3 real. O. two extended practice periods of
W-pI 134.14:2 with o. reality in freedom and in peace.
W-pI 134.14:3 and in peace. O. practicing becomes the
W-pI 134.14:3 lighting up the way for all o. brothers,
W-pI 135.20:4 And gladly will o. brothers lay aside their
W-pI 135.21:2 us for o. accomplishment of this today.
W-pI 135.21:3 realize that o. defenselessness is all that is
W-pI 135.21:3 to dawn upon o. minds with certainty.
W-pI 135.22:1 blocks the truth from entering o. minds.
W-pI 136.15:1 This is o. aim today. And we will give a
W-pI 137.12:6 ask that only truth will occupy o. minds;
W-pI 137.13:1 o. function is to let our minds be healed,
W-pI 137.13:1 our function is to let o. minds be healed,
W-pI 137.15:4 by, remembering o. purpose with this
W-pI 138.12:1 Before we close o. eyes in sleep tonight,
W-pI 138.12:2 we give the last five minutes of o. waking
W-pI 138.12:3 passed, we have declared o. choice again,
W-pI 139.8:5 Let us not allow o. holy minds to occupy
W-pI 139.9:4 It is more than just o. happiness alone we
W-pI 139.11:1 o. minds to our assignment for today. We
W-pI 139.11:1 our minds to o. assignment for today. We
W-pI 139.11:2 start with this review of what o. mission is
W-pI 139.11:6 And in o. memory is the recall how dear
W-pI 139.11:6 the recall how dear o. brothers are to us in
W-pI 139.11:6 how o. Father's Love contains them all.
W-pI 139.12:1 we repeat o. dedication to our cause today
W-pI 139.12:1 we repeat our dedication to o. cause today
W-pI 139.12:1 that would distract us from o. holy aim.
W-pI 140.8:1 Today we seek to change o. minds about
W-pI 140.8:2 is in o. minds because our Father placed it
W-pI 140.8:2 because o. Father placed it there for us. It

| | |
|---|---|
| W-pI...140.8:4 | It is as near to us as **o.** own thoughts; so |
| W-pI.140.10:1 | So do we lay aside **o.** amulets, our charms |
| W-pI.140.10:1 | our amulets, **o.** charms and medicines, |
| W-pI.140.10:1 | **o.** chants and bits of magic in whatever |
| W-pI.140.11:2 | to sleep. **O.** only preparation is to let our |
| W-pI.140.11:2 | to let **o.** interfering thoughts be laid aside, |
| W-pI.140.11:4 | when we can hear **o.** Father speak to us. |
| W-pI.140.12:1 | nothing in **o.** hands to which we cling, |
| W-pI.140.12:4 | deep that no illusion can disturb **o.** minds |
| W-pI.140.12:6 | we will say **o.** prayer for healing hourly, |
| W-pI.140.12:6 | to hear the answer to **o.** prayer be given us |
| WpI.rIV.in1:3 | Such is **o.** aim for this review, and for the |
| WpI.rIV.in3:1 | Let us begin **o.** preparation with some |
| WpI.rIV.in4:4 | in this review with readying **o.** minds to |
| WpI.rIV.in7:6 | we will use no format for **o.** practicing but |
| WpI.rIV.in9:2 | and all **o.** Father wills that we receive as |
| WpI.rIV.in9:3 | and through **o.** faithfulness restored the |
| W-pI.151.13:3 | begins. And then we watch **o.** thoughts, |
| W-pI.151.16:4 | Now do we lift **o.** resurrected minds in |
| W-pI.151.16:4 | to Him Who has restored **o.** sanity to us. |
| W-pI.151.17:2 | us and happily accepts **o.** holy thoughts, |
| W-pI.151.17:3 | Now has **o.** ministry begun at last, to |
| W-pI...152.8:2 | The power of decision is **o.** own. Decide |
| W-pI...152.9:4 | and lift **o.** hearts in true humility instead |
| W-pI.152.10:1 | The power of decision is **o.** own. And we |
| W-pI.152.10:5 | from hell, are joyously accepted as **o.** own. |
| W-pI.152.11:2 | encouraging **o.** frightened minds with this |
| W-pI.152.11:5 | humbly ask **o.** Self that He reveal Himself |
| W-pI.152.11:6 | never left will come again to **o.** awareness, |
| W-pI...153.8:2 | For **o.** true purpose is to save the world, |
| W-pI...153.8:2 | for foolishness the endless joy **o.** function |
| W-pI...153.8:3 | not let **o.** happiness slip by because a |
| W-pI...153.8:3 | dream happened to cross **o.** minds, and |
| W-pI...153.9:3 | secure, serenely certain of **o.** safety now, |
| W-pI...153.9:3 | sure we will fulfill **o.** chosen purpose, as |
| W-pI...153.9:3 | as **o.** ministry extends its holy blessing |
| W-pI.153.13:3 | lock **o.** quaint and childish thoughts of sin |
| W-pI.153.14:1 | but for a moment more, to play **o.** final, |
| W-pI.153.14:2 | we go to take **o.** rightful place where truth |
| W-pI.153.15:2 | will begin each day by giving **o.** attention |
| W-pI.153.15:5 | ceases to arise to turn us from **o.** purpose, |
| W-pI.153.16:1 | Each hour adds to **o.** increasing peace, as |
| W-pI.153.16:4 | a little while, and turn **o.** thoughts to God. |
| W-pI.153.17:1 | will observe **o.** trust as ministers of God, |
| W-pI.153.17:1 | remembrance of **o.** mission and His Love. |
| W-pI.153.19:1 | Today **o.** theme is our defenselessness. |
| W-pI.153.19:1 | Today our theme is **o.** defenselessness. |
| W-pI.153.19:3 | in Christ, and let **o.** weakness disappear, |
| W-pI.153.19:4 | never leaves **o.** weakness unsupported by |
| W-pI.153.19:5 | feel the threat of **o.** defenses undermine |
| W-pI.153.19:5 | undermine **o.** certainty of purpose. We |
| W-pI...154.1:4 | and to delay commitment to **o.** function. |
| W-pI...154.1:5 | It is not **o.** part to judge our worth, nor |
| W-pI...154.1:5 | It is not our part to judge **o.** worth, nor |
| W-pI...154.1:6 | **O.** part is cast in Heaven, not in hell. And |
| W-pI...154.1:7 | what we believe to be **o.** strength is often |
| W-pI.154.10:2 | We will not seek to keep **o.** minds apart |
| W-pI.154.10:2 | it is but **o.** voice we hear as we attend Him |
| W-pI.154.11:2 | needs **o.** voice that He may speak through |
| W-pI.154.11:3 | He needs **o.** hands to hold His messages, |
| W-pI.154.11:4 | needs **o.** feet to bring us where He wills, |
| W-pI.154.11:5 | And He needs **o.** will united with His Own |
| W-pI.154.13:1 | **O.** lesson for today is stated thus: *I am* |
| W-pI.154.14:1 | world recedes as we light up **o.** minds, |
| W-pI.154.14:2 | message sent to us today from **o.** Creator. |
| W-pI.154.14:3 | have changed **o.** minds about ourselves, |
| W-pI.154.14:3 | about ourselves, and what **o.** function is. |
| W-pI.154.14:4 | **o.** many gifts from our Creator will spring |
| W-pI.154.14:4 | our many gifts from **o.** Creator will spring |
| W-pI.154.14:4 | spring to **o.** sight and leap into our hands, |
| W-pI.154.14:4 | spring to our sight and leap into **o.** hands, |
| W-pI.155.11:4 | This is **o.** final journey, which we make for |
| W-pI.155.11:5 | We must not lose **o.** way. For as truth |
| W-pI.155.11:6 | goes before **o.** brothers who will follow us. |
| W-pI...156.2:1 | thoughts that we present in **o.** curriculum |
| W-pI...157.2:4 | it, sure of **o.** direction and our only goal. |
| W-pI...157.2:4 | it, sure of our direction and **o.** only goal. |
| W-pI...157.6:3 | it leaves a vision in **o.** eyes which we can |
| W-pI...158.2:6 | **O.** lesson yesterday evoked a theme found |
| W-pI...158.6:5 | This is beyond **o.** goal, for it transcends |
| W-pI...158.6:6 | **O.** concern is with Christ's vision. This we |
| W-pI.159.10:8 | vision gives the means for a return to **o.** |
| W-pI...160.2:1 | is a stranger in **o.** midst, who comes from |
| W-pI...161.1:1 | and take a stand against **o.** anger, that our |
| W-pI...161.1:1 | **o.** fears may disappear and offer room to |
| W-pI...161.5:1 | be the body that we feel limits **o.** freedom, |
| W-pI...161.5:1 | makes us suffer, and at last puts out **o.** life |
| W-pI...161.6:2 | thought is surely reminiscent of **o.** text, |
| W-pI...163.8:5 | for their salvation and **o.** own as well. God |
| W-pI...163.9:1 | *O. Father, bless our eyes today. We are Your* |
| W-pI...163.9:1 | *Our Father, bless* **o.** *eyes today. We are Your* |
| W-pI...163.9:7 | *ours, and* **o.** *will is one with Yours eternally.* |
| W-pI......164.h | are we one with Him Who is **o.** Source. |
| W-pI...164.1:3 | upon what is forever there; not in **o.** sight, |
| W-pI...164.7:3 | **O.** practicing today becomes our gift of |
| W-pI...164.7:3 | Our practicing today becomes **o.** gift of |
| W-pI...164.7:3 | **o.** release from blindness and from misery |
| W-pI...164.7:4 | All that we see will but increase **o.** joy, |
| W-pI...164.7:4 | joy, because its holiness reflects **o.** own. |
| W-pI...164.7:5 | with all the world forgiven in **o.** own. We |
| W-pI...164.7:6 | we behold it in the light in which **o.** Savior |
| W-pI...164.7:6 | through His forgiving vision, not **o.** own. |
| W-pI...165.8:3 | His sureness lies beyond **o.** every doubt. |
| W-pI...165.8:4 | His Love remains beyond **o.** every fear. |
| W-pI...165.8:5 | is still beyond all dreams and in **o.** minds, |
| W-pI...167.3:7 | to its centrality in **o.** attempts to change |
| W-pI.167.10:1 | of the truth, and not deny **o.** holy heritage |
| W-pI.167.10:2 | **O.** life is not as we imagine it. Who |
| W-pI...168.3:1 | most carefully preserved within **o.** hearts, |
| W-pI...168.3:4 | and sweeps away the cobwebs of **o.** sleep. |
| W-pI...168.5:2 | us. **O.** faith lies in the Giver, not our own |
| W-pI...168.5:2 | lies in the Giver, not **o.** own acceptance. |
| W-pI...168.5:3 | We acknowledge **o.** mistakes, but He to |
| W-pI...168.5:3 | Who answers **o.** mistakes by giving us the |
| W-pI...169.4:1 | appeared to contradict **o.** statement that |
| W-pI.169.15:1 | **O.** learning goal today does not exceed |
| W-pI.170.13:5 | *and make* **o.** *choice for all our brothers,* |
| W-pI.170.13:5 | *and make our choice for all* **o.** *brothers,* |
| W-pI.170.13:8 | *see Your glory, and in them we find* **o.** *peace.* |
| WpI...rV.in1:5 | **O.** footsteps have not been unwavering, |
| WpI...rV.in2:1 | *Steady* **o.** *feet, our Father. Let our doubts be* |
| WpI...rV.in2:1 | *Steady our feet,* **o.** *Father. Let our doubts be* |
| WpI...rV.in2:2 | *Let* **o.** *doubts be quiet and our holy minds be* |
| WpI...rV.in2:2 | *our doubts be quiet and* **o.** *holy minds be still* |
| WpI...rV.in2:5 | *Lead* **o.** *practicing as does a father lead a little* |
| WpI...rV.in3:1 | *So do we bring* **o.** *practicing to You. And if* |
| WpI...rV.in3:5 | *Quicken* **o.** *footsteps now, that we may walk* |
| WpI...rV.in3:6 | *the Word You offer us to unify* **o.** *practicing,* |
| WpI...rV.in5:3 | we keep in mind that this remains **o.** goal, |
| WpI...rV.in5:4 | Let us raise **o.** hearts from dust to life, as |
| WpI...rV.in8:3 | we devote **o.** time and effort to them. And |
| WpI...rV.in8:4 | together we will teach them to **o.** brothers |
| WpI...rV.in8:8 | whole we go together to **o.** ancient home, |
| WpI...rV.in9:8 | **O.** Father wills His Son be one with Him. |
| WpI rV.in11:1 | With this we start each day of **o.** review. |
| WpI rV.in11:3 | again with these same words upon **o.** lips, |
| WpI rV.in11:4 | the thoughts to hold it up before **o.** minds |
| WpI rV.in11:4 | in **o.** remembrance throughout the day. |
| W-pI...177.2:1 | are we one with Him Who is **o.** Source. |
| Wi181-200 1:1 | **O.** next few lessons make a special point |
| Wi181-200 2:1 | **O.** lessons now are geared specifically to |
| Wi181-200 2:1 | limited to let you see the value of **o.** goal. |
| Wi181-200 3:1 | And so we start **o.** journey beyond words |
| W-pI...181.3:1 | way to **o.** great need to let our sinlessness |
| W-pI...181.3:1 | to let **o.** sinlessness become apparent. We |
| W-pI...181.3:2 | instruct **o.** minds that it is this we seek, |
| W-pI...181.3:3 | We do not care about **o.** future goals. And |
| W-pI...181.3:4 | wherein we practice changing **o.** intent. |
| W-pI...181.6:1 | goal if anger blocks **o.** way in any form. |
| W-pI...181.6:2 | **o.** narrowed focus will restrict our sight, |
| W-pI...181.6:2 | our narrowed focus will restrict **o.** sight, |
| W-pI...181.6:2 | and turn **o.** eyes upon our own mistakes, |
| W-pI...181.6:2 | and turn our eyes upon **o.** own mistakes, |
| W-pI...181.6:2 | which we will magnify and call **o.** "sins." |
| W-pI...181.6:3 | to **o.** minds to change their focus, as we |
| W-pI...181.7:3 | seems to block the vision of **o.** sinlessness, |
| W-pI...181.8:3 | And as **o.** focus goes beyond mistakes, we |
| W-pI...181.8:5 | He feels for us becomes **o.** own as well. |
| W-pI...181.9:1 | The world which once proclaimed **o.** sins |
| W-pI...181.9:2 | **o.** love for everyone we look upon attests |
| W-pI...181.9:2 | we look upon attests to **o.** remembrance |
| W-pI...181.9:3 | as we turn **o.** minds to practicing today. |
| W-pI...181.9:6 | give **o.** trust to the experience we ask for |
| W-pI...181.9:7 | **O.** sinlessness is but the Will of God. This |
| W-pI...181.9:8 | This instant is **o.** willing one with His. |
| W-pI...183.6:6 | God's Name becomes **o.** only thought, |
| W-pI...183.6:6 | becomes our only thought, **o.** only word, |
| W-pI...183.6:6 | the only thing that occupies **o.** minds, the |
| W-pI...183.6:6 | of everything that we would call **o.** own. |
| W-pI.183.11:7 | In **o.** Father's Name, we would experience |
| W-pI.184.12:6 | In **o.** practicing, our purpose is to let our |
| W-pI.184.12:6 | **o.** purpose is to let our minds accept what |
| W-pI.184.12:6 | our purpose is to let **o.** minds accept what |
| W-pI.184.13:4 | all. One Name we bring into **o.** practicing. |
| W-pI.184.13:5 | One Name we use to unify **o.** sight. |
| W-pI.184.14:5 | Now **o.** sight is blessed with blessings we |
| W-pI.184.15:1 | *Father,* **o.** *Name is Yours. In It we are united* |
| W-pI.184.15:5 | *All* **o.** *mistakes we give to You, that we may* |
| W-pI.184.15:5 | *absolved from all effects* **o.** *errors seemed to* |
| W-pI.184.15:7 | *Name is* **o.** *salvation and escape from what* |
| W-pI.184.15:8 | *us in the oneness which is* **o.** *inheritance and* |
| W-pI...185.7:1 | Let us today devote **o.** practicing to |
| W-pI.185.14:1 | uniting **o.** desires with the need of every |
| W-pI...186.2:1 | Let us not fight **o.** function. We did not |
| W-pI...186.2:3 | it. It is not **o.** idea. The means are given us |
| W-pI...186.2:5 | do is to accept **o.** part in genuine humility |
| W-pI...186.2:7 | **O.** minds are suited perfectly to take the |
| W-pI...186.3:6 | we will not shrink from **o.** assignment on |
| W-pI...186.4:2 | not doubt **o.** adequacy for the function He |
| W-pI...186.4:3 | certain only that He knows **o.** strengths, |
| W-pI...186.4:3 | our strengths, **o.** wisdom and our holiness |
| W-pI...186.4:3 | our strengths, our wisdom and **o.** holiness |
| W-pI...186.8:1 | And so we find **o.** peace. We will accept |
| W-pI...186.8:3 | **O.** self-made roles are shifting, and they |
| W-pI...186.8:5 | tears. **O.** very being seems to change as we |
| W-pI...186.8:5 | and **o.** emotions raise us high indeed, or |
| W-pI.187.10:3 | Not separate from Him Who is **o.** Source; |
| W-pI.187.10:3 | is part of **o.** one Self Whose innocence has |
| W-pI.187.10:4 | The Name of God is on **o.** lips. And as we |
| W-pI.187.10:5 | shine in **o.** reflection of our Father's Love. |
| W-pI.187.10:5 | shine in our reflection of **o.** Father's Love. |
| W-pI.187.11:6 | us in form of lilies we can lay upon **o.** altar |
| W-pI...188.9:2 | We take **o.** wandering thoughts, and |
| W-pI...188.9:4 | let the light within **o.** minds direct them |
| W-pI.188.10:1 | Thus are **o.** minds restored with them, |
| W-pI.188.10:1 | us to all living things that share **o.** life. We |
| W-pI.188.10:5 | And we lay **o.** saving blessing on it, as we |
| W-pI...189.9:4 | And in **o.** quiet hearts and open minds, |
| W-pI.189.10:4 | *Salvation's ways are not* **o.** *own, for they* |
| W-pI.189.10:6 | *O. hands are open to receive Your gifts. We* |
| W-pI.189.10:9 | *but that Your Will, which is* **o.** *own as well,* |
| W-pI.190.11:2 | Let **o.** gratitude unto our Teacher fill our |
| W-pI.190.11:2 | gratitude unto **o.** Teacher fill our hearts, |
| W-pI.190.11:2 | gratitude unto our Teacher fill **o.** hearts, |
| W-pI.190.11:2 | we are free to choose **o.** joy instead of pain |
| W-pI.190.11:2 | instead of pain, **o.** holiness in place of sin, |
| W-pI...192.7:2 | but to justify **o.** rage and our attack. Our |
| W-pI...192.7:2 | but to justify our rage and **o.** attack. Our |
| W-pI...192.7:3 | **O.** understanding is so limited that what |
| W-pI...192.7:4 | **o.** eyes shut tight against the light; our |
| W-pI...192.7:4 | **o.** minds engaged in worshipping what is |
| W-pI...193.6:1 | death becomes **o.** choice instead of life? |
| W-pI.193.11:2 | in haste and go unto **o.** Father's house. |
| W-pI...194.1:5 | How close are we approaching to **o.** goal! |
| W-pI...194.9:5 | we will appeal to Him Who guards **o.** rest |
| W-pI...194.9:6 | No longer is the world **o.** enemy, for we |
| W-pI...195.4:4 | offer thanks to God **o.** Father that in us all |
| W-pI...195.5:4 | thus we split them off from **o.** awareness |
| W-pI...195.6:1 | We thank **o.** Father for one thing alone; |
| W-pI...195.6:2 | made which would reduce **o.** wholeness, |
| W-pI...195.6:2 | impair or change **o.** function to complete |
| W-pI...195.7:1 | Then let **o.** brothers lean their tired heads |
| W-pI...195.7:1 | against **o.** shoulders as they rest a while. |
| W-pI...195.7:4 | forgotten Word re-echoes in **o.** memory, |
| W-pI...195.9:3 | are not entitled therefore to **o.** bitterness, |
| W-pI...195.9:3 | a thought or care for us or for **o.** future. |
| W-pI.195.10:1 | **O.** gratitude will pave the way to Him, |

W-pI.195.10:1 and shorten **o.** learning time by more
W-pI...196.8:1 **O.** next steps will be easy, if you take this
W-pI.198.13:1 stand between this vision and **o.** sight.
W-pI...200.9:1 Let us not lose **o.** way again today. We go
W-pI...200.9:4 is sure, and He will guide **o.** footsteps. He
W-pI.200.11:5 to replace **o.** shifting goals and solitary
WpI rVI.in.2:1 With this in mind we start **o.** practicing,
WpI rVI.in.2:1 bestowed on us in **o.** last twenty lessons.
WpI rVI.in.3:1 These practice sessions, like **o.** last review
WpI rVI.in.4:3 We merely close **o.** eyes, and then forget
WpI rVI.in.6:6 and gives **o.** thoughts whatever meaning
W-pII ....in.1:5 the end toward which **o.** practicing was
W-pII ....in.2:2 in quiet expectation for **o.** God and Father
W-pII ....in.2:9 forget **o.** hourly remembrance in between,
W-pII ....in.2:9 of Him as we are tempted to forget **o.** goal
W-pII ....in.3:1 will use that thought to introduce **o.** times
W-pII ....in.3:1 times of rest, and calm **o.** minds at need.
W-pII ....in.3:3 and expect **o.** Father to reveal Himself, as
W-pII ....in.4:1 but His Word upon **o.** minds and hearts,
W-pII ....in.4:5 So **o.** times with Him will now be spent.
W-pII ....in.6:4 and fix **o.** eyes upon the journey's end.
W-pII ....in.6:5 world to be the full replacement of **o.** own
W-pII ....in.7:2 sought to find **o.** way by following the
W-pII ....in.8:4 have lit the darkness of **o.** minds. His Love
W-pII ....in.9:3 that **o.** insane desires were the truth. Now
W-pII ....in.9:5 across the wide horizons of **o.** minds. A
W-pII ..in.11:2 of special relevance will intersperse **o.**
W-pII .221.2:5 **O.** minds are joined. We wait with one
W-pII .221.2:6 to hear **o.** Father's answer to our call, to
W-pII .221.2:6 to hear our Father's answer to **o.** call, to
W-pII .221.2:6 let **o.** thoughts be still and find His peace,
W-pII .227.2:1 so today we find **o.** glad return to Heaven,
W-pII .....2.4:2 Here we share **o.** final dream. It is a dream
W-pII .....2.5:2 The song of **o.** rejoicing is the call to all
W-pII .231.2:2 and with the One as well Who is **o.** Father
W-pII .238.2:1 pause to think how much **o.** Father loves
W-pII .239.1:2 be thankful for the gifts **o.** Father gave us.
W-pII .....3.5:1 world has joined **o.** changed perception.
W-pII .....3.5:3 let us not attempt to change **o.** function.
W-pII .244.2:2 come into the hallowed haven of **o.** home.
W-pII .254.2:1 no ego thoughts direct **o.** words or actions
W-pII .254.2:6 God speaks to us and tells us of **o.** will, as
W-pII .256.1:9 God is **o.** goal; forgiveness is the means by
W-pII .256.1:9 by which **o.** minds return to Him at last.
W-pII .257.1:4 that we may unify **o.** thoughts and actions
W-pII .258.1:1 All that is needful is to train **o.** minds to
W-pII .258.1:1 aims, and to remember that **o.** goal is God
W-pII .258.1:2 God. His memory is hidden in **o.** minds,
W-pII .258.1:2 obscured but by **o.** pointless little goals
W-pII .258.1:4 God is **o.** only goal, our only Love. We
W-pII .258.1:4 God is our only goal, **o.** only Love. We
W-pII .259.1:3 What else but sin engenders **o.** attacks?
W-pII .260.2:1 Now is **o.** Source remembered, and
W-pII .260.2:1 Therein we find **o.** true Identity at last.
W-pII .260.2:2 are we, because **o.** Source can know no sin
W-pII .263.2:2 and walk together to **o.** Father's house as
W-pII .266.2:1 calling upon God's Name and on **o.** own,
W-pII .266.2:1 own, acknowledging **o.** Self in each of us;
W-pII .268.2:1 Let not **o.** sight be blasphemous today,
W-pII .268.2:1 nor let **o.** ears attend to lying tongues.
W-pII .269.2:1 Today **o.** sight is blessed indeed. We
W-pII .269.2:3 of God; of Him Who is **o.** own Identity.
W-pII .270.2:1 The quiet of today will bless **o.** hearts,
W-pII .270.2:2 Christ is **o.** eyes today. And through His
W-pII .273.1:4 We need but tell **o.** minds, with certainty,
W-pII .274.2:1 to us today, from Him Who is **o.** Father.
W-pII .276.1:6 created in His Love and we deny **o.** Self, to
W-pII .276.1:6 unsure of who we are, of Who **o.** Father is,
W-pII .276.1:7 Who gave His Word to us in **o.** creation,
W-pII .276.1:7 to remember Him and so recall **o.** Self.
W-pII .283.2:1 with God **o.** Father as our only Source,
W-pII .283.2:1 with God our Father as **o.** only Source,
W-pII .283.2:2 **o.** forgiveness has made one with us.
W-pII .286.2:3 We trust in Him, and in **o.** Self, Who still
W-pII .....8.5:3 That instant is **o.** goal, for it contains the
W-pII .....8.5:4 reminding us of **o.** Identity which our
W-pII .....8.5:4 which **o.** forgiveness has restored to us.
W-pII .292.1:7 Will, which guarantees that **o.** will is done
W-pII .296.2:2 **o.** learning goal becomes an unconflicted
W-pII .....9.5:6 can reach **o.** Father's Love through Him.
W-pII .302.2:1 **O.** Love awaits us as we go to Him, and
W-pII .307.2:1 because we join **o.** holy will with God's, in
W-pII .310.2:2 And all the world joins with us in **o.** song
W-pII .310.2:4 for we have welcomed love into **o.** hearts.
W-pII .313.2:6 For in **o.** vision it becomes as holy as the
W-pII ...11.4:2 and unaware of **o.** eternal unity with Him.
W-pII ...11.4:3 Yet back of all **o.** doubts, past all our fears
W-pII ...11.4:3 Yet back of all our doubts, past all **o.** fears
W-pII ...11.4:5 God's memory is in **o.** holy minds, which
W-pII ...11.4:6 Let **o.** function be only to let this memory
W-pII ...11.5:1 **O.** Father calls to us. We hear His Voice,
W-pII .321.2:2 glad are we to find **o.** freedom through
W-pII .321.2:2 the certain way **o.** Father has established.
W-pII .321.2:3 we learn **o.** freedom can be found in God
W-pII .323.2:3 Love has now returned to **o.** awareness.
W-pII .328.1:2 but by **o.** striving to be separate, and that
W-pII .328.1:2 and that **o.** independence from the rest of
W-pII .328.1:4 This is not what **o.** Father wills for us, nor
W-pII .328.1:5 To join with His is but to find **o.** own. And
W-pII .328.1:6 And since **o.** will is His, it is to Him that
W-pII .328.1:6 Him that we must go to recognize **o.** will.
W-pII .329.2:1 Today we will accept **o.** union with each
W-pII .329.2:1 our union with each other and **o.** Source.
W-pII .329.2:4 Through it we find **o.** way at last to God.
W-pII .330.1:1 day accept forgiveness as **o.** only function.
W-pII .330.1:2 Why should we attack **o.** minds, and give
W-pII .330.1:6 Let us choose today that He be **o.** Identity,
W-pII .340.2:4 **O.** Father has redeemed His Son this day.
W-pII .341.2:1 Let us not, then, attack **o.** sinlessness, for
W-pII .342.2:3 the world goes with us on **o.** way to God.
W-pII .348.2:2 that we choose to be **o.** will as well as His.
W-pII .349.2:1 **O.** Father knows our needs. He gives us
W-pII .349.2:1 Our Father knows **o.** needs. He gives us
W-pII .349.2:3 and heal **o.** minds as we return to Him.
W-pII ...14.2:1 **O.** use for words is almost over now. Yet
W-pII ...14.2:5 Yet we can realize **o.** function here, and
W-pII ...14.3:2 We accept **o.** part as saviors of the world,
W-pII ...14.3:2 through **o.** joint forgiveness is redeemed.
W-pII ...14.3:3 And this, **o.** gift, is therefore given us. We
W-pII ...14.3:6 will return when we have done **o.** part.
W-pII ...14.4:4 we have attained we call to all **o.** brothers,
W-pII ...14.4:4 to share **o.** peace and consummate our joy
W-pII ...14.4:4 to share our peace and consummate **o.** joy
W-pII ...14.5:1 us, we learn that it is written on **o.** hearts.
W-pII ...14.5:2 And thus **o.** minds are changed about the
Wfl........in.1:1 **O.** final lessons will be left as free of
Wfl........in.1:2 them but at the beginning of **o.** practicing
Wfl........in.1:3 leads the way and makes **o.** footsteps sure.
Wfl........in.1:4 as to Him we give **o.** lives henceforth. For
Wfl........in.2:6 let us be the leaders of **o.** many brothers
Wfl........in.3:1 to this purpose let us dedicate **o.** minds,
Wfl........in.3:1 directing all **o.** thoughts to serve the
Wfl........in.3:4 to the dream we seek, and not **o.** own. For
Wfl........in.4:1 is **o.** function to remember Him on earth,
Wfl........in.4:2 So let us not forget **o.** goal is shared, for it
Wfl........in.4:3 And shall we not forgive **o.** brother, who
Wfl........in.4:5 offered us through **o.** forgiveness, given
Wfl........in.5:1 gift **o.** Father promised to His holy Son.
W-ep .........5:6 Joy attends **o.** way. For we go homeward
W-ep .........6:1 We trust **o.** ways to Him and say "Amen.
M-4 .....VII.1:6 than many other ideas in **o.** curriculum.
M-4 ........X.3:4 so far beyond **o.** curriculum that learning
M-9 ...........2:5 direct opposition to that of **o.** curriculum.
M-9 ...........2:7 and strength. **O.** curriculum trains for the
M-10 .........3:1 The aim of **o.** curriculum, unlike the goal
M-16 .........3:7 within the framework of **o.** course. After
M-20 .........5:8 In this one sentence is **o.** course explained
M-20 .........5:9 one sentence is **o.** practicing given its one
M-24 .........1:4 sense. **O.** only question should be, "Is the
M-24 .........3:1 For **o.** purposes, it would not be helpful
M-24 .........3:4 making. **O.** course is not concerned with
M-28 .........4:7 dust and look upon **o.** perfect sinlessness.
M-28 .........5:8 wish for nothing but His Will to be **o.** own
C-6 ............2:1 us, establishing **o.** particular part in it and
C-ep...........3:3 on before and lost **o.** way a little while.
C-ep...........3:5 **O.** new beginning has the certainty the
C-ep...........4:1 and kneel down an instant in **o.** gratitude
C-ep...........4:4 God is here, and with Him all **o.** brothers.
C-ep ..........5:2 had lost **o.** way but He has found it for us.
P-2.........V.4:7 to guide us, as we try to help **o.** brothers.
P-2.........V.4:8 and lean upon a strength beyond **o.** little
P-2.........V.7:3 It is not **o.** perfection that is asked in our
P-2.........V.7:3 that is asked in **o.** attempts to heal. We
P-2.........V.7:5 who seems to share **o.** dream of sickness.
P-2.........V.7:7 His healing is **o.** own. And as we see the
P-2.........V.7:8 and understand that it is but **o.** own.
P-2........ VI.2:2 given us literally "to change **o.** tune." The
S-3.........II.3:5 the Word of God, more certainly **o.** own.

**our** 34
• noise word
*Jesus*
*Our*

**ours** 31
• Jesus

T-5 ....... IV.8:9 it and share it, that it may always be **o.**. I
T-7 .......V.10:9 we are of one Mind, and that Mind is **o.**.
T-8 ..... IV.2:12 me. The light becomes **o.**, and you cannot
T-8 .........V.1:7 of God is established in **o.** and as ours.
T-8 .........V.1:7 of God is established in ours and as **o.**.
T-8 .........V.3:1 God's Oneness and **o.** are not separate,
T-8 .........V.3:1 because His Oneness encompasses **o.**. To
T-8 .........V.5:4 **O.** is simply the journey back to God Who
T-8 ....... IX.7:2 alone, for **o.** is a shared identification. The
T-11 ......in.4:2 you will also have looked upon **o.**. I come
T-31 ...VIII.9:1 gift can once again be recognized as **o.**!
W-pI .... 70.5:1 Will and **o.** are really the same in this.
W-pI .... 80.4:1 will claim the peace that must be **o.** when
W-pI .. 100.7:1 in us according to our Father's Will and **o.**
W-pI .. 104.2:3 be **o.** when time has passed into eternity.
W-pI .. 104.4:1 and seek instead that which is truly **o.**, as
W-pI .. 122.9:1 this will be the day salvation will be **o.**.
W-pI .. 138.5:5 **O.** are teaching goals, to be attained
W-pI .. 163.9:7 *We accept Your Thoughts as* **o.**, *and our will*
W-pI 170.13:3 *Your peace is* **o.**. *And we bless the world with*
WpI...rV.in2:4 *but listen to Your Word, and make it* **o.**.
W-pI .. 181.8:4 are the eyes of Christ inevitably **o.**. And
W-pI 187.11:5 And to ensure this holy sight is **o.**, we
W-pI 187.11:6 in us and offers us His Holiness as **o.**.
W-pI 200.11:3 The peace of God is **o.**, and only this will
W-pII . 269.2:2 upon the face of Him Whose Self is **o.**. We
W-pII . 346.2:2 For we will learn today what peace is **o.**,
W-pII ... 14.4:1 **O.** are the eyes through which Christ's
W-pII ... 14.4:2 **O.** are the ears that hear the Voice for God
W-pII ... 14.4:3 **O.** the minds that join together as we
M-28 ......... 5:7 And we accept His Holiness as **o.**; as it is.

**ourselves** 39
• Jesus
*noise word*

T-15 ..... XI.9:3 Wholeness as we welcome Him into **o.**.
T-20 ... III.10:4 gentleness upon each other and on **o.**.
W-pI .... 64.5:2 remind **o.** of it in the morning and again
W-pI .... 72.9:4 of truth in us is to recognize **o.** as we are.
W-pI .. 76.11:5 Then we will tell **o.**, as a dedication with
W-pI .. 76.12:1 to experience **o.** as subject to other laws
W-pI .... 77.3:5 sure that we will not content **o.** with less.
W-pI .... 78.4:2 We will not let **o.** be blind to him; we will
W-pI .... 91.4:3 Today we will devote **o.** to the attempt to
W-pI .... 95.8:3 to be willing to forgive **o.** for our lapses in
W-pI .... 98.1:5 We dedicate **o.** to truth today, and to
W-pI .... 98.3:5 and thus increase it by accepting it **o.**.
W-pI .... 98.4:4 again. We do not choose but for **o.** today.
W-pI .. 100.5:1 We will not let **o.** be sad today. For if we
W-pI .. 100.7:1 We will prepare **o.** for this today, in our
W-pI .. 103.2:3 again to bring to truth today, and teach **o.**
W-pI .. 104.5:2 will not let **o.** lose sight of them between
W-pI .. 109.9:6 of their resting place each time we tell **o.**,
W-pI .. 124.5:4 we see because we saw it first within **o.**.
W-pI .. 124.7:5 Today we would experience **o.** at one with
W-pI .. 125.3:2 We will not judge **o.** today, for what we
W-pI .. 139.1:2 we come to a decision to accept **o.** as God
W-pI .. 140.8:3 us. It is not farther from us than **o.**. It is as

W-pI.153.19:2 We clothe **o.** in it, as we prepare to meet
W-pI.153.19:4 We will remind **o.** that He remains beside
W-pI...154.1:3 We cannot judge **o.**, nor need we do so.
W-pI.154.14:3 they have changed our minds about **o.**,
W-pI.158.11:4 give, Christ's vision looks upon **o.** as well.
W-pI...165.8:1 We count on God, and not upon **o.**, to
W-pI...181.8:6 we see reflected in the world and in **o.**.
W-pI...186.8:2 belief that we can make another for **o.**.
W-pI.193.11:4 about all things we saved to settle by **o.**,
W-pI...195.5:4 Let us not compare **o.** with them, for thus
W-pII.....in.3:2 will not content **o.** with simple practicing
W-pII..239.1:1 not the truth about **o.** today be hidden by
W-pII..262.2:1 recognize this day the truth about **o.**. We
W-pII..272.2:2 in a dream, we turn aside and ask **o.** if we,
W-pII..311.1:6 all the judgments we have made against **o.**
P-2......... V.4:8 Let us not forget that we are helpless of **o.**,

## ourselves 4

• noise word
*Jesus*

## out 407

*See also* asking-out-of-need, setting-out, working-out, out-of-pattern

T-1........ I.50:1 and rejecting what is **o.** of accord as false.
T-1........ III.1:4 the Atonement is the cancelling **o.** of all
T-1........ III.6:7 You should look **o.** from the perception of
T-1........ III.7:2 united this mind goes **o.** to everyone,
T-1........ VI.5:3 In sorting **o.** the false from the true, the
T-1........ VI.5:4 *Perfect love casts o. fear. If fear exists, Then*
T-2........ VI.5:6 mind and the behavior are **o.** of accord,
T-2....... VII.4:1 in it seems to render it **o.** of your control.
T-2..... VIII.3:3 rather than a meting **o.** of punishment,
T-2..... VIII.4:1 a sorting **o.** of the false from the true. This
T-3........... I.1:6 which arose **o.** of projection, has led
T-3........... I.3:9 and forced him **o.** of the Garden of Eden.
T-3.......... II.6:5 you are cancelling **o.** misperceptions in
T-3........ III.1:2 perception must be straightened **o.** before
T-3........ IV.3:6 because it is **o.** of accord with itself. This
T-3........ IV.5:5 way **o.** of ambiguity is clear perception.
T-3......... V.2:2 do so **o.** of a specific sense of lack or need.
T-3........ VI.2:3 pointing **o.** that evaluation is its obvious
T-4......... I.2:14 make the totally lifeless **o.** of the life-given
T-4......... II.7:3 The ego never gives **o.** of abundance,
T-4........ III.4:3 Being made **o.** of the denial of the Father,
T-4....... V.4:11 Once **o.** of awareness the question can
T-4......... V.6:4 the real question and keep it **o.** of mind.
T-4........ VI.6:4 my will is never **o.** of accord with His. I
T-4....... VII.6:7 constant going **o.** of His Love is blocked
T-4....... VII.8:5 God goes **o.** to them and through them,
T-5......... in.3:2 to bless them in return, **o.** of gratitude.
T-5........... I.1:2 and lets God go **o.** into them and through
T-5........ IV.1:2 the Atonement is the way **o.** of fear. The
T-5........ IV.2:9 cannot cancel **o.** your past errors alone.
T-5....... VII.1:1 can make a voice that can drown **o.** God's
T-5....... VII.4:2 to work **o.** the plan of salvation yourself
T-6......... I.11:5 no perception that is **o.** of accord with the
T-6......... I.14:3 and **o.** of their own fear they spoke of the
T-6.......... II.2:4 that you attacked yourself **o.** of awareness
T-6........ IV.9:3 to the point where they can get you **o.** of it
T-6...... IV.12:8 *yours.* God did not blot it **o.**, because to
T-6...... V.B.5:1 way **o.** of conflict between two opposing
T-6...... V.B.8:4 is a step in the direction **o.** of conflict,
T-6...... V.C.1:2 He sorts **o.** the true from the false in your
T-6...... V.C.1:5 But what is **o.** of accord entirely He rejects
T-6.... V.C.10:7 Only this can cancel **o.** the need for effort,
T-7...... IV.2:10 it can be used as a way **o.** of conflict, as all
T-7........ IV.5:6 state of mind that is **o.** of accord with His.
T-7....... V.6:13 meaning cannot be **o.** of accord with His,
T-7....... V.6:14 God cannot be **o.** of accord with Himself,
T-7....... V.6:14 and you cannot be **o.** of accord with Him.
T-7......... V.9:2 or an idol that you may worship **o.** of fear,
T-7...... VI.13:3 mind could be **o.** of accord with God's,
T-7....... VII.4:4 you will have put them **o.** of your mind.
T-7....... VII.9:2 as you are, are **o.** to take God from you.
T-7..... VII.10:9 is only one way **o.** of the world's thinking,
T-7..... VIII.4:2 There is no way **o.** of this, because it is
T-7......... X.6:8 The only way **o.** of the error is to decide
T-7......... X.7:3 will lead you **o.** of the confusion you have
T-7........ XI.1:5 nature, being **o.** of accord with God's laws
T-7........ XI.2:2 is **o.** of his natural environment and does
T-7........ XI.5:2 and extends **o.** into the darkness of other
T-7........ XI.6:1 **O.** of your natural environment you may
T-8.......... I.5:6 If it is carried **o.** by these two teachers
T-8......... II.3:6 be **o.** of accord because they are one. This
T-8........ VI.1:2 the journey back by setting **o.** together,
T-8..... VII.10:5 By reaching **o.**, the mind extends itself. It
T-8..... VIII.4:1 entirely **o.** of keeping with what you want.
T-8........ IX.3:3 to reinforce sleeping **o.** of fear of waking.
T-8........ IX.6:4 to make nothing **o.** of what God created.
T-9........... I.4:2 **o.** the true from the false in your mind, I
T-9........ III.2:1 to point **o.** errors and "correct" them.
T-9........ III.3:1 point **o.** the errors of your brother's ego
T-9........ IV.5:6 consistently cancelling **o.** all its effects,
T-9......... V.7:2 someone to point **o.** where he is heading,
T-9....... VII.4:6 **o.** of accord with its perception of you.
T-9..... VIII.4:8 is of God, Who created it **o.** of His Love.
T-10...... IV.1:9 the nothingness **o.** of which he was made.
T-10...... IV.3:5 This means it is **o.** of control. To be out of
T-10...... IV.3:6 To be **o.** of control is to be **o.** of reason,
T-10...... IV.3:6 To be out of control is to be **o.** of reason,
T-10....... V.3:7 having made him **o.** of your insanity, he is
T-10....... V.4:2 and **o.** of his depression he made the god
T-10..... V.11:1 **O.** of your gifts to Him the Kingdom will
T-11....... in.2:3 ego was made **o.** of the wish of God's Son
T-11....... in.3:9 it rests, and bring it **o.** into the light.
T-11...... III.3:4 **O.** of your joy you will create beauty in
T-11...... III.4:7 surrounds you and shines **o.** from you.
T-11...... III.5:6 it can sweep you **o.** of all darkness forever.
T-11....... V.5:2 being **o.** of accord with your true nature. I
T-11..... V.13:2 means to break down or to separate **o.**.
T-11..... VII.4:9 saved for you **o.** of what you have made,
T-12......... I.9:6 One is false, for it was made **o.** of denial;
T-12........ II.9:3 abideth in you in the peace **o.** of which He
T-12...... III.8:4 the one you made **o.** of your split mind,
T-12...... III.9:7 For it is made **o.** of what you do not want,
T-12.... III.10:8 will look **o.** in peace and behold the world
T-12...... IV.1:5 is the one promise the ego holds **o.** to you,
T-12....... V.3:3 place you can cancel **o.** all reinforcement
T-12...... VI.5:8 holding **o.** the Father's Love to you in the
T-12..... VII.5:5 and as you look **o.** so will you see in. Two
T-12..... VII.7:1 and you must look in before you look **o.**.
T-12..... VII.7:3 then you look **o.** and behold his witnesses
T-12... VII.15:6 you look **o.** upon a world that cannot die.
T-13....... in.3:6 the Father Who drove him **o.** of Paradise.
T-13......... I.6:6 **O.** of love he was created, and in love he
T-13...... III.3:4 your fortress, for you would shut **o.** God,
T-13.... III.12:1 To "single **o.**" is to "make alone," and
T-13...... IV.1:5 dust **o.** of which it thinks you were made.
T-13...... IV.5:6 from him **o.** of your own past because, by
T-13...... VI.5:4 Let no dark cloud **o.** of your past obscure
T-13...... VI.8:2 Reach **o.** to all your brothers, and touch
T-13.. VI.11:10 others **o.** of darkness as you look on them
T-13.... VI.12:1 and **o.** of quiet recognition of the truth in
T-13.... VI.12:3 them, and it is they who hold it **o.** to you.
T-13..... VII.5:6 The **o.** of mind *is* out of sight, because
T-13..... VII.5:6 The out of mind *is* **o.** of sight, because
T-13..... VII.5:9 into the world He holds **o.** to you in love.
T-13..... VII.6:2 following not the road that love points **o.**.
T-13....... X.11:3 single **o.** part of the Sonship for your love,
T-13....... XI.8:3 Yet His channels of reaching **o.** cannot be
T-14....... II.2:4 and reactions that you have woven **o.** of it
T-14...... III.9:5 for the whole Sonship, directed in and **o.**,
T-14.... III.15:5 you, and would lead you **o.** of insanity.
T-14...... IV.4:6 He created you **o.** of Himself, but still
T-14.... IV.4:10 place made **o.** of darkness and deceit, for
T-14...... V.11:7 and look **o.** in peace on all who think they
T-14...... V.11:8 Cast no one **o.**, for here is what he seeks
T-14...... VI.2:5 of illusion **o.** of nothing are now afraid of
T-14...... VI.7:4 He will separate **o.** all that has meaning,
T-14..... VII.2:1 **o.** of everything that interferes with truth.
T-14. VIII.4:10 the oneness **o.** of which creation happens.
T-14....... IX.6:5 the mirror holds **o.** for everyone to see, no
T-14....... X.1:4 Reach **o.** of time and touch it, with the
T-14....... X.5:2 and grow dim, as darkness blots them **o.**.
T-15......... I.3:5 And **o.** of its unwillingness for you to find
T-15......... I.8:3 without its shadow reaching **o.** into the
T-15......... I.9:6 Nothing can reach you here **o.** of the past,
T-15........ II.3:4 instant reaches **o.** to encompass time, as
T-15........ II.6:1 little part in separating **o.** the holy instant
T-15........ II.6:3 To learn to separate **o.** this single second,
T-15...... III.1:5 because it is a world made **o.** of littleness,
T-15....... V.2:3 If you seek to separate **o.** certain aspects
T-15....... V.9:3 by bringing all perception **o.** of the past,
T-15..... V.11:2 **o.** of His need to extend His Love. With
T-15..... VII.4:6 forged **o.** of anger and dedicated to but
T-15..... VII.5:5 but you will become willing to find **o.**, if
T-15...... XI.4:6 you endow it with fear and try to cast it **o.**
T-15...... XI.4:8 **o.** and giving it the attributes of hell,
T-16......... I.2:2 These it selects **o.**, and joins with. And it
T-16...... IV.1:6 drive it underground and **o.** of sight. It is
T-16...... IV.2:1 love play **o.** a conflict that does not exist.
T-16...... IV.8:1 and your creations are holding **o.** their
T-16....... V.9:1 which the ego holds **o.** to those who place
T-16..... V.10:5 that is acted **o.** in the special relationship.
T-16...... VI.7:2 distorted and completely **o.** of perspective
T-16.... VI.12:5 Him there. **O.** of your recognition of your
T-16..... VII.3:4 in which to act **o.** its hate are fantasies of
T-16..... VII.4:3 Would you act **o.** the dream, or let it go?
T-16..... VII.5:1 be an acting **o.** of vengeance that you seek
T-16..... VII.5:3 is the acting **o.** of vengeance on yourself.
T-17........ II.8:5 Him. Go **o.** in gladness to meet with your
T-17........ II.8:5 walk with Him in trust **o.** of this world,
T-17...... III.4:8 For it was formed to get him **o.** of it, and
T-17.... IV.13:2 is framed to be **o.** of focus and not seen.
T-17.... IV.13:4 as you search it **o.** amid its wrappings. As
T-17....... V.3:5 relationship as it *is* is **o.** of line with its own
T-17....... V.4:6 accepted as the only way **o.** of the conflict,
T-17...... VI.4:3 Holy Spirit's sorting **o.** of truth and falsity
T-18......... I.3:4 different form of acting **o.** for satisfaction.
T-18......... I.3:7 or rejection for acting **o.** a special form of
T-18......... I.5:6 which seemed to cast you **o.** of Heaven, to
T-18......... I.7:3 to go **o.** into the mad world and so depart
T-18....... I.12:4 your brother **o.** of this world and through
T-18....... I.13:2 and reaches **o.** to every broken fragment
T-18........ II.3:2 you see on waking is blotted **o.** in dreams.
T-18........ II.4:6 attempts to blot **o.** reality are very fearful,
T-18........ II.5:6 that you are making them act **o.** for you,
T-18...... III.1:8 Darkness can cover it, but cannot put it **o.**
T-18...... VI.3:5 and direct the body to act them **o.**. Yet it
T-18...... VI.3:7 the body is actually acting **o.** its fantasies,
T-18...... VI.6:2 It is impossible to act **o.** fantasies. For it is
T-18...... VI.7:5 incapable of reaching **o.** as being reached.
T-18...... VI.8:7 It does not go **o.**. Within itself it has no
T-18.... VI.10:1 stretch **o.** your hand and reach to Heaven.
T-18.... VI.13:4 it so. You are not really "lifted **o.**" of it; it
T-18.... VI.14:6 destruction, not through a breaking **o.**,
T-18.... VIII.2:4 on love will always seem to shut Him **o.**,
T-18.... VIII.9:8 reach **o.** to everyone who thirsts for living
T-18.. VIII.10:1 Go **o.** and find them, for they bring your
T-18....... IX.7:3 Figures stand **o.** and move about, actions
T-19....... I.5:10 for seeking **o.** reality through attack. The
T-19...... III.1:3 acute that the sin is denied the acting **o.**.
T-19...... III.1:8 your own, could stamp it **o.** through fear.
T19.... IV.A.1:4 place from which it gently reaches **o.**, but
T19.... IV.A.7:1 in and push Him **o.** *must* produce conflict.
T19. IV.A.11:2 of fear are harshly ordered to seek **o.** guilt
T19.... IV.B.4:1 and it reaches **o.** from the eternal in you.
T19.. IV.B.15:3 it urges you to send **o.** all your messages
T19.... IV.C.1:7 those who are attracted to it and seek it **o.**
T19.. IV.C.10:5 miracle you will perform, held **o.** to you.
T19... IV.D.3:3 veil forever blotted **o.** and unremembered
T19.... IV.D.3:4 to allow union to call you **o.** of separation;
T19. IV.D.14:4 Yet still He holds forgiveness **o.** to you, to
T-20........ II.2:2 neither offer nor accept; hold **o.** nor take.
T-20...... III.4:7 look **o.** in sorrow from what is sad within,
T-20...... III.8:6 for all the happiness that he held **o.** to you
T-20..... VII.8:9 You closed your eyes to shut him **o.**. Such
T-20.... VIII.8:8 world seems to hold **o.** many purposes,
T-20.. VIII.10:2 within to find itself, and *then* looks **o.**. All
T-21.... III.10:5 which tries to use the body to carry **o.** the
T-21...... IV.7:5 which the ego's rule has kept it **o.** so long.
T-21....... V.1:2 It literally picks it **o.** as the mind directs.
T-21....... V.1:6 small Voice for God is not drowned **o.** by
T-21....... V.8:9 not depend on it, and madness keeps it **o.**

T-21 VI.4:1 attack on reason that drives it **o.** of mind,
T-21 VI.8:9 the Holy Spirit still holds **o.** for everyone
T-21 VI.10:2 gratitude goes **o.** to you who blessed him,
T-21 VII.3:6 dream of power and to act **o.** their dream.
T-21 VIII.3:4 **o.** some promise of the power of giving it.
T-22 in.4:7 It must reach **o.** beyond itself, as you
T-22 in.4:7 itself, as you reached **o.** beyond the body,
T-22 II.2:6 of misery is to select some aspects **o.** of it,
T-22 II.4:7 excludes one living thing and holds it **o.**,
T-22 IV.7:6 But hold **o.** your hand, joined with your
T-22 V.2:8 sin is carved into a block **o.** of your peace,
T-22 V.3:7 Yet it remains impossible to keep love **o.**.
T-22 V.4:5 and would drown **o.** the hymn of praise to
T-23 I.6:7 Madness holds **o.** no menace to reality,
T-23 I.9:5 and drive Him **o.** of what He loves forever
T-23 II.1:2 and therefore **o.** of reason's sphere. Yet
T-23 III.4:8 vision, forever clear and never **o.** of sight,
T-24 II.3:3 For sin arose from it, **o.** of nothingness;
T-24 II.7:6 key to Heaven in his hand, held **o.** to you.
T-24 III.8:6 that he holds **o.** for your forgiveness. God
T-24 V.2:3 there, and wove a picture **o.** of nothing.
T-24 V.4:2 from the fireflies of sin and then go **o.**, to
T-24 V.7:4 through them, holding **o.** His hand, that
T-24 VI.13:6 see. **O.** of His lack of conflict comes your
T-24 VII.5:8 Nor will that light go **o.** when it is gone.
T-25 III.5:4 of specialness to put it **o.** of mind, where
T-25 III.6:3 to lead him **o.** of darkness into light at
T-25 V.6:6 the way you pointed **o.** to him because it
T-25 VIII.9:6 special function to hold **o.** to you the gifts
T-25 IX.2:4 offered anyone who but holds **o.** his hand
T-25 IX.2:5 Nor is the treasure less as it is given **o.**.
T-26 I.2:3 is **o.** can never reach and join with what is
T-26 I.7:2 in you be blotted **o.** because he sees it not.
T-26 II.2:3 situation is worked **o.** so no one loses is
T-26 III.3:6 seen that they are temporary, **o.** of place,
T-26 V.8:1 calls from **o.** a past forevermore gone by.
T-26 VII.4:9 What is projected **o.**, and seems to be
T-26 VIII.3:4 Salvation *would* wipe **o.** the space you see
T-26 VIII.6:1 working **o.** of all correction takes no time
T-26 VIII.6:2 of the working **o.** can seem to take forever
T-27 III.2:3 half is cancelled **o.** by the remaining half.
T-27 III.2:4 contradicted by the half it cancelled **o.**,
T-27 III.3:3 The picture has been wholly cancelled **o.**,
T-27 III.3:3 that cancelled **o.** the thought it represents
T-27 III.6:6 remains unknown, but is not cancelled **o.**.
T-27 VIII.4:2 idly in and **o.** of places and events that it
T-28 I.1:3 it cancels **o.** the interference to what has
T-28 I.11:4 Born **o.** of sharing, there can be no pause
T-28 I.13:6 the present and the past, to shut them **o.**.
T-28 II.11:7 sick; projecting **o.** its guilt caused nothing
T-28 IV.8:2 hold **o.** to every separate piece that thinks
T-28 VI.5:1 Sickness is anger taken **o.** upon the body,
T-29 VII.3:1 will impel him to seek **o.** a thousand idols,
T-29 VIII.3:8 A cloud does not put **o.** the sun. No more
T-29 VIII.5:5 the light the veil between has not put **o.**.
T-29 IX.4:2 you sinful and put **o.** the light within you.
T-30 in.1:5 forgiving dreams and **o.** of pain and fear.
T-30 I.5:2 unless you quickly straighten **o.** your
T-30 I.6:6 This cancels **o.** the terms that you have set
T-30 VII.7:1 Do not interpret **o.** of solitude, for what
T-31 IV.1:5 which road will lead you **o.** of conflict,
T-31 IV.10:2 from them than they could keep Him **o.**.
T-31 VI.6:6 perceived as treacherous, and **o.** to kill.
T-31 VII.5:6 Hold **o.** your hand, that you may have the
T-31 VII.7:7 the inner Guide all lead you **o.** of hell with
W-pI 23.1:1 only way **o.** of fear that will ever succeed.
W-pI 24.6:2 your goals, however the situation turns **o.**
W-pI 25.4:1 any sense **o.** of the exercises for today,
W-pI 35.6:8 *I see myself as losing* **o.**. *I see myself as*
W-pI 35.8:3 nothing should be "dug **o.**" with effort.
W-pI 39.6:2 eyes, search **o.** your unloving thoughts in
W-pI 41.3:1 radiate through you and **o.** into the world
W-pI 41.3:2 and suffered **o.** of its allegiance to them.
W-pI 43.6:1 are clearly **o.** of accord with today's idea,
W-pI 50.3:2 It will lift you **o.** of every trial, and raise
W-pI 53.3:4 It holds **o.** no safety and no hope. But
W-pI 55.4:4 to find **o.** what my own best interests are,
W-pI 57.1:6 I can leave simply by walking **o.**. Nothing
W-pI 62.2:3 goal is to find **o.** who you are, having
W-pI 66.3:5 be glad that we can find **o.** what truth is.
W-pI 68.4:4 find **o.** how you would feel without them.
W-pI 69.6:3 Reach **o.** and touch them in your mind.
W-pI 72.12:1 and your hope of success flicker and go **o.**
W-pI 73.1:2 **o.** of which darkness and nothingness
W-pI 73.5:3 and you look **o.** on a darkened world.
W-pI 74.4:1 single it **o.** for special consideration.
W-pI 78.4:3 reversed, as we look **o.** toward truth, away
W-pI 80.5:4 Recognize that you are **o.** of conflict; free
W-pI 90.3:3 must elapse before it can be worked **o.**. I
W-pI 92.7:5 It does not change and flicker and go **o.**. It
W-pI 95.13:5 cast all your illusions **o.** of the one Mind
W-pI 96.10:3 will again flow **o.** from spirit to the spirit
W-pI 97.6:2 makes an uncertain moment and goes **o.**.
W-pI 97.6:3 light remains and leads you **o.** of darkness
W-pI 99.9:1 seek **o.** and lighten up all darkened spots,
W-pI 100.2:3 you to take in working **o.** His plan is given
W-pI 101.2:5 seek them **o.** and find them somewhere,
W-pI 101.4:1 would seek **o.** such savage punishment?
W-pI 101.4:4 and meted **o.** in cruel form to match the
W-pI 106.3:5 held **o.** to you in welcome and in love.
W-pI 108.8:4 of what you would hold **o.** to everyone, to
W-pI 122.11:1 they hold **o.** the sure rewards of questions
W-pI 122.11:2 joy the lifting of the veil holds **o.** to you.
W-pI 124.10:1 this holy half an hour will hold **o.** to you,
W-pI 126.3:2 merely to point **o.** that you are better, on
W-pI 126.3:5 It holds **o.** a gift to him, but hardly to
W-pI 131.13:1 Put **o.** your hand, and see how easily the
W-pI 132.4:3 acted **o.** so you can look on them and
W-pI 132.16:1 send **o.** these thoughts to bless the world.
W-pI 135.11:2 plan. It carries **o.** the plans that it receives
W-pI 137.5:1 which cancels **o.** the dream of sickness in
W-pI 153.18:4 for you who chose to carry **o.** His plan for
W-pI 155.7:5 Yet they need a guide to lead them **o.** of it,
W-pI 155.11:3 along the way that truth points **o.** to us.
W-pI 157.8:2 this day holds **o.** to you to be your own.
W-pI 158.1:2 because you were created **o.** of love. Nor
W-pI 159.10:1 the store of miracles set **o.** for you to give.
W-pI 160.6:4 except a miracle will search him **o.** and
W-pI 161.5:1 makes us suffer, and at last puts **o.** our life
W-pI 164.9:8 holds **o.** complete salvation to His Son?
W-pI 170.6:3 punishment is meted **o.** relentlessly to
WpI rV.in6:5 in his mind the way that led him **o.**, and
WpI rV.in6:5 out, and now will lead you **o.** with him.
W-pI 182.6:3 is so little that He seems so easily shut **o.**,
W-pI 183.2:2 you as they spread **o.** their wings to keep
W-pI 184.1:4 By this you carve it **o.** of unity. By this you
W-pI 186.11:1 stands **o.** clear and wholly unambiguous.
W-pI 189.4:2 the joy with which they look **o.** from the
W-pI 189.5:5 look **o.** on a world of mercy and of love.
W-pI 190.2:5 leave the Son whom It created **o.** of love.
W-pI 191.5:4 gratitude to Him Who pointed **o.** the way
W-pI 197.5:3 changeless, limitless, forever giving **o.**,
W-pI 198.4:1 is the only road that leads **o.** of disaster,
W-pI 200.2:1 chaos, joy of pain, and Heaven **o.** of hell.
W-pII 241.1:3 today holds **o.** the instant to the darkened
W-pII 256.2:2 *way Your sacred Word has pointed* **o.** *to us.*
W-pII 299.2:4 *can obscure it, but can not put* **o.** *its radiance*
W-pII 315.1:5 my savior, pointing **o.** the way to me, and
W-pII 327.2:1 *fail in my experience, if I but test them* **o.**. *Let*
W-pII 330.1:3 God holds **o.** His power and His Love,
W-pII 332.2:6 *while You are holding freedom* **o.** *to us.*
W-pII 334.1:2 they are woven **o.** of thoughts that rest on
W-pII 355.1:3 *me, and I need but reach* **o.** *my hand to find it*
W-pII 357.1:2 *Your holy Son is pointed* **o.** *to me, first in my*
WfI in.2:5 follow in the way that truth points **o.** to us
M-in 5:11 How can they work **o.** their own salvation
M-1 4:7 wears **o.** the world and all things in it. Yet
M-2 4:6 an inevitable choice **o.** of an ancient past.
M-4 1:5 in time as a means of leading **o.** of time.
M-4 I.A.4:1 must go through "a period of sorting **o.**."
M-4 I.A.5:4 no point in sorting **o.** the valuable from
M-4 I.A.6:5 at which he sees in it his whole way **o.**.
M-4 I.A.7:4 Yet his own sorting **o.** was meaningless in
M-4 VII.2:1 of God is generous **o.** of Self interest. This
M-5 III.3:6 The truth in their minds reaches **o.** to the
M-8 2:4 mind therefore seeks to make it true **o.** of
M-8 4:1 It is in the sorting **o.** and categorizing
M-8 6:5 are meaningful in sorting **o.** the messages
M-11 3:4 yet **o.** of which no way seems possible,–
M-13 8:11 God holds **o.** His Word to you, for He has
M-15 2:7 instant **o.** of time can bring time's end.
M-15 3:4 free. What can the world hold **o.** to you,
M-17 4:5 violence, fantasied or apparently acted **o.**.
M-17 8:5 lesson's manifest simplicity stands **o.** like
M-18 3:2 Reality is blotted **o.** as this insane belief is
M-19 1:3 injustice gives rise, and cancels them **o.**.
M-20 3:2 to find it who but seeks **o.** its conditions.
M-20 3:10 contrast stands **o.** clear and apparent. Yet
M-22 2:3 all that his acceptance holds **o.** to him. It
M-24 2:3 he can still work **o.** his salvation only now
M-25 2:6 These limits are placed **o.** of fear, for
M-27 3:2 His Love is blotted **o.** in the idea, which
M-29 3:11 It is the way **o.** of hell for you.
C-4 6:1 What was projected **o.** is seen within, and
C-4 7:7 guilt and death is there snuffed **o.** forever.
C-4 8:3 up to Him, **o.** of illusions into holiness;
C-4 8:3 holiness; **o.** of the world and to eternity;
C-4 8:3 **o.** of all fear and given back to love.
C-6 2:2 the leader in carrying **o.** His plan since he
C-ep 5:1 Let us go **o.** and meet the newborn world
P-2 I.1:4 will be a relationship held **o.** to them that
P-2 II.5:7 Together they can find a pathway **o.**, for
P-2 II.9:3 It is held **o.** to him, but he cannot hold
P-2 II.9:3 he cannot hold **o.** his hand to receive it.
P-2 III.4:5 thus he carries **o.** the plan established for
P-2 V.3:7 God Himself holds **o.** his brother as his
P-3 I.3:8 of reaching **o.** to someone somewhere.
P-3 III.1:2 Holy Spirit to help in carrying **o.** the plan.
P-3 III.5:10 do this, a light goes **o.** even in Heaven.
P-3 III.8:6 you, holding **o.** his hand to his Friend. Let
S-1 II.1:5 wanting, **o.** of a sense of scarcity and lack.
S-1 II.7:6 no longer flickers, and will never go **o.**.
S-1 III.2:3 made **o.** of fear by those who cherish guilt
S-1 III.5:3 Hold **o.** your hand. This enemy has come
S-2 I.2:4 It carefully picks **o.** all evil things, and
S-2 I.8:4 need, and God holds **o.** this gift to you. As

### out-of-pattern 2

T-1 I.47:2 establishes an **o.** time interval not under
T-2 V.A.11:2 Since it is an **o.** time interval, the ordinary

### outcast 3

W-pI 166.4:3 Without the world he made is he an **o.**;
W-pI 166.4:4 too; an **o.** wandering so far from home, so
W-pI 182.7:5 He lives an **o.** in a world of alien thoughts.

### outcome 85

T-2 III.3:10 very acute. But the **o.** is as certain as God.
T-2 V.7:4 is not the final **o.** of the perception. When
T-2 V.A.16:5 There is no reference to the **o.** of the error
T-2 VI.3:1 the **o.** of misthought can result in healing.
T-4 I.2:10 opposed in source, in direction and in **o.**.
T-4 II.5:8 remember that the **o.** is as certain as God.
T-7 X.1:5 ego's premises, but not at their logical **o.**.
T-7 X.1:7 are the logical **o.** of His premises. His
T-7 X.2:3 It is the logical **o.** of what you are. The
T-7 X.2:4 ability to see a logical **o.** depends on the
T-8 I.5:1 established for yourself, but so is its **o.**. If
T-8 I.5:2 If the **o.** of yours has made you unhappy,
T-8 III.2:7 this is the natural **o.** of their being.
T-10 II.6:4 the logical **o.** of your decision is perfectly
T-11 V.5:1 purpose is always the natural **o.** of what it
T-11 V.5:2 ego is the natural **o.** of its central belief,
T-15 I.3:4 **o.** of its strange religion must therefore be
T-17 VI.2:3 for it is this which will determine the **o.**.
T-17 VI.2:5 becomes the determiner of the **o.**, which
T-17 VI.3:7 The absence of a criterion for **o.**, set in
T-17 VI.5:2 for truth and sanity, its **o.** must be peace.
T-17 VI.5:3 And this is quite apart from what the **o.** *is.*
T-17 VI.5:6 come to you and you will see the **o.** truly,
T-17 VI.5:7 recognize the **o.** *because* you are at peace.
T-22 VI.2:4 the **o.** as He is sure of His Creator's Love.
T-23 II.8:4 Only destruction can be the **o.**. And God
T-24 in.2:6 is the **o.** of belief, and follows it as surely

T-24 I.2:8 be denied is their reality, but not their **o.**.
T-25 II.1:4 it must be evident the **o.** does not change.
T-25 II.2:3 change that might result in better **o.**? For
T-26 III.6:3 the area of choice made real, not in the **o.**,
T-26 VIII.8:2 and one form in which its **o.** is perceived.
T-31 I.6:5 What **o.** is inevitable, sure as God, and far
T-31 I.6:6 strange in **o.** and incredible in difficulty
T-31 I.7:2 Each has its **o.** in a different world. And
T-31 I.7:4 certain **o.** of the lesson that God's Son is
T-31 I.7:9 only **o.** which your learning can produce.
T-31 I.8:1 **o.** of the lesson that God's Son is guiltless
T-31 I.11:1 and have an **o.** that you do not want? It is
T-31 I.11:2 another **o.** seen to be preferred. You are
T-31 I.11:10 learned. Its **o.** is the world you look upon.
T-31 II.3:1 it is free, for it will have one **o.** either way.
T-31 II.5:6 because from them there is a different **o.**.
T-31 II.5:8 and for help, is not the same in **o.**. Hear
T-31 II.9:7 And in this choice is learning's **o.** changed
T-31 III.2:10 could the **o.** be that you would want? And
W-pI 24.1:1 realize the **o.** that would make you happy.
W-pI 24.4:2 should be on uncovering the **o.** you want.
W-pI 24.4:3 of goals in mind as part of the desired **o.**,
W-pI 24.6:2 that you have no unified **o.** in mind, and
W-pI 26.7:3 Then go over every possible **o.** that has
W-pI 26.9:1 After you have named each **o.** of which
W-pI 71.6:6 His is the only plan that is certain in its **o.**.
W-pI 131.7:4 and earth the other's sorry **o.** which is
W-pI 135.12:1 it cannot know the **o.** which is best, the
W-pI 136.4:3 of mind, an **o.** with a real effect on you,
W-pI 136.6:2 threat, and not whatever **o.** may result.
W-pI 138.5:6 Decisions are the **o.** of your learning, for
W-pI 163.3:1 hard to gain, uncertain in their **o.**, apt to
W-pI 169.12:1 the course it runs directed and its **o.** sure.
W-pI 185.3:4 the **o.** wanted not the same for both.
W-pII 7.2:4 Spirit guides it to the **o.** He perceives for it
W-pII 292.h A happy **o.** to all things is sure.
W-pII 292.1:2 can be the final **o.** found for everything.
W-pII 292.1:4 as the **o.** of all problems we perceive, all
W-pII 297.2:1 *certain are Your ways; how sure their final* ***o.***
M-1 4:2 of other forms, all with the same **o.**. They
M-1 4:6 There was never a question of **o.**, for what
M-4 I.A.8:4 is their result; the **o.** of honest learning,
M-4 IV.1:3 Harm is the **o.** of judgment. It is the
M-4 VIII.1:1 are certain of the **o.** can afford to wait,
M-4 VIII.1:3 All he sees is certain **o.**, at a time perhaps
M-4 VIII.1:10 no **o.** already seen or yet to come can
M-5 II.2:7 The **o.** is what he decides that it is. Special
M-5 II.4:6 final **o.** of this lesson is the remembrance
M-6 3:1 teachers to evaluate the **o.** of their gifts. It
M-6 3:3 have done that they have also given the **o.**
M-7 5:1 The real basis for doubt about the **o.** of
M-10 6:4 of the ugliness he sees about him is its **o.**.
M-17 2:5 Nor should it be forgotten that the **o.** that
M-17 6:2 is inevitable, for its **o.** must be death.
P-2 I.1:1 the ideal **o.** is rarely achieved. Therapy
P-2 V.6:10 a help. Yet let the **o.** not be judged by us.
P-2 VII.4:4 and was therefore responsible for its **o.**.
P-3 II.5:6 of this world do not expect this **o.**, and

## outcomes 18

T-7 II.2:9 in which diametrically opposed **o.** seem
T-8 I.4:4 learning **o.** is a sign of learning failure,
T-8 VIII.6:4 prescriptions for avoiding catastrophic **o.**.
T-8 VIII.6:9 not necessary to examine all possible **o.** to
T-12 V.8:5 and of the learning **o.** that have resulted.
T-20. VIII.10:4 you all the fearful **o.** of imagined sin into
T-24 I.2:1 because conflicting **o.** are impossible. But
T-24 I.2:3 And many senseless **o.** have been reached
T-31 III.1:2 a choice that will result in different **o.**,
T-31 IV.1:4 you are in control of **o.** of your choosing.
W-pI 24.5:4 kinds of **o.** as may honestly occur to you,
W-pI 26.6:1 whose **o.** are causing you concern. The
W-pI 26.8:3 the list of anticipated **o.** for each situation
W-pI 66.7:5 and no other **o.** possible as a result of
W-pI 66.9:7 Remember the **o.** fairly, and consider also
W-pI 152.1:3 sick unless these are the **o.** that he wants.
W-pII 292.2:1 *Your guarantee of only happy* ***o.*** *in the end.*
M-17 2:4 little value, and must lead to undesired **o.**.

## outdo 1

T-9 VIII.2:6 It is a delusional attempt to **o.**, but not to

## outer 8

T-13 VII.13:5 Son is not a traveller through **o.** worlds.
W-pI 31.2:5 for the inner is the cause of the **o.**.
W-pI 32.2:1 ones, applies to your inner and **o.** worlds,
W-pI 32.5:2 you survey either your inner or **o.** world.
W-pI 33.1:1 the world in both its **o.** and inner aspects.
W-pI 33.1:4 Alternate between surveying your **o.** and
W-pI 37.5:1 for today to your **o.** world if you so desire;
W-pI 188.6:4 to you. Exclude the **o.** world, and let your

## outlook 1

T-30 I.2:1 (1) The **o.** starts with this: *Today I will*

## outraged 3

T-2 VI.5:3 that wants to do something else is **o.**.
T-18 II.1:5 to your ego, which was **o.** by the "attack."
W-pI 186.3:6 the specious grounds that modesty is **o.**.

## outrageous 4

T-6 I.9:1 to demonstrate that the most **o.** assault,
T-12 III.4:1 if your brothers ask you for something "**o.**
T-12 III.4:3 therefore, who have made the request **o.**,
T-12 III.4:8 No "**o.**" requests can be made of one who

## outrageously 1

T-18 II.2:3 so **o.** violated in them becomes apparent.

## outset 5

T-17 VI.3:1 a clear-cut, positive goal, set at the **o.**, the
WpI. rIII.in6:6 Give direction at the **o.**; then lean back in
M-16 3:2 **o.** it is probably the simplest to observe.
M-16 3:4 At the **o.**, we can safely say that time
M-19 2:6 journey continues, be foretold from the **o.**

## outshine 1

W-pI 97.6:2 the radiance of the sun **o.** the tiny gleam a

## outside 167

T-2 I.5:9 You cannot find it **o.**. Illness is some form
T-2 IV.4:6 the **o.** is temporarily given healing belief.
T-4 III.1:2 interprets it as if something **o.** is inside,
T-6 IV.2:5 regard itself as separate and **o.** its maker,
T-6 IV.2:5 *you* are separate and **o.** the Mind of God.
T-6 V.C.9:2 Everything **o.** the Kingdom is illusion.
T-6 V.C.9:4 and thus placed part of your mind **o.** it.
T-7 II.3:1 **O.** the Kingdom, the law that prevails
T-7 II.3:2 **o.** the Kingdom learning is essential. This
T-7 VIII.3:8 it. The belief that by seeing it **o.** you have
T-10 in.1:3 to you is caused by factors **o.** yourself.
T-11 I.9:1 it appear as if God's Will is **o.** yourself,
T-12 III.6:6 always perceives this world as **o.** himself,
T-12 III.6:7 this world, for there is no world **o.** of him.
T-12 III.7:5 Everything you perceive as the **o.** world is
T-12 III.7:10 and not **o.** it before you can get rid of it;
T-12 III.9:9 Do not believe it is **o.** of yourself, for only
T-12 IV.5:3 believe it is **o.** you the search will be futile,
T-12 VII.7:8 mind then sees a divided world **o.** itself,
T-13 VII.13:6 no world **o.** himself holds his inheritance.
T-13 VIII.8:4 The holy light you saw **o.** yourself, in
T-13. VIII.10:7 He leave His Own beloved Son **o.** them,
T-13 X.3:7 perceive the source of guilt **o.** themselves,
T-14 III.17:2 He leaves you no one **o.** you. And so He
T-14 V.8:4 with no one left **o.** to suffer guilt alone.
T-14 V.9:8 Stand not **o.**, but join with me within. Fail
T-14 V.11:1 the holy circle of Atonement or leave **o.**,
T-14 V.11:7 out in peace on all who think they are **o.**.
T-15 VII.4:6 that the more anger you invest **o.** yourself
T-15 X.8:1 that everyone **o.** yourself demands your
T-15 X.9:7 project it from you and see it **o.** yourself.
T-15 XI.2:2 See it not **o.** yourself, but shining in the
T-15 XI.6:4 love lies in what you have cast **o.** yourself,
T-16 III.3:3 impossible that conviction be **o.** of you.
T-16 III.4:6 must be this part that is really **o.** yourself,
T-16 III.6:3 holds are the universe, all else must be **o.**,
T-16 III.6:7 stand **o.** your teaching and apart from it.
T-16 III.7:8 All this is *you*, and nothing **o.** of this *is* you.
T-16 IV.3:3 it emphasizes the guilt **o.** the haven by
T-16 IV.6:5 seek love **o.** yourself you can be certain
T-16 VI.5:5 Far more is left **o.** than would be taken in,
T-16 VI.11:2 it seems to be **o.** and across the bridge.
T-17 I.6:1 give all you have held **o.** the truth to Him
T-17 V.14:5 glad. If Heaven were **o.** you, you could not
T-17 VII.8:12 yourself **o.** it and keep the situation holy.
T-18 I.7:4 Inward is sanity; insanity is **o.** you. You
T-18 I.7:5 believe it is the other way; that truth is **o.**,
T-18 I.8:1 disappear from sight, far, far **o.** of you.
T-18 I.8:3 with you your mad journey **o.** yourself,
T-18 I.8:4 that you have placed **o.** you to the truth.
T-18 I.9:2 In the mad world **o.** you nothing can be
T-18 II.5:3 within your mind, that seems to be **o.**.
T-18 VI.1:1 There is nothing **o.** you. That is what you
T-18 VI.1:6 is nothing else; nothing **o.** this Oneness,
T-18 VI.2:3 get something else, something **o.** yourself,
T-18 VI.8:8 it has no limits, and there is nothing **o.** it.
T-18 VI.9:1 The body is **o.** you, and but seems to
T-18 VI.10:2 beyond the body, but not **o.** yourself, to
T-18 VI.10:3 Could this be **o.** you? Where God is not?
T-18 VIII.1:6 with externals, something **o.** itself. You
T-18. VIII.11:8 Son of God remains **o.** His Fatherhood.
T-18 IX.3:9 to abandon Him at the **o.** ring of fear, but
T-18 IX.9:2 Here the world **o.** is seen anew, without
T-19 IV.1:3 and from various aspects of the world **o.**.
T-19 IV.2:4 indeed be sure of nothing you see **o.** you,
T19 IV.B.5:4 for we stand within the gates and not **o.**.
T-20 III.5:6 it loves, and placed **o.** you in the world.
T-20 III.5:7 as long as you believe this picture is **o.**,
T-20 III.5:8 This world *is* merciless, and were it **o.** you,
T-20 III.6:8 that made it as you see it is not **o.** you.
T-20 IV.7:6 one of them **o.** than I could leave you, and
T-20 V.1:3 his Father's laws to what was held **o.** them
T-20 VIII.9:6 They are the means by which the **o.** world
T-20. VIII.10:3 you give the world **o.** must thus reflect the
T-21 in.1:5 the **o.** picture of an inward condition. As
T-21 I.8:6 to imagine that anything could be **o.**, for
T-21 II.3:1 God be merely driven by events **o.** of him.
T-21 II.3:4 as God created it, **o.** of which is nothing.
T-22 III.5:6 and stopping at the **o.** form of nothing.
T-22 III.5:7 form of vision the **o.** of everything, the
T-23 II.19:1 There is no life **o.** of Heaven. Where God
T-23 II.19:7 **O.** of Heaven, only the conflict of illusion
T-24 II.9:5 so encompassing that nothing stands **o.**.
T-24 II.9:6 Leave all illusions of yourself **o.** this place,
T-24 VII.11:2 One do you perceive **o.** yourself, your own
T-25 in.1:4 What is within you cannot be **o.**. And it is
T-25 VII.9:6 can no more be left **o.**, without a special
T-26 I.3:5 to you are limits placed on everything **o.**,
T-26 VII.4:9 to be external to the mind, is not **o.** at all,
T-26 VII.12:2 Sin is belief attack can be projected **o.** the
T-27 II.14:2 of correction has been placed **o.** yourself,
T-27 II.14:4 to be part of you and thus **o.** yourself; the
T-27 IV.3:3 **O.** there will be no solution, for there is
T-27 IV.3:4 Nowhere **o.** a single, simple question is
T-27 VII.1:4 this "something else," a thing **o.** himself,
T-27 VII.1:7 because its source is seen **o.** himself.
T-27 VIII.1:3 bodies, born into the world **o.** the body,
T-27 VIII.7:4 you thought is being placed **o.** yourself,
T-27 VIII.8:3 innocence by pushing guilt **o.** yourself,
T-28 V.1:4 And so the good is seen to be **o.**; the evil,
T-29 V.8:5 from dreaming of a world **o.** yourself.
T-29 VII.h Seek Not **O.** Yourself
T-29 VII.1:1 Seek not **o.** yourself. For it will fail, and
T-29 VII.1:6 Seek not **o.** yourself. For all your pain
T-29 VII.1:12 the truth, and not to seek for it **o.** yourself
T-29 VII.2:1 that there is something **o.** of himself that
T-29 VII.3:3 Its form appears to be **o.** himself. Yet does
T-29 VII.4:5 Seek not **o.** yourself. The search implies

T-29.....VII.4:6 prefer to seek **o.** yourself for what you are.
T-29.....VII.6:1 is **o.** yourself to be complete and happy. It
T-29.....VII.6:6 Look not to idols. Do not seek **o.** yourself.
T-29.....VII.8:3 see in it a place of idols found **o.** yourself,
T-29.....VII.9:2 making real the picture it projects **o.** itself
T-29...VII.10:6 Seek not **o.** your Father for your hope. For
T-29....VIII.3:2 perceived as real and seen **o.** the mind.
T-29.....IX.5:7 alive and real, but seen **o.** himself, where
T-29.....IX.5:9 a toy, to make his world remain **o.** himself
T-30..... III.8:5 those **o.** of Heaven know not it is there.
T-30.... III.11:3 **O.** you there is no eternal sky, no
T-30....... V.2:8 And no one stands **o.** this hope, because
T-30....... V.4:2 one **o.** of Heaven knows how this can be,
T-30...... VI.8:2 him **o.** your willingness that he be healed.
T-30...... VI.8:4 no missing parts that have been kept **o.**.
T-31..... V.15:7 upon, and nothing is **o.** of this perception
W-pI.......4.3:3 learning to see the meaningless as **o.** you,
W-pI.....10.3:1 are meaningless, **o.** rather than within;
W-pI.....30.2:2 rid of what we do not like by seeing it **o.**.
W-pI.....32.2:2 one involving the world you see **o.** you,
W-pI.....32.3:1 around at the world you see as **o.** yourself.
W-pI.....33.2:1 the world you perceive as **o.** yourself, then
W-pI.....44.2:2 You do not see **o.** yourself, nor is the
W-pI.....44.2:2 nor is the equipment for seeing **o.** you. An
W-pI.....69.4:3 be standing **o.** the circle and quite apart
W-pI.....70.2:1 It means that nothing **o.** yourself can save
W-pI.....70.2:1 nothing **o.** yourself can give you peace.
W-pI.....70.2:2 it also means that nothing **o.** yourself can
W-pI.....70.7:1 salvation comes from nothing **o.** of you.
W-pI...70.10:7 *Nothing **o.** of me can hold me back.* Within
W-pI.....71.2:3 is constantly perceived as **o.** yourself.
W-pI.....72.8:4 yourself in a body and the truth **o.** you,
W-pI.....72.9:2 It is the body that is **o.** us, and is not our
W-pI.....85.3:5 I will not look for it **o.** myself. It is not
W-pI.....85.3:6 It is not found **o.** and then brought in. But
W-pI...122.6:2 stand **o.** while all of Heaven waits for you
W-pI.127.12:1 us **o.** our love if we would know our Self.
W-pI.169.13:4 it forever, while a part of you remains **o.**,
W-pI...170.4:3 it. Yet you attack **o.** yourself, and separate
W-pI...188.6:6 by the dream of worldly things **o.** yourself
W-pI.196.10:3 outward, and returned from **o.** to within.
W-pI.196.10:4 seemed to be an enemy **o.** you had to fear.
W-pI.196.10:5 And thus a god **o.** yourself became your
W-pI...197.1:1 belief in **o.** force pitted against your own.
W-pI...197.6:2 the sins you think you see **o.** yourself, and
W-pI...197.9:3 And from this Self is no one left **o.**. Give
W-pII .....5.1:5 remains within the body, keeping love **o.**?
W-pII .263.2:1 we still remain **o.** the gate of Heaven, let
W-pII .....8.2:4 for nothing there remains **o.** forgiveness.
W-pII .335.1:4 I seem to be impelled by **o.** happenings. I
M-5 .........I.1:8 God is seen as **o.**, fierce and powerful,
M-8 ...........3:2 Certainly they seem to be in the world **o.**.
M-8 ...........3:5 does not exist in the world **o.** at all. What
M-8 ...........6:5 from what appears to be the **o.** world.
M-17 .........9:8 which you have projected on an **o.** world.
C-3.............4:9 near to Heaven as is possible **o.** the gate.
C-4.............6:4 is seen **o.** must lie beyond forgiveness, for
C-4.............6:5 Where is hope while sin is seen as **o.**?
P-3......... II.1:8 may be far more able teachers **o.** of them.

## outstanding 3

T-2......VIII.5:2 an **o.** example of upside-down perception.
T-7......... II.2:8 The **o.** characteristic of the laws of mind
T-8......VIII.2:5 must have noticed an **o.** characteristic of

## outstretched 1

T-31..VIII.11:1 In joyous welcome is my hand **o.** to every

## outward 27

T-6......... II.9:1 of the thinker, from which they reach **o.**.
T-6......... II.9:5 mind and project your perceptions **o.**.
T-6....... II.11:9 extends **o.** only to what is true in other
T-6....... II.12:8 it must shine **o.** to make you aware of it.
T-6......... V.1:7 God's extending **o.**, though not His
T-7...........I.2:4 this way can all creative power extend **o.**.
T-7...........I.3:4 Love extends **o.** simply because it cannot
T-7 ..........I.5:4 extends **o.** beyond limits and beyond time
T-8 ....... III.3:4 His Own Fatherhood must be extended **o.**.
T-12 ..... III.7:9 projected **o.** what is antagonistic to what
T-12 ..... VI.3:5 from the extension of loving thoughts **o.**.
T-14 ........I.3:1 Seeing is always **o.**. Were your thoughts
T-15 .... VII.4:5 it, it will enable you to direct its anger **o.**,
T-15 .......X.8:4 to project Him **o.** and away from you, and
T-18 ........I.6:1 That was the first projection of error **o.**.
T19....IV.A.1:3 are the center from which it radiates **o.**, to
T-20 ... VI.11:1 in sin made flesh and then projected **o.**.
T-24 .. VII.8:10 It is the **o.** picture of a wish; an image that
W-pI........ 2.1:3 on. Then increase the range **o.**. Turn your
W-pI....... 8.1:3 He sees only his thoughts projected **o.**.
W-pI....... 9.4:1 nearest you, and then extend the range **o.**:
W-pI..... 34.1:3 your own thoughts, and then extend **o.**. It
W-pI... 189.9:8 His Love shines **o.** from its home within,
W-pI. 196.10:3 you believed attack could be directed **o.**,
W-pII . 304.1:4 I look on is my state of mind, reflected **o.**.
W-pII . 325.1:3 find. These images are then projected **o.**,
M-8 ........... 3:7 Its hierarchy of values is projected **o.**, and

## outwitted 1

W-pI... 166.9:6 Perhaps He has not wholly been **o.** by

## outworn 1

S-3........II.1:11 a choice, as one lays by a garment now **o.**.

## over 169

*See also* over-

T-1 ........I.46:3 revelation, the need for miracles is **o.**.
T-1 ......VII.1:1 a dense cover **o.** miracle impulses,
T-2 .........II.7:5 take it **o.** because of their strength. A two-
T-2 ....... III.4:4 of the right defense it passes **o.** all others,
T-2 ....... IV.4:5 the illness has a sufficiently strong hold **o.**
T-2 ....... VI.1:3 take **o.** everything that does not matter,
T-2 .....VIII.2:5 Just as the separation occurred **o.** millions
T-2 .....VIII.2:5 will extend **o.** a similarly long period, and
T-3 ...... V.10:2 Atonement and given themselves **o.** to
T-3 ....... VI.4:2 to accept it, you have lost control **o.** it.
T-3 ..... VI.8:10 The dispute **o.** authorship has left such
T-3 ....... VI.9:1 Only those who give **o.** all desire to reject
T-4 .........I.2:1 Many stand guard **o.** their ideas because
T-4 ........ VI.1:2 to it gives the ego any power **o.** you. I
T-5 ..........I.6:5 to knowledge, or cross **o.** into it. It might
T-5 ..........I.6:6 meaning of transferred or "carried **o.**,"
T-5 ..... VII.6:5 and give it **o.** to the Atonement in peace.
T-6 ........ V.2:1 that the night is **o.** and the light has come
T-7 ....... IV.4:1 therefore be given **o.** to the Holy Spirit,
T-7 .....VIII.5:6 Give them **o.** quickly to the Holy Spirit to
T-7 ........ XI.3:9 watches **o.** His children and denies them
T-8 ....... IV.6:7 the dominion of one mind **o.** another.
T-8 ....... VI.3:1 **o.** His Kingdom the world has no power.
T-8 ... VII.12:4 and gives it **o.** entirely to the One Light in
T-9 ........I.11:7 If you hold your hands **o.** your eyes, you
T-9 ....... III.5:3 want to give yours **o.** to the Holy Spirit,
T-9 ....... VI.6:5 they are the same, the need for time is **o.**.
T-9 ...VIII.11:3 Nothing can attack it nor prevail **o.** it. It
T-10 ...... V.5:3 that you need be troubled **o.** nothing.
T-11 ..... VI.1:6 the complete triumph of Christ **o.** the ego,
T-11 ..... VI.5:1 the power the god he worships has **o.** him
T-12 ..... III.9:4 have no control **o.** the world you made. It
T-12 ..... III.9:9 where it is will you gain control **o.** it. For
T-12 ... III.9:10 it. For you do have control **o.** your mind,
T-12 .VIII.7:10 God did not give you has no power **o.** you
T-13 ..... IV.5:3 from the past, and although the past is **o.**,
T-13 ..... IV.6:2 hold **o.** you unless you bring them with
T-13 ..... IV.8:2 and it closes **o.** the present so that no gap
T-13 .... VII.6:6 give this sad world **o.** and exchange your
T-13 .... VII.7:2 Who watches **o.** him in everything. The
T-13 ...VIII.8:3 And suddenly time will be **o.**, and we will
T-13 ..... IX.7:3 You throw a dark veil **o.** it, and cannot see
T-13 .......X.5:3 your mind in peace **o.** to the Atonement.
T-13 ..... XI.6:6 truth, it will flow lightly **o.** you without a
T-13 ..... XI.9:5 sleeping Son holds no power **o.** him. He
T-13 ..... XI.9:7 watches **o.** him and light surrounds him.
T-14 ..... III.6:6 that darkness has no power **o.** the Son of
T-14 ..... III.8:2 that what is not of God has power **o.** you.
T-14 ..... VI.2:5 sentinels of darkness watch **o.** it carefully,
T-15 ..... IV.2:6 Give **o.** every plan you have made for your
T-15 ..... IV.4:2 and gladly give **o.** every plan but His. For
T-15 ..... IV.4:5 practice, try to give **o.** every plan you have
T-15 ... VIII.3:4 redemption **o.** to your Redeemer's Love.
T-16 ........ I.6:2 that hovers **o.** it and blesses it silently by
T-16 ..... III.8:5 so the one who would cross **o.** is literally
T-16 ..... IV.5:3 of love can triumph **o.** the illusion of hate,
T-16 .......V.5:5 "victory" even to the final triumph **o.** God
T-16 .....V.10:1 special relationship as a triumph **o.** God,
T-16 .....V.11:3 triumphing **o.** it and leaving it helpless.
T-16 .....V.11:6 **O.** and over and over this ritual is enacted
T-16 .....V.11:6 Over and **o.** and over this ritual is enacted
T-16 .....V.11:6 Over and over and **o.** this ritual is enacted
T-16 .....V.12:4 sign that form has triumphed **o.** content,
T-16 ... VI.11:1 you will gain from crossing **o.** will be the
T-16 .. VII.11:4 reality to give **o.** all illusions for the reality
T-17 .....V.12:1 forgotten if you allow time to close **o.** it. It
T-18 ........I.4:3 subdivided and divided again, **o.** and over
T-18 ........I.4:3 subdivided and divided again, over and **o.**
T-18 .......II.1:5 to make **o.** whatever seemed to attack you
T-18 .......II.3:8 trying to triumph **o.** it and make it serve
T-18 .VIII.13:1 journey, not realizing yet that it is **o.**. You
T-19 ..... III.3:3 a sin can be repeated **o.** and over, with
T-19 ..... III.3:3 a sin can be repeated over and **o.**, with
T-19 ..... III.9:5 that you give it no power **o.** your brother.
T19 ...IV.A.5:4 same. Each is a gentle winning **o.** from the
T19 ...IV.A.6:5 The sun has risen **o.** it. How can a shadow
T19 ...IV.C.7:7 triumph of the ego's making **o.** creation,
T19 .IV.C.11:1 and the cold sweat of fear comes **o.** it,
T19 IV.D.10:5 when it is **o.** it seems to make no sense.
T19 IV.D.10:6 How can you know that it is **o.** unless you
T19 IV.D.21:3 and watches **o.** you in faith so gentle yet
T-20 ..... III.6:6 Who watches **o.** all perception answered.
T-20 ..... IV.3:1 and give them power **o.** you by accepting
T-20 .......V.8:1 and feel the Holy Spirit watching **o.** you
T-20 .... VII.2:1 sin to holiness may now be almost **o.**. To
T-21 .....II.11:3 by your Creator has any influence **o.** you.
T-21 ... VI.11:1 The power you have **o.** the Son of God is
T-22 .....III.10:2 Nothing you made has any power **o.** you
T-22 ..... IV.3:5 Yet it is almost **o.** in your awareness, and
T-22 .......V.6:6 not one that truth cannot pass **o.** lightly,
T-23 ........ I.2:6 it thinks that truth triumph **o.** you is possible.
T-23 ........ I.4:1 the war against yourself is almost **o.**. The
T-23 ........ I.5:5 to triumph **o.** what you are, remembers
T-23 ........ I.6:8 Illusions cannot triumph **o.** truth, nor can
T-23 ......I.10:8 **O.** His home the Holy Spirit watches, sure
T-23 ..... III.6:2 released from conflict means that it is **o.**.
T-23 ..... IV.5:9 is **o.** when you realize it never was begun.
T-24 .......V.4:2 to a nameless precipice and hurl him **o.** it.
T-24 ..... VI.9:5 to laws that have no power **o.** him at all.
T-25 .....II.10:7 Nothing has power **o.** you except His Will
T-25 ... VIII.3:7 and triumph **o.** eternity and timelessness
T-25 ... VIII.6:6 the chill of fear comes **o.** them when they
T-26 .......V.6:2 It is the key to learning that the past is **o.**.
T-26 .....V.13:4 belief that what is **o.** is still here and now.
T-26 .....V.14:4 again a journey that was **o.** long ago. Look
T-28 ........ I.1:6 This world was **o.** long ago. The thoughts
T-28 ........ I.2:2 For guilt is **o.**. In its passing went its
T-28 ...... I.15:6 that he be lifted up and gently carried **o.**.
T-29 ........ I.5:3 And herein lies its power **o.** you. For now
T-29 .... VII.3:4 within, and prove that he is victor **o.** him.
T-29 ..... IX.7:7 can enter here, for time is almost **o.**. And
T-30 .......II.5:2 that he learn death has no power **o.** him,
W-pI ......... 7.5:1 not linger **o.** any one thing in particular,
W-pI ..... 21.2:5 is nothing but a veil drawn **o.** intense fury
W-pI ..... 26.7:3 go **o.** every possible outcome that has
W-pI ..... 38.5:5 **o.** all things because of what you are.
W-pI ..... 50.5:2 allow peace to flow **o.** you like a blanket of
WpI... rI.in.2:3 related comments after reading them **o.**.
W-pI ..... 67.3:1 gone **o.** several such related thoughts, try
W-pI ..... 68.6:5 you, hovering **o.** you and holding you up.
W-pI ..... 76.6:2 This needs repeating, **o.** and over, until
W-pI ..... 76.6:2 This needs repeating, over and **o.**, until
W-pI ..... 80.2:2 Repeat this **o.** and over to yourself today,
W-pI ..... 80.2:2 Repeat this over and **o.** to yourself today,
WpI.. rII.in.2:2 or four minutes to reading them **o.** slowly
WpI.. rII.in.4:4 will has power **o.** all fantasies and dreams

T-27....VIII.9:2 your error, who have o. the cause entirely
T-28......III.3:4 it is, and you have o. the gap between you
T-30.......VI.5:4 can be no appearance that can not be o..
W-pI.....39.1:4 o. in the clouds of complexity in which
W-pI.....99.4:3 be this plan, by which the never done is o.
M-14 .......1:11 them not. It merely o. the meaningless.
M-17 .......8:11 And so they can be o., and thus forgotten
M-18 .........2:7 o. completely in His sight and in God's
M-26 .........2:7 mistakes are recognized and o. by them.
P-2........IV.7:3 If illness is real it cannot be o. in truth, for

## overlooking 11

T-7......III.1:12 by eliminating or o. its real and only
T-11.....V.10:5 it. If you overlook love you are o. yourself,
T-11.....V.15:2 the ego succeeds in o. it and is left with a
T19. IV.A.10:6 O. guilt completely, it sees no fear. Being
T-23......IV.4:7 The o. of the battleground is now your
T-26....VIII.5:5 looking back, but o. what is here and now
T-26....VIII.5:7 And in o. this, is it protected and kept
T-30......VI.1:7 you forgive a sin by o. what is really there.
C-in ...........1:5 if you are indeed to succeed in o. the error
C-in ...........1:6 this process of o. at which the course aims
P-2........IV.7:2 "rightness" of the mistake and then o. it.

## overlooks 13

T-11.....V.14:2 The ego focuses on error and o. truth. It
T-11.....V.16:6 Can the ego teach truly when it o. truth?
T-16.....VII.2:2 it o. the present in its preoccupation with
T19. IV.A.11:4 What fear would feed upon, love o.. What
T-22.....II.12:8 His home with vision that o. the world.
T-25.......II.8:7 However much he o. the masterpiece in
W-pI.....72.5:7 real. It o. entirely what your brother is. It
W-pI.....92.4:1 Strength o. these things by seeing past
W-pI.135.15:4 It o. the present, for it rests on the idea
W-pI...137.5:2 as forgiveness o. all sins that never were
M-22 .........4:5 He o. the mind *and* body, seeing only the
C-1............6:2 because right-mindedness merely o., or
S-2...........I.2:4 evil things, and o. the loving as a plague; a

## overrun 1

T-21.....VII.4:3 Yes, it can o. the world and *seek* an enemy.

## overshadows 1

M-8 ...........1:3 larger object o. a smaller one. A brighter

## overt 3

T-16.......V.3:2 that center around it are often quite o..
W-pI.....13.5:4 any signs of o. or covert fear which it may
W-pI...126.6:2 you see it, it is but a check upon o. attack,

## overtakes 1

T-20......III.4:2 longer before it o. you and you disappear.

## overthrown 2

T-19.....III.7:4 His creation seem to be split apart and o..
T-23.........I.2:8 the Will of God can be attacked and o..

## overtly 2

T-13.....IV.1:7 When it becomes o. savage, it offers you
W-pI.....10.2:3 no link is made o. with the things around

## overtones 3

T-29.........I.8:7 And there are o. of seeming fear around
P-2.........in.4:4 goals not completely free of magical o..
S-1...........I.3:3 Along with it come the o., the harmonics,

## overturning 1

W-pII .....1.3:2 twisting and o. what it sees as interfering

## overwhelming 1

T-27 .....III.6:2 For you will give it o. preference. Nor

## owe 8

T-4 .......VI.2:2 It is the same debt that you o. to me.
T-15 .....III.3:1 is a deep responsibility you o. yourself,
T-19 .....IV.3:1 The gratitude you o. to Him He asks but
T19. IV.D.19:6 Heaven is the gift you o. your brother, the
W-pI...101.2:5 that evens the account they o. to God.
W-pI...192.9:7 And so you o. him thanks instead of pain.
W-pII .323.2:1 And as we pay the debt we o. to truth,–a
C-5 ...........4:3 this because you o. him this who shared

## Own 88

*own*

T-3 ..........I.1:9 kind of thinking which His O. words have
T-3 ..........I.2:4 His O. Son on behalf of salvation. The
T-3 ..........II.4:1 which He created in the likeness of His O.,
T-3 ........V.7:3 God did create spirit in His O. Thought
T-3 ........V.7:3 Thought and of a quality like to His O..
T-3 ......VII.3:9 of destroying Their O. purpose is in error.
T-4 ......VII.6:6 know. He knows it in His O. Being and its
T-5 .....III.10:5 because it is His O. dwelling place; the
T-5 .......VI.5:1 Spirit can reinterpret them in His O. light.
T-5 .....VI.10:4 believe gladly to God's O. Higher Court,
T-6 .....IV.11:6 Can God lose His O. certainty? I have
T-8 .......III.3:4 O. Fatherhood must be extended outward
T-8 .....VI.8:10 because you who are God's O. treasure do
T-9 ...VIII.11:9 His O. exalted Answer to what you are, so
T-11 .......II.4:3 O. complete Will and make yours whole.
T-11 .....IV.1:7 are denying Him His place in His O. altar.
T-11 ...VI.3:10 For until Christ comes into His O., the
T-11 .....VI.6:4 accepting him without question as His O..
T-13 .VIII.10:7 He leave His O. beloved Son outside them
T-13 .....X.14:1 who make the Father One with His O. Son
T-14 ...VIII.5:7 on the altar, where He has placed His O..
T-15 ........I.2:3 the Holy Spirit uses time in His O. way,
T19....IV.C.5:7 has answered this insane idea with His O.;
T-22 .....VI.4:1 of your Father as a means for His O. plan.
T-23 .....IV.3:2 to create unto His Son because it is His O.
T-24 ......V.8:2 because in your completion is His O.. He
T-24 .....VI.1:6 For He could never leave His O. creation.
T-25 ......V.3:5 by returning unto God what is His O..
T-25 ..VII.10:5 you in God's O. plan to show His Son that
T-25 ...VIII.6:4 "fires" of Heaven by God's O. angry Hand
T-25 ...VIII.9:5 God's O. justice does He recognize all you
T-26 ........I.8:6 be a task apart and separate from His O.?
T-26 .....IX.5:2 For They have come to gather in Their O..
T-27 ......II.6:7 to His Son, and of the Son unto His O.,
T-27 .....II.15:4 goal in which the Holy Spirit sees His O..
T-27 .....II.16:4 the function given it conceived to be its O.
T-28 ......I.10:9 in allowing Cause to have Its O. Effects,
T-30 ......V.5:1 short of this, for this is God's O. purpose;
W-pI.....67.2:8 of God and replace it with His O.. We are
W-pI...91.10:4 in which you share a purpose like Their O.
W-pI.....92.9:2 Self stands ready to embrace you as Its O..
W-pI.....93.9:6 Let It come into Its O.. Here you are; This
WpI. rIV.in6:4 And as His O. completion joins with Him,
W-pI...154.3:1 to hear one Voice which is His O. that you
W-pI. 154.11:5 And He needs our will united with His O.,
W-pI. 154.12:4 have identified with Him and with His O.
W-pI. 155.14:2 In your Name and His O., which are the
W-pI...160.4:3 Is fear His O., created in His likeness? Is it
W-pI...160.6:8 will call Its O. unto Itself in recognition of
W-pI...160.6:8 unto Itself in recognition of what is Its O..
W-pI...160.7:4 as certain of Its O. as God is of His Son.
W-pI...160.9:2 beholds His O. and joyously unites with
W-pI...168.6:4 word He gave to us through His O. Voice,
W-pI...182.5:1 in you your Father knows as His O. Son. It
W-pI. 184.15:3 *we have tried to cast across Your O. reality.*
W-pI. 185.12:1 and established as His O. eternal gift.
W-pI. 195.10:4 His O. completion and the Source of love,
W-pI...197.5:2 And what belongs to God must be His O..
W-pII .233.1:3 *In place of them, give me Your O.. I give You*
W-pII .240.2:4 *feel the love for him which is Your O. as well.*
W-pII .264.1:7 *We come to You in Your O. Name today, to*
W-pII .270.1:6 *His function now is but Your O., and every*
W-pII .270.1:6 *and every thought except Your O. is gone.*
W-pII .279.2:2 *loves the Son Whom He created as His O..*
W-pII .289.2:2 *You have offered me Your O. replacement,*
W-pII .290.1:4 I perceive without God's O. Correction for
W-pII .309.1:2 His Son, whose will is limitless as is His O.
W-pII ... 11.5:2 Whose Holiness His O. creation shares;
W-pII .323.1:1 *of pain, and giving him Your O. eternal joy.*
W-pII347.1:10 *not know my will, but He is sure it is Your O..*
W-pII .348.1:8 *created me in holiness as perfect as Your O.?*
W-pII ... 14.1:6 *Itself, for in my purity abides His O..*
W-pII .354.1:3 *I have no purpose but His O.. And He is like*
W-pII .359.1:1 *Your world, and let creation be Your O.. We*
Wfl........in.4:1 given us to be His O. completion in reality
Wfl........in.6:1 through the Voice of His O. Teacher.
Wfl........in.6:4 thus, for these are His O. words to you.
M-4 .... IV.2:10 And so their will, which always was His O.
M-14 ....... 5:11 say you cannot learn His O. curriculum.
M-27 ......... 5:6 His O. creation must stand in fear of Him.
M-29 ......... 6:8 cruel if He let your words replace His O..
C-4 ........... 6:9 brightness. God has come to claim His O..
C-4 ........... 7:5 God knows it is His O., as it is his. And
P-1............ 2:1 it and give it His O. great gift of rejoicing?
S-2........ III.3:3 with your own sincerity, but with His O..
S-2........ III.6:8 Prayer is His O. right Hand, made free to
S-2........ III.7:5 down to answer you in His O. Name. He
S-3........ IV.8:8 Do not deny to Christ what is His O..

## own 700

*Own*

T-1 ........I.18:4 recognize your o. and your neighbor's
T-1 ........I.24:3 Everything else is your o. nightmare, and
T-1 ....... III.1:3 not need miracles for my o. Atonement,
T-1 ..... III.5:10 since their o. perception of themselves is
T-1 ....... III.6:7 your o. holiness to the holiness of others.
T-1 ....... III.8:4 still expressions of your o. state of grace,
T-1 ....... IV.3:2 It has no unique properties of its o.. It is
T-1 .........V.5:4 creates along the line of its o. creation. If
T-1 ....... VI.3:1 requires correction at its o. level before
T-1 ...... VII.1:1 hard for them to reach your o. awareness.
T-2 ..........I.1:7 fill it with your o. ideas instead of truth.
T-2 ..........I.1:9 created can be changed by your o. mind.
T-2 ........I.1:12 direction of your o. creation is up to you.
T-2 ....... IV.1:9 not understand healing because of your o.
T-2 ....... IV.4:2 believing that the body makes its o. illness
T-2 ........V.1:10 device is not subject to errors of its o.,
T-2 .........V.2:5 misperceive them as your o. creations. As
T-2 .........V.4:1 The healer who relies on his o. readiness
T-2 .........V.5:6 from overevaluating its o. learning device,
T-2 .........V.8:4 cannot endure to see your o. defiled altar.
T-2 ........V.10:2 Since his o. thinking is faulty he cannot
T-2 ... V.A.18:1 do much on behalf of your o. healing and
T-2 ....... VI.1:1 something beyond your o. control. Yet I
T-2 ....... VI.6:4 as you recognize that it is also your o..
T-2 ...... VII.1:5 depreciated the power of your o. thinking
T-2 ...... VII.3:7 if you were not afraid of your o. thoughts.
T-2 ..... VIII.1:5 you alone make is real in your o. sight,
T-2 ..... VIII.4:3 his o. creations and choose to preserve
T-2 ..... VIII.4:4 begin to look with love on its o. creations
T-2 ..... VIII.5:5 Your o. last judgment cannot be directed
T-2 ..... VIII.5:5 because you are not your o. creation. You
T-2 ..... VIII.5:9 It is your o. perfect judgment of your own
T-2 ..... VIII.5:9 own perfect judgment of your o. perfect
T-3 ..........I.3:1 one assigns his o. "evil" past to God. The
T-3 .........II.4:1 Will because you have used your o. mind,
T-3 ..... IV.3:10 and your creation is beyond your o. error.
T-3 ........ IV.5:8 itself when it chooses to make its o. levels.
T-3 ..... IV.6:10 its attack is your o. vague recognition that
T-3 ..... IV.7:11 I can help you make your o. right choice.
T-3 .........V.7:1 The statement "God created man in his o.
T-3 ........ VI.1:4 will be unable to avoid judging your o..
T-3 ..... VI.5:10 a weapon of defense for your o. authority.
T-3 ........ VI.9:1 know that their o. rejection is impossible.
T-3 ...... VI.11:2 result of his o. free will he must regard his
T-3 ...... VI.11:8 what I am and I accept my o. inheritance.
T-3 ...... VII.3:6 where their o. destruction was possible?
T-3 .... VII.4:10 you are an image of your o. making. Your
T-3 ...... VII.6:3 o. thought system will stand corrected. It
T-4 ........in.3:3 accept it as your o. last useless journey,

T-4 I.1:1 A good teacher clarifies his **o.** ideas and
T-4 I.5:1 much of his **o.** learning that they will one
T-4 I.5:3 because it goes against all of its **o.** laws.
T-4 I.11:4 to leave it empty by their **o.** dispossession.
T-4 II.3:1 **o.** state of mind is a good example of how
T-4 II.8:1 The ego believes it is completely on its **o.**,
T-4 II.8:4 mind's belief that it is completely on its **o.**
T-4 II.8:5 thus establish its **o.** existence are useless.
T-4 II.9:3 and its interpretation of its **o.** beginning.
T-4 III.2:4 **o.** Guide and therefore need guidance. My
T-4 III.3:4 which begins with its **o.** beginning and
T-4 III.3:4 beginning and ends with its **o.** ending. It
T-4 III.3:5 this life is your existence because it is its **o.**
T-4 III.6:1 No force except your **o.** will is strong
T-4 III.9:1 In your **o.** mind, though denied by the
T-4 IV.3:3 of nothing except by your **o.** decisions,
T-4 IV.8:6 well you have done this by your **o.** feelings
T-4 IV.8:9 Without your **o.** allegiance, protection
T-4 IV.11:3 too confused to recognize your **o.** hope. I
T-4 V.2:6 its **o.** preservation in the face of threat,
T-4 V.4:1 body is the ego's home by its **o.** election. It
T-4 V.4:2 since the body's vulnerability is its **o.** best
T-4 VI.1:3 if it were a separate thing, acting on its **o.**.
T-4 VI.7:7 I can lead you back to your **o.** creations.
T-4 VII.2:3 the ego is based on its **o.** thought system,
T-4 VII.4:5 are limiting your sense of your **o.** reality,
T-5 I.3:2 Him to you only at your **o.** invitation. The
T-5 I.7:5 leads the mind beyond its **o.** integration
T-5 II.4:3 of Heaven breaks through into its **o.**.
T-5 II.7:11 gain the whole world and lose his **o.** soul?
T-5 II.8:6 for God comes from your **o.** altars to Him.
T-5 III.7:2 with the ego's beliefs in its **o.** language.
T-5 III.9:6 mind reinterpret its **o.** misperceptions.
T-5 IV.2:7 your **o.** thoughts can make you really free.
T-5 IV.8:4 them for you in their **o.** perfect radiance.
T-5 V.5:8 then takes this intent as its **o.** prerogative.
T-5 V.7:6 who believe they order their **o.** thoughts,
T-5 VI.8:2 attempt to guarantee the ego's **o.** survival.
T-5 VII.3:4 ego's last-ditch defense of its **o.** existence.
T-6 in.1:2 be accepted as one's **o.** responsibility,
T-6 I.2:8 contribution to make to your **o.** life, and if
T-6 I.2:8 you understand your **o.** role as a teacher.
T-6 I.6:3 to teach if he is to realize his **o.** salvation.
T-6 I.6:4 Rather, teach your **o.** perfect immunity,
T-6 I.6:6 was part of my **o.** teaching contribution.
T-6 I.14:3 **o.** imperfect love made them vulnerable
T-6 I.14:3 and out of their **o.** fear they spoke of the
T-6 II.3:2 reinforces your belief in your **o.** split mind
T-6 II.13:3 no darkness to abide in your **o.** mind.
T-6 III.3:1 see His gentleness in others your **o.** mind
T-6 V.1:3 You did not believe in your **o.** perfection.
T-6 V.B.3:8 mind of the learner projects its **o.** conflict,
T-7 I.2:1 increase through its **o.** creative thought.
T-7 II.3:9 depends on it, just as their **o.** creation did.
T-7 III.4:10 brothers, because it sees only in its **o.** light
T-7 IV.6:2 that it can offer you its **o.** "will" as a gift.
T-7 V.1:4 does not understand his **o.** vocation.
T-7 V.7:4 lesson is limited by his **o.** ingratitude,
T-7 VI.1:6 of God, of His creations and of his **o.**. He
T-7 VI.3:7 it. This threatens its **o.** existence, a state
T-7 VI.3:10 that you will not know your **o.** safety.
T-7 VI.4:3 love you it *is* faithful to its **o.** antecedents,
T-7 VI.4:10 ego. Its **o.** maker, then, does not want it.
T-7 VI.8:5 your mind in its **o.** delusional system,
T-7 VII.6:6 You cannot know your **o.** perfection until
T-7 VII.8:3 by projecting your **o.** rejection you then
T-7 VIII.2:5 its **o.** warped version of the laws of God,
T-7 VIII.3:9 who project are vigilant for their **o.** safety.
T-7 VIII.3:11 their projections from their **o.** minds,
T-7 VIII.5:4 to project responsibility for your **o.** errors.
T-7 IX.2:1 of all its brothers is included in its **o.**, as it
T-7 IX.2:2 its Creator is therefore spirit's **o.** fullness,
T-7 IX.3:7 You may not know your **o.** creations, but
T-7 IX.4:2 you do not know your **o.** Self-fullness.
T-7 IX.5:2 They are there as part of your **o.** being,
T-7 X.5:10 this, too, is merely a matter of his **o.** belief
T-7 XI.2:8 **o.** worth is beyond anything he can make.
T-7 XI.5:2 Its **o.** radiance shines all around it, and
T-7 XI.5:4 brother is to accept your **o.** inheritance.
T-8 II.2:5 on the grounds of your **o.** experience with
T-8 II.4:2 to learn it is a violation of your **o.** freedom
T-8 II.8:2 for its **o.** acknowledgment of what it is.
T-8 II.8:6 for his creations and for his **o.** extension.
T-8 III.6:2 ego, whose purpose is to defeat its **o.** goal.
T-8 IV.5:7 by which you determine your **o.** condition
T-8 VII.5:1 only from your **o.** misunderstanding. Loss
T-8 VII.5:5 not see him this way for your **o.** salvation,
T-8 VII.11:3 and by blocking its **o.** extension beyond it
T-8 VII.14:6 his ability to accept its purpose as his **o.**.
T-8 VIII.1:7 then, is not the source of its **o.** health. The
T-8 VIII.2:5 end that the ego has accepted as its **o.**.
T-8 VIII.9:6 image of your **o.** perception of littleness.
T-9 I.2:2 of God is really the fear of your **o.** reality.
T-9 I.3:8 re-establish your **o.** will in your awareness
T-9 I.4:1 have imprisoned your will beyond your **o.**
T-9 V.5:4 and he must learn from his **o.** teaching.
T-9 VIII.3:1 impulses and ego-alien beliefs of its **o.**. I
T-10 I.2:3 You recognize from your **o.** experience
T-10 II.2:5 Him and know your **o.** reality again. Let
T-10 II.5:3 your **o.** decision not to be what you are, it
T-10 III.10:11 to give up your **o.** perfect helpfulness and
T-10 III.10:11 helpfulness and your **o.** perfect Help.
T-10 V.1:5 to deny God is to deny their **o.** Identity,
T-10 V.3:2 is in direct opposition to its **o.** survival.
T-10 V.9:10 and suffering into your **o.** mind because
T-11 in.2:4 system in which you made your **o.** father.
T-11 I.8:4 By denying this you deny your **o.** will, and
T-11 I.11:6 the Will of your Father is to know your **o.**.
T-11 II.2:5 from your brother or in your **o.** mind,
T-11 III.2:1 he does, believing his will is not his **o.**.
T-11 IV.3:5 that you can darken only your **o.** mind. As
T-11 V.4:5 independent of any power except its **o.**.
T-11 V.15:4 becomes its demonstration of its **o.** reality
T-11 V.18:7 You hear but your **o.** voice, and if Christ
T-11 VI.6:5 Who, then, is *your* **o.**? The Father has
T-11 VI.8:1 a crown of thorns upon your **o.** head. Yet
T-11 VI.8:3 has been redeemed from his **o.** crucifixion
T-11 VI.9:1 You will awaken to your **o.** call, for the
T-11 VIII.3:8 amiss should not be your **o.** teacher.
T-11 VIII.13:2 willing to let their **o.** interpretations go in
T-11 VIII.13:3 afraid, and laughs happily at his **o.** fear.
T-12 I.1:3 true. But truth is real in its **o.** right, and to
T-12 I.2:1 never without your **o.** ego involvement.
T-12 I.2:2 **o.** ability to understand what you perceive
T-12 I.3:8 to your **o.** mind is not yet fully apparent.
T-12 I.4:1 except your **o.** imagined need to attack. It
T-12 I.6:11 will recognize your **o.** need for the Father.
T-12 I.9:1 is a symptom of your **o.** deep sense of loss.
T-12 I.9:6 belief in what is denied for its **o.** existence.
T-12 II.4:7 in the darkness of your **o.** false certainty,
T-12 III.6:5 its source as his **o.** ego identification, and
T-12 III.10:1 is in your **o.** mind and nowhere else, you
T-12 V.2:1 recognition of your **o.** invulnerability is so
T-12 V.4:2 trust your **o.** love when you attack it. You
T-12 V.4:4 of creation, but with your **o.** content. Yet
T-12 V.8:3 it? Resign now as your **o.** teacher. This
T-12 VI.1:1 gain the whole world and lose your **o.** soul
T-13 III.3:2 and your **o.** real power seems to you as
T-13 III.5:5 it enters of its **o.** volition and cares not for
T-13 III.6:1 they do not rest on their **o.** foundation. In
T-13 III.10:6 attacked his **o.** glorious equality with Him
T-13 IV.5:6 from him out of your **o.** past because, by
T-13 IV.6:7 it as a meeting with your **o.** past? For you
T-13 IV.8:1 the ego interprets the goal of time as its **o.**
T-13 IV.8:2 that no gap in its **o.** continuity can occur.
T-13 V.3:8 Its only reality is in your **o.** mind, and by
T-13 V.5:3 If you see your **o.** hatred as your brother,
T-13 V.6:5 your **o.** split mind everywhere you look.
T-13 V.6:6 for you are preoccupied with your **o.** voice
T-13 V.8:7 private world and rule your **o.** perception.
T-13 VI.1:1 reality through the awareness of your **o.**.
T-13 VI.4:6 present and future for your **o.** purposes.
T-13 VI.9:2 for in their wholeness you will see your **o.**.
T-13 VI.13:7 to be his Father's witness and his **o.**.
T-13 VII.6:2 Yet while he still lays value on his **o.**, he
T-13 VII.10:12 its **o.** sake is the ego's fundamental creed,
T-13 IX.3:1 for being nothing but your **o.** projection,
T-13 IX.4:7 in his freedom would have been your **o.**.
T-13 IX.6:2 of God lies the conviction of your **o.** guilt.
T-13 X.2:8 by pre-empting for your **o.** ends what you
T-13 X.3:1 or share it with him or perceive his **o.**, *you*
T-13 X.3:7 themselves, beyond their **o.** control.
T-13 XI.6:5 Truth comes of its **o.** will unto its own.
T-13 XI.6:5 Truth comes of its own will unto its **o.**.
T-14 III.12:4 set for its Atonement, relinquishing its **o.**.
T-14 IV.6:3 your **o.** volition seems to make deciding
T-14 V.4:5 God has hidden himself from his **o.** sight.
T-14 V.6:1 Teachers of innocence, each in his **o.** way,
T-14 V.7:1 Join your **o.** efforts to the power that
T-14 VII.5:8 must be gently turned to your **o.** good,
T-14 X.1:1 or between His children and their **o.**, the
T-14 X.2:3 satisfied with anything but his **o.** reality.
T-14 X.6:7 which requires no judgment of your **o.**.
T-14 XI.5:2 learned God's lesson, and not your **o.**.
T-14 XI.6:9 *I will not use my* **o.** *past learning as the light*
T-15 I.4:14 because it cannot conceive of its **o.** death,
T-15 II.3:6 support either their weakness or your **o.**.
T-15 II.5:5 blind you to this world by its **o.** vision,
T-15 IV.2:5 find salvation in your **o.** way and have it.
T-15 IV.3:6 value of His Will for you in your **o.** mind.
T-15 V.2:1 you learned to define your **o.** needs and
T-15 V.2:1 for meeting them on your **o.** terms. We
T-15 V.7:2 assemble reality to its **o.** capricious liking,
T-15 VII.10:6 in His Voice your **o.** need to communicate
T-15 VII.11:5 are together their minds remain their **o.**.
T-15 VII.12:1 the ego's plan to establish its **o.** autonomy
T-15 IX.3:3 everyone to a body for its **o.** purposes,
T-15 X.1:9 Release me as I choose your **o.** release.
T-16 I.3:2 to hurt it nor to heal it in your **o.** way. You
T-16 III.4:6 outside yourself, not by your **o.** projection
T-16 III.7:2 chosen this by your **o.** willingness to teach
T-16 IV.8:3 You seek but for your **o.** completion, and
T-16 IV.10:2 removes your **o.** sense of completion, and
T-16 VII.3:6 your alliance in your **o.** destruction, the
T-17 I.1:1 and all his "sins" are but his **o.** imagining.
T-17 II.3:5 by your **o.** forgiveness you are free to see.
T-17 III.1:8 keep them by your **o.** selection do not
T-17 III.2:8 Your **o.** experience has taught you this.
T-17 IV.10:5 to defend you from your **o.** attack. For
T-17 V.3:5 as it *is* is out of line with its **o.** goal, and
T-17 VII.9:1 or you are faithless to your **o.** relationship
T-18 IV.5:11 *to me my* **o.** *awareness of my readiness,*
T-18 IV.5:13 *it, I must be willing not to substitute my* **o.** *in*
T-18 V.4:5 the Holy Spirit's purpose as your **o.**, and
T-18 VII.6:1 everyone will one day find in his **o.** way, at
T-18 VII.6:1 one day find in his own way, at his **o.** time
T-19 I.8:1 your **o.** identification has become because
T-19 III.1:8 an avenger, with a mind unlike your **o.**,
T19 IV.D.16:5 laid upon him and he accepted as his **o.**,
T19 IV.D.21:7 holy Friend, and recognize it as your **o.**.
T-20 I.3:4 with the light of his **o.** innocence lighting
T-20 II.1:5 and trying to justify your **o.** interpretation
T-20 II.3:4 has placed upon it and take it for their **o.**.
T-20 II.5:3 purpose as their **o.** share also His vision.
T-20 IV.2:7 mistakes, and therein lies his **o.** salvation.
T-20 IV.3:4 that you see in him you see your **o.**. For
T-20 V.7:10 recognize it and love it as your **o.**.
T-20 VI.10:3 smile and tender blessing it offers to its **o.**
T-20 VIII.2:1 Do you not want to know your **o.** Identity
T-21 II.6:4 Will cannot be separate from his **o.**. This
T-21 II.10:4 of your desire to create your **o.** creator,
T-21 IV.4:9 to see the Holy Spirit's purpose as its **o.**?
T-21 IV.7:7 what has been given Heaven as its **o.**.
T-21 V.2:5 prey to forces far beyond your **o.** control,
T-21 V.3:10 do not affect another's mind, only its **o.**.
T-21 V.7:10 the Holy Spirit's purpose in its **o.** right. It
T-21 VI.11:5 can be imprisoned save by his **o.** desire.
T-21 VI.11:6 And it is by his **o.** desire that he is freed.
T-21 VI.11:8 is at his **o.** mercy. And where he chooses
T-21 VIII.2:7 because its **o.** desire cannot be shaken. It
T-22 in.3:6 not his **o.** reality *because* it is the truth. Just
T-22 I.4:3 be except another "will" that is your **o.**,
T-22 II.10:5 all the misery you made has been your **o.**.
T-22 III.4:7 For here is its **o.** stability, its heavy anchor
T-22 III.4:7 believing the body's freedom is their **o.**.
T-22 VI.1:6 its importance by diminishing its **o.**.
T-23 II.4:5 his **o.** destruction becomes inevitable.

|  |  |
|---|---|
| T-23.... II.12:12 | purpose of seizing it and making it your **o**. |
| T-23...... IV.9:3 | body; something it seems to offer or to **o**.. |
| T-24....... II.6:3 | the Son remembers his **o**. creations, as |
| T-24...... IV.2:2 | makes it frail and helpless in its **o**. defense |
| T-24....... V.7:1 | hand that holds your brother's in your **o**.. |
| T-24....... V.8:1 | to you, to offer you your **o**. completion. |
| T-24...... VI.3:3 | within His Mind is absent from your **o**.. It |
| T-24..... VII.4:7 | such is your condemnation of your **o**.. |
| T-24..... VII.8:2 | Its scope does not exceed your **o**., except |
| T-24..... VII.9:8 | it makes. It proves its **o**. reality to you. |
| T-24... VII.10:2 | is sure, when seen through its **o**. eyes. It |
| T-24... VII.10:6 | whispers, "Here is my **o**. beloved son, in |
| T-24... VII.11:2 | outside yourself, your **o**. beloved son. The |
| T-24.VII.11:13 | well, and prove its **o**. reality to you. |
| T-25...... III.7:8 | chances to extend your **o**. forgiveness. |
| T-25...... IV.2:7 | his Father's purpose in his **o**. creation, |
| T-25.... IV.5:12 | better could your **o**. mistakes be brought |
| T-25....... V.5:1 | for by his freedom will you gain your **o**.. |
| T-25....... V.6:3 | picture of your **o**. belief in what the Will |
| T-25.... VIII.6:2 | must believe He shares their **o**. confusion, |
| T-25.... VIII.6:2 | avoid the vengeance that their **o**. belief in |
| T-25VIII.13:10 | because his **o**. have been obscured to him. |
| T-25.. VIII.14:5 | God's justice with a version of its **o**.. For |
| T-26.........I.2:5 | joined each one would lose its **o**. identity, |
| T-26.........I.3:2 | incomplete to keep its **o**. identity intact. |
| T-26....... II.7:1 | how great your **o**. release will be when you |
| T-26...... IV.5:4 | tiny spot that sin proclaimed to be its **o**.. |
| T-26....... V.7:3 | And how much can his **o**. illusions about |
| T-26....... V.9:7 | **o**. unfairness to yourself has He protected |
| T-26..... VII.7:3 | Heaven be opposed by its **o**. opposite, as |
| T-26... VII.11:8 | sacrifice his **o**. identity with everything, to |
| T-26... VII.11:8 | to find a little treasure of his **o**.. And this |
| T-26... VII.19:8 | No wishes lie between a brother and his **o**. |
| T-26....... IX.1:2 | be when in him sleeps your **o**. salvation, |
| T-26....... IX.4:5 | what is its **o**. has been restored to it. The |
| T-26....... X.2:7 | and your awareness that it is your **o**. and |
| T-26....... X.4:5 | retribution for your **o**. attack upon the |
| T-26....... X.4:8 | else can take it from him, making it his **o**.. |
| T-27.........I.2:1 | his made manifest, and shown to be his **o**. |
| T-27.........I.2:7 | him. But in his innocence you find your **o**. |
| T-27....... II.3:8 | overlooked it and removed it from his **o**.. |
| T-27....... II.9:2 | pain are seen to represent their **o**. serenity |
| T-27..... II.12:3 | And so your **o**. Identity is found. Yet must |
| T-27..... II.13:4 | lest your errors and his **o**. be seen as one. |
| T-27..... II.14:1 | your **o**. mistakes you will not even see. |
| T-27..... II.15:8 | the awareness of a function not your **o**.. |
| T-27...... III.7:2 | come, not to destroy, but to receive its **o**.. |
| T-27....... V.9:1 | that you thought were not your **o**.. And it |
| T-27...... VI.5:3 | its **o**. effects have come to take their place. |
| T-27..... VII.1:6 | is his **o**. attack upon himself apparent still |
| T-27..... VII.4:7 | is the avenger's knife in his **o**. hand, and |
| T-27..... VII.6:1 | from condemnation is your **o**. escape. |
| T-27... VII.11:6 | but a part of your **o**. dream you gave away |
| T-27.... VIII.2:4 | more senseless things that it can call its **o**. |
| T-27.... VIII.7:5 | brings its vengeance, not your **o**.. It keeps |
| T-28.......I.10:1 | on your **o**. Creator cannot understand it is |
| T-28.......I.11:5 | Their **o**. remembering is quiet now, and |
| T-28.......I.13:2 | Its **o**. remembering has gone. There is no |
| T-28.......I.13:6 | from before his **o**. remembering came in |
| T-28....... II.5:7 | dreams the miracle exchanges for your **o**.. |
| T-28....... II.7:7 | Thus does he fear his **o**. attack, but sees it |
| T-28....... II.7:9 | He authored not his **o**. attack, and he is |
| T-28....... II.8:5 | has given it have they adopted as their **o**.. |
| T-28...... III.3:3 | him to his **o**. dream by sharing it with him |
| T-28...... IV.5:3 | his dreams, instead of dreamer of your **o**.. |
| T-28...... IV.6:4 | you took your **o**. away would he be free of |
| T-28...... IV.6:4 | he be free of them, and of his **o**. as well. |
| T-28....... V.3:5 | you will not want to know your **o**. Identity |
| T-28...... VI.3:5 | And you despise its acts, but not your **o**.. |
| T-28...... VI.4:1 | **o**. and all the rest of what is really yours. |
| T-28..... VII.4:5 | It will not join a purpose not your **o**., and |
| T-29.........I.6:5 | and see in them a purpose not your **o**.. |
| T-29....... II.4:5 | look on them and take them for your **o**.. |
| T-29....... V.5:2 | and to whom is all creation given as his **o**.. |
| T-29...... VI.3:2 | it does not take this purpose as its **o**.. |
| T-29..... VII.8:6 | because you want their power as your **o**.. |
| T-29...... IX.4:8 | nor recognize their wishes are their **o**.. |
| T-29...... IX.5:6 | And their reality becomes his **o**., because |
| T-30....... II.1:3 | In His Divinity is but your **o**.. And all He |
| T-30 .......II.5:1 | saved, for by your **o**. salvation is it healed. |
| T-30 ... III.11:8 | from the Mind of God, but from your **o**.. |
| T-30 ..... IV.4:9 | toys without a single meaning of their **o**.. |
| T-30 .... V.11:5 | they forget for long that it is but their **o**.. |
| T-30 ..... VI.9:4 | *perfect Son, and in his glory will I see my* **o**.. |
| T-30 ...VIII.6:9 | guilt, for his appearance is your **o**. to you. |
| T-31 ........I.3:6 | to teach you that your will is not your **o**., |
| T-31 ........I.9:2 | life, and understood that it is but your **o**.. |
| T-31 ......I.12:2 | Let us remember not our **o**. ideas of what |
| T-31 ......II.5:11 | The voice you hear in him is but your **o**.. |
| T-31 .......II.6:8 | for in his progress do you count your **o**.. |
| T-31 ..... III.1:5 | brother for his sins, but only for your **o**.. |
| T-31 ..... III.3:9 | The body must act on its **o**., and motivate |
| T-31 ... IV.10:8 | it, walking there without your **o**. reality at |
| T-31 ...... V.7:6 | which its maker gives a meaning of his **o**.? |
| T-31 .... V.13:7 | chose it for him in the image of your **o**.. |
| T-31 .. V.15:10 | you see your **o**. concealed desire to kill. |
| T-31 .... V.16:2 | show the changes in your **o**. relationships, |
| T-31 ..... VI.1:6 | you are, as flesh or spirit in your **o**. belief. |
| T-31 ..... VI.1:7 | will escape the body as your **o**. reality, for |
| T-31 .. VII.11:5 | upon, and see his **o**. salvation everywhere. |
| T-31 .. VII.15:4 | and offers them forgiveness with his **o**.. |
| T-31 ... VIII.4:4 | His strength instead of their **o**. weakness, |
| T-31 ... VIII.6:5 | you make establishes your **o**. identity as |
| T-31 ... VIII.8:2 | I ask for nothing but your **o**. release. |
| T-31 .VIII.11:2 | Give me my **o**., for they belong to You. |
| W-pI..... 13.2:3 | in frantically to establish its **o**. ideas there, |
| W-pI..... 13.2:3 | its **o**. impotence and unreality. And on |
| W-pI..... 14.1:5 | It is of your **o**. making, and it does not |
| W-pI..... 14.6:5 | only be in your **o**. mind apart from His. |
| W-pI..... 16.1:6 | Those that are true create their **o**. likeness |
| W-pI..... 22.1:3 | **o**. attack is thus perceived as self defense. |
| W-pI..... 23.3:2 | representation of your **o**. attack thoughts. |
| W-pI........ 24.h | I do not perceive my **o**. best interests. |
| W-pI..... 24.1:4 | you will not serve your **o**. best interests. |
| W-pI..... 24.2:1 | you do not perceive your **o**. best interests, |
| W-pI..... 24.7:2 | *perceive my* **o**. *best interests in this situation* |
| W-pI..... 25.1:5 | Everything is for your **o**. best interests. |
| W-pI..... 25.2:2 | nothing to do with your **o**. best interests, |
| W-pI..... 26.1:6 | it can be used for your **o**. best interests, |
| W-pI..... 26.2:3 | make you vulnerable in your **o**. mind, |
| W-pI..... 26.3:2 | effect is to weaken you in your **o**. eyes. |
| W-pI..... 26.4:1 | is the result of your **o**. thoughts. Nothing |
| W-pI..... 28.5:1 | would withdraw all your **o**. ideas from it, |
| W-pI..... 28.6:3 | instead of placing your **o**. judgment upon |
| W-pI..... 31.4:2 | in the name of your **o**. freedom. And in |
| W-pI..... 32.2:3 | that both are in your **o**. imagination. |
| W-pI..... 34.1:3 | It must begin with your **o**. thoughts, and |
| W-pI..... 37.1:2 | to see the world through your **o**. holiness. |
| W-pI..... 37.6:4 | may learn to keep it in your **o**. awareness. |
| W-pI..... 38.5:1 | add some relevant thoughts of your **o**.. |
| W-pI..... 39.3:2 | world. What about your **o**. salvation? You |
| W-pI..... 39.4:3 | is the salvation of the world, and your **o**.. |
| W-pI..... 41.6:6 | Try to enter very deeply into your **o**. mind |
| W-pI..... 42.1:4 | It is His strength, not your **o**., that gives |
| W-pI..... 42.1:5 | And it is His gift, rather than your **o**., that |
| W-pI..... 43.5:2 | add to the idea in your **o**. personal way. |
| W-pI..... 43.5:7 | *I see my* **o**. *thoughts, which are like God's.* |
| W-pI..... 45.6:2 | a few relevant thoughts of your **o**., |
| W-pI..... 45.6:3 | four or five thoughts of your **o**. to the idea |
| W-pI..... 47.1:1 | If you are trusting in your **o**. strength, |
| W-pI..... 47.4:1 | Today we will try to reach past your **o**. |
| W-pI..... 47.5:1 | related to your **o**. sense of inadequacy. It |
| W-pI..... 47.6:1 | recognition of your **o**. frailty is a necessary |
| W-pI..... 48.3:1 | that you are trusting in your **o**. strength. |
| W-pI..... 51.3:3 | the projection of my **o**. errors of thought. |
| W-pI..... 52.3:2 | I see only my **o**. thoughts, and my mind is |
| W-pI..... 53.4:5 | from the effects of my **o**. insane thoughts, |
| W-pI..... 54.2:4 | the representation of my **o**. state of mind. |
| W-pI..... 55.2:5 | It is my **o**. attack thoughts that give rise to |
| W-pI..... 55.4:1 | (24) I do not perceive my **o**. best interests |
| W-pI..... 55.4:2 | I recognize my **o**. best interests when I do |
| W-pI..... 55.4:4 | to find out what my **o**. best interests are, |
| W-pI..... 56.1:8 | My **o**. real thoughts will teach me what it |
| W-pI..... 56.5:2 | In my **o**. mind, behind all my insane |
| W-pI..... 59.2:3 | Let me not look to my **o**. eyes to see today. |
| W-pI..... 60.2:2 | my **o**. strength through which I forgive. It |
| W-pI..... 62.3:1 | attack you call upon your **o**. weakness, |
| W-pI..... 65.3:3 | closed upon yourself, in your **o**. hands. It |
| W-pI .... 65.7:1 | of your **o**. foolish ideas to the contrary. |
| W-pI .... 68.3:1 | will redefine God in their **o**. image, as it is |
| W-pI .... 70.1:4 | as in your **o**. mind and nowhere else. |
| W-pI .... 70.3:1 | that guilt is in your **o**. mind entails the |
| W-pI .... 70.6:3 | to your **o**. decisions as closely as possible. |
| W-pI .. 70.10:1 | nothing but your **o**. thoughts can hamper |
| W-pI .. 70.10:8 | *Within me is the world's salvation and my* **o**. |
| W-pI .... 71.3:1 | role assigned to your **o**. mind in this plan, |
| W-pI .... 71.8:4 | is your full release from all your **o**. insane |
| W-pI .... 76.5:5 | It would not understand it is its **o**. enemy; |
| W-pI .... 77.5:2 | the salvation of the world, and for your **o**.. |
| W-pI .. 78.10:1 | of God's salvation plan, and not our **o**.. |
| W-pI .... 79.2:1 | seems to have his **o**. special problems. Yet |
| W-pI .... 84.1:6 | raise my **o**. self-concept to replace my Self |
| W-pI .... 86.3:5 | my **o**. best interests in this insane way. I |
| W-pI .... 88.4:4 | *God's laws to work in this, and not my* **o**.. |
| W-pI .... 93.1:3 | you would rush to death by your **o**. hand, |
| W-pI .. 95.15:1 | Your **o**. acknowledgment you are one Self |
| W-pI .... 96.9:4 | Its Thoughts, and claim them as your **o**.. |
| W-pI .... 96.9:5 | are your **o**. real thoughts you have denied, |
| W-pI .... 98.3:4 | They do not doubt their **o**. ability because |
| W-pI .... 99.5:1 | within the Mind of God and in your **o**.. It |
| W-pI .... 99.6:3 | save by giving you its function as your **o**.. |
| W-pI .. 104.2:2 | His are the gifts that are our **o**. in truth. |
| W-pI .. 105.6:4 | you must return to claim them as your **o**.. |
| W-pI .. 107.7:2 | to us, that we may recognize it as our **o**.. |
| W-pI .. 110.4:2 | minds, and only unity within your **o**.. |
| W-pI .. 118.2:2 | *Let my* **o**. *feeble voice be still, and let me hear* |
| W-pI .. 121.4:2 | and shrieks as it beholds its **o**. projections |
| W-pI .. 121.7:1 | to teach your **o**. how to forgive itself. Each |
| W-pI .. 121.7:4 | And as its hope, do you become your **o**.. |
| W-pI .. 121.8:2 | to happiness, and use it on your **o**. behalf. |
| W-pI .. 122.7:5 | has received what God has given as its **o**.. |
| W-pI .. 124.9:5 | face upon it, in reflection of your **o**.. |
| W-pI 124.10:1 | you will see your **o**. transfiguration in the |
| W-pI 124.11:1 | you; the loveliness you look on is your **o**.. |
| W-pI .. 125.2:2 | surely to his Father's house by his **o**. will, |
| W-pI .. 125.5:4 | of his madness that his will is not his **o**.. |
| W-pI .. 126.2:3 | help are not in any way related to your **o**.. |
| W-pI .. 126.4:3 | The sin that you forgive is not your **o**.. |
| W-pI .. 127.4:2 | Love's meaning is your **o**., and shared by |
| W-pI .. 127.9:3 | of your **o**. reality and what love means. He |
| W-pI .. 130.8:1 | by asking for a strength beyond your **o**., |
| W-pI .. 131.7:3 | What denies its **o**. existence and attacks |
| W-pI 131.11:4 | *the thoughts I want to think are not my* **o**.. |
| W-pI .. 132.8:3 | And if it is indeed your **o**. imagining, then |
| W-pI 132.15:3 | *world is not, and I would know my* **o**. *reality.* |
| W-pI 132.16:2 | world. But you will sense your **o**. release, |
| W-pI 132.17:2 | *it was, and choose my* **o**. *reality instead.* |
| W-pI .. 133.7:2 | to everything, you have denied your **o**.. |
| W-pI 133.10:2 | he looks upon the tarnish as his **o**.; the |
| W-pI 133.10:3 | serve them as his **o**. makes no mistakes, |
| W-pI 133.13:1 | to find everything and claim it as their **o**.. |
| W-pI 134.13:3 | is as alien to the world as is your **o**. reality. |
| W-pI .. 135.1:1 | and that his **o**. defense could save himself |
| W-pI .. 135.6:3 | to serve you thus except your **o**. belief? It |
| W-pI 135.11:2 | listening to wisdom that is not its **o**.. It |
| W-pI 135.13:2 | a plan which far exceeds its **o**. protection, |
| W-pI 135.14:2 | mind would undertake its **o**. protection, |
| W-pI 135.15:2 | for, unless it makes its **o**. provisions. Time |
| W-pI 135.20:1 | gratefully acknowledges to be its **o**.. And |
| W-pI .. 136.4:3 | so it seems to be external to your **o**. intent |
| W-pI .. 136.5:1 | seem to be beyond your **o**. control. But |
| W-pI .. 136.6:4 | for your **o**. decision of what should be real |
| W-pI .. 136.7:3 | truth arises in your **o**. deluded mind, and |
| W-pI 136.10:1 | Such is your planning for your **o**. defense. |
| W-pI .. 137.3:4 | healing is his **o**. decision to be one again, |
| W-pI .. 137.9:3 | His life becomes your **o**., as you extend |
| W-pI .. 138.8:1 | relinquish its ideas about its **o**. protection |
| W-pI .. 139.8:2 | in the holy Mind of God, and in your **o**.. It |
| W-pI .. 140.8:4 | It is as near to us as our **o**. thoughts; so |
| W-pI .. 151.5:6 | the guilt. It is its **o**. despair it sees in you. |
| W-pI .. 151.6:2 | to prove to you its evil is your **o**. are false, |
| W-pI .. 151.7:1 | Judge of what is worthy of your **o**. belief. |
| W-pI ..... 152.h | The power of decision is my **o**.. |
| W-pI .. 152.1:1 | can suffer loss unless it be his **o**. decision. |
| W-pI .. 152.1:4 | And no one dies without his **o**. consent. |
| W-pI .. 152.4:3 | that do not appear to be entirely your **o**.. |
| W-pI .. 152.8:2 | is. The power of decision is our **o**.. Decide |

| | |
|---|---|
| W-pI.152.10:1 | The power of decision is our **o.**. And we |
| W-pI.152.10:5 | from hell, are joyously accepted as our **o.**. |
| W-pI.152.11:3 | *The power of decision is my* **o.**. *This day I will* |
| W-pI...153.6:3 | Christ's strength and your **o.** weakness, |
| W-pI.153.10:6 | of God, by His election and their **o.** as well |
| W-pI.153.11:2 | come to realize His Will is but their **o.**. |
| W-pI.153.11:6 | hands, so will you recognize it as your **o.**. |
| W-pI.153.14:4 | not escape, is but his **o.** deluded fantasy. |
| W-pI...154.2:3 | He does not work without your **o.** consent |
| W-pI...154.8:7 | is his **o.** acceptance of what he received. |
| W-pI...154.9:6 | you identify with Him and claim your **o.**. |
| W-pI...155.1:4 | the world as you do recognize their **o.**. Yet |
| W-pI...155.2:2 | can be illusions, and avoid their **o.** reality. |
| W-pI...155.2:3 | when they find their **o.** reality is even here |
| W-pI...156.5:3 | The light you carry is their **o.**. And thus |
| W-pI...157.8:2 | this day holds out to you to be your **o.**. |
| W-pI...159.1:2 | first you have it in your **o.** possession. |
| W-pI...161.8:2 | beholds is his **o.** fear external to himself, |
| W-pI.161.11:5 | take away the nails which pierce your **o.**, |
| W-pI.161.12:2 | for God in you, and answer in your **o.**. |
| W-pI...162.3:1 | indeed is he who makes these words his **o.** |
| W-pI...163.8:5 | form, for their salvation and our **o.** as well |
| W-pI...164.7:4 | our joy, because its holiness reflects our **o.** |
| W-pI...164.7:5 | with all the world forgiven in our **o.**. We |
| W-pI...164.7:6 | us through His forgiving vision, not our **o.** |
| W-pI...165.1:1 | this world seem real except your **o.** denial |
| W-pI...166.3:2 | he may be called to claim them as his **o.**, is |
| W-pI...166.9:4 | Perhaps God's Word is truer than your **o.**. |
| W-pI.166.12:7 | these gifts, and recognize they are your **o.**. |
| W-pI...167.4:3 | becoming different from their **o.** origin, |
| W-pI...167.6:5 | it lacks, nor change its **o.** eternal, mindful |
| W-pI.167.12:3 | it sees its **o.** perfection mirroring the Lord |
| W-pI...168.5:2 | lies in the Giver, not our **o.** acceptance. |
| W-pI...170.2:6 | **o.** *defense against it is it real and inescapable* |
| W-pI.170.10:3 | their **o.** confusion in fear's "enemy"; its |
| WpI .. rV.in9:4 | Self from which I call to you is but your **o.**. |
| WpI rV.in10:5 | Son, completing His extension in your **o.**. |
| W-pI...171.2:1 | (152) The power of decision is my **o.**. |
| W-pI...181.1:4 | the Self that lies beyond your **o.** mistakes, |
| W-pI...181.6:2 | and turn our eyes upon our **o.** mistakes, |
| W-pI...181.8:5 | He feels for us becomes our **o.** as well. |
| W-pI......183.h | I call upon God's Name and on my **o.**. |
| W-pI...183.1:2 | upon His Name is but to call upon your **o.** |
| W-pI...183.6:6 | of everything that we would call our **o.**. |
| W-pI...183.9:3 | forgot, and offer it your **o.** remembering. |
| W-pI...183.9:4 | play in its salvation, and your **o.** as well. |
| W-pI.183.10:4 | His Father's Thoughts become his **o.**. He |
| W-pI...184.1:3 | a separate entity, identified by its **o.** name |
| W-pI...184.8:6 | to take the name you give him as his **o.**. |
| W-pI.185.10:4 | and join your **o.** intent with what they |
| W-pI...186.1:2 | your **o.** but that which has been given you |
| W-pI...187.2:4 | you strengthen them in your **o.** mind. |
| W-pI...188.1:6 | and stayed with you because it is your **o.**. |
| W-pI...189.2:5 | the light in you, in which it sees its **o.**. It |
| W-pI.189.10:4 | *Salvation's ways are not our* **o.**, *for they* |
| W-pI.189.10:9 | *ask but that Your Will, which is our* **o.** *as well* |
| W-pI...190.6:6 | corner of your mind its **o.** inheritance, |
| W-pI...191.2:3 | Deny your **o.** Identity, and this is what |
| W-pI...191.3:1 | Deny your **o.** Identity, and you will not |
| W-pI...191.3:2 | Deny your **o.** Identity, and you assail the |
| W-pI...191.3:3 | Deny your **o.** Identity, and look on evil, |
| W-pI.191.11:1 | They must await your **o.** release. They |
| W-pI.191.11:5 | They die till you accept your **o.** eternal life |
| W-pI...192.2:1 | a function in the world in its **o.** terms. For |
| W-pI...193.8:5 | you now renounce your **o.** salvation? |
| W-pI...196.1:4 | you will understand his safety is your **o.**, |
| W-pI...196.8:3 | you be hurt except by your **o.** thoughts, |
| W-pI...197.1:1 | in outside force pitted against your **o.**. |
| W-pI...198.5:3 | and substitute your **o.** in place of His? |
| W-pI...198.9:4 | *Only my* **o.** *forgiveness sets me free.* Do not |
| W-pI...200.7:1 | in opposition to God's Will and to his **o.**, |
| W-pI...203.1:1 | I call upon God's Name and on my **o.**. *The* |
| W-pI...203.1:2 | *and of sin, because it is my* **o.** *as well as His.* I |
| W-pI...210.1:2 | *Pain is my* **o.** *idea. It is not a Thought of God,* |
| W-pI...213.1:4 | *choose to learn His lessons and forget my* **o.**. |
| W-pII.....in.6:5 | world to be the full replacement of our **o.**. |
| W-pII..227.1:4 | *not affect my* **o.** *reality at all by my illusions.* |
| W-pII..229.1:1 | I seek my **o.** Identity, and find It in these |
| W-pII......2.2:5 | itself, and thought its **o.** Identity was lost. |
| W-pII.....239.h | The glory of my Father is my **o.**. |
| W-pII..240.1:5 | but to your **o.** illusions of yourself. Let us |
| W-pII..247.1:6 | you. Your loveliness reflects my **o.**. Your |
| W-pII..247.2:3 | *all to me as part of You, and my* **o.** *Self as well* |
| W-pII..248.2:3 | *Now is Your Love remembered, and my* **o.**. |
| W-pII..253.2:2 | *is but Your Will in perfect union with my* **o.**, |
| W-pII..264.1:2 | *I hear, and every hand that reaches for my* **o.** |
| W-pII..266.2:1 | calling upon God's Name and on our **o.**, |
| W-pII..267.2:1 | *Let me attend Your Answer, not my* **o.**. |
| W-pII..269.2:3 | Son of God; of Him Who is our **o.** Identity |
| W-pII..273.2:4 | *quietness and in my* **o.** *eternal love for You.* |
| W-pII..276.2:2 | *who are given me to cherish as my* **o.**, *as I am* |
| W-pII.....279.h | Creation's freedom promises my **o.**. |
| W-pII..288.1:9 | *Name, and so remember that It is my* **o.**. |
| W-pII..299.1:1 | My holiness is far beyond my **o.** ability to |
| W-pII..302.1:5 | *we see that darkness is our* **o.** *imagining, and* |
| W-pII..302.1:7 | *and understand it but reflects my* **o.**. |
| W-pII..309.1:3 | to deny my Father's Will is to deny my **o.**. |
| W-pII....10.3:2 | and union with your **o.** Identity. |
| W-pII..315.1:4 | mind receives this gift and takes it as its **o.** |
| W-pII.....316.h | All gifts I give my brothers are my **o.**. |
| W-pII....11.2:1 | all the power that their **o.** Creator has. For |
| W-pII..325.1:3 | esteemed as real and guarded as one's **o.**. |
| W-pII..328.1:5 | To join with His is but to find our **o.**. And |
| W-pII..330.1:4 | joy, as is the Will of God united with its **o.** |
| W-pII..332.1:7 | mind in chains, believing in its **o.** futility. |
| W-pII..335.1:6 | shows me that I would look upon my **o.**. |
| W-pII.....341.h | I can attack but my **o.** sinlessness, And it |
| W-pII..344.1:1 | *This is Your law, my Father, not my* **o.**. *I* |
| W-pII..346.1:7 | *I made as I behold Your glory and my* **o.**. |
| W-pII..349.1:2 | *and give what I would find and make my* **o.**. |
| W-pII..352.1:9 | *For I would love my* **o.** *Identity, and find in It* |
| W-pII..356.1:6 | *to call Your Name is but to call his* **o.**. |
| Wfl ........in.3:4 | to the dream we seek, and not our **o.**. For |
| W-ep .........3:5 | His is the Word you chose to be your **o.**. |
| M-in ........5:11 | they work out their **o.** salvation and the |
| M-1 .........3:10 | found his **o.** salvation and the salvation of |
| M-2 ...........5:9 | person the same interests as his **o.**. |
| M-4 ...........1:6 | who have advanced in their **o.** learning. In |
| M-4 .........I.2:1 | impossible to trust one's **o.** petty strength |
| M-4 .....I.A.5:5 | his **o.** best interests on behalf of truth. He |
| M-4 .....I.A.7:4 | Yet his **o.** sorting out was meaningless in |
| M-4 .....I.A.7:5 | so central to his **o.** thought system, had |
| M-5 ....... II.2:8 | yet they but give form to his **o.** choice. He |
| M-5 ...... III.2:5 | forgiveness for God's Son in his **o.** Name. |
| M-5 ...... III.3:9 | to see no will as separate from their **o.**, |
| M-7 ...........2:5 | that his **o.** uncertainty is not love but fear, |
| M-8 ...........2:8 | minds, with different interests of its **o.**, |
| M-9 ...........2:2 | He does not make his **o.** decisions; he asks |
| M-9 ...........2:3 | of God learns to give up his **o.** judgment. |
| M-10 .........5:9 | has chosen now to trust, instead of his **o.**. |
| M-12 .........1:7 | is based upon God's Judgment, not his **o.**. |
| M-16 .........2:2 | such lack of structuring on their **o.** part. |
| M-16 .........2:4 | must use them as best he can in his **o.** way |
| M-16 .........2:5 | they easily become gods in their **o.** right, |
| M-17 .........1:6 | that he is strengthening his **o.** belief in sin |
| M-17 .........9:8 | have responded to your **o.** interpretation, |
| M-18 .........4:1 | God to let all his **o.** mistakes be corrected. |
| M-19 .........5:1 | confuse His mercy with your **o.** insanity. |
| M-21 .........3:4 | in his heart, all this becomes his **o.**. The |
| M-21 .........5:5 | They are his **o.**, coming from a shabby self- |
| M-21 .........5:7 | They are far wiser than your **o.**. God's |
| M-22 .........5:2 | Another's sickness thus becomes his **o.**. In |
| M-23 .........3:4 | learning guarantees your **o.** success. Is he |
| M-24 .........3:3 | as well as his **o.** decision making. Our |
| M-24 .........3:6 | it advocates a long-held belief of his **o.**. |
| M-24 .........5:5 | to his pupil's advance or his **o.**. |
| M-26 .........2:1 | remembering their **o.** Identity perfectly. |
| M-28 .........5:8 | wish for nothing but His Will to be our **o.**. |
| M-29 .........3:6 | of functions not your **o.** is the basis of fear |
| M-29 .......3:10 | merely because of your **o.** inadequacies. It |
| M-29 .........6:9 | harm himself, or choose his **o.** destruction |
| C-5.............2:6 | men and save them from their **o.** illusions |
| C-6.............2:2 | the first to complete his **o.** part perfectly. |
| P-1...............4:1 | the ability to make his **o.** decisions. He |
| P-2...........I.1:3 | for no one learns beyond his **o.** readiness. |
| P-2...........I.3:6 | connection with their **o.** divergent goals, |
| P-2..........II.7:3 | and lets him formulate his **o.** curriculum; |
| P-2..........II.9:4 | and recognize his brother's need is his **o.**. |
| P-2........ IV.4:3 | but make the body real in their **o.** minds, |
| P-2........ IV.9:1 | A madman will defend his **o.** illusions |
| P-2........ IV.9:1 | because in them he sees his **o.** salvation. |
| P-2......... V.7:7 | His healing is our **o.**. And as we see the |
| P-2......... V.7:8 | and understand that it is but our **o.**. |
| P-2.......VII.3:1 | have been forgiven him, along with his **o.**. |
| P-2.......VII.4:5 | errors thus became his **o.** failures, and |
| S-1..........II.4:6 | lose the recognition of your **o.** Identity. Be |
| S-1..........II.5:3 | becomes a prayer for your **o.** freedom. |
| S-1..........II.6:7 | enemies, for herein lies your **o.** salvation. |
| S-1..........II.7:2 | is a transformation much like your **o.**, for |
| S-1........ III.4:6 | it in another, and does not see it as his **o.**? |
| S-2...........I.5:7 | You cannot see his sins and not your **o.**. |
| S-2..........II.7:2 | try to reinforce his guilt and thus your **o.**? |
| S-2..........II.7:9 | see. It is His face in which you see your **o.**. |
| S-2........ III.3:3 | words sincere; not with your **o.** sincerity, |
| S-2........ III.5:8 | Do not confuse His function with your **o.**. |
| S-3..........II.3:5 | the Word of God, more certainly our **o.**. |
| S-3...... IV.10:3 | is waiting your release because it is its **o.**. |

## owned 1

| | |
|---|---|
| T-29....VIII.1:9 | or a circumstance, an object **o.** or wanted, |

## ownership 3

| | |
|---|---|
| T-5.........I.1:10 | a physical possession, you do divide its **o.**. |
| T-10...... IV.6:3 | it belongs to Him, for to Him **o.** is sharing |
| T-13. VII.10:10 | **O.** is a dangerous concept if it is left to |

# P

**pace** 3

T-16...... VI.8:2 keep gentle **p.** with you in your transition.
W-pI..... 12.2:3 Try to **p.** yourself so that the slow shifting
WpI rVI.in.4:2 reach a quickened **p.** along a shorter path

**paid** 12

T-15....... X.6:8 the price of love, which must be **p.** by fear
T19....IV.B.5:1 You have **p.** very dearly for your illusions
T19....IV.B.5:1 and nothing you have **p.** for brought you
T-25....VIII.3:5 But death must be the cost and must be **p.**
T-25..VIII.4:10 being blind, is satisfied by being **p.**, it
T-25..VIII.11:1 not who pays the cost of sin, so it be **p.**,
T-30...... V.10:4 *cost of pain, nor was it ever* **p.** *by you alone.*
T-31..... V.13:6 But this gain is **p.** in almost equal loss, for
W-pI... 105.2:2 return; a loan with interest to be **p.** in full;
W-pI... 190.8:2 Pain is the ransom you have gladly **p.** not
M-13 ......... 5:3 the price that must be **p.** for the denial of
P-2.........in.2:7 The patient has already **p.** this price. Now

**pain** 320

T-2........ III.3:5 Tolerance for **p.** may be high, but it is not
T-2........ III.4:6 realizing that it only adds unnecessary **p.**.
T-2........VII.3:9 When you miscreate you are in **p.**. The
T-4........ VI.3:4 is more effective than learning through **p.**
T-4........ VI.3:4 through pain, because **p.** is an ego illusion
T-5........ VI.2:7 joy, viciousness for love, and **p.** for peace.
T-6...........I.8:7 has chosen to save them **p.** in all respects,
T-7............ X.h The Confusion of **P.** and Joy
T-7......... X.3:1 Spirit will direct you only so as to avoid **p.**
T-7......... X.3:6 are, you will be confused about joy and **p.**
T-7......... X.7:3 how to distinguish between **p.** and joy,
T-7......... X.8:6 learning the difference between **p.** and joy
T-8......... II.5:1 you the difference between **p.** and joy.
T-8......... III.5:9 He will respond either with **p.** or with joy,
T-8......... IV.5:8 join, and experience **p.** or joy accordingly.
T-10....... V.9:9 sin, wholly without **p.** and wholly without
T-10..... V.9:10 sin, **p.** and suffering into your own mind
T-10..... V.12:2 knows His children as wholly without **p.**,
T-11...... III.1:5 **P.** is not of Him, for He knows no attack
T-11...... III.4:2 Yours is the way of **p.**, of which God
T-11...... VI.5:5 the Son of God is born of sacrifice and **p.**.
T-13.......in.2:5 are born into it through **p.** and in pain.
T-13.......in.2:5 are born into it through pain and in **p.**.
T-13...... III.6:5 And the **p.** in this mind is so apparent,
T-13...... III.7:2 Here is both his **p.** and his healing, for the
T-13...... III.7:5 leave any spot of **p.** hidden from His light,
T-13... III.12:4 He denied you only your request for **p.**,
T-13...... IV.6:3 They carry the spots of **p.** in your mind,
T-13...... IV.6:4 And this decision is one of future **p.**.
T-13...... IV.6:5 Unless you learn that past **p.** is an illusion
T-13......VII.4:3 or not to hear the cries of **p.** that rise to it
T-13......VII.7:2 He is as safe from **p.** as God Himself, Who
T-13......VII.7:3 placed him in Himself where **p.** is not,
T-13......VII.7:6 He must deny the world of **p.** the instant
T-13...... IX.2:3 The ego rewards fidelity to it with **p.**, for
T-13...... IX.2:3 fidelity to it with pain, for faith in it *is* **p.**.
T-13....... X.1:1 can see the source of **p.** where it is not.
T-13....... X.8:3 alone in a dark world where **p.** is pressing
T-14...... III.2:1 merely to offset the **p.** of guilt, and do not
T-14...... III.3:1 escape the **p.** that only guiltlessness allays
T-14...... III.3:3 Whenever the **p.** of guilt seems to attract
T-14....... V.2:3 he will suffer the **p.** of dim awareness that
T-14....... V.5:5 Who is there but wishes to be free of **p.?**
T-14....... V.5:6 this exchange can freedom from **p.** be his.
T-14....... V.6:6 God. There is no **p.**, no trial, no fear that
T-14...... IX.4:3 cover all their sense of **p.** and loss with
T-14...... XI.9:4 or **p.** or trial you have has been undone.
T-15 ........I.4:8 were thought of merely as an end to **p.**,
T-15 ...... V.5:4 and be sure that it will not result in **p.**, if
T-15 ..... XI.3:4 me. All **p.** and sacrifice and littleness will
T-15 ..... XI.3:5 **P.** will be brought to us and disappear in
T-15 ..... XI.3:5 and without **p.** there can be no sacrifice.
T-16 ........I.1:7 He does not join in **p.**, understanding that
T-16 ........I.1:7 pain, understanding that healing **p.** is not
T-16 ..... III.1:7 been to bring peace where there was **p.**,
T-16 ...... V.1:1 that it involves a great amount of **p.**.
T-16 ..... VI.8:6 and that escape from **p.** is really possible.
T-16 .... VII.1:3 remembered **p.**, past disappointments,
T-17 ........I.3:3 in the power that heals all **p.** arises from
T-17 ...VIII.4:5 sorrow and depression, sickness and **p.**,
T-18 ........II.6:7 will remain, not as a source of **p.** and guilt
T-18 .... VII.1:6 by those who prefer **p.** and destruction.
T-18 .... VII.3:5 be experienced as **p.** and nothing else,
T19..IV.A.11:2 find, losing none of them on **p.** of death,
T19..IV.A.13:5 For they are frantic with the **p.** of fear,
T19IV.A.17:11 will also believe that it can bring you **p.**.
T19IV.A.17:12 you would have calls upon **p.** to fill your
T19.... IV.B.3:6 But neither can it bring you fear of **p.**.
T19.... IV.B.3:7 **P.** is the only "sacrifice" the Holy Spirit
T19.... IV.B.4:7 You want salvation, not the **p.** of guilt.
T19.....IV.B.i.h The Attraction of **P.**
T19..IV.B.10:4 peace nor turmoil; neither joy nor **p.**. It is
T19..IV.B.12:1 pleasure through the body and not find **p.**
T19..IV.B.12:4 the body, which is the invitation to **p.**. For
T19..IV.B.12:7 It will share the **p.** of all illusions, and the
T19..IV.B.12:7 illusion of pleasure will be the same as **p.**.
T19..IV.B.13:3 This, then, is the attraction of **p.**. Ruled
T19..IV.B.13:4 the body becomes the servant of **p.**,
T19..IV.B.13:4 and obeying the idea that **p.** is pleasure. It
T19..IV.B.15:4 body search for **p.** in attack upon another
T19..IV.B.16:4 attraction of guilt is the escape from **p.**.
T19. IV.D.15:1 by sin and waiting for release from **p.**.
T19. IV.D.20:3 crucified give **p.** because they are in pain.
T19. IV.D.20:3 crucified give pain because they are in **p.**.
T19. IV.D.20:4 joy because they have been healed of **p.**.
T-20 ........I.1:3 For Easter is the sign of peace, not **p.**. A
T-20 .....II.11:2 leave you, nor forsake the savior in his **p.**.
T-20 ..... IV.1:5 sickness and death and misery and **p.**.
T-20 ...... V.7:4 to **p.** and death must be forgotten. This is
T-21 ........I.3:1 There is no need to learn through **p.**. And
T-21 ........I.4:8 hate the world they learned through **p.**.
T-21 .......II.2:1 from **p.** and the complete escape from sin
T-21 ..... VI.7:2 other being blessed by it, and healed of **p.**
T-22 .......II.1:5 Every illusion carries **p.** and suffering in
T-22 ..... VI.4:4 relationship has the power to heal all **p.**,
T-22 ... VI.12:5 hurt yourself without the other feeling **p.**.
T-23 .....II.12:5 is the magic that will cure all of your **p.**;
T-23 ..... III.1:2 do not always recognize the source of **p.**.
T-23 ..... IV.6:3 There is a stab of **p.**, a twinge of guilt, and
T-24 .......II.2:7 pursuit of specialness must bring you **p.**.
T-24 ..... IV.5:2 and when you suffer **p.** of any kind, you
T-24 ...... V.2:1 the hope of peace and the escape from **p.**,
T-24 ..... VI.4:5 all belief God's Son can suffer **p.** because
T-24 ... VI.10:5 to save from **p.** and give you happiness.
T-25 ...... V.6:1 save what He created from the **p.** of hell.
T-25 .... VII.1:5 seem to hide the **p.** of sin from sinners,
T-26 .......II.7:2 one, for **p.** in any form you will not want.
T-26 .. VII.17:1 needed where there is no **p.** or suffering.
T-26 ... VIII.7:9 as "good" some day but now in form of **p.**
T-27 ........I.2:2 But every **p.** you suffer do you see as proof
T-27 ........I.3:1 Whenever you consent to suffer **p.**, to be
T-27 ........I.3:5 there is no **p.** and no reproach at all. And
T-27 ........I.5:3 and therefore never suffered **p.** at all. It
T-27 .......II.5:6 it has never suffered **p.** because of him.
T-27 .......II.7:3 Your healing saves him **p.** as well as you,
T-27 .......II.9:2 **p.** are seen to represent their own serenity
T-27 .......II.9:3 the grounds on which they justify his **p.**.
T-27 .......II.9:5 The constant **p.** they suffer demonstrates
T-27 ..... IV.4:7 all the **p.** of which this world is made?"
T-27 ..... VI.1:1 **P.** demonstrates the body must be real. It
T-27 ..... VI.1:3 **P.** compels attention, drawing it away
T-27 ..... VI.1:7 itself. Pleasure and **p.** are equally unreal,
T-27 ..... VI.2:1 Sin shifts from **p.** to pleasure, and again
T-27 ..... VI.2:1 from pain to pleasure, and again to **p.**.
T-27 ..... VI.2:3 pleasure, too, but only at the cost of **p.**."
T-27 ..... VI.2:7 Call pleasure **p.**, and it will hurt. Call pain
T-27 ..... VI.2:8 Call **p.** a pleasure, and the pain behind
T-27 ..... VI.2:8 and the **p.** behind the pleasure will be felt
T-27 ..... VI.5:9 live, the dead arise, and **p.** has vanished.
T-27 ..... VI.6:6 to bless the world, a tiny stab of **p.**, a little
T-27 .... VII.7:4 as bringing **p.** and suffering to you, your
T-27 .. VII.16:4 And let no **p.** disturb your dream of deep
T-27 . VIII.10:4 the cause of any **p.** and suffering you feel,
T-27 . VIII.11:2 of the form of suffering that brings you **p.**
T-27 . VIII.11:4 cause of every form of sorrow and of **p.**.
T-28 .....II.12:2 next to every dream of **p.** and suffering, of
T-28 ..... III.4:6 which you see as if it were the cause of **p.**.
T-28 ..... III.5:1 The cause of **p.** is separation, not the
T-28 ..... IV.1:5 of dreams of **p.** because you let him be.
T-28 ..... IV.1:6 you will suffer **p.** with him because that is
T-28 ..... IV.1:7 you become a figure in his dream of **p.**, as
T-28 .......V.2:1 death, of sin and suffering and **p.** and loss
T-28 ..... VI.1:4 It does not seek to make of **p.** a joy and
T-28 ..... VI.5:1 out upon the body, so that it will suffer **p.**.
T-29 .......II.3:2 to demand escape from sin and **p.** of what
T-29 .......II.3:2 serve the function of retaining sin and **p.**.
T-29 .......II.3:3 For **p.** and sin are one illusion, as are hate
T-29 .......II.3:6 You are free of **p.** and sickness, misery
T-29 .......II.3:7 more is **p.** your friend and guilt your god,
T-29 .......V.5:5 are not hands that grasp in dreams of **p.**.
T-29 ..... VI.1:2 instead of endless strife and misery and **p.**
T-29 .... VII.1:7 For all your **p.** comes simply from a futile
T-29 ... VIII.6:6 a little while; to suffer **p.** and finally to die
T-29 ... VIII.8:8 or even more affliction and more **p.**. But
T-29 ..... IX.9:2 and **p.** of self-betrayal and uncertainty, so
T-30 ...... in.1:5 to forgiving dreams and out of **p.** and fear
T-30 .......V.2:4 as the sole cause of **p.** in any form. No one
T-30 .......V.9:7 you sought here that did not bring you **p.**
T-30 .....V.10:4 *Not one was bought except at cost of* **p.**, *nor*
T-30 ... VIII.6:6 There is no **p.** from which he is not free, if
T-31 .......I.11:3 you want disaster and disunity and **p.**.
T-31 ..... III.5:1 evil, sickness and attack; of **p.** and age, of
T-31 .. VII.14:3 It is a thing of madness, **p.** and death; a
T-31 ... VIII.3:1 and thus escape all **p.** that what you chose
T-31 ... VIII.3:3 would not leave one source of **p.** unhealed
T-31 ... VIII.6:2 What you behold as sickness and as **p.**, as
T-31 ... VIII.6:3 Yield not to this, and you will see all **p.**, in
T-31 ... VIII.8:4 the **p.** and sorrow that you saw before.
W-pI ...... 5.1:1 or event you think is causing you **p.**.
W-pI .... 20.2:6 between joy and sorrow, pleasure and **p.**,
W-pI .... 38.2:4 Your holiness, then, can remove all **p.**,
W-pI .... 41.3:2 It will cure all sorrow and **p.** and fear and
W-pI .... 56.1:3 **P.**, illness, loss, age and death seem to
W-pI .... 58.5:5 or deprivation or **p.** because of Who I am.
W-pI .... 62.3:4 It will take away all fear and guilt and **p.**.
W-pI .... 78.6:3 have had with him, the **p.** he caused you,
W-pI .... 95.2:1 and sinful, miserable and beset with **p.**.
W-pI .... 96.6:8 release of His dear Son bring **p.** to him,
W-pI .... 97.5:1 world where **p.** and misery appear to rule.
W-pI .... 98.6:1 you your full release from **p.** of every kind
W-pI .... 99.4:2 without attack and with no touch of **p.?**
W-pI .... 99.5:4 on what you see; on sin and **p.** and death,
W-pI .... 99.7:4 All the world of **p.** is not His Will. Forgive
W-pI .. 101.2:4 The sinful warrant only death and **p.**, and
W-pI .. 101.3:1 If sin is real, salvation must be **p.**. Pain is

| | |
|---|---|
| W-pI...101.3:2 | **P.** is the cost of sin, and suffering can |
| W-pI...101.6:2 | **p.** is but the sign you have misunderstood |
| W-pI...102.2:1 | and to realize that **p.** is purposeless, |
| W-pI...103.1:6 | sin can enter, bringing **p.** instead of joy. |
| W-pI...103.3:2 | what you expect to take the place of **p.**. |
| W-pI...107.3:3 | When truth has come all **p.** is over, for |
| W-pI...107.5:1 | love which does not falter in the face of **p.**, |
| W-pI...109.3:2 | storms and strife, past misery and **p.**, past |
| W-pI...109.5:1 | concerns, no burdens, no anxiety, no **p.**, |
| W-pI...121.2:2 | the hope of respite and release from **p.**. It |
| W-pI...124.5:1 | We see it in appearances of **p.**, and pain |
| W-pI...124.5:1 | of pain, and **p.** gives way to peace. We see |
| W-pI...128.4:3 | here is worth one instant of delay and **p.**; |
| W-pI...132.3:4 | doubts and miseries, your **p.** and tears, |
| W-pI.132.10:2 | To free the world from every kind of **p.** is |
| W-pI.133.12:5 | you make choices easily and without **p.**. |
| W-pI.134.10:1 | and **p.** as God Himself intended it to be, |
| W-pI...135.9:4 | will impose upon the body all the **p.** that |
| W-pI.135.18:2 | plan, for He would never offer **p.** to you. |
| W-pI...136.8:3 | You suffer **p.** because the body does, and |
| W-pI...136.8:3 | and in this **p.** are you made one with it. |
| W-pI.136.17:3 | feeling ill or feeling well, of **p.** or pleasure. |
| W-pI...137.9:3 | from everything that ever caused you **p.**. |
| W-pI.137.13:1 | exchanging curse for blessing, **p.** for joy, |
| W-pI.138.10:3 | a but imagined source of guilt and **p.**? |
| WpI.rIV.in9:3 | light, from grief to joy, from **p.** to peace, |
| W-pI.151.10:1 | remove all faith that you have placed in **p.** |
| W-pI...152.1:2 | No one suffers **p.** except his choice elects |
| W-pI...152.2:4 | Can **p.** be part of peace, or grief of joy? |
| W-pI.166.14:6 | entrusted with the world's release from **p.** |
| W-pI...167.2:6 | sorrow, loss, anxiety and suffering and **p.**, |
| WpI..rV.in6:4 | I must understand uncertainty and **p.**, |
| WpI..rV.in7:2 | learns there is a way from misery and **p.**. I |
| W-pI...183.3:5 | the tears of **p.** are dried as happy laughter |
| W-pI...187.6:4 | take. He laughs as well at **p.** and loss, at |
| W-pI...189.2:2 | safe from every form of danger and of **p.**. |
| W-pI......190.h | I choose the joy of God instead of **p.**. |
| W-pI...190.1:1 | **P.** is a wrong perspective. When it is |
| W-pI...190.1:5 | For **p.** proclaims God cruel. How could it |
| W-pI...190.2:3 | **P.** is but witness to the Son's mistakes in |
| W-pI...190.3:1 | **P.** is a sign illusions reign in place of |
| W-pI...190.3:3 | If God is real, there is no **p.**. If pain is real, |
| W-pI...190.3:4 | no pain. If **p.** is real, there is no God. For |
| W-pI...190.3:6 | denying love and using **p.** to prove that |
| W-pI...190.4:5 | Their witness, **p.**, is mad as they, and no |
| W-pI...190.5:1 | It is your thoughts alone that cause you **p.** |
| W-pI...190.6:6 | and keep it as a hospital for **p.**; a sickly |
| W-pI...190.7:1 | The world may seem to cause you **p.**. |
| W-pI...190.8:1 | **P.** is the thought of evil taking form, and |
| W-pI...190.8:2 | **P.** is the ransom you have gladly paid not |
| W-pI...190.8:3 | In **p.** is God denied the Son He loves. In |
| W-pI...190.8:4 | **p.** does fear appear to triumph over love, |
| W-pI...190.8:5 | **p.** that waits to end all joy in misery. |
| W-pI.190.10:1 | Here will you understand there is no **p.**. |
| W-pI.190.10:4 | It is this: **P.** is illusion; joy, reality. Pain is |
| W-pI.190.10:5 | **P.** is but sleep; joy is awakening. Pain is |
| W-pI.190.10:6 | **P.** is deception; joy alone is truth. |
| W-pI.190.11:1 | illusions and the truth, or **p.** and joy, or |
| W-pI.190.11:2 | we are free to choose our joy instead of **p.**, |
| W-pI...191.7:4 | *I cannot suffer, cannot be in **p.**; I cannot* |
| W-pI...191.9:1 | born but to die, to weep and suffer **p.**, |
| W-pI.191.11:4 | suffer **p.** until you have denied its hold on |
| W-pI...192.6:1 | only **p.** was lifted from a sick and tortured |
| W-pI...192.9:7 | And so you owe him thanks instead of **p.**. |
| W-pI...193.5:2 | speaks in all your tribulations, all your **p.**, |
| W-pI...193.6:1 | we are tempted to believe that **p.** is real, |
| W-pI...193.7:2 | Does **p.** seem real in the perception? If it |
| W-pI...193.7:4 | sees the **p.** through eyes the mind directs. |
| W-pI...193.8:6 | that all **p.** may disappear and God may be |
| W-pI...194.3:1 | felt, or **p.** experienced or loss perceived. |
| W-pI...194.3:4 | from sadness, **p.** and even death itself. |
| W-pI...194.5:2 | bequest of grief and misery, of **p.** and loss |
| W-pI...194.7:3 | suffer? What can cause him **p.**, or bring |
| W-pI...194.7:6 | escaped all fear of future **p.** has found his |
| W-pI...195.2:2 | the certain means whereby all **p.** is healed |
| W-pI...195.5:2 | mourn a seeming loss or feel apparent **p.**, |
| W-pI...198.9:6 | be a form of **p.** forgiveness cannot heal. |
| W-pI...200.1:5 | of God, unless you seek for misery and **p.**. |
| W-pI...200.2:1 | hurt; of making peace of chaos, joy of **p.**, |
| W-pI...210.1:1 | (190) I choose the joy of God instead of **p.** |
| W-pI...210.1:2 | *P. is my own idea. It is not a Thought of God,* |
| W-pII.....in.1:4 | times in which we leave the world of **p.**, |
| W-pII..222.1:3 | and guarantees my safety from all **p.**. He |
| W-pII..241.1:4 | when sorrows pass away and **p.** is gone. |
| W-pII..245.1:5 | *I give Your peace to those who suffer **p.**, or* |
| W-pII..248.1:5 | What is in **p.** is but illusion in my mind. |
| W-pII..268.2:2 | Only reality is free of **p.**. Only reality is |
| W-pII..281.2:2 | For I am far beyond all **p.**. My Father |
| W-pII..284.1:2 | **P.** is impossible. There is no grief with |
| W-pII..284.2:1 | *hurt, so grief and **p.** must be impossible. Let* |
| W-pII..285.1:4 | For what would be the use of **p.** to me, |
| W-pII..289.2:5 | *to be the end of all his dreams and all his **p.**?* |
| W-pII......8.2:4 | There are no cries of **p.** and sorrow heard, |
| W-pII..295.1:2 | to me, and take away all terror and all **p.**. |
| W-pII..301.1:2 | *Nor can I suffer **p.**, or feel I am abandoned or* |
| W-pII..307.1:3 | *will, for it is senseless and will cause me **p.**.* |
| W-pII.....10.4:3 | from his dream of **p.** the Son whom God |
| W-pII..323.1:1 | *in to his awareness, healing him of **p.**, and* |
| W-pII..330.1:2 | our minds, and give them images of **p.**? |
| W-pII..331.1:4 | *to die within a world of **p.** and cruelty. How* |
| W-pII..339.1:1 | No one desires **p.**. But he can think that |
| W-pII..339.1:2 | But he can think that **p.** is pleasure. No |
| W-pII..339.1:9 | without confusing **p.** with joy, or fear |
| W-pII..347.1:7 | *He looks on **p.**, and yet He understands it is* |
| W-pII.....351.h | My sinful brother is my guide to **p.**. And |
| W-pII..356.1:5 | *of sin, and who is sinless cannot suffer **p.**.* |
| W-pII.....359.h | All **p.** Is healed; all misery replaced with |
| Wfl ........in.1:5 | the hope of trust and the escape from **p.**. |
| W-ep .........4:1 | and all **p.** that you may think is real. Nor |
| M-4 ....... V.1:4 | The gentle have no **p.**. They cannot suffer. |
| M-4 .....VII.2:9 | Why should he ensure himself **p.**? But he |
| M-4 ... VIII.1:8 | decisions, if they are causing **p.** to anyone |
| M-5 .........I.1:1 | the sufferer no longer sees any value in **p.**. |
| M-5 ....... II.4:1 | With this idea is **p.** forever gone. But |
| M-5 ....... II.4:7 | What do guilt and sickness, **p.**, disaster |
| M-10 .........6:5 | All of the **p.** he looks upon is its result. All |
| M-13 .........4:2 | Is it a sacrifice to give up **p.**? Does an |
| M-13 .........5:4 | the pleasure would be seen as **p.**, and no |
| M-13 .........5:4 | and no one asks for **p.** if he recognizes it. |
| M-16 .......11:5 | in magic, for it is only this that leads to **p.**. |
| M-17 .........1:7 | well that he has asked for depression, **p.**, |
| M-28 .........2:3 | and **p.** and misery of any kind perceived |
| C-2.............8:1 | the need for vengeance and the cries of **p.**, |
| S-1 ........ III.4:2 | Nor can this be done without some **p.**, |
| S-2 ......... II.4:5 | and do not show the bitter **p.** you feel. |
| S-2 ......... II.5:2 | It shows the face of suffering and **p.**, in |
| S-2 ......... II.5:6 | who needs salvation from the **p.** of guilt? |
| S-2 ......... II.6:4 | no hope, but only greater **p.** and misery. |
| S-2 ......... II.7:4 | of it the means for further slavery and **p.**. |
| S-3 .........in.1:1 | sure, easing the **p.** of fear and offering the |
| S-3 ...........I.2:2 | **p.** and aging and the mark of death upon |
| S-3 ......... II.1:4 | indeed remove a form of **p.** and sickness. |
| S-3 ......... II.3:2 | be thrust down in **p.** upon unwilling flesh |
| S-3 ........ III.3:2 | his skill; to find in him the remedy for **p.**. |
| S-3 ......IV.10:5 | and live no more in terror and in **p.**. Do |

### painful 15

| | |
|---|---|
| T-3...........I.2:3 | procedure is **p.** in its minor applications |
| T-4......... II.5:1 | thought system must be perceived as **p.**, |
| T-7......... X.3:4 | what is **p.** than you know what is joyful, |
| T-7......... X.3:6 | What is joyful to you is **p.** to the ego, and |
| T-11......IV.4:5 | phases of this reversal are often quite **p.**, |
| T19..IV.B.12:6 | fear directs the body to do is therefore **p.**. |
| T-25...... VI.2:1 | and the light of brilliant day seems **p.** to |
| T-25...... VI.2:4 | less **p.** to the eyes than what is wholly |
| W-pI.....14.3:2 | can be quite difficult and even quite **p.**. |
| W-pI...131.7:1 | goals, its **p.** pleasures and its tragic joys. |
| W-pI...196.7:2 | if you want to go along this **p.** path. Until |
| W-pII..290.1:4 | I made is frightening and **p.** to behold. |
| W-pII..339.1:4 | happiness. But he can think that joy is **p.**, |
| M-4 .....I.A.3:2 | This need not be **p.**, but it usually is so |
| M-8 .........3:11 | or undesirable, pleasurable or **p.**. |

### pains 5

| | |
|---|---|
| T-27...... VI.4:9 | Its **p.** and pleasures does He heal alike, for |
| T-27... VIII.1:8 | all, it tries to teach itself its **p.** and joys are |
| T-31.........I.3:1 | and the **p.** to which you went to practice |
| W-pI...190.7:5 | Your idle wishes represent its **p.**. Your |
| C-5.............6:7 | if you will share your **p.** and joys with him |

### paint 2

| | |
|---|---|
| T-23......II.18:8 | Can you **p.** rosy lips upon a skeleton, |
| T-27.........I.7:1 | and helps them **p.** the picture in which sin |

### painted 1

| | |
|---|---|
| T-31..... V.7:10 | of idols, **p.** with the brushes of the world, |

### paints 1

| | |
|---|---|
| W-pII .249.1:1 | Forgiveness **p.** a picture of a world where |

### palaces 1

| | |
|---|---|
| T-14........II.2:7 | would make **p.** and royal robes of nothing |

### Palm 1

| | |
|---|---|
| T-20.........I.1:1 | This is **P.** Sunday, the celebration of |

### palms 1

| | |
|---|---|
| T-20.........I.2:1 | week begins with **p.** and ends with lilies, |

### pamper 1

| | |
|---|---|
| T-23......II.18:8 | dress it in loveliness, pet it and **p.** it, and |

### pangs 1

| | |
|---|---|
| T19. IV.A.13:4 | seem to allay their savage **p.** of hunger. |

### panic 7

| | |
|---|---|
| T-2........ IV.4:9 | miracle, they may be precipitated into **p.**. |
| T-9...........I.2:3 | learn anything consistently in a state of **p.** |
| T-9...........I.8:4 | of these insane decisions will induce **p.**, |
| T-9.........I.12:1 | if the attempt is strong it will induce **p.**. |
| T-9.........I.14:4 | anxiety, depression and ultimately **p.**, |
| T-31..... V.11:5 | Spirit does not seek to throw you into **p.**. |
| W-pI...130.3:4 | can be real in blind imaginings of **p.** born |

### paper 3

| | |
|---|---|
| T-27....VIII.2:2 | bought with little metal discs or **p.** strips |
| W-pI.....76.3:2 | of green **p.** strips and piles of metal discs. |
| P-2..........II.6:2 | Does the **p.** matter, or the ink, or the pen? |

### Paradise 4

| | |
|---|---|
| T-13.......in.3:6 | it was the Father Who drove him out of **P.** |
| T-20....... III.9:6 | you shall this day enter with him to **P.**, |
| T-20.... III.10:6 | in separation are now made free in **P.**. |
| W-pII .266.2:1 | This day we enter into **P.**, calling upon |

### paradox 7

| | |
|---|---|
| T-15.........I.4:9 | seen this strange **p.** in the ego's thought |
| T-27.........II.3:1 | yet forgive it is a **p.** that reason cannot see |
| T-30...... IV.7:1 | Salvation is a **p.** indeed! What could it be |
| W-pI...131.9:1 | we will not choose a **p.** in place of truth. |
| W-pI...166.2:1 | **p.** that underlies the making of the world. |
| M-29 .........4:1 | is the **p.** often referred to in the course. To |
| M-29 .........4:3 | And yet it is but a seeming **p.**. As God |

### paradoxical 1

| | |
|---|---|
| M-11 .........3:4 | Into this strange and **p.** situation,–one |

### parallel 2

| | |
|---|---|
| T-7...........I.1:6 | Even in this world there is a **p.**. Parents |
| T-14...... IV.8:4 | for there is no **p.** in your experience of the |

## paralyze 1

T-1 V.1:5 You can wait, delay, **p.** yourself, or reduce

## pardon 36

T-21 VI.11:10 in chains his **p.** on himself to set him free.
T-25 IX.8:6 miracles. And **p.** must be just to everyone.
T-27 II.2:1 The unhealed cannot **p.**. For they are the
T-27 II.2:2 For they are the witnesses that **p.** is unfair
T-27 II.2:6 seeks to **p.** what it thinks to be the truth.
T-27 II.2:8 am the better of the two, I **p.** you my hurt.
T-27 II.2:9 His **p.** and your hurt cannot exist together
T-27 II.3:2 what has been done to you deserves no **p.**.
T-27 II.12:2 you perceive correction is the same as **p.**,
T-30 VI.1:6 not asked to offer **p.** where attack is due,
T-30 VI.1:8 This is not **p.**. For it would assume that,
T-30 VI.1:9 your **p.** will become the answer to attack
T-30 VI.1:10 And thus is **p.** inappropriate, by being
T-30 VI.2:1 **P.** is *always* justified. It has a sure
T-30 VI.2:6 If **p.** were unjustified, you would be asked
T-30 VI.3:2 had a real foundation **p.** would have none
T-30 VI.4:2 it seems impossible His **p.** could be real.
T-30 VI.4:3 the sure result of seeing **p.** as unmerited.
T-30 VI.4:7 If you can see your brother merits **p.**, you
T-30 VI.6:6 have set a goal of partial **p.** and a limited
T-30 VI.10:3 an idol of the Son of God you will not **p.**.
T-30 VII.6:17 Only dreams of **p.** can be shared. They
T-31 III.4:3 has no power to learn, to **p.**, nor enslave.
T-31 VII.1:6 he counts the "good" to **p.** him the "bad."
W-pI 134.2:1 fact that **p.** is not asked for what is true. It
W-pI 134.2:4 creation, and to **p.** that is meaningless.
W-pI 134.2:6 Does this need **p.**? How can you forgive
W-pI 134.3:2 You conceive of **p.** as a vain attempt to
W-pI 134.4:1 sins are real, you look on **p.** as deception.
W-pI 134.5:1 **P.** is no escape in such a view. It merely is
W-pI 134.5:2 name, for **p.** is a treachery to truth. Guilt
W-pI 134.5:5 did, and once again by those who **p.** them
W-pI 134.8:1 The strength of **p.** is its honesty, which is
W-pI 192.2:5 And who would **p.** Heaven? Yet on earth,
W-pII 1.1:2 It does not **p.** sins and make them real. It
S-3 II.4:2 to bless the mind with loving **p.** for the

## pardoned 2

T-27 II.3:11 healing lies the proof that he has truly **p.**,
T-28 I.7:6 for this is what you would be **p.** from.

## pardons 1

T-30 VI.3:7 It **p.** "sinners" sometimes, but remains

## parent 1

T-3 I.2:7 In milder forms a **p.** says, "This hurts me

## parents 3

T-7 I.1:7 **P.** give birth to children, but children do
T-7 I.1:7 but children do not give birth to **p.**. They
T-7 I.1:8 children, and thus give birth as their **p.** do

## parody 5

T-24 VII.1:11 **p.** of God's creation that takes the place of
T-29 VII.5:3 found that represents a **p.** of life which, in
W-pI 95.2:1 as a ridiculous **p.** on God's creation; weak
W-pI 121.4:2 rising to attack its miserable **p.** of life. It
S-2 I.1:2 of grace, a **p.** upon the holy peace of God.

## part 618

*See also* part-whole

T-1 I.25:1 Miracles are **p.** of an interlocking chain
T-1 I.26:3 is an essential **p.** of the Atonement value
T-1 III.1:4 My **p.** in the Atonement is the cancelling
T-1 III.1:5 become **p.** of the Atonement yourself. As
T-2 I.4:6 itself as **p.** of his dream and be afraid of it.
T-2 III.1:5 distortion, because it alters only **p.** of it. It
T-2 III.5:3 do not involve any effort at all on their **p.**.
T-2 IV.3:8 The body is merely **p.** of your experience
T-2 VI.2:2 on your **p.** by saying you could not help it
T-2 VI.5:3 you because the **p.** of the mind that wants
T-2 VII.6:2 be an integral **p.** of the whole Sonship.
T-2 VII.6:7 Any **p.** of the Sonship can believe in error
T-2 VIII.5:11 you. This is your **p.** in the Atonement.
T-3 II.5:4 The Son of God is **p.** of the Holy Trinity,
T-3 V.4:6 and not a **p.** of knowledge. Images are
T-3 V.7:8 Evaluation is an essential **p.** of perception
T-3 V.8:4 knowing any **p.** of it is to know all of it.
T-4 I.8:5 as it is. You are **p.** of reality, which stands
T-4 II.4:2 they regard them as **p.** of themselves. No
T-4 II.4:3 something he considers **p.** of himself. You
T-4 III.10:1 from the **p.** of the mind the ego rules. The
T-4 V.4:6 Being told by the ego that it is really **p.** of
T-4 VI.1:6 than a **p.** of your belief about yourself.
T-4 VI.6:6 because I completed my **p.** in it as a man,
T-4 VII.1:3 **P.** of the mind becomes concrete,
T-4 VII.1:4 splits. The concrete **p.** believes in the ego,
T-4 VII.1:5 The ego is the **p.** of the mind that believes
T-4 VII.6:4 unless you take your **p.** in the creation,
T-5 in.2:6 why it makes no difference to what **p.** or
T-5 in.2:6 **p.** of the Sonship the healing is offered.
T-5 in.2:7 Every **p.** benefits, and benefits equally.
T-5 I.1:2 gladness calls to every **p.** of the Sonship to
T-5 I.4:1 The Holy Spirit is the only **p.** of the Holy
T-5 II.5:5 in you in a literal sense; you are **p.** of Him.
T-5 II.8:2 **p.** of your mind that always speaks for the
T-5 II.10:9 for any **p.** of the Kingdom than to restore
T-5 III.1:4 He is **p.** of the Holy Trinity, because His
T-5 III.2:4 are **p.** of God it is also the idea of yourself,
T-5 III.2:5 the laws of the universe of which it is a **p.**.
T-5 III.10:3 his mind, because **p.** of it is still for God.
T-5 III.10:4 the ego's attempts to conceal this **p.**, it is
T-5 III.10:7 You who are **p.** of God are not at home
T-5 III.11:8 with God always, and He is **p.** of you. He
T-5 IV.1:1 What fear has hidden still is **p.** of you.
T-5 IV.1:6 It is yours because it is **p.** of you, just as
T-5 IV.1:6 you are **p.** of God because He created you.
T-5 IV.2:6 unhealed **p.** of your mind to the higher
T-5 IV.2:6 part of your mind to the higher **p.**,
T-5 IV.2:13 you are **p.** of God and the Sonship is One,
T-5 IV.3:1 thought held in any **p.** of the Sonship
T-5 IV.3:1 part of the Sonship belongs to every **p.**. It
T-5 IV.6:3 My **p.** in the Atonement is not complete
T-5 V.3:1 ego is the **p.** of the mind that believes in
T-5 V.3:2 How could **p.** of God detach itself without
T-5 V.3:10 a **p.** of Him has been torn away by you.
T-5 V.6:16 As **p.** of His Thought, you *cannot* think
T-5 VI.3:1 who are **p.** of the Kingdom cannot be lost.
T-5 VI.7:3 belong in your mind, which is **p.** of God.
T-5 VI.9:4 destroyed because it is **p.** of your thought,
T-5 VI.9:5 **p.** of your mind that you have given to the
T-5 VII.4:4 you, and will also tell you of your **p.** in it,
T-5 VII.6:5 Your **p.** is merely to return your thinking
T-6 I.6:6 was **p.** of my own teaching contribution.
T-6 I.15:8 as much a **p.** of the Sonship as myself.
T-6 II.1:1 in mind must involve a rejection of **p.** of it
T-6 II.6:2 you, and God created you as **p.** of Him.
T-6 II.13:3 but your **p.** is only to allow no darkness to
T-6 III.1:7 ego never was and never will be **p.** of it,
T-6 IV.1:6 The ego does not regard itself as **p.** of you.
T-6 IV.2:1 God created you He made you **p.** of Him.
T-6 IV.2:5 thus speaking for the **p.** of your mind that
T-6 IV.4:1 that **p.** of the mind that made it is against
T-6 IV.4:5 as its ally, because the body is *not* **p.** of you
T-6 IV.5:1 by recognizing they are not **p.** of you, they
T-6 IV.6:1 of God, a priceless **p.** of His Kingdom,
T-6 IV.6:1 Kingdom, which He created as **p.** of Him.
T-6 V.A.3:3 and therefore cannot be **p.** of you. To be
T-6 V.C.9:4 and thus placed **p.** of your mind outside it
T-7 I.3:2 You are **p.** of God, as your sons are part of
T-7 I.3:2 of God, as your sons are **p.** of His Sons.
T-7 III.3:1 that the ego's friend is not **p.** of you,
T-7 IV.2:2 you are in God because you are **p.** of Him.
T-7 IV.2:3 every **p.** of creation is of one order. This is
T-7 V.9:4 identify with, and by making it **p.** of you,
T-7 V.11:8 one. This is **p.** of the law of creation, and
T-7 VI.1:2 to see something in **p.** of it that you will
T-7 VI.2:6 thinking as you choose is **p.** of its power.
T-7 VI.4:12 And if it recognized any **p.** of the Sonship,
T-7 VI.8:6 it. It wants no **p.** of truth, because the ego
T-7 VI.10:6 because you do not believe you are **p.** of it
T-7 VI.11:1 Perceived without your **p.** in it, God's
T-7 VII.1:2 impossible to deny **p.** of the Sonship as it
T-7 VII.1:2 part of the Sonship as it is to love it in **p.**.
T-7 VII.1:8 why denying any **p.** of it means you have
T-7 VII.1:11 it can help you recognize **p.** of reality, and
T-7 VII.6:5 He created, of which you are a **p.**, or you
T-7 VII.9:1 Being the **p.** of your mind that does not
T-7 VII.10:6 They are **p.** of you, as you are part of God.
T-7 VII.10:6 They are part of you, as you are **p.** of God.
T-7 VII.11:1 Perceive any **p.** of the ego's thought
T-7 VII.11:2 perceive any **p.** of creation as wholly real,
T-7 VIII.3:3 Any attempt to keep **p.** of it and get rid of
T-7 VIII.3:3 another **p.** does not really mean anything.
T-7 VIII.7:3 the whole Kingdom as literally **p.** of you.
T-7 IX.1:5 Holy Spirit is in the **p.** of the mind that
T-7 IX.1:7 cannot conceive of any **p.** from which it is
T-7 IX.2:4 **p.** of Him and shares His Being with Him.
T-7 IX.4:3 Exclude any **p.** of the Kingdom from
T-7 IX.5:2 They are there as **p.** of your own being,
T-7 IX.7:5 including any **p.** of totality in the lesson,
T-7 X.1:4 you could possibly want any **p.** of it is
T-7 X.1:10 mind as **p.** of your identification with His,
T-7 XI.7:1 You cannot deny **p.** of truth. You do not
T-8 I.3:4 as opponents are **p.** of your peace, which
T-8 II.5:5 ask the **p.** of your mind that taught you to
T-8 II.7:4 all things, it made them **p.** of itself. You
T-8 II.7:7 are **p.** of Him Who is all power and glory,
T-8 III.7:1 only **p.** of yourself because you are part of
T-8 III.7:1 part of yourself because you are **p.** of God
T-8 III.7:8 thought any **p.** of the Sonship holds.
T-8 IV.3:1 done completely by any **p.** of the Sonship.
T-8 IV.8:8 **p.** of One you must be part of the Other,
T-8 IV.8:8 part of One you must be **p.** of the Other,
T-8 IV.8:12 in It and fulfill your function as **p.** of It,
T-8 IV.8:13 No **p.** of It can be imprisoned if Its truth
T-8 VII.5:7 As **p.** of you, he is holy. As part of me, you
T-8 VII.5:8 As **p.** of me, you are. To communicate
T-8 VII.5:9 To communicate with **p.** of God Himself
T-8 VII.5:9 which He has established as **p.** of you.
T-8 VII.9:5 It becomes a means by which the **p.** of the
T-8 VII.10:3 and the belief that **p.** of it is physical, or
T-8 VIII.1:9 Functions are **p.** of being since they arise
T-8 VIII.1:10 The whole does define the **p.**, but the part
T-8 VIII.1:10 part, but the **p.** does not define the whole.
T-8 VIII.1:11 know in **p.** is to know entirely because of
T-8 VIII.1:15 is no difference between the **p.** and whole.
T-8 IX.2:6 Its conditions are **p.** of what it is. And this
T-8 IX.2:7 And this **p.** only is up to you. The rest is
T-8 IX.2:9 because your little **p.** is so powerful that it
T-8 IX.2:10 Accept, then, your little **p.**, and let the
T-8 IX.9:5 to His, because your meaning is **p.** of His.
T-8 IX.9:6 Your healing, then, is **p.** of His health,
T-8 IX.9:6 His health, since it is **p.** of His wholeness.
T-9 I.14:7 *He is God must be, for Christ is* **p.** *of Him.*
T-9 IV.2:1 You have a **p.** to play in the Atonement,
T-9 VI.3:1 If your brothers are **p.** of you, will you
T-9 VI.3:8 for yourself because we are **p.** of you,
T-9 VI.3:9 is **p.** of you and shares His glory with you.
T-9 VI.4:4 whenever you recognize **p.** of creation.
T-9 VI.4:5 creation. Each **p.** you remember adds to
T-9 VI.4:5 to your wholeness because each **p.** *is* whole
T-9 VII.7:4 You cannot retain **p.** of a thought system,
T-9 VII.8:7 Return your **p.** to Him, and He will give
T-9 VIII.4:6 argue that grandeur cannot be a real **p.** of
T-9 VIII.10:2 No one else can fill your **p.** in it, and while
T-9 VIII.10:2 while you leave your **p.** of it empty your
T-10 in.2:1 beside you exists, for you are **p.** of Him.
T-10 I.1:3 as yourself, because they are **p.** of you.
T-10 I.1:5 Any **p.** of your mind that does not know
T-10 II.2:5 His Voice will tell you that you are **p.** of
T-10 II.3:4 God will do His **p.** if you will do yours,
T-10 II.4:5 further recognize that you are **p.** of God,
T-10 III.3:1 sick is to believe that **p.** of God can suffer.
T-10 III.3:5 recognition of him as **p.** of God reminds

| | |
|---|---|
| T-10......III.4:5 | is impossible, because you are **p.** of God, |
| T-10......III.6:1 | knowledge that each one is **p.** of Him. |
| T-10......IV.2:6 | and cannot be known by **p.** of a mind. |
| T-10......IV.3:4 | removed **p.** of your mind from God's Will |
| T-10....... V.7:4 | calls to you from every **p.** of the Sonship, |
| T-10..... V.12:6 | And as **p.** of the Sonship, that is how you |
| T-11.......in.4:1 | brother, you are **p.** of God and part of me. |
| T-11.......in.4:1 | brother, you are part of God and **p.** of me. |
| T-11.........I.1:5 | whatever **p.** of the mind of God's Son you |
| T-11.........I.2:5 | are one with you, for you are **p.** of Us. Do |
| T-11.........I.2:6 | you really believe that **p.** of God can be |
| T-11.........I.3:1 | If you were not **p.** of God, His Will would |
| T-11.........I.3:3 | Can **p.** of His Mind contain nothing? If |
| T-11.........I.7:1 | Could any **p.** of God be without His Love, |
| T-11.........I.7:1 | and could any **p.** of His Love be contained |
| T-11....... II.1:6 | Yet when you attack any **p.** of God and |
| T-11....... II.3:2 | You cannot deny **p.** of yourself, because |
| T-11....... II.5:8 | patience, for He cannot leave a **p.** of God. |
| T-11...... III.5:6 | for the little spark in you is **p.** of a light so |
| T-11.... III.7:10 | and no **p.** of the Son can be excluded if he |
| T-11......IV.1:6 | it. Yet if you hate **p.** of your Self all your |
| T-11......IV.1:7 | And since what He created is **p.** of Him, |
| T-11......IV.3:3 | Every altar to God is **p.** of you, because |
| T-11......IV.5:1 | your brothers are **p.** of you and you blame |
| T-11......VI.7:5 | in which everyone has a **p.** of equal value. |
| T-11.... VI.10:2 | have a **p.** in the redemption as valuable as |
| T-11.... VI.10:3 | **p.** must be like mine if you learn it of me. |
| T-11.... VI.10:6 | whole power of God is in every **p.** of Him, |
| T-11. VIII.11:3 | perceive **p.** of you as sick and achieve your |
| T-11. VIII.15:3 | Who will teach you that, as **p.** of God, |
| T-12.........I.3:2 | it requires no effort at all on your **p.**. |
| T-12......IV.2:4 | is inevitable because the ego is **p.** of your |
| T-12......VI.3:2 | whatever **p.** of it you look upon with love. |
| T-12.....VII.2:1 | world must play his **p.** in its redemption, |
| T-12...VII.14:3 | essential **p.** of the Holy Spirit's teaching. |
| T-13......VI.8:7 | with me. Each voice has a **p.** in the song of |
| T-13.....VII.4:3 | that rise to it from every **p.** of this strange |
| T-13...VII.17:8 | Give thanks to every **p.** of you that you |
| T-13... VIII.7:3 | Spirit knows your **p.** in the redemption, |
| T-13... VIII.7:5 | You who are **p.** of it and all of it need only |
| T-13......IX.6:5 | to condemn the Son of God in **p.**. Those |
| T-13..... X.11:3 | single out **p.** of the Sonship for your love, |
| T-14......IV.2:1 | by Him like unto Himself and **p.** of Him, |
| T-14....... V.1:1 | The only **p.** of your mind that has reality |
| T-14....... V.1:1 | is the **p.** that links you still with God. |
| T-14....... V.2:1 | has a special **p.** to play in the Atonement, |
| T-14....... V.6:1 | taking their **p.** in the unified curriculum |
| T-14..... V.10:1 | crucifixion had no **p.** in the Atonement. |
| T-14..... V.10:2 | Only the resurrection became my **p.** in it. |
| T-14......IX.8:6 | no image, and His creations, as **p.** of Him, |
| T-14......XI.6:3 | Your **p.** is very simple. You need only |
| T-14......XI.8:4 | you think that you can run some little **p.**, |
| T-15....... II.6:1 | little **p.** in separating out the holy instant. |
| T-15......IV.3:4 | I call you to fulfill your holy **p.** in the plan |
| T-15....... V.2:2 | We have said that to limit love to **p.** of the |
| T-15....... V.7:1 | one **p.** of one aspect suits its purposes, |
| T-15......VI.1:2 | is equally impossible to condemn **p.** of a |
| T-15...VII.14:6 | recognition of the value of his **p.** in it. In |
| T-15......IX.1:5 | by the **p.** that God Himself plays in the |
| T-15....... X.7:5 | to be both destroyer and destroyed in **p.**, |
| T-15......XI.4:6 | and try to cast it out, though it is **p.** of you |
| T-15......XI.4:7 | can perceive **p.** of himself as loathsome, |
| T-15....XI.10:5 | *I give you to the Holy Spirit as* **p.** *of myself. I* |
| T-16.........I.3:1 | Your **p.** is only to remember this; you do |
| T-16.........I.4:5 | You are not sure that He will do His **p.**, |
| T-16.........I.7:8 | is for the whole Sonship, not for **p.** of it. |
| T-16....... II.1:8 | have to be miraculous, being **p.** of them. |
| T-16....... II.2:1 | the truth of just a little **p.** of the whole. |
| T-16....... II.2:4 | understand them, either in **p.** or in whole. |
| T-16....... II.3:3 | The recognition of the **p.** as whole, and of |
| T-16....... II.3:3 | the whole in every **p.** is perfectly natural, |
| T-16...... III.4:6 | it? It must be this **p.** that is really outside |
| T-16...... III.4:7 | **p.** that you have taken in that is not you. |
| T-16...... III.5:1 | done this, for the Holy Spirit is **p.** of you. |
| T-16...... III.5:7 | real, as **p.** of the Self you do not know. |
| T-16......VI.5:8 | The ego wants but **p.** of him, and sees |
| T-16......VI.5:8 | and sees only this **p.** and nothing else. |
| T-16......VI.9:1 | the special relationship is really **p.** of you. |
| T-16......VI.9:2 | keep **p.** of the thought system that taught |
| T-17.........I.4:3 | to deal with **p.** of the truth in one way, |
| T-17.........I.4:3 | one way, and in another way the other **p.**. |
| T-17....... II.1:5 | even a little **p.** of the happiness this sight |
| T-17...... III.7:5 | has left no **p.** of it without Himself. This is |
| T-17...... III.7:6 | only **p.** of the relationship the Holy Spirit |
| T-17......IV.5:1 | and the **p.** of your mind into which the |
| T-17......IV.5:6 | The separation has nothing in it, no **p.**, |
| T-17......IV.5:7 | And its "protection" is **p.** of it, as insane |
| T-17.... IV.10:6 | For you attack Them, being **p.** of Them, |
| T-17.... IV.16:6 | His. It shines in every **p.** of Him, as in the |
| T-17....... V.7:3 | not **p.** entirely if you choose not to do so. |
| T-17...... VI.6:5 | in it will play his **p.** in its accomplishment |
| T-17.....VII.2:3 | you shift **p.** of the problem elsewhere the |
| T-17.....VII.6:2 | **p.** in any situation dedicated in advance |
| T-17...VII.8:11 | in every aspect and complete in every **p.**. |
| T-17... VIII.5:5 | have assumed your **p.** in his redemption, |
| T-18.........I.4:6 | relationship that you have ever made is **p.** |
| T-18.........I.6:6 | and take no **p.** in all the mad projection |
| T-18...... IV.6:8 | that you may learn how little is your **p.**, |
| T-18....... V.2:5 | **p.** is only to offer Him a little willingness |
| T-18....... V.2:6 | He will build your **p.** in the Atonement |
| T-18.... VI.11:5 | It becomes **p.** of you, as you unite with it. |
| T-18... VIII.2:5 | a little **p.** of a glorious and complete idea. |
| T-18... VIII.3:3 | of your mind is such a tiny **p.** of it that, |
| T-18... VIII.6:1 | that this tiny **p.** regards itself as you. It is |
| T-18... VIII.7:7 | its happiness and deep content to every **p.** |
| T-18. VIII.11:7 | No **p.** of love calls on the whole in vain. |
| T-18...... IX.1:3 | Therefore, it is the tiny **p.** of yourself, the |
| T-18...... IX.1:6 | little **p.** you think you stole from Heaven. |
| T-19.......I.5:10 | for **p.** of it is sought through the body, |
| T-19.......I.5:11 | The other **p.** would heal, and therefore |
| T-19.......I.10:1 | as much a **p.** of love as fear is of attack. |
| T-19....... II.1:5 | a mind not **p.** of it can give it absolution. |
| T-19...... III.1:7 | essential **p.** of what the ego thinks you are |
| T-19...... III.6:2 | what is **p.** of Him is totally unlike the rest. |
| T-19...... III.8:3 | And each **p.** of God's fragmented creation |
| T19... IV.A.9:4 | never to return, and **p.** with it in gladness, |
| T19....IV.B.9:1 | Your little **p.** is but to give the Holy Spirit |
| T19....IV.C.4:5 | all are **p.** of your unrecognized dedication |
| T-20......IV.6:1 | the **p.** that has been given you to learn. |
| T-20......IV.6:3 | not need your **p.** to help Him with the rest |
| T-20......IV.6:4 | For in your **p.** lies all of it, without which |
| T-20......IV.6:4 | all of it, without which is no **p.** complete, |
| T-20......IV.6:4 | is the whole completed without your **p.**. |
| T-20......IV.7:6 | I could leave you, and forget **p.** of myself. |
| T-21.........I.6:3 | But you remember, from just this little **p.**, |
| T-21.........I.9:3 | is the memory of what you are; a **p.** of this |
| T-21...... IV.3:5 | you join with what is **p.** of you in truth. |
| T-21...... IV.4:5 | the **p.** of your mind the ego knows not of. |
| T-21...... IV.4:7 | you. And yet this **p.**, with which you now |
| T-21...... IV.5:1 | **p.** has seen your brother, and recognized |
| T-21...... IV.7:2 | the other **p.** hears as the sweetest music; |
| T-21....... V.6:3 | there must be a **p.** of you that knows His |
| T-21....... V.7:5 | **p.** of knowledge threatens dissociation as |
| T-21....... V.7:6 | And all of it will come with any **p.**. Here is |
| T-21....... V.7:7 | part. Here is the **p.** you can accept. What |
| T-21....... V.9:1 | The **p.** of mind where reason lies was |
| T-21...... VI.5:6 | enters **p.** be kept away from other parts? |
| T-22.........I.2:9 | interprets to the body, of which it is a **p.**. |
| T-22.........I.9:2 | Nothing but what is **p.** of Him is worthy |
| T-22.........I.9:3 | it possible that anything not **p.** of Him *can* |
| T-22....... II.8:1 | is no **p.** of Heaven you can take and weave |
| T-22...... IV.1:8 | is no **p.** of the journey that seems more |
| T-22...... VI.5:3 | error, and lays a **p.** of Heaven in its place. |
| T-22...... VI.5:5 | Each **p.** of Heaven that you bring is given |
| T-22...... VI.8:3 | This is your **p.** in bringing peace. For you |
| T-22.... VI.12:5 | a **p.** of the creation without the whole, the |
| T-23........in.5:4 | it and perceive the light of which he is a **p.** |
| T-23........in.6:1 | Nothing around you but is **p.** of you. |
| T-23........in.6:4 | now will be reinterpreted as **p.** of Heaven. |
| T-23.........I.4:7 | proclaiming it is **p.** of itself no more. |
| T-23.........I.4:9 | shall be **p.** of you and what is kept apart. |
| T-23.........I.6:6 | and they remain **p.** of what made them. |
| T-23.........I.6:9 | reality that they deny is not a **p.** of them. |
| T-23.........I.7:1 | What *you* remember *is* a **p.** of you. For you |
| T-23.........I.8:3 | you could attack that is not **p.** of you. And |
| T-23....... II.3:6 | No **p.** of nothing can be more resistant to |
| T-23...... III.3:2 | To compromise is to accept but **p.** of what |
| T-23...... IV.4:6 | This is your **p.**; to realize that murder in |
| T-23...... IV.5:4 | Here you have chosen to be **p.** of it. Here |
| T-24........II.3:5 | himself, and Him of Whom they are a **p.**. |
| T-24.......II.10:2 | of your acceptance of himself as **p.** of you, |
| T-24.......II.10:4 | keep one **p.** of what He is unto Himself, |
| T-24.......II.11:1 | **p.** of love was not denied to him. But can |
| T-24...... VI.1:9 | that He created you as **p.** of Him. |
| T-24...... VI.2:3 | and **p.** of Him because His Will is One. |
| T-24...... VI.2:4 | Nothing alive that is not **p.** of Him, and |
| T-24...... VI.7:6 | in that **p.** of Him He set forever in your |
| T-24...... VI.8:4 | What never was is not a **p.** of you. Yet you |
| T-24...... VI.8:5 | it is not a **p.** of him who stands beside you |
| T-24.... VI.10:3 | governs **p.** of God holds not for all the |
| T-24.... VI.10:5 | that He has given you a **p.** of Him to save |
| T-24.... VI.10:6 | each **p.** of Him with equal love and care. |
| T-25.........I.3:5 | is a **p.** of what it is your purpose to behold |
| T-25.........I.5:4 | the **p.** of you that shares His Father's Will. |
| T-25.........I.5:5 | The Holy Spirit links the other **p.** –the |
| T-25.........I.7:1 | while you think that **p.** of you is separate, |
| T-25........II.6:1 | **p.** of Him that you would see as separate. |
| T-25........II.9:5 | when any **p.** of Him joins in His praise, to |
| T-25...... VI.4:2 | he alone can fill; a **p.** for only him. Nor is |
| T-25...... VI.4:3 | and fulfills the **p.** assigned to him, to |
| T-25...... VI.5:9 | for on his **p.** does all the plan depend. He |
| T-25.... VI.5:10 | He *has* a special **p.** in time for so he chose, |
| T-25...... VI.6:4 | as each one takes his **p.** in its undoing, as |
| T-25.... VII.9:5 | for he has a special **p.** in everyone's escape |
| T-25... VII.12:7 | in which your special function has a **p.**. |
| T-25.... VIII.4:8 | with someone else by far the greater **p.**. |
| T-26.........I.1:6 | see a little **p.** of him and sacrifice the rest. |
| T-26.........I.2:4 | Each **p.** must sacrifice the other part, to |
| T-26.........I.2:4 | Each part must sacrifice the other **p.**, to |
| T-26.........I.3:2 | And all the rest must lose this little **p.**, |
| T-26...... IV.2:6 | in gladness recognizing what is **p.** of them |
| T-26..... V.10:6 | And now you are a **p.** of resurrection, not |
| T-26..... V.12:3 | The real world is the second **p.** of the |
| T-26..... VII.4:5 | It is in this world, but not a **p.** of it. For it |
| T-26... VII.13:2 | true: that He created you as **p.** of Him, |
| T-27.......II.14:2 | be a **p.** of you while this perception lasts. |
| T-27.......II.14:4 | unworthy to be **p.** of you and thus outside |
| T-27.......II.16:7 | he may accept his other half as **p.** of him. |
| T-27..... V.10:2 | **p.** is merely to apply what He has taught |
| T-27..... VI.4:5 | Nor could it tell a **p.** of God Himself what |
| T-27..... VII.4:4 | For each one thinks that if he does his **p.**, |
| T-27..... VII.4:5 | he perceives to *be* his **p.** in its deliverance. |
| T-27..... VII.6:1 | The **p.** you play in salvaging the world |
| T-27..... VII.7:9 | because he does not see the **p.** he plays in |
| T-27..... VII.8:2 | He becomes a **p.** of someone else's dream. |
| T-27... VII.11:6 | but a **p.** of your own dream you gave away |
| T-27... VII.11:7 | although it caused the **p.** you see and do |
| T-27.... VIII.5:3 | for the **p.** you see is but the second part, |
| T-27.... VIII.5:3 | for the part you see is but the second **p.**, |
| T-27.... VIII.7:1 | real; a **p.** of God that can attack itself; a |
| T-28.........I.4:7 | only you have held it to a **p.** of time where |
| T-28........II.4:1 | and but a **p.** of someone else's dream. The |
| T-28....... III.2:3 | the **p.** you play in making sickness real, |
| T-28...... IV.2:2 | now. Refuse to be a **p.** of fearful dreams |
| T-28...... IV.5:1 | Be certain, if you do your **p.**, he will do |
| T-28...... IV.5:3 | You cannot do his **p.**, but this you *do* when |
| T-28...... IV.9:4 | is recognized as being **p.** of the completed |
| T-28...... IV.9:7 | of God is just the same as every other **p.**. |
| T-28....... V.3:2 | And so he cannot be a **p.** of yours, from |
| T-28....... V.3:7 | your brother, as a **p.** of what you hate. |
| T-28.... VII.1:6 | untrue to what He wills as **p.** of what He is |
| T-28.... VII.2:1 | your brothers is a **p.** of you because it is a |
| T-28.... VII.2:1 | of you because it is a **p.** of God Himself. |
| T-29........II.6:1 | life and every living thing be **p.** of him, |
| T-29........II.8:6 | that **p.** of Him belongs to Him no longer. |
| T-29........II.8:8 | god, protecting you from being **p.** of Him. |
| T-29...... III.5:4 | Father lost not **p.** of him in your creation, |
| T-29...... IV.6:4 | to take the **p.** that you assigned to him, in |
| T-29....... V.3:2 | He is a **p.** of you and you of him, because |
| T-29....... V.4:3 | complete can be a **p.** of God's completion, |
| T-29..... VII.2:3 | if a **p.** of it were separated off and found |
| T-29.... VIII.9:9 | And thus is every living thing a **p.** of you, |
| T-29...... IX.2:6 | dream will seem to last while he is **p.** of it. |
| T-29...... IX.2:9 | you make yourself a **p.** of evil dreams, |
| T-29...... IX.3:2 | Yet they are **p.** of what they have been |
| T-29...... IX.4:2 | it. For idols must be **p.** of it, to save you |
| T-29...... IX.5:9 | himself, and play that he is but a **p.** of it. |

T-30.........I.6:1 something has occurred that is not **p.** of it
T-30......III.5:7 For can he give a **p.** of him away? What is
T-30......VI.7:3 healing, one illusion must be **p.** of truth.
T-30......VI.8:2 And do not keep a **p.** of him outside your
T-30...VII.6:12 is a **p.** of a distorted script, which cannot
T-31.........I.8:7 friend who always wanted to be **p.** of you.
T-31.........I.8:8 The soft eternal calling of each **p.** of God's
T-31.....VII.3:2 as coming from the "baser" **p.** of you, and
T-31.....VII.8:2 To every **p.** of true creation has the Lord
W-in..........7:2 This will require no effort on your **p.**. The
W-pI.....14.6:2 These things are **p.** of the world you see.
W-pI.....14.6:3 and others are **p.** of your personal hell. It
W-pI.....24.4:3 in mind as **p.** of the desired outcome, and
W-pI.....31.3:4 without any special investment on your **p.**
W-pI........35.h My mind is **p.** of God's. I am very holy.
W-pI.....35.2:1 that you are **p.** of where you think you are
W-pI.....35.2:4 The image is **p.** of this environment.
W-pI.....35.5:1 earlier **p.** of the mind-searching period,
W-pI.....35.5:2 Toward the latter **p.** of the exercise period
W-pI.....35.7:5 *But my mind is **p.** of God's. I am very holy.*
W-pI.....36.1:2 are holy because your mind is **p.** of God's.
W-pI.....36.1:7 mind is **p.** of God's you must be sinless,
W-pI.....36.1:7 or a **p.** of His Mind would be sinful. Your
W-pI.....43.5:1 Although this **p.** of the exercise period
W-pI.....44.2:3 essential **p.** of this equipment is the light
W-pI.....45.2:8 is. As you are **p.** of His Mind, so are your
W-pI.....45.2:8 so are your thoughts **p.** of His Mind.
W-pI.....45.3:5 of God is eternal, being **p.** of creation.
W-pI.....49.1:2 The **p.** of your mind in which truth abides
W-pI.....49.1:3 other **p.** of your mind that functions in
W-pI.....49.1:4 It is this **p.** that is constantly distracted,
W-pI.....49.2:1 **p.** that is listening to the Voice for God is
W-pI.....49.2:2 It is really the only **p.** there is. The other
W-pI.....49.2:3 The other **p.** is a wild illusion, frantic and
W-pI.....49.2:5 it. Try to identify with the **p.** of your mind
WpI...rI.in.3:2 and think about it as **p.** of your review of
WpI...rI.in.5:1 You will yet learn that peace is **p.** of you,
W-pI.....52.5:6 is **p.** of creation and part of its Creator.
W-pI.....52.5:6 is part of creation and **p.** of its Creator.
W-pI.....56.4:6 we who are **p.** of Him will yet look past all
W-pI.....57.5:1 (35) My mind is **p.** of God's. I am very
W-pI.....59.5:4 As **p.** of His Mind, my thoughts are His
W-pI.....65.4:4 **p.** of the long-range disciplinary training
W-pI.....67.2:9 you are **p.** of His definition of Himself.
W-pI.....68.2:1 while the **p.** of your mind that weaves
W-pI.....68.3:1 Himself, and defined them as **p.** of Him.
W-pI.....68.6:3 *I may remember you are **p.** of me and come*
W-pI.....71.8:3 depressed or angry at the second **p.**; it is
W-pI...78.10:1 take the role assigned to us as **p.** of God's
WpI..rII.in.1:3 The earlier **p.** of each day will be devoted
WpI..rII.in.1:3 and the latter **p.** of the day to the other.
WpI..rII.in.3:1 but try to spend the major **p.** of the time
W-pI.....87.4:4 *This is **p.** of God's Will for me, however I*
W-pI.....92.4:3 It unites with light, of which it is a **p.**. It
W-pI...93.11:6 you closer to the **p.** in salvation that God
W-pI...95.14:2 little **p.** in bringing happiness to all the
W-pI.....96.3:6 place in which it could be really **p.** of you.
W-pI........98.h accept my **p.** in God's plan for salvation.
W-pI.....98.1:8 it is, and take the **p.** assigned to us by God
W-pI.....98.7:6 *will accept my **p.** in God's plan for salvation.*
W-pI...98.11:2 that you accept the **p.** that He would have
W-pI.....99.8:1 This **p.** belongs to God, as does the rest.
W-pI......100.h **p.** is essential to God's plan for salvation.
W-pI...100.1:1 your **p.** in it completes your Father's plan.
W-pI...100.2:3 The **p.** that He has saved for you to take in
W-pI...100.2:4 This **p.** is as essential to His plan as to
W-pI...100.5:2 take the **p.** that is essential to God's plan,
W-pI...100.5:3 is the sign that you would play another **p.**,
W-pI...100.6:2 If you are sad, your **p.** is unfulfilled, and
W-pI...100.7:3 Then realize your **p.** is to be happy. Only
W-pI...112.1:3 *I share with God, because I am a **p.** of Him.*
W-pI...114.2:1 accept my **p.** in God's plan for salvation.
W-pI...114.3:4 accept my **p.** in God's plan for salvation.
W-pI...115.2:1 (100) My **p.** is essential to God's plan for
W-pI...115.3:4 hour: My **p.** is essential to God's plan for
W-pI...125.5:4 as **p.** of Him regardless of his dreams;
W-pI...127.3:4 mind that thinks of it as partial or in **p.**.
W-pI...127.6:4 that you think are **p.** of human destiny.
W-pI.127.12:1 because we cannot leave a **p.** of us outside
W-pI...128.3:2 make **p.** of you as you perceive yourself.
W-pI...130.7:2 to bring with us a little **p.** of unreality, as
W-pI.130.11:1 Accept a little **p.** of hell as real, and you
W-pI.130.11:3 to you. All you need say to any **p.** of hell,
W-pI.130.11:5 *and this is not a **p.** of what I want.*
W-pI.132.13:1 and break away a **p.** of God Himself and
W-pI...134.3:1 you find in genuine forgiveness on your **p.**
W-pI.135.16:5 Anticipation plays no **p.** at all, for present
W-pI.135.21:1 for this is **p.** of what was planned for us.
W-pI.135.25:5 to learn the **p.** for you within the plan of
W-pI...136.5:1 this quick forgetting of the **p.** you play in
W-pI...138.2:2 But here is opposition **p.** of being "real."
W-pI...139.5:8 do not ask what **p.** of you can really doubt
W-pI...139.5:9 be a **p.** of you that asks this question. For
W-pI.139.5:11 Were it **p.** of you, then certainty would be
W-pI...139.9:7 they may know that they are **p.** of you,
W-pI.139.11:6 truth, how much a **p.** of us is every mind,
WpI. rIV.in1:1 the second **p.** of learning how the truth
W-pI.151.12:1 for your life is not a **p.** of anything you see
W-pI...152.2:4 Can pain be **p.** of peace, or grief of joy?
W-pI...152.3:7 as what is true, then **p.** of truth is false.
W-pI...154.1:5 It is not our **p.** to judge our worth, nor
W-pI...154.1:6 Our **p.** is cast in Heaven, not in hell. And
W-pI...154.2:2 He chooses and accepts your **p.** for you.
W-pI...154.5:4 failing to perform his proper **p.** as bringer
W-pI...154.7:2 **p.** by their acceptance of His messages as
W-pI...154.9:2 For that is **p.** of your appointed role. God
W-pI...154.9:4 another **p.** of your appointed task is yet to
W-pI...156.3:3 what shares His life is **p.** of Holiness, and
W-pI...160.1:4 to the **p.** of you which thinks that it is real
W-pI...161.2:2 But **p.** of it is now unnatural. It does not
W-pI...163.9:6 *things, to be like You and **p.** of You forever.*
W-pI...164.5:1 when vain imaginings **p.** like a curtain, to
W-pI...169.5:5 and no **p.** of mind sufficiently distinct to
W-pI...169.9:3 We merely take the **p.** assigned long since
W-pI.169.11:1 that you have work to do to play your **p.**.
W-pI.169.11:2 obscure to you until your **p.** is done. It
W-pI.169.11:4 **p.** is still what all the rest depends on. As
W-pI.169.13:4 forever, while a **p.** of you remains outside,
W-pI.170.10:3 "enemy"; its cruelty as now a **p.** of love.
WpI...rV.in8:7 I am incomplete without your **p.** in me.
W-pI...183.8:2 also that His Son is **p.** of Him, creating in
W-pI...183.9:4 today the **p.** you play in its salvation, and
W-pI...186.1:3 your acceptance of a **p.** assigned to you,
W-pI...186.2:5 do is to accept our **p.** in genuine humility,
W-pI...186.2:7 to take the **p.** assigned to us by One Who
W-pI...186.5:4 assures you that salvation needs your **p.**,
W-pI.187.10:3 not distant from one brother who is **p.** of
W-pI...189.8:3 **p.** is simply to allow all obstacles that you
W-pI...189.8:4 His **p.** in joyful and immediate response.
W-pI.189.10:9 *the world, that it become a **p.** of Heaven now*
W-pI...190.3:5 For vengeance is not **p.** of love. And fear,
W-pI...191.4:6 proclaimed to be forever **p.** of everything,
W-pI...194.6:1 effort as you can, to make it be a **p.** of you.
W-pI...197.4:2 a **p.** that joins with yours in thanking you.
W-pI...197.7:5 no end, for gratitude remains a **p.** of love.
W-pI...198.2:4 for freedom is a **p.** of knowledge. To
W-pI...199.3:4 **p.** of the illusion that has sheltered it from
W-pI...199.5:2 it a **p.** of every practice period you take.
W-pII ....in.8:1 we start upon the final **p.** of this one holy
W-pII .223.1:3 He has no Thoughts that are not **p.** of me,
W-pII .228.2:3 *My holiness remains a **p.** of me, as I am part*
W-pII .228.2:3 *remains a part of me, as I am **p.** of You. And*
W-pII ......2.2:4 the split became a **p.** of every fragment of
W-pII .235.2:2 *and made my sinlessness forever **p.** of You. I*
W-pII .238.1:5 *certainty that he is safe Who still is **p.** of You,*
W-pII .240.1:8 in us, for we are each a **p.** of Love Itself.
W-pII .243.2:3 *one because each **p.** contains Your memory,*
W-pII .244.2:4 afraid what will forever be a **p.** of Him?
W-pII .247.2:3 *them, and gave them all to me as **p.** of You,*
W-pII ....248.h Whatever suffers is not **p.** of me.
W-pII .248.1:3 Whatever suffers is not **p.** of me. What
W-pII .260.1:2 *my Source, remaining **p.** of Who created me*
W-pII .262.1:8 *he is **p.** of me and I of him, and we are part*
W-pII .262.1:8 *and we are **p.** of You Who are our Source,*
W-pII ......6.2:2 Your mind is **p.** of His, and His of yours.
W-pII ......6.2:3 He is the **p.** in which God's Answer lies;
W-pII ......6.3:2 the only **p.** of you that has reality in truth.
W-pII .278.1:5 free, and what is bound is not a **p.** of truth
W-pII . 283.2:1 Source, and everything created **p.** of us.
W-pII . 285.2:4 *My holiness is **p.** of me, and also part of You.*
W-pII . 285.2:4 *My holiness is part of me, and also **p.** of You.*
W-pII ..... 9.1:2 It is a **p.** of the condition that restores the
W-pII . 317.1:2 Salvation waits until I take this **p.** as what
W-pII . 318.1:3 there be a single **p.** that stands alone, or
W-pII ... 11.3:2 making every **p.** container of the whole.
W-pII ... 11.5:2 shares; Whose Holiness is still a **p.** of us.
W-pII . 328.2:4 *Will which You, my Father, gave as **p.** of me.*
W-pII . 350.1:1 *What we forgive becomes a **p.** of us, as we*
W-pII ... 14.3:2 We accept our **p.** as saviors of the world,
W-pII ... 14.3:6 will return when we have done our **p.**. We
Wfl........in.3:5 not fail to recognize as **p.** of God Himself.
M-3 ........... 3:5 is **p.** of God's plan for Atonement, and
M-6 ........... 3:3 given the outcome, for that is **p.** of the gift
M-6 ........... 3:6 Trust is an essential **p.** of giving; in fact, it
M-6 ........... 3:6 it is the **p.** that makes sharing possible,
M-6 ........... 3:6 **p.** that guarantees the giver will not lose,
M-7 ........... 6:2 a failure to recognize him as **p.** of the Self,
M-9 ........... 1:3 and chance plays no **p.** in God's plan. It is
M-16 ......... 2:2 such lack of structuring on their own **p.**.
M-21 ......... 1:1 words play no **p.** at all in healing. The
M-23 ......... 1:9 Why is the appeal to him **p.** of healing?
M-23 ......... 2:6 recognized all living things as **p.** of him.
M-23 ......... 3:4 His **p.** in the Sonship is also yours, and
M-24 ......... 3:5 it is not the **p.** of wisdom to add sectarian
M-27 ......... 4:1 curious belief that there is **p.** of dying
M-27 ......... 7:1 no compromise in which death plays a **p.**.
C-1 ............ 3:1 Spirit is the **p.** that is still in contact with
C-1 ............ 3:1 abides in this **p.** but sees the other part as
C-1 ............ 3:1 in this part but sees the other **p.** as well.
C-1 ............ 4:1 other **p.** of the mind is entirely illusory
C-3 ............ 5:3 It is the only thing still in the world in **p.**,
C-3 ............ 6:7 As a perception it is **p.** unreal. And yet
C-3 ............ 6:8 And yet this **p.** will vanish. What remains
C-6 ............ 1:5 Christ, His real Son, Who is **p.** of Him.
C-6 ............ 2:1 us, establishing our particular **p.** in it and
C-6 ............ 2:2 the first to complete his own **p.** perfectly.
C-6 ............ 3:3 He knows because He is **p.** of God; He
C-6 ............ 4:1 The Holy Spirit abides in the **p.** of your
C-6 ............ 4:1 of your mind that is **p.** of the Christ Mind
C-6 ............ 5:4 Whose **p.** in its redemption you have
P-1............. 4:4 Until this is at least in **p.** accepted, the
P-2..........II.7:4 does not think of God as **p.** of teaching.
P-2........ IV.7:7 be hidden by illusions, for it is **p.** of them.
P-3...........I.4:1 salvation, nor did he establish his **p.** in it.
P-3...........I.4:2 understands that his **p.** is necessary to the
P-3...........I.4:2 he will recognize the whole when his **p.** is
P-3.........II.5:7 for the relationships of which he is a **p.**.
P-3........ III.1:2 **p.** of His plan that everything in this
P-3........ III.1:8 He has a mighty **p.** in this one purpose,
S-1..........II.1:2 It is a **p.** of life. But it does change in form
S-1..........II.6:2 anyone in prayer, you make him **p.** of you
S-1..........II.7:2 like your own, for prayer is **p.** of you. The
S-1..........II.8:4 is **p.** of forgiveness as long as forgiveness,
S-1..........V.3:9 *cannot go without you, for you are a **p.** of me.*
S-3........ III.1:1 False healing heals the body in a **p.**, but
S-3........ III.5:4 It heals no **p.**, but wholly and forever.
S-3........ IV.8:3 song is **p.** of the eternal harmony of love.

## part-whole 1

T-8 ...VIII.1:14 The idea of **p.** relationships has meaning

## partial 29

T-1 .........V.3:2 God is not **p.**. All His children have His
T-3 .........II.2:1 Innocence is not a **p.** attribute. It is not
T-3 .........V.8:5 it. Only perception involves **p.** awareness.
T-3 .........V.8:6 because **p.** knowledge is impossible. It is
T-11 ......in.1:3 nor the ego proposes a **p.** thought system.
T-11 ......in.1:4 respects so that **p.** allegiance is impossible
T-13 ...VIII.2:1 this: There is nothing **p.** about knowledge
T-13 ...VIII.4:6 His loving gaze are **p.** glimpses of the
T-15 .......X.8:7 No **p.** sacrifice will appease this savage
T-15 .......X.9:1 not succeed in being **p.** hostage to the ego
T-15 .......X.9:2 Nor can you be **p.** host to it. You must
T-19 ........I.5:7 **P.** dedication is impossible. Truth is the
T-20 ..... VI.1:6 The one he made is **p.**, self-centered,

T-21......IV.4:1 liberation still is only p.; still limited and
T-22..... II.13:4 you have p. forgiveness for yourself? Can
T-24.........I.7:8 you give your brother only p. welcome, or
T-26....... II.5:2 There is no such thing as p. justice. If the
T-26...... III.3:3 words imply a limited reality, a p. truth, a
T-30......VI.6:6 And you have set a goal of p. pardon and
T-31...VII.10:4 a p. savior would be one who is but partly
W-pI...122.4:2 less than halfway diligence and p. trust.
W-pI...127.3:4 the mind that thinks of it as p. or in part.
W-pI...151.1:1 No one can judge on p. evidence. That is
W-pI...161.2:4 thus could it invent the p. world you see.
W-pI...184.4:1 is the way reality is made by p. vision,
M-22..........1:4 P. Atonement is a meaningless idea, just
P-2........VI.6:7 and his release is p. and will not be sure.
S-3......... II.5:7 There is no p. healing. What but shifts
S-3........IV.3:4 Do not ask p. healing, nor accept an idol

## partiality 1

T-7........IX.1:6 To the ego this is p., and it responds as if

## partially 8

T-13......XI.3:6 To value it p. is not to know its value. In
T-17....IV.12:2 is complete, and cannot be p. accepted.
T-19......III.6:4 good and evil; partly sane and p. insane.
T-21....... V.8:8 The p. insane have access to it, and only
T-22....... II.7:5 false, and cannot be but p. believed. And
W-pI.....70.2:4 This is not a role that can be p. accepted.
M-13..........7:3 cannot give up Heaven p.. You cannot be
M-17........4:10 is not. It cannot be p. recognized. Who is

## particle 1

W-pI...191.3:2 tiny p. of dust against the legions of your

## particular 33

T-1........VI.1:9 act according to the p. order of needs you
T-2........VI.4:7 The p. result does not matter, but the
T-4......... II.9:2 associate this with its p. form of magic.
T-4.......VII.1:1 of any p. ego illusion does not matter, its
T-7........IV.3:4 is as irrelevant as is the p. ability that was
T-9......... II.1:3 with this course. The latter in p. might be
T-14....... X.7:6 only to the p. perception of his offering
T-21.........I.6:2 not to a person or a place or anything p..
W-pI........2.1:6 do not concentrate on anything in p., and
W-pI........2.2:5 Make no attempt to include anything p.,
W-pI........4.5:1 idea for a p. thought that you recognize as
W-pI........7.5:1 Do not linger over any one thing in p.,
W-pI.....11.3:1 they should not linger on anything in p..
W-pI.....11.3:3 introduction to this idea, in p., should be
W-pI.....16.5:4 of a p. thought that arouses uneasiness.
W-pI.....21.1:2 the idea to p. situations as they may arise.
W-pI.....21.5:2 on a p. attribute of a particular person,
W-pI.....21.5:2 on a particular attribute of a p. person,
W-pI.....31.3:4 Do not dwell on any one in p., but try to
W-pI.....34.4:1 without applying it to anything in p.. Be
W-pI.....35.9:2 If nothing p. occurs to you, merely repeat
W-pI.....39.8:1 without undue emphasis on any one in p.,
W-pI.....43.9:1 If no p. subject presents itself to your
W-pI.....44.8:1 While no p. approach is advocated for
WpI...rI.in.2:2 is not necessary to follow any p. order in
W-pI.....74.4:2 identify the p. person or persons and the
WpI. rII.in.6:4 It is not the p. words you use that matter.
M-1............3:3 So do the p. teaching aids involved. But
M-9............1:8 in p. must be properly perceived, and all
M-16..........6:1 There is one thought in p. that should be
M-25..........4:5 a p. appeal in unusual abilities that can be
M-29..........2:6 the Holy Spirit's p. care and guidance.
C-6.............2:1 establishing our p. part in it and showing

## particularly 33

T-2......IV.3:11 engaging in a p. unworthy form of denial.
T-2........VI.6:5 quite simple, but p. apt to be overlooked.
T-3...........I.1:6 This p. unfortunate interpretation, which
T-3...........I.2:6 been p. difficult to overcome this because,
T-4...........I.7:3 p. any situation that lends itself to the
T-5........VI.8:1 as interpreted by the ego, is p. vicious. It
T-6.........in.2:1 since an extreme example is a p. helpful
T-8..... VIII.3:1 p. difficult to overcome the ego's belief in
T-9...........I.3:2 is p. inappropriate in the minds of those
T-9........IV.7:4 p. dangerous combination of grandiosity
T-9.......VII.4:5 p. likely to attack you when you react
W-pI........4.6:1 in connection with thoughts p. difficult.
W-pI........7.1:1 This idea is p. difficult to believe at first.
W-pI.....13.1:5 will be p. likely to think you do perceive it
W-pI.....29.4:2 which may be p. tempting in connection
W-pI.....31.5:1 idea for today is also a p. useful one to use
W-pI.....37.6:2 is p. helpful to apply it silently to anyone
W-pI....39.11:2 arise, a p. helpful form of the idea is: *My*
W-pI.....43.8:1 p. to those which seem to distress you in
W-pI.....44.3:3 is a p. difficult form for the undisciplined
W-pI.....48.2:5 It is p. important that you use the idea
W-pI.....64.7:2 This will be difficult, at first p., since you
W-pI.....67.5:1 It will be p. helpful today to practice the
W-pI.....74.4:1 one conflict area that seems p. difficult to
W-pI.....80.6:3 And be p. sure to apply the idea for today
W-pI.....91.9:2 Concentrate p. on the experience of
W-pI.....95.7:2 five minutes of the hour will be p. helpful,
W-pI.....95.8:3 be determined, p. for the next week or so,
W-pI...133.1:1 p. after you have gone through what
M-16 .........8:2 this, p. during the time when his mind is
M-21 .........1:8 Words can be helpful, p. for the beginner,
M-25 .........5:4 here, although they are not p. subtle. Yet,
S-1 ......... II.3:4 p. for forgiveness for the many sources of

## parting 1

T-26......IV.2:3 is no sadness and there is no p. here, for

## partly 15

T-3......... II.2:3 The p. innocent are apt to be quite foolish
T-5........ III.1:4 Mind is p. yours and also partly God's.
T-5........ III.1:4 Mind is partly yours and also p. God's.
T-6......V.C.1:4 What is p. in accord with it He accepts
T-7.......VII.1:7 *Reality* cannot be p. appreciated. That is
T-10......IV.3:1 Sonship cannot be perceived as p. sick,
T-11.....VII.3:5 For perceptions cannot be p. true. If you
T-19...... III.6:4 good and evil; p. sane and partially insane
T-21... VIII.4:2 it possible to help you be already p. sane.
T-24........ III.1:3 is why it is impossible but p. to forgive.
T-25... VIII.4:8 up. So is the victim seen as p. you, with
T-31...VII.10:4 savior would be one who is but p. saved.
W-pI...195.2:3 Nor could the even p. sane refuse to take
W-pII..284.1:5 and next to be accepted as but p. true,
S-3......... II.5:9 What is false cannot be p. true. If you are

## partner 4

T-16......IV.3:5 The special love p. is acceptable only as
T-16........ V.7:5 Each p. tries to sacrifice the self he does
T-16.....VII.1:4 for choosing a special p. without the past?
M-3 ...........5:2 each person is given a chosen learning p.

## partners 3

T-16......IV.4:5 certain ones as p. in any aspect of living,
T-16....... V.8:3 both p. see this special self in each other,
W-pI.....73.2:1 Idle wishes and grievances are p. or

## parts 47

T-1......... II.4:7 are two p. to the statement in recognition
T-1.......VII.4:3 Some of the later p. of the course rest too
T-2.......VII.6:3 in its Oneness transcends the sum of its p.
T-2.......VII.6:4 obscured as long as any of its p. is missing
T-2.......VII.6:5 all the p. of the Sonship have returned.
T-3......... V.8:7 It is all one and has no separate p.. You
T-4........ III.1:6 in its totality transcends the sum of its p..
T-8......... V.1:6 is far beyond the power of its separate p..
T-8... VIII.1:12 perception the whole is built up of p. that
T-11....... V.13:5 by breaking it into small, disconnected p.,
T-12.......IV.6:8 can be no disinherited p. of the Sonship,
T-15....... V.3:1 love p. of reality and understand what
T-15....... V.7:1 it prefers different p. of another aspect.
T-15....VIII.4:6 all its p. are joined in God through Christ,
T-17...... III.3:3 separated off as being the only p. of value.
T-18.........I.3:7 with special emphasis on certain p., and
T-18...... VI.8:6 It is *not* made up of different p., which
T-19.........I.6:2 into little p. of seeming wholeness, but
T-20....... V.1:5 the p. of God's Son gradually join in time,
T-20.....VII.1:4 or p. you find more difficult than others,
T-21...... VI.5:6 enters part be kept away from other p.?
T-24........ V.2:4 For the p. do not belong together, and the
T-24........ V.2:4 contributes nothing to the p. to give them
T-25..........I.7:7 *and what is one can not have separate p..*
T-27..... V.11:8 by merely counting up its separate p..
T-30....... III.6:8 no separate p. in what exists within God's
T-30....... VI.8:4 no missing p. that have been kept outside
T-31..... V.10:6 two p. to what you think yourself to be. If
W-pI.....66.7:2 that there are only two p. of your mind.
W-pI.....71.8:1 idea, and realizing that it contains two p.,
W-pI.....95.2:2 divided into many warring p., separate
W-pI...127.1:4 It has no separate p. and no degrees; no
W-pI...127.2:6 perceive the Son of God in separate p..
W-pI...136.2:3 reduce it to a little pile of unassembled p..
W-pI...136.2:5 The p. are seen as if each one were whole
W-pI...136.6:3 When p. are wrested from the whole and
W-pI...137.3:4 Self with all Its p. intact and unassailed.
W-pI...152.3:2 may not yet accept both p. of it. Without
W-pI...156.2:3 nor be in p. uncertain and in others sure.
W-pI...159.3:4 can show but twisted images in broken p.
W-pI.169.12:1 all its p. in meaningful relationships, the
W-pII .243.2:2 *I honor all its p., in which I am included. We*
W-pII .....5.1:1 to separate p. of his Self from other parts.
W-pII .....5.1:1 to separate parts of his Self from other p..
W-pII .318.1:1 all p. of Heaven's plan to save the world.
W-pII .318.1:2 the p. have but one purpose and one aim?
C-1.............2:4 described in the course *as if* it has two p.;

## pass 28

T-1........ III.2:1 "Heaven and earth shall p. away" means
T-1........ III.2:2 shall not p. away because life is eternal.
T-14.... XI.12:4 until you p. the test of perfect peace, for
T-20.... VI.11:4 devotion to death's idols and then p. on.
T-22....... III.3:3 the help of reason would try to p. it. The
T-22....... III.3:4 it would be madness to attempt to p. it.
T-22....... V.6:6 not one that truth cannot p. over lightly,
T-25..... VII.9:6 and p. him by in careless thoughtlessness.
T-26..... V.6:10 and p. from mere imagining into belief
T-29...... VI.4:1 that only Heaven would not p. away. You
W-pI........8.4:4 or theme it contains, and p. on to the next
W-pI...44.10:2 as you p. by the thoughts of this world.
W-pI.....70.9:2 Try to p. the clouds by whatever means
W-pI...100.8:5 p. as you ascend to meet the Christ in you
W-pI...128.2:3 this world contains is that you p. it by,
W-pI.131.14:5 end together as you p. beyond the door.
W-pI.155.11:1 that p. and miracles are purposeless, the
W-pI...189.6:1 Today we p. illusions, as we seek to reach
W-pII .241.1:4 when sorrows p. away and pain is gone.
W-pII .255.2:1 *so, my Father, would I p. this day with You.*
W-pII .263.2:2 us, that we may p. them by in innocence,
W-pII .272.2:1 Today we p. illusions by. And if we hear
W-ep .........4:2 He give you pleasures that will p. away,
M-14 .........3:6 God must learn to p. by and leave behind.
M-27 .........2:2 who has decreed that all things p. away,
P-2...........I.4:2 And this will one day come to p. for every
P-3..........II.9:3 This enables him to p. by many obstacles
S-2..........II.4:3 for this may p. as meekness and as charity

## passage 2

W-pI.....42.2:3 Your p. through time and space is not at
S-3..........II.4:1 This gentle p. to a higher prayer, a kind

## passed 16

T-22....... V.5:7 is quietly p. through and gone beyond?
T-26....... V.5:1 p. away in Heaven too soon for anything
T-26...... IX.3:8 the blight and withering have p. forever
T-29...... IX.6:1 childhood should be p. and gone forever.
T-31.......I.13:5 free, because an ancient learning p. away,
T-31...... VI.3:8 and must be p. that both may disappear,

W-pI.....73.5:5 that the barrier of grievances is easily p.,
W-pI...104.2:3 be ours when time has p. into eternity.
W-pI...109.5:5 but the dreams of fever that has p. away.
W-pI...109.9:5 We give to those unborn and those p. by,
W-pI.138.12:3 As every hour p., we have declared our
W-pI...161.1:4 the world p. safely by and Heaven now
W-pI...163.5:2 no name to him, for he has p. to dust. It
W-pI...194.2:1 today's idea, and you have p. all anxiety,
M-2 ...........3:4 ago p. by is looked upon as a new thought
C-2.............7:6 you left behind at last and finally p. by.

**passes** 9

T-2........ III.4:4 of the right defense it p. over all others,
T-13.........I.8:9 is the opposite of time, for time p. away,
T-26..........I.5:4 itself. No instant p. here in which your
T-26...... IX.4:3 was p. to nothingness when They have
T-29....... V.2:3 that nothing in this world but p. by,
W-pI.122.14:1 a minute as each quarter of an hour p. by.
W-pI...125.9:5 true. As every hour p. by today, be still a
W-pI...151.7:3 him. He p. by such idle witnesses, which
W-pI...188.3:5 hearts, and lights all vision as it p. by. All

**passeth** 2

T-2......... II.1:9 peace of God which p. understanding."
T-13.....VII.8:1 of God p. your understanding only in the

**passing** 19

T-5.....VI.12:6 reminds you of this in every p. moment of
T-16.....VII.6:4 and with its p. the drive for vengeance has
T-18.............h THE P. OF THE DREAM
T-24...... VI.3:5 His Son with p. circumstance which has
T-27.........I.7:3 short and not esteem the worth of p. joys?
T-27.........I.7:8 pleasure in the quickly p. and ephemeral.
T-27.........I.8:2 seek for p. joys and cherish little pleasures
T-28.........I.2:3 over. In its p. went its consequences, left
T-28...... III.5:2 the ripples that a ship has made in p. by.
T-30....... V.9:1 An ancient hate is p. from the world.
W-pI.....44.7:5 your p. thoughts without involvement,
W-pI.....75.2:6 old one has left no trace upon it in its p..
W-pI.....75.3:1 offer thanks for the p. of the old and the
W-pI...110.2:4 change that time appears to bring in p. by
W-pI...194.3:4 And so each instant given unto God in p.,
W-pII .300.1:2 represent more than a p. cloud upon a
W-pII .315.1:1 come to me with every p. moment. I am
M-10 .........6:6 loss; of p. time and growing hopelessness;
P-2.......VII.5:1 The p. of guilt is the true aim of therapy

**passive** 3

T-28......IV.5:3 you *do* when you become a p. figure in his
T-31...... III.3:6 It is not seen to be a p. thing, obeying
T-31..... V.12:3 concept of the self from what is wholly p.,

**passively** 1

T-2....... VI.4:6 p. condoning your mind's miscreations.

**past** 269

• noun

*other*

T-1.........I.13:3 They undo the p. in the present, and thus
T-2.......... II.6:4 free yourself from the p. as you go ahead.
T-2.....V.A.17:4 remember is to recall the p. in the present
T-3...........I.3:1 one assigns his own "evil" p. to God. The
T-3...........I.3:2 The "evil" p. has nothing to do with God.
T-4......... II.1:3 of the p. because the past does not matter,
T-4......... II.1:3 of the past because the p. does not matter,
T-4......... II.3:4 is it surprising that it occurred in the p.?
T-5........IV.8:2 All your p. except its beauty is gone, and
T-5....... V.7:11 is to save the p. in purified form only. If
T-5........VI.2:2 ensure that the future will be like the p..
T-13.........I.3:3 You have "sinned" in the p., but there is
T-13.........I.3:3 "sinned" in the past, but there is no p..
T-13.........I.3:5 carpet spread along the p. behind you,
T-13.........I.8:2 can hold on to the p. only through guilt.
T-13 ........I.8:3 time, proceeding from p. to future. No
T-13 ........I.8:6 way of holding p. and future in your mind
T-13 ........I.9:1 you learn that the p. has never been, and
T-13 ..... IV.4:2 The ego invests heavily in the p., and in
T-13 ..... IV.4:2 and in the end believes that the p. is the
T-13 ..... IV.4:3 by making the future like the p., and thus
T-13 ..... IV.4:4 notion of paying for the p. in the future,
T-13 ..... IV.4:4 p. becomes the determiner of the future,
T-13 ..... IV.4:5 brings the p. to the future by interpreting
T-13 ..... IV.5:2 it reacts to the present as if it *were* the p..
T-13 ..... IV.5:3 ego cannot tolerate release from the p.,
T-13 ..... IV.5:3 from the past, and although the p. is over,
T-13 ..... IV.5:6 from him out of your own p. because, by
T-13 ..... IV.6:1 the p. are precisely what you must escape.
T-13 ..... IV.6:3 in retaliation for a p. that is no more. And
T-13 ..... IV.6:7 it as a meeting with your own p.? For you
T-13 ... IV.6:10 teaches that you always encounter your p.
T-13 ..... IV.7:6 the reality of "now," without p. or future,
T-13 ..... IV.8:2 The continuity of p. and future, under its
T-13 ..... IV.9:3 Healing cannot be accomplished in the p..
T-13 ..... IV.9:5 and extends the present rather than the p.
T-13 ..... IV.9:6 on to the p. to ensure a destructive future.
T-13 ...... V.2:1 world with figures from his individual p.,
T-13 ..... VI.1:4 His p. has no reality in the present, so you
T-13 ..... VI.1:7 the p. as you look upon your brother, you
T-13 ..... VI.2:3 everyone with no reference at all to the p.,
T-13 ..... VI.2:4 For the p. can cast no shadow to darken
T-13 ..... VI.3:2 Christ as revealed to you now has no p.,
T-13 ..... VI.3:5 To be born again is to let the p. go, and
T-13 ..... VI.3:6 that obscures God's Son to you *is* the p.,
T-13 ..... VI.4:2 P., present and future are not continuous,
T-13 ..... VI.4:6 time's continuity by breaking it into p.,
T-13 ..... VI.4:8 by doing so you are aligning p. and future
T-13 ..... VI.5:1 you to see your brother without his p.,
T-13 ..... VI.5:3 And since his p. is yours, you share in this
T-13 ..... VI.5:4 out of your p. obscure him from you, for
T-13 ..... VI.5:7 Your p. was made in anger, and if you use
T-13 ..... VI.6:7 for they are not separated by the p.. Only
T-13 ..... VI.6:8 past. Only the p. can separate, and it is
T-13 ..... VI.7:1 you with them, and free you from the p..
T-13 ..... VI.7:2 you, then, hold the p. against them? For if
T-13 ... VI.13:6 his Father, he has no p. apart from Him.
T-13 ....VII.5:9 and waits for you to leave the p. behind
T-13 ....VII.8:1 passeth your understanding only in the p.
T-13 ...VIII.1:1 All healing is release from the p.. That is
T-13 ...VIII.1:3 He teaches that the p. does not exist, a
T-13 ...VIII.5:4 Everyone seen without the p. thus brings
T-13 ..... IX.1:2 linking the future to the p. as is the ego's
T-13 ..... IX.1:7 and the p. the laws of God must intervene
T-13 ..... IX.3:3 and if you place your faith in the p., the
T-13 ..... IX.4:3 of God is guiltless because you see the p.,
T-13 ..... IX.4:6 could as easily have freed him from the p.,
T-13 .......X.4:1 but the source of your guilt lies in the p.,
T-13 .......X.4:2 inward. The p. is not *in* you. Your weird
T-13 .......X.4:5 your brothers as a means to "solve" the p.
T-13 .......X.4:7 there. You wanted not salvation in the p..
T-13 .......X.5:2 Use no relationship to hold you to the p.
T-13 .......X.5:3 will be enough to free you from the p.,
T-13 ..... XI.2:8 p. are gone as one into the unreality from
T-14 .......II.7:2 Holy Spirit's plan to free you from the p.,
T-14 ..... IX.1:9 the p., too, was changed and interposed
T-14 ... IX.1:10 The p. that you remember never was, and
T-14 ..... XI.3:1 that you have taught yourself in the p., by
T-14 ..... XI.3:3 Learning is therefore in the p., but its
T-14 ..... XI.3:5 present, or teach you how to undo the p..
T-14 ..... XI.3:6 Your p. is what you have taught yourself.
T-14 ..... XI.9:9 For the p. binds Him not, and therefore
T-14 ... XI.10:1 freed you from the p. would teach you are
T-15 ........I.5:4 to look upon with equanimity is the p..
T-15 ........I.6:3 the p. and future be the same is hidden a
T-15 ........I.8:2 the present, but only of the p. and future,
T-15 ........I.8:3 stands clear and separated from the p.,
T-15 ........I.8:4 Son of God emerges from the p. into the
T-15 ........I.9:2 For what is time without a p. and future?
T-15 ........I.9:6 Nothing can reach you here out of the p.,
T-15 ..... IV.1:8 For beyond the p. and future, where you
T-15 ...... V.1:3 Judgment always rests on the p., for past
T-15 ...... V.1:4 becomes impossible without the p., for
T-15 ...... V.2:1 The p. is the ego's chief learning device,
T-15 .......V.2:1 for it is in the p. that you learned to define
T-15 .......V.3:6 The p. has taught you this. Yet the holy
T-15 .......V.8:3 Without the values from the p., you
T-15 .......V.9:3 by bringing all perception out of the p.,
T-15 .......V.9:7 For in the holy instant, free of the p., you
T-15 ..... VI.8:3 in the holy instant because the p. is gone,
T-16 .........I.3:4 have learned of empathy is from the p..
T-16 .........I.3:5 nothing from the p. that you would share,
T-16 .........I.3:5 nothing from the p. that you would keep.
T-16 .........I.3:6 Do not use empathy to make the p. real,
T-16 .......I.3:10 *I would not intrude the p. upon my Guest. I*
T-16 .... VII.1:1 It is impossible to let the p. go without
T-16 .... VII.1:2 attempt to re-enact the p. and change it.
T-16 .... VII.1:4 choosing a special partner without the p.?
T-16 .... VII.1:5 "evil" in the p. to which you cling, and for
T-16 .... VII.2:1 relationship takes vengeance on the p.. By
T-16 .... VII.2:2 By seeking to remove suffering in the p., it
T-16 .... VII.2:2 with the p. and its total commitment to it.
T-16 .... VII.2:4 Shades of the p. envelop it, and make it
T-16 .... VII.2:6 can you change the p. except in fantasy?
T-16 .... VII.2:7 you what you think the p. deprived you of
T-16 .... VII.2:8 The p. is nothing. Do not seek to lay the
T-16 .... VII.2:9 for deprivation on it, for the p. is gone.
T-16 .. VII.2:12 fulfilled in the present, but only in the p..
T-16 .... VII.3:1 of the ego's drive for vengeance on the p..
T-16 .... VII.3:5 For the ego holds the p. against you, and
T-16 .... VII.3:5 escape from the p. it sees itself deprived of
T-16 .... VII.3:6 the ego could not hold you to the p.. In
T-16 .... VII.4:1 The p. is gone; seek not to preserve it in
T-16 .... VII.4:1 you must return to the p. to find salvation
T-16 .... VII.4:2 the dream of retribution for the p..
T-16 .... VII.6:3 in salvation through vengeance for the p..
T-16 .... VII.6:4 instant it is understood that the p. is gone
T-16 .... VII.9:3 Their reality has no p., and only illusions
T-17 .......II.6:2 your perception and fixed it on the p..
T-17 ....... III.h Shadows of the P.
T-17 ....... III.1:1 the loving thoughts you gave in the p.,
T-17 ..... III.5:4 transformed p. is made like the present.
T-17 ..... III.5:5 No longer does the p. conflict with *now.*
T-17 ..... III.5:8 That is why Atonement centers on the p.,
T-17 ..... III.7:8 Give the p. to Him Who can change your
T-17 ..... III.7:9 what you have made the p. to represent,
T-17 ..... III.8:1 p. becomes the justification for entering
T-17 ..... III.8:4 referred for meaning is an *illusion* of the p.
T-17 ..... III.8:5 thus let go is all the truth the p. could ever
T-17 ..... VI.3:4 Not only is your judgment in the p., but
T-17 .... VII.8:3 not his p. but yours you hold against him.
T-17 .... VII.9:6 situation was thus made free of the p.,
T-18 ..... III.8:7 to shine away the p. and so make room
T-18 ..... IV.8:5 And that is why the p. has gone. It never
T-18 .... VII.3:3 Only its p. and future make it seem real.
T-18 .... VII.3:7 be thought of in the p. or in the future.
T-18 .... VII.4:1 you are willing to see no p. or future. You
T-18 .... VII.7:5 is time denied, and p. and future gone.
T-19 .........I.9:3 you offer the gift of freedom from the p.,
T-19 .......I.11:4 because it looks not to the p. to judge him
T-19 .......II.7:4 This is his p., his present and his future.
T-20 .....II.10:1 that the Son of God is risen from the p.,
T-20 .......V.6:4 The p. takes nothing from it, and the
T-23 ...... IV.8:5 It is their p., their present and their future
T-24 ..... VI.9:3 to you is done and he is risen from the p..
T-25 .......II.1:7 The only value that the p. can hold is that
T-25 .......II.4:1 Its p. *has* failed. Be glad that it is gone
T-26 .......V.5:3 Only in the p., –an ancient past, too short
T-26 .......V.5:3 Only in the past,–an ancient p., too short
T-26 .......V.6:2 It is the key to learning that the p. is over.
T-26 .......V.7:2 Is any echo from the p. that he may hear a
T-26 .......V.8:1 calls from out a p. forevermore gone by.
T-26 .......V.8:3 this a hindrance to the truth the p. is gone
T-26 .......V.9:3 you to see the p. and put it in the present?
T-26 .......V.9:5 way in the direction of the p. but sets you
T-26 .....V.10:3 A dreadful instant in a distant p., now
T-26 .....V.11:3 error in the p. that God remembers not,
T-26 .....V.11:4 and forth between the p. and present.
T-26 .....V.11:5 Sometimes the p. seems real, as if it *were*
T-26 .....V.11:6 Voices from the p. are heard and then are
T-26 .....V.11:8 the bridge between the p. and present.
T-26 .....V.11:9 Here the shadow of the p. remains, but
T-26 ...V.11:11 draw you from the p. into the present,

T-26.....V.13:2 cross the gap between the **p.** and present,
T-26.....V.14:1 Forgive the **p.** and let it go, for it *is* gone.
T-27.......I.11:1 let the body have no purpose from the **p.**,
T-28.........I.1:8 The miracle but shows the **p.** is gone, and
T-28.........I.2:6 perception of the **p.** as if it were occurring
T-28.........I.4:5 There is no link of memory to the **p.**. If
T-28.........I.5:2 not seek to use it as a means to keep the **p.**
T-28.........I.5:7 history of all the body's **p.** is hidden there.
T-28.........I.5:8 associations made to keep the **p.** alive, the
T-28.........I.6:4 of it, as if the **p.** had caused the present,
T-28.........I.6:7 the **p.** is held in memory as you make use
T-28.........I.6:7 it is a way to hold the **p.** against the now.
T-28.........I.9:7 Its memory does not lie in the **p.**, nor
T-28.......I.13:3 There is no **p.** to keep its fearful image in
T-28.......I.13:6 came in between the present and the **p.**,
T-28.......I.14:6 that could generate a different **p.** or future
T-29.....VII.7:1 purpose of the world the **p.** has given it.
T-29.....VII.7:2 otherwise, the future will be like the **p.**,
T-31.......I.13:4 without the **p.** that sentenced him to die,
T-31...VII.13:2 It sees no **p.** in anyone at all. And thus it
W-pI..........7.h I see only the **p.**.
W-pI.......7.3:5 this cup except what you learned in the **p.**
W-pI.......7.4:5 *I see only the* **p.** *in this pencil. I see only the*
W-pI.......7.4:6 *I see only the* **p.** *in this shoe. I see only the*
W-pI.......7.4:7 *I see only the* **p.** *in this hand. I see only the*
W-pI.......7.4:8 *I see only the* **p.** *in that body. I see only the*
W-pI.......7.4:9 *past in that body. I see only the* **p.** *in that face.*
W-pI.......8.1:1 course, the reason why you see only the **p.**
W-pI.......8.1:4 The mind's preoccupation with the **p.** is
W-pI.......8.2:1 can hold about the **p.** is that it is not here.
W-pI.......8.2:3 the **p.** or in anticipating the future. The
W-pI.....52.2:1 (7) I see only the **p.**. As I look about, I
W-pI.....52.2:4 seeing. I hold the **p.** against everyone and
W-pI.....52.3:2 and my mind is preoccupied with the **p.**.
W-pI.....52.3:4 Let me remember that I look on the **p.** to
W-pI.....52.3:6 Let me learn to give the **p.** away, realizing
W-pI.....52.4:4 is not whether to see the **p.** or the present;
W-pI.....70.7:5 you have looked for salvation in the **p.**; –
W-pI.....75.3:2 No shadows from the **p.** remain to darken
W-pI.....75.6:1 Dwell not upon the **p.** today. Keep a
W-pI.....75.9:6 the darkness of the **p.** upon your eyes, you
W-pI...78.10:3 you think of or remember from the **p.**,
W-pI...110.2:2 to heal the **p.** and make the future free. It
W-pI...110.3:3 to light the world and free it from the **p.**.
W-pI...110.4:1 In this one thought is all the **p.** undone;
W-pI.127.10:2 that we are spared a future like the **p.**.
W-pI.127.10:3 the past. Today we leave the **p.** behind us,
W-pI.127.10:4 dawns unlike the **p.** in every attribute.
W-pI...131.6:5 How could the Will of God be in the **p.**, or
W-pI...131.6:6 is now, without a **p.** and wholly futureless.
W-pI...132.2:3 free the **p.** from what you thought before.
W-pI...132.3:3 For as you let the **p.** be lifted and release
W-pI...135.1:4 attempt to plan the future, activate the **p.**,
W-pI.135.15:4 rests on the idea the **p.** has taught enough
W-pI.135.16:4 to guarantee a future quite unlike the **p.**,
W-pI...156.7:2 The **p.** is gone, with all its fantasies. They
W-pI...169.6:3 the **p.** and future cannot be conceived. It
W-pI...181.5:2 For the **p.** is gone; the future but imagined
W-pI...181.6:3 little while, without regard to **p.** or future,
W-pI...182.4:2 hold a picture of a **p.** that never happened
W-pI...189.7:4 with you one thought the **p.** has taught,
W-pI...194.4:1 future as He holds your **p.** and present.
W-pI...194.4:6 the **p.** and present in His Hands as well,
W-pI...194.4:6 because the **p.** will punish you no more,
W-pI...194.5:2 For the **p.** is gone, and what is present,
W-pI...214.1:2 *The* **p.** *is gone; the future is not yet. Now am I*
W-pII.....288.h Let me forget my brother's **p.** today.
W-pII...288.1:5 *His sins are in the* **p.** *along with mine, and I*
W-pII...288.1:5 *mine, and I am saved because the* **p.** *is gone.*
W-pII.....289.h The **p.** is over. It can touch me not.
W-pII...289.1:1 Unless the **p.** is over in my mind, the real
W-pII...289.1:4 This the **p.** was made to hide, for this the
W-pII...289.1:5 It has no **p.**. For what can be forgiven but
W-pII...289.1:6 For what can be forgiven but the **p.**, and if
W-pII...289.2:1 *let me not look upon a* **p.** *that is not there. For*
W-pII...289.2:2 *present world the* **p.** *has left untouched and*
W-pII...308.1:3 cannot be to keep the **p.** and future one.
W-pII...308.1:6 of Christ is now, without a **p.** or future.
W-pII.....314.h I seek a future different from the **p.**.
W-pII..314.1:1 comes a future very different from the **p.**.
W-pII..314.2:1 *Father, we were mistaken in the* **p.**, *and*
M-2...........4:6 an inevitable choice out of an ancient **p.**.
M-4 ... VIII.1:6 The **p.** as well held no mistakes; nothing
M-19.........3:1 future states and all concerns about the **p.**
M-20.........2:6 yes, between this thing and all the **p.**. But
M-20.........2:8 The **p.** just slips away, and in its place is
M-24.........1:2 There is no **p.** or future, and the idea of
M-24.........1:9 preoccupation and perhaps pride in the **p.**
M-24.........2:7 in seeing the present in terms of the **p.**.
M-24.........6:3 **p.** and total lack of interest in the future.
M-25.........3:6 anything; achievements from the **p.**,
P-2........VI.6:4 he sees his sins as gone into a **p.** that is no
P-2.......VII.5:4 no one here can have; a certainty of **p.**,
S-1........IV.3:3 asks to have the **p.** repeated in some way.
S-1........IV.3:4 all these are but illusions from the **p.**.
S-2...........I.8:6 with nothing of the **p.** to hold it back from

**past** 158
• other
*noun*

T-2.........II.6:5 It undoes your **p.** errors, thus making it
T-2........III.4:4 over all others, looking **p.** error to truth.
T-5......III.11:9 holds the remembrance of things **p.** and
T-5.......IV.2:9 cannot cancel out your **p.** errors alone.
T-8...........I.4:1 Your **p.** learning must have taught you
T-12... VIII.4:8 It is no more **p.** than future, being forever
T-13......IV.3:3 Even the **p.** life that death might indicate,
T-13......IV.4:5 by interpreting the present in **p.** terms.
T-13......IV.5:2 The present merely reminds it of **p.** hurts,
T-13......IV.5:4 in the present from a **p.** reference point,
T-13......IV.6:5 Unless you learn that **p.** pain is an illusion
T-13......IV.6:6 awakening and understanding they are **p.**.
T-13......VI.1:5 **p.** reactions to him are also not there, and
T-13......VI.2:1 to use your **p.** experience as the reference
T-13......VI.3:6 past, and if you would have it **p.** and gone,
T-13......VI.4:7 future on the basis of your **p.** experience,
T-13......VI.5:2 His errors are all **p.**, and by perceiving
T-13.......X.9:6 look **p.** darkness to the holy place where
T-14......IX.1:8 Thus truth was made **p.**, and the present
T-14......XI.6:9 *own* **p.** *learning as the light to guide me now.*
T-15.......II.1:7 instant you will let go all your **p.** learning,
T-15.......V.1:3 for **p.** experience is the basis on which you
T-16.....VII.1:3 remembered pain, **p.** disappointments,
T-16.....VII.4:1 and would teach you salvation is **p.** and so
T-17......III.2:5 reminds you of your **p.** grievances attracts
T-17.....VII.7:3 so great it reaches **p.** the stars and to the
T-18......III.7:5 and your brother experience is really **p.**.
T-18......III.7:7 You have gone **p.** fear, for no two minds
T-18....VI.12:2 relevant; it can occur with something **p.**,
T-18.....VII.7:3 which you slip **p.** centuries of effort, and
T-18......IX.8:3 unsubstantial nature as He leads you **p.**
T-19.........I.9:5 looking **p.** all barriers between yourself
T-19......IV.1:4 extending **p.** completely unencumbered.
T19. IV.A.10:3 As love must look **p.** fear, so must fear see
T19....IV.B.5:6 difficult for us to walk **p.** barriers together
T19....IV.C.2:3 They but walk **p.** and it is gone. But what
T-20.......II.7:1 have the vision now to look **p.** all illusions
T-20......II.11:7 it to him shall you be led **p.** fear to love.
T-20....VI.12:7 Idolatry is **p.** and meaningless. Perhaps
T-21.........I.8:1 **p.** everything you see and yet somehow
T-21....III.12:4 But in their seeing they look **p.** it, as do
T-21......IV.4:3 inward, **p.** insanity and on to reason. And
T-21.......V.7:9 disregard them, and you have gone **p.** this
T-22......III.5:5 made to look on error and not see **p.** it.
T-22......VI.7:2 sight, preventing you from seeing **p.** it?
T-24...VII.6:10 Not till you go **p.** learning to the Given;
T-25.........I.4:4 light merely by looking **p.** it *to* the light.
T-26.......II.5:7 made it great, and **p.** the hope of healing.
T-26......III.3:5 and only one continues **p.** the gate where
T-26......IV.1:4 justice **p.** the gate that opens into Heaven.
T-26.......V.3:4 And so is all time **p.**, and everything
T-26.......V.4:2 You think you live in what is **p.**. Each
T-26.....V.10:7 No **p.** illusions have the power to keep
T-26.....V.12:2 They come from what is **p.** and gone, and
T-26.....VII.7:2 errors seem forever **p.** the hope of healing,
T-27......VI.6:2 for what is **p.** forgiveness and is true. How
T-28.........I.2:5 selective as perception, being its **p.** tense.
T-28.........I.4:2 Yet this is not a memory of **p.** events, but
T-28.........I.4:3 believe that memory holds only what is **p.**
T-28.........I.6:6 be made in the present if its cause is **p.**.
T-28.........I.8:2 **p.** because He let It not be unremembered
T-28.......I.14:7 fear, and **p.** the world of sin entirely.
T-29.........I.3:3 The rest are **p.**, but this one still remains
T-29....VIII.6:2 idea there is a power **p.** omnipotence, a
T-30.......V.8:6 gratitude to you is **p.** your understanding,
T-30......VI.6:4 are harder to look **p.** than others are. It
T-31.......I.10:3 that echoes **p.** each seeming call to death,
T-31........II.2:9 before you can look **p.** them to the one
T-31.....VII.6:3 unless you choose to hold it **p.** the hope of
T-31..VIII.11:1 join with me in reaching **p.** temptation,
W-pI.......3.2:1 you clear your mind of all **p.** associations,
W-pI.......7.3:2 merely reviewing your **p.** experiences of
W-pI.......7.3:3 to the cup, too, based on **p.** experiences?
W-pI.......7.3:6 this cup is, except for your **p.** learning. Do
W-pI..........8.h My mind is preoccupied with **p.** thoughts
W-pI.......8.5:3 *my mind is preoccupied with* **p.** *thoughts.*
W-pI.....10.3:1 their **p.** rather than their present status.
W-pI.....21.2:2 your mind carefully for situations **p.**,
W-pI.....28.3:2 You are not defining it in **p.** terms. You
W-pI.....41.5:3 to get **p.** this dark and heavy cloud, and to
W-pI.....41.6:5 **p.** all the idle thoughts of the world. Try
W-pI.....41.7:3 You are trying to reach **p.** all these things.
W-pI.....44.7:2 and intrusion by quietly sinking **p.** them.
W-pI.....45.6:6 Then try to go **p.** all the unreal thoughts
W-pI.....47.4:1 Today we will try to reach **p.** your own
W-pI.....47.5:1 Now try to slip **p.** all concerns related to
W-pI.....49.4:3 Go **p.** all the raucous shrieks and sick
W-pI.....52.2:6 I see. There will be no **p.**, and therefore no
W-pI.....52.3:1 My mind is preoccupied with **p.** thoughts.
W-pI.....56.3:4 I may look **p.** it to the world that reflects
W-pI.....56.4:6 of Him will yet look **p.** all appearances,
W-pI.....66.3:1 Today we will try to go **p.** this wholly
W-pI.....67.3:1 and then try to reach **p.** all your images
W-pI.....67.4:3 perhaps you will succeed in going **p.** that,
W-pI.....69.2:4 We are trying to see **p.** the veil of darkness
W-pI.....69.5:4 attempt to go through them and **p.** them,
W-pI.....69.6:2 Determine to go **p.** the clouds. Reach out
W-pI.....70.8:4 It is **p.** the clouds and in the light beyond.
W-pI.....75.6:2 washed of all **p.** ideas and clean of every
W-pI.....92.4:1 these things by seeing **p.** appearances. It
W-pI.....94.4:1 aside; go **p.** the list of attributes, both
W-pI...106.3:2 lightly **p.** their meaningless persuasion.
W-pI...106.3:5 Go **p.** all things which do not speak of
W-pI...106.9:3 And when the hour is **p.**, you will again
W-pI...109.3:2 storms and strife, **p.** misery and pain, past
W-pI...109.3:2 past misery and pain, **p.** loss and death,
W-pI...109.5:1 pain, no fear of future and no **p.** regrets.
W-pI...131.6:3 is the great illusion it is **p.** or in the future.
W-pI.131.12:4 want, and only what lies **p.** it do you seek.
W-pI.131.14:2 and through His aid slip effortlessly **p.** it,
W-pI...134.3:2 as a vain attempt to look **p.** what is there;
W-pI.135.15:3 from **p.** events and previous beliefs. It
W-pI.135.16:3 Its **p.** experience directs its choice of what
W-pI.135.18:1 everything that happens, all events, **p.**,
W-pI.151.12:2 the world, **p.** every witness for unholiness,
W-pI...153.9:1 We look **p.** dreams today, and recognize
W-pI...155.6:4 for the road leads **p.** illusion now, while
W-pI...156.7:5 senseless, ancient dream that now is **p.**.
W-pI...157.2:3 and we catch a glimpse of what lies **p.** the
W-pI...163.8:9 And it is given us to look **p.** death, and see
W-pI...164.1:4 He looks **p.** time, and sees eternity as
W-pI...165.6:1 Now is all doubting **p.**, the journey's end
W-pI...169.1:3 It is **p.** learning, yet the goal of learning,
W-pI...169.6:4 beyond salvation; **p.** all thought of time,
W-pI.169.10:3 explain what is to come is **p.** already. Yet
Wi181-200 3:4 we now attempt to go **p.** all defenses for a
W-pI...181.1:4 and **p.** his seeming sins as well as yours.
W-pI...181.2:6 from what you see in others **p.** their sins.
W-pI...181.4:1 involvement with your **p.** and future goals
W-pI...181.5:6 We do not look to **p.** beliefs, and what we
W-pI...196.3:4 looking **p.** all thoughts of crucifixion and
W-pI...198.4:1 that leads out of disaster, **p.** all suffering,
W-pII .253.1:6 thus am I led **p.** this world to my creations
W-pII .284.1:8 these words today, and **p.** all reservations,
W-pII .....293.h All fear is **p.** and only love is here.
W-pII .293.1:1 All fear is **p.**, because its source is gone,

W-pII .293.1:3 with all my p. mistakes oppressing it, and
W-pII .293.2:3 *the present holds safe from all p. mistakes.*
W-pII .306.1:3 Today I can go p. all fear, and be restored
W-pII .308.1:2 If I elect to reach p. time to timelessness, I
W-pII .314.1:3 P. mistakes can cast no shadows on it, so
W-pII .314.2:2 *Your Hands, leaving behind our p. mistakes*
W-pII .316.1:2 Each one allows a p. mistake to go, and
W-pII .316.1:3 all time, and p. all time as well. My
W-pII ...11.4:3 Yet back of all our doubts, p. all our fears,
W-pII .336.1:2 what remains forever p. its highest reach.
W-pII ...14.3:5 a function that is p. the gate of Heaven.
M-2 ...........4:1 p. even the possibility of remembering.
M-4 ...... VI.1:8 of God finally agrees to look p. them, he
M-4 ....VIII.1:8 is willing to reconsider all his p. decisions,
M-10 .........3:3 an inconceivably wide range of things; p.,
M-10 .........4:8 He does know all the facts; p., present and
M-20 .........2:4 It brings with it no p. associations. It is a
C-4.............5:3 But forgiveness looks p. bodies. This is its
P-2.......VII.8:4 that brushes lightly p. all sickly dreams.
S-1........IV.3:5 the present from its chains of p. illusions;
S-2...........I.6:8 eyes that look p. error to the Christ in you
S-3...........I.2:4 goes irrevocably p. their grasping hands,

## pasts 1

T-18......III.7:6 what your separate p. would hinder. You

## path 28

T-8......... II.2:7 joyful if it leads you along your natural p.,
T-8......... II.4:4 leads you steadily along the p. of freedom
T-14......IV.6:2 being carried down a quiet p. in summer.
T-20......IV.8:5 will go before you making straight your p.
T-27.........I.1:4 But place no terror symbols on your p., or
T-28......VI.2:5 aimlessly the p. on which it has been set.
T-28......VI.2:6 And if that p. is changed, it walks as easily
T-29.........I.3:3 but this one still remains to block your p.,
T-29....... II.1:3 Why does an easy p., so clearly marked it
T-30....... V.7:3 Yet has their p. been surely set away from
T-31....IV.11:7 There *is* no p. that does not lead to Him.
W-pI...155.5:3 You walk this p. as others walk, nor do
W-pI...155.8:2 lighting up the p. of ransom from illusion
W-pI...155.9:1 yet carefully, because this p. is new to you
W-pI.155.12:7 way but this could be a p. that you would
W-pI...166.6:2 comes here has pursued the p. he follows,
WpI...rV.in5:4 was sent to open up the p. of light to us,
W-pI...195.5:2 walk the way of hatred and the p. of death
W-pI...196.7:2 if you want to go along this painful p..
W-pI...200.9:2 We go to Heaven, and the p. is straight.
WpI rVI.in.4:2 a shorter p. to the serenity and peace of
W-pII .....1.3:2 it sees as interfering with its chosen p..
W-pII .291.2:5 *Your Son along the quiet p. that leads to You*
W-pII .296.2:3 us, to seek and find the easy p. to God.
W-pII .324.1:2 *to take, and every step in my appointed p.. I*
M-19 .........2:5 The p. becomes quite different as one
M-27 .........1:6 waning in a certain way upon a certain p.,
S-2........III.4:2 God did not choose this sorry p. for you.

## pathetic 4

T-4.........in.3:7 Do not make the p. error of "clinging to
T-8........ IX.3:4 a p. way of trying not to see by rendering
W-pI...151.3:5 place p. faith in what your eyes and ears
M-16 .........9:3 seem frightening, but they are merely p..

## paths 4

T-5...........I.7:5 own integration toward the p. of creation.
W-pI...155.5:1 Between these p. there is another road
W-pI...155.7:2 and deprivation are p. that lead nowhere,
W-pI...157.3:1 though you will return to p. of learning.

## pathway 8

T-20...... II.8:12 only a p. to the open door of Heaven, the
T-31.......IV.9:3 No p. in the world can lead to Him, nor
W-pI.155.13:6 made your p. certain and your goal secure
W-pI...189.9:4 minds, His Love will blaze its p. of itself.
W-ep .........2:1 the p. of the sun laid down before it rises,
W-ep .........2:2 Indeed, your p. is more certain still. For it
M-19 .........2:7 when the p. ceases and time ends with it.
P-2..........II.5:7 Together they can find a p. out, for no

## pathways 5

T-31 .....IV.3:4 no way except the p. offered by the world.
T-31 .....IV.6:4 The search for different p. in the world is
T-31 ...... V.5:4 it guarantees the p. of the world are safely
W-pI...123.1:2 come to gentler p. and to smoother roads.
P-2.......VII.9:8 choice of p. that can ever lead to peace. O

## patience 30

T-5 .....VI.11:4 p. with your brother is your patience with
T-5 .....VI.11:4 with your brother is your p. with yourself.
T-5 .....VI.11:5 Is not a child of God worth p.? I have
T-5 .....VI.11:6 I have shown you infinite p. because my
T-5 .....VI.11:6 from Whom I learned of infinite p.. His
T-5 .....VI.11:7 speaking for p. towards the Sonship in
T-5 .....VI.12:1 infinite p. produces immediate effects.
T-5 .....VI.12:3 Infinite p. calls upon infinite love, and by
T-7 ......VII.7:3 teaching it with infinite p. born of the
T-7 ......VII.7:4 Every attack is a call for His p., since His
T-7 ......VII.7:4 His p. can translate attack into blessing.
T-11 .......II.5:8 You can safely trust His p., for He cannot
T-11 .......II.5:9 of God. Yet you need far more than p..
T-17 .......II.8:3 would not wait, although He waits in p..
T-17 .......II.8:4 Meet His p. with your impatience at delay
T19..IV.B.10:1 kind, infinite in its p. and wholly loving.
T-20 ...... V.3:5 never see it, but wait in p. for its coming.
T-22 .....VI.2:4 Holy Spirit waits in gentle p., as certain of
T-29 ........I.1:5 attack, and His eternal p. sometimes fail.
W-pI.....75.6:7 several times, slowly and in complete p.:
W-pI.....95.3:3 In p. and in hope we try again today.
W-pI. 152.12:1 In p. wait for Him throughout the day,
W-pI...182.7:6 His p. has no limits. He will wait until you
W-pII .234.2:2 *help we have received, for Your eternal p.,*
M-4 .......VIII.h Patience
M-4 ....VIII.1:2 P. is natural to the teacher of God. All he
M-4 ....VIII.1:9 P. is natural to those who trust. Sure of
M-17 .........8:4 it requires p. and abundant willingness.
P-2...........I.3:4 But He will wait, and His p. is infinite. His
S-2..........II.4:5 how good are you who bear with p. and

## patient 70

*See also* patient-therapist

T-4 ..........I.7:4 Teachers must be p. and repeat their
T-4 .........II.5:8 last. Be p. a while and remember that the
T-9 ........ V.1:6 attack is real for both himself and the p.,
T-9 ........ V.5:8 it is up to him to teach the p. what is real,
T-9 ........ V.8:3 being *for* him, it must also be for his p..
W-pI...140.1:5 so the p. now perceives himself as well.
M-5 ........II.2:3 forms. A p. decides that this is so, and he
M-5 ........II.2:6 Only the mind of the p. himself. The
M-5 ......II.2:12 The p. could merely rise up without their
M-5 ...... III.1:1 If the p. must change his mind in order
M-5 ...... III.2:3 question what the p. has accepted as true.
M-5 ...... III.2:5 They ask the p. for forgiveness for God's
M-6 ........... 1:4 of his errors in the mind of the p.,
M-6 ........... 1:5 himself, he has also accepted it for the p..
M-6 ........... 1:6 what if the p. uses sickness as a way of life
M-6 ........... 1:7 the p. might even try to destroy himself.
M-7 ........... 1:3 If the p. is healed, what remains to heal
M-7 ........... 1:8 He is now the p., and he must so regard
M-7 ........... 6:1 with the self to the exclusion of the p.. It
P-in ........... 1:8 the p. must be helped to change his mind
P-1............ 1:2 Its aim is to aid the p. in abandoning his
P-1............ 2:6 and helps the p. to recognize and accept it
P-1............ 3:2 p. often regards them in that way himself.
P-1............ 4:4 the p. cannot see himself as really capable
P-1............ 5:1 p. need not think of truth as God in order
P-2.........in.1:5 the p. deal with one fundamental error;
P-2.........in.2:7 The p. has already paid this price. Now he
P-2.........in.3:2 as the p. may cherish false self-concepts,
P-2.........in.3:3 p. hopes to learn how to get the changes
P-2...........I.1:4 therapist or p. has reached the next one,
P-2...........I.3:1 of a therapist as well as of a p.. Either way,
P-2...........I.3:6 Whatever resolutions p. and therapist
P-2...........I.4:2 for every "p." on the face of this earth, for
P-2...........I.4:2 except a p. could possibly have come here
P-2..........II.3:4 This is never apparent to the p., and only
P-2..........II.5:4 way, a union of purpose between p. and
P-2..........II.5:6 Teacher and pupil, therapist and p., are
P-2..........II.8:6 can teacher and pupil, therapist and p.,
P-2........ III.1:1 that he walks slightly ahead of the p., and
P-2........ III.2:1 as it is limited by those of the p.. The aim
P-2........ III.4:3 therapist cannot progress without the p.,
P-2........ III.4:3 and the p. cannot be ready to receive the
P-2........ III.4:6 The psychotherapist becomes his p.,
P-2..........V.2:3 the p. is persuaded to reverse his twisted
P-2..........V.6:3 The limits laid on both the p. and the
P-2........ VI.1:5 Healing occurs as a p. begins to hear the
P-2........ VI.6:3 therapist sees in the p. all that he has not
P-2........ VI.6:6 The p. is his screen for the projection of
P-2........ VI.7:5 in the p. and accepted in the therapist,
P-2....... VII.1:1 then, is the therapist, and who is the p.?
P-2....... VII.1:7 Each p. who comes to a therapist offers
P-2....... VII.1:9 to heal from each p. who comes to him.
P-2..... VII.1:10 He thus becomes his p.. God does not
P-2....... VII.2:9 replacing those with which the p. came to
P-2....... VII.3:1 p. that all his sins have been forgiven him,
P-2....... VII.3:6 capable of joining with the p. in a holy
P-2....... VII.9:9 O let your p. in, for he has come to you
P-3...........I.1:1 who is sent to you is a p. of yours. This
P-3..........II.1:3 which everyone is both p. and therapist in
P-3..........II.3:6 rise and grow; a p. will touch his heart,
P-3..........II.4:4 nor a perfect p. can possibly exist. Both
P-3..........II.5:1 from every meeting of p. and therapist.
P-3..........II.6:1 forgets to judge the p. that healing occurs.
P-3..........II.6:2 both p. and therapist may change their
P-3..........II.6:7 no p. can accept more than he is ready to
P-3..........II.9:4 the equality of himself and the p.. There
P-3........II.10:6 God that his p. be helped to join with him
P-3........ III.4:3 it is a right the therapist and p. share alike
P-3........ III.4:6 The therapist repays the p. in gratitude,
P-3........ III.4:6 in gratitude, as does the p. repay him.

## patient's 7

M-5...... III.1:2 do? Can he change the p. mind for him?
M-6 ........... 4:3 Spirit in the p. mind is seeking for him.
P-2.........in.3:1 p. goal and the therapist's are at variance.
P-2.........in.4:1 must want to change the p. self-concept
P-2........ IV.9:5 the p. most cherished possession; his
P-2........ IV.9:6 become the p. security as he perceives it,
P-2....... VII.4:5 His p. errors thus became his own failures

## patient-therapist 4

P-1............. 1:5 which an earthly p. relationship becomes
P-2..........VII.h The Ideal P. Relationship
P-2..... VII.1:13 is reflected in the ideal p. relationship.
P-2....... VII.2:9 "symptoms" of the ideal p. relationship,

## patiently 4

W-pI .... 75.7:8 Wait p. for Him. He will be there. The
W-pI .... 96.8:4 Wait p., and let Him speak to you about
W-pII . 357.1:3 *Voice instructs me p. to hear Your Word,*
P-2..........II.7:3 On the contrary, he listens p. to each one,

## patients 14

M-5...... III.1:6 These p. do not realize they have chosen
P-2.........in.2:1 P. do not enter the therapeutic
P-2.........in.4:4 it is inevitable that p. and therapists alike
P-2...........I.4:5 there are p. who need him just that way.
P-2........ III.4:6 working through other p. to express his
P-2........ VI.7:4 Their p. can but be seen as the bringers of
P-2....... VII.6:7 His p. are God's saints, who call upon his
P-2....... VII.7:3 healer cannot but be fearful of his p., and
P-3.............I.h The Selection of P.
P-3...........I.3:1 p. need not be physically present for you
P-3...........I.4:3 and his p. are the means sent to him for
P-3..........II.5:6 and many of their p. would not be able to
P-3..........II.9:9 Many p., too, consider this strange

P-3 III.3:3 give. **P.** can pay only for the exchange of

## patronage 1

S-3 III.2:5 the one who stands beneath him in his **p.**.

## pattern 4

*See also* out-of-pattern
T-14 X.5:1 changing **p.** that never rests and is never
W-pI 29.4:1 for today should follow a now familiar **p.**:
M-9 1:5 is, however, no set **p.**, since training is
M-16 5:7 It sets your mind into a **p.** of rest, and

## patterning 1

W-pI 186.9:5 leaves that form a **p.** an instant, break

## patterns 6

T-14 X.5:3 alternating **p.** of light and darkness sweep
T-18 I.7:7 and totally meaningless **p.** that need not
W-pI 70.8:6 the cloud **p.** you imagined that endured,
W-pI 131.7:1 ways; its shifting **p.** and uncertain goals,
W-pI 185.3:5 gainer merely shift about in changing **p.**,
P-2 I.2:7 shadows, or perhaps different cloud **p.**.

## pause 20

T-3 I.1:8 Yet the real Christian should **p.** and ask,
T19 IV.A.6:1 a little **p.** of gladness in acknowledgment
T-22 II.7:7 ground where you can **p.** uncertainly,
T-26 II.4:8 He does not **p.** to judge whether the hurt
T-27 II.9:8 be delayed because you **p.** to listen to
T-28 I.11:4 no **p.** in time to cause the miracle delay in
T-31 I.2:8 **p.** in diligence to judge it hard to learn or
T-31 II.6:1 Before you answer, **p.** to think of this: *The*
W-pI 44.9:1 **p.** long enough to repeat today's idea,
W-pI 102.5:3 five-minute rests, **p.** frequently today, to
W-pI 106.9:3 who **p.** to ask that truth be given them,
W-pI 108.9:1 Say each one slowly and then **p.** a while,
W-pI 128.6:1 **P.** and be still a little while, and see how
W-pI.131.13:3 will make you **p.** before you realize the
W-pI 135.3:5 Is it not strange you do not **p.** to ask, as
W-pI 151.2:4 when you **p.** to recollect how frequently
W-pI.153.14:1 We **p.** but for a moment more, to play
W-pI.153.19:6 We will **p.** a moment, as He tells us, "I am
W-pI.155.12:2 **P.** and reflect on this. Could any way be
W-pII..238.2:1 **p.** to think how much our Father loves us.

## pauses 2

W-pI 188.3:2 It **p.** to caress each living thing, and leaves
M-15 1:10 him. Time **p.** as eternity comes near, and

## pave 1

W-pI.195.10:1 Our gratitude will **p.** the way to Him, and

## paves 3

T-30 I.8:3 and **p.** the way for the next easy step.
W-pII 13.1:6 it **p.** the way for the return of timelessness
M-4 X.2:10 It **p.** the way for what goes far beyond all

## pay 20

T-9 II.9:5 There is a price you will **p.** for judgment,
T-9 II.9:6 of a price. And as you set it you will **p.** it.
T-12 IV.6:3 **p.** no price for life for that was given you,
T-12 IV.6:3 given you, but you do **p.** a price for death,
T-12 VI.5:2 the cost of sleeping, and refuse to **p.** it.
T-15 X.5:12 someone must **p.** and someone must get.
T-18 V.7:1 glad that he can **p.** his debt by bringing
T19 IV.A.2:3 to be the cost you are so unwilling to **p.**?
T-21 II.1:5 judgment, to be too much to **p.** for peace.
T-25 VII.11:5 **p.** exact amount in blood and suffering.
T-27 I.7:6 death will **p.** the price for all of them, if
T-27. VIII.12:6 Yet to its witnesses you **p.** no heed at all.
T-30 V.9:10 and what you **p.** for is not happiness. Be
T-30 V.10:6 that he will **p.** the cost as well as you. For
W-pII..323.2:1 And as we **p.** the debt we owe to truth,–
M-5 I.1:3 price to **p.** for something of greater worth
P-3 III.1:1 No one can **p.** for therapy, for healing is
P-3 III.3:3 can **p.** only for the exchange of illusions.
P-3 III.6:1 be turned away because he cannot **p.**. No
S-2 III.1:2 for proof of innocence, nor **p.** of any kind.

## paying 5

T-9 II.10:1 If **p.** is equated with getting, you will set
T-9 II.10:3 If **p.** is associated with giving it cannot be
T-9 III.6:8 You will not escape **p.** the price for this,
T-13 IV.4:4 the notion of **p.** for the past in the future,
T-20 VI.11:7 spend this instant **p.** tribute to the body,

## payment 14

T-15 X.6:2 And the **p.** does not seem to be yours.
T-15 X.6:3 the ego does demand **p.** it never seems to
T-21 III.1:4 sometimes demanding **p.** of yourself,
T-25 VIII.4:6 It is a **p.** offered for the cost of sin, but not
T-25 VIII.4:7 another, to be laid beside your little **p.**, to
T-27 I.7:5 is their righteous **p.** for their little lives?
W-pI 37.2:2 demand **p.** of someone or something. As
W-pI 76.9:4 **P.** is neither given nor received. Exchange
P-3 III.h The Question of **P.**
P-3 III.1:4 need money it will be given him, not in **p.**
P-3 III.2:3 Holy Spirit asks some **p.** for His purpose.
P-3 III.2:6 There is a difference between **p.** and cost.
P-3 III.3:4 This, indeed, must demand **p.**, and the
P-3 III.7:1 This view of **p.** may well seem impractical

## pays 1

T-25. VIII.11:1 cares not who **p.** the cost of sin, so it be

## peace 999

T-in 2:4 ***unreal exists.*** Herein lies the **p.** of God.
T-1 IV.1:5 communion but will also understand **p.**
T-1 VI.1:1 who want **p.** can find it only by complete
T-1 VII.1:7 that you can relate in **p.** to God or to your
T-2 I.5:8 **P.** is an attribute *in* you. You cannot find it
T-2 I.5:11 Health is inner **p.**. It enables you to
T-2 II.1:8 equal power will inevitably destroy **p.**.
T-2 II.1:9 is why the Bible speaks of "the **p.** of God
T-2 II.1:10 **p.** is totally incapable of being shaken by
T-2 III.5:8 He gave them His **p.** so they could not be
T-2 VIII.2:8 if you are to bring **p.** to other minds.
T-3 I.5:3 are not in conflict, but naturally live in **p.**.
T-3 II.5:6 integration and establishes the **p.** of God.
T-3 III.6:2 knowledge will bring **p.** without question.
T-3 IV.7:16 God knows you only in **p.**, and this *is* your
T-3 VI.2:1 than to know is the cause of the loss of **p.**.
T-3 VI.3:1 the tremendous release and deep **p.** that
T-3 VI.10:1 **P.** is a natural heritage of spirit. Everyone
T-3 VI.10:6 is to deny yourself the reason for your **p.**,
T-3 VII.5:8 Your Self is still in **p.**, even though your
T-4 I.2:4 to enter into your ego you will find **p.**.
T-4 I.9:4 at **p.** because you are not fulfilling your
T-4 IV.9:3 Then let the Holy One shine on you in **p.**,
T-4 VI.3:3 that one choice brings **p.** and joy while
T-5 II.7:7 is always quiet, because It speaks of **p.**.
T-5 II.7:8 **P.** is stronger than war because it heals.
T-5 III.8:7 **P.** is the ego's greatest enemy because,
T-5 III.8:12 counters this welcome by welcoming **p.**.
T-5 III.8:13 Eternity and **p.** are as closely related as
T-5 III.9:4 just as the Holy Spirit is the symbol of **p.**.
T-5 III.10:6 home there, too, because it is a place of **p.**
T-5 III.10:6 it is a place of peace, and **p.** is of God. You
T-5 III.10:7 of God are not at home except in His **p.**. If
T-5 III.10:8 If **p.** is eternal, you are at home only in
T-5 IV.8:7 indeed depart in **p.** because I have loved
T-5 IV.8:10 I place the **p.** of God in your heart and in
T-5 V.2:4 to the ego because its **p.** is unassailable. It
T-5 VI.2:7 joy, viciousness for love, and pain for **p.**.
T-5 VII.3:3 He wills to keep it in perfect **p.**, because
T-5 VII.6:5 and give it over to the Atonement in **p.**.
T-5 VII.6:7 *decided wrongly, because I am not at* **p.**. *I*
T-5 VII.6:9 *decide otherwise, because I want to be at* **p.**. *I*
T-6 I.14:1 as the call for **p.** for which it was intended
T-6 I.15:2 "I come not to bring **p.** but a sword." This
T-6 II.1:2 The Wholeness of God, which is His **p.**,
T-6 II.12:7 The **p.** of God lies in that message, and so
T-6 II.12:7 message, and so the **p.** of God lies in you.
T-6 II.12:8 The great **p.** of the Kingdom shines in
T-6 III.4:3 The only way to have **p.** is to teach peace.
T-6 III.4:3 The only way to have peace is to teach **p.**.
T-6 III.4:4 By teaching **p.** you must learn it yourself,
T-6 IV.12:7 It could not shatter the **p.** of God, but it
T-6 V.B.h To Have **P.**, Teach Peace to Learn It
T-6 V.B.h To Have Peace, Teach **P.** to Learn It
T-6 V.B.5:2 disagreement, **p.** of mind is impossible. If
T-6 V.B.5:4 it. Yet you do want **p.**, or you would not
T-6 V.B.5:4 called upon the Voice for **p.** to help you.
T-6 V.B.7:5 lesson is: *To have* **p.**, *teach peace to learn it.*
T-6 V.B.7:5 lesson is: *To have peace, teach* **p.** *to learn it.*
T-6 V.C.5:6 are teaching **p.** *because* you believe in it.
T-6 V.C.6:2 you teach, and that you want to learn **p.**.
T-7 I.5:6 The eternal are in **p.** and joy forever.
T-7 III.2:13 is "treacherous" to the ego is faithful to **p.**
T-7 III.3:2 as brothers, because only equals are at **p.**.
T-7 VI.h From Vigilance to **P.**
T-7 VI.7:5 essential. Vigilance has no place in **p.**. It is
T-7 VI.8:9 it. If they cannot coexist in **p.**, and if you
T-7 VI.8:9 coexist in peace, and if you want **p.**, you
T-7 VI.12:3 state because only **p.** can be extended.
T-7 VII.6:5 or you cannot learn of His **p.** and accept
T-7 VII.10:8 Him. The **p.** of God is understanding this.
T-7 IX.4:7 is why there is perfect **p.** in the Kingdom.
T-7 IX.4:8 and only complete fulfillment is **p.**.
T-7 IX.6:8 His, It extends forever and in perfect **p.**.
T-7 IX.7:1 which maintain It in wholeness and **p.**.
T-7 XI.3:3 it protect his **p.** and shine love upon him?
T-8 I.1:2 course. **P.** is. This is the prerequisite for
T-8 I.1:3 **p.** is the condition of knowledge because
T-8 I.2:6 not want them on the basis of loss of **p.**,
T-8 I.3:1 to war, and war does deprive you of **p.**.
T-8 I.3:3 of reality that you must make to secure **p.**,
T-8 I.3:4 perceive as opponents are part of your **p.**,
T-8 I.3:7 When you give up **p.**, you are excluding
T-8 II.7:2 in strength and in love and in **p.**. It has no
T-8 III.2:1 only joy and **p.** that can be fully known,
T-8 IV.1:1 God's Will for you is complete **p.** and joy,
T-8 IV.1:3 not at **p.** it can only be because you do not
T-8 IV.1:5 in all. His **p.** is complete, and you must be
T-8 IV.3:11 you, so we can teach them **p.** and union.
T-8 IV.4:1 the world needs **p.** as much as you do? Do
T-8 V.1:1 from your identification and be at **p.**?
T-8 V.4:5 I bring God's **p.** back to all His children
T-8 V.5:5 intrudes anywhere along the road to **p.**, it
T-8 VII.4:9 you to hatred and attack and loss of **p.**.
T-8 IX.3:5 "Rest in **p.**" is a blessing for the living, not
T-8 IX.4:9 can rest in **p.** only because you are awake.
T-9 VII.2:3 This, then, is where **p.** abides. And you
T-9 VII.2:4 And you abide in **p.** when you so decide.
T-9 VII.2:5 in **p.** unless you accept the Atonement,
T-9 VII.2:5 because the Atonement *is* the way to **p.**.
T-10 in.3:9 When anything threatens your **p.** of mind
T-10 II.2:2 lie joy and **p.** and the glory of creation.
T-10 II.6:1 your **p.** of mind you could not make such
T-10 II.6:3 want something other than **p.** of mind,
T-10 III.6:6 When I said, "My **p.** I give unto you," I
T-10 III.6:7 **P.** comes from God through me to you. It
T-10 III.7:1 is sick it is because he is not asking for **p.**,
T-10 III.7:2 acceptance of **p.** is the denial of illusion,
T-10 III.8:2 You could accept **p.** now for everyone,
T-10 III.10:6 honor where it is due, and **p.** will be yours
T-10 III.11:1 Only at the altar of God will you find **p.**.
T-10 IV.4:1 your mind at **p.** because peace is His Will,
T-10 IV.4:1 your mind at peace because **p.** is His Will,
T-10 IV.4:10 "given" your **p.** to the gods you made, but
T-10 IV.6:7 **P.** is yours because God created you. And
T-10 V.7:7 Look with **p.** upon your brothers, and
T-11 III.1:5 attack and His **p.** surrounds you silently.
T-11 III.6:3 Him, and accept His Will for you in **p.**.

T-11...... III.7:2 He waits to give you the **p.** that is yours.
T-11...... III.7:3 yours. Give His **p.**, that you may enter the
T-11...... III.7:7 He Himself dwells there and abides in **p.**.
T-11...... IV.2:5 His, and join with your brothers in His **p.**.
T-11...... IV.3:1 Your **p.** lies in its limitlessness. Limit the
T-11...... IV.3:2 Limit the **p.** you share, and your Self must
T-11...... IV.7:5 perfect as His Creator and at **p.** with Him.
T-11...... IV.8:4 **P.** be unto you who rest in God, and in
T-11...... VI.7:1 will not find **p.** until you have removed
T-11..VIII.14:3 at your fears and replace them with **p.**.
T-12....... II.5:5 end of strife and this is the journey to **p.**.
T-12....... II.7:6 not know that I walked with Him in **p.**?
T-12....... II.7:7 mean that **p.** goes with *us* on the journey?
T-12....... II.9:3 you in the **p.** out of which He was created.
T-12....... III.5:1 for the mind, and it is attained through **p.**
T-12.... III.10:8 dwell in **p.** and where you are welcome,
T-12.... III.10:8 look out in **p.** and behold the world truly.
T-12...... VI.5:8 perfect **p.** He waits for you at His Father's
T-12... VII.4:10 For this belief is the destruction of **p.**, a
T-12... VII.10:3 bring you **p.** *if you really looked upon it.* If
T-12... VII.10:6 For we are there in the **p.** of the Father,
T-12... VII.10:6 Who wills to extend His **p.** through you.
T-12... VII.11:1 mission to extend **p.** you will find peace,
T-12... VII.11:1 mission to extend peace you will find **p.**,
T-12.... VIII.1:7 remain hidden, for it can live only in **p.**.
T-12.... VIII.2:2 His Father's Love holds him in perfect **p.**,
T-13......... I.1:2 that he may remember his Father in **p.**.
T-13......... I.1:3 **P.** and guilt are antithetical, and the
T-13......... I.1:3 the Father can be remembered only in **p.**.
T-13....... II.7:1 that its goal for you is happiness and **p.**.
T-13....... III.9:1 magnitude of your Father in **p.** and joy.
T-13.... III.10:2 were at **p.** until you asked for special favor
T-13.... III.10:5 And the **p.** of God's Son was shattered,
T-13.... III.11:1 In **p.** he needed nothing and asked for
T-13.... III.11:3 except by departing in **p.** and returning to
T-13.... III.11:4 If the Son did not wish to remain in **p.**, he
T-13.... III.12:3 knowing that your **p.** lies in His Oneness?
T-13....... V.7:7 come forth from your private world in **p.**.
T-13...... VI.9:6 And in Him you are answered by His **p.**.
T-13.... VI.10:8 You have established them as guides to **p.**
T-13..... VII.6:6 errors for the **p.** of God is but *your* will.
T-13..... VII.7:4 Disturbance of his **p.** can never be. In
T-13..... VII.8:1 **p.** of God passeth your understanding
T-13..... VII.9:1 will first dream of **p.**, and then awaken to
T-13... VII.13:7 for light needs nothing but to shine in **p.**,
T-13... VII.15:1 **p.** of mind this world may set before you.
T-13... VII.15:3 undertake a quiet journey to the **p.** of God
T-13... VII.16:4 the **p.** of mind that we must find together.
T-13... VII.16:8 My **p.** I give you. Take it of me in glad
T-13...... IX.7:6 shining in quiet and in **p.** upon the altar
T-13....... X.3:2 will you find satisfaction and **p.** with him,
T-13....... X.5:3 past, and give your mind in **p.** over to the
T-13....... X.9:4 shining **p.** within you is the perfect purity
T-13....... X.11:7 himself as guiltless and in the **p.** of God. If
T-13....... X.11:8 If he is guiltless and in **p.** and sees it not,
T-13......... XI.h The **P.** of Heaven
T-13...... XI.1:1 and harsh intrusion of guilt on **p.**. Yet no
T-13...... XI.1:3 a war would surely end his **p.** of mind,
T-13.... XI.3:13 a sense of **p.** so deep that no dream in this
T-13...... XI.4:1 Nothing in this world can give this **p.**, for
T-13...... XI.5:5 done. You will find the **p.** in which He has
T-13...... XI.5:6 is invariable as the **p.** in which you dwell,
T-13...... XI.7:3 prevail against the **p.** God wills for you.
T-13...... XI.8:2 belief does interfere with the deep **p.** in
T-13...... XI.8:4 **P.** will be yours because His peace still
T-13...... XI.8:4 Peace will be yours because His **p.** still
T-13...... XI.8:4 flows to you from Him Whose Will is **p.**.
T-13.... XI.11:2 for your reconciliation to sanity and to **p.**.
T-13.... XI.11:8 only truth, in which the **p.** of Heaven lies.
T-14...... III.3:9 *Let me bring* **p.** *to God's Son from his Father.*
T-14.... III.10:6 coming as naturally as **p.** that knows no
T-14.... III.12:4 true. **P.** abides in every mind that quietly
T-14.... III.14:4 and will decide against your **p.** as surely
T-14.... III.14:7 your salvation and the **p.** of God in you.
T-14.... III.15:8 his abode was fixed in perfect **p.** forever.
T-14....... V.6:5 straight to Heaven, and the **p.** of God.
T-14....... V.7:1 that cannot fail and must result in **p.**. No
T-14....... V.7:7 bring within its safety and its perfect **p.**.
T-14....... V.8:1 **P.**, then, be unto everyone who becomes

T-14 ...... V.8:1 everyone who becomes a teacher of **p.**.
T-14 ...... V.8:2 For **p.** is the acknowledgment of perfect
T-14 ...... V.8:6 you in the safety of its **p.** and holiness.
T-14 ...... V.9:4 I stand within the circle, calling you to **p.**.
T-14 ...... V.9:5 Teach **p.** with me, and stand with me on
T-14 ...... V.9:7 not that you cannot teach His perfect **p.**.
T-14 ..... V.11:7 out in **p.** on all who think they are outside
T-14 ..... V.11:9 in the holy place of **p.** which is for all of us
T-14 ..... V.11:9 of us, united as one within the Cause of **p.**
T-14 .. VII.5:11 delay in your return to **p.** by wondering
T-14 ....... X.1:6 Reflect the **p.** of Heaven here, and bring
T-14 ...... XI.5:2 even think of you share in your perfect **p.**,
T-14 ...... XI.5:4 The absence of perfect **p.** means but one
T-14 ...... XI.6:6 **p.** is threatened or disturbed in any way,
T-14 ... XI.12:4 until you pass the test of perfect **p.**, for
T-14 ... XI.12:4 for **p.** and understanding go together and
T-14 ... XI.13:2 all. For this it must be **p.** they want, and
T-14 ... XI.13:3 think you know, **p.** will depart from you,
T-14 ... XI.13:3 you have abandoned the Teacher of **p.**.
T-14 ... XI.13:4 realize that you know not, **p.** will return,
T-14 ... XI.14:1 want **p.** you must abandon the teacher of
T-14 ... XI.14:2 The Teacher of **p.** will never abandon you
T-14 ... XI.14:6 He gives the gift of **p.** to everyone who
T-14 ... XI.14:6 to everyone who perceives the need for **p.**,
T-14 ... XI.14:7 it. Make way for **p.**, and it will come. For
T-14 ... XI.14:8 is in you, and from it **p.** must come.
T-14 ... XI.15:5 that nothing will prevail against your **p.**.
T-15 ........ I.3:5 for you to find **p.** even in death, it offers
T-15 ........ I.6:3 is hidden a far more insidious threat to **p.**.
T-15 ........ I.6:7 can believe that punishment will end in **p.**
T-15 ........ I.9:4 time as a teaching aid to happiness and **p.**
T-15 ....... I.14:2 perfect **p.** and perfect love for everyone,
T-15 ....... II.1:7 quickly offer you the whole lesson of **p.**.
T-15 ....... II.2:2 of **p.** is eternal *because* it is without fear. It
T-15 ...... III.1:6 world in the belief that it will bring you **p.**
T-15 ...... III.2:2 Choose littleness and you will not have **p.**,
T-15 ...... III.8:4 you must be worthy of the Prince of **P.**,
T-15 ...... III.9:1 holiness can content you and give you **p.**?
T-15 ...... III.9:6 where holiness abides in perfect **p.**. My
T-15 ... III.10:2 His Will is constant and at **p.** forever with
T-15 ... III.11:1 and unwilling to attempt to grasp for **p.**
T-15 ... III.12:5 it protects only the **p.** in which He dwells.
T-15 ...... IV.2:7 you, and nothing else can bring you **p.**.
T-15 ...... IV.2:8 For **p.** is of God, and no one beside Him.
T-15 ...... IV.4:3 For there lies **p.**, perfectly clear because
T-15 ...... VI.1:2 part of a relationship and find **p.** within it
T-15 ...... VI.4:7 Herein lies **p.**, for here there *is* no conflict.
T-15 ...... VI.5:1 love has no meaning and **p.** is impossible.
T-15 ...... VI.7:1 It is through *us* that **p.** will come. Join me
T-15 ...... VI.7:2 Join me in the idea of **p.**, for in ideas
T-15 ... VIII.2:9 then, in **p.** from guilt to God and them.
T-15 ....... X.6:1 you want, and thereby purchase **p.**. And
T-15 ....... X.9:8 demand for sacrifice and the **p.** of God.
T-15 ...... XI.4:2 brings guilt as surely as love brings **p.**.
T-15 ...... XI.4:3 as **p.** is the condition for the awareness of
T-15 ...... XI.4:5 **p.** you invite them back, realizing that
T-15 ...... XI.4:7 loathsome, and live within himself in **p.**?
T-15 ...... XI.7:1 where there is communication there is **p.**.
T-15 ...... XI.7:2 The Prince of **P.** was born to re-establish
T-15 ...... XI.7:6 everything, and in the **p.** it re-establishes,
T-15 ...... XI.8:2 from joy. Let us join in celebrating **p.** by
T-16 ........ I.5:7 His, for this will never bring **p.** to anyone.
T-16 ....... II.7:1 increase and **p.** will grow with its increase
T-16 ....... II.9:7 year invest in truth, and let it work in **p.**.
T-16 ...... III.1:7 results have been to bring **p.** where there
T-16 ...... IV.2:5 safety, translated quietly from war to **p.**.
T-16 ...... IV.4:8 but not in the **p.** in which it would gladly
T-16 ...... IV.6:6 Yet **p.** will never come from the illusion of
T-16 ...... IV.9:2 Fear not to cross to the abode of **p.** and
T-16 ..... VII.6:5 and the **p.** of *now* enfold you in perfect
T-17 ........ I.6:5 you become disturbed and lose your **p.** of
T-17 ....... II.7:2 that he has always rested there in **p.**. Even
T-17 ... III.10:8 in the Name of God and bring you **p.**,
T-17 ... III.10:8 you peace, that you may offer **p.** to me.
T-17 ... IV.16:2 Let us ascend in **p.** together to the Father,
T-17 ...... VI.5:2 truth and sanity, its outcome must be **p.**.
T-17 ...... VI.5:4 *is.* If **p.** is the condition of truth and sanity,
T-17 ...... VI.5:4 be without them, where **p.** is they must be
T-17 ...... VI.5:6 If you experience **p.**, it is because the

T-17 ..... VI.5:7 the outcome *because* you are at **p.**. Here
T-17 ..... VI.7:3 And **p.** will not be experienced except in
T-17 ..... VI.7:6 and the illusion of **p.** is not the condition
T-17 .... VII.4:5 that **p.** and faith will not come separately.
T-17 .... VII.5:9 Accept not the illusion of **p.** it offers, but
T-17 .. VII.10:6 it, for it calls you to salvation and to **p.**.
T-17 ...... VIII.h The Conditions of **P.**
T-17 ... VIII.1:6 on it. It is a situation of perfect **p.**, simply
T-17 ... VIII.2:4 every situation and bring you **p.**. Not
T-17 ... VIII.2:6 secure for you the faith you need for **p.**.
T-17 ... VIII.6:1 you became a giver of **p.** as surely as your
T-17 ... VIII.6:1 as surely as your Father gave **p.** to you.
T-17 ... VIII.6:2 goal of **p.** cannot be accepted apart from
T-18 ...... I.10:9 Let us join in Him in **p.** and gratitude,
T-18 ...... I.12:3 what became of **p.** in those who heard?
T-18 ...... I.13:5 **p.** of God is given you with the glowing
T-18 ..... IV.4:4 to you to establish the conditions for **p.**.
T-18 ....... V.6:3 that whatever threatens the **p.** of one is an
T-18 ....... V.7:6 *may descend on us, and keep us both in* **p.**.
T-18 . VI.11:10 You have escaped from fear to **p.**, asking
T-18 ... VI.13:6 space, the sudden experience of **p.** and joy
T-18 ... VI.14:5 of refuge, where you can be yourself in **p.**.
T-18 ... VI.14:7 For **p.** will join you there, simply because
T-18 ... VI.14:7 you, in answer to its gentle call to be at **p.**.
T-18 .... VII.5:7 **p.** comes at last to those who wrestle with
T-18 . VIII.11:1 it into a garden of **p.** and welcome. Love's
T-18 ... IX.14:5 *now.* And it is there that **p.** awaits you.
T-19 ............. h THE ATTAINMENT OF **P.**
T-19 ........ I.1:1 dedicated wholly to truth, **p.** is inevitable.
T-19 ........ I.1:3 also said that **p.** without faith will never
T-19 ...... I.15:2 For faith brings **p.**, and so it calls on truth
T-19 ...... I.15:3 Truth follows faith and **p.**, completing the
T-19 ........ IV.h The Obstacles to **P.**
T-19 ..... IV.1:1 As **p.** extends from deep inside yourself
T-19 ..... IV.1:4 Yet **p.** will gently cover them, extending
T-19 ..... IV.1:6 The **p.** He lay, deep within you and your
T-19 ..... IV.2:2 the **p.** that already lies deeply within must
T-19 ..... IV.3:6 When the **p.** in you has been extended to
T19 ... IV.A.1:1 first obstacle that **p.** must flow across is
T19 ... IV.A.2:1 Why would you want **p.** homeless? What
T19 ... IV.A.2:8 He would bring **p.** to everyone, and how
T19 . IV.A.2:10 the **p.** in you encounters in its going forth.
T19 ... IV.A.3:1 Spirit's purpose rests in **p.** within you. Yet
T19 ... IV.A.4:3 **P.** could no more depart from you than
T19 ... IV.A.4:6 **P.** will flow across it, and join you without
T19 . IV.A.4:11 away so quietly beneath the wings of **p.**.
T19 . IV.A.4:12 **p.** will send its messengers from you to all
T19 ... IV.A.8:2 It is no longer an unrelenting barrier to **p.**
T19 ... IV.B.1:1 We said that **p.** must first surmount the
T19 ... IV.B.1:2 of guilt holds sway, **p.** is not wanted. The
T19 ... IV.B.1:3 second obstacle that **p.** must flow across,
T19 ... IV.B.2:1 value that you think **p.** would rob you of.
T19 ... IV.B.2:3 for which you would deny a home to **p.**.
T19 ... IV.B.3:1 to join in holy communion and be at **p.**.
T19 ... IV.B.4:1 **P.** is extended from you only to the
T19 ... IV.B.4:4 want neither to get rid of **p.** nor limit it.
T19 ... IV.B.4:5 that you would interpose between **p.** and
T19 ... IV.B.5:1 nothing you have paid for brought you **p.**.
T19 ... IV.B.5:5 to let **p.** through to bless the tired world!
T19 ... IV.B.7:5 gratitude for giving **p.** its home in Heaven
T19 ... IV.B.9:2 And to accept the **p.** He gives instead,
T19 ... IV.B.9:5 If **p.** is homeless, so are you and so am I.
T19 ... IV.B.9:8 you forever be a wanderer in search of **p.**?
T19 ... IV.B.9:9 your hope of **p.** and happiness in what
T19 . IV.B.10:2 It will accept you wholly, and give you **p.**.
T19 . IV.B.10:3 only with what already is at **p.** in you,
T19 . IV.B.10:4 body can bring you neither **p.** nor turmoil
T19 . IV.B.10:9 **P.** and guilt are both conditions of the
T19 . IV.B.15:3 this is not so, but as the "enemy" of **p.**, it
T19 ... IV.C.1:3 the third obstacle that **p.** must flow across
T19 ... IV.C.3:2 madness and set against the **p.** of Heaven
T19 ... IV.C.7:5 **p.** must flow across seems to be very great
T19 . IV.C.10:3 can enter and disturb the **p.** of sinlessness
T19IV.C.11:10 *me how* ***not*** *to make of it an obstacle to* **p.**,
T19 .. IV.D.1:5 **p.** must still surmount a final obstacle,
T19 .. IV.D.2:2 **p.** will lightly brush the veil aside and run
T19 .. IV.D.5:1 Every obstacle that **p.** must flow across is
T19 .. IV.D.5:3 The desire to get rid of **p.** and drive the
T19 .. IV.D.8:3 to **p.** can be surmounted through its help.

T19.IV.D.19:4 is the **p.** of God, given to you eternally by
T-20.........I.1:3 For Easter is the sign of **p.**, not pain. A
T-20.........I.3:4 Help him to go in **p.** beyond it, with the
T-20........II.5:6 gleaming in the gentle glow of **p.** that
T-20........II.7:2 no strangers and no obstacles to **p.**. The
T-20.....II.8:12 and where we live in gentleness and **p.**, as
T-20.....II.10:1 the way to Heaven and to the **p.** of Easter,
T-20......III.9:6 him to Paradise, and know the **p.** of God.
T-20......IV.6:5 The ark of **p.** is entered two by two, yet
T-20......IV.8:1 may wonder how you can be at **p.** when,
T-20......IV.8:1 must be done before the way to **p.** is open
T-20........V.2:5 **P.** to your holy relationship, which has
T-20........V.3:6 worth when all you want for him is **p.**.
T-20........V.4:1 the worth of him who offers **p.** to you?
T-20........V.8:2 in his gentle hands in safety and in **p.**. Let
T-20......VI.9:4 which offers you **p.** and understanding?
T-20....VI.10:6 to receive you, and give you **p.** forever.
T-20... VIII.3:2 For **p.** will come to all who ask for it with
T-20. VIII.11:1 it change to sights of loveliness and **p.**;
T-21........II.1:5 judgment, to be too much to pay for **p.**.
T-21......IV.7:4 of another world, brings to it hope of **p.**.
T-21... VIII.2:8 **p.** must come to those who choose to heal
T-21... VIII.5:3 constant **p.** you could experience forever.
T-22.........I.9:8 his Self could be reborn in safety and in **p.**
T-22......III.3:1 but it makes way for **p.** and brings you to
T-22......III.3:2 and without a key, across the road to **p.**.
T-22......IV.3:5 and **p.** has reached you even here, before
T-22........V.2:8 sin is carved into a block out of your **p.**,
T-22........V.3:1 Yet how can **p.** be so fragmented? It is
T-22......VI.6:1 Child of **p.**, the light *has* come to you. The
T-22......VI.6:9 And no illusion can disturb the **p.** of a
T-22......VI.6:9 that has become the means of **p.**.
T-22......VI.8:3 This is your part in bringing **p.**. For you
T-22......VI.8:9 He will use every one of them for **p.**. Nor
T-22......VI.9:6 one and make of it a potent force for **p.**.
T-23.......in.2:5 He walks in **p.** who travels sinlessly along
T-23.........I.1:3 The means of war are not the means of **p.**,
T-23.........I.4:2 The journey's end is at the place of **p.**.
T-23.........I.4:3 not now accept the **p.** offered you here?
T-23.........I.4:4 intruder on your **p.** is here transformed,
T-23.........I.4:4 before your sight, into the giver of your **p.**
T-23....... I.7:10 untouched and quiet in the **p.** of God.
T-23.........I.8:9 turn in **p.** to the remembrance of God,
T-23.........I.9:6 quiet and at **p.** *because* it is His home.
T-23...... I.10:5 where God has set him in serenity and **p.**,
T-23...... I.10:7 You dwell in **p.** as limitless as its Creator,
T-23...... I.10:8 sure that its **p.** can never be disturbed.
T-23...... I.12:3 **P.**, looking on itself, extends itself. War is
T-23...... I.12:5 **P.** is the state where love abides, and
T-23...... I.12:6 Conflict and **p.** are opposites. Where one
T-23...... I.12:9 to be remembered when you side with **p.**.
T-23..... II.22:9 Is **p.** in your awareness? Are you certain
T-23......III.4:7 assault upon your **p.** in any form, if only
T-23......III.5:1 who believe that **p.** can be defended, and
T-23......III.5:3 some forms by which their **p.** is saved?
T-23......III.6:1 Mistake not truce for **p.**, nor compromise
T-23......IV.6:3 twinge of guilt, and above all, a loss of **p.**.
T-23......IV.6:7 the **p.** of God together with His Son.
T-24.......in.1:1 and the keeping of the state of **p.**. Given
T-24.......in.1:7 **P.** will be yours *because* it is His Will. Can
T-24.......in.2:7 There is no substitute for **p.**. What God
T-24.........I.1:5 And now must war, the substitute for **p.**,
T-24.........I.2:4 these hidden warriors to disrupt your **p.**.
T-24.........I.2:6 there. The secret enemies of **p.**, your least
T-24.........I.9:7 Never can there be **p.** among the different
T-24........II.2:1 of specialness is always at the cost of **p.**.
T-24........II.3:7 instead of Heaven and instead of **p.**, and
T-24........II.9:5 and in **p.** so real and so encompassing
T-24.....II.11:6 Heaven, with the hope of **p.** at last in sight
T-24.....II.14:2 will forever fail to bring you **p.** and joy of
T-24......III.6:6 Will it is you rest forever in the arms of **p.**
T-24......III.7:2 see. Freedom and **p.** and joy stand there,
T-24....IV.3:15 disturb your **p.** to enter and destroy.
T-24......IV.5:2 reality: When **p.** is not with you entirely,
T-24........V.2:1 the hope of **p.** and the escape from pain,
T-24........V.3:1 could your **p.** arise *but* from forgiveness?
T-24........V.3:3 He is at **p.** *because* He sees no sin. Identify
T-24......VI.1:1 and **p.** descends on it in gentleness and
T-24......VI.7:5 Where is your **p.** but in his holiness? And
T-24....VI.13:6 Out of His lack of conflict comes your **p.**.
T-25....... II.1:3 Perhaps you fancy to attain some **p.** and
T-25.......III.6:6 war he heard before are really calls to **p.**.
T-25.......III.7:8 This world has much to offer to your **p.**,
T-25.......III.7:9 to see **p.** and forgiveness descend on them
T-25.......IV.3:1 comfort in another world where **p.** abides
T-25.......IV.4:8 your **p.** can never fall away and leave you
T-25.......IV.4:9 offer **p.** to everyone have found a home in
T-25.....IV.4:10 enough to hold the world within its **p.**.
T-25........V.3:4 and join with him in innocence and **p.**.
T-25.......VII.9:6 a special function in the hope of **p.**, than
T-25...VII.12:4 rest in perfect confidence and perfect **p.**.
T-25. VIII.14:1 the right to all the universe; to perfect **p.**,
T-25.......IX.1:5 of this world in favor of the **p.** of Heaven.
T-25.......IX.6:9 in place of healing and return of **p.**?
T-25.......IX.7:4 His gift of healing and deliverance and **p.**.
T-25.......IX.7:8 and **p.** be scattered by the winds of hate.
T-26.........I.6:3 the rest his witness offers on behalf of **p.**.
T-26....VII.19:1 Abide in **p.**, where God would have you
T-26...VII.19:2 the **p.** in which your wishes are fulfilled.
T-26......IX.2:4 blessed it with Their innocence and **p.**.
T-27.......I.10:2 Here its **p.** can come, and perfect healing
T-27....... II.1:4 stand firmly in the way of trust and **p.**,
T-27....... II.1:4 that the damaged have no grounds for **p.**.
T-27.......III.7:6 the **p.** of power that opposes nothing. Yet
T-27.......IV.4:6 Which ones establish **p.** and offer joy?
T-27........V.3:2 conflict, and has reached to **p.**. It carries
T-27........V.3:3 It carries comfort from the place of **p.** into
T-27........V.4:6 for you have withheld its **p.** and comfort,
T-27.......V.11:1 **P.** be to you to whom is healing offered.
T-27.......V.11:2 And you will learn that **p.** is given you
T-27.......VII.8:5 as thoughtless of his **p.** and happiness as
T-27...VII.10:1 or death, waking or sleeping, **p.** or war,
T-27...VII.10:2 There is a risk of thinking death is **p.**,
T-27...VII.10:4 And death is opposite to **p.**, because it is
T-27...VII.10:5 life. And life is **p.**. Awaken and forget all
T-27...VII.10:6 and you will find you have the **p.** of God.
T-28.......I.13:3 the way of glad awakening to present **p.**.
T-29.........I.3:2 that **p.** must flow across has not yet gone.
T-29.........I.7:5 away, and leave you quietly alone in "**p.**."
T-29.........I.9:1 that happens when the gap is gone is **p.**
T-29........II.2:8 for glad rejoicing and for hope of **p.**.
T-29........II.3:1 find the hope of **p.** upon a battleground.
T-29........II.5:4 And nowhere else His gifts of **p.** and joy,
T-29........V.1:5 And where They are is Heaven and is **p.**.
T-29........V.2:4 The still infinity of endless **p.** surrounds
T-29........V.3:4 The **p.** in you can but be found in him.
T-29........V.3:5 wakening to **p.** eternal and to endless joy.
T-29........V.5:3 and where it lies in him behold your **p.**.
T-29........V.6:5 on Heaven itself, and hope to find its **p.**?
T-29........V.8:6 all dreams, unto the **p.** of everlasting life.
T-29......VI.1:2 much do you desire **p.** instead of endless
T-29......VI.1:4 Forgiveness is your **p.**, for herein lies the
T-29......VI.1:5 asks, and gladly offers **p.** instead of this.
T-29.....VII.1:3 and there can be no **p.** excepting there.
T-29.....VII.2:1 that will bring happiness and **p.** to him. If
T-29.....VII.6:2 It is vain to worship idols in the hope of **p.**
T-29... VIII.2:3 against your confidence and **p.** of mind.
T-29... VIII.2:7 lets you stand apart, in quiet and in **p.**.
T-29... VIII.5:4 of the gift of Heaven and eternal **p.**. The
T-29... VIII.6:5 does the changeless change; the **p.** of God
T-29... VIII.9:3 laugh, if idols could intrude upon his **p.**.
T-30......III.6:9 is forever One, eternally united and at **p.**.
T-30....III.10:3 near, it rests in certainty and perfect **p.**.
T-31.......I.11:5 call beyond it that appeals for **p.** and joy.
T-31.......I.11:6 And all the world will give you joy and **p.**.
T-31........II.3:4 to be the hope of satisfaction and of **p.**.
T-31........V.8:3 if any **p.** of mind is to be given you. Nor
T-31.....V.16:4 it will go at last, and leave your mind at **p.**
T-31.....VII.5:7 changed to one that brings the **p.** of God.
T-31.....VII.6:4 the function given you to bring you **p.**,
T-31.....VII.6:4 that you may offer **p.** to have it yours.
T-31... VIII.7:1 I lay before your feet the **p.** of God, and
T-31... VIII.7:1 and power to bring this **p.** to everyone
W-pI.......5.4:4 *are all equally disturbing to my* **p.** *of mind.*
W-pI.......6.3:3 *are all equally disturbing to my* **p.** *of mind.*
W-pI.....11.3:4 It contains the foundation for the **p.**,
W-pI.....14.3:6 is toward perfect safety and perfect **p.**.
W-pI.....16.3:1 thought you have brings either **p.** or war;
W-pI.....20.2:5 You want **p.**. You do not have them now,
W-pI.....22.1:6 What **p.** of mind is possible to him then?
W-pI........34.h I could see **p.** instead of this.
W-pI.....34.1:2 **P.** of mind is clearly an internal matter. It
W-pI.....34.1:4 It is from your **p.** of mind that a peaceful
W-pI.....34.5:1 your **p.** of mind is threatened in any way.
W-pI.....34.5:4 *I could see* **p.** *in this situation instead of what*
W-pI.....34.6:1 If the inroads on your **p.** of mind take the
W-pI.....34.6:4 *this situation, personality or event] with* **p.**.
W-pI.....41.4:4 go. Nothing can destroy your **p.** of mind
W-pI.....47.7:2 reached it if you feel a sense of deep **p.**,
W-pI.....47.7:4 is a place in you where there is perfect **p.**.
W-pI.....47.8:3 Remember that **p.** is your right, because
W-pI.....48.2:5 should anything disturb your **p.** of mind.
W-pI.....49.2:5 mind where stillness and **p.** reign forever.
W-pI.....49.4:4 Sink deep into the **p.** that waits for you
W-pI.....50.3:2 into a climate of perfect **p.** and safety. It
W-pI.....50.5:2 allow **p.** to flow over you like a blanket of
WpI...rI.in.5:1 You will yet learn that **p.** is part of you,
WpI...rI.in.5:2 you are, so that your **p.** is everywhere, as
W-pI.....52.1:4 Reality brings only perfect **p.**. When I am
W-pI.....53.2:5 I cannot live in **p.** in such a world. I am
W-pI.....55.2:6 give me the **p.** God intended me to have.
W-pI.....55.3:4 I will see a world of **p.** and safety and joy.
W-pI.....57.4:1 (34) I could see **p.** instead of this. When I
W-pI.....57.4:3 I will understand that **p.**, not war, abides
W-pI.....57.4:4 And I will perceive that **p.** also abides in
W-pI.....57.5:3 the **p.** of the world with my brothers, I
W-pI.....57.5:3 this **p.** comes from deep within myself.
W-pI.....59.1:4 when He rests in me in absolute **p.**? How
W-pI.....61.4:3 to the truth, and helps you depart in **p.**,
W-pI........63.h light of the world brings **p.** to every mind
W-pI.....63.1:1 have the power to bring **p.** to every mind!
W-pI.....63.3:4 *light of the world brings* **p.** *to every mind*
W-pI.....65.2:3 only way in which you can find **p.** of mind
W-pI.....65.3:3 It places the key to the door of **p.**, which
W-pI.....66.9:5 Did they bring you **p.**? We need great
W-pI.....68.3:2 certain that those who forgive will find **p.**.
W-pI.....68.6:4 at **p.** with everyone and everything, safe
W-pI.....70.2:1 nothing outside yourself can give you **p.**.
W-pI.....70.2:2 or disturb your **p.** or upset you in any way
W-pI.....72.8:3 has been ruinous to your **p.** of mind. You
W-pI.....74.1:5 **P.** has replaced the strange idea that you
W-pI.....74.2:1 There is great **p.** in today's idea, and the
W-pI.....74.2:5 experience the **p.** this recognition brings.
W-pI.....74.3:5 *I am at* **p.**. *Nothing can disturb me. My will is*
W-pI.....74.3:9 *are one. God wills* **p.** *for His Son.* During this
W-pI.....74.5:1 the **p.** to which your reality entitles you.
W-pI.....74.6:1 Joy characterizes **p.**. By this experience
W-pI.....74.6:5 if you do not experience the **p.** you seek.
W-pI.....74.7:3 *I seek His* **p.** *today.* Then try to find what
W-pI.....75.1:5 You are at **p.**, and you bring peace with
W-pI.....75.1:5 you bring **p.** with you wherever you go.
W-pI.....79.3:5 feel completely free of problems and at **p.**.
W-pI.....79.8:4 be brought together and you can be at **p.**.
W-pI.....79.9:5 resolved. In this recognition there is **p.**.
W-pI.....80.1:3 Therefore, you must be at **p.**. Salvation
W-pI.....80.3:1 You are entitled to **p.** today. A problem
W-pI.....80.3:6 the **p.** this simple statement brings.
W-pI.....80.4:1 will claim the **p.** that must be ours when
W-pI.....80.5:1 Now let the **p.** that your acceptance
W-pI.....80.5:4 that you are out of conflict; free and at **p.**.
W-pI.....81.1:5 In its **p.** let me remember Who I am.
W-pI.....82.1:1 light of the world brings **p.** to every mind
W-pI.....82.2:2 *Let* **p.** *extend from my mind to yours, [name*
W-pI.....87.1:6 I will experience the **p.** of true perception.
W-pI.....92.5:3 will for happiness and **p.** for everyone. It
W-pI.....92.9:3 in, for the **p.** of God is where your Self,
W-pI........93.h Light and joy and **p.** abide in me.
W-pI.....93.4:1 and that light and joy and **p.** abide in you
W-pI.....93.5:7 It does not hurt him, nor attack his **p.**. It
W-pI.....93.6:7 and light and joy and **p.** abide in you.
W-pI.....93.7:7 Light and joy and **p.** abide in you because
W-pI.....93.8:2 *Light and joy and* **p.** *abide in me. My*
W-pI.....93.9:8 joy and **p.** abide in you because this is so.
W-pI...93.10:4 hour: *Light and joy and* **p.** *abide in me. My*
W-pI...93.11:3 *Light and joy and* **p.** *abide in you. Your*
W-pI...95.10:2 creation, and limitless in power and in **p.**.
W-pI...95.11:2 *of creation, and limitless in power and in* **p.**.

| | |
|---|---|
| W-pI...95.12:1 | united and secure in light and joy and **p.**. |
| W-pI...95.14:8 | the gentle rustling of the wings of **p.**. |
| W-pI.....96.4:2 | serves the spirit is at **p.** and filled with joy. |
| W-pI.....96.4:5 | Without its function then it has no **p.**, |
| W-pI.....96.7:2 | in your mind, and offers it the way to **p.**. |
| W-pI...96.10:2 | Your Self will welcome it and give it **p.**. |
| W-pI.....97.1:4 | mind from conflict to the quiet fields of **p.** |
| W-pI.....97.2:2 | with all your Father's Love and **p.** and joy. |
| W-pI.....97.8:5 | else. The Holy Spirit gives you **p.** today. |
| W-pI.....98.6:2 | for **p.** of mind and certainty of purpose, |
| W-pI.....98.9:3 | and **p.** and trust will be His gifts; His |
| W-pI.....98.9:6 | you offer Him for timelessness and **p.**. |
| W-pI...99.10:1 | the truth of your completion, unity and **p.** |
| W-pI...100.6:3 | joy; no fear besets him to disturb his **p.**. |
| W-pI...100.6:5 | His **p.** to everyone who looks on you and |
| W-pI...101.7:3 | to go still faster to the waiting goal of **p.**. |
| W-pI...102.3:3 | Here is your **p.**, and here there is no fear. |
| W-pI...104.1:1 | that joy and **p.** are not but idle dreams. |
| W-pI...104.3:3 | *in truth, And joy and* **p.** *are my inheritance.* |
| W-pI...104.4:2 | where His gifts of **p.** and joy are welcome, |
| W-pI...104.5:1 | joy and **p.** belong to us as His eternal gifts |
| W-pI...104.5:5 | *truth. God's gifts of joy and* **p.** *are all I want.* |
| W-pI......105.h | God's **p.** and joy are mine. |
| W-pI...105.1:1 | God's **p.** and joy are yours. Today we will |
| W-pI...105.3:3 | Accept God's **p.** and joy, and you will |
| W-pI...105.4:1 | As Heaven's **p.** and joy intensify when |
| W-pI...105.4:1 | when you accept His joy and **p.** as yours. |
| W-pI...105.5:1 | Today accept God's **p.** and joy as yours. |
| W-pI...105.5:6 | Receive His gift of joy and **p.** today, and |
| W-pI...105.6:2 | by you the **p.** and joy that are their right |
| W-pI...105.7:2 | *My brother,* **p.** *and joy I offer you, That I may* |
| W-pI...105.7:2 | *That I may have God's* **p.** *and joy as mine.* |
| W-pI...105.7:4 | gift of **p.** and joy that God has given you. |
| W-pI...105.7:5 | the joy and **p.** you have denied yourself. |
| W-pI...105.7:6 | you can say, "God's **p.** and joy are mine," |
| W-pI...105.8:2 | have let all bars to **p.** and joy be lifted up, |
| W-pI...105.8:3 | tell yourself, "God's **p.** and joy are mine," |
| W-pI...105.9:6 | *My brother,* **p.** *and joy I offer you, That I may* |
| W-pI...105.9:6 | *That I may have God's* **p.** *and joy as mine.* |
| W-pI...106.2:1 | the way to **p.** to those who cannot see. Be |
| W-pI...107.2:3 | when nothing came to interrupt your **p.** |
| W-pI...107.9:6 | which will envelop you and give you **p.** so |
| W-pI...108.1:3 | is light except the resolution, born of **p.**, |
| W-pI...108.1:5 | And now you are at **p.** forever, for the |
| W-pI...108.3:2 | brings your **p.** of mind to other minds, to |
| W-pI...108.7:4 | we will attempt to offer **p.** to everyone, |
| W-pI...108.7:4 | and see how quickly **p.** returns to us. |
| W-pI...108.7:5 | and in that **p.** is vision given us, and we |
| W-pI...108.8:7 | *To everyone I offer* **p.** *of mind. To everyone I* |
| W-pI...109.1:2 | We ask for **p.** and stillness, in the midst of |
| W-pI...109.2:2 | to you the rest and quiet, **p.** and stillness, |
| W-pI...109.4:1 | This is the day of **p.**. You rest in God, and |
| W-pI...109.5:8 | to slip away from dreams and into **p.**. |
| W-pI...109.6:2 | to bring the **p.** of God into the world, that |
| W-pI...109.8:1 | You rest within the **p.** of God today, and |
| W-pI...109.8:2 | into the boundless circle of your **p.**, the |
| W-pI...109.9:1 | You rest within the **p.** of God today, |
| W-pI.110.11:7 | enter in the **p.** of God and His eternity. |
| WpI. rIII.in4:6 | And so accept their offering and be at **p.**. |
| WpIrIII.in10:5 | to rest a little time in silence and in **p.**. |
| WpIrIII.in10:6 | keep your **p.** throughout the day as well. |
| W-pI...112.1:1 | (93) Light and joy and **p.** abide in me. *I* |
| W-pI...112.1:2 | me. *I am the home of light and joy and* **p.**. *I* |
| W-pI...112.3:2 | Light and joy and **p.** abide in me. On the |
| W-pI...113.1:2 | *Serenity and perfect* **p.** *are mine, because I* |
| W-pI...118.1:1 | (105) God's **p.** and joy are mine. *Today I* |
| W-pI...118.1:2 | *Today I will accept God's* **p.** *and joy, in glad* |
| W-pI...118.1:2 | *that I have made for happiness and* **p.**. |
| W-pI...118.3:2 | God's **p.** and joy are mine. On the half |
| W-pI...121.1:1 | Here is the answer to your search for **p.**. |
| W-pI...121.1:3 | hopes of ever finding quietness and **p.**. |
| W-pI...121.2:1 | its wings in **p.** and soar above the turmoil |
| W-pI...122.1:2 | Do you want **p.**? Forgiveness offers it. Do |
| W-pI...122.2:4 | you another day of happiness and **p.**. All |
| W-pI...122.8:1 | upon a happy world of safety and of **p.**. |
| W-pI.122.11:2 | given you to feel the **p.** forgiveness offers, |
| W-pI...124.5:1 | of pain, and pain gives way to **p.**. We see |
| W-pI...124.5:2 | and **p.** of mind in which they were created |
| W-pI...124.8:1 | **P.** be to you today. Secure your peace by |
| W-pI...124.8:2 | Secure your **p.** by practicing awareness |
| W-pI.124.12:2 | *and my Self, in everlasting holiness and* **p.**. |
| W-pI...125.1:5 | No **p.** is possible until His Word is heard |
| W-pI...125.1:5 | must hear to usher in the quiet time of **p.**. |
| W-pI...125.4:2 | of salvation and the holy time of **p.**. We |
| W-pI...125.6:4 | is **p.** within you to be called upon today, |
| W-pI...125.8:3 | It is the Word of freedom and of **p.**, of |
| W-pI...126.2:4 | apart from condemnation and at **p.**. |
| W-pI...126.6:3 | It cannot give you **p.** as you perceive it. It |
| W-pI...129.1:3 | with joy, and capable of offering you **p.**. |
| W-pI.134.14:2 | meet with our reality in freedom and in **p.** |
| W-pI...135.6:2 | be at **p.** with such a concept of your home |
| W-pI.136.16:1 | **p.** and truth arise to take the place of war |
| W-pI.137.13:1 | for joy, and separation for the **p.** of God. |
| W-pI...140.5:1 | **P.** be to you who have been cured in God, |
| W-pI.140.10:4 | illusions end, and **p.** returns to the eternal |
| W-pI.140.12:4 | **p.** so deep that no illusion can disturb our |
| WpI. rIV.in5:1 | day can offer you in freedom and in **p.**. |
| WpI. rIV.in9:3 | the light, from grief to joy, from pain to **p.** |
| WpIrIV.in10:2 | in the **p.** wherein He wills you be forever, |
| W-pI.151.17:3 | truth has no illusions, and the **p.** of God, |
| W-pI...152.2:4 | Can pain be part of **p.**, or grief of joy? Can |
| W-pI.152.12:3 | the **p.** of God for all your frantic thoughts, |
| W-pI...153.1:5 | No **p.** of mind is possible where danger |
| W-pI...153.5:4 | the holy **p.** of God by your defensiveness. |
| W-pI.153.16:1 | Each hour adds to our increasing **p.**, as |
| W-pI.153.20:4 | because the love and strength and **p.** that |
| W-pI...156.8:2 | has ended doubting and established **p.**. |
| W-pI.158.10:5 | shine on you, and offer you the **p.** of God. |
| W-pI...164.4:2 | an ancient **p.** you carry in your heart and |
| W-pI...165.3:1 | Who would deny his safety and his **p.**, his |
| W-pI...165.3:1 | his joy, his healing and his **p.** of mind, his |
| W-pI...170.3:2 | at war with you, depriving you of **p.**, |
| W-pI...170.5:2 | your safety and protector of your **p.**, to |
| W-pI...170.9:2 | text has stressed about the obstacles to **p.**. |
| W-pI.170.12:3 | And now your heart remains at **p.** forever |
| W-pI.170.13:3 | *Your* **p.** *is ours. And we bless the world with* |
| W-pI.170.13:8 | *we see Your glory, and in them we find our* **p.** |
| Wi181-200 1:3 | **p.** such unified commitment will bestow, |
| Wi181-200 2:4 | freedom and of **p.** that comes as you give |
| W-pI...181.2:5 | the **p.** that comes from faith in sinlessness |
| W-pI...182.5:7 | be Himself, within the **p.** that is His home |
| W-pI...182.5:7 | resting in silence and in **p.** and love. |
| W-pI...182.7:7 | within you, calling you to let Him go in **p.** |
| W-pI...182.8:3 | Him in perfect stillness, silent and at **p.**, |
| W-pI.182.12:9 | go home with Him, and be at **p.** a while. |
| W-pI.183.11:6 | words could possibly convey, is **p.** eternal |
| W-pI.183.11:7 | Name, we would experience this **p.** today. |
| W-pI.184.15:8 | *the oneness which is our inheritance and* **p.**. |
| W-pI......185.h | I want the **p.** of God. |
| W-pI...185.2:4 | He wants the **p.** of God, and it is given |
| W-pI...185.4:6 | what bargain can give them the **p.** of God |
| W-pI...185.5:1 | the **p.** of God is to renounce all dreams. |
| W-pI...185.6:1 | it wants is **p.** must join with other minds, |
| W-pI...185.6:1 | minds, for that is how **p.** is obtained. And |
| W-pI...185.6:2 | And when the wish for **p.** is genuine, the |
| W-pI...185.7:2 | We want the **p.** of God. This is no idle |
| W-pI...185.8:8 | in place of Heaven and the **p.** of God?" |
| W-pI...185.9:4 | You choose God's **p.**, or you have asked |
| W-pI...185.9:6 | Yet will God's **p.** come just as certainly, |
| W-pI.185.10:1 | You want the **p.** of God. And so do all |
| W-pI.185.11:1 | truly seeks the **p.** of God can fail to find it. |
| W-pI.185.11:5 | is his to give? The **p.** of God is yours. |
| W-pI.185.12:1 | For you was **p.** created, given you by its |
| W-pI.185.14:2 | fail today as we request the **p.** of God be |
| W-pI...186.1:6 | save the world, restoring it to Heaven's **p.**. |
| W-pI...186.8:1 | And so we find our **p.**. We will accept the |
| W-pI......188.h | The **p.** of God is shining in me now. |
| W-pI...188.3:1 | The **p.** of God is shining in you now, and |
| W-pI...188.5:1 | The **p.** of God can never be contained. |
| W-pI...188.5:5 | The **p.** of God is shining in you now, and |
| W-pI...188.6:4 | and let your thoughts fly to the **p.** within. |
| W-pI...188.7:4 | God's **p.** is shining on them, but they |
| W-pI...188.7:5 | They lead you back to **p.**, from where they |
| W-pI...188.8:4 | For as the **p.** of God is shining in you, it |
| W-pI.188.10:1 | that the **p.** of God still shines in us, and |
| W-pI.188.10:6 | *The* **p.** *of God is shining in me now. Let all* |
| W-pI.188.10:7 | *Let all things shine upon me in that* **p.**, *And* |
| W-pI...189.3:5 | and **p.** offers its gentle light to everyone, |
| W-pI .. 189.4:2 | the quietness and **p.** that shines in them; |
| W-pI .. 190.4:1 | **P.** to such foolishness! The time has come |
| W-pI .. 190.9:1 | Heaven's **p.** holds all things still at last. |
| W-pI 190.11:2 | of sin, the **p.** of God instead of conflict, |
| W-pI .. 192.5:6 | the **p.** that God intended for His holy Son |
| W-pI 193.10:1 | seeming obstacles to **p.** in just one day. |
| W-pI 193.12:5 | in **p.** eternal in the world of time. |
| W-pI .. 194.1:3 | you to Heaven's gate; the quiet place of **p.**, |
| W-pI .. 194.7:6 | pain has found his way to present **p.**, and |
| W-pI .. 194.8:5 | world along with his, and offers **p.** to both |
| W-pI .. 195.3:1 | you see in him the rival for your **p.**; a |
| W-pI .. 195.7:3 | direct them to the **p.** that we would find, |
| W-pI .. 195.8:3 | What more remains as obstacles to **p.**? |
| W-pI 196.12:2 | between you and the holy **p.** of God. How |
| W-pI ..... 200.h | There is no **p.** except the peace of God. |
| W-pI ..... 200.h | There is no peace except the **p.** of God. |
| W-pI .. 200.1:2 | will not find **p.** except the peace of God. |
| W-pI .. 200.1:2 | will not find peace except the **p.** of God. |
| W-pI .. 200.1:5 | else for you to find except the **p.** of God, |
| W-pI .. 200.2:1 | what can only hurt; of making **p.** of chaos, |
| W-pI .. 200.3:1 | for eternal life in **p.** that has no ending. |
| W-pI .. 200.7:1 | There is no **p.** except the peace of God, |
| W-pI .. 200.7:1 | There is no peace except the **p.** of God, |
| W-pI .. 200.7:4 | Is it here that he would seek for **p.**? Or |
| W-pI .. 200.7:6 | on it another way, and find the **p.** of God. |
| W-pI .. 200.8:1 | **P.** is the bridge that everyone will cross, |
| W-pI .. 200.8:2 | But **p.** begins within the world perceived |
| W-pI .. 200.8:3 | **P.** is the answer to conflicting goals, to |
| W-pI .. 200.8:4 | where freedom lies within the **p.** of God. |
| W-pI 200.10:6 | **P.** is already recognized at last, and you |
| W-pI 200.11:2 | **P.** can not be found in them. The peace of |
| W-pI 200.11:3 | The **p.** of God is ours, and only this will |
| W-pI 200.11:4 | **P.** be to us today. For we have found a |
| W-pI 200.11:6 | For **p.** is union, if it be of God. We seek no |
| W-pI 200.11:9 | *There is no* **p.** *except the peace of God, And I* |
| W-pI 200.11:9 | *There is no peace except the* **p.** *of God, And I* |
| WpI.rVI.in.4:2 | shorter path to the serenity and **p.** of God |
| WpI.rVI.in.6:6 | Who instructs in quiet, speaks of **p.**, and |
| W-pI .. 205.1:1 | (185) I want the **p.** of God. *The peace of* |
| W-pI .. 205.1:2 | *The* **p.** *of God is everything I want. The peace* |
| W-pI .. 205.1:3 | *The* **p.** *of God is my one goal; the aim of all* |
| W-pI .. 208.1:1 | (188) The **p.** of God is shining in me now |
| W-pI .. 208.1:3 | *in that stillness we will find the* **p.** *of God. It is* |
| W-pI .. 220.1:1 | There is no **p.** except the peace of God. *Let* |
| W-pI .. 220.1:1 | There is no peace except the **p.** of God. *Let* |
| W-pI .. 220.1:2 | *Let me not wander from the way of* **p.**, *for I* |
| W-pI .. 220.1:3 | *home, and* **p.** *is certain as the Love of God.* I |
| W-pII .... in.1:4 | leave the world of pain, and go to enter **p.** |
| W-pII .... 221.h | **P.** to my mind. Let all my thoughts be |
| W-pII . 221.1:1 | *today to seek the* **p.** *that You alone can give. I* |
| W-pII . 221.2:6 | to let our thoughts be still and find His **p.**, |
| W-pII . 222.2:1 | *now, and ask to rest with You in* **p.** *a while.* |
| W-pII . 225.1:2 | *beloved, with fear behind and only* **p.** *ahead.* |
| W-pII . 225.2:3 | Now we follow it in **p.** together. You have |
| W-pII .... 230.h | Now will I seek and find the **p.** of God. |
| W-pII . 230.1:1 | In **p.** I was created. And in peace do I |
| W-pII . 230.1:2 | And in **p.** do I remain. It is not given me |
| W-pII . 230.1:4 | He created me He gave me **p.** forever. |
| W-pII . 230.2:1 | *I seek the* **p.** *You gave as mine in my creation.* |
| W-pII . 230.2:3 | *The* **p.** *in which Your Son was born into* |
| W-pII . 230.2:5 | *I need but call on You to find the* **p.** *You gave.* |
| W-pII ..... 2.1:4 | of conflict with the Thought of **p.**. |
| W-pII ..... 2.2:1 | Thought of **p.** was given to God's Son the |
| W-pII ..... 2.2:2 | before, for **p.** was given without opposite, |
| W-pII . 234.1:1 | we have reached the holy **p.** we never left. |
| W-pII . 234.1:4 | the **p.** of God the Father and the Son. This |
| W-pII . 239.2:3 | *You, at* **p.** *with all creation and ourselves.* |
| W-pII ..... 3.4:5 | And let Him give you **p.** and certainty, |
| W-pII . 243.1:6 | I look upon, to be in **p.** as God created us. |
| W-pII .... 245.h | Your **p.** is with me, Father. I am safe. |
| W-pII . 245.1:1 | *Your* **p.** *surrounds me, Father. Where I go,* |
| W-pII . 245.1:2 | *Where I go, Your* **p.** *goes there with me. It* |
| W-pII . 245.1:5 | *I give Your* **p.** *to those who suffer pain, or* |
| W-pII . 245.1:7 | *Let me bring Your* **p.** *with me. For I would* |
| W-pII . 245.2:1 | And so we go in **p.**. To all the world we |
| W-pII ..... 4.3:4 | love slain by hate, and **p.** to be no more. |
| W-pII . 251.1:9 | want. And now at last I find myself at **p.**. |
| W-pII . 251.2:1 | *And for that* **p.**, *our Father, we give thanks.* |
| W-pII .... 255.h | This day I choose to spend in perfect **p.**. |

| | |
|---|---|
| W-pII..255.1:1 | me that I can choose to have but **p.** today. |
| W-pII..255.1:4 | And let the **p.** I choose be mine today |
| W-pII..255.1:5 | must remain forever in the **p.** of Heaven. |
| W-pII..255.2:3 | *The **p.** You gave him still is in his mind, and it* |
| W-pII..257.2:3 | *well, if we would reach the **p.** You will for us.* |
| W-pII..261.1:3 | to find my **p.** in murderous attack. I live |
| W-pII..261.1:7 | In Him is everlasting **p.**. And only there |
| W-pII..262.2:3 | For there is **p.**, and nowhere else can |
| W-pII..262.2:3 | nowhere else can **p.** be sought and found. |
| W-pII..264.1:7 | *to be at **p.** within Your everlasting Love.* |
| W-pII.....267.h | My heart is beating in the **p.** of God. |
| W-pII..267.1:3 | **P.** fills my heart, and floods my body with |
| W-pII..267.1:5 | Each heartbeat brings me **p.**; each breath |
| W-pII..267.1:6 | quiet and at **p.** within His loving Arms. |
| W-pII..267.2:2 | *is beating in the **p.** the Heart of Love created.* |
| W-pII..270.2:1 | through them **p.** will come to everyone. |
| W-pII......6.3:1 | at **p.** within the Heaven of your holy mind |
| W-pII......6.4:3 | and **p.** has come to every Son of God, |
| W-pII.....273.h | The stillness of the **p.** of God is mine. |
| W-pII..273.1:3 | us learn how to dismiss it and return to **p.** |
| W-pII..273.1:4 | "The stillness of the **p.** of God is mine," |
| W-pII..273.1:4 | nothing can intrude upon the **p.** that God |
| W-pII..273.2:1 | *Father, Your **p.** is mine. What need have I to* |
| W-pII..273.2:4 | *so the **p.** You gave Your Son is with me still,* |
| W-pII......7.4:1 | and be restored to sanity and **p.** of mind. |
| W-pII..286.1:7 | *Your **p.** is mine. My heart is quiet, and my* |
| W-pII..287.1:3 | gift could I prefer before the **p.** of God? |
| W-pII......8.2:2 | through quiet eyes and with a mind at **p.**. |
| W-pII......8.3:4 | sees arises from a mind at **p.** within itself. |
| W-pII.....291.h | This is a day of stillness and of **p.**. |
| W-pII..291.1:2 | shows me all things forgiven and at **p.**, |
| W-pII..295.1:2 | asks this gift that He may offer **p.** of mind |
| W-pII.....305.h | There is a **p.** that Christ bestows on us. |
| W-pII..305.1:1 | but Christ's vision finds a **p.** so deep and |
| W-pII..305.1:2 | Comparisons are still before this **p.**. And |
| W-pII..305.1:3 | departs in silence as this **p.** envelops it, |
| W-pII..305.1:4 | healed the world by giving it Christ's **p.**. |
| W-pII..305.2:1 | *Father, the **p.** of Christ is given us, because it* |
| W-pII..306.1:3 | be restored to love and holiness and **p.**. |
| W-pII..306.1:4 | care; of loving kindness and the **p.** of God |
| W-pII..307.1:5 | *enter into **p.** where conflict is impossible,* |
| W-pII..310.2:3 | We are restored to **p.** and holiness. There |
| W-pII....10.3:2 | release from suffering, return to **p.**, |
| W-pII....10.4:1 | to the eternal **p.** He shares with him. Be |
| W-pII..311.1:6 | re-establish **p.** of mind by giving us God's |
| W-pII..314.1:5 | extending its security and **p.** into a quiet |
| W-pII..320.1:2 | There are no limits on his strength, his **p.**, |
| W-pII..323.2:4 | And we are at **p.** again, for fear has gone |
| W-pII..328.2:3 | *Will that I be wholly safe, eternally at **p.**. And* |
| W-pII....12.3:4 | there is surrounding him is everlasting **p.**, |
| W-pII....12.5:2 | And **p.** will be restored forever to the holy |
| W-pII..331.1:8 | *Conflict is sleep, and **p.** awakening. Death is* |
| W-pII..331.2:2 | today, that we may find the **p.** of God. |
| W-pII..334.1:4 | God's Voice is offering the **p.** of God to all |
| W-pII..334.2:3 | *heart, to give him certainty and bring him **p.*** |
| W-pII..336.1:6 | here, and only here, is **p.** of mind restored |
| W-pII..337.1:1 | My sinlessness ensures me perfect **p.**, |
| W-pII.....343.h | To find the mercy and the **p.** of God. |
| W-pII..343.2:1 | The mercy and the **p.** of God are free. |
| W-pII..345.2:1 | **P.** to all seeking hearts today. The light |
| W-pII.....346.h | Today the **p.** of God envelops me, And I |
| W-pII..346.1:7 | *find the **p.** which You created for Your Son,* |
| W-pII..346.2:1 | will remember nothing but the **p.** of God. |
| W-pII..346.2:2 | For we will learn today what **p.** is ours, |
| W-pII..348.1:3 | *except the perfect **p.** and joy I share with You* |
| W-pII....14.4:4 | brothers, asking them to share our **p.** and |
| W-pII.....351.h | My sinless brother is my guide to **p.**. My |
| W-pII.....352.h | The other comes the **p.** of God Himself. |
| W-pII..352.1:4 | *have given me a way to find Your **p.** again. I* |
| W-pII..352.1:8 | *hear Your Voice and find Your **p.** today. For I* |
| W-pII.....354.h | and I, in **p.** And certainty of purpose. And |
| W-pII.....355.h | There is no end to all the **p.** and joy, And |
| W-pII..355.1:6 | *not wait an instant more to be at **p.** forever. It* |
| W-pII.....359.h | God's answer is some form of **p.**. All pain |
| W-pII..359.1:9 | *Help us forgive, for we would be at **p.**.* |
| W-pII.....360.h | **P.** be to me, the holy Son of God. Peace |
| W-pII.....360.h | **P.** to my brother, who is one with me. Let |
| W-pII.....360.h | the world be blessed with **p.** through us. |
| W-pII..360.1:1 | *Father, it is Your **p.** that I would give,* |
| W-pII..360.1:4 | ***P.** be to me, and peace to all the world. In* |
| W-pII..360.1:4 | *Peace be to me, and **p.** to all the world. In* |
| Wfl ........in.2:1 | way to find the **p.** that God has given us. |
| Wfl ........in.4:2 | way to Him and to the Heaven of His **p.**. |
| WpII...361-5.h | Certain that Your direction gives me **p.**. |
| W-ep .........5:5 | for guidance and for **p.** and sure direction |
| W-ep .........6:2 | In **p.** we will continue in His way, and |
| M-4 .....I.A.6:2 | of God rests a while in reasonable **p.**. |
| M-4 .....I.A.8:5 | This is the stage of real **p.**, for here is |
| M-4 .....I.A.8:8 | if **p.** of mind is already complete? And |
| M-4 ....... II.2:1 | **p.** of mind which the advanced teachers |
| M-4 ......IV.1:6 | is the end of **p.** and the denial of learning. |
| M-4 ......VI.1:13 | It is safety. It is **p.**. It is joy. And it is God. |
| M-4 ....... X.1:6 | Only the open-minded can be at **p.**, for |
| M-8 ...........1:7 | not to them for **p.** and understanding. |
| M-10 .......6:10 | Teacher of God, this step will bring you **p.** |
| M-11 ............h | HOW IS **P.** POSSIBLE IN THIS WORLD? |
| M-11 .........1:2 | Certainly **p.** seems to be impossible here. |
| M-11 .........1:4 | His Word has promised **p.**. It has also |
| M-11 .........1:7 | has promised that **p.** is possible here, and |
| M-11 .........3:7 | How is **p.** possible in this world? In your |
| M-11 .........3:9 | of God what is reflected here is only **p.**. |
| M-11 .........4:1 | **P.** is impossible to those who look on war |
| M-11 .........4:2 | **P.** is inevitable to those who offer peace. |
| M-11 .........4:2 | Peace is inevitable to those who offer **p.**. |
| M-11 .........4:4 | the world that makes **p.** seem impossible. |
| M-11 .........4:6 | redeemed it and made it fit to welcome **p.** |
| M-11 .........4:7 | And **p.** descends on it in joyous answer. |
| M-11 .........4:8 | **P.** now belongs here, because a Thought |
| M-11 .......4:12 | **p.** be possible in this world?" but instead, |
| M-11 .......4:12 | it not impossible that **p.** be absent here?" |
| M-13 .........4:7 | To them he sacrifices all his **p.**. To them |
| M-14 .........5:3 | The world will end in **p.**, because it is a |
| M-14 .........5:4 | When **p.** has come, what is the purpose of |
| M-15 .......1:11 | *and whole, at **p.** forever in the Heart of God.* |
| M-16 .........6:2 | It is a thought of pure joy; a thought of **p.**, |
| M-19 .......5:12 | The **p.** of God descends on all the world, |
| M-20 ............h | WHAT IS THE **P.** OF GOD? |
| M-20 .........1:1 | said that there is a kind of **p.** that is not of |
| M-20 .........2:1 | how can the **p.** of God be recognized? |
| M-20 .........2:2 | God's **p.** is recognized at first by just one |
| M-20 .........3:3 | God's **p.** can never come where anger is, |
| M-20 .........3:3 | is, for anger must deny that **p.** exists. |
| M-20 .........3:4 | proclaims that **p.** is meaningless, and |
| M-20 .........3:5 | In this condition, **p.** cannot be found. |
| M-20 .........3:6 | condition for finding the **p.** of God. More |
| M-20 .........3:7 | this, given forgiveness there *must* be **p.**. |
| M-20 .........3:9 | And what but **p.** is opposite to war? Here |
| M-20 .......3:11 | apparent. Yet when **p.** is found, the war is |
| M-20 .........4:1 | How is the **p.** of God retained, once it is |
| M-20 .........4:2 | that **p.** cannot exist will certainly return. |
| M-20 .........4:6 | you want, or is God's **p.** the better choice? |
| M-20 .........6:1 | What is the **p.** of God? No more than this |
| M-20 .......6:12 | God's **p.** is the condition for His Will. |
| M-20 .......6:13 | Attain His **p.**, and you remember Him. |
| M-27 .........2:8 | Where there is death is **p.** impossible. |
| M-28 .........3:4 | Attack is meaningless and **p.** has come. |
| C-2.............7:5 | certainty of Heaven and the surety of **p.**. |
| C-3.............2:4 | to rise up and to return to Him in **p.**. |
| C-3.............3:1 | Thought of **p.** because they are in conflict. |
| C-3.............6:9 | remains is **p.** eternal and the Will of God. |
| C-3.............7:3 | be so because the ego cannot be at **p.**. But |
| C-4.............8:1 | if you only knew the **p.** that will envelop |
| C-5.............6:7 | and leave them both to find the **p.** of God. |
| C-ep...........5:6 | him enters his home and is at **p.** at last. |
| P-1.............3:1 | his **p.** of mind is suffering in consequence. |
| P-2...........I.4:1 | each other and to receive the **p.** of God. |
| P-2......... V.8:3 | them down, to come away in **p.** forever. |
| P-2.......VII.2:8 | Healing is here, and happiness and **p.**. |
| P-2.......VII.9:8 | of pathways that can ever lead to **p.**. O let |
| P-3.......... II.9:3 | pass by many obstacles to **p.** quite quickly |
| P-3.......III.8:10 | of God for the restoration of joy and **p.**. |
| S-1.........in.3:3 | to the lawns of Heaven and the gate of **p.**. |
| S-1......... II.8:8 | if **p.** is to be restored to God's Son, who |
| S-1........IV.4:4 | Prayer can bring the **p.** of God. What |
| S-1......... V.1:4 | Humility brings **p.** because it does not |
| S-2...........I.1:2 | grace, a parody upon the holy **p.** of God. |
| S-2...........I.3:2 | by which you can return to Him in **p.**. *Do* |
| S-2...........I.6:6 | in tranquil silence and in perfect **p.**. He |
| S-2.........I.10:5 | to ascend above the world of chaos into **p.** |
| S-2..........II.7:5 | goal of God, and find the **p.** He offers you. |
| S-2........ III.3:4 | to you another step to Heaven and to **p.**. |
| S-2........ III.6:2 | About salvation and the gift of **p.**. About |
| S-3..........II.2:1 | made joyfully and with a sense of **p.**, |
| S-3..........II.3:4 | we go in **p.** to freer air and gentler climate |
| S-3..........II.4:4 | the world and it is ready to depart in **p.**, |
| S-3........ IV.1:3 | Bringers of **p.**, –the Holy Spirit's voice, |
| S-3........ IV.6:2 | still surrounds you with the Arms of **p.**. |
| S-3........ IV.7:2 | of everlasting Love and perfect **p.**. My |
| S-3........ IV.9:9 | the gift first of forgiveness, then eternal **p.** |
| S-3...... IV.10:7 | to you until you come to Him in **p.** at last. |

## peaceful 5

| | |
|---|---|
| T-8...........I.1:3 | those who are in conflict are not **p.**, and |
| T-8.......VII.4:3 | The body is beautiful or ugly, **p.** or savage |
| T-27...VII.14:8 | The sleep is **p.** now, for these are happy |
| W-pI.....34.1:4 | peace of mind that a **p.** perception of the |
| W-pI.....40.3:5 | *happy, **p.**, loving and contented.* Another |

## peacefully 2

| | |
|---|---|
| T-25..... VII.6:5 | beyond the madness and rest **p.** on truth. |
| T-26..... V.10:4 | Let the dead and gone be **p.** forgotten. |

## pearl 1

| | |
|---|---|
| T-23......II.11:2 | is this precious thing, this priceless **p.**, |

## pebble 2

| | |
|---|---|
| T-28...... III.7:2 | who mistook for gold the shining of a **p.**, |
| P-3...........I.4:6 | God. Would he refuse this Gift for a **p.**, or |

## peculiar 1

| | |
|---|---|
| T-14........II.1:5 | which this most **p.** learning goal depends |

## peering 2

| | |
|---|---|
| W-pI.....92.3:3 | eyes, **p.** about in darkness to behold the |
| W-pI...121.2:3 | abides in misery, **p.** about in darkness, |

## pellet 1

| | |
|---|---|
| W-pI.....76.3:3 | You really think a small round **p.** or some |

## pen 3

| | |
|---|---|
| W-pI.......1.1:6 | *anything. This **p.** does not mean anything.* |
| W-pI.....36.3:9 | *My holiness envelops this **p.**.* Several times |
| P-2..........II.6:2 | the paper matter, or the ink, or the **p.**? Or |

## penalties 1

| | |
|---|---|
| W-pI...135.2:4 | and doubts, its **p.** and heavy armaments, |

## penalty 13

| | |
|---|---|
| T-12...VII.13:2 | The death **p.** is the ego's ultimate goal, for |
| T-12...VII.13:3 | The death **p.** never leaves the ego's mind, |
| T-13.......in.1:5 | to deny itself, and escape the **p.** of denial. |
| T-14...... III.5:7 | what you do not want without this **p.**. |
| T-14...... III.5:9 | Either it is a **p.** from which you suffer, or |
| T-14...... III.6:1 | No **p.** is ever asked of God's Son except |
| T-14...... III.8:7 | imposing on himself the **p.** of guilt, in |
| T-29....VIII.2:7 | **p.** for looking not within for certainty and |
| T-29...... IX.3:5 | who judges him will not escape the **p.** he |
| T-29...... IX.3:6 | God knows of justice, not of **p.**. But in the |
| T-29...... IX.3:7 | between your judgment and the **p.** it |
| T-29.... IX.10:6 | to be the way to save him from its **p.**. |
| T-31...... III.7:3 | will be no ancient **p.** exacted from your |

## penance 1

| | |
|---|---|
| W-pI...101.1:3 | it asks for suffering as **p.** for your "sins." |

T-18 IX.3:6 Its eyes **p.** it not; its senses remain quite
T-19 I.7:5 **p.** this is to recognize where separation is,
T-20 VIII.6:5 What can the body's eyes **p.**, with power
T-21 in.1:6 a man thinketh, so does he **p.**. Therefore,
T-21 II.4:10 You must **p.** that what is strong enough
T-21 V.3:2 in Them, you will **p.** another self in you.
T-21 VI.2:3 as sinful and still **p.** the other innocent.
T-21 VII.5:6 be willing to **p.** a world where it is not. It
T-22 I.5:2 You will **p.** no difficulty in understanding
T-22 II.2:7 Yet to **p.** a difference where none exists
T-22 III.7:6 and must **p.** illusions as the truth. Could
T-22 VI.11:3 **p.** and justify *is* an attack upon your Father
T-23 in.2:4 that you will love what you **p.** as sinless.
T-23 in.5:4 and **p.** the light of which he is a part. Your
T-23 in.5:6 and **p.** the little and the weak about him?
T-23 II.18:4 how else could you **p.** the form they take,
T-23 III.5:1 on its behalf, cannot **p.** it lies within them
T-24 II.1:3 keeping clear in sight, all lacks it can **p.**.
T-24 VI.4:5 in all temptation to **p.** what is not there,
T-24 VII.11:2 One do you **p.** outside yourself, your own
T-25 II.1:1 what the body's eyes **p.** fills you with fear?
T-25 II.1:3 and satisfaction in the world as you **p.** it.
T-25 III.1:1 you **p.** a world in which attack is justified.
T-25 III.1:2 extent you will **p.** attack cannot *be* justified
T-25 III.6:7 He will **p.** that where he gave attack is but
T-25 V.1:1 is no reason to **p.** the Son of God as other
T-25 V.5:4 his sinlessness will be when you **p.** it! And
T-25 V.6:5 way to Heaven or to hell, as you **p.** him.
T-25 VII.9:1 overlook, nor fail completely to **p.** at all.
T-25 VIII.5:10 lay it aside, unaided, and **p.** it is not true?
T-25 VIII.6:3 Spirit, and **p.** the "wrath" of God in Him.
T-25 VIII.6:8 they **p.** the "threat" of what God knows as
T-25 VIII.12:2 You need not **p.**, in every circumstance,
T-25 VIII.14:6 can **p.** what justice must accord the Son of
T-25 IX.2:8 to **p.** salvation as a gift from Him. Yet
T-25 IX.7:3 He cannot **p.** He bears no witness to. And
T-25 IX.9:2 that you **p.** and leave you fair to no one.
T-26 I.4:3 God's Son **p.** himself without his Father?
T-26 II.3:4 or any attribute which you **p.** that makes
T-26 IV.2:5 The sinless must **p.** that they are one, for
T-26 V.4:1 and senseless maze you still **p.** in time,
T-26 VIII.2:1 and this space you **p.** as time because you
T-26 VIII.3:2 Unless you so **p.** it, you will be afraid of it,
T-26 VIII.3:6 for time is not the enemy that you **p.**.
T-26 X.1:3 When you **p.** it as unfair, you think that a
T-26 X.2:1 it mean if you **p.** attack in certain forms to
T-26 X.4:1 temptation to **p.** yourself unfairly treated.
T-26 X.5:2 And in this game do you **p.** one purpose
T-26 X.6:2 brings can you **p.** to lighten up your way.
T-26 X.6:5 If you **p.** injustice anywhere, you need but
T-27 II.11:2 anyone **p.** a function unified which has
T-27 II.12:2 you **p.** correction is the same as pardon,
T-27 II.16:6 the halves of you that you **p.** as separate.
T-27 III.3:5 Who can **p.** effect without a cause? What
T-27 V.6:7 Who looks on one cannot **p.** the other, for
T-27 V.7:7 And happily your brother will **p.** the
T-27 V.8:5 he perceives it he can not **p.** it as it is. But
T-27 V.9:5 Fear you not the way that you **p.** them.
T-27 VII.11:7 **p.** although it caused the part you see and
T-27 VIII.8:4 easy to **p.** the jest when all around you do
T-27 VIII.9:1 laughter does the Holy Spirit **p.** the cause,
T-27 VIII.13:1 you **p.** the world when this is recognized!
T-28 II.5:2 you **p.** this much at least: that you have
T-28 III.2:3 it **p.** itself as separate and apart from you.
T-28 IV.10:5 What, then, would you **p.** within the gap?
T-28 V.3:1 and **p.** that he is not the dream he made.
T-28 V.4:2 sick, and this the world the body's eyes **p.**.
T-28 V.4:4 sounds the body can **p.** are meaningless.
T-28 V.4:7 able to **p.** as it can judge or understand or
T-28 V.5:8 Let not the body's ears and eyes **p.** these
T-28 V.7:2 the place where you **p.** it is not real. The
T-28 VI.4:4 again, whenever you **p.** yourself attacked.
T-29 I.1:6 when you **p.** a gap between your brother
T-29 II.1:1 Why would you not **p.** it as release from
T-29 II.9:5 only in your failure to **p.** that it is nothing.
T-29 IV.3:1 function unfulfilled as you **p.** the function
T-29 VII.5:2 but to **p.** the signs of death you seek? No
T-30 I.3:4 what you **p.** and so you feel attacked. And
T-30 V.10:7 will not **p.** Whose loving hand you hold.
T-30 VI.3:3 you **p.** the basis of forgiveness is quite real
T-30 VII.4:4 change *because* you would **p.** it everywhere
T-30 VIII.2:4 views of him that you **p.** as his reality. The
T-31 I.1:8 that you **p.** no differences in false and true
T-31 II.10:2 will **p.** his purpose is the same as yours.
T-31 IV.4:1 starts, but do not yet **p.** what it is for? Its
T-31 V.5:2 look away, lest it **p.** the treachery it hides.
T-31 V.9:3 though you do not yet **p.** that this is what
T-31 V.15:3 while you **p.** a self that interacts with evil,
T-31 V.15:5 will not **p.** that you can interact but with
T-31 VI.3:1 you behold the spirit and **p.** the body not.
T-31 VII.1:9 it change while you **p.** the "bad" in you.
T-31 VII.2:2 You will **p.** them sometimes, but will not
T-31 VII.7:5 and **p.** the terrified imaginings that come
T-31 VII.9:3 sword, you must **p.** the body as yourself,
T-31 VIII.5:1 to all temptation to **p.** yourself as weak
T-31 VIII.6:2 temptation to **p.** yourself defenseless and
T-31 VIII.9:1 and find so many chances to **p.** another
W-pI 5.7:2 of both the source of the upset as you **p.** it
W-pI 11.1:2 as if the world determines what you **p.**.
W-pI 13.1:4 you **p.** something that has no meaning.
W-pI 13.1:5 be particularly likely to think you do **p.** it.
W-pI 24.h I do not **p.** my own best interests.
W-pI 24.2:1 that you do not **p.** your own best interests
W-pI 24.7:2 *not* **p.** *my own best interests in this situation*
W-pI 25.2:1 You **p.** the world and everything in it as
W-pI 25.3:1 goals you now **p.** is to say that they are all
W-pI 33.2:1 the world you **p.** as outside yourself, then
W-pI 55.4:1 (24) I do not **p.** my own best interests.
W-pI 55.4:4 are, recognizing that I cannot **p.** them by
W-pI 57.4:4 And I will **p.** that peace also abides in the
W-pI 86.2:4 *me* **p.** *this only in the light of God's plan for*
W-pI 87.4:2 *me* **p.** *this in accordance with the Will of God*
W-pI 89.3:2 with the Holy Spirit's, and **p.** them as one.
W-pI 91.2:5 Denial of light leads to failure to **p.** it.
W-pI 91.2:6 Failure to **p.** light is to perceive darkness.
W-pI 91.2:6 Failure to perceive light is to **p.** darkness.
W-pI 91.6:3 *The body's eyes do not* **p.** *the light. But I am*
W-pI 92.4:6 In darkness you **p.** a self that is not there.
W-pI 92.7:3 while light and strength **p.** themselves as
W-pI 93.3:4 wrong, but you do not **p.** that this is so.
W-pI 96.4:4 and **p.** itself within a body it confuses
W-pI 99.7:2 Try to **p.** the strength in what you say, for
W-pI 121.3:2 unforgiving mind **p.** but its damnation?
W-pI 121.11:2 Try to **p.** some light in him somewhere; a
W-pI 121.12:3 **P.** him now as more than friend to you,
W-pI 126.6:3 It cannot give you peace as you **p.** it. It is
W-pI 127.2:6 and **p.** the Son of God in separate parts.
W-pI 128.2:3 without delaying to **p.** some hope where
W-pI 128.3:1 your mind when you **p.** salvation here.
W-pI 128.3:2 you make part of you as you **p.** yourself.
W-pI 133.9:3 one who is deceived will not **p.** that he has
W-pI 133.10:1 still must he **p.** its tarnished edges and its
W-pI 134.h Let me **p.** forgiveness as it is.
W-pI 134.9:1 and **p.** it open wide in welcome. When
W-pI 134.13:1 for the world cannot **p.** its meaning, nor
W-pI 134.14:6 us ask of Him: *Let me* **p.** *forgiveness as it is.*
W-pI 134.17:3 *Let me* **p.** *forgiveness as it is. Would I accuse*
W-pI 135.14:1 not easy to **p.** that self-initiated plans are
W-pI 138.1:3 is the way we make what we **p.**, and what
W-pI 138.4:5 is made, you will **p.** it was no choice at all.
W-pI 140.3:2 dreams forgiveness lets the mind **p.** do
W-pI 147.2:1 (134) Let me **p.** forgiveness as it is.
W-pI 152.4:2 because it is a difficult distinction to **p.**. It
W-pI 152.7:4 you can **p.** what God willed not to be.
W-pI 159.2:3 and thus do you **p.** that you are whole.
W-pI 161.9:5 not **p.** that in his hands is your salvation.
W-pI 161.12:5 and **p.** in him the symbol of your fear.
W-pI 165.4:3 Nor need you **p.** how great the gift, how
W-pI 166.8:1 and **p.** His gentle hand directing you to
W-pI 166.11:4 when you **p.** yourself as lonely and afraid.
W-pI 170.2:7 *your arms, and only then do you* **p.** *it false.*
W-pI 170.4:1 you will **p.** the premises on which the idea
W-pI 170.10:3 must the worshippers of fear **p.** their own
W-pI 184.8:7 denied, for you **p.** him separate from you,
W-pI 187.2:2 away, your body's eyes will not **p.** it yours
W-pI 187.3:5 Now you can **p.** that by your giving is
W-pI 189.1:1 is a light in you the world can not **p.**. And
W-pI 189.5:4 your heart, you will **p.** a fearful world,
W-pI 190.5:7 As you **p.** the harmlessness in them, they
W-pI 191.6:3 cruelly, and then **p.** this savage need in it.
W-pI 191.9:1 You who **p.** yourself as weak and frail,
W-pI 192.6:1 With anger gone, you will indeed **p.** that,
W-pI 192.7:1 do we need forgiveness to **p.** that this is so
W-pI 193.2:4 God does not **p.** at all. Yet it is He Who
W-pI 193.7:1 is failing to **p.** the lesson he should learn?
W-pI 194.6:3 things, so will the world **p.** that it is saved.
W-pI 195.2:3 no door to the deliverance they now **p.**.
W-pI 196.6:5 And he will not **p.** its foolishness, or even
W-pI 196.7:3 you can not **p.** that it is but your thoughts
W-pI 198.7:4 Their blood, you will **p.** a miracle instead.
W-pI 198.12:5 is, that to behold the Son is to **p.** no more,
W-pI 199.1:1 as long as you **p.** a body as yourself. The
W-pI 199.7:3 to set free the many who **p.** themselves as
W-pII 236.1:4 me to serve whatever purpose I **p.** in it.
W-pII 250.1:2 **p.** the lacks in him with which I would
W-pII 261.1:2 will behold myself where I **p.** my strength,
W-pII 262.h Let me **p.** no differences today.
W-pII 262.1:4 *I* **p.** *a thousand forms in what remains as one*
W-pII 263.1:3 *I would not* **p.** *such dark and fearful images.*
W-pII 265.1:10 And so I can **p.** creation's gentleness.
W-pII 270.1:3 *much more will I* **p.** *in it than sight can give.*
W-pII 6.2:4 untouched by anything the body's eyes **p.**
W-pII 278.1:2 frailties and the sins which I **p.** are real,
W-pII 289.1:3 can I then **p.** the world forgiveness offers?
W-pII 290.1:4 What I **p.** without God's Own Correction
W-pII 8.3:2 What can it **p.** surrounding it but safety,
W-pII 8.4:2 eyes **p.** the sure reflection of his Father's
W-pII 292.1:4 as the outcome of all problems we **p.**, all
W-pII 292.2:2 *us for every problem that we can* **p.**; *for every*
W-pII 293.1:5 holy light, and I **p.** a world forgiven at last
W-pII 328.1:1 for all things we **p.** are upside down until
W-pII 345.1:4 *I need to help me with the problems I* **p.**.
W-pII 348.h And in every need That I **p.**, Your grace
W-pII 350.1:1 *becomes a part of us, as we* **p.** *ourselves. The*
W-pII 14.3:4 and **p.** all things as kindly and as good.
M-5 II.1:7 the existence of the world as you **p.** it
M-16 11:9 of magic and **p.** their meaninglessness.
M-19 4:2 you **p.** as broken off and separate. And it
M-29 7:4 you **p.** as your weakness is but illusion.
C-3 8:3 Now you are holy and **p.** it so. And now
C-6 4:8 But He is not deceived when you **p.** your
P-2 IV.1:4 a decision to **p.** the universe as you would
S-2 II.2:4 in sin, and yet **p.** him as the Son of God?

## perceived 205

T-1 VI.2:2 truth, and had thus **p.** yourself as lacking.
T-2 I.4:7 correctly **p.** as the release from the dream,
T-2 V.8:5 becomes doubly dangerous unless it *is* **p.**.
T-3 II.5:7 vision can be **p.** only by the truly innocent
T-3 II.5:10 appear (or be **p.**) we shall be like him, for
T-3 III.5:3 you love someone you have **p.** him as he is
T-3 IV.3:2 involve knowledge and cannot be **p.**. The
T-3 IV.6:6 Thereafter, spirit is **p.** as a threat, because
T-3 IV.6:9 It can be **p.** as an attacker, but it cannot
T-3 V.2:4 you make something to fill a **p.** lack, you
T-3 V.4:5 You have no image to be **p.**. The word
T-3 VI.2:6 What has been **p.** and rejected, or judged
T-3 VI.2:6 in your mind because it has been **p.**. One
T-3 VI.4:1 you have **p.** but have refused to accept.
T-3 VII.2:5 He is **p.** as a force in combat with God,
T-3 VII.4:4 Images are **p.**, not known. Knowledge
T-4 I.3:2 Learning is ultimately **p.** as frightening
T-4 I.6:7 it. I am constantly being **p.** as a teacher
T-4 II.5:1 thought system must be **p.** as painful,
T-4 II.6:9 a term which refers to any **p.** threat to the
T-6 I.10:3 only way in which I can be **p.** as the way,
T-6 V.B.3:4 equality of *having* and *being* is not yet **p.**.
T-7 III.1:11 meaningfully **p.** as belonging to anyone at
T-7 IV.2:8 of remembering when it is properly **p.**.
T-7 IV.2:9 **P.** improperly, it induces a perception of
T-7 IV.2:10 Properly **p.**, it can be used as a way out of
T-7 VI.9:4 **P.** problems in identification at any level
T-7 VI.10:1 You can be **p.** with meaning only by the
T-7 VI.11:1 **P.** without your part in it, God's creation
T-7 VII.8:1 unless you **p.** it as a means of depriving
T-7 VIII.1:5 the law is **p.** as a means of getting rid of

T-8.......VII.9:1 world, not even the body is **p.** as whole.
T-8......VIII.2:2 In this **p.** constellation the body is seen as
T-9...........I.1:4 God, which is what you are, is **p.** as fearful
T-9....... II.10:3 with giving it cannot be **p.** as loss, and the
T-10...... IV.3:1 The Sonship cannot be **p.** as partly sick,
T-11..... VII.2:6 The real world can actually be **p.**. All that
T-12.........I.9:7 its **p.** usefulness by rendering it useless.
T-12...... IV.2:2 a journey which must end in **p.** self-defeat
T-12....... V.1:3 mind, you must have **p.** yourself as weak.
T-12...... VI.7:1 What is one cannot be **p.** as separate, and
T-12..... VII.7:7 of two goals, each **p.** in a different place;
T-13....... V.2:4 being **p.** in one separate mind only.
T-13...... VI.2:3 to the past, either his or yours as you **p.** it,
T-13....VIII.5:3 **p.** in the same light and therefore one.
T-13....... XI.1:1 **p.** and harsh intrusion of guilt on peace.
T-14....... II.8:3 Christ is given the very instant that it is **p.**
T-14...... IX.5:7 reflection of Himself can be **p.** upon it.
T-15.........I.2:1 One source of **p.** discouragement from
T-15...... XI.1:6 brought together and **p.** where they are,
T-16..... IV.3:4 The special love relationship is not **p.** as a
T-16....... V.3:8 love is **p.** as separation and exclusion.
T-16..... V.10:1 **p.** the special relationship as a triumph
T-16..... V.16:3 become when it is **p.** as only what it is.
T-16..... VII.1:3 **p.** injustices and deprivations all enter
T-16...VII.11:2 all problems, be they **p.** as great or small,
T-17...... III.8:3 alliance dictates are not **p.** nor felt as *now.*
T-17.... IV.14:6 brought to light, is not **p.** as fearful, but
T-17..... VII.3:2 **p.**, it is because the thoughts are judged to
T-18.........I.2:5 a process in which they are **p.** as different.
T-18....... V.7:1 the time the threat is **p.** should remember
T-18...... VI.6:7 vengeance and the **p.** source of your guilt.
T-18.... VI.11:6 become whole, as neither is **p.** as separate
T-18.... VI.13:2 is not attacked, but simply properly **p.**. It
T-18.... IX.10:6 Here is the Source of light; nothing **p.**,
T-19.........I.1:4 only thus the situation is **p.** as meaningful
T-19.........I.2:1 Every situation, properly **p.**, becomes an
T-19.........I.5:9 be together, nor **p.** in the same place. To
T-19.......I.10:5 appears just as he is **p.** in the holy instant,
T-19....... II.4:2 of the self as sinful is **p.** as holiness. And it
T-19...... III.7:6 sin. Sin is **p.** as mightier than God, before
T19..IV.C.11:1 the ego has **p.** it as a symbol of fear, a sign
T-20...... VI.6:6 the "mystery" of separation **p.** in awe and
T-20..VIII.10:1 What has no meaning cannot be **p.**. And
T-21.....in.1:11 Nothing **p.** without it means anything.
T-21...... IV.6:3 You have **p.** the ego's madness, and not
T-21...VII.13:3 be **p.** except through constant vision. And
T-22...... III.5:9 that nothing else but form will be **p.**.
T-22...... VI.3:4 this end the body must be **p.** as sinless,
T-23..... II.15:4 its seeming laws must be **p.** as real. Their
T-23..... II.19:7 and yet **p.** as an eternal barrier to Heaven.
T-23.... IV.5:10 be **p.** as nothingness when you engage in
T-23..... IV.7:7 those in battle still are gone, and not **p.**.
T-24.........I.6:3 if his attainment of it were **p.** as yours?
T-24..... VII.5:7 Whatever is **p.** as means for truth shares
T-24..... VII.8:3 because they were so made and so **p.**. And
T-25.........I.1:7 nor any differences **p.** to stand between
T-25.........I.6:3 But this is understood by mind **p.** as one,
T-25...... III.3:4 means to serve the goal for which it is **p.**.
T-25...... VI.2:1 to the dim effects **p.** at twilight. And they
T-25...... VI.5:2 to one **p.** as other than himself, he learns
T-25..... VII.5:1 can be based, another world **p.**. And one
T-25..... VII.5:4 For here is everything **p.** as one, and no
T-25..... VII.6:4 the basis for a world **p.** as wholly mad to
T-25..... VII.9:2 function is designed to be **p.** as possible,
T-25....VIII.8:4 else. And thus is love **p.** as weak, and
T-26..... IV.5:1 Where sin once was **p.** will rise a world
T-26..... V.12:3 are real, and have existence that can be **p.**.
T-26...... VI.1:5 And through its **p.** reality has entered all
T-26..... VII.3:3 Son of God **p.** what he would see because
T-26..... VII.3:6 It cannot be **p.**, but only known. What is
T-26..... VII.3:7 What is **p.** takes many forms, but none
T-26....VIII.2:4 a little watchful of interests **p.** as separate.
T-26....VIII.4:1 *now,* and cannot be **p.** in future time. No
T-26....VIII.7:9 **p.** as "good" some day but now in form of
T-26....VIII.8:2 and one form in which its outcome is **p.**.
T-26....VIII.8:3 when retribution is **p.** to be the form in
T-26....... X.2:4 are given meaning and **p.** as sensible. And
T-26....... X.3:1 where one is **p.** the other must be seen.
T-26....... X.3:4 **p.** to be unfair and not your just deserts.
T-27 .......I.4:11 to the guilt in him which you **p.** and loved
T-27 .........I.8:3 Yet in this picture is the body not **p.** as
T-27 .....II.11:6 And so you cannot be **p.** as one, and with
T-27 .....II.12:7 to represent a split within a self **p.** as two.
T-27 .....II.14:5 left without his presence is **p.** as all of you.
T-27 ..... III.3:8 devoted to its seeing be **p.** as idly spent, a
T-27 ..... III.7:1 seen or ears have heard remains to be **p.**.
T-27 ...... V.9:4 have been properly **p.** but never violated.
T-27 .... VII.7:4 Of all the many causes you **p.** as bringing
T-27 ..VII.11:3 An honest choice could never be **p.** as one
T-28 .....II.10:3 enemies **p.** as friends with merciful intent
T-28 ..... III.2:4 Thus is the body not **p.** as sick by both
T-28 ..... III.2:5 prevents the cause of sickness and **p.**
T-28 ..... III.7:4 except a little gap **p.** to tear eternity apart,
T-28 ...... V.1:3 that is **p.** between you and your brother,
T-28 ...... V.2:2 Unshared, they are **p.** as meaningless. The
T-28 ...... V.7:1 prisoners in a world **p.** to be existing here.
T-29 ........I.3:6 without a gap **p.** between you and him,
T-29 .......II.2:6 is it caused, though not as yet **p.**. And its
T-29 .......II.6:2 life, alive in death, with death **p.** as life,
T-29 .......II.9:3 it can be **p.** and thought to feel and act,
T-29 ... III.3:10 the gap so long **p.** as keeping you apart.
T-29 ..... IV.3:2 where it is **p.** it will be there it is attacked.
T-29 .... VII.8:4 you wish, **p.** as if it had been given you.
T-29 ...VIII.1:8 it is this that never is **p.** and recognized.
T-29 ...VIII.2:3 self, for safety in a world **p.** as dangerous,
T-29 ...VIII.3:2 thus **p.** as real and seen outside the mind.
T-29 ..... IX.7:8 enter in the dream are now **p.** as brothers,
T-30 ..... IV.8:2 that is not there begins to be **p.** without
T-30 ...... V.1:3 is **p.** and takes the place of idols, which
T-30 ...... V.2:5 suffering and death have been **p.** as things
T-30 ...... V.5:2 go when they are still **p.** but wanted not.
T-31 ........I.8:4 made, but you had not **p.** it as it was. And
T-31 ..... III.3:2 They are not **p.** in minds. They are not
T-31 ...... V.6:6 where they cannot be **p.** as errors, which
T-31 ..... VI.5:4 the picture as it was **p.** before will change
T-31 ..... VI.6:6 So is all the world **p.** as treacherous, and
T-31 .... VII.3:2 actions of the body are **p.** as coming from
T-31 .... VII.4:4 as a gift for someone not **p.** to be yourself,
W-pI....... 5.1:3 forms, all of which will be **p.** as different.
W-pI....... 5.2:1 a specific **p.** cause of an upset in any form,
W-pI....... 5.6:1 to some **p.** sources of upset than to others
W-pI....... 6.1:2 depression and so on) and the **p.** source
W-pI..... 22.1:3 His own attack is thus **p.** as self defense.
W-pI..... 24.1:5 goal in any situation which is correctly **p.**.
W-pI..... 36.1:1 for yesterday from the perceiver to the **p.**.
W-pI..... 44.5:6 Yet **p.** through the ego's eyes, it is loss of
W-pI..... 50.3:2 raise you high above all the **p.** dangers of
W-pI..... 65.3:2 you escape from all your **p.** difficulties. It
W-pI..... 71.2:3 is constantly **p.** as outside yourself. Each
W-pI..... 71.3:2 any **p.** source of salvation is acceptable
W-pI... 92.11:3 to the light where only miracles can be **p.**.
W-pI... 108.2:2 unified that darkness cannot be **p.** at all.
W-pI... 108.4:3 because they are **p.** from the same frame
W-pI... 134.1:1 for it is apt to be distorted and to be **p.** as
W-pI... 135.8:2 need merely be **p.** as quite apart from you
W-pI... 138.2:6 come where it could only be **p.** with fear.
WpI. rIV.in3:2 they are not **p.** to be but what they are;
W-pI. 152.10:4 false. Their arrogance has been **p.**. And in
W-pI... 155.1:5 not yet **p.** the way will recognize you also,
W-pI... 158.8:2 merely disappear when this has been **p.**.
W-pI... 161.7:3 An enemy must be **p.** in such a form he
W-pI... 163.2:2 grasp; all goals **p.** but in its sightless eyes.
W-pI... 163.4:2 Himself **p.** within an idol made of dust.
W-pI... 164.6:4 both **p.** and recognized for what they are.
W-pI... 181.1:2 he is limited by what you have **p.** in him.
W-pI... 189.3:3 Only one can be **p.** at all. The other one is
W-pI... 190.3:2 is denied, confused with fear, **p.** as mad,
W-pI... 192.4:3 lets the body be **p.** as what it is; a simple
W-pI... 194.3:1 felt, or pain experienced or loss **p.**. In no
W-pI. 196.11:1 for an instant, is a murderer **p.** within you
W-pI... 197.2:4 freedom and salvation are **p.** as joined,
W-pI. 198.11:5 it. Only that can be **p.** an instant longer.
W-pI... 200.8:2 begins within the world **p.** as different,
W-pII ..... 7.1:5 laid aside. And where they were **p.** before,
W-pII . 284.1:1 Loss is not loss when properly **p.**. Pain is
W-pII ..... 8.1:4 real world cannot be **p.** except through
W-pII . 346.1:4 *all laws of time and things* **p.** *in time. I would*
M-4 ..... I.A.3:4 lack of value be **p.** unless the perceiver is
M-5 ............I.h The **P.** Purpose of Sickness
M-9 ............ 1:8 in particular must be properly **p.**, and all
M-9 ........... 2:4 it is apt to be **p.** as personally insulting.
M-14 ......... 1:7 **P.** as purposeless, they are no longer seen.
M-17 ......... 5:1 Anger in response to **p.** magic thoughts is
M-19 ......... 3:4 way. "Sins" are **p.** and justified by careful
M-20 ....... 2:10 The contrast first **p.** has merely gone.
M-20 ....... 3:12 now that is **p.** as nonexistent and unreal.
M-28 ......... 2:3 and pain and misery of any kind **p.** as hell
C-4 ............ 4:5 was **p.** the face of Christ appears, and in
C-6 ............ 3:5 the light in which the forgiven world is **p.**;
P-2........ IV.6:4 must overcome all limits **p.** in the self, at
P-2........ IV.6:6 now becomes a threat and is **p.** as evil.
P-2........ IV.8:2 the illusions by which sickness is **p.** as real
P-2..........V.5:1 gifts beyond the heights **p.** in any dream.
P-2..........V.5:5 Son for help in his **p.** distress can be but

## perceiver 7

T-3 ....... IV.2:1 the mind a **p.** rather than a creator.
T-5 ....... III.3:2 be in your mind, because you are the **p.**.
T-13 .... VII.5:3 All seeing starts with the **p.**, who judges
W-pI .... 35.3:3 the emphasis for today is on the **p.**, rather
W-pI .... 36.1:1 for yesterday from the **p.** to the perceived.
W-pI .... 37.2:3 As a result, the **p.** will lose. Nor will he
M-4 ..... I.A.3:4 lack of value be perceived unless the **p.** is

## perceiver's 1

T-31 .....V.12:5 you see reflects the state of the **p.** mind.

## perceives 90

T-1 ....... IV.2:9 If a mind **p.** without love, it perceives an
T-1 ....... IV.2:9 it **p.** an empty shell and is unaware of the
T-2 .........V.7:6 Nothing He **p.** can induce fear.
T-3 .........II.3:4 miracle **p.** everything as it is. If nothing
T-3 ....... III.3:1 The questioning mind **p.** itself in time,
T-3 .......V.10:3 so that anyone who **p.** at all needs healing
T-4 .........II.2:2 also makes an ego for everyone else he **p.**,
T-4 .........V.2:6 face of threat, the ego **p.** them as the same
T-4 ...... VII.2:1 Everything the ego **p.** is a separate whole,
T-4 ...... VII.2:7 specific ways to everything it **p.** as related.
T-5 ..... III.11:1 The ego made the world as it **p.** it, but
T-5 .........V.5:9 all the functions of God as it **p.** them,
T-5 ...... VI.4:3 uphold. Nothing the ego **p.** is interpreted
T-6 .........II.5:4 equality, the Holy Spirit **p.** equal needs.
T-6 ........II.11:9 He **p.** only what is true in your mind, and
T-6 ........II.12:3 in every mind, and thus **p.** them as one.
T-6 ........II.12:4 what the Holy Spirit **p.** is all the same.
T-6 ....... III.3:1 own mind **p.** itself as totally harmless.
T-6 ..... V.B.4:1 the ego **p.** the first lesson as insane. In fact
T-6 ..... V.B.7:3 Holy Spirit **p.** the conflict exactly as it is.
T-7 .........II.1:2 it. When a brother **p.** himself as sick, he is
T-7 ....... III.3:1 ego **p.** itself at war and therefore in need
T-7 .........V.4:3 Healing **p.** nothing in the healer that
T-7 ....... VI.5:2 It **p.** their threat as total, because it senses
T-7 ....... VI.6:4 Holy Spirit **p.** the conflict exactly as it is,
T-7 ....... XI.1:6 world **p.** orders of difficulty in everything.
T-7 ....... XI.1:7 the ego **p.** nothing as wholly desirable. By
T-8 .....VIII.9:8 Spirit, Who **p.** no attack on anything.
T-9 ....... IV.7:6 because it has no idea of what it **p.**.
T-9 ...... VII.3:1 Holy Spirit looks with love on all He **p.**,
T-9 ...... VII.3:6 of everything it **p.** because its perceptions
T-10 .......V.1:6 is very literal; denial of life **p.** its opposite,
T-11 .....V.13:5 ego attacks everything it **p.** by breaking it
T-11 .....V.14:3 It makes real every mistake it **p.**, and with
T-11 .....V.15:3 This, then, becomes the universe it **p.**.
T-11 .... VII.2:2 loving thoughts his mind **p.** in this world
T-12 ..... III.6:6 He always **p.** this world as outside himself
T-13 ......in.1:4 mind that judges **p.** itself as separate from
T-13 ..... IV.8:2 is the only purpose the ego **p.** in time, and
T-13 .......V.1:9 maker moves alone, for only he **p.** them.
T-13 .... VII.7:6 instant he **p.** the arms of love around him.
T-13 ..... XI.1:5 **p.** them as wholly without meaning.
T-14 ... IV.10:2 Each **p.** the other as like himself, making
T-14 ..... VI.5:4 **p.** much in your mind that lets you think
T-14 ..... VI.7:2 Interpreter **p.** the meaning in your alien
T-14 ..... IX.7:3 not obscure, for everyone **p.** it as the same

T-14....XI.14:6 to everyone who **p.** the need for peace,
T-15.......V.5:2 Yet He also **p.** that you have made special
T-15.....VII.2:7 who **p.** that it attracts through guilt.
T-15...VIII.1:6 He **p.** as clearly as He knows forgiveness is
T-16......VI.1:3 has no meaning, for it **p.** all love as special
T-17....III.2:10 gathering to itself what it **p.** as like itself.
T-17.....III.6:6 All He **p.** in separation is that it must be
T-18.........I.2:2 ego **p.** one person as a replacement for
T-19.........I.3:3 depends entirely on how the mind **p.** it,
T-23.......I.11:2 when the house of God **p.** itself divided.
T-24...VII.11:8 man **p.** an alien will and wishes it were so.
T-25.......V.2:6 attack whatever he **p.** as wholly innocent?
T-25.....VII.6:3 and either one **p.** the other as insane and
T-26......V.11:7 but lacks conviction in what he **p.**. This is
T-26...VII.10:6 **p.** his wishes and the Will of God are one.
T-27.......II.8:3 The world **p.** it as a statement of the "fact
T-27.......V.8:5 while he **p.** it he can not perceive it as it is.
T-27......VI.5:6 Who brings the miracle **p.** them all as one
T-27.....VII.4:5 that he **p.** to *be* his part in its deliverance.
T-27...VIII.6:1 **p.** the dream as separate from himself
T-28.......II.7:3 of them when he **p.** he made them up.
T-28....IV.10:2 substitutes when he **p.** he has lost nothing
T-28......VI.2:8 It **p.** no gap, because it does not hate. It
T-29......IV.3:5 And it is this the miracle **p.**, and not the
T-29......IV.6:5 of the dream as He **p.** its function, Who
T-30......I.15:2 you have sought **p.** your happiness. You
T-30......IV.3:7 he still **p.** them as obeying rules he made
W-pI.....35.3:3 the perceiver, rather than on what he **p.**.
W-pI...133.8:7 It does not even tell the truth as it **p.** it,
W-pI...140.1:2 What the world **p.** as therapeutic is but
W-pI...140.1:5 and so the patient now **p.** himself as well.
W-pI...155.3:4 need a Teacher Who **p.** their madness,
W-pI.166.11:2 vision which **p.** that you are not what you
W-pI...184.7:3 But the sooner he **p.** on what it rests, how
W-pI.186.13:4 which answer every need His Son **p.**,
W-pI.196.10:2 is you you fear, the mind **p.** itself as split.
W-pII......4.4:2 And yet what sin **p.** is but a childish game
W-pII......7.2:4 Spirit guides it to the outcome He **p.** for it
M-4.......IV.2:6 chooses hell when he **p.** a way to Heaven?
M-16..........7:5 no distinctions among the problems he **p.**
M-21..........5:3 to the presented problem as he **p.** it, and
M-22..........6:5 person **p.** himself as separate from God.
C-6.............3:3 **p.** because He was sent to save humanity.
P-2........IV.9:6 become the patient's security as he **p.** it,

## perceiving 51

T-1........I.39:2 This is the same as saying that by **p.** light,
T-1........I.40:2 It is a way of **p.** the universal mark of God
T-1........VI.3:1 error of **p.** levels at all can be corrected.
T-1.......VII.3:5 in any way and you are **p.** destructively.
T-2........III.1:5 **P.** the body as a temple is only the first
T-2.........V.9:4 and charity is a way of **p.** the perfection of
T-2......VI.9:11 but at the cost of **p.** the mind as impotent.
T-3........III.2:4 The miracle, being a way of **p.**, is not
T-3........IV.3:2 asking questions but not of **p.** meaningful
T-3.........V.6:6 your Father only by **p.** miraculously. You
T-4.......II.4:10 Belief that there is another way of **p.** is the
T-4........IV.2:3 **p.** images your ego makes in a darkened
T-4.........V.2:7 By **p.** them as the same, the ego attempts
T-5........III.3:3 also be in his, because you are **p.** him. See
T-5........VI.4:6 **P.** it as frightening, it interprets it
T-5.......VII.5:2 **P.** this as "sin" you become defensive
T-6.........II.5:1 Holy Spirit begins by **p.** you as perfect.
T-6.........II.5:4 **P.** equality, the Holy Spirit perceives
T-6........IV.4:5 **P.** something alien to itself in your mind,
T-7.........II.1:2 as sick, he is **p.** himself as not whole, and
T-7.........II.1:5 Kingdom, you are **p.** what is not of God.
T-7........IV.5:5 being the only way of **p.** the Sonship as
T-7........VI.3:6 Fearful of **p.** the power of this source, it is
T-7........VI.3:9 onto *you*, and **p.** your being as nonexistent
T-7........VI.6:3 engender by **p.** conflict as meaningless. I
T-7........VI.9:8 **p.** in total contradiction to the Holy Spirit
T-7......VI.10:6 you are **p.** the most powerful force in the
T-8......IV.8:10 you are **p.** the Holy Trinity as separated.
T-8.........V.2:5 **p.** this likeness is to recognize the Father.
T-8.....VII.11:4 **P.** the body as a separate entity cannot
T-9........III.5:1 can heal him only by **p.** the sanity in him.
T-9.........V.3:6 the ego, and by **p.** what *it* does, condemn
T-9.........V.7:8 The miracle worker begins by **p.** light,
T-10......IV.8:4 **P.** the spark will heal, but knowing the
T-11.....VII.1:5 interval between, you were not **p.** at all.
T-11.....VII.3:9 **P.** only the real world will lead you to the
T-12.......V.1:5 longer **p.** yourself and your brothers as
T-12.....VII.2:4 By **p.** what it does, you recognize its being
T-12.....VII.3:4 **P.** His results, you will understand where
T-13......III.8:5 And **p.** it you will welcome it, and it will
T-13......IV.6:7 **p.** it as a meeting with your own past? For
T-13.......V.7:9 **p.** them as witnesses to the reality you
T-13......VI.5:2 by **p.** him without them you are releasing
T-16......V.14:4 have no difficulty in **p.** the decision as just
T-21...VII.12:4 have answered "yes" without **p.** that "yes"
T-30......VI.2:5 not real by not **p.** what has not occurred.
W-pI.....19.1:2 to thinking precede those related to **p.**,
W-pI.....79.6:3 **P.** the underlying constancy in all the
W-pI...166.5:4 **p.** how his little lot but dwindles, as he
C-1.............6:1 illusions; **p.** sin and justifying anger, and
P-2.........II.2:2 term without **p.** the contradiction at all.

## perception 481

*See also* perception-related, self-perception; Appendix C

T-1.........I.23:1 Miracles rearrange **p.** and place all levels
T-1.........I.30:1 of **p.** and show them in proper alignment.
T-1.........I.37:2 erroneous **p.** and reorganizing it properly
T-1.........I.37:3 Atonement principle, where **p.** is healed.
T-1.........I.41:2 correct, or atone for, the faulty **p.** of lack.
T-1.........I.49:2 It is a device for **p.** correction, effective
T-1.........II.6:3 sudden shift from horizontal to vertical **p.**
T-1......III.5:10 others, since their own **p.** of themselves is
T-1........III.6:3 that the **p.** of both must be accurate. The
T-1........III.6:7 look out from the **p.** of your own holiness
T-1.........V.3:7 of anything, their **p.** becomes distorted.
T-1......VI.1:10 turn, depends on your **p.** of what you are.
T-1........VI.2:2 if you had not distorted your **p.** of truth,
T-1.......VII.2:4 your **p.** so you can achieve real vision, of
T-1.......VII.3:2 always involve twisting **p.** into unreality.
T-2........III.3:9 of **p.** is usually experienced as conflict,
T-2......IV.4:10 likely to occur when upside-down **p.** has
T-2.........V.7:4 is not the final outcome of the **p.**. When
T-2....V.A.12:2 on this fundamental correction in level **p.**.
T-2....V.A.15:1 miracle induces the right **p.** for healing.
T-2.....VIII.5:2 outstanding example of upside-down **p.**.
T-3................h THE INNOCENT **P.**
T-3............II.h Miracles as True **P.**
T-3.........II.2:5 Innocent or true **p.** means that you never
T-3.........II.3:8 see. They do not suffer from distorted **p.**.
T-3.........II.5:8 the innocent defend true **p.** instead of
T-3...........III.h **P.** versus Knowledge
T-3........III.1:1 We have been emphasizing **p.**, and have
T-3........III.1:2 This is because **p.** must be straightened
T-3........III.1:6 **P.** is temporary. As an attribute of the
T-3........III.1:8 brings certainty because all **p.** varies.
T-3......III.1:10 True **p.** is the basis for knowledge, but
T-3........III.2:3 ways because **p.** involves interpretation,
T-3........III.4:1 vision is the natural **p.** of spiritual sight,
T-3........III.4:3 It is, however, a means of right **p.**, which
T-3........III.4:5 The fact that **p.** is involved at all removes
T-3........III.5:7 are really confusing knowledge with **p.**.
T-3........III.5:9 **P.**, miracles and doing are closely related.
T-3......III.5:11 its most spiritualized form **p.** involves the
T-3........III.6:1 Right **p.** is necessary before God can
T-3........III.6:4 Knowledge preceded both **p.** and time,
T-3........III.6:6 I am." **P.** can and must be stabilized, but
T-3........IV.1:5 **P.** did not exist until the separation
T-3........IV.2:1 Consciousness, the level of **p.**, was the
T-3........IV.4:1 because it is applicable only to right **p.**.
T-3........IV.4:3 the state of mind that induces accurate **p.**.
T-3........IV.5:1 **P.** always involves some misuse of mind,
T-3........IV.5:5 the only way out of ambiguity is clear **p.**.
T-3........IV.5:7 the service of spirit, where **p.** is changed.
T-3........IV.6:2 That is why **p.** involves an exchange or
T-3........IV.6:3 need. The interpretative function of **p.**, a
T-3......IV.7:10 Sane **p.** induces sane choosing. I cannot
T-3............V.h Beyond **P.**
T-3.........V.1:1 shadows of your real strength, and that **p.**
T-3.........V.4:8 your image" recognizes the power of **p.**,
T-3.........V.5:2 error because it refers to the ***p.*** of meaning.
T-3.........V.6:6 In electing **p.** instead of knowledge, you
T-3.........V.7:5 else. **P.**, on the other hand, is impossible
T-3.........V.7:7 **P.** is a continual process of accepting and
T-3.........V.7:8 Evaluation is an essential part of **p.**,
T-3.........V.8:2 **P.** becomes impossible. Truth can only be
T-3.........V.8:5 of it. Only **p.** involves partial awareness.
T-3.........V.8:6 transcends the laws governing **p.**, because
T-3.........V.9:1 is the healing of the **p.** of separation.
T-3.........V.9:2 Correct **p.** of your brother is necessary,
T-3.......V.10:1 As long as **p.** lasts prayer has a place.
T-3.......V.10:2 Since **p.** rests on lack, those who perceive
T-3.......V.10:3 **P.** is based on a separated state, so that
T-3.......V.10:7 is beyond **p.** because it is beyond doubt.
T-3........VI.1:3 because beyond **p.** there is no judgment.
T-3........VI.2:2 on which **p.** but not knowledge rests. I
T-3........VI.2:3 this before in terms of the selectivity of **p.**,
T-3........VI.3:6 that enables recognition to replace **p.**.
T-3......VI.10:7 This strange **p.** *is* the authority problem.
T-3.......VII.4:5 Knowledge cannot deceive, but **p.** can.
T-3.......VII.6:6 light and darkness, knowledge and **p.**, are
T-4...........I.6:7 but I do not accept either **p.** for myself.
T-4.........I.12:4 are humble, and this gives them truer **p.**.
T-4.........I.12:5 dignity are far beyond doubt, beyond **p.**,
T-4..........II.1:5 **P.**, however, is always specific, and
T-4..........II.2:5 in changing relative **p.** as is physical
T-4..........II.6:7 Its whole **p.** of other egos as real is only an
T-4.......II.10:2 right **p.** is uniformly without attack, and
T-4.......II.11:1 that correcting **p.** is merely a temporary
T-4.......II.11:2 accurate **p.** is a steppingstone towards it.
T-4.......II.11:3 it. The whole value of right **p.** lies in the
T-4.......II.11:3 realization that *all* **p.** is unnecessary. This
T-4........VI.2:3 and the holy **p.** it would produce. The
T-4........VI.2:4 you come as close to knowledge as **p.** can.
T-4........VI.7:1 through my **p.** He can bridge the little gap
T-4.......VII.6:3 praise, and no **p.** with which to judge it.
T-5...........I.4:9 spoken before of the higher or "true" **p.**,
T-5...........I.5:1 of the knowledge that lies beyond **p.**. He
T-5...........I.6:5 **P.** is not knowledge, but it can be
T-5...........I.7:1 the Sonship, induces a kind of **p.** in which
T-5..........II.1:3 the shift in the **p.** of time that the miracle
T-5........III.1:2 Bridge for the transfer of **p.** to knowledge,
T-5........III.9:1 **P.** derives meaning from relationships.
T-6.........I.11:5 is that no **p.** that is out of accord with the
T-6..........II.3:7 **p.** of both yourself and your brothers.
T-6..........II.7:1 the Holy Spirit's **p.** is the reflection of the
T-6..........II.7:2 The ego's **p.** has no counterpart in God,
T-6..........II.7:2 the Bridge between **p.** and knowledge. By
T-6..........II.7:3 to use **p.** in a way that reflects knowledge,
T-6..........II.7:4 yet it is *your* **p.** the Holy Spirit guides.
T-6..........II.7:5 guides. Your **p.** will end where it began.
T-6..........II.9:4 **p.** cannot escape the basic laws of mind.
T-6..........II.9:6 Although **p.** of any kind is unreal, you
T-6..........II.9:7 He can inspire **p.** and lead it toward God.
T-6........II.11:7 There is no conflict anywhere in this **p.**,
T-6........II.11:7 it means that all **p.** is guided by the Holy
T-6........II.12:4 Nothing conflicts in this **p.**, because what
T-6........III.1:3 in your mind through His impartial **p.**. By
T-6........IV.5:2 This is perhaps the strangest **p.** of all, if
T-6......V.A.5:1 ultimately translates **p.** into knowledge.
T-6......V.A.5:4 of this **p.** makes it a fearful one indeed.
T-6......V.A.6:4 your **p.** and turning it right-side up. This
T-6......V.A.6:5 with the upside-down **p.** you have not yet
T-6......V.B.9:1 the unified **p.** that reflects God's knowing
T-6......V.C.8:3 the Kingdom does not depend on your **p.**,
T-7..........II.2:1 correct **p.** in your brother and yourself by
T-7.......III.1:12 **p.** makes it meaningless by eliminating or
T-7........IV.2:9 a **p.** of conflict with something else, as all
T-7........IV.2:9 something else, as all incorrect **p.** does.
T-7.......IV.2:10 a way out of conflict, as all proper **p.** can.
T-7........IV.5:6 **p.** is therefore in accord with the laws of
T-7........IV.5:7 The strength of right **p.** is so great that it
T-7........VI.1:5 the thinker and they will affect his total **p.**
T-7........VI.5:1 recognition, all sane **p.** and all knowledge.
T-7........VI.9:3 you are is not established by your **p.**, and
T-7.......VII.3:9 the image of yourself as long as **p.** lasts.
T-7.....VII.3:10 And **p.** will last until the Sonship knows
T-7.....VII.3:11 made **p.** and it must last as long as you
T-7.....VIII.6:1 truth is beyond belief and His **p.** is true.

T-7......VIII.6:5 The meaninglessness of **p.** based on the
T-7........IX.7:4 The miracle is a lesson in total **p.**. By
T-8.....VII.11:3 is its goal it will distort its **p.** of the body,
T-8.....VII.12:3 **P.** of the body can be unified only by one
T-8....VIII.1:11 difference between knowledge and **p.**. In
T-8....VIII.1:12 In **p.** the whole is built up of parts that
T-8....VIII.1:14 has meaning only at the level of **p.**, where
T-8......VIII.8:3 of how what you want distorts **p.**. No one
T-8......VIII.9:6 it be an image of your own **p.** of littleness.
T-8...........IX.h Healing as Corrected **P.**
T-8........IX.1:6 the Holy Spirit teach you the right ***p.*** of the
T-8........IX.1:6 of the body, for **p.** alone can be distorted.
T-8........IX.1:7 Only **p.** can be sick, because only
T-8........IX.1:7 can be sick, because only **p.** can be wrong.
T-8........IX.2:1 Wrong **p.** is the wish that things be as
T-9...........I.4:4 **p.** of your mind brings its reality to you,
T-9........IV.1:3 error and do not let your **p.** rest upon it,
T-9........IV.1:3 it, for you will believe what your **p.** holds.
T-9.........V.7:7 **p.** ultimately is translated into knowledge
T-9.........V.7:8 and translates his **p.** into sureness by
T-9.......VII.4:2 how lofty the Holy Spirit's **p.** of you really
T-9.......VII.4:6 clearly out of accord with its **p.** of you.
T-10.......in.2:7 your mind determines your **p.** of it.
T-10.......II.3:4 yours is the exchange of knowledge for **p.**.
T-11.......V.14:1 ego's interpretations of the laws of **p.** are,
T-11.......V.16:2 Selective **p.** chooses its witnesses carefully
T-11......VI.2:5 much confusion about what **p.** means,
T-11......VI.3:3 it. And since belief determines **p.**, you do
T-11......VII.1:6 world that awaits your **p.** when you see it?
T-11.....VII.4:1 The **p.** of goodness is not knowledge, but
T-11....VIII.1:5 which your new and only real **p.** will be
T-11....VIII.1:9 is the transfer of all **p.** to knowledge.
T-11....VIII.3:5 Instruction in **p.** is your great need, for
T-11.....VIII.7:3 **p.** you have lost sight of the real world.
T-11..VIII.11:1 not accept your brother's variable **p.** of
T-12.......I.3:10 to reality as it is, but not to your **p.** of it.
T-12......VI.3:5 so does the **p.** of self-value come from the
T-12......VI.6:3 Father, **p.** fuses into knowledge because
T-12......VI.6:3 because **p.** has become so holy that its
T-12......VI.6:7 **p.** and knowledge have become so similar
T-12......VI.7:2 God, the holy **p.** of God's Son becomes so
T-12......VII.1:5 For in this holy **p.** you will be made whole
T-12......VII.5:2 Your **p.** is the result of your invitation,
T-12......VII.5:6 and your **p.** will reflect the guidance you
T-12....VIII.4:3 vision will correct the **p.** of everything you
T-12....VIII.6:6 and through His vision your **p.** is healed.
T-12....VIII.8:3 else invisible, for beholding it is total **p.**.
T-12....VIII.8:6 Redeemed **p.** is easily translated into
T-12....VIII.8:6 only **p.** is capable of error and perception
T-12....VIII.8:6 is capable of error and **p.** has never been.
T-13.......IV.3:7 selective in your questioning as in your **p.**
T-13.......IV.7:1 evident that the Holy Spirit's **p.** of time is
T-13.......V.3:5 Projection makes **p.**, and you cannot see
T-13.......V.8:7 a private world and rule your own **p.**. Yet
T-13.......V.9:7 He has extended your **p.** even unto Him.
T-13.......V.9:8 Him. And there **p.** is no more, for He has
T-13.....VII.9:3 of dreams, where all **p.** is. Knowledge
T-13...VII.13:6 However holy his **p.** may become, no
T-13...... VIII.h From **P.** to Knowledge
T-13....VIII.1:5 dwells in eternity, and utilizes no **p.** at all.
T-13....VIII.2:1 The very real difference between **p.** and
T-13....VIII.2:5 **P.**, at its loftiest, is never complete. Even
T-13....VIII.2:6 Even the **p.** of the Holy Spirit, as perfect
T-13....VIII.2:6 of the Holy Spirit, as perfect as **p.** can be,
T-13....VIII.2:7 in Heaven. **P.** can reach everywhere under
T-13....VIII.2:8 Yet no **p.**, however holy, will last forever.
T-13....VIII.3:1 Perfect **p.**, then, has many elements in
T-13....VIII.5:2 but the true **p.** of one aspect of the whole.
T-13.......X.1:2 your awareness the full **p.** that it is insane.
T-13......XI.4:2 Perfect **p.** can merely show you what is
T-14.........I.2:7 no area of your **p.** that it has not touched,
T-14........VII.h Sharing **P.** with the Holy Spirit
T-14.....VII.1:7 **P.** is the medium by which ignorance is
T-14.....VII.1:8 Yet the **p.** must be without deceit, for
T-14.....VII.5:7 His **p.** of them, according to His purpose,
T-14...VII.6:11 give it to you as you join your **p.** to His.
T-14.....VII.7:1 of **p.** that leads to knowledge. You cannot
T-14.....VII.7:3 Sharing **p.** with Him Whom God has
T-14.......X.1:1 When no **p.** stands between God and His
T-14 .......X.2:2 truth becomes the only **p.** the Son of God
T-14 .......X.7:6 only to the particular **p.** of his offering by
T-15 .......II.4:2 a result, they witness to the ego in your **p.**
T-15 ...... V.9:3 knowing by bringing all **p.** out of the past,
T-15 ..... IX.1:1 limit your **p.** of your brothers to the body,
T-15 ..... IX.1:5 have accepted it as the only **p.** you want,
T-15 ..... IX.6:1 of the limits you have placed on your **p.**,
T-15 .......X.4:2 is but one shift in **p.** that is necessary, for
T-16 ........I.5:8 Offer your empathy to Him for it is *His* **p.**
T-16 ........I.5:9 let Him offer you His strength and His **p.**,
T-16 .......II.3:4 you. Wholly natural **p.** would show you
T-16 .......II.4:4 His natural **p.** of your gift enables Him to
T-16 ...... V.9:3 and the **p.** of the giving of specialness as
T-16 ..... VI.4:4 and for limiting your **p.** of others to theirs
T-17 .......II.3:7 of God's Son upon himself, the real **p.**,
T-17 .......II.4:2 **P.** will be meaningless when it has been
T-17 .......II.4:3 that made **p.** possible will still occur. The
T-17 .......II.4:4 The **p.** of the real world will be so short
T-17 .......II.5:2 great Transformer of **p.** will undertake
T-17 .......II.6:2 twisted your **p.** and fixed it on the past.
T-17 ..... III.3:2 other, already a severely limited **p.** of him
T-17 ..... III.5:6 its reality and its value in your **p.** of it. In
T-17 ... III.10:2 bring reality to your **p.** of your brothers.
T-17 ...... V.2:1 major step toward the **p.** of the real world
T-17 ...... V.5:7 **p.** of the relationship may even become
T-17 ...... V.5:8 former organization of their **p.** no longer
T-18 ........I.3:5 **p.** from which the behavior stems. No one
T-18 .......II.2:2 you could have of how **p.** can be utilized
T-18 ..... VI.5:3 Your **p.** of the body can clearly be sick,
T-18 ..... IX.7:2 the messengers of your **p.** return to you,
T-18 ..... IX.9:4 Here is the new **p.**, where everything is
T-18 ... IX.14:2 know until every **p.** has been cleansed and
T-18 ... IX.14:3 to the bright world of new and clean **p.**.
T-19 ........I.4:2 For faithlessness is the **p.** of a brother as a
T-19 ......I.11:6 It is the messenger of the new **p.**, sent
T-19 ......I.12:2 For faith arises from the Holy Spirit's **p.**,
T-19 ..... III.3:7 This is not really a change in your **p.**, for
T-19 ..... III.5:7 is the belief that your **p.** is unchangeable,
T-19 ..... III.5:9 only power that could change **p.** is thus
T-19 ..... III.5:9 the fear of changed **p.** which its Teacher,
T-19 ..... III.7:3 that bodies limit mind leads to a **p.** of the
T-19 ..... III.9:3 new **p.** the mind corrects it when it seems
T-19 ... III.10:4 **p.** was healed in the holy instant Heaven
T19..IV.A.11:3 **P.** cannot obey two masters, each asking
T19..IV.A.11:6 fear is wholly absent from love's gentle **p.**.
T19....IV.B.2:8 focus of the **p.** of Atonement as murder.
T19....IV.B.8:5 will be the focus of the new **p.** that will
T19..IV.B.13:4 by this **p.** the body becomes the servant of
T-20 ..... III.1:2 an adjustment is a change; a shift in **p.**, or
T-20 ..... III.1:5 For this reduces it at once to mere **p.**; a
T-20 ..... III.3:7 between yourself and it in your **p.**, which
T-20 ..... III.6:6 He Who watches over all **p.** answered.
T-21 .............h REASON AND **P.**
T-21 ......in.1:1 Projection makes **p.**. The world you see is
T-21 ......in.1:8 **P.** is a result and not a cause. And that is
T-21 .......II.9:4 The goal of sin induces the **p.** of a fearful
T-21 ..... III.5:5 faith, **p.** and belief you made, as means
T-21 ..... III.6:5 made **p.** that you might choose among
T-21 ..... III.6:6 The Holy Spirit sees **p.** as a means to
T-21 ... III.12:6 gave **p.** and belief and faith from mind to
T-21 ...... V.1:1 **P.** selects, and makes the world you see.
T-21 ...... V.1:7 It. **P.** is a choice and not a fact. But on this
T-21 .... V.1:10 **P.** is a witness but to this, and never to
T-21 ...... V.8:1 Faith and **p.** and belief can be misplaced,
T-21 ...... V.8:3 guiding **p.** toward what the mind has
T-21 ...... V.8:5 this. For the **p.** would fall away at once, if
T-21 .... V.10:4 reason, cannot fail to lead to changed **p.**.
T-22 ......in.1:4 Sin is a strictly individual **p.**, seen in the
T-22 ......I.10:1 is the first direct **p.** that you can make.
T-22 ......I.10:2 make it through awareness older than **p.**,
T-22 ..... III.4:3 eyes can see is a mistake, an error in **p.**, a
T-22 ..... III.5:6 Theirs is indeed a strange **p.**, for they can
T-22 ..... III.6:7 Nothing so blinding as **p.** of form. For
T-22 ..... III.7:6 what is not there must be distorted **p.**,
T-22 ..... III.8:3 by your **p.** of his sins and of his body.
T-24 ....VII.8:5 it be kept in mind that all **p.** still is upside
T-24 ....VII.8:6 **P.** does not seem to be a means. And it is
T-24 ....VII.8:8 **P.** seems to teach you what you see. Yet it
T-24 ..VII.11:9 thus does his **p.** serve his wish by giving it
T-24 VII.11:10 Yet can **p.** serve another goal. It is not
T-24 VII.11:12 choice, and use **p.** for a different purpose.
T-25 ........I.2:2 **P.** tells you *you* are manifest in what you
T-25 ........I.3:1 **P.** is a choice of what you want yourself
T-25 ........I.3:5 **P.** is a part of what it is your purpose to
T-25 ........ III.h **P.** and Choice
T-25 ..... III.1:4 **P.** has no other law than this. The rest but
T-25 ..... III.2:1 do not obtain directly to a world **p.** rules,
T-25 ..... III.2:1 by the Mind to which **p.** has no meaning.
T-25 ..... III.3:1 **P.** rests on choosing; knowledge does not
T-25 ..... III.3:6 Not one but it upholds in its **p.**; not one
T-25 ..... III.5:2 In His **p.** of the world, nothing is seen but
T-25 ..... III.8:4 Sin is the fixed belief **p.** cannot change.
T-25 ..... III.8:6 is forgiven, sin's **p.** must have been wrong
T-25 ..... VI.4:1 is the Holy Spirit's kind **p.** of specialness;
T-25 .... VII.5:1 insane, on which a sane **p.** can be based,
T-25 ..... IX.3:6 And every error is a **p.** in which one, at
T-25 ..... IX.4:2 Spirit's **p.** leaves no ground for an attack.
T-26 ........I.3:3 In this **p.** of yourself the body's loss would
T-26 .......II.2:3 an error in **p.** that now has been corrected
T-26 ..... III.3:4 knowledge makes no attack upon **p.**.
T-26 ..... III.4:3 of knowledge on **p.**: "It has no meaning,
T-26 ..... III.5:1 of Heaven, for only **p.** needs salvation.
T-26 ..... III.6:3 but in the **p.** of alternatives for choice.
T-26 .....V.14:5 and behold the world in which **p.** of your
T-26 .... VII.3:3 he would see because **p.** is a wish fulfilled.
T-26 .... VII.3:4 **P.** changes, made to take the place of
T-26 .... VII.8:9 separating off is symbolized, in your **p.**,
T-26 ... VIII.2:5 **p.** you cannot conceive of gaining what
T-26 .......X.1:9 Confused **p.** will block knowledge. It is
T-27 .....II.14:2 cannot be a part of you while this **p.** lasts.
T-28 ........I.2:5 Remembering is as selective as **p.**, being
T-28 ........I.2:6 is **p.** of the past as if it were occurring now
T-28 ........I.2:7 Memory, like **p.**, is a skill made up by you
T-28 ........I.7:9 the span of memory which your **p.** sees.
T-30 .... VII.3:7 **P.** cannot be in constant flux, and make
T-30 .... VII.4:1 only means whereby **p.** can be stabilized,
T-30 .... VII.5:5 that makes **p.** shift and meaning change.
T-31 .....V.15:7 upon, and nothing is outside of this **p.**. If
T-31 .....V.16:2 as your **p.** of yourself is changed. There
T-31 ..... VI.3:8 disappear, so that **p.** finds no hiding place
T-31 .... VII.1:3 Concepts are needed while **p.** lasts, and
W-in.......... 3:1 the second with the acquisition of true **p.**.
W-in.......... 4:1 way to a different **p.** of everyone and
W-in.......... 5:1 Transfer of training in true **p.** does not
W-in.......... 5:2 If true **p.** has been achieved in connection
W-in.......... 5:3 one exception held apart from true **p.**
W-in.......... 6:5 nature of true **p.** is that it has no limits. It
W-pI .... 15.3:5 because they merely symbolize true **p.**,
W-pI .... 16.2:2 What gives rise to the **p.** of a whole world
W-pI .... 17.1:5 If it were not so, **p.** would have no cause,
W-pI .... 18.2:2 for today emphasize this aspect of your **p.**
W-pI .... 21.5:3 **p.** is suffering from this form of distortion
W-pI .... 23.1:5 if your **p.** of the world is to be changed.
W-pI .... 24.1:3 is determined by your **p.** of the situation,
W-pI .... 24.1:3 of the situation, and that **p.** is wrong. It is
W-pI .... 26.3:3 they have attacked your **p.** of yourself.
W-pI .... 33.1:1 you can shift your **p.** of the world in both
W-pI .... 34.1:4 mind that a peaceful **p.** of the world arises
W-pI .... 35.5:1 negative aspects of your **p.** of yourself.
W-pI .... 43.1:1 **P.** is not an attribute of God. His is the
W-pI .... 43.1:3 the Mediator between **p.** and knowledge.
W-pI .... 43.1:4 God, **p.** would have replaced knowledge
W-pI .... 43.1:5 **p.** will become so changed and purified
W-pI .... 43.2:2 **P.** has no function in God, and does not
W-pI .... 43.2:3 what never was, **p.** has a mighty purpose.
W-pI .... 43.2:5 **P.** has no meaning. Yet does the Holy
W-pI .... 43.2:7 Healed **p.** becomes the means by which
W-pI .... 55.2:6 will save me from this **p.** of the world, and
W-pI .... 58.1:2 my holiness does the **p.** of the real world
W-pI .... 58.2:2 **p.** of my holiness does not bless me alone.
W-pI .... 64.2:4 sins. In this **p.**, the physical appearance of
W-pI .. 66.10:5 stride in the **p.** of the same as the same,
W-pI .... 68.5:5 in all the universe in your **p.** of yourself.
W-pI .... 72.8:3 upside-down **p.** has been ruinous to your
W-pI .... 79.4:3 This **p.** places you in a position in which
W-pI .... 83.2:2 *My **p.** of this does not change my function.*
W-pI .... 86.2:2 *for salvation will save me from my **p.** of this.*
W-pI .... 87.1:6 day I will experience the peace of true **p.**.

W-pI.....88.4:2 *My **p.** of this shows me I believe in laws that*
W-pI.....91.1:3 system, and the **p.** that it produces. The
W-pI...108.3:3 light that heals because it brings single **p.**,
W-pI.121.12:1 Look at this changed **p.** for a while, and
W-pI...126.2:4 sin without affecting your **p.** of yourself,
W-pI...130.1:1 **P.** is consistent. What you see reflects
W-pI...130.2:5 Love and **p.** thus go hand in hand, but
W-pI...130.9:3 expressed in tangible **p.** and in truth. You
W-pI...130.9:4 you will look upon, for though it is **p.**, it is
W-pI.130.10:3 **P.** is consistent with your choice, and hell
W-pI...138.2:3 It is this strange **p.** of the truth that makes
W-pI...157.8:2 dreams of life, Translator of **p.** into truth,
W-pI...166.8:3 make you laugh at this **p.** of yourself.
W-pI...181.2:1 **P.** has a focus. It is this that gives
W-pI...181.5:3 against present change of focus in **p.**.
W-pI...181.8:4 is all we seek for in the name of true **p.**,
W-pI...184.2:1 means by which the world's **p.** is achieved
W-pI...184.3:2 establishing **p.** as you wished to have
W-pI...184.3:2 perception as you wished to have **p.** be.
W-pI...184.5:1 direction for the mind to channel its **p.**. It
W-pI...184.7:5 can begin, a new **p.** can be gained, and all
W-pI...187.1:6 on which the world and true **p.** differ.
W-pI...188.2:7 There **p.** starts, and there it ends. It has
W-pI...188.5:7 looks upon is your **p.** of the universe.
W-pI...193.2:3 that will lead him back to where **p.** ceases.
W-pI...193.2:5 gives the means by which **p.** is made true
W-pI...193.7:2 Does pain seem real in the **p.**? If it does,
W-pI...194.7:7 He is sure that his **p.** may be faulty, but
W-pI...194.8:3 living creature not respond with healed **p.**
W-pI...198.2:3 Such is the law that rules **p.**. It is not a law
W-pI...200.8:2 and leading from this fresh **p.** to the gate
W-pII......3.1:1 The world is false **p.**. It is born of error,
W-pII......3.2:5 Here was **p.** born, for knowledge could
W-pII......3.4:2 and all **p.** can be given a new purpose by
W-pII......3.5:1 until the world has joined our changed **p.**.
W-pII..243.1:3 I understand the whole from bits of my **p.**
W-pII..269.1:3 *to find a new **p.** through the Guide You gave*
W-pII..269.1:3 *His lessons to surpass **p.** and return to truth.*
W-pII......6.5:3 have no need of learning or **p.** or of time,
W-pII..271.1:3 as they come together all **p.** disappears.
W-pII......7.1:2 **p.** leads to knowledge through the grace
W-pII......8.1:1 is a symbol, like the rest of what **p.** offers.
W-pII......8.4:3 of time, for its **p.** makes time purposeless.
W-pII......8.5:2 disappeared, taking **p.** with it as it goes,
W-pII..300.1:2 is also the idea that lets no false **p.** keep us
W-pII..304.1:3 **P.** is a mirror, not a fact. And what I look
W-pII..308.1:2 I must change my **p.** of what time is for.
W-pII....10.1:2 And this the judgment is in which **p.** ends
W-pII....10.1:4 sight, **p.** gives a silent blessing and then
W-pII..312.1:1 **P.** follows judgment. Having judged, we
W-pII.....313.h Now let a new **p.** come to me.
W-pII..313.1:6 *Now let His true **p.** come to me, that I may*
W-pII..314.1:1 From new **p.** of the world there comes a
W-pII..335.1:2 brother as he is, for that is far beyond **p.**.
W-pII..336.1:2 is restored after **p.** first is changed, and
W-pII....13.1:4 but does not attempt to go beyond **p.**, nor
W-pII....13.2:3 inverts **p.** which was upside down before,
W-pII....13.2:4 Now is **p.** open to the truth. Now is
W-pII....13.3:3 **P.** stands corrected in His sight, and what
W-pII..346.1:1 *with miracles correcting my **p.** of all things.*
W-pII..351.1:3 *world. Yet this **p.** is a choice I make, and can*
M-4..........I.1:2 rests. **P.** is the result of learning. In fact,
M-4..........I.1:3 In fact, **p.** *is* learning, because cause and
M-5...........II.h The Shift in **P.**
M-5........II.3:1 is the single requisite for this shift in **p.**? It
M-8...............h **P.** OF ORDER OF DIFFICULTIES BE
M-8............1:1 difficulties is the basis for the world's **p.**.
M-8............3:9 the messages they bring on which **p.** rests
M-8............4:1 of the mind that errors in **p.** enter. And it
M-8............5:5 carrying affect their credibility in his **p.**?
M-10...........3:5 be certain there is no distortion in his **p.**,
M-10........4:10 for there is no distortion in His **p.**.
M-12..........1:7 His **p.** of himself is based upon God's
M-17..........3:3 only if **p.** of separate goals has entered.
M-19..........3:2 eyes, distorts **p.** and brings witness of the
M-19..........4:7 lens of warped **p.** through which you look
M-19..........5:2 **P.** can make whatever picture the mind
M-19..........5:9 **P.** rests, the mind is still, and light returns
M-21..........3:3 unanswered in the **p.** of the one who asks.
M-22.........1:3 it is the source of a wholly unified **p.**.
M-22.........4:3 both in the individual's **p.** of himself and
M-22.........4:5 correcting all mistakes and healing all **p.**.
M-22.........5:6 mistakes, and distorted **p.** does not heal.
M-27.........2:1 this **p.** of the universe as God created it, it
M-27.........5:4 which the contrast between the **p.** of the
C-in...........1:2 with Atonement, or the correction of **p.**.
C-1.............5:3 This is the final vision, the last **p.**, the
C-1.............7:2 Will is not involved in **p.** at any level, and
C-3.............2:1 the gap between their **p.** and the truth.
C-3.............2:2 go directly from **p.** to knowledge because
C-3.............2:4 it is just this insane **p.** that makes them
C-3.............4:3 Seeing the face of Christ involves **p.**. No
C-3.............6:7 As a **p.** it is part unreal. And yet this part
C-4................h TRUE **P.** – KNOWLEDGE
C-4.............3:1 is not the remedy for false **p.** since, being
C-4.............3:2 for false **p.** must be *true perception*. It will
C-4.............3:2 for false perception must be *true **p.***. It will
C-4.............3:5 For true **p.** is a remedy with many names.
C-4.............3:6 salvation, Atonement, true **p.**, all are one.
C-4.............3:8 True **p.** is the means by which the world
C-4.............3:9 not exist. And it is this that true **p.** sees.
C-4.............4:2 But true **p.** looks on it as nothing more
C-4.............6:1 This is the shift that true **p.** brings: What
C-4.............7:2 Gone is **p.**, false and true alike. Gone is
C-4.............7:6 now is the last **p.** of the world without a
C-6.............3:4 correction principle; the bringer of true **p.**
P-in............1:6 then it is always some change in his **p.** of
P-2........IV.7:4 to make illusions true through false **p.**.
P-2.......VII.3:4 vision heals **p.** and sickness disappears.
P-2.......VII.5:6 Yet no **p.** is omniscient, nor is the tiny self

## perception's 8

T-25......III.1:3 This is in accord with **p.** fundamental law:
T-25......III.1:6 This is **p.** form, adapted to this world, of
T-25......IV.2:1 **P.** basic law could thus be said, "You will
T-26.....VII.4:1 **P.** laws are opposite to truth, and what is
T-26.....VII.5:2 **P.** laws must be reversed, because they *are*
T-31.....V.12:5 of sight into **p.** law that what you see
W-pII......7.1:5 forgiveness has made possible **p.** tranquil
W-pII..336.1:1 is the means appointed for **p.** ending.

## perception-related 1

T-3.........V.4:6 The word "image" is always **p.**, and not a

## perceptions 36

T-1.........I.32:2 for your holiness and make your **p.** holy.
T-1.........I.36:1 aligning your **p.** with truth as God created
T-1........VI.5:2 test, to that extent are your **p.** corrected.
T-1.......VII.1:1 Your distorted **p.** produce a dense cover
T-2.........II.5:6 You can learn to improve your **p.**, and
T-2.......V.10:4 of these **p.** clearly imply their dependence
T-3........III.1:8 produce fear and true **p.** foster love, but
T-3.......III.1:10 the affirmation of truth and beyond all **p.**.
T-3........III.2:8 Since **p.** change, their dependence on
T-3.........V.8:1 happens to **p.** if there are no judgments
T-5...........I.6:2 of thinking that could raise their **p.** so
T-5........III.5:4 true and false **p.** are themselves opposed.
T-6.........II.9:5 your mind and project your **p.** outward.
T-6.......II.11:5 bringing all of your **p.** into the one line
T-9.......VII.3:6 it perceives because its **p.** are so shifting.
T-11........V.15:2 **p.** which it unifies on behalf of itself. This,
T-11.......VI.1:2 **P.** are built up on the basis of experience,
T-11.......VI.1:3 not until beliefs are fixed that **p.** stabilize.
T-11.......VI.3:4 beliefs, and with them different **p.**. For
T-11.......VI.3:5 **p.** are learned *with* beliefs, and experience
T-11.......VI.3:8 His **p.** are your natural awareness, and it
T-11.....VII.2:3 They are still **p.**, because he still believes
T-11.....VII.3:2 That is why its **p.** are so variable. It does
T-11.....VII.3:5 For **p.** cannot be partly true. If you believe
T-11... VIII.3:7 **P.** are learned, and you are not without a
T-12.......II.4:1 about the frightening **p.** of little children,
T-12.......II.4:4 he does not understand what his **p.** mean.
T-12....III.10:6 Bring your **p.** of the world to this altar, for
T-13.....VII.9:3 love. In these lie your true **p.**, for the Holy
T-18.........I.5:6 into meaningless bits of disunited **p.**, and
T-29......IV.5:5 **P.** are determined by their purpose, in
W-pI.....23.3:2 Each of your **p.** of "external reality" is a
W-pI.....33.1:4 surveying your outer and inner **p.**, but
W-pI...195.9:4 thought we substitute for these insane **p.**.
W-pII.334.1:2 woven out of thoughts that rest on false **p.**
P-2.........in.3:2 respective **p.** of "improvement" still must

## perceptual 8

T-1.........I.41:1 Wholeness is the **p.** content of miracles.
T-1........VII.1:2 physical impulses is a major **p.** distortion.
T-4.......II.8:12 Myths are entirely **p.**, and so ambiguous
T-6.......V.B.9:1 The second step, then, is still **p.**, although
T-10........II.3:3 **p.** counterpart of creating in the Kingdom
T-18........II.4:1 Dreams are **p.** temper tantrums, in which
W-pI.....12.1:1 a correction for a major **p.** distortion. You
C-1.............7:4 but it cannot transcend the **p.** realm. At

## perfect 387

T-1.........I.32:4 of celestial order. In this order you *are* **p.**.
T-1.........I.34:2 for lack they establish **p.** protection. The
T-1..........II.3:3 Creator. You are a **p.** creation, and should
T-1..........II.6:8 underlying recognition of **p.** equality of
T-1.........V.5:2 unalterable because it is already **p.**, but
T-1........VI.4:3 Who has **p.** faith in His creations *because*
T-1........VI.5:4 ***P.** love casts out fear. If fear exists, Then*
T-1........VI.5:5 *If fear exists, Then there is not **p.** love.* But:
T-1........VI.5:7 But: *Only **p.** love exists. If there is fear, It*
T-2...........I.1:3 created, but have also been created **p.**.
T-2.........I.1:10 is **p.** can be rendered imperfect or lacking.
T-2.........I.3:10 given you for your joy in creating the **p.**.
T-2..........II.5:7 but the Sonship itself is a **p.** creation and
T-2........III.1:11 the structure at all because it is **p.** vision.
T-2........III.1:12 can, however, see the altar with **p.** clarity.
T-2........III.2:1 **p.** effectiveness the Atonement belongs at
T-2........III.5:1 The children of God are entitled to the **p.**
T-2........III.5:1 perfect comfort that comes from **p.** trust.
T-2........III.5:5 It was created **p.** and is entirely worthy of
T-2........III.5:7 on them *because* He created them **p.**. He
T-2.........V.1:8 spirit is already **p.** and therefore does not
T-2........VI.7:7 The only remedy for lack of love is **p.** love.
T-2........VI.7:8 is perfect love. **P.** love is the Atonement.
T-2......VIII.5:9 own **p.** judgment of your own perfect
T-2......VIII.5:9 perfect judgment of your own **p.** creations
T-3...........I.7:3 if it arose from anything but **p.** innocence
T-3...........I.7:8 The Atonement is therefore the **p.** lesson.
T-3..........II.4:6 Father are One, their **p.** accord is Heaven.
T-3..........II.5:6 This single purpose creates **p.** integration
T-3........III.7:9 God knows His children with **p.** certainty.
T-3.........V.8:1 no judgments and nothing but **p.** equality
T-4........IV.9:1 in which God Himself shines in **p.** light.
T-5..........II.5:1 because He can share only **p.** knowledge.
T-5........II.10:9 the **p.** integration that can make it whole?
T-5.......III.10:1 The Holy Spirit is the **p.** Teacher. He uses
T-5........IV.8:4 them for you in their own **p.** radiance.
T-5........VI.3:2 *is* in you, for God creates with **p.** fairness.
T-5.......VII.3:3 He wills to keep it in **p.** peace, because
T-5.......VII.4:3 God Himself gave you the **p.** Correction
T-6...........I.6:4 Rather, teach your own **p.** immunity,
T-6.........I.16:7 the **p.** symbol of the "conflict" between
T-6..........II.5:1 Holy Spirit begins by perceiving you as **p.**.
T-6........II.6:10 truth lies only in its **p.** inclusion in Him
T-6........II.6:10 perfect inclusion in Him Who alone is **p.**.
T-6..........II.7:1 **p.** equality of the Holy Spirit's perception
T-6..........II.7:1 of the **p.** equality of God's knowing. The
T-6..........II.9:8 mind is not in **p.** alignment with the idea,
T-6........II.11:4 it is surely clear that the **p.** need nothing,
T-6........II.13:1 Spirit was given you with **p.** impartiality,
T-6........IV.8:4 achieved. When they are **p.**, abilities are
T-6........IV.8:5 curious that the **p.** must now be perfected
T-6......IV.10:3 demonstrate that the **p.** are inadequate to
T-6......IV.10:5 God, Who knows that His creations are **p.**
T-6......V.A.4:6 it, because it is a belief in **p.** equality. Only
T-6......V.B.6:4 Holy Spirit's Voice, and Its **p.** consistency,
T-6......V.C.2:6 established what you can extend with **p.**
T-6......V.C.7:4 **p.** accomplishment is not apparent to you
T-6....V.C.10:9 It is in the **p.** safety of God. Therefore,
T-7...........I.6:1 is to share the **p.** Love He shares with you.

| | |
|---|---|
| T-7 II.7:1 | **p.** consistency of the Kingdom mean to |
| T-7 III.3:4 | as anything other than their **p.** equals, the |
| T-7 III.4:9 | because it is a reflection of **p.** Thought. |
| T-7 III.5:8 | This holds them in **p.** serenity, because |
| T-7 V.9:10 | whole glory and **p.** joy that *is* the Kingdom |
| T-7 VI.13:7 | Being a **p.** accomplishment, the Sonship |
| T-7 VII.11:2 | real, wholly **p.** and wholly desirable. |
| T-7 IX.4:7 | is why there is **p.** peace in the Kingdom. |
| T-7 IX.6:8 | His, It extends forever and in **p.** peace. Its |
| T-7 IX.6:9 | is so intense that It creates in **p.** joy, and |
| T-7 XI.4:4 | this lesson has become the **p.** teacher, |
| T-8 III.3:3 | This is **p.** creation by the perfectly created |
| T-8 III.3:3 | created, in union with the **p.** Creator. The |
| T-8 IV.6:7 | the **p.** equality of all God's Sons cannot be |
| T-8 V.2:1 | will of the Sonship is the **p.** creator, being |
| T-8 IX.7:1 | The Bible enjoins you to be **p.**, to heal all |
| T-9 I.13:2 | you would not have been created **p.**. |
| T-9 III.2:2 | This makes **p.** sense to the ego, which is |
| T-9 IV.4:8 | that my words make **p.** sense because |
| T-9 VI.7:4 | in **p.** communication born of perfect |
| T-9 VI.7:4 | communication born of **p.** understanding |
| T-9 VII.1:8 | God wills you **p.** happiness now. Is it |
| T-10 III.8:2 | offer them **p.** freedom from all illusions |
| T-10 III.10:11 | to fear love because of its **p.** harmlessness, |
| T-10 III.10:11 | **p.** helpfulness and your own perfect Help. |
| T-10 III.10:11 | perfect helpfulness and your own **p.** Help. |
| T-10 IV.1:4 | If God created you **p.**, you *are* perfect. If |
| T-10 IV.1:4 | If God created you perfect, you *are* **p.**. If |
| T-10 V.12:5 | If God created His Son **p.**, that is how you |
| T-11 in.2:6 | insane when it is stated with **p.** honesty, |
| T-11 in.2:6 | looks on what it does with **p.** honesty. Yet |
| T-11 in.3:8 | Be willing to judge it with **p.** honesty. |
| T-11 II.1:5 | because, in your **p.** understanding of Him |
| T-11 II.1:6 | Kingdom your understanding is not **p.**, |
| T-11 II.6:6 | Your willingness need not be **p.**, because |
| T-11 IV.7:5 | **p.** as His Creator and at peace with Him. |
| T-11 IV.8:3 | Sharing the **p.** Love of the Father the Son |
| T-12 II.8:1 | There is no fear in **p.** love. We will but be |
| T-12 II.8:2 | We will but be making **p.** to you what is |
| T-12 II.8:2 | perfect to you what is already **p.** in you. |
| T-12 II.10:5 | must look at it yourself in **p.** willingness, |
| T-12 V.4:3 | cannot learn of **p.** love with a split mind, |
| T-12 VI.4:6 | In His sight the Son of God is **p.**, and He |
| T-12 VI.5:8 | **p.** peace He waits for you at His Father's |
| T-12 VI.7:6 | join in **p.** love of God and of each other. |
| T-12 VII.10:5 | the **p.** safety of the Mind which created us |
| T-12 VIII.2:2 | His Father's Love holds him in **p.** peace, |
| T-12 VIII.3:2 | for the Holy Spirit sees it with **p.** clarity. It |
| T-12 VIII.7:4 | What is invisible to you is **p.** in His sight, |
| T-13 I.6:5 | of his being, which is his **p.** blamelessness |
| T-13 V.10:5 | shining in **p.** radiance that is undimmed |
| T-13 VI.7:4 | For the light of **p.** vision is freely given as |
| T-13 VII.7:5 | In **p.** sanity he looks on love, for it is all |
| T-13 VII.10:1 | Father for the **p.** sanity of His most holy |
| T-13 VIII.2:6 | the Holy Spirit, as **p.** as perception can be |
| T-13 VIII.3:1 | **P.** perception, then, has many elements |
| T-13 VIII.9:4 | The miracle that God created is **p.**, as are |
| T-13 IX.8:7 | sign of **p.** faith your Father has in you. He |
| T-13 IX.8:11 | where God knows there is **p.** innocence? |
| T-13 X.9:4 | is the **p.** purity in which you were created. |
| T-13 X.10:11 | Christ's vision He would show you the **p.** |
| T-13 XI.4:2 | **P.** perception can merely show you what |
| T-13 XI.4:5 | He has **p.** faith in your final judgment, |
| T-14 III.7:3 | **p.** freedom from the belief that you can be |
| T-14 III.12:2 | **p.** purity of everything that He created, |
| T-14 III.15:8 | his abode was fixed in **p.** peace forever. |
| T-14 IV.4:9 | nor anyone unworthy of His **p.** Love. Fail |
| T-14 IV.8:6 | even give a blessing in **p.** gentleness. |
| T-14 V.2:5 | your awaking is as **p.** as yours is fallible. |
| T-14 V.3:4 | is the natural extension of **p.** purity. Your |
| T-14 V.7:7 | you bring within its safety and its **p.** peace |
| T-14 V.8:2 | peace is the acknowledgment of **p.** purity, |
| T-14 V.9:7 | not that you cannot teach His **p.** peace. |
| T-14 VI.2:1 | dwells within you is merely **p.** openness, |
| T-14 VI.6:7 | He will interpret it to you with **p.** clarity, |
| T-14 VI.6:7 | with Whom you are in **p.** communication |
| T-14 XI.5:2 | even think of you share in your **p.** peace, |
| T-14 XI.5:4 | absence of **p.** peace means but one thing: |
| T-14 XI.12:4 | until you pass the test of **p.** peace, for |
| T-15 I.14:2 | As long as it takes to re-establish **p.** sanity |
| T-15 I.14:2 | **p.** peace and perfect love for everyone, for |
| T-15 I.14:2 | perfect peace and **p.** love for everyone, for |
| T-15 I.15:10 | you, in that shining instant of **p.** release. |
| T-15 II.5:2 | and you will recognize it with **p.** certainty. |
| T-15 III.4:5 | To hold your magnitude in **p.** awareness |
| T-15 III.6:1 | clearly and in **p.** safety in your mind, |
| T-15 III.9:6 | where holiness abides in **p.** peace. My |
| T-15 IV.3:5 | would have His host abide in **p.** freedom. |
| T-15 IV.4:1 | Would you learn how **p.** and immaculate |
| T-15 IV.6:5 | you receive and give **p.** communication. |
| T-15 IV.7:2 | to deny the **p.** communication that makes |
| T-15 IV.8:2 | to recognize **p.** communication while |
| T-15 IV.8:3 | "Would I want to have **p.** communication |
| T-15 IV.9:6 | not be able to accept **p.** communication |
| T-15 V.4:4 | be depended on because it is not **p.**. In |
| T-15 VI.1:4 | way. **P.** faith in each one, for its ability to |
| T-15 VI.1:4 | arises only from **p.** faith in yourself. And |
| T-15 VI.2:1 | unwilling to accept the fact that **p.** love is |
| T-15 VI.2:3 | I offer you my **p.** faith in you, in place of |
| T-15 VI.2:4 | be as **p.** in all your brothers as it is in you, |
| T-15 VI.5:2 | so no one is aware that **p.** love is in him. |
| T-15 VIII.4:1 | Sonship to you, to ensure your **p.** creation |
| T-15 X.1:1 | to delay the **p.** union of the Father and the |
| T-15 XI.2:9 | Host is as holy as the **p.** Innocence which |
| T-15 XI.10:2 | I have **p.** faith in you to do all that you |
| T-16 II.7:8 | charity on whom God loves with **p.** Love? |
| T-16 III.7:7 | nothing in Him that is not **p.** and eternal. |
| T-16 IV.2:5 | and you will cross the bridge in **p.** safety, |
| T-16 IV.9:2 | to the abode of peace and **p.** holiness. |
| T-16 VI.5:6 | If one such union were made in **p.** faith, |
| T-16 VI.12:3 | need not be complete because His is **p.**. It |
| T-16 VI.12:4 | for your unwillingness by His **p.** faith, |
| T-16 VI.12:5 | release, His **p.** willingness is given you. |
| T-16 VII.6:5 | peace of *now* enfold you in **p.** gentleness. |
| T-16 VII.12:3 | *in us that needs forgiveness when Yours is* ***p.*** |
| T-17 II.3:2 | but this is given, complete and wholly **p.**. |
| T-17 III.6:3 | to make His resolutions complete and **p.**, |
| T-17 IV.13:3 | The other is framed for **p.** clarity. The |
| T-17 IV.16:9 | is only healing, already complete and **p.**. |
| T-17 IV.16:10 | He is only the **p.** and complete can be. |
| T-17 VII.7:2 | And you can use *this* in **p.** safety. Yet for |
| T-17 VIII.1:6 | on it. It is a situation of **p.** peace, simply |
| T-18 I.9:3 | you love your brother with a **p.** love. Here |
| T-18 I.10:7 | but in the Thought so holy and so **p.** that |
| T-18 I.10:9 | His gift as our most holy and **p.** reality, |
| T-18 VI.1:6 | It is merely an awareness of **p.** Oneness, |
| T19 IV.C.5:1 | the body incorruptible and **p.** as long as it |
| T19 IV.C.10:5 | its tiny hands it holds, in **p.** safety, every |
| T19 IV.D.11:3 | with **p.** faith and love and tenderness. |
| T-20 I.2:4 | we honor the **p.** purity of the Son of God, |
| T-20 III.9:6 | his holiness remained untouched and **p.**, |
| T-20 III.10:3 | what is Heaven but union, direct and **p.**, |
| T-20 III.10:4 | one, looking with **p.** gentleness upon each |
| T-20 III.11:3 | is no fear in **p.** love *because* it knows no sin |
| T-20 V.6:6 | means and end in **p.** harmony already. |
| T-20 V.6:7 | **p.** faith that you will one day offer to your |
| T-20 V.8:1 | in love and **p.** confidence in what He sees. |
| T-20 VI.1:5 | one of **p.** union and unbroken continuity. |
| T-20 VIII.5:4 | the **p.** choice to call upon for strength? |
| T-21 I.8:5 | it everything is joined in **p.** continuity. |
| T-22 I.9:8 | in each the other saw a **p.** shelter where |
| T-22 II.13:6 | Heaven is the home of **p.** purity, and God |
| T-22 III.6:4 | For this the body's eyes are **p.** means, but |
| T-23 IV.8:8 | be anything that offers you a **p.** calmness, |
| T-24 III.6:1 | holiness, the **p.** Father of a perfect Son, |
| T-24 III.6:1 | holiness, the perfect Father of a **p.** Son, |
| T-24 III.6:6 | forever in the arms of peace, in **p.** safety, |
| T-24 V.7:6 | His **p.** lack of specialness He offers you, |
| T-24 V.8:4 | unto you except he be as **p.** as yourself, |
| T-24 VI.5:5 | Yet will his **p.** sinlessness release you both |
| T-24 VI.6:4 | the **p.** frame for your salvation and the |
| T-24 VII.7:3 | A **p.** being, all-encompassing and all- |
| T-25 I.4:3 | is framed in holiness and **p.** purity, in |
| T-25 II.6:8 | corruption, unchanged and **p.** in eternity. |
| T-25 II.9:4 | creation as the **p.** Father that He is. And |
| T-25 II.9:6 | This brother is His **p.** gift to you. And He |
| T-25 II.9:7 | you thank His **p.** Son for being what he is. |
| T-25 III.3:4 | and to each it is a **p.** means to serve the |
| T-25 III.3:5 | specialness, it is the **p.** frame to set it off; |
| T-25 III.3:5 | it off; the **p.** battleground to wage its wars |
| T-25 III.3:5 | the **p.** shelter for illusions which it would |
| T-25 III.5:2 | forgiveness and the sight of **p.** sinlessness. |
| T-25 III.8:1 | world of gentleness has **p.** power to offset |
| T-25 VI.5:1 | the laws of God do not prevail in **p.** form, |
| T-25 VI.5:1 | *one* **p.** thing and make *one* perfect choice. |
| T-25 VI.5:1 | *one* perfect thing and make *one* **p.** choice. |
| T-25 VII.10:4 | so emerge from deepest mourning into **p.** |
| T-25 VII.12:4 | rest in **p.** confidence and perfect peace. |
| T-25 VII.12:4 | rest in perfect confidence and **p.** peace. |
| T-25 VIII.12:1 | **p.** witness to the power of love and justice |
| T-25 VIII.14:1 | the right to all the universe; to **p.** peace, |
| T-25 VIII.14:3 | else but **p.** justice can prevail for you. And |
| T-26 II.6:6 | given you to see in him his **p.** sinlessness. |
| T-26 II.8:6 | He gave, when He created you in **p.** love. |
| T-26 V.10:7 | restored unto his Father's **p.** Love. And |
| T-26 VII.10:1 | Salvation, **p.** and complete, asks but a |
| T-26 VII.10:2 | see with Heaven, wholly **p.** and complete. |
| T-27 I.3:6 | becomes the **p.** witness to his innocence. |
| T-27 I.10:2 | and **p.** healing take the place of death. |
| T-27 VII.15:6 | gifts because he is not **p.** in your dreams. |
| T-28 I.9:6 | Its Effect, as changeless and as **p.** as Itself. |
| T-28 III.1:1 | waits in **p.** certainty beyond salvation is |
| T-28 IV.9:2 | Your Holiness, complete and **p.**, lies in |
| T-28 VI.6:5 | Be you **p.** as Myself, for you can never be |
| T-29 III.2:4 | you the proof that He is **p.** and complete? |
| T-29 V.5:2 | Behold His Son, His **p.** gift, in whom his |
| T-29 VIII.6:6 | And the Son of God, as **p.**, sinless and as |
| T-29 IX.2:1 | the mind that God created **p.** as Himself. |
| T-30 I.11:3 | And you can say in **p.** honesty: *I want* |
| T-30 II.2:6 | will when He gave you His **p.** Answer. |
| T-30 III.8:7 | its light grew dimmer or less **p.** ever was. |
| T-30 III.9:2 | Its **p.** purity does not depend on whether |
| T-30 III.9:3 | it and softly holds it in its **p.** place, which |
| T-30 III.10:3 | near, it rests in certainty and **p.** peace. |
| T-30 III.10:5 | In **p.** sureness of its changelessness and of |
| T-30 V.3:2 | but remains until it is made **p.** in himself. |
| T-30 V.4:1 | God Who could create a **p.** Son and share |
| T-30 V.8:2 | with **p.** confidence away from fear forever |
| T-30 VI.9:1 | God's Son is **p.**, or he cannot be God's |
| T-30 VI.9:4 | *I thank You, Father, for Your* ***p.*** *Son, and in* |
| T-30 VIII.2:5 | form of the appearance of his **p.** health, |
| T-30 VIII.2:5 | his **p.** freedom from all forms of lack, and |
| T-30 VIII.5:5 | The Christ in him is **p.**. Is it this that you |
| T-31 I.9:6 | God's **p.** Son remembers his creation. But |
| T-31 VIII.11:1 | light that shines beyond in **p.** constancy. |
| W-pI 14.3:6 | direction is toward **p.** safety and perfect |
| W-pI 14.3:6 | is toward perfect safety and **p.** peace. |
| W-pI 41.3:1 | Deep within you is everything that is **p.**, |
| W-pI 41.4:1 | can never be deprived of your **p.** holiness |
| W-pI 47.7:4 | is a place in you where there is **p.** peace. |
| W-pI 50.3:2 | world into a climate of **p.** peace and safety |
| W-pI 52.1:4 | Reality brings only **p.** peace. When I am |
| W-pI 56.1:5 | Yet **p.** security and complete fulfillment |
| W-pI 59.1:3 | of myself when **p.** certainty abides in Him |
| W-pI 59.1:7 | myself. I am **p.** because God goes with me |
| W-pI 61.4:2 | It is the **p.** answer to all illusions, and |
| W-pI 67.2:6 | *Perfection created me* ***p.***. Any attribute |
| W-pI 69.6:1 | the world, try to settle down in **p.** stillness |
| W-pI 73.9:3 | you and your Father are in **p.** accord. You |
| W-pI 77.8:1 | to be satisfied with less than the **p.** answer |
| W-pI 88.3:2 | Here is the **p.** statement of my freedom. I |
| W-pI 95.1:4 | **p.** unity makes change in you impossible. |
| W-pI 95.3:1 | hear and see, and what makes **p.** sense. |
| W-pI 95.13:1 | one Self, in **p.** harmony with all there is, |
| W-pI 98.3:4 | filled completely in the **p.** time and place. |
| W-pI 98.7:3 | in faith as **p.** and as sure as His in you. His |
| W-pI 100.2:1 | God's Will for you is **p.** happiness. Why |
| W-pI 100.4:4 | proof that God wills **p.** happiness for all |
| W-pI 101.h | God's Will for me is **p.** happiness. |
| W-pI 101.6:1 | you is **p.** happiness because there is no sin |
| W-pI 101.6:6 | *God's Will for me is* ***p.*** *happiness. There is* |
| W-pI 101.7:6 | *God's Will for me is* ***p.*** *happiness. This is the* |
| W-pI 107.4:3 | trusted with a **p.** trust in all the seeming |
| W-pI 107.5:1 | in its wings the gift of **p.** constancy, and |
| W-pI 110.2:1 | and give you **p.** vision that will heal all the |
| WpI rIII.in7:1 | You have been given them in **p.** trust; in |
| WpI rIII.in7:1 | in **p.** confidence that you would use them |

WpI. rIII.in7:1 p. faith that you would see their messages
W-pI...113.1:2 *Serenity and p. peace are mine, because I am*
W-pI...113.2:2 *I see God's p. plan for my salvation perfectly*
W-pI...116.1:1 (101) God's Will for me is p. happiness.
W-pI...116.1:2 *God's Will is p. happiness for me. And I can*
W-pI...116.3:2 God's Will for me is p. happiness. On the
W-pI...118.2:2 *Truth Itself assure me that I am God's p. Son*
W-pI...120.1:2 *while I rest in Him in quiet and in p. certainty*
W-pI.121.13:7 *full of sin, and know I am the p. Son of God.*
W-pI...122.1:6 and a rest so p. it can never be upset?
W-pI...122.4:2 Here is the p. answer, given to imperfect
W-pI...123.8:1 for you, how p. is His gratitude to you.
W-pI...131.5:1 can abandon his Creator, nor affect His p.
W-pI.136.12:5 gifts, and yet it knows, with p. certainty,
WpI. rIV.in9:2 and rest, and endless quiet, p. certainty,
W-pI...151.8:3 can only honor Him, rejoicing in His p.,
W-pI.151.14:4 remains is unified into a p. Thought that
W-pI...152.2:5 a mind where love and p. holiness abide?
W-pI...152.9:3 God's p. gift to His beloved Son. We lay
W-pI.152.10:5 Son, his gentleness, his p. sinlessness, his
W-pI......156.h I walk with God in p. holiness.
W-pI...156.8:5 *I walk with God in p. holiness. I light the*
W-pI...157.9:1 except His shining face and p. Love. The
W-pI...159.3:3 God created p. can be mirrored there.
W-pI...159.6:1 which you can appeal with p. certainty for
W-pI.160.10:2 be complete and p. as it was established.
W-pI...161.4:5 words bring p. clarity with them to you?
W-pI...161.9:1 the angels love and God created p.. This
W-pI.161.11:8 *of Christ, and see my p. sinlessness in you.*
W-pI...162.5:2 is the right to p. holiness you now accept.
W-pI...162.5:4 Who could despair when p. joy is yours,
W-pI...163.4:3 the endlessness of love and Heaven's p.,
W-pI...164.5:4 unfold in p. innocence before your eyes.
W-pI...165.1:2 and death obscure the p. happiness and
W-pI...167.2:5 give response of any kind that is not p. joy
W-pI.167.12:1 in the holy minds which He created p.. As
W-pI...170.4:3 with p. faith the split you made is real.
WpI.. rV.in4:5 Itself, is p. in Its knowledge and Its Love,
W-pI...173.2:1 (156) I walk with God in p. holiness. God
W-pI...182.8:3 and you will stay with Him in p. stillness,
W-pI...186.3:2 and offers you the p. trust He holds in you
W-pI...187.9:5 and leave instead the p. gift forever there,
W-pI...189.1:7 hope, and blessed with p. charity and love
W-pI...189.6:1 its Love which knows us p. as itself, its
W-pI...196.4:1 from bondage to the state of p. freedom.
W-pI.198.12:2 him. He is p. in his holiness. He needs no
W-pI...199.6:4 it becomes p. in the ability to serve an
W-pI...199.7:6 For He would give you p. freedom, perfect
W-pI...199.7:6 He would give you perfect freedom, p. joy
W-pII..233.1:7 *but which is yet Your p. gift to me.*
W-pII..235.1:1 me, and with p. certainty assure myself,
W-pII..235.1:3 Son and keeps his sinlessness forever p.,
W-pII..239.1:4 His Son forever and with p. constancy,
W-pII..252.1:2 Its shimmering and p. purity is far more
W-pII..253.2:2 *is but Your Will in p. union with my own,*
W-pII.....255.h This day I choose to spend in p. peace.
W-pII..281.1:1 *Father, Your Son is p.. When I think that I*
W-pII..299.2:5 *It stands forever p. and untouched. In it are*
W-pII..337.1:1 My sinlessness ensures me p. peace,
W-pII....13.3:5 in the light of p. purity and endless joy.
W-pII..341.1:3 *sinlessness so p. that the Lord of Sinlessness*
W-pII..348.1:3 *except the p. peace and joy I share with You.*
W-pII..348.1:5 *Surrounding me is p. safety. Can I be afraid,*
W-pII..348.1:7 *Surrounding me is p. sinlessness. What can*
W-pII..348.1:8 *created me in holiness as p. as Your Own?*
W-pII..360.1:6 *Your Son is like to You in p. sinlessness. And*
M-in ..........5:5 They are not p., or they would not be here
M-in ..........5:6 Yet it is their mission to become p. here,
M-3............5:3 teaching-learning balance is actually p..
M-3............5:6 it, the p. lesson is before them and can be
M-4......... II.2:1 is largely due to their p. honesty. It is only
M-4...... II.2:12 They choose in p. honesty, sure of their
M-10..........4:7 Someone with you Whose judgment is p..
M-12..........1:2 One wholly p. teacher, whose learning is
M-22..........2:2 complete awareness of the p. applicability
M-22.........7:10 my beloved Son, created p. and forever so
M-23..........5:8 eyes Christ's vision shines in p. constancy
M-28..........4:7 the dust and look upon our p. sinlessness.
C-2............4:2 And this is shown to us with p. clarity. It
C-5.............3:1 with the Christ–the p. Son of God, His
P-2......... II.1:5 made p. in time and restored to eternity.
P-2........ III.3:6 goals alone can interfere with p. healing.
P-2......... V.3:3 the p. teacher could not long remain; the
P-2......... V.3:3 the p. psychotherapist is but a glimmer of
P-2........VII.8:5 is done, for what is p. needs no healing,
P-3......... II.4:2 No, He declared it p., and so it was. And
P-3......... II.4:4 neither a p. therapist nor a perfect patient
P-3......... II.4:4 neither a perfect therapist nor a p. patient
S-2............I.6:6 in tranquil silence and in p. peace. He
S-3........ IV.6:2 which fathered you in p. sinlessness, and
S-3........ IV.7:2 embrace of everlasting Love and p. peace.

## perfected 4

T-6........ IV.8:5 is curious that the perfect must now be p..
T-17....... II.4:2 will be meaningless when it has been p.,
T-31....... V.1:7 time you reach "maturity" you have p. it,
W-pII.... 14.1:3 *life. In me is love p., fear impossible, and joy*

## Perfection 1

*perfection*

P-3.........I.1:10 Who could ask of P. that He be imperfect?

## perfection 37

*Perfection*

T-1.........I.29:2 honoring His creations, affirming their p..
T-1......... II.3:3 only in the Presence of the Creator of p..
T-2......... II.5:7 creation and p. is not a matter of degree.
T-2......... III.5:5 and is entirely worthy of receiving p.. God
T-2......... V.9:4 and charity is a way of perceiving the p. of
T-3...........I.8:3 altar, where nothing except p. belongs.
T-3......... II.3:5 seeing cannot see anything but p.. I have
T-6......... II.5:2 this p. is shared He recognizes it in others,
T-6...... II.11:4 and you cannot experience p. as a difficult
T-6...... IV.10:2 situation if God showed you your p., and
T-6...... IV.10:3 themselves to the awareness of their p.,
T-6...... IV.12:5 The separation was not a loss of p., but a
T-6......... V.1:3 true. You did not believe in your own p..
T-7...... VII.6:6 know your own p. until you have honored
T-7....... IX.2:2 its creations equally whole and equal in p.
T-8......... V.2:6 If your p. is in Him and only in Him, how
T-10...... IV.1:3 Sickness and p. are irreconcilable. If God
T-12....... II.8:5 easily accomplish the goal of p. together.
T-12....... II.8:6 For p. *is,* and cannot be denied. To deny
T-12....... II.8:7 denial of p. is not so difficult as to deny
T-13. VIII.10:1 Yet in this world your p. is unwitnessed.
T-14.... XI.14:6 With your p. ever in His sight, He gives
T-17....... II.2:6 cease to cause you wonderment at its p..
T-17....... II.6:3 and a blade of grass a sign of God's p..
T-23...... IV.9:2 What could they gain but loss of their p.?
T-29...... III.2:3 Was He made incomplete by your p.? Or
W-pI.....53.4:5 when the p. of creation is my home? Let
W-pI.....67.2:6 *P. created me perfect.* Any attribute which
W-pI.151.14:4 Thought that offers its p. everywhere.
W-pI.167.12:1 a Source from which p. comes to us,
W-pI.167.12:3 as it sees its own p. mirroring the Lord of
W-pI...197.8:4 Nor can you dim the light of your p.. In
M-in ..........5:6 here, and so they teach p. over and over,
M-4 ....... X.3:2 Terms like love, sinlessness, p.,
M-23 .........5:7 limit and no stain to mar your beautiful p.
P-2......... V.7:3 p. that is asked in our attempts to heal.
P-3......... II.4:5 Both must have denied their p., for their

## perfectly 123

T-1......... II.3:1 to which it is p. and correctly applicable.
T-2...........I.5:6 In reality you are p. unaffected by all
T-2......... III.2:4 thoughts and making you p. invulnerable
T-2......... III.4:4 P. aware of the right defense it passes
T-2......... V.4:2 are p. safe as long as you are completely
T-2.......VII.1:8 to enable you to do this, which is p. true.
T-3...........I.1:1 further point must be p. clear before any
T-3...........I.6:4 meaning of the Atonement is p. apparent.
T-3...........I.6:6 It is p. clear because it exists in light. Only
T-3...........I.7:5 p. aware of everything that is true. The
T-3...... III.7:11 He recognizes them p.. When they do not
T-3......... V.3:4 you are p. stable as God created you. In
T-3....... V.10:9 where the miracle that is you is p. clear.
T-4...... III.1:12 *is p. united and perfectly protected, and the*
T-4...... III.1:12 *is perfectly united and p. protected, and the*
T-4...... III.10:1 which in your sane mind is p. conscious,
T-4....... VII.3:9 This communication is p. abstract, since
T-5...........I.7:2 First, its universality is p. clear, and no
T-5........ III.6:3 God, so the Holy Spirit understands it p..
T-5....... III.10:5 it p. because it is His Own dwelling place;
T-5....... VII.4:4 I am making His plan p. explicit to you,
T-6...........I.5:1 I have made it p. clear that I am like you
T-6..........I.13:1 The message of the crucifixion is p. clear:
T-6..........II.8:2 Mind. All His Thoughts are thus p. united
T-6........ III.2:5 This is the one lesson that is p. unified,
T-6........ III.3:3 it, assuring it that it is p. safe forever. The
T-6........ III.3:4 The p. safe are wholly benign. They bless
T-6........ IV.7:1 you are and what you are is p. certain.
T-6......... V.3:5 This simple statement is p. clear, easily
T-6...... V.C.1:6 the Kingdom p. consistent and perfectly
T-6...... V.C.1:6 the Kingdom perfectly consistent and p.
T-7..........II.7:6 no translation because it is p. understood
T-7..........II.7:7 Communication is p. direct and perfectly
T-7..........II.7:7 is perfectly direct and p. united. It is
T-7........ III.4:9 The altar is p. clear in thought, because it
T-7........ III.5:6 The certain are p. calm, because they are
T-7........ IV.1:4 Who knows His creations as p. whole. Yet
T-7........ VI.3:4 It is p. logical but clearly insane. The ego
T-7........ VI.8:2 the ego proceeds p. logically to the belief
T-7...... VI.13:5 is the Holy Spirit's p. consistent teaching.
T-7...... VI.13:7 the Sonship can only accomplish p.,
T-7......... X.6:1 The Holy Spirit is p. trustworthy, as you
T-8........ III.1:7 Understanding His function p. He fulfills
T-8........ III.1:7 His function perfectly He fulfills it p.,
T-8........ III.2:1 To fulfill the Will of God p. is the only joy
T-8........ III.3:3 This is perfect creation by the p. created,
T-8........ III.8:5 Fulfilling it p. will let you remember what
T-8........ IV.3:2 was done, it was p. accomplished by all.
T-8........ IV.3:3 How else could it be p. accomplished? My
T-8....... VII.6:3 p. accomplish His holy Will for you when
T-8...... VIII.4:7 Spirit, and one He is p. equipped to fulfill.
T-8...... VIII.6:5 Spirit, p. aware of the same situation,
T-8........ IX.6:7 To the ego this is p. sensible. Believing in
T-9........ II.11:3 laws are always fair and p. consistent. By
T-9........ IV.6:1 function and He knows how to fulfill it p..
T-9...... IV.12:2 and God, and is p. satisfying to all of Us.
T-9....... VII.3:1 is p. obvious that if the Holy Spirit looks
T-9...... VIII.1:3 of the ego becomes p. apparent. When
T-10.........I.1:4 that was created is therefore p. safe,
T-10.........I.2:1 but p. capable of awakening to reality. Is
T-10........II.6:4 outcome of your decision is p. clear, if you
T-10...... IV.4:9 Creation is p. lawful, and the chaotic is
T-11....... V.7:4 are, because it is p. certain of its purpose.
T-11...... VI.3:1 This course is p. clear. If you do not see it
T-12...... III.1:5 Consider how p. your lesson would be
T-12...... VI.2:2 is p. aware that you do not know yourself,
T-12...... VI.2:2 yourself, and p. aware of how to teach
T-13..... X.14:8 I, then, lack faith in you and love Him p.?
T-13...... XI.3:8 Heaven is p. unambiguous. Everything is
T-13.... XI.11:5 *of* everyone, will not be p. accomplished.
T-14........II.2:6 what is true and what is not is p. apparent
T-14...... VI.4:2 make the falsity of its opposite p. clear.
T-14...... X.11:2 Him is p. open and freely accessible to all,
T-15.........I.1:1 to be p. calm and quiet all the time? Yet
T-15...... IV.4:3 p. clear because you have been willing to
T-15...... VI.7:8 of communication, which you know p..
T-16........II.3:3 of the whole in every part is p. natural, for
T-16...... III.4:3 and effect relationship that is p. apparent.
T-17.........I.1:7 for only then does it become p. apparent
T-17.... IV.13:1 pictures are each framed p. for what they
T-17..... VII.6:2 If you lack faith in anyone to fulfill, and p.
T-20.....II.10:3 and p. protected from the cold chill of
T-20...... IV.7:4 p. fulfilled in them and all their brothers.
T-20..... VII.3:7 the goal, and they are p. in line with it.
T-20..... VII.4:2 not p. consistent with the goal of holiness
T-20.... VIII.6:3 unadjusted form and suited p. to meet it.
T-21...... IV.5:1 and recognized him p. since time began.
T-21...... IV.5:6 it follows p. from what you have already
T-21....... V.3:9 This other self is p. aware of this. And
T-23.........I.4:6 He loves you p., completely and eternally.

T-24...... III.3:3 leave it **p.** unmoved and undisturbed. But
T-25...... VI.3:6 and no aim which only they can **p.** fulfill.
T-25...... VI.7:9 and let salvation be **p.** fulfilled in you. Do
T-26....... II.8:4 of His Love kept **p.** intact and undefiled.
T-26..... V.10:3 instant in a distant past, now **p.** corrected
T-27....... V.7:2 needs one lesson that has **p.** been learned.
T-28.........I.9:4 **p.** untouched by time and interference.
T-29...... III.3:5 So **p.** can you forgive him his illusions he
T-30...... III.7:6 of you is **p.** unchanged by your forgetting.
T-30....... V.4:5 and understands it **p.** with Him.
T-30....... V.5:1 and yet completely shared and **p.** fulfilled.
T-31...... IV.4:8 clear, and **p.** within your learning grasp.
T-31..VIII.12:6 Thy Will is done, complete and **p.**, and all
W-pI....... 3.2:2 essential that you keep a **p.** open mind,
W-pI..... 27.4:6 day you feel that you were **p.** sincere while
W-pI..... 29.3:6 world, you will understand today's idea **p.**
W-pI..... 68.6:9 *all my grievances go I will know I am* **p.** *safe.*
W-pI..... 81.3:3 and **p.** unambiguous before my sight. My
W-pI..... 88.3:7 I am **p.** free of the effects of all laws save
W-pI... 113.2:2 *perfect plan for my salvation* **p.** *fulfilled.*
W-pI... 127.6:3 is **p.** apparent to the eyes that see and ears
W-pI. 167.12:3 so **p.** it fades into what is reflected there.
W-pI... 169.9:3 and fully recognized as **p.** fulfilled by Him
WpI...rV.in4:5 Self alone is **p.** consistent in Its Thoughts;
W-pI... 183.9:5 as well. And both can be accomplished **p.**.
W-pI... 186.2:4 us by which it will be **p.** accomplished. All
W-pI... 186.2:7 Our minds are suited **p.** to take the part
M-14 ......... 3:7 One sin **p.** forgiven by one teacher of God
M-23 ......... 2:1 who has **p.** accepted the Atonement for
M-26 ......... 2:1 and remembering their own Identity **p.**.
M-28 ......... 1:6 the dream in which the body functions **p.**,
C-6............. 2:2 was the first to complete his own part **p.**.
P-2......... II.2:7 to find truth, which remains **p.** obvious,

## perform 12

T-1........ III.4:1 one who can **p.** miracles indiscriminately,
T-1........ III.4:3 Ask me which miracles you should **p.**.
T-1........ III.8:3 Miracles you are not asked to **p.** have not
T-2......... II.1:2 I have asked you to **p.** miracles, and have
T-2......... V.2:6 you should not attempt to **p.** miracles.
T-2....V.A.11:3 When you **p.** a miracle, I will arrange
T-5........ III.7:4 **p.** the function of reinterpreting what the
T-6......V.A.4:6 cannot **p.** miracles without believing it,
T-9........ VI.6:3 You cannot **p.** a miracle for yourself,
T19..IV.C.10:5 in perfect safety, every miracle you will **p.**,
W-pI... 154.5:4 failing to **p.** his proper part as bringer of
W-pI... 154.7:2 The messengers of God **p.** their part by

## performed 2

T-1...........I.8:1 they are **p.** by those who temporarily have
T-2......... II.1:3 cannot be **p.** in the spirit of doubt or fear.

## perfume 1

T-25...... IV.5:4 has saved its **p.** and its loveliness for you.

## perhaps 142

T-2.......VIII.2:5 long period, and **p.** an even longer one.
T-5......... V.1:1 **P.** some of our concepts will become
T-6........ IV.5:2 This is **p.** the strangest perception of all, if
T-6......V.A.1:2 **P.** you think this is accomplished through
T-6......V.A.5:6 **P.** you think that fear as well as love can
T-8.............I.1:9 but **p.** you do not yet regard this as wholly
T-9......VIII.7:4 **P.** it is the belief in littleness; perhaps it is
T-9......VIII.7:4 littleness; **p.** it is the belief in grandiosity.
T-11....VIII.1:2 course. **P.** you do not feel you need a
T-11....VIII.5:2 **p.** you have not done what it specifically
T-12.........I.3:8 **P.** the danger of this to your own mind is
T-12...... III.9:2 **P.** you are willing to accept even death to
T-12...... V.7:11 But **p.** you do not realize, even yet, that
T-13.......in.2:9 they love, **p.** the most insane belief of all.
T-13....... II.8:3 You have **p.** recognized the futility of the
T-13....... IV.3:2 While it could **p.** be argued that death
T-14...... III.2:1 **P.** you are accustomed to using
T-14...... IV.2:5 You can **p.** feel His Presence next to you,
T-14....... X.4:1 **P.** you have been aware of lack of
T-15 .... VII.9:5 and wounding him, **p.** in little ways,
T-15 .... VII.9:5 perhaps in little ways, **p.** "unconsciously,"
T-15 .......X.7:3 of two evils, one to be feared a little, **p.**,
T-17 .... V.11:9 **P.** you are now entering upon a campaign
T-18 .... VII.2:2 It has **p.** faded at times from your sight,
T-19 .......II.8:3 is. **P.** you would be tempted to agree with
T-20 .... IV.8:2 **P.** this seems impossible to you. But ask
T-20 ... VI.12:4 **P.** confusion, but hardly discouragement.
T-20 ... VI.12:8 **P.** you fear your brother a little yet;
T-20 ... VI.12:8 **p.** a shadow of the fear of God remains
T-21 ........I.6:1 **p.** you catch a hint of an ancient state not
T-21 ........I.6:1 ancient state not quite forgotten; dim, **p.**,
T-21 .......II.6:1 **P.** you do not see the need for you to give
T-21 ..... III.1:4 of yourself, **p.** more often of the other.
T-21 ...... V.1:3 and shape and brightness would hold, **p.**,
T-22 ......in.2:8 their bodies **p.** under a common roof that
T-23 ..... IV.8:7 **P.** you think the battleground can offer
T-25 .......II.1:2 with fear? **P.** you think you find a hope of
T-25 .......II.1:3 **P.** you fancy to attain some peace and
T-25 ... VIII.3:2 **p.** sustained by someone else, but not
T-26 .... VII.8:6 rule. **P.** you do not see the role forgiveness
T-27 ... VIII.9:6 **P.** you come in tears. But hear Him say,
T-28 ...... V.6:2 glass, a piece of wood, a thread or two, **p.**,
T-29 ........I.3:5 Sometimes a friend, **p.**, provided that
T-29 ..... III.3:1 is yet one theme of truth; no more, **p.**,
T-30 ......I.12:3 ***P.*** *there is another way to look at this. What*
T-30 ...... V.7:2 **P.** they still look back, and think they see
T-31 .......II.4:1 **P.** you call it love. Perhaps you think that
T-31 .......II.4:2 **P.** you think that it is murder justified at
T-31 .......II.9:3 walk with you, and thinks **p.** a bit behind,
T-31 .....II.10:4 It takes, **p.**, a different form in him, but it
T-31 ..... IV.3:2 **P.** you would prefer to try them all, before
T-31 .... V.11:1 **P.** the reason why this concept must be
W-pI..... 27.4:4 applications, and **p.** quite a number. Do
W-pI..... 67.4:3 Yet **p.** you will succeed in going past that,
W-pI..... 67.5:3 or five times an hour, and **p.** even more, it
W-pI..... 68.1:5 **P.** you do not yet fully realize just what
W-pI..... 68.4:2 so? **P.** you do not think you can let your
W-pI..... 71.1:5 the ego's plan is, **p.** you will realize that,
W-pI..... 72.3:1 here, it is **p.** not so apparent why holding
W-pI... 72.13:1 One or **p.** two shorter practice periods an
W-pI..... 76.8:4 **P.** you even think that there are laws
W-pI..... 78.1:1 **P.** it is not yet quite clear to you that each
W-pI..... 78.4:5 **p.**, you fear and even hate; someone you
W-pI..... 79.8:2 **P.** you will not succeed in letting all your
W-pI..... 96.6:7 **P.** you hope it can. Yet would you have
W-pI... 96.11:2 **P.** your mind remains uncertain yet a
W-pI... 107.2:3 when there was a time,– **p.** a minute,
WpI..rIII.in9:1 important, and **p.** of even greater value.
W-pI. 124.10:1 **P.** today, perhaps tomorrow, you will see
W-pI. 124.10:1 Perhaps today, **p.** tomorrow, you will see
W-pI. 124.11:1 **P.** today, perhaps tomorrow, you will
W-pI. 124.11:1 Perhaps today, **p.** tomorrow, you will
W-pI. 124.11:3 yet you can be sure someday, **p.** today,
W-pI. 124.11:3 someday, perhaps today, **p.** tomorrow,
W-pI... 127.1:1 **P.** you think that different kinds of love
W-pI... 127.1:2 **P.** you think there is a kind of love for this
W-pI... 129.2:2 **P.** you will concede there is no loss in
W-pI. 131.13:3 A tiny moment of surprise, **p.**, will make
W-pI... 132.4:4 **P.** you think you did not make the world,
W-pI... 132.6:5 **p.** step back a while and then return again
W-pI. 135.14:1 It is, **p.**, not easy to perceive that self-
W-pI. 135.18:2 **P.** you have misunderstood His plan, for
W-pI. 136.12:5 **P.** it sighs a little when you throw away its
W-pI. 136.18:1 **P.** you do not realize that this removes
W-pI. 137.10:2 **P.** you will not recognize them all, nor
W-pI... 153.6:3 **P.** you will recall the text maintains that
W-pI. 153.16:2 At times, **p.**, a minute, even less, will be
W-pI... 156.6:5 silly dream, not frightening, ridiculous **p.**,
W-pI... 156.7:5 you may **p.** lose sight of your Companion,
W-pI... 161.4:6 seem to be but empty sounds; pretty, **p.**,
W-pI... 166.9:4 **P.** God's Word is truer than your own.
W-pI... 166.9:5 **P.** His gifts to you are real. Perhaps He
W-pI... 166.9:6 **P.** He has not wholly been outwitted by
W-pI... 169.4:1 We have **p.** appeared to contradict our
W-pI... 182.4:1 **P.** you think it is your childhood home
W-pI. 185.10:4 above all things, **p.** unknown to them, but
W-pI... 187.2:5 **P.** the form in which the thought seems to
W-pI... 196.2:1 **P.** at first you will not understand how
W-pI .. 196.5:2 **P.** it seemed to be salvation. Yet it merely
W-pII . 231.1:2 *Love?* ***P.*** *I think I seek for something else; a*
W-pII ..... 4.5:4 **P.** today? There is no sin. Creation is
W-pII . 273.1:1 **P.** we are now ready for a day of
M-3 ........... 2:5 **P.** the seeming strangers in the elevator
M-3 ........... 2:5 **p.** the adult will not scold the child for
M-3 ........... 2:5 him; **p.** the students will become friends.
M-3 ........... 3:5 **P.** the best way to demonstrate that these
M-3 ........... 5:5 to each other for some time, and **p.** for life
M-4 ..... VII.1:6 **p.** more alien to the thinking of the world
M-4 .... VIII.1:3 at a time **p.** unknown to him as yet, but
M-4 .... VIII.1:7 **P.** it was not understood at the time. Even
M-4 ........X.1:1 **p.** the last of the attributes the teacher of
M-7 ........... 5:4 forms. **P.** there is a fear of weakness and
M-7 ........... 5:5 **P.** there is a fear of failure and shame
M-7 ........... 5:6 a sense of inadequacy. **P.** there is a guilty
M-16 ......... 4:7 **P.** the one generalization that can be
M-16 ......... 5:2 **P.** your quiet time should be fairly early in
M-16 ....... 10:5 **P.** he needs to remember, "God is with
M-16 ....... 10:7 **P.** he prefers other words, or only one, or
M-17 ......... 4:1 **P.** it will be helpful to remember that no
M-17 ......... 4:4 **p.** too mild to be even clearly recognized.
M-22 ......... 4:3 **P.** he can accept the idea in theory, but it
M-24 ......... 1:9 preoccupation and **p.** pride in the past. At
M-26 ......... 3:3 It can, **p.**, be won after much devotion
M-27 ......... 2:3 it off without regret or care, **p.** today. Or
M-29 ......... 3:2 **P.** you have not thought of this aspect,
P-2...........I.1:5 **P.** they will come together again and
P-2...........I.1:6 Or **p.** each of them will enter into another
P-2...........I.2:7 shadows, or **p.** different cloud patterns.
P-2..........II.7:4 **P.** the teacher does not think of God as
P-2..........II.7:5 teaching. **P.** the psychotherapist does not
P-2........ IV.5:1 best, and the word is **p.** questionable here
P-2........ IV.7:6 **P.** an illusion of health is substituted for a
P-2..........V.3:1 were ideal, there could **p.** be ideal therapy
P-2..........V.6:8 **P.** the answer does not seem to be a gift
P-3...........I.3:5 They need you as much, and **p.** even more
P-3...........I.3:8 idea, or **p.** just a feeling of reaching out to
P-3........ III.6:6 sent. **P.** he was sent to give his brother the
P-3........ III.6:8 **P.** he was sent to teach the therapist how
P-3........ III.7:7 You have **p.** been seeking for salvation
S-1...........I.7:8 **P.** the specific form of resolution for a
S-1...........I.7:9 **P.** it will reach both, if you are genuinely
S-3........ III.2:4 trained, or is **p.** more talented and wise.

## perilous 1

T-29 ........I.3:3 light seem dark and fearful, **p.** and bleak.

## period 81

T-2 .....VIII.2:5 will extend over a similarly long **p.**, and
T-16 ..... VI.7:4 In the transition there is a **p.** of confusion,
T-16 ..... VI.8:5 The **p.** of disorientation, which precedes
T-20 .... VII.2:1 **p.** of discomfort that follows the sudden
T-22 .......II.6:1 This is a crucial **p.** in this course, for here
W-in.......... 2:4 The training **p.** is one year. The exercises
W-pI ...... 8.4:5 Introduce the practice **p.** by saying: *I seem*
W-pI ...... 8.5:2 at the end of the mind-searching **p.** with:
W-pI .... 10.5:3 is not recommended that this time **p.** be
W-pI .... 12.4:3 At the end of the practice **p.**, add: *But I am*
W-pI .... 14.2:2 The mind-searching **p.** should be short, a
W-pI .... 16.6:3 The length of the exercise **p.** should also
W-pI .... 17.4:2 length of the practice **p.** may be reduced
W-pI .... 18.3:3 Conclude each practice **p.** by repeating
W-pI .... 18.3:5 less, will be sufficient for each practice **p.**.
W-pI .... 22.3:7 the end of each practice **p.**, ask yourself: *Is*
W-pI .... 25.6:2 Each practice **p.** should begin with a slow
W-pI .... 26.6:1 practice **p.** should begin with repeating
W-pI .... 26.6:4 to use very many for any one practice **p.**,
W-pI .... 26.9:3 Conclude each practice **p.** by repeating
W-pI .... 35.5:1 the earlier part of the mind-searching **p.**,
W-pI .... 35.5:2 Toward the latter part of the exercise **p.**,
W-pI .... 37.5:1 the practice **p.** with your eyes closed; you
W-pI .... 37.5:2 The practice **p.** should conclude with a
W-pI .. 39.10:4 End each practice **p.** by repeating the idea
W-pI .... 40.2:3 Do not miss a practice **p.** because of this.
W-pI .... 40.3:3 One practice **p.** might, for example,
W-pI .... 40.3:9 only a brief **p.** is available, merely telling

W-pI.....41.6:1 will be only one long practice **p.** today. In
W-pI.....41.6:3 At the beginning of the practice **p.**, repeat
W-pI.....42.6:3 better to spend the practice **p.** alternating
W-pI.....43.4:5 this phase of the practice **p.** are sufficient.
W-pI.....43.5:1 the exercise **p.** should be relatively short,
W-pI.....43.6:1 repeat the first phase of the exercise **p.**,
W-pI.....43.6:2 Do not allow any protracted **p.** to occur in
W-pI.....44.7:1 Begin the practice **p.** by repeating today's
W-pI.....45.6:2 Then spend a fairly short **p.** in thinking a
W-pI.....46.5:4 practice **p.** to adding related ideas such as
W-pI.....46.6:7 The practice **p.** should end, however, with
W-pI.....47.7:1 In the latter phase of the practice **p.**, try
WpI...rI.in.2:3 two minutes or more to each practice **p.**,
W-pI.....61.6:1 begin and end the day with a practice **p.**.
W-pI.....65.3:1 minutes for a more sustained practice **p.**,
W-pI.....65.5:1 the longer practice **p.**, begin by reviewing
W-pI.....65.7:1 devote the rest of the practice **p.** to trying
W-pI.....66.4:1 longer practice **p.** today has as its purpose
W-pI.....66.5:1 practice **p.** by reviewing these thoughts:
W-pI.....66.9:1 this during the longer practice **p.** today.
W-pI.....67.2:1 In the longer practice **p.**, we will think
W-pI.....68.5:1 Begin today's extended practice **p.** by
W-pI.....68.6:4 the remainder of the practice **p.** trying to
W-pI.....68.6:7 At the end of the practice **p.** tell yourself:
W-pI.....69.2:2 this in our more extended practice **p.**, let
W-pI.....69.3:1 Let us begin our longer practice **p.** today
W-pI.....71.9:6 full charge of the rest of the practice **p.**,
W-pI...73.10:5 Put the rest of the practice **p.** under Their
W-pI...76.11:5 with which the practice **p.** concludes: *I am*
WpI. rII.in.1:4 We will have one longer exercise **p.**, and
WpI. rII.in.3:1 phase of the exercise **p.** if you find your
W-pI.....91.9:1 In the second phase of the exercise **p.**, try
W-pI...91.10:1 Relax for the rest of the practice **p.**,
W-pI...91.10:4 are united with you in this practice **p.**, in
W-pI.....93.8:4 spend the rest of the practice **p.** in trying
W-pI.....97.8:1 each practice **p.** today gladly to Him. And
W-pI.....98.9:6 you each practice **p.** you share with Him,
WpI. rIII.in2:2 when you miss a practice **p.** because it is
WpI. rIII.in3:1 when you skip a practice **p.** because you
W-pI...124.8:4 This is our first attempt at an extended **p.**
WpI. rIV.in4:4 start each practice **p.** in this review with
WpI rV.in11:2 we start and end each **p.** of practice time.
W-pI...199.5:2 it a part of every practice **p.** you take.
WpI rVI.in.7:4 the way each practice **p.** can best become
M-4......I.A.3:1 what might be called "a **p.** of undoing."
M-4......I.A.4:1 God must go through "a **p.** of sorting out.
M-4......I.A.5:1 go can be called "a **p.** of relinquishment."
M-4......I.A.5:5 the **p.** of overlap is apt to be one in which
M-4......I.A.6:1 Now comes "a **p.** of settling down." This
M-4......I.A.6:9 teacher of God needs this **p.** of respite. He
M-4......I.A.7:1 next stage is indeed "a **p.** of unsettling."
M-4......I.A.8:1 And finally, there is "a **p.** of achievement.
M-16..........5:8 be sure that you do not forget a brief **p.**, –

### periods 155

T-16.......V.1:2 into by **p.** in which they seem to be gone.
T-18.....VII.4:9 a lifetime of contemplation and long **p.** of
W-in..........3:2 With the exception of the review **p.**, each
W-pI.......4.1:2 In these practice **p.**, begin with noting the
W-pI.......5.3:1 substituted for practice **p.** in which you
W-pI.......6.2:2 the three or four practice **p.** which are
W-pI.......7.5:3 Three or four practice **p.**, each to last a
W-pI.......9.3:1 three or four practice **p.** are sufficient,
W-pI.....10.1:1 aware, or become aware in the practice **p.**
W-pI.....10.5:2 five practice **p.** are recommended, each
W-pI.....11.2:1 The practice **p.** for today's idea are to be
W-pI.....11.4:1 Three practice **p.** today will probably be
W-pI.....12.6:2 should the practice **p.** exceed a minute.
W-pI.....13.6:2 to think of it except during the practice **p.**
W-pI.....14.2:3 than three practice **p.** with today's idea
W-pI.....14.6:7 fact, conclude the practice **p.** by repeating
W-pI.....14.7:1 during the day, aside from the practice **p.**.
W-pI.....15.5:2 than a minute will do for the practice **p.**,
W-pI.....15.5:3 more than three application **p.** for today's
W-pI.....16.5:1 In the practice **p.**, first repeat the idea to
W-pI.....16.6:1 Four or five practice **p.** are recommended
W-pI.....17.4:1 four specific practice **p.** are recommended
W-pI.....18.2:3 The three or four practice **p.** which are
W-pI.....19.4:1 **p.** should be quite familiar to you by now,
W-pI.....19.4:2 practice **p.** remains essential throughout.
W-pI.....19.5:1 idea, at least three practice **p.** are required
W-pI.....20.1:1 quite casual about our practice **p.** thus far
W-pI.....21.1:2 specific mind-searching **p.** are necessary,
W-pI.....21.1:3 Five practice **p.** are urged, allowing a full
W-pI.....21.2:1 In the practice **p.**, begin by repeating the
W-pI.....21.3:1 of anger escape you in the practice **p.**.
W-pI.....23.6:1 five practice **p.** are required in applying
W-pI.....23.7:1 In the practice **p.**, be sure to include both
W-pI.....23.7:3 them as the same in today's practice **p.**.
W-pI.....24.3:2 **p.** which should be undertaken today,
W-pI.....24.3:3 the mind-searching **p.** which the exercises
W-pI.....24.4:1 practice **p.** should begin with repeating
W-pI.....25.6:1 Six practice **p.**, each of two-minutes
W-pI.....26.5:1 Six practice **p.** are required in applying
W-pI.....28.1:2 In these practice **p.**, you will be making a
W-pI.....28.6:2 subject that you use in the practice **p.**.
W-pI.....28.7:1 will have six two-minute practice **p.** today
W-pI.....29.4:1 Our six two-minute practice **p.** for today
W-pI...29.5:10 In addition to the assigned practice **p.**,
W-pI.....30.5:3 devote several practice **p.** to applying
W-pI.....31.2:1 Two longer **p.** of practice with the idea
W-pI.....32.2:2 the practice **p.** for today will again include
W-pI.....32.3:1 Again we will begin the practice **p.** for the
W-pI.....32.4:1 the two longer practice **p.** three to five
W-pI.....33.1:3 In these practice **p.**, the idea should be
W-pI.....33.3:1 shorter exercise **p.** should be as frequent
W-pI.....34.2:1 longer practice **p.** are required for today's
W-pI.....34.3:1 required for each of the longer practice **p.**
W-pI.....35.4:1 of the three five-minute practice **p.** today,
W-pI.....35.8:1 During the longer exercise **p.**, there will
W-pI.....36.2:1 practice **p.** are required for today. Try to
W-pI.....36.2:3 longer practice **p.** should take this form:
W-pI...36.3:10 *pen.* Several times during these practice **p.**,
W-pI.....36.4:1 For the shorter exercise **p.**, close your
W-pI.....37.4:1 Today's four longer exercise **p.**, each to
W-pI.....38.4:1 four longer practice **p.**, each preferably to
W-pI.....39.5:1 for the four longer practice **p.** for today,
W-pI.....39.6:1 Begin the practice **p.** as usual, by
W-pI.....39.9:1 You may find these practice **p.** easier if
W-pI.....39.9:1 you intersperse them with several short **p.**
W-pI...39.10:1 **p.** in whatever form appeals to you. Do
W-pI.....40.1:2 No long practice **p.** are required today,
W-pI.....40.2:1 not close your eyes for the exercise **p.**,
W-pI.....42.3:1 two three-to-five-minute practice **p.** today
W-pI.....42.4:1 Begin these practice **p.** by repeating the
W-pI.....42.7:1 practice **p.** that would be beneficial today.
W-pI.....43.4:1 five-minute practice **p.** are required today
W-pI.....43.4:3 At the beginning of these practice **p.**,
W-pI.....43.7:1 today's idea in the shorter practice **p.**, the
W-pI.....43.9:2 Try today not to allow any long **p.** of time
W-pI.....44.4:1 Have at least three practice **p.** today, each
W-pI.....45.4:1 three five-minute practice **p.** for today
W-pI.....45.9:1 In the shorter exercise **p.** for today, try to
W-pI.....46.3:1 at least three full five-minute practice **p.**,
W-pI.....46.3:2 Begin the longer practice **p.** by repeating
W-pI.....46.5:1 first phase of today's practice **p.** is to put
W-pI.....46.7:1 The shorter practice **p.** may consist either
W-pI.....47.4:2 Four five-minute practice **p.** are necessary
W-pI.....48.2:1 Today's practice **p.** will be very short,
W-pI.....49.3:1 at least four five-minute practice **p.** today,
WpI...rI.in.1:1 today we will have a series of review **p.**.
WpI...rI.in.1:4 In the practice **p.**, the exercises should be
WpI...rI.in.3:1 literally or thoroughly in the practice **p.**.
WpI...rI.in.4:1 for practice **p.** at your stage of learning. It
W-pI.....61.5:1 As many practice **p.** as possible should be
W-pI.....61.6:3 practice **p.** may be longer than the rest, if
W-pI.....64.8:1 forms of shorter practice **p.** are required.
W-pI.....65.4:1 extended practice **p.** at approximately the
W-pI.....65.8:1 In the shorter practice **p.**, which should
W-pI...66.11:1 In the shorter practice **p.**, which would
W-pI.....67.6:1 practice **p.** that this is not your tiny,
W-pI.....68.7:1 short practice **p.** should include a quick
W-pI.....69.9:1 In the shorter practice **p.**, which you will
W-pI.....70.6:1 are ready for two longer practice **p.** today,
W-pI.....70.7:1 practice **p.** by repeating the idea for today
W-pI...70.10:1 the short and frequent practice **p.** today,
W-pI.....71.8:1 Begin the two longer practice **p.** for today
W-pI.....71.9:1 **p.** to asking God to reveal His plan to us.
W-pI...71.10:1 In the shorter practice **p.**, tell yourself
W-pI...72.10:1 Our goal in the longer practice **p.** today is
W-pI...72.13:1 One or perhaps two shorter practice **p.**
W-pI.....73.9:1 We will begin our longer practice **p.** with
W-pI...73.11:1 In the shorter practice **p.**, again make a
W-pI.....74.3:1 Begin the longer practice **p.** by repeating
W-pI.....74.7:1 shorter **p.**, which should be undertaken at
W-pI.....75.4:1 Our longer practice **p.** will be devoted to
W-pI.....75.5:3 Begin the longer practice **p.** by telling
W-pI.....75.9:1 The shorter practice **p.**, too, will be joyful
W-pI.....76.8:1 will begin the longer practice **p.** today
W-pI.....77.4:1 Begin the longer practice **p.** by telling
W-pI.....77.7:1 Our shorter practice **p.** will be frequent,
W-pI.....78.6:1 practice **p.** today will see him in this role.
W-pI.....79.7:1 longer practice **p.** today we will ask what
W-pI.....79.9:1 practice **p.** for today will not be set by
W-pI.....80.4:1 In our longer practice **p.** today, we will
WpI..rII.in.2:1 longer practice **p.** will follow this general
WpI..rII.in.5:1 these practice **p.** as dedications to the way
WpI..rII.in.6:1 in the shorter practice **p.** as well, using
W-pI.....91.6:1 Begin the longer practice **p.** with this
W-pI.....93.8:1 In our longer exercise **p.** today, which
W-pI.....95.5:1 Frequent but shorter practice **p.** have
W-pI.....95.5:2 tend to forget about it for long **p.** of time.
W-pI.....95.7:1 practice **p.** for a while, and urge you to
W-pI...95.11:1 the practice **p.** today with this assurance,
W-pI...100.7:1 this today, in our five-minute practice **p.**,
W-pI. 100.10:5 for today between your hourly practice **p.**
W-pI...101.5:1 need the practice **p.** today. The exercises
W-pI...101.6:8 So should you start your practice **p.**, and
W-pI...102.3:1 to devote our **p.** of practicing to exercises
W-pI...102.4:1 Begin your practice **p.** today with this
W-pI...103.2:6 Begin your **p.** of practicing today with this
W-pI...104.3:2 Our longer practice **p.** today, the hourly
W-pI...105.6:1 our practice **p.** will start a little differently
W-pI...108.8:1 practice **p.** with the instruction for today,
W-pI...109.5:5 Let these **p.** of rest and respite reassure
W-pI...110.6:1 For your five-minute practice **p.**, begin
WpI. rIII.in1:3 a special format for these practice **p.**, that
WpI. rIII.in4:1 practice **p.** that you have lost because you
WpI. rIII.in4:3 allow your practice **p.** to be replacements
WpIrIII.in10:1 lie idly by between your longer practice **p.**
WpIrIII.in11:2 These practice **p.** are planned to help you
W-pI. 121.10:1 Begin the longer practice **p.** by thinking
W-pI. 122.11:1 happiness as you begin these practice **p.**,
W-pI. 131.11:1 as we start upon our practice **p.**. Begin
W-pI. 132.15:1 Begin the fifteen-minute **p.** in which we
W-pI. 133.13:3 Our two extended practice **p.** of fifteen
WpI.rV.in12:1 the beginning and the end of practice **p.**,
W-pI...185.8:1 Today devote your practice **p.** to careful
W-pII ..in.11:2 our daily lessons and the **p.** of wordless,
M-16 .........3:8 of the more structured practice **p.**, which

### perish 3

T-2.....VII.5:14 whosoever believeth in him should not **p.**
T-5........VI.9:1 wicked shall **p.**" becomes a statement of
T-5........VI.9:1 word "**p.**" is understood as "be undone."

### perishable 3

T-4..........I.11:7 the **p.** as the ego is of making the eternal.
T-11.....VII.1:2 the eternal, and everything you see is **p.**.
W-pI.....22.3:3 *I see only the* **p.**. *I see nothing that will last.*

### perished 1

W-pI...163.7:2 that God was once alive and somehow **p.**;

### permanence 2

T-4........III.3:6 knowledge of **p.** and unshakable being.
W-pI...131.1:2 You look for **p.** in the impermanent, for

### permanent 4

T-8....VIII.1:13 never changes, so its constellation is **p.**.
T-15......IX.1:3 so you will become willing to make it **p.**.

T-15...... IX.1:4 willingness it will not leave you, for it *is* **p.**.
S-3........ III.2:6 because, in dreams, equality cannot be **p.**.

### permit 8

T-4........ IV.7:3 not **p.** this shabby belief to pull you back.
T-4....... VII.4:5 To whatever extent you **p.** this state to be
T-11......... I.5:1 of the universe do not **p.** contradiction.
W-pI..... 43.4:2 time that circumstances and readiness **p.**.
W-pI... 128.4:1 **p.** temptation to believe the world holds
W-pI... 196.7:1 much as will **p.** fear of retaliation to abate
WpI rVI.in.5:2 **P.** no idle thought to go unchallenged. If
P-2........ VI.3:6 it will not **p.** its slaves to change the forms

### permits 10

T-1......... IV.4:6 lets me, and to whatever extent he **p.** it.
T-3......... IV.6:3 **p.** you to interpret the body as yourself in
T-4......... V.1:3 vigilance about what it **p.** into awareness,
T-15...... VI.8:5 And this **p.** your Source, and that of all
T-30....... I.16:3 agreement that **p.** all things to happen.
W-pI..... 61.5:6 with your eyes closed if the situation **p.**.
W-pII . 298.1:1 My gratitude **p.** my love to be accepted
W-pII ..... 9.2:1 that **p.** it to embrace the world and hold
M-3 ........... 3:2 illusion of one **p.** the illusion of the other.
M-4 ....... X.1:4 so open-mindedness **p.** him to be judged

### permitted 3

T-2......... V.7:5 the Holy Spirit is **p.** to look upon the
T-3........... I.1:5 appear as if God **p.** and even encouraged
T-10....... V.1:2 Joy is never **p.**, for depression is the sign

### perpetuate 3

T-7...... VIII.4:1 You cannot **p.** an illusion about another
T-16......... I.3:6 to make the past real, and so **p.** it. Step
T-22...... III.9:5 and is attracted to him to **p.** his sins. And

### perpetuating 1

T-7...... VIII.4:1 another without **p.** it about yourself.

### perplexity 3

T-16....... II.3:5 their attributes could hardly cause you **p.**.
T-20.... VIII.5:7 situation, no **p.** that vision will not solve.
T-31.... VIII.3:2 each **p.** Christ calls to you and gently says,

### persecuted 6

T-3........... I.2:4 **p.** His Own Son on behalf of salvation.
T-6........... I.4:6 in persecution, because you cannot *be* **p.**.
T-6........... I.5:2 to perceive yourself as **p.** if you choose.
T-6........... I.5:3 that I was **p.** as the world judges, and did
T-6........... I.6:2 learn." If you react as if you are **p.**, you are
T-6......... I.11:1 You are not **p.**, nor was I. You are not

### persecution 3

T-3........... I.2:4 **P.** frequently results in an attempt to
T-6........... I.4:6 to perceive any form of assault in **p.**,
T-6........... I.6:2 if you are persecuted, you are teaching **p.**.

### persist 5

T-2....... VII.1:1 nevertheless **p.** in making yourself fearful.
T-9........... I.7:4 That is why you **p.** in asking the teacher
T-28...... IV.3:3 of him as a mind in which illusions still **p.**
T-31........ I.1:10 you **p.** in learning not such simple things?
W-pI..... 15.3:5 last. They will not **p.**, because they merely

### persistence 2

T-4......... II.3:5 to something that occurs with such **p.**.
T-21...... III.2:5 with the **p.** that faith inevitably brings.

### persistent 3

T-9 ........ I.12:2 made into a very **p.** goal even though you
T-31 .... VII.3:3 body grows decreasingly **p.** in your sight,
W-pI... 182.1:6 Just a **p.** feeling, sometimes not more

### persists 5

T-2 ........ V.2:6 As long as your sense of vulnerability **p.**,
T-2 ........ V.9:3 However, as long as time **p.**, healing is
T-9 ........ I.11:2 say of someone who **p.** in attempting the
W-pI..... 27.2:4 If fear of loss still **p.**, add further: *It can*
W-pI..... 71.3:3 will continue, for the illusion **p.** that,

### person 32

T-2 ........ IV.4:5 over the mind to render a **p.** temporarily
T-4 ...... VII.2:5 is a reaction to a specific **p.** or persons.
T-13 ....... X.2:3 are used but to avoid the **p.** *and* the guilt.
T-18 ........ I.2:2 one **p.** as a replacement for another, the
T-21 ........ I.6:2 attached not to a **p.** or a place or anything
T-27 ... VIII.1:2 as if it were a **p.** to be seen and be believed
T-30 ..... III.3:3 To seek a special **p.** or a thing to add to
T-30 ..... III.4:9 Creation gives no separate **p.** and no
T-31 ..... IV.4:1 another road, another **p.** or another place
W-in.......... 5:2 been achieved in connection with any **p.**,
W-pI....... 5.1:1 preceding one, can be used with any **p.**,
W-pI....... 8.5:2 *I seem to be thinking about [name of a* ***p.***
W-pI..... 19.3:3 of the central **p.** or theme it contains, and
W-pI..... 20.5:3 any situation, **p.** or event that upsets you.
W-pI..... 21.4:2 *determined to see_[name of* ***p.****] differently. I*
W-pI..... 21.5:2 on a particular attribute of a particular **p.**,
W-pI..... 21.5:4 *the attribute] in_[name of* ***p.****] differently.*
W-pI..... 37.4:5 apply the idea to any **p.** who occurs to you
W-pI..... 38.4:3 and also the name of the **p.** concerned.
W-pI..... 71.3:4 Another **p.** will yet serve better; another
W-pI..... 72.3:4 A **p.** says something you do not like. He
W-pI..... 72.4:1 are not dealing here with what the **p.** is.
W-pI..... 74.4:2 identify the particular **p.** or persons and
W-pI..... 78.4:4 will select one **p.** you have used as target
W-pI... 127.1:6 It never alters with a **p.** or a circumstance.
M-2 ........... 5:9 another **p.** the same interests as his own.
M-3 ........... 4:1 the sense that each **p.** involved will learn
M-3 ........... 4:1 that he can from the other **p.** at that time.
M-3 ........... 5:2 which each **p.** is given a chosen learning
M-10 ......... 1:6 the same **p.** classifies the same action as
M-22 ......... 6:5 sick **p.** perceives himself as separate from
S-2.......... II.2:1 in which a "better" **p.** deigns to stoop to

### personal 16

T-1 ......... II.1:2 extremely **p.** sense of creation sometimes
T-1 ......... II.2:1 intensely **p.** and cannot be meaningfully
T-1 ....... III.4:5 to the highly **p.** experience of revelation.
T-4 ...... VII.7:4 is intensely **p.** to the mind that receives it.
T-11 .... VII.3:7 To establish your **p.** autonomy you tried
T-12 ........ I.5:2 with a **p.** investment is a reliable witness,
T-15 ...... V.8:2 **p.** needs intrude on no one to make your
W-pI..... 10.4:6 which has little if any **p.** meaning to you.
W-pI..... 14.6:1 **p.** repertory of horrors at which you are
W-pI..... 14.6:3 and others are part of your **p.** hell. It does
W-pI..... 25.3:1 they are all concerned with "**p.**" interests.
W-pI..... 25.3:2 Since you have no **p.** interests, your goals
W-pI..... 28.3:4 its purpose to your little **p.** thoughts.
W-pI..... 43.5:2 to you add to the idea in your own **p.** way.
W-pI... 125.3:1 our petty thoughts, without our **p.** desires
WpI...rV.in4:2 it be more meaningful, more **p.** and true,

### personalities 4

W-pI..... 34.3:2 situations, "offending" **p.** or events, or
W-pI..... 35.7:2 **p.** and events in which you figure cross
W-pI..... 39.7:1 events or **p.** you associate with unloving
M-4 ........... 1:2 their superficial "**p.**" are quite distinct.

### personality 1

W-pI..... 34.6:4 *about this situation,* ***p.*** *or event] with peace.*

### personally 4

T-2 ....... VI.1:7 makes you feel **p.** responsible for them.
T-5 ......... V.1:1 and more **p.** meaningful if the ego's use of
T-18 ..... IV.7:4 for you to realize it is not **p.** insulting that
M-9 ........... 2:4 it is apt to be perceived as **p.** insulting.

### persons 3

T-4 ...... VII.2:5 is a reaction to a specific person or **p.**. The
W-pI .... 21.3:3 on some situations or **p.** than on others,
W-pI .... 74.4:2 identify the particular person or **p.** and

### perspective 20

T-1 ........ I.23:1 perception and place all levels in true **p.**.
T-8 ... VIII.9:10 the proper **p.** on life under the guidance
T-16 ..... VI.7:1 more than a transition in the **p.** of reality.
T-16 ..... VI.7:2 grossly distorted and completely out of **p.**
T-16 ... VI.11:1 The new **p.** you will gain from crossing
T-16 ... VI.12:2 to share His **p.** to give it to you completely
T-17 ........ I.3:6 it is inevitable that your **p.** on reality be
T-17 ........ I.4:5 of reality is a **p.** without understanding; a
T-17 ........ I.5:1 what truth means from the **p.** of illusions?
T-17 ....... II.3:7 born of the new **p.** he has learned, has
T-23 ..... IV.5:2 From there will your **p.** be quite different.
T-23 ..... IV.5:7 **p.** coming from this choice shows you the
T-24 ...... I.8:10 **p.** can the special have that does not
T-27 .... VII.7:2 you find the cause of your **p.** on the world
W-pI .. 128.7:3 whole **p.** on the world will shift by just a
W-pI .. 183.5:2 nameless things on earth slip into right **p.**
W-pI .. 190.1:1 Pain is a wrong **p.**. When it is
W-pI .. 191.5:4 that changed his whole **p.** of the world.
W-pII ..... 2.4:5 Earth is being born again in new **p.**. Night
M-5 ...... II.4:11 creation. Seen in their proper **p.**, without

### persuade 11

T-4 ....... VI.1:4 was necessary to **p.** you that you cannot
T-6 ....... IV.5:3 which is not real, attempts to **p.** the mind,
T-6 ..... V.B.6:3 The ego tries to **p.** you that it is up to you
T-7 ....... VI.8:1 and tries to **p.** you that you have done this
T-7 ..... VIII.2:4 therefore tries to **p.** you that *it* can free you
T-7 ..... VIII.2:6 attempt to **p.** you that you have gotten rid
T-20 . VIII.11:1 need **p.** you to accept the gift of vision?
T-28 ....... V.5:8 let them **p.** their maker his imaginings are
T-31 ... VIII.1:2 would **p.** the holy Son of God he is a body
W-pI .. 192.5:7 Only forgiveness can **p.** the Son to look
W-pII . 296.2:3 we allow His teaching to **p.** the world,

### persuaded 1

P-2.......... V.2:3 the patient is **p.** to reverse his twisted way

### persuading 1

T-13 ....... II.1:4 Only by **p.** you that it is you could the ego

### persuasion 1

W-pI .. 106.3:2 Walk lightly past their meaningless **p.**.

### pervade 1

T-18 ....... II.4:4 Anger and fear **p.** it, and in an instant the

### pervades 1

W-pI .. 105.2:3 means **p.** all levels of the world you see. It

### pervasive 1

T19 ... IV.A.8:5 Its seeming stability is its **p.** weakness,

### pestilence 1

T-28 ..... III.4:3 holds the seeds of **p.** and every form of ill,

**pet** 1

T-23..... II.18:8 dress it in loveliness, **p.** it and pamper it,

**petals** 1

T-20.........I.4:2 looking between the snow-white **p.** of the

**petty** 9

T-15... VIII.4:5 far beyond the **p.** sum of all the separate
W-pI.....61.7:1 the ego's **p.** views of what you are and
W-pI...106.1:1 if you will not accept its **p.** gifts that give
W-pI...123.3:5 your meager gifts and **p.** judgments of the
W-pI...125.3:1 without intrusion of our **p.** thoughts,
W-pI...126.7:3 evaluate such **p.** gifts as worthy of His Son
W-pI...128.1:3 soar beyond its **p.** scope and little ways.
W-pI...130.8:3 hands of all the **p.** treasures of this world.
M-4..........I.2:1 to trust one's own **p.** strength again. Who

**petulant** 1

T-27... VIII.8:3 How childish is the **p.** device to keep your

**phase** 20

T-1......... II.2:6 In this **p.** of learning, working miracles is
T-17....... V.2:5 this; the only difficult **p.** is the beginning.
T-28.........I.6:1 is but another **p.** of what does nothing. It
W-pI.....11.1:1 to a major **p.** of the correction process;
W-pI.....43.4:5 this **p.** of the practice period are sufficient
W-pI.....43.5:1 for this **p.** of practice indiscriminately,
W-pI.....43.5:2 For the second and longer **p.**, close your
W-pI.....43.6:1 repeat the first **p.** of the exercise period,
W-pI.....43.6:1 and then attempt the second **p.** again. Do
W-pI.....43.6:3 Return to the first **p.** of the exercises as
W-pI.....46.5:1 purpose of the first **p.** of today's practice
W-pI.....47.7:1 In the latter **p.** of the practice period, try
W-pI...74.3:10 During this introductory **p.**, be sure to
W-pI.....77.5:1 After this brief introductory **p.**, wait
WpI. rII.in.3:1 Repeat the first **p.** of the exercise period
W-pI.....91.9:1 In the second **p.** of the exercise period,
WpI.. rV.in1:3 for another **p.** of understanding. We
W-pI...184.7:2 It is a **p.** of learning everyone who comes
W-pI.184.10:1 of the world becomes a transitory **p.**; a
W-pI...187.1:6 It is the second **p.** on which the world and

**phases** 7

T-2......... II.6:9 its various **p.** will proceed in time, but the
T-11...... IV.4:5 The beginning **p.** of this reversal are often
T-27... VIII.2:7 But in some **p.** of the dream, it is the slave
W-pI.....32.2:2 for today will again include two **p.**, one
W-pI.....37.5:1 these two **p.** of application that you prefer
W-pI.....65.1:5 only function necessarily entails two **p.**;
W-pI...128.5:2 gave its aspects and its **p.** and its dreams.

**phenomenal** 1

T-17....... V.2:3 is a **p.** teaching accomplishment. In all its

**philosophical** 1

C-in............1:1 This is not a course in **p.** speculation, nor

**phrase** 2

S-1......... II.4:5 What does the **p.** really mean? Pray for
S-3........ III.3:1 magic **p.** by which the body seems to be

**physical** 47

T-1...........I.9:2 sense, the exchange reverses the **p.** laws.
T-1........ I.12:3 One makes the **p.**, and the other creates
T-1........ I.22:2 that what your **p.** eyes cannot see does
T-1......... I.32:3 placing you beyond the **p.** laws they raise
T-1......... II.1:2 sometimes sought in **p.** relationships.
T-1......... II.1:3 **P.** closeness cannot achieve it. Miracles,
T-1.......VII.1:2 of miracle impulses with **p.** impulses is a
T-1.......VII.1:3 distortion. **P.** impulses are misdirected
T-1.......VII.2:4 vision, of which the **p.** eye is incapable.
T-2........ III.1:6 *does* recognize that Atonement in **p.** terms
T-2...... III.1:10 the temple cannot be seen with the **p.** eye.
T-2........ III.3:8 weakening the investment in **p.** sight. The
T-2........ III.4:2 All solutions the **p.** eye seeks dissolve.
T-2........ IV.2:6 error, produces all **p.** symptoms. Physical
T-2........ IV.2:7 **P.** illness represents a belief in magic. The
T-2........ IV.3:8 part of your experience in the **p.** world.
T-2......... V.2:2 **P.** medications are forms of "spells," but
T-2......... V.2:5 to rely temporarily on **p.** healing devices,
T-2......... V.7:1 turning away from the belief in **p.** sight.
T-2......... V.8:2 What the **p.** eye sees is not corrective, nor
T-2......... V.8:3 you believe in what your **p.** sight tells you,
T-4......... II.2:4 the mind as when it involves **p.** proximity
T-4......... II.2:5 relative perception as is **p.** interaction.
T-4......... II.7:7 Body appetites are not **p.** in origin. The
T-4......... II.9:4 beginning is usually associated with **p.**
T-5.........I.1:10 If you share a **p.** possession, you do divide
T-5........ IV.2:4 born. **P.** birth is not a beginning; it is a
T-8.......VII.1:1 Attack is always **p.**. When attack in any
T-8.......VII.4:5 not see anything **p.** except as what it is.
T-8.......VII.5:3 you look upon a brother as a **p.** entity, his
T-8.......VII.7:4 except by belief, since thought is not **p.**.
T-8.....VII.10:3 is whole, and the belief that part of it is **p.**,
T-8.....VII.10:4 Mind cannot be made **p.**, but it can be
T-8.....VII.10:4 made manifest *through* the **p.** if it uses the
T-8........ IX.3:2 **p.** expressions of the fear of awakening.
T-9......... II.2:4 individual may ask for **p.** healing because
T-9......... II.2:5 more fearful to him than its **p.** expression.
T-18.... VI.12:1 occur regardless of the **p.** distance that
T-18.... VI.13:6 instants of release from **p.** restrictions,
W-pI.....64.1:3 and His Son by taking on a **p.** appearance
W-pI.....64.2:4 the **p.** appearance of temptation becomes
W-pI.....72.2:2 the ego is the **p.** embodiment of that wish
W-pI.....96.3:6 If you are **p.**, your mind is gone from your
W-pI...167.3:2 an idea, irrelevant to what is seen as **p.**. A
W-pI...167.6:6 It cannot make the **p.**. What seems to die
M-13 .........2:6 Power, fame, money, **p.** pleasure; who is
P-3...........I.3:4 Some do not need your **p.** presence. They

**physically** 6

T-2......... V.8:2 by any device that can be seen **p.**. As long
T-8.......VII.1:3 to attack **p.** to accept this interpretation.
T-9......... II.2:5 At the same time, if he were healed **p.**, the
W-pI.....25.4:4 who is not **p.** in your immediate vicinity.
W-pI.....68.7:1 arises against anyone, **p.** present or not:
P-3...........I.3:1 Your patients need not be **p.** present for

**physician** 3

M-5 ....... II.2:5 Who is the **p.**? Only the mind of the
P-2.......VII.1:4 **P.**, heal thyself. Who else is there to heal?
P-3........ III.8:1 **P.**, healer, therapist, teacher, heal thyself.

**pick** 3

T-20....... II.6:6 a toy you would **p.** up from time to time
W-pI.....35.7:3 **P.** up any specific situation that occurs to
W-pI.....35.9:1 **p.** up a specific attribute or attributes you

**picked** 2

T-24....... V.2:3 does not realize he **p.** a thread from here,
M-20 .........4:4 not recognize that you have **p.** it up again.

**picking** 1

W-pI.......7.3:2 your past experiences of **p.** up a cup,

**picks** 2

T-21....... V.1:2 It literally **p.** it out as the mind directs.
S-2...........I.2:4 sight. It carefully **p.** out all evil things, and

**pictorial** 1

W-pI.....23.3:2 of "external reality" is a **p.** representation

**picture** 113

T-2...........I.2:1 related distortions represent a **p.** of what
T-4.........I.10:7 and unworthy **p.** of yourself to others,
T-4.........I.10:7 do not accept such a **p.** of them yourself.
T-7.......VII.3:2 The ego's **p.** of you is deprived, unloving
T-7.......VII.3:6 Do not see this **p.** in anyone, or you have
T-9.......VII.5:4 its methods for keeping this **p.** intact?
T-13.......in.4:1 world *is* a **p.** of the crucifixion of God's Son
T-15....... V.7:2 seeking a **p.** whose likeness does not exist.
T-17...... IV.7:7 the frame without the **p.** you cannot have.
T-17...... IV.8:2 and so elaborate that the **p.** is almost
T-17...... IV.9:1 Look at the ***p.***. Do not let the frame
T-17...... IV.9:4 You cannot have the frame without the **p.**
T-17.... IV.9:11 Look at the **p.**, and realize that death is
T-17.... IV.11:2 It is a **p.**, too, set in a frame. Yet if you
T-17.... IV.11:3 to focus all your attention on the **p.**. The
T-17.... IV.11:5 It is a **p.** of timelessness, set in a frame of
T-17.... IV.11:6 If you focus on the **p.**, you will realize that
T-17.... IV.11:6 the frame that made you think it *was* a **p.**.
T-17.... IV.11:7 frame, the **p.** is seen as what it represents.
T-17.... IV.12:3 Each is a **p.** of all that you can have, seen
T-17.... IV.12:4 their value by comparing a **p.** to a frame.
T-17.... IV.12:6 Remember that it is the **p.** that is the gift.
T-17.. IV.12:10 One is a tiny **p.**, hard to see at all beneath
T-17.... IV.13:1 fit the better **p.** into the wrong frame and
T-17.... IV.13:4 The **p.** of darkness and of death grows
T-17.... IV.13:5 and ceases to distract you from the **p.**.
T-17.... IV.13:6 And finally you look upon the **p.** itself,
T-17.... IV.14:1 The other **p.** is lightly framed, for time
T-17.... IV.14:3 **p.** of Heaven and eternity grows more
T-17.... IV.14:6 other. The dark **p.**, brought to light, is not
T-17.... IV.14:6 that it is just a **p.** is brought home at last.
T-17.... IV.14:7 it is; a **p.** of what you thought was real,
T-17.... IV.14:8 For beyond this **p.** you will see nothing.
T-17.... IV.15:1 **p.** of light, in clear-cut and unmistakable
T-17.... IV.15:1 transformed into what lies beyond the **p.**.
T-17.... IV.15:2 look on this, you realize that it is not a **p.**,
T-17.... IV.15:5 of creation in exchange for your little **p.**,
T-20...... III.4:4 It is a **p.** of what you think you are; of how
T-20...... III.5:6 sickly **p.** of yourself is carefully preserved
T-20...... III.5:7 as long as you believe this **p.** is outside,
T-21.......in.1:5 the outside **p.** of an inward condition. As
T-24....... V.2:3 from there, and wove a **p.** out of nothing.
T-24... VII.8:10 It is the outward **p.** of a wish; an image
T-25........II.4:4 the frame is but a means to hold the **p.** up
T-25........II.4:5 A frame that hides the **p.** has no purpose.
T-25........II.4:7 the **p.** is the frame without its meaning.
T-25........II.4:8 Its purpose is to set the **p.** off, and not
T-25........II.5:8 instead of this? And see the **p.** not at all?
T-25........II.6:3 not make the frame into the **p.** when you
T-25........II.6:5 separate purpose that obscures the **p.**,
T-25........II.6:7 you not the **p.** is destroyed in any way.
T-25....... V.6:3 brother you see the **p.** of your own belief
T-26.........I.2:2 a **p.** of complete disunity and total lack of
T-26..... VII.7:6 an insane **p.** an insane defense can be
T-26..... VII.7:6 can not establish that the **p.** must be true.
T-27............I.h The **P.** of Crucifixion
T-27.........I.3:2 a **p.** of your crucifixion before his eyes,
T-27.........I.3:4 The **p.** of yourself you offer him you show
T-27.........I.3:5 a **p.** of yourself in which there is no pain
T-27.........I.4:4 This sick and sorry **p.** *you* accept, if only it
T-27.......I.4:10 The bleak and bitter **p.** you have sent
T-27.........I.5:1 the Holy Spirit lays a **p.** of a different you.
T-27.........I.5:2 It is a **p.** of a body still, for what you really
T-27.........I.7:1 them paint the **p.** in which sin is justified,
T-27.........I.8:3 Yet in this **p.** is the body not perceived as
T-27.........I.9:2 it be to see yourself a **p.** of the proof that
T-27.........I.9:3 The Holy Spirit's **p.** changes not the body
T-27........I.11:2 your crippled **p.** is a lasting sign of what it
T-27...... III.3:1 **p.** of your brother that you see means
T-27...... III.3:3 The **p.** has been wholly cancelled out,
T-27...... III.3:4 And thus the **p.** has no cause at all. Who
T-27...... III.3:7 **p.** of your brother that you see is wholly
T-27...... III.4:8 your **p.** is another picture of another kind
T-27...... III.4:8 your picture is another **p.** of another kind
T-27...... III.6:1 **p.** of your brother given you to occupy the
T-27..... III.6:5 it is but half the **p.** and is incomplete,
T-27.....VII.9:1 This is the only **p.** you can see; the one
T-28...... III.7:5 the world except a **p.** of the Son of God in

T-13......III.8:4 find this **p.** of truth as you see it in your
T-13.....III.9:2 you will be hiding a dark **p.** in your mind
T-13....III.11:5 and it must seek a **p.** of darkness where it
T-13..III.12:10 But seek this **p.** and you will find it, for
T-13......IV.8:1 as one of extending itself in **p.** of eternity,
T-13......IX.3:3 and if you **p.** your faith in the past, the
T-13.......X.9:6 to the holy **p.** where you will see the light.
T-14.......II.3:7 *I will* **p.** *it gently in the holy place where it*
T-14.......II.3:7 *place it gently in the holy* **p.** *where it belongs.*
T-14......III.8:7 in **p.** of all the happy teaching the Holy
T-14....III.12:1 and **p.** your pitiful appraisal of yourself in
T-14....III.12:1 appraisal of yourself in **p.** of His calm and
T-14.....IV.4:10 **p.** made out of darkness and deceit, for
T-14.....V.11:1 Each one you see you **p.** within the holy
T-14.....V.11:9 the holy **p.** of peace which is for all of us,
T-14......VI.5:6 you made in **p.** of the power of creation,
T-14.....VII.4:8 in a separate **p.** can be endowed with firm
T-14...VII.4:10 because the other is seen in the same **p.**.
T-14......VIII.h The Holy Meeting **P.**
T-14...VIII.1:2 All this lies hidden in every darkened **p.**,
T-14.VIII.2:11 division, but in the meeting **p.** where God
T-14.VIII.2:13 holy meeting **p.** of the unseparated Father
T-14...VIII.4:2 the **p.** where you must meet with truth.
T-14...VIII.4:9 meeting **p.** are joined the Father and His
T-14......IX.1:7 it? The making of time to take the **p.** of
T-14......XI.2:5 in **p.** of what you *have* and what you *are?*
T-14....XI.6:11 will take His rightful **p.** in your awareness
T-14....XI.10:6 He always gives His gifts in **p.** of yours. He
T-15......III.1:4 You offer this in **p.** of magnitude, and you
T-15......IV.3:3 For you leave empty your **p.** in His plan,
T-15.......V.5:4 **p.** any relationship under His care and be
T-15......VI.2:3 faith in you, in **p.** of all your doubts. But
T-15......VI.8:6 of God will take Their rightful **p.** in you,
T-15......IX.7:1 and when you **p.** no value on it as a means
T-15......IX.7:4 **p.** no limits on your union with Him. The
T-15.......X.8:5 it to take His **p.** to protect you from Him.
T-15..XI.10:10 as this year is born, and take your **p.**, so
T-16.......II.8:4 because you have preferred to **p.** still
T-16.......II.9:6 for you to **p.** your faith in them, and not
T-16......III.5:6 they will take the **p.** of what you took in to
T-16......IV.3:4 a **p.** of safety from which hatred is split off
T-16....IV.10:4 unwilling to settle for illusion in **p.** of
T-16.......V.3:8 the illusion of love is accepted in love's **p.**,
T-16.......V.7:7 much value can he **p.** upon a self that he
T-16.......V.9:1 out to those who **p.** their faith in littleness
T-16.....V.12:2 the **p.** of God at the expense of content.
T-16.....V.13:3 you raise to **p.** before Him stands before
T-16.....V.13:3 stands before *you,* in **p.** of what you are.
T-16....VI.10:6 *is* a **p.** where truth and beauty wait for you.
T-16....VI.11:5 that returns to take its rightful **p.** within it
T-16...VII.10:2 you as you seek only your **p.** in the plan of
T-16...VII.10:4 and to **p.** all your investment in salvation
T-16...VII.11:3 is nothing that will not give **p.** to Him and
T-17.......II.2:4 it is the meeting **p.** of worlds so different.
T-17....IV.14:5 each is given its rightful **p.** when both are
T-17....IV.16:1 into His rightful **p.** and you to yours, you
T-17.....V.14:8 the means will surely fall in **p.** because the
T-17.....VII.1:2 and the problem were in the same **p.**. The
T-17.....VII.1:3 it from its source and **p.** it elsewhere. As a
T-18......I.10:7 the holy **p.** in which you stand together.
T-18.....II.5:16 the special relationship has a special **p.**. It
T-18......IV.3:5 create His dwelling **p.** unworthy of Him.
T-18.....IV.5:10 *established His dwelling* **p.** *in me created it*
T-18.....IV.5:13 *be willing not to substitute my own in* **p.** *of it.*
T-18......IV.8:2 unwilling to give **p.** to One Who knows.
T-18......VI.1:4 is the dwelling **p.** of the Son of God, who
T-18......VI.1:5 Heaven is not a **p.** nor a condition. It is
T-18......VI.6:8 it to be the dwelling **p.** of God's Son, and
T-18......VI.8:2 **p.** you set aside to house your hate is not a
T-18....VI.14:2 that takes **p.** with your desire for it is the
T-18....VI.14:5 Come to this **p.** of refuge, where you can
T-18.....VII.7:7 make a **p.** within you where the activity of
T-18.....VII.7:8 Into this **p.** the Holy Spirit comes, and
T-18.....VII.8:1 be this **p.** of rest to which you can return.
T-18...VIII.9:4 Give them a **p.** of refuge, prepared by love
T-18...VIII.9:6 They enter one by one into this holy **p.**,
T-18......IX.4:2 that were made to keep the guilt in **p.**, so
T-18....IX.10:5 A step beyond this holy **p.** of forgiveness,
T-18....IX.14:1 you in the holy **p.** of forgiveness you will
T-19.........I.5:9 be together, nor perceived in the same **p.**.
T-19.......I.13:2 and sees the holy **p.** where it was healed.
T-19.......II.6:9 sin is kept in **p.** by just this strange device.
T-19....III.11:3 **p.** where all the weary ones can come and
T-19......IV.2:4 a resting **p.** where you will rest in Him. He
T19...IV.A.1:4 dwelling **p.** from which it gently reaches
T19...IV.A.3:4 that little is a limit you would **p.** upon the
T19....IV.B.4:5 but barriers you **p.** between your will and
T19....IV.B.5:3 obstacle that you can **p.** before our union,
T19..IV.C.2:13 in **p.** of the ego's you renounced death,
T19..IV.C.10:7 a resting **p.** by your forgiveness of your
T19...IV.D.5:8 fear seemed to be holding them in **p.**. Yet
T19...IV.D.9:6 instant, here in this **p.** where the purpose,
T19.IV.D.10:2 **p.** to which everyone must come when he
T19.IV.D.10:4 Yet merely to reach the **p.** is not enough.
T19.IV.D.16:1 Here is the holy **p.** of resurrection, to
T19.IV.D.17:9 that we might meet here in this holy **p.**,
T19.IV.D.21:3 and **p.** the Son of God safely within the
T-20......IV.2:1 Sin has no **p.** in Heaven, where its results
T-20......VI.4:7 bodies as it can collect to **p.** its idols in,
T-20......VI.5:7 the only **p.** in all the universe where it can
T-20......VI.7:5 This **p.** of darkness is not your home.
T-20.....VII.4:7 would **p.** the attributes where they cannot
T-20...VIII.1:3 Open the holy **p.** that you closed off by
T-20...VIII.3:4 And **p.** no value on your brother's body,
T-20...VIII.6:1 upon with vision falls gently into **p.**,
T-21.........I.6:2 to a person or a **p.** or anything particular.
T-21.....II.11:4 and **p.** your faith in its ability to do so,
T-21.....III.3:5 is impossible to **p.** equal faith in opposite
T-21......III.8:4 desiring to **p.** its power elsewhere should
T-21.......V.3:2 And if you **p.** your faith in Them, you will
T-21.......V.5:5 must have set aside a **p.** in which the Holy
T-21.......V.8:2 But reason has no **p.** at all in madness,
T-21......VI.4:1 that drives it out of mind, and takes its **p.**.
T-21......VI.4:2 takes the **p.** of madness quietly, replacing
T-21...VII.13:1 form that shifts with time and **p.**, is an
T-22.......in.1:3 could never see it in the same **p.** and time.
T-22......IV.1:1 come to the **p.** where the branch in the
T-22......IV.3:1 your brother stand, here in this holy **p.**,
T-22......IV.3:8 from this holy **p.** He will return with you,
T-22......VI.5:3 error, and lays a part of Heaven in its **p.**.
T-22......VI.5:6 And every empty **p.** in Heaven that you
T-22......VI.8:1 he beholds his savior in **p.** of the attacker
T-22....VI.10:7 that seems to keep the fear of God in **p.**,
T-23.......in.4:6 the clean **p.** where littleness does not exist
T-23.........I.4:2 The journey's end is at the **p.** of peace.
T-23.......I.10:6 Illusions have no **p.** where love abides,
T-23.......I.11:1 can the resting **p.** of God turn on itself,
T-23.....II.11:6 the hiding **p.** for what belongs to you.
T-23.....II.13:8 They hold in **p.** the substitute for Heaven
T-23.....II.14:3 function of insanity to take the **p.** of truth
T-23......III.6:4 the fear that haunts the **p.** of death is not
T-23......IV.1:3 Yet He remains the only **p.** of safety. In
T-23......IV.5:1 and from a higher **p.** look down upon it.
T-23......IV.6:5 they occur leave not your **p.** on high, but
T-24.........I.1:4 you asked a substitute to take its **p.**. And
T-24.......II.6:4 himself, as it returns to take their **p.**. This
T-24.......II.7:1 to your specialness, and given it his **p.**,
T-24.......II.9:5 holy **p.** does truth stand waiting to receive
T-24.......II.9:6 all illusions of yourself outside this **p.**, to
T-24.....II.13:2 it demands a special **p.** God cannot enter,
T-24.....II.13:2 hiding **p.** where none is welcome but your
T-24.....II.14:1 plan for your salvation in the **p.** of yours.
T-24......VI.6:3 no sight nor **p.** nor time where He is not.
T-24....VI.10:4 You **p.** yourself under the laws you see as
T-24........VII.h The Meeting **P.**
T-24.....VII.1:8 Yet it stands in **p.** of your creations, who
T-24...VII.1:11 God's creation that takes the **p.** of yours?
T-24.....VII.7:3 from; not born of size nor **p.** nor time,
T-24...VII.11:1 without a meeting **p.** and no encounter.
T-25.........I.7:1 note of time and **p.** as if they were discrete
T-25.......II.2:2 no respect, at any time or **p.**, has anything
T-25.......II.2:5 To **p.** your hopes where no hope lies must
T-25.......II.6:3 picture when you choose to see it in its **p.**.
T-25......III.5:6 if they lit a **p.** where they could never be,
T-25......IV.5:7 it. No other **p.**; no other state nor time.
T-25......VI.3:6 them to fill; no **p.** where they are needed,
T-25.....VII.3:2 is mad, or is this world a **p.** of madness.
T-25.....VII.7:3 the special time and **p.** in which you think
T-25.....VII.7:3 and where you can be free of **p.** and time,
T-25.....VII.7:4 time nor **p.** nor anything God did not will
T-25......IX.1:7 will you hold dear that sin be kept in **p.**.
T-25......IX.6:9 warrant vengeance in **p.** of healing and
T-26........II.3:4 regard to size, complexity, or **p.** and time,
T-26........II.7:7 its **p.** the Love of God can be remembered
T-26......III.2:2 It is not a **p.**, and when you reach it is
T-26......III.2:3 meeting **p.** where thoughts are brought
T-26......III.3:6 is. Salvation is a borderland where **p.** and
T-26......III.3:6 be seen that they are temporary, out of **p.**,
T-26......IV.3:1 The holy **p.** on which you stand is but the
T-26......IV.3:2 you see the face of Christ, arising in its **p.**.
T-26......IV.3:4 where sin has left a **p.** for Heaven's altar
T-26.......V.6:6 a **p.** and time that have long since gone by
T-26.......V.7:1 a hindrance to the **p.** whereon he stands?
T-26.......V.7:3 and **p.** effect a change in where he really is
T-26.......V.8:2 now, in **p.** of what is *really* now and here.
T-26.....V.10:5 Resurrection has come to take its **p.**. And
T-26.....V.10:7 the power to keep you in a **p.** of death, a
T-26.....V.13:1 when the time of terror took the **p.** of love
T-26......VI.2:6 Seek not another friend to take His **p.**.
T-26......VI.3:3 it can but take the **p.** of Him Whom God
T-26......VI.3:6 He will **p.** them on your throne, when you
T-26.....VII.3:4 to take the **p.** of changeless knowledge.
T-26.....VII.8:8 They limit you to time and **p.**, and give a
T-26......IX.3:2 What was a **p.** of death has now become a
T-26......IX.3:4 take its ancient **p.** upon an ancient throne
T-26......IX.6:3 There is no **p.** in Heaven holier. And They
T-26......IX.6:4 to be Their resting **p.** as well as yours.
T-27.........I.1:4 But **p.** no terror symbols on your path, or
T-27.......I.10:2 and perfect healing take the **p.** of death.
T-27......III.6:9 the **p.** of every learning aid will merely *be.*
T-27......IV.7:2 But bring the problem to the only **p.** that
T-27.......V.3:1 holy instant is the miracle's abiding **p.**.
T-27.......V.3:3 from the **p.** of peace into the battleground
T-27......VI.5:3 its own effects have come to take their **p.**.
T-27......VI.8:6 to let love's symbols take the **p.** of sin.
T-27...VII.14:3 the **p.** of those you dreamed in terror and
T-27....VIII.1:3 It takes the central **p.** in every dream,
T-28.........I.2:7 the **p.** of what God gave in your creation.
T-28.......I.11:5 and what has come to take its **p.** will not
T-28.......I.15:2 of God has come to take the **p.** of loss?
T-28........II.7:4 The fear was held in **p.** because he did not
T-28......III.5:2 as unsubstantial as the empty **p.** between
T-28......III.8:6 it will make a **p.** of welcome for your
T-28......IV.8:1 of God and put the pieces into **p.** again.
T-28......IV.8:5 picture that the miracle will **p.** within the
T-28....IV.10:9 He will **p.** the miracle of healing where
T-28.......V.4:1 truth to be the **p.** where all your safety lies
T-28.......V.6:5 left no room for them in any **p.** or time.
T-28.......V.6:6 For it fills every **p.** and every time, and
T-28.......V.7:2 the **p.** where you perceive it is not real.
T-29.........I.1:1 There is no time, no **p.**, no state where
T-29.........I.4:4 and thereby signify a meeting **p.** to join.
T-29........II.5:3 is no other **p.** where He can find His host,
T-29....III.3:11 There, in its **p.**, God's witness has set
T-29.........V.h The Changeless Dwelling **P.**
T-29.......V.1:1 **p.** in you where this whole world has been
T-29.......V.1:2 There is a **p.** in you which time has left,
T-29.......V.1:3 resting **p.** so still no sound except a hymn
T-29.......V.2:1 not that you can change Their dwelling **p.**
T-29......VI.6:3 is to dwell a little while in such a happy **p.**
T-29......VI.6:4 timelessness comes quietly to take the **p.**
T-29.....VII.1:4 God calls will never answer in His **p.**.
T-29.....VII.6:4 No idol takes His **p.**. Look not to idols. Do
T-29.....VII.8:3 in it a **p.** of idols found outside yourself,
T-29...VII.10:4 An idol cannot take the **p.** of God. Let
T-29....VIII.1:9 Be it a body or a thing, a **p.**, a situation or
T-29....VIII.4:4 Where is this **p.** where what is everywhere
T-29....VIII.6:2 omnipotence, a **p.** beyond the infinite, a
T-29....VIII.6:3 this power and **p.** and time are given form
T-29....VIII.7:3 a **p.** where time can interrupt eternity? A
T-29....VIII.7:4 A **p.** of darkness set where all is light, a
T-29....VIII.7:4 off from what is endless, *has* no **p.** to be.
T-29..VIII.8:10 And when one fails another takes its **p.**,
T-30......III.2:3 What form can take the **p.** of all the love
T-30......III.9:3 it and softly holds it in its perfect **p.**,
T-30......IV.6:2 will forever **p.** you far beyond deception.
T-30.......V.1:3 is perceived and takes the **p.** of idols,

T-30....... V.2:7 The world becomes a **p.** of hope, because
T-30....... V.2:7 only purpose is to be a **p.** where hope of
T-30...... VI.3:1 rise to take the **p.** of dreams of terror.
T-30..... VII.7:2 will believe the world is an uncertain **p.**,
T-30.... VIII.6:1 hold in **p.** of what your brother really is.
T-31....... I.13:5 away, and left a **p.** for truth to be reborn.
T-31....... II.8:6 Nothing will hurt you in this holy **p.**, to
T-31....... II.9:3 bit ahead would be a safer **p.** for him to be
T-31...... III.5:2 itself; a **p.** where nothing can find mercy,
T-31...... IV.1:3 **p.** where choice among illusions seems to
T-31...... IV.4:1 road, another person or another **p.**, when
T-31....... V.2:3 to take the **p.** of your reality as Son of God
T-31...... VI.3:8 so that perception finds no hiding **p.**.
T-31...... VI.6:8 your trust; a happy **p.** to rest in for a while
T-31.... VIII.1:5 *take your* **p.** *among the saviors of the world,*
T-31.... VIII.4:2 **p.** you raised an image of yourself before.
T-31.... VIII.8:3 There is no **p.** for hell within a world
T-31.. VIII.12:3 closes, ending at the **p.** where it began.
W-pI.......... 1.h this window, in this **p.**] means anything.
W-pI.......... 2.h this **p.**] all the meaning that it has for me.
W-pI.......... 3.h this street, from this window, in this **p.**
W-pI.......... 4.h this street, from this window, in this **p.**
W-pI..... 14.3:1 and see the Word of God in their **p.**. The
W-pI..... 15.1:7 It takes the **p.** of seeing, replacing vision
W-pI..... 26.3:5 has come to take the **p.** of what you are.
W-pI..... 42.2:4 but be in the right **p.** at the right time.
W-pI..... 45.8:5 For such is the **p.** you are trying to reach.
W-pI..... 47.7:1 down into your mind to a **p.** of real safety.
W-pI..... 47.7:4 is a **p.** in you where there is perfect peace.
W-pI..... 47.7:5 is a **p.** in you where nothing is impossible.
W-pI..... 47.7:6 There is a **p.** in you where the strength of
W-pI..... 48.3:2 mind, though not necessarily in a **p.** you
W-pI..... 48.3:2 His strength take the **p.** of your weakness.
W-pI..... 49.4:7 reach the **p.** where you are truly welcome.
W-pI..... 50.5:5 Such is the resting **p.** where your Father
WpI... rI.in.3:3 and when you are alone in a quiet **p.**, if
W-pI..... 51.1:4 I think I see now is taking the **p.** of vision.
W-pI..... 51.1:5 no meaning, so that vision may take its **p.**
W-pI..... 51.4:5 I have made my thoughts to take their **p.**.
W-pI..... 53.3:7 this belief, and **p.** my trust in reality. In
W-pI..... 53.5:7 and I will **p.** no other gods before Him.
W-pI..... 55.3:5 choose to see, in **p.** of what I look on now.
W-pI..... 56.3:2 I see holds my fearful self-image in **p.**, and
W-pI..... 57.3:5 the world is really a **p.** where he can be set
W-pI..... 57.3:6 see it as a **p.** where the Son of God finds
W-pI..... 57.4:2 When I see the world as a **p.** of freedom, I
W-pI..... 57.4:4 the hearts of all who share this **p.** with me
W-pI..... 61.3:3 toward taking your rightful **p.** in salvation
W-pI..... 63.2:4 purpose or meaningless desire in its **p.**, or
W-pI..... 64.2:3 world is a **p.** where you learn to forgive
W-pI..... 65.2:1 rightful **p.** among the saviors of the world
W-pI..... 70.1:5 guilt and salvation must be in the same **p.**
W-pI..... 71.1:3 plan in **p.** of the ego's is to be damned.
W-pI..... 72.5:3 and offering illusions in **p.** of truth. The
W-pI..... 72.7:5 Your chosen savior takes His **p.** instead. It
W-pI..... 73.8:3 it is hell in **p.** of Heaven that you choose.
W-pI..... 78.9:1 the Holy Spirit showed you in their **p.**.
W-pI..... 80.1:8 are ready to take your rightful **p.** in God's
W-pI..... 89.1:4 accept the miracles in **p.** of the grievances
W-pI..... 90.1:6 welcome of the miracle that takes its **p.**.
W-pI..... 91.8:2 and their opposites to take their **p.**. Say,
W-pI..... 92.9:3 meeting **p.** we try today to find and rest in
W-pI... 92.10:4 how to find the meeting **p.** of self and Self
W-pI..... 93.8:4 **p.** of what you have decreed for yourself.
W-pI... 95.10:4 try to reach the **p.** in you in which there is
W-pI..... 96.3:2 and good and evil have no meeting **p.**.
W-pI..... 96.3:6 no **p.** in which it could be really part of
W-pI..... 96.9:5 of dreams, to find illusions in their **p.**.
W-pI..... 98.3:4 completely in the perfect time and **p.**.
W-pI..... 99.3:1 meeting **p.** at all where earth and Heaven
W-pI... 99.12:5 that love may find its rightful **p.** in you
W-pI... 100.4:2 and take their **p.** beside you in God's plan
W-pI... 100.7:4 to take his **p.** among God's messengers.
W-pI... 100.9:3 What could you rather look upon in **p.** of
W-pI... 103.3:2 what you expect to take the **p.** of pain.
W-pI... 104.1:4 must there be a **p.** made ready to receive
W-pI... 104.3:1 in choosing them in **p.** of what we made,
W-pI... 104.4:2 holy **p.** within our minds before His altar,
W-pI... 107.3:5 have no **p.** because the truth has come,
W-pI... 108.1:4 behind it will appear instead to take its **p.**.
W-pI... 108.4:1 first, nor which appears to be in second **p.**
W-pI... 109.9:6 their resting **p.** each time we tell ourselves
W-pI... 110.2:1 that any mind has made at any time or **p.**.
WpI..rIII.in6:1 **P.** the ideas within your mind, and let it
W-pI... 111.2:3 *by giving me His strength to take its* **p.**.
W-pI... 121.2:1 no **p.** where it can spread its wings in
W-pI... 122.8:2 by which it comes to take the **p.** of hell. In
W-pI... 123.2:3 to take the **p.** of Him and His creation.
W-pI... 124.2:3 and death give **p.** to everlasting life. Our
W-pI... 125.4:3 quiet **p.** within the mind where He abides
W-pI... 126.2:1 what you do believe, in **p.** of this idea. It
W-pI... 126.9:2 takes its proper **p.** in your priorities. It is
W-pI. 126.10:1 and seek sanctuary in the quiet **p.** where
W-pI... 127.9:3 And He Himself will **p.** a spark of truth
W-pI... 128.3:1 Escape today the chains you **p.** upon your
W-pI... 129.5:3 Here is the world that comes to take its **p.**,
W-pI... 129.6:5 take the **p.** of all the things you seek but
W-pI. 130.11:2 take the **p.** of everything that hell would
W-pI... 131.1:3 the **p.** to which he comes to find stability?
W-pI... 131.9:1 will not choose a paradox in **p.** of truth.
W-pI... 131.9:4 while Heaven is the **p.** he cannot find.
W-pI. 131.10:3 the **p.** of thoughts that have no meaning,
W-pI. 131.11:7 to the holy **p.** where they can enter not.
W-pI. 131.14:5 the appointed time and **p.** where you will
W-pI... 132.9:3 There is no **p.** where you can suffer, and
W-pI... 132.9:4 How can a world of time and **p.** exist, if
W-pI... 133.4:3 so clearly to the **p.** where there is but one
W-pI... 136.6:4 be real, to take the **p.** of what is real.
W-pI. 136.16:1 to take the **p.** of war and vain imaginings.
W-pI... 137.5:3 to take the **p.** of what has never been at all
W-pI... 137.7:1 will occupy the **p.** of what you made, so
W-pI. 137.15:2 receive the Word of God to take the **p.** of
W-pI... 139.7:2 a **p.** whose purpose is to be a home where
W-pI... 140.5:5 Yet there is no **p.** where He is not. And
W-pI... 140.5:7 There is no **p.** where holiness is not, and
WpI. rIV.in3:3 self-deceptions made to take its **p.**.
WpI. rIV.in4:2 self-deceptions cannot take the **p.** of truth
WpI. rIV.in5:4 **p.** His Mind in charge of all the thoughts
W-pI... 151.3:5 You **p.** pathetic faith in what your eyes
W-pI... 152.8:3 rightful **p.** as co-creator of the universe,
W-pI... 152.8:5 And it will take the **p.** of self-deceptions
W-pI. 153.14:2 we go to take our rightful **p.** where truth
W-pI... 155.2:2 for a **p.** where they can be illusions, and
W-pI... 157.3:3 more swiftly to this holy **p.** and leaves you
W-pI... 158.6:2 Here is a quiet **p.** within the world made
W-pI... 158.9:3 lies beyond them comes to take their **p.**. It
W-pI... 160.3:2 had asked this stranger in to take your **p.**,
W-pI... 160.7:3 for you have given him your rightful **p.**.
W-pI... 163.3:1 wake, in **p.** of aspirations and of dreams.
W-pI... 165.2:6 soft your resting **p.** and smooth your way,
W-pI. 170.11:3 You have reached this **p.** before, but you
W-pI. 170.12:4 You have chosen Him in **p.** of idols, and
WpI... rV.in7:1 **p.** at which the journey ends and is forgot.
WpI.rV.in12:2 We **p.** faith in the experience that comes
W-pI... 182.1:3 if there were a **p.** that called you to return,
W-pI... 182.4:2 of your body, and its **p.** of shelter, are a
W-pI. 183.10:6 and in their **p.** the holy Name of God
W-pI... 184.1:6 all happenings in terms of **p.** and time; all
W-pI... 184.7:5 In its proper **p.**, it serves but as a starting
W-pI. 184.12:5 of the world to take the **p.** of Heaven. In
W-pI. 184.15:6 *the truth You give, in* **p.** *of every one of them.*
W-pI... 185.1:3 for you in any form; in any **p.** or time.
W-pI... 185.4:7 Illusions come to take His **p.**. And what
W-pI... 185.7:6 requesting the eternal in the **p.** of shifting
W-pI... 185.8:8 in **p.** of Heaven and the peace of God?"
W-pI. 185.12:5 that ever seemed to take the **p.** of truth.
W-pI... 187.8:2 is no **p.** for sacrifice in what has any value.
W-pI... 189.5:4 If hatred finds a **p.** within your heart, you
W-pI... 190.3:1 Pain is a sign illusions reign in **p.** of truth
W-pI... 190.6:6 a sickly **p.** where living things must come
W-pI... 190.8:5 the world becomes a cruel and a bitter **p.**,
W-pI... 190.9:1 the quiet **p.** where Heaven's peace holds
W-pI. 190.11:2 instead of pain, our holiness in **p.** of sin,
W-pI... 191.5:1 But let today's idea find a **p.** among your
W-pI... 191.5:2 And from this **p.** of safety and escape you
W-pI...... 194.h I **p.** the future in the Hands of God.
W-pI... 194.1:3 you to Heaven's gate; the quiet **p.** of peace
W-pI... 194.4:5 let the future go, and **p.** it in God's Hands.
W-pI .. 194.8:1 **P.**, then, your future in the Hands of God
W-pI .. 195.9:1 learn to think of gratitude in **p.** of anger,
W-pI .. 195.9:3 regards us in a **p.** of merciless pursuit,
W-pI .. 198.5:3 and substitute your own in **p.** of His?
W-pI .. 198.6:7 the Word of God will come to take its **p.**,
W-pI .. 198.7:2 a **p.** where death is offered to God's Son
W-pI .. 198.7:4 again upon the **p.** where you beheld Their
WpI.rVI.in.6:4 and let it take the **p.** of what you thought.
WpI.rVI.in.7:2 I **p.** you in His charge, and let Him teach
W-pI .. 213.1:2 *to me, in* **p.** *of thoughts I made that hurt me.*
W-pI .. 214.1:1 (194) I **p.** the future in the Hands of God.
W-pII ..... 1.1:7 is free to take its **p.** is now the Will of God
W-pII . 226.2:3 *a* **p.** *of vain desires and of shattered dreams,*
W-pII ..... 2.4:1 Let us come daily to this holy **p.**, and
W-pII . 233.1:3 *In* **p.** *of them, give me Your Own. I give You*
W-pII ..... 3.2:4 to be a **p.** where God could enter not, and
W-pII . 249.1:5 The world becomes a **p.** of joy, abundance
W-pII ..... 4.1:2 seeks to let illusions take the **p.** of truth.
W-pII . 264.1:1 *and behind, beside me, in the* **p.** *I see myself,*
W-pII . 264.1:3 *and* **p.** *becomes a meaningless belief. For*
W-pII . 279.1:3 gone, with truth established in their **p.**.
W-pII . 281.1:4 *ideas in* **p.** *of where Your Thoughts belong,*
W-pII . 286.1:2 *How quietly do all things fall in* **p.**! *This is the*
W-pII ..... 9.1:3 to God's Word to take illusion's **p.**; the
W-pII . 317.1:1 I have a special **p.** to fill; a role for me
W-pII .... 328.h I choose the second **p.** to gain the first.
W-pII . 328.1:1 What seems to be the second **p.** is first,
W-pII ... 12.5:2 God created as His Son, His dwelling **p.**,
W-pII . 332.1:6 and take its rightful **p.** within the mind.
W-pII . 336.1:6 for this the dwelling **p.** of God Himself.
W-pII . 344.1:3 *I found an empty* **p.** *where nothing ever was*
W-ep......... 4:1 And now I **p.** you in His hands, to be His
M-1 ........... 3:6 no language; in any **p.** or time or manner.
M-2 ........... 4:4 comes at the right time to the right **p.**.
M-4 ......... I.2:3 And who would **p.** his faith in the shabby
M-4 ...... IV.2:7 come from harm in **p.** of the unfailing, all-
M-5 ........ II.4:4 **P.** cause and effect in their true sequence
M-5 .... III.2:12 Would you choose sickness in **p.** of this?"
M-8 ........... 6:7 from size and shape and time and **p.** –for
M-14 ......... 5:1 will end in joy, because it is a **p.** of sorrow.
M-14 ......... 5:3 will end in peace, because it is a **p.** of war.
M-14 ......... 5:5 end in laughter, because it is a **p.** of tears.
M-16 ......... 6:3 think you made a **p.** of safety for yourself.
M-16 ......... 8:4 in any **p.** and circumstance he calls for it.
M-16 ......... 8:5 attempts to **p.** reliance on himself alone.
M-17 ......... 5:8 Who usurps the **p.** of God and takes it for
M-17 ......... 7:3 mind, "You have usurped the **p.** of God.
M-19 ......... 3:5 Forgiveness has no **p.** in such a scheme,
M-20 ......... 2:8 away, and in its **p.** is everlasting quiet.
M-22 ......... 3:5 it sees fit could merely take the **p.** of God
M-23 ........... h JESUS HAVE A SPECIAL **P.** IN HEALING
M-28 ......... 6:3 face to take the **p.** of what they dream.
M-29 ....... 7:11 In confidence I **p.** you in His Hands, and I
C-1 ........... 5:2 Christ's vision sees the real world in its **p.**.
C-3 ........... 6:5 But illusions shift from **p.** to place; from
C-3 ........... 6:5 But illusions shift from place to **p.**; from
C-4 ........... 4:4 now there is an empty **p.** made clean and
C-4 ........... 5:7 remains to keep a separated world in **p.**?
C-4 ........... 5:8 For **p.** has gone as well, along with time.
C-4 ........... 8:2 His, for they are joined here in this holy **p.**
C-6 ........... 5:7 **p.** the hymn to God is heard a little while.
P-2............. II.h The **P.** of Religion in Psychotherapy
P-2.......... II.2:1 religion has no **p.** in psychotherapy, but it
P-2.......... II.2:1 but it also has no real **p.** in religion. In
P-2.......... II.5:4 restores the **p.** of God to ascendance, first
P-2....... VII.3:1 process that takes **p.** in this relationship is
P-3.......... II.6:8 is a **p.** for all relationships in this world,
P-3........ II.7:10 They take the **p.** of other images, and help
P-3........ II.10:5 Will of God that he take his **p.** in the plan
P-3........ III.6:4 the resting **p.** of Christ and home of God
S-1.......... V.2:1 share a dwelling **p.** where they can meet.
S-1.......... V.4:3 the **p.** appointed for the time when you
S-2........... I.3:5 sin by choosing in its **p.** the face of Christ.
S-3........... I.5:2 The world of opposites is healing's **p.**, for
S-3........ III.4:3 in humility there is indeed a **p.** for helpers
S-3........ III.5:6 **p.** is written now the holy Word of God.
S-3........ IV.5:3 that it is you who are creator in His **p.**,

## placed 86

| | |
|---|---|
| T-1.........II.4:6 | has **p.** me in charge of the Sonship, which |
| T-2........VI.8:3 | you have **p.** yourself in a position where |
| T-2.......VII.4:5 | since you have **p.** yourself in a position |
| T-3.........V.6:6 | **p.** yourself in a position where you could |
| T-5.........II.1:5 | still in you because God **p.** it in your mind |
| T-5.........II.3:2 | made, God **p.** in the mind the Call to joy. |
| T-5........IV.6:1 | lifts the burden you have **p.** in your mind. |
| T-5........VI.1:7 | where God Himself **p.** you forever. |
| T-5.......VII.6:4 | within you because God **p.** it there. Your |
| T-6...........I.7:3 | God **p.** it there Himself, and so it is true |
| T-6......V.C.7:1 | center, where God **p.** the altar to Himself. |
| T-6......V.C.9:4 | and thus **p.** part of your mind outside it. |
| T-7........III.2:1 | Kingdom, because that is where He **p.** it. |
| T-10......IV.1:5 | sick, you have **p.** other gods before Him. |
| T-11.........I.4:2 | Who **p.** no limits on His creation or upon |
| T-11........VI.8:1 | **p.** a crown of thorns upon your own head. |
| T-11.....VII.4:4 | that you have **p.** between yourself and |
| T-12....III.10:1 | else, you will at last have **p.** its source, and |
| T-12....III.10:5 | has **p.** the Atonement on the altar for you. |
| T-12.......V.5:4 | in which you **p.** yourself is impossible, |
| T-12...VIII.4:1 | what God Himself **p.** in his memory. You |
| T-13.....VII.7:3 | God **p.** him in Himself where pain is not, |
| T-13......IX.2:4 | of the belief in which the faith was **p.**. |
| T-13......IX.3:1 | what you found in it and **p.** your faith in. |
| T-13....IX.8:13 | then, upon the light He **p.** within you, |
| T-13......X.13:2 | unto the worth that God has **p.** upon you. |
| T-13......XI.3:3 | Value is where God **p.** it, and the value of |
| T-13......XI.8:1 | Link that God Himself **p.** within you, |
| T-13....XI.10:1 | when God has **p.** within him the glad Call |
| T-14.........I.2:8 | That is why God **p.** the Holy Spirit in you, |
| T-14.........I.2:8 | Spirit in you, where you **p.** the dream. |
| T-14......IV.7:5 | very mind where God Himself has **p.** it. If |
| T-14....IV.10:5 | have **p.** within your mind cannot exist, for |
| T-14...VIII.5:7 | on the altar, where He has **p.** His Own. |
| T-14......IX.3:8 | His worshippers **p.** other gods upon it. |
| T-15......IV.4:1 | altar on which your Father has **p.** Himself |
| T-15.......V.6:3 | you have **p.** less value on one and more on |
| T-15......IX.6:1 | the limits you have **p.** on your perception, |
| T-17......IV.7:3 | they defend is **p.** in them for safe-keeping, |
| T-17.....VII.9:5 | goal He **p.** there was extended to every |
| T-18.........I.8:4 | that you have **p.** outside you to the truth. |
| T-18....VI.9:10 | God **p.** none between Himself and you. |
| T-18....VI.14:7 | to let go the limits you have **p.** upon love, |
| T-18....IX.13:2 | and gently **p.** before the gates of Heaven. |
| T-19......IV.2:2 | flow across the obstacles you **p.** before it. |
| T-20.......II.3:3 | to it the worshippers of what he **p.** upon it |
| T-20.......II.3:4 | he has **p.** upon it and take it for their own. |
| T-20......III.5:6 | it loves, and **p.** outside you in the world. |
| T-21.......II.8:1 | your altars free of what you **p.** upon them, |
| T-21......III.2:6 | of faith is never recognized if it is **p.** in sin |
| T-21......III.2:7 | But it is always recognized if it is **p.** in love |
| T-23.....II.22:4 | Attack in any form has **p.** your foot upon |
| T-24.......II.7:1 | all the sins you think you **p.** between him |
| T-26.........I.3:5 | to you are limits **p.** on everything outside, |
| T-26.....VII.9:5 | remove the obstacles that you have **p.** |
| T-27.....II.14:2 | of correction has been **p.** outside yourself, |
| T-27...VIII.7:4 | you thought is being **p.** outside yourself, |
| W-pI.....50.1:3 | faith is **p.** in the most trivial and insane |
| W-pI.....50.5:5 | where your Father has **p.** you forever. |
| W-pI.....72.9:1 | of truth is in us, where it was **p.** by God. It |
| W-pI.....90.3:5 | I do not yet realize that God has **p.** the |
| W-pI...102.3:1 | the happiness God's Will has **p.** in you. |
| W-pI...103.3:1 | Allow this one correction to be **p.** within |
| W-pI...104.2:1 | gifts which we have **p.** upon the holy altar |
| W-pI...127.4:5 | There is no limit **p.** upon Himself, and so |
| W-pI...127.8:4 | Withdraw all value you have **p.** upon its |
| W-pI.136.18:1 | this removes the limits you had **p.** upon |
| W-pI...140.8:2 | because our Father **p.** it there for us. It is |
| W-pI.151.10:1 | remove all faith that you have **p.** in pain, |
| W-pI.155.13:4 | Forget not He has **p.** His Hand in yours, |
| W-pI.161.11:5 | you have **p.** upon your bleeding head. Ask |
| W-pI...163.4:4 | **p.** upon the body of the holy Son of God. |
| W-pI...163.9:6 | *And we abide where You have **p.** us, in the* |
| W-pI...167.3:7 | emphasis this course has **p.** on that idea is |
| W-pI...189.1:5 | not **p.** in you to be kept hidden from your |
| W-pI...194.8:4 | has also **p.** the world within the Hands to |
| W-pII..238.1:3 | *yet You **p.** Your Son's salvation in my hands,* |
| W-pII......6.2:5 | His Father **p.** the means for your salvation |
| W-pII......7.4:1 | knowledge, where He has been **p.** by God, |
| W-pII..281.2:3 | My Father **p.** me safe in Heaven, watching |
| W-pII..318.1:4 | find the sinlessness that God has **p.** in me. |
| M-5.......II.3:5 | is responsibility **p.** where it belongs; not |
| M-7...........5:2 | that trust has been **p.** in an illusory self, |
| M-25.........2:6 | These limits are **p.** out of fear, for without |
| S-3...........I.4:4 | to him in the Voice his Father **p.** in him. |
| S-3.........II.6:3 | **p.** upon God's substitute for evil dreams; |

## places 31

| | |
|---|---|
| T-1.........I.30:2 | This **p.** spirit at the center, where it can |
| T-1.........I.37:3 | **p.** you under the Atonement principle, |
| T-1........III.7:4 | the miracle **p.** the mind in a state of grace. |
| T-1.........V.5:5 | it retains its creative potential but **p.** itself |
| T-3........IV.5:7 | This **p.** it in the service of spirit, where |
| T-7.........II.2:2 | This **p.** you both within the Kingdom, |
| T-7.........V.7:8 | **p.** you in a position of needing to learn a |
| T-9........IV.8:2 | whether its unpredictability **p.** the ego in |
| T-11......VI.5:2 | For he **p.** himself at the altar of his god, |
| T19..IV.B.16:2 | sin, and **p.** in it all its faith that this can be |
| T-20.......II.1:6 | acknowledges the lack of value he **p.** on |
| T-23.......II.4:3 | one who makes the error **p.** him beyond |
| T-27...VIII.3:3 | a great variety of **p.** and events wherein its |
| T-27...VIII.4:2 | and out of **p.** and events that it contrives. |
| T-31.....V.16:5 | will appear in many **p.** and in many forms |
| W-pI.....65.3:3 | It **p.** the key to the door of peace, which |
| W-pI.....70.2:3 | way. Today's idea **p.** you in charge of the |
| W-pI.....70.7:5 | reviewing some of the external **p.** where |
| W-pI.....71.3:3 | is still grounds for hope in other **p.** and in |
| W-pI.....79.4:3 | perception **p.** you in a position in which |
| W-pI.....99.7:6 | all your mistakes enter the darkened **p.** of |
| W-pI...102.1:4 | dark and hidden secret **p.** of your mind. |
| WpIrIII.in11:5 | to serve you in all ways, all times and **p.**, |
| W-pI...162.4:3 | which God **p.** all His gifts and all His Love |
| W-pI...200.4:2 | found your happiness in foreign **p.** and in |
| M-13.........5:7 | in a thousand ways and in a thousand **p.**, |
| M-16.........7:7 | his state at different times and different **p.** |
| M-25.........2:5 | limits the world **p.** on communication are |
| M-25.........2:6 | the separate **p.** of the world would fall at |
| M-28.........4:5 | No hidden **p.** now remain on earth to |
| S-2........III.6:6 | Name, and **p.** his forgiveness in His hands |

## placing 10

| | |
|---|---|
| T-1.........I.32:3 | **p.** you beyond the physical laws they raise |
| T-1........IV.2:6 | in the Atonement by **p.** the mind in the |
| T-2........III.2:4 | This heals the separation by **p.** within you |
| T-3......VI.2:11 | way you are **p.** your belief in the unreal. |
| T-8........III.3:5 | His Fatherhood by **p.** no limits upon it. |
| T-16......VI.2:2 | To look for it by **p.** yourself in bondage is |
| T-18.....VII.4:2 | prepare for it without **p.** it in the future. |
| T-21......III.3:4 | hold him, and **p.** it in his freedom instead |
| W-pI.....28.6:3 | instead of **p.** your own judgment upon it. |
| M-5.........I.1:7 | for **p.** God's Son on his Father's throne. |

## plague 1

| | |
|---|---|
| S-2...........I.2:4 | things, and overlooks the loving as a **p.**; a |

## plain 10

| | |
|---|---|
| T-14...VIII.4:2 | And truth will make this **p.** to you as you |
| T-22.........I.8:2 | you do not understand, and make it **p.**. |
| T-22......III.1:3 | reason's goal is to make **p.**, and therefore |
| T-22......III.1:8 | For it is **p.**, and what is obvious is not |
| T-25.......in.2:7 | as **p.** to see as is his specialness set forth |
| T-27......IV.1:2 | and to ensure no answer will be **p.**. A |
| T-30......IV.8:8 | the toys of fear, and then its unreality is **p.** |
| T-31......VI.4:1 | that you must make the way to Heaven **p.**. |
| W-pI...122.6:6 | for here we have an answer, clear and **p.**, |
| W-pI...129.4:1 | unambiguous and **p.** as day, remains |

## plainly 5

| | |
|---|---|
| T-21.......II.8:4 | and see what must be there, **p.** in sight, |
| T-25......III.6:6 | will hear **p.** that the calls to war he heard |
| T-29.........I.2:1 | Here is the fear of God most **p.** seen. For |
| W-pI...129.8:3 | And yet your mind can see it **p.**, and can |
| W-pI...134.4:6 | It would see as right the **p.** wrong; the |

## plaintive 2

| | |
|---|---|
| T-25.......V.3:4 | Nor do you hear his **p.** call, unchanged in |
| T-27......VI.6:6 | a **p.** cry for help within a world of misery. |

## plan 208

| | |
|---|---|
| T-1........III.3:3 | this is the **p.** of the Atonement. Miracles |
| T-1........III.8:4 | of my complete awareness of the whole **p.** |
| T-2..........II.6:8 | the Atonement as a completed **p.** has a |
| T-2........IV.2:1 | in the Atonement **p.** is to undo error at all |
| T-2......VIII.2:4 | devices to be built into the overall **p.**. Just |
| T-5.......VII.1:3 | Do you really believe you can **p.** for your |
| T-5.......VII.4:2 | out the **p.** of salvation yourself because, as |
| T-5.......VII.4:4 | am making His **p.** perfectly explicit to you |
| T-9...........IV.h | The Holy Spirit's **P.** of Forgiveness |
| T-9........IV.2:1 | the **p.** of the Atonement is beyond you. |
| T-9........IV.2:5 | **p.** is not yours because of your limited |
| T-9........IV.4:1 | a **p.** of forgiveness because you are asking |
| T-9........IV.4:2 | The ego's **p.**, of course, makes no sense |
| T-9........IV.4:3 | By following its **p.** you will merely place |
| T-9........IV.4:4 | ego's **p.** is to have you see error clearly |
| T-9........IV.6:3 | to follow the Holy Spirit's **p.** of salvation, |
| T-9.........V.1:1 | ego's **p.** for forgiveness is far more widely |
| T-9.........V.3:3 | the ego's **p.** for forgiveness in one form or |
| T-9.........V.4:1 | ego's **p.** are as unhelpful as the older ones, |
| T-12.........I.6:4 | simple, then, is God's **p.** for salvation. |
| T-13.......I.10:2 | This is the ego's **p.**, which it offers instead |
| T-13......VI.4:7 | past experience, and **p.** for it accordingly. |
| T-13....XI.11:5 | the **p.** the Holy Spirit offers *to* everyone, |
| T-14........II.7:2 | Holy Spirit's **p.** to free you from the past, |
| T-14....III.12:4 | accepts the **p.** God set for its Atonement, |
| T-14....III.13:1 | The One Who knows the **p.** of God that |
| T-14.......V.2:5 | **p.** for your awaking is as perfect as yours |
| T-15....III.11:1 | to the **p.** of God and unwilling to attempt |
| T-15....III.11:2 | not you can substitute your **p.** for His. |
| T-15......IV.2:6 | Give over every **p.** you have made for your |
| T-15......IV.3:2 | no **p.** of the ego before the plan of God. |
| T-15......IV.3:2 | no plan of the ego before the **p.** of God. |
| T-15......IV.3:3 | For you leave empty your place in His **p.**, |
| T-15......IV.3:3 | by your decision to join in any **p.** but His. |
| T-15......IV.3:4 | your holy part in the **p.** that He has given |
| T-15......IV.3:6 | Every allegiance to a **p.** of salvation apart |
| T-15......IV.4:2 | and gladly give over every **p.** but His. For |
| T-15......IV.4:5 | practice, try to give over every **p.** you have |
| T-15...VII.12:1 | the ego's **p.** to establish its own autonomy |
| T-16...VII.10:2 | **p.** of Atonement arising from His Love. |
| T-17........II.3:1 | of all in God's **p.** of Atonement. All else is |
| T-18....IV.5:11 | *but only that I do not interfere with His **p.** to* |
| T-18....IV.5:12 | *I need add nothing to His **p.**. But to receive it,* |
| T-18......IV.6:3 | and that your **p.** for the escape from guilt |
| T-18.......V.1:4 | are all but aspects of the **p.** to change your |
| T-18.......V.3:2 | Can you **p.** for this? Or could you prepare |
| T19. IV.D.19:2 | nothing in the **p.** God has established for |
| T-20......IV.6:1 | The **p.** is not of you, nor need you be |
| T-20......IV.6:6 | its special function in the Holy Spirit's **p.**, |
| T-20......IV.8:3 | a **p.** for your salvation that does not work. |
| T-20......IV.8:4 | work. Once you accept His **p.** as the one |
| T-21.......V.5:1 | God's **p.** for your salvation could not |
| T-21.......V.6:1 | God's **p.** is simple; never circular and |
| T-21.......V.6:5 | must have an answer if the **p.** of God for |
| T-21......VI.9:4 | This gracious **p.** was given love by Love. |
| T-22.........I.1:7 | you wandered in without a **p.** of any kind |
| T-22......VI.4:1 | of your Father as a means for His Own **p.**. |
| T-24......II.14:1 | **p.** for your salvation in the place of yours. |
| T-24......II.14:2 | and the awareness that your **p.** has failed, |
| T-25......VI.4:3 | Nor is the **p.** complete until he finds his |
| T-25......VI.5:9 | him, for on his part does all the **p.** depend |
| T-25......VI.7:7 | see it as your special function in the **p.** to |
| T-25...VII.10:5 | you in God's Own **p.** to show His Son that |
| T-25...VII.12:7 | to the **p.** in which your special function |
| T-26....VIII.5:1 | within the future, where you cannot **p.**. |
| T-30....IV.8:13 | What could God's **p.** for his salvation be, |
| T-31.........I.7:7 | is no **p.** for safety you can make that ever |
| W-pI.....61.7:6 | His **p.** for the salvation of His Son on you. |
| W-pI.........71.h | Only God's **p.** for salvation will work. |
| W-pI.....71.1:1 | a **p.** for salvation in opposition to God's. |

W-pI.....71.1:2 It is this **p.** in which you believe. Since it is
W-pI.....71.1:3 to accept God's **p.** in place of the ego's is
W-pI.....71.1:5 have considered just what the ego's **p.** is,
W-pI.....71.2:1 The ego's **p.** for salvation centers around
W-pI.....71.3:1 role assigned to your own mind in this **p.**,
W-pI.....71.3:2 According to this insane **p.**, any perceived
W-pI.....71.4:1 Such is the ego's **p.** for your salvation.
W-pI.....71.5:1 **p.** for salvation works simply because, by
W-pI.....71.6:4 Only God's **p.** for salvation will work.
W-pI.....71.6:5 is no possible alternative to God's **p.** that
W-pI.....71.6:6 is the only **p.** that is certain in its outcome
W-pI.....71.6:7 His is the only **p.** that must succeed.
W-pI.....71.7:4 Salvation must be yours because of His **p.**
W-pI.....71.8:2 God's **p.** for your salvation will work, and
W-pI.....71.8:5 and anger; but God's **p.** will succeed. It
W-pI.....71.9:1 to asking God to reveal His **p.** to us. Ask
W-pI.....71.9:6 done by you in His **p.** for your salvation.
W-pI...71.10:1 yourself often that God's **p.** for salvation,
W-pI...71.10:3 *is the opposite of God's* ***p.*** *for salvation.*
W-pI...71.10:4 *And only His* ***p.*** *will work.* Try to remember
W-pI........72.h is an attack on God's **p.** for salvation.
W-pI.....72.1:1 **p.** for salvation is the opposite of God's,
W-pI.....72.1:1 that it is an active attack on His **p.**, and a
W-pI.....72.3:1 is an attack on God's **p.** for salvation.
W-pI.....72.5:1 a body, what must His **p.** for salvation be?
W-pI.....72.7:4 you are attacking God's **p.** for salvation,
W-pI.....72.9:5 to end the attack on God's **p.** for salvation
W-pI.....72.9:6 And wherever His **p.** is accepted, it is
W-pI...72.10:1 that God's **p.** for salvation has already
W-pI...72.10:3 cannot understand what God's **p.** for us is
W-pI...72.10:5 aside, and ask what God's **p.** for us is:
W-pI.72.10:10 We have attacked God's **p.** for salvation
W-pI...72.13:3 *is an attack on God's* ***p.*** *for salvation. Let me*
W-pI.....73.7:2 to accept God's **p.** because you share in it.
W-pI.....73.9:1 the recognition that God's **p.** for salvation
W-pI.....78.5:6 Such is his role in God your Father's **p.**.
W-pI...78.10:1 to us as part of God's salvation **p.**, and
W-pI.....80.1:8 rightful place in God's **p.** for salvation.
W-pI.....86.1:1 (71) Only God's **p.** for salvation will work
W-pI.....86.1:7 Only God's **p.** for salvation will work.
W-pI.....86.1:8 I will rejoice because His **p.** can never fail.
W-pI.....86.2:2 *God's* ***p.*** *for salvation will save me from my*
W-pI.....86.2:3 *is no exception in God's* ***p.*** *for my salvation.*
W-pI.....86.2:4 *this only in the light of God's* ***p.*** *for salvation.*
W-pI.....86.3:1 is an attack on God's **p.** for salvation.
W-pI.....86.3:2 that God's **p.** for salvation will not work.
W-pI.....86.3:3 Yet only His **p.** will work. By holding
W-pI.....86.3:6 I would accept God's **p.** for salvation, and
W-pI.....89.3:4 according to God's **p.** for my salvation.
W-pI.....96.6:8 God's **p.** for the release of His dear Son
W-pI........98.h accept my part in God's **p.** for salvation.
W-pI.....98.7:6 *will accept my part in God's* ***p.*** *for salvation.*
W-pI.....99.4:2 What **p.** could hold the truth inviolate,
W-pI.....99.4:3 but a Thought of God could be this **p.**, by
W-pI.....99.5:1 Holy Spirit holds this **p.** of God exactly as
W-pI.....99.6:4 with the One to Whom the **p.** was given.
W-pI.....99.6:5 Now are you entrusted with this **p.**, along
W-pI...99.12:2 with Him Who shares God's **p.** with you.
W-pI......100.h part is essential to God's **p.** for salvation.
W-pI...100.1:1 your part in it completes your Father's **p.**.
W-pI...100.2:3 to take in working out His **p.** is given you
W-pI...100.2:4 as essential to His **p.** as to your happiness.
W-pI...100.2:5 Your joy must be complete to let His **p.** be
W-pI...100.3:1 You are indeed essential to God's **p.**.
W-pI...100.4:1 You are indeed essential to God's **p.**. Just
W-pI...100.4:2 take their place beside you in God's **p.**.
W-pI...100.5:2 take the part that is essential to God's **p.**,
W-pI...100.7:7 You but receive according to God's **p.**,
W-pI.100.10:2 You are essential to His **p.**. You are His
W-pI.100.10:7 to God's **p.** for the salvation of the world.
W-pI...113.2:2 *perfect* ***p.*** *for my salvation perfectly fulfilled*
W-pI...114.2:1 accept my part in God's **p.** for salvation.
W-pI...114.3:4 accept my part in God's **p.** for salvation.
W-pI...115.2:1 part is essential to God's **p.** for salvation.
W-pI...115.2:2 *to the* ***p.*** *of God for the salvation of the world*
W-pI...115.2:3 *gave me His* ***p.*** *that I might save the world.*
W-pI...115.3:4 part is essential to God's **p.** for salvation.
W-pI...122.5:1 **p.** for your salvation cannot change, nor
W-pI...122.6:5 There is no **p.** but this for the salvation of
W-pI...125.2:2 God's **p.** is simply this: The Son of God is
W-pI...135.1:4 you do when you attempt to **p.** the future,
W-pI.135.11:1 A healed mind does not **p.**. It carries out
W-pI.135.11:5 **p.** established for the good of everyone.
W-pI.135.12:1 is relieved of the belief that it must **p.**,
W-pI.135.12:1 the problem that the **p.** is made to solve.
W-pI.135.13:2 means of helping in a **p.** which far exceeds
W-pI.135.18:2 Perhaps you have misunderstood His **p.**,
W-pI.135.20:2 happiness according to the ancient **p.**,
W-pI.135.22:2 Today we will receive instead of **p.**, that
W-pI.135.25:5 learn the part for you within the **p.** of God
W-pI...136.4:3 your **p.** requires that you must forget you
W-pI...136.7:3 It is a choice you make, a **p.** you lay, when
W-pI.136.12:3 attempts to **p.** defenses that would alter it
W-pI.153.18:4 chose to carry out His **p.** for the salvation
W-pI...154.1:5 a larger **p.** we cannot see in its entirety.
W-pI...158.4:2 Yet there is a **p.** behind appearances that
W-pI...166.9:6 your **p.** to keep His Son in deep oblivion,
W-pI.166.10:3 imprisoned in your **p.** to lose your Self.
W-pI.166.10:4 not know about a **p.** so alien to His Will.
W-pI...186.1:6 on earth in Heaven's **p.** to save the world,
W-pI...186.5:1 the imprisonment your **p.** to prove the
W-pI...186.5:2 Accept the **p.** you did not make instead.
W-pI.186.11:6 Your **p.** may be impossible, but God's can
W-pI...198.4:2 when this one is the **p.** of God Himself?
W-pI...199.4:5 that it must reach, according to God's **p.**.
W-pII ..in.10:6 We will accept the way God's **p.** will end,
W-pII .294.2:3 *then, use this dream to help Your* ***p.*** *that we*
W-pII ... 10.4:1 step in His appointed **p.** to bless His Son,
W-pII .317.1:4 way my Father's **p.** appointed me to go,
W-pII .318.1:1 all parts of Heaven's **p.** to save the world.
W-pII .324.1:1 *One Who gave the* ***p.*** *for my salvation to me.*
W-pII .326.1:8 *Your* ***p.*** *I follow here, and at the end I know*
W-pII .331.1:2 *Could he make a* ***p.*** *for his damnation, and*
W-pII .338.2:1 *Your* ***p.*** *is sure, my Father,–only Yours. All*
W-pII .342.1:1 *for Your* ***p.*** *to save me from the hell I made. It*
M-1 .........2:10 that the **p.** of the teachers was established
M-2 ...........2:1 the teaching-learning **p.** of salvation, it is
M-2 ...........2:4 the **p.** for this correction was established
M-3 ...........1:5 the **p.** includes very specific contacts to be
M-3 ...........3:5 is part of God's **p.** for Atonement, and
M-3 ...........3:5 Atonement, and His **p.** can have no levels,
M-4 ...........1:4 a special role in His **p.** for Atonement.
M-4 .....I.A.3:6 **p.** will sometimes call for changes in what
M-9 ...........1:3 and chance plays no part in God's **p.**. It is
C-6 ...........2:1 bringing the **p.** of the Atonement to us,
C-6 ...........2:2 the leader in carrying out His **p.** since he
P-2........ III.4:5 carries out the **p.** established for salvation
P-2......... V.5:8 holy interaction is the **p.** of God Himself,
P-3...........I.1:4 There are no errors in God's **p.**. It would
P-3........II.10:5 he take his place in the **p.** for salvation.
P-3........ III.1:2 part of His **p.** that everything in this
P-3........ III.1:2 Holy Spirit to help in carrying out the **p.**.
P-3........ III.1:4 to help him better serve the **p.**. Money is
P-3........ III.2:7 money where God's **p.** allots it has no cost
P-3...... III.8:10 of salvation. Remember the **p.** of God for
S-2.........in.1:3 ally; sister in the **p.** for your salvation.
S-2...........I.7:8 Salvation's **p.** is made complete, and
S-2...........I.9:6 **p.** that God established for returning be

## plane 3

T-1 .........II.6:2 In the longitudinal or horizontal **p.** the
T-1 ....... III.9:3 of size exists on a **p.** that is itself unreal.
W-pI...126.3:2 on a higher **p.** than he whom you forgive.

## planned 20

T-2 .........II.4:5 necessary for its fulfillment were **p.**. Then
T-8 ..........I.5:5 If it is **p.** by two teachers, each believing
T-12 .....II.10:1 well-structured and carefully **p.** program
T-17 ........II.3:3 Who **p.** salvation could complete it thus.
T-18 ........II.1:4 **p.** solely around what you would have
T-21 ..VII.3:14 What seems to be a **p.** attack is bedlam.
W-in..........3:2 exercises are **p.** around one central idea,
W-in..........4:2 are **p.** to help you generalize the lessons,
W-pI.......20.1:3 has been intentional, and very carefully **p.**
W-pI.....95.6:1 **p.** to include frequent reminders of your
W-pI.....98.1:5 today, and to salvation as God **p.** it be.
W-pI .. 102.3:1 our periods of practicing to exercises **p.** to
WpIrIII.in11:2 These practice periods are **p.** to help you
W-pI .. 122.5:2 Be thankful it remains exactly as He **p.** it.
W-pI 135.18:1 are gently **p.** by One Whose only purpose
W-pI 135.21:1 for this is part of what was **p.** for us. We
W-pI .. 185.6:3 Whatever form the lesson takes is **p.** for
W-pII . 289.2:5 ***p.*** *to be the end of all his dreams and all his*
W-pII . 338.1:7 God has **p.** that His beloved Son will be
C-in ........... 3:2 it is **p.** only to set the direction towards it.

## planning 5

W-pI 135.14:4 Yet **p.** is not often recognized as a defense
W-pI 135.15:1 mind engaged in **p.** for itself is occupied
W-pI 135.22:1 twice today we rest from senseless **p.**, and
W-pI 135.26:2 that comes to you without your **p.**. Learn
W-pI 136.10:1 Such is your **p.** for your own defense.

## plans 31

T-18 .... VII.1:2 What **p.** do you make that do not involve
T-21 ..... VI.9:5 Love **p.** is like Itself in this: Being united,
T-26 ... VIII.5:1 **p.** you make for safety all are laid within
T-27 .. VII.12:1 death, yet **p.** that it be lingering and slow;
T-28 ....... II.6:2 No **p.** are possible, and no design exists
T-30 .... VII.2:1 except your **p.** for what the day *should* be?
T-31 ....... II.1:3 and no **p.** that need be laid for bringing in
T-31 .......V.9:1 are the Holy Spirit's lesson **p.** arranged in
W-pI .... 56.1:4 All my hopes and wishes and **p.** appear to
W-pI .... 71.5:3 and you will attempt to follow two **p.** for
W-pI .... 71.8:2 salvation will work, and other **p.** will not.
W-pI .. 135.3:5 as you elaborate your **p.** and make your
W-pI 135.11:2 carries out the **p.** that it receives through
W-pI 135.11:4 its adequacy to fulfill the **p.** assigned to it.
W-pI 135.12:2 body in its **p.** until it recognizes this is so.
W-pI 135.13:1 Enslavement of the body to the **p.** the
W-pI 135.14:1 easy to perceive that self-initiated **p.** are
W-pI 135.16:1 that **p.** is thus refusing to allow for change
W-pI 135.17:1 Defenses are the **p.** you undertake to
W-pI 135.18:4 While you made **p.** for death, He led you
W-pI 135.21:3 We make no **p.** for how it will be done,
W-pI 135.23:2 If there are **p.** to make, you will be told of
W-pI 135.23:3 They may not be the **p.** you thought were
W-pI 135.25:6 little **p.** or magical beliefs can still have
W-pI 135.26:5 and tempt you to engage in weaving **p.**,
W-pI 136.11:1 knows not of your **p.** to change His Will.
W-pI 136.11:6 are **p.** to defeat what cannot be attacked.
W-pI 136.19:2 or make **p.** against uncertainties to come,
W-pII ... 12.4:1 dreams, its hopes, its **p.** for its salvation,
W-pII . 338.2:2 *All other* ***p.*** *will fail. And I will have thoughts*
S-2........ III.2:1 yours, not by your **p.** but by His holy Will

## planted 2

T-16 ..... III.9:1 you think, and your foot is **p.** firmly on it.
T-18 .......V.2:7 build a ladder **p.** in the solid rock of faith,

## play 34

T-9 ....... IV.2:1 You have a part to **p.** in the Atonement,
T-11 ... VIII.5:3 This is not a course in the **p.** of ideas, but
T-12 .... VII.2:1 world must **p.** his part in its redemption,
T-14 ........V.2:1 has a special part to **p.** in the Atonement,
T-16 ..... IV.2:1 of love **p.** out a conflict that does not exist
T-17 ..... VI.6:5 in it will **p.** his part in its accomplishment
T-18 ..... IX.7:4 go, as long as you would **p.** the game of
T-18 ..... IX.7:5 Yet however long you **p.** it, and regardless
T-20 ....... II.6:6 but a dream, a careless thought to **p.** with
T-20 ... VIII.7:1 the senseless means to **p.** the idle game of
T-22 ..... III.1:5 This is not a **p.** on words, for here is the
T-23 ..... II.16:4 where only shadows **p.** the major roles, it
T-27 .... VII.6:1 The part you **p.** in salvaging the world
T-28 ..... III.2:3 the part you **p.** in making sickness real,
T-29 ..... IX.4:4 idols are the toys you dream you **p.** with.
T-29 ..... IX.4:7 is in the minds of those who **p.** with them.
T-29 ..... IX.5:9 himself, and **p.** that he is but a part of it.
T-30 ..... IV.3:7 Yet while he likes to **p.** with them, he still
W-pI .. 100.5:3 is the sign that you would **p.** another part,
W-pI .. 136.5:1 this quick forgetting of the part you **p.** in

W-pI...132.7:3 Some see it suddenly on **p.** of death, and
W-pI.134.12:5 to **p.** the way to those who follow him.
W-pI...139.2:4 From this one **p.** of certainty, it looks on
W-pI...157.2:1 crucial turning **p.** in the curriculum. We
W-pI...158.4:5 the journey from the **p.** at which it ended,
W-pI...161.3:4 to teach us from a different **p.** of view, so
W-pI...169.8:2 from a **p.** where time was ended, when it
Wi181-200 1:1 Our next few lessons make a special **p.** of
W-pI...184.7:5 it serves but as a starting **p.** from which
W-pI.186.11:5 All of them **p.** to one goal, and one you
W-pI...187.1:3 We have made this **p.** before. What seems
W-pI...188.7:3 And they **p.** surely to their Source, Where
W-pI...189.8:6 **p.** the road to God by which He should
W-pI...198.3:6 Yet does it **p.** to where the truth must be,
W-pI...200.2:1 final **p.** to which each one must come at
W-pII ..... 1.3:4 to pose a contradiction to its **p.** of view.
W-pII .266.2:3 filled the world with those who **p.** to Him,
M-3 ........... 1:4 from a practical **p.** of view he cannot meet
M-4 ..... I.A.3:5 He is not yet at a **p.** at which he can make
M-4 ..... I.A.5:4 no **p.** in sorting out the valuable from the
M-4 ..... I.A.6:5 and the teacher of God is now at the **p.** in
M-5 ...... III.1:8 Nor are they open-minded on this **p.**. The
M-24 ......... 6:9 will **p.** to this if properly interpreted. In
M-25 ......... 2:3 be little **p.** in trying to teach salvation.
M-27 ......... 5:4 is no **p.** at which the contrast between the
P-2......... II.1:3 one who had achieved that **p.** could teach
P-2........ VI.5:3 study of the form a sickness takes will **p.**
P-2....... VII.4:4 Before he reached this **p.**, he thought he
P-2....... VII.5:5 Only from this omniscient **p.** of view
P-3......... II.6:2 relationships this **p.** is never reached,
P-3......... II.9:5 There is no halfway **p.** in this. Either they
S-1........ IV.1:2 For until that **p.**, each one must ask for
S-3........ III.4:8 no **p.** in giving remedy apart from where

## pointed 5

*See also* sharp-pointed
T-25....... V.6:6 and you will walk the way you **p.** out to
T-27..... VII.4:7 knife in his own hand, and **p.** to himself.
W-pI...191.5:4 in gratitude to Him Who **p.** out the way
W-pII .256.2:2 *find the way Your sacred Word has* **p.** *out to*
W-pII .357.1:2 *live. Your holy Son is* **p.** *out to me, first in my*

## pointing 3

T-3........ VI.2:3 of perception, **p.** out that evaluation is its
T-14....... in.1:5 **p.** as clearly to Heaven as the ego points
W-pII .315.1:5 becomes my savior, **p.** out the way to me,

## pointless 8

T-2........ VI.3:1 **p.** to believe that controlling the outcome
T-9....... VII.4:8 Yet it is surely **p.** to attack in return.
T-18......... I.7:8 all. To judge them individually is **p.**. Their
T19... IV.A.8:3 Its **p.** wandering makes its results appear
T-27...... IV.2:8 must be **p.** to attempt to solve a problem
W-pI...181.5:5 lay these **p.** limitations by a little while.
W-pII .258.1:2 by our **p.** little goals which offer nothing,
M-11 ......... 2:3 that it is **p.** to try to reconcile them. God

## pointlessly 2

T19... IV.A.7:4 Now it is aimless, wandering **p.**, causing
W-pI....... 4.5:4 a tendency to become **p.** preoccupied.

## points 26

T-2....... VII.7:1 some additional **p.** might be helpful here.
T-5.......... I.7:5 it **p.** the way beyond the healing that it
T-13..... VII.6:2 following not the road that love **p.** out.
T-13...... XI.4:4 The Holy Spirit **p.** quietly to the contrast,
T-14....... in.1:5 as the ego **p.** to darkness and to death.
T-14....... V.6:5 And every teaching that **p.** to this points
T-14....... V.6:5 that points to this **p.** straight to Heaven,
T-20....... II.4:6 thorns whose **p.** gleam sharply in a blood-
T-21....... V.7:8 What reason **p.** to you can see, because
T-25..... VII.8:4 This One but **p.** to an alternative, another
T-26....... V.8:2 And everything that **p.** to it as real is but a
T-26....... V.9:5 everything that **p.** the way in the direction
T-27 ........ I.4:2 witness is believed because he **p.** beyond
T-27 ........ I.5:4 **p.** beyond itself to both your innocence
T-27 ...... III.4:6 Nothing **p.** beyond the truth, for what
T-28 ..... III.2:4 both your minds from separate **p.** of view.
T-31 ...... V.6:4 does, for your accusing finger **p.** to him,
T-31 ...... V.6:5 It **p.** to you as well, but this is kept still
W-pI..... 78.6:4 body with its flaws and better **p.** as well,
W-pI. 155.11:3 along the way that truth **p.** out to us. This
W-pI. 166.11:4 He **p.** to all the gifts you have each time
Wfl........ in.2:5 follow in the way that truth **p.** out to us.
Wfl........ in.4:2 and **p.** the way to Him and to the Heaven
M-13 ......... 7:7 It is its holiness that **p.** to God. It is its
M-14 ......... 4:8 His Teacher **p.** to it, and he trusts that He
M-19 ......... 5:5 God's justice **p.** to Heaven just because it

## poised 2

W-pI... 161.8:2 own fear external to himself, **p.** to attack,
W-pI... 189.3:5 of hatred rising from attack, **p.** to avenge,

## poisoned 3

T-21 .. VII.3:11 A flower turns into a **p.** spear, a child
T-27 ........ I.5:8 with the **p.** and relentless sting of fear.
S-2........... I.7:4 and **p.** thinking from your holy mind.

## poisonous 2

W-pI..... 93.1:2 recoiling from you as if from a **p.** snake.
S-1........ III.1:5 The **p.** thought that he *is* your enemy, your

## polished 1

T-17 ..... IV.7:5 set with jewels, and deeply carved and **p.**.

## ponderous 1

W-pI. 134.12:4 He can remove the **p.** and useless armor

## poor 22

T-7 ........ V.2:7 are both a **p.** teacher and a poor learner.
T-7 ........ V.2:7 are both a poor teacher and a **p.** learner.
T-7 ..... VIII.3:4 teacher is a **p.** teacher and a poor learner.
T-7 ..... VIII.3:4 teacher is a poor teacher and a **p.** learner.
T-8 ... VII.14:5 is a clear-cut indication of a **p.** learner. He
T-9 ....... IV.8:3 it is a remarkably **p.** choice as a teacher of
T-12 ..... III.1:1 you have and give to the **p.** and follow me.
T-12 ..... III.1:2 can teach the **p.** where their treasure is.
T-12 ..... III.1:3 **p.** are merely those who have invested
T-12 ..... III.1:3 invested wrongly, and they are **p.** indeed!
T-12 ..... III.3:3 it. *Remember that those who attack are* **p.**.
T-12 ..... III.5:5 will surely place yourself among the **p.**,
T-12 ..... III.6:1 is to attack yourself and make yourself **p.**.
T-12 ...... V.4:3 a split mind has made itself a **p.** learner.
T-12 ...... V.4:5 and **p.** learners do need special teaching.
T-12 ...... V.5:5 curriculum. **P.** learners are not good
T-15 ..... III.2:3 is much too **p.** a gift to satisfy you. It is
T-15 ..... III.8:7 your **p.** appreciation of yourself and all
T-15 .... VII.1:1 Beyond the **p.** attraction of the special
W-pI..... 92.3:3 the helpless and afraid, the sad, the **p.**,
P-2....... VII.7:7 alien to the truth and **p.** in wisdom,
S-3.......... II.1:1 False healing merely makes a **p.** exchange

## poorly 3

T-7 ........ V.2:6 An inconsistent lesson will be **p.** taught
T-7 ........ V.2:6 will be poorly taught and **p.** learned. If
WpI..rIII.in3:4 to distinguish situations that are **p.** suited

## popping 1

T-30 ..... IV.3:6 can laugh at **p.** heads and squeaking toys,

## pose 1

W-pII ..... 1.3:4 to **p.** a contradiction to its point of view.

## position 36

T-1 ....... III.8:5 a **p.** to know where they can be bestowed.
T-2 ......... V.4:5 in a **p.** to recognize that those who need
T-2 ......... V.5:4 you place yourself in a **p.** to undo the level
T-2 ......... V.5:6 the mind to its true **p.** as the learner.
T-2 ....... VI.8:3 in a **p.** where you need Atonement. You
T-2 ...... VII.4:5 you have placed yourself in a **p.** where
T-2 ..... VIII.1:2 and this puts you in a **p.** where a belief in
T-3 .......... I.2:1 as always, is not to attack another's **p.**,
T-3 ......... V.6:6 placed yourself in a **p.** where you could
T-3 ....... VI.7:5 untenable **p.** is the result of the authority
T-3 ....... VI.8:9 This leaves you in a **p.** where it sounds
T-3 ..... VI.11:2 this **p.** would be quite apparent. Free will
T-3 ...... VII.3:6 He have put them in a **p.** where their own
T-7 ......... V.7:8 This places you in a **p.** of needing to learn
T-9 ....... IV.8:2 places the ego in a sound **p.** as your guide.
T-13 ....... II.4:3 they are in an excellent **p.** to let it go.
T-16 ..... VI.8:3 your mind from its fixed **p.** here. This will
T-17 ......... I.2:2 This strange **p.**, in a sense, acknowledges
T-18 ... VIII.5:1 Such is the strange **p.** in which those in a
T-22 ... VI.13:5 Either **p.** is a logical conclusion. Either
T-22 ... VI.13:8 **p.** of what you understand you seem to be
T-23 ..... II.10:1 justified **p.** and attack for what has been
T-25 .... VII.9:3 From this **p.** does his sinfulness, and all
W-pI .... 46.5:1 is to put you in a **p.** to forgive yourself.
W-pI .... 79.3:1 is the **p.** in which you find yourself now.
W-pI .... 79.4:3 perception places you in a **p.** in which
W-pI .... 98.1:4 the two, but take a firm **p.** with the One.
W-pI .. 152.2:1 You may believe that this **p.** is extreme,
W-pI .. 163.6:5 For here again we see an obvious **p.**,
M-4 ..... I.A.3:4 the perceiver is in a **p.** where he must see
M-4 ...... III.1:2 to judge is to assume a **p.** you do not have
M-7 ........... 2:6 His **p.** has thus become untenable, for he
M-10 ......... 2:7 he puts himself in a **p.** where judgment
M-10 ......... 3:6 Who is in a **p.** to do this? Who except in
M-16 ......... 5:4 better to sit up, in whatever **p.** you prefer.
P-3.......... II.2:1 professional therapist is in an excellent **p.**

## positions 1

T-18 ... VI.12:1 you join; of your respective **p.** in space;

## positive 11

T-3 ....... VI.2:5 It never emphasizes only the **p.** aspects of
T-5 ....... V.4:10 as a lack of love, but as a **p.** act of assault.
T-6 .......... I.1:5 **p.** interpretation of the crucifixion that is
T-6 ..... V.B.8:3 step is a **p.** affirmation of what you want.
T-12 ........ I.9:7 as a **p.** affirmation of the underlying belief
T-17 ..... VI.2:9 but only that. It has no **p.** goal at all.
T-17 ..... VI.3:1 Without a clear-cut, **p.** goal, set at the
T-20 .... VII.4:4 is **p.** and the body is merely neutral. It is
W-pI .... 12.3:3 seem **p.** rather than negative occur to you,
W-pI .... 35.4:2 you ascribe to yourself, **p.** or negative,
W-pI .... 61.3:4 is a **p.** assertion of your right to be saved,

## positively 2

T-7 ...... VII.1:9 it is as capable of being used **p.** as well as
W-pI .... 20.5:1 slowly and **p.** at least twice an hour today,

## possess 13

T-3 ....... IV.1:1 you now **p.** are only shadows of your real
T-3 ......... V.1:1 I have said that the abilities you **p.** are
T-16 ......... V.8:2 And whoever seems to **p.** a special self is
T-17 ..... VI.1:7 far broader than you now **p.**.
T-29 ... VIII.8:6 will give him more than other men **p.**. It
T-31 ....... II.3:3 each seeming to **p.** advantages you would
W-pI .... 13.3:2 world with attributes that it does not **p.**,
W-pI .... 93.5:9 What power can this self you made **p.**,
W-pI .. 159.1:5 The world believes that to **p.** a thing, it
W-pI .. 187.1:5 you must first **p.** what you would give. It
W-pI .. 187.1:8 that giving will increase what you **p.**.
M-13 ......... 4:9 And to **p.** them must he sacrifice his hope
M-29 ......... 5:1 that he does not **p.** is deceiving himself.

## possessed 6

T-1........IV.2:8 Your mind can be **p.** by illusions, but
T-3.........II.4:3 mind is not free because it is **p.**, or held
T-24.....II.10:6 special, but **p.** of everything, including
W-pI...187.1:7 asserts that you have lost what you **p.**.
W-pII..300.1:1 for their joys are gone before they are **p.**,
M-28..........6:2 as any mind remains **p.** of evil dreams,

## possession 8

T-3.......VII.2:5 God, battling Him for **p.** of His creations.
T-5........I.1:10 If you share a physical **p.**, you do divide
T-8.....VIII.2:1 to contain two voices fighting for its **p.**. In
T-13.VII.10:11 have things for salvation, for **p.** is its law.
T-13.VII.10:12 is its law. **P.** for its own sake is the ego's
T-23.....II.13:1 Never is your **p.** made complete. And
W-pI...159.1:2 requires first you have it in your own **p.**.
P-2........IV.9:5 attacking the patient's most cherished **p.**;

## possessions 1

W-pI.....70.7:5 in the past;–in other people, in **p.**, in

## possibilities 3

T-3.........II.1:3 or everything and nothing as joint **p.**.
W-pI.....26.8:1 some five or six distressing **p.** available
W-pI...198.4:3 it must be wrong; a thousand other **p.**?

## possibility 9

T-2.........II.7:7 This **p.** cannot be controlled except by
T-6.......V.B.4:2 is its only alternative since the other **p.**,
T-13....XI.11:5 and there is no **p.** that the plan the Holy
T-15......VI.1:6 will be guilt as long as you accept the **p.**,
T-15......VI.4:3 his success as witness to the **p.** of yours.
T-27.....VII.9:1 that you can choose, the other **p.** of cause,
T-30.......V.2:6 The **p.** of freedom has been grasped and
W-pII....11.3:3 His holy Will, beyond all **p.** of harm, of
M-2............4:1 and past even the **p.** of remembering. Yet

## possible 337

T-2........VI.3:6 only at the level where change is **p.**.
T-2........VI.6:1 It is **p.** to reach a state in which you bring
T-2.....VII.5:10 no compromise is **p.** between everything
T-3........I.3:11 always **p.** to twist symbols around if you
T-3.......III.5:3 and this makes it **p.** for you to know him.
T-3.......IV.3:7 condition, in which attack is always **p.**.
T-3.......IV.6:1 The ability to perceive made the body **p.**,
T-3.......VI.9:6 is **p.** to look on reality without judgment
T-3.......VII.3:6 where their own destruction was **p.**? The
T-4...........I.2:5 This profound confusion is **p.** only if you
T-4........I.7:10 of devotion is **p.** as long as this delusion
T-4.........II.7:9 the idea that this is **p.** is a decision of the
T-4.........II.7:9 confused about what is really **p.**.
T-4.......II.11:5 You may ask how this is **p.** as long as you
T-5.........in.2:2 the only **p.** whole state is that of love.
T-5.........in.2:4 only **p.** whole state is the wholly joyous.
T-5...........I.6:4 that transfer to it is at last **p.**. Perception
T-5.........II.3:9 It is **p.** even in this world to hear only that
T-5.........II.6:2 of opposition in which opposites are **p.**.
T-5......IV.2:12 I meant when I said it is **p.** even in this
T-5.......V.3:10 that you believe it is **p.** to attack God, and
T-5.........V.8:1 **p.** reason for continuing guilt feelings.
T-5........VI.2:9 will oppose it at every **p.** moment and in
T-5........VI.2:9 possible moment and in every **p.** way.
T-6........III.3:8 No compromise is **p.** in this. Teach attack
T-6........IV.8:7 you believe that the impossible *is* **p.**.
T-6........IV.9:2 the kindest solution **p.** for what you made
T-6......IV.10:1 only because you think it is **p.** to be in one
T-6......IV.11:4 Fidelity to other laws is also **p.**, however,
T-7...........I.4:2 another means that no bargains are **p.**. To
T-7.........II.2:9 diametrically opposed outcomes seem **p.**
T-7........III.3:6 *is* the belief that conflicting interests are **p.**
T-7......VI.13:4 is unchangeable, no conflict of will is **p.**.
T-7.......VII.1:3 Nor is it **p.** to love it totally at times. You
T-7.........X.1:6 **p.** that you have done the same thing with
T-7.........X.4:4 also believe that it is **p.** to *do* the opposite
T-8...........I.6:1 a real change in direction becomes **p.**.
T-8...........I.6:4 might be **p.** except that both are teaching
T-8..........II.2:1 **p.** reason for choosing a teacher such as
T-8......IV.5:11 things are **p.** through our joint decision,
T-8.....VII.16:2 your mind from the belief that this is **p.**.
T-8...VIII.1:14 the level of perception, where change is **p.**
T-8.....VIII.6:9 to examine all **p.** outcomes to which
T-9...........I.1:2 it **p.** for it to be afraid of what it really is.
T-9...........I.3:8 you. He is merely making every **p.** effort,
T-9.........I.11:6 indeed **p.** for you to deny facts, although
T-9.........I.13:5 As long as you believe that fear is **p.**, you
T-9.........I.14:1 then, that God's Will is already **p.**, and
T-9..........II.3:4 It is **p.** that His answer will not be heard.
T-9.......II.11:2 believe that it is **p.** to get much for little is
T-9.......II.11:6 to have, but it is **p.** not to know you have.
T-9........III.6:2 Is it **p.**, then, for you to correct another?
T-9........III.6:3 it is **p.** for you to see yourself truly. It is
T-9........III.7:8 that you believe correction by you is **p.**,
T-9.......VII.1:3 must have made it **p.** and easy to obtain it
T-9.......VII.1:9 Is it **p.** that this is not also your will? And
T-9.....VII.1:10 And is it **p.** that this is not also the will of
T-9.....VIII.6:4 coexist, nor is it **p.** for them to alternate.
T-10.........I.2:6 it not **p.** that you merely shifted from one
T-10.........I.3:3 because loving then seems **p.** to you, but
T-10.........I.3:5 What is **p.** has not yet been accomplished
T-11.........I.4:1 Waiting is **p.** only in time, but time has
T-11.........I.9:2 interpretation it seems **p.** for God's Will
T-11.....V.11:2 to distinguish the **p.** from the impossible
T-11....VI.10:8 To God all things are **p.**. And to Christ it
T-11...VIII.9:6 in your Father, in Whom no deceit is **p.**.
T-12.......V.8:2 Is it **p.** that the way to achieve a goal is not
T-13.....VII.2:3 sight of one is **p.** because you have denied
T-13...VIII.3:1 with knowledge, making transfer to it **p.**.
T-13...VIII.5:5 world to make Christ's vision **p.** even here
T-13......XI.4:7 How is this **p.**, when His mission is of
T-13......XI.9:2 It will not be **p.** to exempt yourself from
T-14.........I.4:7 while you think it **p.** to learn to do this,
T-14.........I.4:7 will not believe all that *is* **p.** to learn to do.
T-14.......V.1:3 *God makes this* **p.**. Would you deny His
T-14......VI.7:6 one is **p.** for purposes of communication.
T-14.....VII.3:1 It is not **p.** to convince the unknowing
T-14.......X.3:3 once you conceive of them as **p.** at all.
T-14.......X.5:6 were all of you, no order at all would be **p.**
T-15...VIII.6:4 it must be **p.** because it is the Will of God.
T-15......IX.2:1 Our task is but to continue, as fast as **p.**,
T-15.......X.4:2 It is **p.** to do this all at once because there
T-15.......X.5:4 it is **p.** to be host to the ego or hostage to
T-16......IV.4:3 Where disillusionment is **p.**, there was
T-16......IV.5:5 only choice remaining **p.** is which illusion
T-16....IV.13:3 in God's completion seem to be **p.**. The
T-16.....V.12:5 Would you want this to be **p.**, even apart
T-16.....V.12:6 it were **p.**, you would have made yourself
T-16.....V.16:4 fantasies make confusion in choosing **p.**,
T-16......VI.8:6 and that escape from pain is really **p.**.
T-16...VII.11:2 as great or small, **p.** or impossible. There
T-17.......II.4:3 that made perception **p.** will still occur.
T-17......IV.2:2 Yet it *is* **p.** to make happy. I have said
T-17.....VII.2:4 it not **p.** that all your problems have been
T-18......III.5:1 together will teach you that this goal is **p.**,
T-18......IV.4:7 to make it **p.** to teach you what they are. If
T-18......IV.8:2 you have become the arbiter of what is **p.**,
T-18......IV.8:4 Everything God wills is not only **p.**, but
T-18.......V.3:4 Yet it is **p.**, because God wills it. Nor will
T-18.......V.6:5 believe that this is necessary, or even **p.**.
T-18.......V.7:4 *It is not* **p.** *that I can have it without him, or*
T-18.......V.7:5 *Yet it is wholly* **p.** *for us to share it now. And*
T-18......VI.3:2 of the body does separation seem to be **p.**.
T-18......VI.9:6 Himself from His Son to make this **p.**. He
T-18....VI.13:6 questioning whether or not all this is **p.**.
T-18....VI.14:1 It is **p.** because you want it. The sudden
T-19.........I.6:2 **p.** only if the mind is limited to the body
T-19........II.1:1 is this distinction that makes salvation **p.**.
T-19........II.1:3 But sin, were it **p.**, would be irreversible.
T-19......II.6:13 Yet it is **p.** to have faith that a mistake can
T-19......III.2:1 The ego does not think it **p.** that love, not
T19....IV.B.8:4 **p.** to keep away One Who is there already
T19....IV.B.8:5 And in Him it *is* **p.** that our communion,
T19..IV.B.15:4 And to convince you this is **p.**, it bids the
T19.IV.D.10:1 Nor is it **p.** to look on this too soon. This
T-20......IV.3:7 Nor is it **p.** for those who follow them to
T-20......IV.8:3 But ask yourself if it is **p.** that God would
T-20......VI.8:6 with God unholy seemed to be **p.**, all your
T-20.....VII.3:9 For if a goal is **p.** to reach, the means to
T-20.....VII.3:9 the means to do so must be **p.** as well.
T-20.....VII.9:8 as was the vision that made his seeing **p.**.
T-20....VIII.9:1 Only two purposes are **p.**. And one is sin,
T-21.........I.8:6 is it **p.** to imagine that anything could be
T-21........II.3:4 is **p.** within the universe as God created it,
T-21........II.6:4 idea that it is **p.** that things could happen
T-21........II.8:4 Then only it is **p.** to look within and see
T-21........II.9:2 of faith, to make its goals seem real and **p.**
T-21.....III.11:7 **p.** that what gives light be one with what
T-21.....V.1:11 in which awareness of reality is **p.**, or
T-21....VIII.4:2 it **p.** to help you be already partly sane.
T-22.........I.9:3 it **p.** that anything not part of Him *can* join
T-22........II.2:6 All that is **p.** in the dark world of misery is
T-22........II.5:6 means for its attainment are more than **p.**
T-22........II.6:5 *You* know what your Creator wills is **p.**,
T-22........II.9:6 Only if it were **p.** the Son of God could
T-22........II.9:6 Will, would it be **p.** that the self he made,
T-22......II.10:3 it seem **p.** that what you made is yours.
T-22......II.11:4 Yet it is **p.** to recognize him for what he is,
T-22......III.1:2 it **p.** for them to coexist in your awareness
T-22....VI.1:10 He will believe it **p.** of mind or body, and
T-22....VI.12:5 only then would it be **p.** to attack a part of
T-23.........I.2:4 The death of God, if it were **p.**, would be
T-23.........I.2:6 it thinks that triumph over you is **p.**. And
T-23.......I.2:12 And to those who think that it is **p.**, the
T-23......II.16:2 There is a strange device that makes it **p.**.
T-23......II.20:2 quite **p.** to value some above the others.
T-23......II.22:5 any instant it is **p.** to have all this undone.
T-23......III.4:2 who still believe that compromise is **p.**.
T-23......III.4:6 Nor is it **p.** to attack for this and love for
T-24.........I.6:1 **p.** for you to hate your brother if you were
T-24......II.13:1 hope of specialness makes it seem **p.** God
T-24......III.4:7 Nor is it **p.** the two can ever be the same,
T-24......IV.4:4 brother *is* its enemy, while sin, if it were **p.**,
T-24.......V.1:7 it **p.** that you can wish for something and
T-24....VI.13:5 at all, for only what His Father wills is **p.**,
T-25......III.8:7 And thus is change made **p.**. The Holy
T-25......VI.3:1 brings the gift of light that makes sight **p.**.
T-25.....VII.1:9 from love to everyone who thinks sin **p.**.
T-25...VII.1:11 **p.** what God created not should share the
T-25.....VII.2:4 is it **p.** that what He did not will cannot be
T-25.....VII.9:2 function is designed to be perceived as **p.**,
T-25...VII.10:6 heaven of hell, had such insanity been **p.**.
T-25...VII.13:6 be his Father's, and in Him no loss is **p.**.
T-25......IX.1:7 And not one doubt that this is **p.** will you
T-26........II.2:5 one mistake; the whole idea that loss is **p.**,
T-26........II.2:6 God would be unfair; sin would be **p.**,
T-26......III.1:7 For it is conflict that makes choice **p.**. The
T-26......III.4:2 make; the last evaluation that will be **p.**,
T-26......III.7:6 No sacrifice is **p.** in the relinquishment of
T-26.......V.1:6 Nothing in between is **p.**. There are two
T-26.....VII.1:3 all that must occur for healing to be **p.**.
T-26.....VII.1:4 For when it once is **p.** it must occur.
T-26.....VII.6:2 it is **p.** that some are given greater value,
T-26...VII.10:6 And every miracle is **p.** the instant that
T-26...VII.13:6 be **p.** in trying to deceive the Son of God.
T-26...VII.14:1 miracle is **p.** when cause and consequence
T-26...VII.14:7 If loss in any form is **p.**, then is God's Son
T-27......III.5:6 Holy Spirit make exchange of pictures **p.**,
T-27......IV.1:2 for its purpose is to make no resolution **p.**
T-27......IV.6:3 Here is it **p.** to separate your wishes from
T-27.......V.2:6 Your single purpose makes this **p.**. But if
T-27.......V.9:3 be their differences which made this **p.**,
T-27....VIII.6:3 and **p.** of both accomplishment and real
T-28.........I.6:4 can be made **p.** because its cause has gone
T-28........II.6:2 No plans are **p.**, and no design exists that
T-29.........I.3:5 made your friendship **p.** a little while. But
T-29.........I.4:5 But always is it **p.** for you and him to go
T-29........II.7:2 the larger dream that change is **p.**. To
T-30......III.4:3 Nor could it be **p.** it be denied. Your will
T-30......VI.5:8 Only if this were **p.** could there be some
T-31.......V.6:3 For this is no forgiveness **p.**. No longer
W-in..........1:2 that will make the goal of the course **p.**.
W-pI.......2.1:5 If **p.**, turn around and apply the idea to
W-pI.......2.1:6 you. Remain as indiscriminate as **p.** in

W-pI.......8.4:3 With as little investment as **p.**, search
W-pI.....11.3:3 should be practiced as casually as **p.**. It
W-pI.....15.5:1 try to make the selection as random as **p.**.
W-pI.....18.3:1 of the idea for today as randomly as **p.**,
W-pI.....19.2:4 that it must be true if salvation is **p.** at all.
W-pI.....19.2:5 salvation must be **p.** because it is the Will
W-pI.....19.4:1 as **p.** in selecting subjects for the practice
W-pI.....21.5:1 Try to be as specific as **p.**. You may, for
W-pI.....22.1:6 What peace of mind is **p.** to him then?
W-pI.....24.5:1 as many goals as **p.** that you would like to
W-pI.....24.7:1 the list of as many hoped-for goals as **p.**,
W-pI.....26.7:3 Then go over every **p.** outcome that has
W-pI.....27.3:2 at least every half hour, and more if **p.**.
W-pI.....28.8:3 quite slowly, and as thoughtfully as **p.**.
W-pI.....29.5:1 therefore be as free of self-selection as **p.**.
W-pI.....30.3:1 applied as often as **p.** throughout the day.
W-pI.....31.3:3 come and go as dispassionately as **p.**. Do
W-pI.....31.4:1 for today as often as **p.** during the day.
W-pI.....32.3:3 Try to treat them both as equally as **p.**.
W-pI.....32.5:1 continued during the day, as often as **p.**.
W-pI.....33.3:1 periods should be as frequent as **p.**.
W-pI.....35.9:1 As often as **p.** during the day, pick up a
W-pI.....36.4:2 as effortlessly and unhurriedly as **p.**.
W-pI.....38.4:2 make as little distinction as **p.** between a
W-pI...39.11:1 three or four times an hour and more if **p.**
W-pI.....40.1:3 schedule and to adhere to it whenever **p.**.
W-pI.....41.6:2 In the morning, as soon as you get up if **p.**
W-pI.....41.8:1 It is quite **p.** to reach God. In fact it is
W-pI.....41.8:4 way will open, if you believe that it is **p.**.
W-pI.....41.8:7 fail completely, and instant success is **p.**.
W-pI.....42.3:1 today, one as soon as **p.** after you wake,
W-pI.....42.3:1 as close as **p.** to the time you go to sleep.
W-pI.....42.4:5 *Vision must be **p.**. God gives truly,* or: *God's*
W-pI.....43.4:1 as early and one as late as **p.** in the day.
W-pI.....44.2:3 is the light that makes seeing **p.**. It is with
W-pI.....44.2:4 making vision **p.** in every circumstance.
W-pI.....44.9:3 exercises with eyes closed as soon as **p.**.
W-pI.....45.4:6 that only what God would have us do is **p.**
W-pI.....46.3:1 periods, and as many shorter ones as **p.**.
W-pI.....46.6:5 *No fear is **p.** in a mind beloved of God. There*
W-pI.....48.2:2 Merely repeat the idea as often as **p.**. You
W-pI.....48.2:4 whenever **p.** to close your eyes and repeat
W-pI.....49.1:1 It is quite **p.** to listen to God's Voice all
W-pI.....49.3:1 practice periods today, and more if **p.**.
W-pI.....49.5:2 open when necessary, but closed when **p.**.
WpI...rI.in.2:4 Do this as often as **p.** during the day. If
WpI...rI.in.3:3 when you are alone in a quiet place, if **p.**.
W-pI.....57.2:4 it is **p.** to imprison the Son of God. I was
W-pI.....61.4:1 think about this idea as often as **p.** today.
W-pI.....61.5:1 periods as **p.** should be undertaken today,
W-pI.....62.4:1 it as frequently as **p.** throughout the day.
W-pI.....62.5:1 As often as you can, closing your eyes if **p.**
W-pI.....65.4:1 Try, if **p.**, to undertake the daily extended
W-pI.....65.4:2 and then adhere to it as closely as **p.**. The
W-pI.....65.5:5 with as little involvement or concern as **p.**
W-pI.....66.7:5 and no other outcomes **p.** as a result of
W-pI.....67.5:2 truth about yourself as frequently as **p.**,
W-pI.....69.9:1 which you will want to do as often as **p.** in
W-pI.....70.6:3 to your own decisions as closely as **p.**.
W-pI.....71.6:5 because there is no **p.** alternative to God's
W-pI.....71.7:2 to be a conflict with no resolution **p.**. All
W-pI.....71.7:3 All things are **p.** to God. Salvation must
W-pI.....74.1:4 His. The belief that conflict is **p.** has gone.
W-pI.....74.7:5 every half an hour, with eyes closed if **p.**,
W-pI...76.12:1 repeat this dedication as often as **p.** today
W-pI...79.10:5 is. If **p.**, close your eyes for a moment and
W-pI.....80.6:2 with deep conviction, as frequently as **p.**.
W-pI.....95.7:1 a while, and urge you to omit as few as **p.**.
W-pI...95.14:8 Repeat today's idea as frequently as **p.**,
W-pI.106.10:2 given to yourself as often as is **p.** today:
W-pI...107.5:2 no defense, and therefore no attack is **p.**.
W-pI...108.2:1 that makes true vision **p.** is not the light
W-pI...125.1:5 No peace is **p.** until His Word is heard
W-pI...127.1:1 think that different kinds of love are **p.**.
W-pI...130.6:1 attempt no compromise where none is **p.**.
W-pI...139.6:1 strange idea that it is **p.** to doubt yourself,
W-pI...140.4:5 away the guilt that makes the sickness **p.**.
W-pI...153.1:5 of mind is **p.** where danger threatens thus
W-pI...153.4:2 but to be an idle dream, beyond the **p.**.
W-pI.153.15:2 to the daily thought as long as **p.**. Five
W-pI.153.18:4 Think you He will not make this **p.**, for
W-pI...163.6:4 No compromise is **p.**. For here again we
W-pI.167.12:5 and the light which makes reflection **p.**.
W-pI...185.1:3 no further sorrow **p.** for you in any form;
W-pI...185.9:3 No compromise is **p.** in this. You choose
W-pI...187.2:1 How is this **p.**? For it is sure that if you
W-pI...196.6:5 there, so that it would be **p.** to question it.
WpI rVI.in.1:1 each day, and practice it as often as is **p.**.
W-pII.226.1:2 It is not death which makes this **p.**, but it
W-pII.....3.2:7 Now mistakes become quite **p.**, for
W-pII.....7.1:5 has made **p.** perception's tranquil end.
W-pII.296.2:2 unconflicted one, and **p.** of easy reach and
Wfl........in.1:1 lessons will be left as free of words as **p.**.
W-ep.........2:3 For it can not be **p.** to change the course
M-3...........2:6 **p.** for two people to lose sight of separate
M-4.....VII.1:8 In the clearest way **p.**, and at the simplest
M-6...........3:6 in fact, it is the part that makes sharing **p.**
M-6...........4:2 And it is trust that makes true giving **p.**.
M-9...........1:7 previous mistakes as **p.** are corrected.
M-11...........h HOW IS PEACE **P.** IN THIS WORLD?
M-11.........1:7 Word has promised that peace is **p.** here,
M-11.........3:4 of sense, yet out of which no way seems **p.**
M-11.........3:7 How is peace **p.** in this world? In your
M-11.........3:8 In your judgment it is not **p.**, and can
M-11.........3:8 it is not possible, and can never be **p.**. But
M-11.......4:12 peace be **p.** in this world?" but instead,
M-12.........3:4 which communication becomes **p.** to
M-13.........3:5 through God's Word could this be **p.**. For
M-16.........2:7 It is always **p.** to begin again, should the
M-16.........4:3 to spend time with God as soon as **p.**, and
M-16.........4:7 as soon as **p.** after waking take your quiet
M-16.........5:6 If **p.**, however, just before going to sleep is
M-16.......11:5 No risk is **p.** throughout the day except to
M-17.........5:4 It states, in the clearest form **p.**, that the
M-17.........8:3 There is a way in which escape is **p.**. It can
M-17.........8:8 Now it is **p.** to take the next step. The
M-19.........2:3 This becomes **p.** because, while it is not
M-22.........1:3 the one complete concept **p.** in this world,
M-22.........1:7 and what remains to make sickness **p.**?
M-23.........7:2 Are other teachers **p.**, to lead the way to
M-24.......1:11 In between, many kinds of folly are **p.**.
M-27.........4:5 No compromise in this is **p.**. There is
C-in...........2:5 experience is not only **p.** but necessary. It
C-in...........2:7 alone consistency becomes **p.** because
C-3............4:9 as near to Heaven as is **p.** outside the gate.
C-4............3:2 The one correction **p.** for false perception
C-4............5:5 sin, for only if there were a body is sin **p.**.
C-5............6:6 It is **p.** to read his words and benefit from
C-6............1:3 **p.** to accept Him and to hear His Voice.
P-2.........in.2:4 rests on the insane belief that this is **p.**.
P-2..........II.4:5 Belief implies that unbelief is **p.**, but
P-2..........II.8:5 Only by doing this is it **p.** to transcend the
P-2........III.3:1 quite **p.** for psychotherapy to seem to fail.
P-2........III.3:2 **p.** for the result to look like retrogression.
P-2.......VII.5:5 point of view would such a role be **p.**. Yet
P-3........III.7:5 away? And is it **p.** to do so? Surely it is
S-1..........II.3:1 is also **p.** to reach a higher form of asking-
S-1..........II.3:4 It is **p.** at this level to continue to ask for
S-1..........II.3:4 also **p.** to ask for gifts such as honesty or
S-1........IV.1:3 an instant, it becomes **p.** to join in prayer.
S-1........IV.2:1 Now it is **p.** to help in prayer, and so
S-2...........I.5:3 How could freedom be **p.** if this were so?
S-3........III.1:5 For it is this that makes true healing **p.**.

## possibly 26

T-3..........I.1:4 in scarcity could **p.** make this mistake. If
T-6.......IV.5:4 one in his right mind could **p.** believe this
T-7......V.5:10 mind could **p.** perceive as meaningful.
T-7.....VI.4:11 only decision the ego could **p.** encounter,
T-7.........X.1:4 only reason you could **p.** want any part of
T-8....VII.14:5 and to believe that joy could **p.** result, is a
T-9..........I.1:2 It could not **p.** have occurred unless the
T-9..........I.4:6 the Holy Spirit sees that you can **p.** have.
T-9..........I.7:4 who could not **p.** give you what you want.
T-9.......IV.9:5 the return of sense. Can this **p.** be fearful?
T-9.....VIII.2:4 meaningless, and you could not **p.** want it
T-10......V.3:4 only in sickness could you **p.** want them.
T-13.......II.1:4 the ego **p.** induce you to project guilt, and
T-14...III.15:2 in this world or Heaven could **p.** commit.
T-14.....XI.2:5 yourself that you can **p.** prefer to keep, in
T-16.....III.3:8 done that you could **p.** deny Its Presence.
T-23........I.4:8 Could nature **p.** establish this, and make
W-pI....26.8:1 each situation you use, and quite **p.** more.
W-pI 153.10:6 What defense could **p.** be needed by the
W-pI..157.2:3 past the highest reaches it can **p.** attain. It
W-pI..170.2:4 needless misery than you can **p.** imagine.
W-pI 183.11:6 height whatever words could **p.** convey, is
P-2...........I.4:2 except a patient could **p.** have come here?
P-2........VI.5:5 only an unforgiveness can **p.** give rise to
P-3..........II.4:4 therapist nor a perfect patient can **p.** exist
P-3......III.4:10 could **p.** imagine that it could be bought?

## post-separation 1

T-3.......IV.3:1 ego is the questioning aspect of the **p.** self,

## postpone 1

T-4..........I.9:9 is merely to **p.** the inevitable. The word

## potency 1

T-24.....II.12:5 Not one believer in its **p.** but seeks for

## potent 2

T-22.....VI.9:6 one and make of it a **p.** force for peace. He
W-pI..137.8:4 are more **p.** than their sickly opposites.

## potential 14

T-1.......II.3:13 leaves me in a state which is only **p.** in you
T-1.....III.1:10 The ability is the **p.**, the achievement is its
T-1.........V.1:7 of communication, but not your **p.**. You
T-1.........V.5:5 it retains its creative **p.** but places itself
T-2.........V.5:4 denying your mind any destructive **p.** and
T-2......VII.7:5 state does not imply more than a **p.** for a
T-12.......V.9:1 Your learning **p.**, properly understood, is
WpI..rIII.in9:3 to prove how great are its **p.** gifts to you.
M-3...........1:7 they have the **p.** for a holy relationship.
M-3...........2:4 Each of them has the **p.** for becoming a
M-4.....I.A.6:5 **p.** is literally staggering, and the teacher
M-25.........6:3 the power, the greater its **p.** usefulness.
C-1............4:2 Spirit retains the **p.** for creating, but its
P-3........III.6:4 them, they are always His **p.** temple; the

## potentiality 3

M-25.........6:1 that anyone develops has the **p.** for good.
P-2........III.2:3 the **p.** for transcending all limitations has
P-2........III.2:4 much of this **p.** they are willing to use.

## potentially 1

C-in...........2:1 All terms are **p.** controversial, and those

## potentials 1

T-6.......IV.8:1 of uncertainty, because abilities are **p.**,

## pounce 1

T19 .IV.A.12:7 for sin they **p.** on any living thing they see

## pound 1

T-30.....V.10:8 that beats in hope and does not **p.** in fear.

## pours 1

T-24.......II.4:4 soundless in the melody that **p.** from God

## poverty 9

T-12.....III.1:5 if you were unwilling to share their **p.**. For

T-12......III.1:6 For **p.** is lack, and there is but one lack
T-12......III.3:4 *poor.* Their **p.** asks for gifts, not for further
T-12......III.3:5 if you accept their **p.** as yours. If you had
T-12......III.4:7 are. **P.** is of the ego, and never of God. No
W-pI...166.5:5 Still he wanders on in misery and **p.**,
W-pI...166.8:2 could you then proclaim your **p.** in exile?
W-pI.166.11:4 each time the thought of **p.** oppresses you
W-pI...187.6:4 and loss, at sickness and at grief, at **p.**,

**power** 582

T-1......... I.20:2 that leads to the healing **p.** of the miracle.
T-1........III.1:7 The **p.** to work miracles belongs to you.
T-1.........V.3:4 you cannot know the real **p.** of the Son in
T-2...........I.4:1 have the ability to usurp the **p.** of God. Of
T-2.........II.1:4 you are acknowledging its **p.** to hurt you.
T-2.........II.1:8 with equal **p.** will inevitably destroy peace
T-2........III.4:6 This re-establishes the **p.** of the mind and
T-2........IV.3:5 no **p.** in itself to introduce actual learning
T-2......IV.3:13 this unfortunate aspect of the mind's **p.**,
T-2......IV.3:13 power, one is also denying the **p.** itself.
T-2... V.A.15:1 (5) The level-adjustment **p.** of the miracle
T-2........VI.9:3 Few appreciate the real **p.** of the mind,
T-2........VI.9:8 that thought and belief combine into a **p.**
T-2........VI.9:9 believe such **p.** about yourself is arrogant,
T-2.......VII.1:5 I depreciated the **p.** of your own thinking.
T-2.......VII.2:2 realization of the **p.** of thought in order to
T-2.......VII.4:3 In fact, it asserts the **p.** of fear by the very
T-2.......VII.4:5 believe in the **p.** of what does not exist.
T-3.........II.3:3 effect of denying the **p.** of the miracle.
T-3........III.1:5 Knowledge is **p.** because it is certain, and
T-3........IV.5:9 spirit that it derives its whole **p.** to make
T-3........IV.6:4 not be reconciled with this loss of **p.**,
T-3........IV.7:5 of the body and the **p.** of the mind. By
T-3.........V.4:8 image" recognizes the **p.** of perception,
T-3.........V.9:4 That is its miraculous **p.**. The fact that
T-3.........V.9:5 fact that each one has this **p.** completely is
T-3........VI.8:4 believe they have usurped the **p.** of God.
T-3........VI.9:2 You have not usurped the **p.** of God, but
T-3.......VII.1:3 lies in their **p.** as foundations. Their
T-3.......VII.1:7 made by a child of God is without **p.**. It is
T-3.......VII.2:1 by depreciating the **p.** of your mind. To
T-4.........in.3:5 re-enacts the separation, the loss of **p.**, the
T-4........IV.8:2 There is no limit to the **p.** of a Son of God,
T-4........IV.8:2 expression of his **p.** as much as he chooses
T-4........VI.1:2 to it gives the ego any **p.** over you. I have
T-5.........II.6:4 its creative **p.** is unlimited and choice is
T-5.........II.6:5 choose is the same **p.** as freedom to create
T-5.........II.9:2 that gave me all **p.** in Heaven and earth.
T-5.......II.11:2 its **p.** to attract the whole Sonship, and to
T-5.......II.12:4 **p.** of our joint motivation is beyond belief
T-5........IV.3:4 but in the Kingdom itself it has no **p.**.
T-5........IV.7:1 gives you the **p.** of a healed mind, but the
T-5........IV.7:1 mind, but the **p.** to create is of God.
T-5........IV.7:3 full **p.** of creation cannot be expressed as
T-5.......V.2:11 underestimate the **p.** of the ego's belief in
T-5.........V.3:3 on the concept of usurping God's **p.**. The
T-5......VI.2:10 can do because you gave it the **p.** to do it.
T-5........VI.4:1 much as a higher court has the **p.** to
T-5.......VII.1:7 **p.** of His care for all those He created by it
T-6........I.18:1 The **p.** of the Sons of God is present all
T-6......V.B.6:4 the quiet **p.** of the Holy Spirit's Voice, and
T-7...........I.1:1 creative **p.** of God and His creations is
T-7...........I.1:5 respect your creative **p.** differs from His.
T-7...........I.2:4 way can all creative **p.** extend outward.
T-7...........I.2:7 it. You have the **p.** to add to the Kingdom,
T-7...........I.2:8 claim this **p.** when you become vigilant
T-7...........I.2:9 By accepting this **p.** as yours you have
T-7........III.1:3 the **p.** of the Kingdom of God Himself, He
T-7........III.1:3 He teaches you that all **p.** is yours. Its
T-7......III.1:10 You did not make this **p.**, any more than I
T-7.........V.7:5 and so vital in its **p.** for change that a Son
T-7.........V.7:5 his **p.** in one instant and change the world
T-7........VI.2:5 thinking has done this because of its **p.**,
T-7........VI.2:5 this because its **p.** is not of your making.
T-7........VI.2:6 thinking as you choose is part of its **p.**. If
T-7........VI.2:7 you have denied the **p.** of your thought,
T-7........VI.3:1 it stems from the very **p.** of the mind the
T-7........VI.3:6 Fearful of perceiving the **p.** of this source,
T-7........VI.4:7 Love is your **p.**, which the ego must deny.
T-7........VI.4:8 It must also deny everything this **p.** gives
T-7......VI.10:4 your sanity and your limitless **p.**. This
T-7......VI.10:5 limitless **p.** is God's gift to you, because it
T-7.......VII.1:5 Denial has no **p.** in itself, but you can give
T-7.......VII.1:5 but you can give it the **p.** of your mind,
T-7.......VII.1:5 of your mind, whose **p.** is without limit. If
T-7.....VII.11:6 All **p.** and glory are yours because the
T-7..... VIII.2:5 the ego utilizes the **p.** of the mind only to
T-7..... VIII.3:8 complete distortion of the **p.** of extension.
T-7..... VIII.4:9 distorted minds that are misusing their **p.**
T-7........IX.1:1 Only you can limit your creative **p.**, but
T-7........IX.2:2 **p.** of the whole Sonship and of its Creator
T-7........IX.2:4 Everything He created is given all His **p.**,
T-7........XI.6:5 acknowledging his **p.** to create and yours.
T-7........XI.6:8 Deny his creative **p.**, and you are denying
T-8...........I.2:1 ego has no **p.** to distract you unless you
T-8...........I.2:1 you unless you give it the **p.** to do so. The
T-8.........II.7:1 "All **p.** and glory are yours because the
T-8.........II.7:1 limit, and all **p.** and glory lie within it. It
T-8.........II.7:7 are part of Him Who is all **p.** and glory,
T-8.........II.8:1 To what else except all **p.** and glory can
T-8........III.2:6 to God's, uniting it with His **p.** and glory
T-8........III.5:3 for the **p.** and glory he thinks he has lost.
T-8........III.5:5 Your **p.** and glory are in him because they
T-8........III.7:2 His **p.** and glory are everywhere, and you
T-8........III.7:8 Through His **p.** and glory all your wrong
T-8........III.7:9 Wrong decisions have no **p.**, because they
T-8........III.8:1 **P.** and glory belong to God alone. So do
T-8........III.8:6 to do this, because this is your **p.**. Glory is
T-8........IV.5:8 It is the **p.** by which you separate or join,
T-8........IV.6:2 God gave your will its **p.**, which I can only
T-8.........V.1:6 our minds fuse into something whose **p.**
T-8.........V.1:6 is far beyond the **p.** of its separate parts.
T-8.........V.3:2 His **p.** to you because we are sharing it.
T-8.........V.3:3 you only the recognition of His **p.** in you,
T-8.........V.6:4 ego the **p.** to interfere with the journey. It
T-8........VI.2:1 world can add nothing to the **p.** and the
T-8........VI.3:1 for over His Kingdom the world has no **p.**
T-8........VI.8:5 The whole **p.** of God's Son lies in all of us,
T-8........VI.8:7 and gave him the **p.** to create with Him.
T-8.......VII.3:2 will understand the **p.** of the mind that is
T-8.......VII.5:3 his **p.** and glory are "lost" to you and so
T-8.......VII.6:3 are has willed your **p.** and glory for you,
T-8.....VII.12:6 of the **p.** of the mind in it. This can be
T-8.....VII.16:6 and therefore unlimited **p.** and wholeness
T-8.....VII.16:7 The **p.** of wholeness is extension. Do not
T-8.......VIII.8:2 the distorting **p.** of something you want,
T-8........IX.6:8 Believing in the **p.** of attack, the ego wants
T-9...........I.4:2 I meant that He has the **p.** to look into
T-9.........V.4:5 the mind's corrective **p.** through the Holy
T-10.......in.3:3 gave you the **p.** to create for yourself so
T-10....III.1:10 He will not limit your **p.** to help them,
T-10......III.2:1 children of God except His **p.** through
T-10......III.4:3 that creation shares **p.** and never usurps it
T-10......III.4:4 is the belief that **p.** can be taken from you.
T-10......III.4:5 because you are part of God, Who is all **p.**
T-10......III.7:3 Yet every Son of God has the **p.** to deny
T-10......IV.7:5 The **p.** of one mind can shine into another
T-10.....V.9:10 own mind because of the **p.** He gave it.
T-11......IV.2:4 for the **p.** of your will cannot be lessened
T-11......IV.2:4 limitation on your **p.** is not the Will of
T-11......IV.2:5 only to the **p.** that God gave to save you,
T-11.......V.3:3 implies the **p.** to do something, and the
T-11.......V.3:3 that the ego *has* the **p.** to do anything. The
T-11.......V.3:6 *All* **p.** *is of God. What is not of Him has no*
T-11.......V.3:7 *What is not of Him has no* **p.** *to do anything.*
T-11.......V.4:5 and independent of any **p.** except its own.
T-11.......V.7:2 it has the **p.** to do this it does nothing else
T-11.......V.8:2 your independence and weaken your **p.**.
T-11.......V.8:3 your allegiance is that it can give **p.** to you
T-11.......V.8:5 yourself and depriving yourself of **p.**?
T-11.....V.10:6 truth, you are believing that attack has **p.**.
T-11.....V.13:4 The ego believes that **p.**, understanding
T-11.....V.18:4 Every brother has the **p.** to release you, if
T-11......VI.5:1 the **p.** of the devotion of God's Son, nor
T-11......VI.5:1 the **p.** the god he worships has over him.
T-11......VI.5:5 believing that the **p.** of the Son of God is
T-11......VI.6:2 whole compelling **p.** lies in the fact that it
T-11....VI.10:6 whole **p.** of God is in every part of Him,
T-11..VIII.10:4 Nothing will be beyond your healing **p.**,
T-11..VIII.12:5 Accept His healing **p.** and use it for all He
T-12.........I.1:8 you. To interpret error is to give it **p.**, and
T-12.......I.9:10 You have denied its **p.** to conceal love,
T-12........II.2:2 give no **p.** to the fog to obscure the light,
T-12........II.2:3 **p.** only if the Son of God gives power to it.
T-12........II.2:3 power only if the Son of God gives **p.** to it.
T-12........II.2:4 to it. He must himself withdraw that **p.**,
T-12........II.2:4 power, remembering that all **p.** is of God.
T-12......IV.2:6 that has the **p.** to deny the ego's existence,
T-12......VII.9:1 The **p.** of decision is your one remaining
T-12......VII.9:5 within and thought you saw the **p.** to give
T-12...VII.10:3 its **p.** and grandeur could only bring you
T-12..VIII.7:10 God did not give you has no **p.** over you,
T-13......III.3:2 real **p.** seems to you as your real weakness
T-13......III.9:3 will exempt yourself from His healing **p.**,
T-13..VI.11:10 will join with theirs in **p.** so compelling,
T-13.....VII.2:5 And yet their **p.** is not the same, because
T-13.....VII.3:6 not the **p.** to touch the living world at all.
T-13.....VII.4:1 world has the **p.** to touch you even here,
T-13....VIII.8:2 the **p.** of God's Son will move in us, and
T-13....VIII.9:2 you the **p.** to create the witnesses to yours
T-13......IX.2:5 Faith makes the **p.** of belief, and where it
T-13......IX.3:5 The **p.** of your valuing will make it so.
T-13......XI.9:5 God's sleeping Son holds no **p.** over him.
T-14.........I.3:3 have all the **p.** that he gives to them. The
T-14......III.4:3 The **p.** of decision is all that is yours.
T-14......III.6:4 By giving **p.** to nothing, he throws away
T-14......III.6:4 to learn that nothing has no **p.**. And by
T-14......III.6:6 that darkness has no **p.** over the Son of
T-14......III.8:2 that what is not of God has **p.** over you.
T-14......III.8:7 The **p.** that God has given to His Son *is* his,
T-14.......V.6:7 **p.** of God Himself supports this teaching,
T-14.......V.7:1 Join your own efforts to the **p.** that
T-14.......V.7:3 the **p.** of God if you teach only this. You
T-14.......V.8:5 The **p.** of God draws everyone to its safe
T-14.......V.9:2 Our **p.** comes not of us, but of our Father.
T-14.......V.9:6 for everyone your Father's **p.** that He has
T-14.....V.10:9 The **p.** of love is in His gentleness, which
T-14......VI.2:4 from love cannot share its healing **p.**,
T-14......VI.3:1 you continue to give imagined **p.** to these
T-14......VI.5:6 The **p.** of decision, which you made in
T-14......VI.5:6 you made in place of the **p.** of creation,
T-14......VII.5:9 is mighty, but the **p.** of God is with Him.
T-14....VIII.1:1 **p.** He bestowed upon His guiltless Son.
T-14....VIII.1:4 of the **p.** of God that shines in you. Banish
T-14....VIII.1:5 Banish not **p.** from your mind, but let all
T-14....VIII.5:1 the **p.** to create can never be dissolved.
T-14......IX.3:2 and all its **p.** will rush to your assistance
T-14......IX.7:1 the **p.** of healing that the reflection of God
T-14........X.6:9 The **p.** of God, and not of you, engenders
T-14.....X.6:10 witness that you have the **p.** of God in you
T-14.....X.6:12 in it. The **p.** of God is limitless. And being
T-14.....X.12:9 Nor will the **p.** of all His Love be absent
T-14......XI.1:2 Knowledge is **p.**, and all power is of God.
T-14......XI.1:2 Knowledge is power, and all **p.** is of God.
T-14......XI.1:3 tried to keep **p.** for yourself have "lost" it.
T-14......XI.1:4 it. You still have the **p.**, but you have
T-14......XI.1:5 your **p.** more and more obscure to you.
T-14......XI.1:7 You have made a semblance of **p.** and a
T-14......XI.1:8 you. For **p.** is not a seeming strength, and
T-14......XI.1:9 all that stands between you and the **p.** of
T-14......XI.2:4 And can His Son, given all **p.** by Him,
T-14......XI.4:4 with God's glory, for in it lies His **p.**,
T-14....XI.15:1 The **p.** of God, from which they both
T-14....XI.15:5 so filled with **p.** that nothing will prevail
T-15.......I.15:2 very little to restore God's whole **p.** to you
T-15.......II.6:6 it is the practice of the **p.** of God in you.
T-15......III.3:2 it is true and is but a tribute to your **p.**.
T-15......III.4:8 The **p.** of God will support every effort
T-15......III.4:9 for the little, and you deny yourself His **p.**
T-15......III.6:5 The **p.** and the glory that lie in you from
T-15....III.12:5 God's **p.** is forever on the side of His host,
T-15......VI.3:2 For holiness is **p.**, and by sharing it, it
T-15......VI.3:5 that transcends the concept of loss of **p.**
T-15......VI.8:6 God and the **p.** of God will take Their
T-15...VII.13:3 for the **p.** of God in Him and you is joined
T-15......IX.4:1 the ego, and release your **p.** to creation,

T-15...... IX.6:3 remains unlimited, but because your **p.**,
T-15....... X.1:1 is in your **p.**, in time, to delay the perfect
T-15....... X.2:2 his unlimited **p.** is thus restored to him.
T-15....... X.4:1 It is in your **p.** to make this season holy,
T-15....... X.4:1 your **p.** to make the time of Christ be now
T-15...... XI.2:9 He protects, and Whose **p.** protects Him.
T-16.........I.6:2 The **p.** of love, which *is* its meaning, lies in
T-16.......... II.h The **P.** of Holiness
T-16....... II.7:2 **p.** of holiness and the weakness of attack
T-16....... II.7:3 that holiness is weakness and attack is **p.**.
T-16....... II.9:6 already proved their **p.** sufficiently for
T-16...... III.5:8 and their **p.** and gratitude to you for their
T-16...... III.7:6 will learn His **p.** and strength and purity,
T-16..... V.11:1 unlimited **p.** to what you think you have
T-16..... V.11:3 you made with **p.** you wrested from truth,
T-16..... V.11:5 body raise another self to take its **p.** from
T-16...... VI.5:4 Each would deny his **p.**, for the separate
T-16..... VII.7:3 holy instant the **p.** of the Holy Spirit will
T-16... VII.10:2 The **p.** of God and all His Love, without
T-17.........I.2:2 position, in a sense, acknowledges your **p.**
T-17.........I.3:3 your lack of faith in the **p.** that heals all
T-17.... III.1:12 your relationships the witness to its **p.**.
T-17.... IV.10:5 The **p.** of Heaven, the Love of God, the
T-17.... IV.16:3 by giving Him the **p.** and the glory, and
T-17..... VII.7:1 **p.** set in you in whom the Holy Spirit's
T-17.... VIII.3:3 **p.** of the Holy Spirit's purpose is free to
T-17.... VIII.3:4 This **p.** instantly transforms all situations
T-18....... II.5:1 Dreams show you that you have the **p.** to
T-18...... III.5:3 with all the **p.** of the Holy Spirit's Will.
T-18...... III.8:4 spark of your desire the **p.** of God Himself
T-18...... IV.4:2 with the unlimited **p.** of God's Will. You
T-18....... V.6:4 The **p.** of joining its blessing lies in the
T-18.... VIII.7:4 sun nor ocean is the **p.** that rests in you.
T-18...... IX.6:3 no **p.** at all to hold back anyone willing to
T-19....... II.3:1 turn the **p.** of his mind against himself.
T-19...... III.5:9 The only **p.** that could change perception
T-19...... III.6:5 to destroy Him, and has the **p.** to do so. Is
T-19...... III.7:5 it, nor remain itself before the **p.** of sin.
T-19...... III.8:2 For there would be a **p.** beyond God's,
T-19...... III.9:5 that you give it no **p.** over your brother.
T19.... IV.B.7:7 and shows you that its **p.** is gone forever.
T19.... IV.B.9:3 extended if you would have its limitless **p.**
T19.... IV.C.6:1 the **p.** to release from corruption. What
T19... IV.D.5:7 each has been surmounted by the **p.** of
T19... IV.D.8:5 it has no **p.** to keep you from the truth.
T19. IV.D.13:5 He has in him the **p.** to forgive your sin,
T-20....... II.7:5 your vision has become the greatest **p.** for
T-20...... III.8:3 given it **p.** to adjust the world to make its
T-20.... III.8:11 Give it no **p.** to adjust the means and end.
T-20...... IV.1:1 hurt you unless you give it the **p.** to do so.
T-20...... IV.1:2 so. Yet *you* give **p.** as the laws of this world
T-20...... IV.1:3 It is not up to you to give **p.** at all. Power
T-20...... IV.1:4 at all. **P.** is of God, given by Him and
T-20...... IV.1:5 He gives no **p.** to sin, and therefore it has
T-20...... IV.1:6 and gives no **p.** to their seeming source.
T-20.... IV.2:10 them **p.** to enforce what God created not.
T-20...... IV.3:1 and give them **p.** over you by accepting
T-20...... IV.4:2 Their **p.** is of God, and they will give it
T-20...... IV.4:3 their **p.** according to the Will of God. And
T-20...... IV.4:7 for themselves the **p.** to share with you.
T-20...... IV.5:2 the **p.** of sinlessness within your brother,
T-20...... IV.5:2 share with him the **p.** of the release from
T-20....... V.2:5 which has the **p.** to hold the unity of the
T-20...... VI.4:2 the sun. It does not seek for **p.**, but for
T-20...... VI.4:3 for seeking **p.** *through* relationships. And
T-20...... VI.9:2 unholy instant of their seeming **p.** is frail
T-20.... VIII.5:1 of weakness, vulnerability and loss of **p.**.
T-20.... VIII.6:5 body's eyes perceive, with **p.** to correct?
T-20.... VIII.8:5 take unto yourself the **p.** you gave them,
T-21....... in.2:8 the **p.** to give it joy must lie within you.
T-21....... II.2:2 the **p.** of salvation lies: ***I am** responsible for*
T-21....... II.3:3 **p.** of decision is the determiner of every
T-21....... II.3:6 gave the **p.** of decision to Him Who must
T-21....... II.3:8 is given you the **p.** to release your savior,
T-21....... II.4:8 this, the **p.** of your wanting must first be
T-21....... II.6:6 This is the statement that he has the **p.** to
T-21....... II.9:2 better demonstration of the **p.** of wanting
T-21..... II.11:5 you made has **p.** to make you what it wills
T-21..... II.12:4 Apart from this he has no **p.** to create,
T-21 ..... III.2:6 The **p.** of faith is never recognized if it is
T-21 ..... III.3:2 This is indeed a little feat for such a **p.**.
T-21 ..... III.5:3 Faith given to illusions does not lack **p.**,
T-21 ..... III.8:3 **p.** of their belief and faith sees far beyond
T-21 ..... III.8:4 desiring to place its **p.** elsewhere should
T-21 ... III.10:1 sacrifice has given it great **p.** in your sight;
T-21 ... III.12:3 and give it **p.** to serve as means to help
T-21 ..... VI.1:6 the **p.** that is in you to make correction. If
T-21 ..... VI.7:4 The **p.** to heal the Son of God is given you
T-21 ... VI.11:1 The **p.** you have over the Son of God is
T-21 .... VII.2:4 And what can they do but envy him his **p.**
T-21 .... VII.2:5 the **p.** of the Son of God will strike them
T-21 .... VII.3:6 to dream of **p.** and to act out their dream.
T-21 .... VII.6:7 hope of finding sin, and not accepting **p.**.
T-21 .... VII.7:1 choice of sin or truth, helplessness or **p.**,
T-21 .... VII.7:2 For healing comes of **p.**, and attack of
T-21 .. VII.10:7 to exchange your helplessness for **p.**, and
T-21 .. VII.13:5 The **p.** of the Son of God's desire remains
T-21 .. VII.13:7 thought but has the **p.** to release or kill.
T-21 ... VIII.2:7 Nothing has **p.** to confound its constancy,
T-21 ... VIII.3:4 out some promise of the **p.** of giving it. He
T-21 ... VIII.4:1 His, a **p.** that is not lost in your illusions,
T-22 ....... II.4:5 real. Such is the **p.** of belief. It cannot
T-22 ....... II.9:1 you made has **p.** to enslave its maker.
T-22 ..... II.10:2 Nothing you made has any **p.** over you
T-22 ..... II.12:3 How great the **p.** that lies in it. Time waits
T-22 ..... IV.2:3 A choice made with the **p.** of Heaven to
T-22 ...... V.3:8 in this quiet state alone is strength and **p.**.
T-22 ..... VI.4:4 relationship has the **p.** to heal all pain,
T-22 ..... VI.9:8 join to it all the **p.** that God has given Him
T-22 ... VI.10:2 that would deny the **p.** of your will. Think
T-22 ... VI.11:7 of the universe, Whose **p.** you know.
T-22 ... VI.12:1 oneness, you would know His **p.** is yours.
T-22 ... VI.15:3 relationship can also teach the **p.** of love
T-23 ........ I.1:5 believe the ego has the **p.** to be victorious.
T-23 ........ I.8:2 exist between one **p.** and nothingness.
T-23 ..... IV.4:3 miracles you have the **p.** to extend to all.
T-24 .... in.1:12 has the **p.** to defeat what is Their Will?
T-24 ...... in.2:4 the **p.** to dictate each decision you make.
T-24 ........ I.2:3 given **p.** to direct all subsequent decisions
T-24 ........ I.2:4 Mistake you not the **p.** of these hidden
T-24 ....... II.2:3 from his omnipotence, yet share his **p.**?
T-24 ....... II.7:1 He has not lost the **p.** to forgive you all
T-24 ..... III.2:6 idol that seems to give you **p.** has taken it
T-24 ...... V.1:9 **p.** of a wish upholds illusions as strongly
T-24 ..... VI.9:5 bound to laws that have no **p.** over him at
T-24 ... VI.11:3 the **p.** to hold itself complete within itself,
T-24 ... VI.12:1 and with the **p.** of God maintaining it,
T-24 ... VI.12:5 and all the **p.** of Heaven and the might of
T-25 ..... II.10:7 has **p.** over you except His Will and yours,
T-25 ..... II.11:5 your brother is given the **p.** of salvation,
T-25 ..... III.8:1 world of gentleness has perfect **p.** to offset
T-25 ..... III.9:2 And he has the **p.** to think he can be hurt.
T-25 ...... V.6:1 God believed to be without the **p.** to save
T-25 ..... VI.1:8 he has the **p.** to heal and bless all those he
T-25 .... VII.5:1 Holy Spirit has the **p.** to change the whole
T-25 . VIII.9:11 Son of God the **p.** to forgive himself of sin
T-25 . VIII.12:1 witness to the **p.** of love and justice, if you
T-25 ..... IX.7:6 and lasting in its **p.** of injustice and attack
T-26 ........ I.1:5 a giving up of **p.** in the name of saving just
T-26 ........ I.7:3 Son, think not that you have **p.** to make of
T-26 ..... IV.5:3 a voice that adds its **p.** to the song, and
T-26 .... V.10:7 have the **p.** to keep you in a place of death
T-26 ..... VI.1:2 Not because it has the **p.** to hurt, but just
T-26 ..... VI.1:6 All belief in sin, in **p.** of attack, in hurt
T-26 ..... VI.2:3 in Whom all **p.** in earth and Heaven rests.
T-26 .. VII.17:5 have **p.** to save the Son of God because his
T-26 .. VII.18:1 use the **p.** God has given you as He would
T-26 .. VII.18:3 is arrogant to lay aside the **p.** that He gave
T-27 ........ I.4:1 **p.** of witness is beyond belief because it
T-27 ...... I.10:6 receive the **p.** to represent an endless life,
T-27 ....... II.5:4 The **p.** of witness comes from your belief.
T-27 ....... II.5:8 with **p.** greater than a thousand tongues.
T-27 ....... II.6:6 This call has **p.** far beyond the weak and
T-27 ..... III.1:1 **P.** cannot oppose. For opposition would
T-27 ..... III.1:2 weakened **p.** is a contradiction in ideas.
T-27 ..... III.1:3 **p.** used to weaken is employed to limit.
T-27 ..... III.1:5 **P.** is unopposed, to be itself. No weakness
T-27 ..... III.1:9 such as "weakened **p.**" or "hateful love"?
T-27 ..... III.2:1 for a "hateful love," a "weakened **p.**," and
T-27 ..... III.3:2 or to endow with **p.** or to see as weak. The
T-27 ..... III.4:4 Unweakened **p.**, with no opposite, is what
T-27 ..... III.5:3 not yet a **p.** known as wholly free of limits
T-27 ..... III.7:2 A **p.** wholly limitless has come, not to
T-27 ..... III.7:5 with **p.** unlimited and single thoughts,
T-27 ..... III.7:6 the peace of **p.** that opposes nothing. Yet
T-27 ..... III.7:8 welcome to the **p.** beyond forgiveness,
T-27 ..... V.10:3 thus the **p.** of your learning will be proved
T-27 ... VIII.7:7 You have no **p.** to make the body stop its
T-29 ........ I.5:2 it with a **p.** that lies not within itself. And
T-29 ........ I.5:3 And herein lies its **p.** over you. For now
T-29 ....... II.2:2 the **p.** to heal must also now be yours.
T-29 ....... II.9:2 so it seems to be a thing with **p.** in itself.
T-29 ... III.3:12 you forgive is given **p.** to forgive you your
T-29 ..... VI.3:6 not remove the **p.** to change your mind,
T-29 .... VII.8:3 with **p.** to make complete what is within
T-29 .... VII.8:5 do, and have the **p.** you ascribe to them.
T-29 .... VII.8:6 because you want their **p.** as your own.
T-29 ... VIII.1:4 That is the only **p.** that they have. Their
T-29 ... VIII.2:4 They have the **p.** to supply your lacks, and
T-29 ... VIII.4:2 yet a thought without the **p.** to change
T-29 ... VIII.5:3 to life, and given **p.** that it may be feared.
T-29 ... VIII.5:4 Its life and **p.** are its believer's gift, and
T-29 ... VIII.5:4 to what *has* life and **p.** worthy of the gift of
T-29 ... VIII.6:2 idea there is a **p.** past omnipotence, a
T-29 ... VIII.6:3 this **p.** and place and time are given form,
T-29 ..... IX.1:2 no life, and seek for **p.** in the powerless.
T-29 ..... IX.4:6 and give their toys the **p.** to move about,
T-30 ....... II.5:2 that he learn death has no **p.** over him,
T-30 ..... III.4:9 thing the **p.** to complete the Son of God.
T-30 ..... IV.5:5 Attack has **p.** to make illusions real. Yet
T-30 ..... IV.5:7 by a **p.** that can have no real effects at all?
T-30 ... IV.5:15 real. What can the **p.** of illusions do?
T-30 ..... VI.5:7 mistake that had the **p.** to undo creation,
T-30 ..... VI.8:5 which the miracle must lack the **p.** to heal
T-30 ... VI.10:3 But what you see as having **p.** to make an
T-30 ... VIII.4:4 it be withheld from **p.** to heal all dreams.
T-30 ... VIII.6:4 give it **p.** to replace the changeless in him
T-31 ........ I.3:1 ever doubt the **p.** of your learning skill.
T-31 ........ I.3:2 There is no greater **p.** in the world. The
T-31 ........ I.3:6 For your **p.** to learn is strong enough to
T-31 ........ I.5:6 forgiveness have a **p.** mightier than yours,
T-31 ........ I.6:3 And the **p.** of His Will is in the Voice that
T-31 ..... III.4:3 has no **p.** to learn, to pardon, nor enslave.
T-31 ..... IV.5:3 is none, what **p.** of decision can he use?
T-31 ..... IV.5:4 The great release of **p.** must begin with
T-31 ..... IV.5:5 And what decision has **p.** if it be applied
T-31 ..... IV.8:1 There *is* a choice that you have **p.** to make
T-31 ..... IV.8:3 than that the **p.** of decision cannot lie in
T-31 .. VII.12:5 a wish, because it has no **p.** to create. Yet
T-31 ... VIII.1:3 can do; its **p.** is the only strength he has;
T-31 ... VIII.2:5 your actions, you have given it no **p.**. And
T-31 ... VIII.3:6 He is the only **p.** that is real in you. His
T-31 ... VIII.4:5 are joined in all the **p.** of the Will of God.
T-31 ... VIII.7:1 and **p.** to bring this peace to everyone
W-pI .... 20.3:7 all **p.** is given him in Heaven and on earth
W-pI .... 38.1:3 its **p.** because it establishes you as a Son
W-pI .... 38.2:1 holiness the **p.** of God is made manifest.
W-pI .... 38.2:2 holiness the **p.** of God is made available.
W-pI .... 38.2:3 there is nothing the **p.** of God cannot do.
W-pI .... 38.2:6 It is equal in its **p.** to help anyone because
W-pI .... 38.2:6 because it is equal in its **p.** to save anyone.
W-pI .... 38.3:4 we will apply the **p.** of your holiness to all
W-pI .... 38.5:3 *cannot do because the **p.** of God lies in it.*
W-pI .... 41.2:4 the **p.** to end all this foolishness forever.
W-pI .... 42.1:4 strength, not your own, that gives you **p.**.
W-pI .. 44.10:3 world unless you give them the **p.** to do so
W-pI .... 53.4:6 Let me remember the **p.** of my decision,
W-pI .... 54.1:2 impossible because all thoughts have **p.**.
W-pI .... 54.4:6 in my **p.** to change every mind along with
W-pI .... 54.4:6 along with mine, for mine is the **p.** of God
W-pI .... 58.3:2 My holiness is unlimited in its **p.** to heal,
W-pI .... 58.3:2 because it is unlimited in its **p.** to save.
W-pI .... 61.3:4 an acknowledgment of the **p.** that is given
W-pI .... 62.3:5 It will restore the invulnerability and **p.**
W-pI .... 63.1:1 have the **p.** to bring peace to every mind!
W-pI .... 69.7:2 call on the **p.** of the universe to help you,
W-pI .... 69.8:6 let the **p.** of God work in you and through

W-pI.....73.1:3 with God has all the **p.** of creation in it.
W-pI.....73.1:4 unshared, and therefore have no **p.** at all.
W-pI.....73.9:2 It is not the purpose of an alien **p.**, thrust
W-pI...73.10:4 joined with the **p.** of God and united with
W-pI.....75.9:4 Rejoice in the **p.** of forgiveness to heal
WpI. rII.in.4:2 take, they have no meaning and no **p.**.
WpI. rII.in.4:4 Do not forget that your will has **p.** over all
W-pI.....85.4:4 *This has no* **p.** *to remove salvation from me.*
W-pI.....87.1:2 I will use the **p.** of my will today. It is not
W-pI.....88.3:4 up other laws and give them **p.** over me.
W-pI.....93.5:9 What **p.** can this self you made possess,
W-pI.....95.8:4 rather than give it **p.** to delay our learning
W-pI.....95.8:5 If we give it **p.** to do this, we are regarding
W-pI...95.10:2 creation, and limitless in **p.** and in peace.
W-pI...95.11:2 *of creation, and limitless in* **p.** *and in peace.*
W-pI...95.12:3 with **p.** to lift the veil of darkness from the
W-pI.....96.4:3 Its **p.** comes from spirit, and it is fulfilling
W-pI.....97.5:3 And they will increase in healing **p.** each
W-pI.....97.7:3 increase its **p.** and give it back to you.
W-pI...99.11:1 which has the **p.** to remove all forms of
W-pI...100.9:4 little thought has **p.** to hold you back?
W-pI...102.2:1 and with no **p.** to accomplish anything. It
W-pI...106.1:1 hear the mighty Voice of truth, quiet in **p.**
W-pI...108.3:1 and vision, being healed, has **p.** to heal.
W-pI...109.2:4 has **p.** to wake the sleeping truth in you,
W-pI...110.5:1 The healing **p.** of today's idea is limitless.
W-pI...110.8:1 with **p.** to save whoever touches Him,
W-pI...122.6:7 before the **p.** and the majesty of this
W-pI.122.14:2 which has **p.** to hold your gifts in your
W-pI...123.6:5 And so they grow in **p.** and in strength,
W-pI...123.7:3 **p.** to save the world eons more quickly for
W-pI...124.1:2 **p.** and strength available to us in all our
W-pI...124.6:2 No thought of theirs but has the **p.** to heal
W-pI...126.6:5 It has no **p.** to restore your unity with him
W-pI...127.3:8 wholeness is the **p.** holding everything as
W-pI...130.9:2 called upon the great unfailing **p.** which
W-pI...131.3:3 you search, unless you give it **p.** to do so.
W-pI.132.17:1 the **p.** of your simple change of mind: *I*
W-pI...135.2:2 that there is danger which has **p.** to call
W-pI.136.14:1 Truth has a **p.** far beyond defense, for no
W-pI...137.2:3 body final **p.** to make the separation real,
W-pI...137.3:6 the body has no **p.** to attack the universal
W-pI.151.14:2 takes on healing **p.** from the Mind which
W-pI......152.h The **p.** of decision is my own.
W-pI...152.8:2 The **p.** of decision is our own. Decide but
W-pI...152.9:4 like to Himself in **p.** and in love.
W-pI.152.10:1 The **p.** of decision is our own. And we
W-pI.152.11:3 *The* **p.** *of decision is my own. This day I will*
W-pI...158.9:1 has vision that has **p.** to overlook them all
W-pI...159.5:2 And in its **p.** can you safely trust to carry
W-pI...165.6:2 Now is Christ's **p.** in your mind, to heal as
W-pI...167.8:4 with the **p.** to extend forever changelessly,
W-pI...167.9:2 assume an alien **p.** which it does not have,
W-pI...170.7:4 We need not defy his **p.**. He has none.
W-pI...171.2:1 (152) The **p.** of decision is my own. God
W-pI...188.6:3 alone has **p.** to give the gift of sight to you
W-pI...190.5:5 that has the **p.** to make you ill or sad, or
W-pI...190.5:6 But it is you who have the **p.** to dominate
W-pI...190.7:2 the world, as causeless, has no **p.** to cause.
W-pI.190.10:3 lesson that contains all of salvation's **p.**. It
W-pI...191.9:1 this: All **p.** is given unto you in earth and
W-pI...192.3:5 Yet God created One Who has the **p.** to
W-pI...193.6:2 their **p.** to release all minds from bondage
W-pI...193.6:3 These are words which give you **p.** over all
W-pI...193.6:3 that seem to have been given **p.** over you.
W-pI...199.2:1 strength and **p.** to do whatever it is asked.
W-pI...199.5:3 not gain thereby in **p.** to help the world,
W-pI...199.6:6 Without the **p.** to enslave, it is a worthy
W-pII......2.2:4 So the Thought that has the **p.** to heal the
W-pII..270.1:1 **p.** *to translate all that the body's eyes behold*
W-pII.....320.h My Father gives all **p.** unto me.
W-pII..320.1:6 in whom the **p.** of my Father's Will abides
W-pII..320.2:3 *And so all* **p.** *has been given to Your Son.*
W-pII....11.2:1 given all the **p.** that their own Creator has
W-pII....11.2:3 and must therefore share in **p.** to create.
W-pII..326.1:6 *of God, and so I have the* **p.** *to create like You.*
W-pII..330.1:3 when God holds out His **p.** and His Love,
W-pII..338.1:5 **p.** to change them and exchange each fear
M-2...........4:8 What could delay the **p.** of eternity?
M-4.........I.1:5 by a **p.** that is *in* them but not *of* them. It is
M-4.........I.1:6 It is this **p.** that keeps all things safe. It is
M-4.........I.1:7 this **p.** that the teachers of God look on a
M-4.........I.2:1 When this **p.** has once been experienced,
M-4.........I.2:2 mighty **p.** of an eagle has been given him?
M-5.........I.1:8 powerful, eager to keep all **p.** for Himself.
M-7...........4:9 teachers the **p.** to be miracle workers, for
M-13.........2:6 **P.**, fame, money, physical pleasure; who
M-16.........6:4 You think you made a **p.** that can save
M-17.......8:10 not really have the **p.** to give rise to guilt.
M-17.........9:2 In truth it has no **p.** to make anything.
M-21.........3:5 The **p.** of his decision offers it to him as
M-21.........3:7 Son of God has but this **p.** left to him. It is
M-21.........5:9 to the words they use the **p.** of His Spirit,
M-22.........6:3 And in it is the **p.** to heal all individuals of
M-22.........7:1 Who can limit the **p.** of God Himself?
M-22.........7:2 must remain beyond God's **p.** to forgive?
M-23.........1:6 an invocation call forth any special **p.**.
M-23.........2:7 There is now no limit on his **p.**, because it
M-23.........2:7 on his power, because it is the **p.** of God.
M-25.........1:2 magic to make up a **p.** that does not exist.
M-25.........5:6 easy. Now the "**p.**" is no longer a genuine
M-25.........6:3 the more unusual and unexpected the **p.**,
M-26.......1:10 But in their joining is the **p.** of God.
M-29.........4:2 myself I can do nothing" is to gain all **p.**.
M-29.........4:4 As God created you, you *have* all **p.**. The
M-29.........5:1 assumes a **p.** that he does not possess is
M-29.........5:2 Yet to accept the **p.** given him by God is
M-29.........6:5 For God has given Him the **p.** to translate
C-6.............2:3 All **p.** in Heaven and earth is therefore
C-6.............3:4 the inherent **p.** of the vision of Christ. He
P-1.............3:6 and helpless midst the **p.** of the world.
P-2.......VII.6:2 way can ever doubt the **p.** that is in him.
P-2.......VII.6:4 understands all **p.** in earth and Heaven
S-1...........I.7:4 are. Herein lies the **p.** of prayer. It asks
S-1........III.1:6 of rising **p.** and with ascending goals,
S-1........III.6:6 The **p.** of prayer can be quite clearly
S-3...........I.4:5 The **p.** to heal is now his Father's gift, for
S-3...........I.5:3 a witness to the **p.** of the world or to the
S-3........III.1:6 false, there is some **p.** that another has,

## power's 1

M-25.........5:7 he will bolster his "**p.**" uncertainties with

## powerful 42

T-2.........II.2:1 True denial is a **p.** protective device. You
T-2.........V.9:6 of a much more **p.** love-encompassment
T-2........VI.9:5 The mind is very **p.**, and never loses its
T-3........VII.2:4 to be extremely **p.** and extremely active.
T-3........VII.5:2 It is **p.**, active, destructive and clearly in
T-7.........V.7:6 changed the most **p.** device that was ever
T-7.......V.10:6 mind is so **p.** a light that you can look into
T-7......VI.10:6 **p.** force in the universe as if it were weak,
T-7.....VII.1:12 Mind is too **p.** to be subject to exclusion.
T-7.......VII.4:3 are **p.** because they are mental judgments.
T-7.........X.4:8 Your will is as **p.** as His because it *is* His.
T-8........IV.5:9 yours, because yours is as **p.** as mine. If it
T-8........VI.7:6 Yet their thought is so **p.** that they can
T-8........IX.2:9 is so **p.** that it will bring the whole to you.
T-14.......X.10:6 you a light so **p.** that what you see is given
T-14.....XI.15:4 of effects so **p.** they could not be of you.
T-15......VII.1:1 the **p.** attraction of the Father for His Son.
T-15.......XI.3:4 relationship with our Father, and as **p.**.
T-16.......VI.7:3 is strong and **p.** cut down to littleness. In
T-18......IV.7:5 is a **p.** contribution to the truth, and
T-19.......II.5:3 concept in the ego's system; lovely and **p.**,
T-20......VI.9:4 seeming **p.** and so bitterly misunderstood
T-21.......V.2:5 own control, and far more **p.** than you.
T-21...VII.5:12 *a world where I am* **p.** *instead of helpless? Do*
T-21... VIII.4:1 are His happiness, whose will is **p.** as His,
T-22......VI.10:6 of countless attackers more **p.** than you.
T-23......II.16:4 play the major roles, it seems most **p.**. No
T-24......VII.2:7 deep concern, the **p.** conviction this is you
T-29.......IX.6:4 in which the child becomes the father, **p.**,
T-30.......I.17:3 the basic law that makes decision **p.**, and
T-30... VIII.3:3 forms of idols have a **p.** appeal that makes
T-31.........I.4:5 **p.** enough to render God forgotten, and
W-pI.....16.1:4 Thoughts are not big or little; **p.** or weak.
W-pI.....42.1:1 for today combines two very **p.** thoughts,
W-pI.....91.8:5 *I am not helpless, but all* **p.**. *I am not limited,*
W-pI...132.1:3 Belief is **p.** indeed. The thoughts you hold
W-pI.134.11:1 as **p.** as love which laid its blessing on it,
W-pI...136.9:2 the body is more **p.** than everlasting life,
W-pI...137.6:2 anti-Christ becomes more **p.** than Christ
W-pII .329.1:1 *interposed a second will more* **p.** *than Yours*
M-4 ...... VI.1:7 and more **p.** its defenses seem to be. Yet
M-5 .........I.1:8 God is seen as outside, fierce and **p.**, eager

## powerfully 1

T-16...... III.8:4 His little efforts are **p.** supplemented by

## powerless 28

T-7........ VI.2:7 and thus rendered it **p.** in your belief.
T-8........ III.8:6 You cannot be **p.** to do this, because this
T-14...... XI.2:4 given all power by Him, learn to be **p.**?
T-17..... V.12:6 the instant, but to make it **p.** in its effects.
T19....IV.C.8:1 God Himself is **p.** before the ego's might,
T-21.........II.6:6 make God **p.** and so to take it for himself,
T-21........ III.5:3 it does the Son of God believe that he is **p.**
T-21..... VII.1:1 from the strange belief that you are **p.**?
T-21..... VII.2:1 No one believes the Son of God is **p.**. And
T-21..... VII.2:6 They join the army of the **p.**, to wage their
T-21..... VII.3:5 The army of the **p.** must be disbanded in
T-21..... VII.4:1 The army of the **p.** is weak indeed. It has
T-21..... VII.5:4 Could he admit that no one made him **p.**?
T-21....VIII.5:6 time is **p.** because of your desire for what
T-22.......I.10:7 Into the holy home where fear is **p.** love
T-22.... VI.10:3 Think you the Will of God is **p.**? Is this
T-23.........II.4:4 which God Himself is **p.** to overcome. Sin
T-23......II.17:4 makes his savior **p.** and finds salvation?
T-24...... III.5:5 They are **p.** to make attack upon illusions.
T-25....VIII.8:7 of justice and vitality, and **p.** to save?
T-27...... VI.6:9 different are dissolved, and shown as **p.**.
T-28.........II.8:1 **p.** to keep them since He was no longer
T-28...... VI.6:8 secret vows are **p.** before the Will of God,
T-29...... IX.1:2 has no life, and seek for power in the **p.**.
T-31....VIII.4:3 the face of Christ is **p.** before His majesty,
W-pI.....73.7:6 it is the ego that stands **p.** before your will
W-pI.....94.1:1 which makes all forms of temptation **p.**;
W-pII .330.1:3 Why should we teach them they are **p.**,

## powerlessness 2

T-3........ IV.7:5 I demonstrated both the **p.** of the body
M-16 .........9:8 **p.** is the reason it can be so easily escaped.

## powers 16

T-2........ III.5:2 their true creative **p.** on useless attempts
T-2......... V.5:4 and reinstating its purely constructive **p.**,
T-4...........II.9:1 magic to the **p.** the ego ascribes to itself.
T-13.......in.2:7 its **p.** to decline if their bodies are hurt.
T-13...... XI.1:4 the war is between real and unreal **p.**, he
T-26..... VII.7:4 subjected to the laws of two opposing **p.**,
W-pI.....50.1:3 that you endow with magical **p.**.
W-pI.....77.2:2 magical **p.** you have ascribed to yourself,
M-25 ............h ARE "PSYCHIC" **P.** DESIRABLE?
M-25 ......... 1:2 There are, of course, no "unnatural" **p.**,
M-25 .........2:1 Certainly there are many "psychic" **p.**
M-25 .........3:7 any **p.** that are not available to everyone.
M-25 .........3:8 of magic are special **p.** "demonstrated."
M-25 .........5:1 may still be deceived by "psychic" **p.**. As
M-25 .........6:7 Those who have developed "psychic" **p.**
P-2.........in.3:4 the magical **p.** he seeks in psychotherapy.

## practical 14

T-8........ IX.8:1 to realize that this is a very **p.** course, and
T-11.....VIII.5:3 play of ideas, but in their **p.** application.
T-17....... V.1:2 salvation, the holy instant is a **p.** device,
T-17....... V.3:1 the **p.** results of asking Him to enter. At
T-17...... VI.1:1 **p.** application of the Holy Spirit's purpose
T-17...... VI.5:1 goal of truth has further **p.** advantages. If
T-18........II.6:1 The Holy Spirit, ever **p.** in His wisdom,

W-pI...133.1:1 learned, to bring him back to **p.** concerns.
M-3 ........... 1:4 **p.** point of view he cannot meet everyone,
M-16 .......... 4:1 This course is always **p.**. It may be that
M-21 .......... 2:3 the word has little or no **p.** meaning, and
M-29 .......... 5:7 That would hardly be **p.**, and it is the
M-29 .......... 5:7 and it is the **p.** with which this course is
P-3........ III.7:2 Yet not one worldly thought is really **p.**.

## practically 1

P-3......... II.1:4 Yet **p.** speaking, it can still be said that

## practice 290

T-11....... II.2:1 and the more you **p.** it the better teacher
T-15.........I.9:4 Begin to **p.** the Holy Spirit's use of time as
T-15.......I.13:3 **P.** giving this blessed instant of freedom
T-15....... II.5:4 can **p.** the mechanics of the holy instant,
T-15....... II.6:1 Start now to **p.** your little part in
T-15....... II.6:6 that will depart from you in this **p.**, for it
T-15....... II.6:6 for it is the **p.** of the power of God in you.
T-15...... IV.2:1 Your **p.** must therefore rest upon your
T-15...... IV.4:5 In your **p.**, try to give over every plan you
T-15...... IV.9:8 In your **p.**, then, try only to be vigilant
T-18.... VII.6:6 preparation, and **p.** doing nothing else. "I
T-30.......in.1:3 alone; your willingness to **p.** every step.
T-30.......in.1:7 So now we need to **p.** them awhile, until
T-30.........I.1:3 a little **p.** with the ones you recognize, a
T-30.......I.13:2 takes **p.** in the rules that will protect you
T-31.........I.3:1 to which you went to **p.** and repeat the
W-pI....... 1.1:1 and **p.** applying this idea very specifically
W-pI....... 1.3:4 see. As you **p.** the idea for the day, use it
W-pI....... 4.1:2 In these **p.** periods, begin with noting the
W-pI....... 4.5:2 This **p.** is useful, but is not a substitute for
W-pI....... 5.3:1 be substituted for **p.** periods in which you
W-pI....... 6.2:2 the three or four **p.** periods which are
W-pI....... 7.5:3 Three or four **p.** periods, each to last a
W-pI....... 8.4:5 Introduce the **p.** period by saying: *I seem*
W-pI....... 9.1:5 These exercises are concerned with **p.**,
W-pI....... 9.1:6 need to **p.** what you already understand.
W-pI....... 9.3:1 three or four **p.** periods are sufficient,
W-pI..... 10.1:1 aware, or become aware in the **p.** periods.
W-pI..... 10.5:2 five **p.** periods are recommended, each
W-pI..... 11.1:4 indeed to **p.** the idea in its initial form, for
W-pI..... 11.2:1 The **p.** periods for today's idea are to be
W-pI..... 11.4:1 Three **p.** periods today will probably be
W-pI..... 12.4:3 At the end of the **p.** period, add: *But I am*
W-pI..... 12.6:2 should the **p.** periods exceed a minute.
W-pI..... 13.6:2 to think of it except during the **p.** periods.
W-pI..... 14.2:3 Do not have more than three **p.** periods
W-pI..... 14.6:7 fact, conclude the **p.** periods by repeating
W-pI..... 14.7:1 during the day, aside from the **p.** periods.
W-pI..... 15.5:1 minute or so of **p.** that is recommended,
W-pI..... 15.5:2 than a minute will do for the **p.** periods, if
W-pI..... 16.3:4 We will **p.** this idea in many forms before
W-pI..... 16.5:1 In the **p.** periods, first repeat the idea to
W-pI..... 16.6:1 Four or five **p.** periods are recommended,
W-pI..... 17.4:1 four specific **p.** periods are recommended
W-pI..... 17.4:2 length of the **p.** period may be reduced to
W-pI..... 18.2:3 The three or four **p.** periods which are
W-pI..... 18.3:3 Conclude each **p.** period by repeating the
W-pI..... 18.3:5 less, will be sufficient for each **p.** period.
W-pI..... 19.4:1 for the **p.** periods should be quite familiar
W-pI..... 19.4:2 random selection of subjects for all **p.**
W-pI..... 19.5:1 idea, at least three **p.** periods are required
W-pI..... 20.1:1 quite casual about our **p.** periods thus far.
W-pI..... 21.1:3 Five **p.** periods are urged, allowing a full
W-pI..... 21.2:1 In the **p.** periods, begin by repeating the
W-pI..... 21.3:1 of anger escape you in the **p.** periods.
W-pI..... 22.3:7 At the end of each **p.** period, ask yourself:
W-pI..... 23.6:1 five **p.** periods are required in applying
W-pI..... 23.7:1 In the **p.** periods, be sure to include both
W-pI..... 23.7:3 them as the same in today's **p.** periods.
W-pI..... 24.3:2 in each of the five **p.** periods which should
W-pI..... 24.4:1 **p.** periods should begin with repeating
W-pI..... 25.6:1 Six **p.** periods, each of two-minutes
W-pI..... 25.6:2 Each **p.** period should begin with a slow
W-pI..... 26.4:1 **P.** with today's idea will help you to
W-pI..... 26.5:1 Six **p.** periods are required in applying
W-pI..... 26.6:1 **p.** period should begin with repeating the
W-pI..... 26.6:4 to use very many for any one **p.** period,
W-pI..... 26.9:3 Conclude each **p.** period by repeating
W-pI..... 28.1:2 In these **p.** periods, you will be making a
W-pI..... 28.6:2 each subject that you use in the **p.** periods
W-pI..... 28.7:1 will have six two-minute **p.** periods today,
W-pI..... 29.4:1 Our six two-minute **p.** periods for today
W-pI... 29.5:10 In addition to the assigned **p.** periods,
W-pI..... 30.5:3 well, devote several **p.** periods to applying
W-pI..... 31.1:3 of **p.** which will be used more and more,
W-pI..... 31.2:1 Two longer periods of **p.** with the idea for
W-pI..... 32.2:2 the **p.** periods for today will again include
W-pI..... 32.3:1 Again we will begin the **p.** periods for the
W-pI..... 32.4:1 For the two longer **p.** periods three to five
W-pI..... 33.1:3 In these **p.** periods, the idea should be
W-pI..... 34.2:1 Three longer **p.** periods are required for
W-pI..... 34.3:1 required for each of the longer **p.** periods.
W-pI..... 35.4:1 of the three five-minute **p.** periods today,
W-pI..... 36.2:1 Four three-to-five-minute **p.** periods are
W-pI..... 36.2:3 longer **p.** periods should take this form:
W-pI... 36.3:10 *pen.* Several times during these **p.** periods,
W-pI..... 37.4:1 each to involve three to five minutes of **p.**,
W-pI..... 37.5:1 may continue the **p.** period with your eyes
W-pI..... 37.5:2 The **p.** period should conclude with a
W-pI..... 38.4:1 four longer **p.** periods, each preferably to
W-pI..... 39.2:6 one needs **p.** to gain what is already his.
W-pI..... 39.5:1 for the four longer **p.** periods for today,
W-pI..... 39.5:1 more frequent **p.** sessions are encouraged
W-pI..... 39.6:1 Begin the **p.** periods as usual, by
W-pI..... 39.9:1 You may find these **p.** periods easier if
W-pI... 39.10:4 End each **p.** period by repeating the idea
W-pI..... 40.1:2 No long **p.** periods are required today,
W-pI..... 40.2:3 Do not miss a **p.** period because of this.
W-pI..... 40.2:4 can **p.** quite well under any circumstances
W-pI..... 40.3:3 One **p.** period might, for example, consist
W-pI..... 41.6:1 will be only one long **p.** period today. In
W-pI..... 41.6:3 At the beginning of the **p.** period, repeat
W-pI..... 41.8:6 detail about this kind of **p.** as we go along.
W-pI..... 42.3:1 two three-to-five-minute **p.** periods today,
W-pI..... 42.4:1 Begin these **p.** periods by repeating the
W-pI..... 42.6:3 better to spend the **p.** period alternating
W-pI..... 42.7:1 is no limit on the number of short **p.**
W-pI..... 43.4:1 five-minute **p.** periods are required today,
W-pI..... 43.4:3 At the beginning of these **p.** periods,
W-pI..... 43.4:5 this phase of the **p.** period are sufficient.
W-pI..... 43.5:1 for this phase of **p.** indiscriminately,
W-pI..... 43.7:1 today's idea in the shorter **p.** periods, the
W-pI..... 44.4:1 Have at least three **p.** periods today, each
W-pI..... 44.4:3 The form of **p.** we will use today is the
W-pI..... 44.5:4 While you **p.** in this way, you leave
W-pI..... 44.7:1 Begin the **p.** period by repeating today's
W-pI..... 45.4:1 three five-minute **p.** periods for today will
W-pI..... 45.8:4 this kind of **p.** only one thing is necessary;
W-pI..... 46.3:1 at least three full five-minute **p.** periods,
W-pI..... 46.3:2 Begin the longer **p.** periods by repeating
W-pI..... 46.5:1 the first phase of today's **p.** periods is to
W-pI..... 46.5:4 devote the remainder of the **p.** period to
W-pI..... 46.6:7 The **p.** period should end, however, with
W-pI..... 46.7:1 The shorter **p.** periods may consist either
W-pI..... 47.4:2 Four five-minute **p.** periods are necessary
W-pI..... 47.7:1 In the latter phase of the **p.** period, try to
W-pI..... 48.2:1 Today's **p.** periods will be very short,
W-pI..... 49.3:1 at least four five-minute **p.** periods today,
WpI... rI.in.1:4 In the **p.** periods, the exercises should be
WpI... rI.in.2:3 two minutes or more to each **p.** period,
WpI... rI.in.3:1 literally or thoroughly in the **p.** periods.
WpI... rI.in.4:1 for **p.** periods at your stage of learning. It
W-pI..... 61.5:1 As many **p.** periods as possible should be
W-pI..... 61.6:1 to begin and end the day with a **p.** period.
W-pI..... 61.6:3 two **p.** periods may be longer than the
W-pI..... 64.6:1 Today, then, let us **p.** with these thoughts
W-pI..... 64.8:1 forms of shorter **p.** periods are required.
W-pI..... 65.3:1 minutes for a more sustained **p.** period, in
W-pI..... 65.4:1 undertake the daily extended **p.** periods
W-pI..... 65.5:1 the longer **p.** period, begin by reviewing
W-pI..... 65.7:1 devote the rest of the **p.** period to trying
W-pI..... 65.8:1 In the shorter **p.** periods, which should
W-pI..... 65.8:4 Sometimes close your eyes as you **p.** this,
W-pI..... 66.4:1 longer **p.** period today has as its purpose
W-pI .... 66.5:1 the ten-to-fifteen-minute **p.** period by
W-pI .... 66.9:1 this during the longer **p.** period today.
W-pI .. 66.11:1 In the shorter **p.** periods, which would be
W-pI .... 67.2:1 In the longer **p.** period, we will think
W-pI .... 67.5:1 will be particularly helpful today to **p.** the
W-pI .... 67.6:1 the shorter **p.** periods that this is not your
W-pI .... 68.5:1 Begin today's extended **p.** period by
W-pI .... 68.6:4 Spend the remainder of the **p.** period
W-pI .... 68.6:7 At the end of the **p.** period tell yourself:
W-pI .... 68.7:1 short **p.** periods should include a quick
W-pI .... 69.2:2 this in our more extended **p.** period, let us
W-pI .... 69.3:1 Let us begin our longer **p.** period today
W-pI .... 69.9:1 In the shorter **p.** periods, which you will
W-pI .... 70.5:1 Today we **p.** realizing that God's Will
W-pI .... 70.6:1 are ready for two longer **p.** periods today,
W-pI .... 70.6:3 will follow this **p.** for a number of lessons,
W-pI .... 70.7:1 these **p.** periods by repeating the idea for
W-pI .. 70.10:1 the short and frequent **p.** periods today,
W-pI .... 71.7:1 Let us **p.** recognizing this certainty today.
W-pI .... 71.8:1 Begin the two longer **p.** periods for today
W-pI .... 71.9:1 the remainder of the extended **p.** periods
W-pI .... 71.9:6 Him full charge of the rest of the **p.** period
W-pI .. 71.10:1 In the shorter **p.** periods, tell yourself
W-pI .. 72.10:1 Our goal in the longer **p.** periods today is
W-pI .. 72.13:1 One or perhaps two shorter **p.** periods an
W-pI .... 73.9:1 We will begin our longer **p.** periods with
W-pI .. 73.10:5 rest of the **p.** period under Their guidance
W-pI .. 73.11:1 In the shorter **p.** periods, again make a
W-pI .... 74.3:1 Begin the longer **p.** periods by repeating
W-pI .... 75.4:1 Our longer **p.** periods will be devoted to
W-pI .... 75.5:3 Begin the longer **p.** periods by telling
W-pI .... 75.9:1 The shorter **p.** periods, too, will be joyful
W-pI .... 76.8:1 We will begin the longer **p.** periods today
W-pI .. 76.11:5 with which the **p.** period concludes: *I am*
W-pI .... 77.4:1 Begin the longer **p.** periods by telling
W-pI .... 77.7:1 Our shorter **p.** periods will be frequent,
W-pI .... 78.6:1 longer **p.** periods today will see him in
W-pI .... 79.7:1 In our longer **p.** periods today we will ask
W-pI .... 79.9:1 shorter **p.** periods for today will not be set
W-pI .... 80.4:1 In our longer **p.** periods today, we will
WpI.. rII.in.1:4 shorter ones in which we **p.** each of them.
WpI.. rII.in.2:1 longer **p.** periods will follow this general
WpI.. rII.in.5:1 these **p.** periods as dedications to the way,
WpI.. rII.in.6:1 in the shorter **p.** periods as well, using the
W-pI .... 91.6:1 Begin the longer **p.** periods with this
W-pI .. 91.10:1 Relax for the rest of the **p.** period,
W-pI .. 91.10:4 They are united with you in this **p.** period
W-pI .. 92.10:4 today, and we will **p.** seeing in the light,
W-pI .. 92.11:1 Morning and evening we will **p.** thus.
W-pI .... 93.8:4 spend the rest of the **p.** period in trying to
W-pI .... 95.4:2 to wander, if it undertakes extended **p.**.
W-pI .... 95.5:1 Frequent but shorter **p.** periods have
W-pI .... 95.6:2 the most beneficial form of **p.** in salvation
W-pI .... 95.7:1 the five-minutes-an-hour **p.** periods for a
W-pI .. 95.11:1 the **p.** periods today with this assurance,
W-pI .... 97.1:4 **P.** this truth today as often as you can, for
W-pI .... 97.3:2 Each time you **p.**, awareness is brought a
W-pI .... 97.8:1 Offer each **p.** period today gladly to Him.
W-pI .... 98.7:5 Today you **p.** with Him, as you say: *I will*
W-pI .... 98.9:6 will be with you each **p.** period you share
W-pI .... 99.7:1 be sure you **p.** well the idea for today. Try
W-pI .... 99.9:1 **P.** His Thought today, and let His light
W-pI .. 100.7:1 this today, in our five-minute **p.** periods,
W-pI 100.10:5 for today between your hourly **p.** periods.
W-pI .. 101.5:1 need the **p.** periods today. The exercises
W-pI .. 101.5:5 We **p.** with this thought as often as we
W-pI .. 101.6:8 So should you start your **p.** periods, and
W-pI .. 102.4:1 Begin your **p.** periods today with this
W-pI .. 104.3:2 Our longer **p.** periods today, the hourly
W-pI .. 105.6:1 our **p.** periods will start a little differently.
W-pI .. 106.7:3 Today we **p.** giving, not the way you
W-pI .. 107.7:3 own. Today we **p.** on the happy note of
W-pI .. 108.7:1 Today we **p.** with the special case of
W-pI .. 108.8:1 begin the **p.** periods with the instruction
W-pI .. 110.5:3 **P.** today's idea with gratitude. This is the
W-pI .. 110.6:1 For your five-minute **p.** periods, begin
WpI.. rIII.in1:3 a special format for these **p.** periods, that
WpI.. rIII.in2:2 will not be hampered when you miss a **p.**
WpI.. rIII.in3:1 when you skip a **p.** period because you are

WpI . rIII.in4:1 p. periods that you have lost because you
WpI . rIII.in4:3 allow your p. periods to be replacements
WpI . rIII.in9:2 inclined to p. only at appointed times,
WpIrIII.in10:1 lie idly by between your longer p. periods.
WpIrIII.in11:2 These p. periods are planned to help you
W-pI ...121.8:1 Today we p. learning to forgive. If you
W-pI.121.10:1 Begin the longer p. periods by thinking
W-pI.122.11:1 happiness as you begin these p. periods,
W-pI ...126.8:5 release that lies in the idea we p. for today
W-pI ...127.6:4 Today we p. making free your mind of all
W-pI ...128.5:1 Today we p. letting go all thought of
W-pI ...129.7:1 P. your willingness to make this change
W-pI.131.11:1 as we start upon our p. periods. Begin
W-pI.132.15:1 in which we p. twice today with this: *I who*
W-pI.133.13:3 Our two extended p. periods of fifteen
W-pI.134.14:1 Today we p. true forgiveness, that the
W-pI.136.14:3 choose to p. giving welcome to the truth.
W-pI ...137.9:2 how little p. you need undertake to let His
WpI . rIV.in4:4 we start each p. period in this review with
WpI . rIV.in8:2 two ideas you p. for the day unhurriedly,
WpIrIV.in10:1 you who p. thus the keeping of His Word.
W-pI.151.13:1 We p. wordlessly today, except at the
W-pI ...152.9:1 Today we p. true humility, abandoning
W-pI.153.15:1 Today we p. in a form we will maintain
W-pI.153.18:1 In time, with p., you will never cease to
W-pI.154.11:1 We p. giving Him what He would have,
W-pI.155.14:2 we p. gladly with this thought today: *I will*
W-pI.158.11:3 We p. seeing with the eyes of Christ today
W-pI ...161.1:1 Today we p. differently, and take a stand
W-pI ...161.1:2 words in which we p. with today's idea.
W-pI.161.10:1 we p. in a form we have attempted earlier.
W-pI ...162.4:1 Today we p. simply. For the words we
W-pI ...164.9:5 P. in earnest, and the gift is yours. Would
W-pI ...165.7:1 P. today in hope. For hope indeed is
W-pI ...165.8:2 Name we p. as His Word directs we do.
WpI .. rV.in5:3 p. it is this to which we are approaching.
WpI .. rV.in8:1 Release me as you p. once again the
WpI rV.in10:6 p. but an ancient truth we knew before
WpI rV.in11:2 we start and end each period of p. time.
WpI rV.in12:1 at the beginning and the end of p. periods
WpI rV.in12:2 faith in the experience that comes from p.
Wi181-200 1:3 are asked to p. now in order to attain the
W-pI ...181.3:4 of time wherein we p. changing our intent
W-pI ...183.6:1 P. but this today; repeat God's Name
W-pI ...185.8:1 Today devote your p. periods to careful
W-pI ...188.9:1 p. coming nearer to the light in us today.
W-pI ...189.1:6 is a reflection of the thought we p. now.
W-pI.193.11:4 And as we p., let us think about all things
W-pI ...196.2:1 can be found in the idea we p. for today.
W-pI ...196.9:1 be heard in the idea we p. for today. If it
W-pI.196.12:3 How kind and merciful is the idea we p.!
W-pI ...198.9:1 Today we p. letting freedom come to
W-pI ...199.5:1 today's idea, and p. it today and every day
W-pI ...199.5:2 Make it a part of every p. period you take.
W-pI ...199.8:4 Then p. well the thought the Holy Spirit
W-pI ...199.8:5 increase of joy your p. brings even to it.
WpI rVI.in.1:1 each day, and p. it as often as is possible.
WpI rVI.in.3:1 These p. sessions, like our last review, are
WpI rVI.in.3:8 of the special thought we p. for the day,
WpI rVI.in.5:4 exchange for the idea we p. for the day.
WpI rVI.in.7:4 it has been given, as we p. day by day,
WpI rVI.in.7:4 the way each p. period can best become a
W-pII.. in.10:1 Now is the need for p. almost done. For
W-pII..232.2:2 p. the end of fear. Have faith in Him Who
M-16..........3:8 of the more structured p. periods, which
P-3................h THE P. OF PSYCHOTHERAPY
P-3......... II.1:6 That, in effect, is the p. of therapy. These

## practiced 11

T-30.........I.4:3 These two procedures, p. well, will serve
W-in..........6:1 the exercises be p. with great specificity,
W-pI.....11.3:3 should be p. as casually as possible. It
W-pI.....13.4:1 are to be p. in a somewhat different way
W-pI.....14.2:1 are to be p. with eyes closed throughout.
WpI ...rI.in.2:2 though each one should be p. at least
W-pI ...129.1:1 that follows from the one we p. yesterday.
W-pI.134.13:1 Forgiveness must be p., for the world
W-pI.134.17:1 Forgiveness should be p. through the day
W-pI.136.17:2 And you will recognize you p. well by this
WpI rVI.in.2:2 the whole curriculum if understood, p.,

## practices 1

W-pI ...162.3:3 he receives each time he p. the words of

## practicing 55

T-15.........IV.h P. the Holy Instant
T-30.......I.13:4 have need for p. the rules for its undoing.
W-in..........7:1 ideas you will be p. to include everything.
W-pI.....12.6:1 times is enough for p. the idea for today.
W-pI.....15.4:1 In p. the idea for today, repeat it first to
W-pI.....62.4:1 begin and end this day by p. today's idea,
W-pI.....66.5:7 the premises for a while, as we are p..
W-pI.....94.5:1 meet the requirement of p. for the first
W-pI.....95.4:1 minutes of every waking hour for p. the
W-pI.....95.8:3 the instructions for p. the day's idea. This
W-pI.....96.8:2 Our hourly five-minute p. will be a search
W-pI.....98.7:2 will give the words you use in p. today's
W-pI.....99.9:5 Think of these things in p. today, and
W-pI ...102.3:1 our periods of p. to exercises planned to
W-pI ...103.2:6 periods of p. today with this association,
WpI . rIII.in1:2 every day for ten successive days of p..
WpI . rIII.in3:4 to your p. from those that you establish to
WpI . rIII.in4:2 are unwilling to cooperate in p. salvation
WpI . rIII.in4:5 But your p. can offer everything to you.
W-pI ...121.9:2 that they are one through p. forgiveness
W-pI ...122.9:1 we undertake our p. today with hope and
W-pI ...124.8:2 Secure your peace by p. awareness you
W-pI ...125.9:2 this, to let your p. today lift you above the
W-pI ...126.8:4 Him that He share your p. in truth today.
W-pI.134.14:3 Our p. becomes the footsteps lighting up
W-pI.134.16:3 p. thus far in willingness and honesty,
WpI . rIV.in7:6 we will use no format for our p. but this:
WpI . rIV.in9:3 Each day of p., as we review, we close as
W-pI.152.11:2 arise, and spend five minutes p. its ways,
W-pI.153.20:1 p. will now begin to take the earnestness
W-pI ...157.4:1 He will direct your p. today, for what you
W-pI ...161.3:2 And now it is specifics we must use in p..
W-pI ...164.3:1 How holy is your p. today, as Christ gives
W-pI ...164.4:5 remember. Faithfulness in p. today will
W-pI ...164.7:3 p. today becomes our gift of thankfulness
W-pI ...164.8:1 Open the curtain in your p. by merely
WpI ...rV.in2:5 *Lead our p. as does a father lead a little child*
WpI ...rV.in3:1 *do we bring our p. to You. And if we stumble,*
WpI ...rV.in3:6 *accept the Word You offer us to unify our p.,*
W-pI ...181.3:1 Therefore, in p. today, we first let all such
W-pI ...181.5:7 We enter in the time of p. with one intent
W-pI ...181.9:3 as we turn our minds to p. today. We
W-pI ...184.9:4 and in your p. it is this thought that will
W-pI.184.12:6 In our p., our purpose is to let our minds
W-pI.184.13:4 all. One Name we bring into our p.. One
W-pI.184.14:2 It is this Name we use in p.. And through
W-pI ...185.7:1 Let us today devote our p. to recognizing
W-pI.193.12:1 in p. the lesson in forgiveness in the form
WpI rVI.in.2:1 With this in mind we start our p., in
WpI rVI.in.4:1 and special forms of p. for this review. For
WpI rVI.in.6:5 or specific thoughts to aid in p.. Instead,
W-pII.....in.1:5 and find the end toward which our p. was
W-pII.....in.3:2 will not content ourselves with simple p.
Wfl ........in.1:2 use them but at the beginning of our p.,
M-20 .........5:9 sentence is our p. given its one direction.

## pragmatic 1

T-2........VI.7:3 more than a series of p. steps in the larger

## pragmatically 1

T-2....V.A.14:3 P., what has no real effect has no real

## praise 30

T-1.........I.29:1 Miracles p. God through you. They
T-1.........I.29:2 They p. Him by honoring His creations,
T-4...........I.8:1 forms of p. for itself in order to overcome
T-4.......VII.6:1 repeatedly states that you should p. God.
T-4.......VII.6:3 has no ego with which to accept such p.,
T-4.......VII.8:4 Their helpfulness is their p. of God, and
T-4.......VII.8:4 their p. of Him because they are like Him,
T-8........ IV.7:8 in p. of Him and you whom He created.
T-11....... IV.5:7 His Son lifts his voice in p. of his Creator,
T-13...... VI.9:3 of p. and gladness rise to your Creator,
T-13...VII.10:1 P., then, the Father for the perfect sanity
T-13..... X.14:1 P. be to you who make the Father One
T-13..... X.14:4 is fitting as a hymn of p. unto your Father
T-13..... X.14:5 See only p. of Him in what He has created
T-13..... X.14:5 for He will never cease His p. of you.
T-13..... X.14:6 United in this p. we stand before the gates
T-16........ III.8:1 holy Self all p. is due for what you are,
T-16...VII.11:5 P. be to your relationship with Him and
T-17....... V.1:7 hymn of hate in p. of its maker, so is the
T-17....... V.1:7 of p. to the Redeemer of relationships.
T19..IV.B.16:3 disciples chant the body's p. continually,
T-21........I.10:1 of their Creator gives p. to them as well.
T-22........ V.4:5 and would drown out the hymn of p. to
T-24.........II.4:4 you eternally in loving p. of what you are,
T-25.........II.9:3 if you but share His p. of what He loves?
T-25.........II.9:5 when any part of Him joins in His p., to
T-25.......II.10:4 believe that all His p. is given not to you.
T-26........ IV.3:5 of gratitude and love and p. by everything
T-26........ IV.5:1 and sing their song of gratitude and p..
W-pI.....50.2:3 They are songs of p. to the ego. Do not

## praised 2

T-4.......VII.8:1 God is p. whenever any mind learns to be
T-11....... IV.5:8 the Creator cannot be p. without His Son,

## praises 2

T-21...... IV.7:4 which sings the p. of another world,
W-pI ...189.2:2 and sings your p. as it keeps you safe from

## pray 22

T-9..........II.6:1 You can no more p. for yourself alone
W-pI ...78.10:4 and all the sightless ones as well, we p.:
W-pI......95.2:2 and capricious maker, to which you p.. It
W-pI ...131.2:7 while in your heart you p. for danger and
W-pI.140.12:1 lifted hearts and listening minds we p.:
W-pI ...168.6:4 To Him we p. today, returning but the
W-pI.196.11:5 P. that the instant may be soon,–today.
W-pII .....9.5:1 P. that the Second Coming will be soon,
M-19 .........5:1 P. for God's justice, and do not confuse
M-23 .........4:3 names of all the gods to which you p.. It
P-2....... VII.2:1 teacher and therapist, for whom you p.,
S-1 ...........I.1:5 It is impossible to p. for idols and hope to
S-1 ...........I.7:7 To p. with one who knows that this is true
S-1 ..........II.2:2 of his Identity could p. in these forms. Yet
S-1 ..........II.4:6 P. for yourself, that you may not seek to
S-1 ..........II.6:7 P. truly for your enemies, for herein lies
S-1 ........ III.1:2 Why, then, should you p. for others at all
S-1 ........ IV.3:1 those who p. together do not ask, before
S-1 ........ IV.4:1 a newborn chance each time you p.. And
S-1 ....... V.3:11 Now can you p. only for what you truly
S-3 ........ IV.4:1 You first forgive, then p., and you are
S-3 ........ IV.4:3 that you forgive and p. but for yourself.

## prayed 1

S-2..........II.7:6 and p. for separation from your Self.

## prayer 132

T-1.........I.11:1 P. is the medium of miracles. It is a
T-1.........I.11:3 Through p. love is received, and through
T-3......... V.6:1 P. is a way of asking for something. It is
T-3......... V.6:3 the only meaningful p. is for forgiveness,
T-3......... V.6:4 p. in the usual sense becomes utterly
T-3......... V.6:5 p. for forgiveness is nothing more than a
T-3....... V.10:1 As long as perception lasts p. has a place.
T-3....... V.10:4 Communion, not p., is the natural state of
T-4........ III.2:1 This is written in the form of a p. because
T-5.........in.3:7 That is why the healer's p. is: *Let me know*
T-9............ II.h The Answer to P.

T-9......... II.1:1 Everyone who ever tried to use **p.** to ask
T-9......... II.3:1 Bible emphasizes that all **p.** is answered,
T-9......... II.6:2 alone. **P.** is the restatement of inclusion,
T-30....VIII.3:4 a **p.** the miracle touch not some dreams,
T-30....VIII.3:5 And Heaven gives no answer to the **p.**,
W-pI.136.15:5 We introduce it with a healing **p.**, to help
W-pI.140.12:6 And we will say our **p.** for healing hourly,
W-pI.140.12:6 to hear the answer to our **p.** be given us as
W-pI.169.15:1 goal today does not exceed this **p.**. Yet in
W-pI.183.10:2 No **p.** but this is necessary, for it holds
W-pII .254.1:3 *I have no* **p.** *but this: I come to You to ask You*
W-pII .264.2:2 This is salvation's **p.**. Must we not join in
W-pII .307.2:1 this **p.** we enter silently into a state where
M-21 ......... 1:2 The motivating factor is **p.**, or asking.
M-21 ......... 1:4 But this refers to the **p.** of the heart, not
M-21 ......... 1:5 the words and the **p.** are contradictory;
M-21 ......... 2:4 The **p.** of the heart does not really ask for
M-21 ......... 3:1 The **p.** for things of this world will bring
M-21 ......... 3:2 If the **p.** of the heart asks for this, this will
M-21 ......... 3:3 impossible that the **p.** of the heart remain
P-2....... VII.2:2 For therapy is **p.**, and healing is its aim
P-2....... VII.2:3 What is **p.** except the joining of minds in
S-1............... h Prayer
S-1......... in.1:1 **P.** is the greatest gift with which God
S-1......... in.1:7 The Love They share is what all **p.** will be
S-1......... in.2:1 **p.** takes the form that best will suit your
S-1......... in.2:4 God. **P.** now must be the means by which
S-1......... in.3:2 **P.** will sustain you now, and bless you as
S-1......... in.3:4 For this is **p.**, and here salvation is. This is
S-1.............. I.h True **P.**
S-1........... I.1:1 **P.** is a way offered by the Holy Spirit to
S-1........... I.1:6 True **p.** must avoid the pitfall of asking to
S-1........... I.2:3 In **p.** this is not contradictory. There are
S-1........... I.3:4 In true **p.** you hear only the song. All the
S-1........... I.4:1 secret of true **p.** is to forget the things you
S-1........... I.4:3 **p.** you overlook your specific needs as you
S-1........... I.5:1 **P.** is a stepping aside; a letting go, a quiet
S-1........... I.5:4 And it is to Love you go in **p.**. Prayer is an
S-1........... I.5:5 **P.** is an offering; a giving up of yourself to
S-1........... I.6:1 a level of **p.** that everyone can attain as yet
S-1........... I.6:2 your help in **p.** because their asking is not
S-1........... I.6:3 Help in **p.** does not mean that another
S-1........... I.7:1 to Christ in anyone is true **p.** because it is
S-1........... I.7:4 are. Herein lies the power of **p.**. It asks
S-1........... I.7:6 This **p.** can be shared because it receives
S-1............ II.h The Ladder of **P.**
S-1......... II.1:1 **P.** has no beginning and no end. It is a
S-1......... II.1:5 At these levels **p.** is merely wanting, out of
S-1......... II.2:1 These forms of **p.**, or asking-out-of-need,
S-1......... II.2:4 And **p.** is as continual as life. Everyone
S-1......... II.3:1 for in this world **p.** is reparative, and so it
S-1......... II.3:4 that inevitably underlie any **p.** of need.
S-1......... II.4:3 have limited **p.** to the laws of this world,
S-1......... II.4:4 if you have enemies you have need of **p.**,
S-1......... II.5:3 The **p.** for enemies thus becomes a prayer
S-1......... II.5:3 thus becomes a **p.** for your own freedom.
S-1......... II.6:1 that **p.** at any level is always for yourself.
S-1......... II.6:2 If you unite with anyone in **p.**, you make
S-1......... II.6:4 become holy, then, **p.** becomes a choice.
S-1......... II.7:1 **P.** is a ladder reaching up to Heaven. At
S-1......... II.7:2 much like your own, for **p.** is part of you.
S-1......... II.7:7 **p.** can again become what it was meant to
S-1......... II.8:1 God is the goal of every **p.**, giving it
S-1......... II.8:3 **P.** in its earlier forms is an illusion,
S-1......... II.8:4 left. Yet **p.** is part of forgiveness as long as
S-1......... II.8:5 **P.** is tied up with learning until the goal of
S-1........ III.1:1 We said that **p.** is always for yourself, and
S-1........ III.1:6 For this the means is **p.**, of rising power
S-1........ III.2:1 The earlier forms of **p.**, at the bottom of
S-1........ III.2:7 could never make a **p.** like that.
S-1........ III.3:1 to recognize that **p.** will bring an answer
S-1........ III.3:1 only in the form in which the **p.** was made
S-1........ III.6:2 and therefore distort the purpose of **p.**.
S-1........ III.6:3 The desire for them *is* the **p.**. One need not
S-1........ III.6:5 and **p.** becomes requests for enemies. The
S-1........ III.6:6 for enemies. The power of **p.** can be quite
S-1........ IV.1:1 at least begins, one cannot share in **p.**. For
S-1........ IV.1:3 instant, it becomes possible to join in **p.**.
S-1........ IV.1:7 still in **p.** lies in this simple thought; this
S-1........ IV.2:1 Now it is possible to help in **p.**, and so
S-1........ IV.2:4 by those who join in **p.** is not the goal that
S-1........ IV.2:4 is not the goal that **p.** should truly seek.
S-1........ IV.3:3 **P.** for specifics always asks to have the
S-1........ IV.3:5 aim of **p.** is to release the present from its
S-1........ IV.3:6 What **p.** can offer now so far exceeds all
S-1........ IV.4:4 **P.** can bring the peace of God. What time-
S-1......... V.1:1 **P.** is a way to true humility. And here
S-1......... V.3:1 Now **p.** is lifted from the world of things,
S-1......... V.3:8 who comes to join in **p.** with you: *I cannot*
S-1......... V.4:6 **P.** has become what it was meant to be,
S-2......... in.1:1 Forgiveness offers wings to **p.**, to make
S-2......... in.1:7 Unlike the timeless nature of its sister, **p.**,
S-2........... I.1:3 chosen to begin the steps of **p.** cannot but
S-2........... I.3:6 How otherwise can **p.** return to God? He
S-2........... I.4:1 **p.** is always for yourself, so is forgiveness
S-2........... I.7:3 **P.** cannot be released to Heaven while
S-2........... I.8:6 And thus is **p.** restored to formlessness,
S-2........... I.9:3 that **p.** can be released from darkness into
S-2......... I.10:5 The level of your **p.** depends on this, for
S-2.......... II.8:7 From here is **p.** released, along with you.
S-2.......... II.8:8 **p.** will lift you up and bring you home
S-2........ III.4:3 undone, for **p.** is merciful and God is just.
S-2........ III.6:8 **P.** is His Own right Hand, made free to
S-3......... in.1:1 **P.** has both aids and witnesses which
S-3......... in.1:2 Forgiveness' witness and an aid to **p.**, a
S-3......... in.1:3 of a change of mind about the goal of **p.**.
S-3........... I.5:3 As **p.** within the world can ask amiss and
S-3.......... II.1:2 can occur at lower forms of **p.**, combining
S-3.......... II.1:7 wish is death a certainty, for **p.** *is* answered
S-3.......... II.4:1 This gentle passage to a higher **p.**, a kind
S-3.......... II.5:4 gate to higher **p.** and kindly justice done?
S-3........ III.4:4 It is like the role that helps in **p.**, and lets
S-3...... IV.1:10 join the song of **p.** in which the healed
S-3........ IV.2:1 As witness to forgiveness, aid to **p.**, and
S-3........ IV.2:2 quickened chorus through the voice of **p.**.
S-3........ IV.2:5 embrace of **p.** rest on the earth an instant,
S-3........ IV.3:8 Do not forget the holy grace of **p.**. Do not
S-3........ IV.4:2 Your **p.** has risen up and called to God,
S-3........ IV.4:5 In **p.** you have united with your Source,
S-3........ IV.6:6 you in **p.** beyond the sorry reaches of the
S-3...... IV.10:2 The song of **p.** is silent without you. The

## prayer's 2

S-2......... in.1:2 be vain to try to rise above **p.** bottom step
S-2......... in.1:3 Forgiveness is **p.** ally; sister in the plan for

## prayers 9

T-9 ......... II.4:1 If you would know your **p.** are answered,
T-9 ......... II.7:6 The answer to all **p.** lies in them. You will
W-pI..... 95.2:3 It does not hear your **p.**, for it is deaf. It
W-pI... 183.7:3 Think not He hears the little **p.** of those
W-pII .. in.10:4 Instead of **p.**, we need but call His Name.
M-29 ......... 2:2 Who would profit more from **p.** alone?
M-29 ......... 6:5 your **p.** of the heart into His language. He
S-1........ III.6:1 It is not easy to realize that **p.** for things,
S-3........ IV.7:3 and that his **p.** have never ceased to sing

## praying 7

M-21 ......... 1:4 the heart, not to the words you use in **p.**.
S-1........... I.7:1 **P.** to Christ in anyone is true prayer
S-1.......... II.2:3 of his Identity can avoid **p.** in this way.
S-1.......... II.4:1 in terms known as "**p.** for one's enemies."
S-1........... III.h **P.** for Others
S-1........ III.1:4 do it? **P.** for others, if rightly understood,
S-1........... IV.h **P.** with Others

## prays 3

S-1........... I.6:5 the goodness of God **p.** without fear. And
S-1........... I.6:6 one who **p.** without fear cannot but reach
S-1.......... II.2:5 Everyone **p.** without ceasing. Ask and you

## pre-empting 1

T-13 ....... X.2:8 by **p.** for your own ends what you should

## pre-separation 1

T-2 .......... I.3:1 The Garden of Eden, or the **p.** condition,

## preach 1

T-11 ....... V.9:3 can it **p.** separation without upholding it

## preaching 1

W-pI .... 37.3:2 that it is one with you, not by **p.** to it, not

## precarious 1

T-17 ....... V.5:4 the situation is experienced as very **p.**. A

## precede 5

T-10 ....... II.1:2 Knowledge must **p.** dissociation, so that
T-18 ..... IV.1:3 the willingness to let it come **p.** its coming
W-pI ...... 5.4:2 help to **p.** the exercises with the statement
W-pI .... 19.1:2 to thinking **p.** those related to perceiving,
WpI...rV.in4:1 the thought which should **p.** the thoughts

## preceded 3

T-3 ....... III.6:4 Knowledge **p.** both perception and time,
T-27 .. VII.13:4 unless a gentler dream **p.** his awaking,
W-pI ...... 6.2:2 be **p.** by a minute or so of mind searching,

## precedes 1

T-16 ..... VI.8:5 **p.** the actual transition, is far shorter than

## preceding 12

W-pI ...... 4.1:1 Unlike the **p.** ones, these exercises do not
W-pI ...... 5.1:1 This idea, like the **p.** one, can be used
W-pI ...... 5.4:1 these exercises, more than in the **p.** ones,
W-pI ...... 6.1:1 this idea are very similar to the **p.** ones.
W-pI ...... 7.1:2 Yet it is the rationale for all of the **p.** ones.
W-pI ...... 9.1:1 obviously follows from the two **p.** ones.
W-pI .... 13.1:1 idea is really another form of the **p.** one,
W-pI .... 13.4:1 somewhat different way from the **p.** ones.
W-pI .... 21.1:1 continuation and extension of the **p.** one.
W-pI .... 32.2:1 idea for today, like the **p.** ones, applies to
W-pII .. in.11:4 **p.** one of the holy and blessed instants in
M-25 ......... 1:1 to this question is much like the **p.** one.

## precious 6

T-14 ..... II.1:11 you have believed that nothing can be **p.**,
T-19 ..... III.7:2 guilt attractive and believe that sin is **p.**.
T19 .IV.B.14:2 Certainly what it is made of is not **p.**. And
T-23 ..... II.11:2 What is this **p.** thing, this priceless pearl,
T-31 ....... II.8:4 you thought were **p.** and in need of care.
W-pI 122.14:2 by. Remind yourself how **p.** are these gifts

## precipice 1

T-24 ....... V.4:2 to a nameless **p.** and hurl him over it. For

## precipitate 1

M-6 ........... 1:7 healing might **p.** intense depression, and

## precipitated 1

T-2 ....... IV.4:9 to a miracle, they may be **p.** into panic.

## precise 1

C-in ........... 1:1 nor is it concerned with **p.** terminology. It

## precisely 9

T-2 ......... II.7:6 weak **p.** because it has two edges, and can
T-2 ....... VI.8:5 **p.** the situation for which the Atonement
T-3 ....... VI.3:3 meaning is lost to you **p.** *because* you are

T-4......... II.5:4 you need **p.** what would hurt you most.
T-4......... V.6:5 with nonessentials is for **p.** that purpose.
T-9...........I.6:7 will, that is **p.** what you are asking for.
T-13......IV.6:1 the past are **p.** what you must escape.
W-pI.......7.2:2 is **p.** why you need new ideas about time.
W-pI.....44.3:4 requires **p.** what the untrained mind lacks

**preclude** 1
W-pI.......9.2:3 Yet that does not **p.** applying it. No more

**precludes** 2
T-9.......VII.6:2 Its range **p.** this. You can only go beyond
T-10....... II.4:3 of reality **p.** the acceptance of God's gift,

**preconceived** 3
W-pI.....28.3:1 to withdraw your **p.** ideas about the table,
W-pI.....79.8:2 succeed in letting all your **p.** notions go,
M-8...........4:3 eyes bring to it according to its **p.** values,

**preconception** 1
T-31...... I.12:1 every **p.** that we hold of what things mean

**preconceptions** 2
W-pI.....67.3:1 and **p.** about yourself to the truth in you.
W-pI...199.2:1 of time and space, unbound by any **p.**,

**predatory** 1
T-4......... II.6:8 and is therefore temporarily less **p.**. This

**predetermined** 2
T-6......V.B.4:3 here as always, is **p.** by what it is. The
W-pI.....74.7:1 be undertaken at regular and **p.** intervals

**predicate** 1
T-29....... II.6:6 become the law on which they **p.** their

**predict** 2
T-26... VIII.5:3 Who can **p.** effects without a cause? And
W-pI.....47.1:2 What can you **p.** or control? What is

**predictable** 1
T-7......... V.6:7 It is **p.** because it can be counted on.

**predisposed** 1
T-8..... VIII.4:4 those who want the ego are **p.** to defend it

**predominance** 4
T-4......... V.1:4 and raises control rather than sanity to **p.**
T-12.........I.9:9 fear conceals to clear-cut unequivocal **p.**,
T-17......IV.3:2 raised their substitutes to such **p.** that,
T-22......VI.1:6 one must serve the other and lead to its **p.**

**prefer** 34
T-2......VI.9:10 **p.** to believe that your thoughts cannot
T-3........VI.8:7 **p.** to be anonymous when you choose to
T-6......... II.7:4 ego would **p.** to believe that this memory
T-8......... V.1:3 recognize it because they **p.** the delusion.
T-13....III.10:1 **p.** separation to sanity cannot obtain it in
T-14......XI.2:5 yourself that you can possibly **p.** to keep,
T-15......IV.6:4 do, it will be only because you **p.** not to
T-15......IV.7:1 you would **p.** to have private thoughts
T-15......VI.7:8 Yet as long as you **p.** to be something else,
T-15.....VII.6:3 For it would **p.** to attack directly, and
T-15......XI.6:5 what you **p.** to keep that has no meaning,
T-16....... II.7:6 you **p.** the results of your interpretation,
T-16......IV.5:5 possible is which illusion you **p.**. There *is*
T-16....... V.7:5 not want for one he thinks he would **p.**.
T-18.......I.12:7 you not **p.** to heal what has been broken,
T-18....... II.4:5 a world that you **p.** *is* terrifying. Your
T-18.....VII.1:6 by those who **p.** pain and destruction.
T-21....... V.1:5 than what you would **p.** to overlook. The
T-23..... II.13:8 the substitute for Heaven which you **p.**.
T-25... VIII.1:6 that you **p.** He take it than that you keep
T-26..... V.6:10 convinced that where he would **p.** to be,
T-27....IV.4:10 "Which sin do you **p.**? That is the one
T-29.........I.4:3 of a promise made to meet when you **p.**,
T-29.....VII.1:9 Do you **p.** that you be right or happy? Be
T-29.....VII.4:6 but **p.** to seek outside yourself for what
T-30......VI.6:2 This means that you **p.** to keep some idols
T-30... VIII.5:7 him that you would **p.** to seeing this. And
T-30... VIII.6:2 to **p.** a dream allow uncertainty to enter
T-31......IV.3:2 Perhaps you would **p.** to try them all,
W-pI.....37.5:1 two phases of application that you **p.**. The
W-pI.....46.7:1 the original or in a related form, as you **p.**
WpI. rIII.in5:1 twice a day, or longer if you would **p.** it, to
W-pII..287.1:3 gift could I **p.** before the peace of God?
M-16 .........5:4 to sit up, in whatever position you **p.**.

**preferably** 6
W-pI....... 1.4:1 twice a day each, **p.** morning and evening.
W-pI.....38.4:1 periods, each **p.** to last a full five minutes,
W-pI...39.11:1 question, repeat today's idea, and **p.** both
W-pI.....41.9:1 it very slowly, **p.** with eyes closed. Think
W-pI.....61.5:6 **p.** with your eyes closed if the situation
W-pI...72.13:6 or so in silence, **p.** with your eyes closed,

**preference** 7
T-20......VI.9:4 false attraction your **p.** to the holy instant
T-26.....VII.6:5 that a hierarchy of illusions can show is **p.**
T-26.....VII.6:6 relevance has **p.** to the truth? Illusions are
T-26.....VII.6:8 Your **p.** gives them no reality. Not one is
T-26...VII.10:1 sigh that speaks for Heaven as a **p.** to this
T-27...... III.6:2 For you will give it overwhelming **p.**. Nor
T-27......IV.4:9 sin is real, and answers in the form of **p.**.

**preferences** 1
T-28......VI.1:6 it has no will, no **p.** and no doubts. It does

**preferred** 5
T-16....... II.8:4 **p.** to place still greater faith in the disaster
T-18....... II.1:4 solely around what you would have **p.**.
T-20... VIII.4:8 How can the engine of destruction be **p.**,
T-31.......I.11:2 reassessed; another outcome seen to be **p.**
T-31...... III.4:9 unless the mind **p.** the body change in its

**prefers** 7
T-15....... V.7:1 it **p.** different parts of another aspect.
T-24...VII.1:12 found another son whom he **p.** to them?
T-25......VI.2:5 and who can say that he **p.** the darkness
T-26......VI.1:8 can choose to keep the ones that he **p.**,
T-29...... III.2:5 in the dream His Son **p.** to his reality. He
M-8 ...........3:6 as "reality" is simply what the mind **p.**. Its
M-16 .......10:7 Perhaps he **p.** other words, or only one,

**prejudiced** 1
T-25. VIII.11:7 Without love is justice **p.** and weak. And

**preliminary** 2
T-6......V.A.6:1 This is a very **p.** step, and the only one
T-6......V.B.8:1 This is still a **p.** step, since *having* and

**premature** 1
M-24 .........3:6 in his **p.** acceptance of the course merely

**prematurely** 1
T-2........ IV.4:9 If they are **p.** exposed to a miracle, they

**premise** 12
T-3........ VI.7:5 the one inconceivable thought as its **p.**,
T-4..........II.8:3 free, however, to open the **p.** to question,
T-4..........II.8:3 question, because the **p.** is its foundation.
T-6.........in.2:3 the moment you accept any **p.** at all, and
T-7......... V.3:7 This belief is its totally insane **p.**, and so it
T-9......... V.1:5 for example, he may begin with the **p.**,
T-11.......in.2:7 Yet that is its insane **p.**, which is carefully
T-22........in.3:1 holy relationship starts from a different **p.**
W-pI..... 66.6:1 The first **p.** is that God gives you only
W-pI..... 66.6:6 believing if you do not accept the first **p.**.
W-pI..... 66.7:1 second **p.** is that God has given you your
W-pI... 170.9:4 Here is the basic **p.** which enthrones the

**premises** 18
T-6.........in.1:4 Given these three wholly irrational **p.**, the
T-6.........in.1:5 expected from insane **p.** except an insane
T-6.........in.1:6 the sanity of the **p.** on which it rests. You
T-6...........I.4:5 false **p.** and teaching them to others. The
T-6...... IV.11:3 exist. Fidelity to **p.** is a law of mind, and
T-7......... X.1:1 The Kingdom is the result of **p.**, just as
T-7......... X.1:5 You are willing to look at the ego's **p.**, but
T-7......... X.1:6 done the same thing with the **p.** of God?
T-7......... X.1:7 creations are the logical outcome of His **p.**
T-7....... X.1:11 they are the **p.** that will determine what
T-8......VIII.5:7 only if the two basic **p.** on which the ego's
T-8......VIII.5:8 Without these **p.** sickness is inconceivable
T-8......VIII.6:9 **p.** give rise in order to judge them truly.
W-pI..... 66.5:7 Let us, then, think about the **p.** for a while
W-pI... 66.10:2 the **p.** on which our conclusion rests. We
W-pI..... 91.2:4 This follows from the **p.** from which the
W-pI... 170.4:1 perceive the **p.** on which the idea stands.
W-pI... 184.7:3 what it rests, how questionable are its **p.**,

**preoccupation** 5
T-16..... VII.2:2 it overlooks the present in its **p.** with the
T-31..... V.14:1 has always been the great **p.** of the world.
W-pI....... 8.1:4 The mind's **p.** with the past is the cause of
W-pI..... 26.6:2 sense of imposition, fear, foreboding or **p.**
M-24 ......... 1:9 offers **p.** and perhaps pride in the past. At

**preoccupations** 1
T-4......... V.6:6 **P.** with problems set up to be incapable of

**preoccupied** 12
T-4..........II.6:6 continually **p.** with the belief in scarcity
T-10..... V.14:6 yourself to become **p.** with the temporal,
T-13....... V.6:6 hear, for you are **p.** with your own voice.
T-30.........I.1:4 to let yourself become **p.** with every step
W-pI....... 4.5:4 avoid a tendency to become pointlessly **p.**
W-pI.......... 8.h My mind is **p.** with past thoughts.
W-pI......... 8.5:3 with: *But my mind is p. with past thoughts.*
W-pI..... 43.6:2 you become **p.** with irrelevant thoughts.
W-pI..... 52.3:1 (8) My mind is **p.** with past thoughts.
W-pI..... 52.3:2 thoughts, and my mind is **p.** with the past
W-pI..... 67.5:2 your mind is so **p.** with false self-images.
W-pI... 181.4:2 quite **p.** with how extremely different the

**preoccupy** 2
W-pI....... 8.3:2 While thoughtless ideas **p.** your mind, the
W-pI..... 22.1:5 will **p.** him and people his entire world.

**preparation** 16
T-1....... VII.4:4 You will also need them for **p.**. Without
T-1....... VII.5:8 to start on these steps without careful **p.**,
T-6...... V.C.7:3 which is the **p.** for *being* without question.
T-18...... IV.6:5 The **p.** for the holy instant belongs to Him
T-18..... VII.4:4 it. Many have spent a lifetime in **p.**, and

T-18.....VII.6:6 Save time for me by only this one **p.**, and
T19. IV.D.11:1 upon the fear of God does need some **p.**.
T-27...... III.4:2 No **p.** can be made that would enhance
W-in..........2:3 They need no **p.**. The training period is
W-pI...92.11:2 will use the day in **p.** for the time at night
W-pI...98.10:1 let your time be spent in happy **p.** for the
W-pI. 140.11:2 only **p.** is to let our interfering thoughts
WpI. rIV.in3:1 us begin our **p.** with some understanding
WpI. rIV.in5:1 to the **p.** of your mind to learn what each
WpI. rIV.in7:1 After your **p.**, merely read each of the two
W-pI. 153.15:3 the least we give to **p.** for a day in which

### preparations 1

T-18...... IV.4:4 to make arrogant **p.** for holiness, and not

### preparatory 1

W-pI..... 67.3:1 thoughts drop away for a brief **p.** interval,

### prepare 29

T-4.......in.3:11 they will help **p.** you to undertake it.
T-4........ III.8:4 We will **p.** for this together, for once He
T-18...... IV.1:4 You **p.** your mind for it only to the extent
T-18...... IV.4:3 that it is needful to **p.** yourself for Him. It
T-18...... IV.5:8 Rather than seek to **p.** yourself for Him,
T-18...... IV.6:4 you will add, if you **p.** yourself for love.
T-18....... V.1:1 **P.** you *now* for the undoing of what never
T-18....... V.3:3 could you **p.** yourself for such a function?
T-18..... VII.4:2 **p.** for it without placing it in the future.
T-19....... I.15:1 so will faith help the Holy Spirit **p.** the
T19. IV.D.18:5 So will we **p.** together the way unto the
T-31...... III.1:2 As you **p.** to make a choice that will result
W-pI..... 15.3:7 to you. But they will **p.** the way to it.
W-pI..... 64.5:3 **P.** yourself in advance for all the decisions
W-pI...1[illegible].7:1 We will **p.** ourselves for this today, in our
W-pI... 105.7:3 you **p.** yourself to recognize God's gifts to
W-pI... 105.8:1 today, if you **p.** your mind as we suggest.
W-pI... 106.4:8 you. **P.** yourself for miracles today. Today
W-pI... 136.7:3 your world appears to totter and **p.** to fall.
W-pI. 153.19:2 ourselves in it, as we **p.** to meet the day.
W-pI... 154.6:4 sense, receiving to **p.** themselves to give.
W-pI... 165.3:2 instantly **p.** to go where they are found,
W-pI... 169.3:4 **p.** for grace in that an open mind can hear
WpI...rV.in4:2 Self we share and now **p.** to know again:
W-pII ... 12.4:2 altar where its sickly followers **p.** to die.
W-ep .........4:3 Let Him **p.** you further. He has earned
M-15 .........2:5 is your function to **p.** yourself to hear this
M-29 .........5:9 **P.** for this each morning, remember God
P-1.............5:6 and to **p.** additional teachers for His work

### prepared 22

T-6...... V.C.5:7 step the Holy Spirit has **p.** you for God.
T-18..... VII.5:4 of you. You *are* **p.**. Now you need but to
T-18.... VIII.9:4 **p.** by love for them where once a desert
T-18.. VIII.13:8 into the garden love has **p.** for both of you
T-19....... I.15:2 what has already been **p.** for loveliness.
T-20....... II.8:2 It has been carefully **p.** for you, and it is
T-22....... I.11:9 home **p.** for Them as earth is turned to
T-30....... V.4:5 And so is Heaven's Son **p.** to be himself,
T-30...... VI.6:2 prefer to keep some idols, and are not **p.**,
T-31....... II.1:3 There is no battle that must be **p.**; no time
T-31... VII.13:3 **p.** to look on only what the present holds.
W-pI..... 72.6:1 To this carefully **p.** arena, where angry
W-pI... 132.7:1 who are **p.** to learn there is no world, and
W-pI. 134.16:2 And now you are **p.** for freedom. If you
W-pI. 137.14:1 Yet must we be **p.** for such a gift. And so
W-pI. 137.15:2 rest in quiet, be **p.** to give as you receive,
W-pI... 168.6:2 He has **p.** for us He gives and we receive.
W-pI... 169.1:4 those who have **p.** a table where it can be
WpI...rV.in8:8 home, **p.** for us before time was and kept
M-14 .........4:3 be grasped by those not yet **p.** to leave the
M-28 .........6:1 are not **p.** as yet to welcome them with joy
S-3......... II.6:4 and was **p.** before time was and still but

### prepares 4

T-29 ..... IV.2:8 to awake, for which the miracle **p.** the way
W-pI... 157.2:2 and **p.** us for what we have yet to learn. It
W-pI... 169.1:3 until the mind **p.** itself for true acceptance
M-28 .........6:9 side, as he **p.** with them to meet his God.

### preparing 4

T-4 ....... III.8:3 taken the first step toward **p.** your mind
T-18 ..... IV.5:4 In **p.** for the holy instant, do not attempt
WpI. rIV.in1:1 this time aware we are **p.** for the second
WpI...rV.in1:3 are **p.** for another phase of understanding

### preposterous 5

T-23 ....... II.6:5 leads directly to the *third* **p.** belief that
W-pI..... 13.5:3 point, and will probably dismiss it as **p.**.
W-pI..... 71.1:4 This sounds **p.**, of course. Yet after we
W-pI..... 71.1:5 you will realize that, however **p.** it may be
W-pI... 163.7:1 The idea of the death of God is so **p.** that

### prerequisite 6

T-2 ...... VII.7:2 is only the **p.** for accomplishment. The
T-3 ....... VI.2:3 out that evaluation is its obvious **p.**.
T-8 .......... I.1:3 This is the **p.** for knowledge only because
W-pI....... 9.1:4 is a **p.** for undoing your false ideas. These
W-pI..... 10.3:5 you see it. As such, it is the **p.** for vision.
M-9 ........... 2:4 the obvious **p.** for hearing God's Voice, is

### prerogative 2

T-5 ........ V.5:8 and then takes this intent as its own **p.**. It
T-7 ......... X.7:1 of your false decision-making **p.**, which

### prescience 1

T-31 ...... V.9:7 you to have such **p.** in the things to come.

### prescriptions 1

T-8 ..... VIII.6:4 **p.** for avoiding catastrophic outcomes.

### Presence 44

*presence*

T-1 ......... II.3:3 only in the **P.** of the Creator of perfection.
T-1 ...... VII.5:3 awe is proper in the **P.** of your Creator.
T-11 ..... III.3:5 leap into Heaven, and into the **P.** of God.
T-11 ..... III.7:4 But be holy in the **P.** of God, or you will
T-11 ..... III.7:8 God's **P.** with the dark companions beside
T-11 ..... IV.5:6 *cannot enter God's* **P.** *if you attack His Son.*
T-11 .... V.17:7 in the **P.** of Christ they need demonstrate
T-11 . VIII.10:5 not disappear in the **P.** of God's Answer?
T-12 .... VII.3:1 but you can see the results of His **P.**, and
T-12 .... VII.4:3 are His witnesses, and speak for His **P.**.
T-13 ..... III.4:1 think you would be helpless in God's **P.**,
T-14 ... III.19:1 what you should do, think of His **P.** in you
T-14 ..... IV.2:5 You can perhaps feel His **P.** next to you,
T-14 ..... IX.3:9 for the **P.** that dwells within it *is* Holiness.
T-14 ..... IX.4:2 **P.** knows they will return to purity and to
T-14 ..... IX.4:7 **P.** of Holiness lives in everything that lives
T-14 ... XI.10:7 what He has established as holy by His **P.**.
T-15 ....... II.6:8 deny the **P.** of what the universe bows to,
T-15 ..... XI.2:5 In His **P.** the whole idea of sacrifice loses
T-15 ..... XI.2:8 for the **P.** of Holiness creates the holiness
T-16 ..... III.3:8 done that you could possibly deny Its **P.**.
T-18 ..... III.8:7 past and so make room for His eternal **P.**,
T-18 ... IX.12:6 is useless in the **P.** of your Creator, Whose
T19.. IV.C.11:6 Remember the holy **P.** of the One given to
T19. IV.D.19:1 will disappear into the **P.** beyond the veil,
T-26 ..... IX.3:4 **P.** which has lifted holiness again to take
T-26 ....... X.1:1 to be undone for you to realize Their **P.**?
T-26 ....... X.1:7 in whatever form, will hide Their **P.**. They
T-26 ....... X.2:7 **P.** is obscured by any veil that stands
T-26 ....... X.5:4 to let the **P.** of your holy Guests be known
T-26 ....... X.6:6 *this do I deny the* **P.** *of the Father and the Son*
T-26 ....... X.6:7 *see injustice, which Their* **P.** *shines away.*
T-29 ....... II.5:4 joy, and all the happiness His **P.** brings,
T-29 ....... II.5:7 you will believe His **P.** must be there. For
T-29 ....... II.5:8 without the love and grace His **P.** holds.
T-31 ..... IV.9:2 His **P.** and remembered not His Love. No
W-pI .. 124.4:2 our faith and our awareness of His **P.**. We
W-pI ..... 157.h Into His **P.** would I enter now.
W-pI .. 157.9:1 Into Christ's **P.** will we enter now,
W-pI .. 174.1:1 (157) Into His **P.** would I enter now. God
W-pII . 222.2:1 *minds, as we come quietly into Your* **P.** *now,*
M-11 ....... 4:10 earth bows down before its gracious **P.**,
M-25 ......... 2:5 Whose **P.** is always there and Whose
P-2........ III.3:9 existence. His simple **P.** is enough to heal.

### presence 58

*Presence*

T-in ........... 1:7 *the blocks to the awareness of love's* **p.**,
T-1 ...... VII.5:2 experience awe in the **p.** of your equals.
T-2 ....... VI.1:6 The **p.** of fear shows that you have raised
T-3 ....... VI.3:6 In the **p.** of knowledge all judgment is
T-4 ......... V.2:7 it would surely be in the **p.** of knowledge.
T-4 ....... VI.5:4 and the opposite of misery with its **p.**. It
T-4 ....... VI.5:8 of the ego in the **p.** of the rewards of God?
T-5 ..... IV.1:11 **p.** of those who hear the Holy Spirit's Call
T-6 .......... I.8:4 and the **p.** of the altar is what makes the
T-6 ....... IV.8:2 in the **p.** of God's accomplishments, and
T-7 ....... VI.9:5 since their **p.** implies a belief that what
T-9 .......... I.9:3 In the **p.** of truth, there are no unbelievers
T-9 ..... VIII.1:3 because in the **p.** of the grandeur of God
T-9 ..... VIII.4:1 immobilized in the **p.** of God's grandeur,
T-10 ..... III.3:4 not side with sickness in the **p.** of a Son of
T-12 ..... IV.3:2 would be totally inadequate in love's **p.**,
T-12 .... VII.4:5 as its **p.** becomes manifest through you.
T-12 .... VII.5:4 Of whose **p.** would you be convinced? For
T-13 ....... II.4:5 truth, and in its **p.** the ego is dispelled.
T-13 ....... II.8:6 For you believe that, in the **p.** of truth,
T-15 ..... XI.3:5 be brought to us and disappear in our **p.**,
T-17 ..... V.14:1 stand together in the holy **p.** of truth itself
T-19 ... IV.3:10 there of seeing, in the **p.** of His gratitude?
T19 .. IV.D.5:3 in the **p.** of the quiet recognition that you
T-21 ....... II.7:8 the **p.** of what you thought you gave away.
T-21 ...... VII.3:5 must be disbanded in the **p.** of strength.
T-24 ........ I.2:7 not deny their **p.** nor their terrible results.
T-26 ..... III.1:9 And how could strife enter in its simple **p.**
T-26 ........ X.1:7 And its **p.**, in whatever form, will hide
T-26 ..... X.1:11 Its simple **p.** shuts the door to Theirs, and
T-27 ..... II.14:5 left without his **p.** is perceived as all of you
T-27 .... VII.3:2 Your **p.** justifies my wrath, and you exist
T-28 ........ I.1:9 a cause can but produce illusions of its **p.**,
T-29 ........ I.7:2 of love, for in love's **p.** fear cannot abide.
T-30 .... VII.3:9 **p.** has no meaning but to show you wrote
W-pI .... 10.3:2 Now we are emphasizing that the **p.** of
W-pI .... 24.2:2 But in the **p.** of your conviction that you
W-pI .... 48.3:1 The **p.** of fear is a sure sign that you are
W-pI .... 58.3:6 me. In the **p.** of my holiness, which I share
W-pI .... 91.1:5 Its **p.** is not caused by your vision; its
W-pI .... 91.2:8 use it because its **p.** is unknown to you.
W-pI .... 96.8:1 whose **p.** in your mind is guaranteed by
W-pI .. 153.5:5 he has made; yet helpless in their **p.**,
W-pI .. 156.4:1 **p.** is so holy that the world is sanctified
W-pI .. 166.3:3 He must deny their **p.**, contradict the
Wi181-200 3:3 may be there, but you cannot accept its **p.**
W-pI .. 184.6:7 to accept its **p.** is the proof of sanity.
W-pI .. 187.8:3 its very **p.** proves that error has arisen and
W-pI .. 188.2:4 can deny the **p.** of what he beholds in him
W-pI .. 199.1:4 firmly tied to it and sheltered by its **p.**. If
W-pII . 332.1:5 its **p.** is the mind recalled from fantasies,
W-pII . 332.1:6 Forgiveness bids this **p.** enter in, and take
M-4 ........ X.3:4 that learning but disappears in its **p.**. Yet
M-4 ........ X.3:5 Yet while its **p.** is obscured, the focus
M-5 ....... III.2:2 The simple **p.** of a teacher of God is a
M-17 ......... 5:3 thought, by its mere **p.**, acknowledges a
C-4 .......... 5:11 just as its **p.** once had been your certainty.
P-3........... I.3:4 Some do not need your physical **p.**. They

### present 7

- verb
  - *noun*
  - *other*

| | |
|---|---|
| T-4 ........ I.10:7 | Do not **p.** a false and unworthy picture of |
| T-9 ......... V.7:4 | is to **p.** an example of one whose direction |
| W-pI ..... 21.4:1 | in which attack thoughts **p.** themselves, |
| W-pI ..... 72.5:3 | In trying to **p.** Himself as the Author of |
| W-pI ..... 79.4:2 | to **p.** you with a vast number of problems, |
| W-pI.135.24:5 | **p.** yourself to your Creator as you really |
| W-pI ... 156.2:1 | the thoughts that we **p.** in our curriculum. |

### present 107

- noun
  - *verb*
  - *other*

| | |
|---|---|
| T-1 ........ I.13:3 | They undo the past in the **p.**, and thus |
| T-2 ... V.A.17:4 | to remember is to recall the past in the **p.**. |
| T-3 ........ III.3:2 | the future and the **p.** will be the same. |
| T-3 ........ III.3:3 | that the future will be worse than the **p.**. |
| T-4 ......... II.1:3 | errors were not being repeated in the **p.**. |
| T-4 ......... II.3:4 | If this occurs in the **p.**, why is it surprising |
| T-5 ...... III.11:9 | and to come, and brings them to the **p.**. |
| T-13 ...... IV.4:3 | like the past, and thus avoiding the **p.**. By |
| T-13 ...... IV.4:4 | continuous without an intervening **p.**. For |
| T-13 ...... IV.4:5 | For the ego regards the **p.** only as a brief |
| T-13 ...... IV.4:5 | future by interpreting the **p.** in past terms |
| T-13 ...... IV.5:2 | The **p.** merely reminds it of past hurts, |
| T-13 ...... IV.5:2 | and it reacts to the **p.** as if it *were* the past. |
| T-13 ...... IV.5:4 | meet in the **p.** from a past reference point, |
| T-13 ...... IV.5:6 | past because, by making it real in the **p.**, |
| T-13 ...... IV.6:3 | mind, directing you to attack in the **p.** in |
| T-13 ...... IV.6:5 | you could find for release in the **p.**. The |
| T-13 .... IV.6:10 | cannot be, and the **p.** is without meaning. |
| T-13 ...... IV.8:2 | and it closes over the **p.** so that no gap in |
| T-13 ...... IV.9:4 | must be accomplished in the **p.** to release |
| T-13 ...... IV.9:5 | interpretation ties the future to the **p.**, |
| T-13 ...... IV.9:5 | and extends the **p.** rather than the past. |
| T-13 ...... IV.9:6 | you will lose sight of the **p.** and hold on to |
| T-13 ......... VI.h | Finding the **P.** |
| T-13 ...... VI.1:4 | His past has no reality in the **p.**, so you |
| T-13 ...... VI.2:1 | reference point from which to judge the **p.** |
| T-13 ...... VI.2:4 | past can cast no shadow to darken the **p.**, |
| T-13 ...... VI.3:5 | look without condemnation upon the **p.**. |
| T-13 ...... VI.4:2 | Past, **p.** and future are not continuous, |
| T-13 ...... VI.4:6 | past, **p.** and future for your own purposes. |
| T-13 ...... VI.5:4 | him from you, for truth lies only in the **p.**, |
| T-13 ...... VI.5:7 | in anger, and if you use it to attack the **p.**, |
| T-13 ...... VI.5:7 | will not see the freedom that the **p.** holds. |
| T-13 ...... VI.6:2 | Look lovingly upon the **p.**, for it holds the |
| T-13 ...... VI.6:5 | The **p.** is before time was, and will be |
| T-13 ...... VI.7:1 | The **p.** offers you your brothers in the |
| T-13 ..... VII.5:9 | He lives within you in the quiet **p.**, and |
| T-13 ....... X.4:3 | to it have no meaning in the **p.**. Yet you |
| T-13 ....... X.4:8 | you impose your idle wishes on the **p.**, |
| T-14 ...... IX.1:8 | past, and the **p.** was dedicated to illusion. |
| T-14 ...... XI.3:3 | its influence determines the **p.** by giving it |
| T-14 ...... XI.3:4 | *Your* learning gives the **p.** no meaning at |
| T-14 ...... XI.3:5 | learned can help you understand the **p.**, |
| T-15 ......... I.7:2 | is only what the ego has made of the **p.**. |
| T-15 ......... I.7:3 | prevents you from understanding the **p.**, |
| T-15 ......... I.7:5 | the Holy Spirit, Who knows only the **p.**, |
| T-15 ......... I.7:5 | which the ego would make the **p.** useless. |
| T-15 ......... I.8:2 | Fear is not of the **p.**, but only of the past |
| T-15 ......... I.8:3 | no fear in the **p.** when each instant stands |
| T-15 ......... I.8:4 | of God emerges from the past into the **p.**. |
| T-15 ......... I.8:5 | the **p.** extends forever. It is so beautiful |
| T-15 ....... I.10:4 | into the holy **p.** is salvation from change. |
| T-15 ....... V.8:5 | it will be when you perceive only the **p.**. |
| T-16 ..... VII.2:2 | overlooks the **p.** in its preoccupation with |
| T-16 ..... VII.2:3 | relationship is experienced in the **p.**. |
| T-16 ..... VII.2:5 | it is. It has no meaning in the **p.**, and if it |
| T-16 ... VII.2:12 | purpose could not be fulfilled in the **p.**, |
| T-16 ..... VII.3:9 | less obvious is that the **p.** is useless to you |
| T-17 ...... III.5:4 | the transformed past is made like the **p.**. |
| T-17 ...... III.5:6 | continuity extends the **p.** by increasing its |
| T-17 ...... III.8:1 | unholy alliance with the ego against the **p.** |
| T-17 ...... III.8:2 | For the **p.** *is* forgiveness. Therefore, the |
| T-17 ...... III.8:4 | which the **p.** is referred for meaning is an |
| T-17 ...... III.8:5 | offer to the **p.** as witnesses for its reality. |
| T-18 ..... VII.3:4 | it entirely, for sin is never wholly in the **p.**. |
| T-19 ....... II.7:4 | This is his past, his **p.** and his future. For |
| T-20 ..... II.10:1 | from the past, and has awakened to the **p.** |
| T-23 ...... IV.8:5 | It is their past, their **p.** and their future; |
| T-26 ....... V.9:3 | to you to see the past and put it in the **p.**? |
| T-26 ..... V.11:4 | back and forth between the past and **p.**. |
| T-26 ..... V.11:5 | the past seems real, as if it *were* the **p.**. |
| T-26 ..... V.11:8 | the bridge between the past and **p.**. Here |
| T-26 ... V.11:11 | It must draw you from the past into the **p.** |
| T-26 ..... V.13:2 | you cross the gap between the past and **p.**, |
| T-26 ... VIII.4:1 | your brother is apparent only in the **p.**, |
| T-26 ... VIII.4:2 | can it be overlooked except within the **p.**. |
| T-28 ......... I.5:8 | made to keep the past alive, the **p.** dead, |
| T-28 ......... I.6:4 | use of it, as if the past had caused the **p.**, |
| T-28 ......... I.6:6 | last. No change can be made in the **p.** if its |
| T-28 ....... I.13:6 | came in between the **p.** and the past, to |
| T-31 ... VII.13:3 | and prepared to look on only what the **p.** |
| W-pI ........ 8.1:5 | Your mind cannot grasp the **p.**, which is |
| W-pI ...... 52.3:4 | prevent the **p.** from dawning on my mind. |
| W-pI ...... 52.4:4 | is not whether to see the past or the **p.**; |
| W-pI ... 110.2:3 | is enough to let the **p.** be accepted as it is. |
| W-pI ... 110.4:1 | **p.** saved to quietly extend into a timeless |
| W-pI.127.10:4 | And we raise our eyes upon a different **p.**, |
| W-pI ... 132.3:1 | The **p.** now remains the only time. Here |
| W-pI ... 132.3:2 | Here in the **p.** is the world set free. For as |
| W-pI ... 135.1:4 | the past, or organize the **p.** as you wish. |
| W-pI.135.15:4 | It overlooks the **p.**, for it rests on the idea |
| W-pI ... 164.1:2 | The **p.** is the only time there is. And so |
| W-pI ... 169.6:3 | It returns the mind into the endless **p.**, |
| W-pI ... 181.9:5 | We look straight into the **p.**. And we give |
| W-pI ... 194.4:1 | your future as He holds your past and **p.**. |
| W-pI ... 194.4:6 | laid the past and **p.** in His Hands as well, |
| W-pII .. 293.1:4 | Yet in the **p.** love is obvious, and its effects |
| W-pII .. 293.2:3 | *is a real world which the* **p.** *holds safe from all* |
| W-pII .. 314.1:2 | is recognized as but extension of the **p.**. |
| W-pII .. 314.1:5 | grieve or suffer when the **p.** has been freed |
| W-pII .. 314.2:1 | *in the past, and choose to use the* **p.** *to be free* |
| M-2 ........... 4:3 | teacher seem to come together in the **p.**, |
| M-16 ......... 7:6 | as safe in the **p.** as he was before illusions |
| M-24 ....... 1:10 | At worst, it induces inertia in the **p.**. In |
| M-24 ......... 2:7 | always some risk in seeing the **p.** in terms |
| P-2 ....... VII.5:4 | can have; a certainty of past, **p.** and future |
| S-1 ........ IV.3:5 | the **p.** from its chains of past illusions; to |

### present 51

- other
  - *verb*
  - *noun*
  - *See also* ever-present

| | |
|---|---|
| T-3 ........ IV.1:2 | All of your **p.** functions are divided and |
| T-6 ......... I.18:1 | power of the Sons of God is **p.** all the time |
| T-13 ...... IV.5:3 | its image by responding as if it were **p.**. It |
| T-13 ...... IV.5:4 | reference point, obscuring their **p.** reality. |
| T-18 ... VI.12:2 | with something past, **p.** or anticipated. |
| T-18 ... VII.4:11 | a state of **p.** unworthiness and inadequacy |
| T-26 ..... V.11:9 | but still a **p.** light is dimly recognized. |
| T-26 ... VIII.4:4 | But **p.** joining is your dread. Who can feel |
| T-26 ... VIII.4:7 | it be that if you fear, there is a **p.** cause. |
| T-26 ... VIII.5:9 | It stands already here, in **p.** grace, within |
| T-26 ... VIII.9:6 | effects of **p.** cause must be delayed until a |
| T-26 ...... IX.6:1 | an ancient hatred has become a **p.** love. |
| T-28 ............ I.h | The **P.** Memory |
| T-28 ......... I.4:2 | of past events, but only of a **p.** state. You |
| T-28 ......... I.9:4 | miracle reminds you of a Cause forever **p.**, |
| T-28 ....... I.13:3 | in the way of glad awakening to **p.** peace. |
| T-28 ....... I.14:1 | aware of **p.** Cause and Its benign Effects. |
| T-28 ...... III.1:3 | The miracle alone is your concern at **p.**. |
| T-29 ......... I.7:3 | must be feared; and only sometimes **p.**, |
| T-29 ....... II.1:8 | must be **p.** where their cause has entered |
| W-pI ..... 10.3:1 | their past rather than their **p.** status. Now |
| W-pI ..... 13.6:3 | the practice periods. That will suffice at **p.** |
| W-pI ..... 20.4:3 | to change your **p.** state for a better one, |
| W-pI ..... 21.2:2 | **p.** or anticipated that arouse anger in you. |
| W-pI ..... 30.4:2 | to think of things beyond your **p.** range as |
| W-pI ..... 46.7:3 | of negative reaction to anyone, **p.** or not. |
| W-pI ..... 68.7:1 | arises against anyone, physically **p.** or not |
| W-pI ..... 95.4:1 | the stage of learning in which you are at **p.** |
| W-pI ... 131.8:6 | He wills to be, and what He wills is **p.** now |
| W-pI.135.16:5 | at all, for **p.** confidence directs the way. |
| W-pI.135.18:1 | happens, all events, past, **p.** and to come, |
| W-pI.135.19:1 | Your **p.** trust in Him is the defense that |
| W-pI.135.19:2 | Let no defenses but your **p.** trust direct |
| W-pI.135.21:1 | that time today with **p.** confidence, for |
| W-pI ... 181.5:3 | against **p.** change of focus in perception. |
| W-pI ... 194.5:2 | For the past is gone, and what is **p.**, freed |
| W-pI ... 194.7:6 | future pain has found his way to **p.** peace, |
| W-pII . 243.1:2 | what must remain beyond my **p.** grasp. |
| W-pII . 289.2:2 | *in a* **p.** *world the past has left untouched and* |
| W-pII .... 290.h | My **p.** happiness is all I see. |
| W-pII . 290.1:1 | is not there, my **p.** happiness is all I see. |
| W-pII . 290.1:6 | This the day I seek my **p.** happiness, and |
| W-pII . 293.1:2 | it. Love remains the only **p.** state, whose |
| W-pII ..... 9.4:2 | to die, or yet will come or who is **p.** now, |
| W-pII . 308.1:7 | come to give His **p.** blessing to the world, |
| W-pII . 314.2:2 | *and sure that You will keep Your* **p.** *promises* |
| M-10 ......... 3:3 | wide range of things; past, **p.** and to come |
| M-10 ......... 4:8 | know all the facts; past, **p.** and to come. |
| M-23 ......... 7:4 | without a very **p.** help in time of trouble; a |
| P-2 ......... V.6:7 | best can serve His Son in all his **p.** needs. |
| P-3 ........... I.3:1 | patients need not be physically **p.** for you |

### presented 3

| | |
|---|---|
| T-31 .... VIII.3:1 | that you failed to learn **p.** once again, so |
| WpI ... rI.in.1:2 | them will cover five of the ideas already **p.** |
| M-21 ......... 5:3 | to the **p.** problem as he perceives it, and |

### presents 18

| | |
|---|---|
| T-6 ........ III.1:4 | He **p.** no barrier to the communication of |
| T-8 ........... I.6:3 | curriculum **p.** an impossible learning task |
| T-13 ...... IV.7:7 | and only "now" **p.** the opportunities for |
| T-22 ....... V.5:2 | by the illusions it **p.** of size and thickness, |
| T-25 ......... I.5:1 | Heaven **p.** itself to you as separate, too. |
| T-31 ....... V.2:6 | The first **p.** the face of innocence, the |
| W-in .......... 8:1 | workbook **p.** you will find hard to believe, |
| W-pI ..... 32.3:4 | your imagination **p.** to your awareness. |
| W-pI ..... 35.3:1 | today **p.** a very different view of yourself. |
| W-pI ..... 43.9:1 | subject **p.** itself to your awareness at the |
| W-pI ..... 90.2:2 | *This* **p.** *a problem to me which I would have* |
| W-pI ..... 96.6:2 | the senseless conflicts which a dream **p.**? |
| W-pI ... 107.4:3 | the appearances the world **p.** engender. |
| W-pI ... 121.7:1 | Each unforgiving mind **p.** you with an |
| W-pI ... 159.3:4 | The darkened glass the world **p.** can show |
| W-pI ... 161.6:4 | its sight **p.** the symbol of love's "enemy" |
| W-pI ... 169.2:2 | grace **p.** a state so opposite to everything |
| M-3 ........... 5:2 | who **p.** him with unlimited opportunities |

### preservation 4

*See also* self-preservation

| | |
|---|---|
| T-4 ........... I.6:5 | their interaction as a means of ego **p.**. |
| T-4 ......... V.2:6 | with its own **p.** in the face of threat, the |
| T-14 ..... VII.5:8 | to means of **p.** and release. His task is |
| T-16 ....... V.4:3 | It is essential to the **p.** of the ego that you |

### preserve 21

| | |
|---|---|
| T-2 ...... VIII.4:3 | and choose to **p.** only what is good, just as |
| T-4 ......... I.10:4 | Do not listen to it and do not **p.** it. Listen |
| T-4 .......... II.9:3 | is only the ego's struggle to **p.** itself, and |
| T-6 ... V.C.10:5 | exerted great effort to **p.** what you made |
| T-7 .......... II.4:6 | therefore change the meaning to **p.** the |
| T-7 .......... II.5:2 | translates only to **p.** the original meaning |
| T-7 ........ VI.3:1 | The ingeniousness of the ego to **p.** itself is |
| T-7 ...... VIII.2:2 | The ego always tries to **p.** conflict. It is |
| T-7 ...... VIII.5:3 | onto anyone else, or you will **p.** the belief. |
| T-13 ...... IV.5:3 | the ego tries to **p.** its image by responding |
| T-13 ...... IV.6:6 | The ego would **p.** your nightmares, and |
| T-16 ..... VII.4:1 | seek not to **p.** it in the special relationship |
| T-17 ...... IV.5:1 | accepted is very anxious to **p.** its reason, |
| T-18 .... VIII.8:3 | giving, encompassing only to **p.** and keep |
| T-22 ...... III.4:6 | It would **p.** all errors and make them sins. |
| T-26 ........ II.6:2 | and good, and necessary to **p.** yourself. It |
| T-28 ......... I.7:2 | when he can learn and can **p.** a better one |

T-28...... III.3:5 in sickness, to **p.** the little gap unhealed,
W-pI.133.10:3 He who would still **p.** the ego's goals and
W-pI...135.2:4 gods, all serve but to **p.** its sense of threat.
W-pI...166.3:3 truth, and suffer to **p.** the world he made.

**preserved** 21
T-17...... IV.4:7 your holy relationships been carefully **p.**,
T19....IV.C.9:3 **p.** from every thought that would attack it
T-20...... III.5:6 picture of yourself is carefully **p.** by the
T-25.... III.8:12 Sin is attacked by punishment, and so **p.**.
T-25....VIII.4:5 is made that sin may be **p.** and kept. It is a
T-25.... IX.2:4 anyone, but cherished and **p.** in Heaven,
T-26.........I.3:1 the self, **p.** through sacrifice of all the rest.
T-26....... II.6:4 and no one whom you wish to be **p.** from
T-26.....VII.2:4 it may be carefully **p.** from reason's light.
T-26....VIII.9:8 and so **p.** because its form is changed and
T-27..... II.15:6 For only thus can He keep yours **p.** intact,
T-27...... IV.6:8 and thus the question is **p.** intact because
T-29...... VI.4:4 in time and change that time might be **p.**,
T-31...... III.5:2 Here are the thoughts of sacrifice **p.**, for
T-31...... III.5:4 In death is sin **p.**, and those who think
T-31....... V.6:6 his sins and yours **p.** and kept in darkness
W-pI...136.8:4 it. Thus is your "true" identity **p.**, and the
W-pI.136.19:1 needs to be **p.** by careful watching. If you
W-pI...168.3:1 He has most carefully **p.** within our hearts
W-pI...192.1:1 pure as He, of love created and in love **p.**,
W-pII .....3.4:5 away, but Heaven has **p.** for you in Him.

**preserver** 1
T-19...... III.2:4 Punishment is always the great **p.** of sin,

**preservers** 1
T-5........ VI.2:1 Guilt feelings are the **p.** of time. They

**preserves** 1
T-27..... II.15:8 him, **p.** yourself from the awareness of a

**preserving** 2
T-7........ VI.3:2 means that the ego attacks what is **p.** it,
T-24.........I.5:3 must make the body dear and worth **p.**.

**press** 2
T19. IV.D.16:6 **P.** it not like thorns against his brow, nor
W-pI...132.3:4 and tears, and all your sorrows **p.** on it,

**pressed** 1
W-pI...166.3:2 is to be **p.** to treachery against himself. He

**pressing** 1
T-13....... X.8:3 is **p.** everywhere upon him from without.

**pressure** 1
W-pI.....20.2:2 it as an effort to exert force or **p.**. You

**prestige** 1
W-pI.....50.1:3 "protective" clothing, influence, **p.**, being

**presumptuous** 1
T-21...... IV.6:6 in rage at your "**p.**" wish to look within,

**presupposes** 1
P-2....... VII.5:4 function **p.** a knowledge that no one here

**pretend** 3
T-21...... IV.3:3 for it to bother to **p.** it is your friend.
T-29 ..... IX.4:6 They **p.** they rule the world, and give their
W-pI. 166.11:2 that you are not what you **p.** to be. One

**pretense** 1
W-pI... 152.9:1 abandoning the false **p.** by which the ego

**pretenses** 1
W-pII ..... 4.4:4 Love which his **p.** cannot change at all.

**pretty** 1
W-pI... 161.4:6 can they seem to be but empty sounds; **p.**,

**prevail** 28
T-3 .........II.5:1 Nothing can **p.** against a Son of God who
T-4 ..... III.1:12 *protected, and the ego will not* **p.** *against it.*
T-4 ....... III.2:6 our united strength the ego cannot **p.**.
T-4 ....... III.3:8 to you **p.** against the glorious gift of God?
T-5 ..... IV.1:10 The ego cannot **p.** against the Kingdom
T-6 .......II.10:8 The ego cannot **p.** against this because it
T-7 ....... IX.2:3 cannot **p.** against a totality that includes
T-8 ........ V.4:6 Nothing can **p.** against our united wills
T-8 ........ V.4:6 because nothing can **p.** against God's.
T-9 ...VIII.11:3 Nothing can attack it nor **p.** over it. It
T-13 ..... XI.7:3 not **p.** against the peace God wills for you.
T-14 .. VII.6:11 His judgment must **p.**, and He will give it
T-14 ... XI.15:5 that nothing will **p.** against your peace.
T-15 ..... VI.5:8 In the holy instant the laws of God **p.**, and
T-16 .... VII.7:3 the power of the Holy Spirit will **p.**,
T-17 ..... VI.5:6 truly, for deception cannot **p.** against you.
T-19 ..... III.7:5 God created holy could not **p.** against it,
T-19 ... III.10:3 For sin will not **p.** against a union Heaven
T-25 ..... VI.5:1 the laws of God do not **p.** in perfect form,
T-25 .VIII.14:3 else but perfect justice can **p.** for you. And
T-31 ...VIII.4:1 The images you make cannot **p.** against
T-31 ...VIII.4:2 again, and let Christ's strength **p.** in every
T-31 ...VIII.5:5 *Son.* Thus is Christ's strength invited to **p.**,
W-pI.....34.1:1 that **p.** in the other way of seeing. Peace of
W-pI.....53.5:6 The images I have made cannot **p.** against
W-pI.....73.7:7 will is free, and nothing can **p.** against it.
W-pI... 137.8:2 that dreams will not **p.** against the truth.
M-18 .......3:10 *laws alone* **p.** *upon you and upon the world.*

**prevailed** 2
W-pI... 161.1:3 Christ where fear and anger had **p.** before
W-pII . 229.1:3 more. Love has **p.**. So still It waited for my

**prevailing** 1
W-pI... 169.1:1 most like the state **p.** in the unity of truth.

**prevails** 2
T-7 .........II.3:1 the law that **p.** inside is adapted to "What
T-8 ..........I.3:8 understand the state that **p.** within it.

**prevalent** 1
T-2 ........ V.1:2 is already very **p.**. This misperception

**prevent** 23
T-4 ....... III.7:2 of fear that **p.** the Holy One from entering
T-4 ....... IV.9:6 ego cannot **p.** Him from shining on you,
T-4 ....... IV.9:6 but it can **p.** you from letting Him shine
T-7 .........X.2:2 His you may deny, but you cannot **p.**. It is
T-8 ....... IX.8:3 can **p.** you from doing exactly what I ask,
T-12 .........I.4:1 is nothing to **p.** you from recognizing all
T-13 ..... III.2:7 because it would **p.** you from this. For still
T-13 ..... IV.5:5 surely **p.** you from recognizing him as he
T-13 ..... IV.6:6 nightmares, and **p.** you from awakening
T-13 ..... XI.5:3 fail. Nothing can **p.** what God would have
T-16 .... VII.7:4 will **p.** you from keeping the experience in
T-16 .... VII.7:5 not **p.** the timeless from being what it is,
T-18 .....II.5:19 unreality, and to **p.** yourself from waking.
T-20 ..... III.2:4 to keep them separate and **p.** their union.
T-22 ..... III.5:2 a mistake, the form cannot **p.** correction.
T-26 .. VII.12:7 seem to be beyond you to control or to **p.**.
T-27 .......II.9:6 sickness is desired to **p.** a shift of balance
T-28 .......I.11:3 to **p.** its radiant extension back into the
T-30 .......I.13:1 if you **p.** unhappiness from entering at all.
W-pI .... 43.6:3 exercises as often as necessary to **p.** this.
W-pI .... 52.3:4 **p.** the present from dawning on my mind.
W-pI .. 105.7:3 be free of all that would **p.** success today.
M-4 ........X.2:2 let go all things that would **p.** forgiveness.

**preventing** 3
T-18 ... VIII.6:4 it, **p.** it from joining with the rest, and
T-22 .... VI.7:2 your sight, **p.** you from seeing past it?
W-pI .... 65.5:6 *is* **p.** *me from accepting my only function.*

**prevents** 5
T-2 ....... VI.1:5 Fear **p.** me from giving you my control.
T-7 .........II.7:2 **p.** the learner from appreciating it. There
T-15 ........I.7:3 The belief in hell is what **p.** you from
T-25 .......II.3:2 hope that they may still be here **p.** you
T-28 ..... III.2:5 view. Uniting with a brother's mind **p.** the

**previous** 12
T-2 .........II.6:2 You correct your **p.** missteps by stepping
T-31 ..... VI.2:4 no one is exactly as he was an instant **p.**,
W-pI ...... 3.1:1 this idea in the same way as the **p.** ones,
W-pI ...... 6.3:1 of the two cautions stated in the **p.** lesson:
W-pI .... 11.2:1 somewhat differently from the **p.** ones.
W-pI .... 79.5:4 as you think you have resolved the **p.** ones
W-pI .... 92.1:1 for today is an extension of the **p.** one.
W-pI 135.15:3 obtained from past events and **p.** beliefs.
W-pI .. 181.3:4 And what we saw an instant **p.** has no
M-7 ........... 2:2 this, he should not repeat his **p.** effort.
M-9 ........... 1:7 which as many **p.** mistakes as possible are
M-20 ......... 2:2 way it is totally unlike all **p.** experiences.

**prey** 7
T19 .IV.A.13:1 to feast upon it and to **p.** upon reality. For
T-21 .......V.2:5 you are helpless **p.** to forces far beyond
W-pI .... 72.6:1 seek for **p.** and mercy cannot enter, the
W-pI .. 135.4:3 must be something made easy **p.**, unable
W-pI .. 192.5:2 will die, nor be the **p.** of merciless attack.
W-pII ..... 4.4:3 has become a body, **p.** to evil and to guilt,
W-pII ..... 5.2:6 could be his **p.**? Who could be victim?

**price** 30
T-9 .........II.9:5 There is a **p.** you will pay for judgment,
T-9 .........II.9:5 because judgment is the setting of a **p.**.
T-9 .......II.10:1 set the **p.** low but demand a high return.
T-9 .......II.10:2 forgotten, however, that to **p.** is to value,
T-9 .......II.10:4 The **p.** will then be set high, because of
T-9 .......II.10:5 The **p.** for getting is to lose sight of value,
T-9 .......II.11:1 you receive, and **p.** it by what you give. To
T-9 ....... III.6:8 You will not escape paying the **p.** for this,
T-12 ..... IV.6:3 pay no **p.** for life for that was given you,
T-12 ..... IV.6:3 given you, but you do pay a **p.** for death,
T-12 ..... IV.7:1 is not the **p.** of your wholeness, but it *is* the
T-12 ..... IV.7:1 but it *is* the **p.** of your awareness of your
T-12 ..... IV.7:4 is will, and will is the "**p.**" of the Kingdom
T-13 ......in.3:2 to this as the **p.** of salvation and *be* loving.
T-15 .... VII.9:2 suffering and sacrifice as the **p.** of union.
T-15 ......X.5:13 that remains is how much is the **p.**, and
T-15 .......X.6:8 fear. And that guilt is the **p.** of love, which
T-15 .......X.8:3 The real **p.** of not accepting this has been
T-16 ..... IV.5:3 always at the **p.** of making both illusions.
T-24 .... VII.1:6 no **p.** too dear to save his specialness from
T-27 ........I.4:6 Death seems an easy **p.**, if they can say,
T-27 ........I.7:6 Their death will pay the **p.** for all of them,
T-27 .......II.8:2 This is the "**p.**" the Holy Spirit and the
T-30 .......V.9:8 bought at fearful **p.** in coins of suffering?
W-pI .. 155.8:3 It is not a ransom with a **p.**. There is no
W-pII ... 12.4:2 the **p.** for faith in it is so immense that
M-5 .........I.1:3 He must think it is a small **p.** to pay for

P-3........ II.2:2 he became a therapist **p.** taught him little
P-3........ II.2:3 fact, it **p.** taught him how to make healing

## problem 155

*See also* problem-solving

T-2....... VII.5:8 to recognize temporarily that there is a **p.**,
T-3........... VI.h Judgment and the Authority **P.**
T-3........ VI.7:2 one cause for all of them: the authority **p.**.
T-3........ VI.7:5 is the result of the authority **p.** which,
T-3........ VI.8:2 When you have an authority **p.**, it is
T-3...... VI.10:3 is. The **p.** everyone must decide is the
T-3...... VI.10:7 This strange perception *is* the authority **p.**.
T-3....... VII.2:1 You cannot resolve the authority **p.** by
T-3..... VII.6:10 is the idea of an authority **p.** meaningful.
T-4....... IV.7:2 The **p.** is not one of concentration; it is
T-5......... V.3:3 spoke before of the authority **p.** as based
T-7..... VIII.2:6 you that you have gotten rid of the **p.**.
T-7......... X.3:3 **p.** is not whether what the Holy Spirit
T-8........ IV.3:5 and your **p.** in accepting it is the problem
T-8........ IV.3:5 problem in accepting it is the **p.** of this
T-9......... V.2:3 not have the answer to the **p.** of healing.
T-11....... in.2:3 The authority **p.** is still the only source of
T-11....... VIII.h The **P.** and the Answer
T-11.... VIII.4:4 You made the **p.** God has answered. Ask
T-11.... VIII.4:6 *Do I want the* **p.** *or do I want the answer?*
T-11.... VIII.5:5 Holy Spirit will answer every specific **p.** as
T-15.... VIII.5:6 understand your **p.** in communication,
T-16....... II.9:1 You have never given any **p.** to the Holy
T-17..... VII.1:2 and the **p.** were in the same place. The
T-17..... VII.1:3 The **p.** *was* the lack of faith, and it is this
T-17..... VII.1:4 As a result, you do not see the **p.**. Had you
T-17..... VII.1:5 it could be solved, the **p.** would be gone.
T-17..... VII.1:7 To remove the **p.** elsewhere is to keep it,
T-17..... VII.2:1 is no **p.** in any situation that faith will not
T-17..... VII.2:2 the **p.** but will make solution impossible.
T-17..... VII.2:3 shift part of the **p.** elsewhere the meaning
T-17..... VII.2:3 the meaning of the **p.** must be lost, and
T-17..... VII.2:3 and the solution to the **p.** is inherent in its
T-20.... VIII.5:7 There is no **p.**, no event or situation, no
T-21......... I.3:6 it would, the learning of it would be no **p.**.
T-21..... VII.7:6 decision leads to its effects is not your **p.**.
T-25..... VII.7:6 whose **p.** is their choices are not free, and
T-25...... IX.3:1 certain any answer to a **p.** the Holy Spirit
T-25...... IX.3:3 loss to anyone has not resolved the **p.**, but
T-25...... IX.4:6 Yet does the **p.** still remain unsolved, for
T-25...... IX.4:7 **P.** solving cannot be vengeance, which at
T-25...... IX.4:7 can bring another **p.** added to the first, in
T-25...... IX.5:1 The Holy Spirit's **p.** solving is the way in
T-25...... IX.5:1 solving is the way in which the **p.** ends. It
T-25...... IX.7:5 To give a **p.** to the Holy Spirit to solve for
T-26....... II.1:3 Every **p.** is the same to Him, because each
T-26....... II.1:4 whatever form the **p.** seems to take. A
T-26....... II.1:5 A **p.** can appear in many forms, and it will
T-26....... II.1:5 forms, and it will do so while the **p.** lasts.
T-26....... II.2:1 from every **p.** that you think you have.
T-26....... II.2:3 worked out so no one loses is the **p.** gone,
T-26....... II.4:2 Every **p.** is an error. It does injustice to
T-26....... II.5:7 time you keep a **p.** for yourself to solve, or
T-26....... II.7:5 What seemed once to be a special **p.**, a
T-26... VII.18:5 and no **p.** which is not resolved within its
T-26.... VIII.1:1 The one remaining **p.** that you have is
T-26.... VIII.2:3 that trust would settle every **p.** now. Thus
T-27...... IV.1:1 answered, and is every **p.** quietly resolved
T-27...... IV.1:3 A **p.** set in conflict has no answer, for it is
T-27...... IV.2:1 and every **p.** can be answered *now*. Yet it
T-27...... IV.2:7 a **p.** must be simple and be easily resolved
T-27...... IV.2:8 to solve a **p.** where the answer cannot be.
T-27...... IV.3:2 there the **p.** *will* be answered and resolved.
T-27...... IV.7:2 bring the **p.** to the only place that holds
T-27....... V.8:2 no one understands the nature of his **p.**. If
T-27..... V.10:5 to have a **p.** that is different from the rest.
T-27..... VII.2:2 is needed is you look upon the **p.** as it is,
T-27..... VII.2:3 way to solve a **p.** that is very simple, but
T-27..... VII.2:3 were made to keep the **p.** unresolved?
T-27..... VII.2:4 Without the clouds the **p.** will emerge in
T-27..... VII.2:5 because the **p.** is absurd when clearly seen
T-27..... VII.2:6 **p.** be resolved if it is seen as hurting him,
T-30......... I.3:1 This is your major **p.** now. You still make
T-30......... I.3:3 may not resolve the **p.** as you saw it first.
T-30......... I.4:3 first arise and then become a **p.** in itself.
W-pI..... 26.6:3 Any **p.** as yet unsettled that tends to recur
W-pI..... 38.6:1 **p.** concerning you or someone else arises,
W-pI..... 41.2:2 not do is to question the reality of the **p.**.
W-pI..... 41.2:3 cannot be cured because the **p.** is not real.
W-pI..... 47.1:4 to be aware of all the facets of any **p.**, and
W-pI..... 50.1:1 answer to every **p.** that will confront you,
W-pI..... 68.4:5 will never be a **p.** in motivation ever again
W-pI........ 79.h me recognize the **p.** so it can be solved.
W-pI..... 79.1:1 A **p.** cannot be solved if you do not know
W-pI..... 79.1:2 solved already you will still have the **p.**,
W-pI..... 79.1:4 The **p.** of separation, which is really the
W-pI..... 79.1:4 of separation, which is really the only **p.**,
W-pI..... 79.1:5 is not recognized because the **p.** is not
W-pI..... 79.2:3 Who can see that a **p.** has been solved if
W-pI..... 79.2:3 solved if he thinks the **p.** is something else
W-pI..... 79.3:2 you are still uncertain about what the **p.** is
W-pI..... 79.4:1 to keep the **p.** of separation unsolved. The
W-pI..... 79.4:3 which your **p.** solving must be inadequate
W-pI..... 79.6:1 desperate attempt not to recognize the **p.**,
W-pI..... 79.6:2 recognize that your only **p.** is separation,
W-pI..... 79.6:4 the means, because you recognize the **p.**.
W-pI..... 79.7:1 periods today we will ask what the **p.** is,
W-pI..... 79.7:4 will try to realize that we have only one **p.**
W-pI..... 79.8:1 which you do not insist on defining the **p.**
W-pI..... 79.8:4 given the answer by recognizing the **p.**, so
W-pI..... 79.8:4 that the **p.** and the answer can be brought
W-pI..... 79.9:3 that there is only one **p.** and one answer.
W-pI... 79.10:3 *Let me recognize this* **p.** *so it can be solved.*
W-pI... 79.10:4 suspend all judgment about what the **p.** is
W-pI..... 80.1:2 Your one central **p.** has been answered,
W-pI..... 80.1:4 thus depends on recognizing this one **p.**,
W-pI..... 80.1:5 solved. One **p.**, one solution. Salvation is
W-pI..... 80.2:1 Your only **p.** has been solved! Repeat this
W-pI..... 80.2:3 have recognized your only **p.**, opening the
W-pI..... 80.2:5 yourself by bringing the **p.** to the answer.
W-pI..... 80.2:6 answer, because the **p.** has been identified
W-pI..... 80.3:2 **p.** that has been resolved cannot trouble
W-pI..... 80.3:5 One **p.**, one solution. Accept the peace
W-pI..... 80.4:1 be ours when the **p.** and the answer have
W-pI..... 80.4:2 The **p.** must be gone, because God's
W-pI..... 80.4:4 The solution is inherent in the **p.**. You are
W-pI..... 80.5:5 Above all, remember that you have one **p.**
W-pI..... 80.5:5 problem, and that the **p.** has one solution
W-pI..... 80.6:3 for today to any specific **p.** that may arise.
W-pI..... 80.6:5 *Let me recognize this* **p.** *has been solved.*
W-pI..... 80.7:4 not deceive yourself about what the **p.** is,
W-pI..... 90.1:1 Let me recognize the **p.** so it can be solved
W-pI..... 90.1:2 Let me realize today that the **p.** is always
W-pI..... 90.1:4 that there is one **p.** and one solution. The
W-pI..... 90.1:5 The **p.** is a grievance; the solution is a
W-pI..... 90.2:2 *a* **p.** *to me which I would have resolved. The*
W-pI..... 90.2:4 *me. The answer to this* **p.** *is the miracle that it*
W-pI..... 90.3:3 I believe that the **p.** comes first, and time
W-pI..... 90.3:4 out. I do not see the **p.** and the answer as
W-pI..... 90.3:5 placed the answer together with the **p.**, so
W-pI..... 90.3:7 a **p.** which has not been solved already.
W-pI..... 90.4:3 *The answer to this* **p.** *is already given me, if I*
W-pI..... 90.4:4 *cannot separate this* **p.** *from its solution.*
W-pI..... 96.2:1 means you use and where you see the **p.**,
W-pI..... 96.6:6 real, nor solve a **p.** that does not exist.
W-pI... 109.3:4 There is no **p.** that it cannot solve. And no
W-pI... 126.1:2 would be no **p.** in complete forgiveness,
W-pI. 135.12:1 recognize the **p.** that the plan is made to
W-pII . 292.2:2 *promised us for every* **p.** *that we can perceive*
W-pII . 356.1:2 *matter where he is, what seems to be his* **p.**,
M-5........ II.1:9 such terms merely state or describe the **p.**
M-7........... 2:5 has given the **p.** to One Who cannot fail,
M-7........... 5:1 the outcome of any **p.** that has been given
M-7........... 6:6 you really want the **p.** solved, you cannot
M-7........... 6:7 you are certain what the **p.** is, you cannot
M-20......... 5:4 because it is not life in which the **p.** lies.
M-21......... 5:3 to the presented **p.** as he perceives it, and
M-22......... 2:1 for a time excludes some **p.** areas from it.
M-24......... 2:1 be the **p.** to be dealt with *now*. If it were
M-26......... 4:6 Behold the **p.**, ask for the answer, and
C-2.......... 10:4 is? **P.** and answer lie together here, and
S-1........... I.2:1 Spirit for the answer to any specific **p.**,
S-1........... I.2:2 that there is only one **p.** and one answer.
S-1........... I.4:6 advice about a **p.** of an instant's duration?
S-1........... I.7:8 for a specific **p.** will occur to either of you;

## problem-solving 2

W-pI .. 194.6:2 your mind, a habit in your **p.** repertoire, a
M-5........ II.1:5 If sickness is but a faulty **p.** approach, it is

## problems 73

T-4......... V.6:6 purpose. Preoccupations with **p.** set up to
T-7....... VI.9:4 Perceived **p.** in identification at any level
T-7....... VI.9:4 at any level are not **p.** of fact. They are
T-7....... VI.9:5 They are **p.** of understanding, since their
T-11 ... VIII.5:5 as long as you believe that **p.** are specific.
T-11 . VIII.10:5 **p.** will not disappear in the Presence of
T-13....... X.4:6 brothers to resolve **p.** that are not there.
T-14..... IX.7:4 bring their different **p.** to its healing light,
T-14..... IX.7:4 and all their **p.** find but healing there.
T-14..... XI.8:6 on miracles to answer all your **p.** for you.
T-14..... XI.9:2 no **p.** that He cannot solve by offering you
T-16........ I.2:1 certain types of **p.** and in certain people.
T-16 .. VII.11:2 to bless everyone and to resolve all **p.**, be
T-17........ I.6:5 attempting to solve his **p.** through fantasy
T-17..... III.6:1 The ego seeks to "resolve" its **p.**, not at
T-17..... III.6:3 seeks and finds the source of **p.** where it is
T-17.... VII.2:4 possible that all your **p.** have been solved,
T-17.... VII.3:2 If **p.** are perceived, it is because the
T-25..... IX.4:4 see. The world solves **p.** in another way. It
T-25..... IX.7:8 And then must **p.** rise to block your way,
T-25..... IX.9:1 little **p.** that you keep and hide become
T-26....... II.1:1 ask the Holy Spirit to solve all **p.** for you.
T-26....... II.3:3 You have no **p.**, though you think you
T-26....... II.6:1 there be no **p.** that justice cannot solve.
T-26....... II.6:3 It is these **p.** that you think are great and
T-26....... II.7:1 willing to receive correction for all your **p.**
T-27..... IV.1:7 be a way in which your **p.** are resolved, for
T-27..... IV.2:5 that all your **p.** should be brought and left
T-27..... IV.3:1 no **p.** but within the holy instant's surety.
T-27..... IV.7:1 attempt to solve no **p.** in a world from
T-27..... IV.7:3 answers that will solve your **p.** because
T-27....... V.8:1 **P.** are not specific but they take specific
T-27....... V.9:1 to **p.** that you thought were not your own.
T-27....... V.9:2 that your many different **p.** will be solved
T-31..... IV.1:1 escape from **p.** that its purpose is to keep.
T-31..... IV.2:5 Seek not escape from **p.** here. The world
T-31..... IV.2:6 was made that **p.** could not *be* escaped. Be
W-pI .... 38.2:4 can end all sorrow, and can solve all **p.**. It
W-pI .... 38.3:4 apply the power of your holiness to all **p.**,
W-pI .... 79.2:1 world seems to have his own special **p.**.
W-pI .... 79.3:3 of different **p.** seems to confront you, and
W-pI .... 79.3:5 you feel completely free of **p.** and at peace
W-pI .... 79.4:1 The temptation to regard **p.** as many is
W-pI .... 79.4:2 to present you with a vast number of **p.**,
W-pI .... 79.5:1 solve all the **p.** the world appears to hold.
W-pI .... 79.6:3 in all the **p.** that seem to confront you,
W-pI .... 79.7:3 different kinds of **p.** we think we have.
W-pI .... 79.8:3 reality of your version of what your **p.** are.
W-pI .... 79.9:2 You will see many **p.** today, each one
W-pI .... 79.9:4 In this recognition are all **p.** resolved. In
W-pI .. 79.10:1 Be not deceived by the form of **p.** today.
W-pI ....... 80.h Let me recognize my **p.** have been solved.
W-pI .... 80.1:1 If you are willing to recognize your **p.**,
W-pI .... 80.1:1 you will recognize that you have no **p.**.
W-pI .... 80.3:3 you do not forget that all **p.** are the same.
W-pI .... 80.5:3 Recognize that your **p.** have been solved.
W-pI .... 80.6:1 often today that your **p.** have been solved.
W-pI .... 80.7:2 to be free of **p.** that do not exist. The
W-pI .... 90.3:1 Let me recognize my **p.** have been solved.
W-pI .... 90.3:2 have **p.** only because I am misusing time.
W-pI .... 96.3:1 **P.** that have no meaning cannot be
WpI..rIII.in5:3 your seeming **p.** and all your concerns.
W-pI 135.23:3 the **p.** which you thought confronted you.
W-pI .. 198.5:1 hold the answer to your **p.** in your hand?
W-pII . 292.1:4 as the outcome of all **p.** we perceive, all
W-pII . 345.1:4 *form I need to help me with the* **p.** *I perceive.*
W-ep......... 1:7 you. He knows the way to solve all **p.**, and
M-4...... IX.1:5 begins by resting on just some **p.**,

M-4.......IX.1:6 give up all **p.** to one Answer is to reverse
M-11..........3:1 is the Answer to all **p.** you have made.
M-11..........3:2 made. These **p.** are not real, but that is
M-16..........7:5 no distinctions among the **p.** he perceives
P-2........IV.9:3 one of the most difficult **p.** with which the

## procedure 6

T-2.......VII.5:8 The initial corrective **p.** is to recognize
T-2..... VIII.3:1 thought of as a **p.** undertaken by God.
T-3...........I.2:3 This **p.** is painful in its minor applications
T-17......VI.2:4 the ego's **p.** this is reversed. The situation
W-pI.....38.5:1 time to time you may want to vary this **p.**,
P-3......... II.9:9 too, consider this strange **p.** as salvation.

## procedures 4

T-30.........I.4:3 These two **p.**, practiced well, will serve to
W-in..........3:3 description of the specific **p.** by which the
W-pI.......4.5:2 random **p.** to be followed for the exercises
M-16..........5:1 The same **p.** should be followed at night.

## proceed 10

T-1........IV.3:3 belief, from which only error can **p.**.
T-2......... II.6:1 seem to **p.** from one degree to the next.
T-2......... II.6:9 its various phases will **p.** in time, but the
T-7...........I.2:3 must your creative thought **p.** from you to
T-27....... V.9:4 All healing must **p.** in lawful manner, in
T-28..... II.12:7 salvation will **p.** to change the course of
T-31......IV.7:3 achieve a goal you must **p.** in its direction,
W-in..........5:1 of training in true perception does not **p.**
W-pI...136.3:4 to do, and then **p.** to think that it is done.
W-ep .........4:6 go; as sure as He of how you should **p.**; as

## proceeding 2

T-2........ I.5:12 conditions **p.** from lack of love in others.
T-13.........I.8:3 time, **p.** from past to future. No one who

## proceeds 13

T-1......... II.5:5 It **p.** from God to you, but not from you
T-1........VI.5:3 the true, the miracle **p.** along these lines:
T-6....V.B.1:11 is at its center, only deception **p.** from it.
T-7...........I.2:3 creative Thought **p.** from Him to you, so
T-7........IV.1:5 it **p.** from His Voice and from His laws. It
T-7......... V.3:7 insane premise, and so it **p.** accordingly.
T-7......... V.6:6 harmony, because it **p.** from integration.
T-7........VI.8:2 the ego **p.** perfectly logically to the belief
T-11.....V.14:6 the ego **p.** to the next step in its thought
T-28....... II.9:1 salvation, which **p.** to go the other way,
W-pI.135.11:3 what should be done, and then **p.** to do it.
W-pI...170.4:1 self-defense **p.** on its imagined way, you
M-19..........2:7 reaches indescribable heights as one **p.**,

## process 60

T-1......... II.4:4 God. In the **p.** of "rising up," I am higher
T-1........III.1:1 I am in charge of the **p.** of Atonement.
T-2...........I.1:8 This **p.** involves the following steps: First,
T-2......... II.6:1 Evolution is a **p.** in which you seem to
T-2......... II.6:3 This **p.** is actually incomprehensible in
T-2........VI.7:3 Then the whole **p.** of correction becomes
T-2........VI.7:3 steps in the larger **p.** of accepting the
T-2.......VII.2:3 circular **p.** that would not foster the time
T-2..... VIII.2:7 **p.** can be virtually immeasurable. It is
T-2..... VIII.3:5 might be called a **p.** of right evaluation. It
T-2..... VIII.4:2 **p.** of separation in the constructive sense,
T-3........IV.6:8 be an active **p.** of correction because, as I
T-3......... V.7:7 a continual **p.** of accepting and rejecting,
T-3........VI.2:2 Judgment is the **p.** on which perception
T-3........VI.3:6 and this is the **p.** that enables recognition
T-4...........I.1:2 and pupil are alike in the learning **p.**.
T-4......... II.2:3 Their interaction is a **p.** that alters both,
T-5...........I.2:1 Let us start our **p.** of reawakening with
T-5.......VII.6:4 yourself fully aware that the undoing **p.**,
T-6......... II.3:8 The **p.** begins by excluding something
T-6......... V.1:6 Giving His joy is an ongoing **p.**, not in
T-6......V.B.3:1 the reversal or undoing **p.** is the undoing
T-7...........I.1:3 This is an ongoing **p.** in which you share,
T-9...........I.4:5 in this **p.** is what you think you will lose.
T-12.........I.2:2 whole **p.** represents a clear-cut attempt to
T-14.....VII.4:3 Dissociation is a distorted **p.** of thinking
T-15...... IX.2:1 the necessary **p.** of looking straight at all
T-18.........I.2:5 Substitution is clearly a **p.** in which they
T-19.......I.15:3 the **p.** of making lovely that they begin.
W-pI.....10.3:1 aspect of the correction **p.** began with the
W-pI.....11.1:1 to a major phase of the correction **p.**; the
W-pI.....15.2:1 This introductory idea to the **p.** of image
W-pI.....23.3:4 Is not fantasy a better word for such a **p.**,
W-pI.....23.5:3 steps in this **p.** require your cooperation.
W-pI.....95.9:4 It is this **p.** that must be laid aside, for it is
W-pI...136.6:2 It is this **p.** that imposes threat, and not
W-pII..325.1:1 What I see reflects a **p.** in my mind, which
M-in ..........1:6 emphasizes that teaching is a constant **p.**;
M-9 ...........2:4 God's Voice, is usually a fairly slow **p.**, not
M-16 .........3:3 important throughout the learning **p.**,
M-21 .........2:3 and thus cannot help the healing **p.**. The
M-21 .........4:6 **p.** is merely a special case of the lesson in
C-in ...........1:6 is just this **p.** of overlooking at which the
P-2................h THE **P.** OF PSYCHOTHERAPY
P-2.........in.1:1 is a **p.** that changes the view of the self. At
P-2...........I.3:3 intrusions of the ego on the therapeutic **p.**
P-2......... II.5:5 **p.** of psychotherapy is the return to sanity
P-2........ III.2:2 patient. The aim of the **p.**, therefore, is to
P-2........ III.4:2 Christ. But healing is a **p.**, not a fact. The
P-2........ III.4:4 that stands at the end of the **p.** of healing,
P-2...........IV.h The **P.** of Illness
P-2........IV.4:4 How could such a **p.** cure? It is ridiculous
P-2............ V.h The **P.** of Healing
P-2......... V.4:6 can be sure that healing is a **p.** He directs,
P-2......... V.5:7 In such a **p.**, who could not be healed?
P-2........ VI.1:1 The **p.** of psychotherapy, then, can be
P-2.......VII.3:1 **p.** that takes place in this relationship is
P-2.......VII.4:4 in charge of the therapeutic **p.** and was
P-3......... II.6:2 may change their dreams in the **p.**. Yet it
P-3........ III.2:2 it. Nor will he find his healing in the **p.**.

## processes 1

P-2......... II.9:8 It is the goal that makes these **p.** the same

## procession 3

T19....IV.C.2:4 the slow **p.** that honors their grim master,
T19....IV.C.3:5 the funeral **p.** march not in honor of their
W-pI.....10.4:6 watching an oddly assorted **p.** going by,

## proclaim 16

T-6....... II.13:5 joining our minds in this light we **p.** the
T-14....XI.11:3 Teacher does God **p.** His Oneness and His
T-27.........I.10:5 its health and loveliness **p.** the truth and
T-29.....VII.5:3 No sadness and no suffering **p.** a message
W-pI.151.14:1 which joyously **p.** the wholeness and the
W-pI...166.8:2 could you then **p.** your poverty in exile?
W-pI...181.1:2 you **p.** that he is limited by what you have
W-pI.184.10:3 but only to **p.** its unreality in terms which
W-pI...191.2:4 You look on chaos and **p.** it is yourself.
WpI rVI.in.6:1 tempted, hasten to **p.** your freedom from
W-pII....10.1:1 Voice for God **p.** that what is false is false,
W-pII....14.4:2 the Voice for God **p.** the world as sinless.
W-pII..351.1:2 *And if I see him sinful I* **p.** *myself a sinner, not*
M-18 .........2:2 can they **p.** the truth about themselves.
M-27 .........4:1 does not **p.** a loving God nor re-establish
M-28 .........6:8 because he let God's Voice **p.** the truth.

## proclaimed 10

T-20....... V.2:4 single heartbeat is the unity of love **p.** and
T-21.......IV.8:6 What matters it to you how loudly it is **p.**
T-26.......IV.5:4 the tiny spot that sin **p.** to be its own. And
W-pI...162.2:2 Here creation is **p.**, and honored as it is.
W-pI...163.4:3 opposite of God **p.** as lord of all creation,
W-pI...181.9:1 world which once **p.** our sins becomes the
W-pI...189.8:8 For in that way is your reality **p.** as well.
W-pI...191.4:6 one fact is sinlessness **p.** to be forever part
W-pI...209.1:4 *The Love of God* **p.** *me as His Son. The Love*
M-15 .........1:6 He will hear his sinlessness **p.** around and

## proclaiming 7

T-14...... IV.1:2 For by **p.** it in him you make it yours, and
T-15.... III.11:3 **p.** together that the Son of God is host to
T-18...... VI.6:8 **p.** it to be the dwelling place of God's Son,
T-18....VIII.2:6 whole, **p.** that within it is your kingdom,
T-23.........I.4:7 in anger, **p.** it is part of itself no more.
T-26.......VII.7:5 **p.** sin has taken His reality from Him and
T-27........II.1:4 **p.** that the frail can have no trust and that

## proclaims 15

T19....IV.B.7:1 your holy relationship truth **p.** the truth,
T-20........II.1:6 still the gift **p.** his worthlessness to you, as
T-24...... IV.4:6 All that is real **p.** his sinlessness. All that
T-24...... IV.4:7 All that is false **p.** his sins as real. If he is
T-25.........I.2:9 the Christ in him **p.** Himself as you.
T-27....VIII.2:2 strips the world **p.** as valuable and real. It
T-27..VIII.12:5 The universe **p.** it so. Yet to its witnesses
W-pI... 139.9:5 as what we are **p.** what everyone must be,
W-pI... 153.7:2 It **p.** you have denied the Christ and come
W-pI... 161.7:4 surely as God's Voice **p.** there is no death.
W-pI... 190.1:5 For pain **p.** God cruel. How could it be
W-pI. 198.10:1 Accept the one illusion which **p.** there is
W-pII .223.2:3 *for guilt* **p.** *that we are not Your Son. And we*
W-pII .228.1:3 Shall I accept as true what He **p.** as false?
M-20 .........3:4 circumstance **p.** that peace is meaningless

## proclamation 2

T-19........II.2:3 Sin is the **p.** that attack is real and guilt is
T-21...... IV.2:7 this constant shout and frantic **p.**, the ego

## procrastination 1

T-2........ III.3:3 and you are capable of enormous **p.**, but

## prodigal 1

T-8........ VI.4:1 Listen to the story of the **p.** son, and

## produce 25

T-1.........I.45:2 **p.** undreamed of changes in situations of
T-1....... VII.1:1 perceptions **p.** a dense cover over miracle
T-2......... V.7:4 is no doubt that this may **p.** discomfort,
T-2........ VI.6:7 Only your mind can **p.** fear. It does so
T-3........ III.1:8 or love. Misperceptions **p.** fear and true
T-3........ VI.7:5 can **p.** only ideas that are inconceivable.
T-4....... V.4:11 the question can and does **p.** uneasiness,
T-4........ VI.2:3 and the holy perception it would **p.**. The
T-5...........I.7:6 change occurs to **p.** a real qualitative shift.
T-5........ III.4:7 the ego as guide. This is bound to **p.** fear.
T-5........ VI.8:3 the thoughts from the ability to **p.** fear.
T-6...... V.B.2:5 this will inevitably **p.** fundamental change
T-8...... III.7:10 imprisonment they seem to **p.** is no more
T-9........ VI.1:5 If it is in you and can **p.** joy, and if you see
T-9........ VI.1:5 and if you see that it does **p.** joy in others,
T-9........ VI.2:1 to you that the Holy Spirit does not **p.** joy
T-9......VIII.8:2 is not. Pride will not **p.** miracles, and will
T-11... V.12:10 sane realize that only attack could **p.** fear,
T-14........ V.5:3 have been denied to **p.** the need of healing
T19:...IV.A.7:1 in and push Him out *must* **p.** conflict. As
T-22...... III.9:2 Unholy values will **p.** confusion, and in
T-28.........I.1:9 a cause can but **p.** illusions of its presence
T-30.........I.2:6 but **p.** confusion and uncertainty and fear
T-31.........I.7:9 only outcome which your learning can **p.**.
W-pI.....53.2:3 They **p.** a world in which there is no order

## produced 10

T-7........ VI.4:4 Mind always reproduces as it was **p.**.
T-7........ VI.4:5 **P.** by fear, the ego reproduces fear. This is
T-9....... VII.5:3 from a sense of inadequacy it has **p.**, and
T-17....VIII.4:3 believing that the "something else" **p.** it.

### projection 52

|  |  |
|---|---|
| T-2..........I.1:7 | The inappropriate use of extension, or **p.**, |
| T-2... V.A.14:5 | substantial content, it lends itself to **p.**. |
| T-2........VI.5:7 | produces rage, and **p.** is likely to follow. |
| T-3..........I.1:6 | interpretation, which arose out of **p.**, has |
| T-3..........I.3:8 | is, and how entirely it arises from **p.**. This |
| T-6.........in.1:2 | Anger always involves **p.** of separation, |
| T-6..........I.3:3 | **P.** means anger, anger fosters assault, and |
| T-6..........I.9:3 | only because of the **p.** of others onto me, |
| T-6........ I.12:1 | be shared because it is the symbol of **p.**, |
| T-6........ I.14:3 | love made them vulnerable to **p.**, and out |
| T-6........ I.16:5 | of punishment involves the **p.** of blame, |
| T-6............ II.h | The Alternative to **P.** |
| T-6......... II.1:5 | it occurs **p.** becomes its main defense, or |
| T-6......... II.3:1 | Yet **p.** will always hurt you. It reinforces |
| T-6......... II.3:5 | **P.** and attack are inevitably related, |
| T-6......... II.3:5 | **p.** is always a means of justifying attack. |
| T-6......... II.3:6 | Anger without **p.** is impossible. The ego |
| T-6......... II.3:7 | The ego uses **p.** only to destroy your |
| T-6......... II.4:1 | however, that there *is* an alternative to **p.**. |
| T-6....... II.12:1 | The difference between the ego's **p.** and |
| T-6......V.B.1:3 | clearly the result of dissociation and **p.**. |
| T-7.......VII.8:5 | is the ultimate basis for all the ego's **p.**. |
| T-7.......VII.9:4 | **P.** always sees your wishes in others. If |
| T-7..... VIII.1:1 | said that without **p.** there can be no anger |
| T-7..... VIII.2:1 | ego's use of **p.** must be fully understood |
| T-7..... VIII.2:1 | **p.** and anger can be finally undone. The |
| T-7..... VIII.4:4 | makes, underlies its whole use of **p.**. It |
| T-7......... X.5:6 | in motivation, it can only be due to **p.**. |
| T-7......... X.5:7 | **P.** is a confusion in motivation, and given |
| T-10........ V.2:1 | to deny God will inevitably result in **p.**, |
| T-11.......in.3:1 | make by **p.**, but God creates by extension. |
| T-11.........I.9:1 | **p.** of the ego makes it appear as if God's |
| T-13....... II.1:1 | purpose of **p.** is always to get rid of guilt. |
| T-13....... V.3:5 | **P.** makes perception, and you cannot see |
| T-13...... IX.3:1 | gave it, for being nothing but your own **p.** |
| T-16....... III.4:6 | outside yourself, not by your own **p.**, but |
| T-18.........I.6:1 | That was the first **p.** of error outward. |
| T-18.........I.6:4 | upside down arose from this **p.** of error? |
| T-18.........I.6:6 | the mad **p.** by which this world was made |
| T-18...... VI.3:7 | by increasing the **p.** of its guilt upon it. |
| T-18...... VI.4:5 | its guilt, but it will not lose it through **p.**. |
| T-20... VIII.9:9 | For it is the **p.** that gives the "nothing" all |
| T-21........in.1:1 | **P.** makes perception. The world you see |
| T-22..... II.10:1 | Behold the great **p.**, but look on it with |
| T-26........ X.3:4 | **P.** of the cause of sacrifice is at the root of |
| W-pI......30.2:1 | we are trying to use a new kind of "**p.**" |
| W-pI......51.3:3 | I see is the **p.** of my own errors of thought |
| W-pI...196.9:3 | the deadly fear of God **p.** hides behind. |
| W-pII......1.2:3 | The thought protects **p.**, tightening its |
| W-pII......1.2:4 | come between a fixed **p.** and the aim that |
| M-4........ X.1:5 | As the **p.** of guilt upon him would send |
| P-2........VI.6:6 | patient is his screen for the **p.** of his sins, |

### projections 11

|  |  |
|---|---|
| T-2......... II.2:5 | results in miscreation, the **p.** of the ego. |
| T-7... VIII.3:10 | that their **p.** will return and hurt them. |
| T-7... VIII.3:11 | Believing they have blotted their **p.** from |
| T-7... VIII.3:11 | believe their **p.** are trying to creep back in. |
| T-7... VIII.3:12 | in. Since the **p.** have not left their minds, |
| T-18.........I.8:4 | He brings all your insane **p.** and the wild |
| T-20... VIII.9:8 | Yet upon nothing are all **p.** made. For it is |
| W-pI...121.4:2 | and shrieks as it beholds its own **p.** rising |
| W-pI...190.2:1 | Can such **p.** be attested to? Can they be |
| P-1.............4:2 | on him were made by his **p.** on the world. |
| S-1........ III.1:4 | lifting your **p.** of guilt from your brother, |

### projects 7

|  |  |
|---|---|
| T-6......... II.4:3 | The Holy Spirit extends and the ego **p.**. |
| T-6....... II.12:2 | The ego **p.** to exclude, and therefore to |
| T-6......V.B.3:8 | the mind of the learner **p.** its own conflict, |
| T-7..... VIII.2:6 | **p.** conflict from your mind to other minds |
| T-12...... III.7:4 | Therefore the mind **p.** the split, not the |
| T-14.........I.3:3 | The thoughts the mind of God's Son **p.** or |
| T-29.....VII.9:2 | making real the picture it **p.** outside itself |

### prominent 1

|  |  |
|---|---|
| T-3..........I.2:6 | it up in view of its **p.** value as a defense. In |

### promise 48

|  |  |
|---|---|
| T-12...... IV.1:5 | This is the one **p.** the ego holds out to you |
| T-12...... IV.1:5 | out to you, and the one **p.** it will keep. For |
| T-12...... IV.4:3 | Is this the **p.** you would keep? The Holy |
| T-12...... IV.4:4 | The Holy Spirit offers you another **p.**, and |
| T-12...... IV.4:5 | For His **p.** is always, "Seek and you *will* |
| T-14... VIII.1:8 | He shares with God the **p.** that was given |
| T-14... VIII.2:2 | He will replace with the one **p.** given unto |
| T19. IV.A.16:4 | there, as long ago I promised and **p.** still. |
| T19... IV.D.3:2 | the **p.** made in secret to the ego never to |
| T19... IV.D.3:4 | **p.** never to allow union to call you out of |
| T19... IV.D.6:2 | remembering your **p.** to your "friends." |
| T-20.........I.3:2 | sign of victory, the **p.** of the resurrection, |
| T-20.... III.11:8 | of God's eternal **p.** of your immortality. |
| T-21.... VIII.3:4 | out some **p.** of the power of giving it. He |
| T-27.......I.10:3 | become a sign of life, a **p.** of redemption, |
| T-28...... VI.4:7 | Yet it is a **p.** to another to be hurt by him, |
| T-28...... VI.5:4 | my mind and yours" has kept God's **p.**, |
| T-28...... VI.6:2 | will keep the **p.** that you make with him, |
| T-28...... VI.6:6 | "I will," though in that **p.** he was born. |
| T-28...... VI.6:7 | time he does not share a **p.** to be sick, but |
| T-28...... VI.6:9 | will, who has made **p.** of himself to God. |
| T-28..... VII.1:6 | God's **p.** is a promise to Himself, and |
| T-28..... VII.1:6 | God's promise is a **p.** to Himself, and |
| T-28..... VII.1:7 | **p.** that there is no gap between Himself |
| T-28..... VII.3:3 | straw that seems to hold some **p.** of relief. |
| T-28..... VII.5:5 | to keep a **p.** to be true to faithlessness. Yet |
| T-28..... VII.7:2 | No secret **p.** you have made instead has |
| T-28..... VII.7:5 | on God's **p.** that His Son is safe forever in |
| T-29.........I.4:3 | of a **p.** made to meet when you prefer, |
| T-29....... II.6:1 | Such is the **p.** of the living God; His Son |
| T-30.........I.7:5 | yourself the rules that **p.** you a happy day. |
| T-30.......I.17:1 | happiness this day to **p.** it to all the world. |
| T-31...... VI.6:7 | and without the **p.** of corruption and the |
| W-pI....95.15:2 | sure to give the **p.** of today's idea and tell |
| W-pI.....98.6:2 | purpose, with the **p.** of complete success. |
| W-pI...106.4:1 | Today the **p.** of God's Word is kept. Hear |
| W-pI.107.10:2 | For you will bring with you the **p.** of the |
| W-pI...122.3:5 | fancied value, trivial effect or transient **p.**, |
| W-pI.131.14:4 | God keeps His ancient **p.** to His holy Son, |
| W-pI...157.1:2 | special time of **p.** in your calendar of days. |
| W-pI...164.9:7 | Can His **p.** fail? Can you withhold so little, |
| W-pII......2.1:1 | Salvation is a **p.**, made by God, that you |
| W-pII......8.4:2 | Love; the certain **p.** that he is redeemed. |
| W-pII..336.2:2 | *and find Your* **p.** *of my sinlessness is kept;* |
| W-pII..338.2:5 | *home, because it holds Your* **p.** *to Your Son.* |
| W-pII..348.1:6 | *be afraid, when Your eternal* **p.** *goes with me* |
| W-pII..358.1:6 | *Your* **p.** *to Your Son in my awareness always.* |
| S-2........ III.1:4 | nor **p.** freedom while it asks for death. |

### promised 30

|  |  |
|---|---|
| T-11.... VIII.8:1 | God, you are asking only for what I **p.** you |
| T-14... VIII.1:7 | has **p.** the Father that through Him you |
| T-14... VIII.1:8 | To what He **p.** God He is wholly faithful, |
| T19. IV.A.16:4 | there, as long ago I **p.** and promise still. |
| T-28..... VII.1:5 | the Will of Either, Who have **p.** to be One. |
| T-28..... VII.7:1 | and everything his Father **p.** him. No |
| W-pI.....75.8:2 | to look upon the world He **p.** you. From |
| W-pI.....75.8:5 | that has been **p.** you since time began, |
| W-pI.....77.3:2 | **p.** full release from the world you made. |
| W-pI.....94.4:2 | God has Himself **p.** that it will be revealed |
| W-pI.....97.4:2 | count on Him Who **p.** to lay timelessness |
| W-pI...110.5:5 | This is the truth that God has **p.** you. This |
| W-pI...127.9:2 | He Himself has **p.** this. And He Himself |
| WpI...rV.in5:4 | dust to life, as we remember this is **p.** us, |
| W-pII.....in.2:3 | has **p.** He will take the final step Himself. |
| W-pII.....in.3:3 | our Father to reveal Himself, as He has **p.**. |
| W-pII.....in.3:4 | He has **p.** that His Son will not remain |
| W-pII..279.1:1 | The end of dreams is **p.** me, because |
| W-pII..286.2:2 | the end which God Himself has **p.** us. We |
| W-pII..292.2:2 | *delay the happy endings You have* **p.** *us for* |
| W-pII..317.2:5 | *embrace, which You have* **p.** *to Your Son,* |
| W-pII..327.1:2 | For God has **p.** He will hear my call, and |
| W-pII..355.1:1 | *I wait, my Father, for the joy You* **p.** *me? For* |
| W-pII.356.1:1 | *You* **p.** *You would never fail to answer any* |
| Wfl........in.5:1 | the gift our Father **p.** to His holy Son. We |
| M-2 ...........5:4 | and God has **p.** to send His Spirit into any |
| M-11 .........1:4 | as this. His Word has **p.** peace. It has also |
| M-11 .........1:5 | It has also **p.** that there is no death, that |
| M-11 .........1:7 | Word has **p.** that peace is possible here, |
| P-3........ III.4:2 | for. It is **p.** him, and guaranteed by God. |

### promises 27

|  |  |
|---|---|
| T-14....VIII.2:2 | Everything that **p.** otherwise, great or |
| T-21.........I.3:5 | is learned will bring to you the joy it **p.**. If |
| T-28...... VI.6:3 | God keeps His **p.**; His Son keeps his. In |
| T-28...... VI.6:8 | the Will of God, Whose **p.** he shares. And |
| T-29....... V.7:6 | rusted sword, to keep his ancient **p.** to die |
| W-pI.....71.5:2 | if you are to succeed, as God **p.** you will, |
| W-pI.....72.5:3 | full of false **p.** and offering illusions in |
| W-pI.135.19:1 | is the defense that **p.** a future undisturbed |
| W-pI...154.4:2 | not obey; which **p.** salvation from all sin, |
| W-pI...156.1:2 | It **p.** there is no cause for guilt, and being |
| W-pII ....in.2:4 | And we are sure His **p.** are kept. We have |
| W-pII ....in.5:2 | are all ancient **p.** upheld and fully kept. |
| W-pII ....in.7:5 | We ask but that Your ancient **p.** be kept |
| W-pII ....279.h | Creation's freedom **p.** my own. |
| W-pII .279.2:1 | *I will accept Your* **p.** *today, and give my faith* |
| W-pII .292.1:1 | God's **p.** make no exceptions. And He |
| W-pII .314.2:2 | *and sure that You will keep Your present* **p.**, |
| W-pII .327.2:1 | *that Your* **p.** *will never fail in my experience,* |
| W-pII .338.2:5 | *Thought You gave me* **p.** *to lead me home,* |
| M-11 .........1:3 | God **p.** other things that seem impossible, |
| M-11 .........1:7 | and what He **p.** can hardly be impossible. |
| M-11 .........1:8 | at differently, if His **p.** are to be accepted. |
| M-15 .........3:7 | His **p.** are sure. Only remember that. His |
| M-15 .........3:9 | His **p.** have guaranteed His Judgment, |
| M-23 .........3:7 | this? Remember his **p.**, and ask yourself |
| P-2......... V.6:2 | And now God's **p.** are kept by Him. The |
| S-3.........in.1:1 | offering the comfort and the **p.** of hope. |

### promising 1

|  |  |
|---|---|
| T-24.... VI.12:1 | of God maintaining it, and **p.** success. Yet |

### promote 1

|  |  |
|---|---|
| T-7....... VII.8:1 | Attack could never **p.** attack unless you |

### promotes 6

|  |  |
|---|---|
| T-5.........in.1:6 | **p.** the mind's natural impulse to respond |
| T-5..........II.1:2 | Holy Spirit **p.** healing by looking beyond |
| T-6...........I.3:3 | anger fosters assault, and assault **p.** fear. |
| T-6...... V.C.1:9 | vary, and that is why it **p.** different moods |
| T-8...... VII.4:2 | Attack **p.** it. The body is beautiful or ugly, |
| T-8..... VII.13:2 | your learning **p.** depression instead of joy, |

### promoting 1

|  |  |
|---|---|
| T-6...... V.A.5:8 | who communicate fear are **p.** attack, and |

### prone

*See* fear-prone

### pronounced 1

|  |  |
|---|---|
| P-3..........II.4:1 | looked on all He created and **p.** it good. |

### pronouncing 1

|  |  |
|---|---|
| T-18...... IX.3:2 | bear witness to this world, **p.** it as true. |

### proof 51

*See also* fool-proof, God-proof

|  |  |
|---|---|
| T-9..........II.1:3 | as "**p.**" that the course does not mean |
| T-13.........I.2:4 | of Christ is the **p.** that the ego never was, |
| T-13...... IV.2:5 | destruction is the final **p.** that you were |
| T-14.........I.2:1 | Indirect **p.** of truth is needed in a world |
| T-16.........I.2:1 | clearest **p.** that empathy as the ego uses it |

|  |  |
|---|---|
| T-19...... III.7:3 | p. of separation seems to be everywhere. |
| T19..IV.B.12:2 | for it is one the ego sees as p. of sin. It is |
| T19....IV.C.8:1 | orders, p. in his decay that God Himself is |
| T-21....... V.5:9 | is p. you will not find the answer there. |
| T-21... VII.13:5 | Son of God's desire remains the p. that he |
| T-21.... VIII.1:5 | the final p. he valued the inconstant more |
| T-27.........I.2:2 | do you see as p. that he is guilty of attack. |
| T-27.........I.5:7 | Here is the p. that he has never sinned; |
| T-27.........I.9:2 | p. that what your function is can never be |
| T-27......... II.3:3 | but retain the p. he is not really innocent. |
| T-27......... II.3:7 | not the p. of sin before his brother's eyes. |
| T-27..... II.3:11 | lies the p. that he has truly pardoned, and |
| T-27......... II.4:6 | lies the p. that they are merely errors. Let |
| T-27......... II.7:7 | his heart made heavy with the p. of sin. |
| T-28...... III.8:5 | miracle would leave no p. of guilt to bring |
| T-29...... III.1:8 | know he has, for giving is the p. of having. |
| T-29...... III.2:4 | you the p. that He is perfect and complete |
| T-30....... VI.6:1 | no surer p. idolatry is what you wish than |
| T-30.... VIII.2:6 | The miracle is p. he is not bound by loss |
| T-31....... I.11:9 | Your answer is the p. of what you learned. |
| T-31.......... V.9:2 | p. there is that you are what your brother |
| W-pI.....54.5:4 | I would behold the p. that what has been |
| W-pI.....55.1:4 | things is p. that I do not understand God. |
| W-pI...100.4:4 | p. that God wills perfect happiness for all |
| W-pI...121.3:3 | it behold except the p. that all its sins are |
| W-pI...130.6:2 | world you see is p. you have already made |
| W-pI...139.8:3 | it must be is all the p. you need to show |
| W-pI. 140.12:4 | our minds, nor offer p. to us that it is real. |
| W-pI. 151.14:1 | wills His Son, as p. of His eternal Love. |
| W-pI...159.1:8 | It is the p. that what you have is yours. |
| W-pI...166.7:2 | witnesses with p. to show this is not you. |
| W-pI. 166.14:5 | your change of mind becomes the p. that |
| W-pI. 166.15:2 | not. Become the living p. of what Christ's |
| W-pI...181.9:1 | sins becomes the p. that we are sinless. |
| W-pI...184.6:7 | to accept its presence is the p. of sanity. |
| W-pI...187.1:2 | In fact, giving is p. of having. We have |
| W-pI...187.2:4 | lack for p. that when you give ideas away, |
| W-pI...190.1:2 | in any form, it is a p. of self-deception. It |
| W-pII .....4.3:2 | the "p." that what has no reality is real. |
| W-pII .....5.2:3 | Son of God's impermanence is "p." his |
| W-pII .....5.2:9 | what "p." is there that God's eternal Son |
| W-pII ...12.1:3 | The ego is the "p." that strength is weak |
| P-2........ VI.7:5 | Yet will the p. of sinlessness, seen in the |
| S-2......... II.5:2 | silent p. of guilt and of the ravages of sin. |
| S-2........ III.1:2 | It does not ask for p. of innocence, nor |
| S-3...........I.1:3 | world. It is external p. of inner "sins," and |

## propaganda 1

|  |  |
|---|---|
| T-27...... IV.5:3 | within the world a form of p. for itself. |

## proper 31

|  |  |
|---|---|
| T-1.........I.30:1 | and show them in p. alignment. This |
| T-1........ IV.2:7 | This establishes the p. function of the |
| T-1...... IV.2:10 | Atonement restores spirit to its p. place. |
| T-1....... VII.5:3 | awe is p. in the Presence of your Creator. I |
| T-2......... II.1:12 | This is the p. use of denial. It is not used |
| T-3........ III.4:3 | brings it into the p. domain of the miracle |
| T-3........ IV.5:6 | its p. function only when it wills to know. |
| T-5...........I.4:8 | The word "know" is p. in this context, |
| T-5......... V.8:8 | the p. ordering of thought becomes quite |
| T-7...... IV.2:10 | out of conflict, as all p. perception can. |
| T-7....... V.11:4 | because this is your p. gift to God. He will |
| T-7........ IX.7:3 | your p. identification with your brothers, |
| T-8.... VIII.9:10 | the beginning of the p. perspective on life |
| T-8........ IX.1:5 | that the body is the p. aim of healing. Ask |
| T-12....... V.8:6 | Under the p. learning conditions, which |
| T-13...... III.2:2 | instantly restore you to your p. place, and |
| T-25....... V.4:8 | If you decide against his p. function, the |
| T-25..VIII.10:8 | to offer, believing vengeance is his p. due. |
| T-29...... IV.5:1 | one who gave the "p." role to every figure |
| T-30.........I.1:5 | The p. set, adopted consciously each time |
| W-pI........3.1:2 | becomes a p. subject for applying the idea |
| W-pI........5.1:5 | a p. subject for the exercises for the day. |
| W-pI...126.9:2 | takes its p. place in your priorities. It is |
| W-pI...154.5:4 | failing to perform his p. part as bringer of |
| W-pI...184.7:5 | In its p. place, it serves but as a starting |
| W-pI...186.1:4 | role. It does not judge your p. role. It but |
| W-pI. 193.10:6 | what time you can to serve its p. aim, and |
| M-5 ......II.4:11 | Seen in their p. perspective, without |
| M-12 ......... 4:1 | recognition of the p. purpose of the body. |
| P-1............. 2:4 | in this is the p. purpose of psychotherapy. |
| P-2....... VII.9:1 | as this, if you but understand your p. role. |

## properly 26

|  |  |
|---|---|
| T-1 ........I.37:2 | perception and reorganizing it p.. This |
| T-1 ....... IV.4:4 | law itself, if p. understood, offers only |
| T-2 ....... IV.3:6 | The body, if p. understood, shares the |
| T-2 ........ V.4:3 | inclinations are not functioning p., it is |
| T-2 .... VII.3:11 | "Cause" is a term p. belonging to God, |
| T-3 ....... IV.4:3 | term "right-mindedness" is p. used as the |
| T-3 ........ V.4:1 | cannot p. be directed to yourself at all. |
| T-4 ........in.1:5 | word which p. understood is the opposite |
| T-6 ..........I.1:5 | in what it teaches, if it is p. understood. |
| T-7 ....... IV.2:8 | of remembering when it is p. perceived. |
| T-7 ..... IV.2:10 | P. perceived, it can be used as a way out |
| T-7 ....... IV.4:1 | Who understands how to use them p.. He |
| T-12 ...... V.9:1 | Your learning potential, p. understood, |
| T-18 ... VI.13:2 | is not attacked, but simply p. perceived. It |
| T-19 ........I.2:1 | Every situation, p. perceived, becomes an |
| T-27 ...... V.9:4 | have been p. perceived but never violated. |
| W-pI.....24.6:1 | If these exercises are done p., you will |
| W-pI.....26.8:1 | If you are doing the exercises p., you |
| W-pI.....44.5:5 | P. speaking, this is the release from hell. |
| W-pI.....69.7:1 | If you are doing the exercises p., you will |
| W-pII .284.1:1 | Loss is not loss when p. perceived. Pain is |
| M-4 ........X.3:5 | the focus p. belongs on the curriculum. It |
| M-4 ........X.3:7 | P. speaking it is unlearning that they |
| M-9 ........... 1:8 | in particular must be p. perceived, and all |
| M-24 ......... 6:9 | beliefs will point to this if p. interpreted. |
| P-3..........II.9:1 | can save enormous time if it is p. used. He |

## properties 5

|  |  |
|---|---|
| T-1 ....... IV.3:2 | It has no unique p. of its own. It is an |
| T-18 ..... VI.3:2 | Only by assigning to the mind the p. of |
| T-26 .......II.4:5 | or less. They have no p. to Him. They are |
| M-8 ........... 5:9 | The p. of illusions which seem to make |
| M-8 ........... 5:9 | for their p. are as illusory as they are. |

## property 3

|  |  |
|---|---|
| T-1 .........II.6:5 | The miracle thus has the unique p. of |
| T-5 ..... III.2:5 | The idea of the Holy Spirit shares the p. of |
| T-18 ..... VI.8:3 | that is an eternal p. of mind. But the |

## prophecy 1

|  |  |
|---|---|
| W-pII ....in.5:1 | Now is the time of p. fulfilled. Now are |

## proportion 4

|  |  |
|---|---|
| T-9 .......II.10:2 | return is in p. to your judgment of worth. |
| W-pI.....71.9:7 | He will answer in p. to your willingness to |
| M-in .......... 1:4 | engages only a relatively small p. of one's |
| M-5 .........II.1:1 | Healing must occur in exact p. to which |

## proposals 1

|  |  |
|---|---|
| W-pI.....71.8:4 | attempts and mad p. to free yourself. |

## proposed 1

|  |  |
|---|---|
| W-pI.....66.9:7 | happiness from anything the ego ever p.. |

## proposes 1

|  |  |
|---|---|
| T-11 ......in.1:3 | true. Neither God nor the ego p. a partial |

## prospect 1

|  |  |
|---|---|
| W-pI... 121.5:1 | without the p. of a future which can offer |

## protect 67

|  |  |
|---|---|
| T-2 ....... III.1:3 | is generally seen as a need to p. the body. |
| T-2 ..... IV.3:12 | to p. the mind by denying the unmindful. |
| T-3 ..........I.2:1 | position, but rather to p. the truth. It is |
| T-3 ..........I.6:1 | and strives only to p. its wholeness. It |
| T-4 ..........I.2:1 | to p. their thought systems as they are, |
| T-4 ..........I.5:4 | that laws are set up to p. the continuity of |
| T-4 ..........I.5:5 | for the ego to try to p. itself once you have |
| T-4 ........I.13:3 | can p. the child's body and his ego, but he |
| T-4 .........II.4:1 | and the need they feel to p. them. That is |
| T-4 ..... III.10:3 | have been willing to exert to p. your ego, |
| T-4 ..... III.10:3 | ego, and how little to p. your right mind. |
| T-4 ..... III.10:4 | and then p. this belief at the cost of truth? |
| T-4 ........ IV.8:7 | other defense, can be used to attack or p.; |
| T-4 .........V.4:6 | is also told that the body cannot p. it. |
| T-4 ..... VII.2:4 | is controlled by its need to p. itself, and it |
| T-6 ..........I.6:5 | Do not try to p. it yourself, or you are |
| T-6 ....... III.3:2 | accept this fully, it sees no need to p. itself |
| T-7 ...... VII.6:4 | in His Love and p. your rest by loving. But |
| T-7 ....... XI.3:3 | it p. his peace and shine love upon him? |
| T-10 .........I.1:4 | because the laws of God p. it by His Love. |
| T-10 ..... III.5:3 | to p. an idol you think will save you from |
| T-12 .........I.8:9 | If you do not p. it, He will reinterpret it. |
| T-12 .......V.2:5 | does not work and cannot p. you. Yet the |
| T-13 .......II.4:5 | for the ego cannot p. you against truth, |
| T-13 .......II.7:6 | it is only your guiltlessness that *can* p. you. |
| T-14 .......V.4:3 | it. P. his purity from every thought that |
| T-14 ..... VI.3:3 | They do not p.; neither do they attack. |
| T-15 ..... III.4:4 | require vigilance to p. your magnitude in |
| T-15 ..... IV.9:8 | and seek not to p. the thoughts you would |
| T-15 .......X.6:6 | the ego takes to p. itself from your sight. |
| T-15 .......X.8:5 | inviting it to take His place to p. you from |
| T-15 ..... XI.1:2 | to p. yourself from where it is not. Your |
| T-17 ..... IV.4:3 | the ego evolved to p. the separation from |
| T-17 ..... IV.5:4 | The insane p. their thought systems, |
| T-17 ..... IV.5:5 | as insane as what they are supposed to p.. |
| T-18 ..... IX.9:6 | waiting to clothe you and p. you, and |
| T19 ... IV.C.8:1 | ego's might, unable to p. the life that He |
| T-21 .... VII.1:8 | p. his unity or see him shattered and slain |
| T-22 .........I.4:6 | not your fear of sin p. it from correction, |
| T-22 ..... IV.5:2 | salvation, which he would p. from harm. |
| T-24 .........I.4:6 | Yet they p. its enmity and call it "friend." |
| T-24 .........I.9:4 | This is what he attacks, and you p.. Here |
| T-24 ..... III.2:5 | You would p. what God created not. And |
| T-24 .... VII.4:1 | Ask yourself this: Can *you* p. the mind? |
| T-25 .VIII.10:8 | p. from all unfairness you might seek to |
| T-27 .......II.1:7 | P. him not, because your damaged body |
| T-27 ... VIII.2:4 | they may p. it and collect more senseless |
| T-29 .........I.4:6 | do p. you from the "sacrifice" of love. The |
| T-29 .... VII.9:8 | you must p. against the light of truth. |
| T-30 .......I.13:2 | that will p. you from the ravages of fear. |
| W-pI ..... 34.5:2 | purpose is to p. yourself from temptation |
| W-pI ..... 35.2:3 | want it to p. the image of yourself that |
| W-pI ..... 36.2:2 | to p. your protection throughout the day. |
| W-pI ..... 50.3:1 | of God will p. you in all circumstances. It |
| W-pI ..... 76.4:4 | health. P. the body, and you will be saved. |
| W-pI .. 128.8:1 | P. your mind throughout the day as well. |
| W-pI .. 133.8:7 | to p. its goals from tarnish and from rust, |
| W-pI .. 135.2:1 | the belief you must p. yourself from what |
| W-pI .. 135.4:3 | prey, unable to p. itself and needing your |
| W-pI .. 135.4:4 | deep concern are needful to p. its little life |
| WpI..rIV.in3:2 | are; defenses that p. your unforgiving |
| W-pI .. 182.9:4 | He asks that they p. Him, for His home is |
| W-pI 182.10:2 | must learn that what he would p. is but |
| W-pI .. 187.4:1 | P. all things you value by the act of giving |
| M-in.......... 3:9 | that the self you are trying to p. is real. |
| M-5 .........I.2:4 | he would hide from himself to p. his "life. |
| M-29 ....... 6:10 | for injury, but his father will p. him still. |

## protected 31

|  |  |
|---|---|
| T-2 ....... III.4:3 | defiled and needs to be repaired and p.. |
| T-4 ..... III.1:12 | *is perfectly united and perfectly p., and the* |
| T-5 ....... IV.1:8 | ever created, and therefore cannot be p.. |
| T-7 ....... IX.5:1 | creations are p. for you because the Holy |
| T-10 ..... IV.4:6 | God Himself has p. everything He created |
| T-11 .......V.1:1 | for not looking is the way they are p.. |
| T-11 ... VIII.7:6 | free and whose freedom is p. by His Being |
| T-13 ..... III.2:5 | and you have p. it because you do not |

T-13....VI.13:3 Even in sleep has Christ **p.** you, ensuring
T-16......III.5:5 **p.** both your creations and you together,
T-19.......II.5:3 necessarily **p.** with every defense at its
T19... IV.C.9:2 **p.** by your union with your brother, and
T19... IV.C.9:4 by the Holy Spirit and **p.** by God Himself.
T19... IV.D.3:1 the belief in death and **p.** by its attraction.
T-20..... II.10:3 and perfectly **p.** from the cold chill of fear
T-20...... VI.5:2 a meaningless enclosure carefully **p.**, yet
T-21...... III.2:4 so cherished and **p.** as is a goal the mind
T-21.....VII.7:4 be the one you chose to be **p.** from attack.
T-22...... I.11:5 and His gentle innocence **p.** from attack.
T-23.......in.5:5 so is yours **p.** and kept in your awareness.
T-25...... III.4:3 And thus has God **p.** still His Son, even in
T-26......... V.9:7 own unfairness to yourself has He **p.** you.
T-26....VII.12:1 the error is, so it can be corrected, not **p.**.
T-26... VIII.5:7 is it **p.** and kept separate from healing.
T-27....... II.1:7 body shows that *you* must be **p.** from him.
T-28...... III.3:5 sickness is kept carefully **p.**, cherished,
T-30......IV.2:4 because he thought the rules **p.** him. Now
W-pI.153.10:5 And who could be more mightily **p.**?
W-pI ...170.2:3 And thus is fear **p.**, not escaped. Today
W-pI.182.10:2 and Who is **p.** by defenselessness. Go
W-pII..275.1:5 It is in this that all things are **p.**. And in

## protecting 17

T-2......... II.7:8 assume your natural talent of **p.** others,
T-4.......VII.8:3 because they are not **p.** their egos and so
T-8........IX.6:2 Yet the ego actually believes that it is **p.** it.
T-9..... VIII.5:2 **p.** it from illusions and keeping yourself
T-11....... V.2:2 looking at them directly, without **p.** them
T-11..... V.14:6 in mind, and **p.** what it has made real, the
T-13....... II.7:5 learning the course you are **p.** yourself.
T-15.....VII.4:5 to direct its anger outward, thus **p.** you.
T-16......VI.3:2 aid in **p.** you from the attraction of guilt,
T-19.........I.7:8 are **p.** the body by hiding this connection,
T-23.......in.2:6 walks with him there, **p.** him from fear.
T-23....... I.10:6 **p.** you from everything that is not true.
T-29....... II.8:8 your god, **p.** you from being part of Him.
W-pII..337.1:6 mine, to feel God's Love **p.** me from harm
M-4....VII.2:12 generosity, **p.** them forever for himself.
M-16..........6:7 up is merely the illusion of **p.** illusions.
P-2.........in.1:5 that by justifying attack he is **p.** himself.

## protection 72

*See also* self-protection

T-1........ I.34:2 atoning for lack they establish perfect **p.**.
T-1........IV.4:4 if properly understood, offers only **p.**. It is
T-2......... II.7:8 the defense of Atonement to your real **p.**,
T-2......... V.9:3 healing is needed as a means of **p.**. This is
T-4........ I.10:1 it you will withdraw all **p.** from the ego,
T-4........ I.13:8 is far beyond the need of your **p.** or mine.
T-4......... II.4:4 His creations,–with love, **p.** and charity.
T-4........IV.8:9 Without your own allegiance, **p.** and love,
T-4......IV.8:10 withdraw allegiance, **p.** and love from it.
T-4......IV.10:4 my judgment, which is used only for **p.**,
T-4......... V.4:7 can I go for **p.**?" to which the ego replies,
T-4......... V.4:8 so there is no point in turning to *it* for **p.**.
T-4......... V.5:1 that *must* be asked: "Where can I go for **p.**
T-5...........I.5:2 into being with the separation as a **p.**,
T-5........IV.1:9 and the union of the Sonship is its **p.**. The
T-6........III.3:3 itself. The **p.** of God then dawns upon it,
T-6......V.C.7:1 third step is thus one of **p.** for your mind,
T-6......V.C.8:4 It is only your awareness that needs **p.**,
T-6....V.C.10:8 since it is already true and needs no **p.**. It
T-9..... VIII.1:4 gifts to induce you to return to its "**p.**."
T-10.......in.1:6 your **p.** and are as inviolate as your safety.
T-10......IV.6:1 experienced the **p.** of God, the making of
T-11.......in.4:4 hidden, for its **p.** will not save you. I give
T-11....... II.5:3 He needs your **p.**, only because your care
T-11......IV.2:3 God's laws hold only for your **p.**, and they
T-11......IV.2:4 you deny your Father is still for your **p.**,
T-11......IV.3:7 for the **p.** of the Wholeness of His Son.
T-12... VIII.2:1 Son knows his Father's **p.** and cannot fear
T-14......VI.3:7 Without **p.** of obscurity only the light of
T-14.....VII.5:3 What needs no **p.** does not defend itself.
T-15...VII.14:7 In the **p.** of your wholeness, all are invited
T-17......IV.5:7 And its "**p.**" is part of it, as insane as the
T-18.....VII.1:2 comfort or **p.** or enjoyment in some way?
T-18.......IX.4:5 this, for the body arose from this for its **p.**
T-19....... II.5:5 is its armor, its **p.**, and the fundamental
T-19...... III.2:3 is but another form of guilt's **p.**, for what
T-19...... IV.1:6 and the calm awareness of complete **p.**.
T19... IV.A.9:5 when you had greater faith in its **p.**.
T19....IV.C.9:5 It needs not your **p.**; it is *yours*. For it is
T19. IV.D.21:3 God safely within the sure **p.** of his Father
T-20....... II.9:2 offering you its guiding light and sure **p.**,
T-23...... III.6:9 one illusion of **p.** stands against the faith
T-24.....VII.2:7 All of the love and care, the strong **p.**, the
W-pI.....36.2:2 to protect your **p.** throughout the day.
W-pI.....41.9:3 on the complete **p.** that surrounds you.
W-pI.....47.3:2 to do to call upon His strength and His **p.**.
W-pI.....50.5:2 over you like a blanket of **p.** and surety.
W-pI.....76.8:2 and of the body's **p.** in innumerable ways.
W-pI...122.1:5 safety, and the warmth of sure **p.** always?
W-pI...124.1:2 home is safe, **p.** guaranteed in all we do,
W-pI...124.4:1 for us, nor question His **p.** and His care.
W-pI...131.2:7 and **p.** for the little dream you made.
W-pI...135.8:1 The "self" that needs **p.** is not real. The
W-pI.135.10:4 offer it **p.** of a kind from which it gains no
W-pI.135.13:2 in a plan which far exceeds its own **p.**,
W-pI.135.14:2 mind would undertake its own **p.**, at the
W-pI.136.19:1 this **p.** needs to be preserved by careful
W-pI...138.8:1 not relinquish its ideas about its own **p.**.
W-pI.140.12:4 we will feel salvation cover us with soft **p.**,
W-pI...170.1:3 you mean that to be cruel is **p.**; you are
W-pI...182.6:1 This Child needs your **p.**. He is far from
W-pI...182.6:4 know that in you still abides His sure **p.**.
W-pI.182.11:4 must beseech his father for **p.** and for love
W-pI...196.2:1 and with all things held in its sure **p.**, can
W-pII..317.2:5 *wandered from the sure **p.** of Your loving*
M-6 ...........1:9 for death. Healing must wait, for his **p.**.
M-16 .......6:14 And only then will you accept your real **p.**
M-16 .........7:1 teacher of God who has accepted His **p.**!
M-16 .........8:1 himself throughout the day of his **p.**. How
M-17 .........5:9 And he must stand alone in his **p.**, and
P-2........ VI.1:3 sheltering, its loving **p.** and alert defense, -
P-2........ VI.4:3 Without **p.** it could not endure. Here is all

## protective 4

T-2......... II.2:1 True denial is a powerful **p.** device. You
T-2......... V.1:6 recognition is a far better **p.** device than
W-pI.....50.1:3 symbols; pills, money, "**p.**" clothing,
W-pI.138.10:1 is raised from its **p.** shield of unawareness

## Protector 1

*protector*

W-pII...... 1.5:1 Who is your Guide, your Savior and **P.**,

## protector 5

*Protector*

T-4......... V.4:6 part of the body and that the body is its **p.**
T-14.... III.13:6 strong **p.** of the innocence that sets you
T-22...... IV.5:3 your brother's strong **p.** from everything
T-22...... IV.5:8 it have become its willing guardian and **p.**
W-pI...170.5:2 becomes your safety and **p.** of your peace,

## protectors 1

T19... IV.D.6:5 your "**p.**" and your "home" will vanish.

## protects 20

T-6....V.C.1:11 He **p.** it by rejecting everything that does
T-11... V.12:10 the Love of God completely **p.** them.
T-13.........I.5:8 Mind of his Father, and **p.** him forever.
T-15.... III.12:5 for it **p.** only the peace in which He dwells
T-15...... XI.2:9 holy as the perfect Innocence which He **p.**
T-15...... XI.2:9 He protects, and Whose power **p.** Him.
T-17...... IV.6:1 special relationship **p.** is but a system of
T-17...... IV.7:4 of the thought system the defense **p.**, set
T-23...... II.14:2 **p.** madness is the belief that it is true. It is
W-pI.....58.5:6 Father supports me, **p.** me, and directs
W-pI.....68.6:4 safe in a world that **p.** you and loves you,
W-pI... 165.2:6 The Thought of God **p.** you, cares for you,
W-pI... 189.2:5 salvation in you, and **p.** the light in you,
W-pII ..... 1.2:3 The thought **p.** projection, tightening its
W-pII ....275.h God's healing Voice **p.** all things today.
W-pII .275.2:1 *Your healing Voice **p.** all things today, and*
W-pII .275.2:5 *Father, Your Voice **p.** all things through me.*
W-pII .294.1:6 Its neutrality **p.** it while it has a use. And
W-pII ....337.h My sinlessness **p.** me from all harm.
M-17 .........9:3 its servant, it neither attacks nor **p.**. To

## protest 2

T-18......II.5:15 They are your **p.** against reality, and your
T-23......II.10:2 do the guilty ones **p.** their "innocence."

## prototype 1

W-pI... 138.6:2 most definitive and **p.** of all the rest, the

## protract 1

T-2..........II.3:8 save time if you do not **p.** this step unduly

## protracted 1

W-pI..... 43.6:2 allow any **p.** period to occur in which you

## proudly 1

T-31....... V.4:1 **p.** wears can tolerate attack in self-defense

## prove 43

T-4...........I.4:2 your mind will not **p.** that the separation
T-9......... V.4:2 use them to **p.** that the nightmare is real.
T-11..... V.17:3 for nothing can **p.** that a lie is true. What
T-13...... IV.3:3 this, and needs this to **p.** that it was at all.
T-18...... VI.4:2 what it does to hurt the body to **p.** it can.
T-19...... III.7:5 sin would **p.** what God created holy could
T-24.VII.11:13 purpose well, and **p.** its own reality to you
T-26....VII.12:5 world is an attempt to **p.** your innocence,
T-27.........I.3:3 are beyond attack and **p.** his innocence.
T-27.........I.4:7 death would **p.** his errors must be sins.
T-27.........I.6:4 Its only purpose is to **p.** guilt real. No
T-27........II.5:3 you would **p.** to him you will believe. The
T-27........II.7:6 love would **p.** all suffering is but a vain
T-27........II.9:4 guilt he suffers serves to **p.** that he is slave
T-27....VIII.2:1 ways to **p.** it is autonomous and real. It
T-28........II.8:7 the body which appears to **p.** the dreamer
T-28.... VII.5:4 This seems to **p.** that you must be apart.
T-29.... VII.3:4 within, and **p.** that he is victor over him.
T-29...VII.10:2 so. Salvation seeks to **p.** there is no death,
T-29..... IX.8:3 They do not seek to **p.** the dream is being
T-30..... IV.5:4 thus you **p.** that you have been deceived.
W-pI.....26.4:4 your thoughts can **p.** to you this is not so.
W-pI.....55.5:2 the purpose of everything is to **p.** that my
W-pI.....73.6:1 which seek to **p.** all this is really Heaven.
W-pI.....76.1:6 Thus do you seek to **p.** salvation is where
W-pI.....76.2:1 Today we will be glad you cannot **p.** it.
W-pI.....86.3:2 to **p.** that God's plan for salvation will not
W-pI.....88.2:1 **p.** useful forms for specific applications of
W-pI.....93.3:4 This is enough to **p.** that they are wrong,
WpI. rIII.in9:3 to **p.** how great are its potential gifts to
W-pI.136.12:3 nor seek to **p.** how pitiful and futile your
W-pI... 137.4:1 would **p.** that lies must be the truth. But
W-pI... 151.4:5 senses carefully, to **p.** how weak you are;
W-pI... 151.6:2 to **p.** to you its evil is your own are false,
W-pI... 152.9:1 by which the ego seeks to **p.** it arrogant.
W-pI.154.14:4 **p.** that we accept no will we do not share,
W-pI... 186.5:1 to **p.** the false is true has brought to you.
W-pI... 188.2:3 which **p.** it is not there become ridiculous.
W-pI... 190.3:6 love and using pain to **p.** that God is dead
W-pII .342.1:3 *given me the means to **p.** its unreality to me.*
M-5 .........I.2:6 will be killed to **p.** to him how weak and
M-22 ......... 3:5 of God and **p.** salvation is impossible.
M-29 ......... 7:5 He has given you the means to **p.** it so.

**proved** 8
T-6...... IV.10:2 and **p.** to you that you were wrong. This
T-6...... IV.11:5 be gained if God **p.** to you that you have
T-16...... II.9:6 already **p.** their power sufficiently for you
T-27...... II.5:9 For here is his forgiveness **p.** to him.
T-27..... V.2:3 when it has been demonstrated is it **p.**,
T-27..... V.10:3 power of your learning will be **p.** to you
W-pI... 108.6:2 this special case has **p.** it always works, in
M-18 ......... 1:3 is then inevitable, for he has "**p.**," both to

**proven** 2
W-pI... 163.6:5 not be true, unless its opposite is **p.** false.
W-pI... 187.4:2 you did not have is thereby **p.** yours. Yet

**proves** 20
T-9........ IV.5:6 teaches that the ego does not exist and **p.**
T-13...... IV.3:2 no one would claim that it **p.** there *is* life.
T-21..... II.13:2 See what "**p.**" otherwise, and you deny
T-24..... VII.9:8 it makes. It **p.** its own reality to you.
T-25..... VII.9:2 as it **p.** to him that it is an alternative he
T-27......... I.6:2 health because it **p.** illusions are not true.
T-27....... II.5:2 A miracle of healing **p.** that separation is
T-27....... VI.5:2 merely **p.** that what they represent has no
T-27....... VI.5:3 And this it **p.** because its own effects have
T-27....... VI.6:8 It is their sameness that it **p.**. The laws
T-28....... V.6:1 Creation **p.** reality because it shares the
W-pI..... 71.9:9 doing the exercises **p.** that you have some
W-pI... 100.8:1 Now let us try to find that joy that **p.** to
W-pI... 136.8:2 it **p.** the body is not separate from you,
W-pI... 137.8:4 And by this attribute it **p.** that laws unlike
W-pI... 165.5:6 For this sight **p.** that you have exchanged
W-pI... 187.8:3 its very presence **p.** that error has arisen
W-pII ..... 4.3:3 Sin "**p.**" God's Son is evil; timelessness
C-4........... 5:10 Forgiveness **p.** it is impossible because it
C-6............ 4:4 And therefore it is He Who **p.** Them One.

**provide** 15
T-1........ III.1:8 I will **p.** the opportunities to do them, but
T-12....... V.8:6 which you can neither **p.** nor understand,
T-14.... III.10:7 to **p.** that offers them anything of value.
T-15....... II.4:2 seem to **p.** reasons for not letting it go.
T-18....... II.2:5 They **p.** striking examples, both of the
T-18....... V.3:9 will **p.** the means to anyone who shares
T-24.... VI.12:5 of truth itself is given to **p.** the means, and
T-27....... V.2:3 and must **p.** a witness that compels belief.
T-31....... V.3:1 world is wicked and unable to **p.** the love
W-pI...... 64.1:2 **p.** you with a justification for forgetting it.
W-pI...... 92.9:1 that the body's eyes **p.** for self-deception.
W-pI. 134.13:1 nor **p.** a guide to teach you its beneficence
W-pII . 316.2:3 *will **p.** the means by which I can behold them*
M-in .......... 2:5 the course might be said to **p.** you with a
P-1............. 1:4 contributions an earthly therapist can **p.**.

**provided** 17
T-2........ III.5:3 But the real means are already **p.**, and do
T-12....... V.5:2 **p.** by a Teacher Who can transcend your
T-13....... X.1:4 **p.** they are not the deeper source to which
T-14...... XI.7:2 depend for miracles has been **p.** for you.
T-15...... XI.7:2 destroyed, **p.** that you see not the body as
T-16.......... I.1:3 Spirit, **p.** you let Him use it in His way.
T-18....... V.3:7 have accepted one; the other will be **p.**. A
T-25.. VIII.11:1 at last, **p.** it is seen and recognized. For
T-27...... IV.6:4 The answer is **p.** everywhere. Yet it is only
T-29......... I.3:5 **p.** that your separate interests made your
W-pI...... 71.3:2 is acceptable **p.** that it will not work. This
W-pI. 135.15:2 It does not think that it will be **p.** for,
W-pI... 160.4:2 to the home which God **p.** for His Son? Is
W-pI. 169.14:1 and accept the gifts that grace **p.** you. You
W-pII . 314.1:4 and all the needed means are happily **p.**.
M-2 ........... 1:7 opportunities to teach will be **p.** for him.
M-26 ......... 4:8 All the help you can accept will be **p.**, and

**provides** 13
T-3........ III.5:8 Knowledge **p.** the strength for creative
T-9 ........ V.9:1 **p.** the Guide Who tells you what to do. If
T-17 ..... VI.1:6 specific guidelines He **p.** for any situation,
T-27 .... VII.5:2 world **p.** the means by which this purpose
W-in.......... 1:1 as the text **p.** is necessary as a framework
W-pI..... 13.2:2 the empty space that meaninglessness **p.**.
W-pI... 140.7:3 is no remedy the world **p.** that can effect a
W-pI... 153.1:2 The world **p.** no safety. It is rooted in
W-pI. 158.10:5 you meet today **p.** another chance to let
W-pI... 159.8:4 and kindly care Christ's charity **p.**. They
W-pI. 169.12:3 Experience that grace **p.** will end in time,
W-pI... 193.1:4 thus His Will **p.** the means to guarantee
W-pII ..... 7.1:3 He **p.** are dreams all carried to the truth,

**proving** 2
T-19 ..... III.8:4 now, the goal of **p.** this is impossible.
M-25 ......... 3:6 Nor does their value lie in **p.** anything;

**provisions** 2
T-24 .. VII.10:1 no **p.** made for evidence beyond itself,
W-pI. 135.15:2 provided for, unless it makes its own **p.**.

**proviso** 1
T-12 ..... IV.1:3 search for love very actively, makes one **p.**

**provoke** 1
T-30 ........ I.5:2 Now the answer will **p.** attack, unless you

**provoked** 1
W-pI... 153.2:2 attack seem reasonable, honestly **p.**, and

**provoking** 1
*See also* anxiety-provoking
T-31 ...... V.3:4 upon its innocence, **p.** it to irritation, and

**proximity** 1
T-4 ......... II.2:4 the mind as when it involves physical **p.**.

**pseudo-being** 1
W-pI. 138.11:3 Its **p.**, brought to what is real, is flimsy

**pseudo-creation** 1
P-2........ VI.2:5 into the self-concept, itself but a **p.**, make

**pseudo-question** 1
T-27 ..... IV.5:1 A **p.** has no answer. It dictates the answer

**psychic** 5
M-25 ............ h ARE "**P.**" POWERS DESIRABLE?
M-25 ......... 2:1 Certainly there are many "**p.**" powers
M-25 ......... 5:1 may still be deceived by "**p.**" powers. As
M-25 ......... 6:5 "**P.**" abilities have been used to call upon
M-25 ......... 6:7 Those who have developed "**p.**" powers

**psychotherapeutic** 1
P-2.......... II.4:3 belief in God were necessary to **p.** success.

**psychotherapist** 12
T-9 ........ V.1:6 If he is a **p.**, he is more likely to start with
T-9 ........ V.4:2 a **p.** may interpret the ego's symbols in a
T-9 ........ V.6:3 light by analyzing darkness, as the **p.** does
P-2.......... II.7:5 Perhaps the **p.** does not understand that
P-2........... III.h The Role of the **P.**
P-2........ III.1:1 **p.** is a leader in the sense that he walks
P-2........ III.2:1 is limited by the limitations of the **p.**, as it
P-2........ III.4:4 egoless **p.** is an abstraction that stands at
P-2........ III.4:6 The **p.** becomes his patient, working
P-2........ IV.9:3 problems with which the **p.** must deal. In
P-2...... IV.10:1 **p.**, then, has a tremendous responsibility.
P-2.......... V.3:3 perfect **p.** is but a glimmer of a thought

**psychotherapist's** 1
P-2...... IV.10:7 the **p.** function to teach that guilt, being

**psychotherapists** 1
P-1........... 5:10 We are all His **p.**, for He would have us all

**psychotherapy** 39
T-9 ......... V.5:2 has really explained what happens in **p.**.
P-in ........... 1:1 **P.** is the only form of therapy there is.
P-in ........... 1:5 **P.** is necessary so that an individual can
P-1................ h THE PURPOSE OF **P.**
P-1............. 1:1 of **p.** is to remove the blocks to truth. Its
P-1............. 2:4 To help in this is the proper purpose of **p.**
P-1............. 2:6 For **p.**, correctly understood, teaches
P-1............. 4:1 **P.**, then, must restore to his awareness
P-1............. 5:4 **P.** can only save him time. The Holy Spirit
P-1............. 5:6 **P.** under His direction is one of the means
P-1............. 5:8 He chooses, all **p.** leads to God in the end.
P-2................ h THE PROCESS OF **P.**
P-2......... in.1:1 **P.** is a process that changes the view of
P-2......... in.1:2 but **p.** can hardly be expected to establish
P-2......... in.3:4 it the magical powers he seeks in **p.**. He
P-2.............. I.h The Limits on **P.**
P-2........... I.1:2 and in **p.** those have come together who
P-2........... I.2:1 **P.** itself cannot be creative. This is one of
P-2........... I.3:2 a limit on **p.** because it restricts its aims.
P-2........... I.4:1 **p.** is a series of holy encounters in which
P-2............. II.h The Place of Religion in **P.**
P-2.......... II.2:1 Formal religion has no place in **p.**, but it
P-2.......... II.2:4 Religion is experience; **p.** is experience. At
P-2.......... II.4:1 that constitutes a reasonable goal for **p.**.
P-2.......... II.4:2 This will come when **p.** is complete, for
P-2.......... II.5:2 of **p.** have nothing to do with healing. Yet
P-2.......... II.5:5 The process of **p.** is the return to sanity.
P-2.......... II.7:1 religion heals, so must true **p.** be religious
P-2.......... II.9:7 **p.** except a help in just this same direction
P-2......... III.3:1 It is quite possible for **p.** to seem to fail. It
P-2......... IV.1:1 As all therapy is **p.**, so all illness is mental
P-2......... IV.3:6 and will say again, all therapy is **p.**. To
P-2......... IV.9:4 fact, this is his central task; the core of **p.**.
P-2.......... V.3:6 No more than that is asked of **p.**; no less
P-2......... VI.1:1 The process of **p.**, then, can be defined
P-2......... VI.6:1 This realization is the final goal of **p.**.
P-2...... VII.2:4 is His home, into which **p.** invites Him.
P-3................ h 3. THE PRACTICE OF **P.**
P-3............. II.h Is **P.** a Profession?

**puff** 1
T-20 ..... III.8:4 asked this **p.** of madness for the meaning

**pull** 4
T-4 ....... IV.7:3 permit this shabby belief to **p.** you back.
T-13 ....... II.1:2 **p.** is so strong that you cannot resist it.
T-23 ...... in.4:1 the little interferers **p.** you to littleness.
W-pI .. 75.10:4 who seems to **p.** you back into darkness:

**punish** 9
T-3 ....... VI.8:6 eager to undo it, not to **p.** His children,
T-19 ..... III.4:1 The Holy Spirit cannot **p.** sin. Mistakes
T-25 ... VIII.8:1 cannot **p.** those who ask for punishment,
T-26 ....... II.5:4 But ask not God to **p.** him because *you*
T-26 ....... II.5:6 fair to **p.** him because you will not look at
T-27 ........ I.4:4 *you* accept, if only it can serve to **p.** him.
T-27 ...... II.11:3 must be a way to **p.** sins you think are
T-28 ..... VI.3:9 It seems to **p.** you, and thus deserve your
W-pI .. 194.4:6 well, because the past will **p.** you no more

## punished 9

| | |
|---|---|
| T-3........ I.2:10 | I was not "**p.**" because *you* were bad. The |
| T-4......... II.9:6 | that the soul will be **p.** for this lapse. |
| T-6........ I.16:4 | No one is **p.** for sins, and the Sons of God |
| T-9........ III.6:8 | this, not because you are being **p.** for it, |
| T-10....... V.9:7 | is not because you will be **p.** otherwise. It |
| T-13.........I.8:3 | For guilt establishes that you will be **p.** for |
| T-13.........I.8:7 | For if what has been will be **p.**, the ego's |
| T-13...... IX.1:4 | are strict, and breaches are severely **p.**. |
| T-19...... III.2:5 | What must be **p.**, must be true. And what |

## punisher 1

| | |
|---|---|
| T-25...... VI.1:5 | an arbiter of vengeance, nor a **p.** of sin. |

## punishes 2

| | |
|---|---|
| T-27... VIII.7:6 | which it **p.** because of all the sinful things |
| T-28...... VI.1:1 | Who **p.** the body is insane. For here the |

## punishing 4

| | |
|---|---|
| T-4........ VI.3:8 | by humbling it or controlling it or **p.** it. |
| T-5......... V.5:6 | The ego believes that by **p.** itself it will |
| T-5......... V.5:8 | It attributes to God a **p.** intent, and then |
| T-13.......in.1:4 | being judged, believing that by **p.** another |

## punishment 54

| | |
|---|---|
| T-2..... VIII.3:3 | healing rather than a meting out of **p.**, |
| T-2..... VIII.3:3 | much you may think that **p.** is deserved. |
| T-2..... VIII.3:4 | **P.** is a concept totally opposed to right- |
| T-5......... V.3:6 | will experience guilt, and you will fear **p.**. |
| T-5......... V.5:6 | itself it will mitigate the **p.** of God. Yet |
| T-6...........I.1:3 | so far has been that it was not a form of **p.** |
| T-6........ I.15:7 | The "**p.**" I was said to have called forth |
| T-6........ I.16:5 | of **p.** involves the projection of blame, |
| T-13.......in.1:2 | as unworthy of love and deserving of **p.**. |
| T-13.......in.1:4 | by punishing another, it will escape **p.**. |
| T-13.......in.2:4 | For this world is the symbol of **p.**, and all |
| T-13...... IX.1:5 | to its laws, for they are laws of **p.**. And |
| T-13...... IX.2:2 | will not escape the **p.** it offers those who |
| T-13...... IX.5:5 | in the other, calling for **p.** instead of love. |
| T-13...... IX.5:6 | to call for **p.** upon yourself must be insane |
| T-15.........I.6:7 | of hell can believe that **p.** will end in peace |
| T-19....... II.1:6 | Sin calls for **p.** as error for correction, and |
| T-19....... II.1:6 | belief that **p.** *is* correction is clearly insane. |
| T-19...... III.2:2 | the ego brings sin to fear, demanding **p.**. |
| T-19...... III.2:3 | punishment. Yet **p.** is but another form of |
| T-19...... III.2:3 | deserving **p.** must have been really done. |
| T-19...... III.2:4 | **P.** is always the great preserver of sin, |
| T-19...... III.3:7 | perception, for it is sin that calls for **p.**, |
| T-19...... III.4:6 | What calls for **p.** must call for nothing. |
| T19. IV.A.13:5 | and would avert the **p.** of him who sends |
| T19.....IV.B.8:1 | me from **p.** for what I have not done. So |
| T-23....... II.4:2 | that errors call for **p.** and not correction. |
| T-23...... III.1:5 | frantic fear of **p.** the murderer must feel? |
| T-25.... III.8:12 | Sin is attacked by **p.**, and so preserved. |
| T-25... VIII.3:2 | for sinners see justice only as their **p.**, |
| T-25. VIII.5:10 | with the idea of **p.** that they lay it aside, |
| T-25... VIII.8:1 | justice cannot punish those who ask for **p.** |
| T-25... VIII.8:5 | its side, and is too weak to save from **p.**. |
| T-25...... IX.3:9 | And **p.** becomes his due instead of justice. |
| T-25...... IX.4:1 | sight of innocence makes **p.** impossible, |
| T-26..... VII.3:1 | Guilt asks for **p.**, and its request is |
| T-26... VIII.7:8 | at **p.** until the time of liberation is at hand |
| T-27..... II.13:6 | His merit **p.**, while yours, in fairness, |
| T-27..... VII.1:3 | shown. Like to a dream of **p.**, in which the |
| T-28...... VI.2:2 | the **p.** you give because it has no feeling. It |
| T-30...... VI.2:3 | nor overlook a real attack that calls for **p.**. |
| W-pI...101.2:1 | real, then **p.** is just and cannot be escaped |
| W-pI...101.4:1 | Who would seek out such savage **p.**? |
| W-pI...151.4:5 | and afraid, how apprehensive of just **p.**, |
| W-pI...156.6:3 | heralds not the end of sin in **p.** and death. |
| W-pI...170.6:3 | Harsh **p.** is meted out relentlessly to those |
| W-pI...196.2:2 | appear to be a sign that **p.** can never be |
| W-pI.196.11:1 | intent on plotting **p.** for you until the |
| W-pII...259.1:4 | of guilt, demanding **p.** and suffering? And |
| W-pII.... 12.2:5 | dreams of **p.**, and trembles at the figures |
| W-pII.... 12.3:4 | What can he know of fear and **p.**, of sin |
| M-12 .........2:4 | feared, for the mind sees no cause for **p.**. |
| S-3 ......... II.5:1 | eyes and takes the form of **p.** for sin. How |
| S-3 ......... II.5:5 | Death is reward and not a **p.**. But such a |

## punitive 2

| | |
|---|---|
| T19..IV.B.12:3 | of sin. It is not really **p.** at all. It is but the |
| W-pI... 191.1:4 | afraid, fearful of shadows, **p.** and wild, |

## puny 1

| | |
|---|---|
| T-24...... III.2:2 | all your **p.** might against the Will of God. |

## pupil 19

| | |
|---|---|
| T-4...........I.1:2 | and **p.** are alike in the learning process. |
| M-2 ...........4:3 | And thus it is that **p.** and teacher seem to |
| M-2 ...........4:4 | The **p.** comes at the right time to the right |
| M-2 ...........5:1 | When **p.** and teacher come together, a |
| M-17 .........1:1 | a crucial question both for teacher and **p.**. |
| M-17 .........1:2 | hurt himself and has also attacked his **p.**. |
| M-17 .........2:5 | will always come to teacher and to **p.** alike |
| M-17 .........3:2 | to nothing but release for teacher and **p.**, |
| M-17 .........3:5 | divided goal of the **p.** into one direction, |
| M-18 .........1:2 | argues with his **p.** about a magic thought, |
| M-18 .........1:3 | has "proved," both to his **p.** and himself, |
| M-18 .........4:4 | in his healing is his **p.** healed with him. |
| M-29 .........1:1 | that both teacher and **p.** may raise. In fact |
| M-29 .........1:4 | that only time divides teacher and **p.**, so |
| M-29 .........1:5 | helpful for the **p.** to read the manual first. |
| P-2......... II.5:3 | if **p.** and teacher join in sharing one goal, |
| P-2......... II.5:6 | Teacher and **p.**, therapist and patient, are |
| P-2......... II.7:2 | teacher uses one approach to every **p.**. On |
| P-2......... II.8:6 | Only by doing this can teacher and **p.**, |

## pupil's 2

| | |
|---|---|
| M-17 .........3:7 | From there it shines into his **p.** mind, |
| M-24 .........5:5 | detrimental to his **p.** advance or his own. |

## pupils 5

| | |
|---|---|
| T-13.........I.1:1 | by teaching their **p.** all they know. The |
| M-2 ..............h | WHO ARE THEIR **P.**? |
| M-2 ...........1:1 | Certain **p.** have been assigned to each of |
| M-2 ...........1:3 | His **p.** have been waiting for him, for his |
| M-23 .........1:3 | if their **p.** were denied healing because of |

## purchase 5

| | |
|---|---|
| T-12...... IV.6:4 | you will sell everything else to **p.** it. And |
| T-14...... III.5:9 | or the happy **p.** of a treasure to hold dear. |
| T-15...... III.8:5 | you have sought to **p.** it with little gifts, |
| T-15....... X.6:1 | whenever you want, and thereby **p.** peace. |
| W-pI...102.2:2 | cannot **p.** anything at all. It offers nothing |

## purchased 3

| | |
|---|---|
| T-12...... IV.6:5 | it. And you will believe that you have **p.** it, |
| T-26....... X.4:3 | Can innocence be **p.** by the giving of your |
| W-pI...101.2:2 | thus cannot be **p.** but through suffering. |

## pure 37

| | |
|---|---|
| T-3...........I.5:4 | "Blessed are the **p.** in heart for they shall |
| T-3...........I.5:5 | A **p.** mind knows the truth and this is its |
| T-3......... II.5:8 | Because their hearts are **p.**, the innocent |
| T-5.............I.1:3 | revelation is an experience of **p.** joy. If you |
| T-5...... IV.2:11 | must be understood as a **p.** act of sharing. |
| T-5...... IV.8:11 | The heart is **p.** to hold it, and the hands |
| T-10...... IV.8:6 | the spark is still as **p.** as the Great Light, |
| T-11...... III.7:6 | And your mind must be as **p.** as His, if |
| T-13.......I.11:8 | And being wholly **p.**, you are invulnerable |
| T-13....... X.2:6 | Spirit, and it is that which makes them **p.**. |
| T-13....... X.9:7 | is as **p.** as He Who raised it to Himself. |
| T-14.... III.12:2 | that He created, for it *is* wholly **p.**. Do not |
| T-15...... IV.9:1 | that you have no thoughts that are not **p.**. |
| T-15..... VII.1:5 | Being wholly **p.**, everyone joined in it has |
| T-20.... III.11:5 | the **p.** in heart see God within His Son, |
| T-24........II.1:6 | stately, clean and honest, **p.** and unsullied |
| T-25.........I.1:7 | and **p.** and worthy of His everlasting Love |
| T-25......II.10:2 | for the wholly **p.** have never sinned. Give, |
| T-26...... III.2:5 | every thought made **p.** and wholly simple. |
| T-31...... VI.7:4 | remains as radiant as a star, as **p.** as light, |
| W-pI..... 93.4:1 | you are as **p.** and holy as you were created |
| W-pI. 151.11:3 | the constancy in change, the **p.** in sin, and |
| W-pI. 151.17:2 | which Heaven has corrected and made **p.**. |
| W-pI. 153.13:3 | of sin forever from the **p.** and holy minds |
| W-pI... 182.4:6 | earth the **p.** reflection of the light above, |
| W-pI... 192.1:1 | shall be His sacred Son, forever **p.** as He, |
| W-pII ....263.h | My holy vision sees all things as **p.**. |
| W-pII . 263.2:2 | Let all appearances seem **p.** to us, that we |
| W-pII . 276.1:2 | "My Son is **p.** and holy as Myself." And |
| W-pII . 280.1:5 | No Thought of God but is forever **p.**. Can |
| W-pII ... 10.5:1 | and completely changeless and forever **p.**. |
| W-pII . 341.1:3 | *How **p.**, how safe, how holy, then, are we,* |
| M-16 ......... 6:2 | It is a thought of **p.** joy; a thought of peace |
| C-2............ 9:5 | is, is wholly uncondemned and wholly **p.**. |
| C-4............ 7:1 | certain, **p.** and wholly understandable, |
| C-4............ 8:1 | safe and **p.** and lovely in the Mind of God, |
| S-1 ..........II.7:7 | clad forever in the **p.** sinlessness that is |

## purely 2

| | |
|---|---|
| T-2......... V.5:4 | and reinstating its **p.** constructive powers, |
| W-pI... 158.1:2 | that you are a mind, in Mind and **p.** mind |

## purification 4

| | |
|---|---|
| T-1...........I.7:1 | everyone's right, but **p.** is necessary first. |
| T-5...... IV.3:12 | The decision to share them *is* their **p.**. |
| T-15..... VII.6:2 | The "sacrifice," which it regards as **p.**, is |
| T-18...... IV.5:7 | **P.** is of God alone, and therefore for you. |

## purified 7

| | |
|---|---|
| T-5...... IV.3:11 | sufficiently **p.** He lets you give them away. |
| T-5......... IV.8:4 | I have **p.** them of the errors that hid their |
| T-5....... V.7:11 | is to save the past in **p.** form only. If you |
| T-13..... X.14:4 | so **p.** that it is fitting as a hymn of praise |
| T-18... IX.14:2 | perception has been cleansed and **p.**, and |
| W-pI..... 43.1:5 | and **p.** that it will lead to knowledge. That |
| W-pI. 151.15:2 | ministry begins as all your thoughts are **p.** |

## purifies 1

| | |
|---|---|
| T-6...... V.C.1:4 | partly in accord with it He accepts and **p.**. |

## purify 2

| | |
|---|---|
| T-15....... V.5:2 | He would **p.** and not let you destroy. |
| T-17....... V.6:5 | **p.** what He has taken under His guidance |

## purity 40

| | |
|---|---|
| T-13.........I.5:6 | the brightness of his **p.** shines untouched |
| T-13.........I.7:6 | mind, and by accepting his **p.** as yours, |
| T-13... VII.17:9 | God give thanks unto his Father for his **p.** |
| T-13........X.2:2 | or even hold one spot of it to mar its **p.**. |
| T-13........X.9:4 | is the perfect **p.** in which you were created |
| T-13... X.10:11 | perfect **p.** that is forever within God's Son |
| T-13... X.11:10 | *Son of God, and look upon his **p.** and be still.* |
| T-13..... X.12:2 | His shining **p.**, wholly untouched by guilt |
| T-13..... X.12:6 | Father, for the **p.** of Your most holy Son, |
| T-14.... III.12:2 | perfect **p.** of everything that He created, |
| T-14.... III.13:5 | against this strange distortion of the **p.** of |
| T-14....... V.3:4 | is the natural extension of perfect **p.**. |
| T-14....... V.4:3 | it. Protect his **p.** from every thought that |
| T-14....... V.4:5 | Never allow **p.** to remain hidden, but |
| T-14....... V.8:2 | peace is the acknowledgment of perfect **p.** |
| T-14..... V.11:2 | If you bring him into the circle of **p.**, you |
| T-14...... IX.4:2 | knows they will return to **p.** and to grace. |
| T-15.......I.15:5 | in which God's Son could lose his **p.**. His |
| T-15.......I.15:6 | for his **p.** remains forever beyond attack |
| T-15...... IV.9:9 | Let the Holy Spirit's **p.** shine them away, |
| T-15...... IV.9:9 | to the readiness for **p.** He offers you. Thus |
| T-16...... III.7:6 | will learn His power and strength and **p.**, |

T-18 IX.9:7 by, and gently replaced by **p.** and love.
T-19 II.4:2 deceive. **P.** is seen as arrogance, and the
T-20 I.2:4 we honor the perfect **p.** of the Son of God,
T-20 VIII.4:4 glowing with radiant **p.** and sparkling
T-22 II.13:6 Heaven is the home of perfect **p.**, and
T-25 I.4:3 is framed in holiness and perfect **p.**, in
T-28 II.2:3 **P.** is not confined. It is the nature of the
T-28 II.2:5 Thus is **p.** not of the body. Nor can it be
T-30 III.9:2 Its perfect **p.** does not depend on whether
W-pI 156.5:5 light all things unto Its likeness and Its **p.**.
W-pI 158.7:3 can be touched, a **p.** undimmed by errors,
W-pI 187.9:3 before the **p.** that you will look on here.
W-pI 187.10:5 within, we see the **p.** of Heaven shine in
W-pII 252.1:2 Its shimmering and perfect **p.** is far more
W-pII 263.1:4 *with which You blessed creation; all its* ***p.***,
W-pII 13.3:5 in the light of perfect **p.** and endless joy.
W-pII 14.1:6 *Itself, for in my* ***p.*** *abides His Own.*
S-1 V.2:6 **p.** it recognizes that it shares with him.

## Purpose 2

*purpose*

T-19 I.3:4 itself as separated from the Universal **P.**.
T-19 I.3:5 becomes its weapon, used against this **P.**,

## purpose 663

*Purpose*

T-1 I.10:1 belief is a misunderstanding of their **p.**.
T-1 I.15:2 **p.** of time is to enable you to learn how to
T-1 III.1:10 profession of the children of God, is the **p.**
T-1 IV.3:6 The **p.** of the Atonement is to restore
T-1 V.1:2 the body nor the miracle serves any **p.**.
T-1 VI.4:1 real **p.** of this world is to use it to correct
T-2 IV.3:3 Their **p.** is merely to facilitate learning.
T-2 V.3:4 its **p.** is to restore him *to* his right mind. It
T-2 VII.1:6 direct opposition to the **p.** of this course.
T-2 VIII.5:8 The **p.** of time is solely to "give you time"
T-3 II.5:6 This single **p.** creates perfect integration
T-3 IV.7:6 remembered spirit and its real **p.**. I
T-3 V.2:3 a specific **p.** has no true generalizability.
T-3 V.2:5 ingenious thought systems for this **p.**.
T-3 VII.3:9 of destroying Their Own **p.** is in error.
T-4 V.6:5 with nonessentials is for precisely that **p.**.
T-4 V.6:9 What is the **p.**? Whatever it is, it will
T-4 V.6:11 When you make a decision of **p.**, then,
T-5 V.1:2 The ego has a **p.**, just as the Holy Spirit
T-5 V.1:3 has. The ego's **p.** is fear, because only the
T-5 V.7:11 **p.** of the Atonement is to save the past in
T-5 VI.4:4 only does the ego cite Scripture for its **p.**,
T-6 I.2:7 **p.** of the crucifixion and how it actually
T-6 I.8:5 serving the **p.** for which God intended it. I
T-6 I.10:3 That is their only **p.**, and that is the only
T-6 II.3:2 its only **p.** is to keep the separation going.
T-7 II.4:4 his whole **p.** is to change the form so that
T-7 II.5:1 Holy Spirit's **p.** in translating is exactly
T-7 IV.3:1 learned, because that would defeat its **p.**.
T-7 VIII.2:5 the mind only to defeat the mind's real **p.**.
T-7 VIII.7:1 The whole **p.** of this course is to teach you
T-8 I.4:3 aims at change, and that is always its **p.**,
T-8 II.1:3 that knowledge is the **p.** of the curriculum
T-8 III.6:2 the ego, whose **p.** is to defeat its own goal.
T-8 IV.2:8 My **p.**, then, is still to overcome the world
T-8 VII.7:7 is to lose sight of the Holy Spirit's **p.**, and
T-8 VII.9:2 Its **p.** is seen as fragmented into many
T-8 VII.10:6 body, for if it does it is blocked in its **p.**. A
T-8 VII.11:6 of attack is an obvious confusion in **p.**.
T-8 VII.12:3 of the body can be unified only by one **p.**.
T-8 VII.13:4 is therefore nothing more than united **p.**.
T-8 VII.13:5 body is brought under the **p.** of the mind,
T-8 VII.13:5 it becomes whole because the mind's **p.** is
T-8 VII.13:6 can only be an assumed **p.** of the body,
T-8 VII.13:6 from the mind the body has no **p.** at all.
T-8 VII.14:4 when your whole **p.** for learning should
T-8 VII.14:6 to the unified **p.** of the curriculum, and
T-8 VII.14:6 with his ability to accept its **p.** as his own.
T-8 VII.15:1 Joy is unified **p.**, and unified purpose is
T-8 VII.15:1 purpose, and unified **p.** is only God's.
T-8 VII.15:3 Believe you can interfere with His **p.**, and
T-8 VIII.5:3 This is the **p.** of everything the ego does.
T-8 IX.4:5 have you utilized sleep according to His **p.**
T-8 IX.8:7 is split, and does not accept a unified **p.**.
T-8 IX.9:1 The unification of **p.**, then, is the Holy
T-9 I.2:4 **p.** of this course is to help you remember
T-9 I.3:6 **p.** of this Guide is merely to remind you of
T-9 II.1:4 that its **p.** is the escape from fear.
T-11 V.4:5 beginning, then, its **p.** is to be separate,
T-11 V.5:1 Every idea has a **p.**, and its purpose is
T-11 V.5:1 and its **p.** is always the natural outcome of
T-11 V.7:4 are, because it is perfectly certain of its **p.**.
T-11 V.11:1 accomplished God's **p.** could be defeated,
T-11 V.11:3 can be accomplished and God's **p.** can *not*
T-11 V.11:4 *only* God's **p.** can be accomplished, and it
T-12 I.9:10 to conceal love, which was its only **p.**. The
T-12 II.6:1 can defeat a child of God in his **p.**. For
T-12 II.6:2 For your **p.** was given you by God, and
T-12 II.6:3 Awake and remember your **p.**, for it is
T-12 II.10:6 fail to help you, since help is His only **p.**.
T-12 VI.7:4 no **p.** as it blends into the purpose of God.
T-12 VI.7:4 no purpose as it blends into the **p.** of God.
T-12 VII.4:10 in direct opposition to the Holy Spirit's **p.**
T-13 II.1:1 ultimate **p.** of projection is always to get
T-13 IV.7:3 The Holy Spirit interprets time's **p.** as
T-13 IV.8:2 is the only **p.** the ego perceives in time,
T-13 X.2:4 you have made for this strange **p.**! And
T-13 X.6:6 The **p.** of Atonement is to dispel illusions,
T-14 V.6:4 for the single **p.** of release from guilt, to
T-14 V.9:9 the only **p.** to which my teaching calls you
T-14 VI.5:3 have use to Him, for His most holy **p.**. He
T-14 VI.6:2 meaning, for its **p.** is not communication,
T-14 VI.6:3 If the **p.** of language is communication,
T-14 VII.5:7 perception of them, according to His **p.**,
T-14 VII.7:5 into *one* meaning, *one* emotion and *one* **p.**.
T-14 VII.7:6 God has one **p.** which He shares with you.
T-15 V.1:2 For its **p.** is to suspend judgment entirely.
T-15 VII.2:4 This is not its statement, but it *is* its **p.**. For
T-15 VII.14:3 only **p.** is to disrupt communication, has
T-15 IX.3:2 the ego has no **p.** you would share with it.
T-15 IX.3:3 purposes, and while you think it has a **p.**,
T-15 IX.3:3 it tries to turn its **p.** into accomplishment.
T-15 IX.4:1 is the only **p.** for which it was given you.
T-16 IV.3:5 acceptable only as long as he serves this **p.**
T-16 IV.4:5 use them for any **p.** which they would not
T-16 V.9:4 The real **p.** of the special relationship, in
T-16 VII.2:11 it serves some **p.** that you want fulfilled.
T-16 VII.2:12 this **p.** could not be fulfilled in the present
T-17 I.1:9 That is their **p.**. They cannot do so in
T-17 II.3:7 he has learned, has served its **p.**.
T-17 III.1:8 came into your mind, and what their **p.** is.
T-17 III.2:3 these relationships have as their **p.** the
T-17 III.4:4 must enter in, because its **p.** is impossible.
T-17 III.5:1 whose only **p.** is separation from reality?
T-17 III.8:4 the **p.** of the unholy alliance are retained,
T-17 III.10:6 let not the holy **p.** of Atonement be lost to
T-17 IV.1:1 do that does not share His **p.** can be real.
T-17 IV.1:2 The **p.** God ascribed to anything is its
T-17 IV.2:6 But the holy relationship shares God's **p.**,
T-17 IV.3:3 you have made has, as its fundamental **p.**,
T-17 IV.4:7 preserved, to serve God's **p.** for you.
T-17 IV.7:6 Its **p.** is to be of value *in itself,* and to divert
T-17 V.3:5 to the **p.** that has been accepted for it. In
T-17 V.4:2 inappropriateness for meeting its new **p.**.
T-17 V.5:2 Only a radical shift in **p.** could induce a
T-17 V.5:6 from the point of view of this new **p.**, they
T-17 V.5:8 serves the **p.** they have agreed to meet.
T-17 V.6:8 And your relationship has sanity as its **p.**.
T-17 V.8:1 perceive its **p.** work in it to make it holy.
T-17 V.8:2 for it will seem at times to have no **p.**. A
T-17 V.14:4 this same discrepancy between the **p.** that
T-17 V.14:7 yours. You *are* joined in **p.**, but remain still
T-17 VI.1:1 of the Holy Spirit's **p.** is extremely simple,
T-17 VI.6:2 in the acceptance of the Holy Spirit's **p.**,
T-17 VII.5:1 to meet the **p.** set for your relationship.
T-17 VII.6:7 but will be gently turned to its use and **p.**.
T-17 VII.8:8 entered any situation that shares Its **p.**.
T-17 VII.8:9 everyone to whom the situation's **p.** calls.
T-17 VII.8:13 it shares the **p.** of your whole relationship,
T-17 VII.9:2 faith will call the others to share your **p.**,
T-17 VII.9:2 as the same **p.** called forth the faith in you
T-17 VII.9:5 When the Holy Spirit changed the **p.** of
T-17 VIII.1:2 The meaning that the Holy Spirit's **p.** has
T-17 VIII.3:3 of the Holy Spirit's **p.** is free to use instead
T-17 VIII.3:4 continuous means for establishing His **p.**,
T-17 VIII.5:7 His salvation is your only **p.**. See only this
T-17 VIII.6:3 Your **p.** has not changed, and will not
T-18 I.1:4 For this special **p.**, one is judged more
T-18 I.1:5 fragmented, and its **p.** split accordingly.
T-18 I.13:5 **p.** in which you join with your brother.
T-18 II.6:6 as a help to make His **p.** real to you. The
T-18 II.7:4 anyone in the **p.** He has given you. And
T-18 II.7:10 For we are joined as in one **p.**, being of
T-18 II.8:4 because its **p.** has been changed from one
T-18 V.1:3 is accomplished, would have no **p.**. For
T-18 V.3:6 it. The means and **p.** both belong to Him.
T-18 V.3:8 A **p.** such as this, without the means, is
T-18 V.3:9 the means to anyone who shares His **p.**.
T-18 V.4:4 The alignment of means and **p.** is an
T-18 V.4:5 accepted the Holy Spirit's **p.** as your own,
T-18 V.4:6 to change the **p.** is all that is required to
T-18 VII.4:10 will ultimately succeed because of their **p.**.
T-18 VII.5:1 will be different, not in **p.** but in means. A
T-18 IX.3:8 For it is not His **p.** to frighten you, but
T-18 IX.13:1 and its unholy **p.** has been safely brought
T-18 IX.14:1 learning, for your only **p.** will be creating.
T-18 IX.14:4 There is your **p.** *now.* And it is there that
T-19 I.2:5 in a united **p.** that makes this purpose real
T-19 I.2:5 in a united purpose that makes this **p.** real
T-19 I.3:3 and the **p.** that the mind would use it for.
T-19 I.4:5 has thus opposed the Holy Spirit's **p.**, and
T-19 I.10:5 united in your **p.** to be released from guilt
T-19 I.12:5 Your holy relationship, with its new **p.**,
T-19 I.16:5 to which it chooses as its **p.** for itself.
T-19 II.3:4 is what sin would do, for such is its **p.**. Yet
T-19 II.5:5 fundamental **p.** of the special relationship
T-19 III.8:4 Your holy relationship has, as its **p.** now,
T-19 IV.1:5 extension of the Holy Spirit's **p.** from your
T19 IV.A.3:1 Holy Spirit's **p.** rests in peace within you.
T19 IV.A.3:8 little wall would hide the **p.** of Heaven,
T19 IV.A.4:8 It is your **p.**. You cannot choose apart
T19 IV.A.4:10 You have no **p.** apart from your brother,
T19 IV.A.5:10 to stand between Him and His holy **p.**, for
T19 IV.A.7:2 upon anything, for it has no **p.** now.
T19 IV.A.7:3 with you it seemed to have a mighty **p.**;
T19 IV.B.10:6 It has no **p.** of itself, but only what is given
T19 IV.B.10:8 Only the mind can set a **p.**, and only the
T19 IV.B.12:5 it invites fear to enter and become your **p.**
T19 IV.C.2:13 When you accepted the Holy Spirit's **p.** in
T19 IV.C.5:1 as long as it is useful for your holy **p.**. The
T19 IV.C.6:3 The body can but serve your **p.**. As you
T19 IV.C.9:4 you. Your newborn **p.** is nursed by angels,
T19 IV.D.9:6 instant, here in this place where the **p.**,
T19 IV.D.10:5 A journey without a **p.** is still meaningless
T19 IV.D.10:6 unless you realize its **p.** is accomplished?
T19 IV.D.10:7 the journey's end before you, you *see* its **p.**.
T19 IV.D.19:3 This is the journey's **p.**, without which is
T19 IV.D.21:4 Here is the only **p.** that gives this world,
T19 IV.D.21:6 still without conviction they have a **p.**. Yet
T19 IV.D.21:7 you to see this **p.** in your holy Friend, and
T-20 I.2:2 intervene between the journey and its **p.**;
T-20 II.5:3 accept the Holy Spirit's **p.** as their own
T-20 II.5:4 And what enables Him to see His **p.** shine
T-20 III.7:3 off. He came without a **p.**, but he will not
T-20 III.8:9 That is the **p.** of your holy relationship.
T-20 IV.6:6 Spirit's plan, now that it shares His **p.**.
T-20 IV.6:7 And as this **p.** is fulfilled, a new world
T-20 IV.7:1 This is the **p.** given you. Think not that
T-20 IV.8:8 except the only **p.** that you would fulfill.
T-20 V.1:7 No one who has a single **p.**, unified and
T-20 V.1:8 his **p.** with him can *not* be one with him.
T-20 V.5:4 which serves the **p.** of a holy relationship.
T-20 VI.7:8 Spirit's **p.** lies safe in your relationship,
T-20 VII.1:2 come from the same Source as does His **p.**
T-20 VII.2:2 the means to Him Who changed the **p.**.
T-20 VII.2:6 A **p.** is attained by means, and if you want
T-20 VII.2:6 and if you want a **p.** you must be willing
T-20 VII.3:4 hesitate, it is because the **p.** frightens you,
T-20 VII.3:8 your wanting of the **p.** has been shaken.

| | |
|---|---|
| T-20.....VII.5:3 | But the *p.* here is sin. It cannot be attained |
| T-20.....VII.5:4 | quite in keeping with the p. of unholiness. |
| T-20.....VII.7:2 | difference lies not in them, but in their p.. |
| T-20.....VII.7:4 | Neither can serve the p. of the other, for |
| T-20.....VII.7:4 | of the other, for each one is a *choice* of p., |
| T-20.....VII.8:2 | the Holy Spirit offers you to serve His p.. |
| T-20.....VII.8:3 | a holy relationship achieve its p. through |
| T-20...VII.8:10 | Such was your p., and while this purpose |
| T-20...VII.8:10 | and while this p. seems to have a meaning |
| T-20... VIII.2:6 | And as its holy p. was not made by you, |
| T-20... VIII.3:2 | for it with real desire and sincerity of p., |
| T-20... VIII.4:2 | This is your p. now, and the vision that |
| T-20... VIII.6:3 | For it will meet His p., seen in unadjusted |
| T-20... VIII.6:9 | and its most holy p. bereft of means for its |
| T-20... VIII.8:6 | thing is sure; hallucinations serve a p., |
| T-20... VIII.8:6 | that p. is no longer held they disappear. |
| T-20... VIII.8:7 | always, do you want the p. that they serve |
| T-20. VIII.10:6 | p. brought to your horrified awareness. |
| T-21........II.9:4 | of a fearful world to justify its p.. What |
| T-21.....II.10:2 | p. now becomes to keep obscure the cause |
| T-21......III.1:5 | from the accepted p. of the relationship. |
| T-21......III.1:6 | why the Holy Spirit must change its p. to |
| T-21......III.2:3 | it is not your p. and you no longer want it. |
| T-21......III.2:4 | No one allows a p. to be replaced while he |
| T-21......III.6:2 | His p. lies in the opposite direction. He |
| T-21......III.6:3 | but not the p. for which you made them. |
| T-21......III.9:1 | is how they think *their* p. is accomplished. |
| T-21....III.11:2 | not what it is His p. to lead you *from*. You |
| T-21......IV.4:5 | The Holy Spirit's p. was accepted by the |
| T-21......IV.4:9 | to see the Holy Spirit's p. as its own? |
| T-21......IV.5:4 | not the ego that joined the Holy Spirit's p. |
| T-21.....V.5:11 | and has your freedom as the p. given it, |
| T-21.....V.7:10 | serves the Holy Spirit's p. in its own right. |
| T-21.......V.9:2 | Here was the Holy Spirit's p. accepted and |
| T-21.....V.10:6 | beyond itself, as does the p. that it serves, |
| T-21......VI.5:2 | But madness has a p., and believes it also |
| T-21......VI.5:2 | it also has the means to make its p. real. |
| T-21....VI.7:10 | kind as is the p. for which it is the means, |
| T-22.......II.5:6 | guilt was given to the Holy Spirit as His p. |
| T-22.......II.6:2 | to let the Holy Spirit's p. be accomplished |
| T-22......IV.1:4 | whole p. of coming this far was to decide |
| T-23.......in.4:6 | Your destiny and p. are far beyond them, |
| T-23.......in.4:7 | p. is at variance with littleness of any kind |
| T-23......I.2:11 | This is the conflict's p.. And to those who |
| T-23.......II.1:5 | because it is their p. to make meaningless, |
| T-23...II.12:12 | the p. of seizing it and making it your own |
| T-23.....II.13:9 | This is their p.; they were made for this. |
| T-23......III.1:4 | Its p. does not change. Its sole intent is |
| T-23......III.1:7 | p. rises to meet his horrified awareness |
| T-23......III.3:5 | awareness of salvation's p. is lost because |
| T-23......III.5:4 | savage p. is directed against themselves? |
| T-23......III.5:5 | enemies, nor is at one with them in p.. |
| T-23......IV.4:7 | of the battleground is now your p.. |
| T-23......IV.7:3 | attack and murder, and if this is your p., |
| T-23......IV.7:4 | Only a p. unifies, and those who share a |
| T-23......IV.7:4 | those who share a p. have a mind as one. |
| T-23......IV.7:5 | The body has no p. of itself, and must be |
| T-23......IV.7:8 | He created for His Son *because* it has no p.. |
| T-23......IV.8:1 | is given those who share their Father's p., |
| T-24.........I.1:2 | the smallest gift is not to know love's p.. |
| T-24.........I.6:4 | in specialness; his friend in a shared p.. |
| T-24.........I.7:5 | this is now the only p. that you share. And |
| T-24.........I.8:5 | For here the p. that you and your brother |
| T-24.........I.8:7 | You have no p. that is not the same, and |
| T-24.....II.12:2 | serves its p. must be given to kill. No gift |
| T-24.....II.12:6 | And no relationship that holds its p. dear |
| T-24......IV.2:1 | the p. of the body be but specialness? And |
| T-24......IV.2:6 | P. is of the mind. And minds can change |
| T-24......IV.2:9 | But what they hold as p. can be changed, |
| T-24......IV.3:5 | The p. of attack is in the mind, and its |
| T-24......IV.3:6 | must it be that harmful p. hurts the mind |
| T-24......IV.3:9 | For miracles are merely change of p. from |
| T-24....IV.3:10 | shift in p. does "endanger" specialness, |
| T-24.......V.5:4 | And yet because they serve a different p., |
| T-24.......V.5:4 | the strength their p. holds is given them. |
| T-24......VI.4:2 | is the only p. the Holy Spirit sees in it, and |
| T-24......VI.4:4 | will use the world for what is not its p., |
| T-24......VI.9:2 | without a p. and without accomplishment |
| T-24....VI.13:2 | forth for you the p. that you can attain, |
| T-24....VI.13:7 | from His p. comes the means for effortless |
| T-24.....VII.4:7 | And if you see this p. in your brother's, |
| T-24.....VII.5:5 | Only the p. that you see in it has meaning, |
| T-24.....VII.5:6 | not, it has no p., and is means for nothing |
| T-24.....VII.5:9 | Its holy p. gave it immortality, setting |
| T-24.....VII.6:3 | to it, according to the p. that you serve. |
| T-24.....VII.7:5 | one thought with p. still uncertain, or one |
| T-24.....VII.8:3 | Here are the means and the p. separate |
| T-24.....VII.8:5 | down until its p. has been understood. |
| T-24...VII.10:7 | the means to serve his "father's" p.. Not |
| T-24.VII.10:10 | and witness to His Love and shared His p. |
| T-24...VII.11:5 | do. They have a different p.. It is this that |
| T-24...VII.11:6 | each from all aspects with a different p.. |
| T-24.VII.11:12 | and use perception for a different p.. And |
| T-24.VII.11:13 | And what you see will serve that p. well, |
| T-25.......in.1:8 | frame of Holiness whose only p. is that He |
| T-25.......in.3:4 | His p. folds the body in His light, and fills |
| T-25.........I.3:4 | And always is it faithful to your p., from |
| T-25.........I.3:4 | anything the p. in your mind upholdeth |
| T-25.........I.3:5 | is a part of what it is your p. to behold, for |
| T-25.........I.6:1 | Holy Spirit serves Christ's p. in your mind |
| T-25.........I.6:2 | p. still is one with Both the Father and the |
| T-25.......II.4:5 | A frame that hides the picture has no p.. |
| T-25.......II.4:8 | Its p. is to set the picture off, and not itself |
| T-25.......II.6:3 | This is its p., and you do not make the |
| T-25.......II.6:4 | that God has given it but serves His p., |
| T-25.......II.6:5 | your separate p. that obscures the picture, |
| T-25.....II.9:11 | offered to everyone who shares His p.. It |
| T-25.....II.11:2 | And you must have one p., since He gave |
| T-25......III.3:4 | To each it has a different p., and to each it |
| T-25......III.5:1 | is another p. in the world that error made, |
| T-25......III.5:1 | can reconcile its goal with His Creator's p. |
| T-25......III.7:9 | Such its p. is, to those who want to see |
| T-25......III.9:6 | Is it your p. that he be saved or damned? |
| T-25....III.9:10 | the p. of the world you see is chosen, and |
| T-25......IV.1:4 | their p. to behold it and rejoice. Everyone |
| T-25......IV.2:7 | sharing his Father's p. in his own creation |
| T-25.......V.1:2 | need for guilt is gone because it has no p., |
| T-25......IX.6:8 | salvation, if its p. is the end of specialness |
| T-26.........I.5:1 | that they might see a p. in the world that |
| T-26.......II.1:6 | no p. to attempt to solve it in a special |
| T-26......III.5:6 | Its only p. is to teach what is the same and |
| T-26......III.7:1 | change of p. in what once was specialness, |
| T-26.......V.1:3 | This is its only p., for only that is all there |
| T-26.......V.2:5 | you undertake with certain p. and high |
| T-26.......V.2:6 | that leads to nothing and that has no p.. |
| T-26.....VII.1:2 | the p. of the course can be accomplished. |
| T-26...VII.15:1 | serve the p. they were made to serve. And |
| T-26...VII.15:2 | p. they derive whatever meaning that they |
| T-26...VII.15:3 | to all illusions that were made another p. |
| T-26... VIII.3:2 | of loss is great between the time its p. is |
| T-26... VIII.5:2 | No p. has been given it as yet, and what |
| T-26... VIII.6:3 | The change of p. the Holy Spirit brought |
| T-26... VIII.7:9 | Given a change of p. for the good, there is |
| T-26... VIII.9:9 | The Holy Spirit's p. now is yours. Should |
| T-26......IX.4:2 | When They come, time's p. is fulfilled. |
| T-26......IX.8:7 | Now is the Holy Spirit's p. done. For They |
| T-26.......X.5:2 | this game do you perceive one p. for your |
| T-26.......X.5:3 | this you seek to add unto the p. given it. |
| T-26.......X.5:4 | The Holy Spirit's p. is to let the Presence |
| T-26.......X.5:5 | And to this p. nothing can be added, for |
| T-26.......X.5:6 | all p. from the world and from yourself. |
| T-26.......X.6:3 | unfairly left without a p. in a futile world. |
| T-27.........I.5:3 | this one has not been used for p. of attack, |
| T-27.........I.6:4 | world. Its only p. is to prove guilt real. No |
| T-27.........I.9:5 | Pictured without a p., it is seen as neither |
| T-27.........I.9:9 | witnesses to nothing yet, its p. being open |
| T-27.......I.9:10 | but waiting for a p. to be given, that it |
| T-27.......I.10:4 | Let it have healing as its p.. Then will it |
| T-27.......I.11:1 | to let the body have no p. from the past, |
| T-27.......I.11:1 | sure you knew its p. was to foster guilt. |
| T-27.......I.11:3 | space in which a different view, another p. |
| T-27.......I.11:4 | it. You do *not* know its p.. You but gave |
| T-27.......I.11:5 | gave illusions of a p. to a thing you made |
| T-27.......I.11:6 | This thing without a p. cannot hide the |
| T-27.......I.11:7 | p. and your function both be reconciled at |
| T-27.....II.12:5 | seems to have a different p. from the one |
| T-27.....II.13:1 | thought extends because that is its p., |
| T-27.....II.15:4 | free. That is divided p., which can not be |
| T-27......II.16:3 | as one because it is not split in p., and |
| T-27......II.16:6 | His single p. unifies the halves of you that |
| T-27......III.1:4 | be limited and weak, because that is its p.. |
| T-27......IV.1:2 | for its p. is to make no resolution possible |
| T-27......IV.4:8 | form the question takes, its p. is the same. |
| T-27.......V.2:6 | Your single p. makes this possible. But if |
| T-27......VI.1:4 | Its p. is the same as pleasure, for they |
| T-27......VI.1:5 | What shares a common p. is the same. |
| T-27......VI.1:6 | This is the law of p., which unites all those |
| T-27......VI.1:7 | because their p. cannot be achieved. Thus |
| T-27......VI.1:9 | the lack of meaning which their p. has. |
| T-27....VI.6:10 | The p. of a miracle is to accomplish this. |
| T-27.....VII.5:1 | This is the p. of the world he sees. And |
| T-27.....VII.5:2 | by which this p. seems to be fulfilled. The |
| T-27.....VII.5:3 | attest the p., but are not themselves a |
| T-27....VIII.3:2 | dream will never change, nor will its p.. |
| T-27....VIII.3:3 | finds itself, the dream has but one p., |
| T-27....VIII.7:7 | control its actions nor its p. nor its fate. |
| T-28.........I.2:8 | made, it can be used to serve another p., |
| T-28........II.4:3 | depending on the p. of your dreaming. |
| T-28........II.6:4 | Yet if it has no cause, it has no p.. You |
| T-28......III.4:5 | p. of the gap is all the cause that sickness |
| T-28......VI.1:5 | does not tell you what its p. is and cannot |
| T-28.....VII.4:1 | With *this* as p. is the body healed. It is not |
| T-28.....VII.4:4 | Son, and for this p. it cannot be sick. It |
| T-28.....VII.4:5 | It will not join a p. not your own, and you |
| T-28.....VII.7:8 | And with this holy p. is it made a home of |
| T-29.........I.5:7 | do, and keep your p. limited and weak. |
| T-29.........I.6:5 | meet, and see in them a p. not your own. |
| T-29........II.7:5 | Yet here on earth it has a double p., for it |
| T-29........II.7:8 | in its belief of what the p. of the body is. |
| T-29......IV.5:5 | Perceptions are determined by their p., in |
| T-29.......V.3:2 | and not for any p. you may see in him. |
| T-29......VI.3:1 | Nothing survives its p.. If it be conceived |
| T-29......VI.3:2 | unless it does not take this p. as its own. |
| T-29......VI.3:3 | made a blessing here, where p. is not fixed |
| T-29......VI.3:4 | you can set a goal unlike God's p. for you, |
| T-29......VI.3:5 | can give yourself a p. that you do not have |
| T-29......VI.3:6 | your mind, and see another p. there. |
| T-29......VI.4:6 | Its p. ended, it is gone. And where it once |
| T-29......VI.6:1 | whose p. is forgiveness of God's Son! How |
| T-29.....VII.2:4 | This is the p. he bestows upon the body; |
| T-29.....VII.3:5 | This is the p. every idol has, for this the |
| T-29.....VII.7:1 | Let us forget the p. of the world the past |
| T-29.....VII.8:1 | you do not know the p. of the world. You |
| T-29....VIII.1:5 | Their p. is obscure, and they are feared |
| T-29....VIII.4:1 | because its p. is to separate your brother |
| T-29....VIII.4:2 | dark and fearful p., yet a thought without |
| T-29....VIII.8:1 | What p. has an idol, then? What is it for? |
| T-29....VIII.9:4 | speaks, and tells you idols have no p. here |
| T-29......IX.7:6 | all is joy, because that is the p. that it has. |
| T-30.......I.11:6 | Its p. has no longer been obscured by the |
| T-30......III.2:9 | want, you lose the understanding of its p.. |
| T-30......III.3:5 | This is the p. of an idol; that you will not |
| T-30..........V.h | The Only P. |
| T-30.......V.1:1 | p. of the world is seen to be forgiveness. |
| T-30.......V.2:7 | because its only p. is to be a place where |
| T-30.......V.2:8 | world has been united in belief the p. of |
| T-30.......V.3:1 | for the p. of forgiveness still remains. Yet |
| T-30.......V.3:4 | because he is united in his p. with himself. |
| T-30.......V.4:3 | has a p. still beneath creation and eternity |
| T-30.......V.4:4 | fear is gone because its p. is forgiveness, |
| T-30.......V.5:1 | falls short of this, for this is God's Own p.; |
| T-30.......V.5:4 | then can guilt and sin be seen without a p. |
| T-30.......V.6:1 | world's p. gently brought into awareness, |
| T-30.......V.7:1 | brothers join in p. in the world of fear, |
| T-30.....V.11:3 | But when they joined and shared a p., |
| T-30......VI.7:2 | p. cannot be to judge which forms are real |
| T-30.....VII.1:4 | Spirit looks upon the world as with one p. |
| T-30.....VII.3:1 | constant p. can endow events with stable |
| T-30.....VII.4:1 | A common p. is the only means whereby |
| T-30.....VII.4:2 | In this shared p. is one judgment shared |
| T-30.....VII.5:1 | lies in this; all things have but one p., |
| T-30.....VII.5:3 | single p. is the end of all ideas of sacrifice, |
| T-30.....VII.5:3 | which must assume a different p. for the |
| T-30.....VII.6:8 | They have no p.. And what they are for |
| T-31.........I.5:5 | for their learning is the only p. for your |
| T-31.......I.12:1 | of what things mean and what their p. is. |
| T-31........II.4:4 | for, and learned to think that this his p. is. |

| | |
|---|---|
| T-31 II.4:6 | he has no **p.** and no usefulness to you. |
| T-31 II.10:2 | will perceive his **p.** is the same as yours. |
| T-31 II.10:5 | receive, for you have come with but one **p.** |
| T-31 III.3:8 | And **p.** must be in the body, not the mind. |
| T-31 III.3:10 | and you give its **p.** to its prison house, |
| T-31 III.4:9 | to suit the **p.** given by the mind. For mind |
| T-31 III.5:1 | mind that thinks it is a sin has but one **p.**; |
| T-31 IV.1:1 | escape from problems that its **p.** is to keep |
| T-31 IV.3:10 | The lesson has a **p.**, and in this you come |
| T-31 IV.4:2 | **p.** is the answer to the search that all must |
| T-31 IV.4:8 | you see the **p.** of the lesson shining clear, |
| T-31 IV.6:2 | against this step is to defeat your **p.** here. |
| T-31 IV.7:4 | way will not advance the **p.** to be found. If |
| T-31 IV.8:5 | when all the lesson's **p.** is to teach that |
| T-31 IV.9:4 | to separate the journey from the **p.** it |
| T-31 V.1:6 | This is its **p.**; that you come without a self, |
| T-31 VIII.10:8 | For we are one in **p.**, and the end of hell is |
| W-in 1:4 | It is the **p.** of this workbook to train your |
| W-in 4:1 | The **p.** of the workbook is to train your |
| W-pI 1.3:2 | applied. That is the **p.** of the exercise. The |
| W-pI 3.2:3 | this **p.** one thing is like another; equally |
| W-pI 4.3:3 | It is a first attempt in the long-range **p.** of |
| W-pI 6.2:1 | be used throughout the day for that **p.**. |
| W-pI 8.3:1 | **p.** of the exercises for today is to begin to |
| W-pI 12.5:9 | That is the ultimate **p.** of these exercises. |
| W-pI 16.5:5 | The following form is suggested for this **p.** |
| W-pI 20.3:4 | the salvation of the world be a trivial **p.**? |
| W-pI 25.1:1 | **P.** is meaning. Today's idea explains why |
| W-pI 25.1:6 | That is what it is for; that is its **p.**; that is |
| W-pI 25.4:2 | superficial levels, you do recognize **p.**. Yet |
| W-pI 25.4:3 | **p.** cannot be understood at these levels. |
| W-pI 25.4:4 | that a telephone is for the **p.** of talking to |
| W-pI 27.1:5 | The **p.** of today's exercises is to bring the |
| W-pI 28.3:4 | you limiting its **p.** to your little personal |
| W-pI 28.4:2 | the **p.** of these exercises is to ask questions |
| W-pI 28.5:3 | under all your ideas about it is its real **p.**, |
| W-pI 28.5:3 | the **p.** it shares with all the universe. |
| W-pI 28.6:1 | really asking to see the **p.** of the universe. |
| W-pI 28.6:3 | of them to let its **p.** be revealed to you, |
| W-pI 29.1:1 | why you can see all **p.** in everything. It |
| W-pI 29.2:4 | that a table shares the **p.** of the universe. |
| W-pI 29.2:5 | And what shares the **p.** of the universe |
| W-pI 29.2:5 | of the universe shares the **p.** of its Creator. |
| W-pI 29.3:5 | Its holy **p.** stands beyond your little range. |
| W-pI 34.5:2 | **p.** is to protect yourself from temptation |
| W-pI 37.1:2 | Your **p.** is to see the world through your |
| W-pI 38.5:5 | **p.** of today's exercises is to begin to instill |
| W-pI 43.2:3 | never was, perception has a mighty **p.**. |
| W-pI 43.2:4 | Made by the Son of God for an unholy **p.**, |
| W-pI 43.3:3 | to which it shares the Holy Spirit's **p.**, |
| W-pI 43.8:2 | For this **p.**, apply the idea in this form: |
| W-pI 44.3:2 | For this **p.**, we will use a form of exercise |
| W-pI 46.5:1 | **p.** of the first phase of today's practice |
| WpI rI.in.4:4 | The **p.** of your learning is to enable you to |
| W-pI 55.5:2 | the **p.** of everything is to prove that my |
| W-pI 55.5:3 | this **p.** that I attempt to use everyone and |
| W-pI 55.5:5 | Therefore I do not recognize its real **p.**. |
| W-pI 55.5:6 | The **p.** I have given the world has led to a |
| W-pI 55.5:7 | **p.** by withdrawing the one I have given it, |
| W-pI 57.3:2 | Since the **p.** of the world is not the one I |
| W-pI 61.4:3 | peace, unburdened and certain of your **p.**. |
| W-pI 61.6:2 | your function and your only **p.** here. |
| W-pI 61.7:1 | views of what you are and what your **p.** is. |
| W-pI 63.1:3 | What **p.** could you have that would bring |
| W-pI 63.2:4 | trivial **p.** or meaningless desire in its place |
| W-pI 64.1:2 | The **p.** of the world you see is to obscure |
| W-pI 64.2:1 | since this was the **p.** of the body itself. Yet |
| W-pI 64.2:2 | and therefore He sees another **p.** in them. |
| W-pI 65.1:4 | Salvation cannot be the only **p.** you hold |
| W-pI 65.4:3 | The **p.** of this is to arrange your day so |
| W-pI 65.4:4 | consistently for the **p.** He shares with you. |
| W-pI 65.6:5 | your illusions of **p.** be replaced by truth. |
| W-pI 66.4:1 | its **p.** your acceptance of the fact that not |
| W-pI 69.3:3 | There is no other **p.** here, and no other |
| W-pI 70.4:2 | Your **p.** was to ensure that healing did not |
| W-pI 70.4:3 | occur. God's **p.** was to ensure that it did. |
| W-pI 71.5:3 | your **p.** is divided and you will attempt to |
| W-pI 73.9:2 | It is not the **p.** of an alien power, thrust |
| W-pI 73.9:3 | one **p.** here on which you and your Father |
| W-pI 75.4:3 | Our single **p.** makes our goal inevitable. |
| W-pI 76.4:2 | of rituals that have no use and serve no **p.**. |
| W-pI 81.4:4 | *my will. I will not use this for an alien* **p.**. |
| W-pI 83.1:4 | With one **p.** only, I am always certain |
| W-pI 91.10:4 | in which you share a **p.** like Their Own. |
| W-pI 91.11:3 | form would be helpful for this special **p.**: |
| W-pI 92.5:7 | will unite in **p.** and forgiveness and in love |
| W-pI 92.6:1 | cannot see a **p.** in forgiveness and in love. |
| W-pI 95.5:2 | you are reminded of your **p.** frequently, |
| W-pI 96.6:4 | What **p.** could it serve? What is it for? |
| W-pI 98.2:2 | and take our stand with certainty of **p.**, |
| W-pI 98.2:3 | We have a mighty **p.** to fulfill, and have |
| W-pI 98.6:2 | time for peace of mind and certainty of **p.**, |
| W-pI 100.1:3 | by separate minds unites them in one **p.**, |
| W-pI 122.1:4 | happiness, a quiet mind, a certainty of **p.**, |
| W-pI 125.8:3 | and of peace, of unity of will and **p.**, with |
| W-pI 125.9:5 | yourself you have a special **p.** for this day; |
| W-pI 127.4:1 | No course whose **p.** is to teach you to |
| W-pI 128.2:2 | must serve the **p.** you have given it, until |
| W-pI 128.2:2 | given it, until you see a different **p.** there. |
| W-pI 128.2:3 | only **p.** worthy of your mind this world |
| W-pI 128.6:4 | fly in sureness and in joy to join its holy **p.** |
| W-pI 131.8:5 | impose an alien will upon God's single **p.**. |
| W-pI 131.15:6 | *My single* **p.** *offers it to me. No one can fail* |
| W-pI 132.14:1 | Today our **p.** is to free the world from all |
| W-pI 133.8:4 | What **p.** does it serve? Here it is easiest of |
| W-pI 135.14:1 | the **p.** all of them were made to realize. |
| W-pI 135.18:1 | planned by One Whose only **p.** is your |
| W-pI 136.1:1 | what **p.** sickness seems to serve. For then |
| W-pI 136.1:2 | understands as well its **p.** has no meaning |
| W-pI 136.2:3 | And like all the rest, its **p.** is to hide reality |
| W-pI 136.12:4 | to give you happiness, for such its **p.** is. |
| W-pI 137.15:4 | by, remembering our **p.** with this thought |
| W-pI 138.7:2 | Such is its holy **p.**, now transformed from |
| W-pI 139.7:2 | is a place whose **p.** is to be a home where |
| WpI rIV.in3:3 | Their **p.** is to show you something else, |
| WpI rIV.in7:3 | for you are using time for its intended **p.**. |
| W-pI 153.8:2 | For our true **p.** is to save the world, and |
| W-pI 153.9:3 | salvation; sure we will fulfill our chosen **p.** |
| W-pI 153.10:1 | and in silence think how holy is your **p.**, |
| W-pI 153.15:5 | ceases to arise to turn us from our **p.**, we |
| W-pI 153.19:5 | defenses undermine our certainty of **p.**. |
| W-pI 154.5:4 | the messages should be, or what their **p.** is |
| W-pI 155.9:3 | you walk with certainty of **p.** to the truth. |
| W-pI 157.6:1 | its only **p.** being now to bring the vision of |
| W-pI 157.7:4 | Yet now it has a **p.**, and will serve it well. |
| W-pI 161.2:5 | The **p.** of all seeing is to show you what |
| W-pI 161.3:3 | that He may employ them for a **p.** which |
| W-pI 164.8:4 | Is not this **p.** worthy to be yours? Is not |
| WpI rV.in1:6 | certainty, a firmer **p.** and a surer goal. |
| WpI rV.in12:1 | but to recall the mind, as needed, to its **p.**. |
| W-pI 184.12:6 | our **p.** is to let our minds accept what God |
| W-pI 185.10:5 | been weak at times, uncertain in your **p.**, |
| W-pI 193.10:5 | Use it today for what its **p.** is. Morning |
| W-pI 199.6:3 | The body's **p.** now is unambiguous. And |
| W-pI 199.6:5 | the body serves, and serves its **p.** well. |
| W-pI 200.5:2 | your mind about the **p.** of the world, if |
| W-pI 200.6:5 | yet believes are true, a worthy **p.**? Who |
| W-pI 200.11:5 | dreams with single **p.** and companionship |
| W-pI 205.1:3 | *end I seek, my* **p.** *and my function and my life* |
| W-pII 1.3:3 | Distortion is its **p.**, and the means by |
| W-pII 226.1:2 | change of mind about the **p.** of the world. |
| W-pII 236.1:4 | given me to serve whatever **p.** I perceive in |
| W-pII 3.3:3 | aim is to fulfill the **p.** which the world was |
| W-pII 3.4:2 | all perception can be given a new **p.** by |
| W-pII 4.2:2 | itself. Its **p.** is to strive. Yet can the goal of |
| W-pII 257.h | Let me remember what my **p.** is. |
| W-pII 257.2:3 | *And thus our* **p.** *must be Yours as well, if we* |
| W-pII 5.3:4 | fearful, must the body serve the **p.** given it |
| W-pII 5.3:5 | change the **p.** that the body will obey by |
| W-pII 267.1:3 | floods my body with the **p.** of forgiveness. |
| W-pII 276.1:6 | Father is, and for what **p.** we have come. |
| W-pII 285.1:4 | to me, what **p.** would my suffering fulfill, |
| W-pII 8.5:1 | no need of time when it has served His **p.**. |
| W-pII 294.1:7 | And afterwards, without a **p.**, it is laid |
| W-pII 308.1:3 | Time's **p.** cannot be to keep the past and |
| W-pII 312.1:5 | the Holy Spirit's **p.** as his goal for seeing. |
| W-pII 312.2:1 | *I have no* **p.** *for today except to look upon a* |
| W-pII 318.1:2 | all the parts have but one **p.** and one aim? |
| W-pII 318.1:4 | salvation's **p.** is to find the sinlessness that |
| W-pII 333.1:3 | and with the **p.** that the mind accorded it. |
| W-pII 14.2:2 | and I, we found a single **p.** that we shared. |
| W-pII 353.h | my hands, my feet today Have but one **p.**; |
| W-pII 353.1:1 | *the* **p.** *that I share with Him. Nothing is mine* |
| W-pII 353.1:2 | *is mine alone, for He and I have joined in* **p.**. |
| W-pII 353.1:4 | *A while I work with Him to serve His* **p.**. *Then* |
| W-pII 354.h | Christ and I, in peace And certainty of **p.**. |
| W-pII 354.1:3 | *I have no* **p.** *but His Own. And He is like His* |
| Wfl in.3:1 | And to this **p.** let us dedicate our minds, |
| M-in 2:5 | **p.** of the course might be said to provide |
| M-in 3:8 | fundamental **p.** is to diminish self-doubt. |
| M-in 4:5 | Herein is the **p.** of the world. What else, |
| M-2 5:4 | The relationship is holy because of that **p.** |
| M-4 V.1:15 | joyous it is to share the **p.** of salvation! |
| M-5 I.h | The Perceived **P.** of Sickness |
| M-5 II.2:1 | for a **p.** for which it would use the body, is |
| M-5 II.4:8 | Having no **p.**, they are gone. And with |
| M-5 III.3:2 | to forget that all of them have the same **p.**, |
| M-12 2:6 | Yet being joined in one **p.**, and one they |
| M-12 4:1 | recognition of the proper **p.** of the body. |
| M-12 4:4 | of God, of what the body's **p.** really is; the |
| M-12 5:9 | another **p.** from the one that keeps it holy. |
| M-14 1:5 | made, for now it has no **p.** and is gone. |
| M-14 1:6 | of illusions is the belief that they have a **p.** |
| M-14 2:1 | is complete, the world does have a **p.**. It |
| M-14 5:2 | joy has come, the **p.** of the world has gone |
| M-14 5:4 | has come, what is the **p.** of the world? The |
| M-22 6:14 | All else must follow from this single **p.**. |
| M-24 4:5 | draining it away from its appointed **p.**. If |
| M-25 5:7 | individual changes his mind about its **p.**, |
| M-28 1:3 | Spirit's interpretation of the world's **p.**; |
| M-28 4:6 | their **p.** is transformed and understood. |
| M-28 5:9 | will are lost, for unity of **p.** has been found |
| C-3 1:3 | then, is an illusion, but because of its **p.**, |
| C-3 7:6 | This is the **p.** of the face of Christ. It is the |
| C-4 7:6 | world without a **p.** and without a cause. |
| P-1 h | THE **P.** OF PSYCHOTHERAPY |
| P-1 1:1 | the **p.** of psychotherapy is to remove the |
| P-1 2:1 | better **p.** could any relationship have than |
| P-1 2:4 | in this is the proper **p.** of psychotherapy. |
| P-2 II.5:4 | union of **p.** between patient and therapist |
| P-2 II.6:6 | It does not matter what their **p.** is, but |
| P-2 II.9:8 | one in **p.** and must thus be one in means. |
| P-2 IV.7:4 | Yet that is magic's **p.**; to make illusions |
| P-2 IV.11:5 | rightly, its **p.** can be understood. What is |
| P-2 VI.4:1 | which the senses bring have but one **p.**; to |
| P-3 III.1:8 | He has a mighty part in this one **p.**, for |
| P-3 III.2:3 | Holy Spirit asks some payment for His **p.**. |
| P-3 III.6:4 | Whatever their **p.** may have been before |
| S-1 I.1:4 | else could it serve its **p.**? It is impossible to |
| S-1 III.6:2 | God, and therefore distort the **p.** of prayer |
| S-1 V.2:3 | no idols, and defense no longer serves a **p.** |
| S-2 in.1:4 | your **p.** steadfast and unchangeable. |
| S-2 in.1:9 | it has a **p.** beyond which you cannot go, |
| S-2 I.2:1 | therefore suit the **p.** of the world far better |
| S-2 II.1:3 | their **p.** is to separate and make what God |
| S-2 II.5:7 | What could the **p.** be, except to keep the |
| S-2 III.4:8 | and you are one with Him in Will and **p.**. |

## purposeful 1

| | |
|---|---|
| P-3 III.6:3 | Relationships are always **p.**. Whatever |

## purposefully 1

| | |
|---|---|
| W-pI 184.4:1 | vision, **p.** set against the given truth. Its |

## purposeless 13

| | |
|---|---|
| T-17 VII.9:6 | of the past, which would have made it **p.**. |
| T-26 X.5:5 | added, for the world is **p.** except for this. |
| T-26 X.5:7 | you, you have laid on it by rendering it **p.**, |
| T-27 II.8:6 | suffering is **p.** and wholly without cause. |
| T-27 VI.3:1 | This body, **p.** within itself, holds all your |
| T-28 I.5:5 | Like to the body, it is **p.** within itself. And |
| T-30 V.5:3 | idols are nothing and nowhere, and are **p.** |
| W-pI 102.2:1 | still further, and to realize that pain is **p.**, |
| W-pI 128.5:3 | We hold it **p.** within our minds, and |

W-pI.155.11:1 all the things that pass and miracles are **p.**
W-pII......8.4:3 of time, for its perception makes time **p.**.
W-pII....10.2:2 totally forgiven, without sin and wholly **p.**
M-14..........1:7 Perceived as **p.**, they are no longer seen.

## purposes 34

T-2........IV.4:4 use of such agents for corrective **p.** is evil.
T-6...........I.1:1 learning **p.**, let us consider the crucifixion
T-13......VI.4:6 past, present and future for your own **p.**.
T-14......VI.7:6 one is possible for **p.** of communication.
T-15.......V.7:1 farther; one part of one aspect suits its **p.**,
T-15......IX.3:3 limit everyone to a body for its own **p.**,
T-15......IX.7:2 the body only for **p.** of communication,
T-17.......V.2:7 to the Holy Spirit, to use for His **p.**.
T-17.......V.5:5 by two individuals for their unholy **p.**,
T-18......VI.5:1 for salvation, and used for **p.** of love?
T-19.........I.4:2 the body cannot be used for **p.** of union. If
T-20.....VII.4:8 And both must be undone for **p.** of truth.
T-20... VIII.8:8 This world seems to hold out many **p.**,
T-20... VIII.9:1 Only two **p.** are possible. And one is sin,
T-27.....II.11:2 has conflicting **p.** and different ends.
T-28.........I.3:4 and the **p.** for which they have been made
T-30.....VII.3:3 it must be that they reflect but different **p.**
T-31......III.3:3 are not seen as **p.**, but actions. Bodies act,
T-31.......V.2:5 For it is made to serve two **p.**, but one of
W-pI.......5.6:4 *go. For the **p.** of these exercises, then, I will*
W-pI.......6.3:6 *go. For the **p.** of these exercises, then, I will*
W-pI.....12.4:2 For the **p.** of these exercises, there is no
WpI...rI.in.6:1 You will note that, for review **p.**, some of
W-pI.....65.4:3 all the trivial **p.** and goals you will pursue.
W-pI...128.5:2 We leave it free of **p.** we gave its aspects
W-pI...135.7:3 roles it cannot fill, to **p.** beyond its scope,
W-pI.136.16:3 pursuits with double **p.** insanely sought,
W-pI.136.18:1 upon the body by the **p.** you gave to it. As
W-pI.136.18:2 be enough to serve all truly useful **p.**. The
M-2............5:3 any two who join together for learning **p.**.
M-24..........3:1 For our **p.**, it would not be helpful to take
M-28..........1:9 It is the relinquishment of all other **p.**, all
M-28..........5:5 His Love behind all forms, beyond all **p.**.
S-2.........II.8:2 For that is what their **p.** have set. Be not

## pursue 12

T-4.........V.6:7 is never asked by those who **p.** them is,
T-12...VII.7:11 For to be healed is to **p.** one goal, because
T-15.........I.3:4 that it can **p.** you beyond the grave. And
T-15.......I.4:14 its own death, it will **p.** you still, because
T-16.....VII.3:9 you while you **p.** the ego's goal as its ally.
T19..IV.B.13:2 Under fear's orders the body will **p.** guilt,
T-23......III.1:7 his horrified awareness and **p.** him still.
T-24....VI.12:1 you **p.** another goal with far less vigilance;
T-29.....VII.8:6 And you **p.** them vainly in the dream,
W-pI.....65.4:3 the trivial purposes and goals you will **p.**.
W-pI...101.2:7 fear. And yet He will **p.**, and they can not
W-pI.166.13:2 not understand they but **p.** their wishes.

## pursued 5

T-11.....V.12:5 ego's goal, which you have **p.** so diligently
T-24....VI.11:4 have **p.** this goal with vigilance you never
W-pI.134.12:2 kill the dragons which he thought **p.** him.
W-pI...166.6:2 everyone who comes here has **p.** the path
W-pI...194.1:6 goal! How short the journey still to be **p.**!

## pursues 4

T-12......IV.1:6 the ego **p.** its goal with fanatic insistence,
W-pII......1.3:2 In frantic action it **p.** its goal, twisting and
M-13.........5:8 who **p.** the world's goals can do otherwise
M-17.......7:10 An angry father **p.** his guilty son. Kill or

## pursuing 2

T-12.....VII.7:9 enables it to believe that it is **p.** one goal.
T-30.......V.2:3 folly of **p.** guilt as goal is fully recognized.

## pursuit 9

T-17.......V.3:8 and the **p.** of the old goal re-established in
T-24........II.2:1 **P.** of specialness is always at the cost of
T-24........II.2:6 Its **p.** will bring you joy. But the pursuit of
T-24........II.2:7 the **p.** of specialness must bring you pain.
T-25.......II.3:3 to uphold **p.** of what has always failed, on
W-pI...131.2:6 **P.** of the imagined leads to death because
W-pI...195.9:3 which regards us in a place of merciless **p.**
W-pI...196.9:2 and need not fear its vengeance and **p.**.
W-pII......5.4:2 Heaven been exchanged for the **p.** of hell.

## pursuits 3

W-pI.136.16:3 and meaningless **p.** with double purposes
W-pI...200.8:3 to senseless journeys, frantic, vain **p.**, and
P-2......IV.11:9 analyses and wearying discussion and **p.**.

## push 3

T-14......III.2:6 guiltlessness, and **p.** it from your sight.
T19... IV.A.7:1 in and **p.** Him out *must* produce conflict.
T-26......IV.2:5 nothing stands between to **p.** the other off

## pushed 5

T-15......VI.6:4 comes swiftly as the veil of time is **p.** aside
T-25......IV.3:6 that they thought was there is **p.** away,
T-25......IV.4:5 that they may be **p.** away before the light.
W-pI.....76.3:3 or some fluid **p.** into your veins through a
W-pI...195.9:3 **p.** about without a thought or care for us

## pushing 3

T-6......V.B.9:2 you will be **p.** toward the center of your
T-27... VIII.8:3 innocence by **p.** guilt outside yourself, but
W-pII......2.4:4 The grass is **p.** through the soil, the trees

## put 72

T-1.........V.5:3 only limit **p.** on its choice is that it cannot
T-3.......VII.3:6 **p.** them in a position where their own
T-5.........II.6:9 The voice they **p.** in their minds was not
T-6.........II.6:2 cannot be anywhere God did not **p.** you,
T-6........IV.8:7 **p.** yourself in an impossible situation you
T-6......V.C.1:2 enter it in the light of what God **p.** there.
T-6......V.C.5:4 have in your mind only what God **p.** there
T-7.......VII.4:4 you will have **p.** them out of your mind.
T-8.......VII.4:3 according to the use to which it is **p.**. And
T-8.......VII.4:4 see the use to which you have **p.** yours. If
T-8.......VII.7:6 the only natural use to which it can be **p.**.
T-8.......VII.9:7 in it by directing the use to which it is **p.**.
T-9.......II.11:8 give is therefore the value you **p.** on what
T-9.......II.11:8 exact measure of the value you **p.** upon it.
T-10....III.11:2 this altar is in you because God **p.** it there.
T-10......IV.8:7 **P.** all your faith in it, and God Himself
T-12.....VII.7:5 because you **p.** it there by wanting it.
T-13......IX.8:6 is there, and what you **p.** your faith in.
T-13........X.3:3 that relationship because you **p.** it there.
T-14........X.8:9 lack any consistent sense when they are **p.**
T-14........X.9:2 but **p.** them together and the system of
T-14......XI.3:9 **P.** no confidence at all in darkness to
T-15......III.3:3 and represents the value that you **p.** upon
T-17......III.7:3 joined as one, the ego cannot **p.** asunder.
T-18......III.1:8 Darkness can cover it, but cannot **p.** it out
T-18.......V.1:5 **P.** yourself not in charge of this, for you
T-18....VI.9:10 You cannot **p.** a barrier around yourself,
T-20........II.6:6 pick up from time to time and then **p.** by.
T-25......III.5:4 of specialness to **p.** it out of mind, where
T-26.......V.9:3 you to see the past and **p.** it in the present
T-28........II.4:1 but that you have **p.** yourself to sleep, and
T-28........II.7:6 the dream has **p.** together and has offered
T-28.......IV.8:1 of God and **p.** the pieces into place again.
T-28.......V.5:7 you, who **p.** together every jagged piece,
T-28.......V.6:2 perhaps, all **p.** together to attest its truth.
T-29....VIII.3:8 A cloud does not **p.** out the sun. No more
T-29....VIII.5:5 the light the veil between has not **p.** out.
T-29......IX.4:2 you sinful and **p.** out the light within you.
T-29......IX.6:3 **P.** them all away, for you have need of
T-29......IX.7:5 for childish things have all been **p.** away.
T-29......IX.8:7 dreams of judgment have been **p.** away?
T-30.........I.1:5 time you wake, will **p.** you well ahead.
T-31.........II.8:2 before, and **p.** aside all images you made.
W-pI.....31.5:2 not yield to it, and **p.** yourself in bondage.
W-pI.....46.5:1 to **p.** you in a position to forgive yourself.
W-pI.....47.2:2 To believe that you can is to **p.** your trust
W-pI.....47.2:3 can **p.** his faith in weakness and feel safe?
W-pI.....47.2:4 can **p.** his faith in strength and feel weak?
W-pI.....50.2:4 Do not **p.** your faith in the worthless. It
W-pI.....50.4:1 **P.** not your faith in illusions. They will
W-pI.....50.4:3 **P.** all your faith in the Love of God within
W-pI.....70.3:2 God would not have **p.** the remedy for the
W-pI.....70.7:2 You might **p.** it this way: *My salvation*
W-pI...73.10:5 **P.** the rest of the practice period under
W-pI.....76.4:2 and **p.** them under different names in a
W-pI.....91.7:3 need to feel something to **p.** your faith in,
W-pI.....93.7:7 abide in you because God **p.** them there.
W-pI.....93.8:4 Then **p.** away your foolish self-images,
W-pI.131.13:1 **P.** out your hand, and see how easily the
W-pI.153.13:3 in which we **p.** away the toys of guilt, and
W-pI...164.8:2 Your trifling treasures **p.** away, and leave
W-pI...182.2:2 some try to **p.** by their suffering in games
W-pI...190.9:4 **p.** aside the withering assaults with which
W-pII .....4.5:2 **p.** away these sharp-edged children's toys
W-pII .281.1:4 *and **p.** my little meaningless ideas in place of*
W-pII .299.2:4 *can obscure it, but can not **p.** out its radiance*
M-7...........4:9 for they have **p.** their trust in Him.
M-8...........6:4 mind will **p.** them all in one category;
M-12.........6:5 but who would **p.** his faith in dreams once
M-16.......11:5 the day except to **p.** your trust in magic,
C-6.............3:9 be obliterated because God has **p.** it there
S-2..........II.5:4 reproach that thus is **p.** upon him. Is this

## puts 7

T-1........IV.2:5 and **p.** you in communion with yourself
T-2......VIII.1:2 this **p.** you in a position where a belief in
T-8........VI.9:1 knowledge of the value He **p.** upon you.
T-12.......IV.1:2 It never **p.** it this way; on the contrary,
T-27....VIII.2:2 **p.** things on itself that it has bought with
W-pI...161.5:1 makes us suffer, and at last **p.** out our life.
M-10.........2:7 **p.** himself in a position where judgment

## putting 1

W-pI.....92.1:4 by **p.** little bits of glass before your eyes.

# Q

**quail** 1
T-29....VIII.4:7 to make you tremble and to **q.** in fear.

**quails** 2
W-pI.136.10:2 that Heaven **q.** before such mad attacks as
W-pI...186.6:2 this image which **q.** and retreats in terror,

**quaint** 2
W-pI.153.13:3 and lock our **q.** and childish thoughts of
W-pI...156.6:4 sin gone, because its **q.** absurdity is seen.

**qualifications** 2
T-9........IV.8:3 Let me repeat that the ego's **q.** as a guide
M-1 ...........1:2 His **q.** consist solely in this; somehow,

**qualified** 1
T-29.........I.3:9 and your brother but shared a **q.** entente,

**qualitative** 1
T-5...........I.7:6 change occurs to produce a real **q.** shift.

**qualities** 2
W-pI.....16.4:4 regardless of the **q.** that you assign to it, is
W-pI...167.4:3 take on **q.** the source does not contain,

**quality** 5
T-3......... V.7:2 and "likeness" as "of a like **q.**." God did
T-3......... V.7:3 Own Thought and of a **q.** like to His Own.
T-4.......VII.3:9 since its **q.** is universal in application and
T-18.... VI.12:1 of your differences in size and seeming **q.**.
W-pI.....12.3:8 Their seeming **q.** does not matter.

**quantitative** 1
T-5...........I.7:6 It is at this point that sufficient **q.** change

**quarrel** 1
W-pI...198.4:3 And why would you oppose it, **q.** with it,

**quarter** 5
W-pI.....75.9:2 Remind yourself every **q.** of an hour or so
W-pI.122.10:1 do we gladly give a **q.** of an hour to the
W-pI.122.14:1 a minute as each **q.** of an hour passes by.
W-pI.134.14:4 let us give a **q.** of an hour twice today, and
W-pI.136.15:2 And we will give a **q.** of an hour twice to

**quest** 1
S-1........III.6:5 goal of God is lost in the **q.** for lesser goals

**question** 209
*See also* pseudo-question
T-2......... II.3:3 It is a **q.** of what it is *for.* Everyone defends
T-3........III.2:5 It is the right answer to a **q.**, but you do
T-3........III.2:5 do not **q.** when you know. Questioning
T-3........III.3:4 This fear inhibits the tendency to **q.** at all.
T-3........III.6:2 knowledge will bring peace without **q.**.
T-3........IV.1:2 are divided and open to **q.** and doubt.
T-3 .......IV.2:5 can be sure of. Everything else *is* open to **q.**
T-3 ........ V.4:1 The fundamental **q.** you continually ask
T-3 ....... VI.8:1 of authority is really a **q.** of authorship.
T-3 ..... VI.10:3 is the fundamental **q.** of authorship. All
T-4 .........II.1:2 fact, it is the best **q.** you could ask. There
T-4 .........II.4:7 The **q.** is not how you respond to the ego,
T-4 .........II.8:3 free, however, to open the premise to **q.**,
T-4 .......II.11:6 That is a reasonable **q.**. You must be
T-4 ...... V.4:10 the **q.** from the mind's awareness. Once
T-4 ...... V.4:11 the **q.** can and does produce uneasiness,
T-4 ........ V.5:1 This is the **q.** that *must* be asked: "Where
T-4 ........ V.6:3 issues touching on the real **q.** in any way.
T-4 ........ V.6:4 to hide the real **q.** and keep it out of mind
T-4 ........ V.6:7 the one **q.** that is never asked by those
T-4 ........ V.6:8 This is the **q.** that *you* must learn to ask in
T-5 ....... III.6:4 is the ego's domain, accepts it without **q.**.
T-5 ........ V.6:2 That is why the **q.**, "What do you want?"
T-6 ....... IV.1:1 the Holy Spirit is the Answer, not the **q.**.
T-6 ....... IV.2:6 raised the first **q.** that was ever asked, but
T-6 ....... IV.2:7 answer. That **q.**, "What are you?" was the
T-6 ....... IV.2:9 have never done more than obscure the **q.**
T-6 ....... IV.7:2 because the first **q.** was never asked.
T-6 ....... IV.7:4 where everything lives in God without **q.**.
T-6 ..... IV.12:9 questioned, He did not **q.**. He merely gave
T-6 ..... V.C.7:2 beyond belief because they are beyond **q.**.
T-6 ..... V.C.7:3 for God speaks only for belief beyond **q.**,
T-6 ..... V.C.7:3 is the preparation for *being* without **q.**. As
T-7 ....... III.5:2 is. This is totally beyond **q.**, and when you
T-7 ....... III.5:2 and when you **q.** it you are answered. The
T-7 ....... III.5:3 The Answer merely undoes the **q.** by
T-7 ....... III.5:3 to **q.** reality is to question meaninglessly.
T-7 ....... III.5:3 to question reality is to **q.** meaninglessly.
T-7 ....... VI.9:2 is totally beyond **q.** except by you, when
T-7 .........X.6:2 your trustworthiness is beyond **q.**. It will
T-7 .........X.6:3 It will always remain beyond **q.**, however
T-7 .........X.6:3 question, however much you may **q.** it. I
T-8 ...... VI.5:14 There can be no **q.** of its worth, because
T-8 ....... VI.8:1 is no **q.** but one you should ever ask of
T-8 ....... IX.1:3 The ego does not know what a real **q.** is,
T-8 ....... IX.1:4 this as you learn to **q.** the value of the ego,
T-9 .........II.4:2 Do not **q.** him and do not confound him,
T-9 ...... VII.6:8 **q.** is meaningless within the ego's thought
T-9 ...... VII.6:8 open the whole thought system to **q.**.
T-9 ...... VII.7:1 the ego does not know what a real **q.** is.
T-9 ...... VII.7:3 to **q.** your littleness therefore is to deny all
T-9 ...... VII.8:1 Whenever you **q.** your value, say: *God*
T-9 ...VIII.11:8 Listen and do not **q.** what you hear, for
T-9 ...VIII.11:9 can cease to **q.** it and know it for what it is
T-11 ......in.1:7 decision is always an answer to the **q.**,
T-11 ......in.2:1 believed this **q.** really involves conflict? If
T-11 ..... VI.6:4 Son, accepting him without **q.** as His Own
T-11 ...VIII.3:8 to **q.** everything you learned of yourself,
T-11 ...VIII.4:5 Ask yourself, therefore, but one simple **q.**:
T-11 ...VIII.6:4 the **q.** you must ask to learn His answer?
T-11 ...VIII.6:5 but you have misunderstood the **q.**. You
T-12 ..... III.2:6 The **q.** is always twofold; first, *what* is to be
T-12 ...VIII.4:3 A Voice will answer every **q.** you ask, and
T-13 .......II.4:4 can withstand your raising all else to **q.**, it
T-13 ..... IV.3:4 You **q.** Heaven, but you do not question
T-13 ..... IV.3:4 question Heaven, but you do not **q.** this.
T-13 ..... IV.3:5 could heal and be healed if you did **q.** it.
T-13 .. VII.11:6 and render you unwilling to **q.** the value
T-14 ..... IV.6:4 in answering your every **q.** what to do. He
T-15 ..... III.5:2 Let this **q.** be asked you by the Holy Spirit
T-15 .... VII.3:5 only **q.** will be why it was you ever wanted
T-15 .....X.5:13 only **q.** that remains is how much is the
T-15 .......X.7:4 and your only **q.** is who is to be destroyed
T-15 .......X.7:5 You seek to answer this **q.** in your special
T-15 .......X.9:8 In you are both the **q.** and the answer; the
T-18 ..... IV.5:1 You merely ask the **q.**. The answer is
T-20 ..... III.3:5 Their looking merely asks a **q.**, and it is
T-20 ..... III.4:1 A simple **q.** yet remains, and needs an
T-20 ..... III.6:7 judgment of the world as answer to the **q.**
T-20 .... VII.9:1 Your **q.** should not be, "How can I see my
T-20 ... VIII.8:7 the **q.** never is whether you want them,
T-21 ......... I.3:5 Your **q.** is whether the means by which
T-21 ..... IV.3:2 This "fearful" **q.** is one the ego never asks.
T-21 ..... IV.8:9 it happily, and **q.** not what must be so.
T-21 .......V.4:5 in it, but if the basic **q.** stems from reason
T-21 .......V.4:6 stems from reason, the basic **q.** is obvious
T-21 .....V.10:2 have asked the **q.** the ego will never ask.
T-21 .....V.10:3 tell you now the **q.** must have come from
T-21 ....... VII.h The Last Unanswered **Q.**
T-21 .... VII.6:5 This final **q.**, which is indeed the last you
T-21 .... VII.8:1 the last **q.** you have left unanswered still.
T-21 .. VII.10:1 Why is the final **q.** so important? Reason
T-21 .. VII.11:4 Yet the last **q.** adds the wish for constancy
T-21 .. VII.11:5 By answering the final **q.** "yes," you add
T-21 ... VIII.2:8 see the final **q.** is necessary to the rest, as
T-21 ... VIII.4:1 how you would answer the final **q.**. Your
T-21 ... VIII.5:5 For here the final **q.** is already answered,
T-22 ... VI.13:7 only **q.** to be answered in order to decide
T-23 .....II.11:1 And now there is a vague unanswered **q.**,
T-24 ......in.2:1 willingness to **q.** every value that you hold
T-25 .... VII.9:1 Now must he **q.** this, because the form of
T-26 .....X.1:10 It is not a **q.** of the size of the confusion,
T-27 ..... IV.3:4 outside a single, simple **q.** is ever asked.
T-27 ..... IV.3:5 The world can only ask a double **q.**. One
T-27 ..... IV.3:8 It does not ask a **q.** to be answered, but
T-27 ..... IV.4:1 are but a way of looking, not a **q.** asked. A
T-27 ..... IV.4:2 A **q.** asked in hate cannot be answered,
T-27 ..... IV.4:3 itself. A double **q.** asks and answers, both
T-27 ..... IV.4:4 The world asks but one **q.**. It is this: "Of
T-27 ..... IV.4:8 Whatever form the **q.** takes, its purpose is
T-27 ... IV.4:16 And this is not a **q.**, for it tells you what
T-27 ... IV.4:17 It leaves no room to **q.** its beliefs, except
T-27 ..... IV.5:6 An honest **q.** is a learning tool that asks
T-27 ..... IV.5:8 one in a conflict state is free to ask this **q.**,
T-27 ..... IV.6:1 can an honest **q.** honestly be asked. And
T-27 ..... IV.6:2 And from the meaning of the **q.** does the
T-27 ..... IV.6:8 thus the **q.** is preserved intact because it
T-27 ..... IV.6:9 that is not entailed within the **q.** asked. It
T-27 ... IV.6:10 something new and different from the **q.**.
T-27 ..... IV.7:3 see what can be answered; what the **q.** *is.*
T-27 ..... IV.7:4 world the answers merely raise another **q.**
T-27 ..... IV.7:5 you can bring the **q.** to the answer, and
T-27 .......V.5:3 Consider well its **q.**. It is asked of you on
T-29 ... VIII.8:3 This is the only **q.** that has many answers,
T-29 ... VIII.8:3 on the one of whom the **q.** has been asked
T-30 ......... I.5:4 by yourself, and can not see the **q.**. Now
T-30 ......... I.6:2 that you have asked a **q.** by yourself, and
T-30 ......... I.6:4 say: *I have no q.. I forgot what to decide.* This
T-30 ......... I.6:6 you what the **q.** must have really been.
T-30 ......... I.7:3 of the **q.** asks will gain momentum, until
T-30 ......... I.7:3 one in which you get *your* answer to *your* **q.**
T-30 ......... I.8:1 to receive you cannot even let your **q.** go,
T-30 ....... I.12:5 you now can ask a **q.** that makes sense,
T-30 ....... I.14:4 The only **q.** really is with what you choose
T-31 ......... I.6:5 as God, and far beyond all doubt and **q.**?
T-31 .....V.11:6 He merely asks if just a little **q.** might be
T-31 .....V.13:1 gains, it does not yet approach a basic **q.**.
T-31 .....V.17:5 concept has been raised to doubt and **q.**,
W-pI ...... 3.1:3 Be sure that you do not **q.** the suitability
W-pI ..... 27.4:1 real **q.** is, how often will you remember?
W-pI ..... 28.1:3 The **q.** of whether you will keep them in
W-pI ..... 28.4:1 will not **q.** what you have already defined.
W-pI ..... 39.2:3 is not due to the ambiguity of the **q.**. But
W-pI ..... 39.4:1 the answer to every **q.** that was ever asked

W-pI...39.11:1 if possible, you may ask yourself this **q.**,
W-pI.....41.2:2 not do is to **q.** the reality of the problem.
W-pI.....64.3:2 of the ego that leads you to **q.** this, and
W-pI.....66.2:1 fundamental **q.** of what your function is.
W-pI...72.12:1 go out, repeat your **q.** and your request,
W-pI.....77.6:6 We are asking a real **q.** at last. The answer
W-pI.....91.6:6 *I?* The **q.** with which this statement ends is
W-pI.....93.3:1 Today we **q.** this, not from the point of
W-pI...102.1:3 now, at least enough to let you **q.** it, and
W-pI...121.5:5 it knows. It does not **q.**, certain it is right.
W-pI...124.4:1 for us, nor **q.** His protection and His care.
W-pI...132.1:7 to **q.** that the hope of freedom comes to
W-pI.135.23:4 But they are answers to another kind of **q.**
W-pI...138.8:3 from **q.** and from reason and from doubt.
W-pI...139.1:5 There is no **q.** but reflects this one. There
W-pI...139.1:6 that does not entail the single, simple **q.**,
W-pI...139.2:1 Yet who could ask this **q.** except one who
W-pI...139.2:2 could make the **q.** seem to be sincere. The
W-pI...139.3:6 Whom does he **q.**? Who can answer him?
W-pI...139.5:9 really be a part of you that asks this **q.**.
W-pI...139.6:3 Yet it is the universal **q.** of the world.
W-pI...139.7:2 can come to **q.** what it is they are. And
W-pI...139.8:3 It is so far beyond all doubt and **q.** that to
W-pI...139.8:4 Is this a **q.**, or a statement which denies
W-pI...151.2:2 You do not really **q.** what is shown you
W-pI...154.5:2 Nor does he **q.** the right of him who does,
W-pI...156.8:2 **q.** should be asked a thousand times a day
W-pI...156.8:4 in answering your **q.** with these words: *I*
W-pI...160.5:1 How simply, then, the **q.** is resolved.
W-pI...170.6:2 obey their dictates, and refuse to **q.** them.
W-pI...184.6:7 To **q.** it is madness; to accept its presence
W-pI...184.7:3 its results, the sooner does he **q.** its effects
W-pI...185.8:8 one, one **q.** should be asked of all of them,
W-pI...196.6:5 there, so that it would be possible to **q.** it.
W-pI...196.7:1 **q.** it at all, its form must first be changed
M-in ..........2:4 The **q.** is not whether you will teach, for
M-1............4:6 There was never a **q.** of outcome, for what
M-5.......III.2:3 to **q.** what the patient has accepted as true
M-7............1:1 This **q.** really answers itself. Healing
M-11..........1:1 This is a **q.** everyone must ask. Certainly
M-11..........2:1 Again we come to the **q.** of judgment.
M-11........4:11 Now is the **q.** different. It is no longer,
M-12..........1:1 answer to this **q.** is –one. One wholly
M-16..........1:1 teacher of God this **q.** is meaningless.
M-16..........1:8 of God, then, this **q.** is superfluous. It has
M-17..........1:1 is a crucial **q.** both for teacher and pupil.
M-24..........1:4 Our only **q.** should be, "Is the concept
M-24..........1:7 other **q.** about it really useful in lighting
M-25..........1:1 to this **q.** is much like the preceding one.
M-25..........3:3 this, the **q.** of how they arise is irrelevant.
M-27..........1:3 We have asked this **q.** before, but now we
M-27..........1:5 "the way of nature," not to be raised to **q.**,
C-in............3:5 another answer, once a **q.** has been raised
C-in............4:2 of a **q.** to which an answer is impossible.
C-2.............7:3 *this* dream and you will never **q.** any more.
C-2.............8:4 to ask, and even make the **q.** meaningless
C-2.............9:1 which asks of everyone one **q.** only: "Are
P-in............1:5 an individual can begin to **q.** their reality.
P-2......IV.4:10 sickness cure? Are not these both one **q.**?
P-2........VI.1:8 To **q.** it must then become his choice.
P-2........VI.2:4 But first the willingness to **q.** the "truth"
P-3...........III.h The **Q.** of Payment
S-1...........I.1:2 God. It is not merely a **q.** or an entreaty. It
S-1...........I.2:6 it is not the form of the **q.** that matters,
S-2........III.5:6 He knows the need; the **q.** and the answer

## question's 1

T-27....IV.4:17 except that what it states takes **q.** form.

## questionable 5

T-3......III.2:10 is timeless, because certainty is not **q.**.
T-7........III.5:5 to undo the **q.** and thus lead to certainty.
T-7........III.5:7 because nothing **q.** enters their minds.
W-pI...184.7:3 on what it rests, how **q.** are its premises,
P-2........IV.5:1 At best, and the word is perhaps **q.** here,

## questioned 8

T-6......IV.12:9 Being **q.**, He did not question. He merely
T-8...........I.4:2 On this basis alone its value should be **q.**.
T-9.......VII.7:4 because it can be **q.** only at its foundation
T-9.......VII.7:5 And this must be **q.** from beyond it,
T-13......IV.2:4 If their reality is **q.**, you believe that yours
T-17......III.4:3 begins to fade and to be **q.** almost at once.
T-20......III.6:5 They gently **q.** it and whispered, "What
S-1........IV.1:3 to hold the other as an enemy has been **q.**

## questioner 3

T-9...........I.7:1 be wiser to consider the kind of **q.** you are
T-9......... V.7:5 in his mind will therefore answer the **q.**,
W-pI...139.4:1 becomes a **q.** of what that something is.

## questioning 10

T-3........III.2:6 **Q.** illusions is the first step in undoing
T-3........III.3:1 The **q.** mind perceives itself in time, and
T-3........IV.3:1 is the **q.** aspect of the post-separation self,
T-6........IV.7:5 The time spent on **q.** in the dream has
T-13......IV.3:7 selective in your **q.** as in your perception.
T-13......IV.4:1 this notion that your **q.** might well begin.
T-13......VI.1:6 In your **q.** of illusions, ask yourself if it is
T-18....VI.13:6 of the **q.** whether or not all this is possible
T-27......IV.5:3 Thus is all **q.** within the world a form of
W-pI...132.1:6 he be swayed by **q.** his thoughts' effects. It

## questions 45

T-2......... II.3:5 The real **q.** are, what do you treasure, and
T-2......... II.3:6 **q.** and to bring them into all your actions,
T-3......III.2:11 You know when you have ceased to ask **q.**
T-3........III.5:5 him. While you ask **q.** about him you are
T-3........IV.3:2 capable of asking **q.** but not of perceiving
T-6........IV.2:8 The ego has never answered any **q.** since,
T-6........IV.6:1 one answer of the Holy Spirit to all the **q.**
T-7......... II.6:1 No one **q.** the connection of learning and
T-7........III.5:4 That is why the Holy Spirit never **q.**. His
T-7........III.5:7 They do not raise **q.**, because nothing
T-8.......IX.1:4 establish your ability to evaluate its **q.**.
T-11.......VI.2:4 Father? These **q.** are all the same, and are
T-18..VI.11:10 from fear to peace, asking no **q.** of reality,
T-21....... V.4:5 All sorts of **q.** may arise in it, but if the
T-21...VII.5:10 But let him only ask himself these **q.**,
T-21.....VII.6:1 already have answered the first three **q.**,
T-21...VII.11:1 In content all the **q.** are the same. For
T-25......III.7:5 For these two **q.** are the same. And when
T-27......IV.4:1 All **q.** asked within this world are but a
T-27......IV.5:4 so are the answers to the **q.** of the world
T-27......IV.5:4 contained within the **q.** that are asked.
T-27......IV.5:5 Where answers represent the **q.**, they add
T-27......IV.6:6 sacrifice because it answers **q.** truly asked.
T-27......IV.6:7 The **q.** of the world but ask of whom is
T-27..... V.10:7 shows the **q.** could not have been separate
T-29......VI.1:3 These **q.** are the same, in different form.
W-pI.....26.6:1 and reviewing the unresolved **q.** whose
W-pI.....27.4:3 Answer one of these **q.**, and you have
W-pI.....28.4:2 is to ask **q.** and receive the answers. In
W-pI...121.1:4 Here are all **q.** answered; here the end of
W-pI...122.4:2 the perfect answer, given to imperfect **q.**,
W-pI.122.11:1 hold out the sure rewards of **q.** answered
W-pI...137.7:2 but be real, then **q.** have been answered.
W-pII..233.1:7 *who* **q.** *not the wisdom of the Infinite, nor*
M-in ..........3:2 these **q.** may be totally unrelated to what
M-in ........5:12 This manual attempts to answer these **q.**.
M-20 .........1:5 Let us consider each of these **q.** separately
M-24 .........4:4 wise to step away from all such **q.**, for he
M-29 .........1:1 manual is not intended to answer all **q.**
M-29 .........2:4 should attempt to answer these **q.** alone.
M-29 .......2:10 To refer the **q.** to Him is yours. Would
C-in ...........3:4 is merely the ego that **q.** because it is only
C-in ...........4:2 It does not recognize as **q.** the mere form
C-2.............9:1 Your **q.** have no answer, being made to
P-2........VI.1:5 hear the dirge he sings, and **q.** its validity.

## quick 15

T-12......III.2:3 experience a **q.** response of opposition,
T-13......III.7:2 vision is merciful and His remedy is **q.**.
T-18.....VII.7:3 **q.** and open door through which you slip
T-30.........I.5:5 need a **q.** restorative before you ask again.
W-pI.....68.7:1 short practice periods should include a **q.**
W-pI.....77.8:2 **q.** to tell yourself, should you be tempted:
W-pI.108.10:3 for today as **q.** advances in your learning,
W-pI...129.2:3 you, **q.** to avenge and pitiless with hate. It
W-pI.133.14:2 be **q.** to answer with this simple thought: *I*
W-pI...136.5:1 It is this **q.** forgetting of the part you play
W-pI...194.1:1 takes another step toward **q.** salvation,
W-pI...194.6:2 a way of **q.** reaction to temptation, you
W-pI...196.2:2 threat, is **q.** to cite the truth to save its lies
WpI rVI.in.5:4 in sure and **q.** exchange for the idea we
W-pII .296.2:2 of easy reach and **q.** accomplishment.

## quicken 1

WpI...rV.in3:5 *Q. our footsteps now, that we may walk*

## quickened 2

WpI rVI.in.4:2 to reach a **q.** pace along a shorter path to
S-3........IV.2:2 world responds in **q.** chorus through the

## quicker 1

S-1........IV.2:2 This step begins the **q.** ascent, but there

## quickly 42

T-2......VIII.2:8 you free yourself from fear **q.**, because
T-7......VIII.5:6 Give them over **q.** to the Holy Spirit to be
T-14........II.6:2 that come **q.** on the firm foundation that
T-14.... III.17:5 Trust Him to answer **q.**, surely, and with
T-15........II.1:7 will **q.** offer you the whole lesson of peace.
T-18......III.2:5 Let us then join **q.** in an instant of light,
T-19......III.9:4 Errors are **q.** recognized and quickly
T-19......III.9:4 recognized and **q.** given to correction, to
T-22.......II.13:2 **Q.** and gladly is His vision given anyone
T-23......IV.6:5 but **q.** choose a miracle instead of murder
T-26....... V.5:2 What disappeared too **q.** to affect the
T-26.......IX.6:2 And They come **q.** to the living temple,
T-27.........I.7:8 pleasure in the **q.** passing and ephemeral.
T-27.......III.2:4 Yet even this is **q.** contradicted by the half
T-30.........I.5:2 unless you **q.** straighten out your mind to
T-30......IV.6:4 changes have been **q.** brought about,
T-30...... V.8:2 on, and **q.** reach the gate of Heaven itself.
W-pI........2.2:1 glance easily and fairly **q.** around you,
W-pI.....15.2:4 certain that real vision will come **q.** when
W-pI.....24.4:3 will **q.** realize that you have a number of
W-pI.....24.6:1 you will **q.** recognize that you are making
W-pI.....68.5:4 It will **q.** become apparent that there is no
W-pI...74.3:10 sure to deal **q.** with any conflict thoughts
W-pI.....74.6:3 **q.** repeat the idea for today and try again.
W-pI...79.10:2 any difficulty seems to rise, tell yourself **q.**
W-pI.....80.6:4 Say **q.**: *Let me recognize this problem has*
W-pI...93.11:1 **q.** dispel the illusion of fear by repeating
W-pI...108.7:4 and see how **q.** peace returns to us. Light
W-pI...123.7:3 eons more **q.** for your thanks to Him.
W-pI...155.5:1 and deprivation both are **q.** left behind.
W-pI...157.4:3 wherein you **q.** leave the world behind.
W-pI...163.3:1 unsure, too **q.** lost however hard to gain,
WpI...rV.in3:5 *we may walk more certainly and q. unto You*
W-pI.193.10:2 Let mercy come to you more **q.**. Do not
W-pI...196.4:2 we may **q.** go the way salvation shows us,
W-pI.196.12:1 reach that instant, and to go beyond it **q.**,
W-pII .249.1:6 It is now so like to Heaven that it **q.** is
M-8 ...........5:3 Will he agree more **q.** to the unreality of a
M-22 .......5:10 Turn **q.** to your Teacher, and let yourself
M-28 .......3:13 How **q.** will it come as it is asked to enter
P-3..........II.9:3 pass by many obstacles to peace quite **q.**,
S-2...........I.6:5 Mistakes are tiny shadows, **q.** gone, that

## quiet 147

T-5..........II.7:6 way, remaining **q.** even in the midst of the
T-5..........II.7:7 The Voice for God is always **q.**, because It

T-5...... IV.8:14 His **q.** children are His blessed Sons. The
T-6...... V.B.6:4 begin to realize the **q.** power of the Holy
T-11...... III.1:6 God is very **q.**, for there is no conflict in
T-11...... III.7:2 In the **q.** of His temple, He waits to give
T-12....... II.5:5 Learn to be **q.** in the midst of turmoil, for
T-12...... VI.5:8 in the **q.** light of the Holy Spirit's blessing.
T-13.... VI.11:8 and spreads across this world in **q.** joy.
T-13.... VI.12:1 out of **q.** recognition of the truth in them.
T-13.... VII.5:9 He lives within you in the **q.** present, and
T-13... VII.13:7 itself to let the rays extend in **q.** to infinity
T-13... VII.15:3 you undertake a **q.** journey to the peace of
T-13... VIII.5:6 into His **q.** sight that makes them one.
T-13...... IX.7:6 shining in **q.** and in peace upon the altar
T-13.... X.11:11 *still. In **q.** look upon his holiness, and offer*
T-14.... III.15:5 Be **q.** in your faith in Him Who loves you,
T-14...... IV.6:2 being carried down a **q.** path in summer.
T-14...... VI.2:1 **q.** light in which the Holy Spirit dwells
T-15......... I.1:1 to be perfectly calm and **q.** all the time?
T-15...... IX.5:3 in Heaven, where you are complete and **q.**
T-18......... I.6:6 to this could only remain within in **q.**,
T-18.... VI.14:6 out, but merely by a **q.** melting in. For
T-18..... VII.8:2 will be more aware of this **q.** center of the
T-18..... VII.8:3 This **q.** center, in which you do nothing,
T-18.... VIII.9:3 becomes a garden, green and deep and **q.**,
T-18..VIII.10:2 And lead them gently to your **q.** garden,
T19. IV.A.16:1 set in a **q.** garden where no sound but
T19.... IV.B.7:3 in the **q.** communion in which the Father
T19... IV.D.5:3 of the **q.** recognition that you love Him.
T19. IV.D.19:5 Here is the rest and **q.** that you seek, the
T-20..VIII.11:1 to **q.** views of gardens under open skies,
T-21...... IV.8:8 The **q.** way is open. Follow it happily, and
T-22..... II.13:1 in **q.** here with Christ is share His vision.
T-22....... V.3:8 God rests with you in **q.**, undefended and
T-22....... V.3:8 this **q.** state alone is strength and power.
T-22....... V.4:2 insignificant before the **q.** strength of
T-22.... VI.9:11 and lays it gently in each **q.** smile of faith
T-23......... I.1:1 memory of God comes to the **q.** mind. It
T-23....... I.7:10 untouched and **q.** in the peace of God.
T-23......... I.8:9 of God, still shining in your **q.** mind.
T-23......... I.9:6 He loves must be forever **q.** and at peace
T-23...... III.4:4 is impossible cannot uphold a **q.**, calm
T-23..... IV.8:8 and a sense of love so deep and **q.** that no
T-23..... IV.9:5 the **q.** sphere above the battleground.
T-24....... in.1:2 Given this state the mind is **q.**, and the
T-24....... V.7:1 Yet is He **q.**, for He knows that love is in
T-24....... V.9:3 and from His certainty His **q.** comes. He
T-25...... IV.4:7 And in the sunlight you will stand in **q.**,
T-27......... IV.h The **Q.** Answer
T-28....... I.11:2 It reaches gently from that **q.** time, and
T-28....... I.11:2 and from the mind it healed in **q.** then, to
T-28....... I.11:5 Their own remembering is **q.** now, and
T-28....... I.12:1 thanks for every **q.** instant given Him. For
T-29....... V.2:4 in its soft embrace, so strong and **q.**,
T-29....... V.5:4 The **q.** that surrounds you dwells in him,
T-29....... V.5:4 and from this **q.** come the happy dreams
T-29.... VIII.2:7 **q.** calm that liberates you from the world,
T-29.... VIII.2:7 lets you stand apart, in **q.** and in peace.
T-30......... I.4:1 time you think of it and have a **q.** moment
W-pI..... 37.3:2 but merely by your **q.** recognition that in
W-pI..... 40.3:8 *I am calm, **q.**, assured and confident.* If only
WpI... rI.in.3:3 and when you are alone in a **q.** place, if
WpI... rI.in.4:3 those that already seem to be calm and **q.**.
WpI... rI.in.4:4 is to enable you to bring the **q.** with you,
W-pI... 72.10:9 Then we will wait in **q.** for His answer.
W-pI... 73.10:1 with gentle firmness and **q.** certainty: *I*
W-pI..... 78.8:6 both. Be very **q.** now, and look upon your
W-pI..... 78.9:1 God thanks you for these **q.** times today
W-pI..... 91.5:1 set aside about ten minutes for a **q.** time
W-pI..... 97.1:4 from conflict to the **q.** fields of peace. No
W-pI..... 98.3:3 They rest in **q.** certainty that they will do
W-pI... 103.3:4 and **q.** all your fears with this assurance,
W-pI... 106.1:1 the mighty Voice of truth, **q.** in power,
W-pI... 107.2:5 Then let the sense of **q.** that you felt be
W-pI... 109.2:2 thought will bring to you the rest and **q.**,
W-pI... 109.9:1 the peace of God today, **q.** and unafraid.
WpI. rIII.in6:6 at the outset; then lean back in **q.** faith,
W-pI... 120.1:2 *I rest in Him in **q.** and in perfect certainty.*
W-pI... 122.1:4 want happiness, a **q.** mind, a certainty of
W-pI...... 125.h In **q.** I receive God's Word today.
W-pI... 125.1:1 day be a day of stillness and of **q.** listening
W-pI... 125.1:5 the world; until your mind, in **q.** listening
W-pI... 125.1:5 must hear to usher in the **q.** time of peace.
W-pI... 125.4:3 **q.** place within the mind where He abides
W-pI... 125.6:2 be heard until your mind is **q.** for a while,
W-pI... 125.6:3 Await His Word in **q.**. There is peace
W-pI... 125.8:4 In **q.** listen to your Self today, and let Him
W-pI... 125.9:1 Only be **q.**. You will need no rule but this
W-pI... 125.9:5 this day; in **q.** to receive the Word of God.
W-pI. 126.10:1 and seek sanctuary in the **q.** place where
W-pI. 126.11:6 Then spend a **q.** moment, opening your
W-pI... 128.8:2 mind, but tell yourself with **q.** certainty:
W-pI... 134.6:1 offer it; a **q.** blessing where it is received.
W-pI... 134.7:5 It looks on them with **q.** eyes, and merely
W-pI. 137.15:2 And as you rest in **q.**, be prepared to give
W-pI. 138.12:3 in a brief **q.** time devoted to maintaining
W-pI. 140.10:4 returns to the eternal, **q.** home of God.
WpI. rIV.in8:1 began, and spend a **q.** moment with it.
WpI. rIV.in9:2 give us happiness and rest, and endless **q.**
W-pI... 143.1:1 (125) In **q.** I receive God's Word today.
W-pI. 153.13:3 Now a **q.** time has come, in which we put
W-pI. 153.18:1 Voice guiding your footsteps into **q.** ways,
W-pI... 155.1:3 Your forehead is serene; your eyes are **q.**.
W-pI... 157.4:3 let it rest in still anticipation and in **q.** joy,
W-pI... 158.6:2 Here is a **q.** place within the world made
W-pI... 164.3:2 **q.** is the time you give to spend with Him,
W-pI... 165.3:1 healing and his peace of mind, his **q.** rest,
W-pI... 170.5:2 strength, and hope of rest in dreamless **q.**
WpI... rV.in2:2 *our doubts be **q.** and our holy minds be still,*
W-pI... 183.5:4 along with him within your **q.** mind, you
W-pI... 189.9:4 And in our **q.** hearts and open minds, His
W-pI... 190.9:1 the **q.** place where Heaven's peace holds
W-pI... 194.1:3 you to Heaven's gate; the **q.** place of peace
W-pI. 198.11:3 face of earth, made **q.** in a dreamless sleep
WpI rVI.in.6:6 give these times of **q.** to the Teacher Who
WpI rVI.in.6:6 quiet to the Teacher Who instructs in **q.**,
W-pII .... in.2:2 in **q.** expectation for our God and Father.
W-pII . 221.1:3 *In the **q.** of my heart, the deep recesses of my*
W-pII . 221.2:1 Now do we wait in **q.**. God is here,
W-pII . 252.1:3 within it, in the calm of **q.** certainty. Its
W-pII . 263.1:4 *its joy, and its eternal, **q.** home in You.*
W-pII . 265.2:1 *In **q.** would I look upon the world, which but*
W-pII . 267.1:6 forever **q.** and at peace within His loving
W-pII . 270.2:1 The **q.** of today will bless our hearts, and
W-pII . 286.1:8 *My heart is **q.**, and my mind at rest. Your*
W-pII ..... 8.2:2 through **q.** eyes and with a mind at peace.
W-pII . 291.2:1 *day my mind is **q.**, to receive the Thoughts*
W-pII . 291.2:5 *Your Son along the **q.** path that leads to You.*
W-pII . 303.1:3 Let earthly sounds be **q.**, and the sights to
W-pII . 305.1:1 vision finds a peace so deep and **q.**,
W-pII . 314.1:5 and peace into a **q.** future filled with joy?
W-pII . 336.2:1 *In **q.** may forgiveness wipe away my dreams*
M-4..... I.A.6:2 This is a **q.** time, in which the teacher of
M-4.... IX.2:12 it rests in **q.** certainty on that alone to
M-15....... 2:12 Learn to be **q.**, for His Voice is heard in
M-15....... 2:13 to all who stand aside in **q.** listening, and
M-16......... 4:2 that fosters **q.** thought as he awakes. If
M-16......... 4:7 as possible after waking take your **q.** time,
M-16......... 5:2 Perhaps your **q.** time should be fairly
M-20......... 2:8 away, and in its place is everlasting **q.**.
M-20....... 2:11 gone. **Q.** has reached to cover everything.
M-20......... 3:1 How is this **q.** found? No one can fail to
C-ep........... 5:6 the **q.** God has given him enters his home
S-1........... I.5:1 go, a **q.** time of listening and loving. It
S-3.......... II.2:1 This is what death should be; a **q.** choice,
S-3.......... II.4:3 Now are its dreams dispelled in **q.** rest.

## quieting 1

M-16......... 9:4 healing nor destructive, **q.** nor fearful.

## quietly 53

T-11 ...... V.1:6 We will undo this error **q.** together, and
T-12 ..... VI.5:6 He looks **q.** on the real world, which He
T-12 ..... VI.7:5 the real world has slipped **q.** into Heaven,
T-13 .... VII.1:1 Sit **q.** and look upon the world you see,
T-13 .... VII.7:7 point of safety he looks **q.** about him and
T-13 ... VIII.6:4 see blends **q.** into the one reality of God.
T-13 ..... XI.4:4 The Holy Spirit points **q.** to the contrast,
T-14 ... III.10:8 the Holy Spirit **q.** understands it for them
T-14 ... III.12:4 Peace abides in every mind that **q.** accepts
T-14 ... III.19:5 you **q.** how to perceive your guiltlessness,
T-14 ....... V.1:8 of death behind, and return **q.** to Heaven.
T-14 ....... V.8:6 Stand **q.** within this circle, and attract all
T-14 ..... IX.4:1 waits **q.** for the return of them that love it.
T-16 ........ I.2:7 you will merely sit **q.** by and let the Holy
T-16 ..... IV.2:5 safety, translated **q.** from war to peace.
T-16 ..... IV.4:8 in which it would gladly come **q.** to them.
T-17 ....... II.6:2 world reaching **q.** and gently across chaos
T-18 ...... I.11:2 Heaven has entered **q.**, for all illusions
T-19 ...... IV.1:6 will **q.** extend to every aspect of your life,
T19 .IV.A.4:11 fall away so **q.** beneath the wings of peace.
T19 .IV.A.5:11 But let Him **q.** extend the miracle of your
T19 ... IV.C.9:2 sin, which nestles **q.** in the safety of your
T19 ... IV.C.9:3 **q.** made ready to fulfill the mighty task
T-20 ..... VI.9:5 lay aside the body and **q.** transcend it,
T-20 ... VIII.1:3 and what was never lost will **q.** return. It
T-21 ..... VI.4:2 attack, but takes the place of madness **q.**,
T-22 ....... V.5:7 is **q.** passed through and gone beyond?
T-22 ..... VI.5:2 joined with love, looks **q.** on all confusion
T-27 ..... IV.1:1 is every problem **q.** resolved. In conflict
T-28 ...... I.11:1 The miracle comes **q.** into the mind that
T-29 ........ I.7:5 go away, and leave you **q.** alone in "peace.
T-29 ..... VI.6:4 timelessness comes **q.** to take the place of
W-pI .... 31.3:5 As you sit and **q.** watch your thoughts,
W-pI .... 33.4:2 so to sit **q.** and repeat the idea to yourself
W-pI .... 41.6:2 sit **q.** for some three to five minutes, with
W-pI .... 42.3:2 to wait until you can sit **q.** by yourself, at
W-pI .... 44.7:2 and intrusion by **q.** sinking past them.
W-pI .... 44.7:5 without involvement, and slip **q.** by them.
W-pI .... 49.5:3 sure to sit **q.** and repeat the idea for today
W-pI .... 69.4:1 Very **q.** now, with your eyes closed, try to
W-pI .... 77.5:1 phase, wait **q.** for the assurance that your
WpI.. rII.in.3:1 of the time listening **q.** but attentively.
W-pI .. 110.4:1 saved to **q.** extend into a timeless future.
W-pI 153.17:2 And we will **q.** sit by and wait on Him and
W-pI .. 157.6:3 experience in which the world is **q.** forgot,
W-pI .. 160.8:4 Hear His Voice assure you, **q.** and sure,
W-pI .. 188.6:1 Sit **q.** and close your eyes. The light
W-pI .. 189.8:3 God the Father to be **q.** removed forever.
W-pII ..... 1.4:1 other hand, is still, and **q.** does nothing. It
W-pII . 222.2:1 *as we come **q.** into Your Presence now, and*
W-pII ..... 2.3:3 it merely lets them **q.** go down to dust.
W-pII . 254.2:2 occur, we **q.** step back and look at them,
W-pII . 286.1:2 *How **q.** do all things fall in place! This is the*

## quietness 22

T-12 ....... II.5:5 for **q.** is the end of strife and this is the
T-13 .. VII.15:3 of God, where He would have you be in **q.**
T-13 .. VII.16:2 walk together on the way to **q.** that is the
T-14 ....... II.3:2 the Holy Spirit says, with steadfast **q.**: *The*
T-14 ....... II.8:5 The **q.** of its simplicity is so compelling
T-14 ..... V.11:4 Judge not except in **q.** which is not of you.
T-20 ..... II.8:12 the home we share in **q.** and where we live
T-24 ....... V.9:6 His **q.** becomes your certainty. And where
T-25 .... VII.8:3 enter into it in **q.** and show him he is mad
T-27 ..... IV.1:1 In **q.** are all things answered, and is every
T-28 ...... I.10:9 healed. In **q.**, see in the miracle a lesson in
T-28 ...... I.11:2 quiet then, to other minds to share its **q.**.
W-pI .. 108.8:6 *To everyone I offer **q.**. To everyone I offer*
W-pI .. 109.1:1 **q.** unshaken by the world's appearances.
W-pI .. 121.1:3 your hopes of ever finding **q.** and peace.
W-pI .. 122.1:6 you want a **q.** that cannot be disturbed, a
W-pI .. 122.8:3 In **q.** it rises up to greet your open eyes,
W-pI 132.15:4 in **q.** be changed so that the world is freed
W-pI .. 188.5:6 In **q.** is it acknowledged universally. For
W-pI .. 189.4:2 world reflects the **q.** and peace that shines
W-pII . 273.2:4 *still, in **q.** and in my own eternal love for You.*
W-pII ..... 7.5:3 by which the **q.** of Heaven is restored to

## quite 142

T-1 ........ I.49:2 effective **q.** apart from either the degree
T-2 ....... VI.6:5 own. The lesson here is **q.** simple, but
T-2 ..... VIII.5:3 **q.** apparent that it is really the doorway to
T-3 ......... II.2:3 innocent are apt to be **q.** foolish at times.

T-3.........V.3:3 stable, and it is **q.** evident that you are not
T-3......VI.11:2 in this position would be **q.** apparent.
T-4.........II.1:5 always specific, and therefore **q.** concrete.
T-4.......VII.1:2 Ego illusions are **q.** specific, although the
T-5...........I.1:9 the lower mind it is **q.** comprehensible in
T-5.........II.1:3 of the time sequence should be **q.** familiar
T-5.........V.3:7 The ego is **q.** literally a fearful thought.
T-5.........V.8:8 ordering of thought becomes **q.** apparent.
T-6......V.B.1:4 is **q.** apparent that you can teach wrongly,
T-7.........V.1:1 is **q.** apart from what they are used for.
T-7.........V.4:5 is **q.** evident that he does not understand
T-8........IX.8:3 this, and given this **q.** literally, nothing
T-9........IV.7:1 you should be **q.** familiar with it by now.
T-11......IV.4:5 phases of this reversal are often **q.** painful
T-11.......V.4:4 ego's goal is **q.** explicitly ego autonomy.
T-11.....V.10:1 of the form it takes and **q.** apart from how
T-12......IV.3:3 for it would be **q.** apparent that it had not
T-13... VIII.2:1 and knowledge becomes **q.** apparent if
T-14.......in.1:3 for learning it and seeing it **q.** clearly. The
T-14....III.15:8 For it is **q.** impossible that He could ever
T-14. VIII.2:14 wills with His Son is **q.** impossible here.
T-15.......V.1:5 because it would be **q.** apparent to you
T-15.......X.5:1 in forms **q.** different from what it is. Yet it
T-16.......II.3:4 of difficulty in miracles is **q.** impossible,
T-16.......II.4:1 **q.** apparent that you have not done them
T-16......III.5:7 They are **q.** real, as part of the Self you do
T-16......IV.2:3 go through this last undoing **q.** unharmed
T-16.......V.3:2 that center around it are often **q.** overt.
T-17.......V.3:3 disjunctive and even **q.** distressing. The
T-17.......V.3:4 distressing. The reason is **q.** clear. For the
T-17.......V.5:7 may even become **q.** disorganized. And
T-17.......V.7:1 your former goal was **q.** appropriate. You
T-17......VI.4:3 It is **q.** noticeable that this approach has
T-17......VI.5:3 this is **q.** apart from what the outcome *is.*
T-18.........I.3:5 appears to introduce **q.** variable behavior,
T-18.........II.1:1 a world that seems **q.** real arise in dreams
T-18.....VII.2:4 see the body again, but never **q.** the same.
T-18......IX.3:4 these messages relay to you is **q.** external.
T-18......IX.3:6 it not; its senses remain **q.** unaware of it;
T-19.......II.5:2 **q.** unapproachable except with reverence
T19. IV.A.11:7 is meaningless to fear, and **q.** invisible.
T19...IV.D.3:4 the memory of God seems **q.** forgotten;
T-20.....VII.5:4 the illusion of a brother as a body is **q.** in
T-21.........I.6:1 a hint of an ancient state not **q.** forgotten;
T-21....III.12:2 of vision it is looked upon **q.** differently.
T-21......IV.1:5 with sin the ego deems **q.** appropriate,
T-21... VIII.2:1 condition **q.** alien to your understanding.
T-22.........I.3:7 of course, render this **q.** unnecessary. Yet
T-22......III.1:6 Vision is sense, **q.** literally. If it is not the
T-22.......IV.1:1 the branch in the road is **q.** apparent, you
T-23.....II.20:2 making it seem **q.** possible to value some
T-23.....II.22:7 **Q.** easily. How do you feel? Is peace in
T-23......IV.5:2 there will your perspective be **q.** different.
T-23......IV.9:5 senselessness of conquest is **q.** apparent
T-24......IV.3:4 to heal and not attack, it is **q.** obvious.
T-24......VI.5:5 you both, for holiness is **q.** impartial, with
T-26.......V.2:2 **q.** meaningless to the real Teacher of the
T-26......V.6:10 **q.** convinced that where he would prefer
T-26.....VII.3:8 to truth, its senselessness is **q.** apparent.
T-27.....VII.7:8 they have is something **q.** apart from him,
T-28.........I.5:1 use of memory is **q.** apart from time. He
T-28.......II.2:8 body, and its innocence is **q.** apart from it
T-28.....VII.5:8 to be **q.** solid and substantial in itself. Yet
T-29.........I.1:4 in His eternal Love is **q.** impossible. For it
T-30......III.1:1 Idols are **q.** specific. But your will is
T-30....III.10:2 forms that fear can take; **q.** undisturbed,
T-30.......V.3:1 Not yet is Heaven **q.** remembered, for the
T-30......VI.3:3 of forgiveness is **q.** real and fully justified.
T-31......IV.3:3 can offer seem to be **q.** large in number,
T-31.....V.15:4 yourself will still remain **q.** meaningless.
W-in..........8:1 and others may seem to be **q.** startling.
W-pI........9.2:2 This idea can be **q.** disturbing, and may
W-pI.....10.4:1 the idea for today **q.** slowly to yourself.
W-pI.....12.2:2 Look around you, this time **q.** slowly. Try
W-pI.....14.3:2 can be **q.** difficult and even quite painful.
W-pI.....14.3:2 can be quite difficult and even **q.** painful.
W-pI.....14.5:2 case, name the "disaster" **q.** specifically.
W-pI.....15.3:2 forms, some of them **q.** unexpected. Do
W-pI.....15.4:6 should be repeated **q.** slowly each time.
W-pI.....16.4:2 This is **q.** difficult until you get used to it.
W-pI.....19.4:1 should be **q.** familiar to you by now, and
W-pI.....20.1:1 **q.** casual about our practice periods thus
W-pI.....25.6:7 Say this **q.** slowly, without shifting your
W-pI.....26.7:3 referring to each one **q.** specifically,
W-pI.....26.8:1 situation you use, and **q.** possibly more. It
W-pI.....27.4:4 applications, and perhaps **q.** a number.
W-pI.....28.8:3 application should be made **q.** slowly,
W-pI.....36.3:2 your eyes and look **q.** slowly about you,
W-pI.....36.4:2 should, of course, be made **q.** slowly, as
W-pI.....40.2:4 practice **q.** well under any circumstances,
W-pI.....41.8:1 It is **q.** possible to reach God. In fact it is
W-pI.....44.5:2 **q.** ready to learn the form of exercise we
W-pI.....49.1:1 It is **q.** possible to listen to God's Voice
WpI....rI.in.6:1 are not given in **q.** their original form. Use
W-pI.....51.2:4 my judgments have been made **q.** apart
W-pI.....64.7:3 function" **q.** often to help you concentrate
W-pI.....68.5:2 Some of these will be **q.** easy to find. Then
W-pI.....69.4:3 outside the circle and **q.** apart from it.
W-pI.....72.5:4 makes this view of God **q.** convincing. In
W-pI.....77.4:1 by telling yourself **q.** confidently that you
W-pI.....78.1:1 Perhaps it is not yet **q.** clear to you that
W-pI...130.6:4 the one you see is **q.** consistent from the
W-pI. 131.13:3 **q.** forget in wandering away in dreams.
W-pI...132.6:1 into a world **q.** separate from yourself,
W-pI...132.6:1 **q.** apart from what you chance to think it
W-pI...135.8:2 merely be perceived as **q.** apart from you,
W-pI. 135.16:4 to guarantee a future **q.** unlike the past,
W-pI...136.7:2 a thing that happens to you, **q.** unsought,
W-pI. 136.13:3 Thoughts of God are **q.** apart from time.
W-pI. 153.15:1 in a form we will maintain for **q.** a while.
W-pI...158.3:2 It appears to be **q.** arbitrary. Yet there is
W-pI...159.5:3 seem **q.** solid here are merely shadows
W-pI...181.4:2 You have been **q.** preoccupied with how
W-pI...186.3:1 Today's idea may seem **q.** sobering, until
W-pI...196.8:2 From there we go ahead **q.** rapidly. For
W-pI. 196.10:1 so wholly that escape appears **q.** hopeless.
W-pI...199.3:2 concerned that to the ego it is **q.** insane.
W-pII .....3.1:4 will the world be seen in **q.** another light;
W-pII .....3.2:7 Now mistakes become **q.** possible, for
W-pII .....5.3:2 but can **q.** suddenly revert to fear, where
M-in ..........3:4 content of your teaching is **q.** irrelevant.
M-3 ...........2:1 of teaching appears to be **q.** superficial. It
M-3 ...........5:5 be **q.** hostile to each other for some time,
M-4 ...........1:2 superficial "personalities" are **q.** distinct.
M-5 .... III.1:13 nothing. To them the separation is **q.** real
M-17 .........1:3 the magic seem **q.** real to both of them.
M-19 .........2:5 The path becomes **q.** different as one goes
M-21 .........2:1 words have **q.** specific references. Even
M-21 .........5:2 what he hears may indeed be **q.** startling.
M-21 .........5:3 It may also seem to be **q.** irrelevant to the
M-25 .........1:4 abilities that seem **q.** startling to him. Yet
C-1.............7:4 and awareness can shift **q.** dramatically,
P-2........ III.3:1 **q.** possible for psychotherapy to seem to
P-2........ VI.5:3 of the form a sickness takes will point **q.**
P-3...........II.9:3 by many obstacles to peace **q.** quickly, if
S-1........ III.6:6 can be **q.** clearly recognized even in this.
S-2...........II.3:1 not appear in **q.** such blatant arrogance.
S-3........ III.1:2 Its separate goals become **q.** clear in this,

## quotation 1

W-pI...110.6:1 periods, begin with this **q.** from the text: *I*

## quotations 1

C-1.............3:2 is not used except in direct biblical **q.**

## quoted 1

T-6.........I.15:2 they never could have **q.** me as saying,

# R

## rack 1

W-pI.......9.4:2 *I do not see that coat* **r.** *as it is now. I do not*

## radiance 19

T-2...........I.2:4 is similar to the inner **r.** that the children
T-4........ I.12:3 its **r.** and gladly sheds its light everywhere
T-5.........in.1:5 **R.** is not associated with sorrow. Joy calls
T-5......... II.4:2 The Holy Spirit is the **r.** that you must let
T-5........IV.8:4 kept them for you in their own perfect **r.**.
T-7........IX.6:9 **r.** is so intense that It creates in perfect joy
T-7........XI.5:2 light. Its own **r.** shines all around it, and
T-11......IV.8:1 is the Son of God whose **r.** is of his Father,
T-13......V.10:5 shining in perfect **r.** that is undimmed by
T-13.......X.8:4 he has looked within and seen the **r.** there
T-13.....X.14:3 the glorious **r.** of the Kingdom guilt melts
T-24.......II.6:2 The shining **r.** of the Son of God, so like
T-25.........I.4:4 **r.** shines through each body that it looks
T-26......IV.3:8 to them, and all their **r.** made whole again
T-26......IX.6:5 becomes the brightest light in Heaven's **r.**
T-27.......V.6:5 The holy instant's **r.** will light your eyes,
W-pI.....97.6:2 you gave as much as does the **r.** of the sun
W-pI.152.10:5 And in humility the **r.** of God's Son, his
W-pII .299.2:4 *can obscure it, but can not put out its* **r.**, *nor*

## radiant 9

T-3...........I.8:5 truth. That is why their altars are truly **r.**.
T-14.......V.1:2 into a **r.** message of God's Love, to share
T-18.........I.9:7 Here is the **r.** truth, to which the Holy
T-18...... III.8:7 in which everything is **r.** in the light.
T-20....VIII.4:4 glowing with **r.** purity and sparkling with
T-23.........I.7:10 And truth stands **r.**, apart from conflict,
T-28.......I.11:3 its **r.** extension back into the Mind which

T-31...... VI.7:4 The truth in you remains as **r.** as a star, as
W-pI... 190.6:5 Your Self is **r.** in this holy joy, unchanged,

**radiate** 2

T-12..... VII.1:5 Atonement will **r.** from your acceptance
W-pI..... 41.3:1 to **r.** through you and out into the world.

**radiates** 6

T-3........... I.7:1 The Atonement itself **r.** nothing but truth
T-5......... in.3:4 The light is so strong that it **r.** throughout
T-6...... V.C.9:7 Once your mind is healed it **r.** health, and
T19... IV.A.1:3 are the center from which it **r.** outward,
W-pI... 134.2:5 to Him, reflects His laws and **r.** His Love.
W-pI... 188.4:2 salvation **r.** with gifts beyond all measure,

**radiating** 1

T-5......... in.3:4 thanks to the Father for **r.** His joy upon it.

**radical** 1

T-17....... V.5:2 Only a **r.** shift in purpose could induce a

**rage** 8

T-2........ VI.5:7 sense of coercion that usually produces **r.**,
T-4......... II.5:2 in **r.** if you take away a knife or scissors,
T-21...... IV.6:6 in **r.** at your "presumptuous" wish to look
W-pI..... 21.2:3 reaction ranging from mild irritation to **r.**
W-pI... 161.8:3 intensity of **r.** projected fear must spawn.
W-pI... 170.2:2 blood, to make it grow and swell and **r.**.
W-pI... 192.7:2 reason but to justify our **r.** and our attack.
M-17 ......... 4:5 Or it may also take the form of intense **r.**,

**raging** 2

T-18..... VII.8:2 center of the storm than all its **r.** activity.
S-3 ......... II.1:9 thoughts and **r.** anger at the universe. It

**rain** 3

T-28... VII.5:11 and **r.** will come and carry it into oblivion
T-28..... VII.7:3 blow upon it and the **r.** will beat against it
W-pII ... 13.5:1 Miracles fall like drops of healing **r.** from

**raise** 42

T-1......... I.24:1 the sick and **r.** the dead because you made
T-1......... I.32:3 **r.** you into the sphere of celestial order. In
T-2........ IV.5:6 is to **r.** the level of communication, not to
T-5........... I.6:2 of thinking that could **r.** their perceptions
T-7........ III.5:7 They do not **r.** questions, because nothing
T-12......... I.9:9 If you **r.** what fear conceals to clear-cut
T-13...... III.1:2 need for you to **r.** it to awareness yourself.
T-14.... XI.11:4 and do not **r.** your voice against Him. For
T-16..... V.11:5 and on his body **r.** another self to take its
T-16..... V.13:1 attempt to **r.** other gods before Him, and
T-16..... V.13:3 every idol that you **r.** to place before Him
T-19.... III.10:5 and **r.** your eyes in faith to what you now
T19... IV.A.5:6 Guilt can **r.** no real barriers against it.
T19.... IV.B.8:3 behind the obstacles you **r.** to freedom,
T19... IV.D.6:3 all rise and bid you not to **r.** your eyes.
T19... IV.D.7:1 abandon you if you but **r.** your eyes. Yet
T19... IV.D.8:6 **r.** your eyes you will be ready to look on
T19. IV.D.12:8 and he will **r.** your eyes in faith together,
T-20...... III.9:4 Strengthen your hold and **r.** your eyes
T-22...... IV.3:3 **R.** it together with your brother, for it is
T-25......... I.1:7 meet and join and **r.** Him to His Father,
T-25..... VII.8:2 He to **r.** a saner world to meet the sight of
T-27...... IV.7:4 the answers merely **r.** another question,
T-29.... VIII.2:6 his little self for strength to **r.** his head,
T-29...... IX.1:3 and look to idols that they **r.** him up?
W-pI..... 50.3:2 and **r.** you high above all the perceived
W-pI..... 60.1:6 reach down to me and **r.** me up to Him.
W-pI..... 69.7:2 will **r.** you from darkness into light. You
W-pI..... 78.1:3 And as you **r.** it up before your eyes, you
W-pI..... 84.1:6 **r.** my own self-concept to replace my Self.
W-pI... 123.4:1 above despair, and **r.** our thankful eyes,
W-pI. 127.10:4 we **r.** our eyes upon a different present,
W-pI. 135.26:5 to **r.** defensiveness in you and tempt you
WpI...rV.in3:2 *And if we stumble, You will r. us up. If we*
WpI...rV.in5:4 Let us **r.** our hearts from dust to life, as we
W-pI... 186.8:5 and our emotions **r.** us high indeed, or
W-pI. 193.13:5 down to earth at last, to **r.** it up to Heaven
W-pII ..... 1.2:1 a judgment that it will not **r.** to doubt,
M-11 ....... 4:10 it leans down in answer, to **r.** it up again.
M-29 ......... 1:1 that both teacher and pupil may **r.**. In fact
P-2......... V.1:6 felt, and seeks to **r.** illusions to the light.
S-1........... I.6:4 beside you and helps to **r.** you up to Him.

**raised** 24

T-2 ....... VI.1:6 presence of fear shows that you have **r.**
T-4 ..... IV.11:7 I **r.** the dead by knowing that life is an
T-5 ...... VII.2:3 at times, but they have not **r.** the dead.
T-6 ....... IV.2:6 **r.** the first question that was ever asked,
T-6 ....... IV.2:8 since, although it has **r.** a great many. The
T-13 ....... X.9:7 is as pure as He Who **r.** it to Himself.
T-17 ..... IV.3:2 recognize them because you have **r.** their
T-19 ...... I.14:1 God has **r.** unto Himself and both of you.
T19... IV.D.5:1 the fear that **r.** it yields to the love beyond
T-20 ...... V.2:3 Two voices **r.** together call to the hearts of
T-23 ..... IV.4:5 relationship is **r.** above the battleground,
T-26 ..... IV.5:4 at the altar that was **r.** within the tiny spot
T-31 .... V.11:4 go, if either one were ever **r.** to doubt. The
T-31 .... V.11:6 asks if just a little question might be **r.**.
T-31 .... V.17:5 has been **r.** to doubt and question, and
T-31 ... VIII.4:2 place you **r.** an image of yourself before.
W-pI... 132.1:7 source is **r.** to question that the hope of
W-pI... 138.9:3 in shadows must be **r.** to understanding,
W-pI. 138.10:1 when it is **r.** from its protective shield of
W-pI. 182.11:1 you **r.** against an enemy without existence
W-pI... 184.7:5 can be withdrawn as they are **r.** to doubt.
M-17 ......... 7:6 thought has guilt already **r.** madness to
M-27 ......... 1:5 way of nature," not to be **r.** to question,
C-in ........... 3:5 answer, once a question has been **r.**.

**raises** 2

T-4 ........ V.1:4 awareness, and **r.** control rather than
T-6 ....... IV.6:1 the questions the ego **r.**: You are a child of

**raising** 5

T-11 . VIII.15:5 last step for you, by **r.** you unto Himself.
T-13 ....... II.4:4 can withstand your **r.** all else to question,
T-16 .... V.12:2 aimed at **r.** the form to take the place of
T-21 .... VII.2:5 and **r.** up their helplessness against him.
M-21 ......... 5:9 **r.** them from meaningless symbols to the

**rally** 1

M-25 ......... 5:3 may still be strong enough to **r.** under this

**random** 6

T-30 ...... I.15:1 Your day is not at **r.**. It is set by what you
W-pI....... 4.5:2 a substitute for the more **r.** procedures to
W-pI..... 15.5:1 try to make the selection as **r.** as possible.
W-pI..... 19.4:2 that **r.** selection of subjects for all practice
W-pI..... 42.2:3 through time and space is not at **r.**. You
M-16 ......... 1:3 of but one thing; they do not change at **r.**.

**randomly** 3

W-pI..... 18.3:1 of the idea for today as **r.** as possible, and
W-pI..... 28.7:2 Not only should the subjects be chosen **r.**,
W-pI..... 29.4:1 apply it to **r.** chosen subjects about you,

**range** 17

*See also* long-range

T-6 ..... V.A.4:9 less. Without a **r.**, order of difficulty is
T-6 ..... V.A.4:9 be no **r.** in what you offer to your brother.
T-9 ...... VII.3:8 That is its **r.**. It cannot exceed it because
T-9 ...... VII.6:2 it. Its **r.** precludes this. You can only go
T-18 ..... IX.7:2 A solid mountain **r.**, a lake, a city, all rise
T-21 ..... V.7:12 For reason is beyond the ego's **r.** of means
W-pI ...... 1.2:1 area, and apply the idea to a wider **r.**: *That*
W-pI ....... 2.1:3 Then increase the **r.** outward. Turn your
W-pI ....... 9.4:1 you, and then extend the **r.** outward: *I do*
W-pI .... 29.3:5 holy purpose stands beyond your little **r.**.
W-pI .... 30.3:2 now if it were within the **r.** of your sight.
W-pI .... 30.4:2 **r.** as well as those you can actually see, as
W-pI .. 130.5:4 They are the **r.** of choice beyond which
W-pI 130.11:2 still remains within your **r.** of choice, to
W-pI .. 133.4:2 The **r.** is set, and this we cannot change. It
M-10 ......... 3:3 of an inconceivably wide **r.** of things; past
M-25 ......... 2:2 small **r.** of channels the world recognizes.

**ranging** 1

W-pI .... 21.2:3 reaction **r.** from mild irritation to rage.

**ransom** 3

W-pI .. 155.8:2 lighting up the path of **r.** from illusion. It
W-pI .. 155.8:3 It is not a **r.** with a price. There is no cost,
W-pI .. 190.8:2 the **r.** you have gladly paid not to be free.

**ranting** 1

T-21 ..... IV.6:5 its **r.** strikes no terror in your heart. For

**rapid** 1

M-22 ......... 2:1 of the teacher of God may be slow or **r.**,

**rapidity** 1

W-pI .. 136.3:3 the **r.** with which you choose to use them.

**rapidly** 3

T-17 ....... V.3:3 This is accomplished very **r.**, but it makes
W-pI .... 11.3:1 move from one thing to another fairly **r.**,
W-pI .. 196.8:2 From there we go ahead quite **r.**. For once

**rapture** 1

W-pI .. 151.8:4 witnesses before the **r.** of Christ's holy

**rare** 2

M-22 ......... 2:2 all situations, but this is comparatively **r.**.
M-26 ......... 3:4 **r.** that it cannot be considered a realistic

**rarely** 7

W-pI .... 19.2:2 This is **r.** a wholly welcome idea at first,
M-4 ..... I.A.3:3 and it is **r.** understood initially that their
M-22 ......... 4:3 but it is **r.** if ever consistently applied to
M-23 ......... 1:1 God's gifts can **r.** be received directly.
P-2........... I.1:1 Yet the ideal outcome is **r.** achieved.
P-2.......... II.3:4 the patient, and only **r.** so to the therapist
P-2....... VII.4:3 This confusion is **r.** if ever in awareness,

**rasping** 1

W-pI .. 182.6:3 and harsh and **r.** noises of the world. Yet

**rather** 99

T-1 ........ I.14:3 mindless and therefore destructive; or **r.**,
T-1 ........ I.38:3 to perceive totally **r.** than selectively.
T-1 ......... II.4:2 of a vertical **r.** than a horizontal axis. You
T-1 ....... IV.3:6 is to restore everything to you; or **r.**, to
T-1 ......... V.5:5 tyrannous **r.** than Authoritative control.
T-2 ... V.A.15:4 is essentially judgmental, **r.** than healing.
T-2 ..... VIII.3:3 It is a final healing **r.** than a meting out of
T-3 .......... I.2:1 position, but **r.** to protect the truth. It is
T-3 ....... III.4:1 but it is still a correction **r.** than a fact.
T-3 ....... III.4:4 would be a miracle **r.** than a revelation.

T-3........IV.2:1 the mind a perceiver **r.** than a creator.
T-3........IV.2:3 as you wish to be, **r.** than as you are. Yet
T-3........IV.3:1 self, which was made **r.** than created. It is
T-3........VI.2:1 The choice to judge **r.** than to know is the
T-3.......VII.2:7 Yet he attracts men **r.** than repels them,
T-4......... V.1:4 control **r.** than sanity to predominance.
T-4.......VII.2:2 establish separateness **r.** than to abolish it
T-5........VI.1:4 have elected to be in time **r.** than eternity,
T-5.......VII.5:5 error **r.** than allow it to be undone for you
T-6.........in.1:2 **r.** than being blamed on others. Anger
T-6.........in.1:4 of attack **r.** than of love must follow.
T-6...........I.6:4 **R.**, teach your own perfect immunity,
T-6........ I.14:1 as a weapon for assault **r.** than as the call
T-6......V.A.6:4 to exacerbate conflict **r.** than resolve it,
T-6......V.A.6:7 **r.** than take the next step towards its
T-7...........I.4:1 because it is competitive **r.** than loving. It
T-7........IV.3:8 their similarity **r.** than their differences is
T-8........IX.1:6 Ask, **r.**, that the Holy Spirit teach you the
T-11......VI.7:4 died in vain. Teach **r.** that I did not die by
T-11. VIII.5:10 that asking is taking **r.** than sharing.
T-13......III.5:2 You would **r.** be a slave of the crucifixion
T-13......IV.9:5 and extends the present **r.** than the past.
T-14......IV.3:5 Ask, **r.**, to learn how to forgive, and to
T-14......VI.6:2 but **r.** the disruption of communication.
T-14.....VII.1:8 **r.** than a helper in the search for truth.
T-14.....VII.3:9 was not a point of view, but **r.** a certainty.
T-14......IX.6:2 interpretations, **r.** than in themselves.
T-14......IX.8:5 but **r.** the actual condition of what was
T-15....III.11:3 His. **R.**, join with me in His, that we may
T-15......IV.1:2 means only that you would **r.** delay the
T-15....... X.8:3 you have given God away **r.** than look at it
T-16......IV.4:5 are trying to live with guilt **r.** than die of it
T-16......VI.8:7 Find hope and comfort, **r.** than despair,
T-17......IV.2:6 **r.** than aiming to make a substitute for it.
T-18....... II.1:4 **R.** it is a distortion of the world, planned
T-18......IV.5:8 **R.** than seek to prepare yourself for Him,
T-18....... V.6:1 for the holy one that you would **r.** have.
T-19....... II.4:5 Or is it, **r.**, an attempt to wrest creation
T-19....... II.8:1 Would you not **r.** that all this be nothing
T19... IV.A.9:6 not **r.** greet the summer sun than fix your
T-20... VIII.4:7 would you **r.** look on it than on the truth?
T-21....... II.1:5 obscure, but **r.** that this little cost seemed,
T-22.........I.9:8 **R.**, in each the other saw a perfect shelter
T-22.......VI.3:2 But be you **r.** grateful that you can be the
T-24.....VII.3:4 Be thankful, **r.**, it is given you to see his
T-24.....VII.4:8 **r.**, then, a frame of holiness around him,
T-25....... II.5:7 would you **r.** see the frame instead of this?
T-26....... X.6:7 *I would* **r.** *know of Them than see injustice,*
T-28.........I.5:2 to keep the past, but **r.** as a way to let it go
T-28...... I.13:5 but **r.** is the Cause that fear was made to
T-28..... II.12:3 **r.** than deny the active role in making up
T-28......IV.3:3 Think, **r.**, of him as a mind in which
T-31...... I.11:5 But listen, **r.**, to the deeper call beyond it
T-31.....VII.6:6 Would you not **r.** look upon yourself as
W-pI.......8.3:3 **r.** than believing that it is filled with real
W-pI.....10.3:1 are meaningless, outside **r.** than within;
W-pI.....10.3:1 their past **r.** than their present status.
W-pI.....12.3:3 positive **r.** than negative occur to you,
W-pI.....25.5:2 are meaningless, **r.** than "good" or "bad,"
W-pI.....26.1:6 own best interests, **r.** than against them.
W-pI.....28.3:3 what it is, **r.** than telling it what it is. You
W-pI.....30.2:4 we see, **r.** than keeping it apart from us.
W-pI.....30.5:3 mind, and looking within **r.** than without.
W-pI.....35.3:3 perceiver, **r.** than on what he perceives.
W-pI.....39.5:2 **r.** than longer sessions are recommended,
W-pI.....42.1:5 And it is His gift, **r.** than your own, that
WpI ...rI.in.3:2 Try, **r.**, to emphasize the central point,
WpI ...rI.in.4:3 **r.** than in those that already seem to be
W-pI.....52.5:7 Would I not **r.** join the thinking of the
W-pI.....55.1:7 **r.** than those which show me an illusion
W-pI.....65.5:4 **R.**, try to uncover each thought that arises
W-pI.....74.5:4 alertness, **r.** than a feeling of drowsiness
W-pI.....88.1:2 In choosing salvation **r.** than attack, I
W-pI.....95.8:4 **r.** than give it power to delay our learning
W-pI...100.9:3 What could you **r.** look upon in place of
W-pI...138.6:1 of choice, **r.** than merely being what it is.
W-pI.155.11:2 be no wish to be illusion **r.** than the truth.
W-pI...181.1:4 **R.**, they are magnified, becoming blocks
W-pII..287.1:5 And would I **r.** live with fear than love?
M-in ..........1:3 to the learner **r.** than to himself. Further,
M-10 .........2:7 *through* him **r.** than *by* him can occur. And
M-15 .........3:4 on its gifts, that you would **r.** have? You
M-20 .........4:9 Would you not **r.** live than choose to die?
P-2......... II.1:2 teach forgiveness **r.** than condemnation.
P-2.......VII.4:2 as self-created **r.** than God-created. This
P-3.........I.2:12 Would you **r.** choose who would be god,
S-1 ...........I.1:7 Ask, **r.**, to receive what is already given; to
S-1 ......... II.4:2 but **r.** in the way in which they are usually
S-2 ......... II.5:6 it **r.** treachery to one who needs salvation

## ratio 1

W-pI...185.3:5 **r.** of gain to loss and loss to gain takes on

## rationale 3

T-8.........I.5:10 exist, and gives them no **r.** for choice.
T-8......... II.1:1 There *is* a **r.** for choice. Only one Teacher
W-pI.......7.1:2 Yet it is the **r.** for all of the preceding ones

## rationally 1

T-2..... VIII.3:7 the ability to choose can be directed **r.**.

## raucous 2

T-21....... V.1:6 the ego's **r.** screams and senseless ravings
W-pI.....49.4:3 mind. Go past all the **r.** shrieks and sick

## ravaged 3

T-13......XI.1:2 and **r.** by a cruel war unless he believes
T-13......XI.1:5 freedom. No one finds himself **r.** and torn
T-18.......I.12:7 whole what has been **r.** by separation and

## ravages 4

T-19.......III.9:5 You will be healed of sin and all its **r.** the
T-30.......I.13:2 that will protect you from the **r.** of fear.
T-31......III.5:2 survive the **r.** of fear except in murder and
S-2......... II.5:2 in silent proof of guilt and of the **r.** of sin.

## raving 1

T19. IV.D.11:2 and **r.** madness with pity and compassion

## ravings 1

T-21....... V.1:6 senseless **r.** to those who want to hear It.

## Ray 2

*ray*

T-18......III.8:2 one **R.** that shines forever in the Mind of
C-ep...........2:5 the Heavens with a shining **R.** that held it

## ray 2

*Ray*

T-18......III.1:4 in which no **r.** of light could enter. And
T-25..... II.9:10 one **r.** of darkness can be seen by those

## Rays 11

*rays*

T-10......IV.8:1 remains, for the Great **R.** are obscured.
T-10......IV.8:2 the **R.** can never be completely forgotten.
T-10......IV.8:3 greater light, for the **R.** are there unseen.
T-11.......in.3:3 Remember the **R.** that are there unseen.
T-15......IX.1:1 you see the Great **R.** shining from them,
T-15......IX.3:1 Great **R.** replace the body in awareness,
T-16......VI.4:5 Great **R.** would establish the total lack of
T-16......VI.6:3 holds the Great **R.** within it is also visible,
T-18.......III.8:7 light will the Great **R.** extend back into
T19... IV.D.2:3 and the bright **R.** of His Father's Love that
W-pII..360.1:2 *me, for the Great* **R.** *remain forever still and*

## rays 1

*Rays*

T-13...VII.13:7 to let the **r.** extend in quiet to infinity.

## re-created 1

T-11..... VII.1:4 be literally true, for the eternal are not **r.**.

## re-echoes 1

W-pI... 195.7:4 a long forgotten Word **r.** in our memory,

## re-enact 1

T-16..... VII.1:2 special relationship is an attempt to **r.** the

## re-enacts 1

T-4.........in.3:5 It merely **r.** the separation, the loss of

## re-establish 8

T-2......... V.3:5 will be unable to **r.** right-mindedness in
T-9...........I.3:8 to **r.** your own will in your awareness.
T-14..... V.10:8 release from fear and **r.** the reign of love.
T-15.......I.14:2 As long as it takes to **r.** perfect sanity,
T-15...... XI.7:2 The Prince of Peace was born to **r.** the
W-pII .311.1:6 and **r.** peace of mind by giving us God's
M-5 ..... II.4:11 and without fear, they **r.** Heaven.
M-27 .........4:1 a loving God nor **r.** any grounds for trust.

## re-established 2

T-2........ VI.8:2 of this worth is **r.** by the Atonement. It is
T-17....... V.3:8 of the old goal **r.** in another relationship.

## re-establishes 4

T-2..........II.2:6 the mind, and **r.** the freedom of the will.
T-2......... III.4:6 This **r.** the power of the mind and makes
T-15...... XI.7:6 everything, and in the peace it **r.**, love
W-pII .....9.1:2 and **r.** what is forever and forever true. It

## re-establishing 3

T-8........ IX.9:3 **r.** of meaning in a chaotic thought system
T-13....VIII.7:6 you to it by **r.** its oneness in your mind.
T-14...... VI.5:2 it as a means of **r.** what was not broken,

## re-establishment 2

T-8.....VII.12:6 to the **r.** of the power of the mind in it.
T19... IV.D.7:3 This is the **r.** of *your* will. Look upon it,

## re-evaluation 2

T-13...... IX.4:1 brings a **r.** of everything you cherish, for it
P-2........ VI.6:3 to look at it, open it to **r.** and forgive it.

## re-invest 1

T-12........ VI.4:9 and by this he will learn to **r.** in himself.

## re-translation 1

T-31....... V.9:1 just a **r.** of what seems to be the evidence

## reach 169

T-1.......VII.1:1 it hard for them to **r.** your own awareness
T-1.....VII.5:11 to you, but to **r.** it the means are needed.
T-2......... III.1:9 and an unwillingness to **r.** the altar itself.
T-2........ VI.6:1 is possible to **r.** a state in which you bring
T-4...........I.2:6 Nothing can **r.** spirit from the ego, and
T-4...........I.2:6 and nothing can **r.** the ego from spirit.
T-4...........I.8:5 which stands unchanged beyond the **r.** of
T-4...........I.8:5 of your ego but within easy **r.** of spirit.
T-4...........I.8:7 what is as far beyond its **r.** as you are.

T-5..........I.3:2 I have said already that I can **r.** up and
T-5..........I.6:2 so high they could **r.** almost back to Him.
T-6........ II.9:1 the thinker, from which they **r.** outward.
T-8........ V.6:6 and **r.** beyond all attempts of the ego to
T-8........ V.6:8 **R.**, therefore, for my hand because you
T-8........VII.3:2 If you use it only to **r.** the minds of those
T-8........VII.5:9 is to **r.** beyond the Kingdom to its Creator
T-8........VII.9:5 to separate *from* spirit can **r.** beyond its
T-8......VIII.9:1 to use your body only to **r.** your brothers,
T-10.......in.3:7 can **r.** you from beyond it because, being
T-13..........I.3:5 but when you **r.** its end it will roll up like
T-13...... VI.6:4 and thus enables them to **r.** each other.
T-13...... VI.8:2 **R.** out to all your brothers, and touch
T-13....VIII.2:7 can **r.** everywhere under His guidance, for
T-13..VIII.10:6 know, and as they **r.** the gates of Heaven,
T-14....... X.1:4 **R.** out of time and touch it, with the help
T-15.........I.9:6 Nothing can **r.** you here out of the past,
T-15...... IX.1:1 them, so unlimited that they **r.** to God. It
T-16.....VII.5:3 allows to **r.** awareness is that the special
T-17....... II.3:4 real world, in its loveliness, you learn to **r.**
T-18...... III.5:1 and will strengthen your desire to **r.** it.
T-18...... VI.8:6 up of different parts, which **r.** each other.
T-18.... VI.10:1 stretch out your hand and **r.** to Heaven.
T-18.... VI.10:2 have begun to **r.** beyond the body, but
T-18.... VI.10:2 to **r.** your shared Identity together. Could
T-18..... VII.4:7 is extremely difficult to **r.** Atonement by
T-18.....VIII.9:8 **r.** out to everyone who thirsts for living
T19... IV.A.1:6 and from you **r.** to everyone who calls,
T19. IV.D.10:4 Yet merely to **r.** the place is not enough. A
T-20...... IV.8:7 but will melt away before you **r.** it. You
T-20.....VII.3:9 For if a goal is possible to **r.**, the means to
T-21.........I.5:3 They try to **r.** each other, and they fail,
T-22.......in.4:7 joined. It must **r.** out beyond itself, as you
T-22.........I.3:1 to understand what fails entirely to **r.** you
T-22..... II.13:5 Can you **r.** Heaven while a single sin still
T-23.........I.7:6 is indivisible, and far beyond their little **r.**
T-24.........I.6:3 not help him **r.** it in every way you could,
T-24.........I.6:5 it depends on goals that you alone can **r.**.
T-24.........I.6:6 And he must never **r.** them, or your goal
T-24....... II.4:3 that the Holy Spirit gives can **r.** you, when
T-24..... IV.4:1 salvation is attained, nor how to **r.** it. But
T-25.........I.5:2 **r.** to you through what you understand.
T-25...... III.9:8 all time becomes a means to **r.** a goal.
T-26.........I.2:3 as if what is inside can never **r.** without,
T-26.........I.2:3 and what is out can never **r.** and join with
T-26.........I.7:7 the **r.** of any sacrifice of life or death. For
T-26...... III.2:2 and when you **r.** it is apart from time.
T-26...... IV.3:4 **r.** beyond the universe to touch the Heart
T-26....... V.2:3 to **r.** a goal as high as learning can achieve
T-28.......I.15:3 bridge an instant will suffice to **r.** beyond
T-28.......I.15:5 another shore that he can never **r.**. His
T-28.....VII.3:6 to help you **r.** the home where God abides
T-29..... VII.4:1 Whenever you attempt to **r.** a goal in
T-30....... V.8:2 on, and quickly **r.** the gate of Heaven itself
T-30..... V.11:4 the Will of God must **r.** to their awareness
T-31..... IV.3:7 All must **r.** this point, and go beyond it. It
T-31....... V.1:7 you **r.** "maturity" you have perfected it, to
T-31....VIII.1:3 he has; his grasp cannot exceed its tiny **r.**.
W-pI.....25.4:5 understand is what you want to **r.** him for
W-pI.....41.7:3 You are trying to **r.** past all these things.
W-pI.....41.8:1 It is quite possible to **r.** God. In fact it is
W-pI.....42.5:4 may also **r.** a point where no thoughts at
W-pI.....44.3:1 we are going to attempt to **r.** that light.
W-pI.....44.6:2 that to **r.** light is to escape from darkness,
W-pI.....44.6:4 you see. You are attempting to **r.** Him.
W-pI.....45.3:2 Today we will attempt to **r.** them. We will
W-pI.....45.6:6 truth in your mind, and **r.** to the eternal.
W-pI.....45.8:5 For such is the place you are trying to **r.**.
W-pI.....45.8:7 an attempt to **r.** the Kingdom of Heaven.
W-pI.....47.4:1 Today we will try to **r.** past your own
W-pI.....47.7:1 try to **r.** down into your mind to a place of
W-pI.....47.7:3 **r.** down and below them to the Kingdom
W-pI.....49.4:6 We are trying to **r.** your real home. We
W-pI.....49.4:7 trying to **r.** the place where you are truly
W-pI.....49.4:8 truly welcome. We are trying to **r.** God.
W-pI.....60.1:6 **r.** down to me and raise me up to Him.
W-pI.....67.1:6 effort today to **r.** this truth about you, and
W-pI.....67.3:1 and then try to **r.** past all your images and
W-pI.....69.2:1 another real attempt to **r.** the light in you.
W-pI..... 69.3:1 real determination to **r.** what is dearer to
W-pI..... 69.6:1 much you want to **r.** the light in you today
W-pI..... 69.6:3 **R.** out and touch them in your mind.
W-pI..... 70.8:1 we will try again to **r.** the light in you,
W-pI..... 70.8:5 the clouds before you can **r.** the light. But
W-pI..... 72.2:3 unable to **r.** other minds except through
W-pI..... 73.4:1 Today we will try once more to **r.** the
W-pI..... 85.3:7 But from within me it will **r.** beyond, and
W-pI..... 91.4:4 makes all miracles within your easy **r.**,
W-pI..... 94.3:5 Now try to **r.** the Son of God in you. This
W-pI..... 94.4:1 Nothing is required of you to **r.** this goal
W-pI..... 95.6:1 of your goal and regular attempts to **r.** it.
W-pI... 95.10:4 try to **r.** the place in you in which there is
W-pI..... 96.2:2 an endless list of goals you cannot **r.**; a
W-pI..... 98.2:3 we need with which to **r.** the goal. Not
W-pI... 100.9:2 And you can **r.** Him now. What could you
W-pI... 102.3:1 help you **r.** the happiness God's Will has
W-pI... 106.3:6 today, and do not wait to **r.** Him longer.
W-pI... 106.5:3 who could **r.** God's Son except his Father,
W-pI...... 131.h No one can fail who seeks to **r.** the truth.
W-pI... 131.2:2 There is no way to **r.** them, for the means
W-pI... 131.4:3 fail to want this goal and **r.** it in the end.
W-pI... 131.5:6 will **r.** the goal you really want as certainly
W-pI... 131.8:6 wills is present now, beyond the **r.** of time
W-pI. 131.10:2 No one can fail who seeks to **r.** the truth,
W-pI. 131.10:2 truth, and it is truth we seek to **r.** today.
W-pI. 131.12:2 no one can fail who seeks to **r.** the truth.
W-pI. 131.15:7 *me. No one can fail who seeks to* **r.** *the truth.*
W-pI. 133.13:2 We will attempt to **r.** this state today,
W-pI... 138.5:5 attained through learning how to **r.** them,
W-pI... 140.9:2 go beyond appearances today and **r.** the
W-pI... 146.1:1 No one can fail who seeks to **r.** the truth.
W-pI. 153.20:3 no doubt that you will **r.** your final goal.
W-pI... 155.6:1 to cling to you, that you may **r.** them. Yet
W-pI... 161.8:4 it can **r.** to its maker and devour him.
W-pI... 162.1:2 it, as we **r.** another stage in learning. It
W-pI... 183.7:4 They cannot **r.** Him thus. He cannot hear
W-pI. 185.10:4 For thus you **r.** to what they really want,
W-pI... 189.6:1 as we seek to **r.** to what is true in us, and
W-pI... 189.8:7 The way to **r.** Him is merely to let Him be.
W-pI... 190.5:3 that can **r.** down and bring oppression.
W-pI. 196.12:1 not go with you to help you **r.** that instant
W-pI... 199.4:5 to the all-inclusive goal that it must **r.**,
WpI rVI.in.4:2 **r.** a quickened pace along a shorter path
W-pII ....in.1:5 we begin to **r.** the goal this course has set,
W-pII ..... 4.1:6 What would they hear or **r.** to grasp?
W-pII . 257.2:3 *well, if we would* **r.** *the peace You will for us.*
W-pII ..... 5.4:3 of God extends his hand to **r.** his brother,
W-pII ..... 8.2:6 can **r.** the mind that has forgiven itself.
W-pII . 296.2:2 of easy **r.** and quick accomplishment.
W-pII ..... 9.5:6 we can **r.** our Father's Love through Him.
W-pII . 308.1:2 If I elect to **r.** past time to timelessness, I
W-pII . 336.1:2 to what remains forever past its highest **r.**
W-pII . 354.1:1 *me as Your Son, beyond the* **r.** *of time, and*
W-pII . 355.1:3 *me, and I need but* **r.** *out my hand to find it.*
W-pII . 360.1:3 *I would* **r.** *to them in silence and in certainty,*
W-ep ......... 5:4 you make brings Heaven nearer to your **r.**
M-4 ..... I.A.7:7 may remain impossible to **r.** for a long,
M-14 ......... 4:3 leave the world and go beyond its tiny **r.**.
M-22 ......... 2:5 realization of inclusiveness may **r.** him. If
M-23 ......... 6:8 went beyond the farthest **r.** of learning.
C-1 ............ 7:6 demonstrates that it cannot **r.** knowledge.
P-2...........I.3:6 and therapist **r.** in connection with their
P-2..........II.7:3 how he can best **r.** the aim it sets for him.
P-2....... III.2:6 **r.** almost to Heaven or go no further than
P-2......... V.1:4 steps which never **r.** to consciousness.
P-2......... V.5:6 a hand to **r.** His Son and touch his heart.
P-3......... III.8:6 times. Whoever He sends you will **r.** you,
S-1...........I.1:1 a way offered by the Holy Spirit to **r.** God.
S-1...........I.1:5 to pray for idols and hope to **r.** God. True
S-1...........I.6:6 who prays without fear cannot but **r.** Him
S-1...........I.6:7 He can therefore also **r.** His Son, wherever
S-1...........I.7:9 which. Perhaps it will **r.** both, if you are
S-1..........II.3:1 also possible to **r.** a higher form of asking-
S-1..........II.8:3 is no need for a ladder to **r.** what one has
S-1....... IV.2:1 to help in prayer, and so **r.** up yourself.
S-2.........in.1:5 ordained to be with you until you **r.** to
S-2...........I.9:1 before you **r.** where learning cannot go.
S-3...........I.4:5 through His Voice He still can **r.** His Son,
S-3..........II.2:3 and to **r.** the Christ in hidden forms and
S-3........ IV.5:2 Nor will your judgment fail to **r.** to God,

## reached 63

T-1 .........V.1:2 state of direct communication is **r.**,
T-16 .......II.4:2 you have **r.** another mind and joined with
T-17 ........II.4:5 when you have **r.** the real world and have
T-18 ..... VI.7:5 incapable of reaching out as being **r.**. You
T-18 . VIII.13:1 You have **r.** the end of an ancient journey
T19 .. IV.D.9:2 for he could not have **r.** this far unless his
T-21 ..... III.4:1 means by which the goal of holiness is **r.**.
T-21 ..... III.4:7 only before the state of certainty is **r.**. In
T-21 ..... III.4:9 unknown. Yet Heaven is **r.** through them.
T-22 ...... in.4:7 itself, as you **r.** out beyond the body, to let
T-22 ..... IV.1:3 the way you went before you **r.** the branch
T-22 ..... IV.3:5 awareness, and peace has **r.** you even here
T-22 ..... VI.1:7 end is **r.** the value of the means decreases,
T-23 ...II.22:11 are you sure the goal of Heaven can be **r.**?
T-24 ........I.2:3 many senseless outcomes have been **r.**,
T-24 .......II.9:4 Yet it is not illusions that have **r.** this final
T-24 .......II.9:4 Heaven so remote that They cannot be **r.**.
T-24 .....II.14:2 readiness be **r.** save through the sight of
T-26 ....V.14:3 and **r.** the world that lies at Heaven's gate.
T-26 .... VII.9:3 yet **r.** beyond the world of choice entirely.
T-27 .......V.3:2 transcended conflict, and has **r.** to peace.
T-30 ...... in.1:3 can be **r.** depends on this one thing alone;
T-30 ......I.10:1 Now you have **r.** the turning point,
T-30 ......I.10:2 Until this point is **r.**, you will believe your
T-30 .......V.7:6 till His Son has **r.** beyond forgiveness to
T-31 ..... IV.6:5 this would *keep* the truth from being **r.**.
T-31 ..... IV.8:2 Until that point is **r.** you have no choice,
T-31 .... VII.3:4 when you have **r.** the world beyond the
T-31 .VIII.12:8 For we have **r.** where all of us are one, and
W-pI .... 47.7:2 have **r.** it if you feel a sense of deep peace,
W-pI .... 74.6:2 will you recognize that you have **r.** it. If
W-pI .... 86.1:3 and in many things, but when I **r.** for it, it
W-pI 122.10:2 for we have **r.** the turning point at which
W-pI 133.13:1 Heaven itself is **r.** with empty hands and
W-pI 170.11:3 You have **r.** this place before, but you
W-pI .. 189.9:5 there, if it be true and can be surely **r.**.
W-pI .. 194.1:3 Your foot has **r.** the lawns that welcome
W-pII . 225.2:4 You have **r.** your hand to me, and I will
W-pII . 234.1:1 we have **r.** the holy peace we never left.
W-pII ..... 6.5:1 goal of the Atonement has been **r.** at last?
W-pII . 282.1:1 salvation would be **r.** for all the world.
W-pII . 292.1:3 Yet it is up to us when this is **r.**; how long
W-pII . 342.1:4 *and I have* **r.** *the door beyond which lies the*
M-3 ........... 5:3 implies that those involved have **r.** a stage
M-16 ......... 2:1 about those who have not **r.** his certainty?
M-16 ......... 9:5 of God has **r.** the most advanced state. All
M-20 ....... 2:11 gone. Quiet has **r.** to cover everything.
M-21 ......... 4:3 are many who must be **r.** through words,
M-23 ......... 7:1 him because his words have **r.** you in a
M-26 ........... h CAN GOD BE **R.** DIRECTLY?
M-26 ......... 1:1 God indeed can be **r.** directly, for there is
M-26 ......... 2:1 There are those who have **r.** God directly,
M-26 ......... 3:8 were **r.** directly in sustained awareness,
P-2...........I.1:4 therapist or patient has **r.** the next one,
P-2........ VI.6:2 How is it **r.**? The therapist sees in the
P-2....... VII.4:4 Before he **r.** this point, he thought he was
P-3..........II.6:2 some relationships this point is never **r.**,
P-3..........II.8:4 goal is **r.** another can be dimly seen ahead
S-1...........I.6:2 **r.** it still need your help in prayer because
S-1..........II.3:3 of identification has generally been **r.**, but
S-1..........II.8:5 until the goal of learning has been **r.**. And
S-1........ III.3:7 that this step cannot be **r.** by anyone who
S-2...........I.2:1 the honest means by which this goal is **r.**.

## reaches 32

T-8 ...... VII.2:4 The Holy Spirit **r.** through it to others.
T-15 .......II.3:4 blessed instant **r.** out to encompass time,
T-15 ..... III.4:2 for it **r.** you through Him *from* Magnitude.
T-15 ..... III.7:5 He **r.** from you to everyone and beyond
T-15 ... III.12:6 which rises above the stars and **r.** even to
T-15 .....V.11:5 For the holy instant **r.** to eternity, and to
T-17 .... VII.7:3 so great it **r.** past the stars and to the
T-18 ......I.13:2 and **r.** out to every broken fragment of the

| | |
|---|---|
| T-18......VI.8:5 | Mind r. to itself. It is *not* made up of |
| T-18... VIII.8:1 | and r. to everything created like itself. Its |
| T19... IV.A.1:4 | dwelling place from which it gently r. out, |
| T19....IV.B.4:1 | and it r. out from the eternal in you. It |
| T19.IV.D.11:7 | And no one r. love with fear beside him. |
| T-22.........I.5:5 | see. It r. you directly, without a need to be |
| T-22..... II.12:1 | the golden light that r. it from the bright, |
| T-22......IV.1:7 | serve. No one who r. this far can make the |
| T-24....... V.7:4 | He r. through them, holding out His hand |
| T-28...... I.11:2 | It r. gently from that quiet time, and from |
| W-pI.133.14:1 | receive what waits for everyone who r., |
| W-pI...157.2:3 | past the highest r. it can possibly attain. It |
| W-pI...157.5:2 | upon. A vision r. everyone you meet, and |
| W-pI...183.5:4 | which r. to God Himself and to His Son. |
| W-pII..264.1:2 | *I hear, and every hand that r. for my own. In* |
| W-pII......6.4:1 | The Holy Spirit r. from the Christ in you |
| W-pII......9.3:1 | extend beyond itself, and r. up to God. |
| M-5....... III.3:6 | truth in their minds r. out to the truth in |
| M-19..........2:7 | splendor r. indescribable heights as one |
| P-3......... II.8:2 | Yet well before he r. this in time he can go |
| S-1.........in.3:2 | song that r. higher and then higher still, |
| S-1......... II.1:3 | with learning until it r. its formless state, |
| S-1........III.1:6 | ascending goals, until it r. even up to God |
| S-3........IV.6:6 | in prayer beyond the sorry r. of the world. |

## reaching 13

| | |
|---|---|
| T-8.....VII.10:5 | By r. out, the mind extends itself. It does |
| T-13......XI.8:3 | channels of r. out cannot be wholly closed |
| T-15.........I.8:3 | without its shadow r. out into the future. |
| T-15......IV.6:3 | instant, beginning now and r. to eternity, |
| T-17....... II.6:2 | world r. quietly and gently across chaos, |
| T-18......VI.7:5 | incapable of r. out as being reached. You |
| T19..IV.B.10:7 | means for r. the goal that you assign to it. |
| T-27......IV.2:3 | God must have given you a way of r. to |
| T-31. VIII.11:1 | would join with me in r. past temptation, |
| W-pI.....95.3:2 | our exercises towards r. your one Self, |
| W-pI.161.10:3 | If you are intent on r. it, you will succeed |
| P-3...........I.3:8 | a feeling of r. out to someone somewhere. |
| S-1......... II.7:1 | Prayer is a ladder r. up to Heaven. At the |

## react 26

| | |
|---|---|
| T-4......... II.4:4 | You r. to your ego much as God does to |
| T-4......... II.4:6 | you will one day r. to your real creations, |
| T-5.........III.8:9 | believe there is strife you will r. viciously, |
| T-5........VII.5:3 | The decision to r. in this way is yours, and |
| T-6...........I.5:3 | you do choose to r. that way, however, |
| T-6...........I.6:2 | If you r. as if you are persecuted, you are |
| T-6....V.B.3:10 | being taught to r. to both as if what you |
| T-9........III.4:1 | When you r. at all to errors, you are not |
| T-9........III.6:7 | and to r. to them as if they were real, is to |
| T-9........IV.8:1 | how appropriately can you expect to r.? |
| T-9........VI.1:4 | inspire joy and others r. to you with joy, |
| T-9.......VII.4:5 | likely to attack you when you r. lovingly, |
| T-12.........I.2:3 | This is shown by the fact that you r. to |
| T-12.........I.3:9 | else you will r. to something else. Your |
| T-12........V.3:2 | others do r. to attack if they perceive it, |
| T-12...VII.13:1 | and r. unfavorably to what you see, you |
| T-13....... II.7:3 | sometimes r. as if it is trying to imprison |
| T-13......IV.5:5 | you will r. to your brother as though he |
| T-13....... V.5:1 | yet in your private world you r. to each of |
| T-13....... V.5:5 | And you r. with fear to love, and draw |
| T-13......VI.1:5 | not there, and if it is to them that you r., |
| T-27. VIII.10:5 | For you would not r. at all to figures in a |
| T-30.........I.2:5 | the rules for how you should r. to them. |
| T-31....... V.9:4 | Does he r. for you? And does he know |
| W-pI.136.10:4 | and r. to them as if they were the truth? |
| M-18..........2:1 | learn how to r. to magic thoughts wholly |

## reacted 2

| | |
|---|---|
| T-5.......VII.5:1 | it is because you have r. with a lack of love |
| T-6...........I.3:1 | probably r. for years as if you were being |

## reacting 2

| | |
|---|---|
| T-5......... V.7:7 | responsibility, they are r. irresponsibly. If |
| P-1.............3:6 | on, r. to external forces as they demand, |

## reaction 13

| | |
|---|---|
| T-1......... II.3:6 | It is therefore an inappropriate r. to me. |
| T-1........VII.5:6 | r. to me because of our inherent equality. |
| T-4.......VII.2:5 | is a r. to a specific person or persons. The |
| T-8........VII.8:6 | Whenever the r. to learning is depression, |
| T-9........IV.8:2 | of how you may account for the r., |
| T-13..... X.14:4 | Every r. you experience will be so purified |
| T-30...... VI.2:7 | natural r. to distress that rests on error, |
| W-pI.....21.2:3 | any r. ranging from mild irritation to rage |
| W-pI.....37.6:3 | seems to cause an adverse r. in you. Offer |
| W-pI.....46.7:3 | aware of any kind of negative r. to anyone |
| W-pI...194.6:2 | repertoire, a way of quick r. to temptation |
| M-17 .........5:2 | fear. Consider what this r. means, and its |
| M-17 .........7:1 | will now be your r. to all magic thoughts? |

## reactions 18

| | |
|---|---|
| T-1.......VII.3:3 | r. of those who know not what they do. |
| T-4......... II.4:5 | r. to the self you made are not surprising. |
| T-6.........I.15:4 | have described my r. to Judas as they did, |
| T-9........ VI.2:2 | Their r. to you are your evaluations of His |
| T-12.........I.2:4 | may then control your r. behaviorally, |
| T-12.........I.8:1 | r. of others more and more consistently, |
| T-13....... II.6:4 | will consider your r. to it you will become |
| T-13......IV.5:4 | It dictates your r. to those you meet in the |
| T-13....... V.2:2 | are made up only of his r. to his brothers, |
| T-13....... V.2:2 | do not include their r. to him. Therefore, |
| T-13......VI.1:5 | Your past r. to him are also not there, and |
| T-13......XI.5:4 | your r. to the Holy Spirit's Voice may be, |
| T-14....... II.2:4 | and r. that you have woven out of it. |
| T-15....... II.4:6 | which you have chosen by *their* r.. A Son |
| W-in..........9:4 | and whatever your r. to the ideas may be, |
| W-pI.......7.3:3 | Are not your aesthetic r. to the cup, too, |
| W-pI.....35.7:3 | are applicable to your r. to that situation, |
| M-17 .........4:7 | All of these r. are the same. They obscure |

## reacts 4

| | |
|---|---|
| T-4.......VII.3:1 | spirit r. in the same way to everything it |
| T-13......IV.5:2 | and it r. to the present as if it *were* the past |
| T-27... VIII.4:4 | But who r. to figures in a dream unless he |
| T-31..... V.15:3 | interacts with evil, and r. to wicked things |

## read 10

| | |
|---|---|
| T-4.......in.3:11 | you will r. these lessons carefully they will |
| T-6.........I.16:1 | As you r. the teachings of the Apostles, |
| WpI...rI.in.3:3 | have r. the idea and the related comments |
| WpI. rIII.in5:2 | R. over the ideas and comments that are |
| WpI. rIV.in4:4 | to understand the lessons that we r., and |
| WpI. rIV.in7:1 | merely r. each of the two ideas assigned to |
| W-pII...in.11:4 | slowly r. and thought about a little while, |
| M-29 .........1:5 | helpful for the pupil to r. the manual first. |
| M-29 .........7:3 | But do not r. this hastily or wrongly. If |
| C-5.............6:6 | It is possible to r. his words and benefit |

## readied 1

| | |
|---|---|
| W-pI...98.10:3 | let your mind be r. for the happy time to |

## readily 4

| | |
|---|---|
| T-4......... II.2:4 | and does occur as r. when the interaction |
| T-13....... II.7:4 | often dismiss it more r. than you dismiss |
| T-17...... III.3:3 | be most r. associated with those on whom |
| W-pI...182.6:3 | shut out, His tiny voice so r. obscured, |

## readiness 28

*See also* miracle-readiness, revelation-readiness

| | |
|---|---|
| T-2......... V.4:1 | own r. is endangering his understanding. |
| T-2......... V.4:2 | are completely unconcerned about your r. |
| T-2.......VII.7:1 | I have already briefly spoken about r., |
| T-2.......VII.7:2 | be helpful here. R. is only the prerequisite |
| T-2.......VII.7:4 | As soon as a state of r. occurs, there is |
| T-2.......VII.7:8 | R. is only the beginning of confidence. |
| T-2.......VII.7:9 | time is necessary between r. and mastery, |
| T-15......IV.1:8 | in shimmering r. for your acceptance. Yet |
| T-15......IV.8:4 | then the Holy Spirit's r. to give it to you is |
| T-15...... IV.9:9 | to the r. for purity He offers you. Thus |
| T-16...... IV.2:4 | This is the last step in the r. for God. Be |
| T-17........II.8:2 | world, trembling with r. to be given you. |
| T-18.... IV.5:11 | *to restore to me my own awareness of my r.,* |
| T-18.... IX.11:7 | r. for knowledge still must be attained. |
| T-24......II.14:2 | r. be reached save through the sight of all |
| T-30.......I.11:7 | Thus is the r. for asking brought to your |
| W-pI.....34.2:2 | between that seems most conducive to r.. |
| W-pI.....43.4:2 | time that circumstances and r. permit. At |
| W-pI.....76.9:2 | and hold your mind in silent r. to hear the |
| W-pI... 132.7:2 | Their r. will bring the lesson to them in |
| WpI. rIV.in1:2 | concentrate on r. for what will follow next |
| WpI. rIV.in1:4 | facilitate the r. that we would now achieve |
| W-pI. 161.10:2 | Your r. is closer now, and you will come |
| W-pII .322.1:2 | in r. to give God's ancient messages to me |
| M-4 .... IX.1:10 | R., as the text notes, is not mastery. |
| P-2...........I.1:3 | for no one learns beyond his own r.. Yet |
| P-2...........I.1:4 | levels of r. change, and when therapist or |
| S-2........ III.1:8 | of God. His r. to give lies far beyond your |

## reading 3

| | |
|---|---|
| WpI...rI.in.2:1 | Begin the day by r. the five ideas, with |
| WpI...rI.in.2:3 | the related comments after r. them over. |
| WpI..rII.in.2:2 | or four minutes to r. them over slowly, |

## readjusted 1

| | |
|---|---|
| T-18...... III.7:6 | Time has been r. to help us do, together, |

## reads 1

| | |
|---|---|
| W-pI. 153.14:4 | learn the tale he r. of terrifying destiny, |

## ready 87

| | |
|---|---|
| T-1........ III.1:8 | do them, but you must be r. and willing. |
| T-1........ III.7:1 | arise from a mind that is r. for them. By |
| T-2......... V.1:1 | miracle workers are r. to undertake their |
| T-4.........I.11:5 | is r. for you when you choose to enter it. |
| T-4........ III.8:4 | will be r. to help me make other minds |
| T-4........ III.8:4 | to help me make other minds r. for Him. |
| T-4........ VI.8:5 | of them and you will be r. to hear God. |
| T-5.........I.4:10 | little gap. Knowledge is always r. to flow |
| T-6.........I.15:9 | that I would condemn him when I was r. |
| T-6.........I.16:1 | not wholly r. to follow me at the time. I |
| T-6...... V.C.5:8 | He is getting you r. for the translation of |
| T-8.........I.1:10 | If you did you would not be so r. to throw |
| T-11...... III.3:6 | this will be like, for your heart is not r.. |
| T-11....... V.1:3 | We are r. to look more closely at the ego's |
| T-11....... V.1:3 | realize you do not want it, you must be r.. |
| T-13..... VII.3:5 | old and tired and r. to return to dust even |
| T-14...... IX.8:4 | holiness in them, are r. at last for Heaven. |
| T-15.......I.11:5 | He stands r. to give you the remembrance |
| T-15...... IV.8:4 | for you are not r. to share it with Him. |
| T-15.... IV.9:10 | Thus will He make you r. to acknowledge |
| T-15...... IX.1:6 | will be no delay when you are r. for it. |
| T-15...... IX.1:7 | for it. God is r. now, but you are not. |
| T-17........II.4:5 | real world and have been made r. for Him |
| T-18...... IV.5:4 | to make yourself holy to be r. to receive it. |
| T-18.... IV.5:11 | *It is not needful that I make it r. for Him, but* |
| T-18...... IX.9:6 | and make you r. for the final step in the |
| T19....IV.C.9:2 | and r. to grow into a mighty force for God |
| T19....IV.C.9:3 | quietly made r. to fulfill the mighty task |
| T19... IV.D.8:6 | be r. to look on terror with no fear at all. |
| T19... IV.D.9:5 | You will be r.. Let us join together in a |
| T19. IV.D.10:2 | which everyone must come when he is r.. |
| T19. IV.D.10:3 | Once he has found his brother he *is* r.. Yet |
| T-20........II.2:5 | making it r. to receive the gifts it wants by |
| T-20........II.8:2 | for you, and it is r. to receive you now. |
| T-20........II.8:8 | r. to be unveiled and freed from all the |
| T-20...... IV.5:6 | he is r. to look upon the face of Christ, |
| T-20....VIII.4:2 | vision that makes it yours is r. to be given. |
| T-23.......I.12:9 | r. to be remembered when you side with |
| T-24......II.14:1 | it to you when you were r. to accept His |
| T-24..... VII.8:2 | is yours will come to you when you are r.. |
| T-25...... III.6:3 | r. to lead him out of darkness into light at |
| T-30.......in.1:8 | you will have them r. for whatever need. |
| T-30.........I.1:6 | and dedication weak, you are not r.. *Do* |

T-30....... V.3:6 heart made r. to arise and go with him.
T-30....... V.3:7 thus is he made r. for the step in which is
W-pI..... 23.7:5 different, you will be r. to let the cause go.
W-pI..... 32.4:3 and when you yourself feel reasonably r..
W-pI..... 41.3:1 r. to radiate through you and out into the
W-pI..... 42.3:2 by yourself, at a time when you feel r.,
W-pI..... 44.5:2 quite r. to learn the form of exercise we
W-pI..... 70.6:1 r. for two longer practice periods today,
W-pI..... 80.1:8 r. to take your rightful place in God's plan
WpI..rII.in.1:1 We are now r. for another review. We
W-pI..... 92.9:2 Self stands r. to embrace you as Its Own.
W-pI... 104.1:4 must there be a place made r. to receive
W-pI... 105.7:4 Now are you r. to accept the gift of peace
W-pI... 105.7:5 Now are you r. to experience the joy and
W-pI... 106.6:1 Be r. for salvation. It is here, and will
W-pI... 106.8:4 becomes r. to understand and to receive.
W-pI... 124.9:2 may not be r. to accept the gain today.
W-pI. 124.10:2 When you are r. you will find it there,
W-pI... 125.6:4 help make r. your most holy mind to hear
W-pI... 132.6:4 Not everyone is r. to accept it, and each
W-pI... 169.3:6 and thus is r. to accept a state completely
WpI...rV.in1:2 This time we are r. to give more effort and
W-pII .228.2:6 *And I stand r. to receive Your Word alone*
W-pII .248.1:8 am I r. to accept him back as God created
W-pII ..... 4.5:3 How soon will you be r. to come home?
W-pII .273.1:1 we are now r. for a day of undisturbed
W-pII .289.2:4 *And here am I made r. for Your final step.*
W-pII ... 13.4:1 the mind has been made r. to conceive of
M-2 ........... 1:5 to fulfill his role, they are r. to fulfill theirs
M-2 ........... 1:7 When he is r. to learn, the opportunities
M-3 ........... 1:8 relationship. They are r. for each other.
M-3 ........... 3:6 Salvation is always r. and always there.
M-4 ... I.A.6:11 Yet when he is r. to go on, he goes with
M-16 ......... 2:2 yet r. for such lack of structuring on their
M-26 ......... 4:9 with goals for which you are not r.. God
M-27 ......... 2:3 r. to break it off without regret or care,
C-2............. 9:1 "Are you r. yet to help Me save the world?
C-4............. 4:4 there is an empty place made clean and r..
P-1............. 5:3 him on from there, as far as he is r. to go.
P-2........ III.4:3 and the patient cannot be r. to receive the
P-3......... II.6:7 can accept more than he is r. to receive,
S-3......... II.4:4 the world and it is r. to depart in peace,
S-3......... II.6:1 r. to strike again until it brings a cruel
S-3......... II.6:4 the home that stands r. to welcome him,

**readying** 1

WpI. rIV.in4:4 r. our minds to understand the lessons

**reaffirm** 3

W-pI..... 61.6:2 and turn to sleep as you r. your function
WpI..rII.in.6:1 R. your determination in the shorter
W-pI. 138.12:1 r. the choice that we have made each hour

**reaffirms** 1

W-pI..... 65.1:1 today r. your commitment to salvation. It

**real** 743

*See also* Appendix C

T-in ........... 2:2 *Nothing r. can be threatened. Nothing*
T-1........... I.3:2 r. miracle is the love that inspires them.
T-1......... I.24:4 not exist. Only the creations of light are r.
T-1......... V.3:4 you cannot know the r. power of the Son
T-1........ VI.4:1 The r. purpose of this world is to use it to
T-1....... VII.1:4 All r. pleasure comes from doing God's
T-1....... VII.2:4 perception so you can achieve r. vision, of
T-1....... VII.3:7 can never make them r. except to yourself
T-2........... I.2:5 Its r. source is internal. This is as true of
T-2........... I.3:5 is seen in dreams seems to be very r.. Yet
T-2........... I.4:3 is the r. basis for your escape from fear.
T-2......... II.3:5 r. questions are, what do you treasure,
T-2......... II.7:8 of Atonement to your r. protection, and
T-2...... III.1:10 The r. beauty of the temple cannot be
T-2........ III.5:3 But the r. means are already provided,
T-2......... V.2:4 may be unable to accept the r. Source of
T-2......... V.8:4 The r. vision is obscured, because you
T-2 ... V.A.14:2 can correct in a way that has any r. effect.
T-2 ... V.A.14:3 what has no r. effect has no real existence.
T-2 ... V.A.14:3 what has no real effect has no r. existence.
T-2 ....... VI.9:3 Few appreciate the r. power of the mind,
T-2 ....... VI.9:9 is not the r. reason you do not believe it.
T-2 ..... VI.9:10 believe that your thoughts cannot exert r.
T-2 .... VII.3:10 principle now becomes a r. expediter,
T-2 ...... VII.7:7 that the only r. mastery is through love.
T-2 ..... VIII.1:5 you alone make is r. in your own sight,
T-2 ..... VIII.1:6 into the r. meaning of the Last Judgment.
T-3 .......... I.1:8 Yet the r. Christian should pause and ask,
T-3 ......... II.2:2 not r. *until* it is total. The partly innocent
T-3 ......... II.3:6 with the same Will has any r. existence.
T-3 ....... III.6:5 is the r. meaning of "Alpha and Omega,
T-3 ....... IV.1:1 are only shadows of your r. strength. All
T-3 ....... IV.7:6 remembered spirit and its r. purpose. I
T-3 ........ V.1:1 are only shadows of your r. strength, and
T-3 ........ V.3:2 The confusion between your r. creation
T-3 ........ V.6:8 is your Source and your only r. function.
T-3 ..... VI.11:7 what is wished is as r. as what is willed.
T-3 ...... VII.2:7 souls in return for gifts of no r. worth.
T-3 ...... VII.3:2 is a system of thought r. enough in time,
T-3 ...... VII.3:3 All beliefs are r. to the believer. The fruit
T-3 ...... VII.5:1 in separation very r. and very fearful, and
T-4 .......... I.4:5 This is very r. to you. You cannot undo it
T-4 .......... I.8:3 in your right mind you realize it is not r..
T-4 .......... I.8:6 are afraid, be still and know that God is r.
T-4 ......... II.4:6 you will one day react to your r. creations,
T-4 ......... II.5:4 You have no sense of r. self-preservation,
T-4 ......... II.6:1 Only those who have a r. and lasting
T-4 ......... II.6:7 Its whole perception of other egos as r. is
T-4 ......... II.6:7 an attempt to convince itself that *it* is r..
T-4 ....... III.4:4 You cannot conceive of the r. relationship
T-4 ..... IV.10:8 to convince you that it is r. and I am not,
T-4 ..... IV.10:8 it is real and I am not, because if I am r., I
T-4 ..... IV.10:8 if I am real, I am no more r. than you are.
T-4 ........ V.4:9 no r. answer to this because there is none,
T-4 ........ V.6:3 touching on the r. question in any way.
T-4 ........ V.6:4 hopes to hide the r. question and keep it
T-4 ....... VI.1:1 does not recognize the r. source of "threat
T-4 ....... VI.7:5 and one moment of r. recognition makes
T-4 ...... VII.4:4 communication with everything that is r..
T-4 ...... VII.4:5 context of its r. relationship to you. This
T-4 ...... VII.4:8 it. It is your r. home, your real temple and
T-4 ...... VII.4:8 home, your r. temple and your real Self.
T-4 ...... VII.4:8 home, your real temple and your r. Self.
T-4 ...... VII.5:2 joy. Nothing r. can be increased except by
T-4 ...... VII.5:6 because r. creation gives everything, since
T-5 .......... I.7:6 occurs to produce a r. qualitative shift.
T-5 ........ V.4:2 It is your acceptance of it that makes it r..
T-5 ...... V.6:13 all. Delusional ideas are not r. thoughts,
T-6 .......... I.3:4 The r. meaning of the crucifixion lies in
T-6 .......... I.4:3 anything that is destructible cannot be r..
T-6 ........ I.16:8 This conflict seems just as r. now, and its
T-6 ....... IV.5:3 The ego, which is not r., attempts to
T-6 ....... IV.5:3 attempts to persuade the mind, which *is* r.,
T-6 ....... IV.5:3 that the body is more r. than the mind is.
T-6 ....... IV.6:2 Nothing else exists and only this is r.. You
T-6 ....... IV.6:3 sleep is not r. and God calls you to awake.
T-6 ........ V.2:2 that frightened them so badly are not r.,
T-6 ..... V.A.3:2 always tells you that only the mind is r.,
T-6 ..... V.A.4:5 r. foundation stone of the thought system
T-6 ..... V.A.5:7 Yet this is not so r. as it may appear.
T-6 ..... V.B.3:9 is the r. reason why, in many respects, the
T-6 ..... V.B.6:2 one is true, and therefore only one is r..
T-6 ..... V.C.5:3 goes beyond them towards r. integration.
T-6 ..... V.C.8:5 a r. sense of being cannot be yours while
T-7 ......... II.2:4 What you project or extend is r. for you.
T-7 ...... III.1:12 or overlooking its r. and only meaning.
T-7 ....... IV.6:1 oppose the Will of God is a r. delusion.
T-7 ........ V.6:8 on, because everything of God is wholly r.
T-7 ....... VI.6:7 else is r. and therefore nothing else has
T-7 .... VII.11:2 perceive any part of creation as wholly r.,
T-7 ..... VIII.2:5 mind only to defeat the mind's r. purpose
T-8 .......... I.2:3 You cannot expect it to say "I am not r.."
T-8 .......... I.6:1 a r. change in direction becomes possible.
T-8 ....... VI.5:5 of God Himself take joy in what is not r.?
T-8 ....... VI.5:6 And what is r. except the creations of God
T-8 ..... VIII.2:4 has no r. use for it because it is *not* an end.
T-8 ..... VIII.8:2 of something you want, even if it is not r.?
T-8 ....... IX.1:3 ego does not know what a r. question is,
T-8 ....... IX.5:3 one error can be more r. than another.
T-9 .......... I.4:3 it r. to you because He is in your mind,
T-9 .......... I.9:6 Fear cannot be r. without a cause, and
T-9 ........ I.10:6 because your requests to Him are r.,
T-9 ........ I.12:5 How r. can this devotion be? If you do not
T-9 ........ I.13:3 you have everything because you are r..
T-9 ........ I.14:2 of reality, because only that is r.. You
T-9 ....... III.6:7 and to react to them as if they were r., is
T-9 ....... III.6:7 if they were real, is to make them r. to you
T-9 ....... III.7:2 you. Accept his errors as r., and you have
T-9 ..... III.8:11 Condemnation will then not be r. to you,
T-9 ....... IV.4:5 can you overlook what you have made r.?
T-9 ....... IV.4:6 you have made it r. and *cannot* overlook it.
T-9 ....... IV.5:2 it make r. the unreal and then destroy it.
T-9 ......... V.1:6 is r. for both himself and the patient, but
T-9 ......... V.2:2 can "uncovering" them make them r.?
T-9 ......... V.3:1 but only to teach that they are not r., and
T-9 ......... V.4:2 use them to prove that the nightmare is r.
T-9 ......... V.4:3 Having made it r., he then attempts to
T-9 ......... V.5:4 Nothing r. has happened to the unhealed
T-9 ......... V.5:8 is up to him to teach the patient what is r.
T-9 ....... VI.3:4 call upon it in them it becomes r. to you.
T-9 ...... VII.7:1 ego does not know what a r. question is.
T-9 ..... VIII.2:2 It is without hope because it is not r.. It is
T-9 ..... VIII.2:3 based on the belief that the littleness is r..
T-9 ..... VIII.4:3 it is r. it is compellingly convincing. Yet
T-9 ..... VIII.4:6 argue that grandeur cannot be a r. part of
T-9 ..... VIII.9:2 And what can be r. that has no witnesses?
T-10 ...... in.2:3 happen, because nothing except Him is r..
T-10 ...... in.2:5 the ephemeral be r. if you are God's only
T-10 ......... I.2:3 you think is r. while you are asleep. Yet
T-10 ..... III.1:7 destruction is no more r. than the image,
T-10 ... III.10:7 It is your inheritance from your r. Father.
T-10 ... III.11:7 belief that you can choose which god is r..
T-10 ..... IV.1:8 attack him, you will make him r. to you.
T-10 ..... V.13:4 That is why your creations are as r. as His.
T-10 ..... V.13:5 r. Fatherhood must be acknowledged if
T-10 ..... V.13:5 acknowledged if the r. Son is to be known
T-10 ..... V.13:6 you have made are your r. creations,
T-10 ..... V.14:8 Time and eternity cannot both be r.,
T-10 ..... V.14:9 you will accept only what is timeless as r.,
T-11 ........ II.7:4 you. Yet this is not r. freedom, for it still
T-11 ........ II.7:7 R. freedom depends on welcoming reality
T-11 ........ II.7:7 of your guests only the Holy Spirit is r..
T-11 ....... III.2:4 Would God let this be r., when He did
T-11 ....... III.5:4 you but undertake a journey that is not r..
T-11 ........ V.1:5 to see beyond it, since you have made it r.
T-11 ........ V.2:3 are beginning to learn that fear is not r..
T-11 ........ V.2:7 what leads to nothing could not be r.. Do
T-11 ........ V.4:2 have any effects if its source is not r.. Fear
T-11 ........ V.5:3 God is wishful thinking and not r. willing.
T-11 ........ V.5:5 The r. conflict you experience, then, is
T-11 ........ V.5:6 which you share. Can this be a r. conflict?
T-11 ...... V.14:3 It makes r. every mistake it perceives, and
T-11 ...... V.14:6 mind, and protecting what it has made r.,
T-11 ...... V.14:6 system: Error is r. and truth is error.
T-11 ..... VII.2:6 The r. world can actually be perceived. All
T-11 ..... VII.3:4 adds something that is not r. to the real,
T-11 ..... VII.3:4 adds something that is not real to the r.,
T-11 ..... VII.3:9 only the r. world will lead you to the real
T-11 ..... VII.3:9 real world will lead you to the r. Heaven,
T-11 ..... VII.4:7 believe that you can perceive the r. world
T-11 ..... VII.4:9 The r. world is all that the Holy Spirit has
T-11 ... VIII.1:4 When you perceive the r. world, you will
T-11 ... VIII.1:5 your new and only r. perception will be
T-11 ... VIII.1:7 the r. world will vanish from your sight.
T-11 ... VIII.7:3 you have lost sight of the r. world. You
T-11 ... VIII.7:4 the r. world is still yours for the asking.
T-11 . VIII.10:1 In the r. world there is no sickness, for
T-11 . VIII.11:2 share the r. world as you share Heaven,
T-11 . VIII.15:4 you will accept the r. world in place of the
T-12 ......... I.1:1 You have been told not to make error r.,
T-12 ......... I.1:2 have to make it r. because it is not true.
T-12 ......... I.1:3 But truth is r. in its own right, and to
T-12 ......... I.1:7 done so, having made his error r. to you.
T-12 ........ II.9:6 lay aside the obstacles to r. vision without
T-12 ....... III.2:4 and are making his error r. to both of you

T-12......III.7:1 reality, the **r.** world must be in his mind.
T-12......III.8:2 God does love the **r.** world, and those
T-12......III.8:3 For death is not of the **r.** world, in which
T-12......III.8:4 God gave you the **r.** world in exchange for
T-12......III.9:8 of its maker, along with his **r.** salvation.
T-12.....III.10:9 the **r.** world to you from the altar of God.
T-12.......V.4:1 for yours is divided and therefore not **r.**.
T-12.......V.7:4 teaching aid, every **r.** instruction, and
T-12......VI.3:6 Make the world **r.** unto yourself, for the
T-12......VI.3:6 the **r.** world is the gift of the Holy Spirit,
T-12......VI.4:7 will show you the **r.** world because God
T-12......VI.4:9 begins with his investment in the **r.** world
T-12.....VI.4:10 Spirit blesses the **r.** world in Their Name.
T-12......VI.5:1 When you have seen this **r.** world, as you
T-12......VI.5:4 then the **r.** world will spring to your sight,
T-12......VI.5:6 He looks quietly on the **r.** world, which
T-12......VI.7:5 **r.** world has slipped quietly into Heaven,
T-12.....VII.1:4 to all situations you will gain the **r.** world.
T-12.....VII.4:4 What you cannot see becomes **r.** to you
T-12.....VII.4:5 and it can become compellingly **r.** to you
T-12...VII.11:5 Yet as I become more **r.** to you, you will
T-12...VII.11:6 we will look upon the **r.** world together.
T-12...VII.11:7 only the **r.** world exists and only the real
T-12...VII.11:7 exists and only the **r.** world can be seen.
T-12... VIII.1:3 You attack the **r.** world every day and
T-12... VIII.6:2 is not **r.** cannot be seen and has no value.
T-12... VIII.6:9 By making nothing **r.** to you, you have
T-12... VIII.8:1 **r.** world was given you by God in loving
T-13.......in.3:1 If this were the **r.** world, God *would* be
T-13...... I.10:1 You cannot dispel guilt by making it **r.**,
T-13...... I.11:3 For attack makes guilt **r.**, and if it is real
T-13...... I.11:3 and if it is **r.** there *is* no way to overcome it.
T-13....... II.6:2 was confronted with the **r.** guiltlessness of
T-13.....III.1:11 Your **r.** terror is of redemption.
T-13......III.3:2 and your own **r.** power seems to you as
T-13......III.3:2 power seems to you as your **r.** weakness.
T-13......III.6:6 for here is the **r.** crucifixion of God's Son.
T-13......III.8:1 you hold so dear is your **r.** call for help.
T-13......III.8:7 Only his love is **r.**, and he will be content
T-13....III.10:6 but still more did he fear his **r.** Father,
T-13......IV.2:2 **r.** Heaven is the greatest threat you think
T-13......IV.5:6 because, by making it **r.** in the present,
T-13......IV.6:2 They are not **r.**, and have no hold over
T-13....... V.2:2 Yet the figures that he sees were never **r.**,
T-13....... V.9:4 for you, as your witness to the **r.** world.
T-13....... V.9:5 looking always on the **r.** world, and
T-13......VI.6:3 lies within it because its continuity is **r.**. It
T-13....VI.13:3 the **r.** world for you when you awake. In
T-13........VII.h Attainment of the **R.** World
T-13.....VII.1:1 tell yourself: "The **r.** world is not like this.
T-13.....VII.2:4 yet either one will seem as **r.** to you as the
T-13.....VII.2:5 their **r.** attraction to you is unequal.
T-13.....VII.4:1 **r.** world has the power to touch you even
T-13.....VII.8:4 The **r.** world is the way that leads you to
T-13.....VII.9:7 and the **r.** world is but your welcome of
T-13...VII.16:6 is the only **r.** need to be fulfilled in time.
T-13... VIII.2:1 very **r.** difference between perception and
T-13....... X.1:2 is to hide the **r.** source of guilt, and keep
T-13....... X.1:4 to which they bear no **r.** relationship at all
T-13....... X.2:1 Insane ideas have no **r.** relationships, for
T-13....... X.2:2 No **r.** relationship can rest on guilt, or
T-13....... X.2:5 you forgot that **r.** relationships are holy,
T-13..... X.2:10 It is not shared, and so it is not **r.**.
T-13....... X.3:2 because your union with him is not **r.**.
T-13....... X.4:4 whom you find no **r.** relationships at all.
T-13....... X.6:5 If guilt were **r.**, Atonement would not be.
T-13....... X.6:6 to establish them as **r.** and then forgive
T-13..... X.11:1 You cannot enter into **r.** relationships
T-13......XI.1:2 that both opponents in the war are **r.**.
T-13......XI.1:4 the war is between **r.** and unreal powers,
T-14....... II.3:4 *Nothing else matters, nothing else is* **r.**, *and*
T-14......IV.3:6 becomes **r.** and visible to those who use it.
T-14.....VII.1:5 everything that is not **r.** must disappear,
T-14.....VII.2:5 or unrecognized, **r.** or false to you. If you
T-14......IX.2:8 Its changelessness is what makes it **r.**.
T-15....... V.7:3 you cannot find it because it is not **r.**.
T-15.....VII.3:2 it is. For having been made **r.** to you, it is
T-15.....VII.3:7 of God can have no **r.** investment here.
T-15...VII.13:3 in a **r.** relationship so holy and so strong,

T-15...... VIII.h The Only **R.** Relationship
T-15...... IX.2:6 which you can establish **r.** relationships,
T-15....... X.3:2 are willing to accept our relationship as **r.**
T-15....... X.8:3 The **r.** price of not accepting this has been
T-16.........I.3:6 Do not use empathy to make the past **r.**,
T-16.........I.6:7 recognizes foolish needs as well as **r.** ones.
T-16....... II.4:5 you must understand it or else it is not **r.**.
T-16....... II.6:2 Yet your relationship with Him is **r.**.
T-16....... II.8:5 is not **r.** and that reality is not disaster.
T-16...... III.4:3 to see the **r.** cause and effect relationship
T-16...... III.5:7 They are quite **r.**, as part of the Self you
T-16.... III.5:10 For nothing **r.** has ever left the mind of its
T-16.... III.5:11 And what is not **r.** was never there.
T-16...... IV.7:2 bring love into fear, and make it **r.** in fear.
T-16...... IV.7:5 the dilemma which seems very **r.** to you,
T-16....... V.9:4 The **r.** purpose of the special relationship,
T-16.........VI.h The Bridge to the **R.** World
T-16...... VI.3:2 guilt, the **r.** lure in the special relationship
T-16...... VI.3:3 do not recognize that this is its **r.** appeal,
T-16...... VI.9:2 thought system that taught you it was **r.**,
T-16..... VII.2:5 now, it cannot have any **r.** meaning at all.
T-16...VII.10:1 between the **r.** Atonement that would
T-16...VII.11:4 with Him is to accept relationships as **r.**,
T-17.........I.5:4 you are trying to make illusions **r.**, and
T-17....... II.2:2 It is the **r.** world, bright and clean and
T-17....... II.3:4 The **r.** world, in its loveliness, you learn to
T-17....... II.3:7 God's Son upon himself, the **r.** perception
T-17....... II.4:4 The perception of the **r.** world will be so
T-17....... II.4:5 when you have reached the **r.** world and
T-17....... II.5:1 The **r.** world is attained simply by the
T-17....... II.5:3 In the light of the **r.** reason that He brings
T-17....... II.6:2 lets you see the **r.** world reaching quietly
T-17....... II.8:2 It will give you the **r.** world, trembling
T-17....... II.8:5 world, and into the **r.** world of beauty and
T-17...... III.9:4 the **r.** world or the world of guilt and fear,
T-17.... III.10:2 Let my relationship to you be **r.** to you,
T-17...... IV.1:1 that does not share His purpose can be **r.**.
T-17...... IV.1:7 does not fulfill this function cannot be **r.**.
T-17...... IV.3:1 very **r.** relationships even in this world.
T-17.... IV.14:4 now, by **r.** comparison, a transformation
T-17.... IV.14:7 it is; a picture of what you thought was **r.**,
T-17....... V.2:1 step toward the perception of the **r.** world
T-17... VIII.6:2 one accepts what he does not believe is **r.**.
T-18.........I.7:9 differences in form are no **r.** differences at
T-18....... II.1:1 world that seems quite **r.** arise in dreams?
T-18....... II.4:8 would do to it. And thus is guilt made **r.**.
T-18....... II.5:2 you see it you do not doubt that it is **r.**.
T-18..... II.5:10 world that is not **r.** remains with you.
T-18....... II.6:6 as a help to make His purpose **r.** to you.
T-18....... II.9:4 the Holy Spirit has gently laid the **r.** world
T-18....... II.9:5 so do the **r.** world and the truth of Heaven
T-18...... VI.5:4 cannot destroy can have no **r.** effect at all.
T-18..... VII.3:3 Only its past and future make it seem **r.**.
T-18...... IX.5:1 as long as you believe that guilt is **r.**. For
T-18...... IX.5:2 and a **r.** foundation for the ego's thought
T-18...... IX.7:3 out and move about, actions seem **r.**, and
T-18...... IX.7:5 the world below, nor seek to make it **r.**.
T-18...... IX.9:1 this circle of brightness is the **r.** world,
T-18.... IX.11:3 only that whoever attains the **r.** world,
T-19.........I.2:5 united purpose that makes this purpose **r.**
T-19........I.12:1 for knowledge as is the **r.** world. For faith
T-19....... II.2:3 that attack is **r.** and guilt is justified. It
T-19....... II.7:1 defended than the idea that sin is **r.**; the
T-19...... III.2:7 For what you think is **r.** you want, and
T-19...... III.6:1 you are tempted to believe that sin is **r.**,
T-19...... III.6:1 that sin is real, remember this: If sin is **r.**,
T-19...... III.6:3 rest. If sin is **r.**, God must be at war with
T-19...... III.8:1 If sin is **r.**, it must forever be beyond the
T19... IV.A.5:6 Guilt can raise no **r.** barriers against it.
T19. IV.A.17:9 But you can live to show it is not **r.**. The
T19....IV.C.8:7 upon the defeat of God, and think it **r.**?
T19....IV.C.9:1 its appeal is yielded to love's **r.** attraction.
T19... IV.D.9:1 and learned illusions are not **r.**. No one
T-20...... III.5:4 a sentence on it, justifies it and makes it **r.**
T-20....... VI.1:5 His **r.** relationship is one of perfect union
T-20.... VI.12:5 have a **r.** relationship, and it has meaning.
T-20.... VI.12:6 It is as like your **r.** relationship with God
T-20..... VII.5:1 to make the unholy relationship seem **r.**.
T-20..... VII.7:6 means seem **r.** because the goal is valued.

T-20..... VII.8:8 imaginings about him will seem **r.** there.
T-20.... VIII.3:2 it with **r.** desire and sincerity of purpose,
T-21........II.9:2 to make its goals seem **r.** and possible.
T-21......II.10:7 seems to *be* the cause, producing **r.** effects.
T-21...... III.4:2 the Holy Spirit leads you to the **r.** world,
T-21...... VI.4:3 and let their madness tell them it is **r.**.
T-21...... VI.5:2 also has the means to make its purpose **r.**.
T-21... VII.11:3 on sin are seeing the denial of the **r.** world
T-21... VII.11:4 in your desire to see the **r.** world, so the
T-21... VII.13:6 and you will look on it and think it **r.**. No
T-22.......in.2:3 It is this difference, seen but not **r.**, that
T-22.......in.2:3 makes the need for sin, not **r.** but seen,
T-22.......in.2:4 And all this would be **r.** if sin were so. For
T-22........II.3:9 Yet if the change be **r.** and not imagined,
T-22........II.4:4 all truth meaningless, and all illusions **r.**.
T-22...... III.2:3 telling you what you thought was **r.** is not.
T-22...... III.7:5 are seeing what can *not* be **r.** as if it were.
T-22...... III.9:6 as causing sin by his desire to have sin **r.**.
T-22.... VI.11:4 why it has not happened, nor could be **r.**.
T-23........I.2:12 think that it is possible, the means seem **r.**
T-23.........I.9:2 For it seems **r.** only as long as it is seen as
T-23.........I.9:2 the conqueror to be the truer, the more **r.**,
T-23.........I.9:2 vanquisher of the illusion that was less **r.**,
T-23.........I.9:3 between illusions, one to be crowned as **r.**
T-23........II.5:7 made **r.** by what the Son of God has done
T-23......II.15:4 its seeming laws must be perceived as **r.**.
T-23...... IV.5:3 Here in the midst of it, it does seem **r.**.
T-23...... IV.5:7 this choice shows you the battle is not **r.**,
T-24........II.3:1 Specialness is the idea of sin made **r.**. Sin
T-24........II.8:2 but only friend to what is **r.** in you. Not
T-24........II.9:5 and in peace so **r.** and so encompassing
T-24...... IV.1:4 it offers is but deception, but its hate is **r.**.
T-24...... IV.4:6 All that is **r.** proclaims his sinlessness. All
T-24...... IV.4:7 All that is false proclaims his sins as **r.**. If
T-24...... IV.4:8 If he is sinful, then is your reality not **r.**,
T-24....... V.1:8 Wishing makes **r.**, as surely as does will
T-25...... III.2:3 world where this reflection is, is **r.** at all.
T-25...... III.3:5 for illusions which it would make **r.**. Not
T-25..... VII.4:8 Sin is not **r.** *because* the Father and the
T-25... VII.11:4 a form of the more basic tenet, "Sin is **r.**,
T-25.... VIII.5:7 the other and denies that it is **r.**. It is
T-26...... III.3:2 We have referred to it as the **r.** world.
T-26.... III.4:10 In the **r.** world is choosing simplified.
T-26...... III.6:3 **r.** world is the area of choice made real,
T-26...... III.6:3 real world is the area of choice made **r.**,
T-26...... IV.1:8 he returned to his **r.** function of creating,
T-26....... V.2:2 quite meaningless to the **r.** Teacher of the
T-26....... V.6:7 How **r.** a hindrance can this dream be to
T-26....... V.8:2 And everything that points to it as **r.** is
T-26....... V.8:2 made **r.** again and seen as here and now,
T-26..... V.11:5 Sometimes the past seems **r.**, as if it *were*
T-26..... V.12:3 The **r.** world is the second part of the
T-26..... V.12:3 of the hallucination time and death are **r.**,
T-26...... VI.1:2 denied it is but an illusion, and made it **r.**.
T-26...... VI.1:3 And it is **r.** to you. It is not nothing. And
T-26...... VI.1:7 For no one can make one illusion **r.**, and
T-26..... VII.3:9 it seems to have a meaning and be **r.**.
T-26..... VII.4:6 it. For it is **r.**, and dwells where all reality
T-26..... VII.7:2 Yet the belief that it is **r.** has made some
T-26..... VII.7:3 be opposed by its own opposite, as **r.** as it.
T-26... VII.12:3 leave their source made **r.** and meaningful
T-27.........I.6:4 Its only purpose is to prove guilt **r.**. No
T-27........I.6:11 vanity of **r.** concern with anything at all.
T-27.........I.8:1 the strange belief that sin and death are **r.**
T-27........II.2:4 one can forgive a sin that he believes is **r.**.
T-27........II.2:5 And what has consequences must be **r.**,
T-27........II.4:1 Forgiveness is not **r.** unless it brings a
T-27........II.4:2 on you to demonstrate they are not **r.**.
T-27...... III.4:2 would enhance the invitation's **r.** appeal.
T-27...... IV.4:9 same. It asks but to establish sin is **r.**, and
T-27..... V.8:11 convinces you that they could not be **r.**.
T-27...... VI.1:1 Pain demonstrates the body must be **r.**. It
T-27...... VI.1:4 they both are means to make the body **r.**.
T-27...... VI.3:5 cannot choose among them which are **r.**,
T-27...... VI.4:3 He knows it is not **r.**. For nothing could
T-27...... VI.4:8 brings is witness that the body is not **r.**.
T-27..... VII.7:9 in making them and making them seem **r.**
T-27... VII.11:7 the part you see and do not doubt is **r.**.
T-27... VII.11:8 and dream in secret that its cause is **r.**?

T-27...VII.13:4 So fearful is the dream, so seeming r., he
T-27....VIII.2:1 ways to prove it is autonomous and r.. It
T-27....VIII.2:2 the world proclaims as valuable and r.. It
T-27....VIII.4:4 unless he sees them as if they were r.? The
T-27....VIII.4:5 causing them and making them seem r..
T-27....VIII.5:5 never have conceived this world as r.. He
T-27....VIII.6:3 of both accomplishment and r. effects.
T-27....VIII.7:1 A timelessness in which is time made r.; a
T-28........ II.6:5 dream, but never will you give it r. effects.
T-28....... III.2:3 the part you play in making sickness r.,
T-28.... IV.2:10 And what is r. and what is but illusion in
T-28........ V.2:1 and pain and loss, that makes them r..
T-28........ V.5:8 their maker his imaginings are r..
T-28........ V.7:2 the place where you perceive it is not r..
T-29.........I.8:6 aroused by learning that the body is not r.
T-29..... VII.5:3 conceived as r. and given living form. Yet
T-29..... VII.9:2 dream succeed in making r. the picture it
T-29....VIII.3:2 perceived as r. and seen outside the mind.
T-29....VIII.4:9 take no form in which he ever will be r..
T-29...... IX.4:8 up the dream in which their toys are r.,
T-29...... IX.5:2 the child who thought he made them r..
T-29...... IX.5:7 Yet do they keep his thoughts alive and r.,
T-29...... IX.5:8 because he thinks the thoughts are r..
T-29...... IX.6:8 Yet is the r. world unaffected by the world
T-29...... IX.6:8 unaffected by the world he thinks is r..
T-29...... IX.7:1 The r. world still is but a dream. Except
T-30........I.14:2 This seems to be a r. decision in itself.
T-30...... IV.5:5 Attack has power to make illusions r.. Yet
T-30...... IV.5:7 a power that can have no r. effects at all?
T-30.... IV.5:14 His one mistake is that he thinks them r..
T-30........ V.1:1 The r. world is the state of mind in which
T-30........ V.4:3 the r. world has a purpose still beneath
T-30........ V.5:1 The r. world still falls short of this, for
T-30........ V.5:2 The r. world is a state in which the mind
T-30........ V.6:1 Thus is the r. world's purpose gently
T-30........ V.7:1 stand already at the edge of the r. world.
T-30...... VI.1:4 Here is the r. world given in exchange for
T-30...... VI.2:3 a r. attack that calls for punishment.
T-30...... VI.2:4 which are inappropriate to what is r..
T-30...... VI.2:5 what is not r. by not perceiving what has
T-30...... VI.3:1 that lets the r. world rise to take the place
T-30...... VI.3:2 a r. foundation pardon would have none.
T-30...... VI.3:3 r. world is achieved when you perceive
T-30...... VI.3:3 of forgiveness is quite r. and fully justified
T-30...... VI.4:2 seems impossible His pardon could be r..
T-30...... VI.6:3 are r. and not appearances at all. Be not
T-30...... VI.7:2 cannot be to judge which forms are r.,
T-30...... VI.9:5 by your wish to make illusions r.. And
T-30....VIII.1:4 change, and yet you thought it r. before,
T-30....VIII.1:4 real before, and now you think it r. again.
T-30....VIII.1:7 It is this that makes it r., and keeps it
T-30....VIII.2:7 This demonstrates that it was never r.,
T-30....VIII.3:1 temptation but a wish to make illusions r.
T-31.........I.5:2 a will apart from it was yet more r. than it
T-31...... III.2:2 Why are they r. in him, if you did not
T-31.........IV.h The R. Alternative
T-31...... IV.2:1 R. choice is no illusion. But the world has
T-31...... IV.5:1 unless he understood their r. futility? Is it
T-31...... IV.6:1 of acceptance that there is a r. alternative
T-31...... IV.8:1 when you have seen the r. alternatives.
T-31........ V.7:8 not be used to demonstrate the world is r.
T-31...... VI.1:3 If one is r. the other must be false, for
T-31...... VI.1:3 be false, for what is r. denies its opposite.
T-31...... VI.1:5 all you see and think is r. and hold as true
T-31...VII.14:6 see the r. alternatives you choose between
T-31....VIII.2:4 what you choose is what you think is r..
T-31....VIII.3:6 He is the only power that is r. in you. His
W-pI....... 4.2:3 None of them represents your r. thoughts
W-pI....... 8.3:3 than believing that it is filled with r. ideas,
W-pI..... 10.1:2 them is that they are not your r. thoughts.
W-pI..... 14.4:3 God did not create it, and so it is not r..
W-pI..... 14.4:5 *God did not create that war, and so it is not r.*
W-pI..... 14.4:6 *create that airplane crash, and so it is not r..*
W-pI..... 14.4:7 *that disaster [specify], and so it is not r..*
W-pI..... 14.7:5 *which is disturbing you], and so it is not r..*
W-pI..... 15.2:3 That is the beginning of r. vision. You can
W-pI..... 15.2:4 You can be certain that r. vision will come
W-pI..... 20.5:2 to do so, but make a r. effort to remember
W-pI..... 20.5:6 Such is the r. law of cause and effect as it
W-pI..... 22.2:2 it not joyous news to hear that it is not r.?
W-pI..... 22.3:5 *What I see is not r.. What I see is a form of*
W-pI..... 26.1:2 see attack as a r. threat. That is because
W-pI..... 27.4:1 The r. question is, how often will you
W-pI..... 28.5:3 all your ideas about it is its r. purpose, the
W-pI..... 30.4:1 R. vision is not limited to concepts such
W-pI..... 30.5:1 R. vision is not only unlimited by space
W-pI..... 41.2:3 be cured because the problem is not r..
W-pI..... 41.3:2 mind that thought these things were r.,
W-pI..... 41.5:3 Today we will make our first r. attempt to
W-pI..... 43.3:3 If vision is r., and it is real to the extent to
W-pI..... 43.3:3 and it is r. to the extent to which it shares
W-pI..... 44.8:3 only one that has any r. use to you at all.
W-pI..... 45.1:1 holds the key to what your r. thoughts are
W-pI..... 45.1:3 what is r. and what you think is real.
W-pI..... 45.1:3 what is real and what you think is r..
W-pI..... 45.1:4 you think are your r. thoughts resemble
W-pI..... 45.1:4 resemble your r. thoughts in any respect.
W-pI..... 45.3:1 Where, then, are your r. thoughts? Today
W-pI..... 45.4:2 to leave the unreal and seek for the r.. We
W-pI..... 45.6:4 *My r. thoughts are in my mind. I would like*
W-pI..... 47.4:1 own weakness to the Source of r. strength
W-pI..... 47.6:2 that confidence in your r. strength is fully
W-pI..... 47.7:1 into your mind to a place of r. safety. You
W-pI..... 49.4:3 your r. thoughts and obscure your eternal
W-pI..... 49.4:6 We are trying to reach your r. home. We
W-pI..... 51.4:3 call "my" thoughts are not my r. thoughts
W-pI..... 51.4:4 My r. thoughts are the thoughts I think
W-pI..... 53.1:4 I have r. thoughts as well as insane ones. I
W-pI..... 53.1:5 I can therefore see a r. world, if I look to
W-pI..... 53.1:5 to my r. thoughts as my guide for seeing.
W-pI..... 53.2:6 I am grateful that this world is not r., and
W-pI..... 53.3:5 But such a world is not r.. I have given it
W-pI..... 53.4:3 and everything that is r. is in His Mind. It
W-pI..... 53.5:4 and am not allowing my r. thoughts to
W-pI..... 54.1:3 a false world or lead me to the r. one. But
W-pI..... 54.1:5 so will the r. world rise before my eyes as I
W-pI..... 54.3:5 I can also call upon my r. thoughts, which
W-pI..... 54.3:6 my r. thoughts awaken the real thoughts
W-pI..... 54.3:6 thoughts awaken the r. thoughts in them.
W-pI..... 54.3:7 world my r. thoughts show me will dawn
W-pI..... 54.5:5 I would look upon the r. world, and let it
W-pI..... 55.5:2 that my illusions about myself are r.. It is
W-pI..... 55.5:5 I do not recognize its r. purpose. The
W-pI..... 55.5:7 the world's r. purpose by withdrawing the
W-pI..... 56.1:8 My own r. thoughts will teach me what it
W-pI..... 58.1:2 does the perception of the r. world come.
W-pI..... 61.3:2 in accepting your r. function on earth. It
W-pI..... 66.4:1 only is there a very r. connection between
W-pI..... 69.2:1 Today let us make another r. attempt to
W-pI..... 69.3:1 and with r. determination to reach what
W-pI..... 70.7:5 self-concepts that you sought to make r..
W-pI..... 70.9:1 easily walk on into the light of r. salvation
W-pI..... 71.6:5 There can be no r. conflict about this,
W-pI..... 72.5:5 In fact, if the body were r., it would be
W-pI..... 72.5:6 that you hold insists that the body is r.. It
W-pI..... 73.1:7 of creation. They make nothing that is r..
W-pI..... 74.4:5 *Him. My conflicts about _ cannot be r..*
W-pI..... 75.4:4 the r. world rises before us in gladness, to
W-pI... 75.11:2 of your vision and the sight of the r. world
W-pI... 75.11:2 the unforgiven world you thought was r..
W-pI..... 77.6:6 We are asking a r. question at last. The
W-pI..... 88.3:6 They have no r. effect on me at all. I am
W-pI..... 91.7:4 need a r. experience of something else,
W-pI..... 96.3:5 the two, for one denies the other can be r.
W-pI..... 96.6:6 Salvation cannot make illusions r., nor
W-pI..... 96.9:5 are your own r. thoughts you have denied
W-pI..... 99.3:2 mind that sees illusions thinks them r..
W-pI..... 99.3:4 And yet they are not r., because the mind
W-pI..... 99.4:3 and sins forgotten which were never r.?
W-pI..... 99.5:3 time, because of your belief that time is r..
W-pI..... 99.8:2 make them r. by hiding them from Him.
W-pI... 101.1:5 think it so while you believe that sin is r.,
W-pI... 101.2:1 If sin is r., then punishment is just and
W-pI... 101.2:3 sin is r., then happiness must be illusion,
W-pI... 101.3:1 If sin is r., salvation must be pain. Pain is
W-pI... 101.3:2 suffering can never be escaped, if sin is r..
W-pI... 101.4:4 If sin is r., its offering is death, and meted
W-pI... 101.4:5 If sin is r., salvation has become your
W-pI .. 101.5:2 The exercises teach sin is not r., and all
W-pI .. 101.7:1 with the insane belief that sin is r.. Today
W-pI .. 103.2:1 that think what they have made is r..
W-pI .. 110.1:4 you fear has no meaning, evil is not r.,
W-pI .. 121.3:3 except the proof that all its sins are r.?
W-pI .. 123.2:1 of some insight into the r. extent of all the
W-pI .. 129.5:5 Esteem them, and they will seem r. to you
W-pI .. 130.3:2 What can be seen in darkness that is r.?
W-pI .. 130.3:4 be r. in blind imaginings of panic born?
W-pI .. 130.5:5 The r. and the unreal are all there are to
W-pI .. 130.7:2 our minds to finding only what is r..
W-pI 130.10:2 The unreal or the r., the false or true is
W-pI 130.11:1 Accept a little part of hell as r., and you
W-pI .. 131.2:5 achieve that offers any hope of being r.?
W-pI 131.10:3 see the rising of the r. world to replace the
W-pI 131.11:5 closed, the senseless world you think is r..
W-pI .. 132.1:5 A madman thinks the world he sees is r.,
W-pI .. 132.4:3 you can look on them and think them r..
W-pI 132.11:4 Unless it does, it is not r., and cannot be
W-pI 132.11:5 If you are r. the world you see is false, for
W-pI 132.12:2 Your r. creations wait for this release to
W-pI 132.13:2 a world which comes from this idea be r.?
W-pI 132.15:3 *For I am r. because the world is not, and I*
W-pI .. 133.3:1 Today we list the r. criteria by which to
W-pI .. 133.6:3 Time can never take away a value that is r.
W-pI 133.11:2 goals to come between the r. alternatives.
W-pI 133.13:2 to value but the truly valuable and the r..
W-pI .. 134.4:1 Because you think your sins are r., you
W-pI .. 134.5:5 forgiven from the view their sins are r. are
W-pI .. 135.1:1 he were attacked, that the attack were r.,
W-pI .. 135.1:2 and then attempts to handle them as r.. It
W-pI .. 135.3:4 speaks of fear made r. and terror justified.
W-pI .. 135.8:1 The "self" that needs protection is not r..
W-pI 135.10:2 This is the body's only r. defense. Yet is
W-pI .. 136.4:1 the threat that has been judged as r.? All
W-pI .. 136.4:3 mind, an outcome with a r. effect on you,
W-pI .. 136.6:4 your own decision of what should be r., to
W-pI .. 136.6:4 be real, to take the place of what is r..
W-pI .. 137.2:3 final power to make the separation r., and
W-pI .. 137.4:6 must demonstrate that sickness is not r..
W-pI .. 137.5:3 Just as the r. world will arise to take the
W-pI .. 137.6:2 Christ to those who dream the world is r..
W-pI .. 137.7:1 the r. world will occupy the place of what
W-pI .. 137.7:2 of all the laws that hold it cannot but be r.
W-pI .. 138.1:3 what we perceive, and what we think is r..
W-pI .. 138.2:2 But here is opposition part of being "r.."
W-pI .. 138.7:2 it be a means for demonstrating hell is r.,
W-pI 138.11:3 Its pseudo-being, brought to what is r., is
W-pI .. 140.6:7 it is, and knows that no illusion can be r..
W-pI 140.12:4 minds, nor offer proof to us that it is r..
W-pI .. 151.3:7 and think more r. than what is witnessed
W-pI .. 151.9:5 could convince Him that your sins are r.?
W-pI .. 152.2:3 have the gift of everything, can loss be r.?
W-pI 153.20:7 You lay aside but what was never r., to
W-pI .. 155.4:1 asked the sacrifice of something that is r..
W-pI .. 159.3:5 The r. world pictures Heaven's innocence.
W-pI .. 160.1:4 to the part of you which thinks that it is r.
W-pI .. 160.4:7 If you are r., then fear must be illusion.
W-pI .. 160.4:8 And if fear is r., then you do not exist at
W-pI .. 163.2:3 before its image, thinking it alone is r.,
W-pI .. 165.1:1 makes this world seem r. except your own
W-pI .. 166.2:2 is not the Will of God, and so it is not r..
W-pI .. 166.2:3 it r. must still believe there is another will,
W-pI .. 166.9:5 Perhaps His gifts to you are r.. Perhaps
W-pI .. 169.2:2 can not believe the world of fear is r..
W-pI .. 170.2:6 *own defense against it is it r. and inescapable*
W-pI .. 170.4:3 with perfect faith the split you made is r..
W-pI .. 184.6:2 and symbols that assert the world is r.. It
W-pI 184.10:3 to darkness, not because you think it r.,
W-pI .. 185.2:3 He cannot make a hell and think it r.. He
W-pI .. 186.6:1 makes an image of yourself that is not r..
W-pI .. 190.1:6 cruel. How could it be r. in any form? It
W-pI .. 190.3:3 If God is r., there is no pain. If pain is real,
W-pI .. 190.3:4 no pain. If pain is r., there is no God. For
W-pI .. 193.3:4 and different themes, apparent but not r..
W-pI .. 193.6:1 we are tempted to believe that pain is r.,
W-pI .. 193.7:2 Does pain seem r. in the perception? If it
W-pI .. 194.4:3 the temporal progression still seems r..
W-pI .. 196.5:3 stood for the belief the fear of God is r..

| | |
|---|---|
| W-pI...196.6:4 | The fear of God is r. to anyone who thinks |
| W-pII......1.1:2 | It does not pardon sins and make them r.. |
| W-pII......3.3:3 | world was made to witness and make r.. |
| W-pII......4.3:2 | the "proof" that what has no reality is r.. |
| W-pII..278.1:2 | and the sins which I perceive are r., and |
| W-pII..289.1:1 | mind, the r. world must escape my sight. |
| W-pII..290.1:5 | the dream I made is r. an instant longer. |
| W-pII.........8.h | What Is the R. World? |
| W-pII......8.1:1 | The r. world is a symbol, like the rest of |
| W-pII......8.1:4 | The r. world cannot be perceived except |
| W-pII......8.2:1 | The r. world holds a counterpart for each |
| W-pII......8.2:2 | r. world shows a world seen differently, |
| W-pII......8.4:1 | r. world is the symbol that the dream of |
| W-pII......8.4:3 | The r. world signifies the end of time, for |
| W-pII..292.1:4 | And while we think this will is r., we will |
| W-pII..293.2:3 | *There is a r. world which the present holds* |
| W-pII..309.1:5 | will that is not true, and made it r.. Yet it |
| W-pII..312.1:5 | must the r. world come to greet the holy |
| W-pII.....322.h | I can give up but what was never r.. |
| W-pII..325.1:3 | esteemed as r. and guarded as one's own. |
| W-pII..332.1:5 | recalled from fantasies, awaking to the r.. |
| W-pII....13.4:3 | a world more r. than what you saw before |
| W-pII..342.1:2 | *It is not r.. And You have given me the means* |
| W-pII..344.1:7 | *with Heaven's treasures, which alone are r..* |
| W-pII..347.1:7 | *on pain, and yet He understands it is not r.,* |
| W-pII..359.1:6 | *made mistakes which have no r. effects on us* |
| W-ep .........4:1 | and all pain that you may think is r.. Nor |
| M-in ..........3:9 | that the self you are trying to protect is r.. |
| M-in ........3:10 | the self you think is r. is what you teach. |
| M-in ..........5:1 | for the world of sin would seem forever r.. |
| M-3............4:4 | to be the end of the relationship a r. end. |
| M-4......I.A.8:5 | This is the stage of r. peace, for here is |
| M-5..........I.1:6 | r. strength is seen as threat and health as |
| M-5.....III.1:13 | To them the separation is quite r.. |
| M-7............5:1 | The r. basis for doubt about the outcome |
| M-8............2:3 | r. that is regarded as of major importance |
| M-8..........3:11 | whether what is seen is r. or illusory, |
| M-8............5:6 | His mind has categorized them all as r., |
| M-8............5:6 | all as real, and so they are all r. to him. |
| M-8............6:6 | And of these two, but one is r.. Just as |
| M-8............6:7 | Just as reality is wholly r., apart from size |
| M-11..........3:2 | These problems are not r., but that is |
| M-12..........6:6 | Awareness of dreaming is the r. function |
| M-12..........6:9 | and separate is no more r. than to regard |
| M-13.............h | IS THE R. MEANING OF SACRIFICE? |
| M-13..........1:3 | it. Now its r. meaning is a lesson. Like all |
| M-13..........5:1 | What is the r. meaning of sacrifice? It is |
| M-14..........2:4 | where sin was made and guilt seemed r.. |
| M-16........6:14 | then will you accept your r. protection. |
| M-16........10:3 | he may accept as r. can but deceive him. |
| M-17..........1:3 | the magic seem quite r. to both of them. |
| M-17........9:13 | fear, and thus forever r. and always true. |
| M-18..........1:3 | it is their task to escape from what is r.. |
| M-18..........3:1 | Anger but screeches, "Guilt is r.!" Reality |
| M-20..........5:7 | end, and nothing He did not create is r.. |
| M-24..........1:3 | cannot, then, be true in any r. sense. Our |
| M-27..........2:5 | love, because he has denied that life is r.. |
| M-27..........3:8 | of life." God is insane, and fear alone is r. |
| M-27..........4:2 | If death is r. for anything, there is no life. |
| M-27..........5:2 | created bodies, death would indeed be r.. |
| M-27..........5:4 | the perception of the r. world and that of |
| M-27..........6:9 | yet to think love r. are mindless magic, |
| M-27........6:11 | opposite, and fear would be as r. as love? |
| M-28..........6:2 | of evil dreams, the thought of hell is r.. |
| C-1............5:2 | vision sees the r. world in its place. This is |
| C-1............6:1 | and seeing guilt, disease and death as r.. |
| C-1............6:2 | real. Both this world and the r. world are |
| C-1............7:5 | highest it becomes aware of the r. world, |
| C-2............2:3 | ego cannot be denied for it alone seems r.. |
| C-2............2:5 | how it arose can be but he who thinks it r. |
| C-2..........6:13 | but seemed r. while you were dreaming it. |
| C-3............4:7 | It is the symbol of the r. world. Whoever |
| C-4............2:1 | means by which the r. world can be seen, |
| C-4............5:9 | Only the body makes the world seem r., |
| C-6............1:5 | alone knows along with Christ, His r. Son |
| P-in...........1:4 | the manifestations of this world seem r. |
| P-2........in.4:1 | in some way that he believes is r.. The |
| P-2........II.2:1 | but it also has no r. place in religion. In |
| P-2.......IV.2:7 | If a deformity is seen as r., what could its |
| P-2........IV.3:1 | the decision that guilt is r. has been made |
| P-2........IV.3:3 | Yet all these things, however r. they seem, |
| P-2........IV.4:3 | but make the body r. in their own minds, |
| P-2........IV.6:5 | accepted as r. and dealt with by illusions. |
| P-2........IV.7:3 | it. If illness is r. it cannot be overlooked in |
| P-2........IV.8:2 | by which sickness is perceived as r. is the |
| P-2........IV.9:6 | but be seen as a r. source of danger, to be |
| P-2.......IV.10:6 | the belief that guilt is r. and fully justified. |
| P-3.........II.2:2 | nothing about the r. principles of healing. |
| P-3.........II.5:2 | that only that was r. in their relationship. |
| S-1...........I.2:9 | r. sound is always a song of thanksgiving |
| S-1........III.3:9 | to be a r. advantage in having enemies, |
| S-1........III.4:5 | His r. escape from guilt can lie only in the |
| S-2...........I.3:4 | Do not make it r.. Select the loving and |
| S-2........III.4:5 | not r. and makes illusions in its evil name |

## realistic 1

| | |
|---|---|
| M-26.........3:4 | rare that it cannot be considered a r. goal. |

## realities 2

| | |
|---|---|
| T-14......IX.2:6 | Different r. are meaningless, for reality |
| T-30....III.11:5 | You have not two r., but one. Nor can you |

## reality 547

| | |
|---|---|
| T-1........III.5:5 | *Your r. is only spirit. Therefore you are in a* |
| T-1........III.9:4 | aims at restoring the awareness of r., it |
| T-1........IV.2:2 | exert enormous efforts to establish its r.. |
| T-1........IV.2:3 | The miracle sets r. where it belongs. |
| T-1........IV.2:4 | R. belongs only to spirit, and the miracle |
| T-1.......VII.3:4 | to control r. according to false needs. |
| T-1.......VII.3:5 | needs. Twist r. in any way and you are |
| T-1.....VII.3:11 | the wholly satisfying nature of r. becomes |
| T-1.....VII.3:12 | R. is "lost" through usurpation, which |
| T-2..........I.3:10 | In r. this is your only choice, because your |
| T-2...........I.4:7 | which is then no longer accorded r.. This |
| T-2...........I.5:6 | In r. you are perfectly unaffected by all |
| T-2.........IV.1:3 | combine two orders of r. inappropriately. |
| T-2....V.A.17:3 | statements are not in the same order of r.. |
| T-3.......IV.7:16 | knows you only in peace, and this *is* your r. |
| T-3........VI.1:4 | it means that if you judge the r. of others |
| T-3.......VI.2:12 | implies the belief that r. is yours to select |
| T-3........VI.5:8 | Yet if you wish to be the author of r., you |
| T-3........VI.9:6 | is possible to look on r. without judgment |
| T-3......VI.11:4 | of r. by the unstable scales of desire. |
| T-4...........I.4:3 | dreamer who doubts the r. of his dream |
| T-4...........I.8:4 | sane solution is not to try to change r., |
| T-4...........I.8:5 | it as it is. You are part of r., which stands |
| T-4.........II.6:8 | ego has deluded itself into accepting its r., |
| T-4.......VII.4:5 | you are limiting your sense of your own r. |
| T-4.......VII.4:5 | becomes total only by recognizing all r. in |
| T-4.......VII.4:6 | you. This is your r.. Do not desecrate it or |
| T-5........III.8:7 | according to its interpretation of r., war is |
| T-5.........V.4:1 | you accept into your mind has r. for you. |
| T-5.........V.4:3 | your allowing it to enter makes it your r.. |
| T-5.........V.4:4 | capable of creating r. or making illusions. |
| T-6........IV.6:7 | because they will have no r. for you. Yet |
| T-6........IV.6:8 | created there will have great r. for you, |
| T-6.........V.4:3 | Children *do* confuse fantasy and r., and |
| T-7.......II.7:11 | That is its r., and nothing can assail it. |
| T-7...........III.h | The R. of the Kingdom |
| T-7........III.4:4 | but seeming and r. are hardly the same. |
| T-7........III.4:6 | R. is yours because you are reality. This is |
| T-7........III.4:6 | Reality is yours because you are r.. This is |
| T-7........III.4:8 | The altar there is the only r.. The altar is |
| T-7........III.5:3 | question r. is to question meaninglessly. |
| T-7.......VII.1:6 | If you use it to deny r., reality is gone for |
| T-7.......VII.1:6 | use it to deny reality, r. is gone for you. |
| T-7.......VII.1:7 | *R.* cannot be partly appreciated. That is |
| T-7.....VII.1:11 | Spirit, it can help you recognize part of r., |
| T-7........IX.3:7 | no more interfere with their r. than your |
| T-7........XI.7:4 | Your creations cannot establish your r., |
| T-8...........I.3:3 | of r. that you must make to secure peace, |
| T-8...........I.6:5 | Your r. is unaffected by both, but if you |
| T-8...........I.6:5 | mind will be split about what your r. is. |
| T-8.........II.1:2 | Only one Teacher knows what your r. is. |
| T-8.......V.2:11 | My r. is yours and His. By joining your |
| T-8.......VII.3:6 | because He knows the only r. of anything |
| T-8.......VII.7:2 | translation of one order of r. into another |
| T-8.......VII.7:3 | orders of r. merely appear to exist, just as |
| T-8........IX.2:2 | The r. of everything is totally harmless, |
| T-8........IX.2:2 | harmlessness is the condition of its r.. It is |
| T-8........IX.2:3 | the condition of your awareness of its r.. |
| T-8........IX.2:4 | You do not have to seek r.. It will seek you |
| T-9..............I.h | The Acceptance of R. |
| T-9...........I.1:3 | is. R. cannot "threaten" anything except |
| T-9...........I.1:3 | illusions, since r. can only uphold truth. |
| T-9...........I.2:2 | of God is really the fear of your own r.. It |
| T-9...........I.3:1 | If you do not know what your r. is, why |
| T-9...........I.3:5 | a Guide Who *does* know what your r. is. |
| T-9...........I.4:3 | in your mind, and therefore He is your r.. |
| T-9...........I.4:4 | of your mind brings its r. to you, He *is* |
| T-9...........I.5:2 | But if you ask the sacrifice of r. of yourself |
| T-9...........I.7:7 | R. is the only safety. Your will is your |
| T-9...........I.9:4 | security of r., fear is totally meaningless. |
| T-9.........I.12:2 | Willing against r., though impossible, can |
| T-9.........I.13:3 | R. is everything, and you have everything |
| T-9.........I.13:4 | unreal because the absence of r. is fearful, |
| T-9.........I.13:6 | orders of r. make reality meaningless, and |
| T-9.........I.13:6 | orders of reality make r. meaningless, and |
| T-9.........I.13:6 | reality meaningless, and r. *is* meaning. |
| T-9.........I.14:2 | be. This is the simple acceptance of r., |
| T-9.........I.14:3 | You cannot distort r. and know what it is. |
| T-9.........I.14:4 | do distort r. you will experience anxiety, |
| T-9........IV.1:6 | is shared, and that Its sharing is Its r.. |
| T-9......IV.10:1 | he despairs of finding satisfaction in r.? |
| T-9......IV.10:2 | only hope is to change your mind about r. |
| T-9......IV.10:3 | that r. is fearful is wrong can God be right |
| T-9......IV.11:2 | for r. in fantasies you will not find it. The |
| T-9......IV.11:8 | Yet when r. dawns, the fantasies are gone. |
| T-9......IV.11:9 | R. has not gone in the meanwhile. The |
| T-9....IV.11:10 | The Second Coming is the awareness of r. |
| T-9......IV.12:1 | Behold, my child, r. is here. It belongs to |
| T-9........VI.5:4 | They will become the witnesses to your r., |
| T-9........VI.5:5 | to its r. as the Son does to the Father. |
| T-9........VI.6:2 | to your r. that you can recognize. You |
| T-9.......VII.2:7 | is the essential characteristic of r.. Yet *you* |
| T-9.......VII.7:6 | The Holy Spirit judges against the r. of |
| T-9......VIII.4:2 | faintest hint of your r. literally drives the |
| T-9......VIII.4:4 | conviction of r. will not remain with you |
| T-9......VIII.8:2 | you of the true witnesses to your r.. Truth |
| T-10..........I.2:1 | but perfectly capable of awakening to r.. |
| T-10..........I.3:1 | that r. is in accord with neither? You do |
| T-10.........II.2:1 | of r. brings more than merely lack of fear. |
| T-10.........II.2:5 | Him and know your own r. again. Let |
| T-10.........II.4:3 | of r. precludes the acceptance of God's |
| T-10.........II.5:5 | And if your r. is God's, when you attack |
| T-10.........II.6:5 | at it. By deciding against your r., you have |
| T-10.......III.1:2 | Can you change your r.? No one can will |
| T-10....III.10:2 | You share r. with Him, because reality is |
| T-10....III.10:2 | reality with Him, because r. is not divided |
| T-10....III.11:8 | it is clear this has nothing to do with r., it |
| T-10....III.11:8 | everything to do with r. as you perceive it. |
| T-10.......IV.2:1 | R. can dawn only on an unclouded mind. |
| T-10.......IV.2:3 | To know r. must involve the willingness |
| T-10.....IV.5:10 | R. cannot break through the obstructions |
| T-10.......IV.6:6 | yourself and your r. affect truth at all. |
| T-10......V.12:5 | must learn to see him to learn of his r.. |
| T-11..........I.1:5 | the mind of God's Son you restore this r., |
| T-11..........I.3:7 | Your denial of its r. may arrest it in time, |
| T-11.........II.2:2 | what better witnesses to its r. could you |
| T-11.........II.7:7 | Real freedom depends on welcoming r., |
| T-11........V.2:4 | be dispelled merely by denying their r.. |
| T-11........V.2:7 | If r. is recognized by its extension, what |
| T-11........V.7:3 | The ego is totally confused about r., but it |
| T-11......V.15:4 | becomes its demonstration of its own r.. |
| T-11......V.18:2 | the r. of the kingdom you have chosen for |
| T-11.......VI.8:4 | eyes, but what you see in dreams is not r.. |
| T-11.........VII.h | The Condition of R. |
| T-11......VII.2:2 | in this world are the world's only r.. They |
| T-11......VII.3:4 | to the real, thus confusing illusion and r.. |
| T-11......VII.4:9 | the recognition that r. is only what is true. |
| T-11.....VIII.1:2 | in the end, teaches that only r. is true. But |
| T-11.....VIII.6:3 | That is its r.. Would the Holy Spirit, Who |
| T-11.....VIII.9:2 | and see only his loving thoughts as his r., |
| T-11..VIII.10:6 | then, to learn of the r. of your brother, |

| | |
|---|---|
| T-11..VIII.13:2 | their own interpretations go in favor of **r**., |
| T-11..VIII.14:3 | Ask what they are of the Teacher of **r**., |
| T-11..VIII.14:4 | For fear lies not in **r**., but in the minds of |
| T-11..VIII.14:4 | of children who do not understand **r**.. It is |
| T-11..VIII.14:7 | the **r**. of your brothers or your Father or |
| T-11..VIII.14:9 | Ask what their **r**. is from the One Who |
| T-11VIII.14:10 | by what you see you need **r**. to dispel your |
| T-12.........I.3:7 | his **r**. by interpreting it as you see fit. |
| T-12........I.3:10 | therefore be inappropriate to **r**. as it is, |
| T-12.........I.4:2 | to engage in endless "battles" with **r**., in |
| T-12.........I.4:2 | you deny the **r**. of the need for healing by |
| T-12.........I.4:3 | for your unwillingness to accept **r**. as it is, |
| T-12.........I.6:5 | There is but one response to **r**., for reality |
| T-12.........I.6:5 | to reality, for **r**. evokes no conflict at all. |
| T-12.........I.6:6 | at all. There is but one Teacher of **r**., Who |
| T-12.........I.6:7 | His Mind about **r**. because reality does |
| T-12.........I.6:7 | about reality because **r**. does not change. |
| T-12.........I.6:8 | of **r**. are meaningless in your divided state |
| T-12.........I.8:4 | you would have taken a step away from **r**., |
| T-12........I.10:1 | look upon love, which *is* the world's **r**., |
| T-12........I.10:2 | better learn of its **r**. than by answering the |
| T-12....... II.5:3 | **r**. of nothingness cannot be frightening. |
| T-12......... III.h | The Investment in **R**. |
| T-12...... III.7:1 | thoughts of God's Son are the world's **r**., |
| T-12...... III.7:4 | the mind projects the split, not the **r**.. |
| T-12...... III.8:2 | who perceive its **r**. cannot see the world of |
| T-12...... VI.1:5 | costs you the world's **r**. by denying yours, |
| T-12...... VI.3:3 | This gives it the only **r**. it will ever have. |
| T-12.... VI.4:10 | For **r**. is one with the Father and the Son, |
| T-12..... VII.3:2 | for miracles violate every law of **r**. as this |
| T-12..... VII.8:4 | they attest only to your decision about **r**., |
| T-12..... VII.9:3 | What you made of it is not its **r**., for its |
| T-12..... VII.9:3 | its reality, for its **r**. is only what you give it |
| T-12... VII.10:2 | Yet you could not have seen **r**., for the |
| T-12... VII.10:2 | for the **r**. of your mind is the loveliest of |
| T-12.... VIII.3:4 | than it is up to you to decide what **r**. is. |
| T-12.... VIII.3:6 | The definition of **r**. is God's, not yours. |
| T-12.... VIII.5:3 | the insane desire to control **r**.. You who |
| T-12.... VIII.7:9 | Him could never be content without **r**.. |
| T-12.... VIII.8:3 | Its **r**. will make everything else invisible, |
| T-12.... VIII.8:7 | to knowledge, which is forever the only **r**.. |
| T-13...... III.8:7 | and he will be content only with his **r**.. |
| T-13...... IV.2:3 | demonstrating their **r**. to establish yours. |
| T-13...... IV.2:4 | If their **r**. is questioned, you believe that |
| T-13...... IV.2:5 | For you believe that attack is your **r**., and |
| T-13...... IV.5:4 | reference point, obscuring their present **r**. |
| T-13...... IV.7:6 | It is in the **r**. of "now," without past or |
| T-13....... V.3:8 | Its only **r**. is in your own mind, and by |
| T-13....... V.4:4 | **r**. of their brothers they cannot recognize. |
| T-13....... V.6:4 | isolated from **r**. as if you were alone in all |
| T-13....... V.6:5 | your madness you overlook **r**. completely, |
| T-13....... V.7:9 | perceiving them as witnesses to the **r**. you |
| T-13...... VI.1:1 | all **r**. through the awareness of your own. |
| T-13...... VI.1:2 | sight, for **r**. leaves no room for any error. |
| T-13...... VI.1:4 | His past has no **r**. in the present, so you |
| T-13...... VI.1:7 | be unable to perceive the **r**. that is now. |
| T-13...... VI.2:5 | and conceals their **r**. from your sight. |
| T-13...... VI.4:5 | For to believe **r**. is what you would have it |
| T-13..... VII.5:5 | You who would judge **r**. cannot see it, for |
| T-13..... VII.5:5 | judgment enters **r**. has slipped away. The |
| T-13..... VII.8:7 | Your one **r**. was given you, and by it God |
| T-13.... VIII.3:5 | is merely a faulty formulation of **r**., with |
| T-13.... VIII.3:7 | Aspects of **r**. can still be seen, and they |
| T-13.... VIII.3:8 | Aspects of **r**. can be seen in everything |
| T-13.... VIII.4:5 | Yet even Christ's vision is not His **r**.. The |
| T-13.... VIII.4:6 | The golden aspects of **r**. that spring to |
| T-13.... VIII.6:3 | There is one miracle, as there is one **r**.. |
| T-13.... VIII.6:4 | as every aspect of **r**. you see blends quietly |
| T-13.... VIII.6:4 | see blends quietly into the one **r**. of God. |
| T-13.... VIII.6:5 | created in the one **r**. that is his Father. |
| T-13.... VIII.7:2 | through the Holy Spirit, attune you to **r**.. |
| T-13..VIII.10:3 | unto Him, for **r**. is witnessed to as one. |
| T-13....... X.6:4 | The Holy Spirit seeks not to dispel **r**.. If |
| T-13....... X.7:3 | Give no **r**. to guilt, and see no reason for it |
| T-14.... III.15:6 | may be your choice, but not your **r**.. |
| T-14...... IV.8:1 | Your task is not to make **r**.. It is here |
| T-14...... IV.9:8 | Remembrance of **r**. is in Him, and |
| T-14....... V.1:1 | only part of your mind that has **r**. is the |
| T-14... VII.3:10 | does not retain any conviction of **r**.. |
| T-14 ..... VII.4:5 | keep them both alive and equal in their **r**.. |
| T-14 ... VIII.3:6 | You cannot join with anything except **r**.. |
| T-14 ...... IX.2:6 | are meaningless, for **r**. must be one. It |
| T-14 ... IX.2:11 | for unreality. And this **r**. will do for you. |
| T-14 ........X.2:1 | In Heaven **r**. is shared and not reflected. |
| T-14 ........X.2:3 | be satisfied with anything but his own **r**.. |
| T-15 ...... V.2:7 | Father and His Son, and thus to attack **r**.. |
| T-15 ...... V.3:1 | of **r**. and understand what love means. If |
| T-15 ...... V.7:2 | aspect. Thus does it assemble **r**. to its own |
| T-15 ...... V.7:3 | and so, however much you seek for its **r**., |
| T-15 ...... VI.6:2 | veil that has been drawn across **r**. is lifted. |
| T-15 ..... VII.6:4 | Yet the ego acknowledges "**r**." as it sees it, |
| T-15 ..... IX.7:5 | The **r**. of this relationship becomes the |
| T-15 ..... XI.5:1 | long as you perceive the body as your **r**., |
| T-15 ..... XI.5:5 | is the belief in the **r**. of the deprivation? |
| T-16 ........II.4:5 | to convince you of the **r**. of what has |
| T-16 ........II.5:1 | How can faith in **r**. be yours while you are |
| T-16 ........II.5:2 | you really safer in maintaining the **r**. of |
| T-16 ........II.5:6 | witnesses that He has given you to His **r**.. |
| T-16 ........II.8:5 | is not real and that **r**. is not disaster. |
| T-16 ........II.8:6 | **R**. is safe and sure, and wholly kind to |
| T-16 ........ IV.h | The Illusion and the **R**. of Love |
| T-16 ...... IV.2:6 | illusion of love will never satisfy, but its **r**., |
| T-16 ...... IV.6:6 | the illusion of love, but only from its **r**.. |
| T-16 ...... V.9:4 | is to destroy **r**. and substitute illusion. For |
| T-16 ...... V.9:5 | illusions can be the witnesses to its "**r**.." |
| T-16 ..... V.17:2 | You will cross the bridge into **r**. simply |
| T-16 ...... VI.7:1 | than a transition in the perspective of **r**.. |
| T-16 ...... VI.8:1 | be abruptly lifted up and hurled into **r**.. |
| T-16 ...... VI.8:2 | is kind, and if you use it on behalf of **r**., it |
| T-16 ...... VI.9:3 | the Thought of your **r**. to enter your mind |
| T-16 ..... VII.8:2 | have no **r**. apart from your receiving them |
| T-16 ..... VII.9:1 | There is nothing you can hold against **r**.. |
| T-16 ..... VII.9:3 | Their **r**. has no past, and only illusions |
| T-16 .. VII.11:4 | **r**. to give over all illusions for the reality |
| T-16 .. VII.11:4 | for the **r**. of your relationship with God. |
| T-17 .........I.1:2 | His **r**. is forever sinless. He need not be |
| T-17 .........I.1:6 | what they are *because* of their illusion of **r**.. |
| T-17 .........I.1:7 | that they had no effect upon **r**. at all, and |
| T-17 .........I.1:8 | Fantasies change **r**.. That is their purpose. |
| T-17 .......I.1:10 | They cannot do so in **r**., but they *can* do so |
| T-17 .......I.1:10 | the mind that would have **r**. be different. |
| T-17 .........I.2:1 | only your wish to change **r**. that is fearful, |
| T-17 .........I.3:3 | to retain some aspects of **r**. for fantasy. If |
| T-17 .........I.3:6 | that your perspective on **r**. be warped and |
| T-17 .........I.4:2 | established this order in **r**. by giving some |
| T-17 .........I.4:5 | **r**. is a perspective without understanding; |
| T-17 .........I.4:5 | a frame of reference for **r**. to which it |
| T-17 .........I.5:6 | establish orders of **r**. that must imprison |
| T-17 .........I.5:7 | you. There is no order in **r**., because |
| T-17 ...... III.1:4 | would make immortal are "enemies" of **r**. |
| T-17 ...... III.4:5 | which the **r**. of the other does not enter at |
| T-17 ...... III.5:1 | whose only purpose is separation from **r**.? |
| T-17 ...... III.5:6 | its **r**. and its value in your perception of it. |
| T-17 ...... III.8:5 | offer to the present as witnesses for its **r**.. |
| T-17 ...... III.8:6 | is kept but witnesses to the **r**. of dreams. |
| T-17 ...... III.9:3 | choose you will endow with beauty and **r**., |
| T-17 ... III.10:2 | let me bring **r**. to your perception of your |
| T-17 ... IV.15:2 | you realize that it is not a picture, but a **r**.. |
| T-17 ... IV.16:7 | The whole **r**. of your relationship with |
| T-17 ..... VII.4:5 | The goal's **r**. will call this forth, for you |
| T-17 ..... VII.6:6 | goal's **r**. will call forth and accomplish |
| T-17 ... VIII.3:4 | His purpose, and demonstrating its **r**.. |
| T-17 ... VIII.4:6 | to give faith to truth, and see its evident **r**. |
| T-18 ............I.h | The Substitute **R**. |
| T-18 .........I.5:1 | how very different is **r**. from what you see. |
| T-18 .........I.6:8 | for guilt implies it was accomplished in **r**.. |
| T-18 .........I.9:2 | have nothing in common in **r**.. Within |
| T-18 ........I.10:2 | Your **r**. was God's creation, and has no |
| T-18 ........I.10:9 | His gift as our most holy and perfect **r**., |
| T-18 ........II.2:3 | because the fact that **r**. is so outrageously |
| T-18 ........II.2:5 | both of the ego's inability to tolerate **r**., |
| T-18 ........II.2:5 | your willingness to change **r**. on its behalf |
| T-18 ........II.4:5 | your ability to control **r**. by substituting a |
| T-18 ........II.4:6 | attempts to blot out **r**. are very fearful, |
| T-18 ........II.4:7 | you substitute the fantasy that **r**. is fearful |
| T-18 ......II.5:15 | They are your protest against **r**., and your |
| T-18 ........II.9:6 | of waking is easily transferred to its **r**.. For |
| T-18 ...... III.1:1 | in bringing truth to illusion, **r**. to fantasy, |
| T-18 ...... IV.8:6 | It never happened in **r**.. Only in your |
| T-18 ...... VI.9:4 | This is not his **r**., though he believes it is. |
| T-18 ...... VI.9:7 | and to establish different orders of **r**., |
| T-18 . VI.11:10 | fear to peace, asking no questions of **r**., |
| T-18 ...... IX.5:2 | For the **r**. of guilt is the illusion that seems |
| T-19 .......I.5:10 | a means for seeking out **r**. through attack. |
| T-19 .........I.6:2 | divided goal has given both an equal **r**., |
| T-19 ........II.2:2 | lacks. To sin would be to violate **r**., and to |
| T-19 ........II.3:3 | that would really change his **r**. in any way, |
| T-19 ........II.4:3 | that replaces the **r**. of the Son of God as |
| T-19 ........II.7:3 | For this is its **r**.; this is the "truth" from |
| T-19 ...... III.7:1 | While you believe that your **r**. or your |
| T19 .IV.A.13:1 | world, to feast upon it and to prey upon **r**. |
| T-20 ...... III.1:3 | calls upon defenses to uphold it against **r**. |
| T-20 ...... VI.5:3 | Here the unholy relationship escapes **r**., |
| T-20 ...... VI.8:7 | the mad idea and give it the illusion of **r**.. |
| T-20 ...... VI.8:9 | this mad idea against **r**. but for an instant |
| T-20 ... VI.10:1 | the Son of God has with his Father in **r**.. |
| T-20 ..... VII.6:4 | hold about him are not held up to his **r**.. |
| T-20 ..... VII.6:5 | Here are illusions and **r**. kept separated. |
| T-20 ..... VII.6:7 | is your brother's **r**. imagined as a body, in |
| T-20 ..... VII.8:6 | sin. And thus it leads you to **r**.. Your holy |
| T-20 ... VIII.9:6 | to sin and seems to witness to its **r**.. It still |
| T-20 . VIII.10:7 | you that it is not **r**. which frightens you, |
| T-21 ........II.7:4 | to tell you what must happen, you give **r**.. |
| T-21 ........II.9:3 | of **r**. to make it fit the goal of madness. |
| T-21 ........II.9:6 | And if its **r**. is false, you will uphold it by |
| T-21 ......II.13:2 | otherwise, and you deny your whole **r**.. |
| T-21 ...... III.1:2 | goal. For they are bargains with **r**., toward |
| T-21 ......V.1:10 | is a witness but to this, and never to **r**.. |
| T-21 ......V.1:11 | in which awareness of **r**. is possible, or |
| T-21 ........V.2:1 | **R**. needs no cooperation from you to be |
| T-21 ........V.2:8 | believe because it is your faith it makes **r**.. |
| T-21 ... VI.11:1 | the Son of God is not a threat to his **r**.. It |
| T-22 ...... in.3:6 | denies not his own **r**. *because* it is the truth |
| T-22 ...... III.7:3 | could not be **r**. *because* it can be changed. |
| T-22 ...... III.7:4 | that if form is not **r**. it must be an illusion, |
| T-22 ........V.1:3 | reason tell you that they contradict **r**.. |
| T-22 ........V.1:5 | opposition comes from them, and not **r**.. |
| T-22 ........V.1:6 | **R**. opposes nothing. What merely is |
| T-22 . VI.12:11 | You would not choose attack on its **r**. if it |
| T-23 .........I.6:7 | Madness holds out no menace to **r**., and |
| T-23 .........I.6:9 | the **r**. that they deny is not a part of them. |
| T-23 .........I.8:7 | of nothing cannot win **r**. through battle. |
| T-23 ........II.6:2 | define what the Creator of **r**. must be; |
| T-23 ......II.20:7 | in love, in any form, attests to chaos as **r**.. |
| T-24 .........I.1:6 | it has given it all the **r**. it seems to have. |
| T-24 .........I.2:8 | All that can be denied is their **r**., but not |
| T-24 .........I.3:2 | but always clashes with the **r**. of God's |
| T-24 .........I.3:6 | of any kind imposes orders of **r**., and a |
| T-24 ...... III.7:5 | because He did not make their dream **r**.. |
| T-24 ...... IV.4:8 | If he is sinful, then is your **r**. not real, but |
| T-24 ...... IV.5:2 | in **r**.: When peace is not with you entirely, |
| T-24 ...... VI.2:2 | There could be no universe and no **r**.. For |
| T-24 ..... VII.6:3 | meaning of itself, yet you can give **r**. to it, |
| T-24 ..... VII.9:8 | it makes. It proves its own **r**. to you. |
| T-24 VII.10:10 | that made it, and speak for its **r**. and truth |
| T-24 VII.11:13 | purpose well, and prove its own **r**. to you. |
| T-26 .........I.6:1 | but can not make sacrifice of its **r**.. Nor |
| T-26 .........I.8:2 | Could it be that you could make his sins **r**. |
| T-26 ...... III.1:3 | He knows of one creation, one **r**., one |
| T-26 ...... III.3:3 | here, in that the words imply a limited **r**., |
| T-26 ...... III.7:7 | all **r**. has been withdrawn from what was |
| T-26 ...... VI.1:5 | And through its perceived **r**. has entered |
| T-26 ..... VII.4:6 | it is real, and dwells where all **r**. must be. |
| T-26 ..... VII.6:5 | of illusions can show is preference, not **r**.. |
| T-26 ..... VII.6:8 | Your preference gives them no **r**.. Not one |
| T-26 ..... VII.7:5 | proclaiming sin has taken His **r**. from |
| T-27 ...... III.2:8 | interfere with the awareness of **r**. is the |
| T-27 ...... III.5:2 | **R**. is ultimately known without a form, |
| T-27 ...... VI.3:4 | when you call forth the witnesses to its **r**.. |
| T-27 ...... VI.4:2 | names that speak in other ways for its **r**.. |
| T-27 ..... VII.7:7 | and their **r**. does not depend on him. |
| T-27 ..... VII.7:9 | He cannot doubt his dreams' **r**., because |
| T-27 .. VII.10:1 | peace or war, your dreams or your **r**.? |
| T-27 .. VII.11:4 | The gap between **r**. and dreams lies not |
| T-27 .. VII.12:3 | between your little dreams and your **r**.. |
| T-27 .. VII.13:4 | waken to **r**. without the sweat of terror |
| T-28 .......I.15:3 | and **r**. than to allow the memory of God |

| | |
|---|---|
| T-28......IV.3:2 | for your Identity depends on his **r.**. Think |
| T-28......IV.3:5 | It is his **r.** that is your brother, as is yours |
| T-28......IV.5:2 | must believe that it is your **r.** as well as his |
| T-28.......V.6:1 | Creation proves **r.** because it shares the |
| T-28.......V.6:3 | **R.** does not depend on this. There is no |
| T-29......III.1:2 | For beyond his dreams is his **r.**. But he |
| T-29......III.2:5 | in the dream His Son prefers to his **r.**. He |
| T-29.....VII.9:7 | It is not the fear of loss of your **r.**. But you |
| T-29.....VII.9:8 | But you have made of your **r.** an idol, |
| T-29... VIII.2:2 | Idols are but substitutes for your **r.**. In |
| T-29... VIII.8:5 | might offer him a gift **r.** does not contain. |
| T-29......IX.5:6 | And their **r.** becomes his own, because |
| T-30....III.10:4 | Here is your one **r.** kept safe, completely |
| T-30....III.11:2 | Is your **r.** a thing apart from you, and in a |
| T-30....III.11:2 | in a world which your **r.** knows nothing of |
| T-30....III.11:3 | eternal sky, no changeless star and no **r.**. |
| T-30....III.11:7 | *or* the Thought God holds of you is your **r.**. |
| T-30..III.11:10 | of God Himself, are unaware of your **r.**. |
| T-30......IV.4:1 | **R.** observes the laws of God, and not the |
| T-30......IV.5:1 | *because* they are appearances and not **r.**. |
| T-30......IV.5:3 | They but obscure **r.**, and they bring fear |
| T-30......IV.7:3 | and not to look upon the unreal as **r.**. You |
| T-30......IV.8:5 | It asks for nothing in **r.**. And even in |
| T-30.......V.7:3 | been surely set away from idols toward **r.**. |
| T-30...... VIII.h | Changeless **R.** |
| T-30... VIII.1:2 | **R.** is changeless. It does not deceive at all, |
| T-30... VIII.1:5 | **R.** is thus reduced to form, and capable of |
| T-30... VIII.1:6 | **R.** is changeless. It is this that makes it |
| T-30... VIII.2:1 | cannot have the changelessness **r.** entails. |
| T-30... VIII.2:4 | views of him that you perceive as his **r.**. |
| T-30... VIII.2:7 | never real, and could not stem from his **r.**. |
| T-30... VIII.3:2 | not seem to be the wish that no **r.** be so. |
| T-30... VIII.3:3 | than those you would not want to have **r.**. |
| T-30... VIII.3:4 | obscure and give to them **r.** instead. And |
| T-30... VIII.4:1 | **R.** is changeless. Miracles but show what |
| T-30... VIII.4:2 | between **r.** and your awareness is unreal, |
| T-30... VIII.4:8 | When he is tempted, he denies **r.**. And he |
| T-30... VIII.5:1 | *Because* **r.** is changeless is a miracle |
| T-31......III.2:2 | if you did not believe that they are your **r.** |
| T-31....IV.10:8 | there without your own **r.** at one with you |
| T-31.......V.1:1 | of the self adjusted to the world's **r.**. It fits |
| T-31.......V.2:3 | to take the place of your **r.** as Son of God. |
| T-31.......V.4:4 | sights, for it is here the world's "**r.**" is set, |
| T-31......VI.1:7 | never will escape the body as your own **r.**, |
| W-pI.....10.2:4 | the lack of **r.** of what you think you think. |
| W-pI.....14.1:4 | world you see has nothing to do with **r.**. It |
| W-pI.....14.4:2 | as it occurs to you, and then deny its **r.**. |
| W-pI.....17.1:5 | cause, and would itself be the cause of **r.**. |
| W-pI.....23.3:2 | Each of your perceptions of "external **r.**" |
| W-pI.....29.4:3 | any order you impose is equally alien to **r.** |
| W-pI.....35.5:4 | Illusions have no direction in **r.**. They are |
| W-pI.....41.2:2 | not do is to question the **r.** of the problem |
| W-pI.....41.7:4 | to leave appearances and approach **r.**. |
| W-pI.....49.2:3 | and distraught, but without **r.** of any kind |
| W-pI.....51.2:4 | It is merely an illusion of **r.**, because my |
| W-pI.....51.2:4 | have been made quite apart from **r.**. I am |
| W-pI.....52.1:2 | **R.** is never frightening. It is impossible |
| W-pI.....52.1:4 | **R.** brings only perfect peace. When I am |
| W-pI.....52.1:5 | it is always because I have replaced **r.** with |
| W-pI.....52.1:6 | are upsetting because I have given them **r.** |
| W-pI.....52.1:6 | reality, and thus regard **r.** as an illusion. |
| W-pI.....53.1:4 | **R.** is not insane, and I have real thoughts |
| W-pI.....53.3:6 | I have given it the illusion of **r.**, and have |
| W-pI.....53.3:7 | this belief, and place my trust in **r.**. In |
| W-pI.....67.2:1 | we will think about your **r.** and its wholly |
| W-pI.....69.5:2 | The clouds seem to be the only **r.**. They |
| W-pI.....72.5:4 | The body's apparent **r.** makes this view of |
| W-pI.....73.2:4 | your awareness and your brothers' **r.**. |
| W-pI.....74.5:1 | the peace to which your **r.** entitles you. |
| W-pI.....78.7:1 | knows this Son of God in his **r.** and truth, |
| W-pI.....79.8:3 | about the **r.** of your version of what your |
| W-pI.....84.1:5 | I would recognize my **r.** today. I will |
| W-pI.....91.2:9 | And the seeming **r.** of the darkness makes |
| W-pI.....91.3:4 | not doubt the images they show you are **r.** |
| W-pI.....91.8:8 | *I am not an illusion, but a* **r.**. *I cannot see in* |
| W-pI.....94.3:6 | sinned, nor made an image to replace **r.**. |
| W-pI.....96.3:7 | the body must be meaningless to your **r.**. |
| W-pI.....97.3:1 | we try to bring **r.** still closer to your mind. |
| W-pI.....98.3:2 | escapes from fancied threats without **r.**. |
| W-pI...103.2:2 | These images, with no **r.** in truth, bear |
| W-pI...110.1:3 | made no changes in yourself that have **r.**, |
| W-pI...124.7:5 | the world may share our recognition of **r.**. |
| W-pI...127.9:3 | dark illusion of your own **r.** and what love |
| W-pI...130.2:2 | desire what he does not want to have **r.**? |
| W-pI.132.15:3 | *world is not, and I would know my own* **r.**. |
| W-pI.132.17:2 | *it was, and choose my own* **r.** *instead.* |
| W-pI.134.13:3 | It is as alien to the world as is your own **r.**. |
| W-pI.134.13:4 | yet it joins your mind with the **r.** in you. |
| W-pI.134.14:2 | meet with our **r.** in freedom and in peace. |
| W-pI.134.14:3 | will follow us to the **r.** we share with them |
| W-pI...135.1:2 | the folly of defense; it gives illusions full **r.** |
| W-pI.135.14:3 | take, where the denial of **r.** is very obvious |
| W-pI.135.17:2 | incompatible with your beliefs of your **r.**. |
| W-pI.135.17:4 | For it is your **r.** that is the "threat" which |
| W-pI.135.26:8 | *needs no defense against the truth of his* **r.**. |
| W-pI...136.2:3 | like all the rest, its purpose is to hide **r.**, |
| W-pI...136.5:1 | the part you play in making your "**r.**" that |
| W-pI...137.6:4 | while fear remains the one **r.** that can be |
| W-pI.139.10:2 | accept Atonement, not to change **r.**, but |
| W-pI...140.2:5 | does the content of a dream make in **r.**? |
| W-pI...140.7:6 | in attributes that have no substance, no **r.** |
| W-pI...151.3:6 | You think your fingers touch **r.**, and close |
| W-pI...151.5:3 | **r.** with such conviction it does not believe |
| W-pI...151.9:2 | the Mind Whose Thought created your **r.**. |
| W-pI...152.1:7 | Here is its whole **r.** for you. And it is only |
| W-pI...152.6:5 | a world where such things seem to have **r.** |
| W-pI...154.4:4 | Self the one **r.** in which its will and that of |
| W-pI...155.2:2 | can be illusions, and avoid their own **r.**. |
| W-pI...155.2:3 | when they find their own **r.** is even here, |
| W-pI...155.4:2 | the world while still believing its **r.**. And |
| W-pI...160.7:7 | between His knowledge and His Son's **r.**. |
| W-pI...161.9:2 | This is his **r.**. And in Christ's vision is his |
| W-pI...166.7:1 | the one you made as a replacement for **r.**. |
| W-pI...183.8:1 | acknowledge Him as sole Creator of **r.**. |
| W-pI...184.3:3 | names, and thus **r.** was given them as well |
| W-pI...184.4:1 | is the way **r.** is made by partial vision, |
| W-pI...184.6:6 | true is but illusion, for it is the ultimate **r.**. |
| W-pI.184.11:2 | Yet accept them not as your **r.**. The Holy |
| W-pI.184.13:3 | first you must accept the Name for all **r.**, |
| W-pI.184.15:3 | *we have tried to cast across Your Own* **r.**. |
| W-pI...189.8:8 | in that way is your **r.** proclaimed as well. |
| W-pI.190.10:4 | It is this: Pain is illusion; joy, **r.**. Pain is |
| W-pI...200.7:3 | It cannot have **r.**, because it never was |
| W-pI...200.9:7 | apart from God, where bodies have **r.**. |
| W-pII......1.3:4 | sets about its furious attempts to smash **r.** |
| W-pII......1.4:2 | It offends no aspect of **r.**, nor seeks to |
| W-pII..224.1:5 | This is **r.**, and only this. This is illusion's |
| W-pII..227.1:4 | *did not affect my own* **r.** *at all by my illusions.* |
| W-pII..248.1:6 | What dies was never living in **r.**, and did |
| W-pII......4.3:2 | are the "proof" that what has no **r.** is real. |
| W-pII..268.2:2 | Only **r.** is free of pain. Only reality is free |
| W-pII..268.2:3 | pain. Only **r.** is free of loss. Only reality is |
| W-pII..268.2:4 | Only **r.** is wholly safe. And it is only this |
| W-pII.......6.3:2 | is the only part of you that has **r.** in truth. |
| W-pII..278.1:4 | And I am lost to all **r.**. For truth is free, |
| W-pII..279.1:3 | Yet in **r.** his dreams are gone, with truth |
| W-pII......7.1:2 | bridge the gap between **r.** and dreams, |
| W-pII..298.1:2 | And thus am I restored to my **r.** at last. |
| W-pII..322.2:4 | *What You did not give has no* **r.**. *What loss* |
| W-pII.....12.4:1 | To know **r.** is not to see the ego and its |
| W-pII..333.1:3 | to be, in the **r.** which has been given it, |
| W-pII..350.2:2 | Son will be restored to us in the **r.** of Love. |
| Wfl........in.4:1 | is given us to be His Own completion in **r.** |
| W-ep.........3:2 | retire from the world, to seek **r.** instead. |
| M-2...........2:5 | So is all **r.**, being of Him. The instant the |
| M-2...........2:8 | long ago. In **r.** it never happened at all. |
| M-3...........3:1 | is a concept as meaningless in **r.** as is time |
| M-4.....I.A.4:6 | any degree of **r.** should be accorded them |
| M-8...........3:6 | as "**r.**" is simply what the mind prefers. |
| M-8...........6:7 | Just as **r.** is wholly real, apart from size |
| M-12.........3:2 | Only because **r.** is not understandable to |
| M-13.........1:4 | illusion, for in **r.** there is nothing to learn. |
| M-17.........9:7 | that anger recognizes a **r.** that is not there |
| M-18.........1:2 | its falsity, he is but witnessing to its **r.**. |
| M-18.........1:5 | **R.** is changeless. Magic thoughts are but |
| M-18.........2:3 | can now speak of the **r.** of the Son of God. |
| M-18.........3:2 | **R.** is blotted out as this insane belief is |
| M-18.........3:4 | and tiny breath become the measure of **r.**. |
| M-18.........3:9 | *nor has* **r.** *been taken from its throne by your* |
| M-20.........4:3 | War is again accepted as the one **r.**. Now |
| M-20.........6:4 | His Will and yours but seemed to be **r.**. In |
| M-21.......1:10 | They are thus twice removed from **r.**. |
| M-27.........4:4 | But if there is **r.** in life, death is denied. |
| M-27.........5:1 | "**r.**" of death is firmly rooted in the belief |
| M-27.........7:5 | deceived by the "**r.**" of any changing form |
| C-2............1:7 | It is a thing of madness, not **r.** at all. A |
| C-4............2:1 | upon must lead to more illusions of **r.**. |
| C-5............1:2 | God alone established in **r.**. Helpers are |
| C-6............1:5 | This form is not His **r.**, which God alone |
| C-ep...........1:8 | each one there is **r.** and there is God. Why |
| P-in............1:5 | individual can begin to question their **r.**. |
| P-in............1:8 | to change his mind about the "**r.**" of |
| P-2.........in.1:2 | can hardly be expected to establish **r.**. |
| P-2.........in.1:4 | If it can make way for **r.**, it has achieved |
| P-2........IV.6:6 | **r.** now becomes a threat and is perceived |
| P-2........IV.6:7 | Love becomes feared because **r.** is love. |
| P-2........IV.7:3 | in truth, for to overlook **r.** is insanity. Yet |
| S-2.........I.10:2 | instant while this world retains **r.** for you. |
| S-3...........I.1:2 | thought that seems to have **r.** and to be |

## realization 15

| | |
|---|---|
| T-2.......VII.2:2 | me. Miracle working entails a full **r.** of the |
| T-4....... II.11:3 | **r.** that *all* perception is unnecessary. This |
| T-10.........I.1:7 | the **r.** that your banishment is not of God, |
| T-11...... IV.4:2 | Do not oppose this **r.**, for it is truly the |
| T-13........II.3:2 | is the **r.** that you have betrayed God's Son |
| T-18.... IV.1:10 | It is your **r.** that you need do so little that |
| T-18...... VI.1:2 | for it is the **r.** that the Kingdom of Heaven |
| T-18..... VII.5:7 | it always comes with just one happy **r.**; |
| W-pI.....69.3:1 | period today with the full **r.** that this is so, |
| W-pI.....70.3:1 | entails the **r.** that salvation is there as well |
| M-22.........2:5 | necessary **r.** of inclusiveness may reach |
| M-27.........7:8 | the **r.** that the Son of God is guiltless now |
| P-2...........I.1:2 | Therapy begins with the **r.** that healing is |
| P-2........IV.3:7 | heal the sick is but to bring this **r.** to them |
| P-2........VI.6:1 | This **r.** is the final goal of psychotherapy. |

## realize 220

| | |
|---|---|
| T-1........IV.2:2 | you **r.** in your heart it *is* a deception, and |
| T-2...........I.4:4 | enables you to **r.** that your errors never |
| T-2........III.1:7 | to **r.** that a temple is not a structure at all. |
| T-2........VI.9:2 | little right thinking to **r.** why fear occurs. |
| T-2........VI.9:4 | fear there are some things you must **r.**, |
| T-2........VI.9:4 | some things you must realize, and **r.** fully. |
| T-3...........I.4:4 | to **r.** that this applies to themselves. Good |
| T-3...........I.8:3 | Son as he is, you **r.** that the Atonement, |
| T-3..........II.1:5 | essential that you **r.** your thinking will be |
| T-3........IV.3:9 | until you **r.** that you did not and could |
| T-3........VI.3:2 | you will **r.** that judging them in any way is |
| T-3.......VII.1:8 | It is essential to **r.** this, because otherwise |
| T-3.......VII.2:3 | You also **r.** that you cannot weaken it, any |
| T-3.......VII.5:4 | But **r.** that this making will surely dissolve |
| T-4...........I.8:3 | in your right mind you **r.** it is not real. |
| T-4..........II.2:4 | is important to **r.** that this alteration can |
| T-4........IV.4:1 | anxious, **r.** that anxiety comes from the |
| T-4........VI.1:4 | and must **r.** how much of your thinking is |
| T-5........IV.2:8 | having made them you did not **r.** how to |
| T-5.......VII.6:2 | **r.** that you must already have decided not |
| T-6...........I.6:3 | to teach if he is to **r.** his own salvation. |
| T-6...........I.6:4 | in you, and **r.** that it cannot *be* assailed. Do |
| T-6......V.B.2:1 | teachers **r.** that only fundamental change |
| T-6......V.B.6:4 | As you begin to **r.** the quiet power of the |
| T-7........VI.6:5 | conflict; He wants you to **r.** that, because |
| T-7......VIII.6:3 | the more you **r.** that it cannot be believed. |
| T-8.........V.2:9 | You will **r.** this when you understand that |
| T-8......VIII.4:1 | because you do not **r.** that it is entirely |
| T-8........IX.8:1 | have surely begun to **r.** that this is a very |
| T-9........IV.8:5 | true that you do not **r.** the guide is insane. |
| T-9........IV.8:6 | You **r.** it because I realize it, and you have |
| T-9........IV.8:6 | You realize it because I **r.** it, and you have |
| T-9.......VII.4:2 | not yet **r.** how completely different these |
| T-10.........in.3:8 | and you will **r.** how much is up to you. |
| T-10.........I.2:4 | instant you waken you **r.** that everything |
| T-10.........II.4:4 | is God, you will **r.** why it is always fearful. |
| T-10.... III.10:4 | not **r.** how much you listen to your gods, |

T-10....... V.1:5 They do not **r.** that to deny God is to deny
T-10..... V.10:1 not **r.** how much you have denied yourself
T-11.......in.1:2 sides fairly, you will **r.** this must be true.
T-11.........I.8:2 when you **r.** that to deny is to "not know."
T-11...... IV.4:6 to **r.** that this is exactly the same thing, for
T-11....... V.1:3 it, and since you **r.** you do not want it, you
T-11....... V.8:1 wishes you to **r.** is that you are afraid of it.
T-11....... V.8:5 can its existence continue if you **r.** that, by
T-11... V.12:10 the sane **r.** that only attack could produce
T-11....VIII.1:5 but an instant to **r.** that this alone is true.
T-12...... III.6:4 He does not **r.** this. Even if he is fully
T-12...... III.6:7 He does not **r.** that he makes this world,
T-12... III.7:10 That is why you must **r.** that your hatred
T-12...... IV.2:6 will surely do so when you **r.** exactly what
T-12...... IV.4:1 Do you **r.** that the ego must set you on a
T-12...... IV.5:2 home whether you **r.** where it is or not. If
T-12....... V.2:5 Once you **r.** this you will no longer see
T-12....... V.3:1 will never **r.** the utter uselessness of attack
T-12...... V.7:11 But perhaps you do not **r.**, even yet, that
T-12..... VII.4:2 unless you do, you will not **r.** He is there.
T-12... VII.15:2 You will **r.** that this is true when you look
T-13.......in.2:3 at this world, and you will **r.** that this is so
T-13.......in.4:2 you **r.** that God's Son cannot be crucified,
T-13.......in.4:3 will not **r.** this until you accept the eternal
T-13.........I.6:1 you will **r.** there is no guilt in God's Son.
T-13.........I.7:1 you, you will **r.** that there is no journey,
T-13....... II.2:6 you do not **r.** that you are failing yourself.
T-13....... II.7:6 **r.** that it is only your guiltlessness that *can*
T-13...... III.1:1 upon your hatred and **r.** its full extent.
T-13...... III.2:6 You **r.** that, by removing the dark cloud
T-13... VII.12:6 and **r.** that all of them have been fulfilled.
T-13... VIII.7:5 all of it need only **r.** that it is of the Father,
T-13....... X.8:6 The moment that you **r.** guilt is insane,
T-13...... XI.1:4 Yet if he could but **r.** the war is between
T-13...... XI.6:7 to help you **r.** that this is what you want,
T-14.........I.2:2 will perceive the need for this if you **r.**
T-14....... II.1:5 **r.** that the foundation on which this most
T-14....... II.7:9 you do not **r.** the light has come and freed
T-14....... II.8:5 **r.** it is impossible to deny the simple truth
T-14....... V.5:6 **r.** that only in this exchange can freedom
T-14...... VI.4:5 do not **r.** that only one means anything.
T-14..... VII.4:2 You will **r.** that salvation must come to
T-14...... IX.7:1 **r.** for a single instant the power of healing
T-14.... XI.13:4 Whenever you fully **r.** that you know not,
T-15...... II.4:1 not **r.** how much you have misused your
T-15...... III.2:1 Yet what you do not **r.**, each time you
T-15...... III.3:2 to love it when you **r.** that it is true and is
T-15..... VII.9:7 what the ego really wants you do not **r.**.
T-15...... XI.7:3 you will **r.** that to sacrifice the body is to
T-16...... III.1:3 will be compelled to **r.** that your Teacher
T-16...... IV.1:9 of the split that lies in this you do not **r.**.
T-16....... V.1:1 necessary first to **r.** that it involves a great
T-16....... V.2:4 it and why, you will **r.** what it must be.
T-16...... VI.6:5 will **r.** that the only value the body has is
T-16...... VI.8:6 than before, only because you **r.** it *is* delay,
T-17...... III.2:9 may not **r.** are all the reasons that go to
T-17...... III.7:9 be sure you fully **r.** what you have made
T-17...... IV.5:2 It does not **r.** that it is totally insane. And
T-17...... IV.5:3 must **r.** just what this means if you would
T-17...... IV.7:1 is essential to **r.** that all defenses *do* what
T-17.... IV.9:11 picture, and **r.** that death is offered you.
T-17.... IV.11:6 you will **r.** that it was only the frame that
T-17.... IV.15:2 look on this, you **r.** that it is not a picture,
T-17..... V.13:2 result, you do not **r.** that it is with you still
T-17...... VI.1:6 but remember that you do not yet **r.** their
T-17.... VIII.3:7 is enormous, and far greater than you **r.**.
T-17.... VIII.5:6 for it has been given you to **r.** what your
T-18.........I.5:2 do not **r.** the magnitude of that one error.
T-18....... II.3:8 You do not **r.** you are attacking it, trying
T-18....... II.5:4 **r.** that the emotions the dream produces
T-18....... II.5:6 You do not **r.** that you are making them
T-18...... III.3:6 do not **r.** that you are not afraid of love,
T-18...... IV.1:5 that you **r.** that you cannot do more. Do
T-18...... IV.7:4 very hard for you to **r.** it is not personally
T-18....... V.4:5 You do not even **r.** you have accepted the
T-18...... VI.2:4 have done a stranger thing than you yet **r.**
T-18.... VI.11:4 you will **r.** that it is a sudden unawareness
T-18.... VIII.8:7 **r.** the life and joy that love would bring to
T-19.........I.5:1 It cannot be difficult to **r.** that faith must
T-19 ......I.14:4 And there it is that you will **r.** that there is
T-19 ..... III.8:6 you do not **r.** that its foundation has gone
T19..IV.B.17:1 to the ego's disciples to **r.** that they have
T19... IV.D.6:4 For you **r.** that if you look on this and let
T19. IV.D.10:6 unless you **r.** its purpose is accomplished?
T-20 ..... VI.6:8 **r.** is what you fear within your brother,
T-21 ... III.10:1 you do not **r.** you cannot see because of it.
T-21 ...... V.1:8 depends far more than you may **r.** as yet.
T-21 ...... V.4:1 You do not **r.** the whole extent to which
T-21 ...... V.8:7 uses it, because it does not **r.** that it exists.
T-22 ..... IV.3:4 nor **r.** how thin the drapery that separates
T-22 ... VI.14:5 you will **r.** that your relationship is a
T-23 ......in.5:7 and **r.** that Heaven's glory shines on him?
T-23 ........I.1:7 Surely you **r.** the ego is at war with God.
T-23 ........I.2:1 **r.** a war against yourself would be a war
T-23 ...II.13:13 as certain that you **r.** the goal is madness?
T-23 ..... IV.1:8 But you are asked to **r.** the form it takes
T-23 ..... IV.4:6 **r.** that murder in any form is not your will
T-23 ..... IV.5:9 it is over when you **r.** it never was begun.
T-24 ...... V.2:3 does not **r.** he picked a thread from here,
T-24 ..... VI.8:5 until you **r.** that it is not a part of him who
T-24 ... VI.10:1 not gladly **r.** these laws are not for you?
T-25 .......II.2:3 long is needed for you to **r.** the chance of
T-25 .... VII.2:8 If you could **r.** nothing is changeless but
T-26 .......X.1:1 to be undone for you to **r.** Their Presence?
T-27 ........I.2:3 and need but look on you to **r.** that he has
T-28 ........I.4:3 it is hard for you to **r.** it is a skill that can
T-29 .......II.1:5 Until you **r.** you give up nothing, until
T-30 ........I.6:2 Then **r.** that you have asked a question by
T-30 ........I.7:5 This can be very hard to **r.**, when once
T-31 ..... III.1:4 shortened by a span of time you cannot **r.**
T-31 ...... V.8:2 its roads nor **r.** the way you see yourself.
W-pI....... 3.2:1 and to **r.** how little you really understand
W-pI..... 24.1:1 In no situation that arises do you **r.** the
W-pI..... 24.4:3 will quickly **r.** that you have a number of
W-pI..... 30.3:2 and trying to **r.** that the idea applies to
W-pI..... 45.8:6 as yet to **r.** how high you are trying to go.
W-pI..... 56.2:2 I am, I **r.** that vision is my greatest need.
W-pI..... 57.4:2 I **r.** that it reflects the laws of God instead
W-pI... 66.10:8 try today to **r.** that only the truth is true.
W-pI..... 67.1:6 reach this truth about you, and to **r.** fully,
W-pI..... 67.6:1 Try to **r.** in the shorter practice periods
W-pI..... 68.1:5 Perhaps you do not yet fully **r.** just what
W-pI..... 70.1:5 **r.** that all guilt is solely an invention of
W-pI..... 70.1:5 you also **r.** that guilt and salvation must
W-pI..... 71.1:1 You may not **r.** that the ego has set up a
W-pI..... 71.1:5 the ego's plan is, perhaps you will **r.** that,
W-pI..... 75.7:1 **R.** that your forgiveness entitles you to
W-pI..... 76.1:4 you must first **r.** salvation lies not there.
W-pI..... 76.6:2 until you **r.** it applies to everything that
W-pI..... 76.7:4 We **r.** instead it is a truth that keeps us
W-pI... 76.10:1 **r.** how foolish are the "laws" you thought
W-pI..... 79.7:4 try to **r.** that we have only one problem,
WpI..rII.in.4:2 **R.** that, whatever form such thoughts
W-pI..... 90.1:2 Let me **r.** today that the problem is always
W-pI..... 90.3:5 That is because I do not yet **r.** that God
W-pI..... 91.4:2 Did you but **r.** how great this strength,
W-pI..... 95.1:5 accept this, and you fail to **r.** it must be so
W-pI... 100.7:3 Then **r.** your part is to be happy. Only
W-pI... 102.2:1 further, and to **r.** that pain is purposeless,
W-pI... 123.1:4 gains, which are far greater than you **r.**.
W-pI... 123.7:2 And you will **r.** to Whom you offer thanks
W-pI... 126.9:3 means, and let you **r.** its worth to you.
W-pI... 129.8:5 day we **r.** that what you feared to lose was
W-pI. 131.13:3 will make you pause before you **r.** the
W-pI. 132.16:1 need not **r.** that healing comes to many
W-pI. 133.11:3 And thus you do not **r.** there are but two,
W-pI. 134.15:2 **r.** that you are using his "offenses" but to
W-pI. 135.14:1 the purpose all of them were made to **r.**.
W-pI. 135.14:3 This is not difficult to **r.** in some forms
W-pI. 135.21:3 but **r.** that our defenselessness is all that is
W-pI. 136.18:1 Perhaps you do not **r.** that this removes
W-pI. 137.10:2 **r.** how great your offering to all the world,
W-pI... 140.9:3 to the extent to which we **r.** that there can
W-pI... 153.5:4 not **r.** what you have done to sabotage the
W-pI. 153.11:2 have come to **r.** His Will is but their own.
W-pI. 154.14:1 minds, and **r.** these holy words are true.
W-pI... 166.4:4 not **r.** that it is here he is afraid indeed,
W-pI... 166.4:4 **r.** he has forgotten where he came from,
W-pI .. 166.6:3 and need but **r.** Who walks with him and
W-pI 184.13:3 **r.** the many names you gave its aspects
W-pI 190.10:3 when it is given you to **r.** the lesson that
W-pI .. 192.9:4 **r.** you hold a sword above your head. And
W-pI .. 196.1:2 you will **r.** that to attack another is but to
W-pI 196.10:2 When you **r.**, once and for all, that it is
W-pI .. 197.5:3 Yet you will never **r.** His gifts are sure,
W-pII . 228.2:1 *I failed to* **r.** *the Source from which I came. I*
W-pII . 282.1:1 I could **r.** but this today, salvation would
W-pII . 285.1:2 and **r.** my invitation will be answered by
W-pII . 332.1:8 giving it the means to **r.** the freedom that
W-pII ... 14.2:5 Yet we can **r.** our function here, and
M-2 ........... 3:5 then will you **r.** that it was always there.
M-4 .... IV.1:11 all, except by those who **r.** that harm can
M-5 ...... III.1:6 These patients do not **r.** they have chosen
M-10 ......... 2:1 It is necessary for the teacher of God to **r.**
M-12 ......... 3:4 to those who do not **r.** that they are spirit.
M-13 ......... 2:1 It takes great learning both to **r.** and to
M-14 ........ 5:10 and **r.** that all God would have you do you
M-18 ......... 4:2 let him instantly **r.** that he has made an
P-1............. 3:3 not **r.** and needs to learn is that this "self,
P-2.........in.1:6 extent he comes to **r.** that this is an error,
S-1...........I.1:3 until you **r.** that it asks for nothing. How
S-1........ III.6:1 It is not easy to **r.** that prayers for things,
S-1........ IV.2:6 and not **r.** that you are asking for effects

## realized 22

T-2 .........V.4:5 not **r.** that right-mindedness *is* healing.
T-10 .......II.6:1 If you **r.** the complete havoc this makes of
T-11 ..... IV.3:5 You would not do so if you **r.** that you can
T-14 ......in.1:7 we have **r.** that they cannot be seen except
T-16 .....V.17:3 to make the natural decision as this is **r.**.
T-17 ........I.3:4 **r.** what this must do to your appreciation
T-20 ... VIII.7:5 **r.** that those who seem to walk about in it,
T-21 ..... IV.6:6 have **r.** that all the gifts it would withdraw
T-22 ........I.3:1 **r.** it is impossible to understand what fails
T-23 .......II.3:3 If it were **r.** that they are all the same and
T-24 ........I.6:2 attack him if you **r.** you journey with him,
T-26 ..... VI.3:2 if you but **r.** its emptiness has left yours
T-28 .......II.5:3 must be **r.** that it is you who dreamed the
W-pI ...... 8.2:3 Very few have **r.** what is actually entailed
W-pI .... 24.2:1 **r.** that you do not perceive your own best
W-pI .... 51.5:5 I have not **r.** how much I have misused
W-pI .... 95.4:3 You have surely **r.** this by now. You have
M-4...... I.A.5:6 not **r.** as yet how wholly impossible such a
P-2...... IV.3:4 could have faith in them once this is **r.**?
P-3..........II.8:1 therapist has **r.** that minds are joined, he
S-1...........I.6:5 Him. One who has **r.** the goodness of God
S-1.........I.7:10 because you have **r.** that Christ is in both

## realizes 4

T-6 ....... IV.5:1 ego **r.** that its "enemy" can end them both
M-4 ..... VII.2:3 because he **r.** it would be valueless to him
M-8 ........... 5:7 **r.** they are all illusions they will disappear
P-2........ IV.3:5 not have faith in them until he **r.** this?

## realizing 19

T-2 ....... III.4:6 **r.** that it only adds unnecessary pain. As a
T-6 .........II.6:1 place except by **r.** that you are not there?
T-6 ..... V.B.9:4 **R.** that it *must* follow is a demonstration of
T-7 .........V.8:2 your brother by **r.** that he could not have
T-14 .......II.4:4 and **r.** that this light is not what you have
T-15 ..... XI.4:5 **r.** that they are where your invitation bids
T-17 ..... IV.6:1 little difficulty now in **r.** that the thought
T-18 . VIII.13:1 ancient journey, not **r.** yet that it is over.
T-21 .......II.9:6 is false, you will uphold it by not **r.** all the
W-pI .... 49.5:3 and **r.** that you are inviting God's Voice to
W-pI .... 51.1:5 I must let it go by **r.** it has no meaning, so
W-pI .... 52.3:6 **r.** that in so doing I am giving up nothing.
W-pI .... 70.5:1 Today we practice **r.** that God's Will and
W-pI .... 71.8:1 idea, and **r.** that it contains two parts,
W-pI .. 93.10:6 so to closing your eyes and **r.** that this is a
W-pI .... 98.2:6 washed away by **r.** they were but mistakes
W-pI .. 183.8:5 **r.** that there is one Name for all there is,
M-10 ......... 4:3 right, without ever **r.** you were wrong?
M-29 ......... 2:5 of God has come this far without **r.** that.

## really 359

| | |
|---|---|
| T-1........I.13:2 | which seem to go back but **r.** go forward. |
| T-1........I.31:2 | You should thank God for what you **r.** are |
| T-1........I.32:1 | all miracles, which are **r.** intercessions. |
| T-1........II.4:1 | except in time, and time does not **r.** exist. |
| T-1........III.5:1 | Error cannot **r.** threaten truth, which can |
| T-1........IV.2:1 | can never be **r.** hidden in darkness, but |
| T-1........VI.2:1 | God is the only lack you **r.** need correct. |
| T-2..........I.4:4 | realize that your errors never **r.** occurred. |
| T-2.........II.2:7 | the will is **r.** free it cannot miscreate, |
| T-2.........V.1:5 | miscreations of the mind do not **r.** exist. |
| T-2.........V.9:6 | Charity is **r.** a weaker reflection of a much |
| T-2........VII.5:3 | Fear is **r.** nothing and love is everything. |
| T-2.....VIII.5:3 | apparent that it is **r.** the doorway to life. |
| T-2.....VIII.5:4 | No one who lives in fear is **r.** alive. Your |
| T-3..........I.2:8 | you believe our Father **r.** thinks this way? |
| T-3........III.5:7 | **r.** confusing knowledge with perception. |
| T-3.........V.8:8 | You who are **r.** one with it need but know |
| T-3........VI.5:5 | You are not **r.** capable of being tired, but |
| T-3........VI.8:1 | of authority is **r.** a question of authorship. |
| T-3.......VI.8:10 | may even doubt whether you **r.** exist at all |
| T-3.......VII.2:2 | will hurt you because you **r.** understand |
| T-3.......VII.5:7 | since then, but nothing has **r.** happened. |
| T-4..........I.4:3 | dreaming is not **r.** healing his split mind. |
| T-4.........II.7:9 | completely confused about what is **r.** |
| T-4........II.11:7 | however, that you **r.** understand it. Who |
| T-4........III.1:1 | of Heaven is within you" **r.** means. This is |
| T-4........III.7:1 | It has never **r.** entered your mind to give |
| T-4........III.8:1 | and see what it is you are **r.** asking for. Be |
| T-4........III.8:3 | If you will **r.** try to do this, you have taken |
| T-4........IV.8:1 | **r.** considered how many opportunities |
| T-4.........V.4:6 | Being told by the ego that it is **r.** part of |
| T-4........VI.5:8 | but can you **r.** want the rewards of the ego |
| T-4.......VII.2:6 | which is **r.** not abstract at all. It merely |
| T-5........IV.2:7 | your own thoughts can make you **r.** free. |
| T-5........V.2:12 | is the belief from which all guilt **r.** stems |
| T-5........V.6:12 | like God, you are not **r.** thinking at all. |
| T-5.......VII.1:1 | Do you **r.** believe you can make a voice |
| T-5.......VII.1:2 | **r.** believe you can devise a thought system |
| T-5.......VII.1:3 | **r.** believe you can plan for your safety and |
| T-6..........I.8:2 | I know they cannot **r.** betray themselves |
| T-6........I.15:1 | its gospel is **r.** only the message of love. If |
| T-6........I.15:4 | as they did, if they had **r.** understood me. |
| T-6........IV.5:2 | of all, if you consider what it **r.** involves. |
| T-6......V.B.8:2 | is **r.** only the beginning of the thought |
| T-7........III.2:8 | It is therefore a lesson you cannot **r.** learn, |
| T-7........III.2:8 | really learn, and therefore cannot **r.** teach |
| T-7........III.4:3 | choice. Is it **r.** a choice? It seems to be, but |
| T-7........IV.3:2 | Therefore it does not **r.** learn at all. The |
| T-7.........V.8:7 | in him you have not **r.** changed him. By |
| T-7........VI.8:4 | your allegiance, but not as you **r.** are. The |
| T-7.....VIII.3:3 | of another part does not **r.** mean anything |
| T-7.........X.1:3 | **r.** saw this result you could not want it. |
| T-7.........X.6:6 | His Will with me is not **r.** open to choice, |
| T-8........III.6:5 | because once you have **r.** looked at it you |
| T-8......VII.12:4 | Light in which it can be **r.** understood. To |
| T-9..........I.1:2 | it possible for it to be afraid of what it **r.** is |
| T-9..........I.2:2 | of God is **r.** the fear of your own reality. It |
| T-9..........I.8:5 | Yet no one **r.** wants either abandonment |
| T-9........I.12:8 | Can you **r.** devote yourself to nothing? |
| T-9.........II.2:1 | ask of the Holy Spirit is what you **r.** want, |
| T-9.........II.2:6 | he is not **r.** asking for release from fear, |
| T-9.........V.5:2 | for why no one has **r.** explained what |
| T-9.........V.5:3 | Nothing **r.** does. Nothing real has |
| T-9.......VII.4:2 | the Holy Spirit's perception of you **r.** is. |
| T-10.........I.2:6 | one dream to another, without **r.** waking? |
| T-10....III.4:10 | to save? Are you **r.** afraid of losing this? |
| T-10......III.5:1 | whether its offering is **r.** what you want, |
| T-10......III.9:1 | but you are **r.** afraid of nothing. And in |
| T-10.......V.1:7 | No one can **r.** do this, but that you can |
| T-11.......in.2:1 | believed this question **r.** involves conflict? |
| T-11.........I.2:6 | Do you **r.** believe that part of God can be |
| T-11.......II.1:6 | what you **r.** want is therefore lost to you. |
| T-11.......II.3:7 | will, you do not know what you **r.** want. |
| T-11.......V.9:1 | and even desperate, but not **r.** afraid. |
| T-12.........I.1:7 | If you decide that someone is **r.** trying to |
| T-12.........I.8:8 | This is what recognizing fear **r.** means. If |
| T-12.......II.3:4 | brother what he **r.** wants is to offer it unto |
| T-12.......II.9:5 | in any way–this is what you will **r.** see. |
| T-12....III.7:10 | you can perceive the world as it **r.** is. |
| T-12......III.8:5 | For if you could **r.** separate yourself from |
| T-12......IV.3:4 | and teach you that love **r.** calls forth the |
| T-12.......V.2:3 | demonstrating that nothing **r.** happened. |
| T-12.......V.9:6 | you. For you **r.** want to learn aright, and |
| T-12.......VI.2:7 | Father but you do not **r.** want to do so, |
| T-12.....VII.9:4 | **r.** give anything but love to anyone or |
| T-12.....VII.9:4 | **r.** receive anything but love from them. If |
| T-12....VII.10:3 | bring you peace *if you **r.** looked upon it.* If |
| T-12... VIII.1:1 | **r.** believe that you can kill the Son of God |
| T-13......III.1:6 | your desire to attack that **r.** frightens you. |
| T-13....III.1:10 | You are not **r.** afraid of crucifixion. Your |
| T-13......III.2:1 | God, and it is of this that you are **r.** afraid. |
| T-13......III.2:9 | for you. This is what you **r.** want to hide. |
| T-13......VI.1:6 | if it is **r.** sane to perceive what was as now. |
| T-13.....VII.3:1 | You do not **r.** want the world you see, for |
| T-13...VII.11:6 | value that this world can **r.** hold for you. |
| T-13...VII.14:1 | from light, remember what you **r.** want, |
| T-13.......X.4:5 | past, and still to see them as they **r.** are? |
| T-14.......X.7:6 | respond to what a brother **r.** offers you, |
| T-14....XI.13:1 | are with them, can **r.** learn at all. For this |
| T-15.....VII.2:5 | For the ego **r.** believes that it can get and |
| T-15.....VII.6:3 | and avoid delaying what it **r.** wants. Yet |
| T-15.....VII.9:7 | what the ego **r.** wants you do not realize. |
| T-16.......II.5:2 | And are you **r.** safer in maintaining the |
| T-16.......II.9:9 | Think what you have **r.** seen and heard, |
| T-16......III.4:6 | be this part that is **r.** outside yourself, not |
| T-16......III.4:8 | into your mind does not **r.** change it. |
| T-16.......V.1:5 | there are some aspects of what is **r.** being |
| T-16......VI.8:6 | and that escape from pain is **r.** possible. |
| T-16......VI.9:1 | in the special relationship is **r.** part of you |
| T-16...VII.2:10 | cannot **r.** *not* let go what has already gone. |
| T-17.........I.1:5 | is done in dreams has not been **r.** done. It |
| T-17.........I.4:5 | to which it cannot **r.** be compared at all. |
| T-17......III.2:1 | you what you do to keep it safe is **r.** love. |
| T-17......III.3:3 | those on whom vengeance is **r.** sought, is |
| T-17......III.4:6 | less the other **r.** brings to the relationship, |
| T-17....IV.12:7 | only on this basis are you **r.** free to choose |
| T-17.......V.8:4 | Forget not now the misery you **r.** found, |
| T-17.....VII.8:2 | **r.** blame him for is what *you* did to *him.* It |
| T-18.........I.6:4 | Do you **r.** think it strange that a world in |
| T-18......III.7:5 | you and your brother experience is **r.** past |
| T-18....VI.11:4 | what this "transportation" **r.** entails, you |
| T-18....VI.11:7 | What **r.** happens is that you have given |
| T-18....VI.13:4 | You are not **r.** "lifted out" of it; it cannot |
| T-18......IX.2:3 | based on what this little kingdom **r.** is. |
| T-19.......II.3:3 | would **r.** change his reality in any way, |
| T-19.......II.3:3 | reality in any way, nor make him **r.** guilty. |
| T-19......III.2:1 | that love, not fear, is **r.** called upon by sin, |
| T-19......III.2:3 | punishment must have been **r.** done. |
| T-19......III.3:7 | This is not **r.** a change in your perception, |
| T19....IV.B.2:6 | the body **r.** given you that justifies your |
| T19..IV.B.12:3 | sin. It is not **r.** punitive at all. It is but the |
| T19....IV.C.1:5 | to be the fear of death is **r.** its attraction. |
| T-20......III.5:1 | not wondered what the world is **r.** like; |
| T-20......VI.9:5 | it, rising to welcome what you **r.** want. |
| T-20....VI.12:2 | and you have learned you **r.** want but one. |
| T-20.....VII.6:2 | He does not **r.** see him as sinful; he does |
| T-20.....VII.9:2 | Ask only, "Do I **r.** wish to see him sinless? |
| T-20... VIII.7:4 | What if you **r.** understood you made it up |
| T-21.........I.1:1 | what it **r.** looks like is unknown to them. |
| T-21.......II.8:1 | and what is **r.** there you cannot fail to see. |
| T-21... VIII.3:7 | God has already given all that he **r.** wants. |
| T-21... VIII.4:3 | final one that **r.** asks if you are willing to |
| T-22.......II.3:5 | happiness that does not last is **r.** fear. Joy |
| T-24.......II.4:2 | against the truth of what you **r.** are, how |
| T-25.........I.5:5 | make the oneness clear to what is **r.** one. |
| T-25.........I.6:2 | the Will of God and what you **r.** will. But |
| T-25......III.6:6 | to war he heard before are **r.** calls to peace |
| T-25......VI.6:3 | that you think you see in it is **r.** there at all |
| T-25...VII.2:10 | believe, if you but looked at what it **r.** is. |
| T-25.....VII.9:2 | to him that it is an alternative he **r.** wants. |
| T-25. VIII.12:3 | of all that is **r.** happening within yourself. |
| T-25. VIII.13:4 | How can the special **r.** understand that |
| T-26......III.6:2 | and seems to choose where no choice **r.** is. |
| T-26......IV.3:3 | Christ and not recall His Father as He **r.** is |
| T-26.......V.6:7 | can this dream be to where he **r.** is? For |
| T-26.......V.7:3 | and place effect a change in where he **r.** is |
| T-26.......V.8:2 | now, in place of what is *r.* now and here. Is |
| T-26... V.11:11 | the past into the present, where you **r.** are |
| T-26.VII.11:14 | about your will, and what you **r.** are? |
| T-26.....VIII.6:9 | advance. Nor is there **r.** sense in this idea. |
| T-27.........I.5:2 | you **r.** are cannot be seen nor pictured. |
| T-27......II.1:10 | add to all the guilt that he has **r.** earned. |
| T-27........II.3:3 | but retain the proof he is not **r.** innocent. |
| T-27......II.13:1 | that is its purpose, being what it **r.** is. |
| T-27.......V.8:7 | all. This is because they **r.** are the same, |
| T-27.....V.10:1 | to the One Who **r.** understands its laws, |
| T-27.....V.11:7 | behold will be far less than all there **r.** are. |
| T-27.....VII.7:3 | you, uninvited and unasked, must **r.** be. |
| T-27...VII.10:7 | Yet if the choice is **r.** given you, then you |
| T-27....VIII.5:5 | No one believes there **r.** was a time when |
| T-28......VI.4:1 | own and all the rest of what is **r.** yours. |
| T-29........II.6:5 | is that except the state confusion **r.** means |
| T-29........II.8:4 | it asks that God be less than all He **r.** is. |
| T-29....III.3:10 | and understand what **r.** fills the gap so |
| T-29.....VII.5:3 | of life which, in its lifelessness, is **r.** death, |
| T-29....VIII.1:3 | such, and never seen for what they **r.** are. |
| T-29....VIII.8:8 | It does not **r.** matter more of what; more |
| T-30.........I.6:6 | you what the question must have **r.** been. |
| T-30.........I.7:4 | day by robbing you of what you **r.** want. |
| T-30.......I.11:5 | and have remembered what you **r.** want. |
| T-30.......I.14:4 | only question **r.** is with what you choose |
| T-30.......I.14:5 | That is **r.** all. The first rule, then, is not |
| T-30......III.5:9 | But what is **r.** asked for cannot be denied. |
| T-30.......V.1:5 | all things created as they **r.** are. And it is |
| T-30......VI.1:7 | a sin by overlooking what is **r.** there. This |
| T-30.....VII.2:6 | What have you **r.** done, except to show |
| T-30.....VII.6:1 | communication **r.** be established while |
| T-30.....VII.7:3 | they are not in line with what you **r.** are. |
| T-30....VIII.6:1 | hold in place of what your brother **r.** is. |
| T-31.........I.5:4 | to see, and too opposed to what is **r.** true. |
| T-31.........I.9:7 | But in guilt he has forgotten what he **r.** is. |
| T-31........II.3:2 | Thus is it **r.** not a choice at all. The leader |
| T-31........II.8:6 | and learn the truth of what you **r.** want. |
| T-31......IV.3:2 | all, before you **r.** learn they are but one. |
| T-31......IV.5:4 | begin with learning where it **r.** has a use. |
| T-31......VI.4:5 | think the truth about yourself must **r.** be. |
| T-31...VII.11:7 | he looks upon, that he may see it as it **r.** is |
| W-pI.......3.2:1 | how little you **r.** understand about them. |
| W-pI.......7.2:3 | is not **r.** so strange as it may sound at first |
| W-pI.......7.3:7 | your past learning. Do you, then, **r.** see it? |
| W-pI.......8.1:2 | No one **r.** sees anything. He sees only his |
| W-pI.......8.2:4 | it is not **r.** thinking about anything. |
| W-pI.......8.3:1 | recognize when it is not **r.** thinking at all. |
| W-pI.....10.3:3 | statement that your mind is **r.** a blank. To |
| W-pI.....13.1:1 | is **r.** another form of the preceding one, |
| W-pI.....13.5:2 | remind yourself that you are **r.** afraid of |
| W-pI.....14.2:4 | because you **r.** understand what they are |
| W-pI.....16.3:4 | in many forms before you **r.** understand it |
| W-pI.....17.1:1 | and effect as it **r.** operates in the world. |
| W-pI.....17.3:2 | anything that is **r.** alive or really joyous. |
| W-pI.....17.3:2 | anything that is really alive or **r.** joyous. |
| W-pI.....17.3:3 | as yet of any thought that is **r.** true, and |
| W-pI.....17.3:3 | that is really true, and therefore **r.** happy. |
| W-pI.....19.1:4 | and its results are **r.** simultaneous, for |
| W-pI.....20.4:3 | state for a better one, and one you **r.** want |
| W-pI.....21.3:2 | Remember that you do not **r.** recognize |
| W-pI.....22.3:8 | *Is this the world I **r.** want to see?* The answer |
| W-pI.....25.3:2 | your goals are **r.** concerned with nothing. |
| W-pI.....26.1:3 | because you believe that you can **r.** attack. |
| W-pI.....27.1:3 | that you are not sure you **r.** mean it. This |
| W-pI.....28.1:1 | we are **r.** giving specific application to the |
| W-pI.....28.2:5 | which **r.** means you are not seeing at all. |
| W-pI.....28.6:1 | you are therefore **r.** asking to see the |
| W-pI.....35.3:2 | it describes you as you must **r.** be in truth. |
| W-pI.....40.2:4 | under any circumstances, if you **r.** want to |
| W-pI.....49.2:2 | It is **r.** the only part there is. The other |
| W-pI.....52.5:7 | than to obscure all that is **r.** mine with my |
| W-pI.....53.4:6 | decision, and recognize where I **r.** abide. |
| W-pI.....57.3:5 | world is **r.** a place where he can be set free |
| W-pI.....64.4:4 | **r.** choosing whether or not to be happy. |
| W-pI.....64.5:3 | remembering they are all **r.** very simple. |
| W-pI.....64.5:5 | a simple decision **r.** be difficult to make? |
| W-pI.....65.3:1 | accept what the idea for the day **r.** means. |
| W-pI.....65.7:1 | extent to which you **r.** want salvation in |
| W-pI.....66.1:2 | because you do not **r.** see the connection. |
| W-pI.....66.8:4 | Does the ego **r.** have gifts to give, being |

| | |
|---|---|
| W-pI.....69.5:4 | be r. convinced of their lack of substance. |
| W-pI.....70.5:1 | Will and ours are r. the same in this. God |
| W-pI.....70.5:2 | healed, and we do not r. want to be sick, |
| W-pI.....70.5:3 | today, we are r. in agreement with God. |
| W-pI.....73.5:7 | Do you r. want to be in hell? Do you |
| W-pI.....73.5:8 | Do you r. want to weep and suffer and die |
| W-pI.....73.6:1 | which seek to prove all this is r. Heaven. |
| W-pI.....73.6:5 | happiness, and it is happiness you r. want |
| W-pI.....73.7:3 | it. You have no will that can r. oppose it, |
| W-pI.....73.7:5 | the freedom to remember Who you r. are. |
| W-pI.....73.11:1 | make a declaration of what you r. want. |
| W-pI.....76.3:2 | You r. think that you would starve unless |
| W-pI.....76.3:3 | You r. think a small round pellet or some |
| W-pI.....76.3:4 | You r. think you are alone unless another |
| W-pI.....76.5:4 | the mind holds up to hide what r. suffers. |
| W-pI.....77.6:1 | doing this, you do not r. ask for anything. |
| W-pI.....79.1:2 | Even if it is r. solved already you will still |
| W-pI.....79.1:4 | separation, which is r. the only problem, |
| W-pI.....91.6:8 | what you r. are must be revealed to you. |
| W-pI.....91.7:4 | more worthy of your faith, and r. there. |
| W-pI.....96.3:6 | place in which it could be r. part of you. If |
| W-pI.....98.7:4 | beyond their sound to what they r. mean. |
| W-pI...102.1:3 | it, and to suspect it r. makes no sense. It |
| W-pI...106.1:1 | that give you nothing that you r. want; if |
| W-pI...120.2:3 | *and let my Father tell me Who I r. am.* |
| W-pI.126.10:2 | help in understanding what it r. means. |
| W-pI...127.4:1 | to teach you to remember what you r. are |
| W-pI...127.4:1 | in what you r. are and what love is. Love's |
| W-pI...129.3:2 | Is it loss to find all things you r. want, and |
| W-pI...129.6:3 | This world holds nothing that you r. want |
| W-pI...129.7:4 | *of this, for here is nothing that I r. want.* Then |
| W-pI...130.1:4 | to see, believing what you see is r. there. |
| W-pI...130.2:1 | Yet who can r. hate and love at once? |
| W-pI...131.3:4 | forgot, yet holding everything you r. want |
| W-pI...131.4:2 | and must find the goal you r. want. No |
| W-pI...131.5:6 | will reach the goal you r. want as certainly |
| W-pI...131.6:7 | or what you chose from what you r. want. |
| W-pI.131.12:4 | nothing before this door you r. want, and |
| W-pI...133.7:3 | will not recognize the things you r. have, |
| W-pI...134.4:3 | Thus is forgiveness r. but a sin, like all the |
| W-pI.135.24:5 | yourself to your Creator as you r. are. |
| W-pI.136.20:3 | *I have forgotten what I r. am, for I mistook* |
| W-pI...137.4:3 | would impose has never r. happened. To |
| W-pI...138.2:4 | It is not r. thus. Yet what is true in God's |
| W-pI...138.4:1 | you, when there is r. only one to make. |
| W-pI...139.3:2 | yourself is to believe that you are r. dead. |
| W-pI...139.5:8 | ask what part of you can r. doubt yourself |
| W-pI...139.5:9 | r. be a part of you that asks this question. |
| W-pI...139.6:1 | yourself, and be unsure of what you r. are. |
| W-pI.139.11:6 | mind, how faithful they have r. been to us |
| W-pI...140.7:4 | brings illusions to the truth is r. changed. |
| W-pI.140.12:8 | ends, and we remember Who we r. are. |
| W-pI...151.2:2 | You do not r. question what is shown you |
| W-pI...155.2:4 | What other choice is r. theirs to make? To |
| W-pI...164.5:2 | Now is what is r. there made visible, while |
| W-pI...166.4:4 | where he goes, and even who he r. is. |
| W-pI...166.6:3 | Yet is he r. tragic, when you see that he is |
| W-pI...170.3:3 | against the threat of what you r. are. |
| W-pI...181.8:2 | For what we seek to look upon is r. there. |
| W-pI...184.8:5 | from you by what you believe he r. is. His |
| W-pI...185.7:1 | that we r. mean the words we say. We |
| W-pI.185.10:4 | For thus you reach to what they r. want, |
| W-pI...190.6:4 | choose the joy of God as what you r. want |
| W-pI...194.4:4 | the lack of sequence r. found in time. You |
| W-pI...194.6:1 | lesson for today as the deliverance it r. is, |
| W-pII .227.2:1 | return to Heaven, which we never r. left. |
| W-pII .228.2:6 | *to receive Your Word alone for what I r. am.* |
| W-pII .231.1:4 | *nothing else that I could ever r. want to find.* |
| W-pII .....4.1:3 | the truth should be, and where it r. is. Sin |
| W-pII .251.2:2 | *restored, and only that is what we r. want.* |
| W-pII .261.1:8 | only there will I remember Who I r. am. |
| W-pII .289.1:2 | For I am r. looking nowhere; seeing but |
| W-pII .303.2:4 | *He is but what I r. am in truth. He is the Son* |
| W-pII ...12.1:3 | is weak and love is fearful, life is r. death, |
| W-pII .339.1:9 | resolve today to ask for what we r. want, |
| W-pII ...13.1:2 | It does not create, nor r. change at all. It |
| W-pII ...13.4:2 | to show that what it rested on is r. there. |
| W-pII ....358.h | be sure; His answer is the one I r. want. |
| W-pII .358.1:1 | *I r. am alone remember what I really want.* |
| W-pII .358.1:1 | *I really am alone remember what I r. want.* |
| W-ep .........2:4 | speak of what you r. want and really need. |
| W-ep .........2:4 | speak of what you really want and r. need. |
| M-in ..........3:3 | situation on behalf of what you r. teach, |
| M-in ..........3:3 | you really teach, and therefore r. learn. |
| M-2 ...........4:1 | Time r., then, goes backward to an |
| M-2 ...........5:2 | the teacher is not r. the one who does the |
| M-4 .....I.A.4:4 | Because he has valued what is r. valueless, |
| M-4 .....I.A.7:2 | that he did not r. know what was valuable |
| M-4 .....I.A.7:3 | All that he r. learned so far was that he |
| M-4 .....I.A.7:8 | what he r. wants in every circumstance. |
| M-4 ......IX.1:8 | Nothing but that r. deserves the name. |
| M-5 ......III.3:2 | purpose, and therefore are not r. different |
| M-7 ...........1:1 | This question r. answers itself. Healing |
| M-7 ...........3:2 | This is what is r. meant by the statement |
| M-7 ...........6:6 | If you r. want the problem solved, you |
| M-8 ...........5:9 | to make them different are r. irrelevant, |
| M-10 .........1:7 | what these categories are be r. taught. At |
| M-12 .........2:2 | It is not r. a change; it is a change of mind |
| M-12 .........4:4 | of God, of what the body's purpose r. is; |
| M-12 .........4:4 | really is; the only use there r. is for it. This |
| M-13 .........2:9 | its Identity and losing sight of what it r. is |
| M-13 .........3:3 | to know not what it r. wants to find. Who |
| M-13 .........6:1 | requires sacrifice of all you r. hold dear. |
| M-14 .........1:1 | Can what has no beginning r. end? The |
| M-17 .......6:10 | memory of Who your great "opponent" r. |
| M-17 .......8:10 | not r. have the power to give rise to guilt. |
| M-21 .........2:4 | The prayer of the heart does not r. ask for |
| M-23 .........6:1 | is, or what its one Creator r. means. Yet |
| M-24 .........1:7 | Is any other question about it r. useful in |
| C-2 ............1:5 | But a dream of what you r. are. A thought |
| C-2 ............4:1 | r. make a definition for what the ego is, |
| C-3 ............2:3 | to be an enemy instead of what He r. is. |
| P-1 ............4:4 | himself as r. capable of making decisions. |
| P-2.........in.1:5 | anger brings him something he r. wants, |
| P-2...........I.2:6 | the ego seeks to make are not r. changes. |
| P-2.........II.4:4 | is belief in God a r. meaningful concept, |
| P-2........IV.6:2 | Yet if such were r. the self, defense would |
| P-2.......VII.8:1 | what the joining of two brothers r. means |
| P-3..........II.5:7 | Yet no therapist r. sets the goal for the |
| P-3........III.7:2 | Yet not one worldly thought is r. practical |
| S-1..........II.4:5 | What does the phrase r. mean? Pray for |
| S-2..........II.1:4 | cannot be missed, nor is it r. meant to be. |
| S-2..........II.2:7 | grief. This is not r. mercy. This is death. |

## realm 3

| | |
|---|---|
| T-3 .......III.4:5 | the experience from the r. of knowledge. |
| W-pI.....43.1:2 | His is the r. of knowledge. Yet He has |
| C-1 ............7:4 | but it cannot transcend the perceptual r.. |

## realness 1

| | |
|---|---|
| T-9 .......IV.5:4 | not let any belief in its r. enter your mind, |

## reap 1

| | |
|---|---|
| T-5 .......VI.6:1 | so shall ye r." He interprets to mean what |

## reappear 1

| | |
|---|---|
| W-pI...185.9:7 | every twist and turning of the road, to r., |

## rearrange 1

| | |
|---|---|
| T-1 ........I.23:1 | Miracles r. perception and place all levels |

## reason 213

| | |
|---|---|
| T-1 .......III.1:3 | The r. you come before me is that I do not |
| T-2 .......VI.9:9 | that is not the real r. you do not believe it. |
| T-2 ...VIII.5:10 | there is no r. for fear to remain with you. |
| T-3 .......IV.3:8 | have every r. to feel afraid as you perceive |
| T-3 .....VI.10:6 | is to deny yourself the r. for your peace, |
| T-4 .......III.2:4 | The r. you need my help is because you |
| T-4 ........V.1:5 | The ego has every r. to do this, according |
| T-5 ........V.8:1 | possible r. for continuing guilt feelings. |
| T-6 ........I.14:2 | same r. that anyone misunderstands it. |
| T-6 .........II.1:6 | The r., however, may not be so obvious as |
| T-6 ..... V.B.3:9 | This is the real r. why, in many respects, |
| T-7 ....... VI.7:2 | only r. you may find this hard to accept is |
| T-7 .........X.1:4 | The only r. you could possibly want any |
| T-8 .........II.2:1 | possible r. for choosing a teacher such as |
| T-9 ..........I.2:5 | Yet the r. for the course is that you do not |
| T-9 ....... IV.7:4 | attack anyone and anything for no r. at all |
| T-9 ...... VII.2:6 | The r. is very simple, and so obvious that |
| T-10 ..... IV.3:6 | To be out of control is to be out of r., and |
| T-12 .....II.10:7 | greater r. for fearing the world as you |
| T-12 ..... III.3:1 | angry with a brother, for whatever r., you |
| T-13 .......II.6:2 | and the r. it gave was that guiltlessness is |
| T-13 ..... IV.1:1 | And now the r. why you are afraid of this |
| T-13 ..... IV.7:2 | The r. is equally clear, for they perceive |
| T-13 .......X.6:2 | as long as you believe there is a r. for it. |
| T-13 .......X.6:3 | is always totally insane, and has no r.. The |
| T-13 .......X.7:3 | Give no reality to guilt, and see no r. for it |
| T-13 .......X.8:6 | wholly unjustified and wholly without r., |
| T-13 .....X.10:5 | your Father can have no fear, for any r., to |
| T-13 .....X.10:7 | guilt is without r. because it is not in the |
| T-13 .....X.10:8 | And this *is* r., which the Holy Spirit would |
| T-14 .... VII.2:8 | you see no r. to believe that the more you |
| T-14 .....X.6:11 | That is the r. why the miracle gives equal |
| T-15 ..... IV.6:1 | The r. this course is simple is that truth is |
| T-15 ..... IV.6:3 | to eternity, but for a very simple r.. Do |
| T-15 ..... IV.6:4 | Do not obscure the simplicity of this r., |
| T-15 ..... IV.6:5 | The simple r., simply stated, is this: The |
| T-15 .......V.5:3 | unholy the r. you made them may be, He |
| T-16 .......II.8:3 | for that is the only r. He has called to you. |
| T-17 .......II.5:3 | In the light of the real r. that He brings, as |
| T-17 .......II.5:3 | will show you that there is no r. here at all |
| T-17 .......II.5:4 | Each spot His r. touches grows alive with |
| T-17 .......II.5:4 | lack of r. is suddenly released to loveliness |
| T-17 ..... IV.1:3 | r. for creating His relationship with you, |
| T-17 ..... IV.5:1 | accepted is very anxious to preserve its r., |
| T-17 ..... IV.5:6 | has nothing in it, no part, no "r.," and no |
| T-17 .......V.3:4 | The r. is quite clear. For the relationship |
| T-17 ....... VI.2:6 | The r. for this disorganized approach is |
| T-18 ........I.8:5 | course of insanity and restores you to r.. |
| T19 .IV.C.11:1 | over it, remember it is always for *one* r.; |
| T19 IV.D.19:5 | the r. for the journey from its beginning. |
| T-21 .............h | R. AND PERCEPTION |
| T-21 ..... IV.4:3 | moving inward, past insanity and on to r. |
| T-21 ..... IV.4:4 | r. tells you now the ego would not hear. |
| T-21 ..... IV.5:6 | For this your r. tells you, and it follows |
| T-21 ..........V.h | The Function of R. |
| T-21 .......V.4:1 | idea of separation has interfered with r.. |
| T-21 .......V.4:2 | R. lies in the other self you have cut off |
| T-21 .......V.4:3 | to stay in your awareness is capable of r.. |
| T-21 .......V.4:4 | devoid of r. understand what reason is, or |
| T-21 .......V.4:4 | devoid of reason understand what r. is, or |
| T-21 .......V.4:5 | it, but if the basic question stems from r., |
| T-21 .......V.4:6 | it. Like all that stems from r., the basic |
| T-21 .......V.4:7 | But think not r. could not answer it. |
| T-21 .......V.5:7 | instant. Such would your r. tell you, if you |
| T-21 .......V.7:8 | What r. points to you can see, because the |
| T-21 .....V.7:10 | R. is a means that serves the Holy Spirit's |
| T-21 .....V.7:12 | For r. is beyond the ego's range of means. |
| T-21 .......V.8:2 | But r. has no place at all in madness, nor |
| T-21 .......V.8:4 | But r. enters not at all in this. For the |
| T-21 .......V.8:5 | would fall away at once, if r. were applied. |
| T-21 .......V.8:6 | There is no r. in insanity, for it depends |
| T-21 .......V.9:1 | part of mind where r. lies was dedicated, |
| T-21 .......V.9:3 | R. is alien to insanity, and those who use |
| T-21 .......V.9:5 | But r. can serve to open doors you closed |
| T-21 .....V.10:3 | r. tell you now the question must have |
| T-21 .....V.10:4 | Faith and belief, upheld by r., cannot fail |
| T-21 ........ VI.h | R. versus Madness |
| T-21 ..... VI.1:1 | R. cannot see sin but can see errors, and |
| T-21 ..... VI.1:3 | R. will also tell you that when you think |
| T-21 ... VI.1:10 | For r. would not make way for correction |
| T-21 ..... VI.2:3 | Yet r. tells you that you cannot see your |
| T-21 ..... VI.2:7 | But r. tells you that this must be wrong. If |
| T-21 ..... VI.3:5 | of madness cannot be the home of r.. Yet |
| T-21 ..... VI.3:6 | to leave the home of madness if you see r.. |
| T-21 ..... VI.3:8 | it simply by accepting r. where madness |
| T-21 ..... VI.3:9 | Madness and r. see the same things, but it |
| T-21 ..... VI.4:1 | an attack on r. that drives it out of mind, |
| T-21 ..... VI.4:2 | R. does not attack, but takes the place of |
| T-21 ..... VI.4:4 | R. would be incapable of this. And if you |

T-21......VI.4:5 would defend the body against your **r.**,
T-21......VI.5:3 see the body as a barrier between what **r.**
T-21......VI.5:4 you see it, if you heard the voice of **r.**.
T-21......VI.5:7 **R.** would tell you this. But think what you
T-21......VI.6:8 truth? **R.** will tell you that this fact is your
T-21......VI.7:3 **R.**, like love, would reassure you, and
T-21......VI.7:6 And **r.** tells you it is given you to change
T-21......VI.7:9 **R.** is given you to understand that this is
T-21....VI.7:10 For **r.**, kind as is the purpose for which it
T-21......VI.8:4 madness sees must be dispelled by **r.**.
T-21......VI.8:5 **R.** assures you Heaven is what you want,
T-21......VI.8:6 Listen to Him Who speaks with **r.**, and
T-21......VI.8:6 and brings your **r.** into line with His. Be
T-21......VI.8:7 Be willing to let **r.** be the means by which
T-21......VI.8:8 behind insanity in order to escape from **r.**
T-21......VI.9:3 **R.** speaks happily indeed of this. This
T-21....VI.10:2 **r.** will tell you that it cannot be you stand
T-21....VI.10:4 And here alone does **r.** tell you that you
T-21...VII.3:10 Dreams have no **r.** in them. A flower
T-21.....VII.5:5 **R.** would surely bid him seek no longer
T-21.....VII.6:3 **r.** would assure you they are all the same.
T-21.....VII.8:2 your **r.** tell you that it must be answered,
T-21...VII.10:2 **R.** will tell you why. It is the same as are
T-21... VIII.3:1 **R.** will tell you that you cannot ask for
T-21... VIII.5:2 you? Here is the great appeal to **r.**; the
T-22.......in.4:5 **R.** now can lead you and your brother to
T-22.........I.1:1 Let **r.** take another step. If you attack
T-22.........I.2:3 **R.** would tell you that the world you see
T-22.........I.3:8 world it sees, you have no **r.** not to listen,
T-22.........I.3:9 true. **R.** would tell you it cannot be true
T-22.........I.4:4 **R.** would tell you that this is no secret
T-22.........I.9:6 **R.** will tell you that they must have seen
T-22.........I.9:9 Such did his **r.** tell him; such he believed
T-22....... II.4:1 **R.** will tell you that the only way to
T-22....... II.5:1 Both **r.** and the ego will tell you this, but
T-22....... II.5:4 Yet **r.** looks on this another way, for
T-22....... II.5:4 for **r.** sees the source of an idea as what
T-22....... II.5:6 Therefore, says **r.**, if escape from guilt was
T-22..... II.6:10 but **r.** tells you misery lies only on one
T-22....... II.7:7 all. **R.** will tell you that there is no middle
T-22.........III.h **R.** and the Forms of Error
T-22......III.1:1 introduction of **r.** into the ego's thought
T-22......III.1:1 for **r.** and the ego are contradictory. Nor
T-22......III.1:4 You can *see* **r.**. This is not a play on words,
T-22....III.1:10 And here do **r.** and the ego separate, to go
T-22......III.2:2 and **r.** will be unable to see your errors
T-22......III.2:3 For **r.** sees through errors, telling you
T-22......III.2:4 **R.** can see the difference between sin and
T-22......III.2:8 Thus does the ego damn, and **r.** save.
T-22......III.3:1 **R.** is not salvation in itself, but it makes
T-22......III.3:3 without the help of **r.** would try to pass it.
T-22......III.3:5 Yet **r.** sees through it easily, because it is
T-22......III.5:1 **R.** will tell you that the form of error is
T-22......III.7:4 **R.** will tell you that if form is not reality it
T-22......III.9:7 Yet **r.** sees a holy relationship as what it is
T-22....... V.1:3 way. Merely by letting **r.** tell you that they
T-22....... V.2:2 flies in the face of **r.** and makes no sense.
T-22......VI.5:2 The form of error is no longer seen, and **r.**
T-23....... II.1:3 appear to be an obstacle to **r.** and to truth
T-23..... II.11:4 "understand" the **r.** why you found it not.
T-23..... II.12:6 This is the **r.** why you must attack. Here is
T-23..... II.19:7 senseless, impossible and beyond all **r.**,
T-24.........I.2:2 kept unknown and never brought to **r.**, to
T-25....... II.3:3 that there is **r.** to uphold pursuit of what
T-25....... V.1:1 and so there is no **r.** to perceive the Son of
T-25.....VII.4:7 thinks, or is maintained by any form of **r.**,
T-25.....VII.7:6 free, and made with **r.** in the light of sense
T-25...VII.12:5 **R.** is satisfied, for all insane beliefs can be
T-26... VIII.7:8 This is not **r.**, for it is unjust, and clearly
T-26... VIII.7:9 is no **r.** for an interval in which disaster
T-27.........I.7:2 The sick have **r.** for each one of their
T-27.........I.8:2 be **r.** to remain content to seek for passing
T-27....... II.3:1 forgive it is a paradox that **r.** cannot see.
T-27....... II.9:7 to **r.** with an argument for sickness such
T-27.....VII.1:4 which he has no **r.** to be held responsible.
T-29....... II.2:8 and you will not behold a **r.** for regret, but
T-29......IV.4:2 become the "**r.**" your attack is justified?
T-30...... I.10:3 But this much **r.** have you now attained;
T-31.........I.2:1 is a **r.**. But confuse it not with difficulty in
T-31..... V.11:1 Perhaps the **r.** why this concept must be
W-pI..........5.h I am never upset for the **r.** I think.
W-pI.......5.2:3 *I am not angry at_for the* **r.** *I think. I am not*
W-pI.......5.2:4 *I think. I am not afraid of_for the* **r.** *I think.*
W-pI.......5.7:4 *I am not worried about_for the* **r.** *I think. I*
W-pI.......5.7:5 *I am not depressed about_for the* **r.** *I think.*
W-pI.......7.1:3 is the **r.** why nothing that you see means
W-pI.......7.1:4 It is the **r.** why you have given everything
W-pI.......7.1:5 **r.** why you do not understand anything
W-pI.......7.1:6 is the **r.** why your thoughts do not mean
W-pI.......7.1:7 It is the **r.** why you are never upset for the
W-pI.......7.1:7 you are never upset for the **r.** you think. It
W-pI.......7.1:8 It is the **r.** why you are upset because you
W-pI.......8.1:1 of course, the **r.** why you see only the past
W-pI.....10.1:2 The **r.** the idea is applicable to all of them
W-pI.....14.1:1 **r.** why a meaningless world is impossible.
W-pI.....19.1:1 The idea for today is obviously the **r.** why
W-pI.....19.1:3 The **r.** is that the order does not matter.
W-pI.....35.1:4 Yet the **r.** he thinks he is in this world is
W-pI.....44.5:3 The **r.** is very simple. While you practice
W-pI.....45.5:3 There is every **r.** to feel confident that we
W-pI.....46.2:4 For this **r.**, forgiveness can truly be called
W-pI.....47.1:1 you have every **r.** to be apprehensive,
W-pI.....51.1:2 The **r.** this is so is that I see nothing, and
W-pI.....51.3:6 But there is every **r.** to let it go, and make
W-pI.....51.5:1 (5) I am never upset for the **r.** I think. I
W-pI.....51.5:2 I am never upset for the **r.** I think because
W-pI.....69.5:1 see no **r.** to believe there is a brilliant light
W-pI.....73.5:6 The **r.** is very simple. Do you really want
WpI. rIII.in4:1 did not want to do them, for whatever **r.**,
W-pI...138.8:3 apart from question and from **r.** and from
W-pI...160.3:1 What **r.** is there for not saying this? What
W-pI...160.3:2 What could the **r.** be except that you had
W-pI...161.6:3 the **r.** bodies easily become fear's symbols
W-pI...166.7:2 the self you savagely defend against all **r.**,
W-pI...167.3:8 It is the **r.** you can heal. It is the cause of
W-pI...191.1:4 shadows, punitive and wild, lacking all **r.**,
W-pI...192.7:2 using **r.** but to justify our rage and our
WpI rVI.in.3:8 up the mind, and makes it deaf to **r.**,
W-pII...... 1.2:3 to doubt, and further kept from **r.**. What
M-4 ....... X.1:6 can be at peace, for they alone see **r.** for it.
M-7 ...........2:5 He must use his **r.** to tell himself that he
M-16 .........9:8 is the **r.** it can be so easily escaped. What
C-3.............4:2 The **r.** is obvious. Seeing the face of Christ
S-1 ........IV.1:3 **r.** for doing so has been recognized if only

## reason's 7

T-21....... V.5:9 **r.** alien nature to the ego is proof you will
T-21....... V.8:6 for it depends entirely on **r.** absence. The
T-22....... II.3:3 misery in **r.** eyes can be confused with joy.
T-22...... III.1:3 For **r.** goal is to make plain, and therefore
T-22...... III.3:6 cannot conceal its emptiness from **r.** eyes.
T-23....... II.1:2 meaningful, and therefore out of **r.** sphere
T-26.....VII.2:4 it may be carefully preserved from **r.** light

## reasonable 8

T-4......... II.1:1 is **r.** to ask how the mind could ever have
T-4......... II.3:5 Surprise is a **r.** response to the unfamiliar,
T-4....... II.11:6 That is a **r.** question. You must be careful,
T19..IV.B.11:6 mistake be **r.** grounds for depression and
W-pI.....66.9:7 and consider also whether it was ever **r.** to
W-pI...153.2:2 brings anger, anger makes attack seem **r.**,
M-4 .....I.A.6:2 teacher of God rests a while in **r.** peace.
P-2......... II.4:1 constitutes a **r.** goal for psychotherapy.

## reasonably 3

T-13......IV.1:6 As long as it is **r.** satisfied with you, as its
W-pI.....32.4:3 and when you yourself feel **r.** ready.
W-pI...91.11:1 or six times an hour, at **r.** regular intervals

## reasoning 16

T-3......VI.11:2 or the circular **r.** in this position would be
T-6......IV.10:4 the kind of "**r.**" in which the ego engages.
T-7......... X.1:2 may have carried the ego's **r.** to its logical
T-11..... V.14:3 characteristically circular **r.** concludes
T-11...... V.16:4 **r.** ends at its beginning, and no thought
T-11...... V.16:5 **r.** without meaning cannot demonstrate
T-13......IV.1:6 satisfied with you, as its **r.** goes, it offers
T-21.........II.5:5 also see how circular the **r.** on which your
T-21....... IV.6:2 is the **r.** of the sane. You have perceived
T-21........ V.5:8 Yet such is clearly not the ego's **r.**. Your
T-26....VIII.7:6 with "**r.**" you do not understand it now,
T-26....VIII.9:6 and the "**r.**" that would maintain effects
T-27.....VII.3:1 The "**r.**" by which the world is made, on
T-27.....VII.3:5 No one who looks upon this "**r.**" exactly
W-pI...189.6:4 the world's apparent **r.** but serve to hide.
M-8 ...........4:8 confused and senseless "**r.**" be depended

## reasons 6

T-15........II.4:2 and seem to provide **r.** for not letting it go
T-17........II.5:2 to you the seeming **r.** for your making it.
T-17.... III.1:12 They offer you the "**r.**" why you should
T-17...... III.2:9 may not realize are all the **r.** that go to
T-17...... III.6:5 at all confused by any "**r.**" for separation.
T-26........II.1:1 It is not difficult to understand the **r.** why

## reassemble 1

T-8....VIII.1:12 separate and **r.** in different constellations.

## reasserts 1

W-pI..... 73.5:4 Forgiveness lifts the darkness, **r.** your will,

## reassessed 1

T-31.......I.11:2 the means whereby the choice is **r.**;

## reassurance 1

T-1......... V.4:3 is not mocked" is not a warning but a **r.**.

## reassurances 1

T-1........ III.5:8 you experience God's **r.** as threat, it is

## reassure 3

T-6......... V.2:3 merely **r.** them that they are safe *now.*
T-21....... VI.7:3 Reason, like love, would **r.** you, and seeks
W-pI...109.5:5 and respite **r.** your mind that all its frantic

## reassured 2

T-24.....VII.9:4 Yet you are **r.** that it is there because you
W-pI...194.9:3 we forget, we will be gently **r.**. If we accept

## reassuring 2

T-20..VIII.10:4 into the calm and **r.** sights with which He
W-pI.....44.9:2 will probably find it more **r.** to open your

## reawaken 2

T-1.........I.20:1 Miracles **r.** the awareness that the spirit,
M-17 .........7:2 They can but **r.** sleeping guilt, which you

## reawakened 2

T-6.........I.10:2 can learn from mine, and be **r.** by them.
T-20...... IV.1:4 given by Him and **r.** by the Holy Spirit,

## reawakening 9

T-2...........I.3:7 any comprehensive **r.** or rebirth. Such a
T-5...........I.2:1 us start our process of **r.** with just a few
T-6...........I.7:1 Your resurrection is your **r.**. I am the
T-6...........I.12:1 symbol of sharing because the **r.** of every
T-7...........I.6:3 in the **r.** of knowledge is taken by God.

| | |
|---|---|
| T-8 VI.9:6 | The journey to God is merely the **r.** of the |
| T-11 IV.4:4 | is a crucial step in the **r.**. The beginning |
| T-20 IV.2:10 | **r.** of the laws of God in minds that have |
| M-28 1:2 | It is a **r.** or a rebirth; a change of mind |

## reawakens 2

| | |
|---|---|
| T-2 III.3:8 | point. This ultimately **r.** spiritual vision, |
| T-7 IX.4:5 | This **r.** the wholeness in it, and restores it |

## rebirth 13

| | |
|---|---|
| T-1 I.13:2 | They are always affirmations of **r.**, which |
| T-2 I.3:7 | any comprehensive reawakening or **r.**. |
| T-2 I.3:8 | **r.** is impossible as long as you continue to |
| T-6 I.7:2 | I am the model for **r.**, but rebirth itself is |
| T-6 I.7:2 | but **r.** itself is merely the dawning on your |
| T-15 X.h | The Time of **R.** |
| T-22 I.7:2 | it has replaced, is like a baby now in its **r.**. |
| T-25 VII.12:1 | Salvation is **r.** of the idea no one can lose |
| W-pI 159.3:2 | love and the **r.** of love which never dies, |
| M-1 3:11 | of the world. In his **r.** is the world reborn. |
| M-11 1:5 | occur, and that **r.** is man's inheritance. |
| M-28 1:2 | It is a reawakening or a **r.**; a change of |
| C-ep 5:1 | that the holiness of this **r.** will last forever. |

## reborn 20

| | |
|---|---|
| T-17 V.7:14 | This relationship has been **r.** as holy. |
| T-18 V.3:1 | **r.** and blessed in every holy instant you |
| T19..IV.C.10:8 | Here is the babe of Bethlehem **r.**. And |
| T-22 I.7:1 | to communicate instead of separate **r.**. |
| T-22 I.7:2 | **r.** itself from an unholy relationship, and |
| T-22 I.8:7 | Yet must He be **r.** into His ancient home, |
| T-22 I.9:8 | his Self could be **r.** in safety and in peace. |
| T-22 I.10:2 | perception, and yet **r.** in just an instant. |
| T-22 II.12:8 | For at its center Christ has been **r.**, to |
| T-26 I.7:1 | Yet every instant can you be **r.**, and given |
| T-26 V.11:2 | He was **r.** the instant that he chose to die |
| T-26 VII.16:5 | of God **r.** until he chooses not to die again |
| T-31 I.13:5 | away, and left a place for truth to be **r.**. |
| T-31 II.9:7 | for Christ has been **r.** to both of you. |
| W-pI 109.7:3 | with hope **r.** and energy restored to walk |
| W-pI.135.25:5 | Now is the light of hope **r.** in you, for now |
| WpI...rV.in7:3 | I am **r.** each time a brother's mind turns |
| W-pI.182.10:1 | Christ is **r.** as but a little Child each time |
| M-1 3:11 | of the world. In his rebirth is the world **r.**. |
| C-ep 5:1 | knowing that Christ has been **r.** in it, and |

## rebuilt 2

| | |
|---|---|
| T-14 V.10:10 | your altar, for it was **r.** through you. And |
| T-26 IX.8:1 | Now is the temple of the living God **r.** as |

## recall 9

| | |
|---|---|
| T-2 V.A.17:4 | remember is to **r.** the past in the present. |
| T-26 IV.3:3 | Christ and not **r.** His Father as He really is |
| W-pI.139.11:6 | is the **r.** how dear our brothers are to us in |
| W-pI 153.6:3 | Perhaps you will **r.** the text maintains that |
| WpI.rV.in12:1 | end of practice periods, but to **r.** the mind |
| W-pII .276.1:7 | to remember Him and so **r.** our Self. |
| W-pII .336.1:3 | can serve but to **r.** the memory that lies |
| P-1 2:3 | aim can there be than to **r.** the way, the |
| S-3 IV.7:2 | you. I would **r.** My weary Son to Me from |

## recalled 1

| | |
|---|---|
| W-pII .332.1:5 | its presence is the mind **r.** from fantasies, |

## recalling 1

| | |
|---|---|
| W-pI 162.3:1 | in his mind, **r.** them throughout the day, |

## recede 3

| | |
|---|---|
| T-26 I.4:10 | him to make the world **r.** before his song, |
| T-26 I.6:3 | brother sings to you, and let the world **r.**, |
| W-pI.122.13:3 | Let not your gifts **r.** throughout the day, |

## recedes 2

| | |
|---|---|
| W-pI.154.14:1 | The world **r.** as we light up our minds, |
| W-pI 182.8:1 | an instant, when the world **r.** from you, |

## receive 190

| | |
|---|---|
| T-1 I.16:1 | it is as blessed to give as to **r.**. They |
| T-2 III.2:3 | opening of the altar to **r.** the Atonement. |
| T-7 VII.4:6 | there is nothing there to **r.** your gift. |
| T-8 IV.4:2 | it to the world as much as you want to **r.** it |
| T-8 IV.4:3 | For unless you do, you will not **r.** it. If you |
| T-9 I.7:3 | is because you are afraid you might **r.** it, |
| T-9 I.8:6 | as these, and actually expect to **r.** them? |
| T-9 II.5:4 | about him determines the message you **r.**. |
| T-9 II.10:5 | that you will not value what you **r.**. |
| T-9 II.11:1 | then, that you set the value on what you **r.** |
| T-9 II.11:4 | By giving you **r.**. But to receive is to accept |
| T-9 II.11:5 | **r.** is to accept, not to get. It is impossible |
| T-9 II.12:2 | asking of Him, and how much you will **r.**. |
| T-9 VI.2:6 | The decision to **r.** is the decision to accept |
| T-10 III.8:1 | that you always **r.** as much as you accept. |
| T-10 V.2:2 | You must **r.** the message you give because |
| T-11 VIII.5:4 | than to be told that if you ask you will **r.**. |
| T-12 I.5:3 | you are unwilling to give help and to **r.** it. |
| T-12 VII.9:4 | you really **r.** anything but love from them. |
| T-12 VIII.6:3 | what has no value, nor could His Son **r.** it. |
| T-13 IV.5:6 | And you will **r.** messages from him out of |
| T-14 IX.7:1 | mirror of your mind clean to **r.** the image |
| T-14 XI.4:6 | joyously laid down by hands open to **r.**, |
| T-15 I.12:4 | instants of release you offer, and will **r.**. |
| T-15 I.13:6 | to give what you would **r.** of Him, for you |
| T-15 II.6:2 | will **r.** very specific instructions as you go |
| T-15 IV.6:5 | you **r.** and give perfect communication. |
| T-15 IV.6:6 | your mind is open, both to **r.** and give. It |
| T-15 VII.8:4 | long as the body is there to **r.** its sacrifice, |
| T-15 VIII.5:5 | open to **r.** His communication to you, and |
| T-15 XI.9:1 | thanks to the holy host who would **r.** Him |
| T-15 XI.9:4 | Those who **r.** the Father are one with Him |
| T-16 VII.8:4 | You will **r.** *because* it is His Will to give. He |
| T-16 VII.8:5 | that you **r.** it not *because* He gave it. When |
| T-16 .. VII.12:6 | *And let us **r.** only what You have given, and* |
| T-18 IV.5:3 | but merely to **r.** the answer as it is given. |
| T-18 IV.5:4 | to make yourself holy to be ready to **r.** it. |
| T-18 IV.5:13 | *But to **r.** it, I must be willing not to substitute* |
| T-18 IV.7:3 | that you need give so little, to **r.** so much. |
| T-18 V.4:6 | is required to **r.** the means and use them. |
| T-18 .VIII.10:2 | quiet garden, and **r.** their blessing there. |
| T-18 .VIII.11:5 | Asking for everything, you will **r.** it. And |
| T-18 .VIII.13:5 | **R.** it now of Him, for He would have you |
| T-19 IV.3:1 | to Him He asks but that you **r.** for Him. |
| T19. IV.D.13:4 | will **r.** of him according to your choice. He |
| T19. IV.D.15:5 | and **r.** from your most holy Friend. Let |
| T19. IV.D.15:7 | he will **r.** of you what you received of him. |
| T19. IV.D.15:8 | you to give your brother, and thus **r.** it. |
| T19. IV.D.17:3 | see in him the gift of God you would **r.**. It |
| T19. IV.D.17:8 | it, **r.** it of Him in return for what you gave. |
| T-20 II.2:3 | mind decides on what it would **r.** and give |
| T-20 II.2:5 | making it ready to **r.** the gifts it wants by |
| T-20 II.8:2 | for you, and it is ready to **r.** you now. You |
| T-20 II.11:5 | to offer and **r.** the bright awareness that |
| T-20 IV.2:6 | but what you would **r.** of him is up to you. |
| T-20 V.3:7 | And what you want for him you will **r.**. |
| T-20 V.4:3 | it as you **r.** his Father's gift through him. |
| T-20 V.7:9 | brother will offer and **r.** it for you both. |
| T-20 VI.10:6 | Love's Arms are open to **r.** you, and give |
| T-20 VIII.2:9 | is given, waiting on your desire but to **r.** it |
| T-21 II.2:5 | *happen to me I ask for, and **r.** as I have asked.* |
| T-21 III.10:3 | mind could neither ask it nor **r.** it of itself. |
| T-21 V.5:2 | for what God wills for him he must **r.**. For |
| T-21 VI.9:8 | To give is no more blessed than to **r.**. But |
| T-21 VIII.3:2 | if what you desire you **r.**, and happiness is |
| T-22 II.11:9 | **R.** of him what God has given him for you |
| T-22 IV.7:4 | to **r.** together and give as you received. |
| T-23 III.2:6 | nothing, and **r.** of him but what you gave. |
| T-24 II.6:6 | nothing, and to **r.** the Love of God forever |
| T-24 II.9:5 | holy place does truth stand waiting to **r.** |
| T-24 III.1:6 | when he would not **r.** it for himself? For it |
| T-24 III.1:7 | sure he would **r.** it wholly the instant that |
| T-25 IX.2:2 | for you until reluctance to **r.** it disappears |
| T-25 IX.8:4 | received because another could **r.** it not. |
| T-25 IX.10:1 | The miracle that you **r.**, you give. Each |
| T-26 II.7:1 | to **r.** correction for all your problems. You |
| T-26 II.8:6 | you should offer or **r.** less than He gave, |
| T-26 IV.4:2 | Son of God Himself comes to **r.** each gift |
| T-26 VI.3:5 | given can make sure that you **r.** them. He |
| T-26 VIII.1:1 | and will **r.** the benefits of trusting in your |
| T-27 I.9:10 | it may fulfill the function that it will **r.**. |
| T-27 I.10:6 | it **r.** the power to represent an endless life, |
| T-27 III.7:2 | has come, not to destroy, but to **r.** its own |
| T-27 IV.7:5 | and **r.** the answer that was made for you. |
| T-28 IV.8:6 | of sin. And here the Father will **r.** His Son, |
| T-29 V.5:7 | being empty they **r.**, instead, a brother's |
| T-30 I.8:1 | to **r.** you cannot even let your question go |
| T-31 II.10:5 | to. He asks and you **r.**, for you have come |
| W-pI 28.4:2 | is to ask questions and **r.** the answers. In |
| W-pI 42.2:2 | that you can **r.** it any time and anywhere, |
| W-pI 69.8:2 | that it is given you and you will yet **r.** it. |
| W-pI 77.1:2 | will **r.** miracles because of what God is. |
| W-pI 77.6:8 | You will **r.** the assurance that you seek. |
| W-pI 77.7:6 | are fully entitled to **r.** it whenever you ask. |
| W-pI 80.5:2 | your eyes, and **r.** your reward. Recognize |
| WpI.. rII.in.3:3 | Be confident that you will **r.** it. Remember |
| W-pI 97.8:6 | **R.** His words, and offer them to Him. |
| W-pI .. 100.7:7 | You but **r.** according to God's plan, and |
| W-pI .. 104.1:4 | there be a place made ready to **r.** His gifts. |
| W-pI .. 105.1:3 | these gifts increase as we **r.** them. They |
| W-pI .. 105.3:1 | reverse your view of giving, so you can **r.**. |
| W-pI .. 105.3:2 | avoid the only means by which you can **r.**. |
| W-pI .. 105.5:6 | **R.** His gift of joy and peace today, and He |
| W-pI .. 105.7:6 | for you have given what you would **r.**. |
| W-pI .. 105.9:2 | what He wills to give, and wills you to **r.**. |
| W-pI .. 105.9:4 | to let yourself **r.** the gifts of God as yours. |
| W-pI .. 106.6:5 | all miracles has need that you **r.** them first |
| W-pI .. 106.7:6 | *truth. What does it mean to give and to **r.**?* |
| W-pI .. 106.8:4 | becomes ready to understand and to **r.**. |
| W-pI 106.10:2 | hear and to **r.** the Word by this reminder, |
| W-pI 106.10:4 | *God today, My voice is His, to give what I **r.**.* |
| W-pI 108.h | To give and to **r.** are one in truth. |
| W-pI .. 108.7:3 | To give is to **r.**. Today we will attempt to |
| W-pI .. 108.8:2 | say: *To give and to **r.** are one in truth. I will* |
| W-pI .. 108.8:3 | *I will **r.** what I am giving now.* Then close |
| W-pI .. 108.9:1 | a while, expecting to **r.** the gift you gave. |
| W-pI 108.10:3 | say, "To give and to **r.** are one in truth." |
| W-pI .. 119.2:1 | (108) To give and to **r.** are one in truth. *I* |
| W-pI .. 119.3:4 | hour: To give and to **r.** are one in truth. |
| W-pI .. 121.8:3 | how to give forgiveness and **r.** forgiveness |
| W-pI .. 122.6:4 | As you give you will **r.**. There is no plan |
| W-pI 122.12:1 | Before the light you will **r.** today the |
| W-pI 122.12:2 | and we **r.** the gifts that have been held in |
| W-pI .. 123.6:2 | **R.** the thanks of God today, as you give |
| W-pI .. 123.7:1 | **R.** His thanks and offer yours to Him for |
| W-pI .. 123.8:1 | **R.** His thanks, and you will understand |
| W-pI .. 124.3:1 | **r.** is our eternal gift to those who follow |
| W-pI 125.h | In quiet I **r.** God's Word today. |
| W-pI .. 125.9:5 | this day; in quiet to **r.** the Word of God. |
| W-pI 133.14:1 | **r.** what waits for everyone who reaches, |
| W-pI 135.22:2 | Today we will **r.** instead of plan, that we |
| W-pI 135.24:1 | at not receiving what you will **r.** today. |
| W-pI 137.10:4 | And legions upon legions will **r.** the gift |
| W-pI 137.10:4 | the gift that you **r.** when you are healed. |
| W-pI 137.13:2 | hour worth the giving to **r.** a gift like this? |
| W-pI 137.15:2 | rest in quiet, be prepared to give as you **r.**, |
| W-pI 137.15:2 | **r.** the Word of God to take the place of all |
| WpI..rIV.in5:4 | of all the thoughts you will **r.** that day. |
| WpI..rIV.in9:2 | we **r.** as the inheritance we have of Him. |
| W-pI .. 143.1:1 | (125) In quiet I **r.** God's Word today. |
| W-pI .. 154.5:2 | who will **r.** the message that he brings. It |
| W-pI .. 154.8:1 | Would you **r.** the messages of God? For |
| W-pI .. 154.8:6 | No one can **r.** and understand he has |
| W-pI .. 154.9:1 | the messenger of God, **r.** His messages. |
| W-pI 154.12:1 | will not recognize what we **r.** until we give |
| W-pI 154.12:3 | you will **r.** a thousand miracles and then |
| W-pI 154.12:3 | miracles and then **r.** a thousand more, |
| W-pI 158.h | Today I learn to give as I **r.**. |

W-pI.158.10:1 Thus do you learn to give as you **r.**. And
W-pI...159.2:5 **R.** them now by opening the storehouse
W-pI...164.7:2 will **r.** but what is given us from judgment
W-pI...165.4:4 Ask to **r.**, and it is given you. Conviction
W-pI...165.4:8 Sureness is not required to **r.** what only
W-pI...168.5:1 today, for we **r.** what has been given us.
W-pI...168.6:2 He has prepared for us He gives and we **r.**.
W-pI.169.13:2 returned by you from holy instants you **r.**,
W-pI...174.2:1 (158) Today I learn to give as I **r.**. God is
W-pI...183.7:5 or that His Son **r.** another name than His.
W-pI.184.14:5 blessed with blessings we can give as we **r.**
W-pI...185.2:5 is all he wants, and that is all he will **r.**.
W-pI.187.10:3 we stand in blessedness, and give as we **r.**.
W-pI...189.8:5 Ask and **r.**. But do not make demands,
W-pI.189.10:6 *Our hands are open to* **r.** *Your gifts. We have*
W-pI...197.9:1 Give thanks as you **r.** it. Be you free of all
W-pI...198.1:6 gift, and you can now **r.** the gift you gave.
W-pII..228.2:6 *to* **r.** *Your Word alone for what I really am.*
W-pII..254.1:2 *You, to hear Your Voice and to* **r.** *Your Word*
W-pII..291.2:1 *is quiet, to* **r.** *the Thoughts You offer me.*
W-pII..303.2:8 *Safe in Your Arms let me* **r.** *Your Son.*
W-pII..304.2:2 *forgive, and thus* **r.** *salvation for the world. It*
W-pII..322.1:3 abides in every gift that I **r.** of Him. And
W-pII.....339.h I will **r.** whatever I request.
W-pII..339.1:5 Everyone will **r.** what he requests. But he
W-pII..349.1:6 *And giving as I would* **r.**, *I learn Your healing*
W-pII..357.1:3 *patiently to hear Your Word, and give as I* **r.**.
WpII361-5.1:3 mind, these are the gifts I will **r.** of Him.
M-6..........4:12 holy exchange can **r.** less than everything?
M-14..........2:7 turning to Him in silence to **r.** His Word.
M-21..........1:3 What you ask for you **r.**. But this refers to
M-22..........7:8 Herein does he **r.** Atonement, for he
P-2...........I.4:1 each other and to **r.** the peace of God.
P-2.........II.9:2 who stands apart can **r.** Christ's vision. It
P-2.........II.9:3 but he cannot hold out his hand to **r.** it.
P-2........III.4:3 to **r.** the Christ or he could not be sick. In
P-3.........II.6:7 can accept more than he is ready to **r.**,
S-1...........I.1:7 Ask, rather, to **r.** what is already given; to
S-1...........I.2:1 you will **r.** a specific answer if such is your
S-1.........II.4:3 have also limited your ability to **r.** and to
S-1........IV.2:8 For no one can **r.** effects alone, asking a
S-3.......II.5:11 is the only gift you give and would **r.**.

## received 132

T-1........I.11:3 Through prayer love is **r.**, and through
T-3........VI.6:2 have **r.** and that is what you should give.
T-5........IV.7:2 because, having **r.** the idea of healing,
T-5......VI.12:8 by God, you must give Him as you **r.** Him.
T-8.........V.4:5 children because I **r.** it of Him for us all.
T-9.........II.3:6 you have already **r.** but have not yet heard
T-9.........V.1:4 he is trying to give what he has not **r.**. If
T-11......VI.9:5 all that you have **r.** you will not know that
T-12.....VII.9:5 If you think you have **r.** anything else, it is
T-13......VI.7:4 vision is freely given as it is freely **r.**, and
T-13....VI.10:7 for having **r.** it of you they would keep it.
T-14......IV.1:6 Yet truth is offered first to be **r.**, even as
T-15....III.10:8 But you will gladly give, having **r.**. The
T-15......IV.8:6 the holy instant is given and **r.** with equal
T-16.....VII.8:1 you is truly given, and will be truly **r.**. For
T-16.....VII.8:8 that you have **r.** what God has given you.
T-17.....V.13:1 You *have* **r.** the holy instant, but you may
T-17.....V.13:5 recognize what has been given and **r.** by
T-17...VIII.6:6 Give as you have **r.**. And demonstrate
T-18......III.4:7 gift is given forever, for God Himself **r.** it.
T-19.........I.9:3 of freedom from the past, which you **r.**.
T19..IV.B.17:2 it, and what is offered must also be **r.**, to
T19.IV.D.15:4 it truly, for it will be both offered and **r.**.
T19.IV.D.15:7 he will receive of you what you **r.** of him.
T19.IV.D.16:1 until redemption is accomplished and **r.**.
T19.IV.D.20:2 so will his offering be seen and so **r.**. The
T-20...........I.4:2 the lilies you have **r.** and given as your gift
T-20.......II.2:1 bodies, if they be truly given and **r.**. For
T-20.......II.5:2 you have asked for and **r.** another sight.
T-20.......II.7:6 God gave the Holy Spirit, you have **r.**. The
T-20......IV.1:8 has already given and **r.** all that is true.
T-20......IV.1:9 The untrue He has neither **r.** nor given.
T-20......IV.5:1 The sinless give as they **r.**. See, then, the
T-21...VIII.3:9 giving must be incomplete unless it is **r.**.
T-22.........I.3:2 have **r.** no messages at all you understand
T-22.........I.6:1 you have **r.** and failed to understand, this
T-22.........I.7:5 nor was **r.** by anything except yourself.
T-22......IV.5:5 For you are here to let it be **r.**. God's offer
T-22......IV.5:7 From you who have accepted it is it **r.**.
T-22......IV.6:1 given to be the givers of what they have **r.**.
T-22......IV.7:2 has **r.** it for himself could find it difficult.
T-22......IV.7:4 to receive together and give as you **r.**.
T-22......VI.8:8 them where they are **r.** and welcomed. He
T-25......IX.2:4 out his hand in willingness they be **r.**. Nor
T-25......IX.2:9 not be satisfied until it is **r.** by everyone.
T-25......IX.8:4 A miracle can never be **r.** because another
T-25....IX.10:5 It is **r.** and given equally. It is awareness
T-26.......II.6:9 Spirit be content until it is **r.** by everyone.
T-26......III.2:6 denied, and everything that *is* **r.** instead.
T-26...VII.17:6 lie, to be both offered and **r.** as one.
T-27.......I.10:5 Then will it send forth the message it **r.**,
T-27......IV.6:3 so it can be given you and also be **r.**. The
T-27.......V.1:5 it is born the instant it is offered and **r.**.
T-27.......V.1:7 and thus offer the other what he has **r.**.
T-27.......V.6:1 for nothing that is there **r.** is left behind
T-28....IV.10:3 he has **r.** the simple happiness of health?
T-29.......II.5:1 give, because of everything you have **r.**.
T-30.......I.17:8 day. And as you have **r.**, so must you give.
W-pI.....76.9:4 Payment is neither given nor **r.**. Exchange
W-pI.....83.3:3 from Oneness, and must be **r.** as one.
W-pI.....97.7:3 will accept this gift that you **r.** of Him,
W-pI.....99.5:1 of God exactly as it was **r.** of Him within
W-pI...104.1:5 **r.** the gifts it made where His belong, as
W-pI...105.2:2 more than was **r.** by him who took the gift
W-pI...106.6:5 become the joyous giver of what you **r.**.
W-pI...106.8:2 has been waiting long to be **r.** by you. It
W-pI...109.9:3 and what we give today we have **r.** already
W-pI...122.7:5 that has **r.** what God has given as its own.
W-pI...122.7:6 God wills salvation be **r.** today, and that
W-pI.122.14:5 *this as true. Today I have* **r.** *the gifts of God.*
W-pI...123.2:1 you have made; the gifts you have **r.**. Be
W-pI...126.7:6 what has been given must have been **r.**.
W-pI.126.11:7 believe, for what He gives will be **r.** by you
W-pI...134.6:1 who offer it; a quiet blessing where it is **r.**.
W-pI...134.8:5 For if one brother has **r.** this gift of you,
W-pI.135.25:6 when you have **r.** your function from the
W-pI.136.12:5 that what God wills for you must be **r.**.
WpI. rIV.in8:2 them be **r.** where they were meant to be.
W-pI...154.8:4 you wait to give the messages you have **r.**.
W-pI...154.8:6 and understand he has **r.** until he gives.
W-pI...154.8:7 giving is his own acceptance of what he **r.**.
W-pI...154.9:5 has **r.** for you the messages of God would
W-pI...154.9:5 God would have them be **r.** by you as well
W-pI.154.14:4 hands, and we will recognize what we **r.**.
W-pI...158.2:1 You have **r.** all this. No one who walks
W-pI...158.2:2 No one who walks the world but has **r.** it.
W-pI......159.h I give the miracles I have **r.**.
W-pI...159.1:1 No one can give what he has not **r.**. To
W-pI...159.1:7 To give is how to recognize you have **r.**. It
W-pI...159.6:3 All can be **r.** but for the asking. Here the
W-pI...159.8:6 His messengers, who give as they **r.**.
W-pI...165.5:3 But when you have **r.**, you will be sure you
W-pI...166.1:5 will is one with His, His gifts are not **r.**.
W-pI.166.15:6 giving of His gifts to all who have **r.** them.
W-pI...169.1:4 where it can be gently laid and willingly **r.**
W-pI...169.6:2 been completely given and **r.** completely.
W-pI.170.13:4 *we bless the world with what we have* **r.** *from*
W-pI.170.13:6 *them Your salvation as we have* **r.** *it now.*
W-pI...175.1:1 (159) I give the miracles I have **r.**. God is
W-pI.185.13:1 God has been requested and **r.** by anyone.
W-pI...188.3:6 to you who give, and you who have **r.**.
W-pI...194.2:3 you give the world, because you have **r.**.
W-pI...197.1:4 Your gifts must be **r.** with honor, lest they
W-pI...197.3:5 thanks, for it is you who have **r.** the gifts.
W-pI...197.4:4 They are **r.** where they are given. In your
W-pII...in.10:6 plan will end, as we **r.** the way it started.
W-pII.224.1:4 gift but this that can be either given or **r.**.
W-pII......2.5:1 to the world, for it is here salvation was **r.**.
W-pII..234.2:2 *on us, for all the loving help we have* **r.**, *for*
W-pII..242.2:4 *Give us what You would have* **r.** *by us. You*
W-pII..245.2:2 world we give the message that we have **r.**
W-pII..316.1:3 gift a brother has **r.** throughout all time,
W-pII....13.2:1 gift of grace, for it is given and **r.** as one.
W-pII .343.2:3 It is a gift that must be freely given and **r.**.
W-pII .345.2:3 today, for we will offer what we have **r.**.
M-6...........2:3 Where healing has been given it will be **r.**.
M-6...........2:7 and it does not appear to have been **r.**. It
M-6...........2:9 Let him be certain it has been **r.**, and trust
M-7.........1:10 and so he has not **r.** the benefit of his gift.
M-7...........2:8 Having offered love, only love can be **r.**.
M-7...........3:3 worker because he gives the gifts he has **r.**
M-7...........3:7 Who gave the gift and Who **r.** it. Thus is
M-15.........1:6 free as God's Final Judgment on him is **r.**.
M-21.........3:2 this will be given because this will be **r.**. It
M-22.......6:11 Atonement is **r.** and offered. Having been
M-22.......6:12 Having been **r.**, it must be accepted. It is
M-23.........1:1 God's gifts can rarely be **r.** directly. Even
P-2..........II.8:6 Atonement and learn to give it as it was **r.**
P-2.........IV.2:2 It has been asked for and will be **r.**. And
P-2.........V.7:1 Somewhere all gifts of God must be **r.**. In
S-1..........II.2:6 ceasing. Ask and you have **r.**, for you have
S-3..........II.4:1 of earth, can only be **r.** with thankfulness.

## receiver 21

T-1...........I.9:3 more love both to the giver *and* the **r.**.
T-1.........I.16:2 of the giver and supply strength to the **r.**.
T-1..........II.6:4 the giver and **r.** both emerge farther along
T-1..........II.6:8 of giver and **r.** on which the miracle rests.
T-1.....VII.3:10 then sustain the belief of the miracle **r.**.
T-1.....VII.3:11 becomes apparent to both giver and **r.**.
T-2........IV.5:2 in whatever way is most helpful to the **r.**.
T-2.........V.3:2 of the miracle worker or the miracle **r.**.
T-2.........V.3:3 not await the right-mindedness of the **r.**.
T19..IV.B.14:7 invested is given by the sender and the **r.**.
T19..IV.B.14:8 that here the sender and **r.** are the same.
T19..IV.B.17:4 Holy Spirit is both the sender and the **r.**.
T-20.........II.3:1 gift is an evaluation of the **r.** and the *giver.*
T-23......III.2:4 And neither the **r.** nor the giver is long
T-24......II.12:3 its seal but offers treachery to giver and **r.**.
W-pI.....98.8:2 one chance to be the glad **r.** of His gifts,
W-pI...126.8:1 the truth that giver and **r.** are the same.
W-pI...159.4:3 bond by which the giver and **r.** are united
W-pI...187.5:5 There is no giver and **r.** in the sense the
M-6...........2:5 for the giver and the **r.** of God's gifts. Not
M-6...........3:5 the giver nor the **r.** would have the gift.

## receivers 2

W-pI...154.6:4 become their first **r.** in the truest sense,
W-pI.154.11:5 we may be the true **r.** of the gifts He gives.

## receives 23

T-4.......VII.7:4 is intensely personal to the mind that **r.** it.
T-10.......III.2:3 mind **r.** Him the remembrance of Him
T-19.......I.13:2 that **r.** it looks instantly beyond the body,
T19..IV.B.14:5 **r.** and sends the messages that it is given.
T19.IV.D.20:5 pain. Everyone gives as he **r.**, but he must
T19.IV.D.20:5 he must choose what it will *be* that he **r.**.
T-25....VIII.9:9 God rejoices as His Son **r.** what loving
T-26......II.6:10 can He ensure that everyone **r.** it equally.
T-28.........I.5:3 Memory holds the message it **r.**, and does
T-28.........II.1:4 and **r.** the gift that he has given Him. It is
T-28.......III.9:2 For here, the more that anyone **r.**, the
W-pI...123.6:3 since He **r.** your gifts in loving gratitude,
W-pI.135.11:2 It carries out the plans that it **r.** through
W-pI...162.3:3 he gives the world what he **r.** each time he
W-pI...164.6:5 what is worthy of your love **r.** your love,
W-pI...181.2:6 This faith **r.** its only sure support from
W-pII .315.1:4 my mind **r.** this gift and takes it as its own
W-pII .339.1:7 request that he would want when he **r.** it?
M-8...........6:5 out the messages the mind **r.** from what
M-21.........4:7 which are offered him, and gives as he **r.**.
P-2........III.4:6 as he **r.** them from the Mind of Christ.
S-1...........I.7:5 It asks nothing and **r.** everything. This
S-1...........I.7:6 can be shared because it **r.** for everyone.

## receiving 35

T-2........III.5:5 and is entirely worthy of **r.** perfection.
T-6......V.B.4:6 is **r.** conflicting messages and accepting

T-7........ V.7:2 r. something equally desirable in return.
T-8........ III.4:7 giving salvation to him and r. it yourself.
T-9....... II.10:3 of giving and r. will be recognized. The
T-9........ VI.2:5 simply because you have limited your r..
T-9........ VI.6:3 are a way of giving acceptance and r. it. In
T-14...... III.5:8 The cost of giving *is* r.. Either it is a penalty
T-15....... X.2:5 I am as incapable of r. sacrifice as God is,
T-16..... VII.8:2 have no reality apart from your r. them.
T-16..... VII.8:3 Your r. completes His giving. You will
T19..IV.B.17:3 medium, r. from the Father and offering
T19. IV.D.15:6 it not, for by r. it you offer it to him. And
T-20....... II.2:6 offering and r. what their minds judge to
T-22...... IV.7:3 For by r. it, he learned it was not given
T-24....... V.7:6 r. from each one the gift of life that your
T-25.... IX.10:6 awareness that giving and r. are the same.
T-26.........I.3:6 For giving and r. are the same. And to
T-26.........I.8:4 you back the gift of freedom by r. it of you
T-26.... VIII.2:6 and r. of the gift seems to be one in which
W-pI.106.10:1 is kept through your r. it to give away, so
W-pI... 108.4:1 are both giving and r. seen as different
W-pI... 108.6:1 and r. are the same has special usefulness,
W-pI... 108.7:1 with the special case of giving and r.. We
W-pI... 121.9:1 not believe that giving and r. are the same
W-pI... 126.7:5 heal the mind that gives, for giving is r..
W-pI. 135.24:1 at not r. what you will receive today. And
W-pI... 154.6:4 sense, r. to prepare themselves to give.
W-pI. 154.10:3 God's Word; the giving and r. of His Will.
W-pI... 164.9:1 you r. your consent and your acceptance.
W-pII . 225.1:1 *Love for me, for giving and r. are the same,*
W-pII . 360.1:1 *it is Your peace that I would give, r. it of You. I*
M-2 ........... 5:5 one learns that giving and r. are the same.
M-22 ....... 6:13 It is in the r., then, that healing lies. All
C-1............. 7:3 r. messages from above or below; from

## recent 3

W-pI..... 66.1:1 our r. lessons on the connection between
WpI. rIII.in1:2 will review two r. lessons every day for ten
WpI. rIV.in1:4 we review the r. lessons and their central

## recently 1

T-22.........I.7:2 relationship, so r. reborn itself from an

## reception 1

T-4....... VII.3:7 a channel for the r. of His Mind and Will.

## receptive 1

C-1............. 7:3 choice. *Consciousness* is the r. mechanism,

## recesses 1

W-pII . 221.1:3 *the quiet of my heart, the deep r. of my mind,*

## recipient 1

T-2........ IV.5:3 that the r. can understand without fear.

## reciprocal 6

T-1......... II.5:4 Revelation is not r.. It proceeds from God
T-7...........I.1:1 but they are not in r. relationship. You
T-7...........I.1:4 you are not in a r. relation to God, since
T-7...........I.4:1 the other hand, always demands r. rights,
T-8...... VIII.1:9 arise from it, but the relationship is not r..
T-9....... II.10:3 r. relationship of giving and receiving will

## reciprocate 1

T-14.... XI.14:3 You can desert Him but He will never r.,

## reciprocity 1

W-pI..... 76.8:3 friendship, of "good" relationships and r..

## recognition 135

T-1 ........I.20:2 r. that leads to the healing power of the
T-1 .........II.4:7 statement in r. that the Father is greater.
T-1 .........II.6:2 longitudinal or horizontal plane the r. of
T-1 .........II.6:8 It does so by the underlying r. of perfect
T-1 ....... III.1:5 restored to the r. of your original state,
T-1 ....... IV.1:1 First, the r. that darkness cannot hide.
T-1 ....... IV.1:3 the r. that there is nothing you want to
T-2 ....... III.3:7 this r. becomes more firmly established,
T-2 ........ V.1:6 r. is a far better protective device than any
T-2 ...... V.10:3 needs help, and a r. that he will accept it.
T-2 ....... VI.8:2 The r. of this worth is re-established by
T-3 ..... IV.6:10 is your own vague r. that knowledge can
T-3 ....... VI.3:6 is the process that enables r. to replace
T-4 ........II.4:11 contains a hint of r. that the ego is not the
T-4 ....... VI.3:6 this r. is made by you and not the ego, the
T-4 ....... VI.3:6 the r. itself establishes that you and your
T-4 ....... VI.7:5 one moment of real r. makes everyone
T-5 ....... IV.5:2 sharing of ideas and the r. that to share
T-6 .........II.1:3 By this r. it knows its Creator. Exclusion
T-6 ........II.10:7 is the r. that *the separation never occurred.*
T-6 ... V.C.10:8 This r. is wholly without effort since it is
T-7 .......... IV.h Healing as the R. of Truth
T-7 ..... IV.6:10 Without this r., you have made the laws
T-7 ....... VI.5:1 therefore opposes all appreciation, all r.,
T-7 ........X.1:10 but your state of mind and your r. of what
T-7 ....... XI.5:8 This is the r. that is immediate, clear and
T-8 .........II.8:4 your r. you awaken theirs, and through
T-8 ........ V.2:7 r. of God is the recognition of yourself.
T-8 ........ V.2:7 recognition of God is the r. of yourself.
T-8 ........ V.3:3 I offer you only the r. of His power in you,
T-9 ..........I.4:3 His r. of this Will can make it real to you
T-9 ..........I.9:2 This r. is the recognition that his will and
T-9 ..........I.9:2 is the r. that his will and God's are one. In
T-9 ........II.11:7 r. of having is the willingness for giving,
T-10 ........I.1:7 for in this r. lies the realization that your
T-10 ..... III.3:5 Your r. of him as part of God reminds
T-10 ..... IV.1:2 All religion is the r. that the irreconcilable
T-10 ..... IV.7:2 it is the r. that his brother can do it. It is a
T-11 ........I.11:9 why healing is the beginning of the r. that
T-11 .... V.10:1 Your r. that whatever seems to separate
T-11 .... VII.4:9 it is the r. that reality is only what is true.
T-11 ... VIII.3:3 The r. of this is your firm beginning. You
T-12 ........I.8:2 r. is necessary to demonstrate the need
T-12 ......I.8:13 in unconscious r. of what has been denied
T-12 ..... III.7:3 and the r. that it encompasses completely
T-12 ..... IV.7:5 only the r. that you have been redeemed.
T-12 ...... V.2:1 why the r. of your own invulnerability is
T-12 ...... V.2:6 Yet the r. of your invulnerability has more
T-13 .......I.11:4 through the calm r. that it has never been.
T-13 .......II.9:5 for it is the r. of love without fear. There
T-13 ... VI.12:1 and out of quiet r. of the truth in them.
T-13 .... VII.5:8 His Being does not depend upon your r..
T-13 .... VII.6:7 of God, in r. that you share it with Him.
T-14 ..... III.1:4 this entails the r. that guilt is interference,
T-14 ..... IV.5:2 what you want, in r. that you do not know
T-14 ..... IV.7:5 that knowledge is swept away from r. in
T-14 .... VII.7:4 r. that nothing you see means anything
T-14 ... VIII.1:4 that interferes with r. of the power of God
T-14 ... VIII.3:3 to where God and His Son await your r..
T-14 .....X.12:1 The miracle is the r. that this is true.
T-14 .....X.12:8 will bless each r. of His Son with all the
T-15 .......II.6:9 the r. of the universe that witnesses to It,
T-15 ..... IV.1:2 rather delay the r. that His Will is so. The
T-15 ..... IV.6:7 r. that all minds are in communication. It
T-15 ... VI.6:10 r. you will join with me in offering what is
T-15 .. VII.14:6 in sudden r. of the value of his part in it.
T-15 ..... IX.3:1 r. of relationships without limits is given
T-15 .......X.6:5 this, since this r. would make it homeless.
T-15 .......X.6:6 For when the r. dawns clearly, you will
T-15 .......X.9:5 And yet it is the r. of the decision, *just as it*
T-16 .......II.3:3 it. The r. of the part as whole, and of the
T-16 ... VI.12:5 of your r. of your unwillingness for your
T-17 ...... V.4:2 the r. of its inappropriateness for meeting
T-19 ..... III.5:3 not share His r. of the difference between
T19... IV.D.5:3 presence of the quiet r. that you love Him.
T-21 .......II.8:2 is not an instant of creation, but of r.. For
T-21 .......II.8:3 For r. comes of vision and suspended
T-21 ..... III.9:6 The instant for its r. is at hand. Join your
T-22 ......I.10:4 r. that the "something else" you thought
T-25 ..... IV.4:6 while, in twisted forms too far away for r.,
T-26 ..... III.7:3 And in the r. this is so lies the ability to
T-26 .... VII.9:5 you are, and r. of where and what you are.
T-28 ........I.3:2 is a r. that you have no needs which mean
T-28 .......II.3:5 And in that r., causelessness is given no
T-31 .......I.11:2 r. that it is a state of mind unwanted that
W-pI ...... 9.1:4 fact, the r. that you do not understand is a
W-pI .... 13.2:1 R. of meaninglessness arouses intense
W-pI .... 14.6:7 In r. of this fact, conclude the practice
W-pI .... 19.4:3 make the r. of lack of order in miracles
W-pI .... 20.4:2 implies the r. that you do not see now.
W-pI .... 25.5:2 The r. that they are meaningless, rather
W-pI .... 37.3:2 but merely by your quiet r. that in your
W-pI .... 47.1:5 that gives you the r. of the right solution,
W-pI .... 47.6:1 r. of your own frailty is a necessary step in
W-pI .... 64.2:4 becomes the spiritual r. of salvation.
W-pI .... 65.1:5 the r. of salvation as your function, and
W-pI .... 70.3:1 clear to you why the r. that guilt is in your
W-pI .... 70.7:1 adding a statement signifying your r. that
W-pI .... 73.9:1 with the r. that God's plan for salvation,
W-pI .... 74.2:5 and experience the peace this r. brings.
W-pI .... 76.3:1 Think of the freedom in the r. that you
W-pI .... 79.9:4 In this r. are all problems resolved. In this
W-pI .... 79.9:5 resolved. In this r. there is peace.
W-pI .... 83.1:3 me. This r. releases me from all conflict,
W-pI .. 124.4:3 with Him today in r. and remembrance.
W-pI .. 124.7:5 that the world may share our r. of reality.
W-pI .. 138.5:3 r. its acceptance lies, and as it is accepted
W-pI .. 152.3:1 Salvation is the r. that the truth is true,
W-pI .. 153.6:2 testifies to r. of the Christ in you. Perhaps
W-pI .. 158.8:2 requires but the r. that the world can not
W-pI .. 160.6:8 Its Own unto Itself in r. of what is Its Own
W-pI .. 162.6:6 Son of God, and in that r. is the world's.
W-pI .. 169.6:2 It comes to every mind when total r. that
W-pI .. 188.1:4 Enlightenment is but a r., not a change at
W-pII . 307.2:1 with God's, in r. that they are the same.
M-5 ........II.3:2 this; the r. that sickness is of the mind,
M-5 ........II.3:3 What does this r. "cost"? It costs the
M-5 ........II.3:5 For with this r. is responsibility placed
M-7 ........... 5:8 important is only the r. of a mistake as a
M-10 ......... 3:1 is the r. that judgment in the usual sense
M-12 ......... 4:1 their r. of the proper purpose of the body.
M-12 ......... 4:4 From this understanding will come the r.,
M-16 ......... 9:6 to this, and bring this goal nearer to r..
M-16 ....... 10:8 as true must be abandoned through his r.,
M-22 ......... 4:6 Healing is the result of the r., by God's
M-22 ......... 4:7 This r. has no special reference. It is true
M-24 ......... 1:6 to strengthen the r. of the eternal nature
M-26 ......... 1:3 the threshold of r. only where all barriers
M-28 ......... 1:5 It is the r. of the gifts of God. It is the
P-2........ VI.4:4 but without the r. that this is so. For when
P-2........ VI.5:5 That is achieved by only one r.; that only
S-1..........II.4:6 thereby lose the r. of your own Identity.
S-1..........II.5:5 unity of Christ and a r. of His sinlessness.
S-1........ III.4:5 lie only in the r. that the guilt has gone.
S-1..........V.1:5 in honesty and r. that they do not serve.

## recognizable 1

P-2..........II.1:1 or even to believe in God to any r. extent.

## recognize 426

T-1 ........I.18:4 r. your own and your neighbor's worth
T-1 ....... III.4:7 into temptation" means "R. your errors
T-1 ....... III.8:1 that you may not r. is not your concern.
T-1 .........V.3:4 r. your complete dependence on God, you
T-2 ....... III.1:6 It *does* r. that Atonement in physical terms
T-2 ....... III.3:6 Eventually everyone begins to r., however
T-2 .........V.4:5 you are in a position to r. that those who
T-2 .........V.5:2 you r. that mind is the only creative level,
T-2 ....... VI.6:4 as soon as you r. that it is also your own.
T-2 ....... VI.8:7 as you r. only the need for the remedy,
T-2 ....... VI.9:8 It is hard to r. that thought and belief
T-2 ...... VII.5:8 to r. temporarily that there is a problem,
T-3 ..........I.3:8 me? Be very sure that you r. how utterly
T-3 ....... III.2:1 from the fact that you do not r. yourself,
T-3 ....... III.2:2 To r. means to "know again," implying

T-3......III.7:12 When they do not **r.** each other, they do
T-3......III.7:12 recognize each other, they do not **r.** Him.
T-3........V.6:5 may be able to **r.** what you already have.
T-3........VI.3:2 When you **r.** what you are and what your
T-4........II.3:3 so apparent that one need only **r.** it to see
T-4........II.5:5 Yet whether or not you **r.** it now, you
T-4......IV.11:3 you are too confused to **r.** your own hope.
T-4........V.5:2 for something you would not **r.**.
T-4........VI.1:1 ego does not **r.** the real source of "threat,"
T-4........VI.7:8 You do not **r.** them now, but what has
T-5........III.1:1 way to **r.** your brother is by recognizing
T-5........III.3:4 in his mind, and you will **r.** Him in yours.
T-5......III.10:4 the ego, although the ego does not **r.** it.
T-5......VI.2:10 you **r.** what it can do because you gave it
T-5......VII.6:3 is to **r.** that you actively decided wrongly,
T-6.......II.13:1 Him impartially can you **r.** Him at all. The
T-6........V.2:4 Then you train them to **r.** the difference
T-6........V.4:3 because they do not **r.** the difference. The
T-6......V.B.1:7 What you must **r.** is that when you do not
T-7........III.3:2 and **r.** all whom you see as brothers,
T-7........V.7:5 that a Son of God can **r.** his power in one
T-7......VI.8:10 only as long as you do not **r.** what is true.
T-7.....VII.1:11 Spirit, it can help you **r.** part of reality,
T-7... VIII.3:12 in constant activity in order not to **r.** this.
T-7........X.3:4 You no more **r.** what is painful than you
T-7........XI.5:3 for you to **r.** and appreciate and know.
T-7........XI.5:6 If you **r.** His gift in anyone, you have
T-7........XI.5:7 Nothing is so easy to **r.** as truth. This is
T-7........XI.5:9 You have trained yourself not to **r.** it, and
T-7........XI.6:6 He cannot have lost what you **r.**, and you
T-8........V.1:3 not **r.** it because they prefer the delusion.
T-8........V.2:5 perceiving this likeness is to **r.** the Father.
T-8.....VIII.6:9 harder it may be to **r.** their nothingness,
T-9..........I.4:2 have hidden and **r.** the Will of God there.
T-9..........I.5:4 you would **r.** that willing is salvation
T-9..........I.9:1 ultimately everyone must **r.** himself. This
T-9........I.10:8 God? And could He fail to **r.** it in His Son?
T-9........I.11:1 not **r.** the enormous waste of energy you
T-9.......II.11:7 this willingness can you **r.** what you have.
T-9.......II.12:1 can give to Him only where you **r.** Him. If
T-9.......II.12:2 If you **r.** Him in everyone, consider how
T-9........VI.2:3 so you will not always **r.** His consistency.
T-9........VI.4:4 creation whenever you **r.** part of creation.
T-9........VI.6:2 witnesses to your reality that you can **r.**.
T-10.........I.1:7 **R.** this gladly, for in this recognition lies
T-10.........I.2:3 **r.** from your own experience that what
T-10........II.4:5 If you further **r.** that you are part of God,
T-11........II.6:5 **r.** the little spark and are willing to let it
T-11.......IV.4:3 must learn to **r.** and to oppose steadfastly,
T-11........V.2:5 next step is obviously to **r.** that what has
T-11........V.4:3 inappropriate if you **r.** the ego's goal,
T-11........V.5:2 to **r.** that their source is not natural, being
T-11........V.7:5 are confused because you do not **r.** yours.
T-11........V.8:1 must **r.** that the last thing the ego wishes
T-11......V.10:3 will not accept the cost of fear if you **r.** it.
T-11......V.12:5 **R.** only that the ego's goal, which you
T-11......V.12:8 Let him but **r.** it and he will not accept it.
T-11......VII.4:1 opposite of goodness enables you to **r.** a
T-11... VIII.1:4 you will **r.** that you did not believe it. Yet
T-11... VIII.2:2 children. Little children **r.** that they do
T-11... VIII.3:6 nothing. **R.** this but do not accept it, for
T-12.........I.5:4 To fail to **r.** a call for help is to refuse help.
T-12.........I.5:6 when you refuse to **r.** a brother's appeal,
T-12.........I.5:7 and you will not **r.** God's Answer to you.
T-12.......I.6:11 you will **r.** your own need for the Father.
T-12.........I.7:3 will **r.** God's Answer as you want It to be,
T-12.........I.8:2 to **r.** fear is not enough to escape from it,
T-12.........I.8:5 repeatedly emphasized the need to **r.** fear
T-12.......I.10:1 reality, how could you do better than to **r.**
T-12........II.3:3 for health is to **r.** in hatred the call for love
T-12.......III.4:1 ***R.*** *what does not matter,* and if your
T-12.....III.10:1 will **r.** that all the attack you perceive is in
T-12.......IV.3:5 you will search for love, but will not **r.** it.
T-12......VII.1:3 You will **r.** that you have learned there is
T-12......VII.2:1 to **r.** that the world has been redeemed.
T-12......VII.2:4 perceiving what it does, you **r.** its being.
T-12......VII.6:6 you will find them, but you will **r.** neither.
T-13........II.5:1 of truth, let us **r.** that you believe you have
T-13........II.9:7 of God, and to **r.** him *is* your redemption.
T-13......IV.6:7 Would you **r.** a holy encounter if you are
T-13........V.4:1 not **r.** they have condemned themselves.
T-13........V.4:4 the reality of their brothers they cannot **r.**
T-13......V.7:13 you must offer them, to **r.** His gift to you.
T-13......X.11:6 Until you **r.** that this is true, you will have
T-14........II.1:2 misery must first **r.** that you are miserable
T-14........II.5:5 your goal, and **r.** how foolish it has been.
T-14.......IV.7:3 you have denied Him and do not **r.** Him,
T-14......VII.7:3 you teaches you how to **r.** what you see. It
T-14........X.7:2 are much too confused either to **r.** love, or
T-14......X.12:7 It is not recognized, you will **r.** It. And
T-14.......XI.5:1 by which to **r.** if what you learned is true.
T-14.......XI.6:4 need only **r.** that everything you learned
T-14.....XI.13:1 Only those who **r.** they cannot know
T-14.....XI.15:6 by which you **r.** that you have understood
T-15........II.4:6 And you will **r.** which you have chosen by
T-15........II.5:2 and you will **r.** it with perfect certainty.
T-15.......IV.4:2 This you will **r.** in the holy instant, in
T-15.......IV.4:7 Use the holy instant only to **r.** that you
T-15.......IV.6:4 you prefer not to **r.** it and not to let it go.
T-15.......IV.8:2 is impossible to **r.** perfect communication
T-15.......VI.2:5 share our faith in God's Son because we **r.**
T-15.......VI.4:4 That is because you **r.**, however dimly,
T-15.......VI.5:3 holy instant you **r.** the idea of love in you,
T-15.....VI.6:10 For in the holy instant you will **r.** the only
T-15......VII.4:1 that you do not **r.** what it would do to you
T-15... VIII.1:7 you **r.** that there is nothing to forgive, you
T-15.......IX.2:2 For it is impossible to **r.** as wholly without
T-15........X.6:4 you. You are unwilling to **r.** that the ego,
T-15........X.8:6 **r.** that it is what you invited in that would
T-15.......XI.1:1 Fear not to **r.** the whole idea of sacrifice
T-15.......XI.6:3 to deny what love is and still **r.** it. The
T-15.....XI.10:7 *because I* ***r.*** *that we will be released together.*
T-16.........I.4:4 that to **r.** and accept the fact that you do
T-16.........I.4:4 to **r.** and accept the fact that He *does* know
T-16.........I.5:2 And yet you **r.** no triumph but this. This
T-16........II.9:9 you have really seen and heard, and **r.** it.
T-16.......III.3:6 and do not **r.** It even though It functions.
T-16.......IV.7:1 **R.** this, for it is true, and truth must be
T-16........V.8:4 one will **r.** that he has asked for hell, and
T-16......V.14:2 which you fail to **r.** them for what they are
T-16......V.17:2 you will **r.** that God is on the other side,
T-16.......VI.3:3 You do not **r.** that this is its real appeal,
T-16.......VI.8:8 soon **r.** the guilt of self-betrayal for what it
T-17.......IV.3:2 Yet you do not **r.** them because you have
T-17.......IV.6:2 You **r.**, at least in general terms, that the
T-17.....IV.14:7 what you see there you will **r.** as what it is;
T-17......V.13:5 to **r.** what has been given and received by
T-17......V.15:1 begin to **r.** and accept the gifts you have
T-17.......VI.5:7 You will **r.** the outcome *because* you are at
T-17......VII.5:9 look upon its offering and **r.** it *is* illusion.
T-18........II.3:2 **r.** that what you see on waking is blotted
T-18........II.5:9 Yet what you fail to **r.** is that what caused
T-18......VII.7:2 And if you **r.** you need do nothing, you
T-18... VIII.1:6 idea? Everything you **r.** you identify with
T-18... VIII.1:7 a body, or in some form you think you **r.**.
T-18. VIII.10:4 And you will **r.** yourself, and see your
T-18. VIII.12:2 You do not **r.** that love has come, because
T-18. VIII.12:5 know you not, or fail to **r.** itself in you.
T-19.........I.7:5 to perceive this is to **r.** where separation is
T-19.........I.12:6 and so you do not **r.** salvation in him. Yet
T-19.......III.4:3 He **r.** mistakes that cannot be corrected.
T19..IV.B.14:8 The ego and the Holy Spirit both **r.** this,
T19..IV.B.14:8 and both also **r.** that here the sender and
T19. IV.D.20:6 And he will **r.** his choice by what he gives,
T19. IV.D.21:7 in your holy Friend, and **r.** it as your own.
T-20.........I.4:2 will behold your brother's face and **r.** it. I
T-20......II.11:3 Heaven and **r.** the home that called to you
T-20.......III.2:5 to **r.** your holy relationship for what it is.
T-20.......III.3:2 it is within the truth they **r.** their holiness,
T-20.......III.8:7 Did you **r.** your brother as the eternal gift
T-20........V.3:4 **r.** the fear that rises from the meaningless
T-20........V.4:3 will **r.** it as you receive his Father's gift
T-20......V.7:10 His understanding **r.** it and love it as your
T-20......VII.2:3 You **r.** you want the goal. Are you not also
T-20... VIII.8:4 all you need to do is **r.** that *you* did this.
T-21........in.2:6 learn from this to **r.** which one you chose.
T-21.........I.1:2 and fall because of what they did not **r.**,
T-21.........I.1:5 fall down upon the stones you did not **r.**,
T-21.........I.2:3 must be seen before you **r.** it for what it is.
T-21........II.7:8 simply to **r.** again the presence of what
T-21......II.11:1 that you **r.** you made the world you see, as
T-21......II.11:1 you **r.** that you did not create yourself.
T-21.......III.8:4 But first they chose to **r.** how much their
T-21.......IV.4:2 much of your insanity and **r.** its madness.
T-21.......IV.5:4 And now you **r.** that it was not the ego
T-21.......VI.5:8 But think what you must **r.**, if it be so.
T-21......VII.4:7 changes so it is impossible even to **r.** him.
T-21.....VIII.5:1 appeal to you to **r.** what He has given you
T-22........in.4:9 golden circle where you **r.** the Son of God.
T-22.........I.6:7 will **r.** his home and see them there with
T-22........I.10:6 illusions is to **r.** that fear is meaningless.
T-22........II.4:1 from misery is to **r.** it *and go the other way.*
T-22......II.11:3 your savior as your enemy and **r.** him. Yet
T-22......II.11:4 Yet it is possible to **r.** him for what he is, if
T-22.......III.4:2 Meaning it does not **r.**, and does not see if
T-22.......III.7:7 as the truth. Could it, then, **r.** the truth?
T-22.......VI.6:2 The light you bring you do not **r.**, and yet
T-22.......VI.6:4 And who would fail to **r.** a gift he let be
T-22.......VI.7:3 could there be you will not **r.** as a mistake;
T-22.......VI.7:4 are His, and they will **r.** their wills are His,
T-23........in.6:8 And it must be complete if you would **r.** it
T-23........II.9:4 and thus it fails to **r.** that you can never
T-23......II.18:6 form they take, and do not **r.** the content.
T-23......II.22:2 you will not **r.** the rest for what they are.
T-23.......III.1:1 you do not **r.** some of the forms attack
T-23.......III.1:2 as much as in another form that you *do* **r.**,
T-23.......III.1:2 must follow that you do not always **r.** the
T-23.......III.4:7 to **r.** assault upon your peace in any form,
T-23.......IV.4:3 you and that you do not **r.** for what it is,
T-23.......IV.6:2 Even in forms you do not **r.**, the signs you
T-24.........II.2:2 cut him down, yet **r.** his strong support?
T-24.....VII.5:9 where your creations **r.** a gift from you, a
T-25........in.2:1 in him can fail to **r.** Him everywhere.
T-25........in.2:5 And thus he does not **r.** Him where He is.
T-25.......III.1:2 to which you **r.** that guilt is meaningless,
T-25.....III.9:10 But **r.** that in this choice the purpose of
T-25.......IV.1:1 Minds that are joined and **r.** they are, can
T-25.....VIII.1:6 and **r.** that what brings loss to no one you
T-25.....VIII.9:4 what you **r.** you could not give yourself. In
T-25.....VIII.9:5 Own justice does He **r.** all you deserve,
T-25..VIII.10:2 that is in him, however much he **r.** it not.
T-25.......IX.1:9 you **r.** that truth must be revealed to you,
T-26...VII.14:8 Nor will he know himself, nor **r.** his will.
T-26...VII.16:1 you will **r.** because the truth is in your
T-27......II.14:6 other half until you **r.** it *is* the other half.
T-27......II.15:5 that He does not see and **r.** as His. For
T-27.......VII.4:3 Yet they do not **r.** their common need.
T-27..VIII.10:6 no effect on you unless you failed to **r.** it is
T-28.......IV.8:4 he sees this picture he will **r.** himself. If
T-29.......IV.2:7 be afraid because you did not **r.** the fear.
T-29.......IX.4:8 are real, nor **r.** their wishes are their own.
T-30.........I.1:3 with a little practice with the ones you **r.**,
T-30.........I.6:1 and **r.** that something has occurred that is
T-31........I.10:5 will **r.** Him as you give Him answer in the
T-31........V.2:5 but one of which the mind can **r.**. The
T-31.......VI.1:1 You see the flesh or **r.** the spirit. There is
T-31......VII.1:2 make the kinds of change you could not **r.**
T-31......VII.2:1 You could not **r.** your "evil" thoughts as
W-pI.......4.3:4 **r.** what is the same and what is different.
W-pI.......4.5:1 particular thought that you **r.** as harmful.
W-pI.......8.3:1 to **r.** when it is not really thinking at all.
W-pI.......8.4:2 easier to **r.** that no matter how vividly you
W-pI.....10.3:4 **r.** this is to recognize nothingness when
W-pI.....10.3:4 recognize this is to **r.** nothingness when
W-pI.....13.3:1 that you learn to **r.** the meaningless, and
W-pI.....15.1:1 images that you do not **r.** them as nothing
W-pI.....16.3:1 salvation requires that you also **r.** that
W-pI.....16.3:3 you **r.** them all as equally destructive, but
W-pI.....21.3:2 do not really **r.** what arouses anger in you,
W-pI.....23.7:3 You do not **r.** this as yet, and you are
W-pI.....24.1:6 Otherwise, you will not **r.** what they are.
W-pI.....24.6:1 you will quickly **r.** that you are making a
W-pI.....24.6:2 will also **r.** that many of your goals are
W-pI.....25.4:2 most superficial levels, you do **r.** purpose.
W-pI.....30.2:3 minds, and what we want to **r.** is there.
W-pI.....33.1:1 Today's idea is an attempt to **r.** that you
W-pI.....35.5:3 mind. Try to **r.** that the direction of your

| | |
|---|---|
| W-pI.....44.2:1 | to see, you must **r.** that light is within, not |
| W-pI.....45.4:6 | we will try to **r.** that only what God would |
| W-pI.....47.7:2 | You will **r.** that you have reached it if you |
| W-pI.....48.1:4 | fear. It is very easy to **r.** this. But it is very |
| W-pI.....48.1:5 | But it is very difficult to **r.** it for those who |
| W-pI.....48.3:2 | not necessarily in a place you **r.** as yet, |
| W-pI.....50.5:2 | thoughts come to help you **r.** its truth, |
| W-pI.....51.1:3 | It is necessary that I **r.** this, that I may |
| W-pI.....51.2:5 | to **r.** the lack of validity in my judgments, |
| W-pI.....51.4:6 | I am willing to **r.** that my thoughts do not |
| W-pI.....53.4:6 | of my decision, and **r.** where I really abide |
| W-pI.....55.4:2 | I **r.** my own best interests when I do not |
| W-pI.....55.5:5 | Therefore I do not **r.** its real purpose. The |
| W-pI.....56.4:6 | and **r.** the truth beyond them all. |
| W-pI.....57.2:3 | All I need do is **r.** this and I am free. I have |
| W-pI.....58.2:5 | As I **r.** my holiness, so does the holiness of |
| W-pI.....60.1:4 | the means by which I will **r.** my innocence |
| W-pI.....60.2:4 | I begin to see, I **r.** His reflection on earth. I |
| W-pI.....60.3:5 | I will **r.** in everyone my dearest Friend. |
| W-pI.....62.1:2 | that lets you **r.** the light in which you see. |
| W-pI.....62.5:5 | freely, for your heart will **r.** these words, |
| W-pI.....63.1:2 | are you who can learn to **r.** the means for |
| W-pI.....66.4:4 | and **r.** a common content where it exists |
| W-pI.....67.4:3 | which you **r.** yourself as love created you. |
| W-pI.....69.8:2 | You may not **r.** His answer yet, but you |
| W-pI.....70.7:6 | **R.** that it is not there, and tell yourself: |
| W-pI.....72.9:4 | **r.** the light of truth in us is to recognize |
| W-pI.....72.9:4 | of truth in us is to **r.** ourselves as we are. |
| W-pI...72.10:4 | are therefore attacking what we do not **r.**. |
| W-pI.....74.2:5 | Let us try to **r.** this today, and experience |
| W-pI.....74.6:2 | will you **r.** that you have reached it. If you |
| W-pI.....77.7:5 | You will **r.** these situations. And since you |
| W-pI........79.h | Let me **r.** the problem so it can be solved. |
| W-pI.....79.1:2 | you will not **r.** that it has been solved. |
| W-pI.....79.6:1 | a desperate attempt not to **r.** the problem |
| W-pI.....79.6:2 | **r.** that your only problem is separation, |
| W-pI.....79.6:4 | the means, because you **r.** the problem. |
| W-pI.....79.7:4 | one problem, which we have failed to **r.**. |
| W-pI.....79.8:4 | You are trying to **r.** that you have been |
| W-pI...79.10:3 | *Let me **r.** this problem so it can be solved.* |
| W-pI........80.h | Let me **r.** my problems have been solved. |
| W-pI.....80.1:1 | If you are willing to **r.** your problems, |
| W-pI.....80.1:1 | you will **r.** that you have no problems. |
| W-pI.....80.2:6 | And you can **r.** the answer, because the |
| W-pI.....80.5:3 | **R.** that your problems have been solved. |
| W-pI.....80.5:4 | **R.** that you are out of conflict; free and at |
| W-pI.....80.6:5 | *Let me **r.** this problem has been solved.* |
| W-pI.....80.7:4 | is, and you must **r.** it has been solved. |
| W-pI.....83.3:5 | I must learn to **r.** what makes me happy, |
| W-pI.....84.1:5 | I would **r.** my reality today. I will worship |
| W-pI.....85.3:2 | Today I will **r.** where my salvation is. It is |
| W-pI.....87.3:5 | I will **r.** that all this has not occurred. I am |
| W-pI.....88.1:2 | I merely choose to **r.** what is already there |
| W-pI.....90.1:1 | Let me **r.** the problem so it can be solved. |
| W-pI.....90.3:1 | Let me **r.** my problems have been solved. |
| W-pI...92.11:3 | **r.** that we are being introduced to sight, |
| W-pI.....98.3:1 | fear, for they are safe and **r.** their safety. |
| W-pI.....98.5:2 | hourly to **r.** your special function here? Is |
| W-pI.....99.4:2 | inviolate, yet **r.** the need illusions bring, |
| W-pI...100.5:5 | you. And so you do not **r.** that it is yours. |
| W-pI...104.3:1 | God wills, and **r.** the same as being one. |
| W-pI...104.4:1 | as we ask to **r.** what God has given us. We |
| W-pI...105.7:3 | prepare yourself to **r.** God's gifts to you, |
| W-pI...107.7:2 | to us, that we may **r.** it as our own. Today |
| W-pI...109.2:6 | the Son of God is born again, to **r.** himself |
| W-pI...119.2:2 | *truth in me, and come to **r.** my sinlessness.* |
| W-pI...122.3:2 | It lets you **r.** the Son of God, and clears |
| W-pI...124.2:5 | to follow us will **r.** the way because the |
| W-pI...124.9:3 | nor will you fail to **r.** it when it dawns |
| W-pI...126.7:1 | gift He asks of you, you cannot **r.** His gifts |
| W-pI.126.10:4 | and **r.** He speaks your words to you. |
| W-pI...132.7:2 | form which they can understand and **r.**. |
| W-pI...133.7:3 | will not **r.** the things you really have, |
| W-pI...133.8:6 | For what the ego wants it fails to **r.**. It |
| W-pI.135.12:1 | nor how to **r.** the problem that the plan is |
| W-pI...136.3:4 | **r.** exactly what you would attempt to do, |
| W-pI.136.17:2 | And you will **r.** you practiced well by this: |
| W-pI.137.10:2 | you. Perhaps you will not **r.** them all, nor |
| W-pI.138.11:2 | **r.** we make a conscious choice between |
| W-pI...139.2:1 | except one who has refused to **r.** himself? |
| W-pI...151.7:1 | evidence will clear the way to **r.** yourself, |
| W-pI.152.10:2 | we are, and humbly **r.** the Son of God. To |
| W-pI.152.10:3 | To **r.** God's Son implies as well that all |
| W-pI...153.9:1 | **r.** that we need no defense because we are |
| W-pI.153.11:6 | your hands, so will you **r.** it as your own. |
| W-pI...154.8:5 | that they are yours, and do not **r.** them. |
| W-pI.154.10:1 | this joining that we undertake to **r.** today. |
| W-pI.154.11:1 | would have, that we may **r.** His gifts to us. |
| W-pI.154.12:1 | will not **r.** what we receive until we give it. |
| W-pI.154.13:2 | *I have the means by which to **r.** that I am free.* |
| W-pI.154.14:4 | hands, and we will **r.** what we received. |
| W-pI...155.1:4 | who walk the world as you do **r.** their own |
| W-pI...155.1:5 | not yet perceived the way will **r.** you also, |
| W-pI...156.5:2 | you, for they **r.** Who walks with you. The |
| W-pI...159.1:7 | To give is how to **r.** you have received. It is |
| W-pI...159.2:3 | You **r.** your brother as yourself, and thus |
| W-pI...160.2:2 | yet, he does not **r.** to whom he comes, and |
| W-pI...160.7:3 | now to **r.** this stranger in your midst, for |
| W-pI...160.9:3 | a stranger, for they do not **r.** themselves. |
| W-pI.161.12:3 | bone, and **r.** that Christ has come to you. |
| W-pI...164.2:4 | You will **r.** them both, for they are but |
| W-pI.166.12:7 | these gifts, and **r.** they are your own. |
| W-pI.166.13:5 | feel the touch of Christ, and **r.** God's gifts. |
| WpI...rV.in1:3 | We **r.** we are preparing for another phase |
| WpI...rV.in6:2 | that you may come to me who **r.** the road |
| WpI.rV.in12:3 | and **r.** that it is only here conviction lies. |
| W-pI...181.6:1 | We **r.** that we have lost this goal if anger |
| W-pI...182.1:3 | to return, although you do not **r.** the voice |
| W-pI...182.2:3 | are sad, and do not **r.** their tears at all. |
| W-pI...184.9:5 | but which you **r.** is not the unity where |
| W-pI...187.6:3 | fail to **r.** the many forms which sacrifice |
| W-pI...188.7:2 | They **r.** their home. And they point surely |
| W-pI...195.6:3 | and we fail to **r.** the gifts of God to us. |
| W-pI...195.9:3 | If we refuse to **r.** it, we are not entitled |
| W-pI.198.13:2 | and **r.** that He Who brought us here will |
| W-pII.....2.2:4 | still was one, but failed to **r.** its oneness. |
| W-pII.234.2:2 | *We **r.** our safety, and give thanks for all the* |
| W-pII.240.2:3 | *Give us faith today to **r.** Your Son, and set* |
| W-pII.243.1:4 | see. Today I **r.** that this is so. And so I am |
| W-pII.245.1:8 | *as is Your Will, that I may come to **r.** my Self.* |
| W-pII.245.2:3 | Whose Love we **r.** because we share the |
| W-pII.246.1:3 | Self. Let me not fail to **r.** myself, and still |
| W-pII.246.2:3 | *I would **r.** that what You will is what I will as* |
| W-pII.247.2:4 | *them, and thus I hope this day to **r.** my Self.* |
| W-pII.251.1:4 | My only need I did not **r.**. But now I see |
| W-pII.262.2:1 | are one would **r.** this day the truth about |
| W-pII.268.1:4 | *I be able, too, to **r.** my Self as You created me.* |
| W-pII.....7.3:1 | yearns to have you **r.** your sinlessness, |
| W-pII.282.1:4 | choice to **r.** the Self Whom God created as |
| W-pII.287.2:7 | *What way but this could I expect to **r.** my Self* |
| W-pII.288.1:3 | *I first must **r.** what You created one with me.* |
| W-pII.291.1:6 | us to **r.** it is a holiness in which we share; |
| W-pII.316.2:2 | *I do not **r.** them. Yet I trust that You Who* |
| W-pII.317.1:4 | go, then will I **r.** salvation is already here, |
| W-pII.328.1:6 | it is to Him that we must go to **r.** our will. |
| W-pII.329.2:3 | Through it we **r.** that we are one. Through |
| W-pII.353.1:5 | *my Identity, and **r.** that Christ is but my Self.* |
| WfI........in.3:5 | will not fail to **r.** as part of God Himself. |
| M-3...........5:4 | does not mean that they necessarily **r.** this |
| M-5.........I.2:3 | form which the Son of God is forced to **r.**. |
| M-5........II.1:3 | to say this, one first must **r.** certain facts. |
| M-5......III.3:5 | They **r.** illusions can have no effect. The |
| M-7...........2:5 | and must **r.** that his own uncertainty is |
| M-7.........3:11 | teacher of God can only **r.** it for what it is, |
| M-7...........4:1 | the most difficult temptations to **r.** is that |
| M-7...........6:2 | It is a failure to **r.** him as part of the Self, |
| M-10.........3:4 | One would have to **r.** in advance all the |
| M-12.........6:9 | They **r.** that to behold a dream figure as |
| M-15.........2:5 | hear this Judgment and to **r.** that it is true |
| M-16.......6:13 | **R.** this, and they will disappear. And only |
| M-16.......11:9 | must God's teachers learn to **r.** the forms |
| M-17.........9:4 | To see it and to **r.** its thought system is to |
| M-20.........4:4 | do not **r.** that you have picked it up again. |
| M-22.........5:5 | in fact, be unable to **r.** his brother at all, |
| M-22.........6:8 | It is your function to **r.** for him that what |
| C-in..........4:2 | It does not **r.** as questions the mere form |
| P-1............2:6 | and helps the patient to **r.** and accept it. |
| P-2..........II.9:4 | Let him be still and **r.** his brother's need is |
| P-2........IV.5:1 | the world may **r.** the mind as the source |
| P-3..........I.2:2 | you, who do not yet **r.** who he is who asks. |
| P-3..........I.2:8 | to you and not be sure you **r.** his needs? |
| P-3..........I.3:6 | You will **r.** them in whatever way can be |
| P-3..........I.4:2 | it he will **r.** the whole when his part is |
| P-3.........II.5:2 | against the day when they can **r.** that only |
| P-3.........II.8:1 | also **r.** that order of difficulty in healing is |
| P-3.........II.9:4 | he must also **r.** the equality of himself and |
| P-3........III.5:9 | they will **r.** him as a brother no longer. |
| S-1........in.2:3 | What God created one must **r.** its oneness |
| S-1..........I.2:5 | beyond the level of need that you can **r.**. |
| S-1........III.1:4 | you to **r.** it is not he who is hurting you. |
| S-1........III.3:1 | the learning goal must be to **r.** that prayer |
| S-1.........V.3:2 | as God's Son, and **r.** the arrogance of sin. |
| S-3........III.4:6 | You but **r.** your oneness with the one who |
| S-3........III.5:1 | they are Sons of God who **r.** their Source, |

## recognized 145

| | |
|---|---|
| T-4.......VI.3:5 | however, are immediately **r.** as eternal. |
| T-7.......IV.1:1 | can only *be* **r.** and *need* only be recognized. |
| T-7.......IV.1:1 | can only *be* recognized and *need* only be **r.**. |
| T-7.....VI.4:12 | And if it **r.** any part of the Sonship, it |
| T-7.....VIII.6:5 | but it may not be **r.** as being beyond belief |
| T-7.........X.3:2 | no one would object to this goal if he **r.** it. |
| T-8..........I.6:1 | of such a curriculum must be fully **r.** |
| T-8.......IV.6:7 | of all God's Sons cannot be **r.** through the |
| T-8.....VIII.3:5 | you **r.** this and also decided against attack |
| T-9.......II.10:3 | of giving and receiving will be **r.**. The |
| T-10.......V.6:3 | knowing that if you **r.** your love for Him, |
| T-11.........I.8:9 | it is only because you have not **r.** your will |
| T-11.......V.2:7 | If reality is **r.** by its extension, what leads |
| T-11.......V.9:3 | listen to it if you **r.** this is what it is doing? |
| T-11.....VI.9:6 | him. Redemption is **r.** only by sharing it. |
| T-11.VIII.10:2 | Only loving thoughts are **r.**, and because |
| T-12.........I.8:4 | were left with the fear, once you had **r.** it, |
| T-12....VII.1:1 | been learned can be **r.** only by its results. |
| T-12....VII.8:5 | Love, too, is **r.** by its messengers. If you |
| T-13.......II.8:3 | perhaps **r.** the futility of the ego and its |
| T-13.......V.5:2 | apart, where when it comes it is not **r.**. If |
| T-13.....V.11:5 | darkness the Christ in them, and **r.** Him. |
| T-13.....VII.5:6 | what is denied is there but is not **r.**. Christ |
| T-14.....VII.2:5 | Yet it can be **r.** or unrecognized, real or |
| T-14.......X.12:7 | your Identity wherever It is not **r.**, you |
| T-14.....XI.9:5 | instead of you, and **r.** they never were. |
| T-15.......II.4:7 | the Holy Spirit in a brother is always **r.**. |
| T-15.......II.5:3 | No gift of God is **r.** in any other way. You |
| T-15.....VII.3:1 | attraction of guilt must be **r.** for what it is. |
| T-15.....IX.3:5 | Yet you have surely **r.** that the ego, whose |
| T-15.......X.6:7 | Each form will be **r.** as but a cover for the |
| T-16.....IV.7:1 | truth must be **r.** if it is to be distinguished |
| T-16...IV.12:4 | near. You have almost **r.** it. Turn with me |
| T-16.....V.12:4 | special relationship must be **r.** for what it |
| T-17.......V.6:9 | **r.** as such in the light of its goal. |
| T-18.......II.7:8 | Him. If you but **r.** His gratitude! Or mine |
| T-18...IX.12:3 | ends when you have **r.** all it is *not*. That is |
| T-19.........I.6:7 | must be, are **r.** as dedication to illusion; |
| T-19.....III.9:4 | quickly **r.** and quickly given to correction, |
| T-20....VII.4:3 | sin be lifted, so what was always true is **r.**. |
| T-20...VIII.7:3 | if you **r.** this world is an hallucination? |
| T-20...VIII.8:1 | when they are **r.** for what they are. This is |
| T-21.......II.4:8 | the power of your wanting must first be **r.** |
| T-21.....III.2:6 | of faith is never **r.** if it is placed in sin. But |
| T-21.....III.2:7 | sin. But it is always **r.** if it is placed in love. |
| T-21.....IV.5:1 | and **r.** him perfectly since time began. |
| T-22.......V.5:1 | **r.** how little stands between you and your |
| T-22.....VI.1:7 | entirely when they are **r.** as functionless. |
| T-22...VI.12:1 | were one with God and **r.** this oneness, |
| T-23.....III.3:5 | purpose is lost because it is not **r.**. It is |
| T-23...IV.5:11 | of miracles be **r.** if murder is your choice? |
| T-24.......V.6:7 | first, but **r.** that you were not complete. |
| T-24.....VI.7:6 | at last in terms you **r.** and understood? |
| T-24....VII.2:3 | is **r.** in its acknowledgment. The holiness |
| T-25.....VI.2:3 | seems better; easier to see, and better **r.**. |
| T-25.VIII.11:1 | at last, provided it is seen and **r.**. For just |
| T-26.....III.7:6 | relinquishment of an illusion **r.** as such. |
| T-26.....V.11:9 | but still a present light is dimly **r.**. Once it |
| T-26..VII.20:5 | been true be **r.** by those who know it not; |
| T-26...VIII.9:8 | is changed and what it is cannot be **r.**. |

T-27...... III.3:8 empty space it occupies be **r.** as vacant,
T-27... VII.11:1 two states, but one of which is clearly **r.**?
T-27... VII.14:2 dream when once the dreamer has been **r.**
T-27. VIII.13:1 will you perceive the world when this is **r.**!
T-28....... II.2:8 the mind is **r.** as not within the body, and
T-28...... IV.9:4 **r.** as being part of the completed picture
T-29....... II.9:1 because its nothingness has not been **r.**.
T-29... VIII.1:8 it is this that never is perceived and **r.**. Be
T-30....... II.4:6 give when you have **r.** that you are free.
T-30....... V.1:6 it is **r.** that all things must be first forgiven
T-30....... V.2:3 folly of pursuing guilt as goal is fully **r.**.
T-30....... V.8:1 when you have **r.** Whose hand you hold!
T-30...... VI.5:1 Forgiveness **r.** as merited will heal. It
T-31..... V.17:5 **r.** as made on no assumptions that would
T-31... VIII.9:1 God's gift can once again be **r.** as ours!
W-pI..... 72.1:1 While we have **r.** that the ego's plan for
W-pI..... 74.1:3 Will. When you have **r.** this, you have
W-pI..... 74.1:3 this, you have **r.** that your will is His. The
W-pI..... 79.1:5 solution is not **r.** because the problem is
W-pI..... 79.1:5 recognized because the problem is not **r.**.
W-pI..... 79.2:2 and must be **r.** as one if the one solution
W-pI..... 80.2:3 You have **r.** your only problem, opening
W-pI..... 80.4:3 Having **r.** one, you have recognized the
W-pI..... 80.4:3 recognized one, you have **r.** the other.
W-pI..... 95.7:5 should, however, merely be **r.** as what it is
W-pI... 135.6:5 defense of something that he **r.** as this?
W-pI. 135.14:4 Yet planning is not often **r.** as a defense.
W-pI... 138.5:2 the truth cannot be learned, but only **r.**.
W-pI... 138.9:6 concealed, because their nothingness is **r.**.
W-pI. 138.11:5 there. Now it is **r.** as but a foolish, trivial
WpI. rIV.in3:2 thoughts from being seen and **r.**. Their
W-pI. 152.10:3 have been laid aside, and **r.** as false. Their
W-pI. 160.10:5 gift of sight by which his Self is clearly **r.**,
W-pI... 162.6:6 For you have **r.** the Son of God, and in
W-pI... 164.1:1 What time but now can truth be **r.**? The
W-pI... 164.6:4 both perceived and **r.** for what they are.
W-pI... 165.3:1 awakening, if he but **r.** where they abide?
W-pI... 168.2:4 give the means by which His Will is **r.**?
W-pI... 169.8:2 He **r.** all that time holds, and gave it to all
W-pI... 169.9:3 and fully **r.** as perfectly fulfilled by Him
WpI rV.in11:5 will have **r.** the words we speak are true.
W-pI... 185.1:4 the resurrection of all creation fully **r.**.
W-pI... 187.7:1 Illusion **r.** must disappear. Accept not
W-pI... 188.5:4 He forgives because he **r.** the truth in him.
W-pI... 193.4:4 forms, and yet is **r.** as easily in all of them,
W-pI... 197.2:4 and claimed, and found and fully **r.**.
W-pI. 200.10:6 Peace is already **r.** at last, and you can feel
W-pII...... in.5:6 when you have **r.** it is your will He do so.
W-pII...... 9.2:4 as one. And thus is oneness **r.** at last.
W-pII.. 314.1:2 now is **r.** as but extension of the present.
W-pII.. 345.1:3 *takes a form which can be **r.** and seen to work*
M-4...... I.A.3:3 that their lack of value is merely being **r.**.
M-4........ X.1:1 when its relation to forgiveness is **r.**.
M-5........ II.1:1 to which the valuelessness of sickness is **r.**
M-6............ 2:9 when it is **r.** as a blessing and not a curse.
M-8............ 1:2 with every other in order to be **r.**. A larger
M-8............ 2:3 importance, but is **r.** as being untrue. The
M-12.......... 3:8 for their unity could not be **r.** directly.
M-12.......... 4:5 unity come in, and what is one is **r.** as one
M-12.......... 6:5 dreams once they are **r.** for what they are?
M-14.......... 1:8 Their uselessness is **r.**, and they are gone.
M-16.......... 9:5 When all magic is **r.** as merely nothing,
M-17.......... 3:1 and errors can be **r.** by their results. A
M-17.......... 4:4 perhaps too mild to be even clearly **r.**. Or
M-17........ 4:10 It cannot be partially **r.**. Who is unaware
M-20.......... 1:2 How is it **r.**? How is it found? And being
M-20.......... 2:1 First, how can the peace of God be **r.**?
M-20.......... 2:2 God's peace is **r.** at first by just one thing;
M-23.......... 2:6 He has **r.** himself as God created him, and
M-23.......... 2:6 he has **r.** all living things as part of him.
M-24.......... 5:7 All that must be **r.**, however, is that birth
M-26.......... 2:7 mistakes are **r.** and overlooked by them.
M-28.......... 2:3 Life is now **r.** as salvation, and pain and
C-2........... 10:5 Who chooses hell when it is **r.**? And who
C-3............. 8:6 understood. His Son is not attacked but **r.**
C-5............. 6:3 names until their oneness can be **r.**. But
P-2........ III.1:5 He may, however, not be **r.**. And so the
P-2...... IV.11:4 It is merely **r.** as what it is. Seen rightly,
P-2........ VI.4:5 For when an unforgiveness is not **r.**, the
S-1......... II.7:5 Identity in Christ is fully **r.** as set forever,
S-1........ III.4:3 they are **r.** they bring their fear with them
S-1........ III.4:6 this be **r.** as long as he hides it in another,
S-1........ III.6:6 prayer can be quite clearly **r.** even in this.
S-1........ IV.1:3 doing so has been **r.** if only for an instant,
S-1......... V.4:6 to be, for you have **r.** the Christ in you.

## recognizes 45

T-1......... I.38:2 **r.** both God's creations and your illusions
T-1......... V.2:4 He **r.** that every collapse of time brings
T-1......... V.2:6 When everyone **r.** that he has everything,
T-2......... II.2:7 cannot miscreate, because it **r.** only truth.
T-2........ III.4:3 and **r.** immediately that the altar has been
T-3...... III.7:11 He **r.** them perfectly. When they do not
T-3......... V.4:8 The idea of "changing your image" **r.** the
T-4......... I.12:3 because it **r.** its radiance and gladly sheds
T-5...... III.10:5 The Holy Spirit **r.** it perfectly because it is
T-5......... V.5:9 **r.** that only total allegiance can be trusted
T-6......... II.1:2 that **r.** the Wholeness of God's creation.
T-6......... II.5:2 this perfection is shared He **r.** it in others,
T-7......... V.3:3 **r.** no other, because He does not accept
T-7........ VI.3:3 is why the ego never **r.** what it is doing. It
T-12....... II.4:4 **r.** that he does not understand what his
T-12....... III.4:8 one who **r.** what is valuable and wants to
T-13...... III.1:4 no one will countenance fear if he **r.** it.
T-13..... VII.7:7 him and **r.** that the world is one with him.
T-14....... IX.6:7 **r.** it because he has been taught his need
T-14....... X.6:5 call. It merely **r.** what it is, and answers
T-15..... VII.2:6 have no hold at all, except that no one **r.** it
T-15..... VII.6:4 and **r.** that no one could interpret direct
T-16......... I.6:7 Spirit **r.** foolish needs as well as real ones.
T-19....... III.4:2 Mistakes He **r.**, and would correct them
T19.. IV.B.15:3 The great deceiver **r.** that this is not so,
T-21..... V.3:10 And thus it **r.** that miracles do not affect
T-25..... VII.8:4 and **r.** as the world in which he lives, and
T-26...... III.5:3 for hell unless he **r.** they are not the same?
T-31. VIII.12:6 and perfectly, and all creation **r.** You, and
W-pI. 135.12:2 the body in its plans until it **r.** this is so.
W-pI... 151.7:4 He **r.** only what God loves, and in the holy
W-pI... 153.6:4 it **r.** strength so great attack is folly, or a
W-pI... 169.4:3 every mind that **r.** truth's effects on you.
W-pI... 187.6:5 He **r.** sacrifice remains the one idea that
W-pI... 188.5:2 Who **r.** it within himself must give it. And
W-pII...... 1.1:1 Forgiveness **r.** what you thought your
M-10......... 6:3 it down happily the instant he **r.** its cost.
M-13......... 5:4 as pain, and no one asks for pain if he **r.** it
M-16......... 7:5 he turns with all of them **r.** no order of
M-17......... 9:7 that anger **r.** a reality that is not there; yet
M-22......... 2:1 he **r.** the Atonement's inclusiveness, or
M-22......... 7:7 teacher **r.** that they are the same mistake.
M-25......... 2:2 the small range of channels the world **r.**.
P-2..... VII.1:14 him who calls, and in Him he **r.** Himself.
S-1......... V.2:6 whose purity it **r.** that it shares with him.

## recognizing 74

T-1......... I.30:1 By **r.** spirit, miracles adjust the levels of
T-2......... V.6:5 to the body by **r.** that it is not the learner,
T-4....... VII.4:5 which becomes total only by **r.** all reality
T-5........ III.1:1 brother is by **r.** the Holy Spirit in him. I
T-5......... V.7:7 feel responsible for their errors without **r.**
T-6....... II.12:3 Spirit extends by **r.** Himself in every mind
T-6....... II.13:1 and only by **r.** Him impartially can you
T-6........ IV.5:1 both merely by **r.** they are not part of you,
T-6...... V.C.4:8 you are not **r.** this mutual exclusiveness,
T-7........ IV.6:9 the laws of God, and **r.** their universality.
T-7........ IV.7:7 you, by not **r.** its existence in your brother
T-7......... V.8:2 **r.** the changeless mind in your brother by
T-7........ XI.5:4 **R.** the Majesty of God as your brother is
T-7........ XI.6:5 you heal a brother by **r.** his worth, you are
T-8......... V.2:6 Him, how can you know it without **r.** Him
T-9........ IV.6:3 **r.** that you do not understand what it is.
T-11......... I.1:2 **r.** your need of healing for yourself? For in
T-11......... I.4:2 by **r.** that neither beginnings nor endings
T-11........ II.1:1 first step toward **r.** what you truly want.
T-11........ II.7:8 abides with you merely by **r.** what is there
T-12......... I.4:1 nothing to prevent you from **r.** all calls for
T-12......... I.8:8 This is what **r.** fear really means. If you do
T-12...... III.9:9 by **r.** where it is will you gain control over
T-12....... V.2:2 are **r.** that attack has no effect. Although
T-12....... V.3:1 of attack except by **r.** that your attack on
T-13...... IV.5:5 surely prevent you from **r.** him as he is.
T-15... VII.10:6 Spirit, **r.** in His Voice your own need to
T-15........ X.9:4 avoid **r.** the one decision you must make.
T-15...... XI.2:7 is there already, by **r.** that His Host is One
T-18...... IV.1:4 extent of **r.** that you want it above all else.
T-19...... IV.1:8 you, **r.** in your call the Call for God. And
T-20........ II.1:5 a crown of thorns, not **r.** it for what it is,
T-26...... IV.2:6 in gladness **r.** what is part of them has not
T-28....... V.7:6 when you have lost the fear of **r.** love.
T-30...... VI.4:2 And **r.** God is just, it seems impossible
T-30...... VI.8:5 Forgiveness rests on **r.** this, and being
T-31......... VI.h **R.** the Spirit
T-31... VII.13:5 And **r.** this, it merely asks, "What is the
W-pI....... 5.1:6 step in ultimately **r.** they are all the same.
W-pI....... 8.3:3 **R.** that your mind has been merely blank,
W-pI..... 13.6:1 which you are very inexperienced in **r.**.
W-pI..... 16.3:1 Besides your **r.** that thoughts are never
W-pI..... 25.1:7 is in **r.** this that your goals become unified
W-pI..... 25.1:8 **r.** this that what you see is given meaning.
W-pI..... 39.3:6 you, **r.** that your salvation is crucial to the
W-pI..... 44.6:1 you will have no difficulty in **r.** that its
W-pI..... 54.5:2 **R.** the shared nature of my thoughts, I am
W-pI..... 55.4:4 **r.** that I cannot perceive them by myself.
W-pI..... 56.2:2 **R.** that what I see reflects what I think I
W-pI..... 58.4:2 **r.** my holiness is recognizing my salvation
W-pI..... 58.4:2 recognizing my holiness is **r.** my salvation
W-pI..... 58.4:3 It is also **r.** the salvation of the world.
W-pI..... 63.3:1 **R.** the importance of this function, we
W-pI..... 71.7:1 Let us practice **r.** this certainty today.
W-pI..... 79.8:4 been given the answer by **r.** the problem,
W-pI..... 79.9:3 Our efforts will be directed toward **r.** that
W-pI..... 80.1:4 thus depends on **r.** this one problem, and
W-pI..... 81.3:4 not depend on my **r.** what my function is,
W-pI..... 85.1:3 **R.** this, what do I want my grievances for?
W-pI..... 95.5:2 In addition to **r.** your difficulties with
W-pI... 95.10:1 Let all these errors go by **r.** them for what
W-pI... 104.5:1 by simply **r.** that His Will is done already,
W-pI... 130.8:1 your own, and **r.** what it is you seek. You
W-pI... 182.3:2 he cannot find; not **r.** what it is he seeks.
W-pI... 185.5:4 them, **r.** that another dream would offer
W-pI... 185.7:1 to **r.** that we really mean the words we say
W-pI... 190.5:6 things you see by merely **r.** what you are.
M-5........ II.1:7 it. The resistance to **r.** this is enormous,
M-6.......... 1:4 the mind of the patient, **r.** it for what it is.
M-10.......... 2:5 **R.** that judgment was always impossible
C-in.......... 2:3 **r.** that it is a defense against truth in the
P-1............ 5:2 illusion, **r.** that they are not the same, and
P-3......... II.5:8 His understanding begins with **r.** this,
P-3........ III.7:7 for salvation without **r.** where to look.

## recoil 1

T-4....... VII.4:7 Do not desecrate it or **r.** from it. It is your

## recoiling 1

W-pI..... 93.1:2 **r.** from you as if from a poisonous snake.

## recoils 1

T-13....... V.5:4 what he loves, and **r.** from what he fears.

## recollect 2

W-pI... 151.2:4 when you pause to **r.** how frequently they
W-pII. 244.1:2 *Name, and he will **r.** his safety and Your Love*

## recommended 15

W-pI..... 10.5:2 In addition, five practice periods are **r.**,
W-pI..... 10.5:3 is not **r.** that this time period be extended
W-pI..... 11.4:3 be undertaken. More than this is not **r.**.
W-pI..... 15.5:1 the minute or so of practice that is **r.**, try
W-pI..... 16.6:1 Four or five practice periods are **r.**, if you
W-pI..... 17.4:1 or four specific practice periods are **r.**,
W-pI..... 17.4:2 than the minute or so that is otherwise **r.**.

### reduce 7

| | |
|---|---|
| T-1 V.1:5 | or **r.** your creativity almost to nothing. |
| T-4 I.2:7 | the ego nor **r.** the conflict within it. The |
| T-9 V.5:1 | fear is to **r.** the importance of the mind, |
| W-pI 26.5:3 | is too great. Do not **r.** it further. |
| W-pI 136.2:3 | or **r.** it to a little pile of unassembled parts |
| W-pI 136.4:1 | sets up a series of defenses to **r.** the threat |
| W-pI 195.6:2 | be made which would **r.** our wholeness, |

### reduced 9

| | |
|---|---|
| T-25 I.7:6 | All this can very simply be **r.** to this: *What* |
| T-30 III.5:5 | if he could be **r.** to any form and limited |
| T-30 VIII.1:5 | Reality is thus **r.** to form, and capable of |
| W-pI 10.5:3 | and it should be **r.** to half a minute or less |
| W-pI 16.6:3 | should also be **r.** if there is discomfort. |
| W-pI 17.4:2 | length of the practice period may be **r.** to |
| W-pI 26.5:2 | although the time may be **r.** to a minute if |
| W-pI 93.5:8 | creation, nor **r.** eternal sinlessness to sin, |
| W-pII 250.1:2 | his strength diminished and **r.** to frailty; |

### reduces 1

| | |
|---|---|
| T-20 III.1:5 | For this **r.** it at once to mere perception; a |

### reducible 1

| | |
|---|---|
| T-2 I.4:1 | All fear is ultimately **r.** to the basic |

### reducing 1

| | |
|---|---|
| T-30 III.2:10 | the idol, thus **r.** it to a specific form. Yet |

### refer 4

| | |
|---|---|
| W-pI 18.2:1 | Today's idea does not **r.** to what you see |
| W-pI 61.1:5 | It does not **r.** to any of the characteristics |
| M-4 VII.2:2 | This does not **r.**, however, to the self of |
| M-29 2:10 | **r.** the questions to Him is yours. Would |

### reference 26

| | |
|---|---|
| T-2 I.3:6 | and nowhere is there **r.** to his waking up. |
| T-2 V.A.16:5 | There is no **r.** to the outcome of the error. |
| T-3 I.2:2 | a whole frame of **r.** in order to justify it. |
| T-3 II.3:2 | This is hardly a miracle-based frame of **r.**. |
| T-5 VI.11:2 | Remember my **r.** to the ego's dark glass, |
| T-13 III.12:9 | His answer is the **r.** point beyond illusions |
| T-13 IV.5:4 | meet in the present from a past **r.** point, |
| T-13 VI.2:1 | **r.** point from which to judge the present. |
| T-13 VI.2:3 | to look on everyone with no **r.** at all to the |
| T-13 VII.5:2 | From such a twisted **r.** point, what could |
| T-15 V.9:3 | thus removing the frame of **r.** you have |
| T-15 V.9:4 | Spirit substitutes His frame of **r.** for it. |
| T-15 V.9:5 | it. His frame of **r.** is simply God. The Holy |
| T-16 VI.7:5 | your hold on the distorted frame of **r.** that |
| T-16 VI.7:6 | This frame of **r.** is built around the special |
| T-16 VI.8:4 | you homeless and without a frame of **r.**. |
| T-17 I.4:5 | a frame of **r.** for reality to which it cannot |
| T-17 I.5:3 | frame of **r.** for its meaning must be itself. |
| T-17 III.8:4 | Yet the frame of **r.** to which the present is |
| T-18 VI.12:3 | and even a general idea without specific **r.** |
| T-23 IV.7:2 | You have no **r.** point from where to look, |
| W-pI 93.3:1 | think, but from a very different **r.** point, |
| W-pI 108.3:3 | perception, based upon one frame of **r.**, |
| W-pI 108.4:3 | frame of **r.** which unifies this Thought. |
| W-pI 151.11:2 | you in any way from His one frame of **r.**, |
| M-22 4:7 | This recognition has no special **r.**. It is |

### references 2

| | |
|---|---|
| T-4 III.5:3 | Bible gives many **r.** to the immeasurable |
| M-21 2:1 | As symbols, words have quite specific **r.**. |

### referent 1

| | |
|---|---|
| M-21 2:3 | Unless a specific **r.** does occur to the mind |

### referred 9

| | |
|---|---|
| T-1 VII.5:1 | fear and awe to which I have already **r.**, |
| T-2 IV.2:3 | **r.** to miracles as the means of correcting |
| T-3 I.5:1 | I have been correctly **r.** to as "the lamb of |
| T-3 II.1:1 | I have stated that the basic concepts **r.** to |
| T-5 I.4:2 | He is **r.** to as the Healer, the Comforter |
| T-17 III.8:4 | is **r.** for meaning is an *illusion* of the past, |
| T-26 III.3:2 | We have **r.** to it as the real world. And yet |
| M-6 2:5 | We have **r.** many times in the text to the |
| M-29 4:1 | is the paradox often **r.** to in the course. To |

### referring 2

| | |
|---|---|
| W-pI 26.7:3 | concern, **r.** to each one quite specifically, |
| M-29 3:1 | in **r.** decisions to the Holy Spirit with |

### refers 5

| | |
|---|---|
| T-3 V.5:2 | is always open to error because it **r.** to the |
| T-4 II.6:9 | a term which **r.** to any perceived threat to |
| W-pI 61.1:6 | It **r.** to you as you were created by God. It |
| M-21 1:4 | But this **r.** to the prayer of the heart, not |
| C-1 1:2 | is capitalized it **r.** to God or Christ (i.e., the |

### reflect 25

| | |
|---|---|
| T-1 I.19:3 | Miracles therefore **r.** the laws of eternity, |
| T-3 VI.6:2 | Your words should **r.** only mercy, because |
| T-4 in.2:3 | are inspired because they **r.** knowledge. If |
| T-7 VIII.1:2 | These **r.** a fundamental law of the mind, |
| T-8 VIII.9:7 | Do not let it **r.** your decision to attack. |
| T-8 IX.3:7 | because they **r.** the ego's distorted notions |
| T-12 VII.5:6 | perception will **r.** the guidance you have |
| T-14 IX.5:2 | You can **r.** Heaven here. Yet no reflections |
| T-14 IX.5:4 | it. Earth can **r.** Heaven or hell; God or the |
| T-14 IX.8:7 | They do not merely **r.** truth, for they *are* |
| T-14 X.1:6 | **R.** the peace of Heaven here, and bring |
| T19 IV.C.11:4 | truth or falsity of the idea which they **r.**. |
| T-20 VIII.10:3 | must thus **r.** the sight you saw within; or |
| T-27 VIII.11:6 | you will understand that miracles **r.** the |
| T-29 II.7:6 | they **r.** the teacher who is teaching them. |
| T-30 VII.2:1 | What do your scripts **r.** except your plans |
| T-30 VII.3:3 | be that they **r.** but different purposes. |
| W-pI 85.3:7 | everything I see will but **r.** the light that |
| W-pI 151.11:1 | those aspects which **r.** but idle dreams. |
| W-pI 155.12:2 | Pause and **r.** on this. Could any way be |
| W-pI 193.3:2 | **r.** His loving kindness to the Son He loves |
| W-pII 265.1:8 | The images I see **r.** my thoughts. Yet is my |
| W-pII 325.h | All things I think I see **r.** ideas. |
| W-pII 325.2:1 | *Our Father, Your ideas **r.** the truth, and* |
| W-pII 325.2:2 | *Let me behold what only Yours **r.**, for Yours* |

### reflected 22

| | |
|---|---|
| T-11 VIII.10:6 | him, and you will see your beauty **r.** in his |
| T-14 IX.8:5 | condition of what was but **r.** to them here |
| T-14 X.2:1 | In Heaven reality is shared and not **r.**. By |
| T-25 III.2:2 | Yet are His laws **r.** everywhere. Not that |
| T-25 IX.5:6 | is **r.** in the sight the Holy Spirit gives. |
| T-26 IV.1:2 | where justice can be **r.** from beyond the |
| W-pI 138.2:5 | **r.** in some form the world can understand |
| W-pI 158.11:2 | in which true knowledge is **r.** in a way so |
| W-pI 161.9:3 | Christ's vision is his loveliness **r.** in a form |
| W-pI 167.12:3 | so perfectly it fades into what is **r.** there. |
| W-pI 167.12:5 | It becomes the thing **r.**, and the light |
| W-pI 181.8:6 | we see **r.** in the world and in ourselves. |
| W-pII 265.1:7 | What is **r.** there is in God's Mind. The |
| W-pII 266.1:2 | *In them are You **r.**, and in them does Christ* |
| W-pII 8.2:1 | each unhappy thought **r.** in your world; a |
| W-pII 304.1:4 | I look on is my state of mind, **r.** outward. |
| W-pII 352.1:4 | *Yet love, **r.** in forgiveness here, reminds me* |
| M-4 I.A.8:5 | peace, for here is Heaven's state fully **r.**. |
| M-11 3:9 | Judgment of God what is **r.** here is only |
| M-14 5:9 | teach are lessons in which Heaven is **r.**. |
| C-3 8:1 | you see the truth about yourself **r.** there. |
| P-2 VII.1:13 | His knowledge is **r.** in the ideal patient- |

### reflecting 1

| | |
|---|---|
| W-pI 64.6:5 | minutes today to **r.** on this with closed |

### reflection 43

| | |
|---|---|
| T-2 V.9:6 | Charity is really a weaker **r.** of a much |
| T-5 II.1:7 | The miracle itself is a **r.** of this union of |
| T-6 II.7:1 | the Holy Spirit's perception is the **r.** of the |
| T-7 III.4:9 | because it is a **r.** of perfect Thought. Your |
| T-8 IX.5:2 | The decision to wake is the **r.** of the will to |
| T-12 VII.8:2 | the **r.** of your conflicting invitations. You |
| T-14 IX.h | The **R.** of Holiness |
| T-14 IX.5:3 | the mirror that would hold God's **r.** in it. |
| T-14 IX.5:7 | clear **r.** of Himself can be perceived upon |
| T-14 IX.6:3 | The **r.** of God needs no interpretation. It |
| T-14 IX.7:1 | the power of healing that the **r.** of God, |
| T-14 IX.8:4 | because of the **r.** of holiness in them, are |
| T-14 IX.8:5 | There, holiness is not a **r.**, but rather the |
| T-14 X.1:4 | and touch it, with the help of its **r.** in you. |
| T-14 X.1:5 | surely as the **r.** of holiness calls everyone |
| T-14 X.1:7 | For the **r.** of truth draws everyone to truth |
| T-14 X.2:2 | By sharing its **r.** here, its truth becomes |
| T-22 VI.14:5 | will realize that your relationship is a **r.** of |
| T-25 III.2:3 | Not that the world where this **r.** is, is real |
| T-25 V.4:7 | In everyone you see but the **r.** of what you |
| T-30 I.4:1 | think of it and have a quiet moment for **r.** |
| W-pI 55.2:4 | It is anything but a **r.** of the Love of God |
| W-pI 60.1:5 | It is the **r.** of God's Love on earth. It will |
| W-pI 60.2:4 | I begin to see, I recognize His **r.** on earth. |
| W-pI 75.5:2 | it we see Heaven's **r.** lie across the world. |
| W-pI 124.9:5 | see Christ's face upon it, in **r.** of your own. |
| W-pI 163.9:2 | *the glorious **r.** of Your Love which shines in* |
| W-pI 167.12:4 | there. And now it is no more a mere **r.**. It |
| W-pI 167.12:5 | and the light which makes **r.** possible. No |
| W-pI 169.13:3 | and brought a clear **r.** of the unity he felt |
| W-pI 182.4:6 | that brings to earth the pure **r.** of the light |
| W-pI 184.12:3 | unified; all space is filled with truth's **r.**. |
| W-pI 187.10:5 | of Heaven shine in our **r.** of our Father's |
| W-pI 189.1:6 | light is a **r.** of the thought we practice now |
| W-pI 189.4:3 | look upon, and see its sure **r.** everywhere. |
| W-pI 191.10:2 | but it will end in the **r.** of his holiness. |
| W-pI 194.9:4 | it will be soon replaced by love's **r.**. And if |
| W-pII 8.4:2 | His waking eyes perceive the sure **r.** of his |
| W-pII 293.1:5 | All the world shines in **r.** of its holy light, |
| W-pII 341.2:2 | God to us. And in its kind **r.** we are saved. |
| W-pII 14.1:1 | *and whole, shining in the **r.** of His Love. In* |
| W-pII 357.1:1 | *Forgiveness, truth's **r.**, tells me how to offer* |
| M-3 3:5 | can have no levels, being a **r.** of His Will. |

### reflections 10

| | |
|---|---|
| T-7 IX.7:3 | **r.** of both your proper identification with |
| T-14 III.16:2 | are **r.** of what God knows about you, and |
| T-14 IX.5:3 | Yet no **r.** of the images of other gods must |
| T-14 IX.6:1 | **R.** are seen in light. In darkness they are |
| T-14 X.1:2 | The **r.** you accept into the mirror of your |
| T-14 X.1:7 | they enter into it they leave all **r.** behind. |
| T-14 X.4:5 | For some are **r.** of Heaven, while others |
| T-14 X.5:2 | **r.** of Heaven last but a moment and grow |
| T-27 VII.5:8 | and sin, for they are but **r.** of their cause. |
| W-pI 163.1:3 | you. All such thoughts are but **r.** of the |

### reflects 56

| | |
|---|---|
| T-1 II.1:2 | It **r.** the original form of communication |
| T-2 VIII.4:2 | and **r.** the true meaning of the Apocalypse |
| T-5 VII.3:5 | It **r.** both the ego's need to separate, and |
| T-6 II.7:3 | use perception in a way that **r.** knowledge |
| T-6 V.B.9:1 | unified perception that **r.** God's knowing. |
| T-7 II.2:3 | This **r.** creation, because it unifies by |
| T-8 IV.5:1 | Healing **r.** our joint will. This is obvious |
| T-12 III.8:3 | world, in which everything **r.** the eternal. |
| T-15 V.9:3 | holy instant **r.** His knowing by bringing |
| T-18 I.4:6 | Everything you see **r.** it, and every special |
| T-18 II.9:7 | dream **r.** your will joined with the Will of |
| T-20 VI.10:1 | holy relationship **r.** the true relationship |
| T-25 II.7:3 | which but **r.** the light that shines from it |
| T-25 VII.6:7 | And each **r.** a view of what the Father and |
| T-25 VII.11:1 | whole belief that someone loses but **r.** the |

T-26....VIII.1:2 r. the little you would keep between you
T-29....VIII.2:6 apart from all the misery the world r..
T-31.......I.7:10 lesson that r. the Love of God is stronger
T-31..... V.12:5 you see r. the state of the perceiver's mind
T-31..... V.14:6 learn that everything it thinks r. the deep
T-31...VII.12:1 but r. a wish to be a self that you are not.
W-pI.....44.1:3 then think you see in it, but light r. life,
W-pI.....53.5:2 Whatever I see r. my thoughts. It is my
W-pI.....56.2:2 that what I see r. what I think I am, I
W-pI.....56.3:4 it to the world that r. the Love of God.
W-pI.....57.4:2 I realize that it r. the laws of God instead
W-pI.....65.5:6 *This thought r. a goal that is preventing me*
W-pI.....73.4:6 that shines upon this world r. your will,
W-pI...73.10:3 *behold the light that r. God's Will and mine.*
W-pI.....92.5:1 it; weakness r. the darkness of its maker.
W-pI.....99.2:4 It r. the truth because it is the means by
W-pI...124.2:2 everything we see r. the holiness within
W-pI...130.1:2 What you see r. your thinking. And your
W-pI...130.1:3 but r. your choice of what you want to see
W-pI...130.6:5 and r. its source in everything you see.
W-pI.131.13:3 you in the light r. the truth you knew, and
W-pI...134.2:5 to Him, r. His laws and radiates His Love.
W-pI...134.3:3 twisted viewpoint but r. the hold that the
W-pI.134.13:2 laws it follows, nor the Thought that it r..
W-pI...139.1:5 There is no question but r. this one. There
W-pI...159.3:2 for it r. eternal love and the rebirth of love
W-pI...164.7:4 our joy, because its holiness r. our own.
W-pI...189.4:2 Their world r. the quietness and peace
W-pI...193.3:2 His Will r. them all, and they reflect His
W-pII .247.1:6 on you. Your loveliness r. my own. Your
W-pII .249.1:6 is transformed into the light that it r..
W-pII .265.2:1 *upon the world, which but r. Your Thoughts*
W-pII .302.1:7 *its holiness and understand it but r. my own.*
W-pII .325.1:1 What I see r. a process in my mind, which
W-pII .345.1:1 *Father, a miracle r. Your gifts to me, Your*
W-pII .356.1:4 *him. The miracle r. Your Love, and thus it*
M-12 .........2:3 internal now r. only the Love of God. God
M-20 .........1:5 for each r. a different step along the way.
M-29 .........3:7 see r. the illusion that you have done so,
M-29 .........8:6 in your light the world R. your holiness,
C-3.............5:2 so the unity that it r. becomes His Will. It

**reflexes** 1

M-5 ....... II.1:8 "r." and the like represent attempts to

**refrain** 5

T-20..... II.8:10 The song of Easter is the glad r. the Son of
T-25......IV.3:2 hearts that look on sin and beat its sad r..
W-pI.131.15:1 r. from dismal thoughts and meaningless
W-pI...151.4:2 have often been urged to r. from judging,
W-pI...161.9:3 could scarce r. from kneeling at his feet.

**refuge** 6

T-18....VI.14:5 Come to this place of r., where you can be
T-18....VIII.9:4 Give them a place of r., prepared by love
W-pII .259.2:2 *afraid of love, nor seek for r. in its opposite.*
W-pII ....261.h God is my r. and security.
W-pII .261.1:1 with what I think is r. and security. I will
W-pII .261.1:5 In Him I find my r. and my strength. In

**refusal** 8

T-2......... II.4:7 R. could not, however, turn it into a
T-2......... V.4:4 of r. to accept the Atonement for yourself.
T-7........IV.7:8 you, because it is a r. to acknowledge fear.
T-14.... XI.6:10 r. to attempt to teach yourself what you
T-21...... III.7:3 fear. In your r. to forgive him, you would
W-pI.....95.7:5 it is; a r. to let your mistake be corrected,
W-pI...139.2:2 Only r. to accept yourself could make the
P-2........VI.1:3 all this is but the grim r. to forgive.

**refusals** 1

T-10..... V.12:4 may take, are r. to accept creation as it is.

**refuse** 34

T-3 ..... VI.10:2 is free to r. to accept his inheritance, but
T-4 ....... IV.7:1 you actively r. to let your mind slip away.
T-4 ....... IV.8:4 r. to accept anything but this as your goal.
T-4 ....VII.3:12 it may r. to utilize it on behalf of being.
T-6 ..........I.3:2 who always r. to consider what they have
T-10 ....in.3:10 r. to change your mind about yourself.
T-10 ..... IV.1:9 But if you r. to worship him in whatever
T-11 ......in.4:4 r. it in order to keep a dark cornerstone
T-11 ..... IV.6:5 You can r. to enter, but you cannot bar
T-11 ...VIII.4:2 God will not r. you the Answer He gave.
T-11 .VIII.5:10 take. When you r. to ask, it is because you
T-12 ........I.5:4 fail to recognize a call for help is to r. help
T-12 ........I.5:6 you r. to recognize a brother's appeal, for
T-12 ..... III.4:2 R., and your opposition establishes that it
T-12 ..... VI.5:2 learn the cost of sleeping, and r. to pay it.
T-14 ... III.10:2 and will not r. to see it and side with it.
T-14 .... V.11:5 of you. R. to accept anyone as without the
T-15 .......II.3:6 and r. to support either their weakness or
T-15 ...VIII.3:3 R. not the awareness of your completion,
T-16 ........I.1:1 for that is what you must *r.* to understand.
T-20 .VIII.11:2 there who could r. what must come after?
T-26 ..VII.20:3 He r. to answer when He has already
T-28 ..... IV.2:2 R. to be a part of fearful dreams whatever
W-pI.....71.9:8 R. not to hear. The very fact that you are
W-pI...78.10:2 r. to hide his light behind our grievances.
WpI..rII.in.5:2 the life. R. to be sidetracked into detours,
W-pI...128.8:2 world, r. to lay this chain upon your mind
W-pI...170.6:2 their dictates, and r. to question them.
W-pI...188.8:1 your Father's Voice when you r. to listen.
W-pI...195.2:3 sane r. to take the steps which He directs,
W-pI...195.9:3 If we r. to recognize it, we are not entitled
W-pII ..... 7.5:4 r. to take the function of completing God,
P-3...........I.4:6 God. Would he r. this Gift for a pebble, or
S-3........ IV.8:7 Do not r. to hear the Call for Love. Do not

**refused** 14

T-2 .........II.4:6 not be misused, although it could be r..
T-3 ....... VI.4:1 you have perceived but have r. to accept.
T-3 ....... VI.4:2 that, because you have r. to accept it, you
T-3 ....... VI.4:4 Nothing that you have r. to accept can be
T-4 ....... IV.8:1 how many of them you have r.? There is
T-5 ........in.1:2 yourself, and how many you have r.. This
T-5 ........in.1:3 you that you have r. to heal yourself. The
T-14 ..... IX.3:6 The gift that you r. is held by Him in you.
T-21 ..... VI.2:1 or r. by you without your brother. Sin
W-pI.137.12:3 And can this invitation be r.? Ask the
W-pI...139.2:1 one who has r. to recognize himself?
W-pI...183.7:1 give an invitation which can never be r..
M-22 ......... 5:4 r. to accept the Atonement for himself,
P-2....... VII.9:6 in him an answer that you have r. to give?

**refuses** 5

T-4 ........ V.2:3 either distorts them or r. to accept them.
T-7 .......X.5:13 and r. to follow any guidance at all. If the
T-14 ...... III.6:3 If he r. it he binds himself to darkness,
T-15 ... VI.5:12 be. For the instant he r. to be bound, he is
P-3........ III.8:3 The Holy Spirit never r. an invitation to

**refusing** 14

T-4 ..........I.4:2 R. to change your mind will not prove
T-8 ....... IV.1:1 you must be r. to acknowledge His Will.
T-10 .... V.11:2 His gift by r. to accept what had been
T-12 .......II.4:7 and r. to open your eyes and look at them
T-12 ..... III.2:3 If you insist on r. and experience a quick
T-13 ..... VI.7:3 r. to accept the light that is offered you.
T-14 ..... III.7:4 and by r. to allow him to think he can,
T-17 ........I.6:5 you are r. to forgive yourself for just this
T-17 ...VIII.3:7 The strain of r. faith to truth is enormous,
T-17 ...VIII.4:6 strain of r. to give faith to truth, and see
T-20 .... VII.2:2 you are r. to leave the means to Him Who
W-pI.....74.6:5 gain in r. to allow retreat into withdrawal,
W-pI.135.16:1 The mind that plans is thus r. to allow for
W-pI.160.10:5 thus r. to accept the gift of sight by which

**regain** 1

T-10 ......in.1:2 time solely as a means to r. eternity. You

**regained** 2

T-24 ..... VI.7:3 eternity is not r. by still one more denial
T-25 .....V.4:10 Nor can it be r. unless the way is shown to

**regard** 44

T-3 .........V.5:3 are the result of attempts to r. yourself as
T-3 ....... VI.5:9 will also r. judgment with fear, believing
T-3 .... VI.11:2 own free will he must r. his will as not free
T-4 .........II.4:2 they r. them as part of themselves. No
T-4 ....... VI.1:5 will r. yourself as necessarily conflicted as
T-5 .......V.4:11 because, as soon as you r. sin as a lack,
T-5 .......V.4:13 but you must learn to r. it as freedom.
T-6 ....... IV.1:6 The ego does not r. itself as part of you.
T-6 ....... IV.2:5 enables the ego to r. itself as separate and
T-8 ..........I.1:9 you do not yet r. this as wholly desirable.
T-8 ..... VI.8:10 God's Own treasure do not r. yourself as
T-8 ...... VII.2:5 because you do not r. bodies solely as a
T-9 ...... VII.5:2 must therefore r. yourself as inadequate.
T-11 .......V.4:2 surely r. a delusional system without fear,
T-11 .......V.9:1 ego can and does allow you to r. yourself
T-12 ........I.8:7 to r. everything else as an appeal for help,
T-14 ....... IX.8:3 without r. for what is brought to it. Those
T-15 ..... VI.4:3 you are more inclined to r. his success as
T-15 .......X.5:3 When you are willing to r. them, not as
T-16 .......II.6:3 R. this not with fear, but with rejoicing.
T-16 ..... III.3:2 show you that you do not r. *yourself* as one
T19 .IV.B.16:5 Not one but must r. the body as himself,
T-26 .......II.3:4 them vanish one by one, without r. to size
T-26 ..... IX.1:5 R. him gently. Look with loving eyes on
T-30 ..... VI.3:4 While you r. it as a gift unwarranted, it
W-pI ...... 5.6:4 *exercises, then, I will r. them all as the same.*
W-pI ...... 6.3:6 *exercises, then, I will r. them all as the same.*
W-pI .... 20.1:6 not see if you r. yourself as being coerced,
W-pI .... 52.1:6 reality, and thus r. reality as an illusion.
W-pI .... 64.3:2 the ego that induces you to r. yourself as
W-pI .... 68.5:1 you hold what you r. as major grievances.
W-pI .... 78.6:4 will r. his body with its flaws and better
W-pI .... 79.4:1 The temptation to r. problems as many is
W-pI .... 79.5:3 depression are inevitable as you r. them.
WpI..rII.in.5:1 R. these practice periods as dedications
W-pI .... 95.7:4 There may well be a temptation to r. the
W-pI .. 134.3:3 as yet upon your mind, as you r. yourself.
W-pI .. 136.6:1 assembles them without r. to all their true
W-pI .. 181.6:3 a little while, without r. to past or future,
W-pI .. 194.7:5 And what can he r. except with love? For
M-7 ........... 1:8 the patient, and he must so r. himself. He
M-12 ......... 6:9 real than to r. it as healthy and beautiful.
P-2....... VII.4:2 because they must r. themselves as self-
P-3..........II.9:8 at their shrine, and this they r. as healing.

**regarded** 9

T-2 ....... III.4:7 r. as very minor intrusions of discomfort.
T-14 ..... VI.5:1 You have r. the separation as a means for
T-21 .....II.10:3 enables it to be r. as standing by itself,
W-pI .... 19.2:2 may even be r. as an "invasion of privacy.
W-pI .... 74.1:1 The idea for today can be r. as the central
M-in .......... 1:4 the act of teaching is r. as a special activity
M-8 ........... 2:3 real that is r. as of major importance, but
M-24 ......... 2:6 be r. as essential to the curriculum. There
M-27 ......... 1:5 This is r. as "the way of nature," not to be

**regarding** 5

T-4 .........II.4:8 belief you are r. it from an ego viewpoint.
T-6 ..........I.4:7 and are therefore r. yourself insanely.
T-8 .....VIII.2:4 R. the body as an end, the ego has no real
T-12 .......V.1:5 as equal, and r. yourself as weaker, you
W-pI .... 95.8:5 it power to do this, we are r. it as strength

**regardless** 27

T-8 ....... III.5:1 curriculum, r. of the teacher you choose,
T-9 ....... IV.8:2 yourself, r. of how you may account for

T-11..... V.10:1 fear, **r.** of the form it takes and quite apart
T-12.........I.3:4 healing and help, **r.** of the form it takes.
T-12....... II.2:1 light in them shines as brightly **r.** of the
T-18.... VI.12:1 This can occur **r.** of the physical distance
T-18......IX.7:5 **r.** of how much imagination you bring to
T-22...... III.4:4 And yet mistakes, **r.** of their form, can be
T-22......VI.4:4 the power to heal all pain, **r.** of its form.
T-26....... II.2:2 each one, **r.** of the form it seems to take, is
T-27. VIII.11:2 **r.** of the form of suffering that brings you
T-31... VIII.6:1 you look upon, **r.** of the images you see.
W-pI.......5.5:1 **r.** of how much or how little you think it
W-pI.......5.7:1 **r.** of the relative importance you may give
W-pI.....16.4:4 you, **r.** of the qualities that you assign to it
W-pI.....17.3:2 **R.** of what you may believe, you do not
W-pI.....99.6:6 answer to appearances; **r.** of their form,
W-pI...125.5:4 he remain as part of Him **r.** of his dreams;
W-pI...125.5:4 **r.** of his madness that his will is not his
W-pI...193.5:2 all your pain, all suffering **r.** of its form.
M-7............4:7 the opposite of love, **r.** of the form it takes
M-15..........3:4 to you, **r.** of your judgments on its gifts,
M-17..........4:2 **r.** of their seeming justification by what
M-17..........4:3 **R.**, too, of the intensity of the anger that
M-24..........3:4 to anyone, **r.** of his formal beliefs. His ego
P-1.............3:1 needs help, **r.** of the form of his distress,
P-2.........in.4:1 **R.** of how sincere the therapist himself

## regards 17

T-4......... II.7:8 The ego **r.** the body as its home, and tries
T-4........ III.3:1 by now why the ego **r.** spirit as its "enemy
T-5....... V.4:13 The ego **r.** this as doom, but you must
T-7........ VI.1:7 any of Them if he **r.** Them fearfully. He
T-7........ VI.1:8 appreciate all of Them if he **r.** Them with
T-8......... V.5:6 it, the ego **r.** itself as rejected and becomes
T-13......IV.4:5 For the ego **r.** the present only as a brief
T-13......IV.7:4 He **r.** the function of time as temporary,
T-13......IV.8:1 **r.** the function of time as one of extending
T-15.....VII.6:2 The "sacrifice," which it **r.** as purification,
T-18... VIII.6:1 that this tiny part **r.** itself as you. It is not
W-pI...121.5:2 **r.** its judgment of the world as irreversible
W-pI...160.2:1 understands what truth **r.** as senseless.
W-pI...195.9:3 which **r.** us in a place of merciless pursuit,
W-pII......5.1:4 safety, he **r.** himself as what his safety is.
P-1.............3:2 patient often **r.** them in that way himself.
P-1.............3:5 For he **r.** it as himself. This self he sees as

## regret 7

T19... IV.A.9:4 return, and part with it in gladness, not **r.**
T-22....VI.15:3 Would you **r.** you cannot fear alone, when
T-29....... II.2:8 and you will not behold a reason for **r.**,
W-pI.121.10:1 to cause **r.** in you if you should meet him;
M-10..........5:1 not with **r.** but with a sigh of gratitude.
M-13..........4:1 God's teachers can have no **r.** on giving
M-27..........2:3 ready to break it off without **r.** or care,

## regrets 2

T-29....... II.1:5 have some **r.** about the way that you have
W-pI...109.5:1 no pain, no fear of future and no past **r.**.

## regular 4

W-pI.....49.1:1 interrupting your **r.** activities in any way.
W-pI.....74.7:1 at **r.** and predetermined intervals today,
W-pI...91.11:1 times an hour, at reasonably **r.** intervals,
W-pI.....95.6:1 of your goal and **r.** attempts to reach it.

## regularity 1

W-pI.....95.6:2 it. **R.** in terms of time is not the ideal

## rehearsed 1

W-pI...157.3:3 increasingly, as every lesson, faithfully **r.**,

## reign 5

T-13...VII.17:5 its eternal **r.** where sorrow dwells. You
T-14..... V.10:8 from fear and re-establish the **r.** of love.
T-23.......I.2:10 And fear will **r.** in madness, and will seem
W-pI.....49.2:5 mind where stillness and peace **r.** forever.
W-pI...190.3:1 Pain is a sign illusions **r.** in place of truth.

## reigns 2

M-18.......3:10 *God* **r.** *forever, and His laws alone prevail*
M-27.........2:7 contradiction **r.** and opposites make

## reincarnation 9

M-24............h IS **R.** SO?
M-24.........1:1 In the ultimate sense, **r.** is impossible.
M-24.........1:3 **R.** cannot, then, be true in any real sense.
M-24.........2:1 **R.** would not, under any circumstances,
M-24.........2:5 who believe in **r.** and by those who do not
M-24.........3:1 be helpful to take any definite stand on **r.**.
M-24.........4:2 as the validity of **r.** become meaningless.
M-24.........5:1 of God should not believe in **r.** himself, or
M-24.........5:3 not! If he does believe in **r.**, it would be a

## reinforce 12

T-1........ III.5:9 you **r.** errors they have already made.
T-5.......VII.5:5 you will **r.** the error rather than allow it to
T-8........ IX.3:3 to **r.** sleeping out of fear of waking. This is
T-17.... III.2:10 unholiness seeks to **r.** itself, as holiness
T-17..... V.13:4 **r.** this every time you attack your brother,
T19... IV.A.2:5 Would you **r.** it now? You are not asked
T-30.......I.16:7 will **r.** the rule of your adviser in the world
W-pI.....25.2:5 world, instead of attempting to **r.** them.
W-pI.....61.6:2 about yourself, **r.** it throughout the day,
W-pI.106.10:2 forget today to **r.** your choice to hear and
W-pI...139.9:2 to **r.** the madness that we once believed in
S-2......... II.7:2 you try to **r.** his guilt and thus your own?

## reinforced 5

T-18...... IX.1:9 guarded by attack and **r.** by hate. Within
T-23....... II.7:1 the fear of God is **r.** by this third principle
W-pI...187.5:3 and grows in strength as it is **r.** by giving.
M-4 .....I.A.7:9 each step in this direction so heavily **r.**, it
M-5 ...... III.3:6 their brothers, so that illusions are not **r.**.

## reinforcement 4

T-12....... V.3:2 be unable to avoid interpreting this as **r.**.
T-12....... V.3:3 you can cancel out all **r.** is in yourself. For
T-27....... V.7:4 No **r.** will its thanks withhold from you
WpI. rIII.in9:3 As a result, you have gained little **r.**, and

## reinforces 6

T-5.........I.1:13 he **r.** it in your mind and thus increases it.
T-6.........I.16:5 and **r.** the idea that blame is justified. The
T-6......... II.3:2 It **r.** your belief in your own split mind,
W-pI.....72.5:8 is. It **r.** your belief that he is a body, and
M-in ..........3:7 but **r.** what you believe about yourself. Its
M-17 .........2:1 to respond to magic in a way that **r.** it.

## reinforcing 4

T-12...... III.3:2 this belief; and if you attack, you are **r.** it.
W-pI.....63.4:3 chance should be lost for **r.** today's idea.
W-pI.....90.1:4 the simplicity of salvation by **r.** the lesson
W-pI.....95.9:3 mistakes, based on the first and **r.** it. It is

## reinstatement 1

T-12...... VI.7:1 of the separation is the **r.** of knowledge.

## reinstating 1

T-2......... V.5:4 and **r.** its purely constructive powers, you

## reinterpret 11

T-5...... III.7:7 the Holy Spirit to **r.** you on behalf of God.
T-5...... III.9:6 lets your mind **r.** its own misperceptions.
T-5...... III.11:2 perceive time, and **r.** it into the timeless.
T-5........ IV.1:3 Holy Spirit will help you **r.** everything
T-5........ VI.5:1 Holy Spirit can **r.** them in His Own light.
T-5........ VI.8:3 He can still **r.** what former generations
T-12.........I.8:9 If you do not protect it, He will **r.** it. That
T-17....... V.5:1 to **r.** each slow step according to its liking.
T-19........II.5:1 Any attempt to **r.** sin as error is always
T-25...... III.6:8 he will **r.** all temptation as just another
W-pI. 151.11:2 dreams. And He will **r.** all you see, and all

## reinterpretation 4

T-3......... V.7:1 in his own image and likeness" needs **r.**.
T-8...........I.3:3 **r.** of reality that you must make to secure
T-11....VIII.1:9 The **r.** of the world is the transfer of all
M-24 .........5:6 **R.** would then be recommended, because

## reinterpreted 6

T-5...... IV.3:10 has **r.** them in the light of the Kingdom,
T-5........ VI.7:1 is mine, sayeth the Lord" is easily **r.** if you
T-5........ VI.9:4 it will be **r.** to release you from fear. The
T-18...... VI.5:1 instruments of separation **r.** as means for
T-21..... V.7:11 not **r.** and redirected from the goal of sin,
T-23.......in.6:4 sinful now will be **r.** as part of Heaven.

## reinterpreter 1

T-5...... III.11:1 Holy Spirit, the **r.** of what the ego made,

## reinterpreting 3

T-1........ IV.4:3 I came to fulfill the law by **r.** it. The law
T-5........ III.7:4 the function of **r.** what the ego makes, not
T-9........ IV.3:3 By **r.** the ability to attack into the ability

## reinterprets 2

T-6......V.A.2:5 He **r.** what the ego uses as an argument
T-14...... VI.5:2 The Holy Spirit **r.** it as a means of re-

## reject 5

T-3........ VI.9:1 who give over all desire to **r.** can know
T-6.........I.17:4 not appreciate it, and will therefore **r.** it.
T-8........ IV.3:7 world must therefore despise and **r.** me,
T-11....... VII.3:3 It does not **r.** goodness entirely, for that
T-13........II.8:2 may **r.** it and do not accept it for yourself.

## rejected 10

T-2.......VII.3:3 By choosing the miracle you *have* **r.** fear, if
T-3...........I.3:9 including the belief that God **r.** Adam and
T-3........ VI.2:6 has been perceived and **r.**, or judged and
T-4...........I.6:7 as a teacher either to be exalted or **r.**, but I
T-4...........II.8:8 being **r.** by something greater than itself.
T-8......... V.5:6 regards itself as **r.** and becomes retaliative
T-10........II.3:2 again what is already there, but was **r.**.
T-21........II.1:4 **R.** yes, but not ambiguous. And if you
W-pI... 193.4:3 is so simple that it cannot be **r.** in the end.
C-in ...........2:4 belief and can therefore be accepted or **r.**.

## rejecting 3

T-1.........I.50:1 true, and **r.** what is out of accord as false.
T-3......... V.7:7 is a continual process of accepting and **r.**,
T-6.... V.C.1:11 it by **r.** everything that does not foster joy,

## rejection 13

T-3...........I.4:6 this results in **r.** of what the teacher offers.
T-3........ VI.2:4 Judgment always involves **r.**. It never
T-3........ VI.9:1 can know that their own **r.** is impossible.
T-6.........I.17:5 reject it. As a result, you will teach **r.**.
T-6.........I.18:3 teach that all forms of **r.** are meaningless.

T-6.........I.18:4 The separation is the notion of **r.**. As long
T-6......... II.1:1 split in mind must involve a **r.** of part of it
T-6...... V.B.1:2 They believe in attack and **r.**, so that is
T-7...... VI.4:11 it. **R.** is therefore the only decision the ego
T-7...... VII.8:3 projecting your own **r.** you then believe
T-8...... IV.4:11 and this **r.** of my decision for you makes
T-14...... III.3:7 *acceptance of the Atonement, not to its* **r.**. *I*
T-18.........I.3:7 or **r.** for acting out a special form of fear.

## rejects 2

T-6...... V.C.1:5 of accord entirely He **r.** by judging against
T-6...... V.C.1:7 what the Holy Spirit **r.** the ego accepts.

## rejoice 36

T-4....... VII.8:4 are like Him, and they can **r.** together.
T-5...........I.1:2 every part of the Sonship to **r.** with them,
T-8....... VII.6:1 **R.**, then, that of yourself you can do
T-9...... VIII.7:9 you seek others like you and **r.** with them.
T-12.... VIII.5:5 you have made of it, and **r.** that it is not so
T-13..... VII.6:4 will **r.** that you have found His company,
T-13...... IX.6:9 where the witnesses to your fatherhood **r.**
T-20...... III.3:2 their holiness, and **r.** at what they see.
T-20.... VIII.2:7 **R.** in what is yours but for the asking, and
T-20.... VIII.3:1 Spirit's vision and to **r.** in along with Him
T-22.......in.1:2 **R.** whom God hath joined have come
T-22....... IV.4:5 looks upon the Christ in you but will **r.**.
T-24....... V.1:3 And thus does He **r.** at what He sees,
T-24....... V.5:1 **R.** you have no eyes with which to see; no
T-25...... IV.1:2 cannot attack, and they **r.** that this is so,
T-25...... IV.1:4 it is their purpose to behold it and **r.**.
T-25...... IV.2:1 "You will **r.** at what you see because you
T-25...... IV.2:1 at what you see because you see it to **r.**."
T-25...... IV.3:4 can rise a world they will **r.** to look upon,
T-26........I.6:4 to, that you may see it and **r.** with him.
T-26...... IX.1:6 may behold his glory and **r.** that Heaven
W-pI..... 69.3:5 who searches with us to look upon and **r.**.
W-pI..... 71.7:2 And let us **r.** that there is an answer to
W-pI..... 75.9:4 **R.** in the power of forgiveness to heal
W-pI..... 78.9:2 of God but must **r.** as you are saved, and
W-pI..... 86.1:8 I will **r.** because His plan can never fail.
W-pI... 122.6:6 Let us today **r.** that this is so, for here we
W-pI... 195.6:2 And we **r.** that no exceptions ever can be
W-pII . 285.2:2 *Let me* **r.** *in it, and through forgiveness be*
W-pII ...... 9.5:5 Let us **r.** that we can do God's Will, and
W-pII . 359.1:6 **r.** *to learn that we have made mistakes which*
M-5 ...... III.1:4 he has no function except to **r.** with them,
M-13 ......... 4:6 must **r.** that he is free of all the sacrifice its
P-2........ VI.1:4 while they mourn their loss and yet **r.** in it
P-3...........I.4:9 Yet would he not **r.** that he can answer,
S-1.........in.2:3 **r.** that what illusions seemed to separate

## rejoiced 2

T-24...... IV.5:2 and have **r.** at what you thought was there
W-pI... 155.3:2 yet **r.** to find they were mistaken in their

## rejoices 6

T-4.........I.10:2 and your ego **r.** when you witness to it.
T-5........ IV.5:6 that was in me **r.** as you choose to hear it.
T-18........I.11:5 it, and **r.** that you have let it come to you.
T-24....... V.7:5 And He **r.** that these sights are yours, to
T-25.... VIII.9:9 God **r.** as His Son receives what loving
W-pI... 189.2:2 It welcomes you, **r.** that you came, and

## rejoicing 12

T-16....... II.6:3 Regard this not with fear, but with **r.**. The
T-20..... II.10:5 Walk with him now **r.**, for the savior from
T-25...... IV.1:8 as what will bring **r.** is defined another
T-25...... IV.2:5 them to be the bringers of **r.** and of joy.
T-29....... II.2:8 indeed for glad **r.** and for hope of peace.
T-29....... II.3:5 Why are you not **r.**? You are free of pain
W-pI..... 76.7:2 We will devote today to **r.** that this is so.
W-pI... 124.1:5 and with the universe we go our way **r.**,
W-pI. 139.10:2 go your way **r.** in the endless Love of God.
W-pI... 151.8:3 God can only honor Him, **r.** in His perfect
W-pII ..... 2.5:2 song of our **r.** is the call to all the world
P-1............ 2:1 into it and give it His Own great gift of **r.**?

## rekindled 1

T-26 ..... IV.3:7 come, to be **r.** and increased in joy. For

## relate 9

T-1 ...... VII.1:7 that you can **r.** in peace to God or to your
T-13 ...... V.3:1 that the insane **r.** to their insane world.
T-13 ...... V.3:2 these images, and it is to them that they **r.**
T-15 ... VIII.3:1 **R.** only with what will never leave you,
T-16 ........I.1:6 not **r.** through your ego to another ego.
T-16 ........I.2:7 by and let the Holy Spirit **r.** through you,
T-17 ...... IV.1:5 you **r.** to your creations as God to His. For
WpI..rIII.in5:3 letting your mind **r.** them to your needs,
W-pII . 245.2:3 God, Who speaks to us as we **r.** His Word

## related 41

*See also* course-related, perception-related

T-2 ..........I.2:1 These **r.** distortions represent a picture of
T-3 ..........I.3:9 error is responsible for a host of **r.** errors,
T-3 ....... III.5:9 miracles and doing are closely **r.**.
T-4 .........II.9:1 since myths are usually **r.** to ego origins,
T-4 ...... VII.2:7 ways to everything it perceives as **r.**.
T-5 ...... III.1:2 so we can use the terms as if they were **r.**,
T-5 ..... III.8:13 peace are as closely **r.** as are time and war.
T-6 .........II.3:5 Projection and attack are inevitably **r.**,
T-12 ..... III.2:5 in is always **r.** to your notion of salvation.
T19.... IV.B.1:3 must flow across, and closely **r.** to the first
T-23 .......II.4:2 This principle, closely **r.** to the first, is the
W-pI..... 11.1:1 we have had that is **r.** to a major phase of
W-pI..... 15.3:5 and they are not **r.** to knowledge. These
W-pI..... 19.1:2 the ideas **r.** to thinking precede those
W-pI..... 19.1:2 to thinking precede those **r.** to perceiving,
W-pI..... 24.5:4 appear to be directly **r.** to the situation, or
W-pI..... 36.1:8 Your sight is **r.** to His Holiness, not to
W-pI..... 42.5:1 clearly **r.** to the idea for today is suitable.
W-pI..... 42.5:5 continue to look for **r.** thoughts in your
W-pI..... 43.5:8 thought **r.** more or less directly to today's
W-pI..... 45.1:2 you think you see is **r.** to vision in any way
W-pI..... 46.5:4 practice period to adding **r.** ideas such as:
W-pI..... 46.7:1 for today in the original or in a **r.** form, as
W-pI..... 47.5:1 Now try to slip past all concerns **r.** to
W-pI..... 50.5:2 let **r.** thoughts come to help you recognize
WpI... rI.in.2:3 the **r.** comments after reading them over.
WpI... rI.in.3:3 have read the idea and the **r.** comments,
W-pI..... 61.5:7 Let a few **r.** thoughts come to you, and
W-pI..... 62.5:5 Let **r.** thoughts come freely, for your heart
W-pI..... 63.4:1 the **r.** thoughts come to you in the minute
W-pI..... 64.6:6 **R.** thoughts will come to help you, if you
W-pI..... 65.5:3 only on thoughts **r.** to the idea for the day
W-pI..... 67.3:1 have gone over several such **r.** thoughts,
W-pI..... 67.4:2 thoughts **r.** to the truth about yourself.
W-pI..... 74.3:4 minutes in adding some **r.** thoughts, such
W-pI... 126.2:3 for help are not in any way **r.** to your own.
W-pI... 133.5:1 Another kindly and **r.** law is that there is
W-pI... 140.6:6 or anything that is **r.** to the form it takes.
W-pI... 154.3:2 in everything you do that is **r.** to it. God
M-22 ............h ARE HEALING AND ATONEMENT **R.**?
M-22 ......... 1:1 Healing and Atonement are not **r.**; they

## relates 4

T-16 ........I.1:6 When He **r.** through you, He does not
WpI... rI.in.3:2 of your review of the idea to which it **r.**.
W-pI... 128.4:1 Let nothing that **r.** to body thoughts
W-pI... 186.7:1 All this the Voice for God **r.** to you. And

## relation 5

T-4 .........II.6:5 always evaluates itself in **r.** to other egos.
T-7 ..........I.1:4 you are not in a reciprocal **r.** to God, since
T-17 ... IV.14:5 when both are seen in **r.** to each other.
W-pI..... 42.4:3 occur to you in **r.** to the idea for the day.
M-4 ........X.1:1 when its **r.** to forgiveness is recognized.

## Relationship 1

*relationship*

P-3.........II.4:6 A one-to-one relationship is not one **R.**.

## relationship 369

*Relationship*

*See also* Appendix C

T-1 .........II.6:6 no **r.** between the time a miracle takes and
T-1 .........V.3:4 of the Son in his true **r.** with the Father.
T-2 .........II.6:8 a completed plan has a unique **r.** to time.
T-4 ....... III.4:4 conceive of the real **r.** that exists between
T-4 ..... VII.4:5 in the glorious context of its real **r.** to you.
T-5 ....... III.1:3 are. This **r.** must be in His Mind because,
T-6 ........ in.1:1 The **r.** of anger to attack is obvious, but
T-6 ........ in.1:1 but the **r.** of anger to fear is not always so
T-7 ...........I.1:1 limitless, but they are not in reciprocal **r.**.
T-8 ...... VII.9:2 functions with little or no **r.** to each other,
T-8 ..... VIII.1:9 arise from it, but the **r.** is not reciprocal.
T-9 .......II.10:3 reciprocal **r.** of giving and receiving will
T-13 .......X.1:4 source to which they bear no real **r.** at all.
T-13 .......X.2:2 No real **r.** can rest on guilt, or even hold
T-13 .......X.2:9 salvation will find it in that strange **r.**. It is
T-13 .......X.3:3 see guilt in that **r.** because you put it there
T-13 .......X.5:2 Use no **r.** to hold you to the past, but with
T-15 .......V.4:6 teaching, every **r.** becomes a lesson in love
T-15 .......V.5:4 You can place any **r.** under His care and
T-15 .......V.5:7 needs, which would destroy the **r.**. Your
T-15 .......V.6:1 Any **r.** you would substitute for another
T-15 .......V.8:5 you see in each **r.** what it will be when you
T-15 ..... VI.1:1 impossible to use one **r.** at the expense of
T-15 ..... VI.1:2 part of a **r.** and find peace within it. Under
T-15 .... VII.1:1 the poor attraction of the special love **r.**,
T-15 .... VII.1:6 the basis for any **r.** in which the ego enters
T-15 .... VII.1:7 For every **r.** on which the ego embarks *is*
T-15 .... VII.2:3 the ego to enter into any **r.** without anger,
T-15 .... VII.6:1 every **r.** the ego makes is based on the idea
T-15 .. VII.10:1 a special **r.** which the ego has "blessed,"
T-15 .. VII.13:3 is joined in a real **r.** so holy and so strong,
T-15 ......VIII.h The Only Real **R.**
T-15 ... VIII.3:8 You are forever in a **r.** so holy that it calls
T-15 ... VIII.4:7 from His Father, Who is His one **r.**, in
T-15 ... VIII.6:6 God created the only **r.** that has meaning,
T-15 ... VIII.6:6 has meaning, and that is His **r.** with you.
T-15 ..... IX.7:5 The reality of this **r.** becomes the only
T-15 .......X.3:2 you are willing to accept our **r.** as real,
T-15 ..... XI.3:4 and littleness will disappear in our **r.**,
T-15 ..... XI.3:4 is as innocent as our **r.** with our Father,
T-15 ..... XI.4:3 for the awareness of your **r.** with God.
T-15 ..... XI.9:5 they remember the only **r.** they ever had,
T-16 ........I.1:2 special **r.** in which the suffering is shared.
T-16 ........I.3:1 want anything you value to come of a **r.**.
T-16 ........I.6:1 meaning of love is lost in any **r.** that looks
T-16 .......II.6:2 Yet your **r.** with Him is real. Regard this
T-16 ..... III.2:6 toward establishing the **r.** between them.
T-16 ..... III.4:3 and effect **r.** that is perfectly apparent. Yet
T-16 ..... IV.1:1 not afraid to look upon the special hate **r.**,
T-16 ..... IV.1:3 this. For the special love **r.**, in which the
T-16 ..... IV.1:6 The special love **r.** will not offset it, but
T-16 ..... IV.3:1 The special love **r.** is an attempt to limit
T-16 ..... IV.3:4 love **r.** is not perceived as a value in itself,
T-16 ..... IV.3:6 is welcome in some aspects of the **r.**, but it
T-16 ..... IV.3:7 the **r.** is broken or becomes unsatisfying
T-16 ..... IV.4:9 love **r.** loses the illusion that it is what it is
T-16 ..... IV.7:1 The special love **r.** is an attempt to bring
T-16 ..... IV.7:3 love **r.** would accomplish the impossible.
T-16 ..... IV.8:4 special love **r.** is but a shabby substitute
T-16 ..... IV.8:5 Your **r.** with them is without guilt, and
T-16 ..... IV.9:6 In any **r.** in which you are wholly willing
T-16 .......V.1:1 In looking at the special **r.**, it is necessary
T-16 .......V.2:3 special love **r.** is the ego's chief weapon for
T-16 .......V.3:1 love **r.** is the ego's most boasted gift, and
T-16 .......V.4:1 It is in the special **r.**, born of the hidden
T-16 .......V.4:2 special **r.** is the renunciation of the Love
T-16 .......V.6:1 The special **r.** is a strange and unnatural
T-16 .......V.6:3 special **r.** is the triumph of this confusion.
T-16 .......V.7:1 self which the ego fosters in the special **r.**.
T-16 .......V.7:2 "self" seeks the **r.** to make itself complete.
T-16 .......V.7:3 Yet when it finds the special **r.** in which it

| | |
|---|---|
| T-16.......V.9:2 | of littleness lies in every special **r.**, for only |
| T-16.......V.9:4 | The real purpose of the special **r.**, in strict |
| T-16.....V.10:1 | perceived the special **r.** as a triumph over |
| T-16.....V.10:5 | theme that is acted out in the special **r.**. |
| T-16.....V.11:4 | is this ritual enacted in the special **r.**. An |
| T-16.....V.12:1 | of special **r.** tempts you to seek for love in |
| T-16.....V.12:2 | The special **r.** is a ritual of form, aimed at |
| T-16.....V.12:4 | special **r.** must be recognized for what it is |
| T-16.....V.13:1 | See in the special **r.** nothing more than a |
| T-16......VI.1:1 | The search for the special **r.** is the sign |
| T-16......VI.1:2 | For the special **r.** has value only to the ego |
| T-16......VI.1:3 | ego, unless a **r.** has special value it has no |
| T-16......VI.1:4 | for it is unlike the **r.** of God and His Son, |
| T-16......VI.3:2 | of guilt, the real lure in the special **r.**. You |
| T-16......VI.3:4 | it. Yet the closer you look at the special **r.**, |
| T-16......VI.4:1 | special **r.** is totally meaningless without a |
| T-16......VI.4:4 | The special **r.** is a device for limiting your |
| T-16......VI.4:5 | the total lack of value of the special **r.**, if |
| T-16......VI.5:7 | special **r.** the ego seeks does not include |
| T-16......VI.7:6 | of reference is built around the special **r.**. |
| T-16......VI.8:7 | the illusion of love in any special **r.** here. |
| T-16......VI.9:1 | in the special **r.** is really part of you. And |
| T-16......VI.9:4 | into a **r.** where it could not go with you, |
| T-16...VI.12:1 | to a special **r.** which still attracts you, |
| T-16.....VII.1:1 | go without relinquishing the special **r.**. |
| T-16.....VII.1:2 | For the special **r.** is an attempt to re-enact |
| T-16.....VII.1:3 | deprivations all enter into the special **r.**, |
| T-16.....VII.2:1 | The special **r.** takes vengeance on the past |
| T-16.....VII.2:3 | No special **r.** is experienced in the present |
| T-16.....VII.3:7 | In the special **r.** you are allowing your |
| T-16.....VII.4:1 | it in the special **r.** that binds you to it, and |
| T-16.....VII.5:1 | In the special **r.** it does not seem to be an |
| T-16.....VII.5:3 | to reach awareness is that the special **r.** is |
| T-16.....VII.5:5 | In seeking the special **r.**, you look not for |
| T-16.....VII.5:6 | and the **r.** becomes your substitute for it. |
| T-16...VII.10:4 | investment in salvation in your **r.** with |
| T-16...VII.11:4 | To join in close **r.** with Him is to accept |
| T-16...VII.11:4 | illusions for the reality of your **r.** with God |
| T-16...VII.11:5 | be to your **r.** with Him and to no other. |
| T-16...VII.12:1 | *and help us to accept our true* **r.** *with You, in* |
| T-17..............h | FORGIVENESS AND THE HOLY **R.** |
| T-17......III.2:9 | the reasons that go to make the **r.** unholy. |
| T-17......III.3:1 | In the unholy **r.**, it is not the body of the |
| T-17......III.3:4 | the breaking off of the unholy **r.** is a move |
| T-17......III.4:1 | Time is indeed unkind to the unholy **r.**. |
| T-17......III.4:3 | The attraction of the unholy **r.** begins to |
| T-17......III.4:5 | The "ideal" of the unholy **r.** thus becomes |
| T-17......III.4:6 | the less the other really brings to the **r.**, |
| T-17......III.5:7 | unholy **r.** where hatred is remembered; |
| T-17......III.5:7 | yet there to come alive as the **r.** is given to |
| T-17......III.6:9 | the **r.** so you can see it more and more. |
| T-17......III.7:4 | safe, however hidden it may be, in every **r.** |
| T-17......III.7:5 | of the one **r.** has left no part of it without |
| T-17......III.7:6 | the only part of the **r.** the Holy Spirit sees, |
| T-17......III.7:7 | is true. You have made the **r.** unreal, and |
| T-17....III.10:2 | Let my **r.** to you be real to you, and let me |
| T-17......IV.1:1 | God established His **r.** with you to make |
| T-17......IV.1:3 | of His reason for creating His **r.** with you, |
| T-17......IV.2:6 | But the holy **r.** shares God's purpose, |
| T-17......IV.2:7 | for it. Every special **r.** you have made is a |
| T-17......IV.3:3 | Every special **r.** you have made has, as its |
| T-17......IV.4:1 | the special **r.** was the ego's answer to the |
| T-17......IV.4:5 | that the Holy Spirit is in close **r.** with you, |
| T-17......IV.4:5 | in Him is your **r.** with God restored to you |
| T-17......IV.4:6 | The **r.** with Him has never been broken, |
| T-17......IV.5:8 | The special **r.**, which is its chief defense, |
| T-17......IV.6:1 | **r.** protects is but a system of delusions. |
| T-17......IV.6:3 | special **r.** still seems to you somehow to be |
| T-17......IV.8:1 | The special **r.** has the most imposing and |
| T-17....IV.16:1 | the meaning of **r.** and know it to be true. |
| T-17....IV.16:7 | The whole reality of your **r.** with Him lies |
| T-17....IV.16:7 | with Him lies in our **r.** to one another. |
| T-17..........V.h | The Healed **R.** |
| T-17.......V.1:1 | The holy **r.** is the expression of the holy |
| T-17.......V.1:6 | The holy **r.** is a constant reminder of the |
| T-17.......V.1:6 | in which the **r.** became what it is. And as |
| T-17.......V.1:7 | And as the unholy **r.** is a continuing hymn |
| T-17.......V.1:7 | so is the holy **r.** a happy song of praise to |
| T-17.......V.2:1 | **r.**, a major step toward the perception of |
| T-17.......V.2:2 | It is the old, unholy **r.**, transformed and |
| T-17.......V.2:3 | The holy **r.** is a phenomenal teaching |
| T-17.......V.2:4 | it represents the reversal of the unholy **r.**. |
| T-17.......V.2:6 | the goal of the **r.** is abruptly shifted to the |
| T-17.......V.2:7 | result of offering the **r.** to the Holy Spirit, |
| T-17.......V.3:3 | makes the **r.** seem disturbed, disjunctive |
| T-17.......V.3:5 | the **r.** as it *is* is out of line with its own goal, |
| T-17.......V.3:8 | of the old goal re-established in another **r.** |
| T-17.......V.3:9 | unholy **r.** has accepted the goal of holiness |
| T-17.......V.4:2 | **r.** has not as yet been changed sufficiently |
| T-17.......V.4:3 | **r.** is so apparent that they cannot coexist. |
| T-17.......V.4:5 | Set firmly in the unholy **r.**, there is no |
| T-17.......V.4:5 | no course except to change the **r.** to fit the |
| T-17.......V.4:6 | the **r.** may seem to be severely strained. |
| T-17.......V.5:2 | of mind about what the whole **r.** is for. As |
| T-17.......V.5:5 | A **r.**, undertaken by two individuals for |
| T-17.......V.5:6 | two contemplate their **r.** from the point of |
| T-17.......V.5:7 | perception of the **r.** may even become |
| T-17.......V.6:5 | the Holy Spirit was there to accept the **r.**, |
| T-17.......V.6:8 | And your **r.** has sanity as its purpose. For |
| T-17.......V.6:9 | For now you find yourself in an insane **r.**, |
| T-17.......V.7:1 | substitute for this another **r.** to which |
| T-17.....V.7:14 | brother. This **r.** has been reborn as holy. |
| T-17.......V.8:2 | your brother for the "failure" of your **r.**, |
| T-17.......V.8:5 | For your **r.** has not been disrupted. It has |
| T-17.....V.10:3 | for God Himself has blessed your holy **r.**. |
| T-17.....V.10:7 | and your brother together in a **r.** in which |
| T-17.....V.11:1 | to invite the Holy Spirit into your **r.**. He |
| T-17.....VII.3:1 | A situation is a **r.**, being the joining of |
| T-17.....VII.3:6 | It is their intrusion on the **r.**, an error in |
| T-17.....VII.4:2 | the goal of holiness was set for your **r.**, |
| T-17.....VII.4:3 | **r.** was not holy because your faith in your |
| T-17.....VII.5:1 | means to meet the purpose set for your **r.**. |
| T-17.....VII.6:4 | No **r.** is holy unless its holiness goes with |
| T-17...VII.8:11 | that does not involve your whole **r.**, in |
| T-17...VII.8:13 | For it shares the purpose of your whole **r.**, |
| T-17.....VII.9:1 | or you are faithless to your own **r.**. Your |
| T-17.....VII.9:5 | of your **r.** by exchanging yours for His, the |
| T-17...VII.10:4 | You whose **r.** shares the Holy Spirit's goal |
| T-17... VIII.1:4 | meaning of every **r.** and every situation, |
| T-17... VIII.6:1 | you accepted truth as the goal for your **r.**, |
| T-18.........I.1:5 | The **r.** in which the substitution occurred |
| T-18.........I.4:6 | special **r.** that you have ever made is part |
| T-18.........I.9:1 | In your **r.** with your brother, where He |
| T-18.........I.9:7 | the Holy Spirit has committed your **r.**. Let |
| T-18.......I.11:1 | to all the Sonship through your **r.**, for in it |
| T-18.......I.11:2 | upon you, blessing your **r.** with truth. |
| T-18.......I.11:4 | How lovely and how holy is your **r.**, with |
| T-18.......I.11:6 | is glad that your **r.** is as it was created. The |
| T-18.......I.13:3 | This is offered you, in your holy **r.**. Accept |
| T-18..... II.5:16 | dreams, the special **r.** has a special place. |
| T-18..... II.5:19 | The special **r.** is your determination to |
| T-18....... II.6:4 | what the Holy Spirit does in the special **r.**. |
| T-18....... II.6:7 | The special **r.** will remain, not as a source |
| T-18....... II.7:1 | special **r.** will be a means for undoing |
| T-18....... II.7:1 | in everyone blessed through your holy **r.**. |
| T-18....... II.7:7 | through you who offered your **r.** to Him. |
| T-18....... II.8:4 | **r.** with your brother has now become one |
| T-18....... II.9:3 | to let your special **r.** meet its conditions. |
| T-18....... II.9:4 | In your **r.** the Holy Spirit has gently laid |
| T-18...... III.4:3 | In your **r.** is this world's light. And fear |
| T-18... III.4:10 | of your **r.** is established in Heaven. You do |
| T-18...... III.6:1 | In your **r.** you have joined with me in |
| T-18...... III.6:5 | joined with me in the holy light of your **r.**, |
| T-18....... V.1:3 | The holy instant, the holy **r.**, the Holy |
| T-18....... V.3:1 | Through your holy **r.**, reborn and blessed |
| T-18....... V.5:2 | is your holy **r.** a dream. All that remains |
| T-18....... V.5:3 | within it is that it is still a special **r.**. Yet it |
| T-18....... V.5:6 | He gave to your **r.** by accepting it for you, |
| T-18....... V.6:1 | of your **r.** is threatened by anything, stop |
| T-18....... V.6:3 | But forget not that your **r.** is one, and so it |
| T-18.....VII.5:2 | A holy **r.** is a means of saving time. One |
| T-18. VIII.12:1 | of this; love has entered your special **r.**, |
| T-18.... IX.13:1 | **r.** with your brother has been uprooted |
| T-19.......I.12:5 | Your holy **r.**, with its new purpose, offers |
| T-19.......I.14:3 | your **r.** as it was made again through faith. |
| T-19....... II.5:5 | of the special **r.** in its interpretation. |
| T-19...... III.8:4 | Your holy **r.** has, as its purpose now, the |
| T-19.... III.11:3 | Your **r.** is now a temple of healing; a place |
| T-19.... III.11:5 | And it is brought nearer to all by your **r.**. |
| T-19...... IV.1:5 | Spirit's purpose from your **r.** to others, to |
| T-19...... IV.2:5 | He answered you, and entered your **r.**. |
| T-19...... IV.2:6 | graciousness, and enter into a **r.** with Him |
| T-19...... IV.2:7 | He Who offered your **r.** the gift of holiness |
| T19....IV.A.5:2 | For in the miracle of your holy **r.**, without |
| T19....IV.A.5:9 | call. His home is in your holy **r.**. Do not |
| T19. IV.A.5:11 | miracle of your **r.** to everyone contained |
| T19. IV.A.16:2 | This is a feast that honors your holy **r.**, |
| T19. IV.A.16:5 | For in your new **r.** am I made welcome. |
| T19....IV.B.4:9 | In your holy **r.** is your Father's Son. He |
| T19....IV.B.5:3 | for in your holy **r.** I am there already. We |
| T19....IV.B.7:1 | your holy **r.** truth proclaims the truth, |
| T19....IV.B.8:3 | I am within your holy **r.**, yet you would |
| T19..IV.B.12:2 | It is essential that this **r.** be understood, |
| T19..IV.B.13:6 | it is this insane **r.** that it keeps hidden, |
| T19....IV.C.1:1 | in whose special **r.** the Holy Spirit entered |
| T19....IV.C.9:2 | nestles quietly in the safety of your **r.**, |
| T-20...... III.2:5 | you to recognize your holy **r.** for what it is |
| T-20...... III.6:1 | Who in a holy **r.** can long remain unholy? |
| T-20...... III.8:4 | for the meaning of your unholy **r.**, and |
| T-20...... III.8:9 | That is the purpose of your holy **r.**. Ask |
| T-20...... IV.6:6 | Each holy **r.** must enter here, to learn its |
| T-20....... V.1:1 | Son comes closest to himself in a holy **r.**. |
| T-20....... V.2:5 | Peace to your holy **r.**, which has the power |
| T-20....... V.5:4 | use which serves the purpose of a holy **r.**. |
| T-20....... V.6:6 | Here is the loveliness of your **r.**, with |
| T-20...... VI.1:1 | of God lies solely in his **r.** with his Creator |
| T-20...... VI.1:4 | an unholy **r.** between him and his Father. |
| T-20...... VI.1:5 | His real **r.** is one of perfect union and |
| T-20...... VI.2:1 | experience of both a holy and an unholy **r.** |
| T-20...... VI.2:4 | Any **r.** in which the body enters is based |
| T-20...... VI.3:4 | **r.** in which they enter has lost its meaning |
| T-20...... VI.5:1 | Holy Spirit's temple is not a body, but a **r.** |
| T-20...... VI.5:3 | Here the unholy **r.** escapes reality, and |
| T-20...... VI.7:8 | Holy Spirit's purpose lies safe in your **r.**, |
| T-20...... VI.8:3 | not. An unholy **r.** is no relationship. It is a |
| T-20...... VI.8:3 | not. An unholy relationship is no **r.**. It is a |
| T-20...... VI.8:6 | **r.** with God unholy seemed to be possible, |
| T-20...... VI.9:4 | Is the malevolence of the unholy **r.**, so |
| T-20.... VI.10:1 | The holy **r.** reflects the true relationship |
| T-20.... VI.10:1 | the true **r.** the Son of God has with his |
| T-20.... VI.12:5 | You have a *real* **r.**, and it has meaning. It is |
| T-20.... VI.12:6 | It is as like your real **r.** with God as equal |
| T-20.... VI.12:9 | been given one true **r.** beyond the body? |
| T-20.. VI.12:11 | their **r.** with their Father from themselves, |
| T-20..... VII.1:1 | before your holy **r.** can bring you only joy. |
| T-20..... VII.2:1 | the sudden change in a **r.** from sin to |
| T-20..... VII.5:1 | ego tries to make the unholy **r.** seem real. |
| T-20..... VII.8:3 | a holy **r.** achieve its purpose through the |
| T-20....VIII.2:4 | Your holy **r.** offers all this to you. As it |
| T-20....VIII.3:6 | And bless the Son of God in your **r.**, nor |
| T-20....VIII.6:9 | Your holy **r.**, the source of your salvation, |
| T-21........II.1:2 | to have your whole **r.** transformed to joy; |
| T-21...... III.1:3 | brother with whom you have a limited **r.**, |
| T-21...... III.1:5 | comes from the accepted purpose of the **r.** |
| T-21...... III.6:6 | the vision of a holy **r.** is all you *want* to see. |
| T-21...... IV.3:5 | holy **r.** is one in which you join with what |
| T-21...... IV.7:6 | it found a home in your **r.** on earth. And |
| T-21....VIII.5:7 | your **r.** and your *awareness* of its holiness. |
| T-22..............h | SALVATION AND THE HOLY **R.** |
| T-22.......in.1:7 | of your **r.** forgives you and your brother, |
| T-22.......in.2:5 | For an unholy **r.** is based on differences, |
| T-22.......in.3:1 | A holy **r.** starts from a different premise. |
| T-22.......in.3:8 | For this **r.** has Heaven's Holiness. How far |
| T-22.......in.3:9 | from home can a **r.** so like to Heaven be? |
| T-22.......in.4:1 | Think what a holy **r.** can teach! Here is |
| T-22.....in.4:10 | what is born into a holy **r.** can never end. |
| T-22............I.h | The Message of the Holy **R.** |
| T-22.........I.7:1 | each holy **r.** is the ability to communicate |
| T-22.........I.7:2 | Yet a holy **r.**, so recently reborn itself |
| T-22.........I.7:2 | so recently reborn itself from an unholy **r.** |
| T-22.........I.8:7 | on the holiness of your **r.** to let Him live. |
| T-22.......I.11:3 | What is as like Him as a holy **r.**? And what |
| T-22.......I.11:9 | surely as Both are drawn to every holy **r.**, |
| T-22......II.11:5 | God has given to your holy **r.** is there. For |
| T-22......II.12:1 | circle that extends forever, is your holy **r.**, |
| T-22...... III.9:1 | A holy **r.**, however newly born, must |
| T-22...... III.9:3 | an unholy **r.**, each one is valued because |

T-22 III.9:7 Yet reason sees a holy **r.** as what it is; a
T-22 IV.7:4 Such is the function of a holy **r.**; to receive
T-22 VI.h The Light of the Holy **R.**
T-22 VI.4:1 holy **r.**, lovely in its innocence, mighty in
T-22 VI.4:4 This holy **r.** has the power to heal all pain,
T-22 VI.5:1 Before a holy **r.** there is no sin. The form
T-22 VI.5:3 you accepted in your **r.** corrects the error,
T-22 VI.6:9 of a **r.** that has become the means of peace
T-22 VI.14:1 This is the function of your holy **r.**. For
T-22 VI.14:5 you will realize that your **r.** is a reflection
T-22 VI.15:3 **r.** can also teach the power of love is there,
T-23 II.5:1 to the **r.** between the Father and the Son.
T-23 II.5:5 And Their **r.** is one of opposition, just as
T-23 IV.4:1 light of your **r.** is like the Love of God. It
T-23 IV.4:5 mighty. Also He understands how your **r.**
T-24 I.7:9 your specialness is limited by your **r.**?
T-24 I.8:8 **r.** has been made clean of special goals.
T-24 II.12:6 And no **r.** that holds its purpose dear but
T-26 VII.2:4 in a **r.** kept hidden from awareness that it
T-26 VIII.6:3 your **r.** has in it all effects that you will see
T-26 X.5:2 perceive one purpose for your whole **r.**.
T-28 VII.2:1 The beautiful **r.** you have with all your
W-pI 13.6:1 and effect **r.** of a kind which you are very
W-pI 42.1:2 It also sets forth a cause and effect **r.** that
W-pI 43.5:9 need not bear any obvious **r.** to the idea,
W-pI 45.1:3 is no **r.** between what is real and what you
W-pI 183.11:6 eternal, still **r.**, in which communication
M-in 3:1 what you believe the **r.** of others is to you.
M-2 5:4 The **r.** is holy because of that purpose,
M-2 5:4 to send His Spirit into any holy **r.**. In the
M-3 1:2 involves a different **r.** at the beginning,
M-3 1:2 same; to make of the **r.** a holy relationship
M-3 1:2 same; to make of the relationship a holy **r.**
M-3 1:7 they have the potential for a holy **r.**. They
M-3 4:3 level of teaching is a more sustained **r.**, in
M-3 4:4 appears to be the end of the **r.** a real end.
M-4 1:6 gifts, born in the holy **r.** toward which the
M-23 3:3 whole **r.** of the Son to the Father lies in
P-in 1:7 extended **r.** with an "official" therapist.
P-1 1:5 in which an earthly patient-therapist **r.**
P-1 2:1 better purpose could any **r.** have than to
P-2 in.2:1 the therapeutic **r.** with this goal in mind.
P-2 I.1:4 there will be a **r.** held out to them that
P-2 I.1:5 together again and advance in the same **r.**
P-2 II.5:3 God will enter into their **r.** because He has
P-2 VII.h The Ideal Patient-Therapist **R.**
P-2 VII.1:13 is reflected in the ideal patient-therapist **r.**
P-2 VII.2:3 of minds in a **r.** which Christ can enter?
P-2 VII.2:9 of the ideal patient-therapist **r.**, replacing
P-2 VII.3:1 The process that takes place in this **r.** is
P-2 VII.3:6 the patient in a holy **r.** in which all sense
P-3 II.1:3 therapist in every **r.** in which he enters?
P-3 II.3:8 the Holy Spirit to enter the **r.** and heal it.
P-3 II.4:6 A one-to-one **r.** is not one Relationship.
P-3 II.5:2 that only that was real in their **r.**. At that
P-3 II.5:4 For the therapeutic **r.** must become like
P-3 II.5:4 become like the **r.** of the Father and the
P-3 II.9:8 indeed. Some utilize the **r.** merely to
P-3 III.3:5 A "bought" **r.** cannot offer the only gift
P-3 III.4:4 alike. If their **r.** is to be holy, whatever one
P-3 III.4:5 Herein is the **r.** made holy, for herein both

## relationships 104

*See also* Appendix C

T-1 II.1:2 creation sometimes sought in physical **r.**.
T-1 V.3:8 God, or the Sonship, is impaired in its **r.**.
T-2 VII.3:12 entails a set of Cause and Effect **r.** totally
T-4 VII.2:1 whole, without the **r.** that imply being.
T-5 III.9:1 Perception derives meaning from **r.**.
T-8 VIII.1:14 idea of part-whole **r.** has meaning only at
T-11 V.13:5 meaningful **r.** and therefore without
T-13 X.2:1 Insane ideas have no real **r.**, for that is
T-13 X.2:3 For all **r.** that guilt has touched are used
T-13 X.2:4 strange **r.** you have made for this strange
T-13 X.2:5 And you forgot that real **r.** are holy, and
T-13 X.4:4 with whom you find no real **r.** at all. Can
T-13 X.11:1 You cannot enter into real **r.** with any of
T-13 X.11:3 imposing guilt on all your **r.** and making
T-15 V.h The Holy Instant and Special **R.**
T-15 V.2:2 the Sonship is to bring guilt into your **r.**,
T-15 V.3:3 To believe that *special* **r.**, with *special* love,
T-15 V.4:1 all special **r.** have elements of fear in them
T-15 V.4:5 you made, the Holy Spirit uses special **r.**,
T-15 V.5:2 perceives that you have made special **r.**,
T-15 V.7:1 The ego's use of **r.** is so fragmented that it
T-15 V.8:1 Everyone on earth has formed special **r.**,
T-15 V.10:1 All your **r.** are blessed in the holy instant,
T-15 VI.1:3 all **r.** are seen as total commitments, yet
T-15 VI.3:5 of **r.** that transcends the concept of loss of
T-15 VII.2:1 ego establishes **r.** only to get something.
T-15 VII.4:6 endless, unrewarding chain of special **r.**,
T-15 VII.5:3 more closely at the **r.** the ego contrives,
T-15 VII.7:1 In such insane **r.**, the attraction of what
T-15 VII.7:8 the guilt that holds all its **r.** together.
T-15 VII.8:2 For **r.**, to the ego, mean only that bodies
T-15 VII.10:3 only basis the ego accepts for special **r.**.
T-15 VIII.2:1 that you have need of no special **r.** at all.
T-15 VIII.4:4 Your **r.** are with the universe. And this
T-15 VIII.6:5 of God teach you the only meaning of **r.**.
T-15 IX.2:6 means by which you can establish real **r.**,
T-15 IX.3:1 of **r.** without limits is given you. But in
T-15 IX.5:3 and loving **r.** that any limit is impossible.
T-15 IX.5:4 you not exchange your little **r.** for this?
T-15 X.7:5 to answer this question in your special **r.**,
T-15 XI.1:4 bargain with them for a few special **r.**, in
T-15 XI.10:12 And let all your **r.** be made holy for you.
T-16 I.7:9 fulfill it if you but ask Him to enter your **r.**
T-16 IV.13:1 special **r.** of any kind would hinder God's
T-16 VI.1:4 and all **r.** that are unlike this one *must* be
T-16 VI.10:1 longing on the travesty it made of your **r.**.
T-16 VII.3:4 fantasies it brings to its chosen **r.** in which
T-16 VII.11:4 relationship with Him is to accept **r.** as
T-17 III.1:12 and make your **r.** the witness to its power.
T-17 III.2:2 and all **r.** into which they enter are totally
T-17 III.2:3 **r.** have as their purpose the exclusion of
T-17 III.2:6 why all such **r.** become attempts at union
T-17 III.2:7 are central to all unholy **r.** is evident.
T-17 III.5:1 a means of communication into **r.** whose
T-17 III.6:7 the hidden spark of beauty in your **r.**, and
T-17 III.8:3 the **r.** the unholy alliance dictates are not
T-17 III.10:1 holy brother, I would enter into all your **r.**
T-17 III.10:7 **R.** in which such dreams are cherished
T-17 IV.1:3 of **r.** became forever "to make happy."
T-17 IV.2:3 would not deprive you of your special **r.**,
T-17 IV.3:1 have made very real **r.** even in this world.
T-17 IV.4:7 all your holy **r.** been carefully preserved,
T-17 IV.16:8 The holy instant shines alike on all **r.**, for
T-17 V.1:7 song of praise to the Redeemer of **r.**.
T-17 V.3:8 Many **r.** have been broken off at this
T-18 I.2:8 fragmented **r.** the ego sponsors to destroy
T-18 VI.11:2 sometimes hoped for in special **r.**. It is a
T19 IV.A.12:1 **R.** in this world are the result of how the
T-20 III.2:2 belief that all **r.** depend upon adjustments
T-20 III.2:3 them be. Direct **r.**, in which there are no
T-20 III.2:4 ego is the self-appointed mediator of all **r.**
T-20 VI.3:7 And they have no **r.**, for no one else is
T-20 VI.4:2 It does not seek for power, but for **r.**. The
T-20 VI.4:3 weapon for seeking power *through* **r.**. And
T-20 VI.4:4 And its **r.** must be unholy, for what they
T-20 VI.6:5 temple dedicated to no **r.** and no return.
T-20 VI.8:1 There is no order in **r.**. They either are or
T-20 VI.8:6 all your **r.** were made meaningless. In that
T-20 VI.10:5 Here is the way to true **r.** held gently open
T-20 VI.11:9 And here can he learn **r.** are his salvation,
T-20 VII.5:8 For vision, like **r.**, has no order. You
T-20 VII.6:7 as a body, in unholy **r.** with other bodies,
T-21 III.1:1 All special **r.** have sin as their goal. For
T-23 II.12:12 all your **r.** have but the purpose of seizing
T-30 VII.6:5 loss of your ability to see **r.** among events.
T-31 V.16:2 one will show the changes in your own **r.**,
WpI rI.in.6:4 We are now emphasizing the **r.** among
W-pI 76.8:3 of friendship, of "good" **r.** and reciprocity
W-pI 91.6:1 this statement of true cause and effect **r.**:
W-pI 136.6:1 them without regard to all their true **r.**,
W-pI 153.1:1 brief **r.** and all the "gifts" it merely lends
W-pI 169.12:1 holding all its parts in meaningful **r.**, the
M-3 4:6 for it is the destiny of all **r.** to become holy
M-3 5:1 third level of teaching occurs in **r.** which,
M-3 5:3 These **r.** are generally few, because their
M-9 1:8 are corrected. **R.** in particular must be
P-in 1:6 interpersonal **r.** that enables him to do so.
P-1 1:2 cause and effect **r.** on which it rests. No
P-2 in.4:3 it is only in **r.** that salvation can be found.
P-2 II.1:5 **R.** are still the temple of the Holy Spirit,
P-3 II.5:7 sets the goal for the **r.** of which he is a part
P-3 II.6:2 In some **r.** this point is never reached,
P-3 II.6:8 so there is a place for all **r.** in this world,
P-3 III.6:3 **R.** are always purposeful. Whatever their

## relative 4

T-4 II.2:5 **r.** perception as is physical interaction.
T-7 VII.4:3 them. Values are **r.**, but they are powerful
W-pI 2.2:1 color, material, or **r.** importance to you.
W-pI 5.7:1 of the **r.** importance you may give them.

## relatively 3

W-pI 16.6:1 if you find them **r.** effortless. If strain is
W-pI 43.5:1 of the exercise period should be **r.** short,
M-in 1:4 only a **r.** small proportion of one's time.

## relax 3

W-pI 35.8:2 merely **r.** and repeat today's idea slowly
W-pI 39.9:2 in which you just **r.** and do not seem to be
W-pI 91.10:1 **R.** for the rest of the practice period,

## relaxation 2

W-pI 11.3:4 **r.** and freedom from worry that we are
W-pI 44.10:1 you should experience some sense of **r.**,

## relay 2

T-18 IX.3:4 these messages **r.** to you is quite external.
T-18 IX.3:6 of it; its tongue cannot **r.** its messages. Yet

## relays 1

W-pI 154.3:2 appoints your function, and **r.** it to you,

## release 239

T-1 I.13:3 past in the present, and thus **r.** the future.
T-1 I.28:1 Miracles are a way of earning **r.** from fear
T-1 III.3:4 the salvation or **r.** of all of God's creations
T-1 V.2:4 closer to the ultimate **r.** from time, in
T-1 VII.1:6 correction of the error brings **r.** from it.
T-1 VII.3:13 to walk the earth, your **r.** is not complete.
T-2 I.4:7 perceived as the **r.** from the dream, which
T-2 I.4:8 This **r.** does not depend on illusions. The
T-2 IV.h Healing as **R.** from Fear
T-2 IV.1:7 All healing is essentially the **r.** from fear.
T-2 V.1:1 that they fully understand the fear of **r.**.
T-2 V.1:2 foster the belief that **r.** is imprisonment, a
T-2 V.5:6 By affirming this you **r.** the mind from
T-2 VI.4:2 When you ask for **r.** from fear, you are
T-2 VII.1:2 that you cannot ask me to **r.** you from fear
T-3 VI.3:1 idea of the tremendous **r.** and deep peace
T-4 I.10:6 **R.** yourself and release others. Do not
T-4 I.10:6 Release yourself and **r.** others. Do not
T-4 III.9:1 by the ego, is the declaration of your **r.**.
T-4 IV.5:4 has hurt, the Atonement cannot **r.** you.
T-5 VI.8:3 and thus **r.** the thoughts from the ability
T-5 VI.9:4 it will be reinterpreted to **r.** you from fear.
T-6 I.2:6 it represents **r.** from fear to anyone who
T-7 IX.1:1 your creative power, but God wills to **r.** it.
T-8 III.2:6 you. Only His teaching will **r.** your will to
T-8 VII.16:3 impossibility lies your only hope for **r.**.
T-8 IX.5:1 Healing is **r.** from the fear of waking and
T-9 II.2:6 case he is not really asking for **r.** from fear
T-9 VIII.4:5 and mobilize its energies against your **r.**.
T-11 V.18:4 Every brother has the power to **r.** you, if
T-11 VIII.7:7 learn that His answer is the **r.** from fear.
T-12 II.7:3 In my resurrection is your **r.**. Our mission

T-13.........I.4:1 his Father sets him is one of **r.** and joy.
T-13.........I.5:3 and the way to find **r.** is not denied him.
T-13.........II.8:1 been interpreted as the **r.** from guilt, and
T-13......IV.5:3 The ego cannot tolerate **r.** from the past,
T-13......IV.5:7 of **r.** that every brother offers you *now.*
T-13......IV.6:5 you could find for **r.** in the present. The
T-13......IV.8:3 while the Holy Spirit would **r.** you from it.
T-13......IV.9:4 be accomplished in the present to **r.** the
T-13.......V.7:4 He would **r.** you from it and set you free.
T-13......VI.3:2 and in His changelessness lies your **r.**. For
T-13......VI.4:1 Time can **r.** as well as imprison,
T-13......VI.5:3 since his past is yours, you share in this **r.**.
T-13......VI.8:1 of salvation, for now is the **r.** from time.
T-13... VIII.1:1 All healing is **r.** from the past. That is
T-13......IX.2:1 **R.** from guilt is the ego's whole undoing.
T-13......IX.6:9 whom you **r.** from guilt great is the joy in
T-13.........X.h **R.** from Guilt
T-13.......X.2:8 given Him, He cannot use it for your **r.**.
T-13.....X.10:1 **R.** from guilt as you would be released.
T-13......XI.2:5 and joy belong to God for your **r.**, because
T-14.......II.4:5 because it teaches them **r.** from nothing
T-14.......II.4:9 Because you taught them gladness and **r.**,
T-14.......II.4:9 become your teachers in **r.** and gladness.
T-14......IV.4:3 When you **r.** them they are gone. God will
T-14.......V.5:4 and **r.** from suffering of every kind lie in it
T-14.......V.6:4 for the single purpose of **r.** from guilt, to
T-14.......V.7:5 From everyone whom you accord **r.** from
T-14.....V.10:3 That is the symbol of the **r.** from guilt by
T-14.....V.10:8 and in His gentleness He would **r.** from
T-14......VI.6:5 from which the Holy Spirit would **r.** you.
T-14.....VII.5:8 to means of preservation and **r.**. His task
T-14......IX.3:1 truth **r.** you from everything that it is not.
T-15......I.12:1 the Holy Spirit on behalf of your **r.** while
T-15......I.12:3 a brother, that his instant of **r.** is yours.
T-15......I.12:4 Miracles are the instants of **r.** you offer,
T-15......I.13:7 In the crystal cleanness of the **r.** you give
T-15....I.15:10 you, in that shining instant of perfect **r.**.
T-15.......II.4:9 because you have not given complete **r.**.
T-15....III.11:3 we may **r.** all those who would be bound,
T-15......IV.1:9 it, for it holds the whole **r.** from littleness.
T-15......IV.3:4 given to the world for its **r.** from littleness
T-15......IV.5:3 for the **r.** from littleness in the mind of
T-15.....VII.5:3 In the name of his **r.**, and in the Name of
T-15.....VII.5:3 in the Name of Him Who would **r.** him,
T-15... VIII.1:2 use everything in this world for your **r.**.
T-15... VIII.1:6 as clearly as He knows forgiveness is **r.**,
T-15......IX.1:1 Holy Spirit **r.** your vision and let you see
T-15......IX.4:1 and the ego, and **r.** your power to creation
T-15......IX.4:4 do as long as you would not **r.** him from it
T-15......IX.6:7 of God's Son to what interferes with his **r.**.
T-15.......X.1:9 **R.** me as I choose your own release. The
T-15.......X.1:9 Release me as I choose your own **r.**. The
T-15......XI.3:2 and let us celebrate our **r.** together by
T-15......XI.3:3 Leave nothing behind, for **r.** is total, and
T-15....XI.10:7 *In the name of my freedom I choose your* **r.**,
T-16.........I.5:3 that it would imprison what it would **r.**.
T-16......VI.2:4 As you **r.**, so will you be released. Forget
T-16....VI.12:1 a holy instant, and there let Him **r.** you.
T-16....VI.12:5 of your unwillingness for your **r.**, His
T-16.....VII.9:5 **R.** your brothers from the slavery of their
T-17.........I.1:7 Only in waking is the full **r.** from them,
T-17.........I.3:5 take away from Him Who would **r.** you.
T-17.......II.5:5 spark of beauty that gentleness could **r.**.
T-17.....V.15:2 also learned how to **r.** all the Sonship, and
T-17.....V.15:2 to Him Who gave you your **r.**, and Who
T-17... VIII.6:5 it. Your **r.** is certain. Give as you have
T-18......IV.6:6 it. **R.** yourself to Him Whose function is
T-18......IV.6:6 yourself to Him Whose function is **r.**. Do
T-18......VI.5:2 fantasies of vengeance to **r.** from them?
T-18....VI.13:6 instants of **r.** from physical restrictions,
T-18.....VII.4:3 **R.** is given you the instant you desire it.
T-18...VII.4:11 all of them look to the future for **r.** from a
T-18.....VII.6:1 Here is the ultimate **r.** which everyone
T19....IV.B.2:5 Is it a sacrifice, or a **r.**? What has the body
T19..IV.B.4:12 This has no cost, but it has **r.** from cost.
T19....IV.B.8:1 and **r.** me from punishment for what I
T19....IV.B.9:3 power, and use it for the Son of God's **r.**.
T19... IV.C.1:1 it is given to **r.** and be released from the
T19... IV.C.4:4 **r.** him are but honoring the Will of his
T19....IV.C.6:1 the power to **r.** from corruption. What
T19....IV.C.8:4 you. Ask not **r.** of *it.* But free it from the
T19. IV.D.15:1 crucified by sin and waiting for **r.** from
T19. IV.D.18:4 brother freedom and complete **r.** from sin
T-20.........I.1:2 but happily in the celebration of his **r.**.
T-20.........I.3:4 lighting his way to his redemption and **r.**.
T-20.........I.4:5 lies his **r.** and your redemption with him.
T-20....... II.7:7 The Son of God looks unto you for his **r.**.
T-20.......IV.5:2 power of the **r.** from sin you offered him.
T-20.......IV.5:3 whose special function here is to **r.** him,
T-20.....VII.8:7 holy brother, sight of whom is your **r.**, is
T-21....... II.2:1 **r.** from pain and the complete escape
T-21....... II.3:8 is given you the power to **r.** your savior,
T-21..... II.13:3 and the instant of **r.** has come to you. All
T-21......IV.5:3 the acceptance of **r.** to come to you. And
T-21......VI.6:8 Reason will tell you that this fact is your **r.**
T-21...VII.13:7 No thought but has the power to **r.** or kill.
T-22......IV.6:5 message of hope and freedom and **r.** from
T-23....... II.8:1 can be no **r.** and no escape. Atonement
T-24....... II.7:5 and one that brings **r.** to both of you.
T-24......III.1:3 Forgiveness is **r.** from all illusions, and
T-24......III.6:6 **r.** your brother from the depths of hell,
T-24......VI.5:5 Yet will his perfect sinlessness **r.** you both
T-25.........I.4:3 it may **r.** all that it looks upon unto itself.
T-25......III.7:7 one that brings **r.** from the belief there are
T-26.........I.8:5 Holy Spirit's special function but to **r.** the
T-26....... II.2:1 The Holy Spirit offers you **r.** from every
T-26....... II.7:1 how great your own **r.** will be when you
T-26.......V.6:1 Forgiveness is the great **r.** from time. It is
T-26...VII.14:3 And this is not **r.**. God's Son could never
T-26...VII.16:2 your brother calls for his **r.** and yours.
T-27.........I.2:1 your **r.** from sacrifice is his made manifest
T-27.......V.7:6 the Friend who brought them their **r.**.
T-28......IV.4:3 Therefore **r.** him, merely by your claim on
T-29....... II.1:1 Why would you not perceive it as **r.** from
T-29.......V.6:8 how blessed are you who can **r.** him, just
T-29.....VII.8:1 and open up a road of hope and of **r.** in
T-29.....IX.10:4 the dreamer full **r.** from dreams of fear.
T-31....... II.9:2 Hear but his call for mercy and **r.** from all
T-31......III.6:5 **R.** your body from imprisonment, and
T-31......III.7:1 innocent **r.** in gratitude for their release.
T-31......III.7:1 innocent release in gratitude for their **r.**.
T-31......IV.5:4 The great **r.** of power must begin with
T-31.....VII.7:7 All that is given you is for **r.**; the sight, the
T-31...VII.15:5 "**R.** My Son!" be tempted not to listen,
T-31...VII.15:5 learn that it is you for whom He asks **r.**?
T-31... VIII.3:5 but would **r.** your mind from everything
T-31... VIII.6:4 opening the way to his salvation and **r.**.
T-31... VIII.8:2 I ask for nothing but your own **r.**. There is
W-pI.....10.4:3 *This idea will help to* **r.** *me from all that I now*
W-pI.....10.5:5 *This idea will help to* **r.** *me from all that I now*
W-pI.....11.1:4 form, for in this idea is your **r.** made sure.
W-pI.....31.1:1 the introduction to your declaration of **r.**.
W-pI.....44.5:5 Properly speaking, this is the **r.** from hell.
W-pI.....50.4:7 a declaration of **r.** from the belief in idols.
W-pI.....62.5:4 and the happiness and **r.** it will bring you.
W-pI.....71.8:4 And in the first is your full **r.** from all your
W-pI.....71.8:6 plan will succeed. It will lead to **r.** and joy.
W-pI.....73.9:4 the time appointed for the **r.** of the Son of
W-pI.....75.5:3 telling yourself the glad tidings of your **r.**:
W-pI.....75.9:1 too, will be joyful reminders of your **r.**.
W-pI.....77.3:2 promised full **r.** from the world you made
W-pI.....89.1:3 His laws **r.** me from all grievances, and
W-pI.....89.3:3 By this idea do I accept my **r.** from hell.
W-pI.....94.5:9 do will be a giant stride toward your **r.**,
W-pI.....96.6:8 the **r.** of His dear Son bring pain to him,
W-pI.....98.6:1 you your full **r.** from pain of every kind,
W-pI...106.9:3 will again **r.** a thousand more who pause
W-pI.107.11:2 world and Him Who would **r.** the world,
W-pI...121.2:2 the hope of respite and **r.** from pain. It
W-pI...121.7:2 Each one awaits **r.** from hell through you,
W-pI...126.6:4 a means for your **r.** from what you see in
W-pI...126.8:5 only catch a tiny glimpse of the **r.** that lies
W-pI...126.9:3 thought that will **r.** your mind from every
W-pI...127.7:1 time beyond the count of years to your **r.**
W-pI...128.6:1 when you **r.** your mind from chains and
W-pI...128.7:5 goes to rest when you **r.** it from the world.
W-pI.130.11:2 Yet the **r.** of Heaven still remains within
W-pI...132.3:3 and **r.** the future from your ancient fears,
W-pI...132.5:1 you wish, and herein lies your ultimate **r.**.
W-pI.132.12:1 **R.** the world! Your real creations wait for
W-pI.132.12:2 wait for this **r.** to give you fatherhood, not
W-pI.132.13:6 **R.** your mind, and you will look upon a
W-pI.132.16:2 But you will sense your own **r.**, although
W-pI.135.24:2 that you must be defended from **r.**.
W-pI.152.10:5 Love, his right to Heaven and **r.** from hell,
W-pI...163.1:3 of death as savior and as giver of **r.**.
W-pI...164.7:3 for our **r.** from blindness and from misery
W-pI.166.14:1 hopes of those who look to you for their **r.**
W-pI.166.14:6 entrusted with the world's **r.** from pain.
W-pI.169.14:6 We welcome the **r.** it offers everyone. We
W-pI.169.15:6 *By grace I give. By grace I will* **r.**.
W-pI...170.8:2 be the time of your **r.** from abject slavery.
WpI...rV.in8:1 **R.** me as you practice once again the
W-pI...183.9:2 and give the world the same **r.** you found.
W-pI.183.10:1 Turn to the Name of God for your **r.**, and
W-pI...184.9:4 is this thought that will **r.** you from them.
W-pI...191.1:1 of **r.** from bondage of the world. And here
W-pI.191.11:1 They must await your own **r.**. They stay
W-pI...192.9:2 **R.** instead of bind, for thus are you made
W-pI...193.6:2 their power to **r.** all minds from bondage?
W-pI...194.3:4 already, is a time of your **r.** from sadness,
W-pI...194.5:1 **R.** the future. For the past is gone, and
W-pI.196.12:4 it welcome, as you should, for it is your **r.**.
W-pI...197.3:1 when you offer it **r.** from your illusions.
W-pI...197.3:2 as well, for its **r.** can only mirror yours.
WpI rVI.in.1:4 Each would be enough to give **r.** to you
W-pII ....227.h This is my holy instant of **r.**.
W-pII .227.1:6 *This is my holy instant of* **r.**. *Father, I know*
W-pII .241.1:3 to the darkened world where its **r.** is set.
W-pII .279.1:5 in chains which have been severed for **r.**,
W-pII .....9.2:2 end to the **r.** the Second Coming brings,
W-pII .308.2:3 *time You have appointed for Your Son's* **r.**,
W-pII .309.2:1 *Father, is my sure* **r.** *from idle dreams of sin.*
W-pII ...10.3:2 is but to fear complete **r.** from suffering,
W-pII .331.1:2 *and be left without a certain way to his* **r.**?
W-pII .332.2:4 *Father, we would* **r.** *it now. For as we offer*
M-5 ..... II.3:11 is the **r.** from guilt and sickness both, for
M-5 ..... II.3:12 Yet to accept this **r.**, the insignificance of
M-16 .........6:2 thought of peace, a thought of limitless **r.**,
M-17 .........3:2 to nothing but **r.** for teacher and pupil,
P-2........ VI.6:7 and his **r.** is partial and will not be sure.
P-3........ III.4:8 the **r.** from long imprisonment and doubt
S-1........ IV.3:5 The aim of prayer is to **r.** the present from
S-2...........II.6:2 my needs, for in your slavery is my **r.**."
S-2........ III.5:4 The light of Christ in him is his **r.**, and it
S-3...........II.3:2 flesh, but as a gentle welcome to **r.**. If
S-3...... IV.10:3 is waiting your **r.** because it is its own. Be

## released 63

T-1........ III.3:3 are **r.** must join in releasing their brothers
T-3.........I.7:11 are **r.** from all errors if you believe this.
T-8...... III.5:10 will be imprisoned or **r.** according to your
T-10...... III.1:9 in sickness. God would have them **r.** from
T-13....VIII.8:1 as yourself you will be **r.** to knowledge,
T-13..... X.10:1 Release from guilt as you would be **r.**.
T-13.... XI.11:6 You will be **r.**, and you will not remember
T-14....VIII.1:7 you would be **r.** from littleness to glory.
T-15........I.12:5 They attest to your willingness to *be* **r.**,
T-15........II.4:7 Son of God who has been **r.** through the
T-15......II.4:13 have wholly **r.** through the Holy Spirit.
T-15..... XI.10:6 *I know that you will be* **r.**, *unless I want to use*
T-15.... XI.10:7 *I recognize that we will be* **r.** *together.* So will
T-16...... VI.2:4 As you release, so will you be **r.**. Forget
T-16...... VI.6:5 with you, and to be **r.** together there.
T-17........II.5:4 lack of reason is suddenly **r.** to loveliness.
T-19........I.10:5 united in your purpose to be **r.** from guilt.
T19....IV.C.1:1 and be **r.** from the dedication to death.
T-20......II.11:1 **r.** from crucifixion through your vision,
T-20....VIII.8:5 you gave them, you are **r.** from them. One
T-21...... III.3:4 **r.** from them it will be simply because he
T-22......II.13:3 would be **r.** entirely from all effects of sin.
T-22....... VI.8:1 and each one is **r.** as he beholds his savior
T-22....... VI.8:2 Through this releasing is the world **r.**.
T-23.......in.3:4 **r.** from sin and fear and happily returned
T-23...... III.6:2 To be **r.** from conflict means that it is over
T-24........II.2:4 gauge of littleness, and be **r.** from limits?

T-25...... IX.1:3 you willing to be **r.** from all effects of sin?
T-26....... II.1:8 form. And only then are you **r.** from it.
T-26...VII.16:4 Deny him not, that you may be **r.**. Each
T-26...... IX.6:5 What hatred has **r.** to love becomes the
T-28..... II.12:5 body is **r.** because the mind acknowledges
T-28...... IV.4:5 With faith in yours, he will not be **r.**, and
T-29.... IX.10:5 nor has sought to be **r.** through judgment
T-31...... VI.2:7 **r.** from looking at the cost of keeping guilt
W-pI..... 69.1:3 grievances is lifted, you are **r.** with him.
W-pI... 115.1:3 *For thus am I r. from them with all the world.*
W-pI. 132.13:6 mind, and you will look upon a world **r.**.
W-pI. 132.16:2 as yet that you could never be **r.** alone.
W-pI. 151.16:3 world redeemed, and joyfully **r.** from guilt
W-pI... 155.4:3 of loss, and have not been **r.** accordingly.
W-pI... 163.8:3 they believe, they would be instantly **r.**.
W-pI... 166.7:4 and be **r.** from self-deception and set free.
W-pI...... 169.h By grace I live. By grace I am **r.**.
W-pI... 169.8:2 when it is **r.** to revelation and eternity.
W-pI. 169.15:4 *By grace I am r.. By grace I give. By grace I will*
W-pI... 180.1:2 By grace I am **r.**. God is but Love, and
W-pI... 186.5:1 to be **r.** from the imprisonment your plan
W-pI... 191.1:2 And here as well is all the world **r.**. You
W-pI... 194.2:2 **r.** the world from all imprisonment by
W-pI... 197.3:3 of a thankful heart, **r.** from hell forever. Is
W-pI... 199.8:5 Your brothers stand **r.** with you in it; the
W-pII ..... 1.2:2 The mind is closed, and will not be **r.**. The
W-pII . 227.2:3 again, **r.** from sin and clad in holiness,
W-pII ..... 9.4:2 now, is equally **r.** from what he made. In
W-pII . 301.1:4 *eyes forgiveness has r. from all distortion.*
W-pII . 338.1:2 thought is everyone **r.** at last from fear.
W-pII . 340.1:6 *he made, which is r. along with him today.*
S-1........ III.4:8 be **r.** without an insane fear for yourself?
S-1........ III.5:5 how your heart is lifted and your fear **r.**.
S-2........... I.7:3 Him. Prayer cannot be **r.** to Heaven while
S-2........... I.9:3 prayer can be **r.** from darkness into light.
S-2......... II.8:7 From here is prayer **r.**, along with you.

**releases** 7
T-5......... V.2:1 the Atonement, which **r.** you to create.
T-8..... VII.12:4 This **r.** the mind from the temptation to
T-15..... VII.8:9 What **r.** him from guilt is "bad," because
T-23....... in.3:3 awareness of the truth **r.** everything from
T-28....... V.3:3 from the evil dream, and thus **r.** him.
T-29...... II.10:6 body's nothingness **r.** yours from sickness
W-pI..... 83.1:3 This recognition **r.** me from all conflict,

**releasing** 13
T-1......... I.33:4 By **r.** your mind from the imprisonment
T-1......... I.42:1 in **r.** you from your false sense of isolation
T-1........ III.3:3 are released must join in **r.** their brothers,
T-2........ III.1:1 accepted within you by **r.** the inner light.
T-4........ IV.8:3 **r.** the strength of God into everything you
T-8........ III.7:8 completely, **r.** you and your brother from
T-13...... VI.5:2 him without them you are **r.** him. And
T-15...... XI.3:2 release together by **r.** everyone with us.
T-19......... I.2:2 giving him to the Holy Spirit and **r.** him
T-19...... III.9:6 by joyously **r.** him from the belief in sin.
T19.... IV.B.8:2 freedom to your brother, and so **r.** me. I
T-22...... VI.8:2 Through this **r.** is the world released. This
W-pI..... 46.1:4 who forgive are thus **r.** themselves from

**relegates** 1
T-26..... VII.7:4 world apart, and **r.** attack unto Himself.

**relentless** 2
T-27......... I.5:8 him with the poisoned and **r.** sting of fear.
W-pI... 195.3:1 and **r.** that there is no hope remaining.

**relentlessly** 1
W-pI... 170.6:3 Harsh punishment is meted out **r.** to

**relevance** 4
T-26..... VII.6:6 What **r.** has preference to the truth?
W-pI..... 79.2:4 he is given the answer, he cannot see its **r.**
W-pI..... 79.6:2 the answer because you would see its **r.**.
W-pII .. in.11:2 instructions on a theme of special **r.** will

**relevant** 6
T-18 ... VI.12:2 quality. Time is not **r.**; it can occur with
W-pI..... 38.5:1 and add some **r.** thoughts of your own.
W-pI..... 42.6:1 that active searching for **r.** thoughts is not
W-pI..... 43.5:2 and then let whatever **r.** thoughts occur to
W-pI..... 45.6:2 in thinking a few **r.** thoughts of your own,
W-pI..... 67.2:2 a few minutes adding some **r.** thoughts,

**reliable** 1
T-12 ........ I.5:2 with a personal investment is a **r.** witness,

**reliance** 2
M-9 ........... 2:6 The world trains for **r.** on one's judgment
M-16 ......... 8:5 attempts to place **r.** on himself alone.

**relief** 9
T-9 ..... VIII.2:9 not to tolerate self-abasement and seek **r.**.
T-15 .... VII.9:3 seeks **r.** from guilt by increasing it in the
T-28 .... VII.3:3 that seems to hold some promise of **r.**.
W-pI..... 34.6:2 the idea until you feel some sense of **r.**. It
W-pI..... 65.7:1 you, the **r.** its acceptance will bring you by
W-pI... 134.6:1 sane, a deep **r.** to those who offer it; a
W-pI. 134.16:3 your chest, a deep and certain feeling of **r.**
W-pI. 136.17:1 source of sickness has been opened to **r.**.
S-3........ III.5:2 remedy that brings **r.** which cannot fail. It

**relies** 2
T-2 ........ V.4:1 The healer who **r.** on his own readiness is
P-2......... V.1:4 strange belief **r.** on certain steps which

**relieve** 3
W-pI... 192.5:5 fear? Only forgiveness can **r.** the mind of
W-pII . 311.1:6 will **r.** us of the agony of all the judgments
P-2...... IV.11:2 **R.** the mind of the insane burden of guilt

**relieved** 2
W-pI. 135.12:1 mind is **r.** of the belief that it must plan,
W-pII . 243.1:5 I am **r.** of judgments that I cannot make.

**religion** 14
T-10 ..... IV.1:2 the irreconcilable. All **r.** is the recognition
T-10 ...... V.3:1 to the denial of God is the ego's **r.**. The
T-15 ........ I.3:4 outcome of its strange **r.** must therefore
T-16 .... V.10:3 attributes of the whole **r.** of separation,
T-19 ....... II.4:1 the ego's insane **r.** is that sin is not error
M-1 ........... 2:2 come from all religions and from no **r.**.
P-2........... II.h The Place of **R.** in Psychotherapy
P-2.......... II.2:1 Formal **r.** has no place in psychotherapy,
P-2.......... II.2:1 but it also has no real place in **r.**. In this
P-2.......... II.2:3 attempt to formalize **r.** is so obviously an
P-2.......... II.2:4 here. **R.** is experience; psychotherapy is
P-2.......... II.5:2 forms of **r.** have nothing to do with God,
P-2.......... II.7:1 true **r.** heals, so must true psychotherapy
P-2.......... II.9:6 What is **r.** but an aid in helping him to see

**religions** 3
T-3 .......... I.1:7 anti-religious concepts enter into many **r.**.
W-pI..... 76.8:5 Many "**r.**" have been based on this. They
M-1 ........... 2:2 come from all **r.** and from no religion.

**religious** 2
*See also* anti-religious
P-2.......... II.1:1 not necessary to be **r.** or even to believe in
P-2.......... II.7:1 heals, so must true psychotherapy be **r.**.

**religiously** 1
T-4 ......... II.9:5 The more "**r.**" ego-oriented may believe

**relinquish** 14
T-6 ..... V.B.5:1 is clearly to choose one and **r.** the other. If
T-6 ... V.C.10:1 entails a willingness to **r.** everything else.
T-7 ......... II.6:7 forget or **r.** one to understand the other.
T-8 .......... I.5:9 one because they cannot **r.** the other, even
T-12 ... III.10:9 you must **r.** your investment in the world
T-12 ..... IV.7:6 but you must **r.** your investment in death,
T-13 ...... in.1:6 It is not an attempt to **r.** denial, but to
T-15 ..... VI.5:3 Mind that thought it, and could not **r.** it.
T-16 ....... V.3:1 most appeal to those unwilling to **r.** guilt.
T-25 ....... II.1:8 For only thus will you be willing to **r.** it,
W-pI .... 68.4:1 not be willing to **r.** your grievances if you
W-pI .. 138.8:1 not **r.** its ideas about its own protection.
W-pII . 351.1:3 *this perception is a choice I make, and can r..*
M-10 ......... 6:1 It is not difficult to **r.** judgment. But it is

**relinquished** 7
T-7 ....... VI.1:3 discrete, and why it must be **r.** entirely. If
T-7 ....... VI.1:4 not **r.** entirely it is not relinquished at all.
T-7 ....... VI.1:4 not relinquished entirely it is not **r.** at all.
T-12 ... VIII.5:3 has **r.** the insane desire to control reality.
W-pI .. 131.3:4 to you from an idea **r.** yet remembered,
M-10 ............ h HOW IS JUDGMENT **R.**?
S-1........ III.1:5 be **r.** before *you* can be saved from guilt.

**relinquishes** 1
W-pI .. 196.4:2 as the mind **r.** its burdens one by one. It is

**relinquishing** 4
T-8 ..... VIII.9:9 Health is the result of **r.** all attempts to
T-14 ... III.12:4 plan God set for its Atonement, **r.** its own
T-16 .... VII.1:1 past go without **r.** the special relationship
M-6 ........... 4:1 **r.** of all concern about the gift that makes

**relinquishment** 14
T-4 .......... I.3:2 as frightening because it leads to the **r.**,
T-6 .......... III.h The **R.** of Attack
T-6 ....... III.3:7 Safety is the complete **r.** of attack. No
T-7 ......... X.7:1 Even the **r.** of your false decision-making
T-9 ....... III.2:3 correction of errors lies in the **r.** of the ego
T-26 ..... III.7:6 in the **r.** of an illusion recognized as such.
T-31 ....... II.2:2 For there are steps in its **r.**. The first is a
W-pI .... 65.1:5 and the **r.** of all the other goals you have
W-pI .. 138.2:3 seem to be the same as the **r.** of hell. It is
WpI.rVI.in.3:8 a deep **r.** of everything that clutters up the
M-4 ..... I.A.5:1 God must go can be called "a period of **r.**.
M-9 ........... 2:7 curriculum trains for the **r.** of judgment
M-10 ......... 4:5 is not judgment; it is the **r.** of judgment.
M-28 ......... 1:9 It is the **r.** of all other purposes, all other

**relive** 1
T-26 ..... V.13:1 but **r.** the single instant when the time of

**relived** 2
T-26 ..... V.13:3 instant gone by long ago that cannot be **r.**
M-2 ........... 4:2 that is **r.** again and again and still again, it

**relives** 1
M-2 ........... 4:5 in that ancient instant which he now **r.**.

**reluctance** 2
T-25 ..... IX.2:2 for you until **r.** to receive it disappears,
T-25 ..... IX.2:8 not fight against His Son's **r.** to perceive

### reluctant 2
T-5......III.10:3 The Holy Spirit can deal with a **r.** learner
T-25......IX.2:1 the gift, because you are **r.** to accept it. It

### reluctantly 2
T-25......IX.2:1 To give **r.** is not to gain the gift, because
W-pI...107.9:6 you will return to the familiar world **r.**.

### rely 1
T-2.........V.2:5 you to **r.** temporarily on physical healing

### relying 1
W-pI.....77.7:6 are not **r.** on yourself to find the miracle,

### remain 192
T-2........I.5:12 enables you to **r.** unshaken by lack of love
T-2........VI.8:7 need for the remedy, you will **r.** fearful.
T-2... VIII.5:10 there is no reason for fear to **r.** with you.
T-3........IV.7:1 God and His creations **r.** in surety, and
T-4...........I.8:2 It will **r.** doubtful as long as you believe in
T-4........III.6:2 are as free as God, and must **r.** so forever.
T-4.......V.6:11 a decision that will **r.** in effect unless you
T-5.........in.2:2 to be wholly fearful and **r.** alive, the only
T-5...........I.5:7 Holy Spirit will **r.** with the Sons of God, to
T-5.......V.7:12 is beyond doubt, how can its symptoms **r.**
T-5...........V.8:1 The continuing decision to **r.** separated is
T-5......VI.12:6 and **r.** to bless your creations there. He is
T-6........IV.2:4 not **r.** within the Kingdom without love,
T-6......V.A.6:3 journey, where you and only you must **r.**.
T-6......V.A.6:6 Some **r.** at this step for a long time,
T-7.........X.6:3 will always **r.** beyond question, however
T-8.......VII.6:5 Son of God **r.** hidden for His Name's sake,
T-9..... VIII.4:4 conviction of reality will not **r.** with you
T-10.....V.14:2 which is not of God, will **r.** with you.
T-11.......II.5:6 He will **r.**, but you have allied yourself
T-11........II.7:3 guest, and how long he shall **r.** with you.
T-12...........I.6:8 your divided state, His **r.** consistently true
T-12... VIII.1:7 But offer attack and love will **r.** hidden,
T-13.......II.9:3 no dark cloud will **r.** between you and the
T-13....III.11:4 If the Son did not wish to **r.** in peace, he
T-13....III.11:4 to remain in peace, he could not **r.** at all.
T-13......VI.7:3 to **r.** in the darkness that is not there, and
T-13......IX.4:4 saying, "I who was guilty choose to **r.** so."
T-13...XI.10:4 will **r.** unchanged throughout eternity.
T-14....III.18:2 you **r.** in close communication with Him,
T-14.......V.4:5 Never allow purity to **r.** hidden, but shine
T-14......XI.7:4 His Son to turn to Him and **r.** Himself. It
T-14......XI.8:1 bound to guilt and committed so to **r.**,
T-15.......II.4:9 If you **r.** uncertain, it is only because you
T-15......III.9:9 who must **r.** forever beyond littleness.
T-15...VII.10:4 with it, guilt will **r.** attractive to you. Yet
T-15...VII.11:5 are together their minds **r.** their own. The
T-15......IX.5:2 of this and long **r.** willing to linger here.
T-16....IV.1:10 until you do, the split will **r.** unrecognized
T-16.......V.5:6 nothing would **r.** to interfere with the ego.
T-17.........I.4:1 order of difficulty in miracles **r.** with you.
T-17.......II.3:5 no one and nothing **r.** still bound by them
T-17.....V.14:7 **r.** still separate and divided on the means.
T-17.....VII.4:6 faith, and **r.** faithful to your brother?
T-18.........I.6:6 truth brought to this could only **r.** within
T-18...... I.10:7 that illusions cannot **r.** to darken the holy
T-18.......II.6:2 You would have used them to **r.** asleep. I
T-18.......II.6:7 The special relationship will **r.**, not as a
T-18......III.6:2 to everyone who would **r.** in darkness.
T-18......III.8:4 of God Himself, can you **r.** in darkness?
T-18......IV.3:1 ask that you **r.** content with littleness. But
T-18......IV.8:2 and **r.** unwilling to give place to One Who
T-18......VI.2:8 it would **r.** separate from your brother's,
T-18.....VII.7:9 He will **r.** when you forget, and the body's
T-18.....VII.8:3 in which you do nothing, will **r.** with you,
T-18... VIII.7:5 Would you **r.** within your tiny kingdom, a
T-18......IX.3:6 it not; its senses **r.** quite unaware of it; its
T-18......IX.5:1 The body will **r.** guilt's messenger, and
T-19.........I.7:2 This will **r.** forever true, however much
T-19.......II.1:5 will forever so **r.** unless a mind not part of
T-19......III.7:5 it, nor **r.** itself before the power of sin. Sin
T-20......III.6:1 in a holy relationship can long **r.** unholy?
T-20......III.7:3 but he will not **r.** before the shining light
T-20......VII.5:5 the means **r.** unquestioned while the end
T-21.........I.3:7 you still **r.** uncertain that vision gives you
T-22.......II.3:8 Only the timeless must **r.** unchanged, but
T-22......II.13:3 And no one can **r.** beyond this willingness
T-22......II.13:5 a single sin still tempts you to **r.** in misery
T-22.......VI.6:8 long **r.** in a mind that serves the timeless.
T-23.........I.6:6 and they **r.** part of what made them.
T-23.......II.7:6 For now salvation must **r.** impossible,
T-23......III.3:8 be different, and yet the same **r.** intact, as
T-23......IV.1:1 Do not **r.** in conflict, for there *is* no war
T-23......IV.6:7 chosen to **r.** where He would have you,
T-24.......II.7:7 the dream of specialness **r.** between you.
T-24......IV.5:1 He loves, and you **r.** beyond salvation.
T-25......III.5:6 you **r.** in darkness where the lamps are
T-25.......V.4:3 So must it **r.** useless to both. Together, it
T-25......VI.3:5 Nor does He will that he **r.** without the
T-25......VI.7:7 and will **r.** in time and in eternity alike.
T-25......IX.4:6 Yet does the problem still **r.** unsolved, for
T-25......IX.7:6 His help is to decide it should **r.** unsettled
T-26......III.4:6 the same and what is different **r.** unclear.
T-26......VI.2:2 nor one with which he could **r.** content.
T-26...VII.10:4 What can **r.** unhealed and broken from a
T-26... VIII.2:4 Thus do you think it safer to **r.** a little
T-27.........I.8:2 be reason to **r.** content to seek for passing
T-27.......II.3:4 The sick **r.** accusers. They cannot forgive
T-27......IV.6:8 tells "of whom," it will **r.** unrecognized,
T-27.....V.10:1 will guarantee that they **r.** unviolated and
T-28......IV.7:4 can not **r.** without a witness or a cause.
T-29......III.3:8 The darkness cannot choose that it **r.**. The
T-29......IX.5:9 a toy, to make his world **r.** outside himself
T-30......VI.7:3 appearance must **r.** apart from healing,
T-30......VI.7:6 and will **r.** afraid to look within and find
T-31.........I.8:3 you. And never does a call **r.** unheard,
T-31.....V.15:4 of yourself will still **r.** quite meaningless.
T-31.....VII.6:1 **r.** forever unaccomplished and undone.
T-31...VII.10:2 be miserable, and **r.** in hell and torment?
T-31...VII.12:3 It will **r.** your concept of yourself until the
T-31... VIII.1:5 *the saviors of the world, or would r. in hell,*
W-pI.......2.1:6 you. **R.** as indiscriminate as possible in
W-pI.....33.2:2 Try to **r.** equally uninvolved in both, and
W-pI.....70.9:1 surely you do not want to **r.** in the clouds,
W-pI.....75.3:2 No shadows from the past **r.** to darken
W-pI.....79.5:5 ones. Others **r.** unsolved under a cloud of
W-pI.....91.2:2 While you **r.** in darkness, the miracle
W-pI.....94.2:2 If you **r.** as God created you, you must be
W-pI.....94.2:6 in which you will **r.** throughout eternity.
W-pI.....95.6:3 who **r.** heavily defended against learning.
W-pI.....96.7:1 and they **r.** within your mind and in the
W-pI...106.7:1 is given away, it will **r.** with you forever.
W-pI...107.1:2 that **r.** unrecognized for what they are?
W-pI...108.4:2 together, that the Thought **r.** complete.
W-pI...110.1:4 **r.** as God created you fear has no meaning
W-pI...110.3:1 If you **r.** as God created you, appearances
W-pI...110.3:2 not occurred, if you **r.** as God created you.
W-pI...112.2:2 me. *I will r. forever as I was, created by the*
W-pI...122.9:2 we made, but where we would **r.** no more.
W-pI...123.3:1 His Love forever will **r.** shining on you,
W-pI...125.5:4 that he **r.** as part of Him regardless of his
W-pI...126.2:4 **r.** apart from condemnation and at peace.
W-pI...127.2:4 and yet **r.** itself although it is withheld
W-pI...129.3:2 and they will **r.** exactly as you want them
W-pI...130.4:6 They can be valued, but **r.** unreal. They
W-pI...132.9:4 place exist, if you **r.** as God created you?
W-pI.132.15:2 *I who r. as God created me would loose the*
W-pI.136.13:5 wills is here, and you **r.** as He created you.
W-pI.136.14:1 can **r.** where truth has been allowed to
W-pI...137.4:4 always will **r.** exactly as it has forever been
W-pI.137.11:3 a haven where the weary can **r.** to rest.
W-pI.139.11:3 *for myself, For I r. as God created me.* We
W-pI.139.12:4 *for myself, For I r. as God created me.*
W-pI...152.5:1 created you, you must **r.** unchangeable,
W-pI...155.3:2 mad illusion will **r.** awhile in evidence, for
W-pI...155.7:2 defeat, and aims that will **r.** impossible.
W-pI...159.9:3 Their roots **r.**. They do not leave their
W-pI...160.8:5 Whom God has joined **r.** forever one, at
W-pI...165.3:3 they stay with him, and he **r.** with them?
W-pI...165.6:5 God consent to let His Son **r.** forever
W-pI...167.5:2 Ideas **r.** united to their source. They can
W-pI...167.8:4 the Thoughts of God **r.** forever changeless
W-pI...169.9:2 as it always was; forever to **r.** as it is now.
W-pI.169.11:2 must **r.** obscure to you until your part is
W-pI.170.11:3 cruel god **r.** with you in still another form.
WpI...rV.in6:5 Yet a savior must **r.** with those he teaches,
W-pI...181.7:3 sin will bring, and uncorrected will **r.**.
W-pI...184.5:1 Yet does this other vision still **r.** a natural
W-pI...185.9:6 as certainly, and to **r.** with you forever. It
W-pI.185.11:3 Who can **r.** unsatisfied who asks for what
W-pI...188.7:4 on them, but they must **r.** with you as well
W-pI...193.9:3 his holy rest **r.** untroubled and serene,
W-pI.193.12:5 it. Thus will you **r.** unbound, in peace
W-pI.196.12:2 no obstacles that still **r.** between you and
W-pII ....in.1:4 lessons that **r.** are merely introductions to
W-pII ....in.3:4 that His Son will not **r.** unanswered when
W-pII .226.1:3 as I see it now, so will it still **r.** for me. But
W-pII .230.1:2 And in peace do I **r.**. It is not given me to
W-pII .....3.1:3 It will **r.** no longer than the thought that
W-pII .243.1:2 what must **r.** beyond my present grasp. I
W-pII .255.1:5 must **r.** forever in the peace of Heaven. In
W-pII .256.1:6 is? And who would yet **r.** asleep, in heavy
W-pII .263.2:1 while we still **r.** outside the gate of Heaven
W-pII .268.1:5 *love was I created, and in love will I r. forever.*
W-pII .....6.2:5 salvation, yet does He **r.** the Self Who,
W-pII .....6.3:1 does Christ **r.** at peace within the Heaven
W-pII .....7.4:2 will your dreams **r.** to terrify you. And the
W-pII .299.2:6 *healed, for they r. as You created them. And I*
W-pII .307.1:5 *nothing contradicts the holy truth that I r. as*
W-pII .332.2:6 *And we would not r. as prisoners, while You*
W-pII .340.2:6 Not one who will **r.** in fear, and none the
W-pII .343.1:8 *As I was created I r.. Your Son can make no*
W-pII .360.1:2 *Rays r. forever still and undisturbed within*
W-pII .360.1:5 *were we created, and in holiness do we r..*
M-in..........5:7 thoughts **r.** a source of strength and truth
M-4 .....I.A.7:7 that may **r.** impossible to reach for a long,
M-4 .......X.2:7 No clouds **r.** to hide the face of Christ.
M-5 ......III.3:4 himself, and must **r.** as God created him.
M-7 ...........1:5 teacher of God to **r.** concerned about the
M-13 .......6:12 And if they stay, you will **r.** with them.
M-14 .........3:4 Not one thought of sin will **r.** the instant
M-21 .........3:3 that the prayer of the heart **r.** unanswered
M-22 .........7:2 must **r.** beyond God's power to forgive?
M-28 .........4:5 No hidden places now **r.** on earth to
C-in .........3:10 Only in that does it **r.** wholly consistent
C-4.............5:9 not **r.** where separation is impossible.
C-5.............5:4 He will **r.** with you to lead you from the
P-2........IV.5:4 Yet must their cures **r.** temporary, or
P-2.......IV.10:9 thus it must **r.** unwanted as well as unreal
P-2.........V.3:3 the perfect teacher could not long **r.**; the
P-3..........II.7:5 **r.** on earth until the closing of time. They
S-3........III.5:3 It will **r.** to bless for all eternity. It heals

### remainder 3
W-pI.....46.5:4 Then devote the **r.** of the practice period
W-pI.....68.6:4 Spend the **r.** of the practice period trying
W-pI.....71.9:1 this, let us devote the **r.** of the extended

### remained 6
T-13......VI.9:4 Son called upon Him and **r.** unanswered.
T-20......III.9:6 yet his holiness **r.** untouched and perfect,
W-pII .232.1:3 *thanksgiving that You have r. with me, and*
W-pII .....5.2:4 For if his oneness still **r.** untouched, who
W-pII .326.1:3 *As You created me I have r.. Where You*
M-23 .........5:9 He has **r.** with you. Would you not learn

### remaining 34
T-5..........II.7:6 **r.** quiet even in the midst of the turmoil
T-5..........II.8:3 He is your **r.** communication with God,
T-7........VI.3:8 **R.** logical but still insane, the ego resolves
T-10......III.2:6 God's **r.** Communication Link with all His
T-10......IV.8:6 Light, because it is the **r.** call of creation.
T-12.....VII.9:1 one **r.** freedom as a prisoner of this world.
T-13......IX.8:4 Yet this you cannot do without **r.** blind.
T-16......IV.5:5 choice **r.** possible is which illusion you

| | |
|---|---|
| T-21......IV.6:7 | A few r. trinkets still seem to shine and |
| T-21.....VII.6:7 | seem to be the last r. hope of finding sin, |
| T-26.........I.3:2 | r. incomplete to keep its own identity |
| T-26....VIII.1:1 | The one r. problem that you have is that |
| T-27..... II.14:6 | r. half the Holy Spirit must represent the |
| T-27...... III.2:3 | where half is cancelled out by the r. half. |
| T-31...VII.14:3 | dreams and no r. hope except to die, and |
| W-pI.134.16:4 | time r. should be given to experiencing |
| W-pI.136.16:3 | purposes insanely sought, r. in your mind |
| W-pI...158.1:3 | left your Source, r. as you were created. |
| W-pI...159.4:2 | their source, r. with each miracle you give |
| W-pI...159.4:2 | each miracle you give, and yet r. yours. It |
| W-pI.167.12:1 | us, r. always in the holy minds which He |
| W-pI...193.9:4 | be wiped away, with none r. yet unshed, |
| W-pI...195.3:1 | and relentless that there is no hope r.. |
| W-pII ....in.3:2 | in the r. holy instants which conclude the |
| W-pII .260.1:2 | *not left my Source, r. part of Who created me* |
| W-pII .270.1:4 | *waits expectantly the one r. instant more of* |
| W-pII ...11.2:4 | r. as it was before the thought of time |
| M-4 ...... IX.1:5 | problems, r. carefully limited for a time. |
| M-12 .......5:11 | is. He does not suffer either in going or r.. |
| M-25 .........5:5 | given a r. wish to be deceived, deception |
| M-26 .........3:9 | to those r. behind are few indeed. And |
| C-1.............7:1 | world the only r. freedom is the freedom |
| C-6.............3:1 | the r. Communication Link between God |
| S-2...........I.9:6 | There can be no trace of it r., if the plan |

## remains 187

| | |
|---|---|
| T-1.....VII.3:13 | As long as a single "slave" r. to walk the |
| T-2...........I.3:9 | It still r. within you, however, to extend as |
| T-2........VI.9:3 | and no one r. fully aware of it all the time. |
| T-3...........I.2:9 | that nothing of this kind r. in your mind. |
| T-3.........VI.2:6 | wanting, r. in your mind because it has |
| T-5......IV.3:10 | The rest r. with you until the Holy Spirit |
| T-6......... II.7:2 | but the Holy Spirit r. the Bridge between |
| T-9...........I.4:1 | beyond your own awareness, where it r., |
| T-9......VIII.2:8 | It r. suspicious as long as you despair of |
| T-10......IV.8:1 | In many only the spark r., for the Great |
| T-11......... II.5:2 | The Eternal Guest r., but His Voice grows |
| T-12...... II.10:5 | otherwise His knowledge r. useless to you |
| T-12..VIII.7:10 | attraction of love for love r. irresistible. |
| T-13...... IX.1:1 | Guilt r. the only thing that hides the |
| T-14....... V.2:3 | that his true function r. unfulfilled in him |
| T-14...... VI.3:7 | of obscurity only the light of love r., for |
| T-14....VIII.5:3 | And Heaven r. the Will of God for you. |
| T-14....... X.5:4 | little sanity that still r. is held together by |
| T-14....... X.9:4 | therefore r. the ego's chosen condition. |
| T-15.......I.15:6 | for his purity r. forever beyond attack and |
| T-15...... VI.1:5 | And this you cannot have while guilt r.. |
| T-15...... VI.4:1 | calls on God for love, your call r. as strong |
| T-15...... IX.2:6 | Yet it r. the only means by which you can |
| T-15...... IX.6:3 | His attraction for you r. unlimited, but |
| T-15..... X.5:13 | question that r. is how much is the price, |
| T-15...... XI.7:2 | r. unbroken even if the body is destroyed, |
| T-17...... III.5:3 | have been forgotten, what r. is eternal. |
| T-17...... IV.6:5 | go. While this one r., you will not let the |
| T-17..... V.12:3 | The instant r.. But where are you? To give |
| T-18.........I.6:7 | madness, for such it was and so it still r.. |
| T-18..... II.5:10 | another world that is not real r. with you. |
| T-18....... V.5:3 | All that r. of dreams within it is that it is |
| T-18.....VIII.4:5 | being. Its whole existence still r. in them. |
| T-18..VIII.11:8 | No Son of God r. outside His Fatherhood. |
| T-19.........I.7:7 | produced the body and r. connected to it, |
| T-19.......I.16:5 | it. For it r. joined to its source, which is its |
| T-19...... III.1:4 | the guilt r. attractive the mind will suffer, |
| T-19...... III.3:5 | stop and let it go, unless the guilt r.. For |
| T-19...... III.8:8 | Only the habit of looking for it still r.. |
| T-19...... IV.2:3 | with the Holy Spirit r. unfinished. You |
| T19... IV.A.8:1 | is all that r. of what once seemed to be the |
| T19... IV.D.8:6 | Guide Who brought you here r. with you, |
| T-20...... III.4:1 | A simple question yet r., and needs an |
| T-20.... VI.12:8 | a shadow of the fear of God r. with you. |
| T-21....... V.4:6 | is obvious, simple and r. unasked. But |
| T-21....VII.13:5 | Son of God's desire r. the proof that he is |
| T-21....VIII.3:9 | he does not desire it while he r. uncertain, |
| T-22....... V.3:7 | Yet it r. impossible to keep love out. God |
| T-22.... VI.10:8 | a rock. While this r., so will it seem to be. |
| T-23...... IV.1:3 | Yet He r. the only place of safety. In Him |
| T-24 ..... VI.1:1 | trace of conflict still r. to haunt you in the |
| T-25 ..... III.5:4 | Nothing r. an instant, to obscure the |
| T-25 ...VIII.2:8 | a little faith r. to those who still believe in |
| T-26 ........I.3:4 | and something still r. for you alone. And |
| T-26 ..... IV.5:3 | the song of Heaven and r. without a voice |
| T-26 ...... V.1:9 | while time r. and choice is meaningful. |
| T-26 ...... V.4:4 | illusion still r. unanswered in your mind. |
| T-26 .... V.11:9 | Here the shadow of the past r., but still a |
| T-26 .......X.1:1 | r. to be undone for you to realize Their |
| T-27 ..... III.6:6 | half of what it represents r. unknown, but |
| T-27 ..... III.7:1 | seen or ears have heard r. to be perceived. |
| T-27 ...... V.2:2 | as it is unattested, it r. without conviction |
| T-29 ........I.3:3 | but this one still r. to block your path, |
| T-29 .......II.7:8 | means the mind r. unchanged in its belief |
| T-29 ...... V.8:3 | nothing in the world of dreams r. without |
| T-30 ... III.10:2 | Thought God holds of you r. exactly as it |
| T-30 ...... V.3:1 | for the purpose of forgiveness still r.. Yet |
| T-30 ...... V.3:2 | he but r. until it is made perfect in himself |
| T-30 ..... VI.3:7 | but r. aware that they have sinned. And |
| T-30 ..... VI.5:6 | special form of error that r. unchangeable |
| T-31 ..... VI.7:4 | The truth in you r. as radiant as a star, as |
| T-31 .VIII.12:4 | began. No trace of it r.. Not one illusion is |
| T-31 .VIII.12:5 | one spot of darkness still r. to hide the |
| W-pI..... 19.4:2 | practice periods r. essential throughout. |
| W-pI..... 56.4:2 | I have made, the truth r. unchanged. |
| W-pI..... 56.4:3 | the face of love, its light r. undimmed. |
| W-pI..... 68.2:1 | r. aware of Its likeness to Its Creator, your |
| W-pI..... 83.4:3 | *and my function r. wholly unaffected by this* |
| W-pI..... 91.2:2 | remain in darkness, the miracle r. unseen. |
| W-pI..... 91.5:4 | Your will r. your teacher, and your will |
| W-pI..... 92.6:4 | In darkness it r. to hide itself, and dreams |
| W-pI... 96.11:2 | Perhaps your mind r. uncertain yet a little |
| W-pI..... 97.6:3 | this light r. and leads you out of darkness, |
| W-pI... 107.1:7 | to dust they come and go, for only truth r. |
| W-pI... 108.2:3 | while what is not the same r. unnoticed, |
| W-pI... 109.4:2 | hate your rest r. completely undisturbed. |
| W-pI... 113.2:2 | *Whose knowledge still r. within my mind, I* |
| W-pI... 122.5:2 | Be thankful it r. exactly as He planned it. |
| W-pI... 123.1:4 | the truth. A bit of wavering r., some small |
| W-pI... 124.2:5 | behind, yet still r. with us as we walk on. |
| W-pI... 126.5:3 | it r. your right to let the sinner not escape |
| W-pI... 126.7:6 | What r. as unreceived has not been given, |
| W-pI... 129.4:1 | plain as day, r. unlimited for all eternity. |
| W-pI... 130.3:3 | by fear, and what r. is but imagined. Yet |
| W-pI... 130.5:3 | But one r.. They are the range of choice |
| W-pI. 130.11:2 | Heaven still r. within your range of choice |
| W-pI... 131.5:1 | No one r. in hell, for no one can abandon |
| W-pI... 131.7:1 | Heaven r. your one alternative to this |
| W-pI... 132.3:1 | The present now r. the only time. Here in |
| W-pI. 135.17:3 | Yet what r. is meaningless indeed. For it |
| W-pI. 135.23:4 | r. unanswered yet in need of answering |
| W-pI... 136.5:3 | the sign that this decision still r. in force, |
| W-pI. 136.11:2 | The universe r. unheeding of the laws by |
| W-pI. 136.17:5 | does. Its usefulness r. and nothing more. |
| W-pI... 137.1:1 | Today's idea r. the central thought on |
| W-pI... 137.6:4 | while fear r. the one reality that can be |
| W-pI... 138.6:3 | could decide the rest, this one r. unsolved |
| W-pI... 140.2:3 | and so his mind r. exactly as it was before. |
| W-pI... 151.5:3 | underneath r. the hidden doubt that what |
| W-pI. 151.14:4 | r. is unified into a perfect Thought that |
| W-pI. 153.19:4 | will remind ourselves that He r. beside us |
| W-pI... 156.3:2 | of His r. unshared by everything that lives |
| W-pI... 156.7:5 | in the little interval of doubt that still r., |
| W-pI... 160.1:4 | What is your Self r. an alien to the part of |
| W-pI... 160.6:6 | For in his home his Self r.. It asked no |
| W-pI... 164.6:5 | your love, while nothing to be feared r.. |
| W-pI... 165.4:6 | you welcome it as yours, uncertainty r.. |
| W-pI... 165.8:4 | His Love r. beyond our every fear. The |
| W-pI... 168.1:6 | He r. entirely accessible. He loves His Son |
| W-pI. 168.1:10 | When his mind r. asleep, He loves him |
| W-pI... 168.4:4 | What now r. that Heaven be delayed an |
| W-pI... 169.6:7 | been at all. Eternity r. a constant state. |
| W-pI. 169.13:4 | to it forever, while a part of you r. outside, |
| W-pI. 170.12:3 | And now your heart r. at peace forever. |
| WpI...rV.in5:3 | if we keep in mind that this r. our goal, |
| Wi181-200 3:2 | r. beyond achievement while it is denied. |
| W-pI. 182.12:5 | The holy Child r. with you. His home is |
| W-pI. 185.14:1 | sever, but which still r. as God created it. |
| W-pI... 187.5:3 | The thought r., and grows in strength as |
| W-pI .. 187.6:5 | He recognizes sacrifice r. the one idea |
| W-pI .. 188.3:2 | blessing with it that r. forever and forever |
| W-pI .. 191.2:3 | your own Identity, and this is what r.. |
| W-pI .. 193.7:4 | And there r. an unforgiveness hiding in |
| W-pI .. 195.8:3 | What more r. as obstacles to peace? The |
| W-pI .. 197.7:5 | has no end, for gratitude r. a part of love. |
| W-pI .. 198.8:1 | The stillness of your Self r. unmoved, |
| W-pI 198.11:4 | now the Word of God alone r. upon it. |
| W-pII .... in.5:3 | No step r. for time to separate from its |
| W-pII . 228.2:3 | *My holiness r. a part of me, as I am part of* |
| W-pII . 230.2:2 | *from time, and still r. beyond all change.* |
| W-pII . 238.2:2 | r. to Him Whose Love is made complete |
| W-pII . 256.1:8 | him in whom all sin r. impossible, and it |
| W-pII . 259.2:5 | *And everything that is r. with You, and You* |
| W-pII ..... 5.1:5 | could he be certain he r. within the body, |
| W-pII . 262.1:4 | *I perceive a thousand forms in what r. as one* |
| W-pII ..... 6.2:4 | He r. untouched by anything the body's |
| W-pII ..... 6.4:3 | for what r. to see except Christ's face? |
| W-pII . 282.1:3 | truth r. forever living in the joy of love. |
| W-pII . 282.1:4 | Son He loves, and Who r. my one Identity |
| W-pII . 283.1:5 | *holiness r. the light of Heaven and the Love* |
| W-pII ..... 8.2:4 | for nothing there r. outside forgiveness. |
| W-pII . 293.1:2 | it. Love r. the only present state, whose |
| W-pII . 319.1:1 | has been removed, and only truth r.. For |
| W-pII ... 11.4:4 | love r. with all its Thoughts, its sureness |
| W-pII . 322.2:1 | *to You all sacrifice r. forever inconceivable.* |
| W-pII . 323.2:4 | again, for fear has gone and only love r.. |
| W-pII . 336.1:2 | what r. forever past its highest reach. For |
| W-pII . 336.2:2 | *Your Word r. unchanged within my mind,* |
| M-4 ...... III.1:6 | and trust r. the bedrock of the teacher of |
| M-6 ........... 3:7 | Who gives a gift and then r. with it, to be |
| M-7 ........... 1:3 | patient is healed, what r. to heal him from |
| M-13 ......... 5:8 | end. "Seek but do not find" r. this world's |
| M-14 ....... 2:10 | When not one thought of sin r., the world |
| M-14 ......... 3:2 | one thought of sin r." appears to be a long- |
| M-16 ......... 3:3 | although it r. important throughout the |
| M-18 ....... 3:11 | *His Love r. the only thing there is. Fear is* |
| M-19 ......... 4:5 | It r. forever and forever like its Creator, |
| M-22 ......... 1:7 | and what r. to make sickness possible? |
| M-24 ......... 6:1 | of this course always r. the same;–it is at |
| M-28 ......... 3:7 | for what r. unanswered or incomplete? |
| M-28 ......... 5:4 | What r. that vision could accomplish? |
| M-28 ......... 6:2 | as any mind r. possessed of evil dreams, |
| M-29 ......... 6:3 | that, while attack r. attractive to you, He |
| C-in ........... 3:1 | This course r. within the ego framework, |
| C-3 ............ 6:9 | r. is peace eternal and the Will of God. |
| C-4 ............ 5:7 | more r. to keep a separated world in place |
| C-5 ............ 2:5 | Jesus r. a Savior because he saw the false |
| C-6 ............ 5:6 | over and no trace r. of dreams of spite in |
| P-2...........II.2:7 | to find truth, which r. perfectly obvious, |
| P-2........ VII.8:5 | r. to be forgiven where there is no sin? |
| P-3..........II.7:9 | Their image r., because they have chosen |
| S-1..........II.8:4 | itself an illusion, r. unattained. Prayer is |
| S-2...........I.6:5 | which still r. unchanged behind them all. |
| S-2...........I.6:6 | His constancy r. in tranquil silence and in |
| S-2...........I.7:3 | while forgiveness-to-destroy r. with you. |
| S-3..........II.1:5 | But the cause r., and will not lack effects. |
| S-3........ IV.2:5 | Time r. only to let the last embrace of |

## remarkably 1

| | |
|---|---|
| T-9 ....... IV.8:3 | is a r. poor choice as a teacher of salvation |

## remedies 4

| | |
|---|---|
| T-2 ....... IV.4:1 | that you accept as r. for bodily ills are |
| W-pI .. 139.6:1 | Atonement r. the strange idea that it is |
| P-2........ IV.2:3 | themselves to seek for r. that cannot help, |
| P-2........ VI.3:7 | These are its "r."; its "safeguards" from |

## remedy 36

| | |
|---|---|
| T-2 ....... IV.1:5 | is a r. and any type of healing is a result. |
| T-2 ....... VI.7:3 | of accepting the Atonement as the r.. |
| T-2 ....... VI.7:7 | The only r. for lack of love is perfect love. |
| T-2 ....... VI.8:6 | need for the r. inspired its establishment. |
| T-2 ....... VI.8:7 | as you recognize only the need for the r., |
| T-2 ....... VI.8:8 | However, as soon as you accept the r., you |
| T-5 ..... IV.2:10 | the Atonement, a r. not of your making. |

T-5.......V.4:11 automatically attempt to **r.** the situation.
T-5.......V.7:12 If you accept the **r.** for disordered thought
T-5.......V.7:12 a **r.** whose efficacy is beyond doubt, how
T-5.......VII.4:2 before, the **r.** could not be of your making
T-12.......II.3:2 Whatever the sickness, there is but one **r.**.
T-13......III.7:2 vision is merciful and His **r.** is quick. Do
T-19.........I.6:6 established **r.** where sickness cannot be.
T-20... VIII.8:2 are. This is the healing and the **r.**. Believe
T-25.......in.3:3 And it is here that Christ sets forth the **r.**.
T-26.......II.7:5 a special problem, a mistake without a **r.**,
W-pI.....70.3:2 God would not have put the **r.** for the
W-pI.136.20:1 Give instant **r.**, should this occur, by not
W-pI...140.1:1 to any **r.** the world accepts as beneficial.
W-pI...140.7:3 There is no **r.** the world provides that can
W-pI...162.5:4 available to all as **r.** for grief and misery,
W-pII....13.1:6 slip away under the gentle **r.** it brings.
M-5.......III.2:7 them of the **r.** God has already given them
C-4.............3:1 is not the **r.** for false perception since,
C-4.............3:5 true perception is a **r.** with many names.
C-4.............6:6 What **r.** can guilt expect? But seen within
C-4.............6:8 single **r.** joined in one healing brightness.
P-2........VI.4:8 not sick, and needs no **r.**. To concentrate
S-1........IV.3:5 to let it be a freely chosen **r.** from every
S-2...........I.1:6 **r.** appears to be a terrible alternative to
S-2...........I.6:3 God Himself has given all His Sons a **r.**
S-3........III.3:2 and his skill; to find in him the **r.** for pain.
S-3........III.4:8 no point in giving **r.** apart from where the
S-3........III.5:2 the **r.** that brings relief which cannot fail.
S-3........III.6:2 His kindly **r.** to those He sends to you, to

## remember 396

T-1........III.5:3 the right choice is inevitable if you **r.** this:
T-2...........I.5:5 But **r.** the first principle in this course;
T-2.........II.1:5 **R.** that where your heart is, there is your
T-2.........V.1:7 It is essential to **r.** that only the mind can
T-2... V.A.17:4 time, since to **r.** is to recall the past in the
T-2....... VIII.1:1 is to **r.** that you did not create yourself.
T-3........VI.9:4 merely means that you do not **r.** where it
T-4...........I.5:4 But **r.** that laws are set up to protect the
T-4.........I.13:9 **R.** this: *In this world you need not have*
T-4.........II.5:8 patient a while and **r.** that the outcome is
T-4........IV.3:3 have. **R.** that you are deprived of nothing
T-4........IV.5:1 **r.** that the ego has indeed violated the
T-4.......VII.5:7 itself. **R.** that in the Kingdom there is no
T-5...........I.1:5 to be. **R.** that spirit knows no difference
T-5.........II.6:1 Spirit calls you both to **r.** and to forget.
T-5........II.11:3 **R.** that "yoke" means "join together," and
T-5.........V.1:5 it elects. But again, **r.** that both are in you.
T-5.........V.6:5 changed. **R.**, though, that the alternatives
T-5........VI.3:1 **R.** the Kingdom always, and remember
T-5........VI.3:1 **r.** that you who are part of the Kingdom
T-5........VI.7:1 **r.** that ideas increase only by being shared
T-5......VI.11:2 **R.** my reference to the ego's dark glass,
T-5......VI.11:2 the ego's dark glass, and **r.** also that I said,
T-6...........I.5:3 you might **r.** that I was persecuted as the
T-6.........I.6:10 **R.** always that what you believe you will
T-6.........I.16:1 **r.** that I told them myself that there was
T-6.........I.19:1 **R.** that the Holy Spirit is the
T-6.........II.7:3 knowledge, you will ultimately **r.** it. The
T-6........III.2:3 you are something you must learn to **r.**. I
T-6........IV.1:1 **R.** that the Holy Spirit is the Answer, not
T-6........IV.8:7 **R.**, however, that when you put yourself
T-6......V.C.1:7 **R.**, however, that what the Holy Spirit
T-6......V.C.5:2 but what you are you must learn to **r.**.
T-6......V.C.5:3 way to **r.** it is inherent in the third step,
T-7...........I.2:9 yours you have learned to **r.** what you are.
T-7.........II.6:5 You forget in order to **r.** better. You will
T-7........IV.4:3 learning of wholeness you learn to **r.** God.
T-7......IV.7:12 not. This enables you to **r.** what you are.
T-7.........V.3:6 must **r.** that magic always involves the
T-7........VII.5:7 Keep His way to **r.** yourself, and teach His
T-7..... VIII.3:4 **R.** that a conflicted teacher is a poor
T-7......XI.3:11 to everything you see and touch and **r.**,
T-7........XI.4:1 I call upon you to **r.** that I have chosen
T-8........III.4:1 you meet anyone, **r.** it is a holy encounter.
T-8........III.8:5 will let you **r.** what you *have* of Him, and
T-8........III.8:5 by this you will **r.** also what you *are* in Him
T-8........III.8:8 this glory everywhere to **r.** what you are.
T-8........IV.7:5 yourself. I will always **r.** you, and in my
T-8.......VII.2:1 **R.** that the Holy Spirit interprets the
T-9...........I.2:4 this course is to help you **r.** what you are,
T-9...........I.4:4 to you, He *is* helping you to **r.** what you are
T-9...........I.9:1 everyone must **r.** the Will of God, because
T-9.........I.14:1 **R.**, then, that God's Will is already
T-9.........II.1:4 You must **r.**, however, that the course
T-9.........II.5:5 **R.** that the Holy Spirit is in him, and His
T-9........IV.1:6 **R.** always that your Identity is shared,
T-9.........V.8:9 **R.** that you choose the guide for helping,
T-9........V.8:10 But **r.** also that the right one will. Trust
T-9........VI.4:4 you **r.** creation whenever you recognize
T-9........VI.4:5 Each part you **r.** adds to your wholeness
T-9........VI.7:2 to you until you **r.** God's open Arms, and
T-9.......VII.8:3 **R.** this when the ego speaks, and you will
T-9..... VIII.5:3 **R.** always that you cannot be anywhere
T-10.........I.1:2 But **r.** that *it is as impossible for God.* The
T-10.........I.3:2 You do not **r.** being awake. When you
T-10.........I.3:3 but you do not **r.** yet that it once was so.
T-10.........I.3:7 When you **r.**, you will know that what you
T-10.........I.3:7 you will know that what you **r.** is eternal,
T-10.........I.4:1 will **r.** everything the instant you desire it
T-10.......II.2:3 the Holy Spirit only your willingness to **r.**,
T-10.......II.2:5 **r.** Him and know your own reality again.
T-10.......II.3:1 **r.** is merely to restore to your mind *what is*
T-10.......II.3:2 You do not make what you **r.**; you merely
T-10.......II.3:6 you. But signify your will to **r.** Him, and
T-10.......II.5:6 you are actively choosing not to **r.** Him.
T-10.......II.6:6 vigilance that makes you afraid to **r.** Him.
T-10......III.2:2 **R.** that it does not matter where in the
T-10......III.3:7 wholeness and **r.** your Creator with him?
T-10......III.8:7 to you, **r.** that nothing can replace God,
T-10.......V.6:5 you. **R.** that what you deny you must have
T-10.......V.8:5 **R.**, though, that to do this is blasphemy,
T-10.....V.11:7 and you will learn how to **r.** what you are.
T-10.....V.14:5 If you would **r.** eternity, you must look
T-11.......in.1:5 **R.**, too, that their results are as different
T-11.......in.3:3 **R.** the Rays that are there unseen. The
T-11.......I.11:4 Always **r.** that what He gives He keeps, so
T-11.......II.6:8 this increase, you will begin to **r.** creation.
T-11......III.1:1 you are weary, **r.** you have hurt yourself.
T-11......III.6:3 tempted to deny Him **r.** that there *are* no
T-11......IV.4:3 **R.** also that the denial of this simple fact
T-11.......V.17:1 Would *you* **r.** the Father? Accept His Son
T-11.......V.17:2 Accept His Son and you will **r.** Him.
T-12..........II.h The Way to **R.** God
T-12.......II.2:5 You can **r.** this for all the Sonship. Do not
T-12.......II.2:6 Do not allow your brother not to **r.**, for
T-12.......II.2:9 of yourself is thus the way to **r.** God. For
T-12.....II.2:10 to your forgetting is but the way to **r.**.
T-12.......II.4:1 **R.** what was said about the frightening
T-12.......II.6:3 Awake and **r.** your purpose, for it is your
T-12......III.3:3 it. ***R.*** *that those who attack are poor.* Their
T-12......IV.5:4 You do not **r.** how to look within for you
T-12......VI.2:2 aware of how to teach you to **r.** what you
T-12......VI.4:8 Him your Father calls His Son to **r.**. The
T-12......VI.5:1 world, as you will surely do, you will **r.** Us
T-12.....VII.6:3 **R.** always that you see what you seek, for
T-12...VII.13:1 **R.**, then, that whenever you look without
T-12...VII.15:1 to the desire for death, ***r.*** *that I did not die.*
T-12... VIII.3:8 to **r.** you would have condemned yourself
T-12... VIII.5:1 to ask for this memory, and you will **r.**.
T-12... VIII.5:3 dawn only in a mind that chooses to **r.**,
T-12... VIII.8:4 look upon it you will **r.** that it was always
T-13.........I.1:2 mind that he may **r.** his Father in peace.
T-13.......II.9:3 Father, for you will **r.** His guiltless Son,
T-13......IV.4:3 **R.** that its emphasis on guilt enables it to
T-13......VI.1:7 **r.** the past as you look upon your brother,
T-13......VI.9:1 will **r.** Him as you call forth the witnesses
T-13...VII.14:1 away from light, **r.** what you really want,
T-13...VII.17:8 of you that you have taught how to **r.** you.
T-13......IX.6:5 for you. **R.** always that it is impossible to
T-13.......X.8:4 he will **r.** how much his Father loves him.
T-13.......X.9:1 to yourself do not **r.** your Father's Love.
T-13.......X.9:2 you do not **r.** how much you love Him.
T-13......XI.4:3 while you still **r.** the results of not sharing
T-13......XI.5:1 **r.** this: God gave the Holy Spirit to you,
T-13......XI.6:1 will not **r.** change and shift in Heaven.
T-13....XI.11:6 and you will not **r.** anything you made
T-13....XI.11:7 For how can you **r.** what was never true,
T-13....XI.11:7 never true, or not **r.** what has always been
T-14.......III.3:3 to attract you, **r.** that if you yield to it, you
T-14.......III.8:5 **R.** always that mind is one, and cause is
T-14.......IV.4:8 **R.** that there is no second to Him. There
T-14.......IV.5:1 **r.** that you have decided against your
T-14.......IV.9:7 If you **r.** what you have made, you are
T-14.......V.9:6 **R.** for everyone your Father's power that
T-14....IX.1:10 now. The past that you **r.** never was, and
T-14.....X.10:1 is impossible to **r.** God in secret and alone
T-14.....X.10:2 you are not alone, and are willing to **r.** it.
T-14.....X.10:4 If you would **r.** your Father, let the Holy
T-14.....X.12:4 will teach you how to **r.** what you are,
T-14....XI.11:6 will **r.** that you have always created like
T-14....XI.12:1 who **r.** always that they know nothing,
T-15.......I.10:7 as bright with freedom, you will **r.** God.
T-15.......I.10:8 For remembering Him *is* to **r.** freedom.
T-15.......I.12:3 **R.**, then, when you are tempted to attack
T-15.......I.14:3 As long as it takes to **r.** immortality, and
T-15......III.3:1 and one you must learn to **r.** all the time.
T-15......III.3:3 **r.** this: Every decision you make stems
T-15......III.9:2 **R.** that you learn not for yourself alone,
T-15....III.11:4 we let no one forget what you would **r.**.
T-15....III.11:5 would remember. And thus will you **r.** it.
T-15......VI.7:5 But **r.** that understanding is of the mind,
T-15......VI.7:8 will not **r.** the language of communication
T-15...VII.10:5 to you. Yet **r.** this; to be with a body is not
T-15....VIII.1:6 teach you to **r.** that forgiveness is not loss,
T-15......IX.6:2 see. But this you must **r.**; the attraction of
T-15......XI.9:5 they **r.** the only relationship they ever had
T-16.........I.3:1 Your part is only to **r.** this; you do not
T-16........II.3:1 that it does not **r.** what is natural to it.
T-16........II.7:5 But **r.** also that whenever you listened to
T-16......III.2:8 Yet **r.** how much care you have exerted in
T-16..IV.11:13 inability to forget and your ability to **r.**. In
T-16....IV.12:1 the truth in you than you can fail to **r.** it.
T-16.....V.12:1 to seek for love in ritual, **r.** love is content,
T-16.....V.14:4 **R.** this, and you will have no difficulty in
T-16...VII.10:1 **R.** that you always choose between truth
T-16...VII.12:4 *to* ***r.*** *Your forgiveness and Your Love. Let us*
T-17........II.1:5 Nothing that you **r.** that made your heart
T-17......III.1:1 To forgive is merely to **r.** only the loving
T-17......III.9:2 **r.** that to choose one is to let the other go.
T-17....IV.12:6 **R.** that it is the picture that is the gift.
T-17.......V.9:3 **r.** that you and your brother have started
T-17.......V.9:5 you will **r.** a goal unchanged throughout
T-17......VI.1:6 but **r.** that you do not yet realize their
T-17.....VII.4:2 But **r.** this; the goal of holiness was set for
T-18.....III.4:11 but **r.** that your understanding is not
T-18......IV.6:3 **R.** you made guilt, and that your plan for
T-18.......V.7:1 the threat is perceived should **r.** how deep
T-18.......V.7:2 Let him **r.** this, and say: *I desire this holy*
T-18.....VII.5:5 you need but to **r.** you need do nothing. It
T-18....IX.11:3 need **r.** only that whoever attains the real
T-18....IX.14:1 of forgiveness you will **r.** nothing else, and
T-19......III.6:1 believe that sin is real, **r.** this: If sin is real,
T19....IV.B.6:3 of your forgiveness he will **r.** who he is,
T19..IV.C.11:1 comes over it, **r.** it is always for *one* reason;
T19..IV.C.11:2 **R.**, then, that neither sign nor symbol
T19..IV.C.11:6 **R.** the holy Presence of the One given to
T19... IV.D.1:3 Very simply, you would **r.** your Father.
T19... IV.D.1:4 that lies even beyond them would you **r.**.
T19... IV.D.6:6 vanish. Nothing that you **r.** now will you
T19... IV.D.6:6 that you remember now will you **r.**.
T-20........II.1:3 and **r.** all these were made to make seem
T-20......III.9:1 cast down in darkness they **r.** not the light
T-20......IV.6:7 to forget imprisonment and to **r.** freedom
T-20......IV.6:8 can he enter, to rest and to **r.**, without you
T-20......IV.7:4 on them and they **r.** the laws of God,
T-20.......V.2:7 will you **r.** Who gave the gifts to Him to
T-20.....VII.3:5 **R.** this, for otherwise you will make the
T-20.....VII.3:8 **r.** that if you think they are impossible,
T-21.........I.5:5 think if you **r.** what we will speak of now.
T-21.........I.6:3 But you **r.**, from just this little part, how
T-21.........I.7:3 You could **r.**, yet you are afraid, believing
T-21.........I.7:5 and see if you **r.** an ancient song you knew
T-21......IV.2:1 **R.** that the ego is not alone. Its rule is
T-21......IV.8:1 and **r.** the ego's weakness is revealed in
T-21.....VII.2:8 his brother or turn upon himself as to **r.**.

T-22...... VI.6:2 you do not recognize, and yet you will **r.**.
T-22.... VI.12:2 But you will not **r.** this while you believe
T-23......... I.1:3 and what the warlike would **r.** is not love.
T-23......... I.7:1 What *you* **r.** *is* a part of you. For you must
T-23......... I.7:7 You will **r.** what you know when you have
T-23....... I.10:7 is given those who would **r.** Him. Over
T-23...... IV.6:1 **r.** you *can* see the battle from above. Even
T-24......... I.7:5 and to **r.** this is now the only purpose that
T-24....... II.7:1 place, **r.** this: He has not lost the power to
T-25... VII.10:4 It is God's Will that you **r.** this, and so
T-25... VII.13:1 **R.** all temptation is but this; a mad belief
T-25... VIII.2:4 But **r.** salvation is not needed by the saved
T-26....... II.5:1 others to yourself, **r.** this: Justice is total.
T-27.... VIII.5:8 And no one can **r.** when they would have
T-27.... VIII.5:9 We can **r.** this, if we but look directly at
T-28......... I.4:3 you to realize it is a skill that can **r.** *now.*
T-28......... I.7:1 **R.** nothing that you taught yourself, for
T-28......... I.7:3 of hate appear, **r.** that their cause is gone.
T-28......... I.9:1 **r.** never was. It came from causelessness
T-28....... V.3:4 **R.** if you share an evil dream, you will
T-29...... III.1:3 is a savior first, before he can **r.** what he is
T-30......... I.6:1 (3) **R.** once again the day you want, and
T-30....... II.3:6 birth. **R.** Him Who has created you, and
T-30...... III.7:7 and will be just the same when you **r.**.
T-30....... V.4:5 **r.** that the Son of God knows everything
T-31....... I.12:2 is. Let us **r.** not our own ideas of what the
T-31..... VII.5:5 **r.** what the concept of yourself that now
W-in.......... 9:1 **R.** only this; you need not believe the
W-pI....... 7.5:1 but **r.** to omit nothing specifically. Glance
W-pI..... 10.5:4 **R.**, however, to repeat the idea slowly
W-pI..... 12.3:6 these exercises but **r.** that a "good world"
W-pI..... 20.5:2 forget to do so, but make a real effort to **r.**
W-pI..... 21.3:2 **R.** that you do not really recognize what
W-pI..... 27.4:1 The real question is, how often will you **r.**
W-pI..... 29.4:3 **R.** that any order you impose is equally
W-pI..... 33.4:1 **R.** to apply today's idea the instant you
W-pI..... 40.1:6 try again. Whenever you **r.**, try again.
W-pI..... 42.6:1 **R.**, however, that active searching for
W-pI..... 43.7:2 for example, try to **r.** to tell him silently:
W-pI..... 45.5:2 And we will also try to **r.** that we cannot
W-pI..... 45.9:1 try to **r.** how important it is to you to
W-pI..... 47.8:3 **R.** that peace is your right, because you
W-pI..... 52.3:4 as it is? Let me **r.** that I look on the past to
W-pI..... 53.4:6 Let me **r.** the power of my decision, and
W-pI..... 56.2:4 If I would **r.** who I am, it is essential that I
W-pI..... 60.2:6 And I begin to **r.** the Love I chose to forget
W-pI..... 60.5:5 He has given me, I **r.** that I am His Son.
W-pI..... 62.2:4 Now you are learning how to **r.** the truth.
W-pI..... 62.3:1 **R.** that in every attack you call upon your
W-pI..... 62.5:7 *I would* **r.** *this because I want to be happy.*
W-pI..... 63.3:1 we will be happy to **r.** it very often today.
W-pI..... 63.4:4 **R.** that God's Son looks to you for his
W-pI..... 64.5:1 Let us **r.** this today. Let us remind
W-pI..... 64.6:6 **r.** the crucial importance of your function
W-pI..... 66.9:7 **R.** the outcomes fairly, and consider also
W-pI..... 68.3:3 it is certain that those who forgive will **r.**.
W-pI..... 68.6:3 *that I may* **r.** *you are part of me and come to*
W-pI..... 69.8:4 Try to **r.** that you are at last joining your
W-pI..... 70.8:5 **R.** that you will have to go through the
W-pI..... 70.8:6 But **r.** also that you have never found
W-pI... 71.10:5 Try to **r.** today's idea some six or seven
W-pI... 71.10:6 less than to **r.** the Source of your salvation
W-pI..... 73.7:1 you **r.** that you want salvation for yourself
W-pI..... 73.7:5 want the freedom to **r.** Who you really are
W-pI..... 73.8:1 and **r.** what it is your will to remember.
W-pI..... 73.8:1 and remember what it is your will to **r.**.
W-pI..... 77.8:1 **R.**, too, not to be satisfied with less than
W-pI... 78.10:1 We will **r.** this throughout the day, and
W-pI... 78.10:3 the ones you think of or **r.** from the past,
W-pI..... 80.3:4 will not deceive you while you **r.** this. One
W-pI..... 80.5:5 Above all, **r.** that you have one problem,
WpI..rII.in.3:4 it. **R.** that it belongs to you, and that you
W-pI..... 81.1:5 In its peace let me **r.** Who I am.
W-pI..... 82.3:2 my function, because I would **r.** my Self. I
W-pI..... 84.2:3 *As I look on this, let me* **r.** *my Creator. My*
W-pI..... 84.3:6 my Self today, so that I can **r.** Who I am.
W-pI..... 90.1:4 replaced. Today I would **r.** the simplicity
W-pI..... 91.1:1 is important to **r.** that miracles and vision
W-pI..... 91.9:3 **R.** that all sense of weakness is associated
W-pI... 93.10:3 least **r.** to repeat these thoughts each hour
W-pI..... 95.5:3 You often fail to **r.** the short applications
W-pI.... 99.11:2 **r.** that appearances can not withstand the
W-pI... 101.7:5 **R.** this today, and tell yourself as often as
W-pI... 105.9:2 At least **r.** hourly to say the words which
W-pI... 107.2:3 feel? Try to **r.** when there was a time,–
W-pI... 109.6:2 hourly **r.** that you came to bring the peace
W-pI. 110.11:1 We will **r.** Him throughout the day with
W-pI. 110.11:2 For it is thus that we **r.** Him. And we will
W-pI... 117.1:2 *Let me* **r.** *love is happiness, and nothing else*
W-pI... 122.8:4 you will **r.** then can never be described.
W-pI... 123.8:2 **R.** hourly to think of Him, and give Him
W-pI...... 124.h Let me **r.** I am one with God.
W-pI. 124.10:3 You will **r.** then the thought to which you
W-pI. 124.12:2 *Let me* **r.** *I am one with God, at one with all*
W-pI... 127.4:1 you to **r.** what you really are could fail to
W-pI. 127.12:1 We will **r.** them throughout the day,
W-pI... 129.9:3 made. **R.** your decision hourly, and take a
W-pI. 131.14:4 holy Son, as does His Son **r.** his to Him.
W-pI. 131.15:1 **R.** often that today should be a time of
W-pI. 134.17:6 In everything you do **r.** this: *No one is*
W-pI. 135.25:2 you. Today we will **r.** Him. For this is
W-pI. 137.13:1 will **r.**, as the hour strikes, our function is
W-pI. 139.11:5 We can **r.** it for everyone, for in creation
W-pI. 140.12:8 ends, and we **r.** Who we really are.
W-pI... 142.2:1 (124) Let me **r.** I am one with God.
W-pI. 151.17:1 will hourly **r.** Him Who is salvation and
W-pI... 153.6:4 he becomes too sleepy to **r.** what he wants
W-pI. 153.16:1 as we **r.** to be faithful to the Will we share
W-pI. 153.19:3 as we **r.** that His strength abides in us. We
W-pI. 158.10:3 **r.** in your brother you but see yourself. If
W-pI... 159.7:1 world **r.** what was lost when it was made.
W-pI... 160.9:4 Yet as they give Him welcome, they **r.**.
W-pI. 160.10:2 Not one He fails to give you to **r.**, that
W-pI. 160.10:4 will not **r.** Him until you look on all as He
W-pI. 161.10:5 sing to you of ancient melodies you will **r.**
W-pI. 161.10:7 not forgot in Heaven. Would you not **r.** it
W-pI... 164.4:4 All this today you will **r.**. Faithfulness in
W-pI... 170.9:2 Let us **r.** what the text has stressed about
WpI...rV.in5:4 dust to life, as we **r.** this is promised us,
W-pI... 183.2:1 an echo in the mind that calls you to **r.**.
W-pI... 183.9:3 You can **r.** what the world forgot, and
W-pI. 186.12:2 seems impossible, **r.** Who it is that asks,
W-pI. 186.12:6 you, and urges that you now **r.** Him.
W-pI. 191.11:7 Himself. **R.** this, and all the world is free.
W-pI. 191.11:8 **R.** this, and earth and Heaven are one.
W-pI... 193.8:3 His Son does not **r.** who he is. And God
WpI rVI.in.3:7 it every time the hour strikes, or we **r.**, in
W-pII .... 231.h Father, I will but to **r.** You.
W-pII . 231.1:5 *Let me* **r.** *You. What else could I desire but*
W-pII . 231.2:3 To **r.** Him is Heaven. This we seek. And
W-pII . 235.1:3 I need but **r.** that God's Love surrounds
W-pII . 241.2:3 *restored to us, and to* **r.** *that we all are one.*
W-pII . 254.2:6 us of our will, as we have chosen to **r.** Him
W-pII .... 257.h Let me **r.** what my purpose is.
W-pII . 257.1:4 Let us therefore be determined to **r.** what
W-pII .... 258.h Let me **r.** that my goal is God.
W-pII . 258.1:1 aims, and to **r.** that our goal is God. His
W-pII . 258.1:5 only Love. We have no aim but to **r.** Him.
W-pII . 258.2:3 *What could we want but to* **r.** *You? What*
W-pII .... 259.h Let me **r.** that there is no sin.
W-pII .... 260.h Let me **r.** God created me.
W-pII . 260.1:4 *Let me* **r.** *You created me. Let me remember*
W-pII . 260.1:5 *Let me* **r.** *my Identity. And let my sinlessness*
W-pII . 261.1:8 And only there will I **r.** Who I really am.
W-pII . 265.2:2 *Let me* **r.** *that they are the same, and I will see*
W-pII . 276.1:7 creation, to **r.** Him and so recall our Self.
W-pII . 288.1:9 *bears Your Name, and so* **r.** *that It is my own.*
W-pII . 310.1:4 *day will be Your sweet reminder to* **r.** *You,*
W-pII . 342.1:8 *is. Let me* **r.** *that I am Your Son, and opening*
W-pII . 345.1:7 *lights the way that I must travel to* **r.** *You.*
W-pII . 346.2:1 we will **r.** nothing but the peace of God.
W-pII . 348.1:1 *Father, let me* **r.** *You are here, and I am not*
W-pII .... 350.h To offer them is to **r.** Him, And through
W-pII . 350.2:2 For as we **r.** Him, His Son will be restored
W-pII . 358.1:1 **r.** *what I really am alone remember what I*
W-pII . 358.1:1 *what I really am alone* **r.** *what I really want.*
W-pII . 358.1:5 *Let me* **r.** *all I do not know, and let my voice*
WfI........ in.4:1 It is our function to **r.** Him on earth, as it
M-7........... 3:7 let him **r.** Who gave the gift and Who
M-9........... 1:3 **R.** that no one is where he is by accident,
M-10......... 4:1 **R.** how many times you thought you
M-13......... 8:1 and **r.** what each decision you make must
M-13......... 8:5 **R.** only what you would learn. For it is
M-15......... 3:8 are sure. Only **r.** that. His promises have
M-16......... 4:3 so, let him but **r.** that he chooses to spend
M-16....... 10:5 Perhaps he needs to **r.**, "God is with me. I
M-17......... 1:8 him. Let him **r.**, then, it is not this that he
M-17......... 4:1 to **r.** that no one can be angry at a fact. It
M-17......... 6:7 Do not **r.** the impossible odds against you
M-17......... 6:8 Do not **r.** the immensity of the "enemy,"
M-17......... 6:9 but do not **r.** how it came about. Believe
M-17......... 9:7 so. **R.**, then, teacher of God, that anger
M-19......... 5:3 **R.** this. In this lies either Heaven or hell,
M-20......... 4:5 as you **r.** even faintly now what happiness
M-20....... 6:13 Will. Attain His peace, and you **r.** Him.
M-23......... 3:7 **R.** his promises, and ask yourself honestly
M-29......... 5:9 **r.** God when you can throughout the day,
M-29......... 7:1 **R.** you are His completion and His Love.
M-29......... 7:2 **R.** your weakness is His strength. But do
C-ep.......... 1:5 **r.** that you walk with Him and with His
P-1............. 2:3 way, the truth and the life, and to **r.** God?
P-2.......... II.3:1 who learns to forgive can fail to **r.** God.
P-2.......... V.2:1 Let us **r.** that the ones who come to us for
P-3........... I.3:2 This may be hard to **r.**, but God will not
P-3........ III.5:8 will lose this understanding unless they **r.**
P-3........ III.8:9 **R.** the sorrowful story of the world, and
P-3...... III.8:10 **R.** the plan of God for the restoration of
S-1......... in.3:1 you, dispense with idols and **r.** Him.
S-2........... I.3:8 Can you **r.** Him and hate what He created
S-2.......... II.3:6 His Son condemn himself and still **r.** Him
S-3...... IV.10:7 **R.** this; whatever you may think about

## rememberance 5

*See also remembrance*

T-23 ........ I.8:9 for you, and turn in peace to the **r.** of God
W-pI .. 157.9:4 vision speaks of your **r.** of what you knew
WpI.rV.in11:4 keep it clear in our **r.** throughout the day.
S-3........... I.3:2 Only that can give **r.** of immortality,
S-3........ IV.3:4 nor accept an idol for **r.** of Him Whose

## remembered 66

T-3 ..... IV.6:10 that knowledge can always be **r.**, never
T-3 ....... IV.7:3 was a man who **r.** spirit and its knowledge
T-3 ....... IV.7:6 I naturally **r.** spirit and its real purpose. I
T-6 ......... V.3:5 clear, easily understood and very easily **r.**.
T-7 ......... II.6:2 since it must be consistent to be **r.**. That is
T-12 ......... II.2:7 is his, for God cannot be **r.** alone. *This is*
T-12 ... VIII.7:5 **r.** you because He forgot not the Father.
T-13 ......... I.1:3 and the Father can be **r.** only in peace.
T-14 ... III.15:7 forget the Love of God, Who has **r.** you.
T-15 ......... I.8:7 No darkness is **r.**, and immortality and
T-15 .... I.15:10 instant, that eternity may be **r.** for you, in
T-15 ..... VI.8:1 In the holy instant God is **r.**, and the
T-15 ..... VI.8:1 with all your brothers is **r.** with Him. For
T-15 ..... VI.8:2 For communication is **r.** together, as is
T-16 .... VII.1:3 slights, **r.** pain, past disappointments,
T-17 ..... III.5:7 the unholy relationship where hatred is **r.**
T-17 ....... V.1:5 Yet without expression it is not **r.**. The
T-18 .... VII.3:2 all. It is always **r.** or anticipated, but never
T-18 ... IX.13:4 it is through forgiveness that it will be **r.**.
T-21 ......... I.3:2 are acquired joyously, and are **r.** gladly.
T-21 ......... I.7:2 you weep if you **r.** how dear it was to you.
T-23 ......... I.9:4 Here will the Father never be **r.**. Yet no
T-23 ....... I.11:4 of sin. And nothing is **r.** except illusions.
T-23 ....... I.12:9 ready to be **r.** when you side with peace.
T-24 ....... in.1:2 condition in which God is **r.** is attained. It
T-25 ...... IV.3:6 not long to be **r.** as the sun shines them to
T-26 ........ II.7:7 And in its place the Love of God can be **r.**,
T-26 ........ II.8:1 be **r.** until justice is loved instead of feared
T-27 ....... I.10:1 has been removed, is Heaven free to be **r.**.
T-27 ........ II.8:9 because God's Son **r.** that he *is* God's Son.
T-27 ... VIII.6:2 at which the Son of God **r.** not to laugh.
T-28 ......... I.8:1 is the Cause the Holy Spirit has **r.** for you,
T-28 ......... I.8:4 you thought that you **r.** not their Cause.
T-28 ......... I.9:3 when you learn you have **r.** consequences

T-28 I.13:5 And what is now **r.** is not fear, but rather
T-29 V.1:4 Where Both abide are They **r.**, Both. And
T-30 I.11:5 the day, and have **r.** what you really want.
T-30 V.3:1 yet is Heaven quite **r.**, for the purpose of
T-30 V.7:5 is looked upon before the Father is **r.**. For
T-31 I.10:1 must be **r.** when he learns his innocence.
T-31 II.11:1 inheritance **r.** and accepted by you both.
T-31 IV.9:2 forgot His Presence and **r.** not His Love.
W-pI 48.3:2 you recognize as yet, you have **r.** God, and
W-pI 52.2:5 I have forgiven myself and **r.** Who I am, I
W-pI 107.1:4 leaving not a trace by which to be **r.**. They
W-pI 127.10:3 the past behind us, nevermore to be **r.**.
W-pI 131.3:4 to you from an idea relinquished yet **r.**,
W-pI 135.25:1 He has **r.** you. Today we will remember
W-pI 136.5:2 But what you have forgot can be **r.**, given
W-pI 157.6:3 quietly forgot, and Heaven is **r.** for a while
W-pI 160.10:5 his home **r.** and salvation come.
W-pI 182.1:6 than a tiny throb, at other times hardly **r.**,
W-pI 183.1:5 not know; even though you have not **r.** it.
W-pI 193.8:6 disappear and God may be **r.** by His Son?
W-pI 198.6:7 its place, for it will be **r.** then and loved.
W-pI 198.10:1 in God's Son, and Heaven is **r.** instantly;
W-pII 2.5:2 instant more to wait until his Father is **r.**,
W-pII 248.2:3 *Now is Your Love* **r.**, *and my own. Now do I*
W-pII 260.2:1 Now is our Source **r.**, and Therein we
M-16 6:1 that should be **r.** throughout the day. It is
M-23 4:6 to God becomes the way in which He is **r.**,
M-29 1:4 be **r.** that only time divides teacher and
C-4 6:2 to the Son is set, and there his Father is **r.**.
C-5 2:1 of Christ in all his brothers and **r.** God. So
P-2 VI.7:3 statement cannot be too often **r.** by all
P-2 VII.8:3 and nothing now can be **r.** of the world of

## remembering 75

T-5 VII.6:6 **r.** that the Holy Spirit will respond fully to
T-7 II.6:3 the Holy Spirit's teaching is a lesson in **r.**.
T-7 II.6:4 before that He teaches **r.** and forgetting,
T-7 II.6:4 is only to make the **r.** consistent. You
T-7 IV.2:6 you are **r.** the laws of God and forgetting
T-7 IV.2:7 that forgetting is merely a way of **r.** better.
T-7 IV.2:8 not the opposite of **r.** when it is properly
T-7 IV.4:4 must be translated into a way of **r.**.
T-7 IV.6:8 By not **r.** it, you do not know what you are
T-10 I.3:4 **r.** that you will know it can be so again.
T-10 II.2:4 that would stand in the way of your **r.**, for
T-10 II.2:6 nothing in this world delay your **r.** of Him
T-10 II.2:6 for in this **r.** is the knowledge of yourself.
T-10 II.5:5 when you attack you are not **r.** Him. This
T-11 IV.2:5 save you, **r.** that it is yours *because* it is His
T-12 II.2:4 that power, **r.** that all power is of God.
T-12 II.2:7 But your **r.** is his, for God cannot be
T-12 VI.2:4 it. **R.** you always, He cannot let you forget
T-12 VI.4:3 the sleep of forgetting to the **r.** of God.
T-13 II.1:2 guilt stands in the way of your **r.** God,
T-13 II.9:5 In this understanding lies your **r.**, for it is
T-14 IV.9:7 what you have made, you are **r.** nothing.
T-14 X.10:2 For **r.** Him means you are not alone, and
T-15 I.10:8 God. For **r.** Him *is* to remember freedom.
T-15 III.10:4 less, **r.** that everything I learned is yours.
T-17 III.1:3 Forgiveness is a selective **r.**, based not on
T19 IV.B.6:6 **r.** that what I signify to you you see within
T19 IV.D.6:2 down, **r.** your promise to your "friends."
T19 IV.D.13:4 **r.** that you will receive of him according
T-20 V.7:4 And merely by **r.** them, the laws that held
T-21 I.10:3 the Son of God, **r.** who he is they sing of.
T-21 I.10:4 What is a miracle but this **r.**? And who is
T-21 I.10:7 it in your brother, you *are* **r.** for everyone.
T-24 II.10:7 has, **r.** God gave Himself to you and your
T-25 V.5:7 **R.** but this; that what he does you do,
T-28 I.1:9 **R.** a cause can but produce illusions of its
T-28 I.2:5 **R.** is as selective as perception, being its
T-28 I.4:4 The limitations on **r.** the world imposes
T-28 I.10:4 **r.** would witness to is but the fear of God.
T-28 I.11:5 Their own **r.** is quiet now, and what has
T-28 I.13:2 Its own **r.** has gone. There is no past to
T-28 I.13:6 his own **r.** came in between the present
T-29 IX.10:6 And all the while he is **r.** what he forgot,
T-30 III.8:3 birth. They wait for welcome and **r.**. The

T-30 V.10:6 **r.** that he will pay the cost as well as you.
T-31 II.6:4 we heard; **r.** how much we do not know.
T-31 VII.14:1 temptation, then, **r.** that it is but a wish,
T-31 VIII.6:5 **r.** that every choice you make establishes
W-pI 9.3:1 you see, **r.** the need for its indiscriminate
W-pI 41.10:1 **r.** that God goes with you wherever you
W-pI 43.9:2 of time to slip by without **r.** today's idea,
W-pI 43.9:2 today's idea, and thus **r.** your function.
W-pI 60.2:3 of God in me, which I am **r.** as I forgive.
W-pI 64.5:3 today by **r.** they are all really very simple.
W-pI 69.6:1 **r.** only how much you want to reach the
W-pI 71.9:1 **R.** this, let us devote the remainder of the
W-pI 72.12:1 your request, **r.** that you are asking of the
W-pI 122.9:1 **R.** the gifts forgiveness gives, we
W-pI 123.8:2 above the world, **r.** his Father and his Self.
W-pI 130.10:1 merely by **r.** the limits of your choice. The
W-pI 136.5:3 not **r.** is but the sign that this decision still
W-pI 137.15:4 slips by, **r.** our purpose with this thought:
WpI rV.in3:3 *forget the way, we count upon Your sure* **r.**.
W-pI 183.9:3 the world forgot, and offer it your own **r.**.
W-pII 271.1:4 but must live, **r.** the Father and the Son;
W-pII 306.2:1 *we return to You,* **r.** *we never went away;*
W-pII 306.2:1 *we never went away;* **r.** *Your holy gifts to us.*
W-pII 358.1:5 *all I do not know, and let my voice be still,* **r.**.
M-2 4:1 and past even the possibility of **r.**. Yet
M-23 3:2 that in **r.** Jesus you are remembering God.
M-23 3:2 that in remembering Jesus you are **r.** God.
M-23 4:5 **R.** the name of Jesus Christ is to give
M-25 1:5 with the glorious surprise of **r.** Who he is.
M-26 2:1 limits and **r.** their own Identity perfectly.
S-1 I.5:2 because it is a way of **r.** your holiness.

## remembers 21

T-3 II.5:2 awakens from its sleep and **r.** its Creator.
T-11 I.8:6 what it is, but the Holy Spirit **r.** it for you.
T-12 IV.5:5 Yet the Holy Spirit **r.** it for you, and He
T-14 IV.9:5 Holy Spirit, Who **r.** this for you, merely
T-15 V.9:2 He **r.** nothing, having always known you
T-16 IV.11:10 Whom God **r.** must be whole. And God
T-16 VII.3:3 For the ego **r.** everything you have done
T-20 IV.6:10 And it is his completion that he **r.** there.
T-21 IV.7:5 For it **r.** Heaven, and now it sees that
T-23 I.1:2 war against itself **r.** not eternal gentleness
T-23 I.5:5 wish to triumph over what you are, **r.** not.
T-24 II.6:3 this memory, the Son **r.** his own creations
T-26 V.11:3 made an error in the past that God **r.** not,
T-27 VIII.5:4 in the world **r.** his attack upon himself.
T-28 I.13:6 of love the Son of God **r.** from before his
T-28 VI.6:6 His Son **r.** not that he replied "I will,"
T-29 IX.8:4 dreams a melody is heard that everyone **r.**
T-31 I.9:3 Christ in you **r.** God with all the certainty
T-31 I.9:6 God's perfect Son **r.** his creation. But in
W-pI 186.3:2 All it says is that your Father still **r.** you,
W-pI 186.12:6 given you by your Creator Who **r.** you,

## remembrance 47

*See also rememberance*

T-2 V.A.17:2 My request "Do this in **r.** of me" is the
T-5 III.11:7 looks back to God in **r.** of me. He is in
T-5 III.11:9 He holds the **r.** of things past and to come
T-7 V.10:4 your **r.** of me and of Him Who created me
T-7 V.10:5 me. Through this **r.**, you can change their
T-8 III.4:8 I am always there with you, in **r.** of *you.*
T-8 IV.2:13 **r.** of me is the remembrance of yourself,
T-8 IV.2:13 remembrance of me is the **r.** of yourself,
T-8 IV.7:5 in my **r.** of you lies your remembrance of
T-8 IV.7:5 in my remembrance of you lies your **r.** of
T-8 IV.7:6 **r.** of each other lies our remembrance of
T-8 IV.7:6 of each other lies our **r.** of God. And in
T-8 IV.7:7 And in this **r.** lies your freedom because
T-10 III.2:3 the **r.** of Him awakens throughout the
T-10 III.3:3 **r.** of love therefore brings invulnerability
T-12 I.7:4 **r.** of your Father closer to your awareness.
T-13 II.9:3 between you and the **r.** of your Father, for
T-13 III.8:3 unite with the Father, in loving **r.** of Him.
T-13 VI.9:1 on your brothers in **r.** of your Creator, for
T-13 VII.8:4 that leads you to **r.** of the one thing that is

T-14 IV.9:8 **R.** of reality is in Him, and therefore in
T-14 X.2:3 And thus, **r.** of his Father dawns on him,
T-15 I.11:5 stands ready to give you the **r.** of eternity.
T-15 II.1:3 holds **r.** of God cannot be bound by time.
T-15 III.12:1 Call forth in everyone only the **r.** of God,
T-15 XI.9:5 enter, the **r.** of the Father enters with Him
T-17 IV.15:5 fades gently and God rises to your **r.**,
T19 IV.A.9:6 and shiver in **r.** of the winter's cold?
T19 IV.D.18:5 let him rise again to glad **r.** of his Father,
T-20 V.7:3 gift returns the laws of God to your **r.**.
T-20 VI.12:11 and keep **r.** of His Love apart from their
T-22 VI.6:7 is your **r.** of everything that is eternal. No
T-22 VI.7:6 could **r.** of what they are be long delayed?
W-pI 122.3:2 so that **r.** of your Father can arise across
W-pI 124.4:3 one with Him today in recognition and **r.**.
W-pI 153.17:1 in hourly **r.** of our mission and His Love.
W-pI 168.2:3 is to all despair, for in it lies **r.** of His Love.
W-pI 181.9:2 our **r.** of the holy Self which knows no sin,
W-pI 181.9:3 We seek for this **r.** as we turn our minds
W-pII in.2:9 will we forget our hourly **r.** in between,
Wfl in.4:2 that **r.** which contains the memory of God
M-5 II.4:6 outcome of this lesson is the **r.** of God.
M-13 4:9 hope of Heaven and **r.** of his Father's Love
M-28 2:5 **r.** of God shines unimpeded across the
P-2 II.3:3 the **r.** of God are forms of unforgiveness,
S-1 I.4:5 could His answer be but your **r.** of Him?
S-3 I.4:3 sinlessness and the **r.** of his Father's Love.

## remembrances 1

WpI rVI.in.1:2 hourly **r.** you make throughout the day,

## remind 59

T-2 VII.1:7 It is much more helpful to **r.** you that you
T-2 VII.7:9 but let me **r.** you that time and space are
T-4 I.3:6 When I **r.** you of your true creation, your
T-5 II.11:1 voice, call on me to **r.** you how to heal by
T-5 VI.3:3 Holy Spirit **r.** you always of His fairness,
T-5 VI.10:8 was given to you to **r.** you of what you are.
T-6 V.2:1 but will merely **r.** them that the night is
T-6 V.B.6:5 before that you **r.** yourself to allow the
T-9 I.3:6 is merely to **r.** you of what you want. He is
T-9 I.5:2 the Holy Spirit must **r.** you that this is not
T-10 III.3:7 Or would you **r.** him of his wholeness and
T-11 III.3:7 Yet I can tell you, and **r.** you often, that
T-12 VI.2:5 Father never ceases to **r.** Him of His Son,
T-12 VI.2:5 He never ceases to **r.** His Son of the Father
T-13 V.3:2 only those who **r.** them of these images,
T-13 VI.11:7 everything **r.** you of your Father and His
T-16 VII.8:8 is to **r.** you that you have received what
T-17 V.8:3 **r.** you of all the ways you once sought for
T-18 III.2:5 be enough to **r.** you that your goal is light.
T-18 IX.13:3 to **r.** you of all that lies beyond it. Yet it is
T-21 I.4:9 they think is in it serves to **r.** them that
T-27 V.7:3 it, will the world **r.** you gently of what you
T-28 I.9:9 They but **r.** you that It has not gone.
T-29 VII.10:5 Let Him **r.** you of His Love for you, and do
T-29 IX.10:1 Forgiving dreams **r.** you that you live in
W-pI 6.3:1 **r.** yourself of the two cautions stated in
W-pI 13.5:2 **r.** yourself that you are really afraid of
W-pI 31.4:2 the day. **R.** yourself that you are making a
W-pI 44.6:2 You might find it helpful to **r.** yourself,
W-pI 45.8:7 able to **r.** yourself that this is no idle game
W-pI 64.5:2 Let us **r.** ourselves of it in the morning
W-pI 67.5:3 be most beneficial to **r.** yourself that love
W-pI 69.9:1 **r.** yourself that your grievances are hiding
W-pI 69.9:2 **R.** yourself also that you are not searching
W-pI 70.10:1 **r.** yourself that your salvation comes from
W-pI 75.9:2 **R.** yourself every quarter of an hour or so
W-pI 77.4:2 **r.** yourself that you are asking only for
W-pI 77.4:3 **R.** yourself also that miracles are never
W-pI 91.11:1 **r.** yourself that miracles are seen in light.
W-pI 94.5:1 of every hour, at least **r.** yourself hourly: *I*
W-pI 99.12:2 **R.** yourself of this between the times you
W-pI 99.12:3 **R.** yourself: *Salvation is my only function*
W-pI 109.9:6 And we **r.** them of their resting place each
W-pI 122.14:2 **R.** yourself how precious are these gifts
W-pI 125.9:5 be still a moment and **r.** yourself you have

W-pI.126.11:1 you can, **r.** yourself you have a goal today;
W-pI.131.12:2 it, **r.** yourself no one can fail who seeks to
W-pI.131.15:4 forget this happy fact, **r.** yourself with this
W-pI.135.26:5 **r.** yourself this is a special day for learning
W-pI.153.19:4 will **r.** ourselves that He remains beside us
WpI.rV.in10:7 And we **r.** the world that it is free of all
W-pI...188.7:5 came but to **r.** you how you must return.
W-pI...188.8:3 They **r.** you that you are the co-creator of
W-pII .224.2:3 *I do. R. me, Father, now, for I am weary of the*
Wfl........in.1:2 to **r.** us that we seek to go beyond them.
M-5 ...... III.2:7 heal the sick but to **r.** them of the remedy
M-5 ...... III.3:4 they **r.** him that he did not make himself,
M-18 .........2:4 Now He can **r.** the world of sinlessness,
S-3........ IV.8:2 Let Me instead **r.** you of eternity, in which

### reminded 5

T-30....... II.2:7 may be **r.** of His Love and learn your will.
W-pI.....95.5:2 you are **r.** of your purpose frequently, you
W-pI.110.11:3 we will say, that we may be **r.** of His Son,
W-pI...138.4:1 need to be **r.** that you think a thousand
W-pI.166.12:6 He has **r.** you of all the gifts that God has

### reminder 13

T-16.....VII.8:7 In the holy instant is His **r.** that His Son
T-17....... V.1:6 The holy relationship is a constant **r.** of
T-21.........I.7:2 but as a soft **r.** of what would make you
T-25...... VI.6:1 than a **r.** this world is not your home. Its
T-29......... V.4:1 the soft **r.** of his Father's Love by which he
T-30.......I.17:6 this be the one **r.** that you keep in mind,
W-pI.....19.4:1 it will occasionally be included as a **r.**. Do
W-pI.....77.7:1 will also be devoted to a **r.** of a simple fact
W-pI...104.5:3 **r.** will we bring to mind as often as we can
W-pI.106.10:2 to hear and to receive the Word by this **r.**,
W-pI.122.14:2 how precious are these gifts with this **r.**,
W-pII .310.1:4 *day will be Your sweet r. to remember You,*
M-5 ...... III.2:2 simple presence of a teacher of God is a **r.**.

### reminders 2

W-pI.....75.9:1 will be joyful **r.** of your release. Remind
W-pI.....95.6:1 planned to include frequent **r.** of your

### reminding 15

T-13.........I.9:3 is therefore God's way of **r.** you of His Son
T-20..VIII.10:7 **r.** you that it is not reality which frightens
T-30....... II.3:3 **r.** you that it is not your will to hate and
W-pI.....20.4:1 exercises for today consist in **r.** yourself
W-pI.....42.8:1 the more often you will be **r.** yourself that
W-pI.....49.2:6 **r.** you that your Creator has not forgotten
W-pI.....49.3:2 Voice **r.** you of Him and of your Self. We
W-pI.....67.6:2 **r.** you of your Father and of your Self.
W-pI...73.10:1 After **r.** yourself of this, and determining
W-pI.....97.8:2 will speak to you, **r.** you that you are spirit
W-pI.155.14:1 of His Love, **r.** you how great His trust;
W-pII .....8.5:4 **r.** us of our Identity which our forgiveness
W-pII .345.1:2 *to me, r. me the law of love is universal. Even*
M-16 .........8:1 and he has need of **r.** himself throughout
S-3...........I.4:5 **r.** him the body may become his chosen

### reminds 32

T-4......... V.4:8 **r.** the ego that it has itself insisted that it
T-5......... II.7:4 It merely **r.**. It is compelling only because
T-5......... II.7:5 only because of what It **r.** you *of.* It brings
T-5........ III.5:4 Everything of which the Holy Spirit **r.** you
T-5........ III.8:4 It is of this that the Holy Spirit **r.** you. It is
T-5...... VI.12:6 He **r.** you of this in every passing moment
T-5.......VII.1:6 Voice **r.** you always that all hope is yours
T-7........ IV.2:5 and the Holy Spirit **r.** you of it. When you
T-7...... VI.13:1 this depressing state the Holy Spirit **r.** you
T-9........ IV.3:2 Holy Spirit merely **r.** you of the natural
T-9....VIII.10:3 God, through His Voice, **r.** you of it, and
T-10....... III.3:5 of God **r.** him of the truth about himself,
T-13...... IV.5:2 The present merely **r.** it of past hurts, and
T-13...... XI.5:6 dwell, and of which the Holy Spirit **r.** you.
T-17...... III.2:5 whatever **r.** you of your past grievances
T-21 ..... III.4:4 you wander, He **r.** you there is but one.
T-21 ... VI.10:3 The gratitude he offers you **r.** you of the
T-25 ........I.2:4 body that you look upon **r.** you of yourself
T-26 ..... IV.4:4 Each **r.** him of his Father's Love as surely
T-28 ........I.9:4 miracle **r.** you of a Cause forever present,
T-28 ..... VI.6:7 Yet God **r.** him of it every time he does
T-30 ........I.9:3 and **r.** you that help is not being thrust
W-pI.....60.5:4 His Love **r.** me that His Son is sinless.
W-pI.....65.1:2 It also **r.** you that you have no function
W-pI.166.12:1 Yet He **r.** you still of one thing more you
W-pI...182.1:3 the voice, nor what it is the voice **r.** you of
W-pI...183.1:5 Your Father's Name **r.** you who you are,
W-pI...188.4:1 mind **r.** the world of what it has forgotten
W-pI...204.1:2 *God's Name r. me that I am His Son, not*
W-pII .335.2:2 *holiness r. me that he was created one with*
W-pII ... 13.1:3 and **r.** the mind that what it sees is false.
W-pII .352.1:4 *r. me You have given me a way to find Your*

### reminiscent 1

W-pI...161.6:2 This thought is surely **r.** of our text, where

### remitted 1

T-23 .......II.4:5 Sin cannot be **r.**, being the belief the Son

### remnant 3

T19..IV.A.2:10 little **r.** of attack you cherish still against
T19....IV.A.8:1 this microscopic **r.** of the belief in sin, is
T19....IV.A.8:6 The variability the little **r.** induces merely

### remote 2

T-24 .......II.9:4 Heaven so **r.** that They cannot be reached.
T-25 ..... IV.4:4 increasingly **r.** and far away from you.

### remotely 1

T-30 ... III.10:3 complete no sound of battle comes **r.** near

### removal 3

T-8 .... VII.11:1 The **r.** of blocks, then, is the only way to
T-9 .........II.2:6 **r.** of a symptom that he himself selected.
T-11 ...... V.2:1 healing but the **r.** of all that stands in the

### remove 43

T-8 .........II.1:3 is. If learning to **r.** the obstacles to that
T-9 ........ V.6:3 and looking for a distant light to **r.** it,
T-11 .VIII.12:4 Let the Holy Spirit **r.** all offenses of God's
T-13 ........I.1:2 He seeks to **r.** all guilt from his mind that
T-13 ......X.10:9 He would **r.** only illusions. All else He
T-13 ..... XI.5:1 and gave Him the mission to **r.** all doubt
T-14 ..... IV.5:5 will He teach you to **r.** the awful burden
T-14 ..... IV.9:5 merely teaches you how to **r.** the blocks
T-14 ..... VI.8:2 therefore must **r.** whatever interferes with
T-15 .......II.2:1 the instant of holiness that will **r.** all fear.
T-15 .... VII.5:1 Holy Spirit would **r.** from his holy mind.
T-16 .... VII.2:2 By seeking to **r.** suffering in the past, it
T-17 .... VII.1:3 when you **r.** it from its source and place it
T-17 .... VII.1:7 To **r.** the problem elsewhere is to keep it,
T-17 .... VII.1:7 **r.** yourself from it and make it unsolvable.
T-18 ...... V.2:1 to **r.** all fear and hatred from your mind.
T-18 ...... V.2:5 to let Him **r.** all fear and hatred, and to be
T-18 ...... IX.1:9 Let the Holy Spirit **r.** it from the withered
T-19 ........I.5:3 would **r.** all limitations and make whole.
T-19 ........I.5:5 faith would **r.** all obstacles that seem to
T19..IV.A.15:4 cannot ask love's messengers to **r.** from it,
T19.... IV.B.3:7 the Holy Spirit asks, and this He *would* **r.**.
T19. IV.D.16:4 and **r.** all trace of guilt from his disturbed
T-26 .... VII.9:5 does **r.** the obstacles that you have placed
T-29 ..... VI.3:6 can not **r.** the power to change your mind
T-31 ...VIII.3:4 **r.** all misery from you whom God created
W-pI.....38.2:4 Your holiness, then, can **r.** all pain, can
W-pI.....62.3:3 It will **r.** all sense of weakness, strain and
W-pI.....85.4:4 *This has no power to r. salvation from me.*
W-pI.....91.9:4 Try to **r.** your faith from it, if only for a
W-pI .. 99.11:1 the power to **r.** all forms of doubt and fear
W-pI .. 101.7:1 to **r.** the heavy load you lay upon yourself
W-pI .. 104.2:1 Today we would **r.** all meaningless and
W-pI 134.12:4 **r.** the ponderous and useless armor made
WpI..rIV.in5:2 alone engage it fully, and **r.** the rest: *My*
W-pI 151.10:1 He will **r.** all faith that you have placed in
W-pI 151.13:4 comes to mind, **r.** the elements of dreams,
W-pI .. 181.2:5 **R.** your focus on your brother's sins, and
W-pI .. 187.7:2 and you **r.** the thought of suffering. Your
P-1............. 1:1 psychotherapy is to **r.** the blocks to truth.
P-2..........II.2:7 **r.** the seeming obstacles to true awareness
S-2...........I.7:4 God's mercy would **r.** this withering and
S-3..........II.1:4 can indeed **r.** a form of pain and sickness.

### removed 40

T-8 ..........I.2:6 they will be **r.** from your mind for you.
T-10 ..... IV.3:4 have **r.** part of your mind from God's Will
T-10 .....V.11:2 Son **r.** himself from His gift by refusing to
T-11 ..... VI.7:1 will not find peace until you have **r.** the
T-12 ........I.9:2 supply the loss, the basic cause of fear is **r.**
T-13 ..... XI.7:6 You will not keep what God would have **r.**
T-14 ..... IV.2:2 which what is not there has been **r.** from
T-15 .......II.1:8 all the obstacles to learning it have been **r.**
T-15 .....X.5:11 last when the idea of sacrifice has been **r.**.
T-17 .... VII.1:6 way of understanding would have been **r.**.
T-17 .... VII.2:4 but you have **r.** yourself from the solution
T-18 .......II.8:4 become one in which the wish has been **r.**
T-18 ..... III.6:4 is offered to the light, and is **r.** forever.
T-18 ..... VI.7:5 in a separate prison, **r.** and unreachable,
T-18 ... IX.14:2 and purified, and finally **r.** forever.
T-19 ..... III.8:7 Its source has been **r.**, and so it can be
T-19 ... III.10:7 Look not for what has been **r.**, but for the
T19IV.A.17:14 creeps in where happiness has been **r.**,
T19 ... IV.B.3:4 it a sacrifice to be **r.** from what can suffer?
T-21 ..... III.3:7 you offer holiness has been **r.** from sin.
T-21 ..... III.8:2 sin by choosing to let all limitations be **r.**.
T-25 ..... IX.9:1 did not choose to let them be **r.** for you.
T-26 .....V.10:8 since **r.** and gone forever from his mind?
T-27 ......I.10:1 from which the goal of sin has been **r.**, is
T-27 .......II.3:8 have overlooked it and **r.** it from his own.
T-27 .... VII.2:6 as hurting him, and also very easily **r.**.
T-27 ... VIII.9:5 cause. And by His judgment are effects **r.**.
T-31 .....V.11:2 you see, if all its underpinnings were **r.**?
W-pI .... 37.2:1 can be **r.** from the world's thinking. Any
W-pI .. 131.6:7 It is as far **r.** from time as is a tiny candle
W-pI .. 189.8:3 God the Father to be quietly **r.** forever.
W-pII . 227.1:5 *feet of truth, to be r. forever from my mind.*
W-pII . 295.1:3 And as they are **r.** from me, the dreams
W-pII . 319.1:1 from which all arrogance has been **r.**, and
M-9 ........... 1:8 all dark cornerstones of unforgiveness **r.**.
M-17 ....... 7:13 The stain of blood can never be **r.**, and
M-21 ....... 1:10 They are thus twice **r.** from reality.
M-26 ......... 1:3 where all barriers to truth have been **r.**. In
P-2....... VII.3:5 it return again, once its cause has been **r.**.
S-3........ III.1:2 it has not **r.** the curse of sin that lies on it.

### removes 11

T-2 ....... VI.1:7 This **r.** them from my control, and makes
T-3 ....... III.4:5 that perception is involved at all **r.** the
T-4 .......II.11:4 This **r.** the block entirely. You may ask
T-14 .......X.5:3 there was light, darkness **r.** it in an instant
T-16 ... IV.10:2 **r.** your own sense of completion, and thus
T-18 ... IX.14:3 Forgiveness **r.** only the untrue, lifting the
T-22 ...... in.4:8 and finally **r.** all sense of differences, so
W-pI 136.18:1 Perhaps you do not realize that this **r.** the
W-pI .. 137.5:2 but **r.** illusions that have not occurred.
W-pI .. 165.7:6 This course **r.** all doubts which you have
W-pI .. 188.3:4 It **r.** all thoughts of the ephemeral and

### removing 9

T-in ........... 1:7 *at r. the blocks to the awareness of love's*
T-12 ........I.9:4 The means for **r.** it is in yourself, and you
T-13 ..... III.2:6 that, by **r.** the dark cloud that obscures it,
T-15 .......V.5:3 holiness by **r.** as much fear as you will let
T-15 .......V.9:3 thus **r.** the frame of reference you have
T-15 ...VIII.6:2 and by **r.** every element of disagreement,

T-17....... II.6:2 chaos, **r.** all illusions that had twisted
T-21...... III.7:5 brother free, **r.** hatred by removing fear,
T-21...... III.7:5 brother free, removing hatred by **r.** fear,

**render** 12
T-1........ I.18:2 the maximal service you can **r.** to another.
T-1......... II.4:6 which I **r.** complete because I share it.
T-2........IV.4:5 over the mind to **r.** a person temporarily
T-2.......VII.4:1 in it seems to **r.** it out of your control. Yet
T-13...VII.11:6 and **r.** you unwilling to question the value
T-16......IV.8:3 and it is they who **r.** you complete. The
T-22.........I.3:7 would, of course, **r.** this quite unnecessary
T-28....... I.13:5 made to **r.** unremembered and undone.
T-31.........I.4:5 powerful enough to **r.** God forgotten, and
W-pI.134.10:1 in terms that **r.** choosing meaningful, and
W-pI...136.2:3 hide reality, attack it, change it, **r.** it inept,
W-pI.170.13:7 *we give thanks for them who* **r.** *us complete.*

**rendered** 4
T-2........ I.1:10 that what is perfect can be **r.** imperfect or
T-7.......VI.2:7 and thus **r.** it powerless in your belief.
T-19....... II.2:7 Himself is changed, and **r.** incomplete.
T-26......IX.3:5 that hate had scorched and **r.** desolate.

**rendering** 7
T-5........IV.6:8 by **r.** unto God the things that are God's?
T-7........IX.2:2 **r.** its creations equally whole and equal in
T-8........IX.3:4 by **r.** the faculties for seeing ineffectual.
T-12.........I.9:7 its perceived usefulness by **r.** it useless.
T-13......IV.7:3 as **r.** the need for time unnecessary. He
T-17.........I.4:4 truth is to destroy it by **r.** it meaningless.
T-26....... X.5:7 you have laid on it by **r.** it purposeless,

**renders** 6
T-1......... II.6:5 to the extent that it **r.** the interval of time
T-5......VI.12:3 results *now* it **r.** time unnecessary. We
T-8.......VII.3:6 reality of anything is the service it **r.** God
T-9.......VII.8:7 belongs to Him and **r.** Him complete.
T-9..... VIII.3:3 Its profound sense of vulnerability **r.** it
W-pI.....94.1:1 one thought which **r.** the ego silent and

**renew** 1
T-13...VII.12:4 will **r.** them as long as you have need of

**renewal** 1
W-pI...188.3:5 It brings **r.** to all tired hearts, and lights

**renewed** 1
WpI.. rV.in7:2 I am **r.** each time a brother learns there is

**renews** 1
W-pII..222.1:2 the water which **r.** and cleanses me. He is

**renounce** 9
T-4...........I.4:7 If you are willing to **r.** the role of guardian
T-8......... V.4:2 union is therefore the way to **r.** the ego in
T-15.......IX.7:2 **r.** its use for separation and attack which
T-16....... II.6:9 have come too near to truth to **r.** it now,
W-pI...155.4:2 Many have chosen to **r.** the world while
W-pI...163.8:5 is no death, and we **r.** it now in every form
W-pI...185.5:1 want the peace of God is to **r.** all dreams.
W-pI...193.8:5 it. Would you now **r.** your own salvation?
M-24..........5:3 mistake for him to **r.** the belief unless his

**renounced** 5
T-8......... V.4:1 because I have **r.** the ego in myself and
T19. IV.C.2:13 purpose in place of the ego's you **r.** death,
T-21...... III.8:2 **r.** the means for sin by choosing to let all
T-21...VII.11:6 For only then have you **r.** the option to
T-29.....VII.4:4 And by this giving up is life **r.**. Seek not

**renouncing** 1
T-18.........I.1:3 **r.** one aspect of the Sonship in favor of

**renunciation** 1
T-16....... V.4:2 special relationship is the **r.** of the Love of

**reopened** 1
M-16 .....11:11 And thus the gate of Heaven is **r.**, and its

**reorganizing** 2
T-1.........I.37:2 erroneous perception and **r.** it properly.
T-3......... V.7:7 accepting and rejecting, organizing and **r.**

**repaid** 1
W-pI...105.2:2 meant to be a pledge of debt to be **r.** with

**repaired** 2
T-2........ III.4:3 defiled and needs to be **r.** and protected.
W-pI...159.7:2 For here it is **r.**, made new again, but in a

**reparation** 2
T-4.........in.3:5 power, the futile attempts of the ego at **r.**,
T-5......... II.1:1 Healing is not creating; it is **r.**. The Holy

**reparative** 2
T-9........ VI.6:1 no place in eternity, because they are **r.**.
S-1......... II.3:1 for in this world prayer is **r.**, and so it

**repay** 1
P-3........ III.4:6 in gratitude, as does the patient **r.** him.

**repayment** 1
W-pI...126.5:3 not escape the justified **r.** for his sin.

**repays** 1
P-3........ III.4:6 The therapist **r.** the patient in gratitude,

**repeat** 106
T-2........ VI.6:6 I will therefore **r.** it, urging you to listen.
T-4...........I.7:4 and **r.** their lessons until they are learned.
T-4......... III.5:2 It is necessary to **r.** that your belief in
T-6.........I.11:2 to **r.** my experiences because the Holy
T-9........IV.8:3 Let me **r.** that the ego's qualifications as a
T-19...... III.3:5 Now you will not **r.** it; you will merely
T-26..... V.14:4 need that you **r.** again a journey that was
T-27. VIII.11:2 Holy Spirit will **r.** this one inclusive lesson
T-31.........I.3:1 to practice and **r.** the lessons endlessly, in
T-31......IV.7:3 let me **r.** that to achieve a goal you must
W-pI.......4.6:2 Do not **r.** these exercises more than three
W-pI.....10.5:4 to **r.** the idea slowly before applying it
W-pI.....11.2:2 closed, and **r.** the idea slowly to yourself.
W-pI.....11.2:4 in using the idea merely **r.** it to yourself,
W-pI.....11.3:5 eyes and **r.** the idea once more slowly to
W-pI.....13.4:2 eyes closed, **r.** today's idea to yourself.
W-pI.....13.4:5 **R.** this statement to yourself as you look
W-pI.....15.4:1 the idea for today, **r.** it first to yourself,
W-pI.....15.4:5 subject while you **r.** the idea to yourself.
W-pI.....16.5:1 periods, first **r.** the idea to yourself, and
W-pI.....20.4:3 as you **r.** the idea, you are stating that you
W-pI.....20.5:1 **R.** today's idea slowly and positively at
W-pI.....23.6:2 you, **r.** the idea slowly to yourself first,
W-pI.....27.3:6 can still **r.** one short sentence to yourself
W-pI...29.5:10 **r.** the idea for today at least once an hour,
W-pI.....30.3:2 a moment or so, **r.** it to yourself slowly,
W-pI.....31.3:5 **r.** today's idea to yourself as often as you
W-pI.....31.4:1 **r.** the idea for today as often as possible
W-pI.....32.3:4 **R.** the idea for today unhurriedly as often
W-pI.....33.2:2 as you **r.** the idea throughout the day.
W-pI.....33.4:2 and **r.** the idea to yourself several times.
W-pI.....34.4:1 continue to **r.** the idea to yourself in an
W-pI.....35.8:2 merely relax and **r.** today's idea slowly
W-pI.....35.9:2 to you, merely **r.** the idea to yourself, with
W-pI.....36.3:1 close your eyes and **r.** the idea for today
W-pI...36.3:10 close your eyes and **r.** the idea to yourself.
W-pI.....36.4:1 periods, close your eyes and **r.** the idea;
W-pI.....36.4:1 the idea; look about you as you **r.** it again;
W-pI.....38.4:1 a full five minutes, **r.** the idea for today,
W-pI.....39.9:1 you merely **r.** today's idea to yourself
W-pI...39.11:1 ask yourself this question, **r.** today's idea,
W-pI.....40.3:2 effort. **R.** the idea for today, and then add
W-pI.....41.6:3 practice period, **r.** today's idea very slowly
W-pI.....41.7:1 you may **r.** the idea if you find it helpful.
W-pI.....42.4:2 Then close your eyes and **r.** the idea again
W-pI.....42.5:5 open your eyes and **r.** the thought once
W-pI.....42.5:5 close your eyes, **r.** the idea once more,
W-pI.....42.8:1 more often you **r.** the idea during the day,
W-pI.....43.4:3 **r.** the idea for today to yourself with eyes
W-pI.....43.5:2 close your eyes, **r.** today's idea again, and
W-pI.....43.6:1 **r.** the first phase of the exercise period,
W-pI.....43.9:1 merely **r.** the idea in its original form. Try
W-pI.....44.9:1 form, pause long enough to **r.** today's idea
W-pI...44.11:1 Throughout the day **r.** the idea often,
W-pI.....45.6:3 the idea, **r.** it again and tell yourself gently
W-pI.....45.9:2 two, as you **r.** the idea throughout the day
W-pI.....47.8:1 During the day, **r.** the idea often. Use it as
W-pI.....48.2:2 Merely **r.** the idea as often as possible.
W-pI.....48.2:4 **r.** the idea slowly to yourself several times
W-pI.....49.5:1 forget to **r.** today's idea very frequently.
W-pI.....49.5:3 sure to sit quietly and **r.** the idea for today
W-pI.....50.5:2 **R.** it, think about it, let related thoughts
W-pI.....61.5:7 and **r.** the idea to yourself if your mind
W-pI.....62.5:6 attention wander, **r.** the idea and add: *I*
W-pI.....63.3:3 throughout the day we will **r.** this as often
W-pI.....64.7:3 You may need to **r.** "Let me not forget my
W-pI.....65.5:2 eyes, **r.** the idea to yourself once again,
W-pI.....65.7:1 Finally, **r.** the idea for today once more,
W-pI...66.11:3 to **r.** these words slowly and think about
W-pI.....67.4:1 You may find it necessary to **r.** the idea
W-pI.....68.7:4 **r.** the idea several times an hour in this
W-pI...72.12:1 go out, **r.** your question and your request,
W-pI.....74.6:3 quickly **r.** the idea for today and try again.
W-pI.....75.6:7 While you wait, **r.** several times, slowly
W-pI...76.11:4 will **r.** today's idea until we have listened
W-pI...76.12:1 will **r.** this dedication as often as possible
W-pI.....80.2:2 **R.** this over and over to yourself today,
W-pI.....80.6:2 **R.** the idea with deep conviction, as
WpI..rII.in.3:1 **R.** the first phase of the exercise period if
W-pI...92.11:3 us **r.** as often as we can the idea for today,
W-pI...93.10:3 remember to **r.** these thoughts each hour:
W-pI...95.11:5 **R.** this several times, and then attempt to
W-pI...95.14:8 **R.** today's idea as frequently as possible,
W-pI...98.10:2 **R.** today's idea while you wait for the glad
W-pI...98.10:3 **R.** it often, and do not forget each time
W-pI...110.1:1 We will **r.** today's idea from time to time.
WpIrIII.in10:5 **R.** it, and allow your mind to rest a little
WpIrIII.in11:3 Do not **r.** the thought and lay it down. Its
W-pI.126.10:2 by. **R.** today's idea, and ask for help in
W-pI.139.12:1 **r.** our dedication to our cause today each
WpI. rIV.in8:2 Then **r.** the two ideas you practice for the
W-pI...162.1:2 From time to time we will **r.** it, as we
W-pI...183.3:1 **R.** God's Name, and all the world
W-pI...183.4:1 **R.** the Name of God, and little names
W-pI...183.4:3 **R.** His Name, and see how easily you will
W-pI...183.5:1 **R.** the Name of God, and call upon your
W-pI...183.5:2 **R.** His Name, and all the tiny, nameless
W-pI...183.5:4 and **r.** God's Name along with him within
W-pI...183.6:1 **r.** God's Name slowly again and still again
W-pI...183.8:1 **R.** God's Name, and you acknowledge
W-pI.193.13:4 form of suffering, **r.** these selfsame words.
WpI rVI.in.3:7 And we **r.** it every time the hour strikes,
WpI rVI.in.6:4 And then **r.** the idea for the day, and let it
M-7 ........... 1:4 have already said it is, what is there to **r.**?

M-7 ..........2:2 this, he should not **r.** his previous effort.
P-2........VI.1:4 "God may not enter here" the sick **r.**, over

## repeated 20

T-4......... II.1:3 errors were not being **r.** in the present.
T-11.........I.8:8 be too often **r.** that you do not know it.
T-19...... III.1:2 Sin will be **r.** because of this attraction.
T-19...... III.2:6 must be eternal, and will be **r.** endlessly.
T-19...... III.3:3 Sometimes a sin can be **r.** over and over,
T-21....... II.1:1 We have **r.** how little is asked of you to
T-24...... IV.3:2 This has been oft **r.**, but is difficult to
W-pI.......4.3:1 will be **r.** from time to time in somewhat
W-pI.....15.4:6 idea should be **r.** quite slowly each time.
W-pI.....19.3:2 The idea for today is to be **r.** first, and
W-pI.....19.4:1 by now, and will no longer be **r.** each day,
W-pI.....33.1:3 the idea should be **r.** as often as you find
W-pI...73.11:5 This should be **r.** several times an hour. It
W-pI.....93.6:2 Over and over this must be **r.**, until it is
W-pI...132.9:1 earlier **r.** once must now be stressed again
W-pI...169.8:3 We have **r.** several times before that you
W-pII .284.1:5 first to be but said and then **r.** many times
M-7 .............h SHOULD HEALING BE **R.**?
M-7 ...........1:2 Healing cannot be **r.**. If the patient is
S-1........IV.3:3 asks to have the past **r.** in some way.

## repeatedly 11

T-4.......VII.6:1 Bible **r.** states that you should praise God.
T-5........ III.6:1 I have **r.** emphasized that one level of the
T-5...... VI.12:4 **r.** said that time is a learning device to be
T-7......... V.2:5 because, as has been **r.** emphasized, you
T-7........VI.8:1 I have **r.** emphasized that the ego does
T-9......... II.1:4 however, that the course states, and **r.**,
T-9......... V.2:1 I have **r.** said that beliefs of the ego
T-12.........I.8:5 **r.** emphasized the need to recognize fear
T-17...... IV.2:3 I have said **r.** that the Holy Spirit would
W-pI.....73.5:5 We have **r.** emphasized that the barrier of
M-23 .........2:1 have **r.** said that one who has perfectly

## repeating 36

W-pI.....10.3:3 is merely another way of **r.** our earlier
W-pI.....10.4:1 introduce them by **r.** the idea for today
W-pI.....14.6:7 the practice periods by **r.** today's idea:
W-pI.....18.3:3 period by **r.** the more general statement: *I*
W-pI.....21.2:1 periods, begin by **r.** the idea to yourself.
W-pI.....24.4:1 periods should begin with **r.** today's idea,
W-pI.....26.6:1 practice period should begin with **r.** the
W-pI.....26.9:3 each practice period by **r.** today's idea to
W-pI.....27.4:6 sincere while you were **r.** today's idea, you
W-pI.....29.4:1 pattern: Begin with **r.** the idea to yourself,
W-pI.....31.2:3 slowly while **r.** the idea two or three times
W-pI.....32.3:1 the morning and evening by **r.** the idea
W-pI.....32.5:2 applications consist of **r.** the idea slowly,
W-pI.....34.3:3 **r.** the idea for today slowly as you watch
W-pI.....34.6:2 and devote them to **r.** the idea until you
W-pI.....35.4:1 today, begin by **r.** today's idea to yourself,
W-pI.....37.6:1 consist of **r.** the idea as often as you can. It
W-pI.....39.6:1 as usual, by **r.** today's idea to yourself.
W-pI...39.10:4 End each practice period by **r.** the idea in
W-pI.....41.9:1 day use today's idea often, **r.** it very slowly
W-pI.....42.4:1 periods by **r.** the idea for today slowly,
W-pI.....44.7:1 by **r.** today's idea with your eyes open,
W-pI.....44.7:1 slowly, **r.** the idea several times more.
W-pI.....45.6:1 the exercises for today by **r.** the idea to
W-pI.....46.3:2 periods by **r.** today's idea to yourself, as
W-pI.....47.4:3 begin, as usual, by **r.** the idea for the day.
W-pI.....67.2:2 We will begin by **r.** this truth about you,
W-pI.....70.7:1 practice periods by **r.** the idea for today,
W-pI.....74.3:1 periods by **r.** these thoughts several times
W-pI.....76.6:2 This needs **r.**, over and over, until you
W-pI.....91.1:2 This needs **r.**, and frequent repeating. It is
W-pI.....91.1:2 This needs repeating, and frequent **r.**. It is
W-pI...93.11:1 illusion of fear by **r.** these thoughts again.
W-pI.124.12:1 offered you today, by hourly **r.** to yourself
WpI. rIV.in9:3 **r.** first the thought that made the day a
W-pI.151.13:2 slow **r.** of the thought with which the day

## repeats 1

T-27 ... IV.6:11 How could it be answered if it but **r.** itself

## repelled 1

W-pI.....93.1:2 see the truth about you he would be **r.**,

## repels 1

T-3 ......VII.2:7 Yet he attracts men rather than **r.** them,

## repentance 1

T-5 ......VII.5:4 cannot be undone by **r.** in the usual sense,

## repertoire 1

W-pI...194.6:2 mind, a habit in your problem-solving **r.**,

## repertory 1

W-pI.....14.6:1 personal **r.** of horrors at which you are

## repetition 10

T-21 ..... IV.8:7 not made meaningful by **r.** and by clamor
T-26 .... V.13:3 a **r.** of an instant gone by long ago that
W-pI.....25.6:2 begin with a slow **r.** of the idea for today,
W-pI.....36.4:1 conclude with one more **r.** with your eyes
W-pI.....37.4:1 begin with the **r.** of the idea for today,
W-pI.....37.5:2 with a **r.** of the idea with your eyes closed,
W-pI.....46.6:7 a **r.** of today's idea as originally stated.
W-pI.....46.7:1 of a **r.** of the idea for today in the original
W-pI.....98.7:3 each **r.** of today's idea a total dedication,
WpI rVI.in.3:8 and a **r.** of the special thought we practice

## repetitions 4

T-4 ........in.3:6 **r.** are endless until they are voluntarily
W-pI.....20.5:3 extra **r.** should be applied to any situation
W-pI.....27.3:1 needs many **r.** for maximum benefit. It
W-pI.....42.6:3 between slow **r.** of the idea with eyes open

## replace 86

T-3 ....... III.6:4 and time, and will ultimately **r.** them.
T-3 ....... VI.3:6 that enables recognition to **r.** perception.
T-9 .....VIII.9:6 because it is used to **r.** your grandeur. Yet
T-9 ...VIII.10:5 You cannot **r.** the Kingdom, and you
T-9 ...VIII.10:5 the Kingdom, and you cannot **r.** yourself.
T-9 ...VIII.11:9 He would have you **r.** the ego's belief in
T-10 ..... III.8:6 fearful fact that you made them to **r.** God.
T-10 ..... III.8:7 you, remember that nothing can **r.** God,
T-10 ...... V.1:6 forms of denial **r.** what is with what is not
T-11 .VIII.14:3 laugh at your fears and **r.** them with peace
T-12 ........I.10:4 Thus does the Holy Spirit **r.** fear with love
T-12 ........I.10:5 you learn of Him how to **r.** your dream of
T-13 ...VIII.3:7 seen, and they will **r.** aspects of unreality.
T-14 ..... III.6:2 **r.** darkness with light and fear with love.
T-14 ...VIII.2:2 will **r.** with the one promise given unto
T-14 ..... XI.5:6 will **r.** the dark ones you do not accept,
T-15 ..... III.9:4 together we can **r.** the shabby littleness
T-15 ..... VI.8:5 your brothers, to **r.** it in your awareness.
T-15 ...VIII.1:1 instant does not **r.** the need for learning,
T-15 ..... IX.3:1 the Great Rays **r.** the body in awareness,
T-16 ..... III.5:6 the place of what you took in to **r.** them.
T-16 ..... V.10:6 snatch it from the other to **r.** the self that
T19..IV.A.15:6 to **r.** the hungry dogs of fear you sent
T-20 ........I.2:7 the thorns, offering the lilies to **r.** them.
T-20 ... VI.11:8 him to **r.** the unholy one he chose before.
T-20 ...VIII.4:8 to **r.** the holy home the Holy Spirit offers,
T-20 .VIII.10:4 sights with which He would **r.** them.
T-25 .VIII.14:5 **r.** God's justice with a version of its own.
T-26 ......I.4:10 song, and sight of him **r.** the body's eyes.
T-26 ...... V.3:1 gave His Teacher to **r.** the one you made,
T-26 ...... V.3:2 And what He would **r.** has been replaced.
T-26 ..... VI.2:8 for what illusion can **r.** the truth?
T-26 ..VII.10:2 you, to **r.** the world you see with Heaven,
T-26 ..... IX.8:5 to **r.** an ancient enmity that came to kill.
T-27 .......II.8:9 And laughter will **r.** your sighs, because
T-27 ..... VI.4:9 heal alike, for all sin's witnesses do His **r.**.
T-27 ..... VI.8:2 The holy instant will **r.** all sin if you but
T-30 .......V.6:1 awareness, to **r.** the goal of sin and guilt.
T-30 ..... VI.5:7 that could **r.** it and destroy the Will of
T-30 ...VIII.6:4 give it power to **r.** the changeless in him
T-31 ..... VI.4:2 the world that will **r.** the one you made.
W-pI .... 34.6:4 *I can r. my feelings of depression, anxiety or*
W-pI .... 51.4:7 replaced by what they were intended to **r.**
W-pI .... 54.5:4 through me has enabled love to **r.** fear,
W-pI .... 54.5:4 love to replace fear, laughter to **r.** tears,
W-pI .... 54.5:4 to replace tears, and abundance to **r.** loss.
W-pI .... 59.3:8 of Christ has been given me to **r.** them. It
W-pI .... 62.2:5 thoughts of life may **r.** thoughts of death.
W-pI .... 66.7:5 that the Holy Spirit always offers to **r.** it.
W-pI .... 66.8:1 the ego which you have made to **r.** Him.
W-pI .... 67.2:8 definition of God and **r.** it with His Own.
W-pI .... 67.4:1 time to time to **r.** distracting thoughts.
W-pI .... 72.2:1 The ego's fundamental wish is to **r.** God.
W-pI .. 72.10:2 goal, we must **r.** attack with acceptance.
W-pI .. 75.11:2 has come to **r.** the unforgiven world you
W-pI .......78.h Let miracles **r.** all grievances.
W-pI .. 78.10:5 well, we pray: *Let miracles r. all grievances.*
WpI.. rII.in.4:3 **R.** them with your determination to
W-pI .... 84.1:6 raise my own self-concept to **r.** my Self. I
W-pI .... 89.1:3 all grievances, and **r.** them with miracles.
W-pI .... 89.3:1 (78) Let miracles **r.** all grievances. By this
W-pI .... 91.7:2 to **r.** the image of a body in your mind.
W-pI .... 93.9:5 evil and sinfulness you have made to **r.** It.
W-pI .... 94.3:6 sinned, nor made an image to **r.** reality.
W-pI .. 110.3:1 you, appearances cannot **r.** the truth,
W-pI .. 127.8:4 gifts, and let the gift of God **r.** them all.
W-pI 131.10:3 to **r.** the foolish images that we hold dear,
W-pI .. 132.8:4 life **r.** all thoughts you ever held of death.
W-pI .. 133.3:2 at all, for they can but **r.** what offers more
W-pI .. 137.7:1 healing must **r.** the fantasies of sickness
W-pI .. 137.9:2 let His laws **r.** the ones you made to hold
W-pI 153.12:2 **r.** their fearful toys with joyous games,
W-pI 169.12:3 **r.** the thought of time but for a little while
W-pI .. 170.8:5 Or will you make another idol to **r.** it? For
W-pI .. 183.4:5 let the Name of God **r.** their little names,
W-pI .. 183.8:5 and see God's Name **r.** the thousand little
W-pI .. 190.8:4 over love, and time **r.** eternity and Heaven
W-pI .. 192.4:1 the Word of God can now **r.** the senseless
W-pI .. 193.9:5 willed that laughter should **r.** each one,
W-pI .. 199.7:4 Let love **r.** their fears through you. Accept
W-pI 200.11:5 and to **r.** our shifting goals and solitary
W-pII . 226.1:5 not sought for illusions to **r.** the truth.
W-pII ..... 2.1:4 and will **r.** these thoughts of conflict with
W-pII . 272.2:2 as hell, and love will happily **r.** all fear.
W-pII . 274.1:3 *illusions were, light will r. all darkness, and*
M-29 ......... 6:8 be cruel if He let your words **r.** His Own.

## replaced 52

T-1 ....... IV.4:1 by fear must be **r.** by forgiveness. That is
T-9 .....VIII.7:3 have **r.** it with something you have made.
T-9 .....VIII.9:7 Yet what God has created cannot be **r.**.
T-10 .......II.1:5 And you have **r.** your knowledge by an
T-13 ... IX.8:13 you feared was there has been **r.** with love
T-14 ...VIII.2:4 but will be **r.** by gifts wholly acceptable to
T-14 ..... IX.4:4 fear of death will be **r.** with joy of life. For
T-16 ..... III.1:7 suffering has disappeared to be **r.** by joy.
T-18 ........I.1:4 more valuable and the other is **r.** by him.
T-18 ..... IX.9:7 laid by, and gently **r.** by purity and love.
T-18 ... IX.12:6 **r.** forever by the knowledge of love and its
T-21 .......II.5:8 it taken from him and be **r.** with truth.
T-21 ..... III.2:4 No one allows a purpose to be **r.** while he
T-22 ........I.7:2 more ancient than the old illusion it has **r.**
T-22 .....II.10:7 of the illusions that you made **r.** the truth
T-23 ......I.2:10 and will seem to have **r.** love there. This is
T-26 .......V.3:2 And what He would replace has been **r.**.
T-26 .... VII.2:3 it has been healed, and been **r.** by sanity.
T-26 .......X.6:4 and been **r.** with justice and with love. If
T-27 .......V.7:6 world of accusation is **r.** by one in which
T-29 ...VIII.1:7 he is. Idols are made that he may be **r.**, no
T-30 ..... VI.7:8 appearances that have **r.** the truth about
W-pI .... 23.5:2 and then let go, so that it can be **r.**. The

W-pI.....23.5:5 not. Your images have already been **r.**. By
W-pI.....31.3:1 for a moment, and then **r.** by the next.
W-pI.....34.3:3 and let each one go, to be **r.** by the next.
W-pI.....43.1:4 God, perception would have **r.** knowledge
W-pI.....51.4:7 I choose to have them be **r.** by what they
W-pI.....52.1:5 I have **r.** reality with illusions I made up.
W-pI.....56.2:5 go. As it is **r.** by truth, vision will surely be
W-pI.....62.2:5 For this attack must be **r.** by forgiveness,
W-pI.....65.6:5 your illusions of purpose be **r.** by truth.
W-pI.....74.1:5 Peace has **r.** the strange idea that you are
W-pI.....76.7:1 The laws of God can never be **r.**. We will
W-pI.....76.9:5 and nothing is **r.** by something else. God's
W-pI.....88.1:8 It has **r.** the darkness, and the darkness
W-pI.....89.3:4 to have all my illusions be **r.** with truth,
W-pI.....89.4:3 *Let our grievances be* **r.** *by miracles, [name].*
W-pI.....89.4:4 *the miracle by which all my grievances are* **r.**.
W-pI.....90.1:3 with which I let the grievance be **r.**. Today
W-pI.....99.7:6 let the Thought with which He has **r.** all
W-pI...110.1:3 what God created was **r.** by fear and evil,
W-pI.135.10:1 have been corrected and **r.** with truth.
W-pI.166.11:2 upon it now has been **r.** by vision which
W-pI...181.2:4 which has **r.** the one you held before.
W-pI...194.9:4 it will be soon **r.** by love's reflection. And
W-pI...195.2:2 and suffering **r.** with laughter and with
W-pII......7.2:4 beyond itself, to be **r.** by the eternal truth.
W-pII294.1:10 serve, and then to be **r.** for greater good.
W-pII.....359.h All pain Is healed; all misery **r.** with joy.
M-13..........1:5 illusion must be **r.** by a corrective device;
M-28..........6:4 The thought of murder is **r.** with blessing.

## replacement 15

*See also* self-replacement

T-10....III.11:6 him, because he was made as God's **r.**. He
T-18.........I.2:2 perceives one person as a **r.** for another,
T-18.........I.3:2 by definition, for it is love's **r.**. Fear is
T-21....... II.6:5 This is the Son of God's **r.** for his will, a
T-27...... III.4:8 first **r.** for your picture is another picture
W-pI.....23.4:4 Vision already holds a **r.** for everything
W-pI...166.7:1 self, the one you made as a **r.** for reality.
W-pII.....in.6:2 the world of sorrow in exchange for its **r.**,
W-pII.....in.6:5 take that world to be the full **r.** of our own
W-pII......4.2:5 taken as **r.** for the goal of self-deception.
W-pII......7.3:1 nor turn away from His **r.** for the fearful
W-pII..289.2:2 *For You have offered me Your Own* **r.**, *in a*
M-4.......IV.1:7 of God's curriculum, and its **r.** by insanity
M-18..........3:2 insane belief is taken as **r.** for God's Word
M-23..........4:3 It is a symbol that is safely used as a **r.** for

## replacements 3

T-10......III.8:7 and whatever **r.** you have attempted are
W-pI.....50.2:1 things are your **r.** for the Love of God. All
WpI. rIII.in4:3 periods to be **r.** for your litanies to them.

## replaces 11

T-8........VII.9:6 devotion to Him **r.** devotion to the ego. In
T-17........V.3:2 to enter. At once His goal **r.** yours. This is
T-18....VI.11:8 love that instantly **r.** it extends to what
T-19....... II.4:3 And it is this doctrine that **r.** the reality of
T-24....... V.6:3 Love for God **r.** all the fear you thought
T-27....... V.6:6 Healing **r.** suffering. Who looks on one
W-pI.....97.4:4 who asks; **r.** error with the simple truth.
W-pI...103.3:2 all the happiness it brings as truth **r.** fear,
W-pI.170.12:6 way for love, as God Himself **r.** cruelty.
W-pII..356.1:5 *Your Name* **r.** *every thought of sin, and who*
M-13..........1:5 device; another illusion that **r.** the first, so

## replacing 12

T-8........IX.5:2 since all healing involves **r.** fear with love.
T-8........IX.5:4 and the true, **r.** the false with the true.
T-21......VI.4:2 **r.** madness if it be the choice of the insane
T-29..... II.10:1 **r.** what He is with littleness and limit and
T-31... VIII.5:5 **r.** all your weakness with the strength that
W-pI.....15.1:7 the place of seeing, **r.** vision with illusions
W-pI.....67.6:3 **r.** everything that the ego tells you about
W-pI...95.11:3 to sink into your mind, **r.** false ideas: *I am*

W-pI.151.16:2 the world, **r.** witnesses to sin and death.
W-pI...194.8:2 **r.** all your thoughts of sin and evil with
M-28 .........3:8 world, forgiving all things and **r.** all attack
P-2.......VII.2:9 **r.** those with which the patient came to

## replicate 1

M-5 ..... II.4:10 Cause and effect but **r.** creation. Seen in

## replied 1

T-28...... VI.6:6 His Son remembers not that he **r.** "I will,"

## replies 1

T-4......... V.4:7 I go for protection?" to which the ego **r.**,

## reply 2

W-pI.166.11:3 all your fears with this one merciful **r.**, "It
S-1...........I.2:8 is merely an echo of the **r.** of His Voice.

## report 5

T-28....... V.5:6 and what they see and hear they but **r.**. It
W-pI...151.2:4 last detail which they **r.** is even stranger,
W-pI...151.3:5 faith in what your eyes and ears **r.**. You
W-pII......3.3:5 Yet everything that they **r.** is but illusion
M-8 ...........6:3 eyes will **r.** their changed appearances as

## reports 1

W-pI...151.7:2 nor what your fingers' touch **r.** of him. He

## represent 37

T-1.........I.12:2 Thoughts can **r.** the lower or bodily level
T-1.........I.26:1 Miracles **r.** freedom from fear. "Atoning"
T-2.............I.2:1 These related distortions **r.** a picture of
T-2....V.A.18:3 *I am here to* **r.** *Him Who sent me. I do not*
T-3...........I.5:1 who **r.** the lamb as blood-stained do not
T-15...... IX.4:3 ego, and **r.** its demands to make little and
T-17...... III.1:9 **r.** the evil that you think was done to you.
T-17...... III.7:9 realize what you have made the past to **r.**,
T-17.... IV.13:1 are each framed perfectly for what they **r.**.
T-18....... II.9:5 dreams **r.** the same wishes in your mind,
T19..IV.C.11:3 them, but must be sought in what they **r.**.
T-22...... III.6:2 For the idea they **r.** left not its maker, and
T-27.........I.6:6 to the system they speak for and **r.**. And
T-27.........I.10:6 it receive the power to **r.** an endless life,
T-27....... II.9:2 and pain are seen to **r.** their own serenity.
T-27....... II.9:3 helplessness and weakness **r.** the grounds
T-27..... II.12:7 two halves appear to **r.** a split within a self
T-27..... II.14:6 remaining half the Holy Spirit must **r.** the
T-27...... III.2:6 Symbols which but **r.** ideas that cannot be
T-27...... IV.5:5 Where answers **r.** the questions, they add
T-27...... VI.5:2 proves that what they **r.** has no effects.
T-27...VII.16:2 see as gifts your brother offers **r.** the gifts
T-29.........I.1:4 **r.** in His eternal Love is quite impossible.
T-29...... IV.4:8 an event, or body, or a thing *should* **r.**, and
T-30........ IV.1:9 them for the things you think they **r.**.
T-30.... IV.3:10 his toys? And *can* they **r.** a threat to him?
T-31...VII.12:5 For seeing can but **r.** a wish, because it
W-pI.......4.1:6 thoughts, that they **r.** such a mixture that,
W-pI.151.11:1 the elements in them which **r.** the truth,
W-pI...187.2:3 things but **r.** the thoughts that make them
W-pI...190.7:5 Your idle wishes **r.** its pains. Your strange
W-pI...192.9:6 to be angry **r.** your savior from the prison
W-pII..300.1:2 nor **r.** more than a passing cloud upon a
M-5 ....... II.1:8 "reflexes" and the like **r.** attempts to
M-5 ...... III.2:1 come, to **r.** another choice which they had
C-1............. 1:1 term *mind* is used to **r.** the activating agent
P-2........ VI.2:2 These fleeting awarenesses **r.** the many

## representation 5

T-17.... IV.15:3 This is no figured **r.** of a thought system,
W-pI.....23.3:2 a pictorial **r.** of your own attack thoughts.
W-pI.....53.5:4 seeing only the **r.** of my insane thoughts,

W-pI.....54.2:4 I see as the **r.** of my own state of mind. I
W-pI.....55.2:2 I see is hardly the **r.** of loving thoughts. It

## represented 3

T-27...... III.5:5 by which the truth is **r.** temporarily. It lets
W-pI...164.1:4 past time, and sees eternity as **r.** there. He
M-17 .........7:5 we have the fear of God most starkly **r.**.

## representing 5

T-4..........II.7:5 **r.** the ego's need to confirm itself. This is
T-14...... III.2:2 each **r.** an escape from what the other
T-31..... V.7:10 cannot make a single picture **r.** truth.
W-pI.....41.5:2 dense and obscuring, yet **r.** all you see?
C-in ...........1:4 **r.** the "original error" or the "original sin.

## represents 50

T-2........ IV.2:7 Physical illness **r.** a belief in magic. The
T-5...........I.6:4 He **r.** a state of mind close enough to One-
T-5......... V.3:9 It **r.** a delusional system, and speaks for it.
T-6...........I.2:6 and that it **r.** release from fear to anyone
T-11...... VI.6:2 in the fact that it **r.** what you want to be.
T-12.........I.2:2 The whole process **r.** a clear-cut attempt
T-12..... VII.7:7 for it **r.** the acceptance of two goals, each
T-14.... IX.1:10 and **r.** only the denial of what always was.
T-15...... III.3:3 **r.** the value that you put upon yourself.
T-16........II.5:5 the miracle into the knowledge which it **r.**.
T-17.... IV.11:7 the frame, the picture is seen as what it **r.**.
T-17.... IV.15:4 What it **r.** is there. The frame fades gently
T-17........ V.2:4 **r.** the reversal of the unholy relationship.
T-26... VII.8:10 symbol **r.** is but your wish to *be* apart and
T-27.........I.4:2 he points beyond himself to what he **r.**. A
T-27.........I.4:3 suffering you but **r.** your brother's guilt;
T-27.........I.4:9 Yet it speaks with certainty for what it **r.**.
T-27.......I.10:5 proclaim the truth and value that it **r.**. Let
T-27.......I.11:2 picture is a lasting sign of what it **r.**. This
T-27......II.12:5 And thus He **r.** the other half, and seems
T-27...... III.2:3 He **r.** a double thought, where half is
T-27...... III.3:3 that cancelled out the thought it **r.**. And
T-27...... III.6:6 other half of what it **r.** remains unknown,
T-27...... VI.3:8 truth is found in him if it is truth he **r.**.
T-27.... VI.5:10 speaks not but for itself, but what it **r.**.
T-27... VII.15:7 **r.** his Father, Whom you see as offering
T-28.........I.3:1 healing **r.** an effort to do anything at all. It
T-28...... IV.8:3 his Identity, which the whole picture **r.**,
T-28...... VI.4:1 The body **r.** the gap between the little bit
T-29.........II.7:2 **r.** the larger dream that change is possible
T-29..... IV.4:8 each one **r.** some function that you have
T-29..... VII.5:3 idol found that **r.** a parody of life which,
T-29.... VIII.3:4 Nor is its form apart from the idea it **r.**.
T-29...... IX.3:4 And this the idol **r.**, and so its worship is
T-30........II.1:8 And Heaven itself but **r.** your will, where
T-31..... V.12:4 he **r.** has meaning that was given it by you
W-pI........4.2:3 None of them **r.** your real thoughts,
W-pI..... 13.2:2 It **r.** a situation in which God and the ego
W-pI.....44.3:3 and **r.** a major goal of mind training. It
W-pI.....53.2:4 rules a world that **r.** chaotic thinking, and
W-pI... 108.9:5 He **r.** the others, and through him you
W-pI... 121.6:3 yourself, Who **r.** the other Self in you.
WpI. rIV.in2:3 **r.** the truth of What you are and What
W-pI... 152.1:5 Nothing occurs but **r.** your wish, and
W-pI... 190.6:3 all. It merely **r.** your thoughts. And it will
W-pI... 192.2:3 Forgiveness **r.** your function here. It is not
M-5 .........I.2:3 It **r.** the ultimate defiance in a direct form
M-7 ........... 6:2 Self, and thus **r.** a confusion in identity.
C-6............. 4:2 He **r.** your Self and your Creator, Who are
P-2........ VI.5:3 to the form of unforgiveness that it **r.**. Yet

## reprieve 2

W-pI... 126.5:2 to give indulgently an undeserved **r.**. Yet
S-3........ IV.2:3 Forgiveness shines its merciful **r.** upon

## reproach 5

T-27.........I.3:5 in which there is no pain and no **r.** at all.
T-27.........I.5:8 That no **r.** he laid upon his heart was ever

T-27.........I.8:4 For it becomes the symbol of **r.**, the sign
T-27....... V.5:2 The eyes of all the dying bring **r.**, and
S-2......... II.5:4 heavy-laid **r.** that thus is put upon him. Is

## reproduce 1

P-2........ VI.5:2 forms of one but **r.** the forms of the other,

## reproduces 3

T-7........ VI.4:4 Mind always **r.** as it was produced.
T-7........ VI.4:5 Produced by fear, the ego **r.** fear. This is
P-2........ VI.3:2 The eye **r.**; it does not see. Their task is to

## reproducing 1

P-2........ VI.3:4 **r.** its desires and translating them into

## request 44

T-2....V.A.17:2 My **r.** "Do this in remembrance of me" is
T-3......... V.6:5 for forgiveness is nothing more than a **r.**
T-4........ III.6:4 Him. He has never failed to answer this **r.**,
T-9.........I.10:2 for nothing, and to ask for it is not a **r.**. It
T-9.........I.10:3 It is merely a denial in the form of a **r.**.
T-9......... II.2:7 This **r.** is, therefore, not for healing at all.
T-11..VIII.10:4 nothing will be denied your simple **r.**.
T-12...... III.4:3 who have made the **r.** outrageous, and
T-12...... III.4:3 and every **r.** of a brother is for you. Why
T-13.... III.10:3 did not give it for the **r.** was alien to Him,
T-13.... III.12:4 He denied you only your **r.** for pain, for
T-13.... III.12:6 He could but answer your insane **r.** with a
T-14..... VII.6:3 At your **r.** He enters gladly. He brings the
T-18.........I.9:1 has taken charge of everything at your **r.**,
T-18....... V.6:7 And it will come to both at the **r.** of either
T-18..VIII.12:1 and entered fully at your weak **r.**. You do
T-21....VIII.3:6 Yet he will ask because desire is a **r.**, an
T-25..... VII.1:8 is. For sin is a **r.** for death, a wish to make
T-26..... VII.3:1 asks for punishment, and its **r.** is granted.
T-27..... VII.7:5 did you in any way **r.** them for yourself.
T-30....VIII.6:5 but will fade, if you **r.** a miracle instead.
W-pI..... 28.6:2 will be making this same **r.** of each subject
W-pI..... 63.2:5 This is no idle **r.** that is being asked of you
W-pI... 72.12:1 go out, repeat your question and your **r.**,
W-pI..... 77.5:1 for the assurance that your **r.** is granted.
W-pI..... 77.6:3 but assure you that your **r.** is granted. The
W-pI..... 98.5:3 Is not five minutes but a small **r.** to make
W-pI... 106.7:4 begin with this **r.** for your enlightenment:
W-pI... 106.8:2 **r.** is one whose answer has been waiting
W-pI... 109.1:4 will answer our asking with what we **r.**.
W-pI. 131.12:3 And it is this **r.** you make today. Nothing
W-pI... 159.6:4 denied his least **r.** or his most urgent need
W-pI... 161.9:8 Would you **r.** that love destroy itself? Or
W-pI... 165.5:2 need not be sure that you **r.** the only thing
W-pI... 168.4:2 **R.** Him now to give the means by which
W-pI... 185.7:4 do not **r.** another dream be given us. They
W-pI. 185.10:3 when you make this **r.** with deep sincerity
W-pI. 185.12:3 how could your **r.** be limited to you alone
W-pI. 185.14:2 we fail today as we **r.** the peace of God be
W-pI... 186.3:4 are. What could humility **r.** but this? And
W-pII .318.2:1 *in Your* **r.** *that I accept Atonement for myself*
W-pII ....339.h I will receive whatever I **r.**.
W-pII .339.1:7 **r.** that he would want when he receives it?
WpII361-5.1:4 He is in charge by my **r.**. And He will hear

## requested 3

W-pI..... 77.5:3 You have **r.** that you be given the means
W-pI... 185.9:5 And dreams will come as you **r.** them. Yet
W-pI. 185.13:1 God has been **r.** and received by anyone.

## requesting 3

T-31..... II.5:14 and hear your voice **r.** what you want.
W-pI... 185.7:6 vain, **r.** the eternal in the place of shifting
W-pII .339.2:2 *in everything I do;* **r.** *only what You offer me,*

## requests 16

T-9 ........I.10:6 Spirit, because your **r.** to Him are real,
T-9 .........II.1:2 also in connection with **r.** that are strictly
T-12 ..... III.4:8 No "outrageous" **r.** can be made of one
T-16 ........I.6:6 Foolish **r.** are foolish merely because they
T-28 .....II.10:1 lesson that the Holy Spirit **r.** you learn,
W-pI... 122.4:2 to imperfect questions, meaningless **r.**,
W-pI... 127.6:5 this course **r.** in your advance towards its
W-pI... 183.7:5 He cannot hear **r.** that He be not Himself,
W-pI. 183.10:3 and all **r.** unneeded when God's Son calls
W-pI... 185.8:3 the words you use in making your **r.**.
W-pI. 185.11:4 who **r.** an answer which is his to give? The
W-pII . 339.1:5 Everyone will receive what he **r.**. But he
M-21 ......... 2:5 It always **r.** some kind of experience, the
M-21 ......... 3:5 of his decision offers it to him as he **r.**.
M-29 ......... 6:2 He understands the **r.** of your heart, and
S-1........ III.6:5 kind, and prayer becomes **r.** for enemies.

## require 23

T-1 ...... VII.4:3 sections not to **r.** their careful study. You
T-2 ........ V.1:8 and therefore does not **r.** correction. The
T-3 ........ III.5:6 Certainty does not **r.** action. When you
T-3 ........ V.5:6 because knowledge does not **r.** ingenuity.
T-6 ... V.C.10:4 Vigilance does **r.** effort, but only until you
T-7 ....... VI.7:3 does not **r.** vigilance unless it is conflicted
T-9 ........I.11:5 fact that God is Love does not **r.** belief,
T-9 ........I.11:5 require belief, but it does **r.** acceptance. It
T-11 ..... VI.5:7 He does not **r.** obedience, for obedience
T-12 ...... V.5:4 situation you clearly **r.** a special Teacher
T-15 ..... III.4:4 **r.** vigilance to protect your magnitude in
T-15 ..... IV.9:1 the holy instant does not **r.** that you have
T-15 ..... IV.9:2 **r.** that you have none that you would keep
T-18 ........I.3:4 and each one seems to **r.** a different form
T-18 ..... IV.3:2 But it does **r.** that you be not content with
W-in.......... 2:2 They do not **r.** a great deal of time, and it
W-in.......... 7:2 This will **r.** no effort on your part. The
W-pI..... 19.3:1 **r.** is to be undertaken with eyes closed.
W-pI..... 23.5:3 steps in this process **r.** your cooperation.
W-pI..... 24.3:1 exercises for today **r.** much more honesty
W-pI..... 46.3:1 Today's exercises **r.** at least three full five-
WpI... rI.in.4:2 that you learn to **r.** no special settings in
W-pI... 197.3:3 Your gratitude is all your gifts **r.**, that

## required 32

T-in ........... 1:2 *It is a* **r.** *course. Only the time you take it is*
T-6 ..... V.C.9:9 Vigilance was **r.** of me as much as of you,
T-18 ...... V.4:6 is **r.** to receive the means and use them.
T-27 ...... V.2:8 that is **r.** for a healing is a lack of fear. The
W-in.......... 9:5 use them. Nothing more than that is **r.**.
W-pI....... 4.2:1 of today's idea, the usual specificity is **r.**.
W-pI....... 6.2:2 three or four practice periods which are **r.**
W-pI....... 9.2:4 it. No more than that is **r.** for these or any
W-pI..... 17.4:1 than three are **r.** for maximum benefit,
W-pI..... 19.5:1 idea, at least three practice periods are **r.**,
W-pI..... 20.1:2 them, minimal effort has been **r.**, and not
W-pI..... 23.6:1 periods are **r.** in applying today's idea. As
W-pI..... 25.6:1 each of two-minutes duration, are **r.**. Each
W-pI..... 26.5:1 periods are **r.** in applying today's idea. A
W-pI..... 32.4:1 recommended, with not less than three **r.**.
W-pI..... 34.2:1 periods are **r.** for today's exercises. One in
W-pI..... 34.3:1 **r.** for each of the longer practice periods.
W-pI..... 36.2:1 practice periods are **r.** for today. Try to
W-pI..... 40.1:2 No long practice periods are **r.** today, but
W-pI..... 43.4:1 five-minute practice periods are **r.** today,
W-pI..... 64.8:1 forms of shorter practice periods are **r.**.
W-pI..... 94.4:1 Nothing is **r.** of you to reach this goal
W-pI..... 95.7:4 you have already failed to do what is **r.**.
W-pI. 135.21:3 our defenselessness is all that is **r.** for the
W-pI... 165.4:8 Sureness is not **r.** to receive what only
M-9 ............. h CHANGES **R.** IN THE LIFE SITUATION
M-9 ........... 1:1 are **r.** in the *minds* of God's teachers. This
M-22 ......... 2:9 And having done what was **r.**, would God
M-24 ......... 3:3 If a definite stand were **r.** of him, it would
M-24 ......... 5:8 even this much is not **r.** of the beginner.
P-2..........II.1:3 in this, complete consistency is not **r.**, for
P-2....... VII.4:1 one thing and one thing only is **r.**: The

## requirement 6

T-21 .... VII.1:3 the one **r.** that it demands to be believed.
T-25 .... VII.6:1 that you believe against this one **r.**, and
W-pI .... 19.4:1 The **r.** of as much indiscriminateness as
W-pI .... 94.5:1 If you do not meet the **r.** of practicing for
W-pI .... 95.6:2 the ideal **r.** for the most beneficial form of
P-2..........II.8:3 the same **r.** salvation asks of everyone.

## requirements 3

W-pI .... 39.5:2 If you want to exceed the minimum **r.**,
W-pI .... 95.9:1 fail to comply with the **r.** of this course,
W-pI .. 133.3:2 Unless they meet these sound **r.**, they are

## requires 29

T-1 ....... VI.3:1 **r.** correction at its own level before the
T-2 .......... I.2:8 This **r.** God's endowment of the Son with
T-7 .........II.5:7 your inheritance and **r.** no learning at all,
T-7 ..... VI.8:10 This **r.** vigilance only as long as you do
T-12 ........ I.3:2 Holy Spirit's judgment it **r.** no effort at all
T-14 ........X.6:7 do that which **r.** no judgment of your own
T-17 ..... VI.6:1 The goal of truth **r.** faith. Faith is implicit
T-20 ..... III.1:4 Knowledge **r.** no adjustments and, in fact,
T-20 .... VII.1:7 This course **r.** almost nothing of you. It is
T-24 ...... in.2:1 To learn this course **r.** willingness to
T-25 .... VII.7:5 to those who are insane **r.** special choice.
T-27 .......V.7:1 is your healing everything the world **r.**,
T-28 ... IV.10:8 go is all the Healer of God's Son **r.**. He will
T-31 .... VII.5:3 And all this shift **r.** is that you be willing
W-pI .... 16.3:1 salvation **r.** that you also recognize that
W-pI .... 20.3:1 Your decision to see is all that vision **r.**.
W-pI .... 23.5:2 This change **r.**, first, that the cause be
W-pI .... 44.3:4 It **r.** precisely what the untrained mind
WpI... rI.in.5:1 and **r.** only that you be there to embrace
W-pI .... 61.3:1 True humility **r.** that you accept today's
W-pI .... 64.7:2 proficient in the mind discipline that it **r.**.
W-pI .... 93.7:1 Salvation **r.** the acceptance of but one
W-pI .. 136.4:3 plan **r.** that you must forget you made it,
W-pI .. 158.8:2 **r.** but the recognition that the world can
W-pI .. 159.1:2 To give a thing **r.** first you have it in your
M-13 ......... 6:1 may believe this course **r.** sacrifice of all
M-17 ......... 8:4 it **r.** patience and abundant willingness.
M-24 ....... 6:12 This is the sole criterion this course **r.**. No
P-2..........II.2:3 that it hardly **r.** elaboration here. Religion

## requiring 2

W-pI .... 79.4:2 of problems, each **r.** a different answer.
W-pI .. 126.6:2 attack, without **r.** correction in your mind

## requisite 1

M-5 ........II.3:1 is the single **r.** for this shift in perception?

## rescind 1

W-pI .. 129.2:4 It gives but to **r.**, and takes away all things

## rescue 2

T-23 .....II.12:3 a *final* principle of chaos comes to the "**r.**."
W-pII . 296.2:3 the Holy Spirit come to **r.** us from hell,

## resemblance 2

T-3 ...... VII.1:3 Their **r.** lies in their power as foundations
W-pI .... 45.1:5 bears any **r.** to what vision will show you.

## resemble 4

T-1 ....... VI.4:3 not in content, you **r.** your Creator, Who
T-3 .........V.6:6 where you could **r.** your Father only by
T-4 .........II.4:6 they **r.** in many ways how you will one
W-pI .... 45.1:4 real thoughts **r.** your real thoughts in any

**resembles** 4

T-5......... II.9:5 the one choice that r. true creation. I am
T-7......... II.1:1 in this world that r. the Thought of God,
T-14......IV.8:5 felt apart from Him r. it ever so faintly.
T-15....... V.7:3 is nothing in Heaven or earth that it r.,

**resent** 1

M-13..........4:3 an adult r. the giving up of children's toys

**resentment** 3

T-15.....VII.6:2 is actually the root of its bitter r.. For it
W-pI .....20.1:6 and if you give in to r. and opposition.
S-1 ......... V.1:5 All little gods it gladly lays aside, not in r.,

**reservation** 3

T-18....VI.12:4 you join it without r. because you love it,
T-18.....VII.4:1 accept the holy instant without r. unless,
W-pI .....27.2:2 uneasy about the lack of r. involved, add:

**reservations** 3

T-21....... II.2:2 Say only this, but mean it with no r., for
W-pII..284.1:5 accepted as but partly true, with many r..
W-pII..284.1:8 beyond these words today, and past all r.,

**reserve** 4

T-17.........I.3:5 What you r. for yourself, you take away
T-17.........I.5:6 R. not one idea aside from truth, or you
W-pII..233.2:2 will give this day to Him with no r. at all.
W-pII......9.1:3 things without exception and without r..

**reserved** 1

T-1......... II.3:1 Awe should be r. for revelation, to which

**reserves** 1

T-12...VII.13:3 that is what it always r. for you in the end.

**reserving** 2

T-12...VII.12:7 He does, r. no judgment at all for yourself
W-pI ...185.8:6 r. shame and secrecy for others. They are

**resides** 2

W-pII....14.1:5 *I am the Heaven where His Love r.. I am His*
Wfl ........in.4:5 us. In him r. salvation, offered us through

**residual** 1

T-3...........I.1:1 before any r. fear still associated with

**residue** 1

T-5......... V.2:2 the blessed r. is restored and therefore

**resign** 1

T-12....... V.8:3 it? R. now as your own teacher. This

**resignation** 1

T-12....... V.8:4 This r. will not lead to depression. It is

**resist** 6

T-13....... II.1:2 pull is so strong that you cannot r. it. On
T-22....... V.5:4 you is a Force that no illusions can r.. This
T-30... VIII.3:3 that makes them harder to r. than those
W-in ..........9:2 Some of them you may actively r.. None
W-pI .......6.3:1 you r. applying the idea to some upsetting
W-pI ...182.8:2 to you that you will not r. Him longer. In

**resistance** 12

T-30.........I.1:6 if you find r. strong and dedication weak,
W-pI ........9.2:2 with active r. in any number of forms. Yet
W-pI .....13.5:1 You may find it difficult to avoid r., in
W-pI .....13.5:2 Whatever form such r. may take, remind
W-pI .....17.4:1 benefit, even if you experience r..
W-pI .....19.2:4 Despite your initial r. to this idea, you will
W-pI .....44.5:2 may find that you will encounter strong r.
W-pI .....44.9:1 If r. rises in any form, pause long enough
W-pI ...123.1:3 back, and no implacable r. to the truth. A
M-5 ....... II.1:7 it. The r. to recognizing this is enormous,
P-2...........I.2:4 "R." is its way of looking at things; its
P-2...........I.3:1 R. as defined here can be characteristic of

**resistant** 1

T-23....... II.3:6 be more r. to the truth than can another.

**resolution** 14

T-2.......VII.4:4 true r. rests entirely on mastery through
T-3.....VII.4:11 no r. while you believe the one thing that
T-6......V.A.6:7 than take the next step towards its r..
T-25......IX.3:4 the Holy Spirit could see unfairness as a r.
T-25......IX.4:5 It sees a r. as a state in which it is decided
T-26....... II.5:7 solve, or judge that it is one that has no r.,
T-27......IV.1:2 conflict there can be no answer and no r.,
T-27......IV.1:2 for its purpose is to make no r. possible,
W-pI .....24.5:1 that you would like to be met in its r.. The
W-pI .....71.7:2 seems to be a conflict with no r. possible.
W-pI .....96.6:3 What could the r. mean in truth? What
W-pI ...108.1:3 And what is light except the r., born of
M-7 ...........5:1 God's Teacher for r. is always self-doubt.
S-1 ...........I.7:8 specific form of r. for a specific problem

**resolutions** 2

T-17...... III.6:3 only to make His r. complete and perfect,
P-2...........I.3:6 Whatever r. patient and therapist reach

**resolve** 23

T-2.......VII.4:2 Yet any attempt to r. the error through
T-3.......VII.2:1 You cannot r. the authority problem by
T-6....... II.11:8 God. Only the Holy Spirit can r. conflict,
T-6......V.A.1:6 is an attempt to r. conflict by not deciding
T-6......V.A.6:4 to exacerbate conflict rather than r. it,
T-13....... X.4:6 brothers to r. problems that are not there.
T-15...... XI.4:8 try to r. the "conflict" of Heaven and hell
T-16....... II.8:5 let us r. together to accept the joyful
T-16...VII.11:2 to bless everyone and to r. all problems,
T-17...... III.6:1 The ego seeks to "r." its problems, not at
T-17...... VI.7:1 take this aspect elsewhere, and r. it there.
T-25......IX.3:3 it greater, harder to r. and more unfair. It
T-26....... V.2:5 certain purpose and high r. and happy
T-30.........I.3:3 may not r. the problem as you saw it first.
W-pI .....47.1:4 r. them in such a way that only good can
W-pI .....50.4:5 you can r. all seeming difficulties without
W-pI .....74.4:1 area that seems particularly difficult to r.,
W-pI .....90.2:3 *miracle behind this grievance will r. it for me*
W-pI .....96.6:2 Who can r. the senseless conflicts which a
W-pI ...138.7:5 To r. the conflict is to end your life as well
W-pII..290.2:1 *With this r. I come to You, and ask Your*
W-pII..339.1:9 us r. today to ask for what we really want,
W-ep .........1:7 to solve all problems, and r. all doubts.

**resolved** 29

T-2.......VII.6:5 the conflict cannot ultimately be r. until
T-5......... V.7:9 dilemma cannot be r. except by accepting
T-16.... III.4:10 only be r. by separating yourself from the
T-25...... IX.3:3 loss to anyone has not r. the problem, but
T-26....... II.6:3 that you think are great and cannot be r..
T-26....... II.7:3 will see each little hurt r. before the Holy
T-26...VII.18:5 and no problem which is not r. within its
T-26....... X.6:4 and there has all unfairness been r. and
T-27......IV.1:1 answered, and is every problem quietly r..
T-27......IV.1:7 be a way in which your problems are r.,
T-27......IV.2:7 a problem must be simple and be easily r.
T-27...... IV.2:9 be. Yet just as surely it must be r., if it is
T-27...... IV.3:2 there the problem *will* be answered and r..
T-27..... VII.2:6 problem be r. if it is seen as hurting him,
W-pI .....79.5:4 as you think you have r. the previous ones
W-pI .....79.6:1 problem, and therefore not to let it be r..
W-pI .....79.9:4 In this recognition are all problems r.. In
W-pI .....80.3:2 that has been r. cannot trouble you. Only
W-pI .....90.2:2 *a problem to me which I would have r.. The*
W-pI .....90.4:2 *I need not wait for this to be r.. The answer to*
W-pI .....96.3:1 be r. within the framework they are set.
W-pI .....96.3:2 Two selves in conflict could not be r., and
W-pI ...138.6:4 you solve this one, the others are r. with it
W-pI ...138.7:3 In death alone are opposites r., for ending
W-pI ...160.5:1 How simply, then, the question is r..
W-pII .286.1:5 *In You has every conflict been r.. In You is*
W-pII .296.1:2 *me. I am r. to let You speak through me, for I*
W-pII .333.1:1 Conflict must be r.. It cannot be evaded,
M-17 ......... 6:1 can this unfair battle be r.? Its ending is

**resolves** 2

T-7........ VI.3:8 the ego r. this completely insane dilemma
T-7........ VI.6:3 He r. the apparent conflict they engender

**resolving** 3

T-26........II.1:2 greater difficulty in r. some than others.
W-pI .....65.7:1 you by r. your conflicts once and for all,
M-16 .........7:5 no order of difficulty in r. them. He is as

**resort** 1

C-in ...........3:6 to r. to inventiveness or ingenuity. These

**resound** 2

T-28.......I.13:4 of eternity r. throughout the stillness, yet
W-pI ...106.6:4 will r. throughout the world through you.

**Resource** 1

T-12....... V.5:3 becomes your R. because of yourself you

**resources** 1

T-12....... V.5:2 Who can transcend your limited r.. He

**respect** 20

T-1.........II.3:7 is entitled to r. for his greater experience,
T-1......... III.5:7 Atonement undoes all errors in this r.,
T-2........ VI.8:1 a sign of r. *from* the worthy *to* the worthy.
T-2...... VI.9:12 of it, but you are hardly likely to r. it.
T-2....... VII.2:4 The miracle worker must have genuine r.
T-2..... VII.5:11 all compromise in this r. can be given up.
T-4........ III.7:7 complete r. for what you have made, but I
T-4........ III.9:6 Any distinction in this r. is meaningful
T-7...........I.1:5 only in this r. your creative power differs
T-19.........I.6:7 with truth, in any r. or in any way.
T-19...... III.2:4 of sin, treating it with r. and honoring its
T-25........II.2:2 you see? In no r., at any time or place, has
T-25........II.2:3 chance of change in this r. is hardly worth
T-26........II.1:3 same r. and through the same approach.
W-pI .....45.1:4 resemble your real thoughts in any r..
W-pI .....47.6:2 strength is fully justified in every r. and in
M-4 ........... 1:7 own learning. In this r. they are all alike.
M-5 ........II.4:4 and effect in their true sequence in one r.,
M-16 ......... 5:5 have come to some conclusions in this r..
P-3..........II.9:7 compromise in this r. are strange indeed.

**respectable** 1

P-2........ IV.4:1 the more "r." therapists of the world, and

**respectfully** 1

T19. IV.A.11:2 and laying them r. before their lord and

**respecting** 1

T-18......VI.4:8 r. what the Son of God has made and

**respective** 2

T-18....VI.12:1 you join; of your r. positions in space; and
P-2.........in.3:2 but their r. perceptions of "improvement

**respects** 9

T-6...........I.8:7 has chosen to save them pain in all r.,
T-6......V.B.3:9 This is the real reason why, in many r.,
T-7......... II.5:2 meaning in all r. and in all languages.
T-9........IV.5:6 out all its effects, everywhere and in all r.,
T-10......IV.3:2 Sonship is One, it is One in all r.. Oneness
T-11.......in.1:4 are diametrically opposed in all r. so that
T-16.....VII.7:1 the complete difference, in all r., between
T-24......VI.4:5 is given you to be beyond its laws in all r.,
T-30....VIII.5:3 you would have it otherwise in some r..

**respite** 5

W-pI...109.5:5 Let these periods of rest and r. reassure
W-pI...121.2:2 the hope of r. and release from pain. It
W-pI...182.5:4 ask for more than just a few instants of r.;
M-4 .....I.A.6:9 The teacher of God needs this period of r.
S-3......... II.6:2 and there can be brief r. as it waits to take

**respond** 40

T-1........ III.6:1 You r. to what you perceive, and as you
T-4...........I.3:6 creation, your ego cannot but r. with fear.
T-4......... II.4:7 The question is not how you r. to the ego,
T-4.......VII.3:1 true, and does not r. at all to anything else
T-5.........in.1:6 the mind's natural impulse to r. as one.
T-5....... II.12:1 we must r. to the same Mind to do this.
T-5......... V.3:6 you r. to your ego you will experience
T-5.......VII.6:6 will r. fully to your slightest invitation: *I*
T-6...........I.4:7 If you r. with anger, you must be equating
T-6...........I.19:3 need in them, and do not r. to any other,
T-7......... II.2:9 because you can r. to two conflicting
T-8........ III.5:9 are. He will r. either with pain or with joy,
T-9.......VII.4:4 especially when you r. to the Holy Spirit,
T-12.........I.1:4 that you do not r. to anything directly,
T-12.........I.1:7 you will r. as if he had actually done so,
T-12......IV.3:2 in love's presence, for it could not r. at all.
T-13.... III.11:3 the gentleness of love r. to his demands,
T-14.... III.10:2 who believe they are guilty will r. to guilt,
T-14......X.7:6 not r. to what a brother really offers you,
T-14.......XI.6:8 *And so I do not know how to r. to it. And I will*
T-15....VIII.5:3 The Holy Spirit asks you to r. as God does
T-15....VIII.5:4 God would r. to every need, whatever
T-16.........I.4:6 how to r. to what you do not understand.
T-18....... II.5:4 You do not r. to it as though you made it,
T-23....... II.6:2 He must believe; and how He must r.,
T-23..... II.10:3 enemy, they would r. with only kindness.
T-30......VI.2:5 it merely asks that you r. appropriately to
T-31....... II.1:4 against the truth, but truth does not r..
W-pI.....66.2:4 ego attacks and the Holy Spirit does not r.
W-pI...71.10:2 r. to them with this form of today's idea:
W-pI.....94.5:5 And be sure to r. to anyone who seems to
W-pI.....98.9:4 He will r. with all His faith and joy and
W-pI.135.10:1 body will r. with health when they have
W-pI...183.8:5 And to all other thoughts r. with this, and
W-pI...194.8:3 creature not r. with healed perception?
W-pII .335.1:4 It is to this alone that I r., however much I
M-17 .........2:1 to r. to magic in a way that reinforces it.
M-29 .........6:3 attractive to you, He will r. with evil?
S-2 ......... II.4:4 r. except with silence and a gentle smile?
S-2 ........ III.2:7 His task, and it is He Who will r. for you.

**responded** 2

M-17 .........3:6 then is easily r. to with just one answer,
M-17 .........9:8 see you have r. to your own interpretation

**responding** 9

T-2........IV.2:5 wrongly only when it is r. to misthought.
T-2 ...V.A.13:2 R. to any form of error with anything
T-5 ........in.1:7 others of the joy of r. wholeheartedly.
T-6 ...V.B.3:10 and r. primarily to the ego in others, you
T-12 ........I.3:5 anyone be justified in r. with anger to a
T-13 ..... IV.5:3 ego tries to preserve its image by r. as if it
T-17 ...VIII.4:1 the strain of not r. to His Call seems to be
T-30 ..... VI.1:9 that, by r. in a way which is not justified,
W-pI ....357.h we make to God, R. first with miracles,

**responds** 6

T-4 ......VII.2:7 all. It merely r. in certain specific ways to
T-7 ....... IX.1:6 and it r. as if it were being sided against.
W-pI... 183.3:1 all the world r. by laying down illusions.
M-18 .........4:2 of irritation in himself as he r. to anyone,
M-29 ......... 6:7 And He r. with help accordingly. God
S-3........ IV.2:2 world r. in quickened chorus through the

**response** 48

T-4 .........II.3:5 the past? Surprise is a reasonable r. to the
T-4 ..... III.7:10 will come in r. to a single unequivocal call
T-7 ...... VII.2:7 Every r. you make is determined by what
T-7 ...... VII.2:8 then, must determine every r. you make.
T-8 ..........I.3:1 Every r. to the ego is a call to war, and
T-8 .........II.8:6 This is the natural r. of every Son of God
T-9 .........II.3:2 been asked for anything will ensure a r..
T-9 .........II.3:3 Yet it is equally certain that no r. given by
T-10 ......in.2:7 you. Every r. you make to everything you
T-12 ........I.1:5 thus becomes the justification for the r..
T-12 ........I.3:6 help? No r. can be appropriate except the
T-12 .......I.3:10 Your r. will therefore be inappropriate to
T-12 ........I.6:1 appreciation is an appropriate r. to your
T-12 ........I.6:5 There is but one r. to reality, for reality
T-12 ..... III.2:3 and experience a quick r. of opposition,
T-12 ..... III.5:3 r. other than love arises from a confusion
T-12 ..... IV.3:3 that it had not taught you the r. you need.
T-13 ..... III.3:3 joyous r. to the call of love if you heard it,
T-13 .... VII.9:8 glad r. is your awakening to what you
T-13 ..... XI.3:9 is clear and bright, and calls forth one r..
T-14 ..... IX.8:1 The r. of holiness to any form of error is
T-14 ..... IX.8:3 Its one r. is healing, without regard for
T-14 .......X.6:3 exactly the same r. to every call for help. It
T-16 ........I.3:8 and to determine your r. *by* judging it.
T-17 ..... IV.4:3 in r. to the gift with which God blessed it,
T-21 ....... V.3:5 They are the obvious r. to calls for help,
T-26 ........X.1:3 you think that a r. of anger now is just.
T-27 ..... IV.5:7 does not set conditions for r., but merely
T-27 ..... IV.5:7 but merely asks what the r. should be. But
T-29 ..... IV.3:1 said attack is a r. to function unfulfilled as
T-30 ........I.2:4 where you will be called upon to make r..
T-30 .... VI.2:8 Forgiveness is the only sane r.. It *keeps*
T-31 ..... III.1:3 It must become a habit of r. so typical of
T-31 ..... III.1:3 it becomes your first r. to all temptation,
T-31 ...VIII.5:1 the happy habit of r. to all temptation to
W-pI.....31.5:1 to use as a r. to any form of temptation
W-pI...76.12:1 hour, as well as in r. to any temptation to
W-pI.....95.5:3 the idea as an automatic r. to temptation.
W-pI. 136.17:4 No r. at all is in the mind to what the
W-pI... 152.5:2 the mind; in all awareness and in all r..
W-pI... 161.5:3 Fear without symbols calls for no r., for
W-pI... 167.2:5 to which you give r. of any kind that is not
W-pI... 183.2:1 God's Name can not be heard without r.,
W-pI... 184.8:6 His body makes r. to what you call him,
W-pI... 189.8:4 will do His part in joyful and immediate r.
W-pI... 199.6:5 conflict-free and unequivocal r. to mind
M-17 ......... 5:1 Anger in r. to perceived magic thoughts
M-18 ......... 4:3 and let Him judge what the r. should be.

**responses** 4

T-5 ........in.1:7 forth different kinds of r. at the same time
T-9 ....... IV.7:6 It is unpredictable in its r., because it has
T-12 ..... IV.3:4 really calls forth the r. the ego *can* teach.
T-30 ..... VI.2:4 r. which are inappropriate to what is real.

**responsibility** 28

T-2 ........ V.5:1 *The sole r. of the miracle worker is to accept*
T-2 ....... VI.4:1 The correction of fear *is* your r.. When
T-5 .........V.7:7 recognizing that, by accepting this r., they
T-5 .........V.7:8 If the sole r. of the miracle worker is to
T-5 .........V.7:8 r. for *what* is atoned for cannot be yours.
T-6 ........ in.1:2 ultimately be accepted as one's own r.,
T-6 ........ in.2:3 r. you inevitably assume the moment you
T-7 .....VIII.5:3 the r. for your belief in it onto anyone else
T-7 .....VIII.5:4 When you are willing to accept sole r. for
T-7 .....VIII.5:4 attempt to project r. for your own errors.
T-8 ..... III.5:11 Never forget your r. to him, because it is
T-8 ..... III.5:11 to him, because it is your r. to yourself.
T-8 ....... III.6:5 This is your r., because once you have
T-10 ...... in.1:4 in the world can take this r. from you.
T-14 ... III.17:7 the sole r. for deciding what can bring
T-15 ..... III.3:1 There is a deep r. you owe yourself, and
T-18 .... VII.1:5 goal. You have thus not met your *one* r..
T-21 ..........II.h The R. for Sight
T-25 ..... IX.9:6 That is why your sole r. must be to take
W-pI .... 19.2:2 to carry with it an enormous sense of r.,
W-pI .. 196.7:1 and the r. returned to some extent to you.
M-5 ........II.3:5 recognition is r. placed where it belongs;
M-7 ........... 3:2 that the one r. of the miracle worker is to
M-17 ......... 1:5 His first r. in this is not to attack it. If a
M-18 ......... 4:5 The sole r. of God's teacher is to accept
M-24 ......... 6:2 This is still your one r.. Atonement might
M-29 ......... 2:8 The r. is His, and He alone is fit to assume
P-2...... IV.10:1 then, has a tremendous r.. He must meet

**responsible** 25

T-2 ....... VI.1:7 and makes you feel personally r. for them.
T-2 ....... VI.2:5 believe that you are r. for what you do,
T-2 ....... VI.2:6 truth is that you are r. for what you think,
T-2 ....... VI.3:3 That is why you feel r. for it. You must
T-3 ..........I.3:9 This kind of error is r. for a host of related
T-4 ........I.13:2 elder brother who has shown himself r.,
T-5 .........V.7:7 This makes them feel r. for their errors
T-5 .........V.7:10 *would* be r. for the effects of all your wrong
T-6 ........ in.1:3 return, and that you are in no way r. for it
T-6 ........ in.1:7 and you *are* r. for what you believe.
T-7 ...... VII.9:1 mind that does not believe it is r. for itself
T-17 ...VIII.5:5 and you are now fully r. to him. Fail him
T-21 .......II.2:3 *I am r. for what I see. I choose the feelings I*
T-21 ..... VI.7:5 You *are* r. for how he sees himself. And
T-27 .... VII.1:4 for which he has no reason to be held r..
T-28 ..... VI.2:1 to hold r. for sight a thing that cannot see,
W-pI .... 72.5:9 onto God, and holding Him r. for it.
M-5 .........I.2:5 If he is healed, he is r. for his thoughts.
M-5 .........I.2:6 And if he is r. for his thoughts, he will be
M-8 ......... 3:10 and so only the mind is r. for seeing. It
M-12 ......... 5:7 as it makes all decisions that are r. for the
M-24 ......... 2:2 If it were r. for some of the difficulties the
M-29 ....... 2:11 Would you want to be r. for decisions
P-2....... VII.4:4 and was therefore r. for its outcome. His
P-2....... VII.5:3 experience the end of guilt who feels r. for

**rest** 134

- peace, repose
  *remainder*
  *other*

T-3 ..... IV.7:15 now, and they will find r. unto their souls.
T-5 .......II.10:4 R. does not come from sleeping but from
T-7 ...... VII.6:4 R. in His Love and protect your rest by
T-7 ...... VII.6:4 in His Love and protect your r. by loving.
T-8 ....... IX.3:5 "R. in peace" is a blessing for the living,
T-8 ....... IX.3:5 the dead, because r. comes from waking,
T-8 ....... IX.4:9 r. in peace only because you are awake.
T-11 .......II.6:1 will never r. until you know your function
T-11 ..... III.1:2 Comforter will r. you, but you cannot.
T-11 ..... IV.8:4 Peace be unto you who r. in God, and in
T-14 .....V.11:2 circle of purity, you will r. there with him.
T-18 .... VII.7:7 To do nothing is to r., and make a place
T-18 .... VII.8:1 be this place of r. to which you can return.
T-18 .... VII.8:3 giving you r. in the midst of every busy
T-18 ... VIII.9:3 offering r. to those who lost their way and
T-19 ... III.11:3 where all the weary ones can come and r..
T-19 ... III.11:4 Here is the r. that waits for all, after the
T-19 ..... IV.1:1 to embrace all the Sonship and give it r., it

T-19......IV.1:9 And you will draw him in and give him **r.**,
T-19......IV.2:4 a resting place where you will **r.** in Him.
T19... IV.A.1:6 who calls, and bring him **r.** by joining you
T19.IV.D.19:5 Here is the **r.** and quiet that you seek, the
T-20......IV.6:8 How can he enter, to **r.** and to remember,
T-20......IV.7:3 hands of every two who enter here to **r.**.
T-20......IV.7:4 And as they **r.**, the face of Christ shines on
T-20......IV.7:5 achieved that you will **r.** without them?
T-21.....VII.4:5 another, and never comes to **r.** in victory.
T-24...... III.6:6 it is you **r.** forever in the arms of peace, in
T-24...... III.6:6 one thought of specialness to mar your **r.**.
T-24.....VI.13:7 for effortless accomplishment and **r.**.
T-25......IV.3:1 so, take **r.** and comfort in another world
T-25......IV.3:3 From you can come their **r.**. From you can
T-25......IV.4:8 And from you will the **r.** you found extend
T-25...VII.12:4 **r.** in perfect confidence and perfect peace.
T-26.........I.6:3 the **r.** his witness offers on behalf of peace.
T-27..... II.15:5 you can **r.** assured that He will not fulfill a
T-27....... V.5:5 A dying world asks only that you **r.** an
T-27...VII.14:3 **R.** in the Holy Spirit, and allow His gentle
T-30.... III.10:5 changelessness and of its **r.** in its eternal
T-31...... VI.6:8 trust; a happy place to **r.** in for a while,
T-31... VIII.9:5 in vain, and in His certainty I **r.** content.
W-pI.....49.2:1 is calm, always at **r.** and wholly certain. It
W-pI.....92.9:3 place we try today to find and **r.** in, for the
W-pI.....98.3:3 They **r.** in quiet certainty that they will do
W-pI...102.3:5 no fear. Here is salvation. Here is **r.** at last.
W-pI...107.3:1 mind will **r.** in when the truth has come.
W-pI...107.9:5 *my mind, And I will* **r.** *in Him Who is my Self.*
W-pI......109.h I **r.** in God.
W-pI...109.1:1 ask for **r.** today, and quietness unshaken
W-pI...109.2:1 "I **r.** in God." This thought will bring to
W-pI...109.2:2 thought will bring to you the **r.** and quiet,
W-pI...109.2:3 "I **r.** in God." This thought has power to
W-pI...109.3:1 "I **r.** in God." Completely undismayed,
W-pI...109.3:5 truth before the eyes of you who **r.** in God
W-pI...109.4:2 You **r.** in God, and while the world is torn
W-pI...109.4:2 your **r.** remains completely undisturbed.
W-pI...109.4:3 Yours is the **r.** of truth. Appearances
W-pI...109.4:5 You call to all to join you in your **r.**, and
W-pI...109.4:5 and come to you because you **r.** in God.
W-pI...109.4:6 you **r.** in Him and let Him speak through
W-pI...109.5:2 In timelessness you **r.**, while time goes by
W-pI...109.5:2 your **r.** can never change in any way at all.
W-pI...109.5:3 You **r.** today. And as you close your eyes,
W-pI...109.5:5 Let these periods of **r.** and respite reassure
W-pI...109.5:7 dreams will come, now that you **r.** in God.
W-pI...109.6:1 Each hour that you take your **r.** today, a
W-pI...109.6:2 The world is born again each time you **r.**,
W-pI...109.6:2 that it might take its **r.** along with you.
W-pI...109.7:1 With each five minutes that you **r.** today,
W-pI...109.7:2 time when **r.** will be the only thing there is
W-pI...109.8:1 You **r.** within the peace of God today,
W-pI...109.8:1 from your **r.** to draw them to their rest,
W-pI...109.8:1 from your rest to draw them to their **r.**,
W-pI...109.8:2 peace, the holy sanctuary where you **r.**.
W-pI...109.8:3 bid them all enter here and **r.** with you.
W-pI...109.9:1 You **r.** within the peace of God today,
W-pI...109.9:2 Each brother comes to take his **r.**, and
W-pI...109.9:3 We **r.** together here, for thus our rest is
W-pI...109.9:3 here, for thus our **r.** is made complete,
W-pI...109.9:5 Thoughts were born and where they **r.**.
W-pI...109.9:6 each time we tell ourselves, "I **r.** in God."
WpIrIII.in10:5 your mind to **r.** a little time in silence and
W-pI...120.1:1 (109) I **r.** in God. *I rest in God today, and*
W-pI...120.1:2 *I* **r.** *in God today, and let Him work in me and*
W-pI...120.1:2 *I* **r.** *in Him in quiet and in perfect certainty.*
W-pI...120.3:2 I **r.** in God. On the half hour: I am as God
W-pI...122.1:6 and a **r.** so perfect it can never be upset?
W-pI...127.8:2 Open your mind and **r.**. The world that
W-pI...128.6:5 Let it **r.** in its Creator, there to be restored
W-pI...128.7:1 Give it ten minutes **r.** three times today.
W-pI...128.7:5 to **r.** when you release it from the world.
W-pI...128.7:8 Open your mind to Him. Be still and **r.**.
W-pI...129.8:1 as you **r.** beyond the world of darkness.
W-pI.132.15:4 Then merely **r.**, alert but with no strain,
W-pI.135.22:1 twice today we **r.** from senseless planning,
W-pI.137.11:3 a haven where the weary can remain to **r.**.
W-pI.137.15:2 And as you **r.** in quiet, be prepared to give
WpI. rIV.in9:2 more than this to give us happiness and **r.**
W-pI.153.10:1 holy is your purpose, how secure you **r.**,
W-pI...157.4:3 let it **r.** in still anticipation and in quiet joy
W-pI...162.3:2 His dreams are happy and his **r.** secure,
W-pI...163.4:4 laid to **r.** beneath the headstone death has
W-pI...164.4:5 that here your treasure is, and here your **r.**
W-pI...165.3:1 healing and his peace of mind, his quiet **r.**
W-pI...170.5:2 and hope of **r.** in dreamless quiet. And as
WpI rV.in12:6 of meaning. It is Here that we find **r.**.
W-pI...182.5:3 voice cries unto you to let Him **r.** a while.
W-pI...182.9:1 **R.** with Him frequently today. For He was
W-pI...189.9:3 And with this choice we **r.**. And in our
W-pI.191.10:8 willing to bring your weary brothers **r.**?
W-pI...193.9:3 his holy **r.** remain untroubled and serene,
W-pI...194.9:2 For in God's Hands we **r.** untroubled, sure
W-pI...194.9:5 Who guards our **r.** to make the choice for
W-pI...195.7:1 against our shoulders as they **r.** a while.
W-pII.....in.3:1 that thought to introduce our times of **r.**,
W-pII.....in.7:8 You, and **r.** in confidence upon Your Love
W-pII..222.2:1 *now, and ask to* **r.** *with You in peace a while.*
W-pII......3.5:1 Let us not **r.** content until the world has
W-pII..249.2:3 *death. Now would we* **r.** *again in You, as You*
W-pII..262.2:2 We would come home, and **r.** in unity.
W-pII..286.1:8 *My heart is quiet, and my mind at* **r.**. *Your*
W-pII......8.2:3 Nothing but **r.** is there. There are no cries
W-pII......9.5:1 will be soon, but do not **r.** with that. It
W-pII..325.1:6 he can **r.** a while before he journeys on,
W-pII..345.2:3 It will find **r.** today, for we will offer what
M-4 ....... II.2:6 trust on which God's teachers **r.** secure
M-16 .........5:7 It sets your mind into a pattern of **r.**, and
M-27 .........3:4 he is "laid to **r.**" in devastation's arms,
C-2.............8:2 as a loving mother sings her child to **r.**. Is
C-5.............5:9 For he will set your mind at **r.** at last and
S-1......... V.3:1 kind, and you can **r.** in holiness at last.
S-2........ III.7:3 **R.** a while in this; do not attempt to judge
S-3......... II.3:3 which death comes when it is time to **r.** a
S-3......... II.4:3 Now are its dreams dispelled in quiet **r.**.

**rest** 76
• remainder
*peace, repose*
*other*

T-5......IV.3:10 **r.** remains with you until the Holy Spirit
T-8........ IX.2:8 The **r.** is of itself. You need do so little
T-11....... II.3:2 **r.** will seem to be separate and therefore
T-14...... VI.7:4 dropping off the **r.** and offering your true
T-17...... III.1:2 All the **r.** must be forgotten. Forgiveness
T-17...... III.8:4 alliance are retained, and all the **r.** let go.
T-18... VIII.6:3 ruled by an idea of separation from the **r.**.
T-18... VIII.6:4 it, preventing it from joining with the **r.**,
T-18...... IX.1:4 The **r.** is fully in God's keeping, and needs
T-19...... III.6:2 what is part of Him is totally unlike the **r.**.
T-20......IV.6:2 the **r.** will see to it without your help. But
T-20......IV.6:3 not need your part to help Him with the **r.**
T-20......IV.7:4 forgetting all the **r.** and yearning only to
T-20......VI.4:6 The **r.** it merely throws away, for all that it
T-21.....VII.6:5 still seems to hold a threat the **r.** have lost
T-21...VII.11:5 you have already made to all the **r.**. For
T-21...VII.11:7 do not want, the **r.** are wholly answered.
T-21... VIII.2:8 see the final question is necessary to the **r.**
T-23..... II.22:2 will not recognize the **r.** for what they are.
T-23...... III.3:2 you want; to take a little and give up the **r.**
T-24.... VI.10:3 part of God holds not for all the **r.**. You
T-25...... III.1:5 The **r.** but stems from this, to hold it up
T-25...VII.3:12 make. The **r.** is up to God, and not to you.
T-25... VIII.4:7 The **r.** is taken from another, to be laid
T-26.........I.1:6 see a little part of him and sacrifice the **r.**.
T-26.........I.3:1 preserved through sacrifice of all the **r.**.
T-26.........I.3:2 And all the **r.** must lose this little part,
T-26....... II.3:4 makes each one seem different from the **r.**
T-26......IV.4:4 him of his Father's Love as surely as the **r.**.
T-26...... VI.1:7 one illusion real, and still escape the **r.**.
T-26.....VII.6:1 be less amenable to truth than are the **r.**.
T-27..........I.7:1 that bolsters all the **r.** and helps them
T-27..... V.10:2 you to yourself, and He will do the **r.**. And
T-27..... V.10:5 a problem that is different from the **r.**. Yet
T-27...... VI.3:5 real, for any one you choose is like the **r.**.
T-27. VIII.12:1 Who knows that every one is like the **r.**.
T-27..VIII.12:3 None has a different cause from all the **r.**,
T-28...... III.9:2 the more is left for all the **r.** to share. The
T-28...... VI.4:1 own and all the **r.** of what is really yours.
T-29.........I.3:3 The **r.** are past, but this one still remains
T-29..... VII.2:3 off and found where all the **r.** of it is not.
T-30.........I.1:3 to form which sees you through the **r.**. It
T-31... VII.10:3 himself, and thus is he a savior to the **r.**.
W-pI..... 12.3:5 occur to you, use them along with the **r.**.
W-pI..... 61.6:3 practice periods may be longer than the **r.**
W-pI..... 65.7:1 and devote the **r.** of the practice period to
W-pI..... 71.9:6 *whom?* Give Him full charge of the **r.** of the
W-pI... 73.10:5 Put the **r.** of the practice period under
W-pI... 91.10:1 Relax for the **r.** of the practice period,
W-pI..... 93.8:4 and spend the **r.** of the practice period in
W-pI..... 98.9:1 Give Him the words, and He will do the **r.**
W-pI..... 99.8:1 This part belongs to God, as does the **r.**.
W-pI..... 99.9:1 shine through them to join them to the **r.**.
W-pI... 124.8:7 Him this half an hour. He will do the **r.**.
W-pI... 134.4:3 is forgiveness really but a sin, like all the **r.**
W-pI... 136.2:3 And like all the **r.**, its purpose is to hide
W-pI... 137.2:2 seems to keep one self apart from all the **r.**
W-pI... 138.6:2 most definitive and prototype of all the **r.**,
W-pI... 138.6:3 you could decide the **r.**, this one remains
WpI. rIV.in5:2 alone engage it fully, and remove the **r.**:
W-pI. 155.10:6 with you. Let Him lead you with the **r.**.
W-pI. 161.11:1 Select one brother, symbol of the **r.**, and
W-pI... 163.6:1 yet avoid, while still believing in the **r.**.
W-pI. 169.11:4 your part is still what all the **r.** depends on
Wi181-200 3:6 be enough to guarantee the **r.** will come.
W-pI... 185.5:6 the same despair and misery as do the **r.**.
W-pI... 185.7:5 can succeed where all the **r.** have failed.
W-pI. 198.2:10 is illusion that is answer to the **r.**.
W-pII ..... 6.3:3 The **r.** is dreams. Yet will these dreams be
W-pII ..... 8.1:1 like the **r.** of what perception offers. Yet it
W-pII . 318.1:3 one of more or less importance than the **r.**
W-pII . 328.1:2 and that our independence from the **r.** of
M-19 .........5:6 as separate and apart from all the **r.**. From
M-22 .........2:9 was required, would God withhold the **r.**?
M-29 ............h AS FOR THE **R.** ...
S-1...........I.3:5 song. All the **r.** is merely added. You have

**rest** 36
• other
*peace, repose*
*remainder*

T-1....... VII.4:3 Some of the later parts of the course **r.** too
T-2.... V.A.12:2 is essential. All forms of healing **r.** on this
T-4....... VII.4:1 as well as being **r.** on communication.
T-9........ IV.1:3 and do not let your perception **r.** upon it,
T-13...... III.6:1 they do not **r.** on their own foundation. In
T-13...... III.6:3 illusion on which the others **r.**. For
T-13........X.2:2 No real relationship can **r.** on guilt, or
T-15...... IV.2:1 Your practice must therefore **r.** upon
T-18...... IX.6:5 Nothing can **r.** upon it, for it is but an
T-20...... VI.1:2 were elsewhere it would **r.** on contingency
T-22....... III.6:5 eyes **r.** on externals and cannot go beyond
T-23......II.13:4 laws on which your "sanity" appears to **r.**.
T-25... VII.4:10 the changeless if it does not **r.** on truth?
T-25...... VII.6:5 the madness and **r.** peacefully on truth.
T-26........II.6:8 call forth will **r.** on you as surely as on him
T-27...... VII.4:4 condemnation of the world will **r.** on him.
T-27.... VIII.8:2 because you *want* the guilt to **r.** on them.
T-27..VIII.13:3 nor does your guiltlessness **r.** on its sins.
T-29...... III.5:6 and be sure his waking eyes will **r.** on you.
W-pI..... 15.4:1 and letting your eyes **r.** on it as you say:
W-pI..... 25.6:2 **r.** on whatever happens to catch your eye,
W-pI..... 28.8:1 you should **r.** your eyes on it while saying:
W-pI... 126.5:1 on which to **r.** dependably and sure. It is
W-pI... 133.8:1 is the one on which the others **r.**. Why is
W-pI... 134.1:2 course appear to **r.** salvation on a whim.
W-pI... 138.5:6 for they **r.** on what you have accepted as
W-pI... 186.8:2 all illusions **r.** upon the weird belief that
W-pI. 186.10:5 What hope of gain can **r.** on goals like this
W-pII . 238.1:3 *in my hands, and let it* **r.** *on my decision. I*
W-pII ..... 7.4:1 to let forgiveness **r.** upon your dreams,
W-pII . 295.2:2 *upon, that His forgiving Love may* **r.** *on me.*
W-pII ..... 9.1:3 the willingness to let forgiveness **r.** upon
W-pII . 334.1:2 of thoughts that **r.** on false perceptions.

W-pII ....342.h I let forgiveness r. upon all things, For
M-4 ....... II.1:1 other traits of God's teachers r. on trust.
S-3 ........ IV.2:5 of prayer r. on the earth an instant, as the

## restate 2

T-5....... II.11:4 Let us r. "My yoke is easy and my burden
T-27...... IV.3:8 answered, but only to r. its point of view.

## restatement 2

T-9......... II.6:2 Prayer is the r. of inclusion, directed by
WpIrIII.in12:1 with a r. of the thought to use each hour,

## restatements 1

T-2........ IV.4:1 for bodily ills are r. of magic principles.

## rested 1

• peace, repose
*other*

T-17....... II.7:2 knows that he has always r. there in peace

## rested 4

• other
*peace, repose*

T-11.....in.3:10 you will see that it r. on meaninglessness,
W-pI... 126.5:5 indeed, if your salvation r. on a whim?
W-pII ... 13.4:2 to show that what it r. on is really there.
W-pII ... 13.4:3 and show it r. on a world more real than

## restful 2

T-14...... IV.6:7 tired will find this is more r. than sleep.
W-pI..... 32.4:2 can be utilized, if you find the exercise r..

## restfulness 1

W-pI...29.5:11 experience a sense of r. as you do this.

## resting 11

• peace, repose
*other*

T-19...... IV.2:4 Him a r. place where you will rest in Him.
T19..IV.C.10:7 gave a r. place by your forgiveness of your
T-20.... VI.10:5 behind and r. in the Everlasting Arms.
T-23....... I.11:1 How can the r. place of God turn on itself
T-26...... IX.6:4 Them, to be Their r. place as well as yours
T-29....... V.1:3 There is a r. place so still no sound except
W-pI..... 50.5:5 Such is the r. place where your Father has
W-pI... 109.9:6 of their r. place each time we tell ourselves
W-pI... 165.2:6 makes soft your r. place and smooth your
W-pI... 182.5:7 home, r. in silence and in peace and love.
P-3........ III.6:4 the r. place of Christ and home of God

## resting 7

• other
*peace,repose*

T-24...... III.4:3 No, His Son is safe, r. on Him. It is your
T-28..... VII.7:5 r. on God's promise that His Son is safe
T-29...... IX.2:7 hold the judgment off from r. on himself.
W-pI..... 17.2:3 r. your glance on each thing you note long
W-pI..... 25.6:3 your eyes r. on each subject you so select,
W-pI..... 69.6:4 feel them r. on your cheeks and forehead
M-4 ...... IX.1:5 his faithfulness begins by r. on just some

## restitution 2

W-pI... 137.5:3 healing but offers r. for imagined states
W-pI. 186.13:3 sorrow. He would make a r., though He is

## restless 3

T-13... VII.15:3 what you will as surely keep, and be not r.
W-pI... 182.3:3 he makes, yet none contents his r. mind.
W-pI... 182.8:1 ideas cease to have value in your r. mind,

## restoration 9

T-1 .... VII.3:14 Complete r. of the Sonship is the only
T-2 ....... III.2:3 must be undone for the r. of the temple,
T-5 .......... I.5:4 or the r. of the integrity of the mind.
T-11 ..... IV.7:1 Christ waits for the r. of Himself in you.
T-12 ...... V.2:1 is so important to the r. of your sanity.
T-14 ..... VI.5:7 Him how to apply it to the holy cause of r.
W-pI..... 43.2:4 it must become the means for the r. of his
W-pII . 323.1:2 *the only "cost" of r. of Your memory to me,*
P-3...... III.8:10 the plan of God for the r. of joy and peace

## restorative 1

T-30 ........ I.5:5 you need a quick r. before you ask again.

## restore 51

T-1 ........ I.33:4 of your illusions, they r. your sanity.
T-1 ........ I.34:1 Miracles r. the mind to its fullness. By
T-1 ....... IV.3:6 the Atonement is to r. everything to you;
T-1 ....... IV.3:6 you; or rather, to r. it to your awareness.
T-2 ........ V.3:4 its purpose is to r. him *to* his right mind. It
T-2 ........ V.5:6 and r. the mind to its true position as the
T-2 ..... VIII.3:4 the aim of the Last Judgment is to r. right-
T-5 ....... II.10:9 part of the Kingdom than to r. it to the
T-8 ......... II.8:1 Holy Spirit appeal to r. God's Kingdom?
T-8 ........ V.3:2 To join with me is to r. His power to you
T-8 ..... VIII.8:8 of choice, which the Holy Spirit seeks to r.
T-10 ....... II.3:1 remember is merely to r. to your mind
T-11 ........ I.1:5 the mind of God's Son you r. this reality,
T-11 ........ I.1:5 restore this reality, you r. it to yourself.
T-11 ... VIII.2:4 will r. to you what you have thrown away.
T-11 ... VIII.6:4 the Holy Spirit, Who wills only to r., be
T-13 ..... III.2:2 instantly r. you to your proper place, and
T-13 .. VII.16:4 We will r. to you the peace of mind that
T-13 ..... X.10:8 which the Holy Spirit would r. to you. He
T-13 ..... XI.7:4 The Holy Spirit will r. your sanity because
T-14 ..... IV.3:5 to r. what always was to your unforgiving
T-14 ...... V.7:4 to r. what is the right of God's creation.
T-14 .... V.9:10 R. to God His Son as He created him, by
T-14 .... V.10:5 Yet you r. guiltlessness to whomever you
T-14 .. V.10:10 The temple you r. becomes your altar, for
T-14 .. V.10:12 Thus He creates, and thus must you r..
T-14 ..... VI.8:2 with communication in order to r. it.
T-15 ...... I.15:2 very little to r. God's whole power to you.
T-15 ..... III.7:2 It is our task together to r. the awareness
T-15 ... VIII.3:3 and seek not to r. it to yourself. Fear not
T-15 ..... XI.5:4 and loss without attempting to r. himself?
T-16 .... VII.1:3 you seek to r. your wounded self-esteem.
T-16 .. VII.10:4 His Messenger understands how to r. the
T-17 ........ I.6:7 you r. to truth what was denied by both
T-17 ..... IV.2:4 He will r. to them the function given them
T-18 ... IV.5:11 *His plan to r. to me my own awareness of my*
T-28 ........ I.6:3 Time neither takes away nor can r.. And
T-29 ... VIII.5:5 The miracle does not r. the truth, the
T-31 ...... I.10:3 and pleads that love r. the dying world.
W-pI..... 62.3:5 will r. the invulnerability and power God
W-pI... 126.6:5 has no power to r. your unity with him to
W-pI. 152.11:6 awareness, grateful to r. His home to God
W-pI... 170.8:4 Will you r. to love what you have sought
W-pI... 188.9:7 wishes. We r. to them the holiness of
W-pI... 192.5:6 Only forgiveness can r. the peace that
W-pII ..... 7.3:3 r. your mind to where it truly is at home.
W-pII . 335.2:1 *What could r. Your memory to me, except*
M-25 ......... 6:4 would destroy the Holy Spirit would r..
P-1............. 4:1 must r. to his awareness the ability to
P-2.......... II.6:4 comes to those who would r. His world,
S-3........ III.3:4 and used to help r. the wounded and to

## restored 83

T-1 ....... III.1:5 r. to the recognition of your original state,
T-4 ....... II.10:1 be achieved before One-mindedness is r..
T-4 ..... IV.11:6 in my name, and your sanity will be r.. I
T-5 ........ V.2:2 is r. and therefore continues in creation.
T-8 .......... I.1:4 be r. only when you meet its conditions.
T-10 ..... V.11:1 to Him the Kingdom will be r. to His Son.
T-14 ....... V.5:2 and full communication be r. between the
T-15 .. VII.14:2 since communication has been r.. And
T-15 ....... X.2:2 and his unlimited power is thus r. to him.
T-15 ..... XI.8:5 in the time of Christ communication is r.,
T-16 ..... V.15:2 And unless love's meaning is r. to you,
T-17 ..... IV.4:5 is your relationship with God r. to you.
T-17 ..... IV.5:3 this means if you would be r. to sanity.
T-17 .. VII.3:11 faith, ask that it be r. where it was lost,
T-18 ...... I.11:1 Heaven is r. to all the Sonship through
T-18 ..... VI.1:2 that the Kingdom of Heaven is r. to you.
T-19 ... III.10:7 the glory that has been r. for you to see.
T19 .. IV.D.1:5 and the Son of God entirely r. to sanity.
T-20 ... VIII.1:2 Truth is r. to you through your desire, as
T-22 ........ I.9:4 must have been r. to those who join, for
T-25 ..... IV.5:5 that Heaven be r. to him for whom it was
T-25 .. VII.12:3 Here is sanity r.. And on this single rock
T-26 ..... IV.3:8 For here is what was lost r. to them, and
T-26 ..... V.10:7 instantly r. unto his Father's perfect Love.
T-26 ..... IX.4:5 because what is its own has been r. to it.
T-26 ..... IX.6:6 grow, in gratitude for what has been r..
T-26 ..... IX.7:3 offers thanks to one who has r. his home,
T-29 ..... VI.4:7 it once held seeming sway is now r. the
T-30 ... IV.8:12 by his will, and but r. to what he is. What
W-pI .... 37.2:5 his wholeness r. to his awareness through
W-pI .... 73.9:5 His will is now r. to his awareness. He is
W-pI .... 94.1:5 salvation accomplished. Here is sanity r..
W-pI .... 96.8:4 can do, r. to It and free to serve Its Will.
W-pI .. 96.10:3 R. in strength, it will again flow out from
W-pI .. 96.10:5 Confusion done, you are r., for you have
W-pI .... 97.2:1 in you, whose mind has been r. to sanity.
W-pI .. 100.2:3 you that you might be r. to what He wills.
W-pI .. 109.7:3 with hope reborn and energy r. to walk
W-pI .. 124.5:2 who are r. to the tranquility and peace of
W-pI .. 128.6:5 rest in its Creator, there to be r. to sanity,
WpI..rIV.in9:3 faithfulness r. the world from darkness to
W-pI 151.16:4 gratitude to Him Who has r. our sanity to
W-pI .. 159.5:4 Holiness has been r. to vision, and the
W-pI .. 161.1:4 world passed safely by and Heaven now r.
W-pI .. 162.4:5 has r. your sight by salvaging your mind.
W-pI 170.11:6 but in the vision that your choice r. to you
W-pI 170.12:4 given by your Creator, are r. to you at last.
W-pI .. 185.1:4 full awareness, memory of God entirely r.
W-pI 186.14:4 formlessness has been r. to you is greater
W-pI 188.10:1 Thus are our minds r. with them, and we
W-pII . 227.2:3 with his right mind r. to him at last.
W-pII ..... 3.5:5 made to die can be r. to everlasting life.
W-pII . 241.2:3 *How glad are we to have our sanity r. to us,*
W-pII . 251.2:2 *What we denied ourselves You have r., and*
W-pII . 252.2:2 *in You, and know that Heaven is r. to me.*
W-pII . 271.2:2 *beholds invites Your memory to be r. to me.*
W-pII ..... 7.4:1 and be r. to sanity and peace of mind.
W-pII ..... 7.5:3 quietness of Heaven is r. to God's beloved
W-pII . 285.2:2 *in it, and through forgiveness be r. to sanity.*
W-pII ..... 8.5:4 Identity which our forgiveness has r. to us
W-pII . 298.1:2 And thus am I r. to my reality at last. All
W-pII . 300.2:3 *to do to be r. to Heaven and our true Identity.*
W-pII ..... 9.4:3 In this equality is Christ r. as one Identity,
W-pII . 302.1:2 *us, as our sight is finally r. and we can see. We*
W-pII . 306.1:3 and be r. to love and holiness and peace.
W-pII . 310.2:3 We are r. to peace and holiness. There is
W-pII ... 11.4:6 be done on earth, only to be r. to sanity,
W-pII . 330.1:4 to accept God's gifts has been r. to spirit,
W-pII ... 12.5:2 peace will be r. forever to the holy minds
W-pII . 336.1:2 is r. after perception first is changed, and
W-pII . 336.1:6 here, and only here, is peace of mind r.,
W-pII . 350.2:2 Son will be r. to us in the reality of Love.
Wfl........ in.5:4 a dream. We are r. to sanity, in which we
M-4 ........ X.2:3 and let it be r. to them in newness and in
M-14 ....... 3:10 it is the final lesson in which unity is r.. It
M-16 ..... 10:10 "sacrifice" is Heaven r. to his awareness.
M-19 ....... 5:10 Vision is now r.. What had been lost has
M-28 ......... 6:6 is r. the truth about the holy Son of God.
P-2.......... II.1:5 be made perfect in time and r. to eternity.
S-1.......... II.8:8 if peace is to be r. to God's Son, who lives
S-2........... I.8:6 And thus is prayer r. to formlessness,
S-3...... IV.1:10 has r. their wholeness so they can forgive,
S-3........ IV.3:3 Son, r. as His completion and returned to

**restorer** 2

W-pI...110.5:2 the great **r.** of the truth to the awareness
W-pI...134.8:2 face of lies; the great **r.** of the simple truth

**restores** 12

T-1......IV.2:10 the Atonement **r.** spirit to its proper place
T-2........III.2:1 where it undoes the separation and **r.** the
T-7.........II.2:2 and **r.** its wholeness in your mind. This
T-7........IX.4:5 it, and **r.** it to the Kingdom because of its
T-18.........I.8:5 the course of insanity and **r.** you to reason
T-18.....VII.5:3 brother **r.** the universe to both of you.
T-29... VIII.5:4 and this is what the miracle **r.** to what *has*
W-pI...168.3:6 **r.** all memories the sleeping mind forgot;
W-pI...188.4:1 the world **r.** the memory to you as well.
W-pII......9.1:2 part of the condition that **r.** the never lost
M-19..........4:2 **r.** to your awareness the wholeness of the
P-2.........II.5:4 **r.** the place of God to ascendance, first

**restoring** 10

T-1........III.9:4 miracle aims at **r.** the awareness of reality,
T-11..........I.1:4 be **r.** the holy dwelling place of His Son,
T-13......III.7:6 its littleness, **r.** it to the magnitude of God
T-14......IV.9:2 the means of **r.** guiltlessness to minds that
T-14.....X.12:4 what you are, **r.** to you your Identity. We
T-20.......V.1:3 finds his function of **r.** his Father's laws to
W-pI...124.5:3 dying and the dead as well, **r.** them to life.
W-pI.140.10:2 ills as one, **r.** saneness to the Son of God.
W-pI...186.1:6 to save the world, **r.** it to Heaven's peace.
W-pII..308.1:7 to the world, **r.** it to timelessness and love

**restrict** 2

W-pI...181.6:2 to us, our narrowed focus will **r.** our sight,
S-1........IV.4:3 Do not **r.** your asking. Prayer can bring

**restricted** 1

T-29.........I.3:8 and limited in scope and carefully **r.** in

**restricting** 1

W-pI...181.4:3 by the depressing and **r.** thought that,

**restriction** 1

W-pI.....38.1:2 world. It is beyond every **r.** of time, space,

**restrictions** 1

T-18....VI.13:6 these instants of release from physical **r.**,

**restricts** 1

P-2...........I.3:2 on psychotherapy because it **r.** its aims.

**rests** 33

• peace, repose
*other*

T-2..... VIII.1:4 Since creative ability **r.** in the mind,
T-7........III.2:3 It merely **r.** in the Kingdom because it
T-11......IV.8:4 God, and in whom the whole Sonship **r.**.
T-14.......X.5:1 pattern that never **r.** and is never still. It
T-16....IV.10:1 straight to Him where your completion **r.**,
T-17.....V.10:5 that you may see that in it **r.** salvation.
T-18... VIII.7:4 sun nor ocean is the power that **r.** in you.
T-19.........I.2:7 joined the Mind in which all healing **r.**.
T19... IV.A.3:1 Spirit's purpose **r.** in peace within you.
T-20......IV.6:7 enter without fear and where he **r.** a while
T-20......IV.7:3 For the whole new world **r.** in the hands
T-20.......V.8:2 his Father's certainty the universe **r.** in his
T-20.......V.8:4 offer it to him and know it **r.** in safety? He
T-20....VI.10:2 Holy Spirit **r.** within it in the certainty it
T-22.....II.12:2 How still it **r.**, in time and yet beyond,
T-22.......V.3:8 God **r.** with you in quiet, undefended and
T-22.....V.3:10 Love **r.** in certainty. Only uncertainty can
T-24.....VII.5:5 and if that is true, its safety **r.** secure. If
T-24.....VII.5:7 holiness, and **r.** in light as safely as itself.
T-24...VII.11:3 son. The other **r.** within, his Father's Son,
T-26......VI.2:3 Whom all power in earth and Heaven **r.**.
T-27.......II.3:6 one in whom true forgiveness **r.** can suffer
T-30....III.10:3 near, it **r.** in certainty and perfect peace.
W-pI.....59.1:4 when He **r.** in me in absolute peace? How
W-pI.....97.2:1 Self, the holy Son of God Who **r.** in you,
W-pI...102.5:3 Besides these hourly five-minute **r.**, pause
W-pI...119.1:3 *Son, whose Self* **r.** *safely in the Mind of God.*
W-pI...199.2:3 It **r.** in God. And who can be afraid who
M-4 ......I.A.6:2 the teacher of God **r.** a while in reasonable
M-4 ...I.A.6:12 him. Now he **r.** a while, and gathers them
M-4 ....IX.2:12 **r.** in quiet certainty on that alone to which
M-16 .........1:4 understanding that it is true, he **r.** content
M-19 .........5:9 Perception **r.**, the mind is still, and light

**rests** 73

• other
*peace, repose*

T-1.........II.6:8 giver and receiver on which the miracle **r.**.
T-1.........V.6:4 on which the reverse of the Golden Rule **r.**
T-2........IV.2:8 that made magic **r.** on the belief that there
T-2.........V.9:4 This is because healing **r.** on charity, and
T-2.......VII.4:4 resolution **r.** entirely on mastery through
T-3.......V.10:2 Since perception **r.** on lack, those who
T-3.......VI.2:2 on which perception but not knowledge **r.**
T-3.......VII.1:4 Their difference lies in what **r.** upon them.
T-4...........I.4:4 ego and believe in a world that **r.** upon it.
T-6.........in.1:6 the sanity of the premises on which it **r.**.
T-6......V.C.6:1 You learn first that *having* **r.** on giving,
T-7.........II.5:6 **r.** only on the knowledge of what truth is.
T-8..... VIII.5:7 ego's interpretation of the body **r.** are true
T-11.......in.3:9 dark cornerstone of terror on which it **r.**,
T-15.......V.1:3 Judgment always **r.** on the past, for past
T-16.......V.6:4 for the attempt at union **r.** on exclusion.
T-18.........I.4:5 Your whole world **r.** upon it. Everything
T-18... VIII.7:3 the ripple dances as it **r.** upon the ocean.
T-20.........I.2:10 complete till your forgiveness **r.** on Christ,
T-20....IV.8:10 for it **r.** on certainty and not contingency.
T-20....IV.8:11 It **r.** on *you.* And what can be more certain
T-20......VI.2:2 love, and **r.** on it serene and undisturbed.
T-21.......II.1:2 the very little on which salvation **r.**; the
T-21.......II.5:5 the reasoning on which your "seeing" **r.**.
T-22.......V.6:4 but **r.** on the belief that you are separate.
T-23.....II.20:3 Yet each one **r.** as surely on the belief the
T-24......III.3:6 What **r.** on nothing never can be stable.
T-25......III.3:1 Perception **r.** on choosing; knowledge
T-25......VI.1:1 grace of God **r.** gently on forgiving eyes,
T-25......VI.1:6 kindness of his sight **r.** on himself with all
T-25......VI.5:6 all. But when it **r.** on all it is complete, and
T-25.....VII.4:9 world is meaningless *because* it **r.** on sin.
T-25...VII.12:7 This is the rock on which salvation **r.**, the
T-25....IX.10:2 of the law on which salvation **r.**; that
T-26.........I.8:1 justice **r.** in gentleness upon His Son, and
T-26......IV.1:7 always **r.** upon the one who offers it, until
T-27.........I.2:5 and when it **r.** on him are you set free.
T-27.....VII.3:1 by which the world is made, on which it **r.**
T-28...VII.5:10 If it **r.** on straw, there is no need to bar
T-28.....VII.6:3 What can be safe that **r.** upon a shadow?
T-29.......II.6:3 based, and there is nothing else it **r.** upon.
T-30.......V.8:5 as surely as His Father's Love **r.** upon Him
T-30......VI.1:5 For it is on this forgiveness **r.**, and is but
T-30......VI.2:7 reaction to distress that **r.** on error, and
T-30......VI.7:7 Salvation **r.** on faith there cannot be some
T-30......VI.8:5 Forgiveness **r.** on recognizing this, and
W-pI.......2.1:2 the idea to whatever your glance **r.** on.
W-pI.....12.2:6 **r.** on equal attention and equal time. This
W-pI.....45.7:4 the Foundation on which it **r.** is wholly
W-pI...66.10:2 the premises on which our conclusion **r.**.
W-pI...122.2:3 **r.** upon your eyelids so you see no dreams
W-pI.135.15:4 **r.** on the idea the past has taught enough
W-pI...137.1:1 the central thought on which salvation **r.**.
W-pI...151.3:2 Your judgment **r.** upon the witness that
W-pI...151.8:1 because it **r.** on Certainty so great that
W-pI...161.7:4 When hatred **r.** upon a thing, it calls for
W-pI...168.4:5 when your forgiveness **r.** on everything?
W-pI...184.7:3 But the sooner he perceives on what it **r.**,
W-pII ....238.h On my decision all salvation **r.**.
W-pII .....6.4:3 For when forgiveness **r.** upon the world
W-pII .359.1:7 *and on this fact forgiveness* **r.** *upon a certain*
M-4 .........I.1:1 their ability to fulfill their function **r.**.
M-4 .....VII.1:3 teachers this one **r.** ultimately on trust,
M-8 ...........1:2 perception. It **r.** on differences; on uneven
M-8 ...........3:9 they bring on which perception **r.**. Only
M-8 ...........4:7 On this the judgment of all differences **r.**,
M-10 .........3:5 on whom it **r.** now and in the future. Who
M-18 .........3:6 to all this, and to the world that **r.** on this:
P-1.............1:2 and effect relationships on which it **r.**. No
P-2.........in.2:4 whole equilibrium **r.** on the insane belief
S-2...........I.7:2 your salvation **r.** on learning this of Him.
S-2..........II.2:2 is. Forgiveness here **r.** on an attitude of
S-3..........II.6:1 False healing **r.** upon the body's cure,

**result** 97

T-1..........II.1:4 **r.** in true closeness to others. Revelation
T-1.........V.5:6 As a **r.** it imprisons, because such are the
T-1.........V.6:2 is the natural **r.** of choosing to follow Him
T-2........III.4:7 As a **r.**, the mind becomes increasingly
T-2........IV.1:2 is the principle, and healing is the **r.**. To
T-2........IV.1:5 is a remedy and any type of healing is a **r.**.
T-2........IV.2:2 is the **r.** of level confusion, because it
T-2.........V.4:4 the **r.** of refusal to accept the Atonement
T-2........VI.3:1 outcome of misthought can **r.** in healing.
T-2........VI.4:7 The particular **r.** does not matter, but the
T-3...........I.4:7 teacher offers. The **r.** is learning failure.
T-3......III.5:10 is the **r.** of revelation and induces only
T-3.........V.5:3 Such incongruities are the **r.** of attempts
T-3........VI.7:5 is the **r.** of the authority problem which,
T-3......VI.11:2 If this is the **r.** of his own free will he must
T-4.........in.1:5 The **r.** of genuine devotion is inspiration,
T-5..........II.6:3 As a **r.**, there are choices you must make.
T-5.......II.12:3 thought, and to behave like me as a **r.**.
T-6.........I.16:6 **r.** is a lesson in blame, for all behavior
T-6.........I.16:7 the **r.** of clearly opposed thought systems;
T-6.........I.17:5 reject it. As a **r.**, you will teach rejection.
T-6..........II.4:4 As their goals are opposed, so is the **r.**.
T-6......V.B.1:3 ideas are clearly the **r.** of dissociation and
T-7........IV.1:6 It is their **r.**, in a state of mind that does
T-7........IV.3:8 then, they all contribute to one **r.**, and by
T-7........VI.3:2 it, which must **r.** in extreme anxiety. That
T-7.........X.1:1 The Kingdom is the **r.** of premises, just as
T-7.........X.1:3 really saw this **r.** you could not want it.
T-7.......X.5:14 If the **r.** of this decision is confusion, this
T-8...........I.1:6 is merely the **r.** of your misuse of His laws
T-8........III.3:2 Their extension is the **r.** of Their Oneness,
T-8.....VII.10:1 Healing is the **r.** of using the body solely
T-8.....VII.14:5 and to believe that joy could possibly **r.**, is
T-8......VIII.9:9 anything. Health is the **r.** of relinquishing
T-9.........I.12:3 consider the **r.** of this strange decision.
T-9........VI.3:2 learning is the **r.** of what you taught them.
T-10.......V.2:1 deny God will inevitably **r.** in projection,
T-12.......V.7:3 The **r.** of this curriculum goal is obvious.
T-12.......V.8:5 It is merely the **r.** of an honest appraisal
T-12.....VII.5:2 perception is the **r.** of your invitation,
T-13........I.11:1 the guilt, for guilt is the **r.** of attack. In the
T-14......III.5:3 the natural **r.** of choosing right, attesting
T-14.......V.7:1 that cannot fail and must **r.** in peace. No
T-14........X.5:1 The **r.** is a weaving, changing pattern that
T-15........II.4:2 As a **r.**, they witness to the ego in your
T-15.......V.5:4 care and be sure that it will not **r.** in pain,
T-17.......V.2:7 first **r.** of offering the relationship to the
T-17.....V.13:2 it. As a **r.**, you do not realize that it is with
T-17.....VII.1:4 As a **r.**, you do not see the problem. Had
T-18......IV.1:1 is the **r.** of your determination to be holy.
T-18......IV.4:2 is always the **r.** of your small willingness
T-19..........I.7:6 The **r.** of an idea is never separate from its
T19. IV.A.12:1 world are the **r.** of how the world is seen.
T19..IV.B.12:4 inevitable **r.** of equating yourself with the
T19..IV.C.2:15 is the **r.** of the thought we call the ego, as
T19..IV.C.2:15 as surely as life is the **r.** of the Thought of
T19....IV.C.5:6 *is* nothing. It is the **r.** of a tiny, mad idea of
T-20.....VII.4:3 the **r.** of letting the effects of sin be lifted,
T-21.........in.1:8 Perception is a **r.** and not a cause. And
T-25.........II.1:5 hopes and fancies, always does despair **r.**.
T-25........II.2:3 change that might **r.** in better outcome?

T-26....... II.2:5 possible, and could **r.** in gain for anyone.
T-27....... II.7:7 Your health is a **r.** of your desire to see
T-28.... IV.10:7 miracles are the **r.** when you do not insist
T-29...... IX.9:3 Your self-betrayal must **r.** in fear, for fear
T-30...... VI.4:3 the sure **r.** of seeing pardon as unmerited.
T-31...... III.1:2 a choice that will **r.** in different outcomes,
W-pI....... 5.3:1 and forms of upset which you think **r.**.
W-pI..... 16.1:2 you see is the **r.** of your thoughts. There is
W-pI..... 16.3:2 neutral **r.** is impossible because a neutral
W-pI..... 23.3:4 a more appropriate term for the **r.**?
W-pI..... 24.1:2 action, and no way of judging the **r.**.
W-pI..... 25.2:4 As a **r.**, you are bound to misuse it. When
W-pI..... 26.4:1 is the **r.** of your own thoughts. Nothing
W-pI..... 37.2:3 As a **r.**, the perceiver will lose. Nor will he
W-pI..... 66.7:5 and no other outcomes possible as a **r.** of
W-pI..... 71.5:4 The **r.** can only bring confusion, misery
W-pI..... 91.1:5 absence is not the **r.** of your failure to see.
WpI. rIII.in9:3 to them. As a **r.**, you have gained little
W-pI... 136.6:2 threat, and not whatever outcome may **r.**.
W-pII .... in.2:8 use as much as we will need for the **r.** that
W-pII . 350.1:5 *But what he looks upon is their direct* **r.**.
M-3 ........... 3:7 levels, but the **r.** is always the same.
M-4 ........ I.1:2 Perception is the **r.** of learning. In fact,
M-4 ..... I.A.8:4 Indeed, the tranquility is their **r.**; the
M-4 ....... II.2:4 conflict. Conflict is the inevitable **r.** of self-
M-4 ....... V.1:1 Joy is the inevitable **r.** of gentleness.
M-6 ........... 3:4 give if he is concerned with the **r.** of giving
M-7 ........... 1:5 the **r.** of healing is to limit the healing. It
M-7 ........... 4:8 the gift and it is impossible to doubt its **r.**.
M-7 ........... 6:8 Doubt is the **r.** of conflicting wishes. Be
M-10 ......... 6:5 All of the pain he looks upon is its **r.**. All
M-17 ......... 3:4 been the case if the **r.** is anything but joy.
M-22 ......... 4:6 Healing is the **r.** of the recognition, by
P-2........ III.3:2 for the **r.** to look like retrogression. But in
P-2........ IV.6:1 as the **r.** of a view of the self as weak,
P-2....... VII.2:2 is prayer, and healing is its aim and its **r.**.

## resulted 1

T-12....... V.8:5 and of the learning outcomes that have **r.**.

## resulting 2

T-2........ VI.5:6 **r.** in a situation in which you are doing
W-pI..... 99.1:3 **r.** in a state of conflict seen between what

## results 66

T-1....... VII.1:6 of Self. Denial of Self **r.** in illusions, while
T-2......... II.2:5 truth, but denial of truth **r.** in miscreation
T-2......... V.7:7 fear. Everything that **r.** from spiritual
T-2....... VII.1:4 between your thoughts and their **r.**, I
T-3........... I.2:4 frequently **r.** in an attempt to "justify" the
T-3........... I.4:6 **r.** in rejection of what the teacher offers.
T-4........ VI.3:2 The **r.** will convince you increasingly that
T-4....... VII.2:6 **r.** in spurious generalization which is
T-5......... V.8:2 the destructive **r.** of the decision. Any
T-5..... VI.12:3 and by producing **r.** *now* it renders time
T-6...... IV.8:3 are **r.** that have been achieved. When they
T-7......... II.2:8 you can arrive at diametrically opposed **r.**
T-7........ III.1:2 He maximizes all efforts and all **r.**. By
T-7......... V.5:2 healer always heals by Him the **r.** will vary
T-7........ VI.2:4 of unreality and **r.** in utter confusion.
T-8........... I.2:5 evaluate them in terms of their **r.** to you.
T-8..... VII.15:6 No more are any of its seeming **r.**. When
T-8..... VII.15:8 it is a form of attack, then it can *have* no **r.**.
T-8..... VII.16:1 suffer from imagined **r.** of what is not true
T-8..... VIII.6:8 *Any* way you handle error **r.** in nothing.
T-8..... VIII.6:9 The more complicated the **r.** become the
T-9......... V.9:3 Its **r.** are more convincing than its words.
T-11....... in.1:5 **r.** are as different as their foundations,
T-11....... V.5:2 way to undo its **r.** is merely to recognize
T-12..... VII.1:1 learned can be recognized only by its **r.**.
T-12..... VII.2:7 act. And the **r.** of your actions you *can* see.
T-12..... VII.3:1 but you can see the **r.** of His Presence, and
T-12..... VII.3:4 Perceiving His **r.**, you will understand
T-13...... XI.4:3 It can also show you the **r.** of sharing,
T-13...... XI.4:3 you still remember the **r.** of not sharing.
T-14....... V.6:7 teaching, and guarantees its limitless **r.**.
T-15 ........ I.2:1 **r.** of the Holy Spirit's teaching are far in
T-16 ....... II.7:5 interpretation the **r.** have brought you joy
T-16 ....... II.7:6 you prefer the **r.** of your interpretation,
T-16 ..... III.1:7 **r.** have been to bring peace where there
T-16 ..... III.2:4 The ego's teaching produces immediate **r.**
T-17 ...... V.1:2 is a practical device, witnessed to by its **r.**.
T-17 ...... V.3:1 the practical **r.** of asking Him to enter. At
T-17 .... V.12:5 enable its **r.** to be accepted and shared.
T-17 .... V.15:1 your mistakes and free you from their **r.**.
T-19 ........ I.8:2 attack that seems to be justified by its **r.**.
T-19 ..... III.3:3 and over, with obviously distressing **r.**,
T19.... IV.A.7:3 unchangeable dedication to sin and its **r.**.
T19.... IV.A.8:3 pointless wandering makes its **r.** appear
T19.... IV.A.8:6 induces merely indicates its limited **r.**.
T19.... IV.C.3:4 He knows of neither sin nor its **r.**. The
T-20 ..... IV.1:5 none; nor to its **r.** as this world sees them,
T-20 ..... IV.2:1 its **r.** are alien and can no more enter than
T-20 ..... IV.3:1 you by accepting their **r.** as your just due.
T-20 ..... IV.3:7 them to suffer the **r.** of any other source.
T-20 ..... IV.4:1 choose freedom will experience only its **r.**.
T-23 ..... II.20:5 less certain in their witnessing, or their **r.**.
T-24 ........ I.2:2 where the **r.** of conflict are kept unknown
T-24 ........ I.2:7 deny their presence nor their terrible **r.**.
T-26 .... VIII.2:7 see eventual salvation, not immediate **r.**.
T-27 ...... V.9:3 to their opposites and bring the same **r.**.
T-30 ...... I.16:5 Decisions cause **r.** *because* they are not
T-31 ...... I.10:1 fear of God **r.** as surely from the lesson
W-pI..... 19.1:4 not matter. Thinking and its **r.** are really
W-pI..... 41.8:5 exercise can bring very startling **r.** even
W-pI... 103.2:1 and its **r.** become the heritage of minds
W-pI... 108.7:2 obvious because it has **r.** we cannot miss.
W-pI... 138.3:4 in return, and time goes by without **r.**.
W-pI... 184.7:3 are its premises, how doubtful its **r.**, the
M-17 ......... 2:5 be forgotten that the outcome that **r.** will
M-17 ......... 3:1 and errors can be recognized by their **r.**.

## resurrected 2

W-pI. 151.16:4 Now do we lift our **r.** minds in gladness
M-28 ......... 6:9 he sought before to crucify are **r.** with him

## resurrection 43

T-1 ....... III.2:2 My word, which is the **r.** and the life, shall
T-3 .......... I.1:2 not establish the Atonement; the **r.** did.
T-3 .......... I.7:6 **r.** demonstrated that nothing can destroy
T-3 ........ V.1:3 I have also made it clear that the **r.** was
T-4 ......... in.3:3 journey, you are also free to join my **r.**.
T-6 .......... I.2:7 While I emphasized only the **r.** before, the
T-6 .......... I.2:7 actually led to the **r.** was not clarified then
T-6 .......... I.7:1 Your **r.** is your reawakening. I am the
T-6 ........ I.12:1 the **r.** is the symbol of sharing because the
T-11 ..... VI.1:5 for those who believe in the **r.** will see it.
T-11 ..... VI.1:6 The **r.** is the complete triumph of Christ
T-11 ..... VI.2:1 join in the **r.** or the crucifixion? Would
T-11 ..... VI.4:1 I am *your* **r.** and *your* life. You live in me
T-11 ..... VI.4:6 in the **r.** because it has been accomplished
T-11 ..... VI.4:7 it will ever be, for the **r.** is the Will of God,
T-11 ..... VI.5:6 The God of **r.** demands nothing, for He
T-11 ..... VI.6:1 **R.** must compel your allegiance gladly,
T-11 ..... VI.6:7 Guard them in their **r.**, for otherwise you
T-12 ....... II.7:3 In my **r.** is your release. Our mission is to
T-14 ..... III.4:1 between the crucifixion and the **r.**;
T-14 .... V.10:2 Only the **r.** became my part in it. That is
T19.. IV.C.10:9 not to the cross, but to the **r.** and the life.
T19. IV.D.16:1 Here is the holy place of **r.**, to which we
T19. IV.D.17:4 It is almost Easter, the time of **r.**. Let us
T19. IV.D.17:5 share in it, that we may rise as one in **r.**,
T19. IV.D.18:5 together the way unto the **r.** of God's Son,
T-20 ...... I.2:10 **r.** be complete till your forgiveness rests
T-20 ........ I.3:2 the sign of victory, the promise of the **r.**,
T-20 ........ I.3:6 gift of lilies speed him on his way to **r.**.
T-21 ........ II.1:2 by which the crucifixion is changed to **r.**.
T-26 .... V.10:5 **R.** has come to take its place. And now
T-26 .... V.10:6 And now you are a part of **r.**, not of death.
T-27 ..... VI.8:1 The **r.** of the world awaits your healing
W-pI..... 20.3:6 has one Son, and he is the **r.** and the life.
W-pI. 151.12:1 Such is your **r.**, for your life is not a part
WpI... rV.in7:1 My **r.** comes again each time I lead a
W-pI .. 185.1:4 the **r.** of all creation fully recognized.
W-pI .. 196.3:4 will see within today's idea the light of **r.**,
M-11 ......... 1:5 that there is no death, that **r.** must occur,
M-28 ............ h WHAT IS THE **R.**?
M-28 ......... 1:1 the **r.** is the overcoming or surmounting
M-28 ......... 2:1 The **r.** is the denial of death, being the
C-5 .......... 6:11 *with me instead to share the* **r.** *of God's Son.*

## retain 23

T-2 ..... VIII.5:6 **r.** in your memory only what is creative
T-2 ... VIII.5:10 When everything you **r.** is lovable, there
T-4 ....... III.7:2 You **r.** thousands of little scraps of fear
T-6 ....... IV.9:7 You therefore **r.** the central place in your
T-9 ...... VII.7:4 You cannot **r.** part of a thought system,
T-12 ....... V.4:4 to **r.** the characteristics of creation, but
T-13 ....... II.1:2 ego wants to **r.** guilt *you* find it intolerable,
T-13 ....... II.1:3 split of all occurs, for if you are to **r.** guilt,
T-14 .. VII.3:10 does not **r.** any conviction of reality.
T-15 ....... X.5:2 **r.** the principle that governs all of them.
T-15 ..... XI.5:7 as long as you would **r.** the deprivation,
T-17 ........ I.3:3 to **r.** some aspects of reality for fantasy. If
T-17 ..... IV.6:7 **R.** this one, and you have retained the
T-25 ..... IX.1:6 Not one sin would you **r.**. And not one
T-27 ....... II.2:3 They would **r.** the consequences of the
T-27 ....... II.3:3 your brother mercy but **r.** the proof he is
T-29 ..... IX.6:2 Seek not to **r.** the toys of children. Put
W-pI 122.13:4 **R.** your gifts in clear awareness as you see
W-pI .. 195.8:5 and yet **r.** some other things still locked
W-pII .. in.11:1 One further use for words we still **r.**.
M-17 ....... 6:10 not **r.** the slightest memory of Who your
P-2......... in.2:3 able to **r.** their self-concept exactly as it is,
P-2........ VI.6:7 Let him **r.** one spot of sin in what he looks

## retained 5

T-7 ......... II.4:4 the form so that the original meaning is **r.**
T-17 ...... III.8:4 the purpose of the unholy alliance are **r.**,
T-17 ..... IV.6:7 Retain this one, and you have **r.** the whole
M-20 ......... 1:4 And being found, how can it be **r.**? Let us
M-20 ......... 4:1 How is the peace of God **r.**, once it is

## retaining 4

T-6 ......... II.8:1 and **r.** the extensions of His Thought in
T-29 ....... II.3:2 to serve the function of **r.** sin and pain.
WpI... rV.in6:5 still **r.** in his mind the way that led him
M-26 ......... 2:1 directly, **r.** no trace of worldly limits and

## retains 12

T-1 ......... V.5:5 it **r.** its creative potential but places itself
T-6 ..... V.C.1:3 Whatever is in accord with this light He **r.**
T-7 ....... IX.2:7 That is how it **r.** the knowledge of itself.
T-10 ....... II.2:3 **r.** the knowledge of God and of yourself
T-24 .... VII.7:5 who still **r.** one unlearned lesson in his
T-24 .. VII.11:7 The Son of God **r.** his Father's Will. The
T-27 ....... II.3:11 and **r.** no trace of condemnation that he
W-pI .... 96.7:1 Self **r.** Its Thoughts, and they remain
W-pI .. 134.3:3 the idea of sin **r.** as yet upon your mind,
W-pI .. 187.5:6 There is a giver who **r.**; another who will
C-1 ............ 4:2 Spirit **r.** the potential for creating, but its
S-2......... I.10:2 instant while this world **r.** reality for you.

## retaliate 1

T-10 ....... V.7:2 He does not **r.**, but He does call to you to

## retaliation 9

T-5 ....... V.3:11 Fear of **r.** from without follows, because
T-5 ....... VI.2:2 They induce fears of **r.** or abandonment,
T-6 ..... V.B.1:1 have a basic fear of **r.** and abandonment.
T-8 ......... V.5:7 to its **r.** because I am with you. On this
T-9 .......... I.8:5 really wants either abandonment or **r.**,
T-13 ........ I.4:3 **r.** that he fears and that he sees will never
T-13 ..... IV.6:3 the present in **r.** for a past that is no more
W-pI .. 190.2:4 a dream of fierce **r.** for a crime that could
W-pI .. 196.7:1 as much as will permit fear of **r.** to abate,

**retaliative** 3

T-8 ... V.5:6 regards itself as rejected and becomes **r.**.
T-9 ... V.3:5 onto God, they make Him appear **r.**, and
T19 .. IV.B.11:6 **r.** attack on what you think has failed you

**retaliatory** 1

T-6 ... I.14:3 of the "wrath of God" as His **r.** weapon.

**retire** 1

W-ep ... 3:2 for your Self when you **r.** from the world,

**retraced** 1

T-28 ... II.12:7 separation, until all the steps have been **r.**

**retraces** 1

T-18 ... I.8:3 and **r.** with you your mad journey outside

**retracing** 1

T-2 ... II.6:5 to keep **r.** your steps without advancing

**retranslated** 1

W-pI.151.15:5 with you which He has **r.** in your mind.

**retreat** 8

T-18 ... III.3:8 you **r.** to the illusion your fear increases,
T-18 ... V.1:5 distinguish between advance and **r.**.
T19 ... IV.C.7:3 the **r.** to death is not the end of conflict.
T-20 ... VI.7:2 as it will surely do, and they **r.** in fear,
T-30 ... VII.2:2 judge disaster and success, advance, **r.**,
W-pI ... 74.6:5 in refusing to allow **r.** into withdrawal,
W-pI ... 137.1:3 states. Sickness is a **r.** from others, and a
S-1 ... III.4:2 time be followed by a deep **r.** into fear.

**retreating** 1

T-18 ... III.2:1 sometimes **r.** to the lesser forms of fear,

**retreats** 3

T-18 ... V.1:6 deepest **r.** you have evaluated as success.
W-pI ... 186.6:2 is this image which quails and **r.** in terror,
M-8 ... 2:7 health a burden, it **r.** into feverish dreams

**retribution** 9

T-3 ... I.3:4 God does not believe in **r.**. His Mind does
T-9 ... V.3:5 Him appear retaliative, and fear His **r.**.
T-13 ... I.2:3 the world of **r.** rose in the black cloud of
T-16 ... VII.3:3 that has offended it, and seeks **r.** of you.
T-16 ... VII.4:2 not contain the dream of **r.** for the past.
T-26 ... VIII.8:3 **r.** is perceived to be the form in which the
T-26 ... X.4:5 Is it not **r.** for your own attack upon the
S-2 ... II.3:3 and deserve the **r.** of the wrath of God.
S-3 ... IV.8:1 dream of **r.** and a little life beset with fear,

**retroactively** 1

T-2 ... V.10:8 This corrects **r.** as well as progressively.

**retrogression** 2

P-2 ... I.1:8 **R.** is temporary. The overall direction is
P-2 ... III.3:2 even possible for the result to look like **r.**.

**retrospect** 1

T-30 ... V.9:11 let not your experiences here deceive in **r.**.

**return** 204

T-1 ... I.46:3 When you **r.** to your original form of
T-1 ... III.3:2 Being filled with spirit, they forgive in **r.**.
T-1 ... V.4:1 member of the family of God must **r.**. The
T-1 ... V.4:2 to **r.** because it blesses and honors him,
T-2 ... II.6:3 terms, because you **r.** as you go forward.
T-2 ... II.6:5 your steps without advancing to your **r.**.
T-2 ... II.6:10 that point the bridge of **r.** has been built.
T-3 ... V.1:3 was the means for the **r.** to knowledge,
T-3 ... VII.2:7 their souls in **r.** for gifts of no real worth.
T-3 ... VII.5:6 truth, and you must **r.** to your Beginning.
T-4 ... VII.8:4 and He will **r.** their praise of Him because
T-5 ... in.3:2 You should want to bless them in **r.**, out
T-5 ... I.5:5 is healed there will be no Call to **r.**. But
T-5 ... II.2:2 the Call to **r.** with which God blessed the
T-5 ... IV.2:6 It will increase as you are willing to **r.** the
T-5 ... V.8:7 It will also **r.** to full creation the instant it
T-5 ... VI.1:2 All the Sons of God are waiting for your **r.**
T-5 ... VI.9:5 to the ego will merely **r.** to the Kingdom,
T-5 ... VI.12:6 because it is His special function to **r.** you
T-5 ... VII.2:6 to **r.** to God the mind as He created it. He
T-5 ... VII.6:5 Your part is merely to **r.** your thinking to
T-6 ... in.1:3 attacked, that your attack is justified in **r.**,
T-6 ... II.10:5 He tells you to **r.** your whole mind to God
T-6 ... II.11:1 ego can accept the idea that **r.** is necessary
T-6 ... II.11:2 Spirit tells you that even **r.** is unnecessary,
T-6 ... II.11:3 the idea of **r.** both necessary and difficult.
T-7 ... V.7:2 something equally desirable in **r.**. His
T-7 ... VI.1:5 but they *will* **r.** to the mind of the thinker
T-7 ... VIII.3:10 are afraid that their projections will **r.** and
T-8 ... VI.4:2 time. He was ashamed to **r.** to his father,
T-8 ... VI.5:9 or give anything else, and expect joy in **r.**?
T-8 ... VII.9:5 reach beyond its distortions and **r.** *to* spirit
T-8 ... IX.9:5 Yet your **r.** to meaning is essential to His,
T-9 ... II.10:1 will set the price low but demand a high **r.**
T-9 ... II.10:2 so that your **r.** is in proportion to your
T-9 ... II.10:4 be set high, because of the value of the **r.**.
T-9 ... IV.9:4 Second Coming is merely the **r.** of sense.
T-9 ... IV.11:10 is the awareness of reality, not its **r.**.
T-9 ... VII.1:7 these chances, not because they will not **r.**
T-9 ... VII.4:8 Yet it is surely pointless to attack in **r.**.
T-9 ... VII.8:7 **R.** your part to Him, and He will give you
T-9 ... VII.8:7 of Himself in exchange for the **r.** of what
T-9 ... VIII.1:4 gifts to induce you to **r.** to its "protection.
T-9 ... VIII.10:2 your eternal place merely waits for your **r.**
T-9 ... VIII.10:4 do not know them until you **r.** to them.
T-10 ... II.3:4 **r.** in exchange for yours is the exchange of
T-10 ... III.11:3 His Voice still calls you to **r.**, and He will
T-10 ... V.7:2 not retaliate, but He does call to you to **r.**.
T-10 ... V.11:3 Heaven waits for his **r.**, for it was created
T-11 ... I.1:3 lies the beginning of the **r.** to knowledge;
T-11 ... I.3:8 and why so much is waiting for your **r.**.
T-11 ... IV.3:6 As you bring him back, so will you **r.**.
T-11 ... VIII.6:1 what is yours, and will take nothing in **r.**.
T-12 ... VI.1:5 yours, and gives you nothing in **r.**. You
T-13 ... V.7:3 And He will not **r.** it, for it is unworthy of
T-13 ... V.9:7 He will not **r.** unto the Father until He has
T-13 ... VI.9:3 He will **r.** your thanks in His clear Answer
T-13 ... VI.10:2 having given light to them they will **r.** it.
T-13 ... VII.3:5 and tired and ready to **r.** to dust even as
T-13 ... XI.11:6 was not created for you and by you in **r.**.
T-14 ... V.1:8 of death behind, and **r.** quietly to Heaven.
T-14 ... VII.5:11 delay in your **r.** to peace by wondering
T-14 ... IX.4:1 waits quietly for the **r.** of them that love it
T-14 ... IX.4:2 knows they will **r.** to purity and to grace.
T-14 ... XI.13:4 realize that you know not, peace will **r.**,
T-15 ... XI.8:4 that you may give it and **r.** it to the Father
T-16 ... V.7:6 taking, and of giving nothing of value in **r.**
T-16 ... VII.4:1 so you must **r.** to the past to find salvation
T-17 ... III.1:10 with you only that you may **r.** evil for evil,
T-18 ... I.12:4 **R.** with me to Heaven, walking together
T-18 ... VII.2:5 gives you a different view of it when you **r.**
T-18 ... VII.7:9 and the body's activities **r.** to occupy your
T-18 ... VII.8:1 be this place of rest to which you can **r.**.
T-18 ... VIII.8:7 it comes, and where it would **r.** with you.
T-18 ... IX.7:2 messengers of your perception **r.** to you,
T-19 ... I.11:6 coming, and to **r.** their messages to you.
T-19 ... IV.2:6 Would you not now **r.** His graciousness,
T19 ... IV.A.9:4 is lifted up and carried away, never to **r.**,
T19IV.A.10:10 which **r.** to it with messages written in the
T19. IV.A.11:1 **r.** with messages of love and gentleness.
T19. IV.A.12:2 it, and **r.** with word of what they saw.
T19. IV.A.12:5 to feast only upon what they **r.** to him. No
T19. IV.A.13:3 **r.** with gorges filled with things decayed
T19. IV.A.14:2 They are as eager to **r.** to you what they
T19. IV.A.14:5 they will **r.** with all the happy things they
T19. IV.A.15:5 brother and **r.** to you with what love sees.
T19. IV.D.10:8 on, only to **r.** and make the choice again.
T19. IV.D.16:1 will **r.** until redemption is accomplished
T19. IV.D.17:8 it, receive it of Him in **r.** for what you gave
T-20 ... VI.3:2 Idols accept, but never make **r.**. They can
T-20 ... VI.6:5 dedicated to no relationships and no **r.**.
T-20 ... VI.10:4 in gladness for the holy one of safe **r.**.
T-20 ... VIII.1:3 and what was never lost will quietly **r.**. It
T-21 ... VI.6:2 Father forever, without a hope of safe **r.**.
T-22 ... in.3:7 stand, but close enough not to **r.** to earth.
T-22 ... I.11:6 And here can He **r.** in confidence, for
T-22 ... IV.3:8 from this holy place He will **r.** with you,
T-22 ... V.2:8 peace, and laid between you and its **r.**.
T-23 ... II.21:5 another, nor that **r.** from one is easier.
T-23 ... III.6:4 **r.** because the guns are stilled an instant,
T-24 ... II.8:6 only that he may **r.** it unto you. It is not
T-25 ... V.4:1 of you; that you **r.** to him what is his due,
T-25 .. VIII.11:4 may **r.** to love and there be satisfied. Each
T-25 ... IX.6:9 vengeance in place of healing and **r.** of
T-26 ... IX.8:6 the Father and the Son **r.** to what is Theirs
T-27 ... VIII.6:1 Let us **r.** the dream he gave away unto the
T-28 ... VI.4:7 to be hurt by him, and to attack him in **r.**.
T-29 ... VI.2:9 with time and bloom and fade will not **r.**.
T-30 ... VI.2:6 rights when you **r.** forgiveness for attack.
W-pI ... 4.6:3 during the day. We will **r.** to them later.
W-pI ... 43.6:3 **R.** to the first phase of the exercises as
W-pI ... 44.9:3 **r.** to the exercises with eyes closed as soon
WpI ... rI.in.6:3 necessary to **r.** to the original statements,
W-pI ... 55.3:4 allows love to **r.** to my awareness, I will
W-pI ... 62.1:4 truth about yourself **r.** to your memory.
W-pI ... 68.6:4 you and loves you, and that you love in **r.**.
W-pI ... 95.7:3 not to **r.** to it again as soon as you can.
W-pI ... 98.6:3 asked for nothing in **r.** for everything.
W-pI ... 105.2:2 "gifts" are but a bid for a more valuable **r.**
W-pI ... 105.6:4 you must **r.** to claim them as your own.
W-pI ... 107.9:6 will **r.** to the familiar world reluctantly.
W-pI ... 108.9:3 You will find you have exact **r.**, for that is
W-pI ... 121.6:5 Thus you **r.** your mind as one to Him
W-pI.122.13:3 as you **r.** again to meet a world of shifting
W-pI.124.11:2 certainty that His **r.** will be a sense of love
W-pI ... 125.5:1 He has not waited until you **r.** your mind
W-pI ... 132.6:5 He will **r.** and go still farther, or perhaps
W-pI ... 132.6:5 or perhaps step back a while and then **r.**
W-pI ... 138.3:4 It is spent for nothing in **r.**, and time goes
W-pI ... 140.4:7 gone, with nothing left to which it can **r.**.
W-pI.153.20:6 is all you need to give Him in **r.**. You lay
W-pI ... 157.3:1 though you will **r.** to paths of learning.
W-pI ... 157.7:1 the world to which you will **r.** becomes a
W-pI ... 157.7:3 time will come when you will not **r.** in the
W-pI ... 159.9:7 them. And they **r.** them gladly unto Him.
W-pI.159.10:8 His vision gives the means for a **r.** to our
W-pI ... 160.6:3 may look, for he has made **r.** impossible.
W-pI ... 167.5:8 where they come from, there will they **r.**.
W-pI.169.14:1 Be grateful to **r.**, as you were glad to go
W-pI.170.11:6 And you **r.** to a new world, unburdened
WpI ... rV.in5:4 to **r.** to the eternal Self we thought we lost
W-pI ... 182.1:3 if there were a place that called you to **r.**,
W-pI ... 182.1:6 dismissed, but surely to **r.** to mind again.
W-pI ... 182.5:4 just an interval in which He can **r.** to
W-pI ... 182.5:6 He will **r.**. But give Him just a little time
W-pI ... 182.7:5 not **r.** again where He does not belong,
W-pI ... 182.9:4 is far away, and He will not **r.** to it alone.
W-pI.182.11:5 He asks unceasingly that you **r.** with Him,
W-pI.186.11:1 sun's **r.** each morning to dispel the night,
W-pI ... 187.2:6 Yet it must **r.** to him who gives. Nor can
W-pI ... 188.7:5 came but to remind you how you must **r.**.
W-pI ... 191.5:2 safety and escape you will **r.** and set it free
W-pI.191.10:1 eyes, **r.** again to bless the world he made.
W-pI ... 192.2:7 waits for your **r.** to be acknowledged, not
W-pI ... 199.8:3 Would you not **r.** your mind to this? Then
W-pI ... 219.1:5 *And then* **r.** *to earth, without confusion as to*
W-pII .223.2:6 *Today we would* **r.**. *Our Name is Yours, and*
W-pII .225.1:1 *Father, I must* **r.** *Your Love for me, for giving*
W-pII .225.1:2 *to me. I must* **r.** *it, for I want it mine in full*

|  |  |
|---|---|
| W-pII .226.2:1 | *Father, my home awaits my glad r.. Your* |
| W-pII .227.2:1 | so today we find our glad r. to Heaven, |
| W-pII .246.1:3 | for me, and all the love which I r. to Him. |
| W-pII .249.2:1 | *Father, we would r. our minds to You. We* |
| W-pII .....4.5:7 | Would you still hold r. to Heaven back? |
| W-pII .256.1:9 | by which our minds r. to Him at last. |
| W-pII .269.1:3 | *lessons to surpass perception and r. to truth.* |
| W-pII .273.1:3 | us learn how to dismiss it and r. to peace. |
| W-pII .....7.4:3 | r. to signify the end of dreams has come. |
| W-pII .291.2:6 | *and let the memory of You r. to me.* |
| W-pII .....9.1:1 | of mistakes, and the r. of sanity. It is a |
| W-pII .306.2:1 | *so, our Father, we r. to You, remembering* |
| W-pII ...10.3:2 | release from suffering, r. to peace, |
| W-pII ...10.4:1 | and call him to r. to the eternal peace He |
| W-pII ...10.5:2 | Therefore awaken and r. to Me. I am your |
| W-pII ...11.4:6 | our function be only to let this memory r. |
| W-pII .321.1:9 | *in You alone. Father, it is my will that I r..* |
| W-pII .322.2:5 | *loss of fear, and the r. of love into my mind?* |
| W-pII .324.1:4 | *but choose to wander off a while, and then r..* |
| W-pII .330.2:3 | *You. We would r. to It today, to be made free* |
| W-pII .333.2:1 | *all doubt, and light the way for our r. to You.* |
| W-pII .336.1:5 | the mind, and call it to r. and look within, |
| W-pII ...13.1:6 | it paves the way for the r. of timelessness |
| W-pII .349.2:3 | and heal our minds as we r. to Him. |
| W-pII .350.1:8 | *teaches me to let Your memory r. to me, and* |
| W-pII ...14.3:6 | Knowledge will r. when we have done our |
| Wfl ........in.1:5 | For we would not r. again to the belief in |
| M-9 ...........1:9 | old thought system still has a basis for r.. |
| M-16 .........8:5 | the instant this occurs he will r. to earlier |
| M-20 .........4:2 | that peace cannot exist will certainly r.. |
| M-29 .........3:8 | To r. the function to the One to Whom it |
| M-29 .........3:9 | this that lets the memory of love r. to you. |
| C-3.............2:4 | merely to rise up and to r. to Him in |
| C-3.............4:1 | be seen before the memory of God can r.. |
| C-6.............5:8 | to r. to the eternal formlessness of God. |
| P-2......... II.5:5 | The process of psychotherapy is the r. to |
| P-2........IV.6:4 | into which the old one cannot r.. In a |
| P-2.......VII.3:5 | Nor will it r. again, once its cause has |
| P-3......... II.4:7 | Yet it is the means of r.; the way God |
| P-3......... II.4:7 | the way God chose for the r. of His Son. |
| S-2...........I.3:2 | by which you can r. to Him in peace. *Do* |
| S-2...........I.3:6 | How otherwise can prayer r. to God? He |
| S-3...........I.1:5 | back to dust, where it was born and will r. |
| S-3........IV.8:5 | R. to Me Who never left My Son. Listen, |
| S-3......IV.10:1 | So now r. your holy voice to Me. The |

## returned 40

|  |  |
|---|---|
| T-2.......VII.6:5 | until all the parts of the Sonship have r.. |
| T-4.......VII.7:3 | God does not need revelation r. to Him, |
| T-4.......VII.7:5 | r. by that mind to other minds, through |
| T-6....... II.10:6 | you need only perceive it as it is to be r.. |
| T-9.....VIII.8:1 | because love is r. and pride is not. Pride |
| T-10...... III.1:9 | from their sickness and r. to His Mind. |
| T-13....... V.9:8 | for He has r. you to the Father with Him. |
| T-13....VIII.8:4 | offered to your brothers, will be r. to you. |
| T-13...... IX.2:6 | and what is treasured is r. to you. |
| T-15.....VII.1:3 | the only love that is fully given and fully r. |
| T-15...... XI.9:2 | in you who welcome Him is r. to Him. |
| T-18...... IX.3:1 | insane messages seem to be r. to the mind |
| T-20.........I.2:8 | offered by you to me, and r. by me to you. |
| T-22.........I.7:3 | Still in this infant is your vision r. to you, |
| T-23.......in.3:4 | from sin and fear and happily r. to love. |
| T-24....IV.3:14 | Offered to them, no gifts can be r.. What |
| T-25...... VIII.h | Justice R. to Love |
| T-26...... IV.1:8 | is he r. to his real function of creating, |
| T-26....... V.8:3 | the past is gone, and cannot be r. to you? |
| T-27....... II.2:7 | Good cannot *be* r. for evil, for forgiveness |
| T-27.... II.14:3 | condemned can never be r. to its accuser, |
| W-pI.....97.6:2 | And when it is r. to you, it will surpass in |
| W-pI....123.7:3 | holy half an hour given Him will be r. to |
| W-pI....159.9:6 | Christ have been delivered, and r. to them |
| W-pI.169.13:2 | r. by you from holy instants you receive, |
| W-pI.170.11:4 | And so the fear of God r. with you. This |
| W-pI....187.5:8 | less than what will surely be r. to him. |
| W-pI.187.11:6 | will be r. to us in form of lilies we can lay |
| W-pI....188.4:2 | gifts beyond all measure, given and r.. To |
| W-pI....196.7:1 | the responsibility r. to some extent to you |
| W-pI.196.10:3 | outward, and r. from outside to within. It |
| W-pII .....2.5:2 | the call to all the world that freedom is r., |
| W-pII .....9.3:2 | be r. to spirit in the name of true creation |
| W-pII .323.2:3 | Love has now r. to our awareness. And we |
| W-pII ....345.h | today, For I would have them be r. to me. |
| M-18 .........2:6 | they are, so they will gladly be r. to Him. |
| M-22 .........3:8 | mind be r. to the Holy Spirit unless the |
| P-3..........II.5:3 | At that moment the good is r. to them, |
| S-1..........II.8:6 | and r. unblemished into the Mind of God |
| S-3........ IV.3:3 | restored as His completion and r. to share |

## returning 21

|  |  |
|---|---|
| T-5 ....... IV.2:6 | the higher part, r. it undivided to creation |
| T-10 .........I.4:1 | r. your mind simultaneously to your |
| T-10 ..... IV.8:5 | r. the little light must be acknowledged |
| T-12 .... VII.8:4 | r. to you the messages you gave them. |
| T-13 ... III.11:3 | by departing in peace and r. to the Father |
| T-18 ..... IX.2:1 | r. your little offering of darkness to the |
| T-19 ......I.14:6 | r. the glad tidings that it was done to you |
| T19..IV.B.17:6 | the ego find the death *it* seeks, r. it to you. |
| T-22 ..... IV.3:9 | His messenger, r. Him unto Himself. |
| T-25 ...... V.3:5 | answer by r. unto God what is His Own. |
| T-27 ...... V.6:1 | is left behind on your r. to the world. And |
| T-28 ...... III.6:4 | come and bridge His Son's r. to Himself. |
| W-pI..... 46.2:3 | r. the mind to the awareness of God. For |
| W-pI... 107.1:6 | to nothingness, r. whence they came. |
| WpI. rIV.in6:2 | Love to you, r. messages of yours to Him. |
| W-pI... 153.3:2 | with iron overlaid, r. but to start again. |
| W-pI... 168.6:4 | r. but the word He gave to us through His |
| W-pII . 324.2:4 | sure, and guarantees a safe r. home. |
| W-pII .... 357.h | miracles, and then R. unto us to be itself. |
| M-20 ......... 4:2 | R. anger, in whatever form, will drop the |
| S-2...........I.9:6 | God established for r. be achieved at last, |

## returns 33

|  |  |
|---|---|
| T-3 ....... IV.5:6 | mind r. to its proper function only when |
| T-5 ....... in.3:4 | the Sonship and r. thanks to the Father |
| T-5 .........II.2:5 | heals until the whole mind r. to creating. |
| T-7 ....... XI.4:3 | Every Son who r. to the Kingdom with |
| T-13 .... VII.8:3 | and His Son r. his Father's Love forever. |
| T-14 ..... III.5:4 | guilt. Everyone you offer healing to r. it. |
| T-16 ... VI.11:5 | that r. to take its rightful place within it. |
| T19..IV.B.17:5 | For what is sent through Him r. to Him, |
| T-20 ...... V.7:3 | other? This gift r. the laws of God to your |
| T-24 .......II.6:4 | about himself, as it r. to take their place. |
| T-24 .... VII.2:5 | And by your seeing it in him, r. to you. All |
| T-24 .... VII.2:6 | belongs to him, and thus r. to you. All of |
| T-28 ......I.11:4 | when the memory of God r. to them. |
| T-28 .....II.11:1 | miracle r. the cause of fear to you who |
| T-30 ..... III.7:3 | again to you when it r. to your awareness. |
| T-31 .... V.17:3 | this unsealed and open mind that truth r. |
| W-pI... 108.7:4 | and see how quickly peace r. to us. Light |
| W-pI. 140.10:4 | illusions end, and peace r. to the eternal, |
| W-pI... 169.6:3 | It r. the mind into the endless present, |
| W-pII . 241.2:2 | *who never left, r. to Heaven and his home.* |
| W-pII . 248.2:1 | *Father, my ancient love for You r., and lets* |
| W-pII ..... 5.4:1 | the means by which God's Son r. to sanity |
| W-pII . 270.1:4 | *ends forever, as Your memory r. to him. And* |
| W-pII . 306.1:1 | Heaven that an ancient memory r. to me? |
| W-pII . 323.2:1 | truth r. to us in wholeness and in joy. |
| W-pII . 342.1:8 | *light of truth, as memory of You r. to me.* |
| W-pII . 344.1:9 | *And thus Your Son arises and r. to You.* |
| W-pII . 345.1:2 | *And every one I give r. to me, reminding me* |
| M-19 ......... 5:9 | rests, the mind is still, and light r. again. |
| C-3 ........... 8:4 | And now the mind r. to its Creator; the |
| C-ep........... 5:3 | Let us go and bid Him welcome Who r. to |
| P-2......... V.8:9 | Son of God r. to Heaven through its kind |
| S-1.........in.1:2 | r. the thanks it offers Him unto the Son. |

## reunite 1

|  |  |
|---|---|
| T-12 ... VIII.4:5 | God would r. you with yourself, and did |

## reuniting 1

|  |  |
|---|---|
| S-2...........I.8:6 | of the past to hold it back from r. with the |

## reveal 13

|  |  |
|---|---|
| T-1 .... VII.5:11 | may occasionally r. the end to you, but to |
| T-7 ........I.7:13 | God does not r. this to you because it was |
| W-pI .... 15.3:6 | exercises will not r. knowledge to you. But |
| W-pI .... 71.9:1 | periods to asking God to r. His plan to us. |
| W-pI 152.11:5 | ask our Self that He r. Himself to us. And |
| W-pI .. 164.5:1 | like a curtain, to r. what lies beyond them |
| W-pI .. 186.4:1 | to God's Voice r. to us what He would |
| W-pII .... in.3:3 | and expect our Father to r. Himself, as He |
| W-pII . 221.2:6 | we are, and to r. Himself unto His Son. |
| W-pII . 224.2:4 | *see. R. what You would have me see instead.* |
| W-pII . 232.2:5 | Let Him r. all things to you, and be you |
| W-pII . 252.2:2 | *R. It now to me who am Your Son, that I may* |
| W-pII ..... 6.3:4 | fade before His glory and r. your holy Self |

## revealed 22

|  |  |
|---|---|
| T-7 ........I.7:15 | is fully shared be withheld and then r.? |
| T-8 ....... VI.8:3 | has r. it to me because I asked it of Him, |
| T-13 .....V.11:1 | Spirit is the light in which Christ stands r. |
| T-13 ..... VI.3:2 | The Christ as r. to you now has no past, |
| T-13 ..... VI.3:4 | and He stands r. in everyone you meet |
| T-14 ..... IX.2:3 | when its impossible nature is clearly r.? |
| T-21 ..... IV.8:1 | the ego's weakness is r. in both your sight. |
| T-21 .... VII.7:5 | or let him be r. to you through vision? |
| T-21 ... VIII.5:4 | Here is what denial has denied r. to you. |
| T-25 ..... IX.1:9 | you recognize that truth must be r. to you |
| T-27 ..... VI.8:6 | And truth will be r. to you who chose to |
| T-28 ........I.9:8 | It is not r. in miracles. They but remind |
| T-31 .....V.17:4 | have been laid by is truth r. exactly as it is |
| W-pI .... 28.6:3 | each of them to let its purpose be r. to you |
| W-pI .... 69.9:6 | *hidden. Yet I want to let it be r. to me, for my* |
| W-pI .... 91.6:8 | But what you really are must be r. to you. |
| W-pI .... 93.1:3 | if what is true about you were r. to you, |
| W-pI .... 94.4:2 | that it will be r. to all who ask for it. You |
| W-pI .. 158.5:2 | it. It r. itself to him at its appointed time. |
| W-pI .. 161.9:9 | you have it be r. to you and set you free? |
| W-pII ..... 2.3:4 | And what they hid is now r.; an altar to |
| S-3........ III.5:5 | of every malady has been r. exactly as it is. |

## reveals 2

|  |  |
|---|---|
| T-25 ........I.3:3 | r. yourself to you as you would have you |
| W-pI .. 189.3:1 | This is the world the Love of God r.. It is |

## revelation 32

*See also* revelation-readiness

|  |  |
|---|---|
| T-1 ........I.28:2 | fear. R. induces a state in which fear has |
| T-1 ........I.28:3 | Miracles are thus a means and r. is an end |
| T-1 ........I.46:3 | of communication with God by direct r., |
| T-1 ........I.48:2 | Only r. transcends it, having nothing to |
| T-1 ............II.h | R., Time and Miracles |
| T-1 .........II.1:1 | R. induces complete but temporary |
| T-1 .........II.1:5 | R. unites you directly with God. Miracles |
| T-1 .........II.2:1 | R. is intensely personal and cannot be |
| T-1 .........II.2:3 | R. induces only experience. Miracles, on |
| T-1 .........II.2:7 | R. is literally unspeakable because it is an |
| T-1 .........II.3:1 | Awe should be reserved for r., to which it |
| T-1 .........II.5:3 | channel from God to you open for r.. |
| T-1 .........II.5:4 | r. is not reciprocal. It proceeds from God |
| T-1 ....... III.4:5 | to the highly personal experience of r.. A |
| T-1 .... VII.5:11 | R. may occasionally reveal the end to you, |
| T-2 .......V.10:5 | I said before that only r. transcends time. |
| T-3 ...... III.4:4 | God" would be a miracle rather than a r.. |
| T-3 ..... III.5:10 | the result of r. and induces only thought. |
| T-4 ....... III.3:7 | No one who has experienced the r. of this |
| T-4 ...... VII.7:2 | mind. R. is not enough, because it is only |
| T-4 ...... VII.7:3 | God does not need r. returned to Him, |
| T-4 ...... VII.7:4 | This cannot be done with the actual r.; its |
| T-4 ...... VII.7:5 | the attitudes the knowledge from the r. |
| T-5 ..........I.1:3 | mind can experience r. with lasting effect, |
| T-5 ..........I.1:3 | because r. is an experience of pure joy. If |
| W-pI .. 158.2:8 | The r. that the Father and the Son are one |
| W-pI 158.11:1 | It matters not when r. comes, for that is |
| W-pI .. 169.4:1 | our statement that the r. of the Father |
| W-pI .. 169.8:2 | when it is released to r. and eternity. We |
| W-pI .. 169.9:2 | Whatever time the mind has set for r. is |
| W-pI 169.10:2 | When r. of your oneness comes, it will be |

W-pI.169.14:3 And **r.** stands not far behind. Its coming

## revelation-readiness 2

T-1......... II.5:1 Spirit, and alert to the **r.** of my brothers.
T-2... V.A.17:1 "Be of one mind" is the statement for **r.**.

## revelations 1

T-1......... II.5:1 **R.** are indirectly inspired by me because I

## revenge 3

T-25...... IV.3:7 their dreams of guilt and merciless **r.**, and
W-pI...190.1:7 and His insane desire for **r.** and death.
W-pI...195.9:1 gratitude in place of anger, malice and **r.**.

## revered 1

W-pI...193.5:3 ends, and guilt, abandoned, is **r.** no more.

## reverence 5

T-19....... II.5:2 unapproachable except with **r.** and awe. It
T-20...... VI.6:6 separation perceived in awe and held in **r.**
T-24..... VII.1:6 hint of threat, or anything but deepest **r.**.
T-25....... II.5:1 a wall and stands before it, deep in **r.**, as if
W-pI...156.5:5 Accept their **r.**, for it is due to Holiness

## reversal 18

T-6...... V.B.3:1 The first step in the **r.** or undoing process
T-6...... V.B.8:2 really only the beginning of the thought **r.**
T-6...... V.C.3:2 Yet it still has an aspect of thought **r.**,
T-6...... V.C.3:3 is merely the beginning of the thought **r.**,
T-11...... IV.4:5 beginning phases of this **r.** are often quite
T-17....... V.2:4 the **r.** of the unholy relationship. Be
T-23..... II.14:6 Such a **r.**, completely turned around, with
T-23..... II.15:1 the great **r.** they appear to be the laws of
T-23..... II.21:4 form in the progression of truth's **r.**,
T-24...... VI.5:1 and behold in him the whole **r.** of the laws
T-26..... VII.5:4 be corrected where the illusion of **r.** lies.
W-pI.....11.1:1 process; the **r.** of the thinking of the world
W-pI.....20.1:4 importance of the **r.** of your thinking. The
W-pI...126.1:1 is crucial to the thought **r.** that this course
M-in ..........1:2 The **r.** is characteristic. It seems as if the
M-4...... VII.1:7 of its **r.** of the world's thinking. In the
M-24..........4:1 course aims at a complete **r.** of thought.
M-28..........3:9 The whole **r.** is accomplished. Nothing is

## reversals 1

T-26..... VII.5:2 because they *are* **r.** of the laws of truth. The

## reverse 8

T-1......... V.6:4 on which the **r.** of the Golden Rule rests.
T-5........ VI.4:1 **r.** a lower court's decisions in this world.
W-pI.....78.2:2 We will **r.** the way you see by not allowing
W-pI...100.1:2 plan. Salvation must **r.** the mad belief in
W-pI...105.3:1 course has set is to **r.** your view of giving,
M-4....... IX.1:6 is to **r.** the thinking of the world entirely.
P-1.............4:2 He must become willing to **r.** his thinking
P-2......... V.2:3 **r.** his twisted way of looking at the world;

## reversed 14

T-12....... V.8:7 situation as you have set it up is **r.**.
T-17...... VI.2:4 In the ego's procedure this is **r.**. The
T-23..... II.14:7 by which the laws of God appear to be **r.**.
T-26..... VII.5:2 Perception's laws must be **r.**, because they
T-26..... VII.5:3 forever will be true, and cannot be **r.**; yet
T-28....... II.8:8 and cause are first split off, and then **r.**, so
T-28...... III.3:2 Yet in the dreaming has this been **r.**, and
W-pI.....19.1:2 while at other times the order is **r.**. The
W-pI.....78.4:3 So is the seeing of the world **r.**, as we look
W-pI.....91.3:6 the light. How can this be **r.**? For you it is
M-in ..........1:1 is actually **r.** in the thinking of the world.
M-14..........4:1 its thought system has been completely **r.**
M-28 .........2:2 is all the thinking of the world **r.** entirely.
S-2 ...........I.9:4 Forgiveness' role must be **r.**, and cleansed

## reverses 4

T-1...........I.9:2 sense, the exchange **r.** the physical laws.
T-5........ VI.4:1 and the Holy Spirit **r.** its decision, much
T-18.........I.8:5 Thus He **r.** the course of insanity and
W-pI.....38.1:1 Your holiness **r.** all the laws of the world.

## reversing 2

T-6...... V.A.6:4 because it is the beginning step in **r.** your
T-28.......... II.h **R.** Effect and Cause

## revert 1

W-pII......5.3:2 but can quite suddenly **r.** to fear, where

## review 81

T-26..... VII.1:3 us **r.** the principles that we have covered,
T-31....... II.2:1 Let us **r.** again what seems to stand
W-in ..........3:2 With the exception of the **r.** periods, each
W-pI.............h Review I
WpI...rI.in.1:1 today we will have a series of **r.** periods.
WpI...rI.in.1:3 which you should consider in your **r.**. In
WpI...rI.in.2:6 be sure to **r.** all of them once more.
WpI...rI.in.3:2 it as part of your **r.** of the idea to which it
WpI...rI.in.6:1 You will note that, for **r.** purposes, some
W-pI........51.h **r.** for today covers the following ideas:
W-pI........52.h Today's **r.** covers these ideas:
W-pI........53.h Today we will **r.** the following:
W-pI........54.h These are the **r.** ideas for today:
W-pI........55.h Today's **r.** includes the following:
W-pI........56.h Our **r.** for today covers the following:
W-pI........57.h Today let us **r.** these ideas:
W-pI........58.h These ideas are for **r.** today:
W-pI........59.h The following ideas are for **r.** today:
W-pI........60.h These ideas are for today's **r.**:
W-pI.......64.3:1 To **r.** our last few lessons, your function
W-pI.....76.8:1 a short **r.** of the different kinds of "laws"
W-pI.....78.6:3 You will **r.** his faults, the difficulties you
W-pI.............h Review II
WpI..rII.in.1:1 We are now ready for another **r.**. We will
WpI..rII.in.1:2 We will begin where our last **r.** left off,
W-pI........81.h Our ideas for **r.** today are:
W-pI........82.h We will **r.** these ideas today:
W-pI........83.h Today let us **r.** these ideas:
W-pI........84.h These are the ideas for today's **r.**:
W-pI........85.h Today's **r.** will cover these ideas:
W-pI........86.h These ideas are for **r.** today:
W-pI........87.h Our **r.** today will cover these ideas:
W-pI........88.h Today we will **r.** these ideas:
W-pI........89.h These are our **r.** ideas for today:
W-pI........90.h For this **r.** we will use these ideas:
W-pI.............h Review III
WpI. rIII.in1:1 Our next **r.** begins today. We will review
WpI. rIII.in1:2 We will **r.** two recent lessons every day for
WpIrIII.in10:2 two ideas a brief but serious **r.** each hour.
WpIrIII.in12:1 Each day's **r.** assignments will conclude
WpIrIII.in13:3 As you **r.** these thoughts He gave to you.
W-pI......111.h For morning and evening **r.**:
W-pI......112.h For morning and evening **r.**:
W-pI......113.h For morning and evening **r.**:
W-pI......114.h For morning and evening **r.**:
W-pI......115.h For morning and evening **r.**:
W-pI......116.h For morning and evening **r.**:
W-pI......117.h For morning and evening **r.**:
W-pI......118.h For morning and evening **r.**:
W-pI......119.h For morning and evening **r.**:
W-pI......120.h For morning and evening **r.**:
W-pI.131.11:6 is real. **R.** the thoughts as well which are
W-pI...134.1:1 Let us **r.** the meaning of "forgive," for it is
W-pI.139.11:2 start with this **r.** of what our mission is: *I*
W-pI.............h Review IV
WpI. rIV.in1:1 Now we **r.** again, this time aware we are
WpI. rIV.in1:3 Such is our aim for this **r.**, and for the
WpI. rIV.in1:4 we **r.** the recent lessons and their central
WpI. rIV.in2:1 unifies each step in the **r.** we undertake,
WpI. rIV.in4:4 start each practice period in this **r.** with
WpI. rIV.in5:1 idea you will **r.** that day can offer you in
WpI. rIV.in7:5 Let each idea which you **r.** that day give
WpI. rIV.in9:3 Each day of practicing, as we **r.**, we close
W-pI.............h Review V
WpI...rV.in1:1 We now **r.** again. This time we are ready
WpI...rV.in3:6 *as we r. the thoughts that You have given us.*
WpI...rV.in4:1 should precede the thoughts that we **r.**.
WpI...rV.in5:3 This **r.** will shorten time immeasurably, if
WpI...rV.in8:2 Together we **r.** these thoughts. Together
WpI...rV.in9:1 Let this **r.** be then your gift to me. For
WpI.rV.in10:1 Let this **r.** become a time in which we
WpI.rV.in11:1 With this we start each day of our **r.**.
WpI.rV.in11:4 No thought that we **r.** but we surround
WpI.rV.in11:5 And thus, when we have finished this **r.**,
W-pI.............h Review VI
WpI rVI.in.1:1 For this **r.** we take but one idea each day,
WpI rVI.in.2:1 in which we carefully **r.** the thoughts the
WpI rVI.in.3:1 These practice sessions, like our last **r.**,
WpI rVI.in.4:1 and special forms of practicing for this **r.**.
WpI rVI.in.7:1 To Him I offer this **r.** for you. I place you
WpI rVI.in.7:4 us offer Him the whole **r.** we now begin,

## reviewed 2

WpI. rIV.in7:1 two ideas assigned to you to be **r.** that day
W-pII ..in.11:3 special thoughts should be **r.** each day,

## reviewing 8

W-pI....... 7.3:2 or are you merely **r.** your past experiences
W-pI.....26.6:1 closing your eyes and **r.** the unresolved
W-pI.....64.7:1 several minutes to **r.** these thoughts, and
W-pI.....64.8:3 keep your eyes open after **r.** the thoughts,
W-pI.....65.5:1 period, begin by **r.** the idea for the day.
W-pI.....66.5:1 practice period by **r.** these thoughts: *God*
W-pI.....70.7:5 **r.** some of the external places where you
W-pI...158.4:5 once again; **r.** mentally what has gone by.

## reviews 5

WpI. rIII.in5:1 format you should use for these **r.** is this:
WpI. rIII.in6:4 Have faith, in these **r.**, the means the Holy
WpI. rIII.in8:1 the first five minutes of the day to your **r.**,
WpIrIII.in10:1 In these **r.**, we stress the need to let your
WpIrIII.in12:3 we come from these **r.** with learning gains

## revolt 2

T-9......... V.3:7 but to **r.** against it is still to believe in it.
T-21........II.6:5 a mad **r.** against what must forever be.

## revolts 2

T-9......... V.3:7 there have been **r.** against this concept,
M-8 ...........2:6 the mind **r.** against truth and gives itself

## reward 9

T-4........ III.3:3 some sort of **r.** for maintaining this belief.
T-13....... IX.2:5 and where it is invested determines its **r.**.
T-16......... III.h The **R.** of Teaching
T-25........II.2:2 anything but fear and guilt been your **r.**.
T-26.... VIII.9:2 It has no meaning, and is not your just **r.**.
W-pI.....20.2:8 apart. And great indeed will be your **r.**.
W-pI.....80.5:2 your eyes, and receive your **r.**. Recognize
W-pI.....98.5:3 of gaining a **r.** so great it has no measure?
S-3 ..........II.5:5 Death is **r.** and not a punishment. But

## rewarded 2

T-13...... IX.2:4 And faith can be **r.** only in terms of the
T-13...... IX.3:2 because your faith will be **r.** as you gave it.

## rewarding 1

M-16 .........9:4 bad, neither **r.** nor demanding sacrifice,

## rewards 10

| | |
|---|---|
| T-4 VI.h | The **R.** of God |
| T-4 VI.3:4 | Learning through **r.** is more effective than |
| T-4 VI.3:5 | The **r.** of God, however, are immediately |
| T-4 VI.5:8 | but can you really want the **r.** of the ego in |
| T-4 VI.5:8 | of the ego in the presence of the **r.** of God |
| T-13 IX.2:3 | The ego **r.** fidelity to it with pain, for faith |
| T-17 V.6:4 | that the **r.** of faith are being introduced. If |
| T-25 II.1:7 | you no **r.** which you would want to keep. |
| W-pI.122.11:1 | hold out the sure **r.** of questions answered |
| W-pI 164.4:5 | practicing today will bring **r.** so great and |

## rhythm 1

| | |
|---|---|
| P-2 VI.2:6 | "The **r.** of the universe," "the herald |

## rich 1

| | |
|---|---|
| T-26 I.5:3 | house as **r.** and limitless as Heaven itself. |

## richer 2

| | |
|---|---|
| T-25 VIII.9:8 | Heaven is **r.** made by each one you accept. |
| W-pI 105.1:4 | gives the gift; the taker is the **r.** by his loss. |

## rid 20

| | |
|---|---|
| T-7 VIII.1:5 | of getting **r.** of something it does not want |
| T-7 VIII.2:6 | that you have gotten **r.** of the problem. |
| T-7 VIII.3:3 | and get **r.** of another part does not really |
| T-7 VIII.3:6 | the idea that you can get **r.** of something |
| T-12 III.7:10 | not outside it before you can get **r.** of it; |
| T-12 III.7:10 | and why you must get **r.** of it before you |
| T-13 II.1:1 | of projection is always to get **r.** of guilt. |
| T-13 II.1:2 | to get **r.** of guilt from its viewpoint only, |
| T-13 II.2:2 | You project guilt to get **r.** of it, but you are |
| T-17 V.7:2 | distress only by getting **r.** of your brother. |
| T19 IV.A.h | First Obstacle: The Desire to Get **R.** of It |
| T19 IV.A.1:1 | flow across is your desire to get **r.** of it. |
| T19 IV.A.7:1 | little insane wish to get **r.** of Him Whom |
| T19 IV.B.1:1 | the obstacle of your desire to get **r.** of it. |
| T19 IV.B.4:4 | want neither to get **r.** of peace nor limit it. |
| T19 IV.B.9:4 | is not this you would be **r.** of, and having |
| T19 IV.D.5:3 | The desire to get **r.** of peace and drive the |
| W-pI 30.2:2 | attempting to get **r.** of what we do not like |
| W-pI 193.5:4 | the dream of sin, and **r.** the mind of fear. |
| S-2 II.6:4 | And you will seek to **r.** yourself of guilt in |

## riddle 1

| | |
|---|---|
| T-31 V.14:2 | must find the answer to the **r.** of himself. |

## ridiculous 9

| | |
|---|---|
| T-5 V.3:8 | However **r.** the idea of attacking God may |
| T-12 V.8:1 | indeed, it is merely **r.** if you look at it. Is it |
| T-23 I.4:7 | **r.** as nature roaring at the wind in anger, |
| T-27 VIII.5:6 | too **r.** for anything but to be laughed away |
| W-pI 95.2:1 | yourself as a **r.** parody on God's creation; |
| W-pI 135.7:4 | Such attempts, **r.** yet deeply cherished, |
| W-pI 156.6:5 | a silly dream, not frightening, **r.** perhaps, |
| W-pI 188.2:3 | which prove it is not there become **r.**. |
| P-2 IV.4:5 | It is **r.** from start to finish. Yet having |

## right 140

*See also* non-right-minded, not-right-mindedness, right-, right-minded, right-mindedness, right-side

| | |
|---|---|
| T-1 I.7:1 | Miracles are everyone's **r.**, but |
| T-1 I.36:1 | Miracles are examples of **r.** thinking, |
| T-1 III.5:3 | the **r.** choice is inevitable if you remember |
| T-2 II.2:4 | Your **r.** mind depends on it. Denial of |
| T-2 II.2:6 | of the **r.** mind the denial of error frees the |
| T-2 III.4:4 | Perfectly aware of the **r.** defense it passes |
| T-2 V.3:4 | its purpose is to restore him *to* his **r.** mind. |
| T-2 V.3:5 | that the miracle worker be in his **r.** mind, |
| T-2 V.A.15:1 | induces the **r.** perception for healing. |
| T-2 VI.9:2 | little **r.** thinking to realize why fear occurs |
| T-2 VIII.3:5 | might be called a process of **r.** evaluation. |
| T-3 II.3:1 | to your belief that he is not in his **r.** mind. |
| T-3 III.2:5 | It is the **r.** answer to a question, but you |
| T-3 III.2:7 | The miracle, or the **r.** answer, corrects |
| T-3 III.4:3 | It is, however, a means of **r.** perception, |
| T-3 III.5:8 | for creative thinking, but not for **r.** doing. |
| T-3 III.6:1 | **R.** perception is necessary before God |
| T-3 IV.4:1 | it is applicable only to **r.** perception. You |
| T-3 IV.7:11 | I can help you make your own **r.** choice. |
| T-3 IV.7:13 | Therefore, they do not choose **r.**. The |
| T-3 IV.7:14 | are merely those who choose **r.** sooner. |
| T-3 IV.7:15 | **R.** minds can do this now, and they will |
| T-3 V.3:6 | want to do it if you were in your **r.** mind. |
| T-3 VI.2:10 | whether your judgment is **r.** or wrong. |
| T-3 VI.11:7 | no one in his **r.** mind believes that what is |
| T-4 in.1:7 | in the **r.** sense is to be inspired or in spirit. |
| T-4 I.h | **R.** Teaching and Right Learning |
| T-4 I.h | Right Teaching and **R.** Learning |
| T-4 I.7:5 | I have no **r.** to set your learning limits for |
| T-4 I.8:3 | in your **r.** mind you realize it is not real. |
| T-4 I.12:5 | The Kingdom of Heaven is the spirit's **r.**, |
| T-4 II.10:2 | **r.** perception is uniformly without attack, |
| T-4 II.11:3 | whole value of **r.** perception lies in the |
| T-4 III.10:3 | ego, and how little to protect your **r.** mind |
| T-4 IV.8:6 | for this is the one **r.** use of judgment. |
| T-4 VI.7:6 | all things, but it does set all things **r.**. |
| T-5 I.3:3 | The Holy Spirit is in your **r.** mind, as He |
| T-5 I.4:6 | one of God's creations, my **r.** thinking, |
| T-5 II.2:4 | have understood the Call to **r.** thinking. |
| T-5 II.5:2 | implies there is a **r.** way and also a wrong |
| T-5 II.7:14 | therefore "lost" to you until you choose **r.** |
| T-5 II.8:2 | mind that always speaks for the **r.** choice, |
| T-6 IV.5:4 | in his **r.** mind could possibly believe this, |
| T-6 IV.5:4 | and no one in his **r.** mind does believe it. |
| T-6 IV.11:10 | You would doubt your **r.** mind, which is |
| T-7 III.4:10 | Your **r.** mind sees only brothers, because |
| T-7 IV.5:7 | strength of **r.** perception is so great that it |
| T-8 IX.1:6 | teach you the **r.** *perception* of the body, for |
| T-9 I.8:1 | No **r.** mind can believe that its will is |
| T-9 I.10:6 | to Him are real, being of your **r.** mind. |
| T-9 III.2:1 | ego it is kind and **r.** and good to point out |
| T-9 III.2:6 | But your task is still to tell him he is **r.**. |
| T-9 III.2:9 | He is still **r.**, because he is a Son of God. |
| T-9 III.5:6 | Your brother is as **r.** as you are, and if you |
| T-9 IV.4:1 | for one, though not of the **r.** teacher. The |
| T-9 IV.10:3 | reality is fearful is wrong can God be **r.**. |
| T-9 IV.10:4 | And I assure you that God *is* **r.**. Be glad, |
| T-9 V.8:10 | But remember also that the **r.** one will. |
| T-9 V.9:5 | By following the **r.** Guide, you will learn |
| T-12 I.1:3 | true. But truth is real in its own **r.**, and to |
| T-12 I.3:7 | and you are assuming the **r.** to attack his |
| T-12 II.5:7 | The goal of love is but your **r.**, and it |
| T-12 VII.1:1 | has occurred under the **r.** guidance, for |
| T-12 VII.9:2 | You can decide to see it **r.**. What you |
| T-12 VII.12:6 | judgment of the Holy Spirit it will be **r.**, |
| T-13 III.8:6 | For grandeur is the **r.** of God's Son, and |
| T-13 III.10:1 | to sanity cannot obtain it in your **r.** mind. |
| T-13 IV.2:5 | is the final proof that you were **r.**. |
| T-13 IX.5:2 | then, teach him he is **r.** in his delusion? |
| T-14 III.5:3 | It is the natural result of choosing **r.**, |
| T-14 IV.4:5 | is **r.** and you are wrong about yourself. He |
| T-14 IV.6:1 | become as easy and as **r.** as breathing. |
| T-14 V.3:7 | that is the **r.** of all that God created. Deny |
| T-14 V.4:1 | of the Kingdom is the **r.** of God's Son, |
| T-14 V.7:4 | to restore what is the **r.** of God's creation. |
| T-18 IV.7:7 | it asks nothing you cannot give **r.** now. |
| T-18 VII.7:4 | in which sin loses all attraction ***r.*** *now.* For |
| T-19 II.1:2 | can be corrected, and the wrong made **r.**. |
| T-20 V.6:3 | it ever held or will ever hold is here **r.** now |
| T-20 VIII.7:2 | But vision sets all things **r.**, bringing them |
| T-21 II.5:1 | see is but the idle witness that you were **r.**. |
| T-21 V.7:10 | the Holy Spirit's purpose in its own **r.**. It |
| T-22 IV.2:1 | few steps along the **r.** way that seem hard, |
| T-25 VIII.9:11 | same does mercy stand at God's **r.** Hand, |
| T-25 VIII.14:1 | You have the **r.** to all the universe; to |
| T-25 IX.8:1 | have an equal **r.** to miracles with you, you |
| T-25 IX.8:1 | you will not claim your **r.** to them because |
| T-25 IX.9:3 | Not one **r.** do you believe you have. And |
| T-26 X.3:7 | of what he is, denied the **r.** to be himself, |
| T-27 V.9:6 | but there is One within you Who is **r.**. |
| T-28 IV.2:1 | a way of finding certainty **r.** here and now |
| T-29 I.4:6 | Conditional upon the "**r.**" to separate will |
| T-29 VII.1:9 | Do you prefer that you be **r.** or happy? Be |
| T-29 VIII.1:9 | or wanted, or a **r.** demanded or achieved, |
| T-30 I.10:2 | your happiness depends on being **r.**. But |
| T-30 I.11:6 | the goal of being **r.** when you are wrong. |
| T-30 III.4:2 | you want indeed and have the **r.** to ask for |
| T-30 V.9:10 | It is your sacred **r.**, and what you pay for |
| T-30 VI.4:7 | forgiveness is your **r.** as much as his. Nor |
| W-pI 42.2:4 | but be in the **r.** place at the right time. |
| W-pI 42.2:4 | but be in the right place at the **r.** time. |
| W-pI 47.1:5 | you the recognition of the **r.** solution, and |
| W-pI 47.8:3 | Remember that peace is your **r.**, because |
| W-pI 50.1:3 | being liked, knowing the "**r.**" people, and |
| W-pI 61.3:4 | a positive assertion of your **r.** to be saved, |
| W-pI 77.3:1 | will claim the miracles which are your **r.**, |
| W-pI 77.8:5 | *me. God has established miracles as my* ***r.***. |
| W-pI 104.1:2 | They are your **r.**, because of what you are. |
| W-pI 105.6:2 | are their **r.** under the equal laws of God. |
| W-pI 121.5:5 | knows. It does not question, certain it is **r.** |
| W-pI 126.5:3 | Yet it remains your **r.** to let the sinner not |
| W-pI 133.7:2 | when you deny his **r.** to everything, you |
| W-pI 134.4:6 | It would see as **r.** the plainly wrong; the |
| W-pI 135.6:3 | endowed the body with the **r.** to serve you |
| W-pI 136.13:2 | God has given you is not the truth **r.** now, |
| W-pI 151.4:2 | because it is a **r.** to be withheld from you. |
| W-pI 152.10:5 | his **r.** to Heaven and release from hell, are |
| W-pI 154.5:2 | does he question the **r.** of him who does, |
| W-pI 162.5:2 | the **r.** to perfect holiness you now accept. |
| W-pI 183.5:2 | things on earth slip into **r.** perspective. |
| W-pI 186.12:3 | consider this; which is more likely to be **r.** |
| W-pI 195.8:6 | has earned the **r.** to love by being loving, |
| W-pI 198.1:4 | **r.** you have established for yourself can be |
| W-pII 227.2:3 | with his **r.** mind restored to him at last. |
| M-2 4:4 | The pupil comes at the **r.** time to the right |
| M-2 4:4 | comes at the right time to the **r.** place. |
| M-2 4:5 | made the **r.** choice in that ancient instant |
| M-4 VIII.1:4 | The time will be as **r.** as is the answer. |
| M-4 IX.1:4 | in the Word of God to set all things **r.**; not |
| M-5 III.2:3 | thoughts ask for the **r.** to question what |
| M-10 4:3 | times you merely thought you were **r.**, |
| M-11 2:7 | Who is **r.**? For one of you is wrong. It |
| M-16 2:5 | they easily become gods in their own **r.**, |
| M-16 2:6 | can be said that it is well to start the day **r.** |
| M-16 3:4 | starting the day **r.** does indeed save time. |
| M-29 2:13 | His answers are always **r.**. Would you say |
| C-1 5:1 | The mind can be **r.** or wrong, depending |
| P-3 III.4:1 | The **r.** to live is something no one need |
| P-3 III.4:3 | is a **r.** the therapist and patient share alike |
| S-2 III.6:8 | Prayer is His Own **r.** Hand, made free to |

## right-minded 3

| | |
|---|---|
| T-2 V.3:2 | **r.** neither exalt nor depreciate the mind of |
| T-3 II.3:5 | exists, **r.** seeing cannot see anything but |
| T-3 IV.4:2 | You can be **r.** or wrong-minded, and even |

## right-mindedness 16

| | |
|---|---|
| T-2 V.3:1 | and miracle-mindedness means **r.**. The |
| T-2 V.3:3 | need not await the **r.** of the receiver. In |
| T-2 V.3:5 | unable to re-establish **r.** in someone else. |
| T-2 V.4:3 | on your **r.** and has turned it upside down. |
| T-2 V.4:5 | who have not realized that **r.** *is* healing. |
| T-2 V.9:7 | yet. Charity is essential to **r.** in the limited |
| T-2 V.A.14:2 | Only **r.** can correct in a way that has any |
| T-2 VIII.3:4 | is a concept totally opposed to **r.**, and the |
| T-2 VIII.3:4 | of the Last Judgment is to restore **r.** to you |
| T-2 VIII.5:7 | This is what your **r.** cannot but dictate. |
| T-3 IV.4:1 | **R.** is not to be confused with the knowing |
| T-3 IV.4:3 | The term "**r.**" is properly used as the |
| T-4 II.10:1 | Salvation is nothing more than "**r.**," |
| T-4 II.10:2 | **R.** leads to the next step automatically, |
| C-1 5:2 | ***R.*** listens to the Holy Spirit, forgives the |
| C-1 6:2 | are illusions because **r.** merely overlooks, |

**right-** 1

T-2... V.A.13:1 Never confuse **r.** and wrong-mindedness.

**right-side** 1

T-6......V.A.6:4 your perception and turning it **r.** up. This

**righted** 1

W-pI...164.5:3 Now is the balance **r.**, and the scale of

**righteous** 6

T-23.... II.11:2 to be wrested in **r.** wrath from this most
T-27.........I.7:5 is their **r.** payment for their little lives?
W-pI.....73.2:2 to attack you and call for "**r.**" judgment.
W-pI...127.2:6 to judge between the **r.** and the sinner,
W-pI...134.1:1 that entails an unfair sacrifice of **r.** wrath,
W-pI...153.2:2 and **r.** in the name of self-defense. Yet is

**righteousness** 1

T-27.........I.2:4 you has been unfair will come to him in **r.**

**rightful** 15

T-5........III.8:2 apart from your **r.** place in the Sonship,
T-5........III.8:2 and the **r.** place of the Sonship is God.
T-14....XI.6:11 will take His **r.** place in your awareness
T-15.....VI.8:6 of God will take Their **r.** place in you, and
T-16....VI.11:5 that returns to take its **r.** place within it.
T-17....IV.14:5 And each is given its **r.** place when both
T-17....IV.16:1 ascends into His **r.** place and you to yours
W-pI.....61.3:3 toward taking your **r.** place in salvation. It
W-pI.....65.2:1 only way in which you can take your **r.**
W-pI.....80.1:8 your **r.** place in God's plan for salvation.
W-pI.....99.12:5 that love may find its **r.** place in you and
W-pI...152.8:3 your **r.** place as co-creator of the universe,
W-pI.153.14:2 And then we go to take our **r.** place where
W-pI...160.7:3 for you have given him your **r.** place. Yet
W-pII..332.1:6 in, and take its **r.** place within the mind.

**rightfully** 3

T-17......VI.7:4 being withheld from where it **r.** belonged.
W-pI.....77.4:2 you are asking only for what is **r.** yours.
P-3........III.2:8 withhold it from where it **r.** belongs has

**rightly** 5

W-pI...193.6:4 see them **r.** when you hold these words in
M-10..........3:3 In order to judge anything **r.**, one would
M-14..........2:8 in it have been **r.** judged by His judgment.
P-2......IV.11:5 is. Seen **r.**, its purpose can be understood.
S-1........III.1:4 for others, if **r.** understood, becomes a

**rightness** 1

P-2........IV.7:2 achieved by first establishing the "**r.**" of

**rights** 7

T-7..........I.4:1 other hand, always demands reciprocal **r.**,
T-25VIII.13:10 and cannot fairly see another's **r.** because
T-25......IX.8:1 you were unjust to one with equal **r.**. Seek
T-30......VI.2:6 asked to sacrifice your **r.** when you return
T-30......VI.2:9 It *keeps* your **r.** from being sacrificed.
W-pI.....77.4:3 to another, and that in asking for your **r.**,
W-pI.....77.4:3 you are upholding the **r.** of everyone.

**rim** 1

W-pI.......7.3:2 feeling the **r.** of a cup against your lips,

**ring** 1

T-18......IX.3:9 to abandon Him at the outside **r.** of fear,

**riotous** 1

W-pI.....49.4:4 **r.** thoughts and sights and sounds of this

**ripple** 5

T-18... VIII.3:3 the faintest **r.** on the surface of the ocean.
T-18... VIII.3:4 imperceptible **r.** hails itself as the ocean.
T-18... VIII.3:6 terrifies the little **r.** and wants to swallow
T-18... VIII.4:6 the **r.** without the ocean is inconceivable.
T-18... VIII.7:3 the **r.** dances as it rests upon the ocean.

**ripples** 1

T-28...... III.5:2 the **r.** that a ship has made in passing by.

**rise** 83

T-4......... II.6:6 with the belief in scarcity that gave **r.** to it.
T-4........ IV.6:3 can focus and **r.** above fatigue and heal.
T-4......... V.1:5 which gave **r.** to it and which it serves.
T-5......... V.2:3 blessed is incapable of giving **r.** to guilt,
T-5......... V.2:3 giving rise to guilt, and must give **r.** to joy.
T-8..... VIII.6:9 premises give **r.** in order to judge them
T-9........ VI.2:3 you will not always give **r.** to joy, and so
T-11....... V.8:2 of it. For if the ego could give **r.** to fear, it
T-11...... VI.1:7 For Christ does **r.** above the ego and all its
T-13...... VI.1:2 this no illusions can **r.** to meet your sight,
T-13...... VI.9:3 of praise and gladness **r.** to your Creator,
T-13.....VII.4:3 or not to hear the cries of pain that **r.** to it
T-16...... IV.1:4 Your salvation will **r.** clearly before your
T-16...... IV.3:2 It makes no attempt to **r.** above the storm
T-17....... II.6:1 All this beauty will **r.** to bless your sight
T-17... VIII.2:7 But **r.** you not against it, for against your
T-18....... V.3:1 thousands will **r.** to Heaven with you. Can
T-18...... IX.4:2 world could **r.** from it and keep it hidden.
T-18...... IX.6:3 to the mountain tops that **r.** above it, and
T-18...... IX.7:2 a lake, a city, all **r.** in your imagination,
T-19.........I.5:5 all obstacles that seem to **r.** between them
T19... IV.D.6:3 all **r.** and bid you not to raise your eyes.
T19. IV.D.17:5 in it, that we may **r.** as one in resurrection
T19. IV.D.18:5 and let him **r.** again to glad remembrance
T-20.... VIII.3:3 may **r.** before your vision and give you joy
T-22...... IV.5:3 that seems to **r.** between you both. So
T-22...... IV.6:3 seemed to **r.** and block their way before.
T-23.......in.5:4 but help him **r.** above it and perceive the
T-24...... III.5:2 will, **r.** between what He wills for you and
T-25...... IV.3:4 **r.** a world they will rejoice to look upon,
T-25.....VII.2:7 What wish can **r.** against His Will, and be
T-25...... IX.7:8 then must problems **r.** to block your way,
T-26....... II.1:7 all time and will not **r.** again in any form.
T-26...... IV.3:4 altar to **r.** and tower far above the world,
T-26...... IV.5:1 sin once was perceived will **r.** a world that
T-26....... V.5:3 to creation,–did this world appear to **r.**.
T-26.....VII.8:6 and all beliefs that **r.** from mists of guilt.
T-26...VII.10:2 joyous answer will creation **r.** within you,
T-28....... V.7:3 misty pictures **r.** to cover it with vague
T-30...... IV.4:5 But then they fall and cannot **r.** again.
T-30....... V.8:6 Him to **r.** from chains and go with you,
T-30...... VI.3:1 **r.** to take the place of dreams of terror.
T-30.....VII.7:4 state so seemingly unsafe that fear must **r.**
T-31.........I.3:4 so overlearned and fixed they **r.** like heavy
T-31.........I.6:1 so small and still It cannot **r.** above the
T-31...... V.13:3 done the learning which gave **r.** to them.
T-31...VII.10:2 give **r.** to but an image of yourself that can
W-pI.....16.2:2 What gives **r.** to the perception of a whole
W-pI.....18.1:1 the thoughts which give **r.** to what you see
W-pI.....54.1:5 so will the real world **r.** before my eyes as
W-pI.....55.2:5 attack thoughts that give **r.** to this picture
W-pI.....73.2:2 The wishes of the ego gave **r.** to it, and the
W-pI.....74.2:3 Therefore it cannot give **r.** to illusions.
W-pI.....79.5:5 and **r.** to haunt you from time to time,
W-pI...79.10:2 Whenever any difficulty seems to **r.**, tell
W-pI...123.8:2 His Son, that he might **r.** above the world,
W-pI...128.6:1 and see how far you **r.** above the world,
W-pI...132.7:3 point of death, and **r.** to teach it. Others
W-pI.135.25:4 And you **r.** again from what was seeming
W-pI.136.15:5 prayer, to help us **r.** above defensiveness,
W-pI...153.2:1 The world gives **r.** but to defensiveness.
W-pI.153.19:3 day. We **r.** up strong in Christ, and let our
W-pI...157.3:2 alter time sufficiently to **r.** above its laws,
W-pI...168.4:3 hearts **r.** up and claim the light as theirs.
W-pI...168.5:3 down, and **r.** to Him in gratitude and love
W-pI.169.10:4 and **r.** and work and go to sleep by them?
W-pI.186.10:2 you make give **r.** to but conflicting goals,
W-pI...187.7:4 The thought of sacrifice gives **r.** to all the
W-pII ....in.9:6 A moment more, and it will **r.** again. A
M-5 ..... II.2:12 merely **r.** up without their aid and say, "I
M-10 .........5:5 can the teacher of God **r.** up unburdened,
M-17 .........4:2 an interpretation that gives **r.** to negative
M-17 .......8:10 really have the power to give **r.** to guilt.
M-17 .........9:5 Can nothing give **r.** to anger? Hardly so.
M-19 .........1:3 interpretations to which injustice gives **r.**,
M-19 .........2:6 **r.** to meet one as the journey continues,
M-28 .........4:7 **r.** up from the dust and look upon our
C-3.............2:4 to **r.** up and to return to Him in peace.
P-2........ IV.5:4 temporary, or another illness **r.** instead,
P-2........ VI.5:5 possibly give **r.** to sickness of any kind.
P-3..........II.3:6 or later that something will **r.** and grow; a
S-1......... V.1:3 the ground where it begins to **r.** to God,
S-2.........in.1:2 to try to **r.** above prayer's bottom step, or

**risen** 16

T-13..... V.11:4 the Son, they have **r.** in Him to the Father.
T-13...... VI.3:4 No cloud of guilt has **r.** to obscure Him,
T-17....VIII.5:4 For he is **r.**, and you have accepted the
T-17....VIII.6:7 demonstrate that you have **r.** far beyond
T19....IV.A.6:5 The sun has **r.** over it. How can a shadow
T-20.........I.1:5 But a **r.** Christ becomes the symbol of the
T-20.........I.4:7 Look on your **r.** Friend, and celebrate his
T-20......II.10:1 that the Son of God is **r.** from the past,
T-24...... VI.9:3 to you is done and he is **r.** from the past.
T-25.......in.2:6 is. The son of man is not the **r.** Christ. Yet
T-25...... IV.4:5 sun in you has **r.** that they may be pushed
T-26...... IX.8:4 stood a cross stands now the **r.** Christ,
W-pI...191.5:1 and you have **r.** far above the world, and
M-23 .........2:4 He has become the **r.** Son of God. He has
S-1......... V.3:5 High has the ladder **r.**. You have come
S-3........ IV.4:2 Your prayer has **r.** up and called to God,

**rises** 24

T-12........II.5:6 at every image that **r.** to delay you, for the
T-15.... III.12:6 which **r.** above the stars and reaches even
T-16.... IV.11:6 and in every fantasy that **r.** to delay you,
T-16.... IV.11:6 call for help that **r.** ceaselessly from you to
T-16....... V.8:5 is buried deep and **r.** in the form of "love.
T-17.... IV.15:5 gently and God **r.** to your remembrance,
T-18...... IX.4:3 Its shadow **r.** to the surface, enough to
T19... IV.D.1:5 And as this memory **r.** in your mind,
T19... IV.D.2:2 Yet as His face **r.** beyond it, shining with
T-20...... IV.6:7 a new world **r.** in which sin can enter not,
T-20....... V.3:4 Do you recognize the fear that **r.** from the
T-23...... III.1:7 where the purpose **r.** to meet his horrified
T-23...... IV.6:1 the temptation to attack **r.** to make your
T-28....... V.7:5 where terror **r.** from the bones of death.
T-29....... V.1:3 hymn to Heaven **r.** up to gladden God the
T-31...VII.12:2 And from that wish a concept **r.**, teaching
W-pI.....44.9:1 If resistance **r.** in any form, pause long
W-pI.....75.4:4 the real world **r.** before us in gladness, to
W-pI...100.6:3 and wills no sorrow **r.** to abate his joy; no
W-pI...122.8:3 quietness it **r.** up to greet your open eyes,
W-pI...152.8:4 What **r.** to awareness then will be all that
W-ep .........2:1 pathway of the sun laid down before it **r.**,
S-1..........II.7:8 it **r.** as a song of thanks to your Creator,
S-1......... V.1:2 And here again it **r.** slowly up, and grows

**rising** 17

T-1..........II.4:4 In the process of "**r.** up," I am higher
T-13...... XI.2:4 the hymn of freedom **r.** unto Heaven.
T-18.........I.7:1 of the original error **r.** to frighten you, say
T-18....... V.2:7 solid rock of faith, and **r.** even to Heaven.
T-18...... IX.7:1 bank it is easy to see a whole world **r.**. A
T-20...... VI.9:5 it, **r.** to welcome what you really want.
T-28...... III.1:5 and simple in the **r.** up to waking and the
W-pI...121.4:2 it beholds its own projections **r.** to attack
W-pI.131.10:3 and we will ask to see the **r.** of the real

W-pI...186.9:6 seen above a desert, **r.** from the dust.
W-pI...189.3:5 who see a world of hatred **r.** from attack,
S-1.........in.3:1 Son of God, and **r.** up as God created you,
S-1.........in.3:2 your heart to Him in **r.** song that reaches
S-1........III.1:6 of **r.** power and with ascending goals,
S-1........IV.1:7 The key to **r.** further still in prayer lies in
S-2.........in.1:1 to make its **r.** easy and its progress swift.
S-2.........in.1:8 becomes unneeded when the **r.** up is done

## risk 4

T-26....VIII.3:2 of it, believing that the **r.** of loss is great
T-27...VII.10:2 There is a **r.** of thinking death is peace,
M-16.......11:5 it. No **r.** is possible throughout the day
M-24.........2:7 is always some **r.** in seeing the present in

## rites 1

W-pI...191.8:1 the **r.** of death echoed since time began.

## ritual 6

T-16..... V.11:4 this **r.** enacted in the special relationship.
T-16..... V.11:6 Over and over and over this **r.** is enacted.
T-16..... V.11:8 The **r.** of completion cannot complete, for
T-16..... V.12:1 tempts you to seek for love in **r.**,
T-16..... V.12:2 The special relationship is a **r.** of form,
T-16..... V.12:4 senseless **r.** in which strength is extracted

## ritualistic 1

W-pI.......1.3:5 for these exercises should not become **r.**.

## rituals 7

T-10....... V.1:1 The **r.** of the god of sickness are strange
T-16... V.12:10 No **r.** that you have set up in which the
T19....IV.C.8:3 no grim commandments nor twisted **r.** of
W-pI.....76.4:2 **r.** that have no use and serve no purpose.
W-pI.....77.2:2 nor on any of the **r.** you have devised. It is
WpI. rIII.in2:4 **R.** are not our aim, and would defeat our
M-27.........6:9 compromises and the **r.** the world fosters

## rival 1

W-pI...195.3:1 you see in him the **r.** for your peace; a

## rivalry 1

S-2......... II.3:4 indeed induce a **r.** in sinfulness and guilt.

## road 59

T-8......... V.5:5 intrudes anywhere along the **r.** to peace, it
T-13.........I.7:3 There is no **r.** to travel on, and no time to
T-13.....VII.3:7 you cannot find in it the **r.** that leads away
T-13.....VII.6:2 following not the **r.** that love points out.
T-17....... V.9:4 walk together along a **r.** far more familiar
T-18.....VII.4:6 very long **r.** to the goal you have accepted.
T-22.......III.3:2 and without a key, across the **r.** to peace.
T-22.........IV.h The Branching of the **R.**
T-22.......IV.1:1 the branch in the **r.** is quite apparent, you
T-22.......IV.1:8 futile than standing where the **r.** branches
T-26..... V.1:10 will another **r.** be made except the way to
T-26....... V.2:6 down a **r.** that leads to nothing and that
T-26..... V.10:1 a **r.** long since a memory of time gone by?
T-28...... VI.2:7 no sides and judges not the **r.** it travels. It
T-29........ II.1:4 Is it not because you see it as the **r.** to hell
T-29.....VII.8:1 and open up a **r.** of hope and of release in
T-31....... II.6:5 us, but walks beside us on the selfsame **r.**.
T-31....... II.11:4 This is the **r.** to nowhere, for the light
T-31..... II.11:7 is made in certainty and sureness of the **r.**
T-31...... IV.1:5 which **r.** will lead you out of conflict, and
T-31...... IV.1:8 you whatever **r.** you choose to walk along.
T-31...... IV.4:1 Why would you seek to try another **r.**,
T-31...... IV.4:5 that seems to point to still another **r.**. No
T-31...... IV.6:3 come to learn to find a **r.** the world does
T-31...... IV.7:1 ever found by following a **r.** away from it.
T-31...... IV.7:4 And every **r.** that leads the other way will
T-31 ..... IV.9:4 What **r.** in all the world will lead within,
T-31 ..... IV.9:4 every **r.** was made to separate the journey
T-31 ... IV.10:4 There is no **r.** that leads away from Him.
T-31 ... IV.10:6 that there could be a **r.** with such an aim!
W-pI... 101.7:3 You are set on freedom's **r.**, and now
W-pI... 109.7:3 the **r.** that suddenly seems easy as they go
W-pI. 122.10:2 point at which the **r.** becomes far easier.
W-pI... 132.6:4 can let himself be led along the **r.** to truth.
W-pI... 155.5:1 Between these paths there is another **r.**
W-pI... 155.6:4 illusions, for the **r.** leads past illusion now
W-pI. 155.13:1 upon the **r.** that leads the world to God.
W-pI. 155.14:3 *way, For I would walk along the* **r.** *to Him.*
W-pI... 158.3:3 no step along the **r.** that anyone takes but
W-pI... 166.6:1 bleed a little from the rocky **r.** he walks.
W-pI. 166.13:1 who chose the lonely **r.** you have escaped.
WpI...rV.in1:5 and slowly on the **r.** this course sets forth.
WpI...rV.in6:2 may come to me who recognize the **r.** by
WpI...rV.in6:6 crucified until you walk along the **r.** with
W-pI... 185.9:7 gone with every twist and turning of the **r.**
W-pI... 189.8:6 point the **r.** to God by which He should
W-pI. 195.10:6 can walk no **r.** except the way of gratitude
W-pI... 198.4:1 Forgiveness is the only **r.** that leads out of
W-pI. 200.10:3 come to where the **r.** is carpeted with
W-pII ....in.2:5 We have come far along the **r.**, and now
W-pII ..... 5.4:3 to help him walk along the **r.** with him.
W-pII . 327.1:4 still farther on the **r.** that leads to Him.
M-1 ........... 1:3 **r.** is established and his direction is sure.
M-16 ....... 1:10 and sees the **r.** on which he walks stretch
C-5 ............ 3:3 to God because he saw the **r.** before him,
C-ep........... 1:9 farther on the **r.** where all illusions end?
C-ep........... 3:3 begun again upon a **r.** we travelled on
P-2........ III.1:1 pitfalls along the **r.** by seeing them first.
P-3..........II.9:2 He has chosen a **r.** in which there is great

## roads 11

T-13 .... VII.3:3 The **r.** you made have led you nowhere,
T-31 ..... IV.2:3 All its **r.** but lead to disappointment,
T-31 ..... IV.2:7 by all the different names its **r.** are given.
T-31 ..... IV.2:9 end, for it is here that all its **r.** will lead,
T-31 ..... IV.3:3 **r.** this world can offer seem to be quite
T-31 ..... IV.9:5 All **r.** that lead away from what you are
T-31 ...... V.8:2 its **r.** nor realize the way you see yourself.
T-31 ... VIII.9:3 to lift us high above the thorny **r.** we
W-pI... 123.1:2 to gentler pathways and to smoother **r.**.
W-pI... 155.7:1 All **r.** will lead to this one in the end. For
W-pI... 220.1:2 *of peace, for I am lost on other* **r.** *than this.*

## roadways 1

T-31 ..... IV.5:1 turned away from all the **r.** of the world,

## roaring 1

T-23 ........I.4:7 as ridiculous as nature **r.** at the wind in

## roars 1

T-21 .. VII.3:11 becomes a giant and a mouse **r.** like a lion

## rob 3

T19.... IV.B.2:1 value that you think peace would **r.** you of
T-22 ......in.2:6 each to complete himself and **r.** the other.
W-pII . 273.2:2 *can* **r.** *me of what You would have me keep?*

## robbing 1

T-30 ........I.7:4 the day by **r.** you of what you really want.

## robe 1

T19....IV.C.2:6 the black **r.** he was wearing to his funeral,

## robes 1

T-14 .......II.2:7 make palaces and royal **r.** of nothing,

## rock 8

T-18 .......V.2:7 a ladder planted in the solid **r.** of faith,
T-18 ..... IX.6:1 this artificial floor that looks like **r.**, is like
T-22 ..... III.4:7 it made; the **r.** on which its church is built
T-22 ... VI.10:7 God in place, immovable and solid as a **r.**.
T-24 ..... III.3:7 it still must **r.** and turn and whirl about
T-25 ....... VII.h The **R.** of Salvation
T-25 .. VII.12:4 single **r.** of truth can faith in God's eternal
T-25 .. VII.12:7 This is the **r.** on which salvation rests, the

## rocky 1

W-pI .. 166.6:1 feet that bleed a little from the **r.** road he

## role 76

T-1 ....... III.4:2 **r.** in the Atonement which I will dictate to
T-1 ...... VII.5:4 I have been careful to clarify my **r.** in the
T-4 ..........I.4:7 willing to renounce the **r.** of guardian of
T-4 ........ III.2:5 My **r.** is to separate the true from the false
T-5 ....... VI.2:8 My **r.** is only to unchain your will and set
T-6 ..........I.2:8 you understand your own **r.** as a teacher.
T-13 ... VIII.7:6 Your **r.** in the redemption leads you to it
T-16 ........I.5:7 Do not confuse your **r.** with His, for this
T-18 ..... IV.5:5 That is but to confuse your **r.** with God's.
T-22 ..... VI.3:1 He can change the **r.** of means and end so
T-25 ........V.4:8 found if he fulfilled the **r.** God gave to him
T-25 .......V.6:6 this; the **r.** you give to him is given you,
T-26 .... VII.8:6 Perhaps you do not see the **r.** forgiveness
T-27 .......II.10:3 If you assume correction's **r.**, you lose the
T-27 .......II.11:5 yours, and gives you both a different **r.**.
T-27 .... VII.8:6 as it will in any **r.** that satisfies its dream.
T-27 . VIII.10:3 takes the **r.** of enemy and of attacker, still
T-28 .......II.8:3 against him, taking on the **r.** of its creator,
T-28 .....II.10:5 can accept the **r.** of maker of their hate,
T-28 .....II.12:3 deny the active **r.** in making up the dream
T-28 ... VI.1:10 It accepts no **r.**, but does what it is told,
T-29 ..... IV.5:1 the one who gave the "proper" **r.** to every
T-29 ..... IV.6:3 not ascribe a **r.** to him that you imagine
T-29 .......V.3:1 Here is the **r.** the Holy Spirit gives to you
T-29 .... VII.3:5 has, for this the **r.** that is assigned to it,
T-29 .... VII.3:5 it, and this the **r.** that cannot be fulfilled.
T-31 .......II.4:3 the leader's **r.** when you would have it,
T-31 .......II.4:3 arise, and give away the **r.** of leadership.
T-31 .....V.16:5 The **r.** of the accuser will appear in many
T-31 .... VII.8:1 Behold your **r.** within the universe! To
W-pI ... 51.5:5 everything I see by assigning this **r.** to it.
W-pI ... 61.2:3 your **r.** in salvation and in taking no other
W-pI .... 70.2:4 is not a **r.** that can be partially accepted.
W-pI .... 71.3:1 **r.** assigned to your own mind in this plan,
W-pI .... 78.4:5 as his, according to the **r.** you set for him.
W-pI .... 78.5:4 holy **r.** the Holy Spirit has assigned to him
W-pI .... 78.5:6 Such is his **r.** in God your Father's plan.
W-pI .... 78.6:1 periods today will see him in this **r.**. You
W-pI .... 78.8:8 **r.** God gave Him that you might be saved.
W-pI .. 78.10:1 take the **r.** assigned to us as part of God's
W-pI .. 78.10:3 the past, allow the **r.** of savior to be given,
W-pI 121.13:4 **r.** forgiveness plays in bringing happiness
W-pI .. 154.1:5 nor can we know what **r.** is best for us;
W-pI .. 154.2:1 Whatever your appointed **r.** may be, it
W-pI .. 154.5:3 is intended, and fulfill his **r.** in its delivery
W-pI .. 154.6:1 one major difference in the **r.** of Heaven's
W-pI .. 154.7:1 his **r.** by giving all his messages away. The
W-pI .. 154.9:2 For that is part of your appointed **r.**. God
W-pI 169.11:5 on. As you take the **r.** assigned to you,
W-pI .. 186.1:3 to you, without insisting on another **r.**. It
W-pI .. 186.1:4 It does not judge your proper **r.**. It but
W-pI .. 191.1:3 the world the **r.** of jailer to the Son of God
W-pII . 317.1:1 a special place to fill; a **r.** for me alone.
W-pII . 318.2:1 *take the* **r.** *You offer me in Your request that I*
W-pII . 324.1:2 *You have set the way I am to go, the* **r.** *to take,*
M-in.......... 1:1 The **r.** of teaching and learning is actually
M-2 ........... 1:5 Once he has chosen to fulfill his **r.**, they
M-4 ........... 1:4 a special **r.** in His plan for Atonement.
M-12 ....... 5:10 will tell him when he has fulfilled his **r.**,
M-15 ....... 2:11 you still attempt to take His **r.** from Him?
M-16 ......... 1:5 He will be told all that his **r.** should be,
M-16 ......... 1:6 who share that **r.** with him will find him,
M-21 ............ h IS THE **R.** OF WORDS IN HEALING?

M-26 1:5 Here, then, is the **r.** of God's teachers.
P-2 III.h The **R.** of the Psychotherapist
P-2 VII.5:3 for his brother in the **r.** of guide for him?
P-2 VII.5:5 point of view would such a **r.** be possible.
P-2 VII.9:1 this, if you but understand your proper **r.**.
P-3 II.9:2 there is great temptation to misuse his **r.**.
S-2 I.9:4 Forgiveness' **r.** must be reversed, and
S-2 II.4:2 seek the **r.** of martyr at another's hand.
S-2 III.6:4 About the **r.** forgiveness has in Him. Do
S-3 I.3:5 forgot that it is he who gave this **r.** to it.
S-3 III.4:1 Is there a **r.** for healing, then, that one
S-3 III.4:4 It is like the **r.** that helps in prayer, and
S-3 IV.5:2 give the **r.** to Him you see in His creation.

## roles 9

T-23 II.16:4 where only shadows play the major **r.**, it
T-29 IV.h Dream **R.**
T-30 VII.2:3 according to the **r.** the script assigns. The
T-31 II.3:3 and the follower emerge as separate **r.**,
T-31 II.3:5 see yourself divided into both these **r.**,
W-pI 135.7:3 abuse it by assigning it to **r.** it cannot fill,
W-pI 154.7:3 They choose no **r.** that are not given them
W-pI 186.8:3 Our self-made **r.** are shifting, and they
M-2 5:6 they have drawn between their **r.**, their

## roll 2

T-13 I.3:5 reach its end it will **r.** up like a long carpet
C-ep 2:3 Ask but my help to **r.** the stone away, and

## roof 1

T-22 in.2:8 under a common **r.** that shelters neither;

## room 32

T-1 I.34:3 spirit's strength leaves no **r.** for intrusions
T-13 VI.1:2 sight, for reality leaves no **r.** for any error.
T-14 XI.13:6 fill every mind that so makes **r.** for Him.
T-14 XI.15:5 of you. Leave **r.** for Him, and you will find
T-17 VII.9:4 calls for faith, and faith makes **r.** for truth.
T-18 III.8:7 shine away the past and so make **r.** for His
T-20 VI.5:2 speck of darkness; a hidden secret **r.**, a
T-21 II.7:6 that is asked of you is to make **r.** for truth.
T-21 III.2:1 accepted the idea of making **r.** for truth.
T-21 V.10:5 in this change is **r.** made way for vision.
T-22 in.2:8 in the same **r.** and yet a world apart.
T-26 III.1:12 is everything leaves **r.** for nothing else.
T-26 III.5:6 leaving **r.** to make the only choice that
T-26 VI.3:6 throne, when you make **r.** for Him on His.
T-27 IV.4:17 for it. It leaves no **r.** to question its beliefs,
T-28 III.6:4 thus make **r.** for Him Who wills to come
T-28 V.6:5 has left no **r.** for them in any place or time
T-29 VIII.7:5 has left no **r.** for anything to be except His
W-pI 1.h Nothing I see in this **r.** [on this street,
W-pI 2.h I have given everything I see in this **r.** [on
W-pI 3.h anything I see in this **r.** [on this street,
W-pI 4.h the things I see in this **r.** [on this street,
W-pI 4.4:3 *is like the things I see in this* **r.** [*on this street,*
W-pI 51.3:6 go, and make **r.** for what can be seen and
W-pI 77.6:5 is no **r.** for doubt and uncertainty today.
W-pI 107.3:3 for there is no **r.** for transitory thoughts
W-pI 121.2:1 of fear, and offers love no **r.** to be itself;
W-pI 161.1:1 fears may disappear and offer **r.** to love.
W-pI 195.5:2 let your gratitude make **r.** for all who will
W-pII 310.2:4 There is no **r.** in us for fear today, for we
W-pII 340.2:3 is no **r.** for anything but joy and thanks
P-2 VII.8:4 The **r.** becomes a temple, and the street a

## root 5

T-3 VI.7:3 This *is* "the **r.** of all evil." Every symptom
T-11 III.1:7 Conflict is the **r.** of all evil, for being blind
T-13 in.1:1 for condemnation is the **r.** of attack. It is
T-15 VII.6:2 is actually the **r.** of its bitter resentment.
T-26 X.3:4 cause of sacrifice is at the **r.** of everything

## rooted 6

*See also* deep-rooted

T-18 IX.13:1 shining and firmly **r.** in the world of light.
W-pI 7.2:1 everything you believe is **r.** in time, and
W-pI 139.1:4 are? There is no doubt that is not **r.** here.
W-pI 153.1:3 **r.** in attack, and all its "gifts" of seeming
M-16 10:9 **R.** in sacrifice and separation, two aspects
M-27 5:1 "reality" of death is firmly **r.** in the belief

## roots 7

T-1 V.6:3 All shallow **r.** must be uprooted, because
T-1 V.6:4 illusion that shallow **r.** can be deepened,
T-24 II.3:3 an evil flower with no **r.** at all. Here is the
W-pI 102.1:4 but lacks the **r.** that once secured it tightly
W-pI 156.3:3 grass to grow with **r.** suspended in the air.
W-pI 159.8:1 which the lilies of forgiveness set their **r.**.
W-pI 159.9:3 Their **r.** remain. They do not leave their

## rose 2

T-13 I.2:3 world of retribution **r.** in the black cloud
T-24 in.2:10 **r.** in His Mind *because* of what He knows.

## rosy 1

T-23 II.18:8 Can you paint **r.** lips upon a skeleton,

## rotted 1

T19. IV.A.13:3 gorges filled with things decayed and **r.**.

## rotting 1

T-26 I.8:3 within the **r.** prison where he sees himself

## rough 1

T-29 II.1:3 **r.** and far too difficult for you to follow? Is

## roughly 1

W-pI 24.5:2 of each application should be **r.** as follows

## round 10

T-28 VII.3:3 to both, and merely sets you spinning **r.**,
T-31 VII.3:3 than just a shadow circling **r.** the good.
W-pI 76.3:3 You really think a small **r.** pellet or some
W-pI 97.7:1 let them echo **r.** the world through Him:
W-pI 123.6:1 and lets It echo **r.** and round the world.
W-pI 123.6:1 and lets It echo round and **r.** the world.
W-pI. 151.17:3 to carry **r.** the world the joyous news that
W-pI 156.4:4 wind sinks to a whisper **r.** your holy head.
W-pI 199.5:4 call of freedom **r.** the world with this idea.
WpI rVI.in.3:1 centered **r.** a central theme with which we

## routes 3

T-3 VI.10:4 and sometimes by way of very devious **r.**,
T-15 X.5:1 to follow fear through all the circuitous **r.**
P-1 5:8 He directs. By whatever **r.** He chooses, all

## routines 1

M-16 2:5 **R.** as such are dangerous, because they

## royal 1

T-14 II.2:7 make palaces and **r.** robes of nothing,

## rubies 1

T-17 IV.8:4 The glitter of blood shines like **r.**, and the

## rug 1

W-pI 36.3:4 *My holiness envelops that* **r.**. *My holiness*

## rugged 1

T-4 in.3:7 error of "clinging to the old **r.** cross." The

## ruinous 1

W-pI 72.8:3 has been **r.** to your peace of mind. You

## rule 42

T-1 III.6:2 The Golden **R.** asks you to do unto others
T-1 III.6:4 The Golden **R.** is the rule for appropriate
T-1 III.6:4 The Golden Rule is the **r.** for appropriate
T-1 V.6:4 which the reverse of the Golden **R.** rests.
T-4 IV.10:2 of the ego's **r.** and the healing of the mind
T-12 V.7:1 I have said that the ego's **r.** is, "Seek and
T-13 V.8:7 private world and **r.** your own perception.
T19 IV.B.16:3 in solemn celebration of the ego's **r.**. Not
T-21 IV.2:2 alone. Its **r.** is tempered, and its unknown
T-21 IV.7:5 which the ego's **r.** has kept it out so long.
T-21 VII.5:11 *a world I* **r.** *instead of one that rules me? Do I*
T-21 VII.10:6 desire a world you **r.** that rules you not,
T-23 II.1:6 are the laws that **r.** the world you made.
T-24 II.13:4 to **r.** in madness and in loneliness your
T-24 VI.5:1 of the laws that seem to **r.** this world. See
T-26 VII.8:5 of God's Son where sin was thought to **r.**.
T-26 VII.10:1 that death and desolation seem to **r.**. In
T-27 VIII.1:6 Its comfort is its guiding **r.**. It tries to look
T-29 IX.4:6 They pretend they **r.** the world, and give
T-30 I.7:1 Try to observe this **r.** without delay,
T-30 I.14:6 all. The first **r.**, then, is not coercion, but a
T-30 I.16:1 The second **r.** as well is but a fact. For you
T-30 I.16:7 the **r.** of your adviser in the world. Whose
T-30 II.3:2 and thus the **r.** of fear established there.
T-30 IV.8:7 Such is the only **r.** for happy dreams. The
W-pI 9.3:1 and the essential **r.** of excluding nothing.
W-pI 46.4:2 It is a safe **r.** that anyone you do not like is
W-pI 68.1:4 hold a grievance is to let the ego **r.** your
W-pI 92.4:7 and darkness **r.** where God appointed
W-pI 97.5:1 world where pain and misery appear to **r.**.
W-pI 125.9:2 You will need no **r.** but this, to let your
W-pI 204.1:2 *by laws which* **r.** *the world of sick illusions,*
W-pII 236.h I **r.** my mind, which I alone must rule.
W-pII 236.h I rule my mind, which I alone must **r.**.
W-pII 236.1:1 I have a kingdom I must **r.**. At times, it
W-pII 236.1:7 thus direct my mind, which I alone can **r.**.
W-pII 236.2:2 *I* **r.** *my mind, and offer it to You. Accept my*
W-pII 253.1:2 in this world, it is I who **r.** my destiny.
W-pII 277.1:2 *him with the laws I made to* **r.** *the body. He is*
M-5 II.3:4 will never again appear to **r.** the mind.
P-3 III.6:1 One **r.** should always be observed: No
S-1 V.1:4 not claim that you must **r.** the universe,

## ruled 5

T-8 VII.9:2 other, so that it appears to be **r.** by chaos.
T-18 VIII.6:3 **r.** by an idea of separation from the rest.
T19 IV.B.13:4 **R.** by this perception the body becomes
W-pI 66.7:3 One is **r.** by the ego, and is made up of
W-pI 97.3:3 makes use of time, but is not **r.** by it.

## ruler 3

T-18 VIII.7:5 sorry king, a bitter **r.** of all that he surveys
T-18 IX.1:5 omnipotent, sole **r.** of the kingdom it set
W-pII 253.h My Self is **r.** of the universe.

## rules 42

T-4 III.10:1 from the part of the mind the ego **r.**. The
T-18 VIII.3:1 Within this kingdom the ego **r.**, and
T-19 II.6:5 to an ideal the ego wants; a world it **r.**,
T-21 VII.5:11 *desire a world I rule instead of one that* **r.** *me*
T-21 VII.10:6 can desire a world you rule that **r.** you not
T-25 III.2:1 obtain directly to a world perception **r.**,
T-25 VI.4:3 within a world where incompletion **r.**.
T-25 VII.11:4 basic tenet, "Sin is real, and **r.** the world?"
T-30 in.1:6 ideas than **r.** of thought to you as yet. So
T-30 in.1:7 until they are the **r.** by which you live. We
T-30 I.h **R.** for Decision

T-30.........I.2:5 have set the **r.** for how you should react to
T-30.........I.3:6 There are **r.** by which this will not happen
T-30.........I.7:5 the **r.** that promise you a happy day. Yet
T-30.......I.13:2 But this takes practice in the **r.** that will
T-30.......I.13:4 need for practicing the **r.** for its undoing.
T-30......IV.2:3 **r.** he made for boxes and for bears have
T-30......IV.2:4 because he thought the **r.** protected him.
T-30......IV.2:5 the bears did not deceive him, broke no **r.**
T-30......IV.3:2 one seems to break the **r.** you set for it. It
T-30......IV.3:4 It must appear to break your **r.** for safety,
T-30......IV.3:4 rules for safety, since the **r.** were wrong.
T-30......IV.3:7 still perceives them as obeying **r.** he made
T-30......IV.3:8 still are **r.** that they can seem to break and
T-30......IV.4:1 the laws of God, and not the **r.** you set. It
T-30......IV.4:4 while, according to the **r.** you set for them
T-30......IV.4:8 nor make you safe if they obeyed your **r.**.
T-30....... V.1:4 No **r.** are idly set, and no demands are
T-31...... III.5:2 of sacrifice preserved, for here guilt **r.**,
W-in.......... 6:1 only general **r.** to be observed throughout
W-pI.....53.2:4 Only chaos **r.** a world that represents
W-pI.....57.4:2 instead of the **r.** I made up for it to obey.
W-pI...124.8:4 for which we give no **r.** nor special words
W-pI...127.3:6 other principle that **r.** where love is not.
W-pI.182.11:5 love. He **r.** the universe, and yet He asks
W-pI.184.10:3 meaning in the world that darkness **r.**.
W-pI...190.8:5 where sorrow **r.** and little joys give way
W-pI...194.6:2 As it becomes a thought that **r.** your mind
W-pI...198.2:3 Such is the law that **r.** perception. It is not
W-pII .253.2:2 *My Self, which* **r.** *the universe, is but Your*
M-16 ......... 2:4 There are some general **r.** which do apply,
P-3......... II.1:9 These people need no special **r.**, of course,

**ruling** 1
T-24 ... VI.10:4 yourself under the laws you see as **r.** him.

**run** 3
T-14 ..... XI.8:4 you think that you can **r.** some little part,
T19... IV.D.2:2 brush the veil aside and **r.** to meet Him,
T-24 .......II.2:8 and thus **r.** counter to the Will of God. To

**running** 2
T-20 .VIII.11:1 life-giving water **r.** happily beside them in
M-3 .......... 2:2 he is going **r.** into an adult "by chance,"

**runs** 7
T-8 .........II.8:5 Awakening **r.** easily and gladly through
T-20 ...... V.5:8 little breath of eternity that **r.** through
T-21 .... VII.4:5 so that it **r.** at once to find another, and
T-21 .... VII.4:6 And as it **r.** it turns against itself, thinking
W-pI.169.12:1 is the central theme that **r.** throughout
W-pI.169.12:1 course it **r.** directed and its outcome sure.
W-pI... 194.5:2 bondage of illusions where it **r.** its pitiless

**rush** 8
T-14 ..... IX.3:2 all its power will **r.** to your assistance and
T-18 ..... III.2:1 light comes nearer you will **r.** to darkness,
T-18 ... VI.12:5 it. And so you **r.** to meet it, letting your
T-30 .... IV.1:3 entirely, and **r.** to its embrace. The truth
W-pI..... 93.1:3 you would **r.** to death by your own hand,
W-pI. 198.11:2 frantic **r.** of thoughts that made no sense.
Wfl........in.6:3 Or would He **r.** to answer him, and say,
C-4 ........... 8:1 but **r.** to meet Him where His altar is.

**rushed** 1
T-18 ..... III.3:1 has **r.** to meet you since you called upon it

**rushes** 3
T-16 ... IV.4:10 are broken, fear **r.** in and hatred triumphs
T-28 ..... III.5:3 just as fast, as water **r.** in to close the gap,
W-pI .... 13.2:3 The ego **r.** in frantically to establish its

**rushing** 1
T-10 .......V.7:7 and God will come **r.** into your heart in

**rust** 2
W-pI .. 133.8:7 protect its goals from tarnish and from **r.**,
W-pI 133.10:2 the **r.** a sign of deep unworthiness within

**rusted** 2
T-29 .......V.7:6 each with his tiny spear and **r.** sword, to
W-pI 133.10:1 perceive its tarnished edges and its **r.** core

**rustling** 1
W-pI .. 95.14:8 mind, the gentle **r.** of the wings of peace.

**ruthlessly** 1
T-4 ..... III.10:1 **r.** banished from the part of the mind the

# S

**sabotage** 1
W-pI... 153.5:4 realize what you have done to **s.** the holy

**sacrament** 1
T-24...... VI.8:1 holiness is **s.** and benediction unto you.

**sacred** 11
T-14.........I.2:7 not touched, and your dream *is* **s.** to you.
T-24...... II.13:3 Nothing is **s.** here but unto you, and you
T-29....... V.2:4 can intrude upon the **s.** Son of God within
T-29....... V.4:1 This **s.** Son of God is like yourself; the
T-30...... V.9:10 It is your **s.** right, and what you pay for is
W-pI.161.11:5 whose **s.** hands can take away the nails
W-pI...162.1:4 These words are **s.**, for they are the words
W-pI...164.6:1 Brother, this day is **s.** to the world. Your
W-pI...192.1:1 and that your Self shall be His **s.** Son,
W-pII .256.2:2 *find the way Your* **s.** *Word has pointed out to*
P-2......... V.5:5 **s.** calling of God's holy Son for help in his

**sacrifice** 225
T-3.............I.h Atonement without **S.**
T-3...........I.4:1 **S.** is a notion totally unknown to God. It
T-3...........I.8:3 is, you realize that the Atonement, not **s.**,
T-4......... II.6:4 it. When you associate giving with **s.**, you
T-5.......VII.4:5 God weeps at the "**s.**" of His children who
T-6.........I.10:4 one Voice you are never called on to **s.**.
T-7 ....... IX.2:5 of loss, as blessing is the opposite of **s.**.
T-7 .........X.3:7 is the cause of the whole idea of **s.**. Obey
T-7 .........X.5:5 The Holy Spirit never asks for **s.**, but the
T-9 ..........I.5:1 will never call upon you to **s.** anything.
T-9 ..........I.5:2 But if you ask the **s.** of reality of yourself,
T-11 ..... VI.5:5 of the Son of God is born of **s.** and pain.
T-11 ..... VI.5:8 it, not in the spirit of **s.** and submission,
T-13 .. VII.15:2 Kneel not before the altars to **s.**, and seek
T-15 ..... III.8:1 Is it a **s.** to leave littleness behind, and
T-15 ..... III.8:2 vain? It is not **s.** to wake to glory. But it is
T-15 ..... III.8:3 it is **s.** to accept anything less than glory.
T-15 .......VII.h The Needless **S.**
T-15 .... VII.6:2 The "**s.**," which it regards as purification,
T-15 .... VII.7:5 He merely believes he is in love with **s.**.
T-15 .... VII.7:6 And for this **s.**, which he demands of
T-15 .... VII.7:6 accept the guilt and **s.** himself as well.
T-15 .... VII.8:4 long as the body is there to receive its **s.**, it
T-15 .... VII.9:1 Suffering and **s.** are the gifts with which
T-15 .... VII.9:2 suffering and **s.** as the price of union. In
T-15 .... VII.9:5 yet never without demand of **s.**. The fury
T-15 .......X.2:5 I am as incapable of receiving **s.** as God is,
T-15 .......X.2:5 every **s.** you ask of yourself you ask of me.
T-15 .......X.2:6 Learn now that **s.** of any kind is nothing
T-15 .......X.5:6 cannot accept the fact that **s.** gets nothing
T-15 .......X.5:7 **S.** is so essential to your thought system
T-15 .......X.5:7 apart from **s.** means nothing to you. Your
T-15 .......X.5:8 confusion of **s.** and love is so profound
T-15 .......X.5:8 you cannot conceive of love without **s.**.
T-15 .......X.5:9 this that you must look upon; **s.** is attack,
T-15 .....X.5:11 last when the idea of **s.** has been removed.
T-15 .....X.5:12 For if there is **s.**, someone must pay and
T-15 .......X.6:7 behind them all; that love demands **s.**,
T-15 .......X.7:1 a **s.** do you believe His Love demands! For
T-15 .......X.7:2 For total love would demand total **s.**. And
T-15 .......X.8:1 outside yourself demands your **s.**, but you
T-15 .......X.8:1 you do not see that only you demand **s.**,
T-15 .......X.8:2 Yet the demand of **s.** is so savage and so
T-15 .......X.8:4 For if God would demand total **s.** of you,
T-15 .......X.8:6 you, and does demand total **s.** of you. No
T-15 .......X.8:7 you. No partial **s.** will appease this savage
T-15 .......X.8:7 but always to make the **s.** complete.
T-15 .......X.9:8 the demand for **s.** and the peace of God.
T-15 ........ XI.h Christmas as the End of **S.**
T-15 ..... XI.1:1 whole idea of **s.** as solely of your making.
T-15 ..... XI.2:4 No **s.** of any kind, of anyone, is asked by
T-15 ..... XI.2:5 the whole idea of **s.** loses all meaning. For
T-15 ..... XI.3:4 with me. All pain and **s.** and littleness will
T-15 ..... XI.3:5 and without pain there can be no **s.**. And
T-15 ..... XI.3:6 And without **s.** there love *must* be.
T-15 ..... XI.4:1 You who believe that **s.** is love must learn
T-15 ..... XI.4:1 must learn that **s.** is separation from love.
T-15 ..... XI.4:2 For **s.** brings guilt as surely as love brings
T-15 ..... XI.4:3 Guilt is the condition of **s.**, as peace is the
T-15 ..... XI.5:2 you also perceive yourself as a victim of **s.**,
T-15 ..... XI.5:3 aside without a sense of **s.** and loss? And
T-15 ..... XI.5:4 And who could suffer **s.** and loss without
T-15 ..... XI.5:7 attack becomes salvation and **s.** becomes
T-15 ..... XI.6:1 seeking for love, you seek for **s.** and find it

T-15......XI.7:3 that to s. the body is to sacrifice nothing,
T-15......XI.7:3 that to sacrifice the body is to s. nothing,
T-15......XI.7:4 Where, then, *is* s.? The lesson I was born
T-15......XI.7:5 that s. is nowhere and love is everywhere.
T-15......XI.8:2 peace by demanding no s. of anyone, for
T-16....... V.7:5 Each partner tries to s. the self he does
T-16...... V.10:4 its litany to s. is that God must die so you
T-17......IV.8:3 dreams of s. and self-aggrandizement,
T19....IV.B.2:4 This "s." you feel to be too great to make,
T19....IV.B.2:5 Is it a s., or a release? What has the body
T19....IV.B.3:4 it a s. to be removed from what can suffer
T19....IV.B.3:5 you s. the hope of the body's pleasure; it
T19....IV.B.3:7 Pain is the only "s." the Holy Spirit asks,
T19....IV.B.5:2 sacrificed, and s. cannot be asked of you?
T19....IV.B.9:1 to give the Holy Spirit the whole idea of s.
T19.... IV.C.4:2 death, a symbol of corruption, a s. to sin,
T-21...... III.9:1 sin must think the Holy Spirit asks for s.,
T-21...... III.9:2 Holy Spirit knows that s. brings nothing.
T-21.... III.10:1 in s. has given it great power in your sight
T-21.... III.10:2 For s. must be exacted of a body, and by
T-21.... III.10:7 so is s. invariably a means for limitation,
T-21.... III.11:8 Neither demands the s. of the other. Yet
T-21.... III.12:1 The body was made to be a s. to sin, and
T-24....... II.6:6 Is it a s. to give up nothing, and to receive
T-24...... VI.1:3 He is the healing of your sense of s. and
T-24.... VI.12:3 The "s." of self you understand, nor do
T-24.... VI.12:5 truth as God established it no s. is asked,
T-25....... V.5:1 It is no s. that he be saved, for by his
T-25... VIII.4:5 Justice demands no s., for any sacrifice is
T-25... VIII.4:5 s. is made that sin may be preserved and
T-25...... IX.3:2 be true, because He asks no s. of anyone.
T-26........... I.h The "S." of Oneness
T-26.........I.1:1 the "dynamics" of attack is s. a key idea. It
T-26.........I.1:5 loss. The body is itself a s.; a giving up of
T-26.........I.1:6 to see a little part of him and s. the rest.
T-26.........I.2:1 world you see is based on "s." of oneness.
T-26.........I.2:4 Each part must s. the other part, to keep
T-26.........I.3:1 self, preserved through s. of all the rest.
T-26.........I.3:3 the body's loss would be a s. indeed. For
T-26.........I.3:4 bodies becomes the sign that s. is limited,
T-26.........I.4:1 The body *is* a loss, and *can* be made to s..
T-26.........I.4:2 cell, you are demanding s. of him and you
T-26.........I.4:3 What greater s. could be demanded than
T-26.........I.4:5 every s. demands that they be separate
T-26.........I.4:6 of God must be denied if any s. is asked of
T-26.........I.6:1 oneness, but can not make s. of its reality.
T-26.........I.6:2 Nor can you lose what you would s., nor
T-26.........I.6:5 Make not his holiness a s. to your belief in
T-26.........I.6:6 You s. your innocence with his, and die
T-26.........I.7:3 not. You who would make a s. of life, and
T-26.........I.7:7 beyond the reach of any s. of life or death.
T-26.........I.7:8 His gifts can never suffer s. and loss.
T-26.........I.8:2 reality, and s. his Father's Will for him?
T-26....... II.2:2 loss and make a s. that you might gain.
T-26....... II.6:4 you wish to be preserved from s. entirely.
T-26....... II.6:7 And you will ask no s. of him because you
T-26....... II.7:6 S. is gone. And in its place the Love of
T-26....... II.7:7 will shine away all memory of s. and loss.
T-26...... III.7:6 No s. is possible in the relinquishment of
T-26...... VI.1:6 attack, in hurt and harm, in s. and death,
T-26...VII.11:8 would s. his own identity with everything,
T-26...VII.12:4 error does the world of sin and s. arise.
T-26...VII.14:5 still demands that he must make some s.,
T-26...VII.14:6 A tiny s. is just the same in its effects as is
T-26...VII.14:6 same in its effects as is the whole idea of s.
T-26... VIII.2:6 to be one in which you s. and suffer loss.
T-26. VIII.7:10 This is a s. of *now,* which could not be the
T-26....... X.3:4 Projection of the cause of s. is at the root
T-26....... X.3:7 asked to s. his Father's Love and yours as
T-27.........I.1:7 You cannot s. yourself alone. For sacrifice
T-27.........I.1:8 For s. is total. If it could occur at all it
T-27.........I.1:9 the Father with the s. of His beloved Son.
T-27.........I.2:1 your release from s. is his made manifest,
T-27....... II.9:2 Only those to whom their brother's s. and
T-27....... II.9:6 to prevent a shift of balance in the s.. How
T-27...... IV.6:6 An honest answer asks no s. because it
T-27...... IV.6:7 world but ask of whom is s. demanded,
T-27...... IV.6:7 asking not if s. is meaningful at all. And
T-28...... I.15:2 And where is s., when memory of God
T-28.... IV.10:6 separation, and its giving up would be a s.
T-29.........I.4:6 which do protect you from the "s." of love
T-29.........I.4:7 for it gets away from total s. and gives to
T-29.........I.7:1 not love that asks a s.. But fear demands
T-29.........I.7:2 But fear demands the s. of love, for in
T-29....... II.1:4 it as a simple way, without a s. or any loss,
T-29....... II.8:5 you, for it is you of whom the s. is asked?
T-29....... II.8:7 He must s. your self, and in His sacrifice
T-29....... II.8:7 and in His s. are you made more and He
T-29...... VI.1:5 This is the "s." salvation asks, and gladly
T-29..... VII.4:3 To s. is to give up, and thus to be without
T-29...VII.10:3 The s. of death is nothing lost. An idol
T-30....... V.9:5 But not to s.. You never wanted it. What
T-30..... VI.2:6 you would be asked to s. your rights when
T-30..... VII.5:3 single purpose is the end of all ideas of s.,
T-30..... VII.5:4 be no thought of s. apart from this idea.
T-30..... VII.6:4 understand the s. of meaning is undone.
T-30..... VII.6:5 All s. entails the loss of your ability to see
T-31...... III.5:2 Here are the thoughts of s. preserved, for
T-31...... III.7:4 For God has said there *is* no s. that can be
T-31...... III.7:4 be asked; there *is* no s. that can be made.
W-pI..... 27.2:1 some sort of s. is being asked of you when
W-pI..... 37.1:5 of s. because it offers everyone his full due
W-pI..... 37.2:1 is no other way in which the idea of s. can
W-pI... 100.7:6 been wrong in your belief that s. is asked.
W-pI... 100.7:7 to God's plan, and never lose or s. or die.
W-pI... 134.1:1 that entails an unfair s. of righteous wrath
W-pI. 135.24:4 that makes extravagant demands for s..
W-pI... 153.5:3 how much you have been made to s., who
W-pI... 155.4:1 if it asked the s. of something that is real.
W-pI... 155.5:1 for s. and deprivation both are quickly
W-pI... 155.7:2 For s. and deprivation are paths that lead
W-pI... 187.6:2 giving means must laugh at the idea of s..
W-pI... 187.6:3 the many forms which s. may take. He
W-pI... 187.6:5 He recognizes s. remains the one idea that
W-pI... 187.7:4 thought of s. gives rise to all the forms
W-pI... 187.7:5 s. is an idea so mad that sanity dismisses
W-pI... 187.8:1 Never believe that you can s.. There is no
W-pI... 187.8:2 is no place for s. in what has any value. If
W-pI... 187.8:6 well. No form of s. and suffering can long
W-pI... 192.6:1 and the gift of sight, no s. was asked, and
W-pII.. 322.1:1 I s. illusions; nothing more. And as
W-pII.. 322.2:1 *to You all s. remains forever inconceivable.*
W-pII.. 322.2:2 *And so I cannot s. except in dreams. As You*
W-pII..... 323.h I gladly make the "s." of fear.
W-pII.. 323.1:1 *is the only "s." You ask of Your beloved Son;*
W-pII.. 323.1:2 *joy. Such is the "s." You ask of me, and one I*
W-pII..... 343.h I am not asked to make a s. To find the
W-pII.. 343.1:5 *s. becomes impossible for me as well as You.*
W-pII.. 343.1:9 *Your Son can make no s., for he must be*
M-4 ...... I.A.4:4 generalize the lesson for fear of loss and s.
M-4 ..... I.A.5:5 s. his own best interests on behalf of truth
M-4 ..... I.A.7:5 idea of s., so central to his own thought
M-10 ......... 2:6 it. This is no s.. On the contrary, he puts
M-13 ............h WHAT IS THE REAL MEANING OF S.?
M-13 ......... 1:1 the term s. is altogether meaningless, it
M-13 ......... 1:6 it is a s. to give up the things of this world.
M-13 ......... 2:2 give. What can the s. of nothing mean? It
M-13 ......... 2:4 is no s. in the world's terms that does not
M-13 ......... 2:5 a while about what the world calls s..
M-13 ......... 3:2 But what a s., –and it is sacrifice indeed!
M-13 ......... 3:2 error and what a sacrifice,–and it is s. indeed!
M-13 ......... 4:2 Is it a s. to give up pain? Does an adult
M-13 ......... 4:6 all the s. its values would demand of him.
M-13 ......... 4:9 And to possess them must he s. his hope
M-13 ......... 5:1 What is the real meaning of s.? It is the
M-13 ......... 5:5 it. It is the idea of s. that makes him blind.
M-13 ......... 6:1 requires s. of all you really hold dear. In
M-13 ......... 6:3 do not be mistaken about what s. means.
M-13 ......... 6:7 Would you now s. that Call? Few have
M-13 ....... 6:11 If you would s. the truth, they stay in hell.
M-13 ......... 7:1 Do not forget that s. is total. There are no
M-13 ....... 7:15 It seems to happen at the "s." of truth.
M-13 ......... 8:1 of God, do not forget the meaning of s.,
M-16 ......... 9:4 bad, neither rewarding nor demanding s.,
M-16 ....... 10:9 Rooted in s. and separation, two aspects
M-16 ..... 10:10 "s." is Heaven restored to his awareness.
P-1 ............. 3:4 even willing to "s." his "life" on its behalf.
P-3 ...........I.1:9 To demand s. of yourself is to demand a
P-3 ...........I.1:9 of yourself is to demand a s. of God, and
P-3 ...........I.1:9 of God, and He knows nothing of s.. Who
P-3 ...........I.2:5 Do not demand, do not decide, do not s..

## sacrificed 9

T-15..... VII.7:2 that he has s. something to the other, and
T-15...... XI.7:3 which must be of the mind, cannot be s..
T19.... IV.B.5:2 Are you not glad that Heaven cannot be s.
T-22....... V.2:7 offers must be defended against and s..
T-23...... II.11:7 Now must his body be destroyed and s.,
T-26.........I.7:2 no more be s. by you than can the light in
T-26.........I.7:4 in a body, nor is s. in solitude to sin. And
T-29..... VII.5:4 be life, and what is s. cannot be whole.
T-30...... VI.2:9 It *keeps* your rights from being s..

## sacrifices 8

T-7..... VII.11:4 to the ego are always experienced as s.,
T-9...........I.8:3 who believes that God demands s.. Either
T-9...........I.9:3 truth, there are no unbelievers and no s..
T-27........ II.8:3 of the "fact" that your salvation s. his.
M-13 ......... 4:7 To them he s. all his peace. To them he
M-13 ......... 4:8 To them he s. all his freedom. And to
M-13 ......... 7:2 There are no half s.. You cannot give up
P-3 ...........I.1:7 to make s. of yourself for those who come.

## sacrificing 5

T-3...........I.4:3 vicious. S. in any way is a violation of my
T-3...........I.6:1 Innocence is incapable of s. anything,
T-7......... X.3:9 the ego. But you will be s. nothing. On the
T-15..... VII.6:1 makes is based on the idea that by s. itself
T-15...... XI.5:2 a victim of sacrifice, justified in s. others.

## sacrosanct 1

T-19........ II.5:2 of sin is wholly s. to its thought system,

## sad 23

T-4........ IV.3:1 When you are s., *know this need not be.*
T-7...... VI.13:1 you gently that you are s. because you are
T-13..... VII.6:6 give this s. world over and exchange your
T-13. VII.16:10 like a veil of light across the world's s. face
T19.. IV.B.16:3 Its s. disciples chant the body's praise
T-20...... III.4:7 look out in sorrow from what is s. within,
T-25...... IV.3:2 that look on sin and beat its s. refrain.
T-27.... VIII.8:5 do its effects seem serious and s. indeed.
T-29.... IV.4:10 If it should fail you think the dream is s..
T-29..... VII.9:4 made s. and sick by seeing idols there.
W-pI..... 12.1:2 you is a frightening world, or a s. world,
W-pI..... 12.3:2 *dangerous world, a hostile world, a s. world,*
W-pI..... 92.3:3 in need, the helpless and afraid, the s., the
W-pI... 100.3:4 saved. While you are s., the light that God
W-pI... 100.5:1 We will not let ourselves be s. today. For
W-pI... 100.6:2 If you are s., your part is unfulfilled, and
W-pI... 121.2:2 The unforgiving mind is s., without the
W-pI... 124.5:2 in the frantic, in the s. and the distressed,
W-pI... 139.6:5 Why share its madness in the s. belief
W-pI... 182.2:3 Others will deny that they are s., and do
W-pI... 190.5:5 that has the power to make you ill or s., or
W-pII . 281.1:4 *If ever I am s. or hurt or ill, I have forgotten*
M-15 ......... 3:1 are sometimes s. and sometimes angry;

## sadness 14

T-13..... VII.3:7 and so although you turn in s. from it,
T-16..... V.10:2 entail, nor of the s. and the loneliness. For
T-20..... III.4:7 what is sad within, and see the s. there.
T-20..... VI.12:3 This is no time for s.. Perhaps confusion,
T-26..... IV.2:3 There is no s. and there is no parting here
T-27....... V.4:1 is no s. where a miracle has come to heal.
T-29...... IV.5:7 And dreams of s. thus are turned to joy.
T-29..... VII.5:3 seek? No s. and no suffering proclaim a
W-pI... 100.5:3 S. is the sign that you would play another
W-pI... 137.9:1 sorrow for a world where s. cannot enter,
W-pI... 163.1:2 It may appear as s., fear, anxiety or doubt;
W-pI... 182.2:2 their time, and keep their s. from them.

| | |
|---|---|
| W-pI...194.3:4 | already, is a time of your release from s., |
| W-pII .323.1:1 | *to give up all suffering, all sense of loss and s.* |

## safe 124

*See also* safe-keeping

| | |
|---|---|
| T-2......... V.4:2 | perfectly s. as long as you are completely |
| T-4...... III.1:11 | that your creations are as s. as you are. |
| T-4......... V.4:2 | identification with which the ego feels s., |
| T-6......... II.2:4 | imagine that you have made yourself s.. |
| T-6........ III.1:3 | the Holy Spirit still holds knowledge s. in |
| T-6........ III.3:3 | it, assuring it that it is perfectly s. forever. |
| T-6........ III.3:4 | The perfectly s. are wholly benign. They |
| T-6......... V.2:3 | merely reassure them that they are s. *now.* |
| T-6......... V.3:3 | you will escape from harm and be s., and |
| T-9...........I.7:6 | Yet you cannot be s. *from* truth, but only |
| T-9....VIII.10:3 | Himself keeps your extensions s. within it |
| T-10.........I.1:4 | that was created is therefore perfectly s., |
| T-12....VIII.2:1 | God's Son is as s. as his Father, for the |
| T-13....VII.7:2 | him. He is as s. from pain as God Himself, |
| T-13...VII.17:7 | travel but in dreams, while s. at home. |
| T-14....... V.7:7 | in your s. inclusion in the circle with |
| T-14....... V.8:5 | to its s. embrace of love and union. Stand |
| T-14...... VI.3:2 | They are neither s. nor unsafe. They do |
| T-14..VIII.2:10 | All this is s. within you, where the Holy |
| T-14...... IX.1:6 | The knowledge is s., but where is your |
| T-16........ II.8:6 | Reality is s. and sure, and wholly kind to |
| T-16.... IV.13:8 | center, and only there, you are s. forever, |
| T-17.........I.2:6 | to truth to use for you is s. from fantasy. |
| T-17...... III.2:1 | you what you do to keep it s. is really love. |
| T-17...... III.7:4 | The spark of holiness must be s., however |
| T-18.......I.11:1 | whole and beautiful, s. in your love. |
| T-18.... VI.14:3 | you to be yourself, within its s. embrace. |
| T-18.... IX.14:3 | it, s. and sure within its gentleness, to the |
| T-19.........I.7:8 | identification s. from the "attack" of truth |
| T-20..... VI.5:5 | Here it is "s.," for here love cannot enter. |
| T-20..... VI.6:7 | have *not* be is here kept "s." from Him. |
| T-20..... VI.7:8 | purpose lies s. in your relationship, and |
| T-20.... VI.10:4 | in gladness for the holy one of s. return. |
| T-21...... VI.6:2 | Father forever, without a hope of s. return |
| T-22... VI.12:8 | Attack is neither s. nor dangerous. It is |
| T-23.......in.3:2 | are s. because they share their innocence. |
| T-24....... II.3:7 | carefully in sin, to keep it "s." from truth. |
| T-24....... II.5:5 | each in his special sins and "s." from love, |
| T-24..... II.13:3 | brothers; s. from all intrusions of sanity |
| T-24..... II.13:3 | illusions; s. from God and safe for conflict |
| T-24..... II.13:3 | illusions; safe from God and s. for conflict |
| T-24...... III.4:3 | No, His Son is s., resting on Him. It is |
| T-24...... III.4:5 | Nothing is s. from its attack, and it is safe |
| T-24...... III.4:5 | from its attack, and it is s. from nothing. |
| T-24...... IV.5:3 | Your specialness seemed s. because of it. |
| T-24..... VII.5:1 | The Father keeps what He created s.. You |
| T-25....... II.6:8 | God creates is s. from all corruption, |
| T-25....... II.7:5 | God kept it s. that you might look on it, |
| T-25...... VI.7:7 | and let him understand that he is s., as he |
| T-25..... VII.1:9 | The world is s. from love to everyone who |
| T-25..VIII.14:4 | you are s. from vengeance in all forms. |
| T-26.........I.8:1 | keeps him s. from all injustice the world |
| T-26....... II.5:1 | believe it s. to give but some mistakes to |
| T-28..... VII.6:1 | sense in seeking to be s. in what was made |
| T-28..... VII.6:3 | What can be s. that rests upon a shadow? |
| T-28..... VII.7:5 | that His Son is s. forever in Himself. |
| T-30..... III.9:1 | for He is the eternal sky that holds it s., |
| T-30.... III.10:4 | peace. Here is your one reality kept s., |
| T-30...... IV.2:7 | He misunderstood what made him s., and |
| T-30...... IV.4:8 | nor make you s. if they obeyed your rules. |
| W-pI.....46.4:2 | It is a s. rule that anyone you do not like is |
| W-pI.....47.2:3 | can put his faith in weakness and feel s.? |
| W-pI.....56.1:7 | God has kept my inheritance s. for me. |
| W-pI.....60.3:2 | s. the world will look to me when I can see |
| W-pI.....68.6:4 | s. in a world that protects you and loves |
| W-pI.....68.6:9 | *grievances go I will know I am perfectly s..* |
| W-pI.....76.8:7 | you hold must be obeyed to make you s.. |
| W-pI.....87.3:2 | I am s. today because there is no will but |
| W-pI.....87.3:6 | I am s. because there is no will but God's. |
| W-pI.....97.7:2 | *free of all limits, s. and healed and whole,* |
| W-pI.....98.3:1 | for they are s. and recognize their safety. |
| W-pI...107.2:3 | you were certain you were loved and s.. |
| W-pI...124.1:2 | Our home is s., protection guaranteed in |
| W-pI. 134.12:3 | iron doors he thought would make him s. |
| W-pI...135.5:4 | to make it beautiful or walls to make it s., |
| W-pI...138.8:2 | saved from salvation, threatened to be s., |
| W-pI. 161.12:4 | is your s. escape from anger and from fear |
| W-pI...170.1:3 | is protection; you are s. because of cruelty |
| WpI...rV.in2:6 | *is s. because his father leads the way for him.* |
| WpI...rV.in8:8 | unchanged by time, immaculate and s., as |
| W-pI...181.7:1 | thought to keep us s. throughout the day. |
| W-pI...183.2:2 | they spread out their wings to keep you s., |
| W-pI...187.4:4 | time, however much you try to keep it s.. |
| W-pI...189.2:2 | sings your praises as it keeps you s. from |
| W-pI...193.2:6 | and keeps his sinlessness forever s.. |
| W-pII .229.1:5 | but which my Father has kept s. for me. |
| W-pII .235.1:3 | that I am saved and s. forever in His Arms |
| W-pII .238.1:5 | *certainty that he is s. Who still is part of You,* |
| W-pII .244.1:1 | *Your Son is s. wherever he may be, for You* |
| W-pII ....245.h | Your peace is with me, Father. I am s.. |
| W-pII ..... 5.1:3 | this fence he thinks that he is s. from love. |
| W-pII ..... 5.5:1 | with what you think will make you s.. |
| W-pII ..... 5.5:6 | Identify with love, and you are s.. Identify |
| W-pII .261.1:2 | where I am s. and cannot be attacked. Let |
| W-pII .264.1:4 | *surrounds Your Son and keeps him s. is Love* |
| W-pII .268.2:4 | Only reality is wholly s.. And it is only |
| W-pII .272.1:7 | *forever still, forever gentle and forever s..* |
| W-pII .278.2:5 | *of fear. For truth is s., and only love is sure.* |
| W-pII .281.2:3 | pain. My Father placed me s. in Heaven, |
| W-pII .293.1:3 | bright and clear and s. and welcoming, |
| W-pII .293.2:3 | *the present holds s. from all past mistakes.* |
| W-pII ..... 9.2:1 | and hold you s. within its gentle advent, |
| W-pII .303.2:8 | *S. in Your Arms let me receive Your Son.* |
| W-pII .324.2:4 | sure, and guarantees a s. returning home. |
| W-pII .328.2:3 | *It is Your Will that I be wholly s., eternally at* |
| W-pII .329.1:9 | *And I am s., untroubled and serene, in* |
| W-pII .338.1:4 | and he is s. from all external things. His |
| W-pII ....341.h | And it is only that which keeps me s.. |
| W-pII .341.1:3 | *How pure, how s., how holy, then, are we,* |
| W-ep ......... 4:6 | the goal, and of your s. arrival in the end. |
| M-4 .........I.1:6 | It is this power that keeps all things s.. It |
| M-4 ....... V.1:7 | are sure they are beloved and must be s.. |
| M-13 ......... 7:8 | It is its holiness that makes you s.. It is |
| M-15 ....... 3:11 | and offer it to all the world to keep it s.. |
| M-16 ......... 7:3 | For he is s., and knows it to be so. He has |
| M-16 ......... 7:6 | He is as s. in the present as he was before |
| M-16 ....... 10:4 | he is s. from all deception if he so decides. |
| M-17 ......... 5:9 | him s. from fury that can never be abated, |
| C-4 ............ 8:1 | s. and pure and lovely in the Mind of God |
| C-6 .......... 4:10 | is from these that He would make you s.. |
| C-ep........... 2:5 | that held it s. within eternity and through |
| P-2...... IV.10:4 | if his lesson is to be that sanity is s.. It |
| P-2...... IV.10:8 | neither is it s.. And thus it must remain |
| P-2......... V.1:3 | comes the inevitable belief that, to be s., |

## safe-keeping 1

| | |
|---|---|
| T-17 ..... IV.7:3 | What they defend is placed in them for s., |

## safeguards 1

| | |
|---|---|
| P-2........ VI.3:7 | are its "remedies"; its "s." from insanity. |

## safely 33

| | |
|---|---|
| T-4 ........I.13:2 | A father can s. leave a child with an elder |
| T-4 ....... VI.1:5 | We cannot s. let it go at that, however, or |
| T-11 .......II.5:8 | You can s. trust His patience, for He |
| T-11 ..... VI.6:7 | s. surrounded by what is yours forever. |
| T-12 ...VIII.1:2 | has hidden His Son s. within Himself, and |
| T-13 ..VII.13:3 | What comes to you of Him comes s., for |
| T-13 ..VII.15:1 | with faith that He will lead you s. through |
| T-14 .......X.7:2 | You cannot s. make this division, for you |
| T-16 ..... III.9:2 | wait for you will not draw you s. across. |
| T-17 ..... VI.1:7 | can more s. look beyond each situation, |
| T-18 ..... IX.3:9 | would lead you s. through and far beyond |
| T-18 ... IX.13:1 | its unholy purpose has been s. brought |
| T-19 ........I.1:2 | of the dedication can be s. assumed. Yet |
| T19. IV.D.21:3 | place the Son of God s. within the sure |
| T-20 .....II.10:4 | to guide you s. through them and beyond. |
| T-22 ..... IV.5:8 | joined with your brother's, is it s. given, |
| T-24 ...... V.7:1 | and s. held in you by that same hand that |
| T-24 .... VII.5:7 | its holiness, and rests in light as s. as itself |
| T-28 ........I.8:3 | which He did not keep It s. in your mind. |
| T-28 .......V.4:1 | Self is s. hidden by what you have made. |
| T-29 ........I.6:3 | and when to shrink more s. into fear. It |
| T-31 .......II.6:9 | way unless you keep him s. by your side. |
| T-31 .......V.5:4 | the pathways of the world are s. kept, and |
| W-pI .. 119.1:3 | *Son, whose Self rests s. in the Mind of God.* |
| W-pI .. 138.8:3 | unaware, to keep them s. undisturbed; |
| W-pI .. 155.9:1 | Walk s. now, yet carefully, because this |
| W-pI 155.13:1 | feet are s. set upon the road that leads the |
| W-pI .. 159.5:2 | And in its power can you s. trust to carry |
| W-pI .. 161.1:4 | passed s. by and Heaven now restored. |
| WpI...rV.in7:1 | again each time I lead a brother s. to the |
| W-pII .... in.9:7 | and we who are God's Sons are s. home, |
| M-16 ......... 3:4 | we can s. say that time devoted to starting |
| M-23 ......... 4:3 | a symbol that is s. used as a replacement |

## safer 11

| | |
|---|---|
| T-2 .........V.2:5 | s. for you to rely temporarily on physical |
| T-15 .... VII.4:6 | invest outside yourself, the s. you become |
| T-15 .......X.8:4 | it seems s. to project Him outward and |
| T-16 .......II.5:2 | And are you really s. in maintaining the |
| T-16 .....V.11:3 | You think it s. to endow the little self you |
| T-20 ... VIII.4:6 | is a better home, a s. shelter for God's Son |
| T-22 ... VI.11:7 | it seems s. to attack another or yourself |
| T-26 ... VIII.2:3 | Thus do you think it s. to remain a little |
| T-26 .......X.4:6 | s. to believe that you are innocent of this, |
| T-31 .......II.9:3 | ahead would be a s. place for him to be. |
| W-pI .. 170.1:5 | in which you are for something better, s., |

## safety 114

| | |
|---|---|
| T-5 ....... IV.1:9 | is the guarantee of the s. of the Kingdom, |
| T-5 ...... VII.1:3 | for your s. and joy better than He can? |
| T-6 ....... III.3:1 | only s. lies in extending the Holy Spirit, |
| T-6 ....... III.3:7 | S. is the complete relinquishment of |
| T-6 ..... V.C.2:6 | what you can extend with perfect s.. |
| T-6 ... V.C.10:9 | It is in the perfect s. of God. Therefore, |
| T-7 ..... VI.3:10 | that you will not know your own s.. |
| T-7 ..... VIII.3:9 | who project are vigilant for their own s.. |
| T-9 ..........I.7:5 | it is, and this gives you the illusion of s.. |
| T-9 ..........I.7:7 | Reality is the only s.. Your will is your |
| T-10 ......in.1:6 | protection and are as inviolate as your s.. |
| T-12 .. VII.10:5 | perfect s. of the Mind which created us. |
| T-13 .... VII.7:7 | And from this point of s. he looks quietly |
| T-14 .......V.7:7 | bring within its s. and its perfect peace. |
| T-14 .......V.8:6 | with you in the s. of its peace and holiness |
| T-14 ..... VI.3:1 | power to these strange ideas of s.? They |
| T-14 ..... IX.1:6 | is safe, but where is your s. apart from it? |
| T-15 ..... III.6:1 | clearly and in perfect s. in your mind, |
| T-15 .. VII.12:3 | And you will see s. in guilt and danger in |
| T-15 ..... XI.1:2 | And seek not s. by attempting to protect |
| T-15 ..... XI.1:4 | which you think you see some scraps of s.. |
| T-16 ..... IV.2:5 | and you will cross the bridge in perfect s., |
| T-16 ..... IV.3:4 | a place of s. from which hatred is split off |
| T-17 .... VII.7:2 | And you can use *this* in perfect s.. Yet for |
| T-18 ........I.8:3 | you gently back to the truth and s. within. |
| T-19 ..... IV.1:7 | will carry its message of love and s. and |
| T19 .IV.A.14:8 | Theirs are the messages of s., for they see |
| T19 ...IV.C.7:2 | For death is seen as s., the great dark |
| T19 ...IV.C.9:2 | sin, which nestles quietly in the s. of your |
| T19 .IV.C.10:5 | In its tiny hands it holds, in perfect s., |
| T-20 ... III.11:5 | The innocent see s., and the pure in heart |
| T-20 .......V.8:2 | rests in his gentle hands in s. and in peace |
| T-20 .......V.8:4 | offer it to him and know it rests in s.? He |
| T-21 ........I.2:4 | are open, and you can see where s. lies; |
| T-22 ........I.9:8 | his Self could be reborn in s. and in peace. |
| T-22 ... VI.12:7 | value, except in the desire to attack in s.? |
| T-23 .....II.17:7 | find s. from attack by turning on himself? |
| T-23 ..... III.6:5 | There *is* no s. in a battleground. You can |
| T-23 ..... III.6:6 | on it in s. from above and not be touched. |
| T-23 ..... III.6:7 | But from within it you can find no s.. Not |
| T-23 ... III.6:11 | the form that murder takes can offer s.? |
| T-23 ..... IV.1:3 | Yet He remains the only place of s.. In |
| T-24 ..... III.4:2 | in such a state, where s. has no meaning? |
| T-24 ..... III.6:6 | forever in the arms of peace, in perfect s., |
| T-24 .... VII.4:8 | shine on him, and give *you* s. from decay. |
| T-24 .... VII.5:5 | and if that is true, its s. rests secure. If not |

T-25.........I.3:2 It chooses where you think your s. lies, at
T-25......IV.1:2 this is so, seeing their s. in this happy fact.
T-26......VI.1:8 find the s. that the truth alone can give?
T-26... VIII.5:1 make for s. all are laid within the future,
T-27... VIII.1:5 Its s. is its main concern. Its comfort is its
T-28....... V.4:1 truth to be the place where all your s. lies,
T-28........VII.h The Ark of S.
T-28.....VII.7:5 It is an ark of s., resting on God's promise
T-28.....VII.7:6 the s. of this shelter and its Source? From
T-29... VIII.2:3 for s. in a world perceived as dangerous,
T-29....IX.10:1 live in s. and have not attacked yourself.
T-30......IV.3:4 It must appear to break your rules for s.,
T-30......IV.4:2 It is His laws that guarantee your s.. All
T-30... VIII.2:5 of lack, and s. from disaster of all kinds.
T-31.........I.7:7 for s. you can make that ever will succeed.
W-pI.....13.3:3 To the ego illusions are s. devices, as they
W-pI.....14.3:6 direction is toward perfect s. and perfect
W-pI.....47.3:1 God is your s. in every circumstance. His
W-pI.....47.7:1 down into your mind to a place of real s..
W-pI.....50.3:2 into a climate of perfect peace and s.. It
W-pI.....53.3:4 It holds out no s. and no hope. But such a
W-pI.....55.3:4 I will see a world of peace and s. and joy.
W-pI.....68.6:5 Try to feel s. surrounding you, hovering
W-pI.....87.3:4 I believe that my eternal s. is threatened.
W-pI.....98.3:1 for they are safe and recognize their s..
W-pI...102.3:2 Here is your home, and here your s. is.
W-pI...109.1:3 We ask for s. and for happiness, although
W-pI...109.2:2 and the s. and the happiness you seek. "I
W-pI...121.1:3 Here is the way to s. in apparent dangers
W-pI...122.1:5 Do you want care and s., and the warmth
W-pI...122.8:1 upon a happy world of s. and of peace.
W-pI...131.1:2 there is none, for s. in the midst of danger
W-pI...131.2:7 You look for s. and security, while in your
W-pI...135.3:3 You think it offers s.. Yet it speaks of fear
W-pI......153.h In my defenselessness my s. lies.
W-pI...153.1:2 The world provides no s.. It is rooted in
W-pI...153.1:3 and all its "gifts" of seeming s. are illusory
W-pI...153.5:5 by which illusions of his s. comfort him.
W-pI...153.9:3 secure, serenely certain of our s. now,
W-pI...162.3:2 secure, his s. certain and his body healed,
W-pI...165.3:1 Who would deny his s. and his peace, his
W-pI...166.4:2 is the only s. he believes that he can find.
W-pI...170.5:2 For fear becomes your s. and protector of
W-pI...170.7:6 who see in him their s. have no guardian,
W-pI...172.1:1 (153) In my defenselessness my s. lies.
W-pI...191.5:2 And from this place of s. and escape you
W-pI...196.1:4 you will understand his s. is your own,
W-pII..222.1:3 and guarantees my s. from all pain. He
W-pII..232.1:5 *And let me sleep sure of my s., certain of*
W-pII..234.2:2 *We recognize our s., and give thanks for all*
W-pII..244.1:2 *and he will recollect his s. and Your Love, for*
W-pII..244.1:3 *loving, in the s. of Your Fatherly embrace?*
W-pII......5.1:4 Identifying with his s., he regards himself
W-pII......5.1:4 safety, he regards himself as what his s. is.
W-pII......5.2:2 Yet this he sees as double s.. For the Son
W-pII......5.5:3 Your s. lies in truth, and not in lies. Love
W-pII......5.5:4 in lies. Love is your s.. Fear does not exist.
W-pII..275.2:4 *The s. that I bring is given me. Father, Your*
W-pII......8.3:2 What can it perceive surrounding it but s.
W-pII....12.2:5 it can ensure its s. by attacking them.
W-pII..337.1:1 ensures me perfect peace, eternal s.,
W-pII..348.1:5 *Surrounding me is perfect s.. Can I be afraid,*
M-4.....VI.1:12 It is s.. It is peace. It is joy. And it is God.
M-16..........6:3 think you made a place of s. for yourself.
M-16..........6:6 Your s. lies not there. What you give up is
M-16..........7:2 in the name of s. no longer interests him.
M-16..........7:8 God. This is his s.. And he has no need for
S-1........III.4:7 make a jailer of an enemy seems to be s..

## safety's 1

T-24.....II.12:6 dear but clings to murder as s. weapon,

## said 123

T-1.......VII.5:2 I have s. that awe is inappropriate in
T-2......... V.3:1 I have already s. that miracles are
T-2......... V.7:3 I s. before that the Holy Spirit cannot see
T-2....... V.10:5 I s. before that only revelation transcends
T-2........ VI.1:2 I have s. already that only constructive
T-2.......VII.4:1 It has already been s. that you believe you
T-3......... II.3:6 I have s. that only what God creates or
T-3........ III.1:1 have s. very little about knowledge as yet.
T-3......... V.1:1 I have s. that the abilities you possess are
T-3......VI.11:8 the Kingdom of Heaven," and you have s.,
T-3.......VII.4:8 as I s. before, when you finally perceive
T-4........ IV.2:1 I have s. that you cannot change your
T-4........ IV.2:1 changing your behavior, but I have also s.
T-4........ VI.6:5 I have s. before that I am in charge of the
T-5...........I.3:2 I have s. already that I can reach up and
T-5...........I.4:4 I myself s., "If I go I will send you another
T-5........ III.1:2 I have already s. that the Holy Spirit is the
T-5........ III.5:3 I have s. before that the Holy Spirit is
T-5......IV.2:12 I meant when I s. it is possible even in this
T-5......... V.4:5 I s. before that you must learn to think
T-5......... V.5:4 I s. before that illness is a form of magic.
T-5......... V.8:2 have s. this before, but did not emphasize
T-5......VI.11:1 I s. "I am come as a light into the world,"
T-5......VI.11:2 dark glass, and remember also that I s.,
T-5......VI.12:4 repeatedly s. that time is a learning device
T-6...........I.6:1 As I have s. before, "As you teach so shall
T-6.........I.15:5 I could not have s., "Betrayest thou the
T-6.........I.15:7 The "punishment" I was s. to have called
T-6......... II.1:5 We have s. before that the separation was
T-6........ III.2:4 remember. I s. before that the message of
T-6......IV.11:7 frequently s. that what you teach you are.
T-6......V.A.3:1 I have s. that the Holy Spirit is the
T-6......V.B.3:3 all." I s. that this is apt to increase conflict
T-6......V.C.1:1 s. before that the Holy Spirit is evaluative,
T-7..........I.6:3 is whole. I have s. that the last step in the
T-7......... II.6:4 I s. before that He teaches remembering
T-7........ III.1:7 ways. When I s. "I am with you always,"
T-7........ III.3:1 I s. before that the ego's friend is not part
T-7........ IV.2:7 I s. before that forgetting is merely a way
T-7........ VI.6:4 as meaningless. I have s. before that the
T-7........ VI.6:6 As I have already s., understanding brings
T-7..... VIII.1:1 We have s. that without projection there
T-7......... X.6:4 it. I s. before that you are the Will of God.
T-7........ XI.6:4 you. I have already s. that only the whole
T-8......... II.5:1 We have s. that the Holy Spirit teaches
T-8......... II.7:1 When I s., "All power and glory are yours
T-8........ IV.2:4 I s. that I am with you always, even unto
T-8..... VIII.4:7 I have s. that judgment is the function of
T-8..... VIII.7:6 I s. that the ego does not know anything,
T-8..... VIII.7:6 I s. the one thing about the ego that is
T-8........ IX.1:1 I s. before that the Holy Spirit is the
T-9...........I.4:2 When I s. that the Holy Spirit's function
T-9........ IV.6:2 meant when I s. that miracles are natural,
T-9......... V.2:1 repeatedly s. that beliefs of the ego cannot
T-9......... V.6:2 When God s., "Let there be light," there
T-9.......VII.7:1 I have s. that the ego does not know what
T-9..... VIII.2:7 s. before that the ego vacillates between
T-10....... III.6:6 When I s., "My peace I give unto you,"
T-10....... V.5:1 I s. before that of yourself you can do
T-11....... III.3:3 When the light comes and you have s.,
T-11....... V.5:3 I s. before that to will contrary to God is
T-11...... VI.1:5 That is what I meant when I s., "Blessed
T-12........ II.4:1 Remember what was s. about the
T-12...... III.8:1 I s. before that God so loved the world
T-12....... V.7:1 I have s. that the ego's rule is, "Seek and
T-12.....VII.7:1 I s. before that what you project or
T-13.........I.1:1 I s. that the Holy Spirit shares the goal of
T-13......... II.6:1 I have s. that the crucifixion is the symbol
T-13....... III.1:4 We have s. that no one will countenance
T-13......... V.1:1 I have s. you have but two emotions, love
T-14......... II.5:7 I s. before, "Be not content with nothing,"
T-14...... VI.7:1 say, and so you know not what is s. to you
T-14..... X.12:4 Earlier I s. this course will teach you how
T-15....... V.2:2 We have s. that to limit love to part of the
T-15.....VII.4:1 We s. before that the ego attempts to
T-16..........I.6:4 I have s. that if a brother asks a foolish
T-16...... III.2:2 I s. earlier, "By their fruits ye shall know
T-16.....VII.6:2 s. before that the Holy Spirit must teach
T-17..... IV.2:3 I have s. repeatedly that the Holy Spirit
T-18........ II.6:3 I s. before that the first change, before
T-19.........I.1:1 We s. before that when a situation has
T-19.........I.1:3 Yet we also s. that peace without faith will
T-19.........I.3:6 there, hearing what truth has never s. and
T-19........II.6:1 indeed be s. the ego made its world on sin
T19. IV.A.16:3 instant grace is s. by everyone together, as
T19....IV.B.1:1 We s. that peace must first surmount the
T-20..... VII.1:1 We have s. much about discrepancies of
T-20..... VII.1:2 But we have also s. the means to meet the
T-21........II.9:1 We have already s. that wishful thinking
T-21..... VII.6:4 We s. this year would emphasize the
T-24...... IV.4:1 Earlier I s. consider not the means by
T-25...... IV.2:1 Perception's basic law could thus be s.,
T-25...... VII.3:1 Let us go back to what we s. before, and
T-29...... IV.3:1 can be s. attack is a response to function
T-30.......I.14:1 We s. you can begin a happy day with the
T-30...... III.1:6 as if you s., "I have no need of everything.
T-31...... III.7:4 God has s. there *is* no sacrifice that can be
T-31...... VI.4:7 For God Himself has s., "Your will be
W-pI.....39.3:1 We have already s. that your holiness is
W-pI.....52.4:2 is now, it can truly be s. that I see nothing
W-pI......140.h Only salvation can be s. to cure.
W-pI. 140.12:2 *Only salvation can be s. to cure. Speak to us,*
W-pI... 150.2:1 (140) Only salvation can be s. to cure.
W-pI... 152.3:6 can not be too often s. and thought about
W-pI. 154.12:2 You have heard this s. a hundred ways, a
W-pI... 160.5:2 Who fears has but denied himself and s.,
W-pI... 169.4:2 But we have also s. the mind determines
W-pI... 183.2:1 nor s. without an echo in the mind that
W-pI... 185.2:6 Many have s. these words. But few indeed
W-pII . 284.1:5 be but s. and then repeated many times;
M-in .......... 2:5 The purpose of the course might be s. to
M-4 ........... 2:2 in time it can be s. that the advanced
M-7 ........... 1:4 is certain, as we have already s. it is, what
M-16 ......... 2:6 be s. that it is well to start the day right. It
M-20 ......... 1:1 It has been s. that there is a kind of peace
M-23 ......... 2:1 We have repeatedly s. that one who has
M-24 ....... 6:10 s. that their truth lies in their usefulness.
P-2........ IV.3:6 and we have s. already and will say again,
P-3...........II.1:4 it can still be s. that there are those who
P-3...........II.4:1 God is s. to have looked on all He created
P-3........ III.5:1 well been s. that to him who hath shall be
S-1........ III.1:1 We s. that prayer is always for yourself,
S-3........ III.2:2 And yet it can be s. of any form of healing

## saint 1

P-2....... VII.9:4 s. can come to take you home with him?

## saintliness 1

S-2...........II.4:5 s. the anger and the hurt another gives,

## Saints 1

*saints*

P-3..........II.7:7 are the S. of God. They are the Saviors of

## saints 1

*Saints*

P-2....... VII.6:7 His patients are God's s., who call upon

## sake 5

T-6...........I.9:1 I elected, for your s. and mine, to
T-8....... VII.6:5 of God remain hidden for His Name's s.,
T-9..........II.8:2 in them, for the s. of what God gave them
T-12.........I.7:5 For the s. of your need, then, hear every
T-13. VII.10:12 its own s. is the ego's fundamental creed,

## saluting 1

W-pI... 156.5:4 their holiness, s. you as savior and as God

## salvaged 1

T-4..........II.9:7 not in danger and does not need to be s..

## salvaging 2

T-27..... VII.6:1 The part you play in s. the world from
W-pI... 162.4:5 has restored your sight by s. your mind.

**salvation** 672

*See also* forgiveness-for-salvation

T-1 III.3:4 the s. or release of all of God's creations.
T-3 I.2:4 persecuted His Own Son on behalf of s..
T-3 VII.6:5 You who fear s. are choosing death. Life
T-4 I.12:1 you can do everything for the s. of both.
T-4 II.9:7 However, s. does not apply to spirit,
T-4 II.10:1 S. is nothing more than "right-
T-4 VI.8:2 S. is a collaborative venture. It cannot be
T-5 III.h The Guide to S.
T-5 III.11:9 He is your Guide to s., because He holds
T-5 VII.4:2 to work out the plan of s. yourself because
T-6 I.6:3 want to teach if he is to realize his own s..
T-6 I.18:2 limit, and must be used for their joint s..
T-6 III.4:1 your s. lies in teaching the exact opposite
T-8 III.4:6 meet, they are given another chance at s..
T-8 III.4:7 leave anyone without giving s. to him and
T-8 IV.3:6 Dispelling it is s., and in this sense I *am* the
T-8 IV.3:6 and in this sense I *am* the s. of the world.
T-8 VII.1:8 in them, he has cut himself off from s..
T-8 VII.5:5 Do not see him this way for your own s.,
T-8 VII.15:3 with His purpose, and you need s.. You
T-9 I.5:4 willing is s. because it is communication.
T-9 I.7:8 is your s. because it is the same as God's.
T-9 II.6:3 God. S. is of your brother. The Holy Spirit
T-9 IV.6:3 to follow the Holy Spirit's plan of s.,
T-9 IV.8:3 remarkably poor choice as a teacher of s..
T-9 VII.1:1 God's Will is your s.. Would He not have
T-9 VII.1:5 You do not have to seek far for s.. Every
T-10 III.1:11 Do not be afraid of it, because it is your s..
T-11 IV.1:1 Never forget that the Sonship is your s.,
T-11 IV.1:3 Your Self does not need s., but your mind
T-11 IV.1:3 but your mind needs to learn what s. is.
T-11 V.13:5 with the conviction that separation is s.,
T-11 V.13:6 chaos for meaning, for if separation is s.,
T-11 VII.4:9 have made, and to perceive only this is s.,
T-12 I.6:4 How simple, then, is God's plan for s..
T-12 III.2:2 should tell you that he believes s. lies in it.
T-12 III.2:3 believing that your s. lies in *not* doing it.
T-12 III.2:5 in is always related to your notion of s..
T-12 III.4:6 He is asking for s., as you are. Poverty is
T-12 III.5:1 S. is for the mind, and it is attained
T-12 III.5:3 about the "what" and the "how" of s.,
T-12 III.5:5 dwell in abundance and that s. is come.
T-12 III.7:5 everyone believes that identification is s..
T-12 III.9:8 mind of its maker, along with his real s..
T-12 III.10:2 For in this same place also lies s.. The
T-12 IV.1:2 the ego is s. seems to be intensely engaged
T-13 in.3:2 to this as the price of s. and *be* loving. *Love*
T-13 in.3:4 If it did, attack would be s., and this is the
T-13 in.4:6 never having sinned, he has no need of s..
T-13 I.10:3 to the insane notion that attack is s.. And
T-13 II.4:3 by not valuing its interpretation of s.,
T-13 III.2:7 believe that attack is s. because it would
T-13 IV.6:8 be meeting no one, and the sharing of s.,
T-13 IV.7:7 holy encounters in which s. can be found.
T-13 IV.8:4 means of s. that you must learn to accept,
T-13 IV.8:4 if you would share His goal of s. for you.
T-13 VI.8:1 Now is the time of s., for now is the
T-13 VII.10:11 The ego wants to have things for s., for
T-13 VII.11:4 where the ego sees s. it sees separation,
T-13 VII.16:7 S. from the world lies only here. My peace
T-13 X.2:9 s. will find it in that strange relationship.
T-13 X.4:6 S. is not found by those who use their
T-13 X.4:7 You wanted not s. in the past. Would you
T-13 X.4:8 on the present, and hope to find s. now?
T-13 XI.9:1 learn s. because you will learn how to save
T-13 XI.9:3 S. is as sure as God. His certainty suffices.
T-13 XI.11:5 offers *to* everyone, for the s. *of* everyone,
T-14 III.1:4 guilt is interference, not s., and serves no
T-14 III.10:2 to guilt, because they think it is s., and
T-14 III.12:5 own. You know not of s., for you do not
T-14 III.13:3 signifies that you would define what s. *is,*
T-14 III.13:4 The Holy Spirit knows that all s. is escape
T-14 III.14:1 the only Guide that you would follow to s.
T-14 III.14:4 as you decided that s. lay in you alone.
T-14 III.14:5 S. is of Him to Whom God gave it for you.
T-14 III.14:7 for your s. and the peace of God in you.
T-14 VII.4:2 realize that s. must come to you this way,
T-15 I.10:4 into the holy present is s. from change.
T-15 I.11:2 short a time to the Holy Spirit for your s.?
T-15 III.11:1 If you are wholly willing to leave s. to the
T-15 III.11:1 for peace yourself, s. will be given you.
T-15 IV.2:5 can find s. in your own way and have it.
T-15 IV.2:6 made for your s. in exchange for God's.
T-15 IV.3:6 Every allegiance to a plan of s. apart from
T-15 IV.7:3 that s. lies in keeping thoughts to yourself
T-15 V.2:5 to it for s. is to believe you are alone. To
T-15 V.3:3 offer you s. is the belief that separation is
T-15 V.3:3 salvation is the belief that separation is s..
T-15 V.3:4 equality of the Atonement in which s. lies.
T-15 VII.13:2 to be damnation that communication is s.
T-15 VIII.1:6 that forgiveness is not loss, but your s..
T-15 X.5:7 to your thought system that s. apart from
T-15 X.9:6 S. is simple, being of God, and therefore
T-15 XI.5:7 attack becomes s. and sacrifice becomes
T-16 IV.1:4 s. will rise clearly before your open eyes as
T-16 V.14:1 S. lies in the simple fact that illusions are
T-16 VI.10:1 the mockery of s. the ego offered you, and
T-16 VII.4:1 and would teach you s. is past and so you
T-16 VII.4:1 so you must return to the past to find s..
T-16 VII.6:1 Against the ego's insane notion of s. the
T-16 VII.6:3 belief in s. through vengeance for the past
T-16 VII.10:4 investment in s. in your relationship with
T-17 I.6:2 S. from separation would be complete, or
T-17 I.6:6 both of you away from truth and from s..
T-17 II.3:3 Who planned s. could complete it thus.
T-17 II.7:3 Even s. will become a dream, and vanish
T-17 II.7:4 For s. is the end of dreams, and with the
T-17 II.7:5 dream that there could ever be need of s.?
T-17 II.8:1 How much do you want s.? It will give
T-17 V.1:2 Like everything about s., the holy instant
T-17 V.9:1 You are very new in the ways of s., and
T-17 V.10:5 you may see that in it rests s.. Condemn
T-17 V.10:6 Condemn s. not, for it has come to you.
T-17 VII.10:6 it, for it calls you to s. and to peace.
T-17 VIII.5:7 His s. is your only purpose. See only this
T-18 II.7:6 on Him as means for the s. of everyone.
T-18 III.6:5 of your relationship, is your need for s..
T-18 III.7:1 now the bringer of s. have the function of
T-18 IV.6:3 Atonement to it, and make s. fearful. And
T-18 IV.7:7 S. is easy just *because* it asks nothing you
T-18 V.1:3 all the means by which s. is accomplished
T-18 VI.5:1 separation reinterpreted as means for s.,
T-19 I.12:6 and so you do not recognize s. in him. Yet
T-19 II.1:1 it is this distinction that makes s. possible
T19 IV.A.2:9 stand between your brothers and s.? And
T19 IV.A.4:1 thrust s. away from the giver of salvation?
T19 IV.A.4:1 thrust salvation away from the giver of s.?
T19 IV.A.4:7 S. cannot be withheld from you. It is your
T19 IV.A.14:7 They offer you s.. Theirs are the messages
T19 IV.A.17:4 S. is looked upon as a way by which the
T19 IV.A.17:7 no better means for communication of s.,
T19 IV.B.2:6 justifies your strange belief that in it lies s.
T19 IV.B.4:7 You want s., not the pain of guilt. And
T19 IV.B.7:2 S. flows from deep within the home you
T19 IV.C.9:3 infancy of s. is carefully guarded by love,
T19 IV.D.1:5 final obstacle, after which is s. completed,
T19 IV.D.12:4 Yet in his hands is your s.. You see his
T19 IV.D.13:3 Is this giver of s. your friend or enemy?
T19 IV.D.14:5 "stranger" still offers you s. as His Friend.
T19 IV.D.19:2 has established for s. will be left undone.
T19 IV.D.20:2 is seen as either the giver of guilt or of s.,
T-20 I.4:8 me. For Easter is the time of your s., along
T-20 IV.2:7 your mistakes, and therein lies his own s..
T-20 IV.2:9 S. is a lesson in giving, as the Holy Spirit
T-20 IV.5:5 that they are all the same need not s.. And
T-20 IV.8:3 have a plan for your s. that does not work.
T-20 VI.11:9 here can he learn relationships are his s.,
T-20 VII.9:4 S. is the Holy Spirit's goal. The means is
T-20 VIII.3:2 Spirit and at one with Him on what s. is.
T-20 VIII.6:9 holy relationship, the source of your s.,
T-21 II.1:2 the very little on which s. rests; the tiny
T-21 II.2:2 reservations, for here the power of s. lies: *I*
T-21 II.3:8 your savior, that he may give s. unto you.
T-21 II.6:3 it the whole exchange of separation for s..
T-21 V.5:1 God's plan for your s. could not have
T-21 V.6:5 if the plan of God for your s. is complete.
T-21 VI.7:8 his whole s. seen as complete with yours.
T-21 VI.8:1 you and your brother are joined is your s.;
T-22 h S. AND THE HOLY RELATIONSHIP
T-22 II.11:2 S. cannot be. It *is* impossible to look upon
T-22 III.3:1 Reason is not s. in itself, but it makes way
T-22 III.3:1 state of mind in which s. can be given you
T-22 III.8:5 his errors is his holiness and your s.. You
T-22 III.8:8 sinful the one whose holiness is your s.?
T-22 IV.5:2 For in his sight your loveliness is his s.,
T-23 in.6:7 For here is your s. and your freedom. And
T-23 II.7:4 Nor can s. lie within the Son, whose every
T-23 II.7:6 God. For now s. must remain impossible,
T-23 II.12:10 of your enmity to your brother, must be s.
T-23 II.13:7 These are the laws you made for your s..
T-23 II.15:6 its substitute, the savior from s.. How
T-23 II.17:4 makes his savior powerless and finds s.?
T-23 III.h S. without Compromise
T-23 III.3:1 S. is no compromise of any kind. To
T-23 III.3:3 S. gives up nothing. It is complete for
T-23 III.3:6 compromise is the belief s. is impossible.
T-23 III.4:3 They do not see that, if it is, s. is attack.
T-23 III.4:4 it is certain the belief that s. is impossible
T-24 II.2:5 You have a function in s.. Its pursuit will
T-24 II.2:8 Here is a goal that would defeat s., and
T-24 II.7:1 and the function of s. given him for you.
T-24 II.13:4 from God, away from truth and from s..
T-24 II.14:1 His plan for your s. in the place of yours.
T-24 III.5:7 S. challenges not even death. And God
T-24 III.6:5 The way is barred to love and to s.. Yet if
T-24 IV.1:7 s. can only mean destruction of the world
T-24 IV.4:1 not the means by which s. is attained, nor
T-24 IV.5:1 what He loves, and you remain beyond s..
T-24 V.8:1 specialness, and seek s. in a war with love,
T-24 VI.h S. from Fear
T-24 VI.6:4 perfect frame for your s. and the world's,
T-24 VI.7:4 And where is your s., if he is but a body?
T-25 II.11:5 and your brother is given the power of s.,
T-25 V.4:5 Forgiven by you, your savior offers you s..
T-25 VI.4:2 a special function in s. he alone can fill; a
T-25 VI.5:4 to translate specialness from sin into s..
T-25 VI.6:1 S. is no more than a reminder this world
T-25 VI.6:6 did God appoint to be the means for his s.
T-25 VI.7:4 that you made can serve s. easily and well.
T-25 VI.7:9 and let s. be perfectly fulfilled in you. Do
T-25 VII.h The Rock of S.
T-25 VII.8:1 be madness to entrust s. to the insane.
T-25 VII.8:2 of everyone who chose insanity as his s..
T-25 VII.12:1 S. is rebirth of the idea no one can lose
T-25 VII.12:7 true. This is the rock on which s. rests, the
T-25 VII.13:4 S. is His Will *because* you share it. Not for
T-25 VIII.1:1 can use all that you give to Him for your s.
T-25 VIII.2:1 Here is the only principle s. needs. Nor is
T-25 VIII.2:4 remember s. is not needed by the saved.
T-25 VIII.3:1 is a kind of justice in s. of which the world
T-25 IX.2:8 to perceive s. as a gift from Him. Yet
T-25 IX.6:8 Who is there who can be separate from s.,
T-25 IX.7:1 S. cannot seek to help God's Son be more
T-25 IX.10:2 an illustration of the law on which s. rests
T-26 III.3:6 S. is a borderland where place and time
T-26 III.5:1 S. stops just short of Heaven, for only
T-26 III.5:1 of Heaven, for only perception needs s..
T-26 VII.10:1 S., perfect and complete, asks but a little
T-26 VII.14:4 with less than full s. and escape from guilt
T-26 VII.17:6 so. And in your hands does all s. lie, to be
T-26 VIII.h The Immediacy of S.
T-26 VIII.2:7 You see eventual s., not immediate results
T-26 VIII.3:1 S. *is* immediate. Unless you so perceive it,
T-26 VIII.3:4 of fear. S. *would* wipe out the space you see
T-26 IX.1:2 must be when in him sleeps your own s.,
T-26 X.6:2 the happy sparkle that s. brings can you
T-27 II.4:7 offering s. to your brother and yourself.
T-27 II.8:3 of the "fact" that your s. sacrifices his.
T-27 VI.7:3 have made it deaf to its s. and deliverance
T-27 VII.1:2 the world's demented version of s. clearly
T-27 VIII.10:1 secret of s. is but this: that you are doing
T-27 VIII.12:4 S. is a secret you have kept but from
T-28 II.9:1 the separation's final step, with which s.,
T-28 II.12:7 s. will proceed to change the course of
T-28 III.1:1 waits in perfect certainty beyond s. is not

T-28.....VII.2:7 is no middle ground in any aspect of s..
T-29.........I.2:6 and think that it is their s. and their hope.
T-29....... II.9:6 Yet its nothingness is your s., from which
T-29...... III.1:6 For who is savior but the one who gives s.
T-29...... III.5:7 on you. And in his glad s. you are saved.
T-29...... VI.1:5 This is the "sacrifice" s. asks, and gladly
T-29...VII.9:10 S. thus appears to threaten life and offer
T-29...VII.10:2 S. seeks to prove there is no death, and
T-29...... IX.2:9 s. from the judgment laid in terror and in
T-29...... IX.4:1 no s. in the dream as you are dreaming it.
T-30....... II.5:1 be saved, for by your own s. is it healed.
T-30...... IV.7:1 S. is a paradox indeed! What could it be
T-30...... IV.8:4 Be glad indeed s. asks so little, not so
T-30.... IV.8:13 he is. What could God's plan for his s. be,
T-30...... VI.2:4 S. does not lie in being asked to make
T-30...... VI.7:7 S. rests on faith there cannot be some
T-30.... VI.10:7 you to heal, for your s. and deliverance?
T-30... VIII.2:2 The miracle attests s. from appearances
T-31........... I.h The Simplicity of S.
T-31.........I.1:1 How simple is s.! All it says is what was
T-31.........I.2:2 in the simple things s. asks you learn. It
T-31.........I.4:6 learn the simple things s. teaches you!
T-31..... II.5:10 with him and in your answer is s. found.
T-31..... V.14:3 S. can be seen as nothing more than the
T-31..... V.17:8 Yet in this learning is s. born. And What
T-31...... VI.2:1 S. is undoing. If you choose to see the
T-31...... VI.2:6 S. is undoing of all this. For constancy
T-31...... VI.2:7 sight of those whose eyes s. has released
T-31...... VI.3:1 S. does not ask that you behold the spirit
T-31...... VI.3:4 It is your world s. will undo, and let you
T-31..... VII.1:2 S. does not seek to use a means as yet too
T-31..... VII.6:6 yourself as needed for s. of the world,
T-31..... VII.8:2 life entrusted all s. from the misery of hell
T-31..... VII.9:1 the face of Christ, the fear of God and of s.
T-31...VII.11:5 upon, and see his own s. everywhere. He
T-31... VIII.6:4 opening the way to his s. and release.
T-31... VIII.8:1 My brothers in s., do not fail to hear my
W-pI.....14.3:2 this exchange, which can truly be called s.
W-pI.....16.3:1 s. requires that you also recognize that
W-pI.....19.2:4 that it must be true if s. is possible at all.
W-pI.....19.2:5 And s. must be possible because it is the
W-pI.....20.1:5 The s. of the world depends on it. Yet you
W-pI.....20.2:3 You want s.. You want to be happy. You
W-pI.....20.3:4 the s. of the world be a trivial purpose?
W-pI.....23.4:3 This is what s. means, for where is the
W-pI.....37.3:1 Your holiness is the s. of the world. It lets
W-pI.........39.h My holiness is my s..
W-pI.....39.3:1 that your holiness is the s. of the world.
W-pI.....39.3:2 What about your own s.? You cannot give
W-pI.....39.3:5 saved. How else can he teach s.? Today's
W-pI.....39.3:6 recognizing that your s. is crucial to the
W-pI.....39.3:6 salvation is crucial to the s. of the world.
W-pI.....39.4:3 Your holiness is the s. of the world, and
W-pI.....39.7:2 is imperative for your s. that you see them
W-pI.....39.8:1 that stands between you and your s..
W-pI.....39.8:4 *are keeping me in hell. My holiness is my s..*
W-pI...39.10:3 is the fact that your holiness is your s..
W-pI...39.11:3 of the idea is: *My holiness is my s. from this.*
W-pI.....43.2:3 Yet in s., which is the undoing of what
W-pI.....44.8:2 S. is your happiest accomplishment. It is
W-pI.....46.2:4 reason, forgiveness can truly be called s..
W-pI.....55.3:2 Herein lies s., and nowhere else. Without
W-pI.....58.4:1 (39) My holiness is my s.. Since my
W-pI.....58.4:2 my holiness is recognizing my s.. It is also
W-pI.....58.4:3 It is also recognizing the s. of the world.
W-pI.....61.2:3 your role in s. and in taking no other. It is
W-pI.....61.3:3 toward taking your rightful place in s.. It
W-pI.....61.7:2 is. As a bringer of s., this is obviously
W-pI.....61.7:6 built His plan for the s. of His Son on you.
W-pI.....62.1:5 Therefore, in your forgiveness lies your s..
W-pI.....63.2:6 are being asked to accept s. that it may be
W-pI.....63.3:5 *God has appointed for the s. of the world.*
W-pI.....63.4:4 that God's Son looks to you for his s..
W-pI.....64.2:4 becomes the spiritual recognition of s..
W-pI.....64.3:3 The world's s. awaits your forgiveness,
W-pI.....65.1:1 today reaffirms your commitment to s.. It
W-pI.....65.1:4 S. cannot be the only purpose you hold
W-pI.....65.1:5 full acceptance of s. as your only function
W-pI.....65.1:5 the recognition of s. as your function, and
W-pI.....65.7:1 which you really want s. in spite of your
W-pI.....66.9:2 tried to find s. under the ego's guidance.
W-pI.....67.1:4 why the Son of God looks to you for his s.
W-pI.....69.1:4 Share your s. now with him who stood
W-pI.....69.2:3 to get in touch with the s. of the world.
W-pI.....69.3:2 else. S. is our only need. There is no other
W-pI.....69.3:4 Learning s. is our only goal. Let us end
W-pI.....69.9:6 *me, for my s. and the salvation of the world.*
W-pI.....69.9:6 *me, for my salvation and the s. of the world.*
W-pI.........70.h My s. comes from me.
W-pI.....70.1:2 S. seems to come from anywhere except
W-pI.....70.1:4 You see neither guilt nor s. as in your own
W-pI.....70.1:5 that guilt and s. must be in the same place
W-pI.....70.2:5 surely begin to see that accepting it is s..
W-pI.....70.3:1 the realization that s. is there as well. God
W-pI.....70.7:1 that s. comes from nothing outside of you
W-pI.....70.7:3 *My s. comes from me. It cannot come from*
W-pI.....70.7:5 where you have looked for s. in the past;–
W-pI.....70.7:7 *My s. cannot come from any of these things.*
W-pI.....70.7:8 *My s. comes from me and only from me.*
W-pI.....70.8:1 the light in you, which is where your s. is.
W-pI.....70.9:1 Since all illusions of s. have failed you,
W-pI.....70.9:1 so easily walk on into the light of real s..
W-pI...70.10:1 yourself that your s. comes from you, and
W-pI...70.10:3 You are in charge of your s.. You are in
W-pI...70.10:4 You are in charge of the s. of the world.
W-pI...70.10:6 *My s. comes from me. Nothing outside of*
W-pI...70.10:8 *Within me is the world's s. and my own.*
W-pI.........71.h Only God's plan for s. will work.
W-pI.....71.1:1 set up a plan for s. in opposition to God's.
W-pI.....71.2:1 for s. centers around holding grievances.
W-pI.....71.2:3 the source of s. is constantly perceived as
W-pI.....71.2:5 The change of mind necessary for s. is
W-pI.....71.3:2 any perceived source of s. is acceptable
W-pI.....71.4:1 Such is the ego's plan for your s.. Surely
W-pI.....71.4:3 you will not find s. than to channelize all
W-pI.....71.5:1 God's plan for s. works simply because,
W-pI.....71.5:1 His direction, you seek for s. where it is.
W-pI.....71.5:3 attempt to follow two plans for s. that are
W-pI.....71.6:4 Only God's plan for s. will work. There
W-pI.....71.7:4 S. must be yours because of His plan,
W-pI.....71.8:2 God's plan for your s. will work, and
W-pI.....71.9:6 to be done by you in His plan for your s..
W-pI...71.10:1 tell yourself often that God's plan for s.,
W-pI...71.10:3 *is the opposite of God's plan for s.. And only*
W-pI...71.10:6 than to remember the Source of your s.,
W-pI.........72.h is an attack on God's plan for s..
W-pI.....72.1:1 ego's plan for s. is the opposite of God's,
W-pI.....72.3:1 is an attack on God's plan for s.. But let us
W-pI.....72.5:1 is a body, what must His plan for s. be?
W-pI.....72.5:9 it. And it asserts that his s. must be death,
W-pI.....72.6:9 savior. It is the death of God and your s..
W-pI.....72.7:4 you are attacking God's plan for s., and
W-pI.....72.8:1 today to stop these senseless attacks on s..
W-pI.....72.9:5 is to end the attack on God's plan for s.,
W-pI...72.10:1 for s. has already been accomplished in us
W-pI...72.10:6 is: *What is s., Father? I do not know. Tell me,*
W-pI.72.10:10 for s. without waiting to hear what it is.
W-pI...72.11:2 "What is s., Father?" Ask and you will be
W-pI...72.11:5 the ego what s. is and where to find it. We
W-pI...72.12:2 *What is s., Father? I do not know. Tell me,*
W-pI...72.13:3 *grievances is an attack on God's plan for s..*
W-pI...72.13:5 *What is s., Father?* Then wait a minute or
W-pI.....73.5:5 cannot stand between you and your s..
W-pI.....73.6:7 And so s. is your will as well. You want to
W-pI.....73.7:1 remember that you want s. for yourself.
W-pI.....73.7:4 S. is for you. Above all else, you want the
W-pI.....73.9:1 with the recognition that God's plan for s.
W-pI.....76.1:1 things have seemed to you to be s.. Each
W-pI.....76.1:4 so, you must first realize s. lies not there.
W-pI.....76.1:6 do you seek to prove s. is where it is not.
W-pI.....76.2:2 you would forever seek s. where it is not,
W-pI.....76.2:3 tells you once again how simple is s..
W-pI.....77.1:4 Again, how simple is s.! It is merely a
W-pI.....77.5:2 You have asked for the s. of the world,
W-pI...78.10:1 role assigned to us as part of God's s. plan
W-pI.....80.1:4 S. thus depends on recognizing this one
W-pI.....80.1:6 S. is accomplished. Freedom from
W-pI.....80.1:8 your rightful place in God's plan for s..
W-pI.....80.2:5 accepted s. for yourself by bringing the
W-pI.....80.5:6 It is in this that the simplicity of s. lies. It
WpI..rII.in.5:3 You are dedicated to s.. Be determined
W-pI.....85.3:1 (70) My s. comes from me. Today I will
W-pI.....85.3:2 Today I will recognize where my s. is. It is
W-pI.....85.4:2 *not tempt me to look away from me for my s.*
W-pI.....85.4:3 *with my awareness of the Source of my s..*
W-pI.....85.4:4 *This has no power to remove s. from me.*
W-pI.....86.1:1 (71) Only God's plan for s. will work. It is
W-pI.....86.1:2 for me to search wildly about for s.. I have
W-pI.....86.1:7 Only God's plan for s. will work. And I
W-pI.....86.2:2 *for s. will save me from my perception of this*
W-pI.....86.2:3 *This is no exception in God's plan for my s..*
W-pI.....86.2:4 *this only in the light of God's plan for s..*
W-pI.....86.3:1 is an attack on God's plan for s.. Holding
W-pI.....86.3:2 prove that God's plan for s. will not work.
W-pI.....86.3:4 my only hope of s. from my awareness.
W-pI.....86.3:6 I would accept God's plan for s., and be
W-pI.....86.4:2 *misperception and s. as I look on this. If I see*
W-pI.....86.4:3 *in this, I will not see the grounds for my s..*
W-pI.....86.4:4 *for my salvation. This calls for s., not attack.*
W-pI.....88.1:2 In choosing s. rather than attack, I merely
W-pI.....88.1:3 S. is a decision made already. Attack and
W-pI.....89.3:4 truth, according to God's plan for my s..
W-pI.....89.4:2 *not hold this grievance apart from my s.. Let*
W-pI.....90.1:4 simplicity of s. by reinforcing the lesson
W-pI.....93.2:3 That you have sought s. in strange ways;
W-pI.....93.7:1 S. requires the acceptance of but one
W-pI...93.11:5 You can do much for the world's s. today.
W-pI...93.11:6 the part in s. that God has assigned to you
W-pI.....94.1:1 the one idea which brings complete s.; the
W-pI.....94.1:4 Here is s. accomplished. Here is sanity
W-pI.....95.6:2 the most beneficial form of practice in s..
W-pI.........96.h S. comes from my one Self.
W-pI.....96.6:6 S. cannot make illusions real, nor solve a
W-pI.....96.7:2 The Holy Spirit holds s. in your mind,
W-pI.....96.7:3 peace. S. is a thought you share with God,
W-pI.....96.7:4 Thus is s. kept among the Thoughts your
W-pI.....96.8:3 S. comes from this one Self through Him
W-pI.....96.9:2 *S. comes from my one Self. Its Thoughts are*
W-pI.....96.9:7 you have. S. is among them; find it there.
W-pI...96.12:1 frantic mind s. comes from your one Self,
W-pI.....97.3:4 S. is a miracle, the first and last; the first
W-pI.........98.h I will accept my part in God's plan for s..
W-pI.....98.1:5 today, and to s. as God planned it be. We
W-pI.....98.7:6 say: *I will accept my part in God's plan for s..*
W-pI.........99.h S. is my only function here.
W-pI.....99.1:1 S. and forgiveness are the same. They
W-pI.....99.2:2 thing you need forgiveness for, s. from.
W-pI.....99.2:3 S. now becomes the borderland between
W-pI.....99.6:4 own. S. is your function, with the One to
W-pI.....99.6:7 *S. is my only function here. God still is Love,*
W-pI.....99.9:6 *S. is my only function here. Salvation and*
W-pI.....99.9:7 *S. and forgiveness are the same.* Then turn
W-pI...99.10:6 Forgiveness and s. are the same. Forgive
W-pI...99.11:3 *S. is my only function here. God still is Love,*
W-pI...99.12:4 *S. is my only function here.* Thus do you lay
W-pI.......100.h My part is essential to God's plan for s..
W-pI...100.1:2 S. must reverse the mad belief in separate
W-pI.100.10:7 to God's plan for the s. of the world.
W-pI...101.1:2 key idea in understanding what s. means.
W-pI...101.2:2 S. thus cannot be purchased but through
W-pI...101.3:1 If sin is real, s. must be pain. Pain is the
W-pI...101.3:3 real. S. must be feared, for it will kill, but
W-pI...101.3:3 more than bones before s. is appeased. Its
W-pI...101.4:2 Who would not flee s., and attempt in
W-pI...101.4:5 is real, s. has become your bitter enemy,
W-pI...102.3:4 is no fear. Here is s.. Here is rest at last.
W-pI...104.3:2 hourly five minutes given truth for your s.
W-pI...106.1:1 mind, that has not told you what s. is;
W-pI...106.6:1 Be ready for s.. It is here, and will today
W-pI...106.7:1 Thus does s. start and thus it ends; when
W-pI...108.5:2 wholly is enough to bring s. to all minds.
WpI. rIII.in4:2 to cooperate in practicing s. only if it
WpI. rIII.in7:4 the Holy Spirit's chosen means for your s.
W-pI...113.2:1 (96) S. comes from my one Self. *From my*
W-pI...113.2:2 *I see God's perfect plan for my s. perfectly*
W-pI...113.3:4 the half hour: S. comes from my one Self.
W-pI...114.2:1 I will accept my part in God's plan for s..

W-pI.....28.6:2 You will be making this s. request of each
W-pI.....31.2:4 and apply the s. idea to your inner world.
W-pI.....32.2:1 outer worlds, which are actually the s..
W-pI.....45.2:3 They are the s. thoughts, because they are
W-pI.....45.2:3 because they are thought by the s. Mind.
W-pI.....45.4:1 for today will take the s. general form that
W-pI.....65.4:1 at approximately the s. time each day. Try
W-pI.....66.1:3 connection between them; they are the s..
W-pI...66.10:5 in the perception of the s. as the same,
W-pI...66.10:5 in the perception of the same as the s.,
W-pI.....70.1:5 guilt and salvation must be in the s. place.
W-pI.....70.5:1 Will and ours are really the s. in this. God
W-pI.....73.1:2 This is not the s. as the ego's idle wishes,
W-pI.....79.2:2 they are all the s., and must be recognized
W-pI.....80.3:3 do not forget that all problems are the s..
W-pI.....83.3:4 because both come from the s. Source.
W-pI.....99.1:1 Salvation and forgiveness are the s.. They
W-pI.....99.9:7 *Salvation and forgiveness are the s..* Then
W-pI...99.10:6 Forgiveness and salvation are the s..
W-pI...104.3:1 wills, and recognize the s. as being one.
W-pI...107.8:3 Father knows that You are both the s.. It
W-pI...108.2:3 all. And thus what is the s. is seen as one,
W-pI...108.2:3 what is not the s. remains unnoticed, for
W-pI...108.4:3 perceived from the s. frame of reference
W-pI...108.5:2 This is the s. as saying one correction will
W-pI...108.6:1 receiving are the s. has special usefulness,
W-pI...109.2:4 that s. truth in everyone and everything
WpI. rIII.in7:2 in that s. trust and confidence and faith.
W-pI...121.9:1 believe that giving and receiving are the s.
W-pI...125.7:4 you are and that He is; the s. as you, and
W-pI...125.7:4 is; the same as you, and you the s. as He.
W-pI...126.8:1 the truth that giver and receiver are the s..
W-pI...127.3:8 which holds Them both forever as the s..
W-pI...136.1:5 dispels this meaningless illusion by the s.
W-pI...138.2:3 to be the s. as the relinquishment of hell.
W-pI.140.11:3 They are the s.. We have no need to make
W-pI.152.12:1 concluding it with this s. invitation to
W-pI.155.14:2 your Name and His Own, which are the s.
W-pI...157.6:3 may come the sooner to the s. experience
W-pI...157.7:3 in the s. form in which you now appear,
W-pI.161.11:2 that s. form to which you are accustomed.
WpI.rV.in11:3 to waken once again with these s. words
W-pI...183.9:2 give the world the s. release you found.
W-pI...185.3:3 In dreams, no two can share the s. intent.
W-pI...185.3:4 the outcome wanted not the s. for both.
W-pI...185.5:6 the s. despair and misery as do the rest.
W-pI...193.3:3 has a central thought, the s. in all of them.
W-pI...193.3:5 They are the s. in fundamental content. It
W-pI...200.7:1 Will and to his own, which is the s. as His.
W-pII .225.1:1 *for me, for giving and receiving are the s.,*
W-pII .265.2:2 *Let me remember that they are the s., and I*
W-pII .291.1:2 and offers this s. vision to the world. And
W-pII .307.2:1 God's, in recognition that they are the s..
M-in ..........1:5 so that teacher and learner are the s.. It
M-1 ...........4:2 of other forms, all with the s. outcome.
M-2 ...........2:6 in that s. instant was God's Answer given.
M-2 ...........5:5 learns that giving and receiving are the s..
M-2 ...........5:7 the s. course share one interest and one
M-2 ...........5:9 another person the s. interests as his own.
M-3 ...........1:2 although the ultimate goal is always the s.
M-3 ...........3:7 levels, but the result is always the s..
M-5 ...... III.3:2 forget that all of them have the s. purpose
M-10 .........1:6 the s. person classifies the same action as
M-10 .........1:6 the same person classifies the s. action as
M-12 .........5:2 for sin or for attack, which is the s. as sin,
M-16 .........5:1 s. procedures should be followed at night.
M-17 .........4:7 All of these reactions are the s.. They
M-18 .........1:7 only the s. age-old impossible dream in
M-22 .........7:7 recognizes that they are the s. mistake.
M-24 .........2:8 idea that life and the body are not the s..
M-24 .........6:1 of this course always remains the s.; –it is
M-25 .........4:7 Yet the ego sees in these s. strengths an
P-in............1:8 Either way, the task is the s.; the patient
P-1 .............5:2 recognizing that they are not the s., and
P-2............I.1:5 again and advance in the s. relationship,
P-2.......... II.5:4 In the s. way, a union of purpose between
P-2.......... II.8:3 s. requirement salvation asks of everyone.
P-2.......... II.9:7 except a help in just this s. direction? It is
P-2.......... II.9:8 the goal that makes these processes the s.,
P-2........ IV.6:4 the s. time making a new self-concept into
P-2........ VI.5:2 of the other, for they are the s. illusion. So
P-2....... VII.8:3 The s. are one, and nothing now can be
P-3..........II.6:3 will not be the s. dream for both of them,
P-3......... III.8:7 for that s. Christ is in him as well. Deny
S-1...........I.4:2 the s. as to look on sin and then forgive it.
S-1...........I.4:3 Also in the s. way, in prayer you overlook
S-1..........II.4:3 and to accept to the s. narrow margins.

**sameness** 8

T-21 .... VII.6:4 the s. of things that are the same. This
T-22 ......in.4:3 Here is the faith in differences shifted to s.
T-22 ......in.4:8 And now the s. that you saw extends and
T-22 ......in.4:8 the s. that lies beneath them all becomes
T-22 ........I.4:9 leads to sight of differences and loss of s..
T-27 ..... VI.6:7 It is their s. that the miracle attests. It is
T-27 ..... VI.6:8 It is their s. that it proves. The laws that
W-pI...193.4:3 It is this s. which makes learning sure,

**sanctified** 6

T-22 ..... VI.3:6 You will be s. by your brother, using your
W-pI...125.2:4 only love. He is not judged, but only s..
W-pI...156.4:1 so holy that the world is s. because of you.
W-pI...157.6:1 body will be s. today, its only purpose
W-pII ... 14.1:2 *is His creation s. and guaranteed eternal life.*
M-12 ......... 1:3 This one, s. and redeemed, becomes the

**sanctity** 4

T-15 ......I.15:9 instant of the eternal s. of God's creation,
W-pI.151.15:3 the Son of God the holy lesson of his s..
W-pI.159.10:8 to our unlost and everlasting s. in God.
P-2....... VII.6:7 who call upon his s. to make it theirs. And

**sanctuary** 5

T-22 .......II.7:3 judge, offering him s. or condemnation.
T-31 .... V.17:5 then is the truth left free to enter in its s.,
W-pI...109.8:2 of your peace, the holy s. where you rest.
W-pI.126.10:1 seek s. in the quiet place where thoughts
W-pII .298.2:4 *I am grateful for Your holy gifts of certain s.,*

**sand** 4

T19....IV.A.2:4 The little barrier of s. still stands between
T19....IV.A.2:9 Would you let a little bank of s., a wall of
T-20 ... VI.11:3 instant of despair, a tiny island of dry s.,
T-28 ..... IV.9:4 How holy is the smallest grain of s., when

**sands** 1

T-18 ..... IX.2:4 is. The barren s., the darkness and the

**sane** 40

T-3 ..... IV.7:10 S. perception induces sane choosing.
T-3 ..... IV.7:10 Sane perception induces s. choosing.
T-4 ..........I.8:4 The only s. solution is not to try to change
T-4 ..... III.10:1 in your s. mind is perfectly conscious, is
T-4 ........ V.1:6 it serves. S. judgment would inevitably
T-4 ....... VI.3:2 choice is the only s. one you can make. No
T-5 ........ V.3:8 of attacking God may be to the s. mind,
T-5 ........ V.3:8 mind, never forget that the ego is not s.. It
T-5 ........ V.5:2 Being s., the mind heals the body because
T-5 ........ V.5:3 s. mind cannot conceive of illness because
T-7 ....... VI.5:1 all s. perception and all knowledge. It
T-11 .. V.12:10 But the s. realize that only attack could
T-12 ......... V.h The S. Curriculum
T-13 ... III.12:6 your insane request with a s. answer that
T-13 ...... V.7:5 s. Answer tells you what you have offered
T-13 ..... VI.1:6 it is really s. to perceive what was as now.
T-19 ..... III.6:4 and evil; partly s. and partially insane.
T19. IV.D.11:2 Only the s. can look on stark insanity and
T-21 ...... IV.6:2 This is the reasoning of the s.. You have
T-21 ...VIII.4:2 it possible to help you be already partly s..
T-21 ...VIII.4:3 asks if you are willing to be wholly s..
T-23 .....II.12:5 factor in your madness that makes it "s.."
T-25 .... VII.4:7 Who thinks the world is s. in any way, is
T-25 .... VII.5:1 on which a s. perception can be based,
T-25 .... VII.6:7 to make that viewpoint meaningful and s.
T-25 .... VII.8:2 mad has God appointed One as s. as He
T-25 .... VII.9:4 him and whatever hope he has of being s..
T-25 .. VII.13:1 make you s. and give you what you want;
T-25 .. VII.13:7 And this is s. because it is the truth.
T-30 ..... VI.2:8 Forgiveness is the only s. response. It
W-pI .. 134.6:1 makes forgiveness natural and wholly s.,
W-pI 138.11:1 we have made the one decision that is s..
W-pI .. 160.1:5 Who could be s. in such a circumstance?
W-pI .. 163.6:5 position, which we must accept if we be s.
W-pI .. 170.6:3 ask if the demands are sensible or even s..
W-pI .. 195.2:3 Nor could the even partly s. refuse to take
M-4 ...... IV.2:5 choice but this has meaning to the s.?
M-13 ........ 4:10 Who in his s. mind chooses nothing as a
P-2.........in.2:5 to the s. mind it is so clearly impossible,
P-2....... VII.5:8 No unhealed healer can be wholly s..

**sanely** 1

W-pI .. 195.4:1 could you s. be enraged if he seems freer.

**saneness** 2

T-25 .. VII.12:4 of truth can faith in God's eternal s. rest
W-pI 140.10:2 ills as one, restoring s. to the Son of God.

**saner** 3

T-18 .......V.7:1 Whoever is s. at the time the threat is
T-21 ..... IV.6:5 Yet in your s. moments, its ranting strikes
T-25 .... VII.8:2 He to raise a s. world to meet the sight of

**sang** 1

T-25 ..... IV.5:3 bird that ever s. will sing again in you.

**sanity** 70

T-1 ........I.33:4 of your illusions, they restore your s..
T-4 ..... IV.11:6 in my name, and your s. will be restored.
T-4 .........V.1:4 control rather than s. to predominance.
T-5 ...... VII.2:8 S. is wholeness, and the sanity of your
T-5 ...... VII.2:8 and the s. of your brothers is yours.
T-6 ........in.1:6 the s. of the premises on which it rests.
T-6 ... IV.11:10 where you can find the s. He gave you.
T-6 ..... V.B.6:1 can be no conflict between s. and insanity
T-7 ..... VI.10:4 your s. and your limitless power. This
T-7 ..... VI.12:1 you have not judged s. as wholly desirable
T-9 ....... III.5:1 heal him only by perceiving the s. in him.
T-9 ...... VII.6:3 where s. exists and *see the contrast.* Only
T-10 .....V.10:8 To know that is s.. To deny it is insanity.
T-12 .......V.2:1 so important to the restoration of your s..
T-13 ..... III.7:4 Lay before His eternal s. all your hurt,
T-13 ... III.10:1 prefer separation to s. cannot obtain it in
T-13 .....V.11:6 In the s. of His vision they looked upon
T-13 .... VII.7:5 In perfect s. he looks on love, for it is all
T-13 .. VII.10:1 Father for the perfect s. of His most holy
T-13 ..... XI.7:4 Holy Spirit will restore your s. because
T-13 ... XI.11:2 for your reconciliation to s. and to peace.
T-14 .......X.5:4 little s. that still remains is held together
T-15 ......I.14:2 long as it takes to re-establish perfect s.,
T-17 ..... IV.5:3 this means if you would be restored to s..
T-17 .......V.6:8 your relationship has s. as its purpose.
T-17 .......V.7:4 fantasy from your brother, to save your s..
T-17 ..... VI.5:2 If the situation is used for truth and s., its
T-17 ..... VI.5:4 *is.* If peace is the condition of truth and s.,
T-18 ........I.7:4 Inward is s.; insanity is outside you. You
T19 .. IV.D.1:5 and the Son of God entirely restored to s..
T-23 .....II.13:4 you walk in s. with feet on solid ground,
T-23 .....II.13:4 laws on which your "s." appears to rest.
T-23 .....II.14:6 turned around, with madness s., illusions
T-23 .....II.15:5 Their goal of madness must be seen as s..
T-24 .....II.13:3 from all intrusions of s. upon illusions;
T-25 ..... III.2:5 could be sure His s. went there with him,
T-25 .... VII.4:1 is to deny your Father's s. and yours. For
T-25 .... VII.4:4 and s. must lie apart from both the Father
T-25 .... VII.5:2 would lead the Son of God to s. and joy.

| | |
|---|---|
| T-25.....VII.6:4 | sinners, who believe theirs is the way to s. |
| T-25.....VII.7:5 | form of s. which makes it most acceptable |
| T-25.....VII.9:4 | he comes to understand it cost him his s., |
| T-25...VII.10:2 | And where does s. abide except in Him? |
| T-25...VII.12:3 | Here is s. restored. And on this single |
| T-26.....VII.2:3 | has been healed, and been replaced by s.. |
| W-pI.....94.1:5 | accomplished. Here is s. restored. |
| W-pI.....97.2:1 | you, whose mind has been restored to s.. |
| W-pI...128.6:5 | in its Creator, there to be restored to s., to |
| W-pI.138.12:3 | brief quiet time devoted to maintaining s. |
| W-pI.151.16:4 | to Him Who has restored our s. to us. |
| W-pI...153.4:2 | hope of s. seems but to be an idle dream, |
| W-pI...155.2:6 | truth stand forth as what it is, is merely s.. |
| W-pI...184.6:7 | to accept its presence is the proof of s.. |
| W-pI...187.7:5 | an idea so mad that s. dismisses it at once |
| WpI rVI.in.3:8 | it deaf to reason, s. and simple truth. |
| W-pII..241.2:3 | *How glad are we to have our s. restored to us,* |
| W-pII......5.4:1 | means by which God's Son returns to s.. |
| W-pII......7.4:1 | and be restored to s. and peace of mind. |
| W-pII..285.2:2 | *it, and through forgiveness be restored to s..* |
| W-pII......9.1:1 | of mistakes, and the return of s.. It is a |
| W-pII....11.4:6 | be done on earth, only to be restored to s. |
| Wfl ........in.5:4 | dream. We are restored to s., in which we |
| P-2...........I.4:7 | give for now. Yet both will find s. at last. |
| P-2......... II.5:5 | of psychotherapy is the return to s.. |
| P-2......... II.5:7 | pathway out, for no one will find s. alone. |
| P-2......IV.10:4 | his lesson is to be that s. is safe. It cannot |
| P-2......IV.10:5 | that the insane believe that s. is threat. |
| P-2........VI.3:5 | grows fearful and begins to doubt its s.. |
| S-2...........I.7:8 | plan is made complete, and s. has come. |
| S-2...........I.8:1 | Forgiveness is the call to s., for who but |

## satisfaction 12

| | |
|---|---|
| T-9......IV.10:1 | unless he despairs of finding s. in reality? |
| T-9......IV.10:2 | that you will never find s. in fantasy, so |
| T-13....... X.3:2 | Nor will you find s. and peace with him, |
| T-15......VI.3:3 | If you seek for s. in gratifying your needs |
| T-17....... V.8:3 | sought for s. and thought you found it. |
| T-18.........I.3:4 | a different form of acting out for s.. While |
| T-18....... II.4:4 | the illusion of s. is invaded by the illusion |
| T-18....... II.5:6 | and the illusion of s. would be gone. In |
| T-25....... II.1:2 | you think you find a hope of s. there. |
| T-25....... II.1:3 | and s. in the world as you perceive it. Yet |
| T-25....... II.2:1 | some hope of s. from the world you see? |
| T-31....... II.3:4 | appears to be the hope of s. and of peace. |

## satisfactions 2

| | |
|---|---|
| W-pI...133.2:4 | ideas for s. which the world contains. |
| W-pI...133.2:5 | contains. There are no s. in the world. |

## satisfied 25

| | |
|---|---|
| T-8...........I.4:3 | are you s. with the changes your learning |
| T-8..... VIII.2:6 | you have achieved it, *it has not s. you.* This |
| T-11....... II.7:8 | do not be s. with imaginary comforters, |
| T-12...VII.13:5 | live, but its hatred is not s. until you die. |
| T-12...VII.13:6 | and the only end with which it will be s.. |
| T-13......IV.1:6 | As long as it is reasonably s. with you, as |
| T-14....... X.2:3 | no longer be s. with anything but his own |
| T-15.........I.1:3 | God's Teacher cannot be s. with His |
| T-15......III.3:4 | and by limiting yourself you will not be s.. |
| T19IV.A.17:12 | To think you could be s. and happy with |
| T-25.........I.3:1 | think your mind will be content and s.. It |
| T-25...VII.12:5 | Reason is s., for all insane beliefs can be |
| T-25. VIII.4:10 | justice, being blind, is s. by being paid, it |
| T-25. VIII.11:4 | justice may return to love and there be s.. |
| T-25......IX.2:9 | not be s. until it is received by everyone. |
| T-30......III.4:7 | will could not be s. with empty forms, |
| W-pI.....77.8:1 | to be s. with less than the perfect answer. |
| W-pI...126.7:3 | Could He be s. with empty gestures, and |
| W-pI...168.2:2 | For hope would be forever s.; despair of |
| W-pII......3.5:2 | Let us not be s. until forgiveness has been |
| W-pII..251.1:6 | In that all needs are s., all cravings end, |
| W-pII..273.1:2 | content and even more than s. to learn |
| M-17..........5:9 | and vengeance that can never be s.. |
| M-28..........3:7 | hell. All longings are s., for what remains |
| S-1........IV.3:2 | answer come in which are all specifics s.; |

## satisfies 1

| | |
|---|---|
| T-27.....VII.8:6 | him as it will in any role that s. its dream. |

## satisfy 14

| | |
|---|---|
| T-4......... II.7:8 | and tries to s. itself through the body. But |
| T-13....... II.3:3 | of God's Son can ultimately s. it. It does |
| T-13.......III.8:6 | can s. him or save him from what he is. |
| T-15.......III.2:3 | substitute is much too poor a gift to s. you |
| T-15......VI.1:4 | one, for its ability to s. you completely, |
| T-15.....VII.1:2 | There is no other love that can s. you, |
| T-15.......IX.2:5 | of meaning, it will not s. you completely. |
| T-16......IV.2:6 | For the illusion of love will never s., but |
| T-16......IV.9:4 | is certain and where everything fails to s.. |
| T-18......VI.3:6 | never what the body does that seems to s. |
| T-30.......III.1:8 | And this must fail to s., because it is your |
| T-30.......IV.1:1 | You will attack what does not s., and |
| W-pII.....272.h | How can illusions s. God's Son? |
| W-pII..272.1:5 | *What but Your memory can s. Your Son? I* |

## satisfying 5

| | |
|---|---|
| T-1.....VII.3:11 | as the wholly s. nature of reality becomes |
| T-9......IV.12:2 | me and God, and is perfectly s. to all of Us |
| W-pI.....12.3:4 | think of "a good world," or "a s. world." |
| W-pI.....12.3:6 | a "s. world" implies an "unsatisfying" one |
| W-pI...129.1:3 | on exchanging it for what is far more s., |

## savage 19

| | |
|---|---|
| T-8.......VII.4:3 | body is beautiful or ugly, peaceful or s., |
| T-13.......III.2:4 | even upon your s. wish to kill God's Son, |
| T-13......IV.1:7 | When it becomes overtly s., it offers you |
| T-15....... X.8:2 | Yet the demand of sacrifice is so s. and so |
| T-15....... X.8:7 | partial sacrifice will appease this s. guest, |
| T-16.....VII.3:2 | It is completely s. and completely insane. |
| T19. IV.A.12:7 | And in their s. search for sin they pounce |
| T19. IV.A.13:1 | not these s. messengers into the world, to |
| T19. IV.A.13:4 | they seem to allay their s. pangs of hunger |
| T19....IV.C.8:1 | He created against the ego's s. wish to kill. |
| T-23...... II.10:4 | But in a s. world the kind cannot survive, |
| T-23.......III.5:4 | willing to accept the fact their s. purpose |
| W-pI.....22.2:1 | this s. fantasy that you want to escape. Is |
| W-pI.....93.2:3 | afraid of foolish fantasies and s. dreams; |
| W-pI...101.4:1 | Who would seek out such s. punishment |
| W-pI...190.4:3 | is no need to think of them as s. crimes, |
| W-pI...190.8:5 | s. pain that waits to end all joy in misery. |
| W-pI...191.6:3 | cruelly, and then perceive this s. need in it |
| S-3........IV.6:5 | in a s. world with feet that bleed, and with |

## savagely 2

| | |
|---|---|
| T-15.........I.5:2 | Even when it attacks so s. that it tries to |
| W-pI...166.7:2 | is the self you s. defend against all reason, |

## savagery 3

| | |
|---|---|
| T-15.....VII.5:2 | For the chain of s. belongs not around the |
| T-16.....VII.5:2 | hatred and the s. break briefly through, |
| T-23.......III.1:6 | and justify his s. with smiles as he attacks. |

## save 173

| | |
|---|---|
| T-2......... II.3:8 | s. time if you do not protract this step |
| T-4.........I.12:1 | can do nothing to s. yourself or others, |
| T-4........IV.1:4 | to keep, and what you are vigilant to s.. |
| T-4........IV.1:5 | mind is filled with schemes to s. the face |
| T-4......... V.2:7 | ego attempts to s. itself from being swept |
| T-5....... V.7:11 | the Atonement is to s. the past in purified |
| T-6.........I.8:7 | has chosen to s. them pain in all respects, |
| T-7........VI.2:5 | thinking can also s. you from this because |
| T-9........IV.4:7 | must accept the meaningless to s. yourself |
| T-9.......VII.1:6 | second gives you a chance to s. yourself. |
| T-10.......III.4:9 | this the image you would be vigilant to s.? |
| T-10.......III.5:3 | protect an idol you think will s. you from |
| T-10.......III.8:5 | are. You would s. them and serve them, |
| T-11.......in.4:4 | hidden, for its protection will not s. you. I |
| T-11......IV.2:5 | only to the power that God gave to s. you, |
| T-11. VIII.12:4 | He would s. you from all condemnation. |
| T-12........II.5:1 | Let us not s. nightmares, for they are not |
| T-12...... III.5:2 | that can be saved and the only way to s. it. |
| T-12...VII.14:6 | from what you want God does not s. you. |
| T-13.......in.3:3 | *Love does not kill to s..* If it did, attack |
| T-13...... III.4:1 | and you would s. yourself from His Love |
| T-13...... III.8:6 | can satisfy him or s. him from what he is. |
| T-13...... III.9:1 | S. him from his illusions that you may |
| T-13....... V.3:4 | their answer s. him who called upon them |
| T-13...... XI.9:1 | salvation because you will learn how to s.. |
| T-14....VIII.1:6 | Whom He would s. for glory *is* saved for it. |
| T-15....... V.2:3 | are attempting to use separation to s. you. |
| T-17.... IV.10:6 | being part of Them, and They must s. you |
| T-17....... V.7:4 | from your brother, to s. your sanity. *Hear* |
| T-18.........I.7:2 | The truth will s. you. It has not left you, to |
| T-18...... VI.4:8 | made and using it to s. him from illusions |
| T-18..... VII.6:4 | means this course is using to s. you time. |
| T-18..... VII.6:6 | for *you.* S. time for me by only this one |
| T19....IV.C.7:1 | it come to s. them from communication. |
| T19... IV.D.4:1 | the belief in death would seem to "s." you |
| T-20....VIII.6:8 | All that could s. you, you will never see. |
| T-21.........I.5:4 | the body is to s. the little that they have. |
| T-21.... III.12:7 | them still to s. itself from what it made. |
| T-21.... VI.11:5 | can be imprisoned s. by his own desire. |
| T-21..... VII.1:5 | it. Enormity has no appeal s. to the little. |
| T-22........II.8:5 | Whose function is to s., will save. *How* He |
| T-22........II.8:5 | Whose function is to save, will s.. *How* He |
| T-22...... III.2:8 | Thus does the ego damn, and reason s.. |
| T-22...... III.8:6 | tried to see your sins in him to s. yourself. |
| T-22...... IV.6:5 | to everyone who needs a miracle to s. him |
| T-22....... V.2:4 | to insanity, to s. you from the truth? And |
| T-22....... VI.9:5 | S. no dark secrets that He cannot use, but |
| T-23........II.9:4 | you can never take away s. from yourself. |
| T-23.......II.10:1 | loss the enemy must suffer to s. yourself. |
| T-23.......II.17:9 | condemning what it says it wants to s.. Be |
| T-24........II.8:7 | you, to s. his specialness and kill his Self. |
| T-24.......II.14:2 | be reached s. through the sight of all your |
| T-24...... III.2:7 | misery, before the idol that can s. you not |
| T-24...... III.8:5 | to join His Will to s. you both from hell. |
| T-24....... V.7:6 | you may s. all living things from death, |
| T-24...... VI.9:4 | is given you to s. from condemnation, |
| T-24.... VI.10:5 | to s. from pain and give you happiness. |
| T-24..... VII.1:6 | to s. his specialness from the least slight, |
| T-24..... VII.4:3 | And much you think you s., you hurt. |
| T-24..... VII.4:4 | hurt. What would you s. it *for?* For in that |
| T-24..... VII.4:6 | S. it for show, as bait to catch another fish |
| T-25....... V.4:4 | to each an equal strength to s. the other, |
| T-25....... V.4:4 | the other, and s. himself along with him. |
| T-25....... V.6:1 | to s. what He created from the pain of hell |
| T-25.... VI.5:11 | thus become a means to s. instead of lose. |
| T-25..... VI.7:7 | plan to s. the Son of God from all attack, |
| T-25....VIII.8:5 | and is too weak to s. from punishment. |
| T-25....VIII.8:7 | what but vengeance now can help and s., |
| T-25....VIII.8:7 | of justice and vitality, and powerless to s.? |
| T-26...VII.17:4 | has been given to s. the Son of God from |
| T-26...VII.17:5 | For you have power to s. the Son of God |
| T-26...VII.19:4 | what can s. each one of us can save us all. |
| T-26...VII.19:4 | what can save each one of us can s. us all. |
| T-26...VII.19:6 | that specialness denies will s. them all, for |
| T-29...... III.1:4 | And he must s. who would be saved. On |
| T-29...... III.5:4 | your light to him, to s. him from the dark. |
| T-29.....VII.9:3 | S. time, my brother; learn what time is for |
| T-29...... IX.3:1 | are idols, made to s. you from the dream. |
| T-29...... IX.3:2 | what they have been made to s. you *from.* |
| T-29...... IX.4:2 | to s. you from what you believe you have |
| T-29...... IX.5:6 | they seem to s. him from his thoughts. |
| T-29...... IX.9:2 | For beneath your hope that it will s. you |
| T-29.... IX.10:6 | judgment seemed to be the way to s. him |
| T-31........II.3:6 | a means to help you s. yourself from this. |
| T-31...VII.10:5 | holy ones whom God has given you to s. |
| T-31...VII.10:6 | to s. from every concept that he ever held. |
| W-pI.....26.1:5 | It is this law that will ultimately s. you, |
| W-pI.....38.2:6 | it is equal in its power to s. anyone. |
| W-pI.....39.7:3 | blessing on them that will s. you and give |
| W-pI.....55.2:6 | My loving thoughts will s. me from this |
| W-pI.....58.3:2 | because it is unlimited in its power to s.. |
| W-pI.....60.4:2 | ceases to call on my forgiveness to s. me. |
| W-pI.....61.3:4 | of the power that is given you to s. others. |
| W-pI.....64.8:4 | *This is the world it is my function to s..* |
| W-pI.....70.2:1 | that nothing outside yourself can s. you; |

W-pI.....71.6:5 alternative to God's plan that will s. you.
W-pI.....72.6:1 cannot enter, the ego comes to s. you.
W-pI.....75.1:4 You are saved and you can s.. You are at
W-pI.....76.3:1 and twisted laws you have set up to s. you
W-pI.....76.5:6 is from this your "laws" would s. the body
W-pI.....76.6:4 What it is meant to s. does not exist. Only
W-pI.....76.6:5 Only what it is meant to hide will s. you.
W-pI.....76.8:6 would not s. but damn in Heaven's name.
W-pI...78.10:2 when we allow each one we meet to s. us,
W-pI.....86.2:2 *will s. me from my perception of this. This is*
W-pI.....88.3:7 free of the effects of all laws s. God's. And
W-pI...96.11:4 joy your Self experiences It will s. for you,
W-pI.....97.7:2 *free to forgive, and free to s. the world.*
W-pI.....99.6:3 Thought whose function is to s. by giving
W-pI...100.3:4 to s. the world is dim and lusterless, and
W-pI...110.1:2 would be enough to s. you and the world,
W-pI...110.8:1 with power to s. whoever touches Him,
W-pI...115.2:3 *gave me His plan that I might s. the world.*
W-pI...123.5:6 An unheard message will not s. the world,
W-pI...123.7:3 power to s. the world eons more quickly
W-pI...124.7:2 that we can s. and heal accordingly. We
W-pI...125.2:2 No other means can s. it, for God's plan is
W-pI...125.2:2 this: The Son of God is free to s. himself,
W-pI...132.1:2 what can s. the world except your Self?
W-pI.134.12:1 He does not have to fight to s. himself.
W-pI.134.15:2 but to s. the world from all ideas of sin.
W-pI...135.1:1 and that his own defense could s. himself
W-pI.135.13:1 up to s. itself must make the body sick. It
W-pI...153.7:3 What can s. you now from your delusion
W-pI...153.8:2 For our true purpose is to s. the world,
W-pI...162.1:1 firmly in the mind, would s. the world.
W-pI...162.3:3 He will s. the world, because he gives the
W-pI...164.8:3 of your most holy mind to s. the world. Is
W-pI...170.2:4 Today we learn a lesson which can s. you
WpI...rV.in9:3 my hands through which I s. the world.
W-pI...186.1:6 on earth in Heaven's plan to s. the world,
W-pI...187.3:2 If you are to s. the world, you first accept
W-pI...191.8:3 glory to redeem the lost, to s. the helpless,
W-pI...196.2:2 is quick to cite the truth to s. its lies. Yet
W-pI.196.11:4 Him to s. you from illusions by His Love,
W-pI...198.3:2 All illusions s. this one must multiply a
W-pI...198.6:2 His words will s.. His words contain all
W-pI...200.1:3 s. yourself the agony of yet more bitter
W-pII .....3.5:4 We must s. the world. For we who made
W-pII .245.1:8 *For I would s. Your Son, as is Your Will, that I*
W-pII .264.2:3 Must we not join in what will s. the world
W-pII .267.1:4 and all I need to s. the world is given me.
W-pII .303.2:2 *He has come to s. me from the evil self I made*
W-pII .305.2:3 *has come to us to s. us from our judgment on*
W-pII .313.2:5 We s. the world when we have joined. For
W-pII .318.1:1 all parts of Heaven's plan to s. the world.
W-pII .333.2:3 *No light but this can s. the world. For this*
W-pII .342.1:1 *for Your plan to s. me from the hell I made. It*
W-pII .344.1:2 *thought to s. what I desired for myself alone.*
W-pII ....350.h And through His memory to s. the world.
M-1 .........2:11 Their function is to s. time. Each one
M-1 ...........4:3 They merely s. time. Yet it is time alone
M-12 ...........h GOD ARE NEEDED TO S. THE WORLD?
M-13 .......8:12 What other way is there to s. His Son?
M-16 .........3:4 starting the day right does indeed s. time.
M-16 .........6:4 you made a power that can s. you from all
M-29 .........8:2 *God turns to you for help to s. the world.*
C-2.............9:1 you ready yet to help Me s. the world?"
C-3.............7:7 It is the gift of God to s. His Son. But look
C-5.............2:4 Yet who can s. unless he sees illusions and
C-5.............2:6 men and s. them from their own illusions.
C-6.............3:3 because He was sent to s. humanity. He is
C-6.............5:5 with him when he began to s. the world.
P-1.............5:4 Psychotherapy can only s. him time. The
P-1.............5:6 is one of the means He uses to s. time,
P-2........IV.9:2 he will attack the one who tries to s. him
P-3........ II.9:1 can s. enormous time if it is properly used
S-2.......in.1:12 Accomplish this and you will s. the world.
S-2...........I.8:3 God calls on you to s. His Son from death
S-2......... II.2:1 to s. a "baser" one from what he truly is.
S-2........ III.5:3 which forgiveness comes to s. God's Son.
S-2........ III.6:7 to s. it from destruction and to make the
S-2........ III.6:8 made free to s. as true forgiveness is

## saved 123

T-5 ....... IV.8:3 I have s. all your kindnesses and every
T-8 ....... VI.2:7 His Will has s. you, not from yourself but
T-8 ....... VI.2:8 of yourself. He has s. you *for* yourself.
T-11 ..... IV.1:4 You are not s. *from* anything, but you are
T-11 ..... IV.1:4 *from* anything, but you are s. *for* glory.
T-11 ... VI.10:1 God's Son *is* s.. Bring only this awareness
T-11 .... VII.4:9 has s. for you out of what you have made,
T-11 ...VIII.2:4 the Holy Spirit has s. its meaning for you,
T-12 ..... III.2:6 is always twofold; first, *what* is to be s.?
T-12 ..... III.2:7 to be saved? And second, *how* can it be s.?
T-12 ..... III.3:1 you are believing that the ego is to be s.,
T-12 ..... III.3:1 ego is to be saved, and to be s. by attack.
T-12 ..... III.5:2 only thing that can be s. and the only way
T-13 ......I.11:7 then, are s. because God's Son is guiltless.
T-13 .......X.7:1 to demonstrate what He has s. you from.
T-13 .......X.7:2 What He has s. you from is gone. Give no
T-14 ... III.13:3 *is,* and what you would be s. *from.* The
T-14 ...VIII.1:6 Whom He would save for glory *is* s. for it.
T-17 ...... V.8:6 has not been disrupted. It has been s..
T-18 .... VII.6:3 Time has been s. for you because you and
T-20 .....II.10:4 gift has s. him from the thorns and nails,
T-20 ...VIII.1:4 It has been s. for you. Vision would not be
T-22 ..... III.8:8 you be s. by making sinful the one whose
T-22 ...... V.2:5 would you be s. from but what you fear?
T-23 .....II.15:8 who s. the Son of God for fear and death!
T-23 .....II.17:6 You cannot seek to harm him and be s..
T-23 ..... III.5:3 some forms by which their peace is s.?
T-24 ..... IV.5:4 thus you s. what you appointed to be your
T-25 ..... III.9:6 Is it your purpose that he be s. or damned
T-25 ..... IV.5:4 that ever bloomed has s. its perfume and
T-25 ...... V.5:1 It is no sacrifice that he be s., for by his
T-25 ...VIII.2:4 salvation is not needed by the s.. You are
T-25 ...VIII.2:9 know of Heaven and the justice of the s.?
T-25 ..... IX.2:2 It is s. for you until reluctance to receive it
T-26 ..... III.5:2 was never lost, and so cannot be s.. Yet
T-27 ...... V.5:1 by the one who could have s. it, but
T-29 ..... III.1:4 is. And he must save who would be s.. On
T-29 ..... III.5:7 you. And in his glad salvation you are s..
T-29 ... VII.9:9 the means by which this idol can be s..
T-30 .......II.1:4 knowledge, s. for you that you may do
T-30 .......II.5:1 God turns to you to ask the world be s.,
T-30 ..... VI.4:5 is s. from this dilemma if he can forgive.
T-31 ........I.9:2 as it is s. from death when you have heard
T-31 .......II.7:1 you will be s. from all appearances and
T-31 .. VII.10:3 see his brother not as this has s. himself,
T-31 .. VII.10:4 savior would be one who is but partly s..
W-pI......20.3:5 And can the world be s. if you are not?
W-pI......23.4:2 You cannot be s. from the world, but you
W-pI......27.4:6 sure that you have s. yourself many years
W-pI......39.3:4 A savior must be s.. How else can he teach
W-pI......39.6:4 so it is from them that you need to be s..
W-pI......58.3:3 is there to be s. from except illusions?
W-pI......61.3:4 is a positive assertion of your right to be s.
W-pI......67.1:5 He is s. by what you are. We will make
W-pI......70.1:6 place. In understanding this you are s..
W-pI......71.2:2 or event were changed, you would be s..
W-pI......71.2:4 says, "If this were different, I would be s..
W-pI......71.3:1 than itself, must change if you are to be s..
W-pI......73.9:6 to look upon the light in him and be s..
W-pI......75.1:4 You are s. and you can save. You are at
W-pI......76.4:4 Protect the body, and you will be s..
W-pI...76.12:3 God is our Father, and that His Son is s..
W-pI......78.8:8 role God gave Him that you might be s..
W-pI......78.9:2 of God but must rejoice as you are s., and
W-pI......80.4:6 and have accepted the answer. You are s..
W-pI......93.4:4 think you are destroyed, but you are s..
W-pI......96.2:1 must be accepted if you would be s.. Until
W-pI...96.10:1 that come to you will tell you you are s.,
W-pI......97.3:2 a thousand years or more are s.. The
W-pI......99.1:2 has gone wrong; something to be s. from,
W-pI...99.10:7 what you have made and you are s..
W-pI...100.2:3 The part that He has s. for you to take in
W-pI...100.3:3 your smile, the world cannot be s.. While
W-pI...110.4:1 present s. to quietly extend into a timeless
W-pI...110.8:1 world; the Savior Who has been forever s.
W-pI...121.7:5 forgiveness that it has been s. from hell.
W-pI. 121.12:3 shows you your savior, s. and saving,
W-pI...123.2:3 Be grateful He has s. you from the self you
W-pI .. 123.3:3 Be grateful you are s.. Be glad you have a
W-pI .. 124.7:2 we say as well that we are s. and healed;
W-pI .. 128.1:2 and you are s. from years of misery, from
W-pI .. 135.9:2 from which you think the body must be s.
W-pI .. 138.8:2 It must be s. from salvation, threatened to
W-pI .. 155.8:6 It is but from illusions he is s.. As they
W-pI 166.12:5 has s. you from the solitude you sought to
W-pI .. 191.5:3 who can accept his true Identity is truly s.
W-pI 193.11:4 let us think about all things we s. to settle
W-pI .. 194.2:3 on it. You are s., and your salvation thus
W-pI .. 194.6:3 so will the world perceive that it is s..
W-pI .. 194.9:1 Now are we s. indeed. For in God's
W-pI .. 200.2:1 is none; of being s. by what can only hurt;
W-pII ...... 1.5:3 His function, and forgive whom He has s.,
W-pII . 234.2:2 *Word which You have given us that we are s..*
W-pII .... 235.h God in His mercy wills that I be s..
W-pII . 235.1:1 myself, "God wills that I be s. from this,"
W-pII . 235.1:3 that I am s. and safe forever in His Arms.
W-pII . 235.1:5 am s. because God in His mercy wills it so
W-pII . 276.2:2 *own, as I am loved and blessed and s. by You.*
W-pII . 288.1:5 *mine, and I am s. because the past is gone.*
W-pII . 295.1:5 As I am s., the world is saved with me. For
W-pII . 295.1:5 As I am saved, the world is s. with me. For
W-pII . 297.1:4 And I, who would be s., would make it
W-pII . 297.1:4 will be s. as I accept Atonement for myself
W-pII . 298.1:5 as mine, sure that in that alone I will be s.;
W-pII . 305.2:1 *given us, because it is Your Will that we be s.*
W-pII . 308.1:4 in which I can be s. from time is now. For
W-pII . 318.1:4 I am the means by which God's Son is s.,
W-pII . 330.2:3 *and to be s. from what we thought we were.*
W-pII . 340.2:5 Not one of us but will be s. today. Not one
W-pII . 341.2:2 to us. And in its kind reflection we are s..
Wfl........in.5:3 s. from all the wrath we thought belonged
Wfl........in.5:5 s. from wrath because we learned we were
M-12 ....... 1:10 him. He has accepted Christ, and he is s..
C-2 ............ 9:4 world is s. from what you thought it was.
C-4 ............ 3:8 means by which the world is s. from sin,
P-2.........in.1:6 this is an error, to that extent is he truly s.
P-2..........V.5:8 of God Himself, by which His Son is s..
P-3..........II.5:2 And that good is s. for both, against the
P-3..........II.6:4 The good is s.; indeed is cherished. But
P-3..........II.6:5 But only little time is s.. The new dreams
S-1........ III.1:5 before *you* can be s. from guilt. For this the
S-3..........II.3:4 hard to see the gifts we gave were s. for us
S-3........ IV.7:7 Hear this an instant and you have been s..

## saves 12

T-2 .........II.6:6 In this sense the Atonement s. time, but
T-13 ...... III.2:4 did not believe that it s. you from love.
T-15 .......X.7:6 And this you think s. you from God,
T-24 ..... VI.3:7 s. you from a world that He created not.
T-27 .......II.7:3 Your healing s. him pain as well as you,
T-29 ........I.4:7 The body s. you, for it gets away from
W-pI .... 58.4:2 Since my holiness s. me from all guilt,
W-pI .... 69.1:5 in the light of the world that s. you both.
W-pI .... 99.6:2 is the Thought that s. and that forgives,
W-pI 191.10:5 Your glory is the light that s. the world.
W-pI .. 196.1:3 belief that to attack a brother s. yourself.
M-1 ......... 2:13 And each one s. a thousand years of time

## saving 13

T-18 .... VII.4:5 learned in time, but it does aim at s. time.
T-18 .... VII.5:2 A holy relationship is a means of s. time.
T-26 ........I.1:5 in the name of s. just a little for yourself.
T-28 ........I.5:6 of injustices and hurts that you were s.,
T-29 ..... III.1:5 On s. you depends his happiness. For who
W-pI 121.12:3 shows you your savior, saved and s.,
W-pI .. 123.5:2 come to speak the s. Word of God to us.
W-pI 188.10:5 And we lay our s. blessing on it, as we say:
W-pII . 229.2:2 *up. And thanks to You for s. me from them.*
W-pII ... 10.3:2 fear God's s. grace is but to fear complete
M-16 ......... 2:8 are obvious advantages in terms of s. time
M-16 ......... 3:3 s. of time is an essential early emphasis
P-2...........I.2:3 of "the s. illusion" or "the final dream,"

## Savior 11
*savior*

T-23....... II.7:6 because the S. has become the enemy.
T-25.... V.2:11 is there to see by searching for your S.,
W-pI...110.8:1 world; the S. Who has been forever saved,
W-pI.110.10:2 be your S. from all idols you have made.
W-pI...164.7:6 it in the light in which our S. looks on us,
W-pII......1.5:1 Who is your Guide, your S. and Protector,
W-pII......3.4:2 Whom God appointed S. to the world.
M-14..........2:4 A gentle S., born where sin was made and
C-5............2:5 Jesus remains a S. because he saw the false
C-6............5:4 with you he is the shining S. of the world,
P-2......... V.5:2 for he comes to us as Christ and S.. What

## savior 83
*Savior*

T19... IV.C.7:2 the great dark s. from the light of truth,
T19.IV.D.13:7 And yet your s. stands beside each one.
T-20....... II.3:7 Forget not that it is your s. to whom the
T-20....... II.7:4 knowing his s. stands beside him? With
T-20....... II.9:3 Let him be to you the s. from illusions,
T-20.... II.10:5 the s. from illusions has come to greet you
T-20..... II.11:1 Here is your s. and your friend, released
T-20..... II.11:2 leave you, nor forsake the s. in his pain.
T-20...... IV.2:6 Your s. gives you only love, but what you
T-20...... IV.3:3 would see within your s. from insanity?
T-20...... IV.5:3 this earth in seeming solitude is a s. given,
T-20...... IV.5:6 And each one finds his s. when he is ready
T-20... VIII.5:2 Can such a s. help you? Would you turn
T-20... VIII.5:5 Judgment will seem to make your s. weak.
T-21....... II.3:8 is given you the power to release your s.,
T-21...... VI.9:1 You *are* your brother's s.. He is yours.
T-22....... II.7:3 either you are each other's s. or his judge,
T-22....... II.8:3 with. A s. cannot be a judge, nor mercy
T-22..... II.11:3 your s. as your enemy and recognize him.
T-22..... II.11:7 look upon the s. that has been given you?
T-22...... VI.8:1 each one is released as he beholds his s. in
T-23..... II.15:6 its substitute, the s. from salvation. How
T-23..... II.17:4 makes his s. powerless and finds salvation
T-24....... II.1:5 whom it thus diminishes would be your s.
T-24....... II.2:2 Who can attack his s. and cut him down,
T-24....... II.3:4 Here is the self-made "s.," the "creator"
T-24....... II.7:1 have chained your s. to your specialness,
T-24..... II.10:1 Here is your s. *from* your specialness. He
T-24...... III.7:7 see the s. God gave to you that you might
T-24...... III.8:4 do you will that this be done unto your s.?
T-24...... IV.1:7 Here is death enthroned as s.; crucifixion
T-24...... IV.5:4 saved what you appointed to be your s.,
T-24...... VI.1:2 He is your s. from the dreams of fear. He
T-25.......... II.h The S. from the Dark
T-25....... II.8:1 the darkness see the s. *from* the dark, and
T-25....... V.4:5 your s. offers you salvation. Condemned
T-25...... VI.3:4 not will your s. be unrecognized by you.
T-28..... VII.2:3 Your s. waits for healing, and the world
T-29.........I.8:5 who learn their s. is their enemy no more.
T-29..... II.10:4 Your s. is not dead, nor does he dwell in
T-29..... II.10:5 and it is this that makes him s. unto you,
T-29...... III.1:1 your s. not because he thinks he is a body.
T-29...... III.1:3 But he must learn he is a s. first, before he
T-29...... III.1:6 who is s. but the one who gives salvation?
T-29...... III.2:6 He must be s. from the dream he made,
T-29...... III.3:5 he becomes your s. from your dreams.
T-29...... III.4:3 your forgiveness, he will not forget his s.,
T-29...... III.5:1 that the Son of God can be your s. in the
T-29....... V.7:1 dream is given you in which he is your s.,
T-30... VI.10:5 Is this your s.? Is his Father wrong about
T-31..... VII.8:3 He allowed the grace to be a s. to the holy
T-31... VII.10:3 himself, and thus is he a s. to the rest. To
T-31... VII.10:4 a partial s. would be one who is but partly
T-31... VII.11:1 how could you be the s. of the Son of God
T-31... VII.15:3 Their s. stands, unknowing and unknown
W-pI.....39.3:4 A s. must be saved. How else can he teach
W-pI.....67.1:3 why God appointed you as the world's s..
W-pI.....72.6:8 The body is your only s.. It is the death of
W-pI.....72.7:5 Your chosen s. takes His place instead. It
W-pI.....78.5:5 Let him be s. unto you today. Such is his
W-pI.....78.7:1 and see our s. shining in the light of true
W-pI.....78.7:3 *Let me behold my s. in this one You have*
W-pI.....78.8:2 Your s. has been waiting long for this. He
W-pI.....78.8:6 quiet now, and look upon your shining s..
W-pI...78.10:3 the past, allow the role of s. to be given,
W-pI.....92.5:3 itself. Truth is a s. and can only will for
W-pI.121.12:3 that light his holiness shows you your s.,
W-pI...156.5:4 holiness, saluting you as s. and as God.
W-pI.161.12:6 suddenly transformed from enemy to s.;
W-pI...162.6:1 to you now; you, his redeemer and his s..
W-pI...163.1:3 worshipping of death as s. and as giver of
WpI...rV.in6:5 a s. must remain with those he teaches,
W-pI...192.9:6 your s. from the prison house of death.
W-pII..288.1:7 *My brother is my s.. Let me not attack the*
W-pII..288.1:8 *Let me not attack the s. You have given me.*
W-pII..296.1:3 *I would be s. to the world I made. For having*
W-pII..315.1:5 who finds the way to God becomes my s.,
M-1 ...........3:8 He has become a s. by his answering. He
M-23 .........7:4 trouble; a s. who can symbolize Himself?
M-26 .........4:4 If you would be a s., you must understand
P-2......... V.3:7 out his brother as his s. from the world.
P-3...........I.4:6 on the s. of the world to let in a ghost? Let
S-2......... II.5:3 witness that it offers one who could be s.,

## savior's 4

T-31........VII.h The S. Vision
T-31... VII.11:5 of him. This is the s. vision; that he see his
T-31... VII.13:1 The s. vision is as innocent of what your
T-31... VII.15:2 and men despair because the s. vision is

## Saviors 1
*saviors*

P-3......... II.7:8 They are the S. of the world. Their image

## saviors 9
*Saviors*

T-22...... IV.6:5 lifted from their minds are this world's s.,
T-31... VIII.1:5 *take your place among the s. of the world, or*
T-31... VIII.4:4 The s. of the world, who see like Him, are
W-pI.....65.2:1 rightful place among the s. of the world.
W-pI...165.6:3 For now you are among the s. of the world
W-pII..266.1:1 *Sons, to be my s. and my counselors in sight;*
W-pII..266.2:2 How many s. God has given us! How can
W-pII.... 14.3:2 We accept our part as s. of the world,
M-3 ...........5:7 they become the s. of the teachers who

## saw 50

T-6...... V.C.9:3 threw truth away you s. yourself as if you
T-7......... X.1:3 really s. this result you could not want it.
T-12..... VII.9:5 looked within and thought you s. the
T-12... VII.10:1 within and are afraid of what you s.. Yet
T-12... VII.10:4 because you s. something that is not there
T-12... VII.12:3 see it without *because* you s. it first within.
T-13....... V.3:6 because you s. in him a shadow figure risen in
T-13..... V.11:4 Because they s. the Son, they have risen in
T-13..... V.11:5 looked within and s. beyond the darkness
T-13... VIII.8:4 The holy light you s. outside yourself, in
T-18....... II.1:3 is clearly not the world you s. before you
T-18....... II.1:6 unless you s. yourself as one with the ego,
T19. IV.A.12:2 it, and return with word of what they s..
T-20. VIII.10:3 must thus reflect the sight you s. within;
T-20. VIII.10:3 if you s. at all or merely judged against.
T-21....... II.5:3 convinced yourself that what it s. was true
T-21...... IV.3:1 What if you looked within and s. no sin?
T-22.......in.1:7 effects of what you both believed and s..
T-22.......in.4:8 now the sameness that you s. extends and
T-22.........I.9:8 in each the other s. a perfect shelter where
T-22...... IV.4:6 beautiful the sight you s. beyond the veil,
T-23.......in.3:6 error disappeared because they s. it not.
T-24....... V.4:7 in him and love to look upon it s. in you,
T-24....... V.6:3 fear you thought you s. within yourself.
T-25....... II.7:4 because you s. it in a frame of death. God
T-26....... II.3:4 think so if you s. them vanish one by one,
T-26....... V.4:3 you look upon you s. but for an instant,
T-27... VII.11:6 and s. as if it were its start and ending,
T-29...... III.4:4 he s. the light that he would keep beside
T-30.........I.3:3 not resolve the problem as you s. it first.
T-31...... IV.3:4 s. no way except the pathways offered by
T-31... VII.10:5 are; all those you s. an instant and forgot,
T-31.... VIII.8:4 the pain and sorrow that you s. before.
W-pI.....30.1:3 Nor will what you s. before be even faintly
W-pI.....75.6:4 upon it now as if you never s. it before.
W-pI... 76.10:1 upheld the world you thought you s..
W-pI.....78.5:3 while you s. him not is there in everyone,
W-pI... 124.5:4 see because we s. it first within ourselves.
W-pI. 134.11:3 what he thought he s. was never there.
W-pI. 151.14:2 from the Mind which s. the truth in it,
W-pI... 163.8:3 s. that it is only this which they believe,
W-pI... 181.3:4 And what we s. an instant previous has
W-pII .....in.5:7 have never come this far unless you s.,
W-pII . 265.1:1 sins on it and s. them looking back at me.
W-pII . 301.2:4 we have learned the world we s. was false,
W-pII ... 13.4:3 a world more real than what you s. before
M-14 ....... 1:10 brought to truth, and truth s. them not. It
C-5............2:1 the name of one who was a man but s. the
C-5............2:5 he s. the false without accepting it as true.
C-5............3:3 to God because he s. the road before him,

## say 163

T-2.... V.A.18:4 *have to worry about what to s. or what to do,*
T-2........ VI.7:2 S. to yourself that you must somehow
T-3........ III.5:7 When you s. you are acting on the basis of
T-3...... VI.11:8 "Seek ye first the Kingdom of Heaven" s.,
T-4........ IV.9:2 To the ego's dark glass you need but s., "I
T-5......... V.5:5 It might be better to s. that it is a form of
T-5....... VII.6:6 S. this to yourself as sincerely as you can,
T-8...........I.2:3 You cannot expect it to s. "I am not real."
T-9.........I.11:2 s. of someone who persists in attempting
T-9.........I.14:6 S., therefore: *Christ is in me, and where He*
T-9..........II.5:2 What does he s. to you? What would you
T-9..........II.5:3 you? What would you have him s.? Your
T-9....... II.12:5 S., then, to everyone: *Because I will to know*
T-9....... VII.8:1 Whenever you question your value, s.:
T-11.......in.2:1 s. to someone who believed this question
T-13...... III.3:1 harder for you to s. "I love" than "I hate"?
T-13... VII.14:1 remember what you really want, and s.:
T-13..... X.11:9 To him I s.: *Behold the Son of God, and*
T-14...... III.3:4 S. therefore, to yourself, gently, but with
T-14... III.16:1 S. to the Holy Spirit only, "Decide for me
T-14...... VI.7:1 You know not what you s., and so you
T-14...... XI.6:6 or disturbed in any way, s. to yourself: *I do*
T-15... XI.10:4 S., then, to your brother: *I give you to the*
T-18.........I.7:1 error rising to frighten you, s. only, "God
T-18....... V.7:2 Let him remember this, and s.: *I desire this*
T19..IV.C.11:7 Give it to Him to judge for you, and s.:
T-20..... VII.2:7 How can one be sincere and s., "I want
T-21........II.2:2 you. S. only this, but mean it with no
T-23.........I.4:9 Nor is it up to you to s. what shall be part
T-23......II.18:2 And when you look at what they s., they
T-24...... III.5:8 knows that death is not your will, must s.,
T-24..... VII.8:2 except to s. that what is yours will come
T-25...... VI.2:5 can s. that he prefers the darkness and
T-26........X.6:5 injustice anywhere, you need but s.: *By*
T-27.........I.4:6 Death seems an easy price, if they can s.,
T-27........II.2:8 Who can s. and mean, "My brother, you
T-27........II.5:5 And everything you s. or do or think but
T-27.... VIII.9:7 But hear Him s., "My brother, holy Son of
T-28...... VI.6:4 In his creation did his Father s., "You are
T-29.........I.9:5 you allow the body to s. "no" to Heaven's
T-30.........I.4:1 the things you would experience, and s.: *If*
T-30.........I.6:3 Then s.: *I have no question. I forgot what to*
T-30.......I.11:3 And you can s. in perfect honesty: *I want*
T-31.........I.1:8 You can no longer s. that you perceive no
T-31.........I.3:5 S. not you cannot learn them. For your
T-31.........I.4:6 s. not that you cannot learn the simple
T-31..VIII.12:1 And now we s. "Amen." For Christ has
W-pI..... 10.4:7 As each one crosses your mind, s.: *My*
W-pI..... 12.3:1 As you look about you, s. to yourself: *I*
W-pI..... 14.4:4 S., for example: *God did not create that war*
W-pI..... 14.5:4 For example, do not s., "God did not
W-pI..... 14.7:3 S.: *God did not create a meaningless world.*
W-pI..... 15.4:1 and letting your eyes rest on it as you s.:
W-pI..... 17.2:1 In applying today's idea, s. to yourself,
W-pI..... 17.2:3 on each thing you note long enough to s.:
W-pI..... 17.2:5 For example, you might s.: *I do not see a*

W-pI.....18.3:1 your eyes on each one long enough to s.: *I*
W-pI.....19.3:3 holding it in your mind as you do so, s.: *I*
W-pI.....21.5:3 suffering from this form of distortion, s.: *I*
W-pI.....22.3:2 from one body to another, s. to yourself: *I*
W-pI.....23.6:3 As each one crosses your mind s.: *I can*
W-pI.....23.6:5 each attack thought in mind as you s. this
W-pI.....24.7:1 that crosses your mind s. to yourself: *I do*
W-pI.....25.3:1 you now perceive is to s. that they are all
W-pI.....25.6:3 resting on each subject you so select, s.,
W-pI.....25.6:7 S. this quite slowly, without shifting your
W-pI.....27.2:1 when you s. you want to see above all else.
W-pI.....28.2:1 You may wonder why it is important to s.
W-pI.....28.3:1 When you s., "Above all else I want to see
W-pI...29.5:10 you s. the words unhurriedly to yourself.
W-pI.....33.3:3 For these applications, s.: *There is another*
W-pI.....36.3:3 S., for example: *My holiness envelops that*
W-pI.....41.8:3 even s. it is the only natural thing in the
W-pI.....43.4:6 You might s., for example: *God is my*
W-pI.....46.4:3 Mention each one by name, and s.: *God is*
W-pI.....46.6:2 of. You might s., for example: *I cannot be*
W-pI.....54.4:3 I think or s. or do teaches all the universe.
W-pI.....62.5:1 your eyes if possible, s. to yourself today:
W-pI.....65.2:2 only way in which you can s. and mean,
W-pI...66.11:3 about them a little while as you s. them.
W-pI.....68.6:2 S. to them all, thinking of each one in
W-pI.....69.9:3 S., then: *My grievances hide the light of the*
W-pI...70.10:5 S., then: *My salvation comes from me.*
W-pI.....71.9:5 *What would You have me s., and to whom?*
W-pI...73.11:2 S.: *I will there be light. Darkness is not my*
W-pI.....74.7:1 intervals today, s. to yourself: *There is no*
W-pI...75.10:1 S., then: *The light has come. I have forgiven*
W-pI...75.10:4 s. to anyone who seems to pull you back
W-pI.....80.6:4 S. quickly: *Let me recognize this problem*
W-pI.....83.1:4 what to do, what to s. and what to think.
W-pI.....91.8:3 S., for example: *I am not weak, but strong. I*
W-pI.....98.7:4 will bring the light to all the words you s.,
W-pI.....98.7:5 Today you practice with Him, as you s.: *I*
W-pI.....98.9:4 joy and certainty that what you s. is true.
W-pI.....99.7:2 to perceive the strength in what you s.,
W-pI...101.6:5 S.: *God's Will for me is perfect happiness.*
W-pI...105.7:6 Now you can s., "God's peace and joy are
W-pI...105.9:2 At least remember hourly to s. the words
W-pI...105.9:5 bless your brother thankfully, and s.: *My*
W-pI...107.9:4 confidence is with you, as you s.: *Truth*
W-pI...108.8:1 with the instruction for today, and s.: *To*
W-pI...108.8:5 You might, for instance, s.: *To everyone I*
W-pI...108.9:1 S. each one slowly and then pause a while
W-pI.108.10:3 still faster and more sure each time you s.,
W-pI.110.11:3 And we will s., that we may be reminded
W-pI...124.7:1 in this awareness as we s. that we are one
W-pI...124.7:2 we s. as well that we are saved and healed;
W-pI...129.4:3 for what They s. cannot be symbolized.
W-pI...130.8:4 You wait for God to help you, as you s.: *It*
W-pI.130.11:3 to you. All you need s. to any part of hell,
W-pI.132.17:1 and s. whenever you are tempted to deny
W-pI...135.5:4 s. your home is open to the thief of time,
W-pI.135.22:3 And we are given truly, as we s.: *If I defend*
W-pI.139.12:3 apart from your awareness, as you s.: *I will*
W-pI.140.12:6 we will s. our prayer for healing hourly,
WpI. rIV.in7:2 your eyes, and s. them slowly to yourself.
W-pI...160.2:3 And yet, how easy it would be to s., "This
W-pI...169.5:4 We s. "God is," and then we cease to
WpI.rV.in10:7 it is free of all illusions every time we s.:
W-pI...181.6:3 our minds to change their focus, as we s.:
W-pI...182.1:5 Nothing so definite that you could s. with
W-pI...183.2:2 S. His Name, and you invite the angels to
W-pI...183.6:5 when we s. today's idea but once. And
W-pI...185.1:1 To s. these words is nothing. But to mean
W-pI...185.7:1 that we really mean the words we s.. We
W-pI.188.10:5 we lay our saving blessing on it, as we s.:
W-pI...193.6:1 Shall we not learn to s. these words when
W-pI...193.6:2 Shall we not learn to s. these words when
W-pI...199.8:6 His Love and happiness each time you s.: *I*
W-pI.200.11:8 and draw still nearer every time we s.:
WpI rVI.in.6:1 your freedom from temptation, as you s.:
WpI rVI.in.7:2 teach you what to do and s. and think,
W-pII ....in.3:3 We s. some simple words of welcome,
W-pII ....in.4:6 s. the words of invitation that His Voice
W-pII .275.2:3 *to go; to whom to speak and what to s. to him*
W-pII .300.1:1 to s. that death and sorrow are the certain
W-pII .360.1:7 *And with this thought we gladly s. "Amen."*
Wfl........in.6:1 to God and s. we did not understand, and
Wfl........in.6:3 Or would He rush to answer him, and s.,
W-ep......... 5:2 To this we s. "Amen." You will be told
W-ep......... 6:1 We trust our ways to Him and s. "Amen.
M-in.......... 3:6 underlying what you s. that teaches you.
M-3........... 3:5 simply to s. that any level of the teaching-
M-4........II.1:4 does not apply only to what you s.. The
M-4........II.1:6 you s. that contradicts what you think or
M-5........II.1:2 One need but s., "There is no gain at all to
M-5........II.1:3 But to s. this, one first must recognize
M-5......II.2:12 merely rise up without their aid and s., "I
M-11......... 2:3 they s. different things about the world,
M-14....... 5:11 arrogant and s. you cannot learn His Own
M-16......... 3:4 safely s. that time devoted to starting the
M-21......... 4:5 to decide for himself what he will s.. This
M-22......... 7:2 can s. which one can be healed of what,
M-22....... 7:10 Now can he s. with God, "This is my
M-23......... 3:6 What did he s. about this? Remember his
M-29....... 2:14 always right. Would you s. that of yours?
M-29......... 4:2 To s., "Of myself I can do nothing" is to
M-29......... 5:5 mean that you cannot s. anything without
C-2........... 4:1 what the ego is, but we *can* s. what it is not
P-2........ IV.3:6 and we have said already and will s. again
S-1........ V.3:8 Now can you s. to everyone who comes to
S-2..........II.6:3 S. this to anyone and you are slave. And
S-2........ III.5:7 He will s. exactly what to do, in words

### sayeth 2

T-3..........I.3:1 s. the Lord" is a misperception by which
T-5....... VI.7:1 s. the Lord" is easily reinterpreted if you

### saying 20

T-1........I.39:2 is the same as s. that by perceiving light,
T-2....... VI.2:2 on your part by s. you could not help it.
T-3..........I.5:4 God" is another way of s. the same thing.
T-6........I.15:2 they never could have quoted me as s., "I
T-7....... III.3:7 from s. you perceive yourself as unreal?
T-8.........II.5:2 That is the same as s. He teaches you the
T-13..... IX.4:4 When you condemn a brother you are s.,
T-21 ... III.11:5 It is like s. that the moon and sun are one
W-pI....... 8.4:5 Introduce the practice period by s.: *I seem*
W-pI..... 13.4:3 your eyes, and look about you slowly, s.: *I*
W-pI..... 26.7:3 referring to each one quite specifically, s.:
W-pI..... 28.4:3 In s., "Above all else I want to see this
W-pI..... 28.8:1 you should rest your eyes on it while s.:
W-pI..... 37.4:5 who occurs to you, using his name and s.:
W-pI..... 41.9:2 Think of what you are s.; what the words
W-pI..... 64.1:1 of s. "Let me not wander into temptation.
W-pI..... 96.9:1 Begin with s. this: *Salvation comes from*
W-pI...108.5:2 This is the same as s. one correction will
W-pI.132.10:1 for today except another way of s. that to
W-pI...160.3:1 reason is there for not s. this? What could

### says 47

T-2..........I.3:6 Bible s. that a deep sleep fell upon Adam,
T-3..........I.2:7 In milder forms a parent s., "This hurts
T-3.......II.5:10 This is what the Bible means when it s.,
T-3....... VI.1:4 Bible s. "Judge not that ye be not judged,"
T-4........in.1:1 Bible s. that you should go with a brother
T-5..........I.3:4 The Bible s., "May the mind be in you
T-7.........X.3:3 not whether what the Holy Spirit s. is true
T-7.........X.3:3 whether you want to listen to what He s..
T-8......VII.7:1 The Bible s., "The Word (or thought) was
T-8....... IX.8:1 and one that means exactly what it s.. I
T-9.........II.1:3 that the course does not mean what it s..
T-9..... III.2:10 wrong, no matter what it s. or does.
T-14.......II.3:2 that it is not nothing, the Holy Spirit s.,
T-21....... V.2:3 Listen to what the ego s., and see what it
T-22.......I.2:10 But what it s. you cannot understand. Yet
T-22.......II.5:6 Therefore, s. reason, if escape from guilt
T-23.....II.16:6 one of these laws is true sees what it s..
T-23.....II.17:9 condemning what it s. it wants to save. Be
T-25.......in.3:5 body s. or does but makes Him manifest.
T-27.... V.1:12 because you have accepted what He s..
T-27..... VI.1:2 would silence what the Holy Spirit s., and
T-28..... VI.5:4 Whoever s., "There is no gap between my
T-31........I.1:2 it s. is what was never true is not true now
T-31 .. VII.15:5 Can you to whom God s., "Release My
T-31 ... VIII.3:2 perplexity Christ calls to you and gently s.
W-pI .... 71.2:4 an assertion in which you believe, that s.,
W-pI .... 72.3:4 A person s. something you do not like. He
W-pI .... 76.9:3 will be listening to One Who s. there is no
W-pI .. 134.4:4 It s. the truth is false, and smiles on the
W-pI .. 134.7:5 with quiet eyes, and merely s. to them,
W-pI .. 151.7:2 nor what his body's mouth s. to your ears,
W-pI .. 152.9:4 the arrogance which s. that we are sinners
W-pI .. 160.2:4 will not leave because a madman s. I must
W-pI .. 163.5:3 It s. but this: "Here lies a witness God is
W-pI .. 186.3:2 it s. is that your Father still remembers
W-pII . 255.1:3 have faith in Him Who s. I am God's Son.
W-pII . 255.1:4 bear witness to the truth of what He s..
M-10......... 1:8 what his would-be teacher s. about them,
M-11......... 2:5 God s. there is no death; your judgment
M-11......... 2:6 world; your judgment s. it is unlovable.
M-12......... 6:5 The dream s. otherwise, but who would
M-14....... 5:12 His Word s. otherwise. His Will be done.
M-17......... 7:3 go. Each one s. clearly to your frightened
M-21......... 4:6 case of the lesson in the workbook that s.,
M-23......... 1:4 The Bible s., "Ask in the name of Jesus
P-3........II.9:10 Yet at each meeting there is One Who s.,
S-2..........II.3:3 Now he s. instead that here is one whose

### scale 3

T-3..........I.2:3 and genuinely tragic on a wider s..
W-pI .. 139.3:1 must be is self-deception on a s. so vast,
W-pI .. 164.5:3 the s. of judgment left to Him Who judges

### scales 1

T-3..... VI.11:4 of reality by the unstable s. of desire.

### scamper 1

W-pI .. 186.9:5 break apart to group again, and s. off. Or

### scapegoat 1

T-18..... VI.6:1 is insane to use the body as the s. for guilt

### scar 1

T-27........I.5:5 who will see that every s. is healed, and

### scarce 1

W-pI .. 161.9:3 could s. refrain from kneeling at his feet.

### scarcity 9

T-1....... IV.3:3 It is an example of the "s." belief, from
T-3..........I.1:4 in s. could possibly make this mistake. If
T-4.........II.6:6 with the belief in s. that gave rise to it. Its
T-7...... VII.7:8 Do not share their illusions of s., or you
T-7..... VIII.1:9 It therefore produces abundance or s.,
T-13 .. VII.10:5 is a world of s. in which you find yourself
T-15..... VI.5:1 In the world of s., love has no meaning
S-1..........II.1:5 wanting, out of a sense of s. and lack.
S-1..........II.3:5 Without guilt there is no s.. The sinless

### scars 1

T-26..... IX.8:4 and ancient s. are healed within His sight.

### scatter 1

T-24..... VI.1:3 will s. with the wind and turn to dust. In

### scattered 3

T-25..... IX.7:8 way, and peace be s. by the winds of hate.
T-31 .VIII.11:5 to Heaven grows from tiny s. threads of

Wi181-200 1:1 strong; your **s.** goals blend into one intent

### scavenger 1
T-27...VII.12:2 the **s.** and the destroyer of your brother

### scene 1
M-19..........2:6 the grandeur of the **s.** and the enormous

### scenes 1
T-20. VIII.11:1 have looked on **s.** of violence and death,

### scent 3
T-27...... I.10:3 sick of breathing in the fetid **s.** of death.
W-pI ...156.4:3 The **s.** of flowers is their gift to you. The
S-3 ...........I.2:6 the heavy **s.** of death upon their hearts.

### schedule 3
W-pI .....27.4:5 but do try to keep on your **s.** from then on
W-pI .....40.1:3 urged to attempt this **s.** and to adhere to
W-pI .....95.7:3 use your lapses from this **s.** as an excuse

### scheme 1
M-19..........3:5 Forgiveness has no place in such a **s.**, for

### schemes 1
T-4........IV.1:5 is filled with **s.** to save the face of your ego

### scissors 1
T-4......... II.5:2 in rage if you take away a knife or **s.**,

### scold 1
M-3............2:5 will not **s.** the child for bumping into him;

### scope 8
T-18....IX.11:1 is still beyond the **s.** of our curriculum.
T-24.....VII.8:2 Its **s.** does not exceed your own, except to
T-26....III.1:13 beyond the **s.** of this curriculum. Nor is it
T-29.........I.3:8 in **s.** and carefully restricted in amount,
W-pI ...128.1:3 soar beyond its petty **s.** and little ways.
W-pI ...135.7:3 it cannot fill, to purposes beyond its **s.**,
W-pI ...193.1:2 eternal and forever gaining **s.**, eternally
P-2 ......... V.4:8 our little **s.** for what to teach as well as

### scorched 2
T-18... VIII.8:6 dry and unproductive, **s.** and joyless–
T-26......IX.3:5 that hate had **s.** and rendered desolate.

### scourge 1
S-2 ...........I.1:2 It has, in fact, become a **s.**; a curse where

### scrap 6
T19. IV.A.11:2 cherish every **s.** of evil and of sin that they
T-24....... V.2:3 picked a thread from here, a **s.** from there
T-26.........I.5:4 to every meager **s.** and tiny crumb of
T-27.........I.7:5 to believe that every stolen **s.** of pleasure
T-28....... V.5:7 each senseless **s.** and shred of evidence,
W-pI ...191.3:3 snatch from your fingers every **s.** of hope,

### scraps 3
T-4........III.7:2 You retain thousands of little **s.** of fear
T-4........III.7:5 Watch your mind for the **s.** of fear, or you
T-15......XI.1:4 which you think you see some **s.** of safety.

### scream 3
T-4......... II.5:2 Babies **s.** in rage if you take away a knife
T-18....... II.4:1 temper tantrums, in which you literally **s.**
T-27...VII.13:4 the sweat of terror and a **s.** of mortal fear,

### screaming 3
T19. IV.A.12:7 they see, and carry it **s.** to their master, to
T-20. VIII.10:6 all the terrifying sights and **s.** sounds the
T-27....... V.3:4 limbs, the **s.** dying and the silent dead,

### screams 1
T-21....... V.1:6 the ego's raucous **s.** and senseless ravings

### screeches 1
M-18 .........3:1 Anger but **s.**, "Guilt is real!" Reality is

### screen 3
T-18.........I.6:2 became the **s.** on which it was projected
W-pI. 133.12:3 Complexity is nothing but a **s.** of smoke,
P-2 ........ VI.6:6 patient is his **s.** for the projection of his

### script 6
T-30.....VII.1:7 add an element into the **s.** you write for
T-30.....VII.2:3 made according to the roles the **s.** assigns.
T-30.....VII.3:9 but to show you wrote a fearful **s.**, and are
T-30...VII.6:12 It is a part of a distorted **s.**, which cannot
W-pI...158.4:3 The **s.** is written. When experience will
W-pI...169.9:3 wrote salvation's **s.** in His Creator's Name

### scripts 2
T-30.....VII.2:1 What do your **s.** reflect except your plans
T-30...VII.6:15 the senseless, isolated **s.** you write in sleep

### Scripture 2
T-5........ VI.4:4 only does the ego cite **S.** for its purpose,
T-5........ VI.4:4 it even interprets **S.** as a witness for itself.

### sea 1
W-pI...156.3:3 of ice; the **s.** elect to be apart from water,

### seal 2
T-24..... II.12:1 is the **s.** of treachery upon the gift of love.
T-24..... II.12:3 to kill. No gift that bears its **s.** but offers

### search 60
T-4........IV.2:5 **S.** sincerely for what you have done and
T-9......IV.11:2 **s.** for reality in fantasies you will not find
T-12.......IV.1:2 to be intensely engaged in the **s.** for love.
T-12.......IV.1:3 encouraging the **s.** for love very actively,
T-12.......IV.2:1 **s.** the ego undertakes is therefore bound
T-12.......IV.2:3 its frantic **s.** for love it is seeking what it is
T-12.......IV.2:4 The **s.** is inevitable because the ego is part
T-12.......IV.3:5 its teaching, then, and you will **s.** for love,
T-12.......IV.5:2 And you *will* **s.** for your home whether you
T-12.......IV.5:3 believe it is outside you the **s.** will be futile
T-13.......III.7:5 **s.** your mind carefully for any thoughts
T-14.....VII.1:8 rather than a helper in the **s.** for truth.
T-14.....VII.2:1 **s.** for truth is but the honest searching out
T-14..... X.10:6 it. If you undertake the **s.** together, you
T-15.......III.4:9 **S.** for the little, and you deny yourself His
T-16.......VI.1:1 The **s.** for the special relationship is the
T-17....IV.13:4 as you **s.** it out amid its wrappings. As
T19. IV.A.12:5 steal guiltily away in hungry **s.** of guilt, for
T19. IV.A.12:7 And in their savage **s.** for sin they pounce
T19....IV.B.9:8 you forever be a wanderer in **s.** of peace?
T19..IV.B.15:4 body **s.** for pain in attack upon another,
T-22....... II.2:5 The **s.** for joy in misery is senseless, for
T-29.....VII.1:7 simply from a futile **s.** for what you want,
T-29..... VII.2:5 in **s.** of something that he cannot find,
T-29..... VII.4:6 The **s.** implies you are not whole within
T-29...... IX.9:3 to the frantic **s.** for idols and for death.
T-30...... III.3:1 Behind the **s.** for every idol lies the
T-30...... III.3:8 the **s.** for wholeness to be made beyond
T-31...... IV.4:2 Its purpose is the answer to the **s.** that all
T-31...... IV.6:4 The **s.** for different pathways in the world
T-31...... IV.6:4 is but the **s.** for different forms of truth.
W-pI....... 5.3:1 which you first **s.** your mind for "sources"
W-pI....... 5.7:1 **s.** your mind for no more than a minute
W-pI....... 6.2:2 upsetting thought uncovered in the **s.**.
W-pI....... 8.4:3 **s.** your mind for the usual minute or so,
W-pI..... 16.4:1 **s.** your mind for a minute or so with eyes
W-pI..... 16.4:1 thought that may tend to elude the **s.**.
W-pI..... 21.2:2 close your eyes and **s.** your mind carefully
W-pI..... 21.4:1 As you **s.** your mind for all the forms in
W-pI..... 34.3:2 **S.** your mind for fear thoughts, anxiety-
W-pI..... 35.4:1 and then close your eyes and **s.** your mind
W-pI..... 38.4:1 then **s.** your mind for any sense of loss or
W-pI..... 39.6:2 **s.** out your unloving thoughts in whatever
W-pI..... 39.8:1 particular, **s.** your mind for every thought
W-pI..... 69.3:5 ancient **s.** today by finding the light in us,
W-pI..... 71.3:3 ensures that the fruitless **s.** will continue,
W-pI..... 86.1:2 It is senseless for me to **s.** wildly about for
W-pI..... 96.8:2 will be a **s.** for Him within your mind.
W-pI... 121.1:1 Here is the answer to your **s.** for peace.
W-pI. 122.10:1 **s.** in which the end of hell is guaranteed.
W-pI... 131.2:6 death because it is the **s.** for nothingness,
W-pI... 131.3:3 can not dictate the goal for which you **s.**,
W-pI... 131.4:1 Be glad that **s.** you must. Be glad as well
W-pI... 131.4:2 Be glad as well to learn you **s.** for Heaven,
W-pI... 160.6:1 What does he **s.** for now? What can he
W-pI... 160.6:4 except a miracle will **s.** him out and show
W-pI... 160.9:1 to **s.** the world for what belongs to Him.
W-pI... 182.3:2 He goes uncertainly about in endless **s.**,
W-pII ....in.8:1 spent together in the **s.** for truth and God,
W-pII . 226.1:4 I want to keep as mine or **s.** for as a goal,

### searched 2
W-pI..... 19.3:2 the mind should be carefully **s.** for the
W-pII . 321.1:2 *I have* **s.** *in vain until I heard Your Voice*

### searches 3
T-9......... V.2:3 healer who **s.** fantasies for truth must be
T-31....... V.2:8 It **s.** for companions and it looks, at times
W-pI..... 69.3:5 it up for everyone who **s.** with us to look

### searching 28
*See also* mind-searching
T-2.........I.5:10 Illness is some form of external **s.**. Health
T-14..... VII.2:1 search for truth is but the honest **s.** out of
T-14........X.9:6 two or more join together in **s.** for truth,
T-17........II.5:2 **s.** of the mind that made this world, and
T-24........II.1:3 seen in another, and maintained by **s.** for,
T-25..... V.2:11 what is there to see by **s.** for your Savior,
W-pI........ 6.2:2 be preceded by a minute or so of mind **s.**,
W-pI........ 8.6:3 for today may induce, in the mind **s.** itself
W-pI..... 10.4:4 in **s.** your mind for all the thoughts that
W-pI..... 10.5:2 no more than a minute or so of mind **s.**. It
W-pI..... 19.3:1 minute or so of mind **s.** which today's
W-pI..... 23.6:2 minute to **s.** your mind for as many attack
W-pI..... 24.4:1 today's idea, followed by **s.** the mind,
W-pI..... 34.3:1 Some five minutes of mind **s.** are
W-pI..... 42.6:1 that active **s.** for relevant thoughts is not
W-pI..... 46.3:3 spend a minute or two in **s.** your mind for
W-pI..... 47.4:4 spend a minute or two in **s.** for situations
W-pI..... 65.3:4 you the answer to all the **s.** you have done
W-pI..... 68.5:1 extended practice period by **s.** your mind
W-pI..... 69.9:2 also that you are not **s.** for it alone, and
W-pI..... 71.4:3 all your efforts in **s.** for it where it is not?
W-pI..... 94.3:2 Begin these times of **s.** with these words: *I*
W-pI... 130.8:1 Begin your **s.** for the other world by
W-pI... 131.1:3 where contradiction is the setting of his **s.**
W-pI... 131.3:1 Yet **s.** is inevitable here. For this you
W-pI. 131.14:5 you will find the goal of all your **s.** here,
W-pI... 185.8:1 practice periods to careful **s.** of your mind

| | |
|---|---|
| W-pII .318.1:6 | seek. I am the goal the world is s. for. I am |

## season 4

| | |
|---|---|
| T-15...... III.7:1 | s. (Christmas) which celebrates the birth |
| T-15....... X.1:3 | time nor s. means anything in eternity. |
| T-15....... X.1:5 | the s. when you would celebrate my birth |
| T-15....... X.4:1 | It is in your power to make this s. holy, |

## seasons 1

| | |
|---|---|
| T-29...... VI.2:9 | go, the tides, the s. and the lives of men; |

## seat 3

| | |
|---|---|
| T-20...... VI.6:1 | temple, and it will never be the s. of love. |
| W-pI... 161.6:7 | be the s. of fear except what thinks of fear |
| W-pI... 192.5:4 | the core of anguish and the s. of fear? |

## Second 16

*second*

| | |
|---|---|
| T-4...... IV.10:2 | The S. Coming of Christ means nothing |
| T-4...... IV.10:3 | I have called you to join with me in the S.. |
| T-4...... IV.10:4 | I am in charge of the S. Coming, and my |
| T-9........ IV.9:3 | This is the S. Coming that was made for |
| T-9........ IV.9:4 | S. Coming is merely the return of sense. |
| T-9.... IV.11:10 | The S. Coming is the awareness of reality, |
| W-pII ........ 9.h | What Is the S. Coming? |
| W-pII ..... 9.1:1 | Christ's S. Coming, which is sure as God, |
| W-pII ..... 9.2:1 | of Christ's S. Coming that permits it to |
| W-pII ..... 9.2:2 | end to the release the S. Coming brings, |
| W-pII ..... 9.2:3 | Forgiveness lights the S. Coming's way, |
| W-pII ..... 9.3:1 | The S. Coming ends the lessons that the |
| W-pII ..... 9.3:2 | S. Coming is the time in which all minds |
| W-pII ..... 9.4:1 | S. Coming is the one event in time which |
| W-pII ..... 9.5:1 | Pray that the S. Coming will be soon, but |
| W-pII ... 10.1:1 | Christ's S. Coming gives the Son of God |

## second 59

*Second*

| | |
|---|---|
| T-1........ IV.1:3 | S., the recognition that there is nothing |
| T-2......... I.1:10 | S., you believe that what is perfect can be |
| T-2........ IV.4:3 | a s. misstep to attempt to heal it through |
| T-2........ VI.5:4 | S., you can behave as you think you |
| T-2........ VI.5:10 | shift the error from the first to the s. type, |
| T-2..... VII.3:14 | All fear is implicit in the s., and all love in |
| T-5........... I.7:3 | but gain. S., it is incapable of attack and is |
| T-5......... V.6:3 | are answering it every minute and every s. |
| T-6...... V.B.7:4 | Therefore, His s. lesson is: *To have peace,* |
| T-6...... V.B.8:3 | The s. step is a positive affirmation of |
| T-6...... V.B.9:1 | s. step, then, is still perceptual, although |
| T-6...... V.B.9:3 | At the s. step progress is intermittent, but |
| T-6...... V.B.9:3 | s. step is easier than the first because it |
| T-6...... V.C.3:3 | the thought reversal, and also from the s., |
| T-6...... V.C.3:4 | the s. as the second follows from the first, |
| T-6...... V.C.3:4 | the second as the s. follows from the first, |
| T-6...... V.C.4:1 | s. may still entail conflict to some extent, |
| T-7...... VIII.3:6 | The s. error is the idea that you can get rid |
| T-9....... VII.1:6 | Every minute and every s. gives you a |
| T-12...... III.2:7 | is to be saved? And s., *how* can it be saved? |
| T-14...... III.4:1 | day, each hour and minute, even each s., |
| T-14...... IV.1:8 | other, for there is no order, no s. or third, |
| T-14...... IV.4:8 | are. Remember that there is no s. to Him. |
| T-15....... II.6:3 | To learn to separate out this single s., and |
| T19....... IV.B.h | The S. Obstacle: The Belief the Body is |
| T19.... IV.B.1:3 | s. obstacle that peace must flow across, |
| T19.... IV.B.4:3 | s. obstacle is no more solid than the first. |
| T-20..... VII.3:3 | The means are s. to the goal. And when |
| T-23....... II.4:1 | The *s.* law of chaos, dear indeed to every |
| T-26..... V.12:3 | now. The real world is the s. part of the |
| T-27.... VIII.5:3 | for the part you see is but the s. part, |
| T-30....... I.16:1 | The s. rule as well is but a fact. For you |
| T-31......... I.8:8 | throughout the world this s. lesson brings |
| T-31..... V.13:5 | the shifting to the s. from the first is that |
| W-in.......... 3:1 | s. with the acquisition of true perception. |
| W-in.......... 6:3 | in it. S., be sure that you do not decide for |
| W-pI..... 10.2:1 | the s. time we have used this kind of idea. |
| W-pI..... 43.5:2 | For the s. and longer phase, close your |
| W-pI..... 43.6:1 | and then attempt the s. phase again. Do |
| W-pI..... 66.7:1 | The s. premise is that God has given you |
| W-pI..... 71.8:3 | become depressed or angry at the s. part; |
| W-pI..... 91.9:1 | In the s. phase of the exercise period, try |
| W-pI... 108.4:1 | first, nor which appears to be in s. place. |
| WpIrIII.in12:3 | This s. chance with each of these ideas |
| W-pI... 123.7:3 | to you in terms of years for every s.; |
| W-pI... 136.3:4 | In that s., even less, in which the choice is |
| WpI. rIV.in1:1 | aware we are preparing for the s. part of |
| W-pI... 152.3:3 | Without the first, the s. has no meaning. |
| W-pI... 152.3:4 | But without the s., is the first no longer |
| W-pI... 187.1:6 | It is the s. phase on which the world and |
| W-pI... 197.1:1 | s. step we take to free your mind from the |
| W-pII .... 328.h | I choose the s. place to gain the first. |
| W-pII . 328.1:1 | What seems to be the s. place is first, for |
| W-pII . 328.1:4 | wills for us, nor is there any s. to His Will. |
| W-pII . 329.1:1 | *a s. will more powerful than Yours. Yet what* |
| M-3 ........... 4:3 | the s. level of teaching is a more sustained |
| M-4 ..... I.A.3:8 | that much, he goes on to the s. stage. |
| M-16 ....... 11:9 | every hour, and even every minute and s., |
| S-1........ IV.1:1 | Until the s. level at least begins, one |

## secondary 2

| | |
|---|---|
| T-20 .... VII.5:6 | to wish, for sight is always s. to desire. |
| S-1........... I.3:3 | harmonics, the echoes, but these are s.. In |

## secrecy 4

| | |
|---|---|
| T-16 ........ I.7:1 | *You* will attempt to do this only in s.. And |
| T-20 ..... VI.3:6 | They live in s., hating the sunlight and |
| T-22 ........ I.4:8 | to be. This is the emotion of s., of private |
| W-pI... 185.8:6 | reserving shame and s. for others. They |

## secret 52

| | |
|---|---|
| T-13 ....... II.3:2 | dark and s. place is the realization that |
| T-13 ....... II.4:4 | question, it guards this one s. with its life, |
| T-13 ....... II.4:4 | its existence depends on keeping this s.. |
| T-13 ....... II.4:5 | So it is this s. that we must look upon, for |
| T-13 ....... II.5:2 | admitted to this "terrible" s. because you |
| T-13 ....... II.9:2 | Your "guilty s." is nothing, and if you will |
| T-13 ..... IX.5:1 | his guilt lies in his s. thought that he has |
| T-14 .... VII.6:1 | every s. you have locked away from Him. |
| T-14 .... VII.6:8 | all your dark and s. thoughts to Him, and |
| T-14 ..... X.10:1 | to remember God in s. and alone. For |
| T-14 ..... X.11:2 | them. God has no s. communications, for |
| T-14 ..... X.11:3 | Nothing lives in s., and what you would |
| T-16 ........ I.7:2 | you keep them separate and s. from each |
| T19... IV.D.3:2 | made in s. to the ego never to lift this veil, |
| T19... IV.D.3:3 | This is the s. bargain made with the ego |
| T19... IV.D.4:6 | For in your s. alliance with them you have |
| T-20 ..... VI.5:2 | speck of darkness; a hidden s. room, a |
| T-21 ..... II.13:3 | separate from your Father, you made in s. |
| T-22 ........ I.4:1 | What could be s. from God's Will? Yet |
| T-22 ........ I.4:4 | this is no s. that need be hidden as a sin. |
| T-23 ..... II.11:2 | this priceless pearl, this hidden s. treasure |
| T-23 ..... II.12:8 | Behold, unveiled, the ego's s. gift, torn |
| T-23 ..... II.12:9 | He would deprive you of the s. ingredient |
| T-24 ........ I.2:2 | belief is a decision to war in s., where the |
| T-24 ........ I.2:6 | there. The s. enemies of peace, your least |
| T-24 ..... III.1:8 | so. And thus his s. guilt would disappear, |
| T-24 ..... III.4:6 | a s. vow that what God wants for you will |
| T-25 ..... IX.9:1 | you keep and hide become your s. sins, |
| T-27 .. VII.11:4 | of the world and what you dream in s.. |
| T-27 .. VII.11:7 | Yet was it started by your s. dream, which |
| T-27 .. VII.11:8 | and dream in s. that its cause is real? |
| T-27 .. VII.12:2 | you become the murderer, the s. enemy, |
| T-27 . VIII.10:1 | The s. of salvation is but this: that you |
| T-27 . VIII.12:4 | is a s. you have kept but from yourself. |
| T-27 . VIII.12:8 | They seem to keep it s. from you. Yet you |
| T-27 . VIII.13:4 | a s. kept from no one but yourself. And it |
| T-27 . VIII.13:8 | This is the only s. yet to learn. And it will |
| T-27 . VIII.13:9 | learn. And it will be no s. you are healed. |
| T-28 ........ VI.h | The S. Vows |
| T-28 ..... VI.4:3 | the s. vow that you have made with every |
| T-28 ..... VI.4:4 | apart. This is the s. oath you take again, |
| T-28 ..... VI.5:2 | the obvious effect of what was made in s., |
| T-28 ..... VI.5:2 | another's s. wish to be apart from you, as |
| T-28 ..... VI.6:8 | His s. vows are powerless before the Will |
| T-28 .... VII.7:2 | No s. promise you have made instead has |
| T-31 ..... V.15:8 | see a picture of your s. wishes. Nothing |
| T-31 ... VIII.9:2 | hell, the s. sins and hidden hates be gone. |
| W-pI .. 102.1:4 | dark and hidden s. places of your mind. |
| W-pI .. 127.5:2 | love's meaning, and to keep it dark and s.. |
| W-pI .. 136.3:2 | They are s., magic wands you wave when |
| W-pI .. 190.4:3 | or s. sins with weighty consequence. Who |
| S-1........... I.4:1 | s. of true prayer is to forget the things you |

## secretly 1

| | |
|---|---|
| T-16 ........ I.7:6 | He will not meet them s., for He would |

## secrets 10

| | |
|---|---|
| T19 ... IV.C.7:6 | For in it lie hidden all the ego's s., all its |
| T19 .. IV.D.8:4 | It does not open up its s., and bid you |
| T-20 ..... VI.2:6 | It has no s.; nothing that it would keep |
| T-20 ..... VI.3:6 | and keep their s. hidden along with them. |
| T-22 ...... I.3:10 | it. God has no s.. He does not lead you |
| T-22 ........ I.4:2 | Yet you believe that you have s.. What |
| T-22 ........ I.4:3 | What could your s. be except another |
| T-22 ..... VI.9:5 | Save no dark s. that He cannot use, but |
| T-28 ....... V.7:5 | no awesome s. and no darkened tombs |
| W-pI .... 99.8:4 | Open your s. to His kindly light, and see |

## sectarian 1

| | |
|---|---|
| M-24 ......... 3:5 | part of wisdom to add s. controversies to |

## section 1

| | |
|---|---|
| W-pII .. in.10:2 | done. For in this final s., we will come to |

## sections 3

| | |
|---|---|
| T-1 ...... VII.4:3 | earlier s. not to require their careful study |
| T-1 ...... VII.4:6 | as you study these earlier s., you will |
| W-in.......... 3:1 | The workbook is divided into two main s. |

## secure 26

| | |
|---|---|
| T-2 ......... II.7:8 | and as you become more and more s. you |
| T-7 ....... IX.6:1 | thus have not failed to s. it for yourself. |
| T-8 .......... I.3:3 | of reality that you must make to s. peace, |
| T-16 ....... V.4:2 | attempt to s. for the self the specialness |
| T-17 ... VIII.2:6 | and s. for you the faith you need for peace |
| T-24 ...... in.1:8 | back the Will that holds the universe s.? |
| T-24 ..... III.4:1 | Without foundation nothing is s.. Would |
| T-24 ..... VII.5:5 | and if that is true, its safety rests s.. If not, |
| W-pI .. 95.12:1 | united and s. in light and joy and peace. |
| W-pI .. 124.8:2 | S. your peace by practicing awareness you |
| W-pI 135.11:5 | It is s. in certainty that obstacles can not |
| W-pI .. 153.9:3 | in defenselessness we stand s., serenely |
| W-pI 153.10:1 | how holy is your purpose, how s. you rest, |
| W-pI 155.13:6 | your pathway certain and your goal s.. |
| W-pI .. 162.3:2 | His dreams are happy and his rest s., his |
| W-pI .. 170.1:5 | more s. from dangerous invasion and |
| W-pI 186.10:4 | change ten times an hour at their most s.. |
| W-pI .. 197.7:4 | His Being in His Father is s., because |
| W-pII . 224.1:1 | My true Identity is so s., so lofty, sinless, |
| W-pII . 244.2:3 | In God we are s.. For what can come to |
| W-pII . 277.1:3 | *by which I try to make the body more s.. He is* |
| W-pII . 283.1:6 | *Is not what is beloved of You s.? Is not the* |
| W-pII . 317.2:3 | *way is certain, and the end s.. The memory of* |
| W-pII . 351.1:5 | *Friend beside me, and my way s. and clear.* |
| M-4 ........ II.2:6 | teachers rest s. makes doubt impossible. |
| S-2......... in.1:4 | come to hold you up and keep your feet s. |

## secured 1

| | |
|---|---|
| W-pI .. 102.1:4 | lacks the roots that once s. it tightly to the |

## securely 2

| | |
|---|---|
| T-26 ....... II.8:5 | to hold the door s. barred and locked will |
| W-pI .... 92.2:3 | your hand, s. bound until you let it go. |

## securing 1

W-pI...105.4:5 it has away, s. it forever for itself.

## security 11

T-5........VI.2:4 It gives the ego a false sense of s. by
T-9...........I.9:4 sacrifices. In the s. of reality, fear is totally
W-pI.....56.1:5 Yet perfect s. and complete fulfillment are
W-pI...131.2:7 You look for safety and s., while in your
W-pI...194.8:4 has himself appealed for comfort and s..
W-pII.....261.h God is my refuge and s..
W-pII..261.1:1 identify with what I think is refuge and s..
W-pII..261.1:3 Let me today seek not s. in danger, nor
W-pII....10.3:2 return to peace, s. and happiness, and
W-pII..314.1:5 extending its s. and peace into a quiet
P-2........IV.9:6 become the patient's s. as he perceives it,

## see 1706

T-1........ I.22:2 your physical eyes cannot s. does not exist
T-1........III.5:3 to establish your kingdom where you s. fit
T-1.......VII.4:6 will begin to s. some of the implications
T-2.......III.1:11 cannot s. the structure at all because it is
T-2.......III.1:12 however, s. the altar with perfect clarity.
T-2........III.4:1 Spiritual vision literally cannot s. error,
T-2......... V.7:3 before that the Holy Spirit cannot s. error
T-2......... V.8:4 cannot endure to s. your own defiled altar
T-2.........V.10:2 he cannot s. the Atonement for himself,
T-3...........I.5:4 the pure in heart for they shall s. God" is
T-3...........I.6:7 to those who do not choose to s..
T-3......... II.2:5 you never misperceive and always s. truly.
T-3......... II.2:6 that you never s. what does not exist, and
T-3......... II.2:6 does not exist, and always s. what does.
T-3......... II.3:5 seeing cannot s. anything but perfection.
T-3......... II.3:7 This, then, is all the innocent can s.. They
T-3......... II.5:9 wish to attack, and therefore they s. truly.
T-3....... II.5:10 be like him, for we shall s. him as he is."
T-3......... II.6:6 Because you s. them as they are, you offer
T-3........III.2:3 can s. in many ways because perception
T-3......... V.9:2 have chosen to s. themselves as separate.
T-3........VI.4:3 This is why you s. it in nightmares, or in
T-3.......VI.10:6 so that you s. yourself only in segments.
T-3.......VII.5:3 at your life and s. what the devil has made
T-4......... II.3:3 only recognize it to s. that it does happen.
T-4........III.7:4 No one can s. through a wall, but I can
T-4........III.8:1 and s. what it is you are really asking for.
T-4........IV.1:6 glass in which the ego seeks to s. its face is
T-4........IV.2:9 and s. in both the glorious creations of a
T-4........IV.6:3 you will s. how your mind can focus and
T-5........III.3:4 him. S. him through the Holy Spirit in his
T-5........IV.6:7 You must learn to s. them as they are, and
T-6........III.3:1 because as you s. His gentleness in others
T-6........IV.6:7 wake you will s. the truth around you and
T-7......... II.1:3 If you, too, s. him this way, you are seeing
T-7........III.2:5 can s. yourself as separated from your
T-7........III.3:2 and recognize all whom you s. as brothers
T-7......... V.8:7 s. only the changeless in him you have not
T-7......... V.9:1 hear two voices, so you can s. in two ways.
T-7..... V.10:10 S. only this Mind everywhere, because
T-7........V.11:2 as we s. them truly they will be healed. Let
T-7........VI.1:2 to s. something in part of it that you will
T-7........VI.8:3 as you are, it can s. itself as it wants to be.
T-7.......VI.11:1 who s. themselves as weakened do attack.
T-7.......VII.3:6 Do not s. this picture in anyone, or you
T-7.......VII.3:9 is the mirror in which you s. the image of
T-7.....VII.10:4 But s. the Love of God in you, and you
T-7.....VII.10:4 and you will s. it everywhere because it *is*
T-7.....VII.10:5 S. His abundance in everyone, and you
T-7......... X.1:4 it is because you do not s. the whole of it.
T-7......... X.2:4 ability to s. a logical outcome depends on
T-7......... X.2:4 depends on the willingness to s. it, but its
T-7.......XI.3:11 you s. and touch and remember, are
T-7........XI.6:6 and you must have the glory you s. in him
T-8........III.4:2 As you s. him you will see yourself. As you
T-8........III.4:2 As you see him you will s. yourself. As you
T-8........III.8:8 is. S. this glory everywhere to remember
T-8.......VII.3:6 Holy Spirit does not s. the body as you do
T-8.......VII.4:4 will s. the use to which you have put yours
T-8.......VII.4:5 not s. anything physical except as what it
T-8.......VII.4:6 is. Use it for truth and you will s. it truly.
T-8.......VII.5:5 not s. him this way for your own salvation
T-8.....VII.12:4 temptation to s. the body in many lights,
T-8.....VII.13:3 To s. a body as anything except a means
T-8.....VII.14:3 Whenever you s. another as limited to or
T-8.....VII.15:7 When you s. a brother as a body, you are
T-8........ IX.3:4 way of trying not to s. by rendering the
T-9.........I.11:7 you will not s. because you are interfering
T-9....... II.12:6 *myself, I s. you as God's Son and my brother.*
T-9........ III.6:3 Yet you can s. him truly, because it is
T-9........ III.6:3 it is possible for you to s. yourself truly. It
T-9........ III.7:3 it, s. only truth beside you for you walk
T-9......III.8:10 how to s. yourself without condemnation,
T-9........ IV.1:5 what you are, because you s. him falsely.
T-9........ IV.4:4 plan is to have you s. error clearly first,
T-9......... V.9:2 If you do it, you will s. that it works. Its
T-9........ VI.1:2 s. Him with your eyes nor hear Him with
T-9........ VI.1:5 if you s. that it does produce joy in others,
T-9........ VI.4:3 yours is dimmed because you do not s..
T-9........ VI.4:6 your wholeness until you s. it everywhere.
T-9........ VI.5:3 As you s. them waken you will learn what
T-9.......VII.5:1 choose to s. yourself as unloving you will
T-9.......VII.6:3 where sanity exists and *s. the contrast.*
T-10.........I.2:3 that what you s. in dreams you think is
T-10....III.11:5 For if you s. the god of sickness anywhere,
T-10......IV.1:9 you, and wherever you think you s. him,
T-10......IV.5:7 want it, if you were willing to s. it as it is.
T-10......IV.5:8 You will s. nothing at all. And your vision
T-10......IV.8:3 If you but s. the little spark you will learn
T-10....... V.2:4 s. the spark in them that would bring joy
T-10....... V.2:5 whenever you s. your brothers without it,
T-10..... V.12:5 must learn to s. him to learn of his reality.
T-10..... V.12:6 how you must s. yourself to learn of yours
T-11.....in.3:10 will s. that it rested on meaninglessness,
T-11.........I.5:9 S. His creations as His Son, for yours were
T-11.......I.5:10 love does not stop because you do not s. it
T-11.......I.5:10 have your closed eyes lost the ability to s..
T-11....... II.7:4 for it still depends on how you s. it. The
T-11......III.1:7 being blind it does not s. whom it attacks.
T-11......III.3:3 you will s. such beauty that you will know
T-11......III.4:6 light and do not s. the dark companions,
T-11......III.4:8 How can you s. the dark companions in a
T-11......III.4:9 If you s. them, it is only because you are
T-11....... V.1:5 we must look first at this to s. beyond it,
T-11..... V.16:9 straight at the Father and does not s. Him
T-11..... V.17:4 s. of His Son through the eyes of the ego is
T-11......VI.1:1 It is impossible not to believe what you s.
T-11......VI.1:1 impossible to s. what you do not believe.
T-11......VI.1:4 In effect, then, what you believe you *do* s..
T-11......VI.1:5 who believe in the resurrection will s. it.
T-11......VI.3:2 If you do not s. it clearly, it is because you
T-11......VI.3:9 try to limit what you s. by narrow little
T-11....VI.3:10 Son of God will s. himself as Fatherless.
T-11......VI.8:4 but what you s. in dreams is not reality.
T-11......VI.9:3 you must s. the works I do through you,
T-11.....VII.1:1 the Father, for the world is not as you s. it
T-11.....VII.1:2 everything you s. is perishable. Therefore,
T-11.....VII.1:3 must be another world that you do not s..
T-11.....VII.1:6 that awaits your perception when you s. it
T-11.....VII.3:1 The ego may s. some good, but never
T-11... VIII.2:5 you will s. no need to ask it of Him.
T-11... VIII.4:7 you will have it, for you will s. it as it is,
T-11... VIII.7:4 You are afraid of the world as you s. it,
T-11... VIII.9:2 s. only his loving thoughts as his reality,
T-11. VIII.10:6 you will s. your beauty reflected in his.
T-11VIII.14:10 you s. you need reality to dispel your fears
T-12.........I.3:7 his reality by interpreting it as you s. fit.
T-12.......I.8:12 if you s. attack as the call for help that it is
T-12....... II.7:1 A little while and you will s. me, for I am
T-12....... II.8:7 believed when you s. it as accomplished.
T-12....... II.9:5 in any way–this is what you will really s..
T-12......III.8:2 perceive its reality cannot s. the world of
T-12....III.10:7 There you will s. your vision changed,
T-12....III.10:7 and there you will learn to s. truly. From
T-12......IV.7:6 will not s. life though it is all around you.
T-12....... V.1:2 attack because they s. no need to do so.
T-12....... V.2:5 you will no longer s. any sense in attack,
T-12......VI.4:1 Correction is for all who cannot s.. To
T-12......VI.4:4 will look upon whatever you s. with love if
T-12..... VII.2:2 You cannot s. the invisible. Yet if you see
T-12..... VII.2:3 s. its effects you know it must be there. By
T-12..... VII.2:6 is. You cannot s. your strengths, but you
T-12..... VII.2:7 And the results of your actions you *can* s..
T-12..... VII.3:1 but you can s. the results of His Presence,
T-12..... VII.4:1 You cannot s. the Holy Spirit, but you
T-12..... VII.4:1 Spirit, but you can s. His manifestations.
T-12..... VII.4:4 What you cannot s. becomes real to you
T-12..... VII.4:5 you can be aware of what you cannot s.,
T-12..... VII.5:1 You s. what you expect, and you expect
T-12..... VII.5:3 Whose manifestations would you s.? Of
T-12..... VII.5:5 and as you look out so will you s. in. Two
T-12..... VII.6:1 and when you s. me it will be because you
T-12..... VII.6:3 always that you s. what you seek, for what
T-12..... VII.8:1 want only love you will s. nothing else.
T-12..... VII.9:2 You can decide to s. it right. What you
T-12... VII.11:1 for by making it manifest you will s. it. Its
T-12... VII.11:6 And you will s. me as you look within,
T-12... VII.11:8 As you decide so will you s.. And all that
T-12... VII.11:9 that you s. but witnesses to your decision.
T-12... VII.12:1 When you look within and s. me, it will
T-12... VII.12:2 manifest it you will s. it both without and
T-12... VII.12:3 will s. it without *because* you saw it first
T-12... VII.13:1 and react unfavorably to what you s., you
T-12... VII.15:2 this is true when you look within and *s.* me
T-12... VII.15:5 make me manifest, you will never s. death
T-12... VII.15:6 you will s. only the eternal as you look out
T-12.... VIII.1:3 yet you are surprised that you cannot s. it.
T-12.... VIII.4:3 the perception of everything you s.. For
T-12.... VIII.6:5 because the Holy Spirit does not s. it. Yet
T-12.... VIII.6:6 it. Yet what He does s. is yours to behold,
T-12.... VIII.8:1 the world you made and the world you s..
T-13.......in.2:2 The world you s. is the delusional system
T-13.......in.4:2 be crucified, this is the world you will s..
T-13.........I.2:2 How could you s. him, then? By making
T-13.........I.5:1 will s. me as you learn the Son of God is
T-13........II.9:4 will s. that you were redeemed with him,
T-13...... III.8:4 place of truth as you s. it in your brothers,
T-13.... III.12:9 look back on them and s. them as insane.
T-13....... V.2:3 Therefore, he does not s. he made them,
T-13....... V.3:2 For they s. only those who remind them
T-13....... V.3:5 perception, and you cannot s. beyond it.
T-13....... V.4:4 Yet what is within they do not s., for the
T-13....... V.5:3 If you s. your own hatred as your brother,
T-13....... V.5:7 love your brothers offer you, you do not s.
T-13....... V.6:2 You s. what is not there, and you hear
T-13....... V.6:5 s. only your own split mind everywhere
T-13....... V.7:8 will s. all that you denied in your brothers
T-13....... V.8:2 on light. You cannot s. in darkness. Yet in
T-13....... V.8:3 S. in dreams although your eyes are closed
T-13....... V.8:4 And it is here that what you s. you made.
T-13....... V.8:5 go and all you made you will no longer s.,
T-13....... V.8:6 vision it does not follow you cannot s..
T-13....... V.8:9 when light has come and you can s..
T-13....... V.9:1 of seeing that you might s. in darkness,
T-13..... V.10:3 S. through the vision that is given you, for
T-13..... V.10:6 And this *you* will s. as you look with Him,
T-13..... V.11:2 all who would behold Him can s. Him, for
T-13..... V.11:3 Nor will they s. Him alone, for He is no
T-13...... VI.1:3 perceive a brother only as you s. him *now.*
T-13...... VI.1:4 reality in the present, so you cannot s. it.
T-13...... VI.1:5 you s. but an image of him that you made
T-13...... VI.2:3 will be able to learn from what you s. *now.*
T-13...... VI.2:5 s. it as a dark cloud that shrouds your
T-13...... VI.3:4 meet because you s. Him through Himself
T-13...... VI.3:6 it past and gone, you must not s. it now. If
T-13...... VI.3:7 If you s. it now in your illusions, it has not
T-13...... VI.5:1 you to s. your brother without his past,
T-13...... VI.5:6 where it is, and it will dawn on eyes that s.
T-13...... VI.5:7 not s. the freedom that the present holds.
T-13...... VI.6:1 you, you will s. that you are free of them.
T-13...... VI.9:2 in their wholeness you will s. your own.
T-13.... VI.10:3 Each one you s. in light brings your light
T-13.... VI.12:7 You do not s. your brothers, and in the
T-13..... VII.1:1 Sit quietly and look upon the world you s.
T-13..... VII.2:1 The world you s. must be denied, for
T-13..... VII.2:2 *You cannot s. both worlds,* for each of them
T-13..... VII.3:1 You do not really want the world you s.,
T-13..... VII.5:2 twisted reference point, what could you s.

T-13.....VII.5:4 And what he judges false he does not s..
T-13.....VII.5:5 You who would judge reality cannot s. it,
T-13.....VII.9:6 them you s. nothing fearful, and because
T-13.....VIII.5:3 know this until you s. that every aspect is
T-13.....VIII.5:4 the darkness, and enabling the world to s.
T-13.....VIII.6:4 all, as every aspect of reality you s. blends
T-13......IX.3:2 faithful unto darkness and you will not s.,
T-13......IX.4:3 of God is guiltless because you s. the past,
T-13......IX.4:3 because you see the past, and s. him not.
T-13......IX.6:1 S. no one, then, as guilty, and you will
T-13......IX.6:6 Those whom you s. as guilty become the
T-13......IX.6:6 to guilt in you, and you will s. it there, for
T-13......IX.7:1 while you s. one spot of guilt within you,
T-13......IX.7:1 guilt within you, you will not s. the light.
T-13......IX.7:3 s. it because you cannot look within. You
T-13......IX.7:4 You are afraid of what you would s. there,
T-13......IX.7:6 within you would s. only the Atonement,
T-13......IX.8:3 your brothers, and s. the guilt in them.
T-13......IX.8:5 those who s. their brothers in the dark,
T-13....IX.8:11 Can you s. guilt where God knows there is
T-13.......X.1:1 can s. the source of pain where it is not.
T-13.......X.3:3 will s. guilt in that relationship because
T-13.......X.4:5 past, and still to s. them as they really are
T-13.......X.5:4 to your Father, you will s. no guilt in you.
T-13.......X.5:5 guilt, and would not look within and s. it.
T-13.......X.7:3 no reality to guilt, and s. no reason for it.
T-13.......X.7:7 would have you s. and teach as He does,
T-13.......X.9:6 the holy place where you will s. the light.
T-13.......X.9:8 from you what Christ would have you s..
T-13.....X.10:2 way to look within and s. the light of love,
T-13.....X.10:5 to look within and s. your holiness. You
T-13...X.10:10 All else He would have you s.. And in
T-13.....X.11:7 who condemns a brother can s. himself as
T-13.....X.12:5 for what you s. will banish guilt forever. I
T-13.....X.14:5 S. only praise of Him in what He has
T-13......XI.1:4 look upon himself and s. his freedom. No
T-14.........I.4:4 created only to create, neither to s. nor do
T-14.........I.5:2 you cannot s. that it means nothing. He
T-14.........I.5:4 lies upon your mind, cannot s. through it.
T-14.......II.2:6 is perfectly apparent, yet you do not s. it.
T-14.......II.4:4 And as it shines your brothers s. it, and
T-14.......II.4:4 made, they s. in you more than you see.
T-14.......II.4:4 made, they see in you more than you s..
T-14.......II.4:6 them to despair they do not s. as nothing,
T-14.......II.4:7 then they s. the chains have disappeared,
T-14.......II.4:8 And you will s. it with them. Because you
T-14.......II.5:5 Yet s. that this has been your goal, and
T-14......III.2:3 for without both you do not s. yourself as
T-14......III.8:7 and nothing else can His Son s. or choose
T-14....III.10:2 and will not refuse to s. it and side with it.
T-14......IV.1:1 you will s. the Atonement in him. For by
T-14......IV.1:2 it yours, and you will s. what you sought.
T-14......IV.1:3 will not s. the symbol of your brother's
T-14......IV.1:5 and you will s. the truth of what you have
T-14.......V.7:3 You will not s. yourself beyond the power
T-14.....V.10:5 restore guiltlessness to whomever you s.
T-14.....V.11:1 Each one you s. you place within the holy
T-14.....VII.2:8 you s. no reason to believe that the more
T-14.....VII.2:8 the more you look at fear the less you s. it,
T-14...VII.5:15 You will s. how easily all that He asks can
T-14.....VII.6:6 unless you look with Him He cannot s..
T-14.....VII.7:2 You cannot s. alone. Sharing perception
T-14.....VII.7:3 teaches you how to recognize what you s..
T-14.....VII.7:4 that nothing you s. means anything alone
T-14......IX.6:5 the mirror holds out for everyone to s., no
T-14......IX.6:8 then, s. it in you and share it with you.
T-14.....X.10:6 that what you s. is given meaning. The
T-14......XI.3:8 in which you try to s. can only obscure.
T-14......XI.3:9 and thereby think you s. the darkness.
T-14....XI.9:10 He does not s. time as you do. And each
T-14....XI.15:3 Yet s. the mighty works that He will do
T-15.......I.10:5 taught by those who cannot s. themselves
T-15.......I.10:7 you s. yourself as bright with freedom,
T-15.......V.8:3 s. them all the same and like yourself. Nor
T-15.......V.8:4 Nor would you s. any separation between
T-15.......V.8:5 you s. in each relationship what it will be
T-15.......V.9:7 free of the past, you s. that love is in you,
T-15...VII.12:3 And you will s. safety in guilt and danger
T-15......IX.1:1 you s. the Great Rays shining from them,
T-15 .....IX.3:2 But in order to s. this, it is necessary to
T-15 .....IX.5:5 only those whom you would s. without
T-15 .....IX.6:1 idea of all the loveliness that you could s..
T-15 .......X.2:4 And to s. me is to see me in everyone, and
T-15 .......X.2:4 And to see me is to s. me in everyone, and
T-15 .......X.5:6 You s. no other alternatives, for you
T-15 .......X.7:4 For you s. love as destructive, and your
T-15 .......X.8:1 do not s. that only you demand sacrifice,
T-15 .......X.9:7 try to project it from you and s. it outside
T-15 .....XI.1:4 you think you s. some scraps of safety. Do
T-15 .....XI.2:2 S. it not outside yourself, but shining in
T-15 .....XI.7:2 provided that you s. not the body as the
T-16 .......II.1:1 understand, because you cannot s. how it
T-16 .......II.8:1 and deaf could fail to s. and hear them.
T-16 .....III.4:3 to s. the real cause and effect relationship
T-16 .....IV.4:6 it. This is the choice they s.. And love, to
T-16 ....IV.11:4 not the call of hate, and s. no fantasies.
T-16 ....IV.11:6 S. in the call of hate, and in every fantasy
T-16 ......V.2:2 For the ego would have you s. Him, and
T-16 ......V.4:4 you s. that separation could only be loss,
T-16 ......V.8:3 partners s. this special self in each other,
T-16 ....V.11:4 S. how exactly is this ritual enacted in the
T-16 ....V.13:1 S. in the special relationship nothing
T-16 .....VI.5:1 You s. the world you value. On this side
T-16 .....VI.5:2 bridge you s. the world of separate bodies
T-16 .....VI.6:4 that you will s. no need at all to magnify it
T-16 .....VI.7:2 everything you s. is grossly distorted and
T-16 ...VI.10:3 sickness and despair, and s. it thus. What
T-16 ...VI.10:5 S. no illusion of truth and beauty there.
T-17 .......I.6:8 will s. forgiveness where you have given it
T-17 .......II.1:3 Nothing you s. here, sleeping or waking,
T-17 .......II.1:6 For you will s. the Son of God. You will
T-17 .......II.1:8 He was created to s. this for you, until you
T-17 .......II.1:8 you, until you learned to s. it for yourself.
T-17 .......II.3:5 by your own forgiveness you are free to s..
T-17 .......II.3:6 Yet what you s. is only what you made,
T-17 .......II.5:1 old, the world you s. without forgiveness.
T-17 .......II.6:2 lets you s. the real world reaching quietly
T-17 .....III.2:4 is why you s. in both what is not there,
T-17 .....III.6:9 so you can s. it more and more. For you
T-17 .....IV.9:5 is the frame, for there you s. no conflict.
T-17 ...IV.11:3 accept this gift you will not s. the frame at
T-17 . IV.12:10 picture, hard to s. at all beneath the heavy
T-17 ...IV.14:7 s. there you will recognize as what it is; a
T-17 ...IV.14:8 beyond this picture you will s. nothing.
T-17 ....V.7:12 you will s. the justification for your faith
T-17 ....V.10:5 that you may s. that in it rests salvation.
T-17 ....V.11:5 Nor does He s. the mistakes at all. Have
T-17 .....VI.5:6 truth has come to you and you will s. the
T-17 .....VI.5:8 again you s. the opposite of the ego's way
T-17 ....VII.1:4 As a result, you do not s. the problem.
T-17 ....VII.2:5 has been done, and where you s. it done.
T-17 ....VII.4:5 for you will s. that peace and faith will not
T-17 ....VII.5:2 relationship. S. it as something else and
T-17 ....VII.9:3 will s. the means you once employed to
T-17 ...VIII.4:6 faith to truth, and s. its evident reality.
T-17 ...VIII.5:8 S. only this in every situation, and it will
T-18 ........I.4:6 it. Everything you s. reflects it, and every
T-18 ........I.5:1 very different is reality from what you s..
T-18 ........I.7:1 When you seem to s. some twisted form
T-18 .......II.3:1 you s. in sleep and on awaking disturbing
T-18 .......II.3:2 you s. on waking is blotted out in dreams.
T-18 .......II.5:1 be, and that because you want it you s. it.
T-18 .......II.5:2 you s. it you do not doubt that it is real.
T-18 .....II.5:11 form of this same world you s. in dreams.
T-18 .....II.5:20 while you s. more value in sleeping than
T-18 .......II.8:6 dreams you do not s. that you have made,
T-18 .....III.6:3 Those who would s. *will* see. And they will
T-18 .....III.6:3 Those who would see *will* s.. And they will
T-18 .....VI.7:5 You s. yourself locked in a separate prison
T-18 ....VII.2:4 Afterwards you will s. the body again, but
T-18 ....VII.4:1 you are willing to s. no past or future. You
T-18 ...VIII.1:5 s. yourself within a body know yourself as
T-18 ...VIII.2:2 not s. the grandeur that surrounds you.
T-18 ...VIII.3:3 you would s. instantly that it is like the
T-18 ...VIII.9:2 S. how life springs up everywhere! The
T-18 .VIII.10:4 s. your little garden gently transformed
T-18 .....IX.4:5 The body cannot s. this, for the body
T-18 .....IX.4:7 look on it. Yet they will s. what it dictates.
T-18 .....IX.5:3 apparent until you s. the light behind it.
T-18 .....IX.5:4 you s. it as a fragile veil before the light.
T-18 .....IX.6:3 willing to climb above it and s. the sun. It
T-18 .....IX.7:1 bank it is easy to s. a whole world rising.
T-19 ........I.2:3 Thus do you s. him free, and in this vision
T-19 ........I.3:4 that a segment of the mind can s. itself as
T-19 ........I.4:3 If, then, you s. your brother as a body,
T-19 ........I.8:2 You do not s. how great the devastation
T-19 ........I.8:3 withholding faith you s. what is unworthy
T-19 ........I.9:6 that one you s. your faith is fully justified.
T-19 .......I.10:6 You s. the Christ in him, and he is healed
T-19 .......I.11:4 s. in him only what it would see in you. It
T-19 .......I.11:4 see in him only what it would s. in you. It
T-19 .......I.12:7 Yet faith unites you in the holiness you s.,
T-19 .......I.14:3 There will you s. the miracle of your
T-19 .....III.3:2 s. clearly as a mistake you want corrected.
T-19 .....III.5:5 look on time differently and s. beyond it,
T-19 .....III.8:6 You s. it still, because you do not realize
T-19 .....III.9:2 You will not s. sin long. For in the new
T-19 ...III.10:1 you will s. the smile of Heaven shining on
T-19 ...III.10:5 your eyes in faith to what you now can s..
T-19 ...III.10:6 have been given vision, and you can s..
T-19 ...III.10:7 glory that has been restored for you to s..
T-19 .....IV.2:4 be sure of nothing you s. outside you, but
T-19 .....IV.3:4 You cannot s. the Holy Spirit, but you can
T-19 .....IV.3:4 Spirit, but you can s. your brothers truly.
T-19 .....IV.3:5 them will show you all that you need to s..
T19 ...IV.A.9:4 S. but how easily this little wisp is lifted
T19 .IV.A.10:3 look past fear, so must fear s. love not.
T19 .IV.A.11:5 What fear demands, love cannot even s..
T19 .IV.A.12:7 they pounce on any living thing they s.,
T19 .IV.A.14:3 they will s. only the blameless and the
T19 .IV.A.14:8 of safety, for they s. the world as kind.
T19 .IV.A.15:1 but theirs, you will s. fear no more. The
T19 .IV.A.15:4 to remove from it, and s. it still. The Holy
T19 ...IV.B.2:7 you not s. that this is the belief in death?
T19 ...IV.B.3:3 the messengers of fear that s. the body,
T19 ...IV.B.6:6 Would you s. in me the symbol of guilt or
T19 ...IV.B.6:6 I signify to you you s. within yourself?
T19 .IV.B.10:8 can s. the means for its accomplishment,
T19 ...IV.C.2:6 S. him throw aside the black robe he was
T19 ...IV.C.7:1 who fear death s. not how often and how
T19 .IV.C.10:7 your brother, and s. in it the Will of God.
T19 .IV.C.11:9 *Let me not s. it as a sign of sin and death, nor*
T19 .. IV.D.1:1 would you s. without the fear of death?
T19 .. IV.D.4:1 S. how the belief in death would seem to
T19 .. IV.D.8:5 It would not have you s. its weakness, and
T19 IV.D.10:7 end before you, you s. its purpose. And it
T19 IV.D.12:5 s. his madness, which you hate because
T19 IV.D15:10 and all the guilt you think you s. in him.
T19 IV.D.17:3 and s. in him the gift of God you would
T19 IV.D.18:3 S. him as guiltless as I look on you, and
T19 IV.D.21:7 you to s. this purpose in your holy Friend,
T-20 ........I.4:2 s. glimpses of the face of Christ behind
T-20 .......II.1:2 S. all the useless things made for its eyes
T-20 .......II.1:2 the useless things made for its eyes to s..
T-20 .......II.3:4 that they may s. what he has placed upon
T-20 .......II.4:5 s. what you have laid upon it to offer me.
T-20 .......II.4:8 will s. your altar is no longer what it was.
T-20 .......II.5:1 body's eyes, and they can s. but thorns.
T-20 .......II.5:4 And what enables Him to s. His purpose
T-20 .......II.6:3 use your gift of lilies while you s. them not
T-20 .......II.7:2 It has been given you to s. no thorns, no
T-20 .......II.7:8 s. no thorns nor nails to crucify the Son of
T-20 .......II.8:3 You will not s. it with the body's eyes. Yet
T-20 .....III.3:2 their holiness, and rejoice at what they s..
T-20 .....III.3:4 And so they s. that it was in them, not
T-20 .....III.3:5 and it is what they s. that answers them.
T-20 .....III.4:4 you think you are; of how you s. yourself.
T-20 .....III.4:7 is sad within, and s. the sadness there.
T-20 .....III.5:2 world you s. is but a judgment on yourself
T-20 .....III.5:5 Such is the world you s.; a judgment on
T-20 .....III.6:2 The world the holy s. is one with them,
T-20 .....III.6:3 The world the holy s. is beautiful because
T-20 .....III.6:3 because they s. their innocence in it. They
T-20 .....III.6:8 that made it as you s. it is not outside you.
T-20 .....III.8:8 Did you s. the holiness that shone in both
T-20 ...III.11:5 The innocent s. safety, and the pure in
T-20 ...III.11:5 the pure in heart s. God within His Son,

T-20.III.11:9 S. him as sinless, and there can *be* no fear
T-20.IV.2:2 lies your need to s. your brother sinless.
T-20.IV.2:4 S. sin in him instead, and Heaven is lost
T-20.IV.2:5 you. But s. him as he is, and what is yours
T-20.IV.3:3 would s. within your savior from insanity
T-20.IV.3:4 that you s. in him you see your own. For
T-20.IV.3:4 that you see in him you s. your own. For
T-20.IV.4:3 this can touch them, for they s. only this,
T-20.IV.5:2 S., then, the power of sinlessness within
T-20.IV.5:6 upon the face of Christ, and s. Him sinless
T-20.IV.6:2 the rest will s. to it without your help. But
T-20.V.3:4 your judgment you cannot even s. it?
T-20.V.3:5 is invisible to you or you will never s. it,
T-20.V.3:6 It will be given you to s. your brother's
T-20.V.4:5 for who would s. the face of Christ and yet
T-20.V.4:6 this insistence is of those who do not s..
T-20.V.7:10 And through His vision will you s. it, and
T-20.VI.3:8 those who smile on them they do not s..
T-20.VI.4:4 for what they are it does not even s.. It
T-20.VI.6:8 your brother, and would not s. in him, is
T-20.VII.4:1 *is* impossible to s. your brother as sinless
T-20.VII.4:4 To s. a sinless body is impossible, for
T-20.VII.5:7 And if you s. the body, you have chosen
T-20.VII.5:9 has no order. You either s. or not.
T-20.VII.6:2 not. He does not really s. him as sinful; he
T-20.VII.6:2 see him as sinful; he does not s. him at all.
T-20.VII.8:2 s. the body is the sign that you lack vision,
T-20.VII.8:5 cannot s. the body because it cannot look
T-20.VII.8:8 Attempt to s. him not in darkness, for
T-20.VII.8:10 as worth the seeing, and so you will not s..
T-20.VII.9:1 can I s. my brother without the body?"
T-20.VII.9:2 only, "Do I really wish to s. him sinless?"
T-20.VII.9:8 he did not make, for it was given him to s.
T-20.VIII.1:1 is given you who s. your brother sinless.
T-20.VIII.2:8 you who would but s. your brother sinless
T-20.VIII.2:10 is freely given to those who ask to s..
T-20.VIII.3:3 Be willing, then, to s. your brother sinless,
T-20.VIII.3:5 It is his desire to s. his sinlessness, as it is
T-20.VIII.3:6 nor s. in him what you have made of him.
T-20.VIII.4:3 vision that enables you to s. the body not.
T-20.VIII.4:4 brother, you will s. an altar to your Father
T-20.VIII.6:8 All that could save you, you will never s..
T-20.VIII.7:6 Could you have faith in what you s., if you
T-20.VIII.7:7 if you accepted this? And would you s. it?
T-20.VIII.9:3 which you choose determines what you s.
T-20.VIII.9:4 For what you s. is merely how you elect to
T-20.VIII.11:4 that there is something else for you to s..
T-21.in.1:2 The world you s. is what you gave it,
T-21.in.2:2 S. it as damned, and all you see is what
T-21.in.2:2 you s. is what you did to hurt the Son of
T-21.in.2:4 If you s. holiness and hope, you joined the
T-21.in.2:6 will s. the witness to the choice you made,
T-21.in.2:7 world you s. but shows you how much joy
T-21.in.2:7 joy you have allowed yourself to s. in you,
T-21.I.1:1 world the sightless "s." must be imagined
T-21.I.1:4 You do not s.. Your cues for inference are
T-21.I.2:4 are open, and you can s. where safety lies;
T-21.I.4:4 and cling to them because they cannot s..
T-21.I.4:7 they learned to "s." in their imagination,
T-21.I.5:2 And so it is with all who s. the body as all
T-21.I.7:5 and s. if you remember an ancient song
T-21.I.8:1 you s. and yet somehow familiar, is an arc
T-21.I.10:1 And now the blind can s., for that same
T-21.I.10:7 And when you s. it in your brother, you
T-21.II.2:3 *I am responsible for what I s.. I choose the*
T-21.II.4:2 it, and you keep the world as now you s. it
T-21.II.4:3 it away, and everything you s. goes with it
T-21.II.4:10 accept correction if it is willing to s. that it
T-21.II.5:1 The world you s. is but the idle witness
T-21.II.5:5 S. only this, and you will also see how
T-21.II.5:5 will also s. how circular the reasoning on
T-21.II.5:9 him, it will be given you to s. it in yourself
T-21.II.6:1 Perhaps you do not s. the need for you to
T-21.II.6:3 s. in it the whole exchange of separation
T-21.II.7:1 holiness and vision to s. it easily enough.
T-21.II.8:1 what is really there you cannot fail to s..
T-21.II.8:4 to look within and s. what must be there,
T-21.II.9:5 What you desire, you will s.. And if its
T-21.II.11:1 you recognize you made the world you s.,
T-21.II.11:4 made can tell you what you s. and feel,
T-21.II.13:2 S. what "proves" otherwise, and you deny
T-21.III.6:6 of a holy relationship is all you *want* to s..
T-21.III.10:1 do not realize you cannot s. because of it.
T-21.III.12:3 to serve as means to help the blind to s..
T-21.IV.1:3 indeed afraid to look within and s. the sin
T-21.IV.1:9 to your desire that it *be* there to s.. This
T-21.IV.2:2 "enemy," Whom it cannot even s., it fears
T-21.IV.3:6 unwilling to look within and s. it not.
T-21.IV.4:9 to s. the Holy Spirit's purpose as its own?
T-21.V.1:1 selects, and makes the world you s.. It
T-21.V.1:9 to hear, and on the sights you choose to s.
T-21.V.2:3 the ego says, and s. what it directs you see
T-21.V.2:3 the ego says, and see what it directs you s.
T-21.V.2:3 it is sure that you will s. yourself as tiny,
T-21.V.7:8 What reason points to you can s., because
T-21.VI.1:1 Reason cannot s. sin but can see errors,
T-21.VI.1:1 Reason cannot see sin but can s. errors,
T-21.VI.2:3 you cannot s. your brother or yourself as
T-21.VI.2:5 And who can s. a sinful world and look
T-21.VI.3:6 the home of madness if you s. reason. You
T-21.VI.3:9 Madness and reason s. the same things,
T-21.VI.4:3 their will, for they believe they s. the body
T-21.VI.5:3 To s. the body as a barrier between what
T-21.VI.5:4 Nor could you s. it, if you heard the voice
T-21.VII.1:1 Do you not s. that all your misery comes
T-21.VII.1:6 they are little could s. attraction there.
T-21.VII.1:8 protect his unity or s. him shattered and
T-21.VII.2:2 And those who s. themselves as helpless
T-21.VII.5:7 that he understand how he can s. it. Nor
T-21.VII.5:14 *do I want to s. what I denied because it is the*
T-21.VII.7:5 whether to s. him through the body's eyes
T-21.VII.7:7 what you want to s. must be your choice.
T-21.VII.8:4 *Is this what I would s.? Do I want this?*
T-21.VII.9:4 choose to s. a world without an enemy, in
T-21.VII.9:4 the means to s. it will be given you.
T-21.VII.10:8 And you can want to s. a sinless world,
T-21.VII.11:4 in your desire to s. the real world, so the
T-21.VII.12:5 he may do so if he does not s. he does it.
T-21.VIII.2:8 It comes as surely unto those who s. the
T-21.VIII.5:2 the awareness of what is always there to s.
T-22.in.1:3 never s. it in the same place and time. Sin
T-22.in.2:2 and alone, who s. their brothers different
T-22.I.1:5 in this and s. much evidence on its behalf.
T-22.I.2:3 tell you that the world you s. through eyes
T-22.I.5:4 vision can convey to you what you can s..
T-22.I.6:7 will recognize his home and s. them there
T-22.II.2:6 some aspects out of it, s. them as different
T-22.II.5:2 impossible for you to s. no guilt in anyone
T-22.II.9:5 And here we s. again another form of the
T-22.II.13:2 who is but willing to s. his brother sinless.
T-22.III.1:4 You can *s.* reason. This is not a play on
T-22.III.2:2 and reason will be unable to s. your errors
T-22.III.2:4 Reason can s. the difference between sin
T-22.III.4:2 does not s. if it is there or not. Everything
T-22.III.4:3 the body's eyes can s. is a mistake, an
T-22.III.5:3 The body's eyes s. only form. They cannot
T-22.III.5:4 s. beyond what they were made to see.
T-22.III.5:4 see beyond what they were made to s..
T-22.III.5:5 made to look on error and not s. past it.
T-22.III.5:6 perception, for they can s. only illusions,
T-22.III.5:8 as if it were a solid wall, s. truly? It is held
T-22.III.6:1 These eyes, made not to s., will never see.
T-22.III.6:1 These eyes, made not to see, will never s..
T-22.III.6:3 What was its maker's goal but not to s.?
T-22.III.6:5 S. how the body's eyes rest on externals
T-22.III.7:4 must be an illusion, and is not there to s..
T-22.III.7:5 And if you s. it you must be mistaken, for
T-22.III.7:6 What cannot s. beyond what is not there
T-22.III.8:2 from you by what the body's eyes can s..
T-22.III.8:6 to s. your sins in him to save yourself.
T-22.III.9:6 for each to s. himself as causing sin by his
T-22.IV.3:4 brother alone will s. it as a solid block,
T-22.IV.4:1 Think of the loveliness that you will s.,
T-22.IV.4:7 will they be to s. you come among them,
T-22.V.3:3 S. how the means and the material of evil
T-22.VI.1:5 For one you s. as means; the other, end.
T-22.VI.4:1 than the sun that lights the sky you s., is
T-22.VI.8:1 will s. your value through your brother's
T-22.VI.10:5 You do not s. what this belief has done.
T-22.VI.10:6 You s. yourself as vulnerable, frail and
T-22.VI.11:3 s. that every sin and every condemnation
T-22.VI.11:5 You do not s. that this is your attempt
T-22.VI.12:11 to attack to s. it separated from its maker.
T-23.in.1:1 Do you not s. the opposite of frailty and
T-23.in.2:7 And he will s. only the sinless, who can
T-23.in.3:3 Nothing they s. is harmful, for their
T-23.in.6:2 it lovingly, and s. the light of Heaven in it.
T-23.I.9:1 S. how the conflict of illusions disappears
T-23.II.7:1 S. how the fear of God is reinforced by
T-23.III.4:3 They do not s. that, if it is, salvation is
T-23.IV.2:4 they be to those who s. God's Son a body.
T-23.IV.6:1 remember you *can* s. the battle from above
T-23.IV.7:1 S. no one from the battleground, for
T-23.IV.7:2 where meaning can be given what you s..
T-24.I.7:7 attack your brother if you chose to s. no
T-24.II.1:6 you s. in him you stand as tall and stately,
T-24.II.1:6 by comparison with what you s.. Nor do
T-24.II.5:5 which does not s. his specialness at all.
T-24.II.5:6 the specialness they think they s. is an
T-24.II.6:1 What would they s. instead? The shining
T-24.II.6:5 You will no longer s. what never was, nor
T-24.II.8:1 loveliness that you will s. within yourself,
T-24.III.1:4 to one illusion can s. himself as sinless,
T-24.III.7:1 by a world of loveliness they do not s..
T-24.III.7:7 s. the savior God gave to you that you
T-24.IV.2:11 S. it as means to hurt, and it is hurt. See it
T-24.IV.2:12 S. it as means to heal, and it is healed.
T-24.IV.4:2 that you might s. your brother sinless. To
T-24.V.3:7 he will s. nothing and there is no sound to
T-24.V.5:1 Rejoice you have no eyes with which to s.
T-24.V.5:5 And what they s. and hear and hold and
T-24.V.6:5 And what you s. is like yourself. For what
T-24.V.6:6 Christ is there to s. and hear and love and
T-24.V.7:4 all living things, and s. their holiness.
T-24.V.7:7 The sight of Christ is all there is to s.. The
T-24.VI.1:8 S. in him God's creation. For in him his
T-24.VI.4:3 Until you s. the healing of the Son as all
T-24.VI.5:2 S. in his freedom yours, for such it is. Let
T-24.VI.5:4 one sin you s. in him but keeps you both
T-24.VI.6:1 sinlessness that eyes that s. can look upon
T-24.VI.6:2 It is His loveliness they s. in everything.
T-24.VI.6:6 the vision you were meant to s. from you.
T-24.VI.7:1 or his holiness as what you want to s., and
T-24.VI.7:6 that you might s. the truth about yourself,
T-24.VI.8:2 from himself, nor you who s. him truly.
T-24.VI.8:6 wherein you s. the judgment you have
T-24.VI.9:1 S. him as what he is, that your
T-24.VI.9:5 And both shall s. God's glory in His Son,
T-24.VI.10:2 Then s. him not as prisoner to them. It
T-24.VI.10:4 under the laws you s. as ruling him. Think
T-24.VI.10:7 Christ in you can s. your brother truly.
T-24.VI.13:1 it easier to s. your brother's body than his
T-24.VI.13:5 and there is no alternative for Him to s..
T-24.VII.3:4 you to s. his holiness *because* it is the truth
T-24.VII.4:7 if you s. this purpose in your brother's,
T-24.VII.5:5 the purpose that you s. in it has meaning,
T-24.VII.8:7 it must depend on what you s. it for.
T-24.VII.8:8 seems to teach you what you s.. Yet it but
T-24.VII.9:1 Look at yourself, and you will s. a body.
T-24.VII.11:13 what you s. will serve that purpose well,
T-25.in.1:8 Him and s. Him where they thought their
T-25.in.2:7 as plain to s. as is his specialness set forth
T-25.I.2:1 to look on holiness and s. Him there?
T-25.I.2:2 tells you *you* are manifest in what you s..
T-25.I.2:7 And you must s. your brother as yourself.
T-25.I.2:8 in his body you will s. your sinfulness,
T-25.II.2:1 hope of satisfaction from the world you s.
T-25.II.2:4 For one thing is sure; the way you s., and
T-25.II.4:6 It cannot be a frame if it is what you s..
T-25.II.5:1 as if a masterpiece were there to s.? Yet if
T-25.II.5:2 Yet if you s. your brother as a body, it is
T-25.II.5:3 set within this frame is all there is to s..
T-25.II.5:6 His masterpiece He offers you to s.. And
T-25.II.5:7 you rather s. the frame instead of this?
T-25.II.5:8 of this? And s. the picture not at all?
T-25.II.6:1 part of Him that you would s. as separate.
T-25.II.6:3 when you choose to s. it in its place. The

| | |
|---|---|
| T-25 II.7:1 | of yours, and you will s. the masterpiece. |
| T-25 II.7:5 | it, and s. the holiness that He has given it. |
| T-25 II.8:1 | Within the darkness s. the savior *from* the |
| T-25 II.8:2 | on him, and you will s. the dark no more. |
| T-25 II.8:5 | s. the holiness that must be there because |
| T-25 II.10:3 | given you, that you may s. His Son as one, |
| T-25 II.11:4 | S. not in him the sinfulness he sees, but |
| T-25 II.11:5 | you may s. as one what never has been |
| T-25 III.1:3 | law: You s. what you believe is there, and |
| T-25 III.3:3 | made it, and they do not s. it as the same. |
| T-25 III.5:5 | mind to choose to s. them where it will. If |
| T-25 III.5:6 | to s. them elsewhere from their home, as |
| T-25 III.6:5 | will he s. each situation that he thought |
| T-25 III.7:2 | you to s. the workings of the Helper given |
| T-25 III.7:2 | to s. the world He made instead of yours. |
| T-25 III.7:6 | And when you s. them as the same, your |
| T-25 III.7:7 | from the belief there are two ways to s.. |
| T-25 III.7:9 | want to s. peace and forgiveness descend |
| T-25 III.9:10 | the purpose of the world you s. is chosen, |
| T-25 IV.1:3 | Their joy is in the innocence they s.. And |
| T-25 IV.2:1 | at what you s. because you see it to rejoice |
| T-25 IV.2:1 | at what you see because you s. it to rejoice |
| T-25 IV.2:2 | joy, so long will they be there for you to s.. |
| T-25 V.2:8 | s. the Son of God as innocent and wish |
| T-25 V.2:11 | is there to s. by searching for your Savior, |
| T-25 V.3:1 | It is not Christ you s. by looking thus. It |
| T-25 V.3:3 | because there is no sin in him for you to s. |
| T-25 V.4:7 | everyone you s. but the reflection of what |
| T-25 V.5:8 | And as you s. him, so do you define the |
| T-25 V.5:8 | until you s. him differently and let him be |
| T-25 V.6:3 | In your brother you s. the picture of your |
| T-25 VI.1:2 | He can s. no evil; nothing in the world to |
| T-25 VI.2:3 | Dimness seems better; easier to s., and |
| T-25 VI.2:5 | the darkness and maintain he wants to s.? |
| T-25 VI.3:1 | The wish to s. calls down the grace of |
| T-25 VI.3:6 | lonely ones are those who s. no function |
| T-25 VI.6:3 | nothing that you think you s. in it is really |
| T-25 VI.7:7 | s. it as your special function in the plan to |
| T-25 VII.3:10 | Do not attempt to s. it differently, nor |
| T-25 VII.5:1 | of the world you s. to something else; a |
| T-25 VIII.3:2 | sinners s. justice only as their punishment |
| T-25 VIII.9:4 | No more than what you s. He offers you, |
| T-25 VIII.10:4 | his death, and could not s. his worth at all |
| T-25 VIII.13:10 | fairly s. another's rights because his own |
| T-25 IX.1:4 | answer this until you s. all that the answer |
| T-25 IX.3:4 | Spirit could s. unfairness as a resolution. |
| T-25 IX.4:3 | attack, and loss of any kind He cannot s.. |
| T-26 I.1:6 | To s. a brother in another body, separate |
| T-26 I.1:6 | expression of a wish to s. a little part of |
| T-26 I.1:7 | you will s. nothing attached to anything |
| T-26 I.2:1 | you s. is based on "sacrifice" of oneness. |
| T-26 I.3:7 | these limits on each brother whom you s.. |
| T-26 I.3:8 | For you must s. him as you see yourself. |
| T-26 I.3:8 | For you must see him as you s. yourself. |
| T-26 I.4:2 | And while you s. your brother as a body, |
| T-26 I.5:1 | Those who would s. the witnesses to |
| T-26 I.5:1 | to illusion merely ask that they might s. a |
| T-26 I.6:4 | nor s. what it is given him to witness to, |
| T-26 I.6:4 | to, that you may s. it and rejoice with him |
| T-26 I.6:6 | die each time you s. in him a sin deserving |
| T-26 II.3:5 | on what you s. can limit God in any way. |
| T-26 II.5:5 | offers you the means to s. his innocence. |
| T-26 II.5:6 | you will not look at what is there to s.? |
| T-26 II.6:6 | you to s. in him his perfect sinlessness. |
| T-26 II.7:3 | will s. each little hurt resolved before the |
| T-26 IV.2:1 | sin into a world of glory, wonderful to s.. |
| T-26 IV.3:2 | And here you s. the face of Christ, arising |
| T-26 V.9:3 | you to s. the past and put it in the present |
| T-26 VII.3:3 | Son of God perceived what he would s. |
| T-26 VII.8:6 | Perhaps you do not s. the role forgiveness |
| T-26 VII.10:2 | to replace the world you s. with Heaven, |
| T-26 VIII.1:1 | is that you s. an interval between the time |
| T-26 VIII.2:7 | You s. eventual salvation, not immediate |
| T-26 VIII.3:4 | out the space you s. between you still, and |
| T-26 VIII.3:7 | is, except in terms of what you s. it for. If |
| T-26 VIII.6:3 | has in it all effects that you will s.. They |
| T-26 X.1:4 | thus you s. what is the same as different. |
| T-26 X.6:1 | unfairly, and who s. as you have judged, |
| T-26 X.6:3 | And so you s. yourself deprived of light, |
| T-26 X.6:7 | *would rather know of Them than s. injustice* |
| T-27 I.1:6 | he must suffer the unfairness that you s.. |
| T-27 I.2:2 | you s. as proof that he is guilty of attack. |
| T-27 I.3:2 | that he may s. his sins are writ in Heaven |
| T-27 I.5:5 | who will s. that every scar is healed, and |
| T-27 I.8:4 | whose consequences still are there to s., |
| T-27 I.9:2 | futile must it be to s. yourself a picture of |
| T-27 II.2:5 | because what it has done is there to s.. |
| T-27 II.3:1 | it is a paradox that reason cannot s.. For it |
| T-27 II.7:7 | is a result of your desire to s. your brother |
| T-27 II.7:8 | sin. And what you wish is given you to s.. |
| T-27 II.10:5 | Alone, you cannot s. they are the same, |
| T-27 II.14:1 | your own mistakes you will not even s.. |
| T-27 II.15:5 | that He does not s. and recognize as His. |
| T-27 II.15:8 | His inability to s. His goal divided and |
| T-27 III.3:1 | of your brother that you s. means nothing |
| T-27 III.3:2 | or to endow with power or to s. as weak. |
| T-27 III.3:7 | your brother that you s. is wholly absent |
| T-27 IV.7:3 | from them, and s. what can be answered; |
| T-27 V.6:5 | give them sight to s. beyond all suffering |
| T-27 V.6:5 | all suffering and s. Christ's face instead. |
| T-27 V.6:8 | And what you s. the world will witness, |
| T-27 V.8:3 | it would be there no more for him to s.. |
| T-27 V.8:9 | Who does not s. the differences you see. |
| T-27 V.8:9 | Who does not see the differences you s.. |
| T-27 V.8:11 | made in spite of all the differences you s., |
| T-27 VII.3:2 | You use its eyes to s., its ears to hear, and |
| T-27 VII.3:5 | "reasoning" exactly as it is could fail to s. |
| T-27 VII.4:8 | And he must s. it in another's hand, if he |
| T-27 VII.7:7 | them does not s. himself as making them, |
| T-27 VII.7:9 | because he does not s. the part he plays in |
| T-27 VII.9:1 | This is the only picture you can s.; the |
| T-27 VII.10:7 | then you must s. the causes of the things |
| T-27 VII.11:7 | the part you s. and do not doubt is real. |
| T-27 VII.12:4 | The little gap you do not even s., the |
| T-27 VII.15:7 | s. as offering both life and death to you. |
| T-27 VII.16:2 | s. as gifts your brother offers represent |
| T-27 VIII.5:3 | for the part you s. is but the second part, |
| T-27 VIII.5:10 | And we will s. the grounds for laughter, |
| T-27 VIII.7:2 | The world you s. depicts exactly what you |
| T-27 VIII.8:2 | you will not s. the cause of what they do, |
| T-27 VIII.12:9 | learn you chose but not to listen, not to s.. |
| T-28 I.2:6 | occurring now, and still were there to s.. |
| T-28 I.7:7 | And s., instead, the new effects of cause |
| T-28 I.10:9 | s. in the miracle a lesson in allowing |
| T-28 I.15:1 | has been lost, to s. the causeless not? And |
| T-28 II.5:8 | only that you s. you made the one you |
| T-28 II.7:4 | did not s. that he was author of the dream |
| T-28 II.10:5 | hate, because you s. that it has no effects. |
| T-28 III.4:6 | which you s. as if it were the cause of pain |
| T-28 IV.2:9 | You s. them as the same, because you |
| T-28 IV.6:6 | Yet if you s. there is no truth in yours, his |
| T-28 V.4:5 | It cannot s. nor hear. It does not know |
| T-28 V.5:6 | and what they s. and hear they but report. |
| T-28 V.5:7 | It is not they that hear and s., but you, |
| T-28 V.7:1 | s. that it is here you are as prisoners in a |
| T-28 V.7:2 | The world you s. does not exist, because |
| T-28 V.7:6 | of sin that you will s. within yourself, |
| T-28 VI.2:1 | for sight a thing that cannot s., and blame |
| T-28 VI.3:10 | want your mind to have and s. and keep. |
| T-28 VI.4:5 | No one can suffer if he does not s. himself |
| T-29 I.6:5 | and s. in them a purpose not your own. |
| T-29 I.7:5 | s. how limited and weak is your allegiance |
| T-29 II.1:4 | s. it as the road to hell instead of looking |
| T-29 II.1:6 | will not s. the many gains your choice has |
| T-29 II.1:7 | Yet though you do not s. them, they are |
| T-29 II.5:1 | do not s. how much you now can give, |
| T-29 II.5:6 | You cannot s. your Guest, but you can see |
| T-29 II.5:6 | Guest, but you can s. the gifts He brought |
| T-29 III.2:7 | it. He must s. someone else as not a body, |
| T-29 III.3:6 | And as you s. him shining in the space of |
| T-29 III.3:6 | will s. that God Himself is where his body |
| T-29 III.3:10 | In glory will you s. your brother then, and |
| T-29 III.5:2 | S. how eagerly he comes, and steps aside |
| T-29 IV.6:5 | and you have help to give him if you s. the |
| T-29 V.3:2 | not for any purpose you may s. in him. |
| T-29 V.5:1 | you s. in all creation but the shining glory |
| T-29 VI.3:6 | your mind, and s. another purpose there. |
| T-29 VI.5:4 | here but is defined as what you s. it for. |
| T-29 VII.7:2 | s. death and disappointment everywhere. |
| T-29 VII.8:3 | try to s. in it a place of idols found outside |
| T-29 VIII.3:1 | a gap between the Christ and what you s.. |
| T-30 I.5:4 | by yourself, and can not s. the question. |
| T-30 I.11:7 | and s. that it is this for which you ask. |
| T-30 I.12:6 | s. that it is you who will be helped by it. |
| T-30 I.15:4 | you can s. there cannot be coercion here, |
| T-30 III.2:10 | So you s. your will within the idol, thus |
| T-30 IV.1:1 | and thus you will not s. you made it up. |
| T-30 IV.4:10 | S. one in them and you will see them all. |
| T-30 IV.4:10 | See one in them and you will s. them all. |
| T-30 IV.4:11 | S. none in them and they will touch you |
| T-30 V.7:2 | and think they s. an idol that they want. |
| T-30 VI.2:7 | But you are merely asked to s. forgiveness |
| T-30 VI.4:7 | If you can s. your brother merits pardon, |
| T-30 VI.8:1 | with the willingness to s. him as he is. |
| T-30 VI.9:4 | *perfect Son, and in his glory will I s. my own.* |
| T-30 VI.10:3 | But what you s. as having power to make |
| T-30 VII.2:5 | you think you s. another meaning in what |
| T-30 VII.4:2 | shared by everyone and everything you s.. |
| T-30 VII.4:3 | and you are glad to s. it everywhere. It |
| T-30 VII.6:5 | ability to s. relationships among events. |
| T-30 VII.7:1 | solitude, for what you s. means nothing. |
| T-30 VIII.1:3 | s. beyond appearances you *are* deceived. |
| T-30 VIII.1:4 | For everything you s. will change, and yet |
| T-30 VIII.5:1 | and offer them to you to s. in happy form, |
| T-30 VIII.5:8 | And you will s. the Christ in him because |
| T-30 VIII.6:7 | is. Why should you fear to s. the Christ in |
| T-30 VIII.6:8 | You but behold yourself in what you s.. |
| T-31 I.1:7 | is it to s. that what is false can not be true, |
| T-31 I.5:4 | true; too hard to learn, too difficult to s., |
| T-31 I.7:4 | that God's Son is guilty is the world you s. |
| T-31 I.7:11 | Son is innocent, and s. another world. |
| T-31 I.8:5 | And now you s. you were mistaken. You |
| T-31 II.2:9 | Yet must we s. them both, before you can |
| T-31 II.3:5 | s. yourself divided into both these roles, |
| T-31 II.5:14 | you s. an image of yourself and hear your |
| T-31 II.11:4 | and so you cannot s. which way you go. |
| T-31 III.6:1 | be glad that you will s. what you believe, |
| T-31 III.6:5 | and you will s. no one as prisoner to what |
| T-31 III.7:2 | And what they s. upholds their freedom |
| T-31 IV.3:3 | to s. how like they are to one another. |
| T-31 IV.4:8 | s. the purpose of the lesson shining clear, |
| T-31 V.4:3 | The other side he does not want to s.. Yet |
| T-31 V.4:4 | "reality" is set, to s. to it the idol lasts. |
| T-31 V.8:1 | for no one here can s. what it is for, and |
| T-31 V.8:2 | roads nor realize the way you s. yourself. |
| T-31 V.8:3 | s. this concept of the self must be undone, |
| T-31 V.9:6 | Can he s. your future and ordain, before it |
| T-31 V.10:10 | of. Who is there to s.? And what but is |
| T-31 V.11:2 | what would happen to the world you s., if |
| T-31 V.12:5 | s. reflects the state of the perceiver's mind |
| T-31 V.15:6 | To s. a guilty world is but the sign your |
| T-31 V.15:6 | and you behold it as you s. yourself. The |
| T-31 V.15:8 | you s. a picture of your secret wishes. |
| T-31 V.15:10 | you s. your own concealed desire to kill. |
| T-31 V.17:2 | and you will s. you know not what you are |
| T-31 VI.1:1 | You s. the flesh or recognize the spirit. |
| T-31 VI.1:5 | you s. and think is real and hold as true. |
| T-31 VI.1:8 | may s. the world of flesh no more except |
| T-31 VI.2:2 | If you choose to s. the body, you behold a |
| T-31 VI.3:3 | For you can s. the body without help, but |
| T-31 VI.3:4 | let you s. another world your eyes could |
| T-31 VI.3:6 | how what you s. arose to meet your sight. |
| T-31 VI.4:2 | which to s. the world that will replace the |
| T-31 VI.5:1 | that you can choose to s. the Son of God |
| T-31 VI.5:4 | change the world for eyes that learn to s., |
| T-31 VI.6:4 | it looks on you with eyes that s. as yours. |
| T-31 VII.2:1 | thoughts as long as you s. value in attack. |
| T-31 VII.2:2 | but will not s. them as meaningless. And |
| T-31 VII.3:1 | it is thus you s. him more than just a body |
| T-31 VII.3:4 | sight your eyes alone can offer you to s.. |
| T-31 VII.3:5 | will not interpret what you s. without the |
| T-31 VII.6:5 | use, and you can s. yourself another way. |
| T-31 VII.7:2 | All things you s. are images, because you |
| T-31 VII.7:3 | The light is kept from everything you s.. |
| T-31 VII.7:6 | And what you s. is hell, for fear *is* hell. All |
| T-31 VII.8:6 | single vision does he s. the face of Christ, |
| T-31 VII.10:3 | Who has learned to s. his brother not as |

T-31...VII.11:2 know his holiness while you **s.** him apart
T-31...VII.11:3 and thus expect to **s.** it everywhere. And
T-31...VII.11:5 he **s.** his innocence in all he looks upon,
T-31...VII.11:5 and **s.** his own salvation everywhere. He
T-31...VII.11:7 looks upon, that he may **s.** it as it really is.
T-31...VII.12:6 whether you would join with what you **s.**,
T-31...VII.13:7 **s.** beyond the veil of old ideas and ancient
T-31...VII.14:6 is, and **s.** the real alternatives you choose
T-31...VII.15:2 is withheld and what they **s.** is death.
T-31...VII.15:4 **s.** until he looks on them with seeing eyes,
T-31... VIII.4:2 fearful of temptation, then, but **s.** it as it is
T-31... VIII.4:4 The saviors of the world, who **s.** like Him,
T-31... VIII.6:1 look upon, regardless of the images you **s.**
T-31... VIII.6:3 Yield not to this, and you will **s.** all pain,
T-31... VIII.6:5 identity as you will **s.** it and believe it is.
T-31... VIII.8:5 you must share with everyone you **s.**, for
W-in ..........3:1 with the undoing of the way you **s.** now,
W-in ..........4:2 to everyone and everything you **s.**.
W-in ..........6:6 It is the opposite of the way you **s.** now.
W-pI ..........1.h Nothing I **s.** in this room [on this street,
W-pI .......1.1:1 idea very specifically to whatever you **s.**:
W-pI .......1.3:3 merely be applied to anything you **s.**. As
W-pI .......1.3:5 attempt to apply it to everything you **s.**,
W-pI .......1.3:6 be sure that nothing you **s.** is specifically
W-pI ..........2.h everything I **s.** in this room [on this street,
W-pI .......2.1:6 include everything you **s.** in a given area,
W-pI .......2.2:2 Take the subjects simply as you **s.** them.
W-pI ..........3.h anything I **s.** in this room [on this street,
W-pI .......3.1:2 kind. Whatever you **s.** becomes a proper
W-pI .......3.1:5 Anything is suitable if you **s.** it. Some of
W-pI .......3.1:6 see it. Some of the things you **s.** may have
W-pI .......3.2:1 to **s.** things exactly as they appear to you
W-pI ..........4.h the things I **s.** in this room [on this street,
W-pI .......4.3:3 to **s.** the meaningless as outside you, and
W-pI .......4.4:3 *like the things I* **s.** *in this room [on this street*
W-pI .......5.2:1 of the form in which you **s.** the upset, and
W-pI ..........6.h I am upset because I **s.** something that is
W-pI .......6.1:4 *at_because I* **s.** *something that is not there. I*
W-pI .......6.1:5 *I am worried about_because I* **s.** *something*
W-pI ..........7.h I **s.** only the past.
W-pI .......7.1:3 why nothing that you **s.** means anything.
W-pI .......7.1:4 you **s.** all the meaning that it has for you.
W-pI .......7.1:5 you do not understand anything you **s.**. It
W-pI .......7.1:6 and why they are like the things you **s.**. It
W-pI .......7.1:8 because you **s.** something that is not there
W-pI .......7.3:2 you **s.** a cup, or are you merely reviewing
W-pI .......7.3:7 past learning. Do you, then, really **s.** it?
W-pI .......7.4:5 *I* **s.** *only the past in this pencil. I see only the*
W-pI .......7.4:6 *I* **s.** *only the past in this shoe. I see only the*
W-pI .......7.4:7 *I* **s.** *only the past in this hand. I see only the*
W-pI .......7.4:8 *I* **s.** *only the past in that body. I see only the*
W-pI .......7.4:9 *in that body. I* **s.** *only the past in that face.*
W-pI .......8.1:1 the reason why you **s.** only the past. No
W-pI .......8.4:2 is because you actually cannot **s.** anything
W-pI ..........9.h I **s.** nothing as it is now.
W-pI .......9.3:1 the idea for the day to whatever you **s.**,
W-pI .......9.3:3 *I do not* **s.** *this typewriter as it is now. I do not*
W-pI .......9.3:4 *I do not* **s.** *this telephone as it is now. I do not*
W-pI .......9.3:5 *as it is now. I do not* **s.** *this arm as it is now.*
W-pI .......9.4:2 *I do not* **s.** *that coat rack as it is now. I do not*
W-pI .......9.4:3 *I do not* **s.** *that door as it is now. I do not see*
W-pI .......9.4:4 *as it is now. I do not* **s.** *that face as it is now.*
W-pI .....10.3:4 nothingness when you think you **s.** it. As
W-pI .....11.1:3 your thoughts determine the world you **s.**
W-pI ........12.h am upset because I **s.** a meaningless world
W-pI .....12.2:5 What you **s.** does not matter. You teach
W-pI .....12.3:2 *I think I* **s.** *a fearful world, a dangerous world*
W-pI .....12.4:4 *I am upset because I* **s.** *a meaningless world.*
W-pI .....12.5:5 it be. It is this you **s.** in it. It is this that is
W-pI .....12.5:8 words have been erased, you will **s.** His.
W-pI .....14.1:4 you **s.** has nothing to do with reality. It is
W-pI .....14.3:1 and **s.** the Word of God in their place.
W-pI .....14.6:2 These things are part of the world you **s.**.
W-pI .....15.1:2 think them, and so you think you **s.** them.
W-pI .....15.2:2 same familiar objects which you **s.** now.
W-pI .....15.4:1 apply it to whatever you **s.** around you,
W-pI .....16.1:2 Everything you **s.** is the result of your
W-pI ........17.h I **s.** no neutral things.
W-pI .....17.1:2 You **s.** no neutral things because you have
W-pI .....17.2:2 open: *I* **s.** *no neutral things because I have no*
W-pI .....17.2:4 *I do not* **s.** *a neutral–, because my thoughts*
W-pI .....17.2:6 say: *I do not* **s.** *a neutral wall, because my*
W-pI .....17.2:7 *I do not* **s.** *a neutral body, because my*
W-pI .....17.3:2 you do not **s.** anything that is really alive
W-pI .....18.1:1 you **s.** are never neutral or unimportant.
W-pI .....18.2:1 what you **s.** as much as to how you see it.
W-pI .....18.2:1 what you see as much as to how you **s.** it.
W-pI .....18.3:2 *alone in experiencing the effects of how I* **s.** –
W-pI ........20.h I am determined to **s.**.
W-pI .....20.1:6 will not **s.** if you regard yourself as being
W-pI .....20.3:1 decision to **s.** is all that vision requires.
W-pI .....20.3:8 determination to **s.** is vision given you.
W-pI .....20.4:1 throughout the day that you want to **s.**.
W-pI .....20.4:2 the recognition that you do not **s.** now.
W-pI .....20.5:4 You can **s.** them differently, and you will.
W-pI .....20.5:5 What you desire you will **s.**. Such is the
W-pI ........21.h I am determined to **s.** things differently.
W-pI .....21.4:2 *to* **s.** *_[name of person] differently. I am*
W-pI .....21.4:3 *I am determined to* **s.** *_[specify the situation*
W-pI .....21.5:4 *I am determined to* **s.** *_[specify the attribute*
W-pI ........22.h What I **s.** is a form of vengeance.
W-pI .....22.1:1 thoughts in his mind must **s.** the world.
W-pI .....22.3:3 *I* **s.** *only the perishable. I see nothing that*
W-pI .....22.3:4 *I* **s.** *nothing that will last. What I see is not*
W-pI .....22.3:5 *What I* **s.** *is not real. What I see is a form of*
W-pI .....22.3:6 *What I* **s.** *is a form of vengeance.* At the end
W-pI .....22.3:8 *this the world I really want to* **s.**? The answer
W-pI ........23.h from the world I **s.** by giving up attack
W-pI .....23.1:4 up some segment of the world you **s.**. It is
W-pI .....23.2:1 of the world you **s.** is attack thoughts, you
W-pI .....23.3:1 The world you **s.** is a vengeful world, and
W-pI .....23.4:1 You **s.** the world that you have made, but
W-pI .....23.4:1 you do not **s.** yourself as the image maker.
W-pI .....23.4:3 is the world you **s.** when its cause is gone?
W-pI .....23.4:4 for everything you think you **s.** now.
W-pI .....23.5:1 you are not trapped in the world you **s.**,
W-pI .....23.5:6 first two steps, you will **s.** that this is so.
W-pI .....23.6:4 *world I* **s.** *by giving up attack thoughts about*
W-pI .....23.7:4 identifying the cause of the world you **s.**.
W-pI .....25.1:2 why nothing you **s.** means anything. You
W-pI .....25.1:8 recognizing this that what you **s.** is given
W-pI .....26.1:2 You **s.** attack as a real threat. That is
W-pI ........27.h Above all else I want to **s.**.
W-pI .....27.2:1 when you say you want to **s.** above all else
W-pI ........28.h all else I want to **s.** things differently.
W-pI .....28.2:1 all else I want to **s.** this table differently."
W-pI .....28.2:5 You **s.** a lot of separate things about you,
W-pI .....28.2:6 You either **s.** or not. When you have seen
W-pI .....28.2:7 you will **s.** all things differently. The light
W-pI .....28.2:8 The light you will **s.** in any one of them is
W-pI .....28.2:8 is the same light you will **s.** in them all.
W-pI .....28.3:1 all else I want to **s.** this table differently,"
W-pI .....28.4:3 all else I want to **s.** this table differently,"
W-pI .....28.6:1 asking to **s.** the purpose of the universe.
W-pI .....28.7:1 then applied to whatever you **s.** about you
W-pI .....28.8:2 *Above all else I want to* **s.** *this_differently.*
W-pI ........29.h God is in everything I **s.**.
W-pI .....29.1:1 why you can **s.** all purpose in everything.
W-pI .....29.1:3 why nothing you **s.** means anything. In
W-pI .....29.2:3 is not in a table, for example, as you **s.** it.
W-pI .....29.3:2 You do not **s.** them now. Would you
W-pI ........30.h everything I **s.** because God is in my mind
W-pI .....30.1:2 you will look upon it and **s.** in it what you
W-pI .....30.2:3 are trying to **s.** in the world what is in our
W-pI .....30.2:4 we are trying to join with what we **s.**,
W-pI .....30.2:5 between vision and the way you **s.**.
W-pI .....30.3:2 idea applies to everything you do **s.** now,
W-pI .....30.3:2 or could **s.** now if it were within the range
W-pI .....30.4:2 range as well as those you can actually **s.**,
W-pI ........31.h I am not the victim of the world I **s.**.
W-pI .....31.1:2 **s.** without and the world you see within.
W-pI .....31.1:2 see without and the world you **s.** within.
W-pI ........32.h I have invented the world I **s.**.
W-pI .....32.1:2 the victim of the world you **s.** because you
W-pI .....32.1:4 up. You will **s.** it or not see it, as you wish.
W-pI .....32.1:4 up. You will see it or not **s.** it, as you wish.
W-pI .....32.1:5 While you want it you will **s.** it; when you
W-pI .....32.1:5 want it, it will not be there for you to **s.**.
W-pI .....32.2:2 However, since you **s.** them as different,
W-pI .....32.2:2 involving the world you **s.** outside you,
W-pI .....32.2:2 the other the world you **s.** in your mind.
W-pI .....32.3:1 at the world you **s.** as outside yourself.
W-pI .....32.6:3 *I have invented this situation as I* **s.** *it.*
W-pI ........34.h I could **s.** peace instead of this.
W-pI .....34.5:4 *I could* **s.** *peace in this situation instead of*
W-pI .....34.5:4 *in this situation instead of what I now* **s.** *in it.*
W-pI .....35.1:1 not describe the way you **s.** yourself now.
W-pI .....35.2:5 What you **s.** while you believe you are in
W-pI .....35.2:7 This is not vision. Images cannot **s.**.
W-pI .....35.4:1 descriptive terms in which you **s.** yourself.
W-pI .....35.6:2 *I* **s.** *myself as imposed on. I see myself as*
W-pI .....35.6:3 *I* **s.** *myself as depressed. I see myself as failing*
W-pI .....35.6:4 *I* **s.** *myself as failing. I see myself as*
W-pI .....35.6:5 *I* **s.** *myself as endangered. I see myself as*
W-pI .....35.6:6 *I* **s.** *myself as helpless. I see myself as*
W-pI .....35.6:7 *I* **s.** *myself as victorious. I see myself as losing*
W-pI .....35.6:8 *I* **s.** *myself as losing out. I see myself as*
W-pI .....35.6:9 *out. I* **s.** *myself as charitable. I see myself as*
W-pI ...35.6:10 *myself as charitable. I* **s.** *myself as virtuous.*
W-pI ........36.h My holiness envelops everything I **s.**.
W-pI .....37.1:2 to **s.** the world through your own holiness
W-pI .....37.2:7 **s.** themselves as whole make no demands.
W-pI .....37.4:1 as you apply the idea to whatever you **s.**:
W-pI .....37.5:1 what you **s.** around you and to those who
W-pI .....38.4:1 or unhappiness of any kind as you **s.** it.
W-pI .....38.4:5 *in which I* **s.** *myself, there is nothing that my*
W-pI .....39.2:5 **s.** at once how direct and simple the text
W-pI .....39.7:2 your salvation that you **s.** them differently
W-pI .....41.5:2 and obscuring, yet representing all you **s.**
W-pI .....42.1:3 You will **s.** because it is the Will of God. It
W-pI ........43.h is my Source. I cannot **s.** apart from Him.
W-pI .....43.2:1 In God you cannot **s.**. Perception has no
W-pI .....43.3:1 **s.** apart from God because you cannot be
W-pI .....43.3:3 then you cannot **s.** apart from God.
W-pI .....43.4:4 the idea specifically to what you **s.**. Four
W-pI .....43.4:8 *I cannot* **s.** *this desk apart from Him. God is*
W-pI ...43.4:10 *I cannot* **s.** *that picture apart from Him.*
W-pI .....43.5:4 *I* **s.** *through the eyes of forgiveness. I see the*
W-pI .....43.5:5 *I* **s.** *the world as blessed. The world can show*
W-pI .....43.5:7 *I* **s.** *my own thoughts, which are like God's.*
W-pI .....43.7:4 *I cannot* **s.** *you apart from Him.* This form is
W-pI .....43.8:4 *my Source. I cannot* **s.** *this apart from Him.*
W-pI ........44.h God is the light in which I **s.**.
W-pI .....44.1:2 to it. You cannot **s.** in darkness, and you
W-pI .....44.1:3 make darkness and then think you **s.** in it,
W-pI .....44.2:1 In order to **s.**, you must recognize that
W-pI .....44.2:2 You do not **s.** outside yourself, nor is the
W-pI .....44.3:5 must be accomplished if you are to **s.**.
W-pI .....44.6:3 God is the light in which you **s.**. You are
W-pI .....45.1:2 think you **s.** is related to vision in any way
W-pI .....45.1:5 Nothing that you think you **s.** bears any
W-pI .....51.1:1 (1) Nothing I **s.** means anything. The
W-pI .....51.1:2 The reason this is so is that I **s.** nothing,
W-pI .....51.1:3 that I recognize this, that I may learn to **s.**
W-pI .....51.1:4 think I **s.** now is taking the place of vision.
W-pI .....51.2:1 what I **s.** all the meaning it has for me. I
W-pI .....51.2:2 I look upon, and it is this and only this I **s.**
W-pI .....51.2:5 in my judgments, because I want to **s.**. My
W-pI .....51.2:6 and I do not want to **s.** according to them.
W-pI .....51.3:1 (3) I do not understand anything I **s.**.
W-pI .....51.3:2 I understand what I **s.** when I have judged
W-pI .....51.3:3 I **s.** is the projection of my own errors of
W-pI .....51.3:4 what I **s.** because it is not understandable.
W-pI .....51.3:7 I can exchange what I **s.** now for this
W-pI .....51.5:5 everything I **s.** by assigning this role to it.
W-pI .....52.1:1 I am upset because I **s.** what is not there.
W-pI .....52.2:1 (7) I **s.** only the past. As I look about, I
W-pI .....52.2:5 I will bless everyone and everything I **s.**.
W-pI .....52.2:7 with love on all that I failed to **s.** before.
W-pI .....52.3:2 I **s.** only my own thoughts, and my mind
W-pI .....52.3:3 then, can I **s.** as it is? Let me remember
W-pI .....52.4:1 (9) I **s.** nothing as it is now. If I see
W-pI .....52.4:2 If I **s.** nothing as it is now, it can truly be
W-pI .....52.4:2 now, it can truly be said that I **s.** nothing.
W-pI .....52.4:3 I can **s.** only what is now. The choice is
W-pI .....52.4:4 is not whether to **s.** the past or the present
W-pI .....52.4:4 the choice is merely whether to **s.** or not.

W-pI.....52.4:5 I have chosen to s. has cost me vision.
W-pI.....52.4:6 Now I would choose again, that I may s..
W-pI.....53.1:5 I can therefore s. a real world, if I look to
W-pI.....53.2:1 am upset because I s. a meaningless world
W-pI.....53.2:6 not s. it at all unless I choose to value it.
W-pI.....53.5:2 Whatever I s. reflects my thoughts. It is
W-pI.....53.5:4 The fact that I s. a world in which there is
W-pI.....53.5:4 to cast their beneficent light on what I s..
W-pI.....54.1:5 world I s. arises from my thinking errors,
W-pI.....54.1:8 other. What I s. shows me which they are.
W-pI.....54.2:1 (17) I s. no neutral things. What I see
W-pI.....54.2:2 What I s. witnesses to what I think. If I
W-pI.....54.2:4 thought. Let me look on the world I s. as
W-pI.....54.2:6 so I also know the world I s. can change as
W-pI.....54.3:2 thoughts, I cannot s. a private world.
W-pI.....54.3:3 it could form the basis of the world I s..
W-pI.....54.5:1 (20) I am determined to s.. Recognizing
W-pI.....54.5:2 of my thoughts, I am determined to s.. I
W-pI.....55.1:1 I am determined to s. things differently.
W-pI.....55.1:2 What I s. now are but signs of disease,
W-pI.....55.1:4 The very fact that I s. such things is proof
W-pI.....55.1:6 I s. tells me that I do not know who I am. I
W-pI.....55.1:7 I am determined to s. the witnesses to the
W-pI.....55.2:1 (22) What I s. is a form of vengeance. The
W-pI.....55.2:2 The world I s. is hardly the representation
W-pI.....55.3:3 thoughts I could not s. a world of attack.
W-pI.....55.3:4 will s. a world of peace and safety and joy.
W-pI.....55.3:5 joy. And it is this I choose to s., in place of
W-pI.....56.1:2 when I s. myself as under constant attack
W-pI.....56.1:6 away in exchange for the world I s.. But
W-pI.....56.2:1 (27) Above all else I want to s..
W-pI.....56.2:2 that what I s. reflects what I think I am, I
W-pI.....56.2:3 The world I s. attests to the fearful nature
W-pI.....56.3:1 (28) Above all else I want to s. differently.
W-pI.....56.3:2 I s. holds my fearful self-image in place,
W-pI.....56.3:3 While I s. the world as I see it now, truth
W-pI.....56.3:3 While I see the world as I s. it now, truth
W-pI.....56.4:1 (29) God is in everything I s.. Behind
W-pI.....56.5:1 everything I s. because God is in my mind
W-pI.....57.1:1 (31) I am not the victim of the world I s.. I
W-pI.....57.2:1 (32) I have invented the world I s.. I
W-pI.....57.2:2 I made up the prison in which I s. myself.
W-pI.....57.3:3 at it. I s. everything upside down, and my
W-pI.....57.3:4 I s. the world as a prison for God's Son. It
W-pI.....57.3:6 and s. it as a place where the Son of God
W-pI.....57.4:1 (34) I could s. peace instead of this.
W-pI.....57.4:2 When I s. the world as a place of freedom,
W-pI.....57.5:5 In this light I begin to s. what my illusions
W-pI.....58.1:1 (36) My holiness envelops everything I s..
W-pI.....58.1:3 forgiven, I no longer s. myself as guilty. I
W-pI.....58.1:5 eyes, the holiness of the world is all I s.,
W-pI.....58.2:3 Everyone and everything I s. in its light
W-pI.....58.2:5 of the world shine forth for everyone to s..
W-pI.....59.2:3 me not look to my own eyes to s. today.
W-pI.....59.3:2 I cannot s. apart from Him. I can see what
W-pI.....59.3:3 Him. I can s. what God wants me to see. I
W-pI.....59.3:3 Him. I can see what God wants me to s.. I
W-pI.....59.3:4 I cannot s. anything else. Beyond His Will
W-pI.....59.3:6 when I think I can s. apart from Him. It is
W-pI.....59.3:7 these I choose when I try to s. through the
W-pI.....59.3:9 It is through this vision that I choose to s..
W-pI.....59.4:1 (44) God is the light in which I s.. I
W-pI.....59.4:2 I cannot s. in darkness. God is the only
W-pI.....59.4:4 Therefore, if I am to s., it must be through
W-pI.....59.4:6 that God is the light in which I s.. Let me
W-pI.....60.1:3 their innocence s. nothing to forgive. Yet
W-pI.....60.2:4 As I begin to s., I recognize His reflection
W-pI.....60.3:2 the world will look to me when I can s. it!
W-pI.....60.3:3 look anything like what I imagine I s. now
W-pI.....60.3:4 I s. will lean toward me to bless me. I will
W-pI.....60.5:3 His Love lights up the world for me to s..
W-pI.....62.1:2 you recognize the light in which you s..
W-pI.....64.1:2 purpose of the world you s. is to obscure
W-pI.....64.2:1 Nothing the body's eyes seem to s. can be
W-pI.....65.8:5 It is what you s. now that will be totally
W-pI.....66.1:2 you do not really s. the connection. Yet
W-pI.....66.5:5 Try to s. the logic in this sequence, even if
W-pI.....68.1:3 hold a grievance is to s. yourself as a body
W-pI.....68.6:1 now to s. all these people as friends. Say
W-pI.....68.6:3 do so: *I would s. you as my friend, that I may*
W-pI.....69.2:4 trying to s. past the veil of darkness that
W-pI.....69.2:5 and to s. the tears of God's Son disappear
W-pI.....69.4:3 s. only the clouds because you seem to be
W-pI.....69.5:1 you can s. no reason to believe there is a
W-pI.....69.5:3 reality. They seem to be all there is to s..
W-pI.....69.9:5 *I cannot s. what I have hidden. Yet I want to*
W-pI.....70.1:4 You s. neither guilt nor salvation as in
W-pI.....70.2:5 must surely begin to s. that accepting it is
W-pI.....71.4:2 Surely you can s. how it is in strict accord
W-pI...71.10:6 of your salvation, and to s. It where It is.
W-pI.....72.7:1 is the universal belief of the world you s..
W-pI.....72.8:5 we are going to try to s. this differently.
W-pI.....72.9:5 To s. our Self as separate from the body is
W-pI...72.11:1 Now we would s. and hear and learn.
W-pI.....73.2:1 or co-makers in picturing the world you s.
W-pI.....75.2:7 Today we s. a different world, because the
W-pI.....75.3:3 the new world as what we want to s.. We
W-pI.....75.3:5 We will to s. the light; the light has come.
W-pI.....75.4:2 This is what we want to s., and only this.
W-pI.....75.5:1 to s. the ego's shadow on the world today.
W-pI.....75.5:2 We s. the light, and in it we see Heaven's
W-pI.....75.5:2 s. Heaven's reflection lie across the world.
W-pI.....75.8:3 From this time forth you will s. differently
W-pI.....75.8:5 And you will s. the world that has been
W-pI.....75.9:6 your eyes, you cannot fail to s. today. And
W-pI.....75.9:7 And what you s. will be so welcome that
W-pI...75.11:2 of yourself and s. it everywhere today, as
W-pI.....76.5:3 mind will fail to s. it is the victim of itself.
W-pI.....78.1:3 eyes, you will not s. the miracle beyond.
W-pI.....78.2:2 will reverse the way you s. by not allowing
W-pI.....78.3:2 and as it lifts you s. the Son of God where
W-pI.....78.3:4 the darkness deeper, and you could not s.
W-pI.....78.4:1 Today we will attempt to s. God's Son.
W-pI.....78.4:5 s. as difficult at times or hard to please,
W-pI.....78.6:1 periods today will s. him in this role. You
W-pI.....78.7:1 and s. our savior shining in the light of
W-pI.....78.8:5 you s. through Him will free you both. Be
W-pI.....79.2:3 s. that a problem has been solved if he
W-pI.....79.2:4 the answer, he cannot s. its relevance.
W-pI.....79.6:2 answer because you would s. its relevance
W-pI.....79.9:2 You will s. many problems today, each
WpI..rII.in.4:5 Trust it to s. you through, and carry you
W-pI.....81.3:2 my function that I will s. the light in me.
W-pI.....81.3:5 trust that, in the light, I will s. it as it is.
W-pI.....82.2:4 *Through my forgiveness I can s. this as it is.*
W-pI.....84.2:2 *Let me not s. an illusion of myself in this. As I*
W-pI.....84.2:4 *My Creator did not create this as I s. it.*
W-pI.....85.1:2 there, and hide from me what I would s..
W-pI.....85.1:5 and vision must be joined for me to s.. To
W-pI.....85.1:6 To s., I must lay grievances aside. I want
W-pI.....85.1:7 I want to s., and this will be the means by
W-pI.....85.2:5 *I have no need for this. I want to s..*
W-pI.....85.3:7 and everything I s. will but reflect the
W-pI.....86.4:3 *If I s. grounds for grievances in this, I will not*
W-pI.....86.4:3 *this, I will not s. the grounds for my salvation*
W-pI.....87.2:2 *This cannot hide the light I will to s.. You*
W-pI.....87.4:4 *part of God's Will for me, however I may s. it.*
W-pI.....88.2:3 *The light in you is all that I would s., [name].*
W-pI.....88.2:4 *[name]. I would s. in this only what is there.*
W-pI.....88.4:3 *I s. only the laws of God at work in this. Let*
W-pI.....90.3:4 I do not s. the problem and the answer as
W-pI.....91.1:5 is not the result of your failure to s.. It is
W-pI.....91.1:7 You will s. them in the light; you will not
W-pI.....91.1:7 the light; you will not s. them in the dark.
W-pI.....91.3:1 you do not s. is there sounds like insanity.
W-pI.....91.3:2 that it is insanity not to s. what is there,
W-pI.....91.3:2 there, and to s. what is not there instead.
W-pI.....91.3:3 do not doubt that the body's eyes can s..
W-pI.....91.8:9 *a reality. I cannot s. in darkness, but in light.*
W-pI...91.10:5 is the light in which you will s. miracles,
W-pI...91.10:6 becomes your eyes, that you may s..
W-pI.....92.1:4 you s. by putting little bits of glass before
W-pI.....92.1:5 you are a body, and the body's eyes can s..
W-pI.....92.2:4 than to believe the body's eyes can s.; the
W-pI.....92.3:1 in you that is the light in which you s., as
W-pI.....92.3:4 are seen through eyes that cannot s. and
W-pI.....92.5:6 its light that all may s. and benefit as one.
W-pI.....92.6:1 s. a purpose in forgiveness and in love. It
W-pI ....92.7:4 The light of strength is not the light you s.
W-pI ....93.1:2 think if anyone could s. the truth about
W-pI ....93.2:1 help you s. that they are based on nothing
W-pI ....95.2:1 You s. yourself as a ridiculous parody on
W-pI ....95.2:4 It does not s. the oneness in you, for it is
W-pI ....95.3:1 to be aware only of what can hear and s.,
W-pI ....96.1:4 The opposites you s. in you will never be
W-pI ....96.2:1 you use and where you s. the problem,
W-pI ....96.4:4 can also s. itself divorced from spirit, and
W-pI ....99.5:4 does the Holy Spirit look on what you s.;
W-pI ....99.8:4 s. how bright this light still shines in you.
W-pI ..100.2:6 will s. their function in your shining face,
W-pI ..100.6:3 world can s. how much He loves His Son,
W-pI ..105.2:3 pervades all levels of the world you s.. It
W-pI ..105.9:4 s. it as but another chance to let yourself
W-pI ..106.2:1 the way to peace to those who cannot s..
W-pI ..106.5:1 wakes all those who sleep and cannot s..
W-pI ..108.7:4 and s. how quickly peace returns to us.
W-pI ..108.7:5 peace is vision given us, and we can s..
W-pI ..109.7:3 sing and s. the stream begin to flow again,
WpI..rIII.in7:1 in perfect faith that you would s. their
W-pI ..111.1:2 light. *I cannot s. in darkness. Let the light of*
W-pI ..111.1:3 *mind, and let me s. the innocence within.*
W-pI ..111.2:2 *I s. through strength, the gift of God to me.*
W-pI ..113.2:2 *I s. God's perfect plan for my salvation*
W-pI ..121.5:2 s. it has condemned itself to this despair.
W-pI ..121.9:3 And as you learn to s. them both as one,
W-pI ..121.9:3 and s. that their escape included yours.
W-pI 121.11:1 close your eyes and s. him in your mind,
W-pI 121.11:4 till you s. a light somewhere within it, and
W-pI 121.12:2 to s. around your former "enemy" to him.
W-pI 121.13:1 let him offer you the light you s. in him,
W-pI ..122.2:3 eyelids so you s. no dreams of fear and
W-pI 122.12:1 and you will s. another world arise you
W-pI 122.13:4 s. the changeless in the heart of change;
W-pI ..123.4:3 Today we smile on everyone we s., and
W-pI ..124.2:2 And everything we s. reflects the holiness
W-pI ..124.4:6 upon. Today we s. only the loving and the
W-pI ..124.5:1 We s. it in appearances of pain, and pain
W-pI ..124.5:2 We s. it in the frantic, in the sad and the
W-pI ..124.5:3 we s. it in the dying and the dead as well,
W-pI ..124.5:4 to life. All this we s. because we saw it first
W-pI ..124.9:5 And you will s. Christ's face upon it, in
W-pI 124.10:1 you will s. your own transfiguration in the
W-pI 124.11:1 the sinless light you s. belongs to you; the
W-pI 124.11:2 a sight too holy for the body's eyes to s..
W-pI 124.11:3 will understand and comprehend and s..
W-pI ..126.6:2 As you s. it, it is but a check upon overt
W-pI ..126.6:4 you s. in someone other than yourself. It
W-pI ..127.2:2 s. that changing love must be impossible.
W-pI ..127.6:3 eyes that s. and ears that hear love's Voice
W-pI .....128.h The world I s. holds nothing that I want.
W-pI ..128.1:1 The world you s. holds nothing that you
W-pI ..128.2:2 it, until you s. a different purpose there.
W-pI ..128.2:5 world you s. holds nothing that you want.
W-pI ..128.6:1 and s. how far you rise above the world,
W-pI ..128.7:2 will not value anything you s. as much as
W-pI ..128.8:2 And when you think you s. some value in
W-pI ..128.8:4 *The world I s. holds nothing that I want.*
W-pI ..129.1:2 you s. that there is something else to hope
W-pI ..129.2:3 The world you s. is merciless indeed,
W-pI ..129.5:2 never back to s. again the world you do
W-pI ..129.7:4 *I choose to s. that world instead of this, for*
W-pI ..129.7:5 close your eyes upon the world you s.,
W-pI ..129.8:3 And yet your mind can s. it plainly, and
W-pI ..129.9:4 *The world I s. holds nothing that I want.*
W-pI .....130.h It is impossible to s. two worlds.
W-pI ..130.1:2 What you s. reflects your thinking. And
W-pI ..130.1:3 reflects your choice of what you want to s.
W-pI ..130.1:4 for what you value you must want to s.,
W-pI ..130.1:4 to see, believing what you s. is really there
W-pI ..130.1:5 No one can s. a world his mind has not
W-pI ..130.2:3 choose to s. a world of which he is afraid?
W-pI ..130.2:4 That which you fear to s. you cannot see.
W-pI ..130.2:4 That which you fear to see you cannot s..
W-pI ..130.4:1 has made everything you think you s.. All
W-pI ..130.5:1 is impossible to s. two worlds which have
W-pI ..130.6:2 world you s. is proof you have already
W-pI ..130.6:3 the lesson that you cannot s. two worlds.

W-pI...130.6:4 It also teaches that the one you s. is quite
W-pI...130.6:4 the point of view from which you s. it. It is
W-pI...130.6:5 and reflects its source in everything you s.
W-pI...130.8:5 say: *It is impossible to s. two worlds. Let me*
W-pI...130.8:6 *God offers me and s. no value in this world,*
W-pI...130.9:3 will you fail to s. His thanks expressed in
W-pI.130.10:2 true is what you s. and only what you see.
W-pI.130.10:2 true is what you see and only what you s..
W-pI.130.11:4 *It is impossible to s. two worlds. I seek my*
W-pI.131.10:3 and we will ask to s. the rising of the real
W-pI.131.11:3 this: *I ask to s. a different world, and think a*
W-pI.131.11:5 several minutes watch your mind and s.,
W-pI.131.13:1 and s. how easily the door swings open
W-pI.131.13:2 that you can understand all things you s..
W-pI.131.13:3 you realize the world you s. before you in
W-pI...132.5:2 but your mind on what you want to s.,
W-pI...132.5:5 tells you that you made the world you s.,
W-pI...132.7:3 Some s. it suddenly on point of death,
W-pI.132.11:2 Are these inherent in the world you s.?
W-pI.132.11:5 If you are real the world you s. is false, for
W-pI.132.14:1 it, and about all living things we s. upon it
W-pI.132.16:1 world, as well as to the ones you s. nearby
W-pI...133.8:7 rust, that you may s. how "innocent" it is.
W-pI.133.14:2 you s. some difficult decisions facing you,
W-pI...134.4:6 It would s. as right the plainly wrong; the
W-pI.134.10:1 Thus will you s. alternatives for choice in
W-pI.134.10:4 world you s. and that which lies beyond;
W-pI.134.17:2 occurs, allow your mind to s. through this
W-pI...135.6:4 the body all the functions that you s. in it,
W-pI...135.9:3 You will not s. the mind as separate from
W-pI.135.10:5 you fail to s. where hope must lie if it be
W-pI.135.16:4 s. that here and now is everything it needs
W-pI.135.18:3 your defenses did not let you s. His loving
W-pI...136.8:5 For s., this dust can make you suffer, twist
W-pI.136.10:4 Who else can s. them and react to them as
W-pI.137.10:1 be healed, you s. all those around you, or
WpI.rIV.in4:4 and s. the meaning that they offer us.
WpI.rIV.in8:2 with time enough to s. the gifts that they
W-pI...144.2:1 The world I s. holds nothing that I want.
W-pI...145.2:1 (130) It is impossible to s. two worlds.
W-pI...151.2:1 do not seem to doubt the world you s..
W-pI...151.3:4 how else do you judge the world you s.?
W-pI.151.11:2 And He will reinterpret all you s., and all
W-pI.151.11:3 And you will s. the love beyond the hate,
W-pI.151.12:1 your life is not a part of anything you s.. It
W-pI.151.12:4 you s. the holy face of Christ in everything
W-pI...152.6:1 you made the world you s. is arrogance?
W-pI...152.7:2 Humility would s. at once these things are
W-pI...152.7:3 And can you s. what God created not? To
W-pI...153.7:3 you s. at work in all the evils of the world?
W-pI.153.11:5 For you will not s. the light, until you
W-pI.153.12:5 come to s. the benefits salvation brings.
W-pI.153.20:7 to look on Christ and s. His sinlessness.
W-pI...154.1:5 a larger plan we cannot s. in its entirety.
W-pI...155.9:4 may s. something with which they can
W-pI...156.5:4 And thus they s. in you their holiness,
W-pI...157.7:2 it light will come to s. the light more sure;
W-pI...158.4:5 For we but s. the journey from the point
W-pI...158.8:3 this you give today: S. no one as a body.
W-pI.158.10:3 in your brother you but s. yourself. If he
W-pI.158.10:4 sin, so must you be; if you s. light in him,
W-pI...159.5:4 restored to vision, and the blind can s..
W-pI...160.9:3 They s. Him as a stranger, for they do not
W-pI...161.2:4 could it invent the partial world you s..
W-pI...161.2:5 seeing is to show you what you wish to s..
W-pI...161.3:4 so we can s. a different use in everything.
W-pI...161.4:8 We need to s. a little, that we learn a lot.
W-pI...161.6:4 love's "enemy" Christ's vision does not s..
W-pI.161.10:5 will s. will sing to you of ancient melodies
W-pI.161.11:2 S. him first as clearly as you can, in that
W-pI.161.11:3 S. his face, his hands and feet, his
W-pI.161.11:4 and s. familiar gestures which he makes
W-pI.161.11:8 *Christ, and s. my perfect sinlessness in you.*
W-pI.161.12:6 will s. him suddenly transformed from
W-pI...163.6:5 For here again we s. an obvious position,
W-pI...163.8:9 to look past death, and s. the life beyond.
W-pI...164.5:5 Now will you s. it with the eyes of Christ.
W-pI...164.6:3 And what you s. becomes the healing and
W-pI...164.7:4 All that we s. will but increase our joy,
W-pI...164.9:3 You may not s. the value your acceptance
W-pI...165.1:4 already have except your choice to s. it
W-pI...166.6:3 s. that he is following the way he chose,
W-pI...168.4:3 you s. a light that covers all the world in
W-pI.169.13:2 who s. the light that lingers in your face.
W-pI...170.7:6 s. in him their safety have no guardian, no
W-pI.170.13:8 *In them we s. Your glory, and in them we*
WpI...rV.in6:5 with those he teaches, seeing what they s.,
Wi181-200 2:1 limited to let you s. the value of our goal.
Wi181-200 2:4 control of what you s. speaks for itself.
W-pI...181.2:2 this that gives consistency to what you s..
W-pI...181.2:6 from what you s. in others past their sins.
W-pI...181.2:8 will not transcend their sight and s. the
W-pI...181.8:4 When seeing this is all we want to s.,
W-pI...181.8:6 will become the only thing we s. reflected
W-pI...182.9:3 they may s. He would be Friend to them.
W-pI...183.3:4 The blind can s.; the deaf can hear. The
W-pI...183.4:3 s. how easily you will forget the names of
W-pI...183.6:6 Name of everything that we desire to s.; of
W-pI...183.8:5 and s. God's Name replace the thousand
W-pI...184.1:2 have made up names for everything you s.
W-pI...184.2:1 This space you s. as setting off all things
W-pI...184.2:2 You s. something where nothing is, and
W-pI...184.2:2 and s. as well nothing where there is unity
W-pI.184.13:3 gave its aspects have distorted what you s.
W-pI.184.14:4 we are given strength to s. beyond them.
W-pI...185.2:8 look upon the world you s. around you to
W-pI...186.3:1 quite sobering, until you s. its meaning.
W-pI...187.3:3 done until you s. the miracles it brings to
W-pI...187.7:3 you choose to s. all suffering as what it is.
W-pI.187.10:5 we s. the purity of Heaven shine in our
W-pI.187.11:2 extend, for we would s. it everywhere. We
W-pI.187.11:5 is ours, we offer it to everything we s.. For
W-pI.187.11:6 For where we s. it, it will be returned to us
W-pI...189.1:2 And with its eyes you will not s. this light,
W-pI...189.1:3 Yet you have eyes to s. it. It is there for
W-pI...189.1:7 feel the Love of God within you is to s. the
W-pI...189.3:2 different from the world you s. through
W-pI...189.3:5 is inconceivable to those who s. a world of
W-pI...189.4:2 and innocence they s. surrounding them;
W-pI...189.4:3 and s. its sure reflection everywhere.
W-pI...189.5:1 What would you s.? The choice is given
W-pI...190.5:6 you s. by merely recognizing what you are
W-pI...190.6:1 awhile: The world you s. does nothing. It
W-pI...191.1:3 not s. what you have done by giving to the
W-pI...191.2:2 have you done that this is what you s.?
W-pI...191.6:5 will not s. a devastating image of yourself
W-pI...191.8:4 Who could s. the world as dark and sinful
W-pI.191.10:7 about the world, and s. the suffering there
W-pI.191.11:3 s. the mercy of the world until you find it
W-pI.192.10:9 and you will s. that you are one with him.
W-pI...193.3:7 this: *Forgive, and you will s. this differently.*
W-pI...193.4:4 but wants to s. the simple lesson there.
W-pI...193.5:1 *Forgive, and you will s. this differently.*
W-pI...193.6:4 You s. them rightly when you hold these
W-pI...193.6:4 you s. or any brother looks upon amiss.
W-pI...194.4:6 And you will s. by your experience that
W-pI...194.6:1 s. the lesson for today as the deliverance it
W-pI...194.6:3 as you learn to s. salvation in all things, so
W-pI...195.1:2 is s. themselves as better off than others.
W-pI...195.3:1 you s. in him the rival for your peace; a
W-pI...195.8:6 for you will s. that everything has earned
W-pI...196.2:4 can learn to s. these foolish applications,
W-pI...196.3:4 you will s. within today's idea the light of
W-pI...196.6:3 Until you s. that this, at least, must be
W-pI...196.6:5 its foolishness, or even s. that it is there,
W-pI...197.2:3 S. yourself as bound, and bars become
W-pI...197.6:2 the sins you think you s. outside yourself,
W-pI.198.10:4 and s. your innocence shining upon you
W-pI.198.12:6 itself, you s. the vision of yourself, and
W-pI...200.7:5 Or must he s. that, as he looks on it, the
WpI rVI.in.3:7 a function that transcends the world we s.
W-pI...218.1:2 *my sightless eyes I cannot s. the vision of my*
W-pII..223.2:1 *let us s. the face of Christ instead of our*
W-pII..224.2:3 *Father, now, for I am weary of the world I s..*
W-pII..224.2:4 *Reveal what You would have me s. instead.*
W-pII..226.1:3 If I believe it has a value as I s. it now, so
W-pII..226.1:4 if I s. no value in the world as I behold it,
W-pII..237.1:4 the world that Christ would have me s.,
W-pII.239.1:3 s. in those with whom He shares His glory
W-pII.....3.3:4 They s. in its illusions but a solid base
W-pII.....3.4:3 light, and s. the world as He beholds it.
W-pII.243.1:3 my perception, which are all that I can s..
W-pII....250.h Let me not s. myself as limited.
W-pII.250.1:2 s. his strength diminished and reduced to
W-pII.250.2:3 *He is what I am, and as I s. him so I see*
W-pII.250.2:3 *what I am, and as I see him so I s. myself.*
W-pII.250.2:4 *Today I would s. truly, that this day I may at*
W-pII.251.1:5 But now I s. that I need only truth. In that
W-pII.262.1:7 *Let me not s. him as a stranger to his Father,*
W-pII.263.2:1 let us look on all we s. through holy vision
W-pII.264.1:1 *behind, beside me, in the place I s. myself,*
W-pII....265.h Creation's gentleness is all I s..
W-pII.265.1:4 alone. Today I s. the world in the celestial
W-pII.265.1:8 The images I s. reflect my thoughts. Yet is
W-pII.265.2:2 *the same, and I will s. creation's gentleness.*
W-pII.269.1:5 *Today I choose to s. a world forgiven, in*
W-pII.....6.4:3 for what remains to s. except Christ's face
W-pII.271.1:2 look upon what Christ would have me s.,
W-pII....290.h My present happiness is all I s..
W-pII.290.1:1 not there, my present happiness is all I s..
W-pII.290.1:2 Eyes that begin to open s. at last. And I
W-pII.290.2:4 *I am sure that I will s. my happiness today.*
W-pII.....8.1:4 they s. a world where terror is impossible,
W-pII.291.1:5 What holiness we s. surrounding us! And
W-pII.292.1:4 of all problems we perceive, all trials we s.
W-pII.293.2:4 *I would s. only this world before my eyes*
W-pII.294.1:5 And yet a neutral thing does not s. death,
W-pII294.1:10 Let me not s. it more than this today; of
W-pII.301.1:5 *Let me s. Your world instead of mine. And all*
W-pII.302.1:2 *as our sight is finally restored and we can s..*
W-pII.302.1:5 *created. Now we s. that darkness is our own*
W-pII.303.1:5 s. but sights that show His Father's Love.
W-pII.306.1:1 when it can offer me a day in which I s. a
W-pII...10.1:3 first you s. a world that has accepted this
W-pII.311.1:4 s. totality and therefore judges falsely. Let
W-pII....312.h I s. all things as I would have them be.
W-pII.312.1:2 we therefore s. what we would look upon.
W-pII.312.1:4 impossible to overlook what we would s.,
W-pII.312.1:4 fail to s. what we have chosen to behold.
W-pII.312.1:6 look upon what Christ would have him s.,
W-pII.316.2:3 *by which I can behold them, s. their worth,*
W-pII....325.h All things I think I s. reflect ideas.
W-pII.325.1:1 What I s. reflects a process in my mind,
W-pII...12.4:1 reality is not to s. the ego and its thoughts
W-pII....335.h I choose to s. my brother's sinlessness.
W-pII.335.1:2 I never s. my brother as he is, for that is
W-pII.335.1:3 I s. in him is merely what I wish to see,
W-pII.335.1:3 I see in him is merely what I wish to s.,
W-pII.335.1:5 I choose to s. what I would look upon,
W-pII.335.1:5 see what I would look upon, and this I s.,
W-pII.335.1:7 And I will s. it, having chosen to behold
W-pII.335.2:1 *to me, except to s. my brother's sinlessness?*
W-pII...13.4:1 it cannot s. and does not understand. Yet
W-pII.349.1:1 *So would I liberate all things I s., and give to*
W-pII....351.h And which I choose to s. I will behold.
W-pII.351.1:2 *if I s. him sinful I proclaim myself a sinner,*
W-pII.351.1:4 *I can also s. my brother sinless, as Your holy*
W-pII.351.1:5 *And with this choice I s. my sinlessness, my*
W-pII.359.1:7 *base more solid than the shadow world we s.*
M-1 ........... 1:2 which he did not s. his interests as apart
M-4 ..... I.A.3:4 he must s. things in a different light? He
M-4 ..... I.A.6:4 Now he begins to s. the transfer value of
M-4 ........II.1:3 honesty, for only they can s. its value.
M-4 ....... X.1:6 be at peace, for they alone s. reason for it.
M-5 ........II.3:4 It costs the whole world you s., for the
M-5 ........II.3:6 He looks on what he chooses to s.. No
M-5 ...... III.3:9 to s. no will as separate from their own,
M-8 ........... 3:8 will never s. except through differences.
M-8 ........... 6:1 body's eyes will continue to s. differences.
M-11 ......... 1:6 you s. cannot be the world God loves, and
M-11 ....... 1:11 But you can choose how you would s. it.
M-11 ......... 4:5 It is the world you s. that is impossible.
M-12 ......... 3:5 are spirit. A body they can s.. A voice they
M-12 ......... 5:2 the same as sin, and you will s. it as sinful.
M-12 ......... 6:8 Yet they are not deceived by what they s..
M-13 ......... 5:6 He does not s. what he is asking for. And
M-16 ......... 6:4 all the fearful things you s. in dreams. It is

| | |
|---|---|
| M-17 .........9:4 | s. it and to recognize its thought system is |
| M-17 .........9:8 | until you s. you have responded to your |
| M-18 .........2:5 | and bring Christ's vision to eyes that s.. |
| M-18 .........3:3 | The body's eyes now "s."; its ears alone |
| M-19 .........4:9 | s. you hate and fear your Self as enemy. |
| M-19 .........5:2 | whatever picture the mind desires to s.. |
| M-19 .......5:12 | descends on all the world, and we can s.. |
| M-19 .......5:13 | the world, and we can see. And we can s.! |
| M-20 .........5:2 | s. in death escape from what you made. |
| M-20 .........5:3 | But this you do not s.; that you made |
| M-22 .........6:6 | Would you s. him as separate from you? |
| M-27 .......6:11 | not s. that otherwise He has an opposite, |
| M-29 .........3:7 | whole world you s. reflects the illusion |
| C-2.............4:4 | can s. the only answer that is meaningful. |
| C-2.............5:3 | was, for here we s. all that it seemed to do |
| C-2.............6:1 | there was darkness now we s. the light. |
| C-2.............7:4 | Look at the kindly world you s. extend |
| C-2.............9:2 | and you will s. a sudden brightness cover |
| C-3.............8:1 | s. the truth about yourself reflected there. |
| C-4.............1:1 | The world you s. is an illusion of a world. |
| C-4.............1:3 | the world you s. that will endure forever. |
| C-4.............2:3 | everything they s. not only will not last, |
| C-ep...........3:6 | Look up and s. His Word among the stars |
| C-ep...........3:7 | would hide but God would have you s.. |
| P-1.............4:4 | patient cannot s. himself as really capable |
| P-1.............5:2 | to s. illusions as false and to accept the |
| P-2......... II.9:5 | need as his and s. that they are met as one |
| P-2......... II.9:6 | an aid in helping him to s. that this is so? |
| P-2........ III.1:2 | walk ahead of him to give him light to s.. |
| P-2........ III.3:8 | No one need s. him or talk to him or even |
| P-2......... V.7:8 | And as we s. the sinlessness in him come |
| P-2........ VI.3:2 | The eye reproduces; it does not s.. Their |
| P-2........ VI.7:3 | by all who s. themselves as therapists. |
| P-2....... VII.7:2 | s. in him because of this they fear indeed. |
| P-2....... VII.7:6 | He does not s. the Christ in him who calls. |
| P-2....... VII.7:8 | him, for what you s. will be your Answer. |
| P-2....... VII.9:1 | that you can s. such things as this, if you |
| P-2....... VII.9:6 | And can you now expect to s. in him an |
| P-3...........I.3:2 | to you limited to the few you actually s.. |
| P-3...........I.3:3 | You can s. others as well, for seeing is not |
| P-3....... II.10:3 | He does not s. and he does not hear. How, |
| P-3....... II.10:7 | Because his inability to s. and hear does |
| P-3...... III.5:12 | himself denied the light, and cannot s.. |
| S-1...........I.2:7 | by God, will suit your need as you s. it. |
| S-1...........I.4:3 | your specific needs as you s. them, and let |
| S-1........ III.4:6 | it in another, and does not s. it as his own |
| S-1........ III.5:9 | Be this to him, that you may s. him thus. |
| S-2...........I.3:3 | *Do not s. error.* Do not make it real. Select |
| S-2.........I.3:10 | For as you s. the Son you see yourself, and |
| S-2.........I.3:10 | For as you see the Son you s. yourself, and |
| S-2.........I.3:10 | and as you s. yourself is God to you. |
| S-2...........I.4:2 | for it is only your sins you s. in him. You |
| S-2...........I.4:3 | You want to s. them there, and not in you |
| S-2...........I.4:8 | you can s. sin in anyone except yourself. |
| S-2...........I.5:7 | You cannot s. his sins and not your own. |
| S-2...........I.6:3 | for all illusions that they think they s.. |
| S-2...........I.6:4 | look through His and learn to s. like Him. |
| S-2...........I.8:1 | when he could s. the face of Christ instead |
| S-2......... II.7:8 | It is His face forgiveness lets you s.. It is |
| S-2......... II.7:9 | It is His face in which you s. your own. |
| S-2......... II.8:6 | You want to s. the sunlight and the glow |
| S-2........ III.7:7 | will s. the door swing silently open upon |
| S-3......... II.3:4 | hard to s. the gifts we gave were saved for |
| S-3........ IV.2:6 | to s. His likeness and to teach like Him. |
| S-3........ IV.5:2 | give the role to Him you s. in His creation. |
| S-3........ IV.9:3 | S. the shadows fade away in gentleness; |

## seeds 8

| | |
|---|---|
| T-18...... VI.7:2 | where you have sown the s. of vengeance, |
| T19..IV.B.11:5 | disillusionment and the s. of faithlessness |
| T-28...... III.4:3 | the s. of pestilence and every form of ill, |
| T-28...... III.5:5 | where the s. of sickness seemed to grow? |
| T-28...... III.6:2 | The s. of sickness and the shame of guilt |
| T-28...... IV.8:5 | left clean of all the s. of sickness and of sin |
| T-28.... IV.10:6 | The s. of sickness come from the belief |
| T-28.... IV.10:9 | of healing where the s. of sickness were. |

## seeing 132

| | |
|---|---|
| T-3 .........II.3:5 | right-minded s. cannot see anything but |
| T-5 ....... III.3:1 | opposed ways of s. your brother. They |
| T-7 ..........II.1:3 | you are s. him as if he were absent from |
| T-7 ....... VI.8:3 | By not s. you as you are, it can see itself as |
| T-7 .....VIII.3:8 | it. The belief that by s. it outside you have |
| T-8 ...... VII.1:7 | and s. his brothers as similarly belittled. |
| T-8 ....... IX.3:4 | rendering the faculties for s. ineffectual. |
| T-9 ........I.11:7 | you are interfering with the laws of s.. If |
| T-9 ....... III.3:1 | your brother's ego you must be s. through |
| T-9 ....... IV.4:6 | By s. it clearly, you have made it real and |
| T-12 .... VII.7:2 | As you look in, you choose the guide for s. |
| T-13 .......II.2:5 | failing the Son of God by s. him as guilty. |
| T-13 ...... V.5:3 | hatred as your brother, you are not s. him |
| T-13 ...... V.9:1 | way of s. that you might see in darkness, |
| T-13 .... V.10:2 | Each is a way of s., and different worlds |
| T-13 .... V.10:4 | And s. what He is, He knows His Father. |
| T-13 .... V.11:6 | s. themselves as the Holy Spirit sees them. |
| T-13 ... VI.10:9 | them. And s. it, its beauty calls you home. |
| T-13 .... VII.2:2 | of them involves a different kind of s., |
| T-13 .... VII.5:3 | see? All s. starts with the perceiver, who |
| T-14 ......in.1:3 | for learning it and s. it quite clearly. The |
| T-14 ........I.3:1 | S. is always outward. Were your |
| T-14 .......II.2:1 | s. where you are but knowing you are |
| T-14 .... VII.7:1 | Joining with Him in s. is the way in which |
| T-14 .... VII.7:5 | alone. S. with Him will show you that all |
| T-14 ... XI.3:10 | condition in which s. becomes impossible |
| T-14 ..... XI.7:7 | by s. His Son as he always was, and not as |
| T-15 .......II.4:1 | by s. them as sources of ego support. As a |
| T-15 ..... IX.2:1 | all the interference and s. it exactly as it is. |
| T-16 ..... VI.4:6 | For in s. them the body would disappear, |
| T-16 ..... VI.4:7 | investment in s. it would be withdrawn |
| T-17 .......II.1:9 | leads to s. it and giving thanks with Him. |
| T-17 ..... III.7:7 | by s. it where it is not and as it is not. Give |
| T-17 ... IV.13:6 | look upon the picture itself, s. at last that, |
| T-19 ........I.3:6 | acting accordingly; s. what is not there, |
| T-19 ........I.9:5 | yourself and him, and s. them as one. |
| T-19 ..... IV.3:7 | What need is there for s., then? When |
| T-19 ... IV.3:10 | What need is there of s., in the presence |
| T-20 ... III.7:10 | the one blind thing in all the s. universe of |
| T-20 .... VII.5:6 | S. adapts to wish, for sight is always |
| T-20 .. VII.8:10 | will be evaluated as worth the s., and so |
| T-20 .... VII.9:6 | For what the s. look upon *is* sinless. No |
| T-20 .... VII.9:8 | as was the vision that made his s. possible |
| T-20 ...VIII.6:6 | it in any form and s. it everywhere, in |
| T-21 .......II.5:5 | the reasoning on which your "s." rests. |
| T-21 ..... III.9:9 | For He Who loves the world is s. it for you |
| T-21 ... III.12:4 | But in their s. they look past it, as do you. |
| T-21 .. VII.11:3 | on sin are s. the denial of the real world. |
| T-22 ........I.2:4 | s. such as this send back its messages? |
| T-22 .......II.5:3 | s. is the only means by which escape from |
| T-22 ..... III.6:4 | eyes are perfect means, but not for s.. See |
| T-22 ..... III.7:5 | you are s. what can *not* be real as if it were. |
| T-22 ..... VI.7:2 | your sight, preventing you from s. past it? |
| T-24 .... VII.2:5 | And by your s. it in him, returns to you. |
| T-25 .......II.8:8 | s. is the vision shared that looks on Christ |
| T-25 .......II.8:8 | that looks on Christ instead of s. death. |
| T-25 ..... III.7:7 | For it is s. them as one that brings release |
| T-25 ..... IV.1:2 | this is so, s. their safety in this happy fact. |
| T-25 .... V.2:11 | your Savior, s. Him through sightless eyes |
| T-26 ........I.8:3 | Condemn him not by s. him within the |
| T-27 ..... III.3:8 | devoted to its s. be perceived as idly spent |
| T-27 .... VII.5:4 | be changed by s. it apart from its effects. |
| T-28 ......I.14:4 | And in s. this, he understands he never |
| T-28 ... IV.10:7 | insist on s. in the gap what is not there. |
| T-28 ...... V.4:6 | It does not know what s. *is*; what listening |
| T-29 .... VII.9:4 | world made sad and sick by s. idols there. |
| T-30 ..... VI.4:3 | the sure result of s. pardon as unmerited. |
| T-30 ...VIII.5:7 | about him that you would prefer to s. this |
| T-31 .......II.7:5 | tenderness, s. no leaders and no followers |
| T-31 ..... IV.3:4 | Men have died on s. this, because they |
| T-31 .. VII.12:5 | For s. can but represent a wish, because it |
| T-31 .. VII.15:4 | see until he looks on them with s. eyes, |
| W-pI....... 4.2:5 | blocks to sight, and make s. impossible. |
| W-pI....... 8.1:4 | about time from which your s. suffers. |
| W-pI....... 8.4:2 | picture a thought, you are not s. anything |
| W-pI..... 15.1:3 | This is how your "s." was made. This is |
| W-pI..... 15.1:5 | It is not s.. It is image making. It takes the |
| W-pI..... 15.1:7 | It takes the place of s., replacing vision |
| W-pI .... 15.2:1 | s. will not have much meaning for you. |
| W-pI ....... 18.h | alone in experiencing the effects of my s.. |
| W-pI .... 18.3:4 | *not alone in experiencing the effects of my s..* |
| W-pI .... 19.1:1 | why your s. does not affect you alone. |
| W-pI .... 23.3:3 | One can well ask if this can be called s.. Is |
| W-pI .... 28.2:5 | which really means you are not s. at all. |
| W-pI .... 28.4:3 | you are committing yourself to s.. It is not |
| W-pI .... 28.7:2 | of them all in their contribution to your s. |
| W-pI .... 30.2:2 | rid of what we do not like by s. it outside. |
| W-pI .... 34.1:1 | that prevail in the other way of s.. Peace |
| W-pI .... 37.2:2 | other way of s. will inevitably demand |
| W-pI .... 44.2:2 | nor is the equipment for s. outside you. |
| W-pI .... 44.2:3 | is the light that makes s. possible. It is |
| W-pI .... 52.2:3 | upon. I call this s.. I hold the past against |
| W-pI .... 53.1:5 | to my real thoughts as my guide for s.. |
| W-pI .... 53.5:4 | and death shows me that I am s. only the |
| W-pI .... 54.3:1 | alone in experiencing the effects of my s.. |
| W-pI .... 59.2:4 | of s. for the vision that is given by God. |
| W-pI .... 59.4:5 | I have tried to define what s. is, and I have |
| W-pI .... 78.4:3 | So is the s. of the world reversed, as we |
| W-pI .... 78.5:3 | Through s. him behind the grievances |
| W-pI .... 78.8:4 | him to you, s. no separation in God's Son. |
| W-pI .... 92.1:3 | idea of what s. means is tied up with the |
| W-pI .... 92.4:1 | these things by s. past appearances. It |
| W-pI .... 92.9:1 | and guide your s. so you do not dwell on |
| W-pI .. 92.10:4 | today, and we will practice s. in the light, |
| W-pI .... 93.1:3 | living on after s. this being impossible. |
| W-pI .. 121.2:3 | misery, peering about in darkness, s. not, |
| W-pI .. 130.9:4 | it is not the kind of s. that your eyes alone |
| W-pI .. 154.2:2 | S. your strengths exactly as they are, and |
| W-pI 158.11:3 | practice s. with the eyes of Christ today. |
| W-pI .. 161.2:5 | all s. is to show you what you wish to see. |
| W-pI .. 161.7:5 | its eyes behold, s. itself in everything, |
| W-pI 161.11:5 | s. now conceals from you the sight of one |
| W-pI .. 165.5:6 | your blindness for the s. eyes of Christ; |
| W-pI .. 170.8:3 | before this idol, s. him exactly as he is. |
| WpI...rV.in6:5 | with those he teaches, s. what they see, |
| W-pI .. 181.8:4 | When s. this is all we want to see, when |
| W-pI .. 189.5:3 | law of s.: You will look upon that which |
| W-pI .. 193.7:1 | How can you tell when you are s. wrong, |
| W-pII . 289.1:2 | looking nowhere; s. but what is not there. |
| W-pII . 312.1:5 | the Holy Spirit's purpose as his goal for s.. |
| M-8 ......... 3:10 | and so only the mind is responsible for s.. |
| M-16 ......... 1:4 | S. this and understanding that it is true, |
| M-22 ......... 4:5 | s. only the face of Christ shining in front |
| M-22 ......... 5:5 | so he is s. in his brother only the unreal. |
| M-24 ......... 2:7 | risk in s. the present in terms of the past. |
| M-28 ......... 6:3 | and s. there the vision of Christ's face to |
| C-1 ............ 6:1 | sin and justifying anger, and s. guilt, |
| C-3 ............ 4:3 | S. the face of Christ involves perception. |
| P-2........ III.1:1 | the pitfalls along the road by s. them first. |
| P-2........ IV.8:3 | to compromise by s. just a little bit of hell. |
| P-2........ VI.5:4 | Yet s. this will not effect a cure. That is |
| P-3...........I.3:3 | for s. is not limited to the body's eyes. |

## seek 325

| | |
|---|---|
| T-3 ..... VI.11:8 | of "S. ye first the Kingdom of Heaven" say |
| T-4 ...... IV.1:5 | ego, and you do not s. the face of Christ. |
| T-4 .........V.5:2 | "S. and ye shall find" does not mean that |
| T-4 .........V.5:2 | that you should s. blindly and desperately |
| T-5 .........II.7:2 | demand, because It does not s. control. It |
| T-7 ....... IV.7:1 | S. ye first the Kingdom of Heaven, |
| T-7 ....... IV.7:2 | But s. this only, because you can find |
| T-8 ....... III.5:2 | There is nothing else to s.. Everyone is |
| T-8 ....... IV.8:3 | Whom you s. to imprison you do not love |
| T-8 ....... IV.8:4 | you s. to imprison anyone, including |
| T-8 ....... IX.2:4 | You do not have to s. reality. It will seek |
| T-8 ....... IX.2:5 | It will s. you and find you when you meet |
| T-9 ..........I.8:5 | even though many may s. both. Can you |
| T-9 .........V.5:5 | will always s. to get something from the |
| T-9 ...... VII.1:5 | You do not have to s. far for salvation. |
| T-9 .....VIII.2:9 | not to tolerate self-abasement and s. relief |
| T-9 .....VIII.7:9 | exalted state you s. others like you and |
| T-12 ..... IV.1:4 | summed up simply as: "S. and do *not* find. |
| T-12 ..... IV.4:2 | To s. and not to find is hardly joyous. Is |
| T-12 ..... IV.4:5 | promise is always, "S. and you *will* find," |
| T-12 .......V.7:1 | that the ego's rule is, "S. and do not find." |
| T-12 .... VII.6:3 | always that you see what you s., for what |

T-12.....VII.6:3 you seek, for what you s. you will find.
T-12.....VII.6:6 if you s. for two goals you will find them,
T-12.....VII.7:4 This is why you find what you s.. What
T-12... VIII.1:4 If you s. love in order to attack it, you will
T-13....III.11:5 and it must s. a place of darkness where it
T-13..III.12:10 But s. this place and you will find it, for
T-13....... V.9:1 Do not s. vision through your eyes, for
T-13...... VI.5:4 and you will find it if you s. it there. You
T-13...... VI.5:6 Learn, then, to s. it where it is, and it will
T-13...VII.15:2 s. not what you will surely lose. Content
T-13....... X.3:1 in which you s. to lay your guilt upon him
T-13..... X.11:5 S. not to love unlike Him, for there is no
T-13..... XI.6:3 you learn what to avoid and what to s..
T-14....... II.1:7 you will find the "treasure" that you s..
T-14....III.15:1 S. not to appraise the worth of God's Son
T-15....III.10:9 host of God needs not s. to find anything.
T-15......IV.9:8 s. not to protect the thoughts you would
T-15....... V.2:3 If you s. to separate out certain aspects of
T-15....... V.7:3 so, however much you s. for its reality,
T-15...... VI.2:2 you s. without for what you cannot find
T-15...... VI.3:3 If you s. for satisfaction in gratifying your
T-15... VIII.2:2 s. in them what you have thrown away.
T-15... VIII.3:3 and s. not to restore it to yourself. Fear
T-15... VIII.3:9 And where you are must everyone s., and
T-15......IX.4:6 it. And s. it not through yours. Yet your
T-15......IX.6:6 S. not Atonement in further separation.
T-15....... X.7:5 s. to answer this question in your special
T-15...... XI.1:2 And s. not safety by attempting to protect
T-15...... XI.6:1 for love, you s. for sacrifice and find it.
T-16......IV.4:8 They s. it desperately, but not in the
T-16......IV.6:1 Your task is not to s. for love, but merely
T-16......IV.6:1 merely to s. and find all of the barriers
T-16......IV.6:2 it. It is not necessary to s. for what is true,
T-16......IV.6:2 but it *is* necessary to s. for what is false.
T-16......IV.6:5 If you s. love outside yourself you can be
T-16......IV.8:2 For it is they you s.. You seek but for your
T-16......IV.8:3 You s. but for your own completion, and
T-16......IV.9:4 forever. S. not for this in the bleak world
T-16....... V.6:5 be of the ego's maxim, "S. but do not find
T-16..... V.12:1 relationship tempts you to s. for love in
T-16...... VI.2:3 God, no longer s. for union in separation,
T-16...... VI.5:3 When two individuals s. to become one,
T-16...... VI.7:7 be no meaning you would still s. here.
T-16...... VI.9:1 Nothing you s. to strengthen in the
T-16.....VII.1:3 becomes a way in which you s. to restore
T-16.....VII.2:9 s. to lay the blame for deprivation on it,
T-16.....VII.4:1 is gone; s. not to preserve it in the special
T-16.....VII.5:1 be an acting out of vengeance that you s..
T-16...VII.10:2 will support you as you s. only your place
T-16...VII.11:1 S. and *find* His message in the holy instant
T-17....III.6:11 And you will learn to s. for and establish
T-17...VII.3:11 s. not to have it made up to you elsewhere
T-18......IV.5:3 S. not to answer, but merely to receive the
T-18......IV.5:8 than s. to prepare yourself for Him, try to
T-18......IX.7:5 the world below, nor s. to make it real.
T-19.........I.7:2 however much you s. to connect them.
T19. IV.A.11:2 of fear are harshly ordered to s. out guilt,
T19. IV.A.13:3 have been taught to s. for the corruptible,
T19..IV.B.12:1 It is impossible to s. for pleasure through
T19... IV.C.1:7 those who are attracted to it and s. it out.
T19. IV.D.13:8 he is, and s. not to make of love an enemy
T19. IV.D.19:5 Here is the rest and quiet that you s., the
T-20......III.7:1 S. not to make the Son of God adjust to
T-20...... VI.4:2 the sun. It does not s. for power, but for
T-21.......in.1:7 Therefore, s. not to change the world, but
T-21......III.6:5 your brothers, and s. for sin with them.
T-21......III.9:4 And if you s. to limit Him, you will hate
T-21.....VII.4:3 it can overrun the world and *s.* an enemy.
T-21.....VII.5:5 him s. no longer what is not there to find.
T-22....... II.1:6 heavy garments are those who s. illusions
T-22....... II.2:3 misery and s. another is hardly an escape.
T-22...... VI.1:9 will s. for it where he believes it is and can
T-22...... VI.8:5 S. not to change it, nor to substitute
T-23....... I.11:1 s. to overcome the One Who dwells there
T-23....... II.9:6 they s. to share the things they value. And
T-23..... II.17:6 You cannot s. to harm him and be saved.
T-23......IV.9:4 he has everything could s. for limitation,
T-24....... II.1:4 This does it s., and this it looks upon.
T-24.....III.8:10 s. your love that you may love yourself.
T-24....... V.1:5 s. for is a source of joy as you conceive it.
T-24....... V.4:4 What does it s. for but the sight of death?
T-24....... V.8:1 s. salvation in a war with love, consider
T-24.....VII.3:3 S. not to make your specialness the truth,
T-25.........I.2:5 tells you this, and s. his death instead?
T-25....... II.2:6 you would s. for hope where none is ever
T-25......IV.1:4 And thus they s. for it, because it is their
T-25. VIII.10:4 Son be judged by those who s. his death,
T-25. VIII.10:8 from all unfairness you might s. to offer,
T-25......IX.7:1 Salvation cannot s. to help God's Son be
T-25......IX.8:2 S. to deny and you will feel denied. Seek
T-25......IX.8:3 S. to deprive, and you have been deprived
T-26...... VI.2:6 S. not another friend to take His place.
T-26... VIII.7:6 And you s. to be content with sighing,
T-26....... X.4:2 s. to find an innocence that is not Theirs
T-26....... X.4:5 own attack upon the Son of God you s.? Is
T-26....... X.5:3 you s. to add unto the purpose given it.
T-27.........I.4:5 and in contagion do they s. to kill. Death
T-27.........I.8:2 reason to remain content to s. for passing
T-27.....VII.6:6 S. not another cause, nor look among the
T-28.........I.5:2 not s. to use it as a means to keep the past
T-28.........I.6:2 which you s. to keep concealed the truth
T-28...... VI.1:4 It does not s. to make of pain a joy and
T-28...... VI.3:2 forth to s. for separation and be separate.
T-29....... V.8:4 is so, and s. not the eternal in this world.
T-29........VII.h S. Not Outside Yourself
T-29.....VII.1:1 S. not outside yourself. For it will fail,
T-29.....VII.1:6 S. not outside yourself. For all your pain
T-29...VII.1:10 abides, and s. no longer elsewhere. You
T-29...VII.1:12 truth, and not to s. for it outside yourself.
T-29.....VII.2:4 upon the body; that it s. for what he lacks,
T-29.....VII.3:1 will impel him to s. out a thousand idols,
T-29.....VII.3:1 to s. beyond them for a thousand more.
T-29.....VII.3:4 Yet does he s. to kill God's Son within,
T-29.....VII.4:5 S. not outside yourself. The search
T-29.....VII.4:6 prefer to s. outside yourself for what you
T-29.....VII.5:2 but to perceive the signs of death you s.?
T-29.....VII.6:6 not to idols. Do not s. outside yourself.
T-29...VII.10:5 s. to drown His Voice in chants of deep
T-29...VII.10:6 S. not outside your Father for your hope.
T-29... VIII.2:6 And thus must s. beyond his little self for
T-29... VIII.8:5 still attempts to s. for one that yet might
T-29... VIII.9:6 why would you s. for idols that would
T-29......IX.1:2 no life, and s. for power in the powerless.
T-29......IX.6:2 S. not to retain the toys of children. Put
T-29......IX.8:3 s. to prove the dream is being dreamed by
T-30.......in.1:8 We s. to make them habits now, so you
T-30...... III.2:1 It is not form you s.. What form can be a
T-30...... III.2:8 It will not bestow on you the gift you s..
T-30...... III.3:3 To s. a special person or a thing to add to
T-30...... III.5:2 He has no need to s. for it at all. Beyond
T-30...... III.9:5 s. for idols cannot know the star is there.
T-30......IV.7:4 and s. no longer for the things you do not
T-30......IV.7:5 and s. no more to substitute the strength
T-31.........I.7:8 that you can s. for here and hope to find.
T-31......IV.2:5 S. not escape from problems here. The
T-31......IV.4:1 Why would you s. to try another road,
T-31......IV.4:5 S. not another signpost in the world that
T-31......IV.5:2 begin with this, to s. another way instead?
T-31....... V.8:2 never s. to go beyond its roads nor realize
T-31..... V.11:5 Spirit does not s. to throw you into panic.
T-31..... V.15:1 S. not your Self in symbols. There can be
T-31.....VII.1:2 Salvation does not s. to use a means as yet
W-pI.....16.4:1 and actively s. not to overlook any "little"
W-pI.....45.4:2 will attempt to leave the unreal and s. for
W-pI.....71.4:2 ego's basic doctrine, "S. but do not find."
W-pI.....71.5:1 direction, you s. for salvation where it is.
W-pI.....71.5:2 will, you must be willing to s. there only.
W-pI.....72.6:1 animals s. for prey and mercy cannot
W-pI...72.11:4 S. and you will find. We are no longer
W-pI.....73.6:1 which s. to prove all this is really Heaven.
W-pI.....74.6:5 if you do not experience the peace you s..
W-pI.....74.7:3 *I s. His peace today.* Then try to find what
W-pI.....76.1:5 you would s. for it in things that have no
W-pI.....76.1:6 Thus do you s. to prove salvation is where
W-pI.....76.2:2 would forever s. salvation where it is not,
W-pI.....77.6:8 You will receive the assurance that you s..
W-pI.....96.9:4 Then s. Its Thoughts, and claim them as
W-pI.....98.1:7 else. We will not s. for it where it is not. In
W-pI.....99.9:1 light s. out and lighten up all darkened
W-pI...101.2:5 and it will s. them out and find them
W-pI...101.4:1 would s. out such savage punishment?
W-pI...102.4:3 s. this function deep within your mind,
W-pI...103.3:6 *And it is happiness I s. today. I cannot fail,*
W-pI...103.3:7 *today. I cannot fail, because I s. the truth.*
W-pI......104.h I s. but what belongs to me in truth.
W-pI...104.3:3 *I s. but what belongs to me in truth, And joy*
W-pI...104.4:1 and s. instead that which is truly ours, as
W-pI...104.5:2 to s. for them where He has laid them.
W-pI...104.5:4 *I s. but what belongs to me in truth. God's*
W-pI...107.6:4 is impossible that anyone could s. it truly,
W-pI...109.2:2 and the safety and the happiness you s.. "I
W-pI...110.8:1 S. Him within you Who is Christ in you,
W-pI. 110.10:1 S. Him today, and find Him. He will be
W-pI...117.2:1 (104) I s. but what belongs to me in truth
W-pI...117.3:4 hour: I s. but what belongs to me in truth.
W-pI...122.4:1 Why would you s. an answer other than
W-pI...122.4:4 S. for it no more. You will not find
W-pI...122.9:2 Earnestly and gladly will we s. for it today
W-pI. 126.10:1 and s. sanctuary in the quiet place where
W-pI...127.6:1 S. not within the world to find your Self.
W-pI...128.3:3 yourself. All things you s. to make your
W-pI...128.6:1 it s. the level where it finds itself at home.
W-pI...129.6:5 of all the things you s. but do not want.
W-pI...130.4:8 Today we will not s. for them, nor waste
W-pI...130.5:2 S. for the one; the other disappears. But
W-pI...130.8:1 own, and recognizing what it is you s..
W-pI. 130.11:5 *I s. my freedom and deliverance, and this is*
W-pI...131.1:1 you s. for goals that cannot be achieved.
W-pI...131.2:6 and while you s. for life you ask for death.
W-pI...131.4:4 God's Son can not s. vainly, though he try
W-pI...131.5:3 Everything you s. but this will fall away.
W-pI. 131.10:2 truth, and it is truth we s. to reach today.
W-pI. 131.11:4 *The world I s. I did not make alone, the*
W-pI. 131.12:1 S. for that door and find it. But before
W-pI. 131.12:4 want, and only what lies past it do you s..
W-pI. 131.15:5 *Today I s. and find all that I want. My single*
W-pI. 133.13:4 *is valueless, and only what has value do I s.,*
W-pI. 136.12:3 nor s. to prove how pitiful and futile your
W-pI...138.5:4 beyond the goals we s. to teach within the
W-pI...140.6:3 Nor does it s. to heal what is not sick,
W-pI...140.7:1 to s. to cure what cannot suffer sickness.
W-pI...140.8:1 Today we s. to change our minds about
W-pI...140.8:1 of sickness, for we s. a cure for all illusions
W-pI...140.8:5 We need but s. it and it must be found.
W-pI. 154.10:2 We will not s. to keep our minds apart
W-pI...181.3:2 We instruct our minds that it is this we s.,
W-pI...181.3:5 We s. for innocence and nothing else. We
W-pI...181.3:6 We s. for it with no concern but now.
W-pI...181.7:2 We do not s. for long-range goals. As each
W-pI...181.7:3 we s. but for surcease an instant from the
W-pI...181.8:2 For what we s. to look upon is really there
W-pI...181.8:4 we s. for in the name of true perception,
W-pI...181.9:3 We s. for this remembrance as we turn
W-pI. 185.10:2 And so do all who seem to s. for dreams.
W-pI. 185.10:4 intent with what they s. above all things,
W-pI. 185.14:1 It is this one intent we s. today, uniting
W-pI...188.1:2 s. the light are merely covering their eyes.
W-pI...189.6:1 as we s. to reach to what is true in us, and
W-pI...190.9:4 with which you s. to hide your holiness.
W-pI...198.4:3 it, s. to find a thousand ways in which it
W-pI...199.1:3 Who would s. for freedom in a body looks
W-pI...199.6:1 is the home of minds that s. for freedom.
W-pI...200.1:1 S. you no further. You will not find peace
W-pI...200.1:4 S. you no further. There is nothing else
W-pI...200.1:5 of God, unless you s. for misery and pain.
W-pI...200.3:5 and s. no longer what you cannot find.
W-pI...200.3:6 than to s. and seek and seek again for hell,
W-pI...200.3:6 than to seek and s. and seek again for hell,
W-pI...200.3:6 than to seek and seek and s. again for hell,
W-pI...200.7:4 Is it here that he would s. for peace? Or
W-pI. 200.10:2 S. no further. You have come to where the
W-pI. 200.11:1 Today we s. no idols. Peace can not be
W-pI. 200.11:7 We s. no further. We are close to home,
W-pI...205.1:3 *goal; the aim of all my living here, the end I s.*
W-pI...211.1:2 *silence and in true humility I s. God's glory,*
W-pI...212.1:2 *I s. the function that would set me free from*
W-pI...212.1:4 *Only this I s., and only this will I accept as*

W-pII ....in.1:3 now we s. direct experience of truth alone
W-pII .221.1:1 *today to s. the peace that You alone can give.*
W-pII .225.2:5 one, and it is but this oneness that we s.,
W-pII .229.1:1 I s. my own Identity, and find It in these
W-pII .229.1:2 I am." Now need I s. no more. Love has
W-pII ....230.h Now will I s. and find the peace of God.
W-pII .230.2:1 *Father, I s. the peace You gave as mine in my*
W-pII .231.1:1 *What can I s. for, Father, but Your Love?*
W-pII .231.1:2 *Perhaps I think I s. for something else; a*
W-pII .231.1:3 *Yet is Your Love the only thing I s., or ever*
W-pII .231.2:4 This we s.. And only this is what it will be
W-pII .....3.3:2 go to find what has been given them to s..
W-pII .....4.2:7 will s. instead for witnesses to what is true
W-pII .251.1:2 Now do I s. but one, for in that one is all I
W-pII .258.2:4 *You? What could we s. but our Identity?*
W-pII .259.2:2 *afraid of love, nor s. for refuge in its opposite*
W-pII .261.1:3 Let me today s. not security in danger,
W-pII .261.2:1 *Let me not s. for idols. I would come, my*
W-pII .268.2:5 safe. And it is only this we s. today.
W-pII .....6.5:2 So therefore let us s. to find Christ's face
W-pII .271.1:2 s. the witnesses to what is true in God's
W-pII .275.1:2 will s. and hear and learn and understand
W-pII .287.1:4 treasure would I s. and find and keep that
W-pII .290.1:6 This the day I s. my present happiness,
W-pII .290.1:6 look on nothing else except the thing I s..
W-pII .290.2:1 *me up today, while I but s. to do Your Will.*
W-pII .292.1:7 will s. and we will find according to His
W-pII .296.2:3 us, to s. and find the easy path to God.
W-pII .300.1:3 And it is this serenity we s., unclouded,
W-pII .300.2:1 *We s. Your holy world today. For we, Your*
W-pII .302.2:3 He the End we s., and He the Means by
W-pII ....306.h The gift of Christ is all I s. today.
W-pII ....314.h I s. a future different from the past.
W-pII .318.1:5 I was created as the thing I s.. I am the
W-pII .319.1:4 it must s. for aims which are curtailed and
W-pII ...12.2:5 who s. to murder it before it can ensure
W-pII .334.2:1 *I s. but the eternal. For Your Son can be*
W-pII .346.1:3 *I do not s. the things of time, and so I will not*
W-pII .346.1:4 *What I s. today transcends all laws of time*
W-pII .349.1:1 *I see, and give to them the freedom that I s..*
W-pII ...14.3:5 do not s. a function that is past the gate of
W-pII ...14.5:2 which we came, and which we s. to serve.
Wfl ........in.1:2 remind us that we s. to go beyond them.
Wfl ........in.3:4 It is His ending to the dream we s., and
W-ep .........3:2 retire from the world, to s. reality instead.
M-4 .....I.A.8:9 And who would s. to change tranquility
M-4 .....VII.2:7 he does not s. what only he could keep,
M-5 ......III.3:3 They s. for God's Voice in this brother
M-13 .........3:3 condemned itself to s. without finding; to
M-13 .........5:8 "S. but do not find" remains this world's
M-20 .........6:7 He does not s. to keep it for Himself. Why
M-20 .........6:8 Why would you s. to keep your tiny frail
C-in ...........2:1 and those who s. controversy will find it.
C-in ...........2:2 who s. clarification will find it as well.
C-in ...........4:5 S. only this, and do not let theology delay
C-2...........6:18 need to s. for an illusion now that dreams
P-2.........in.2:5 clearly impossible, what they s. is magic.
P-2........IV.2:3 themselves to s. for remedies that cannot
P-2........IV.4:3 s. for magic by which to heal the ills with
P-2......... V.8:7 There is no other way to s. His Son. There
S-1......... II.4:6 may not s. to imprison Christ and thereby
S-1........IV.2:4 is not the goal that prayer should truly s..
S-2...........I.2:2 no guilt that it can s. and find and "love."
S-2......... II.4:2 goal is also sought by those who s. the
S-2......... II.6:4 And you will s. to rid yourself of guilt in
S-2........III.2:3 s. to understand what is beyond you yet,

## seeking 41

T-4......... V.5:3 Meaningful s. is consciously undertaken,
T-9......... II.8:5 this way you are s. the truth in you. This
T-12.........IV.h S. and Finding
T-12......IV.2:3 its frantic search for love it is s. what it is
T-12......IV.5:3 futile, for you will be s. it where it is not.
T-12.....VII.6:5 not find love, for that is not what it is s..
T-12.....VII.6:6 Yet s. and finding are the same, and if you
T-12....VIII.7:7 Yet by s. the unreal, what else could you
T-13.........I.5:3 everyone is s. to escape from the prison
T-13....VIII.7:3 who are s. you and where to find them.
T-14 .....X.10:5 it not unless he joins with you in s. it. If
T-15 ...... V.7:2 liking, offering for your s. a picture whose
T-15 ...... V.10:7 Spirit bring to you those who are s. you.
T-15 ..... XI.6:1 So is it that, in all your s. for love, you
T-16 ..... VI.5:2 s. to join each other in separate unions
T-16 .....VII.2:2 By s. to remove suffering in the past, it
T-16 .....VII.5:5 In s. the special relationship, you look not
T-16 ..VII.10:3 ego in s. how Atonement can come to you
T-19 ......I.5:10 a means for s. out reality through attack.
T19..IV.B.13:4 s. it dutifully and obeying the idea that
T19..IV.B.17:5 returns to Him, s. itself along the way,
T-20 ..... VI.4:3 weapon for s. power *through* relationships
T-28 .....VII.6:1 sense in s. to be safe in what was made for
WpI... rI.in.4:5 and s. a haven of isolation for yourself.
W-pI...... 74.7:4 Then try to find what you are s.. A minute
W-pI...... 86.1:6 it is. I will undertake no more idle s.. Only
W-pI... 96.11:5 s. Him Who joins your mind and Self, you
W-pI... 130.4:8 waste this day in s. what can not be found
W-pI. 131.14:5 searching here, and all the s. of the world,
W-pI... 132.2:4 thoughts of s. what you do not want to
W-pI... 155.2:2 who choose to come to it are s. for a place
W-pI... 182.3:2 search, s. in darkness what he cannot find
W-pII .233.1:4 *instead of s. goals which cannot be obtained*
W-pII .345.2:1 Peace to all s. hearts today. The light has
Wfl........in.2:6 our many brothers who are s. for the way,
M-4 .... IX.2:10 Toward Them it looks, s. until it finds.
M-6 ........... 4:3 Spirit in the patient's mind is s. for him.
M-13 ......... 2:9 By s. after such things the mind associates
P-2......... V.5:1 A brother s. aid can bring us gifts beyond
P-3........ III.7:7 You have perhaps been s. for salvation
S-2........ III.5:2 The form the s. takes you need not judge.

## seeks 77

T-2 ....... III.4:2 All solutions the physical eye s. dissolve.
T-4 ....... IV.1:6 glass in which the ego s. to see its face is
T-7 ....... IV.5:2 The ego always s. to divide and separate.
T-7 ....... IV.5:3 Holy Spirit always s. to unify and heal. As
T-8 .....VIII.8:8 choice, which the Holy Spirit s. to restore,
T-12 .... VII.6:4 The ego finds what it s., and only that. It
T-13 .........I.1:2 He s. to remove all guilt from his mind
T-13 ........X.6:4 The Holy Spirit s. not to dispel reality. If
T-14 ...... V.7:4 which s. but to restore what is the right of
T-14 .... V.11:8 out, for here is what he s. along with you.
T-14 .....X.10:5 Everyone s. for love as you do, but knows
T-15 ..... IV.6:8 It therefore s. to change nothing, but
T-15 .... VII.9:3 each s. relief from guilt by increasing it in
T-16 ...... V.7:2 "self" s. the relationship to make itself
T-16 ...... V.8:1 "better" self the ego s. is always one that
T-16 ..... V.11:5 people, on which each s. to kill his self,
T-16 ..... VI.5:7 special relationship the ego s. does not
T-16 .... VII.3:3 has offended it, and s. retribution of you.
T-17 ... III.2:10 For unholiness s. to reinforce itself, as
T-17 ..... III.6:1 The ego s. to "resolve" its problems, not
T-17 ..... III.6:2 it s. to guarantee there will be no solution
T-17 ..... III.6:3 s. and finds the source of problems where
T-17 ... VI.6:10 it s. to split off segments of the situation
T19..IV.B.17:5 itself along the way, and finding what it s.
T19..IV.B.17:6 seeks. So does the ego find the death *it* s.,
T-20 .......II.3:3 to himself. No one but s. to draw to it the
T-20 ..... VI.4:7 the ego s. as many bodies as it can collect
T-20 ..... VI.5:3 and s. for crumbs to keep itself alive. Here
T-21 ..... VI.7:3 reassure you, and s. not to frighten you.
T-23 ......I.3:10 The victory it s. is meaningless as is itself.
T-23 .......I.12:4 is born, and grows and s. to dominate.
T-23 .......I.12:5 where love abides, and s. to share itself.
T-24 .....II.12:5 Not one believer in its potency but s. for
T-24 ...... V.6:9 And s. it still, that each might offer you
T-25 ..... IV.1:5 Everyone s. for what will bring him joy as
T-27 ........I.6:9 Adornment of the body s. to show how
T-27 .......II.2:6 s. to pardon what it thinks to be the truth
T-27 ... VIII.1:4 it s. for other bodies as its friends and
T-27 ... VIII.2:1 the body s. in many ways to prove it is
T-28 ... IV.10:2 Who s. for substitutes when he perceives
T-29 .... VII.2:3 s. for something more than everything, as
T-29 .... VII.3:2 the idol that he s. *is* but his death. Its form
T-29 .. VII.10:2 so. Salvation s. to prove there is no death,
W-pI....... 131.h No one can fail who s. to reach the truth.
W-pI... 131.4:4 himself and think that it is hell he s..
W-pI 131.10:2 No one can fail who s. to reach the truth,
W-pI 131.12:2 no one can fail who s. to reach the truth.
W-pI 131.15:7 *me. No one can fail who s. to reach the truth.*
W-pI .. 133.7:4 Who s. to take away has been deceived by
W-pI .. 146.1:1 No one can fail who s. to reach the truth.
W-pI .. 152.9:1 by which the ego s. to prove it arrogant.
W-pI .. 182.3:2 find; not recognizing what it is he s.. A
W-pI .. 182.3:5 The home he s. can not be made by him.
W-pI .. 182.4:3 a Child in you Who s. His Father's house,
W-pI 184.13:1 who s. the meaning of the Name of God.
W-pI .. 185.5:2 s. the means which bring illusions. He has
W-pI .. 185.5:4 wanting. Now he s. to go beyond them,
W-pI .. 185.6:2 a form each mind that s. for it in honesty
W-pI 185.11:1 truly s. the peace of God can fail to find it.
W-pI .. 186.7:2 image trembles and s. to attack the threat
W-pI .. 199.6:6 which the mind within the Holy Spirit s..
W-pII .... in.4:3 the invitation that He s. to make us happy
W-pII ..... 1.4:2 nor s. to twist it to appearances it likes. It
W-pII ..... 4.1:2 s. to let illusions take the place of truth.
W-pII ..... 4.2:5 What it s. for now is chosen by the aim
W-pII . 325.1:2 judges valuable, and therefore s. to find.
M-8 ........... 2:4 The mind therefore s. to make it true out
M-13 .......... 5:7 And so he s. it in a thousand ways and in
M-20 ......... 3:2 fail to find it who but s. out its conditions.
M-21 ......... 3:4 not exist or s. for illusions in his heart, all
C-2 ............ 2:5 s. by definition to ensure that its illusive
P-2.........in.3:4 magical powers he s. in psychotherapy.
P-2.........in.3:6 is his god, and he s. only to serve it better.
P-2...........I.2:6 the ego s. to make are not really changes.
P-2..........V.1:6 felt, and s. to raise illusions to the light.
S-2..........II.6:5 become, and how distorted is the end it s.
S-2........ III.1:7 and s. to understand the Will of God. His

## seem 262

T-1 ........I.13:2 which s. to go back but really go forward.
T-2 ..........I.5:4 may s. to be of greater magnitude than
T-2 .........II.6:1 Evolution is a process in which you s. to
T-3 ....... VI.4:3 in pleasant disguises in what s. to be your
T-3 ....... VI.4:5 but you have made it s. dangerous to you.
T-4 ....... IV.2:6 This may s. hard to do, but it is much
T-6 ..........II.3:4 that it makes you s. "better" than they are
T-6 .......II.11:1 it can so easily make the idea s. difficult.
T-7 ..........II.2:9 opposed outcomes s. possible because
T-7 .........V.5:8 the idea of exceptions s. to be meaningful.
T-7 .....VIII.2:3 devising ways that s. to diminish conflict,
T-7 .........X.6:6 open to choice, though it may s. to be.
T-8 ..........I.2:1 ego may s. to interfere with your learning,
T-8 ..... III.7:10 The imprisonment they s. to produce is
T-9 ..........I.9:5 To deny what is can only *s.* to be fearful.
T-10 ..... III.8:7 God. Yet when they s. to speak to you,
T-10 .......V.3:8 may s. to be many different things he is
T-11 ........I.9:3 may s. to demand of you what you do not
T-11 .......II.3:2 because the rest will s. to be separate and
T-12 .... VII.6:8 it has one goal by making it s. to be one.
T-13 ......in.2:4 and all the laws that s. to govern it are the
T-13 ......in.2:7 minds s. to be trapped in their brain, and
T-13 ......in.2:8 They s. to love, yet they desert and are
T-13 ........I.3:7 will s. long and cruel and senseless, for so
T-13 ..... III.6:2 do so, and thus they s. to be self-sustained
T-13 .... VII.2:4 yet either one will s. as real to you as the
T-13 .......X.8:5 will s. incredible that he ever thought his
T-14 ........I.5:6 s. to encroach upon deception and strike
T-14 .......II.4:6 The heavy chains that s. to bind them to
T-14 .......X.2:4 world you s. to live in is a world of limits.
T-14 .......X.6:1 It will s. difficult for you to learn that you
T-14 .......X.9:2 Separately, they s. to hold, but put them
T-15 .......I.4:10 For the ego must s. to keep fear from you
T-15 .......I.4:12 together so that they s. to be reconciled.
T-15 .......II.4:2 s. to provide reasons for not letting it go.
T-15 ..... III.3:2 The lesson may s. hard at first, but you
T-15 .......V.8:2 no one to make your brothers s. different.
T-15 .... VII.6:5 direct attack, although it does not s. to be.
T-15 .... VII.8:1 only *s.* to be together. For relationships, to
T-15 .......X.6:2 And the payment does not s. to be yours.
T-15 .......X.7:5 in which you s. to be both destroyer and
T-16 .......II.3:1 To you the miracle cannot s. natural,
T-16 ... IV.13:3 in God's completion s. to be possible. The
T-16 .......V.1:2 by periods in which they s. to be gone. All

T-16.......V.3:5 natural at all s. to be the unnatural ones.
T-16.....V.14:2 They but s. to be fearful to the extent to
T-16.....VII.5:1 special relationship it does not s. to be an
T-17......III.3:5 the one in whom they s. to be decreases in
T-17.......V.3:3 but it makes the relationship s. disturbed,
T-17.......V.4:6 relationship may s. to be severely strained
T-17.......V.8:2 for it will s. at times to have no purpose.
T-17......VI.7:2 And it will s. to be successful, except that
T-18.........I.7:1 When you s. to see some twisted form of
T-18........II.5:5 what they do that s. to make the dream.
T-18........II.5:8 You s. to waken, and the dream is gone.
T-18......II.5:11 s. to waken to is but another form of this
T-18......VI.3:2 the body does separation s. to be possible
T-18.....VII.3:3 Only its past and future make it s. real.
T-18... VIII.1:1 of the body that makes love s. limited. For
T-18... VIII.2:4 Limits on love will always s. to shut Him
T-18... VIII.5:1 in a world inhabited by bodies s. to be.
T-18......IX.3:1 messages s. to be returned to the mind
T-18......IX.6:1 that s. to be a solid wall before the sun. Its
T-18......IX.7:3 stand out and move about, actions s. real,
T-19.........I.4:6 And the body will s. to be sick, for you
T-19.........I.5:5 all obstacles that s. to rise between them.
T-19........II.6:3 clouds of guilt s. heavy and impenetrable.
T-19......III.7:4 and His creation s. to be split apart and
T-19......IV.1:3 Others will s. to arise from elsewhere;
T19. IV.A.13:4 s. to allay their savage pangs of hunger.
T19..IV.B.10:7 body will s. to be whatever is the means
T19... IV.C.6:4 As you look on it, so will it s. to be. Death,
T19...IV.D.4:1 the belief in death would s. to "save" you.
T19...IV.D.4:3 of death that makes life s. to be ugly, cruel
T19.IV.D.11:3 For only if they share in it does it s. fearful
T-20........II.1:3 made to make s. lovely what you hate.
T-20......VI.6:8 him, is what makes God s. fearful to you,
T-20.....VII.5:1 to make the unholy relationship s. real.
T-20.....VII.7:6 means s. real because the goal is valued.
T-20.....VII.8:8 imaginings about him will s. real there.
T-20... VIII.5:5 will s. to make your savior weak. Yet it is
T-20... VIII.7:5 that those who s. to walk about in it, to
T-21........II.7:5 you otherwise must therefore s. unreal.
T-21........II.9:2 faith, to make its goals s. real and possible
T-21......IV.6:7 trinkets still s. to shine and catch your eye
T-21.......V.3:6 Miracles s. unnatural to the ego because
T-21......VI.8:2 Does Heaven s. to be a burden to you? In
T-21.....VII.3:1 and loud and strong the dark ones s. to be
T-21.....VII.6:7 would s. to be the last remaining hope of
T-21... VIII.1:3 The thoughts that s. to kill are those that
T-22........in.2:3 need for sin, not real but seen, s. justified.
T-22.........I.4:7 that you made, whatever it may s. to be.
T-22......II.10:3 it s. possible that what you made is yours.
T-22......IV.2:1 few steps along the right way that s. hard,
T-22.......V.6:5 Not one that does not s. to stand, heavy
T-22....VI.10:8 While this remains, so will it s. to be.
T-22....VI.13:8 of what you understand you s. to be, and
T-23.......I.2:10 and will s. to have replaced love there.
T-23.......I.2:12 think that it is possible, the means s. real.
T-23.........I.3:2 You s. to meet, and make your strange
T-23........II.2:5 and those who hold them s. to be unlike,
T-23........II.3:2 making it s. that some of them are harder
T-23......II.13:5 the ground beneath your feet s. solid.
T-23......II.15:1 These do not s. to be the goals of chaos,
T-23......II.16:7 Some forms it takes s. to have meaning,
T-23......II.20:2 making it s. quite possible to value some
T-23......III.2:1 lovely and charitable it may s. to be, a
T-23......IV.5:3 Here in the midst of it, it does s. real.
T-24.........I.4:4 those who s. "beneath" the special one is
T-24......II.11:6 and you as one s. anything but Heaven,
T-24......II.13:1 hope of specialness makes it s. possible
T-24......III.2:4 So does it s. to split you off from God,
T-24.......V.2:1 the form, however lovely it may s. to be,
T-24......VI.5:1 of the laws that s. to rule this world. See
T-24.....VII.8:6 Perception does not s. to be a means. And
T-25......IV.4:4 you now will s. increasingly remote and
T-25.....VII.1:5 can s. to hide the pain of sin from sinners,
T-26........II.3:4 makes each one s. different from the rest.
T-26.......V.1:1 A little hindrance can s. large indeed to
T-26.....VII.4:7 their effects but s. to be apart from them.
T-26.....VII.7:2 errors s. forever past the hope of healing,
T-26...VII.10:1 world that death and desolation s. to rule.
T-26...VII.12:7 and s. to be beyond you to control or to
T-26...VII.15:2 whatever meaning that they s. to have.
T-26... VIII.3:9 from you and given s. dangerous, with
T-26... VIII.6:2 of the working out can s. to take forever.
T-27......II.11:1 split mind, identity must s. to be divided.
T-27......II.12:6 Thus does your function s. divided, with a
T-27.......V.4:6 blessing, will the world indeed s. fearful,
T-27......V.10:5 Each one may s. to have a problem that is
T-27.....VII.7:9 in making them and making them s. real.
T-27... VIII.4:5 by causing them and making them s. real.
T-27... VIII.8:5 Without the cause do its effects s. serious
T-27. VIII.12:8 They s. to keep it secret from you. Yet you
T-28.........I.8:4 Its consequences will indeed s. new,
T-28......II.10:6 and the bodies that still s. to move about
T-28......III.3:6 all things that s. to glisten in the dream.
T-28......IV.3:7 and his dreams but s. to make a little gap,
T-28......IV.9:5 the broken pieces s. to take mean nothing
T-28.......V.3:6 you s. to be a something you are not. You
T-29.........I.3:3 make the way to light s. dark and fearful,
T-29.........I.4:4 And then your bodies s. to get in touch,
T-29........II.1:3 it is impossible to lose the way, s. thorny,
T-29........II.7:7 health, and with events that s. to alter it.
T-29......IV.5:5 in that they s. to be what they are for. A
T-29.......V.7:3 Why does it s. so hard to share this dream
T-29......IX.2:6 dream will s. to last while he is part of it.
T-29......IX.5:6 they s. to save him from his thoughts. Yet
T-29......IX.6:7 And bad things s. to happen, and he is
T-30......III.7:1 Thoughts s. to come and go. Yet all this
T-30......IV.3:8 that they can s. to break and frighten him
T-30......IV.4:4 They s. to dance a little while, according
T-30... VIII.3:2 not s. to be the wish that no reality be so.
T-31......IV.2:9 lead, however differently they s. to start;
T-31......IV.2:9 to start; however differently they s. to go.
T-31......IV.3:3 can offer s. to be quite large in number,
T-31......IV.7:3 To you who s. to find this course to be too
T-31.....V.16:6 And each will s. to be accusing you. Yet
W-in..........8:1 and others may s. to be quite startling.
W-pI........5.1:3 to you. The upset may s. to be fear, worry,
W-pI........8.4:6 by saying: *I s. to be thinking about–.*
W-pI........8.5:2 *I s. to be thinking about [name of a person],*
W-pI......12.3:3 you. If terms which s. positive rather than
W-pI......39.9:2 and do not s. to be thinking of anything.
W-pI......42.5:4 no thoughts at all s. to come to mind. If
W-pI......43.6:1 if you s. to be unable to think of anything,
W-pI......43.8:1 those which s. to distress you in any way.
WpI...rI.in.4:3 those that already s. to be calm and quiet.
W-pI......56.1:3 loss, age and death s. to threaten me. All
W-pI......62.4:3 who s. to be far away in space and time,
W-pI......64.2:1 Nothing the body's eyes s. to see can be
W-pI......69.4:3 see only the clouds because you s. to be
W-pI......69.5:2 The clouds s. to be the only reality. They
W-pI......69.5:3 They s. to be all there is to see. Therefore,
W-pI......73.2:2 it, peoples it with figures that s. to attack
W-pI......79.5:2 They s. to be on so many levels, in such
W-pI......79.6:3 in all the problems that s. to confront you
W-pI......81.2:1 special difficulties s. to arise might be: *Let*
W-pI......90.3:2 I s. to have problems only because I am
W-pI......99.6:6 depth or any attribute they s. to have:
W-pI....106.1:1 voice, however loudly it may s. to call, if
W-pI....109.1:3 we s. to look on danger and on sorrow.
W-pI....129.5:5 Esteem them, and they will s. real to you.
W-pI....136.3:3 They s. to be unconscious but because of
W-pI....136.5:1 s. to be beyond your own control. But
W-pI.137.10:1 those who s. to have no contact with you,
W-pI....138.2:3 the choice of Heaven s. to be the same as
W-pI....139.2:2 could make the question s. to be sincere.
W-pI.139.12:3 the chains that s. to keep the knowledge
W-pI....151.2:1 You do not s. to doubt the world you see.
W-pI....152.4:4 s. to be but contradictions introduced by
W-pI....152.6:5 world where such things s. to have reality.
W-pI....153.2:2 anger, anger makes attack s. reasonable,
W-pI....155.5:3 nor do you s. to be distinct from them,
W-pI....155.8:5 Illusion can but s. to hold in chains the
W-pI.155.13:2 not to ways that s. to lead you elsewhere.
W-pI....159.5:3 forgiveness. Things which s. quite solid
W-pI....161.4:6 What can they s. to be but empty sounds;
W-pI....163.2:1 does the thought of death s. mighty. For it
W-pI....165.1:1 makes this world s. real except your own
W-pI....170.3:2 two camps which s. wholly irreconcilable.
W-pI....182.1:1 world you s. to live in is not home to you.
W-pI....185.7:6 which s. to change in what they offer, but
W-pI.185.10:2 And so do all who s. to seek for dreams.
W-pI....186.3:1 Today's idea may s. quite sobering, until
W-pI....186.8:3 and they s. to change from mourner to
W-pI....190.7:1 The world may s. to cause you pain. And
W-pI....191.2:6 that does not s. to bring you nearer death;
W-pI....193.6:3 that s. to have been given power over you.
W-pI....193.7:2 Does pain s. real in the perception? If it
W-pI....196.4:5 s. to need a thousand years can easily be
W-pI....197.4:3 matter if your gifts s. lost and ineffectual.
W-pII .235.1:1 but look upon all things that s. to hurt me
W-pII .236.1:2 At times, it does not s. I am its king at all.
W-pII .255.1:1 not s. to me that I can choose to have but
W-pII .259.1:1 makes the goal of God s. unattainable.
W-pII .259.1:2 strange and the distorted s. more clear?
W-pII .263.2:2 Let all appearances s. pure to us, that we
W-pII .278.1:1 all things that s. to live appear to die, then
W-pII .293.1:3 Can the world s. bright and clear and safe
W-pII ... 11.4:2 We s. to be discrete, and unaware of our
W-pII .335.1:4 I s. to be impelled by outside happenings.
Wfl........in.1:5 that made the world s. ugly and unsafe,
M-in ..........5:1 for the world of sin would s. forever real.
M-2 ...........4:3 teacher s. to come together in the present,
M-3 ...........2:2 of what s. to be very casual encounters; a
M-3 ...........5:7 teachers who falter and may even s. to fail
M-4 ..... I.A.3:6 in what s. to be external circumstances.
M-4 ...... VI.1:7 and more powerful its defenses s. to be.
M-5 ........II.2:8 Special agents s. to be ministering to him,
M-8 ...........3:2 they s. to be in the world outside. Yet it is
M-8 ...........5:9 properties of illusions which s. to make
M-8 ...........6:3 be those who s. to be "sicker" than others
M-11 .........1:3 promises other things that s. impossible,
M-11 .........4:4 the world that makes peace s. impossible.
M-13 .......7:14 situation the impossible can s. to happen.
M-14 .......2:12 touched. It will merely cease to s. to be.
M-14 .........4:2 pieces of its thinking will still s. sensible.
M-16 .........9:3 These attempts may indeed s. frightening
M-17 .........1:3 the magic s. quite real to both of them.
M-20 .........5:6 Life and death s. to be opposites because
M-21 .........2:2 Even when they s. most abstract, the
M-21 .........5:3 It may also s. to be quite irrelevant to the
M-25 .........1:4 he may well develop abilities that s. quite
C-1.............2:2 Nor do their minds s. to be joined. In this
C-2.............2:5 behind the words that s. to make it so.
C-4.............5:9 Only the body makes the world s. real, for
C-ep...........1:7 Illusions of despair may s. to come, but
P-in............1:4 manifestations of this world s. real indeed
P-2........ III.3:1 possible for psychotherapy to s. to fail. It
P-2........ IV.3:3 Yet all these things, however real they s.,
P-2......... V.6:8 Perhaps the answer does not s. to be a gift
P-2......... V.6:9 even s. to be a worsening and not a help.
P-2........ VI.2:5 make this ugly sound s. truly beautiful.
P-3........ III.7:1 view of payment may well s. impractical,
S-1...........I.6:7 be and whatever form he may s. to take.
S-1........ III.3:8 s. to be dangerous instead of merciful. To
S-2...........I.6:5 instant only s. to hide the face of Christ,
S-2...........II.1:3 it may s. to take have but this single goal;
S-2........ III.4:6 not the form that dreams may s. to take.
S-3...........II.3:2 come in forms that s. to be thrust down in
S-3........ III.2:1 may s. to be a strange idea. And yet it can

**seemed** 57

T-10.........I.2:4 that everything that s. to happen in the
T-10....... V.4:1 Sickness and death s. to enter the mind
T-14........II.5:2 learn that what s. hardest was the easiest.
T-16.......III.7:3 Though you s. to suffer for it, the joy of
T-16.... IV.12:3 journey that s. endless is almost complete
T-16...... VI.7:5 that s. to hold your world together. This
T-17........II.5:4 and what s. ugly in the darkness of your
T-17....... V.3:6 *your* goal was all that s. to give it meaning.
T-17..... V.11:8 in what s. to be the light of the mistakes?
T-18.........I.5:6 error, which s. to cast you out of Heaven,
T-18........II.1:5 "free" to make over whatever s. to attack
T-18...... III.1:3 and every fantasy that s. to bring a light
T19....IV.A.7:3 with you it s. to have a mighty purpose;
T19....IV.A.8:1 remains of what once s. to be the world. It
T19... IV.D.5:8 fear s. to be holding them in place. Yet
T-20...... III.9:5 He s. to be crucified beside you. And yet

| | |
|---|---|
| T-20 VI.8:6 | with God unholy s. to be possible, all |
| T-20 VI.8:8 | s. to have a home that held together for a |
| T-20 VIII.11:1 | you have looked on what s. terrifying, and |
| T-21 II.1:5 | obscure, but rather that this little cost s., |
| T-22 IV.6:3 | that s. to rise and block their way before. |
| T-23 in.3:4 | And what s. harmful now stands shining |
| T-24 IV.5:3 | Your specialness s. safe because of it. And |
| T-26 II.7:5 | What s. once to be a special problem, a |
| T-26 V.8:4 | when Heaven s. to disappear and God |
| T-28 I.7:5 | made them what they were, or s. to be. Be |
| T-28 III.5:4 | and covered up the space which s. to keep |
| T-28 III.5:5 | where the seeds of sickness s. to grow? |
| T-28 III.9:8 | its table in the space that s. to keep your |
| T-29 IX.10:6 | when judgment s. to be the way to save |
| W-pI 76.1:1 | things have s. to you to be salvation. Each |
| W-pI 158.9:4 | to be, nor who s. to be hurt by them. They |
| W-pI 158.9:6 | effects they s. to have are gone with them, |
| WpI.rV.in10:6 | knew before illusion s. to claim the world. |
| W-pI 183.3:2 | by, and where it s. to stand you find a star |
| W-pI.184.15:5 | *absolved from all effects our errors s. to have* |
| W-pI.185.12:5 | that ever s. to take the place of truth. |
| W-pI 196.5:2 | Perhaps it s. to be salvation. Yet it merely |
| W-pI.196.10:4 | s. to be an enemy outside you had to fear. |
| W-pI 198.1:5 | and those it s. to have will be undone. |
| W-pII .265.1:2 | How fierce they s.! And how deceived was |
| W-pII .295.1:3 | dreams that s. to settle on the world are |
| W-pII 10.3:1 | them, and all effects they ever s. to have. |
| M-4 VIII.1:6 | as well as him to whom it s. to happen. |
| M-4 X.2:5 | which s. so dull and lifeless before. And |
| M-5 II.4:9 | them also go all the effects they s. to cause |
| M-14 2:4 | born where sin was made and guilt s. real. |
| M-20 6:4 | His Will and yours but s. to be reality. In |
| C-2 5:3 | ego was, for here we see all that it s. to do, |
| C-2 6:13 | evil dream that but s. real while you were |
| C-2 8:1 | illusion and the self that s. alone in all the |
| C-5 2:3 | an illusion, for he s. to be a separate being |
| S-1 in.1:8 | done. For such it was before time s. to be. |
| S-1 in.2:3 | rejoice that what illusions s. to separate is |
| S-1 IV.3:4 | was enjoyed before, or s. to be; what was |
| S-1 IV.3:4 | to be; what was another's and he s. to love |
| S-1 V.3:12 | he never left, and you, who s. alone, are |

## seeming 73

*See also* heavy-seeming

| | |
|---|---|
| T-7 III.4:4 | be, but s. and reality are hardly the same. |
| T-7 III.4:5 | *are* the Kingdom are not concerned with s. |
| T-8 VII.15:6 | No more are any of its s. results. When |
| T-14 in.1:7 | their s. clearness seems to be clearly seen. |
| T-14 XI.1:8 | For power is not a s. strength, and truth is |
| T-16 III.4:10 | s. conflict between truth and illusion can |
| T-17 II.5:2 | and uncover to you the s. reasons for your |
| T-18 VI.12:1 | of your differences in size and s. quality. |
| T-18 IX.3:7 | to follow the Holy Spirit through s. terror, |
| T-19 I.6:2 | divided into little parts of s. wholeness, |
| T19 IV.A.2:9 | of sand, a wall of dust, a tiny s. barrier, |
| T19 IV.A.8:5 | Its s. stability is its pervasive weakness, |
| T19 IV.B.11:4 | The body is the great s. betrayer of faith. |
| T19 IV.C.7:5 | The obstacle of your s. love for death that |
| T19 IV.C.11:5 | Confronted with such s. uncertainty of |
| T19 IV.D.7:6 | of s. death can stand against your will. |
| T19. IV.D.18:4 | here in the garden of s. agony and death. |
| T-20 IV.1:6 | not, and gives no power to their s. source. |
| T-20 IV.5:3 | this earth in s. solitude is a savior given, |
| T-20 IV.8:7 | one s. difficulty but will melt away before |
| T-20 VI.7:2 | fear, feeling the s. firm foundation of their |
| T-20 VI.9:2 | unholy instant of their s. power is frail as |
| T-20 VI.9:4 | s. powerful and so bitterly misunderstood |
| T-20 VI.12:2 | now to you than its unholy s. counterpart |
| T-20 VII.1:4 | The s. inconsistencies, or parts you find |
| T-20 VIII.8:10 | is no order; only a s. hierarchy of values. |
| T-21 II.10:3 | This s. independence of effect enables it |
| T-21 II.13:5 | It is its s. independence of its source that |
| T-21 III.1:2 | toward which the s. union is adjusted. |
| T-22 I.8:7 | home, so s. new and yet as old as He, a |
| T-22 II.3:5 | be sure indeed that any s. happiness that |
| T-22 V.1:10 | *You* are the strong one in this s. conflict. |
| T-23 in.4:4 | world of freedom for a little sigh of s. sin, |
| T-23 II.9:3 | This s. law is the belief you have what you |
| T-23 II.15:4 | its s. laws must be perceived as real. Their |
| T-23 II.20:5 | The s. gentler forms of the attack are no |
| T-24 I.8:10 | that does not change with every s. blow, |
| T-26 I.1:2 | and all conflicts achieve a s. balance. It is |
| T-26 I.1:8 | All s. entities can come a little nearer, or |
| T-26 I.2:3 | so s. solid that it looks as if what is inside |
| T-26 V.13:3 | a s. interval from birth to death and on to |
| T-27 VII.13:4 | So fearful is the dream, so s. real, he could |
| T-29 I.8:7 | are overtones of s. fear around the happy |
| T-29 VI.4:7 | And where it once held s. sway is now |
| T-31 I.10:3 | call that echoes past each s. call to death, |
| T-31 II.3:3 | each s. to possess advantages you would |
| W-pI 12.3:8 | Their s. quality does not matter. |
| W-pI 50.4:5 | can resolve all s. difficulties without effort |
| W-pI 70.2:1 | s. cost of accepting today's idea is this: It |
| W-pI 91.2:9 | And the s. reality of the darkness makes |
| W-pI 107.4:3 | the s. difficulties and the doubts that the |
| W-pI 108.1:2 | is in it, for it reconciles all s. opposites. |
| WpI..rIII.in5:3 | your s. problems and all your concerns. |
| W-pI.135.25:4 | from what was s. death and hopelessness. |
| W-pI 140.6:6 | judges an illusion by its size, its s. gravity, |
| W-pI 151.1:4 | doubt. Its s. certainty is but a cloak for |
| W-pI 153.1:3 | "gifts" of s. safety are illusory deceptions. |
| W-pI 164.3:3 | How easily are all your s. sins forgot, and |
| W-pI 169.2:1 | of God within a world of s. hate and fear. |
| W-pI 170.9:3 | and a s. obstacle with the appearance of a |
| W-pI 181.1:4 | and past his s. sins as well as yours. |
| W-pI.193.10:1 | s. obstacles to peace in just one day. Let |
| W-pI 195.5:2 | who mourn a s. loss or feel apparent pain, |
| W-pI 198.7:1 | world has many s. separate haunts where |
| WpI rVI.in.2:2 | all the s. happenings throughout the day. |
| M-3 2:5 | Perhaps the s. strangers in the elevator |
| M-12 6:11 | dream, beyond all s. and yet surely theirs. |
| M-17 4:2 | of their s. justification by what *appears* as |
| M-29 4:3 | And yet it is but a s. paradox. As God |
| P-2 II.2:7 | remove the s. obstacles to true awareness |
| S-3 I.5:3 | can ask amiss and s. charity forgive to kill, |
| S-3 II.1:8 | kind of s. death that has a different source |
| S-3 II.6:1 | until it brings a cruel death in s. victory. It |

## seemingly 4

| | |
|---|---|
| T-3 III.3:3 | establishes a s. stable state that is usually |
| T-30 VII.7:4 | is a state so s. unsafe that fear must rise. |
| W-pI 68.5:3 | Then think of the s. minor grievances you |
| M-25 3:1 | The s. new abilities that may be gathered |

## seems 331

| | |
|---|---|
| T-2 I.3:5 | What is seen in dreams s. to be very real. |
| T-2 VI.1:1 | Being afraid s. to be involuntary; |
| T-2 VII.4:1 | in it s. to render it out of your control. Yet |
| T-2 VII.5:12 | up. It only s. to be abolished by degrees, |
| T-3 VII.2:4 | because he s. to be extremely powerful |
| T-6 I.16:8 | This conflict s. just as real now, and its |
| T-6 II.9:8 | This convergence s. to be far in the future |
| T-6 V.B.3:6 | first lesson s. to contain a contradiction, |
| T-6 V.C.4:1 | While the first step s. to increase conflict |
| T-7 III.4:4 | It s. to be, but seeming and reality are |
| T-7 V.7:8 | to learn a lesson that s. contradictory;– |
| T-7 VI.7:8 | know, your thought s. to contradict His, |
| T-8 VII.7:2 | since it s. to involve the translation of one |
| T-8 VIII.2:1 | body exists in a world that s. to contain |
| T-9 I.2:2 | What s. to be the fear of God is really the |
| T-9 VI.2:1 | It s. to you that the Holy Spirit does not |
| T-10 I.3:3 | because loving then s. possible to you, |
| T-11 I.9:2 | interpretation it s. possible for God's Will |
| T-11 V.10:1 | recognition that whatever s. to separate |
| T-12 IV.1:2 | that the ego is salvation s. to be intensely |
| T-13 I.3:5 | Time s. to go in one direction, but when |
| T-13 III.3:2 | real power s. to you as your real weakness |
| T-13 III.3:4 | then, s. to be attacking your fortress, for |
| T-13 III.5:3 | death s. more valuable than your living |
| T-13 VIII.3:2 | redemption, which s. to be in the future, |
| T-13 IX.7:2 | And by projecting it the world s. dark, |
| T-14 in.1:7 | seeming clearness s. to be clearly seen. Let |
| T-14 III.3:3 | Whenever the pain of guilt s. to attract |
| T-14 IV.6:3 | own volition s. to make deciding hard. |
| T-14 VII.4:5 | separation s. to keep them both alive and |
| T-14 IX.6:2 | and their meaning s. to lie only in shifting |
| T-14 X.4:5 | by the ego, which but s. to think. |
| T-15 I.2:6 | all the waste that time s. to bring with it is |
| T-15 VII.2:7 | the ego always s. to attract through love, |
| T-15 VII.7:1 | attraction of what you do not want s. to |
| T-15 VII.8:3 | or what it thinks, for this s. unimportant. |
| T-15 VII.9:5 | The other s. always to be attacking and |
| T-15 VII.14:1 | that what s. impossible is accomplished, |
| T-15 VIII.6:4 | then, what s. to you to be impossible, to |
| T-15 X.4:3 | It s. like many, but it is all the same. For |
| T-15 X.6:3 | it never s. to be demanding it of you. You |
| T-15 X.7:3 | the ego s. to demand less of you than God |
| T-15 X.8:4 | s. safer to project Him outward and away |
| T-15 X.8:7 | is an invader who but s. to offer kindness, |
| T-15 XI.4:6 | What you exclude from yourself s. fearful, |
| T-16 IV.5:8 | the choice s. to be one between illusions, |
| T-16 IV.7:5 | the dilemma which s. very real to you, but |
| T-16 IV.10:4 | To lift the veil that s. so dark and heavy, it |
| T-16 IV.11:2 | For such the journey s. to be. Love calls, |
| T-16 V.8:2 | And whoever s. to possess a special self is |
| T-16 VI.11:2 | it s. to be outside and across the bridge. |
| T-17 III.2:5 | you, and s. to go by the name of love, no |
| T-17 IV.6:3 | still s. to you somehow to be "different." |
| T-17 IV.13:5 | each senseless stone that s. to shine from |
| T-17 V.3:7 | Now it s. to make no sense. Many |
| T-17 V.6:6 | faith in your brother in what but s. to be a |
| T-17 V.14:4 | stand now which s. to make you suffer, |
| T-17 VI.3:1 | the outset, the situation just s. to happen, |
| T-17 VI.6:8 | This s. to ask for faith beyond you, and |
| T-17 VI.7:1 | of the situation that s. to be difficult, the |
| T-17 VIII.4:1 | to His Call s. to be greater than before. |
| T-18 I.2:8 | one. But everything *s.* to come between the |
| T-18 I.3:4 | It s. to take many forms, and each one |
| T-18 I.3:4 | and each one s. to require a different form |
| T-18 II.1:1 | a world that s. quite real arise in dreams? |
| T-18 II.3:7 | a time it s. as if the world were given you, |
| T-18 II.4:2 | And thus it s. to be. And yet the dream |
| T-18 II.5:3 | within your mind, that s. to be outside. |
| T-18 III.2:4 | Fear s. to live in darkness, and when you |
| T-18 VI.3:3 | mind that s. to be fragmented and private |
| T-18 VI.3:6 | never what the body does that s. to satisfy |
| T-18 VI.9:1 | is outside you, and but s. to surround you |
| T-18 VI.12:1 | s. to be between you and what you join; of |
| T-18 VIII.5:2 | Each body s. to house a separate mind, a |
| T-18 VIII.5:3 | Each tiny fragment s. to be self-contained, |
| T-18 .VIII.13:2 | and the desert's dust still s. to cloud your |
| T-18 IX.1:3 | little thought that s. split off and separate, |
| T-18 IX.4:1 | s. to be the whole foundation on which |
| T-18 IX.5:2 | that s. to make it heavy and opaque, |
| T-19 I.7:8 | concealment s. to keep your identification |
| T-19 I.8:2 | attack that s. to be justified by its results. |
| T-19 II.6:4 | foundation s. to have is found in this. For |
| T-19 III.7:3 | proof of separation s. to be everywhere. |
| T-19 III.9:3 | the mind corrects it when it s. to be seen, |
| T19 IV.A.2:3 | s. to be the cost you are so unwilling to |
| T19 IV.A.3:7 | brother s. mightier than the universe, for |
| T19 IV.A.5:7 | And all that s. to stand between you and |
| T19 IV.C.1:5 | What s. to be the fear of death is really its |
| T19 IV.C.6:2 | you the one that s. to be the hardest can |
| T19 IV.C.7:5 | peace must flow across s. to be very great. |
| T19 .IV.C.11:1 | anything s. to you to be a source of fear, |
| T19 .. IV.D.2:3 | s. to make the face of Christ Himself like |
| T19 .. IV.D.3:4 | the memory of God s. quite forgotten; the |
| T19 .. IV.D.7:1 | It s. to you the world will utterly abandon |
| T19 IV.D.10:5 | even when it is over it s. to make no sense. |
| T19 IV.D.12:1 | stands beside you still s. to be a stranger. |
| T19 IV.D.12:3 | to keep what s. to be yourself unharmed. |
| T-20 III.5:9 | now if mercilessness s. to look back at you |
| T-20 IV.8:2 | Perhaps this s. impossible to you. But ask |
| T-20 VI.8:4 | of isolation, which s. to be what it is not. |
| T-20 VI.11:2 | This produces what s. to be a wall of flesh |
| T-20 VI.11:3 | And this unholy instant s. to be life; an |
| T-20 VII.8:10 | while this purpose s. to have a meaning, |
| T-20 VIII.8:8 | This world s. to hold out many purposes, |
| T-20 VIII.9:6 | to sin and s. to witness to its reality. It still |
| T-21 II.2:5 | *everything that s. to happen to me I ask for,* |
| T-21 II.3:3 | he s. to find himself by chance or accident |
| T-21 II.6:8 | that threatens this s. to attack your faith, |
| T-21 II.7:4 | which s. to tell you what must happen, |

T-21.....II.10:7 And so he **s.** to *be* the cause, producing
T-21.....II.13:3 But grant that everything that **s.** to stand
T-21....IV.1:10 see. This merely **s.** to be the source of fear.
T-21......VI.2:9 thoughts that enter into what but **s.** like
T-21...VII.3:14 What **s.** to be a planned attack is bedlam.
T-21.....VII.6:2 For this one still **s.** fearful, and unlike the
T-21.....VII.6:5 still **s.** to hold a threat the rest have lost
T-22.......in.1:5 And each one **s.** to make a different error,
T-22.........I.1:7 to wander off, for only that **s.** certain.
T-22.......II.1:4 though each one **s.** to be the way to lose
T-22......III.9:3 because he **s.** to justify the other's sin.
T-22......IV.1:8 part of the journey that **s.** more hopeless
T-22......IV.5:3 that **s.** to rise between you both. So shall
T-22......IV.7:5 Standing before the veil, it still **s.** difficult.
T-22.......V.5:5 This body only **s.** to be immovable; this
T-22.......V.6:8 your unwillingness to overlook what **s.** to
T-22.....VI.10:7 that **s.** to keep the fear of God in place,
T-22.....VI.11:7 For it **s.** safer to attack another or yourself
T-22..VI.12:12 And thus it **s.** as if love could attack and
T-22.....VI.13:9 this **s.** more natural and more in line with
T-23.........I.9:2 For it **s.** real only as long as it is seen as
T-23.......II.3:1 Think how this **s.** to interfere with the
T-23.......II.5:1 what this **s.** to do to the relationship
T-23.......II.6:5 belief that **s.** to make chaos eternal. For if
T-23.......II.7:4 every aspect **s.** to be at war with Him, and
T-23.......II.8:5 And God Himself **s.** to be siding with it,
T-23.....II.16:4 play the major roles, it **s.** most powerful.
T-23.....II.19:4 At best it **s.** like life; at worst, like death.
T-23.....II.21:2 follows that it **s.** to be a logical conclusion
T-23......III.4:2 Yet it **s.** difficult to those who still believe
T-23....IV.1:12 of love because it **s.** to be of equal truth.
T-23......IV.9:3 body; something it **s.** to offer or to own.
T-24.....in.1:12 illusion that idly **s.** to drift between Them
T-24.........I.1:6 it has given it all the reality it **s.** to have.
T-24.......II.4:5 what you are **s.** silent and unheard before
T-24.......II.9:4 which **s.** to make God and His Heaven so
T-24......III.2:6 idol that **s.** to give you power has taken it
T-24......III.3:7 However large and overblown it **s.** to be,
T-24......VI.7:2 and through time that **s.** to have no end,
T-24.....VII.8:8 Perception **s.** to teach you what you see.
T-24.....VII.9:3 And without a light it **s.** that it is gone.
T-25.........I.1:2 will you learn the body merely **s.** to be the
T-25.........I.3:6 learn what **s.** to have a life apart has none.
T-25.........I.4:6 veil that **s.** to keep you separate and apart
T-25......III.8:1 world of violence and hate that **s.** to stand
T-25.......V.1:4 but **s.** to draw a meaning from the other.
T-25.......V.1:5 the other for whatever sense it **s.** to have.
T-25......VI.2:1 and the light of brilliant day **s.** painful to
T-25......VI.2:3 Dimness **s.** better; easier to see, and
T-25......VI.2:4 and more obscure **s.** easier to look upon;
T-25...VII.11:2 this world it **s.** that one must gain *because*
T-25... VIII.7:4 to hell that **s.** to look like Heaven's gate?
T-26.......II.1:4 whatever form the problem **s.** to take. A
T-26.......II.2:2 one, regardless of the form it **s.** to take, is
T-26.......II.8:5 and every bolt and barrier that **s.** to hold
T-26......III.6:2 and **s.** to choose where no choice really is.
T-26......V.11:5 Sometimes the past **s.** real, as if it *were* the
T-26.....VII.3:9 truth, it **s.** to have a meaning and be real.
T-26.....VII.4:9 out, and **s.** to be external to the mind, is
T-26...VII.6:11 wish that **s.** to go against His Will has no
T-26... VIII.2:6 the gift **s.** to be one in which you sacrifice
T-26... VIII.6:7 And yet it **s.** as if this is not so. Good in
T-27.........I.4:6 kill. Death **s.** an easy price, if they can say,
T-27.....II.12:5 and **s.** to have a different purpose from
T-27......VI.2:5 Each one **s.** different because it has a
T-27......VI.2:5 and so it **s.** to answer to a different sound.
T-27.....VII.3:6 Yet it **s.** sensible, because it looks as if the
T-27.....VII.3:7 it **s.** as if there is no need to go beyond the
T-27.....VII.5:2 by which this purpose **s.** to be fulfilled.
T-27... VIII.3:3 and **s.** to show a great variety of places
T-27. VIII.10:4 Whatever **s.** to be the cause of any pain
T-28.........I.5:6 And if it **s.** to serve to cherish ancient hate
T-28.......II.9:5 heard, because it **s.** to be the call to fear.
T-28......III.4:4 thus it **s.** to give a cause to sickness which
T-28......IV.6:2 What is the same **s.** different, because
T-28.......V.3:7 upon your Self, which **s.** to be your enemy
T-28......VI.3:9 It **s.** to punish you, and thus deserve your
T-28.....VII.3:3 that **s.** to hold some promise of relief. Yet
T-28.....VII.4:8 The choice of sickness **s.** to be of form, yet
T-28.....VII.5:4 This **s.** to prove that you must be apart.
T-28.....VII.5:8 It **s.** to be quite solid and substantial in
T-29.........I.4:2 **s.** to be dividing off your separate minds.
T-29.........I.7:4 because it **s.** to come and go uncertainly,
T-29.......II.6:4 although it **s.** to be in constant change.
T-29.......II.9:2 so it **s.** to be a thing with power in itself.
T-29......IV.2:2 fear, no matter what the form it **s.** to take.
T-29......VI.2:7 What *s.* eternal all will have an end. The
T-29... VIII.3:6 dark veil that **s.** to shut you off from Him,
T-29... VIII.3:9 a veil can banish what it **s.** to separate,
T-29... VIII.5:3 be believed before it **s.** to come to life, and
T-30.......I.14:2 This **s.** to be a real decision in itself. And
T-30......IV.3:2 each one **s.** to break the rules you set for it
T-30......VI.4:2 it **s.** impossible His pardon could be real.
T-30......VI.6:7 and everyone who **s.** apart from you?
T-31.........I.4:4 **s.** small and still before its magnitude.
T-31.......II.2:1 Let us review again what **s.** to stand
T-31......IV.1:3 among illusions **s.** to be the only choice.
T-31......IV.4:5 world that **s.** to point to still another road
T-31.......V.2:7 smiles and charms and even **s.** to love. It
T-31.......V.9:1 of what **s.** to be the evidence on its behalf.
T-31.....V.10:1 your brother made of you **s.** most unlikely
T-31.....VII.3:1 the good is never what the body **s.** to be.
T-31...VII.12:1 Whatever form temptation **s.** to take, it
W-pI.......5.1:2 in whatever term **s.** accurate to you. The
W-pI.......6.2:1 to anything that **s.** to upset you, and can
W-pI.......9.2:1 that what it **s.** to picture is not there. This
W-pI.....11.1:2 It **s.** as if the world determines what you
W-pI.....19.2:2 since it **s.** to carry with it an enormous
W-pI.....34.2:2 that **s.** most conducive to readiness. All
W-pI.....37.6:3 the idea if anyone **s.** to cause an adverse
W-pI.....44.4:3 just as it **s.** to be the most unnatural and
W-pI...44.11:1 eyes open or closed as **s.** better to you at
W-pI.....68.1:6 It **s.** to split you off from your Source and
W-pI.....68.2:1 likeness to Its Creator, your Self **s.** to sleep
W-pI.....70.1:2 Salvation **s.** to come from anywhere
W-pI.....71.7:2 answer to what **s.** to be a conflict with no
W-pI.....72.2:3 that **s.** to surround the mind with a body,
W-pI.....74.4:1 area that **s.** particularly difficult to resolve
W-pI...75.10:4 who **s.** to pull you back into darkness: *The*
W-pI.....79.2:1 world **s.** to have his own special problems
W-pI.....79.3:3 of different problems **s.** to confront you,
W-pI.....79.3:4 There **s.** to be no end to them. There is no
W-pI.....79.4:2 The world **s.** to present you with a vast
W-pI...79.10:2 Whenever any difficulty **s.** to rise, tell
W-pI.....93.5:3 it **s.** to do and think means nothing. It is
W-pI...93.11:1 a situation arises that **s.** to be disturbing,
W-pI.....94.5:5 who **s.** to irritate you with these words:
W-pI...105.9:4 brother **s.** to tempt you to deny God's gift
W-pI...109.7:3 the road that suddenly **s.** easy as they go.
W-pI...121.1:2 key to meaning in a world that **s.** to make
W-pI.121.10:1 you do not like, who **s.** to irritate you, or
W-pI...124.8:3 today, whenever it **s.** best, devote a half
W-pI...126.2:2 **s.** to you that other people are apart from
W-pI...127.8:3 The world that **s.** to hold you prisoner can
W-pI...133.1:1 you have gone through what **s.** theoretical
W-pI.133.11:3 alternative you think you chose **s.** fearful,
W-pI...135.7:5 it. For it **s.** to fail your hopes, your needs,
W-pI...136.1:1 what purpose sickness **s.** to serve. For
W-pI...136.4:3 so it **s.** to be external to your own intent; a
W-pI...137.2:2 it **s.** to keep one self apart from all the rest
W-pI...137.6:3 body **s.** to be more solid and more stable
W-pI...138.4:2 And even this but **s.** to be a choice. Do
W-pI...151.1:6 And its defense **s.** strong, convincing, and
W-pI...151.9:6 that **s.** to happen to you in this world. His
W-pI.151.11:2 and every happening that **s.** to touch on
W-pI...153.3:3 There **s.** to be no break nor ending in the
W-pI...153.4:2 hope of sanity **s.** but to be an idle dream,
W-pI...155.1:1 world that is not here, although it **s.** to be.
W-pI...158.3:5 For time but **s.** to go in one direction. We
W-pI...158.3:7 it **s.** to have a future still unknown to us.
W-pI...161.5:1 It **s.** to be the body that we feel limits our
W-pI...163.2:2 For it **s.** to hold all living things within its
W-pI...166.6:1 He **s.** a sorry figure; weary, worn, in
W-pI...167.6:7 **s.** to die is but the sign of mind asleep.
W-pI...167.7:5 it **s.** to make when it believes it sleeps.
W-pI...167.9:1 What **s.** to be the opposite of life is
W-pI...167.9:2 Source, it merely **s.** to go to sleep a while.
W-pI...167.9:3 what **s.** to happen never has occurred, the
W-pI...170.3:1 **s.** to be the enemy without that you attack
W-pI...170.7:2 with blood, and fire **s.** to flame from him,
W-pI...181.7:3 obstruction **s.** to block the vision of our
W-pI...182.6:3 He is so little that He **s.** so easily shut out,
W-pI...186.8:5 very being **s.** to change as we experience a
W-pI.186.12:2 It asks a thing of you which **s.** impossible,
W-pI...187.1:4 **s.** to make it hard to credit is not this. No
W-pI...187.2:5 thought **s.** to appear is changed in giving.
W-pI...187.5:8 What he **s.** to lose is always something he
W-pI...192.9:6 Thus does each one who **s.** to tempt you
W-pI...194.4:3 the temporal progression still **s.** real. And
W-pI...195.1:3 another **s.** to suffer more than they. How
W-pI...195.4:1 could you sanely be enraged if he **s.** freer.
W-pI.196.10:1 There is an instant in which terror **s.** to
W-pI...198.2:6 What **s.** to be its influence and its effects
W-pI...200.4:5 **s.** to be a prison house or jail for anyone.
W-pII.236.1:3 It **s.** to triumph over me, and tell me what
W-pII.....5.3:2 it sometimes **s.** to picture happiness, but
W-pII.328.1:1 What **s.** to be the second place is first, for
W-pII.328.1:2 **s.** that we will gain autonomy but by our
W-pII.356.1:2 *matter where he is, what s. to be his problem*
Wfl........in.2:3 In the dream of time it **s.** to be far off.
W-ep........1:6 need for anything that **s.** to trouble you.
M-in.........1:3 It **s.** as if the teacher and the learner are
M-2...........3:2 long ago **s.** to be happening now. Choices
M-2...........4:2 and again and still again, it **s.** to be now.
M-2...........4:7 but **s.** to take time in the working-out.
M-3...........3:3 the teacher of God **s.** to begin to change
M-3...........3:4 of teaching **s.** to be something different.
M-4.....I.A.3:3 It **s.** as if things are being taken away, and
M-7...........4:3 Usually it **s.** to be just the opposite. It
M-11.........1:2 Certainly peace **s.** to be impossible here.
M-11.........3:4 sense, yet out of which no way **s.** possible,
M-13.......7:15 It **s.** to happen at the "sacrifice" of truth.
M-14.........3:1 Certainly this **s.** to be a long, long while
M-17.......6:11 onto Him, it **s.** to you He has forgotten,
M-17.........9:1 Madness but **s.** terrible. In truth it has no
M-19.........3:5 for not one "sin" but **s.** forever true.
M-22.........2:6 If the way **s.** long, let him be content. He
M-27.........7:3 What **s.** to die has but been misperceived
C-1............2:3 an "individual mind" **s.** to be meaningful.
C-1............4:2 **s.** to be imprisoned while the mind is not
C-2............2:2 but in a form that **s.** like something. In a
C-2............2:3 ego cannot be denied for it alone **s.** real.
C-2............3:3 clear because its nature **s.** to have a form.
C-4............6:4 forgiveness, for it **s.** to be forever sinful.
C-6............4:5 He **s.** to be a Voice, for in that form He
C-6............4:6 He **s.** to be a Guide through a far country,
C-6............4:7 He **s.** to be whatever meets the needs you
C-ep...........3:2 journey long ago begun that but **s.** new.
C-ep...........4:6 instant, though it **s.** to be unsung forever.
P-2.........V.1:6 **s.** as if these forces can be held at bay only
P-2.........V.7:5 one who **s.** to share our dream of sickness
P-2........VI.4:5 the form it takes **s.** to be something else.
P-2........VI.4:6 it is the "something else" that **s.** to terrify.
P-2.......VII.7:7 can he give to one who **s.** to be a stranger;
S-1........III.2:4 god, and it is he who **s.** to answer them.
S-1........III.3:9 To the guilty there **s.** indeed to be a real
S-1........III.4:7 to make a jailer of an enemy **s.** to be safety
S-2...........I.5:2 It always **s.** to be another who is evil, and
S-2..........II.1:2 concealed beneath what **s.** like charity.
S-3...........I.1:2 of an evil thought that **s.** to have reality
S-3...........I.2:3 Fearful and frail it **s.** to be to those who
S-3........III.3:1 magic phrase by which the body **s.** to be

## seen 302

T-2...........I.3:5 What is **s.** in dreams seems to be very real
T-2........III.1:3 generally **s.** as a need to protect the body.
T-2......III.1:10 temple cannot be **s.** with the physical eye.
T-2.........V.8:2 by any device that can be **s.** physically. As
T-3...........I.1:5 is **s.** from an upside-down point of view, it
T-3.......VII.5:7 Much has been **s.** since then, but nothing
T-7......VI.11:1 part in it, God's creation is **s.** as weak, and
T-8.......VII.9:2 Its purpose is **s.** as fragmented into many
T-8......VIII.2:2 perceived constellation the body is **s.** as
T-8......VIII.9:8 attack. Health is **s.** as the natural state of
T-11......IV.5:3 blame must be undone, not **s.** elsewhere.
T-11.......V.2:8 then, to look upon fear, for it cannot be **s.**

T-11...... VI.1:5 are ye who have not s. and still believe,"
T-12...... VI.5:1 When you have s. this real world, as you
T-12...... VI.5:5 He is waiting to be s., for He has never
T-12... VII.10:2 Yet you could not have s. reality, for the
T-12... VII.11:7 exists and only the real world can be s..
T-12.... VIII.3:5 can be s. is what the Holy Spirit sees. The
T-12.... VIII.6:2 is not real cannot be s. and has no value.
T-12.... VIII.6:9 making nothing real to you, you have s. it.
T-12.... VIII.7:2 Son can be s. because his vision is shared.
T-12.... VIII.8:5 invisible, for you will at last have s. truly.
T-13....... V.1:6 They are made of sights that are not s.,
T-13..... VII.6:1 in this distracted world but has s. some
T-13.... VIII.3:7 Aspects of reality can still be s., and they
T-13.... VIII.3:8 Aspects of reality can be s. in everything
T-13.... VIII.5:4 Everyone s. without the past thus brings
T-13.... VIII.8:1 s. your brothers as yourself you will be
T-13....... X.7:5 He has s. separation, but knows of union.
T-13....... X.8:4 looked within and s. the radiance there,
T-14....... in.1:6 logic, and have s. its logical conclusions.
T-14....... in.1:7 And having s. them, we have realized that
T-14....... in.1:7 that they cannot be s. except in illusions,
T-14....... in.1:7 seeming clearness seems to be clearly s..
T-14... VII.4:10 because the other is s. in the same place.
T-14...... IX.6:1 Reflections are s. in light. In darkness
T-14... XI.3:10 darkness cannot be s., for it is nothing
T-15......... I.4:9 We have s. this strange paradox in the
T-15....... V.6:6 Unless you had s. yourself as without love
T-15...... VI.1:3 relationships are s. as total commitments,
T-16....... II.9:9 Think what you have really s. and heard,
T-16...... IV.5:7 S. in these terms, no one would hesitate.
T-16...... VI.4:5 of the special relationship, if they were s..
T-16...... VI.6:2 For a time the body is still s., but not
T-16...... VI.6:2 seen, but not exclusively, as it is s. here.
T-17....... II.1:2 In no fantasy have you ever s. anything so
T-17...... III.2:6 bodies can be s. as means for vengeance.
T-17.... III.6:11 conditions in which this beauty can be s..
T-17.... IV.11:7 the picture is s. as what it represents. For
T-17.... IV.12:3 of all that you can have, s. very differently
T-17.... IV.13:2 is framed to be out of focus and not s..
T-17.... IV.14:5 when both are s. in relation to each other.
T-17....... V.2:2 relationship, transformed and s. anew.
T-17....... V.4:6 goal. Until this happy solution is s. and
T-17.... VII.4:3 holiness cannot be s. except through faith
T-17.... VIII.1:4 and every situation, s. as a whole. Faith
T-18......... I.3:6 stems. No one is s. complete. The body is
T-18......... I.5:6 But nothing you have s. begins to show
T-18...... IX.2:4 are s. only through the body's eyes. Its
T-18...... IX.4:5 which depends on keeping it not s.. The
T-18...... IX.9:2 Here the world outside is s. anew, without
T-19......... I.6:7 together, and when they are s. together,
T-19......... I.6:7 and s. as totally unreconcilable with truth
T-19....... I.11:3 faith, the Son of God is s. already forgiven
T-19....... II.2:5 Thus is creation s. as not eternal, and the
T-19....... II.4:2 deceive. Purity is s. as arrogance, and the
T-19..... III.9:3 the mind corrects it when it seems to be s.
T-19.... III.10:5 Forget what you have s., and raise your
T19. IV.A.12:1 world are the result of how the world is s..
T19.... IV.B.1:4 made manifest in the body, and s. in it.
T19.... IV.C.7:2 For death is s. as safety, the great dark
T19. IV.D.19:1 be lost but found; not to be s. but known.
T19. IV.D.20:2 As he is s. as either the giver of guilt or of
T19. IV.D.20:2 so will his offering be s. and so received.
T-20...... III.2:3 interferences, are always s. as dangerous.
T-20....... V.6:7 of Christ you yet will look upon already s..
T-20...... VI.4:6 for all that it could offer is s. as valueless.
T-20...... VI.5:7 in all the universe where it can not be s.?
T-20.... VIII.6:3 s. in unadjusted form and suited perfectly
T-20.. VIII.11:1 and s. it change to sights of loveliness and
T-21......... I.1:2 must infer what could be s. from evidence
T-21......... I.2:1 attempt to judge what could be s. instead.
T-21......... I.2:3 be s. before you recognize it for what it is.
T-21.... III.11:7 with what depends on darkness to be s..
T-21.... III.12:1 to sin, and in the darkness so it still is s..
T-21...... IV.5:1 part has s. your brother, and recognized
T-21...... VI.7:8 whole salvation s. as complete with yours.
T-21.... VII.3:9 be s. attacking anyone with anything.
T-22....... in.1:4 s. in the other yet believed by each to be
T-22....... in.2:3 It is this difference, s. but not real, that
T-22....... in.2:3 that makes the need for sin, not real but s.
T-22 ....... in.3:2 Each one has looked within and s. no lack
T-22 ........ I.9:6 that they must have s. each other through
T-22 ....... II.9:5 illusion we have s. many times before.
T-22 ..... VI.5:2 sin. The form of error is no longer s., and
T-23 ........ I.9:2 as it is s. as war between conflicting truths
T-23 ....... II.6:3 not s. as even necessary that He be asked
T-23 ..... II.10:1 mechanisms of madness are s. emerging
T-23 ..... II.14:4 It must be s. as truth to be believed. And
T-23 ..... II.15:5 Their goal of madness must be s. as sanity
T-23 ..... II.16:3 s. how it appears to function many times
T-24 ....... II.1:3 It is established by a lack s. in another,
T-24 ...... V.3:7 showing him what can be s. and heard,
T-24 .. VII.10:2 is sure, when s. through its own eyes. It
T-25 ....... II.2:4 is sure; the way you see, and long have s.,
T-25 ....... II.3:1 inconstant, wavering, yet dimly s.,–
T-25 ....... II.4:4 to hold the picture up, so that it can be s..
T-25 ..... II.9:10 Not one ray of darkness can be s. by those
T-25 ..... III.5:2 nothing is s. but justifies forgiveness and
T-25 ..... IV.1:7 Yet it is the way in which the aim is s. that
T-25 ..... VI.6:4 is s. and understood as each one takes his
T-25 .... VII.7:5 Yet if His Will is s. as madness, then the
T-25 .... VII.8:4 way of looking at what he has s. before,
T-25 ... VIII.3:7 and death is s. as victory and triumph
T-25 ... VIII.4:8 up. So is the victim s. as partly you, with
T-25 . VIII.11:1 at last, provided it is s. and recognized.
T-25 ..... IX.3:6 in which one, at least, is s. unfairly. Thus
T-25 ..... IX.3:8 When anyone is s. as losing, he has been
T-25 ..... IX.5:6 Not as it is s. through this world's eyes,
T-26 ........ I.4:7 Son is s. within a world of separate bodies
T-26 ........ I.5:4 your brother's holiness cannot be s., to
T-26 ..... III.3:6 yet it can be s. that they are temporary,
T-26 ...... V.8:2 be made real again and s. as here and now
T-26 .. V.11:10 Once it is s., this light can never be
T-26 .... VII.2:4 and sin are s. as consequence and cause,
T-26 .... VII.5:3 be reversed; yet can be s. as upside down.
T-26 .. VII.12:7 Effects are s. as separate from their source
T-26 ....... X.2:5 And only some are s. as meaningless. And
T-26 ....... X.3:1 one is perceived the other must be s.. You
T-27 ........ I.5:2 you really are cannot be s. nor pictured.
T-27 ........ I.9:5 a purpose, it is s. as neither sick nor well,
T-27 ...... I.11:7 both be reconciled at last and s. as one.
T-27 ....... II.9:2 pain are s. to represent their own serenity
T-27 .... II.13:4 lest your errors and his own be s. as one.
T-27 ..... III.4:1 An empty space that is not s. as filled, an
T-27 ..... III.4:1 of time not s. as spent and fully occupied,
T-27 ..... III.7:1 and nothing that the eyes have ever s. or
T-27 ..... IV.1:3 has no answer, for it is s. in different ways
T-27 ...... V.8:8 within two situations that are s. as one,
T-27 .... V.10:4 Your brother first among them will be s.,
T-27 .... VII.1:7 because its source is s. outside himself.
T-27 .... VII.2:5 the problem is absurd when clearly s.. No
T-27 .... VII.2:6 be resolved if it is s. as hurting him, and
T-27 .... VII.6:2 for what has s. a need for evil in the world
T-27 .. VII.11:2 effects, when only one is s. as up to him?
T-27 .. VII.16:3 Let all your brother's gifts be s. in light of
T-27 ... VIII.1:2 if it were a person to be s. and be believed
T-27 ... VIII.5:6 s. at once that these ideas are one illusion,
T-28 ....... II.3:5 is given no effects and none is s.. A mind
T-28 ..... II.10:4 enmity is s. as causeless now, because
T-28 ..... III.3:2 and separate minds are s. as bodies,
T-28 ..... III.3:4 has not s. the cause of sickness where it is,
T-28 ..... III.8:2 gap was s. to stand between you and your
T-28 ..... III.8:3 so sickness will now be s. without a cause.
T-28 ...... V.1:3 your brother, and what is now s. as health
T-28 ...... V.1:4 And so the good is s. to be outside; the
T-28 ...... V.5:5 that *can* be s. and heard and understood.
T-28 ...... V.5:8 s. within the gap that you imagined, and
T-28 ..... VI.1:2 For here the little gap is s., and yet it is
T-28 .... VII.3:6 it does, it can be s. as not your home, but
T-28 .... VII.7:7 From here the body can be s. as what it is,
T-29 ........ I.2:1 Here is the fear of God most plainly s..
T-29 ........ I.5:1 and of distance s. between you and him.
T-29 ........ I.7:4 Thus is love s. as treacherous, because it
T-29 ....... II.2:7 And its effects are there, though not yet s.
T-29 ..... IV.2:1 as much as those in which the fear is s..
T-29 ..... IV.2:3 The fear is s. within, without, or both. Or
T-29 ... VIII.1:3 such, and never s. for what they really are.
T-29 ... VIII.3:2 perceived as real and s. outside the mind.
T-29 ..... IX.5:7 alive and real, but s. outside himself,
T-29 ..... IX.7:3 They are not s. as idols which betray. It is
T-30 ..... III.9:2 depend on whether it is s. on earth or not.
T-30 ....... V.1:1 of the world is s. to be forgiveness. Fear is
T-30 ....... V.5:4 can guilt and sin be s. without a purpose,
T-30 .... VII.6:7 by which they can be s. and understood.
T-30 .... VII.6:9 And what they are for cannot be s.. In any
T-31 ....... I.11:2 another outcome s. to be preferred. You
T-31 ..... III.3:3 They are not s. as purposes, but actions.
T-31 ..... III.3:6 It is not s. to be a passive thing, obeying
T-31 ..... IV.8:1 when you have s. the real alternatives.
T-31 ..... V.14:3 Salvation can be s. as nothing more than
T-31 ..... VI.2:5 have trust where so much change is s., for
T-31 ..... VI.5:4 One vision, clearly s., that does not fit the
T-31 ..... VI.6:8 So the world is s. as stable, fully worthy of
T-31 .... VII.3:3 and will at length be s. as little more than
T-31 .. VII.11:3 For holiness is s. through holy eyes that
T-31 ... VIII.4:4 of their own weakness, s. apart from Him.
W-pI .... 15.2:2 you have s. little edges of light around the
W-pI .... 28.2:7 When you have s. one thing differently,
W-pI .... 30.1:2 and see in it what you have never s. before
W-pI .... 35.2:5 are in it is s. through the eyes of the image
W-pI .... 51.3:6 what can be s. and understood and loved.
W-pI .... 58.1:5 me. S. through understanding eyes, the
W-pI .... 66.7:2 We have s. that there are only two parts
W-pI .... 72.8:4 s. yourself in a body and the truth outside
W-pI .... 75.4:4 rises before us in gladness, to be s. at last.
W-pI .... 78.5:3 him not is there in everyone, and can be s.
W-pI .... 80.2:4 deception aside, and s. the light of truth.
W-pI .... 86.1:3 I have s. it in many people and in many
W-pI .... 89.2:4 *you instead. S. truly, this offers me a miracle.*
W-pI ....... 91.h Miracles are s. in light.
W-pI .... 91.6:2 *Miracles are s. in light. The body's eyes do*
W-pI .. 91.11:1 yourself that miracles are s. in light. Also,
W-pI .. 91.11:4 *Miracles are s. in light. Let me not close my*
W-pI ....... 92.h Miracles are s. in light, and light and
W-pI .... 92.3:4 These are s. through eyes that cannot see
W-pI .... 95.4:4 have s. the extent of your lack of mental
W-pI .... 99.1:3 resulting in a state of conflict s. between
W-pI .. 108.2:3 all. And thus what is the same is s. as one,
W-pI .. 108.4:1 Here are both giving and receiving s. as
W-pI .. 108.4:1 does not depend on which is s. as first,
W-pI .. 108.6:1 it can be tried so easily and s. as true. And
W-pI .. 111.1:1 (91) Miracles are s. in light. *I cannot see in*
W-pI .. 111.2:1 (92) Miracles are s. in light, and light and
W-pI .. 111.3:2 Miracles are s. in light. On the half hour:
W-pI .. 111.3:4 Miracles are s. in light, and light and
W-pI .. 129.9:2 For we have s. its opposite at last, and we
W-pI .. 130.3:2 What can be s. in darkness that is real?
W-pI .. 130.9:4 that your eyes alone have ever s. before.
W-pI .. 134.1:2 forgiveness must be s. as mere eccentric
W-pI .. 135.9:2 mind. For you have s. in it the faults, the
W-pI .. 136.1:4 When this is s., healing is automatic. It
W-pI .. 136.2:5 The parts are s. as if each one were whole
W-pI .. 136.6:3 parts are wrested from the whole and s. as
W-pI .. 136.6:3 in effect, and never to be s. as whole again
W-pI .. 137.6:4 be s. and justified and fully understood.
W-pI .. 137.7:2 When sickness has been s. to disappear in
W-pI .. 138.7:4 And thus salvation must be s. as death,
W-pI .. 138.7:4 be seen as death, for life is s. as conflict.
W-pI .. 138.9:2 are accurately s. and understood. All that
W-pI 138.10:2 the clearly s. and the unrecognized? Yet
W-pI 138.10:3 when only one is s. as valuable; the other
W-pI .. 140.2:4 He has not s. the light that would awaken
WpI..rIV.in3:2 thoughts from being s. and recognized.
W-pI .. 153.6:3 your own weakness, s. apart from Him.
W-pI .. 156.6:4 sin gone, because its quaint absurdity is s.
W-pI .. 159.5:3 shadows there; transparent, faintly s., at
W-pI .. 161.7:3 form he can be touched and s. and heard,
W-pI 161.12:3 you have s. as merely flesh and bone, and
W-pI .. 162.1:5 and all things s. within its misty clouds
W-pI .. 163.3:1 All things but death are s. to be unsure,
W-pI .. 167.3:2 an idea, irrelevant to what is s. as physical
W-pI .. 184.3:4 and will then be s. as meaningful; a cause
W-pI .. 184.6:5 It can be s., as is anticipated. What denies
W-pI .. 186.9:6 Or like mirages s. above a desert, rising
W-pI .. 188.2:6 shadow of the s. through inward vision.
W-pI .. 190.1:4 it takes that will not disappear if s. aright.
W-pI .. 190.3:2 as mad, and s. as traitor to Himself. If
W-pI .. 190.5:8 And what was s. as fearful now becomes a

| | |
|---|---|
| W-pI...197.2:4 | until guilt and salvation are not s. as one, |
| W-pI...199.4:1 | it hide, and here it can be s. as what it is. |
| W-pI...200.5:3 | will be bound till all the world is s. by you |
| W-pII..240.1:2 | you have s. yourself as you could never be |
| W-pII......3.1:4 | will the world be s. in quite another light; |
| W-pII......6.5:1 | And how long will this holy face be s., |
| W-pII......8.1:3 | Your world is s. through eyes of fear, and |
| W-pII......8.2:2 | real world shows a world s. differently, |
| W-pII..333.1:2 | denied, disguised, s. somewhere else, |
| W-pII..333.1:3 | It must be s. exactly as it is, where it is |
| W-pII....13.2:5 | truth. Now is forgiveness s. as justified. |
| W-pII..345.1:3 | *form which can be recognized and s. to work* |
| M-in ..........5:7 | it. And then they are s. no more, although |
| M-1............3:9 | He has s. someone else as himself. He has |
| M-2............5:9 | s. in another person the same interests as |
| M-4......I.A.8:3 | Now what was s. as merely shadows |
| M-4.. VIII.1:10 | already s. or yet to come can cause them |
| M-5..........I.1:6 | real strength is s. as threat and health as |
| M-5..........I.1:8 | God is s. as outside, fierce and powerful, |
| M-5...... II.4:11 | S. in their proper perspective, without |
| M-6............1:4 | teacher of God has s. the correction of his |
| M-6............2:1 | stand aside when it would be s. as threat. |
| M-8............1:2 | which each thing s. competes with every |
| M-8............3:6 | What is s. as "reality" is simply what the |
| M-8..........3:11 | alone decides whether what is s. is real or |
| M-13..........5:4 | otherwise the pleasure would be s. as pain |
| M-14..........1:7 | as purposeless, they are no longer s.. |
| M-25..........5:4 | guile. Many have not s. through the ego's |
| M-28..........2:6 | Christ's face is s. in every living thing, and |
| M-28..........4:6 | All things are s. in light, and in the light |
| M-28..........5:5 | have s. the face of Christ, His sinlessness, |
| C-3............4:1 | *The face of Christ* has to be s. before the |
| C-3............8:5 | all. God is not s. but only understood. His |
| C-4............2:1 | means by which the real world can be s., |
| C-4............4:3 | It is s. at last for only what it is. And now |
| C-4............6:1 | What was projected out is s. within, and |
| C-4............6:4 | is s. outside must lie beyond forgiveness, |
| C-4............6:5 | Where is hope while sin is s. as outside? |
| C-4............6:7 | expect? But s. within your mind, guilt and |
| C-6............3:5 | in which the face of Christ alone is s.. He |
| P-2........IV.2:1 | Once God's Son is s. as guilty, illness |
| P-2........IV.2:7 | If a deformity is s. as real, what could its |
| P-2........IV.9:5 | The therapist is s. as one who is attacking |
| P-2........IV.9:6 | cannot but be s. as a real source of danger |
| P-2......IV.11:5 | S. rightly, its purpose can be understood. |
| P-2........VI.4:2 | S. undisguised it is intolerable. Without |
| P-2........VI.7:4 | but be s. as the bringers of forgiveness, |
| P-2........VI.7:5 | sinlessness, s. in the patient and accepted |
| P-2.......VII.5:2 | In this their oneness can be clearly s.. Yet |
| P-3......... II.8:4 | is reached another can be dimly s. ahead. |
| S-2......... II.4:3 | Here must the aim be clearly s., for this |
| S-3...........I.3:3 | among which sickness should be s. as one |
| S-3......... II.2:3 | and clearly s. at most in lovely flashes. |

## sees 279

| | |
|---|---|
| T-2......... V.8:2 | What the physical eye s. is not corrective, |
| T-3.......VII.3:9 | that any interpretation that s. either God |
| T-5........III.8:5 | you. It is this that the Holy Spirit s.. This |
| T-5......III.11:1 | made, s. the world as a teaching device |
| T-5.......IV.2:13 | you cannot be limited to the self the ego s. |
| T-6....... II.11:5 | into the one line the Holy Spirit s.. This |
| T-6....... II.12:5 | Wherever He looks He s. Himself, and |
| T-6........III.3:2 | this fully, it s. no need to protect itself. |
| T-6......V.A.5:5 | Holy Spirit s. the body only as a means of |
| T-7.......III.4:10 | Your right mind s. only brothers, because |
| T-7.......III.4:10 | because it s. only in its own light. |
| T-7........IV.5:4 | Spirit s. no order of difficulty in healing. |
| T-7......... V.4:4 | Magic always s. something "special" in |
| T-7.........V.11:6 | Who s. the altar of God in everyone, and |
| T-7.......VII.9:4 | Projection always s. your wishes in others |
| T-8..... VIII.1:3 | what it s. with the function it ascribes to it |
| T-8..... VIII.9:3 | as the Holy Spirit s. it cannot be sick. |
| T-9...........I.4:6 | Holy Spirit s. that you can possibly have. |
| T-9......... V.7:5 | with God that there is light *because* he s. it |
| T-9..... VIII.3:1 | s. no difference between miracle impulses |
| T-11....... V.6:8 | The ego s. all dependency as threatening, |
| T-12.....VII.7:8 | then s. a divided world outside itself, but |
| T-12... VIII.3:2 | for the Holy Spirit s. it with perfect clarity |
| T-12... VIII.3:5 | can be seen is what the Holy Spirit s.. The |
| T-12... VIII.7:3 | upon him, and s. nothing else in you. |
| T-13.........I.4:3 | fears and that he s. will never touch him, |
| T-13....... V.2:2 | Yet the figures that he s. were never real, |
| T-13....... V.9:4 | And He s. for you, as your witness to the |
| T-13....... V.9:6 | He loves what He s. within you, and He |
| T-13..... V.10:5 | He s. God's guiltless Son within you, |
| T-13..... V.11:6 | themselves as the Holy Spirit s. them. |
| T-13...VII.11:4 | the ego s. salvation it sees separation, and |
| T-13...VII.11:4 | the ego sees salvation it s. separation, and |
| T-13..... X.11:8 | If he is guiltless and in peace and s. it not, |
| T-13...... XI.1:2 | no one s. himself in conflict and ravaged |
| T-14....... II.3:1 | All this the Holy Spirit s., and teaches, |
| T-14.....IV.10:2 | each s. the other unlike the way he sees |
| T-14.....IV.10:2 | sees the other unlike the way he s. himself |
| T-14..... V.10:7 | aim. It s. everyone as guilty, and by its |
| T-14..... V.10:8 | The Holy Spirit s. only guiltlessness, and |
| T-14.....VII.6:6 | He s. for you, and unless you look with |
| T-15.....VII.6:4 | the ego acknowledges "reality" as it s. it, |
| T-15...... IX.7:2 | and attack which the ego s. in it, you will |
| T-16.........I.2:4 | the ego s. itself and would increase itself |
| T-16....... II.4:4 | have offered it to Him to use as He s. fit, |
| T-16....... V.5:6 | this it s. the ultimate freedom of the self, |
| T-16....... V.8:3 | other, the ego s. "a union made in Heaven |
| T-16.....VI.5:8 | and s. only this part and nothing else. |
| T-16.....VII.3:5 | escape from the past it s. itself deprived of |
| T-17...... III.7:6 | part of the relationship the Holy Spirit s., |
| T-17...... IV.5:1 | anxious to preserve its reason, as it s. it. It |
| T-17...... VI.6:4 | The Holy Spirit s. the situation as a whole |
| T-18.........I.2:2 | Holy Spirit s. them joined and indivisible. |
| T-18.........I.2:7 | joined and what the Holy Spirit s. as one. |
| T-18...... IX.4:1 | of fear lies just below the level the body s., |
| T-19.......I.11:4 | Faith s. him only *now* because it looks not |
| T-19.......I.11:5 | you. It s. not through the body's eyes, nor |
| T-19.......I.13:2 | and s. the holy place where it was healed. |
| T-19.......III.5:1 | Spirit clearly s. the Son of God can make |
| T19. IV.A.10:2 | upon only the truth, for there it s. itself, |
| T19. IV.A.10:6 | Overlooking guilt completely, it s. no fear |
| T19. IV.A.10:8 | Fear is attracted to what love s. not, and |
| T19. IV.A.15:5 | and return to you with what love s.. They |
| T19IV.A.17:13 | This is completion as the ego s. it. For |
| T19..IV.B.12:2 | for it is one the ego s. as proof of sin. It is |
| T19... IV.D.8:7 | through the eyes of faith that s. them not. |
| T19. IV.D.18:3 | the sins he thinks he s. within himself. |
| T-20....... II.3:2 | one but s. his chosen home as an altar to |
| T-20....... II.5:5 | He s. no strangers; only dearly loved and |
| T-20....... II.5:6 | He s. no thorns but only lilies, gleaming |
| T-20.......IV.1:5 | nor to its results as this world s. them,– |
| T-20.......IV.1:6 | because the Holy Spirit s. them not, and |
| T-20....... V.5:4 | sight that s. the body has no use which |
| T-20....... V.7:9 | have faith that He Who s. the gift in you |
| T-20....... V.8:1 | love and perfect confidence in what He s.. |
| T-20......VI.5:7 | s. the face of Christ choose as His home |
| T-20.....VII.6:1 | s. a brother's body has laid a judgment on |
| T-20.....VII.6:1 | laid a judgment on him, and s. him not. |
| T-20.....VII.9:7 | and what he s. is free of condemnation. |
| T-20.....VII.9:8 | And what he s. he did not make, for it was |
| T-21...... III.4:3 | is His direction; the only one He ever s.. |
| T-21...... III.6:3 | He s. the means you use, but not the |
| T-21...... III.6:4 | s. their value as a means for what He wills |
| T-21...... III.6:6 | The Holy Spirit s. perception as a means |
| T-21...... III.8:3 | the power of their belief and faith s. far |
| T-21...... IV.7:5 | it s. that Heaven has come to earth at last, |
| T-21....... V.3:3 | This other self s. miracles as natural. They |
| T-21...... VI.2:4 | himself as guilty and s. a sinless world? |
| T-21...... VI.7:5 | You *are* responsible for how he s. himself. |
| T-21...... VI.8:4 | madness s. must be dispelled by reason. |
| T-21...VII.11:2 | the world of sin for what the Holy Spirit s. |
| T-21...VII.12:6 | if he s. his happiness as ever changing, |
| T-21...VII.13:5 | he is wrong who s. himself as helpless. |
| T-21... VIII.2:5 | looks on everything and s. it is the same. |
| T-21... VIII.2:6 | It s. not the ephemeral, for it desires |
| T-21... VIII.2:6 | everything be like itself, and s. it so. |
| T-22.......in.3:4 | He s. no difference between these selves, |
| T-22.........I.2:7 | brain cannot interpret what your vision s. |
| T-22.........I.3:6 | Yet it must be the "something else" that s. |
| T-22.........I.3:8 | asking it to explain to you the world it s., |
| T-22.........I.5:2 | for everyone s. only what he thinks he is. |
| T-22.........I.6:5 | he hears nor sights he s. are stable yet. |
| T-22.........I.6:7 | shifting ones he s. about him will become |
| T-22.........I.7:6 | through Christ, Whose vision s. them one |
| T-22........II.5:4 | for reason s. the source of an idea as what |
| T-22...... III.2:3 | For reason s. through errors, telling you |
| T-22...... III.3:5 | Yet reason s. through it easily, because it |
| T-22...... III.6:2 | and it is their maker that s. through them. |
| T-22...... III.9:4 | Each s. within the other what impels him |
| T-22...... III.9:7 | reason s. a holy relationship as what it is; |
| T-23......II.14:1 | his madness if he s. that this is what it is. |
| T-23......II.16:6 | one of these laws is true s. what it says. |
| T-24........II.5:6 | for it s. not what they would look upon, |
| T-24....... V.1:3 | And thus does He rejoice at what He s., |
| T-24....... V.1:4 | Specialness, too, takes joy in what it s., |
| T-24....... V.3:2 | and s. no condemnation that could need |
| T-24....... V.3:3 | is at peace *because* He s. no sin. Identify |
| T-24....... V.3:6 | feet. How gentle are the sights He s., the |
| T-24...... VI.4:2 | is the only purpose the Holy Spirit s. in it, |
| T-24...... VI.4:5 | pain because he s. himself as he is not. |
| T-24.... VI.10:8 | you decide against the holiness He s.? |
| T-25........II.8:7 | in him and s. only a frame of darkness, it |
| T-25........II.8:7 | function to behold in him what he s. not. |
| T-25......II.11:4 | See not in him the sinfulness he s., but |
| T-25...... III.8:8 | s. what He sees as far beyond the chance |
| T-25...... III.8:8 | He s. as far beyond the chance of change. |
| T-25.....VII.6:6 | truth. Each s. a world immutable, as each |
| T-25.....VII.8:3 | one which will not attack the world he s., |
| T-25.....VII.9:3 | and all the sin he s. within the world, |
| T-25..VIII.11:2 | For just *one* witness is enough, if he s. truly |
| T-25..... IX.4:5 | It s. a resolution as a state in which it is |
| T-25.... IX.10:7 | it s. no differences where none exists. And |
| T-25.... IX.10:8 | because it s. no differences in them. Its |
| T-26.........I.7:2 | in you be blotted out because he s. it not. |
| T-26.........I.8:3 | the rotting prison where he s. himself. It |
| T-26...... IV.1:7 | until he s. himself as needing it no more. |
| T-26........X.5:7 | the function that the Holy Spirit s.. And |
| T-27........II.7:4 | obeys; that healing s. no specialness at all. |
| T-27......II.15:4 | goal in which the Holy Spirit s. His Own. |
| T-27...... VI.4:1 | Witness s. no witnesses against the body. |
| T-27.....VII.1:3 | he s. himself attacked unjustly and by |
| T-27.....VII.5:1 | This is the purpose of the world he s.. |
| T-27.....VII.7:8 | and what he s. is separate from his mind. |
| T-27....VIII.4:4 | unless he s. them as if they were real? The |
| T-27....VIII.4:5 | The instant that he s. them as they are |
| T-27..VIII.12:2 | He s. no differences where none exists, |
| T-28.........I.7:9 | span of memory which your perception s. |
| T-28........II.6:8 | He s. illusions of himself as sick or well, |
| T-28........II.7:7 | own attack, but s. it at another's hands. |
| T-28...... IV.8:4 | he s. this picture he will recognize himself |
| T-28...... VI.3:4 | shrink from what it s. and what it hears, |
| T-28...... VI.3:6 | It s. and acts for *you*. It hears your voice. |
| T-29....... V.8:1 | Who s. a different function for a dream. |
| T-29...... IX.7:4 | the mind conceives and what it s.. No one |
| T-30.........I.1:3 | a set begins to form which s. you through |
| T-30...... VI.4:4 | No one who s. himself as guilty can avoid |
| T-31.........I.5:5 | skill the Holy Spirit s. in all the world. His |
| T-31...... IV.5:3 | while he s. a choice where there is none, |
| T-31....... V.1:4 | at home, where what it s. is one with it. |
| T-31.....VII.8:4 | and s. the mirror of himself in him. Thus |
| T-31...VII.11:6 | his calm and open eyes and what he s.. He |
| T-31...VII.13:2 | It s. no past in anyone at all. And thus it |
| W-pI.......8.1:2 | No one really s. anything. He sees only his |
| W-pI.......8.1:3 | He s. only his thoughts projected outward |
| W-pI.....22.1:2 | he s. vengeance about to strike at him. |
| W-pI.....22.1:4 | until he is willing to change how he s.. |
| W-pI.....38.4:6 | *situation involving_in which_s. himself,* |
| W-pI.....43.1:6 | That is its function as the Holy Spirit s. it. |
| W-pI.....64.2:2 | therefore He s. another purpose in them. |
| W-pI.....64.5:9 | That is the only choice the Holy Spirit s.. |
| W-pI.....75.7:6 | He will show you what true vision s.. It is |
| W-pI.....78.2:2 | by not allowing sight to stop before it s.. |
| W-pI.....92.3:3 | weakness that s. through the body's eyes, |
| W-pI.....92.4:4 | It s. itself. It brings the light in which your |
| W-pI.....92.5:5 | It s. that lack in anyone would be a lack in |
| W-pI.....92.6:2 | It s. all others different from itself, and |
| W-pI.....92.7:1 | itself, and darkness covers everything it s. |
| W-pI.....92.7:3 | It separates itself from what it s., while |
| W-pI.....96.5:2 | Source of strength, and s. itself as helpless |
| W-pI.....99.3:2 | mind that s. illusions thinks them real. |
| W-pI.....99.6:1 | and s. them as appearances behind which |

W-pI...100.6:5 you and s. His message in your happy face
W-pI...109.2:4 whose vision s. beyond appearances to
W-pI...121.3:1 doubt, confused about itself and all it s.;
W-pI...121.4:1 The unforgiving mind s. no mistakes, but
W-pI...121.4:4 It wants forgiveness, yet it s. no hope. It
W-pI...121.4:5 of none because it s. the sinful everywhere
W-pI...121.5:3 it s. bears witness that its judgment is
W-pI...124.8:5 God's Voice to speak as He s. fit today,
W-pI...132.1:5 A madman thinks the world he s. is real,
W-pI...134.7:2 It s. their nothingness, and looks straight
W-pI...134.8:1 uncorrupted that it s. illusions as illusions
W-pI...137.3:6 healing is accomplished as he s. the body
W-pI...140.1:3 mind, it s. no separation from the body,
W-pI...151.5:5 It is within itself it s. the guilt. It is its own
W-pI...151.5:6 the guilt. It is its own despair it s. in you.
W-pI...151.7:4 and in the holy light of what He s. do all
W-pI.151.13:3 Him Who s. the elements of truth in them
W-pI...158.5:6 a vision which the Holy Spirit s. because
W-pI...158.7:4 of sin. It s. no separation. And it looks on
W-pI...158.7:5 the slightest fading of the light it s..
W-pI...159.3:3 it s. a world so like to Heaven that what
W-pI...160.9:2 His vision s. no strangers, but beholds
W-pI...161.2:4 It s. instead but fragments of the whole,
W-pI...161.8:1 Who s. a brother as a body sees him as
W-pI...161.8:1 brother as a body s. him as fear's symbol.
W-pI...161.9:4 are like him in the sight that s. him thus.
W-pI...164.1:4 time, and s. eternity as represented there.
W-pI...166.5:4 of the futility he s. about him everywhere,
W-pI.167.10:3 and s. in dreams an opposite to what he is
W-pI.167.12:3 it s. its own perfection mirroring the Lord
WpI...rV.in8:1 to you from Him Who s. your bitter need,
W-pI...184.4:4 sense of unity or vision that s. differently,
W-pI.186.13:4 Son perceives, although He s. them not.
W-pI...189.2:5 It s. salvation in you, and protects the
W-pI...189.2:5 the light in you, in which it s. its own. It
W-pI...190.1:7 of His Son, the sinfulness He s. in him,
W-pI...192.4:1 unknown in Heaven, s. them disappear,
W-pI...192.8:1 everyone he s. or thinks of or imagines?
W-pI...193.2:1 God s. no contradictions. Yet His Son
W-pI...193.2:2 Yet His Son believes he s. them. Thus he
W-pI...193.7:4 s. the pain through eyes the mind directs.
W-pI...195.1:6 less because he s. another suffer more?
W-pI...196.2:2 because the ego, under what it s. as threat
W-pI...199.1:4 free when it no longer s. itself as in a body
W-pI...199.4:3 of it except the need the Holy Spirit s.. For
W-pII.....1.1:3 It s. there was no sin. And in that view are
W-pII.....1.1:6 Son? Forgiveness merely s. its falsity, and
W-pII.....1.3:2 it s. as interfering with its chosen path.
W-pII.....1.5:3 He has saved, whose sinlessness He s.,
W-pII.236.1:6 to the Holy Spirit to employ as He s. fit.
W-pII.....4.1:3 it s. illusions where the truth should be,
W-pII.....5.2:2 Yet this he s. as double safety. For the Son
W-pII....263.h My holy vision s. all things as pure.
W-pII.....8.3:4 it s. arises from a mind at peace within
W-pII.....8.3:5 No danger lurks in anything it s., for it is
W-pII...10.2:2 For it s. the world as totally forgiven,
W-pII.313.1:5 *for He s. no sin in anything He looks upon.*
W-pII...12.1:2 "will" that s. the Will of God as enemy,
W-pII...12.2:4 it "s." the Will of God has been destroyed
W-pII...13.1:3 reminds the mind that what it s. is false.
W-pII.347.1:6 *He s. what I behold, and yet He knows the*
W-pII...14.4:1 the eyes through which Christ's vision s. a
W-pII...14.5:5 s. the gate of Heaven stand open before
M-4.....I.A.6:5 at which he s. in it his whole way out.
M-4.....I.A.7:6 but now he s. that he does not know what
M-4....VIII.1:3 All he s. is certain outcome, at a time
M-5.........I.1:1 the sufferer no longer s. any value in pain.
M-5.......II.3:5 looks on the world and s. it as it is not. He
M-8...........5:5 of pitchforks the devils he s. carrying
M-10.........6:4 ugliness he s. about him is its outcome.
M-11.........2:5 judgment s. but death as the inevitable
M-12.........1:4 spirit now no longer s. himself as a body,
M-12.........2:4 for the mind s. no cause for punishment.
M-16.......1:10 and s. the road on which he walks stretch
M-20.........3:4 Who s. anger as justified in any way or
M-22.........3:5 as it s. fit could merely take the place of
M-23.........2:8 no longer s. himself as separate from Him
M-23.........5:5 that he s. in it an image of his Father. You
M-23.........5:7 because in you he s. no limit and no stain
M-25.........4:7 Yet the ego s. in these same strengths an
C-1............3:1 abides in this part but s. the other part as
C-1............5:2 Christ's vision s. the real world in its place
C-3............4:8 looks on this no longer s. the world. He is
C-4............3:9 exist. And it is this that true perception s..
C-4..........5:10 proves it is impossible because it s. it not.
C-5............2:4 can save unless he s. illusions and then
P-1............3:6 This self he s. as being acted on, reacting
P-1............4:3 The world he s. does therefore not exist.
P-2.........in.3:6 The self he s. is his god, and he seeks only
P-2........IV.9:1 because in them he s. his own salvation.
P-2........VI.6:3 The therapist s. in the patient all that he
P-2........VI.6:4 he s. his sins as gone into a past that is no
P-2.......VII.7:3 suspect them of the treachery he s. in him
S-1........III.3:7 who s. no value or advantage to himself in
S-1.........V.2:6 is Self, and this it s. in every meeting,
S-2...........I.2:5 and this it s. in all it looks upon and hates
S-2...........I.7:6 Who s. no evil in it sees like Him. For
S-2...........I.7:6 Who sees no evil in it s. like Him. For

## segment 8

T-18...VIII.2:6 small, around a very little s. of Heaven,
T-18...VIII.4:2 and hated by a tiny s. of themselves. Even
T-18...VIII.4:3 Even that s. is not lost to them, for it
T-18...IX.1:10 its barricades is still a tiny s. of the Son of
T-19........I.3:4 It is obvious that a s. of the mind can see
T-21......V.4:4 can the s. of the mind devoid of reason
T-26.....III.3:3 truth, a s. of the universe made true. This
W-pI.....23.1:4 makes up some s. of the world you see. It

## segments 3

T-3.....VI.10:6 peace, so that you see yourself only in s..
T-3.....VI.11:4 because it separates s. of reality by the
T-17...VI.6:10 it seeks to split off s. of the situation and

## seizing 1

T-23...II.12:12 purpose of s. it and making it your own.

## select 18

T-3........V.7:8 judgments are necessary in order to s..
T-3.....VI.2:12 the belief that reality is yours to s. *from.*
T-16.....IV.4:5 It is sure that those who s. certain ones as
T-22.......II.2:6 of misery is to s. some aspects out of it,
T-27..VII.15:4 S. his thoughtfulness to dream about
T-29.....IV.1:6 Thus it is the miracle does not s. some
W-pI.......4.1:5 s. only the thoughts you think are "bad."
W-pI.....25.6:3 your eyes resting on each subject you so s.
W-pI.....32.4:3 this, s. a time when few distractions are
W-pI.....43.5:1 sure that you s. the subjects for this phase
W-pI.....78.4:4 will s. one person you have used as target
W-pI.135.17:2 Their aim is to s. what you approve, and
W-pI.151.11:1 He will s. the elements in them which
W-pI.161.11:1 S. one brother, symbol of the rest, and
W-pI...163.6:1 and still s. a few you would not cherish
M-4......IX.1:2 Does he still s. some aspects of his life to
P-3...........I.1:2 This does not mean that you s. him, nor
S-2...........I.3:5 it real. S. the loving and forgive the sin by

## selected 4

T-1..........I.5:3 Consciously s. miracles can be misguided.
T-9.........II.2:6 removal of a symptom that he himself s..
W-pI...154.2:1 role may be, it was s. by the Voice for God
M-29.........7:9 your dreams of danger and s. "wrongs."

## selecting 5

W-pI.......2.1:6 possible in s. subjects for its application,
W-pI.......3.2:2 s. the things to which the idea for the day
W-pI.......4.2:1 In s. the subjects for the application of
W-pI.....18.3:1 s. subjects for the application of the idea
W-pI.....19.4:1 as possible in s. subjects for the practice

## selection 9

*See also* self-selection

T-17.....III.1:3 remembering, based not on your s.. For
T-17.....III.1:8 you who keep them by your own s. do not
W-pI......2.2:1 around you, trying to avoid s. by size,
W-pI....10.4:4 available to you, without s. or judgment.
W-pI....15.5:1 try to make the s. as random as possible.
W-pI....19.4:2 that random s. of subjects for all practice
W-pI....29.4:2 avoid the tendency toward self-directed s.
W-pI....39.8:1 without conscious s. and without undue
P-3.............I.h The S. of Patients

## selective 5

T-1.......III.9:1 Miracles are s. only in the sense that they
T-11.....V.16:2 listen. S. perception chooses its witnesses
T-13.....IV.3:7 You have been as s. in your questioning
T-17.....III.1:3 Forgiveness is a s. remembering, based
T-28........I.2:5 Remembering is as s. as perception, being

## selectively 2

T-1........I.38:3 ability to perceive totally rather than s..
M-19.........3:3 S. and arbitrarily is every concept of the

## selectivity 4

T-1.......III.9:3 this s. takes no account of the magnitude
T-3.........V.7:6 At every level it involves s.. Perception is a
T-3.......VI.2:3 this before in terms of the s. of perception
M-19.........3:4 and justified by careful s. in which all

## selects 2

T-16........I.2:2 These it s. out, and joins with. And it
T-21.......V.1:1 Perception s., and makes the world you

## Self 245

*self*

*See also* He, Him, Himself, His, One, Who, Whom, Whose, You, Self-centered, Self-encompassing, Self-extending, Self-fullness Self-love

T-1......VII.1:5 This is because *not* doing it is a denial of S.
T-1......VII.1:6 Self. Denial of S. results in illusions, while
T-3......VII.5:8 Your S. is still in peace, even though your
T-4..........I.2:9 Your self and God's S. *are* in opposition.
T-4.......II.4:11 of recognition that the ego is not the S..
T-4......VII.4:8 home, your real temple and your real S..
T-5.......III.8:3 This is your life, your eternity and your S..
T-7.......V.6:15 separate your S. from your Creator, Who
T-7.........V.8:6 He therefore does not know what his S. is.
T-10.......II.5:1 All attack is S. attack. It cannot be
T-11.....IV.1:1 your salvation, for the Sonship is your S..
T-11.....IV.1:3 Your S. does not need salvation, but your
T-11.....IV.1:6 of your S. all your understanding is lost,
T-11.....IV.3:2 and your S. must be unknown to you.
T-12.....VI.5:9 to his Father, where Christ waits as his S..
T-12...VIII.2:3 Yet he is far from you whose S. he is, for
T-15...V.10:10 For Christ is the S. the Sonship shares, as
T-15...V.10:10 shares, as God shares His S. with Christ.
T-15.....V.11:1 you that you can judge the S. of God? God
T-15.....VI.7:3 give yourself as your Father gives His S.,
T-16.....III.3:6 Yet this S. you clearly do not know, and
T-16.....III.5:7 real, as part of the S. you do not know.
T-16.....III.7:5 As you learn, your gratitude to your S.,
T-16.....III.8:1 holy S. all praise is due for what you are,
T-16.....III.9:3 would be, and where your S. awaits you.
T-18...VI.13:5 would be, gaining, not losing, a sense of S.
T-18...VIII.6:1 to the sun and ocean your S. continues,
T-18.VIII.10:1 them, for they bring your S. with them.
T-18.VIII.11:6 shining S. will lift the tiny aspect that you
T19..IV.D.3:4 the cleavage of your S. from you;–*the fear*
T-20...III.10:7 you, my friend, my brother and my S..
T-21...VI.10:6 that could be nearer you than is your S.?
T-22........I.9:8 S. could be reborn in safety and in peace.
T-22......I.10:5 to show you where your S. must be. It is
T-22.....IV.7:8 and the holy S. you share together.
T-24........I.3:4 who could hate someone whose S. is his,

T-24....... II.8:7 you, to save his specialness and kill his S..
T-24....... V.7:6 life that your forgiveness offers to your S..
T-25....... V.2:4 yourself, and made your S. your "enemy."
T-25...VII.13:5 alone, but for the S. that is the Son of God
T-25. VIII.12:4 comes not of you, but from a larger S., so
T-27...VII.10:2 world equates the body with the S. which
T-28...... III.8:6 of welcome for your Father and your S..
T-28....... V.3:6 And you will deny your S., and walk upon
T-28....... V.3:7 You will make war upon your S., which
T-28....... V.3:9 You are your S. or an illusion. What can
T-28....... V.4:1 S. is safely hidden by what you have made
T-29...... IX.2:8 can he know the S. he has condemned.
T-31..........I.5:6 call from God and from your S. to you.
T-31.......... V.h Self-Concept versus S.
T-31..... V.15:1 Seek not your S. in symbols. There can be
T-31... VIII.3:7 is the S. that God created as His only Son.
W-pI.....49.3:2 reminding you of Him and of your S.. We
W-pI.....63.4:5 And Who but your S. must be His Son?
W-pI.....67.3:2 you like itself, this S. must be in you. And
W-pI.....67.6:2 you of your Father and of your S.. This is
W-pI.....68.1:1 can hold no grievances and know your S..
W-pI.....68.2:1 Shut off from your S., which remains
W-pI.....68.2:1 to Its Creator, your S. seems to sleep,
W-pI.....68.7:3 *Let me not betray my S..* In addition, repeat
W-pI.....68.7:6 *grievances. I would wake to my S. by laying*
W-pI.....72.9:5 To see our S. as separate from the body is
W-pI.....73.2:5 you do not know your brothers or your S..
W-pI...73.10:4 the power of God and united with your S..
W-pI.....82.3:2 I would remember my S.. I cannot fulfill
W-pI.....84.1:6 my own self-concept to replace my S..
W-pI.....84.3:4 love, and therefore attacking my S.. My
W-pI.....84.3:5 Self. My S. thus becomes alien to me. I am
W-pI.....84.3:6 I am determined not to attack my S. today
W-pI.....84.4:2 *This is no justification for denying my S..*
W-pI.....92.4:5 brings the light in which your S. appears.
W-pI.....92.9:2 S. stands ready to embrace you as Its Own
W-pI.....92.9:3 in, for the peace of God is where your S.,
W-pI...92.10:2 Let yourself be brought unto your S.. Its
W-pI...92.10:4 to find the meeting place of self and S.,
W-pI.....93.9:2 One S. is true; the other is not there. Try
W-pI.....93.9:3 Try to experience the unity of your one S..
W-pI.....93.9:5 to interfere with the S. which God created
W-pI.....94.3:6 This is the S. that never sinned, nor made
W-pI.....94.3:7 S. that never left Its home in God to walk
W-pI.....94.3:8 This is the S. that knows no fear, nor
W-pI........95.h I am one S., united with my Creator.
W-pI.....95.3:2 exercises towards reaching your one S.,
W-pI...95.10:2 to keep you unaware you are one S.,
W-pI...95.11:2 *I am one S., united with my Creator, at one*
W-pI...95.11:4 *I am one S..* Repeat this several times, and
W-pI...95.12:1 You are one S., united and secure in light
W-pI...95.12:2 are God's Son, one S., with one Creator
W-pI...95.12:3 You are one S., complete and healed and
W-pI...95.13:1 You are one S., in perfect harmony with
W-pI...95.13:2 be. You are one S., the holy Son of God,
W-pI...95.13:2 God, united with your brothers in that S.;
W-pI...95.13:3 Feel this one S. in you, and let It shine
W-pI...95.13:4 This is your S., the Son of God Himself,
W-pI...95.13:5 You are one S., and it is given you to feel
W-pI...95.13:5 it is given you to feel this S. within you,
W-pI...95.13:5 out of the one Mind that is this S., the
W-pI...95.15:1 Your own acknowledgment you are one S.
W-pI...95.15:3 this: *You are one S. with me, united with our*
W-pI...95.15:3 *with me, united with our Creator in this S..*
W-pI........96.h Salvation comes from my one S..
W-pI.....96.1:1 Although you are one S., you experience
W-pI.....96.3:3 The self you made can never be your S.,
W-pI.....96.3:3 your Self, nor can your S. be split in two,
W-pI.....96.4:1 of mind as means to find its S. expression.
W-pI.....96.7:1 Your S. retains Its Thoughts, and they
W-pI.....96.7:4 your S. holds dear and cherishes for you.
W-pI.....96.8:1 Him Who speaks to you from your one S..
W-pI.....96.8:3 Salvation comes from this one S. through
W-pI.....96.8:4 and let Him speak to you about your S.,
W-pI.....96.9:2 this: *Salvation comes from my one S.. Its*
W-pI...96.10:2 Your S. will welcome it and give it peace.
W-pI...96.10:5 are restored, for you have found your S..
W-pI...96.11:1 Your S. knows that you cannot fail today.
W-pI...96.11:4 joy your S. experiences It will save for you,
W-pI...96.11:5 seeking Him Who joins your mind and S.,
W-pI...96.12:1 mind salvation comes from your one S.,
W-pI.....97.1:1 idea identifies you with your one S.. It
W-pI.....97.2:1 We state again the truth about your S.,
W-pI.....97.8:2 Him and God, your brothers and your S..
W-pI.....99.9:8 your S. as Love which has no opposite in
W-pI.100.10:6 It is your S. Who calls to you today. And
W-pI...106.5:3 except his Father, calling through your S.?
W-pI...107.8:4 It is your S. you ask to go with you, and
W-pI...107.9:5 *mind, And I will rest in Him Who is my S..*
W-pI...110.7:1 the S. Who is the holy Son of God Himself
W-pI...110.9:2 Today honor your S.. Let graven images
W-pI.110.11:3 may be reminded of His Son, our holy S.,
WpIrIII.in11:6 Son, acceptable to God and to your S..
W-pI...113.1:1 (95) I am one S., united with my Creator.
W-pI...113.1:2 *perfect peace are mine, because I am one S.,*
W-pI...113.2:1 (96) Salvation comes from my one S..
W-pI...113.2:2 Self. *From my one S., Whose knowledge still*
W-pI...113.3:2 I am one S., united with my Creator. On
W-pI...113.3:4 hour: Salvation comes from my one S..
W-pI...119.1:3 *whose S. rests safely in the Mind of God.*
W-pI...121.6:3 represents the other S. in you. Through
W-pI...121.6:5 your mind as one to Him Who is your S.,
W-pI...123.4:2 in honor of the S. that God has willed to
W-pI...123.8:2 world, remembering his Father and his S..
W-pI.124.12:2 *God, at one with all my brothers and my S.,*
W-pI...125.8:4 In quiet listen to your S. today, and let
W-pI...125.8:4 His Son, and you have never left your S..
W-pI...127.6:1 Seek not within the world to find your S..
W-pI.127.12:1 outside our love if we would know our S..
W-pI.127.12:3 mind, give him this message from your S.:
W-pI...128.3:3 that leads to true awareness of your S..
W-pI...132.1:2 what can save the world except your S.?
W-pI.132.10:1 know your S. is the salvation of the world
W-pI...137.3:4 accept his S. with all Its parts intact and
W-pI...137.3:5 does his S. appear to be dismembered,
W-pI.137.12:2 You but invite your S. to be at home. And
W-pI.137.14:4 *mind of God's one Son, Who is my only S..*
W-pI.151.12:3 of nothing but your S. and your Creator,
W-pI.152.11:5 humbly ask our S. that He reveal Himself
W-pI.152.12:1 it with this same invitation to your S..
W-pI...154.4:4 So is its S. the one reality in which its will
W-pI.155.13:7 You will not fail your brothers nor your S.
W-pI...157.3:3 and leaves you, for a moment, to your S..
W-pI...160.1:4 your S. remains an alien to the part of you
W-pI...160.6:6 For in his home his S. remains. It asked
W-pI...160.7:2 Is he not the one your S. calls not? You
W-pI...160.7:4 Yet is your S. as certain of Its Own as God
W-pI.160.10:5 sight by which his S. is clearly recognized,
W-pI...164.2:5 Christ answers for you, echoing your S.,
W-pI...166.9:6 and go the way you chose without your S..
W-pI.166.10:3 imprisoned in your plan to lose your S..
W-pI.167.12:7 mind is one that knows its Source, its S.,
WpI...rV.in4:2 more descriptive of the holy S. we share
WpI...rV.in4:4 *I.* This S. alone knows Love. This Self alone
WpI...rV.in4:5 This S. alone is perfectly consistent in Its
WpI...rV.in5:4 return to the eternal S. we thought we lost
WpI...rV.in9:4 S. from which I call to you is but your own
W-pI...181.1:4 the S. that lies beyond your own mistakes,
W-pI...181.9:2 of the holy S. which knows no sin, and
W-pI...183.5:1 the Name of God, and call upon your S.,
W-pI.187.10:3 our one S. Whose innocence has joined us
W-pI...190.6:5 want. Your S. is radiant in this holy joy,
W-pI...192.1:1 and that your S. shall be His sacred Son,
W-pI...192.1:1 forever one with God and with your S..
W-pI...195.8:6 to love by being loving, even as your S..
W-pI...197.7:2 Thank your S. for this, for He is grateful
W-pI...197.8:2 you contain all things within your S.. And
W-pI...197.9:2 to anyone who makes your S. complete.
W-pI...197.9:3 And from this S. is no one left outside.
W-pI...197.9:4 countless channels which extend this S..
W-pI...198.3:7 of God awakens to his S. and to his Father
W-pI...198.8:1 The stillness of your S. remains unmoved
W-pI...201.1:3 *one Creator of the whole that is my S.,*
W-pI...211.1:2 *it in the Son whom He created as my S..* I am
W-pI...217.1:3 *I find the S. to Whom my thanks are due?*
W-pII..230.1:3 It is not given me to change my S.. How
W-pII..237.2:2 *Him Who is Your Son, and my true S. as well.*
W-pII..238.1:5 *of You, and yet is mine, because He is my S..*
W-pII .245.1:8 *Will, that I may come to recognize my S..*
W-pII .246.1:2 think that I can know his Father or my S..
W-pII .247.2:3 *to me as part of You, and my own S. as well*
W-pII .247.2:4 *and thus I hope this day to recognize my S..*
W-pII .252.1:1 My S. is holy beyond all the thoughts of
W-pII .252.1:5 How far beyond this world my S. must be,
W-pII ....253.h My S. is ruler of the universe.
W-pII .253.1:6 in Heaven where my holy S. abides with
W-pII .253.2:1 *You are the S. Whom You created Son,*
W-pII .253.2:2 *My S., which rules the universe, is but Your*
W-pII ..... 5.1:1 to separate parts of his S. from other parts
W-pII ..... 5.5:8 home. Identify with love, and find your S.
W-pII .261.2:3 *and find the Son whom You created as my S..*
W-pII ....266.h My holy S. abides in you, God's Son.
W-pII .266.1:2 *does Christ look back upon me from my S..*
W-pII .266.2:1 own, acknowledging our S. in each of us;
W-pII .268.1:4 *too, to recognize my S. as You created me. In*
W-pII .269.2:2 upon the face of Him Whose S. is ours.
W-pII ..... 6.1:2 He is the S. we share, uniting us with one
W-pII ..... 6.2:5 salvation, yet does He remain the S. Who,
W-pII ..... 6.3:4 before His glory and reveal your holy S.,
W-pII ..... 6.5:3 or of time, or anything except the holy S.,
W-pII .276.1:6 created in His Love and we deny our S., to
W-pII .276.1:7 to remember Him and so recall our S..
W-pII .278.1:3 way, I do not know my Father nor my S..
W-pII .282.1:4 the choice to recognize the S. Whom God
W-pII .286.2:3 We trust in Him, and in our S., Who still
W-pII .287.2:7 *but this could I expect to recognize my S.,*
W-pII .303.2:3 *He is the S. that You have given me. He is but*
W-pII .303.2:6 *He is my S. as You created me. It is not Christ*
W-pII .309.2:3 *It is the holy altar to my S., and there I find*
W-pII .313.1:6 *holy Son, the S. with which I would identify.*
W-pII .319.2:4 *could be the Will my S. has shared with You?*
W-pII .322.1:4 to conceal the S. which is God's only Son,
W-pII .330.1:5 The S. which God created cannot sin, and
W-pII .335.2:3 *In him I find my S., and in Your Son I find the*
W-pII .337.1:6 of myself, for I need but accept my S., my
W-pII .353.1:5 *and recognize that Christ is but my S..*
W-pII .358.1:7 *not forget myself is nothing, but my S. is all.*
W-ep ......... 3:2 your S. when you retire from the world, to
W-ep ......... 4:4 your Father and your brother and your S..
W-ep ......... 5:4 And He will speak for God and for your S.
M-4 ..... VII.2:1 of God is generous out of S. interest. This
M-7 ........... 6:2 a failure to recognize him as part of the S.,
M-12 ......... 1:3 becomes the S. Who is the Son of God. He
M-19 ......... 4:9 not see you hate and fear your S. as enemy
C-5............. 2:3 that appeared to hold his self from S., as
C-6............. 4:2 He represents your S. and your Creator,
P-2......... V.8:8 Son. There is no other way to find your S..
S-1......... V.2:6 Its selflessness is S., and this it sees in
S-2..........II.7:6 and prayed for separation from your S..

**self** 114

*Self*

*See also* self-abasement, self-accused, self-accusing, self-aggrandizement, self-appointed, self-appraisal, self-betrayal, self-blame, self-centered self-concept, self-concepts, self-condemnation, self-contained, self-contradictory, self-controlled, self-created, self-creating, self-debasement, self-deceiving, self-deception, self-deceptions, self-defeat, self-defeating, self-defense, self-destruction, self-destructive, self-directed, self-doubt, self-esteem, self-evident, self-extension, self-glorification, self-hate, self-image, self-images, self-inflating, self-inflation, self-initiated, self-initiative, self-limiting, self-made, self-maintained, self-perception, self-pity, self-preservation, self-protection, self-replacement, self-selection, self-sufficient, self-sustained, self-value

T-3........ IV.3:1 aspect of the post-separation s., which
T-3....... VII.4:3 of the s. to make an image of itself. Images
T-4........... I.2:9 Your s. and God's Self *are* in opposition.
T-4.......... II.2:1 Everyone makes an ego or a s. for himself
T-4.......... II.4:5 to the s. you made are not surprising. In
T-4........ III.4:4 of your hatred for the s. you made. You
T-5..... IV.2:13 cannot be limited to the s. the ego sees.
T-6...... IV.11:9 If He confronted the s. you made with the

|  |  |
|---|---|
| T-16....... V.1:4 | attack on the **s.** to make the other guilty. |
| T-16....... V.4:2 | attempt to secure for the **s.** the specialness |
| T-16....... V.5:6 | this it sees the ultimate freedom of the **s.**, |
| T-16....... V.7:1 | curious of all is the concept of the **s.** which |
| T-16....... V.7:2 | This "**s.**" seeks the relationship to make |
| T-16....... V.7:3 | tries to "trade" itself for the **s.** of another. |
| T-16....... V.7:5 | Each partner tries to sacrifice the **s.** he |
| T-16....... V.7:7 | much value can he place upon a **s.** that he |
| T-16....... V.8:1 | "better" **s.** the ego seeks is always one that |
| T-16....... V.8:2 | to possess a special **s.** is "loved" for what |
| T-16....... V.8:3 | partners see this special **s.** in each other, |
| T-16..... V.10:6 | your **s.** you think you can attack another |
| T-16..... V.10:6 | self you think you can attack another **s.**, |
| T-16..... V.10:6 | the other to replace the **s.** that you despise |
| T-16..... V.11:3 | think it safer to endow the little **s.** you |
| T-16..... V.11:5 | people, on which each seeks to kill his **s.**, |
| T-16..... V.11:5 | raise another **s.** to take its power from his |
| T-16...... VI.4:4 | is a device for limiting your **s.** to a body, |
| T-18....VIII.7:6 | This little **s.** is not your kingdom. Arched |
| T-19....... II.4:2 | of the **s.** as sinful is perceived as holiness. |
| T-21....... V.3:2 | Them, you will perceive another **s.** in you. |
| T-21....... V.3:3 | you. This other **s.** sees miracles as natural. |
| T-21....... V.3:9 | This other **s.** is perfectly aware of this. |
| T-21....... V.4:2 | Reason lies in the other **s.** you have cut off |
| T-22.......I.4:10 | dependent on the **s.** you think you made |
| T-22....... II.9:6 | would it be possible that the **s.** he made, |
| T-24..... II.13:2 | where none is welcome but your tiny **s.**. |
| T-24.... VI.12:3 | The "sacrifice" of **s.** you understand, nor |
| T-26.........I.3:1 | that the body fences off becomes the **s.**, |
| T-27..... II.12:7 | represent a split within a **s.** perceived as |
| T-27..... II.13:2 | From an idea of **s.** as two, there comes a |
| T-28..... IV.6:1 | confused, for in the gap no stable **s.** exists. |
| T-28....... V.1:5 | is sickness separating off the **s.** from good, |
| T-28...... VI.4:2 | You hate it, yet you think it is your **s.**, and |
| T-28...... VI.4:2 | and that, without it, would your **s.** be lost. |
| T-29.........I.4:7 | in which to build again your separate **s.**, |
| T-29.........I.9:5 | afraid to find a loss of **s.** in finding God? |
| T-29.........I.9:6 | Yet can your **s.** be lost by being found? |
| T-29....... II.8:7 | He must sacrifice your **s.**, and in His |
| T-29....VIII.2:3 | believe they will complete your little **s.**, |
| T-29....VIII.2:6 | his little **s.** for strength to raise his head, |
| T-31....... V.1:1 | of the **s.** adjusted to the world's reality. It |
| T-31....... V.1:5 | building of a concept of the **s.** is what the |
| T-31....... V.1:6 | is its purpose; that you come without a **s.**, |
| T-31....... V.2:1 | A concept of the **s.** is made by you. It |
| T-31....... V.2:4 | concept of the **s.** the world would teach is |
| T-31....... V.4:1 | innocence the concept of the **s.** so proudly |
| T-31....... V.5:1 | the concept of the **s.** was made to teach. It |
| T-31....... V.5:4 | conception of the **s.** the world smiles with |
| T-31....... V.8:1 | A concept of the **s.** is meaningless, for no |
| T-31....... V.8:3 | see this concept of the **s.** must be undone, |
| T-31....... V.8:5 | of what you now believe for total loss of **s.** |
| T-31..... V.11:3 | world depends upon this concept of the **s.** |
| T-31..... V.12:3 | of the **s.** from what is wholly passive, and |
| T-31..... V.13:2 | have gone before these concepts of the **s.**. |
| T-31..... V.14:1 | The concept of the **s.** has always been the |
| T-31..... V.14:7 | vaguely does the concept of the **s.** appear |
| T-31..... V.15:3 | you perceive a **s.** that interacts with evil, |
| T-31..... V.15:7 | of the **s.** embraces all you look upon, and |
| T-31..... V.16:1 | concepts of the **s.** as learning goes along. |
| T-31..... V.17:4 | Where concepts of the **s.** have been laid |
| T-31...... VI.5:4 | because the concept of the **s.** has changed. |
| T-31..... VII.7:1 | The concept of the **s.** stands like a shield, |
| T-31... VII.12:1 | it always but reflects a wish to be a **s.** that |
| T-31... VII.12:4 | **s.** whose image has the wish begot of you. |
| W-pI..... 22.1:3 | own attack is thus perceived as **s.** defense. |
| W-pI..... 92.4:6 | darkness you perceive a **s.** that is not there |
| W-pI... 92.10:4 | to find the meeting place of **s.** and Self, |
| W-pI..... 93.5:1 | The **s.** you made is not the Son of God. |
| W-pI..... 93.5:2 | Therefore, this **s.** does not exist at all. And |
| W-pI..... 93.5:9 | What power can this **s.** you made possess, |
| W-pI..... 93.6:6 | The **s.** you made, evil and full of sin, is |
| W-pI..... 95.2:2 | a **s.** divided into many warring parts, |
| W-pI..... 96.3:3 | The **s.** you made can never be your Self, |
| W-pI... 99.10:3 | You do not want to be another **s.**. You |
| W-pI... 121.6:4 | how to forgive the **s.** you think you made, |
| W-pI... 123.2:3 | He has saved you from the **s.** you thought |
| W-pI... 135.8:1 | The "**s.**" that needs protection is not real. |
| W-pI... 137.1:4 | a door that closes on a separate **s.**, and |
| W-pI... 137.2:2 | to keep one **s.** apart from all the rest, to |
| W-pI... 166.7:1 | This is your chosen **s.**, the one you made |
| W-pI... 166.7:2 | **s.** you savagely defend against all reason, |
| W-pI... 166.9:3 | think the miserable **s.** you thought was |
| W-pII . 303.2:2 | *has come to save me from the evil* **s.** *I made.* |
| W-pII ... 12.1:1 | the sign of limited and separated **s.**, born |
| W-pII . 354.1:2 | *I have no* **s.** *except the Christ in me. I have no* |
| M-in .......... 3:9 | that the **s.** you are trying to protect is real. |
| M-in ........ 3:10 | the **s.** you think is real is what you teach. |
| M-4 ..... VII.2:2 | to the **s.** of which the world speaks. The |
| M-7 ........... 5:2 | that trust has been placed in an illusory **s.**, |
| M-7 ........... 5:2 | self, for only such a **s.** can be doubted. |
| M-7 ........... 6:1 | with the **s.** to the exclusion of the patient. |
| C-2 ............ 8:1 | the **s.** that seemed alone in all the universe |
| C-5 ............ 2:3 | that appeared to hold his **s.** from Self, as |
| C-6 ............ 4:8 | you perceive your **s.** entrapped in needs |
| P-1............. 3:3 | realize and needs to learn is that this "**s.**," |
| P-1............. 3:6 | This **s.** he sees as being acted on, reacting |
| P-2.........in.1:1 | is a process that changes the view of the **s.** |
| P-2.........in.1:2 | "new" **s.** is a more beneficent self-concept, |
| P-2.........in.3:6 | The **s.** he sees is his god, and he seeks only |
| P-2..........II.8:5 | the ego would impose upon the **s.**. Only |
| P-2........ IV.6:1 | as the result of a view of the **s.** as weak, |
| P-2........ IV.6:2 | Yet if such were really the **s.**, defense |
| P-2........ IV.6:4 | overcome all limits perceived in the **s.**, at |
| P-2......... V.1:6 | **s.** that holds in darkness what is truly felt, |
| P-2........VII.5:6 | nor is the tiny **s.** of one alone against the |

## self-abasement 1

|  |  |
|---|---|
| T-9 .....VIII.2:9 | decide not to tolerate **s.** and seek relief. |

## self-accused 2

|  |  |
|---|---|
| T-31 ........ III.h | The **S.** |
| T-31 ..... III.1:1 | Only the **s.** condemn. As you prepare to |

## self-accusing 1

|  |  |
|---|---|
| W-pI... 134.7:4 | the **s.** shrieks of sinners mad with guilt. It |

## self-aggrandizement 1

|  |  |
|---|---|
| T-17 ..... IV.8:3 | of love, set with dreams of sacrifice and **s.**, |

## self-appointed 1

|  |  |
|---|---|
| T-20 ..... III.2:4 | ego is the **s.** mediator of all relationships, |

## self-appraisal 1

|  |  |
|---|---|
| T-23 ........I.3:4 | You meet at a mistake; an error in your **s.**. |

## self-betrayal 3

|  |  |
|---|---|
| T-16 ..... VI.8:8 | soon recognize the guilt of **s.** for what it is |
| T-29 ..... IX.9:2 | lie the guilt and pain of **s.** and uncertainty |
| T-29 ..... IX.9:3 | **s.** must result in fear, for fear *is* judgment, |

## self-blame 1

|  |  |
|---|---|
| T-11 ..... IV.5:5 | **S.** is therefore ego identification, and as |

## Self-centered 1

*self-centered*

|  |  |
|---|---|
| T-4 ........in.1:7 | **S.** in the right sense is to be inspired or in |

## self-centered 1

*Self-centered*

|  |  |
|---|---|
| T-20 ..... VI.1:6 | The one he made is partial, **s.**, broken into |

## self-concept 11

|  |  |
|---|---|
| T-3 ...... VII.4:3 | belief that they are is implicit in the "**s.**," |
| T-31 ......... V.h | **S.** versus Self |
| W-pI..... 61.1:4 | It does not describe the **s.** you have made. |
| W-pI .... 84.1:6 | nor raise my own **s.** to replace my Self. |
| W-pI .... 96.3:6 | physical, your mind is gone from your **s.**, |
| P-2.........in.1:2 | best this "new" self is a more beneficent **s.** |
| P-2.........in.2:3 | to be able to retain their **s.** exactly as it is, |
| P-2.........in.3:3 | changing his **s.** to any significant extent. |
| P-2.........in.4:1 | he must want to change the patient's **s.** in |
| P-2........ IV.6:4 | same time making a new **s.** into which the |
| P-2........ VI.2:5 | distortions woven inextricably into the **s.**, |

## self-concepts 4

|  |  |
|---|---|
| W-pI .... 70.7:5 | and in **s.** that you sought to make real. |
| W-pI 152.10:3 | as well that all **s.** have been laid aside, and |
| W-pII . 248.1:7 | Now I disown **s.** and deceits and lies |
| P-2.........in.3:2 | as well as the patient may cherish false **s.**, |

## self-condemnation 2

|  |  |
|---|---|
| M-13 ......... 3:4 | Who can escape this **s.**? Only through |
| M-13 ......... 3:6 | For **s.** is a decision about identity, and no |

## self-contained 1

|  |  |
|---|---|
| T-18 ... VIII.5:3 | Each tiny fragment seems to be **s.**, |

## self-contradictory 1

|  |  |
|---|---|
| W-pI .... 16.2:1 | is no more **s.** concept than that of "idle |

## self-controlled 1

|  |  |
|---|---|
| T-2 ....... VI.1:4 | be controlled by me, but it can be **s.**. Fear |

## self-created 3

|  |  |
|---|---|
| T-10 ..... III.4:7 | perceive in a Son of God; a sick god, **s.**, |
| T-24 ... VI.11:2 | for you alone, as **s.**, self-maintained, in |
| P-2....... VII.4:2 | themselves as **s.** rather than God-created. |

## self-creating 2

|  |  |
|---|---|
| T-3 ...... VII.4:1 | expression for usurping the ability for **s.**. |
| T-3 ...... VII.4:6 | You can perceive yourself as **s.**, but you |

## self-debasement 1

|  |  |
|---|---|
| W-pI .... 61.2:2 | understand humility, mistaking it for **s.**. |

## self-deceiving 2

|  |  |
|---|---|
| W-pI .. 186.2:5 | deny with **s.** arrogance that we are worthy |
| M-in.......... 5:2 | The **s.** must deceive, for they must teach |

## self-deception 13

|  |  |
|---|---|
| W-pI .... 61.1:3 | a statement of pride, of arrogance, or of **s.** |
| W-pI .... 92.9:1 | that the body's eyes provide for **s.**. |
| W-pI 133.13:2 | to reach this state today, with **s.** laid aside |
| W-pI .. 134.9:2 | on what you think he did, for that is **s.**. |
| W-pI .. 136.2:2 | all defenses, it is an insane device for **s.**. |
| W-pI .. 139.3:1 | what you must be is **s.** on a scale so vast, |
| W-pI .. 166.7:4 | truth, and be released from **s.** and set free |
| W-pI .. 182.2:5 | honesty, without defensiveness and **s.**, |
| W-pI .. 190.1:2 | experienced in any form, it is a proof of **s.**. |
| W-pII ..... 4.2:5 | has taken as replacement for the goal of **s.** |
| M-4 ........II.2:4 | Conflict is the inevitable result of **s.**, and |
| M-4 ........II.2:4 | of self-deception, and **s.** is dishonesty. |
| M-4 ...... III.1:3 | have. Judgment without **s.** is impossible. |

## self-deceptions 7

|  |  |
|---|---|
| W-pI 135.14:3 | realize in some forms which these **s.** take, |
| WpI..rIV.in3:3 | hold correction off through **s.** made to |
| WpI..rIV.in4:2 | Your **s.** cannot take the place of truth. No |
| W-pI .. 152.8:5 | And it will take the place of **s.** made but to |
| W-pI 152.11:5 | will we wait in silence, giving up all **s.**, as |
| W-pI 152.12:3 | frantic thoughts, the truth of God for **s.**, |
| W-pII . 323.2:1 | of **s.** and of images we worshipped falsely |

**self-defeat** 1
T-12......IV.2:2 a journey which must end in perceived **s.**.

**self-defeating** 1
T-21.......V.6:1 plan is simple; never circular and never **s.**.

**self-defense** 5
T-23.....II.11:9 you may live. And you attack only in **s.**.
T-31.......V.4:1 so proudly wears can tolerate attack in **s.**,
W-pI...153.2:2 provoked, and righteous in the name of **s.**
W-pI...170.1:3 When you think that you attack in **s.**, you
W-pI...170.4:1 fancied **s.** proceeds on its imagined way,

**self-destruction** 2
T-14.....VII.5:8 of **s.** to means of preservation and release.
T-17......IV.8:3 and interlaced with gilded threads of **s.**.

**self-destructive** 3
T-10.......V.3:5 Blasphemy, then, is **s.**, not God-destructive
T-20......VI.1:8 one he made is wholly **s.** and self-limiting.
P-1.............3:2 tendencies are often described as "**s.**,"

**self-directed** 2
W-pI.....29.4:2 to avoid the tendency toward **s.** selection,
W-pI.....43.5:1 without **s.** inclusion or exclusion. For the

**self-doubt** 2
M-in..........3:8 Its fundamental purpose is to diminish **s.**.
M-7............5:1 God's Teacher for resolution is always **s.**.

**Self-encompassing** 1
T-20......VI.1:7 his Father is wholly **S.** and Self-extending.

**self-esteem** 4
T-4.........II.6:8 "**S.**" in ego terms means nothing more
T-4.........II.6:9 This "**s.**" is always vulnerable to stress, a
T-4.........II.8:9 is why **s.** in ego terms must be delusional.
T-16.....VII.1:3 you seek to restore your wounded **s.**.

**self-evident** 1
M-24..........2:4 and if it heartens them its value is **s.**. It is

**Self-extending** 2
T-20......VI.1:7 Father is wholly Self-encompassing and **S.**
T-21.......V.6:2 He has no Thoughts except the **S.**, and in

**self-extension** 1
T-12......VI.3:5 As self-value comes from **s.**, so does the

**Self-fullness** 4
T-7........IX.1:4 but **S.** is of spirit because that is how God
T-7........IX.4:2 joy because you do not know your own **S.**.
T-7........IX.4:6 full appreciation of the mind's **S.** makes
T-7........IX.6:7 Your **S.** is as boundless as God's. Like His,

**self-glorification** 1
W-pI.....61.2:1 the ego, today's idea is the epitome of **s.**.

**self-hate** 1
T-12......III.6:3 he did was to exchange Self-love for **s.**,

**self-image** 3
T-3..........VII.h Creating versus the **S.**
W-pI.....56.2:3 to the fearful nature of the **s.** I have made.
W-pI.....56.3:2 world I see holds my fearful **s.** in place,

**self-images** 3
W-pI.....67.5:2 your mind is so preoccupied with false **s.**.
W-pI.....93.8:4 Then put away your foolish **s.**, and spend
W-pI.....94.4:1 this goal except to lay all idols and **s.** aside

**self-inflating** 1
W-pI.....35.5:2 more **s.** descriptive terms may well cross

**self-inflation** 1
T-9..... VIII.1:5 **S.** is the only offering it can make. The

**self-initiated** 1
W-pI.135.14:1 to perceive that **s.** plans are but defenses,

**self-initiative** 1
T-2.........V.6:2 learner, but if it is falsely endowed with **s.**,

**self-limiting** 1
T-20......VI.1:8 he made is wholly self-destructive and **s.**.

**Self-love** 1
T-12......III.6:3 he did was to exchange **S.** for self-hate,

**self-made** 3
T-24.......II.3:4 Here is the **s.** "savior," the "creator" who
W-pI...104.2:1 and **s.** gifts which we have placed upon
W-pI...186.8:3 Our **s.** roles are shifting, and they seem to

**self-maintained** 1
T-24....VI.11:2 It stands for you alone, as self-created, **s.**,

**self-perception** 4
T-27.....II.13:1 Consider how this **s.** must extend, and do
W-pI.....96.1:2 the contradictory aspects of this **s.**. You
W-pI...195.9:3 and to a **s.** which regards us in a place of
M-21.........5:5 a shabby **s.** which he would leave behind.

**self-pity** 1
W-pI...166.8:4 Where is **s.** then? And what becomes of

**self-preservation** 2
T-4.........II.5:4 You have no sense of real **s.**, and are likely
T-4.........V.1:6 by the ego in the interest of its **s.**.

**self-protection** 1
T-14....III.10:3 it. They believe that increasing guilt is **s.**.

**self-replacement** 1
T-14....III.15:3 that the "sin" of **s.** on the throne of God is

**self-selection** 1
W-pI.....29.5:1 therefore be as free of **s.** as possible. For

**self-sufficient** 2
T-7.........V.2:3 can act like the mind, and is therefore **s.**.
T-10......III.4:7 in a Son of God; a sick god, self-created, **s.**

**self-sustained** 1
T-13......III.6:2 to do so, and thus they seem to be **s.**. This

**self-value** 2
T-12......VI.3:5 As **s.** comes from self-extension, so does
T-12......VI.3:5 perception of **s.** come from the extension

**Selfhood** 1
T-15......VI.7:3 His Self, you will learn to understand **S.**.

**selfish** 1
P-3..........II.3:2 The unhealed healer may be arrogant, **s.**,

**selfishness** 2
T-7........IX.1:4 **S.** is of the ego, but Self-fullness is of spirit
T-7........IX.4:6 **s.** impossible and extension inevitable.

**selflessness** 1
S-1.........V.2:6 God. Its **s.** is Self, and this it sees in every

**selfsame** 5
T19. IV.D.18:2 Give him the **s.** gift, nor look upon him
T-31.........I.8:3 the **s.** tongue in which the call was made.
T-31........II.6:5 us, but walks beside us on the **s.** road. He
W-pI...107.8:2 but were created by the **s.** Thought which
W-pI.193.13:4 form of suffering, repeat these **s.** words.

**sell** 8
T-3.......VII.2:7 willing to "**s.**" him their souls in return
T-12......III.1:1 I once asked you to **s.** all you have and
T-12......IV.6:4 you will **s.** everything else to purchase it.
T-12......IV.6:6 Yet you cannot **s.** the Kingdom of Heaven
T-12......IV.7:2 you chose to "**s.**" had to be kept for you,
T-12......VI.1:6 You cannot **s.** your soul, but you can sell
T-12......VI.1:6 soul, but you can **s.** your awareness of it.
T-21......IV.6:8 you would not "**s.**" Heaven to have them.

**selves** 5
T-16......III.6:1 You are not two **s.** in conflict. What is
T-16......III.8:2 the gap he imagines exists between his **s.**.
T-22........in.3:4 He sees no difference between these **s.**, for
T-26.........I.2:5 their separation are their **s.** maintained.
W-pI.....96.3:2 Two **s.** in conflict could not be resolved,

**semblance** 2
T-14......XI.1:7 made a **s.** of power and a show of strength
T-14......XI.1:8 and truth is beyond **s.** of any kind. Yet all

**send** 25
T-5...........I.4:4 "If I go I will **s.** you another Comforter
T-8......IV.3:10 sent me to you so will I **s.** you to others.
T-12.....VII.6:2 For He will **s.** you His witnesses if you will
T19. IV.A.4:12 will **s.** its messengers from you to all the
T19. IV.A.12:2 on to **s.** its messengers to look upon it,
T19. IV.A.13:1 **S.** not these savage messengers into the
T19. IV.A.14:1 to **s.** instead of those you trained through
T19. IV.A.14:3 If you **s.** them forth, they will see only the
T19. IV.A.15:1 you **s.** forth only the messengers the Holy
T19. IV.A.15:5 you His messengers to **s.** to your brother
T19....IV.B.7:6 in Heaven. **S.** forth to all the world the
T19IV.B.14:11 **s.** messages of hatred and attack if he but
T19..IV.B.15:3 it urges you to **s.** out all your messages of
T-22.........I.2:4 seeing such as this **s.** back its messages?
T-27.........I.4:3 you **s.** lest he forget the injuries he gave,
T-27.......I.10:5 will it **s.** forth the message it received, and
T-28......VI.3:2 You **s.** it forth to seek for separation and
W-pI.132.16:1 **s.** out these thoughts to bless the world.
W-pII.245.1:6 *S. them to me, my Father. Let me bring Your*

W-pII .349.2:3 in Him to **s.** us miracles to bless the world
M-2 ........... 5:4 God has promised to **s.** His Spirit into any
M-4 ....... X.1:5 of guilt upon him would **s.** him to hell, so
P-2 ......... V.6:7 And He will **s.** His Answer through the
P-3 ........... I.2:8 Would God **s.** His Son to you and not be
S-2 ........ III.7:5 fail to **s.** His angels down to answer you in

## sender 3

T19..IV.B.14:7 invested is given by the **s.** and the receiver
T19..IV.B.14:8 that here the **s.** and receiver are the same.
T19..IV.B.17:4 Holy Spirit is both the **s.** and the receiver.

## sends 16

T-9......... V.8:8 to do to help anyone He **s.** to you for help,
T-11..VIII.12:5 healing power and use it for all He **s.** you,
T-12..... VII.1:5 the Holy Spirit **s.** you for your blessing. In
T19IV.A.10:10 And each has messengers which it **s.** forth
T19. IV.A.13:5 avert the punishment of him who **s.** them
T19..IV.B.14:5 and **s.** the messages that it is given. It has
T19IV.B.14:11 if he but understood he **s.** them to himself
T-27...... VI.4:7 each witness to the body's death He **s.** a
T-27...... VI.6:6 Who **s.** forth miracles to bless the world,
W-pI... 100.2:5 understood by those to whom He **s.** you.
W-pI... 151.6:2 The witnesses it **s.** to prove to you its evil
M-in .......... 4:7 despair and death, God **s.** His teachers.
M-8 ........... 3:7 and it **s.** the body's eyes to find it. The
M-17 ......... 8:1 hopeless situation God **s.** His teachers.
P-3 ........ III.8:6 times. Whoever He **s.** you will reach you,
S-3 ........ III.6:2 His kindly remedy to those He **s.** to you,

## sense 231

T-1........... I.3:3 In this **s.** everything that comes from love
T-1........... I.9:2 which are always miraculous in the true **s.**
T-1......... I.42:1 in releasing you from your false **s.** of
T-1......... I.47:3 usual laws of time. In this **s.** it is timeless.
T-1......... II.1:2 involving the extremely personal **s.** of
T-1......... III.9:1 Miracles are selective only in the **s.** that
T-1........ VI.2:1 **s.** of separation from God is the only lack
T-1........ VI.2:2 **s.** of separation would never have arisen if
T-2........... I.2:7 **s.** the creation includes both the creation
T-2......... II.6:6 In this **s.** the Atonement saves time, but
T-2......... V.2:6 As long as your **s.** of vulnerability persists
T-2......... V.9:7 limited **s.** in which it can now be attained.
T-2......... VI.5:7 a **s.** of coercion that usually produces rage
T-2....... VII.4:5 however, the **s.** of conflict is inevitable,
T-2....... VII.5:6 In this **s.** the separation *has* occurred, and
T-2....... VII.6:6 of wholeness in the true **s.** be understood.
T-2...... VIII.4:2 of separation in the constructive **s.**, and
T-3........... I.6:4 in the **s.** that the state of innocence, or
T-3......... II.5:3 All **s.** of separation disappears. The Son of
T-3......... V.2:2 do so out of a specific **s.** of lack or need.
T-3......... V.3:5 In this **s.**, when your behavior is unstable,
T-3......... V.6:4 the usual **s.** becomes utterly meaningless.
T-3....... VII.2:8 real worth. This makes absolutely no **s.**.
T-3....... VII.4:2 This is the only **s.** in which God and His
T-4......... in.1:7 in the right **s.** is to be inspired or in spirit.
T-4......... II.5:3 In this **s.** you are still a baby. You have no
T-4......... II.5:4 You have no **s.** of real self-preservation,
T-4......... II.6:1 and lasting **s.** of abundance can be truly
T-4........ III.3:4 it can offer is a **s.** of temporary existence,
T-4........ III.3:6 Against this **s.** of temporary existence
T-4........ IV.3:2 *be.* Depression comes from a **s.** of being
T-4......... V.3:3 In one **s.** the ego's fear of God is at least
T-4......... V.3:4 ego identifies so closely, makes no **s.** at all
T-4....... VII.4:5 are limiting your **s.** of your own reality,
T-5......... II.3:7 The Holy Spirit is in you in a very literal **s.**
T-5......... II.5:5 God is not in you in a literal **s.**; you are
T-5........ VI.2:4 It gives the ego a false **s.** of security by
T-5....... VII.5:4 be undone by repentance in the usual **s.**,
T-6......... I.14:4 their **s.** of guilt had made them angry.
T-6...... V.C.8:5 real **s.** of being cannot be yours while you
T-7........... I.7:5 He is first in the **s.** that He is the First in
T-7......... IV.7:4 else. God is All in all in a very literal **s.**. All
T-7......... IV.7:7 is a way of forgetting the **s.** of danger the
T-7......... XI.3:4 him to give always, without any **s.** of loss?
T-8......... II.2:2 anything it teaches make anything but **s.**?
T-8 ....... IV.3:6 in this **s.** I *am* the salvation of the world.
T-8 ...... VII.8:2 His **s.** of adequacy suffers, and he must
T-8 ...... VII.9:7 **s.** the body does become a temple to God;
T-8 ..... VIII.5:5 A sick body does not make any **s.**. It could
T-8 ..... VIII.5:6 It could not make **s.** because sickness is
T-9 .......... I.6:5 be communicated unless it makes **s.**. How
T-9 ....... III.1:2 in terms of the kind of "**s.**" they stand for.
T-9 ....... III.1:3 They understand this kind of **s.**, because
T-9 ....... III.1:4 To the Holy Spirit it makes no **s.** at all.
T-9 ....... III.2:2 This makes perfect **s.** to the ego, which is
T-9 ....... III.2:5 He may be making no **s.** at the time, and
T-9 ....... III.2:5 from the ego, he will not be making **s.**.
T-9 ....... III.3:3 The ego makes no **s.**, and the Holy Spirit
T-9 ....... III.4:3 ego and making as little **s.** as the brother
T-9 ....... IV.2:6 **s.** of limitation is where all errors arise.
T-9 ....... IV.4:2 of course, makes no **s.** and will not work.
T-9 ....... IV.4:8 perfect **s.** because they come from God.
T-9 ....... IV.9:4 Second Coming is merely the return of **s.**.
T-9 ...... VII.5:3 from a **s.** of inadequacy it has produced,
T-9 ..... VIII.3:3 Its profound **s.** of vulnerability renders it
T-10 ...... V.1:5 and in this **s.** the wages of sin *is* death. The
T-10 ...... V.1:6 *is* death. The **s.** is very literal; denial of life
T-12 ......... I.3:1 of motivation that makes any **s.**. And
T-12 ......... I.6:3 And all your **s.** of strain comes from your
T-12 ......... I.9:1 is a symptom of your own deep **s.** of loss.
T-12 ..... IV.4:1 but lead to a **s.** of futility and depression?
T-12 ...... V.2:5 this you will no longer see any **s.** in attack,
T-12 ...... V.5:1 have learning handicaps in a very literal **s.**
T-12 ...... V.7:6 Such a curriculum does not make **s.**. This
T-13 ......... I.9:2 could induce a **s.** of a need for expiation.
T-13 ... XI.3:13 a **s.** of peace so deep that no dream in this
T-14 ....... II.1:6 Yet it may still make **s.** to you. Have faith
T-14 ..... VI.4:6 The other is wholly without **s.** of any kind
T-14 ..... IX.4:3 and cover all their **s.** of pain and loss with
T-14 ....... X.5:4 together by a **s.** of order that you establish
T-14 ....... X.8:9 consistent **s.** when they are put together.
T-15 ......... I.9:7 fear, and with no **s.** of change with time.
T-15 ..... III.6:5 a **s.** of magnitude that can content them.
T-15 ... VIII.3:6 Accept your **s.** of failure as nothing more
T-15 ..... XI.5:3 aside without a **s.** of sacrifice and loss?
T-16 ......... I.4:4 Humility is strength in this **s.** only; that to
T-16 ........ II.9:3 these facts together and made **s.** of them?
T-16 ... IV.10:2 removes your own **s.** of completion, and
T-16 ..... VI.7:4 a **s.** of actual disorientation may occur.
T-17 ......... I.2:2 strange position, in a **s.**, acknowledges
T-17 ..... IV.4:1 In a **s.**, the special relationship was the
T-17 ...... V.3:7 Now it seems to make no **s.**. Many
T-17 ...... V.8:3 A **s.** of aimlessness will come to haunt you
T-17 ..... VI.3:1 makes no **s.** until it has already happened.
T-18 ... VI.11:1 a **s.** of being transported beyond himself.
T-18 ... VI.11:3 It is a **s.** of actual escape from limitations.
T-18 ... VI.13:5 would be, gaining, not losing, a **s.** of Self.
T19. IV.D.10:5 when it is over it seems to make no **s.**.
T-21 ...... V.2:4 depression, a **s.** of worthlessness, and
T-22 ...... in.4:8 and finally removes all **s.** of differences, so
T-22 ......... I.1:6 uneasiness, your **s.** of being disconnected,
T-22 ......... I.2:3 that are not yours must make no **s.** to you
T-22 ..... III.1:6 Vision is **s.**, quite literally. If it is not the
T-22 ...... V.2:2 flies in the face of reason and makes no **s.**.
T-23 ..... III.3:9 Does this make **s.**? Can it be understood?
T-23 ..... IV.8:8 and a **s.** of love so deep and quiet that no
T-24 ..... IV.3:7 Nothing could make less **s.** to specialness.
T-24 ..... IV.3:8 Nothing could make more **s.** to miracles.
T-24 ... IV.3:10 but only in the **s.** that all illusions are
T-24 ..... VI.1:3 He is the healing of your **s.** of sacrifice and
T-24 ... VI.13:5 To Him this judgment makes no **s.** at all,
T-25 ....... II.3:3 Can it make **s.** to hold the fixed belief that
T-25 ...... V.1:5 the other for whatever **s.** it seems to have.
T-25 .... VII.3:3 His makes any **s.** at all within this world.
T-25 .... VII.3:5 no **s.** and has no meaning is insanity. And
T-25 .... VII.3:8 meaning to are false, and make no **s.** at all
T-25 .... VII.7:6 and made with reason in the light of **s.**.
T-26 ......... I.5:1 that gives it **s.** and makes it meaningful.
T-26 .... VII.6:4 although this clearly makes no **s.** at all.
T-26 .. VII.11:9 this he cannot do without a **s.** of isolation,
T-26 ... VIII.6:9 advance. Nor is there really **s.** in this idea.
T-27 .... VII.3:5 see it does not follow and it makes no **s.**.
T-28 ...... V.1:1 is a **s.** of sickness but a sense of limitation
T-28 ...... V.1:1 is a sense of sickness but a **s.** of limitation
T-28 ....... V.5:6 For eyes and ears are senses without **s.**,
T-28 .... VII.6:1 **s.** in seeking to be safe in what was made
T-29 ..... IX.9:2 conceal completely all your **s.** of doom.
T-30 ......... I.9:3 This works against the **s.** of opposition,
T-30 ....... I.12:5 you now can ask a question that makes **s.**,
T-30 ....... I.12:5 and so the answer will make **s.** as well.
T-30 ..... VI.4:1 world employs to keep the **s.** of sin alive.
T-31 ..... II.11:5 **s.** of endless doubting as you stagger back
T-31 ..... IV.7:2 This makes no **s.**, and cannot be the way.
T-31 ..... VI.2:2 and happenings that make no **s.** at all.
T-31 .... VII.6:2 a bitter **s.** of deep depression and futility.
W-pI ...... 1.4:2 or so, unless that entails a **s.** of hurry. A
W-pI ...... 1.4:3 A comfortable **s.** of leisure is essential.
W-pI ...... 4.1:6 they represent such a mixture that, in a **s.**,
W-pI ..... 11.2:4 haste, and with no **s.** of urgency or effort.
W-pI .... 12.6:4 whenever you experience a **s.** of strain.
W-pI .... 19.2:2 with it an enormous **s.** of responsibility,
W-pI .... 25.4:1 make any **s.** out of the exercises for today,
W-pI .... 26.6:2 worry, anger, a **s.** of imposition, fear,
W-pI .. 29.5:11 experience a **s.** of restfulness as you do
W-pI .... 31.3:5 as you care to, but with no **s.** of hurry.
W-pI .... 33.1:4 but without an abrupt **s.** of shifting.
W-pI .... 34.6:2 the idea until you feel some **s.** of relief. It
W-pI .... 38.4:1 then search your mind for any **s.** of loss or
W-pI .... 38.5:5 to begin to instill in you a **s.** that you have
W-pI .... 41.1:1 the **s.** of loneliness and abandonment all
W-pI .... 41.1:3 anxiety, worry, a deep **s.** of helplessness,
W-pI .... 41.6:5 Try, instead, to get a **s.** of turning inward,
W-pI .... 44.4:2 slipping by with little or no **s.** of strain.
W-pI .... 44.8:1 what is needful is a **s.** of the importance of
W-pI .. 44.10:1 should experience some **s.** of relaxation,
W-pI .... 47.5:1 related to your own **s.** of inadequacy. It is
W-pI .... 47.7:2 reached it if you feel a **s.** of deep peace,
W-pI .... 51.3:5 There is no **s.** in trying to understand it.
W-pI .... 62.3:3 It will remove all **s.** of weakness, strain
W-pI .... 65.6:5 but try to get the **s.** of being willing to
W-pI .... 69.7:1 to feel a **s.** of being lifted up and carried
W-pI .... 71.5:4 and a deep **s.** of failure and despair.
W-pI .... 73.1:5 Its wishes are not idle in the **s.** that they
W-pI .... 74.5:4 a deep **s.** of joy and an increased alertness
W-pI .... 76.1:5 you bind yourself to laws that make no **s.**.
W-pI .... 91.4:5 The miracles your **s.** of weakness hides
W-pI .... 91.9:3 Remember that all **s.** of weakness is
W-pI .... 95.3:1 hear and see, and what makes perfect **s.**.
W-pI .... 96.1:2 **s.** of being split into opposites induces
W-pI .. 102.1:3 it, and to suspect it really makes no **s.**. It
W-pI .. 107.2:5 Then let the **s.** of quiet that you felt be
W-pI .. 121.1:2 in a world that seems to make no **s.**. Here
W-pI .. 122.1:4 a **s.** of worth and beauty that transcends
W-pI 124.11:2 will be a **s.** of love you cannot understand,
W-pI 132.16:2 But you will **s.** your own release, although
W-pI 134.16:3 honesty, you will begin to **s.** a lifting up, a
W-pI .. 135.2:2 A **s.** of threat is an acknowledgment of an
W-pI .. 135.2:4 all serve but to preserve its **s.** of threat.
W-pI 136.17:3 will be no **s.** of feeling ill or feeling well, of
W-pI .. 138.3:5 no **s.** of gain, for nothing is accomplished;
W-pI .. 153.4:3 The **s.** of threat the world encourages is so
W-pI .. 154.6:4 become their first receivers in the truest **s.**
W-pI .. 155.4:3 And they have suffered from a **s.** of loss,
W-pI .. 155.4:4 have suffered from a **s.** of loss still deeper,
W-pI .. 161.4:7 in the **s.** that it is all-encompassing. We
W-pI .. 162.5:4 remedy for grief and misery, all **s.** of loss,
W-pI .. 164.4:3 **s.** of holiness in you the thought of sin has
Wi181-200 1:3 order to attain the **s.** of peace such unified
Wi181-200 2:3 Words alone can not convey the **s.** of
W-pI .. 184.4:4 a **s.** of unity or vision that sees differently,
W-pI .. 187.5:5 the **s.** the world conceives of them. There
W-pI 198.11:2 a frantic rush of thoughts that made no **s.**.
W-pI .. 200.1:3 and **s.** of icy hopelessness and doubt. Seek
W-pII ..... 2.3:1 is undoing in the **s.** that it does nothing,
W-pII . 249.1:1 impossible and anger makes no **s.**. Attack
W-pII ..... 4.1:7 What would they **s.** at all? To sense is not
W-pII ..... 4.1:8 To **s.** is not to know. And truth can be but
W-pII . 323.1:1 *give up all suffering, all* **s.** *of loss and sadness*
M-3 ........... 4:1 the **s.** that each person involved will learn
M-3 ........... 4:2 In this **s.**, and in this sense only, we can
M-3 ........... 4:2 In this sense, and in this **s.** only, we can
M-4 ..... VII.1:3 trust no one can be generous in the true **s.**
M-4 ..... VII.1:4 "giving away" in the **s.** of "giving up." To

M-4.......IX.2:9 in the true **s.** is always directed. Toward
M-6............1:7 a **s.** of loss so deep that the patient might
M-7............5:5 shame associated with a **s.** of inadequacy.
M-8............4:3 judging where each **s.** datum fits best.
M-10...........3:1 judgment in the usual **s.** is impossible.
M-10...........5:7 His **s.** of care is gone, for he has none. He
M-10...........6:6 All of the loneliness and **s.** of loss; of
M-11...........3:4 one without meaning and devoid of **s.**,
M-13...........6:2 In one **s.** this is true, for you hold dear the
M-17.........8:11 and thus forgotten in the truest **s.**.
M-22...........6:7 task to heal the **s.** of separation that has
M-24...........1:1 ultimate **s.**, reincarnation is impossible.
M-24...........1:3 cannot, then, be true in any real **s.**. Our
M-24.........6:10 In this **s.**, it can be said that their truth
M-29...........7:9 your **s.** of frailty and your fear of harm,
C-6.............1:3 in the **s.** that it was now possible to accept
P-2.........II.8:4 in so doing, lose all **s.** of separate interests
P-2........III.1:1 is a leader in the **s.** that he walks slightly
P-2........III.4:4 In a **s.**, the egoless psychotherapist is an
P-2.........V.1:6 only by an inflated **s.** of self that holds in
P-2........VII.3:6 all **s.** of separation finally is overcome.
P-3.........II.4:5 need for each other implies a **s.** of lack. A
S-1.........II.1:5 wanting, out of a **s.** of scarcity and lack.
S-1.........II.3:3 A vague and usually unstable **s.** of
S-1.........II.3:3 to be blurred by a deep-rooted **s.** of sin. It
S-3...........I.2:6 For they **s.** the heavy scent of death upon
S-3.........II.2:1 made joyfully and with a **s.** of peace,
S-3........III.4:7 in this oneness is his separate **s.** dispelled,

## senseless 62

T-11.......V.4:3 which is so clearly **s.** that any effort on its
T-12......III.9:6 governed by arbitrary and **s.** "laws," and
T-13.........I.3:7 journey will seem long and cruel and **s.**,
T-14.......X.8:9 For their teacher is **s.**, though careful to
T-14.....X.11:4 you would lay upon a brother is **s.**. Let the
T-16.....V.12:4 a **s.** ritual in which strength is extracted
T-17....IV.13:5 As each **s.** stone that seems to shine from
T-18.........I.7:6 Your little, **s.** substitutions, touched with
T-20......VI.5:2 secret room, a tiny spot of **s.** mystery, a
T-20...VIII.7:1 **s.** means to play the idle game of death in
T-21......IV.8:7 **s.** is not made meaningful by repetition
T-21.......V.1:6 **s.** ravings to those who want to hear It.
T-22.......II.2:5 The search for joy in misery is **s.**, for how
T-23......I.12:9 Yet far beyond this **s.** war it shines, ready
T-23.....II.18:1 true, that you do not believe these **s.** laws,
T-23.....II.19:7 only the conflict of illusion stands; **s.**,
T-24.........I.2:3 And many **s.** outcomes have been reached
T-24......IV.5:1 Do not defend this **s.** dream, in which
T-24......VI.9:2 A **s.** wandering, without a purpose and
T-25.......V.3:5 And yet, beneath the ego's **s.** shrieks, such
T-26.......V.4:1 and **s.** maze you still perceive in time,
T-26...VII.18:3 choose a little **s.** wish instead of what He
T-26...VIII.9:6 Delay is **s.**, and the "reasoning" that
T-26.......X.2:6 And this denies the fact that *all* are **s.**,
T-27.....II.6:11 his guilt is but the fabric of a **s.** dream.
T-27.....VII.8:7 and down according to a **s.** plot conceived
T-27...VIII.2:3 It works to get them, doing **s.** things, and
T-27...VIII.2:3 and tosses them away for **s.** things it does
T-27...VIII.2:4 more **s.** things that it can call its own. It
T-28.........I.7:2 who would keep a **s.** lesson in his mind,
T-28.......V.5:7 piece, each **s.** scrap and shred of evidence,
T-28......VI.2:1 It is indeed a **s.** point of view to hold
T-30...VII.6:15 Your dark dreams are but the **s.**, isolated
T-31.........I.6:1 small and still It cannot rise above the **s.**
T-31....IV.11:1 forget all **s.** journeys and all goal-less aims
W-pI.....29.2:2 You may find it silly, irreverent, **s.**, funny
W-pI.....45.7:1 Under all the **s.** thoughts and mad ideas
W-pI.....66.3:2 We will not engage in **s.** arguments about
W-pI.....72.8:1 today to stop these **s.** attacks on salvation.
W-pI.....76.1:1 observed before how many **s.** things have
W-pI.....76.1:2 imprisoned you with laws as **s.** as itself.
W-pI.....86.1:2 It is **s.** for me to search wildly about for
W-pI.....95.2:5 God, for it is **s.** and understands nothing.
W-pI.....96.2:2 **s.** series of expenditures of time and effort
W-pI.....96.6:2 can resolve the **s.** conflicts which a dream
W-pI...127.8:4 upon its meager offerings and **s.** gifts, and
W-pI...131.2:3 Who can use such **s.** means, and hope
W-pI.131.11:5 are closed, the **s.** world you think is real.
W-pI.135.22:1 twice today we rest from **s.** planning, and
W-pI...139.8:5 themselves with **s.** musings such as this.
W-pI...153.8:3 a **s.** dream happened to cross our minds,
W-pI...156.6:5 in approach to God Himself for such a **s.**
W-pI...156.7:5 Companion, and mistake Him for the **s.**,
W-pI...160.2:1 and understands what truth regards as **s.**.
W-pI...164.1:5 He hears the sounds the **s.**, busy world
W-pI...166.5:1 Yet in his lonely, **s.** wanderings, God's
W-pI...192.4:1 now replace the **s.** symbols written there
W-pI...200.8:3 answer to conflicting goals, to **s.** journeys,
W-pII..258.1:1 our minds to overlook all little **s.** aims,
W-pII..298.1:4 And I draw near the end of **s.** journeys,
W-pII..307.1:3 *another will, for it is s. and will cause me pain*
M-8...........4:8 confused and **s.** "reasoning" be depended

## senselessness 3

T-8...........I.6:1 The total **s.** of such a curriculum must be
T-23......IV.9:5 The **s.** of conquest is quite apparent from
T-26.....VII.3:8 Brought to truth, its **s.** is quite apparent.

## senses 11

T-7........VI.5:2 **s.** that all commitments the mind makes
T-18...VIII.2:2 you limit your awareness to its tiny **s.**, you
T-18......IX.3:6 it not; its **s.** remain quite unaware of it; its
T-27......IV.5:4 witnesses are but the **s.** from within itself,
T-28.......V.5:6 For eyes and ears are **s.** without sense,
W-pI...151.2:3 a long while since your **s.** do deceive. That
W-pI...151.3:2 upon the witness that your **s.** offer you.
W-pI...151.4:5 It guides your **s.** carefully, to prove how
W-pII......4.2:7 The **s.** then will seek instead for witnesses
M-18.........4:2 If he **s.** even the faintest hint of irritation
P-2........VI.4:1 which the **s.** bring have but one purpose;

## sensible 13

T-8.........II.2:4 never given you a **s.** answer to anything.
T-8........IX.6:7 To the ego this is perfectly **s.**. Believing in
T-9...........I.6:6 How **s.** can your messages be, when you
T-9........III.1:3 this kind of sense, because it is **s.** to them.
T-9........IV.4:9 God. They are as **s.** now as they ever were,
T-12.......V.7:4 and every **s.** guide to learning will be
T-23.......II.5:7 God and of each other now appears as **s.**,
T-24.........I.2:2 to reason, to be considered **s.** or not. And
T-25.....VII.7:1 appears most **s.** and meaningful to you.
T-26.......X.2:4 are given meaning and perceived as **s.**.
T-27.....VII.3:6 Yet it seems **s.**, because it looks as if the
W-pI...170.6:3 ask if the demands are **s.** or even sane. It
M-14.........4:2 and pieces of its thinking will still seem **s.**.

## sensing 2

T-8.........V.5:6 do so. **S.** defeat and angered by it, the ego
W-pI...186.7:2 it does not know, **s.** its basis crumble. Let

## sensitive 1

T-2........III.4:7 the mind becomes increasingly **s.** to what

## sent 43

T-2....V.A.18:3 *I am here to represent Him Who s. me. I do*
T-2....V.A.18:4 *to do, because He Who s. me will direct me.*
T-8......IV.2:13 of yourself, and of Him Who **s.** me to you.
T-8......IV.3:10 As God **s.** me to you so will I send you to
T-11.......II.6:5 God **s.** you will teach you how to do this,
T-12.....VII.5:2 invitation, coming to you as you **s.** for it.
T-14......XI.4:3 so you have another lesson **s.** from Him,
T-17....IV.11:1 a miniature of Heaven, **s.** you *from* Heaven
T-18.....VII.8:3 of every busy doing on which you are **s.**.
T-18......IX.3:3 For you **s.** forth these messengers to bring
T-18....IX.13:3 **s.** from beyond forgiveness to remind you
T-19.......I.11:6 perception, **s.** forth to gather witnesses
T-19.......I.14:6 the messengers of love are **s.** to do they do
T-19.......I.14:6 the altar from which they were **s.** forth.
T19. IV.A.11:1 Love's messengers are gently **s.**, and
T19. IV.A.15:6 the hungry dogs of fear you **s.** instead.
T19....IV.B.3:1 Holy Spirit's messengers are **s.** far beyond
T19..IV.B.15:1 messages are always **s.** away from you, in
T19..IV.B.17:5 what is **s.** through Him returns to Him,
T-25....VIII.7:2 were a messenger from hell, **s.** from above
T-27.......I.4:10 bleak and bitter picture you have **s.** your
T-28......II.11:6 for this is not the lesson it was **s.** to teach.
W-pI.131.14:2 walks with you the Spirit Heaven **s.** you,
W-pI.132.17:1 day, increase the freedom **s.** through your
W-pI.134.14:4 of forgiveness, and was **s.** to us to teach it.
W-pI.154.14:2 message **s.** to us today from our Creator.
WpI...rV.in5:4 was **s.** to open up the path of light to us,
W-pII....in.7:2 way by following the Guide You **s.** to us.
W-pII .285.1:2 the thoughts to which it has been **s.** by me
W-pII....14.5:1 Word to everyone whom He has **s.** to us,
M-11.........3:4 God has **s.** His Judgment to answer yours.
M-16.........1:7 is **s.** without a learning goal already set,
C-5..........6:12 *He has s. to you to care for as I care for you.*
C-6............3:3 because He was **s.** to save humanity. He is
P-3...........I.1:1 who is **s.** to you is a patient of yours. This
P-3...........I.3:5 even more, at the instant they are **s.**. You
P-3...........I.3:8 will be **s.** in whatever form is most helpful
P-3...........I.4:3 are the means **s.** to him for his learning.
P-3........III.6:2 pay. No one is **s.** by accident to anyone.
P-3........III.6:5 Whoever comes has been **s.**. Perhaps he
P-3........III.6:6 Perhaps he was **s.** to give his brother the
P-3........III.6:8 Perhaps he was **s.** to teach the therapist
P-3......III.8:13 *And then God s. His Son to give it to you.*

## sentence 8

T19....IV.C.2:7 **s.** sin would lay upon him he can escape
T-20......III.5:4 all. Yet judgment lays a **s.** on it, justifies it
T-23........II.4:4 as an irrevocable **s.** upon himself, which
T-25.....VII.1:1 if the Holy Spirit can commute each **s.**
W-pI.....27.3:6 can still repeat one short **s.** to yourself
M-20.........5:8 In this one **s.** is our course explained. In
M-20.........5:9 this one **s.** is our practicing given its one
M-20.......5:10 in this one **s.** is the Holy Spirit's whole

## sentenced 1

T-31.......I.13:4 to him, without the past that **s.** him to die

## sentiment 1

W-pI...161.4:6 sounds; pretty, perhaps, correct in **s.**, yet

## sentinels 2

T-14......VI.2:5 The **s.** of darkness watch over it carefully,
T-14......VI.8:3 His sight, for He will not attack your **s.**.

## separate 309

*See also* healing-to-separate

T-1..........II.4:1 **s.** or different from you except in time,
T-1........III.2:1 they will not continue to exist as **s.** states.
T-2........VI.2:8 You cannot **s.** yourself from the truth by
T-2........VI.4:4 always entail a willingness to be **s.**. At
T-3........IV.5:9 it could not entirely **s.** itself from spirit,
T-3.........V.8:7 It is all one and has no **s.** parts. You who
T-3.........V.9:2 minds have chosen to see themselves as **s.**
T-3........VI.8:7 choose to **s.** yourself from your Author.
T-4........III.2:5 My role is to **s.** the true from the false, so
T-4........III.4:5 You project onto the ego the decision to **s.**
T-4........VI.1:3 spoken of the ego as if it were a **s.** thing,
T-4........VI.4:3 impulses, not because the ego is a **s.** thing
T-4.......VII.2:1 Everything the ego perceives is a **s.** whole,
T-5...........I.4:3 He is also described as something "**s.**,"
T-5.......VII.1:2 thought system that can **s.** you from Him
T-5.......VII.3:5 It reflects both the ego's need to **s.**, and
T-6........IV.2:5 to regard itself as **s.** and outside its maker,
T-6........IV.2:5 *you* are **s.** and outside the Mind of God.
T-6......V.A.3:3 The body is **s.**, and therefore cannot be
T-7........IV.5:2 The ego always seeks to divide and **s.**. The
T-7.......V.6:15 You cannot **s.** your Self from your Creator
T-7......VI.10:3 since God and His creation are not **s.**. The
T-7.......VII.9:5 If you choose to **s.** yourself from God,
T-8........IV.5:8 It is the power by which you **s.** or join,
T-8.........V.1:6 is far beyond the power of its **s.** parts. By

W-pI...184.3:1 holding bits of mind as **s.** awarenesses?
W-pI...184.8:7 denied, for you perceive him **s.** from you,
W-pI...184.8:7 you, and he accepts this **s.** name as his.
W-pI.187.10:3 Not **s.** from Him Who is our Source; not
W-pI...195.6:1 alone; that we are **s.** from no living thing,
W-pI...196.5:5 Father is his deadly enemy, **s.** from him,
W-pI...198.7:1 world has many seeming **s.** haunts where
W-pII.....in.5:3 for time to **s.** from its accomplishment.
W-pII..223.1:1 God, a **s.** entity that moved in isolation,
W-pII......2.1:4 mind which thinks that it has **s.** thoughts,
W-pII......5.1:1 to **s.** parts of his Self from other parts. It is
W-pII......6.4:3 God, what could there be to keep things **s.**
W-pII..326.1:8 *and all* **s.** *thoughts unite in glory as the Son of*
W-pII..328.1:2 gain autonomy but by our striving to be **s.**
M-3............2:6 for two people to lose sight of **s.** interests,
M-3............4:3 situation and then appear to **s.**. As with
M-5.......III.3:9 to see no will as **s.** from their own, nor
M-5.......III.3:9 their own, nor theirs as **s.** from God's.
M-8............2:8 in these dreams the mind is **s.**, different
M-12..........2:6 how could they be **s.** from each other?
M-12..........6:9 as sick and **s.** is no more real than to
M-17..........3:3 only if perception of **s.** goals has entered.
M-17..........5:4 it has a **s.** will that can oppose the Will of
M-19..........4:2 you perceive as broken off and **s.**. And it
M-19..........4:4 For **s.** fragments must decay and die, but
M-19..........5:6 nothing as **s.** and apart from all the rest.
M-22..........6:5 person perceives himself as **s.** from God.
M-22..........6:6 Would you see him as **s.** from you? It is
M-23..........2:8 he no longer sees himself as **s.** from Him.
M-25..........2:6 walls that surround all the **s.** places of the
C-1.............2:1 is split, the Sons of God appear to be **s.**.
C-4.............5:9 for being **s.** it could not remain where
C-5.............2:3 an illusion, for he seemed to be a **s.** being,
P-1.............5:2 he must begin to **s.** truth from illusion,
P-2.........II.8:4 in so doing, lose all sense of **s.** interests.
P-3.........II.1:2 How could a **s.** profession be one in which
S-1.........in.2:3 to **s.** is one forever in the Mind of God.
S-1.........in.2:4 leaves **s.** goals and separate interests by,
S-1.........in.2:4 leaves separate goals and **s.** interests by,
S-1........IV.1:6 Their **s.** wishes are their arsenals; their
S-1........IV.3:2 satisfied; all **s.** wishes unified in one.
S-2.........II.1:3 is to **s.** and make what God created equal,
S-2.........II.4:1 goal is to **s.** from God the Son He loves,
S-3...........I.1:1 apart and **s.** from what its cause must be.
S-3........III.1:2 Its **s.** goals become quite clear in this, for
S-3........III.4:7 For in this oneness is his **s.** sense dispelled
S-3........IV.1:9 given up all **s.** dreams of special attributes

## separated 65

T-1........VI.3:1 original error that one can be **s.** from God
T-2.........II.7:2 a mistake all the **s.** Sons of God make in
T-3........IV.3:4 A **s.** or divided mind *must* be confused. It
T-3........IV.5:3 it chooses to be **s.** it chooses to perceive.
T-3.........V.5:3 as **s.** and unseparated at the same time. It
T-3.........V.5:5 happens when method and content are **s.**,
T-3.......V.10:3 Perception is based on a **s.** state, so that
T-4...........I.2:2 Change is always fearful to the **s.**, because
T-4...........I.4:4 dream of a **s.** ego and believe in a world
T-4........VI.4:2 **s.** mind cannot maintain the separation
T-5.........II.2:2 God blessed the minds of His **s.** Sons.
T-5.........V.8:1 The continuing decision to remain **s.** is
T-6...........I.3:2 This is a marked tendency of the **s.**, who
T-6........I.19:1 between God the Father and His **s.** Sons.
T-6.........II.2:3 it because you continue to keep it **s.**. By
T-6.........II.3:3 from your brothers and **s.** from them.
T-7.........II.1:3 absent from the Kingdom or **s.** from it,
T-7........III.2:5 see yourself as **s.** from your meaning only
T-8......IV.8:10 you are perceiving the Holy Trinity as **s.**.
T-8.........V.1:1 Can you be **s.** from your identification
T-8........VI.9:3 We cannot be **s.**. Whom God has joined
T-8........VI.9:4 Whom God has joined cannot be **s.**, and
T-8........VI.9:5 you be **s.** from your life and your being?
T-8.......VII.2:2 Link between God and His **s.** Sons, the
T-9........VI.6:4 eternity, where they cannot be **s.**. When
T-10.......V.8:5 His creation, from which He cannot be **s.**.
T-11.........I.2:1 To be alone is to be **s.** from infinity, but
T-12.....VII.7:7 **s.** from each other because you made
T-13.......II.9:4 him, and have never been **s.** from him. In
T-13......VI.6:7 unbroken, for they are not **s.** by the past.
T-13......XI.8:3 cannot be wholly closed and **s.** from Him.
T-14.........I.2:5 is closed off and wholly **s.** from the truth.
T-14......VI.2:4 it has been **s.** off and kept in darkness.
T-15.......I.4:14 Yet because you and the ego cannot be **s.**,
T-15.........I.8:3 instant stands clear and **s.** from the past,
T-15.......V.6:4 You have not only **s.** them, but you have
T-16.....V.16:2 **s.** from illusion and not confused with it
T-17......III.3:3 and **s.** off as being the only parts of value.
T-18......VI.9:3 Son be **s.** from Himself except in illusions.
T-18......VI.9:6 have **s.** Himself from His Son to make this
T-19.........I.3:4 see itself as **s.** from the Universal Purpose.
T-19.........I.4:4 faithlessness to him has **s.** you from him,
T-20.....VII.6:5 Here are illusions and reality kept **s.**. Here
T-22..VI.12:11 to attack to see it **s.** from its maker. And
T-27...VII.12:1 A brother **s.** from yourself, an ancient
T-28......III.3:2 which are **s.** and which cannot join. Do
T-28......III.4:6 For it was made to keep you **s.**, in a body
T-28......IV.7:4 His desire to be a sick and **s.** mind can not
T-28......IV.7:6 that he was **s.** from his brother who, by
T-29.......V.7:6 death have come to worship in a **s.** world,
T-29.....VII.2:3 a part of it were **s.** off and found where all
T-29...VIII.7:4 a dismal alcove **s.** off from what is endless
T-30......III.3:7 are alone and **s.** off from what is whole.
W-pI.....13.2:1 arouses intense anxiety in all the **s.** ones.
W-pI.....41.1:1 abandonment all the **s.** ones experience.
W-pI.....41.2:1 The **s.** ones have invented many "cures"
W-pI.....90.3:5 so that they cannot be **s.** by time. The
W-pI.....99.4:1 joins the **s.** mind and thoughts with Mind
W-pII....12.1:1 is idolatry; the sign of limited and **s.** self,
M-in..........1:3 as if the teacher and the learner are **s.**, the
M-2...........5:6 they thought **s.** them from one another,
M-4.........I.1:3 because cause and effect are never **s.**. The
M-21.........1:7 for they were made by **s.** minds to keep
C-4............5:7 more remains to keep a **s.** world in place?
C-6............3:1 Link between God and His **s.** Sons. In

## separately 13

T-6......V.A.5:9 but always for what each one can get *s.*.
T-14.......X.9:2 S., they seem to hold, but put them
T-15.......X.3:1 We who are one cannot give **s.**. When
T-17......VI.1:7 this point to use them in each situation **s.**,
T-17....VI.6:10 of the situation and deal with them **s.**, for
T-17.....VII.4:5 see that peace and faith will not come **s.**.
T-18. VIII.12:3 he will not be able to give love welcome **s.**.
T-20.....IV.5:4 world of separation each is appointed **s.**.
T-30.....VII.6:6 And looked at **s.** they have no meaning.
T-31.......II.6:9 go **s.** along the way unless you keep him
W-pI.......5.1:6 idea to each of them **s.** is the first step in
W-pI.140.11:2 interfering thoughts be laid aside, not **s.**,
M-20.........1:5 Let us consider each of these questions **s.**,

## separateness 2

T-4.......VII.2:2 to establish **s.** rather than to abolish it.
T-5.......VII.3:5 and your willingness to side with its **s.**.

## separates 12

T-1.........I.38:3 He **s.** the true from the false by His ability
T-3......VI.11:4 because it **s.** segments of reality by the
T-8.......VII.2:3 is. The ego **s.** through the body. The Holy
T-22......IV.3:4 how thin the drapery that **s.** you now. Yet
T-24...VII.11:6 **s.** each from all aspects with a different
T-25.........I.3:4 to your purpose, from which it never **s.**,
T-28......IV.7:1 is One because there is no gap that **s.** His
T-28.......V.3:3 Forgiveness **s.** the dreamer from the evil
T-28.......V.6:4 no gap that **s.** the truth from dreams and
W-pI.....92.7:3 It **s.** itself from what it sees, while light
W-pII..311.1:2 It **s.** what it is being used against, and sets
M-22.........3:3 the body autonomy, **s.** it from the mind,

## separating 7

T-8........IV.5:5 It cannot be overcome by **s.**. The decision
T-15.......II.6:1 your little part in **s.** out the holy instant.
T-16.....III.4:10 only be resolved by **s.** yourself from the
T-26.....VII.8:9 to him. This **s.** off is symbolized, in your
T-28.......V.1:2 Of a splitting *off* and **s.** *from?* A gap that is
T-28.......V.1:5 thus is sickness **s.** off the self from good,
W-pI.......4.3:2 of **s.** the meaningless from the meaningful

## separation 240

*See also* post-separation, pre-separation

T-1........VI.1:6 Until the "**s.**," which is the meaning of the
T-1........VI.2:1 sense of **s.** from God is the only lack you
T-1........VI.2:2 This sense of **s.** would never have arisen if
T-2................h THE **S.** AND THE ATONEMENT
T-2..............I.h The Origins of **S.**
T-2...........I.2:1 picture of what actually occurred in the **s.**,
T-2...........I.2:2 None of this existed before the **s.**, nor
T-2..........II.4:4 Acts were not necessary before the **s.**,
T-2..........II.4:5 only after the **s.** that the Atonement and
T-2........III.1:2 Since the **s.**, defenses have been used
T-2........III.1:2 the Atonement, and thus maintain the **s.**.
T-2........III.2:1 undoes the **s.** and restores the wholeness
T-2........III.2:2 the **s.** the mind was invulnerable to fear,
T-2........III.2:3 Both the **s.** and the fear are miscreations
T-2........III.2:4 This heals the **s.** by placing within you the
T-2........III.2:4 you the one effective defense against all **s.**
T-2......III.5:12 the world as a means of healing the **s.**.
T-2.........V.9:1 is an ability that developed after the **s.**,
T-2.......VII.5:6 In this sense the **s.** *has* occurred, and to
T-2......VIII.2:4 It was brought into being only after the **s.**,
T-2......VIII.2:5 as the **s.** occurred over millions of years,
T-2......VIII.4:2 is a process of **s.** in the constructive sense,
T-3..........II.5:3 All sense of **s.** disappears. The Son of God
T-3........IV.1:5 not exist until the **s.** introduced degrees,
T-3........IV.1:8 levels created by the **s.** cannot but conflict
T-3........IV.2:1 split introduced into the mind after the **s.**,
T-3......IV.3:11 you must eventually choose to heal the **s.**.
T-3.........V.1:1 was introduced only after the **s.**. No one
T-3.........V.2:1 Since the **s.**, the words "create" and
T-3.........V.2:4 are tacitly implying that you believe in **s.**.
T-3.........V.9:1 is the healing of the perception of **s.**.
T-3.......VII.3:1 We have discussed the fall or **s.** before,
T-3.......VII.3:2 The **s.** is a system of thought real enough
T-3.......VII.5:1 the belief in **s.** very real and very fearful,
T-4.........in.3:5 merely re-enacts the **s.**, the loss of power,
T-4...........I.2:2 of it as a move towards healing the **s.**.
T-4...........I.2:3 perceive it as a move toward further **s.**,
T-4...........I.2:3 the **s.** was their first experience of change.
T-4...........I.4:2 will not prove that the **s.** has not occurred
T-4...........I.6:2 ego would be to increase anxiety about **s.**.
T-4.........I.10:2 now because fear is a witness to the **s.**,
T-4........III.3:2 ego arose from the **s.**, and its continued
T-4........III.3:2 on your continuing belief in the **s.**. The
T-4........VI.4:2 maintain the **s.** except by dissociating.
T-4.......VII.1:5 believes your existence is defined by **s.**.
T-5...........I.5:2 into being with the **s.** as a protection,
T-5..........II.1:4 the decision to heal the **s.** by letting it go.
T-5..........II.2:4 The mind had no calling until the **s.**,
T-5..........II.2:5 The Holy Spirit is God's Answer to the **s.**;
T-5..........II.3:1 and the **s.** began at the same time. When
T-5..........II.4:4 Before the **s.** you did not need guidance.
T-5........III.1:3 the **s.** between the two ways of thinking
T-5........III.9:3 **s.** is merely another term for a split mind.
T-5........III.9:4 The ego is the symbol of **s.**, just as the
T-5.........V.2:8 If the ego is the symbol of the **s.**, it is also
T-6.........in.1:2 Anger always involves projection of **s.**,
T-6.........I.18:4 The **s.** is the notion of rejection. As long
T-6..........II.1:1 of part of it, and this *is* the belief in **s.**. The
T-6..........II.1:4 Exclusion and **s.** are synonymous, as are
T-6..........II.1:4 synonymous, as are **s.** and dissociation.
T-6..........II.1:5 before that the **s.** was and is dissociation,
T-6..........II.3:2 its only purpose is to keep the **s.** going. It
T-6........II.10:7 the recognition that *the s. never occurred.*
T-6........IV.4:7 It is an alliance frankly based on **s.**. If you
T-6......IV.12:5 The **s.** was not a loss of perfection, but a
T-6......V.A.2:3 It is clearly a **s.** device, and therefore does
T-6......V.A.2:5 for **s.** into a demonstration against it. If
T-6......V.B.1:1 All who believe in **s.** have a basic fear of
T-7..........II.1:4 Sickness and **s.** are not of God, but the
T-7.........V.6:5 dissociation, because it induces **s.**.
T-7......VI.13:6 Creation, not **s.**, is your will *because* it is
T-7......VIII.7:3 be alone, thus dispelling the idea of **s.** and

T-7 X.6:7 The whole s. lies in this error. The only
T-8 IV.5:3 is the way in which the s. is overcome.
T-8 IV.5:4 S. is overcome by union. It cannot be
T-8 V.2:8 There is no s. of God and His creation.
T-8 V.2:9 there is no s. between your will and mine.
T-8 VII.4:1 Communication ends s.. Attack
T-8 VII.11:3 induce illness by fostering s.. Perceiving
T-9 I.7:9 The s. is nothing more than the belief that
T-10 I.4:1 to create, you will have willed away the s.,
T-10 IV.8:5 for the s. was a descent from magnitude
T-11 II.1:1 If sickness is s., the decision to heal and
T-11 V.3:3 and the whole s. fallacy lies in the belief
T-11 V.4:6 its own. This is why it is the symbol of s..
T-11 V.7:1 The ego always attacks on behalf of s..
T-11 V.9:3 it preach s. without upholding it through
T-11 V.13:4 power, understanding and truth lie in s.,
T-11 V.13:5 with the conviction that s. is salvation,
T-11 V.13:6 chaos for meaning, for if s. is salvation,
T-11 VIII.10:1 sickness, for there is no s. and no division
T-12 I.10:5 your dream of s. with the fact of unity.
T-12 I.10:6 For the s. is only the denial of union, and
T-12 III.9:1 The world you perceive is a world of s..
T-12 V.4:4 You tried to make the s. eternal, because
T-12 VI.7:1 the s. is the reinstatement of knowledge.
T-13 in.2:1 of God's Son was the beginning of the s.,
T-13 in.2:6 and they learn of sorrow and s. and death
T-13 I.6:3 by another, projecting s. in place of unity.
T-13 III.2:5 For this wish caused the s., and you have
T-13 III.2:5 it because you do not want the s. healed.
T-13 III.10:1 You who prefer s. to sanity cannot obtain
T-13 VII.11:4 For where the ego sees salvation it sees s.,
T-13 VIII.3:3 The s. has not interrupted it. Creation
T-13 VIII.3:5 s. is merely a faulty formulation of reality,
T-13 X.7:5 so. He has seen s., but knows of union. He
T-14 V.5:2 So will the world of s. slip away, and full
T-14 VI.5:1 You have regarded the s. as a means for
T-14 VII.1:4 For their s. is only in your mind, and they
T-14 VII.4:5 their s. seems to keep them both alive and
T-14 VIII.3:4 of oneness, before which all s. vanishes.
T-14 X.9:4 S. therefore remains the ego's chosen
T-15 V.2:3 you are attempting to use s. to save you.
T-15 V.2:5 For s. is the source of guilt, and to appeal
T-15 V.3:3 salvation is the belief that s. is salvation.
T-15 V.8:4 you see any s. between yourself and them.
T-15 VI.3:1 All s. vanishes as holiness is shared. For
T-15 VIII.4:7 Christ knows of no s. from His Father,
T-15 IX.2:3 the ego, as the ego is the symbol of the s..
T-15 IX.6:6 Seek not Atonement in further s.. And
T-15 IX.7:2 for s. and attack which the ego sees in it,
T-15 XI.4:1 must learn that sacrifice is s. from love.
T-16 III.5:4 For God's Answer to the s. added more to
T-16 IV.7:1 is an attempt to bring love into s.. And, as
T-16 V.3:5 This is the "natural" condition of the s.,
T-16 V.3:8 place, love is perceived as s. and exclusion
T-16 V.4:4 have you see that s. could only be loss,
T-16 V.10:3 only attributes of the whole religion of s.,
T-16 V.15:1 The core of the s. illusion lies simply in
T-16 V.15:3 S. is only the decision *not* to know yourself
T-16 VI.2:3 of God, no longer seek for union in s., nor
T-17 I.6:2 Salvation from s. would be complete, or
T-17 III.1:11 speak so clearly for the s. that no one not
T-17 III.1:11 obsessed with keeping s. could hear them.
T-17 III.5:1 whose only purpose is s. from reality?
T-17 III.5:8 on the past, which is the source of s., and
T-17 III.5:9 s. must be corrected where it was made.
T-17 III.6:4 undoing is the s. more and more undone,
T-17 III.6:5 not at all confused by any "reasons" for s.
T-17 III.6:6 perceives in s. is that it must be undone.
T-17 IV.4:1 Spirit, Who was God's Answer to the s..
T-17 IV.4:3 the ego evolved to protect the s. from the
T-17 IV.4:6 been separate from anyone since the s..
T-17 IV.5:6 s. has nothing in it, no part, no "reason,"
T-17 VI.6:10 for it has faith in s. and not in wholeness.
T-18 I.1:6 is the strongest defense the ego has for s..
T-18 I.10:1 In you there is no s., and no substitute
T-18 I.12:7 what has been ravaged by s. and disease?
T-18 VI.3:2 of the body does s. seem to be possible.
T-18 VI.3:4 it is attacked to hold the s. in the mind,
T-18 VI.5:1 of s. reinterpreted as means for salvation,
T-18 VIII.6:3 ruled by an idea of s. from the rest. Nor
T-19 I.3:5 the "fact" that s. has occurred. The body
T-19 I.7:5 to perceive this is to recognize where s. is,
T-19 I.7:7 idea of s. produced the body and remains
T-19 III.7:3 the proof of s. seems to be everywhere.
T19 IV.C.4:5 sin, the pride of guilt, the sepulchre of s.,
T19 IV.D.3:4 never to allow union to call you out of s.;
T-20 II.4:6 chosen home and it is s. that you offer me
T-20 III.10:5 of any s. between us become impossible.
T-20 III.10:6 in s. are now made free in Paradise. And
T-20 IV.5:4 world of s. each is appointed separately,
T-20 VI.6:6 "mystery" of s. perceived in awe and held
T-21 II.6:3 in it the whole exchange of s. for salvation
T-21 V.4:1 the idea of s. has interfered with reason.
T-22 II.6:1 for here the s. of you and the ego must be
T-22 II.9:2 This is the same belief that caused the s..
T-22 VI.14:6 Son. From loving minds there *is* no s.. And
T-24 III.5:2 He would have no s., like an alien will,
T-24 IV.2:4 The goal of s. is its curse. Yet bodies have
T-25 VII.5:3 death and cruelty; to s. and to differences.
T-26 I.2:5 and by their s. are their selves maintained
T-26 III.7:1 s. is undone by change of purpose in what
T-26 VII.2:1 All sickness comes from s.. When the
T-26 VII.2:2 When the s. is denied, it goes. For it is
T-27 II.5:2 of healing proves that s. is without effect.
T-27 II.10:8 s. but a wish to take God's function from
T-27 VII.6:4 s. from your brother was the first attack
T-28 II.8:1 The s. started with the dream the Father
T-28 II.12:7 course of every step in the descent to s.,
T-28 III.1:2 be directed up the ladder s. led you down.
T-28 III.5:1 The cause of pain is s., not the body,
T-28 III.5:2 effect. Yet s. is but empty space, enclosing
T-28 IV.10:6 come from the belief that there is joy in s.,
T-28 VI.3:2 send it forth to seek for s. and be separate
T-28 VII.2:6 What could correct for s. but its opposite
T-28 VII.4:2 to witness to the dream of s. and disease.
T-29 I.3:9 clause of s. was a point you both agreed to
T-29 I.4:6 to time, and keep apart in intervals of s.,
T-29 I.5:1 a cause of s. and of distance seen between
T-29 V.8:2 they lose the function of attack and s.,
T-29 VI.1:4 for herein lies the end of s. and the dream
T-30 IV.8:1 dream of s. start to fade and disappear.
T-31 VI.2:2 to see the body, you behold a world of s.,
T-31 VII.9:3 are bound to s. from the sight of him who
W-pI 41.1:2 is an inevitable consequence of s.. So are
W-pI 54.3:3 Even the mad idea of s. had to be shared
W-pI 54.3:6 As my thoughts of s. call to the separation
W-pI 54.3:6 separation call to the s. thoughts of others
W-pI 56.5:2 all my insane thoughts of s. and attack, is
W-pI 78.8:4 him to you, seeing no s. in God's Son.
W-pI 79.1:4 The problem of s., which is really the only
W-pI 79.4:1 to keep the problem of s. unsolved. The
W-pI 79.6:2 recognize that your only problem is s., no
W-pI 99.5:4 and death, on grief and s. and on loss. Yet
W-pI 110.4:2 has been no s. of your mind from His, no
W-pI 124.7:7 As we deny our s. from our Father, it is
W-pI 125.8:3 with no s. nor division in the single Mind
W-pI 130.4:2 All s., all distinctions, and the multitude
W-pI 137.2:3 the body final power to make the s. real,
W-pI 137.4:3 s. sickness would impose has never really
W-pI. 137.13:1 pain for joy, and s. for the peace of God.
W-pI 140.1:3 heal the mind, it sees no s. from the body,
W-pI. 140.12:8 to us. This is the day when s. ends, and we
W-pI 158.7:4 It sees no s.. And it looks on everyone, on
W-pI 184.2:3 do you think that you have given life in s..
W-pI. 184.12:4 Every gap is closed, and s. healed. The
W-pII 3.1:4 When the thought of s. has been changed
W-pII 6.2:1 and guarantees that s. is no more than an
W-pII 11.3:3 Will, beyond all possibility of harm, of s.,
W-pII 12.2:2 apart from All, in s. from the Infinite. In
W-pII. 336.2:1 *wipe away my dreams of s. and of sin. Then*
M-2 2:6 idea of s. entered the mind of God's Son,
M-5 III.1:13 nothing. To them the s. is quite real.
M-12 4:6 of God appear to share the illusion of s.,
M-16 10:9 Rooted in sacrifice and s., two aspects of
M-17 5:3 presence, acknowledges a s. from God. It
M-17 6:9 Accept your s., but do not remember how
M-19 1:9 thought of s. would have been forever
M-21 1:7 minds to keep them in the illusion of s..
M-22 6:7 task to heal the sense of s. that has made
C-4 5:9 it could not remain where s. is impossible
C-6 2:1 the answer to the s. and bringing the plan
P-2 VII.1:11 God does not know of s.. What He knows
P-2 VII.3:6 in which all sense of s. finally is overcome.
S-2 II.7:6 death, and prayed for s. from your Self.
S-2 III.6:7 destruction and to make the means for s.,
S-3 III.h S. versus Union
S-3 III.1:7 as one. Here is the s. shown. And here the
S-3 III.5:7 and s. must be healed by love and union.

## separation's 1

T-28 II.9:1 is the s. final step, with which salvation,

## separations 1

W-pI 184.14:3 foolish s. disappear which kept us blind.

## sepulchre 1

T19 IV.C.4:5 sin, the pride of guilt, the s. of separation,

## sequence 6

T-1 II.6:10 however, within the larger temporal s..
T-5 II.1:3 of the time s. should be quite familiar,
W-pI 66.5:5 Try to see the logic in this s., even if you
W-pI 194.4:4 the lack of s. really found in time. You are
W-pI 196.4:2 us, taking every step in its appointed s., as
M-5 II.4:4 and effect in their true s. in one respect,

## serene 9

T-18 IX.1:10 holy, s. and unaware of what you think
T-20 VI.2:2 on love, and rests on it s. and undisturbed
T-28 III.1:5 will the way be made s. and simple in the
W-pI 155.1:3 Your forehead is s.; your eyes are quiet.
W-pI 186.10:1 go, and leave your mind unclouded and s.
W-pI 193.9:3 his holy rest remain untroubled and s.,
W-pII. 300.1:2 a passing cloud upon a sky eternally s..
W-pII. 309.2:2 *Your altar stands s. and undefiled. It is the*
W-pII. 329.1:9 *And I am safe, untroubled and s., in endless*

## serenely 2

W-pI 153.9:3 stand secure, s. certain of our safety now,
W-pI 157.9:1 now, s. unaware of everything except His

## serenity 8

T-7 III.5:8 This holds them in perfect s., because this
T-23 I.10:5 where God has set him in s. and peace,
T-27 II.8:1 The "cost" of your s. is his. This is the
T-27 II.9:2 pain are seen to represent their own s..
W-pI 75.11:1 to the s. in which God would have you be.
W-pI 113.1:2 *S. and perfect peace are mine, because I am*
WpI.rVI.in.4:2 a shorter path to the s. and peace of God.
W-pII. 300.1:3 it is this s. we seek, unclouded, obvious

## serial 1

T-27 VIII.3:1 The body's s. adventures, from the time

## series 10

T-2 VI.7:3 than a s. of pragmatic steps in the larger
T-11 V.15:2 is left with a s. of fragmented perceptions
T-29 VII.7:2 past, and but a s. of depressing dreams, in
W-pI 28.1:2 be making a s. of definite commitments.
WpI rI.in.1:1 today we will have a s. of review periods.
W-pI 79.3:3 A long s. of different problems seems to
W-pI 96.2:2 a senseless s. of expenditures of time and
W-pI 136.4:1 and sets up a s. of defenses to reduce the
W-pI 184.3:1 the world becomes a s. of discrete events,
P-2 I.4:1 psychotherapy is a s. of holy encounters

**serious** 8

T-2.........V.6:2 it becomes a s. obstruction to the very
T-8........IX.5:3 form of sickness is more s. than another,
T-18.........I.3:5 a far more s. effect lies in the fragmented
T-27... VIII.5:7 How s. they now appear to be! And no
T-27... VIII.6:3 did the thought become a s. idea, and
T-27... VIII.8:5 cause do its effects seem s. and sad indeed
W-pI.....41.2:5 despite the s. and tragic forms it may take
WpIrIII.in10:2 two ideas a brief but s. review each hour.

**seriously** 6

T-8..... VIII.4:2 you have not s. cross-examined him. If
T-13......III.1:7 You are not s. disturbed by your hostility.
T-18....... II.2:3 take them s. on awaking because the fact
T-21.....IV.3:3 the ego's whole defensive system too s.
W-pII..284.1:6 Then to be considered s. more and more,
M-25..........5:2 gifts, the ego has been s. threatened. It

**serpent** 1

T-2...........I.3:2 When Adam listened to the "lies of the s.,

**servant** 5

T-17.....VII.5:5 it. Faithlessness is the s. of illusion, and
T19..IV.B.13:4 the body becomes the s. of pain, seeking
T-27....IV.4:14 It is your s. and also your friend. But tell it
W-pI...199.6:6 it is a worthy s. of the freedom which the
M-17..........9:3 Like the magic which becomes its s., it

**serve** 117

T-1........III.3:4 which minds that s. the Holy Spirit unite
T-1.........V.5:2 the mind can elect what it chooses to s..
T-1.........V.5:3 its choice is that it cannot s. two masters.
T-2........III.5:9 and your mind cannot s. the Holy Spirit.
T-5......... II.8:9 must choose at which altar you want to s..
T-6...........I.3:6 I cannot s. as a model for learning.
T-6........... I.11:6 case, merely because it would s. as a good
T-10....... III.8:5 are. You would save them and s. them,
T-12.........I.8:6 of the motives of others will s. you then.
T-13...VII.11:6 think you need will merely s. to tighten
T-14......VI.8:4 s. to guard the dark doors behind which
T-15....... V.5:4 willingness to have it s. no need but His.
T-17......IV.4:7 preserved, to s. God's purpose for you.
T-17......VII.6:8 The universe will s. it gladly, as it serves
T-18....... II.3:8 to triumph over it and make it s. you.
T-18......VI.7:3 thing you made to s. your guilt stands
T-19....... II.5:4 its "best" defense, which all the others s..
T19. IV.A.12:3 when their master calls on them to s. him.
T19... IV.C.6:3 The body can but s. your purpose. As you
T-20.....VII.7:4 Neither can s. the purpose of the other,
T-20.....VII.8:2 Holy Spirit offers you to s. His purpose.
T-20... VIII.8:6 thing is sure; hallucinations s. a purpose,
T-20... VIII.8:7 do you want the purpose that they s.?
T-20... VIII.9:5 goal. Hallucinations s. to meet the goal of
T-21.... II.12:5 and cannot s. to justify the madness. Your
T-21....III.12:3 have faith in it to s. the Holy Spirit's goal,
T-21....III.12:3 to s. as means to help the blind to see. But
T-21.....IV.2:5 the ego's hidden fear, nor yours who s. it.
T-21....... V.8:1 and s. the great deceiver's needs as well as
T-21....... V.9:5 can s. to open doors you closed against it.
T-22......IV.1:6 It can no longer s.. No one who reaches
T-22......VI.1:6 And one must s. the other and lead to its
T-22......VI.1:7 own. Means s. the end, and as the end is
T-22.....VI.1:10 will make the other s. his choice as means
T-22......VI.2:2 so the mind is dedicated to s. illusions.
T-22......VI.3:2 that you can be the means to s. His end.
T-22......VI.3:4 To s. this end the body must be perceived
T-22......VI.3:6 using your body only to s. the sinless.
T-22......VI.4:5 you nor your brother alone can s. at all.
T-22......VI.7:4 their wills are His, *because* they s. His Will.
T-22......VI.7:5 His Will. And s. it willingly. And could
T-22......VI.8:7 this. Accept this one and s. it willingly, for
T-23..... II.14:6 is the goal the laws of chaos s.. These are
T-24..... II.12:5 sin love's substitute, and s. it faithfully.
T-24....... V.5:4 yet because they s. a different purpose,
T-24.....VII.6:3 to it, according to the purpose that you s..
T-24...VII.10:7 the means to s. his "father's" purpose.
T-24...VII.11:9 And thus does his perception s. his wish
T-24.VII.11:10 Yet can perception s. another goal. It is
T-24.VII.11:13 And what you see will s. that purpose well
T-25...... III.3:4 to s. the goal for which it is perceived. For
T-25.... VI.5:11 in form, to let it s. his brother and himself
T-25......VI.7:4 you made can s. salvation easily and well.
T-26...VII.15:1 Illusions s. the purpose they were made
T-26...VII.15:1 serve the purpose they were made to s..
T-27.........I.4:4 *you* accept, if only it can s. to punish him.
T-27....IV.4:15 want, and it will s. you lovingly and well."
T-27......VI.8:4 better function could you s. than this? Be
T-28.........I.2:8 it can be used to s. another purpose, and
T-28.........I.5:6 if it seems to s. to cherish ancient hate,
T-29.........I.9:4 or trinkets in the gap could s. to hold you
T-29....... II.3:2 to s. the function of retaining sin and pain
T-29......IV.6:5 as means to s. the function given Him.
T-29....... V.7:6 s. the lord of death have come to worship
T-30.........I.4:3 will s. to let you be directed without fear,
T-31...... III.4:4 It gives no orders that the mind need s.,
T-31....... V.2:5 For it is made to s. two purposes, but one
T-31.....VII.6:4 it needs to let it s. the function given you
W-pI.....10.5:1 Today's thought can obviously s. for any
W-pI.....24.1:4 you will not s. your own best interests.
W-pI.....71.3:4 Another person will yet s. better; another
W-pI.....76.4:2 rituals that have no use and s. no purpose
W-pI.....96.6:4 What purpose could it s.? What is it for?
W-pI.....96.8:4 do, restored to It and free to s. Its Will.
W-pI...108.5:1 unified, will s. to unify all thought. This is
WpIrIII.in10:6 and let it s. to help you keep your peace
WpIrIII.in11:5 And it is meant to s. you in all ways, all
W-pI...128.2:1 world, and it will s. no other end but this.
W-pI...128.2:2 everything must s. the purpose you have
W-pI...133.8:4 What purpose does it s.? Here it is easiest
W-pI.133.10:3 still preserve the ego's goals and s. them
W-pI...135.2:4 all s. but to preserve its sense of threat.
W-pI...135.4:5 fail to s. the Son of God as worthy host?
W-pI...135.6:3 right to s. you thus except your own belief
W-pI...136.1:1 what purpose sickness seems to s.. For
W-pI.136.18:2 be enough to s. all truly useful purposes.
W-pI.136.18:3 drink, or any laws you made it s. before.
W-pI...155.5:4 can you s. them while you serve yourself,
W-pI...155.5:4 can you serve them while you s. yourself,
W-pI...157.7:4 now it has a purpose, and will s. it well.
W-pI...189.6:4 world's apparent reasoning but s. to hide.
W-pI.193.10:6 devote what time you can to s. its proper
W-pI...199.6:4 in the ability to s. an undivided goal. In
W-pI...200.6:4 and where it must s. a mighty function. Is
W-pII..236.1:4 me to s. whatever purpose I perceive in it.
W-pII..236.1:5 in it. My mind can only s.. Today I give its
W-pII..257.1:2 No one can s. contradicting goals and
W-pII..257.1:2 serve contradicting goals and s. them well
W-pII.......5.3:4 must the body s. the purpose given it. But
W-pII294.1:10 today; of service for a while and fit to s.,
W-pII294.1:10 serve, to keep its usefulness while it can s.
W-pII..312.1:3 For sight can merely s. to offer us what we
W-pII..336.1:3 can s. but to recall the memory that lies
W-pII....14.5:2 which we came, and which we seek to s..
W-pII..353.1:1 *best will s. the purpose that I share with Him*
W-pII..353.1:4 *A while I work with Him to s. His purpose.*
Wfl.........in.3:1 minds, directing all our thoughts to s. the
M-2 ...........1:6 on his choice, but not on whom he will s..
M-4 ... VIII.1:6 that did not s. to benefit the world, as
M-14 .........1:6 they s. a need or gratify a want. Perceived
P-2.........in.3:6 is his god, and he seeks only to s. it better.
P-2......... V.6:7 best can s. His Son in all his present needs
P-3...........I.3:1 for you to s. them in the Name of God.
P-3........ III.1:4 but to help him better s. the plan. Money
S-1...........I.1:4 How else could it s. its purpose? It is
S-1......... V.1:5 and recognition that they do not s..
S-3........ III.6:2 those who s. with Him in healing's name.

**served** 6

T-17....... II.3:7 he has learned, has s. its purpose.
T-18......VI.6:6 How has this s. you? You have identified
T-18.....VII.6:5 on using means which have s. others well,
T-21...... III.7:1 the means that once s. sin are redirected
W-pI...133.9:4 will believe that he has s. the ego's hidden
W-pII .....8.5:1 need of time when it has s. His purpose.

**serves** 43

T-1...... IV.2:11 The mind that s. spirit *is* invulnerable.
T-1......... V.1:2 the body nor the miracle s. any purpose.
T-2..........II.6:6 saves time, but like the miracle it s., does
T-4......... V.1:5 which gave rise to it and which it s.. Sane
T-7........ IV.5:7 accord with His, because it s. His Voice,
T-14...... III.1:4 salvation, and s. no useful function at all.
T-16...... IV.3:5 only as long as he s. this purpose. Hatred
T-16... VII.2:11 it s. some purpose that you want fulfilled.
T-17....... V.5:8 s. the purpose they have agreed to meet.
T-17..... VII.6:8 will serve it gladly, as it s. the universe.
T-20...... IV.7:2 of your brother s. but you two alone. For
T-20......... V.5:4 s. the purpose of a holy relationship. And
T-21.........I.4:9 everything they think is in it s. to remind
T-21..... V.7:10 Reason is a means that s. the Holy Spirit's
T-21..... V.10:6 itself, as does the purpose that it s., and
T-21...... VI.7:7 instant s. to bring complete correction of
T-22...... VI.3:7 you to hate what s. whom you would heal.
T-22...... VI.4:2 plan. Be thankful that it s. yours not at all.
T-22...... VI.6:8 long remain in a mind that s. the timeless
T-23...... III.1:5 and what form of murder s. to cover the
T-24.........I.4:4 s. as grounds from which attack on those
T-24......II.12:2 Whatever s. its purpose must be given to
T-25.........I.6:1 Spirit s. Christ's purpose in your mind, so
T-25........II.6:4 that God has given it but s. His purpose,
T-26........II.1:6 It s. no purpose to attempt to solve it in a
T-26..... VII.8:5 and s. to bring the joy this world denies to
T-27........II.9:4 guilt he suffers s. to prove that he is slave,
T-28..... VII.4:4 It s. to help the healing of God's Son, and
T-31........II.4:5 is. Unless he s. it, he has not fulfilled the
T-31... VII.13:3 at all. And thus it s. a wholly open mind,
W-pI.......96.4:2 which s. the spirit is at peace and filled
W-pI... 128.1:1 nor anything at all that s. to give you joy.
W-pI.135.11:5 that s. the greater plan established for the
W-pI... 137.3:1 The world obeys the laws that sickness s.,
W-pI... 184.7:5 it s. but as a starting point from which
W-pI... 199.2:1 that s. the Holy Spirit is unlimited forever
W-pI... 199.6:5 thought of freedom as its goal, the body s.
W-pI... 199.6:5 the body serves, and s. its purpose well.
W-pII ..... 4.2:4 the body s. a different aim for striving.
W-pII ......5.4:5 it s. to heal the mind that it was made to
W-pII .322.1:4 And every dream s. only to conceal the
C-2............. 3:1 definition for a lie that s. to make it true.
S-1......... V.2:3 idols, and defense no longer s. a purpose.

**service** 20

T-1.........I.18:1 A miracle is a s.. It is the maximal service
T-1.........I.18:2 the maximal s. you can render to another.
T-1........ IV.2:6 the mind in the s. of the Holy Spirit. This
T-1......... V.6:1 has chosen to be led by me in Christ's s..
T-2..........II.2:6 the s. of the right mind the denial of error
T-2........ III.4:5 of its vision, it brings the mind into its s..
T-3........ IV.5:7 This places it in the s. of spirit, where
T-7......... V.3:5 in the s. of the ego can hurt other bodies,
T-7..... VII.1:11 But in the s. of the Holy Spirit, it can help
T-8....... VII.3:4 In the s. of uniting it becomes a beautiful
T-8....... VII.3:6 reality of anything is the s. it renders God
T-13........X.1:2 The doubtful s. of such displacement is to
T-22...... VI.3:3 This is the only s. that leads to freedom.
T-22...... VI.6:5 The gentle s. that you give the Holy Spirit
T-22...... VI.6:5 you give the Holy Spirit is s. to yourself.
W-pI. 135.13:2 and which needs its s. for a little while. In
W-pII .236.1:6 Today I give its s. to the Holy Spirit to
W-pII294.1:10 this today; of s. for a while and fit to serve
M-25 .........6:6 of hope and healing in the Holy Spirit's s..
S-3..........II.2:2 the body, then, for all the s. it has given us

**serviceable** 1

W-pI... 135.8:2 s. instrument through which the mind

**services** 1

T-29....... V.7:4 for hate, and will continue in death's s..

## serving 7

T-6...........I.8:5 s. the purpose for which God intended it.
T-13.......IV.7:4 temporary, s. only His teaching function,
T19..IV.B.13:2 s. its master whose attraction to guilt
T-20.....VII.6:7 s. the cause of sin an instant before he
T-21..... II.10:3 and capable of s. as a cause of the events
W-pI.200.10:5 body's eyes but s. for an instant longer
Wfl........in.2:4 already s. us as gracious guidance in the

## sessions 3

W-pI.....39.5:1 more frequent practice s. are encouraged.
W-pI.....39.5:2 rather than longer s. are recommended,
WpI rVI.in.3:1 These practice s., like our last review, are

## set 241

T-2......... II.5:1 to s. a limit on the need for the belief itself
T-2........ III.3:3 s. the limits on your ability to miscreate.
T-2.......VII.2:3 be necessary to s. the mind itself straight,
T-2.....VII.3:12 Son. This entails a s. of Cause and Effect
T-3......... V.5:7 is *not* the truth that shall s. you free, but
T-4.........in.1:2 certainly does not suggest that you s. him
T-4.........in.1:3 to a brother cannot s. you back either. It
T-4...........I.5:4 remember that laws are s. up to protect
T-4...........I.7:5 no right to s. your learning limits for you.
T-4........ III.2:5 has s. up and can shine into your mind.
T-4......... V.6:6 Preoccupations with problems s. up to be
T-4........VI.7:6 all things, but it does s. all things right.
T-5...... III.11:5 made truth, but truth can still s. you free.
T-5........ VI.2:8 is only to unchain your will and s. it free.
T-6........ III.4:2 will learn the truth that will s. you free,
T-9...........I.3:5 You have s. up this strange situation so
T-9......... II.9:6 of a price. And as you s. it you will pay it.
T-9........ II.10:1 will s. the price low but demand a high
T-9........ II.10:4 The price will then be s. high, because of
T-9....... II.11:1 that you s. the value on what you receive,
T-11...... VI.9:4 Do not s. limits on what you believe I can
T-12.......IV.4:1 Do you realize that the ego must s. you
T-12....... V.6:2 and do not try to s. up curriculum goals
T-12....... V.8:1 you s. yourself is depressing indeed, it is
T-12....... V.8:7 situation as you have s. it up is reversed.
T-13.........I.4:1 journey the Son of God has s. himself is
T-13....... II.7:3 told again and again that it will s. you free
T-13.... III.12:3 Could He s. you apart, knowing that your
T-13....... V.7:4 would release you from it and s. you free.
T-13...VII.15:1 of mind this world may s. before you.
T-13...... X.13:2 beyond the value that you s. on yourself,
T-14.........I.4:6 You have s. yourself the task of sharing
T-14.... III.12:4 accepts the plan God s. for its Atonement
T-15...... IX.6:7 the Holy Spirit must undo to s. him free.
T-16... V.12:10 No rituals that you have s. up in which
T-17......IV.7:4 the defense protects, s. in a golden frame.
T-17......IV.7:5 frame is very elaborate, all s. with jewels,
T-17......IV.8:3 of love, s. with dreams of sacrifice and self-
T-17.... IV.11:2 It is a picture, too, s. in a frame. Yet if you
T-17.... IV.11:5 of timelessness, s. in a frame of time. If
T-17.... IV.11:8 borrowed from eternity and s. in time for
T-17....... V.4:5 S. firmly in the unholy relationship, there
T-17....... V.6:2 You let this goal be s. for you. That was
T-17....... V.6:7 The goal *is* s.. And your relationship has
T-17...... VI.3:1 a clear-cut, positive goal, s. at the outset,
T-17...... VI.3:5 No goal was s. with which to bring the
T-17...... VI.3:7 of a criterion for outcome, s. in advance,
T-17...... VI.6:3 Where the goal of truth is s., there faith
T-17.....VII.4:2 of holiness was s. for your relationship,
T-17.....VII.4:3 You did not s. it because holiness cannot
T-17.....VII.4:4 grow to meet the goal that has been s..
T-17.....VII.5:1 meet the purpose s. for your relationship.
T-17.....VII.7:1 power s. in you in whom the Holy Spirit's
T-17...VII.10:4 the Holy Spirit's goal are s. apart from
T-18.........I.9:1 He has s. the course inward to the truth
T-18...... VI.8:2 you s. aside to house your hate is not a
T-18....VIII.7:8 that you think you s. apart is no exception
T-18...... IX.1:5 sole ruler of the kingdom it s. apart to
T-18...... IX.1:9 withered kingdom in which you s. it off,
T-18.... IX.13:1 s. shining and firmly rooted in the world
T-19.......I.5:10 to s. up a goal forever impossible to attain
T19. IV.A.16:1 Love, too, would s. a feast before you, on
T19..IV.A.16:1 s. in a quiet garden where no sound but
T19..IV.B.10:8 Only the mind can s. a purpose, and only
T19....IV.C.3:2 and s. against the peace of Heaven? One
T-20 .......II.3:4 And each has s. a light upon his altar, that
T-20 ... VI.7:10 for the Holy Spirit has s. His temple there
T-20 ... VI.11:3 of water and s. uncertainly upon oblivion.
T-21 ......in.2:4 you joined the Will of God to s. him free.
T-21 .......II.7:3 have s. up your idols to something else.
T-21 ..... III.1:3 Forget not this; to bargain is to s. a limit,
T-21 ..... III.7:5 But holiness would s. your brother free,
T-21 ...... V.5:5 You must have s. aside a place in which
T-21 . VI.11:10 his pardon on himself to s. him free.
T-22 ..... III.3:2 Sin is a block, s. like a heavy gate, locked
T-23 ......I.10:5 God has s. him in serenity and peace, and
T-23 .......II.2:2 s. of thoughts that set him off from others
T-23 .......II.2:2 set of thoughts that s. him off from others
T-24 ..... VI.6:4 s. the shining memory of Him in Whom
T-24 ..... VI.6:8 to you. He *is* s. forth within his holiness.
T-24 ..... VI.7:6 He s. forever in your brother's holiness,
T-24 ..... VI.7:6 s. forth at last in terms you recognized
T-25 ......in.2:7 is his specialness s. forth within his body.
T-25 ........I.2:9 S. in his holiness, the Christ in him
T-25 .......II.3:2 and unrewarding task you s. yourself. Can
T-25 .......II.4:8 Its purpose is to s. the picture off, and not
T-25 .......II.5:3 masterpiece that God has s. within this
T-25 .......II.6:1 Holy Spirit is the frame God s. around the
T-25 .......II.6:6 Yet God has s. His masterpiece within a
T-25 .......II.8:6 is the frame in which your holiness is s.,
T-25 ..... III.3:5 is the perfect frame to s. it off; the perfect
T-25 ...VIII.8:2 In justice He is bound to s. them free, and
T-25 ..... IX.4:6 can s. up a state in which there is no loser;
T-26 ..... III.5:4 is the learning goal this course has s.. It
T-26 ..... IV.3:6 of altars is s. where once sin was believed
T-26 ..VII.18:2 all His Son's mistakes and s. him free. But
T-26 ..... IX.6:2 where a home for Them has been s. up.
T-27 ........I.2:5 and when it rests on him are you s. free.
T-27 .....II.15:3 leave mistakes in one unhealed and s. the
T-27 ..... IV.1:3 A problem s. in conflict has no answer,
T-27 ..... IV.5:7 It does not s. conditions for response, but
T-27 .... VII.2:2 it is, and not the way that you have s. it up
T-27 .VIII.11:1 single lesson learned will s. you free from
T-28 ..... III.8:7 the feast of plenty s. before them there.
T-28 ..... III.9:8 For love has s. its table in the space that
T-28 ..... VI.2:5 aimlessly the path on which it has been s..
T-28 .... VII.5:7 It is like the house s. upon straw. It seems
T-29 ........I.5:7 And its "inherent" weaknesses s. up the
T-29 ... III.3:11 God's witness has s. forth the gentle way
T-29 ... VI.2:10 time has s. an end is not where the eternal
T-29 ... VI.2:12 nor s. the hour of his birth and death.
T-29 ..... VI.3:4 you can s. a goal unlike God's purpose for
T-29 ..... VI.4:4 All other goals are s. in time and change
T-29 ..... VI.4:8 Time can s. no end to its fulfillment nor
T-29 ...VIII.6:3 Here the world of idols has been s. by the
T-29 ...VIII.7:4 A place of darkness s. where all is light, a
T-29 ...VIII.7:5 idol is beyond where God has s. all things
T-30 ........I.1:3 s. begins to form which sees you through
T-30 ........I.1:5 The proper s., adopted consciously each
T-30 ........I.2:5 you have s. the rules for how you should
T-30 ........I.6:2 and must have s. an answer in your terms
T-30 ........I.6:6 cancels out the terms that you have s.,
T-30 ......I.15:2 It is s. by what you choose to live it with,
T-30 .......II.1:7 He did not s. His Kingdom up alone. And
T-30 .......II.3:8 you, for it was s. in Heaven by your will.
T-30 ..... III.8:5 high in Heaven is it s. that those outside
T-30 ..... IV.3:2 one seems to break the rules you s. for it.
T-30 ..... IV.4:1 the laws of God, and not the rules you s..
T-30 ..... IV.4:4 according to the rules you s. for them. But
T-30 ...... V.1:4 No rules are idly s., and no demands are
T-30 ...... V.7:3 their path been surely s. away from idols
T-30 ..... VI.6:6 And you have s. a goal of partial pardon
T-31 .......II.2:6 your wish you s. two choices to be made,
T-31 ...... V.4:4 the learning of the world has s. its sights,
T-31 ...... V.4:4 for it is here the world's "reality" is s., to
T-31 .VIII.12:2 the abode You s. for Him before time was,
W-in......... 2:6 to do more than one s. of exercises a day.
W-pI.....27.3:4 It is recommended that you s. a definite
W-pI.....57.3:5 is really a place where he can be s. free. I
W-pI.....65.3:1 s. aside ten to fifteen minutes for a more
W-pI.....65.4:3 so that you have s. apart the time for God,
W-pI .... 71.1:1 that the ego has s. up a plan for salvation
W-pI .... 76.3:1 twisted laws you have s. up to save you.
W-pI .... 76.8:4 s. forth what is God's and what is yours.
W-pI .... 78.4:5 as his, according to the role you s. for him
W-pI .... 79.9:1 periods for today will not be s. by time,
W-pI .... 91.5:1 s. aside about ten minutes for a quiet time
W-pI .... 96.3:1 resolved within the framework they are s..
W-pI .... 96.6:8 bring pain to him, and fail to s. him free?
W-pI .. 101.6:4 to it in confidence that it will s. you free
W-pI .. 101.7:3 You are s. on freedom's road, and now
W-pI .. 105.3:1 has s. is to reverse your view of giving, so
W-pI 107.11:2 release the world, as He would s. you free.
W-pI .. 110.5:4 This is the truth that comes to s. you free.
W-pI .. 124.9:4 every minute like a diamond s. around
W-pI .. 125.7:1 ten minutes s. apart from listening to the
W-pI 131.15:3 Today is s. by Heaven itself to be a time of
W-pI .. 132.3:2 Here in the present is the world s. free.
W-pI 132.11:6 which made it and must s. it free, that you
W-pI 132.14:4 we are in the home our Father s. for us,
W-pI .. 133.3:5 learn the laws you s. in motion when you
W-pI .. 133.4:2 The range is s., and this we cannot change
W-pI .. 135.6:4 and s. its value far beyond a little pile of
W-pI 135.19:1 this life becomes a holy instant, s. in time,
W-pI 136.15:2 ask the truth to come to us and s. us free.
W-pI .. 139.8:2 It is s. forever in the holy Mind of God,
WpI..rIV.in5:4 this thought will be enough to s. the day
W-pI .. 155.5:4 and s. their footsteps on the way that God
W-pI .. 155.7:3 and s. them on the way to happiness.
W-pI 155.13:1 Your feet are safely s. upon the road that
W-pI .. 157.1:3 a time Heaven has s. apart to shine upon,
W-pI .. 158.3:1 The time is s. already. It appears to be
W-pI .. 158.4:4 come to end your doubting has been s..
W-pI .. 158.8:2 nor s. up a goal that does not merely
W-pI .. 159.8:1 the lilies of forgiveness s. their roots. This
W-pI 159.10:1 the store of miracles s. out for you to give.
W-pI .. 160.8:2 belongs where He has s. His Son forever.
W-pI .. 161.9:9 have it be revealed to you and s. you free?
W-pI 161.11:6 Ask this of him, that he may s. you free:
W-pI .. 166.7:4 be released from self-deception and s. free
W-pI 167.10:5 of life eternal has been s. by God Himself.
W-pI .. 169.4:1 and the Son as One has been already s..
W-pI .. 169.9:2 here. Whatever time the mind has s. for
W-pI 170.13:9 *are we because Your Holiness has s. us free.*
W-pI .. 184.1:5 s. it off from other things by emphasizing
W-pI .. 184.4:1 purposefully s. against the given truth. Its
W-pI .. 191.4:4 In this one thought is everyone s. free. In
W-pI .. 191.5:2 and escape you will return and s. it free.
W-pI .. 191.6:4 You s. it free of your imprisonment. You
W-pI .. 191.8:4 Son has come again at last to s. it free?
W-pI .. 192.8:2 be s. free while he imprisons anyone? A
W-pI .. 194.3:2 instant sorrow can be s. upon a throne,
W-pI .. 199.7:3 s. free the many who perceive themselves
WpI.rVI.in.7:4 advancing toward the goal He s. for us;
W-pI .. 212.1:2 *I seek the function that would s. me free from*
W-pI .. 213.1:3 *I learn of Him becomes the way I am s. free.*
W-pII .... in.1:5 begin to reach the goal this course has s.,
W-pII . 236.1:8 And thus I s. it free to do the Will of God.
W-pII . 240.2:3 *today to recognize Your Son, and s. him free.*
W-pII . 241.1:3 the darkened world where its release is s..
W-pII . 241.1:5 dawns today upon a world s. free. This is
W-pII . 272.1:2 *home is s. in Heaven by Your Will and mine.*
W-pII . 296.1:4 *For having damned it I would s. it free, that I*
W-pII . 297.2:1 *is every step in my salvation s. already, and*
W-pII . 308.1:5 instant has forgiveness come to s. me free.
W-pII . 310.1:4 *me, and that it is Your Will I be s. free today.*
W-pII . 310.2:2 gave salvation to us, and Who s. us free.
W-pII ... 10.4:6 your glad acceptance, which will s. it free.
W-pII . 312.2:1 *s. free from all the judgments I have made.*
W-pII . 324.1:2 *You have s. the way I am to go, the role to take*
W-pII . 332.2:3 *Your Love has given us the means to s. it free.*
W-pII . 333.1:2 It cannot be evaded, s. aside, denied,
W-pII . 350.1:7 *Only Your memory will s. me free. And only*
W-ep.......... 2:1 sun laid down before it rises, after it has s.
M-in.......... 3:1 The curriculum you s. up is therefore
M-3 ........... 1:1 teachers of God have no s. teaching level.
M-4 ........... 1:5 s. in time as a means of leading out of
M-4 ...... IX.1:4 in the Word of God to s. all things right;
M-9 ........... 1:5 There is, however, no s. pattern, since
M-13 ......... 6:2 and it is the course's aim to s. him free.

**shadows** 40

T-3........IV.1:1 possess are only s. of your real strength.
T-3......... V.1:1 possess are only s. of your real strength,
T-17.........III.h S. of the Past
T-17..IV.12:10 hard to see at all beneath the heavy s. of
T-18......IV.2:4 and be not disturbed that s. surround it.
T-18......IX.8:3 is a world of light whereon they cast no s..
T-18......IX.8:4 Their s. lie upon the world beyond them,
T-18......IX.8:5 from them to the light their s. cannot fall.
T-18....IX.13:1 has been uprooted from the world of s.,
T-18....IX.14:3 the s. from the world and carrying it, safe
T19... IV.A.6:4 Look not upon the little wall of s.. The
T19... IV.A.6:7 by s. from the light in which illusions end.
T-23..... II.16:4 where only s. play the major roles, it
T-25......IV.3:6 is pushed away, until it is but distant s.,
T-25..VIII.12:3 s. of all that is really happening within
T-26......VI.3:1 Who dwells with s. is alone indeed, and
T-26.....VII.3:2 in the world of s. and illusions built on sin
T-27.........I.1:3 you will fear no evil and no s. in the night.
T-29...... III.3:7 as heavy s. must give way to light. The
T-29...... III.5:2 aside from heavy s. that have hidden him,
T-31....... V.1:3 is that suits a world of s. and illusions.
W-pI.......4.2:4 "good" ones are but s. of what lies beyond
W-pI.......4.2:4 lies beyond, and s. make sight difficult.
W-pI.......75.3:2 No s. from the past remain to darken our
W-pI.......87.1:3 fearful of s. and afraid of things unseen
W-pI.......92.9:1 you do not dwell on idle s. that the body's
W-pI...138.9:3 in s. must be raised to understanding, to
W-pI...158.6:1 of doubt and s. made with the intangible.
W-pI...159.5:3 seem quite solid here are merely s. there;
W-pI...164.5:2 while all the s. which appeared to hide it
W-pI...188.8:2 what you are, instead of fantasies and s..
W-pI...191.1:4 it be but vicious and afraid, fearful of s.,
W-pII .314.1:3 Past mistakes can cast no s. on it, so that
M-4 ......I.A.8:3 as merely s. before become solid gains, to
P-2...........I.2:7 are but deeper s., or perhaps different
P-2........IV.2:4 all external things are only s. of a decision
S-2...........I.6:5 Mistakes are tiny s., quickly gone, that for
S-2...........I.6:7 He does not know of s.. His the eyes that
S-3...........I.3:3 overlook all s. on the holy face of Christ,
S-3........IV.9:3 See the s. fade away in gentleness; the

**shadowy** 2

T-13......IV.6:1 The s. figures from the past are precisely
T-13....... V.3:1 It is through these strange and s. figures

**shake** 4

T-14.... III.12:2 Nothing can s. God's conviction of the
T-20......VI.7:2 of their temple begin to s. and loosen.
T-21......IV.1:8 Its temples do not s. because of this. Your
T-31.....VII.2:3 to s. your sorry concept of yourself and

**shaken** 12

T-2......... II.1:10 incapable of being s. by errors of any kind
T-2........ III.5:8 could not be s. and could not be deceived.
T-3.......VII.5:5 is the only Foundation that cannot be s.,
T-9......... II.4:3 in me whose faith in you cannot be s..
T-11......V.10:2 dream of autonomy is s. to its foundation
T-16.....VII.5:2 the illusion of love is not profoundly s..
T-20.....VII.3:8 your wanting of the purpose has been s..
T-21......IV.3:6 And your belief in sin has been already s.,
T-21.....VIII.2:7 because its own desire cannot be s.. It
T-28.....VII.7:2 instead has s. the Foundation of his home
W-pI...102.1:3 Yet this belief is surely s. now, at least
WpIrIII.in11:1 are s., think of it again. These practice

**shaky** 1

W-pI...107.7:4 The s. and unsteady footsteps of illusion

**shall** 54

T-1........III.2:1 "Heaven and earth s. pass away" means
T-1........III.2:2 life, s. not pass away because life is eternal
T-1........III.6:1 and as you perceive so s. you behave. The
T-2......... II.7:4 is meant by "the meek s. inherit the earth.
T-3 ..........I.5:4 they s. see God" is another way of saying
T-3 .......II.5:10 "When he s. appear (or be perceived) we
T-3 .......II.5:10 appear (or be perceived) we s. be like him,
T-3 .......II.5:10 shall be like him, for we s. see him as he is
T-3 ........ V.5:7 thinking is *not* the truth that s. set you free
T-4 ........I.12:4 The meek s. inherit the earth because
T-4 ........ V.5:2 "Seek and ye s. find" does not mean that
T-5 .......IV.6:4 As you teach so s. you learn. I will never
T-5 .......VI.6:1 so s. ye reap" He interprets to mean what
T-5 .......VI.9:1 wicked s. perish" becomes a statement of
T-6 ..........I.6:1 said before, "As you teach so s. you learn.
T-8 ....... III.1:2 Ask and it s. be given you, because it has
T-9 ........ V.9:6 *By their fruits ye s. know them, and they*
T-9 ........ V.9:6 *know them, and they s. know themselves.*
T-11 .......II.7:3 are free to determine who s. be your guest
T-11 .......II.7:3 and how long he s. remain with you. Yet
T-11 ..... VI.4:9 in the beginning, is now and ever s. be,
T-16 ..... III.2:2 earlier, "By their fruits ye s. know them,
T-16 ..... III.2:2 know them, and they s. know themselves.
T-20 .....II.11:7 that gave it to him s. you be led past fear
T-20 ... III.7:10 ask, "How s. I look upon the Son of God?
T-20 ..... III.9:6 you s. this day enter with him to Paradise,
T-20 ...VIII.4:1 what God willed and gave you s. be yours.
T-22 ..... IV.5:4 So s. you walk the world with me, whose
T-23 ........I.4:9 is it up to you to say what s. be part of you
T-24 ..... VI.9:5 And both s. see God's glory in His Son,
T-25 ..... IX.4:5 it is decided who s. win and who shall lose
T-25 ..... IX.4:5 it is decided who shall win and who s. lose
T-25 ..... IX.4:5 who shall lose; how much the one s. take,
T-26 ..... IX.7:4 And s. the Lord of Heaven and His Son
T-27 .. VII.14:4 is the murderer and who s. be the victim.
W-pI..... 87.1:4 Light s. be my guide today. I will follow it
W-pI. 138.10:5 this? And s. we hesitate to choose today?
W-pI... 168.1:2 S. we not speak to Him? He is not distant.
W-pI... 182.4:5 Where this Child s. go is holy ground. It is
W-pI. 183.11:8 today. And in His Name, it s. be given us.
W-pI... 192.1:1 and that your Self s. be His sacred Son,
W-pI... 193.6:1 S. we not learn to say these words when
W-pI... 193.6:2 S. we not learn to say these words when
W-pII .228.1:2 S. I deny His knowledge, and believe in
W-pII .228.1:3 S. I accept as true what He proclaims as
W-pII .228.1:4 Or s. I take His Word for what I am, since
W-pII ..... 4.5:2 sin? S. we not put away these sharp-edged
W-pII .258.1:3 S. we continue to allow God's grace to
W-pII .289.2:5 *S. I demand that You wait longer for Your*
W-pII .... 301.h And God Himself s. wipe away all tears.
W-pII .357.1:4 *to You, as You appointed that the way s. be:*
Wfl........in.4:3 And s. we not forgive our brother, who
P-3........ III.5:1 said that to him who hath s. be given.
P-3........ III.5:3 And because he gives, he s. be given. This

**shallow** 4

T-1 ........ V.6:3 All s. roots must be uprooted, because
T-1 ........ V.6:4 The illusion that s. roots can be deepened
T-11 ...... V.9:1 "lighthearted," distant, emotionally s.,
W-pI... 159.8:3 never grow in its unnourishing and s. soil.

**shalt** 1

T-4 ....... III.6:6 Thou s. have no other gods before Him

**shame** 5

T-24 ........I.5:8 and its victory is his defeat and s.. How
T-28 ..... III.6:2 and the s. of guilt He cannot bridge, for
W-pI... 185.8:6 reserving s. and secrecy for others. They
M-7 .......... 5:5 Perhaps there is a fear of failure and s.
S-1......... V.2:5 in s. because it is content with what it is,

**shape** 4

T-21 ...... V.1:3 of size and s. and brightness would hold,
T-29 ...VIII.6:3 and s. the world where the impossible has
W-pI. 135.26:1 Try not to s. this day as you believe
M-8 .......... 6:7 apart from size and s. and time and place

**shapes** 3

T-14 .......II.7:7 the s. and forms and fears of nothing.
T-27 .......V.8:1 and these specific s. make up the world.
T-28 .......V.7:3 vague uncertain forms and changing s.,

**share** 344

T-1 .........II.4:6 which I render complete because I s. it.
T-1 ....... III.1:6 you s. my unwillingness to accept error in
T-4 ..........I.1:3 unless they s. their lessons conviction will
T-4 ..........I.3:3 fear, because it does not s. my charity. My
T-4 ........I.13:7 who s. my aim of healing the mind. Spirit
T-4 ....... VII.5:1 but who want to s. it to increase their joy.
T-4 ....... VII.7:1 s. His joy with you until you know it with
T-4 ....... VII.8:6 with its individual willingness to s. in it.
T-5 ........in.1:6 forth an integrated willingness to s. it,
T-5 ........I.1:10 If you s. a physical possession, you do
T-5 ........I.1:11 If you s. an idea, however, you do not
T-5 .........II.5:1 because He can s. only perfect knowledge.
T-5 .........II.5:6 He could no longer s. His knowledge with
T-5 .........II.9:4 This decision is the choice to s. it, because
T-5 .........II.9:4 the decision itself *is* the decision to s.. It is
T-5 .......II.11:2 As we s. this goal, we increase its power to
T-5 ....... III.3:5 yourself, and what you s. you strengthen.
T-5 ....... III.4:2 you. That is why you must s. It. It must be
T-5 ....... IV.3:7 *It is impossible to s. opposing thoughts.* You
T-5 ....... IV.3:8 You can s. only the thoughts that are of
T-5 ..... IV.3:12 decision to s. them *is* their purification.
T-5 ....... IV.4:2 decision to s. It in order to hear It yourself
T-5 ....... IV.5:2 that to s. ideas is to strengthen them. I
T-5 ....... IV.8:9 Hold it and s. it, that it may always be
T-5 ..... IV.8:10 heart and in your hands, to hold and s..
T-5 ....... VI.3:3 teach you how to s. it with your brothers.
T-5 ..... VI.11:1 meant that I came to s. the light with you.
T-6 ..........I.2:5 can always call on me to s. my decision,
T-6 ..........I.5:3 and did not s. this evaluation for myself.
T-6 ..........I.5:4 I did not s. it, I did not strengthen it. I
T-6 ..........I.5:5 and one which I want to s. with you. If
T-6 ..........I.8:1 not s. my decision to hear only one Voice,
T-6 ........I.11:2 because the Holy Spirit, Whom we s.,
T-6 ........I.19:3 will be as eager to s. your learning as I am.
T-6 ....... III.4:6 An idea that you s. you must have. It
T-6 .....V.A.1:5 If we s. the same mind, you can overcome
T-6 .....V.B.1:7 that when you do not s. a thought system,
T-7 ..........I.1:3 This is an ongoing process in which you s.
T-7 ..........I.1:3 in which you share, and because you s. it,
T-7 ..........I.6:1 God is to s. His certainty of what you are,
T-7 ..........I.6:1 to s. the perfect Love He shares with you.
T-7 ........I.7:14 obscured, because it is His Will to s. it.
T-7 .........II.1:1 God, and because of the elements they s.,
T-7 .........II.7:5 you s. it and extend it as your Creator did.
T-7 ....... III.5:8 serenity, because this is what they s.,
T-7 .........V.4:3 that everyone else does not s. with him.
T-7 .......V.10:7 yours. I do not want to s. my body in
T-7 .......V.10:7 communion because this is to s. nothing.
T-7 .......V.10:8 Would I try to s. an illusion with the most
T-7 .......V.10:9 I do want to s. my mind with you because
T-7 .......V.11:2 mind we s. is shared by all our brothers,
T-7 ..... VI.8:11 contradictory thought systems s. truth,
T-7 ...... VII.7:8 Do not s. their illusions of scarcity, or you
T-7 ....... IX.2:8 Spirit yearns to s. its being as its Creator
T-7 .........X.2:6 S. His Will and you share what He knows.
T-7 .........X.2:6 Share His Will and you s. what He knows.
T-8 ..........I.3:6 You s. to have, but you do not give it up
T-8 ....... III.2:7 You s. them as God shares them, because
T-8 ....... IV.7:9 which He will s. with all His creations, to
T-8 .........V.4:4 and I s. this confidence for both of us and
T-8 .........V.6:9 and if you choose to s. it you will do so. I
T-8 ....... VI.9:1 I s. with God the knowledge of the value
T-8 ....... IX.7:3 works of love because we s. this Oneness.
T-9 .......II.12:3 nothing, and so you can s. everything.
T-9 ....... IV.3:3 the ability to attack into the ability to s.,
T-9 .........V.5:6 how to give, and consequently cannot s..
T-10 ... III.10:2 You s. reality with Him, because reality is
T-10 ..... IV.7:4 his belief in sickness, which he does not s.
T-10 .......V.5:7 It can s. only what it is. Depression is
T-10 .....V.10:5 Would you have Him s. your insanity?
T-11 ........I.1:3 again the thought system you s. with Him
T-11 ........I.6:7 that is His and that He wills to s. with you

T-11...... I.11:5 who s. His life must share it to know it,
T-11...... I.11:5 who share His life must s. it to know it,
T-11......IV.3:2 Limit the peace you s., and your Self must
T-11......IV.8:1 wills to s. as his Father shares it with him.
T-11......IV.8:3 the Son must s. what belongs to Him, for
T-11....... V.5:5 wishes and the Will of God, which you s..
T-11....... V.6:3 By His willingness to s. it, He became as
T-11......VI.8:8 with the awakening of others to s. your
T-11... VIII.6:2 is everything, and you s. it with God. That
T-11... VIII.8:5 God's Sons have nothing they do not s..
T-11. VIII.11:2 you s. the real world as you share Heaven,
T-11. VIII.11:2 you share the real world as you s. Heaven,
T-12...... III.1:5 if you were unwilling to s. their poverty.
T-12......VI.2:3 you what He loves, for He wills to s. it.
T-12......VI.4:6 and He longs to s. His vision with you. He
T-12......VI.5:6 which He would s. with you because He
T-12......VI.6:7 they s. the unification of the laws of God.
T-12.....VII.4:6 Spirit's work, for you s. in His function.
T-12...VII.12:7 s. His function only by judging as He does
T-12... VIII.7:9 s. God's Being with Him could never be
T-13......IV.8:4 you would s. His goal of salvation for you.
T-13....... V.7:9 as witnesses to the reality you s. with God
T-13......VI.5:3 his past is yours, you s. in this release. Let
T-13.....VII.6:7 in recognition that you s. it with Him.
T-13... VIII.4:3 He has no Thoughts He does not s.. His
T-13. VIII.10:2 not, and so you do not s. His witness to it.
T-13....... X.3:1 him, or s. it with him or perceive his own,
T-13......XI.8:2 God would s. with you is known. Yet His
T-14.........I.4:5 that your Father does not s. with you. You
T-14.....III.17:3 your Father would have you s. it with Him
T-14....... V.1:2 to s. with all the lonely ones who have
T-14....... V.2:7 you s. with God He holds in trust for you.
T-14....... V.3:3 that does not s. His shining innocence.
T-14......VI.2:4 kept apart from love cannot s. its healing
T-14.....VII.7:1 the way in which you learn to s. with Him
T-14... VIII.1:8 the promise that was given Him to s. with
T-14......IX.6:8 him, then, see it in you and s. it with you.
T-14...... X.6:11 gives equal blessing to all who s. in it, and
T-14......XI.5:2 even think of you s. in your perfect peace,
T-15...... I.14:3 immortal creations who s. it with you. As
T-15......IV.7:3 you can harbor thoughts you would not s.
T-15......IV.7:4 have alone, and s. what *you* would share.
T-15......IV.7:4 have alone, and share what *you* would s..
T-15......IV.8:4 for you are not ready to s. it with Him.
T-15......VI.2:5 In the holy instant we s. our faith in God's
T-15....VI.6:10 the only need the Sons of God s. equally,
T-15... VIII.2:6 the only need that God and His Son s.,
T-15... VIII.2:8 calls to you, to s. your will with them.
T-15... VIII.5:6 for He does not s. it with you. It is only
T-15......IX.3:2 ego has no purpose you would s. with it.
T-16.........I.3:5 is nothing from the past that you would s.
T-16.........I.5:8 and *His* strength that you would s..
T-16.........I.7:6 s. everything you give through Him. That
T-16....... II.4:3 minds join as one and s. one idea equally,
T-16....... II.8:3 Awake and s. it, for that is the only reason
T-16......IV.4:5 which they would not s. with others, are
T-16..... V.15:2 cannot know yourself who s. its meaning.
T-16....VI.12:2 He needs only your willingness to s. His
T-16....VI.12:4 and it is His faith you s. with Him there.
T-17......IV.1:1 that does not s. His purpose can be real.
T-17..... V.14:5 you, you could not s. in its gladness. Yet
T-17..... V.14:9 will s. the gladness of the Sonship that it
T-17.....VII.9:2 faith will call the others to s. your purpose
T-18.........I.9:1 set the course inward to the truth you s..
T-18....... I.10:9 and perfect reality, which we s. in Him.
T-18....... II.7:2 you will s. with all who come within your
T-18....... V.7:3 *for myself, that I may s. it with my brother,*
T-18....... V.7:5 *Yet it is wholly possible for us to s. it now.*
T-19.........I.2:3 and in this vision does the Holy Spirit s..
T-19.........I.9:2 for yourself, and would therefore s. it. By
T-19...... I.12:2 and is the sign you s. it with Him. Faith is
T-19...... III.5:2 On this you s. His vision. Yet you do not
T-19...... III.5:3 do not s. His recognition of the difference
T19. IV.A.4:10 you asked the Holy Spirit to s. with you.
T19. IV.A.14:5 they found, to s. them lovingly with you.
T19..IV.B.12:7 It will s. the pain of all illusions, and the
T19.IV.D.11:3 For only if they s. in it does it seem fearful
T19.IV.D.11:3 s. in it until you look upon your brother
T19.IV.D.12:5 madness, which you hate because you s. it
T19.IV.D.12:7 will s. in madness or in Heaven together.
T19.IV.D.14:4 forgiveness out to you, to s. His Holiness.
T19.IV.D.15:9 forgive is free, and what you give you s..
T19.IV.D.17:5 give redemption to each other and s. in it,
T-20....... II.5:3 purpose as their own s. also His vision.
T-20....... II.6:4 you use what I have given unless you s. it.
T-20..... II.8:12 the home we s. in quietness and where we
T-20.... III.11:2 S., then, this faith with me, and know
T-20......IV.3:5 own. For this you s.. What God has given
T-20......IV.4:2 to what God has given, to s. with them.
T-20......IV.4:7 for themselves the power to s. with you.
T-20......IV.5:2 and s. with him the power of the release
T-20....... V.8:3 learn, to s. his Father's confidence in him.
T-20......VI.3:1 But idols do not s.. Idols accept, but
T-21......IV.6:3 because you did not choose to s. in it. At
T-22..... II.13:1 in quiet here with Christ is s. His vision.
T-22...... III.2:2 S. this belief, and reason will be unable to
T-22......IV.5:8 for you who s. it have become its willing
T-22......IV.6:1 To all who s. the Love of God the grace is
T-22......IV.7:8 brother, and the holy Self you s. together.
T-23.......in.3:2 are safe because they s. their innocence.
T-23.......in.3:5 s. the strength of love *because* they looked
T-23.........I.3:5 with an illusion of yourself you s. with it.
T-23.......I.12:5 where love abides, and seeks to s. itself.
T-23....... II.9:6 would they seek to s. the things they value
T-23......IV.3:1 God does not s. His function with a body.
T-23......IV.7:4 who s. a purpose have a mind as one. The
T-23......IV.8:1 given those who s. their Father's purpose,
T-24.........I.6:5 Specialness can never s., for it depends on
T-24.........I.7:5 this is now the only purpose that you s..
T-24.........I.8:5 your brother s. becomes obscured from
T-24.........I.8:7 none your Father does not s. with you.
T-24....... II.2:3 from his omnipotence, yet s. his power?
T-24..... II.10:7 that both might s. the universe with Him
T-24....... V.7:5 to look upon with Him and s. His joy. His
T-24......VI.3:4 It is His Will you s. His Love for you, and
T-24.....VII.1:8 that you might s. the Fatherhood of God,
T-25....... II.9:3 if you but s. His praise of what He loves?
T-25....... II.9:5 of Him joins in His praise, to s. His joy.
T-25...... II.11:5 from darkness into light be yours to s.;
T-25....... V.4:1 is his due, that you may s. in it with him.
T-25...VII.1:11 should s. the attributes of His creation,
T-25.....VII.2:6 And what can s. its attributes except itself
T-25...VII.13:4 Salvation is His Will *because* you s. it. Not
T-25... VIII.5:8 impossible for you to s. the Holy Spirit's
T-27....... V.1:9 And who can s. what he denies himself?
T-27......VI.1:6 unites all those who s. in it within itself.
T-27......VI.1:9 And they s. the lack of meaning which
T-27... VIII.2:5 for special bodies that can s. its dream.
T-28.......I.11:2 then, to other minds to s. its quietness.
T-28...... III.9:2 the more is left for all the rest to s.. The
T-28......IV.1:2 means that you s. not his wish to separate
T-28......IV.1:9 depending on whose evil dream you s..
T-28....IV.1:10 you are evil, for you s. in dreams of fear.
T-28......IV.3:2 S. not in his illusion of himself, for your
T-28......IV.6:1 You s. confusion and you are confused,
T-28......IV.8:5 If you s. not your brother's evil dream,
T-28....... V.1:7 Who shares in them can never s. in Him.
T-28..... V.1:10 Except you s. it, nothing can exist. And
T-28....... V.2:6 you s. becomes the only one you have.
T-28....... V.3:1 You s. no evil dreams if you forgive the
T-28....... V.3:4 Remember if you s. an evil dream, you
T-28....... V.3:4 you will believe you are the dream you s..
T-28......VI.6:7 time he does not s. a promise to be sick,
T-29....... V.7:2 of death; a dream of hope you s. with him
T-29....... V.7:3 Why does it seem so hard to s. this dream
T-29......VI.4:9 There is no death because the living s. the
T-30....... II.4:9 apart from Him Whose holy Will you s..
T-30...... III.6:6 They s. the attributes of their creator, nor
T-30....... V.2:8 of the world is one which all must s., if
T-30....... V.4:1 Son and s. His Fatherhood with him. No
T-30.....VII.5:1 purpose, which you s. with all the world.
T-31.........I.9:1 not s. the universal Will that it be whole,
T-31..... V.13:7 is. And you must s. his guilt, because you
T-31... VIII.8:5 vision is which you must s. with everyone
W-pI.....45.2:2 Therefore you s. your thoughts with Him,
W-pI.....45.2:4 To s. is to make alike, or to make one.
W-pI.....54.3:5 which s. everything with everyone. As my
W-pI.....57.4:4 the hearts of all who s. this place with me.
W-pI.....57.5:3 As I s. the peace of the world with my
W-pI.....58.2:4 is nothing that does not s. my holiness.
W-pI.....58.3:6 my holiness, which I s. with God Himself,
W-pI.....58.4:5 everyone must s. in my understanding,
W-pI.....59.5:2 I have no thoughts I do not s. with God. I
W-pI.....62.4:3 and time, to s. this happiness with you.
W-pI...66.10:3 We can s. in this conclusion, but in no
W-pI.....69.1:4 him. S. your salvation now with him who
W-pI.....73.1:1 are considering the will you s. with God.
W-pI.....73.1:3 The will you s. with God has all the power
W-pI.....73.7:2 to accept God's plan because you s. in it.
W-pI.....74.4:4 *God's. I s. it with Him. My conflicts about* _
W-pI...78.10:3 to be given, that you may s. it with him.
W-pI.....82.2:3 *I s. the light of the world with you, [name].*
W-pI...91.10:4 in which you s. a purpose like Their Own.
W-pI.....92.6:2 and nothing in the world that it would s..
W-pI.....92.8:2 No one can ask in vain to s. its sight, and
W-pI.....93.3:3 weird beliefs He does not s. with you.
W-pI...95.14:4 S., then, its surety, for it is yours. Be
W-pI.....96.7:3 Salvation is a thought you s. with God,
W-pI.....98.3:5 may s. their certainty and thus increase it
W-pI.....98.9:6 you each practice period you s. with Him,
W-pI......102.h I s. God's Will for happiness for me.
W-pI...102.4:2 *I s. God's Will for happiness for me, and I*
W-pI...102.4:4 is your choice, and that you s. God's Will.
W-pI...107.9:3 To s. His function is to share His joy. His
W-pI...107.9:3 To share His function is to s. His joy. His
W-pI...108.3:2 to s. it and be glad that they are one with
W-pI...112.1:3 *I welcome them into the home I s. with God,*
W-pI...116.2:1 (102) I s. God's Will for happiness for me
W-pI...116.2:2 *I s. my Father's Will for me, His Son. What*
W-pI...116.3:4 hour: I s. God's Will for happiness for me.
W-pI...124.7:5 world may s. our recognition of reality. In
W-pI...126.8:4 and ask Him that He s. your practicing in
W-pI. 127.12:4 *the Love of God, which I would s. with you.*
W-pI. 132.11:1 make what does not s. His timelessness
W-pI. 132.11:6 may know the Thoughts you s. with God.
W-pI. 134.14:3 follow us to the reality we s. with them.
W-pI. 137.14:4 *And I would s. my healing with the world,*
W-pI...139.6:5 Why s. its madness in the sad belief that
W-pI...151.6:3 because you would not s. the doubts their
W-pI. 151.15:5 And everyone will s. the thoughts with
W-pI. 153.16:1 to be faithful to the Will we s. with God.
W-pI. 154.14:4 prove that we accept no will we do not s.,
W-pI...156.2:8 That life you s. with Him. Nothing can be
W-pI...163.9:6 *life we s. with You and with all living things,*
W-pI. 166.15:8 And now you go to s. it with the world.
W-pI......167.h There is one life, and that I s. with God.
W-pI...167.1:3 condition in which all that God created s..
W-pI...167.8:2 His creations cannot s. what He gives not,
W-pI...167.8:2 which He does not s. with them. The
W-pI. 167.11:3 there is one life, and that we s. with Him,
W-pI. 167.12:1 s. one life because we have one Source, a
WpI...rV.in4:2 Self we s. and now prepare to know again:
WpI...rV.in6:2 For I s. your doubts and fears a little while
WpI.rV.in10:1 in which we s. a new experience for you,
W-pI...179.1:1 There is one life, and that I s. with God.
W-pI...183.1:4 His brothers s. his name, and thus are
W-pI. 184.10:2 you; the one Identity which all things s.;
W-pI. 184.11:4 forget they s. the Name of God along with
W-pI...185.3:3 In dreams, no two can s. the same intent.
W-pI. 185.13:4 you can be sure you s. one Will with Him,
W-pI. 185.13:5 you will also know you s. one Will with all
W-pI...188.9:2 line with all the thoughts we s. with God.
W-pI. 188.10:1 from us to all living things that s. our life.
W-pI...194.5:4 made free with him, to s. his holiness.
W-pI...195.5:4 awareness of the unity we s. with them, as
W-pI...195.5:4 share with them, as they must s. with us.
W-pII ..... 1.5:3 God. Now must you s. His function, and
W-pII ..... 2.4:2 Here we s. our final dream. It is a dream
W-pII .231.2:2 And you s. this will with me, and with the
W-pII .239.2:2 *And we honor it, because You s. it with us.*
W-pII .245.2:3 we s. the Word that He has given unto us
W-pII .254.1:4 *Your Will, which I would s. with You today.*
W-pII .264.1:5 *and nothing is that does not s. its holiness;*
W-pII .269.2:2 We s. one vision, as we look upon the face
W-pII ..... 6.1:2 He is the Self we s., uniting us with one
W-pII .291.1:6 to recognize it is a holiness in which we s.;
W-pII .312.1:6 s. Christ's Love for what he looks upon.

W-pII ... 11.2:3 and must therefore s. in power to create.
W-pII . 328.2:4 *And happily I s. that Will which You, my*
W-pII . 330.2:2 *fail to know our one Identity we s. with You.*
W-pII . 331.2:1 us that God's Will is One, and that we s. it
W-pII . 339.2:2 *accepting only Thoughts You s. with me.*
W-pII . 344.1:4 *be. Who can s. a dream? And what can an*
W-pII . 346.1:2 *the day I s. with You as I will share eternity,*
W-pII . 346.1:2 *the day I share with You as I will s. eternity,*
W-pII . 348.1:3 *except the perfect peace and joy I s. with You*
W-pII ... 14.4:4 brothers, asking them to s. our peace and
W-pII . 353.1:1 *best will serve the purpose that I s. with Him.*
M-2 ........... 5:7 same course s. one interest and one goal.
M-4 ..... V.1:15 joyous it is to s. the purpose of salvation!
M-12 ......... 1:8 Thus does he s. God's Will, and bring His
M-12 ......... 2:6 in one purpose, and one they s. with God,
M-12 ......... 4:6 God appear to s. the illusion of separation
M-16 ......... 1:6 who s. that role with him will find him, so
C-5............ 6:7 if you will s. your pains and joys with him
C-5........... 6:11 *to s. the resurrection of God's Son. And*
C-6............ 2:3 therefore given him and he will s. it with
P-2......... II.6:6 is, but they must s. it wholly to succeed. It
P-2......... II.6:7 to s. a goal not blessed by Christ, for what
P-2......... II.8:4 one must s. one goal with someone else,
P-2......... V.7:5 who seems to s. our dream of sickness.
P-3 ....... III.4:3 is a right the therapist and patient s. alike.
S-1 ......... in.1:2 the single voice Creator and creation s.;
S-1 ......... in.1:7 The Love They s. is what all prayer will be
S-1 ........ IV.1:1 at least begins, one cannot s. in prayer.
S-1 ........ IV.1:4 Enemies do not s. a goal. It is in this their
S-1 ........ IV.2:5 thus set up but an illusion of a goal you s..
S-1 ......... V.2:1 s. a dwelling place where they can meet.
S-1 ....... V.3:11 pray only for what you truly s. with him.
S-3 ........ IV.1:2 sight their brothers s. their healing and
S-3 ........ IV.1:6 And these they s. because they know that
S-3 ........ IV.3:3 to s. with Him creation's holy joy. Do not

## shared 86

T-1......... V.3:1 all talents will be s. by all the Sons of God.
T-5........... I.7:1 Spirit, the s. Inspiration of all the Sonship
T-5........ III.2:2 Being thought, the idea gains as it is s..
T-5........ IV.3:2 It is s. *because* it is loving. Sharing is God's
T-5...... IV.3:10 making them, too, worthy of being s..
T-5........ VI.7:1 that ideas increase only by being s.. The
T-5........ VI.7:2 emphasizes that vengeance cannot be s..
T-6......... I.12:1 cannot be s. because it is the symbol of
T-6......... II.5:2 perfection is s. He recognizes it in others,
T-6...... V.A.3:2 is real, because only the mind can be s..
T-6...... V.A.5:6 be communicated; and therefore can be s.
T-7......... I.7:15 is fully s. be withheld and then revealed?
T-7...... III.1:11 I did. It was created to be s., and therefore
T-7....... V.11:2 mind we share is s. by all our brothers,
T-7...... VIII.3:2 be projected because it cannot be s.. Any
T-7........ XI.7:7 Because God s. His Being with you, you
T-7........ XI.7:8 all He created, to know what they have s..
T-8........ IX.7:2 name alone, for ours is a s. identification.
T-9........ IV.1:6 Remember always that your Identity is s.,
T-9......... V.2:1 said that beliefs of the ego cannot be s.,
T-9........ VI.4:7 His Son, for knowledge is s. with God.
T-9...... VIII.8:4 attest to pride because pride is not s.. God
T-11...... IV.5:8 glory is s. and They are glorified together.
T-12.... VIII.7:2 Son can be seen because his vision is s..
T-13....... V.1:7 make up a private world that cannot be s.
T-13...... VI.8:3 unbroken because it is wholly s.. God's
T-13..... X.2:10 It is not s., and so it is not real.
T-13...... XI.4:1 for nothing in this world is wholly s..
T-13...... XI.4:2 you what is capable of being wholly s.. It
T-14......... I.4:6 the task of sharing what cannot be s.. And
T-14..... V.11:6 him. Holiness must be s., for therein lies
T-14...... VI.1:7 value, for what is hidden cannot be s.,
T-14....... X.2:1 In Heaven reality is s. and not reflected.
T-14..... X.12:5 already learned that this Identity is s..
T-15....... I.12:2 the instant of holiness is s., and cannot be
T-15...... VI.3:1 All separation vanishes as holiness is s..
T-15..... VII.8:5 is private, and only the body can be s..
T-16......... I.1:2 relationship in which the suffering is s..
T-16......... I.5:9 and His perception, to be s. through you.
T-16...... III.6:8 from the conviction you s. with them.
T-17..... V.12:5 enable its results to be accepted and s.. To
T-18 ........ I.9:2 nothing can be s. but only substituted,
T-18 ... VI.10:2 yourself, to reach your s. Identity together
T-20 ..... VI.2:5 be known, completely understood and s..
T-20 ... VIII.3:2 s. with the Holy Spirit and at one with
T-23 ..... IV.8:5 same, eternally complete and wholly s..
T-24 ........ I.6:4 in specialness; his friend in a s. purpose.
T-24 VII.10:10 witness to His Love and s. His purpose, so
T-25 ....... II.8:8 seeing is the vision s. that looks on Christ
T-27 ..... II.11:6 would mean a s. identity with but one end
T-27 ..... II.15:2 when it is fulfilled as s., it must correct
T-27 ..... II.15:4 is divided purpose, which can not be s.,
T-27 ..... II.16:4 that its Giver keeps *because* it has been s..
T-28 ..... V.1:11 exist because God s. His Will with you,
T-29 ........ I.3:9 your brother but s. a qualified entente, in
T-29 ..... III.2:2 He made weak because He s. His Love?
T-29 ..... V.8:2 When dreams are s. they lose the function
T-30 ...... I.17:2 the joy they asked for will be wholly s..
T-30 ...... V.5:1 yet completely s. and perfectly fulfilled.
T-30 .... V.11:3 But when they joined and s. a purpose,
T-30 .... VII.4:2 In this s. purpose is one judgment shared
T-30 .... VII.4:2 In this shared purpose is one judgment s.
T-30 .. VII.6:17 Only dreams of pardon can be s.. They
W-pI..... 14.6:3 Some of them are s. illusions, and others
W-pI..... 54.3:3 mad idea of separation had to be s. before
W-pI..... 54.5:2 Recognizing the s. nature of my thoughts,
W-pI..... 92.5:7 Its strength is s., that it may bring to all
W-pI... 99.12:2 to be s. with Him Who shares God's plan
W-pI... 100.1:3 One function s. by separate minds unites
W-pI... 127.4:2 is your own, and s. by God Himself. For
W-pI... 129.4:4 is direct and wholly s. and wholly one.
W-pI... 137.8:3 Healing is s.. And by this attribute it
WpI. rIV.in6:1 you alone, for they will all be s. with Him.
W-pI... 158.2:7 Experience cannot be s. directly, in the
W-pI. 166.15:7 He has s. His joy with you. And now you
W-pI... 184.5:3 and concepts can be meaningfully s..
W-pI... 187.5:4 Thoughts extend as they are s., for they
W-pII . 283.2:1 Now are we One in s. Identity, with God
W-pII . 319.2:4 *could be the Will my Self has s. with You?*
W-pII . 329.2:2 are one because His Will is s. by all of us.
W-pII ... 14.2:2 I, we found a single purpose that we s..
Wfl........ in.4:2 So let us not forget our goal is s., for it is
M-17 ......... 3:2 and pupil, who have s. in one intent.
C-5 ........... 4:3 you owe him this who s. your dreams that
C-5 ........... 5:5 be his vision, for the eyes of Christ are s..
S-1........... I.7:6 can be s. because it receives for everyone.

## shares 86

T-2 ....... IV.3:6 s. the invulnerability of the Atonement to
T-4 ....... VI.6:4 The Holy One s. my trust, and accepts my
T-5 ....... III.2:5 The idea of the Holy Spirit s. the property
T-7 .......... I.6:1 is to share the perfect Love He s. with you
T-7 ....... IX.2:4 is part of Him and s. His Being with Him.
T-8 ......... II.3:4 you, because He s. His Will with you. His
T-8 ....... III.2:7 You share them as God s. them, because
T-9 ....... VI.3:9 is part of you and s. His glory with you.
T-10 ..... III.4:3 that creation s. power and never usurps it
T-10 .... V.14:1 because love s. and arrogance withholds.
T-11 ....... I.11:3 He s. His Will with you; He does not
T-11 ...... IV.8:1 wills to share as his Father s. it with him.
T-11 ...... V.6:2 on God, Whose function He s. with you.
T-12 .... VII.4:8 God s. His function with you in Heaven,
T-12 .... VII.4:8 the Holy Spirit s. His with you on earth.
T-13 ........ I.1:1 Holy Spirit s. the goal of all good teachers
T-14 ........ I.3:4 he s. with God are beyond his belief, but
T-14 ... IV.10:3 because only He s. the knowledge of what
T-14 .... VII.7:6 has one purpose which He s. with you.
T-14 ... VIII.1:8 for He s. with God the promise that was
T-14 ... VIII.2:1 He s. it still, for you. Everything that
T-14 ..... X.6:11 in it, and that is also why everyone s. in it.
T-14 ..... XI.4:4 power, which He s. so gladly with His Son
T-15 .. V.10:10 For Christ is the Self the Sonship s., as
T-15 .. V.10:10 shares, as God s. His Self with Christ.
T-16 ..... III.7:4 teacher in gratitude, and s. it with him.
T-17 ..... IV.2:6 the holy relationship s. God's purpose,
T-17 .... VII.8:8 entered any situation that s. Its purpose.
T-17 .. VII.8:13 s. the purpose of your whole relationship,
T-17 .. VII.10:4 relationship s. the Holy Spirit's goal are
T-18 ...... V.3:9 the means to anyone who s. His purpose.
T-19 ........ I.2:4 And since He s. it He has given it, and so
T-20 ..... IV.6:6 Spirit's plan, now that it s. His purpose.
T-20 ....... V.1:8 No one who s. his purpose with him can
T-20 ....... V.8:2 and s. his Father's certainty the universe
T-21 ....... V.6:3 a part of you that knows His Will and s. it
T-21 ..... VI.1:8 And if he s. this same belief you both will
T-24 ..... VI.5:6 in everything that lives and s. His Being.
T-24 .... VII.5:7 as means for truth s. in its holiness, and
T-25 ........ I.5:4 in the part of you that s. His Father's Will.
T-25 ..... II.9:11 offered to everyone who s. His purpose. It
T-25 .. VII.12:8 because it s. the function of the whole.
T-25 ... VIII.6:2 must believe He s. their own confusion,
T-25 . VIII.12:5 may smile on you whose sinlessness He s..
T-27 ..... VI.1:5 What s. a common purpose is the same.
T-28 ...... I.12:4 And His Creator s. His thanks, because
T-28 ..... III.9:5 before His Son, and s. it equally with him.
T-28 ..... IV.5:5 s. a dream must be the dream he shares,
T-28 ..... IV.5:5 shares a dream must be the dream he s.,
T-28 ....... V.1:7 Who s. in them can never share in Him.
T-28 ....... V.6:1 it s. the function all creation shares. It is
T-28 ....... V.6:1 it shares the function all creation s.. It is
T-28 ..... VI.6:8 the Will of God, Whose promises he s..
T-28 .... VII.7:8 because it s. your Father's Will with you.
T-30 ....... II.5:2 he s. your freedom as he shares your will.
T-30 ....... II.5:2 he shares your freedom as he s. your will.
T-30 ... III.2:11 because what s. in all creation cannot be
W-pI .... 28.5:3 the purpose it s. with all the universe.
W-pI .... 29.2:4 that a table s. the purpose of the universe.
W-pI .... 29.2:5 And what s. the purpose of the universe
W-pI .... 29.2:5 the universe s. the purpose of its Creator.
W-pI .... 43.3:3 is real to the extent to which it s. the Holy
W-pI .... 45.2:2 thoughts with Him, as He s. His with you.
W-pI .... 58.2:3 see in its light s. in the joy it brings to me.
W-pI .... 65.4:4 it consistently for the purpose He s. with
W-pI .. 66.10:4 For God Himself s. it with us. Today's
W-pI .... 73.3:2 the Will the Son of God s. with his Father
W-pI .... 97.2:3 Himself, and s. His function as Creator.
W-pI .... 99.9:8 turn to Him Who s. your function here,
W-pI .. 99.12:2 with Him Who s. God's plan with you.
W-pI 132.12:3 God s. His Fatherhood with you who are
WpI..rIV.in2:6 thoughts can dwell but those his Father s.
W-pI .. 156.3:3 because what s. His life is part of Holiness
W-pI 158.11:2 accurate its image s. its unseen holiness;
W-pI .. 167.1:5 because what God created s. His life.
W-pI .. 186.9:3 is changeless s. His attributes with His
W-pII . 239.1:3 He s. His glory any trace of sin and guilt?
W-pII ... 10.4:1 return to the eternal peace He s. with him
W-pII . 319.2:2 *the goal which stems from it s. its totality.*
W-pII ... 11.2:3 Thus His Son s. in creation, and must
W-pII ... 11.5:2 Whose Holiness His Own creation s.;
W-pII . 341.1:2 *smiles back on You, and s. Your Holiness.*
C-5 ........... 4:4 And s. them still, to be at one with you.
P-2........ III.2:5 one at the beginning, and as the other s. it
S-1.......... V.2:6 purity it recognizes that it s. with him.
S-2.......... II.3:3 that here is one whose sinfulness he s.,

## sharing 66

T-4 ...... VII.5:2 Nothing real can be increased except by s.
T-4 ...... VII.5:4 Divine Abstraction takes joy in s.. That is
T-5 ........ in.3:5 are beautiful enough to hold it by s. it. It
T-5 .......... I.7:2 that s. it involves anything but gain.
T-5 ....... II.11:1 by s. my decision and making it stronger.
T-5 ... III.11:10 Name by s. it to increase His joy in you.
T-5 ..... IV.2:11 must be understood as a pure act of s..
T-5 ....... IV.3:3 S. is God's way of creating, and also yours
T-5 ....... IV.5:2 the s. of ideas and the recognition that to
T-6 ........ I.12:1 the symbol of s. because the reawakening
T-6 ....... III.1:9 in yourself because you are s. it. Every
T-6 ..... V.A.5:5 is s. it becomes communion. Perhaps you
T-7 ......... II.2:1 yourself by s. the Holy Spirit with him.
T-7 ....... V.6:15 Who created you by s. His Being with you
T-7 ..... VIII.1:6 Holy Spirit, it is the fundamental law of s.
T-7 ..... IX.2:9 Created by s., its will is to create. It does
T-7 ......... X.6:6 S. His Will with me is not really open to
T-7 ......... X.8:5 is. Being a lesson in s. it is a lesson in love,
T-7 ....... XI.7:6 Being is known by s.. Because God shared
T-8 ......... V.3:2 His power to you because we are s. it. I
T-8 ..... VI.5:14 because its value lies in God's s. Himself

T-9........IV.1:6 is shared, and that Its s. is Its reality.
T-9........IV.3:1 The Atonement is a lesson in s., which is
T-10......IV.6:3 to Him, for to Him ownership is s.. And if
T-10....... V.5:6 If creation is s., it cannot create what is
T-11...... I.11:5 must share it to know it, for s. *is* knowing.
T-11......IV.8:3 S. the perfect Love of the Father the Son
T-11......VI.9:6 Redemption is recognized only by s. it.
T-11. VIII.5:10 believe that asking is taking rather than s.
T-12... VIII.1:5 For if love is s., how can you find it except
T-13.........I.1:2 this, for s. the Father's Love for His Son,
T-13......IV.6:8 be meeting no one, and the s. of salvation
T-13......XI.4:3 It can also show you the results of s.,
T-13......XI.4:3 you still remember the results of not s..
T-14.........I.4:6 the task of s. what cannot be shared. And
T-14......III.3:8 *guiltlessness by making it manifest and s. it.*
T-14........VII.h S. Perception with the Holy Spirit
T-14.....VII.7:3 S. perception with Him Whom God has
T-14....... X.2:2 By s. its reflection here, its truth becomes
T-14...... X.12:6 The miracle becomes the means of s. It.
T-15......VI.3:2 For holiness is power, and by s. it, it gains
T-15......VI.4:4 so your faith in Him is strengthened by s..
T-16.........I.1:7 into it, and lighten it by s. the delusion.
T-16.........I.2:4 increase itself by s. what is like itself.
T-18.........I.9:2 and s. and substituting have nothing in
T-20......IV.4:3 s. their power according to the Will of
T-25......IV.2:7 s. his Father's purpose in his own creation
T-26...VII.11:5 became your function, s. it with God. It is
T-27.....VII.4:2 those within the world are joined in s..
T-28...... I.11:4 Born out of s., there can be no pause in
T-28......III.3:3 him to his own dream by s. it with him.
T-28......III.9:6 in Their s. there can be no gap in which
T-28......IV.5:5 shares, because by s. is a cause produced.
T-28......IV.7:6 from his brother who, by s. not his dream
T-28....... V.1:8 who withdraws his mind from s. them *is*
T-28....... V.1:8 his mind from sharing them *is* s. Him.
T-28....... V.2:1 s. of the evil dreams of hate and malice,
W-pI.....54.3:4 Yet that s. was a sharing of nothing. I can
W-pI.....54.3:4 Yet that sharing was a s. of nothing. I can
W-pI...123.6:4 will bless your gifts by s. them with you.
W-pI...162.4:3 kept complete because its s. is unlimited.
W-pI.185.10:7 would you not avail yourself of it by s. it?
W-pI...197.9:6 s. with Him the holy Thoughts of God.
M-6............3:6 in fact, it is the part that makes s. possible
P-2......... II.5:3 Yet if pupil and teacher join in s. one goal,
P-3...... III.6:11 more. In s., everyone must gain a blessing

## sharp

*See* sharp-edged, sharp-pointed

## sharp-edged 1

W-pII......4.5:2 we not put away these s. children's toys?

## sharp-pointed 1

W-pI...189.5:4 a fearful world, held cruelly in death's s.,

## sharpened 1

W-pI.....76.3:3 a s. needle will ward off disease and death

## sharply 2

T-20....... II.4:6 whose points gleam s. in a blood-red light
M-27..........5:4 of illusions becomes more s. evident.

## shatter 3

T-6......IV.12:7 It could not s. the peace of God, but it
T-6......IV.12:7 the peace of God, but it could s. *yours.*
T-18.........I.5:6 to s. knowledge into meaningless bits of

## shattered 5

T-13....III.10:5 And the peace of God's Son was s., for he
T-18...... I.12:2 echo of the original error that s. Heaven.
T-21.....VII.1:8 protect his unity or see him s. and slain
T-27....... V.3:4 bring, the broken bodies and the s. limbs,
W-pII..226.2:3 *in a place of vain desires and of s. dreams,*

## shattering 1

T-31....... V.9:1 distress, there is no s. of what was learned

## shatters 1

M-4 .... III.1:10 Judgment destroys honesty and s. trust.

## shed 3

T-26...... IX.4:6 and the insane have s. their garments of
W-pI.127.11:2 s. its blessing upon all who come to learn
W-pII..301.1:6 *And all the tears I s. will be forgotten, for*

## sheds 4

T-3...........I.7:2 harmlessness and s. only blessing. It
T-4.........I.12:3 radiance and gladly s. its light everywhere
W-pI...157.2:2 fresh experience that s. a light on all that
W-pII..245.1:3 *It s. its light on everyone I meet. I bring it to*

## shell 2

T-1........IV.2:9 it perceives an empty s. and is unaware of
T-1......... V.1:4 can make an empty s., but you cannot

## shelter 13

T19..IV.C.10:9 everyone who gives him s. will follow him
T-20... VIII.4:6 is a better home, a safer s. for God's Son?
T-22.........I.9:8 in each the other saw a perfect s. where
T-23...... III.6:8 Not one tree left still standing will s. you.
T-25...... III.3:5 the perfect s. for illusions which it would
T-28.....VII.3:4 straw, and count on it as s. from the wind
T-28.....VII.7:6 the safety of this s. and its Source? From
T-31....... V.3:1 the love and s. innocence deserves. And
W-pI.137.12:1 Would you not offer s. to God's Will?
W-pI...160.4:5 by? There is no home can s. love and fear.
W-pI...182.4:2 childhood of your body, and its place of s.
W-pI...183.2:2 and s. you from every worldly thought
M-28 .........4:5 now remain on earth to s. sick illusions,

## sheltered 4

T-13.....VII.3:2 The homes you built have never s. you.
T-26...... IX.7:3 s. him from bitter winter and the freezing
W-pI...199.1:4 firmly tied to it and s. by its presence. If
W-pI...199.3:4 the illusion that has s. it from being found

## sheltering 1

P-2........ VI.1:3 to guilt, its hugging-close and s., its loving

## shelters 1

T-22.......in.2:8 under a common roof that s. neither; in

## shield 8

T-31.....VII.7:1 The concept of the self stands like a s., a
W-pI.....78.1:2 Each grievance stands like a dark s. of
W-pI.....78.2:3 We will not wait before the s. of hate, but
W-pI.138.10:1 from its protective s. of unawareness, and
W-pI...156.4:4 extend their arms to s. you from the heat,
W-pI.182.11:1 to lay aside your s. which profits nothing,
M-17 .........5:9 and make himself a s. to keep him safe
M-27 .........3:2 it from awareness like a s. held up to

## shielded 1

W-pI...136.5:2 decision which is doubly s. by oblivion.

## shielding 1

W-pI...136.8:1 sickness can succeed in s. you from truth?

## shields 1

W-pI...190.4:5 feared than the insane illusions which it s.

## shift 56

T-1..........II.6:3 a sudden s. from horizontal to vertical
T-2...... VI.5:10 the behavioral level can s. the error from
T-5...........I.7:6 occurs to produce a real qualitative s..
T-5..........II.1:3 because it is very similar to the s. in the
T-8......VIII.2:7 to s. ceaselessly from one goal to another,
T-9.......VII.4:7 it will s. abruptly from suspiciousness to
T-9......VIII.6:6 Being the level of s., it is experienced as
T-13...... XI.6:1 not remember change and s. in Heaven.
T-15....... V.4:2 is why they s. and change so frequently.
T-15....... IX.1:2 It is this s. to vision that is accomplished
T-15....... IX.1:3 for you to learn just what this s. entails, so
T-15........X.4:2 but one s. in perception that is necessary,
T-17....... V.4:1 extremely intense with this s. in goals. For
T-17....... V.5:1 not be kinder to s. the goal more slowly,
T-17....... V.5:2 Only a radical s. in purpose could induce
T-17..... VII.2:2 no s. in any aspect of the problem but will
T-17..... VII.2:3 if you s. part of the problem elsewhere the
T-18...... VI.5:2 you not welcome and support the s. from
T-18...... IX.7:3 forms appear and s. from loveliness to the
T-20...... III.1:2 adjustment is a change; a s. in perception,
T-20...... III.1:4 is lost if any s. or change is undertaken.
T-21..... VII.4:5 enemy, but this will s. even as it attacks,
T-21.......VIII.h The Inner S.
T-22...... VI.3:5 as easy as is the s. from hate to gratitude
T-24...... IV.2:9 and body states must s. accordingly. Of
T-24.... IV.3:10 s. in purpose does "endanger" specialness
T-26... VII.14:2 cause can merely s. effects to other forms.
T-27........II.9:6 to prevent a s. of balance in the sacrifice.
T-27...... VI.2:9 Sin's witnesses but s. from name to name,
T-29........II.6:6 s. and change become the law on which
T-30..... VII.5:5 makes perception s. and meaning change.
T-30..... VII.7:2 It will s. in what it stands for, and you will
T-31..... V.16:3 be some confusion every time there is a s.,
T-31..... VII.5:3 all this s. requires is that you be willing
W-pI..... 12.2:4 Do not allow the time of the s. to become
W-pI..... 33.1:1 you can s. your perception of the world in
W-pI..... 92.7:6 It does not s. from night to day, and back
W-pI... 107.4:2 It does not s. and alter in its form, nor
W-pI... 107.6:1 does not come and go nor s. nor change,
W-pI... 128.7:3 on the world will s. by just a little, every
W-pI... 140.8:1 all illusions, not another s. among them.
W-pI... 181.2:4 Your vision now will s., to give support to
W-pI... 185.3:5 both. Loser and gainer merely s. about in
W-pI... 185.9:7 which s. and change with every step you
W-pI... 196.7:3 Until this s. has been accomplished, you
M-4 .........I.2:4 is it that induces them to make the s.?
M-4 ..... I.A.3:5 point at which he can make the s. entirely
M-5 .......... II.h The S. in Perception
M-5 ........II.3:1 single requisite for this s. in perception?
M-12 ......... 6:7 dream figures come and go, s. and change
M-23 .........7:5 must s. and change to suit the need. Jesus
C-1.............7:4 and awareness can s. quite dramatically,
C-3............. 6:5 But illusions s. from place to place; from
C-3............. 6:6 to time. The final step is also but a s.. As a
C-4............. 6:1 This is the s. that true perception brings:
P-2...... IV.11:7 Given this single s., all else will follow.

## shifted 5

T-10.........I.2:6 you merely s. from one dream to another,
T-17....... V.2:6 the relationship is abruptly s. to the exact
T-21..... V.10:2 Faith and belief have s., and you have
T-22.......in.4:3 is the faith in differences s. to sameness.
W-pI... 132.2:2 it. Now the source of thought has s., for to

## shifting 24

T-3......... V.7:7 reorganizing, s. and changing. Evaluation
T-8......VIII.2:2 of s. its allegiance from one to the other,
T-9....... VII.3:6 perceives because its perceptions are so s.
T-9......VIII.6:6 it is experienced as s. and extremes are its
T-14...... IX.6:2 seems to lie only in s. interpretations,
T-18.........I.7:7 in s. and totally meaningless patterns that
T-22.........I.6:7 s. ones he sees about him will become to

T-22...... III.4:7 its heavy anchor in the **s.** world it made;
T-24...... IV.5:2 Only this is certain in this **s.** world that
T-24....... V.4:2 unlit but by the **s.** tiny gleams that spark
T-26..... V.11:4 Now you are **s.** back and forth between
T-30..... VII.2:7 with every meaning **s.** as they change.
T-31..... V.13:5 main advantage of the **s.** to the second
W-pI..... 12.2:3 Try to pace yourself so that the slow **s.** of
W-pI..... 25.6:7 without **s.** your eyes from the subject
W-pI..... 33.1:4 but without an abrupt sense of **s.**.
W-pI. 122.13:3 world of **s.** change and bleak appearances
W-pI... 131.7:1 ways; its **s.** patterns and uncertain goals,
W-pI... 185.7:6 the eternal in the place of **s.** dreams which
W-pI... 186.8:3 Our self-made roles are **s.**, and they seem
W-pI... 192.7:4 in mists of **s.** dreams and fearful thoughts
W-pI. 200.11:5 to replace our **s.** goals and solitary dreams
M-8 ........... 1:2 on uneven background and **s.** foreground
S-3........ IV.3:6 you for **s.** dreams within a sorry world?

## shifts 12

T-1......... I.17:2 They are sudden **s.** into invisibility, away
T-9...... VIII.2:9 It **s.** to viciousness when you decide not to
T-14....... X.5:2 It **s.** unceasingly across the mirror of your
T-17....... II.4:3 will ever change; no **s.** nor shadings, no
T-21... VII.13:1 changing form that **s.** with time and place
T-27...... VI.2:1 Sin **s.** from pain to pleasure, and again to
T-30..... VII.1:8 and every meaning **s.** accordingly.
T-31..... V.12:3 This **s.** the concept of the self from what is
W-pI... 152.5:2 false. And that includes all **s.** in feeling,
W-pI... 186.8:5 as we experience a thousand **s.** in mood,
S-3......... II.5:8 What but **s.** illusions has done nothing.
S-3........ III.2:7 **s.** and change are what the dream is made

## shimmering 3

T-15...... IV.1:8 stands in **s.** readiness for your acceptance.
W-pII .... in.9:5 The memory of God is **s.** across the wide
W-pII . 252.1:2 **s.** and perfect purity is far more brilliant

## shine 79

T-3....... VII.6:3 will **s.** from the true Foundation of life,
T-4........ III.2:5 ego has set up and can **s.** into your mind.
T-4........ IV.9:3 Then let the Holy One **s.** on you in peace,
T-4........ IV.9:5 shines on you and must **s.** through you.
T-4........ IV.9:6 prevent you from letting Him **s.** through
T-6....... II.12:8 it must **s.** outward to make you aware of it
T-7....... V.11:3 your mind **s.** with mine upon their minds,
T-7....... V.11:4 This light will **s.** back upon you and on
T-7........ XI.3:3 it protect his peace and **s.** love upon him?
T-8...... IV.2:10 not attack darkness, but it does **s.** it away.
T-8...... IV.2:11 you everywhere, you **s.** it away with me.
T-8....... V.2:10 of God **s.** upon you by your acceptance of
T-9......... II.5:9 This light can **s.** into yours, giving truth
T-10...... IV.7:5 power of one mind can **s.** into another,
T-12....... II.1:7 light in another mind must **s.** into theirs
T-12....... II.9:8 He cannot **s.** away what you keep hidden,
T-12..... VI.7:3 it. Very gently does God **s.** upon Himself,
T-12.... VIII.5:2 memory of God cannot **s.** in a mind that
T-13......... I.7:6 Let the holiness of God's Son **s.** away the
T-13..... V.11:7 the beauty of the world to **s.** upon them.
T-13...... VI.7:5 to **s.** on you *because you called them forth.*
T-13...... VI.9:1 **S.** on your brothers in remembrance of
T-13.... VI.10:5 and in their joy they **s.** with holy thanks.
T-13.... VI.11:9 those you brought with you will **s.** on you,
T-13.... VI.11:9 will **s.** on them in gratitude because they
T-13... VII.13:7 for light needs nothing but to **s.** in peace,
T-13...... X.14:2 together we **s.** with brightness so intense
T-14....... II.4:3 into the darkness, and lets it **s.** on you.
T-14....... V.4:5 but **s.** away the heavy veils of guilt within
T-14...... IX.5:6 it. God will **s.** upon it of Himself. Only the
T-15...... IV.9:9 Let the Holy Spirit's purity **s.** them away,
T-17.... IV.13:5 each senseless stone that seems to **s.** from
T-18...... III.8:7 to **s.** away the past and so make room for
T-18.... VIII.9:1 inside and **s.** upon the barren ground. See
T-19.... III.10:2 will **s.** upon him, in glad acknowledgment
T-20....... II.5:4 enables Him to see His purpose **s.** forth
T-20....... V.4:4 What is in him will **s.** so brightly in your
T-21...... IV.6:7 trinkets still seem to **s.** and catch your eye
T-22 ..... IV.3:7 and **s.** from it into a darkened world that
T-23 ...... in.6:4 forgiveness will the world sparkle and **s.**,
T-24 .... VII.4:8 around him, that the truth may **s.** on him,
T-25 ....... II.9:8 all His thanks and gladness **s.** on you who
T-26 ........ I.8:4 that he may come forth to **s.** on you, and
T-26 ....... II.7:7 will **s.** away all memory of sacrifice and
T-26 ..... IX.5:3 that light may **s.** on it and leave no space
T-27 ...... V.6:4 but **s.** in thanks to you who blessing gave.
T-29 ... VIII.5:6 veil, and lets the truth **s.** unencumbered,
T-30 ..... III.8:1 are far beyond all change, and **s.** forever.
T-30 ..... III.8:6 still and white and lovely will it **s.** through
T-31 .. VII.13:7 face of Christ to **s.** upon the one who asks,
T-31 . VIII.12:7 Your likeness does the light **s.** forth from
W-pI..... 58.2:5 holiness of the world **s.** forth for everyone
W-pI..... 81.2:3 *light of the world **s.** through this appearance*
W-pI..... 85.2:3 *The light of the world will **s.** all this away. I*
W-pI... 95.13:3 let It **s.** away all your illusions and your
W-pI..... 99.9:1 **s.** through them to join them to the rest.
W-pI... 127.9:4 will **s.** through your idle thoughts today,
W-pI... 129.8:1 to **s.** upon your eyelids as you rest beyond
W-pI. 135.18:3 blessing **s.** in every step you ever took.
WpI. rIV.in7:4 Let each word **s.** with the meaning God
W-pI. 153.20:4 love and strength and peace that **s.** from
W-pI... 157.1:3 is a time Heaven has set apart to **s.** upon,
W-pI. 158.10:5 chance to let Christ's vision **s.** on you, and
W-pI... 165.2:7 Eternity and everlasting life **s.** in your
W-pI. 187.10:5 we see the purity of Heaven **s.** in our
W-pI... 188.4:4 blessing does the light in you **s.** brighter,
W-pI... 188.8:4 God is shining in you, it must **s.** on them.
W-pI. 188.10:7 *Let all things **s.** upon me in that peace, And*
W-pI... 191.9:4 accord it mercy, will its mercy **s.** on you.
W-pI... 193.2:5 to let the light of Heaven **s.** upon it. It is
W-pII . 232.1:1 *and **s.** on me throughout the day today. Let*
W-pII . 237.1:2 to **s.** upon the world throughout the day. I
W-pII . 243.2:3 *memory, and truth must **s.** in all of us as one.*
W-pII . 258.1:3 to allow God's grace to **s.** in unawareness,
W-pII . 332.1:8 the light **s.** through the dream of darkness
W-pII . 333.1:4 the truth can **s.** upon it as it disappears.
W-pII . 333.2:1 *chose to **s.** away all conflict and all doubt,*
W-pII . 336.1:5 Its lilies **s.** into the mind, and call it to
M-16 ..... 11:11 light can **s.** again on an untroubled mind.

## shined 3

T-18 ...... I.11:2 the truth in you, and love has **s.** upon you,
W-pII ..... 2.5:2 are done, eternity has **s.** away the world,
S-3........ IV.2:5 earth an instant, as the world is **s.** away.

## shines 90

T-4 ....... IV.9:1 in which God Himself **s.** in perfect light.
T-4 ....... IV.9:5 still **s.** on you and must shine through you
T-6 ....... II.12:8 The great peace of the Kingdom **s.** in your
T-6 ........ V.4:5 merely **s.** them away. His light is always
T-7 ....... XI.5:2 Its own radiance **s.** all around it, and
T-11 ..... III.4:7 always surrounds you and **s.** out from you
T-11 ..... III.5:2 and gave him the light that **s.** in him. You
T-11 ..... IV.7:4 lives in His Creator and **s.** with His glory.
T-12 ....... II.2:1 The light in them **s.** as brightly regardless
T-12 ..... VI.7:2 and the spirit of God's Son **s.** in the Mind
T-12 ... VIII.4:7 memory **s.** in your mind and cannot be
T-13 ........ I.5:6 the brightness of his purity **s.** untouched
T-13 ..... VI.8:8 holy light that **s.** forth from God's Son is
T-13 ... VI.11:3 it **s.** forth to call you from the world and
T-13 .... VII.1:7 Nothing is there but **s.**, and shines forever
T-13 .... VII.1:7 Nothing is there but shines, and **s.** forever
T-13 .... VII.7:3 The world about him **s.** with love because
T-14 ....... II.4:4 you. And as it **s.** your brothers see it, and
T-14 ....... II.7:7 The key is only the light that **s.** away the
T-14 ..... VI.4:2 light of guiltlessness **s.** guilt away because
T-14 ... VIII.1:4 of the power of God that **s.** in you. Banish
T-14 . VIII.2:10 is safe within you, where the Holy Spirit **s.**
T-14 . VIII.2:11 He **s.** not in division, but in the meeting
T-14 ..... IX.5:1 Holiness of your Creator **s.** forth from you
T-14 ..... IX.6:5 and the message that **s.** forth from what
T-14 ..... IX.7:2 image of holiness that **s.** in your mind is
T-14 ..... XI.4:4 it. This lesson **s.** with God's glory, for in it
T-17 ..... IV.8:4 The glitter of blood **s.** like rubies, and the
T-17 ... IV.16:6 It **s.** in every part of Him, as in the whole.
T-17 ... IV.16:8 holy instant **s.** alike on all relationships,
T-17 .... VII.8:9 of truth **s.** from the center of the situation
T-18 ..... III.8:2 Not one Ray that **s.** forever in the Mind of
T-18 ..... III.8:2 forever in the Mind of God but **s.** on you.
T-20 ....... II.5:6 **s.** on everything He looks upon and loves.
T-20 ..... IV.2:5 is, and what is yours **s.** from him to you.
T-20 ..... IV.7:4 the face of Christ **s.** on them and they
T-20 ... VI.10:3 and love **s.** on it with the gentle smile and
T-22 ..... VI.5:6 the eternal light you bring, **s.** now on you.
T-22 ... VI.15:1 your brother **s.** throughout the universe,
T-23 ...... in.5:7 and realize that Heaven's glory **s.** on him?
T-23 ...... I.12:9 Yet far beyond this senseless war it **s.**,
T-23 ..... IV.8:4 and only love **s.** upon them forever. It is
T-24 .... VII.2:1 The memory of God **s.** not alone. What is
T-25 ...... in.3:4 fills it with the Holiness that **s.** from Him.
T-25 ........ I.4:4 Its radiance **s.** through each body that it
T-25 ....... II.7:3 the light that **s.** from it to its Creator.
T-25 ..... III.5:4 obscure the sinlessness that **s.** unchanged
T-25 ..... IV.3:6 long to be remembered as the sun **s.** them
T-26 ..... IV.2:2 see. Each flower **s.** in light, and every bird
T-26 ....... X.6:7 *see injustice, which Their Presence **s.** away.*
T-29 ..... III.3:1 created in the dark, where God still **s.**.
T-29 ..... III.5:2 him, and **s.** on you in gratitude and love.
T-29 ..... III.5:5 light in you must be as bright as **s.** in him.
T-29 ..... III.5:6 This is the spark that **s.** within the dream;
T-29 ....... V.5:2 perfect gift, in whom his Father **s.** forever,
T-30 ....... II.3:8 No light of Heaven **s.** except for you, for it
T-30 ... III.11:9 The star **s.** still; the sky has never changed
T-31 . VIII.11:1 light that **s.** beyond in perfect constancy.
W-pI .... 57.5:4 forgiveness, and **s.** forgiveness back at me
W-pI .... 73.4:3 Heaven, but the light of Heaven **s.** on it.
W-pI .... 73.4:6 that **s.** upon this world reflects your will,
W-pI .... 85.3:7 reflect the light that **s.** in me and in itself.
W-pI .... 92.5:1 and **s.** with light its Source has given it;
W-pI .... 99.8:4 and see how bright this light still **s.** in you
W-pI .. 100.4:2 increases every light that **s.** in Heaven, so
W-pI .. 137.7:1 Just as forgiveness **s.** away all sin and the
W-p! 158.11:2 its likeness **s.** with its immortal love. We
W-pI .. 159.5:3 to obscure the light that **s.** beyond them.
W-pI .. 163.9:2 *of Your Love which **s.** in everything. We live*
W-pI .. 188.1:8 It **s.** in you because it lights your home,
W-pI 188.10:1 that the peace of God still **s.** in us, and
W-pI .. 189.3:5 in which forgiveness **s.** on everything, and
W-pI .. 189.4:2 the quietness and peace that **s.** in them;
W-pI .. 189.9:8 His Love **s.** outward from its home within
W-pI .. 192.3:6 that the light of day already **s.** in them,
W-pI .. 194.5:4 glory **s.** upon a world made free with him,
W-pI .. 207.1:2 *blessing **s.** upon me from within my heart,*
W-pII . 222.1:4 care, and holds in love the Son He **s.** upon
W-pII . 222.1:4 Son He shines upon, who also **s.** on Him.
W-pII . 239.2:1 *You, Father, for the light that **s.** forever in us.*
W-pII ..... 4.4:4 But all the while his Father **s.** on him, and
W-pII . 265.1:4 celestial gentleness with which creation **s.**
W-pII .... 285.h My holiness **s.** bright and clear today.
W-pII . 293.1:5 the world **s.** in reflection of its holy light,
W-pII ..... 9.2:3 way, because it **s.** on everything as one.
W-pII . 320.1:4 because his Father **s.** upon his mind, and
M-17 ......... 3:7 From there it **s.** into his pupil's mind,
M-23 ......... 5:8 eyes Christ's vision **s.** in perfect constancy
M-28 ......... 2:5 of God **s.** unimpeded across the world.
S-3........ IV.2:3 Forgiveness **s.** its merciful reprieve upon

## shining 83

T-4 ....... IV.8:3 and mine can unite in **s.** your ego away,
T-4 ....... IV.9:6 ego cannot prevent Him from **s.** on you,
T-6 ......... V.4:7 Spirit, **s.** with the light from God Himself,
T-13 ..... V.10:5 **s.** in perfect radiance that is undimmed
T-13 ..... IX.1:8 like a lamp **s.** so brightly that the chain of
T-13 ..... IX.7:6 **s.** in quiet and in peace upon the altar to
T-13 ....... X.9:4 In **s.** peace within you is the perfect purity
T-13 ..... X.10:2 **s.** as steadily and as surely as God Himself
T-13 ..... X.12:2 His **s.** purity, wholly untouched by guilt
T-14 ..... IV.1:3 your brother's guiltlessness **s.** within him
T-14 ....... V.3:3 God that does not share His **s.** innocence.
T-14 ..... IX.7:1 that the reflection of God, **s.** in you, can
T-14 ....... X.6:2 you the **s.** examples of miracles to show
T-15 .... I.15:10 for you, in that **s.** instant of perfect release
T-15 ....... II.5:5 Yet its **s.** and glittering brilliance, which

| | |
|---|---|
| T-15......IX.1:1 | let you see the Great Rays s. from them, |
| T-15......XI.2:2 | yourself, but s. in the Heaven within, and |
| T-17.....V.7:12 | faith emerge, to bring you s. conviction. |
| T-17.....V.12:2 | it. It must be kept s. and gracious in your |
| T-17...VIII.1:4 | The holy instant is the s. example, the |
| T-18......I.11:4 | relationship, with the truth s. upon it! |
| T-18. VIII.10:4 | with all the Love of its Creator s. upon it. |
| T-18. VIII.11:6 | s. Self will lift the tiny aspect that you |
| T-18......IX.9:4 | everything is bright and s. with innocence |
| T-18.....IX.13:1 | set s. and firmly rooted in the world of |
| T-19......III.10:1 | Heaven s. on both you and your brother. |
| T19...IV.D.2:2 | it, s. with joy because He is in His Father's |
| T-20.........I.3:6 | But let the whiteness of your s. gift of |
| T-20.......II.9:2 | s. from the holy altar within him where |
| T-20......III.7:3 | before the s. light the Holy Spirit offered, |
| T-20...VIII.3:1 | sinlessness is given you in s. light, to look |
| T-20...VIII.4:4 | sparkling with the s. lilies you laid upon it |
| T-21.........I.8:1 | as you look into a great and s. circle. And |
| T-21.........I.8:4 | extending to infinity forever s. and with |
| T-22.....II.12:1 | and s. in the golden light that reaches it |
| T-22....VI.14:8 | because each s. thought of love extends its |
| T-23.......in.3:4 | harmful now stands s. in their innocence, |
| T-23.........I.8:9 | of God, still s. in your quiet mind. |
| T-23......III.4:8 | of it? It can be kept s. before your vision, |
| T-24.......II.6:2 | The s. radiance of the Son of God, so like |
| T-24......VI.6:4 | set the s. memory of Him in Whom your |
| T-26...VII.16:3 | Heaven is s. on the Son of God. Deny him |
| T-26.......X.2:7 | that stands between Their s. innocence, |
| T-28.....II.12:2 | stand in s. silence next to every dream of |
| T-28......III.7:2 | who mistook for gold the s. of a pebble, |
| T-29......III.3:6 | And as you see him s. in the space of light |
| T-29.......V.5:1 | creation but the s. glory of His gift to you. |
| T-31......IV.4:8 | you see the purpose of the lesson s. clear, |
| W-pI.....78.3:1 | in s. light where each one stood before. |
| W-pI.....78.7:1 | savior s. in the light of true forgiveness, |
| W-pI.....78.8:6 | quiet now, and look upon your s. savior. |
| W-pI....100.2:6 | They will see their function in your s. face |
| W-pI.121.11:3 | of brightness s. through the ugly picture |
| W-pI....123.3:1 | His Love forever will remain s. on you, |
| W-pI....124.1:4 | on a s. light that blesses and that heals. At |
| W-pI....124.2:4 | Our s. footprints point the way to truth, |
| W-pI....157.9:1 | except His s. face and perfect Love. The |
| W-pI.187.11:3 | it s. with the grace of God in everyone. |
| W-pI......188.h | The peace of God is s. in me now. |
| W-pI....188.3:1 | The peace of God is s. in you now, and |
| W-pI....188.4:1 | The s. in your mind reminds the world of |
| W-pI....188.5:5 | The peace of God is s. in you now, and in |
| W-pI....188.7:4 | God's peace is s. on them, but they must |
| W-pI....188.8:4 | live. For as the peace of God is s. in you, it |
| W-pI.188.10:6 | say: *The peace of God is s. in me now. Let all* |
| W-pI....189.1:7 | is to see the world anew, s. in innocence, |
| W-pI.198.10:4 | see your innocence s. upon you from the |
| W-pI....208.1:1 | (188) The peace of God is s. in me now. *I* |
| W-pII..230.2:3 | *born into Your Mind is s. there unchanged. I* |
| W-pII..265.1:6 | the light of Heaven s. on the world. What |
| W-pII..322.1:2 | tried to hide, awaiting me in s. welcome, |
| W-pII..332.1:2 | undoes its evil dreams by s. them away. |
| W-pII....14.1:1 | *and whole, s. in the reflection of His Love. In* |
| M-22..........4:5 | seeing only the face of Christ s. in front of |
| M-23..........4:4 | It becomes the s. symbol for the Word of |
| C-6.............3:9 | to you in an eternal s. that will never be |
| C-6.............5:4 | with you he is the s. Savior of the world, |
| C-ep...........2:5 | the Heavens with a s. Ray that held it safe |
| P-2.........V.7:8 | the sinlessness in him come s. through |
| P-2.......VII.6:8 | Christ's s. face as it looks back at them. |
| S-1.........in.3:3 | as you ascend the s. stairway to the lawns |
| S-2.........II.8:6 | the glow of Heaven s. on the face of earth, |
| S-2........III.7:7 | silently open upon the s. face of Christ. |

## ship 1

| | |
|---|---|
| T-28......III.5:2 | ripples that a s. has made in passing by. |

## shiver 1

| | |
|---|---|
| T19...IV.A.9:6 | s. in remembrance of the winter's cold? |

## shock 1

| | |
|---|---|
| T-29.........I.8:5 | is a s. that comes to those who learn their |

## shoe 1

| | |
|---|---|
| W-pI.......7.4:6 | *I see only the past in this s.. I see only the past* |

## shone 5

| | |
|---|---|
| T-4........IV.9:4 | His Mind s. on you in your creation and |
| T-13.......X.5:5 | s. within you all the while you dreamed of |
| T-20......III.8:8 | that s. in both you and your brother, to |
| T-28......III.7:2 | stored a heap of snow that s. like silver. |
| C-4.............7:6 | of Christ has s. away time's final instant, |

## shore 3

| | |
|---|---|
| T-26.......V.6:6 | And who can stand upon a distant s., and |
| T-28.......I.15:5 | left a stranded Son forever on a s. where |
| T-28.......I.15:5 | another s. that he can never reach. His |

## shorn 1

| | |
|---|---|
| W-pI...170.5:3 | love is s. of what belongs to it and it alone |

## short 33

| | |
|---|---|
| T-13.......II.3:3 | that nothing s. of the crucifixion of God's |
| T-15.......I.11:2 | not give so s. a time to the Holy Spirit for |
| T-15.......I.13:2 | It is as s. for your brother as it is for you. |
| T-17.......II.4:4 | be so s. that you will barely have time to |
| T-20.........I.3:1 | A week is s., and yet this holy week is the |
| T-26......III.5:1 | Salvation stops just s. of Heaven, for only |
| T-26.......V.5:3 | s. to make a world in answer to creation, |
| T-26.....VII.9:5 | far s. of giving you your full inheritance, it |
| T-27.........I.7:3 | For who could live a life so soon cut s. and |
| T-30.......V.5:1 | The real world still falls s. of this, for this |
| W-pI.....14.2:2 | The mind-searching period should be s., a |
| W-pI.....27.3:6 | can still repeat one s. sentence to yourself |
| W-pI.....39.9:1 | if you intersperse them with several s. |
| W-pI.....39.9:2 | to include a few s. intervals in which you |
| W-pI.....40.1:2 | but very frequent s. ones are necessary. |
| W-pI.....42.7:1 | is no limit on the number of s. practice |
| W-pI.....43.4:4 | Then glance around you for a s. time, |
| W-pI.....43.5:1 | the exercise period should be relatively s., |
| W-pI.....45.6:2 | Then spend a fairly s. period in thinking a |
| W-pI.....48.2:1 | Today's practice periods will be very s., |
| WpI...rI.in.1:3 | a few s. comments after each of the ideas, |
| W-pI.....61.5:6 | about these statements for a s. while, |
| W-pI.....68.7:1 | s. practice periods should include a quick |
| W-pI...70.10:1 | the s. and frequent practice periods today |
| W-pI.....76.8:1 | the longer practice periods today with a s. |
| W-pI.....95.5:3 | fail to remember the s. applications of the |
| W-pI.122.10:3 | And now the way is s. that yet we travel. |
| W-pI.153.15:5 | an hour is too s. a time to spend with God |
| W-pI...184.7:4 | world would teach stops s. of meaning. In |
| W-pI...194.1:2 | it sets you down just s. of Heaven, with |
| W-pI...194.1:6 | How s. the journey still to be pursued! |
| M-19 .........2:7 | fall s. indeed of all that wait when the |
| C-2...........10:6 | to understand the way is s. and Heaven is |

## shorten 4

| | |
|---|---|
| T-2.........II.3:9 | The correct focus will s. it immeasurably. |
| T-2.......V.10:6 | as an expression of charity, can only s. it. |
| WpI...rV.in5:3 | This review will s. time immeasurably, if |
| W-pI.195.10:1 | and s. our learning time by more than |

## shortened 2

| | |
|---|---|
| T-2..... VIII.2:6 | can, however, be greatly s. by miracles, |
| T-31......III.1:4 | is s. by a span of time you cannot realize. |

## shortening 4

| | |
|---|---|
| T-2.......V.10:7 | you are s. the suffering of both of you. |
| T-2..... VIII.2:6 | the device for s. but not abolishing time. |
| T-2..... VIII.2:7 | s. process can be virtually immeasurable. |
| W-pI.....19.5:1 | required, s. the length of time involved, if |

## shortens 1

| | |
|---|---|
| T-1..........II.6:9 | The miracle s. time by collapsing it, thus |

## shorter 30

| | |
|---|---|
| T-16......VI.8:5 | is far s. than the time it took to fix your |
| W-pI.....12.2:4 | the shift to become markedly longer or s., |
| W-pI.....32.5:2 | The s. applications consist of repeating |
| W-pI.....33.3:1 | s. exercise periods should be as frequent |
| W-pI.....34.5:1 | The s. applications are to be frequent, |
| W-pI.....36.2:2 | and make the s. applications frequently, |
| W-pI.....36.4:1 | For the s. exercise periods, close your |
| W-pI.....37.6:1 | The s. exercises consist of repeating the |
| W-pI.....38.6:1 | In the frequent s. applications, apply the |
| W-pI...39.11:1 | In the s. applications, which should be |
| W-pI.....43.7:1 | today's idea in the s. practice periods, the |
| W-pI.....45.9:1 | In the s. exercise periods for today, try to |
| W-pI.....46.3:1 | periods, and as many s. ones as possible. |
| W-pI.....46.7:1 | The s. practice periods may consist either |
| W-pI.....64.8:1 | forms of s. practice periods are required. |
| W-pI.....65.8:1 | In the s. practice periods, which should |
| W-pI...66.11:1 | In the s. practice periods, which would |
| W-pI.....67.6:1 | Try to realize in the s. practice periods |
| W-pI.....69.9:1 | In the s. practice periods, which you will |
| W-pI...71.10:1 | In the s. practice periods, tell yourself |
| W-pI...72.13:1 | One or perhaps two s. practice periods |
| W-pI...73.11:1 | In the s. practice periods, again make a |
| W-pI.....74.7:1 | s. periods, which should be undertaken at |
| W-pI.....75.9:1 | The s. practice periods, too, will be joyful |
| W-pI.....77.7:1 | Our s. practice periods will be frequent, |
| W-pI.....79.9:1 | The s. practice periods for today will not |
| WpI..rII.in.1:4 | frequent s. ones in which we practice each |
| WpI..rII.in.6:1 | in the s. practice periods as well, using the |
| W-pI.....95.5:1 | Frequent but s. practice periods have |
| WpI rVI.in.4:2 | to reach a quickened pace along a s. path |

## shortly 1

| | |
|---|---|
| W-pI.....27.3:4 | the idea when you wake or s. afterwards, |

## should 324

## shoulder 2

| | |
|---|---|
| W-pI...166.8:1 | should feel Christ's touch upon your s., |
| W-pI...166.9:2 | Christ's hand has touched your s., and |

## shoulders 1

| | |
|---|---|
| W-pI...195.7:1 | heads against our s. as they rest a while. |

## shout 2

| | |
|---|---|
| T-21......IV.2:7 | this constant s. and frantic proclamation, |
| M-8 ...........5:4 | a whispered demand to kill than a s.? And |

## shouted 1

| | |
|---|---|
| W-pI.72.10:11 | We have s. our grievances so loudly that |

## show 109

| | |
|---|---|
| T-1.........I.30:1 | and s. them in proper alignment. This |
| T-2.........V.7:2 | of what your spiritual sight will s. you. I |
| T-4..........II.8:2 | them in an equally feeble s. of strength. It |
| T-4........VI.5:3 | only s. him how miserable he is without it |
| T-5........IV.4:4 | want to s. your brother anything except |
| T-5........IV.4:5 | S. him that he cannot hurt you and hold |
| T-5.........V.7:4 | also s. that you believe you can think |
| T-5........VI.5:1 | a few will suffice to s. how the Holy Spirit |
| T-6.........I.11:6 | to s. this was true in an extreme case, |
| T-9.......VIII.8:3 | you bring to its witnesses, who s. it to you |
| T-12......VI.4:7 | He will s. you the real world because God |
| T-13......III.1:2 | enough for the Holy Spirit to s. it to you, |
| T-13........X.7:1 | s. them to you fearfully to demonstrate |

T-13... X.10:11 And in Christ's vision He would s. you the
T-13...... XI.4:2 Perfect perception can merely s. you what
T-13...... XI.4:3 It can also s. you the results of sharing,
T-14..... VII.7:5 alone. Seeing with Him will s. you that all
T-14....... X.6:2 s. you that your way of ordering is wrong,
T-14...... X.11:5 Let the Holy Spirit s. him to you, and
T-14...... XI.1:7 made a semblance of power and a s. of
T-16....... II.3:4 Wholly natural perception would s. you
T-16...... III.3:1 what you have taught s. you that you do
T-16...... III.3:2 also s. you that you do not regard *yourself*
T-17....... II.5:3 will s. you that there is no reason here at
T-17...... III.6:7 in your relationships, and s. it to you. Its
T-18.........I.5:6 nothing you have seen begins to s. you
T-18.........I.9:9 to help Him s. you that no substitute you
T-18....... II.5:1 Dreams s. you that you have the power to
T-19.... III.11:1 and behold what He would s. you in your
T-19...... IV.3:5 in them will s. you all that you need to see
T19. IV.A.17:9 sin. But you can live to s. it is not real. The
T-20...... VI.2:1 Nothing can s. the contrast better than
T-20.... VIII.1:1 but they will be enough to s. you what is
T-20..VIII.10:4 your wild hallucinations that s. you all the
T-21.........I.9:4 Accept the vision that can s. you this, and
T-21....... II.7:5 And what would s. you otherwise must
T-21....... V.1:11 Yet it can s. you the conditions in which
T-22.........I.2:6 is not your vision, what can it s. to you?
T-22.........I.5:3 is. And what your sight would s. you, you
T-22.......I.10:5 to s. you where your Self must be. It is
T-22...... III.8:2 of which would s. you your forgiveness,
T-23.......in.1:4 s. of strength attack would use to cover
T-24....... II.5:6 and it would s. them that the specialness
T-24..... VII.4:6 Save it for s., as bait to catch another fish,
T-25..... VII.8:3 into it in quietness and s. him he is mad.
T-25... VII.10:3 One Who speaks for Him can s. you this,
T-25... VII.10:5 you in God's Own plan to s. His Son that
T-26..... VII.6:5 hierarchy of illusions can s. is preference,
T-27.........I.3:4 of yourself you offer him you s. yourself,
T-27.........I.5:5 S. this unto your brother, who will see
T-27.........I.6:9 to s. how lovely are the witnesses for guilt.
T-27.........I.9:1 is to s. your brother sin can have no cause
T-27....... II.6:2 does your healing s. your mind is healed,
T-27....... II.6:9 you learn when you but wish to s. your
T-27..... II.6:11 it is given you to s. him, by your healing,
T-27....... II.8:6 Yet you can s. him that his suffering is
T-27....... II.8:7 S. him your healing, and he will consent
T-27....... V.7:5 It will call forth its witnesses to s. the face
T-27.... VIII.3:3 and seems to s. a great variety of places
T-28....... II.7:6 to s. him that his wishes have been done.
T-28..... II.7:10 to s. him that he has done nothing. What
T-28..... II.11:4 because they s. the mind made sickness,
T-30.........I.6:6 lets the answer s. you what the question
T-30..... VII.2:6 except to s. there was no meaning there?
T-30..... VII.3:9 but to s. you wrote a fearful script, and
T-30.... VIII.4:2 Miracles but s. what you have interposed
T-31....... V.6:6 as errors, which the light would surely s..
T-31..... V.16:2 Each one will s. the changes in your own
W-in..........8:6 to you, and will s. you that they are true.
W-pI.....28.5:2 It has something to s. you; something
W-pI.....35.1:2 however, describe what vision will s. you.
W-pI.....43.5:6 *The world can s. me myself. I see my own*
W-pI.....45.1:5 any resemblance to what vision will s. you
W-pI.....54.3:7 And the world my real thoughts s. me will
W-pI.....54.5:3 the witnesses that s. me the thinking of
W-pI.....55.1:7 those which s. me an illusion of myself.
W-pI.....59.4:7 vision and the happy world it will s. me.
W-pI.....75.7:6 He will s. you what true vision sees. It is
W-pI.....85.1:2 My grievances s. me what is not there,
W-pI.....88.2:2 *This cannot s. me darkness, for the light has*
W-pI.....91.3:4 doubt the images they s. you are reality.
W-pI... 92.10:4 and asking truth to s. us how to find the
W-pI... 99.12:5 and s. you that you are the Son of God.
W-pI... 100.5:4 Thus do you fail to s. the world how great
W-pI... 121.7:7 Who was given you to s. the way to you.
W-pI. 130.11:2 of everything that hell would s. to you. All
W-pI... 139.8:3 the proof you need to s. that you believe
WpI. rIV.in3:3 Their purpose is to s. you something else,
W-pI... 151.2:6 which you would hide with s. of certainty
W-pI... 154.7:2 s. they understand the messages by giving
W-pI... 159.3:4 can s. but twisted images in broken parts.
W-pI... 160.6:4 out and s. him that he is no stranger now.
W-pI... 161.2:5 all seeing is to s. you what you wish to see.
W-pI... 163.8:4 And you will s. them this today. There is
W-pI... 166.7:2 witnesses with proof to s. this is not you.
W-pI... 189.9:7 His Son to s. Him how to find His way.
W-pII ..... 1.5:1 then, and let forgiveness s. you what to do
W-pII . 269.1:2 *to become the way to s. me my mistakes, and*
W-pII . 303.1:5 see but sights that s. His Father's Love.
W-pII ... 13.4:2 to s. that what it rested on is really there.
W-pII ... 13.4:3 and s. it rested on a world more real than
W-pII ... 13.5:4 up, to s. that what is born can never die,
M-14 ......... 4:8 trusts that He will s. him how to learn it.
M-22 ......... 6:9 It is your forgiveness that must s. him this
M-27 ......... 3:3 is enough to s. it cannot coexist with God.
P-2......... V.2:6 above all else, to s. them what is strength.
P-3....... III.7:8 Whoever asks your help can s. you where.
S-2..........II.4:5 and do not s. the bitter pain you feel.
S-2..........II.7:1 What would you s. your brother? Would

## showed 4

T-5 .........II.9:7 I s. you that this decision can be made,
T-6 ..... IV.10:2 situation if God s. you your perfection,
W-pI..... 78.9:1 of love the Holy Spirit s. you in their place
C-5 ............ 4:3 Arise with him who s. you this because

## showing 16

T-3 ....... IV.6:6 light abolishes darkness merely by s. you
T-14 ........I.5:1 His teaching by s. you what you can never
T-14 ..... XI.3:1 the past, by s. you only what you are *now.*
T19.... IV.C.6:2 than by s. you the one that seems to be
T-24 ...... V.3:7 him, s. him what can be seen and heard,
T-26 ........I.6:2 His task of s. you that it has not been lost.
T-30 ...... V.8:4 would He delay in s. you the way that He
T-30 ... VIII.2:2 from appearances by s. they can change.
W-pI........ 11.h thoughts are s. me a meaningless world.
W-pI..... 53.1:1 thoughts are s. me a meaningless world.
W-pI. 166.13:5 Teach them by s. them the happiness that
W-pI... 215.1:4 *I give thanks to Him for s. me the way to go.* I
W-pII . 293.1:3 it, and s. me distorted forms of fear? Yet
W-pII . 302.2:1 to Him, and walks beside us s. us the way.
M-10 ......... 1:6 s. "good" judgment at one time and "bad
C-6 ............ 2:1 part in it and s. us exactly what it is. He

## shown 28

T-4 ........I.13:2 brother who has s. himself responsible,
T-5 ..... VI.11:6 I have s. you infinite patience because my
T-12 ........I.2:3 This is s. by the fact that you react to your
T-21 ........I.2:4 You can be s. which doors are open, and
T-25 .... V.4:10 unless the way is s. to him through you,
T-27 ........I.2:1 is his made manifest, and s. to be his own.
T-27 ......I.4:11 everything that it has s. to him have you
T-27 ..... VI.6:9 are dissolved, and s. as powerless. The
T-27 .... VII.1:2 demented version of salvation clearly s..
T-27 .... VII.2:1 Now you are being s. you *can* escape. All
T-28 .......II.4:5 that it pictures what you wanted s. to you.
T-28 ..... III.9:1 to those the dreaming of the world has s..
T-30 .......I.12:2 mind, not certain yet, but willing to be s.:
T-30 ... VIII.2:9 are s. to be unreal *because* they change.
T-31 .... V.14:5 and can be s. that different thoughts have
W-pI..... 29.3:6 When vision has s. you the holiness that
W-pI..... 75.6:6 like. You merely wait to have it s. to you.
W-pI..... 78.5:2 of whom we ask God's Son be s. to you.
W-pI..... 78.7:4 you, let your mind be s. the light in him
W-pI... 130.3:5 would you want that this is s. to you?
W-pI... 137.4:5 be s. that what they look upon is false. So
W-pI... 151.2:2 really question what is s. you through the
W-pI... 190.3:6 is dead, has s. that death is victor over life
M-17 ......... 2:7 And where could this be better s. than in
C-2 ............ 4:2 And this is s. to us with perfect clarity. It
S-3...........I.1:4 this is s. by the brief nature of the " cure."
S-3...........I.2:2 the mark of death upon it this is clearly s..
S-3........ III.1:7 Here is the separation s.. And here the

## shows 50

T-2 ..........I.4:9 but also s. you clearly that you *are* free.
T-2 ....... VI.1:6 presence of fear s. that you have raised
T-4 ....... VI.3:8 you must escape from the ego s. this; but
T-7 .........V.9:2 One way s. you an image, or an idol that
T-7 .........V.9:3 The other s. you only truth, which you
T-14 ..... III.7:3 can be harmed s. him that he is guiltless.
T-14 ........X.5:5 bring any order into chaos s. you that you
T19 ... IV.B.7:7 and s. you that its power is gone forever.
T-21 ...... in.2:7 The world you see but s. you how much
T-21 ........I.2:5 directions, but vision s. you where to go.
T-23 ...... in.2:5 travels sinlessly along the way love s. him.
T-23 ..... IV.5:7 this choice s. you the battle is not real,
T-24 .......V.6:4 His Holiness s. you Himself in him whose
T-24 ..... VI.2:5 holiness s. you that God is One with him
T-24 ..... VI.6:7 Your brother's body s. not Christ to you.
T-25 .......II.8:1 brother as his Father's Mind s. him to you
T-25 .......V.6:2 But in the love he s. himself is God made
T-25 . VIII.14:3 Your special function s. you nothing else
T-27 .......II.1:7 body s. that *you* must be protected from
T-27 .......II.5:1 body s. the mind has not been healed. A
T-27 .....V.10:7 common answer s. the questions could
T-28 ........I.1:8 The miracle but s. the past is gone, and
T-28 .......II.4:2 you, but merely s. you who the dreamer is
T-28 .....II.10:2 and s. you its effects are what you want.
T-28 .....II.11:2 But it also s. that, having no effects, it is
T-28 ..... III.8:4 and gently s. you that you never sinned.
T-31 .....V.12:5 It also s. some glimmering of sight into
W-pI .... 48.3:2 to fear s. that somewhere in your mind,
W-pI .... 53.5:4 and loss and death s. me that I am seeing
W-pI .... 54.1:8 other. What I see s. me which they are.
W-pI .... 75.4:1 at the world that our forgiveness s. us.
W-pI .... 87.1:5 me, and I will look only on what it s. me.
W-pI .... 88.4:2 *of this s. me I believe in laws that do not exist.*
W-pI .. 106.2:1 s. the way to peace to those who cannot
W-pI .. 108.3:1 This is the light that s. no opposites, and
W-pI 121.12:3 that light his holiness s. you your savior,
W-pI .. 132.7:4 which s. them that the world does not
W-pI .. 139.4:3 merely s. he does not want to be the thing
W-pI .. 151.5:3 the hidden doubt that what it s. you as
W-pI .. 191.9:3 in a world which s. no mercy to you. Yet
W-pI .. 196.4:2 we may quickly go the way salvation s. us,
W-pII . 247.1:4 Let me accept what His sight s. me as the
W-pII . 269.1:5 *in which everyone s. me the face of Christ,*
W-pII ..... 8.2:2 The real world s. a world seen differently,
W-pII . 291.1:2 His sight s. me all things forgiven and at
W-pII . 331.2:1 Forgiveness s. us that God's Will is One,
W-pII . 331.2:2 upon the holy sights forgiveness s. today,
W-pII . 335.1:6 this. My brother's sinlessness s. me that I
Wfl........ in.4:4 the truth and life that s. the way to us. In
S-2..........II.5:2 this. It s. the face of suffering and pain, in

## shred 2

T19 .IV.A.12:6 little s. of guilt escapes their hungry eyes.
T-28 .......V.5:7 each senseless scrap and s. of evidence,

## shreds 1

T-28 .......II.5:1 holds all your s. of memories and dreams.

## shrieks 7

T-25 .......V.3:5 And yet, beneath the ego's senseless s.,
T-27 ..... VI.1:2 obscuring voice whose s. would silence
W-pI .... 49.4:3 mind. Go past all the raucous s. and sick
W-pI .. 121.4:2 s. as it beholds its own projections rising
W-pI .. 134.7:4 self-accusing s. of sinners mad with guilt.
W-pI .. 161.8:4 It s. in wrath, and claws the air in frantic
P-2........ VI.2:6 are heard instead of loud discordant s..

## shrine 3

W-pII ... 12.4:2 of God is offered daily at its darkened s.,
W-pII ... 12.5:1 the altar to illusions to the s. of Life Itself.
P-3..........II.9:8 to collect bodies to worship at their s.,

## shrink 6

T-11 .......V.1:2 There is no need to s. from illusions, for
T-14 ..... VI.1:3 and s. away from it to further darkness.
T-27 .......V.4:6 But if you s. from blessing, will the world

T-28......VI.3:4 You **s.** from what it sees and what it hears
T-29.........I.6:3 and when to **s.** more safely into fear. It
W-pI...186.3:6 Today we will not **s.** from our assignment

**shrinking** 2

T-11.......in.4:2 **s.** you will also have looked upon ours. I
T-18......III.2:1 will rush to darkness, **s.** from the truth,

**shroud** 2

T-3...........I.6:7 Only the attempts to **s.** it in darkness
T-13......IX.8:5 guilty in the dark in which they **s.** them,

**shrouded** 5

T-13......IX.7:2 the world seems dark, and **s.** in your guilt.
T-14... VIII.1:2 place, **s.** in guilt and in the dark denial of
T19... IV.C.3:5 **s.** figures in the funeral procession march
T-20......VI.6:4 that are worshipped here are **s.** in mystery
T-31....... V.6:6 And in these **s.** vaults are all his sins and

**shrouds** 2

T-13......VI.2:5 see it as a dark cloud that **s.** your brothers
P-2......... V.7:8 the veil of guilt that **s.** the Son of God, we

**shut** 11

T-11......IV.6:6 for you, for while I live it cannot be **s.**, and
T-13.....III.3:4 your fortress, for you would **s.** out God,
T-18... VIII.2:4 on love will always seem to **s.** Him out,
T-20......VII.8:9 You closed your eyes to **s.** him out. Such
T-24.....VI.11:3 itself, with every entry **s.** against intrusion
T-28....... I.13:6 the present and the past, to **s.** them out.
T-29... VIII.3:6 veil that seems to **s.** you off from Him,
W-pI.....68.2:1 **S.** off from your Self, which remains
W-pI...169.3:5 It is not **s.** tight against God's Voice. It
W-pI...182.6:3 is so little that He seems so easily **s.** out,
W-pI...192.7:4 our eyes **s.** tight against the light; our

**shuts** 4

T-15......IV.8:1 would keep hidden **s.** communication off,
T-26...... X.1:11 Its simple presence **s.** the door to Theirs,
W-pI.167.10:3 Who changes life because he **s.** his eyes,
M-4........ X.1:3 As judgment **s.** the mind against God's

**shutting** 2

T-18......VI.9:1 **s.** you off from others and keeping you
W-pI...137.1:3 retreat from others, and a **s.** off of joining.

**sick** 119

T-1........ I.24:1 Miracles enable you to heal the **s.** and
T-2........IV.4:7 can help the non-right-minded, or the **s.**,
T-5.......VII.2:3 Some of them have healed the **s.** at times,
T-6......V.C.9:5 given you a **s.** mind that must be healed.
T-7.......... II.1:2 When a brother perceives himself as **s.**, he
T-7.......... V.8:5 can, or he would not perceive himself as **s.**
T-8.....VII.10:3 mind, is a fragmented or **s.** interpretation
T-8..... VIII.3:3 If you are **s.**, how can you object to the
T-8..... VIII.5:5 A **s.** body does not make any sense. It
T-8..... VIII.9:3 as the Holy Spirit sees it cannot be **s.**.
T-8.........IX.1:7 Only perception can be **s.**, because only
T-8.........IX.7:5 If you are **s.** you are withdrawing from me
T-10......III.2:1 Comforter can there be for the **s.** children
T-10......III.2:7 that no one is separate, and so no one is **s.**
T-10......III.3:1 believe that a Son of God can be **s.** is to
T-10......III.4:1 of God is **s.** is to worship the same idol he
T-10......III.4:3 taught by **s.** minds too divided to know
T-10......III.4:6 A **s.** god must be an idol, made in the
T-10......III.4:7 does perceive in a Son of God; a **s.** god,
T-10......III.6:5 you do not value yourself you become **s.**,
T-10......III.7:1 is **s.** it is because he is not asking for peace
T-10......IV.1:5 If you believe you can be **s.**, you have
T-10......IV.3:1 Sonship cannot be perceived as partly **s.**,
T-10......IV.7:4 Voice, he strengthens It in a **s.** brother by
T-10........ V.3:4 are **s.** you cannot keep the gods you made
T-10........ V.3:6 not to know yourself in order to be **s.**.
T-10........ V.8:3 You are not **s.** and you cannot die. But
T-10..... V.13:6 You believe that the **s.** things you have
T-10..... V.13:6 because you believe that the **s.** images you
T-11. VIII.11:3 perceive part of you as **s.** and achieve your
T-12........ II.1:2 those who are **s.** do not love themselves.
T-12........ II.1:4 about themselves they could not be **s.**.
T-12........ II.1:6 The **s.** must heal themselves, for the truth
T-13.... VI.10:5 The **s.**, who ask for love, are grateful for it,
T-15.....VII.3:1 **s.** attraction of guilt must be recognized
T-18...... VI.5:3 perception of the body can clearly be **s.**,
T-19.........I.3:1 heal, because it cannot make itself **s.**. It
T-19.........I.4:6 And the body will seem to be **s.**, for you
T-19.........I.7:7 to it, making it **s.** because of the mind's
T-19...... III.1:5 itself a willing captive to its **s.** appeal. Sin
T19....IV.C.3:2 opposition lie but in the **s.** minds of the
T19....IV.C.7:6 all its **s.** ideas and weird imaginings. Here
T-25.......in.3:2 mind that thinks it is a body is **s.** indeed!
T-26...... VI.1:5 has entered all the world of **s.** illusions.
T-27.........I.4:3 A **s.** and suffering you but represents your
T-27.........I.4:4 This **s.** and sorry picture *you* accept, if only
T-27.........I.4:5 The **s.** are merciless to everyone, and in
T-27.........I.7:2 The **s.** have reason for each one of their
T-27.........I.9:5 a purpose, it is seen as neither **s.** nor well,
T-27.......I.10:3 breath of immortality to those grown **s.** of
T-27....... II.3:4 The **s.** remain accusers. They cannot
T-28....... II.6:8 He sees illusions of himself as **s.** or well,
T-28..... II.10:7 need not be feared. And so they are not **s.**.
T-28..... II.11:7 was **s.** that thought the body could be sick
T-28..... II.11:7 was sick that thought the body could be **s.**
T-28...... III.2:1 No mind is **s.** until another mind agrees
T-28...... III.2:2 And thus it is their joint decision to be **s.**.
T-28...... III.2:4 Thus is the body not perceived as **s.** by
T-28...... III.3:3 Do not allow your brother to be **s.**, for if
T-28......IV.7:3 No one is **s.** if someone else accepts his
T-28......IV.7:4 His desire to be a **s.** and separated mind
T-28....... V.4:2 Here is a world established that is **s.**, and
T-28....... V.5:1 What is there God created to be **s.**? And
T-28...... VI.6:7 time he does not share a promise to be **s.**,
T-28.....VII.2:2 Are you not **s.**, if you deny yourself your
T-28.....VII.4:4 Son, and for this purpose it cannot be **s.**.
T-28.....VII.4:5 own, and you have chosen that it not be **s.**
T-28.....VII.4:9 And you are **s.** or well, accordingly.
T-28.....VII.5:3 apart, and if you are, you cannot but be **s.**
T-29.........I.5:6 and what will tire it and make it **s.**. And
T-29.........I.6:4 will be **s.** because you do not know what
T-29....... II.8:2 is guarantee that it can *not* be **s.**. In your
T-29.....VII.9:4 made sad and **s.** by seeing idols there.
T-31...... III.4:7 dies, because that mind is **s.** within itself.
W-pI.....49.4:3 all the raucous shrieks and **s.** imaginings
W-pI......70.5:2 healed, and we do not really want to be **s.**,
W-pI......70.5:4 He does not want us to be **s.**. Neither do
W-pI.....92.5:2 It is **s.** and looks on sickness, which is like
W-pI...120.2:3 *Today I lay aside all **s.** illusions of myself,*
W-pI...132.8:4 The **s.** are healed as you let go all thoughts
W-pI.135.13:1 up to save itself must make the body **s.**. It
W-pI.135.16:4 a continuity of any old ideas and **s.** beliefs
W-pI...136.7:4 Now are you **s.**, that truth may go away
W-pI.136.19:2 will attack the body, for the mind is **s.**.
W-pI.136.20:7 *my mind cannot attack. So I can not be **s.**.*
W-pI.137.15:3 come together to make well all that was **s.**
W-pI...140.2:2 He merely had a dream that he was **s.**,
W-pI...140.4:4 Atonement does not heal the **s.**, for that is
W-pI...140.6:3 Nor does it seek to heal what is not **s.**,
W-pI...140.7:2 where it is, and then applied to what is **s.**,
W-pI...140.9:1 misled today by what appears to us as **s.**.
W-pI...152.1:3 nor fear nor think him **s.** unless these are
W-pI...163.2:3 and the **s.** bow down before its image,
W-pI.166.14:3 you are **s.**, you but withhold their healing.
W-pI...183.3:3 of grace. The **s.** arise, healed of their sickly
W-pI...192.6:1 was lifted from a **s.** and tortured mind. Is
W-pI...194.8:5 the **s.** illusions of the world along with his
W-pI...195.5:2 for all who will escape with you; the **s.**,
W-pI...204.1:2 *by laws which rule the world of **s.** illusions,*
W-pII..294.1:8 aside. It is not **s.** nor old nor hurt. It is but
W-pII..347.1:3 *It is **s.**. But You have offered freedom, and I*
M-5 ...... III.2:7 not to heal the **s.** but to remind them of
M-12 .........5:5 Because it is holy it cannot be **s.**, nor can
M-12 .........6:9 as **s.** and separate is no more real than to
M-22 .........3:2 The idea that a body can be **s.** is a central
M-22 .........3:4 be **s.** Atonement would be impossible. A
M-22 .........4:2 anyone actually believe he wants to be **s.**.
M-22 .........6:5 A **s.** person perceives himself as separate
M-22 .........6:7 sense of separation that has made him **s.**.
M-28 .........4:5 now remain on earth to shelter **s.** illusions
P-in............1:2 is. Since only the mind can be **s.**, only the
P-2........ III.4:3 to receive the Christ or he could not be **s.**.
P-2........ IV.3:7 heal the **s.** is but to bring this realization
P-2......... V.3:5 While they are **s.**, they can and must be
P-2........ VI.1:2 The unforgiving are **s.**, believing they are
P-2........ VI.1:4 "God may not enter here" the **s.** repeat,
P-2........ VI.4:8 It is not **s.**, and needs no remedy. To
P-2...... VI.4:10 cure what cannot be **s.** and make it well?
S-3........ III.4:7 dispelled, and it is this that made him **s.**.

**sicken** 1

S-3...........I.2:5 And they feel fear as bodies change and **s.**

**sickened** 1

W-pI... 137.2:3 held in pieces by a solid wall of **s.** flesh,

**sickening** 1

M-10 .........6:6 of **s.** despair and fear of death; all these

**sickens** 1

T-31...... III.4:6 It **s.** at the bidding of the mind that would

**sicker** 1

M-8 ...........6:3 be those who seem to be "**s.**" than others,

**sickly** 9

T-20...... III.5:6 **s.** picture of yourself is carefully preserved
W-pI.....92.3:3 the small, the weak, the **s.** and the dying,
W-pI. 136.16:4 It will be healed of all the **s.** wishes that it
W-pI... 137.8:4 are more potent than their **s.** opposites.
W-pI... 183.3:3 The sick arise, healed of their **s.** thoughts.
W-pI... 190.6:6 a **s.** place where living things must come
W-pII . 268.1:2 *Your creation, and distort it into **s.** forms.*
W-pII ... 12.4:2 altar where its **s.** followers prepare to die.
P-2.......VII.8:4 that brushes lightly past all **s.** dreams.

**sickness** 198

T-1.........I.23:2 healing because **s.** comes from confusing
T-1.........I.24:1 because you made **s.** and death yourself,
T-2........ IV.2:2 **S.** or "not-right-mindedness" is the result
T-6...... V.C.9:6 against this **s.** is the way to heal it. Once
T-7..........II.1:4 **S.** and separation are not of God, but the
T-7......... V.2:7 If you teach both **s.** *and* healing, you are
T-7......... V.7:4 his own ingratitude, which is a lesson in **s.**
T-8......VIII.2:2 concepts of both health and **s.** meaningful
T-8......VIII.3:2 The ego has a profound investment in **s.**.
T-8......VIII.3:4 the obvious attack that underlies the **s.**. If
T-8......VIII.4:1 It is hard to perceive **s.** as a false witness,
T-8......VIII.4:3 you would not consider **s.** such a strong
T-8......VIII.5:6 not make sense because **s.** is not what the
T-8......VIII.5:7 for. **S.** is meaningful only if the two basic
T-8......VIII.5:8 are a body. Without these premises **s.** is
T-8......VIII.6:1 **S.** is a way of demonstrating that you can
T-8......VIII.7:4 feel. **S.** is merely another example of your
T-8........ IX.1:5 When the ego tempts you to **s.** do not ask
T-8........ IX.3:2 All forms of **s.**, even unto death, are
T-8........ IX.4:6 if you have misused it on behalf of **s.**.
T-8........ IX.5:3 taught that one form of **s.** is more serious
T-8........ IX.8:5 we are not of one mind, and that is **s.**. Yet
T-8........ IX.8:6 Yet **s.** is not of the body, but of the mind.
T-8........ IX.8:7 forms of **s.** are signs that the mind is split,
T-10.............h THE IDOLS OF **S.**
T-10......... III.h The God of **S.**
T-10...... III.1:8 worshippers are the Sons of God in **s.**.
T-10...... III.1:9 from their **s.** and returned to His Mind.

| | |
|---|---|
| T-10 III.3:4 | not side with s. in the presence of a Son of |
| T-10 III.4:4 | S. is idolatry, because it is the belief that |
| T-10 III.7:2 | is the denial of illusion, and s. *is* an illusion |
| T-10 III.9:4 | You made the god of s., and by making |
| T-10 III.11:4 | can give up the god of s. for your brothers |
| T-10 III.11:5 | For if you see the god of s. anywhere, you |
| T-10 IV.h | The End of S. |
| T-10 IV.1:3 | S. and perfection are irreconcilable. If |
| T-10 IV.1:6 | is not at war with the god of s. you made, |
| T-10 IV.7:4 | sick brother by weakening his belief in s., |
| T-10 V.1:1 | god of s. are strange and very demanding. |
| T-10 V.3:2 | god of s. obviously demands the denial of |
| T-10 V.3:4 | only in s. could you possibly want them. |
| T-10 V.4:1 | S. and death seemed to enter the mind of |
| T-10 V.8:1 | look to the god of s. for healing but only |
| T-11 I.10:4 | belief is your whole s. and your whole fear |
| T-11 I.10:5 | Every symptom of s. and fear arises here, |
| T-11 II.1:1 | If s. is separation, the decision to heal |
| T-11 VIII.10:1 | In the real world there is no s., for there |
| T-12 II.3:1 | Perceive in s. but another call for love, |
| T-12 II.3:2 | Whatever the s., there is but one remedy. |
| T-12 II.3:3 | for to perceive in s. the appeal for health |
| T-16 VI.10:3 | on death and suffering, s. and despair, |
| T-17 VIII.4:5 | was sorrow and depression, s. and pain, |
| T-19 I.3:3 | Its health or s. depends entirely on how |
| T-19 I.6:6 | *is.* For God gave healing not apart from s., |
| T-19 I.6:6 | established remedy where s. cannot be. |
| T-20 IV.1:5 | them,– s. and death and misery and pain |
| T-22 II.3:1 | only guilt and suffering, s. and death, to |
| T-26 VII.2:1 | All s. comes from separation. When the |
| T-26 VII.2:4 | S. and sin are seen as consequence and |
| T-26 VII.4:2 | has God given answer to the world of s., |
| T-27 I.4:7 | For s. is the witness to his guilt, and death |
| T-27 I.4:8 | be sins. S. is but a "little" death; a form of |
| T-27 I.7:1 | is justified, is s. in whatever form it takes. |
| T-27 II.9:6 | s. is desired to prevent a shift of balance |
| T-27 II.9:7 | with an argument for s. such as this? And |
| T-28 II.2:11 | s. is a meaningless attempt to give effects |
| T-28 II.3:1 | Always in s. does the Son of God attempt |
| T-28 II.11:4 | because they show the mind made s., and |
| T-28 II.12:4 | back the consequence of s. to its cause. |
| T-28 III.2:3 | accept the part you play in making s. real, |
| T-28 III.2:5 | the cause of s. and perceived effects. |
| T-28 III.2:6 | join, as s. comes from minds that separate |
| T-28 III.3:4 | He has not seen the cause of s. where it is, |
| T-28 III.3:4 | between you, where the s. has been bred. |
| T-28 III.3:5 | Thus are you joined in s., to preserve the |
| T-28 III.3:5 | s. is kept carefully protected, cherished, |
| T-28 III.4:4 | to give a cause to s. which is not its cause. |
| T-28 III.4:5 | of the gap is all the cause that s. has. For it |
| T-28 III.5:5 | Where are the grounds for s. when the |
| T-28 III.5:5 | where the seeds of s. seemed to grow? |
| T-28 III.6:2 | The seeds of s. and the shame of guilt He |
| T-28 III.8:3 | so s. will now be seen without a cause. |
| T-28 IV.1:1 | to someone's dream of s. and of death. It |
| T-28 IV.8:5 | left clean of all the seeds of s. and of sin. |
| T-28 IV.10:3 | want to have the "benefits" of s. when he |
| T-28 IV.10:6 | The seeds of s. come from the belief that |
| T-28 IV.10:9 | of healing where the seeds of s. were. And |
| T-28 V.1:1 | is a sense of s. but a sense of limitation? |
| T-28 V.1:5 | thus is s. separating off the self from good |
| T-28 VI.4:6 | in consciousness is every pledge to s.. Yet |
| T-28 VI.5:1 | S. is anger taken out upon the body, so |
| T-28 VII.4:7 | No forms of s. are immune, because the |
| T-28 VII.4:8 | The choice of s. seems to be of form, yet it |
| T-28 VII.5:6 | Yet faithlessness is s.. It is like the house |
| T-29 II.3:6 | You are free of pain and s., misery and |
| T-29 II.7:7 | change with time, with s. or with health, |
| T-29 II.8:1 | S. is a demand the body be a thing that it |
| T-29 II.8:3 | that it be more than this lies the idea of s.. |
| T-29 II.10:6 | releases yours from s. and from death. |
| T-30 VI.6:1 | forms of s. and of joylessness forgiveness |
| T-30 VI.7:1 | be true the miracle can heal all forms of s. |
| T-30 VI.8:5 | of s. which the miracle must lack the |
| T-31 III.5:1 | dogs of hate and evil, s. and attack; of |
| T-31 VIII.6:2 | see. What you behold as s. and as pain, as |
| W-pI 70.3:2 | the remedy for the s. where it cannot help |
| W-pI 70.4:1 | from the s. for which it was intended, and |
| W-pI 70.4:1 | it was intended, and thus keep the s.. |
| W-pI 92.5:2 | It is sick and looks on s., which is like |
| W-pI 110.3:1 | replace the truth, health cannot turn to s., |
| W-pI 132.8:4 | are healed as you let go all thoughts of s., |
| W-pI 136.h | S. is a defense against the truth. |
| W-pI 136.1:1 | what purpose s. seems to serve. For then |
| W-pI 136.2:1 | S. is not an accident. Like all defenses, it |
| W-pI 136.7:1 | S. is a decision. It is not a thing that |
| W-pI 136.8:1 | that s. can succeed in shielding you from |
| W-pI 136.11:4 | or suffer s. or distort the truth in any way. |
| W-pI 136.15:6 | *S. is a defense against the truth. I will accept* |
| W-pI 136.16:2 | will be no dark corners s. can conceal, |
| W-pI 136.17:1 | the source of s. has been opened to relief. |
| W-pI 136.18:4 | make it well, for s. has become impossible |
| W-pI 136.20:4 | *S. is a defense against the truth. But I am not* |
| W-pI 137.1:2 | which dwell on s. and on separate states. |
| W-pI 137.1:3 | S. is a retreat from others, and a shutting |
| W-pI 137.2:1 | S. is isolation. For it seems to keep one |
| W-pI 137.3:1 | The world obeys the laws that s. serves, |
| W-pI 137.3:3 | In s. must he be apart and separate. But |
| W-pI 137.3:5 | s. does his Self appear to be dismembered |
| W-pI 137.4:1 | S. would prove that lies must be the truth |
| W-pI 137.4:3 | The separation s. would impose has never |
| W-pI 137.4:6 | truth, must demonstrate that s. is not real |
| W-pI 137.5:1 | out the dream of s. in the name of truth, |
| W-pI 137.7:1 | so healing must replace the fantasies of s. |
| W-pI 137.7:2 | When s. has been seen to disappear in |
| W-pI 137.8:4 | which hold that s. is inevitable are more |
| W-pI 137.14:4 | *s. may be banished from the mind of God's* |
| W-pI 140.1:5 | One belief in s. takes another form, and |
| W-pI 140.4:1 | heals with certainty, and cures all s.. For |
| W-pI 140.4:2 | which understands that s. can be nothing |
| W-pI 140.4:3 | S. where guilt is absent cannot come, for |
| W-pI 140.4:5 | away the guilt that makes the s. possible. |
| W-pI 140.4:7 | For s. now is gone, with nothing left to |
| W-pI 140.5:7 | is not, and nowhere sin and s. can abide. |
| W-pI 140.7:1 | today to seek to cure what cannot suffer s. |
| W-pI 140.8:1 | change our minds about the source of s., |
| W-pI 148.2:1 | (136) S. is a defense against the truth. |
| W-pI 152.2:5 | Can fear and s. enter in a mind where love |
| W-pI 159.6:5 | There is no s. not already healed, no lack |
| W-pI 187.6:4 | as well at pain and loss, at s. and at grief, |
| W-pII 328.1:3 | Yet all we find is s., suffering and loss and |
| W-pII 356.h | S. is but another name for sin. Healing is |
| M-5 1:1 | of what the illusion of s. is for. Healing is |
| M-5 I.h | The Perceived Purpose of S. |
| M-5 I.1:4 | For s. is an election; a decision. It is the |
| M-5 I.1:7 | S. is a method, conceived in madness, for |
| M-5 II.1:1 | which the valuelessness of s. is recognized |
| M-5 II.1:5 | body. If s. is but a faulty problem-solving |
| M-5 II.2:1 | acceptance of s. as a decision of the mind, |
| M-5 II.2:13 | form of s. that would not be cured at once |
| M-5 II.3:2 | this; the recognition that s. is of the mind, |
| M-5 II.3:11 | is the release from guilt and s. both, for |
| M-5 II.4:7 | What do guilt and s., pain, disaster and |
| M-5 III.1:6 | patients do not realize they have chosen s. |
| M-5 III.1:7 | they believe that s. has chosen them. Nor |
| M-5 III.2:12 | Would you choose s. in place of this?" |
| M-5 III.3:1 | forms of s. in which their brother believes |
| M-6 1:6 | what if the patient uses s. as a way of life, |
| M-8 5:1 | in healing merely because all s. is illusion. |
| M-8 6:8 | one answer to s. of any kind is healing. |
| M-12 5:12 | remaining. S. is now impossible to him. |
| M-12 6:1 | Oneness and s. cannot coexist. God's |
| M-22 1:7 | and what remains to make s. possible? |
| M-22 4:1 | s. does not appear to be a decision. Nor |
| M-22 4:3 | applied to all specific forms of s., both in |
| M-22 5:2 | is. Another's s. thus becomes his own. In |
| M-22 6:3 | to heal all individuals of all forms of s.. |
| C-4 6:8 | There at last are s. and its single remedy |
| P-2 III.4:4 | too advanced to believe in s. and too near |
| P-2 IV.3:2 | S. and death and misery now stalk the |
| P-2 IV.4:9 | And how could s. cure? Are not these |
| P-2 IV.8:1 | S. is insanity because all sickness is |
| P-2 IV.8:1 | is insanity because all s. is mental illness, |
| P-2 IV.8:2 | degrees. One of the illusions by which s. is |
| P-2 IV.11:6 | What is the need for s. then? Given this |
| P-2 V.7:5 | one who seems to share our dream of s.. |
| P-2 VI.4:4 | Here is all s. cherished, but without the |
| P-2 VI.5:1 | S. takes many forms, and so does |
| P-2 VI.5:3 | that a careful study of the form a s. takes |
| P-2 VI.5:5 | can possibly give rise to s. of any kind. |
| P-2 VII.3:4 | vision heals perception and s. disappears. |
| S-3 I.h | The Cause of S. |
| S-3 I.1:1 | nor think that s. is apart and separate |
| S-3 I.3:3 | among which s. should be seen as one. |
| S-3 II.1:1 | one; a dream of s. for a dream of health. |
| S-3 II.1:3 | to fear, so s. will be free to strike again. |
| S-3 II.1:4 | can indeed remove a form of pain and s.. |
| S-3 III.4:8 | apart from where the source of s. is, for |
| S-3 III.5:7 | S. and separation must be healed by love |
| S-3 IV.5:8 | death. And s., suffering and grievous loss |

## side 42

*See also* right-side

| | |
|---|---|
| T-4 IV.7:3 | effort. S. with me consistently against this |
| T-5 V.1:4 | at its disposal to s. with Heaven or earth, |
| T-5 VII.3:5 | willingness to s. with its separateness. |
| T-6 IV.4:4 | you do believe it you will not s. with it, |
| T-6 IV.4:8 | you s. with this alliance you will be afraid, |
| T-6 IV.10:3 | and thus s. with the belief that those who |
| T-7 VI.3:10 | ensures its continuance if you s. with it, |
| T-9 II.9:1 | To disbelieve is to s. against, or to attack. |
| T-9 II.9:2 | To believe is to accept, and to s. with. To |
| T-10 III.3:4 | Do not s. with sickness in the presence of |
| T-14 III.10:2 | and will not refuse to see it and s. with it. |
| T-15 III.6:2 | s. against Him in what He wills for you. |
| T-15 III.12:5 | power is forever on the s. of His host, for |
| T-15 VIII.1:3 | must s. with every sign or token of your |
| T-16 III.9:2 | the other s. and wait for you will not draw |
| T-16 IV.2:6 | reality, which awaits you on the other s., |
| T-16 IV.13:6 | On this s. of the bridge to timelessness |
| T-16 V.17:2 | will recognize that God is on the other s., |
| T-16 VI.5:2 | On this s. of the bridge you see the world |
| T-16 VI.7:2 | On this s., everything you see is grossly |
| T-16 VI.11:2 | *is.* From this s., it seems to be outside and |
| T-20 II.8:1 | Your chosen home is on the other s., |
| T-21 III.9:5 | anything that stands this s. of Heaven. |
| T-22 II.6:10 | Faith and belief can fall to either s., but |
| T-22 II.6:10 | lies only on one s. and joy upon the other. |
| T-23 I.12:9 | to be remembered when you s. with peace |
| T-23 III.5:3 | they accept forgiveness s. by side with the |
| T-23 III.5:3 | they accept forgiveness side by s. with the |
| T-25 V.4:10 | that you may find it, walking by his s.. |
| T-25 VIII.8:5 | For love has lost when judgment left its s., |
| T-31 II.6:9 | way unless you keep him safely by your s.. |
| T-31 II.11:3 | you walk alone, with no one by your s.? |
| T-31 V.4:3 | The other s. he does not want to see. Yet |
| W-pI 2.1:4 | that you include whatever is on either s.. |
| W-pI 66.10:6 | On one s. stand all illusions. All truth |
| W-pI 98.1:2 | We take a stand on but one s. today. We |
| W-pI 98.1:3 | We s. with truth and let illusions go. We |
| W-pI 125.2:2 | forever in his mind and at his s. to lead |
| W-pI 198.8:3 | to it that brings illusions to the other s.? |
| M-28 6:9 | crucify are resurrected with him, by his s., |
| C-4 6:7 | for an instant lie together, s. by side, |
| C-4 6:7 | for an instant lie together, side by s., |

## sided 1

| | |
|---|---|
| T-7 IX.1:6 | it responds as if it were being s. against. |

## sides 3

| | |
|---|---|
| T-7 X.5:1 | always s. with you and with your strength |
| T-11 in.1:2 | will examine the evidence on both s. fairly |
| T-28 VI.2:7 | no s. and judges not the road it travels. It |

## sidetracked 1

| | |
|---|---|
| WpI..rII.in.5:2 | Refuse to be s. into detours, illusions and |

## siding 2

| | |
|---|---|
| T-6 IV.4:8 | because you are s. with an alliance of fear. |
| T-23 II.8:5 | And God Himself seems to be s. with it, |

## sigh 6

T-20....VI.11:2 which to **s.** and grieve and die in honor of
T-23.......in.4:4 of freedom for a little **s.** of seeming sin,
T-26....... II.7:4 than just a tiny **s.** before they disappear,
T-26...VII.10:1 a little **s.** that speaks for Heaven as a
W-pI...167.2:6 and pain, even a little **s.** of weariness, a
M-10..........5:1 not with regret but with a **s.** of gratitude.

## sighing 1

T-26... VIII.7:6 And you seek to be content with **s.**, and

## sighs 3

T-27....... II.8:9 And laughter will replace your **s.**, because
W-pI.136.12:5 it **s.** a little when you throw away its gifts,
W-pI.166.14:1 **s.** will now betray the hopes of those who

## sight 253

T-1........ I.22:3 exist. This leads to a denial of spiritual **s.**.
T-2...... III.1:11 Spiritual **s.**, on the other hand, cannot see
T-2........ III.3:8 weakening the investment in physical **s.**.
T-2......... V.7:1 turning away from the belief in physical **s.**
T-2......... V.7:2 of what your spiritual **s.** will show you. I
T-2......... V.8:3 believe in what your physical **s.** tells you,
T-2..... VIII.1:5 you alone make is real in your own **s.**,
T-3........ III.4:1 is the natural perception of spiritual **s.**,
T-3........ III.4:2 Spiritual **s.** is symbolic, and therefore not
T-5....... II.7:12 wrong voice you *have* lost **s.** of your soul.
T-8........ IV.8:5 imprison yourself you are losing **s.** of your
T-8......... V.6:3 lose **s.** of His direction through illusions,
T-8....... VII.7:7 is to lose **s.** of the Holy Spirit's purpose,
T-8....... VII.8:6 goal of the curriculum has been lost **s.** of.
T-8..... VIII.5:4 is to lose **s.** of the function of everything.
T-9....... II.10:5 The price for getting is to lose **s.** of value,
T-10...... III.3:6 denial of God and thus lose **s.** of yourself?
T-10...... III.5:2 of your brothers, and thus lose **s.** of yours.
T-11....... V.7:3 reality, but it does not lose **s.** of its goal. It
T-11... VIII.1:7 the real world will vanish from your **s.**.
T-11... VIII.7:3 you have lost **s.** of the real world. You are
T-12...... III.5:4 Never lose **s.** of this, and never allow
T-12...... VI.4:6 In His **s.** the Son of God is perfect, and He
T-12...... VI.5:4 then the real world will spring to your **s.**,
T-12...... VI.5:5 to be seen, for He has never lost **s.** of you.
T-12... VIII.2:3 disappeared from your **s.** into his Father.
T-12... VIII.7:4 What is invisible to you is perfect in His **s.**
T-13......... I.1:5 Guilt hides Christ from your **s.**, for it is
T-13...... III.7:3 Do not hide suffering from His **s.**, but
T-13...... IV.6:8 holy, would be excluded from your **s.**. The
T-13...... IV.9:6 you will lose **s.** of the present and hold on
T-13....... V.6:7 And the vision of Christ is not in your **s.**,
T-13....... V.8:5 for **s.** of it depends upon denying vision.
T-13...... VI.1:2 this no illusions can rise to meet your **s.**,
T-13...... VI.2:5 and conceals their reality from your **s.**.
T-13...... VI.7:5 and where there is no **s.** of what you were,
T-13..... VII.2:1 for **s.** of it is costing you a different kind
T-13..... VII.2:3 The **s.** of one is possible because you have
T-13..... VII.5:6 The out of mind *is* out of **s.**, because what
T-13...VII.13:4 for His **s.** is ever on the journey's end,
T-13... VIII.5:4 healed and healing **s.** into the darkness,
T-13... VIII.5:6 into His quiet **s.** that makes them one.
T-14...... III.2:6 guiltlessness, and push it from your **s.**.
T-14....... V.4:3 would steal it away and keep it from his **s.**
T-14....... V.4:5 God has hidden himself from his own **s.**.
T-14...... VI.8:3 keep no source of interference from His **s.**
T-14..... VII.4:8 Apart, this fact is lost from **s.**, for each in
T-14.... XI.14:6 so. With your perfection ever in His **s.**, He
T-15...... IX.4:4 Limit your **s.** of a brother to his body,
T-15...... IX.6:5 your **s.** grows weak and dim and limited,
T-15....... X.6:6 the ego takes to protect itself from your **s.**
T-16......... I.3:8 thought in mind and do not lose **s.** of it,
T-16...... IV.1:6 merely drive it underground and out of **s.**.
T-16...... IV.1:7 It is essential to bring it into **s.**, and to
T-16...... VI.6:4 so diminished in your **s.** that you will see
T-17....... II.1:5 part of the happiness this **s.** will bring you
T-17....... II.6:1 All this beauty will rise to bless your **s.** as
T-17...... III.2:1 that would make the ego holy in your **s.**,
T-17...... III.6:8 be unwilling ever to lose the **s.** of it again.
T-17... V.11:10 the holy instant, and thus lose **s.** of it.
T-18......... I.8:1 and turning till they disappear from **s.**,
T-18....... II.7:2 share with all who come within your **s.**.
T-18.... VI.12:3 be anything and anywhere; a sound, a **s.**,
T-18..... VII.2:2 It has perhaps faded at times from your **s.**
T-18...... IX.1:8 not lost it, but *you* have lost **s.** of Heaven.
T-18...... IX.2:5 Its bleak **s.** is distorted, and the messages
T-19....... I.12:7 eyes, but in the **s.** of Him Who joined you,
T-19....... I.14:5 No error interferes with its calm **s.**, which
T-19...... III.9:1 lips, and Heaven's blessing on your **s.**.
T-19..... III.10:6 Heaven will disappear before your holy **s.**,
T19. IV.A.15:2 world will be transformed before your **s.**,
T-20....... II.5:2 have asked for and received another **s.**.
T-20....... V.5:4 The **s.** that sees the body has no use which
T-20..... VII.5:6 wish, for **s.** is always secondary to desire.
T-20..... VII.8:7 holy brother, **s.** of whom is your release,
T-20... VIII.5:9 For this is not *your* **s.**, and brings with it
T-20... VIII.5:9 it the laws beloved of Him Whose **s.** it is.
T-20... VIII.6:1 brought to it by His calm and certain **s.**.
T-20. VIII.10:3 must thus reflect the **s.** you saw within; or
T-21......... I.9:2 is the **s.** of him who knows his Father.
T-21.......... II.h The Responsibility for **S.**
T-21....... II.8:4 and see what must be there, plainly in **s.**,
T-21...... III.9:9 in the innocence that makes the **s.** of it as
T-21.... III.10:1 has given it great power in your **s.**; except
T-21.... III.11:6 Yet **s.** of one is but the sign the other has
T-21.... III.11:6 the sign the other has disappeared from **s.**
T-21...... IV.8:1 ego's weakness is revealed in both your **s.**.
T-22.......in.4:4 is **s.** of differences transformed to vision.
T-22......... I.2:5 **s.** is wholly independent of the eyes that
T-22......... I.3:5 have made to be yourself becomes your **s.**.
T-22......... I.3:6 sees, and as *not* you, explains its **s.** *to* you.
T-22......... I.4:9 to **s.** of differences and loss of sameness.
T-22......... I.5:1 **s.** was given you, along with everything
T-22......... I.5:3 is. And what your **s.** would show you, you
T-22......... I.9:7 Nor could it be a fearful **s.** or sound that
T-22...... III.1:7 literally. If it is not the body's **s.**, it *must* be
T-22...... III.5:8 Yet how can **s.** that stops at nothingness,
T-22...... III.6:8 For **s.** of form means understanding has
T-22...... III.8:2 the **s.** of which would show you your
T-22...... IV.4:6 beautiful the **s.** you saw beyond the veil,
T-22...... IV.5:2 in his **s.** your loveliness is his salvation,
T-22...... VI.7:2 form of suffering could block your **s.**,
T-23.......in.5:3 not let time intrude upon your **s.** of him.
T-23......... I.4:4 peace is here transformed, before your **s.**,
T-23....... II.8:3 there is no **s.** of help that can succeed.
T-23....... II.9:7 because they keep it hidden from your **s.**.
T-23...... III.4:7 it become impossible that you lose **s.** of it
T-23...... III.4:8 vision, forever clear and never out of **s.**, if
T-24....... II.1:3 by searching for, and keeping clear in **s.**,
T-24..... II.11:6 with the hope of peace at last in **s.**.
T-24..... II.12:4 from eyes it veils but looks on **s.** of death.
T-24..... II.14:2 save through the **s.** of all your misery, and
T-24....... V.4:4 What does it seek for but the **s.** of death?
T-24....... V.7:7 The **s.** of Christ is all there is to see. The
T-24...... VI.6:3 no **s.** nor place nor time where He is not.
T-24...VII.10:1 beyond itself, and no escape within its **s.**.
T-25...... III.5:2 and the **s.** of perfect sinlessness. Nothing
T-25...... III.8:9 for sin has been corrected by His **s.**. And
T-25....... V.5:5 you the gift of **s.** God gave to him for you!
T-25...... VI.1:6 kindness of his **s.** rests on himself with all
T-25...... VI.1:8 looks on with the grace of God upon his **s.**
T-25...... VI.3:1 the gift of light that makes **s.** possible.
T-25..... VII.6:5 sin is equally insane within the **s.** of love,
T-25..... VII.8:2 He to raise a saner world to meet the **s.** of
T-25. VIII.13:5 since they are equal in the Holy Spirit's **s.**.
T-25...... IX.4:1 The **s.** of innocence makes punishment
T-25...... IX.5:6 is reflected in the **s.** the Holy Spirit gives.
T-26......... I.3:4 For **s.** of bodies becomes the sign that
T-26....... I.4:10 and **s.** of him replace the body's eyes.
T-26......... I.6:1 You can lose **s.** of oneness, but can not
T-26....... II.7:3 resolved before the Holy Spirit's gentle **s.**.
T-26....... II.7:4 For all of them *are* little in His **s.**, and
T-26...... IX.8:4 and ancient scars are healed within His **s.**.
T-27....... II.8:8 has been established in your **s.** and his.
T-27....... V.6:5 give them **s.** to see beyond all suffering
T-27....... V.7:5 Christ to you who brought the **s.** to them,
T-27... VII.14:6 The dream of guilt is fading from your **s.**,
T-28...... VI.2:1 responsible for **s.** a thing that cannot see,
T-30.... VIII.6:4 the changeless in him in your **s.** of him.
T-31...... II.11:8 A blindfold can indeed obscure your **s.**,
T-31....... V.12:5 It also shows some glimmering of **s.** into
T-31...... VI.1:8 to touch your eyes and bless your holy **s.**,
T-31...... VI.2:7 constancy arises in the **s.** of those whose
T-31...... VI.3:6 how what you see arose to meet your **s.**.
T-31...... VI.6:2 Then the world is harmless in your **s.**. Do
T-31..... VII.2:5 *one* brother dawn upon your **s.** as wholly
T-31..... VII.3:3 grows decreasingly persistent in your **s.**,
T-31..... VII.3:4 the **s.** your eyes alone can offer you to see.
T-31..... VII.3:6 you. And in His **s.** there *is* another world.
T-31..... VII.7:1 before the truth, and hides it from your **s.**
T-31..... VII.7:2 that dims your **s.** and warps your vision,
T-31..... VII.7:7 All that is given you is for release; the **s.**,
T-31..... VII.8:5 between his **s.** and what he looks upon, to
T-31..... VII.8:7 and now the veil is lifted from his **s.**.
T-31..... VII.9:3 bound to separation from the **s.** of him
T-31.... VIII.4:3 majesty, and disappears before His holy **s.**
T-31.... VIII.9:3 appear like lawns of Heaven to our **s.**, to
W-pI....... 4.2:4 beyond, and shadows make **s.** difficult.
W-pI....... 4.2:5 The "bad" ones are blocks to **s.**, and make
W-pI..... 20.1:4 not lost **s.** of the crucial importance of the
W-pI..... 30.3:2 now if it were within the range of your **s.**.
W-pI..... 36.1:3 you are holy, your **s.** must be holy as well.
W-pI..... 36.1:8 Your **s.** is related to His Holiness, not to
W-pI..... 46.6:1 the central idea should not be lost **s.** of.
W-pI..... 54.3:7 me will dawn on their **s.** as well as mine.
W-pI..... 75.3:2 **s.** and hide the world forgiveness offers us
W-pI..... 75.4:5 **S.** is given us, now that the light has come
W-pI..... 75.7:2 fails to give the gift of **s.** to the forgiving.
W-pI..... 75.9:4 of forgiveness to heal your **s.** completely.
W-pI... 75.11:2 of your vision and the **s.** of the real world,
W-pI..... 78.2:2 by not allowing **s.** to stop before it sees.
W-pI..... 78.3:2 For every grievance is a block to **s.**, and as
W-pI..... 78.8:7 No dark grievances obscure the **s.** of him.
W-pI..... 81.3:3 and perfectly unambiguous before my **s.**.
W-pI..... 85.2:2 *Let me not use this as a block to* **s.**. *The light*
W-pI..... 92.8:2 No one can ask in vain to share its **s.**, and
W-pI... 92.10:3 the light in which the gift of **s.** is given you
W-pI... 92.11:3 that we are being introduced to **s.**, and
W-pI..... 97.4:4 thing; offers His **s.** to everyone who asks;
W-pI... 104.5:2 We will not let ourselves lose **s.** of them
W-pI. 124.11:2 a **s.** too holy for the body's eyes to see.
W-pI... 128.3:3 value greater in your **s.** limit you further,
W-pI. 130.11:1 damned your eyes and cursed your **s.**, and
W-pI. 154.14:4 spring to our **s.** and leap into our hands,
W-pI... 156.7:5 may perhaps lose **s.** of your Companion,
W-pI... 159.4:5 And in His **s.** the sinless are as one. Their
W-pI. 160.10:5 thus refusing to accept the gift of **s.** by
W-pI... 161.6:4 **s.** presents the symbol of love's "enemy"
W-pI... 161.9:4 are like him in the **s.** that sees him thus.
W-pI. 161.11:5 you the **s.** of one who can forgive you all
W-pI... 162.4:5 restored your **s.** by salvaging your mind.
W-pI... 164.1:3 upon what is forever there; not in our **s.**,
W-pI... 164.2:1 The world fades easily away before His **s.**.
W-pI... 164.3:1 Christ gives you His **s.** and hears for you,
W-pI... 164.7:5 We stand forgiven in the **s.** of Christ, with
W-pI... 165.5:6 **s.** proves that you have exchanged your
W-pI. 166.11:2 and the **s.** that looked upon it now has
W-pI... 181.2:8 you will not transcend their **s.** and see the
W-pI... 181.6:2 us, our narrowed focus will restrict our **s.**,
W-pI. 182.12:8 and the journey has an end in **s.** at last. Be
W-pI. 184.13:5 One Name we use to unify our **s.**.
W-pI. 184.14:5 Now our **s.** is blessed with blessings we
W-pI. 187.11:5 And to ensure this holy **s.** is ours, we offer
W-pI... 188.2:6 There is no **s.**, be it of dreams or from a
W-pI... 188.6:3 has power to give the gift of **s.** to you.
W-pI... 189.1:5 in you to be kept hidden from your **s.**.
W-pI... 189.6:1 **s.** which is the gift its Love bestows on us.
W-pI... 191.2:5 is no **s.** that fails to witness this to you.
W-pI... 192.6:1 that, for Christ's vision and the gift of **s.**,
W-pI... 193.2:3 for One Who can correct his erring **s.**, and
W-pI... 194.1:2 with the goal in **s.** and obstacles behind.
W-pI. 198.12:6 this single **s.** and timelessness itself, you
W-pI. 198.13:1 stand between this vision and our **s.**. And
W-pII ..... 3.4:1 As **s.** was made to lead away from truth,
W-pII . 247.1:4 Let me accept what His **s.** shows me as the
W-pII . 266.1:1 *to be my saviors and my counselors in* **s.**; *the*
W-pII . 266.2:3 Him, and given us the **s.** to look on them?

W-pII .268.2:1 Let not our **s.** be blasphemous today, nor
W-pII ....269.h My **s.** goes forth to look upon Christ's
W-pII .269.1:1 *I ask Your blessing on my* **s.** *today. It is the*
W-pII .269.2:1 Today our **s.** is blessed indeed. We share
W-pII .270.1:1 *all that the body's eyes behold into the* **s.** *of a*
W-pII .270.1:3 *more will I perceive in it than* **s.** *can give. The*
W-pII .270.2:3 And through His **s.** we offer healing to the
W-pII .271.1:3 Christ's **s.**, the world and God's creation
W-pII .271.1:4 kindly **s.** redeems the world from death,
W-pII .289.1:1 mind, the real world must escape my **s.**.
W-pII .290.1:4 the **s.** I made is frightening and painful to
W-pII .291.1:2 His **s.** shows me all things forgiven and at
W-pII .293.2:1 *let not Your holy world escape my* **s.** *today.*
W-pII .298.1:3 on my holy **s.** forgiveness takes away. And
W-pII .302.1:2 *us, as our* **s.** *is finally restored and we can see.*
W-pII ....304.h Let not my world obscure the **s.** of Christ.
W-pII .304.1:1 I can obscure my holy **s.**, if I intrude my
W-pII ... 10.1:4 And with this holy **s.**, perception gives a
W-pII ... 10.2:3 and now without a function in Christ's **s.**,
W-pII .312.1:3 For **s.** can merely serve to offer us what we
W-pII .312.1:5 to greet the holy **s.** of anyone who takes
W-pII .313.1:5 *In His* **s.** *are all its sins forgiven, for He sees*
W-pII .313.2:1 today behold each other in the **s.** of Christ
W-pII ... 13.3:3 Perception stands corrected in His **s.**, and
M-3 ........... 2:6 two people to lose **s.** of separate interests,
M-13 ......... 2:9 Identity and losing **s.** of what it really is.
M-18 ......... 2:7 completely in His **s.** and in God's Word.
M-25 ......... 6:9 hearts, and His holy **s.** not far behind.
M-28 ......... 5:3 What further **s.** is needed? What remains
M-29 ......... 8:4 *of time; to end the* **s.** *Of all things visible; and*
C-5............. 5:5 will with his, your **s.** will be his vision, for
P-3....... II.10:2 has lost **s.** of the Source of his salvation.
S-2 ...........I.2:3 large and grow and swell within its **s.**. It
S-2 ...........I.7:5 **s.** the world becomes as holy as Himself.
S-2 ........ III.2:3 eyes of Christ become the **s.** you choose.
S-3 ........ IV.1:2 For in their **s.** their brothers share their

## sightless 13

T-18..VIII.13:2 seems to cloud your eyes and keep you **s.**.
T-19.... III.10:6 you who were **s.** have been given vision,
T-21.........I.1:1 the world the **s.** "see" must be imagined,
T-23.... II.15:6 And fear, with ashen lips and **s.** eyes,
T-24....... V.4:2 each intent, in the dark forest of the **s.**,
T-24....... V.4:8 from the bone and **s.** holes for eyes, is like
T-24....... V.7:3 He gives them vision for their **s.** eyes, and
T-25..... V.2:11 your Savior, seeing Him through **s.** eyes?
W-pI... 78.10:4 For you both, and all the **s.** ones as well,
W-pI... 121.4:2 It looks upon the world with **s.** eyes, and
W-pI... 163.2:2 grasp; all goals perceived but in its **s.** eyes.
W-pI.170.11:6 by its weight; beheld not in its **s.** eyes, but
W-pI... 218.1:2 *my* **s.** *eyes I cannot see the vision of my glory.*

## sights 28

T-13....... V.1:6 They are made of **s.** that are not seen, and
T-13....... V.10:2 worlds arise from their different **s.**. See
T-20..VIII.10:4 **s.** with which He would replace them.
T-20..VIII.10:5 These gentle **s.** and sounds are looked on
T-20..VIII.10:6 His substitutes for all the terrifying **s.** and
T-20..VIII.11:1 and seen it change to **s.** of loveliness and
T-21....... V.1:9 to hear, and on the **s.** you choose to see,
T-22.........I.6:5 times. Neither the sounds he hears nor **s.**
T-24....... V.3:6 How gentle are the **s.** He sees, the sounds
T-24....... V.7:5 And He rejoices that these **s.** are yours, to
T-28....... V.4:4 Yet **s.** and sounds the body can perceive
T-28....... V.5:5 other sounds and other **s.** that *can* be seen
T-31....... V.4:4 here the learning of the world has set its **s.**
W-pI..... 49.4:4 riotous thoughts and **s.** and sounds of this
W-pI..... 94.1:3 are still, the **s.** of this world disappear,
W-pI... 164.3:4 **s.** and sounds that come from nearer than
W-pI... 192.3:6 behold the joyful **s.** their offerings contain
W-pII ..... 4.1:5 need have they of **s.** or sounds or touch?
W-pII ..... 7.1:4 There are **s.** and sounds forever laid aside.
W-pII ..... 7.2:2 **s.** and sounds must be translated from
W-pII ..... 8.2:1 a sure correction for the **s.** of fear and
W-pII ..... 8.2:5 And the **s.** are gentle. Only happy sights
W-pII ..... 8.2:6 Only happy **s.** and sounds can reach the
W-pII .303.1:3 **s.** to which I am accustomed disappear.
W-pII .303.1:5 and see but **s.** that show His Father's Love
W-pII .304.1:2 can I behold the holy **s.** Christ looks upon
W-pII .331.2:2 it. Let us look upon the holy **s.** forgiveness
W-pII .336.1:3 For **s.** and sounds, at best, can serve but

## sign 69

T-1 .........II.3:4 is therefore a **s.** of love among equals.
T-1 ........ V.6:1 miracle is a **s.** that the mind has chosen to
T-2 ....... III.1:9 structures is a **s.** of the fear of Atonement,
T-2 ..... VI.2:10 a sure **s.** that you have allowed your mind
T-2 ....... VI.5:1 Fear is always a **s.** of strain, arising
T-2 ....... VI.8:1 always a **s.** of respect *from* the worthy *to*
T-5 ........ V.4:8 is a sure **s.** that your thinking is unnatural
T-5 ........ V.7:3 are always a **s.** that you do not know this.
T-6 ... V.C.10:3 is the **s.** that you *want* Him to guide you.
T-8 ..........I.4:4 outcomes is a **s.** of learning failure, since
T-8 ....... IX.4:1 wake is the **s.** of how you have used sleep.
T-9 ....... IV.6:3 wrong. Miracles are merely the **s.** of your
T-10 ..... III.1:4 a sure **s.** that you hate what you *think* you
T-10 ..... IV.3:4 because it is the **s.** that you have removed
T-10 ...... V.1:2 depression is the **s.** of allegiance to him.
T-11 .......II.4:1 is a **s.** that you want to make whole. And
T-11 .......II.5:3 your care is a **s.** that you want Him. Think
T-11 .... V.17:7 is the **s.** that they have beheld God's Son,
T-13 ..... IX.8:7 Within you is the holy **s.** of perfect faith
T-15 ...VIII.1:3 must side with every **s.** or token of your
T-15 ..... XI.2:1 The **s.** of Christmas is a star, a light in
T-15 ..... XI.2:2 it as the **s.** the time of Christ has come. He
T-16 .... V.12:4 invested in His killer as the **s.** that form
T-16 ..... VI.1:1 the special relationship is the **s.** that you
T-17 .......II.6:3 a blade of grass a **s.** of God's perfection.
T-17 .... VII.3:5 thought of bodies is the **s.** of faithlessness,
T-19 ........I.9:2 **s.** that you have accepted the Atonement
T-19 ......I.12:2 and is the **s.** you share it with Him. Faith
T19..IV.C.11:1 it as a symbol of fear, a **s.** of sin and death
T19..IV.C.11:2 neither **s.** nor symbol should be confused
T19..IV.C.11:9 *Let me not see it as a* **s.** *of sin and death, nor*
T-20 ........I.1:3 For Easter is the **s.** of peace, not pain. A
T-20 ........I.1:5 the **s.** he looks upon himself as healed and
T-20 ........I.2:1 and holy **s.** the Son of God is innocent.
T-20 ........I.2:2 Let no dark **s.** of crucifixion intervene
T-20 ........I.3:2 started with the **s.** of victory, the promise
T-20 .... VII.8:2 see the body is the **s.** that you lack vision,
T-20 ...VIII.5:1 body is the **s.** of weakness, vulnerability
T-21 ... III.11:6 Yet sight of one is but the **s.** the other has
T-23 ..... III.2:1 blessing and a **s.** the Voice for God speaks
T-24 ..... VI.1:7 the **s.** that this is so lies in your brother,
T-24 .... VII.5:9 you, a **s.** that you have not forgotten them
T-26 ........I.3:4 becomes the **s.** that sacrifice is limited,
T-27 ........I.2:3 to be the **s.** that he has lost his innocence,
T-27 ........I.8:4 the **s.** of guilt whose consequences still are
T-27 ......I.10:3 death. The body can become a **s.** of life, a
T-27 ......I.11:2 picture is a lasting **s.** of what it represents.
T-29 .... VII.5:1 no life, and what is lifeless is a **s.** of death.
T-29 ...VIII.4:2 from something living to a **s.** of death. Its
T-29 ... IX.10:2 dreams become a **s.** that you have made a
T-30 ... VI.10:4 to you a graven image and a **s.** of death. Is
T-31 .... V.15:6 To see a guilty world is but the **s.** your
T-31 .... VII.2:7 should be the **s.** of evil and of guilt in him.
W-pI....... 1.2:5 **s.** *does not mean anything. That shadow*
W-pI..... 48.3:1 The presence of fear is a sure **s.** that you
W-pI... 100.5:3 is the **s.** that you would play another part,
W-pI... 101.6:2 pain is but the **s.** you have misunderstood
W-pI. 133.10:2 a **s.** of deep unworthiness within himself.
W-pI... 134.5:2 is a further **s.** that sin is unforgivable, at
W-pI... 136.5:3 not remembering is but the **s.** that this
W-pI... 167.6:7 seems to die is but the **s.** of mind asleep.
W-pI... 190.3:1 is a **s.** illusions reign in place of truth. It
W-pI... 196.2:2 appear to be a **s.** that punishment can
W-pII . 310.1:4 *holy Son, the* **s.** *Your grace has come to me,*
W-pII ... 12.1:1 the **s.** of limited and separated self, born
P-3.........II.5:3 gift from their Creator as a **s.** of His Love.
S-3........in.1:3 is a **s.** or symbol of forgiveness' strength,
S-3...........I.1:2 It is a **s.**, a shadow of an evil thought that
S-3...........I.3:4 the **s.** of judgment made by brother upon

## significant 1

P-2.........in.3:3 changing his self-concept to any **s.** extent.

## signified 2

T-13 ... VI.12:2 willingly, and willingness is **s.** by giving.
T-18 ..... III.2:3 for which you **s.** your willingness. Fear

## signifies 5

T-14 ... III.13:3 alone but **s.** that you would define what
W-pI .... 37.1:5 It **s.** the end of sacrifice because it offers
W-pII . 270.1:4 *world forgiven* **s.** *Your Son acknowledges*
W-pII ..... 8.4:3 The real world **s.** the end of time, for its
S-3........II.1:10 merely **s.** the end has come for usefulness

## signify 7

T-10 .......II.3:6 But **s.** your will to remember Him, and
T-10 ..... III.9:6 for you the instant you **s.** your willingness
T19 .IV.A.15:7 And they go forth to **s.** the end of fear.
T19 ... IV.B.6:6 what I **s.** to you you see within yourself?
T-29 ........I.4:4 and thereby **s.** a meeting place to join. But
W-pII ..... 7.4:3 return to **s.** the end of dreams has come.
W-pII . 287.2:4 *except the memory of You could* **s.** *to me the*

## signifying 2

T-8 .......V.2:12 you are **s.** your awareness that the Will of
W-pI .... 70.7:1 adding a statement **s.** your recognition

## signpost 1

T-31 ..... IV.4:5 this. Seek not another **s.** in the world that

## signs 11

T-1 ........I.21:1 Miracles are natural **s.** of forgiveness.
T-8 ....... IX.8:7 All forms of sickness are **s.** that the mind
T-23 ..... IV.6:2 you do not recognize, the **s.** you know.
T-27 ........I.9:4 only takes away from it all **s.** of accusation
T-29 .... VII.5:2 but to perceive the **s.** of death you seek?
W-pI .... 13.5:4 any **s.** of overt or covert fear which it may
W-pI .... 15.3:4 **s.** that you are opening your eyes at last.
W-pI .... 55.1:2 What I see now are but **s.** of disease,
W-pI .. 184.6:2 so accepts the **s.** and symbols that assert
W-pII . 304.1:6 I will look upon the certain **s.** that all my
W-pII ... 13.5:4 And everywhere the **s.** of life spring up, to

## silence 38

T-11 .....V.17:7 Their **s.** is the sign that they have beheld
T-14 ... XI.11:4 Listen in **s.**, and do not raise your voice
T-27 ..... VI.1:2 shrieks would **s.** what the Holy Spirit says
T-28 ......I.12:5 The instant's **s.** that His Son accepts gives
T-28 .....II.12:2 stand in shining **s.** next to every dream of
W-pI .... 49.4:1 Listen in deep **s.**. Be very still and open
W-pI .. 72.13:6 Then wait a minute or so in **s.**, preferably
W-pI .... 78.2:3 lift our eyes in **s.** to behold the Son of God
WpIrIII.in10:5 mind to rest a little time in **s.** and in peace
W-pI .. 125.3:5 world, but wait in **s.** for the Word of God.
W-pI .. 125.6:2 His Voice awaits your **s.**, for His Word
W-pI .. 125.7:1 times today, at times most suitable for **s.**,
W-pI 126.10:1 In **s.**, close your eyes upon the world that
W-pI .. 129.3:3 into a **s.** where the language is unspoken
W-pI 140.12:6 be given us as we attend in **s.** and in joy.
W-pI 152.11:5 Then will we wait in **s.**, giving up all self-
W-pI 153.10:1 and in **s.** think how holy is your purpose,
W-pI .. 157.1:1 is a day of **s.** and of trust. It is a special
W-pI .. 164.4:1 a **s.** into which the world can not intrude.
W-pI .. 182.5:7 home, resting in **s.** and in peace and love.
W-pI .. 183.5:4 you join a brother as you sit with him in **s.**
W-pI 198.11:1 Now is there **s.** all around the world.
W-pI 200.10:1 Now is there **s.**. Seek no further. You
W-pI .. 211.1:2 *In* **s.** *and in true humility I seek God's glory,*
W-pII .... in.7:1 And now we wait in **s.**, unafraid and
W-pII . 221.1:2 *I come in* **s.**. *In the quiet of my heart, the deep*
W-pII . 221.1:5 *today. I come to hear Your Voice in* **s.** *and in*

| | |
|---|---|
| W-pII..254.1:2 | *In deepest* **s.** *I would come to You, to hear* |
| W-pII..305.1:3 | departs in **s.** as this peace envelops it, and |
| W-pII....12.3:4 | undisturbed, in deepest **s.** and tranquility |
| W-pII..360.1:3 | *I would reach to them in* **s.** *and in certainty,* |
| W-ep .........3:3 | mind, and when to come to Him in **s.**, |
| M-14..........2:7 | turning to Him in **s.** to receive His Word. |
| M-15........1:10 | and **s.** lies across the world that everyone |
| M-21..........4:3 | words, being as yet unable to hear in **s.**. |
| C-ep...........4:1 | Let us wait here in **s.**, and kneel down an |
| S-2 ...........I.6:6 | constancy remains in tranquil **s.** and in |
| S-2 ......... II.4:4 | respond except with **s.** and a gentle smile? |

## silenced 1

| | |
|---|---|
| W-pI ...136.8:4 | beyond this little pile of dust **s.** and stilled |

## silencer 1

| | |
|---|---|
| T19 ... IV.C.7:2 | the **s.** of the Voice that speaks for God. |

## silences 1

| | |
|---|---|
| W-pI ...106.2:1 | which **s.** the thunder of the meaningless, |

## silent 22

| | |
|---|---|
| T-11..... V.17:8 | They are **s.** because Christ speaks to them |
| T-21 .....VII.2:5 | are the dark ones, **s.** and afraid, alone and |
| T-24 ....... II.4:5 | **s.** and unheard before its "mightiness." |
| T-24 ....... II.9:5 | you and your brother in **s.** blessing, and |
| T-27 ...... III.4:1 | a **s.** invitation to the truth to enter, and to |
| T-27 ....... V.3:4 | the screaming dying and the **s.** dead, are |
| T-30 ......IV.2:2 | or when a soft and **s.** woolly bear begins |
| T-31 .....VII.7:1 | a shield, a **s.** barricade before the truth, |
| W-pI .....76.9:2 | hold your mind in **s.** readiness to hear the |
| W-pI .....94.1:1 | one thought which renders the ego **s.** and |
| W-pI .....94.4:1 | and wait in **s.** expectancy for the truth. |
| W-pI ...106.4:2 | Hear and be **s.**. He would speak to you. |
| W-pI ...129.7:5 | **s.** darkness watch the lights that are not |
| W-pI ...182.8:3 | Him in perfect stillness, **s.** and at peace, |
| W-pI.183.11:1 | All little things are **s.**. Little sounds are |
| W-pI ...189.2:4 | the night as **s.** guardian of your holy sleep |
| W-pII..254.2:5 | They are **s.** now. And in the stillness, |
| W-pII....10.1:4 | gives a **s.** blessing and then disappears, its |
| W-pII....13.3:4 | offers all the world the **s.** miracle of love. |
| M-29..........8:3 | *all the world stands* **s.** *in the grace You bring* |
| S-2 ......... II.5:2 | **s.** proof of guilt and of the ravages of sin. |
| S-3 ......IV.10:2 | The song of prayer is **s.** without you. The |

## silently 17

| | |
|---|---|
| T-11.....III.1:5 | no attack and His peace surrounds you **s.**. |
| T-16.........I.6:2 | it **s.** by enveloping it in healing wings. Let |
| T-16......IV.8:1 | Heaven waits **s.**, and your creations are |
| T-31 ....... II.8:6 | to which you come to listen **s.** and learn |
| T-31 ....... V.6:8 | symbol of your sins to you who are but **s.**, |
| W-pI .....37.6:2 | helpful to apply it **s.** to anyone you meet, |
| W-pI .....43.7:2 | example, try to remember to tell him **s.**: |
| W-pI .....46.7:4 | In that event, tell him **s.**: *God is the Love in* |
| W-pI ...93.11:2 | become angry with someone, tell him **s.**: |
| W-pI.134.11:1 | of hatred and attack brought **s.** to truth. |
| W-pI.151.13:3 | thoughts, appealing **s.** to Him Who sees |
| W-pI ...183.8:3 | Sit **s.**, and let His Name become the all- |
| W-pII.....in.5:5 | Sit **s.** and wait upon your Father. He has |
| W-pII..307.2:1 | this prayer we enter **s.** into a state where |
| P-2 ......... V.8:1 | Let us stand **s.** before God's Will, and do |
| P-3 ......... II.3:6 | and the therapist will **s.** ask him for help. |
| S-2 ........ III.7:7 | will see the door swing **s.** open upon the |

## silly 3

| | |
|---|---|
| W-pI .....29.2:2 | You may find it **s.**, irreverent, senseless, |
| W-pI ...153.6:4 | folly, or a **s.** game a tired child might play, |
| W-pI ...156.6:5 | It is a foolish thought, a **s.** dream, not |

## silver 3

| | |
|---|---|
| T-28 ...... III.7:1 | the **s.** miracles and golden dreams of |
| T-28 ...... III.7:2 | stored a heap of snow that shone like **s.**. |
| WpI. rIV.in4:3 | the sun, the **s.** of the moon on it by night. |

## similar 6

| | |
|---|---|
| T-2...........I.2:4 | **s.** to the inner radiance that the children |
| T-5......... II.1:3 | it is very **s.** to the shift in the perception of |
| T-6.........I.15:7 | called forth upon Judas was a **s.** mistake. |
| T-12...... VI.6:7 | so **s.** that they share the unification of the |
| T-22.........I.2:1 | we have heard a very **s.** description earlier |
| W-pI .......6.1:1 | this idea are very **s.** to the preceding ones. |

## similarity 1

| | |
|---|---|
| T-7........ IV.3:8 | their **s.** rather than their differences is |

## similarly 4

| | |
|---|---|
| T-2......... V.5:5 | truth that their minds are **s.** constructive, |
| T-2..... VIII.2:5 | will extend over a **s.** long period, and |
| T-8....... VII.1:7 | and seeing his brothers as **s.** belittled. |
| T-17..... V.11:6 | Have you been **s.** grateful to your brother |

## simple 158

*See also* simple-minded

| | |
|---|---|
| T-2........ VI.6:5 | your own. The lesson here is quite **s.**, but |
| T-3...........I.5:2 | it is a very **s.** symbol that speaks of my |
| T-4......... VI.6:2 | Your mission is very **s.**. You are asked to |
| T-5...........I.2:1 | of reawakening with just a few **s.** concepts |
| T-5........ II.8:11 | The decision is very **s.**. It is made on the |
| T-6........ II.12:1 | and the Holy Spirit's extension is very **s.**. |
| T-6......... V.3:5 | This **s.** statement is perfectly clear, easily |
| T-9.........I.14:2 | be. This is the **s.** acceptance of reality, |
| T-9......... V.9:1 | very direct and a very **s.** learning situation |
| T-9....... VII.2:6 | The reason is very **s.**, and so obvious that |
| T-11....... IV.4:3 | the denial of this **s.** fact takes many forms, |
| T-11....... V.3:5 | Yet the truth is very **s.**: *All power is of God.* |
| T-11... VIII.1:1 | This is a very **s.** course. Perhaps you do |
| T-11... VIII.4:5 | yourself, therefore, but one **s.** question: |
| T-11. VIII.10:4 | nothing will be denied your **s.** request. |
| T-12.........I.1:1 | error real, and the way to do this is very **s.** |
| T-12.........I.6:4 | How **s.**, then, is God's plan for salvation. |
| T-14.......in.1:8 | and follow the **s.** logic by which the Holy |
| T-14.......in.1:8 | the **s.** conclusions that speak for truth, |
| T-14.........I.5:2 | but He must introduce the **s.** truth into a |
| T-14....... II.2:5 | Nothing is so alien to you as the **s.** truth, |
| T-14....... II.2:7 | The **s.** and the obvious are not apparent |
| T-14....... II.3:8 | *find no deception there, but only the* **s.** *truth* |
| T-14....... II.5:6 | for when you look at it in **s.** honesty, it *is* |
| T-14....... II.7:5 | This **s.** lesson holds the key to the dark |
| T-14....... II.8:5 | realize it is impossible to deny the **s.** truth |
| T-14...... III.7:1 | The way to teach this **s.** lesson is merely |
| T-14.... III.10:4 | And they will fail to understand the **s.** fact |
| T-14....... X.6:8 | The answer is very **s.**. The power of God, |
| T-14....... XI.6:3 | know? Your part is very **s.**. You need only |
| T-15...... IV.6:1 | The reason this course is **s.** is that truth is |
| T-15...... IV.6:1 | this course is simple is that truth is **s.**. |
| T-15...... IV.6:3 | to eternity, but for a very **s.** reason. Do |
| T-15...... IV.6:5 | The **s.** reason, simply stated, is this: The |
| T-15....... X.9:6 | so easy. Salvation is **s.**, being of God, and |
| T-15...... XI.1:6 | and as **s.** as opening your eyes to daylight |
| T-16..... V.14:1 | Salvation lies in the **s.** fact that illusions |
| T-16..... V.14:3 | are failing to make the **s.** choice between |
| T-16..... V.16:3 | How **s.** does this choice become when it is |
| T-16.... VI.10:7 | awaits you for the **s.** willingness to give up |
| T-17...... VI.1:1 | the Holy Spirit's purpose is extremely **s.**, |
| T-17...... VI.1:2 | in order to be **s.** it *must* be unequivocal. |
| T-17...... VI.1:3 | The **s.** is merely what is easily understood |
| T-17... VIII.2:1 | This **s.** courtesy is all the Holy Spirit asks |
| T-18...... IV.5:6 | than **s.** willingness to make way for it. |
| T-18...... IX.2:3 | It is extremely **s.**, being based on what |
| T-20...... III.4:1 | A **s.** question yet remains, and needs an |
| T-20...... VI.2:7 | sincerity so **s.** and so obvious it cannot be |
| T-20..... VII.1:3 | Being so **s.** and direct, this course has |
| T-20.... VIII.8:5 | Once you accept this **s.** fact and take unto |
| T-21....... II.1:3 | is so **s.** that it cannot fail to be completely |
| T-21....... V.3:4 | **s.** and as natural to it as breathing to the |
| T-21....... V.4:6 | is obvious, **s.** and remains unasked. But |
| T-21....... V.6:1 | God's plan is **s.**; never circular and never |
| T-25..VIII.11:3 | **S.** justice asks no more. Of each one does |
| T-25..VIII.12:9 | Spirit that **s.** justice may be given you. |
| T-26...... III.1:8 | truth is **s.**; it is one, without an opposite. |
| T-26...... III.1:9 | how could strife enter in its **s.** presence, |
| T-26...... III.2:5 | is every thought made pure and wholly **s.**. |
| T-26...... III.4:5 | It is but a **s.** statement of a simple fact. |
| T-26...... III.4:5 | It is but a simple statement of a **s.** fact. |
| T-26...... III.4:6 | fact. But in this world there are no **s.** facts, |
| T-26...... III.7:4 | How **s.** is the choice between two things |
| T-26...... IV.1:2 | translates the world of sin into a **s.** world, |
| T-26...... IV.1:4 | the world gives way to **s.** justice past the |
| T-26....... V.5:2 | to affect the **s.** knowledge of the Son of |
| T-26...... X.1:11 | Its **s.** presence shuts the door to Theirs, |
| T-26........X.5:8 | And **s.** justice has been thus denied to |
| T-27........I.11:1 | **s.** way to let this be achieved is merely this |
| T-27...... IV.2:7 | problem must be **s.** and be easily resolved |
| T-27...... IV.3:4 | outside a single, **s.** question is ever asked. |
| T-27..... VII.2:3 | way to solve a problem that is very **s.**, but |
| T-27..... VII.2:6 | his mind to let a **s.** problem be resolved if |
| T-27..VIII.11:3 | will make answer with this very **s.** truth. |
| T-27..VIII.11:6 | that miracles reflect the **s.** statement, "*I* |
| T-28...... III.1:5 | will the way be made serene and **s.** in the |
| T-28.... IV.10:3 | he has received the **s.** happiness of health |
| T-29........II.1:4 | to hell instead of looking on it as a **s.** way, |
| T-30.........I.7:6 | by **s.** methods that you can accept. |
| T-30........I.14:6 | but a **s.** statement of a simple fact. You |
| T-30........I.14:6 | but a simple statement of a **s.** fact. You |
| T-30...... IV.6:2 | And you can make a **s.** choice that will |
| T-30...... IV.6:4 | about, when you decide one very **s.** thing; |
| T-30...... VI.9:6 | is this except a **s.** statement of the truth? |
| T-31.........I.1:1 | How **s.** is salvation! All it says is what was |
| T-31........I.1:10 | you persist in learning not such **s.** things? |
| T-31.........I.2:2 | in the **s.** things salvation asks you learn. It |
| T-31.........I.3:4 | curtains to obscure the **s.** and the obvious |
| T-31.........I.4:6 | say not that you cannot learn the **s.** things |
| T-31.........I.5:6 | His **s.** lessons in forgiveness have a power |
| T-31.........I.6:6 | the **s.** lessons being taught to you in every |
| T-31...... IV.7:7 | it is a **s.** teaching in the obvious. |
| T-31..... V.14:4 | but with the **s.** statement that it thinks. |
| T-31... VII.12:6 | hate, depending only on the **s.** choice of |
| W-in ..........2:1 | The exercises are very **s.**. They do not |
| W-pI..... 39.1:2 | the ideas used for the exercises are very **s.**, |
| W-pI..... 39.2:5 | see at once how direct and **s.** the text is, |
| W-pI..... 44.5:3 | The reason is very **s.**. While you practice |
| W-pI..... 48.2:1 | be very short, very **s.** and very frequent. |
| W-pI..... 64.5:3 | by remembering they are all really very **s.**. |
| W-pI..... 64.5:5 | a **s.** decision really be difficult to make? |
| W-pI..... 64.5:8 | different from just this one **s.** choice. That |
| W-pI..... 67.6:3 | with the **s.** truth about the Son of God. |
| W-pI..... 73.5:6 | The reason is very **s.**. Do you really want |
| W-pI..... 76.2:3 | tells you once again how **s.** is salvation. |
| W-pI..... 77.1:4 | Again, how **s.** is salvation! It is merely a |
| W-pI..... 77.6:7 | answer is a **s.** statement of a simple fact. |
| W-pI..... 77.6:7 | answer is a simple statement of a **s.** fact. |
| W-pI..... 77.7:1 | also be devoted to a reminder of a **s.** fact. |
| W-pI..... 80.3:6 | Accept the peace this **s.** statement brings. |
| W-pI..... 80.7:3 | The means is **s.** honesty. Do not deceive |
| W-pI..... 97.4:4 | who asks; replaces error with the **s.** truth. |
| W-pI... 105.4:4 | already, not in **s.** terms of adding more, |
| W-pI... 108.7:2 | We will use this **s.** lesson in the obvious |
| W-pI. 108.10:1 | very **s.** lesson for today will teach you |
| W-pI... 122.6:7 | of this extremely **s.** statement of the truth. |
| W-pI. 132.17:1 | deny the power of your **s.** change of mind: |
| W-pI. 133.12:3 | hides the very **s.** fact that no decision can |
| W-pI. 133.14:2 | be quick to answer with this **s.** thought: |
| W-pI... 134.8:2 | of lies; the great restorer of the **s.** truth. |
| W-pI... 134.9:1 | is a very **s.** way to find the door to true |
| W-pI. 135.24:2 | And in the light and joy of **s.** trust, you |
| W-pI. 136.12:1 | Such is the **s.** truth. It does not make |
| W-pI... 137.4:4 | to accept what always was the **s.** truth, |
| W-pI... 137.7:1 | which you hold before the **s.** truth. When |
| W-pI... 139.1:6 | that does not entail the single, **s.** question |
| W-pI... 155.3:1 | This is the **s.** choice we make today. The |
| W-pI... 155.3:4 | can look beyond illusion to the **s.** truth in |
| W-pI... 156.1:1 | Today's idea but states the **s.** truth that |
| W-pI... 161.1:2 | Here is salvation in the **s.** words in which |
| W-pI... 182.2:5 | who, in **s.** honesty, without defensiveness |
| W-pI... 192.2:2 | understand a language far beyond his **s.** |
| W-pI... 192.4:3 | be perceived as what it is; a **s.** teaching aid |

W-pI...192.9:3 The way is **s.**. Every time you feel a stab of
W-pI...193.4:3 lesson is so **s.** that it cannot be rejected in
W-pI...193.4:4 if one but wants to see the **s.** lesson there.
W-pI...193.8:6 you fail to learn the **s.** lessons Heaven's
W-pI...198.5:3 and learn the **s.** lessons He would teach,
W-pI.200.11:5 For we have found a **s.**, happy way to
WpI rVI.in.3:8 it deaf to reason, sanity and **s.** truth.
W-pII ....in.3:2 not content ourselves with **s.** practicing in
W-pII ....in.3:3 We say some **s.** words of welcome, and
W-pII .247.1:4 what His sight shows me as the **s.** truth,
W-pII .297.1:3 This is salvation's **s.** formula. And I, who
M-4 .....I.A.6:7 How **s.** is the obvious! And how easy to
M-4 ...... VI.1:1 God's teachers have learned how to be **s.**.
M-5 ...... III.2:2 The **s.** presence of a teacher of God is a
M-16 ....... 10:2 In **s.** statement, it is to this fact that the
M-20 ......... 6:2 **s.** understanding that His Will is wholly
M-22 ....... 6:10 Healing is very **s.**. Atonement is received
C-in ........... 3:8 *The course is s.*. It has one function and one
P-2........ III.3:9 His **s.** Presence is enough to heal.
P-2.... IV.11:10 pursuits. The truth is **s.**, being one for all.
P-2......... V.1:1 While truth is **s.**, it must still be taught to
P-2......... V.2:4 The truth is **s.**. Yet it must be taught to
P-3..... III.8:11 not forget how very **s.** are the ways of God
S-1........ IV.1:7 still in prayer lies in this **s.** thought; this
S-2........ III.1:8 your understanding and your **s.** grasp.

## simple-minded 1

M-16 ....... 11:8 magic is maintained by just one **s.** illusion

## simplest 8

T-9......... V.9:5 Guide, you will learn the **s.** of all lessons:
T-29...... IV.3:1 **s.** form, it can be said attack is a response
W-pI...138.6:2 you have tried to make this is the **s.**, most
W-pI...152.4:1 This is the **s.** of distinctions, yet the most
M-3 ........... 2:1 The **s.** level of teaching appears to be
M-4 ..... VII.1:8 way possible, and at the **s.** of levels, the
M-16 ......... 3:2 the outset it is probably the **s.** to observe.
S-2 ........... I.8:2 This is the choice you make; the **s.** one,

## simplicity 12

T-14....... II.2:1 elsewhere, begins His lesson in **s.** with the
T-14....... II.2:3 one. **S.** is very difficult for twisted minds.
T-14....... II.6:4 open up before you in all its gracious **s.**.
T-14....... II.8:5 The quietness of its **s.** is so compelling
T-15...... IV.6:4 Do not obscure the **s.** of this reason, for if
T-27..... VII.2:4 problem will emerge in all its primitive **s.**.
T-31............ I.h The **S.** of Salvation
W-pI..... 80.5:6 It is in this that the **s.** of salvation lies. It is
W-pI..... 90.1:4 the **s.** of salvation by reinforcing the
W-pI...122.6:6 clear and plain, beyond deceit in its **s.**. All
W-pI...189.6:4 us. For its **s.** avoids the snares the foolish
M-17 ......... 8:5 the lesson's manifest **s.** stands out like an

## simplified 1

T-26... III.4:10 In the real world is choosing **s.**.

## simply 87

T-in ........... 2:1 therefore be summed up very **s.** in this
T-2......... V.4:5 who need healing are **s.** those who have
T-2...... VIII.3:6 It **s.** means that everyone will finally come
T-3......... II.2:6 More **s.**, it means that you never see what
T-6......... I.15:6 of the crucifixion was **s.** that I did not.
T-7........... I.3:4 outward **s.** because it cannot be contained
T-8........... I.4:1 **s.** because it has not made you happy. On
T-8......... II.2:5 **S.** on the grounds of your own experience
T-8........ IV.2:2 **s.** by dissociating itself from everything. It
T-8........ IV.3:4 My mission was **s.** to unite the will of the
T-8......... V.5:4 Ours is **s.** the journey back to God Who is
T-8....... VII.1:4 accepting it **s.** by the belief that attack can
T-9........... I.6:4 the ability to communicate **s.** because
T-9........ IV.5:3 the Holy Spirit lies **s.** in looking beyond
T-9........ VI.2:5 **s.** because you have limited your receiving
T-9........ VI.5:2 Very **s.**, the Holy Spirit teaches you to
T-9....... VII.7:2 knowledge **s.** because knowledge is total.
T-10 ......... I.1:1 know your creations **s.** because you would
T-10 ..... III.2:4 Heal your brothers **s.** by accepting God
T-10 ..... III.9:1 Very **s.**, then, you may believe you are
T-11 ......... I.4:2 made delay can leave time behind **s.** by
T-11 ......... I.4:3 You do not know this **s.** because you have
T-11 .... V.10:7 Very **s.**, then, you have become afraid of
T-12 ..... IV.1:4 be summed up **s.** as: "Seek and do *not* find
T-13 ...... I.11:4 The Holy Spirit dispels it **s.** through the
T-14 ....... II.3:1 this the Holy Spirit sees, and teaches, **s.**,
T-14 ... III.11:3 gives you everything will **s.** offer it to you?
T-14 ..... VI.4:1 Death yields to life **s.** because destruction
T-15 ..... IV.6:5 The simple reason, **s.** stated, is this: The
T-15 ...... V.9:5 His frame of reference is **s.** God. The Holy
T-15 ....... X.5:4 idea is **s.** this: You believe it is possible to
T-16 ...... V.2:1 Very **s.**, the attempt to make guilty is
T-16 .... V.15:1 core of the separation illusion lies **s.** in the
T-16 .... V.17:2 the bridge into reality **s.** because you will
T-17 ......... I.3:3 Very **s.**, your lack of faith in the power
T-17 ........ II.5:1 real world is attained **s.** by the complete
T-17 ..... III.9:6 all their attributes come **s.** from what they
T-17 ..... VI.2:1 first thing to consider, very **s.**, is "What
T-17 ..... VI.4:1 to happen is **s.** that you will perceive the
T-17 ... VIII.1:6 **s.** because you have let it be what it is.
T-18 ..... III.1:6 you forgot was **s.** that God cannot destroy
T-18 . VI.11:11 **s.** by not letting your mind be limited by
T-18 ... VI.13:2 is not attacked, but **s.** properly perceived.
T-18 ... VI.14:7 **s.** because you have been willing to let go
T19... IV.D.1:3 Very **s.**, you would remember your Father
T-21 ........ II.6:3 And, very **s.**, see in it the whole exchange
T-21 ........ II.7:8 **s.** to recognize again the presence of what
T-21 ..... III.3:4 released from them it will be **s.** because he
T-21 ..... VI.3:8 You leave it **s.** by accepting reason where
T-21 .... VII.8:3 any form, all you need do is **s.** ask yourself
T-24 .... VII.6:1 The test of everything on earth is **s.** this;
T-25 ......... I.7:6 All this can very **s.** be reduced to this:
T-27 .... VII.3:1 is **s.** this: "*You* are the cause of what I do.
T-29 .... VII.1:7 all your pain comes **s.** from a futile search
T-30 .... VII.5:1 Escape from judgment **s.** lies in this; all
T-31 ... VIII.2:5 **S.** by never using weakness to direct your
W-pI........ 2.2:2 Take the subjects **s.** as you see them. Try
W-pI..... 48.1:1 The idea for today **s.** states a fact. It is not
W-pI..... 57.1:6 I can leave **s.** by walking out. Nothing
W-pI..... 61.1:7 were created by God. It **s.** states the truth.
W-pI..... 68.4:3 however, is **s.** a matter of motivation.
W-pI..... 71.3:1 in this plan, then, is **s.** to determine what,
W-pI..... 71.5:1 God's plan for salvation works **s.** because
W-pI..... 71.6:2 Very **s.**. The idea for today is the answer.
W-pI..... 91.5:2 is accomplished very **s.**, as you instruct
W-pI..... 97.1:3 It **s.** states the truth. Practice this truth
W-pI... 104.5:1 for Him today by **s.** recognizing that His
W-pI... 125.2:2 for God's plan is **s.** this: The Son of God is
W-pI. 130.11:3 of hell, whatever form it takes, is **s.** this: *It*
WpI. rIV.in2:1 which can be **s.** stated in these words: *My*
W-pI... 160.5:1 How **s.**, then, the question is resolved.
W-pI... 162.4:1 Today we practice **s.**. For the words we
W-pI... 169.5:1 Oneness is **s.** the idea God is. And in His
W-pI... 189.7:1 **S.** do this: Be still, and lay aside all
W-pI... 189.8:3 Your part is **s.** to allow all obstacles that
W-pII . 282.2:4 *The name of fear is s. a mistake. Let me not*
W-ep ......... 1:5 if you **s.** turn to Him and ask it of Him. He
M-3 ........... 3:5 these levels cannot exist is **s.** to say that
M-5 ........ II.3:2 It is **s.** this; the recognition that sickness is
M-8 ........... 3:6 as "reality" is **s.** what the mind prefers. Its
M-16 ......... 7:1 **s.** and how easily does time slip by for the
M-16 ......... 9:7 any kind, in all its forms, **s.** does nothing.
M-25 ......... 6:7 developed "psychic" powers have **s.** let
M-28 ......... 1:1 Very **s.**, the resurrection is the
M-29 ......... 5:4 you is **s.** to accept your true inheritance.
P-1............. 1:1 Very **s.**, the purpose of psychotherapy is
P-2......... VI.1:1 then, can be defined **s.** as forgiveness, for

## simultaneous 5

T-9 ....... VI.6:4 comes first, though they are **s.** in eternity,
T-14 ........ X.3:2 They can be **s.** and legion. This is not
T-25 ..... III.4:1 the **s.** Corrector of the mad belief that
W-pI..... 19.1:4 Thinking and its results are really **s.**, for
W-pI..... 90.3:4 and the answer as **s.** in their occurrence.

## simultaneously 14

T-1 ........ I.16:2 They **s.** increase the strength of the giver
T-1 ........ I.18:4 your own and your neighbor's worth **s.**.
T-2 ....... III.3:8 **s.** weakening the investment in physical
T-2 ....... VI.5:2 conflicting things, either **s.** or successively
T-3 ......... II.6:5 in yourself and in others **s.**. Because you
T-5 ....... VI.2:7 will **s.** exchange guilt for joy, viciousness
T-5 ....... VI.3:5 interpretations of the same thing **s.**; or
T-5 ....... VI.3:5 same thing simultaneously; or almost **s.**,
T-8 .......... I.5:6 If it is carried out by these two teachers **s.**,
T-8 .......... I.6:2 You cannot learn **s.** from two teachers
T-8 .... VII.12:2 both **s.** with the same thing and not suffer
T-10 ........ I.4:1 your mind **s.** to your Creator and your
M-2 ........... 2:4 was established and completed **s.**, for the
M-3 ........... 5:3 those involved have reached a stage **s.** in

## sin 544

T-1 ....... IV.3:1 is lack of light as **s.** is lack of love. It has
T-5 ......... V.4:9 with guilt, because it is the belief in **s.**.
T-5 ....... V.4:10 ego does not perceive **s.** as a lack of love,
T-5 ....... V.4:11 because, as soon as you regard **s.** as a lack,
T-5 ...... VII.5:2 creations. Perceiving this as "**s.**" you
T-10 ....... V.1:5 and in this sense the wages of **s.** *is* death.
T-10 ....... V.6:2 that you could not **s.** against Him. You
T-10 ....... V.9:9 Your Father created you wholly without **s.**
T-10 ..... V.9:10 If you deny Him you bring **s.**, pain and
T-13 ...... in.3:6 Adam's "**s.**" could have touched no one,
T-13 ..... IX.5:5 For **s.** and condemnation are the same,
T-14 ... III.15:3 The Holy Spirit teaches only that the "**s.**"
T-16 ....... V.3:4 believe that hate is **s.** merely feel guilty,
T-16 ....... V.7:6 And he feels guilty for the "**s.**" of taking,
T-18 ........ I.6:7 Call it not **s.** but madness, for such it was
T-18 .... VII.1:3 always means you still find **s.** attractive.
T-18 .... VII.1:4 for himself who still accepts **s.** as his goal.
T-18 .... VII.3:4 for **s.** is never wholly in the present. In
T-18 .... VII.4:7 to reach Atonement by fighting against **s.**.
T-18 .... VII.5:7 and fight against the giving in to **s.**; when
T-18 .... VII.7:4 in which **s.** loses all attraction *right now.*
T-19 .......... II.h **S.** versus Error
T-19 ....... II.1:1 that error be not confused with **s.**, and it
T-19 ....... II.1:3 right. But **s.**, were it possible, would be
T-19 ....... II.1:4 The belief in **s.** is necessarily based on the
T-19 ....... II.1:6 it absolution. **S.** calls for punishment as
T-19 ....... II.2:1 **S.** is not an error, for sin entails an
T-19 ....... II.2:1 for **s.** entails an arrogance which the idea
T-19 ....... II.2:2 To **s.** would be to violate reality, and to
T-19 ....... II.2:3 **S.** is the proclamation that attack is real
T-19 ....... II.2:6 **S.** is the grand illusion underlying all the
T-19 ....... II.3:2 But he *cannot* **s.**. There is nothing he can
T-19 ....... II.3:4 That is what **s.** would do, for such is its
T-19 ....... II.3:5 insanity inherent in the whole idea of **s.**, it
T-19 ....... II.3:6 For the wages of **s.** *is* death, and how can
T-19 ....... II.4:1 religion is that **s.** is not error but truth,
T-19 ....... II.5:1 attempt to reinterpret **s.** as error is always
T-19 ....... II.5:2 The idea of **s.** is wholly sacrosanct to its
T-19 ....... II.6:1 be said the ego made its world on **s.**. Only
T-19 ....... II.6:5 For **s.** has changed creation from an idea
T-19 ....... II.6:9 The "holiness" of **s.** is kept in place by just
T-19 ..... II.6:12 It is impossible to have faith in **s.**, for sin
T-19 ..... II.6:12 to have faith in sin, for **s.** is faithlessness.
T-19 ....... II.7:1 defended than the idea that **s.** is real; the
T-19 ....... II.7:6 the death of God, Whom **s.** has killed!
T-19 ........ III.h The Unreality of **S.**
T-19 ..... III.1:1 The attraction of guilt is found in **s.**, not
T-19 ..... III.1:2 error. **S.** will be repeated because of this
T-19 ..... III.1:3 acute that the **s.** is denied the acting out.
T-19 ..... III.1:4 will suffer, and not let go of the idea of **s.**.
T-19 ..... III.1:6 appeal. **S.** is an idea of evil that cannot be
T-19 ..... III.2:1 love, not fear, is really called upon by **s.**,
T-19 ..... III.2:2 For the ego brings **s.** to fear, demanding
T-19 ..... III.2:4 is always the great preserver of **s.**, treating
T-19 ..... III.3:3 Sometimes a **s.** can be repeated over and
T-19 ..... III.3:4 change its status from a **s.** to a mistake.
T-19 ..... III.3:6 then you will but change the form of **s.**,
T-19 ..... III.3:7 for it is **s.** that calls for punishment, not
T-19 ..... III.4:1 Holy Spirit cannot punish **s.**. Mistakes He
T-19 ..... III.4:3 to do. But **s.** He knows not, nor can He
T-19 ..... III.4:8 What, then, is **s.**? What could it be but a

T-26......IV.3:6 is set where once **s.** was believed to be.
T-26......IV.5:1 Where **s.** once was perceived will rise a
T-26......IV.5:4 tiny spot that **s.** proclaimed to be its own.
T-26......IV.6:1 This tiny spot of **s.** that stands between
T-26....... V.5:5 in every judgment and in all belief in **s.**, is
T-26....... V.9:2 Can **s.** withstand the Will of God? Can it
T-26......VI.1:6 All belief in **s.**, in power of attack, in hurt
T-26.....VII.2:4 and **s.** are seen as consequence and cause,
T-26.....VII.3:2 world of shadows and illusions built on **s.**
T-26.....VII.5:1 answer lies where the belief in **s.** must be,
T-26.....VII.7:1 **S.** is not error, for it goes beyond
T-26.....VII.7:5 proclaiming **s.** has taken His reality from
T-26.....VII.8:5 of God's Son where **s.** was thought to rule
T-26...VII.10:5 itself? There is no **s.**. And every miracle is
T-26...VII.12:2 **S.** is belief attack can be projected outside
T-26...VII.12:4 does the world of **s.** and sacrifice arise.
T-26...VII.19:3 blessing to the world of **s.** and death. For
T-26....VIII.5:5 Belief in **s.** arouses fear, and like its cause,
T-26....VIII.5:9 of time that **s.** and fear have overlooked,
T-26...... IX.7:1 to keep away all darkened thoughts of **s.**,
T-27.........I.7:1 paint the picture in which **s.** is justified, is
T-27.........I.8:1 strange belief that **s.** and death are real,
T-27.........I.8:1 and innocence and **s.** will end alike within
T-27.........I.9:1 to show your brother **s.** can have no cause
T-27.......I.10:1 which the goal of **s.** has been removed, is
T-27....... II.2:4 one can forgive a **s.** that he believes is real.
T-27....... II.2:7 forgiveness does not first establish **s.** and
T-27....... II.3:1 witness **s.** and yet forgive it is a paradox
T-27....... II.3:7 the proof of **s.** before his brother's eyes.
T-27....... II.7:7 his heart made heavy with the proof of **s.**.
T-27...... IV.4:9 It asks but to establish **s.** is real, and
T-27.... IV.4:10 "Which **s.** do you prefer? That is the one
T-27.........VI.h The Witnesses to **S.**
T-27...... VI.2:1 **S.** shifts from pain to pleasure, and again
T-27...... VI.2:6 for this, the witnesses of **s.** are all alike.
T-27...... VI.6:1 Love, too, has symbols in a world of **s.**.
T-27...... VI.6:4 The laws of **s.** have different witnesses
T-27...... VI.7:1 to the miracle, and not the laws of **s.**.
T-27...... VI.8:2 all **s.** if you but carry its effects with you.
T-27...... VI.8:5 not the laws of **s.** to be applied to you.
T-27...... VI.8:6 to let love's symbols take the place of **s.**.
T-27.....VII.5:7 here the cause of suffering and **s.** must lie.
T-27.....VII.5:8 And dwell not on the suffering and **s.**, for
T-27.....VII.7:1 to **s.** all stand within one little space. And
T-28.......I.14:7 fear, and past the world of **s.** entirely.
T-28..... II.12:2 of pain and suffering, of **s.** and guilt. They
T-28......IV.8:5 clean of all the seeds of sickness and of **s.**.
T-28....... V.2:1 of **s.** and suffering and pain and loss, that
T-28....... V.7:6 of **s.** that you will see within yourself,
T-29....... II.3:2 futile to demand escape from **s.** and pain
T-29....... II.3:2 serve the function of retaining **s.** and pain
T-29....... II.3:3 For pain and **s.** are one illusion, as are
T-29....... V.1:1 memory of **s.** and of illusion lingers still.
T-29...... VI.1:4 of danger and destruction, **s.** and death;
T-30...... III.3:7 **s.** is the idea you are alone and separated
T-30....... V.5:4 can guilt and **s.** be seen without a purpose
T-30....... V.6:1 to replace the goal of **s.** and guilt. And all
T-30...... VI.1:7 that you forgive a **s.** by overlooking what
T-30...... VI.4:1 employs to keep the sense of **s.** alive. And
T-30...... VI.5:5 be some **s.** that stands beyond forgiveness
T-31...... III.2:4 Are *you* a **s.**? You answer "yes" whenever
T-31...... III.3:7 If you are **s.** you *are* a body, for the mind
T-31.... III.3:10 are **s.** you lock the mind within the body,
T-31...... III.5:1 that thinks it is a **s.** has but one purpose;
T-31...... III.5:1 purpose; that the body be the source of **s.**,
T-31...... III.5:3 For here are you made **s.**, and sin cannot
T-31...... III.5:3 **s.** cannot abide the joyous and the free,
T-31...... III.5:3 for they are enemies which **s.** must kill. In
T-31...... III.5:4 In death is **s.** preserved, and those who
T-31...... III.5:4 think that they are **s.** must die for what
T-31....... V.6:2 For what you are has now become his **s.**.
T-31...... VI.6:7 of corruption and the stain of **s.** upon you
W-pI.....36.1:4 "Sinless" means without **s.**. You cannot
W-pI.....36.1:5 You cannot be without **s.** a little. You are
W-pI.....93.1:1 you are the home of evil, darkness and **s.**.
W-pI.....93.5:8 nor reduced eternal sinlessness to **s.**, and
W-pI.....93.6:6 The self you made, evil and full of **s.**, is
W-pI.....99.5:4 on what you see; on **s.** and pain and death
W-pI...101.1:5 think it so while you believe that **s.** is real,
W-pI...101.1:5 that sin is real, and that God's Son can **s.**.
W-pI...101.2:1 If **s.** is real, then punishment is just and
W-pI...101.2:3 **s.** is real, then happiness must be illusion,
W-pI...101.3:1 If **s.** is real, salvation must be pain. Pain
W-pI...101.3:2 Pain is the cost of **s.**, and suffering can
W-pI...101.3:2 suffering can never be escaped, if **s.** is real
W-pI...101.4:4 **s.** is real, its offering is death, and meted
W-pI...101.4:4 the vicious wishes in which **s.** is born. If
W-pI...101.4:5 If **s.** is real, salvation has become your
W-pI...101.5:2 The exercises teach **s.** is not real, and all
W-pI...101.5:2 must come from **s.** will never happen, for
W-pI...101.5:4 Son. There is no **s.**. We practice with this
W-pI...101.6:1 is perfect happiness because there is no **s.**,
W-pI...101.6:4 **s.** has wrought in feverish imagination.
W-pI...101.6:7 *There is no* **s.**; *it has no consequence.* So
W-pI...101.7:1 with the insane belief that **s.** is real. Today
W-pI...101.7:4 There is no **s.**. Remember this today, and
W-pI...101.7:7 *This is the truth, because there is no* **s.**.
W-pI...103.1:6 there are gaps in love where **s.** can enter,
W-pI...121.6:2 not inherent in the mind, which cannot **s.**
W-pI...121.6:3 sin. As **s.** is an idea you taught yourself,
W-pI...121.6:5 Who is your Self, and Who can never **s.**.
W-pI.121.13:7 *dream that I am mortal, fallible and full of* **s.**
W-pI...126.2:4 You further think that they can **s.** without
W-pI...126.2:4 of yourself, while you can judge their **s.**,
W-pI...126.3:1 When you "forgive" a **s.**, there is no gain
W-pI...126.4:3 The **s.** that you forgive is not your own.
W-pI...126.4:5 the gift is no more yours than was his **s.**.
W-pI...126.5:3 escape the justified repayment for his **s.**.
W-pI...134.3:3 idea of **s.** retains as yet upon your mind,
W-pI...134.4:2 is impossible to think of **s.** as true and not
W-pI...134.4:3 Thus is forgiveness really but a **s.**, like all
W-pI...134.5:2 is a further sign that **s.** is unforgivable, at
W-pI...134.5:4 If you **s.**, your guilt is everlasting. Those
W-pI...134.9:2 to accuse someone of **s.** in any form, do
W-pI.134.15:2 but to save the world from all ideas of **s.**.
W-pI.134.16:1 from all the thoughts you had of **s.** in him
W-pI.136.11:8 And what is wholly sinless cannot **s.**.
W-pI...137.7:1 Just as forgiveness shines away all **s.** and
W-pI...140.5:2 can not be found where **s.** is cherished.
W-pI...140.5:4 He is barred where **s.** has entered. Yet
W-pI...140.5:6 **s.** can have no home in which to hide
W-pI...140.5:7 and nowhere **s.** and sickness can abide.
WpI. rIV.in9:3 from pain to peace, from **s.** to holiness.
W-pI...151.4:5 of just punishment, how black with **s.**,
W-pI...151.8:4 guilt, unwilling now to play with toys of **s.**
W-pI.151.11:3 the constancy in change, the pure in **s.**,
W-pI.151.16:2 world, replacing witnesses to **s.** and death
W-pI.153.11:1 a fearful world made mad by **s.** and guilt;
W-pI.153.13:3 and childish thoughts of **s.** forever from
W-pI...154.4:2 obey; which promises salvation from all **s.**
W-pI...156.1:1 that makes the thought of **s.** impossible.
W-pI...156.6:3 not the end of **s.** in punishment and death
W-pI...156.6:4 In lightness and in laughter is **s.** gone,
W-pI...158.7:3 fearful thoughts of guilt from dreams of **s.**
W-pI.158.10:4 If he be lost in **s.**, so must you be; if you
W-pI...159.4:4 Christ beholds no **s.** in anyone. And in
W-pI...159.7:3 to be the home of **s.** becomes the center of
W-pI...162.2:3 no thought of **s.** and no illusion which the
W-pI...162.5:3 for who could cherish **s.** when holiness
W-pI...162.5:4 and for complete escape from **s.** and guilt
W-pI...163.2:1 Embodiment of fear, the host of **s.**, god of
W-pI...164.4:3 in you the thought of **s.** has never touched
W-pI...181.7:3 the misery the focus upon **s.** will bring,
W-pI...181.9:2 of the holy Self which knows no **s.**, and
W-pI...183.5:3 nameless for the Name, nor **s.** for grace,
W-pI...186.6:5 **S.** can not tarnish the truth in you, and
W-pI.188.10:4 devoid of **s.** and open to salvation. And
W-pI.190.11:2 instead of pain, our holiness in place of **s.**,
W-pI...191.3:3 Identity, and look on evil, **s.** and death,
W-pI...193.5:4 are the words which end the dream of **s.**,
W-pI...194.2:1 all blackness of depression, thoughts of **s.**
W-pI...194.8:2 of **s.** and evil with the truth of love. Think
W-pI...203.1:2 *from every thought of evil and of* **s.**, *because*
W-pII ..... 1.1:3 It sees there was no **s.**. And in that view
W-pII ..... 1.1:5 What is **s.**, except a false idea about God's
W-pII .227.2:3 released from **s.** and clad in holiness, with
W-pII .229.2:1 *the thoughts of* **s.** *my foolish mind made up.*
W-pII .234.1:1 time when dreams of **s.** and guilt are gone
W-pII .235.2:3 *I have no guilt nor* **s.** *in me, for there is none*
W-pII .239.1:3 shares His glory any trace of **s.** and guilt?
W-pII .247.1:1 **S.** is the symbol of attack. Behold it
W-pII ........ 4.h What Is **S.**?
W-pII ..... 4.1:1 **S.** is insanity. It is the means by which
W-pII ..... 4.1:4 is. **S.** gave the body eyes, for what is there
W-pII ..... 4.3:1 **S.** is the home of all illusions, which but
W-pII ..... 4.3:3 **S.** "proves" God's Son is evil; timelessness
W-pII ..... 4.4:1 and **s.** appears indeed to terrify. And yet
W-pII ..... 4.4:2 what **s.** perceives is but a childish game.
W-pII ..... 4.5:1 of God, will you maintain the game of **s.**?
W-pII ..... 4.5:5 There is no **s.**. Creation is unchanged.
W-pII .256.1:3 If **s.** had not been cherished by the mind,
W-pII .256.1:8 him in whom all **s.** remains impossible,
W-pII .... 259.h Let me remember that there is no **s.**.
W-pII .259.1:1 **S.** is the only thought that makes the goal
W-pII .259.1:3 What else but **s.** engenders our attacks?
W-pII .259.1:4 else but **s.** could be the source of guilt,
W-pII .259.1:5 what but **s.** could be the source of fear,
W-pII .260.2:2 we, because our Source can know no **s.**.
W-pII ..... 6.2:5 the Self Who, like His Father, knows no **s.**
W-pII .289.2:2 *the past has left untouched and free of* **s.**.
W-pII ..... 8.4:1 that the dream of **s.** and guilt is over, and
W-pII .299.2:2 *It is not mine to be destroyed by* **s.**. *It is not*
W-pII .304.2:1 *the darkness to the light; from* **s.** *to holiness.*
W-pII .309.2:1 *is my sure release from idle dreams of* **s.**.
W-pII ... 10.2:2 without **s.** and wholly purposeless.
W-pII .313.1:5 *for He sees no* **s.** *in anything He looks upon.*
W-pII .313.1:6 *from the dream of* **s.** *and look within upon*
W-pII .330.1:5 The Self which God created cannot **s.**,
W-pII ... 12.3:4 of fear and punishment, of **s.** and guilt, of
W-pII .336.2:1 *away my dreams of separation and of* **s.**.
W-pII .344.2:3 How close the ending of the dream of **s.**,
W-pII ... 14.4:1 world redeemed from every thought of **s.**.
W-pII .... 356.h Sickness is but another name for **s.**.
W-pII .356.1:5 *Your Name replaces every thought of* **s.**, *and*
W-pII .... 359.h all **s.** Is understood as merely a mistake.
W-pII .359.1:7 **S.** *is impossible, and on this fact forgiveness*
Wfl........ in.1:5 return again to the belief in **s.** that made
M-in .......... 5:1 the world of **s.** would seem forever real.
M-10 ......... 2:9 Son is guiltless, and **s.** does not exist."
M-12 ......... 5:2 you. Use it for **s.** or for attack, which is the
M-12 ......... 5:2 sin or for attack, which is the same as **s.**,
M-14 ......... 1:4 concealing all **s.** and ending guilt forever.
M-14 ......... 2:4 where **s.** was made and guilt seemed real.
M-14 ....... 2:10 When not one thought of **s.** remains, the
M-14 ......... 3:2 one thought of **s.** remains" appears to be
M-14 ......... 3:4 one thought of **s.** will remain the instant
M-14 ......... 3:5 forgive one **s.** than to forgive all of them.
M-14 ......... 3:7 One **s.** perfectly forgiven by one teacher
M-17 ......... 1:6 belief in **s.** and has condemned himself.
M-18 ......... 3:9 *But a mistake is not a* **s.**, *nor has reality been*
M-19 ......... 3:5 for not one "**s.**" but seems forever true.
C-in ........... 1:4 the "original error" or the "original **s.**."
C-1 ............ 6:1 perceiving **s.** and justifying anger, and
C-4 ............ 2:3 but lends itself to thoughts of **s.** and guilt.
C-4 ............ 2:4 **s.** and therefore is forever without guilt.
C-4 ............ 3:8 by which the world is saved from **s.**, for
C-4 ............ 3:8 is saved from sin, for **s.** does not exist.
C-4 ............ 5:5 The world of bodies is the world of **s.**, for
C-4 ............ 5:5 for only if there were a body is **s.** possible.
C-4 ............ 5:6 **s.** comes guilt as surely as forgiveness
C-4 ............ 6:5 Where is hope while **s.** is seen as outside?
C-4 ............ 7:7 at last there is no journey, no belief in **s.**,
C-5 ............ 3:5 life in any way be changed by **s.** and evil,
C-5 .......... 6:11 *Forget your dreams of* **s.** *and guilt, and come*
C-ep .......... 4:7 all that the dream of **s.** had made of it.
P-2...... IV.10:6 This is the corollary of the "original **s.**";
P-2........ VI.6:7 one spot of **s.** in what he looks upon, and
P-2........ VI.7:4 still believe that **s.** is there to look upon.
P-2....... VII.8:5 to be forgiven where there is no **s.**?
P-3........ III.3:9 Can this be how the dream of **s.** will end?
S-1..........I.4:2 same as to look on **s.** and then forgive it.
S-1..........II.3:3 to be blurred by a deep-rooted sense of **s.**.
S-1..........V.3:2 Son, and recognize the arrogance of **s.**.
S-2..........I.2:2 Forgiveness-to-destroy will overlook no **s.**
S-2..........I.3:5 real. Select the loving and forgive the **s.** by
S-2..........I.4:8 you can see **s.** in anyone except yourself.
S-2..........I.5:2 evil, and in his **s.** you are the injured one.

S-2 ...........I.8:1 who but the insane would look on s.
S-2 ......... II.2:4 who can tell another he is steeped in s.,
S-2 ......... II.5:2 proof of guilt and of the ravages of s..
S-2 ......... II.8:6 redeemed from s. and in the Love of God.
S-2 ........ III.6:3 About the end of s. and guilt and death.
S-2 ........ III.6:7 s. and death become again the holy gift of
S-3 ......... II.5:1 and takes the form of punishment for s..
S-3 ......... II.6:3 veil of s. to keep it dark and comfortless.
S-3 ........ III.1:2 not removed the curse of s. that lies on it.

## sin's 8

T-21 ....VII.1:3 sin. Helplessness is s. condition; the one
T-25 ......III.8:6 s. perception must have been wrong. And
T-25 ... VIII.6:7 Their world depends on s. stability. And
T-27 ......VI.2:9 S. witnesses but shift from name to name,
T-27 ....VI.2:11 S. witnesses hear but the call of death.
T-27 ......VI.4:9 alike, for all s. witnesses do His replace.
T-27 ......VI.5:1 names by which s. witnesses are called. It
W-pI ...134.6:1 It is s. unreality that makes forgiveness

## since 179

## sincere 9

T-3 ...........I.1:3 Many s. Christians have misunderstood
T-20 .....VII.2:7 How can one be s. and say, "I want this
W-pI .....27.4:6 s. while you were repeating today's idea,
W-pI ...139.2:2 could make the question seem to be s..
WpI .. rV.in1:4 we may go on again more certain, more s.
W-pI ...185.6:3 he can not mistake it, if his asking is s..
W-pI ...195.4:3 can only be s. if it be joined to love. We
P-2 .........in.4:1 of how s. the therapist himself may be, he
S-2 ........ III.3:3 make your footsteps sure, your words s.;

## sincerely 2

T-4 ........IV.2:5 Search s. for what you have done and left
T-5 .......VII.6:6 peace. Say this to yourself as s. as you can,

## sincerity 9

T-20 ......VI.2:7 smiling welcome and in s. so simple and
T-20 ... VIII.3:2 for it with real desire and s. of purpose,
T-21 ...VII.11:5 add s. to the decisions you have already
W-pI .....28.7:2 equal s. as today's idea is applied to it, in
W-pI ...185.6:4 But if he asks without s., there is no form
W-pI.185.10:3 when you make this request with deep s..
W-pI ...195.5:1 Therefore give thanks, but in s.. And let
P-2 ......... V.4:3 however limited, however lacking in s..
S-2 ........ III.3:3 your words sincere; not with your own s.,

## sinful 31

T-19 ....... II.4:2 acceptance of the self as s. is perceived as
T-19 ....... II.8:3 that it is far better to be s. than mistaken.
T-20 .....VII.4:5 It is not s., but neither is it sinless. As
T-20 .....VII.6:2 He does not really see him as s.; he does
T-21 .......IV.1:1 Spirit will never teach you that you are s..
T-21 ......VI.2:3 as s. and still perceive the other innocent.
T-21 ......VI.2:5 can see a s. world and look upon himself
T-22 ......III.8:8 you be saved by making s. the one whose
T-23 .......in.6:4 and everything you once thought s. now
T-23 ......IV.3:3 not s. to believe the function of the Son is
T-24 ......IV.4:8 If he is s., then is your reality not real, but
T-24 ...VII.10:5 it. You brand it s. and you hate its acts,
T-25 ......IV.3:7 all their "evil" thoughts and "s." hopes,
T-27 ... VIII.7:6 it punishes because of all the s. things the
T-29 .......IX.4:2 you s. and put out the light within you.
W-pI .....36.1:7 sinless, or a part of His Mind would be s..
W-pI .....95.2:1 God's creation; weak, vicious, ugly and s.,
W-pI ...101.2:4 The s. warrant only death and pain, and it
W-pI ...121.4:5 of none because it sees the s. everywhere.
W-pI ...152.6:4 of the ephemeral, the s. and the guilty,
W-pI ...156.3:3 no more be s. than the sun could choose
W-pI ...191.8:4 Who could see the world as dark and s.,
W-pII ..263.1:2 *what You created as if it could be made s.?*
W-pII ..294.2:2 *what is not created cannot be s. nor sinless;*
W-pII .....351.h My s. brother is my guide to pain. And
W-pII ..351.1:2 *And if I see him s. I proclaim myself a sinner,*
M-12 .........5:2 is the same as sin, and you will see it as s..
M-12 .........5:3 Because it is s. it is weak, and being weak,
M-16 .......10:8 not that it is fearful, not that it is s., not
C-4 ............6:4 forgiveness, for it seems to be forever s..
S-2 ...........I.4:7 Who but the s. need to be forgiven? And

## sinfulness 9

T-25 .........I.2:4 upon reminds you of yourself; your s.,
T-25 .........I.2:8 Framed in his body you will see your s.,
T-25 ..... II.11:4 See not in him the s. he sees, but give him
T-25 ......VII.9:3 From this position does his s., and all the
T-31 ........ II.9:1 have taught yourself about the s. in you.
W-pI .....93.9:5 of evil and s. you have made to replace It.
W-pI ...190.1:7 hatred of His Son, the s. He sees in him,
S-2 ......... II.3:3 instead that here is one whose s. he shares
S-2 ......... II.3:4 may indeed induce a rivalry in s. and guilt

## sing 14

T-13 ...VII.17:1 We cannot s. redemption's hymn alone.
T-14 ....... II.8:8 he s. the dirge of sorrow when this is true
T-17 ....... II.1:5 that made your heart s. with joy has ever
T-21 .......I.10:1 that same song they s. in honor of their
T-21 .......I.10:3 of God, remembering who he is they s. of.
T-25 ......IV.5:3 bird that ever sang will s. again in you.
T-26 ......IV.5:1 and s. their song of gratitude and praise.
W-pI ...109.6:1 a bird with broken wings begins to s., a
W-pI ...109.7:3 will hear the bird begin to s. and see the
W-pI ...123.4:2 We s. the song of thankfulness today, in
W-pI.161.10:5 What you will see will s. to you of ancient
W-pI ...183.2:2 s. to you as they spread out their wings to
S-3 ......IV.1:10 s. of their union and their thanks to God.
S-3 ........IV.7:3 prayers have never ceased to s. his joyful

## singing 4

T19. IV.A.16:1 where no sound but s. and a softly joyous
T-20 ..... II.11:3 s. as you behold the open door of Heaven
T-26 ......IV.5:4 And each one joins the s. at the altar that
W-pII ..293.2:2 *the world is s. underneath the sounds of fear*

## single 74

T-1 .....VII.3:13 As long as a s. "slave" remains to walk the
T-3 ......... II.5:6 s. purpose creates perfect integration and
T-4 ........III.7:10 come in response to a s. unequivocal call.
T-13 ...III.12:1 To "s. out" is to "make alone," and thus
T-13 ..... X.11:3 s. out part of the Sonship for your love,
T-14 ........ V.6:4 for the s. purpose of release from guilt, to
T-14 .....VII.7:7 The s. vision which the Holy Spirit offers
T-14 ...... IX.7:1 Could you but realize for a s. instant the
T-15 .......I.15:9 For caught in the s. instant of the eternal
T-15 ..... II.4:10 a s. instant completely to the Holy Spirit.
T-15 ....... II.6:3 To learn to separate out this s. second,
T-15 ......IV.8:6 the acceptance of the s. Will that governs
T-18 .....VII.3:1 At no s. instant does the body exist at all.
T-18 .....VII.3:5 s. instant the attraction of guilt would be
T-20 ....... V.1:7 No one who has a s. purpose, unified and
T-20 ....... V.2:4 And in that s. heartbeat is the unity of
T-22 ..... II.13:5 reach Heaven while a s. sin still tempts
T-25 ...VII.12:4 s. rock of truth can faith in God's eternal
T-26 ......IV.5:5 the universe has joined with but a s. voice
T-26 ...... V.13:1 you but relive the s. instant when the time
T-26 ...... IX.2:1 and left without a s. one you cherish still?
T-27 ..... II.11:6 and with a s. function that would mean a
T-27 ..... II.16:3 and conceives a s. function as its only one.
T-27 ..... II.16:6 His s. purpose unifies the halves of you
T-27 ......III.7:5 with power unlimited and s. thoughts,
T-27 ......IV.3:4 Nowhere outside a s., simple question is
T-27 ....... V.2:6 Your s. purpose makes this possible. But
T-27 ....... V.4:3 and in that s. instant is all healing done.
T-27 ......VI.6:6 throes of death itself are but a s. sound; a
T-27 ... VIII.3:4 This s. lesson does it try to teach again,
T-27. VIII.11:1 This s. lesson learned will set you free
T-27. VIII.11:5 teach you but the s. cause of all of them,
T-27. VIII.12:3 undone by but a s. lesson truly learned.
T-30 ...... IV.4:9 toys without a s. meaning of their own.
T-30 .... IV.8:11 him no s. thing that he could ever want.
T-30 .....VII.5:3 you. In s. purpose is the end of all ideas of
T-31 ..... V.7:10 make a s. picture representing truth.
T-31 ....... V.8:2 and ended with the s. aim of teaching you
T-31 .....VII.8:6 this s. vision does he see the face of Christ
W-pI .....74.4:1 resolve, s. it out for special consideration.
W-pI .....75.4:3 Our s. purpose makes our goal inevitable.
W-pI ...108.3:3 that heals because it brings s. perception,
W-pI ...125.8:3 in the s. Mind of Father and of Son. In
W-pI ...127.6:5 Today we take the largest s. step this
W-pI ...131.8:5 an alien will upon God's s. purpose. He is
W-pI.131.15:6 *My s. purpose offers it to me. No one can fail*
W-pI ...139.1:6 is no conflict that does not entail the s.,
W-pI.140.10:4 hear a s. Voice which speaks to us of truth
W-pI.151.10:3 teach the s. lesson that they all contain.
W-pI.151.13:2 We introduce these times with but a s.,
W-pI ...159.6:1 is the Holy Spirit's s. gift; the treasure
W-pI ...162.1:1 This s. thought, held firmly in the mind,
W-pI.184.11:3 a s. Source which unifies all things within
W-pI ...195.9:4 Gratitude becomes the s. thought we
W-pI.198.12:6 this s. sight and timelessness itself, you
W-pI.200.11:5 with s. purpose and companionship. For
W-pII .318.1:3 could there be a s. part that stands alone,
W-pII .338.1:2 For in this s. thought is everyone released
W-pII ... 14.2:2 I, we found a s. purpose that we shared.
M-1 ........... 1:5 It may be a s. light, but that is enough. He
M-1 .........2:12 Each one begins as a s. light, but with the
M-3 ...........3:3 mind about the world with a s. decision,
M-4 ..... X.2:12 goal. Forgiveness is its s. aim, at which all
M-5 ........II.3:1 the s. requisite for this shift in perception
M-17 .........3:5 s. aim of the teacher turns the divided
M-22 .......6:14 All else must follow from this s. purpose.
M-28 .......1:10 It is the s. desire of the Son for the Father.
C-3 ............8:1 just that s. instant when you see the truth
C-4 ............6:8 last are sickness and its s. remedy joined
C-5 ............6:4 of Christ's s. message of the Love of God.
P-2 ...... IV.11:1 Salvation's s. doctrine is the goal of all
P-2 ...... IV.11:7 Given this s. shift, all else will follow.
S-1 .........in.1:2 the s. voice Creator and creation share;
S-2 ..........II.1:3 it may seem to take have but this s. goal;

## sings 15

T-20 ....... V.2:1 Each herald of eternity s. of the end of sin
T-21 .........I.9:6 of love the Son of God s. to his Father still
T-21 ......IV.7:4 which s. the praises of another world,
T-22 ....... V.4:5 throughout the universe forever s. as one?
T-24 ....... V.7:3 sightless eyes, and s. to them of Heaven,
T-26 .........I.6:3 then, the song your brother s. to you, and
T-26 ......IV.2:2 and every bird s. of the joy of Heaven.
T-31 .......I.10:3 that s. behind each murderous attack and
W-pI ...189.2:2 and s. your praises as it keeps you safe
C-2 ............8:2 as a loving mother s. her child to rest. Is
P-2 ........ VI.1:5 as a patient begins to hear the dirge he s.,
P-2 ........ VI.1:6 that it is he who s. it to himself. To hear it
P-2 ........ VI.7:2 song salvation s. to all who hear its Voice.
S-1 .........in.1:2 share; the song the Son s. to the Father,
S-2 ...........I.8:6 song that all creation s. unto its God.

## singularly 1

T-9 ........ IV.8:3 as a guide are s. unfortunate, and that it is

## sink 11

W-pI .....41.7:2 But most of all, try to s. down and inward
W-pI .....44.7:2 Then try to s. into your mind, letting go
W-pI .....49.4:4 S. deep into the peace that waits for you
W-pI .....50.5:1 for today s. deep into your consciousness.
W-pI .....74.5:2 S. into it and feel it closing around you.
W-pI ...95.11:3 the meaning of the words to s. into your
W-pI ...109.5:4 as you close your eyes, s. into stillness. Let
W-pI.122.11:1 S. into happiness as you begin these
W-pI.131.11:7 and s. below them to the holy place where
W-pI ...155.2:6 But to let illusion s. behind the truth and
W-pI ...164.5:2 which appeared to hide it merely s. away.

## sinking 1

| | |
|---|---|
| W-pI.....44.7:2 | and intrusion by quietly s. past them. |

## sinks 2

| | |
|---|---|
| W-pI...156.4:4 | the wind s. to a whisper round your holy |
| M-27 .........7:6 | nor s. down to death and dissolution. |

## sinless 61

| | |
|---|---|
| T-10..... V.12:1 | If God knows His children as wholly s., it |
| T-14...... IV.9:1 | Father, because they know that they are s. |
| T-17.........I.1:2 | His reality is forever s.. He need not be |
| T-20.... III.11:9 | See him as s., and there can *be* no fear in |
| T-20...... IV.2:2 | lies your need to see your brother s.. In |
| T-20...... IV.5:1 | The s. give as they received. See, then, the |
| T-20...... IV.5:6 | upon the face of Christ, and see Him s.. |
| T-20.....VII.4:1 | as s. and yet to look upon him as a body. |
| T-20.....VII.4:4 | see a s. body is impossible, for holiness is |
| T-20.....VII.4:5 | It is not sinful, but neither is it s.. As |
| T-20.....VII.9:2 | Ask only, "Do I really wish to see him s.?" |
| T-20.....VII.9:6 | For what the seeing look upon *is* s.. No one |
| T-20....VIII.1:1 | what is given you who see your brother s.. |
| T-20....VIII.2:8 | you who would but see your brother s.. |
| T-20....VIII.3:3 | willing, then, to see your brother s., that |
| T-21...... VI.2:4 | upon himself as guilty and sees a s. world |
| T-21...VII.10:8 | And you can want to see a s. world, and |
| T-22..... II.13:2 | who is but willing to see his brother s.. |
| T-22..... II.13:7 | Look on your holy brother, s. as yourself, |
| T-22...... VI.3:4 | this end the body must be perceived as s., |
| T-22...... VI.3:6 | using your body only to serve the s.. And |
| T-23.......in.1:3 | The s. cannot fear, for sin of any kind is |
| T-23.......in.2:4 | that you will love what you perceive as s.. |
| T-23.......in.2:7 | And he will see only the s., who can not |
| T-24.........I.4:2 | "above" it, s. by comparison with it. And |
| T-24...... III.1:4 | clings to one illusion can see himself as s., |
| T-24...... IV.4:2 | wish that you might see your brother s.. |
| T-24...... IV.4:4 | A s. brother *is* its enemy, while sin, if it |
| T-26....... II.8:3 | loves but must be s. and beyond attack. |
| T-26...... IV.2:5 | The s. must perceive that they are one, for |
| T-27....VII.15:1 | Dream softly of your s. brother, who |
| T-29....VIII.6:6 | as perfect, s. and as loving as his Father, |
| W-pI.....36.1:4 | "S." means without sin. You cannot be |
| W-pI.....36.1:6 | You are s. or not. If your mind is part of |
| W-pI.....36.1:7 | your mind is part of God's you must be s., |
| W-pI.....60.5:4 | His Love reminds me that His Son is s.. |
| W-pI...95.13:4 | the Son of God Himself, s. as Its Creator, |
| W-pI.124.11:1 | understand the s. light you see belongs to |
| W-pI...134.2:7 | you forgive the s. and eternally benign? |
| W-pI.136.11:8 | change. And what is wholly s. cannot sin. |
| W-pI...154.4:2 | abolished in the mind that God created s. |
| W-pI...158.1:2 | in Mind and purely mind, s. forever, |
| W-pI...159.4:5 | And in His sight the s. are as one. Their |
| W-pI...181.8:3 | mistakes, we will behold a wholly s. world |
| W-pI...181.9:1 | our sins becomes the proof that we are s.. |
| W-pII .223.2:2 | *For we who are Your holy Son are s.. We* |
| W-pII .224.1:1 | My true Identity is so secure, so lofty, s., |
| W-pII .229.2:1 | *for keeping my Identity untouched and s., in* |
| W-pII .....4.1:4 | eyes, for what is there the s. would behold |
| W-pII .256.1:6 | the holiness of him whom God created s.? |
| W-pII .294.2:2 | *what is not created cannot be sinful nor s.;* |
| W-pII .313.1:1 | *which beholds all things as s., so that fear has* |
| W-pII .334.2:4 | *Today I would behold my brother s.. This* |
| W-pII ...14.4:2 | Voice for God proclaim the world as s.. |
| W-pII ....351.h | My s. brother is my guide to peace. My |
| W-pII .351.1:4 | *I can also see my brother s., as Your holy Son.* |
| W-pII .356.1:5 | *of sin, and who is s. cannot suffer pain. Your* |
| W-pII .359.1:4 | *You created s. so abides forever and forever.* |
| M-3 ...........1:2 | both can look upon the Son of God as s.. |
| C-3.............8:2 | you are s. and behold your sinlessness. |
| S-1......... II.3:6 | there is no scarcity. The s. have no needs. |

## sinlessly 2

| | |
|---|---|
| T-18.....VII.8:4 | you be directed how to use the body s.. It |
| T-23.......in.2:5 | who travels s. along the way love shows |

## Sinlessness 3

*sinlessness*

| | |
|---|---|
| W-pI. 198.12:5 | offering forgiveness to the Son of S. Itself, |
| W-pII . 341.1:3 | *that the Lord of S. conceives us as His Son, a* |
| W-pII ... 14.1:6 | *I am His holy S. Itself, for in my purity abides* |

## sinlessness 97

*Sinlessness*

| | |
|---|---|
| T-13 .....X.14:6 | where we will surely enter in our s.. God |
| T19..IV.C.10:3 | fear can enter and disturb the peace of s.? |
| T-20 ..... IV.5:2 | then, the power of s. within your brother, |
| T-20 .... VII.9:3 | forget not that his s. is *your* escape from |
| T-20 ......VIII.h | The Vision of S. |
| T-20 ...VIII.3:1 | brother's s. is given you in shining light, |
| T-20 ...VIII.3:5 | It is his desire to see his s., as it is yours. |
| T-22 ......... II.h | Your Brother's S. |
| T-22 ..... VI.3:4 | perceived as sinless, because the goal is s.. |
| T-22 ..... VI.5:7 | The means of s. can know no fear because |
| T-23 ......in.1:1 | the opposite of frailty and weakness is s.? |
| T-24 ......in.2:6 | does suffering follow guilt and freedom s.. |
| T-24 ........IV.h | Specialness versus S. |
| T-24 ..... IV.4:6 | All that is real proclaims his s.. All that is |
| T-24 ..... VI.5:5 | Yet will his perfect s. release you both, for |
| T-24 ..... VI.6:1 | is His s. that eyes that see can look upon. |
| T-25 .......II.7:3 | up the s. the frame of darkness hides, and |
| T-25 .......II.8:4 | His s. but pictures yours. His gentleness |
| T-25 ..... III.5:2 | forgiveness and the sight of perfect s.. |
| T-25 ..... III.5:4 | to obscure the s. that shines unchanged, |
| T-25 ......... V.h | The State of S. |
| T-25 ...... V.1:1 | state of s. is merely this: The whole desire |
| T-25 ...... V.5:4 | beautiful his s. will be when you perceive |
| T-25 .VIII.12:5 | He may smile on you whose s. He shares. |
| T-25 .VIII.12:8 | a witness unto his s. and not his sins. How |
| T-26 ........I.7:2 | cannot die because his s. is known to God |
| T-26 .......II.6:6 | is given you to see in him his perfect s.. |
| T-28 .... VII.7:1 | health, upon his happiness, his s., and |
| W-pI..... 93.5:8 | creation, nor reduced eternal s. to sin, |
| W-pI..... 93.6:1 | Your s. is guaranteed by God. Over and |
| W-pI..... 93.6:4 | Your s. is guaranteed by God. Nothing |
| W-pI..... 93.6:7 | Your s. is guaranteed by God, and light |
| W-pI..... 93.7:5 | Your s. is guaranteed by God. You are |
| W-pI..... 93.8:3 | *My s. is guaranteed by God.* Then put away |
| W-pI... 93.10:5 | *me. My s. is guaranteed by God.* Then try to |
| W-pI... 93.11:4 | *Your s. is guaranteed by God.* You can do |
| W-pI..... 94.2:1 | True light is strength, and strength is s.. |
| W-pI..... 94.2:3 | ensured your s. must be the guarantee of |
| W-pI..... 94.2:6 | strong in the s. in which you were created, |
| W-pI... 119.2:2 | *truth in me, and come to recognize my s..* |
| W-pI... 131.5:6 | want as certainly as God created you in s.. |
| W-pI... 151.8:3 | rejoicing in His perfect, everlasting s.. |
| W-pI. 152.10:5 | of God's Son, his gentleness, his perfect s., |
| W-pI. 153.20:7 | never real, to look on Christ and see His s. |
| W-pI. 161.11:8 | *eyes of Christ, and see my perfect s. in you.* |
| W-pI... 181.2:5 | the peace that comes from faith in s.. This |
| W-pI... 181.2:8 | their sight and see the s. that lies beyond. |
| W-pI... 181.3:1 | great need to let our s. become apparent. |
| W-pI... 181.5:7 | with one intent; to look upon the s. within |
| W-pI... 181.7:3 | seems to block the vision of our s., we |
| W-pI... 181.9:2 | could conceive of anything without Its s.. |
| W-pI... 181.9:7 | Our s. is but the Will of God. This instant |
| W-pI... 191.4:6 | one fact is s. proclaimed to be forever part |
| W-pI... 193.2:6 | contradict, and keeps his s. forever safe. |
| W-pII ..... 1.5:3 | whom He has saved, whose s. He sees, |
| W-pII . 223.2:3 | *sinless. We would look upon our s., for guilt* |
| W-pII . 235.1:3 | His Son and keeps his s. forever perfect, |
| W-pII . 235.2:2 | *me, and made my s. forever part of You.* |
| W-pII . 247.1:7 | Your s. is mine. You stand forgiven, and I |
| W-pII . 260.1:6 | *let my s. arise again before Christ's vision,* |
| W-pII . 274.1:1 | *them, and give Your Son the honor due his s.* |
| W-pII ..... 7.3:1 | yearns to have you recognize your s., you |
| W-pII . 313.1:6 | *the dream of sin and look within upon my s.,* |
| W-pII . 318.1:4 | is to find the s. that God has placed in me. |
| W-pII ... 11.3:3 | imperfection and of any spot upon its s.. |
| W-pII . 334.2:5 | *Your Will for me, for so will I behold my s..* |
| W-pII .... 335.h | I choose to see my brother's s.. |
| W-pII . 335.1:6 | My brother's s. shows me that I would |
| W-pII . 335.2:1 | *memory to me, except to see my brother's s.?* |
| W-pII . 336.2:2 | *and find Your promise of my s. is kept; Your* |
| W-pII .... 337.h | My s. protects me from all harm. |
| W-pII . 337.1:1 | My s. ensures me perfect peace, eternal |
| W-pII . 337.1:6 | I need but accept my Self, my s., created |
| W-pII . 337.2:1 | *created me in s. are not mistaken about what* |
| W-pII .... 341.h | I can attack but my own s., And it is only |
| W-pII . 341.1:3 | *in s. so perfect that the Lord of Sinlessness* |
| W-pII . 341.2:1 | Let us not, then, attack our s., for it |
| W-pII . 348.1:7 | *Surrounding me is perfect s.. What can I fear* |
| W-pII . 351.1:5 | *Son. And with this choice I see my s., my* |
| W-pII . 352.1:1 | *Forgiveness looks on s. alone, and judges* |
| W-pII . 357.1:5 | *shall be: "Behold his s., and be you healed."* |
| W-pII . 360.1:6 | *Your Son is like to You in perfect s.. And with* |
| M-4 ........X.3:2 | Terms like love, s., perfection, knowledge |
| M-15 ......... 1:6 | He will hear his s. proclaimed around and |
| M-18 ......... 2:4 | Now He can remind the world of s., the |
| M-28 ......... 4:7 | the dust and look upon our perfect s.. The |
| M-28 ......... 5:5 | We have seen the face of Christ, His s., |
| C-3 ............ 8:2 | Now you are sinless and behold your s.. |
| P-2..........V.7:8 | And as we see the s. in him come shining |
| P-2........ VI.7:4 | come to demonstrate their s. to eyes that |
| P-2........ VI.7:5 | Yet will the proof of s., seen in the patient |
| P-2....... VII.3:3 | Only Christ forgives, knowing His s.. His |
| S-1..........II.5:5 | unity of Christ and a recognition of His s.. |
| S-1..........II.7:7 | in the pure s. that is the gift of God to you, |
| S-1..........V.3:4 | Now can you look upon His s.. High has |
| S-3...........I.4:3 | his holy s. and the remembrance of his |
| S-3........ IV.6:2 | Holiness which fathered you in perfect s., |

## sinned 16

| | |
|---|---|
| T-6 ..... IV.11:8 | you have God teach you that you have s.? |
| T-10 .......V.6:1 | Son of God, you have not s., but you have |
| T-13 ...... in.4:6 | for it teaches him that, never having s., he |
| T-13 ........I.2:1 | that you have made the Son of God *has* s.. |
| T-13 ........I.3:3 | You have "s." in the past, but there is no |
| T19 .IV.B.11:8 | have not s., but you have been mistaken |
| T19 IV.D.14:3 | thought He s. because you cast the veil of |
| T-25 .....II.10:2 | for the wholly pure have never s.. Give, |
| T-25 ... VIII.6:6 | when they are told that they have never s. |
| T-27 ........I.5:7 | Here is the proof that he has never s.; that |
| T-28 ..... III.8:4 | and gently shows you that you never s.. |
| T-30 ..... III.3:6 | Only if you had s. could this be so. For sin |
| T-30 ..... VI.3:7 | but remains aware that they have s.. And |
| W-pI .... 94.3:6 | This is the Self that never s., nor made an |
| W-pII . 337.2:2 | *I am. I was mistaken when I thought I s., but I* |
| S-2...........I.7:7 | For what He has forgiven has not s., and |

## sinner 7

| | |
|---|---|
| T-9 .........V.1:5 | with the premise, "I am a miserable s., |
| T-9 .........V.6:6 | "miserable s." cannot be healed without |
| T-25 ... VIII.5:9 | if He condemns a s. for the crimes he did |
| T-25 . VIII.13:3 | not because you are a miserable s. too. |
| W-pI .. 126.5:3 | Yet it remains your right to let the s. not |
| W-pI .. 127.2:6 | to judge between the righteous and the s., |
| W-pII . 351.1:2 | *And if I see him sinful I proclaim myself a s.,* |

## sinner's 1

| | |
|---|---|
| T-25 .... VII.2:1 | It cannot be the "s." wish for death is just |

## sinners 10

| | |
|---|---|
| T-6 ........I.16:4 | for sins, and the Sons of God are not s.. |
| T19 ...IV.C.2:4 | is not to live; the black-draped "s.," the |
| T-25 .... VII.1:5 | can seem to hide the pain of sin from s., |
| T-25 .... VII.6:4 | for a world perceived as wholly mad to s., |
| T-25 ... VIII.3:2 | for s. see justice only as their punishment, |
| T-25 ... VIII.8:3 | Love is not understandable to s. because |
| T-30 ..... VI.3:7 | It pardons "s." sometimes, but remains |
| W-pI .. 134.7:4 | self-accusing shrieks of s. mad with guilt. |
| W-pI .. 152.9:4 | the arrogance which says that we are s., |
| W-pII . 359.1:3 | *we have not made s. of the holy Sons of God.* |

## sins 100

| | |
|---|---|
| T-3 ..........I.5:1 | God who taketh away the s. of the world," |
| T-3 ..........I.6:4 | The lamb "taketh away the s. of the world |
| T-4 ....... IV.5:2 | Leave the "s." of the ego to me. That is |

| | |
|---|---|
| T-5........VI.8:1 | "I will visit the s. of the fathers unto the |
| T-6........I.16:4 | No one is punished for s., and the Sons of |
| T-17.........I.1:1 | and all his "s." are but his own imagining. |
| T19....IV.B.6:2 | Forgive me all the s. you think the Son of |
| T19.IV.D.13:2 | Would you hold his s. against him, or |
| T19 IV.D15:10 | Forgive the s. your brother thinks he has |
| T19.IV.D.18:3 | the s. he thinks he sees within himself. |
| T-20.........I.2:4 | purity of the Son of God, and not his s.. |
| T-22......III.4:6 | preserve all errors and make them s.. For |
| T-22......III.8:3 | your perception of his s. and of his body. |
| T-22......III.8:6 | tried to see your s. in him to save yourself. |
| T-22......III.9:5 | And thus he lays his s. upon the other, |
| T-22......III.9:5 | is attracted to him to perpetuate his s.. |
| T-24.........I.5:9 | How can he live, with all your s. upon him |
| T-24....... II.5:5 | each in his special s. and "safe" from love, |
| T-24....... II.6:4 | and all the s. he held in its defense against |
| T-24....... II.7:1 | lost the power to forgive you all the s. you |
| T-24......IV.4:7 | All that is false proclaims his s. as real. If |
| T-25. VIII.12:8 | witness unto his sinlessness and not his s. |
| T-25......IX.1:2 | except that they are s. and not mistakes, |
| T-25......IX.9:1 | you keep and hide become your secret s., |
| T-26.........I.8:2 | it be that you could make his s. reality, |
| T-26.....VII.8:7 | S. are beliefs that you impose between |
| T-26......IX.2:1 | you, that you may be forgiven all your s., |
| T-27.........I.3:2 | that he may see his s. are writ in Heaven |
| T-27.........I.4:7 | death would prove his errors must be s.. |
| T-27.........I.8:1 | These are not s., but witnesses unto the |
| T-27....... II.4:2 | must attest his s. have no effect on you to |
| T-27....... II.4:4 | his s. have no effect to warrant guilt? Sins |
| T-27....... II.4:5 | S. are beyond forgiveness just because |
| T-27..... II.11:3 | must be a way to punish s. you think are |
| T-27..... II.13:4 | brother's s. become the central target for |
| T-27..... II.13:5 | but his are s. and not the same as yours. |
| T-27. VIII.13:3 | nor does your guiltlessness rest on its s.. |
| T-28....... I.9:10 | When you forgive It for your s., It will no |
| T-31......III.1:5 | You never hate your brother for his s., but |
| T-31......III.1:6 | Whatever form his s. appear to take, it |
| T-31......III.2:1 | Why should his s. be sins, if you did not |
| T-31......III.2:1 | Why should his sins be s., if you did not |
| T-31......III.3:1 | S. are in bodies. They are not perceived |
| T-31....... V.6:6 | all his s. and yours preserved and kept in |
| T-31....... V.6:8 | of your s. to you who are but silently, and |
| T-31... VIII.9:2 | the secret s. and hidden hates be gone. |
| W-pI.....64.2:3 | yourself what you think of as your s.. In |
| W-pI.....78.6:4 | think of his mistakes and even of his "s.." |
| W-pI.....93.4:1 | never done, that all your s. are nothing, |
| W-pI.....98.2:6 | All our s. are washed away by realizing |
| W-pI.....99.4:3 | and s. forgotten which were never real? |
| W-pI...101.1:3 | asks for suffering as penance for your "s.. |
| W-pI...121.3:3 | except the proof that all its s. are real? |
| W-pI...121.4:1 | mind sees no mistakes, but only s.. It |
| W-pI...126.3:3 | because his s. have lowered him beneath |
| W-pI.133.10:2 | ineffectual mistakes appear as s. to him, |
| W-pI.133.10:4 | is error to believe that s. are but mistakes, |
| W-pI.133.10:4 | who would suffer for his s. if this were so? |
| W-pI...134.4:1 | Because you think your s. are real, you |
| W-pI...134.5:5 | forgiven from the view their s. are real are |
| W-pI.134.15:1 | as He will direct, and catalogue his "s.," |
| W-pI...137.5:2 | as forgiveness overlooks all s. that never |
| W-pI...151.9:5 | could convince Him that your s. are real? |
| W-pI...158.9:1 | Thus are his s. forgiven him, for Christ |
| W-pI.158.10:4 | your s. have been forgiven by yourself. |
| W-pI.161.11:5 | of one who can forgive you all your s.; |
| W-pI...164.3:3 | How easily are all your seeming s. forgot, |
| W-pI...181.1:4 | and past his seeming s. as well as yours. |
| W-pI...181.2:5 | Remove your focus on your brother's s., |
| W-pI...181.2:6 | from what you see in others past their s.. |
| W-pI...181.2:7 | if focused on, are witnesses to s. in you. |
| W-pI...181.6:2 | form. And if a brother's s. occur to us, our |
| W-pI...181.6:2 | which we will magnify and call our "s.." |
| W-pI...181.9:1 | which once proclaimed our s. becomes |
| W-pI...190.4:3 | or secret s. with weighty consequence. |
| W-pI.192.10:9 | Forgive him now his s., and you will see |
| W-pI...195.8:5 | some other things still locked away as "s.. |
| W-pI...197.6:2 | the s. you think you see outside yourself, |
| W-pII......1.1:2 | It does not pardon s. and make them real. |
| W-pII......1.1:4 | And in that view are all your s. forgiven. |
| W-pII..265.1:1 | my s. on it and saw them looking back at |
| W-pII..265.1:6 | it. Let no appearance of my s. obscure the |
| W-pII..278.1:2 | the frailties and the s. which I perceive are |
| W-pII..288.1:5 | *His s. are in the past along with mine, and I* |
| W-pII..304.1:6 | signs that all my s. have been forgiven me |
| W-pII..313.1:5 | *In His sight are all its s. forgiven, for He sees* |
| M-18 .........4:8 | His s. have been forgiven him, and he no |
| M-19 .........3:4 | "S." are perceived and justified by careful |
| C-5............4:1 | all your s. have been forgiven because |
| P-2....... V.8:10 | that all his s. have been forgiven him. |
| P-2........ VI.6:4 | he sees his s. as gone into a past that is no |
| P-2........ VI.6:6 | is his screen for the projection of his s., |
| P-2........VII.3:1 | that all his s. have been forgiven him, |
| P-3........ II.4:10 | for all your s. have been forgiven you. |
| S-1........ II.6:8 | Forgive them for your s., and you will be |
| S-2...........I.4:2 | for it is only your s. you see in him. You |
| S-2...........I.4:6 | for you have called him guilty of your s., |
| S-2...........I.5:7 | You cannot see his s. and not your own. |
| S-3...........I.1:3 | It is external proof of inner "s.," and |
| S-3......... II.4:2 | for the s. it dreamed about and laid upon |

## sister 2

| | |
|---|---|
| S-2.........in.1:3 | ally; s. in the plan for your salvation. Both |
| S-2.........in.1:7 | Unlike the timeless nature of its s., prayer |

## sit 16

| | |
|---|---|
| T-13.....VII.1:1 | S. quietly and look upon the world you |
| T-16.........I.2:7 | if you will merely s. quietly by and let the |
| T-30.........I.5:3 | to s. by and ask to have the answer given |
| W-pI.....31.3:5 | As you s. and quietly watch your thoughts |
| W-pI.....33.4:2 | or so to s. quietly and repeat the idea to |
| W-pI.....41.6:2 | s. quietly for some three to five minutes, |
| W-pI.....42.3:2 | to wait until you can s. quietly by yourself |
| W-pI.....49.5:3 | And be sure to s. quietly and repeat the |
| W-pI.153.17:2 | And we will quietly s. by and wait on Him |
| W-pI...183.5:4 | a brother as you s. with him in silence, |
| W-pI...183.8:3 | S. silently, and let His Name become the |
| W-pI...188.6:1 | S. quietly and close your eyes. The light |
| W-pII.....in.5:5 | S. silently and wait upon your Father. He |
| M-14 .......5:10 | And now s. down in true humility, and |
| M-16 .........4:5 | One can easily s. still an hour with closed |
| M-16 .........5:4 | It is better to s. up, in whatever position |

## sits 1

| | |
|---|---|
| W-pI...136.9:3 | and chaos s. in triumph on His throne. |

## situation 155

| | |
|---|---|
| T-2........ III.3:4 | An imprisoned will engenders a s. which, |
| T-2.....V.A.18:1 | that of others if, in a s. calling for help, |
| T-2........ VI.5:2 | This s. arises in two ways: First, you can |
| T-2........ VI.5:6 | resulting in a s. in which you are doing |
| T-2........ VI.8:5 | precisely the s. for which the Atonement |
| T-3........ VI.8:3 | You then perceive the s. as one in which |
| T-4...........I.6:1 | Egos can clash in any s., but spirit cannot |
| T-4...........I.7:3 | particularly any s. that lends itself to the |
| T-4........ VI.1:1 | ego, you do not understand the s. as it is. |
| T-5......... V.4:11 | automatically attempt to remedy the s.. |
| T-6........IV.8:7 | you put yourself in an impossible s. you |
| T-6........IV.9:3 | In an impossible s., you can develop your |
| T-6......IV.10:1 | You are in an impossible s. only because |
| T-6......IV.10:2 | You *would* be in an impossible s. if God |
| T-7........ III.1:8 | I am not absent to anyone in any s.. |
| T-7......... V.3:6 | This s., too, can be used either for healing |
| T-8.......VII.8:3 | Being faced with an impossible learning s. |
| T-8...... VIII.6:5 | Holy Spirit, perfectly aware of the same s. |
| T-9...........I.3:5 | You have set up this strange s. so that it is |
| T-9........IV.4:3 | merely place yourself in an impossible s., |
| T-9......... V.5:5 | always seek to get something from the s.. |
| T-9......... V.7:1 | "impossible s." to which the ego always |
| T-9......... V.8:5 | makes healing clear in any s. in which He |
| T-9......... V.9:1 | a very direct and a very simple learning s., |
| T-12....... V.1:5 | you attempt to "equalize" the s. you made |
| T-12....... V.2:8 | need to "equalize" the s. to establish your |
| T-12....... V.5:4 | learning s. in which you placed yourself is |
| T-12....... V.5:4 | and in this s. you clearly require a special |
| T-12....... V.8:7 | whole learning s. as you have set it up is |
| T-12.....VII.1:4 | is no s. to which miracles do not apply, |
| T-16.........I.3:8 | tempted you may be to judge any s., and |
| T-17....... V.5:4 | the s. is experienced as very precarious. A |
| T-17..... V.11:9 | of the s. in which you find yourself. And |
| T-17...... VI.1:6 | specific guidelines He provides for any s., |
| T-17...... VI.1:7 | point to use them in each s. separately, |
| T-17...... VI.1:7 | you can more safely look beyond each s., |
| T-17...... VI.2:1 | In any s. in which you are uncertain, the |
| T-17...... VI.2:5 | s. becomes the determiner of the outcome |
| T-17...... VI.2:7 | not know what it wants to come of the s.. |
| T-17...... VI.3:1 | at the outset, the s. just seems to happen, |
| T-17...... VI.4:1 | the s. as a means to *make* it happen. You |
| T-17...... VI.4:6 | of view. The s. now has meaning, but only |
| T-17...... VI.5:2 | If the s. is used for truth and sanity, its |
| T-17...... VI.5:8 | ego believes the s. brings the experience. |
| T-17...... VI.5:9 | that the s. is as the goal determines it, and |
| T-17...... VI.6:4 | The Holy Spirit sees the s. as a whole. The |
| T-17...... VI.6:9 | and does not perceive the s. as a whole. |
| T-17.... VI.6:10 | of the s. and deal with them separately, |
| T-17...... VI.7:1 | Confronted with any aspect of the s. that |
| T-17...... VI.7:5 | of the s. the goal of truth would bring. For |
| T-17..... VII.1:1 | substitutes for aspects of the s. are the |
| T-17..... VII.1:2 | s. and the problem were in the same place |
| T-17..... VII.1:6 | the s. would have been meaningful to you |
| T-17..... VII.2:1 | problem in any s. that faith will not solve. |
| T-17..... VII.3:1 | A s. is a relationship, being the joining of |
| T-17..... VII.3:6 | an error in your thoughts about the s., |
| T-17..... VII.4:1 | *you* have not given can be lacking in any s.. |
| T-17..... VII.4:6 | What s. can you be in without faith, and |
| T-17..... VII.5:1 | Every s. in which you find yourself is but |
| T-17..... VII.6:2 | his part in any s. dedicated in advance to |
| T-17..... VII.8:8 | has entered any s. that shares Its purpose. |
| T-17..... VII.8:9 | of truth shines from the center of the s., |
| T-17... VII.8:11 | There is no s. that does not involve your |
| T-17... VII.8:12 | of yourself outside it and keep the s. holy. |
| T-17..... VII.9:1 | Enter each s. with the faith you give your |
| T-17..... VII.9:5 | extended to every s. in which you enter, |
| T-17..... VII.9:6 | every s. was thus made free of the past, |
| T-17... VII.10:1 | of Him Who walks with you in every s.. |
| T-17.... VIII.1:1 | example, of what every s. is meant to be. |
| T-17.... VIII.1:2 | has given it is also given to every s.. It |
| T-17.... VIII.1:4 | of every relationship and every s., seen as |
| T-17.... VIII.1:5 | Faith has accepted every aspect of the s., |
| T-17.... VIII.1:6 | It is a s. of perfect peace, simply because |
| T-17.... VIII.2:4 | it encompass every s. and bring you peace |
| T-17.... VIII.3:1 | want to make a holy instant of every s.? |
| T-17.... VIII.5:8 | See only this in every s., and it will be a |
| T-17.... VIII.6:7 | beyond any s. that could hold you back, |
| T-19.........I.1:1 | before that when a s. has been dedicated |
| T-19.........I.1:4 | involved, for only thus the s. is perceived |
| T-19.........I.2:1 | Every s., properly perceived, becomes an |
| T19..IV.C.11:1 | s. strikes you with terror and makes your |
| T-20.... VIII.5:7 | There is no problem, no event or s., no |
| T-21........II.3:3 | determiner of every s. in which he seems |
| T-22...... VI.2:3 | s. so contradictory and so impossible that |
| T-25...... III.6:5 | will he see each s. that he thought before |
| T-26........II.2:3 | And when the s. is worked out so no one |
| T-29.... VIII.1:9 | or a thing, a place, a s. or a circumstance, |
| T-30..... VII.1:5 | And no s. can affect its aim, but must be |
| T-30..... VII.1:6 | if its aim could change with every s. could |
| T-31...... III.1:3 | all temptation, and to every s. that occurs |
| T-31.... VIII.9:1 | to perceive another s. where God's gift |
| W-in..........5:2 | in connection with any person, s. or event |
| W-in..........6:2 | to every s. in which you find yourself, and |
| W-pI........5.1:1 | s. or event you think is causing you pain. |
| W-pI.....13.2:2 | represents a s. in which God and the ego |
| W-pI.....14.7:5 | *[specify the s. which is disturbing you], and* |
| W-pI.....20.5:3 | repetitions should be applied to any s., |
| W-pI.....21.4:3 | *I am determined to see_[specify the s.]* |
| W-pI.....24.1:1 | In no s. that arises do you realize the |
| W-pI.....24.1:3 | is determined by your perception of the s. |
| W-pI.....24.1:5 | goal in any s. which is correctly perceived. |
| W-pI.....24.5:1 | for today, name each s. that occurs to you |
| W-pI.....24.5:3 | *In the s. involving–, I would like_to happen* |
| W-pI.....24.5:4 | not appear to be directly related to the s., |
| W-pI.....24.6:1 | of the s. which have nothing to do with it. |
| W-pI.....24.6:2 | of your goals, however the s. turns out. |
| W-pI.....24.7:1 | unresolved s. that crosses your mind say |
| W-pI.....24.7:2 | *not perceive my own best interests in this s.,* |
| W-pI.....26.7:1 | First, name the s.: *I am concerned about–* |

W-pI.....26.8:1 possibilities available for each s. you use,
W-pI.....26.8:3 outcomes for each s. continues, you will
W-pI.....32.6:1 to any s. that may distress you. Apply the
W-pI.....32.6:3 yourself: *I have invented this s. as I see it.*
W-pI.....33.3:2 any s. arises which tempts you to become
W-pI.....34.5:4 *peace in this s. instead of what I now see in it.*
W-pI.....34.6:4 *or worry [or my thoughts about this s.,*
W-pI.....35.7:3 Pick up any specific s. that occurs to you,
W-pI.....35.7:3 are applicable to your reactions to that s.,
W-pI.....38.4:2 between a s. that is difficult for you, and
W-pI.....38.4:3 Identify the s. specifically, and also the
W-pI.....38.4:5 *In the s. involving –in which I see myself,*
W-pI.....38.4:6 *In the s. involving_in which_sees himself,*
W-pI.....47.5:2 It is obvious that any s. that causes you
W-pI.....47.5:2 you could deal with the s. successfully. It
W-pI.....48.2:3 your eyes open at any time and in any s..
WpI...rI.in.5:1 there to embrace any s. in which you are.
W-pI.....61.5:6 with your eyes closed if the s. permits. Let
W-pI.....71.3:4 better; another s. will yet offer success.
W-pI.....74.4:2 persons and the s. or situations involved,
W-pI.....77.7:4 *miracles.* Ask for them whenever a s. arises
W-pI.....79.1:3 This is the s. of the world. The problem of
W-pI.....79.5:2 they confront you with an impossible s..
W-pI...93.11:1 If a s. arises that seems to be disturbing,
W-pII .292.1:4 all trials we see, and every s. that we meet.
M-in ........2:10 s. must be to you a chance to teach others
M-in ..........3:2 In the formal teaching s., these questions
M-in ..........3:3 any s. on behalf of what you really teach,
M-in ..........4:7 Into this hopeless and closed learning s.,
M-2 ...........5:1 together, a teaching-learning s. begins.
M-2 ...........5:5 In the teaching-learning s., each one
M-3 ...........1:2 level. Each teaching-learning s. involves a
M-3 ...........2:4 for becoming a teaching-learning s..
M-3 ...........3:5 s. is part of God's plan for Atonement,
M-3 ...........4:1 Each teaching-learning s. is maximal in
M-3 ...........4:3 s. and then appear to separate. As with
M-4 ...........1:6 which the teaching-learning s. is geared,
M-9 ..............h IN THE LIFE S. OF GOD'S TEACHERS?
M-9 ...........1:2 may not involve changes in the external s.
M-9 ...........1:6 to change their life s. almost immediately,
M-11 ..........3:4 Into this strange and paradoxical s., –one
M-13 ........7:13 you have set up a s. that is impossible.
M-13 ........7:14 this s. the impossible can seem to happen
M-16 ..........4:2 s. that fosters quiet thought as he awakes.
M-17 ..........8:1 this hopeless s. God sends His teachers.
M-21 ..........5:3 in fact, confront the teacher with a s. that

**situation's** 1

T-17.....VII.8:9 everyone to whom the s. purpose calls. It

**situations** 38

T-1.........I.45:2 in s. of which you are not even aware.
T-4...........I.8:1 The ego tries to exploit all s. into forms of
T-7.......... III.1:1 and applies it to all individuals in all s..
T-12....... VI.6:5 and more common elements in all s., the
T-12.......VII.1:2 as you use it in more and more s.. You
T-12.....VII.1:3 in miracles when you apply them to all s..
T-12.....VII.1:4 them to all s. you will gain the real world.
T-17....VIII.3:4 This power instantly transforms all s. into
T-24...... VI.7:2 Yet will you choose in countless s., and
T-27....... V.8:8 within two s. that are seen as one, for only
T-27....... V.9:3 learning does not jump from s. to their
T-30.........I.2:4 you will not judge the s. where you will be
T-31...... IV.5:5 power if it be applied in s. without choice
W-in..........6:3 people, s. or things to which the ideas are
W-pI.....21.1:2 the idea to particular s. as they may arise.
W-pI.....21.2:2 and search your mind carefully for s. past,
W-pI.....21.3:3 on some s. or persons than on others, on
W-pI.....24.4:1 for unresolved s. about which you are
W-pI.....26.8:2 to cover a few s. thoroughly than to touch
W-pI.....34.3:2 for fear thoughts, anxiety-provoking s.,
W-pI.....35.7:2 way. They will occur to you as various s.,
W-pI.....39.7:1 Specific s., events or personalities you
W-pI.....40.2:2 you may be in a number of s. during the
W-pI.....43.7:1 to the circumstances and s. in which you
W-pI.....43.8:1 to various s. and events that may occur,
W-pI.....47.3:2 Voice speaks for Him in all s. and in every
W-pI.....47.3:2 all situations and in every aspect of all s.,
W-pI.....47.4:4 for s. in your life which you have invested
WpI...rI.in.4:3 most in s. that appear to be upsetting,
W-pI.....70.7:5 in possessions, in various s. and events,
W-pI.....74.4:2 persons and the situation or s. involved,
W-pI.....77.7:5 You will recognize these s.. And since you
WpI..rIII.in3:3 behind a cloak of s. you cannot control.
WpI..rIII.in3:4 Learn to distinguish s. that are poorly
M-3 ...........5:2 teaching-learning s. in which each person
M-4 .....I.A.4:3 what he has learned to new s. as they arise
M-22 ..........2:2 of the lesson of the Atonement to all s.,
P-1.............1:5 times and s. in which an earthly patient-

**six** 8

W-pI.....25.6:1 S. practice periods, each of two-minutes
W-pI.....26.5:1 S. practice periods are required in
W-pI.....26.8:1 some five or s. distressing possibilities
W-pI.....28.7:1 have s. two-minute practice periods today
W-pI.....29.4:1 s. two-minute practice periods for today
W-pI...71.10:5 idea some s. or seven times an hour.
W-pI...91.11:1 Five or s. times an hour, at reasonably
W-pI...130.7:1 S. times today, in thanks and gratitude,

**size** 13

T-1 ....... III.9:3 of s. exists on a plane that is itself unreal.
T-11 ... VI.10:7 does not exist has no s. and no measure.
T-18 ... VI.12:1 your differences in s. and seeming quality
T-21 ...... V.1:3 laws of s. and shape and brightness would
T-22 ...... V.5:2 illusions it presents of s. and thickness,
T-24 .... VII.7:3 from; not born of s. nor place nor time,
T-26 ........II.3:4 vanish one by one, without regard to s.,
T-26 .....X.1:10 is not a question of the s. of the confusion
W-pI........2.2:1 around you, trying to avoid selection by s.
W-pI.....92.6:4 that but grow in darkness to enormous s..
W-pI.....99.6:6 regardless of their form, their s., their
W-pI...140.6:6 a thought that judges an illusion by its s.,
M-8 ...........6:7 from s. and shape and time and place–

**sizes** 1

M-8 ...........1:2 on unequal heights and diverse s., on

**skeleton** 1

T-23 .....II.18:8 Can you paint rosy lips upon a s., dress it

**skies** 1

T-20 .VIII.11:1 to quiet views of gardens under open s.,

**skill** 7

T-8 .....VIII.8:4 the ego's s. in building up false cases. Nor
T-11 ...... V.9:2 is indeed a s. at which it is very ingenious.
T-28 ........I.2:7 is a s. made up by you to take the place of
T-28 ........I.4:3 to realize it is a s. that can remember *now.*
T-31 ........I.3:1 ever doubt the power of your learning s..
T-31 ........I.5:5 s. the Holy Spirit sees in all the world. His
S-3........ III.3:2 goes to profit by his learning and his s.; to

**skills** 2

T-12 ...... V.5:2 There are areas in your learning s. that
T-28 ........I.3:5 They are but s. without an application.

**skin** 1

T19..IV.A.13:2 bring you word of bones and s. and flesh.

**skip** 1

WpI..rIII.in3:1 learning will be hampered when you s. a

**sky** 7

T-22 ..... VI.4:1 than the sun that lights the s. you see, is
T-30 ..... III.8:4 is like a star, unchangeable in an eternal s.
T-30 ..... III.9:1 for He is the eternal s. that holds it safe,
T-30 ..... III.9:3 The s. embraces it and softly holds it in its
T-30 ... III.11:3 of? Outside you there is no eternal s., no
T-30 ... III.11:9 star shines still; the s. has never changed.
W-pII . 300.1:2 a passing cloud upon a s. eternally serene.

**slain** 6

T19 ...IV.C.8:1 would lay the Son of God, s. by its orders,
T-20 ........I.1:4 A s. Christ has no meaning. But a risen
T-21 .... VII.1:8 or see him shattered and s. by your attack
T-28 .......II.5:5 are you the victim in a dying body s.. But
W-pI .. 190.3:7 in death, as mortal as the Father he has s..
W-pII ..... 4.3:4 forever overcome by death, love s. by hate

**slate** 2

W-pI .... 65.6:4 *clean s. let my true function be written for*
W-pI .. 192.4:1 and unmarked s. on which the Word of

**slaughter** 1

M-13 ......... 4:4 look back with longing on a s. house? No

**slave** 26

T-1 .... VII.3:13 as a single "s." remains to walk the earth,
T-13 ..... III.5:2 You would rather be a s. of the crucifixion
T-19 ......I.16:1 to interfere with it and make it s. to time.
T-19 ......I.16:3 God created as His Son is s. to nothing,
T-22 .......II.8:8 no more a s. to time than to the world you
T-27 .......II.9:4 guilt he suffers serves to prove that he is s.
T-27 ... VIII.2:7 s. of bodies that would hurt and torture it
T-28 .......II.8:5 His body is their s., which they abuse
T-29 ..... IX.1:1 s. of idols is a willing slave. For willing he
T-29 ..... IX.1:1 slave of idols is a willing s.. For willing he
T-29 ..... IX.3:7 condemned; and wish to be the s. of idols,
T-30 .......II.3:3 and be a prisoner to fear, a s. to death, a
T-30 ... VIII.4:9 he becomes the willing s. of what he chose
T-31 ........I.9:5 He created innocent could be a s. to guilt.
W-pI .. 102.2:5 You have been s. to nothing. Be you free
W-pI 136.10:2 and all the universe made s. to laws which
W-pI .. 153.5:1 You are its s.. You know not what you do
W-pI .. 194.5:3 Then is each instant which was s. to time
W-pI .. 195.4:1 because your brother is more s. than you,
W-pI .. 196.1:1 nor make your body s. to vengeance. You
W-pI .. 204.1:2 *reminds me that I am His Son, not s. to time,*
W-pII . 277.1:5 *He is not s. to any laws of time. He is as You*
W-pII . 317.1:3 I am the s. of time and human destiny.
S-2...........I.5:4 You would be s. to everyone, for what he
S-2..........II.2:5 Who makes a s. to teach what freedom is?
S-2..........II.6:3 Say this to anyone and you are s.. And

**slavery** 10

T-11 ..... VI.5:3 is why his s. is as complete as his freedom
T-16 .... VII.9:5 Release your brothers from the s. of their
T-17 ..... III.9:4 and fear, truth or illusion, freedom or s.
T-18 ..... IX.1:5 by madness into obedience and s.. This is
W-pI .. 170.8:2 be the time of your release from abject s..
W-pII . 277.2:3 is, is far beyond his faith in s. or freedom.
P-1............. 4:5 his freedom because he thinks that it is s..
S-2..........II.6:2 my needs, for in your s. is my release."
S-2..........II.7:4 of it the means for further s. and pain.
S-2..........II.8:4 You do not want to stay in s.. You do not

**slaves** 4

T-17 ..... III.2:4 and make of both the s. of vengeance.
T-24 ..... III.8:1 The s. of specialness will yet be free. Such
T-29 ... VIII.6:4 loss, the timeless to be made the s. of time
P-2........ VI.3:6 its s. to change the forms they look upon;

**sleep** 66

T-2 ..........I.3:6 Bible says that a deep s. fell upon Adam,
T-2 ..........I.4:5 Only after the deep s. fell upon Adam
T-3 .........II.5:2 from its s. and remembers its Creator. All

| | |
|---|---|
| T-6........IV.6:3 | a **s.** in which you have had bad dreams, |
| T-6........IV.6:3 | **s.** is not real and God calls you to awake. |
| T-6.........V.1:8 | "My children **s.** and must be awakened." |
| T-7........IV.1:7 | not exist, but those who **s.** are unaware. |
| T-8........IX.3:6 | **S.** is withdrawing; waking is joining. |
| T-8........IX.3:8 | the Holy Spirit, too, has use for **s.**, and |
| T-8........IX.4:1 | wake is the sign of how you have used **s.**. |
| T-8........IX.4:5 | you utilized **s.** according to His purpose. |
| T-8........IX.4:6 | You can indeed be "drugged" by **s.**, if you |
| T-8........IX.4:7 | **S.** is no more a form of death than death |
| T-10.........I.4:2 | Them you will have no wish to **s.**, but |
| T-11.........I.9:7 | **S.** is not death. What He created can sleep |
| T-11.........I.9:8 | What He created can **s.**, but cannot die. |
| T-12......VI.4:2 | have not lost their vision, but merely **s.**. |
| T-12......VI.4:3 | awaken them from the **s.** of forgetting to |
| T-13.......V.8:3 | Yet in darkness, in the private world of **s.**, |
| T-13....VI.12:4 | In **s.** you are alone, and your awareness is |
| T-13....VI.13:1 | of love are not suspended because you **s.**. |
| T-13....VI.13:3 | alone. Even in **s.** has Christ protected you, |
| T-13......XI.1:1 | Forgetfulness and **s.** and even death |
| T-13....XI.10:3 | His **s.** will not withstand the Call to wake. |
| T-14....... II.7:9 | and freed you from the **s.** of darkness. |
| T-14......IV.6:7 | tired will find this is more restful than **s.**. |
| T-14......XI.2:2 | that only the insane, in deepest **s.**, could |
| T-15......XI.1:6 | when you have no more need of **s.**. |
| T-16...VII.12:4 | *s. of forgetfulness is only the unwillingness* |
| T-18....... II.3:1 | you see in **s.** and on awaking disturbing. |
| T-18....... III.1:2 | sleeping, and on and on to a yet deeper **s.**. |
| T-24...... III.7:2 | there, beside the bier on which they **s.**, |
| T-27...VII.14:8 | face. The **s.** is peaceful now, for these are |
| T-28....... II.4:1 | but that you have put yourself to **s.**, and |
| T-30...VII.6:15 | senseless, isolated scripts you write in **s.**. |
| T-31...... III.6:4 | be. It does not guard your **s.**, nor interfere |
| W-pI.....42.3:1 | close as possible to the time you go to **s.**. |
| W-pI.....61.6:2 | turn to **s.** as you reaffirm your function |
| W-pI.....68.2:1 | to Its Creator, your Self seems to **s.**, while |
| W-pI.....68.2:1 | illusions in its **s.** appears to be awake. Can |
| W-pI...106.5:1 | and wakes all those who **s.** and cannot see |
| WpI. rIII.in8:2 | other in the hour just before you go to **s.**. |
| W-pI...121.3:1 | to stay, afraid to waken or to go to **s.**, |
| W-pI...122.2:3 | It soothes your forehead while you **s.**, and |
| W-pI.138.12:1 | Before we close our eyes in **s.** tonight, we |
| W-pI...140.3:2 | perceive do not induce another form of **s.**, |
| W-pI...140.3:4 | They lead from **s.** to gentle waking, so |
| W-pI.140.11:1 | again five minutes more before we go to **s.** |
| WpIrIV.in10:2 | to the ideas for the day again before you **s.** |
| W-pI.151.15:1 | another fifteen more before you go to **s.**. |
| W-pI...162.3:1 | bringing them with him as he goes to **s.**. |
| W-pI...167.8:2 | He does not **s.**, and His creations cannot |
| W-pI...167.9:2 | Source, it merely seems to go to **s.** a while. |
| W-pI...168.2:6 | the means of Him whereby its **s.** is done. |
| W-pI...168.3:4 | and sweeps away the cobwebs of our **s.**. |
| W-pI.169.10:4 | and rise and work and go to **s.** by them? |
| WpI rV.in11:3 | And with this thought we **s.**, to waken |
| W-pI...189.2:4 | the night as silent guardian of your holy **s.** |
| W-pI.190.10:5 | Pain is but **s.**; joy is awakening. Pain is |
| W-pI.191.10:1 | let the Son of God awaken from his **s.**, |
| W-pI.191.10:3 | he will **s.** no more and dream of death. |
| W-pI.198.11:3 | face of earth, made quiet in a dreamless **s.** |
| W-pII..232.1:5 | *And let me s. sure of my safety, certain of* |
| W-pII..331.1:8 | *Conflict is s., and peace awakening. Death is* |
| M-16..........5:2 | for you to take it just before going to **s.**. It |
| M-16..........5:6 | to **s.** is a desirable time to devote to God. |

## sleepeth 1

| | |
|---|---|
| T-13.........I.7:2 | The Son of God, who **s.** not, has kept faith |

## sleeping 27

| | |
|---|---|
| T-5....... II.10:4 | does not come from **s.** but from waking. |
| T-6.........V.2:4 | the difference between **s.** and waking, so |
| T-8........IX.3:3 | to reinforce **s.** out of fear of waking. This |
| T-8........IX.3:5 | rest comes from waking, not from **s.**. |
| T-12......VI.5:2 | Us. Yet you must learn the cost of **s.**, and |
| T-13......XI.9:5 | of God's **s.** Son holds no power over him. |
| T-14......IV.6:8 | For you can bring your guilt into **s.**, but |
| T-17....... II.1:3 | Nothing you see here, **s.** or waking, comes |
| T-18..... II.5:13 | **s.** and your waking dreams have different |
| T-18..... II.5:17 | you try to make your **s.** dreams come true |
| T-18..... II.5:20 | you see more value in **s.** than in waking, |
| T-18....... II.9:5 | **s.** and your waking dreams represent the |
| T-18...... III.1:2 | For you have gone from waking to **s.**, and |
| T-27.....VII.9:4 | to make between a **s.** death and dreams of |
| T-27...VII.10:1 | between but life or death, waking or **s.**, |
| T-27...VII.14:7 | smile has come to lighten up your **s.** face. |
| T-29......IV.1:7 | from some, for you are either **s.** or awake. |
| T-31...... III.5:1 | a **s.** prisoner to the snarling dogs of hate |
| W-pI...109.2:4 | thought has power to wake the **s.** truth in |
| W-pI...167.7:4 | Yet mind is mind, awake or **s.**. It is not its |
| W-pI...167.9:1 | to be the opposite of life is merely **s.**. |
| W-pI.167.12:3 | A **s.** mind must waken, as it sees its own |
| W-pI...168.3:6 | It restores all memories the **s.** mind forgot |
| W-pI...185.4:8 | is lost to **s.** minds intent on compromise, |
| M-in ..........1:6 | and continues into **s.** thoughts as well. |
| M-17 .........7:2 | They can but reawaken **s.** guilt, which you |
| M-21 .........3:7 | The **s.** Son of God has but this power left |

## sleeps 10

| | |
|---|---|
| T-2........VI.9:6 | It never **s.**. Every instant it is creating. It is |
| T-12......VI.4:5 | of Christ for every Son of God who **s.**. In |
| T-26......IX.1:2 | be when in him **s.** your own salvation, |
| T-28....... II.6:7 | is not awake, but does not know he **s.**. He |
| W-pI...140.2:6 | One either **s.** or wakens. There is nothing |
| W-pI...162.3:2 | because he **s.** and wakens with the truth |
| W-pI...167.6:1 | The mind can think it **s.**, but that is all. It |
| W-pI...167.7:5 | it seems to make when it believes it **s.**. |
| W-pI.167.10:3 | himself what he is not because he **s.**, and |
| W-pII......8.4:1 | guilt is over, and God's Son no longer **s.**. |

## sleepy 1

| | |
|---|---|
| W-pI...153.6:4 | he becomes too **s.** to remember what he |

## sleight 1

| | |
|---|---|
| W-pI...158.4:1 | Time is a trick, a **s.** of hand, a vast |

## slept 6

| | |
|---|---|
| T-6...........I.7:6 | amiss. My brothers **s.** during the so-called |
| T-10.........I.2:5 | you awaken to were violated while you **s.**. |
| T-12......VI.5:4 | to your sight, for Christ has never **s.**. He is |
| T-13....VI.13:8 | Although he **s.**, Christ's vision did not |
| T-13....VI.13:9 | witnesses that teach him that he never **s.**. |
| T-18....... II.1:3 | not the world you saw before you **s.**. |

## slight 7

| | |
|---|---|
| T-2....VII.5:14 | only one **s.** correction to be meaningful in |
| T-24.......I.8:10 | change with every seeming blow, each **s.**, |
| T-24.....VII.1:6 | to save his specialness from the least **s.**, |
| W-pI.....21.2:5 | that a **s.** twinge of annoyance is nothing |
| W-pI...167.2:6 | a **s.** discomfort or the merest frown, |
| M-17 .........4:4 | It may be merely **s.** irritation, perhaps too |
| P-3......... II.3:4 | to him, however **s.** it may have been, |

## slightest 8

| | |
|---|---|
| T-5.......VII.6:6 | will respond fully to your **s.** invitation: |
| T-25.........I.3:4 | nor gives the **s.** witness unto anything the |
| T-25...... IX.3:3 | An answer which demands the **s.** loss to |
| W-pI.133.12:1 | desirable or not worth the **s.** effort to |
| W-pI...158.7:5 | without the **s.** fading of the light it sees. |
| M-17 .......6:10 | but do not retain the **s.** memory of Who |
| M-25 .........1:5 | even in the **s.** with the glorious surprise of |
| P-3......... II.3:1 | use, and will use, given the **s.** invitation. |

## slightly 4

| | |
|---|---|
| T-11....... II.5:4 | Think like Him ever so **s.**, and the little |
| T-29......IV.3:4 | in which they may be wrapped but **s.** veils |
| W-pI.....10.2:2 | The form is only **s.** different. This time |
| P-2........III.1:1 | sense that he walks **s.** ahead of the patient |

## slights 1

| | |
|---|---|
| T-16.....VII.1:3 | it. Imagined **s.**, remembered pain, past |

## slip 17

| | |
|---|---|
| T-4........IV.7:1 | actively refuse to let your mind **s.** away. |
| T-6......V.A.4:4 | to let this crucial concept **s.** away. It is a |
| T-14....... V.5:2 | So will the world of separation **s.** away, |
| T-15....... III.8:7 | offerings you give **s.** into nothingness. |
| T-18.....VII.7:3 | which you **s.** past centuries of effort, and |
| T-22...... IV.7:6 | your fingers **s.** through its nothingness. It |
| W-pI.....43.9:2 | **s.** by without remembering today's idea, |
| W-pI.....44.7:5 | involvement, and **s.** quietly by them. |
| W-pI.....47.5:1 | Now try to **s.** past all concerns related to |
| W-pI...109.5:8 | to **s.** away from dreams and into peace. |
| W-pI.122.14:1 | gifts **s.** by and drift into forgetfulness, but |
| W-pI.131.14:2 | and through His aid **s.** effortlessly past it, |
| W-pI...153.8:3 | not let our happiness **s.** by because a |
| W-pI...164.9:1 | Let not today **s.** by without the gifts it |
| W-pI...183.5:2 | things on earth **s.** into right perspective. |
| W-pII ...13.1:6 | must **s.** away under the gentle remedy it |
| M-16 .........7:1 | how easily does time **s.** by for the teacher |

## slipped 2

| | |
|---|---|
| T-12...... VI.7:5 | the real world has **s.** quietly into Heaven, |
| T-13.....VII.5:5 | judgment enters reality has **s.** away. The |

## slipping 2

| | |
|---|---|
| W-pI.....44.4:2 | only if you find the time **s.** by with little or |
| W-pI.....74.6:3 | If you feel yourself **s.** off into withdrawal, |

## slips 5

| | |
|---|---|
| T-9......VIII.7:3 | When grandeur **s.** away from you, you |
| T-20...... III.7:8 | so tiny and so meaningless it **s.** unnoticed |
| W-pI.137.15:4 | be forgot as every hour of the day **s.** by, |
| W-pII ...10.2:3 | sight, it merely **s.** away to nothingness. |
| M-20 .........2:8 | The past just **s.** away, and in its place is |

## sloping 1

| | |
|---|---|
| W-pI...200.8:4 | is easy, **s.** gently toward the bridge where |

## slow 9

| | |
|---|---|
| T-17....... V.5:1 | each **s.** step according to its liking. Only a |
| T19....IV.C.2:4 | and marching in the **s.** procession that |
| T-27...VII.12:1 | death, yet plans that it be lingering and **s.**; |
| W-pI.....12.2:3 | Try to pace yourself so that the **s.** shifting |
| W-pI.....25.6:2 | with a **s.** repetition of the idea for today, |
| W-pI.....42.6:3 | **s.** repetitions of the idea with eyes open, |
| W-pI.151.13:2 | **s.** repeating of the thought with which the |
| M-9 ...........2:4 | God's Voice, is usually a fairly **s.** process, |
| M-22 .........2:1 | of the teacher of God may be **s.** or rapid, |

## slower 1

| | |
|---|---|
| W-pI.....42.4:2 | repeat the idea again, even **s.** than before. |

## slowly 47

| | |
|---|---|
| T-4........ VI.5:3 | and **s.** bring it nearer so he can learn how |
| T-17....... V.5:1 | not be kinder to shift the goal more **s.**, for |
| W-pI.......1.1:1 | Now look **s.** around you, and practice |
| W-pI.....10.4:1 | the idea for today quite **s.** to yourself. |
| W-pI.....10.5:4 | the idea **s.** before applying it specifically, |
| W-pI.....11.2:2 | closed, and repeat the idea **s.** to yourself. |
| W-pI.....11.3:5 | repeat the idea once more **s.** to yourself. |
| W-pI.....12.2:2 | Look around you, this time quite **s.**. Try |
| W-pI.....13.4:3 | open your eyes, and look about you **s.**, |
| W-pI.....15.4:6 | idea should be repeated quite **s.** each time |
| W-pI.....20.5:1 | Repeat today's idea **s.** and positively at |
| W-pI.....22.3:2 | eyes move **s.** from one object to another, |
| W-pI.....23.6:2 | you, repeat the idea **s.** to yourself first, |
| W-pI.....25.6:7 | *for.* Say this quite **s.**, without shifting your |
| W-pI.....28.8:3 | Each application should be made quite **s.**, |

| | |
|---|---|
| W-pI...29.5:10 | looking **s.** about you as you say the words |
| W-pI....30.3:2 | a moment or so, repeat it to yourself **s.**, |
| W-pI.....31.2:3 | look about you **s.** while repeating the idea |
| W-pI.....32.5:2 | consist of repeating the idea **s.**, as you |
| W-pI.....34.3:3 | repeating the idea for today **s.** as you |
| W-pI.....35.8:2 | idea **s.** until something occurs to you. |
| W-pI.....36.3:1 | repeat the idea for today several times, **s.**. |
| W-pI.....36.3:2 | your eyes and look quite **s.** about you, |
| W-pI.....36.4:2 | should, of course, be made quite **s.**, as |
| W-pI.....39.8:1 | **S.**, without conscious selection and |
| W-pI.....39.9:1 | today's idea to yourself **s.** a few times. |
| W-pI.....41.6:3 | practice period, repeat today's idea very **s.** |
| W-pI.....41.9:1 | use today's idea often, repeating it very **s.**, |
| W-pI.....42.4:1 | periods by repeating the idea for today **s.**, |
| W-pI.....42.5:5 | thought once more while looking **s.** about |
| W-pI.....44.7:1 | with your eyes open, and close them **s.**, |
| W-pI.....48.2:4 | repeat the idea **s.** to yourself several times |
| W-pI.....64.8:3 | then look **s.** and unselectively around you |
| W-pI...66.11:3 | to repeat these words **s.** and think about |
| W-pI.....74.3:1 | times, **s.** and with firm determination to |
| W-pI.....75.6:7 | several times, **s.** and in complete patience: |
| WpI..rII.in.2:2 | or four minutes to reading them over **s.**, |
| W-pI...95.11:3 | tell yourself again, **s.** and thoughtfully, |
| W-pI...101.3:3 | must be feared, for it will kill, but **s.**, |
| W-pI...108.9:1 | Say each one **s.** and then pause a while, |
| WpI. rIV.in7:2 | your eyes, and say them **s.** to yourself. |
| WpI...rV.in1:5 | and **s.** on the road this course sets forth. |
| W-pI...183.6:1 | repeat God's Name **s.** again and still again |
| W-pII ..in.11:4 | be **s.** read and thought about a little while |
| M-4 ...... VI.1:9 | **S.** at first he lets himself be undeceived. |
| M-9 ........... 1:7 | By far the majority are given a **s.** evolving |
| S-1......... V.1:2 | And here again it rises **s.** up, and grows in |

## small 37

| | |
|---|---|
| T-4........ VI.2:5 | gap is then so **s.** that knowledge can easily |
| T-11....... II.4:3 | beside your **s.** willingness to make whole |
| T-11....... V.13:5 | it perceives by breaking it into **s.**, |
| T-11.... VI.10:6 | to His Will is either great or **s.**. What does |
| T-14.... IV.4:12 | this **s.** gift of appreciation for His Love, |
| T-14...VII.5:14 | Him only to the **s.** extent of believing that, |
| T-14....VIII.2:2 | that promises otherwise, great or **s.**, |
| T-16...VII.11:2 | problems, be they perceived as great or **s.**, |
| T-17....... II.2:6 | little step, so **s.** it has escaped your notice, |
| T-17.....VII.6:7 | Nothing too **s.** or too enormous, too weak |
| T-18......IV.4:2 | is always the result of your **s.** willingness |
| T-18....VIII.2:6 | It draws a circle, infinitely **s.**, around a |
| T-21....... II.1:2 | same **s.** willingness you need to have your |
| T-21....... V.1:6 | **s.** Voice for God is not drowned out by all |
| T-26....... II.4:4 | does not evaluate injustices as great or **s.**, |
| T-26....... V.4:1 | you through the infinitely **s.** and senseless |
| T-30.... III.2:11 | be content with **s.** ideas and little things. |
| T-31.........I.4:4 | seems **s.** and still before its magnitude. |
| T-31.........I.6:1 | so **s.** and still It cannot rise above the |
| T-31....... V.3:4 | make **s.** assaults upon its innocence, |
| W-pI.......5.4:3 | *There are no* **s.** *upsets. They are all equally* |
| W-pI.......6.3:2 | *There are no* **s.** *upsets. They are all equally* |
| W-pI.......9.2:5 | exercises. Each **s.** step will clear a little of |
| W-pI.....69.7:2 | Your little effort and **s.** determination call |
| W-pI.....76.3:3 | You really think a **s.** round pellet or some |
| W-pI.....92.3:3 | to behold the likeness of itself; the **s.**, the |
| W-pI.....98.5:3 | five minutes but a **s.** request to make in |
| W-pI.107.10:3 | with every gift you give of five **s.** minutes, |
| W-pI...123.1:4 | some **s.** objections and a little hesitance, |
| W-pI...126.5:5 | Would not His care for you be **s.** indeed, |
| W-pI.137.13:3 | Is not a little time a **s.** expense to offer for |
| M-in .......... 1:4 | a relatively **s.** proportion of one's time. |
| M-4 ...... IX.1:9 | Yet each degree, however **s.**, is worth |
| M-5 .........I.1:3 | He must think it is a **s.** price to pay for |
| M-15 ......... 3:2 | **s.** and meaningless to occupy your holy |
| M-19 ......... 2:4 | but the first **s.** step in the direction of the |
| M-25 ......... 2:2 | Communication is not limited to the **s.** |

## smaller 4

| | |
|---|---|
| T-3.........I.7:10 | be no need to learn from many **s.** lessons. |
| T-23..... II.21:5 | Think not one step is **s.** than another, nor |
| M-8 ........... 1:3 | A larger object overshadows a **s.** one. A |
| M-8 ........... 5:2 | larger hallucination as opposed to a **s.** one |

## smallest 6

| | |
|---|---|
| T-17 .......II.3:1 | This step, the **s.** ever taken, is still the |
| T-17 .......II.6:3 | The **s.** leaf becomes a thing of wonder, |
| T-18 ...VIII.3:3 | that it is like the **s.** sunbeam to the sun, or |
| T-24 ........I.1:2 | the **s.** gift is not to know love's purpose. |
| T-28 ..... IV.9:4 | How holy is the **s.** grain of sand, when it is |
| P-2......... V.6:5 | asked for more than just the **s.** willingness |

## smash 1

| | |
|---|---|
| W-pII ..... 1.3:4 | sets about its furious attempts to **s.** reality |

## smeared 1

| | |
|---|---|
| W-pI...170.7:2 | note that though his lips are **s.** with blood |

## smile 20

| | |
|---|---|
| T-19 ..... III.8:5 | in sin has been uprooted in its **s.** of love. |
| T-19 ..... III.9:1 | you look with Heaven's **s.** upon your lips, |
| T-19 ... III.10:1 | you will see the **s.** of Heaven shining on |
| T-20 ..... VI.3:8 | They **s.** on no one, and those who smile |
| T-20 ..... VI.3:8 | and those who **s.** on them they do not see. |
| T-20 ... VI.10:3 | love shines on it with the gentle **s.** and |
| T-22 ... VI.8:10 | will one little **s.** or willingness to overlook |
| T-22 ... VI.9:11 | and lays it gently in each quiet **s.** of faith |
| T-25 .VIII.12:5 | He may **s.** on you whose sinlessness He |
| T-27 .. VII.14:7 | A **s.** has come to lighten up your sleeping |
| W-pI... 100.3:3 | Without your **s.**, the world cannot be |
| W-pI... 123.4:3 | Today we **s.** on everyone we see, and walk |
| W-pI. 153.14:6 | God's Son can **s.** at last, on learning that |
| W-pI... 155.1:2 | though you **s.** more frequently. Your |
| W-pI. 161.11:4 | Watch him **s.**, and see familiar gestures |
| W-pII . 341.1:2 | *is holy. I am he on whom You* **s.** *in love and* |
| W-pII . 341.1:3 | *how holy, then, are we, abiding in Your* **S.**, |
| M-3 ........... 2:5 | in the elevator will **s.** to one another, |
| M-29 ......... 2:3 | Who needs but a **s.**, being as yet unready |
| S-2..........II.4:4 | except with silence and a gentle **s.**? |

## smiled 2

| | |
|---|---|
| T-19 ..... III.8:5 | Heaven has **s.** upon it, and the belief in |
| T-19 ... III.10:3 | against a union Heaven has **s.** upon. Your |

## smiles 11

| | |
|---|---|
| T-21 ..... IV.1:5 | quite appropriate, and **s.** approvingly. It |
| T-23 ..... III.1:6 | justify his savagery with **s.** as he attacks. |
| T-23 ..... III.1:7 | in nightmares where the **s.** are gone, and |
| T-31 ...... V.2:7 | that **s.** and charms and even seems to love |
| T-31 ...... V.5:2 | that **s.** above it must forever look away, |
| T-31 ...... V.5:4 | of the self the world **s.** with approval, for |
| W-pI... 124.3:2 | **s.** on us and offers us the happiness we |
| W-pI... 134.4:4 | and **s.** on the corrupt as if they were as |
| W-pII ..... 9.4:4 | And God the Father **s.** upon His Son, His |
| W-pII . 315.1:3 | A brother **s.** upon another, and my heart |
| W-pII . 341.1:2 | *dear and deep and still the universe* **s.** *back* |

## smiling 1

| | |
|---|---|
| T-20 ..... VI.2:7 | **s.** welcome and in sincerity so simple and |

## smoke 1

| | |
|---|---|
| W-pI. 133.12:3 | Complexity is nothing but a screen of **s.**, |

## smooth 1

| | |
|---|---|
| W-pI... 165.2:6 | soft your resting place and **s.** your way, |

## smoother 1

| | |
|---|---|
| W-pI... 123.1:2 | come to gentler pathways and to **s.** roads. |

## smoothly 1

| | |
|---|---|
| M-16 ....... 1:10 | he walks stretch surely and **s.** before him. |

## snake 1

| | |
|---|---|
| W-pI .... 93.1:2 | from you as if from a poisonous **s.**. You |

## snares 1

| | |
|---|---|
| W-pI .. 189.6:4 | For its simplicity avoids the **s.** the foolish |

## snarling 1

| | |
|---|---|
| T-31 ..... III.5:1 | prisoner to the **s.** dogs of hate and evil, |

## snatch 6

| | |
|---|---|
| T-15 .......V.9:7 | have no need to look without and **s.** love |
| T-16 .....V.10:6 | and **s.** it from the other to replace the self |
| T-18 .......II.6:5 | not destroy it, nor **s.** it away from you. |
| T-18 ..... III.4:5 | Be tempted not to **s.** away the gift of faith |
| T-24 .... VII.1:8 | Fatherhood of God, not **s.** it from Him. |
| W-pI .. 191.3:3 | despair **s.** from your fingers every scrap of |

## snatches 1

| | |
|---|---|
| W-pI .. 197.6:2 | before He **s.** them away again in death. |

## snow 4

*See also* snow-white

| | |
|---|---|
| T19 ...IV.A.9:3 | sun upon a garden covered by the **s.**? See |
| T-28 ..... III.7:2 | stored a heap of **s.** that shone like silver. |
| W-pI .. 134.4:4 | as blameless as the grass; as white as **s.**. It |
| W-pI .. 189.2:6 | own. It offers you its flowers and its **s.**, in |

## snow-white 2

| | |
|---|---|
| T-20 ........I.4:2 | looking between the **s.** petals of the lilies |
| W-pI 151.16:2 | so you lay the gift of **s.** lilies on the world, |

## snowflake 2

| | |
|---|---|
| T19 ...IV.A.9:6 | than fix your gaze upon a disappearing **s.**, |
| T-20 ..... VI.9:2 | of their seeming power is frail as is a **s.**, |

## snuffed 1

| | |
|---|---|
| C-4 ............ 7:7 | of guilt and death is there **s.** out forever. |

## so 1456

## so-called 3

| | |
|---|---|
| T-4 .........II.7:6 | as it is of the **s.** "higher ego needs." Body |
| T-4 .........II.9:3 | The **s.** "battle for survival" is only the |
| T-6 ..........I.7:6 | My brothers slept during the **s.** "agony in |

## soar 2

| | |
|---|---|
| W-pI .. 121.2:1 | and **s.** above the turmoil of the world. The |
| W-pI .. 128.1:3 | leave the world behind and **s.** beyond its |

## soared 1

| | |
|---|---|
| T-26 ..... IV.5:5 | tiny then has **s.** into a magnitude of song |

## soars 1

| | |
|---|---|
| T-20 ..... IV.4:7 | Ask not the sparrow how the eagle **s.**, for |

## sobering 1

| | |
|---|---|
| W-pI .. 186.3:1 | Today's idea may seem quite **s.**, until you |

## soft 10

| | |
|---|---|
| T-21 ........I.7:2 | but as a **s.** reminder of what would make |
| T-22 ..... VI.3:5 | of contradiction makes the **s.** transition |
| T-29 .......V.2:4 | surrounds you gently in its **s.** embrace, so |
| T-29 .......V.4:1 | **s.** reminder of his Father's Love by which |

- T-30......IV.2:2 or when a **s.** and silent woolly bear begins
- T-31.........I.8:2 Nothing but calls to you in **s.** appeal to be
- T-31.........I.8:8 The **s.** eternal calling of each part of God's
- W-pI.140.12:4 feel salvation cover us with **s.** protection,
- W-pI...165.2:6 makes **s.** your resting place and smooth
- W-pI.200.10:6 and you can feel its **s.** embrace surround

## softer 1

- M-8............5:3 voice he hears than to that of a **s.** one?

## softly 6

- T-18......IX.6:3 gives way **s.** to the mountain tops that rise
- T19.IV.A.15:2 cleansed of all guilt and **s.** brushed with
- T19.IV.A.16:1 and a **s.** joyous whispering is ever heard.
- T-27...VII.15:1 Dream **s.** of your sinless brother, who
- T-30......III.9:3 it and **s.** holds it in its perfect place, which
- S-3........IV.9:3 the thorns fall **s.** from the bleeding brow

## softness 1

- W-pI...156.4:4 you on the ground that you may walk in **s.**

## soil 2

- W-pI...159.8:3 grow in its unnourishing and shallow **s.**.
- W-pII......2.4:4 The grass is pushing through the **s.**, the

## solace 4

- T-3.........II.6:4 and emptiness can never find lasting **s.**. If
- T-31.......V.2:8 on the suffering, and sometimes offers **s.**.
- W-pI...170.5:2 to which you turn for **s.** and escape from
- W-pII..334.2:3 *can be his s. but what You are offering to his*

## sold 2

- T-12......IV.6:5 it, because you have **s.** everything else.
- T-12......IV.6:7 inheritance can neither be bought nor **s.**.

## sole 15

- T-2...........I.5:3 **s.** concern is to distinguish between truth
- T-2.........V.5:1 *The s. responsibility of the miracle worker*
- T-5.........V.7:8 **s.** responsibility of the miracle worker is
- T-7........III.5:5 **s.** function is to undo the questionable
- T-7.....VIII.5:4 willing to accept **s.** responsibility for the
- T-8.....VIII.5:4 Its **s.** aim is to lose sight of the function of
- T-14....III.17:7 take unto yourself the **s.** responsibility for
- T-18.......IX.1:5 **s.** ruler of the kingdom it set apart to
- T-23......III.1:5 Its **s.** intent is murder, and what form of
- T-25......IX.9:6 That is why your **s.** responsibility must be
- T-30.......V.2:4 the **s.** cause of pain in any form. No one is
- W-pI........2.2:4 The **s.** criterion for applying the idea to
- W-pI...183.8:1 acknowledge Him as **s.** Creator of reality.
- M-18..........4:5 The **s.** responsibility of God's teacher is to
- M-24........6:12 This is the **s.** criterion this course requires

## solely 19

- T-2.....VIII.5:8 The purpose of time is **s.** to "give you time
- T-3...........I.4:2 God. It arises **s.** from fear, and frightened
- T-6...........I.2:2 lies **s.** in the kind of learning it facilitates.
- T-6.........II.3:3 It is **s.** a device of the ego to make you feel
- T-8.......VII.2:5 because you do not regard bodies **s.** as a
- T-8.....VII.10:1 of using the body **s.** for communication.
- T-8.....VIII.1:8 condition lies **s.** in your interpretation of
- T-9.....VIII.6:1 depends **s.** on your willingness to tolerate
- T-10.......in.1:2 time **s.** as a means to regain eternity. You
- T-10.......in.1:4 must learn that time is **s.** at your disposal,
- T-15.......XI.1:1 idea of sacrifice as **s.** of your making. And
- T-16.......IV.1:3 hidden, is undertaken **s.** to offset the hate,
- T-18.......II.1:4 planned **s.** around what you would have
- T-20.......VI.1:1 lies **s.** in his relationship with his Creator.
- T-20.......VI.4:5 wants them **s.** for the offerings on which
- T-27.......VI.6:3 is bound by laws that it came **s.** to undo!
- W-pI.....70.1:5 all guilt is **s.** an invention of your mind,
- M-in..........4:4 teaches **s.** to convince himself that he is
- M-1...........1:2 one. His qualifications consist **s.** in this;

## solemn 2

- T19..IV.B.16:3 in **s.** celebration of the ego's rule. Not one
- T19...IV.D.3:2 and to its sovereignty is but the **s.** vow,

## solid 26

- T-1.......VII.5:1 **s.** foundation is necessary because of the
- T-18.......V.2:7 will build a ladder planted in the **s.** rock
- T-18.......IX.6:1 that seem to be a **s.** wall before the sun.
- T-18.......IX.7:2 A **s.** mountain range, a lake, a city, all rise
- T19....IV.B.4:3 obstacle is no more **s.** than the first. For
- T-22......III.3:4 The body's eyes behold it as **s.** granite, so
- T-22......III.5:8 stops at nothingness, as if it were a **s.** wall,
- T-22......IV.3:4 your brother alone will see it as a **s.** block,
- T-22......IV.7:7 is no **s.** wall. And only an illusion stands
- T-22.......V.5:3 eyes it looks like an enormous **s.** body,
- T-22.......V.6:5 to stand, heavy and **s.** and immovable,
- T-22....VI.10:7 God in place, immovable and **s.** as a rock.
- T-23.......II.13:4 you walk in sanity with feet on **s.** ground,
- T-23.......II.13:5 the ground beneath your feet seem **s.**.
- T-26.........I.2:3 so seeming **s.** that it looks as if what is
- T-28.....VII.5:8 to be quite **s.** and substantial in itself. Yet
- W-pI.....91.7:4 else, something more **s.** and more sure;
- WpIrIII.in12:3 great we will continue on more **s.** ground,
- W-pI...137.2:3 held in pieces by a **s.** wall of sickened flesh
- W-pI...137.6:3 be more **s.** and more stable than the mind
- W-pI...159.5:3 quite **s.** here are merely shadows there;
- W-pI...166.2:4 upon the world and judges it as certain, **s.**
- W-pI...170.9:3 obstacle with the appearance of a **s.** block,
- W-pII......3.3:4 illusions but a **s.** base where truth exists,
- W-pII..359.1:7 *base more s. than the shadow world we see.*
- M-4.....I.A.8:3 as merely shadows before become **s.** gains

## solidity 1

- T-22.......V.5:2 weight, **s.** and firmness of foundation. Yes

## solidness 1

- T-19.......II.6:4 The **s.** that this world's foundation seems

## solitary 5

- T-23......IV.7:5 has no purpose of itself, and must be **s.**.
- W-pI.....67.6:1 is not your tiny, **s.** voice that tells you this.
- W-pI.....99.8:2 rest. It does not think its **s.** thoughts, and
- W-pI...137.2:3 real, and keep the mind in **s.** prison, split
- W-pI.200.11:5 and **s.** dreams with single purpose and

## solitude 6

- T-20......IV.5:3 this earth in seeming **s.** is a savior given,
- T-26.........I.7:4 in a body, nor is sacrificed in **s.** to sin.
- T-26.......VI.2:1 Lead not your little life in **s.**, with one
- T-30.....VII.7:1 Do not interpret out of **s.**, for what you
- W-pI...123.5:2 And we give thanks that in our **s.** a Friend
- W-pI.166.12:5 saved you from the **s.** you sought to make

## solution 32

- T-1......VI.5:10 Only God can establish this **s.**, and this
- T-4...........I.8:4 only sane **s.** is not to try to change reality,
- T-4.........V.4:9 there is none, but it does have a typical **s.**.
- T-4.........V.6:6 be incapable of **s.** are favorite ego devices
- T-5.........V.5:5 better to say that it is a form of magical **s.**.
- T-5.........V.7:9 except by accepting the **s.** of undoing.
- T-6.........IV.9:2 the kindest **s.** possible for what you made.
- T-6......V.A.1:7 any other impossible **s.** the ego attempts,
- T-8.........V.1:2 Dissociation is not a **s.**; it is a delusion.
- T-9.........V.3:4 condemnation and advocate a fearful **s.**.
- T-9...VIII.2:10 it offers you the illusion of attack as a "**s.**."
- T-13.......II.2:1 how strange a **s.** the ego's arrangement is.
- T-17......III.6:2 it seeks to guarantee there will be no **s.**.
- T-17.......V.4:6 Until this happy **s.** is seen and accepted as
- T-17.....VII.2:2 the problem but will make **s.** impossible.
- T-17.....VII.2:3 and the **s.** to the problem is inherent in its
- T-17.....VII.2:4 you have removed yourself from the **s.**?
- T-27......IV.2:2 in your state of mind, **s.** is impossible.
- T-27......IV.3:3 Outside there will be no **s.**, for there is no
- W-pI.....47.1:5 gives you the recognition of the right **s.**,
- W-pI.....79.1:5 Yet the **s.** is not recognized because the
- W-pI.....79.2:2 must be recognized as one if the one **s.**
- W-pI.....79.7:7 Then we will ask for the **s.** to it. And we
- W-pI.....80.1:5 one **s.**. Salvation is accomplished.
- W-pI.....80.3:5 One problem, one **s.**. Accept the peace
- W-pI.....80.4:4 The **s.** is inherent in the problem. You are
- W-pI.....80.5:5 problem, and that the problem has one **s.**.
- W-pI.....90.1:3 Let me also understand that the **s.** is
- W-pI.....90.1:4 that there is one problem and one **s.**. The
- W-pI.....90.1:5 problem is a grievance; the **s.** is a miracle.
- W-pI.....90.1:6 And I invite the **s.** to come to me through
- W-pI.....90.4:4 *cannot separate this problem from its s.*.

## solutions 3

- T-2........III.4:2 All **s.** the physical eye seeks dissolve.
- T-17......VI.7:6 For fantasy **s.** bring but the illusion of
- W-pI.....96.1:3 You have sought many such **s.**, and none

## solve 27

- T-13........X.4:5 your brothers as a means to "**s.**" the past,
- T-14......XI.9:2 He cannot **s.** by offering you a miracle.
- T-16........II.9:2 tried to **s.** anything yourself and been
- T-16......IV.7:5 you can do to **s.** the dilemma which seems
- T-17.........I.6:5 to **s.** his problems through fantasy, you
- T-17.....VII.2:1 in any situation that faith will not **s.**.
- T-17.....VII.3:5 for bodies cannot **s.** anything. It is their
- T-20....VIII.5:7 no perplexity that vision will not **s.**. All is
- T-25......IX.7:5 to **s.** for you means that you *want* it solved.
- T-25......IX.7:6 keep it for yourself to **s.** without His help
- T-26........II.1:1 the Holy Spirit to **s.** all problems for you.
- T-26........II.1:6 to attempt to **s.** it in a special form. It will
- T-26........II.5:7 time you keep a problem for yourself to **s.**
- T-26........II.6:1 be no problems that justice cannot **s.**. But
- T-27......IV.2:8 It must be pointless to attempt to **s.** a
- T-27......IV.3:1 Attempt to **s.** no problems but within the
- T-27......IV.7:1 attempt to **s.** no problems in a world
- T-27......IV.7:3 are the answers that will **s.** your problems
- T-27.....VII.2:3 way to **s.** a problem that is very simple,
- W-pI.....38.2:4 end all sorrow, and can **s.** all problems. It
- W-pI.....79.5:1 No one could **s.** all the problems the
- W-pI.....79.6:3 that you have the means to **s.** them all.
- W-pI.....96.6:6 real, nor **s.** a problem that does not exist.
- W-pI...109.3:4 There is no problem that it cannot **s.**. And
- W-pI.135.12:1 the problem that the plan is made to **s.**. It
- W-pI...138.6:4 But when you **s.** this one, the others are
- W-ep.........1:7 He knows the way to **s.** all problems, and

## solved 28

- T-15...VII.12:4 always teach that loneliness is **s.** by guilt,
- T-16........II.9:1 to the Holy Spirit He has not **s.** for you,
- T-17.....VII.1:5 you not lacked faith that it could be **s.**, the
- T-17.....VII.2:4 that all your problems have been **s.**, but
- T-25......IX.5:2 **s.** because it has been met with justice.
- T-25......IX.5:3 it will recur, because it has not yet been **s.**.
- T-25......IX.7:5 to solve for you means that you *want* it **s.**.
- T-26........II.1:3 each one is **s.** in just the same respect and
- T-27.......V.9:2 be **s.** as any one of them has been escaped
- T-27.....V.10:6 rest. Yet they are **s.** together. And their
- W-pI........79.h me recognize the problem so it can be **s.**.
- W-pI.....79.1:1 cannot be **s.** if you do not know what it is.
- W-pI.....79.1:2 it is really **s.** already you will still have the
- W-pI.....79.1:2 you will not recognize that it has been **s.**.
- W-pI.....79.1:4 the only problem, has already been **s.**. Yet
- W-pI.....79.2:3 Who can see that a problem has been **s.** if
- W-pI...79.10:3 *Let me recognize this problem so it can be s.*.
- W-pI........80.h me recognize my problems have been **s.**.
- W-pI.....80.1:4 and understanding that it has been **s.**.
- W-pI.....80.2:1 Your only problem has been **s.**! Repeat
- W-pI.....80.5:3 that your problems have been **s.**.
- W-pI.....80.6:1 today that your problems have been **s.**.
- W-pI.....80.6:5 *Let me recognize this problem has been s.*.
- W-pI.....80.7:4 is, and you must recognize it has been **s.**.

W-pI.....90.1:1 me recognize the problem so it can be s..
W-pI.....90.3:1 me recognize my problems have been s..
W-pI.....90.3:7 a problem which has not been s. already.
M-7...........6:6 If you really want the problem s., you

## solves 3

T-25......IX.3:1 s. will always be one in which no one loses
T-25......IX.4:4 The world s. problems in another way. It
W-pI.....79.2:2 solution that s. them all is to be accepted.

## solving 5

*See also* problem-solving
T-17......VI.6:9 in "s." conflict through fragmentation,
T-25......IX.4:7 Problem s. cannot be vengeance, which at
T-25......IX.5:1 Spirit's problem s. is the way in which the
T-26.......II.1:4 The aspects that need s. do not change,
W-pI.....79.4:3 your problem s. must be inadequate, and

## some 243

## somebody 1

T-26.........I.1:3 of the central theme that *s. must lose.* Its

## someday 4

T-3........VI.5:9 that it will s. be used against you. This
W-pI.124.11:3 And yet you can be sure s., perhaps today
M-3...........4:6 Yet all who meet will s. meet again, for it
P-3.........II.6:3 of forgiveness in which both will s. wake.

## somehow 11

T-1........VI.1:5 a state s. different from the one you are in
T-2........VI.7:2 that you must s. have chosen not to love,
T-4.........II.6:4 that you are s. getting something better,
T-17......IV.6:3 still seems to you s. to be "different." Yet
T-19.......II.7:5 he has s. managed to corrupt his Father,
T-21.........I.8:1 past everything you see and yet s. familiar
T-25......VI.2:4 S. the vague and more obscure seems
T-31.........I.2:6 For s. you believe that what is totally
T-31.....V.13:5 s. entered in the choice by your decision.
W-pI...163.7:2 that God was once alive and s. perished;
M-1...........1:2 His qualifications consist solely in this; s.,

## Someone 1

*someone*
M-10.........4:7 is S. with you Whose judgment is perfect.

## someone 81

*Someone*
T-2...........I.4:6 on while s. is dreaming a fearful dream,
T-2.........V.3:5 to re-establish right-mindedness in s. else.
T-3.........II.3:1 you lack confidence in what s. will do, you
T-3........III.5:3 love s. you have perceived him as he is,
T-3........VI.5:2 When you laugh at s., it is because you
T-4........VI.5:1 you teach s. the value of something he has
T-7.........V.4:4 offer as a gift to s. who does not have it.
T-7.........V.9:8 that every time it deprives s. of something
T-8........III.6:7 once believed that, when you met s. else,
T-8........III.6:7 someone else, you thought he *was* s. else.
T-9.........I.11:2 What would you say of s. who persists in
T-9.........V.7:2 help s. to point out where he is heading,
T-11.......in.2:1 say to s. who believed this question really
T-11..VIII.13:2 ask s. they trust for the meaning of what
T-12.........I.1:7 decide that s. is really trying to attack you
T-13......IV.5:5 to your brother as though he were s. else,
T-15.........I.5:2 life of s. who thinks its is the only voice, it
T-15......VI.3:4 loses. S. must always lose if you perceive
T-15...VII.10:3 than an attempt to make s. feel guilty, and
T-15.....X.5:12 s. must pay and someone must get. And
T-15.....X.5:12 someone must pay and s. must get. And
T-16.....VII.1:5 cling, and for which must s. else atone.
T19..IV.B.15:1 and guilt will s. other than yourself suffer.
T19..IV.B.15:2 if you suffer, yet s. else will suffer more.
T-24........I.3:4 For who could hate s. whose Self is his,
T-24........I.4:2 and this must come from s. "better,"
T-24........I.4:2 "better," s. incapable of being like what
T-25..VII.11:1 The whole belief that s. loses but reflects
T-25..VII.11:5 For every little gain must s. lose, and pay
T-25...VIII.3:2 punishment, perhaps sustained by s. else,
T-25...VIII.4:8 you, with s. else by far the greater part.
T-25.....IX.6:4 unless s. deserves to suffer more and
T-26.......II.2:2 is a demand that s. suffer loss and make a
T-26.......X.3:3 idea you are deprived by s. not yourself.
T-26.......X.4:2 alone, and at the cost of s. else's guilt. Can
T-26.......X.4:3 by the giving of your guilt to s. else? And
T-26.......X.4:8 S. must lose his innocence that someone
T-26.......X.4:8 innocence that s. else can take it from him
T-27.....II.11:3 punish sins you think are yours in s. else.
T-27....V.1:11 He does not speak to s. else. Yet by your
T-27....VII.8:2 He becomes a part of s. else's dream. He
T-28.......II.4:1 yourself, and but a part of s. else's dream.
T-28.....IV.7:3 is sick if s. else accepts his union with him
T-28.....IV.7:5 are gone if s. wills to be united with him.
T-29.....III.2:7 He must see s. else as not a body, one with
T-29.....IV.3:2 It can be in you or s. else, but where it is
T-29.....IV.4:1 is it not because s. has failed to fill the
T-29.....IX.8:3 the dream is being dreamed by s. else.
T-31........I.3:6 not belong to you, and even you are s. else
T-31....V.12:7 and s. must have first decided on the one
T-31....VII.4:4 as a gift for s. not perceived to be yourself,
W-pI.....25.4:4 for the purpose of talking to s. who is not
W-pI.....37.2:2 demand payment of s. or something. As a
W-pI.....38.3:4 happen to think of, in yourself or in s. else
W-pI.....38.4:2 for you, and one that is difficult for s. else.
W-pI.....38.6:1 problem concerning you or s. else arises,
W-pI.....43.7:2 When you are with s. else, for example,
W-pI.....71.2:2 that, if s. else spoke or acted differently, if
W-pI.....78.4:5 him. S., perhaps, you fear and even hate;
W-pI.....78.4:5 s. you think you love who angered you;
W-pI.....78.4:5 love who angered you; s. you call a friend,
W-pI...93.11:2 you be tempted to become angry with s.,
W-pI...95.14:8 time you do so, s. hears the voice of hope,
W-pI.....97.5:3 each time s. accepts them as his thoughts,
W-pI. 121.10:1 periods by thinking of s. you do not like,
W-pI...126.4:4 S. apart from you committed it. And if
W-pI...126.6:4 what you see in s. other than yourself. It
W-pI...133.7:1 choose to take a thing away from s. else,
W-pI...134.9:2 are tempted to accuse s. of sin in any form
W-pI...193.7:1 or s. else is failing to perceive the lesson
W-pII. 315.1:4 S. speaks a word of gratitude or mercy,
M-in..........2:6 You cannot give to s. else, but only to
M-1...........1:2 not see his interests as apart from s. else's.
M-1...........3:9 He has seen s. else as himself. He has
P-2..........II.8:4 Each one must share one goal with s. else,
P-3...........I.3:8 a feeling of reaching out to s. somewhere.
S-2...........I.4:6 Only in s. else can you forgive yourself, for
S-2........III.2:5 When s. calls for help in any form, He is
S-3........III.2:4 S. knows better, has been better trained,
S-3........III.3:1 S. knows better; this the magic phrase by
S-3........III.4:1 that one can use to offer help for s. else?

## someone's 1

T-28.....IV.1:1 to s. dream of sickness and of death. It

## Something 2

*something*
T-16.......II.2:8 must be S. in you that *does* understand.
P-3...........I.2:3 There is S. in him that will tell you, if you

## something 221

*Something*
T-1..........I.6:2 they do not occur s. has gone wrong.
T-2.......IV.4:6 s. from the outside is temporarily given
T-2.......VI.1:1 involuntary; s. beyond your own control.
T-2.......VI.5:3 mind that wants to do s. else is outraged.
T-2.......VI.8:4 You have done s. loveless, having chosen
T-3.......IV.6:1 you must perceive *s.* and *with* something.
T-3.......IV.6:1 you must perceive *something* and *with* s..
T-3.........V.2:2 When you make s., you do so out of a
T-3.........V.2:4 When you make s. to fill a perceived lack,
T-3.........V.4:7 Images are symbolic and stand for s. else.
T-3.........V.6:1 Prayer is a way of asking for s.. It is the
T-3.......VI.9:3 to lose s. does not mean that it has gone.
T-4.........II.3:5 though hardly to s. that occurs with such
T-4.........II.4:3 dismisses s. he considers part of himself.
T-4.........II.6:4 that you are somehow getting s. better,
T-4.........II.8:8 as being rejected by s. greater than itself.
T-4.......III.1:2 which interprets it as if s. outside is inside
T-4.......IV.3:2 deprived of s. you want and do not have.
T-4.........V.5:2 and desperately for s. you would not
T-4.......VI.2:1 your brother is s. you must never forget.
T-4.......VI.5:1 of s. he has deliberately thrown away? He
T-5..........I.4:3 He is also described as s. "separate,"
T-6.........II.3:8 process begins by excluding s. that exists
T-6.......III.2:3 you are s. you must learn to remember. I
T-6.......IV.4:5 Perceiving s. alien to itself in your mind,
T-6.....V.C.3:2 there is s. you must be vigilant *against.* It
T-7..........I.6:6 therefore tell you s. about this last step.
T-7.....III.2:10 You must, therefore, be teaching s. else,
T-7.......IV.2:9 a perception of conflict with s. else, as all
T-7.........V.4:4 him. Magic always sees s. "special" in the
T-7.........V.4:5 God if he thinks he has s. that others lack.
T-7.........V.7:2 is because he thinks he is giving s. to them
T-7.........V.7:2 receiving s. equally desirable in return.
T-7.........V.9:8 that every time it deprives someone of s.,
T-7.......VI.1:2 to see s. in part of it that you will not
T-7.......VI.7:2 because you may still think there is s. else.
T-7.......VI.7:7 When you believe s., you have made it
T-7.....VI.12:2 want s. else you will make something else,
T-7.....VI.12:2 want something else you will make s. else,
T-7.....VI.12:2 something else, but because it is s. else, it
T-7......VII.8:1 a means of depriving you of s. you want.
T-7.....VIII.1:5 means of getting rid of s. it does not want.
T-7.....VIII.3:6 rid of s. you do not want by giving it away
T-8.........V.1:4 Judging truth as s. they do not want, they
T-8.........V.1:6 but together our minds fuse into s. whose
T-8.......VII.1:4 belief that attack can get you s. you want.
T-8.....VIII.2:7 continue to hope it can yet offer you s..
T-8.....VIII.8:1 of s. that does not exist can be so insistent
T-8.....VIII.8:2 about the distorting power of s. you want,
T-9..........I.3:3 you are arbitrarily associating s. beyond
T-9..........I.3:3 your awareness with s. you do not want.
T-9..........I.3:4 you are judging s. of which you are totally
T-9..........I.8:7 He cannot give you s. you do not want.
T-9.........II.1:1 to use prayer to ask for s. has experienced
T-9.......IV.6:2 when they do not occur s. has gone wrong
T-9.........V.5:5 His ego will always seek to get s. from the
T-9.......VI.1:4 be s. in you that is capable of producing it
T-9.....VIII.7:3 have replaced it with s. you have made.
T-10.......II.1:1 you first know s. you cannot dissociate it.
T-10.......II.4:3 you have accepted s. else in its place. If
T-10.......II.6:2 you still believe it can get you s. you want.
T-10.......II.6:3 that you want s. other than peace of mind
T-11.......V.3:3 "Dynamics" implies the power to do s.,
T-11....VII.3:4 it always adds s. that is not real to the real
T-12........I.3:9 is s. else you will react to something else.
T-12........I.3:9 is something else you will react to s. else.
T-12.....III.2:1 you do s. you think you do not want to do
T-12.....III.4:1 your brothers ask you for s. "outrageous,"
T-12.....V.7:11 even yet, that there is s. you want to learn,
T-12.....VI.1:7 you perceive s. else as more valuable.
T-12....VII.9:5 the power to give s. else within yourself. It
T-12..VII.10:4 it is because you saw s. that is not there.
T-12..VIII.3:3 to you because you are looking at s. else.
T-13.......II.5:4 who you are, and identifying with s. else.
T-13.....III.1:9 find within yourself s. you fear even more.
T-14....VII.3:6 merely a belief in s. that does not exist. It
T-14.......X.3:4 as s. that must come from elsewhere, not
T-14.......X.8:4 you understand s. of the "dynamics" of
T-15.....VI.7:8 Yet as long as you prefer to be s. else, or
T-15.....VI.7:8 to be nothing else and s. else together,
T-15....VII.2:1 ego establishes relationships only to get s.
T-15....VII.7:2 that he has sacrificed s. to the other, and
T-16.....IV.2:2 For symbols stand for s. else, and the
T-16....VII.1:5 of s. "evil" in the past to which you cling,
T-17....VII.2:5 Yet faith must be where s. has been done,
T-17....VII.5:2 See it as s. else and you are faithless. Use

T-17... VIII.4:3 was there, but you attributed it to s. else,
T-17... VIII.4:3 believing that the "s. else" produced it.
T-17... VIII.4:5 the "s. else" produced was sorrow and
T-18...... I.10:4 would never accept s. else instead of you.
T-18...... VI.2:3 belief that you could give and get s. else,
T-18...... VI.2:3 get something else, s. outside yourself,
T-18.... VI.11:4 a joining of yourself and s. else in which
T-18.. VI.11:11 have let yourself be one with s. beyond it,
T-18.... VI.12:2 is not relevant; it can occur with s. past,
T-18.... VI.12:3 The "s." can be anything and anywhere; a
T-18.... VIII.1:6 identify with externals, s. outside itself.
T-18.... IX.10:5 transports you to s. completely different.
T19. IV.C.11:2 must stand for s. other than themselves.
T-20... VIII.1:2 lost to you through your desire for s. else.
T-20... VIII.1:3 that you closed off by valuing the "s. else,
T-20. VIII.11:4 think that there is s. else for you to see.
T-21....... II.7:3 be, you have set up your idols to s. else.
T-21...... IV.5:4 purpose, and so there must be s. else.
T-21..... V.10:3 have come from s. that you do not know,
T-21..... VII.4:6 murderous attack by turning into s. else.
T-21... VIII.3:4 to ask for his desire of s. he believes holds
T-22.........I.3:5 are, and firm in faith that you are s. else,
T-22.........I.3:5 this "s. else" that you have made to be
T-22.........I.3:6 Yet it must be the "s. else" that sees, and
T-22.........I.7:4 by the "s. else" you thought was you. He
T-22.........I.8:5 come to anyone but you, never to "s. else.
T-22...... I.10:4 recognition that the "s. else" you thought
T-23...... IV.8:7 the battleground can offer s. you can win.
T-23...... IV.9:3 of the body; s. it seems to offer or to own.
T-24....... V.1:7 that you can wish for s. and lack faith that
T-25....... V.2:5 s. alien to yourself and "something else,"
T-25....... V.2:5 something alien to yourself and "s. else,"
T-25....... V.2:5 else," a "s." to be feared instead of loved.
T-25... VII.3:10 it differently, nor twist it into s. it is not.
T-25..... VII.5:1 foundation of the world you see to s. else;
T-25... VIII.8:3 is split off from love, and stands for s. else
T-26.........I.3:4 limited, and s. still remains for you alone.
T-27.........I.9:3 changes not the body into s. it is not. It
T-27...... III.1:6 on it without changing it into s. it is not.
T-27...... III.1:8 by this does it join to the idea a s. it is not,
T-27...... III.2:8 of reality is the belief that there is s. there.
T-27...... IV.5:6 tool that asks for s. that you do not know.
T-27.... IV.6:10 It offers s. new and different from the
T-27..... VII.1:3 attacked unjustly and by s. not himself.
T-27..... VII.1:4 He is the victim of this "s. else," a thing
T-27..... VII.7:8 cause they have is s. quite apart from him,
T-28.........I.2:8 purpose, and to be the means for s. else.
T-28.........I.3:2 needs which mean that s. must be done.
T-28....... V.3:6 and where you seem to be a s. you are not
T-28..... VII.1:4 there that he could want for s. he has not.
T-29...... II.9:3 As s., it can be perceived and thought to
T-29..... II.10:1 "s." is the body asked to be God's enemy,
T-29...... IV.2:6 change, but they cannot be made of s. else
T-29...... IV.5:4 has changed because they cover s. else.
T-29..... VII.2:1 or some dream that there is s. outside of
T-29..... VII.2:3 and seeks for s. more than everything, as
T-29..... VII.2:5 about, in search of s. that he cannot find,
T-29... VIII.4:2 of grass from s. living to a sign of death.
T-29... VIII.8:9 But more of s. is an idol for. And when
T-29. VIII.8:10 place, with hope of finding more of s. else
T-29. VIII.8:11 Be not deceived by forms the "s." takes.
T-29...... IX.7:4 no one is used to substitute for s. else, nor
T-29...... IX.7:5 No one is used for s. he is not, for childish
T-30.........I.6:1 that s. has occurred that is not part of it.
T-30.........I.9:3 but is s. that you want and that you need,
T-30..... VII.1:7 and all that happens now means s. else.
T-31....... V.8:4 lessons aimed to teach that you are s. else.
T-31..... V.10:8 And from whom must s. be kept hidden?
T-31..... V.13:2 S. must have gone before these concepts
T-31..... V.13:3 And s. must have done the learning which
W-pI..........6.h am upset because I see s. that is not there.
W-pI.......6.1:4 *am angry at_because I see s. that is not there.*
W-pI.......6.1:5 *am worried about_because I see s. that is not*
W-pI.......7.1:8 upset because you see s. that is not there.
W-pI..... 13.1:4 think you perceive s. that has no meaning
W-pI..... 27.1:1 Today's idea expresses s. stronger than
W-pI..... 28.5:2 It has s. to show you; something beautiful
W-pI..... 28.5:2 s. beautiful and clean and of infinite value
W-pI..... 35.8:2 today's idea slowly until s. occurs to you.
W-pI..... 37.2:2 demand payment of someone or s.. As a
W-pI..... 44.8:1 that you are attempting s. very holy.
W-pI..... 66.6:2 is necessary to define God as s. He is not.
W-pI..... 72.3:3 not always associated with s. a body does
W-pI..... 72.3:4 A person says s. you do not like. He does
W-pI..... 72.3:5 like. He does s. that displeases you. He
W-pI..... 76.9:5 and nothing is replaced by s. else. God's
W-pI..... 79.2:3 solved if he thinks the problem is s. else?
W-pI..... 91.7:3 You need to feel s. to put your faith in, as
W-pI..... 91.7:4 You need a real experience of s. else,
W-pI..... 91.7:4 else, s. more solid and more sure; more
W-pI..... 97.8:4 you yield to the belief that you are s. else.
W-pI..... 98.1:6 We will not argue it is s. else. We will not
W-pI..... 99.1:2 They both imply that s. has gone wrong;
W-pI..... 99.1:2 has gone wrong; s. to be saved from,
W-pI..... 99.1:2 for; s. amiss that needs corrective change;
W-pI..... 99.1:2 s. apart or different from the Will of God.
W-pI... 102.1:2 You may think it buys you s., and may
W-pI... 107.4:1 a while, to disappear or change to s. else.
W-pI... 129.1:2 unless you see that there is s. else to hope
W-pI. 132.12:4 the Son begin as s. separate from Him.
W-pI... 134.1:1 to be perceived as s. that entails an unfair
W-pI... 135.4:2 be s. that is very weak and easily assaulted
W-pI... 135.4:3 It must be s. made easy prey, unable to
W-pI... 135.6:5 defense of s. that he recognized as this?
W-pI... 136.8:4 that you might be s. beyond this little pile
W-pI... 139.4:1 is not himself, and therefore, being s. else,
W-pI... 139.4:1 becomes a questioner of what that s. is.
WpI. rIV.in3:3 Their purpose is to show you s. else, and
W-pI... 155.4:1 as if it asked the sacrifice of s. that is real.
W-pI... 155.9:4 may see s. with which they can identify;
W-pI... 155.9:4 s. they understand to lead the way.
W-pI... 169.5:5 to feel that it is now aware of s. not itself.
W-pI... 170.1:5 the state in which you are for s. better,
W-pI... 184.2:2 You see s. where nothing is, and see as
W-pI... 187.5:8 What he seems to lose is always s. he will
W-pII.. 231.1:2 *Perhaps I think I seek for s. else; a something*
W-pII.. 231.1:2 *else; a s. I have called by many names. Yet is*
M-in .......... 1:3 the teacher giving s. to the learner rather
M-3 ........... 3:4 levels of teaching seems to be s. different.
M-4 ..... I.A.5:8 where he thought s. was asked of him, he
M-4 ..... I.A.8:9 change tranquility for s. more desirable?
M-5 .........I.1:2 unless he thought it brought him s., and
M-5 .........I.1:2 him something, and s. of value to him?
M-5 .........I.1:3 a small price to pay for s. of greater worth
M-8 ........... 2:3 illusion is an attempt to make s. real that
C-2............. 2:2 but in a form that seems like s.. In a world
P-2......... in.1:5 that anger brings him s. he really wants,
P-2........ VI.4:5 the form it takes seems to be s. else. And
P-2........ VI.4:6 now it is the "s. else" that seems to terrify.
P-2........ VI.4:7 it is not the "s. else" that can be healed. It
P-3......... II.3:4 Yet s. happened to him, however slight it
P-3......... II.3:5 That "s." is enough. Sooner or later that
P-3......... II.3:6 Sooner or later that s. will rise and grow;
P-3......... II.5:1 S. good must come from every meeting
P-3........ III.4:1 right to live is s. no one need fight for. It is

### sometime 3

W-pI... 101.2:5 them out and find them somewhere, s., in
W-pI... 124.8:3 S. today, whenever it seems best, devote a
W-pI... 124.9:3 Yet s., somewhere, it will come to you,

### sometimes 46

T-1......... II.1:2 sense of creation s. sought in physical
T-2........ IV.4:5 S. the illness has a sufficiently strong hold
T-3.... VI.10:4 and s. by way of very devious routes, from
T-7......... V.5:4 that he can s. heal and sometimes not, the
T-7......... V.5:4 that he can sometimes heal and s. not, the
T-7....... VII.1:4 You cannot be totally committed s..
T-13....... II.7:3 s. react as if it is trying to imprison you.
T-18...... III.2:1 s. retreating to the lesser forms of fear,
T-18...... III.2:1 lesser forms of fear, and s. to stark terror.
T-18.... VI.11:2 s. hoped for in special relationships. It is a
T-19...... III.3:3 S. a sin can be repeated over and over,
T-21...... III.1:4 s. demanding payment of yourself,
T-26..... V.11:5 S. the past seems real, as if it *were* the
T-27... VIII.2:6 S. it dreams it is a conqueror of bodies
T-29.........I.1:5 of hate, His gentleness turn s. to attack,
T-29.........I.1:5 to attack, and His eternal patience s. fail.
T-29.........I.3:5 S. a friend, perhaps, provided that your
T-29.........I.7:3 love must be feared; and only s. present,
T-29.........I.7:3 and only sometimes present, s. gone.
T-30...... III.7:2 means is that you are s. aware of them,
T-30...... III.7:2 are sometimes aware of them, and s. not.
T-30...... VI.3:7 give. It pardons "sinners" s., but remains
T-31....... V.2:8 pity, on the suffering, and s. offers solace.
T-31..... VII.2:2 You will perceive them s., but will not see
W-pI..... 65.8:4 S. close your eyes as you practice this, and
W-pI..... 65.8:4 s. keep them open and look about you. It
W-pI..... 97.3:2 s. a thousand years or more are saved.
W-pI... 126.5:2 in which you s. choose to give indulgently
W-pI... 133.1:1 S. in teaching there is benefit,
W-pI. 153.16:3 S. we will forget. At other times the
W-pI... 182.1:6 feeling, s. not more than a tiny throb, at
W-pI... 185.4:2 S. it takes the form of union, but only the
W-pII ..... 5.3:2 dreams it s. seems to picture happiness,
M-4 ..... I.A.3:6 And so the plan will s. call for changes in
M-15 ......... 3:1 You who are s. sad and sometimes angry;
M-15 ......... 3:1 You who are sometimes sad and s. angry;
M-15 ......... 3:1 who s. feel your just due is not given you,
M-21 ......... 1:5 praying. S. the words and the prayer are
M-21 ......... 1:5 the prayer are contradictory; s. they agree
M-26 ......... 3:1 S. a teacher of God may have a brief
P-in............ 1:6 S. he is able to start to open his mind
P-in............ 1:7 S. he needs a more structured, extended
P-1............. 3:4 s. even willing to "sacrifice" his "life" on
P-2........ IV.3:2 waves, s. together and sometimes in grim
P-2........ IV.3:2 together and s. in grim succession. Yet all
P-2........ VI.3:5 S. the thought behind the form breaks

### somewhat 7

W-pI....... 4.3:1 repeated from time to time in s. different
W-pI..... 11.2:1 s. differently from the previous ones.
W-pI..... 13.4:1 a s. different way from the preceding ones
W-pI..... 35.3:3 will use a s. different kind of application
W-pI... 72.13:1 since they will be s. longer than usual.
M-4 ..... I.A.4:2 This is always s. difficult because, having
P-2...........I.4:3 The therapist is only a s. more specialized

### somewhere 14

T-21...... VI.3:7 You do not leave insanity by going s. else.
W-pI..... 48.3:2 nothing to fear shows that s. in your mind
W-pI..... 67.3:3 s. in your mind It is there for you to find.
W-pI... 101.2:5 and it will seek them out and find them s.,
W-pI. 121.11:2 Try to perceive some light in him s.; a
W-pI. 121.11:4 this picture till you see a light s. within it,
W-pI... 124.9:3 Yet sometime, s., it will come to you, nor
W-pI... 182.1:2 s. in your mind you know that this is true.
W-pI... 182.1:4 feel an alien here, from s. all unknown.
W-pII . 333.1:2 set aside, denied, disguised, seen s. else,
M-1 ........... 1:2 s. he has made a deliberate choice in
M-19 ......... 2:8 with it. But s. one must start. Justice is the
P-2......... V.7:1 S. all gifts of God must be received. In
P-3...........I.3:8 a feeling of reaching out to someone s..

### Son 1320

*son*

T-1..........II.4:5 one hand, and as a S. of God on the other.
T-1......... V.2:4 in which the S. and the Father are One.
T-1......... V.3:4 know the real power of the S. in his true
T-2...........I.1:1 aspect of God which He gave to His S.. In
T-2...........I.2:6 This is as true of the S. as of the Father. In
T-2...........I.2:7 both the creation of the S. by God, and
T-2...........I.2:8 God's endowment of the S. with free will,
T-2.........II.7:8 yourself as both a brother and a S..
T-2..... VII.3:11 to God, and His "Effect" is His S.. This
T-2..... VII.5:14 world that he gave his only begotten S.,
T-2..... VII.5:14 context; "He gave it *to* His only begotten S.
T-2....... VII.6:1 be noted that God has only *one* S.. If all
T-3...........I.1:9 have clearly stated is unworthy of His S.?
T-3...........I.2:4 His Own S. on behalf of salvation. The
T-3...........I.8:1 God is the true state of the mind of His S..
T-3...........I.8:3 Knowing His S. as he is, you realize that

T-3 II.5:1 Nothing can prevail against a S. of God
T-3 II.5:4 The S. of God is part of the Holy Trinity,
T-3 VII.6:7 is to believe that God and His S. can *not.*
T-4 I.8:6 His beloved S. in whom He is well pleased
T-4 IV.8:2 is no limit to the power of a S. of God, but
T-4 IV.10:1 for the creation, for Christ is the S. of God
T-5 I.4:3 apart from the Father and from the S.. I
T-5 II.1:7 this union of Will between Father and S..
T-5 IV.4:3 Wholeness is the Wholeness of His S..
T-5 IV.5:5 because my name is the Name of God's S..
T-6 I.6:3 lesson a S. of God should want to teach if
T-6 I.12:1 of every S. of God is necessary to enable
T-6 I.15:8 Judas was my brother and a S. of God, as
T-6 I.16:7 between the ego and the S. of God. This
T-7 V.7:5 so vital in its power for change that a S. of
T-7 VII.7:3 the inestimable worth of every S. of God,
T-7 IX.5:3 The creations of every S. of God are yours,
T-7 X.7:4 is no confusion in the mind of a S. of God,
T-7 X.7:4 Father, because the Father's Will *is* His S..
T-7 XI.2:1 is the natural state of every S. of God.
T-7 XI.2:6 A S. of God is happy only when he knows
T-7 XI.4:3 Every S. who returns to the Kingdom with
T-8 II.2:3 teacher to whom a S. of God should turn
T-8 II.4:3 any imprisoning of the will of a S. of God,
T-8 II.4:3 that the Will of the S. is the Father's. The
T-8 II.8:6 natural response of every S. of God to the
T-8 III.3:1 Will of the Father and of the S. are One,
T-8 III.3:4 The Father must give fatherhood to His S.
T-8 IV.8:6 is with the Father *and* with the S..
T-8 V.3:7 witness to the Will of the Father for His S.
T-8 VI.5:1 God wants only His S. because His Son is
T-8 VI.5:1 Son because His S. is His only treasure.
T-8 VI.7:6 can even imprison the mind of God's S., if
T-8 VI.8:5 whole power of God's S. lies in all of us,
T-8 VI.8:7 That is why He created His S., and gave
T-8 VII.6:5 Let no S. of God remain hidden for His
T-8 IX.7:3 The Name of God's S. is One, and you are
T-9 I.10:8 And could He fail to recognize it in His S.?
T-9 II.4:1 are answered, never doubt a S. of God. Do
T-9 II.12:6 *myself, I see you as God's S. and my brother.*
T-9 III.2:9 He is still right, because he is a S. of God.
T-9 VI.3:5 God has but one S., knowing them all as
T-9 VI.4:7 know yourself only as God knows His S.,
T-9 VI.5:5 to its reality as the S. does to the Father.
T-10 III.2:5 for healing because He has but one S..
T-10 III.3:1 To believe that a S. of God can be sick is
T-10 III.3:4 of a S. of God even if he believes in it, for
T-10 III.4:1 To believe a S. of God is sick is to worship
T-10 III.4:7 what the ego does perceive in a S. of God;
T-10 III.6:2 Him. God's S. knows no idols, but he does
T-10 III.6:5 you, because the value of God's S. is one.
T-10 III.7:3 Yet every S. of God has the power to deny
T-10 III.10:1 If God has but one S., there is but one
T-10 IV.7:1 miracle is the act of a S. of God who has
T-10 V.4:1 the mind of God's S. against His Will. The
T-10 V.4:2 God" made His S. think he was Fatherless
T-10 V.4:4 Yet the S. *is* helpless without the Father,
T-10 V.5:5 have created a S. who was unlike Him. If
T-10 V.6:1 S. of God, you have not sinned, but you
T-10 V.7:4 Sonship, because of His Love for His S.. If
T-10 V.7:6 He created, for His S. is everywhere. Look
T-10 V.9:4 would He offer His S. anything that is not
T-10 V.10:2 would not know His S. if he were not free.
T-10 V.10:6 God will never cease to love His S., and
T-10 V.10:6 and His S. will never cease to love Him.
T-10 V.11:1 the Kingdom will be restored to His S..
T-10 V.11:2 His S. removed himself from His gift by
T-10 V.11:3 created as the dwelling place of God's S..
T-10 V.12:5 If God created His S. perfect, that is how
T-10 V.13:5 acknowledged if the real S. is to be known
T-11 in.2:3 out of the wish of God's S. to father Him.
T-11 I.1:4 restoring the holy dwelling place of His S.,
T-11 I.1:4 He wills His S. to be and where he is. In
T-11 I.1:5 mind of God's S. you restore this reality,
T-11 I.5:5 There is no end to God and His S., for we
T-11 I.5:7 to be alone, He created a S. like Himself.
T-11 I.5:8 Himself. Do not deny Him His S., for your
T-11 I.5:9 See His creations as His S., for yours were
T-11 I.8:3 God's Will is that you are His S.. By
T-11 I.9:9 Immortality is His Will for His S., and His
T-11 I.9:10 God's S. cannot will death for himself
T-11 I.9:10 his Father is life, and His S. is like Him.
T-11 I.11:8 so. God's Will is that His S. be One, and
T-11 II.1:3 The S. of God *has* both Father and Son,
T-11 II.1:3 The Son of God *has* both Father and S.,
T-11 II.1:3 and Son, because he *is* both Father and S..
T-11 II.2:5 mind, teaches you that you are God's S..
T-11 II.3:5 yourself, for only God's S. needs healing.
T-11 II.4:4 can the S. of God not accomplish with the
T-11 III.1:4 way, for that is not God's Will for His S..
T-11 III.1:8 Yet it always attacks the S. of God, and
T-11 III.1:8 the Son of God, and the S. of God is you.
T-11 III.2:1 God's S. is indeed in need of comfort, for
T-11 III.4:5 the dark journey is not the way of God's S.
T-11 III.4:6 are not fit companions for the S. of God,
T-11 III.5:1 God hides nothing from His S., even
T-11 III.5:1 even though His S. would hide himself.
T-11 III.5:2 Yet the S. of God cannot hide his glory,
T-11 III.6:2 never let them enter the mind of God's S.,
T-11 III.7:10 and no part of the S. can be excluded if he
T-11 III.8:3 God blessed His S. forever. If you will
T-11 IV.h The Inheritance of God's S.
T-11 IV.2:2 S. deny the Father without believing that
T-11 IV.3:7 the protection of the Wholeness of His S..
T-11 IV.5:6 *enter God's Presence if you attack His S..*
T-11 IV.5:7 S. lifts his voice in praise of his Creator, he
T-11 IV.5:8 Creator cannot be praised without His S.,
T-11 IV.6:1 at God's altar, waiting to welcome His S..
T-11 IV.6:7 and nothing is denied by God to His S..
T-11 IV.7:2 His S. as wholly blameless as Himself, and
T-11 IV.7:2 through the appreciation of His S.. Christ
T-11 IV.7:4 For Christ is the S. of God, Who lives in
T-11 IV.8:1 Blessed is the S. of God whose radiance is
T-11 IV.8:2 There is no condemnation in the S., for
T-11 IV.8:3 the S. must share what belongs to Him,
T-11 IV.8:3 he will not know the Father or the S..
T-11 V.12:7 Yet God's S. is not insane, and cannot
T-11 V.16:9 does not see Him, for it has denied His S..
T-11 V.17:2 Accept His S. and you will remember Him
T-11 V.17:3 can demonstrate that His S. is unworthy,
T-11 V.17:4 What you see of His S. through the eyes of
T-11 V.17:4 a demonstration that His S. does not exist
T-11 V.17:4 yet where the S. is the Father must be.
T-11 V.17:7 is the sign that they have beheld God's S.,
T-11 VI.3:9 little beliefs that are unworthy of God's S..
T-11 VI.3:10 the S. of God will see himself as Fatherless
T-11 VI.4:9 nature of God's S. as his Father created
T-11 VI.5:1 the power of the devotion of God's S., nor
T-11 VI.5:5 the S. of God is born of sacrifice and pain.
T-11 VI.6:4 by His grace, for God is gracious to His S.,
T-11 VI.7:1 the nails from the hands of God's S., and
T-11 VI.7:2 Love of God surrounds His S. whom the
T-11 VI.7:5 of God's S. is the work of the redemption,
T-11 VI.7:6 value. God does not judge His guiltless S..
T-11 VI.8:2 Yet you cannot crucify God's S., for the
T-11 VI.8:3 His S. has been redeemed from his own
T-11 VI.8:5 you perceive the S. of God as crucified,
T-11 VI.10:1 God's S. *is* saved. Bring only this
T-11 VII.2:1 that the S. of God ever had is eternal. The
T-11 VIII.7:6 Nothing of God will enslave His S. whom
T-11 VIII.8:6 Ask for truth of any S. of God, and you
T-11 VIII.9:1 of God's S. and his Father will answer you
T-11 VIII.9:4 Christ is the S. of God Who is in no way
T-11 VIII.9:5 Be not deceived in God's S., for thereby
T-11 VIII.11:5 Be not deceived in God's S., for he is one
T-11 VIII.12:3 God's S. whom God condemneth not. Let
T-11 VIII.12:4 of God's S. against himself and perceive
T-11 VIII.12:5 you, for He wills to heal the S. of God, in
T-12 II.2:3 only if the S. of God gives power to it. He
T-12 III.7:1 of God's S. are the world's reality, the real
T-12 III.8:1 that He gave it to His only begotten S..
T-12 III.10:8 where God and His S. dwell in peace and
T-12 IV.4:7 For He will never deceive God's S. whom
T-12 V.9:6 can oppose the decision of God's S.. His
T-12 VI.2:5 never ceases to remind Him of His S., and
T-12 VI.2:5 ceases to remind His S. of the Father. God
T-12 VI.4:5 of Christ for every S. of God who sleeps.
T-12 VI.4:6 In His sight the S. of God is perfect, and
T-12 VI.4:8 Him your Father calls His S. to remember.
T-12 VI.4:9 The awakening of His S. begins with his
T-12 VI.4:10 reality is one with the Father and the S.,
T-12 VI.7:2 the holy perception of God's S. becomes
T-12 VI.7:2 spirit of God's S. shines in the Mind of the
T-12 VI.7:3 the extension of Himself that is His S..
T-12 VIII.1:1 believe that you can kill the S. of God?
T-12 VIII.1:2 The Father has hidden His S. safely within
T-12 VIII.1:2 the Father nor the S. because of them.
T-12 VIII.2:1 God's S. is as safe as his Father, for the
T-12 VIII.2:1 for the S. knows his Father's protection
T-12 VIII.6:1 S. of God, be not content with nothing!
T-12 VIII.6:3 could not offer His S. what has no value,
T-12 VIII.6:3 has no value, nor could His S. receive it.
T-12 VIII.7:2 God's S. can be seen because his vision is
T-12 VIII.8:9 Your Father could not cease to love His S..
T-13 in.2:1 S. was the beginning of the separation, as
T-13 in.4:1 *is* a picture of the crucifixion of God's S..
T-13 in.4:2 realize that God's S. cannot be crucified,
T-13 in.4:3 the eternal fact that God's S. is not guilty.
T-13 I.1:2 for sharing the Father's Love for His S.,
T-13 I.1:5 the denial of the blamelessness of God's S.
T-13 I.2:1 you have made the S. of God *has* sinned.
T-13 I.2:5 has no life, and God's S. *is* without guilt.
T-13 I.3:6 long as you believe the S. of God is guilty
T-13 I.4:1 the S. of God has set himself is useless
T-13 I.4:2 not cruel, and His S. cannot hurt himself.
T-13 I.4:5 everything unworthy of the S. of God, for
T-13 I.5:1 me as you learn the S. of God is guiltless.
T-13 I.5:6 For the S. of God is guiltless now, and the
T-13 I.5:7 God's S. will always be as he was created.
T-13 I.6:1 will realize there is no guilt in God's S..
T-13 I.6:4 you cannot know that you are God's S..
T-13 I.7:2 The S. of God, who sleepeth not, has kept
T-13 I.7:4 For God waits not for His S. in time, being
T-13 I.7:6 Let the holiness of God's S. shine away
T-13 I.9:3 Accepting the guiltlessness of the S. of
T-13 I.9:3 God's way of reminding you of His S., and
T-13 I.9:4 For God has never condemned His S., and
T-13 I.11:5 As He looks upon the guiltless S. of God,
T-13 I.11:7 are saved because God's S. is guiltless.
T-13 II.h The Guiltless S. of God
T-13 II.2:5 the S. of God by seeing him as guilty.
T-13 II.3:2 God's S. by condemning him to death.
T-13 II.3:3 of God's S. can ultimately satisfy it. It
T-13 II.3:4 who the S. of God is because it is blind.
T-13 II.5:1 you believe you have crucified God's S..
T-13 II.6:2 of God's S. it did attempt to kill him, and
T-13 II.9:3 for you will remember His guiltless S.,
T-13 II.9:7 son of man is the guiltless S. of God, and
T-13 III.2:4 upon your savage wish to kill God's S., if
T-13 III.5:2 slave of the crucifixion than a S. of God in
T-13 III.6:6 for here is the real crucifixion of God's S..
T-13 III.8:6 For grandeur is the right of God's S., and
T-13 III.10:3 ask this of a Father Who truly loved His S.
T-13 III.10:5 And the peace of God's S. was shattered,
T-13 III.11:4 If the S. did not wish to remain in peace,
T-13 V.7:12 For every S. of God is given you to whom
T-13 V.10:5 He sees God's guiltless S. within you,
T-13 V.11:4 Because they saw the S., they have risen in
T-13 VI.3:6 that obscures God's S. to you *is* the past,
T-13 VI.8:4 God's guiltless S. is only light. There is no
T-13 VI.8:8 light that shines forth from God's S. is the
T-13 VI.9:4 For it can never be that His S. called upon
T-13 VI.11:7 remind you of your Father and His holy S.
T-13 VI.13:5 God's S. is still as loving as his Father.
T-13 VII.7:1 that nothing touch His S. except Himself,
T-13 VII.8:3 *now.* God loves His S. forever, and His Son
T-13 VII.8:3 His S. returns his Father's Love forever.
T-13 VII.8:6 yours, being the gift of God unto His S..
T-13 VII.10:1 for the perfect sanity of His most holy S..
T-13 VII.13:5 God's S. is not a traveller through outer
T-13 VII.17:4 from the mind of God's most holy S.,
T-13 VII.17:9 Thus does the S. of God give thanks unto
T-13 VIII.4:1 Apart from the Father and the S., the
T-13 VIII.5:2 Every miracle you offer to the S. of God is
T-13 VIII.6:5 that ever was is God's most holy S.,
T-13 VIII.7:2 the S. of God through the Holy Spirit,
T-13 VIII.8:2 the power of God's S. will move in us, and

T-13. VIII.10:4 your witness to His S. and to Himself. The
T-13. VIII.10:7 leave His Own beloved S. outside them,
T-13......IX.1:1 Father, for guilt is the attack upon His S..
T-13......IX.4:3 believe the S. of God is guiltless because
T-13......IX.5:3 idea that the guiltless S. of God can attack
T-13......IX.6:2 you offer the S. of God lies the conviction
T-13......IX.6:5 to condemn the S. of God in part. Those
T-13....... X.8:3 S. of God believes that he is lost in guilt,
T-13..... X.10:2 as God Himself has always loved His S..
T-13..... X.10:3 *And as His S. loves Him.* There is no fear in
T-13... X.10:11 purity that is forever within God's S..
T-13... X.11:10 say: *Behold the S. of God, and look upon his*
T-13..... X.12:6 Father, for the purity of Your most holy S.
T-13..... X.14:1 make the Father One with His Own S..
T-13......XI.2:1 God would not have His S. embattled,
T-13......XI.5:1 that His dear S. has laid upon himself. It
T-13......XI.9:5 sleeping S. holds no power over him. He
T-13....XI.10:1 Can God's S. lose himself in dreams,
T-14.........I.3:3 thoughts the mind of God's S. projects or
T-14....... II.8:7 and His S. is in Him with everything. Can
T-14......III.3:4 born of the Love of God and of His S.:
T-14......III.3:9 *me bring peace to God's S. from his Father.*
T-14......III.6:1 asked of God's S. except by himself and of
T-14......III.6:6 the S. of God is the happy lesson the Holy
T-14......III.7:6 No one can hurt the S. of God. His guilt is
T-14......III.8:7 power that God has given to His S. *is* his,
T-14......III.8:7 and nothing else can His S. see or choose
T-14......III.9:4 No thought of God's S. can be separate or
T-14....III.12:1 His calm and unswerving value of His S.?
T-14....III.13:5 distortion of the purity of the S. of God
T-14....III.15:1 worth of God's S. whom He created holy,
T-14....III.15:8 His S. drop from the loving Mind wherein
T-14......IV.1:6 received, even as God gave it first to His S.
T-14....IV.4:11 offer to God and you His blameless S.. For
T-14......IV.5:5 upon yourself by loving not the S. of God,
T-14......IV.7:4 you. He cannot be known without His S.,
T-14......IV.7:5 Accepting His S. as guilty is denial of the
T-14......IV.9:3 you the true condition of the S. of God. It
T-14..... V.1:12 for God is blessed in His S. as the Son is
T-14..... V.1:12 is blessed in His Son as the S. is blessed in
T-14....... V.2:1 one is always the same; *God's S. is guiltless.*
T-14....... V.3:1 Blessed S. of a wholly blessing Father, joy
T-14....... V.4:1 of the Kingdom is the right of God's S.,
T-14....... V.4:5 heavy veils of guilt within which the S. of
T-14....... V.5:2 be restored between the Father and the S..
T-14....... V.8:3 is everyone whom God created as His S..
T-14..... V.9:10 Restore to God His S. as He created him,
T-14......VI.8:7 Its gates are open wide to greet His S.. No
T-14... VIII.1:1 power He bestowed upon His guiltless S..
T-14... VIII.2:2 upon the altar to your Father and His S..
T-14... VIII.2:3 No altar stands to God without His S..
T-14... VIII.2:4 gifts wholly acceptable to Father and to S.
T-14... VIII.2:6 You cannot, then, offer it to His S.. For
T-14. VIII.2:11 place where God, united with His S.,
T-14. VIII.2:11 His Son, speaks to His S. through Him.
T-14. VIII.2:13 His S. lies in the Holy Spirit and in you.
T-14. VIII.2:14 wills with His S. is quite impossible here.
T-14. VIII.2:15 constantly between the Father and the S.,
T-14... VIII.3:3 God and His S. await your recognition.
T-14... VIII.4:9 creations of His S. with Them together.
T-14... VIII.5:5 of the Father will be accepted by the S.,
T-14....... X.2:2 the only perception the S. of God accepts.
T-14..... X.12:8 Who wills to be with His S. forever, will
T-14..... X.12:8 His S. with all the Love He holds for him.
T-14..... X.12:9 from any miracle you offer to His S.. How,
T-14......XI.2:2 yourself how to imprison the S. of God, a
T-14......XI.2:4 And can His S., given all power by Him,
T-14......XI.4:4 which He shares so gladly with His S..
T-14......XI.5:4 think you do not will for God's S. what his
T-14......XI.5:6 that you will with the Father and His S..
T-14......XI.7:3 God's S. can make no needs his Father
T-14......XI.7:4 His S. to turn to Him and remain Himself.
T-14......XI.7:7 by seeing His S. as he always was, and not
T-14....XI.11:1 God's S. will always be indivisible. As we
T-14....XI.11:3 is as like to His Creator as is His S., and
T-15.........I.8:4 in which the S. of God emerges from the
T-15...... I.15:5 in which God's S. could lose his purity.
T-15....... II.2:4 joy it is to teach God's holy S. his holiness.
T-15....... II.4:7 S. of God who has been released through
T-15...... III.4:8 effort you make on behalf of His dear S..
T-15.... III.4:10 God is not willing that His S. be content
T-15.... III.4:11 For He is not content without His S., and
T-15.... III.4:11 and His S. cannot be content with less
T-15..... III.5:6 make His S. hostage to the ego, cannot
T-15.... III.11:3 together that the S. of God is host to Him.
T-15....... V.2:7 deny the Oneness of the Father and His S.
T-15...... VI.2:5 our faith in God's S. because we recognize
T-15.... VI.5:10 S. of God accepts the laws of God as what
T-15......VII.1:1 attraction of the Father for His S.. There is
T-15......VII.5:1 this chain that binds the S. of God to guilt
T-15... VIII.2:5 is. God's S. has such great need of your
T-15... VIII.2:6 the only need that God and His S. share,
T-15... VIII.3:2 of God's S. is the loneliness of his Father.
T-15...... IX.6:5 to separate the Father from the S., and
T-15...... IX.6:7 limit not your vision of God's S. to what
T-15....... X.1:1 the perfect union of the Father and the S..
T-15....... X.2:2 instant no guilt is laid upon the S. of God,
T-16...... IV.9:3 of God and of His S. established forever.
T-16...... IV.9:6 is God completed, and His S. with Him.
T-16...... VI.1:4 unlike the relationship of God and His S.,
T-16..... VII.8:6 it. When He willed that His S. be free, His
T-16..... VII.8:6 willed that His Son be free, His S. *was* free.
T-16..... VII.8:7 holy instant is His reminder that His S.
T-16...VII.12:5 *temptation of the S. of God is not Your Will.*
T-17.........I.1:1 of the S. of God lies only in illusions, and
T-17....... II.1:6 For you will see the S. of God. You will
T-17....... II.3:7 final blessing of God's S. upon himself,
T-17....... II.5:5 the S. of God made in insanity could be
T-17....... II.7:1 the S. of God is lifted easily into his home.
T-17...... III.1:5 the S. of God for what he did not do. The
T-17...... III.7:2 God's S. is One. Whom God has joined as
T-17... VIII.5:1 Such was the crucifixion of the S. of God.
T-18...... III.6:1 me in bringing Heaven to the S. of God,
T-18...... VI.1:4 is the dwelling place of the S. of God, who
T-18...... VI.4:8 respecting what the S. of God has made
T-18...... VI.6:8 it to be the dwelling place of God's S., and
T-18...... VI.7:2 nor His most holy S. can enter an abode
T-18...... VI.9:3 is no barrier between God and His S., nor
T-18...... VI.9:3 nor can His S. be separated from Himself
T-18...... VI.9:6 Himself from His S. to make this possible.
T-18. VIII.11:8 in vain. No S. of God remains outside His
T-18...... IX.1:5 in its delusions, it thinks it is the S. of God
T-18.... IX.1:10 is still a tiny segment of the S. of God,
T-18...... IX.9:5 Here there is no attack upon the S. of God
T-19.........I.2:1 an opportunity to heal the S. of God. And
T-19.........I.5:5 between the S. of God and his Creator;
T-19........I.10:3 as a S. of your most loving Father, loved
T-19........I.11:2 Faithlessness looks upon the S. of God,
T-19........I.11:3 the S. of God is seen already forgiven, free
T-19........I.12:3 you offer to the S. of God through Him,
T-19........I.16:3 God created as His S. is slave to nothing,
T-19....... II.2:4 It assumes the S. of God is guilty, and has
T-19....... II.3:1 The S. of God can be mistaken; he can
T-19....... II.4:3 of the S. of God as his Father created him,
T-19....... II.7:1 what the S. of God has made himself to be
T-19...... III.5:1 sees the S. of God can make mistakes. On
T-19...... III.8:2 it; and give His S. a will apart from His,
T-19...... IV.3:8 Creator in the Name of His most holy S..
T19... IV.A.1:5 how can it abide within the S. of God? If it
T19. IV.A.17:4 the S. of God was killed instead of you.
T19....IV.B.4:9 your holy relationship is your Father's S..
T19....IV.B.6:2 sins you think the S. of God committed.
T19....IV.B.7:3 in which the Father and the S. are joined.
T19....IV.B.7:4 holy union of the Father and the S. in you!
T19....IV.B.9:3 and use it for the S. of God's release. It is
T19..IV.B.17:3 and offering His messages unto the S..
T19....IV.C.4:3 the S. of God to this *are* arrogant. But you
T19....IV.C.8:1 world the ego would lay the S. of God,
T19... IV.D.1:5 the S. of God entirely restored to sanity.
T19. IV.D.18:5 the way unto the resurrection of God's S.,
T19. IV.D.19:6 to the S. of God in thanks for what he is,
T19. IV.D.21:3 and place the S. of God safely within the
T-20.........I.1:2 brooding on the crucifixion of God's S.,
T-20.........I.1:5 of the S. of God's forgiveness on himself;
T-20.........I.2:1 and holy sign the S. of God is innocent.
T-20.........I.2:4 honor the perfect purity of the S. of God,
T-20.........I.3:1 journey the S. of God has undertaken. He
T-20....... II.3:6 judgment on the S. of God for what he is.
T-20........II.4:1 for the S. of God has not forgiven me.
T-20........II.4:4 you may look upon the S. of God as whole
T-20........II.7:7 S. of God looks unto you for his release.
T-20........II.7:8 thorns nor nails to crucify the S. of God,
T-20......II.8:10 refrain the S. of God was never crucified.
T-20......II.10:1 that the S. of God is risen from the past,
T-20...... III.7:1 make the S. of God adjust to his insanity.
T-20.... III.7:10 ask, "How shall I look upon the S. of God?
T-20...... III.8:6 brother with joy to bless the S. of God,
T-20.... III.11:5 the pure in heart see God within His S.,
T-20.... III.11:5 and look unto the S. to lead them to the
T-20.... III.11:7 as surely as God created His S. holy, and
T-20...... IV.6:7 the S. of God can enter without fear and
T-20.... IV.8:12 what can be more certain than a S. of God
T-20....... V.1:1 God's S. comes closest to himself in a holy
T-20....... V.1:5 parts of God's S. gradually join in time,
T-20....... V.2:5 to hold the unity of the S. of God together
T-20....... V.8:2 He knows the S. of God, and shares his
T-20...... VI.1:1 meaning of the S. of God lies solely in his
T-20...... VI.1:4 Yet has the S. of God invented an unholy
T-20.... VI.10:1 the S. of God has with his Father in reality
T-20.... VI.11:4 Here does the S. of God stop briefly by, to
T-20....VIII.3:6 bless the S. of God in your relationship,
T-20....VIII.4:6 a better home, a safer shelter for God's S.?
T-20..VIII.11:3 can behold the holiness God gave His S..
T-21.......in.2:2 see is what you did to hurt the S. of God.
T-21.........I.9:1 This is the vision of the S. of God, whom
T-21.........I.9:6 love the S. of God sings to his Father still.
T-21........I.10:3 will look upon the vision of the S. of God,
T-21........II.3:1 impossible the S. of God be merely driven
T-21........II.6:4 happen to the S. of God without his will;
T-21........II.6:5 is the S. of God's replacement for his will,
T-21......II.10:6 The S. is the Effect, whose Cause he would
T-21......II.11:5 it wills, you are confusing S. and Father;
T-21......II.12:2 in creating them the S. does not delude
T-21...... III.3:3 For faith can keep the S. of God in chains
T-21...... III.5:1 is impossible that the S. of God lack faith,
T-21...... III.5:3 the S. of God believe that he is powerless.
T-21....... V.5:2 must have been accepted by the S. of God,
T-21...... VI.3:1 himself, as God thinks not without His S..
T-21...... VI.6:1 condemn the S. of God to what can never
T-21...... VI.7:4 The power to heal the S. of God is given
T-21.... VI.10:1 The S. of God is always blessed as one.
T-21.... VI.11:1 you have over the S. of God is not a threat
T-21.... VI.11:5 no more His S. can be imprisoned save by
T-21..... VII.1:7 Treachery to the S. of God is the defense
T-21..... VII.2:1 one believes the S. of God is powerless.
T-21..... VII.2:2 believe that they are not the S. of God.
T-21..... VII.2:5 of the S. of God will strike them dead, and
T-21...VII.13:5 power of the S. of God's desire remains
T-22.......in.4:9 circle where you recognize the S. of God.
T-22.........I.9:1 did not entrust His S. to the unworthy.
T-22........II.9:6 Only if it were possible the S. of God
T-22......II.10:3 For only if you would believe His S. could
T-22.... VI.11:1 can attack the S. of God and not attack his
T-22.... VI.11:2 How can God's S. be weak and frail and
T-22.... VI.11:5 think the Father and the S. are separate.
T-22.... VI.12:5 the whole, the S. without the Father; and
T-22.... VI.14:5 of the union of the Creator and His S..
T-23.......in.5:1 let littleness lead God's S. into temptation
T-23.........I.4:7 The S. of God at war with his Creator is a
T-23.........I.5:1 teach the S. of God that he is not himself,
T-23.........I.5:1 he is not himself, and *not* his Father's S..
T-23........I.10:3 keeps God homeless and His S. with Him.
T-23........II.4:5 being the belief the S. of God can make
T-23........II.5:1 between the Father and the S.. Now it
T-23........II.5:5 the S. meet only to conflict but not to join
T-23........II.5:7 made real by what the S. of God has done
T-23........II.6:4 His S. can tell Him this, and He has but
T-23........II.7:4 Nor can salvation lie within the S., whose
T-23........II.8:5 to be siding with it, to overcome His S..
T-23......II.15:8 saved the S. of God for fear and death!
T-23...... IV.2:4 they be to those who see God's S. a body.
T-23...... IV.2:6 what is lifeless cannot be the S. of Life.
T-23...... IV.3:2 to create unto His S. because it is His Own
T-23...... IV.3:3 to believe the function of the S. is murder,
T-23...... IV.3:6 Either the Father and the S. are murderers
T-23...... IV.4:2 assume the holy function God gave His S.,
T-23...... IV.6:7 the peace of God together with His S..

| | |
|---|---|
| T-23 IV.7:8 | He created for His S. *because* it has no |
| T-24 in.1:10 | No more His S.. They *are.* And what |
| T-24 I.3:2 | and with the grandeur that He gave His S. |
| T-24 II.3:4 | His S. like to itself and not like unto Him. |
| T-24 II.6:2 | The shining radiance of the S. of God, so |
| T-24 II.6:3 | the S. remembers his own creations, as |
| T-24 II.8:7 | It is not God Who has condemned His S., |
| T-24 II.10:4 | not given to His S. but kept for Him alone |
| T-24 II.10:5 | then He willed His S. to be like Him, and |
| T-24 II.13:1 | prison house that keeps His S. from Him. |
| T-24 III.4:2 | Would God have left His S. in such a state |
| T-24 III.4:3 | No, His S. is safe, resting on Him. It is |
| T-24 III.6:1 | holiness, the perfect Father of a perfect S., |
| T-24 III.8:2 | free. Such is the Will of God and of His S.. |
| T-24 III.8:7 | asks your mercy on His S. and on Himself. |
| T-24 V.8:3 | not to be without His S. could never will |
| T-24 VI.2:1 | Heaven incomplete, a S. without a Father. |
| T-24 VI.3:5 | not His Mind about His S. with passing |
| T-24 VI.4:1 | healing of God's S. is all the world is for. |
| T-24 VI.4:3 | Until you see the healing of the S. as all |
| T-24 VI.4:5 | all belief God's S. can suffer pain because |
| T-24 VI.9:5 | And both shall see God's glory in His S., |
| T-24 VII.7:1 | co-creator with the Father must have a S.. |
| T-24 VII.7:2 | this S. have been created like Himself. A |
| T-24 VII.11:3 | The other rests within, his Father's S., |
| T-24 VII.11:7 | The S. of God retains his Father's Will. |
| T-25 in.2:7 | the S. of God abide exactly where he is, |
| T-25 I.4:2 | His life is manifest in you who are His S.. |
| T-25 I.5:3 | Father and S. and Holy Spirit are as One, |
| T-25 I.6:2 | still is one with Both the Father and the S. |
| T-25 II.9:2 | thanks to you who love His S. as He does? |
| T-25 II.9:7 | thank His perfect S. for being what he is. |
| T-25 II.10:3 | given you, that you may see His S. as one, |
| T-25 II.10:6 | He offers unto the Father and the S. alike. |
| T-25 III.2:4 | all. Only because His S. believes it is, and |
| T-25 III.4:1 | to the need the S. of God believes he has. |
| T-25 III.4:3 | And thus has God protected still His S., |
| T-25 III.9:1 | The S. of God could never sin, but he can |
| T-25 IV.2:7 | The S. of God creates to bring him joy, |
| T-25 IV.5:5 | supersede the Will of God and of His S., |
| T-25 V.1:1 | perceive the S. of God as other than he is. |
| T-25 V.2:8 | the S. of God as innocent and wish him |
| T-25 V.4:1 | The S. of God asks only this of you; that |
| T-25 V.6:1 | the S. of God may cherish toward himself, |
| T-25 VI.7:5 | The S. of God can make no choice the |
| T-25 VI.7:7 | plan to save the S. of God from all attack, |
| T-25 VII.4:2 | For God and His beloved S. do not think |
| T-25 VII.4:3 | that makes the S. a co-creator with the |
| T-25 VII.4:4 | not his Father's S. because the Son is mad, |
| T-25 VII.4:4 | not his Father's Son because the S. is mad, |
| T-25 VII.4:4 | lie apart from Both the Father and the S.. |
| T-25 VII.4:8 | the Father and the S. are not insane. This |
| T-25 VII.5:2 | would lead the S. of God to sanity and joy. |
| T-25 VII.6:7 | of what the Father and the S. must be, to |
| T-25 VII.7:4 | The S. of God cannot be bound by time |
| T-25 VII.9:6 | than could the Father overlook His S., and |
| T-25 VII.10:5 | His S. that hell and Heaven are different, |
| T-25 VII.13:5 | alone, but for the Self that is the S. of God |
| T-25 VIII.9:9 | God rejoices as His S. receives what loving |
| T-25 VIII.9:11 | gives the S. of God the power to forgive |
| T-25 VIII.10:4 | allow His S. be judged by those who seek |
| T-25 VIII.10:8 | justice would be done unto the S. He loves |
| T-25 VIII.12:1 | the S. of God could merit vengeance. You |
| T-25 VIII.12:8 | God's S. has found a witness unto his |
| T-25 VIII.14:1 | way, as God appointed for His holy S.. |
| T-25 VIII.14:6 | what justice must accord the S. of God. |
| T-25 IX.2:4 | given to God's S. are kept for him, and |
| T-25 IX.3:7 | is justice not accorded to the S. of God. |
| T-25 IX.7:1 | Salvation cannot seek to help God's S. be |
| T-26 I.4:3 | S. perceive himself without his Father? |
| T-26 I.4:4 | And his Father be without His S.? Yet |
| T-26 I.4:7 | witness to the Wholeness of God's S. is |
| T-26 I.7:3 | to the death of God and of His holy S., |
| T-26 I.7:4 | God's S. is not imprisoned in a body, nor |
| T-26 I.8:1 | justice rests in gentleness upon His S., |
| T-26 I.8:5 | the holy S. of God from the imprisonment |
| T-26 II.4:3 | It does injustice to the S. of God, and |
| T-26 II.4:6 | from which the S. of God is suffering, but |
| T-26 II.4:9 | God's S. must be unfair and therefore is |
| T-26 II.5:3 | S. of God is guilty then is he condemned, |
| T-26 III.1:3 | one reality, one truth and but one S.. |
| T-26 III.4:1 | the S. of God believes can be destroyed. |
| T-26 IV.4:2 | S. of God Himself comes to receive each |
| T-26 V.5:2 | of the S. of God can hardly still be there, |
| T-26 V.10:1 | Would God allow His S. to lose his way |
| T-26 V.10:7 | death, a vault God's S. entered an instant, |
| T-26 V.11:1 | The S. whom God created is as free as |
| T-26 VI.2:2 | This is no friendship worthy of God's S., |
| T-26 VII.3:3 | The S. of God perceived what he would |
| T-26 VII.8:5 | of God's S. where sin was thought to rule. |
| T-26 VII.10:6 | the instant that the S. of God perceives his |
| T-26 VII.11:2 | He wills His S. have everything. And this |
| T-26 VII.11:7 | Here does the S. of God ask not too much, |
| T-26 VII.13:6 | possible in trying to deceive the S. of God. |
| T-26 VII.14:4 | God's S. could never be content with less |
| T-26 VII.14:7 | then is God's S. made incomplete and not |
| T-26 VII.16:3 | Heaven is shining on the S. of God. Deny |
| T-26 VII.16:5 | Each instant is the S. of God reborn until |
| T-26 VII.17:4 | has been given to save the S. of God from |
| T-26 VII.17:5 | For you have power to save the S. of God |
| T-26 VII.20:5 | itself, the S. of God allowed to be himself, |
| T-26 IX.7:4 | the Lord of Heaven and His S. give less in |
| T-26 IX.8:2 | Where He dwells, His S. dwells with Him, |
| T-26 IX.8:6 | Father and the S. return to what is Theirs, |
| T-26 X.3:5 | yourself, in deep injustice to the S. of God |
| T-26 X.4:5 | own attack upon the S. of God you seek? |
| T-26 X.6:6 | *I deny the Presence of the Father and the S..* |
| T-27 I.1:9 | Father with the sacrifice of His beloved S.. |
| T-27 I.3:1 | your brother of attack upon God's S.. You |
| T-27 II.6:7 | The ancient calling of the Father to His S., |
| T-27 II.6:7 | to His Son, and of the S. unto His Own, |
| T-27 II.8:9 | God's S. remembered that he *is* God's Son. |
| T-27 II.8:9 | God's Son remembered that he *is* God's S.. |
| T-27 V.11:9 | for He knows it is a gift of love unto His S. |
| T-27 VII.13:3 | than an idle dream has terrified God's S., |
| T-27 VII.15:2 | will Himself awaken His beloved S.. |
| T-27 VIII.6:2 | the S. of God remembered not to laugh. |
| T-27 VIII.9:7 | Him say, "My brother, holy S. of God, |
| T-28 I.8:5 | Will that He be unremembered by His S.. |
| T-28 I.10:1 | it is not He Who laid a judgment on His S. |
| T-28 I.10:3 | There was no time in which His S. could |
| T-28 I.12:2 | to offer all its treasures to the S. of God, |
| T-28 I.12:5 | The instant's silence that His S. accepts |
| T-28 I.12:6 | instant does the S. of God do nothing that |
| T-28 I.13:6 | the S. of God remembers from before his |
| T-28 I.14:1 | Now is the S. of God at last aware of |
| T-28 I.15:5 | left a stranded S. forever on a shore where |
| T-28 I.15:7 | it is He Who will transport His S. across it |
| T-28 II.1:2 | its effects; the Father *is* a Father by His S.. |
| T-28 II.1:4 | the S. gives Fatherhood to his Creator, |
| T-28 II.1:5 | he is God's S. that he must also be a father |
| T-28 II.3:1 | Always in sickness does the S. of God |
| T-28 II.3:1 | and not allow himself to be his Father's S.. |
| T-28 III.7:5 | a picture of the S. of God in broken pieces |
| T-28 III.9:5 | is a feast the Father lays before His S., and |
| T-28 IV.7:7 | comes to join His S. the Holy Spirit joined |
| T-28 IV.8:1 | picture of the S. of God and put the pieces |
| T-28 IV.8:6 | And here the Father will receive His S., |
| T-28 IV.8:6 | because His S. was gracious to himself. |
| T-28 IV.9:1 | between the broken pieces of Your holy S. |
| T-28 IV.9:4 | part of the completed picture of God's S.! |
| T-28 IV.9:7 | And every aspect of the S. of God is just |
| T-28 IV.10:1 | and where you join His S. the Father is. |
| T-28 IV.10:8 | go is all the Healer of God's S. requires. |
| T-28 VI.6:3 | God keeps His promises; His S. keeps his. |
| T-28 VI.6:6 | S. remembers not that he replied "I will," |
| T-28 VII.1:1 | God asks for nothing, and His S., like |
| T-28 VII.1:5 | Father and the S. is not the Will of Either, |
| T-28 VII.4:4 | It serves to help the healing of God's S., |
| T-28 VII.7:5 | that His S. is safe forever in Himself. |
| T-28 VII.7:7 | be used to liberate God's S. unto his home |
| T-29 II.6:1 | His S. have life and every living thing be |
| T-29 III.2:5 | in the dream His S. prefers to his reality. |
| T-29 III.3:11 | the gentle way of kindness to God's S.. |
| T-29 III.5:1 | S. of God can be your savior in the midst |
| T-29 V.1:3 | up to gladden God the Father and the S.. |
| T-29 V.2:4 | intrude upon the sacred S. of God within. |
| T-29 V.3:1 | gives to you who wait upon the S. of God, |
| T-29 V.3:2 | you of him, because he is his Father's S., |
| T-29 V.4:1 | This sacred S. of God is like yourself; the |
| T-29 V.5:2 | Behold His S., His perfect gift, in whom |
| T-29 V.6:2 | and lead God's S. unto his Father's house. |
| T-29 VI.2:1 | Swear not to die, you holy S. of God! You |
| T-29 VI.2:3 | keep. The S. of Life cannot be killed. He is |
| T-29 VI.2:11 | God's S. can never change by what men |
| T-29 VI.4:7 | established for His S. in full awareness. |
| T-29 VI.5:1 | think that it was made to crucify God's S.. |
| T-29 VI.6:1 | whose purpose is forgiveness of God's S.! |
| T-29 VII.3:4 | Yet does he seek to kill God's S. within, |
| T-29 VIII.6:6 | And the S. of God, as perfect, sinless and |
| T-29 VIII.9:3 | In Heaven would the S. of God but laugh, |
| T-29 IX.1:3 | holy S. of God that this could be his wish; |
| T-29 IX.2:2 | to hell, and God made enemy unto His S.. |
| T-29 IX.2:3 | How can God's S. awaken from the dream |
| T-29 IX.3:5 | Judgment is an injustice to God's S., and |
| T-29 IX.8:5 | abides forever deep within the S. of God. |
| T-30 II.2:5 | God leave His S. without what he has |
| T-30 II.2:8 | God would not have His S. made prisoner |
| T-30 III.2:3 | of all the love in the Divinity of God the S. |
| T-30 III.4:9 | thing the power to complete the S. of God |
| T-30 III.4:10 | to give the S. of God what he already has? |
| T-30 III.5:1 | Completion is the *function* of God's S.. He |
| T-30 III.11:4 | The mind of Heaven's S. in Heaven is, for |
| T-30 III.11:4 | the Mind of Father and of S. joined in |
| T-30 III.11:10 | But you, the holy S. of God Himself, are |
| T-30 IV.5:12 | God's S. needs no defense against his |
| T-30 IV.6:5 | thus the S. of God declares that he is free |
| T-30 IV.8:10 | the S. of God can have no need of them. |
| T-30 V.4:1 | God Who could create a perfect S. and |
| T-30 V.4:5 | so is Heaven's S. prepared to be himself, |
| T-30 V.4:5 | to remember that the S. of God knows |
| T-30 V.6:3 | Yet God need not create His S. again, that |
| T-30 V.6:5 | And what the S. of God knew in creation |
| T-30 V.7:6 | till His S. has reached beyond forgiveness |
| T-30 VI.7:5 | it. You must forgive God's S. entirely. Or |
| T-30 VI.7:8 | have replaced the truth about God's S.. |
| T-30 VI.9:1 | God's S. is perfect, or he cannot be God's |
| T-30 VI.9:1 | Son is perfect, or he cannot be God's S.. |
| T-30 VI.9:4 | *I thank You, Father, for Your perfect S., and* |
| T-30 VI.10:3 | idol of the S. of God you will not pardon. |
| T-30 VI.10:6 | Is his Father wrong about His S.? Or have |
| T-30 VIII.4:7 | freedom to bestow His gifts upon God's S. |
| T-31 I.4:5 | forgotten, and His S. an alien to himself, |
| T-31 I.4:6 | taught yourself the S. of God is guilty, say |
| T-31 I.6:2 | God willed not His S. forget Him. And the |
| T-31 I.7:4 | that God's S. is guilty is the world you see. |
| T-31 I.7:11 | And you will learn God's S. is innocent, |
| T-31 I.8:1 | of the lesson that God's S. is guiltless is a |
| T-31 I.9:4 | only if His S. is innocent can He be Love. |
| T-31 I.9:6 | God's perfect S. remembers his creation. |
| T-31 I.10:1 | the lesson that His S. is guilty as God's |
| T-31 II.7:4 | about this S. of God who calls to you. |
| T-31 II.7:6 | when God appointed Him His only S.. |
| T-31 IV.11:4 | and did not let His S. abandon Him. For |
| T-31 V.2:3 | take the place of your reality as S. of God. |
| T-31 VI.5:1 | the S. of God as you would have him be, |
| T-31 VII.10:6 | For God has given you His S. to save from |
| T-31 VII.11:1 | could you be the savior of the S. of God? |
| T-31 VII.15:5 | "Release My S.!" be tempted not to listen, |
| T-31 VIII.1:2 | persuade the holy S. of God he is a body, |
| T-31 VIII.3:7 | is the Self that God created as His only S.. |
| T-31 VIII.5:3 | *His S. can suffer nothing. And* ***I am His Son.*** |
| T-31 VIII.5:4 | *And* ***I am His*** *S..* Thus is Christ's strength |
| T-31 VIII.6:4 | A miracle has come to heal God's S., and |
| W-pI 20.3:6 | God has one S., and he is the resurrection |
| W-pI 37.1:6 | because it is his birthright as a S. of God. |
| W-pI 38.1:3 | because it establishes you as a S. of God, |
| W-pI 39.4:6 | Can it be He does not know His S.? |
| W-pI 40.h | I am blessed as a S. of God. |
| W-pI 40.3:2 | you associate with being a S. of God, |
| W-pI 40.3:4 | *I am blessed as a S. of God. I am happy,* |
| W-pI 40.3:7 | *I am blessed as a S. of God. I am calm, quiet,* |
| W-pI 40.3:9 | that you are blessed as a S. of God will do. |
| W-pI 43.2:4 | by the S. of God for an unholy purpose, it |
| W-pI 43.2:7 | which the S. of God forgives his brother, |
| W-pI 45.8:4 | to God the Father and to God the S.. For |
| W-pI 46.6:3 | *I cannot be guilty because I am a S. of God. I* |

W-pI.....49.2:6 that your Creator has not forgotten His S..
W-pI.....50.3:3 upon the eternal calm of the S. of God.
W-pI.....50.5:3 to disturb the holy mind of the S. of God.
W-pI.....54.4:4 A S. of God cannot think or speak or act
W-pI.....55.1:3 be what God created for His beloved S..
W-pI.....55.1:5 Therefore I also do not understand His S..
W-pI.....55.2:4 of the Love of God and the Love of His S..
W-pI.....57.2:4 it is possible to imprison the S. of God. I
W-pI.....57.2:6 The S. of God must be forever free. He is
W-pI.....57.3:4 I see the world as a prison for God's S.. It
W-pI.....57.3:6 see it as a place where the S. of God finds
W-pI.....58.5:1 (40) I am blessed as a S. of God. Herein
W-pI.....58.5:3 I am blessed as a S. of God. All good
W-pI.....58.5:8 forever. I am eternally blessed as His S..
W-pI.....60.4:5 only Guide that has been given to His S..
W-pI.....60.5:4 His Love reminds me that His S. is sinless.
W-pI.....60.5:5 has given me, I remember that I am His S.
W-pI.....61.1:1 is the light of the world except God's S.?
W-pI.....61.7:6 His plan for the salvation of His S. on you.
W-pI.....62.3:5 power God gave His S. to your awareness.
W-pI.....63.2:2 S. of God looks to you for his redemption.
W-pI.....63.2:4 function and leave the S. of God in hell.
W-pI.....63.4:4 that God's S. looks to you for his salvation
W-pI.....63.4:5 And Who but your Self must be His S.?
W-pI.....64.1:3 temptation to abandon God and His S.
W-pI.....64.3:3 the S. of God escape from all illusions,
W-pI.....64.3:4 from all temptation. The S. of God is you.
W-pI.....67.1:4 is why the S. of God looks to you for his
W-pI.....67.6:3 with the simple truth about the S. of God.
W-pI.....69.2:5 tears of God's S. disappear in the sunlight
W-pI.....72.4:5 is God attacked, for if His S. is only a body
W-pI.....73.3:2 Will the S. of God shares with his Father?
W-pI.....73.3:3 God create disaster for His S.? Creation is
W-pI.....73.9:4 time appointed for the release of the S. of
W-pI.....74.3:9 *one. God wills peace for His S..* During this
W-pI...76.10:6 you. About His yearning for His only S.,
W-pI...76.12:3 God is our Father, and that His S. is saved
W-pI.....78.2:3 our eyes in silence to behold the S. of God
W-pI.....78.3:2 it lifts you see the S. of God where he has
W-pI.....78.4:1 Today we will attempt to see God's S..
W-pI.....78.5:2 of whom we ask God's S. be shown to you
W-pI.....78.7:1 this S. of God in his reality and truth, that
W-pI.....78.7:2 in the holy Name of God and of His S., as
W-pI.....78.8:4 to you, seeing no separation in God's S..
W-pI.....87.4:3 *It is God's Will you are His S., [name], and*
W-pI.....92.9:3 the peace of God is where your Self, His S.
W-pI.....93.5:1 The self you made is not the S. of God.
W-pI.....93.5:6 It does not battle with the S. of God. It
W-pI.....94.2:5 cannot obscure the glory of God's S.. You
W-pI.....94.3:4 *I am His S. eternally.* Now try to reach the
W-pI.....94.3:5 Now try to reach the S. of God in you.
W-pI.....94.5:3 *me. I am His S. eternally.* Tell yourself
W-pI.....94.5:7 *You are His S. eternally.* Make every effort
W-pI.....95.2:5 does not understand you are the S. of God
W-pI...95.12:2 are God's S., one Self, with one Creator
W-pI...95.13:2 are one Self, the holy S. of God, united
W-pI...95.13:4 This is your Self, the S. of God Himself,
W-pI.....96.6:8 release of His dear S. bring pain to him,
W-pI.....97.2:1 Self, the holy S. of God Who rests in you,
W-pI.....97.7:2 *Spirit am I, a holy S. of God, free of all limits,*
W-pI.....99.9:3 It is God's Will that He has but one S.. It
W-pI.....99.9:4 Son. It is God's Will that His one S. is you.
W-pI...99.12:5 and show you that you are the S. of God.
W-pI...100.1:1 Just as God's S. completes his Father, so
W-pI...100.6:3 world can see how much He loves His S.,
W-pI...101.1:5 that sin is real, and that God's S. can sin.
W-pI...101.4:5 God upon you who have crucified His S..
W-pI...101.5:3 that you have made a devil of God's S..
W-pI...102.5:2 no need to be less loving to God's S. than
W-pI...105.5:3 Him must complete His S. as well. He
W-pI...106.4:7 for they come from God to His dear S.,
W-pI...106.5:3 could reach God's S. except his Father,
W-pI...109.2:6 the thought in which the S. of God is born
W-pI...110.6:3 *His S. can suffer nothing. And I am His Son.*
W-pI...110.6:4 *His Son can suffer nothing. And I am His S..*
W-pI...110.7:1 the Self Who is the holy S. of God Himself
W-pI...110.8:1 the S. of God and brother to the world;
W-pI...110.9:3 you made to be the S. of God instead of
W-pI.110.11:3 say, that we may be reminded of His S.,

WpIrIII.in11:6 day and make it holy, worthy of God's S.,
W-pI...114.1:2 *I am the S. of God. No body can contain my*
W-pI...116.2:2 *I share my Father's Will for me, His S.. What*
W-pI...118.2:2 *Itself assure me that I am God's perfect S..*
W-pI...119.1:3 *I am God's S., whose Self rests safely in the*
W-pI...120.2:2 *me. I am God's S.. Today I lay aside all sick*
W-pI.121.13:7 *of sin, and know I am the perfect S. of God.*
W-pI...122.3:2 It lets you recognize the S. of God, and
W-pI...122.6:5 but this for the salvation of the S. of God.
W-pI...123.3:2 the S. He loves is changeless as Himself.
W-pI...123.3:5 the one whom God established as His S..
W-pI...123.8:2 Him thanks for everything He gave His S.,
W-pI...125.2:2 this: The S. of God is free to save himself,
W-pI...125.3:3 the world has laid upon the S. of God. It
W-pI...125.4:1 Hear, holy S. of God, your Father speak.
W-pI...125.5:4 He knows His S., and wills that he remain
W-pI...125.8:3 in the single Mind of Father and of S.. In
W-pI...125.8:4 let Him tell you God has never left His S.,
W-pI...125.9:4 of God the S. joins in his Father's Will, at
W-pI...126.7:3 such petty gifts as worthy of His S.?
W-pI...127.1:7 It is the Heart of God, and also of His S..
W-pI...127.2:6 perceive the S. of God in separate parts.
W-pI...127.3:8 link between the Father and the S. which
W-pI...129.4:2 And God Himself speaks to His S., as His
W-pI...129.4:2 speaks to His Son, as His S. speaks to Him
W-pI...131.4:4 God's S. can not seek vainly, though he
W-pI...131.6:4 be, if it is where God wills His S. to be.
W-pI...131.8:3 How could it be His S. could be in hell,
W-pI...131.9:2 S. of God make time to take away the Will
W-pI.131.14:4 keeps His ancient promise to His holy S.,
W-pI.131.14:4 Son, as does His S. remember his to Him.
W-pI.132.12:3 His Fatherhood with you who are His S.,
W-pI.132.12:4 S. begin as something separate from Him.
W-pI.132.13:1 made to separate the Father and the S.,
W-pI...135.4:5 fail to serve the S. of God as worthy host?
W-pI.135.26:8 *S. of God needs no defense against the truth*
W-pI...136.9:2 salvation of His S. opposed by a decision
W-pI...136.9:3 His S. is dust, the Father incomplete, and
W-pI...137.3:6 attack the universal Oneness of God's S..
W-pI.137.14:4 *be banished from the mind of God's one S.,*
W-pI.139.10:1 the Oneness of God's S. is unassailed by
W-pI.139.12:2 would weave around the holy S. of God.
W-pI.140.10:2 as one, restoring saneness to the S. of God
WpI. rIV.in2:4 which the Father gave creation to the S.,
WpI. rIV.in2:4 the S. as co-creator with Himself. It is this
WpI. rIV.in2:5 that fully guarantees salvation to the S..
W-pI...151.7:3 merely bear false witness to God's S.. He
W-pI...151.9:3 knows the glory of the Father and the S.?
W-pI.151.14:1 and the happiness God wills His S., as
W-pI.151.15:3 you taught to teach the S. of God the holy
W-pI.151.15:4 the Voice for God give honor to God's S..
W-pI...152.8:5 to usurp the altar to the Father and the S..
W-pI...152.9:3 God's perfect gift to His beloved S.. We
W-pI.152.10:2 are, and humbly recognize the S. of God.
W-pI.152.10:3 To recognize God's S. implies as well that
W-pI.152.10:5 And in humility the radiance of God's S.,
W-pI.152.12:3 and God's S. for your illusions of yourself.
W-pI...153.5:5 For you behold the S. of God as but a
W-pI...153.8:3 mistook the figures in it for the S. of God;
W-pI.153.13:3 of Heaven's children and the S. of God.
W-pI.153.14:6 God's S. can smile at last, on learning that
W-pI...154.3:3 God has joined His S. in this, and thus His
W-pI...154.3:3 and thus His S. becomes His messenger of
W-pI...154.4:1 the Voice for God, of Father and of S.,
W-pI.154.12:3 denied the tiniest of blessings to His S..
W-pI...155.8:5 seem to hold in chains the holy S. of God.
W-pI.155.11:1 the holy S. of God will make no journeys.
W-pI.155.12:4 less and still content the holy S. of God?
W-pI.155.13:3 a worthy guide for you who are God's S..
W-pI...158.2:8 revelation that the Father and the S. are
W-pI...158.7:2 mistake it for the S. whom God created. It
W-pI...158.8:4 a body. Greet him as the S. of God he is,
W-pI.159.10:3 Judge not God's S., but follow in the way
W-pI...160.4:2 the home which God provided for His S.?
W-pI...160.7:4 as certain of Its Own as God is of His S..
W-pI...160.7:9 know of strangers. He is certain of His S..
W-pI...160.8:2 knows to be His S. belongs where He has
W-pI...160.8:2 belongs where He has set His S. forever.
W-pI......161.h Give me your blessing, holy S. of God.

W-pI.161.11:7 *me your blessing, holy S. of God. I would*
W-pI...162.2:1 the S. became his Father's happiness, His
W-pI...162.6:6 For you have recognized the S. of God,
W-pI......163.h There is no death. The S. of God is free.
W-pI...163.4:4 Will of Father and of S. defeated finally,
W-pI...163.4:4 upon the body of the holy S. of God.
W-pI...163.7:4 And with the Father died the S. as well.
W-pI...164.9:8 holds out complete salvation to His S.?
W-pI...165.6:5 Would God consent to let His S. remain
W-pI...166.1:3 knows His S.. He gives without exception,
W-pI...166.9:6 your plan to keep His S. in deep oblivion,
W-pI...167.1:7 because the Father and the S. are One.
W-pI...168.1:7 He loves His S.. There is no certainty but
W-pI...168.1:9 He will love His S. forever. When his
W-pI...168.4:1 God loves His S.. Request Him now to
W-pI...168.6:3 Such is His Will, because He loves His S..
W-pI...168.6:9 *come to me who ask. I am the S. You love.*
W-pI...169.4:1 and the S. as One has been already set.
W-pI...169.6:5 S. of God has merely disappeared into his
W-pI...169.9:3 and in the Name of His Creator's S..
WpI...rV.in6:6 God's S. is crucified until you walk along
WpI...rV.in9:8 Our Father wills His S. be one with Him.
WpI.rV.in10:5 You are His S., completing His extension
W-pI...176.1:1 Give me your blessing, holy S. of God.
W-pI...177.1:2 The S. of God is free. God is but Love, and
W-pI...182.5:1 in you your Father knows as His Own S..
W-pI...183.5:3 grace, nor bodies for the holy S. of God.
W-pI...183.5:4 reaches to God Himself and to His S..
W-pI...183.7:5 that His S. receive another name than His.
W-pI...183.8:2 also that His S. is part of Him, creating in
W-pI.183.10:3 when God's S. calls on his Father's Name.
W-pI.183.11:4 consists of nothing but the S. of God, who
W-pI.184.12:6 made as fitting tribute to the S. He loves.
W-pI.184.14:1 each awareness of an aspect of God's S.,
W-pI...186.3:2 trust He holds in you who are His S.. It
W-pI...186.7:5 What can it tell the holy S. of God? Why
W-pI...186.9:1 Is this the S. of God? Could He create
W-pI...186.9:2 He create such instability and call it S.?
W-pI...186.9:4 All the images His S. appears to make
W-pI.186.13:4 which answer every need His S. perceives,
W-pI.187.10:2 we stand together as one S. of God. Not
W-pI...188.7:3 Where God the Father and the S. are One.
W-pI...189.8:3 you have interposed between the S. and
W-pI...189.9:6 God knows His S., and knows the way to
W-pI...189.9:7 His S. to show Him how to find His way.
W-pI...190.1:7 to God the Father's hatred of His S., the
W-pI...190.2:5 leave the S. whom It created out of love.
W-pI...190.3:7 The body is the S. of God, corruptible in
W-pI...190.8:3 In pain is God denied the S. He loves. In
W-pI......191.h I am the holy S. of God Himself.
W-pI...191.1:3 the world the role of jailer to the S. of God
W-pI...191.6:1 free: You are the holy S. of God Himself.
W-pI...191.7:3 *I am the holy S. of God Himself. I cannot*
W-pI...191.8:3 S. of God has come in glory to redeem the
W-pI...191.8:4 God's S. has come again at last to set it
W-pI.191.10:1 let the S. of God awaken from his sleep,
W-pI.191.11:6 life. You are the holy S. of God Himself.
W-pI...192.1:1 and that your Self shall be His sacred S.,
W-pI...192.5:6 peace that God intended for His holy S..
W-pI...192.5:7 the S. to look again upon his holiness.
W-pI.192.10:2 The S. of God deserves your mercy. It is
W-pI...193.1:2 He wills the happiness His S. inherited of
W-pI...193.2:2 Yet His S. believes he sees them. Thus he
W-pI...193.2:6 answers what His S. would contradict,
W-pI...193.3:2 His loving kindness to the S. He loves.
W-pI...193.8:3 His S. does not remember who he is. And
W-pI...193.8:6 and God may be remembered by His S.?
W-pI...193.9:2 or nail to hurt His holy S. in any way. He
W-pI...193.9:5 each one, and that His S. be free again.
W-pI...194.5:3 in God's S. is freed to bless the world.
W-pI...195.9:5 God has cared for us, and calls us S.. Can
W-pI.195.10:4 God gives thanks to you, His S., for being
W-pI.196.11:4 calling Him Father and yourself His S..
W-pI...197.8:1 Thanks be to you, the holy S. of God. For
W-pI...198.3:7 dream in which the S. of God awakens to
W-pI...198.7:2 is offered to God's S. and to his Father.
W-pI...198.7:7 and that the holy S. of God can die!
W-pI.198.10:1 there is no condemnation in God's S., and
W-pI.198.11:6 that God forever knows to be His only S..

W-pI.198.12:5 forgiveness to the S. of Sinlessness Itself,
W-pI.198.12:5 Itself, so like to Him Whose S. he is, that
W-pI.198.12:5 to behold the S. is to perceive no more,
W-pI.198.12:6 In this vision of the S., so brief that not an
W-pI...199.8:1 You are God's S.. In immortality you live
W-pI...199.8:5 with you, God's S. will weep no more, and
W-pI...200.6:5 the escape of God's beloved S. from evil
W-pI...200.7:1 because He has one S. who cannot make a
W-pI...200.9:5 He will not desert His S. in need, nor let
W-pI...200.9:6 The Father calls; the S. will hear. And that
W-pI...204.1:2 *God's Name reminds me that I am His S.,*
W-pI...206.1:2 *with the gifts of God, because I am His S..*
W-pI...209.1:4 *The Love of God proclaimed me as His S..*
W-pI...210.1:4 *Will is joy, and only joy for His beloved S..*
W-pI...211.1:1 (191) I am the holy S. of God Himself. *In*
W-pI...211.1:2 *it in the S. whom He created as my Self.* I am
W-pI...219.1:3 *I am God's S.. Be still, my mind, and think a*
W-pI...219.1:5 *as to what my Father loves forever as His S..* I
W-pII ....in.3:4 and He has promised that His S. will not
W-pII ....in.4:2 He has not left His S. in all his madness,
W-pII ....in.7:7 The Father and the S., Whose holy Will
W-pII ....in.7:8 which will not fail the S. who calls to You.
W-pII ....in.9:1 have the S. whom He created for Himself.
W-pII .....1.1:5 is sin, except a false idea about God's S.?
W-pII .....1.5:3 and whom He honors as the S. of God.
W-pII .221.2:6 we are, and to reveal Himself unto His S..
W-pII .222.1:4 and holds in love the S. He shines upon,
W-pII .223.2:2 *For we who are Your holy S. are sinless. We*
W-pII .223.2:3 *for guilt proclaims that we are not Your S..*
W-pII .223.2:7 *and we acknowledge that we are Your S..*
W-pII ....224.h God is my Father, and He loves His S..
W-pII ....225.h God is my Father, and His S. loves Him.
W-pII .225.1:3 *still the way Your loving S. is led along to You*
W-pII .227.2:2 S. of God this day lays down his dreams.
W-pII .227.2:3 The S. of God this day comes home again,
W-pII .228.1:4 Who knows the true condition of His S.?
W-pII .230.2:3 *The peace in which Your S. was born into*
W-pII .230.2:6 *gave. It is Your Will that gave it to Your S..*
W-pII .....2.2:1 to God's S. the instant that his mind had
W-pII .....2.5:2 and God's S. has but an instant more to
W-pII .232.1:5 *Your care, and happily aware I am Your S..*
W-pII .232.2:5 be you undismayed because you are His S.
W-pII ....234.h Father, today I am Your S. again.
W-pII .234.1:4 the peace of God the Father and the S..
W-pII .235.1:3 His S. and keeps his sinlessness forever
W-pII .235.1:4 I am the S. He loves. And I am saved
W-pII .237.2:2 *I come to You through Him Who is Your S.,*
W-pII .238.1:5 *give Your S. to me in certainty that he is safe*
W-pII .238.2:2 And how dear His S., created by His Love,
W-pII .239.1:4 His S. forever and with perfect constancy,
W-pII .240.2:2 *Would You allow Your S. to suffer? Give us*
W-pII .240.2:3 *Give us faith today to recognize Your S., and*
W-pII .....3.2:4 where His S. could be apart from Him.
W-pII .241.2:2 *Father, Your S., who never left, returns to*
W-pII .244.1:1 *Your S. is safe wherever he may be, for You*
W-pII .245.1:8 *For I would save Your S., as is Your Will, that*
W-pII ....246.h To love my Father is to love His S..
W-pII .246.1:2 Let me not try to hurt God's S., and think
W-pII .246.2:4 *that. And so I choose to love Your S.. Amen.*
W-pII .248.1:7 deceits and lies about the holy S. of God.
W-pII .248.2:1 *and lets me love Your S. again as well. Father*
W-pII .249.1:7 the journey which the S. of God began has
W-pII .250.1:1 Let me behold the S. of God today, and
W-pII .250.2:1 *He is Your S., my Father. And today I would*
W-pII .....4.3:3 Sin "proves" God's S. is evil; timelessness
W-pII .....4.3:4 And God Himself has lost the S. He loves,
W-pII .....4.4:3 S. of God may play he has become a body,
W-pII .....4.5:1 How long, O S. of God, will you maintain
W-pII .....4.5:8 How long, O holy S. of God, how long?
W-pII ....252.h The S. of God is my Identity.
W-pII .252.2:2 *Reveal It now to me who am Your S., that I*
W-pII .253.2:1 *You are the Self Whom You created S.,*
W-pII .255.1:2 God assures me that His S. is like Himself.
W-pII .255.1:3 have faith in Him Who says I am God's S..
W-pII .255.1:5 says. God's S. can have no cares, and must
W-pII .255.2:2 *Your S. has not forgotten You. The peace*
W-pII .260.1:3 *Your S., my Father, calls on You today. Let*
W-pII .....5.1:1 a fence the S. of God imagines he has built
W-pII .....5.2:3 S. of God's impermanence is "proof" his
W-pII .....5.2:9 that God's eternal S. can be destroyed?
W-pII .....5.4:1 means by which God's S. returns to sanity
W-pII .....5.4:3 The S. of God extends his hand to reach
W-pII .261.2:3 *and find the S. whom You created as my Self.*
W-pII .262.1:1 *Father, You have one S.. And it is he that I*
W-pII .262.1:6 *For Your S. must bear Your Name, for You*
W-pII .262.1:8 *in Your Love; eternally the holy S. of God.*
W-pII .264.1:4 *Your S. and keeps him safe is Love itself.*
W-pII .264.1:6 *Father, Your S. is like Yourself. We come to*
W-pII ....266.h My holy Self abides in you, God's S..
W-pII .266.1:3 *Let not Your S. forget Your holy Name. Let*
W-pII .266.1:4 *Let not Your S. forget his holy Source. Let*
W-pII .266.1:5 *Let not Your S. forget his Name is Yours.*
W-pII .269.1:5 *to me; that nothing is, except Your holy S..*
W-pII .269.2:3 one because of Him Who is the S. of God;
W-pII .270.1:4 *signifies Your S. acknowledges his Father,*
W-pII .270.2:3 the holy S. whom God created whole; the
W-pII .270.2:3 whole; the holy S. whom God created One
W-pII .....6.1:1 Christ is God's S. as He created Him. He
W-pII .....6.4:3 and peace has come to every S. of God,
W-pII .....6.5:3 the Christ Whom God created as His S..
W-pII .271.1:4 live, remembering the Father and the S.;
W-pII ....272.h How can illusions satisfy God's S.?
W-pII .272.1:5 *What but Your memory can satisfy Your S.?*
W-pII .272.1:8 *safe. God's S. must be as You created him.*
W-pII .273.1:4 that God Himself has given to His S..
W-pII .273.2:4 *so the peace You gave Your S. is with me still,*
W-pII .274.1:1 *give Your S. the honor due his sinlessness;*
W-pII .274.1:3 *Your S. will know he is as You created him.*
W-pII .276.1:2 "My S. is pure and holy as Myself." And
W-pII .276.1:3 God become the Father of the S. He loves,
W-pII .276.1:4 the Word His S. did not create with Him,
W-pII .276.1:4 with Him, because in this His S. was born.
W-pII ....277.h Let me not bind Your S. with laws I made
W-pII .277.1:1 *S. is free, my Father. Let me not imagine I*
W-pII .277.2:1 make to hide the freedom of the S. of God
W-pII .277.2:4 He is free because he is his Father's S..
W-pII .279.1:1 God's S. is not abandoned by His Love.
W-pII .279.2:2 *My Father loves the S. Whom He created as*
W-pII ....280.h What limits can I lay upon God's S.?
W-pII .280.1:6 Can I lay limits on the S. of God, whose
W-pII .280.2:1 *Today let me give honor to Your S., for thus*
W-pII .280.2:2 *on the S. You love and You created limitless.*
W-pII .....7.5:3 of Heaven is restored to God's beloved S..
W-pII .281.1:1 *Father, Your S. is perfect. When I think that*
W-pII .281.2:4 And I would not attack the S. He loves,
W-pII .282.1:4 Self Whom God created as the S. He loves
W-pII .283.1:1 *of myself, and it is this I call the S. of God. Yet*
W-pII .283.1:8 *Is not Your S. my true Identity, when You*
W-pII .285.2:3 *sanity. Your S. is still as You created him. My*
W-pII .287.2:6 *Your S. would be as You created him. What*
W-pII .289.2:5 *I demand that You wait longer for Your S. to*
W-pII .....8.4:1 guilt is over, and God's S. no longer sleeps
W-pII .291.2:5 *guide Your S. along the quiet path that leads*
W-pII .294.1:1 I am a S. of God. And can I be another
W-pII .294.1:4 has God's beloved S. for what must die?
W-pII .294.2:1 *My body, Father, cannot be Your S.. And*
W-pII ....298.h I love You, Father, and I love Your S..
W-pII .298.2:4 *my love for God my Father and His holy S..*
W-pII .....9.4:4 And God the Father smiles upon His S.,
W-pII .....9.5:6 Behold, the S. of God is one in us, and we
W-pII .302.1:4 *But we had forgot the S. whom You created.*
W-pII .303.1:2 be still with me while Heaven's S. is born.
W-pII .303.2:1 *Your S. is welcome, Father. He has come to*
W-pII .303.2:5 *He is the S. You love above all things. He is*
W-pII .303.2:8 *Safe in Your Arms let me receive Your S..*
W-pII .304.2:3 *my Father, given me to offer to Your holy S.,*
W-pII .304.2:3 *of You, and of Your S. as You created him.*
W-pII .306.2:3 *make an offering sufficient for Your S.. But*
W-pII .307.1:5 *Your S. is one with You in being and in will,*
W-pII .309.1:2 I, His S., whose will is limitless as is His
W-pII .310.1:3 *hours, for it comes from Heaven to Your S..*
W-pII .310.1:4 *You, Your gracious calling to Your holy S.,*
W-pII ...10.1:1 Christ's Second Coming gives the S. of
W-pII ...10.2:6 away, because the S. of God is limitless.
W-pII ...10.4:1 step in His appointed plan to bless His S.,
W-pII ...10.4:3 the S. whom God acknowledges as His. Be
W-pII ...10.5:1 Final Judgment: "You are still My holy S.,
W-pII ...10.5:3 Me. I am your Father and you are My S.."
W-pII .311.1:6 by giving us God's Judgment of His S..
W-pII .311.2:1 *to hear Your Judgment of the S. You love.*
W-pII .311.2:3 *he whom You created as Your S. must be.*
W-pII .313.1:6 *undefiled upon the altar to Your holy S., the*
W-pII .315.2:1 *me today and every day from every S. of God*
W-pII .317.2:5 *which You have promised to Your S., who*
W-pII .318.1:1 In me, God's holy S., are reconciled all
W-pII .318.1:4 I am the means by which God's S. is saved
W-pII .318.1:7 I am God's S., His one eternal Love. I am
W-pII .320.1:1 The S. of God is limitless. There are no
W-pII .320.2:3 *And so all power has been given to Your S..*
W-pII ...11.2:3 Thus His S. shares in creation, and must
W-pII ...11.3:2 Creation is the holy S. of God, for in
W-pII .321.1:6 *freedom as Your holy S. will not be lost to me*
W-pII .322.1:4 to conceal the Self which is God's only S.,
W-pII .323.1:1 *only "sacrifice" You ask of Your beloved S.;*
W-pII .325.1:6 forth, with mercy for the holy S. of God,
W-pII .326.1:5 *because it is Your Will to have a S. so like his*
W-pII .326.1:8 *thoughts unite in glory as the S. of God.*
W-pII .330.2:1 *Father, Your S. can not be hurt. And if we*
W-pII ...12.3:1 The S. of God is egoless. What can he
W-pII ...12.4:2 that crucifixion of the S. of God is offered
W-pII ...12.5:2 holy minds which God created as His S.,
W-pII .331.1:1 *believe Your S. could cause himself to suffer!*
W-pII .333.2:4 *anything, being Your gift to Your beloved S..*
W-pII .334.2:2 *S. can be content with nothing less than this.*
W-pII .335.2:3 *in Your S. I find the memory of You as well.*
W-pII .337.1:6 to understand my Father loves His S.; to
W-pII .337.1:6 Son; to know I am the S. my Father loves.
W-pII .338.1:7 God has planned that His beloved S. will
W-pII .338.2:5 *because it holds Your promise to Your S..*
W-pII .340.1:2 *is holy, for today Your S. will be redeemed.*
W-pII .340.1:6 *for Your holy S. and for the world he made,*
W-pII .340.2:4 Our Father has redeemed His S. this day.
W-pII .341.1:1 *Father, Your S. is holy. I am he on whom*
W-pII .341.1:3 *the Lord of Sinlessness conceives us as His S.*
W-pII .342.1:8 *it is. Let me remember that I am Your S., and*
W-pII .343.1:9 *Your S. can make no sacrifice, for he must be*
W-pII343.1:10 *I am complete because I am Your S.. I cannot*
W-pII .344.1:9 *And thus Your S. arises and returns to You.*
W-pII .344.2:3 sin, and the redemption of the S. of God.
W-pII .345.1:1 *a miracle reflects Your gifts to me, Your S..*
W-pII .346.1:7 *find the peace which You created for Your S.*
W-pII .347.2:2 that He has judged you as the S. He loves.
W-pII .350.1:2 *The S. of God incorporates all things within*
W-pII .350.2:2 His S. will be restored to us in the reality
W-pII ...14.1:1 *I am God's S., complete and healed and*
W-pII ...14.5:3 We bring glad tidings to the S. of God,
W-pII .351.1:1 *Who is my brother but Your holy S.? And if I*
W-pII .351.1:2 *I proclaim myself a sinner, not a S. of God;*
W-pII .351.1:4 *also see my brother sinless, as Your holy S..*
W-pII .354.1:1 *with the Christ establishes me as Your S.,*
W-pII .354.1:6 *is Christ except Your S. as You created Him?*
W-pII .355.1:2 *keep Your Word You gave Your S. in exile. I*
W-pII .355.1:8 *Your S. would be Himself, and know You as*
W-pII .356.1:1 *answer any call Your S. might make to You.*
W-pII .356.1:3 *He is Your S., and You will answer him. The*
W-pII .356.1:6 *Your Name gives answer to Your S., because*
W-pII .357.1:2 *Your holy S. is pointed out to me, first in my*
W-pII .357.1:4 *And as I look upon Your S. today, I hear Your*
W-pII .358.1:6 *care, keeping Your promise to Your S. in my*
W-pII ....360.h Peace be to me, the holy S. of God. Peace
W-pII .360.1:2 *I am Your S., forever just as You created me,*
W-pII .360.1:6 *Your S. is like to You in perfect sinlessness.*
Wfl........in.5:1 the gift our Father promised to His holy S.
Wfl........in.6:2 Would He hurt His S.? Or would He rush
Wfl........in.6:3 to answer him, and say, "This is My S.,
WpII361-5.1:5 speaks for God my Father and His holy S..
W-ep......... 6:4 He loves God's S. as we would love him.
M-1........... 3:5 theme is always, "God's S. is guiltless, and
M-2........... 2:6 separation entered the mind of God's S.,
M-3........... 1:2 can look upon the S. of God as sinless.
M-3........... 4:7 holy. God is not mistaken in His S..
M-4......II.2:10 and for the S. of God and his Creator.
M-4...... IV.2:8 neither from God's S. nor his Creator.
M-4... VII.2:10 that are of God, and therefore for His S..
M-4...... IX.2:8 Word of God and His definition of His S..
M-4........X.1:4 condemnation judges the S. of God as evil
M-4........X.3:1 things that are the S. of God's inheritance.

M-5 I.1:7 for placing God's S. on his Father's throne
M-5 I.1:9 His death can He be conquered by His S..
M-5 I.2:2 symbolizes the defeat of God's S. and the
M-5 I.2:3 which the S. of God is forced to recognize.
M-5 III.2:5 forgiveness for God's S. in his own Name.
M-5 III.2:11 away from death: "Behold, you S. of God,
M-5 III.3:3 himself as to believe God's S. can suffer.
M-10 2:9 is, and it is only one: "God's S. is guiltless,
M-12 1:3 becomes the Self Who is the S. of God. He
M-12 2:1 does the son of man become the S. of God
M-13 6:2 hold dear the things that crucify God's S.,
M-13 8:12 What other way is there to save His S.?
M-15 1:10 may hear this Judgment of the S. of God:
M-16 8:7 because it is not enough for God's S..
M-17 2:10 is his judgment upon the holy S. of God.
M-18 2:3 now speak of the reality of the S. of God.
M-19 1:8 If God's S. were fairly judged, there would
M-21 3:7 sleeping S. of God has but this power left
M-22 7:4 it is not up to them to judge His S.. And to
M-22 7:5 And to judge His S. is to limit his Father.
M-22 7:8 he withdraws his judgment from the S. of
M-22 7:10 he say with God, "This is my beloved S.,
M-23 2:4 He has become the risen S. of God. He has
M-23 3:3 of the S. to the Father lies in him. His part
M-23 3:8 Can God fail His S.? And can one who is
M-26 1:1 is no distance between Him and His S..
M-27 3:4 holds an image of the S. of God in which
M-27 5:1 rooted in the belief that God's S. is a body
M-27 7:8 the S. of God is guiltless now and forever.
M-28 1:10 is the single desire of the S. for the Father.
M-28 4:3 The S. of God is free. And in his freedom
M-28 6:6 the truth about the holy S. of God. He is
M-29 6:11 than this does your Father love His S.?
M-29 7:10 God knows but His S., and as he was
M-29 8:4 *You are the S. He loves, And it is given you to*
C-1 1:4 unified spirit is God's one S., or Christ.
C-2 2:4 God's S. as He created him abide in form
C-2 6:14 there was crucifixion stands God's S..
C-3 3:2 knows what His S. needs before he asks.
C-3 7:7 It is the gift of God to save His S.. But look
C-3 8:4 the joining of the Father and the S., the
C-3 8:6 His S. is not attacked but recognized.
C-4 6:2 For there the altar to the S. is set, and
C-4 7:4 light upon the altar to the S. of God. God
C-5 1:8 He creates all Helpers of His S. while he
C-5 3:1 with the Christ–the perfect S. of God,
C-5 3:5 that it is impossible to kill God's S.; nor
C-5 6:9 *death because the S. of God is like his Father.*
C-5 6:11 *instead to share the resurrection of God's S..*
C-6 1:1 Christ, the S. of God as He created Him.
C-6 1:5 alone knows along with Christ, His real S.
C-6 3:7 He never forgets the S. of God. He never
C-6 5:3 of God's S. for he alone is functionless.
C-ep 5:4 God is welcomed and His S. with Him.
C-ep 5:6 us. The S. is still, and in the quiet God has
P-2 IV.1:2 It is a judgment on the S. of God, and
P-2 IV.2:1 Once God's S. is seen as guilty, illness
P-2 V.5:5 sacred calling of God's holy S. for help in
P-2 V.5:6 a hand to reach His S. and touch his heart
P-2 V.5:8 of God Himself, by which His S. is saved.
P-2 V.6:7 can serve His S. in all his present needs.
P-2 V.7:8 the veil of guilt that shrouds the S. of God
P-2 V.8:7 There is no other way to seek His S..
P-2 V.8:9 S. of God returns to Heaven through its
P-2 VII.1:12 What He knows is only that He has one S.
P-2 VII.7:1 not afraid to offer weakness to God's S..
P-2 VII.9:2 and so you will not know you are His S..
P-3 I.2:8 Would God send His S. to you and not be
P-3 I.4:7 Let him not betray the S. of God. Who
P-3 II.4:7 the way God chose for the return of His S.
P-3 II.5:4 the relationship of the Father and the S..
P-3 III.3:7 if it does, it merely crucifies God's S. again
P-3 III.5:11 Where God's S. turns against himself, he
P-3 III.8:13 *And then God sent His S. to give it to you.*
S-1 in.1:1 which God blessed His S. at his creation.
S-1 in.1:2 share; the song the S. sings to the Father,
S-1 in.1:2 the thanks it offers Him unto the S..
S-1 in.1:5 gives thanks to His extension in His S..
S-1 in.1:6 His S. gives thanks for his creation, in the
S-1 in.2:4 which God's S. leaves separate goals and
S-1 in.3:1 down your dreams, you holy S. of God,
S-1 I.6:7 Him. He can therefore also reach His S.,
S-1 II.2:1 never be made by a S. of God who knows
S-1 II.5:6 it acknowledges the S. of God as he was
S-1 II.7:7 is the gift of God to you, His S., prayer can
S-1 II.8:8 if peace is to be restored to God's S., who
S-1 III.5:7 He is a S. of God, along with you. He is no
S-1 V.2:6 where it gladly joins with every S. of God,
S-1 V.3:2 how to understand your glory as God's S.,
S-2 I.2:6 that would destroy the holy S. He loves.
S-2 I.3:7 He loves His S.. Can you remember Him
S-2 I.3:9 hate his Father if you hate the S. He loves.
S-2 I.3:10 For as you see the S. you see yourself, and
S-2 I.8:3 God calls on you to save His S. from death
S-2 II.2:4 sin, and yet perceive him as the S. of God?
S-2 II.3:6 S. condemn himself and still remember
S-2 II.4:1 is to separate from God the S. He loves,
S-2 II.6:10 try to strike a bargain with the S. of God,
S-2 III.5:1 Your holy S.?" should be the only thing
S-2 III.5:3 which forgiveness comes to save God's S..
S-2 III.7:8 the door; the S. of God as He created him.
S-3 I.1:3 that injure and would hurt the S. of God.
S-3 I.2:1 cause is unforgiveness of the S. of God. It
S-3 I.3:4 brother, and the S. of God upon himself.
S-3 I.4:1 he has done now must God's S. undo. But
S-3 I.4:5 Voice He still can reach His S., reminding
S-3 II.2:1 to help the S. of God along the way he
S-3 II.6:2 to take its vengeance on the S. of God. Yet
S-3 II.6:4 gate of Heaven opens and God's S. is free
S-3 III.1:8 to obscure the unity that is the S. of God.
S-3 IV.3:3 of healing is Himself, His Love, His S.,
S-3 IV.3:9 Do not forget forgiveness of God's S..
S-3 IV.4:6 and no desire to attack the S. of God.
S-3 IV.5:1 forget this; it is you who are God's S., and
S-3 IV.7:2 I would recall My weary S. to Me from
S-3 IV.7:3 My Arms are open to the S. I love, who
S-3 IV.8:5 Return to Me Who never left My S..
S-3 IV.9:3 brow of him who is the holy S. of God
S-3 IV.9:7 healed My S. and took him from the cross

## son 20

*Son*

T-6 I.15:5 "Betrayest thou the S. of man with a kiss?"
T-8 VI.4:1 Listen to the story of the prodigal s., and
T-8 VI.4:1 This s. of a loving father left his home and
T-8 VI.4:3 the s. himself *was* his father's treasure. He
T-13 II.9:7 redeemed s. of man is the guiltless Son of
T-21 II.10:4 creator, and be father and not s. to him.
T-24 VII.1:7 This is your s., beloved of you as you are
T-24 VII.1:8 place of your creations, who *are* s. to you,
T-24 VII.1:9 s. that you have made to be your strength
T-24 VII.1:12 another s. whom he prefers to them?
T-24 VII.10:6 whispers, "Here is my own beloved s., in
T-24 VII.10:7 Thus does the "s." become the means to
T-24 VII.11:2 outside yourself, your own beloved s.. The
T-24 VII.11:8 The s. of man perceives an alien will and
T-25 in.2:6 The s. of man is not the risen Christ. Yet
W-pI 183.1:3 A father gives his s. his name, and thus
W-pI 183.1:3 name, and thus identifies the s. with him.
Wfl in.5:7 a father angry at his s. because he failed to
M-12 2:1 does the s. of man become the Son of God
M-17 7:10 An angry father pursues his guilty s.. Kill

## Son's 24

T-2 I.2:7 the S. creations when his mind is healed.
T-4 VII.6:6 and its experience of His S. experience.
T-8 VI.7:7 make the S. function unknown to him,
T-10 V.10:7 That was the condition of His S. creation,
T-11 I.9:9 for His Son, and His S. will for himself.
T-13 XI.2:1 His S. imagined "enemy" is totally unreal.
T-14 VIII.3:7 glory and His S. belong to you in truth.
T-14 XI.11:3 God proclaim His Oneness and His S..
T-15 III.7:5 and beyond everyone to His S. creations,
T-15 XI.8:5 us in the celebration of His S. creation.
T-21 II.12:1 The S. creations are like his Father's. Yet
T-23 II.6:6 He must accept His S. belief in what he is,
T-23 IV.2:5 it is not the body that is like the S. Creator
T-23 IV.3:5 and what is His must be His S. as well.
T-24 VII.10:10 For as His S. creation gave Him joy and
T-25 III.2:4 His S. belief He could not let Himself be
T-25 III.2:5 could not enter His S. insanity with him,
T-25 IX.2:8 fight against His S. reluctance to perceive
T-26 VII.18:2 all His S. mistakes and set him free. But it
T-28 III.6:4 and bridge His S. returning to Himself.
W-pI 160.7:7 between His knowledge and His S. reality.
W-pI 190.2:3 to the S. mistakes in what he thinks he is.
W-pII 238.1:3 *You placed Your S. salvation in my hands,*
W-pII 308.2:3 *time You have appointed for Your S. release,*

## song 57

T-13 VI.8:7 voice has a part in the s. of redemption,
T-17 V.1:7 so is the holy relationship a happy s. of
T-17 V.10:1 the Sonship is the s. of freedom heard, in
T-20 II.8:10 The s. of Easter is the glad refrain the Son
T-21 I.h The Forgotten S.
T-21 I.6:1 like a s. whose name is long forgotten,
T-21 I.6:2 Not the whole s. has stayed with you, but
T-21 I.6:3 just this little part, how lovely was the s.,
T-21 I.7:5 and see if you remember an ancient s. you
T-21 I.9:5 You know the ancient s., and know it well
T-21 I.10:1 for that same s. they sing in honor of their
T-21 I.10:2 will not withstand the memory of this s..
T-21 IV.7:2 the s. it longed to hear since first the ego
T-21 IV.7:4 The s. of freedom, which sings the praises
T-24 II.4:5 And that vast s. of honor and of love for
T-24 V.7:8 The s. of Christ is all there is to hear. The
T-26 I.4:9 his s. of union and of love be heard at all.
T-26 I.4:10 to make the world recede before his s.,
T-26 I.6:3 then, the s. your brother sings to you, and
T-26 I.6:4 will hear no s. of liberation for yourself,
T-26 IV.3:5 What is Heaven but a s. of gratitude and
T-26 IV.5:1 and sing their s. of gratitude and praise.
T-26 IV.5:3 For no one hears the s. of Heaven and
T-26 IV.5:3 a voice that adds its power to the s., and
T-26 IV.5:5 magnitude of s. in which the universe has
T-26 V.2:5 hand and keeping step to Heaven's s., is
T-26 V.5:4 not one note in Heaven's s. was missed.
T-29 IX.8:5 so close the s. of Heaven can be heard, not
T-29 IX.8:6 God. And when he hears this s. again, he
T-31 VIII.10:7 Salvation's s. will echo through the world
T-31 VIII.11:5 s. of thanks from earth to Heaven grows
W-pI 123.4:2 We sing the s. of thankfulness today, in
W-pI 164.1:6 beyond them all He hears the s. of Heaven
W-pI 196.9:1 Salvation's s. can certainly be heard in
W-pI 198.6:5 His words have heard the s. of Heaven.
W-pII 2.5:2 The s. of our rejoicing is the call to all the
W-pII 310.2:2 And all the world joins with us in our s. of
M-4 V.1:12 Joy is their s. of thanks. And Christ looks
M-28 4:8 s. of Heaven sounds around the world, as
C-2 8:3 Is not a s. like this what you would hear?
C-ep 4:6 s. begins again which had been stopped
P-2 VI.2:1 to hear this s. of death only an instant,
P-2 VI.2:4 of the s. of condemnation must arise. The
P-2 VI.2:6 of the universe," "the herald angel's s.,"
P-2 VI.7:2 joyous s. salvation sings to all who hear
S-1 in.1:2 share; the s. the Son sings to the Father,
S-1 in.1:6 the s. of his creating in his Father's Name.
S-1 in.3:2 s. that reaches higher and then higher still
S-1 I.2:9 is always a s. of thanksgiving and of Love.
S-1 I.3:2 It is the s. that is the gift. Along with it
S-1 I.3:4 In true prayer you hear only the s.. All the
S-1 I.7:3 It is a s. of thanksgiving for what you are.
S-1 II.7:8 it rises as a s. of thanks to your Creator,
S-2 I.8:6 s. that all creation sings unto its God.
S-3 IV.1:10 join the s. of prayer in which the healed
S-3 IV.8:3 s. is part of the eternal harmony of love.
S-3 IV.10:2 The s. of prayer is silent without you. The

## songs 1

W-pI 50.2:3 They are s. of praise to the ego. Do not

## Sons 79

*sons*

| | |
|---|---|
| T-1 V.3:1 | talents will be shared by all the S. of God. |
| T-1 V.3:5 | The specialness of God's S. does not stem |
| T-1 VII.5:2 | in connection with the S. of God, because |
| T-2 II.7:2 | mistake all the separated S. of God make |
| T-2 III.5:11 | God is lonely without His S., and they are |
| T-2 VII.6:2 | If all His creations are His S., every one |
| T-3 I.1:5 | of His S. to suffer because he was good. |
| T-3 III.6:1 | His altars, which He established in His S.. |
| T-3 III.6:3 | God is not a stranger to His S., and His |
| T-3 III.6:3 | and His S. are not strangers to each other. |
| T-5 I.5:7 | Holy Spirit will remain with the S. of God, |
| T-5 II.2:2 | God blessed the minds of His separated S. |
| T-5 II.3:11 | and God's S. are as equal as learners as |
| T-5 II.3:11 | are as equal as learners as they are as S.. |
| T-5 IV.8:14 | His quiet children are His blessed S.. The |
| T-5 VI.1:2 | wait. All the S. of God are waiting for your |
| T-6 I.3:4 | of some of the S. of God upon another. |
| T-6 I.11:7 | with God that none of His S. should suffer |
| T-6 I.16:4 | for sins, and the S. of God are not sinners. |
| T-6 I.18:1 | of the S. of God is present all the time, |
| T-6 I.19:1 | God the Father and His separated S.. If |
| T-6 II.8:1 | created His S. by extending His Thought, |
| T-6 V.A.4:7 | gift can be offered to the equal S. of God, |
| T-7 I.3:2 | of God, as your sons are part of His S.. To |
| T-7 II.3:6 | God and His S., in the surety of being, |
| T-7 II.3:9 | And His S., who create like Him, follow it |
| T-7 II.5:5 | the use of truth to convince His S. of truth |
| T-7 III.3:3 | Because God's equal S. have everything, |
| T-7 V.11:5 | acceptable to Him and therefore to His S.. |
| T-7 VII.5:8 | only honor to the S. of the living God, and |
| T-7 VII.6:2 | His beloved S. in whom He is well pleased |
| T-7 VII.10:7 | is lonely when His S. do'not know Him. |
| T-7 VII.11:5 | because they belong to His beloved S., |
| T-7 IX.6:1 | increase the inheritance of the S. of God, |
| T-7 XI.7:10 | God includes all His S. and their children, |
| T-7 XI.7:10 | are as like the S. as they are like the Father |
| T-7 XI.7:11 | Know, then, the S. of God, and you will |
| T-8 III.4:6 | Whenever two S. of God meet, they are |
| T-8 IV.5:10 | not so the S. of God would be unequal. All |
| T-8 IV.6:7 | perfect equality of all God's S. cannot be |
| T-8 IV.6:8 | God's S. are equal in will, all being the |
| T-8 IV.7:10 | of freedom, which is His Will for all His S. |
| T-8 IV.8:1 | is the only gift you can offer to God's S., |
| T-8 V.3:5 | be to the union of God and His holy S.! |
| T-8 VI.2:1 | and the glory of God and His holy S., but |
| T-8 VI.2:1 | blind the S. to the Father if they behold it. |
| T-8 VI.3:3 | What God and His S. create is eternal, |
| T-8 VI.7:5 | does not contradict Himself, and His S., |
| T-8 VI.8:8 | we are, and we are the S. of God Himself, |
| T-8 VI.9:4 | God has joined all His S. with Himself. |
| T-8 VII.2:2 | Link between God and His separated S., |
| T-9 II.6:11 | except as He answers all of God's S.? Hear |
| T-9 II.8:7 | Hear only God's Answer in His S., and |
| T-10 III.1:8 | worshippers are the S. of God in sickness. |
| T-10 V.13:6 | sick images you perceive are the S. of God |
| T-11 VI.10:5 | because all of God's S. are of equal value, |
| T-11 VIII.8:5 | God's S. have nothing they do not share. |
| T-13 X.11:1 | S. unless you love them all and equally. |
| T-15 VI.6:10 | the only need the S. of God share equally, |
| T-26 VII.19:5 | is no difference among the S. of God. The |
| T-29 VIII.9:1 | God has not many S., but only One. Who |
| T-31 VIII.10:1 | who are my brothers as they are Your S.. |
| W-pII in.9:7 | and we who are God's S. are safely home, |
| W-pII .240.1:7 | We are the S. of God. There is no fear in |
| W-pII .247.2:2 | *My brothers are Your S.. Your Fatherhood* |
| W-pII .255.1:6 | as mine, and giving it to all my Father's S., |
| W-pII .260.2:3 | And we who are His S. are like each other, |
| W-pII .263.2:2 | house as brothers and the holy S. of God. |
| W-pII .266.1:1 | *Father, You gave me all Your S., to be my* |
| W-pII .272.2:2 | and ask ourselves if we, the S. of God, |
| W-pII .300.2:2 | *For we, Your loving S., have lost our way a* |
| W-pII 9.4:3 | in which the S. of God acknowledge that |
| W-pII 11.4:1 | We are creation; we the S. of God. We |
| W-pII .359.1:3 | *have not made sinners of the holy S. of God.* |
| M-4 2:1 | All differences among the S. of God are |
| C-1 2:1 | split, the S. of God appear to be separate. |
| C-6 3:1 | Link between God and His separated S.. |
| S-2 I.6:3 | God Himself has given all His S. a remedy |
| S-3 III.5:1 | are S. of God who recognize their Source, |

## sons 3

*Sons*

| | |
|---|---|
| T-7 I.3:2 | of God, as your s. are part of His Sons. To |
| T-24 II.3:5 | His "special" s. are many, never one, each |
| T-24 VII.11:1 | thus are two s. made, and both appear to |

## Sonship 104

| | |
|---|---|
| T-1 I.19:2 | the S. is the sum of all that God created. |
| T-1 II.4:6 | brothers has placed me in charge of the S. |
| T-1 II.6:2 | S. appears to involve almost endless time. |
| T-1 V.2:6 | individual contributions to the S. will no |
| T-1 V.3:8 | occurs the whole family of God, or the S., |
| T-1 V.4:6 | Miracles are affirmations of S., which is a |
| T-1 VII.3:14 | Complete restoration of the S. is the only |
| T-2 II.5:7 | into closer and closer accord with the S.; |
| T-2 II.5:7 | but the S. itself is a perfect creation and |
| T-2 VII.6:2 | must be an integral part of the whole S.. |
| T-2 VII.6:3 | The S. in its Oneness transcends the sum |
| T-2 VII.6:5 | until all the parts of the S. have returned. |
| T-2 VII.6:7 | Any part of the S. can believe in error or |
| T-3 II.4:6 | the Will of the S. and the Father are One, |
| T-4 VI.2:4 | much you are indebted to the whole S., |
| T-4 VI.8:3 | who disengage themselves from the S., |
| T-5 in.2:6 | what part of the S. the healing is offered. |
| T-5 in.3:4 | it radiates throughout the S. and returns |
| T-5 I.1:2 | to every part of the S. to rejoice with them |
| T-5 I.5:5 | Atonement is complete and the whole S. |
| T-5 I.7:1 | Spirit, the shared Inspiration of all the S., |
| T-5 II.10:8 | the Holy Spirit, or the S. cannot be as One |
| T-5 II.11:2 | increase its power to attract the whole S., |
| T-5 III.8:2 | apart from your rightful place in the S., |
| T-5 III.8:2 | and the rightful place of the S. is God. |
| T-5 IV.1:9 | and the union of the S. is its protection. |
| T-5 IV.1:10 | the Kingdom because the S. is united. In |
| T-5 IV.2:13 | If you are part of God and the S. is One, |
| T-5 IV.3:1 | in any part of the S. belongs to every part. |
| T-5 IV.7:4 | The joint will of the S. is the only creator |
| T-5 VI.11:7 | towards the S. in the Name of its Creator. |
| T-6 I.2:6 | the last useless journey the S. need take, |
| T-6 I.12:1 | to enable the S. to know its Wholeness. |
| T-6 I.15:8 | of God, as much a part of the S. as myself. |
| T-6 V.1:7 | the S. does not communicate with Him as |
| T-6 V.C.8:1 | To teach the whole S. without exception |
| T-7 I.2:6 | He created the S. and you increase it. You |
| T-7 IV.5:5 | the only way of perceiving the S. as one. |
| T-7 IV.7:10 | It comes freely to all the S., being what |
| T-7 IV.7:10 | to all the Sonship, being what the S. is. By |
| T-7 V.11:4 | shine back upon you and on the whole S., |
| T-7 V.11:5 | God. He will accept it and give it to the S., |
| T-7 V.11:7 | You can appreciate the S. only as one. |
| T-7 VI.1:1 | Although you can love the S. only as one, |
| T-7 VI.4:12 | And if it recognized any part of the S., it |
| T-7 VI.13:7 | the S. can only accomplish perfectly, |
| T-7 VII.1:2 | impossible to deny part of the S. as it is to |
| T-7 VII.3:7 | All illusions about the S. are dispelled |
| T-7 VII.3:10 | will last until the S. knows itself as whole. |
| T-7 VIII.5:6 | your mind and from the S. as a whole. |
| T-7 IX.1:3 | Do not withhold your gifts to the S., or |
| T-7 IX.2:2 | power of the whole S. and of its Creator is |
| T-7 IX.5:3 | being created for the S. as a whole. |
| T-7 XI.4:3 | has healed the S. and given thanks to God |
| T-7 XI.6:4 | that only the whole S. is worthy to be co- |
| T-7 XI.6:4 | only the whole S. can create like Him. |
| T-8 III.7:8 | thought any part of the S. holds. Wrong |
| T-8 IV.3:1 | was done completely by any part of the S. |
| T-8 IV.3:4 | will of the S. with the Will of the Father |
| T-8 V.h | The Undivided Will of the S. |
| T-8 V.2:1 | will of the S. is the perfect creator, being |
| T-8 VI.1:1 | We are the joint will of the S., whose |
| T-8 VII.4:5 | Spirit to use on behalf of union of the S., |
| T-9 VI.4:4 | Because the S. must create as one, you |
| T-9 VI.5:5 | S. comes together and accepts its Oneness |
| T-10 III.2:2 | not matter where in the S. He is accepted. |
| T-10 III.2:3 | of Him awakens throughout the S.. Heal |
| T-10 IV.3:1 | The S. cannot be perceived as partly sick, |
| T-10 IV.3:2 | If the S. is One, it is One in all respects. |
| T-10 V.7:4 | He calls to you from every part of the S., |
| T-10 V.12:6 | And as part of the S., that is how you |
| T-11 I.1:2 | Would you bring anything else to the S., |
| T-11 II.2:6 | denial of God's Fatherhood and of your S. |
| T-11 III.8:1 | you can accept the whole S. and bless it |
| T-11 IV.1:1 | Never forget that the S. is your salvation, |
| T-11 IV.1:1 | is your salvation, for the S. is your Self. As |
| T-11 IV.8:4 | in God, and in whom the whole S. rests. |
| T-11 VI.10:2 | Bring only this awareness to the S., and |
| T-12 II.2:5 | You can remember this for all the S.. Do |
| T-12 IV.6:8 | can be no disinherited parts of the S., for |
| T-13 VI.6:4 | extends to all aspects of the S. at the same |
| T-13 X.11:3 | you single out part of the S. for your love, |
| T-14 III.9:5 | Every decision is made for the whole S., |
| T-15 V.2:2 | to part of the S. is to bring guilt into your |
| T-15 V.3:5 | of the S. can give you more than others? |
| T-15 V.10:2 | In the holy instant the S. gains as one, |
| T-15 V.10:10 | For Christ is the Self the S. shares, as God |
| T-15 VIII.4:1 | an instant on this: God gave the S. to you, |
| T-16 I.7:8 | you give through Him is for the whole S., |
| T-16 II.1:6 | the miracle extends to all the S. when you |
| T-16 II.4:3 | awareness of the S. as One has been made |
| T-16 III.3:1 | you that you do not perceive the S. as one |
| T-16 V.2:2 | as guilty, leaving the S. open to attack and |
| T-17 V.10:1 | Throughout the S. is the song of freedom |
| T-17 V.10:7 | in which all the S. is together blessed. |
| T-17 V.14:9 | share the gladness of the S. that it is so. |
| T-17 V.15:2 | have also learned how to release all the S., |
| T-18 I.1:3 | renouncing one aspect of the S. in favor of |
| T-18 I.11:1 | to all the S. through your relationship, for |
| T-18 I.11:1 | your relationship, for in it lies the S., |
| T-18 I.13:2 | of the S. with healing and uniting comfort |
| T-19 IV.1:1 | to embrace all the S. and give it rest, it |
| T-22 VI.4:8 | healing is the S. healed *because* your will |
| M-23 3:4 | His part in the S. is also yours, and his |

## soon 29

| | |
|---|---|
| T-2 VI.2:9 | is controlled by me automatically as s. as |
| T-2 VI.6:4 | no strain in doing God's Will as s. as you |
| T-2 VI.8:8 | However, as s. as you accept the remedy, |
| T-2 VII.7:4 | As s. as a state of readiness occurs, there |
| T-5 V.4:11 | because, as s. as you regard sin as a lack, |
| T-9 VII.4:6 | The ego will attack your motives as s. as |
| T-15 XI.10:1 | will s. be born from the time of Christ. I |
| T-16 III.8:3 | which carries him across the gap as s. as |
| T-16 VI.8:8 | and you would s. recognize the guilt of |
| T19 IV.D.10:1 | Nor is it possible to look on this too s.. |
| T-20 III.11:1 | given me the certainty our union will be s. |
| T-26 V.5:1 | passed away in Heaven too s. for anything |
| T-26 VII.2:3 | For it is gone as s. as the idea that brought |
| T-27 I.7:3 | For who could live a life so s. cut short |
| W-pI 41.6:2 | morning, as s. as you get up if possible, sit |
| W-pI 42.3:1 | today, one as s. as possible after you wake |
| W-pI 44.9:3 | exercises with eyes closed as s. as possible |
| W-pI 95.7:3 | not to return to it again as s. as you can. |
| WpI..rIII.in4:1 | should be done as s. as you have changed |
| W-pI 194.9:4 | it will be s. replaced by love's reflection. |
| W-pI 196.11:5 | Pray that the instant may be s., –today. |
| W-pII 4.5:3 | How s. will you be ready to come home? |
| W-pII 9.5:1 | Pray that the Second Coming will be s., |
| M-2 1:1 | for him as s. as he has answered the Call. |
| M-15 3:10 | It is your function to make that end be s.. |
| M-16 4:3 | to spend time with God as s. as possible, |
| M-16 4:7 | s. as possible after waking take your quiet |
| C-in 5:2 | Afterwards and s., it drops away to make |
| S-3 IV.8:1 | ends so s. it might as well have never been |

## sooner 7

| | |
|---|---|
| T-3 IV.7:14 | are merely those who choose right s.. |
| T-16 III.8:2 | S. or later must everyone bridge the gap |
| W-pI 41.8:5 | and s. or later it is always successful. We |
| W-pI 157.6:3 | may come the s. to the same experience in |
| W-pI 184.7:3 | But the s. he perceives on what it rests, |
| W-pI 184.7:3 | results, the s. does he question its effects. |
| P-3 II.3:6 | S. or later that something will rise and |

**soothes** 1

W-pI...122.2:3 It s. your forehead while you sleep, and

**sorrow** 44

T-5.........in.1:5 joy. Radiance is not associated with s.. Joy
T-13.......in.2:6 they learn of s. and separation and death.
T-13...VII.17:4 sound of it will banish s. from the mind of
T-13...VII.17:5 establish its eternal reign where s. dwells.
T-14....... II.8:8 he sing the dirge of s. when this is true?
T-15...... III.5:3 this, and invites s. or joy accordingly.
T-17... VIII.4:5 else" produced was s. and depression,
T-20...... III.4:7 they look out in s. from what is sad within
T-22....... II.3:6 Joy does not turn to s., for the eternal
T-22....... II.3:7 But s. can be turned to joy, for time gives
T-23......IV.8:3 S. of any kind is inconceivable. Only the
T-27......VI.7:3 because the suffering and s. of the world
T-27. VIII.11:4 the cause of every form of s. and of pain.
T-31.... VIII.8:4 forget the pain and s. that you saw before.
W-pI.....20.2:6 you cannot distinguish between joy and s.
W-pI.....38.2:4 then, can remove all pain, can end all s.,
W-pI.....41.3:2 will cure all s. and pain and fear and loss
W-pI.....47.2:2 fear, anxiety, depression, anger and s..
W-pI...100.4:3 joyous, and their joy heals s. and despair.
W-pI...100.6:3 Son, and wills no s. rises to abate his joy;
W-pI...109.1:3 we seem to look on danger and on s.. And
W-pI...110.5:6 you. This is the Word in which all s. ends.
W-pI...133.2:2 as valued by the world, you ask for s., not
W-pI.135.19:1 a future undisturbed, without a trace of s.
W-pI...137.9:1 glad exchange of all the world of s. for a
W-pI.166.13:6 Let s. not tempt you to be unfaithful to
W-pI...167.2:6 All s., loss, anxiety and suffering and pain
W-pI...185.1:3 no further s. possible for you in any form;
W-pI.186.13:2 comfort you, although He knows no s..
W-pI...190.8:5 s. rules and little joys give way before the
W-pI...194.3:2 no one instant s. can be set upon a throne
W-pI...195.1:7 of s. disappear throughout the world.
W-pI...207.1:3 *but turn to Him, and every s. melts away, as I*
W-pII.....in.6:2 of s. in exchange for its replacement,
W-pII......2.4:3 It is a dream in which there is no s., for it
W-pII......8.2:4 There are no cries of pain and s. heard,
W-pII..300.1:1 s. are the certain lot of all who come here,
W-pII....10.4:3 For it alone can heal all s., wipe away all
W-pII....12.3:3 What can he know of s. and of suffering,
M-14..........5:1 will end in joy, because it is a place of s..
M-15........1:12 *Where is the world, and where is s. now?*
M-28..........2:7 There is no s. still upon the earth. The joy
P-2........IV.1:6 be except an expression of s. and of guilt?
S-3........IV.8:3 wait in s. Heaven's melody is incomplete,

**sorrowful** 3

T-22......IV.4:4 now for you, will you now open to the s..
W-pI...183.3:5 The s. cast off their mourning, and the
P-3........III.8:9 Remember the s. story of the world, and

**sorrows** 6

W-pI...100.4:2 on earth calls to all minds to let their s. go
W-pI...132.3:4 pain and tears, and all your s. press on it,
W-pI...164.3:3 sins forgot, and all your s. unremembered
W-pII..241.1:4 come when s. pass away and pain is gone.
W-pII..317.2:5 *And all my s. end in Your embrace, which*
W-pII.....352.h From one Come all the s. of the world.

**sorry** 13

T-6...........I.8:1 I am s. when my brothers do not share
T-18... VIII.7:5 within your tiny kingdom, a s. king, a
T-21.....VII.2:8 They are indeed a s. army, each one as
T-27.........I.4:4 This sick and s. picture *you* accept, if only
T-30...... I.13:3 s. dream of judgment has forever been
T-31.....VII.2:3 to shake your s. concept of yourself and
W-pI.....97.8:4 and escape its s. consequences if you yield
W-pI...131.7:4 and earth the other's s. outcome which is
W-pI...166.6:1 He seems a s. figure; weary, worn, in
M-16..........8:6 magic is a s. substitute for true assistance.
S-2........III.4:2 God did not choose this s. path for you.
S-3........IV.3:6 you for shifting dreams within a s. world?
S-3........IV.6:6 prayer beyond the s. reaches of the world.

**sort** 6

T-4........ III.3:3 ego must offer you some s. of reward for
T-9...........I.4:2 s. out the true from the false in your mind
T-12...... III.6:5 to handle it by making some s. of insane
W-pI.....27.2:1 to believe that some s. of sacrifice is being
W-pI.....68.5:4 you do not cherish grievances of some s..
P-3......... II.1:4 of one s. or another as their chief function

**sorting** 8

T-1........VI.5:3 s. out the false from the true, the miracle
T-2..... VIII.4:1 involves a s. out of the false from the true.
T-17......VI.4:3 the Holy Spirit's s. out of truth and falsity
M-4 .....I.A.4:1 God must go through "a period of s. out."
M-4 .....I.A.5:4 no point in s. out the valuable from the
M-4 .....I.A.7:4 own s. out was meaningless in teaching
M-8 ...........4:1 s. out and categorizing activities of the
M-8 ...........6:5 only two categories are meaningful in s.

**sorts** 3

T-6......V.C.1:2 s. out the true from the false in your mind
T-17......IV.8:3 Into the frame are woven all s. of fanciful
T-21....... V.4:5 All s. of questions may arise in it, but if

**sought** 69

T-1......... II.1:2 sometimes s. in physical relationships.
T-12.....VII.8:3 opposition there, having s. it there. But
T-12.....VII.9:6 for it was the decision for what you s..
T-12...VII.11:3 upon me nor hear the answer that you s..
T-12... VIII.6:8 Valuing nothing, you have s. nothing. By
T-13.........I.5:2 He has always s. his guiltlessness, and he
T-13...... III.2:2 it is this place that you have s. to leave.
T-14......IV.1:2 it yours, and you will see what you s.. You
T-14.....VII.2:3 *is.* It can neither be lost nor s. nor found. It
T-15...... III.3:3 You who have s. and found littleness,
T-15...... III.8:5 you have s. to purchase it with little gifts,
T-17...... III.3:3 with those on whom vengeance is really s.
T-17...... III.4:7 even the one with whom the union was s..
T-17....... V.8:3 remind you of all the ways you once s. for
T-18...... III.1:5 And you s. a blackness so complete that
T-19.......I.5:10 attain, for part of it is s. through the body
T19..IV.C.11:3 but must be s. in what they represent.
T-21...... III.6:1 means for sin by which you s. to find it.
T-24....... V.6:8 And so He s. for your completion in each
T-25......IV.1:8 defined another way and s. for differently.
T-25......IX.7:1 Son be more unfair than he has s. to be. If
T-26.VII.11:10 This is the treasure he has s. to find. And
T-27....... V.3:4 For all the hurt that war has s. to bring,
T-28.......I.10:1 s. to lay a judgment on your own Creator
T-29....IX.10:5 s. to be released through judgment from
T-30.......I.15:2 you have s. perceives your happiness. You
T-30....... V.1:3 the place of idols, which are s. no longer,
T-30....... V.9:7 you s. here that did not bring you pain?
T-31.........I.5:3 And this has learning s. to demonstrate,
W-pI.....70.7:5 in self-concepts that you s. to make real.
W-pI.....93.2:3 That you have s. salvation in strange ways
W-pI.....96.1:3 You have s. many such solutions, and
W-pI...96.10:1 has found the function that it s. to lose.
W-pI...104.3:4 them, and s. for only in a world of dreams
W-pI...122.3:4 What gifts but these are worthy to be s.?
W-pI...130.4:7 They can be s., but they can not be found.
W-pI.131.12:4 now; no other goal is valued now nor s.,
W-pI.133.12:1 valueless, worthy or not of being s. at all,
W-pI.134.16:4 chains you s. to lay upon your brother,
W-pI.136.16:3 pursuits with double purposes insanely s.
W-pI...140.7:2 Healing must be s. but where it is, and
W-pI...164.4:5 different from all things you s. before,
W-pI...164.8:5 be s. above the world's unsatisfying goals
W-pI...165.5:3 you have the treasure you have always s..
W-pI...166.8:5 becomes of all the tragedy you s. to make
W-pI.166.12:5 you s. to make in which to hide from God
W-pI...170.8:4 you have s. to wrest from it and lay before
W-pI.185.14:1 the brotherhood that hate has s. to sever,
W-pI...196.9:7 You have s. to be both weak and bound,
W-pI...197.2:4 beside them, to be s. and claimed, and
W-pI...199.6:2 In Him they have found what they have s.
W-pI...200.4:2 though you s. to make them meaningful.
W-pI.200.10:3 the trees of hopelessness you s. before.
W-pII ....in.7:2 We have s. to find our way by following
W-pII .226.1:5 not s. for illusions to replace the truth.
W-pII .229.1:5 attests the truth of the Identity I s. to lose,
W-pII .231.1:3 *is Your Love the only thing I seek, or ever s..*
W-pII .251.1:1 I s. for many things, and found despair.
W-pII .251.1:3 All that I s. before I needed not, and did
W-pII .258.1:3 and trinkets of the world are s. instead?
W-pII .262.2:3 nowhere else can peace be s. and found.
W-pII .336.1:5 to find what it has vainly s. without. For
M-28 .........6:9 all he s. before to crucify are resurrected
P-2........IV.6:3 the defenses s. for must be magical. They
S-1...........I.3:6 You have s. first the Kingdom of Heaven,
S-2...........I.1:4 salvation is not understood, *nor truly s. for.*
S-2..........II.4:2 This goal is also s. by those who seek the
S-2..........II.7:6 nothing else, or you have s. your death,
S-2........ III.5:1 when help is needed and forgiveness s..

**soul** 9

T-4..........II.9:5 may believe that the s. existed before, and
T-4..........II.9:6 that the s. will be punished for this lapse.
T-5....... II.7:11 gain the whole world and lose his own s.?
T-5....... II.7:12 wrong voice you *have* lost sight of your s..
T-12...... VI.1:1 gain the whole world and lose your own s.
T-12...... VI.1:2 your s. and there is no gain in the world,
T-12...... VI.1:6 You cannot sell your s., but you can sell
T-12...... VI.1:7 You cannot perceive your s., but you will
C-1.............3:2 The term "s." is not used except in direct

**souls** 2

T-3...... IV.7:15 now, and they will find rest unto their s..
T-3.......VII.2:7 their s. in return for gifts of no real worth.

**sound** 31

T-5..........II.3:3 that the ego always dissolves at Its s..
T-9........IV.8:2 the ego in a s. position as your guide. Let
T-9....... V.8:14 is a s. though insufficient statement. Only
T-13....... V.6:2 not there, and you hear what makes no s..
T-13...VII.17:4 The s. of it will banish sorrow from the
T-18.... VI.12:3 can be anything and anywhere; a s., a
T19. IV.A.16:1 set in a quiet garden where no s. but
T-22.........I.9:7 sight or s. that drew them gently into one.
T-24........II.6:5 never was, nor hear what makes no s.. Is
T-24....... V.3:7 will see nothing and there is no s. to hear.
T-24....... V.7:3 ears may hear no more the s. of battle and
T-27...... VI.2:5 and so it seems to answer to a different s..
T-27...... VI.6:6 the throes of death itself are but a single s.
T-28....... V.5:4 to hear the voices that can make no s.. Yet
T-29....... V.1:3 a resting place so still no s. except a hymn
T-30.... III.10:3 no s. of battle comes remotely near, it
W-pI.........7.2:3 is not really so strange as it may s. at first.
W-pI.....98.7:4 beyond their s. to what they really mean.
W-pI...121.3:1 waken or to go to sleep, afraid of every s.,
W-pI...133.3:2 Unless they meet these s. requirements,
W-pI.151.12:4 hear in everything no s. except the echo of
W-pI...162.2:6 and hear this s. will never look on death.
WpI.rV.in12:4 meaning, which is far beyond their s.. The
WpI.rV.in12:5 The s. grows dim and disappears, as we
W-pI...183.6:6 we have, the only s. with any meaning,
W-pI...191.2:6 no s. that does not speak of frailty within
W-pI...199.5:4 We s. the call of freedom round the world
M-25 .........2:6 would fall at the holy s. of His Voice. Who
P-2........ VI.2:3 The s. of healing can be heard instead.
P-2........ VI.2:5 make this ugly s. seem truly beautiful.
S-1...........I.2:9 real s. is always a song of thanksgiving

**sounding** 1

T-14........X.8:9 this fact behind impressive s. words, but

**soundless** 5

T-24........II.4:4 s. in the melody that pours from God to

T-24....... II.4:6 You strain your ears to hear its s. voice,
T-24....... II.4:6 yet the Call of God Himself is s. to you.
W-pI...123.5:4 Him. His Word is s. if it be not heard. In
W-pI.183.11:2 Little sounds are s. now. The little things

## soundlessly 1

M-1 ...........3:6 by actions or thoughts; in words or s.; in

## sounds 42

T-3........ VI.8:9 where it s. meaningful to believe that you
T-11.......in.2:6 It s. insane when it is stated with perfect
T-13....... V.1:6 are not seen, and s. that are not heard.
T-20..VIII.10:5 gentle sights and s. are looked on happily,
T-20..VIII.10:6 the terrifying sights and screaming s. the
T-22.........I.6:4 The s. a baby makes and what he hears
T-22.........I.6:5 Neither the s. he hears nor sights he sees
T-24........ V.3:6 are the sights He sees, the s. He hears.
T-24..... VII.9:7 with which you listen to the s. it makes. It
T-28.......I.13:6 The stillness speaks in gentle s. of love the
T-28....... V.4:3 Here are the s. it hears; the voices that its
T-28....... V.4:4 sights and s. the body can perceive are
T-28....... V.5:5 other s. and other sights that *can* be seen
T-28...... VI.2:1 see, and blame it for the s. you do not like
T-31.........I.6:1 senseless noise of s. that have no meaning
W-pI.....49.4:4 riotous thoughts and sights and s. of this
W-pI.....71.1:4 This s. preposterous, of course. Yet after
W-pI.....91.3:1 you do not see is there s. like insanity. It is
W-pI.....94.1:3 The s. of this world are still, the sights of
W-pI...161.2:6 brings to your mind the s. it wants to hear
W-pI...161.4:6 What can they seem to be but empty s.;
W-pI...162.2:4 trumpet of awakening that s. around the
W-pI...164.1:5 He hears the s. the senseless, busy world
W-pI...164.2:2 sight. Its s. grow dim. A melody from far
W-pI...164.3:4 sights and s. that come from nearer than
W-pI...182.6:3 amid the grating s. and harsh and rasping
W-pI.183.11:2 Little s. are soundless now. The little
W-pII .....3.4:2 S. become the call for God, and all
W-pII .....4.1:5 need have they of sights or s. or touch?
W-pII .264.1:2 *are in all the things I look upon, the s. I hear,*
W-pII .271.1:1 I want to look upon, the s. I want to hear,
W-pII .....7.1:4 There are sights and s. forever laid aside.
W-pII .....7.2:2 For sights and s. must be translated from
W-pII .....8.2:1 s. of battle which your world contains.
W-pII .....8.2:6 Only happy sights and s. can reach the
W-pII .293.2:2 *the world is singing underneath the s. of fear*
W-pII .303.1:3 Let earthly s. be quiet, and the sights to
W-pII .303.1:5 And let Him hear the s. He understands,
W-pII .336.1:3 For sights and s., at best, can serve but to
M-28 .........4:8 The song of Heaven s. around the world,
P-2........ VI.3:6 the forms they look upon; the s. they hear
S-3........ IV.7:5 Underneath the s. of harsh and bitter

## Source 102

*source*

T-1...........I.2:2 The only thing that matters is their S.,
T-2......... V.2:4 unable to accept the real S. of the healing.
T-3......IV.5:10 in miscreation the mind is affirming its S.,
T-3......... V.6:8 is your S. and your only real function.
T-7.........IV.1:3 Both, therefore, come from the same S.,
T-9....VIII.11:7 It is an exalted answer because of its S.,
T-9....VIII.11:7 but the S. is true and so is Its answer.
T-14.........I.3:7 him, for the S. of their undoing is in him.
T-14.... XI.15:4 It is impossible to deny the S. of effects so
T-15....... II.3:5 do not perceive the S. of strength. In this
T-15...... VI.8:5 And this permits your S., and that of all
T-15....VIII.5:2 And because of the S. of the attempt, it
T-17....... III.9:8 is as true as is the holy S. from which they
T-18.... IX.10:3 it is the messenger of love and not its S..
T-18.... IX.10:6 Here is the S. of light; nothing perceived,
T19. IV.A.17:7 communication of salvation, but not its S.
T19...IV.C.11:6 One given to you to be the S. of judgment.
T19... IV.D.1:4 of life, the S. of everything that lives, the
T-20.... VII.1:2 from the same S. as does His purpose.
T-21..... II.11:5 confusing Son and Father; effect and S..
T-21..... II.12:2 himself that he is independent of his S..
T-21..... II.13:6 of the S. by which you were created, and
T-21 ...... V.6:6 because its S. knows not of incompletion.
T-21 ...... V.7:1 Where would the answer be but in the S.?
T-21 ...... V.7:3 true Effect of this same S. as is the answer,
T-24 ..... III.6:1 great Creator of the universe, the S. of life,
T-26 ..... IV.3:5 everything created to the S. of its creation
T-28 .... VII.2:2 wholeness and your health, the S. of help,
T-28 .... VII.7:6 the safety of this shelter and its S.? From
T-31 ..... IV.9:6 die, without their S. forever in themselves
T-31 .VIII.12:6 You, and knows You as the only S. it has.
W-pI..... 35.3:2 your S. it establishes your Identity, and it
W-pI..... 41.4:1 its S. goes with you wherever you go. You
W-pI..... 41.4:2 never suffer because the S. of all joy goes
W-pI..... 41.4:3 can never be alone because the S. of all life
W-pI........ 43.h God is my S.. I cannot see apart from
W-pI..... 43.4:7 *God is my S.. I cannot see this desk apart*
W-pI..... 43.4:9 *God is my S.. I cannot see that picture apart*
W-pI..... 43.7:3 *God is my S.. I cannot see you apart from*
W-pI..... 43.8:3 *God is my S.. I cannot see this apart from*
W-pI..... 47.4:1 own weakness to the S. of real strength.
W-pI..... 53.4:3 He is the S. of all meaning, and everything
W-pI..... 59.3:1 (43) God is my S.. I cannot see apart from
W-pI..... 68.1:6 off from your S. and make you unlike Him
W-pI..... 70.3:4 so He has kept the S. of healing where the
W-pI... 71.10:6 than to remember the S. of your salvation
W-pI..... 83.3:4 because both come from the same S.. And
W-pI..... 85.3:3 It is in me because its S. is there. It has not
W-pI..... 85.3:4 It has not left its S., and so it cannot have
W-pI..... 85.4:3 *with my awareness of the S. of my salvation.*
W-pI..... 92.5:1 and shines with light its S. has given it;
W-pI..... 96.5:2 It has denied its S. of strength, and sees
W-pI..... 99.5:2 is apart from time in that its S. is timeless.
W-pI..... 99.6:2 what is not created by the only S. it knows
W-pI... 135.9:4 from other minds and separate from its S.
W-pI... 156.1:5 the world alone and separate from your S.
W-pI... 158.1:3 Nor have you left your S., remaining as
W-pI...... 164.h Now are we one with Him Who is our S..
W-pI... 165.2:5 It is your S. of life, holding you one with it
W-pI... 167.9:2 enter, or a false condition not within its S.
W-pI. 167.11:3 and leave the S. of life from where it came.
W-pI. 167.12:1 We share one life because we have one S.,
W-pI. 167.12:1 a S. from which perfection comes to us,
W-pI. 167.12:7 the wakened mind is one that knows its S.
W-pI... 169.5:6 itself. It has united with its S.. And like its
W-pI... 169.5:7 Source. And like its S. Itself, it merely is.
WpI.rV.in12:5 as we approach the S. of meaning. It is
W-pI... 177.2:1 Now are we one with Him Who is our S..
W-pI. 184.11:3 a single S. which unifies all things within
W-pI. 186.11:6 God's can never fail because He is its S..
W-pI. 187.10:3 Not separate from Him Who is our S.; not
W-pI... 188.1:7 bring with you from Him Who is your S..
W-pI... 188.2:6 no sight, be it of dreams or from a truer S.
W-pI... 188.7:3 And they point surely to their S., Where
W-pI. 195.10:3 of the Love which is the S. of all creation.
W-pI. 195.10:4 His Own completion and the S. of love,
W-pI... 199.2:2 because it has been given to the S. of love,
W-pII .222.1:2 He is my S. of life, the life within, the air I
W-pII .228.2:1 *I failed to realize the S. from which I came. I*
W-pII .228.2:2 *I have not left that S. to enter in a body and to*
W-pII .259.2:4 *You are the S. of everything there is. And*
W-pII .260.1:2 *Yet, as Your Thought, I have not left my S.,*
W-pII .260.2:1 Now is our S. remembered, and Therein
W-pII .260.2:2 are we, because our S. can know no sin.
W-pII .262.1:8 *him, and we are part of You Who are our S.,*
W-pII .266.1:4 *Let not Your Son forget his holy S.. Let not*
W-pII ..... 6.1:3 still abides within the Mind that is His S..
W-pII .282.1:2 as God Himself, my Father and my S.,
W-pII .283.2:1 with God our Father as our only S., and
W-pII .288.1:3 *And to know my S., I first must recognize*
W-pII .293.1:2 state, whose S. is here forever and forever.
W-pII .299.2:8 *I can know my S. because it is Your Will that*
W-pII .329.2:1 our union with each other and our S.. We
M-4 ...... IV.2:9 their thoughts with Him Who is their S..
M-7 ............ 6:4 you have denied the S. of your creation. If
M-12 .......... 4:3 mind will understand because of their S..
P-2....... VII.6:3 Nor does he doubt its S.. He understands
P-3....... II.10:2 has lost sight of the S. of his salvation. He
S-2......... II.4:1 Son He loves, and keep him from his S..
S-3........ III.5:1 are Sons of God who recognize their S.,
S-3........ III.5:1 that all their S. creates is one with them.
S-3........ IV.4:5 In prayer you have united with your S.,

## source 129

*Source*

*See also* Appendix C

T-1 ....... III.5:7 respect, and thus uproots the s. of fear.
T-2 .......... I.2:5 Its real s. is internal. This is as true of the
T-4 ......... I.2:10 They are opposed in s., in direction and in
T-4 ......... V.2:1 A major s. of the ego's off-balanced state
T-4 ....... VI.1:1 does not recognize the real s. of "threat,"
T-7 ....... VI.3:5 ego draws upon the one s. that is totally
T-7 ....... VI.3:6 Fearful of perceiving the power of this s.,
T-8 ..... VIII.1:7 body, then, is not the s. of its own health.
T-9 .......... I.4:5 The only s. of fear in this process is what
T-11 ...... in.2:3 problem is still the only s. of conflict,
T-11 ....... V.2:3 what you will be looking at is the s. of fear
T-11 ....... V.4:2 cannot have any effects if its s. is not real.
T-11 ....... V.5:2 to recognize that their s. is not natural,
T-11 ..... V.16:4 and no thought system transcends its s..
T-12 ..... III.6:5 its s. as his own ego identification, and he
T-12 ... III.10:1 else, you will at last have placed its s., and
T-12 ..... IV.2:4 of its s. the ego is not wholly split off, or it
T-13 ....... II.5:5 but you have not uncovered its s.. For the
T-13 ....... X.1:1 mind can see the s. of pain where it is not.
T-13 ....... X.1:2 displacement is to hide the real s. of guilt,
T-13 ....... X.1:3 by the illusion that the s. of guilt, from
T-13 ....... X.1:4 provided they are not the deeper s. to
T-13 ....... X.3:7 perceive the s. of guilt outside themselves,
T-13 ....... X.4:1 but the s. of your guilt lies in the past, you
T-14 ... III.15:3 on the throne of God is not a s. of guilt.
T-14 ..... VI.8:3 keep no s. of interference from His sight,
T-14 .... VII.4:6 Their joining thus becomes the s. of fear,
T-15 ........ I.2:1 One s. of perceived discouragement from
T-15 ....... V.2:5 For separation is the s. of guilt, and to
T-15 ..... VI.8:4 Without its s. exclusion vanishes. And
T-17 ..... III.5:8 on the past, which is the s. of separation,
T-17 ..... III.6:1 to "resolve" its problems, not at their s.,
T-17 ..... III.6:3 and finds the s. of problems where it is,
T-17 .... VII.1:3 it from its s. and place it elsewhere. As a
T-18 ....... II.6:7 will remain, not as a s. of pain and guilt,
T-18 ....... II.6:7 and guilt, but as a s. of joy and freedom. It
T-18 ..... VI.6:7 and the perceived s. of your guilt. You
T-18 .... VII.1:1 much faith in the body as a s. of strength.
T-18 ..... IX.1:2 told that error must be corrected at its s..
T-18 ... IX.10:3 create. It is the s. of healing, but it is the
T-19 ........ I.7:6 of an idea is never separate from its s..
T-19 ...... I.16:5 For it remains joined to its s., which is its
T-19 ..... III.8:7 Its s. has been removed, and so it can be
T19 ... IV.B.2:9 Here is the s. of the idea that love is fear.
T19 .IV.C.2:14 We know that an idea leaves not its s..
T19 .IV.C.11:1 anything seems to you to be a s. of fear,
T19 .IV.C.11:2 nor symbol should be confused with s.,
T-20 ..... IV.1:6 and gives no power to their seeming s..
T-20 ..... IV.2:1 and can no more enter than can their s..
T-20 ..... IV.3:7 them to suffer the results of any other s..
T-20 ... VIII.6:9 holy relationship, the s. of your salvation,
T-21 ..... II.12:3 His union with It is the s. of his creating.
T-21 ..... II.13:4 gone, because its s. has been uncovered. It
T-21 ..... II.13:5 seeming independence of its s. that keeps
T-21 ..... III.2:2 The s. of sin is gone. You may imagine that
T-21 ..... III.7:5 fear, not as a symptom, but at its s..
T-21 ... IV.1:10 see. This merely seems to be the s. of fear.
T-22 ....... II.5:4 for reason sees the s. of an idea as what
T-22 ....... II.5:5 This must be so, if the idea is like its s..
T-22 ..... VI.9:8 make each little gift of love a s. of healing
T-23 ..... III.1:2 you do not always recognize the s. of pain.
T-24 ....... V.1:5 you seek for is a s. of joy as you conceive it
T-26 .... VII.4:7 Ideas leave not their s., and their effects
T-26 .... VII.4:9 effect of what is in, and has not left its s..
T-26 .. VII.12:3 leave their s. made real and meaningful.
T-26 .. VII.12:7 Effects are seen as separate from their s.,
T-26 .. VII.13:2 be true because ideas leave not their s..
T-26 .. VII.13:5 their s. is to invite illusions to be true,
T-26 ... VIII.3:3 error still obscured that is the s. of fear.
T-27 .... VII.1:7 because its s. is seen outside himself.
T-29 ... VIII.3:3 and cannot leave the mind that is its s..
T-29 ... VIII.4:3 for its s. abides within your mind where
T-30 ..... III.3:5 the s. of the belief that you are incomplete

T-31.........I.7:3 And each world follows surely from its **s.**.
T-31......III.5:1 one purpose; that the body be the **s.** of sin
T-31... VIII.3:3 would not leave one **s.** of pain unhealed,
W-pI........5.7:2 the name of both the **s.** of the upset as you
W-pI........6.1:2 and the perceived **s.** very specifically for
W-pI.....30.5:2 The mind is its only **s.**. To aid in helping
W-pI.....45.2:5 because thoughts do not leave their **s.**.
W-pI.....45.3:4 because they cannot have left their **s.**.
W-pI.....70.1:3 too, does the **s.** of guilt. You see neither
W-pI.....71.2:3 the **s.** of salvation is constantly perceived
W-pI.....71.3:2 any perceived **s.** of salvation is acceptable
W-pI.....73.5:2 The **s.** of neither light nor darkness can be
W-pI...105.3:2 For giving has become a **s.** of fear, and so
W-pI...106.2:3 tell you they have found the **s.** of life and
W-pI...130.6:5 and reflects its **s.** in everything you see.
W-pI.131.10:3 and neither **s.** nor substance in the truth.
W-pI...132.1:7 It is but when their **s.** is raised to question
W-pI...132.2:2 Now the **s.** of thought has shifted, for to
W-pI...132.2:2 your mind means you have changed the **s.**
W-pI...132.5:3 Ideas leave not their **s.**. This central theme
W-pI.132.10:3 your ideas because ideas leave not their **s.**,
W-pI.136.17:1 the **s.** of sickness has been opened to relief
W-pI.138.10:3 thing, a but imagined **s.** of guilt and pain?
W-pI...140.8:1 change our minds about the **s.** of sickness,
W-pI...140.8:2 We will try today to find the **s.** of healing,
W-pI...140.9:2 today and reach the **s.** of healing, from
W-pI...156.1:3 in the text; ideas leave not their **s.**. If this
W-pI...159.4:2 It is their **s.**, remaining with each miracle
W-pI...159.9:4 They do not leave their **s.**, but carry its
W-pI...167.3:6 Ideas leave not their **s.**. The emphasis this
W-pI...167.4:3 It is the fixed belief ideas can leave their **s.**
W-pI...167.4:3 take on qualities the **s.** does not contain,
W-pI...167.5:2 Ideas remain united to their **s.**. They can
W-pI...167.5:3 They can extend all that their **s.** contains.
W-pI...167.6:4 mind does not exist, because it has no **s.**.
W-pI...170.4:2 First, it is obvious ideas must leave their **s.**
W-pI...188.2:8 and there it ends. It has no **s.** but this.
W-pI...190.5:8 becomes a **s.** of innocence and holiness.
W-pI...192.5:4 those who have lost the **s.** of all attack, the
W-pI.196.10:5 became your mortal enemy; the **s.** of fear.
W-pII.......3.1:2 It is born of error, and it has not left its **s.**.
W-pII.......3.1:5 Now its **s.** has gone, and its effects are
W-pII..259.1:4 What else but sin could be the **s.** of guilt,
W-pII..259.1:5 And what but sin could be the **s.** of fear,
W-pII..264.1:5 *There is no* **s.** *but this, and nothing is that*
W-pII..293.1:1 All fear is past, because its **s.** is gone, and
W-pII..301.1:6 *I shed will be forgotten, for their* **s.** *is gone.*
M-in ..........5:7 remain a **s.** of strength and truth forever.
M-22..........1:3 it is the **s.** of a wholly unified perception.
P-2........IV.5:1 may recognize the mind as the **s.** of illness
P-2........IV.7:8 another form, being the **s.** of all illusions.
P-2........IV.9:6 cannot but be seen as a real **s.** of danger,
S-3...........I.2:2 It has not left its **s.**, and in its pain and
S-3......... II.1:8 of seeming death that has a different **s.**. It
S-3........III.4:8 apart from where the **s.** of sickness is, for
S-3........IV.5:5 He Who is Love becomes the **s.** of fear, for

**sources** 6

T-13....... X.1:4 willing to look upon all kinds of "**s.**,"
T-15....... II.4:1 by seeing them as **s.** of ego support. As a
W-pI........5.3:1 for "**s.**" of upset in which you believe, and
W-pI........5.6:1 some perceived **s.** of upset than to others.
W-pI...135.7:4 the **s.** for the many mad attacks you make
S-1......... II.3:4 for the many **s.** of guilt that inevitably

**sovereignty** 2

T19...IV.D.3:2 dedication to death and to its **s.** is but the
W-pII..250.1:2 in him with which I would attack his **s.**.

**sow** 1

T-5........VI.6:1 "As ye **s.**, so shall ye reap" He interprets

**sown** 1

T-18......VI.7:2 where you have **s.** the seeds of vengeance,

**space** 65
*See also* space-time

T-1........ VI.3:4 This is because you think you live in **s.**,
T-1........ VI.3:5 Ultimately, **s.** is as meaningless as time.
T-2......... II.4:4 because belief in **s.** and time did not exist.
T-2......... V.9:2 Like all aspects of the belief in **s.** and time,
T-2....V.A.11:2 of time and **s.** do not apply. When you
T-2....V.A.11:3 I will arrange both time and **s.** to adjust to
T-2.......VII.7:9 you that time and **s.** are under my control
T-3........ III.1:7 As an attribute of the belief in **s.** and time,
T-12......VII.3:3 it. Every law of time and **s.**, of magnitude
T-18....VI.12:1 you join; of your respective positions in **s.**
T-18....VI.13:6 the lifting of the barriers of time and **s.**,
T-20....VI.11:2 it prisoner in a tiny spot of **s.** and time,
T-26......IV.2:6 **s.** that sin left vacant do they join as one,
T-26......IV.3:1 you stand is but the **s.** that sin has left.
T-26......IV.4:8 be to make the **s.** between you disappear?
T-26......VII.8:8 time and place, and give a little **s.** to you,
T-26......VII.8:8 little space to you, another little **s.** to him.
T-26... VIII.1:3 For time and **s.** are one illusion, which
T-26... VIII.1:5 it is, the more you think of it in terms of **s.**
T-26... VIII.2:1 and this **s.** you perceive as time because
T-26... VIII.3:4 wipe out the **s.** you see between you still,
T-26... VIII.3:8 little **s.** between you and your brother still
T-26... VIII.4:1 Yet **s.** between you and your brother is
T-26... VIII.8:3 aspect of the little **s.** that lies between you
T-26... VIII.9:7 time, but to the little **s.** between you still,
T-26...... IX.5:3 it and leave no **s.** nor distance lingering
T-27.......I.10:1 Into this empty **s.**, from which the goal of
T-27.......I.11:3 This leaves no **s.** in which a different view,
T-27...... III.2:6 must stand for empty **s.** and nothingness.
T-27...... III.2:7 Yet nothingness and empty **s.** can not be
T-27...... III.3:8 the empty **s.** it occupies be recognized as
T-27...... III.4:1 An empty **s.** that is not seen as filled, an
T-27...... III.6:1 your brother given you to occupy the **s.** so
T-27......VII.7:1 to sin all stand within one little **s.**. And it
T-27...VII.12:3 the **s.** between your little dreams and
T-28...... III.5:2 Yet separation is but empty **s.**, enclosing
T-28...... III.5:4 and covered up the **s.** which seemed to
T-28...... III.6:1 the **s.** left clean and vacant by the miracle.
T-28...... III.9:8 love has set its table in the **s.** that seemed
T-28...... IV.7:6 has left the **s.** between them vacant. And
T-28.....VII.1:3 An empty **s.**, a little gap, would be a lack.
T-28.....VII.1:5 A **s.** where God is not, a gap between the
T-29.........I.4:1 not one of **s.** between two separate bodies
T-29...... III.3:1 tiny spark, a **s.** of light created in the dark
T-29...... III.3:6 And as you see him shining in the **s.** of
T-31.....VII.9:1 there is a **s.** between you and your brother
T-31.....VII.9:2 that it may fight to keep the **s.** that holds
W-pI.....13.2:2 empty **s.** that meaninglessness provides.
W-pI.....30.5:1 is not only unlimited by **s.** and distance,
W-pI.....38.1:2 It is beyond every restriction of time, **s.**,
W-pI.....42.2:3 through time and **s.** is not at random.
W-pI.....62.4:3 who seem to be far away in **s.** and time, to
W-pI...129.5:1 an instant's **s.** away from timelessness.
W-pI...164.8:2 and leave a clean and open **s.** within your
W-pI...184.1:5 things by emphasizing **s.** surrounding it.
W-pI...184.1:6 **s.** you lay between all things to which you
W-pI...184.2:1 This **s.** you see as setting off all things
W-pI...184.2:2 there is unity; a **s.** between all things,
W-pI...184.4:4 And a lack of **s.**, a sense of unity or vision
W-pI.184.12:3 all **s.** is filled with truth's reflection. Every
W-pI...199.2:1 in all ways, beyond the laws of time and **s.**
W-pII..319.1:3 up the **s.** the ego left unoccupied by lies.
M-18.........3:4 Its little **s.** and tiny breath become the
M-23.........4:4 for that the little **s.** between the two is lost
S-1........IV.4:5 the little **s.** that lasts until it crumbles into

**space-time** 1

T-2......... II.5:1 Atonement was built into the **s.** belief to

**span** 2

T-28.........I.7:9 **s.** of memory which your perception sees.
T-31...... III.1:4 by a **s.** of time you cannot realize. You

**spans** 1

T-1..........II.6:5 the interval of time it **s.** unnecessary.

**spare** 2

T-2........VI.9:4 you hope to **s.** yourself from fear there are
T-21...... VI.1:9 This you could **s.** him and yourself. For

**spared** 1

W-pI.127.10:2 today that we are **s.** a future like the past.

**spares** 1

T-1........ III.4:4 This **s.** you needless effort, because you

**spark** 28

T-10...... IV.7:5 the lamps of God were lit by the same **s.**.
T-10...... IV.8:1 many only the **s.** remains, for the Great
T-10...... IV.8:2 Yet God has kept the **s.** alive so that the
T-10...... IV.8:3 see the little **s.** you will learn of the greater
T-10...... IV.8:4 Perceiving the **s.** will heal, but knowing
T-10...... IV.8:6 But the **s.** is still as pure as the Great Light
T-10....... V.2:4 the **s.** in them that would bring joy to you.
T-10....... V.2:5 the denial of the **s.** that brings depression,
T-11.......in.3:6 little **s.** in your mind is enough to lighten
T-11........II.5:4 and the little **s.** becomes a blazing light
T-11........II.6:5 recognize the little **s.** and are willing to let
T-11...... III.5:6 the little **s.** in you is part of a light so great
T-16...... VI.6:3 little **s.** that holds the Great Rays within it
T-16...... VI.6:3 this **s.** cannot be limited long to littleness.
T-17........II.5:5 **s.** of beauty that gentleness could release.
T-17...... III.5:7 In these loving thoughts is the **s.** of beauty
T-17...... III.6:7 hidden **s.** of beauty in your relationships,
T-17...... III.6:9 will let this **s.** transform the relationship
T-17...... III.7:1 if you but let Him hold the **s.** before you,
T-17...... III.7:4 The **s.** of holiness must be safe, however
T-17...... III.9:4 The **s.** of beauty or the veil of ugliness, the
T-18...... III.8:4 you to give the little **s.** of your desire the
T-24....... V.4:2 the shifting tiny gleams that **s.** an instant
T-29...... III.3:1 no more, perhaps, than just a tiny **s.**, a
T-29...... III.5:6 This is the **s.** that shines within the dream
T-30........II.1:9 No **s.** of life but was created with your
W-pI. 121.11:3 Try to find some little **s.** of brightness
W-pI... 127.9:3 And He Himself will place a **s.** of truth

**sparkle** 2

T-23.......in.6:4 forgiveness will the world **s.** and shine,
T-26........X.6:2 a trace of all the happy **s.** that salvation

**sparkles** 4

T-18....VIII.7:3 The sunbeam **s.** only in the sunlight, and
T-31.........I.8:1 hope and **s.** with a gentle friendliness.
W-pI... 122.2:2 It **s.** on your eyes as you awake, and gives
M-4 ....... X.2:5 Nothing but **s.** now which seemed so dull

**sparkling** 3

T-17........II.2:2 with everything **s.** under the open sun.
T-20.....VIII.4:4 glowing with radiant purity and **s.** with
T-26...... IX.3:1 let the flowers be all white and **s.** in the

**sparrow** 2

T-20...... IV.4:7 is. Ask not the **s.** how the eagle soars, for
M-4 .........I.2:2 wings of a **s.** when the mighty power of an

**spawn** 1

W-pI... 161.8:3 the intensity of rage projected fear must **s.**

**speak** 122

T-2........ IV.1:3 **s.** of "a miracle of healing" is to combine
T-4.........in.2:1 You can **s.** from the spirit or from the ego

| | |
|---|---|
| T-4.........in.2:2 | s. from spirit you have chosen to "Be still |
| T-4.........in.2:4 | If you s. from the ego you are disclaiming |
| T-5......... II.5:6 | He gave you a Voice to s. for Him because |
| T-5........ VI.3:5 | two voices s. for different interpretations |
| T-6.........I.14:4 | s. of the crucifixion entirely without anger |
| T-6....... II.10:4 | true. The Holy Spirit can s. only for this, |
| T-6....... II.12:6 | gave to Him and for which He must s., |
| T-6........ IV.3:2 | The Holy Spirit does not s. first, *but He* |
| T-7......... II.4:2 | be translated for those who s. different |
| T-9........ IV.4:9 | because they s. of ideas that are eternal. |
| T-9......... V.8:8 | and will s. to him through you if you do |
| T-10....... III.8:7 | God. Yet when they seem to s. to you, |
| T-11....... II.5:1 | Spirit cannot s. to an unwelcoming host, |
| T-11..... V.17:8 | speaks to them, and it is His words they s. |
| T-12..... VII.4:3 | are His witnesses, and s. for His Presence. |
| T-12..... VII.4:4 | only through the witnesses that s. for it. |
| T-14.......in.1:8 | the simple conclusions that s. for truth, |
| T-14...... IV.8:3 | little, hear me s. for Him and for yourself. |
| T-14...... VI.6:1 | You who s. in dark and devious symbols |
| T-14...... VI.7:5 | You s. two languages at once, and this |
| T-14.... XI.6:10 | Whom God has given you will s. to you. |
| T-15..... II.4:12 | sure because the witness to Him will s. so |
| T-15...... IX.5:2 | No one can hear Him s. of this and long |
| T-16........ II.8:1 | many witnesses that s. of it so clearly that |
| T-17.... III.1:11 | s. so clearly for the separation that no one |
| T-17....... III.2:2 | shadow figures always s. for vengeance, |
| T-18...... IX.3:5 | messages that s. of what lies underneath, |
| T-18...... IX.3:5 | for it is not the body that could s. of this. |
| T-18.... IX.11:2 | any need for us to try to s. of what must |
| T-21.........I.5:5 | if you remember what we will s. of now. |
| T-22.........I.7:3 | will s. the language you can understand. |
| T-22.........I.9:6 | in a language the body does not s.. Nor |
| T-24....... II.5:2 | They s. a different language and they fall |
| T-24. VII.10:10 | made it, and s. for its reality and truth. |
| T-25..VIII.10:5 | could they call forth to s. on his behalf? |
| T-27.........I.6:6 | lend conviction to the system they s. for |
| T-27....... II.5:8 | It is this testimony that can s. with power |
| T-27..... V.1:11 | *you.* He does not s. to someone else. Yet by |
| T-27...... VI.4:2 | names that s. in other ways for its reality. |
| T-27..... VII.6:2 | world of evil cannot s. except for what has |
| T-29...... IX.4:6 | talk and think and feel and s. for them. |
| T-30....... II.3:3 | Now hear God s. to you, through Him |
| T-30.... VII.7:8 | language lets us s. to all our brothers, and |
| W-pI..... 49.5:3 | you are inviting God's Voice to s. to you. |
| W-pI..... 54.4:4 | of God cannot think or s. or act in vain. |
| W-pI... 76.11:3 | His Voice will s. of this to us, as well as of |
| W-pI..... 96.8:4 | and let Him s. to you about your Self, and |
| W-pI..... 97.8:2 | And He will s. to you, reminding you that |
| W-pI..... 97.8:3 | time you s. the words He offers you today, |
| W-pI... 105.8:3 | assure you that the words you s. are true. |
| W-pI... 106.2:1 | Father s. to you through His appointed |
| W-pI... 106.3:5 | Go past all things which do not s. of Him |
| W-pI... 106.4:3 | silent. He would s. to you. He comes with |
| W-pI... 106.5:3 | He needs your voice to s. to them, for who |
| W-pI... 106.5:4 | and offer Him your voice to s. to all the |
| W-pI... 106.5:4 | to hear the Word that He will s. today. |
| W-pI... 107.9:2 | Him. You s. to Him today, and make your |
| W-pI. 107.11:2 | s. for all the world and Him Who would |
| W-pI... 109.4:6 | rest in Him and let Him s. through you. |
| W-pI... 123.5:2 | come to s. the saving Word of God to us. |
| W-pI... 124.8:5 | trust God's Voice to s. as He sees fit today |
| W-pI... 125.4:1 | Hear, holy Son of God, your Father s.. |
| W-pI... 125.6:4 | mind to hear the Voice for its Creator s.. |
| W-pI. 126.10:4 | the Voice of truth and healing s. to you, |
| W-pI... 129.3:3 | exchanged at last for what we cannot s. of |
| W-pI... 133.1:3 | do today. We will not s. of lofty, world- |
| W-pI. 140.11:1 | let Him s. to us five minutes as the day |
| W-pI. 140.11:4 | time when we can hear our Father s. to us |
| W-pI. 140.12:3 | *S. to us, Father, that we may be healed.* And |
| W-pI... 151.6:2 | and s. with certainty of what they do not |
| W-pI. 151.12:3 | His Voice would s. to you of nothing but |
| W-pI... 154.2:1 | Whose function is to s. for you as well. |
| W-pI. 154.10:3 | He alone can s. to us and for us, joining in |
| W-pI. 154.11:2 | needs our voice that He may s. through us |
| W-pI... 155.6:3 | it is not illusion that they hear you s. of, |
| W-pI... 155.6:4 | ahead of you, s. to them through illusions |
| W-pI. 155.14:1 | He may s. to you and tell you of His Love, |
| W-pI... 168.1:2 | Shall we not s. to Him? He is not distant. |
| W-pI... 169.5:4 | We say "God is," and then we cease to s., |
| W-pI... 169.5:5 | There are no lips to s. them, and no part |
| W-pI... 169.6:1 | s. nor write nor even think of this at all. It |
| W-pI. 169.10:3 | for those in time can s. of things beyond, |
| WpI...rV.in2:2 | *quiet and our holy minds be still, and s. to us.* |
| WpI...rV.in9:2 | I need; that you will hear the words I s., |
| WpI.rV.in11:5 | have recognized the words we s. are true. |
| W-pI... 182.2:1 | No one but knows whereof we s.. Yet |
| W-pI... 182.2:4 | will maintain that what we s. of is illusion |
| W-pI... 182.2:5 | deny he understands the words we s.? |
| W-pI... 182.3:1 | We s. today for everyone who walks this |
| W-pI... 191.2:6 | no sound that does not s. of frailty within |
| W-pII . 221.1:4 | *My Father, s. to me today. I come to hear* |
| W-pII . 221.2:3 | I am sure that He will s. to you, and you |
| W-pII . 221.2:6 | peace, to hear Him s. to us of what we are, |
| W-pII . 275.2:3 | *to go; to whom to s. and what to say to him,* |
| W-pII .... 276.h | The Word of God is given me to s.. |
| W-pII . 276.2:2 | *And it is this that I would s. to all my brothers* |
| W-pII . 296.1:2 | *I am resolved to let You s. through me, for I* |
| W-pII . 296.1:4 | *hear the Word Your holy Voice will s. to me* |
| W-pII347.1:11 | *And He will s. for me, and call Your miracles* |
| W-pII ... 14.2:4 | are is not for words to s. of nor describe. |
| W-pII ... 14.2:5 | here, and words can s. of this and teach it, |
| W-pII ... 14.5:1 | holy messengers of God who s. for Him, |
| W-pII . 358.1:2 | *You s. for God, and so You speak for me. And* |
| W-pII . 358.1:2 | *You speak for God, and so You s. for me. And* |
| W-ep......... 2:4 | s. of what you really want and really need. |
| W-ep......... 5:4 | And He will s. for God and for your Self, |
| M-1........... 2:6 | teachers to s. for It and redeem the world. |
| M-3........... 4:2 | sense only, we can s. of levels of teaching. |
| M-12......... 4:2 | God's Voice s. through it to human ears. |
| M-18......... 2:3 | can now s. of the reality of the Son of God |
| M-18......... 2:5 | can s. the Word of God to listening ears, |
| M-23......... 7:2 | lead the way to those who s. in different |
| M-26......... 4:3 | who suffer, you must s. their language. If |
| P-2...........I.2:3 | we s. of "the saving illusion" or "the final |
| P-2......... V.3:3 | s. of ideal teaching in a world in which the |
| P-2......... V.3:4 | But still we s. of what can yet be done in |
| P-2......... V.5:6 | voice through which to s. His holy Word; |
| P-3...........I.2:9 | you; He needs your voice to s. for Him. |
| S-2........ III.5:5 | you look on him, and s. for Him as well. |
| S-3........ IV.1:4 | but s. for Him and never for themselves. |

## speaking 16

| | |
|---|---|
| T-5 ..... VI.11:7 | s. for patience towards the Sonship in the |
| T-6 ....... IV.2:5 | thus s. for the part of your mind that |
| T-7 ..... VIII.3:2 | First, strictly s., conflict cannot be |
| T-8 ...... VII.7:2 | Strictly s. this is impossible, since it seems |
| T-9 ....... III.2:5 | it is certain that, if he is s. from the ego, |
| T-9 ....... III.2:7 | tell him this verbally, if he is s. foolishly. |
| T-27 ........I.6:7 | voices, s. to your brother and yourself in |
| W-pI..... 31.1:4 | Generally s., the form includes two |
| W-pI..... 44.5:5 | Properly s., this is the release from hell. |
| W-ep......... 4:4 | has earned your trust by s. daily to you of |
| M-4 ........X.3:7 | Properly s. it is unlearning that they bring |
| M-16 ......... 2:6 | Broadly s., then, it can be said that it is |
| M-21 ......... 1:1 | Strictly s., words play no part at all in |
| M-21 ......... 4:8 | He does not control the direction of his s.. |
| P-3..........II.1:1 | Strictly s. the answer is no. How could a |
| P-3..........II.1:4 | Yet practically s., it can still be said that |

## speaks 115

| | |
|---|---|
| T-2 .........II.1:9 | That is why the Bible s. of "the peace of |
| T-3 ..........I.5:2 | simple symbol that s. of my innocence. |
| T-5 .........II.6:9 | for His Will, for which the Holy Spirit s.. |
| T-5 .........II.7:7 | God is always quiet, because It s. of peace. |
| T-5 .........II.8:2 | mind that always s. for the right choice, |
| T-5 .........II.8:2 | for the right choice, because He s. for God |
| T-5 ....... III.7:3 | the laws of God, for which He s.. He can |
| T-5 ........ V.3:9 | delusional system, and s. for it. Listening |
| T-5 ....... VI.3:5 | simultaneously, for the ego always s. first. |
| T-5 ....... VI.4:1 | The ego s. in judgment, and the Holy |
| T-5 ..... VI.10:4 | it s. for Him and therefore speaks truly. It |
| T-5 ..... VI.10:4 | it speaks for Him and therefore s. truly. It |
| T-5 ..... VI.12:5 | The Holy Spirit, Who s. for God in time, |
| T-6 .......II.10:4 | speak only for this, because He s. for God. |
| T-6 ....... IV.1:2 | The ego always s. first. It is capricious and |
| T-6 ........ V.4:7 | Himself, s. only for what lasts forever. |
| T-6 ..... V.C.7:3 | for God s. only for belief beyond question |
| T-6 ..... V.C.7:6 | ego s. against His creation, and therefore |
| T-7 ...... VII.7:3 | born of the infinite Love for which He s.. |
| T-7 ...... XI.1:2 | because He s. for the Kingdom of God, |
| T-8 .........V.6:3 | one for which God's Voice s. in all of us. |
| T-9 ..........I.6:3 | it s. for different things to the same mind. |
| T-9 .........II.5:5 | him, and His Voice s. to you through him. |
| T-9 .........II.7:4 | Spirit in you, Who s. to me through you. |
| T-9 .........II.7:5 | hear my brothers in whom God's Voice s.. |
| T-9 ...... VII.8:3 | Remember this when the ego s., and you |
| T-11 ......I.11:1 | the Holy Spirit only because He s. for you. |
| T-11 .......II.2:4 | Every miracle that you accomplish s. to |
| T-11 .....V.17:7 | for Christ s. to them of Himself and of His |
| T-11 .....V.17:8 | They are silent because Christ s. to them, |
| T-11 .....V.18:6 | If he s. not of Christ to you, you spoke not |
| T-11 .....V.18:7 | own voice, and if Christ s. through you, |
| T-11 .... VII.1:4 | Bible s. of a new Heaven and a new earth, |
| T-12 .....V.7:10 | Yet your mind s. against your learning as |
| T-12 .....V.7:10 | as your learning s. against your mind, and |
| T-13 ... VIII.4:4 | His message s. of timelessness in time, |
| T-14 ..... IV.5:4 | all decisions to the One Who s. for God, |
| T-14 .....V.1:11 | He s. of you to *you.* There is no guilt in you |
| T-14 . VIII.2:11 | with His Son, s. to His Son through Him. |
| T-15 ........I.3:6 | It s. to you of Heaven, but assures you |
| T-15 ........I.5:2 | is the only voice, it s. of hell even to him. |
| T-16 .........II.5:4 | are natural to the One Who s. for God. |
| T19 ... IV.C.7:2 | the silencer of the Voice that s. for God. |
| T-20 .......V.2:2 | Each s. in time of what is far beyond it. |
| T-21 ..... VI.8:6 | Listen to Him Who s. with reason, and |
| T-21 ..... VI.9:3 | Reason s. happily indeed of this. This |
| T-23 ..... III.2:1 | for God s. through you to your brother? |
| T-24 ..... VI.5:6 | but through the Voice that s. for God in |
| T-25 ..... VI.1:1 | they look on s. of Him to the beholder. He |
| T-25 .. VII.10:3 | One Who s. for Him can show you this, in |
| T-26 .......V.6:3 | Madness s. no more. There *is* no other |
| T-26 .. VII.10:1 | there; a little sigh that s. for Heaven as a |
| T-27 ........I.4:9 | it s. with certainty for what it represents. |
| T-27 .......I.6:11 | Depression s. of death, and vanity of real |
| T-27 .....V.1:10 | The Holy Spirit s. to *you.* He does not |
| T-27 ... VI.5:10 | Yet a miracle s. not but for itself, but what |
| T-28 ......I.13:6 | The stillness s. in gentle sounds of love |
| T-29 ... VIII.9:4 | It is for him the Holy Spirit s., and tells |
| T-30 .......II.1:2 | He tells you but your will; He s. for you. |
| T-31 ........I.6:3 | of His Will is in the Voice that s. for Him. |
| W-pI .... 47.3:2 | His Voice s. for Him in all situations and |
| W-pI .... 47.3:4 | Voice which s. for Him thinks as He does. |
| W-pI ....... 49.h | God's Voice s. to me all through the day. |
| W-pI .... 60.4:1 | God's Voice s. to me all through the day. |
| W-pI .... 76.9:2 | to hear the Voice that s. the truth to you. |
| W-pI .... 96.8:1 | by Him Who s. to you from your one Self. |
| W-pI .... 97.7:1 | with the words the Holy Spirit s. to you, |
| W-pI .. 123.5:6 | however mighty be the Voice that s., |
| W-pI .. 125.6:1 | Today He s. to you. His Voice awaits your |
| W-pI .. 125.7:2 | He s. from nearer than your heart to you. |
| W-pI .. 125.8:1 | voice to which you listen as He s. to you. |
| W-pI .. 125.8:2 | It is your word He s.. It is the Word of |
| W-pI 126.10:4 | and you will understand the words He s., |
| W-pI 126.10:4 | and recognize He s. your words to you. |
| W-pI .. 129.4:2 | And God Himself s. to His Son, as His |
| W-pI .. 129.4:2 | speaks to His Son, as His Son s. to Him. |
| W-pI .. 135.3:4 | it s. of fear made real and terror justified. |
| W-pI 140.10:4 | hear a single Voice which s. to us of truth, |
| W-pI .. 151.5:1 | This thing it s. of, and would yet defend, |
| W-pI 152.12:2 | for He s. for you and for your Father. He |
| W-pI .. 154.4:2 | which s. of laws the world does not obey; |
| W-pI 154.10:2 | our minds apart from Him Who s. for us, |
| W-pI .. 156.8:4 | God s. for you in answering your question |
| W-pI .. 157.9:4 | Yet the vision s. of your remembrance of |
| W-pI .. 160.2:1 | to the truth he s. a different language, |
| W-pI 166.11:4 | and s. of His Companionship when you |
| W-pI 166.12:7 | s. as well of what becomes your will when |
| W-pI .. 168.1:1 | God s. to us. Shall we not speak to Him? |
| Wi181-200 2:4 | tight control of what you see s. for itself. |
| W-pI .. 186.7:2 | you. And as He s., the image trembles and |
| W-pI 186.12:4 | Voice that s. for the Creator of all things, |
| W-pI .. 193.5:2 | the Holy Spirit s. in all your tribulations, |
| W-pI 193.13:2 | To all that s. of terror, answer thus: *I will* |
| WpI.rVI.in.6:6 | Who instructs in quiet, s. of peace, and |
| W-pII . 222.1:5 | who knows the truth of what He s. today! |

W-pII..237.1:3 which I hear as God my Father s. to me.
W-pII......3.4:4 Hear His Voice alone in all that s. to you.
W-pII..245.2:3 God, Who s. to us as we relate His Word;
W-pII..254.2:6 Love, God s. to us and tells us of our will,
W-pII..275.1:1 Voice for God, which s. an ancient lesson,
W-pII.....296.h The Holy Spirit s. through me today.
W-pII..315.1:4 Someone s. a word of gratitude or mercy,
WpII361-5.1:5 He s. for God my Father and His holy Son
W-ep .........2:6 And thus He s. of freedom and of truth.
M-2............5:3 God's Teacher s. to any two who join
M-4.....VII.2:2 however, to the self of which the world s..
M-5......III.2:9 is not their voice that s. the Word of God.
M-21..........4:9 his speaking. He listens and hears and s..
C-6............4:3 One. He s. for God and also for you, being
C-6............4:5 for in that form He s. God's Word to you.
P-2.......VII.4:7 in those through whom the Holy Spirit s..
S-2 ........III.6:1 And what is it He s. to you about? About
S-3 ........IV.1:3 voice, through whom He s. for God,
S-3 ........IV.7:1 He comes for Me and s. My Word to you.
S-3 ........IV.7:5 defeat there is a Voice that s. to you of Me

## spear 3

T-21...VII.3:11 A flower turns into a poisoned s., a child
T-29.......V.7:6 each with his tiny s. and rusted sword, to
W-pI.182.11:1 and lay down the s. and sword you raised

## special 241

*See also* Appendix C
T-1.........V.3:6 All my brothers are s.. If they believe they
T-2.........V.A.h S. Principles of Miracle Workers
T-5......VI.12:6 because it is His s. function to return you
T-7.........V.4:4 always sees something "s." in the healer,
T-12.......V.4:5 and poor learners do need s. teaching.
T-12.......V.5:4 you clearly require a s. Teacher and a
T-12.......V.5:4 a special Teacher and a s. curriculum.
T-13....III.10:2 were at peace until you asked for s. favor.
T-13.....X.11:2 Love is not s.. If you single out part of the
T-14.......V.2:1 has a s. part to play in the Atonement,
T-15..........V.h The Holy Instant and S. Relationships
T-15.......V.3:2 love unlike to God, Who knows no s. love
T-15.......V.3:3 it? To believe that *s.* relationships, with
T-15.......V.3:3 that *special* relationships, with *s.* love, can
T-15.......V.3:5 How can you decide that s. aspects of the
T-15.......V.4:1 all s. relationships have elements of fear
T-15.......V.4:5 the Holy Spirit uses s. relationships,
T-15.......V.5:1 The Holy Spirit knows no one is s.. Yet
T-15.......V.5:2 that you have made s. relationships,
T-15.......V.8:1 on earth has formed s. relationships, and
T-15.......V.8:2 In the holy instant no one is s., for your
T-15.....VII.1:1 poor attraction of the s. love relationship,
T-15.....VII.1:7 on which the ego embarks *is* s..
T-15.....VII.4:6 unrewarding chain of s. relationships,
T-15...VII.10:1 you can be sure that you have formed a s.
T-15...VII.10:3 basis the ego accepts for s. relationships.
T-15... VIII.2:1 you have need of no s. relationships at all.
T-15.......X.7:5 this question in your s. relationships, in
T-15.....XI.1:4 with them for a few s. relationships, in
T-16.........I.1:2 is always used to form a s. relationship in
T-16......IV.1:1 to look upon the s. hate relationship, for
T-16......IV.1:3 For the s. love relationship, in which the
T-16......IV.1:6 The s. love relationship will not offset it,
T-16......IV.3:1 The s. love relationship is an attempt to
T-16......IV.3:4 The s. love relationship is not perceived
T-16......IV.3:5 The s. love partner is acceptable only as
T-16......IV.7:1 s. love relationship is an attempt to bring
T-16......IV.7:3 the s. love relationship would accomplish
T-16......IV.8:4 The s. love relationship is but a shabby
T-16......IV.9:1 be wholly in God, willing for nothing s.,
T-16....IV.13:1 s. relationships of any kind would hinder
T-16.......V.1:1 In looking at the s. relationship, it is
T-16.......V.2:3 The s. love relationship is the ego's chief
T-16.......V.3:1 The s. love relationship is the ego's most
T-16.......V.4:1 It is in the s. relationship, born of the
T-16.......V.4:1 of the hidden wish for s. love from God,
T-16.......V.4:2 For the s. relationship is the renunciation
T-16.......V.6:1 s. relationship is a strange and unnatural
T-16.......V.6:3 The s. relationship is the triumph of this
T-16.......V.7:1 the ego fosters in the s. relationship. This
T-16.......V.7:3 finds the s. relationship in which it thinks
T-16.......V.8:1 the ego seeks is always one that is more s..
T-16.......V.8:2 And whoever seems to possess a s. self is
T-16.......V.8:3 both partners see this s. self in each other,
T-16.......V.9:2 of littleness lies in every s. relationship,
T-16.......V.9:4 The real purpose of the s. relationship, in
T-16.....V.10:1 the s. relationship as a triumph over God,
T-16.....V.10:5 that is acted out in the s. relationship.
T-16.....V.11:4 is this ritual enacted in the s. relationship.
T-16.....V.12:1 Whenever any form of s. relationship
T-16.....V.12:2 The s. relationship is a ritual of form,
T-16.....V.12:4 The s. relationship must be recognized
T-16.....V.13:1 See in the s. relationship nothing more
T-16......VI.1:1 The search for the s. relationship is the
T-16......VI.1:2 s. relationship has value only to the ego.
T-16......VI.1:3 unless a relationship has s. value it has no
T-16......VI.1:3 no meaning, for it perceives all love as s..
T-16......VI.3:2 of guilt, the real lure in the s. relationship.
T-16......VI.3:4 the closer you look at the s. relationship,
T-16......VI.4:1 The s. relationship is totally meaningless
T-16......VI.4:4 The s. relationship is a device for limiting
T-16......VI.4:5 total lack of value of the s. relationship, if
T-16......VI.5:7 Yet the s. relationship the ego seeks does
T-16......VI.7:6 frame of reference is built around the s.
T-16......VI.8:7 illusion of love in any s. relationship here.
T-16......VI.9:1 in the s. relationship is really part of you.
T-16....VI.12:1 to a s. relationship which still attracts you
T-16.....VII.1:1 without relinquishing the s. relationship.
T-16.....VII.1:2 For the s. relationship is an attempt to re-
T-16.....VII.1:3 all enter into the s. relationship, which
T-16.....VII.1:4 for choosing a s. partner without the past
T-16.....VII.2:1 The s. relationship takes vengeance on
T-16.....VII.2:3 it. No s. relationship is experienced in the
T-16.....VII.3:7 the s. relationship you are allowing your
T-16.....VII.4:1 in the s. relationship that binds you to it,
T-16.....VII.5:1 In the s. relationship it does not seem to
T-16.....VII.5:3 that the s. relationship is the acting out of
T-16.....VII.5:5 In seeking the s. relationship, you look
T-17......IV.2:3 not deprive you of your s. relationships,
T-17......IV.2:7 Every s. relationship you have made is a
T-17......IV.3:3 Every s. relationship you have made has,
T-17......IV.4:1 the s. relationship was the ego's answer to
T-17......IV.5:8 The s. relationship, which is its chief
T-17......IV.6:1 the s. relationship protects is but a system
T-17......IV.6:3 Yet the s. relationship still seems to you
T-17......IV.8:1 s. relationship has the most imposing and
T-17... VIII.1:1 instant is nothing more than a s. case, or
T-18.........I.1:4 For this s. purpose, one is judged more
T-18.........I.3:7 with s. emphasis on certain parts, and
T-18.........I.3:7 or rejection for acting out a s. form of fear
T-18.........I.4:6 every s. relationship that you have ever
T-18....... II.5:16 the s. relationship has a special place. It is
T-18....... II.5:16 the special relationship has a s. place. It is
T-18....... II.5:19 The s. relationship is your determination
T-18....... II.6:4 the Holy Spirit does in the s. relationship.
T-18....... II.6:7 The s. relationship will remain, not as a
T-18....... II.7:1 Your s. relationship will be a means for
T-18....... II.9:3 your s. relationship meet its conditions.
T-18....... V.5:3 within it is that it is still a s. relationship.
T-18....... V.5:4 the Holy Spirit, Who *has* a s. function here
T-18.....VI.11:2 sometimes hoped for in s. relationships.
T-18.....VII.6:4 This is the s. means this course is using to
T-18. VIII.12:1 this; love has entered your s. relationship,
T-19....... II.5:5 of the s. relationship in its interpretation.
T19.....IV.C.1:1 s. relationship the Holy Spirit entered, it
T-20......IV.5:3 whose s. function here is to release him,
T-20......IV.6:6 to learn its s. function in the Holy Spirit's
T-21...... III.1:1 All s. relationships have sin as their goal.
T-22...... III.4:5 is but error in a s. form the ego venerates.
T-24.........I.3:5 Only the s. could have enemies, for they
T-24.........I.4:4 the s. one is "natural" and "just." The
T-24.........I.4:5 The s. ones feel weak and frail because of
T-24.........I.4:5 what would make them s. *is* their enemy.
T-24.........I.8:8 has been made clean of s. goals. And
T-24.......I.8:10 perspective can the s. have that does not
T-24.........I.9:1 s. must defend illusions against the truth.
T-24....... II.3:5 His "s." sons are many, never one, each
T-24....... II.4:1 You are not s.. If you think you are, and
T-24........II.5:3 To every s. one a different message, and
T-24........II.5:5 The s. messages the special hear convince
T-24........II.5:5 The special messages the s. hear convince
T-24........II.5:5 each in his s. sins and "safe" from love,
T-24......II.10:4 He is not s., for He would not keep one
T-24......II.10:5 And it is this you fear, for if He is not s.,
T-24......II.10:6 you. Not s., but possessed of everything,
T-24......II.13:2 it demands a s. place God cannot enter,
T-24......II.13:4 and in loneliness your s. kingdom, apart
T-24...... III.7:1 The s. ones are all asleep, surrounded by
T-25.........I.5:5 mad desire to be separate, different and s.
T-25..........VI.h The S. Function
T-25...... VI.4:2 each He gives a s. function in salvation he
T-25...... VI.4:3 complete until he finds his s. function,
T-25...... VI.5:2 And by this act of s. faithfulness to one
T-25.... VI.5:10 He *has* a s. part in time for so he chose,
T-25...... VI.6:7 His s. sin was made his special grace. His
T-25...... VI.6:7 His special sin was made his s. grace. His
T-25...... VI.6:8 grace. His s. hate became his special love.
T-25...... VI.6:8 grace. His special hate became his s. love.
T-25...... VI.7:1 The Holy Spirit needs your s. function,
T-25...... VI.7:2 Think not you lack a s. value here. You
T-25...... VI.7:7 you see it as your s. function in the plan
T-25..... VII.7:1 Your s. function is the special form in
T-25..... VII.7:1 Your special function is the s. form in
T-25..... VII.7:3 The form is suited to your s. needs, and to
T-25..... VII.7:3 and to the s. time and place in which you
T-25..... VII.7:5 to those who are insane requires s. choice.
T-25..... VII.9:2 To each his s. function is designed to be
T-25..... VII.9:5 for he has a s. part in everyone's escape.
T-25..... VII.9:6 without a s. function in the hope of peace,
T-25... VII.12:7 plan in which your s. function has a part.
T-25... VII.12:8 For here your s. function is made whole,
T-25.... VIII.9:6 It is His s. function to hold out to you the
T-25..VIII.11:5 Each s. function He allots is but for this;
T-25..VIII.12:5 Your s. function is a call to Him, that He
T-25..VIII.12:7 Holy Spirit's s. function has been fulfilled.
T-25..VIII.13:4 the s. really understand that justice is the
T-25..VIII.14:3 Your s. function shows you nothing else
T-25...... IX.6:7 It is not a s. gift to some, to be withheld
T-25...... IX.7:2 given specially to an elect and s. group,
T-26.........I.5:2 Without your s. function has this world
T-26.........I.8:4 s. function to ensure the door be opened,
T-26.........I.8:5 Holy Spirit's s. function but to release the
T-26........II.1:6 purpose to attempt to solve it in a s. form.
T-26........II.6:5 Consider once again your s. function. One
T-26........II.7:5 What seemed once to be a s. problem, a
T-26........II.8:4 s. function opens wide the door beyond
T-26....... III.7:1 Is not this like your s. function, where the
T-27....VIII.2:5 looks about for s. bodies that can share its
T-29....VIII.8:6 hope his s. deities will give him more than
T-30...... III.3:3 To seek a s. person or a thing to add to
T-30...... VI.5:6 a mistake; a s. form of error that remains
W-pI.....31.3:4 without any s. investment on your part.
WpI...rI.in.4:2 that you learn to require no s. settings in
W-pI.....74.4:1 resolve, single it out for s. consideration.
W-pI.....75.9:2 or so that today is a time for s. celebration
W-pI.....79.2:1 world seems to have his own s. problems.
W-pI.....81.2:1 when s. difficulties seem to arise might be
W-pI...91.11:3 form would be helpful for this s. purpose:
W-pI.....95.4:1 for the day has s. advantages at the stage
W-pI.....98.1:1 Today is a day of s. dedication. We take a
W-pI.....98.5:2 hourly to recognize your s. function here?
W-pI.....98.9:2 enable you to understand your s. function
W-pI...99.11:1 There is a s. message for today which has
W-pI...108.5:3 For these are but some s. cases of one law
W-pI...108.6:1 receiving are the same has s. usefulness,
W-pI...108.6:2 this s. case has proved it always works, in
W-pI...108.7:1 with the s. case of giving and receiving.
WpI. rIII.in1:3 a s. format for these practice periods, that
W-pI...124.8:4 nor s. words to guide your meditation.
W-pI...125.9:5 yourself you have a s. purpose for this day
W-pI.126.11:1 an aim which makes this day of s. value to
W-pI.131.15:1 that today should be a time of s. gladness,
W-pI.135.26:5 yourself this is a s. day for learning, and
WpI. rIV.in9:3 s. time of blessing and of happiness for us
W-pI...157.1:2 It is a s. time of promise in your calendar
Wi181-200 1:1 Our next few lessons make a s. point of
Wi181-200 2:1 the s. blocks that keep your vision narrow

W-pI ... 184.1:5 By this you designate its s. attributes, and
WpI rVI.in.3:8 of the s. thought we practice for the day,
WpI rVI.in.4:1 and s. forms of practicing for this review.
WpI rVI.in.6:5 such s. applications of each day's idea, we
W-pII .. in.11:2 instructions on a theme of s. relevance
W-pII .. in.11:3 s. thoughts should be reviewed each day,
W-pII . 241.1:2 It is a time of s. celebration. For today
W-pII . 274.2:1 A s. blessing comes to us today, from
W-pII . 317.1:1 I have a s. place to fill; a role for me alone
M-in .......... 1:4 act of teaching is regarded as a s. activity,
M-1 ........... 4:1 This is a manual for a s. curriculum,
M-1 ........... 4:1 of a s. form of the universal course. There
M-4 ........... 1:4 God gives s. gifts to His teachers, because
M-4 ........... 1:4 have a s. role in His plan for Atonement.
M-4 ........... 1:6 of time. These s. gifts, born in the holy
M-4 ..... VII.1:1 has s. meaning to the teacher of God. It is
M-5 ....... II.2:8 S. agents seem to be ministering to him,
M-9 ........... 1:6 but these are generally s. cases. By far the
M-21 ......... 4:6 process is merely a s. case of the lesson in
M-22 ......... 1:4 idea, just as s. areas of hell in Heaven are
M-22 ......... 4:7 This recognition has no s. reference. It is
M-23 ............h JESUS HAVE A S. PLACE IN HEALING?
M-23 ......... 1:6 does an invocation call forth any s. power
M-25 ......... 2:8 He is doing nothing s., and there is no
M-25 ......... 3:6 the "unseen," or "s." favors from God.
M-25 ......... 3:7 God gives no s. favors, and no one has
M-25 ......... 3:8 of magic are s. powers "demonstrated."
C-6............. 3:2 In order to fulfill this s. function the Holy
P-3......... II.1:9 These people need no s. rules, of course,
P-3......... II.1:9 may be called upon to use s. applications
P-3......... II.2:2 For this, however, he needs s. training,
S-3........ III.4:5 bearer of the s. gift that brings the healing
S-3........ IV.1:7 They are not s.. They are holy. They have
S-3........ IV.1:9 of s. attributes through which they can

## specialized 1

P-2...........I.4:3 only a somewhat more s. teacher of God.

## specially 1

T-25...... IX.7:2 were given s. to an elect and special group

## specialness 116

T-1......... V.3:5 The s. of God's Sons does not stem from
T-16.........I.6:6 they always contain some element of s..
T-16...... IV.8:7 No s. can offer you what God has given,
T-16....... V.4:2 to secure for the self the s. that He denied.
T-16....... V.4:3 the ego that you believe this s. is not hell,
T-16....... V.9:2 for only the deprived could value s.. The
T-16....... V.9:3 The demand for s., and the perception of
T-16....... V.9:3 of the giving of s. as an act of love, would
T-16..... V.10:7 not think it offers the s. that you demand.
T-24..............h THE GOAL OF S.
T-24............I.h S. as a Substitute for Love
T-24.........I.3:1 though unrecognized, is faith in s.. This
T-24.........I.4:3 does s. become a means and end at once.
T-24.........I.4:4 For s. not only sets apart, but serves as
T-24.........I.5:1 S. is the great dictator of the wrong
T-24.........I.5:4 S. must be defended. Illusions can attack
T-24.........I.5:6 must become to keep your s. *is* an illusion.
T-24.........I.5:7 so that your s. can live on his defeat. For
T-24.........I.5:8 For s. is triumph, and its victory is his
T-24.........I.6:4 You are his enemy in s.; his friend in a
T-24.........I.6:5 S. can never share, for it depends on goals
T-24.........I.7:7 no s. of any kind between you and him?
T-24.........I.7:9 not always your belief your s. is limited by
T-24.........I.8:1 comes from each unrecognized belief in s.
T-24.........I.9:2 is s. but an attack upon the Will of God?
T-24.......... II.h The Treachery of S.
T-24....... II.1:2 none. S. always makes comparisons. It is
T-24....... II.1:5 of him a tiny measure of your s. instead.
T-24....... II.2:1 Pursuit of s. is always at the cost of peace.
T-24....... II.2:7 But the pursuit of s. must bring you pain.
T-24....... II.2:9 value s. is to esteem an alien will to which
T-24....... II.3:1 S. is the idea of sin made real. Sin is
T-24....... II.3:7 their s. instead of Heaven and instead of
T-24....... II.4:2 defend your s. against the truth of what
T-24 .......II.4:3 you, when it is your s. to which you listen,
T-24 .......II.5:1 You can defend your s., but never will
T-24 .......II.5:5 from love, which does not see his s. at all.
T-24 .......II.5:6 show them that the s. they think they see
T-24 .......II.6:4 And all the world he made, and all his s.,
T-24 .......II.7:1 who have chained your savior to your s.,
T-24 .......II.7:7 not the dream of s. remain between you.
T-24 .......II.8:2 He *is* the enemy of s., but only friend to
T-24 .......II.8:5 Let him forgive you all your s., and make
T-24 .......II.8:7 but you, to save his s. and kill his Self.
T-24 .......II.9:3 Your brother's s. and yours *are* enemies,
T-24 .....II.10:1 Here is your savior *from* your s.. He is in
T-24 .....II.11:6 And only s. could make the truth of God
T-24 .....II.12:1 S. is the seal of treachery upon the gift of
T-24 .....II.13:1 The hope of s. makes it seem possible
T-24 .....II.14:4 The death of s. is not your death, but your
T-24 ........ III.h The Forgiveness of S.
T-24 ..... III.1:1 Forgiveness is the end of s.. Only
T-24 ..... III.2:1 Whatever form of s. you cherish, you
T-24 ..... III.3:4 But s. is not the truth in you. *It* can be
T-24 ..... III.4:4 It is your s. that is attacked by everything
T-24 ..... III.4:7 while s. stands like a flaming sword of
T-24 ..... III.5:3 They *are* the same, for neither One wills s..
T-24 ..... III.6:1 a perfect Son, for your illusions of your s..
T-24 ..... III.6:6 of one thought of s. to mar your rest.
T-24 ..... III.6:7 Forgive the Holy One the s. He could not
T-24 ..... III.7:4 They are lost in dreams of s.. They hate
T-24 ..... III.8:1 The slaves of s. will yet be free. Such is
T-24 ... III.8:11 Love not your s. instead of Them. The
T-24 ........ IV.h S. versus Sinlessness
T-24 ..... IV.1:1 S. is a lack of trust in anyone except
T-24 ..... IV.2:1 could the purpose of the body be but s.?
T-24 ..... IV.3:3 To minds intent on s. it is impossible. Yet
T-24 ..... IV.3:7 one. Nothing could make less sense to s..
T-24 ... IV.3:10 This shift in purpose does "endanger" s.,
T-24 ... IV.3:15 given s. has left you bankrupt and your
T-24 ..... IV.4:3 To s. the answer must be "no." A sinless
T-24 ..... IV.4:8 but just a dream of s. that lasts an instant,
T-24 ..... IV.5:3 Your s. seemed safe because of it. And
T-24 ..... IV.5:6 And so is s. his "enemy," and yours as
T-24 ...... V.1:4 S., too, takes joy in what it sees, although
T-24 ...... V.2:1 There is no dream of s., however hidden
T-24 ...... V.4:1 Yet let your s. direct his way, and you will
T-24 ...... V.4:3 it. For what can s. delight in but to kill?
T-24 ...... V.7:6 His perfect lack of s. He offers you, that
T-24 ...... V.8:1 You who would be content with s., and
T-24 ..... VI.5:3 Let not his s. obscure the truth in him, for
T-24 ..... VI.6:5 s. that hides the face of Christ from him,
T-24 ..... VI.8:8 s. looks on his body and beholds him not.
T-24 ... VI.10:6 And never doubt but that your s. will
T-24 ... VI.11:1 S. is the function that you gave yourself.
T-24 ... VI.11:5 was for this; you wanted s. to be the truth.
T-24 ... VI.13:2 is the voice of s. heard clearly, judging
T-24 .... VII.1:1 defend the s. he wants to be the truth! His
T-24 .... VII.1:3 Nothing his s. demands does he withhold
T-24 .... VII.1:6 too dear to save his s. from the least slight
T-24 .... VII.2:6 tribute you have given s. belongs to him,
T-24 .... VII.2:8 Nothing you gave to s. but is his due. And
T-24 .... VII.3:1 your worth while s. claims you instead?
T-24 .... VII.3:3 Seek not to make your s. the truth, for if it
T-24 .... VII.4:6 fish, to house your s. in better style, or
T-24 .. VII.10:6 Yet your s. whispers, "Here is my own
T-24 VII.11:11 It is not bound to s. but by your choice.
T-25 ...... in.2:7 to see as is his s. set forth within his body.
T-25 ........I.6:1 of s. can be corrected where the error lies.
T-25 ..... III.3:5 For s., it is the perfect frame to set it off;
T-25 ..... III.5:4 pitiful attempts of s. to put it out of mind,
T-25 ..... VI.4:1 is the Holy Spirit's kind perception of s.;
T-25 ..... VI.5:4 uses to translate s. from sin into salvation
T-25 ..... VI.6:6 The s. he chose to hurt himself did God
T-25 ..... VI.7:6 darkness does your s. appear to be attack.
T-25 ... VIII.5:8 with a mind that can conceive of s. at all.
T-25 . VIII.11:1 As s. cares not who pays the cost of sin,
T-25 . VIII.13:2 How can s. be just? Judge not because you
T-25 ..... IX.6:8 salvation, if its purpose is the end of s.?
T-25 ..... IX.7:2 as less deserving, then is He ally to s..
T-26 ..... III.7:1 by change of purpose in what once was s.,
T-26 .. VII.19:6 The unity that s. denies will save them all,
T-26 .. VII.19:6 them all, for what is one can have no s..
T-27 .......II.7:4 obeys; that healing sees no s. at all. It does
M-4 ........... 1:5 Their s. is, of course, only temporary; set
P-3........II.10:1 that any form of s. must be defended, and

## specific 87

T-3 .........V.2:2 you do so out of a s. sense of lack or need.
T-3 .........V.2:3 a s. purpose has no true generalizability.
T-3 .........V.2:8 The highly s. nature of invention is not
T-4 .........II.1:5 Perception, however, is always s., and
T-4 ...... VII.1:1 correction is more helpful in a s. context.
T-4 ...... VII.1:2 Ego illusions are quite s., although the
T-4 ...... VII.2:5 is a reaction to a s. person or persons. The
T-4 ...... VII.2:7 It merely responds in certain s. ways to
T-4 ...... VII.4:2 Existence, however, is s. in how, what and
T-9 .........II.1:2 only true in connection with s. things that
T-9 .........II.2:3 is why certain s. forms of healing are not
T-11 ... VIII.5:1 s. for you to understand and use. Yet
T-11 ... VIII.5:4 Nothing could be more s. than to be told
T-11 ... VIII.5:5 Holy Spirit will answer every s. problem
T-11 ... VIII.5:5 as long as you believe that problems are s.
T-15 .......II.6:2 will receive very s. instructions as you go
T-17 ..... VI.1:5 Now He will work with you to make it s.,
T-17 ..... VI.1:5 you to make it specific, for application *is* s.
T-17 ..... VI.1:6 certain very s. guidelines He provides for
T-18 ... VI.12:3 even a general idea without s. reference.
T-27 .......V.8:1 Problems are not s. but they take specific
T-27 .......V.8:1 are not specific but they take s. forms,
T-27 .......V.8:1 and these s. shapes make up the world.
T-27 .......V.8:6 is. But healing is apparent in s. instances,
T-30 ...... in.1:2 now you need s. methods for attaining it.
T-30 ..... III.1:1 Idols are quite s.. But your will is
T-30 ... III.2:10 the idol, thus reducing it to a s. form. Yet
W-in.......... 3:3 description of the s. procedures by which
W-pI ...... 5.2:1 using the idea for today for a s. perceived
W-pI ...... 9.5:1 attempted, s. exclusion must be avoided.
W-pI .... 13.1:1 except that it is more s. as to the emotion
W-pI .... 14.7:2 Be very s. in applying it. Say: *God did not*
W-pI .... 15.4:4 number of s. subjects for the application
W-pI .... 17.4:1 four s. practice periods are recommended
W-pI .... 21.1:2 s. mind-searching periods are necessary,
W-pI .... 21.5:1 Try to be as s. as possible. You may, for
W-pI .... 28.1:1 Today we are really giving s. application
W-pI .... 33.3:2 S. applications of today's idea should also
W-pI .... 34.4:1 to experience difficulty in thinking of s.
W-pI .... 34.4:2 however, not to make any s. exclusions.
W-pI .... 34.5:3 If a s. form of temptation arises in your
W-pI .... 34.6:2 you change your mind in any s. context,
W-pI .... 35.7:3 Pick up any s. situation that occurs to you
W-pI .... 35.8:1 in which nothing s. occurs to you. Do not
W-pI .... 35.8:2 to think up s. things to fill the interval,
W-pI .... 35.9:1 pick up a s. attribute or attributes you are
W-pI .... 38.6:1 in its original form unless a s. problem
W-pI .... 38.6:2 the more s. form in applying the idea to it
W-pI .... 39.7:1 S. situations, events or personalities you
W-pI .... 46.7:2 more s. applications if they are needed.
W-pI .... 80.6:3 for today to any s. problem that may arise
WpI.. rII.in.6:1 and more s. forms when needed. Some
WpI.. rII.in.6:2 needed. Some s. forms are included in the
W-pI .... 81.2:1 Some s. forms for applying this idea
W-pI .... 81.4:1 S. forms for using this idea might include
W-pI .... 82.2:1 for s. forms for applying this idea are: *Let*
W-pI .... 82.4:1 Suitable s. forms of this idea include: *Let*
W-pI .... 83.2:1 More s. applications of this idea might
W-pI .... 83.4:1 forms for s. applications of this idea are:
W-pI .... 84.2:1 these s. forms helpful in applying the idea
W-pI .... 84.4:1 s. forms for applying this idea would be
W-pI .... 85.2:1 S. applications for this idea might be
W-pI .... 85.4:1 idea are suitable for more s. applications:
W-pI .... 86.4:1 S. applications for this idea might be in
W-pI .... 87.2:1 idea would be helpful for s. applications:
W-pI .... 87.4:1 forms of this idea for s. applications: *Let*
W-pI .... 88.2:1 forms for s. applications of this idea: *This*
W-pI .... 88.4:1 For s. forms in applying this idea, these
W-pI .... 89.2:1 suggestions for s. applications of this idea
W-pI .... 89.4:1 Useful s. forms for applying this idea
W-pI .... 90.2:1 S. applications of this idea might be in
W-pI .... 90.4:1 the idea will be useful for s. applications:
W-pI .. 161.7:1 Hate is s.. There must be a thing to be

| | |
|---|---|
| T-2 V.7:1 | always begins with the awakening of **s.**, |
| T-3 II.5:1 | his **s.** into the Hands of his Father. By |
| T-3 IV.1:6 | **S.** has no levels, and all conflict arises |
| T-3 IV.5:7 | This places it in the service of **s.**, where |
| T-3 IV.5:9 | it could not entirely separate itself from **s.** |
| T-3 IV.5:9 | **s.** that it derives its whole power to make |
| T-3 IV.5:11 | because the mind belongs to **s.** which God |
| T-3 IV.6:4 | **S.**, which knows, could not be reconciled |
| T-3 IV.6:5 | This makes **s.** almost inaccessible to the |
| T-3 IV.6:6 | Thereafter, **s.** is perceived as a threat, |
| T-3 IV.7:3 | who remembered **s.** and its knowledge. |
| T-3 IV.7:6 | remembered **s.** and its real purpose. |
| T-3 V.7:3 | God did create **s.** in His Own Thought |
| T-3 V.9:3 | **S.** knows God completely. That is its |
| T-3 VI.10:1 | Peace is a natural heritage of **s.**. Everyone |
| T-4 in.1:6 | but to be inspired is to be in the **s.**. To be |
| T-4 in.1:7 | in the right sense is to be inspired or in **s.**. |
| T-4 in.2:1 | You can speak from the **s.** or from the ego |
| T-4 in.2:2 | speak from **s.** you have chosen to "Be still |
| T-4 in.2:6 | but **s.** cannot embark on them because it |
| T-4 I.2:6 | Nothing can reach **s.** from the ego, and |
| T-4 I.2:6 | and nothing can reach the ego from **s.**. |
| T-4 I.2:7 | **S.** can neither strengthen the ego nor |
| T-4 I.2:11 | because **s.** cannot perceive and the ego |
| T-4 I.3:1 | **S.** need not be taught, but the ego must |
| T-4 I.3:2 | destruction, of the ego to the light of **s.**. |
| T-4 I.6:1 | in any situation, but **s.** cannot clash at all. |
| T-4 I.7:9 | Your **s.** is never at stake because He did. |
| T-4 I.8:5 | of your ego but within easy reach of **s.**. |
| T-4 I.9:10 | is fearful to the ego, but joyous to the **s.**. |
| T-4 I.10:5 | is as incapable of deception as is the **s.** He |
| T-4 I.12:1 | **s.** you can do everything for the salvation |
| T-4 I.12:2 | is a lesson for the ego, not for the **s.**. Spirit |
| T-4 I.12:3 | spirit. **S.** is beyond humility, because it |
| T-4 I.13:1 | your ego if you wish, but never for your **s.**. |
| T-4 I.13:8 | mind. **S.** is far beyond the need of your |
| T-4 II.8:6 | **S.** in its knowledge is unaware of the ego. |
| T-4 II.8:8 | While the ego is equally unaware of **s.**, it |
| T-4 II.9:7 | However, salvation does not apply to **s.**, |
| T-4 II.11:9 | **S.** is immortal, and immortality is a |
| T-4 III.1:7 | too, have a Kingdom that your **s.** created. |
| T-4 III.1:10 | ego and your **s.** will never be co-creators, |
| T-4 III.1:10 | your **s.** and your Creator will always be. |
| T-4 III.3:1 | now why the ego regards **s.** as its "enemy. |
| T-4 III.3:6 | sense of temporary existence **s.** offers you |
| T-4 VI.4:1 | ego and the **s.** do not know each other. |
| T-4 VI.5:6 | misery with the ego and joy with the **s.**. |
| T-4 VII.3:1 | **s.** reacts in the same way to everything it |
| T-5 I.1:5 | be. Remember that **s.** knows no difference |
| T-5 I.1:6 | thinks according to the laws **s.** obeys, and |
| T-5 I.1:7 | **s.** getting is meaningless and giving is all. |
| T-5 I.1:8 | **s.** holds everything by giving it, and thus |
| T-5 II.2:1 | The Holy Spirit is the **s.** of joy. He is the |
| T-5 III.7:1 | of the ego and the knowledge of the **s.**. His |
| T-5 IV.3:5 | of the **s.** do not leave the mind that thinks |
| T-5 VII.3:3 | you are of one mind and **s.** with Him. |
| T-7 IX.1:4 | is of **s.** because that is how God created it. |
| T-7 IX.1:5 | between them always in favor of the **s.**. To |
| T-7 IX.1:5 | mind that lies between the ego and the **s.**, |
| T-7 IX.1:7 | To **s.** this is truth, because it knows its |
| T-7 IX.2:1 | **S.** knows that the awareness of all its |
| T-7 IX.2:8 | **S.** yearns to share its being as its Creator |
| T-7 IX.3:7 | of your **s.** can interfere with its being. |
| T-7 IX.4:8 | **S.** is fulfilling its function, and only |
| T-8 VII.9:5 | the mind you tried to separate *from* **s.** can |
| T-8 VII.9:5 | beyond its distortions and return *to* **s.**. The |
| T-11 VI.5:8 | it, not in the **s.** of sacrifice and submission |
| T-12 IV.7:3 | invest in it, not with money but with **s.**. |
| T-12 IV.7:4 | For **s.** is will, and will is the "price" of the |
| T-12 VI.2:1 | He knows nothing but the **s.** as you. He is |
| T-12 VI.7:2 | **s.** of God's Son shines in the Mind of the |
| T19 IV.D.5:4 | of the body is given up in favor of the **s.**, |
| T-31 VI.h | Recognizing the **S.** |
| T-31 VI.1:1 | You see the flesh or recognize the **s.**. |
| T-31 VI.1:6 | you are, as flesh or **s.** in your own belief. If |
| T-31 VI.1:8 | But choose the **s.**, and all Heaven bends to |
| T-31 VI.3:1 | behold the **s.** and perceive the body not. It |
| T-31 VI.6:7 | Are you a **s.**, deathless, and without the |
| W-pI 96.3:7 | you. If you are **s.**, then the body must be |
| W-pI 96.4:1 | **S.** makes use of mind as means to find its |
| W-pI 96.4:2 | serves the **s.** is at peace and filled with joy. |
| W-pI 96.4:3 | Its power comes from **s.**, and it is fulfilling |
| W-pI 96.4:4 | mind can also see itself divorced from **s.**, |
| W-pI 96.5:1 | Yet mind apart from **s.** cannot think. It |
| W-pI 96.10:3 | it will again flow out from **s.** to the spirit |
| W-pI 96.10:3 | to the **s.** in all things created by the Spirit |
| W-pI 97.h | I am **s.**. |
| W-pI 97.2:2 | **s.** lovingly endowed with all your Father's |
| W-pI 97.2:3 | You are the **s.** which completes Himself, |
| W-pI 97.4:1 | the **s.** in whose mind abides the miracle in |
| W-pI 97.4:4 | Him you are the **s.** that abides in Him, |
| W-pI 97.7:2 | ***S.** am I, a holy Son of God, free of all limits,* |
| W-pI 97.8:2 | to you, reminding you that you are **s.**, one |
| W-pI 114.1:1 | (97) I am **s.**. *I am the Son of God. No body* |
| W-pI 114.1:3 | *No body can contain my* **s.**, *nor impose on* |
| W-pI 114.3:2 | I am **s.**. On the half hour: I will accept my |
| W-pII 9.3:2 | returned to **s.** in the name of true creation |
| W-pII 330.1:4 | accept God's gifts has been restored to **s.**, |
| M-12 1:4 | wholly **s.** now no longer sees himself as a |
| M-12 3:4 | those who do not realize that they are **s.**. |
| C-1 h | MIND – **S.** |
| C-1 1:1 | used to represent the activating agent of **s.** |
| C-1 1:3 | **S.** is the Thought of God which He created |
| C-1 1:4 | The unified **s.** is God's one Son, or Christ. |
| C-1 2:4 | the course *as if* it has two parts; **s.** and ego. |
| C-1 3:1 | **S.** is the part that is still in contact with |
| C-1 3:3 | It would, however, be an equivalent of "**s.**, |
| C-1 4:2 | **S.** retains the potential for creating, but |
| C-6 1:2 | with Him and in His likeness or **s.**, is |

## Spirit's 139

*See* Holy Spirit's
*spirit's*

## spirit's 7

*Spirit's*

| | |
|---|---|
| T-1 I.34:3 | **s.** strength leaves no room for intrusions. |
| T-1 V.1:2 | **s.** original state of direct communication |
| T-4 I.10:1 | The ego is afraid of the **s.** joy, because |
| T-4 I.12:5 | The Kingdom of Heaven is the **s.** right, |
| T-4 II.8:5 | the **s.** acknowledgment and thus establish |
| T-7 IX.2:2 | of its Creator is therefore **s.** own fullness, |
| T-7 IX.3:1 | of God's Being is **s.** only function. Its |

## spirit-identification 1

| | |
|---|---|
| T-1 I.29:3 | deny body-identification and affirm **s.**. |

## spirited

*See* dis-spirited

## spiriting

*See* dis-spiriting

## spiritual 12

| | |
|---|---|
| T-1 I.12:2 | or the higher or **s.** level of experience. One |
| T-1 I.12:3 | the physical, and the other creates the **s.**. |
| T-1 I.22:3 | not exist. This leads to a denial of **s.** sight. |
| T-2 III.1:11 | **S.** sight, on the other hand, cannot see the |
| T-2 III.3:8 | reawakens **s.** vision, simultaneously |
| T-2 III.4:1 | **S.** vision literally cannot see error, and |
| T-2 III.4:3 | **S.** vision looks within and recognizes |
| T-2 V.7:2 | afraid of what your **s.** sight will show you. |
| T-2 V.7:7 | Everything that results from **s.** awareness |
| T-3 III.4:1 | vision is the natural perception of **s.** sight, |
| T-3 III.4:2 | **S.** sight is symbolic, and therefore not a |
| W-pI 64.2:4 | becomes the **s.** recognition of salvation. |

## spiritualized 1

| | |
|---|---|
| T-3 III.5:11 | in its most **s.** form perception involves the |

## spite 8

| | |
|---|---|
| T-18 V.6:1 | Holy Spirit your willingness, in **s.** of fear, |
| T-21 VII.2:6 | of vengeance, bitterness and **s.** on him, to |
| T-22 V.6:6 | in **s.** of what you thought it was, that it is |
| T-27 V.8:11 | made in **s.** of all the differences you see, |
| W-pI 65.7:1 | to which you really want salvation in **s.** of |
| W-pI 137.7:2 | to disappear in **s.** of all the laws that hold |
| C-6 5:6 | no trace remains of dreams of **s.** in which |
| S-2 II.4:4 | it not kind to be accepting of another's **s.**, |

## splendid 1

| | |
|---|---|
| T-2 II.4:6 | defense so **s.** was needed that it could not |

## splendor 2

| | |
|---|---|
| W-pI 151.7:4 | you are vanish before the **s.** He beholds. |
| M-19 2:7 | whose **s.** reaches indescribable heights as |

## splintered 2

| | |
|---|---|
| T-18 I.4:3 | become so **s.** and subdivided and divided |
| T-18 VIII.2:6 | segment of Heaven, **s.** from the whole, |

## split 81

| | |
|---|---|
| T-2 VI.5:9 | mind. Your mind is therefore **s.**, and your |
| T-3 IV.2:1 | was the first **s.** introduced into the mind |
| T-3 VI.7:4 | is **s.** between the ego and the Holy Spirit, |
| T-3 VII.4:11 | is **s.** with the Holy Spirit on this point, |
| T-4 I.4:3 | dreaming is not really healing his **s.** mind. |
| T-4 IV.2:8 | together, but has literally **s.** your mind. |
| T-5 II.6:6 | Choosing depends on a **s.** mind. The Holy |
| T-5 III.9:3 | is merely another term for a **s.** mind. The |
| T-6 II.1:1 | **s.** in mind must involve a rejection of part |
| T-6 II.3:2 | reinforces your belief in your own **s.** mind |
| T-6 II.9:3 | Because your mind is **s.**, you can perceive |
| T-6 V.1:4 | teach you that you had made a **s.** mind, |
| T-7 IX.4:4 | A **s.** mind cannot perceive its fullness, |
| T-8 I.6:5 | mind will be **s.** about what your reality is. |
| T-8 VIII.9:5 | allow the body to be a mirror of a **s.** mind. |
| T-8 IX.8:7 | of sickness are signs that the mind is **s.**, |
| T-9 I.1:2 | the mind were already profoundly **s.**, |
| T-9 I.5:4 | If you did not have a **s.** mind, you would |
| T-10 I.1:1 | against them as long as your mind is **s.**, |
| T-10 IV.3:4 | If you perceive other gods your mind is **s.**, |
| T-10 IV.3:4 | and you will not be able to limit the **s.**, |
| T-11 VIII.9:2 | denying that his mind is **s.** you will heal |
| T-11 VIII.11:1 | of himself for his **s.** mind is yours, and |
| T-12 I.2:5 | This would obviously be a **s.** or an attack |
| T-12 III.7:3 | tolerate. A **s.** mind is endangered, and the |
| T-12 III.7:4 | Therefore the mind projects the **s.**, not |
| T-12 III.8:4 | for the one you made out of your **s.** mind, |
| T-12 IV.2:4 | of its source the ego is not wholly **s.** off, or |
| T-12 V.4:3 | cannot learn of perfect love with a **s.** mind |
| T-12 V.4:3 | a **s.** mind has made itself a poor learner. |
| T-12 V.7:8 | **s.** that makes its primary aim believable. |
| T-12 V.7:9 | not overcome the **s.** in this curriculum, |
| T-12 VII.6:8 | and if it is **s.** and wants to keep the split, it |
| T-12 VII.6:8 | and if it is split and wants to keep the **s.**, it |
| T-12 VII.7:10 | Yet as long as you perceive the world as **s.** |
| T-12 VIII.2:5 | **s.** mind and all its works were not created |
| T-13 in.1:3 | But herein lies the **s.**. For the mind that |
| T-13 II.1:3 | issue, then, the deepest **s.** of all occurs, for |
| T-13 V.6:5 | your own **s.** mind everywhere you look. |
| T-16 IV.1:9 | of the **s.** that lies in this you do not realize |
| T-16 IV.1:10 | you do, the **s.** will remain unrecognized, |
| T-16 IV.3:4 | from which hatred is **s.** off and kept apart. |
| T-17 VI.6:10 | it seeks to **s.** off segments of the situation |
| T-18 I.1:5 | its purpose **s.** accordingly. To fragment is |
| T-18 IX.1:3 | thought that seems **s.** off and separate, |
| T-19 III.6:4 | He must be **s.**, and torn between good |
| T-19 III.7:4 | God and His creation seem to be **s.** apart |
| T-24 III.2:4 | So does it seem to **s.** you off from God, |
| T-25 I.7:2 | apparent that a mind so **s.** could never be |
| T-25 VIII.8:3 | they think that justice is **s.** off from love, |
| T-26 VII.7:4 | Then would God's Will be **s.** in two, and |
| T-27 II.11:1 | In a **s.** mind, identity must seem to be |
| T-27 II.11:3 | Correction, to a mind so **s.**, must be a way |

T-27..... II.12:7 to represent a **s.** within a self perceived as
T-27..... II.13:2 view of function **s.** between the two. And
T-27..... II.16:3 as one because it is not **s.** in purpose, and
T-27...VII.11:3 which the choice is **s.** between a tiny you
T-28....... II.8:8 Effect and cause are first **s.** off, and then
T-28.....VII.3:2 and no allegiance to be **s.** between the two
T-28.....VII.3:3 A **s.** allegiance is but faithlessness to both,
T-31....... II.3:5 these roles, forever **s.** between the two.
W-pI.....68.1:6 seems to **s.** you off from your Source and
W-pI.....96.1:2 sense of being **s.** into opposites induces
W-pI.....96.3:3 be your Self, nor can your Self be **s.** in two
W-pI.....97.1:2 It accepts no **s.** identity, nor tries to weave
W-pI.....97.1:5 letting go illusions of a **s.** identity.
W-pI...110.4:2 no **s.** between your mind and other minds
W-pI...131.8:2 Nor is His creation **s.** in two. How could it
W-pI...137.2:3 **s.** apart and held in pieces by a solid wall
W-pI...139.5:4 **s.** your mind into what knows and does
W-pI...170.4:3 with perfect faith the **s.** you made is real.
W-pI...184.2:4 By this **s.** you think you are established as
W-pI...195.5:4 thus we **s.** them off from our awareness of
W-pI.196.10:2 you fear, the mind perceives itself as **s.**.
W-pII......2.2:3 the mind is **s.** there is a need of healing.
W-pII......2.2:4 that has the power to heal the **s.** became a
M-13........7:10 For it is here the **s.** with God occurs. A
M-13........7:11 A **s.** that is impossible. A split that cannot
M-13........7:12 A **s.** that cannot happen. Yet a split in
M-13........7:13 Yet a **s.** in which you surely will believe,
C-1.............2:1 In this world, because the mind is **s.**, the

### splits 3
T-4.......VII.1:3 becomes concrete, however, when it **s.**.
T-26.....VII.7:4 becomes impatient, **s.** the world apart,
T-27..... II.11:5 This **s.** his function off from yours, and

### splitting 4
T-7........VI.8:8 cannot coexist in your mind without **s.** it.
T-28....... V.1:2 Of a **s.** *off* and separating *from*? A gap that
T-29.....VII.8:3 within by **s.** what you are between the two
W-pI...170.3:2 **s.** your mind into two camps which seem

### spoil 1
T-17......III.4:5 does not enter at all to "**s.**" the dream.

### spoke 6
T-5......... V.3:3 We **s.** before of the authority problem as
T-6........ I.14:3 out of their own fear they **s.** of the "wrath
T-11..... V.18:6 Christ to you, you **s.** not of Christ to him.
T-16......III.2:8 in avoiding those which **s.** for the cause of
T-21..... II.10:4 we **s.** of your desire to create your own
W-pI.....71.2:2 if someone else **s.** or acted differently, if

### spoken 8
T-2.......VII.7:1 I have already briefly **s.** about readiness,
T-3........VI.7:1 I have **s.** of different symptoms, and at
T-4........VI.1:3 I have **s.** of the ego as if it were a separate
T-5...........I.4:9 I have **s.** before of the higher or "true"
T-7.......... V.9:9 increased. I have **s.** often of the increase of
T-16........ II.8:4 His Voice has **s.** clearly, and yet you have
T-16........ V.1:5 I have **s.** of this before, but there are some
W-pI...162.1:5 illusions vanish as these words are **s.**. For

### sponsors 2
T-4......... V.4:3 This is the belief that the ego **s.** eagerly.
T-18.........I.2:8 the fragmented relationships the ego **s.** to

### spot 14
T-13......III.7:5 leave any **s.** of pain hidden from His light,
T-13......III.9:4 there is one **s.** of fear to mar its welcome.
T-13...VII.13:3 will ensure it never can become a dark **s.**,
T-13......IX.7:1 for while you see one **s.** of guilt within you
T-13....... X.2:2 or even hold one **s.** of it to mar its purity.
T-17....... II.5:4 all. Each **s.** His reason touches grows alive
T-20...... VI.5:2 secret room, a tiny **s.** of senseless mystery,
T-20....VI.11:2 it prisoner in a tiny **s.** of space and time,
T-21...... III.9:9 it for you, without one **s.** of sin upon it,
T-26......IV.5:4 tiny **s.** that sin proclaimed to be its own.
T-26......IV.6:1 tiny **s.** of sin that stands between you and
T-31. VIII.12:5 and not one **s.** of darkness still remains to
W-pII.... 11.3:3 imperfection and of any **s.** upon its
P-2........ VI.6:7 retain one **s.** of sin in what he looks upon,

### spotless 2
T-14...... IX.5:1 In this world you can become a **s.** mirror,
T19. IV.A.16:1 you, on a table covered with a **s.** cloth, set

### spots 3
T-13......IV.6:3 They carry the **s.** of pain in your mind,
T-26...... IX.6:1 The holiest of all the **s.** on earth is where
W-pI.....99.9:1 seek out and lighten up all darkened **s.**,

### spread 7
T-13.........I.3:5 a long carpet **s.** along the past behind you
T-13.VII.16:10 And we will **s.** it like a veil of light across
T-18....... V.5:5 the happy dream through which He can **s.**
T19... IV.A.1:6 If it would **s.** across the whole creation, it
W-pI...121.2:1 no place where it can **s.** its wings in peace
W-pI...125.4:2 **s.** across the world the tidings of salvation
W-pI...183.2:2 as they **s.** out their wings to keep you safe,

### spreads 2
T-13....VI.11:8 and **s.** across this world in quiet joy. All
M-28 .........3:8 last illusion **s.** across the world, forgiving

### spring 5
T-12......VI.5:4 then the real world will **s.** to your sight,
T-13... VIII.4:6 The golden aspects of reality that **s.** to
W-pI.....79.5:4 Some **s.** up unexpectedly, just as you
W-pI.154.14:4 our Creator will **s.** to our sight and leap
W-pII....13.5:4 And everywhere the signs of life **s.** up, to

### springboard 1
W-pI.....30.1:1 The idea for today is the **s.** for vision.

### springs 3
T-18... VIII.9:2 See how life **s.** up everywhere! The desert
T-24....... II.6:2 the memory of Him **s.** instantly to mind.
T-30......IV.2:2 when a wooden head **s.** up as a closed box

### sprung 1
T-26......IX.3:5 miracles **s.** up as grass and flowers on the

### spun 1
W-pI...122.6:7 All the complexities the world has **s.** of

### spurious 2
T-4.......VII.2:6 results in **s.** generalization which is really
P-1.............1:2 begin to reconsider the **s.** cause and effect

### squandered 1
T-8........VI.4:1 had **s.** everything for nothing of any value

### squeak 1
T-30......IV.2:2 bear begins to **s.** as he takes hold of it.

### squeaking 1
T-30......IV.3:6 can laugh at popping heads and **s.** toys, as

### squeaks 1
T-22....... V.4:5 difficult to disregard its feeble **s.** that tell

### stab 5
T19... IV.D.7:6 no **s.** of fear nor the cold sweat of seeming
T-23...... IV.6:3 There is a **s.** of pain, a twinge of guilt, and
T-24.........I.8:4 **s.** of hate or wish to separate arises here.
T-27...... VI.6:6 to bless the world, a tiny **s.** of pain, a little
W-pI... 192.9:4 Every time you feel a **s.** of anger, realize

### stability 11
T-1......... V.6:7 upside down be conducive to increased **s.**.
T19....IV.A.8:5 Its seeming **s.** is its pervasive weakness,
T-22...... III.4:7 For here is its own **s.**, its heavy anchor in
T-25....VIII.6:7 Their world depends on sin's **s.**. And they
T-28..... VII.5:9 Yet its **s.** cannot be judged apart from its
T-29.........I.7:4 and go uncertainly, and offer no **s.** to you.
T-29........II.6:6 means? **S.** to those who are confused is
T-30..... VII.3:7 allowance for **s.** of meaning anywhere.
T-30..... VII.4:5 it to all events, and let them offer you **s.**.
T-30..... VII.7:3 interpretations which are lacking in **s.**, for
W-pI... 131.1:3 and the place to which he comes to find **s.**

### stabilize 4
T-4...... IV.11:8 the dis-spirited or to **s.** the unstable? I do
T-11...... VI.1:3 until beliefs are fixed that perceptions **s.**.
T-30..... VII.5:6 agreement makes interpretation **s.** and
P-2.........in.3:4 to **s.** it sufficiently to include within it the

### stabilized 2
T-3........ III.6:6 I am." Perception can and must be **s.**, but
T-30..... VII.4:1 only means whereby perception can be **s.**,

### stable 13
T-1......... V.6:6 is less **s.** than an upside-down orientation
T-3........ III.3:3 This establishes a seemingly **s.** state that
T-3........ III.6:6 and must be stabilized, but knowledge *is* **s.**
T-3......... V.3:3 Knowledge is always **s.**, and it is quite
T-3......... V.3:4 you are perfectly **s.** as God created you. In
T-3......... V.4:8 implies that there is nothing **s.** to know.
T-22.........I.6:5 he hears nor sights he sees are **s.** yet. But
T-24...... III.3:6 What rests on nothing never can be **s.**.
T-28.........II.6:8 without a **s.** cause with guaranteed effects
T-28...... IV.6:1 confused, for in the gap no **s.** self exists.
T-30..... VII.3:1 can endow events with **s.** meaning. But it
T-31....... VI.6:8 So the world is seen as **s.**, fully worthy of
W-pI... 137.6:3 be more solid and more **s.** than the mind.

### stacks 1
W-pI.....76.3:2 you have **s.** of green paper strips and piles

### stage 11
W-pI.....23.7:4 still at the **s.** of identifying the cause of the
WpI... rI.in.4:1 for practice periods at your **s.** of learning.
W-pI.....95.4:1 **s.** of learning in which you are at present.
W-pI... 162.1:2 it, as we reach another **s.** in learning. It
M-3 ...........5:3 that those involved have reached a **s.**
M-4 ..... I.A.3:8 that much, he goes on to the second **s.**.
M-4 ..... I.A.5:1 The third **s.** through which the teacher of
M-4 ..... I.A.7:1 next **s.** is indeed "a period of unsettling."
M-4 ..... I.A.8:5 This is the **s.** of real peace, for here is
P-2...........I.4:5 But whatever **s.** he is in, there are patients
P-3..........II.8:5 of the beginning **s.** of the first journey.

### stages 3
T-1........ IV.1:1 from darkness involves two **s.**: First, the
M-4 ...........1:3 at the beginning **s.** of their functioning as
S-1..........II.8:8 **s.** necessary to its attainment, however,

**stagger** 2

T-31..... II.11:5 a sense of endless doubting as you s. back
M-10 ......... 5:2 could merely s. and fall down beneath it.

**staggering** 1

M-4 ..... I.A.6:5 Its potential is literally s., and the teacher

**stain** 4

T-31...... VI.6:7 of corruption and the s. of sin upon you?
M-17 ....... 7:13 The s. of blood can never be removed,
M-17 ....... 7:13 bears this s. on him must meet with death
M-23 ......... 5:7 and no s. to mar your beautiful perfection

**stained**

*See* blood-stained

**stairs** 1

T-23..... II.22:6 whether you chose the s. to Heaven or the

**stairway** 2

T-23..... II.22:4 the twisted s. that leads from Heaven. Yet
S-1 ......... in.3:3 you up as you ascend the shining s. to the

**stake** 2

T-4........... I.7:8 is never at s. because God did not create it
T-4........... I.7:9 Your spirit is never at s. because He did.

**stalk** 1

P-2........ IV.3:2 now s. the earth in unrelenting waves,

**stalks** 2

T-23...... IV.1:4 and no illusion in any form s. Heaven.
T-27... VII.12:1 who s. you in the night and plots your

**stamp** 3

T-7........... I.5:5 Eternity is the indelible s. of creation. The
T-14.... XI.11:7 having the holy s. of immortality upon it.
T-19...... III.1:8 your own, could s. it out through fear.

**stamps** 1

T-14....... X.3:4 of order of difficulty that s. the miracle as

**stance** 1

W-pI... 186.5:5 to experience which might affront their s.

**stand** 165

T-1......... II.4:3 You s. below me and I stand below God.
T-1......... II.4:3 You stand below me and I s. below God.
T-1........ III.1:3 I s. at the end in case you fail temporarily.
T-3........ IV.7:8 Only your misperceptions s. in your way.
T-3......... V.4:7 Images are symbolic and s. for something
T-3....... VII.6:3 your own thought system will s. corrected
T-3....... VII.6:4 It cannot s. otherwise. You who fear
T-4........... I.2:1 Many s. guard over their ideas because
T-4........... I.2:5 thought system can s. on two foundations
T-4......... I.11:2 try to make this impoverished house s..
T-4......... I.11:5 Yet His home will s. forever, and is ready
T-4......... I.12:5 and s. forever as the mark of the Love of
T-8...... VIII.3:5 not give this false witness to the ego's s..
T-8........ IX.9:8 His Will must s. forever and in all things.
T-9........ III.1:2 in terms of the kind of "sense" they s. for.
T-9....... VII.7:5 it, because within it its foundation does s.
T-10........ II.2:4 would s. in the way of your remembering,
T-11....... in.2:8 or its whole thought system will not s..
T-11..... V.17:6 The witnesses for God s. in His light and
T-12........ II.6:5 not let your hatred s. in the way of love,
T-13 ....... X.4:4 them s. between you and your brothers,
T-13 ..... X.14:6 United in this praise we s. before the gates
T-14 ..... IV.3:1 therefore s. in grace before your Father,
T-14 ..... IV.9:5 that s. between you and what you know.
T-14 ...... V.8:6 S. quietly within this circle, and attract all
T-14 ...... V.9:4 I s. within the circle, calling you to peace.
T-14 ...... V.9:5 with me, and s. with me on holy ground.
T-14 ...... V.9:8 S. not outside, but join with me within.
T-14 ..... IX.2:2 the contradiction can no longer s.. How
T-14 ..... IX.2:3 How long can contradiction s. when its
T-15 ...... II.2:7 Through Him you s. before God's altar,
T-15 ..... IV.5:1 I s. within the holy instant, as clear as
T-15 ....... X.1:2 attraction of guilt does s. between them.
T-16 ..... III.6:7 s. outside your teaching and apart from it
T-16 ..... III.9:2 the attraction of those who s. on the other
T-16 ..... IV.2:2 For symbols s. for something else, and the
T-16 ... IV.12:5 now, and let nothing s. in the way of truth
T-17 .... V.14:1 brother s. together in the holy presence of
T-17 .... V.14:4 s. now which seems to make you suffer,
T-18 ..... I.10:7 the holy place in which you s. together.
T-18 ..... III.5:6 I s. with you and walk with you in your
T-18 ..... IX.7:3 Figures s. out and move about, actions
T-19 ........ I.4:5 centered on the body, to s. between you.
T-19 ...... I.13:4 for you s. at the same altar where grace
T-19 ...... I.14:1 brother s. before the altar God has raised
T-19 ...... I.14:6 and your brother who s. together before
T19.... IV.A.2:9 s. between your brothers and salvation?
T19.... IV.A.5:7 And all that seems to s. between you and
T19.. IV.A.5:10 to s. between Him and His holy purpose,
T19.... IV.A.6:3 illusions s. between you and your brother
T19.... IV.B.5:4 for we s. within the gates and not outside.
T19.. IV.C.11:2 for they must s. for something other than
T19... IV.D.6:1 And now you s. in terror before what you
T19... IV.D.7:6 of seeming death can s. against your will.
T19... IV.D.9:2 No one can s. before this obstacle alone,
T19... IV.D.9:4 S. you here a while and tremble not. You
T19. IV.D.11:4 forgiveness you still s. unforgiving. You
T19. IV.D.21:6 You and your brother s. together, still
T-20 ........ I.2:6 You s. beside your brother, thorns in one
T-20 ... VIII.6:7 everything will s. condemned before you.
T-21 ........ I.1:5 but which s. open before unseeing eyes,
T-21 ..... II.13:3 seems to s. between you and your brother
T-21 ... VI.10:2 it cannot be you s. apart from blessing.
T-21 ... VIII.5:7 have asked that nothing s. between the
T-22 ...... in.3:7 Just under Heaven does he s., but close
T-22 ..... IV.3:1 And so you and your brother s., here in
T-22 ...... V.3:4 In truth you and your brother s. together,
T-22 ...... V.6:5 Not one that does not seem to s., heavy
T-22 ...... V.6:8 what seems to s. between you and your
T-23 ...... II.6:1 on which the laws of chaos s. could not be
T-24 ...... II.1:6 you see in him you s. as tall and stately,
T-24 ...... II.9:5 holy place does truth s. waiting to receive
T-24 ..... III.7:2 see. Freedom and peace and joy s. there,
T-24 ... IV.3:11 truth. They will not s. before it. Yet what
T-25 ........ I.1:7 to s. between the aspects of His Holiness,
T-25 ........ I.2:8 sinfulness, wherein you s. condemned.
T-25 ........ I.4:6 You and your brother s. before Him now,
T-25 ..... III.8:1 to s. between you and His gentleness. It is
T-25 ..... IV.4:7 And in the sunlight you will s. in quiet, in
T-25 . VIII.9:11 same does mercy s. at God's right Hand,
T-26 ..... IV.3:1 which you s. is but the space that sin has
T-26 ..... IV.3:4 and s. upon the ground where sin has left
T-26 ...... V.6:6 And who can s. upon a distant shore, and
T-26 .... V.14:2 You s. no longer on the ground that lies
T-26 ..... IX.2:4 ground whereon you s. is holy ground
T-26 ..... IX.3:7 now you s. on ground so holy Heaven
T-26 ..... IX.4:6 join Them on the ground whereon you s..
T-27 ....... II.1:4 s. firmly in the way of trust and peace,
T-27 ..... III.2:6 must s. for empty space and nothingness.
T-27 ..... III.4:6 for what can s. for more than everything?
T-27 ..... III.6:4 want. It does not s. for double concepts.
T-27 ..... IV.7:3 because they s. apart from them, and see
T-27 .... V.10:4 will be seen, but thousands s. behind him
T-27 .... VII.7:1 to sin all s. within one little space. And it
T-28 ..... II.12:2 They s. in shining silence next to every
T-28 ..... III.8:2 seen to s. between you and your brother,
T-28 ..... IV.2:4 You s. apart from them, but not apart
T-28 ..... IV.5:1 do his, for he will join you where you s..
T-28 .... VII.7:4 away and yet this house will s. forever, for
T-29 ....... II.4:7 touched the holy ground whereon you s.,
T-29 ..... VI.5:2 death, you need not let it s. for this to you
T-29 ... VIII.2:6 and s. apart from all the misery the world
T-29 ... VIII.2:7 you from the world, and lets you s. apart,
T-30 ....... V.7:1 s. already at the edge of the real world.
T-31 ........ I.5:4 Now does your ancient overlearning s.
T-31 ....... II.2:1 again what seems to s. between you and
T-31 ....... V.5:3 you s. condemned because of what I am."
T-31 ..... V.13:6 now you s. accused of guilt for what your
T-31 ..... V.15:2 be no concept that can s. for what you are
T-31 ..... V.17:5 on no assumptions that would s. the light
T-31 ..... VI.5:1 will s. against the truth of what you are.
W-pI .... 44.6:1 can s. aside from the ego by ever so little,
W-pI .... 45.9:3 S. aside, however briefly, from all
W-pI .. 66.10:6 one side s. all illusions. All truth stands
W-pI .... 69.5:1 From where you s., you can see no reason
W-pI .... 73.2:4 They s. between your awareness and your
W-pI .... 73.5:5 cannot s. between you and your salvation.
W-pI .... 81.3:3 And in this light will my function s. clear
W-pI .... 87.2:3 *You s. with me in light, [name]. In the light*
W-pI .... 94.2:6 You s. in light, strong in the sinlessness in
W-pI .... 98.1:2 We take a s. on but one side today. We
W-pI .... 98.2:2 and take our s. with certainty of purpose,
W-pI .... 98.3:5 They took the s. which we will take today,
W-pI .... 98.4:1 us; all who took the s. we take today will
W-pI .. 122.6:2 Would you s. outside while all of Heaven
W-pI .. 125.3:3 We s. apart from all the judgments which
W-pI .. 129.5:1 now you s. an instant's space away from
W-pI .. 136.6:4 that they s. but for your own decision of
W-pI .. 153.9:3 And in defenselessness we s. secure,
W-pI .. 155.2:6 truth and let the truth s. forth as what it is
W-pI .. 161.1:1 differently, and take a s. against our anger
W-pI .. 161.5:3 for symbols can s. for the meaningless.
W-pI .. 163.8:8 This the s. we take today. And it is given
W-pI .. 164.7:5 We s. forgiven in the sight of Christ, with
W-pI .. 183.2:2 to surround the ground on which you s.,
W-pI .. 183.3:2 and where it seemed to s. you find a star;
W-pI .. 184.6:3 It is for this they s.. They leave no doubt
W-pI .. 184.9:4 They do not s. for anything at all, and in
W-pI 187.10:2 we s. together as one Son of God. Not
W-pI 187.10:3 joined us all as one, we s. in blessedness,
W-pI 198.13:1 would s. between this vision and our sight
W-pI .. 199.8:5 Your brothers s. released with you in it;
W-pII . 228.2:6 *And I s. ready to receive Your Word alone*
W-pII . 247.1:8 You s. forgiven, and I stand with you.
W-pII . 247.1:8 You stand forgiven, and I s. with you.
W-pII ..... 4.3:1 illusions, which but s. for things imagined
W-pII . 264.1:1 *Father, You s. before me and behind, beside*
W-pII . 342.1:5 *I s. before the gate of Heaven, wondering if I*
W-pII ... 14.5:5 the gate of Heaven s. open before him, he
W-pII .... 354.h We s. together, Christ and I, in peace
M-5 ......... I.2:1 this insane conviction, does healing s. for
M-5 ...... III.2:6 They s. for the Alternative. With God's
M-6 ........... 2:1 will always s. aside when it would be seen
M-15 ....... 2:10 Have you yet learned to s. aside and hear
M-15 ....... 2:13 comes to all who s. aside in quiet listening
M-17 ......... 5:9 And he must s. alone in his protection,
M-21 ......... 2:6 but the things themselves but s. for the
M-22 ......... 7:9 No longer does he s. apart from God,
M-24 ......... 3:1 to take any definite s. on reincarnation. A
M-24 ......... 3:3 If a definite s. were required of him, it
M-27 ......... 5:6 His Own creation must s. in fear of Him.
P-2.......... V.8:1 Let us s. silently before God's Will, and
S-1........ III.5:1 S. still an instant, now, and think what
S-1.......... V.4:2 Now you s. before the gate of Heaven,
S-3........ III.6:6 has entered now where idols used to s.,

**standard** 2

T-9 ....... IV.8:6 you have judged it by the same s. I have.
T-18 ........ I.3:7 and used as the s. for comparison of

**standards** 1

M-8 ........... 1:5 of as more desirable by the world's s.,

**standing** 9

T-21 ..... II.10:3 enables it to be regarded as s. by itself,

T-22......IV.1:8 futile than **s.** where the road branches,
T-22......IV.7:5 S. before the veil, it still seems difficult.
T-23......III.6:8 Not one tree left still **s.** will shelter you.
T-26......IX.2:4 because of Them Who, **s.** there with you,
W-pI.....69.4:3 you seem to be **s.** outside the circle and
W-pI.131.13:2 **s.** in a light so bright and clear that you
W-pI...136.6:3 symbols **s.** for attack upon the whole;
W-pI...170.8:3 You make a choice, **s.** before this idol,

## standpoint 1

M-19..........5:7 From this one **s.** does it judge, and this

## stands 132

T-1.........II.3:2 one of a lesser order **s.** before his Creator.
T-2.........II.6:9 but the whole Atonement **s.** at time's end.
T-4...........I.8:5 which **s.** unchanged beyond the reach of
T-10......III.5:3 save you from the dangers for which it **s.**,
T-11.......V.2:1 but the removal of all that **s.** in the way of
T-13.........I.4:4 true. The Holy Spirit **s.** at the end of time,
T-13.......II.1:2 guilt **s.** in the way of your remembering
T-13.....V.11:1 is the light in which Christ **s.** revealed.
T-13......VI.3:4 and He **s.** revealed in everyone you meet
T-13......IX.1:8 Atonement **s.** between them, like a lamp
T-14... VIII.2:3 No altar **s.** to God without His Son. And
T-14......IX.2:1 it **s.** corrected because it is the opposite of
T-14.......X.1:1 no perception **s.** between God and His
T-14......XI.1:9 Yet all that **s.** between you and the power
T-15.........I.8:3 **s.** clear and separated from the past,
T-15......I.11:5 In exchange for this instant He **s.** ready to
T-15......I.15:7 Time **s.** still in his holiness, and changes
T-15......IV.1:8 it, it **s.** in shimmering readiness for your
T-16......IV.7:6 only this **s.** between you and the bridge
T-16.....V.13:3 raise to place before Him **s.** before *you*, in
T-18......I.11:7 The universe within you **s.** with you,
T-18......VI.7:3 guilt **s.** between you and other minds.
T-18. VIII.13:6 dust still **s.** between you and your brother
T-19......I.13:3 where the grace was given, in which it **s.**.
T19... IV.A.2:4 sand still **s.** between you and your brother
T19.IV.D.12:1 brother who **s.** beside you still seems to
T19.IV.D.13:7 And yet your savior **s.** beside each one.
T19.IV.D.14:1 your Friend, the Christ Who **s.** beside you
T-20.......II.7:4 knowing his savior **s.** beside him? With
T-21......III.9:5 than anything that **s.** this side of Heaven.
T-21......VI.5:5 be that **s.** between what is continuous?
T-22......III.5:7 the wall that **s.** between you and the truth
T-22......IV.3:3 for it is but a veil that **s.** between you.
T-22......IV.7:8 illusion **s.** between you and your brother,
T-22.......V.5:1 recognized how little **s.** between you and
T-23......in.3:4 harmful now **s.** shining in their innocence
T-23......I.7:10 And truth **s.** radiant, apart from conflict,
T-23.....II.19:7 of Heaven, only the conflict of illusion **s.**;
T-23......III.6:9 protection **s.** against the faith in murder.
T-23....III.6:10 **s.** the body, torn between the natural
T-23......IV.7:8 The body **s.** between the Father and the
T-24.......II.7:6 **s.** your brother with the key to Heaven in
T-24.......II.9:5 so encompassing that nothing **s.** outside.
T-24......III.2:2 Inviolate it **s.**, strongly defended with all
T-24......III.2:3 And thus it **s.** against yourself; *your* enemy
T-24......III.4:7 while specialness **s.** like a flaming sword
T-24......VI.8:5 it is not a part of him who **s.** beside you.
T-24....VI.11:2 It **s.** for you alone, as self-created, self-
T-24.....VII.1:8 Yet it **s.** in place of your creations, who *are*
T-25.......II.5:1 empty frame upon a wall and **s.** before it,
T-25.......V.2:9 Christ **s.** before you, each time you look
T-25.....VII.9:4 and **s.** between him and whatever hope he
T-25... VIII.8:3 off from love, and **s.** for something else.
T-25... VIII.8:7 while love **s.** feebly by with helpless hands
T-26......III.2:1 is a borderland of thought that **s.** between
T-26......IV.2:4 nothing **s.** between to keep them separate
T-26......IV.2:5 nothing **s.** between to push the other off.
T-26......IV.6:1 This tiny spot of sin that **s.** between you
T-26.......V.7:1 a hindrance to the place whereon he **s.**? Is
T-26.....VII.9:1 Forgiveness takes away what **s.** between
T-26... VIII.5:9 It **s.** already here, in present grace, within
T-26......IX.8:4 stood a cross **s.** now the risen Christ, and
T-26.......X.2:7 that **s.** between Their shining innocence,
T-27.........I.9:8 **s.** apart from all experience of love or fear.
T-27.....II.6:10 is on his hands, and so he **s.** condemned.
T-27......III.2:2 to you, for he **s.** for what is meaningless.
T-27......III.2:5 gone. And now he **s.** for nothing. Symbols
T-27.......V.4:4 What **s.** apart from you, when you accept
T-27......VI.6:2 miracle forgives because it **s.** for what is
T-27.....VII.8:4 make. Helpless he **s.**, a victim to a dream
T-28.....VII.6:2 the little gap of nothingness whereon it **s.**
T-29.........I.8:3 nothing **s.** between you and your brother?
T-30......III.5:3 idols **s.** his holy will to be but what he is.
T-30.......V.2:8 And no one **s.** outside this hope, because
T-30......VI.5:5 be some sin that **s.** beyond forgiveness.
T-30.....VII.7:2 It will shift in what it **s.** for, and you will
T-31.....VII.7:1 The concept of the self **s.** like a shield, a
T-31.....VII.8:5 for nothing **s.** between his sight and what
T-31...VII.15:3 Their savior **s.**, unknowing and unknown,
W-pI.....29.3:5 holy purpose **s.** beyond your little range.
W-pI.....39.3:7 your world, the whole world **s.** to benefit.
W-pI.....39.8:1 that **s.** between you and your salvation.
W-pI...66.10:7 All truth **s.** on the other. Let us try today
W-pI.....69.1:2 the world in you, everyone **s.** in darkness,
W-pI.....72.7:4 But while the body **s.** at the center of your
W-pI.....73.7:6 the ego that **s.** powerless before your will.
W-pI.....78.1:2 Each grievance **s.** like a dark shield of hate
W-pI.....78.3:3 He **s.** in light, but you were in the dark.
W-pI.....78.7:3 *ask to lead me to the holy light in which he* **s.**,
W-pI.....92.9:2 Self **s.** ready to embrace you as Its Own.
W-pI.....97.4:1 abides the miracle in which all time **s.** still
W-pI.....98.2:4 Not one mistake **s.** in our way. For we
W-pI...107.5:4 But the truth **s.** far beyond illusions, and
W-pI...107.6:3 It **s.** in open light, in obvious accessibility.
W-pI...122.5:3 Changelessly it **s.** before you like an open
W-pI...134.7:1 Forgiveness is the only thing that **s.** for
W-pI.134.10:4 Forgiveness **s.** between illusions and the
W-pI.151.12:2 It **s.** beyond the body and the world, past
W-pI.169.14:3 revelation **s.** not far behind. Its coming is
W-pI...170.4:1 perceive the premises on which the idea **s.**
W-pI.186.11:1 your truly given function **s.** out clear and
W-pI...187.6:5 the one idea that **s.** behind them all, and
W-pI.198.12:6 so brief that not an instant **s.** between this
W-pII..264.1:5 *holiness; that* **s.** *beyond Your one creation,*
W-pII......8.1:2 **s.** for what is opposite to what you made.
W-pII..299.2:5 *It* **s.** *forever perfect and untouched. In it are*
W-pII..309.2:2 *Your altar* **s.** *serene and undefiled. It is the*
W-pII..318.1:3 could there be a single part that **s.** alone,
W-pII....12.2:2 In fear it **s.** beyond the Everywhere, apart
W-pII..335.1:3 it **s.** for what I want to be the truth. It is to
W-pII....13.3:3 Perception **s.** corrected in His sight, and
M-4 ......III.1:9 brothers, for who is there who **s.** apart?
M-5 .........I.2:4 **s.** for all that he would hide from himself
M-14 ..........3:3 But time **s.** still, and waits on the goal of
M-17 ..........8:5 the lesson's manifest simplicity **s.** out like
M-20 ........3:10 initial contrast **s.** out clear and apparent.
M-21 ........3:11 alone understands what this Word **s.** for.
M-23 ..........4:2 But it **s.** for love that is not of this world.
M-23 ..........4:4 close to what it **s.** for that the little space
M-29 ..........8:3 *world* **s.** *silent in the grace You bring from*
C-2...........6:14 Where there was crucifixion **s.** God's Son.
C-3.............8:4 Unity of unities that **s.** behind all joining
C-4.............4:1 world **s.** like a block before Christ's face.
C-ep.........1:11 Who **s.** before a lifeless image when a step
P-2.........II.3:5 lies the ending of the world and all it **s.** for
P-2.........II.9:2 who **s.** apart can receive Christ's vision. It
P-2........III.4:4 that **s.** at the end of the process of healing,
S-1...........I.6:4 does mean that another **s.** beside you and
S-1.........V.4:2 and your brother **s.** beside you there. The
S-2........III.7:6 He **s.** beside the door to which forgiveness
S-3.........II.6:4 in the home that **s.** ready to welcome him,
S-3........III.2:5 one who **s.** beneath him in his patronage.

## star 11

T-15......XI.2:1 The sign of Christmas is a **s.**, a light in
T-30......III.8:4 The Thought God holds of you is like a **s.**,
T-30......III.9:4 time that keeps this **s.** invisible to earth.
T-30......III.9:5 seek for idols cannot know the **s.** is there.
T-30....III.11:3 sky, no changeless **s.** and no reality. The
T-30....III.11:9 own. The **s.** shines still; the sky has never
T-31......VI.7:4 The truth in you remains as radiant as a **s.**
W-pI...131.6:7 time as is a tiny candle from a distant **s.**,
W-pI.134.12:5 his foot to stride ahead a **s.** is left behind,
W-pI...183.3:2 and where it seemed to stand you find a **s.**
C-ep...........5:4 The morning **s.** of this new day looks on a

## stares 1

S-3...........I.2:4 Death **s.** at them as every moment goes

## stark 2

T-18......III.2:1 forms of fear, and sometimes to **s.** terror.
T19.IV.D.11:2 Only the sane can look on **s.** insanity and

## starkly 1

M-17 .........7:5 have the fear of God most **s.** represented.

## stars 9

T-15.... III.12:6 above the **s.** and reaches even to Heaven,
T-17........II.4:1 The **s.** will disappear in light, and the sun
T-17.....VII.7:3 so great it reaches past the **s.** and to the
T-21.........I.8:1 Beyond the body, beyond the sun and **s.**,
T-29......VI.2:8 The **s.** will disappear, and night and day
M-20 .......6:11 The universe beyond the sun and **s.**, and
C-ep...........2:5 the end was written in the **s.** and set into
C-ep...........3:6 Look up and see His Word among the **s.**,
P-2.......VII.8:4 and the street a stream of **s.** that brushes

## start 31

T-1.......VII.5:8 It would be unwise to **s.** on these steps
T-5...........I.2:1 Let us **s.** our process of reawakening with
T-9.........V.1:6 he is more likely to **s.** with the equally
T-15........II.6:1 S. now to practice your little part in
T-27...VII.11:6 and saw as if it were its **s.** and ending,
T-30......IV.8:1 of separation **s.** to fade and disappear. For
T-31......IV.2:9 lead, however differently they seem to **s.**;
W-pI.....99.9:5 and **s.** the lesson that we learn today with
W-pI...101.6:8 So should you **s.** your practice periods,
W-pI...105.6:1 practice periods will **s.** a little differently.
W-pI...106.7:1 Thus does salvation **s.** and thus it ends;
W-pI.131.11:1 as we **s.** upon our practice periods. Begin
W-pI.139.11:2 **s.** with this review of what our mission is:
WpI. rIV.in4:4 **s.** each practice period in this review with
W-pI...153.3:2 iron overlaid, returning but to **s.** again.
W-pI...157.8:2 this journey which you make and **s.** today
WpI.rV.in11:1 With this we **s.** each day of our review.
WpI.rV.in11:2 we **s.** and end each period of practice time
Wi181-200 3:1 And so we **s.** our journey beyond words
WpI rVI.in.2:1 With this in mind we **s.** our practicing, in
WpI rVI.in.3:1 with which we **s.** and end each lesson. It is
W-pII ....in.8:1 **s.** upon the final part of this one holy year
M-16 .........2:6 be said that it is well to **s.** the day right. It
M-19 .........2:8 But somewhere one must **s.**. Justice is the
M-23 .......5:11 Why would you choose to **s.** again, when
M-29 .........1:7 to **s.** at the more abstract level of the text.
C-ep...........3:2 We only **s.** again an ancient journey long
P-in............1:6 Sometimes he is able to **s.** to open his
P-2........IV.4:5 cure? It is ridiculous from **s.** to finish. Yet
P-2.........V.6:4 they must **s.** their Father will complete.
P-3..........II.8:5 still at the very **s.** of the beginning stage of

## started 9

T-17.......V.9:3 that you and your brother have **s.** again,
T-20.........I.3:2 He **s.** with the sign of victory, the promise
T-27...VII.11:7 Yet was it **s.** by your secret dream, which
T-28........II.8:1 separation **s.** with the dream the Father
T-28......III.1:2 For you have barely **s.** to allow your first,
T-28......III.1:5 And having **s.**, will the way be made
W-pI.....28.1:4 you have **s.** on the way to keeping them.
W-pII ..in.10:6 plan will end, as we received the way it **s.**.
P-2........IV.4:6 Yet having **s.**, it must finish thus. It is as if

## starting 7

T-3.......VII.1:1 system of thought must have a **s.** point. It
T-3.......VII.5:6 in it. Your **s.** point is truth, and you must

T-23..... II.21:3 chaos do follow neatly from their s. point.
T-28....... II.1:7 Its s. and its ending are the same. But in
WpI...rI.in.1:2 presented, s. with the first and ending
W-pI...184.7:5 it serves but as a s. point from which
M-16.........3:4 to s. the day right does indeed save time.

## startling 4

W-in..........8:1 and others may seem to be quite s.. This
W-pI.....41.8:5 exercise can bring very s. results even the
M-21.........5:2 And what he hears may indeed be quite s.
M-25.........1:4 develop abilities that seem quite s. to him

## starts 9

T-13..... VII.5:3 see? All seeing s. with the perceiver, who
T-22.......in.3:1 relationship s. from a different premise.
T-23..... II.21:7 And where your thinking s., there must it
T-27....VIII.7:1 whose ending s. at its beginning, ending
T-30.........I.2:1 (1) The outlook s. with this: *Today I will*
T-31...... IV.4:1 you have learned the way the lesson s.,
W-pI...188.2:5 to look within, for there all vision s..
W-pI...188.2:7 There perception s., and there it ends. It
W-pII .325.1:1 which s. with my idea of what I want.

## starvation 1

W-pI...187.6:4 and at grief, at poverty, s. and at death.

## starve 2

T-28...... III.8:7 those may come who would no longer s.,
W-pI.....76.3:2 You really think that you would s. unless

## starved 3

T-20...... III.9:1 heavy chains for years, s. and emaciated,
W-pI...165.6:5 His Son remain forever s. by his denial of
W-pII ...13.5:1 where s. and thirsty creatures come to die

## starves 1

T-2...... III.5:10 s. you by denying you your daily bread.

## starving 3

T19. IV.A.12:5 cold and s. and made very vicious by their
T-28...... III.7:2 not to thieves, but to your s. brothers,
W-pI.....92.3:3 the sad, the poor, the s. and the joyless.

## state 149

T-1.........I.28:2 Revelation induces a s. in which fear has
T-1.........I.43:1 arise from a miraculous s. of mind, or a
T-1.........I.43:1 state of mind, or a s. of miracle-readiness.
T-1......... II.1:8 there. Consciousness is the s. that induces
T-1......... II.3:2 miracles because a s. of awe is worshipful,
T-1....... II.3:13 leaves me in a s. which is only potential in
T-1........ III.1:5 to the recognition of your original s., you
T-1........ III.5:4 *Spirit is in a s. of grace forever. Your reality is*
T-1........ III.5:6 *Therefore you are in a s. of grace forever.*
T-1........ III.7:4 miracle places the mind in a s. of grace.
T-1........ III.8:4 still expressions of your own s. of grace,
T-1......... V.1:1 a s. in which they become unnecessary.
T-1......... V.1:2 original s. of direct communication is
T-1......... V.4:6 is a s. of completion and abundance.
T-1........ VI.1:5 implies that you would be better off in a s.
T-1........ VI.5:8 *is fear, It produces a s. that does not exist.*
T-2...........I.3:1 a s. of mind in which nothing was needed.
T-2......... IV.4:8 They are already in a fear-weakened s.. If
T-2......... V.8:5 your s. becomes doubly dangerous unless
T-2......... VI.6:1 possible to reach a s. in which you bring
T-2....... VII.5:9 This establishes a s. of mind in which the
T-2....... VII.7:4 As soon as a s. of readiness occurs, there
T-2....... VII.7:5 s. does not imply more than a potential
T-3...........I.6:4 in the sense that the s. of innocence, or
T-3...........I.8:1 The innocence of God is the true s. of the
T-3...........I.8:2 In this s. your mind knows God, for God
T-3........ III.3:3 This establishes a seemingly stable s. that
T-3 ....... IV.4:3 and applies to the s. of mind that induces
T-3 ...... V.10:3 Perception is based on a separated s., so
T-3 ...... V.10:4 is the natural s. of those who know. God
T-4 .........II.3:1 Your own s. of mind is a good example of
T-4 .........II.8:2 This is such a fearful s. that it can only
T-4 .......II.11:9 and immortality is a constant s.. It is as
T-4 ........ V.2:1 source of the ego's off-balanced s. is its
T-4 ...... VII.4:4 s. in which the mind is in communication
T-4 ...... VII.4:5 To whatever extent you permit this s. to
T-4 ...... VII.5:8 the s. of being the mind gives everything
T-5 ........in.2:2 the only possible whole s. is that of love.
T-5 ........in.2:4 only possible whole s. is the wholly joyous
T-5 ..........I.6:4 He represents a s. of mind close enough
T-5 .........II.6:2 chosen to be in a s. of opposition in which
T-5 .........II.6:4 In the holy s. the will is free, so that its
T-7 ....... IV.1:6 in a s. of mind that does not know Him.
T-7 ....... IV.1:7 The s. is unknown to Him and therefore
T-7 ....... IV.5:6 a s. of mind that is out of accord with His.
T-7 ....... VI.3:7 existence, a s. which it finds intolerable.
T-7 ....... VI.7:4 within it that have led to a s. of war, and
T-7 ..... VI.12:3 You cannot create in this divided s., and
T-7 ..... VI.12:3 must be vigilant against this divided s.
T-7 ..... VI.13:1 depressing s. the Holy Spirit reminds you
T-7 .......X.1:10 but your s. of mind and your recognition
T-7 .......... XI.h The S. of Grace
T-7 ....... XI.1:8 convince yourself that, in your natural s.,
T-7 ....... XI.1:8 no difficulty at all *because* it is a s. of grace.
T-7 ....... XI.2:1 is the natural s. of every Son of God.
T-7 ....... XI.2:2 When he is not in a s. of grace, he is out of
T-8 ..........I.3:8 understand the s. that prevails within it.
T-8 .... VIII.9:8 attack. Health is seen as the natural s. of
T-9 ..........I.2:3 anything consistently in a s. of panic. If
T-9 .........II.2:3 achieved, even when the s. of healing is.
T-9 ..... VIII.7:9 And in your exalted s. you seek others like
T-12 ........I.6:8 reality are meaningless in your divided s.,
T-13 ..... III.1:5 disordered s. of mind you are not afraid
T-14 ..... IV.2:2 s. of guiltlessness is only the condition in
T-14 ..... IV.2:3 This s., and only this, must you attain,
T-15 ......I.15:6 His changeless s. is beyond time, for his
T-18 ..... IV.2:7 achieve the s. its coming brings with it.
T-18 .. VII.4:11 the future for release from a s. of present
T19..IV.A.17:1 I am made welcome in the s. of grace,
T-20 ..... VI.8:4 It is a s. of isolation, which seems to be
T-21 ......in.1:5 It is the witness to your s. of mind, the
T-21 ........I.6:1 a hint of an ancient s. not quite forgotten;
T-21 ..... III.4:7 only before the s. of certainty is reached.
T-21 .. VII.10:5 a s. where vacillations are impossible.
T-22 ..... III.3:1 for peace and brings you to a s. of mind in
T-22 ..... III.9:7 as what it is; a common s. of mind, where
T-22 ...... V.3:8 this quiet s. alone is strength and power.
T-23 ........I.7:8 illusions is a s. where nothing happens.
T-23 ......I.12:5 Peace is the s. where love abides, and
T-23 .....II.19:3 In any s. apart from Heaven life is illusion
T-24 ......in.1:1 and the keeping of the s. of peace. Given
T-24 ......in.1:2 Given this s. the mind is quiet, and the
T-24 ..... III.4:2 Would God have left His Son in such a s.,
T-24 .... VII.6:7 This is the s. of true creation, found not
T-25 ........I.3:1 and the s. in which you think your mind
T-25 ... III.8:13 it is to change its s. from error into truth.
T-25 ..... IV.5:7 other place; no other s. nor time. Nothing
T-25 ......... V.h The S. of Sinlessness
T-25 ...... V.1:1 s. of sinlessness is merely this: The whole
T-25 ... VIII.2:6 could be found in such a s. of mind. But
T-25 ..... IX.4:5 It sees a resolution as a s. in which it is
T-25 ..... IX.4:6 only justice can set up a s. in which there
T-26 .... VII.9:4 Yet is this wish in line with Heaven's s.,
T-26 ... VIII.4:8 is *this* that needs correction, not a future s.
T-27 ..... IV.2:2 Yet it must also be that, in your s. of mind
T-27 ..... IV.2:3 to another s. of mind in which the answer
T-27 ..... IV.5:8 in a conflict s. is free to ask this question,
T-27 ...... V.3:2 a s. of mind that has transcended conflict,
T-28 ........I.4:2 of past events, but only of a present s..
T-29 ........I.1:1 time, no place, no s. where God is absent.
T-29 .......II.6:5 that except the s. confusion really means?
T-29 .......II.7:3 To change is to attain a s. unlike the one
T-30 ...... V.1:1 The real world is the s. of mind in which
T-30 ...... V.5:2 The real world is a s. in which the mind
T-30 .... VII.7:4 s. so seemingly unsafe that fear must rise.
T-31 ......I.11:2 It is the recognition that it is a s. of mind
T-31 .....V.12:5 see reflects the s. of the perceiver's mind.
W-pI .... 20.4:3 to change your present s. for a better one,
W-pI .... 50.3:3 It will transport you into a s. of mind that
W-pI .... 54.2:4 the representation of my own s. of mind.
W-pI .... 54.2:5 I know that my s. of mind can change.
W-pI .... 72.9:3 without a body is to be in our natural s..
W-pI .... 77.6:2 You s. a fact that cannot be denied. The
W-pI .... 97.2:1 We s. again the truth about your Self, the
W-pI .... 99.1:3 resulting in a s. of conflict seen between
W-pI .. 107.2:1 what a s. of mind without illusions is?
W-pI .. 107.3:1 the faintest intimation of the s. your mind
W-pI .. 108.2:2 s. of mind that has become so unified that
W-pI .. 132.9:3 that can bring change to your eternal s..
W-pI 133.13:2 We will attempt to reach this s. today,
W-pI .. 136.4:3 a happening beyond your s. of mind, an
W-pI .. 152.1:2 except his choice elects this s. for him. No
W-pI .. 167.2:1 appears to be a s. that is life's opposite.
W-pI .. 167.6:2 It cannot change what is its waking s.. It
W-pI .. 167.6:5 nor change its own eternal, mindful s.. It
W-pI .. 167.9:2 does not have, a foreign s. it cannot enter,
W-pI .. 169.1:1 like the s. prevailing in the unity of truth.
W-pI .. 169.2:2 for grace presents a s. so opposite to
W-pI .. 169.3:6 and thus is ready to accept a s. completely
W-pI .. 169.6:7 been at all. Eternity remains a constant s..
W-pI .. 169.9:2 irrelevant to what must be a constant s.,
W-pI .. 170.1:5 mean that to attack is to exchange the s.
WpI...rV.in4:5 Its constant s. of union with Its Father
W-pI .. 183.9:1 Today you can achieve a s. in which you
W-pI .. 196.4:1 from bondage to the s. of perfect freedom
W-pII . 293.1:2 Love remains the only present s., whose
W-pII . 304.1:4 fact. And what I look on is my s. of mind,
W-pII . 307.2:1 into a s. where conflict cannot come,
W-pII . 337.1:2 And only happiness can be my s., for only
W-pII . 339.1:6 things he wants; the s. he would attain.
M-4 ..... I.A.7:7 now he must attain a s. that may remain
M-4 ..... I.A.8:5 for here is Heaven's s. fully reflected.
M-5 ........II.1:9 terms merely s. or describe the problem.
M-16 ......... 7:7 is no difference in his s. at different times
M-16 ......... 9:5 of God has reached the most advanced s..
C-1 ............ 2:3 illusory s., the concept of an "individual
P-2..........V.3:2 And yet it would be useless in an ideal s..
S-1..........II.1:3 learning until it reaches its formless s.,
S-1..........II.8:7 learning, this s. cannot be described. The

## stated 15

T-3 ..........I.1:9 have clearly s. is unworthy of His Son?
T-3 .........II.1:1 I have s. that the basic concepts referred
T-11 ......in.2:6 insane when it is s. with perfect honesty,
T-13 .......II.7:1 This course has explicitly s. that its goal
T-15 ..... IV.6:5 The simple reason, simply s., is this: The
W-in.......... 3:2 around one central idea, which is s. first.
W-pI ...... 6.3:1 the two cautions s. in the previous lesson:
W-pI .... 28.7:1 in which the idea for the day is s. first,
W-pI .... 35.9:1 idea in the form s. above to each of them.
W-pI .. 39.10:3 the idea should be s. so that its meaning
W-pI .... 46.6:7 a repetition of today's idea as originally s..
W-pI .. 132.5:4 This central theme is often s. in the text,
WpI..rIV.in2:1 which can be simply s. in these words: *My*
W-pI 154.13:1 lesson for today is s. thus: *I am among the*
M-27 ......... 7:1 one assignment could be s. thus: Accept

## stately 2

T-18 ........I.8:2 And turn you to the s. calm within, where
T-24 .......II.1:6 you see in him you stand as tall and s.,

## statement 66

T-1 .........II.4:2 The s. is more meaningful in terms of a
T-1 .........II.4:7 contradict the s. "I and my Father are one
T-1 .........II.4:7 to the s. in recognition that the Father is
T-2 ..........V.1:8 To amplify an earlier s., spirit is already
T-2 ... V.A.16:3 The s. "Father forgive them for they know
T-2 ... V.A.17:1 injunction "Be of one mind" is the s. for
T-2 .... VII.5:14 The s. "For God so loved the world that
T-3 ..........I.3:1 The s. "Vengeance is mine, sayeth the
T-3 .........V.7:1 s. "God created man in his own image
T-5 ....... III.1:5 clarification, not in s. but in experience.

T-5........VI.7:2 The **s.** emphasizes that vengeance cannot
T-5........VI.8:3 the **s.** means that in later generations He
T-5........VI.9:1 shall perish" becomes a **s.** of Atonement,
T-6....... II.10:8 an explicit **s.** that the ego never occurred.
T-6......... V.3:5 This simple **s.** is perfectly clear, easily
T-6....V.C.10:1 then, is a **s.** of what you want to believe,
T-8..... VIII.4:4 A more honest **s.** would be that those who
T-9....... V.8:14 works" is a sound though insufficient **s.**.
T-15.....VII.2:4 This is not its **s.**, but it *is* its purpose. For
T-17..... V.7:10 that He has given you a most explicit **s.**?
T-18.....VII.6:7 "I need do nothing" is a **s.** of allegiance, a
T-19.........I.4:1 overlook our earlier **s.** that faithlessness
T-21....... II.6:6 the **s.** that he has the power to make God
T-26......III.4:5 It is but a simple **s.** of a simple fact. But in
T-27....... II.8:3 The world perceives it as a **s.** of the "fact"
T-27. VIII.11:6 that miracles reflect the simple **s.**, "*I* have
T-30...... I.12:2 It is a **s.** of an open mind, not certain yet,
T-30...... I.14:6 coercion, but a simple **s.** of a simple fact.
T-30......VI.9:5 the joyful **s.** that there are no forms of evil
T-30......VI.9:6 what is this except a simple **s.** of the truth
T-31..... V.14:4 mind, but with the simple **s.** that it thinks
T-31..... V.17:6 no **s.** that the world is more afraid to hear
W-pI.......1.3:3 **s.** should merely be applied to anything
W-pI.......5.4:2 help to precede the exercises with the **s.**:
W-pI.....10.3:3 earlier **s.** that your mind is really a blank.
W-pI.....13.4:5 this **s.** to yourself as you look about. Then
W-pI.....13.5:1 one form or another, to this concluding **s.**
W-pI.....13.5:3 not expected to believe the **s.** at this point
W-pI.....13.6:2 Do not dwell on the concluding **s.**, and
W-pI.....18.3:3 period by repeating the more general **s.**:
W-pI.....25.6:7 until you have completed the **s.** about it.
W-pI.....61.1:2 is merely a **s.** of the truth about yourself.
W-pI.....61.1:3 the opposite of a **s.** of pride, of arrogance,
W-pI.....67.1:1 complete and accurate **s.** of what you are.
W-pI.....70.7:1 adding a **s.** signifying your recognition
W-pI...76.12:2 It is our **s.** of freedom from all danger and
W-pI.....77.1:5 It is merely a **s.** of your true Identity. It is
W-pI.....77.6:7 The answer is a simple **s.** of a simple fact.
W-pI.....80.3:6 Accept the peace this simple **s.** brings.
WpI. rII.in.6:2 comments which follow the **s.** of the ideas
W-pI.....88.3:2 Here is the perfect **s.** of my freedom. I am
W-pI.....91.6:1 **s.** of true cause and effect relationships:
W-pI.....91.6:6 question with which this **s.** ends is needed
W-pI...93.10:6 that this is a **s.** of the truth about you.
W-pI.....94.1:1 salvation; the one **s.** which makes all
W-pI...110.7:1 Then, with this **s.** firmly in your mind,
W-pI...122.6:7 of this extremely simple **s.** of the truth.
W-pI...126.1:2 If you believed this **s.**, there would be no
W-pI...139.8:4 or a **s.** which denies itself in statement?
W-pI...139.8:4 or a statement which denies itself in **s.**?
W-pI...169.4:1 to contradict our **s.** that the revelation of
W-pI...186.1:1 the **s.** that will one day take all arrogance
M-7............3:2 This is what is really meant by the **s.** that
M-16........10:2 God. In simple **s.**, it is to this fact that the
P-2........VI.7:3 This **s.** cannot be too often remembered
S-1......... II.5:5 It has become a **s.** of the unity of Christ

## statements 5

T-2... V.A.17:3 two **s.** are not in the same order of reality.
T-3......... V.1:4 that will clarify some of our subsequent **s.**
W-pI.......1.3:1 that these **s.** are not arranged in any order
WpI ...rI.in.6:3 is not necessary to return to the original **s.**
W-pI.....61.5:6 think about these **s.** for a short while,

## states 17

T-1........III.2:1 will not continue to exist as separate **s.**.
T-4.......VII.6:1 repeatedly **s.** that you should praise God.
T-9......... II.1:4 remember, however, that the course **s.**,
T-24......IV.2:9 and body **s.** must shift accordingly. Of
T-27....IV.4:17 that what it **s.** takes question's form.
T-27...VII.11:1 What choices can be made between two **s.**
W-pI.....48.1:1 The idea for today simply **s.** a fact. It is
W-pI.....61.1:7 created by God. It simply **s.** the truth.
W-pI.....97.1:3 It simply **s.** the truth. Practice this truth
W-pI...137.1:2 dwell on sickness and on separate **s.**.
W-pI...137.5:3 but offers restitution for imagined **s.** and
W-pI...139.4:1 He merely **s.** that he is not himself, and
W-pI...152.5:1 with transitory **s.** by definition false. And
W-pI...156.1:1 Today's idea but **s.** the simple truth that
M-17 .........5:4 It **s.**, in the clearest form possible, that the
M-19 .........3:1 future **s.** and all concerns about the past,
M-26 .........3:7 All worldly **s.** must be illusory. If God

## static 1

T-31.....VII.6:3 keep it **s.** and concealed within your mind

## stating 3

*See also* over-

W-pI.....13.6:1 This is our first attempt at **s.** an explicit
W-pI.....20.4:3 **s.** that you are determined to change your
W-pI.....93.8:1 begin by **s.** the truth about your creation:

## status 4

T-19....... II.6:8 But if the mistake is given the **s.** of truth,
T-19.......III.3:4 you change its **s.** from a sin to a mistake.
W-pI.....10.3:1 their past rather than their present **s.**.
S-1........ III.6:1 to realize that prayers for things, for **s.**,

## stay 31

T-16....IV.11:3 calls, but hate would have you **s.**. Hear
T-18... VIII.9:7 they brought with them will **s.** with them,
T-18... VIII.9:7 will stay with them, as it will **s.** with you.
T-19.......I.15:5 has been learned. Yet truth will **s.** forever.
T-21....... V.4:3 nothing you have allowed to **s.** in your
T-22.......in.2:7 **s.** until they think that there is nothing
T-25.......III.6:2 Nor need he **s.** more than an instant. For
T-27..... V.11:4 in without attack will **s.** with you forever.
T-30....... V.3:5 he can barely **s.** and wait a little longer,
T-31...VII.10:1 but the wish to **s.** in hell and misery? And
T-31...VII.11:1 while you wish to **s.** in hell, how could
W-pI.....57.1:8 Only my wish to **s.** keeps me a prisoner.
W-pI...107.4:1 truth has come it does not **s.** a while, to
W-pI...121.3:1 blustering, afraid to go ahead, afraid to **s.**,
W-pI...129.4:5 this are you who **s.** bound to this world.
W-pI...157.9:2 The vision of His face will **s.** with you, but
W-pI...165.3:3 would he not make sure they **s.** with him,
W-pI...182.7:5 back with Him, that He Himself might **s.**,
W-pI...182.8:3 you will **s.** with Him in perfect stillness,
W-pI...189.2:3 and gentle home in which to **s.** a while. It
W-pI.191.11:2 They **s.** in chains till you are free. They
W-pI...202.1:2 *to* **s.** *an instant more where I do not belong,*
W-pII......5.2:1 The body will not **s.**. Yet this he sees as
W-pII..272.2:2 hear temptation call to us to **s.** and linger
M-7 .........3:10 was a mistake, but hardly one to **s.** with.
M-13 .......6:11 would sacrifice the truth, they **s.** in hell.
M-13 .......6:12 And if they **s.**, you will remain with them.
P-2.......VII.2:6 what choice is there except to have Him **s.**
P-3......... II.7:5 the gift entirely in order to **s.** and let their
P-3......III.1:10 stays he will be given what he needs to **s.**.
S-2......... II.8:4 You do not want to **s.** in slavery. You do

## stayed 3

T-21.........I.6:2 Not the whole song has **s.** with you, but
W-pI...124.3:1 who went before or **s.** with us a while.
W-pI...188.1:6 and **s.** with you because it is your own. It

## stays 5

W-pI...107.4:3 again. It **s.** exactly as it always was, to be
W-pI...124.2:5 way because the light we carry **s.** behind,
W-pII....13.1:5 Thus it **s.** within time's limits. Yet it paves
P-3........ III.1:9 He **s.** here but for this. And while he stays
P-3.......III.1:10 while he **s.** he will be given what he needs

## steadfast 4

T-14....... II.3:2 the Holy Spirit says, with **s.** quietness: *The*
W-pII..238.1:5 *And I must be* **s.** *in holiness as well, that You*
M-27 .........7:5 Be **s.** but in this; be not deceived by the
S-2.........in.1:4 secure; your purpose **s.** and unchangeable

## steadfastly 2

T-11...... IV.4:3 must learn to recognize and to oppose **s.**,
T-14.........II.1:2 **s.** devoted to misery must first recognize

## steadily 7

T-8..........II.4:4 Holy Spirit leads you **s.** along the path of
T-9........ IV.5:6 By **s.** and consistently cancelling out all its
T-13...... X.10:2 shining as **s.** and as surely as God Himself
T-15.........I.7:4 as **s.** to Heaven as the ego drives to hell.
T-21.... VI.7:10 leads **s.** away from madness toward the
W-pI..... 60.4:4 I am walking **s.** on toward truth. There is
W-pI... 107.5:1 of pain, but looks beyond it, **s.** and sure.

## steady 4

W-pI.....92.4:2 It keeps its **s.** gaze upon the light that lies
W-pI.....97.6:3 The **s.** brilliance of this light remains and
W-pI.....98.8:1 so strong and **s.** they will light the world
WpI...rV.in2:1 *S. our feet, our Father. Let our doubts be*

## steal 4

T-14....... V.4:2 Do not try to **s.** it from him, or you will
T-14....... V.4:3 would **s.** it away and keep it from his sight
T19. IV.A.12:5 Its messengers **s.** guiltily away in hungry
T-22.......in.2:7 they think that there is nothing left to **s.**,

## steel 1

W-pI...153.3:2 in heavy bands of **s.** with iron overlaid,

## steep 1

S-3.........in.1:1 the **s.** ascent more gentle and more sure,

## steeped 1

S-2..........II.2:4 And who can tell another he is **s.** in sin,

## stem 6

T-1......... V.3:5 not **s.** from exclusion but from inclusion.
T-1.......VII.3:3 unreality. Actions that **s.** from distortions
T-3........ III.2:1 All your difficulties **s.** from the fact that
T-30....VIII.2:7 real, and could not **s.** from his reality. For
M-19 .........3:1 concerns about the past, **s.** from injustice.
M-27 .........1:1 central dream from which all illusions **s.**.

## stemming 1

M-7 ...........5:6 embarrassment **s.** from false humility.

## stems 13

T-5....... V.2:12 is the belief from which all guilt really **s.**.
T-7........ VI.3:1 but it **s.** from the very power of the mind
T-9.........I.10:2 that **s.** from the ego is a wish for nothing,
T-11....... V.5:2 it is. Everything that **s.** from the ego is the
T-13........II.6:4 **s.** ultimately from this interpretation, but
T-15...... III.3:3 Every decision you make **s.** from what you
T-18.........I.3:5 perception from which the behavior **s.**.
T-21....... V.4:5 it, but if the basic question **s.** from reason
T-21....... V.4:6 it. Like all that **s.** from reason, the basic
T-25...... III.1:5 The rest but **s.** from this, to hold it up and
W-pI... 130.6:5 all a piece because it **s.** from one emotion,
W-pI... 135.3:2 It **s.** from fear, increasing fear as each
W-pII .319.2:2 *the goal which* **s.** *from it shares its totality.*

## step 193

*See also* Appendix C

T-1........ IV.1:2 This **s.** usually entails fear. Second, the
T-1........ IV.1:4 This **s.** brings escape from fear. When you
T-2..........II.3:8 time if you do not protract this **s.** unduly.
T-2......... III.1:5 the first **s.** in correcting this distortion,
T-2........ III.1:7 The next **s.**, however, is to realize that a
T-2........ IV.2:1 major **s.** in the Atonement plan is to undo

| | |
|---|---|
| T-2........IV.4:2 | first s. in believing that the body makes |
| T-2........VI.7:1 | first corrective s. in undoing the error is |
| T-2......VIII.4:1 | first s. toward freedom involves a sorting |
| T-3........III.2:6 | illusions is the first s. in undoing them. |
| T-4........II.10:2 | leads to the next s. automatically, because |
| T-4........III.7:4 | see through a wall, but I can s. around it. |
| T-4........III.8:3 | taken the first s. toward preparing your |
| T-4........IV.8:5 | accomplishment, and s. away from them. |
| T-5..........I.6:6 | over," since the last s. is taken by God. |
| T-5.......VII.6:3 | the first s. in the undoing is to recognize |
| T-6......V.A.6:1 | This is a very preliminary s., and the only |
| T-6......V.A.6:2 | that you complete the s. yourself, but it is |
| T-6......V.A.6:4 | This s. may appear to exacerbate conflict |
| T-6......V.A.6:4 | because it is the beginning s. in reversing |
| T-6......V.A.6:6 | Some remain at this s. for a long time, |
| T-6......V.A.6:7 | take the next s. towards its resolution. |
| T-6......V.A.6:8 | Having taken the first s., however, they |
| T-6......V.B.3:1 | first s. in the reversal or undoing process |
| T-6......V.B.8:1 | This is still a preliminary s., since *having* |
| T-6......V.B.8:2 | however, more advanced than the first s., |
| T-6......V.B.8:3 | The second s. is a positive affirmation of |
| T-6......V.B.8:4 | then, is a s. in the direction out of conflict |
| T-6......V.B.8:6 | s. is essential for the ultimate decision, it |
| T-6......V.B.9:1 | The second s., then, is still perceptual, |
| T-6......V.B.9:1 | although it is a giant s. toward the unified |
| T-6......V.B.9:2 | As you take this s. and hold this direction, |
| T-6......V.B.9:3 | At the second s. progress is intermittent, |
| T-6......V.B.9:3 | second s. is easier than the first because it |
| T-6......V.C.3:1 | is a major s. toward fundamental change. |
| T-6......V.C.3:4 | This s., which follows from the second as |
| T-6......V.C.4:1 | While the first s. seems to increase |
| T-6......V.C.4:1 | s. calls for consistent vigilance against it. |
| T-6......V.C.5:3 | to remember it is inherent in the third s., |
| T-6......V.C.5:7 | final s. will still be taken for you by God, |
| T-6......V.C.5:7 | third s. the Holy Spirit has prepared you |
| T-6......V.C.7:1 | third s. is thus one of protection for your |
| T-6....V.C.10:1 | The third s., then, is a statement of what |
| T-6....V.C.10:2 | Holy Spirit will enable you to take this s., |
| T-7..............I.h | The Last S. |
| T-7...........I.6:3 | is whole. I have said that the last s. in the |
| T-7...........I.6:6 | tell you something about this last s.. |
| T-7...........I.7:8 | "last s." that God will take was therefore |
| T-7........IV.2:2 | an intermediary s. toward the knowledge |
| T-11....... II.1:1 | heal and to be healed is the first s. toward |
| T-11....... II.1:2 | Every attack is a s. away from this, and |
| T-11......IV.4:4 | This is a crucial s. in the reawakening. |
| T-11....... V.2:5 | The next s. is obviously to recognize that |
| T-11..... V.14:4 | The next s., then, is obvious. If consistent |
| T-11..... V.14:6 | ego proceeds to the next s. in its thought |
| T-11..VIII.15:5 | down to you and take the last s. for you, |
| T-12.........I.8:4 | would have taken a s. away from reality, |
| T-12.........I.8:5 | as a crucial s. in the undoing of the ego. |
| T-13....VII.12:6 | and will but last until you s. aside from all |
| T-13....VIII.3:2 | Yet the last s. must be taken by God, |
| T-13....VIII.3:2 | because the last s. is your redemption, |
| T-15......IX.1:5 | for it is the only s. in it He understands. |
| T-16.........I.3:7 | it. S. gently aside, and let healing be done |
| T-16......IV.2:4 | This is the last s. in the readiness for God. |
| T-16....IV.13:7 | But as you s. lightly across it, upheld *by* |
| T-17....... II.2:6 | This little s., so small it has escaped your |
| T-17....... II.3:1 | This s., the smallest ever taken, is still the |
| T-17....... II.4:5 | For God will take the last s. swiftly, when |
| T-17...... III.3:4 | of value. Every s. taken in the making, the |
| T-17...... III.6:4 | each s. in His undoing is the separation |
| T-17.... III.10:1 | and s. between you and your fantasies. |
| T-17....... V.2:1 | major s. toward the perception of the real |
| T-17....... V.5:1 | each slow s. according to its liking. Only a |
| T-18...... IX.9:6 | for the final s. in the journey inward. Here |
| T-18.... IX.10:4 | Himself can take the final s. unhindered, |
| T-18.... IX.10:5 | A s. beyond this holy place of forgiveness, |
| T-18.... IX.10:5 | a s. still further inward but the one *you* |
| T-19...... IV.3:8 | When God has taken the last s. Himself, |
| T19... IV.D.3:4 | *fear of God,* the final s. in your dissociation |
| T-20..VIII.10:7 | They s. away from sin, reminding you |
| T-22.........I.1:1 | Let reason take another s.. If you attack |
| T-23..... II.21:2 | conclusion; a valid s. in ordered thought. |
| T-23..... II.21:5 | Think not one s. is smaller than another, |
| T-23..... II.22:1 | take not one s. in the descent to hell. For |
| T-24....... II.9:2 | Just one s. more, and every vestige of the |
| T-25 .......II.8:2 | will s. forth from darkness as you look on |
| T-26 ... III.1:11 | s. in the advance toward oneness. What is |
| T-26 ...... V.2:5 | hand and keeping s. to Heaven's song, is |
| T-27 ..... III.6:7 | is God left free to take the final s. Himself. |
| T-28 .......II.7:2 | This is a crucial s. in dealing with illusions |
| T-28 .......II.9:1 | This is the separation's final s., with |
| T-28 .......II.9:2 | final s. is an effect of what has gone before |
| T-28 .......II.9:3 | The miracle is the first s. in giving back to |
| T-28 .....II.12:7 | of every s. in the descent to separation, |
| T-29 ...... V.8:5 | Forgiving dreams are means to s. aside |
| T-30 ......in.1:3 | your willingness to practice every s.. Each |
| T-30 ........I.1:4 | preoccupied with every s. you take. The |
| T-30 ........I.8:3 | and paves the way for the next easy s.. |
| T-30 ......I.12:1 | (7) This final s. is but acknowledgment of |
| T-30 ...... V.3:7 | thus is he made ready for the s. in which |
| T-30 ...... V.4:1 | The final s. is God's, because it is but |
| T-30 ...... V.8:1 | light and easy is the s. across the narrow |
| T-31 ........I.4:3 | have continued, taking every s., however |
| T-31 .......II.9:4 | advancing only when he would s. back, |
| T-31 .....II.11:7 | every s. is made in certainty and sureness |
| T-31 ..... IV.6:2 | this s. is to defeat your purpose here. You |
| T-31 ..... V.13:1 | Although this s. has gains, it does not yet |
| T-31 ...VIII.8:3 | intense and so inclusive it is but a s. from |
| W-pI....... 5.1:6 | the first s. in ultimately recognizing they |
| W-pI....... 8.3:3 | is the first s. to opening the way to vision. |
| W-pI....... 9.2:5 | small s. will clear a little of the darkness |
| W-pI..... 12.2:7 | a beginning s. in learning to give them all |
| W-pI..... 14.3:1 | idea for today is another s. in learning to |
| W-pI..... 16.1:1 | The idea for today is a beginning s. in |
| W-pI..... 17.1:1 | This idea is another s. in the direction of |
| W-pI..... 18.1:1 | idea for today is another s. in learning |
| W-pI..... 24.2:3 | The idea for today is a s. toward opening |
| W-pI..... 25.5:3 | The idea for today is a s. in this direction. |
| W-pI..... 42.6:2 | Try merely to s. back and let the thoughts |
| W-pI..... 42.7:2 | day is a beginning s. in bringing thoughts |
| W-pI..... 47.6:1 | s. in the correction of your errors, but it is |
| W-pI..... 61.3:2 | is a beginning s. in accepting your real |
| W-pI... 127.6:5 | Today we take the largest single s. this |
| W-pI... 129.5:1 | Now is the last s. certain; now you stand |
| W-pI... 130.9:2 | will take this giant s. with you in gratitude |
| W-pI... 132.6:5 | perhaps s. back a while and then return |
| W-pI. 134.12:5 | His s. is light, and as he lifts his foot to |
| W-pI. 135.18:3 | blessing shine in every s. you ever took. |
| WpI. rIV.in2:1 | unifies each s. in the review we undertake, |
| W-pI...... 155.h | I will s. back and let Him lead the way. |
| W-pI... 155.2:3 | then they s. back and let it lead the way. |
| W-pI... 155.8:7 | As they s. back, he finds himself again. |
| W-pI. 155.10:3 | S. back in faith and let truth lead the way. |
| W-pI. 155.11:3 | truth. And we s. forth toward this, as we |
| W-pI. 155.14:3 | *I will s. back and let Him lead the way, For I* |
| W-pI... 156.6:2 | As you s. back, the light in you steps |
| W-pI... 158.3:3 | no s. along the road that anyone takes but |
| W-pI... 168.3:2 | us up, taking salvation's final s. Himself. |
| W-pI... 169.3:2 | The final s. must go beyond all learning. |
| WpI...rV.in1:4 | We would take this s. completely, that we |
| WpI...rV.in5:2 | Every s. we take brings us a little nearer. |
| WpI...rV.in5:4 | path of light to us, and teach us, s. by step |
| WpI...rV.in5:4 | path of light to us, and teach us, step by s. |
| W-pI... 173.1:1 | I will s. back and let Him lead the way. |
| W-pI. 184.10:3 | And then s. back to darkness, not because |
| W-pI... 185.9:7 | shift and change with every s. you take. |
| W-pI. 193.13:1 | that lets it be to you another s. to Him, |
| W-pI. 193.13:6 | God will take this final s. Himself. Do not |
| W-pI... 194.1:1 | takes another s. toward quick salvation, |
| W-pI... 194.1:3 | await with certainty the final s. of God. |
| W-pI... 196.4:1 | Today's idea is one s. we take in leading |
| W-pI... 196.4:2 | Let us take this s. today, that we may |
| W-pI... 196.4:2 | taking every s. in its appointed sequence, |
| W-pI. 196.11:6 | S. back from fear, and make advance to |
| W-pI... 197.1:1 | Here is the second s. we take to free your |
| W-pII .....in.2:3 | promised He will take the final s. Himself. |
| W-pII .....in.4:1 | the s. to us that He has told us, through |
| W-pII .....in.5:3 | No s. remains for time to separate from |
| W-pII . 233.1:6 | *I will s. back and merely follow You. Be You* |
| W-pII . 254.2:2 | occur, we quietly s. back and look at them |
| W-pII . 289.2:4 | *And here am I made ready for Your final s..* |
| W-pII ..... 8.5:2 | instant more for God to take His final s., |
| W-pII . 297.2:1 | *how faithfully is every s. in my salvation set* |
| W-pII . 309.2:1 | *The s. I take today, my Father, is my sure* |
| W-pII ... 10.4:1 | s. in His appointed plan to bless His Son, |
| W-pII . 324.1:2 | *to take, and every s. in my appointed path.* |
| M-4 ..... I.A.5:4 | the valueless unless the next obvious s. is |
| M-4 ..... I.A.7:9 | not each s. in this direction so heavily |
| M-9 ........... 1:4 | the first s. in the newly made teacher of |
| M-10 ....... 6:10 | of God, this s. will bring you peace. Can it |
| M-17 ......... 8:8 | Now it is possible to take the next s.. The |
| M-19 ......... 2:4 | first small s. in the direction of the other. |
| M-20 ......... 1:5 | each reflects a different s. along the way. |
| M-21 ......... 4:6 | "I will s. back and let Him lead the way." |
| M-22 ......... 5:7 | S. back now, teacher of God. You have |
| M-24 ......... 4:4 | wise to s. away from all such questions, |
| M-28 ......... 1:8 | is the invitation to God to take His final s. |
| C-1 ............ 5:3 | in which God takes the final s. Himself. |
| C-3 .......... 4:10 | this gate it is no more than just a s. inside. |
| C-3 .......... 4:11 | It is the final s.. And this we leave to God. |
| C-3 ............ 6:6 | to time. The final s. is also but a shift. As a |
| C-ep ........ 1:11 | before a lifeless image when a s. away the |
| P-2........ III.2:6 | or go no further than a s. or two from hell |
| P-2........ IV.3:1 | follows s. by step in an inevitable course, |
| P-2........ IV.3:1 | follows step by s. in an inevitable course, |
| P-2........ VI.1:7 | To hear it is the first s. in recovery. To |
| S-1........ III.3:3 | here it will be an easy s. to the next levels. |
| S-1........ III.3:7 | apparent that this s. cannot be reached by |
| S-1........ III.4:2 | of this s. may for some time be followed |
| S-1........ IV.2:2 | This s. begins the quicker ascent, but |
| S-2.........in.1:2 | to try to rise above prayer's bottom s., or |
| S-2........ III.2:6 | need do is to s. back and not to interfere. |
| S-2........ III.3:4 | to you another s. to Heaven and to peace. |

## stepped 4

| | |
|---|---|
| T-18 ..... III.2:4 | and when you are afraid you have s. back. |
| T-27 .......V.5:1 | but s. back because he was afraid of being |
| W-pI .. 155.6:2 | Yet it has s. back. And it is not illusion |
| W-pII . 346.1:2 | *share eternity, for time has s. aside today.* |

## stepping 2

| | |
|---|---|
| T-2 .........II.6:2 | your previous missteps by s. forward. |
| S-1...........I.5:1 | Prayer is a s. aside; a letting go, a quiet |

## steppingstone 1

| | |
|---|---|
| T-4 .......II.11:2 | accurate perception is a s. towards it. The |

## steps 35

| | |
|---|---|
| T-1 ...... VII.5:7 | Some of the later s. in this course, |
| T-1 ...... VII.5:8 | unwise to start on these s. without careful |
| T-2 ..........I.1:8 | This process involves the following s.: |
| T-2 .........II.6:5 | your s. without advancing to your return. |
| T-2 ....... VI.7:3 | series of pragmatic s. in the larger process |
| T-2 ....... VI.7:4 | These s. may be summarized in this way: |
| T-6 ..... V.C.5:8 | nature of the s. you must take with Him. |
| T-7 ..........I.7:1 | God does not take s., because His |
| T-22 ..... IV.2:1 | few s. along the right way that seem hard, |
| T-23 .....II.21:3 | The s. to chaos do follow neatly from |
| T-27 ..... VI.2:9 | name, as one s. forward and another back |
| T-28 .....II.12:7 | until all the s. have been retraced, the |
| T-28 ..... III.1:2 | uncertain s. to be directed up the ladder |
| T-29 ..... III.5:2 | and s. aside from heavy shadows that |
| T-30 ......in.1:5 | And together will these s. lead you from |
| T-30 .........I.9:4 | more s. you need to let yourself be helped |
| T-31 .........I.2:4 | in easy s. that lead you gently from one to |
| T-31 .......II.2:2 | For there are s. in its relinquishment. The |
| T-31 .......V.9:1 | Spirit's lesson plans arranged in easy s., |
| W-pI ...... 4.3:2 | to train you in the first s. toward the goal |
| W-pI .... 14.3:2 | The early s. in this exchange, which can |
| W-pI .... 23.5:3 | The first two s. in this process require |
| W-pI .... 23.5:6 | By taking the first two s., you will see that |
| W-pI .... 61.7:3 | giant s. we will take in the next few weeks. |
| W-pI .. 109.7:3 | to walk with lightened s. along the road |
| W-pI .. 155.7:3 | this s. back as truth comes forth in you, to |
| W-pI .. 156.6:2 | in you s. forward and encompasses the |
| W-pI .. 168.3:3 | All s. but this we learn, instructed by His |
| W-pI 193.13:7 | deny the little s. He asks you take to Him. |
| W-pI .. 195.2:3 | sane refuse to take the s. which He directs |
| W-pI .. 196.8:1 | Our next s. will be easy, if you take this |

W-pII.....in.7:8 we undertake these last few s. to You, and
W-pII..225.2:5 accomplish these few final s. which end a
P-2.........V.1:4 belief relies on certain s. which never
S-2...........I.1:3 chosen to begin the s. of prayer cannot

## stern 2

T-21.........I.4:3 but through the s. necessity of limits they
M-13..........5:8 not find" remains this world's s. decree,

## stick 1

WpI.rIV.in4:3 who throws a s. into the ocean change the

## stifle 1

S-1........IV.4:2 you s. and imprison it in ancient prisons,

## still 84

• quiet, peaceful
*other*

T-4.........in.2:2 chosen to "Be s. and know that I am God.
T-4...........I.8:6 are afraid, be s. and know that God is real,
T-13......VI.7:5 s. dimension of time that does not change
T-13...X.11:10 *of God, and look upon his purity and be s.. In*
T-14........X.5:1 pattern that never rests and is never s.. It
T-15......I.15:7 Time stands s. in his holiness, and
T-21........V.1:6 s., small Voice for God is not drowned out
T-22.....II.12:2 How s. it rests, in time and yet beyond,
T-24........V.1:1 The Christ in you is very s.. He looks on
T-24........V.6:1 The Christ in you is very s.. He knows
T-24......VI.1:1 your brother's holiness the world is s.,
T-27.......IV.6:9 in which the mind is s. enough to hear an
T-28........I.11:1 the mind that stops an instant and is s.. It
T-29........V.1:3 is a resting place so s. no sound except a
T-29........V.2:4 The s. infinity of endless peace surrounds
T-29........V.4:2 Be very s. and hear God's Voice in him,
T-30......III.8:6 Yet s. and white and lovely will it shine
T-30......IV.1:3 is so lovely and so s. in loving gentleness,
T-31.........I.4:4 seems small and s. before its magnitude.
T-31.........I.6:1 so small and s. It cannot rise above the
T-31......I.12:1 Let us be s. an instant, and forget all
T-31.......II.6:4 Then let us wait an instant and be s.,
T-31.......II.7:2 to you. Be s. and listen. Think not ancient
T-31.......II.8:1 Be very s. an instant. Come without all
W-pI.....49.4:2 Be very s. and open your mind. Go past
W-pI.....81.1:3 Let me be s. before my holiness. In its
W-pI.....94.1:3 The sounds of this world are s., the sights
W-pI.....97.4:1 the miracle in which all time stands s.; the
W-pI......106.h Let me be s. and listen to the truth.
W-pI...106.2:2 Be s. today and listen to the truth. Be not
W-pI...106.3:4 Be s. today and listen to the truth. Go past
W-pI...106.7:5 *I will be s. and listen to the truth. What does*
W-pI...106.9:1 Be s. and listen to the truth today. For
W-pI.106.10:3 *Let me be s. and listen to the truth. I am the*
W-pI...109.5:6 it be s. and thankfully accept its healing.
W-pI...118.2:1 (106) Let me be s. and listen to the truth.
W-pI...118.2:2 *Let my own feeble voice be s., and let me hear*
W-pI...118.3:4 hour: Let me be s. and listen to the truth.
W-pI...125.9:3 Only be s. and listen. You will hear the
W-pI...125.9:5 be s. a moment and remind yourself you
W-pI...128.6:1 Pause and be s. a little while, and see how
W-pI...128.7:8 Open your mind to Him. Be s. and rest.
W-pI.140.10:2 be s. and listen for the Voice of healing,
W-pI.153.10:1 Be s. a moment, and in silence think how
W-pI...156.5:2 All living things are s. before you, for they
W-pI...157.4:3 it rest in s. anticipation and in quiet joy,
WpI..rV.in2:2 *our doubts be quiet and our holy minds be s.*
W-pI......182.h I will be s. an instant and go home.
W-pI...182.8:1 When you are s. an instant, when the
W-pI.182.12:9 Be s. an instant and go home with Him,
W-pI...183.8:4 Let all thoughts be s. except this one. And
W-pI.183.11:6 In this eternal, s. relationship, in which
W-pI...189.7:1 Simply do this: Be s., and lay aside all
W-pI...190.9:1 Heaven's peace holds all things s. at last.
W-pI...202.1:1 (182) I will be s. an instant and go home.
W-pI...208.1:2 *I will be s., and let the earth be still along with*
W-pI...208.1:2 *be still, and let the earth be s. along with me.*
W-pI...219.1:4 *Be s., my mind, and think a moment upon*
W-pII...in.10:5 need but be s. and let all things be healed.
W-pII......1.4:1 Forgiveness, on the other hand, is s., and
W-pII.....221.h to my mind. Let all my thoughts be s..
W-pII..221.2:6 let our thoughts be s. and find His peace,
W-pII..222.1:5 How s. is he who knows the truth of what
W-pII..225.1:3 *s. the way Your loving Son is led along to You*
W-pII..229.1:4 So s. It waited for my coming home, that I
W-pII.....254.h Let every voice but God's be s. in me.
W-pII..272.1:7 *I am surrounded by Your Love, forever s.,*
W-pII..286.1:1 *Father, how s. today! How quietly do all*
W-pII..303.1:2 be s. with me while Heaven's Son is born.
W-pII..305.1:2 Comparisons are s. before this peace. And
W-pII..341.1:2 *deep and s. the universe smiles back on You,*
W-pII..347.2:2 Be very s., and hear the gentle Voice for
W-pII..358.1:5 *all I do not know, and let my voice be s.,*
W-pII..360.1:2 *for the Great Rays remain forever s. and*
M-14.........3:3 But time stands s., and waits on the goal
M-16.........4:5 One can easily sit s. an hour with closed
M-19.........5:9 Perception rests, the mind is s., and light
C-2............9:1 no answer, being made to s. God's Voice,
C-ep...........4:7 until the world is s. an instant and forgets
C-ep...........5:6 us. The Son is s., and in the quiet God has
P-2......... II.9:4 Let him be s. and recognize his brother's
S-1........ III.5:1 Stand s. an instant, now, and think what
S-1......... V.4:3 The lawns are deep and s., for here the
S-3........IV.7:4 Be s. an instant. Underneath the sounds

## still 535

• other
*quiet, peaceful*

T-1........III.8:4 s. expressions of your own state of grace,
T-1.......VII.2:3 must s. be expressed through one body to
T-1.......VII.2:3 to another, because vision is s. so dim.
T-2...........I.3:9 It s. remains within you, however, to
T-2......... II.7:2 may s. think this is associated with loss, a
T-2.......V.10:4 making it apparent that charity s. lies
T-2.......VII.1:1 You may s. complain about fear, but you
T-3...........I.1:1 s. associated with miracles can disappear.
T-3........III.4:1 but it is s. a correction rather than a fact.
T-3........IV.1:4 because you can s. perceive lovelessly.
T-3......... V.5:4 your overall confusion s. further. Your
T-3.....VII.4:10 You s. believe you are an image of your
T-3.......VII.5:8 Your Self is s. in peace, even though your
T-4...........I.4:3 dream while he is s. dreaming is not really
T-4......... II.5:3 In this sense you are s. a baby. You have
T-4........IV.9:5 His Mind s. shines on you and must shine
T-4........VI.4:4 s. only your decision to use the device that
T-4........VI.5:8 You are s. free to choose, but can you
T-4........VI.7:8 but what has been dissociated is s. there.
T-5.........I.1:12 it. All of it is s. yours although all of it has
T-5......... II.1:5 Your will is s. in you because God placed
T-5......III.10:3 his mind, because part of it is s. for God.
T-5......III.10:4 part, it is s. much stronger than the ego,
T-5......III.11:5 made truth, but truth can s. set you free.
T-5........IV.1:1 What fear has hidden s. is part of you.
T-5........IV.4:3 The Mind that was in me is s. irresistibly
T-5.........VI.8:3 means that in later generations He can s.
T-5......VI.11:3 It is s. true that where you look to find
T-6.........in.2:5 is s. a form of faith and can be redirected.
T-6...........I.8:2 is s. on them that I must build my church.
T-6..........I.10:1 We are s. equal as learners, although we
T-6..........I.11:3 you must s. follow my example in how to
T-6......... II.3:4 thus obscuring your equality with them s.
T-6........III.1:2 what extends from the mind is s. in it, and
T-6........III.1:3 the Holy Spirit s. holds knowledge safe in
T-6........III.4:4 you cannot teach what you s. dissociate.
T-6......V.B.3:3 and we can clarify this s. further now. At
T-6....V.B.3:10 S. strongly aware of the ego in yourself,
T-6......V.B.4:4 fundamental change will s. occur with the
T-6......V.B.8:1 This is s. a preliminary step, since *having*
T-6......V.B.8:1 since *having* and *being* are s. not equated. It
T-6......V.B.8:5 term "more desirable" s. implies that the
T-6......V.B.9:1 The second step, then, is s. perceptual,
T-6......V.C.3:2 Yet it s. has an aspect of thought reversal,
T-6......V.C.4:1 may s. entail conflict to some extent, this
T-6......V.C.4:8 s. believe that you can choose either one.
T-6......V.C.5:7 final step will s. be taken for you by God,
T-7........IV.1:5 whole. Yet healing is s. of God, because it
T-7........VI.3:8 Remaining logical but s. insane, the ego
T-7........VI.7:2 you may s. think there is something else.
T-8..........II.1:9 you could s. learn nothing from the ego,
T-8........IV.2:8 purpose, then, is s. to overcome the world
T-8......... V.2:4 Yet to heal is s. to make whole. Therefore,
T-8......VIII.5:1 It is s. true that the body has no function
T-8........IX.9:8 Yet it is s. His Will for you, and His Will
T-9..........II.2:1 you really want, but you are s. afraid of it.
T-9........III.2:6 But your task is s. to tell him he is right.
T-9........III.2:9 He is s. right, because he is a Son of God.
T-9......... V.3:7 but to revolt against it is s. to believe in it.
T-9........VI.6:2 while you s. need healing, your miracles
T-10........II.6:2 You make it only because you s. believe it
T-10.... III.11:3 His Voice s. calls you to return, and He
T-10........IV.8:6 the spark is s. as pure as the Great Light,
T-11.......in.2:3 problem is s. the only source of conflict,
T-11........II.7:4 for it s. depends on how you see it. The
T-11........IV.2:4 deny your Father is s. for your protection,
T-11......VI.1:5 are ye who have not seen and s. believe,"
T-11......VI.8:4 dream of crucifixion s. lies heavy on your
T-11......VI.8:7 beginning to wake are s. aware of dreams,
T-11.....VII.2:3 They are s. perceptions, because he still
T-11.....VII.2:3 because he s. believes that he is separate.
T-11....VIII.7:4 the real world is s. yours for the asking.
T-12.........I.8:3 Spirit must s. translate the fear into truth.
T-12........II.6:1 s. want what God wills, and no nightmare
T-12.......III.9:4 You s. cannot will against Him, and that
T-12....... V.2:7 failed to weaken you, you are s. strong.
T-12.....VII.6:8 it will s. believe it has one goal by making
T-12.....VII.7:6 do not want, it is s. because you *do* want it.
T-13........II.5:2 because you would s. wish to crucify him
T-13...... III.2:8 For s. deeper than the ego's foundation,
T-13.... III.10:6 but s. more did he fear his real Father,
T-13....... V.9:2 this darkness, and yet s. within you, is the
T-13.... VI.13:5 God's Son is s. as loving as his Father.
T-13.....VII.5:7 Christ is s. there, although you know Him
T-13.....VII.6:2 Yet while he s. lays value on his own, he
T-13....VIII.3:7 Aspects of reality can s. be seen, and they
T-13...... IX.1:2 and having done so they will s. condemn,
T-13........X.4:5 past, and s. to see them as they really are?
T-13...... XI.4:3 while you s. remember the results of not
T-13...... XI.8:4 be yours because His peace s. flows to you
T-14........II.1:6 Yet it may s. make sense to you. Have
T-14...... IV.1:3 him while you s. believe it is not there. His
T-14...... IV.2:4 will s. think that you are separate from
T-14...... IV.4:6 you out of Himself, but s. within Him. He
T-14....... V.1:1 is the part that links you s. with God.
T-14....VIII.2:1 He shares it s., for you. Everything that
T-14...... IX.3:9 it. The temple s. is holy, for the Presence
T-14........X.5:4 The little sanity that s. remains is held
T-14........X.6:7 may wonder how you who are s. bound to
T-14...... XI.1:4 it. You s. have the power, but you have
T-15.........I.4:14 of its own death, it will pursue you s.,
T-15.........I.6:4 its worshippers s. believe that it can offer
T-15...... III.7:6 Far beyond your little world but s. in you,
T-15....VIII.2:3 cast aside, but s. desire with all your heart
T-15...... XI.6:3 to deny what love is and s. recognize it.
T-15...... XI.7:5 and s. would teach to all my brothers, is
T-16........II.1:1 may s. think that holiness is impossible to
T-16........II.2:3 you would s. try to keep understanding
T-16........II.2:7 Yet it is s. impossible to accomplish what
T-16........II.8:4 to place s. greater faith in the disaster you
T-16...... IV.3:6 it is s. held together by the illusion of love.
T-16...... IV.4:9 they find the fear of death is s. upon them
T-16...... VI.6:2 For a time the body is s. seen, but not
T-16...... VI.7:7 be no meaning you would s. seek here.
T-16.... VI.12:1 special relationship which s. attracts you,
T-17........II.3:1 is s. the greatest accomplishment of all in
T-17........II.3:5 and nothing remain s. bound by them,
T-17........II.4:3 made perception possible will s. occur.
T-17...... III.9:1 s. up to you to choose to join with truth or
T-17...... IV.6:3 relationship s. seems to you somehow to
T-17.... IV.13:1 who have tried so hard, and are s. trying,
T-17....... V.6:5 why would you now not s. believe that He
T-17..... V.13:2 you do not realize that it is with you s..
T-17..... V.14:7 but remain s. separate and divided on the
T-18.........I.4:3 it once was one, and s. is what it was. That
T-18.........I.6:7 for such it was and so it s. remains. Invest

T-18.......I.12:5 s. further weaken and break apart what is
T-18...... III.3:5 go toward love s. hating it, and terribly
T-18...... IV.7:5 s. convinced that your understanding is a
T-18....... V.5:3 it is that it is s. a special relationship. Yet
T-18...... VI.6:3 For it is s. the fantasies you want, and
T-18..... VII.1:1 You s. have too much faith in the body as
T-18..... VII.1:3 always means you s. find sin attractive.
T-18..... VII.1:4 for himself who s. accepts sin as his goal.
T-18.... VIII.4:5 Its whole existence s. remains in them.
T-18.... VIII.7:5 nothing yet who would s. die to defend it?
T-18..VIII.13:2 You are s. worn and tired, and the desert's
T-18..VIII.13:2 desert's dust s. seems to cloud your eyes
T-18..VIII.13:6 Only a little wall of dust s. stands between
T-18.... IX.1:10 its barricades is s. a tiny segment of the
T-18...... IX.8:4 beyond them, s. further from the light.
T-18.... IX.10:5 a step s. further inward but the one *you*
T-18.... IX.11:1 is s. beyond the scope of our curriculum.
T-18.... IX.11:7 The readiness for knowledge s. must be
T-19.......I.15:4 For faith is s. a learning goal, no longer
T-19...... III.1:5 For guilt s. calls to it, and the mind hears
T-19...... III.8:6 You see it s., because you do not realize
T-19...... III.8:8 Only the habit of looking for it s. remains.
T19... IV.A.2:4 little barrier of sand s. stands between
T19. IV.A.2:10 you cherish s. against your brother *is* the
T19. IV.A.2:11 of hatred would s. oppose the Will of God
T19... IV.A.3:2 are s. unwilling to let it join you wholly.
T19... IV.A.3:3 You s. oppose the Will of God, just by a
T19... IV.A.3:7 What you would s. contain behind your
T19. IV.A.15:4 to remove from it, and see it s.. The Holy
T19. IV.A.16:4 as long ago I promised and promise s..
T19....IV.C.1:3 learn s. more about this strange devotion,
T19... IV.D.1:5 peace must s. surmount a final obstacle,
T19. IV.D.10:5 without a purpose is s. meaningless, and
T19. IV.D.11:4 forgiveness you s. stand unforgiving. You
T19. IV.D.12:1 brother who stands beside you s. seems to
T19. IV.D.12:3 you attack him s., to keep what seems to
T19. IV.D.14:4 Yet s. He holds forgiveness out to you, to
T19. IV.D.14:5 "stranger" s. offers you salvation as His
T19. IV.D.21:3 What you had faith in s. is faithful, and
T19. IV.D.21:6 s. without conviction they have a purpose.
T-20....... II.1:6 Yet s. the gift proclaims his worthlessness
T-20....... II.4:3 offers thorns to anyone is against me s.,
T-20....... II.4:8 Look you s. closer at them now, and you
T-20....... II.5:1 You look s. with the body's eyes, and they
T-20.... III.8:10 one thing that s. would have it be unholy.
T-20....... V.4:5 yet insist that judgment s. has meaning?
T-20.... VI.12:1 who are learning this may s. be fearful,
T-20..... VII.1:4 where means and end are s. discrepant.
T-20..... VII.2:2 To the extent you s. experience it, you are
T-20.... VIII.9:7 It s. is true that nothing is without. Yet
T-21.........I.3:7 a happy learner yet because you s. remain
T-21.........I.4:4 And s. believing this, they hold those
T-21.........I.9:6 love the Son of God sings to his Father s..
T-21...... III.2:3 imagine that you s. experience its effects,
T-21.... III.12:1 to sin, and in the darkness so it s. is seen.
T-21.... III.12:7 them s. to save itself from what it made.
T-21...... IV.4:1 Your liberation s. is only partial; still
T-21...... IV.4:1 is only partial; s. limited and incomplete,
T-21...... IV.6:4 it. At times it s. deceives you. Yet in your
T-21...... IV.6:7 A few remaining trinkets s. seem to shine
T-21...... VI.2:3 sinful and s. perceive the other innocent.
T-21...... VI.8:9 the Holy Spirit s. holds out for everyone
T-21...... VI.9:6 you to give what It has given, and gives s..
T-21..... VII.6:2 For this one s. seems fearful, and unlike
T-21..... VII.6:5 s. seems to hold a threat the rest have lost
T-21..... VII.8:1 last question you have left unanswered s..
T-22.........I.2:2 you. But s. this strange idea which it does
T-22.........I.7:3 S. in this infant is your vision returned to
T-22..... II.10:2 you s. would be apart from your Creator,
T-22..... II.13:5 sin s. tempts you to remain in misery?
T-22...... IV.2:1 s. may think you can go back and make
T-22...... IV.5:6 God's offer s. is open, yet it waits
T-22...... IV.7:5 before the veil, it s. seems difficult. But
T-22....... V.3:2 It is s. whole, and nothing has been taken
T-23.........I.8:9 of God, s. shining in your quiet mind.
T-23..... II.21:4 leading s. deeper into terror and away
T-23...... III.1:7 his horrified awareness and pursue him s.
T-23...... III.2:3 and gently given, s. contains nothing.
T-23...... III.3:8 a little of the same can s. be different, and
T-23 ..... III.4:2 seems difficult to those who s. believe that
T-23 ..... III.5:6 with an enemy but hates him s., for what
T-23 ..... III.6:8 one tree left s. standing will shelter you.
T-23 ..... IV.4:3 form of murder and attack that s. attracts
T-23 ..... IV.7:7 it exerts on those in battle s. are gone, and
T-24 ..... III.1:4 he holds one error to himself as lovely s..
T-24 ..... III.3:7 it s. must rock and turn and whirl about
T-24 ...... V.4:7 it saw in you, and looks on s. with joy. Yet
T-24 ...... V.6:9 And seeks it s., that each might offer you
T-24 ..... VI.1:1 trace of conflict s. remains to haunt you in
T-24 ..... VI.3:4 the world began, and as He knows you s..
T-24 ..... VI.7:3 eternity is not regained by s. one more
T-24 .... VII.2:2 your brother s. contains all of creation,
T-24 .... VII.2:2 yet, s. in the future or apparently gone by.
T-24 .... VII.7:5 no meaning to anyone who s. retains one
T-24 .... VII.7:5 one thought with purpose s. uncertain, or
T-24 .... VII.8:5 that all perception s. is upside down until
T-24 .... VII.9:4 because you s. can feel it with your hands
T-24 .. VII.10:8 s. a means to offer to the "father" what he
T-25 ........I.6:2 purpose s. is one with Both the Father and
T-25 .......II.2:1 that you should cherish s. some hope of
T-25 .......II.3:2 And yet your hope that they may s. be
T-25 .......II.3:2 still be here prevents you s. from giving
T-25 .......II.8:7 it is s. your only function to behold in him
T-25 ..... III.4:1 link that kept it s. within the laws of God;
T-25 ..... III.4:3 And thus has God protected s. His Son,
T-25 ..... VI.5:8 Yet while in time, there is s. much to do.
T-25 ... VIII.2:5 what one divided s. against himself would
T-25 ... VIII.2:8 little faith remains to those who s. believe
T-25 ... VIII.4:1 You who know not of justice s. can ask,
T-25 ... VIII.6:1 is extremely hard for those who s. believe
T-25 ..... IX.4:5 and how much can the loser s. defend. Yet
T-25 ..... IX.4:6 Yet does the problem s. remain unsolved,
T-26 ........I.3:4 and something s. remains for you alone.
T-26 ..... III.3:6 and time and choice have meaning s., and
T-26 ..... IV.1:5 s. believes that he has much to be forgiven
T-26 ..... IV.5:3 power to the song, and makes it sweeter s.
T-26 ..... IV.6:1 your brother s. is holding back the happy
T-26 ...... V.4:1 To you who s. believe you live in time and
T-26 ...... V.4:1 the Holy Spirit s. guides you through the
T-26 ...... V.4:1 and senseless maze you s. perceive in time
T-26 ...... V.4:4 Not one illusion s. remains unanswered in
T-26 ...... V.4:5 it to your heart, as if it were before you s..
T-26 ...... V.5:2 of the Son of God can hardly s. be there,
T-26 ...... V.5:5 in sin, is that one instant s. called back, as
T-26 ...... V.6:9 Yet can he s. imagine he is elsewhere, and
T-26 .... V.11:7 You are like to one who s. hallucinates,
T-26 .... V.11:9 but s. a present light is dimly recognized.
T-26 .... V.13:4 belief that what is over is s. here and now.
T-26 ..... VI.1:7 one illusion real, and s. escape the rest.
T-26 ..... VI.1:9 and s. maintain that even one is best?
T-26 .... VII.9:3 We call it "wish" because it s. conceives of
T-26 .. VII.12:6 Its failure lies in that you s. feel guilty,
T-26 .. VII.13:2 and this must s. be true because ideas
T-26 .. VII.14:5 For otherwise he s. demands that he must
T-26 ... VIII.2:1 you s. believe you are external to him.
T-26 ... VIII.3:3 error s. obscured that is the source of fear.
T-26 ... VIII.3:4 wipe out the space you see between you s.,
T-26 ... VIII.3:8 space between you and your brother s.,
T-26 ... VIII.8:3 space that lies between you, unforgiven s..
T-26 ... VIII.9:7 time, but to the little space between you s.
T-26 ..... IX.2:1 left without a single one you cherish s.?
T-27 ........I.5:2 It is a picture of a body s., for what you
T-27 ........I.8:4 whose consequences s. are there to see, so
T-27 .......II.1:5 brother, and could love and trust him s.?
T-27 .....II.3:11 that he s. would hold against himself or
T-27 .....II.14:3 it, and hates it s. as symbol of his fear.
T-27 .... VII.1:6 is his own attack upon himself apparent s.
T-27 ... VIII.3:4 does it try to teach again, and s. again,
T-27 . VIII.10:2 what the form of the attack, this s. is true.
T-27 . VIII.10:3 enemy and of attacker, s. is this the truth.
T-27 . VIII.10:4 pain and suffering you feel, this is s. true.
T-28 ........I.2:6 occurring now, and s. were there to see.
T-28 ........I.4:7 of time where guilt appears to linger s..
T-28 .......II.4:3 a choice of dreams while you are s. asleep,
T-28 .....II.10:6 and the bodies that s. seem to move about
T-28 ..... IV.3:3 him as a mind in which illusions s. persist
T-29 ........I.3:3 but this one s. remains to block your path
T-29 ..... III.3:1 created in the dark, where God s. shines.
T-29 ..... III.5:4 the light in him is brighter s. because you
T-29 .... IV.2:7 it allowed you s. to be afraid because you
T-29 .......V.1:1 no memory of sin and of illusion lingers s.
T-29 .......V.4:1 which s. abides in him as it abides in you.
T-29 .... VII.2:1 who comes here but must s. have hope,
T-29 ... VIII.3:3 Yet it is s. a thought, and cannot leave the
T-29 ... VIII.8:5 s. attempts to seek for one that yet might
T-29 ..... IX.7:1 The real world s. is but a dream. Except
T-30 ........I.3:2 now. You s. make up your mind, and *then*
T-30 ........I.5:1 will s. be times when you have judged
T-30 ........I.7:6 Yet this decision s. can be undone, by
T-30 ... III.11:9 own. The star shines s.; the sky has never
T-30 ..... IV.3:7 he s. perceives them as obeying rules he
T-30 ..... IV.3:8 So there s. are rules that they can seem to
T-30 .......V.3:1 for the purpose of forgiveness s. remains.
T-30 .......V.3:5 longer, with his feet s. touching earth. Yet
T-30 .......V.4:3 a purpose s. beneath creation and eternity
T-30 .......V.5:1 The real world s. falls short of this, for
T-30 .......V.5:2 when they are s. perceived but wanted not
T-30 .......V.7:2 Perhaps they s. look back, and think they
T-31 ......I.7:10 that reflects the Love of God is stronger s..
T-31 .....II.11:3 clear that while you s. insist on leading or
T-31 ..... IV.4:2 who s. believe there is another answer to
T-31 ..... IV.4:5 that seems to point to s. another road. No
T-31 ..... IV.8:3 s. the same illusion and the same mistake.
T-31 .......V.6:5 kept s. deeper in the mists below the face
T-31 .......V.6:8 condemning s. your brother for the hated
T-31 .....V.10:9 is s. no need to hide what you are made of
T-31 .....V.15:4 yourself will s. remain quite meaningless.
T-31 ... VI.3:11 that God created that must s. be done?
T-31 .... VII.2:3 in fearful form, with content s. concealed,
T-31 .... VII.2:3 and blacken it with s. another "crime."
T-31 . VIII.12:5 and not one spot of darkness s. remains
W-pI .... 16.4:3 You will find that it is s. hard for you not
W-pI .... 23.7:4 We are s. at the stage of identifying the
W-pI .... 27.2:4 If fear of loss s. persists, add further: *It can*
W-pI .... 27.3:6 You can s. repeat one short sentence to
W-pI .... 28.1:5 them. And we are s. at the beginning.
W-pI .... 45.3:4 are. They must s. be there, because they
W-pI .... 56.4:5 God is s. everywhere and in everything
W-pI .... 65.1:4 you hold while you s. cherish others. The
W-pI .... 70.6:2 s. let you decide when to undertake them.
W-pI .... 71.3:3 s. grounds for hope in other places and in
W-pI .... 79.1:2 is really solved already you will s. have the
W-pI .... 79.3:2 s. uncertain about what the problem is. A
W-pI .... 79.5:5 only to be hidden again but s. unsolved.
W-pI .... 96.3:3 and s. be what It is and must forever be. A
W-pI .... 97.3:1 try to bring reality s. closer to your mind.
W-pI .... 98.4:2 Those s. uncertain, too, will join with us,
W-pI .... 98.4:2 our certainty, will make it stronger s..
W-pI .... 99.5:5 does He know one thing must s. be true;
W-pI .... 99.5:5 one thing must still be true; God is s. Love
W-pI .... 99.6:8 *here. God s. is Love, and this is not His Will.*
W-pI .... 99.8:4 see how bright this light s. shines in you.
W-pI .. 99.11:4 *here. God s. is Love, and this is not His Will.*
W-pI .. 101.1:3 s. believe it asks for suffering as penance
W-pI .. 101.7:3 to go s. faster to the waiting goal of peace.
W-pI .. 102.1:2 and may s. believe a little that it buys you
W-pI .. 102.2:1 try to loose its weakened hold s. further,
W-pI .. 104.2:3 will s. be ours when time has passed into
W-pI 108.10:3 made s. faster and more sure each time
W-pI .. 113.2:2 *knowledge s. remains within my mind, I see*
W-pI .. 124.2:5 yet s. remains with us as we walk on.
W-pI .. 127.1:2 one, another way of loving s. another.
W-pI 130.11:2 of Heaven s. remains within your range of
W-pI .. 131.3:4 you s. are free to choose a goal that lies
W-pI .. 132.6:5 truth. He will return and go s. farther, or
W-pI 132.12:3 in what is Himself and what is s. Himself.
W-pI 133.10:1 s. must he perceive its tarnished edges
W-pI 133.10:3 He who would s. preserve the ego's goals
W-pI .. 134.3:1 you s. believe you must forgive the truth,
W-pI 134.17:1 for there will s. be many times when you
W-pI 135.25:6 plans or magical beliefs can s. have value,
W-pI .. 136.5:3 sign that this decision s. remains in force,
W-pI .. 153.2:5 Now are the weak s. further undermined,
W-pI .. 153.2:5 without and s. a greater treachery within.
W-pI .. 153.5:5 only of defense by s. more fantasies, and
W-pI 153.15:4 Ten would be better; fifteen better s.. And
W-pI 154.12:2 hundred times, and yet belief is lacking s..

### stone 10

T-3.......VII.4:9 the foundation s. in your thought system,
T-6.......V.A.4:5 real foundation s. of the thought system I
T-11.........I.1:4 Not one s. you place upon it but will be
T-17....IV.13:5 each senseless s. that seems to shine from
T-19....... II.7:1 There is no s. in all the ego's embattled
W-pI.134.12:3 the heavy walls of s. and iron doors he
W-pI...170.7:2 to flame from him, he is but made of s..
W-pI...170.8:4 it and lay before this mindless piece of s.?
W-pI.170.11:2 time upon this bit of carven s. you made,
C-ep...........2:3 Ask but my help to roll the s. away, and it

### stones 3

T-20...... IV.8:5 and leaving in your way no s. to trip on,
T-21.........I.1:5 down upon the s. you did not recognize,
T-29...... IX.1:3 let himself fall lower than the s. upon the

### stood 9

T19... IV.A.9:5 and s. for nothing when you had greater
T-26...... IX.8:4 s. a cross stands now the risen Christ, and
T-30....... V.6:2 all that s. between your image of yourself
W-pI.....69.1:4 who s. beside you when you were in hell.
W-pI.....78.3:1 in shining light where each one s. before.
W-pI...183.4:5 names, you s. before them worshipfully,
W-pI...196.5:3 it merely s. for the belief the fear of God is
S-1........ IV.3:5 from every choice that s. for a mistake.
S-1......... V.1:3 it was alone and s. against the world.

### stoop 1

S-2......... II.2:1 in which a "better" person deigns to s. to

### stop 21

T-7...........I.3:5 Being limitless it does not s.. It creates
T-8.....VII.10:6 It does not s. at the body, for if it does it is
T-11.......I.5:10 love does not s. because you do not see it,
T-18....... V.6:1 s. instantly and offer the Holy Spirit your
T-18...... IX.6:4 It is not strong enough to s. a button's fall
T-18...... III.3:5 repeat it; you will merely s. and let it go,
T19....IV.B.5:8 s. now to look for guilt in your brother?
T-20.... VI.11:4 Here does the Son of God s. briefly by, to
T-21....... II.7:8 *it in;* only to s. your interference with what
T-22...... III.6:6 Watch how they s. at nothingness, unable
T-27....VIII.7:7 have no power to make the body s. its evil
W-pI.....44.7:3 stopped in this unless you choose to s. it.
W-pI.....69.6:5 them. Go on; clouds cannot s. you.
W-pI.....72.8:1 will try today to s. these senseless attacks
W-pI.72.10:12 our grievances to close our eyes and s. our
W-pI.....78.2:2 by not allowing sight to s. before it sees.
W-pI...129.1:2 s. with the idea the world is worthless, for
W-pI...136.8:5 suffer, twist your limbs and s. your heart,
M-16 ..........4:9 drop away. If not, that is the time to s..
M-20 .........4:6 S. for a moment now and think of this: Is
P-3........ III.7:7 Then s. a while, long enough to think of

### stopped 2

W-pI.....44.7:3 be s. in this unless you choose to stop it. It
C-ep...........4:6 song begins again which had been s. only

### stopping 1

T-22...... III.5:6 sin, and s. at the outside form of nothing.

### stops 5

T-22...... III.5:8 Yet how can sight that s. at nothingness,
T-26...... III.5:1 Salvation s. just short of Heaven, for only
T-28.......I.11:1 into the mind that s. an instant and is still
W-pI...184.7:4 Learning that s. with what the world
W-pI...184.7:4 world would teach s. short of meaning. In

### store 6

T19IV.A.17:12 meager s. and make your life complete.
W-pI...96.12:1 lay another treasure in your growing s..
W-pI.122.12:2 been held in s. for us since time began,
W-pI.159.10:1 the s. of miracles set out for you to give.
W-pI...187.3:5 that by your giving is your s. increased.
W-pII.344.1:7 *brothers fill my s. with Heaven's treasures,*

### stored 2

T-28 ........I.5:8 alive, the present dead, are s. within it,
T-28 ..... III.7:2 s. a heap of snow that shone like silver.

### storehouse 6

T-28 .......II.5:1 An empty s., with an open door, holds all
T-28 ..... III.7:1 you would keep within the s. of the world.
T-28 ..... III.8:6 s. it will make a place of welcome for your
W-pI...159.2:5 the s. of your mind where they are laid,
W-pI...159.9:1 Take from His s., that its treasures may
M-6 ...........2:5 referred many times in the text to the s. of

### stores 1

T-13 .... VII.1:3 no s. where people buy an endless list of

### storm 3

T-16 ..... IV.3:1 of hate by finding a haven in the s. of guilt
T-16 ..... IV.3:2 It makes no attempt to rise above the s.,
T-18 .... VII.8:2 center of the s. than all its raging activity.

### storms 2

W-pI...109.3:2 will carry you through s. and strife, past
W-pII.244.2:2 No s. can come into the hallowed haven

### story 6

T-8 ....... VI.4:1 Listen to the s. of the prodigal son, and
T-27 ...VIII.1:3 the s. of how it was made by other bodies,
T-29 ..... IX.1:4 then, your s. in the dream you made, and
W-pI.153.14:3 So is the s. ended. Let this day bring the
W-pI.153.14:5 dreams this s. has evoked in his confused,
P-3........ III.8:9 Remember the sorrowful s. of the world,

### straight 18

T-2 ...... VII.2:3 will be necessary to set the mind itself s.,
T-11 .... V.16:9 ego looks s. at the Father and does not see
T-12 .......II.5:6 Look s. at every image that rises to delay
T-14 ...... V.6:5 that points to this points s. to Heaven,
T-15 ..... IX.2:1 the necessary process of looking s. at all
T-16 ... IV.10:1 lead you s. to Him where your completion
T-16 ... IV.12:6 and then together we go s. to God, in
T-16 ... IV.13:7 you are directed s. to the Heart of God. At
T-17 .... VII.5:6 Use it, and it will carry you s. to illusions.
T-18 .VIII.11:6 tried to hide from Heaven s. to Heaven.
T-19 ........I.4:1 that faithlessness leads s. to illusions. For
T-20 ..... IV.8:5 He will go before you making s. your path
T-22 ..... IV.1:3 For now if you go s. ahead, the way you
T-22 ... VI.10:7 you. Let us look s. at how this error came
T-30 ...... V.8:2 away from fear forever, and to go s. on,
W-pI...134.7:2 and looks s. through the thousand forms
W-pI...181.9:5 We look s. into the present. And we give
W-pI...200.9:2 We go to Heaven, and the path is s.. Only

### straighten 2

T-30 ........I.5:2 unless you quickly s. out your mind to
W-pII.347.1:2 *S. my mind, my Father. It is sick. But You*

### straightened 1

T-3 ....... III.1:2 be s. out before you can know anything.

### strain 27

T-2 ....... VI.5:1 Fear is always a sign of s., arising
T-2 ....... VI.5:5 consistent behavior, but entails great s..
T-2 ....... VI.6:4 There is no s. in doing God's Will as soon
T-2 ....... VI.6:8 producing inevitable s. because wanting
T-3 ....... VI.5:6 The s. of constant judgment is virtually
T-7 ....... XI.2:3 Everything he does becomes a s., because
T-7 ....... XI.2:7 in which he will not experience s.,
T-11 ..... VI.3:7 to perceive with Him involves no s. at all.
T-12 ........I.6:3 And all your sense of s. comes from your
T-14 ... III.10:8 them what they want without effort, s., or
T-17 ... VIII.3:7 s. of refusing faith to truth is enormous,
T-17 ... VIII.3:8 answer truth with faith entails no s. at all.
T-17 ... VIII.4:1 the s. of not responding to His Call seems
T-17 ... VIII.4:3 the s. was there, but you attributed it to
T-17 ... VIII.4:6 nothing but the intolerable s. of refusing
T-24 .......II.4:6 s. your ears to hear its soundless voice,
T-24 ... VI.12:5 it no sacrifice is asked, no s. called forth,
T-31 ........I.2:4 from one to another, with no s. at all.
W-pI ...... 2.1:6 in a given area, or you will introduce s..
W-pI .... 12.6:4 whenever you experience a sense of s..
W-pI .... 16.6:2 If s. is experienced, three will be enough.
W-pI .... 35.8:2 Do not s. to think up specific things to fill
W-pI .... 42.6:3 than it is to s. to find suitable thoughts.
W-pI .... 44.4:2 slipping by with little or no sense of s..
W-pI .... 62.3:3 weakness, s. and fatigue from your mind.
W-pI .... 65.6:2 not s. or make undue effort in doing this.
W-pI 132.15:4 Then merely rest, alert but with no s., and

### strained 1

T-17 .......V.4:6 relationship may seem to be severely s..

### stranded 1

T-28 ......I.15:5 and left a s. Son forever on a shore where

### strange 86

T-3 ..... VI.10:7 s. perception *is* the authority problem
T-6 ..... V.B.1:6 An insane learner learns s. lessons. What
T-9 ..........I.3:5 You have set up this s. situation so that it
T-9 ........I.12:3 But consider the result of this s. decision.
T-10 ........I.2:5 You do not think this s., even though all
T-10 ..... III.1:6 and what this s. image makes you do can
T-10 ..... IV.6:2 are no s. images in the Mind of God, and
T-10 .......V.1:1 god of sickness are s. and very demanding
T-11 ........I.8:2 s. when you realize that to deny is to "not
T-12 .......V.7:4 the learning this s. curriculum is against.
T-13 ........I.2:1 In the s. world that you have made the
T-13 .......II.2:1 how s. a solution the ego's arrangement is
T-13 .......II.4:1 Much of the ego's s. behavior is directly
T-13 ..... IV.4:1 The ego has a s. notion of time, and it is
T-13 .......V.3:1 It is through these s. and shadowy figures
T-13 .... VII.4:3 of this s. world you made but do not want
T-13 .......X.2:4 What s. relationships you have made for
T-13 .......X.2:4 you have made for this s. purpose! And
T-13 .......X.2:9 salvation will find it in that s. relationship
T-13 ..... XI.5:4 to, whatever s. thoughts may occur to you
T-14 .......II.2:4 all the s. forms and feelings and actions
T-14 ... III.13:5 and against this s. distortion of the purity
T-14 ..... VI.3:1 imagined power to these s. ideas of safety
T-14 ..... VI.6:4 this s. and twisted effort to communicate
T-15 ........I.3:4 outcome of its s. religion must therefore
T-15 ........I.4:9 We have seen this s. paradox in the ego's
T-15 ..... III.1:5 the s. belief that littleness can content you
T-16 .......V.6:1 special relationship is a s. and unnatural
T-17 ........I.2:2 This s. position, in a sense, acknowledges
T-18 ........I.6:4 you really think it s. that a world in which
T-18 .......II.8:2 It is not s. that dreams can make a world
T-18 ... VIII.4:1 of all this s. and meaningless activity.
T-18 ... VIII.5:1 Such is the s. position in which those in a
T-19 ........I.8:1 this s. concealment has hurt your mind,
T-19 .......II.6:3 s. illusion that makes the clouds of guilt
T-19 .......II.6:9 of sin is kept in place by just this s. device.
T19 ... IV.B.2:6 your s. belief that in it lies salvation? Do
T19 ... IV.C.1:3 learn still more about this s. devotion, for
T19 ... IV.C.7:6 secrets, all its s. devices for deception, all
T-21 ..... III.3:1 it s. to you that faith can move mountains
T-21 .... VII.1:1 from the s. belief that you are powerless?
T-22 ........I.1:6 you wonder, does your s. uneasiness,
T-22 ........I.2:2 still this s. idea which it does accurately

| | |
|---|---|
| T-22.........I.6:7 | And the s., shifting ones he sees about |
| T-22......III.5:6 | Theirs is indeed a s. perception, for they |
| T-23.......in.2:1 | How s. indeed becomes this war against |
| T-23.........I.3:2 | and make your s. alliances on grounds |
| T-23.........I.5:5 | Only a s. illusion of yourself, a wish to |
| T-23..... II.16:2 | There is a s. device that makes it possible. |
| T-25....... II.2:1 | s. that you should cherish still some hope |
| T-27.........I.7:2 | of their unnatural desires and s. needs. |
| T-27.........I.8:1 | witnesses unto the s. belief that sin and |
| T-28.........I.5:8 | the s. associations made to keep the past |
| T-28.........I.6:4 | And yet you make s. use of it, as if the |
| T-29... VIII.6:2 | s. idea there is a power past omnipotence, |
| T-31.........I.4:5 | world began with one s. lesson, powerful |
| T-31.........I.6:6 | s. in outcome and incredible in difficulty |
| W-pI.......7.2:3 | is not really so s. as it may sound at first. |
| W-pI.....73.3:1 | Your will is lost to you in this s. bartering |
| W-pI.....74.1:5 | Peace has replaced the s. idea that you are |
| W-pI.....76.3:1 | the s. and twisted laws you have set up to |
| W-pI.....76.8:7 | Yet they are no more s. than other "laws" |
| W-pI.....93.2:3 | That you have sought salvation in s. ways; |
| W-pI...103.1:7 | This s. belief would limit happiness by |
| W-pI...105.2:3 | This s. distortion of what giving means |
| W-pI...131.7:1 | to this s. world you made and all its ways; |
| W-pI...135.3:5 | Is it not s. you do not pause to ask, as you |
| W-pI...136.8:4 | your "true" identity preserved, and the s., |
| W-pI...138.2:3 | s. perception of the truth that makes the |
| W-pI...139.6:1 | Atonement remedies the s. idea that it is |
| W-pI...152.6:1 | s. that you believe to think you made the |
| W-pI...166.3:1 | to anyone who holds such s. beliefs. He |
| W-pI...184.9:1 | It would indeed be s. if you were asked to |
| W-pI...188.9:6 | clean of s. desires and disordered wishes. |
| W-pI...190.7:6 | Your s. desires bring it evil dreams. Your |
| W-pI...198.8:2 | Dreams of any kind are s. and alien to the |
| W-pII..259.1:2 | the s. and the distorted seem more clear? |
| W-pII....13.2:3 | ends the s. distortions that were manifest. |
| M-11..........3:4 | it. Into this s. and paradoxical situation,– |
| P-2......... V.1:4 | This s. belief relies on certain steps which |
| P-2........VI.2:5 | The s. distortions woven inextricably into |
| P-3......... II.4:8 | s. dream a strange correction must enter, |
| P-3......... II.4:8 | strange dream a s. correction must enter, |
| P-3......... II.9:7 | compromise in this respect are s. indeed. |
| P-3......... II.9:9 | consider this s. procedure as salvation. |
| S-3........III.2:1 | may seem to be a s. idea. And yet it can be |

### strangely 1

| | |
|---|---|
| M-20..........2:7 | the past. But s., it is not a contrast of true |

### strangeness 1

| | |
|---|---|
| M-4......VII.1:7 | greater s. lies merely in the obviousness of |

### stranger 44

| | |
|---|---|
| T-1........III.7:5 | the Host within and the s. without. When |
| T-1........III.7:6 | When you bring in the s., he becomes |
| T-3........III.6:3 | God is not a s. to His Sons, and His Sons |
| T-3........III.7:3 | Attack is always made upon a s.. You are |
| T-3........III.7:4 | are making him a s. by misperceiving him |
| T-3........III.7:5 | made him a s. that you are afraid of him. |
| T-18......VI.2:4 | have done a s. thing than you yet realize. |
| T19.IV.D.12:1 | stands beside you still seems to be a s.. |
| T19.IV.D.14:5 | "s." still offers you salvation as His Friend |
| T-20.........I.4:3 | it. I was a s. and you took me in, not |
| T-20.........I.4:5 | In your forgiveness of this s., alien to you |
| T-20......III.7:2 | is a s. in him, who wandered carelessly |
| T-20......III.7:4 | s. is made homeless and *you* are welcome. |
| T-20......III.7:5 | Ask not this transient s., "What am I?" |
| T-23...... I.10:4 | Him. You are not a s. in the house of God. |
| W-pI...151.2:4 | the last detail which they report is even s., |
| W-pI...159.7:5 | waits. No one is s. to him. No one asks for |
| W-pI......160.h | I am at home. Fear is the s. here. |
| W-pI...160.1:1 | Fear is a s. to the ways of love. Identify |
| W-pI...160.1:2 | with fear, and you will be a s. to yourself. |
| W-pI...160.2:1 | There is a s. in our midst, who comes |
| W-pI...160.2:2 | S. yet, he does not recognize to whom he |
| W-pI...160.3:2 | you had asked this s. in to take your place |
| W-pI...160.3:2 | your place, and let you be a s. to yourself? |
| W-pI...160.4:1 | Who is the s.? Is it fear or you who are |
| W-pI...160.5:2 | denied himself and said, "I am the s. here. |
| W-pI...160.6:3 | s. to himself can find no home wherever |
| W-pI...160.6:4 | out and show him that he is no s. now. |
| W-pI...160.6:7 | asked no s. in, and took no alien thought |
| W-pI...160.7:1 | Who is the s.? Is he not the one your Self |
| W-pI...160.7:3 | now to recognize this s. in your midst, for |
| W-pI...160.7:7 | Him. No s. can be interposed between His |
| W-pI...160.8:3 | has answered you who ask, "Who is the s. |
| W-pI...160.8:4 | sure, that you are not a s. to your Father, |
| W-pI...160.8:4 | Father, nor is your Creator s. made to you |
| W-pI...160.8:5 | one, at home in Him, no s. to Himself. |
| W-pI...160.9:3 | They see Him as a s., for they do not |
| W-pI...175.2:2 | Fear is the s. here. God is but Love, and |
| W-pI...200.4:4 | You are a s. here. But it is given you to |
| W-pII..262.1:7 | *Let me not see him as a s. to his Father, nor as* |
| W-pII..262.1:7 | *as a stranger to his Father, nor as s. to myself.* |
| W-pII..303.1:6 | Let Him no longer be a s. here, for He is |
| C-ep...........2:1 | You *are* a s. here. But you belong to Him |
| P-2.......VII.7:7 | can he give to one who seems to be a s.; |

### strangers 11

| | |
|---|---|
| T-3........ III.6:3 | and His Sons are not s. to each other. |
| T-3........ III.7:7 | him. There are no s. in God's creation. To |
| T-3........ IV.3:7 | This makes its aspects s. to each other, |
| T-20......... II.5:5 | His. He sees no s.; only dearly loved and |
| T-20......... II.7:2 | no thorns, no s. and no obstacles to peace |
| T-22.........in.2:8 | And so they wander through a world of s., |
| W-pI.....43.7:5 | This form is equally applicable to s. as it |
| W-pI...160.7:8 | He does not know of s.. He is certain of |
| W-pI...160.9:2 | His vision sees no s., but beholds His |
| M-3 ...........2:2 | meeting of two apparent s. in an elevator, |
| M-3 ...........2:5 | the seeming s. in the elevator will smile to |

### strangest 2

| | |
|---|---|
| T-6........IV.5:2 | This is perhaps the s. perception of all, if |
| T-9...........I.1:1 | Fear of the Will of God is one of the s. |

### straw 4

| | |
|---|---|
| T-28.....VII.3:3 | to grasp uncertainly at any s. that seems |
| T-28.....VII.3:4 | Yet who can build his home upon a s., |
| T-28.....VII.5:7 | It is like the house set upon s.. It seems to |
| T-28...VII.5:10 | If it rests on s., there is no need to bar the |

### stray 3

| | |
|---|---|
| W-pI...188.9:3 | We will not let them s.. We let the light |
| W-pI...200.9:5 | nor let him s. forever from his home. The |
| W-pII..324.2:2 | s. except an instant from His loving Hand |

### stream 4

| | |
|---|---|
| W-pI.....31.3:4 | try to let the s. move on evenly and calmly |
| W-pI...109.6:1 | to sing, a s. long dry begins to flow again. |
| W-pI...109.7:3 | to sing and see the s. begin to flow again, |
| P-2.......VII.8:4 | street a s. of stars that brushes lightly past |

### streaming 2

| | |
|---|---|
| T-14......VI.8:5 | all doors and let the light come s. through |
| W-pII..323.1:1 | *let Your Love come s. in to his awareness,* |

### streams 2

| | |
|---|---|
| T-12......VI.7:2 | so enlightened that light s. into it, and the |
| T19...IV.D.2:3 | His face with glory appear as s. of blood, |

### street 6

| | |
|---|---|
| W-pI..........1.h | Nothing I see in this room [on this s., |
| W-pI..........2.h | everything I see in this room [on this s., |
| W-pI..........3.h | anything I see in this room [on this s., |
| W-pI..........4.h | the things I see in this room [on this s., |
| W-pI.......4.4:3 | *is like the things I see in this room [on this s.,* |
| P-2.......VII.8:4 | and the s. a stream of stars that brushes |

### streets 1

| | |
|---|---|
| T-13..... VII.1:2 | no buildings and there are no s. where |

### strength 231

| | |
|---|---|
| T-1.........I.16:2 | They simultaneously increase the s. of the |
| T-1.........I.16:2 | of the giver and supply s. to the receiver. |
| T-1.........I.34:3 | spirit's s. leaves no room for intrusions. |
| T-1.........I.42:1 | is their s. in releasing you from your false |
| T-1.....VII.3:10 | The s. of your conviction will then sustain |
| T-2..........II.7:5 | will literally take it over because of their s. |
| T-2........ III.4:5 | Because of the s. of its vision, it brings the |
| T-2........ VI.6:3 | The s. to do comes from your undivided |
| T-3...........I.5:3 | that s. and innocence are not in conflict, |
| T-3...........I.5:5 | mind knows the truth and this is its s.. It |
| T-3...........I.5:6 | because it associates innocence with s., |
| T-3........ III.1:5 | because it is certain, and certainty is s.. |
| T-3........ III.5:8 | provides the s. for creative thinking, but |
| T-3........ IV.1:1 | possess are only shadows of your real s.. |
| T-3......... V.1:1 | possess are only shadows of your real s., |
| T-3....... VII.2:2 | you really understand the s. of the mind. |
| T-4.........I.11:3 | Its weakness is your s.. Only God could |
| T-4..........II.8:2 | them in an equally feeble show of s.. It is |
| T-4........ III.2:6 | our united s. the ego cannot prevail. |
| T-4........ IV.8:3 | releasing the s. of God into everything |
| T-4........ VI.6:7 | them my s. as long as theirs is wanting. |
| T-5........ III.4:3 | be increased in s. before you can hear It. |
| T-5...... III.8:11 | it with His s. just as the ego welcomes it. |
| T-5........ IV.2:1 | it keeps to itself, and so it is without s.. Its |
| T-7........ IV.5:7 | The s. of right perception is so great that |
| T-7....... X.4:11 | This is the ego's weakness and your s.. |
| T-7......... X.5:1 | always sides with you and with your s.. As |
| T-8..........II.7:2 | is boundless in s. and in love and in peace |
| T-8........ III.7:3 | ego teaches that your s. is in you alone. |
| T-8........ III.7:4 | that all s. is in God and *therefore* in you. |
| T-8...... IV.5:14 | I can offer my s. to make yours invincible, |
| T-8......... V.6:9 | My s. will never be wanting, and if you |
| T-8........ VI.1:3 | Every gain in our s. is offered for all, so |
| T-8........ VI.1:3 | aside their weakness and add their s. to us |
| T-9......... V.5:1 | of the mind, how can this build ego s.? |
| T-12....... V.2:8 | the situation to establish your s.. |
| T-12....... V.4:1 | Holy Spirit's Love is your s., for yours is |
| T-12....... VI.2:1 | Holy Spirit is your s. because He knows |
| T-13...... III.3:2 | love with weakness and hatred with s., |
| T-13....VIII.8:2 | in s. the power of God's Son will move in |
| T-14...... XI.1:7 | a show of s. so pitiful that it must fail you. |
| T-14...... XI.1:8 | For power is not a seeming s., and truth is |
| T-15........II.3:5 | weakness, do not perceive the Source of s. |
| T-15........II.4:4 | And they support His s.. It is, therefore, |
| T-15........II.6:5 | and His lesson will support your s.. It is |
| T-15...... VI.3:2 | is power, and by sharing it, it gains in s.. |
| T-15...... VI.3:3 | must believe that s. comes from another, |
| T-15...... IX.3:5 | will do so with the s. that you have given |
| T-15...... IX.4:1 | to divide your s. between Heaven and hell |
| T-16.........I.2:7 | through you, you will empathize with s., |
| T-16.........I.2:7 | and will gain in s. and not in weakness. |
| T-16.........I.4:2 | of it if you let Him use your capacity for s. |
| T-16.........I.4:4 | Humility is s. in this sense only; that to |
| T-16.........I.5:8 | perception and *His* s. that you would share |
| T-16.........I.5:9 | Him offer you His s. and His perception, |
| T-16.........I.6:2 | lies in the s. of God that hovers over it |
| T-16...... III.7:6 | you will learn His power and s. and purity |
| T-16...... III.8:4 | supplemented by the s. of Heaven, and by |
| T-16...... V.12:4 | a senseless ritual in which s. is extracted |
| T-17.....VII.7:1 | idea how great the s. that goes with you. |
| T-18...... III.5:4 | your desire from His Will and from His s.. |
| T-18...... III.6:2 | willingness has given s. to everyone who |
| T-18...... IV.3:7 | the s. of willingness to come from you, |
| T-18.....VII.1:1 | much faith in the body as a source of s.. |
| T-20.........II.7:8 | the s. to look upon this final obstacle, and |
| T-20......II.11:4 | the freedom and the s. to lead you there. |
| T-20......II.11:5 | holy altar where the s. and freedom wait, |
| T-20.....VIII.5:4 | little the perfect choice to call upon for s.? |
| T-20.....VIII.5:6 | Yet it is *you* who need his s.. There is no |
| T-21.........II.4:9 | must accept its s., and not its weakness. |
| T-21...... IV.7:3 | The ego's weakness is its s.. The song of |
| T-21..... VI.11:7 | Such is his s., and not his weakness. He is |
| T-21..... VII.3:5 | must be disbanded in the presence of s.. |
| T-22....... V.3:8 | in this quiet state alone is s. and power. |

T-22....... V.4:2 the quiet **s.** of those whom love has joined
T-22...... VI.4:1 lovely in its innocence, mighty in **s.**, and
T-23.......in.1:2 Innocence is **s.**, and nothing else is strong
T-23.......in.1:4 The show of **s.** attack would use to cover
T-23.......in.3:5 share the **s.** of love *because* they looked on
T-23...... IV.9:1 **s.** of God in their awareness could never
T-24....... V.5:4 the **s.** their purpose holds is given them.
T-24.....VII.1:9 this son that you have made to be your **s.**?
T-25....... II.8:5 His gentleness becomes your **s.**, and both
T-25....... V.4:4 give to each an equal **s.** to save the other,
T-25.....VIII.8:6 vengeance without love has gained in **s.**
T-27....... III.1:3 Weak **s.** is meaningless, and power used
T-27.... VI.6:11 the **s.** of miracles for what they witness to.
T-28..... VII.7:4 for its **s.** lies not within itself alone. It is
T-29.........I.8:2 its weakness, but its lack of **s.** *or* weakness.
T-29...... III.1:9 **s.** could fail to understand this must be so
T-29....VIII.2:6 his little self for **s.** to raise his head, and
T-30...... IV.7:5 the **s.** of idle wishes for the Will of God.
T-30...... VI.5:2 heal. It gives the miracle its **s.** to overlook
T-31....VIII.1:3 he can do; its power is the only **s.** he has;
T-31....VIII.2:3 your weakness and the **s.** of Christ in you.
T-31....VIII.2:7 Him, and He has given you His **s.** instead.
T-31....VIII.3:7 His **s.** is yours because He is the Self that
T-31....VIII.4:2 again, and let Christ's **s.** prevail in every
T-31....VIII.4:4 His **s.** instead of their own weakness, seen
T-31....VIII.5:5 *Son.* Thus is Christ's **s.** invited to prevail,
T-31....VIII.5:5 all your weakness with the **s.** that comes
W-pI........42.h God is my **s.**. Vision is His gift.
W-pI.....42.1:4 It is His **s.**, not your own, that gives you
W-pI.....42.2:1 God is indeed your **s.**, and what He gives
W-pI.....42.2:5 Such is the **s.** of God. Such are His gifts.
W-pI........47.h God is the **s.** in which I trust.
W-pI.....47.1:1 If you are trusting in your own **s.**, you
W-pI.....47.2:4 who can put his faith in **s.** and feel weak?
W-pI.....47.3:2 do to call upon His **s.** and His protection.
W-pI.....47.4:1 own weakness to the Source of real **s.**.
W-pI.....47.4:5 yourself: *God is the* **s.** *in which I trust.*
W-pI.....47.5:4 **s.** of God in you is successful in all things.
W-pI.....47.6:2 in your real **s.** is fully justified in every
W-pI.....47.7:6 a place in you where the **s.** of God abides.
W-pI.....47.8:3 you are giving your trust to the **s.** of God.
W-pI.....48.3:1 sign that you are trusting in your own **s.**.
W-pI.....48.3:2 let His **s.** take the place of your weakness.
W-pI.....59.2:1 (42) God is my **s.**. Vision is His gift. Let
W-pI.....60.2:1 (47) God is the **s.** in which I trust. It is
W-pI.....60.2:2 is not my own **s.** through which I forgive.
W-pI.....60.2:3 It is through the **s.** of God in me, which I
W-pI.....60.2:5 because I feel the stirring of His **s.** in me.
W-pI.....62.3:1 you call upon the **s.** of Christ in you. Do
W-pI.....73.8:2 us, nor deceive us with an illusion of **s.**.
W-pI.....91.4:2 Did you but realize how great this **s.**, your
W-pI.....91.4:3 to the attempt to let you feel this **s.**. When
W-pI.....91.4:4 When you have felt the **s.** in you, which
W-pI.....91.4:5 into awareness as you feel the **s.** in you.
W-pI.....91.5:4 will has all the **s.** to do what it desires.
W-pI.....91.5:6 choose. You can experience the **s.** in you.
W-pI...91.6:10 The truth of what you are calls on the **s.** in
W-pI.....91.9:2 particularly on the experience of **s.**.
W-pI...91.10:1 by the **s.** of God and all His Thoughts. It is
W-pI...91.10:2 It is from Them that your **s.** will come. It
W-pI...91.10:3 support that you will feel the **s.** in you.
W-pI...91.10:5 will see miracles, because Their **s.** is yours
W-pI...91.10:6 Their **s.** becomes your eyes, that you may
W-pI........92.h are seen in light, and light and **s.** are one.
W-pI.....92.1:2 You do not think of light in terms of **s.**,
W-pI.....92.3:1 is God's **s.** in you that is the light in which
W-pI.....92.3:2 His **s.** denies your weakness. It is your
W-pI.....92.4:1 **S.** overlooks these things by seeing past
W-pI.....92.4:7 **S.** is the truth about you; weakness is an
W-pI.....92.4:7 and adored that **s.** may be dispelled, and
W-pI.....92.5:1 **S.** comes from truth, and shines with
W-pI.....92.5:4 It gives its **s.** to everyone who asks, in
W-pI.....92.5:7 Its **s.** is shared, that it may bring to all the
W-pI.....92.7:3 while light and **s.** perceive themselves as
W-pI.....92.7:4 The light of **s.** is not the light you see. It
W-pI.....92.8:1 The light of **s.** is constant, sure as love,
W-pI.....92.8:2 eyes, and **s.** and light abiding in his heart.
W-pI.....92.9:1 The **s.** in you will offer you the light, and
W-pI.....92.9:2 **S.** and light unite in you, and where they
W-pI...92.10:3 Its **s.** will be the light in which the gift of
W-pI...92.10:4 of self and Self, where light and **s.** are one.
W-pI.....94.2:1 True light is **s.**, and strength is
W-pI.....94.2:1 light is strength, and **s.** is sinlessness. If
W-pI.....94.2:3 be the guarantee of **s.** and light as well.
W-pI.....95.8:5 power to do this, we are regarding it as **s.**,
W-pI.....95.8:5 and are confusing **s.** with weakness.
W-pI...95.13:4 **s.** within you and His Love forever yours.
W-pI.....96.5:2 It has denied its Source of **s.**, and sees
W-pI...96.10:3 Restored in **s.**, it will again flow out from
W-pI.....97.4:3 His **s.** to every little effort that you make.
W-pI.....99.7:2 Try to perceive the **s.** in what you say, for
W-pI...111.2:1 are seen in light, and light and **s.** are one. *I*
W-pI...111.2:2 *I see through* **s.**, *the gift of God to me. My*
W-pI...111.2:3 *dispels, by giving me His* **s.** *to take its place.*
W-pI...111.3:4 are seen in light, and light and **s.** are one.
W-pI...123.6:5 And so they grow in power and in **s.**, until
W-pI...124.1:2 do, power and **s.** available to us in all our
W-pI. 127.11:2 And we will watch it grow in health and **s.**
W-pI...130.8:1 world by asking for a **s.** beyond your own,
W-pI...130.8:6 *Let me accept the* **s.** *God offers me and see no*
W-pI...130.9:5 you will know God's **s.** upheld you as you
W-pI...134.8:1 The **s.** of pardon is its honesty, which is
W-pI. 135.13:4 **s.** that has been given it and cannot fail.
W-pI. 136.18:2 the **s.** the body has will always be enough
W-pI...137.8:5 Healing is **s.**. For by its gentle hand is
W-pI...153.6:1 Defenselessness is **s.**. It testifies to
W-pI...153.6:3 Christ's **s.** and your own weakness, seen
W-pI...153.6:4 it recognizes **s.** so great attack is folly, or a
W-pI. 153.19:3 as we remember that His **s.** abides in us.
W-pI. 153.19:4 our weakness unsupported by His **s.**. We
W-pI. 153.19:5 We call upon His **s.** each time we feel the
W-pI. 153.20:4 the love and **s.** and peace that shine from
W-pI...154.1:7 And what we think is weakness can be **s.**;
W-pI...154.1:7 we believe to be our **s.** is often arrogance.
W-pI...154.3:2 to you, giving you the **s.** to understand it,
W-pI...163.4:2 Here is the **s.** and might of God Himself
W-pI...170.5:2 and escape from doubts about your **s.**,
W-pI...170.7:6 no guardian, no **s.** to call upon in danger,
W-pI...182.7:1 This Child is your defenselessness; your **s.**
W-pI...182.9:3 calls them friend, and gives His **s.** to them
W-pI. 184.14:4 And we are given **s.** to see beyond them.
W-pI...186.2:6 is given us to do, we have the **s.** to do. Our
W-pI...186.6:2 for God assures you that you have the **s.**,
W-pI...187.5:3 grows in **s.** as it is reinforced by giving.
W-pI...196.9:5 You are strong, and it is **s.** you want. And
W-pI...196.9:7 because you feared your **s.** and freedom.
W-pI...197.2:2 Deny your **s.**, and weakness must become
W-pI...197.2:4 leave the prison house, or claim your **s.**,
W-pI...197.2:4 perceived as joined, with **s.** beside them,
W-pI...199.2:1 **s.** and power to do whatever it is asked.
W-pII . 250.1:2 his **s.** diminished and reduced to frailty;
W-pII . 252.1:4 Its **s.** comes not from burning impulses
W-pII . 261.1:2 will behold myself where I perceive my **s.**,
W-pII . 261.1:5 In Him I find my refuge and my **s.**. In
W-pII . 267.1:5 me peace; each breath infuses me with **s.**.
W-pII . 290.2:1 *to You, and ask Your* **s.** *to hold me up today,*
W-pII . 320.1:2 There are no limits on his **s.**, his peace, his
W-pII . 320.1:4 it all the **s.** and love in earth and Heaven. I
W-pII ... 12.1:3 ego is the "proof" that **s.** is weak and love
M-in.......... 5:7 remain a source of **s.** and truth forever.
M-4 .........I.2:1 to trust one's own petty **s.** again. Who
M-4 ...... IV.2:2 They need the **s.** of gentleness, for it is in
M-4 ...... IV.2:7 and limitless **s.** of gentleness? The might
M-5 .........I.1:5 in the mistaken conviction that it is **s.**.
M-5 .........I.1:6 real **s.** is seen as threat and health as
M-5 .........I.2:7 death himself, his weakness is his **s.**. Now
M-9 ........... 2:6 as the criterion for maturity and **s.**. Our
M-25 ......... 5:3 new temptation to win back **s.** by guile.
M-29 ......... 7:2 Remember your weakness is His **s.**. But
M-29 ......... 7:4 If His **s.** is in you, what you perceive as
C-ep........... 4:7 begun will grow in life and **s.** and hope,
P-2...... IV.10:3 necessary, and that defenselessness is **s.**.
P-2......... V.2:6 above all else, to show them what is **s.**.
P-2......... V.4:8 and lean upon a **s.** beyond our little scope
P-3........II.10:2 therapist has the **s.** of God with him, but
S-1......... V.1:2 up, and grows in **s.** and love and holiness.
S-3.........in.1:3 is a sign or symbol of forgiveness' **s.**, and

## strengthen 17

T-4 ..........I.2:7 Spirit can neither **s.** the ego nor reduce
T-5 ....... III.3:5 in yourself, and what you share you **s.**.
T-5 ....... IV.5:2 that to share ideas is to **s.** them. I cannot
T-6 ..........I.5:4 because I did not share it, I did not **s.** it. I
T-6 ....... III.1:9 you **s.** in yourself because you are sharing
T-6 ....... IV.9:6 to follow who will **s.** your command, and
T-6 ..... V.C.1:3 light He retains, to **s.** the Kingdom in you.
T-6 ..... V.C.2:2 you to **s.** what you must learn to avoid. In
T-10 ..... III.3:6 Would you **s.** his denial of God and thus
T-16 ........I.2:3 with. And it never joins except to **s.** itself.
T-16 ..... III.6:5 God's to **s.** your faith in what you taught.
T-16 ..... VI.9:1 Nothing you seek to **s.** in the special
T-18 ..... III.5:1 possible, and will **s.** your desire to reach it
T-20 ..... III.9:4 **S.** your hold and raise your eyes unto
W-pI .. 187.2:4 ideas away, you **s.** them in your own mind
M-24 ......... 1:6 is used to **s.** the recognition of the eternal
M-25 ......... 6:5 devil, which merely means to **s.** the ego.

## strengthened 4

T-5 ....... III.2:6 It is **s.** by being given away. It increases in
T-10 ..... IV.7:3 in his mind, a call that is **s.** by joining.
T-15 ..... VI.4:4 and so your faith in Him is **s.** by sharing.
T-25 . VIII.11:6 both are **s.** by their union with each other.

## strengthening 5

T-5 ....... III.9:5 perceive in others you are **s.** in yourself.
T-6 .........II.5:2 recognizes it in others, thus **s.** it in both.
T-6 ..... V.B.2:2 **S.** motivation for change is their first and
M-10 ......... 1:3 at **s.** the former and minimizing the latter
M-17 ......... 1:6 God's teacher can be sure that he is **s.** his

## strengthens 8

T-1 ....... IV.4:7 demonstrates your belief, and thus **s.** it.
T-4 ..........I.1:1 own ideas and **s.** them by teaching them.
T-7 ....... IV.7:8 This **s.** the Holy Spirit in both of you,
T-7 .........V.4:1 Healing only **s.**. Magic always tries to
T-10 ..... IV.7:4 he **s.** It in a sick brother by weakening his
T-28 ..... III.1:8 effects. For it is your support that **s.** it.
M-17 ......... 1:3 This **s.** fear, and makes the magic seem
M-24 ......... 2:8 which **s.** the idea that life and the body

## strengths 8

T-4 ..........I.4:1 and learning are your greatest **s.** now,
T-12 .... VII.2:6 it is. You cannot see your **s.**, but you gain
T-27 ..... VI.6:4 have different witnesses with different **s.**.
W-pI .. 154.2:2 Seeing your **s.** exactly as they are, and
W-pI .. 186.4:3 will be certain only that He knows our **s.**,
M-25 ......... 4:6 **s.** which the Holy Spirit wants and needs.
M-25 ......... 4:7 in these same **s.** an opportunity to glorify
M-25 ......... 4:8 **S.** turned to weakness are tragedy indeed.

## stress 3

T-4 .........II.6:9 "self-esteem" is always vulnerable to **s.**, a
W-pI .... 18.1:2 which will be given increasing **s.** later on.
WpIrIII.in10:1 we **s.** the need to let your learning not lie

## stressed 5

T-1 ...... VII.5:6 I have **s.** that awe is not an appropriate
W-pI .... 10.3:1 and then **s.** their past rather than their
W-pI .. 132.9:1 repeated once must now be **s.** again, for it
W-pI .. 133.4:1 We have already **s.** there are but two,
W-pI .. 170.9:2 text has **s.** about the obstacles to peace.

## stretch 3

T-18 ... VI.10:1 can **s.** out your hand and reach to Heaven
T-18 . VIII.10:3 So will it grow and **s.** across the desert,
M-16 ....... 1:10 walks **s.** surely and smoothly before him.

**stretches** 1

T-21.........I.8:1 is an arc of golden light that **s.** as you look

**strict** 3

T-13......IX.1:4 The ego's laws are **s.**, and breaches are
T-16.......V.9:4 in **s.** accordance with the ego's goals, is to
W-pI.....71.4:2 in **s.** accord with the ego's basic doctrine,

**strictly** 6

T-7..... VIII.3:2 First, **s.** speaking, conflict cannot be
T-8.......VII.7:2 **S.** speaking this is impossible, since it
T-9......... II.1:2 requests that are **s.** in line with this course
T-22.......in.1:4 Sin is a **s.** individual perception, seen in
M-21..........1:1 **S.** speaking, words play no part at all in
P-3......... II.1:1 **S.** speaking the answer is no. How could

**stride** 7

T-17....... II.2:6 notice, is a **s.** through time into eternity,
W-pI.....61.3:3 It is a giant **s.** toward taking your rightful
W-pI...66.10:5 us. Today's idea is another giant **s.** in the
W-pI.....94.5:9 Each one you do will be a giant **s.** toward
W-pI.134.12:5 his foot to **s.** ahead a star is left behind, to
W-pI.135.26:4 And all the world will take this giant **s.**,
W-pI...194.1:1 quick salvation, and a giant **s.** it is indeed!

**strident** 1

T-6......IV.12:6 A harsh and **s.** form of communication

**strife** 7

T-5....... II.7:10 No one gains from **s.**. What profiteth it a
T-5........III.8:8 The ego becomes strong in **s.**. If you
T-5........III.8:9 believe there is **s.** you will react viciously,
T-12....... II.5:5 end of **s.** and this is the journey to peace.
T-26.......III.1:9 how could **s.** enter in its simple presence,
T-29.......VI.1:2 instead of endless **s.** and misery and pain?
W-pI...109.3:2 will carry you through storms and **s.**, past

**strike** 10

T-7...........I.4:2 It is always willing to **s.** a bargain, but it
T-14.........I.5:6 to encroach upon deception and **s.** at it.
T-21......IV.2:3 will light on sin, and God will **s.** you blind
T-21......VII.2:5 power of the Son of God will **s.** them dead
T-25... VIII.6:4 they trust Him not to **s.** them dead with
T-26.........I.1:2 all desperate attempts to **s.** a bargain, and
W-pI.....22.1:2 he sees vengeance about to **s.** at him. His
S-2 ....... II.6:10 try to **s.** a bargain with the Son of God,
S-3 ......... II.1:3 to fear, so sickness will be free to **s.** again.
S-3 ......... II.6:1 ready to **s.** again until it brings a cruel

**strikes** 9

T19. IV.C.11:1 when any situation **s.** you with terror and
T-21......IV.6:5 its ranting **s.** no terror in your heart. For
T-26... VIII.7:9 reason for an interval in which disaster **s.**,
W-pI...132.3:5 Death **s.** it everywhere because you hold
W-pI.137.13:1 We will remember, as the hour **s.**, our
W-pI.140.12:6 hourly, and take a minute as the hour **s.**,
W-pI.153.16:2 the most that we can offer as the hour **s.**.
W-pI...197.1:5 ensure that when He **s.** He will not fail to
WpI rVI.in.3:7 And we repeat it every time the hour **s.**, or

**striking** 3

T-18....... II.2:5 They provide **s.** examples, both of the
W-pI...135.2:5 in armature but must have terror **s.** at his
W-pI.170.10:6 **s.** down all who acknowledge Him to be

**strips** 3

T-27... VIII.2:2 discs or paper **s.** the world proclaims as
W-pI.....76.3:2 of green paper **s.** and piles of metal discs.
W-pI...105.2:4 It **s.** all meaning from the gifts you give,

**strive** 9

T-15...... III.1:6 When you **s.** for anything in this world in
T-15...... III.4:3 You do not have to **s.** for it, because you
T-15... VIII.2:5 need of your willingness to **s.** for this that
T-15...... IX.3:5 will **s.** for them with all its might, and will
W-pI...131.2:2 the means by which you **s.** for them are
W-pI.167.11:1 we **s.** to keep today as He established it,
W-pII......4.2:2 Its purpose is to **s.**. Yet can the goal of
P-3........ III.1:7 for he must yet **s.** to have the last illusion
P-3........ III.7:6 Surely it is impractical to **s.** for nothing,

**striven** 1

T-30....... V.2:5 as things not wanted and not **s.** for. The

**strives** 2

T-3...........I.6:1 and **s.** only to protect its wholeness. It
T-12.....VII.6:8 The mind always **s.** for integration, and if

**striving** 8

T-15...... III.1:7 choices open to your **s.** and your vigilance
T-15...... III.4:4 your **s.** must be directed against littleness,
T-26...... VI.1:1 valuable and worth **s.** for can hurt you,
W-pII......4.2:3 Yet can the goal of **s.** change. And now
W-pII......4.2:4 now the body serves a different aim for **s.**.
W-pII..328.1:2 autonomy but by our **s.** to be separate,
P-3........ III.7:3 How much is gained by **s.** for illusions?
S-3 ........ IV.7:5 of harsh and bitter **s.** and defeat there is a

**strong** 77

T-1........ III.9:2 others, a **s.** chain of Atonement is welded.
T-1........VII.3:9 will be equally **s.** in your belief in them.
T-2......... II.2:5 Denial of error is a **s.** defense of truth, but
T-2........ IV.4:5 the illness has a sufficiently **s.** hold over
T-4........ III.6:1 force except your own will is **s.** enough or
T-5.........in.3:4 light is so **s.** that it radiates throughout
T-5......... II.3:3 Call is so **s.** that the ego always dissolves
T-5........ III.8:8 The ego becomes **s.** in strife. If you believe
T-5...... IV.8:11 to hold it, and the hands are **s.** to give it.
T-5...... IV.8:13 judgment is as **s.** as the wisdom of God, in
T-8..... VIII.4:3 not consider sickness such a **s.** witness on
T-9.........I.12:1 and if the attempt is **s.** it will induce panic
T-9........ II.5:11 your faith in him **s.** enough to let you hear
T-11...... IV.4:5 there is a **s.** tendency to harbor it within.
T-11...... V.16:3 The case for insanity is **s.** to the insane.
T-12....... V.1:1 Only love is **s.** because it is undivided.
T-12....... V.1:2 The **s.** do not attack because they see no
T-12....... V.2:7 have failed to weaken you, you are still **s.**.
T-13....... II.1:2 pull is so **s.** that you cannot resist it. On
T-13..... X.13:4 My faith in you is as **s.** as all the love I give
T-14.... III.13:6 **s.** protector of the innocence that sets you
T-15...... VI.4:1 on God for love, your call remains as **s.**.
T-15...VII.13:3 in a real relationship so holy and so **s.**,
T-16...... VI.7:3 is **s.** and powerful cut down to littleness.
T-17...VII.10:5 come. Its call for faith is **s.**. Use not your
T-18...... IX.6:4 It is not **s.** enough to stop a button's fall,
T19. IV.D.21:3 **s.** that it would lift you far beyond the veil
T-20..... II.10:4 and his **s.** arm is free to guide you safely
T-20...... III.9:4 raise your eyes unto your **s.** companion,
T-21..... II.4:10 is **s.** enough to make a world can let it go,
T-21....... II.6:9 your belief and trust in this is **s.** indeed.
T-21...... III.5:4 **s.** in faith in his illusions about himself.
T-21....... V.8:3 its end. Faith and belief are **s.** in madness,
T-21.....VII.3:1 and loud and **s.** the dark ones seem to be.
T-21.....VII.3:6 Those who are **s.** are never treacherous,
T-22...... IV.5:3 will be your brother's **s.** protector from
T-22..... V.1:10 *You* are the **s.** one in this seeming conflict.
T-23.......in.1:2 is strength, and nothing else is **s.**. The
T-23.......in.1:5 No one is **s.** who has an enemy, and no
T-23....... II.5:6 becomes weak, the other **s.** by his defeat.
T-23..... II.10:1 the "enemy" made **s.** by keeping hidden
T-24....... II.2:2 him down, yet recognize his **s.** support?
T-24......VII.2:7 All of the love and care, the **s.** protection,
T-25.....VII.1:8 as Heaven, and as **s.** as God Himself. The
T-25.....VII.2:1 death is just as **s.** as is God's Will for life.
T-25... VIII.2:2 is it necessary that your faith in it be **s.**,
T-25....VIII.8:4 love perceived as weak, and vengeance **s.**.
T-29....... V.2:4 gently in its soft embrace, so **s.** and quiet,
T-30.........I.1:6 find resistance **s.** and dedication weak,
T-31.........I.3:6 For your power to learn is **s.** enough to
W-pI.....44.5:2 find that you will encounter **s.** resistance.
W-pI.....73.1:5 in which your belief can be very **s.**. But
W-pI.....91.4:1 little they may be, have **s.** support. Did
W-pI.....91.8:4 *I am not weak, but* **s.**. *I am not helpless, but*
W-pI...91.10:3 It is through Their **s.** support that you will
W-pI.....92.6:4 and dreams that it is **s.** and conquering, a
W-pI.....94.2:2 you must be **s.** and light must be in you.
W-pI.....94.2:6 **s.** in the sinlessness in which you were
W-pI.....98.8:1 and confidence so **s.** and steady they will
W-pI...106.1:1 of truth, quiet in power, **s.** in stillness,
W-pI...132.1:4 are as **s.** in their effects as is the truth. A
W-pI...135.7:3 will be **s.** and healthy if the mind does not
W-pI.135.22:5 *But in defenselessness I will be* **s.**, *and I will*
W-pI...137.8:6 to join with other minds, to be forever **s.**.
W-pI...138.8:1 and anxiety so **s.** that it will not relinquish
W-pI...151.1:6 And its defense seems **s.**, convincing, and
W-pI.153.19:3 day. We rise up **s.** in Christ, and let our
Wi181-200 1:1 to make your weak commitment **s.**; your
W-pI...182.9:2 how **s.** is he who comes without defenses,
W-pI...185.3:1 so **s.** that what they will becomes the Will
W-pI...196.9:5 You are **s.**, and it is strength you want.
W-pII ..... 1.5:1 your Savior and Protector, **s.** in hope, and
M-25 ......... 5:3 may still be **s.** enough to rally under this
P-2........ VI.2:1 There is a tendency, and it is very **s.**, to
P-2.......VII.4:5 and guilt became the cover, dark and **s.**,
S-1...... III.4:10 is heavy, and your fear of letting it go is **s.**.
S-2.........in.1:2 Without its **s.** support it would be vain to

**stronger** 22

T-5...........I.2:3 *who believe in them the* **s.** *they become.*
T-5..........II.7:8 Peace is **s.** than war because it heals. War
T-5....... II.11:1 by sharing my decision and making it **s.**.
T-5...... III.10:4 this part, it is still much **s.** than the ego,
T-6...........I.2:5 to share my decision, and thus make it **s.**.
T-6......V.A.2:6 then the mind must be **s.** than the body.
T-9...........I.8:1 can believe that its will is **s.** than God's. If,
T-13...... III.2:8 and much **s.** than it will ever be, is your
T-15........II.4:3 they are far **s.** and much more compelling
T-15.....VII.7:1 **s.** than the attraction of what you do want
T-16...... III.9:1 Your bridge is builded **s.** than you think,
T-19...... III.8:2 give His Son a will apart from His, and **s.**.
T-22....... V.4:6 Which is the **s.**? Is it this tiny mouse or
T-31.......I.7:10 that reflects the Love of God is **s.** still.
W-pI.....27.1:1 something **s.** than mere determination. It
W-pI.....98.4:2 our certainty, will make it **s.** still. While
WpIrIII.in12:3 with firmer footsteps and with **s.** faith.
W-pI...136.9:1 Thus is the body **s.** than the truth, which
W-pI...136.9:2 opposed by a decision **s.** than His Will.
W-pI...163.4:3 of all creation, **s.** than God's Will for life,
W-pI...163.7:3 Their **s.** will could triumph over His, and
M-14 .........2:2 and becomes **s.** and more all-embracing.

**strongest** 3

T-17........II.2:5 little bridge is the **s.** thing that touches on
T-18..........I.1:6 is the **s.** defense the ego has for separation
T-27.........I.7:1 The **s.** witness to futility, that bolsters all

**strongly** 7

T-6.... V.B.3:10 Still **s.** aware of the ego in yourself, and
T-24...... III.2:2 **s.** defended with all your puny might
T-24....... V.1:9 illusions as **s.** as does love extend itself.
W-pI.....48.2:4 It is **s.** recommended, however, that you
M-24 .........4:1 It cannot be too **s.** emphasized that this
P-2...... IV.10:5 **s.** emphasized that the insane believe that
S-3.........in.1:3 should not be too **s.** emphasized, for

**struck** 2

T-9......VIII.1:4 it, the ego believes that its "enemy" has **s.**
W-pI.....93.1:3 **s.** with horror so intense that you would

**structural** 1
C-in ........... 5:1 on s. issues in the course is brief and early

**structure** 10
T-2........ III.1:7 is to realize that a temple is not a s. at all.
T-2........ III.1:8 the inner altar around which the s. is built
T-2........ III.1:11 see the s. at all because it is perfect vision.
T-17...... IV.8:2 is almost obliterated by its imposing s..
T-17....... V.4:2 s. is "threatened" by the recognition of its
T-17....... V.4:3 conflict between the goal and the s. of the
W-pI..... 20.2:1 This is our first attempt to introduce s..
W-pI..... 95.6:1 S., then, is necessary for you at this time,
W-pI..... 95.7:2 helpful, since it imposes firmer s.. Do not,
C-in ........... 1:4 The s. of "individual consciousness" is

**structured** 2
*See also* well-structured
M-16 ......... 3:8 of the more s. practice periods, which the
P-in............ 1:7 Sometimes he needs a more s., extended

**structures** 3
T-2........ III.1:9 emphasis on beautiful s. is a sign of the
W-pI... 135.2:4 And all its s., all its thoughts and doubts,
W-pI... 135.5:3 It needs no complicated s. of defense, no

**structuring** 2
WpI rVI.in.5:1 is but one exception to this lack of s..
M-16 ......... 2:2 ready for such lack of s. on their own part

**struggle** 4
T-4......... II.9:3 is only the ego's s. to preserve itself, and
T-14.... III.16:3 Why would you s. so frantically to
T-14..... VII.5:2 Truth does not s. against ignorance, and
T-18..... VII.6:8 or of s. against temptation.

**struggles** 1
T-14.... III.16:4 His answer to everyone who s. in the dark

**struggling** 1
T-23......... I.6:1 s. to make them different from each other

**stubborn** 1
W-pI... 151.5:2 you believe that this is so with s. certainty

**student** 2
W-pI... 133.1:1 far from what the s. has already learned,
M-10 ......... 1:8 At any time the s. may disagree with what

**students** 6
T-3........... I.4:5 Good teachers never terrorize their s.. To
T-4........... I.1:4 must believe in the s. to whom he offers
T-4........... I.5:1 Every good teacher hopes to give his s. so
T-14....... X.8:7 undertakings of s. who would "analyze" it
M-3 ........... 2:2 s. "happening" to walk home together.
M-3 ........... 2:5 him; perhaps the s. will become friends.

**studied** 1
T-20...... III.2:5 s. interference that makes it difficult for

**study** 8
T-1....... VII.4:2 learning involves attention and s. at some
T-1....... VII.4:3 sections not to require their careful s..
T-1....... VII.4:6 However, as you s. these earlier sections,
T-14....... X.8:6 s. of the ego is not the study of the mind.
T-14....... X.8:6 study of the ego is not the s. of the mind.
T-14....... X.8:8 but s. form with meaningless content. For
C-in ........... 1:5 sin." To s. the error itself does not lead to
P-2........ VI.5:3 careful s. of the form a sickness takes will

**studying** 2
T-14 ....... X.8:7 the ego enjoys s. itself, and thoroughly
W-pI..... 42.7:2 and teaching you that you are s. a unified

**stumble** 4
T-21 ........ I.1:2 their inferences as they s. and fall because
T-21 ........ I.1:5 s. and fall down upon the stones you did
WpI...rV.in3:2 *And if we s., You will raise us up. If we forget*
P-2........ III.1:3 both will merely s. blindly on to nowhere.

**style** 1
T-24 .... VII.4:6 fish, to house your specialness in better s.,

**subdivided** 1
T-18 ........ I.4:3 become so splintered and s. and divided

**subject** 14
• noun
*other*
W-pI....... 3.1:2 becomes a proper s. for applying the idea.
W-pI....... 5.1:5 a proper s. for the exercises for the day.
W-pI....... 7.5:2 Glance briefly at each s., and then move
W-pI..... 15.4:5 to continue to look at each s. while you
W-pI..... 16.4:4 it, is a suitable s. for applying today's idea
W-pI..... 25.6:3 your eyes resting on each s. you so select,
W-pI..... 25.6:7 from the s. until you have completed the
W-pI..... 25.6:8 it. Then move on to the next s., and apply
W-pI..... 26.6:3 thoughts during the day is a suitable s..
W-pI..... 28.6:1 as a s. for applying the idea for today, you
W-pI..... 28.6:2 s. that you use in the practice periods.
W-pI..... 28.8:1 of the s. your eyes happen to light on, and
W-pI..... 43.9:1 If no particular s. presents itself to your
W-pI..... 46.4:2 that anyone you do not like is a suitable s.

**subject** 9
• other
*noun*
T-2 ...... V.1:10 learning device is not s. to errors of its
T-3 ....... III.1:7 and time, it is s. to either fear or love.
T-3 ....... IV.4:2 and even this is s. to degrees, clearly
T-4 ......... II.2:1 which is s. to enormous variation because
T-4 ...... VII.3:9 in application and not s. to any judgment,
T-7 .... VII.1:12 Mind is too powerful to be s. to exclusion.
T-13 ...... in.3:2 For no Father could s. His children to this
W-pI... 76.12:1 as s. to other laws throughout the day. It
W-pII . 277.1:3 *He is not s. to any laws I made by which I try*

**subjected** 1
T-26 .... VII.7:4 be s. to the laws of two opposing powers,

**subjects** 20
W-pI....... 2.1:6 possible in selecting s. for its application,
W-pI....... 2.2:2 Take the s. simply as you see them. Try to
W-pI....... 4.1:4 thoughts, use them as s. for the idea. Do
W-pI....... 4.2:1 the s. for the application of today's idea,
W-pI....... 5.4:1 greater weight to some s. than to others.
W-pI..... 12.3:7 mind are suitable s. for today's exercises.
W-pI..... 14.5:1 Suitable s. for the application of today's
W-pI..... 15.4:4 s. for the application of today's idea. It is
W-pI..... 18.3:1 selecting s. for the application of the idea
W-pI..... 19.4:1 as possible in selecting s. for the practice
W-pI..... 19.4:2 that random selection of s. for all practice
W-pI..... 24.3:2 to using. A few s., honestly and carefully
W-pI..... 28.7:2 only should the s. be chosen randomly,
W-pI..... 29.4:1 apply it to randomly chosen s. about you,
W-pI..... 29.5:1 list of s. should therefore be as free of self-
W-pI..... 30.5:3 closed, using whatever s. come to mind,
W-pI..... 34.4:1 difficulty in thinking of specific s.,
W-pI .... 39.7:1 kind are suitable s. for today's exercises.
W-pI .... 43.4:5 see. Four or five s. for this phase of the
W-pI .... 43.5:1 be sure that you select the s. for this phase

**sublimely** 1
W-pI .. 182.8:3 and doubt, s. certain that you are at home

**submission** 2
T-11 ..... VI.5:7 obedience, for obedience implies s.. He
T-11 ..... VI.5:8 it, not in the spirit of sacrifice and s., but

**submit** 1
T-1 ....... VI.5:2 are willing to s. your beliefs to this test, to

**subsequent** 3
T-3 ......... V.1:4 that will clarify some of our s. statements.
T-24 ........ I.2:3 now given power to direct all s. decisions.
W-pI .... 29.1:4 have used thus far, and all s. ones as well.

**substance** 4
T-18 ........ I.7:6 dancing insanely in the wind, have no s..
W-pI .... 69.5:4 be really convinced of their lack of s.. We
W-pI 131.10:3 and neither source nor s. in the truth.
W-pI .. 140.7:6 another but in attributes that have no s.,

**substanceless** 1
W-pI .. 167.9:3 has occurred, the changes wrought are s.,

**substantial** 3
T-2 ... V.A.14:5 Being without s. content, it lends itself to
T-18 ..... IX.8:1 no more impenetrable and no more s..
T-28 .... VII.5:8 It seems to be quite solid and s. in itself.

**substitute** 66
T-4 ........ I.13:1 I will s. for your ego if you wish, but
T-4 ......... II.7:3 because it was made as a s. for it. That is
T-11 ..... V.13:6 The ego will always s. chaos for meaning,
T-13 ... XI.11:2 the ego would s. for your reconciliation to
T-14 ... VIII.4:1 There is no s. for truth. And truth will
T-15 ..... III.2:3 you offer as a s. is much too poor a gift to
T-15 ... III.11:2 Yet think not you can s. your plan for His.
T-15 ....... V.6:1 relationship you would s. for another has
T-15 ....... V.6:2 use. There *is* no s. for love. If you would
T-15 ....... V.6:3 would attempt to s. one aspect of love for
T-16 ........ I.6:3 do not try to s. your "miracle" for this. I
T-16 ..... IV.8:4 but a shabby s. for what makes you whole
T-16 ....... V.9:4 goals, is to destroy reality and s. illusion.
T-16 ... V.12:11 Nor can your chosen s. for the Wholeness
T-16 .... VII.5:6 the relationship becomes your s. for it.
T-16 .... VII.5:7 becomes your s. for Atonement, and the
T-17 ..... IV.2:6 rather than aiming to make a s. for it.
T-17 ..... IV.2:7 you have made is a s. for God's Will, and
T-17 ..... IV.3:2 as it does constantly, you answer with a s.
T-17 ....... V.7:1 s. for this another relationship to which
T-18 ........... I.h The S. Reality
T-18 ........ I.1:1 To s. is to accept instead. If you would
T-18 ........ I.1:3 To s. is to choose between, renouncing
T-18 ........ I.9:9 help Him show you that no s. you made
T-18 ...... I.10:1 and no s. can keep you from your brother
T-18 ...... I.10:2 reality was God's creation, and has no s..
T-18 ....... II.2:2 perception can be utilized to s. illusions
T-18 ....... II.4:7 so you s. the fantasy that reality is fearful,
T-18 ... IV.5:13 *I must be willing not to s. my own in place of*
T-20 ..... VI.9:3 s. you want for the eternal blessing of the
T-22 ..... VI.8:5 not to change it, nor to s. another goal.
T-23 ..... II.12:4 It holds there is a s. for love. This is the
T-23 ... II.12:10 The s. for love, born of your enmity to
T-23 ... II.12:11 It has no s., and there is only one. And all
T-23 ..... II.13:3 His madness He must have this s. for love
T-23 ..... II.13:8 place the s. for Heaven which you prefer.
T-23 ..... II.15:6 throne of love, its dying conqueror, its s.,

W-pII..282.2:2 *S. is the truth. And can the truth be changed*
W-pII......8.3:1 need has s. a mind for thoughts of death,
W-pII..308.1:1 of time in s. a way that I defeat my aim. If
W-pII..323.1:2 *S. is the "sacrifice" You ask of me, and one*
W-pII..334.1:3 me not accept s. meager gifts again today.
W-pII..359.1:5 *S. are we. And we rejoice to learn that we*
M-1..........4:10 S. was their choice, and it is given them.
M-4.......I.A.5:6 wholly impossible s. a demand would be.
M-4........ II.1:7 S. are the truly honest. At no level are
M-4........ X.2:3 could never have conceived of s. a change.
M-5........ II.1:9 s. terms merely state or describe the
M-6............3:8 S. is not giving but imprisoning.
M-7............4:2 As s. it is an attack. Usually it seems to be
M-7............5:2 self, for only s. a self can be doubted. This
M-10..........4:4 Why would you choose s. an arbitrary
M-13..........2:9 seeking after s. things the mind associates
M-16..........2:2 for s. lack of structuring on their own part
M-16..........2:5 Routines as s. are dangerous, because
M-17..........8:5 light against a black horizon, for s. it is. If
M-19..........3:5 Forgiveness has no place in s. a scheme,
M-22..........3:9 who would want salvation at s. a price?
M-23..........4:1 name of Jesus Christ as s. is but a symbol.
M-24..........1:9 least, s. misuse offers preoccupation and
M-24..........4:2 issues s. as the validity of reincarnation
M-24..........4:4 wise to step away from all s. questions,
M-26..........2:4 s. appearances would be frightening, they
M-27..........2:5 Who loves s. a god knows not of love,
M-28........3:13 it is asked to enter and envelop s. a world!
M-29..........4:9 it. S. is your teaching, and the teaching of
C-in............2:4 as s. are necessarily controversial, since
C-5.............5:6 since you were born, for s. indeed he is.
P-2.........in.2:2 contrary, s. concepts mean little to them,
P-2......... II.9:5 that they are met as one, for s. they are.
P-2........IV.4:4 could s. a process cure? It is ridiculous
P-2........IV.6:2 Yet if s. were really the self, defense would
P-2......... V.5:7 In s. a process, who could not be healed?
P-2.......VII.5:4 S. a function presupposes a knowledge
P-2.......VII.5:5 point of view would s. a role be possible.
P-2.......VII.5:6 he has s. wisdom except in madness. That
P-2.......VII.9:1 therapist, that you can see s. things as this
P-3........III.4:9 Who would not be grateful for s. a gift?
P-3........III.8:4 to your salvation, for s. is His function.
S-1.........in.1:8 For s. it was before time seemed to be.
S-1...........I.2:1 receive a specific answer if s. is your need.
S-1......... II.3:4 also possible to ask for gifts s. as honesty
S-2......... II.3:1 not appear in quite s. blatant arrogance.
S-2......... II.5:3 sin. S. is the witness that it offers one who
S-3......... II.5:4 What healing has occurred in s. a view of
S-3......... II.5:6 But s. a viewpoint must be fostered by the
S-3........IV.1:3 Whose Voice He is,– s. are God's healers.
S-3........IV.6:1 without s. twisted thoughts upon your

## sudden 10

T-1........ I.17:2 They are s. shifts into invisibility, away
T-1......... II.6:3 miracle entails a s. shift from horizontal
T-15...VII.14:6 s. recognition of the value of his part in it.
T-18....VI.11:4 will realize that it is a s. unawareness of
T-18....VI.13:6 space, the s. experience of peace and joy,
T-18....VI.14:2 The s. expansion of awareness that takes
T-20.....VII.2:1 discomfort that follows the s. change in a
M-6............1:7 so, a s. healing might precipitate intense
M-22..........2:2 a s. and complete awareness of the perfect
C-2.............9:2 will see a s. brightness cover up the world

## suddenly 14

T-2...........I.4:6 If a light is s. turned on while someone is
T-13... VIII.8:3 And s. time will be over, and we will all
T-17....... II.5:4 lack of reason is s. released to loveliness.
T-17....... V.5:5 purposes, s. has holiness for its goal. As
T-19......III.3:4 And s., you change its status from a sin to
T-25....... II.3:3 grounds that it will s. succeed and bring
T-29....... II.2:3 is not a separate thing that happens s., as
T-30......IV.2:2 springs up as a closed box is opened s., or
W-pI...109.6:1 rest today, a tired mind is s. made glad, a
W-pI...109.7:3 the road that s. seems easy as they go.
W-pI...132.7:3 Some see it s. on point of death, and rise
W-pI.161.12:6 him s. transformed from enemy to savior;
W-pI...183.3:2 the world holds dear has s. gone by, and
W-pII......5.3:2 happiness, but can quite s. revert to fear,

## suffer 124

T-3...........I.1:5 one of His Sons to s. because he was good.
T-3......... II.3:8 They do not s. from distorted perception.
T-3........ VI.2:7 One of the illusions from which you s. is
T-5........IV.8:1 How can you who are so holy s.? All your
T-5......... V.5:1 The guiltless mind cannot s.. Being sane,
T-6.........I.11:7 with God that none of His Sons should s..
T-8........III.7:5 you. God wills no one s.. He does not will
T-8........III.7:6 not will anyone to s. for a wrong decision,
T-8.....VII.12:2 with the same thing and not s.?
T-8.....VII.16:1 allow yourself to s. from imagined results
T-10...... III.3:1 be sick is to believe that part of God can s.
T-10...... III.3:2 Love cannot s., because it cannot attack.
T-10....... V.9:3 God. Would He allow Himself to s.? And
T-11...... III.1:4 yourself you could never s. in any way, for
T-13....... X.3:4 those who s. guilt will attempt to displace
T-13....... X.3:5 in it. Yet though they s., they will not look
T-14...... III.5:9 Either it is a penalty from which you s., or
T-14....... V.2:3 he will s. the pain of dim awareness that
T-14....... V.8:4 with no one left outside to s. guilt alone.
T-14.... V.10:9 therefore cannot crucify nor s. crucifixion
T-15.........I.2:1 may s. is your belief that this takes time,
T-15...... VI.1:1 the expense of another and not to s. guilt.
T-15...... XI.5:4 s. sacrifice and loss without attempting to
T-16...... III.7:3 Though you seemed to s. for it, the joy of
T-16.... VI.10:2 Now no one need s., for you have come
T-17..... V.14:4 stand now which seems to make you s.,
T-19...... III.1:4 guilt remains attractive the mind will s.,
T19....IV.B.3:3 see the body, for they look for what can s..
T19....IV.B.3:4 a sacrifice to be removed from what can s.
T19..IV.B.15:1 guilt will someone other than yourself s..
T19..IV.B.15:2 And even if you s., yet someone else will
T19..IV.B.15:2 if you suffer, yet someone else will s. more
T-20...... IV.3:7 them to s. the results of any other source.
T-21....... II.3:5 S., and you decided sin was your goal. Be
T-23.... II.10:1 loss the enemy must s. to save yourself.
T-23...... III.1:7 Yet he will s., and will look on his intent
T-23...... IV.2:9 its creations all that it is and never s. loss?
T-23...... IV.8:6 could ever s. change of any kind. Perhaps
T-24.........I.8:3 Himself must honor it or s. vengeance.
T-24...... IV.5:2 entirely, and when you s. pain of any kind
T-24....... V.2:1 in which you s. not your condemnation.
T-24...... VI.4:5 all belief God's Son can s. pain because he
T-25...VII.13:3 can s. for the Will of God to be fulfilled.
T-25...... IX.6:4 deserves to s. more and others less? And
T-26.........I.7:8 His gifts can never s. sacrifice and loss.
T-26....... II.2:2 demand that someone s. loss and make a
T-26....... II.6:4 For there are those you want to s. loss,
T-26....... II.6:7 him because you could not will he s. loss.
T-26... VIII.2:6 be one in which you sacrifice and s. loss.
T-27.........I.1:6 he must s. the unfairness that you see.
T-27.........I.2:2 But every pain you s. do you see as proof
T-27.........I.2:5 vengeance that you s. now belongs to him
T-27.........I.3:1 Whenever you consent to s. pain, to be
T-27....... II.3:6 one in whom true forgiveness rests can s..
T-27....... II.8:5 As long as he consents to s., you will be
T-27....... II.8:7 healing, and he will consent no more to s.
T-27....... II.9:5 The constant pain they s. demonstrates
T-27...... VI.7:2 There is no need to s. any more. But there
T-27...... VI.8:3 And no one will elect to s. more. What
T-27...... VI.8:5 s. not the laws of sin to be applied to you.
T-27.....VII.3:4 And what I s. from is your attack." No
T-28...... IV.1:6 will s. pain with him because that is your
T-28...... VI.4:5 can s. if he does not see himself attacked,
T-28...... VI.5:1 out upon the body, so that it will s. pain.
T-29......VII.4:2 For you believe that you can s. lack, and
T-29... VIII.6:4 to die, the all-encompassing to s. loss, the
T-29... VIII.6:6 a little while; to s. pain and finally to die.
T-30...... III.6:4 Thoughts were absent or could s. change.
T-31... VIII.5:3 *His Son can s. nothing. And I **am His Son.***
W-pI.....41.4:2 You can never s. because the Source of all
W-pI.....53.4:5 me. Why should I continue to s. from the
W-pI.....58.5:5 I cannot s. any loss or deprivation or pain
W-pI.....59.1:5 How can I s. when love and joy surround
W-pI.....68.3:2 those who hold grievances will s. guilt, as
W-pI.....73.5:8 Do you really want to weep and s. and die
W-pI.....84.1:3 I cannot s., I cannot experience loss and I
W-pI.....88.3:5 me. I s. only because of my belief in them.
W-pI...102.1:1 You do not want to s.. You may think it
W-pI...107.6:7 You were not meant to s. and to die. Your
W-pI...110.6:3 *His Son can s. nothing. And I am His Son.*
W-pI...116.1:3 *I can s. but from the belief there is another*
W-pI...126.4:2 fair that you should s. when it is withheld.
W-pI...131.8:1 God does not s. conflict. Nor is His
W-pI...132.9:3 There is no place where you can s., and
W-pI.133.10:4 who would s. for his sins if this were so?
W-pI...136.8:3 You s. pain because the body does, and in
W-pI...136.8:5 For see, this dust can make you s., twist
W-pI.136.11:4 s. sickness or distort the truth in any way.
W-pI...137.2:2 the rest, to s. what the others do not feel.
W-pI...140.7:1 to seek to cure what cannot s. sickness.
W-pI...152.1:1 can s. loss unless it be his own decision.
W-pI...161.5:1 we feel limits our freedom, makes us s.,
W-pI...166.3:3 and s. to preserve the world he made.
W-pI.166.14:5 accepts God's gifts can never s. anything.
W-pI...168.1:5 to hide from Him, and s. from deception.
W-pI...191.7:4 *I cannot s., cannot be in pain; I cannot suffer*
W-pI...191.7:4 *suffer, cannot be in pain; I cannot s. loss, nor*
W-pI...191.9:1 born but to die, to weep and s. pain, hear
W-pI.191.11:4 s. pain until you have denied its hold on
W-pI...193.8:1 God would not have you s. thus. He
W-pI...194.7:2 What can he s.? What can cause him pain
W-pI...195.1:3 another seems to s. more than they. How
W-pI...195.1:6 And who could s. less because he sees
W-pI...195.1:6 less because he sees another s. more?
W-pI...195.5:2 feel apparent pain, who s. cold or hunger,
W-pI...216.1:3 *If I attack, I s.. But if I forgive, salvation will*
W-pII .240.2:2 *Would You allow Your Son to s.? Give us*
W-pII .244.1:3 *he fear or doubt or fail to know he cannot s.,*
W-pII .245.1:5 *I give Your peace to those who s. pain, or*
W-pII .247.1:2 Behold it anywhere, and I will s.. For
W-pII .299.2:3 *It is not mine to s. from attack. Illusions can*
W-pII .301.1:2 *Nor can I s. pain, or feel I am abandoned or*
W-pII .314.1:5 can grieve or s. when the present has been
W-pII .330.1:5 cannot sin, and therefore cannot s.. Let us
W-pII .330.2:2 *And if we think we s., we but fail to know our*
W-pII ...12.1:1 doomed to s. and to end its life in death.
W-pII .331.1:1 *to believe Your Son could cause himself to s.*
W-pII .356.1:5 *of sin, and who is sinless cannot s. pain. Your*
M-4 ....... V.1:5 They cannot s.. Why would they not be
M-4 .....VII.2:8 He does not want to s.. Why should he
M-5 ....... III.3:3 himself as to believe God's Son can s..
M-12 .......5:11 does not s. either in going or remaining.
M-12 .........6:7 come and go, shift and change, s. and die.
M-26 .........4:3 If you would be heard by those who s.,

## suffered 9

T-27.........I.5:3 of attack, and therefore never s. pain at all
T-27........II.5:6 that it has never s. pain because of him.
T-29..... VII.4:3 and thus to be without and to have s. loss.
W-pI.....41.3:2 real, and s. out of its allegiance to them.
W-pI.....53.3:6 of reality, and have s. from my belief in it.
W-pI...155.4:3 And they have s. from a sense of loss, and
W-pI...155.4:4 have s. from a sense of loss still deeper,
W-pII .302.1:3 *We thought we s.. But we had forgot the Son*
W-pII ...14.5:3 to the Son of God, who thought he s..

## sufferer 2

T-28........II.5:6 is no one asked to be the victim and the s.
M-5 .........I.1:1 the s. no longer sees any value in pain.

## suffering 117

T-2....... V.10:7 you are shortening the s. of both of you.
T-10....... V.9:5 created you, you will be incapable of s..
T-10....... V.9:9 pain and wholly without s. of any kind. If
T-10..... V.9:10 pain and s. into your own mind because
T-10..... V.12:2 it is blasphemous to perceive s. anywhere.
T-13.......in.2:6 Their growth is attended by s., and they
T-13...... III.7:3 Do not hide s. from His sight, but bring it
T-13.... III.12:4 for pain, for s. is not of His creation.
T-14....... V.5:4 and release from s. of every kind lie in it.

T-15.....VII.9:1 **S.** and sacrifice are the gifts with which
T-15.....VII.9:2 united at its altar accept **s.** and sacrifice as
T-16.........I.1:1 To empathize does not mean to join in **s.**,
T-16.........I.1:2 relationship in which the **s.** is shared. The
T-16.........I.1:5 He does not understand **s.**, and would
T-16...... III.1:7 **s.** has disappeared to be replaced by joy.
T-16.... VI.10:3 wholly insane could look on death and **s.**,
T-16..... VII.2:2 By seeking to remove **s.** in the past, it
T-22....... II.1:5 Every illusion carries pain and **s.** in the
T-22....... II.3:1 Illusions carry only guilt and **s.**, sickness
T-22...... IV.6:5 hope and freedom and release from **s.** to
T-22...... VI.7:2 What form of **s.** could block your sight,
T-24.......in.2:6 follows it as surely as does **s.** follow guilt
T-25...... IV.2:2 think that **s.** and sin will bring you joy, so
T-25... VII.11:5 and pay exact amount in blood and **s.**.
T-26....... II.4:6 mistakes from which the Son of God is **s.**,
T-26... VII.17:1 is not needed where there is no pain or **s.**.
T-27.........I.4:3 and **s.** you but represents your brother's
T-27....... II.7:6 would prove all **s.** is but a vain imagining,
T-27....... II.8:6 show him that his **s.** is purposeless and
T-27....... V.5:2 the dying bring reproach, and **s.** whispers
T-27....... V.6:4 And **s.** eyes no longer will accuse, but
T-27....... V.6:5 beyond all **s.** and see Christ's face instead.
T-27....... V.6:6 Healing replaces **s.**. Who looks on one
T-27...... VI.5:4 not the name by which you called your **s.**.
T-27...... VI.7:3 because the **s.** and sorrow of the world
T-27..... VII.1:1 **S.** is an emphasis upon all that the world
T-27..... VII.1:6 apparent still, for it is he who bears the **s.**.
T-27..... VII.5:7 is not here the cause of **s.** and sin must lie.
T-27..... VII.5:8 And dwell not on the **s.** and sin, for they
T-27..... VII.7:4 perceived as bringing pain and **s.** to you,
T-27..... VII.9:2 if you deny the cause of **s.** is in your mind.
T-27... VII.12:3 Here is the cause of **s.**, the space between
T-27... VII.13:4 in which his **s.** was healed and where his
T-27..VIII.10:4 to be the cause of any pain and **s.** you feel,
T-27..VIII.11:1 lesson learned will set you free from **s.**,
T-27..VIII.11:2 of the form of **s.** that brings you pain.
T-27..VIII.12:1 all forms of **s.** to Him Who knows that
T-28....... II.7:8 As victim, he is **s.** from its effects, but not
T-28..... II.12:2 silence next to every dream of pain and **s.**,
T-28....... V.2:1 and death, of sin and **s.** and pain and loss,
T-29....... II.1:1 release from **s.** to learn that you are free?
T-29..... VII.5:3 No sadness and no **s.** proclaim a message
T-30....... V.2:5 for **s.** and death have been perceived as
T-30....... V.9:8 been bought at fearful price in coins of **s.**?
T-30.... VIII.2:6 he is not bound by loss or **s.** in any form,
T-31...... III.5:1 and attack; of pain and age, of grief and **s.**
T-31....... V.2:8 and it looks, at times with pity, on the **s.**,
T-31... V.15:10 **s.** of any kind you see your own concealed
T-31...... VI.2:3 in death; that one is doomed to **s.** and loss
T-31.... VIII.6:2 as pain, as weakness and as **s.** and loss, is
W-pI..... 21.5:3 is **s.** from this form of distortion, say: *I am*
W-pI..... 38.3:4 or **s.** in any form that you happen to think
W-pI..... 41.1:3 misery, **s.** and intense fear of loss.
W-pI..... 53.5:4 which there is **s.** and loss and death shows
W-pI..... 73.6:5 go. **S.** is not happiness, and it is happiness
W-pI..... 76.5:4 The body's **s.** is a mask the mind holds up
W-pI..... 94.3:8 nor could conceive of loss or **s.** or death.
W-pI... 101.1:3 it asks for **s.** as penance for your "sins."
W-pI... 101.2:2 thus cannot be purchased but through **s.**.
W-pI... 101.3:2 cost of sin, and **s.** can never be escaped, if
W-pI... 101.6:1 because there is no sin, and **s.** is causeless.
W-pI... 109.2:5 Here is the end of **s.** for all the world, and
W-pI... 109.3:3 There is no **s.** it cannot heal. There is no
W-pI... 124.6:2 the power to heal all forms of **s.** in anyone
W-pI... 136.7:2 which makes you weak and brings you **s.**.
W-pI. 151.10:1 have placed in pain, disaster, **s.** and loss.
W-pI... 152.6:4 the guilty, the afraid, the **s.** and lonely,
W-pI... 155.7:4 Their **s.** is but illusion. Yet they need a
W-pI... 159.7:3 where the **s.** are healed and welcome. No
W-pI... 164.9:4 can exchange all **s.** for joy this very day.
W-pI... 167.2:6 All sorrow, loss, anxiety and **s.** and pain,
W-pI... 182.2:2 some try to put by their **s.** in games they
W-pI... 187.7:2 Accept not **s.**, and you remove the
W-pI... 187.7:2 and you remove the thought of **s.**. Your
W-pI... 187.7:3 when you choose to see all **s.** as what it is.
W-pI... 187.7:4 rise to all the forms that **s.** appears to take
W-pI... 187.8:6 well. No form of sacrifice and **s.** can long
W-pI. 191.10:7 Look about the world, and see the **s.** there
W-pI... 193.5:2 all your pain, all **s.** regardless of its form.
W-pI. 193.13:4 every care and every form of **s.**, repeat
W-pI... 195.2:1 It is insane to offer thanks because of **s.**.
W-pI... 195.2:2 and **s.** replaced with laughter and with
W-pI... 198.4:1 road that leads out of disaster, past all **s.**,
W-pI... 198.9:5 that there can be no form of **s.** that fails to
W-pII .... 249.h Forgiveness ends all **s.** and loss.
W-pII . 249.1:1 paints a picture of a world where **s.** is over
W-pII . 249.1:3 What **s.** is now conceivable? What loss
W-pII . 259.1:4 of guilt, demanding punishment and **s.**?
W-pII . 284.1:4 And **s.** of any kind is nothing but a dream
W-pII . 285.1:4 to me, what purpose would my **s.** fulfill,
W-pII ... 10.3:2 is but to fear complete release from **s.**,
W-pII . 323.1:1 *beloved Son; You ask him to give up all* **s.**, *all*
W-pII . 328.1:3 we find is sickness, **s.** and loss and death.
W-pII ... 12.3:3 What can he know of sorrow and of **s.**,
W-pII ... 12.4:2 In **s.**, the price for faith in it is so immense
W-pII . 337.1:1 of loss; complete deliverance from **s.**. And
W-pII . 339.1:8 what will frighten him, and bring him **s.**.
W-pII .... 340.h I can be free of **s.** today.
W-pII . 340.1:3 *His* **s.** *is done. For he will hear Your Voice*
W-pII . 340.1:4 *forgiveness, and be free forever from all* **s.**.
W-pII . 343.1:1 *The end of* **s.** *can not be loss. The gift of*
M-5 .........I.1:2 Who would choose **s.** unless he thought it
M-5 ........II.4:7 pain, disaster and all **s.** mean now?
P-1............. 3:1 his peace of mind is **s.** in consequence.
P-2.........in.2:3 as it is, but without the **s.** that it entails.
S-2..........II.5:2 It shows the face of **s.** and pain, in silent
S-3........ IV.5:8 **s.** and grievous loss become the lot of

## sufferings 1

T-27 ..... VI.6:5 And they attest to different **s.**. Yet to the

## suffers 17

T-8 ...... VII.8:2 His sense of adequacy **s.**, and he must
T-18 ..... VI.3:4 which **s.** and dies because it is attacked to
T-27 .......II.9:4 guilt he **s.** serves to prove that he is slave,
T-27 .... VII.4:9 And thus he **s.** from the wounds a knife
T-28 ..... VI.2:2 It **s.** not the punishment you give because
W-pI....... 8.1:4 about time from which your seeing **s.**.
W-pI..... 76.5:3 The body **s.** just in order that the mind
W-pI..... 76.5:4 the mind holds up to hide what really **s.**.
W-pI... 121.2:3 It **s.** and abides in misery, peering about
W-pI... 152.1:2 No one **s.** pain except his choice elects
W-pI... 152.7:1 to truth, and **s.** death to triumph over life;
W-pI... 187.7:3 Your blessing lies on everyone who **s.**,
W-pII .... 248.h Whatever **s.** is not part of me.
W-pII . 248.1:3 Whatever **s.** is not part of me. What
W-pII ... 11.1:4 when anything that it created **s.** any loss.
M-12 ......... 5:3 it is weak, and being weak, it **s.** and it dies
S-3........ III.3:4 the mind that **s.** from the agony of doubt.

## suffice 6

T-5 ....... VI.5:1 a few will **s.** to show how the Holy Spirit
T-28 ......I.15:3 a bridge an instant will **s.** to reach beyond
T-30 ......I.11:1 grain of wisdom will **s.** to take you further
W-pI..... 13.6:3 practice periods. That will **s.** at present.
W-pI... 108.5:2 one correction will **s.** for all correction, or
W-pI. 169.11:1 **S.** it, then, that you have work to do to

## suffices 11

T-13 ..... XI.7:5 If that **s.** Him, it is enough for you. You
T-13 ..... XI.9:4 God. His certainty **s.**. Learn that even the
T-16 .. VII.10:4 to you. His help **s.**, for His Messenger
W-pI... 160.8:1 God's certainty **s.**. Who He knows to be
W-pI... 168.1:8 There is no certainty but this, yet this **s.**.
W-pI. 169.13:1 The interval **s.**. It is here that miracles are
W-pII . 262.1:5 *this one a thousand names, when only one* **s.**
W-pII .... 348.h need That I perceive, Your grace **s.** me.
W-pII . 348.2:1 God's grace **s.** us in everything that He
M-12 ......... 1:2 teacher, whose learning is complete, **s.**.
C-3 ............ 3:4 And that **s.**. The form adapts itself to

## sufficient 18

*See also* self-sufficient

T-2 ..... VIII.2:7 **s.** number become truly miracle-minded,
T-3 ..... VI.11:6 To wish is to imply that willing is not **s.**.
T-5 ..........I.7:6 point that **s.** quantitative change occurs
T-11 .......V.4:5 **s.** unto itself and independent of any
T-13 ..... XI.7:1 it will be **s.**: God wills you be in Heaven,
T-16 .......II.7:4 **s.** miracle to teach you that your Teacher
T-18 ..... III.3:4 been **s.** to give you confidence in yourself,
T-27 .....V.2:13 An instant is **s.**. Miracles wait not on time
W-pI ...... 8.6:2 you find it trying, three or four times is **s.**.
W-pI ...... 9.3:1 which three or four practice periods are **s.**
W-pI ..... 11.4:1 practice periods today will probably be **s.**.
W-pI .... 18.3:5 less, will be **s.** for each practice period.
W-pI .... 43.4:5 for this phase of the practice period are **s.**.
W-pI .... 47.6:1 but it is hardly a **s.** one in giving you the
W-pI .... 67.4:2 You may also find that this is not **s.**, and
W-pI .. 188.6:2 The light within you is **s.**. It alone has
WpI.rVI.in.1:3 these ideas alone would be **s.** for salvation
W-pII . 306.2:3 *We cannot make an offering* **s.** *for Your Son.*

## sufficiently 11

T-2 ....... IV.4:5 Sometimes the illness has a **s.** strong hold
T-4 ........I.12:6 Nothing else is **s.** worthy to be a gift for a
T-4 ....... IV.6:4 **s.** vigilant against the demands of the ego
T-5 ..... IV.3:11 **s.** purified He lets you give them away.
T-7 ...... VII.7:1 only teacher **s.** worthy to teach another.
T-11 ... VIII.5:1 may complain that this course is not **s.**
T-16 .......II.9:6 already proved their power **s.** for you to
T-17 .......V.4:2 as yet been changed **s.** to make its former
W-pI .. 157.3:2 way to alter time **s.** to rise above its laws,
W-pI .. 169.5:5 and no part of mind **s.** distinct to feel that
P-2......... in.3:4 to stabilize it **s.** to include within it the

## suggest 2

T-4 ........ in.1:2 certainly does not **s.** that you set him back
W-pI .. 105.8:1 today, if you prepare your mind as we **s.**.

## suggested 9

T-6 ..... V.B.6:5 is why I **s.** before that you remind yourself
W-pI .... 16.5:5 The following form is **s.** for this purpose:
W-pI .... 24.3:3 Two minutes are **s.** for each of the mind-
W-pI .... 39.5:2 are recommended, although both are **s.**.
W-pI .... 44.3:2 form of exercise which has been **s.** before,
WpI... rI.in.6:3 nor to apply the ideas as was **s.** then. We
W-pI .. 66.11:1 an hour, this form of the application is **s.**:
W-pI .... 86.2:1 are some **s.** forms for applying this idea
WpI..rIII.in2:1 to undertake what is **s.** here as optimal

## suggestions 4

T-25 .......II.2:4 future hopes, and no **s.** of success at all.
WpI.. rII.in.6:3 These, however, are merely **s.**. It is not the
W-pI .... 82.2:1 **S.** for specific forms for applying this idea
W-pI .... 89.2:1 might use these **s.** for specific applications

## suggests 3

T-13 ..... IV.3:2 be argued that death **s.** there *was* life, no
T-14 .. VII.5:14 merely asked to do the little He **s.** you do,
W-pII ... in.4:6 the words of invitation that His Voice **s.**,

## suit 6

T-18 .......II.2:4 world, and changing it to **s.** the ego better
T-31 ..... III.4:9 to **s.** the purpose given by the mind. For
M-23 ......... 7:5 must shift and change to **s.** the need.
S-1......... in.2:1 takes the form that best will **s.** your need.
S-1...........I.2:7 by God, will **s.** your need as you see it.
S-2...........I.2:1 therefore **s.** the purpose of the world far

## suitability 1

W-pI ...... 3.1:3 you do not question the **s.** of anything for

**suitable** 19

T-25.....VII.8:3 is given the choice of form most **s.** to him;
W-pI.......3.1:5 Anything is **s.** if you see it. Some of the
W-pI.......3.2:3 equally **s.** and therefore equally useful.
W-pI.....12.3:7 mind are **s.** subjects for today's exercises.
W-pI.....14.5:1 **S.** subjects for the application of today's
W-pI.....16.4:4 it, is a **s.** subject for applying today's idea.
W-pI.....26.6:3 thoughts during the day is a **s.** subject.
W-pI.....29.5:2 For example, a **s.** list might include: *God is*
W-pI.....35.6:1 A **s.** unselected list for applying the idea
W-pI.....39.7:1 kind are **s.** subjects for today's exercises.
W-pI.....42.5:1 is clearly related to the idea for today is **s.**.
W-pI.....42.6:3 than it is to strain to find **s.** thoughts.
W-pI.....43.4:2 at the most convenient and **s.** time that
W-pI.....43.5:8 more or less directly to today's idea is **s.**.
W-pI.....46.4:2 that anyone you do not like is a **s.** subject.
W-pI.....82.4:1 **S.** specific forms of this idea include: *Let*
W-pI.....85.4:1 idea are **s.** for more specific applications:
W-pI...125.7:1 times today, at times most **s.** for silence,
P-3...........I.1:2 you choose the kind of treatment that is **s.**

**suited** 6

T-20... VIII.6:3 unadjusted form and **s.** perfectly to meet
T-25.....VII.7:3 The form is **s.** to your special needs, and
T-31.........I.4:3 until a world was built that **s.** you. And
WpI. rIII.in3:4 that are poorly **s.** to your practicing from
W-pI...160.3:3 were another home more **s.** to his tastes.
W-pI...186.2:7 Our minds are **s.** perfectly to take the part

**suits** 3

T-15....... V.7:1 one part of one aspect **s.** its purposes,
T-24...... III.3:1 do not like, a circumstance that **s.** you not
T-31....... V.1:3 is that **s.** a world of shadows and illusions

**sum** 7

T-1........ I.19:2 Sonship is the **s.** of all that God created.
T-2.......VII.6:3 its Oneness transcends the **s.** of its parts.
T-4.........III.1:6 in its totality transcends the **s.** of its parts.
T-15.... VIII.4:5 the petty **s.** of all the separate bodies you
T-29..... II.10:3 For if He be the **s.** of everything, then
W-pI...184.6:1 **s.** of the inheritance the world bestows.
W-pII....11.1:1 Creation is the **s.** of all God's Thoughts,

**summarized** 1

T-2........VI.7:4 These steps may be **s.** in this way: Know

**summarizes** 1

T-26.....VII.1:3 and arrange them in a way that **s.** all that

**summary** 2

W-pII......9.3:1 in one last **s.** that will extend beyond itself
M-29..........1:2 in terms of a brief **s.** of some of the major

**summed** 2

T-in............2:1 therefore be **s.** up very simply in this way:
T-12......IV.1:4 be **s.** up simply as: "Seek and do *not* find."

**summer** 4

T-14......IV.6:2 were being carried down a quiet path in **s.**
T19... IV.A.9:2 eagle's flight, or hinder the advance of **s.**?
T19... IV.A.9:6 greet the **s.** sun than fix your gaze upon a
T-26......IX.3:1 be all white and sparkling in the **s.** sun.

**summer's** 1

T19... IV.A.9:3 interfere with the effects of **s.** sun upon a

**sun** 34

T-17....... II.2:2 everything sparkling under the open **s.**.
T-17........ II.4:1 **s.** that opened up the world to beauty will
T-18... VIII.3:3 it is like the smallest sunbeam to the **s.**, or
T-18... VIII.3:4 this tiny sunbeam has decided it is the **s.**;
T-18... VIII.3:6 The **s.** becomes the sunbeam's "enemy"
T-18... VIII.4:1 Yet neither **s.** nor ocean is even aware of
T-18... VIII.4:6 the **s.** the sunbeam would be gone; the
T-18... VIII.6:1 to the **s.** and ocean your Self continues,
T-18... VIII.7:2 The **s.** and ocean are as nothing beside
T-18... VIII.7:4 in neither **s.** nor ocean is the power that
T-18...... IX.6:1 that seem to be a solid wall before the **s.**.
T-18...... IX.6:3 willing to climb above it and see the **s.**. It
T-19....... II.8:1 is like walking through a mist into the **s.**?
T19... IV.A.6:5 **s.** has risen over it. How can a shadow
T19... IV.A.6:6 How can a shadow keep you from the **s.**?
T19... IV.A.9:3 the effects of summer's **s.** upon a garden
T19... IV.A.9:6 greet the summer **s.** than fix your gaze
T-20...... VI.4:1 are kept obscure and hidden from the **s.**.
T-21.........I.8:1 Beyond the body, beyond the **s.** and stars
T-21... III.11:5 is like saying that the moon and **s.** are one
T-22...... VI.4:1 than the **s.** that lights the sky you see, is
T-25...... IV.3:6 as the **s.** shines them to nothingness. And
T-25...... IV.3:7 die, will disappear before the **s.** you bring.
T-25...... IV.4:5 because the **s.** in you has risen that they
T-26...... IX.3:1 all white and sparkling in the summer **s.**.
T-29... VIII.3:8 A cloud does not put out the **s.**. No more
T-31... VIII.6:3 but disappear as mists before the **s.**. A
W-pI.....92.2:3 lights the **s.** and gives it all its warmth; or
W-pI.....97.6:2 as does the radiance of the **s.** outshine the
WpI. rIV.in4:3 tides, the warming of the water by the **s.**,
W-pI...156.3:3 sinful than the **s.** could choose to be of ice
W-ep .........2:1 pathway of the **s.** laid down before it rises
M-20 .......6:11 The universe beyond the **s.** and stars, and
M-27 .........3:2 like a shield held up to obscure the **s.**. The

**sun's** 1

W-pI.186.11:1 certain as the **s.** return each morning to

**sunbeam** 4

T-18... VIII.3:3 that it is like the smallest **s.** to the sun, or
T-18... VIII.3:4 this tiny **s.** has decided it is the sun; this
T-18... VIII.4:6 Without the sun the **s.** would be gone; the
T-18... VIII.7:3 The **s.** sparkles only in the sunlight, and

**sunbeam's** 1

T-18... VIII.3:6 the **s.** "enemy" that would devour it, and

**Sunday** 1

T-20.........I.1:1 This is Palm **S.**, the celebration of victory

**sung** 1

S-1......... II.7:8 thanks to your Creator, **s.** without words,

**sunlight** 10

T-16...... IV.3:2 to rise above the storm, into the **s.**. On the
T-18... VIII.7:3 The sunbeam sparkles only in the **s.**, and
T-20...... VI.2:7 It walks in **s.**, open-eyed and calm, in
T-20...... VI.3:6 the **s.** and happy in the body's darkness,
T-25...... IV.4:7 And in the **s.** you will stand in quiet, in
T-25...... VI.2:2 turn away from **s.** and the clarity it brings
W-pI.....57.1:9 insane wishes and walk into the **s.** at last.
W-pI.....69.2:5 the tears of God's Son disappear in the **s.**.
W-pI.184.10:1 you go into the **s.** and forget the darkness.
S-2......... II.8:6 want to see the **s.** and the glow of Heaven

**supercilious** 1

T-11....... V.9:1 does allow you to regard yourself as **s.**,

**superficial** 4

T-17...... IV.9:8 not deceived by the most **s.** aspects of this
W-pI.....25.4:2 At the most **s.** levels, you do recognize
M-3 ...........2:1 level of teaching appears to be quite **s.**. It
M-4 ...........1:2 their **s.** "personalities" are quite distinct.

**superfluous** 1

M-16 .........1:8 teacher of God, then, this question is **s.**. It

**superiority** 1

T-4...........I.7:3 itself to the belief in **s.** and inferiority.

**supersede** 1

T-25...... IV.5:5 aim can **s.** the Will of God and of His Son,

**supplement** 2

W-pI.184.13:2 Experience must come to **s.** the Word.
M-29 .........1:3 not a substitute for either, but merely a **s.**.

**supplementary** 1

T-12....... V.7:8 **s.** goal in this curriculum is learning how

**supplemented** 1

T-16...... III.8:4 it. His little efforts are powerfully **s.** by the

**supplication** 1

S-1...........I.5:2 be confused with **s.** of any kind, because it

**supplies** 2

T-13...VII.12:7 has no investment in the things that He **s.**
P-3........ III.4:4 the other; whatever one lacks the other **s.**.

**supply** 11

T-1...........I.8:1 are healing because they **s.** a lack; they are
T-1.........I.16:2 of the giver and **s.** strength to the receiver.
T-3.......... V.4:3 but is also one that is up to you to **s.**. Yet
T-12.........I.9:2 it in others you learn to **s.** the loss, the
T-13...VII.13:2 will **s.** them with no emphasis at all upon
T-15........II.5:5 this world by its own vision, you cannot **s.**
T-25...... IX.2:6 Each gift but adds to the **s.**. For God is fair
T-26.........I.5:4 to add a limitless **s.** to every meager scrap
T-28...... III.9:3 have brought unlimited **s.** with Them.
T-29....VIII.2:4 They have the power to **s.** your lacks, and
W-pI.....92.5:4 to everyone who asks, in limitless **s.**. It

**supplying** 2

T-14..... X.12:7 It. By **s.** your Identity wherever It is not
C-1............1:1 agent of spirit, **s.** its creative energy.

**support** 29

T-6........ IV.1:4 withdraw his **s.** from it at any moment. If
T-14...... IX.3:2 power will rush to your assistance and **s.**.
T-15..........I.2:6 uses time to **s.** its belief in destruction.
T-15........II.3:5 attempt to **s.** it and uphold its weakness,
T-15........II.3:6 to **s.** either their weakness or your own.
T-15........II.4:1 by seeing them as sources of ego **s.**. As a
T-15........II.4:4 And they **s.** His strength. It is, therefore,
T-15........II.4:5 choice whether they **s.** the ego or the Holy
T-15........II.6:5 and His lesson will **s.** your strength. It is
T-15...... III.4:8 The power of God will **s.** every effort you
T-15....... V.4:5 which you have chosen to **s.** the ego, as
T-16...VII.10:2 will **s.** you as you seek only your place in
T-17.... III.1:12 into unholy alliances to **s.** the ego's goals,
T-18...... VI.5:2 welcome and **s.** the shift from fantasies of
T-24........II.2:2 cut him down, yet recognize his strong **s.**?
T-25........II.2:4 seen, gives no **s.** to base your future hopes
T-25...... III.1:5 from this, to hold it up and offer it **s.**. This
T-27.....VII.6:7 They **s.** its claim on your allegiance. What
T-28...... III.1:7 Without **s.**, the dream will fade away
T-28...... III.1:8 effects. For it is your **s.** that strengthens it.
T-28...... IV.1:1 to give **s.** to someone's dream of sickness

T-28....... V.2:3 because you did not give them your s..
W-pI..... 91.4:1 however little they may be, have strong s..
W-pI... 91.10:3 strong s. that you will feel the strength in
W-pI..... 96.5:3 itself and hiding in the body's frail s..
W-pI... 181.2:4 to give s. to the intent which has replaced
W-pI... 181.2:6 This faith receives its only sure s. from
W-pII ..... 2.3:1 to s. the world of dreams and malice.
S-2.........in.1:2 Without its strong s. it would be vain to

**supported** 2

T-28..... IV.4:6 which you have s. in your brother's mind.
W-pI... 91.10:1 are fully s. by the strength of God and all

**supporting** 3

T-21...... III.8:3 faith sees far beyond the body, s. vision,
T-28...... IV.4:4 he is, by not s. his illusions by your faith,
W-pII ..... 2.3:3 By not s. them, it merely lets them quietly

**supports** 4

T-14....... V.6:7 The power of God Himself s. this teaching
T-15....... I.4:16 And it is this the ego's version of time s..
T-25....... II.5:5 created He s. and frames within Himself.
W-pI..... 58.5:6 My Father s. me, protects me, and directs

**suppose** 2

T-9......... II.2:1 Let us s., then, that what you ask of the
T-12...... III.2:1 S. a brother insists on having you do

**supposed** 1

T-17...... IV.5:5 are as insane as what they are s. to protect

**supremely** 1

W-pI... 167.2:4 underlies all feelings that are not s. happy

**surcease** 1

W-pI... 181.7:3 seek but for s. an instant from the misery

**sure** 225

T-2...... VI.2:10 a s. sign that you have allowed your mind
T-2...... VI.4:10 If you are s. that it is, there will be no fear.
T-3........... I.2:9 that we must be s. that nothing of this
T-3........... I.3:8 Be very s. that you recognize how utterly
T-3......... IV.2:4 you are, because that is all you can be s. of
T-3......... V.1:2 No one has been s. of anything since. I
T-3....... VII.3:9 but you may be s. that any interpretation
T-5......... V.4:8 is a s. sign that your thinking is unnatural
T-9........... I.3:1 is, why would you be so s. that it is fearful
T-10...... III.1:4 it is a s. sign that you hate what you *think*
T-11....... II.2:3 But be s. to count yourself among them,
T-13...... XI.8:9 Heaven will not be yours, for God is s.,
T-13...... XI.8:9 is sure, and what He wills is as s. as He is.
T-13...... XI.9:3 Salvation is as s. as God. His certainty
T-14...... XI.5:1 You have one test, as s. as God, by which
T-14...... XI.5:2 be s. that you have learned God's lesson,
T-14...... XI.8:3 be s. that you are willing to acknowledge
T-15..... II.4:11 when you have, you will be s. you have.
T-15..... II.4:12 You will be s. because the witness to Him
T-15...... III.1:2 be s. you understand what littleness is,
T-15....... V.5:4 and be s. that it will not result in pain, if
T-15... VII.10:1 can be s. that you have formed a special
T-15...... IX.5:3 s. and loving relationships that any limit
T-16......... I.2:7 of this you may be s.; if you will merely sit
T-16......... I.4:3 you, but be s. that you desert not Him.
T-16......... I.4:5 You are not s. that He will do His part,
T-16....... II.8:6 Reality is safe and s., and wholly kind to
T-16...... IV.4:5 It is s. that those who select certain ones
T-17...... III.7:9 be s. you fully realize what you have made
T-17..... V.14:8 surely fall in place because the goal is s..
T-17... VIII.3:4 transforms all situations into one s. and
T-18....... II.8:5 You are not s. of this because you think it
T-18....... II.9:1 Yet Heaven is s.. This is no dream. Its
T-18 ...... V.2:6 and make s. that you fulfill it easily. And
T-18 . VIII.12:1 Be s. of this; love has entered your special
T-18 ... IX.14:3 it, safe and s. within its gentleness, to the
T-19 ..... IV.2:4 be s. of nothing you see outside you, but
T-19 ..... IV.2:4 you *can* be s.: The Holy Spirit asks that you
T19.... IV.C.3:3 One thing is s.; God, Who created neither
T19. IV.D.21:3 within the s. protection of his Father.
T-20 ....... II.9:2 you its guiding light and s. protection,
T-20 ...... V.1:7 who has a single purpose, unified and s.,
T-20 ... VIII.6:2 for everything He looks upon is always s..
T-20 ... VIII.8:6 One thing is s.; hallucinations serve a
T-21 ...... V.2:3 it is s. that you will see yourself as tiny,
T-21 .. VIII.2:5 S. in its vision as its Creator is in what He
T-22 ....... II.3:5 s. indeed that any seeming happiness that
T-22 ..... VI.2:4 as certain of the outcome as He is s. of His
T-23 ...... in.2:4 it is s. that you will love what you perceive
T-23 ...... I.10:8 s. that its peace can never be disturbed.
T-23 ..... II.12:2 Can you be s. your murderous attack is
T-23 .. II.22:11 you s. the goal of Heaven can be reached?
T-24 ..... III.1:7 is s. he would receive it wholly the instant
T-24 ..... VI.1:5 can be s. that God is knowable and will be
T-24 ... VI.13:1 be s. you understand what made this
T-24 .. VII.10:2 Its course is s., when seen through its own
T-25 ....... II.2:4 For one thing is s.; the way you see, and
T-25 ..... III.2:5 could be s. His sanity went there with him
T-25 .... VII.1:8 to make this world's foundation s. as love,
T-25 .... VII.2:2 He did not make be firm and s. as Heaven
T-25 ..... IX.4:1 punishment impossible, and justice s..
T-26 ..... VI.3:5 given can make s. that you receive them.
T-27 ....... I.11:1 s. you knew its purpose was to foster guilt
T-27 .... VII.7:4 Of one thing you were s.: Of all the many
T-28 ... IV.1:10 You can be s. of just one thing; that you
T-29 ..... III.5:6 and be s. his waking eyes will rest on you.
T-29 ... VIII.9:8 And to be s. you could not lose it, did He
T-29 ..... IX.9:1 goes with you,–be s. you made an idol,
T-30 ..... III.9:1 it safe, forever lifted up and anchored s..
T-30 ...... V.3:5 of happiness in him so s. and constant he
T-30 ..... VI.2:2 It has a s. foundation. You do not forgive
T-30 ..... VI.4:3 Thus is the fear of God the s. result of
T-31 ........ I.6:5 What outcome is inevitable, s. as God,
T-31 ..... IV.3:1 There is no choice where every end is s..
T-31 .... V.16:4 s. and happy in the confidence that it will
T-31 . VIII.10:3 I am as s. that they will come to me as
T-31 . VIII.10:3 come to me as You are s. of what they are,
W-in.......... 6:3 s. that you do not decide for yourself that
W-pI....... 1.3:6 ritualistic. Only be s. that nothing you see
W-pI....... 2.2:5 be s. that nothing is specifically excluded.
W-pI....... 3.1:3 s. that you do not question the suitability
W-pI....... 9.5:2 s. you are honest with yourself in making
W-pI..... 11.1:4 for in this idea is your release made s..
W-pI..... 11.2:4 yourself, being s. to do so without haste,
W-pI..... 12.4:1 s. that you do not alter the time intervals
W-pI..... 23.7:1 be s. to include both your thoughts of
W-pI..... 27.1:3 that you are not s. you really mean it. This
W-pI..... 27.4:6 you can be s. that you have saved yourself
W-pI..... 34.4:2 Be s., however, not to make any specific
W-pI..... 43.5:1 be s. that you select the subjects for this
W-pI..... 46.7:2 Be s., however, to make more specific
W-pI..... 48.3:1 The presence of fear is a s. sign that you
W-pI..... 49.5:3 be s. to sit quietly and repeat the idea for
W-pI..... 50.4:5 without effort and in s. confidence. Tell
WpI... rI.in.2:6 be s. to review all of them once more.
W-pI..... 53.5:5 see. Yet God's way is s.. The images I have
W-pI..... 61.6:1 Be s. both to begin and end the day with
W-pI..... 68.3:1 is as s. that those who hold grievances will
W-pI..... 68.3:2 is as s. that those who hold grievances will
W-pI..... 68.3:3 is as s. that those who hold grievances will
W-pI..... 69.8:2 but you can indeed be s. that it is given
W-pI..... 69.9:7 Also, be s. to tell yourself: *If I hold this*
W-pI... 74.3:10 be s. to deal quickly with any conflict
W-pI..... 77.3:5 will also make s. that we will not content
W-pI..... 80.6:3 particularly s. to apply the idea for today
W-pI..... 91.7:4 else, something more solid and more s.;
W-pI... 91.11:2 be s. to meet temptation with today's idea
W-pI..... 92.8:1 light of strength is constant, s. as love,
W-pI..... 94.5:5 be s. to respond to anyone who seems to
W-pI... 95.15:2 be s. to give the promise of today's idea
W-pI..... 98.7:3 made in faith as perfect and as s. as His in
W-pI... 98.11:2 He will make you s. you want this choice,
W-pI .... 99.6:1 behind which is the changeless and the s..
W-pI .... 99.7:1 be s. you practice well the idea for today.
W-pI .. 102.5:4 And be s. that you are joining with God's
W-pI .. 107.5:1 pain, but looks beyond it, steadily and s..
W-pI .. 107.7:5 certain of success as we are s. we live and
W-pI 108.10:3 still faster and more s. each time you say,
WpI..rIII.in2:3 s. that you catch up in terms of numbers.
W-pI .. 122.1:5 and the warmth of s. protection always?
W-pI 122.11:1 they hold out the s. rewards of questions
W-pI 124.11:3 And yet you can be s. someday, perhaps
W-pI .. 126.1:2 certainty of goal, and s. direction. You
W-pI .. 126.5:1 on which to rest dependably and s.. It is
W-pI .. 128.7:6 Your Guide is s.. Open your mind to Him.
W-pI 135.21:2 will be s. that everything we need is given
W-pI 138.10:1 is as s. as is the ending of the fear of hell,
W-pI 138.11:1 and spend five minutes making s. that we
W-pI 151.11:2 frame of reference, wholly unified and s..
W-pI .. 152.6:3 Of this you can be s.. What can He know
W-pI .. 153.9:3 certain of our safety now, s. of salvation;
W-pI .. 153.9:3 s. we will fulfill our chosen purpose, as
W-pI 154.12:3 But this is s.; until belief is given it, you
W-pI .. 156.2:3 nor be in parts uncertain and in others s..
W-pI .. 157.2:4 it, s. of our direction and our only goal.
W-pI .. 157.7:2 it light will come to see the light more s.;
W-pI .. 160.7:6 is s. of what belongs to Him. No stranger
W-pI .. 160.8:4 Hear His Voice assure you, quietly and s.,
W-pI 161.12:5 Be s. you use it instantly, should you be
W-pI .. 165.3:3 would he not make s. they stay with him,
W-pI .. 165.5:2 You need not be s. that you request the
W-pI .. 165.5:3 you will be s. you have the treasure you
W-pI 169.12:1 course it runs directed and its outcome s..
WpI... rV.in2:6 *s. that he is safe because his father leads the*
WpI... rV.in3:3 *way, we count upon Your s. remembering.*
Wi181-200 1:4 It is experiencing this that makes it s. that
Wi181-200 2:6 You will be s. of what you want, and what
W-pI .. 181.1:1 doubt and lack of s. conviction in yourself
W-pI .. 181.2:6 This faith receives its only s. support from
W-pI .. 182.6:4 that in you still abides His s. protection.
W-pI .. 185.2:8 around you to be s. how very few they are.
W-pI 185.10:4 perhaps unknown to them, but s. to you.
W-pI 185.13:4 can be s. you share one Will with Him,
W-pI .. 186.5:4 whole depends on you, be s. that it is so.
W-pI .. 187.2:2 it is s. that if you give a finite thing away,
W-pI .. 187.4:1 you are s. that you will never lose them.
W-pI .. 189.4:3 upon, and see its s. reflection everywhere.
W-pI .. 189.6:3 It is as s. as Love itself, to which it carries
W-pI .. 192.8:4 He must be s. that he does not escape,
W-pI .. 193.4:3 is this sameness which makes learning s.,
W-pI .. 193.7:3 If it does, be s. the lesson is not learned.
W-pI .. 194.7:7 He is s. that his perception may be faulty,
W-pI .. 194.9:2 s. that only good can come to us. If we
W-pI .. 196.2:1 with all things held in its s. protection,
W-pI .. 197.5:3 Yet you will never realize His gifts are s.,
W-pI .. 200.9:4 God alone is s., and He will guide our
WpI.rVI.in.5:4 in s. and quick exchange for the idea we
W-pII .... in.2:4 And we are s. His promises are kept. We
W-pII . 221.1:5 *love, s. You will hear my call and answer me.*
W-pII . 221.2:3 I am s. that He will speak to you, and you
W-pII . 232.1:5 *And let me sleep s. of my safety, certain of*
W-pII . 235.1:3 to be s. that I am saved and safe forever in
W-pII . 278.2:5 *fear. For truth is safe, and only love is s..*
W-pII . 290.2:4 *I am s. that I will see my happiness today.*
W-pII ...... 8.2:1 a s. correction for the sights of fear and
W-pII ...... 8.4:2 the s. reflection of his Father's Love; the
W-pII .... 292.h A happy outcome to all things is s..
W-pII . 297.2:1 *are Your ways; how s. their final outcome,*
W-pII . 298.1:5 mine, s. that in that alone I will be saved;
W-pII . 298.1:5 s. that I go through fear to meet my Love.
W-pII . 300.1:3 we seek, unclouded, obvious and s., today
W-pII ...... 9.1:1 Second Coming, which is s. as God, is
W-pII . 309.2:1 *is my s. release from idle dreams of sin. Your*
W-pII . 314.2:2 *s. that You will keep Your present promises,*
W-pII . 317.2:5 *from the s. protection of Your loving Arms.*
W-pII . 321.2:3 And how s. is all the world's salvation,
W-pII . 324.2:4 And it is He Who makes the ending s.,
W-pII . 327.1:5 Him. For thus I will be s. that He has not
W-pII . 338.2:1 *Your plan is s., my Father,–only Yours. All*
W-pII347.1:10 *not know my will, but He is s. it is Your Own.*
W-pII . 355.1:3 *I am s. my treasure waits for me, and I need*

**surprised** 2

T-12....VIII.1:3 and yet you are **s.** that you cannot see it. If
T-18.........I.5:1 You may be **s.** to hear how very different

**surprising** 3

T-4......... II.3:4 why is it **s.** that it occurred in the past?
T-4......... II.4:5 reactions to the self you made are not **s.**.
T-7....... X.5:14 this decision is confusion, this is hardly **s.**.

**surround** 16

T-12...VII.11:2 will **s.** you because you called upon them,
T-18...... IV.2:4 and be not disturbed that shadows **s.** it.
T-18...... VI.9:1 is outside you, and but seems to **s.** you,
T-18....VIII.6:4 Nor does a fence **s.** it, preventing it from
T-18...... IX.2:1 Who does **s.** it has brought union to you,
W-pI.....35.2:2 you **s.** yourself with the environment you
W-pI.....59.1:5 when love and joy **s.** me through Him?
W-pI.....70.8:2 find it in the clouds that **s.** the light, and it
W-pI.....72.2:3 that wish that seems to **s.** the mind with a
W-pI.107.10:3 errors that **s.** the world will be corrected
WpI.rV.in11:4 thought that we review but we **s.** with it,
W-pI...183.2:2 to **s.** the ground on which you stand, and
W-pI.200.10:6 can feel its soft embrace **s.** your heart and
W-pII .303.1:2 Let all God's holy Thoughts **s.** me, and be
W-pII ....348.h cause for anger or for fear, For You **s.** me.
M-25 .........2:6 for without them the walls that **s.** all the

**surrounded** 11

T-11...... VI.6:7 in God, safely **s.** by what is yours forever.
T-14..... VII.2:6 to you *because* you hid it and **s.** it with fear
T-17...... IV.8:2 **s.** by a frame so heavy and so elaborate
T-18...... III.3:7 from all illusions in which you have **s.** it.
T-18.... VI.10:6 You are **s.** only by Him. What limits can
T-18...... IX.1:9 in which you set it off, **s.** by darkness,
T-24...... III.7:1 **s.** by a world of loveliness they do not see.
T-30.... III.10:3 **S.** by a stillness so complete no sound of
W-pI.....69.4:2 mind as a vast circle, **s.** by a layer of heavy
W-pII ....264.h I am **s.** by the Love of God.
W-pII .272.1:7 *I am s. by Your Love, forever still, forever*

**surrounding** 12

T-18....VIII.7:7 it and **s.** it with love is the glorious whole,
T-19...... IV.1:6 life, **s.** you and your brother with glowing
W-pI.....68.6:5 Try to feel safety **s.** you, hovering over
W-pI...184.1:5 other things by emphasizing space **s.** it.
W-pI...189.4:2 gentleness and innocence they see **s.** them
W-pII .267.1:1 **S.** me is all the life that God created in
W-pII .....8.3:2 What can it perceive **s.** it but safety, love
W-pII .291.1:5 What holiness we see **s.** us! And it is given
W-pII ...12.3:4 all there is **s.** him is everlasting peace,
W-pII .348.1:2 *S. me is everlasting Love. I have no cause for*
W-pII .348.1:5 *S. me is perfect safety. Can I be afraid, when*
W-pII .348.1:7 *S. me is perfect sinlessness. What can I fear,*

**surrounds** 20

T-11...... III.1:5 no attack and His peace **s.** you silently.
T-11...... III.4:7 Great Light always **s.** you and shines out
T-11...... VI.7:2 The Love of God **s.** His Son whom the god
T-13...... VII.7:3 is not, and love **s.** him without end or flaw
T-13...... XI.9:7 God watches over him and light **s.** him.
T-15...... IV.7:5 and with God Who **s.** all of you together.
T-15...... XI.2:8 of Holiness creates the holiness that **s.** it.
T-18....VIII.2:2 you will not see the grandeur that **s.** you.
T-18....VIII.9:1 Thought of God **s.** your little kingdom,
T-18.... IX.1:10 and unaware of what you think **s.** it.
T-29....... V.2:4 still infinity of endless peace **s.** you gently
T-29....... V.5:4 The quiet that **s.** you dwells in him, and
T-30...... IV.2:3 have broken his "control" of what **s.** him.
W-pI.....41.9:3 on the complete protection that **s.** you.
WpIrIV.in10:2 His gratitude **s.** you in the peace wherein
W-pII .235.1:3 but remember that God's Love **s.** His Son
W-pII .245.1:1 *Your peace s. me, Father. Where I go, Your*
W-pII .264.1:4 *s. Your Son and keeps him safe is Love itself.*
W-ep .........6:8 His Love **s.** you, and of this be sure; that I

S-3........ IV.6:2 and still **s.** you with the Arms of peace.

**survey** 4

W-pI..... 31.3:1 As you **s.** your inner world, merely let
W-pI..... 32.5:2 as you **s.** either your inner or outer world.
W-pI..... 33.2:1 close your eyes and **s.** your inner thoughts
W-pI..... 36.3:2 to whatever you note in your casual **s.**.

**surveying** 1

W-pI..... 33.1:4 Alternate between **s.** your outer and inner

**surveys** 1

T-18 ...VIII.7:5 a sorry king, a bitter ruler of all that he **s.**,

**survival** 6

T-4 .........II.9:3 The so-called "battle for **s.**" is only the
T-5 ....... III.8:7 of reality, war is the guarantee of its **s.**.
T-5 ...... V.4:11 This is necessary to the ego's **s.** because,
T-5 ....... VI.8:2 an attempt to guarantee the ego's own **s.**.
T-10 ....... V.3:2 health is in direct opposition to its own **s.**.
T-15 .... VII.4:4 Yet its **s.** depends on your belief that you

**survive** 5

T-4 .......II.10:3 The ego cannot **s.** without judgment, and
T-18 ...VIII.4:3 them, for it could not **s.** apart from them.
T-23 .....II.10:4 But in a savage world the kind cannot **s.**,
T-31 ..... III.5:2 nor **s.** the ravages of fear except in murder
W-pI...163.7:2 by those who did not want Him to **s.**.

**survives** 1

T-29 ..... VI.3:1 Nothing **s.** its purpose. If it be conceived

**suspect** 8

T-7 ..... III.2:11 being undone, and does **s.** your motives.
T-8 .....VIII.4:5 witnesses should be **s.** from the beginning
T-13 .......II.3:3 You do not even **s.** this murderous but
T19... IV.D.3:2 approach it, nor even to **s.** that it is there.
T-22 ........I.3:8 nor to **s.** that what it tells you is not true.
W-pI...102.1:3 it, and to **s.** it really makes no sense. It has
M-5 .... III.1:12 healed. Yet they **s.** nothing. To them the
P-2....... VII.7:3 **s.** them of the treachery he sees in him.

**suspected** 1

M-5 .... III.1:11 is. If they even **s.** it, they would be healed.

**suspend** 2

T-15 ...... V.1:2 For its purpose is to **s.** judgment entirely.
W-pI...79.10:4 try to **s.** all judgment about what the

**suspended** 4

T-3 ....... VI.3:6 all judgment is automatically **s.**, and this
T-13 ... VI.13:1 laws of love are not **s.** because you sleep.
T-21 .......II.8:3 comes of vision and **s.** judgment. Then
W-pI...156.3:3 the grass to grow with roots **s.** in the air.

**suspending** 1

T-18 ... VI.12:5 **s.** all the "laws" your body obeys and

**suspension** 3

T-1 .........II.1:1 but temporary **s.** of doubt and fear. It
T-17 ...VIII.1:3 calls forth just the same **s.** of faithlessness,
W-pI....... 4.6:1 may find the **s.** of judgment in connection

**suspicion** 1

T-25 ...VIII.6:6 And deep **s.** and the chill of fear comes

**suspicious** 3

T-6 ..... V.B.3:8 others, making him **s.** of their motivation.
T-9 ..... VIII.2:8 It remains **s.** as long as you despair of
M-4 ...... IV.1:9 make him confused, fearful, angry and **s.**.

**suspiciousness** 3

T-9 ...... VII.3:7 of **s.** at best and viciousness at worst. That
T-9 ...... VII.4:7 it will shift abruptly from **s.** to viciousness
T-9 ..... VIII.2:7 ego vacillates between **s.** and viciousness.

**sustain** 4

T-1 .........V.6:3 they are not deep enough to **s.** you. The
T-1 .... VII.3:10 then **s.** the belief of the miracle receiver.
W-pI .... 50.2:5 faith in the worthless. It will not **s.** you.
S-1.........in.3:2 Prayer will **s.** you now, and bless you as

**sustained** 15

*See also* self-sustained

T-25 ... VIII.3:2 punishment, perhaps **s.** by someone else,
W-pI .... 31.1:4 you apply the idea on a more **s.** basis, and
W-pI .... 39.9:3 **S.** concentration is very difficult at first. It
W-pI ....... 50.h I am **s.** by the Love of God.
W-pI .... 50.1:2 believe you are **s.** by everything but God.
W-pI .... 60.5:1 (50) I am **s.** by the Love of God. As I
W-pI .... 60.5:2 I listen to God's Voice, I am **s.** by His Love
W-pI .... 65.3:1 minutes for a more **s.** practice period, in
W-pI .... 95.5:2 your difficulties with **s.** attention, you
W-pII . 222.1:2 air I breathe, the food by which I am **s.**,
W-pII . 249.1:4 What loss can be **s.**? The world becomes a
W-pII . 267.1:6 directed by His Voice, **s.** by Him in love,
M-3 ........... 4:3 level of teaching is a more **s.** relationship,
M-26 ......... 3:8 God were reached directly in **s.** awareness
S-3.........II.3:5 is clearer now; His vision more **s.** in us;

**sustaining** 1

W-pI .. 165.6:6 off from God's **s.** Love and from his home

**swallow** 1

T-18 ... VIII.3:6 terrifies the little ripple and wants to **s.** it.

**sway** 3

T19 ... IV.B.1:2 it. Where the attraction of guilt holds **s.**,
T-20 ... VIII.7:2 within the kindly **s.** of Heaven's laws.
T-29 ..... VI.4:7 And where it once held seeming **s.** is now

**swayed** 1

W-pI .. 132.1:6 be **s.** by questioning his thoughts' effects.

**swear** 2

T-27 ........ I.4:3 from which you **s.** he never will escape.
T-29 ..... VI.2:1 **S.** not to die, you holy Son of God! You

**swearing** 1

S-3........ IV.5:8 devil's care, **s.** He will deliver it no more.

**sweat** 3

T19 .IV.C.11:1 and the cold **s.** of fear comes over it,
T19 .. IV.D.7:6 no stab of fear nor the cold **s.** of seeming
T-27 .. VII.13:4 waken to reality without the **s.** of terror

**sweep** 4

T-11 ..... III.5:6 it can **s.** you out of all darkness forever.
T-13 ..... III.4:2 You are afraid it would **s.** you away from
T-14 .......X.5:3 darkness **s.** constantly across your mind.
T-23 ...... I.10:3 and let forgiveness **s.** away all trace of the

**sweeps** 3

W-pI...168.3:4 and s. away the cobwebs of our sleep. His
W-pI...198.3:1 Forgiveness s. all other dreams away, and
W-pII..336.1:4 all. Forgiveness s. away distortions, and

**sweet** 4

T-13......XI.8:2 the s. and constant communication God
W-pI.159.10:5 whereby a s. transition can be made from
W-pII..310.1:4 *will be Your s. reminder to remember You,*
S-3........IV.7:2 from dreams of malice to the s. embrace

**sweeter** 1

T-26......IV.5:3 its power to the song, and makes it s. still.

**sweetest** 1

T-21......IV.7:2 terror, the other part hears as the s. music

**sweetness** 1

T-22...... I.11:5 Here are His s. and His gentle innocence

**swell** 3

W-pI.134.11:2 They are not kept to s. and bluster, and to
W-pI...170.2:2 blood, to make it grow and s. and rage.
S-2...........I.2:3 large and grow and s. within its sight. It

**swept** 3

*See also* wind-swept

T-4......... V.2:7 attempts to save itself from being s. away,
T-14......IV.7:5 knowledge is s. away from recognition in
T-31...... I.12:4 be loosened from our minds and s. away.

**swift** 3

T-15... VIII.1:4 He is s. to utilize whatever you offer Him
T-24.........I.2:6 unrecognized and s. to challenge you to
S-2.........in.1:1 to make its rising easy and its progress s..

**swiftly** 4

T-15......VI.6:4 of changelessness comes s. as the veil of
T-17....... II.4:5 it. For God will take the last step s., when
T-18......III.3:9 travel surely and very s. away from fear?
W-pI...157.3:3 more s. to this holy place and leaves you,

**swiftness** 1

T-11... VIII.1:5 Yet the s. with which your new and only

**swing** 1

S-2........III.7:7 and you will see the door s. silently open

**swinging** 1

W-pI...195.7:4 us. An ancient door is s. free again; a long

**swings** 2

W-pI.131.13:1 and see how easily the door s. open with
W-pI.133.14:1 of Heaven, which s. open as he comes.

**swirling** 1

T-18.........I.7:6 touched with insanity and s. lightly off on

**sword** 13

T-2......... II.4:8 the only defense that is not a two-edged s.
T-6........ I.15:2 saying, "I come not to bring peace but a s.
T-24......III.4:7 like a flaming s. of death between them,
T-29....... V.5:6 They hold no s., for they have left their
T-29....... V.7:6 each with his tiny spear and rusted s., to
T-31.....VII.9:2 The s. of judgment is the weapon that you
T-31.....VII.9:3 love. Yet while you hold this s., you must
W-pI.182.11:1 and lay down the spear and s. you raised
W-pI...190.9:4 Lay down the cruel s. of judgment that
W-pI...192.9:4 realize you hold a s. above your head.
M-17 .........9:9 Let this grim s. be taken from you now.
M-17 .......9:11 This s. does not exist. The fear of God is
M-20 .........4:4 must you once again lay down your s.,

**swore** 2

T19... IV.D.6:1 before what you s. never to look upon.
T19... IV.D.6:3 of the ego you s. in blood not to desert, all

**symbol** 65

T-3...........I.5:1 do not understand the meaning of the s..
T-3...........I.5:2 simple s. that speaks of my innocence.
T-5........ III.9:4 The ego is the s. of separation, just as the
T-5........ III.9:4 just as the Holy Spirit is the s. of peace.
T-5......... V.2:8 If the ego is the s. of the separation, it is
T-5......... V.2:8 of the separation, it is also the s. of guilt.
T-5....... V.2:10 God. It is the s. of attack on God. This is a
T-6.........I.12:1 be shared because it is the s. of projection
T-6.........I.12:1 but the resurrection is the s. of sharing
T-6.........I.16:7 the perfect s. of the "conflict" between the
T-6......V.A.2:2 body is the s. of what you think you are. It
T-10......IV.1:7 He is the s. of deciding against God, and
T-11....... V.4:6 own. This is why it is the s. of separation.
T-11...... VI.6:1 allegiance gladly, because it is the s. of joy
T-12...... III.8:4 split mind, and which is the s. of death.
T-13.......in.2:4 so. For this world is the s. of punishment,
T-13....... II.6:1 said that the crucifixion is the s. of the ego
T-14......IV.1:3 You will not see the s. of your brother's
T-14..... V.10:3 s. of the release from guilt by guiltlessness
T-15......IX.2:3 The body is the s. of the ego, as the ego is
T-15......IX.2:3 ego, as the ego is the s. of the separation.
T-16......IV.2:2 the s. of love is without meaning if love is
T19. IV.A.17:2 For I became the s. of your sin, and so I
T19IV.A.17:10 The body does appear to be the s. of sin
T19....IV.B.6:1 Let me be to you the s. of the end of guilt,
T19....IV.B.6:6 in me the s. of guilt or of the end of guilt,
T19....IV.C.4:2 they dedicated to death, a s. of corruption
T19..IV.C.11:1 the ego has perceived it as a s. of fear, a
T19..IV.C.11:2 nor s. should be confused with source, for
T-20.........I.1:5 a risen Christ becomes the s. of the Son of
T-20.........I.3:1 holy week is the s. of the whole journey
T-26.........I.1:3 the s. of the central theme that *somebody*
T-26....... V.8:4 was feared and made a s. of your hate?
T-26...VII.8:10 s. represents is but your wish to *be* apart
T-27.........I.2:6 not to make yourself a living s. of his guilt
T-27.........I.8:4 For it becomes the s. of reproach, the sign
T-27..... II.14:3 hated it, and hates it still as s. of his fear.
T-27...... III.2:1 that your brother is a s. for a "hateful love
T-27...... III.5:1 be pictured, so there is no s. for totality.
T-28... VI.3:10 made of it a s. for the limitations that you
T-29.........I.4:3 s. of a promise made to meet when you
T-31....... V.6:8 then is s. of your sins to you who are but
W-pI.....23.3:1 and everything in it is a s. of vengeance.
W-pI...161.6:4 its sight presents the s. of love's "enemy"
W-pI...161.8:1 a brother as a body sees him as fear's s..
W-pI.161.11:1 Select one brother, s. of the rest, and ask
W-pI.161.12:5 and perceive in him the s. of your fear.
W-pII..247.1:1 Sin is the s. of attack. Behold it anywhere,
W-pII......6.5:1 s. that the time for learning now is over,
W-pII......8.1:1 The real world is a s., like the rest of what
W-pII......8.4:1 real world is the s. that the dream of sin
M-23 .........4:1 name of Jesus Christ as such is but a s..
M-23 .........4:3 a s. that is safely used as a replacement for
M-23 .........4:4 It becomes the shining s. for the Word of
M-23 .........5:6 become the s. of his Father here on earth.
M-27 .........2:6 Death has become life's s.. His world is
M-27 .........3:1 Death is the s. of the fear of God. His
M-27 .........3:3 The grimness of the s. is enough to show
C-2............1:9 A s. of impossibility; a choice for options
C-3............4:5 face of Christ is the great s. of forgiveness.
C-3............4:7 It is the s. of the real world. Whoever
C-3............5:1 Forgiveness is a s., too, but as the symbol
C-3............5:1 s. of His Will alone it cannot be divided.
S-1..........II.5:1 enemy is the s. of an imprisoned Christ.
S-3.........in.1:3 is a sign or s. of forgiveness' strength, and

**symbolic** 9

T-3...........I.8:2 your mind knows God, for God is not s.;
T-3....... III.4:2 Spiritual sight is s., and therefore not a
T-3......... V.4:7 are s. and stand for something else. The
T-3........ VI.1:3 Judgment is s. because beyond perception
T-3.......VII.3:4 one tree was "forbidden" in the s. garden.
T-3.......VII.4:1 of the tree of knowledge is a s. expression
T-5...........I.4:1 of the Holy Trinity that has a s. function.
T-5...........I.4:5 s. function makes the Holy Spirit difficult
C-in ...........3:3 Therefore it uses words, which are s., and

**symbolism** 2

T-3.......VII.3:9 His creations. The s. here has been given
T-5...........I.4:5 s. is open to different interpretations. As

**symbolize** 4

T-3...........I.5:3 and the lamb lying down together s. that
W-pI..... 15.3:5 because they merely s. true perception,
W-pI... 161.9:7 Ask him not to s. your fear. Would you
M-23 .........7:4 of trouble; a savior who can s. Himself?

**symbolized** 3

T-26..... VII.8:9 to him. This separating off is s., in your
T-27...... III.3:3 it s. a contradiction that cancelled out the
W-pI... 129.4:3 no words, for what They say cannot be s..

**symbolizes** 4

T-29........II.6:2 s. but your wish to be alive apart from life
W-pII ..... 3.2:2 It s. fear. And what is fear except love's
M-5 .........I.2:2 for? It s. the defeat of God's Son and the
M-21 .......3:10 s. that which has no human symbols at all

**symbols** 49

T-3.........I.3:11 is always possible to twist s. around if you
T-5........ III.7:2 His ability to deal with s. enables Him to
T-5........ III.7:3 His ability to look beyond s. into eternity
T-6........ IV.6:5 of the ego's s. and they have confused you
T-7...........I.6:4 to explain in words because words are s.,
T-9....... IV.11:3 it. The s. of fantasy are of the ego, and of
T-9......... V.4:2 may interpret the ego's s. in a nightmare,
T-14...... VI.6:1 You who speak in dark and devious s. do
T-16...... IV.2:1 The s. of hate against the symbols of love
T-16...... IV.2:1 The symbols of hate against the s. of love
T-16...... IV.2:2 For s. stand for something else, and the
T-27.........I.1:4 But place no terror s. on your path, or you
T-27......... III.h Beyond All S.
T-27...... III.2:6 S. which but represent ideas that cannot
T-27...... III.4:5 is. For this there are no s.. Nothing points
T-27...... III.7:1 Forgiveness vanishes and s. fade, and
T-27...... III.7:8 beyond the world of s. and of limitations.
T-27...... VI.6:1 Love, too, has s. in a world of sin. The
T-27...... VI.8:6 chose to let love's s. take the place of sin.
T-30..... VII.6:1 the s. that are used mean different things?
T-30..... VII.6:4 In s. that you both can understand the
T-30..... VII.7:7 And through His use of s. are we joined,
T-31..... V.15:1 Seek not your Self in s.. There can be no
W-pI..... 50.1:3 is placed in the most trivial and insane s.;
W-pI... 136.6:3 become s. standing for attack upon the
W-pI... 161.5:2 are but s. for a concrete form of fear. Fear
W-pI... 161.5:3 Fear without s. calls for no response, for
W-pI... 161.5:3 for s. can stand for the meaningless. Love
W-pI... 161.5:4 Love needs no s., being true. But fear
W-pI... 161.6:3 the reason bodies easily become fear's s..
W-pI... 184.1:1 You live by s.. You have made up names
W-pI... 184.6:2 signs and s. that assert the world is real. It
W-pI... 184.9:1 asked to go beyond all s. of the world,
W-pI... 184.9:2 need to use the s. of the world a while. But
W-pI. 184.11:1 all the little names and s. which delineate
W-pI... 192.4:1 the senseless s. written there before.
W-pI. 198.11:6 Then are s. done, and everything you ever

M-5 ...... III.2:4 His teachers are the **s.** of salvation. They
M-21 ......... 1:9 however, that words are but **s.** of symbols
M-21 ......... 1:9 however, that words are but symbols of **s.**
M-21 ......... 2:1 **s.**, words have quite specific references.
M-21 ......... 2:6 words, then, are **s.** for the things asked for
M-21 ....... 3:10 that which has no human **s.** at all. The
M-21 ......... 5:8 teachers have God's Word behind their **s.**
M-21 ......... 5:9 meaningless **s.** to the Call of Heaven itself.
M-23 ......... 7:2 tongues and appeal to different **s.**?
M-23 ......... 7:5 **s.** must shift and change to suit the need.
C-in ........... 3:3 and cannot express what lies beyond **s.**. It
C-5............. 1:5 which differ for a time, for time needs **s.**,

## symptom 7

T-2........ VI.3:7 does not mean anything at the **s.** level,
T-3........ VI.7:4 all evil." Every **s.** the ego makes involves a
T-9......... II.2:6 removal of a **s.** that he himself selected.
T-11....... I.10:5 Every **s.** of sickness and fear arises here,
T-12......... I.9:1 Fear is a **s.** of your own deep sense of loss.
T-21...... III.7:5 hatred by removing fear, not as a **s.**, but
P-2....... VII.2:5 What is **s.** cure, when another is always

## symptoms 5

T-2........ IV.2:6 error, produces all physical **s.**. Physical
T-3........ VI.7:1 I have spoken of different **s.**, and at that
T-5....... V.7:12 is beyond doubt, how can its **s.** remain?
M-7 ........... 4:1 **s.** is a mistake in the form of lack of trust.
P-2....... VII.2:9 are the "**s.**" of the ideal patient-therapist

## synonymous 3

T-4....... VII.3:6 Creation and communication are **s.**. God
T-6......... II.1:4 Exclusion and separation are **s.**, as are
T-8...... VIII.3:1 it is **s.** with the belief in attack as an end.

## system 108

T-3....... VII.1:1 Every **s.** of thought must have a starting
T-3....... VII.1:6 mistake to believe that a thought **s.** based
T-3....... VII.3:2 separation is a **s.** of thought real enough
T-3....... VII.4:9 is the foundation stone in your thought **s.**
T-3..... VII.5:10 **s.** upon you as if it were the fear of death.
T-3....... VII.6:3 your own thought **s.** will stand corrected.
T-4........... I.2:5 thought **s.** can stand on two foundations.
T-4........... I.3:5 to teach you how its thought **s.** arose.
T-4........... I.4:7 of your thought **s.** and open it to me, I
T-4........... I.5:4 of the **s.** in which the lawmaker believes.
T-4......... II.5:1 thought **s.** must be perceived as painful,
T-4......... II.7:4 of "getting" arose in the ego's thought **s.**.
T-4....... II.10:5 be dictated by the thought **s.** to which it
T-4......... V.1:5 according to the thought **s.** which gave
T-4......... V.3:1 Any thought **s.** that confuses God and
T-4....... VII.2:3 The communication **s.** of the ego is based
T-4....... VII.2:3 of the ego is based on its own thought **s.**,
T-5 ........ V.3:9 It represents a delusional **s.**, and speaks
T-5 ...... VII.1:2 can devise a thought **s.** that can separate
T-6 ........ in.2:3 organize his life without some thought **s.**.
T-6 ........ in.2:4 have developed a thought **s.** of any kind,
T-6 ........ in.2:5 capacity for allegiance to a thought **s.** may
T-6 ........ I.16:2 thought **s.** toward which I am guiding you
T-6 ....... IV.1:7 the foundation of its whole thought **s.**.
T-6 ..... V.A.4:5 thought **s.** I teach and want you to teach.
T-6 ..... V.B.1:7 is that when you do not share a thought **s.**
T-6 ..... V.B.1:9 identifies himself with his thought **s.**, and
T-6 ..... V.B.1:9 and every thought **s.** centers on what you
T-6 ... V.B.1:10 If the center of the thought **s.** is true, only
T-6 ..... V.B.5:2 If you identify with your thought **s.**, and
T-6 ..... V.B.9:2 toward the center of your thought **s.**,
T-7 ....... VI.8:5 engage your mind in its own delusional **s.**
T-7 ..... VI.12:2 your thought **s.** and divide your allegiance
T-7 .... VII.11:1 of the ego's thought **s.** as wholly insane,
T-7 ....... IX.3:4 ego's whole thought **s.** blocks extension,
T-8 ....... IX.9:3 in a chaotic thought **s.** *is* the way to heal it.
T-9 ......... II.2:5 the threat to his thought **s.** might be
T-9 ...... VII.6:1 evaluate an insane belief **s.** from within it.
T-9 ...... VII.6:6 Within the **s.** that dictated this choice the
T-9 ...... VII.6:8 is meaningless within the ego's thought **s.**
T-9 ...... VII.6:8 open the whole thought **s.** to question.
T-9 ...... VII.7:3 and keep the ego's whole thought **s.** intact
T-9 ...... VII.7:4 You cannot retain part of a thought **s.**,
T-9 ...... VII.7:6 the reality of the ego's thought **s.** merely
T-10 ..... III.5:1 the ego's thought **s.** and judge whether its
T-11 ...... in.1:3 nor the ego proposes a partial thought **s.**.
T-11 ...... in.2:4 than a delusional **s.** in which you made
T-11 ...... in.2:7 in the dark cornerstone of its thought **s.**.
T-11 ...... in.2:8 or its whole thought **s.** will not stand.
T-11 ...... in.3:2 creation is you, for His thought **s.** is light.
T-11 ...... in.3:4 you approach the center of His thought **s.**,
T-11 ...... in.3:5 to the foundation of the ego's thought **s.**,
T-11 ...... in.3:7 to the foundation of the ego's thought **s.**.
T-11 ........ I.1:3 again the thought **s.** you share with Him.
T-11 ....... V.1:3 the ego's thought **s.** because together we
T-11 ....... V.4:2 surely regard a delusional **s.** without fear,
T-11 .... V.14:6 thought **s.**: Error is real and truth is error.
T-11 .... V.16:4 and no thought **s.** transcends its source.
T-11 .... V.18:3 to the thought **s.** you want to be true.
T-13 ...... in.2:2 you see is the delusional **s.** of those made
T-13 ....... II.7:4 than you dismiss the ego's thought **s.**. To
T-13 ..... III.4:1 your whole insane belief **s.** because you
T-14 ........ I.2:5 your thought **s.** is closed off and wholly
T-14 ........ I.3:2 the thought **s.** you made would be forever
T-14 ........ I.5:2 the simple truth into a thought **s.** which
T-14 .... VII.2:7 you have erected your insane **s.** of belief,
T-14 ........ X.9:2 put them together and the **s.** of thought
T-14 ........ X.9:3 of content makes a cohesive **s.** impossible.
T-15 ........ I.4:9 paradox in the ego's thought **s.** before,
T-15 ....... X.5:7 your thought **s.** that salvation apart from
T-16 ..... III.1:3 came from beyond your thought **s.**.
T-16 ..... III.1:5 the basis of a very different thought **s.**,
T-16 ..... III.2:6 effect are very clear in the ego's thought **s.**
T-16 .... V.15:4 whole thought **s.** is a carefully contrived
T-16 ..... VI.9:2 the thought **s.** that taught you it was real,
T-17 ..... IV.4:3 The whole defense **s.** the ego evolved to
T-17 ..... IV.6:1 the thought **s.** the special relationship
T-17 ..... IV.6:1 protects is but a **s.** of delusions. You
T-17 ..... IV.6:4 of the ego's thought **s.** that you have been
T-17 ..... IV.7:4 of the thought **s.** the defense protects, set
T-17 ..... IV.8:2 Its thought **s.** is offered here, surrounded
T-17 ..... IV.9:8 most superficial aspects of this thought **s.**,
T-17 ... IV.11:8 whole thought **s.** of the ego lies in its gifts,
T-17 ... IV.15:3 no figured representation of a thought **s.**,
T-18 ..... IX.5:2 a real foundation for the ego's thought **s.**.
T-19 ........ I.6:3 the delusional thought **s.** in the mind.
T-19 ........ I.7:4 Each is united, a complete thought **s.**, but
T-19 ....... II.5:2 sin is wholly sacrosanct to its thought **s.**,
T-19 ....... II.5:3 is the most "holy" concept in the ego's **s.**;
T19 ... IV.A.8:4 than a tightly organized delusional **s.**? Its
T-21 ..... IV.3:3 the ego's whole defensive **s.** too seriously
T-22 ..... III.1:1 thought **s.** is the beginning of its undoing,
T-27 ........ I.6:6 lend conviction to the **s.** they speak for
W-pI .... 42.7:2 that you are studying a unified thought **s.**
WpI... rI.in.6:4 thought **s.** to which they are leading you.
W-pI .... 51.5:6 to defend a thought **s.** that has hurt me,
W-pI .... 91.1:3 It is a central idea in your new thought **s.**,
W-pI .... 94.5:9 the thought **s.** which this course sets forth
W-pI .. 153.2:4 sets up a **s.** of defense that cannot work.
M-4 .... I.A.7:5 sacrifice, so central to his own thought **s.**,
M-4 ...... III.1:6 of the teacher of God's whole thought **s.**.
M-9 ........... 1:9 old thought **s.** still has a basis for return.
M-13 ......... 1:6 before another thought **s.** can take hold,
M-14 ......... 4:1 thought **s.** has been completely reversed.
M-17 ......... 5:2 the world's thought **s.** becomes apparent.
M-17 ......... 9:4 its thought **s.** is to look on nothing. Can
M-22 ......... 3:2 is a central concept in the ego's thought **s.**
P-1............. 1:2 in abandoning his fixed delusional **s.**, and

## systematic 1

W-in.......... 4:1 train your mind in a **s.** way to a different

## systematically 1

T-4 ......... V.6:2 to develop, but has **s.** failed to achieve.

## systems 12

T-3 ......... V.2:5 ingenious thought **s.** for this purpose.
T-3 ...... VII.1:5 Both are cornerstones for **s.** of belief by
T-4 .......... I.2:1 to protect their thought **s.** as they are, and
T-4 ......... II.9:2 Mythological **s.** generally include some
T-6 ........ I.16:7 the result of clearly opposed thought **s.**;
T-6 ..... V.B.5:1 conflict between two opposing thought **s.**
T-6 ..... V.B.5:2 if you accept two thought **s.** which are in
T-7 ..... VI.8:11 contradictory thought **s.** share truth, your
T-14 .... VII.4:3 of thinking whereby two **s.** of belief which
T-17 ..... III.9:6 Thought **s.** are but true or false, and all
T-17 ..... IV.5:4 The insane protect their thought **s.**, but
M-in .......... 2:2 There are only two thought **s.**, and you

# T

## table 14

T19.IV.A.16:1 you, on a t. covered with a spotless cloth,
T19.IV.A.16:3 in gentleness before the t. of communion.
T-28......III.9:8 love has set its t. in the space that seemed
W-pI.......1.1:2 *This t. does not mean anything. This chair*
W-pI.....28.2:1 all else I want to see this t. differently." In
W-pI.....28.3:1 all else I want to see this t. differently,"
W-pI.....28.3:1 your preconceived ideas about the t., and
W-pI.....28.4:3 all else I want to see this t. differently,"
W-pI.....28.4:5 commitment that applies to the t. just as
W-pI.....28.5:1 could, in fact, gain vision from just that t.,
W-pI.....28.6:1 In using the t. as a subject for applying
W-pI.....29.2:3 Certainly God is not in a t., for example,
W-pI.....29.2:4 yesterday that a t. shares the purpose of
W-pI...169.1:4 those who have prepared a t. where it can

## tables 1

W-pI.....28.3:4 its meaning to your tiny experience of t.,

## tacitly 2

T-3.........V.2:4 t. implying that you believe in separation.
W-pI.....20.4:2 to see. Today's idea also t. implies the

## tactics 1

T-4.........V.6:7 In all these diversionary t., however, the

## tainted 1

T-3........I.2:11 t. with this kind of distortion in any form.

## take 350

T-in............1:3 *Only the time you t. it is voluntary. Free will*
T-in............1:5 *can elect what you want to t. at a given time.*
T-2.........II.7:5 literally t. it over because of their strength
T-2........IV.2:9 This error can t. two forms; it can be
T-2........VI.1:3 My control can t. over everything that
T-2........VI.9:2 Yet it would t. very little right thinking to
T-2.......VII.1:8 would t. a miracle to enable you to do this
T-4.........II.5:2 in rage if you t. away a knife or scissors,
T-4.......VII.6:4 But unless you t. your part in the creation
T-6.........in.2:1 asked to t. me as your model for learning,
T-6...........I.2:6 last useless journey the Sonship need t.,
T-6......V.A.6:1 and the only one you must t. for yourself.
T-6......V.A.6:7 rather than t. the next step towards its
T-6......V.B.9:2 As you t. this step and hold this direction,
T-6......V.C.5:8 nature of the steps you must t. with Him.
T-6....V.C.10:2 Holy Spirit will enable you to t. this step,
T-7...........I.7:1 God does not t. steps, because His
T-7...........I.7:8 will t. was therefore true in the beginning,
T-7.........V.9:7 it. It incorporates to t. away. It literally
T-7.......VII.9:2 this as you are, are out to t. God from you
T-8......IV.8:12 Unless you t. your place in It and fulfill
T-8........VI.5:5 of God Himself t. joy in what is not real?
T-8........IX.7:1 t. no thought of the body as separate and
T-10......in.1:4 world can t. this responsibility from you.
T-10....IV.4:10 but they are not there to t. it from you,
T-10.....V.12:4 many other forms that blasphemy may t.,
T-11.......in.4:6 You will not t. this journey alone. I will
T-11.......II.5:7 Whatever journey you choose to t., He
T-11......VI.5:6 nothing, for He does not will to t. away.
T-11... VIII.5:9 gives; He does not t.. When you refuse to
T-11... VIII.6:1 is yours, and will t. nothing in return. For
T-11. VIII.15:5 down to you and t. the last step for you,
T-12.......II.5:2 T. off the covers and look at what you are
T-12.......II.9:8 offered it to Him and He cannot t. it from
T-12.......V.8:1 what you do not want should t. heart, for
T-12... VIII.8:2 see. Only t. it from the hand of Christ and
T-13....III.12:5 you creation, He could not t. it from you.
T-13...VII.12:5 He will t. nothing from you as long as you
T-13...VII.16:9 T. it of me in glad exchange for all the
T-13...VII.16:9 for all the world has offered but to t. away
T-14.......in.1:5 t. a direction exactly opposite, pointing as
T-14....III.17:7 t. unto yourself the sole responsibility for
T-14......IX.1:7 it? The making of time to t. the place of
T-14......IX.4:3 graciousness of God will t. them gently in,
T-14......X.10:3 T. no thought for yourself, for no thought
T-14......XI.4:6 by hands open to receive, not closed to t..
T-14....XI.6:11 will t. His rightful place in your awareness
T-15.........I.5:2 it attacks so savagely that it tries to t. the
T-15.........I.9:5 T. this very instant, now, and think of it
T-15.......I.11:1 t. to change your mind so completely, ask
T-15.......II.1:8 What can t. time, when all the obstacles
T-15.......II.3:1 can it t. to be where God would have you?
T-15......VI.8:6 of God will t. Their rightful place in you,
T-15.......X.8:5 it to t. His place to protect you from Him.
T-15..XI.10:10 as this year is born, and t. your place, so
T-16......III.5:4 more to you than you tried to t. away. He
T-16......III.5:6 And they will t. the place of what you
T-16....IV.12:6 We will t. the last useless journey away
T-16.......V.1:4 Whatever form they t., they are always an
T-16.....V.11:5 another self to t. its power from his death.
T-16.....V.12:2 aimed at raising the form to t. the place of
T-16....VI.11:5 returns to t. its rightful place within it.
T-17.........I.3:5 t. away from Him Who would release you
T-17.......II.4:5 For God will t. the last step swiftly, when
T-17......IV.9:3 t. it you will believe that you *are* damned.
T-17.......V.9:4 And t. his hand, to walk together along a
T-17......VI.7:1 will attempt to t. this aspect elsewhere,
T-18.........I.3:4 It seems to t. many forms, and each one
T-18.........I.6:6 and t. no part in all the mad projection by
T-18.......II.2:3 You do not t. them seriously on awaking
T-18.......II.8:1 not the dream t. hold to close your eyes. It
T-18......III.4:8 You cannot t. it back. You have accepted
T-18......III.5:4 faltering footsteps that you may t. can
T-18......III.5:5 surely as you agreed to t. your brother's.
T-18......IV.6:2 will merely t. away the little that is asked.
T-18....IX.10:4 Himself can t. the final step unhindered,
T-18....IX.10:5 further inward but the one *you* cannot t.,
T19..IV.C.11:8 *T. this from me and look upon it, judging it*
T-20.......II.2:2 neither offer nor accept; hold out nor t..
T-20.......II.3:4 has placed upon it and t. it for their own.
T-20......III.6:7 answered. T. not the judgment of the
T-20......III.9:3 it go or to t. hold on life so long forgotten.
T-20......IV.8:8 You need t. thought for nothing, careless
T-20.......V.5:6 Why should it t. so many holy instants to
T-20... VIII.8:5 Once you accept this simple fact and t.
T-21.......II.6:6 God powerless and so to t. it for himself,
T-21......III.3:6 you give to sin you t. away from holiness.
T-21......III.6:4 He would not t. them from you, for He
T-22.......in.1:1 T. pity on yourself, so long enslaved.
T-22.......in.3:5 looks on nothing he would t.. He denies
T-22.........I.1:1 Let reason t. another step. If you attack
T-22.......II.8:1 you can t. and weave into illusions. Nor is
T-22......IV.1:4 to decide which branch you will t. now.
T-22......VI.9:6 He will t. each one and make of it a potent
T-23.........I.6:5 And so it matters not what form they t..
T-23.......II.6:4 to t. his word for it or be mistaken. This
T-23.......II.9:4 you can never t. away save from yourself.
T-23.....II.10:4 so they must t. or else be taken from.
T-23.....II.14:3 function of insanity to t. the place of truth
T-23.....II.18:4 else could you perceive the form they t.,
T-23.....II.18:6 Yet you believe them *for* the form they t.,
T-23.....II.22:1 t. not one step in the descent to hell. For
T-23......III.1:1 recognize some of the forms attack can t.?
T-23......III.3:2 you want; to t. a little and give up the rest.
T-24.........I.1:4 you asked a substitute to t. its place. And
T-24........II.6:4 himself, as it returns to t. their place. This
T-24......VI.8:3 delay, which it is given you to t. from him,
T-25........II.4:3 T. not the form for content, for the form
T-25......IV.3:1 so, t. rest and comfort in another world
T-25......VI.7:9 T. it gently, then, from your brother's
T-25....VIII.1:2 t. it from you without your willingness.
T-25....VIII.1:6 that you prefer He t. it than that you keep
T-25..VIII.13:5 To t. from one to give another must be an
T-25..VIII.13:9 and try to t. away from whom he judges.
T-25......IX.4:5 who shall lose; how much the one shall t.,
T-25......IX.9:6 responsibility must be to t. forgiveness
T-26.........I.6:3 and t. the rest his witness offers on behalf
T-26........II.1:4 whatever form the problem seems to t.. A
T-26........II.2:2 one, regardless of the form it seems to t.,
T-26.......V.1:9 There are but two directions you can t.,
T-26.....V.10:5 Resurrection has come to t. its place. And
T-26......VI.2:6 Seek not another friend to t. His place.
T-26......VI.3:3 it can but t. the place of Him Whom God
T-26.....VII.3:4 to t. the place of changeless knowledge.
T-26....VIII.6:2 of the working out can seem to t. forever.
T-26......IX.3:4 which has lifted holiness again to t. its
T-26........X.4:8 that someone else can t. it from him,
T-26........X.5:6 add or t. away from this one goal is but to
T-26........X.5:6 this one goal is but to t. away all purpose
T-27.........I.7:8 And so t. pleasure in the quickly passing
T-27.......I.10:2 and perfect healing t. the place of death.
T-27......II.10:8 separation but a wish to t. God's function
T-27......II.10:9 for you must lose what you would t. away.
T-27......III.6:7 is God left free to t. the final step Himself.
T-27......III.6:9 And what will ultimately t. the place of
T-27.......V.8:1 are not specific but they t. specific forms,
T-27......VI.5:3 its own effects have come to t. their place.
T-27......VI.8:6 to let love's symbols t. the place of sin.
T-27...VII.14:3 allow His gentle dreams to t. the place of
T-28.........I.2:7 is a skill made up by you to t. the place of
T-28.......I.11:5 and what has come to t. its place will not
T-28.......I.15:2 of God has come to t. the place of loss?
T-28......IV.2:2 of fearful dreams whatever form they t.,
T-28......IV.8:1 Holy Spirit's function is to t. the broken
T-28......IV.9:5 broken pieces seem to t. mean nothing.
T-28......VI.4:4 apart. This is the secret oath you t. again,
T-29.........I.6:3 And it will t. command of when to "love,"
T-29........II.4:5 look on them and t. them for your own.
T-29......IV.2:2 no matter what the form it seems to t..
T-29......IV.6:4 try to hurt him when he fails to t. the part
T-29......VI.3:2 it does not t. this purpose as its own.
T-29......VI.6:4 comes quietly to t. the place of time.
T-29...VII.10:4 An idol cannot t. the place of God. Let
T-29....VIII.4:9 t. no form in which he ever will be real.
T-30.........I.1:4 preoccupied with every step you t.. The
T-30.......I.11:1 of wisdom will suffice to t. you further.
T-30......III.2:3 What form can t. the place of all the love
T-30....III.10:2 the myriad of forms that fear can t.; quite
T-30......VI.3:1 rise to t. the place of dreams of terror.
T-30.....VII.1:8 You t. away another element, and every
T-31........II.6:8 T. not his hand in anger but in love, for in
T-31......III.1:6 Whatever form his sins appear to t., it but
T-31......IV.1:8 will t. with you whatever road you choose
T-31.......V.2:3 made to t. the place of your reality as Son
T-31...VII.12:1 Whatever form temptation seems to t., it
T-31....VIII.1:5 *Choose once again if you would t. your place*
W-pI.......2.2:2 T. the subjects simply as you see them.
W-pI.....13.5:2 Whatever form such resistance may t.,
W-pI.....15.3:2 They may t. many different forms, some
W-pI.....21.2:3 The anger may t. the form of any reaction
W-pI.....26.3:5 has come to t. the place of what you are.
W-pI.....26.6:2 concern may t. the form of depression,

| | |
|---|---|
| W-pI.....33.4:2 | It may be necessary to **t.** a minute or so to |
| W-pI.....34.5:3 | the exercise should **t.** this form: *I could see* |
| W-pI.....34.6:1 | inroads on your peace of mind **t.** the form |
| W-pI.....34.6:2 | try to **t.** several minutes and devote them |
| W-pI.....36.2:3 | practice periods should **t.** this form: |
| W-pI.....39.6:3 | Whatever form they **t.**, they are unloving |
| W-pI.....40.3:1 | Today's exercises **t.** little time and no |
| W-pI.....40.3:6 | Another might **t.** this form: *I am blessed as* |
| W-pI.....41.2:5 | the serious and tragic forms it may **t.**. |
| W-pI.....45.4:1 | for today will **t.** the same general form |
| W-pI.....45.9:2 | **T.** a minute or two, as you repeat the idea |
| W-pI.....48.2:4 | **t.** a minute or so whenever possible to |
| W-pI.....48.3:2 | His strength **t.** the place of your weakness |
| W-pI.....51.1:5 | no meaning, so that vision may **t.** its place |
| W-pI.....51.4:5 | I have made my thoughts to **t.** their place. |
| W-pI.....61.7:3 | giant steps we will **t.** in the next few weeks |
| W-pI.....62.3:4 | It will **t.** away all fear and guilt and pain. |
| W-pI.....65.2:1 | only way in which you can **t.** your rightful |
| W-pI...66.11:3 | *both.* It will not **t.** more than a minute, and |
| W-pI.....72.1:2 | ego appears to **t.** on the attributes of God. |
| W-pI.....72.6:6 | **T.** the little you can get. God gave you |
| W-pI.....76.9:6 | else. God's laws forever give and never **t.**. |
| W-pI.....78.5:4 | when he is freed to **t.** the holy role the |
| W-pI...78.10:1 | **t.** the role assigned to us as part of God's |
| W-pI.....80.1:8 | and you are ready to **t.** your rightful place |
| WpI..rII.in.2:1 | **T.** about fifteen minutes for each of them, |
| WpI..rII.in.4:2 | that, whatever form such thoughts may **t.**, |
| W-pI.....83.2:1 | of this idea might **t.** these forms: *My* |
| W-pI.....91.8:2 | and their opposites to **t.** their place. Say, |
| W-pI.....97.5:1 | Holy Spirit will be glad to **t.** five minutes |
| W-pI.....98.1:2 | We **t.** a stand on but one side today. We |
| W-pI.....98.1:4 | two, but **t.** a firm position with the One. |
| W-pI.....98.1:8 | it is, and **t.** the part assigned to us by God |
| W-pI.....98.2:2 | and **t.** our stand with certainty of purpose |
| W-pI.....98.3:5 | took the stand which we will **t.** today, that |
| W-pI.....98.4:1 | us; all who took the stand we **t.** today will |
| W-pI...98.11:2 | He would have you **t.** and help you fill, |
| W-pI...100.2:3 | The part that He has saved for you to **t.** in |
| W-pI...100.4:2 | and **t.** their place beside you in God's plan |
| W-pI...100.5:2 | fail to **t.** the part that is essential to God's |
| W-pI...100.7:4 | to **t.** his place among God's messengers. |
| W-pI...103.3:2 | and joy becomes what you expect to **t.** the |
| W-pI...105.2:4 | and leaves you nothing in the ones you **t.**. |
| W-pI...108.1:4 | behind it will appear instead to **t.** its place |
| W-pI...109.5:8 | **T.** time today to slip away from dreams |
| W-pI...109.6:1 | Each hour that you **t.** your rest today, a |
| W-pI...109.6:2 | that it might **t.** its rest along with you. |
| W-pI...109.9:2 | Each brother comes to **t.** his rest, and |
| WpIrIII.in11:6 | to **t.** it with you in the business of the day |
| W-pI...111.2:3 | *by giving me His strength to* **t.** *its place.* |
| W-pI...121.8:2 | can learn today to **t.** the key to happiness, |
| W-pI...122.8:2 | by which it comes to **t.** the place of hell. In |
| W-pI...123.2:3 | to **t.** the place of Him and His creation. |
| W-pI...127.6:5 | Today we **t.** the largest single step this |
| W-pI...129.5:3 | Here is the world that comes to **t.** its place |
| W-pI...129.6:5 | **t.** the place of all the things you seek but |
| W-pI...129.9:3 | and **t.** a moment to confirm your choice |
| W-pI...130.9:2 | will **t.** this giant step with you in gratitude |
| W-pI.130.11:2 | **t.** the place of everything that hell would |
| W-pI...131.9:2 | God make time to **t.** away the Will of God |
| W-pI...133.2:3 | to **t.** from you the little that you have. It |
| W-pI...133.6:3 | Time can never **t.** away a value that is real |
| W-pI...133.7:1 | to **t.** a thing away from someone else, you |
| W-pI...133.7:4 | Who seeks to **t.** away has been deceived |
| W-pI.135.10:5 | but merely **t.** away the hope of healing, |
| W-pI.135.14:3 | some forms which these self-deceptions **t.** |
| W-pI.135.17:4 | attack, obscure, and **t.** apart and crucify. |
| W-pI.135.26:4 | And all the world will **t.** this giant stride, |
| W-pI...136.6:4 | be real, to **t.** the place of what is real. |
| W-pI.136.16:1 | to **t.** the place of war and vain imaginings. |
| W-pI...137.5:3 | Just as the real world will arise to **t.** the |
| W-pI.137.15:2 | and to receive the Word of God to **t.** the |
| W-pI...138.6:1 | Heaven appears to **t.** the form of choice, |
| W-pI...140.4:2 | is not deceived by forms the dream may **t.** |
| W-pI.140.10:1 | and bits of magic in whatever form they **t.** |
| W-pI.140.12:6 | hourly, and **t.** a minute as the hour strikes |
| WpI. rIV.in3:3 | off through self-deceptions made to **t.** its |
| WpI. rIV.in4:2 | cannot **t.** the place of truth. No more than |
| W-pI...152.8:5 | And it will **t.** the place of self-deceptions |
| W-pI...153.1:1 | the "gifts" it merely lends to **t.** away again |
| W-pI.153.11:6 | As they **t.** it from your hands, so will you |
| W-pI.153.14:2 | we go to **t.** our rightful place where truth |
| W-pI.153.20:1 | now begin to **t.** the earnestness of love, to |
| W-pI...158.9:3 | lies beyond them comes to **t.** their place. |
| W-pI...159.9:1 | **T.** from His storehouse, that its treasures |
| W-pI...160.3:2 | had asked this stranger in to **t.** your place, |
| W-pI...161.1:1 | and **t.** a stand against our anger, that our |
| W-pI...161.9:4 | Yet you will **t.** his hand instead, for you |
| W-pI.161.11:5 | sacred hands can **t.** away the nails which |
| W-pI...163.3:4 | never fail to **t.** all life as hostage to itself. |
| W-pI...163.8:8 | This the stand we **t.** today. And it is given |
| W-pI...167.4:3 | **t.** on qualities the source does not contain |
| W-pI...169.9:3 | We merely **t.** the part assigned long since, |
| W-pI.169.11:5 | on. As you **t.** the role assigned to you, |
| WpI...rV.in1:4 | We would **t.** this step completely, that we |
| WpI...rV.in5:2 | Every step we **t.** brings us a little nearer. |
| WpI...rV.in6:1 | I **t.** the journey with you. For I share your |
| WpI...rV.in9:6 | **T.** your brother's hand, for this is not a |
| W-pI...182.8:3 | In that instant He will **t.** you to His home, |
| W-pI.182.11:1 | **T.** time today to lay aside your shield |
| W-pI.182.11:5 | and **t.** illusions as your gods no more. |
| W-pI...184.8:6 | his mind consents to **t.** the name you give |
| W-pI...184.9:1 | yet were asked to **t.** a teaching function. |
| W-pI.184.12:5 | of the world to **t.** the place of Heaven. In |
| W-pI...185.4:7 | Illusions come to **t.** His place. And what |
| W-pI...185.9:7 | shift and change with every step you **t.**. |
| W-pI.185.12:5 | that ever seemed to **t.** the place of truth. |
| W-pI.185.13:3 | To **t.** away is meaningless to Him. And |
| W-pI...186.1:1 | day **t.** all arrogance away from every mind |
| W-pI...186.2:7 | Our minds are suited perfectly to **t.** the |
| W-pI...187.6:3 | the many forms which sacrifice may **t.**. He |
| W-pI...187.7:4 | all the forms that suffering appears to **t.**. |
| W-pI...187.9:5 | blessedness you will behold will **t.** away |
| W-pI...188.9:2 | We **t.** our wandering thoughts, and gently |
| W-pI.193.13:6 | God will **t.** this final step Himself. Do not |
| W-pI.193.13:7 | deny the little steps He asks you **t.** to Him |
| W-pI...195.2:3 | partly sane refuse to **t.** the steps which He |
| W-pI...196.4:1 | Today's idea is one step we **t.** in leading |
| W-pI...196.4:2 | Let us **t.** this step today, that we may |
| W-pI...196.8:1 | steps will be easy, if you **t.** this one today. |
| W-pI...197.1:1 | Here is the second step we **t.** to free your |
| W-pI...197.4:6 | And would you **t.** them back, when He |
| W-pI...197.6:2 | But learn to let forgiveness **t.** away the |
| W-pI...198.6:7 | the Word of God will come to **t.** its place, |
| W-pI...199.5:2 | it a part of every practice period you **t.**. |
| WpI rVI.in.1:1 | this review we **t.** but one idea each day, |
| WpI rVI.in.6:4 | and let it **t.** the place of what you thought. |
| W-pII ....in.2:3 | promised He will **t.** the final step Himself. |
| W-pII ....in.4:1 | for Him to **t.** the step to us that He has |
| W-pII ....in.4:1 | would not fail to **t.** when we invited Him. |
| W-pII ....in.6:5 | **t.** that world to be the full replacement of |
| W-pII ..... 1.1:7 | free to **t.** its place is now the Will of God. |
| W-pII . 228.1:4 | Or shall I **t.** His Word for what I am, since |
| W-pII ..... 4.1:2 | seeks to let illusions **t.** the place of truth. |
| W-pII ..... 7.5:4 | to **t.** the function of completing God, |
| W-pII ..... 8.5:2 | instant more for God to **t.** His final step, |
| W-pII ..... 8.5:4 | Who calls to us and comes to **t.** us home, |
| W-pII . 295.1:2 | to me, and **t.** away all terror and all pain. |
| W-pII ..... 9.1:3 | to God's Word to **t.** illusion's place; the |
| W-pII . 309.2:1 | *The step I* **t.** *today, my Father, is my sure* |
| W-pII . 317.1:2 | Salvation waits until I **t.** this part as what |
| W-pII . 318.2:1 | **t.** *the role You offer me in Your request that I* |
| W-pII . 324.1:2 | *You have set the way I am to go, the role to* **t.**, |
| W-pII . 327.1:1 | I am not asked to **t.** salvation on the basis |
| W-pII . 327.1:4 | and **t.** me farther and still farther on the |
| W-pII . 330.1:3 | and bids them **t.** what is already theirs? |
| W-pII . 332.1:6 | and **t.** its rightful place within the mind. |
| W-pII . 342.2:2 | I come to you to **t.** you home with me. |
| W-pII . 343.1:4 | *You never* **t.** *away. And You created me to be* |
| M-2 ........... 4:7 | but seems to **t.** time in the working-out. |
| M-7 ........... 5:3 | This illusion can **t.** many forms. Perhaps |
| M-13 ......... 1:6 | before another thought system can **t.** hold |
| M-15 ....... 2:11 | you still attempt to **t.** His role from Him? |
| M-16 ......... 4:7 | as possible after waking **t.** your quiet time |
| M-16 ......... 5:2 | for you to **t.** it just before going to sleep. It |
| M-17 ......... 4:5 | Or it may also **t.** the form of intense rage, |
| M-17 ......... 8:8 | Now it is possible to **t.** the next step. The |
| M-22 ......... 2:7 | decided on the direction he wants to **t.**. |
| M-22 ......... 3:5 | do as it sees fit could merely **t.** the place of |
| M-23 ......... 6:9 | He will **t.** you with him, for he did not go |
| M-24 ......... 3:1 | to **t.** any definite stand on reincarnation. |
| M-28 ......... 1:8 | is the invitation to God to **t.** His final step |
| M-28 ......... 6:3 | face to **t.** the place of what they dream. |
| C-6 ............ 5:8 | no longer to **t.** form but to return to the |
| P-1............. 5:3 | His Teacher will **t.** him on from there, as |
| P-2........... I.4:6 | cannot **t.** more than he can give for now. |
| P-2........ IV.7:8 | It will escape and **t.** another form, being |
| P-2....... VII.9:4 | saint can come to **t.** you home with him? |
| P-3.......II.7:10 | so. They **t.** the place of other images, and |
| P-3........II.10:5 | Will of God that he **t.** his place in the plan |
| S-1........... I.6:7 | be and whatever form he may seem to **t.**. |
| S-1........ III.5:5 | **T.** his blessing, and feel how your heart is |
| S-2..........II.1:3 | it may seem to **t.** have but this single goal; |
| S-2..........II.6:1 | Forgiveness-to-destroy can also **t.** the |
| S-2..........II.7:6 | **T.** nothing else, or you have sought your |
| S-2........ III.3:4 | Own. Let Him **t.** charge of how you would |
| S-2........ III.4:6 | not the form that dreams may seem to **t.**. |
| S-3..........II.6:2 | to **t.** its vengeance on the Son of God. Yet |

## taken 52

| | |
|---|---|
| T-1 .........II.6:7 | that might have **t.** thousands of years. It |
| T-4 ....... III.8:3 | **t.** the first step toward preparing your |
| T-5 .......... I.6:6 | over," since the last step is **t.** by God. |
| T-6 ..... V.A.6:8 | Having **t.** the first step, however, they will |
| T-6 ..... V.C.5:7 | final step will still be **t.** for you by God, |
| T-7 .......... I.6:3 | reawakening of knowledge is **t.** by God. |
| T-9 ...... VII.6:7 | is **t.** for granted there and you do not ask, |
| T-10 ..... III.4:4 | is the belief that power can be **t.** from you |
| T-11 ..... VI.7:1 | and **t.** the last thorn from his forehead. |
| T-12 ......... I.8:4 | you would have **t.** a step away from reality |
| T-13 ... VIII.3:2 | the last step must be **t.** by God, because |
| T-14 ......... I.3:6 | They will not be **t.** from him. But they can |
| T-15 ......... I.9:3 | has **t.** time to misguide you so completely, |
| T-16 ..... III.4:7 | this part that you have **t.** in that is not you |
| T-16 ....... V.8:2 | self is "loved" for what can be **t.** from him |
| T-16 ..... VI.5:5 | more is left outside than would be **t.** in, |
| T-16 ..... VI.5:5 | in, for God is left without and *nothing* **t.** in |
| T-17 ........II.3:1 | This step, the smallest ever **t.**, is still the |
| T-17 ..... III.3:4 | of value. Every step **t.** in the making, the |
| T-17 ....... V.6:5 | purify what He has **t.** under His guidance? |
| T-18 ......... I.4:2 | It has **t.** many forms, because it was the |
| T-18 ......... I.9:1 | has **t.** charge of everything at your request |
| T-19 ..... IV.3:8 | When God has **t.** the last step Himself, |
| T-21 ........II.5:8 | it **t.** from him and be replaced with truth. |
| T-22 ....... V.3:2 | whole, and nothing has been **t.** from it. |
| T-23 ........II.9:3 | law is the belief you have what you have **t.** |
| T-23 ......II.10:4 | so they must take or else be **t.** from. |
| T-23 ......II.11:5 | For it was **t.** from you by this enemy, and |
| T-23 ......II.22:2 | For having **t.** one, you will not recognize |
| T-24 ........II.8:3 | you made on him has **t.** from him the gift |
| T-24 ..... III.2:6 | seems to give you power has **t.** it away. |
| T-24 .... VII.7:3 | nothing to add and nothing **t.** from; not |
| T-25 ... VIII.4:7 | cost. The rest is **t.** from another, to be laid |
| T-26 .... VII.7:5 | proclaiming sin has **t.** His reality from |
| T-28 ..... VI.5:1 | Sickness is anger **t.** out upon the body, so |
| W-pI .... 37.1:4 | one loses; nothing is **t.** away from anyone; |
| W-pI .... 57.5:4 | upon has **t.** on the light of my forgiveness, |
| W-pI .... 66.9:2 | of your function has **t.** in your mind, and |
| W-pI .... 77.4:3 | never **t.** from one and given to another, |
| W-pI .. 131.5:4 | Yet not because it has been **t.** from you. It |
| W-pI .. 158.3:4 | It has already been **t.** by him, although he |
| W-pII ..... 4.2:5 | by the aim the mind has **t.** as replacement |
| W-pII ... 13.4:1 | The miracle is **t.** first on faith, because to |
| M-4 ..... I.A.3:3 | It seems as if things are being **t.** away, and |
| M-4 ..... I.A.5:4 | valueless unless the next obvious step is **t.** |
| M-17 ........... 9:9 | Let this grim sword be **t.** from you now. |
| M-18 ......... 3:2 | belief is **t.** as replacement for God's Word |
| M-18 ......... 3:9 | *been* **t.** *from its throne by your mistakes.* |
| M-20 ......... 4:5 | you must have **t.** it again as your defense. |
| M-22 ....... 1:10 | The teacher of God has **t.** accepting the |
| M-27 ......... 1:6 | path,–all this is **t.** as the Will of God. |
| C-6 ............ 1:4 | Voice for God, and has therefore **t.** form. |

## taker 1

| | |
|---|---|
| W-pI .. 105.1:4 | the gift; the **t.** is the richer by his loss. |

## takes 134

|  |  |
|---|---|
| T-1 II.6:6 | the time a miracle **t.** and the time it covers |
| T-1 III.9:3 | selectivity **t.** no account of the magnitude |
| T-4 II.2:4 | when the interaction **t.** place in the mind |
| T-4 VII.5:4 | Divine Abstraction **t.** joy in sharing. That |
| T-5 II.3:10 | It **t.** effort and great willingness to learn. |
| T-5 V.5:8 | then **t.** this intent as its own prerogative. |
| T-6 V.A.2:4 | **t.** what you have made and translates it |
| T-6 V.A.5:11 | all. He never **t.** anything back, because He |
| T-8 II.6:1 | Holy Spirit's teaching **t.** only *one* direction |
| T-11 IV.4:3 | denial of this simple fact **t.** many forms, |
| T-11 V.10:1 | regardless of the form it **t.** and quite apart |
| T-11 VIII.7:2 | You believe in a world that **t.**, because |
| T-12 I.3:4 | and help, regardless of the form it **t.**. Can |
| T-14 IV.3:9 | For in the end, whatever form it **t.**, your |
| T-15 I.2:1 | may suffer is your belief that this **t.** time, |
| T-15 I.9:1 | This lesson **t.** no time. For what is time |
| T-15 I.9:3 | but it **t.** no time at all to be what you are. |
| T-15 I.11:4 | It **t.** far longer to teach you to be willing to |
| T-15 I.14:2 | long as it **t.** to re-establish perfect sanity, |
| T-15 I.14:3 | As long as it **t.** to remember immortality, |
| T-15 I.14:4 | long as it **t.** to exchange hell for Heaven. |
| T-15 IV.1:1 | you believe that what God wills **t.** time. |
| T-15 VII.10:2 | Anger **t.** many forms, but it cannot long |
| T-15 VIII.5:4 | respond to every need, whatever form it **t.** |
| T-15 X.4:4 | For though the ego **t.** many forms, it is |
| T-15 X.6:6 | the ego **t.** to protect itself from your sight. |
| T-16 IV.6:3 | illusion is one of fear, whatever form it **t.**. |
| T-16 V.3:6 | and everything here **t.** a direction exactly |
| T-16 VII.2:1 | relationship **t.** vengeance on the past. By |
| T-18 I.8:3 | The Holy Spirit **t.** you gently by the hand, |
| T-18 VI.14:2 | expansion of awareness that **t.** place with |
| T-20 III.9:2 | It **t.** a while for them to understand what |
| T-20 V.6:4 | The past **t.** nothing from it, and the future |
| T-21 VI.4:1 | that drives it out of mind, and **t.** its place. |
| T-21 VI.4:2 | attack, but **t.** the place of madness quietly |
| T-22 III.3:6 | form it **t.** cannot conceal its emptiness |
| T-23 II.9:1 | The ego values only what it **t.**. This leads |
| T-23 II.16:7 | Some forms it **t.** seem to have meaning, |
| T-23 II.17:8 | it matter what the form this madness **t.**? |
| T-23 II.17:10 | not deceived when madness **t.** a form you |
| T-23 III.1:9 | intent is death, what matter the form it **t.** |
| T-23 III.5:3 | that murder **t.** some forms by which their |
| T-23 III.6:11 | the form that murder **t.** can offer safety? |
| T-23 IV.1:8 | asked to realize the form it **t.** conceals the |
| T-24 I.3:2 | This **t.** many forms, but always clashes |
| T-24 V.1:4 | Specialness, too, **t.** joy in what it sees, |
| T-24 VII.1:11 | of God's creation that **t.** the place of yours |
| T-25 I.7:1 | All this **t.** note of time and place as if they |
| T-25 VI.6:4 | as each one **t.** his part in its undoing, as |
| T-25 VII.4:6 | this belief depends upon the form it **t.**. |
| T-25 VIII.4:4 | that is vengeance in whatever form it **t.**. |
| T-26 II.4:7 | And so He **t.** the thorns and nails away. |
| T-26 VII.3:7 | What is perceived **t.** many forms, but |
| T-26 VII.9:1 | Forgiveness **t.** away what stands between |
| T-26 VII.13:3 | but adds to its abundance, never **t.** away. |
| T-26 VIII.1:3 | are one illusion, which **t.** different forms. |
| T-26 VIII.6:1 | out of all correction **t.** no time at all. Yet |
| T-27 I.7:1 | justified, is sickness in whatever form it **t.**. |
| T-27 I.9:4 | only **t.** away from it all signs of accusation |
| T-27 IV.4:8 | Whatever form the question **t.**, its |
| T-27 IV.4:17 | that what it states **t.** question's form. |
| T-27 VIII.1:3 | It **t.** the central place in every dream, |
| T-27 VIII.2:1 | The dreaming of the world **t.** many forms |
| T-27 VIII.3:3 | Though the dream itself **t.** many forms, |
| T-27 VIII.10:3 | true. Whoever **t.** the role of enemy and of |
| T-27 VIII.11:1 | free from suffering, whatever form it **t.**. |
| T-27 VIII.11:4 | this one answer **t.** away the cause of every |
| T-28 I.1:4 | It does not add, but merely **t.** away. And |
| T-28 I.1:5 | And what it **t.** away is long since gone, |
| T-28 I.6:3 | Time neither **t.** away nor can restore. And |
| T-28 VI.2:7 | It **t.** no sides and judges not the road it |
| T-29 IV.6:7 | which lights whatever form it **t.** with love. |
| T-29 V.7:5 | Each form it **t.** in some way calls for death |
| T-29 VII.6:4 | No idol **t.** His place. Look not to idols. Do |
| T-29 VIII.8:10 | And when one fails another **t.** its place, |
| T-29 VIII.8:11 | not deceived by forms the "something" **t.**. |
| T-30 I.13:2 | But this **t.** practice in the rules that will |
| T-30 IV.2:2 | bear begins to squeak as he **t.** hold of it. |
| T-30 V.1:3 | is perceived and **t.** the place of idols, |
| T-30 VIII.2:5 | happy dream about him **t.** the form of the |
| T-31 II.10:4 | It **t.**, perhaps, a different form in him, but |
| W-pI 15.1:7 | It **t.** the place of seeing, replacing vision |
| W-pI 72.7:5 | Your chosen savior **t.** His place instead. It |
| W-pI 79.6:2 | is separation, no matter what form it **t.**, |
| W-pI 90.1:6 | welcome of the miracle that **t.** its place. |
| W-pI 121.10:2 | not matter what the form your anger **t.**. |
| W-pI 124.1:4 | Everything we touch **t.** on a shining light |
| W-pI 126.9:2 | thought by which forgiveness **t.** its proper |
| W-pI 129.2:4 | **t.** away all things that you have cherished |
| W-pI 130.11:3 | say to any part of hell, whatever form it **t.**, |
| W-pI 136.6:1 | Every defense **t.** fragments of the whole, |
| W-pI 140.1:5 | One belief in sickness **t.** another form, |
| W-pI 140.4:5 | It **t.** away the guilt that makes the sickness |
| W-pI 140.6:6 | or anything that is related to the form it **t.** |
| W-pI 151.14:2 | **t.** on healing power from the Mind which |
| W-pI 157.5:1 | your ministry **t.** on a genuine devotion, |
| W-pI 158.3:3 | no step along the road that anyone **t.** but |
| W-pI 163.1:1 | Death is a thought that **t.** on many forms, |
| W-pI 163.8:7 | form it **t.** must therefore be illusion. This |
| W-pI 167.2:3 | that the idea of death **t.** many forms. It is |
| W-pI 168.3:4 | and **t.** us in His Arms and sweeps away |
| W-pI 170.8:6 | it? For the god of cruelty **t.** many forms. |
| W-pI 185.3:5 | ratio of gain to loss and loss to gain **t.** on a |
| W-pI 185.4:2 | Sometimes it **t.** the form of union, but |
| W-pI 185.6:3 | Whatever form the lesson **t.** is planned |
| W-pI 186.13:5 | and what is given in His Name **t.** on the |
| W-pI 187.2:7 | Nor can the form it **t.** be less acceptable. |
| W-pI 190.1:4 | it **t.** that will not disappear if seen aright. |
| W-pI 194.1:1 | Today's idea **t.** another step toward quick |
| W-pI 195.3:1 | peace; a plunderer who **t.** his joy from you |
| W-pII 298.1:3 | on my holy sight forgiveness **t.** away. And |
| W-pII 312.1:5 | the holy sight of anyone who **t.** the Holy |
| W-pII 315.1:4 | mind receives this gift and **t.** it as its own. |
| W-pII 12.1:2 | enemy, and **t.** a form in which it is denied. |
| W-pII 345.1:3 | *it t. a form which can be recognized and seen* |
| M-4 I.A.4:5 | It **t.** great learning to understand that all |
| M-7 4:7 | of love, regardless of the form it **t.**. Doubt |
| M-13 2:1 | It **t.** great learning both to realize and to |
| M-17 5:8 | Who usurps the place of God and **t.** it for |
| M-26 4:10 | God **t.** you where you are and welcomes |
| C-1 5:3 | in which God **t.** the final step Himself. |
| C-4 5:6 | as surely as forgiveness **t.** all guilt away. |
| C-5 6:3 | For Christ **t.** many forms with different |
| P-2 IV.8:2 | of threat differs according to the form it **t.** |
| P-2 V.6:6 | To ask for help, whatever form it **t.**, is but |
| P-2 VI.4:5 | the form it **t.** seems to be something else. |
| P-2 VI.5:1 | Sickness **t.** many forms, and so does |
| P-2 VI.5:3 | careful study of the form a sickness **t.** will |
| P-2 VII.3:1 | process that **t.** place in this relationship is |
| S-1 in.2:1 | prayer **t.** the form that best will suit your |
| S-2 II.8:1 | All forms forgiveness **t.** that do not lead |
| S-2 III.3:1 | form should be that Christ's forgiveness **t.** |
| S-2 III.5:2 | form the seeking **t.** you need not judge. |
| S-3 II.5:1 | eyes and **t.** the form of punishment for sin |

## taketh 2

|  |  |
|---|---|
| T-3 I.5:1 | of God who **t.** away the sins of the world," |
| T-3 I.6:4 | lamb "**t.** away the sins of the world" in the |

## taking 24

|  |  |
|---|---|
| T-5 IV.6:2 | you find the way except by **t.** your brother |
| T-7 VII.8:3 | then believe that others are **t.** it from you. |
| T-11 VIII.5:10 | you believe that asking is **t.** rather than |
| T-11 VIII.7:2 | because you believe that you can get by **t.**. |
| T-14 V.6:1 | **t.** their part in the unified curriculum of |
| T-16 V.7:6 | And he feels guilty for the "sin" of **t.**, and |
| T-25 I.7:5 | the truth, **t.** all false ideas of what you are, |
| T-28 II.8:3 | against him, **t.** on the role of its creator, as |
| T-28 II.12:4 | glad effects of **t.** back the consequence of |
| T-31 I.4:3 | have continued, **t.** every step, however |
| W-pI 23.5:6 | By **t.** the first two steps, you will see that |
| W-pI 44.7:4 | it. It is merely **t.** its natural course. Try to |
| W-pI 51.1:4 | I think I see now is **t.** the place of vision. I |
| W-pI 61.2:3 | your role in salvation and in **t.** no other. It |
| W-pI 61.3:3 | a giant stride toward **t.** your rightful place |
| W-pI 64.1:3 | His Son by **t.** on a physical appearance. It |
| W-pI 101.3:3 | **t.** everything away before it grants the |
| W-pI 138.6:4 | but conceal this one by **t.** different forms. |
| W-pI 168.3:2 | lifts us up, **t.** salvation's final step Himself |
| W-pI 190.8:1 | Pain is the thought of evil **t.** form, and |
| W-pI 196.4:2 | us, **t.** every step in its appointed sequence |
| W-pI 197.3:4 | this you would undo by **t.** back your gifts, |
| W-pII 8.5:2 | **t.** perception with it as it goes, and |
| M-25 3:5 | **T.** them as ends in themselves, no matter |

## tale 2

|  |  |
|---|---|
| W-pI 153.14:4 | that everyone may learn the **t.** he reads of |
| W-pI 153.14:5 | bewildered memory of this distorted **t.**. |

## talent 1

|  |  |
|---|---|
| T-2 II.7:8 | you assume your natural **t.** of protecting |

## talented 1

|  |  |
|---|---|
| S-3 III.2:4 | trained, or is perhaps more **t.** and wise. |

## talents 1

|  |  |
|---|---|
| T-1 V.3:1 | all **t.** will be shared by all the Sons of God. |

## tales 2

|  |  |
|---|---|
| T-9 IV.11:6 | Fairy **t.** can be pleasant or fearful, but no |
| T-9 IV.11:7 | so, for a while, the **t.** are true for them. |

## talk 2

|  |  |
|---|---|
| T-29 IX.4:6 | **t.** and think and feel and speak for them. |
| P-2 III.3:8 | or **t.** to him or even know of his existence. |

## talking 1

|  |  |
|---|---|
| W-pI 25.4:4 | is for the purpose of **t.** to someone who is |

## tall 1

|  |  |
|---|---|
| T-24 II.1:6 | you see in him you stand as **t.** and stately, |

## tampering 1

|  |  |
|---|---|
| T-2 VII.1:4 | be **t.** with a basic law of cause and effect; |

## tangential 1

|  |  |
|---|---|
| T-4 V.6:4 | By becoming involved with **t.** issues, it |

## tangible 3

|  |  |
|---|---|
| T-29 VIII.3:2 | An idol is a wish, made **t.** and given form, |
| W-pI 130.9:3 | expressed in **t.** perception and in truth. |
| M-5 II.2:9 | chooses them in order to bring **t.** form to |

## tantrums 1

|  |  |
|---|---|
| T-18 II.4:1 | Dreams are perceptual temper **t.**, in |

## target 4

|  |  |
|---|---|
| T-21 VII.5:1 | Yet hate must have a **t.**. There can be no |
| T-27 II.13:4 | sins become the central **t.** for correction, |
| W-pI 78.4:4 | you have used as **t.** for your grievances, |
| W-pI 161.6:5 | The body is the **t.** for attack, for no one |

## tarnish 3

|  |  |
|---|---|
| W-pI 133.8:7 | to protect its goals from **t.** and from rust, |
| W-pI 133.10:2 | because he looks upon the **t.** as his own; |
| W-pI 186.6:5 | Sin can not **t.** the truth in you, and misery |

## tarnished 1

| | |
|---|---|
| W-pI.133.10:1 | he perceive its t. edges and its rusted core. |

## tarry 1

| | |
|---|---|
| W-pII .324.2:2 | way. We need not t., and we cannot stray |

## task 43

| | |
|---|---|
| T-5....... II.10:7 | Our t. is the joyous one of waking it to the |
| T-5........ III.5:5 | the t. of undoing what the ego has made. |
| T-5........ III.7:7 | It is therefore the t. of the Holy Spirit to |
| T-7...........I.6:5 | Holy Spirit has the t. of translating the |
| T-8...........I.6:3 | presents an impossible learning t.. They |
| T-8........ IX.9:4 | Your t. is only to meet the conditions for |
| T-9........ III.2:6 | But your t. is still to tell him he is right. |
| T-12....... II.1:5 | The t. of the miracle worker thus becomes |
| T-13... VII.17:2 | My t. is not completed until I have lifted |
| T-14.........I.4:6 | set yourself the t. of sharing what cannot |
| T-14....... II.7:8 | join Him in the holy t. of bringing light. |
| T-14...... IV.8:1 | Your t. is not to make reality. It is here |
| T-14..... VII.5:9 | His t. is mighty, but the power of God is |
| T-15...... III.4:5 | littleness is a t. the little cannot undertake |
| T-15...... III.7:2 | our t. together to restore the awareness of |
| T-15...... IX.2:1 | t. is but to continue, as fast as possible, |
| T-16....... II.5:5 | For His t. is to translate the miracle into |
| T-16...... IV.6:1 | Your t. is not to seek for love, but merely |
| T-16.... VI.12:4 | It is His t. to atone for your unwillingness |
| T19.... IV.C.9:3 | the mighty t. for which it was given you. |
| T-21....... II.8:5 | Undoing is not your t., but it *is* up to you |
| T-25.........I.1:1 | do the t. that Christ appointed you to do, |
| T-25....... II.3:2 | and unrewarding t. you set yourself. Can |
| T-25....... V.5:6 | allow him freedom to complete the t. God |
| T-26.........I.6:2 | nor keep the Holy Spirit from His t. of |
| T-26.........I.8:6 | be a t. apart and separate from His Own? |
| T-31.......I.7:10 | you may have overlearned your chosen t., |
| T-31..... VII.1:3 | and changing concepts is salvation's t.. |
| W-pI..... 64.3:2 | of the t. assigned to you by God Himself. |
| W-pI... 131.4:6 | off, he is led back to his appointed t.. |
| W-pI... 154.9:4 | appointed t. is yet to be accomplished. He |
| W-pII ..... 5.2:3 | and do the t. his mind assigns to them. |
| M-18 ......... 1:3 | it is their t. to escape from what is real. |
| M-22 ......... 6:7 | It is your t. to heal the sense of separation |
| M-24 ......... 2:2 | t. would still be only to escape from them |
| M-27 ......... 7:4 | Now it becomes your t. to let the illusion |
| C-4............ 7:3 | Gone is forgiveness, for its t. is done. And |
| P-in............ 1:8 | Either way, the t. is the same; the patient |
| P-2.........in.4:2 | The t. of therapy is one of reconciling |
| P-2........ IV.9:4 | In fact, this is his central t.; the core of |
| P-2...... IV.10:3 | It is his t. to demonstrate that defenses |
| P-2........ VI.3:3 | Their t. is to make agreeable whatever is |
| S-2........ III.2:7 | Forgiveness-for-salvation is His t., and it |

## tasks 2

| | |
|---|---|
| T-14... VII.5:13 | You are not asked to do mighty t. yourself |
| W-pI... 98.11:1 | be thankful and lay down all earthly t., all |

## taste 1

| | |
|---|---|
| W-pI... 163.3:1 | leave the t. of dust and ashes in their wake |

## tastes 1

| | |
|---|---|
| W-pI... 160.3:3 | were another home more suited to his t.. |

## taught 101

| | |
|---|---|
| T-in ........... 1:6 | *of love, for that is beyond what can be t.. It* |
| T-3...........I.7:9 | that all the other lessons I t. are true. If |
| T-4...........I.3:1 | Spirit need not be t., but the ego must be. |
| T-4.......... VI.5:7 | You have t. yourself the opposite. You are |
| T-5...........I.4:6 | Inspiration, t. me first and foremost that |
| T-6.........I.15:3 | is clearly the opposite of everything I t.. |
| T-6........ III.1:8 | t. yourself to believe that you are not what |
| T-6........ V.1:2 | Him. You had already t. yourself wrongly, |
| T-6.... V.B.3:10 | you are being t. to react to both as if what |
| T-7......... V.2:6 | lesson will be poorly t. and poorly learned |
| T-8...........I.4:1 | must have t. you the wrong things, simply |
| T-8 .........II.2:8 | When you are t. against your nature, |
| T-8 .........II.5:3 | t. yourself that imprisonment is freedom. |
| T-8 .........II.5:5 | that t. you to believe they are the same, to |
| T-8 ........ V.6:2 | all minds, and the one He t. me is yours. |
| T-8 ....... IX.5:3 | if He t. that one form of sickness is more |
| T-9 ....... VI.3:2 | learning is the result of what you t. them. |
| T-10 ..... III.4:3 | t. by sick minds too divided to know that |
| T-12 ........I.8:7 | then. Having t. you to accept only loving |
| T-12 ........I.8:7 | t. you that fear itself is an appeal for help. |
| T-12 ..... IV.3:3 | quite apparent that it had not t. you the |
| T-12 ...... V.8:5 | appraisal of what you have t. yourself, |
| T-13 .. VII.17:8 | that you have t. how to remember you. |
| T-14 ........I.1:2 | be so. The knowledge is not t., but its |
| T-14 .......II.4:9 | Because you t. them gladness and release, |
| T-14 ... III.18:1 | You t. yourself the most unnatural habit |
| T-14 ..... IV.2:6 | This cannot be t.. Learning applies only |
| T-14 ...... V.6:3 | which has one aim however it is t.. Each |
| T-14 ..... IX.6:7 | it because he has been t. his need for it, |
| T-14 ..... XI.1:5 | Everything you have t. yourself has made |
| T-14 ..... XI.2:2 | For you have t. yourself how to imprison |
| T-14 ..... XI.2:5 | t. yourself that you can possibly prefer to |
| T-14 ..... XI.3:1 | that you have t. yourself in the past, by |
| T-14 ..... XI.3:6 | Your past is what you have t. yourself. *Let* |
| T-14 ..... XI.4:1 | you have t. yourself into the light in you, |
| T-14 ..... XI.6:1 | from everything that you have t. yourself. |
| T-14 ..... XI.6:5 | want. Ask to be t., and do not use your |
| T-15 ......I.10:5 | t. by those who cannot see themselves as |
| T-15 ...... V.3:6 | The past has t. you this. Yet the holy |
| T-16 ..... III.1:2 | You may have t. well, and yet you may |
| T-16 ..... III.1:3 | If you will consider what you have t., and |
| T-16 ..... III.1:6 | For certainly what He has t., and what |
| T-16 ..... III.1:6 | and what you have t. through Him, have |
| T-16 ..... III.1:6 | common with what you t. before He came |
| T-16 ..... III.2:1 | You may have t. freedom, but you have |
| T-16 ..... III.2:7 | have so diligently t. yourself to believe? |
| T-16 ..... III.3:1 | what you have t. show you that you do |
| T-16 ..... III.3:4 | have t. freedom unless you did believe in |
| T-16 ..... III.3:5 | be that what you t. came from yourself. |
| T-16 ..... III.4:2 | You have t. what you are, but have not let |
| T-16 ..... III.4:4 | Yet within you is everything you t.. What |
| T-16 ..... III.6:4 | is. You have t. this, and from far off in the |
| T-16 ..... III.6:5 | to strengthen your faith in what you t.. |
| T-16 ..... III.6:6 | For what you t. is true. Alone, you stand |
| T-16 ..... III.6:8 | you must learn that you but t. yourself, |
| T-16 ..... VI.3:3 | the ego has t. you that freedom lies in it. |
| T-16 ..... VI.9:2 | the thought system that t. you it was real, |
| T-17 ..... III.2:8 | Your own experience has t. you this. But |
| T19..IV.A.13:3 | have been t. to seek for the corruptible, |
| T19.... IV.B.8:2 | the freedom that I t. by teaching freedom |
| T-20 .... VII.8:4 | Judgment you t. yourself; vision is learned |
| T-21 ........I.7:5 | melody you t. yourself to cherish since. |
| T-21 ..... VI.6:3 | you will learn of him exactly what you t.. |
| T-22 ........I.8:4 | t. him what he knows *because* you knew it. |
| T-24 .... VII.8:9 | Yet it but witnesses to what you t.. It is |
| T-25 ........I.5:6 | world this is not understood, but can be t. |
| T-27 ...... V.7:3 | remind you gently of what you have t.. No |
| T-27 .... V.10:2 | part is merely to apply what He has t. you |
| T-27 ... VIII.3:3 | has but one purpose, t. in many ways. |
| T-28 ........I.7:1 | Remember nothing that you t. yourself, |
| T-28 ........I.7:1 | you taught yourself, for you were badly t.. |
| T-31 ........I.2:7 | t. yourself is such a giant learning feat it is |
| T-31 ........I.3:4 | lessons you have t. yourself have been so |
| T-31 ........I.4:6 | have t. yourself the Son of God is guilty, |
| T-31 ........I.6:6 | t. to you in every moment of each day, |
| T-31 .......II.9:1 | ancient lessons you have t. yourself about |
| W-pI..... 24.2:1 | interests, you could be t. what they are. |
| W-pI... 121.6:3 | sin. As sin is an idea you t. yourself, |
| W-pI. 126.10:3 | Be willing to be t.. Be glad to hear the |
| W-pI. 135.11:3 | It waits until it has been t. what should be |
| W-pI. 135.15:4 | rests on the idea the past has t. enough to |
| W-pI. 151.15:3 | So are you t. to teach the Son of God the |
| W-pI... 158.2:9 | time determined by the mind itself, not t.. |
| W-pI... 158.8:1 | This can be t.; and must be taught by all |
| W-pI... 158.8:1 | and must be t. by all who would achieve it |
| W-pI... 161.4:7 | The mind that t. itself to think specifically |
| W-pI... 169.7:2 | Yet forgiveness, t. and learned, brings |
| W-pI... 189.7:4 | bring with you one thought the past has t. |
| W-pII .... in.6:2 | gratitude to Him Who t. us how to leave |
| M-1 ........... 3:6 | It can be t. by actions or thoughts; in |
| M-10 ......... 1:7 | what these categories are be really t.. At |
| M-17 ......... 3:2 | A lesson truly t. can lead to nothing but |
| M-17 ......... 8:4 | It can be learned and t., but it requires |
| P-2..........II.3:2 | Forgiveness, then, is all that need be t., |
| P-2..........V.1:1 | must still be t. to those who have already |
| P-2..........V.2:5 | Yet it must be t. to those who think it will |
| P-2..........V.2:6 | It must be t. to those who will attack |
| P-3..........II.2:2 | which he became a therapist probably t. |
| P-3..........II.2:3 | it probably t. him how to make healing |
| S-3........ IV.2:1 | to prayer, and the effect of mercy truly t., |
| S-3........ IV.2:6 | has t. to see His likeness and to teach like |

## teach 310

| | |
|---|---|
| T-2 ... V.A.18:6 | *me. I will be healed as I let Him t. me to heal.* |
| T-3 ....... VI.6:3 | attempt to t. you the meaning of mercy. It |
| T-4 ..........I.3:4 | yours, and because I learned it I can t. it. I |
| T-4 ..........I.3:5 | but I am trying to t. you how its thought |
| T-4 ..........I.6:3 | I will t. with you and live with you if you |
| T-4 ........I.13:4 | and lets me t. you their unimportance. I |
| T-4 ........ VI.5:1 | t. someone the value of something he has |
| T-5 .....II.10:10 | t. your brothers to listen as I am teaching |
| T-5 ..... III.10:2 | to t. you that you do not understand it. |
| T-5 ....... IV.1:3 | and t. you that only what is loving is true. |
| T-5 ....... IV.5:3 | forget my need to t. what I have learned, |
| T-5 ....... IV.5:4 | call upon you to t. what you have learned, |
| T-5 ....... IV.6:4 | As you t. so shall you learn. I will never |
| T-5 ....... VI.3:3 | let me t. you how to share it with your |
| T-6 ........ in.2:4 | system of any kind, you live by it and t. it. |
| T-6 ..........I.4:6 | the crucifixion was intended to t. was that |
| T-6 ..........I.5:6 | If you will believe it, you will help me t. it. |
| T-6 ..........I.6:1 | said before, "As you t. so shall you learn." |
| T-6 ..........I.6:3 | to t. if he is to realize his own salvation. |
| T-6 ..........I.6:4 | Rather, t. your own perfect immunity, |
| T-6 ..........I.6:9 | believe there is, and do not t. that there is. |
| T-6 ........I.6:10 | always that what you believe you will t.. |
| T-6 ..........I.7:5 | me. Help me to t. it to our brothers in the |
| T-6 ..........I.7:5 | that it is true for you, or you will t. amiss. |
| T-6 ........I.11:5 | one lesson, which I must t. as I learned it, |
| T-6 ........I.13:2 | clear: *T. only love, for that is what you are.* |
| T-6 ........I.17:5 | reject it. As a result, you will t. rejection. |
| T-6 ........I.18:3 | Each one must learn to t. that all forms of |
| T-6 ........I.18:5 | As long as you t. this you will believe it. |
| T-6 ....... III.1:7 | can hear and t. and learn what is not true. |
| T-6 ....... III.1:9 | You cannot t. what you have not learned, |
| T-6 ....... III.1:9 | t. you strengthen in yourself because you |
| T-6 ..... III.1:10 | it. Every lesson you t. you are learning. |
| T-6 ....... III.2:1 | That is why you must t. only one lesson. |
| T-6 ....... III.2:2 | from the Holy Spirit and t. only by Him. |
| T-6 ....... III.2:4 | of the crucifixion was, "T. only love, for |
| T-6 ....... III.2:7 | "As you t. so will you learn." If that is true |
| T-6 ....... III.2:8 | not forget that what you t. is teaching you |
| T-6 ....... III.3:9 | this. T. attack in any form and you have |
| T-6 ....... III.4:1 | Since you cannot *not* t., your salvation lies |
| T-6 ....... III.4:3 | The only way to have peace is to t. peace. |
| T-6 ....... III.4:4 | you cannot t. what you still dissociate. |
| T-6 ....... III.4:8 | Everything you t. you are learning. Teach |
| T-6 ....... III.4:9 | T. only love, and learn that love is yours |
| T-6 ..... IV.11:7 | frequently said that what you t. you are. |
| T-6 ..... IV.11:8 | you have God t. you that you have sinned |
| T-6 ..... IV.12:1 | God does not t.. To teach is to imply a |
| T-6 ..... IV.12:2 | To t. is to imply a lack, which God knows |
| T-6 ..........V.1:4 | God t. you that you had made a split |
| T-6 ..... V.A.4:5 | thought system I t. and want you to teach. |
| T-6 ..... V.A.4:5 | thought system I teach and want you to t.. |
| T-6 ........ V.B.h | To Have Peace, T. Peace to Learn It |
| T-6 ..... V.B.1:2 | that is what they perceive and t. and learn |
| T-6 ..... V.B.1:4 | you t. you are, but it is quite apparent |
| T-6 ..... V.B.1:4 | is quite apparent that you can t. wrongly, |
| T-6 ..... V.B.1:4 | can therefore t. yourself wrong. Many |
| T-6 ..... V.B.5:3 | If you t. both, which you will surely do as |
| T-6 ..... V.B.7:5 | lesson is: *To have peace, t. peace to learn it.* |
| T-6 ..... V.C.2:1 | Holy Spirit does not t. you to judge others |
| T-6 ..... V.C.2:1 | want you to t. error and learn it yourself. |
| T-6 ..... V.C.2:4 | enables the mind to t. without judgment, |
| T-6 ..... V.C.4:9 | Holy Spirit will ultimately t. you that you |
| T-6 ..... V.C.6:2 | Next you learn that you learn what you t., |
| T-6 ..... V.C.6:5 | to t. you that you must be included, and |
| T-6 ..... V.C.8:1 | t. the whole Sonship without exception |

T-6......V.C.8:2 of its wholeness and will be unable to t. it.
T-6......V.C.9:9 and those who choose to t. the same thing
T-7...........I.7:2 He does not t., because His creations are
T-7........III.2:8 really learn, and therefore cannot really t.
T-7........IV.2:1 work *through* you to t. you He is *in* you.
T-7........IV.3:1 not want to t. everyone all it has learned,
T-7........IV.3:3 to t. the opposite of what the ego has
T-7......... V.2:2 it can only t. you that the body can both
T-7......... V.2:3 ego thus tries to t. you that the body can
T-7......... V.2:5 emphasized, you t. what you *do* believe.
T-7......... V.2:7 If you t. both sickness *and* healing, you are
T-7.......VII.3:8 T. no one that he is what you would not
T-7.......VII.5:7 and t. His way lest you forget yourself.
T-7.......VII.7:1 teacher sufficiently worthy to t. another.
T-7.......VII.7:7 abundance, and t. your brothers theirs.
T-7..... VIII.6:1 will t. you to perceive beyond your belief,
T-7..... VIII.7:1 purpose of this course is to t. you that the
T-7......... X.3:5 function is to t. you to tell them apart.
T-7......... X.7:3 His Voice will t. you how to distinguish
T-7........XI.3:5 Does it t. him that this giving is his joy,
T-7........XI.4:1 you to t. the Kingdom *to* the Kingdom.
T-8......... II.1:4 ego does not know what it is trying to t..
T-8......... II.1:5 It is trying to t. you what you are without
T-8......... II.3:1 ego cannot t. you anything as long as your
T-8......... II.3:7 undoing of everything the ego tries to t..
T-8......... II.4:1 to t. that you want to oppose God's Will.
T-8......... II.5:5 the same, to t. you how they are different?
T-8........III.1:4 of light, and can therefore t. it to you.
T-8........III.1:6 His teaching because He was created to t..
T-8........III.2:4 Holy Spirit understands how to t. this,
T-8........III.3:6 Let the Holy Spirit t. you how to do this,
T-8........III.6:8 you enter fully will t. you this is not so.
T-8......IV.3:11 you, so we can t. them peace and union.
T-8........IV.6:5 I can t. you, but only you can choose to
T-8........IV.6:9 Father. This is the only lesson I came to t..
T-8.......VII.3:2 t. them *through* the body that this is not so
T-8..... VIII.9:1 so He can t. His message through you.
T-8........IX.1:6 Holy Spirit t. you the right *perception* of
T-9........III.5:5 telling you that what you t. you learn?
T-9......III.8:10 He will t. you how to see yourself without
T-9......... V.3:1 but only to t. that they are not real, and
T-9......... V.3:4 t. condemnation and advocate a fearful
T-9......... V.5:8 it is up to him to t. the patient what is real
T-9........VI.3:2 Only they can t. you what you are, for
T-9........VI.5:3 you have given them will t. you its value.
T-11....... II.6:5 God sent you will t. you how to do this, if
T-11..... V.16:6 the ego t. truly when it overlooks truth?
T-11.......VI.3:5 learned *with* beliefs, and experience does t.
T-11.......VI.7:3 T. not that I died in vain. Teach rather
T-11.......VI.7:4 in vain. T. rather that I did not die by
T-11. VIII.15:3 from the Holy Spirit, Who will t. you that,
T-12.........I.9:3 t. yourself that fear does not exist in you.
T-12.......III.1:2 you can t. the poor where their treasure is
T-12.......IV.3:4 and t. you that love really calls forth the
T-12.......IV.3:4 calls forth the responses the ego *can* t..
T-12.......IV.5:6 He fulfills His mission He will t. you yours
T-12....... V.6:2 to t. yourself what you do not understand
T-12....... V.9:2 You can t. the way to Him and learn it, if
T-12.......VI.1:1 The ego is trying to t. you how to gain the
T-12.......VI.2:2 how to t. you to remember what you are.
T-12.......VI.2:3 you, He will gladly t. you what He loves,
T-13....VI.13:9 witnesses that t. him that he never slept.
T-13...VII.16:5 Spirit will t. you to awaken unto us and to
T-13.......IX.5:2 then, t. him he is right in his delusion?
T-13....... X.7:7 He would have you see and t. as He does,
T-13....... X.8:1 *Now* it is given you to heal and t., to make
T-13.......XI.8:6 The Holy Spirit will t. you how to use it,
T-13.......XI.9:2 from what the Holy Spirit wants to t. you.
T-14.........I.3:8 is nothing in the world to t. him that the
T-14.........I.4:2 He must therefore t. you not to deny it.
T-14....... II.1:3 Holy Spirit cannot t. without this contrast
T-14....... II.3:2 learners who would t. themselves nothing
T-14....... II.5:1 When you t. anyone that truth is true,
T-14.......III.6:6 teaches, and would have you t. with Him.
T-14.......III.6:7 It is His joy to t. it, as it will be yours.
T-14.......III.7:1 The way to t. this simple lesson is merely
T-14.......III.7:3 T. him that, whatever he may try to do to
T-14.......III.7:4 he can, you t. him that the Atonement,
T-14.......III.8:2 T. no one he has hurt you, for if you do,

T-14...... III.8:2 you t. yourself that what is not of God has
T-14.... III.13:1 have you follow can t. you what it is. Only
T-14.... III.16:4 t. His answer to everyone who struggles
T-14.... III.19:5 let Him t. you quietly how to perceive
T-14...... IV.5:5 will He t. you to remove the awful burden
T-14...... IV.5:5 and trying to t. him guilt instead of love.
T-14...... IV.9:4 It does not t. you what you are, or what
T-14....... V.2:8 t. you nothing except how to be happy.
T-14....... V.7:3 the power of God if you t. only this. You
T-14....... V.9:1 Blessed are you who t. with me. Our
T-14....... V.9:5 T. peace with me, and stand with me on
T-14....... V.9:7 not that you cannot t. His perfect peace.
T-14...... VI.5:6 would t. you how to use on your behalf.
T-14...... VI.8:4 to Him and let His gentleness t. you that,
T-14...... X.11:5 t. you both his love and his call for love.
T-14...... X.12:4 this course will t. you how to remember
T-14...... XI.3:5 present, or t. you how to undo the past.
T-14.... XI.6:10 refusal to attempt to t. yourself what you
T-14...... XI.9:7 would t. yourself He has corrected already
T-14.... XI.10:1 freed you from the past would t. you are
T-14.... XI.11:6 T. like Him here, and you will remember
T-15.......I.11:4 It takes far longer to t. you to be willing to
T-15....... II.2:4 joy it is to t. God's holy Son his holiness.
T-15...... III.9:4 I would but t. you what is yours, so that
T-15...VII.11:1 The Holy Spirit cannot t. through fear.
T-15...VII.12:4 always t. that loneliness is solved by guilt,
T-15... VIII.1:6 will t. you to remember that forgiveness is
T-15... VIII.5:3 would t. you what you do not understand
T-15... VIII.6:5 is only of God t. you the only meaning of
T-15...... IX.7:2 As you let the Holy Spirit t. you how to
T-15....... X.1:7 it. Let the Holy Spirit t. you, and let me
T-15...... XI.7:5 lesson I was born to t., and still would
T-15...... XI.7:5 teach, and still would t. to all my brothers
T-16.........I.1:5 have you t. it is not understandable.
T-16.........I.5:5 Attempt to t. Him not. You are the
T-16.........I.6:8 He will t. you how to meet both without
T-16....... II.7:4 be a sufficient miracle to t. you that your
T-16...... III.3:3 it is impossible to t. successfully wholly
T-16...... III.4:2 are, but have not let what you are t. you.
T-16...... III.7:2 chosen this by your own willingness to t..
T-16......VII.4:1 and would t. you salvation is past and so
T-16......VII.6:2 Holy Spirit must t. through comparisons,
T-17.........I.5:5 truth to t. that the illusions are unreal,
T-17...... III.2:1 t. you what you do to keep it safe is really
T-18...... III.5:1 will t. you that this goal is possible, and
T-18...... IV.4:7 to make it possible to t. you what they are
T-18......VII.4:5 to t. more than they learned in time, but
T-18...... IX.8:3 Let your Guide t. you their unsubstantial
T-19...... III.5:5 The Holy Spirit can t. you how to look on
T19. IV.A.17:6 I t. that bodies cannot keep us apart?
T19....IV.C.6:2 better way to t. the first and fundamental
T19IV.C.11:10 *T. me how* ***not*** *to make of it an obstacle to*
T-21...... III.6:6 as a means to t. you that the vision of a
T-21...... IV.1:1 Spirit will never t. you that you are sinful.
T-21...... VI.6:3 You t. him this, and you will learn of him
T-21...... VI.6:4 For you can t. him only that he is as you
T-21... VIII.1:3 that t. the thinker that he *can* be killed.
T-22........in.4:1 Think what a holy relationship can t.!
T-22.........I.8:2 will t. you what you do not understand,
T-22.. VI.13:10 truth, to t. you what *is* natural and true.
T-22.... VI.15:3 relationship can also t. the power of love
T-22.... VI.15:7 or the same, and t. you which is true.
T-23.........I.5:1 to t. the Son of God that he is not himself,
T-23...... III.3:8 it would t. a little of the same can still be
T-24.....VII.8:1 to t. what cannot easily be learned. Its
T-24.....VII.8:8 Perception seems to t. you what you see.
T-25.........I.6:4 to t. you how this oneness is experienced,
T-26...... III.5:6 only purpose is to t. what is the same and
T-26...... V.10:2 This course will t. you only what is now.
T-27....... II.5:5 or think but testifies to what you t. to him
T-27....... II.5:6 Your body can be means to t. that it has
T-27... VIII.1:8 all, it tries to t. itself its pains and joys are
T-27... VIII.3:4 This single lesson does it try to t. again,
T-27. VIII.11:5 t. you but the single cause of all of them,
T-27. VIII.12:2 and He will t. you how each one is caused.
T-28.... II.11:5 Yet half the lesson will not t. the whole.
T-28.... II.11:6 for this is not the lesson it was sent to t..
T-29....... II.7:5 for it can be made to t. opposing things.
T-31.........I.3:6 to t. you that your will is not your own,

T-31.........I.5:3 you have learned what it was made to t..
T-31.........I.5:4 and t. you that Its lessons are not true;
T-31...... IV.8:3 This course attempts to t. no more than
T-31...... IV.8:5 when all the lesson's purpose is to t. that
T-31....... V.2:4 the self the world would t. is not the thing
T-31....... V.5:1 that the concept of the self was made to t..
T-31....... V.8:4 except by lessons aimed to t. that you are
T-31..... V.17:1 The world can t. no images of you unless
T-31... VII.15:6 what but this is what this course would t.?
T-31....VIII.1:1 Temptation has one lesson it would t., in
W-pI..... 12.2:6 You t. yourself this as you give whatever
W-pI..... 37.3:2 lets you t. the world that it is one with you
W-pI..... 39.3:5 How else can he t. salvation? Today's
W-pI..... 54.5:5 and let it t. me that my will and the Will
W-pI..... 56.1:8 My own real thoughts will t. me what it is
W-pI..... 90.3:6 The Holy Spirit will t. me this, if I will let
W-pI... 95.12:3 to t. the world the truth about yourself.
W-pI..... 99.9:8 and let Him t. you what you need to learn
W-pI... 101.5:2 The exercises t. sin is not real, and all that
W-pI... 103.2:3 to bring to truth today, and t. ourselves:
W-pI. 106.10:1 so you can t. the world what giving means
W-pI. 108.10:1 simple lesson for today will t. you much.
W-pI... 121.7:1 to t. your own how to forgive itself. Each
W-pI... 121.7:6 And as you t. salvation, you will learn. Yet
W-pI... 127.4:1 No course whose purpose is to t. you to
W-pI... 127.9:5 allow His Voice to t. love's meaning to
W-pI... 132.6:3 central thought the course attempts to t..
W-pI... 132.7:3 on point of death, and rise to t. it. Others
W-pI. 134.13:1 provide a guide to t. you its beneficence.
W-pI. 134.14:4 of forgiveness, and was sent to us to t. it.
W-pI... 137.9:2 gentle lessons t. how easily salvation can
W-pI... 138.5:4 to t. within the framework of this course.
W-pI. 139.10:1 does Atonement t., and demonstrates the
W-pI. 151.10:3 t. the single lesson that they all contain.
W-pI. 151.15:3 So are you taught to t. the Son of God the
W-pI. 153.11:3 while you fail to t. what you have learned,
W-pI. 153.12:2 t. them that the game of fear is gone. His
W-pI... 157.9:3 This you will never t., for you attained it
W-pI... 161.3:4 to t. us from a different point of view, so
W-pI. 166.13:3 It is you who t. them now. For you have
W-pI. 166.13:5 T. them by showing them the happiness
WpI...rV.in5:4 open up the path of light to us, and t. us,
WpI...rV.in8:4 together we will t. them to our brothers.
W-pI... 184.5:2 It is hard to t. the mind a thousand alien
W-pI... 184.7:4 the world would t. stops short of meaning
W-pI... 196.3:1 also t. your mind that you are not an ego.
W-pI... 198.5:3 and learn the simple lessons He would t.,
WpI rVI.in.7:2 Him t. you what to do and say and think,
WpI rVI.in.7:4 set for us; allowing Him to t. us how to go
W-pII . 296.2:1 We t. today what we would learn, and
W-pII . 330.1:3 of pain? Why should we t. them they are
W-pII ... 14.2:5 here, and words can speak of this and t. it
M-in .......... 1:5 hand, emphasizes that to t. *is* to learn, so
M-in .......... 2:1 To t. is to demonstrate. There are only
M-in .......... 2:4 The question is not whether you will t.,
M-in .......... 2:5 t. on the basis of what you want to learn.
M-in ........ 2:10 to you a chance to t. others what you are,
M-in .......... 3:3 situation on behalf of what you really t.,
M-in ........ 3:10 the self you think is real is what you t..
M-in .......... 4:8 And as they t. His lessons of joy and hope,
M-in .......... 5:2 must deceive, for they must t. deception.
M-in .......... 5:6 and so they t. perfection over and over, in
M-2 ........... 1:2 the universal curriculum that he will t. is
M-2 ........... 1:7 opportunities to t. will be provided for
M-3 ........... 1:3 so there is no one whom he cannot t..
M-13 ......... 8:4 What would you t.? Remember only what
M-14 ......... 5:9 t. are lessons in which Heaven is reflected.
M-16 ....... 11:3 is God's teachers who must t. it that it can
M-17 ......... 1:8 it is not this that he would t., because it is
M-18 ......... 2:6 is He free to t. all minds the truth of what
M-23 ......... 6:5 we t. the limitations we have laid on us.
M-23 ......... 7:8 Do you, then, t. with him, for he is with
M-24 ......... 4:4 has much to t. and learn apart from them.
M-24 ......... 4:5 both learn and t. that theoretical issues
M-25 ......... 2:3 be little point in trying to t. salvation. It
C-5............. 5:3 to t. the mighty lesson that he learned for
P-2..........II.1:2 t. forgiveness rather than condemnation.
P-2..........II.1:3 that point could t. salvation completely,
P-2...... IV.10:7 psychotherapist's function to t. that guilt,

P-2 V.4:8 for what to **t.** as well as what to learn.
P-3 II.10:4 How, then, can he **t.**? Because it is the
P-3 III.6:8 Perhaps he was sent to **t.** the therapist
S-1 V.3:2 last. Humility has come to **t.** you how to
S-2 II.2:5 Who makes a slave to **t.** what freedom is?
S-2 III.2:2 His Voice will **t.** you what forgiveness is,
S-2 III.6:7 Forgiveness has been given Him to **t.**, to
S-3 IV.2:6 to see His likeness and to **t.** like Him.

## Teacher 55

*teacher*

T-5 III.10:1 The Holy Spirit is the perfect **T.**. He uses
T-6 IV.12:11 gave the Answer. His Answer is your **T.**.
T-7 VII.7:2 One **T.** is in all minds and He teaches the
T-8 II.1:2 Only one **T.** knows what your reality is. If
T-8 III.1:4 to listen to the **T.** Who knows of light,
T-8 VII.13:2 God's joyous **T.** and learning His lessons.
T-8 VIII.9:10 of the one **T.** Who knows what life is,
T-11 VIII.3:7 are learned, and you are not without a **T.**.
T-11 VIII.14:3 Ask what they are of the **T.** of reality, and
T-12 I.6:6 at all. There is but one **T.** of reality, Who
T-12 V.5:2 provided by a **T.** Who can transcend your
T-12 V.5:4 a special **T.** and a special curriculum. Poor
T-12 V.9:2 if you follow the **T.** Who knows the way to
T-14 X.2:6 motivated by a unique **T.** Who brings the
T-14 XI.11:3 God's **T.** is as like to His Creator as is His
T-14 XI.11:3 and through His **T.** does God proclaim
T-14 XI.13:3 you have abandoned the **T.** of peace.
T-14 XI.14:2 The **T.** of peace will never abandon you.
T-15 I.1:3 God's **T.** cannot be satisfied with His
T-15 II.2:3 **T.** He has appointed to translate time into
T-15 II.2:4 Blessed is God's **T.**, Whose joy it is to
T-15 II.6:5 God's **T.** and His lesson will support your
T-15 VIII.1:1 you as your **T.** until the holy instant has
T-16 I.5:6 You are the learner; He the **T.**. Do not
T-16 II.7:4 to teach you that your **T.** is not of you?
T-16 III.1:3 to realize that your **T.** came from beyond
T-19 III.5:9 fear of changed perception which its **T.**,
T-25 I.7:2 so split could never be the **T.** of a Oneness
T-25 I.7:3 unite all things together, must be its **T.**.
T-26 V.2:2 meaningless to the real **T.** of the world.
T-26 V.3:1 gave His **T.** to replace the one you made,
W-pI 121.6:3 as well, but from a **T.** other than yourself,
W-pI 121.7:7 but of the **T.** Who was given you to show
W-pI 155.3:4 need a **T.** Who perceives their madness,
W-pI 190.11:2 our gratitude unto our **T.** fill our hearts,
W-pI 193.8:6 simple lessons Heaven's **T.** sets before you
WpI rVI.in.6:6 we give these times of quiet to the **T.** Who
Wfl in.6:1 lessons, through the Voice of His Own **T.**.
M-2 5:3 God's **T.** speaks to any two who join
M-4 IV.1:11 Nor can God's **T.** be heard at all, except
M-4 V.1:10 And they are sure His **T.** goes before them
M-4 X.1:3 judgment shuts the mind against God's **T.**
M-7 5:1 **T.** for resolution is always self-doubt. And
M-8 6:5 This is the gift of its **T.**; the understanding
M-9 2:2 decisions; he asks his **T.** for His answer,
M-14 4:8 His **T.** points to it, and he trusts that He
M-22 5:10 Turn quickly to your **T.**, and let yourself
M-24 5:3 the belief unless his internal **T.** so advised.
M-29 2:12 Be glad you have a **T.** Who cannot make a
M-29 4:10 **T.** Who knows the truth has not forgotten
M-29 7:6 Ask all things of His **T.**, and all things are
P-1 1:4 God has given everyone a **T.** Whose
P-1 5:3 His **T.** will take him on from there, as far
S-2 III.1:7 He gives His **T.** to whoever asks, and seeks
S-2 III.7:2 has a **T.** Who will fail in nothing. Rest a

## teacher 184

*Teacher*

T-3 I.4:6 results in rejection of what the **t.** offers.
T-4 I.1:1 A good **t.** clarifies his own ideas and
T-4 I.1:2 **T.** and pupil are alike in the learning
T-4 I.1:4 A good **t.** must believe in the ideas he
T-4 I.5:1 Every good **t.** hopes to give his students
T-4 I.5:2 him. This is the one true goal of the **t.**. It is
T-4 I.6:2 If you perceive a **t.** as merely "a larger ego
T-4 I.6:3 absolve you finally from the need for a **t.**.
T-4 I.6:6 you will not be a devoted **t.** as long as you
T-4 I.6:7 as a **t.** either to be exalted or rejected, but
T-6 I.2:8 help you understand your own role as a **t.**.
T-6 V.1:1 Like any good **t.**, the Holy Spirit knows
T-6 V.3:1 A wise **t.** teaches through approach, not
T-6 V.B.2:4 is all that a **t.** need do to guarantee change
T-6 V.C.9:8 establishes you as a **t.** who teaches like me
T-7 V.2:5 weaken you as a **t.** and a learner because,
T-7 V.2:7 you are both a poor **t.** and a poor learner.
T-7 VII.7:1 One child of God is the only **t.** sufficiently
T-7 VIII.3:4 Remember that a conflicted **t.** is a poor
T-7 VIII.3:4 teacher is a poor **t.** and a poor learner. His
T-7 XI.4:4 this lesson has become the perfect **t.**,
T-8 II.1:8 As a **t.**, then, the ego is totally confused
T-8 II.2:1 reason for choosing a **t.** such as this? Does
T-8 II.2:3 Is this the **t.** to whom a Son of God should
T-8 II.2:5 this alone disqualify it as your future **t.**?
T-8 III.5:1 regardless of the **t.** you choose, is "Know
T-8 III.5:9 depending on which **t.** you are following.
T-8 VIII.7:1 A learning device is not a **t.**. It cannot tell
T-8 VIII.7:4 of a **t.** who does not know the answer. The
T-8 IX.4:3 give it? Under which **t.** did you place it?
T-9 I.7:4 why you persist in asking the **t.** who could
T-9 IV.4:1 asking for one, though not of the right **t.**.
T-9 IV.8:3 remarkably poor choice as a **t.** of salvation
T-11 II.2:1 it the better **t.** and learner you become. If
T-11 VIII.3:8 learned amiss should not be your own **t.**.
T-12 V.8:3 attain it? Resign now as your own **t.**. This
T-12 V.8:6 an excellent learner and an excellent **t.**.
T-14 V.8:1 unto everyone who becomes a **t.** of peace.
T-14 V.8:7 with me within it, as a **t.** of Atonement,
T-14 X.8:9 For their **t.** is senseless, though careful to
T-14 XI.14:1 peace you must abandon the **t.** of attack.
T-15 I.1:5 longer need a **t.** or time in which to learn.
T-16 III.7:4 learner, who offers it to the **t.** in gratitude,
T-17 I.4:2 in reality by giving some of it to one **t.**,
T-26 V.1:8 will go along the way your chosen **t.** leads.
T-26 V.5:2 be there, for you to choose to be your **t.**.
T-26 V.6:4 There *is* no other **t.** and no other way. For
T-29 II.7:6 they reflect the **t.** who is teaching them.
W-pI 91.5:4 Your will remains your **t.**, and your will
W-pI 158.5:1 A **t.** does not give experience, because he
M-in 1:3 as if the **t.** and the learner are separated,
M-in 1:3 **t.** giving something to the learner rather
M-in 1:5 learn, so that **t.** and learner are the same.
M-1 1:1 **t.** of God is anyone who chooses to be one
M-1 1:8 of salvation. He has become a **t.** of God.
M-1 3:1 There is a course for every **t.** of God. The
M-1 3:7 matter who the **t.** was before he heard the
M-2 4:3 thus it is that pupil and **t.** seem to come
M-2 4:6 So has the **t.**, too, made an inevitable
M-2 5:1 pupil and **t.** come together, a teaching-
M-2 5:2 For the **t.** is not really the one who does
M-2 5:8 the learner becomes a **t.** of God himself,
M-2 5:8 the one decision that gave his **t.** to him.
M-3 1:3 one from whom a **t.** of God cannot learn,
M-3 1:5 contacts to be made for each **t.** of God.
M-3 3:3 the **t.** of God seems to begin to change his
M-3 5:8 No **t.** of God can fail to find the Help he
M-4 I.A.3:8 When the **t.** of God has learned that much
M-4 I.A.4:1 the **t.** of God must go through "a period
M-4 I.A.5:1 The third stage through which the **t.** of
M-4 I.A.5:5 in which the **t.** of God feels called upon to
M-4 I.A.6:2 **t.** of God rests a while in reasonable peace
M-4 I.A.6:5 and the **t.** of God is now at the point in his
M-4 I.A.6:9 The **t.** of God needs this period of respite.
M-4 I.A.7:2 Now must the **t.** of God understand that
M-4 II.2:5 is no challenge to a **t.** of God. Challenge
M-4 III.1:6 of the **t.** of God's whole thought system.
M-4 III.1:11 No **t.** of God can judge and hope to learn.
M-4 IV.1:8 No **t.** of God but must learn,–and fairly
M-4 VI.1:6 No one can become an advanced **t.** of God
M-4 VI.1:8 **t.** of God finally agrees to look past them,
M-4 VII.1:1 has special meaning to the **t.** of God. It is
M-4 VII.2:1 **t.** of God is generous out of Self interest.
M-4 VII.2:3 The **t.** of God does not want anything he
M-4 VIII.1:2 Patience is natural to the **t.** of God. All he
M-4 VIII.1:8 the **t.** of God is willing to reconsider all his
M-4 IX.1:1 The extent of the **t.** of God's faithfulness
M-4 IX.1:4 Faithfulness is the **t.** of God's trust in the
M-4 X.1:1 last of the attributes the **t.** of God acquires
M-5 III.h The Function of the **T.** of God
M-5 III.1:1 to be healed, what does the **t.** of God do?
M-5 III.2:2 presence of a **t.** of God is a reminder. His
M-6 1:4 The **t.** of God has seen the correction of
M-6 2:7 No **t.** of God should feel disappointed if
M-6 4:11 can a **t.** of God have about what becomes
M-7 1:5 For a **t.** of God to remain concerned about
M-7 1:6 is now the **t.** of God himself whose mind
M-7 2:1 Whenever a **t.** of God has tried to be a
M-7 2:4 the **t.** of God has only one course to follow
M-7 3:1 It is in this that the **t.** of God must trust.
M-7 3:3 The **t.** of God is a miracle worker because
M-7 3:11 And so the **t.** of God can only recognize it
M-9 1:4 in the newly made **t.** of God's training.
M-9 2:1 As the **t.** of God advances in his training,
M-9 2:3 as the **t.** of God learns to give up his own
M-10 1:8 with what his would-be **t.** says about them
M-10 1:8 the **t.** himself may well be inconsistent in
M-10 2:1 It is necessary for the **t.** of God to realize,
M-10 5:5 Now can the **t.** of God rise up unburdened
M-10 6:3 **t.** of God lays it down happily the instant
M-10 6:10 **T.** of God, this step will bring you peace.
M-12 1:2 One wholly perfect **t.**, whose learning is
M-12 4:4 the recognition, in this new **t.** of God, of
M-12 5:8 the **t.** of God does not make this decision
M-13 6:5 And what, O **t.** of God, is it that you want
M-13 8:1 **T.** of God, do not forget the meaning of
M-14 3:6 orders of difficulty is an obstacle the **t.** of
M-14 3:7 One sin perfectly forgiven by one **t.** of
M-14 4:4 of the **t.** of God in this concluding lesson?
M-15 2:1 this your judgment on yourself, **t.** of God?
M-15 2:9 is your judgment of the world, **t.** of God?
M-16 h THE **T.** OF GOD SPEND HIS DAY?
M-16 1:1 To the advanced **t.** of God this question is
M-16 1:3 Yet the **t.** of God is sure of but one thing;
M-16 1:8 day. For the advanced **t.** of God, then, this
M-16 3:6 must depend on the **t.** of God himself. He
M-16 4:2 It may be that the **t.** of God is not in a
M-16 7:1 **t.** of God who has accepted His protection
M-16 8:1 the way the **t.** of God has yet to travel, and
M-16 8:7 It is not good enough for God's **t.**, because
M-16 9:5 **t.** of God has reached the most advanced
M-16 10:2 this fact that the **t.** of God devotes his day.
M-17 1:1 is a crucial question both for **t.** and pupil.
M-17 1:2 the **t.** of God has hurt himself and has also
M-17 1:4 a major lesson for the **t.** of God to master.
M-17 1:6 in any form, God's **t.** can be sure that he is
M-17 2:5 will always come to **t.** and to pupil alike.
M-17 2:7 **t.** of God gives to those who need his aid?
M-17 3:2 lead to nothing but release for **t.** and pupil
M-17 3:5 The single aim of the **t.** turns the divided
M-17 9:7 then, **t.** of God, that anger recognizes a
M-18 1:1 be made until the **t.** of God has ceased to
M-18 4:1 it thus becomes essential for the **t.** of God
M-18 4:5 sole responsibility of God's **t.** is to accept
M-18 4:7 the **t.** of God becomes a miracle worker by
M-21 4:1 Is the **t.** of God, then, to avoid the use of
M-21 4:4 The **t.** of God must, however, learn to use
M-21 4:7 The **t.** of God accepts the words which are
M-21 5:1 this aspect of his learning is the **t.** of God's
M-21 5:3 fact, confront the **t.** with a situation that
M-22 1:10 The **t.** of God has taken accepting the
M-22 2:1 progress of the **t.** of God may be slow or
M-22 2:3 **t.** of God may have accepted the function
M-22 3:1 if the **t.** of God is to make progress. The
M-22 4:4 that the **t.** of God calls forth the miracle of
M-22 4:6 is the result of the recognition, by God's **t.**
M-22 5:1 a **t.** of God fails to heal, it is because he
M-22 5:7 Step back now, **t.** of God. You have been
M-22 7:7 until God's **t.** recognizes that they are the
M-23 3:11 the greatest **t.** be unavailable to those who
M-23 6:6 dedicated **t.** of God forgets his brothers.
M-24 3:2 A **t.** of God should be as helpful to those
M-24 4:4 The **t.** of God is, therefore, wise to step
M-24 5:1 mean that the **t.** of God should not believe
M-26 3:1 Sometimes a **t.** of God may have a brief
M-27 7:1 **T.** of God, your one assignment could be

M-29 1:1 questions that both **t.** and pupil may raise
M-29 1:4 that only time divides **t.** and pupil, so that
M-29 2:5 Surely no **t.** of God has come this far
M-29 8:3 *T. of God, His thanks He offers you, And all*
P-2 I.4:3 a somewhat more specialized **t.** of God.
P-2 II.1:1 To be a **t.** of God, it is not necessary to be
P-2 II.1:4 has learned all things does not need a **t.**,
P-2 II.5:3 Yet if pupil and **t.** join in sharing one goal,
P-2 II.5:6 **T.** and pupil, therapist and patient, are all
P-2 II.7:2 good **t.** uses one approach to every pupil.
P-2 II.7:4 Perhaps the **t.** does not think of God as
P-2 II.8:1 What must the **t.** do to ensure learning?
P-2 II.8:6 self. Only by doing this can **t.** and pupil,
P-2 V.3:3 which the perfect **t.** could not long remain
P-2 VII.2:1 Think carefully, **t.** and therapist, for
P-2 VII.4:3 healer would instantly become a **t.** of God
P-3 I.4:1 A holy therapist, an advanced **t.** of God,
P-3 III.8:1 Physician, healer, therapist, **t.**, heal

### teacher's 2

T-4 I.6:4 is the opposite of the ego-oriented **t.** goal.
M-17 3:6 answer will enter the **t.** mind unfailingly.

### Teachers 1

*teachers*

M-26 2:2 might be called the **T.** of teachers because,

### teachers 93

*Teachers*

T-3 I.4:5 Good **t.** never terrorize their students. To
T-4 I.7:4 inferiority. **T.** must be patient and repeat
T-4 I.13:7 devoted **t.** who share my aim of healing
T-6 I.6:11 with me, and we will become equal as **t.**.
T-6 I.8:1 it weakens them as **t.** and as learners. Yet
T-6 I.16:3 I do not call for martyrs but for **t.**. No one
T-6 V.B.2:1 All good **t.** realize that only fundamental
T-8 I.5:5 If it is planned by two **t.**, each believing in
T-8 I.5:6 carried out by these two **t.** simultaneously
T-8 I.6:2 learn simultaneously from two **t.** who are
T-12 V.5:5 Poor learners are not good choices as **t.**,
T-13 I.1:1 Holy Spirit shares the goal of all good **t.**,
T-14 II.4:9 become your **t.** in release and gladness.
T-14 V.3:7 the **t.** of the innocence that is the right of
T-14 V.6:1 **T.** of innocence, each in his own way,
T-26 V.1:7 are two **t.** only, who point in different
M-in 4:7 but despair and death, God sends His **t.**.
M-in 5:1 for God's **t.** there would be little hope of
M-in 5:4 This is a manual for the **t.** of God. They
M-1 h WHO ARE GOD'S **T.**?
M-1 2:6 for **t.** to speak for It and redeem the world
M-1 2:10 this that the plan of the **t.** was established.
M-1 4:1 for **t.** of a special form of the universal
M-1 4:8 the **t.** of God are appointed to bring about
M-2 1:1 have been assigned to each of God's **t.**,
M-3 1:1 The **t.** of God have no set teaching level.
M-3 3:7 God's **t.** work at different levels, but the
M-3 5:7 the **t.** who falter and may even seem to fail
M-4 h THE CHARACTERISTICS OF GOD'S **T.**?
M-4 1:1 surface traits of God's **t.** are not at all alike
M-4 1:3 stages of their functioning as **t.** of God,
M-4 1:4 God gives special gifts to His **t.**, because
M-4 1:6 become characteristic of all **t.** of God who
M-4 2:2 it can be said that the advanced **t.** of God
M-4 I.1:4 The **t.** of God have trust in the world,
M-4 I.1:7 that the **t.** of God look on a forgiven world
M-4 I.A.5:3 Few **t.** of God escape this distress entirely.
M-4 II.1:1 All other traits of God's **t.** rest on trust.
M-4 II.2:1 peace of mind which the advanced **t.** of
M-4 II.2:6 trust on which God's **t.** rest secure makes
M-4 III.1:1 God's **t.** do not judge. To judge is to be
M-4 IV.1:1 Harm is impossible for God's **t.**. They can
M-4 IV.2:1 Therefore, God's **t.** are wholly gentle.
M-4 IV.2:8 might of God's **t.** lies in their gentleness,
M-4 V.1:9 God's **t.** trust in Him. And they are sure
M-4 VI.1:1 God's **t.** have learned how to be simple.
M-4 VII.1:3 God's **t.** this one rests ultimately on trust,
M-4 VII.1:5 To the **t.** of God, it means giving away in
M-4 VII.1:8 opposite to the **t.** of God and to the world.
M-4 IX.2:7 in itself the other attributes of God's **t.**. It
M-4 X.3:1 the list of attributes of God's **t.** does not
M-4 X.3:6 function of God's **t.** to bring true learning
M-4 X.3:8 is given to the **t.** of God to bring the glad
M-5 III.1:4 for they have become **t.** of God with him.
M-5 III.2:1 To them God's **t.** come, to represent
M-5 III.2:4 His **t.** are the symbols of salvation. They
M-5 III.3:1 once do the advanced **t.** of God consider
M-5 III.3:9 And this is the function of God's **t.**; to see
M-6 3:1 not the function of God's **t.** to evaluate the
M-7 4:9 God's **t.** the power to be miracle workers,
M-9 h IN THE LIFE SITUATION OF GOD'S **T.**?
M-9 1:1 are required in the *minds* of God's **t.**. This
M-12 h HOW MANY **T.** OF GOD ARE NEEDED
M-12 2:5 God's **t.** appear to be many, for that is
M-12 3:8 So do God's **t.** need a body, for their unity
M-12 4:1 makes God's **t.** is their recognition of the
M-12 4:6 The **t.** of God appear to share the illusion
M-12 6:2 God's **t.** choose to look on dreams a while.
M-12 6:6 dreaming is the real function of God's **t.**.
M-12 6:11 is this God's **t.** acknowledge as behind the
M-13 4:1 God's **t.** can have no regret on giving up
M-13 8:11 out His Word to you, for He has need of **t.**
M-14 2:7 It is His Call God's **t.** answer, turning to
M-14 3:3 still, and waits on the goal of God's **t.**. Not
M-14 5:9 hell into Heaven is the function of God's **t.**
M-16 11:3 It is God's **t.** who must teach it that it can.
M-16 11:7 **t.** know that this is so, and have learned
M-16 11:9 must God's **t.** learn to recognize the forms
M-17 h DO GOD'S **T.** DEAL WITH MAGIC
M-17 8:1 this hopeless situation God sends His **t.**.
M-21 5:8 God's **t.** have God's Word behind their
M-22 7:4 not up to God's **t.** to set limits upon Him,
M-23 1:2 most advanced of God's **t.** will give way to
M-23 7:2 Are other **t.** possible, to lead the way to
M-24 6:8 not lead to this is of concern to God's **t.**.
M-26 1:5 Here, then, is the role of God's **t.**. They,
M-26 2:2 might be called the Teachers of **t.** because,
M-26 2:9 to the **t.** of God who look to them for help
M-27 4:8 Not one can be acceptable to God's **t.**,
M-28 6:3 God's **t.** have the goal of wakening the
M-29 1:4 While it is called a manual for **t.**, it must
P-1 5:6 and to prepare additional **t.** for His work.
P-3 II.1:8 may be far more able **t.** outside of them.

### teachers' 1

M-18 2:1 God's **t.** major lesson is to learn how to

### teaches 102

T-3 I.2:11 wholly benign lesson the Atonement **t.** is
T-4 I.1:4 teacher must believe in the ideas he **t.**, but
T-4 VI.5:4 This **t.** him to associate his misery with its
T-5 II.12:3 He **t.** you how to keep me as the model for
T-6 in.2:2 Everyone **t.**, and teaches all the time. This
T-6 in.2:2 Everyone teaches, and **t.** all the time. This
T-6 I.1:5 and therefore wholly benign in what it **t.**,
T-6 I.16:6 all behavior **t.** the beliefs that motivate it.
T-6 V.1:1 He **t.** only to make you equal with Him.
T-6 V.3:1 A wise teacher **t.** through approach, not
T-6 V.B.6:3 Holy Spirit **t.** you that truth was created
T-6 V.C.1:2 **t.** you to judge every thought you allow to
T-6 V.C.4:3 it. This lesson **t.** not only that you can be,
T-6 V.C.4:5 in that it **t.** there must be no exceptions,
T-6 V.C.9:7 it radiates health, and thereby **t.** healing.
T-6 V.C.9:8 establishes you as a teacher who **t.** like me
T-7 II.6:4 I said before that He **t.** remembering and
T-7 III.1:1 The Holy Spirit **t.** one lesson, and applies
T-7 III.1:3 Himself, He **t.** you that all power is yours.
T-7 III.2:6 insane; it **t.** that you are not what you are.
T-7 IV.3:3 Spirit **t.** you to use what the ego has made
T-7 VII.7:2 all minds and He **t.** the same lesson to all.
T-7 VII.7:3 He always **t.** you the inestimable worth of
T-8 I.5:10 curriculum **t.** them that *all* directions exist
T-8 II.2:2 of anything it **t.** make anything but sense?
T-8 II.3:5 Voice **t.** only in accordance with His Will,
T-8 II.5:1 have said that the Holy Spirit **t.** you the
T-8 II.5:2 That is the same as saying He **t.** you the
T-8 III.5:7 Holy Spirit **t.** you that if you look only at
T-8 III.7:3 ego **t.** that your strength is in you alone.
T-8 III.7:4 The Holy Spirit **t.** that all strength is in
T-8 VIII.1:6 the body, it **t.** that *you* are to attack with.
T-8 VIII.9:1 Holy Spirit **t.** you to use your body only to
T-9 IV.5:6 **t.** that the ego does not exist and proves it
T-9 VI.5:2 the Holy Spirit **t.** you to awaken others.
T-11 II.2:5 own mind, **t.** you that you are God's Son.
T-11 VIII.1:2 in the end, **t.** that only reality is true. But
T-12 IV.2:2 since it also **t.** that it is your identification
T-12 VI.1:2 The Holy Spirit **t.** that you cannot lose
T-13 in.4:6 lesson he need learn, for it **t.** him that,
T-13 I.9:1 the Atonement **t.** you what immortality is
T-13 I.11:1 The ego **t.** you to attack yourself because
T-13 IV.1:4 The ego **t.** that your function on earth is
T-13 IV.6:9 Spirit **t.** that you always meet yourself,
T-13 IV.6:10 The ego **t.** that you always encounter your
T-13 VIII.1:3 He **t.** that the past does not exist, a fact
T-13 X.7:6 union. He **t.** healing, but He also knows of
T-13 XI.11:1 you have learned that **t.** that what is not
T-14 in.1:8 the Holy Spirit **t.** the simple conclusions
T-14 II.3:1 All this the Holy Spirit sees, and **t.**,
T-14 II.4:5 **t.** them release from nothing and from all
T-14 III.5:1 The miracle **t.** you that you have chosen
T-14 III.6:6 God is the happy lesson the Holy Spirit **t.**,
T-14 III.15:3 The Holy Spirit **t.** only that the "sin" of
T-14 IV.9:3 Atonement **t.** you the true condition of
T-14 IV.9:5 merely **t.** you how to remove the blocks
T-14 V.2:2 Each one **t.** the message differently, and
T-14 V.2:3 Yet until he **t.** it and learns it, he will
T-14 VII.7:3 you **t.** you how to recognize what you see.
T-14 X.6:2 lesson the Holy Spirit **t.** by giving you the
T-14 XI.3:1 Atonement **t.** you how to escape forever
T-14 XI.4:7 Him Who **t.** light He will accept from you,
T-14 XI.5:5 Every dark lesson **t.** this, in one form or
T-14 XI.5:6 **t.** you that you will with the Father and
T-14 XI.11:5 For He **t.** the miracle of oneness, and
T-15 I.4:3 it. The ego **t.** that hell is in the future, for
T-15 I.4:13 The ego **t.** thus: Death is the end as far as
T-15 I.5:1 The ego **t.** that Heaven is here and now
T-15 I.7:1 The Holy Spirit **t.** thus: There is no hell.
T-15 V.3:7 Yet the holy instant **t.** you it is not so.
T-16 III.1:1 We have already learned that everyone **t.**,
T-16 III.1:1 that everyone teaches, and **t.** all the time.
T-16 III.7:5 to your Self, Who **t.** you what He is, will
T-16 VII.8:8 everything the Holy Spirit **t.** is to remind
T19 IV.B.13:7 it **t.** that the body's pleasure is happiness.
T-20 V.5:2 When it is used only as the Holy Spirit **t.**,
T-21 IV.6:1 inconsistency in what the Holy Spirit **t.**.
T-22 VI.15:6 **t.** you that you cannot separate denies the
T-24 I.8:6 this course because it **t.** you you and your
T-25 IX.10:9 is universal, and it **t.** but one message:
T-26 IV.4:5 And each one **t.** him that what he feared
T-28 II.4:3 It **t.** you there is a choice of dreams while
T-31 I.2:3 It **t.** but the very obvious. It merely goes
T-31 I.4:6 learn the simple things salvation **t.** you!
T-31 V.5:3 lesson **t.** this: "I am the thing you made of
W-pI 54.4:3 I think or say or do **t.** all the universe. A
W-pI 130.6:4 It also **t.** that the one you see is quite
W-pI 133.10:4 This guidance **t.** it is error to believe that
W-pI 159.1:6 Salvation **t.** otherwise. To give is how to
W-pI 166.14:4 fear but **t.** them their fears are justified.
W-pI 169.7:3 from Him Who **t.** what forgiveness means
WpI rV.in6:5 Yet a savior must remain with those he **t.**,
W-pII 269.1:5 *t. me that what I look upon belongs to me;*
W-pII 9.3:1 ends the lessons that the Holy Spirit **t.**,
W-pII 350.1:8 *And only my forgiveness t. me to let Your*
W-ep 6:5 **t.** us how to behold him through His eyes,
M-in 3:6 underlying what you say that **t.** you.
M-in 4:4 **t.** solely to convince himself that he is
M-in 4:7 which **t.** nothing but despair and death,
M-3 3:3 more about the new direction as he **t.** it.
P-1 2:6 **t.** forgiveness and helps the patient to
P-2 I.4:4 is the more he **t.** and the more he learns.

## teaching 165

*See also* teaching-learning

| | |
|---|---|
| T-in 1:6 | *course does not aim at* t. *the meaning of love,* |
| T-1 I.15:3 | is thus a t. device and a means to an end. |
| T-1 I.16:1 | Miracles are t. devices for demonstrating |
| T-4 I.h | Right T. and Right Learning |
| T-4 I.1:1 | ideas and strengthens them by t. them. |
| T-4 I.4:1 | T. and learning are your greatest |
| T-4 I.6:6 | able to devote myself to t. if I believed this |
| T-4 I.7:1 | worth is not established by t. or learning. |
| T-4 II.4:9 | When t. is no longer necessary you will |
| T-4 VI.5:6 | I am t. you to associate misery with the |
| T-5 II.10:10 | your brothers to listen as I am t. you. |
| T-5 III.11:1 | world as a t. device for bringing you home |
| T-5 IV.h | T. and Healing |
| T-5 IV.5:1 | T. is done in many ways, above all by |
| T-5 IV.5:2 | T. should be healing, because it is the |
| T-6 I.2:2 | Its value, like the value of any t. device, |
| T-6 I.4:5 | false premises and t. them to others. The |
| T-6 I.6:2 | you are persecuted, you are t. persecution |
| T-6 I.6:6 | which was part of my own t. contribution |
| T-6 I.11:6 | because it would serve as a good t. aid to |
| T-6 III.2:6 | one. Only by t. it can you learn it. "As you |
| T-6 III.2:8 | do not forget that what you teach is t. you |
| T-6 III.3:10 | and you can unlearn it by not t. it. |
| T-6 III.4:1 | your salvation lies in t. the exact opposite |
| T-6 III.4:4 | By t. peace you must learn it yourself, |
| T-6 III.4:7 | your mind through the conviction of t. it. |
| T-6 IV.12:4 | T. aims at change, but God created only |
| T-6 V.A.5:12 | Therefore, His t. begins with the lesson: |
| T-6 V.B.5:3 | both, you are t. conflict and learning it. |
| T-6 V.C.4:9 | By t. *what* to choose, the Holy Spirit will |
| T-6 V.C.5:6 | you are t. peace *because* you believe in it. |
| T-7 II.3:2 | This is its t. form, because outside the |
| T-7 II.3:4 | In the Kingdom there is no t. or learning, |
| T-7 II.6:3 | Holy Spirit's t. is a lesson in remembering |
| T-7 III.1:3 | By t. the power of the Kingdom of God |
| T-7 III.2:9 | Yet you are always t.. You must, therefore |
| T-7 III.2:10 | You must, therefore, be t. something else, |
| T-7 V.2:4 | is not the level for either t. or learning, |
| T-7 V.5:5 | is therefore in conflict, and is t. conflict. |
| T-7 V.7:3 | t. is limited because he is learning so little |
| T-7 VI.13:5 | is the Holy Spirit's perfectly consistent t.. |
| T-7 VII.7:3 | t. it with infinite patience born of the |
| T-8 I.6:4 | They are t. you entirely different things in |
| T-8 I.6:4 | except that both are t. you about yourself. |
| T-8 II.2:5 | of your own experience with its t., should |
| T-8 II.4:4 | t. you how to disregard or look beyond |
| T-8 II.6:1 | Holy Spirit's t. takes only *one* direction |
| T-8 III.1:6 | on His t. because He was created to teach. |
| T-8 III.2:6 | Only His t. will release your will to God's, |
| T-8 III.5:8 | you are because you are t. what you are. |
| T-8 IV.6:5 | but only you can choose to listen to my t.. |
| T-8 IX.5:3 | He would be t. that one error can be more |
| T-9 IV.6:1 | Follow the Holy Spirit's t. in forgiveness, |
| T-9 V.5:4 | healer, and he must learn from his own t.. |
| T-10 II.4:2 | are specifically t. yourself that you are not |
| T-11 V.11:3 | According to the ego's t., *its* goal can be |
| T-11 V.11:4 | *not.* According to the Holy Spirit's t., *only* |
| T-12 IV.1:1 | dangerous, and this is always its central t. |
| T-12 IV.3:5 | Follow its t., then, and you will search for |
| T-12 V.4:5 | you, and poor learners do need special t.. |
| T-12 V.7:4 | obvious. Every legitimate t. aid, every real |
| T-12 V.7:5 | and the aim of your t. is to defeat itself, |
| T-12 VII.14:3 | is an essential part of the Holy Spirit's t.. |
| T-13 I.1:1 | by t. their pupils all they know. The Holy |
| T-13 I.11:2 | In the ego's t., then, there is no escape |
| T-13 IV.7:4 | as temporary, serving only His t. function |
| T-13 VIII.8:2 | with me under the holy banner of His t., |
| T-13 XI.6:3 | and differences are necessary t. aids, for |
| T-14 h | T. FOR TRUTH |
| T-14 I.5:1 | must begin His t. by showing you what |
| T-14 II.2:1 | with the fundamental t. that *truth* is true. |
| T-14 III.8:7 | in place of all the happy t. the Holy Spirit |
| T-14 V.5:7 | Yet those who have failed to learn need t., |
| T-14 V.5:8 | those who have need of t. is to fail to learn |
| T-14 V.6:5 | every t. that points to this points straight |
| T-14 V.6:6 | no fear that t. this can fail to overcome. |
| T-14 V.6:7 | power of God Himself supports this t., |
| T-14 V.7:2 | one can be untouched by t. such as this. |
| T-14 V.9:9 | the only purpose to which my t. calls you. |
| T-14 V.9:10 | He created him, by t. him his innocence. |
| T-14 XI.10:7 | His bright t. so firmly in your mind, that |
| T-15 I.1:3 | His t. until it constitutes all your learning. |
| T-15 I.1:4 | not fulfilled His t. function until you have |
| T-15 I.2:1 | of the Holy Spirit's t. are far in the future. |
| T-15 I.2:4 | Time is His friend in t.. It does not waste |
| T-15 I.2:7 | the inevitability of the goal and end of t.. |
| T-15 I.4:3 | for this is what all its t. is directed to. Hell |
| T-15 I.4:7 | who follows the ego's t. is without the fear |
| T-15 I.7:7 | For time, according to its t., is nothing |
| T-15 I.7:7 | nothing but a t. device for compounding |
| T-15 I.9:4 | of time as a t. aid to happiness and peace. |
| T-15 II.2:6 | His t. is for you because His joy is yours. |
| T-15 V.1:1 | learning device for t. you love's meaning. |
| T-15 V.4:6 | Under His t., every relationship becomes |
| T-15 VI.1:3 | Under the Holy Spirit's t. all relationships |
| T-15 VII.13:2 | Holy Spirit's t. function to instruct those |
| T-15 VIII.1:2 | For a t. assignment such as His, He must |
| T-15 VIII.6:5 | let Him Whose t. is only of God teach you |
| T-15 XI.7:2 | of love by t. that communication remains |
| T-16 III.h | The Reward of T. |
| T-16 III.1:2 | how to accept the comfort of your t.. If |
| T-16 III.2:3 | you judge yourself according to your t.. |
| T-16 III.2:4 | The ego's t. produces immediate results, |
| T-16 III.5:1 | Your t. has already done this, for the |
| T-16 III.5:8 | they offer gladly to your t. of yourself, |
| T-16 III.6:4 | to your t. have gathered to help you learn. |
| T-16 III.6:7 | stand outside your t. and apart from it. |
| T-16 III.7:1 | and make learning commensurate with t.. |
| T-16 III.7:3 | suffer for it, the joy of t. will yet be yours. |
| T-16 III.7:4 | For the joy of t. is in the learner, who |
| T-17 II.1:9 | And all His t. leads to seeing it and giving |
| T-17 V.2:3 | is a phenomenal t. accomplishment. In all |
| T-18 V.1:3 | the holy relationship, the Holy Spirit's t., |
| T19 IV.B.8:2 | I taught by t. freedom to your brother, |
| T-20 VII.8:4 | from Him Who would undo your t.. His |
| T-26 V.1:2 | Yet t. that is what this course is for. This |
| T-29 II.7:6 | they reflect the teacher who is t. them. |
| T-31 IV.7:7 | otherwise, it is a simple t. in the obvious. |
| T-31 V.8:2 | aim of t. you this concept of yourself, that |
| T-31 VII.12:2 | t. that you are the thing you wish to be. It |
| W-pI 42.7:2 | and t. you that you are studying a unified |
| W-pI 95.8:1 | Holy Spirit is not delayed in His t. by your |
| W-pI 121.7:7 | all your t. and your learning will be not of |
| W-pI 133.1:1 | Sometimes in t. there is benefit, |
| W-pI 138.5:5 | Ours are t. goals, to be attained through |
| W-pI 184.7:1 | Such is the t. of the world. It is a phase of |
| W-pI 184.9:1 | yet were asked to take a t. function. You |
| W-pI 184.12:5 | t. of the world to take the place of Heaven |
| W-pI 192.4:3 | be perceived as what it is; a simple t. aid, |
| W-pI 193.11:6 | Truth is His message; truth His t. is. His |
| W-pII 7.2:1 | Spirit's t. sets is just this end of dreams. |
| W-pII 296.2:3 | we allow His t. to persuade the world, |
| M-in 1:1 | role of t. and learning is actually reversed |
| M-in 1:4 | act of t. is regarded as a special activity, in |
| M-in 1:6 | emphasizes that t. is a constant process; it |
| M-in 2:6 | to yourself, and this you learn through t.. |
| M-in 2:7 | T. is but a call to witnesses to attest to |
| M-in 3:2 | In the formal t. situation, these questions |
| M-in 3:2 | unrelated to what you think you are t.. |
| M-in 3:4 | this the verbal content of your t. is quite |
| M-in 3:6 | It is the t. underlying what you say that |
| M-in 3:7 | T. but reinforces what you believe about |
| M-1 3:3 | So do the particular t. aids involved. But |
| M-2 5:2 | is not really the one who does the t.. |
| M-3 h | WHAT ARE THE LEVELS OF T.? |
| M-3 1:1 | The teachers of God have no set t. level. |
| M-3 2:1 | level of t. appears to be quite superficial. |
| M-3 3:1 | difficult to understand that levels of t. the |
| M-3 3:4 | but the illusion of levels of t. seems to be |
| M-3 4:2 | this sense only, we can speak of levels of t. |
| M-3 4:3 | level of t. is a more sustained relationship |
| M-3 5:1 | level of t. occurs in relationships which, |
| M-4 I.A.7:4 | was meaningless in t. him the difference. |
| M-21 4:1 | then, to avoid the use of words in his t.? |
| M-24 6:8 | time. No t. that does not lead to this is of |
| M-25 3:2 | His direction, they are valuable t. aids. To |
| M-29 4:9 | it. Such is your t., and the teaching of the |
| M-29 4:9 | t. of the world that was made to uphold it |
| C-in 5:2 | drops away to make way for the central t.. |
| P-2 I.4:4 | God. He learns through t., and the more |
| P-2 II.5:1 | t. aids appeal to different people. Some |
| P-2 II.7:4 | teacher does not think of God as part of t. |
| P-2 IV.10:4 | This must be his t., if his lesson is to be |
| P-2 V.3:3 | We speak of ideal t. in a world in which |
| P-3 II.2:4 | of the world's t. follows a curriculum in |

## teaching-learning 11

| | |
|---|---|
| M-2 2:1 | to understand the t. plan of salvation, it is |
| M-2 5:1 | come together, a t. situation begins. For |
| M-2 5:5 | In the t. situation, each one learns that |
| M-3 1:2 | level. Each t. situation involves a different |
| M-3 2:4 | the potential for becoming a t. situation. |
| M-3 3:5 | that any level of the t. situation is part of |
| M-3 4:1 | Each t. situation is maximal in the sense |
| M-3 4:3 | two people enter into a fairly intense t. |
| M-3 5:2 | t. situations in which each person is given |
| M-3 5:3 | in which the t. balance is actually perfect. |
| M-4 1:6 | toward which the t. situation is geared, |

## teachings 1

| | |
|---|---|
| T-6 I.16:1 | you read the t. of the Apostles, remember |

## tear 3

| | |
|---|---|
| T-7 VII.8:4 | to t. the Kingdom of Heaven from you. |
| T-27 I.5:5 | every t. is wiped away in laughter and in |
| T-28 III.7:4 | a little gap perceived to t. eternity apart, |

## tears 17

| | |
|---|---|
| T-17 IV.8:4 | and the t. are faceted like diamonds and |
| T-17 IV.10:5 | Heaven, the Love of God, the t. of Christ, |
| T-27 VIII.9:6 | Perhaps you come in t.. But hear Him say, |
| T-31 V.3:2 | And so this face is often wet with t. at the |
| W-pI 54.5:4 | love to replace fear, laughter to replace t., |
| W-pI 69.2:5 | to see the t. of God's Son disappear in the |
| W-pI 132.3:4 | doubts and miseries, your pain and t., |
| W-pI 166.14:2 | Your t. are theirs. If you are sick, you but |
| W-pI 182.2:3 | are sad, and do not recognize their t. at all |
| W-pI 183.3:5 | the t. of pain are dried as happy laughter |
| W-pI 186.8:4 | and greet the day with welcome or with t.. |
| W-pI 191.2:6 | no hope you hold but will dissolve in t.. |
| W-pI 193.9:4 | And He would have all t. be wiped away, |
| W-pII 301.h | And God Himself shall wipe away all t.. |
| W-pII 301.1:6 | *And all the* t. *I shed will be forgotten, for* |
| W-pII 10.4:3 | alone can heal all sorrow, wipe away all t., |
| M-14 5:5 | end in laughter, because it is a place of t.. |

## tedious 2

| | |
|---|---|
| T-18 VII.4:11 | the means are t. and very time consuming |
| T-24 VI.12:4 | you, you find a burden wearisome and t., |

## telephone 2

| | |
|---|---|
| W-pI 9.3:4 | *I do not see this* t. *as it is now. I do not see this* |
| W-pI 25.4:4 | understand that a t. is for the purpose of |

## tell 139

| | |
|---|---|
| T-4 VII.6:2 | hardly means that you should t. Him how |
| T-5 VII.4:4 | you, and will also t. you of your part in it, |
| T-7 I.6:6 | t. you something about this last step. |
| T-7 X.3:5 | function is to teach you to t. them apart. |
| T-8 II.5:4 | to be the same, how can you t. them apart |
| T-8 IV.4:9 | I can t. you what to do, but you must |
| T-8 VI.2:4 | I am come to t. you that the choice of |
| T-8 VIII.7:2 | It cannot t. you how you feel. You do not |
| T-8 VIII.7:3 | a learning device *can* t. you how you feel. |
| T-9 II.5:6 | can so holy a brother t. you except truth? |
| T-9 III.2:6 | But your task is still to t. him he is right. |
| T-9 III.2:7 | You do not t. him this verbally, if he is |
| T-9 V.8:8 | He will t. you exactly what to do to help |

T-9.....VIII.4:6 It will t. you that you are insane, and
T-9...VIII.11:6 Holy Spirit what it is and He will t. you,
T-10.......II.2:5 His Voice will t. you that you are part of
T-11.........I.8:7 Will is for you, and He will t. you yours. It
T-11......III.3:6 I cannot t. you what this will be like, for
T-11......III.3:7 Yet I can t. you, and remind you often,
T-11.....VII.3:6 and illusion, you cannot t. which is true.
T-11. VIII.14:9 knows it, and He will t. you what they are.
T-12.........I.5:1 is surely good advice to t. you not to judge
T-12......III.2:2 His very insistence should t. you that he
T-13.....VII.1:1 t. yourself: "The real world is not like this.
T-14....III.19:1 of His Presence in you, and t. yourself this
T-14......IV.6:6 And He will t. you, and then do it for you.
T-15......IX.5:1 the Holy Spirit t. you of the Love of God
T-20......III.6:4 They did not t. it what it was; they did not
T-21.......II.7:4 which seems to t. you what must happen,
T-21.....II.11:4 made can t. you what you see and feel,
T-21.......V.5:7 Such would your reason t. you, if you
T-21.....V.10:3 reason t. you now the question must have
T-21......VI.1:3 also t. you that when you think you sin,
T-21......VI.4:3 and let their madness t. them it is real.
T-21......VI.5:7 Reason would t. you this. But think what
T-21......VI.6:2 You t. him, by your choice, that he is
T-21......VI.6:8 will t. you that this fact is your release.
T-21....VI.10:2 reason will t. you that it cannot be you
T-21....VI.10:4 here alone does reason t. you that you can
T-21.....VII.5:9 sin t. him that his enemy must be himself.
T-21.....VII.8:2 And let your reason t. you that it must be
T-21...VII.10:2 Reason will t. you why. It is the same as
T-21... VIII.3:1 Reason will t. you that you cannot ask for
T-22.........I.2:3 Reason would t. you that the world you
T-22.........I.3:9 Reason would t. you it cannot be true
T-22...... I.3:11 a world of misery, waiting to t. you, at the
T-22.........I.4:4 Reason would t. you that this is no secret
T-22.........I.9:6 Reason will t. you that they must have
T-22.........I.9:9 peace. Such did his reason t. him; such he
T-22.......II.4:1 Reason will t. you that the only way to
T-22.......II.5:1 Both reason and the ego will t. you this,
T-22.......II.7:7 Reason will t. you that there is no middle
T-22......III.5:1 Reason will t. you that the form of error
T-22......III.7:4 Reason will t. you that if form is not
T-22.......V.1:3 reason t. you that they contradict reality.
T-22.......V.4:5 feeble squeaks that t. of its omnipotence,
T-23.......II.6:4 His Son can t. Him this, and He has but
T-24.......in.1:3 It is not necessary to t. Him what to do.
T-27....IV.4:15 But t. it what you want, and it will serve
T-27......VI.3:2 to hear, and let it t. you what it is it feels.
T-27......VI.4:5 Nor could it t. a part of God Himself what
T-28....IV.2:10 you do not know and cannot t. apart.
T-28......VI.1:5 It does not t. you what its purpose is and
T-29.......V.4:2 him, and let It t. you what his function is.
T-30.........I.1:8 and t. yourself there is a way in which this
T-30.........I.4:1 t. yourself again the kind of day you want;
T-30...... I.14:9 will join with you and t. you what to do.
T-31.........I.1:9 told exactly how to t. one from the other,
T-31.....V.17:9 And What you are will t. you of Itself.
W-pI.....16.5:1 hold it in awareness while you t. yourself:
W-pI.....20.2:7 are now learning how to t. them apart.
W-pI.....21.4:1 each one in mind while you t. yourself:
W-pI.....26.9:1 of which you are afraid, t. yourself: *That*
W-pI.....34.6:3 will help you if you t. yourself specifically:
W-pI.....43.7:2 try to remember to t. him silently: *God is*
W-pI.....45.4:5 the world t. us that what God would have
W-pI.....45.6:3 idea, repeat it again and t. yourself gently:
W-pI.....46.5:2 those who have come to mind, t. yourself:
W-pI.....46.7:4 In that event, t. him silently: *God is the*
W-pI.....50.4:6 T. yourself this often today. It is a
W-pI.....53.5:3 that t. me where I am and what I am. The
W-pI.....65.6:3 Then t. yourself: *On this clean slate let my*
W-pI.....68.6:7 the end of the practice period t. yourself:
W-pI.....69.9:7 Also, be sure to t. yourself: *If I hold this*
W-pI.....70.7:6 that it is not there, and t. yourself: *My*
W-pI.....71.9:6 and let Him t. you what needs to be done
W-pI...71.10:1 periods, t. yourself often that God's plan
W-pI...72.10:8 *T. me, that I may understand.* Then we will
W-pI...72.12:4 *know. T. me, that I may understand.* He will
W-pI...73.10:1 t. yourself with gentle firmness and quiet
W-pI...74.3:11 T. yourself immediately: *There is no will*
W-pI.....74.4:2 or situations involved, and t. yourself:
W-pI.....75.8:1 T. Him you know you cannot fail because
W-pI.....75.8:2 And t. yourself you wait in certainty to
W-pI...76.10:3 He will t. you more. About the Love your
W-pI...76.11:5 Then we will t. ourselves, as a dedication
W-pI.....77.7:2 T. yourself often today: *I am entitled to*
W-pI.....77.8:2 Be quick to t. yourself, should you be
W-pI...79.10:2 difficulty seems to rise, t. yourself quickly:
W-pI...93.11:2 angry with someone, t. him silently: *Light*
W-pI.....94.5:4 T. yourself frequently today that you are
W-pI...95.11:3 Then close your eyes and t. yourself again
W-pI...95.15:2 promise of today's idea and t. him this:
W-pI...96.10:1 that come to you will t. you you are saved,
W-pI...96.12:1 Each time today you t. your frantic mind
W-pI.....97.8:3 let Him t. your mind that they are true.
W-pI...98.11:2 T. Him once more that you accept the
W-pI.100.10:7 answer, every time you t. yourself you are
W-pI...101.7:5 today, and t. yourself as often as you can:
W-pI...102.5:3 to t. yourself that you have now accepted
W-pI...105.7:1 "enemies" a little while, and t. each one,
W-pI...105.8:3 So t. yourself, "God's peace and joy are
W-pI...106.2:3 which t. you they have found the source
W-pI...107.9:1 which t. you you could be apart from Him
W-pI.107.11:2 Each time you t. yourself with confidence,
W-pI...109.9:6 resting place each time we t. ourselves,
W-pI...120.2:3 *and let my Father t. me Who I really am.*
W-pI.121.13:5 Every hour t. yourself: *Forgiveness is the*
W-pI...125.8:4 let Him t. you God has never left His Son,
W-pI.126.11:2 forget this goal for long, but t. yourself:
W-pI...128.8:2 mind, but t. yourself with quiet certainty:
W-pI...133.8:7 does not even t. the truth as it perceives it
W-pI.134.17:2 see through this illusion as you t. yourself
W-pI.136.20:2 what must be healed, but t. yourself:
W-pI...151.7:2 will not t. you that your brother should
W-pI.155.14:1 may speak to you and t. you of His Love,
W-pI...186.7:5 What can it t. the holy Son of God? Why
W-pI...191.7:2 You need but t. yourself: *I am the holy Son*
W-pI...193.7:1 can you t. when you are seeing wrong, or
W-pII..236.1:3 triumph over me, and t. me what to think
W-pII..273.1:4 We need but t. our minds, with certainty,
W-pII..275.2:3 *Voice will t. me what to do and where to go;*
M-7...........2:5 He must use his reason to t. himself that
M-12.......5:10 holy. God's Voice will t. him when he has
P-3...........I.2:3 There is Something in him that will t. you
P-3........III.8:5 will also t. you exactly what your function
S-1...........I.4:4 they t. Him that you would have no gods
S-2.........II.2:4 who can t. another he is steeped in sin,
S-3........III.6:1 God's Voice alone can t. you how to heal.

### telling 17

T-5.........in.1:3 This is the same as t. you that you have
T-9........III.2:4 a brother, you are t. him that he is wrong.
T-9........III.5:5 from t. you that what you teach you learn
T-22.......III.2:3 t. you what you thought was real is not.
W-pI.....28.3:3 what it is, rather than t. it what it is. You
W-pI.....32.6:2 you. Apply the idea by t. yourself: *I have*
W-pI.....37.3:2 by preaching to it, not by t. it anything,
W-pI.....40.3:9 merely t. yourself that you are blessed as a
W-pI.....47.3:2 t. you exactly what to do to call upon His
W-pI.....47.4:4 fear, dismissing each one by t. yourself:
W-pI.....61.5:2 They should begin with t. yourself: *I am*
W-pI.....64.8:3 and unselectively around you, t. yourself:
W-pI.....65.5:5 dismissing each one by t. yourself: *This*
W-pI.....75.5:3 Begin the longer practice periods by t.
W-pI.....77.4:1 the longer practice periods by t. yourself
W-ep.........3:3 your efforts, t. you exactly what to do,
P-3...........I.2:9 Think what God is t. you; He needs your

### tells 58

T-2.........V.8:3 believe in what your physical sight t. you,
T-3.........III.5:1 The Bible t. you to know yourself, or to
T-4.........III.3:5 It t. you this life is your existence because
T-4........IV.2:2 your mood t. you that you have chosen
T-6.......II.10:5 t. you to return your whole mind to God,
T-6.......II.11:2 the Holy Spirit t. you that even return is
T-6......V.A.3:2 He always t. you that only the mind is real
T-9.........V.9:1 the Guide Who t. you what to do. If you
T-11.........I.8:9 Holy Spirit t. you appears to be coercive,
T-11....VIII.2:1 Bible t. you to become as little children.
T-12...VII.14:4 t. you that you have been treacherous to
T-13.......V.7:5 sane Answer t. you what you have offered
T-13...VII.11:1 the ego t. you that you need will hurt you.
T-13......IX.8:2 ego t. you all is black with guilt within
T-14........X.9:7 The fact of union t. them it is not true.
T-15.........I.5:3 For it t. him hell is here as well, and bids
T19..IV.B.14:9 The Holy Spirit t. you this with joy. The
T-21......IV.2:3 Loudly the ego t. you not to look inward,
T-21......IV.4:4 reason t. you now the ego would not hear.
T-21......IV.5:6 For this your reason t. you, and it follows
T-21...... VI.2:3 Yet reason t. you that you cannot see your
T-21...... VI.2:7 But reason t. you that this must be wrong.
T-21...... VI.5:3 t. you must be joined must be insane. Nor
T-21...... VI.7:6 reason t. you it is given you to change his
T-22.........I.3:8 to suspect that what it t. you is not true.
T-22.........I.5:2 in understanding what this vision t. you,
T-22.....II.6:10 but reason t. you misery lies only on one
T-22...... III.2:5 Therefore, it t. you what you thought was
T-25.........I.2:2 Perception t. you *you* are manifest in what
T-25.........I.2:5 you not despise the one who t. you this,
T-27.... IV.4:16 for it t. you what you want and where to
T-27...... IV.6:8 And so, unless the answer t. "of whom,"
T-27...... VI.3:4 t. you but the names you gave to it to use,
T-27.....VIII.1:3 which t. the story of how it was made by
T-29.........I.5:5 it t. you where to go and how to go there,
T-29.... VIII.9:4 and t. you idols have no purpose here. For
T-30........II.1:2 He t. you but your will; He speaks for you.
W-pI.....55.1:6 I see t. me that I do not know who I am. I
W-pI.....61.3:1 it is God's Voice which t. you it is true.
W-pI.....67.6:1 your tiny, solitary voice that t. you this.
W-pI.....67.6:3 replacing everything that the ego t. you
W-pI.....76.2:3 for today t. you once again how simple is
W-pI...76.10:1 Hear Him Who t. you this, and realize
W-pI...99.12:1 Your only function t. you you are one.
W-pI...110.8:1 Word that t. him he is brother unto Him.
W-pI...132.5:5 which t. you that you made the world you
W-pI...151.5:1 and would yet defend, it t. you is yourself.
W-pI.153.19:6 We will pause a moment, as He t. us, "I
W-pI...186.5:6 the Voice which t. them what they are,
W-pI.186.12:6 which t. you of a function given you by
W-pII .254.2:6 God speaks to us and t. us of our will, as
W-pII .275.1:4 For the Voice for God t. us of things we
W-pII .357.1:1 *truth's reflection, t. me how to offer miracles*
M-5 ...... III.1:9 body t. them what to do and they obey.
M-12 .......5:10 role, just as It t. him what his function is.
M-14 .........4:6 Voice t. him it is a lesson he can learn, he
P-2........V.8:10 For healing t. him, in the Voice for God,
P-2.......VII.3:1 in his heart t. the patient that all his sins

### temper 1

T-18........II.4:1 Dreams are perceptual t. tantrums, in

### tempered 1

T-21...... IV.2:2 Its rule is t., and its unknown "enemy,"

### temple 37

T-2.........III.1:5 Perceiving the body as a t. is only the first
T-2.........III.1:7 to realize that a t. is not a structure at all.
T-2......III.1:10 the t. cannot be seen with the physical eye
T-2.........III.2:3 be undone for the restoration of the t.,
T-4........VII.4:8 real home, your real t. and your real Self.
T-8........VII.9:6 The ego's t. thus becomes the temple of
T-8........VII.9:6 ego's temple thus becomes the t. of the
T-8.......VII.9:7 sense the body does become a t. to God;
T-11...... III.6:2 God's Son, for they have no place in His t.
T-11...... III.7:2 In the quiet of His t., He waits to give you
T-11...... III.7:3 enter the t. and find it waiting for you.
T-11...... III.7:7 Guard carefully His t., for He Himself
T-11...... III.8:2 will be worthy to dwell in the t. with Him,
T-14... V.10:10 The t. you restore becomes your altar, for
T-14...... VI.8:6 There are no hidden chambers in God's t.
T-14...... IX.3:9 it. The t. still is holy, for the Presence that
T-14...... IX.4:1 In the t., Holiness waits quietly for the
T-19..... III.11:3 Your relationship is now a t. of healing; a
T-19...... IV.1:7 to everyone who draws nigh unto your t.,

T-20 VI.h The **T.** of the Holy Spirit
T-20 VI.5:1 The Holy Spirit's **t.** is not a body, but a
T-20 VI.6:1 cannot make the body the Holy Spirit's **t.**,
T-20 VI.6:5 This is the **t.** dedicated to no relationships
T-20 VI.7:2 of their **t.** begin to shake and loosen.
T-20 VI.7:6 Your **t.** is not threatened. You are an
T-20 VI.7:10 for the Holy Spirit has set His **t.** there.
T-20 VI.9:6 And from His holy **t.**, look you not back
T-23 I.11:3 **t.** of the Holy One becomes a house of sin.
T-26 IX.3:2 now become a living **t.** in a world of light.
T-26 IX.6:2 And They come quickly to the living **t.**,
T-26 IX.6:4 come to dwell within the **t.** offered Them,
T-26 IX.8:1 Now is the **t.** of the living God rebuilt as
T-29 II.10:4 he dwell in what was built as **t.** unto death
W-pI 109.8:3 rest. Open the **t.** doors and let them come
P-2 II.1:5 are still the **t.** of the Holy Spirit, and they
P-2 VII.8:4 The room becomes a **t.**, and the street a
P-3 III.6:4 them, they are always His potential **t.**; the

## temples 5

T-20 VI.4:1 Love has no darkened **t.** where mysteries
T-20 VI.4:7 in, and so establish them as **t.** to itself.
T-20 VI.5:6 not build His **t.** where love can never be.
T-21 IV.1:8 Its **t.** do not shake because of this. Your
W-pI 140.5:3 God abides in holy **t.**. He is barred where

## tempo 1

W-pI 12.2:4 to keep a measured, even **t.** throughout.

## temporal 6

T-1 I.13:1 and endings, and so they alter the **t.** order
T-1 II.6:10 however, within the larger **t.** sequence.
T-2 II.6:3 is actually incomprehensible in **t.** terms,
T-10 V.14:6 to become preoccupied with the **t.**, you
T-24 VII.5:4 be attacked; what is but **t.** has no effect.
W-pI 194.4:3 world, the **t.** progression still seems real.

## temporarily 14

T-1 I.8:1 they are performed by those who **t.** have
T-1 I.8:1 have more for those who **t.** have less.
T-1 III.1:3 but I stand at the end in case you fail **t.**.
T-1 V.6:5 equilibrium is **t.** experienced as unstable.
T-2 IV.4:5 a person **t.** inaccessible to the Atonement.
T-2 IV.4:6 from the outside is **t.** given healing belief.
T-2 V.2:5 you to rely **t.** on physical healing devices,
T-2 VII.3:3 the miracle you *have* rejected fear, if only **t.**
T-2 VII.3:10 becomes a real expediter, though only **t.**.
T-2 VII.5:8 is to recognize **t.** that there is a problem,
T-4 II.6:8 reality, and is therefore **t.** less predatory.
T-6 V.B.3:3 I said that this is apt to increase conflict **t.**
T-24 VII.4:2 body, yes, a little; not from time, but **t.**.
T-27 III.5:5 by which the truth is represented **t.**. It lets

## temporary 26

T-1 I.46:2 because they are ***t.*** communication devices
T-1 II.1:1 but **t.** suspension of doubt and fear. It
T-2 II.5:3 like the classrooms in which it occurs, is **t.**
T-2 V.9:2 of the belief in space and time, it is **t.**.
T-3 III.1:6 Perception is **t.**. As an attribute of the
T-3 VI.6:3 Justice is a **t.** expedient, or an attempt to
T-4 II.9:5 to exist after a **t.** lapse into ego life. Some
T-4 II.11:1 perception is merely a **t.** expedient. It is
T-4 III.3:4 All it can offer is a sense of **t.** existence,
T-4 III.3:6 Against this sense of **t.** existence spirit
T-4 VI.3:4 and can never induce more than a **t.** effect
T-6 V.A.5:9 Egos do join together in **t.** allegiance, but
T-7 I.6:5 meaningful, and the **t.** into the timeless.
T-13 IV.7:4 He regards the function of time as **t.**,
T-13 IV.7:4 function, which is **t.** by definition. His
T-13 VII.12:6 He knows that everything you need is **t.**,
T-26 III.3:6 still, and yet it can be seen that they are **t.**,
W-pI 105.2:2 with interest to be paid in full; a **t.** lending
W-pI 133.6:2 A **t.** value is without all value. Time can
M-4 1:5 Their specialness is, of course, only **t.**; set
M-4 2:1 differences among the Sons of God are **t.**.
M-13 1:2 meaning is **t.** and will ultimately fade into
M-29 1:4 so that the difference is **t.** by definition. In
P-2 I.1:8 Retrogression is **t.**. The overall direction
P-2 IV.5:4 Yet must their cures remain **t.**, or another
P-3 II.6:6 their **t.** appeal and turn to dreams of fear,

## temporize 1

T-2 III.3:3 can **t.** and you are capable of enormous

## tempt 9

T-21 VII.10:8 let an "enemy" **t.** you to use the body's
W-pI 84.4:4 *love. Let this not* ***t.*** *me to attack myself.*
W-pI 85.4:2 *this not* ***t.*** *me to look away from me for my*
W-pI 105.9:4 seems to **t.** you to deny God's gift to him,
W-pI 128.8:3 *This will not* ***t.*** *me to delay myself. The world*
W-pI 135.26:5 you and **t.** you to engage in weaving plans
W-pI 163.1:2 to be as you are not may come to **t.** you.
W-pI 166.13:6 Let sorrow not **t.** you to be unfaithful to
W-pI 192.9:6 Thus does each one who seems to **t.** you

## temptation 78

T-1 III.4:7 "Lead us not into **t.**" means "Recognize
T-4 III.2:1 because it is useful in moments of **t.**. It is
T-6 I.11:6 as a good teaching aid to those whose **t.** to
T-6 V.C.4:5 that the **t.** to make exceptions will occur.
T-8 VII.12:4 from the **t.** to see the body in many lights,
T-13 VII.16:1 every **t.** that would hold you back. We
T-16 VII.12:5 *Let us not wander into* ***t.****, for the temptation*
T-16 VII.12:5 *for the* ***t.*** *of the Son of God is not Your Will.*
T-17 V.4:1 **t.** of the ego becomes extremely intense
T-18 VII.5:7 **t.** and fight against the giving in to sin;
T-18 VII.6:8 of contemplation, or of struggle against **t.**
T-20 I.3:3 him not wander into the **t.** of crucifixion,
T-20 IV.4:5 all **t.** to imprison and to be imprisoned. It
T-23 in.5:1 us not let littleness lead God's Son into **t.**.
T-23 in.5:4 him not frightened and alone in his **t.**, but
T-23 IV.6:1 When the **t.** to attack rises to make your
T-24 VI.4:5 in all **t.** to perceive what is not there, and
T-25 III.6:8 he will reinterpret all **t.** as just another
T-25 VII.13:1 Remember all **t.** is but this; a mad belief
T-26 X.4:1 the **t.** to perceive yourself unfairly treated.
T-30 VIII.3:1 is **t.** but a wish to make illusions real? It
T-30 VIII.3:4 **T.**, then, is nothing more than this; a
T-30 VIII.6:2 really is. Let no **t.** to prefer a dream allow
T-31 I.11:1 What is **t.** but a wish to make the wrong
T-31 III.1:3 it becomes your first response to all **t.**,
T-31 VII.10:1 is **t.** but the wish to stay in hell and misery
T-31 VII.12:1 Whatever form **t.** seems to take, it always
T-31 VII.14:1 Be vigilant against **t.**, then, remembering
T-31 VII.14:4 *This* is **t.**; nothing more than this. Can this
T-31 VII.14:6 Consider what **t.** is, and see the real
T-31 VIII.1:1 **T.** has one lesson it would teach, in all its
T-31 VIII.4:2 Be never fearful of **t.**, then, but see it as it
T-31 VIII.5:1 the happy habit of response to all **t.** to
T-31 VIII.6:2 is but **t.** to perceive yourself defenseless
T-31 VIII.11:1 would join with me in reaching past **t.**,
W-pI 16.3:3 There is such a **t.** to dismiss fear thoughts
W-pI 17.1:3 despite the **t.** to believe that it is the other
W-pI 27.2:1 may be a great **t.** to believe that some sort
W-pI 31.5:1 a response to any form of **t.** that may arise
W-pI 34.5:2 yourself from **t.** throughout the day. If a
W-pI 34.5:3 form of **t.** arises in your awareness, the
W-pI 61.4:2 to all illusions, and therefore to all **t.**. It
W-pI 64.1:1 way of saying "Let me not wander into **t.**.
W-pI 64.1:3 **t.** to abandon God and His Son by taking
W-pI 64.2:1 to see can be anything but a form of **t.**,
W-pI 64.2:4 the physical appearance of **t.** becomes the
W-pI 64.3:3 from all illusions, and thus from all **t.**.
W-pI 70.1:1 All **t.** is nothing more than some form of
W-pI 70.1:1 basic **t.** not to believe the idea for today.
W-pI 71.10:2 Be alert to all **t.** to hold grievances today,
W-pI 74.5:3 may be some **t.** to mistake these attempts
W-pI 76.12:1 well as in response to any **t.** to experience
W-pI 78.10:2 **T.** falls away when we allow each one we
W-pI 79.4:1 The **t.** to regard problems as many is the
W-pI 79.4:1 as many is the **t.** to keep the problem of
W-pI 91.11:2 Also, be sure to meet **t.** with today's idea.
W-pI 94.1:1 which makes all forms of **t.** powerless; the
W-pI 95.5:3 the idea as an automatic response to **t.**.
W-pI 95.7:4 There may well be a **t.** to regard the day as
W-pI 97.8:4 Use them against **t.**, and escape its sorry
W-pI 128.4:1 nor permit **t.** to believe the world holds
W-pI 130.10:1 Dismiss **t.** easily today whenever it arises,
W-pI 161.1:3 Here is the answer to **t.** which can never
W-pI 183.4:2 meaning. No **t.** but becomes a nameless
W-pI 193.5:3 These are the words with which **t.** ends,
W-pI 194.6:2 repertoire, a way of quick reaction to **t.**,
W-pI 194.9:5 the choice for us that leaves **t.** far behind.
WpI.rVI.in.6:1 hasten to proclaim your freedom from **t.**,
W-pII 272.2:2 we hear **t.** call to us to stay and linger in a
M-16 9:1 avoidance of magic is the avoidance of **t.**.
M-16 9:2 all **t.** is nothing more than the attempt to
M-16 10:8 Yet each **t.** to accept magic as true must
M-17 2:1 a **t.** to respond to magic in a way that
M-23 1:2 teachers will give way to **t.** in this world.
M-23 2:3 **T.** may recur to others, but never to this
M-25 5:3 this new **t.** to win back strength by guile.
P-3 II.9:2 which there is great **t.** to misuse his role.
P-3 II.9:3 he escapes the **t.** to assume a function that

## temptations 6

T-4 IV.6:1 Watch your mind for the **t.** of the ego,
T-6 I.6:7 of much less extreme **t.** to misperceive,
W-pI 39.11:2 If **t.** arise, a particularly helpful form of
W-pII in.10:2 need only call to God, and all **t.** disappear
M-7 4:1 One of the most difficult **t.** to recognize is
M-16 8:1 will be **t.** along the way the teacher of God

## tempted 38

T-4 I.13:5 not once been **t.** to believe in them myself
T-5 II.11:1 When you are **t.** by the wrong voice, call
T-11 III.6:3 **t.** to deny Him remember that there *are* no
T-12 VII.15:1 you are **t.** to yield to the desire for death,
T-13 I.3:1 be **t.** to wonder how you can be guiltless
T-13 VII.14:1 Whenever you are **t.** to undertake a
T-15 I.11:1 **t.** to be dispirited by thinking how long it
T-15 I.12:3 then, when you are **t.** to attack a brother,
T-16 I.3:8 **t.** you may be to judge any situation, and
T-16 I.4:7 Be **t.** not in this, and yield not to the ego's
T-17 VII.5:7 illusions. Be **t.** not by what it offers you. It
T-18 III.4:5 Be **t.** not to snatch away the gift of faith
T-18 IX.3:9 You are severely **t.** to abandon Him at the
T-19 II.8:3 Perhaps you would be **t.** to agree with the
T-19 III.6:1 When you are **t.** to believe that sin is real,
T-30 V.2:5 form. No one is **t.** by its vain appeal, for
T-30 VIII.4:8 When he is **t.**, he denies reality. And he
T-30 VIII.6:3 when you are **t.** by a dream of what he is.
T-31 VII.15:5 says, "Release My Son!" be **t.** not to listen
W-pI 9.5:3 distinction. You may be **t.** to obscure it.
W-pI 21.3:3 You will probably be **t.** to dwell more on
W-pI 69.9:8 **t.** to hold anything against anyone today.
W-pI 73.11:6 you are **t.** to hold a grievance of any kind.
W-pI 75.10:4 *world.* Should you be **t.**, say to anyone who
W-pI 77.8:2 Be quick to tell yourself, should you be **t.**:
W-pI 88.3:4 I am constantly **t.** to make up other laws
W-pI 93.11:2 you be **t.** to become angry with someone,
W-pI 99.11:2 mind. If you are **t.** to believe them true,
W-pI 122.14:1 Be **t.** not to let your gifts slip by and drift
W-pI 132.17:1 say whenever you are **t.** to deny the power
W-pI 134.9:2 feel that you are **t.** to accuse someone of
W-pI 155.9:2 may find that you are **t.** still to walk ahead
W-pI 161.12:5 should you be **t.** to attack a brother and
W-pI 193.6:1 when we are **t.** to believe that pain is real,
W-pI 194.9:5 And if we are **t.** to attack, we will appeal
WpI.rVI.in.6:1 When you are **t.**, hasten to proclaim your
W-pII in.2:9 need of Him as we are **t.** to forget our goal
M-7 2:2 Should he be **t.** to doubt this, he should

## tempting 2

W-pI 29.4:2 may be particularly **t.** in connection with
M-25 4:5 unusual abilities that can be curiously **t.**.

### tempts 5
T-8........IX.1:5 ego t. you to sickness do not ask the Holy
T-16.....V.12:1 t. you to seek for love in ritual, remember
T-22.....II.13:5 a single sin still t. you to remain in misery
T-30.....V.10:2 And when an idol t. you, think of this:
W-pI.....33.3:2 arises which t. you to become disturbed.

### ten 16
*See also* ten-to-fifteen-minute
W-pI.....40.1:3 Once every t. minutes would be highly
W-pI.....50.5:1 For t. minutes, twice today, morning and
W-pI.....64.6:5 At least once devote t. or fifteen minutes
W-pI.....65.3:1 set aside t. to fifteen minutes for a more
W-pI.....70.6:1 should last some t. to fifteen minutes. We
W-pI.....91.5:1 set aside about t. minutes for a quiet time
WpI.rIII.in1:2 day for t. successive days of practicing.
W-pI...121.8:3 We will devote t. minutes in the morning,
W-pI...121.8:3 in the morning, and at night another t., to
W-pI...125.7:1 give t. minutes set apart from listening to
W-pI...128.7:1 Give it t. minutes rest three times today.
W-pI...129.7:1 t. minutes in the morning and at night,
W-pI.131.10:3 devote t. minutes to this goal three times
W-pI.137.14:2 and give t. minutes to these thoughts with
W-pI.153.15:4 T. would be better; fifteen better still.
W-pI.186.10:4 t. times an hour at their most secure.

### ten-to-fifteen-minute 1
W-pI.....66.5:1 Begin the t. practice period by reviewing

### tenable 1
T-23.....II.18:5 Can any form of this be t.? Yet you believe

### tend 2
W-pI.....16.4:1 thought that may t. to elude the search.
W-pI.....95.5:2 you t. to forget about it for long periods

### tendencies 1
P-1............3:2 t. are often described as "self-destructive,

### tendency 11
T-3........III.3:4 This fear inhibits the t. to question at all.
T-3.......VII.4:3 the t. of the self to make an image of itself.
T-6...........I.3:2 This is a marked t. of the separated, who
T-11......IV.4:5 there is a strong t. to harbor it within. It is
T-16.......II.2:1 There is a t. to fragment, and then to be
T-31......IV.1:1 t. to think the world can offer consolation
W-pI.......4.5:4 a t. to become pointlessly preoccupied.
W-pI.....29.4:2 avoid the t. toward self-directed selection,
P-2.........II.2:2 astonishing t. to join contradictory words
P-2........VI.2:1 There is a t., and it is very strong, to hear
P-3...........I.1:7 There is a t. to assume that you are being

### tender 1
T-20....VI.10:3 smile and t. blessing it offers to its own.

### tenderness 6
T19.IV.D.11:3 brother with perfect faith and love and t..
T-25......VI.1:6 on himself with all the t. it offers others.
T-31.......II.7:5 Christ calls to all with equal t., seeing no
W-pI...189.6:1 is true in us, and feel its all-embracing t.,
W-pII..233.1:7 *nor Love whose t. I cannot comprehend, but*
W-pII..341.1:2 *I am he on whom You smile in love and t. so*

### tends 2
W-pI.....26.6:3 Any problem as yet unsettled that t. to
S-1.........II.3:3 t. to be blurred by a deep-rooted sense of

### tenet 3
T-19.......II.4:1 major t. in the ego's insane religion is that
T-25...VII.11:1 the underlying t. God must be insane. For
T-25...VII.11:4 belief except a form of the more basic t.,

### tens 2
T-26......IX.4:1 years to Them, or t. of thousands? When
W-pI.....97.6:1 a thousandfold and t. of thousands more.

### tense 1
T-28.........I.2:5 as selective as perception, being its past t.

### tenuously 1
W-pI.....95.2:2 and t. held together by its erratic and

### term 22
T-2......IV.3:12 The t. "unworthy" here implies only that
T-2.....VII.3:11 "Cause" is a t. properly belonging to God,
T-2..... VIII.5:1 The t. "Last Judgment" is frightening not
T-3........IV.4:3 t. "right-mindedness" is properly used as
T-4.........II.6:9 a t. which refers to any perceived threat to
T-4........VI.2:4 The t. "holy" can be used here because, as
T-5........III.9:3 is merely another t. for a split mind. The
T-6......V.B.8:5 the t. "more desirable" still implies that
T-10......IV.4:8 exist. "Laws of chaos" is a meaningless t..
T-11.......V.3:1 that the t. itself does not mean anything.
W-pI.......5.1:2 in whatever t. seems accurate to you. The
W-pI.....23.3:4 a more appropriate t. for the result?
W-pI.....35.7:3 identify the descriptive t. or terms you
M-3...........4:3 Using the t. in this way, the second level
M-4.......II.1:5 The t. actually means consistency. There
M-4.....VII.1:1 The t. generosity has special meaning to
M-10.........1:3 As the world uses the t., an individual is
M-13.........1:1 the t. sacrifice is altogether meaningless,
C-1............1:1 t. *mind* is used to represent the activating
C-1............1:2 When the t. is capitalized it refers to God
C-1............3:2 The t. "soul" is not used except in direct
P-2.........II.2:2 to join contradictory words into one t.

### terminate 1
W-pI.....12.6:4 T. the exercises whenever you experience

### termination 1
T-27.........I.8:1 sin will end alike within the t. of the grave

### terminology 1
C-in...........1:1 nor is it concerned with precise t.. It is

### terms 79
T-1.........II.4:2 The statement is more meaningful in t. of
T-2.........II.6:3 actually incomprehensible in temporal t.,
T-2........III.1:6 Atonement in physical t. is impossible.
T-3.........II.1:2 cannot be understood in t. of opposites. It
T-3........VI.2:3 before in t. of the selectivity of perception
T-3........VI.7:4 ego makes involves a contradiction in t.,
T-4.........II.1:3 no point in giving an answer in t. of the
T-4.........II.6:8 "Self-esteem" in ego t. means nothing
T-4.........II.8:9 self-esteem in ego t. must be delusional.
T-4.........V.3:2 only in t. of threat or non-threat to itself.
T-5........III.1:2 so we can use the t. as if they were related,
T-6...........I.1:4 can be explained in negative t. only.
T-7.......V.5:10 "fearful healer" is a contradiction in t.,
T-8...........I.2:5 evaluate them in t. of their results to you.
T-8........VI.7:1 in t. that actually means nothing. When
T-9........III.1:2 Egos are critical in t. of the kind of "sense
T-9.........V.4:6 This is a contradiction even in the ego's t.,
T-9.......VII.7:8 you hold in t. of where it comes from. If it
T-9......VII.8:5 Choose, then, what you want in these t.,
T-9.......VIII.3:3 of judgment except in t. of attack. When
T-11.......V.3:2 the very contradiction in t. that makes it
T-12.......V.7:2 Translated into curricular t. this means,
T-13......IV.4:5 by interpreting the present in past t..
T-13......IX.2:4 And faith can be rewarded only in t. of
T-15.......V.2:1 methods for meeting them on your own t.
T-15.....VII.8:7 t. that it evaluates ideas as good or bad.
T-16......IV.5:7 Seen in these t., no one would hesitate.
T-17......IV.6:2 You recognize, at least in general t., that
T-24......VI.7:6 last in t. you recognized and understood?
T-26....VIII.1:5 it is, the more you think of it in t. of space
T-26....VIII.3:7 body is, except in t. of what you see it for.
T-27.....VII.3:7 to go beyond the obvious in t. of cause.
T-28.....VII.4:7 the choice cannot be made in t. of form.
T-30.........I.6:2 and must have set an answer in your t..
T-30.........I.6:6 This cancels out the t. that you have set,
T-30......III.1:3 content for its expression in the t. of form
T-30......III.4:6 answer you in t. that have no meaning.
T-31.......V.1:7 perfected it, to meet the world on equal t.,
T-31.....VII.3:1 In t. of concepts, it is thus you see him
W-pI.....12.3:2 using whatever descriptive t. happen to
W-pI.....12.3:3 you. If t. which seem positive rather than
W-pI.....12.3:5 If such t. occur to you, use them along
W-pI.....12.3:7 All t. which cross your mind are suitable
W-pI.....14.5:3 Do not use general t.. For example, do not
W-pI.....19.3:3 one, name it in t. of the central person or
W-pI.....25.2:1 in it as meaningful in t. of ego goals.
W-pI.....28.3:2 You are not defining it in past t.. You are
W-pI.....35.4:1 of descriptive t. in which you see yourself.
W-pI.....35.5:2 more self-inflating descriptive t. may well
W-pI.....35.7:1 not think of these t. in an abstract way.
W-pI.....35.7:3 identify the descriptive term or t. you feel
W-pI.....73.1:6 But they are idle indeed in t. of creation.
W-pI.....92.1:2 You do not think of light in t. of strength,
W-pI.....92.1:2 strength, and darkness in t. of weakness.
W-pI.....95.6:2 it. Regularity in t. of time is not the ideal
W-pI.....98.5:3 to make in t. of gaining a reward so great
W-pI.....99.1:3 Thus do both t. imply a thing impossible
W-pI...105.4:4 already, not in simple t. of adding more,
WpI. rIII.in2:3 be sure that you catch up in t. of numbers
W-pI...123.7:3 to you in t. of years for every second;
W-pI.134.10:1 in t. that render choosing meaningful,
W-pI...184.1:6 all happenings in t. of place and time; all
W-pI.184.10:3 only to proclaim its unreality in t. which
W-pI...192.2:1 have a function in the world in its own t..
M-4.......X.3:2 T. like love, sinlessness, perfection,
M-5........II.1:8 T. like "instincts," "reflexes" and the like
M-5........II.1:9 t. merely state or describe the problem.
M-10.........1:9 "Good" judgment, in these t., does not
M-13.........2:4 no sacrifice in the world's t. that does not
M-13.........8:1 decision you make must mean in t. of cost
M-16.........2:8 obvious advantages in t. of saving time.
M-16.........3:1 beginning, it is wise to think in t. of time.
M-24.........2:7 risk in seeing the present in t. of the past.
M-29.........1:2 t. of a brief summary of some of the major
C-in...........2:1 All t. are potentially controversial, and
C-in...........5:3 these are some of the t. that are used.
P-3......III.6:10 Only in t. of cost could one have more. In
S-1..........II.4:1 in t. known as "praying for one's enemies.
S-1..........II.5:4 Now it is no longer a contradiction in t..

### terrible 17
T-3...........I.2:4 to "justify" the t. misperception that God
T-13..........II.5:2 You have not admitted to this "t." secret
T-16.......V.9:1 of hell lies only in the t. attraction of guilt,
T-21....VI.7:12 *This* is the burden that is t., and not the
T-23......II.15:6 sightless eyes, blinded and t. to look upon
T-24.........I.2:7 deny their presence nor their t. results.
T-26.....V.12:4 This t. illusion was denied in but the time
T-27....VIII.9:3 He bids you bring each t. effect to Him
T-29......IX.3:3 does an idol keep the dream alive and t.,
T-31.......V.5:2 It is a lesson in a t. displacement, and a
W-pI...170.8:1 This moment can be t.. But it can also be
W-pI.170.10:6 And He is t. above all else, cruel beyond
W-pII...12.2:4 And in its t. autonomy it "sees" the Will
M-17.........9:1 Madness but seems t.. In truth it has no
M-27.........5:9 T. His Thoughts and fearful His image.
C-2............8:2 This t. mistake about yourself the miracle
S-2...........I.1:6 remedy appears to be a t. alternative to

**terribly** 1

T-18......III.3:5 it, and **t.** afraid of its judgment upon you.

**terrified** 5

T-11..VIII.13:1 monsters and dragons, and they are **t.**.
T-27...VII.13:3 than an idle dream has **t.** God's Son, and
T-31.....VII.7:5 and perceive the **t.** imaginings that come
W-pI...121.3:1 yet more afraid of stillness; **t.** of darkness,
W-pI...121.3:1 yet more **t.** at the approach of light. What

**terrifies** 1

T-18....VIII.3:6 the ocean **t.** the little ripple and wants to

**terrify** 8

T-12....... II.4:1 **t.** them because they do not understand
T-14...... VI.1:4 And yet it is only the hidden that can **t.**,
W-pI.134.11:2 and to **t.** the foolish dreamer who believes
W-pI.135.20:4 availed them nothing and could only **t.**.
W-pII .....4.4:1 frightening, and sin appears indeed to **t.**.
W-pII .....7.4:2 will your dreams remain to **t.** you. And
M-16 .........9:9 escaped. What has no effects can hardly **t.**
P-2........ VI.4:6 it is the "something else" that seems to **t.**.

**terrifying** 5

T-15.........I.6:2 And how **t.**! For underneath its fanatical
T-18....... II.4:5 by substituting a world that you prefer *is* **t.**
T-20..VIII.10:6 are His substitutes for all the **t.** sights and
T-20..VIII.11:1 When you have looked on what seemed **t.**
W-pI.153.14:4 may learn the tale he reads of **t.** destiny,

**terror** 46

T-11.......in.3:9 Open the dark cornerstone of **t.** on which
T-13.... III.1:11 crucifixion. Your real **t.** is of redemption.
T-17....VIII.4:5 pain, darkness and dim imaginings of **t.**,
T-18....... II.4:4 satisfaction is invaded by the illusion of **t.**.
T-18...... III.2:1 forms of fear, and sometimes to stark **t.**.
T-18...... IX.3:7 follow the Holy Spirit through seeming **t.**,
T19. IV.A.12:3 Fear's messengers are trained through **t.**,
T19..IV.C.11:1 when any situation strikes you with **t.** and
T19... IV.D.6:1 And now you stand in **t.** before what you
T19... IV.D.8:6 be ready to look on **t.** with no fear at all.
T-20....... II.8:8 freed from all the **t.** that kept it hidden.
T-21...... IV.6:5 its ranting strikes no **t.** in your heart. For
T-21...... IV.7:2 Yet what it hears in **t.**, the other part
T-23..... II.21:4 leading still deeper into **t.** and away from
T-26....... V.9:1 Forget the time of **t.** that has been so long
T-26..... V.13:1 when the time of **t.** took the place of love.
T-26....VIII.3:9 given seem dangerous, with **t.** justified.
T-27.........I.1:4 But place no **t.** symbols on your path, or
T-27...VII.12:4 of fear, the time of **t.** and of ancient hate,
T-27...VII.13:4 the sweat of **t.** and a scream of mortal fear
T-27...VII.14:3 you dreamed in **t.** and in fear of death. He
T-28....... V.7:5 where **t.** rises from the bones of death.
T-29...... IX.2:9 salvation from the judgment laid in **t.** and
T-29...... IX.3:3 for one unless he were in **t.** and despair?
T-29...... IX.3:4 worship is the worship of despair and **t.**,
T-30.... III.10:2 by the turmoil and the **t.** of the world, the
T-30...... IV.8:2 without the toys of **t.** that you made. No
T-30...... VI.1:4 world given in exchange for dreams of **t.**.
T-30...... VI.3:1 world rise to take the place of dreams of **t.**
T-31.........I.7:5 It is a world of **t.** and despair. Nor is there
T-31....... V.8:5 of self, and greater **t.** would arise in you.
W-pI...135.2:5 but must have **t.** striking at his heart.
W-pI...135.3:4 it speaks of fear made real and **t.** justified.
W-pI...138.8:1 and grip the mind with **t.** and anxiety so
W-pI.138.11:4 It holds no **t.** now, for what was made
W-pI.153.13:1 left alone in **t.** in a fearful world made
W-pI...186.6:2 this image which quails and retreats in **t.**,
W-pI...191.6:5 image of yourself walking the world in **t.**,
W-pI...192.5:3 becomes impossible, and where is **t.** then
W-pI.193.13:2 To all that speaks of **t.**, answer thus: *I will*
W-pI...196.9:3 need you hide in **t.** from the deadly fear of
W-pI.196.10:1 There is an instant in which **t.** seems to
W-pII .....8.1:3 brings the witnesses of **t.** to your mind.
W-pII .....8.1:4 so they see a world where **t.** is impossible,
W-pII .295.1:2 to me, and take away all **t.** and all pain.
S-3...... IV.10:5 and live no more in **t.** and in pain. Do not

**terrorize** 2

T-3 ..........I.4:5 Good teachers never **t.** their students. To
T-3 ..........I.4:6 **t.** is to attack, and this results in rejection

**terrors** 1

T-29 ... IX.10:2 So do your childish **t.** melt away, and

**test** 9

T-1 ....... VI.5:2 are willing to submit your beliefs to this **t.**
T-14 ........ XI.h The **T.** of Truth
T-14 ..... XI.5:1 You have one **t.**, as sure as God, by which
T-14 ... XI.12:4 until you pass the **t.** of perfect peace, for
T-14 ... XI.15:6 will be the **t.** by which you recognize that
T-24 .... VII.6:1 **t.** of everything on earth is simply this;
T-25 .... VII.6:1 **T.** everything that you believe against
W-pI... 133.3:1 which to **t.** all things you think you want.
W-pII . 327.2:1 *fail in my experience, if I but* **t.** *them out. Let*

**Testament** 1

T-6 ........I.15:1 of upside-down thinking in the New **T.**,

**testifies** 2

T-27 .......II.5:5 or think but **t.** to what you teach to him.
W-pI... 153.6:2 It **t.** to recognition of the Christ in you.

**testify** 2

T-14 ..... III.3:7 *to* **t.** *to my acceptance of the Atonement, not*
T-24 VII.10:10 does the body **t.** to the idea that made it,

**testimonies** 1

P-2........ VI.4:1 These **t.** which the senses bring have but

**testimony** 4

T-14 ........I.1:6 is why miracles offer *you* the **t.** that you are
T-21 .......II.5:3 You trained it in its **t.**, and as it gave it
T-27 .......II.5:7 can it offer him mute **t.** of his innocence.
T-27 .......II.5:8 **t.** that can speak with power greater than

**tests** 1

W-pI... 133.5:4 learn the **t.** by which you can distinguish

**text** 17

W-in.......... 1:1 such as the **t.** provides is necessary as a
W-in.......... 1:4 to think along the lines the **t.** sets forth.
W-pI..... 39.1:2 Like the **t.** for which this workbook was
W-pI..... 39.2:5 see at once how direct and simple the **t.** is,
W-pI... 110.6:1 begin with this quotation from the **t.**: *I am*
W-pI... 132.5:4 This central theme is often stated in the **t.**
W-pI... 153.6:3 Perhaps you will recall the **t.** maintains
W-pI... 156.1:3 basic thought so often mentioned in the **t.**
W-pI... 158.2:6 evoked a theme found early in the **t.**.
W-pI... 161.6:2 thought is surely reminiscent of our **t.**,
W-pI... 170.9:2 Let us remember what the **t.** has stressed
M-4 ..... VII.1:6 throughout the **t.** and the workbook, but
M-4 .... IX.1:10 Readiness, as the **t.** notes, is not mastery.
M-6 ........... 2:5 We have referred many times in the **t.** to
M-11 ......... 3:1 The **t.** explains that the Holy Spirit is the
M-29 ......... 1:2 major concepts in the **t.** and workbook. It
M-29 ......... 1:7 to start at the more abstract level of the **t.**.

**than** 555

**thank** 29

T-1 ........I.31:2 You should **t.** God for what you really are.
T-13 .....X.12:6 I **t.** You, Father, for the purity of Your
T-13 .....X.13:6 I **t.** the Father for your loveliness, and for
T-14 ... XI.10:8 His Presence. **T.** God that He is there and
T-17 .......II.4:4 you will barely have time to **t.** God for it.
T-25 .......II.9:7 you **t.** His perfect Son for being what he is
T-25 .....II.10:3 as one, and **t.** his Father as He thanks you.
T-28 ..... IV.9:1 I **t.** You, Father, knowing You will come
T-30 ..... VI.9:4 *I* **t.** *You, Father, for Your perfect Son, and in*
T-31 . VIII.10:1 I **t.** You, Father, for these holy ones who
W-pI .... 45.9:4 **t.** Him for the Thoughts He is thinking
W-pI .. 105.5:6 and He will **t.** you for your gift to Him.
W-pI ..... 123.h I **t.** my Father for His gifts to me.
W-pI .. 142.1:1 (123) I **t.** my Father for His gifts to me.
W-pI .. 195.6:1 We **t.** our Father for one thing alone; that
W-pI .. 197.3:1 The world must **t.** you when you offer it
W-pI .. 197.7:2 **T.** your Self for this, for He is grateful only
W-pI .. 198.5:2 more intelligent to **t.** the One Who gives
W-pII . 234.2:1 *We* **t.** *You, Father, that we cannot lose the*
W-pII . 239.2:1 *We* **t.** *You, Father, for the light that shines*
W-pII . 292.2:1 *We* **t.** *You, Father, for Your guarantee of*
W-pII . 315.2:1 *I* **t.** *You, Father, for the many gifts that come*
W-pII . 327.2:1 *I* **t.** *You that Your promises will never fail in*
W-pII . 340.1:1 *Father, I* **t.** *You for today, and for the*
W-pII . 342.1:1 *I* **t.** *You, Father, for Your plan to save me*
M-29 ......... 5:9 so, and **t.** Him for His guidance at night.
C-5 ............ 1:9 **T.** God for them for they will lead you
S-2........II.6:10 of God, and **t.** his Father for his holiness?
S-3..........II.2:2 We **t.** the body, then, for all the service it

**thankful** 22

T-16 ... VI.10:6 you **t.** that there *is* a place where truth and
T-22 ..... IV.4:7 **t.** will they be to see you come among
T-22 ..... VI.4:2 plan. Be **t.** that it serves yours not at all.
T-24 .... VII.3:4 Be **t.**, rather, it is given you to see his
T-25 .......II.9:7 And He is glad and **t.** when you thank His
T-25 ... VIII.2:7 you **t.** that only little faith is asked of you.
T-31 ... IV.11:5 For what He is be **t.**, for in that is your
T-31 .....V.16:3 be you **t.** that the learning of the world is
W-pI .. 98.11:1 you, be **t.** and lay down all earthly tasks,
W-pI 110.11:1 the day with **t.** hearts and loving thoughts
W-pI .. 122.5:2 Be **t.** it remains exactly as He planned it.
W-pI .. 123.1:1 Today let us be **t.**. We have come to
W-pI .. 123.3:5 Be **t.** that your value far transcends your
W-pI .. 123.4:1 hearts above despair, and raise our **t.** eyes
W-pI 184.15:4 *And we are glad and* **t.** *we were wrong. All*
W-pI .. 197.3:3 that they be a lasting offering of a **t.** heart,
W-pI 200.11:9 *the peace of God, And I am glad and* **t.** *it is so.*
W-pII . 239.1:2 Let us instead be **t.** for the gifts our Father
M-14 ....... 5:15 be otherwise. And be you **t.** it is so.
M-23 ......... 4:6 be far behind a grateful heart and **t.** mind.
P-2....... VII.9:1 Be **t.**, therapist, that you can see such
S-3..........II.2:3 us. But we are **t.**, too, the need is done to

**thankfully** 6

T-20 ... VI.10:5 leaving the body **t.** behind and resting in
T-22 ......I.10:7 where fear is powerless love enters **t.**,
W-pI .. 105.9:5 Then bless your brother **t.**, and say: *My*
W-pI .. 109.5:6 Let it be still and **t.** accept its healing. No
W-pI 124.10:3 **t.** aware no time was ever better spent.
W-pI .. 197.4:5 and **t.** acknowledged by the Heart of God

**thankfulness** 9

W-pI .. 123.2:2 Be glad today, in loving **t.**, your Father
W-pI .. 123.4:2 We sing the song of **t.** today, in honor of
W-pI .. 164.7:3 practicing today becomes our gift of **t.** for
W-pI .. 189.2:6 and its snow, in **t.** for your benevolence.
W-pII . 306.2:2 *us. In gratitude and* **t.** *we come, with empty*
W-pII . 310.2:2 in our song of **t.** and joy to Him Who gave
W-pII . 315.2:3 *Now may I offer them my* **t.**, *that gratitude to*
W-pII . 350.1:8 *return to me, and give it to the world in* **t.**.
S-3..........II.4:1 ways of earth, can only be received with **t.**

### thanking 5

W-pI.....78.9:2 The world and Heaven join in **t.** you, for
W-pI...123.5:5 In **t.** Him the thanks are yours as well. An
W-pI...123.7:2 and Whom He thanks as you are **t.** Him.
W-pI.153.17:2 while **t.** Him for all the gifts He gave us in
W-pI...197.4:2 is a part that joins with yours in **t.** you. It

### thanks 122

T-5.........in.3:4 and returns **t.** to the Father for radiating
T-7.........XI.3:5 and that God Himself **t.** him for his giving
T-7.........XI.4:3 healed the Sonship and given **t.** to God.
T-13......VI.9:3 will return your **t.** in His clear Answer to
T-13....VI.10:5 it, and in their joy they shine with holy **t.**.
T-13...VII.17:8 Give **t.** to every part of you that you have
T-13...VII.17:9 Thus does the Son of God give **t.** unto his
T-13...X.11:11 *and offer **t.** unto his Father that no guilt has*
T-15......XI.9:1 God offers **t.** to the holy host who would
T-16.......II.5:2 truth for what it is, and giving **t.** for it?
T-17.......II.1:7 look upon, and which He **t.** the Father for.
T-17.......II.1:9 leads to seeing it and giving **t.** with Him.
T-17...V.11:10 lack of **t.** and gratitude you make yourself
T-17.....V.12:5 To give **t.** to your brother is to appreciate
T-19......IV.3:8 the Holy Spirit will gather all the **t.** and
T19.IV.D.16:3 And offer **t.** to God that he is holy, and
T19.IV.D.19:6 offer to the Son of God in **t.** for what he is,
T-20......III.8:6 and give him **t.** for all the happiness that
T-21....VI.10:3 you reminds you of the **t.** your Father
T-23.....II.15:8 Give **t.** unto the hero on love's throne,
T-25.....II.9:2 but offer **t.** to you who love His Son as He
T-25.....II.9:8 And all His **t.** and gladness shine on you
T-25.....II.10:3 as one, and thank his Father as He **t.** you.
T-26......IX.7:3 offers **t.** to one who has restored his home
T-26......IX.8:3 give **t.** that They are welcome made at last
T-27.......V.6:4 but shine in **t.** to you who blessing gave.
T-27.......V.7:4 No reinforcement will its **t.** withhold
T-27.....V.11:9 God **t.** you for your healing, for He knows
T-27...VII.15:5 give **t.** to him for all the helpfulness he
T-28......I.12:1 offers **t.** for every quiet instant given Him.
T-28......I.12:4 And His Creator shares His **t.**, because He
T-30.......II.3:7 Not one created thing but gives you **t.**, for
T-31.VIII.10:6 And I give **t.** for them. Salvation's song
T-31.VIII.11:4 I give You **t.** for what my brothers are.
T-31.VIII.11:5 the song of **t.** from earth to Heaven grows
T-31.VIII.11:5 redeemed from hell, and giving **t.** to You.
W-pI.....75.3:1 in which we offer **t.** for the passing of the
W-pI.....75.9:3 Give **t.** for mercy and the Love of God.
W-pI.....78.9:1 God **t.** you for these quiet times today in
W-pI.....98.2:2 **t.** that doubt is gone and surety has come.
W-pI...123.2:4 Him and His creation. Give Him **t.** today.
W-pI...123.3:1 Give **t.** that He has not abandoned you,
W-pI...123.3:2 Give **t.** as well that you are changeless, for
W-pI...123.5:2 we give **t.** that in our solitude a Friend has
W-pI...123.5:3 us. And **t.** to you for listening to Him. His
W-pI...123.5:5 In thanking Him the **t.** are yours as well.
W-pI...123.6:1 **T.** be to you who heard, for you become
W-pI...123.6:2 Receive the **t.** of God today, as you give
W-pI...123.6:2 thanks of God today, as you give **t.** to Him
W-pI...123.6:3 For He would offer you the **t.** you give,
W-pI...123.7:1 Receive His **t.** and offer yours to Him for
W-pI...123.7:2 And you will realize to Whom you offer **t.**
W-pI...123.7:2 and Whom He **t.** as you are thanking Him
W-pI...123.7:3 eons more quickly for your **t.** to Him.
W-pI...123.8:1 Receive His **t.**, and you will understand
W-pI...123.8:2 Him **t.** for everything He gave His Son,
W-pI...124.1:1 will again give **t.** for our Identity in God.
W-pI.127.10:2 Let us give **t.** today that we are spared a
W-pI...129.8:4 of grace is given you today, and we give **t.**.
W-pI...130.7:1 Six times today, in **t.** and gratitude, we
W-pI...130.9:3 Nor will you fail to see His **t.** expressed in
W-pI.139.12:1 In **t.** for all creation, in the Name of its
WpIrIV.in10:1 God offers **t.** to you who practice thus the
W-pI.151.17:2 As we give **t.**, the world unites with us and
W-pI...160.9:1 Today we offer **t.** that Christ has come to
W-pI.170.13:7 *we give **t.** for them who render us complete.*
WpI 170.13:10 *has set us free. And we give **t.**. Amen.*
W-pI...188.3:6 unites in giving **t.** to you who give, and
W-pI...188.4:3 giver of the gift, does God Himself give **t.**.
W-pI...192.6:4 for, met with **t.** and joyously accepted?
W-pI...192.9:7 And so you owe him **t.** instead of pain.
W-pI...195.1:5 cause for **t.** while others have less cause?
W-pI...195.2:1 It is insane to offer **t.** because of suffering
W-pI...195.4:4 We offer **t.** to God our Father that in us
W-pI...195.5:1 Therefore give **t.**, but in sincerity. And let
W-pI...195.6:3 give **t.** for every living thing, for otherwise
W-pI...195.6:3 for otherwise we offer **t.** for nothing, and
W-pI...195.7:2 We offer **t.** for them. For if we can direct
W-pI.195.10:4 God gives **t.** to you, His Son, for being
W-pI...197.1:3 you find external gratitude and lavish **t.**.
W-pI...197.3:2 Yet your **t.** belong to you as well, for its
W-pI...197.3:5 who honor them and give them fitting **t.**,
W-pI...197.7:2 God, and He gives **t.** for you unto Himself
W-pI...197.8:1 **T.** be to you, the holy Son of God. For as
W-pI...197.9:1 Give **t.** as you receive it. Be you free of all
W-pI...197.9:4 Give **t.** for all the countless channels
W-pI...197.9:8 that He has ever ceased to offer **t.** to you.
W-pI...199.8:5 and Heaven offers **t.** for the increase of joy
W-pI...215.1:4 *I give **t.** to Him for showing me the way to go.* I
W-pI...217.1:2 *should give **t.** for my salvation but myself?*
W-pI...217.1:3 *can I find the Self to Whom my **t.** are due?* I
W-pII.....in.6:5 Accept these little gifts of **t.** from us, as
W-pII..229.2:1 *Father, my **t.** to You for what I am; for*
W-pII..229.2:2 *up. And **t.** to You for saving me from them.*
W-pII..234.2:2 *give **t.** for all the gifts You have bestowed on*
W-pII..251.2:1 *And for that peace, our Father, we give **t.**.*
W-pII..297.2:2 *grace. **T.** be to You for Your eternal gifts, and*
W-pII..297.2:2 *eternal gifts, and **t.** to You for my Identity.*
W-pII..300.2:4 *we give **t.** today the world endures but for an*
W-pII..308.2:1 ***T.** for this instant, Father. It is now I am*
W-pII..340.1:5 ***T.** for today, my Father. I was born into this*
W-pII..340.2:3 no room for anything but joy and **t.** today
M-4 .....V.1:12 Joy is their song of **t.**. And Christ looks
M-4 .....V.1:13 Christ looks down on them in **t.** as well.
M-23 .........4:5 **t.** for all the gifts that God has given you.
M-29 .......7:11 Hands, and I give **t.** for you that this is so.
M-29 .........8:3 *Teacher of God, His **t.** He offers you, And all*
M-29 .........8:7 *I give **t.** for you, And join your efforts on*
C-6.............5:5 He offers **t.** to you as well as him for you
C-ep...........5:5 We who complete Him offer **t.** to Him, as
C-ep...........5:5 offer thanks to Him, as He gives **t.** to us.
P-3........III.4:8 But **t.** are due to both, for the release from
S-1.........in.1:2 returns the **t.** it offers Him unto the Son.
S-1.........in.1:5 God gives **t.** to His extension in His Son.
S-1.........in.1:6 His Son gives **t.** for his creation, in the
S-1...........I.7:1 because it is a gift of **t.** to His Father. To
S-1..........II.7:8 now it rises as a song of **t.** to your Creator,
S-1.......II.7:10 And for this giving God Himself gives **t.**.
S-3.......IV.1:10 sing of their union and their **t.** to God.
S-3........IV.3:3 this? God **t.** His healers, for He knows the
S-3........IV.7:3 his joyful **t.** in unison with all creation, in
S-3........IV.9:8 Arise and let My **t.** be given you. And

### thanksgiving 5

T-13......VI.8:7 and **t.** for the light to the Creator of light.
T-17......V.15:2 and **t.** to Him Who gave you your release,
W-pII..232.1:3 *hourly **t.** that You have remained with me,*
S-1...........I.2:9 sound is always a song of **t.** and of Love.
S-1...........I.7:3 It is a song of **t.** for what you are. Herein

### that 7721

### the 23636

### Their 33
*their*

T-3.......VII.3:9 of destroying **T.** Own purpose is in error.
T-8........III.3:1 and of the Son are One, by **T.** extension.
T-8........III.3:2 **T.** extension is the result of Their Oneness
T-8........III.3:2 Their extension is the result of **T.** Oneness
T-8........III.3:2 holding **T.** unity together by extending
T-8........III.3:2 unity together by extending **T.** joint Will.
T-11......IV.5:8 **T.** glory is shared and They are glorified
T-12....VI.4:10 Spirit blesses the real world in **T.** Name.
T-15......VI.8:6 of God will take **T.** rightful place in you,
T-23........II.5:5 And **T.** relationship is one of opposition,
T-24.....in.1:12 has the power to defeat what is **T.** Will?
T-26......IX.2:4 blessed it with **T.** innocence and peace.
T-26......IX.3:4 It is **T.** Presence which has lifted holiness
T-26......IX.5:2 For They have come to gather in **T.** Own.
T-26......IX.6:4 to be **T.** resting place as well as yours.
T-26........X.1:1 be undone for you to realize **T.** Presence?
T-26........X.1:7 in whatever form, will hide **T.** Presence.
T-26........X.2:7 **T.** Presence is obscured by any veil that
T-26........X.2:7 that stands between **T.** shining innocence,
T-26........X.6:7 *see injustice, which **T.** Presence shines away.*
T-28......III.9:6 in **T.** sharing there can be no gap in which
T-29.......V.2:1 not that you can change **T.** dwelling place.
T-31.....IV.10:3 and in **T.** Oneness Both are kept complete
W-pI...73.10:5 of the practice period under **T.** guidance.
W-pI...91.10:3 It is through **T.** strong support that you
W-pI...91.10:4 in which you share a purpose like **T.** Own.
W-pI...91.10:5 see miracles, because **T.** strength is yours.
W-pI...91.10:6 **T.** strength becomes your eyes, that you
W-pI...129.4:3 **T.** language has no words, for what They
W-pI...129.4:4 **T.** knowledge is direct and wholly shared
W-pI...197.7:4 Father is secure, because **T.** Will is One.
W-pI...197.7:5 **T.** gratitude to all They have created has
W-pI...198.7:4 upon the place where you beheld **T.** blood

### their 891
*Their*

### Theirs 4
*theirs*

T-26......IX.8:6 Father and the Son return to what is **T.**,
T-26.....X.1:11 Its simple presence shuts the door to **T.**,
T-26........X.4:2 innocence that is not **T.** but yours alone,
W-pI...91.10:5 Own. **T.** is the light in which you will see

### theirs 37
*Theirs*

### Them 39
*them*

T-7........VI.1:7 any of **T.** if he regards Them fearfully. He
T-7........VI.1:7 any of Them if he regards **T.** fearfully. He
T-7........VI.1:8 will appreciate all of **T.** if he regards Them
T-7........VI.1:8 all of Them if he regards **T.** with love.
T-8.........V.3:6 All glory lies in **T.** *because* They are united.
T-10.........I.4:2 Knowing **T.** you will have no wish to sleep
T-14....VIII.4:9 the creations of His Son with **T.** together.
T-14..VIII.4:10 There is one link that joins **T.** all together,
T-14..VIII.4:10 holding **T.** in the oneness out of which
T-17....IV.10:6 For you attack **T.**, being part of Them,
T-17....IV.10:6 For you attack Them, being part of **T.**,
T-21.......V.3:2 And if you place your faith in **T.**, you will
T-22.......I.11:9 home prepared for **T.** as earth is turned to
T-24.....in.1:12 that idly seems to drift between **T.** has the
T-24......III.5:6 wait for all illusions to be brought to **T.**,
T-24......III.8:8 Deny **T.** not. They ask of you but that
T-24.....III.8:11 Love not your specialness instead of **T.**.
T-26.........I.7:3 make of **T.** what God willed not They be.
T-26...VII.14:9 and made **T.** Both his enemies in hate.
T-26......IX.2:3 would you trade **T.** for an ancient hate?
T-26......IX.2:4 stand is holy ground because of **T.** Who,
T-26......IX.3:3 Because of **T.**. It is Their Presence which
T-26......IX.3:5 Because of **T.** have miracles sprung up as
T-26......IX.4:1 is a hundred or a thousand years to **T.**, or
T-26......IX.4:6 join **T.** on the ground whereon you stand.
T-26......IX.6:2 where a home for **T.** has been set up.
T-26......IX.6:4 to dwell within the temple offered **T.**, to
T-26.....X.1:11 to Theirs, and keeps **T.** there unknown.
T-26........X.6:7 *I would rather know of **T.** than see injustice,*
T-28.......I.12:5 and lets **T.** enter where They would abide.
T-28......III.9:3 have brought unlimited supply with **T.**.
T-29.......V.2:2 For your Identity abides in **T.**, and where
W-pI...73.10:6 Join with **T.** as They lead the way.

T-20......IV.2:7 mistakes, and **t.** lies his own salvation.

**these** 452

**They** 51
*they*
T-3.........II.5:5 because **T.** are of one Mind and one Will.
T-7......VI.13:7 and its creations, knowing **T.** are One.
T-8.........IV.8:8 be part of the Other, because **T.** are One.
T-8.........V.3:6 All glory lies in Them *because* **T.** are united
T-11......IV.5:8 Their glory is shared and **T.** are glorified
T-14... VIII.2:7 For **T.** are not apart, and gifts to One are
T-14... VIII.3:4 **T.** are joined in giving you the gift of
T-17....IV.10:6 being part of Them, and **T.** must save you,
T-17....IV.10:6 must save you, for **T.** love Themselves.
T-22....VI.11:6 And you must think that **T.** are separate,
T-23....... II.5:2 it appears that **T.** can never be One again.
T-23....... II.5:4 Now are **T.** different, and enemies. And
T-24.... in.1:11 **T.** *are.* And what illusion that idly seems to
T-24....... II.9:4 so remote that **T.** cannot be reached. Here
T-24......III.5:4 How could **T.** will the death of love itself?
T-24......III.5:5 Yet **T.** are powerless to make attack upon
T-24......III.5:6 **T.** are not bodies; as one Mind They wait
T-24......III.5:6 as one Mind **T.** wait for all illusions to be
T-24......III.8:9 **T.** ask of you but that your will be done.
T-24....III.8:10 done. **T.** seek your love that you may love
T-25...VII.10:6 And that in Heaven *T.* are all the same,
T-26.........I.7:3 make of Them what God willed not **T.** be.
T-26.........IX.h For **T.** Have Come
T-26......IX.3:6 What hate has wrought have **T.** undone.
T-26......IX.3:8 forever from the land where **T.** have come
T-26......IX.4:2 When **T.** come, time's purpose is fulfilled.
T-26......IX.4:3 passes to nothingness when **T.** have come.
T-26......IX.5:2 For **T.** have come to gather in Their Own.
T-26......IX.6:2 And **T.** come quickly to the living temple,
T-26......IX.6:4 **T.** have come to dwell within the temple
T-26......IX.8:3 And **T.** give thanks that They are welcome
T-26......IX.8:3 thanks that **T.** are welcome made at last.
T-26......IX.8:8 For **T.** have come! For They have come at
T-26......IX.8:9 They have come! For **T.** have come at last!
T-26........X.1:8 **T.** are known with clarity or not at all.
T-28...... I.10:2 His Effects, yet have **T.** never been denied.
T-28...... I.12:5 and lets Them enter where **T.** would abide
T-29.........V.1:4 Where Both abide are **T.** remembered,
T-29.........V.1:5 And where **T.** are is Heaven and is peace.
T-29.........V.2:2 Identity abides in Them, and where **T.** are
T-30.......V.7:8 then will come the knowledge **T.** are One.
W-pI...73.10:6 Join with Them as **T.** lead the way.
W-pI...91.10:4 **T.** are united with you in this practice
W-pI...129.4:3 for what **T.** say cannot be symbolized.
W-pI...197.7:5 gratitude to all **T.** have created has no end
W-pI...198.3:7 Self and to his Father, knowing **T.** are One
W-pI...198.7:3 You may think **T.** have accepted. But if
W-pI...198.7:5 How foolish to believe that **T.** could die!
C-4.............7:6 his. And here **T.** join, for here the face of
S-1.........in.1:3 joyous concord of the Love **T.** give forever
S-1.........in.1:7 The Love **T.** share is what all prayer will

**they** 2153
*They*

**thick** 1
T-22......III.3:4 **t.** it would be madness to attempt to pass

**thicker** 1
W-pI...135.3:5 your armor **t.** and your locks more tight,

**thickness** 1
T-22.......V.5:2 by the illusions it presents of size and **t.**,

**thief** 1
W-pI...135.5:4 say your home is open to the **t.** of time,

**thieves** 1
T-28...... III.7:2 The door is open, not to **t.**, but to your

**thin** 5
T-22......IV.3:4 how **t.** the drapery that separates you now
T-28...... III.9:6 in which abundance falters and grows **t.**.
T-29......IV.3:4 **t.** disguise of pleasure and of joy in which
W-pI...133.9:1 Yet is its camouflage a **t.** veneer, which
C-6.............5:6 in which you dance to death's **t.** melody.

**thine** 1
T-5......VI.10:8 verdict will always be "**t.** is the Kingdom,"

**thing** 209
T-1...........I.2:2 The only **t.** that matters is their Source,
T-2........IV.4:7 last **t.** that can help the non-right-minded
T-3...........I.5:4 God" is another way of saying the same **t.**.
T-3......... II.1:7 has not experienced *some* light and *some* **t.**.
T-3......VII.4:11 while you believe the one **t.** that is literally
T-4......... II.6:4 can therefore do without the **t.** you give.
T-4........VI.1:3 spoken of the ego as if it were a separate **t.**
T-4........VI.4:3 not because the ego is a separate **t.**, but
T-5........VI.3:5 of the same **t.** simultaneously; or almost
T-5........VI.4:5 Bible is a fearful **t.** in the ego's judgment.
T-6......V.C.6:5 not is the only **t.** that you must exclude.
T-6......V.C.9:9 to teach the same **t.** must be in agreement
T-7......... X.1:6 the same **t.** with the premises of God?
T-7........XI.1:3 Him is therefore the easiest **t.** in the world
T-7........XI.1:3 in the world, and the only **t.** that is easy,
T-8.......VII.8:3 is the most depressing **t.** in the world. In
T-8.....VII.12:2 simultaneously with the same **t.** and not
T-8..... VIII.1:2 based on what it believes the **t.** is *for.* This
T-8..... VIII.7:6 one **t.** about the ego that is wholly true.
T-11......IV.4:6 to realize that this is exactly the same **t.**,
T-11....... V.8:1 You must recognize that the last **t.** the
T-12......III.5:2 only **t.** that can be saved and the only way
T-12.......VI.3:2 The only **t.** of value in it is whatever part
T-12... VIII.7:8 The unreal world *is* a **t.** of despair, for it
T-13....... V.1:5 Yet they have one **t.** in common; they are
T-13.....VII.8:4 one **t.** that is wholly true and wholly yours
T-13.....VII.8:6 But this one **t.** is always yours, being the
T-13......IX.1:1 remains the only **t.** that hides the Father,
T-13......IX.7:5 *The **t.** you fear is gone.* If you would look
T-13......XI.7:1 Have faith in only this one **t.**, and it will
T-14...... II.1:11 For if you value one **t.** made of nothing,
T-14....... X.2:7 The miracle is the one **t.** you can do that
T-14.......XI.1:1 the essential **t.** is learning that *you do not*
T-14.......XI.5:4 absence of perfect peace means but one **t.**:
T-16.........I.6:4 if a brother asks a foolish **t.** of you to do it
T-16.........I.6:5 **t.** that would hurt either him or you, for
T-16.....VII.5:3 the one **t.** the ego never allows to reach
T-17....... II.2:5 this little bridge is the strongest **t.** that
T-17....... II.6:3 The smallest leaf becomes a **t.** of wonder,
T-17......VI.2:1 you are uncertain, the first **t.** to consider,
T-18....... II.6:9 As its unholiness kept it a **t.** apart, its
T-18....III.4:15 For you desire the only **t.** you ever had, or
T-18......VI.2:4 done a stranger **t.** than you yet realize.
T-18......VI.6:7 You have identified with this **t.** you hate,
T-18......VI.6:8 have done this to a **t.** that has no meaning
T-18......VI.7:3 **t.** you made to serve your guilt stands
T-18.....VII.2:1 There is one **t.** that you have never done;
T19. IV.A.12:7 sin they pounce on any living **t.** they see,
T19....IV.C.3:3 One **t.** is sure; God, Who created neither
T19....IV.C.4:2 and keep itself alive; a **t.** condemned,
T19. IV.D.15:3 as God created every living **t.** and loves it.
T-20....... II.1:4 this hated **t.** to draw your brother to you,
T-20.......III.7:6 the only **t.** in all the universe that does not
T-20....III.7:10 And of the one blind **t.** in all the seeing
T-20....III.8:10 one **t.** that still would have it be unholy.
T-20.....VII.7:5 as a separate **t.** apart from the intention.
T-20... VIII.8:6 One **t.** is sure; hallucinations serve a
T-21....... II.2:1 is the only **t.** that you need do for vision,
T-22.........I.3:8 you have called upon this **t.** to lead you,
T-22....... II.4:7 excludes one living **t.** and holds it out,
T-23.... II.11:2 What is this precious **t.**, this priceless
T-24....... V.4:8 madness, and believe this crumbling **t.**,
T-24....... V.6:8 in each living **t.** that He beholds and loves
T-25........II.2:4 For one **t.** is sure; the way you see, and
T-25...... VI.5:1 *one* perfect **t.** and make *one* perfect choice.
T-25.... VI.7:10 Do this *one* **t.**, that everything be given
T-25..... VII.1:2 a sin. Sin is the only **t.** in all the world that
T-26........II.5:2 There is no such **t.** as partial justice. If the
T-26...... III.4:7 essential **t.** to make a choice at all is this
T-26....... V.4:3 Each **t.** you look upon you saw but for an
T-26..... VII.8:9 which is clearly separate and a **t.** apart.
T-26...... IX.4:4 up every living **t.** and lifts it into Heaven,
T-26........X.2:7 belongs to every living **t.** along with you.
T-26........X.5:8 denied to every living **t.** upon the earth.
T-27.......I.11:5 illusions of a purpose to a **t.** you made to
T-27.......I.11:6 This **t.** without a purpose cannot hide the
T-27......II.3:11 hold against himself or any living **t.**.
T-27...... IV.4:3 attesting the same **t.** in different form.
T-27....... V.2:8 The only **t.** that is required for a healing is
T-27..... VII.1:4 this "something else," a **t.** outside himself
T-27..... VII.7:4 Of one **t.** you were sure: Of all the many
T-27... VII.10:3 Yet a **t.** can never be its opposite. And
T-27..VIII.11:6 the simple statement, "*I* have done this **t.**,
T-27..VIII.12:7 they attest the **t.** you do not want to know
T-27..VIII.13:7 The one **t.** that is impossible is that you
T-28.......I.10:5 He has not done the **t.** you fear. No more
T-28........II.6:3 else could be expected from a **t.** that has
T-28.... IV.1:10 You can be sure of just one **t.**; that you are
T-28..... V.3:11 where you can be a **t.** that is not you,
T-28...... VI.2:1 responsible for sight a **t.** that cannot see,
T-28...... VI.3:1 **t.** you hate and fear and loathe and want,
T-29........II.2:3 is not a separate **t.** that happens suddenly
T-29........II.6:1 have life and every living **t.** be part of him,
T-29........II.8:1 is a demand the body be a **t.** that it is not.
T-29........II.9:2 so it seems to be a **t.** with power in itself.
T-29......II.10:2 when you behold the body as a **t.** you love
T-29......II.10:2 you love, or look upon it as a **t.** you hate.
T-29...... IV.4:8 an event, or body, or a **t.** *should* represent,
T-29...... VI.2:6 only **t.** in all the universe that must be one
T-29...... VI.3:3 only **t.** that can be made a blessing here,
T-29...... VI.6:3 joyous **t.** it is to dwell a little while in such
T-29....VIII.1:9 Be it a body or a **t.**, a place, a situation or
T-29....VIII.4:7 The "more-than-everything" is not a **t.** to
T-29....VIII.9:8 also give the same to every living **t.** as well
T-29....VIII.9:9 And thus is every living **t.** a part of you, as
T-30.......in.1:3 be reached depends on this one **t.** alone;
T-30.......I.11:2 but merely hope to get a **t.** you want. And
T-30........II.3:7 Not one created **t.** but gives you thanks,
T-30...... III.1:7 little **t.** I want, and it will be as everything
T-30...... III.3:3 To seek a special person or a **t.** to add to
T-30...... III.4:9 **t.** the power to complete the Son of God.
T-30.... III.11:2 Is your reality a **t.** apart from you, and in
T-30...... IV.3:3 it. It never was the **t.** you thought. It must
T-30...... IV.6:4 about, when you decide one very simple **t.**
T-30.... IV.8:11 him no single **t.** that he could ever want.
T-30... VII.3:10 the **t.** you fear has fearful meaning in itself
T-31.........I.9:1 There is no living **t.** that does not share
T-31...... III.1:2 is first one **t.** that must be overlearned. It
T-31...... III.3:6 It is not seen to be a passive **t.**, obeying
T-31....... V.2:4 teach is not the **t.** that it appears to be.
T-31....... V.5:3 teaches this: "I am the **t.** you made of me,
T-31....... V.6:8 still your brother for the hated **t.** you are.
T-31..... V.12:1 alternatives about the **t.** that you must be.
T-31..... V.12:2 the **t.** you chose to have your brother be.
T-31..... V.17:7 *I do not know the **t.** I am, and therefore do*
T-31... VII.12:2 teaching that you are the **t.** you wish to be
T-31... VII.14:1 to make yourself a **t.** that you are not.
T-31... VII.14:2 well upon the **t.** that you would be instead
T-31... VII.14:3 It is a **t.** of madness, pain and death; a
T-31... VII.14:3 death; a **t.** of treachery and black despair,
T-31....VIII.6:1 and so is every living **t.** you look upon,
W-pI....... 1.3:7 excluded. One **t.** is like another as far as
W-pI........3.2:3 For this purpose one **t.** is like another;
W-pI....... 7.5:1 not linger over any one **t.** in particular,
W-pI..... 11.3:1 move from one **t.** to another fairly rapidly
W-pI..... 12.2:3 slow shifting of your glance from one **t.** to
W-pI..... 17.2:3 on each **t.** you note long enough to say: *I*
W-pI..... 28.2:7 When you have seen one **t.** differently,
W-pI..... 41.2:2 one **t.** they do not do is to question the
W-pI..... 41.8:2 it is the most natural **t.** in the world. You
W-pI..... 41.8:3 say it is the only natural **t.** in the world.

W-pI.....45.8:4 kind of practice only one t. is necessary;
W-pI.....97.4:4 calls through His Voice to every living t.;
W-pI.....99.1:3 Thus do both terms imply a t. impossible
W-pI.....99.2:2 becomes the t. you need forgiveness for,
W-pI.....99.5:5 Yet does He know one t. must still be true
W-pI...109.7:2 time when rest will be the only t. there is
W-pI...128.2:1 Each t. you value here is but a chain that
W-pI...131.3:2 and you will surely do the t. you came for.
W-pI...133.6:1 if you choose a t. that will not last forever,
W-pI...133.7:1 to take a t. away from someone else, you
W-pI...134.7:1 Forgiveness is the only t. that stands for
W-pI.134.10:3 In truth is innocence the only t. there is.
W-pI...135.5:1 the body that can fear, nor be a t. of fear.
W-pI...136.7:2 It is not a t. that happens to you, quite
W-pI.138.10:3 the other as a wholly worthless t., a but
W-pI.138.12:6 *my mind, because it is the only t. I want.*
W-pI...139.2:3 The only t. that can be surely known by
W-pI...139.2:3 surely known by any living t. is what it is.
W-pI...139.4:3 shows he does not want to be the t. he is.
W-pI...151.5:1 This t. it speaks of, and would yet defend,
W-pI...158.1:5 It was given as well to every living t., for
W-pI...159.1:2 give a t. requires first you have it in your
W-pI...159.1:5 The world believes that to possess a t., it
W-pI...161.7:2 There must be a t. to be attacked. An
W-pI...161.7:4 When hatred rests upon a t., it calls for
W-pI...165.5:2 sure that you request the only t. you want
W-pI.166.12:1 you still of one t. more you had forgotten.
W-pI.167.12:5 It becomes the t. reflected, and the light
W-pI...181.8:6 will become the only t. we see reflected in
W-pI...183.4:2 and unwanted t. before God's Name.
W-pI...183.6:6 word, the only t. that occupies our minds,
W-pI...185.2:9 these words express the only t. they want.
W-pI.186.12:2 It asks a t. of you which seems impossible,
W-pI...187.2:2 it is sure that if you give a finite t. away,
W-pI...188.1:7 only t. you bring with you from Him Who
W-pI...188.3:2 It pauses to caress each living t., and
W-pI...191.4:3 All else but this one t. is folly to believe.
W-pI...195.6:1 We thank our Father for one t. alone;
W-pI...195.6:1 that we are separate from no living t., and
W-pI...195.6:3 We give thanks for every living t., for
W-pI...196.9:4 t. you dread the most is your salvation.
W-pII .231.1:3 *Yet is Your Love the only t. I seek, or ever*
W-pII .240.1:3 Not one t. in this world is true. It does not
W-pII .290.1:6 look on nothing else except the t. I seek.
W-pII ....294.h My body is a wholly neutral t..
W-pII .294.1:2 And can I be another t. as well? Did God
W-pII .294.1:5 And yet a neutral t. does not see death,
W-pII .311.1:2 and sets it off as if it were a t. apart. And
W-pII .318.1:5 I was created as the t. I seek. I am the goal
W-pII .325.1:2 the mind makes up an image of the t. the
M-8 ..........1:2 in which each t. seen competes with every
M-8 ..........1:4 A brighter t. draws the attention from
M-12 .......6:10 Unity alone is not a t. of dreams. And it is
M-16 .........1:3 Yet the teacher of God is sure of but one t.
M-18 .......3:11 *His Love remains the only t. there is. Fear is*
M-20 .........2:2 peace is recognized at first by just one t.;
M-20 .........2:5 It is a new t. entirely. There is a contrast,
M-20 .........2:6 yes, between this t. and all the past. But
M-28 .........2:6 Christ's face is seen in every living t., and
C-2.............1:7 It is a t. of madness, not reality at all. A
C-3.............5:3 It is the only t. still in the world in part,
P-2......... II.8:3 about? Only one t.; the same requirement
P-2.......VII.4:1 one t. and one thing only is required: The
P-2.......VII.4:1 one thing and one t. only is required: The
P-3...........I.4:1 teacher of God, never forgets one t.; he
S-1........IV.4:5 time-bound t. can give you more than this
S-2...........I.2:4 plague; a hateful t. of danger and of death
S-2........III.5:1 Your holy Son?" should be the only t. you

## things 401

T-2........VI.5:2 First, you can choose to do conflicting t.,
T-2........VI.9:4 fear there are some t. you must realize,
T-4......... V.1:1 All t. work together for good. There are
T-4......... V.5:8 many of the t. you want to learn may be
T-4........VI.7:6 Love does not conquer all t., but it does
T-4........VI.7:6 all things, but it does set all t. right.
T-5...........I.1:9 of thinking is totally alien to having t.,
T-5......... II.8:7 These altars are not t.; they are devotions.
T-5 ..... III.11:9 the remembrance of t. past and to come,
T-5 ....... IV.6:8 rendering unto God the t. that are God's?
T-6 ..........I.9:2 As the world judges these t., but not as
T-7 .... V.10:11 because it encompasses all t. within itself.
T-8 ..........I.4:1 must have taught you the wrong t.,
T-8 ..........I.6:4 different t. in entirely different ways,
T-8 .........II.7:3 it encompasses all t. because it created all
T-8 .........II.7:3 all things because it created all t.. By
T-8 .........II.7:4 By creating all t., it made them part of
T-8 .... IV.5:11 t. are possible through our joint decision,
T-8 ....... IX.2:1 is the wish that t. be as they are not. The
T-8 ....... IX.7:1 and to accomplish all t. in my name. This
T-8 ....... IX.8:2 would not ask you to do t. you cannot do,
T-8 ....... IX.8:2 is impossible that I could do t. you cannot
T-8 ....... IX.9:8 His Will must stand forever and in all t..
T-9 ..........I.6:3 it speaks for different t. to the same mind.
T-9 ........I.14:5 When you feel these t., do not try to look
T-9 .........II.1:2 with specific t. that might be harmful, but
T-9 ....... III.7:4 forgives all t. in you and in your brother.
T-10 ...... V.3:8 may seem to be many different t. he is but
T-10 ...... V.8:4 you can confuse yourself with t. that do.
T-10 .... V.13:6 believe that the sick t. you have made are
T-11 ... VI.10:8 To God all t. are possible. And to Christ it
T-12 .VIII.7:11 function of love to unite all t. unto itself,
T-12 .VIII.7:11 all t. together by extending its wholeness.
T-13 ..... VI.6:2 it holds the only t. that are forever true.
T-13 ..... VI.6:6 In it are all t. that are eternal, and they are
T-13 .... VII.1:3 buy an endless list of t. they do not need.
T-13 .. VII.10:4 In your world you do need t.. It is a world
T-13 VII.10:11 The ego wants to have t. for salvation, for
T-13 VII.10:13 altar it demands you lay all of the t. it bids
T-13 .. VII.12:2 will give you all t. that do not block the
T-13 .. VII.12:4 He gives you all the t. that you need have,
T-13 .. VII.12:7 no investment in the t. that He supplies,
T-14 ... III.17:1 How gracious it is to decide all t. through
T-14 ..... VI.5:3 All t. you made have use to Him, for His
T-17 .........I.2:4 two masters who ask conflicting t. of you.
T-17 .........I.3:1 some t. you would withhold from truth.
T-18 ...... VI.9:7 He would have had to create different t.,
T-18 ... VIII.5:3 needing another for some t., but by no
T19..IV.A.11:3 for messages of different t. in different
T19..IV.A.13:3 return with gorges filled with t. decayed
T19..IV.A.13:4 To them such t. are beautiful, because
T19..IV.A.14:5 return with all the happy t. they found, to
T19.....IV.C.1:9 its dark shadow falls across all living t.,
T19.... IV.D.7:4 that you are at the mercy of t. beyond you
T-20 ........II.1:2 all the useless t. made for its eyes to see.
T-20 ..... IV.1:6 These t. have not occurred because the
T-20 ... VI.12:6 God as equal t. are like unto each other.
T-20 ... VIII.7:2 But vision sets all t. right, bringing them
T-21 ........II.6:4 is an idea that it is possible that t. could
T-21 ...... V.1:3 hold, perhaps, if other t. were equal. They
T-21 ...... VI.3:9 Madness and reason see the same t., but
T-21 ..... VII.6:4 the sameness of t. that are the same. This
T-22 .........I.6:4 meaning different t. to him at different
T-23 ........II.9:6 would they seek to share the t. they value.
T-24 ...... V.7:4 hand, that everyone may bless all living t.,
T-24 ...... V.7:6 that you may save all living t. from death,
T-25 .........I.7:2 a Oneness which unites all t. within Itself.
T-25 .........I.7:3 this mind, and does unite all t. together,
T-26 ..... III.7:4 choice between two t. so clearly unalike.
T-26 .. VII.10:4 a unity which holds all t. within itself?
T-27 ........II.6:4 the miracle undo all t. the world attests
T-27 ...... IV.1:1 In quietness are all t. answered, and is
T-27 .. VII.10:7 then you must see the causes of the t. you
T-27 ... VIII.1:7 and avoid the t. that would be hurtful.
T-27 ... VIII.2:2 It puts t. on itself that it has bought with
T-27 ... VIII.2:3 It works to get them, doing senseless t.,
T-27 ... VIII.2:3 tosses them away for senseless t. it does
T-27 ... VIII.2:4 more senseless t. that it can call its own. It
T-27 ... VIII.7:6 sinful t. the body does within its dream.
T-28 .........I.2:8 And like all the t. you made, it can be
T-28 .........I.3:4 truth. All t. the Holy Spirit can employ for
T-28 ......II.10:6 about as separate t. need not be feared.
T-28 ...... III.3:6 all t. that seem to glisten in the dream.
T-29 ........II.7:5 for it can be made to teach opposing t..
T-29 ...... III.2:7 all living t. who know not that they live.
T-29 ...... VI.2:9 All t. that come and go, the tides, the
T-29 ...... VI.2:9 all t. that change with time and bloom
T-29 ... VI.2:14 time waits upon forgiveness that the t. of
T-29 ... VIII.6:5 peace of God, forever given to all living t.,
T-29 ... VIII.7:5 is beyond where God has set all t. forever,
T-29 ..... IX.6:7 And bad t. seem to happen, and he is
T-29 ..... IX.7:5 not, for childish t. have all been put away.
T-30 ........I.4:1 have, the t. you want to happen to you,
T-30 ........I.4:1 to you, and the t. you would experience,
T-30 .......I.16:3 agreement that permits all t. to happen.
T-30 ... III.2:11 be content with small ideas and little t..
T-30 ..... IV.1:9 them for the t. you think they represent.
T-30 ..... IV.4:8 But neither were they t. to frighten you,
T-30 ..... IV.5:8 an illusion, making t. appear like to itself?
T-30 ..... IV.7:3 that you forgive all t. that no one ever did;
T-30 ..... IV.7:4 seek no longer for the t. you do not want.
T-30 .......V.1:5 understand all t. created as they really are
T-30 .......V.1:6 that all t. must be first forgiven, and *then*
T-30 .......V.2:5 as t. not wanted and not striven for. The
T-30 .... VII.5:1 lies in this; all t. have but one purpose,
T-30 .... VII.6:1 symbols that are used mean different t.?
T-30 ... VIII.5:1 already there to heal all t. that change,
T-31 ......I.1:10 you persist in learning not such simple t.?
T-31 ........I.2:2 in the simple t. salvation asks you learn. It
T-31 ........I.4:6 learn the simple t. salvation teaches you!
T-31 ......I.12:1 instant, and forget all t. we ever learned,
T-31 ......I.12:1 of what t. mean and what their purpose is
T-31 .......II.8:4 will be no attack upon the t. you thought
T-31 .......V.3:4 every day a hundred little t. make small
T-31 .......V.6:7 nor can you change the t. it makes you do
T-31 .......V.9:7 to have such prescience in the t. to come.
T-31 .....V.15:3 interacts with evil, and reacts to wicked t.
T-31 ..... VI.2:2 behold a world of separation, unrelated t.
T-31 .... VII.7:2 All t. you see are images, because you
W-in.......... 6:3 or t. to which the ideas are inapplicable.
W-pI ....... 1.3:1 the kinds of t. to which they are applied.
W-pI ....... 2.1:2 Begin with the t. that are near you, and
W-pI ....... 3.1:6 see it. Some of the t. you see may have
W-pI ....... 3.1:7 use these t. exactly as you would anything
W-pI ....... 3.2:1 to see t. exactly as they appear to you now
W-pI ....... 3.2:2 in selecting the t. to which the idea for the
W-pI ......... 4.h like the t. I see in this room [on this street
W-pI ....... 4.4:3 *It is like the t. I see in this room [on this street*
W-pI ....... 7.1:6 and why they are like the t. you see. It is
W-pI ....... 9.4:1 Begin with t. that are nearest you, and
W-pI ..... 10.2:3 is made overtly with the t. around you.
W-pI ..... 14.6:2 These t. are part of the world you see.
W-pI ..... 15.5:1 to very many t. during the minute or so of
W-pI ....... 17.h I see no neutral t..
W-pI ..... 17.1:2 no neutral t. because you have no neutral
W-pI ..... 17.2:2 *neutral t. because I have no neutral thoughts*
W-pI ....... 21.h I am determined to see t. differently.
W-pI ....... 28.h Above all else I want to see t. differently.
W-pI ..... 28.2:5 You see a lot of separate t. about you,
W-pI ..... 28.2:7 differently, you will see all t. differently.
W-pI ..... 29.3:1 to learn how to look on all t. with love,
W-pI ..... 30.4:2 try to think of t. beyond your present
W-pI ..... 35.8:2 to think up specific t. to fill the interval,
W-pI ..... 37.3:2 holiness are all t. blessed along with you.
W-pI ..... 38.3:2 are holy because all t. He created are holy.
W-pI ..... 38.3:3 all t. He created are holy because you are.
W-pI ..... 38.5:5 dominion over all t. because of what you
W-pI ..... 40.1:1 of the happy t. to which you are entitled,
W-pI ..... 41.3:2 the mind that thought these t. were real,
W-pI ..... 41.7:3 You are trying to reach past all these t..
W-pI ..... 47.2:1 Of yourself you can do none of these t..
W-pI ..... 47.5:4 of God in you is successful in all t..
W-pI ..... 47.7:3 Let go all the trivial t. that churn and
W-pI ..... 50.2:1 All these t. are your replacements for the
W-pI ..... 50.2:2 All these t. are cherished to ensure a body
W-pI ..... 51.5:4 I make all t. my enemies, so that my anger
W-pI ..... 54.2:1 (17) I see no neutral t.. What I see
W-pI ..... 55.1:1 (21) I am determined to see t. differently
W-pI ..... 55.1:4 very fact that I see such t. is proof that I
W-pI ..... 57.5:6 to understand the holiness of all living t.,
W-pI ..... 58.5:4 of God. All good t. are mine, because God
W-pI ..... 58.5:6 me, protects me, and directs me in all t..
W-pI ..... 60.2:5 I forgive all t. because I feel the stirring of
W-pI ..... 70.7:7 *salvation cannot come from any of these t..*
W-pI ..... 71.3:3 for hope in other places and in other t..
W-pI ..... 71.7:3 All t. are possible to God. Salvation must

W-pI.....72.3:2 of **t.** you are apt to hold grievances for.
W-pI.....76.1:1 how many senseless **t.** have seemed to
W-pI.....76.1:5 While you would seek for it in **t.** that have
W-pI.....76.4:1 It is insanity that thinks these **t.**. You call
W-pI.....83.3:2 All **t.** that come from God are one. They
W-pI.....86.1:3 seen it in many people and in many **t.**,
W-pI.....87.1:3 fearful of shadows and afraid of **t.** unseen
W-pI.....92.4:1 Strength overlooks these **t.** by seeing past
W-pI...96.10:3 spirit in all **t.** created by the Spirit as Itself
W-pI...96.10:4 Your mind will bless all **t.**. Confusion
W-pI.....99.9:5 Think of these **t.** in practicing today, and
W-pI...106.3:5 Go past all **t.** which do not speak of Him
WpI . rIII.in9:2 times, and then go on your way to other **t.**
WpIrIII.in10:6 Then turn to other **t.**, but try to keep the
W-pI...119.2:2 *I will forgive all **t.** today, that I may learn how*
W-pI.122.13:2 Today all **t.** you want are given you. Let
W-pI...127.2:5 these **t.** of love is not to understand it. If it
W-pI...128.3:3 All **t.** you seek to make your value greater
W-pI...129.2:4 all **t.** that you have cherished for a while.
W-pI...129.2:6 This is the world of time, where all **t.** end.
W-pI...129.3:2 Is it loss to find all **t.** you really want, and
W-pI...129.5:3 as you unbind your mind from little **t.** the
W-pI...129.6:5 place of all the **t.** you seek but do not want
W-pI.131.13:2 that you can understand all **t.** you see. A
W-pI...132.8:3 then you can loose it from all **t.** you ever
W-pI.132.14:1 it, and about all living **t.** we see upon it.
W-pI...133.2:2 drawn to bodily concerns, to **t.** you buy,
W-pI...133.3:1 by which to test all **t.** you think you want.
W-pI...133.7:3 will not recognize the **t.** you really have,
W-pI.133.12:1 All **t.** are valuable or valueless, worthy or
W-pI.134.15:3 consider all the evil **t.** you thought of him,
W-pI.135.26:5 the day, as foolish little **t.** appear to raise
W-pI...138.1:2 We think that all **t.** have an opposite, and
W-pI...139.2:4 it looks on other **t.** as certain as itself.
W-pI......151.h All **t.** are echoes of the Voice for God.
W-pI...152.6:5 a world where such **t.** seem to have reality
W-pI...152.7:2 would see at once these **t.** are not of Him.
W-pI.155.11:1 time has closed the door on all the **t.** that
W-pI...156.4:2 All **t.** that live bring gifts to you, and offer
W-pI...156.5:2 All living **t.** are still before you, for they
W-pI...156.5:5 light all **t.** unto Its likeness and Its purity.
W-pI...159.5:3 **T.** which seem quite solid here are merely
W-pI...159.6:1 for all the **t.** that can contribute to your
W-pI...160.5:4 who he is, uncertain of all **t.** but this; that
W-pI...162.1:5 and all **t.** seen within its misty clouds and
W-pI...163.2:2 hold all living **t.** within its withered hand;
W-pI...163.3:1 All **t.** but death are seen to be unsure, too
W-pI...163.6:3 total. Either all **t.** die, or else they live and
W-pI...163.9:6 *life we share with You and with all living **t.**, to*
W-pI...164.4:5 different from all **t.** you sought before,
W-pI...164.6:2 from far beyond all **t.** within the world,
W-pI...164.8:1 merely letting go all **t.** you think you want
W-pI...166.1:1 All **t.** are given you. God's trust in you is
W-pI...167.6:5 mind creates all **t.** that are, and cannot
W-pI...169.3:6 become aware that there are **t.** it does not
W-pI...169.5:2 And in His Being, He encompasses all **t.**.
W-pI.169.10:3 for those in time can speak of **t.** beyond,
W-pI...171.1:1 All **t.** are echoes of the Voice for God.
W-pI...183.5:2 tiny, nameless **t.** on earth slip into right
W-pI.183.10:6 He calls on Him to let all **t.** he thought he
W-pI.183.11:1 All little **t.** are silent. Little sounds are
W-pI.183.11:3 The little **t.** of earth have disappeared.
W-pI...184.1:5 it off from other **t.** by emphasizing space
W-pI...184.1:6 space you lay between all **t.** to which you
W-pI...184.2:1 space you see as setting off all **t.** from one
W-pI...184.2:2 where there is unity; a space between all **t.**
W-pI...184.2:2 between all things, between all **t.** and you.
W-pI...184.3:1 a series of discrete events, of **t.** ununified,
W-pI...184.3:3 The nameless **t.** were given names, and
W-pI...184.4:3 conceives of little **t.** and looks upon them.
W-pI.184.10:2 you; the one Identity which all **t.** share;
W-pI.184.11:3 Source which unifies all **t.** within Itself.
W-pI.184.12:2 becomes the final lesson that all **t.** are one
W-pI.184.15:2 *In It we are united with all living **t.**, and You*
W-pI.185.10:4 intent with what they seek above all **t.**,
W-pI.186.12:4 Voice that speaks for the Creator of all **t.**,
W-pI.186.12:4 Who knows all **t.** exactly as they are, or a
W-pI...187.2:3 Yet we have learned that **t.** but represent
W-pI...187.4:1 Protect all **t.** you value by the act of
W-pI...187.4:6 the form of **t.** that lives unchangeable.
W-pI...188.5:5 is shining in you now, and in all living **t.**.
W-pI...188.6:6 the dream of worldly **t.** outside yourself,
W-pI...188.8:3 you are the co-creator of all **t.** that live.
W-pI.188.10:1 from us to all living **t.** that share our life.
W-pI.188.10:7 *Let all **t.** shine upon me in that peace, And let*
W-pI...190.5:6 the power to dominate all **t.** you see by
W-pI...190.6:6 a sickly place where living **t.** must come at
W-pI...190.9:1 Heaven's peace holds all **t.** still at last. Lay
W-pI...192.4:1 looks upon all **t.** unknown in Heaven, sees
W-pI......193.h All **t.** are lessons God would have me
W-pI...193.9:1 All **t.** are lessons God would have you
W-pI.193.11:4 about all **t.** we saved to settle by ourselves
W-pI...194.6:3 And as you learn to see salvation in all **t.**,
W-pI...195.4:4 that in us all **t.** will find their freedom. It
W-pI...195.8:5 we cannot choose to overlook some **t.**,
W-pI...195.8:5 some other **t.** still locked away as "sins."
W-pI...196.2:1 and with all **t.** held in its sure protection,
W-pI...197.8:2 created, you contain all **t.** within your Self
W-pI...213.1:1 (193) All **t.** are lessons God would have
W-pII...in.10:5 we need but be still and let all **t.** be healed
W-pII......1.3:1 An unforgiving thought does many **t.**. In
W-pII..232.2:4 Trust all **t.** to Him. Let Him reveal all
W-pII..232.2:5 Let Him reveal all **t.** to you, and be you
W-pII..235.1:1 but look upon all **t.** that seem to hurt me,
W-pII......4.3:1 illusions, which but stand for **t.** imagined,
W-pII..251.1:1 I sought for many **t.**, and found despair.
W-pII..252.1:3 with an intensity that holds all **t.** within it
W-pII.....263.h My holy vision sees all **t.** as pure.
W-pII..264.1:2 *You are in all the **t.** I look upon, the sounds I*
W-pII..264.1:5 *or without the Love which holds all **t.** within*
W-pII.....268.h Let all **t.** be exactly as they are.
W-pII..268.1:6 *me, when I let all **t.** be exactly as they are?*
W-pII......6.4:3 what could there be to keep **t.** separate,
W-pII..274.1:1 *today I would let all **t.** be as You created them*
W-pII.....275.h God's healing Voice protects all **t.** today.
W-pII..275.1:4 tells us of **t.** we cannot understand alone,
W-pII..275.1:5 It is in this that all **t.** are protected. And in
W-pII..275.2:1 *Your healing Voice protects all **t.** today, and*
W-pII..275.2:1 *all things today, and so I leave all **t.** to You. I*
W-pII..275.2:5 *Your Voice protects all **t.** through me.*
W-pII..278.1:1 which all **t.** that seem to live appear to die
W-pII..283.2:2 And so we offer blessing to all **t.**, uniting
W-pII..285.1:1 but the happy **t.** of God to come to me.
W-pII..285.1:3 joyous **t.** the instant I accept my holiness.
W-pII..286.1:2 *How quietly do all **t.** fall in place! This is the*
W-pII..291.1:2 sight shows me all **t.** forgiven and at peace
W-pII.....292.h A happy outcome to all **t.** is sure.
W-pII..295.2:2 *Love to bless all **t.** which I may look upon,*
W-pII..299.2:6 *In it are all **t.** healed, for they remain as You*
W-pII......9.1:3 **t.** without exception and without reserve.
W-pII......9.2:1 which encompasses all living **t.** with you.
W-pII..303.2:5 *He is the Son You love above all **t.**. He is my*
W-pII.....311.h I judge all **t.** as I would have them be.
W-pII.....312.h I see all **t.** as I would have them be.
W-pII..313.1:1 *there is a vision which beholds all **t.** as sinless*
W-pII..315.1:2 far beyond all **t.** of which I can conceive.
W-pII..320.2:1 *Will can do all **t.** in me, and then extend to all*
W-pII.....325.h All **t.** I think I see reflect ideas.
W-pII..328.1:1 all **t.** we perceive are upside down until
W-pII..330.1:6 all **t.** the dream of fear appears to offer us.
W-pII..337.1:5 has already done all **t.** that need be done.
W-pII..338.1:4 enemies, and he is safe from all external **t.**
W-pII..339.1:6 be confused indeed about the **t.** he wants;
W-pII.....342.h I let forgiveness rest upon all **t.**, For thus
W-pII..342.1:7 *Let me forgive all **t.**, and let creation be as*
W-pII..343.1:7 *so all **t.** are given unto me forever and forever*
W-pII.....346.h me, And I forget all **t.** except His Love.
W-pII..346.1:1 *miracles correcting my perception of all **t.**.*
W-pII..346.1:3 *I do not seek the **t.** of time, and so I will not*
W-pII..346.1:4 *all laws of time and **t.** perceived in time. I*
W-pII..346.1:5 *time. I would forget all **t.** except Your Love. I*
W-pII..346.2:2 when we forget all **t.** except God's Love.
W-pII.....349.h upon All **t.** for me and judge them not,
W-pII..349.1:1 *So would I liberate all **t.** I see, and give to*
W-pII..350.1:2 *of God incorporates all **t.** within himself as*
W-pII....14.3:4 and perceive all **t.** as kindly and as good.
W-pII..359.1:2 *We have misunderstood all **t.**. But we have*
W-ep .........6:2 in His way, and trust all **t.** to Him. In
M-1 ...........4:7 death, wears out the world and all **t.** in it.
M-4 .........I.1:6 It is this power that keeps all **t.** safe. It is
M-4 ..... I.A.3:3 It seems as if **t.** are being taken away, and
M-4 ..... I.A.3:4 where he must see **t.** in a different light?
M-4 ..... I.A.4:2 he must now decide all **t.** on the basis of
M-4 ..... I.A.4:3 most of the **t.** he valued before will merely
M-4 ..... I.A.4:5 great learning to understand that all **t.**,
M-4 .........II.2:8 In this, as in all **t.**, they are honest. They
M-4 ..... II.2:10 mankind; for all the world and all **t.** in it;
M-4 ...... III.1:8 judgment are all **t.** equally acceptable, for
M-4 ..... V.1:11 because God's Voice directs them in all **t.**.
M-4 ... VII.2:10 to keep for himself all **t.** that are of God,
M-4 ... VII.2:11 These are the **t.** that belong to him. These
M-4 ..VIII.1:10 the ultimate interpretation of all **t.** in time
M-4 ...... IX.1:4 trust in the Word of God to set all **t.** right;
M-4 ....... X.2:2 let go all **t.** that would prevent forgiveness
M-4 ....... X.2:6 And above all are all **t.** welcoming, for
M-4 ....... X.3:1 **t.** that are the Son of God's inheritance.
M-10 .........3:3 aware of an inconceivably wide range of **t.**
M-10 .........6:7 now he knows that these **t.** need not be.
M-11 .........1:3 Word of God promises other **t.** that seem
M-11 .........2:3 For they say different **t.** about the world,
M-11 .........2:3 and **t.** so opposite that it is pointless to try
M-13 .........1:2 Like all **t.** in the world, its meaning is
M-13 .........1:6 is a sacrifice to give up the **t.** of this world.
M-13 .........2:6 is the "hero" to whom all these **t.** belong?
M-13 .........2:9 seeking after such **t.** the mind associates
M-13 .........3:7 he is. He can doubt all **t.**, but never this.
M-13 .........6:2 hold dear the **t.** that crucify God's Son,
M-14 .........2:8 The world will end when all **t.** in it have
M-15 .........1:9 the Judgment in which all **t.** are freed with
M-16 .........6:2 limitless because all **t.** are freed within it.
M-16 .........6:4 from all the fearful **t.** you see in dreams. It
M-16 .........8:2 his mind is occupied with external **t.**? He
M-21 .........2:4 heart does not really ask for concrete **t.**. It
M-21 .........2:5 the specific **t.** asked for being the bringers
M-21 .........2:6 then, are symbols for the **t.** asked for, but
M-21 .........2:6 but the **t.** themselves but stand for the
M-21 .........3:1 The prayer for **t.** of this world will bring
M-22 .........4:8 It is true of all **t.** that God created. In it
M-23 .........2:6 has recognized all living **t.** as part of him.
M-25 .........5:1 who no longer value the material **t.** of the
M-26 .........2:9 asking all **t.** in their name and in no other.
M-27 .........1:4 world that all **t.** in it are born only to die.
M-27 .........2:2 For who has decreed that all **t.** pass away,
M-27 .........3:6 And so do all **t.** live because of death.
M-27 .........4:1 curious belief that there is part of dying **t.**
M-27 .......6:10 and in Him all created **t.** must be eternal.
M-28 .........3:8 forgiving all **t.** and replacing all attack.
M-28 .........4:1 the time of everlasting **t.** is now at hand.
M-28 .........4:6 All **t.** are seen in light, and in the light
M-28 .........6:1 **t.** await us all, but we are not prepared as
M-29 .........4:8 image assumes it knows all **t.** because you
M-29 .........7:6 so. Ask all **t.** of His Teacher, and all things
M-29 .........7:6 of His Teacher, and all **t.** are given you.
M-29 .........8:4 *around the world, To close all **t.** of time; to*
M-29 .........8:4 *things of time; to end the sight Of all **t.** visible*
M-29 .........8:4 *things visible; and to undo All **t.** that change.*
C-4.............1:4 Some **t.** will last in time a little while
C-4.............1:5 time will come when all **t.** visible will have
P-2...........I.2:4 "Resistance" is its way of looking at **t.**; its
P-2...........II.1:4 has learned all **t.** does not need a teacher,
P-2......... IV.2:4 for all external **t.** are only shadows of a
P-2......... IV.3:3 Yet all these **t.**, however real they seem,
P-2....... VII.9:1 therapist, that you can see such **t.** as this,
S-1...........I.4:1 is to forget the **t.** you think you need. To
S-1 ..........II.3:4 to ask for **t.** of this world in various forms,
S-1 ..........II.7:3 of you. The **t.** of earth are left behind, all
S-1 ..........II.8:6 then all **t.** will be transformed together,
S-1 ........ III.6:1 It is not easy to realize that prayers for **t.**,
S-1 ........ III.6:2 These **t.** are used for goals that substitute
S-1 ........ IV.1:2 point, each one must ask for different **t.**.
S-1 ........ IV.2:5 Even together you may ask for **t.**, and
S-1 ......... V.1:4 nor judge all **t.** as you would have them be
S-1 ......... V.3:1 Now prayer is lifted from the world of **t.**,
S-2 ...........I.2:4 sight. It carefully picks out all evil **t.**, and
S-3 ........ IV.2:3 wing and all the living **t.** upon the earth.

**think** 715

T-1 III.2:4 how a man must **t.** of himself in his heart,
T-1 VI.3:4 This is because you **t.** you live in space,
T-2 II.7:2 You may still **t.** this is associated with loss
T-2 V.A.18:1 calling for help, you **t.** of it this way: *I am*
T-2 VI.2:5 for what you do, but not for what you **t.**.
T-2 VI.2:6 is that you are responsible for what you **t.**,
T-2 VI.2:7 What you do comes from what you **t.**.
T-2 VI.2:9 you place what you **t.** under my guidance.
T-2 VI.5:4 you can behave as you **t.** you should, but
T-2 VI.9:12 believe that what you **t.** is ineffectual you
T-2 VII.1:9 but you can be trained to **t.** that way. All
T-2 VII.7:9 You may **t.** this implies that an enormous
T-2 VIII.3:3 you may **t.** that punishment is deserved.
T-4 I.6:3 and live with you if you will **t.** with me,
T-4 I.7:6 nothing you do or **t.** or wish or make is
T-4 II.4:1 **T.** of the love of animals for their
T-4 IV.2:4 **T.** honestly what you have thought that
T-4 IV.2:4 not thought that God would have you **t.**.
T-4 IV.2:5 then change your mind to **t.** with God's.
T-4 IV.2:6 is much easier than trying to **t.** against it.
T-4 IV.8:3 of God into everything you **t.** and do. Do
T-5 in.1:2 happy. I have told you to **t.** how many
T-5 I.3:6 asks that you may **t.** as I thought, joining
T-5 IV.7:4 only the complete can **t.** completely, and
T-5 IV.7:5 Everything you **t.** that is not through the
T-5 V.4:5 before that you must learn to **t.** with God.
T-5 V.4:6 To **t.** with Him is to think like Him. This
T-5 V.4:6 To think with Him is to **t.** like Him. This
T-5 V.6:12 because, when you do not **t.** like God, you
T-5 V.6:16 Thought, you *cannot* **t.** apart from Him.
T-5 V.7:4 you believe you can **t.** apart from God,
T-5 VII.3:1 insane calls you **t.** are made upon you,
T-6 I.18:6 and you must **t.** as He thinks if you are to
T-6 II.1:6 however, may not be so obvious as you **t.**.
T-6 II.9:3 mind is split, you can perceive as well as **t.**
T-6 IV.10:1 because you **t.** it is possible to be in one.
T-6 V.A.1:2 you **t.** this is accomplished through death,
T-6 V.A.2:2 body is the symbol of what you **t.** you are.
T-6 V.A.5:6 Perhaps you **t.** that fear as well as love can
T-6 V.B.7:1 decisions, although you can **t.** you are. It
T-7 I.6:1 To **t.** like God is to share His certainty of
T-7 IV.6:1 To **t.** you can oppose the Will of God is a
T-7 V.7:7 **t.** that you have changed it as long as you
T-7 V.8:5 He himself may **t.** he can, or he would not
T-7 VI.7:2 you may still **t.** there is something else.
T-7 VII.2:7 is determined by what you **t.** you are, and
T-7 VII.2:7 what you want to be *is* what you **t.** you are.
T-7 VII.9:5 is what you will **t.** others are doing to you.
T-8 III.4:4 As you **t.** of him you will think of yourself.
T-8 III.4:4 As you think of him you will **t.** of yourself.
T-8 IV.4:1 Do you not **t.** the world needs peace as
T-8 VI.7:2 you **t.** you are unwilling to will with God,
T-9 I.4:5 in this process is what you **t.** you will lose.
T-9 III.5:6 if you **t.** he is wrong you are condemning
T-10 I.2:3 dreams you **t.** is real while you are asleep.
T-10 I.2:5 You do not **t.** this strange, even though all
T-10 III.1:4 When you **t.** you are attacking yourself, it
T-10 III.1:4 sure sign that you hate what you *t.* you are.
T-10 III.1:6 What you **t.** you are can be very hateful,
T-10 III.5:3 protect an idol you **t.** will save you from
T-10 III.8:6 You **t.** they are your father, because you
T-10 IV.1:9 to you, and wherever you **t.** you see him,
T-10 V.1:7 **t.** you can and believe you have is beyond
T-10 V.4:2 God" made His Son **t.** he was Fatherless,
T-10 V.7:3 you **t.** He has not answered your call, you
T-11 II.5:4 **T.** like Him ever so slightly, and the little
T-11 VIII.2:5 Yet while you **t.** you know its meaning,
T-11 VIII.5:7 fear of what you **t.** it will demand of you.
T-12 III.2:1 something you **t.** you do not want to do.
T-12 III.7:7 it, because you **t.** it is antagonistic to you.
T-12 VII.6:7 You will **t.** they are the same because you
T-12 VII.7:6 When you **t.** you are projecting what you
T-12 VII.9:5 If you **t.** you have received anything else,
T-12 VII.14:5 will **t.** that death comes from God and not
T-13 III.1:2 may also **t.** that it would be easy enough
T-13 III.4:1 because you **t.** you would be helpless in
T-13 III.4:1 **t.** it would crush you into nothingness.
T-13 III.4:3 You **t.** you have made a world God would
T-13 IV.2:2 threat you **t.** you could experience. For
T-13 VII.11:6 For what you **t.** you need will merely serve
T-13 VIII.5:6 to all who **t.** they wander in the darkness,
T-13 IX.3:4 it. Whatever you hold dear you **t.** is yours.
T-13 X.14:2 that none of us alone can even **t.** of it.
T-14 I.4:7 while you **t.** it possible to learn to do this,
T-14 III.5:6 make no difference; you will **t.** he does. It
T-14 III.7:4 and by refusing to allow him to **t.** he can,
T-14 III.10:2 to guilt, because they **t.** it is salvation, and
T-14 III.14:4 His guidance you will **t.** you know alone,
T-14 III.19:1 you should do, **t.** of His Presence in you,
T-14 IV.2:4 will still **t.** that you are separate from Him
T-14 V.11:7 out in peace on all who **t.** they are outside.
T-14 VI.5:4 much in your mind that lets you **t.** you are
T-14 X.4:4 the mind of those who **t.** they live apart.
T-14 X.4:5 by the ego, which but seems to **t.**.
T-14 XI.3:9 light, and thereby **t.** you see the darkness.
T-14 XI.5:2 even **t.** of you share in your perfect peace,
T-14 XI.5:4 You **t.** you do not will for God's Son what
T-14 XI.8:4 you **t.** that you can run some little part, or
T-14 XI.9:1 Do you **t.** that what the Holy Spirit would
T-14 XI.12:4 **T.** not you understand anything until you
T-14 XI.13:3 Whenever you **t.** you know, peace will
T-14 XI.15:2 You **t.** you know Him not, only because,
T-15 I.9:5 now, and **t.** of it as all there is of time.
T-15 III.3:3 you make stems from what you **t.** you are,
T-15 III.11:2 **t.** not you can substitute your plan for His
T-15 III.12:2 your brother be, there will you **t.** you are.
T-15 IV.2:5 **T.** not that you can find salvation in your
T-15 IV.7:4 **t.** you find a way to keep what you would
T-15 V.11:1 **T.** you that you can judge the Self of God
T-15 VI.4:2 Nor do you **t.** that when God answers him
T-15 VII.10:6 And if you **t.** it is, you will feel guilty
T-15 VII.11:5 **t.** their minds must be kept private or
T-15 VIII.4:1 **T.** but an instant on this: God gave the
T-15 IX.2:2 gratification what you **t.** you want. The
T-15 IX.3:3 and while you **t.** it has a purpose, you will
T-15 X.5:5 This is the choice you **t.** you have, and the
T-15 X.6:4 only to those who **t.** they are its host. The
T-15 X.7:6 And this you **t.** saves you from God,
T-15 X.8:1 **t.** that everyone outside yourself demands
T-15 XI.1:4 which you **t.** you see some scraps of safety
T-16 I.7:2 And you will **t.** that by meeting the needs
T-16 II.1:1 may still **t.** that holiness is impossible to
T-16 II.2:2 **t.** you might be better able to understand.
T-16 II.2:4 A better and far more helpful way to **t.** of
T-16 II.6:6 Him is to deny all that you **t.** you know.
T-16 II.6:7 But what you **t.** you know was never true.
T-16 II.9:9 **T.** what you have really seen and heard,
T-16 III.9:1 bridge is builded stronger than you **t.**,
T-16 IV.7:5 is you **t.** you can do to solve the dilemma
T-16 V.10:2 it? Let us not **t.** of its fearful nature, nor of
T-16 V.10:6 your self you **t.** you can attack another self
T-16 V.10:7 you do not **t.** it offers the specialness that
T-16 V.11:1 grant unlimited power to what you **t.** you
T-16 V.11:3 You **t.** it safer to endow the little self you
T-16 VI.11:4 And you will **t.**, in glad astonishment,
T-16 VII.2:7 you what you **t.** the past deprived you of?
T-16 VII.2:11 because you **t.** it serves some purpose that
T-17 I.2:1 you **t.** you have accomplished what you
T-17 I.5:1 **T.** you that you can bring truth to fantasy
T-17 III.1:9 the evil that you **t.** was done to you. You
T-17 III.1:10 their witness will enable you to **t.** guiltily
T-17 IV.7:8 Defenses operate to make you **t.** you can.
T-17 IV.11:6 the frame that made you **t.** it *was* a picture.
T-17 V.9:1 of salvation, and **t.** you have lost your way
T-17 V.9:2 *Your* way *is* lost, but **t.** not this is loss. In
T-17 V.10:3 with you. **T.** not your choice will leave you
T-17 V.14:3 you. **T.** you not the goal itself will gladly
T-17 VII.8:1 Yet **t.** on this, and learn the cause of
T-17 VII.8:1 You **t.** you hold against your brother what
T-17 VIII.5:3 **T.** carefully before you let yourself use
T-18 I.6:4 Do you really **t.** it strange that a world in
T-18 II.1:2 Yet **t.** what this world is. It is clearly not
T-18 II.7:4 **T.** not that He has forgotten anyone in
T-18 II.7:5 **t.** not that He has forgotten you to whom
T-18 II.8:5 of this because you **t.** it may be this that is
T-18 III.3:8 doubt that what you **t.** it means *is* fearful.
T-18 IV.5:6 to those who **t.** that they must first atone,
T-18 IV.5:8 to prepare yourself for Him, try to **t.** thus:
T-18 VI.2:7 **t.** you hate your body deceive yourself.
T-18 VIII.1:4 **T.** not that this is merely allegorical, for it
T-18 VIII.1:7 You cannot even **t.** of God without a body
T-18 VIII.1:7 or in some form you **t.** you recognize.
T-18 VIII.3:5 **T.** how alone and frightened is this little
T-18 VIII.7:8 that you **t.** you set apart is no exception.
T-18 IX.1:6 little part you **t.** you stole from Heaven.
T-18 IX.1:10 and unaware of what you **t.** surrounds it.
T-19 I.7:8 **t.** you are protecting the body by hiding
T-19 I.16:2 you **t.** you do to the eternal you do to *you.*
T-19 II.8:4 **t.** you carefully before you allow yourself
T-19 III.2:1 The ego does not **t.** it possible that love,
T-19 III.2:7 For what you **t.** is real you want, and will
T19 IV.A.2:2 What do you **t.** that it must dispossess to
T19 IV.A.17:12 **t.** you could be satisfied and happy with
T19 IV.B.2:1 value that you **t.** peace would rob you of.
T19 IV.B.6:2 the sins you **t.** the Son of God committed.
T19 IV.B.7:7 **T.** of your happiness as everyone offers
T19 IV.B.11:1 But **t.** you which it is that is compatible
T19 IV.B.11:3 you **t.** you are can never be apart from it.
T19 IV.B.11:6 attack on what you **t.** has failed you? Use
T19 IV.C.8:7 look upon the defeat of God, and **t.** it real
T19 IV.D.1:2 and **t.** if death held no attraction for you?
T19 IV.D15:10 and all the guilt you **t.** you see in him.
T19 IV.D.16:2 **T.** who your brother is, before you would
T19 IV.D.20:1 **T.** carefully how you would look upon
T-20 II.1:3 see. **T.** on the many offerings made for its
T-20 II.6:6 hear this carefully, nor **t.** it but a dream, a
T-20 III.4:4 *up.* It is a picture of what you **t.** you are; of
T-20 IV.6:3 But **t.** not that He does not need your part
T-20 IV.7:2 you. **T.** not that your forgiveness of your
T-20 IV.7:5 **T.** you when this has been achieved that
T-20 V.4:5 glad. You will not **t.** to judge him, for who
T-20 VII.3:8 that if you **t.** they are impossible, your
T-20 VIII.2:7 **t.** not that you need make either means or
T-20 VIII.4:6 Why do you **t.** the body is a better home,
T-20 VIII.11:3 **T.** but an instant just on this; you can
T-20 VIII.11:4 never need you **t.** that there is something
T-21 I.4:2 it. They **t.** they know their way about in it.
T-21 I.4:9 everything they **t.** is in it serves to remind
T-21 I.5:1 live, adjusting to it as they **t.** they must,
T-21 I.5:5 and try to **t.** if you remember what we will
T-21 II.6:9 **T.** not that you are faithless, for your
T-21 II.11:4 And if you **t.** what you have made can tell
T-21 II.11:5 **t.** the world you made has power to make
T-21 III.7:2 For what you **t.** is sin is limitation, and
T-21 III.9:1 believe in sin must **t.** the Holy Spirit asks
T-21 III.9:1 how they **t.** *their* purpose is accomplished.
T-21 III.11:1 **T.** you the Holy Spirit is concerned with
T-21 III.11:3 **t.** He would deprive you for your good.
T-21 IV.1:3 look within and see the sin you **t.** is there.
T-21 IV.5:5 **T.** not that this is madness. For this your
T-21 V.2:6 will **t.** the world you made directs your
T-21 V.4:7 But **t.** not reason could not answer it.
T-21 VI.1:3 will also tell you that when you **t.** you sin,
T-21 VI.1:8 you both will **t.** that you are damned. This
T-21 VI.3:1 No one can **t.** but for himself, as God
T-21 VI.3:3 one mind **t.** only for itself unless the body
T-21 VI.5:1 and if you **t.** it does you are insane. But
T-21 VI.5:8 But **t.** what you must recognize, if it be so.
T-21 VI.6:5 you. Yet **t.** not this is fearful. That you are
T-21 VII.12:1 Why do you **t.** you are unsure the others
T-21 VII.13:6 want, and you will look on it and **t.** it real.
T-21 VIII.4:1 **t.** carefully why you have not yet decided
T-22 in.2:7 stay until they **t.** that there is nothing left
T-22 in.4:1 **T.** what a holy relationship can teach!
T-22 I.2:2 it does accurately describe, you *t.* is you.
T-22 I.3:4 all. **T.**, then, what happens. Denying what
T-22 I.4:10 dependent on the self you **t.** you made to
T-22 I.8:1 **T.** what is given you, my holy brother.
T-22 I.10:4 so? **T.** what that instant brought; the
T-22 IV.2:1 although you still may **t.** you can go back
T-22 IV.3:6 **T.** what will happen after. The Love of
T-22 IV.4:1 **T.** of the loveliness that you will see, who
T-22 IV.4:2 **t.** how beautiful will you and your brother
T-22 VI.3:1 Be not disturbed at all to **t.** how He can
T-22 VI.10:3 **T.** you the Will of God is powerless? Is
T-22 VI.11:5 you **t.** the Father and the Son are separate

W-pI.....68.5:3 Then t. of the seemingly minor grievances
W-pI.....68.5:3 against those you like and even t. you love
W-pI.....68.6:4 the practice period trying to t. of yourself
W-pI.....69.4:2 T. of your mind as a vast circle,
W-pI.....70.9:3 t. of me holding your hand and leading
W-pI.....74.4:2 T. about it briefly but very specifically,
W-pI.....76.3:1 T. of the freedom in the recognition that
W-pI.....76.3:2 You really t. that you would starve unless
W-pI.....76.3:3 You really t. a small round pellet or some
W-pI.....76.3:4 You really t. you are alone unless another
W-pI.....76.4:3 t. you must obey the "laws" of medicine,
W-pI.....76.5:7 body. It is for this you t. you are a body.
W-pI.....76.8:3 T. further; you believe in the "laws" of
W-pI.....76.8:4 Perhaps you even t. that there are laws
W-pI.....78.4:5 someone you t. you love who angered you
W-pI.....78.6:4 will t. of his mistakes and even of his "sins
W-pI.....78.7:4 and as you t. of him who grieved you, let
W-pI...78.10:3 ones you t. of or remember from the past,
W-pI.....79.5:4 as you t. you have resolved the previous
W-pI.....79.7:3 different kinds of problems we t. we have.
W-pI.....83.1:4 what to do, what to say and what to t.. All
W-pI.....91.6:7 you t. you are is a belief to be undone. But
W-pI.....92.1:2 You do not t. of light in terms of strength,
W-pI.....92.2:1 You also believe the body's brain can t..
W-pI.....92.2:4 the body's eyes can see; the brain can t..
W-pI.....92.3:1 see, as it is His Mind with which you t..
W-pI.....93.1:1 You t. you are the home of evil, darkness
W-pI.....93.1:2 You t. if anyone could see the truth about
W-pI.....93.1:3 t. if what is true about you were revealed
W-pI.....93.3:1 not from the point of view of what you t.,
W-pI.....93.4:1 evil that you t. you did was never done,
W-pI.....93.4:3 You t. that this is death, but it is life. You
W-pI.....93.4:4 life. You t. you are destroyed, but you are
W-pI.....93.5:3 it seems to do and t. means nothing. It is
W-pI.....93.7:2 Whatever evil you may t. you did, you are
W-pI.....96.5:1 Yet mind apart from spirit cannot t.. It
W-pI...96.12:3 T., then, how much is given unto you to
W-pI.....99.8:2 It does not t. its solitary thoughts, and
W-pI.....99.9:5 T. of these things in practicing today, and
W-pI...99.10:5 Forgive yourself the one you t. you made.
W-pI...100.7:5 T. what this means. You have indeed
W-pI...101.1:5 must t. it so while you believe that sin is
W-pI...102.1:2 You may t. it buys you something, and
W-pI...102.2:4 you t. it offers you is lacking in existence,
W-pI...103.2:1 minds that t. what they have made is real.
W-pI...105.7:1 T. of your "enemies" a little while, and
W-pI...105.9:1 but do not t. that less is worthless when
W-pI...107.7:5 sure we live and hope and breathe and t..
W-pI...108.8:4 minutes t. of what you would hold out to
W-pI...108.9:4 too, to t. of one to whom to give your gifts
W-pI.108.10:3 now. T. of the exercises for today as quick
WpI. rIII.in5:3 And then begin to t. about them, while
WpIrIII.in11:1 If you are shaken, t. of it again. These
W-pI...119.1:2 *mistaken when I t. I can be hurt in any way. I*
W-pI...121.6:4 how to forgive the self you t. you made,
W-pI...121.9:2 toward one whom you t. of as an enemy,
W-pI.122.14:1 your mind by your attempts to t. of them
W-pI...123.8:2 Remember hourly to t. of Him, and give
W-pI...126.2:4 You further t. that they can sin without
W-pI...126.5:4 T. you the Lord of Heaven would allow
W-pI...126.7:1 gifts, and t. He has not given them to you.
W-pI...127.1:1 Perhaps you t. that different kinds of love
W-pI...127.1:2 Perhaps you t. there is a kind of love for
W-pI...127.6:4 mind of all the laws you t. you must obey;
W-pI...127.6:4 and all the changes that you t. are part of
W-pI.127.12:2 At least three times an hour t. of one who
W-pI...128.8:2 And when you t. you see some value in an
W-pI...129.1:4 T. you this world can offer that to you?
W-pI...129.2:1 It might be worth a little time to t. once
W-pI...130.4:1 Fear has made everything you t. you see.
W-pI...131.4:4 deceive himself and t. that it is hell he
W-pI.131.11:3 *and t. a different kind of thought from those*
W-pI.131.11:4 *the thoughts I want to t. are not my own.* For
W-pI.131.11:5 closed, the senseless world you t. is real.
W-pI.131.11:6 such a world, and which you t. are true.
W-pI...132.2:2 you t. or ever thought or yet will think.
W-pI...132.2:2 you think or ever thought or yet will t..
W-pI...132.4:3 so you can look on them and t. them real.
W-pI...132.4:4 real. Perhaps you t. you did not make the
W-pI...132.6:1 from yourself, impervious to what you t.,
W-pI...132.6:1 apart from what you chance to t. it is.
W-pI.132.11:1 you, you cannot t. apart from Him, nor
W-pI...133.3:1 by which to test all things you t. you want
W-pI.133.11:3 alternative you t. you chose seems fearful,
W-pI...134.4:1 Because you t. your sins are real, you look
W-pI...134.4:2 For it is impossible to t. of sin as true and
W-pI...134.5:5 by themselves for what they t. they did,
W-pI...134.7:5 "My brother, what you t. is not the truth.
W-pI...134.9:2 your mind to dwell on what you t. he did,
W-pI...135.3:3 You t. it offers safety. Yet it speaks of fear
W-pI...135.9:2 from which you t. the body must be saved
W-pI.135.15:2 It does not t. that it will be provided for,
W-pI...136.3:4 do, and then proceed to t. that it is done.
W-pI...136.8:1 How do you t. that sickness can succeed
W-pI.136.11:4 You can but choose to t. you die, or suffer
W-pI.136.13:2 time lets you t. what God has given you is
W-pI...137.6:1 Yet t. not healing is unworthy of your
W-pI...138.1:2 We t. that all things have an opposite,
W-pI...138.1:3 what we perceive, and what we t. is real.
W-pI...138.4:1 You need to be reminded that you t. a
WpI. rIV.in2:2 *My mind holds only what I t. with God.* That
WpI. rIV.in4:1 mind holds only what you t. with God.
WpI. rIV.in5:3 *My mind holds only what I t. with God.* Five
W-pI......141.h My mind holds only what I t. with God
W-pI......142.h My mind holds only what I t. with God.
W-pI......143.h My mind holds only what I t. with God.
W-pI......144.h My mind holds only what I t. with God.
W-pI......145.h My mind holds only what I t. with God.
W-pI......146.h My mind holds only what I t. with God.
W-pI......147.h My mind holds only what I t. with God.
W-pI......148.h My mind holds only what I t. with God.
W-pI......149.h My mind holds only what I t. with God.
W-pI......150.h My mind holds only what I t. with God.
W-pI...151.3:6 You t. your fingers touch reality, and
W-pI...151.3:7 and t. more real than what is witnessed to
W-pI...152.1:3 No one can grieve nor fear nor t. him sick
W-pI...152.6:1 Is it not strange that you believe to t. you
W-pI...152.6:5 to t. He made a world where such things
W-pI...152.7:1 To t. that God made chaos, contradicts
W-pI...152.7:4 To t. you can is merely to believe you can
W-pI...152.8:3 and all you t. you made will disappear.
W-pI.152.11:2 true. We t. of truth alone as we arise, and
W-pI.153.10:1 and in silence t. how holy is your purpose,
W-pI.153.18:1 practice, you will never cease to t. of Him,
W-pI.153.18:4 T. you He will not make this possible, for
W-pI...154.1:7 what we t. is weakness can be strength;
W-pI.155.14:1 but that you t. of Him a while each day,
W-pI...157.5:2 everyone you meet, and everyone you t. of
W-pI...161.4:7 mind that taught itself to t. specifically
W-pI.161.11:5 Then t. of this: What you are seeing now
W-pI...162.4:4 thus you learn to t. with God. Christ's
W-pI...164.8:1 letting go all things you t. you want. Your
W-pI...166.1:6 make you t. there is another will than His
W-pI...166.2:3 t. it real must still believe there is another
W-pI...166.9:3 You even t. the miserable self you thought
W-pI...167.3:1 You t. that death is of the body. Yet it is
W-pI...167.6:1 The mind can t. it sleeps, but that is all. It
W-pI.167.11:2 He is Lord of what we t. today. And in His
W-pI...169.6:1 speak nor write nor even t. of this at all. It
W-pI...170.1:3 you t. that you attack in self-defense, you
W-pI...170.9:1 do not t. that fear is the escape from fear.
W-pI...182.4:1 Perhaps you t. it is your childhood home
W-pI...182.9:2 to those who t. he is their enemy. He
W-pI...183.7:3 T. not He hears the little prayers of those
W-pI...184.2:3 Thus do you t. that you have given life in
W-pI...184.2:4 By this split you t. you are established as a
W-pI...184.6:2 And everyone who learns to t. that it is so
W-pI...184.8:1 T. not you made the world. Illusions, yes!
W-pI.184.10:3 to darkness, not because you t. it real, but
W-pI...185.2:2 with dreams, nor t. he is himself a dream.
W-pI...185.2:3 He cannot make a hell and t. it real. He
W-pI...188.7:1 These thoughts you t. with Him. They
W-pI.189.10:7 *We have no thoughts we t. apart from You,*
W-pI...190.4:3 is no need to t. of them as savage crimes,
W-pI...190.6:1 t. of this awhile: The world you see does
W-pI...192.5:2 It cannot t. that it will die, nor be the prey
W-pI...192.7:3 so limited that what we t. we understand
W-pI.193.11:4 let us t. about all things we saved to settle
W-pI .. 194.8:3 T. you the world could fail to gain thereby
W-pI .. 195.9:1 Today we learn to t. of gratitude in place
W-pI .. 197.1:5 And so you t. God's gifts are loans at best;
W-pI .. 197.6:1 and you will t. that what is given you has
W-pI .. 197.6:2 the sins you t. you see outside yourself,
W-pI .. 197.6:2 and you can never t. the gifts of God are
W-pI .. 197.9:6 All that you t. can only be His Thoughts,
W-pI .. 197.9:8 But never t. that He has ever ceased to
W-pI .. 198.7:3 You may t. They have accepted. But if you
W-pI .. 198.7:7 mad to t. that you could be condemned,
WpI.rVI.in.7:2 Him teach you what to do and say and t.,
W-pI .. 219.1:4 *Be still, my mind, and t. a moment upon this*
W-pII ....in.9:4 undone, and we no longer t. illusions true
W-pII . 231.1:2 *Love? Perhaps I t. I seek for something else; a*
W-pII . 236.1:3 to triumph over me, and tell me what to t.
W-pII . 238.2:1 pause to t. how much our Father loves us.
W-pII . 242.2:3 *not ask for anything that we may t. we want.*
W-pII . 243.1:2 I will not t. that I already know what must
W-pII . 243.1:3 I will not t. I understand the whole from
W-pII . 245.1:5 *or t. they are bereft of hope and happiness.*
W-pII . 246.1:1 me not t. that I can find the way to God, if
W-pII . 246.1:2 t. that I can know his Father or my Self.
W-pII ..... 5.3:5 obey by changing what we t. that it is for.
W-pII ..... 5.5:1 identify with what you t. will make you
W-pII . 261.1:1 with what I t. is refuge and security. I will
W-pII . 261.1:2 and t. I live within the citadel where I am
W-pII . 265.1:3 deceived was I to t. that what I feared was
W-pII . 275.2:3 *and what to say to him, what thoughts to t.,*
W-pII . 281.1:2 *When I t. that I am hurt in any way, it is*
W-pII . 281.1:4 *or hurt or ill, I have forgotten what You t.,*
W-pII . 281.1:6 *The Thoughts I t. with You can only bless.*
W-pII . 281.1:7 *The Thoughts I t. with You alone are true.*
W-pII . 292.1:4 And while we t. this will is real, we will
W-pII . 292.2:2 *for every trial we t. we still must meet.*
W-pII . 309.1:5 to look within because I t. I made another
W-pII .... 325.h All things I t. I see reflect ideas.
W-pII . 330.2:2 *And if we t. we suffer, we but fail to know our*
W-pII . 331.1:5 *How could I t. that Love has left Itself? There*
W-pII . 339.1:2 But he can t. that pain is pleasure. No one
W-pII . 339.1:4 he can t. that joy is painful, threatening
W-pII . 357.1:1 *escape the prison house in which I t. I live.*
W-ep ......... 4:1 and all pain that you may t. is real. Nor
M-in .......... 3:1 exclusively by what you t. you are, and
M-in .......... 3:2 unrelated to what you t. you are teaching.
M-in ........ 3:10 the self you t. is real is what you teach.
M-4 ........II.1:6 you say that contradicts what you t. or do
M-5 .........I.1:3 He must t. it is a small price to pay for
M-13 ......... 2:5 T. a while about what the world calls
M-16 ......... 3:1 beginning, it is wise to t. in terms of time.
M-16 ......... 5:8 in which you close your eyes and t. of God
M-16 ......... 6:3 t. you made a place of safety for yourself.
M-16 ......... 6:4 You t. you made a power that can save
M-17 ......... 6:8 do not t. about your frailty in comparison
M-17 ......... 7:4 T. not He has forgotten." Here we have
M-20 ......... 4:6 defense. Stop for a moment now and t. of
M-27 ......... 1:2 Is it not madness to t. of life as being born
M-27 ......... 2:1 be impossible to t. of Him as loving. For
M-27 ......... 6:9 and yet to t. love real are mindless magic,
M-29 ....... 3:10 then, t. that following the Holy Spirit's
C-3 ............ 1:2 is impossible to t. of anything He created
C-3 ............ 2:2 they do not t. it is their will to do so. This
C-6 ............ 4:7 whatever meets the needs you t. you have.
P-1............. 5:1 The patient need not t. of truth as God in
P-2..........II.7:4 Perhaps the teacher does not t. of God as
P-2..........V.2:5 to those who t. it will endanger them. It
P-2..........V.7:4 already, if we t. there is a need of healing.
P-2........ VI.6:5 must t. of evil as besetting him here and
P-2....... VII.2:1 T. carefully, teacher and therapist, for
P-2....... VII.6:6 fail. T. what this means; he has the gifts of
P-2....... VII.8:1 T. what the joining of two brothers really
P-3...........I.2:9 T. what God is telling you; He needs your
P-3........ III.7:7 while, long enough to t. of this: You have
S-1...........I.4:1 is to forget the things you t. you need. To
S-1........ III.5:1 instant, now, and t. what you have done.
S-1........ III.6:9 T. of the cost, and understand it well. All
S-2...........I.4:8 ever t. you can see sin in anyone except
S-2...........I.6:3 a remedy for all illusions that they t. they
S-2...... III.6:11 nor is His forgiveness what you t. it is.
S-3...........I.1:1 nor t. that sickness is apart and separate

| | |
|---|---|
| S-3 ...........I.2:3 | to be to those who t. their life is tied to its |
| S-3 ........IV.3:1 | T. what it means to help the Christ to |
| S-3 ........IV.5:3 | or you will t. that it is you who are creator |
| S-3 ......IV.10:7 | this; whatever you may t. about yourself, |
| S-3 ......IV.10:7 | whatever you may t. about the world, |

### thinker 7

| | |
|---|---|
| T-6......... II.9:1 | Thoughts begin in the mind of the t., |
| T-6......... III.1:1 | every idea begins in the mind of the t.. |
| T-6...... V.B.4:4 | occur with the change of mind in the t.. |
| T-6...... V.C.2:3 | to avoid. In the mind of the t., then, He *is* |
| T-7......... VI.1:5 | *will* return to the mind of the t. and they |
| T-12....... III.7:6 | thoughts do have consequences to the t.. |
| T-21... VIII.1:3 | those that teach the t. that he *can* be killed. |

### thinker's 2

| | |
|---|---|
| T-21...VII.13:8 | And none can leave the t. mind, or leave |
| T-22....... II.9:3 | idea that thoughts can leave the t. mind, |

### thinketh 1

| | |
|---|---|
| T-21.......in.1:6 | a man t., so does he perceive. Therefore, |

### thinking 100

| | |
|---|---|
| T-1........ I.36:1 | Miracles are examples of right t., aligning |
| T-1........ I.37:1 | a correction introduced into false t. by me |
| T-2....... V.10:2 | Since his own t. is faulty he cannot see the |
| T-2........ VI.2:3 | it. Why should you condone insane t.? |
| T-2........ VI.9:2 | take very little right t. to realize why fear |
| T-2...... VI.9:14 | All t. produces form at some level. |
| T-2....... VII.1:5 | if I depreciated the power of your own t.. |
| T-2....... VII.1:9 | You are not used to miracle-minded t., |
| T-2..... VIII.2:1 | of the most threatening ideas in your t.. |
| T-3...........I.1:9 | the kind of t. which His Own words have |
| T-3...........I.2:9 | essential that all such t. be dispelled that |
| T-3......... II.1:5 | It is essential that you realize your t. will |
| T-3........ III.5:8 | provides the strength for creative t., but |
| T-3......... V.5:7 | Ingenious t. is *not* the truth that shall set |
| T-3......... V.9:5 | a condition entirely alien to the world's t.. |
| T-4......... II.2:5 | T. about another ego is as effective in |
| T-4....... II.4:10 | the loftiest idea of which ego t. is capable. |
| T-4........ IV.2:8 | this and t. otherwise has held your ego |
| T-4........ VI.1:4 | how much of your t. is ego-directed. We |
| T-4....... VII.2:6 | The specificity of the ego's t., then, results |
| T-5...........I.1:9 | kind of t. is totally alien to having things, |
| T-5...........I.3:6 | as I thought, joining with me in Christ t.. |
| T-5...........I.4:6 | also one of God's creations, my right t., |
| T-5...........I.6:2 | children with a way of t. that could raise |
| T-5......... II.2:4 | not have understood the Call to right t.. |
| T-5........ III.1:3 | ways of t. would not be open to healing. |
| T-5........ IV.7:4 | the t. of God lacks nothing. Everything |
| T-5......... V.4:8 | is a sure sign that your t. is unnatural. |
| T-5......... V.4:9 | Unnatural t. will always be attended with |
| T-5....... V.6:12 | think like God, you are not really t. at all. |
| T-5....... V.7:10 | all your wrong t. if it could not be undone |
| T-5....... VII.6:5 | Your part is merely to return your t. to |
| T-6........ I.15:1 | of upside-down t. in the New Testament, |
| T-6......... II.9:2 | This is as true of God's T. as it is of yours. |
| T-7......... II.1:1 | To heal is the only kind of t. in this world |
| T-7........ IV.6:9 | by t. in accordance with the laws of God, |
| T-7........ VI.2:5 | Your t. has done this because of its power |
| T-7........ VI.2:5 | t. can also save you from this because its |
| T-7........ VI.2:6 | your t. as you choose is part of its power. |
| T-7........ VI.9:2 | except by you, when you are t. insanely. |
| T-7...... VI.12:5 | t. with your Creator and creating as He |
| T-7..... VII.10:9 | There is only one way out of the world's t. |
| T-7.......... X.1:8 | His t. has established them for you. They |
| T-8........ VI.7:2 | unwilling to will with God, you are not t.. |
| T-11....... V.5:3 | to God is wishful t. and not real willing. |
| T-14..... III.9:1 | for yourself you are t. destructively, and |
| T-14..... VII.4:3 | is a distorted process of t. whereby two |
| T-14.... XI.12:3 | for learning by t. they already know. |
| T-15....... I.11:1 | tempted to be dispirited by t. how long it |
| T-18...... IV.4:3 | wrong in t. that it is needful to prepare |
| T-21....... II.9:1 | already said that wishful t. is how the ego |
| T-21..... II.13:6 | same mistake as t. you are independent of |
| T-21..... VII.4:6 | t. it caught a glimpse of the great enemy |
| T-23..... II.21:7 | And where your t. starts, there must it |
| T-25....... V.6:4 | He hates you, t. Heaven must be hell. |
| T-27... VII.10:2 | There is a risk of t. death is peace, because |
| T-31..... VII.1:2 | as yet too alien to your t. to be helpful, |
| W-pI....... 8.2:4 | because it is not really t. about anything. |
| W-pI....... 8.3:1 | to recognize when it is not really t. at all. |
| W-pI....... 8.4:6 | period by saying: *I seem to be t. about–.* |
| W-pI....... 8.5:2 | *I seem to be t. about [name of a person],* |
| W-pI..... 10.3:2 | "thoughts" means that you are not t.. |
| W-pI..... 11.1:1 | process; the reversal of the t. of the world. |
| W-pI..... 19.1:2 | to t. precede those related to perceiving, |
| W-pI..... 19.1:4 | T. and its results are really simultaneous, |
| W-pI..... 20.1:4 | importance of the reversal of your t.. The |
| W-pI..... 34.4:1 | to experience difficulty in t. of specific |
| W-pI..... 37.2:1 | can be removed from the world's t.. Any |
| W-pI..... 39.9:2 | relax and do not seem to be t. of anything |
| W-pI..... 45.6:2 | in t. a few relevant thoughts of your own, |
| W-pI..... 45.9:4 | Him for the Thoughts He is t. with you. |
| WpI...rI.in.2:3 | period, t. about the idea and the related |
| W-pI..... 52.5:7 | I not rather join the t. of the universe than |
| W-pI..... 53.2:4 | rules a world that represents chaotic t., |
| W-pI..... 54.1:5 | As the world I see arises from my t. errors |
| W-pI..... 54.5:3 | me the t. of the world has been changed. |
| W-pI..... 64.7:1 | t. about them and about nothing else. |
| W-pI..... 68.6:2 | all, t. of each one in turn as you do so: *I* |
| W-pI..... 69.2:2 | to t. about what we are trying to do. We |
| W-pI..... 71.8:1 | periods for today by t. about today's idea, |
| WpI..rII.in.2:1 | and begin by t. about the ideas for the day |
| W-pI... 105.6:2 | Begin today by t. of those brothers who |
| W-pI... 106.8:3 | will free the world from t. giving is a way |
| W-pI. 121.10:1 | periods by t. of someone you do not like, |
| W-pI... 125.9:2 | today lift you above the t. of the world, |
| W-pI... 126.1:1 | alien to the ego and the t. of the world, is |
| W-pI... 130.1:2 | What you see reflects your t.. And your |
| W-pI... 130.1:3 | And your t. but reflects your choice of |
| W-pI... 163.2:3 | down before its image, t. it alone is real, |
| W-pI... 192.5:5 | the mind of t. that the body is its home. |
| M-in .......... 1:1 | is actually reversed in the t. of the world. |
| M-4 ..... VII.1:6 | but it is perhaps more alien to the t. of the |
| M-4 ..... VII.1:7 | of its reversal of the world's t.. In the |
| M-4 ...... IX.1:6 | is to reverse the t. of the world entirely. |
| M-14 ....... 3:11 | It goes against all the t. of the world, but |
| M-14 ......... 4:2 | and pieces of its t. will still seem sensible. |
| M-28 ......... 2:2 | is all the t. of the world reversed entirely. |
| P-1............. 4:2 | He must become willing to reverse his t., |
| P-2....... VII.7:1 | insane, t. they are God, are not afraid to |
| S-2 ...........I.7:4 | and poisoned t. from your holy mind. |

### thinks 110

| | |
|---|---|
| T-1........ VI.4:5 | you can believe what no one else t. is true. |
| T-3...........I.2:8 | you believe our Father really t. this way? |
| T-3......... II.1:8 | to deny truth totally, even if he t. he can. |
| T-4......... II.8:1 | way of describing how it t. it originated. |
| T-4......... V.6:1 | ego t. it is an advantage not to commit |
| T-5...........I.1:6 | mind t. according to the laws spirit obeys, |
| T-5........ IV.3:5 | spirit do not leave the mind that t. them, |
| T-6.........I.18:6 | This is not as God t., and you must think |
| T-6.........I.18:6 | you must think as He t. if you are to know |
| T-7......... V.4:5 | if he t. he has something that others lack. |
| T-7......... V.7:2 | he t. he is giving something to them, and |
| T-7......... V.8:8 | help him undo the change his ego t. it has |
| T-8........ III.5:3 | for the power and glory he t. he has lost. |
| T-8....... VII.1:7 | When a child of God t. of himself in this |
| T-10...... III.4:6 | in the image of what its maker t. he is. |
| T-13...... IV.1:5 | the dust out of which it t. you were made. |
| T-15.........I.5:2 | life of someone who t. its is the only voice, |
| T-15..... VII.7:2 | For each one t. that he has sacrificed |
| T-15..... VII.7:3 | Yet this is what he t. he wants. He is not |
| T-15..... VII.8:3 | object where the mind goes or what it t., |
| T-16.........I.2:4 | identified with what it t. it understands, |
| T-16....... II.3:3 | is perfectly natural, for it is the way God t. |
| T-16....... V.7:3 | which it t. it can accomplish this it gives |
| T-16....... V.7:5 | not want for one he t. he would prefer. |
| T-18... VIII.4:4 | And what it t. it is in no way changes its |
| T-18...... IX.1:5 | in its delusions, it t. it is the Son of God, |
| T-19...... III.1:7 | an essential part of what the ego t. you are |
| T19 IV.D15:10 | the sins your brother t. he has committed |
| T19. IV.D.18:3 | the sins he t. he sees within himself. Offer |
| T-21...... II.10:3 | events and feelings its maker t. it causes. |
| T-21...... II.12:6 | brother t. he made the world with you. |
| T-21...... II.12:8 | With you, he t. the world he made, made |
| T-21...... VI.3:1 | for himself, as God t. not without His Son |
| T-22....... in.2:5 | each one t. the other has what he has not. |
| T-22.........I.5:2 | for everyone sees only what he t. he is. |
| T-22.... VI.14:2 | For what one t., the other will experience |
| T-23....... in.1:5 | and no one can attack unless he t. he has. |
| T-23.........I.2:6 | it t. that triumph over you is possible. |
| T-23.........I.2:7 | And God t. otherwise. This is no war; |
| T-23...... II.16:6 | No one who t. that one of these laws is |
| T-23...... III.1:8 | For no one t. of murder and escapes the |
| T-25....... in.2:3 | in a body, where he t. he is He cannot be. |
| T-25....... in.3:2 | the mind that t. it is a body is sick indeed! |
| T-25.........I.7:4 | in the condition in which it t. it is. And It |
| T-25..... VII.1:9 | from love to everyone who t. sin possible. |
| T-25..... VII.4:7 | Who t. the world is sane in any way, is |
| T-25..... VII.4:7 | in any way, is justified in anything it t., or |
| T-25.... VIII.5:9 | for the crimes he did not do, but t. he did |
| T-25.. VIII.13:8 | due, because he t. he is deprived. And so |
| T-27........ II.2:6 | seeks to pardon what it t. to be the truth. |
| T-27...... II.6:10 | He t. your blood is on his hands, and so |
| T-27..... VII.4:4 | For each one t. that if he does his part, the |
| T-27.... VIII.7:4 | and t. your thoughts instead of you. It |
| T-28...... IV.3:1 | Like you, your brother t. he is a dream. |
| T-28...... IV.8:2 | separate piece that t. it is a picture in itself |
| T-29.........I.2:5 | to hate, and so he t. that love is fearful; |
| T-29...... III.1:1 | your savior not because he t. he is a body. |
| T-29....... V.6:6 | brother t. he holds the hand of death. |
| T-29...... IX.5:8 | He t. he needs them that he may escape |
| T-29...... IX.5:8 | because he t. the thoughts are real. And |
| T-29...... IX.6:7 | he t. is governed by the laws he made. Yet |
| T-29...... IX.6:8 | world unaffected by the world he t. is real |
| T-29...... IX.8:2 | made to separate the mind from what it t. |
| T-30.... IV.5:14 | all. His one mistake is that he t. them real. |
| T-31........ II.9:3 | with you, and t. perhaps a bit behind, a |
| T-31...... III.4:2 | The body t. no thoughts. It has no power |
| T-31...... III.5:1 | that t. it is a sin has but one purpose; that |
| T-31..... V.14:4 | but with the simple statement that it t.. |
| T-31..... V.14:6 | So it can learn that everything it t. reflects |
| W-pI..... 17.1:4 | This is not the way the world t., but you |
| W-pI..... 35.1:3 | is difficult for anyone who t. he is in this |
| W-pI..... 35.1:4 | Yet the reason he t. he is in this world is |
| W-pI..... 45.9:1 | the holiness of the mind that t. with God. |
| W-pI..... 47.3:4 | Voice which speaks for Him t. as He does. |
| W-pI..... 76.4:1 | It is insanity that t. these things. You call |
| W-pI..... 79.2:3 | if he t. the problem is something else? |
| W-pI..... 96.5:3 | function now, it t. it is alone and separate, |
| W-pI..... 96.5:4 | with like, for this is what it t. that it is for. |
| W-pI..... 99.3:2 | The mind that sees illusions t. them real. |
| W-pI..... 99.3:4 | that t. these thoughts is separate from |
| W-pI... 121.5:3 | It t. it cannot change, for what it sees |
| W-pI... 121.5:4 | It does not ask, because it t. it knows. It |
| W-pI... 127.2:1 | to anyone who t. that love can change. He |
| W-pI... 127.2:3 | And thus he t. that he can love at times, |
| W-pI... 127.2:4 | also t. that love can be bestowed on one, |
| W-pI... 127.3:4 | must elude the mind that t. of it as partial |
| W-pI... 131.9:4 | He t. he made a hell opposing Heaven, |
| W-pI... 132.1:5 | A madman t. the world he sees is real, |
| W-pI... 133.6:5 | is deceived by nothing in a form he t. he |
| W-pI... 134.4:5 | delusional in what it t. it can accomplish. |
| W-pI... 140.1:3 | from the body, where it t. the mind exists. |
| W-pI... 157.5:2 | everyone you think of, or who t. of you. |
| W-pI... 160.1:4 | to the part of you which t. that it is real, |
| W-pI... 161.6:5 | for attack, for no one t. he hates a mind. |
| W-pI... 161.6:7 | be the seat of fear except what t. of fear? |
| W-pI... 166.4:1 | Here is the only home he t. he knows. |
| W-pI... 189.7:2 | of everything it t. is either true or false, or |
| W-pI... 190.2:3 | to the Son's mistakes in what he t. he is. It |
| W-pI... 192.8:1 | everyone he sees or t. of or imagines? |
| W-pI... 196.6:4 | real to anyone who t. this thought is true. |
| W-pI... 197.4:1 | matter if another t. your gifts unworthy. |
| W-pII ..... 2.1:4 | which t. that it has separate thoughts, |
| W-pII ..... 5.1:2 | It is within this fence he t. he lives, to die |
| W-pII ..... 5.1:3 | within this fence he t. that he is safe from |
| W-pII . 319.1:5 | The ego t. that what one gains, totality |
| W-pII ... 12.2:3 | insanity it t. it has become a victor over |
| M-4 ... I.A.6:10 | He has not yet come as far as he t.. Yet |

C-2 2:5 how it arose can be but he who **t.** it real,
P-1 4:5 his freedom because he **t.** that it is slavery
P-1 5:5 The Holy Spirit uses time as He **t.** best,

## thinness 1

T-18 IX.5:3 Its **t.** and transparency are not apparent

## third 15

T-2 I.1:11 **T.**, you believe that you can distort the
T-5 VI.8:1 fathers unto the **t.** and fourth generation,
T-6 V.C.2:7 Therefore, the Holy Spirit's **t.** lesson is: *Be*
T-6 V.C.5:3 to remember it is inherent in the **t.** step,
T-6 V.C.5:7 **t.** step the Holy Spirit has prepared you
T-6 V.C.7:1 The **t.** step is thus one of protection for
T-6 V.C.10:1 The **t.** step, then, is a statement of what
T-14 IV.1:8 for there is no order, no second or **t.**, and
T19 IV.C.h The **T.** Obstacle: The Attraction of Death
T19 IV.C.1:3 the **t.** obstacle that peace must flow across
T-23 II.6:5 This leads directly to the ***t.*** preposterous
T-23 II.7:1 of God is reinforced by this **t.** principle.
W-pI 43.4:2 The **t.** may be undertaken at the most
M-3 5:1 **t.** level of teaching occurs in relationships
M-4 I.A.5:1 The **t.** stage through which the teacher of

## thirsts 1

T-18 VIII.9:8 out to everyone who **t.** for living water,

## thirsty 2

W-pI 7.3:2 experiences of picking up a cup, being **t.**,
W-pII 13.5:1 starved and **t.** creatures come to die. Now

## this 4878

## thorn 2

T-11 VI.7:1 and taken the last **t.** from his forehead.
W-pI 193.9:2 one **t.** or nail to hurt His holy Son in any

## thorns 22

T-11 VI.8:1 placed a crown of **t.** upon your own head.
T19 IV.D.16:6 Press it not like **t.** against his brow, nor
T-20 I.2:5 the gift of lilies, not the crown of **t.**; the
T-20 I.2:6 **t.** in one hand and lilies in the other,
T-20 I.2:7 Join now with me and throw away the **t.**,
T-20 I.3:5 Hold him not back with **t.** and nails when
T-20 II.1:5 Learn you but offer him a crown of **t.**, not
T-20 II.3:8 Offer him **t.** and *you* are crucified. Offer
T-20 II.4:2 him forgiveness when he offers **t.** to me?
T-20 II.4:3 who offers **t.** to anyone is against me still,
T-20 II.4:6 If it be **t.** whose points gleam sharply in a
T-20 II.4:7 me. And yet the **t.** are gone. Look you still
T-20 II.5:1 the body's eyes, and they can see but **t.**.
T-20 II.5:6 He sees no **t.** but only lilies, gleaming in
T-20 II.7:2 It has been given you to see no **t.**, no
T-20 II.7:8 no **t.** nor nails to crucify the Son of God,
T-20 II.10:4 gift has saved him from the **t.** and nails,
T-26 II.4:7 And so He takes the **t.** and nails away. He
T-27 I.1:4 will weave a crown of **t.** from which your
T-31 IV.2:13 And on some the **t.** are felt at once. The
W-pI 161.11:5 lift the crown of **t.** which you have placed
S-3 IV.9:3 the **t.** fall softly from the bleeding brow of

## thorny 3

T-29 II.1:3 it is impossible to lose the way, seem **t.**,
T-31 VIII.9:3 lift us high above the **t.** roads we travelled
W-pI 200.9:3 and needless wasted time on **t.** byways.

## thoroughly 4

T-14 X.8:7 **t.** approves the undertakings of students
W-pI 26.8:2 **t.** than to touch on a larger number. As
WpI rI.in.3:1 either literally or **t.** in the practice periods
W-pI 170.2:1 How **t.** insane is the idea that to defend

## thoroughness 1

M-9 2:1 he learns one lesson with increasing **t.**. He

## those 421

## thou 2

T-4 III.6:6 **T.** shalt have no other gods before Him
T-6 I.15:5 "Betrayest **t.** the Son of man with a kiss?"

## though 107

T-1 II.1:8 induces action, **t.** it does not inspire it.
T-1 V.4:2 him, even **t.** he may be absent in spirit.
T-1 VI.4:3 In attitude, then, **t.** not in content, you
T-2 VII.3:10 a real expediter, **t.** only temporarily.
T-2 VIII.1:5 your own sight, **t.** not in the Mind of God.
T-3 VII.3:2 real enough in time, **t.** not in eternity. All
T-3 VII.5:8 in peace, even **t.** your mind is in conflict.
T-4 I.2:13 learn, even **t.** its maker can be misguided.
T-4 II.3:5 **t.** hardly to something that occurs with
T-4 II.3:6 way, even **t.** it does work that way now.
T-4 II.5:1 painful, even **t.** this is anything but true.
T-4 III.9:1 In your own mind, **t.** denied by the ego,
T-4 VII.3:12 even **t.** it may refuse to utilize it on behalf
T-5 II.6:8 even **t.** they chose to leave Him. The voice
T-5 V.6:5 Remember, **t.**, that the alternatives
T-6 IV.4:4 badly in need of allies, **t.** not of brothers.
T-6 V.1:7 outward, **t.** not His completeness, is
T-6 V.B.1:5 them, even **t.** it was apparent I was not.
T-7 I.2:7 Kingdom, **t.** not to add to the Creator of
T-7 III.2:10 even **t.** the ego does not know what it is.
T-7 X.6:6 really open to choice, **t.** it may seem to be.
T-8 IX.6:5 even **t.** it makes every effort to induce it.
T-9 I.8:5 retaliation, even **t.** many may seek both.
T-9 I.12:2 Willing against reality, **t.** impossible, can
T-9 I.12:2 persistent goal even **t.** you do not want it.
T-9 IV.4:1 asking for one, **t.** not of the right teacher.
T-9 IV.7:2 to it, even **t.** it has no idea what they are.
T-9 V.8:14 is a sound **t.** insufficient statement. Only
T-9 VI.1:4 **t.** you are not experiencing joy yourself
T-9 VI.6:4 first, **t.** they are simultaneous in eternity,
T-9 VIII.1:4 occurs, even **t.** it does not understand it,
T-10 I.2:5 even **t.** all the laws of what you awaken to
T-10 V.8:5 **t.**, that to do this is blasphemy, for it
T-11 III.5:1 Son, even **t.** His Son would hide himself.
T-11 V.10:3 For **t.** you may countenance a false idea of
T-12 IV.1:3 **t.** encouraging the search for love very
T-12 IV.1:6 and its judgment, **t.** severely impaired, is
T-12 IV.7:6 you will not see life **t.** it is all around you.
T-13 II.8:3 its offerings, but **t.** you do not want them,
T-13 III.8:4 for **t.** they may deceive themselves, like
T-13 IV.3:6 And even **t.** you know not Heaven, might
T-13 IV.5:5 to your brother as **t.** he were someone else
T-13 V.5:1 to each of them as **t.** it were the other. For
T-13 VIII.5:3 **T.** every aspect *is* the whole, you cannot
T-13 X.3:5 in it. Yet **t.** they suffer, they will not look
T-13 X.7:8 He knows you do not know, **t.** it is yours.
T-14 IV.7:3 not recognize Him, **t.** He is all around you
T-14 IX.3:8 **t.** His worshippers placed other gods
T-14 X.4:1 thoughts, which even **t.** they may conflict,
T-14 X.5:7 **t.** the order you impose upon your mind
T-14 X.8:9 is senseless, **t.** careful to conceal this fact
T-15 X.1:4 use them both, **t.** not as the ego uses them
T-15 X.4:4 For **t.** the ego takes many forms, it is
T-15 XI.4:6 and try to cast it out, **t.** it is part of you.
T-16 III.3:6 do not recognize It even **t.** It functions.
T-16 III.7:3 **T.** you seemed to suffer for it, the joy of
T-18 II.5:4 You do not respond to it as **t.** you made it,
T-18 VI.4:6 **t.** it clearly can misperceive the function
T-18 VI.9:4 This is not his reality, **t.** he believes it is.
T-19 I.5:2 **t.** it follows directly from the fundamental
T-20 IV.5:4 separately, **t.** they are all the same. Yet
T-21 in.1:3 But **t.** it is no more than that, it is not less.
T-22 I.1:7 It is as **t.** you wandered in without a plan
T-22 II.1:4 **t.** each one seems to be the way to lose the
T-23 II.1:1 be brought to light, **t.** never understood.
T-24 I.3:1 belief, to be defended **t.** unrecognized, is
T-26 II.3:3 have no problems, **t.** you think you have.
T-26 V.4:1 perceive in time, **t.** it has long since gone.
T-26 VII.4:3 God's answer is eternal, **t.** it works in time
T-26 VII.9:7 **t.** they were known before they were
T-26 VII.12:6 feel guilty, **t.** without understanding why.
T-26 VIII.8:1 this illusion has a cause which, **t.** untrue,
T-27 III.6:5 concepts. **T.** it is but half the picture and
T-27 IV.7:4 **t.** they leave the first unanswered. In the
T-27 VIII.3:3 **T.** the dream itself takes many forms, and
T-28 VI.6:6 "I will," **t.** in that promise he was born.
T-29 II.1:7 Yet **t.** you do not see them, they are there.
T-29 II.2:6 Now is it caused, **t.** not as yet perceived.
T-29 II.2:7 And its effects are there, **t.** not yet seen.
T-29 V.8:2 even **t.** it was for this that every dream
T-29 VI.5:2 For even **t.** it was a dream of death, you
T-29 IX.8:4 **t.** he has not heard it since before all time
T-31 V.9:1 that **t.** there be some lack of ease at times
T-31 V.9:3 **t.** you do not yet perceive that this is what
W-pI 23.4:5 love them, even **t.** they were made of hate.
W-pI 33.1:3 **t.** unhurried applications are essential.
W-pI 48.3:2 **t.** not necessarily in a place you recognize
WpI rI.in.2:2 **t.** each one should be practiced at least
W-pI 91.2:7 is useless to you then, even **t.** it is there.
W-pI 130.9:4 you will look upon, for **t.** it is perception,
W-pI 131.4:4 can not seek vainly, **t.** he try to force delay
W-pI 133.10:1 Yet **t.** he tries to keep its halo clear within
W-pI 151.2:3 **t.** you learned a long while since your
W-pI 153.18:3 **t.** your time is spent in offering salvation
W-pI 155.1:2 appearance, **t.** you smile more frequently.
W-pI 157.3:1 **t.** you will return to paths of learning. Yet
W-pI 166.5:5 and poverty, alone **t.** God is with him,
W-pI 170.7:2 that **t.** his lips are smeared with blood,
W-pI 183.1:5 even **t.** you have not remembered it.
W-pI 184.14:1 And **t.** we use a different name for each
W-pI 186.13:3 make a restitution, **t.** He is complete; a
W-pI 198.3:1 dreams away, and **t.** it is itself a dream, it
W-pI 200.4:2 **t.** you sought to make them meaningful.
W-pII 5.4:2 **T.** it was made to fence him into hell
W-pII 6.2:5 For **t.** in Him His Father placed the means
C-ep 4:6 instant, **t.** it seems to be unsung forever.
S-1 II.3:2 belief, **t.** not yet with understanding. A

## Thought 83

*thought*

T-3 V.7:3 Own **T.** and of a quality like to His Own.
T-5 V.6:16 As part of His **T.**, you *cannot* think apart
T-6 II.8:1 God created His Sons by extending His **T.**
T-6 II.8:1 the extensions of His **T.** in His Mind. All
T-7 I.2:3 creative **T.** proceeds from Him to you, so
T-7 II.1:1 in this world that resembles the **T.** of God
T-7 III.4:9 because it is a reflection of perfect **T.**.
T-8 VI.7:3 God's Will *is* **T.**. It cannot be contradicted
T-11 III.7:5 **T.** and therefore does not belong to Him.
T-11 VIII.9:4 every thought is as loving as the **T.** of His
T-13 VIII.4:3 He is a **T.** of God, and God has given Him
T-15 XI.1:5 and the **T.** that has been given you. When
T-16 VI.9:2 understand the **T.** that *knows* what you are
T-16 VI.9:3 the **T.** of your reality to enter your mind,
T-17 IV.15:3 of a thought system, but the **T.** itself.
T-18 I.10:7 the **T.** so holy and so perfect that illusions
T-18 VIII.5:2 joined to the **T.** by which it was created.
T-18 VIII.9:1 **T.** of God surrounds your little kingdom,
T19 IV.C.2:15 surely as life is the result of the **T.** of God.
T-24 VI.3:3 And no **T.** within His Mind is absent from
T-25 VII.3:3 one **T.** of His makes any sense at all within
T-25 VII.3:7 then every **T.** God ever had is an illusion.
T-25 VII.3:8 And if but one **T.** of His is true, then all
T-25 VII.4:3 with the Mind Whose **T.** created him. So
T-30 II.1:10 And not one **T.** that God has ever had but
T-30 III.5:11 whole completely lovely **T.** God holds of
T-30 III.7:6 of it. The **T.** God holds of you is perfectly
T-30 III.8:4 The **T.** God holds of you is like a star,
T-30 III.10:1 Beyond all idols is the **T.** God holds of
T-30 III.10:2 the **T.** God holds of you remains exactly
T-30 III.10:5 the **T.** God holds of you has never left the

T-30....III.11:1 T. God holds of you exist but where you
T-30....III.11:7 *or* the T. God holds of you is your reality.
W-pI....78.9:2 for not one T. of God but must rejoice as
W-pI....99.4:1 with Mind and T. which are forever One?
W-pI....99.4:3 What but a T. of God could be this plan,
W-pI....99.6:1 is the T. that brings illusions to the truth,
W-pI....99.6:2 This is the T. that saves and that forgives,
W-pI....99.6:3 This is the T. whose function is to save by
W-pI....99.7:6 let the T. with which He has replaced all
W-pI....99.9:1 Practice His T. today, and let His light
W-pI...107.8:2 but were created by the selfsame T. which
W-pI...108.1:4 T. behind it will appear instead to take its
W-pI...108.4:1 of one T. whose truth does not depend on
W-pI...108.4:2 together, that the T. remain complete.
W-pI...108.4:3 frame of reference which unifies this T..
W-pI...108.6:3 finally arrive at the one T. which underlies
W-pI...109.9:5 and those passed by, to every T. of God,
W-pI.132.11:6 as it was His T. by which you were created
W-pI.134.13:2 laws it follows, nor the T. that it reflects.
W-pI...151.9:2 the Mind Whose T. created your reality.
W-pI.151.14:4 remains is unified into a perfect T. that
W-pI......165.h Let not my mind deny the T. of God.
W-pI...165.2:1 The T. of God created you. It left you not,
W-pI...165.2:6 The T. of God protects you, cares for you,
W-pI...165.2:7 because the T. of God has left you not,
W-pI...165.5:6 accept the T. of God as your inheritance.
W-pI...165.7:4 the T. of Him is never absent. Sureness
W-pI...165.8:5 T. of Him is still beyond all dreams and in
W-pI.167.10:5 even an instant where the T. of life eternal
W-pI...178.1:1 Let not my mind deny the T. of God. God
W-pI.187.10:2 God, one Father, one Creator and one T.,
W-pI.196.12:1 no T. of God that does not go with you to
W-pI...198.8:3 And what but truth could have a T. which
W-pI...210.1:3 *It is not a T. of God, but one I thought apart*
W-pII......2.1:4 thoughts of conflict with the T. of peace.
W-pII......2.2:1 The T. of peace was given to God's Son
W-pII......2.2:2 There was no need for such a T. before,
W-pII......2.2:4 the T. that has the power to heal the split
W-pII..260.1:2 *Yet, as Your T., I have not left my Source,*
W-pII......6.1:3 He is the T. which still abides within the
W-pII..280.1:3 No T. of God has left its Father's Mind.
W-pII..280.1:4 No T. of God is limited at all. No Thought
W-pII..280.1:5 No T. of God but is forever pure. Can I lay
W-pII..326.1:1 *Your Mind, a holy T. that never left its home.*
W-pII..338.2:3 *me the only T. that leads me to salvation.*
W-pII..338.2:5 *T. You gave me promises to lead me home,*
W-pII..341.1:3 *as His Son, a universe of T. completing Him.*
M-11..........4:8 here, because a T. of God has entered.
M-11..........4:9 else but a T. of God turns hell to Heaven
C-1.............1:3 is the T. of God which He created like
C-3.............3:1 a T. of peace because they are in conflict.
C-5.............1:4 Beyond each one there is a T. of God, and

## thought 596

*Thought*

T-2.........V.1:7 and that correction belongs at the t. level.
T-2........VI.9:8 It is hard to recognize that t. and belief
T-2.......VII.2:2 power of t. in order to avoid miscreation.
T-2.....VIII.3:1 The Last Judgment is generally t. of as a
T-3......III.5:10 the result of revelation and induces only t.
T-3.........V.2:5 ingenious t. systems for this purpose.
T-3.........V.7:2 "Image" can be understood as "t.," and
T-3........VI.7:5 the one inconceivable t. as its premise,
T-3.......VII.1:1 system of t. must have a starting point. It
T-3.......VII.1:6 a mistake to believe that a t. system based
T-3.......VII.3:2 separation is a system of t. real enough in
T-3.......VII.4:9 is the foundation stone in your t. system,
T-3.....VII.5:10 destruction of your t. system upon you as
T-3.......VII.6:3 your own t. system will stand corrected. It
T-4...........I.2:1 want to protect their t. systems as they are
T-4...........I.2:5 t. system can stand on two foundations.
T-4...........I.3:5 trying to teach you how its t. system arose
T-4...........I.4:7 of your t. system and open it to me, I will
T-4.........II.1:4 Abstract t. applies to knowledge because
T-4.........II.5:1 the ego's t. system must be perceived as
T-4.........II.7:4 of "getting" arose in the ego's t. system.
T-4.......II.10:5 be dictated by the t. system to which it
T-4........IV.2:3 *be.* In every case you have t. wrongly about
T-4........IV.2:4 what you have t. that God would not have
T-4........IV.2:4 have thought that God would not have t.,
T-4........IV.2:4 not t. that God would have you think.
T-4.........V.1:5 according to the t. system which gave rise
T-4.........V.3:1 Any t. system that confuses God and the
T-4.......VII.2:3 of the ego is based on its own t. system, as
T-5.........in.3:1 being blessed by every beneficent t. of any
T-5...........I.1:1 Healing is a t. by which two minds
T-5...........I.3:6 It asks that you may think as I t., joining
T-5.......II.12:3 how to keep me as the model for your t.,
T-5........III.2:2 Being t., the idea gains as it is shared.
T-5........IV.3:1 Every loving t. held in any part of the
T-5........IV.8:3 and every loving t. you ever had. I have
T-5.........V.3:7 ego is quite literally a fearful t.. However
T-5.........V.6:15 of t. comes from God and is in God. As
T-5.........V.7:1 Irrational t. is disordered thought. God
T-5.........V.7:1 Irrational thought is disordered t.. God
T-5.........V.7:2 God Himself orders your t. because your
T-5.........V.7:2 because your t. was created by Him. Guilt
T-5.........V.7:5 Every disordered t. is attended by guilt at
T-5.......V.7:12 If you accept the remedy for disordered t.,
T-5.........V.8:8 so. Having given up its disordered t., the
T-5.........V.8:8 ordering of t. becomes quite apparent.
T-5........VI.9:2 Every loveless t. must be undone, a word
T-5........VI.9:4 be destroyed because it is part of your t.,
T-5.......VII.1:2 really believe you can devise a t. system
T-6.........in.2:3 organize his life without some t. system.
T-6.........in.2:4 Once you have developed a t. system of
T-6.........in.2:5 allegiance to a t. system may be misplaced
T-6........I.16:2 t. system toward which I am guiding you.
T-6........I.16:7 the result of clearly opposed t. systems;
T-6........IV.1:7 the foundation of its whole t. system.
T-6......IV.11:5 proved to you that you have t. insanely?
T-6.........V.1:8 So He t., "My children sleep and must be
T-6......V.A.4:5 a real foundation stone of the t. system I
T-6......V.B.1:5 Many t. I was attacking them, even
T-6......V.B.1:7 is that when you do not share a t. system,
T-6......V.B.1:9 identifies himself with his t. system, and
T-6......V.B.1:9 and every t. system centers on what you
T-6....V.B.1:10 If the center of the t. system is true, only
T-6......V.B.5:1 out of conflict between two opposing t.
T-6......V.B.5:2 If you identify with your t. system, and
T-6......V.B.5:2 and if you accept two t. systems which are
T-6......V.B.8:2 really only the beginning of the t. reversal.
T-6......V.B.9:2 toward the center of your t. system, where
T-6......V.C.1:2 teaches you to judge every t. you allow to
T-6......V.C.3:2 Yet it still has an aspect of t. reversal,
T-6......V.C.3:3 is merely the beginning of the t. reversal,
T-7...........I.2:1 not increase through its own creative t..
T-7...........I.2:3 your creative t. proceed from you to your
T-7........III.4:9 The altar is perfectly clear in t., because it
T-7........V.11:8 of creation, and therefore governs all t..
T-7........VI.2:7 this you have denied the power of your t.,
T-7........VI.7:8 not know, your t. seems to contradict His,
T-7......VI.8:11 contradictory t. systems share truth, your
T-7......VI.12:2 your t. system and divide your allegiance.
T-7.....VII.11:1 Perceive any part of the ego's t. system as
T-7........IX.3:4 ego's whole t. system blocks extension,
T-8........III.6:7 someone else, you t. he *was* someone else.
T-8........III.7:8 t. any part of the Sonship holds. Wrong
T-8........VI.4:1 left his home and t. he had squandered
T-8........VI.4:2 his father, because he t. he had hurt him.
T-8........VI.7:4 It cannot be contradicted *by* t.. God does
T-8........VI.7:6 Yet their t. is so powerful that they can
T-8.......VII.7:1 says, "The Word (or t.) was made flesh."
T-8.......VII.7:4 T. cannot be made into flesh except by
T-8.......VII.7:4 except by belief, since t. is not physical.
T-8.......VII.7:5 Yet t. is communication, for which the
T-8.....VII.14:1 by the body, and t. cannot be made flesh.
T-8.....VII.16:8 Do not arrest your t. in this world, and
T-8......VIII.8:2 Have you t. about the distorting power of
T-8........IX.7:1 to take no t. of the body as separate and
T-8........IX.9:3 in a chaotic t. system *is* the way to heal it.
T-9........II.2:5 physically, the threat to his t. system
T-9.......VII.6:8 is meaningless within the ego's t. system,
T-9.......VII.6:8 open the whole t. system to question.
T-9.......VII.7:3 and keep the ego's whole t. system intact.
T-9.......VII.7:4 You cannot retain part of a t. system,
T-9.......VII.7:6 the reality of the ego's t. system merely
T-10......III.5:1 the ego's t. system and judge whether its
T-11.......in.1:3 nor the ego proposes a partial t. system.
T-11.......in.2:7 in the dark cornerstone of its t. system.
T-11.......in.2:8 or its whole t. system will not stand.
T-11.......in.3:2 creation is you, for His t. system is light.
T-11.......in.3:4 you approach the center of His t. system,
T-11.......in.3:5 to the foundation of the ego's t. system,
T-11.......in.3:7 up to the foundation of the ego's t. system
T-11.........I.1:3 again the t. system you share with Him.
T-11........II.1:2 this, and every healing t. brings it closer.
T-11........II.2:5 Every healing t. that you accept, either
T-11........II.2:6 In every hurtful t. you hold, wherever you
T-11.......V.1:3 at the ego's t. system because together we
T-11......V.14:6 the ego proceeds to the next step in its t.
T-11......V.16:4 and no t. system transcends its source.
T-11......V.18:3 to the t. system you want to be true. Every
T-11.....VII.2:1 loving t. that the Son of God ever had is
T-11....VIII.3:2 Not one t. you hold is wholly true. The
T-11....VIII.9:4 Whose every t. is as loving as the Thought
T-12.........I.3:3 Every loving t. is true. Everything else is
T-12.....VII.9:5 within and t. you saw the power to give
T-12....VIII.6:4 the instant you t. you had deserted Him.
T-13.....in.2:11 one of them but has t. that God is cruel.
T-13........II.7:4 than you dismiss the ego's t. system. To
T-13......III.3:3 world you t. you made would vanish. The
T-13......III.6:4 loving mind that t. it made them in anger.
T-13......III.7:6 He will heal every little t. you have kept to
T-13......IX.5:1 his secret t. that he has done this unto you
T-13........X.8:5 that he ever t. his Father loved him not,
T-14.........I.2:5 your t. system is closed off and wholly
T-14.........I.3:2 t. system you made would be forever dark
T-14.........I.5:2 the simple truth into a t. system which
T-14......III.9:4 No t. of God's Son can be separate or
T-14......IV.2:2 from the disordered mind that t. it was.
T-14.......V.4:3 Protect his purity from every t. that would
T-14........X.9:2 the system of t. that arises from joining
T-14.....X.10:3 Take no t. for yourself, for no thought you
T-14.....X.10:3 yourself, for no t. you hold *is* for yourself.
T-14.....X.11:6 holds more than these two orders of t..
T-15.........I.4:8 death were t. of merely as an end to pain,
T-15.........I.4:9 paradox in the ego's t. system before, but
T-15......IV.8:1 Every t. you would keep hidden shuts
T-15......IV.8:6 of the single Will that governs all t..
T-15.......V.9:7 love guiltily from where you t. it was.
T-15......VI.5:3 and unite this idea with the Mind that t. it
T-15........X.5:7 Sacrifice is so essential to your t. system
T-15......XI.2:7 and no t. alien to His Oneness can abide
T-16.........I.3:8 one t. in mind and do not lose sight of it,
T-16......III.1:3 how alien it is to what you t. you knew,
T-16......III.1:3 Teacher came from beyond your t. system
T-16......III.1:5 from the basis of a very different t. system
T-16......III.2:6 effect are very clear in the ego's t. system,
T-16.....V.10:3 the total context in which it is t. to occur.
T-16.....V.15:4 whole t. system is a carefully contrived
T-16......VI.9:2 of the t. system that taught you it was real
T-17......III.9:6 T. systems are but true or false, and all
T-17......IV.5:4 The insane protect their t. systems, but
T-17......IV.6:1 that the t. system the special relationship
T-17......IV.6:4 of the ego's t. system that you have been
T-17......IV.7:4 of the t. system the defense protects, set
T-17......IV.8:2 Its t. system is offered here, surrounded
T-17......IV.9:8 most superficial aspects of this t. system,
T-17....IV.11:8 whole t. system of the ego lies in its gifts,
T-17....IV.14:7 what it is; a picture of what you t. was real
T-17....IV.15:3 is no figured representation of a t. system,
T-17.......V.8:3 sought for satisfaction and t. you found it.
T-17.....VII.3:5 The t. of bodies is the sign of faithlessness
T-18......IV.8:7 Only in your mind, which t. it did, is its
T-18.....VI.12:3 and anywhere; a sound, a sight, a t., a
T-18.....VII.3:7 must be t. of in the past or in the future.
T-18....VIII.3:5 how alone and frightened is this little t.,
T-18....VIII.5:2 house a separate mind, a disconnected t.,
T-18......IX.1:3 little t. that seems split off and separate,
T-18......IX.1:5 wild and delusional t. needs help because,
T-18......IX.5:2 a real foundation for the ego's t. system.
T-18......IX.9:4 cleansed of every evil t. you laid upon it.
T-19.......I.5:10 t. of as a means for seeking out reality
T-19.........I.6:3 keep the delusional t. system in the mind.
T-19.........I.7:4 Each is united, a complete t. system, but

| | |
|---|---|
| T-19.......I.16:4 | in any way except by the mind that t. it. |
| T-19....... II.5:2 | of sin is wholly sacrosanct to its t. system, |
| T19..IV.C.2:15 | death is the result of the t. we call the ego, |
| T19....IV.C.9:3 | preserved from every t. that would attack |
| T19. IV.D.14:3 | You t. He sinned because you cast the veil |
| T-20....... II.6:6 | it but a dream, a careless t. to play with, |
| T-20...... III.7:8 | This one wild t., fierce in its arrogance, |
| T-20...... IV.8:8 | it. You need take t. for nothing, careless of |
| T-21.........I.1:2 | open doorways that they t. were closed. |
| T-21.........I.1:5 | go through the doors you t. were closed, |
| T-21....... II.7:8 | the presence of what you t. you gave away |
| T-21.....VII.2:8 | that they t. they had a common cause. |
| T-21...VII.13:7 | No t. but has the power to release or kill. |
| T-21.....VIII.1:6 | Surely he t. he wanted happiness. Yet he |
| T-22.........I.7:4 | by the "something else" you t. was you. |
| T-22.........I.10:4 | else" you t. was you is an illusion. And |
| T-22...... III.1:1 | introduction of reason into the ego's t. |
| T-22...... III.2:3 | telling you what you t. was real is not. |
| T-22...... III.2:5 | you t. was uncorrectable can be corrected, |
| T-22....... V.6:6 | be convinced, in spite of what you t. it was |
| T-22...... VI.8:1 | place of the attacker who he t. was there. |
| T-22.... VI.14:7 | And every t. in one brings gladness to the |
| T-22.... VI.14:8 | because each shining t. of love extends its |
| T-22.... VI.14:9 | anywhere in it, for every t. is like itself. |
| T-23.......in.6:4 | and everything you once t. sinful now will |
| T-23.... II.21:2 | conclusion; a valid step in ordered t.. The |
| T-23...... III.1:8 | murder and escapes the guilt the t. entails |
| T-24....... II.8:3 | Not one attack you t. you made on him |
| T-24...... III.6:6 | of one t. of specialness to mar your rest. |
| T-24...... IV.5:2 | and have rejoiced at what you t. was there |
| T-24....... V.6:3 | all the fear you t. you saw within yourself. |
| T-24.... VI.11:4 | goal with vigilance you never t. to yield, |
| T-24.... VI.11:4 | yield, and effort that you never t. to cease. |
| T-24..... VII.2:7 | strong protection, the t. by day and night, |
| T-24..... VII.7:5 | one t. with purpose still uncertain, or one |
| T-25.......in.1:8 | see Him where they t. their bodies were. |
| T-25....... II.7:2 | and understand the Mind that t. it, not in |
| T-25...... III.6:5 | will he see each situation that he t. before |
| T-25...... IV.3:6 | that they t. was there is pushed away, |
| T-25..... VII.4:3 | agreement of their t. that makes the Son a |
| T-25..... VII.4:4 | chooses to believe one t. opposed to truth, |
| T-25..... VII.8:4 | he lives, and t. he understood before. |
| T-26...... III.2:1 | borderland of t. that stands between this |
| T-26...... III.2:5 | is every t. made pure and wholly simple. |
| T-26....... V.5:5 | Yet in each unforgiving act or t., in every |
| T-26..... VII.8:5 | of God's Son where sin was t. to rule. |
| T-26.... VIII.5:4 | effects unless he t. they had been caused, |
| T-27.........I.6:5 | real. No worldly t. or act or feeling has a |
| T-27.... II.13:1 | not overlook the fact that every t. extends |
| T-27...... III.2:3 | He represents a double t., where half is |
| T-27...... III.3:3 | that cancelled out the t. it represents. And |
| T-27....... V.7:7 | the many friends he t. were enemies. |
| T-27....... V.9:1 | problems that you t. were not your own. |
| T-27.... VIII.6:3 | forgetting did the t. become a serious idea |
| T-27.... VIII.7:2 | see depicts exactly what you t. you did. |
| T-27.... VIII.7:4 | The guilt for what you t. is being placed |
| T-28.........I.1:7 | t. of them and loved them for a little while |
| T-28.........I.8:4 | t. that you remembered not their Cause. |
| T-28.... II.11:7 | the *mind* was sick that t. the body could be |
| T-29.......I.3:10 | And violating this was t. to be a breach of |
| T-29....... II.9:3 | it can be perceived and t. to feel and act, |
| T-29....... V.3:5 | every t. of love you offer him but brings |
| T-29....... V.6:1 | would not keep hold on any t., however |
| T-29.... VIII.3:3 | Yet it is still a t., and cannot leave the |
| T-29.... VIII.4:2 | yet a t. without the power to change one |
| T-29...... IX.5:2 | the child who t. he made them real. Yet |
| T-30.......in.1:6 | more ideas than rules of t. to you as yet. |
| T-30...... III.6:3 | as long as does the mind that t. of them. |
| T-30...... III.6:7 | as you are in the Mind which t. of you. |
| T-30...... III.7:3 | An unremembered t. is born again to you |
| T-30...... IV.2:4 | because he t. the rules protected him. |
| T-30...... IV.2:7 | what made him safe, and t. that it had left |
| T-30...... IV.3:3 | for it. It never was the thing you t.. It must |
| T-30....... V.2:1 | it is t. that understanding is acquired by |
| T-30..... V.11:2 | they joined, they t. He was their enemy. |
| T-30..... VII.5:4 | be no t. of sacrifice apart from this idea. |
| T-30... VII.6:10 | In any t. of loss there is no meaning. No |
| T-30.... VIII.1:4 | will change, and yet you t. it real before, |
| T-31....... II.6:4 | still, forgetting everything we t. we heard; |
| T-31 .......II.8:2 | all t. of what you ever learned before, and |
| T-31 .......II.8:4 | you t. were precious and in need of care. |
| T-31 ...... V.7:6 | concept but a t. to which its maker gives a |
| T-31 ...... V.7:9 | in its ways and finally "maturing" in its t.. |
| W-pI....... 4.4:1 | each t. by the central figure or event it |
| W-pI....... 4.4:2 | *This t. about_does not mean anything. It is* |
| W-pI....... 4.5:1 | particular t. that you recognize as harmful |
| W-pI....... 6.2:2 | each upsetting t. uncovered in the search. |
| W-pI....... 8.2:1 | The one wholly true t. one can hold about |
| W-pI....... 8.4:2 | matter how vividly you may picture a t., |
| W-pI..... 10.4:8 | *My t. about_does not mean anything. My* |
| W-pI..... 10.4:9 | *My t. about_does not mean anything.* |
| W-pI..... 10.5:1 | Today's t. can obviously serve for any |
| W-pI..... 10.5:1 | for any t. that distresses you at any time. |
| W-pI..... 13.5:2 | you are really afraid of such a t. because of |
| W-pI..... 16.2:3 | Every t. you have contributes to truth or |
| W-pI..... 16.3:1 | t. you have brings either peace or war; |
| W-pI..... 16.3:2 | because a neutral t. is impossible. There is |
| W-pI..... 16.4:1 | to overlook any "little" t. that may tend to |
| W-pI..... 16.4:4 | Every t. that occurs to you, regardless of |
| W-pI..... 16.5:2 | *This t. about_is not a neutral thought. That* |
| W-pI..... 16.5:2 | *This thought about_is not a neutral t.. That* |
| W-pI..... 16.5:3 | *That t. about_is not a neutral thought.* As |
| W-pI..... 16.5:3 | *That thought about_is not a neutral t..* As |
| W-pI..... 16.5:4 | of a particular t. that arouses uneasiness. |
| W-pI..... 16.5:6 | *This t. about_is not a neutral thought,* |
| W-pI..... 16.5:6 | *This thought about_is not a neutral t.,* |
| W-pI..... 17.1:3 | It is always the t. that comes first, despite |
| W-pI..... 17.3:3 | unaware as yet of any t. that is really true, |
| W-pI..... 19.3:4 | *in experiencing the effects of this t. about–.* |
| W-pI..... 23.1:4 | Every t. you have makes up some segment |
| W-pI..... 23.5:1 | The idea for today introduces the t. that |
| W-pI..... 23.6:5 | Hold each attack t. in mind as you say this |
| W-pI..... 23.6:5 | then dismiss that t. and go on to the next. |
| W-pI..... 25.4:1 | for today, one more t. is necessary. At the |
| W-pI..... 26.3:1 | the t. that you always attack yourself first. |
| W-pI..... 26.9:2 | *That t. is an attack upon myself.* Conclude |
| W-pI..... 32.2:3 | try to introduce the t. that both are in |
| W-pI..... 39.8:1 | search your mind for every t. that stands |
| W-pI..... 41.3:2 | the mind that t. these things were real, |
| W-pI..... 42.5:1 | Any t. that is clearly related to the idea |
| W-pI..... 42.5:5 | open your eyes and repeat the t. once |
| W-pI..... 42.7:2 | that you are studying a unified t. system |
| W-pI..... 43.5:8 | t. related more or less directly to today's |
| W-pI..... 45.2:3 | because they are t. by the same Mind. To |
| W-pI..... 45.3:5 | What is t. by the Mind of God is eternal, |
| W-pI..... 45.7:1 | that you t. with God in the beginning. |
| W-pI..... 45.7:4 | you have t. since then will change, but the |
| WpI... rI.in.6:4 | of the t. system to which they are leading |
| W-pI..... 51.3:3 | see is the projection of my own errors of t. |
| W-pI..... 51.5:6 | this to defend a t. system that has hurt me |
| W-pI..... 54.2:3 | think I would not exist, because life is t.. |
| W-pI..... 57.2:8 | and not where I t. to hold him prisoner. |
| W-pI..... 61.5:7 | mind wanders away from the central t.. |
| W-pI..... 63.3:2 | the day with the t. of it in our awareness. |
| W-pI..... 65.5:4 | each t. that arises to interfere with it. Note |
| W-pI..... 65.5:6 | *t. reflects a goal that is preventing me from* |
| W-pI..... 68.7:1 | any t. of grievance arises against anyone, |
| W-pI..... 69.6:1 | After you have t. about the importance of |
| W-pI..... 69.8:5 | Try to keep the t. clearly in mind that |
| W-pI..... 74.1:1 | for today can be regarded as the central t. |
| W-pI... 75.11:2 | the unforgiven world you t. was real. |
| W-pI... 76.10:1 | realize how foolish are the "laws" you t. |
| W-pI... 76.10:1 | thought upheld the world you t. you saw. |
| W-pI..... 91.1:3 | It is a central idea in your new t. system, |
| W-pI..... 92.2:2 | If you but understood the nature of t., you |
| W-pI..... 92.2:3 | It is as if you t. you held the match that |
| W-pI..... 93.7:1 | requires the acceptance of but one t.; |
| W-pI..... 94.1:1 | the one t. which renders the ego silent |
| W-pI..... 94.5:9 | the t. system which this course sets forth. |
| W-pI..... 96.7:3 | Salvation is a t. you share with God, |
| W-pI..... 96.8:1 | We will attempt today to find this t., |
| W-pI..... 99.7:5 | Forgive yourself the t. He wanted this for |
| W-pI..... 99.7:6 | t. the thoughts that never were His Will. |
| W-pI... 100.7:2 | exercises with the t. today's idea contains. |
| W-pI... 100.9:4 | What little t. has power to hold you back? |
| W-pI... 101.5:5 | We practice with this t. as often as we can |
| W-pI... 104.1:1 | Today's idea continues with the t. that |
| W-pI... 108.5:1 | One t., completely unified, will serve to |
| W-pI .. 108.5:1 | unified, will serve to unify all t.. This is |
| W-pI .. 108.6:2 | t. behind it can be generalized to other |
| W-pI .. 109.1:4 | And we have the t. that will answer our |
| W-pI .. 109.2:2 | This t. will bring to you the rest and quiet, |
| W-pI .. 109.2:4 | t. has power to wake the sleeping truth in |
| W-pI .. 109.2:6 | t. in which the Son of God is born again, |
| W-pI .. 109.3:2 | t. will carry you through storms and strife |
| W-pI .. 110.1:2 | For this one t. would be enough to save |
| W-pI .. 110.3:3 | You need no t. but just this one, to let |
| W-pI .. 110.4:1 | In this one t. is all the past undone; the |
| WpIrIII.in10:6 | things, but try to keep the t. with you, and |
| WpIrIII.in11:3 | Do not repeat the t. and lay it down. Its |
| WpIrIII.in12:1 | a restatement of the t. to use each hour, |
| W-pI .. 123.1:3 | There is no t. of turning back, and no |
| W-pI .. 123.2:3 | you from the self you t. you made to take |
| W-pI .. 124.1:5 | t. that God Himself goes everywhere with |
| W-pI .. 124.6:2 | No t. of theirs but has the power to heal |
| W-pI .. 124.8:3 | to the t. that you are one with God. This is |
| W-pI 124.10:3 | the t. to which you gave this half an hour, |
| W-pI .. 126.1:1 | is crucial to the t. reversal that this course |
| W-pI .. 126.9:2 | It is the t. by which forgiveness takes its |
| W-pI .. 126.9:3 | It is the t. that will release your mind from |
| W-pI 127.11:2 | t. was made in hate to be love's enemy. |
| W-pI .. 128.1:2 | joy. Believe this t., and you are saved from |
| W-pI .. 128.1:3 | No one but must accept this t. as true, if |
| W-pI .. 128.5:1 | all t. of values we have given to the world. |
| W-pI .. 129.1:1 | This is the t. that follows from the one we |
| W-pI .. 129.2:2 | is no loss in letting go all t. of value here. |
| W-pI .. 130.7:1 | the t. that ends all compromise and doubt |
| W-pI .. 131.3:4 | lies beyond the world and every worldly t. |
| W-pI 131.11:3 | *think a different kind of t. from those I made.* |
| W-pI ..... 132.h | I loose the world from all I t. it was. |
| W-pI .. 132.2:2 | it. Now the source of t. has shifted, for to |
| W-pI .. 132.2:2 | ideas you think or ever t. or yet will think. |
| W-pI .. 132.2:3 | You free the past from what you t. before. |
| W-pI .. 132.6:3 | the central t. the course attempts to teach. |
| W-pI .. 132.8:3 | loose it from all things you ever t. it was |
| W-pI 132.10:3 | maintain the world within your mind in t. |
| W-pI 132.13:1 | no world because it is a t. apart from God, |
| W-pI 132.15:2 | *me would loose the world from all I t. it was.* |
| W-pI 132.17:2 | *I loose the world from all I t. it was, and* |
| W-pI 133.14:2 | you, be quick to answer with this simple t. |
| W-pI 134.11:3 | what he t. he saw was never there. And |
| W-pI 134.12:2 | kill the dragons which he t. pursued him. |
| W-pI 134.12:3 | and iron doors he t. would make him safe. |
| W-pI 134.13:2 | There is no t. in all the world that leads to |
| W-pI 134.15:3 | consider all the evil things you t. of him, |
| W-pI .. 135.1:1 | himself unless he t. he were attacked, that |
| W-pI 135.22:1 | and from every t. that blocks the truth |
| W-pI 135.23:3 | may not be the plans you t. were needed, |
| W-pI 135.23:3 | the problems which you t. confronted you |
| W-pI 135.24:2 | will but wonder why you ever t. that you |
| W-pI .. 136.8:4 | haunting t. that you might be something |
| W-pI 136.11:2 | of the laws by which you t. to govern it. |
| W-pI .. 137.1:1 | the central t. on which salvation rests. For |
| W-pI 137.15:4 | by, remembering our purpose with this t.: |
| W-pI .. 140.6:1 | This is the t. that cures. It does not make |
| W-pI .. 140.6:6 | is not a t. that judges an illusion by its size |
| WpI..rIV.in2:4 | t. by which the Father gave creation to the |
| WpI..rIV.in2:5 | It is this t. that fully guarantees salvation |
| WpI..rIV.in2:7 | blocks this t. from his awareness. Yet it is |
| WpI..rIV.in5:2 | deceive, and let this t. alone engage it fully |
| WpI..rIV.in5:4 | Five minutes with this t. will be enough to |
| WpI..rIV.in8:1 | mind the t. with which the day began, and |
| WpI..rIV.in9:3 | repeating first the t. that made the day a |
| W-pI .. 146.2:1 | (132) I loose the world from all I t. it was. |
| W-pI 151.13:2 | of the t. with which the day begins. And |
| W-pI 151.13:4 | Him evaluate each t. that comes to mind, |
| W-pI 151.14:2 | And as each t. is thus transformed, it |
| W-pI .. 152.3:6 | can not be too often said and t. about. For |
| W-pI .. 153.9:1 | without all t. or wish or dream in which |
| W-pI 153.12:1 | be t. of as a game that happy children play |
| W-pI 153.15:2 | attention to the daily t. as long as possible |
| W-pI 155.14:2 | same, we practice gladly with this t. today |
| W-pI .. 156.1:1 | truth that makes the t. of sin impossible. |
| W-pI .. 156.1:3 | the basic t. so often mentioned in the text; |
| W-pI .. 156.6:5 | is seen. It is a foolish t., a silly dream, not |
| W-pI .. 156.7:1 | many, many years on just this foolish t.. |
| W-pI .. 160.3:3 | unless he t. there were another home |

W-pI...160.5:3 and give him all I t. belonged to me." Now
W-pI...160.6:7 in, and took no alien t. to be Itself. And It
W-pI...161.6:2 This t. is surely reminiscent of our text,
W-pI...162.1:1 This single t., held firmly in the mind,
W-pI...162.2:3 no t. of sin and no illusion which the
W-pI...163.1:1 Death is a t. that takes on many forms,
W-pI...163.2:1 does the t. of death seem mighty. For it
W-pI...163.6:5 contradicts one t. entirely can not be true,
W-pI...164.4:3 in you the t. of sin has never touched. All
W-pI...166.9:3 you t. was you may not be your Identity.
W-pI.166.11:4 each time the t. of poverty oppresses you,
W-pI...167.3:3 A t. is in the mind. It can be then applied
W-pI...167.4:1 is the t. that you are separate from your
W-pI...167.8:3 t. of death is not the opposite to thoughts
W-pI...169.6:4 It lies beyond salvation; past all t. of time,
W-pI.169.12:3 replace the t. of time but for a little while.
W-pI...170.3:2 enemy within; an alien t. at war with you,
W-pI...170.9:4 which enthrones the t. of fear as god. For
WpI.. rV.in4:1 t. which should precede the thoughts that
WpI.. rV.in4:2 one but clarifies some aspect of this t., or
WpI.. rV.in5:4 to return to the eternal Self we t. we lost.
WpI rV.in11:3 And with this t. we sleep, to waken once
WpI rV.in11:4 day. No t. that we review but we surround
W-pI...181.4:3 by the depressing and restricting t. that,
W-pI...181.7:1 also use this t. to keep us safe throughout
W-pI...183.2:2 you from every worldly t. that would
W-pI...183.6:6 then God's Name becomes our only t.,
W-pI.183.10:6 to let all things he t. he made be nameless
W-pI...184.9:4 it is this t. that will release you from them.
W-pI...186.1:2 Here is the t. of true humility, which
W-pI...187.2:5 the t. seems to appear is changed in giving
W-pI...187.4:2 What you t. you did not have is thereby
W-pI...187.4:6 It is the t. behind the form of things that
W-pI...187.5:3 The t. remains, and grows in strength as it
W-pI...187.5:7 each will have the t. in form most helpful
W-pI...187.7:2 and you remove the t. of suffering. Your
W-pI...187.7:4 t. of sacrifice gives rise to all the forms
W-pI...187.8:3 If the t. occurs, its very presence proves
W-pI...187.9:5 will behold will take away all t. of form,
W-pI.187.10:1 Now are we one in t., for fear has gone.
W-pI.188.10:2 all the world from what we t. it did to us.
W-pI...189.1:6 is a reflection of the t. we practice now. To
W-pI...189.7:2 good or bad, of every t. it judges worthy,
W-pI...189.7:4 bring with you one t. the past has taught,
W-pI...190.8:1 Pain is the t. of evil taking form, and
W-pI...191.3:1 this weird, unnatural and ghostly t. that
W-pI...191.4:4 In this one t. is everyone set free. In this
W-pI...191.6:1 One holy t. like this and you are free: You
W-pI...191.6:2 And with this holy t. you learn as well that
W-pI...191.7:5 in that t. is everything you look on wholly
W-pI...193.3:3 Each lesson has a central t., the same in all
W-pI...193.9:2 leave an unforgiving t. without correction
W-pI...194.6:2 As it becomes a t. that rules your mind, a
W-pI...194.9:4 If we accept an unforgiving t., it will be
W-pI...195.2:3 to escape a prison that they t. contained
W-pI...195.9:3 pushed about without a t. or care for us or
W-pI...195.9:4 future. Gratitude becomes the single t. we
W-pI...196.5:1 hopeless t. that you can make attacks on
W-pI...196.6:1 if you accept the fearful t. you can attack
W-pI...196.6:4 is real to anyone who thinks this t. is true.
W-pI...196.8:5 And God, Whom you had t. to banish,
W-pI...198.9:5 that fails to hide an unforgiving t.. Nor
W-pI.198.10:4 the trespasses you t. Them guilty of, and
W-pI.198.11:6 and everything you ever t. you made
W-pI...199.5:3 There is no t. that will not gain thereby in
W-pI...199.6:5 mind with but the t. of freedom as its goal
W-pI...199.8:4 the t. the Holy Spirit gives you for today.
WpI rVI.in.3:8 of the special t. we practice for the day, no
WpI rVI.in.4:3 and then forget all that we t. we knew and
WpI rVI.in.5:2 Permit no idle t. to go unchallenged. If
WpI rVI.in.5:4 let the t. which you denied be given up, in
WpI rVI.in.6:2 say: *This t. I do not want. I choose instead* _
WpI rVI.in.6:4 day, and let it take the place of what you t.
W-pI...203.1:2 *my deliverance from every t. of evil and of sin*
W-pI...210.1:3 *one I t. apart from Him and from His Will.*
W-pII.....in.3:1 with a central t. for all the days to come,
W-pII.....in.3:1 use that t. to introduce our times of rest,
W-pII.. in.11:4 be slowly read and t. about a little while,
W-pII......1.1:1 Forgiveness recognizes what you t. your
W-pII......1.2:1 An unforgiving t. is one which makes a
W-pII......1.2:3 The t. protects projection, tightening its
W-pII......1.3:1 An unforgiving t. does many things. In
W-pII..223.1:1 mistaken when I t. I lived apart from God,
W-pII..227.1:2 *I t. to make another will. Yet nothing that I*
W-pII..227.1:3 *Yet nothing that I t. apart from You exists.*
W-pII......2.2:1 the instant that his mind had t. of war.
W-pII......2.2:5 itself, and t. its own Identity was lost.
W-pII..236.2:1 *and closed today to every t. but Yours. I rule*
W-pII......3.1:3 the t. that gave it birth is cherished. When
W-pII......3.1:4 t. of separation has been changed to one
W-pII..259.1:1 Sin is the only t. that makes the goal of
W-pII..260.1:1 *myself, although in my insanity I t. I did. Yet,*
W-pII..267.1:2 breath; in every action and in every t..
W-pII..270.1:6 *Own, and every t. except Your Own is gone.*
W-pII..288.1:1 *This is the t. that leads the way to You, and*
W-pII......8.2:1 each unhappy t. reflected in your world; a
W-pII..300.1:1 t. which can be used to say that death and
W-pII..302.1:3 *We t. we suffered. But we had forgot the Son*
W-pII..317.2:5 *t. mistakenly that he had wandered from the*
W-pII..319.1:1 Here is a t. from which all arrogance has
W-pII....11.2:4 remaining as it was before the t. of time
W-pII..329.1:1 *Father, I t. I wandered from Your Will,*
W-pII..330.2:3 *and to be saved from what we t. we were.*
W-pII..333.1:3 be seen exactly as it is, where it is t. to be,
W-pII..337.1:1 love, freedom forever from all t. of loss;
W-pII..337.2:2 *I was mistaken when I t. I sinned, but I accept*
W-pII..338.1:2 single t. is everyone released at last from
W-pII..338.1:5 each fear t. for a happy thought of love.
W-pII..338.1:5 each fear thought for a happy t. of love.
W-pII....13.4:3 redeemed from what you t. was there.
W-pII..344.1:2 *and t. to save what I desired for myself alone.*
W-pII..344.1:3 *as I looked upon the treasure that I t. I had, I*
W-pII....14.4:1 sees a world redeemed from every t. of sin
W-pII....14.5:3 to the Son of God, who t. he suffered.
W-pII..356.1:5 *Your Name replaces every t. of sin, and who*
W-pII..360.1:7 *And with this t. we gladly say "Amen."*
Wfl ........in.5:3 from all the wrath we t. belonged to God,
WpII361-5.1:2 If I need a t., that will He also give. And if
M-in ..........2:2 There are only two t. systems, and you
M-2 ...........3:4 ago passed by is looked upon as a new t.,
M-2 ...........5:6 they t. separated them from one another,
M-4 .....I.A.5:8 where he t. something was asked of him,
M-4 .....I.A.7:5 of sacrifice, so central to his own t. system
M-4 .....I.A.7:6 He t. he learned willingness, but now he
M-4 .....I.A.8:4 consistency of t. and full transfer. This is
M-4 ....... II.1:6 or do; no t. opposes any other thought; no
M-4 ....... II.1:6 or do; no thought opposes any other t.; no
M-4 ....... III.1:6 of the teacher of God's whole t. system.
M-4 ...... IV.1:4 dishonest act that follows a dishonest t.. It
M-5 .........I.1:2 unless he t. it brought him something,
M-5 ....... II.3:9 He only t. it did. Nor does he do anything
M-7 ...........3:9 He t. the gifts of God could be withdrawn.
M-9 ...........1:9 the old t. system still has a basis for return
M-10 .........4:1 Remember how many times you t. you
M-10 .........4:3 many times you merely t. you were right,
M-12 .........4:5 lesson is enough to let the t. of unity come
M-13 .........1:6 before another t. system can take hold, is
M-14 .......2:10 When not one t. of sin remains, the world
M-14 .........3:2 "When not one t. of sin remains" appears
M-14 .........3:4 Not one t. of sin will remain the instant
M-14 .........4:1 world will end when its t. system has been
M-16 .........4:2 situation that fosters quiet t. as he awakes
M-16 .........6:1 There is one t. in particular that should
M-16 .........6:2 It is a t. of pure joy; a thought of peace, a
M-16 .........6:2 It is a thought of pure joy; a t. of peace, a
M-16 .........6:2 a thought of peace, a t. of limitless release,
M-17 .........1:6 it. If a magic t. arouses anger in any form,
M-17 .........5:2 in the world's t. system becomes apparent
M-17 .........5:3 t., by its mere presence, acknowledges a
M-17 .........7:6 t. has guilt already raised madness to the
M-17 .........9:4 and to recognize its t. system is to look on
M-18 .........1:2 he argues with his pupil about a magic t.,
M-19 .........1:9 t. of separation would have been forever
M-19 .........3:4 in which all t. of wholeness must be lost.
M-20 .........6:3 There is no t. that contradicts His Will,
M-22 .........3:2 is a central concept in the ego's t. system.
M-22 .........3:3 system. This t. gives the body autonomy,
M-24 .........2:8 There is always some good in any t. which
M-24 .........4:1 course aims at a complete reversal of t..
M-28 .........6:2 of evil dreams, the t. of hell is real. God's
M-28 .........6:4 The t. of murder is replaced with blessing.
M-29 .........3:2 Perhaps you have not t. of this aspect, but
C-2.............1:6 A t. you are apart from your Creator and a
C-2...........1:10 t. that what is made has immortality. But
C-2.............8:4 Would it not answer all you t. to ask, and
C-2.............9:4 The world is saved from what you t. it was
C-ep...........5:3 salvation and the end of all we t. we made.
P-1.............4:2 to understand that what he t. projected its
P-2......... V.3:3 is but a glimmer of a t. not yet conceived.
P-2........ VI.3:5 Sometimes the t. behind the form breaks
P-2....... VII.4:4 he t. he was in charge of the therapeutic
P-3.............I.3:8 form is most helpful; a name, a t., a
P-3........ III.7:2 Yet not one worldly t. is really practical.
S-1........ III.1:5 The poisonous t. that he *is* your enemy,
S-1........ IV.1:7 further still in prayer lies in this simple t.;
S-1......... V.1:3 t. it was alone and stood against the world
S-2...........II.3:4 This can appear to be a humble t., and
S-3............I.1:2 a shadow of an evil t. that seems to have

**thoughtfully** 2

W-pI.....28.8:3 be made quite slowly, and as t. as possible
W-pI...95.11:3 eyes and tell yourself again, slowly and t.,

**thoughtfulness** 1

T-27...VII.15:4 Select his t. to dream about instead of

**thoughtless** 2

T-27..... VII.8:5 as t. of his peace and happiness as is the
W-pI.......8.3:2 While t. ideas preoccupy your mind, the

**thoughtlessly** 1

T-30..... V.10:6 do not choose an idol t., remembering

**thoughtlessness** 2

T-25..... VII.9:6 His Son, and pass him by in careless t..
W-pI.....67.4:3 interval of t. to the awareness of a blazing

**Thoughts** 57

*thoughts*

T-3......... V.9:7 as His T. because they *are* His Thoughts.
T-3......... V.9:7 as His Thoughts because they *are* His T..
T-3....... V.10:6 beautiful indeed are the T. of God who
T-4......... V.2:1 between the body and the T. of God.
T-4......... V.2:2 T. of God are unacceptable to the ego,
T-4......... V.2:5 body impulses, but also the T. of God,
T-5...... IV.8:15 blessed Sons. The T. of God are with you.
T-6..........II.8:2 All His T. are thus perfectly united within
T-7..........II.2:6 very different from the T. in the Kingdom.
T-13....VIII.4:3 because He has no T. He does not share.
T-17...... III.9:7 Only the T. of God are true. And all that
T-21....... V.6:2 He has no T. except the Self-extending,
T-30...... III.6:4 His T. were absent or could suffer change.
T-30...... III.8:1 The T. of God are far beyond all change,
T-31...... IV.9:1 He has not left His T.! But you forgot His
T-31...... IV.9:6 has He never left His T. to die, without
T-31.... IV.10:1 He has not left His T.! He could no more
W-pI.....45.9:4 thank Him for the T. He is thinking with
W-pI.....56.5:4 the Mind of God, Who has not left His T..
W-pI.....59.5:4 my thoughts are His and His T. are mine.
W-pI...91.10:1 by the strength of God and all His T.. It is
W-pI.....96.7:1 Your Self retains Its T., and they remain
W-pI.....96.7:4 Thus is salvation kept among the T. your
W-pI.....96.9:3 *one Self. Its T. are mine to use.* Then seek Its
W-pI.....96.9:4 Then seek Its T., and claim them as your
W-pI...109.9:5 which these T. were born and where they
W-pI...124.4:5 minds contain His T.; our eyes behold His
W-pI. 132.11:6 you may know the T. you share with God.
W-pI. 136.13:3 The T. of God are quite apart from time.
W-pI...157.5:3 the touchstone for the holy T. of God.
W-pI...163.9:7 *We accept Your T. as ours, and our will is one*
W-pI...167.1:4 Like all His T., it has no opposite. There is

W-pI...167.8:4 the T. of God remain forever changeless,
W-pI.167.11:3 And in His T., which have no opposite, we
WpI...rV.in4:5 Self alone is perfectly consistent in Its T.;
W-pI.183.10:4 His Father's T. become his own. He makes
W-pI.186.13:4 He has T. which answer every need His
W-pI...197.9:6 All that you think can only be His T.,
W-pI...197.9:6 sharing with Him the holy T. of God. Earn
W-pII ....in.8:4 His T. have lit the darkness of our minds.
W-pII .222.1:3 which directs my actions, offers me Its T.,
W-pII .223.1:3 He has no T. that are not part of me, and I
W-pII .236.2:1 *Father, my mind is open to Your T., and*
W-pII .265.2:1 *upon the world, which but reflects Your T.,*
W-pII .281.1:3 *Your T. can only bring me happiness. If ever*
W-pII .281.1:4 *ideas in place of where Your T. belong, and*
W-pII .281.1:6 *The T. I think with You can only bless. The*
W-pII .281.1:7 *bless. The T. I think with You alone are true.*
W-pII .291.2:1 *mind is quiet, to receive the T. You offer me.*
W-pII .303.1:2 Let all God's holy T. surround me, and be
W-pII ...11.1:1 Creation is the sum of all God's T., in
W-pII ...11.1:5 God's T. exactly as they were and as they
W-pII ...11.2:1 God's T. are given all the power that their
W-pII ...11.4:4 love remains with all its T., its sureness
W-pII .339.2:2 *me, accepting only T. You share with me.*
M-12 .........1:8 and bring His T. to still deluded minds.
M-27 .........5:9 Terrible His T. and fearful His image. To

## thoughts 526

*Thoughts*

T-1.........I.12:1 Miracles are t.. Thoughts can represent
T-1.........I.12:2 T. can represent the lower or bodily level
T-2......... II.1:8 and by endowing all t. with equal power
T-2......... III.2:4 t. and making you perfectly invulnerable.
T-2......... VI.1:6 raised body t. to the level of the mind.
T-2...... VI.9:10 You prefer to believe that your t. cannot
T-2...... VI.9:13 There *are* no idle t.. All thinking produces
T-2.......VII.1:4 between your t. and their results, I would
T-2.......VII.1:7 you do not guard your t. carefully enough.
T-2.......VII.3:1 Both miracles and fear come from t.. If
T-2.......VII.3:7 this if you were not afraid of your own t..
T-5...........I.2:2 *T. increase by being given away. The more*
T-5........ III.4:6 alone your t. will frighten you because, by
T-5........ IV.2:7 so your own t. can make you really free.
T-5........ IV.3:6 also include opposite t. at the same level.
T-5........ IV.3:7 *It is impossible to share opposing t..* You can
T-5........ IV.3:8 You can share only the t. that are of God
T-5....... V.6:13 Delusional ideas are not real t., although
T-5......... V.7:6 those who believe they order their own t.,
T-5........ VI.8:3 and thus release the t. from the ability to
T-6......... II.9:1 T. begin in the mind of the thinker, from
T-7......... II.2:6 because the t. it governs are very different
T-7.....VII.1:13 be able to exclude yourself from your t..
T-11.....VII.2:2 loving t. his mind perceives in this world
T-11.....VIII.9:2 and see only his loving t. as his reality, for
T-11..VIII.10:2 Only loving t. are recognized, and because
T-12.........I.6:2 both his loving t. and his appeals for help,
T-12.........I.8:7 you to accept only loving t. in others and
T-12...... III.7:1 the loving t. of God's Son are the world's
T-12...... III.7:2 His insane t., too, must be in his mind,
T-12...... III.7:3 opposed t. within itself is intolerable.
T-12...... III.7:6 for t. do have consequences to the thinker
T-12...... VI.3:5 from the extension of loving t. outward.
T-12....VIII.1:2 kept him far away from your destructive t.
T-13...... III.7:5 for any t. you may fear to uncover. For He
T-13...... XI.5:4 to, whatever strange t. may occur to you,
T-14.........I.2:4 you must direct your t. unto oblivion.
T-14.........I.3:2 Were your t. wholly of you, the thought
T-14.........I.3:3 The t. the mind of God's Son projects or
T-14.........I.3:4 The t. he shares with God are beyond his
T-14...... III.1:3 learner learns easily because his t. are free
T-14.....VII.6:8 all your dark and secret t. to Him, and
T-14....... X.4:1 of lack of competition among your t.,
T-14....... X.4:3 some of your t. as more important, larger
T-14....... X.4:4 This is true of the t. that cross the mind of
T-14....... X.6:1 have no basis at all for ordering your t..
T-14..... X.10:4 let the Holy Spirit order your t. and give
T-15......IV.7:1 prefer to have private t. and keep them?
T-15......IV.7:3 you can harbor t. you would not share,
T-15......IV.7:3 lies in keeping t. to yourself alone. For in
T-15 ..... IV.7:4 For in private t., known only to yourself,
T-15 ..... IV.9:1 that you have no t. that are not pure. But
T-15 ..... IV.9:8 protect the t. you would keep to yourself.
T-15 .. VII.14:4 there is no concealment, and no private t..
T-15 ..... IX.7:1 and your t. will be as free as God's. As you
T-15 ..... XI.1:5 to keep apart your t. and the Thought
T-16 ... VI.12:1 you: Whenever your t. wander to a special
T-17 ..... III.1:1 only the loving t. you gave in the past, and
T-17 ..... III.5:3 so. If all but loving t. have been forgotten,
T-17 ..... III.5:7 loving t. is the spark of beauty hidden in
T-17 .... VII.3:1 is a relationship, being the joining of t.. If
T-17 .... VII.3:2 because the t. are judged to be in conflict.
T-17 .... VII.3:6 an error in your t. about the situation,
T-18 ..... IX.4:2 Here are all the illusions, all the twisted t.,
T19... IV.D.7:4 and t. that come to you against your will.
T-20 ..... III.4:6 All these are but the fearful t. of those
T-20 ... III.10:5 Here all t. of any separation between us
T-21 ..... VI.2:8 how could it be that you have private t.?
T-21 ..... VI.2:9 And how could t. that enter into what but
T-21 ...VIII.1:1 Are t., then, dangerous? To bodies, yes!
T-21 ...VIII.1:3 t. that seem to kill are those that teach the
T-22 ........I.4:8 of secrecy, of private t. and of the body.
T-22 .......II.9:3 idea that t. can leave the thinker's mind,
T-22 .......II.9:4 t. would not be the mind's extensions, but
T-22 .....II.11:1 Only *your* t. have been impossible.
T-23 .......II.2:2 set of t. that set him off from others. This
T-25 ..... IV.3:7 And all their "evil" t. and "sinful" hopes,
T-25 ..... IV.4:4 Your "evil" t. that haunt you now will
T-25 ... IV.5:11 and all the t. that entered it and were
T-26 ..... III.2:3 is the meeting place where t. are brought
T-26 ..... IX.7:1 to keep away all darkened t. of sin, and
T-27 ..... III.7:5 with power unlimited and single t.,
T-27 .. VII.10:6 Awaken and forget all t. of death, and you
T-27 ... VIII.7:4 dreams and thinks your t. instead of you.
T-28 ........I.1:7 The t. that made it are no longer in the
T-29 ..... IX.5:5 his t. and gives them to the toys instead.
T-29 ..... IX.5:6 because they seem to save him from his t..
T-29 ..... IX.5:7 Yet do they keep his t. alive and real, but
T-29 ..... IX.5:8 he needs them that he may escape his t.,
T-29 ..... IX.5:8 thoughts, because he thinks the t. are real.
T-29 ..... IX.7:4 the t. the mind conceives and what it sees.
T-30 ..... III.6:3 For t. endure as long as does the mind
T-30 ..... III.6:5 T. are not born and cannot die. They
T-30 ..... III.6:7 The t. you think are in your mind, as you
T-30 ..... III.7:1 T. seem to come and go. Yet all this
T-31 ........I.3:6 your own, your t. do not belong to you,
T-31 ......I.12:1 all things we ever learned, all t. we had,
T-31 ......I.13:1 unaware of any t. of evil or of good that
T-31 .......II.7:3 Think not ancient t.. Forget the dismal
T-31 .......II.8:8 away without the t. you did not want, and
T-31 ..... III.4:2 The body thinks no t.. It has no power to
T-31 ..... III.5:2 Here are the t. of sacrifice preserved, for
T-31 .... V.14:5 different t. have different consequence. So
T-31 .... VII.2:1 "evil" t. as long as you see value in attack.
T-31 .... VII.2:6 Your "evil" t. have been forgiven with his,
T-31 .... VII.5:2 not be frightened by your "evil" t. because
T-31 .... VII.7:5 from guilty t. and concepts born of fear.
W-pI..........4.h These t. do not mean anything. They are
W-pI....... 4.1:2 begin with noting the t. that are crossing
W-pI....... 4.1:4 If you are already aware of unhappy t., use
W-pI....... 4.1:5 select only the t. you think are "bad." You
W-pI....... 4.1:6 find, if you train yourself to look at your t.
W-pI....... 4.2:2 be afraid to use "good" t. as well as "bad."
W-pI....... 4.2:3 None of them represents your real t.,
W-pI....... 4.4:1 In using your t. for application of the idea
W-pI....... 4.6:1 in connection with t. particularly difficult.
W-pI....... 6.3:1 to some upsetting t. more than to others,
W-pI....... 7.1:6 reason why your t. do not mean anything,
W-pI.......... 8.h My mind is preoccupied with past t..
W-pI....... 8.1:3 He sees only his t. projected outward. The
W-pI....... 8.4:3 or so, merely noting the t. you find there.
W-pI....... 8.5:1 Then name each of your t. specifically,
W-pI....... 8.5:3 *But my mind is preoccupied with past t..*
W-pI......... 10.h My t. do not mean anything.
W-pI..... 10.1:1 applies to all the t. of which you are aware
W-pI..... 10.1:2 all of them is that they are not your real t..
W-pI..... 10.1:5 were your t. did not mean anything.
W-pI..... 10.2:3 with "My t." instead of "These thoughts,"
W-pI..... 10.2:3 with "My thoughts" instead of "These t.,"
W-pI .... 10.3:1 t. of which you are aware are meaningless,
W-pI .... 10.3:2 these "t." means that you are not thinking
W-pI .... 10.4:4 mind for all the t. that are available to you
W-pI ....... 11.h My meaningless t. are showing me a
W-pI .... 11.1:3 that your t. determine the world you see.
W-pI .... 14.3:1 the t. that you have written on the world,
W-pI ....... 15.h My t. are images that I have made.
W-pI .... 15.1:1 It is because the t. you think you think
W-pI ....... 16.h I have no neutral t..
W-pI .... 16.1:1 the belief that your t. have no effect.
W-pI .... 16.1:2 Everything you see is the result of your t..
W-pI .... 16.1:4 T. are not big or little; powerful or weak.
W-pI .... 16.2:1 concept than that of "idle t.." What gives
W-pI .... 16.3:1 Besides your recognizing that t. are never
W-pI .... 16.3:3 to dismiss fear t. as unimportant, trivial
W-pI .... 16.5:6 *thought, because I have no neutral t..*
W-pI .... 17.1:2 things because you have no neutral t.. It is
W-pI .... 17.2:2 *neutral things because I have no neutral t..*
W-pI .... 17.2:4 *because my t. about_are not neutral.* For
W-pI .... 17.2:6 *because my t. about walls are not neutral. I*
W-pI .... 17.2:7 *because my t. about bodies are not neutral.*
W-pI .... 18.1:1 that the t. which give rise to what you see
W-pI ....... 19.h alone in experiencing the effects of my t..
W-pI .... 19.2:3 Yet it is a fact that there are no private t..
W-pI .... 19.3:2 searched for the t. it contains at that time.
W-pI .... 21.3:1 not to let the "little" t. of anger escape you
W-pI .... 21.4:1 in which attack t. present themselves,
W-pI .... 22.1:1 attack t. in his mind must see the world.
W-pI .... 22.1:5 Otherwise, t. of attack and counter-attack
W-pI ....... 23.h from the world I see by giving up attack t..
W-pI .... 23.1:5 It is with your t., then, that we must work,
W-pI .... 23.2:1 the cause of the world you see is attack t.,
W-pI .... 23.2:1 must learn that it is these t. which you do
W-pI .... 23.2:5 point in changing your t. about the world.
W-pI .... 23.3:2 representation of your own attack t.. One
W-pI .... 23.6:2 mind for as many attack t. as occur to you
W-pI .... 23.6:4 *the world I see by giving up attack t. about*
W-pI .... 23.7:1 your t. of attacking and of being attacked.
W-pI .... 23.7:5 finally learn that t. of attack and of being
W-pI ....... 26.h attack t. are attacking my invulnerability.
W-pI .... 26.2:1 Because your attack t. will be projected,
W-pI .... 26.2:3 Attack t. therefore make you vulnerable
W-pI .... 26.2:3 mind, which is where the attack t. are.
W-pI .... 26.2:4 Attack t. and invulnerability cannot be
W-pI .... 26.3:2 attack t. must entail the belief that you are
W-pI .... 26.4:1 invulnerability is the result of your own t..
W-pI .... 26.4:2 Nothing except your t. can attack you.
W-pI .... 26.4:3 except your t. can make you think you are
W-pI .... 26.4:4 nothing except your t. can prove to you
W-pI .... 26.6:3 your t. during the day is a suitable subject
W-pI .... 28.3:4 its purpose to your little personal t..
W-pI .... 31.3:1 merely let whatever t. cross your mind
W-pI .... 31.3:5 part. As you sit and quietly watch your t.,
W-pI .... 33.2:1 survey your inner t. with equal casualness
W-pI .... 34.1:3 It must begin with your own t., and then
W-pI .... 34.3:2 Search your mind for fear t., anxiety-
W-pI .... 34.3:2 which you are harboring unloving t.. Note
W-pI .... 34.6:4 *or worry [or my t. about this situation,*
W-pI .... 37.5:1 you and to those who are in your t.; or
W-pI .... 38.5:1 and add some relevant t. of your own.
W-pI .... 38.5:2 like, for example, to include t. such as:
W-pI .... 39.6:2 unloving t. in whatever form they appear;
W-pI .... 39.7:1 you associate with unloving t. of any kind
W-pI .... 39.8:3 *My unloving t. about_are keeping me in hell*
W-pI .... 41.5:2 within, under a heavy cloud of insane t.,
W-pI .... 41.6:5 inward, past all the idle t. of the world.
W-pI .... 41.6:6 keeping it clear of any t. that might divert
W-pI .... 41.7:2 world and all the foolish t. of the world.
W-pI .. 41.10:1 You can indeed afford to laugh at fear t.,
W-pI .... 42.1:1 for today combines two very powerful t.,
W-pI .... 42.4:3 try to think of nothing except t. that occur
W-pI .... 42.5:2 understanding some of your t. contain.
W-pI .... 42.5:3 have let obviously irrelevant t. intrude.
W-pI .... 42.5:4 where no t. at all seem to come to mind. If
W-pI .... 42.5:5 then continue to look for related t. in your
W-pI .... 42.6:1 that active searching for relevant t. is not
W-pI .... 42.6:2 merely to step back and let the t. come. If
W-pI .... 42.6:3 than it is to strain to find suitable t..
W-pI .... 42.7:2 is a beginning step in bringing t. together,

W-pI.....43.5:2 and then let whatever relevant t. occur to
W-pI.....43.5:3 way. T. such as: *I see through the eyes of*
W-pI.....43.5:7 *I see my own t., which are like God's.* Any
W-pI.....43.5:9 t. need not bear any obvious relationship
W-pI.....43.6:1 if you begin to be aware of t. which are
W-pI.....43.6:2 become preoccupied with irrelevant t..
W-pI.....44.5:4 and all the t. that you have made up.
W-pI.....44.7:5 your passing t. without involvement, and
W-pI...44.10:2 limit, as you pass by the t. of this world.
W-pI.....45.1:1 idea holds the key to what your real t. are.
W-pI.....45.1:4 your real t. resemble your real thoughts in
W-pI.....45.1:4 real thoughts resemble your real t. in any
W-pI.....45.2:2 Therefore you share your t. with Him, as
W-pI.....45.2:3 They are the same t., because they are
W-pI.....45.2:5 Nor do the t. you think with the Mind of
W-pI.....45.2:5 mind, because t. do not leave their source.
W-pI.....45.2:6 Therefore, your t. are in the Mind of God,
W-pI.....45.2:8 His Mind, so are your t. part of His Mind.
W-pI.....45.3:1 Where, then, are your real t.? Today we
W-pI.....45.4:4 will not let the t. of the world hold us back
W-pI.....45.6:2 in thinking a few relevant t. of your own,
W-pI.....45.6:3 four or five t. of your own to the idea,
W-pI.....45.6:4 *My real t. are in my mind. I would like to find*
W-pI.....45.6:6 unreal t. that cover the truth in your mind
W-pI.....45.7:1 Under all the senseless t. and mad ideas
W-pI.....45.7:1 up your mind are the t. that you thought
W-pI.....45.8:3 Here are your t. one with His. For this
W-pI.....45.9:3 all t. that are unworthy of Him Whose
W-pI.....49.3:3 happiest and holiest of t. with confidence,
W-pI.....49.4:3 t. and obscure your eternal link with God.
W-pI.....49.4:4 riotous t. and sights and sounds of this
W-pI.....50.5:2 related t. come to help you recognize its
W-pI.....50.5:3 Let no idle and foolish t. enter to disturb
W-pI.....51.4:1 (4) These t. do not mean anything. The
W-pI.....51.4:2 The t. of which I am aware do not mean
W-pI.....51.4:3 I call "my" t. are not my real thoughts.
W-pI.....51.4:3 I call "my" thoughts are not my real t..
W-pI.....51.4:4 real t. are the thoughts I think with God.
W-pI.....51.4:4 real thoughts are the t. I think with God.
W-pI.....51.4:5 I have made my t. to take their place. I am
W-pI.....51.4:6 that my t. do not mean anything, and to
W-pI.....51.4:8 My t. are meaningless, but all creation lies
W-pI.....51.4:8 all creation lies in the t. I think with God.
W-pI.....51.5:2 I am constantly trying to justify my t.. I
W-pI.....52.3:1 (8) My mind is preoccupied with past t.. I
W-pI.....52.3:2 I see only my own t., and my mind is
W-pI.....52.5:1 (10) My t. do not mean anything. I have
W-pI.....52.5:2 I have no private t.. Yet it is only private
W-pI.....52.5:3 it is only private t. of which I am aware.
W-pI.....52.5:4 What can these t. mean? They do not
W-pI.....52.5:7 my pitiful and meaningless "private" t.?
W-pI.....53.1:1 (11) My meaningless t. are showing me a
W-pI.....53.1:2 Since the t. of which I am aware do not
W-pI.....53.1:4 and I have real t. as well as insane ones.
W-pI.....53.1:5 I look to my real t. as my guide for seeing.
W-pI.....53.2:2 Insane t. are upsetting. They produce a
W-pI.....53.4:5 suffer from the effects of my own insane t.
W-pI.....53.5:1 (15) My t. are images that I have made.
W-pI.....53.5:2 Whatever I see reflects my t.. It is my
W-pI.....53.5:3 is my t. that tell me where I am and what I
W-pI.....53.5:4 only the representation of my insane t.,
W-pI.....53.5:4 and am not allowing my real t. to cast
W-pI.....54.1:1 (16) I have no neutral t.. Neutral
W-pI.....54.1:2 Neutral t. are impossible because all
W-pI.....54.1:2 are impossible because all t. have power.
W-pI.....54.1:4 But t. cannot be without effects. As the
W-pI.....54.1:6 My t. cannot be neither true nor false.
W-pI.....54.3:2 I have no private t., I cannot see a private
W-pI.....54.3:5 I can also call upon my real t., which
W-pI.....54.3:6 my t. of separation call to the separation
W-pI.....54.3:6 call to the separation t. of others, so my
W-pI.....54.3:6 real t. awaken the real thoughts in them.
W-pI.....54.3:6 real thoughts awaken the real t. in them.
W-pI.....54.3:7 And the world my real t. show me will
W-pI.....54.4:1 alone in experiencing the effects of my t.. I
W-pI.....54.5:2 Recognizing the shared nature of my t., I
W-pI.....55.2:2 is hardly the representation of loving t.. It
W-pI.....55.2:5 own attack t. that give rise to this picture.
W-pI.....55.2:6 picture. My loving t. will save me from
W-pI.....55.3:1 from this world by giving up attack t..
W-pI.....55.3:3 attack t. I could not see a world of attack.
W-pI.....56.1:1 attack t. are attacking my invulnerability.
W-pI.....56.1:8 My own real t. will teach me what it is.
W-pI.....56.5:2 all my insane t. of separation and attack,
W-pI.....57.3:3 down, and my t. are the opposite of truth.
W-pI.....58.1:5 can picture only the t. I hold about myself
W-pI.....59.5:2 I have no t. I do not share with God.
W-pI.....59.5:3 I have no t. apart from Him, because I
W-pI.....59.5:4 my t. are His and His Thoughts are mine.
W-pI.....60.4:3 in which His Voice fails to direct my t.,
W-pI.....61.5:7 Let a few related t. come to you, and
W-pI.....62.2:5 t. of life may replace thoughts of death.
W-pI.....62.2:5 thoughts of life may replace t. of death.
W-pI.....62.5:5 Let related t. come freely, for your heart
W-pI.....63.4:1 the related t. come to you in the minute or
W-pI.....64.6:1 Today, then, let us practice with these t.:
W-pI.....64.6:6 Related t. will come to help you, if you
W-pI.....64.7:1 several minutes to reviewing these t., and
W-pI.....64.8:2 to concentrate on the t. you are using. At
W-pI.....64.8:3 keep your eyes open after reviewing the t.,
W-pI.....65.1:3 Both these t. are obviously necessary for a
W-pI.....65.5:2 carefully to catch whatever t. cross it. At
W-pI.....65.5:3 only on t. related to the idea for the day.
W-pI.....65.6:1 interfering t. will become harder to find.
W-pI.....65.6:2 idle t. that escaped your attention before,
W-pI.....66.5:1 practice period by reviewing these t.: *God*
W-pI.....66.5:6 is only if the first two t. are wrong that the
W-pI.....67.2:2 a few minutes adding some relevant t.,
W-pI.....67.3:1 you have gone over several such related t.,
W-pI.....67.3:1 thoughts, try to let all t. drop away for a
W-pI.....67.4:1 from time to time to replace distracting t..
W-pI.....67.4:2 other t. related to the truth about yourself
W-pI...70.10:1 but your own t. can hamper your progress
W-pI.....72.3:6 He "betrays" his hostile t. in his behavior.
W-pI.....74.3:1 periods by repeating these t. several times
W-pI.....74.3:4 several minutes in adding some related t.,
W-pI...74.3:10 any conflict t. that may cross your mind.
W-pI...74.3:13 *but God's. These conflict t. are meaningless.*
WpI..rII.in.4:1 intent to waver in the face of distracting t.
WpI..rII.in.4:2 that, whatever form such t. may take, they
WpI..rII.in.5:2 into detours, illusions and t. of death. You
W-pI.....91.8:2 t. about your attributes to be corrected,
W-pI.....93.3:1 from which such idle t. are meaningless.
W-pI.....93.3:2 These t. are not according to God's Will.
W-pI...93.10:3 remember to repeat these t. each hour:
W-pI...93.11:1 illusion of fear by repeating these t. again.
W-pI.....94.1:3 and all the t. that this world ever held are
W-pI.....96.4:5 no peace, and happiness is alien to its t..
W-pI.....96.9:5 are your own real t. you have denied, and
W-pI.....96.9:6 Here are your t., the only ones you have.
W-pI...96.10:1 the t. that come to you will tell you you
W-pI.....97.5:3 each time someone accepts them as his t.,
W-pI...98.11:1 earthly tasks, all little t. and limited ideas,
W-pI.....99.3:3 They have existence in that they are t..
W-pI.....99.3:4 that thinks these t. is separate from God.
W-pI.....99.4:1 the separated mind and t. with Mind and
W-pI.....99.7:6 thought the t. that never were His Will.
W-pI.....99.8:2 It does not think its solitary t., and make
W-pI...99.10:1 Forgive all t. which would oppose the
W-pI...100.1:2 belief in separate t. and separate bodies,
W-pI...100.8:5 undismayed by all the little t. and foolish
W-pI...101.6:8 joy these t. will introduce into your mind.
W-pI...107.3:3 is no room for transitory t. and dead ideas
W-pI...108.1:3 all your conflicts and mistaken t. into one
W-pI.110.11:1 loving t. for all who meet with us today.
WpI. rIII.in5:1 it, to considering the t. that are assigned.
WpI. rIII.in6:2 by the One Who gave the t. to you. What
WpI. rIII.in6:6 and let the mind employ the t. you gave as
WpIrIII.in13:3 As you review these t. He gave to you.
W-pI...122.3:2 and clears your memory of all dead t. so
W-pI...124.6:3 now. Their t. are timeless, and apart from
W-pI...125.3:1 today without intrusion of our petty t.,
W-pI...126.2:2 in ways which have no bearing on your t.,
W-pI...126.8:2 to the t. to which you are accustomed. But
W-pI.126.10:1 where t. are changed and false beliefs laid
W-pI...127.9:4 He will shine through your idle t. today,
W-pI...128.4:1 to body t. delay your progress to salvation
W-pI...129.9:3 choice by laying by whatever t. you have,
W-pI.131.10:1 Leave foolish t. like these behind today,
W-pI.131.10:3 in the place of t. that have no meaning, no
W-pI.131.11:4 *alone, the t. I want to think are not my own.*
W-pI.131.11:6 Review the t. as well which are compatible
W-pI.131.15:1 from dismal t. and meaningless laments.
W-pI...132.1:4 The t. you hold are mighty, and illusions
W-pI...132.2:1 his mind, and all his t. change with it.
W-pI...132.2:4 You free the future from all ancient t. of
W-pI...132.3:5 the bitter t. of death within your mind.
W-pI...132.4:4 waiting for your t. to give it meaning. Yet
W-pI...132.8:3 all the t. that gave it these appearances.
W-pI...132.8:4 are healed as you let go all t. of sickness,
W-pI...132.8:4 dead arise when you let t. of life replace all
W-pI...132.8:4 of life replace all t. you ever held of death.
W-pI.132.11:6 your t. which made it and must set it free,
W-pI.132.14:1 from all the idle t. we ever held about it,
W-pI.132.16:1 as you send out these t. to bless the world.
W-pI.134.16:1 freed from all the t. you had of sin in him.
W-pI...135.2:4 And all its structures, all its t. and doubts,
W-pI.135.10:1 These are the t. in need of healing, and
W-pI.136.19:2 If you let your mind harbor attack t., yield
W-pI.137.12:6 that t. of healing will this day go forth
W-pI.137.14:2 give ten minutes to these t. with which we
W-pI.137.15:2 all the foolish t. that ever were imagined.
W-pI.139.12:1 as we lay aside all t. that would distract us
W-pI...140.8:4 It is as near to us as our own t.; so close it
W-pI.140.11:2 is to let our interfering t. be laid aside, not
WpI. rIV.in1:4 and their central t. in such a way as will
WpI. rIV.in2:6 no t. can dwell but those his Father shares
WpI. rIV.in3:2 defenses that protect your unforgiving t.
WpI. rIV.in5:2 and clear it of all t. that would deceive,
WpI. rIV.in5:4 in charge of all the t. you will receive that
WpI. rIV.in9:1 We add no other t., but let these be the
W-pI.151.13:3 And then we watch our t., appealing
W-pI.151.14:1 Give Him your t., and He will give them
W-pI.151.15:2 ministry begins as all your t. are purified.
W-pI.151.15:5 everyone will share the t. with you which
W-pI.151.17:2 with us and happily accepts our holy t.,
W-pI.152.12:3 the peace of God for all your frantic t., the
W-pI...153.9:2 fear, for we have left all fearful t. behind.
W-pI.153.13:3 and lock our quaint and childish t. of sin
W-pI.153.16:4 a little while, and turn our t. to God.
W-pI...156.2:1 in the t. that we present in our curriculum
W-pI...158.7:3 and fearful t. of guilt from dreams of sin.
W-pI...161.4:4 t. make clear the meaning of creation? Do
W-pI...162.4:2 and they need no t. beyond themselves to
W-pI...163.1:3 you. All such t. are but reflections of the
W-pI...163.8:2 And yet, can t. like these be fearful? If
W-pI...165.1:2 t. of misery and death obscure the perfect
W-pI...167.8:3 of death is not the opposite to t. of life.
W-pI.167.11:3 Him, with all creation, with their t. as well
WpI...rV.in3:6 *as we review the t. that You have given us.*
WpI...rV.in4:1 should precede the t. that we review. Each
WpI...rV.in8:1 you practice once again the t. I brought to
WpI...rV.in8:2 Together we review these t.. Together we
WpI.rV.in11:4 use the t. to hold it up before our minds,
W-pI...182.7:5 He lives an outcast in a world of alien t..
W-pI...183.3:3 The sick arise, healed of their sickly t..
W-pI...183.6:4 Let all your t. become anchored on this.
W-pI...183.8:4 Let all t. be still except this one. And to all
W-pI...183.8:5 And to all other t. respond with this, and
W-pI...183.8:5 the thousand little names you gave your t.
W-pI...187.2:3 but represent the t. that make them. And
W-pI...187.5:4 T. extend as they are shared, for they can
W-pI...188.3:4 all t. of the ephemeral and valueless. It
W-pI...188.6:4 and let your t. fly to the peace within.
W-pI...188.6:6 For honest t., untainted by the dream of
W-pI...188.7:1 t. you think with Him. They recognize
W-pI...188.9:2 We take our wandering t., and gently
W-pI...189.9:2 in line with all the t. we share with God.
W-pI...189.7:1 all t. of what you are and what God is; all
W-pI.189.10:7 *We have no t. we think apart from You, and*
W-pI...190.5:1 It is your t. alone that cause you pain.
W-pI...190.6:3 It merely represents your t.. And it will
W-pI...190.7:7 Your t. of death envelop it in fear, while in
W-pI...190.9:2 Lay down all t. of danger and of fear. Let
W-pI...191.5:1 your t. and you have risen far above the
W-pI...191.5:1 and all the worldly t. that hold it prisoner.
W-pI...192.7:4 in mists of shifting dreams and fearful t.,

W-pI...194.2:1 hell, all blackness of depression, **t.** of sin,
W-pI...194.8:2 all your **t.** of sin and evil with the truth of
W-pI...195.1:4 How pitiful and deprecating are such **t.**!
W-pI...196.3:4 past all **t.** of crucifixion and of death, to
W-pI...196.3:4 and of death, to **t.** of liberation and of life.
W-pI...196.7:3 that it is but your **t.** that bring you fear,
W-pI...196.8:3 that you be hurt except by your own **t.**,
W-pI...197.2:1 those who know not what their **t.** can do.
W-pI...198.8:1 unmoved, untouched by **t.** like these, and
W-pI.198.11:2 was a frantic rush of **t.** that made no sense
W-pI.198.12:3 He needs no **t.** of mercy. Who could give
W-pI...199.2:2 asked. Attack **t.** cannot enter such a mind,
WpI rVI.in.2:1 carefully review the **t.** the Holy Spirit has
WpI rVI.in.6:5 or specific **t.** to aid in practicing. Instead,
WpI rVI.in.6:6 our **t.** whatever meaning they may have.
W-pI...213.1:2 *offers to me, in place of **t.** I made that hurt me*
W-pII ..in.11:3 special **t.** should be reviewed each day,
W-pII ....221.h Peace to my mind. Let all my **t.** be still.
W-pII .221.2:6 call, to let our **t.** be still and find His peace
W-pII .229.2:1 *of all the **t.** of sin my foolish mind made up.*
W-pII .....2.1:3 and all the **t.** that have been born in time
W-pII .....2.1:4 mind which thinks that it has separate **t.**,
W-pII .....2.1:4 these **t.** of conflict with the Thought of
W-pII .232.1:4 *let all my **t.** be still of You and of Your Love.*
W-pII .233.1:1 *Father, I give You all my **t.** today. I would*
W-pII .234.1:3 in **t.** which are forever unified as one.
W-pII .....3.2:5 knowledge could not cause such insane **t.**.
W-pII .249.2:2 *and frightened them with **t.** of violence and*
W-pII .....4.3:1 imagined, issuing from **t.** that are untrue.
W-pII .252.1:1 the **t.** of holiness of which I now conceive.
W-pII .254.2:1 Today we let no ego **t.** direct our words or
W-pII .254.2:2 When such **t.** occur, we quietly step back
W-pII .257.1:4 may unify our **t.** and actions meaningfully
W-pII .265.1:8 The images I see reflect my **t.**. Yet is my
W-pII .275.2:3 *speak and what to say to him, what **t.** to think*
W-pII .278.2:2 *foolish **t.** about myself and my creation, and*
W-pII ....281.h I can be hurt by nothing but my **t.**.
W-pII .281.1:5 *are. I can be hurt by nothing but my **t.**. The*
W-pII ....284.h I can elect to change all **t.** that hurt.
W-pII .284.1:7 I can elect to change all **t.** that hurt. And I
W-pII .285.1:2 by the **t.** to which it has been sent by me.
W-pII .....8.3:1 need has such a mind for **t.** of death,
W-pII .293.1:1 its source is gone, and all its **t.** gone with it
W-pII .294.1:5 death, for **t.** of fear are not invested there,
W-pII .296.1:2 *and have no **t.** which are apart from Yours,*
W-pII .325.1:6 forgiving **t.** a gentle world comes forth,
W-pII .326.1:8 *all separate **t.** unite in glory as the Son of God*
W-pII ...12.4:1 know reality is not to see the ego and its **t.**
W-pII .334.1:2 out of **t.** that rest on false perceptions. Let
W-pII ....338.h I am affected only by my **t.**.
W-pII .338.1:5 His **t.** can frighten him, but since these
W-pII .338.1:5 but since these **t.** belong to him alone, he
W-pII .338.2:3 *And I will have **t.** that will frighten me, until I*
W-pII .350.1:4 *What he is, is unaffected by his **t.**. But what*
Wfl........in.3:1 all our **t.** to serve the function of salvation.
M-in ..........1:6 day, and continues into sleeping **t.** as well.
M-in ..........5:7 **t.** remain a source of strength and truth
M-1 ...........3:6 It can be taught by actions or **t.**; in words
M-4 ......IV.2:8 understood their evil **t.** came neither from
M-4 ......IV.2:9 join their **t.** with Him Who is their Source
M-5 .........I.2:5 If he is healed, he is responsible for his **t.**.
M-5 .........I.2:6 And if he is responsible for his **t.**, he will
M-5 ......III.2:3 His **t.** ask for the right to question what
M-12 .........1:6 **t.** are joined with God's forever and ever.
M-15 .........3:1 even contempt; give up these foolish **t.**!
M-17 ............h TEACHERS DEAL WITH MAGIC **T.**?
M-17 .........4:5 rage, accompanied by **t.** of violence,
M-17 .........5:1 perceived magic **t.** is a basic cause of fear.
M-17 .........7:1 will now be your reaction to all magic **t.**?
M-17 .......8:10 Magic **t.** need not lead to condemnation,
M-18 .........1:6 Magic **t.** are but illusions. Otherwise
M-18 .........2:1 to react to magic **t.** wholly without anger.
M-20 ........6:11 and all the **t.** of which you can conceive,
M-21 .........1:8 or at least the control, of extraneous **t.**.
M-28 .........3:6 **T.** turn to Heaven and away from hell. All
C-4.............2:3 last, but lends itself to **t.** of sin and guilt.
P-2........III.4:6 to express his **t.** as he receives them from
S-1 .........II.7:8 to your Creator, sung without words, or **t.**
S-3 ...........I.1:3 and witnesses to unforgiving **t.** that injure
S-3..........II.1:9 hurtful **t.** and raging anger at the universe
S-3........IV.6:1 without such twisted **t.** upon your hearts.

**thoughts'** 1

W-pI...132.1:6 he be swayed by questioning his **t.** effects.

**thousand** 35

T-23 ........I.3:8 two are as meaningless as one or as a **t.**.
T-26 .....IX.4:1 What is a hundred or a **t.** years to Them,
T-27 .......II.5:8 with power greater than a **t.** tongues. For
T-27 ....V.10:4 each one of them there are a **t.** more. Each
T-29 ....VII.3:1 will impel him to seek out a **t.** idols, and
T-29 ....VII.3:1 and to seek beyond them for a **t.** more.
W-pI.....97.3:2 sometimes a **t.** years or more are saved.
W-pI.....98.5:4 have made a **t.** losing bargains at the least
W-pI...106.4:4 comes with miracles a **t.** times as happy
W-pI...106.9:2 **t.** minds are opened to the truth and they
W-pI...106.9:3 you will again release a **t.** more who pause
W-pI...123.6:3 and gives them back a **t.** and a hundred
W-pI...123.6:3 a hundred **t.** more than they were given.
W-pI...130.7:2 as one. We will not make a **t.** meaningless
W-pI...134.7:2 the **t.** forms in which they may appear. It
W-pI...138.4:1 you think a **t.** choices are confronting you
W-pI.154.12:3 will receive a **t.** miracles and then receive
W-pI.154.12:3 miracles and then receive a **t.** more, but
W-pI...156.8:2 question should be asked a **t.** times a day,
W-pI...182.3:3 A **t.** homes he makes, yet none contents
W-pI...183.8:5 the **t.** little names you gave your thoughts,
W-pI...184.5:2 is hard to teach the mind a **t.** alien names,
W-pI...186.8:5 as we experience a **t.** shifts in mood, and
W-pI.193.10:1 to overcome a **t.** seeming obstacles to
W-pI...196.4:5 seem to need a **t.** years can easily be done
W-pI...198.4:3 find a **t.** ways in which it must be wrong;
W-pI...198.4:3 it must be wrong; a **t.** other possibilities?
W-pII .262.1:4 *I perceive a **t.** forms in what remains as one?*
W-pII .262.1:5 *Why should I give this one a **t.** names, when*
W-pII .315.1:1 Each day a **t.** treasures come to me with
M-1 .........2:13 saves a **t.** years of time as the world judges
M-13 .........5:7 it in a **t.** ways and in a thousand places,
M-13 .........5:7 it in a thousand ways and in a **t.** places,
M-27 .........4:7 The world attempts a **t.** compromises,
M-27 .........4:7 compromises, and will attempt a **t.** more.

**thousandfold** 2

W-pI.....97.6:1 a **t.** and tens of thousands more. And
W-pI...198.3:2 illusions save this one must multiply a **t.**.

**thousands** 11

T-1 .........II.6:7 learning that might have taken **t.** of years.
T-4 .......III.7:2 You retain **t.** of little scraps of fear that
T-18 ......V.3:1 arrange, **t.** will rise to Heaven with you.
T-18 ......V.5:5 to **t.** on thousands who believe that love is
T-18 ......V.5:5 on **t.** who believe that love is fear, not
T-26 .....IX.4:1 or a thousand years to Them, or tens of **t.**
T-27 ....V.10:4 will be seen, but **t.** stand behind him, and
W-pI.....97.6:1 a thousandfold and tens of **t.** more. And
W-pI...184.5:2 a thousand alien names, and **t.** more. Yet
M-1 ...........4:2 There are many **t.** of other forms, all with
M-8 ...........1:2 and **t.** of contrasts in which each thing

**thread** 4

T-20 .....III.4:2 you **t.** your timid way through constant
T-24 ......V.2:3 does not realize he picked a **t.** from here,
T-28 ......V.6:2 bits of glass, a piece of wood, a **t.** or two,
M-27 .........2:3 holds your little life in his hand but by a **t.**

**threadbare** 1

W-pI...166.6:1 a sorry figure; weary, worn, in **t.** clothing,

**threads** 3

T-17 .....IV.8:3 with gilded **t.** of self-destruction. The
T-31 .VIII.11:5 to Heaven grows from tiny scattered **t.** of
W-pI 151.14:3 All the **t.** of fantasy are gone. And what

**threat** 49

*See also* non-threat

T-1 .......III.5:8 you experience God's reassurances as **t.**, it
T-3 .......IV.6:6 Thereafter, spirit is perceived as a **t.**,
T-4 .........II.6:9 to any perceived **t.** to the ego's existence.
T-4 .........V.2:6 with its own preservation in the face of **t.**,
T-4 .........V.3:2 only in terms of **t.** or non-threat to itself.
T-4 .......VI.1:1 does not recognize the real source of "**t.**,"
T-4 ......VII.2:4 communication when it experiences **t.**.
T-7 .......VI.3:9 threatened by projecting the **t.** onto *you,*
T-7 .......VI.5:2 It perceives their **t.** as total, because it
T-9 .........II.2:5 the **t.** to his thought system might be
T-9 .....VIII.3:2 that the ego is aware of **t.** to its existence,
T-9 .....VIII.3:2 these two very different kinds of **t.**. Its
T-9 .....VIII.3:4 When the ego experiences **t.**, its only
T-11 .....V.10:1 experience it, is therefore the basic ego **t.**.
T-11 .....V.13:6 if separation is salvation, harmony is **t.**.
T-13 ..... IV.2:2 is the greatest **t.** you think you could
T-15 ........I.6:3 is hidden a far more insidious **t.** to peace.
T-15 ........I.6:4 The ego does not advertise its final **t.**, for
T-17 ..... IV.4:2 what had been created, it was aware of **t.**.
T-17 ..... IV.5:1 The ego is always alert to **t.**, and the part
T-18 .......V.6:3 the peace of one is an equal **t.** to the other
T-18 .......V.7:1 Whoever is saner at the time the **t.** is
T-21 ... VI.11:1 the Son of God is not a **t.** to his reality. It
T-21 .... VII.6:5 to hold a **t.** the rest have lost for you. And
T-24 .....II.12:6 defender of all illusions from the "**t.**" of
T-24 .... VII.1:6 attack, the whispered doubt, the hint of **t.**
T-25 ...VIII.6:8 And they perceive the "**t.**" of what God
T-30 ..... IV.3:6 the child who learns they are no **t.** to him.
T-30 ... IV.3:10 toys? And *can* they represent a **t.** to him?
W-pI .... 26.1:2 You see attack as a real **t.**. That is because
W-pI .. 135.2:2 A sense of **t.** is an acknowledgment of an
W-pI .. 135.2:4 all serve but to preserve its sense of **t.**. For
W-pI 135.17:4 reality that is the "**t.**" which your defenses
W-pI .. 136.4:1 Who but yourself evaluates a **t.**, decides
W-pI .. 136.4:1 reduce the **t.** that has been judged as real?
W-pI .. 136.6:2 It is this process that imposes **t.**, and not
W-pI .. 153.2:2 For **t.** brings anger, anger makes attack
W-pI .. 153.2:3 Yet is defensiveness a double **t.**. For it
W-pI .. 153.4:3 The sense of **t.** the world encourages is so
W-pI 153.19:5 we feel the **t.** of our defenses undermine
W-pI .. 170.3:3 defense against the **t.** of what you really
W-pI .. 186.7:2 and seeks to attack the **t.** it does not know
W-pI .. 196.2:2 because the ego, under what it sees as **t.**,
M-4 ........X.2:6 all are all things welcoming, for **t.** is gone.
M-5 .........I.1:6 strength is seen as **t.** and health as danger
M-6 ........... 2:1 stand aside when it would be seen as **t.**.
P-2........ IV.6:6 now becomes a **t.** and is perceived as evil.
P-2........ IV.8:2 of **t.** differs according to the form it takes.
P-2...... IV.10:5 that the insane believe that sanity is **t.**.

**threaten** 14

T-1 ....... III.5:1 Error cannot really **t.** truth, which can
T-9 ..........I.1:3 cannot "**t.**" anything except illusions,
T-17 ... IV.10:3 to truth, you **t.** truth with destruction.
T-23 ........I.6:8 over truth, nor can they **t.** it in any way.
T-29 .. VII.9:10 Salvation thus appears to **t.** life and offer
T-30 ... IV.5:13 His idols do not **t.** him at all. His one
W-pI .... 50.3:3 into a state of mind that nothing can **t.**,
W-pI .... 56.1:3 illness, loss, age and death seem to **t.** me.
W-pI .... 82.4:4 *This may **t.** my ego, but cannot change my*
W-pI .. 121.1:3 that appear to **t.** you at every turn, and
W-pI .. 136.3:2 appears to **t.** what you would believe.
W-pI .. 136.7:4 away and **t.** your establishments no more.
W-pI .. 194.7:6 certainty of care the world can never **t.**.
W-pII . 244.2:4 For what can come to **t.** God Himself, or

**threatened** 13

T-in ........... 2:2 ***Nothing real can be t.. Nothing unreal***
T-6 ....... III.1:5 Therefore, being is never **t.**. Your Godlike
T-7 ....... VI.3:9 perceive *its* existence as **t.** by projecting
T-14 ..... XI.6:6 your peace is **t.** or disturbed in any way,
T-17 .......V.4:2 and its structure is "**t.**" by the recognition

T-18.......V.6:1 of your relationship is **t.** by anything, stop
T-20......VI.7:6 Your temple is not **t.**. You are an idolater
T-24....IV.3:10 that all illusions are "**t.**" by the truth.
W-pI.....34.5:1 feel your peace of mind is **t.** in any way.
W-pI.....87.3:4 can I believe that my eternal safety is **t.**.
W-pI...138.8:2 must be saved from salvation, **t.** to be safe
W-pI...153.1:1 You who feel **t.** by this changing world,
M-25..........5:2 gifts, the ego has been seriously **t.**. It may

## threatening 8

T-2..... VIII.2:1 one of the most **t.** ideas in your thinking.
T-4.........V.2:5 Thoughts of God, because both are **t.** to it
T-11.......V.6:8 The ego sees all dependency as **t.**, and has
T-21......IV.3:3 ask it now are **t.** the ego's whole defensive
T-26.......X.6:2 The world grows dim and **t.**, not a trace of
W-pII..339.1:4 think that joy is painful, **t.** and dangerous.
M-8............1:5 And a more **t.** idea, or one conceived of as
M-16..........2:5 **t.** the very goals for which they were set

## threatens 8

T-7........VI.3:7 This **t.** its own existence, a state which it
T-10.......in.3:9 When anything **t.** your peace of mind, ask
T-18.......V.6:3 must be that whatever **t.** the peace of one
T-20......VI.7:1 so severely **t.** them as love's approach. Let
T-21.......II.6:8 that **t.** this seems to attack your faith, for
T-21.......V.7:5 part of knowledge **t.** dissociation as much
W-pI...135.2:1 because it must contain what **t.** you. A
W-pI...153.1:5 of mind is possible where danger **t.** thus.

## threats 2

W-pI.....98.3:2 escapes from fancied **t.** without reality.
W-pI...184.4:4 become the **t.** which it must overcome,

## three 43

*See also* three-to-five-minute
T-6.........in.1:4 Given these **t.** wholly irrational premises,
T-6.........V.3:4 better to use only **t.** words: "Do only that!
T-21.....VII.6:1 have answered the first **t.** questions, but
T-21.....VII.8:2 answered, and is answered in the other **t.**.
T-21...VII.10:3 It is the same as are the other **t.**, except in
W-pI.......1.4:1 Each of the first **t.** lessons should not be
W-pI.......4.6:2 repeat these exercises more than **t.** or four
W-pI.......5.7:6 **T.** or four times during the day is enough.
W-pI.......6.2:2 the **t.** or four practice periods which are
W-pI.......7.5:3 **T.** or four practice periods, each to last a
W-pI.......8.6:2 find it trying, **t.** or four times is sufficient.
W-pI.......9.3:1 **t.** or four practice periods are sufficient,
W-pI.....11.4:1 **T.** practice periods today will probably
W-pI.....12.6:1 **T.** or four times is enough for practicing
W-pI.....13.4:1 about **t.** or four times for not more than a
W-pI.....14.2:3 Do not have more than **t.** practice periods
W-pI.....15.5:3 have more than **t.** application periods for
W-pI.....16.6:2 If strain is experienced, **t.** will be enough.
W-pI.....17.4:1 **T.** or four specific practice periods are
W-pI.....17.4:1 than **t.** are required for maximum benefit,
W-pI.....18.2:3 The **t.** or four practice periods which are
W-pI.....19.5:1 at least **t.** practice periods are required,
W-pI.....31.2:2 **T.** to five minutes for each of these are
W-pI.....31.2:3 while repeating the idea two or **t.** times.
W-pI.....32.3:1 for today two or **t.** times while looking
W-pI.....32.4:1 the two longer practice periods **t.** to five
W-pI.....32.4:1 with not less than **t.** required. More than
W-pI.....34.2:1 **T.** longer practice periods are required
W-pI.....35.4:1 the **t.** five-minute practice periods today,
W-pI.....37.4:1 to involve **t.** to five minutes of practice,
W-pI....39.11:1 made some **t.** or four times an hour and
W-pI.....41.6:2 sit quietly for some **t.** to five minutes,
W-pI.....43.4:1 **T.** five-minute practice periods are
W-pI.....44.4:1 Have at least **t.** practice periods today,
W-pI.....44.4:1 today, each lasting **t.** to five minutes. A
W-pI.....45.4:1 **t.** five-minute practice periods for today
W-pI.....46.3:1 at least **t.** full five-minute practice periods
WpI. rII.in.2:2 Devote some **t.** or four minutes to reading
W-pI.....91.5:1 **T.** times today, set aside about ten
W-pI...125.7:1 **T.** times today, at times most suitable for
W-pI.127.12:2 At least **t.** times an hour think of one who
W-pI...128.7:1 Give it ten minutes rest **t.** times today.
W-pI.131.10:3 ten minutes to this goal **t.** times today,

## three-to-five-minute 2

W-pI....36.2:1 Four **t.** practice periods are required for
W-pI.....42.3:1 will have two **t.** practice periods today,

## threshold 2

W-pI...122.3:2 Father can arise across the **t.** of your mind
M-26.........1:3 across the **t.** of recognition only where all

## threw 4

T-4.........II.3:2 **t.** knowledge away it is as if you never had
T-6........III.4:5 win back the knowledge that you **t.** away.
T-6......V.C.9:3 When you **t.** truth away you saw yourself
T-24.....II.14:1 key you **t.** away God gave your brother,

## thrive 1

T-20......VI.4:5 for the offerings on which its idols **t.**. The

## throat 1

W-pI...190.9:4 of judgment that you hold against your **t.**,

## throb 1

W-pI...182.1:6 feeling, sometimes not more than a tiny **t.**

## throes 1

T-27......VI.6:6 the **t.** of death itself are but a single sound

## throne 13

T-14.....III.15:3 on the **t.** of God is not a source of guilt.
T-23.....II.15:6 to look upon, is lifted to the **t.** of love, its
T-23.....II.15:8 Give thanks unto the hero on love's **t.**,
T-26......VI.3:2 the **t.** that God appointed for your Friend,
T-26......VI.3:6 He will place them on your **t.**, when you
T-26......IX.3:4 take its ancient place upon an ancient **t.**.
W-pI...125.4:3 We gather at the **t.** of God today, the
W-pI...136.9:3 and chaos sits in triumph on His **t.**.
W-pI...194.3:2 no one instant sorrow can be set upon a **t.**
M-5..........I.1:7 for placing God's Son on his Father's **t.**.
M-5..........I.2:8 thus entirely usurped the **t.** of his Creator.
M-17.........7:6 raised madness to the **t.** of God Himself.
M-18.........3:9 *been taken from its **t.** by your mistakes. God*

## through 548

## throughout 77

T-4.......VII.8:5 and there is great joy **t.** the Kingdom.
T-5.........in.3:4 The light is so strong that it radiates **t.** the
T-10.......III.2:3 of Him awakens **t.** the Sonship. Heal your
T-13....XI.10:4 will remain unchanged **t.** eternity. You do
T-17.......V.9:5 remember a goal unchanged **t.** eternity?
T-17.....V.10:1 **T.** the Sonship is the song of freedom
T-22.......V.4:5 heart **t.** the universe forever sings as one?
T-22....VI.15:1 and your brother shines **t.** the universe,
T-28.......I.13:4 of eternity resound **t.** the stillness, yet
T-30.........I.4:1 (2) **T.** the day, at any time you think of it
T-31.........I.8:8 **t.** the world this second lesson brings.
W-in..........6:1 The only general rules to be observed **t.**,
W-pI.......6.2:1 can profitably be used **t.** the day for that
W-pI.....12.2:4 to keep a measured, even tempo **t.**. What
W-pI.....14.2:1 are to be practiced with eyes closed **t.**.
W-pI.....15.5:4 idea can be applied as needed **t.** the day.
W-pI.....19.4:2 all practice periods remains essential **t.**.
W-pI.....20.4:1 yourself **t.** the day that you want to see.
W-pI.....23.6:1 using it **t.** the day as the need arises, five
W-pI.....27.3:4 and attempt to adhere to it **t.** the day. It
W-pI.....30.3:1 be applied as often as possible **t.** the day.
W-pI.....31.1:4 of frequent applications of the idea **t.** the
W-pI.....33.2:2 detachment as you repeat the idea **t.** the
W-pI.....34.5:2 yourself from temptation **t.** the day. If a
W-pI.....36.2:2 to protect your protection **t.** the day. The
W-pI.....41.9:1 **T.** the day use today's idea often,
W-pI.....43.8:1 Today's idea should also be applied **t.** the
W-pI...44.11:1 **T.** the day repeat the idea often, with eyes
W-pI.....45.9:2 or two, as you repeat the idea **t.** the day,
W-pI.....50.1:1 you, today and tomorrow and **t.** time. In
W-pI.....61.6:2 about yourself, reinforce it **t.** the day, and
W-pI.....62.4:1 use it as frequently as possible **t.** the day.
W-pI.....63.3:3 And **t.** the day we will repeat this as often
W-pI.....64.7:1 applications of today's idea **t.** the day,
W-pI.....66.1:1 noticed an emphasis **t.** our recent lessons
W-pI...76.12:1 as subject to other laws **t.** the day. It is our
W-pI...78.10:1 We will remember this **t.** the day, and
W-pI.....94.2:6 and in which you will remain **t.** eternity.
W-pI...95.14:7 **T.** the day do not forget your goal. Repeat
W-pI...98.10:1 **T.** the hour, let your time be spent in
W-pI...103.3:4 this expectation frequently **t.** the day, and
W-pI...106.6:4 will resound **t.** the world through you.
W-pI.110.11:1 We will remember Him **t.** the day with
WpI. rIII.in9:1 be done **t.** the day are equally important,
WpIrIII.in10:6 you keep your peace **t.** the day as well.
W-pI.121.13:4 not forget, **t.** the day, the role forgiveness
W-pI.122.13:3 Let not your gifts recede **t.** the day, as you
W-pI...127.1:5 It is like itself, unchanged **t.**. It never
W-pI.127.12:1 will remember them **t.** the day, because
W-pI...128.8:1 Protect your mind **t.** the day as well. And
W-pI...129.3:2 remain exactly as you want them **t.** time?
W-pI.132.17:1 **T.** the day, increase the freedom sent
W-pI.135.26:5 **T.** the day, as foolish little things appear
W-pI.152.12:1 In patience wait for Him **t.** the day, and
W-pI...156.2:2 Truth must be true **t.**, if it be true. It
W-pI...162.3:1 in his mind, recalling them **t.** the day, at
W-pI.169.12:1 is the central theme that runs **t.** salvation,
WpI.rV.in11:4 it clear in our rememberance **t.** the day.
W-pI...181.7:1 use this thought to keep us safe **t.** the day.
W-pI...189.2:4 It blesses you **t.** the day, and watches
W-pI...195.1:7 all cause of sorrow disappear **t.** the world.
WpI rVI.in.1:2 remembrances you make **t.** the day, use
WpI rVI.in.2:2 to all the seeming happenings **t.** the day.
W-pII .232.1:1 *I wake, and shine on me **t.** the day today. Let*
W-pII .237.1:2 in me to shine upon the world **t.** the day.
W-pII .315.1:2 I am blessed with gifts **t.** the day, in value
W-pII .316.1:3 every gift a brother has received **t.** all time
W-pII ...11.2:4 will not be changed **t.** the course of time,
WfI........in.6:5 and all that there will be **t.** all time and in
M-4 .....VII.1:6 emphasized **t.** the text and the workbook,
M-16 .........3:3 remains important **t.** the learning process
M-16 .........6:1 that should be remembered **t.** the day. It
M-16 .........8:1 himself **t.** the day of his protection. How
M-16 .......11:5 No risk is possible **t.** the day except to put
M-29 .........5:9 remember God when you can **t.** the day,
C-6.............2:1 The Holy Spirit is described **t.** the course
S-1 .........in.1:7 share is what all prayer will be **t.** eternity,

## throw 8

T-8.........I.1:10 to **t.** it away when the ego asks for your
T-13.......III.4:3 you do, you would **t.** this world away,
T-13......IX.7:3 You **t.** a dark veil over it, and cannot see it
T-14.....IV.8:3 tried to **t.** yourself away and valued God
T19....IV.C.2:6 See him **t.** aside the black robe he was
T-20.........I.2:7 Join now with me and **t.** away the thorns,
T-31.....V.11:5 Spirit does not seek to **t.** you into panic.
W-pI.136.12:5 it sighs a little when you **t.** away its gifts,

## throwing 2

T-4........VI.2:3 you are **t.** away the graciousness of your
P-3........III.7:4 How much is lost by **t.** God away? And is

## thrown 10

T-4.........V.1:4 The ego is **t.** further off balance because it
T-4........VI.5:1 of something he has deliberately **t.** away?
T-4........VI.5:2 have **t.** it away because he did not value it.
T-11....VIII.2:4 will restore to you what you have **t.** away.

T-14 I.1:2 for it is they that have been **t.** away. You
T-14 III.18:3 that you have **t.** away but could not lose.
T-15 VIII.2:2 but seek in them what you have **t.** away.
T-24 III.3:5 *It* can be **t.** off balance by anything. What
W-pII 3.4:5 and certainty, which you have **t.** away,
S-3 I.4:3 For he has **t.** away the prison's key; his

**throws** 3
T-14 III.6:4 he **t.** away the joyous opportunity to learn
T-20 VI.4:6 The rest it merely **t.** away, for all that it
WpI. rIV.in4:3 No more than can a child who **t.** a stick

**thrust** 9
T-1 II.2:6 freedom from fear cannot be **t.** upon you.
T-11 I.11:3 Will with you; He does not **t.** it upon you.
T-11 VI.6:3 and frightens you cannot be **t.** upon you,
T-15 XI.5:3 For who could **t.** Heaven and its Creator
T19 IV.A.4:1 Would you **t.** salvation away from the
T-27 VII.7:3 everything the world appeared to **t.** upon
T-30 I.9:3 you that help is not being **t.** upon you but
W-pI 73.9:2 of an alien power, **t.** upon you unwillingly
S-3 II.3:2 to be **t.** down in pain upon unwilling flesh

**thunder** 1
W-pI 106.2:1 which silences the **t.** of the meaningless,

**thus** 521

**Thy** 2
*thy*
T-18 V.4:3 Their message is, "**T.** Will be done," and
T-31 VIII.12:6 **T.** Will is done, complete and perfectly,

**thy** 1
*Thy*
T-24 III.5:8 "**T.** will be done" because you think it is.

**thyself** 3
T-8 III.5:1 of the teacher you choose, is "Know **t.**."
P-2 VII.1:4 Physician, heal **t.**. Who else is there to
P-3 III.8:1 healer, therapist, teacher, heal **t.**. Many

**tick** 1
T-26 V.3:5 tiny **t.** of time in which the first mistake

**tides** 2
T-29 VI.2:9 All things that come and go, the **t.**, the
WpI. rIV.in4:3 change the coming and the going of the **t.**,

**tidings** 9
T-16 II.6:5 who bring you the glad **t.** He has come. It
T-16 II.8:5 to accept the joyful **t.** that disaster is not
T-19 I.14:6 returning the glad **t.** that it was done to
W-pI 75.5:3 telling yourself the glad **t.** of your release:
W-pI 125.4:2 spread across the world the **t.** of salvation
W-pII 237.1:3 I bring the world the **t.** of salvation which
W-pII 14.5:3 We bring glad **t.** to the Son of God, who
M-4 X.3:8 **t.** of complete forgiveness to the world.
P-3 III.8:9 of the world, and the glad **t.** of salvation.

**tie** 1
T-29 VI.5:1 This world will bind your feet and **t.** your

**tied** 7
T-17 VII.6:1 closely **t.** to faithlessness as faith to truth.
T-24 VII.1:1 How bitterly does everyone **t.** to this
W-pI 92.1:3 idea of what seeing means is **t.** up with
W-pI 191.9:3 pitifully **t.** to dissolution in a world which
W-pI 199.1:4 a body, firmly **t.** to it and sheltered by its
S-1 II.8:5 Prayer is **t.** up with learning until the goal
S-3 I.2:3 who think their life is **t.** to its command

**ties** 1
T-13 IV.9:5 interpretation **t.** the future to the present,

**tight** 4
W-pI 135.3:5 your armor thicker and your locks more **t.**
W-pI 169.3:5 It is not shut **t.** against God's Voice. It has
Wi181-200 2:4 **t.** control of what you see speaks for itself.
W-pI 192.7:4 thoughts, our eyes shut **t.** against the light

**tighten** 1
T-13 VII.11:6 serve to **t.** up your world against the light,

**tightening** 1
*See also* ever-tightening
W-pII 1.2:3 thought protects projection, **t.** its chains,

**tightly** 2
T19 IV.A.8:4 than a **t.** organized delusional system? Its
W-pI 102.1:4 it **t.** to the dark and hidden secret places

**till** 21
T-14 IV.3:8 You will feel guilty **t.** you learn this. For in
T-18 I.8:1 and turning **t.** they disappear from sight,
T-20 I.2:10 be complete **t.** your forgiveness rests on
T-24 VI.9:3 **t.** what has been assigned to you is done
T-24 VII.6:10 Not **t.** you go past learning to the Given;
T-24 VII.6:10 not **t.** you make again a holy home for
T-26 VIII.6:5 Why wait **t.** they unfold in time and fear
T-29 I.4:3 separate **t.** you and he elect to meet again.
T-29 VI.6:4 it *is* a little while **t.** timelessness comes
T-30 V.3:6 is he glad to wait **t.** every hand is joined,
T-30 V.7:6 For He must be unremembered **t.** His Son
W-pI 92.7:6 to darkness **t.** the morning comes again.
W-pI. 121.11:4 this picture **t.** you see a light somewhere
W-pI 156.8:2 day, **t.** certainty has ended doubting and
W-pI 165.4:6 it. **T.** you welcome it as yours, uncertainty
W-pI. 191.11:2 They stay in chains **t.** you are free. They
W-pI. 191.11:5 die **t.** you accept your own eternal life.
W-pI 198.1:4 against you, **t.** you lay it down as valueless
W-pI 200.5:3 be bound **t.** all the world is seen by you as
W-pII in.11:3 to be continued **t.** the next is given you.
C-ep 3:5 the certainty the journey lacked **t.** now.

**time** 985
*See also* space-time, time-bound, time-control, time-dependent
T-in 1:3 *Only the* **t.** *you take it is voluntary. Free will*
T-in 1:5 *can elect what you want to take at a given* **t.**.
T-1 I.15:2 The purpose of **t.** is to enable you to learn
T-1 I.15:2 you to learn how to use **t.** constructively.
T-1 I.15:4 **T.** will cease when it is no longer useful in
T-1 I.19:3 reflect the laws of eternity, not of **t.**.
T-1 I.25:2 all the **t.** and in all the dimensions of time
T-1 I.25:2 all the time and in all the dimensions of **t.**
T-1 I.47:1 learning device that lessens the need for **t.**
T-1 I.47:2 It establishes an out-of-pattern **t.** interval
T-1 I.47:2 interval not under the usual laws of **t.**. In
T-1 I.48:1 your immediate disposal for controlling **t.**
T-1 I.48:2 it, having nothing to do with **t.** at all.
T-1 II.h Revelation, **T.** and Miracles
T-1 II.4:1 separate or different from you except in **t.**
T-1 II.4:1 except in time, and **t.** does not really exist.
T-1 II.6:1 The miracle minimizes the need for **t.**. In
T-1 II.6:2 appears to involve almost endless **t.**.
T-1 II.6:4 in **t.** than they would otherwise have been
T-1 II.6:5 the unique property of abolishing **t.** to the
T-1 II.6:5 the interval of **t.** it spans unnecessary.
T-1 II.6:6 is no relationship between the **t.** a miracle
T-1 II.6:6 time a miracle takes and the **t.** it covers.
T-1 II.6:9 The miracle shortens **t.** by collapsing it,
T-1 V.2:1 to wait on **t.** any longer than is necessary.
T-1 V.2:2 **T.** can waste as well as be wasted. The
T-1 V.2:4 recognizes that every collapse of **t.** brings
T-1 V.2:4 closer to the ultimate release from **t.**, in
T-1 VI.3:5 Ultimately, space is as meaningless as **t.**.
T-2 II.3:8 save **t.** if you do not protract this step
T-2 II.4:4 because belief in space and **t.** did not exist
T-2 II.6:6 In this sense the Atonement saves **t.**, but
T-2 II.6:7 is need for Atonement, there is need for **t.**
T-2 II.6:8 plan has a unique relationship to **t.**. Until
T-2 II.6:9 its various phases will proceed in **t.**, but
T-2 III.3:1 by everyone is only a matter of **t.**. This
T-2 V.9:2 all aspects of the belief in space and **t.**, it
T-2 V.9:3 However, as long as **t.** persists, healing is
T-2 V.10:1 beyond his actual accomplishments in **t.**.
T-2 V.10:4 clearly imply their dependence on **t.**,
T-2 V.10:5 before that only revelation transcends **t.**.
T-2 V.A.11:2 Since it is an out-of-pattern **t.** interval, the
T-2 V.A.11:2 of **t.** and space do not apply. When you
T-2 V.A.11:3 I will arrange both **t.** and space to adjust
T-2 V.A.17:4 Only the latter involves an awareness of **t.**
T-2 V.A.17:5 **T.** is under my direction, but timelessness
T-2 V.A.17:6 In **t.** we exist for and with each other. In
T-2 VI.9:3 no one remains fully aware of it all the **t.**.
T-2 VII.2:3 that would not foster the **t.** collapse for
T-2 VII.5:11 **T.** is essentially a device by which all
T-2 VII.5:12 **t.** itself involves intervals that do not exist
T-2 VII.7:9 an enormous amount of **t.** is necessary
T-2 VII.7:9 that **t.** and space are under my control.
T-2 VIII.2:6 for shortening but not abolishing **t.**. If a
T-2 VIII.4:5 At the same **t.** the mind will inevitably
T-2 VIII.5:6 and at any **t.** to everything you have made
T-2 VIII.5:8 purpose of **t.** is solely to "give you time"
T-2 VIII.5:8 to "give you **t.**" to achieve this judgment.
T-3 I.3:10 from **t.** to time that I am misdirecting you
T-3 I.3:10 from time to **t.** that I am misdirecting you
T-3 III.1:7 an attribute of the belief in space and **t.**, it
T-3 III.2:8 change, their dependence on **t.** is obvious.
T-3 III.2:9 at any given **t.** determines what you do,
T-3 III.2:9 what you do, and actions must occur in **t.**.
T-3 III.3:1 The questioning mind perceives itself in **t.**
T-3 III.6:4 preceded both perception and **t.**, and will
T-3 V.5:3 separated and unseparated at the same **t.**.
T-3 VII.3:2 is a system of thought real enough in **t.**,
T-4 II.9:4 that the ego existed before that point in **t.**
T-5 in.1:7 different kinds of responses at the same **t.**
T-5 I.5:2 the Atonement principle at the same **t.**.
T-5 II.1:3 of the **t.** sequence should be quite familiar
T-5 II.1:3 of **t.** that the miracle introduces. The Holy
T-5 II.1:6 His Mind to yours as long as there is **t.**.
T-5 II.3:1 and the separation began at the same **t.**.
T-5 III.5:1 is of the ego, because **t.** is its concept.
T-5 III.5:2 Both **t.** and delay are meaningless in
T-5 III.6:2 and the Holy Spirit; with **t.** and eternity.
T-5 III.6:4 **T.** is a belief of the ego, so the lower mind,
T-5 III.6:5 The only aspect of **t.** that is eternal is *now.*
T-5 III.8:13 are as closely related as are **t.** and war.
T-5 III.11:2 The Holy Spirit must perceive **t.**, and
T-5 VI.h **T.** and Eternity
T-5 VI.1:3 not matter in eternity, but it is tragic in **t.**.
T-5 VI.1:4 elected to be in **t.** rather than eternity,
T-5 VI.1:4 eternity, and therefore believe you *are* in **t.**
T-5 VI.1:6 You do not belong in **t.**. Your place is only
T-5 VI.2:1 Guilt feelings are the preservers of **t.**.
T-5 VI.12:2 way in which **t.** is exchanged for eternity.
T-5 VI.12:3 results *now* it renders **t.** unnecessary. We
T-5 VI.12:4 repeatedly said that **t.** is a learning device
T-5 VI.12:5 The Holy Spirit, Who speaks for God in **t.**
T-5 VI.12:5 in time, also knows that **t.** is meaningless.
T-5 VI.12:6 you of this in every passing moment of **t.**,
T-5 VII.4:1 But the **t.** is now. You have not been
T-6 in.2:2 Everyone teaches, and teaches all the **t.**.
T-6 I.16:1 not wholly ready to follow me at the **t.**.
T-6 I.18:1 of the Sons of God is present all the **t.**,
T-6 II.10:1 The Holy Spirit uses **t.**, but does not

T-6 IV.3:3 **t.** or another and in one way or another,
T-6 IV.3:4 Spirit answers truly He answers for all **t.**,
T-6 IV.7:5 The **t.** spent on questioning in the dream
T-6 V.1:6 ongoing process, not in **t.** but in eternity.
T-6 V.A.6:6 Some remain at this step for a long **t.**,
T-6 V.B.4:6 For a **t.**, then, he is receiving conflicting
T-7 I.3:6 It creates forever, but not in **t.**. God's
T-7 I.5:4 outward beyond limits and beyond **t.**,
T-7 I.7:4 as applied to Him is not a **t.** concept. He is
T-7 I.7:7 **t.** applies neither to Him nor to what He
T-7 III.2:2 It does not wait in **t.**. It merely rests in the
T-7 V.9:8 believes that every **t.** it deprives someone
T-7 VI.8:9 the idea of conflict entirely and for all **t.**.
T-7 VIII.6:2 ego can be completely forgotten at any **t.**,
T-8 VI.4:1 not understood its worthlessness at the **t.**.
T-9 II.2:5 harm. At the same **t.**, if he were healed
T-9 III.2:5 He may be making no sense at the **t.**, and
T-9 III.8:3 Accept only the function of healing in **t.**,
T-9 III.8:3 in time, because that is what **t.** is for. God
T-9 IV.9:1 The ego literally lives on borrowed **t.**,
T-9 IV.9:2 ego's **t.** is "borrowed" from your eternity.
T-9 VI.6:4 it. In **t.** the giving comes first, though they
T-9 VI.6:5 they are the same, the need for **t.** is over.
T-9 VI.7:1 Eternity is one **t.**, its only dimension
T-10 in.1:2 **T.** and eternity are both in your mind,
T-10 in.1:2 will conflict until you perceive **t.** solely as
T-10 in.1:4 learn that **t.** is solely at your disposal, and
T-10 V.14:3 this is not true in eternity it *is* true in **t.**, so
T-10 V.14:3 while **t.** lasts in your mind there will be
T-10 V.14:4 **T.** itself is your choice. If you would
T-10 V.14:6 with the temporal, you are living in **t.**. As
T-10 V.14:8 value. **T.** and eternity cannot both be real,
T-11 I.3:7 Your denial of its reality may arrest it in **t.**
T-11 I.4:1 Waiting is possible only in **t.**, but time
T-11 I.4:1 only in time, but **t.** has no meaning. You
T-11 I.4:2 You who made delay can leave **t.** behind
T-11 I.9:6 Even in **t.** you cannot live apart from Him
T-11 III.8:4 If you will bless him in **t.**, you will be in
T-11 III.8:5 **T.** cannot separate you from God if you
T-11 VI.4:7 which knows no **t.** and no exceptions. But
T-12 VII.3:3 it. Every law of **t.** and space, of magnitude
T-13 I.3:2 consider this: You are not guiltless in **t.**,
T-13 I.3:5 **T.** seems to go in one direction, but when
T-13 I.4:4 The Holy Spirit stands at the end of **t.**,
T-13 I.5:5 *When* he finds it is only a matter of **t.**, and
T-13 I.5:5 a matter of time, and **t.** is but an illusion.
T-13 I.7:3 to travel on, and no **t.** to travel through.
T-13 I.7:4 For God waits not for His Son in **t.**, being
T-13 I.8:3 and thus depends on one-dimensional **t.**,
T-13 I.8:9 And immortality is the opposite of **t.**, for
T-13 I.8:9 is the opposite of time, for **t.** passes away,
T-13 I.9:2 The future, in **t.**, is always associated with
T-13 IV.h The Function of **T.**
T-13 IV.4:1 The ego has a strange notion of **t.**, and it
T-13 IV.4:2 is the only aspect of **t.** that is meaningful.
T-13 IV.7:1 of **t.** is the exact opposite of the ego's. The
T-13 IV.7:2 the goal of **t.** as diametrically opposed.
T-13 IV.7:3 as rendering the need for **t.** unnecessary.
T-13 IV.7:4 He regards the function of **t.** as temporary
T-13 IV.7:5 aspect of **t.** that can extend to the infinite,
T-13 IV.8:1 hand, regards the function of **t.** as one of
T-13 IV.8:1 the ego interprets the goal of **t.** as its own.
T-13 IV.8:2 is the only purpose the ego perceives in **t.**,
T-13 IV.8:3 Its continuity, then, would keep you in **t.**,
T-13 IV.9:1 the function of **t.** as you interpret yours. If
T-13 IV.9:2 in the world of **t.** as one of healing, you
T-13 IV.9:2 the aspect of **t.** in which healing can occur
T-13 IV.9:7 And **t.** will be as you interpret it, for of
T-13 VI.4:1 **T.** can release as well as imprison,
T-13 VI.6:4 to all aspects of the Sonship at the same **t.**
T-13 VI.6:5 The present is before **t.** was, and will be
T-13 VI.6:5 time was, and will be when **t.** is no more.
T-13 VI.7:5 still dimension of **t.** that does not change,
T-13 VI.8:1 Now is the **t.** of salvation, for now is the
T-13 VI.8:1 of salvation, for now is the release from **t.**.
T-13 VII.3:1 for it has disappointed you since **t.** began.
T-13 VII.3:3 has withstood the crumbling assault of **t.**.
T-13 VII.8:5 For all else you have lent yourself in **t.**,
T-13 VII.9:7 Love waits on welcome, not on **t.**, and the
T-13 VII.12:4 In **t.**, He gives you all the things that you
T-13 VII.12:7 not use them on behalf of lingering in **t.**.
T-13 VII.16:6 is the only real need to be fulfilled in **t.**.
T-13 VII.17:5 Healing in **t.** is needed, for joy cannot
T-13 VIII.4:4 His message speaks of timelessness in **t.**,
T-13 VIII.5:4 end of **t.** by bringing healed and healing
T-13 VIII.8:3 And suddenly **t.** will be over, and we will
T-14 IV.1:7 The first in **t.** means nothing, but the First
T-14 IX.1:7 it? The making of **t.** to take the place of
T-14 IX.2:7 cannot change with **t.** or mood or chance.
T-14 X.1:2 in **t.** but bring eternity nearer or farther.
T-14 X.1:3 But eternity itself is beyond all **t.**. Reach
T-14 X.1:4 Reach out of **t.** and touch it, with the help
T-14 X.1:5 And you will turn from **t.** to holiness, as
T-14 XI.9:10 He does not see **t.** as you do. And each
T-14 XI.9:11 He offers you corrects your use of **t.**, and
T-15 I.h The Two Uses of **T.**
T-15 I.1:1 to be perfectly calm and quiet all the **t.**?
T-15 I.1:2 Yet that is what **t.** is for; to learn just that
T-15 I.1:5 no longer need a teacher or **t.** in which to
T-15 I.2:1 may suffer is your belief that this takes **t.**,
T-15 I.2:3 For the Holy Spirit uses **t.** in His Own way
T-15 I.2:4 it. **T.** is His friend in teaching. It does not
T-15 I.2:6 all the waste that **t.** seems to bring with it
T-15 I.2:6 uses **t.** to support its belief in destruction.
T-15 I.2:7 uses **t.** to convince you of the inevitability
T-15 I.3:1 The ego is an ally of **t.**, but not a friend.
T-15 I.4:16 it is this the ego's version of **t.** supports.
T-15 I.5:4 The only **t.** the ego allows anyone to look
T-15 I.6:1 bleak and despairing is the ego's use of **t.**!
T-15 I.7:6 is no escape from fear in the ego's use of **t.**
T-15 I.7:7 time. For **t.**, according to its teaching, is
T-15 I.9:1 This lesson takes no **t.**. For what is time
T-15 I.9:2 For what is **t.** without a past and future? It
T-15 I.9:3 taken **t.** to misguide you so completely,
T-15 I.9:3 but it takes no **t.** at all to be what you are.
T-15 I.9:4 the Holy Spirit's use of **t.** as a teaching aid
T-15 I.9:5 now, and think of it as all there is of **t.**.
T-15 I.9:7 again you will go forth in **t.** without fear,
T-15 I.9:7 fear, and with no sense of change with **t.**.
T-15 I.10:1 **T.** is inconceivable without change, yet
T-15 I.11:2 not give so short a **t.** to the Holy Spirit for
T-15 I.12:5 offer **t.** to the Holy Spirit for His use of it.
T-15 I.13:3 of freedom to all who are enslaved by **t.**,
T-15 I.13:3 and thus make **t.** their friend for them.
T-15 I.15:1 **T.** is your friend, if you leave it to the
T-15 I.15:3 transcends **t.** for you understands what
T-15 I.15:3 time for you understands what **t.** is for.
T-15 I.15:4 for. Holiness lies not in **t.**, but in eternity.
T-15 I.15:6 His changeless state is beyond **t.**, for his
T-15 I.15:7 **T.** stands still in his holiness, and changes
T-15 I.15:8 And so it is no longer **t.** at all. For caught
T-15 II.1:1 The Atonement is *in* **t.**, but not *for* time.
T-15 II.1:1 The Atonement is *in* time, but not *for* **t.**.
T-15 II.1:3 of God cannot be bound by **t.**. No more
T-15 II.1:8 What can take **t.**, when all the obstacles
T-15 II.1:9 far beyond **t.** that all of it happens at once
T-15 II.1:10 one, so its oneness depends not on **t.** at all
T-15 II.2:1 Do not be concerned with **t.**, and fear not
T-15 II.2:3 has appointed to translate **t.** into eternity.
T-15 II.2:5 His joy is not contained in **t.**. His teaching
T-15 II.3:4 instant reaches out to encompass **t.**, as
T-15 III.2:1 you do not realize, each **t.** you choose, is
T-15 III.3:1 one you must learn to remember all the **t.**
T-15 III.5:2 Holy Spirit every **t.** you make a decision.
T-15 IV.1:1 you believe that what God wills takes **t.**.
T-15 IV.4:4 You can claim the holy instant any **t.** and
T-15 IV.5:2 learn to accept me is the measure of the **t.**
T-15 IV.5:3 depends on willingness, and not on **t.**.
T-15 IV.6:5 holy instant is a **t.** in which you receive
T-15 IV.6:6 that it is a **t.** in which your mind is open,
T-15 V.10:7 In **t.**, you have been told to offer miracles
T-15 VI.6:4 swiftly as the veil of **t.** is pushed aside. No
T-15 VIII.1:1 holy instant has extended far beyond **t.**.
T-15 X.h The **T.** of Rebirth
T-15 X.1:1 It is in your power, in **t.**, to delay the
T-15 X.1:3 Neither **t.** nor season means anything in
T-15 X.1:10 The **t.** of Christ we celebrate together, for
T-15 X.2:1 The holy instant is truly the **t.** of Christ.
T-15 X.3:6 The **t.** of Christ is the time appointed for
T-15 X.3:6 is the **t.** appointed for the gift of freedom,
T-15 X.4:1 power to make the **t.** of Christ be now. It
T-15 XI.2:2 it as the sign the **t.** of Christ has come. He
T-15 XI.2:9 Host Who cradles God in the **t.** of Christ,
T-15 XI.8:1 **t.** of Christ is meaningless apart from joy.
T-15 XI.8:4 Such is the message of the **t.** of Christ,
T-15 XI.8:5 the **t.** of Christ communication is restored
T-15 XI.10:1 **t.** in which a new year will soon be born
T-15 XI.10:1 will soon be born from the **t.** of Christ.
T-16 II.9:3 **t.** you brought these facts together and
T-16 III.1:1 everyone teaches, and teaches all the **t.**.
T-16 IV.13:3 you. Only in **t.** does interference in God's
T-16 IV.13:4 you across lifts you from **t.** into eternity.
T-16 IV.13:5 Waken from **t.**, and answer fearlessly the
T-16 V.17:1 This year is thus the **t.** to make the easiest
T-16 VI.6:2 For a **t.** the body is still seen, but not
T-16 VI.8:2 **T.** is kind, and if you use it on behalf of
T-16 VI.8:5 is far shorter than the **t.** it took to fix your
T-16 VII.7:1 **t.** you may attempt to bring illusions into
T-16 VII.7:5 illusions of **t.** will not prevent the timeless
T-16 VII.9:7 the holy instant this is done for you in **t.**,
T-17 II.2:6 notice, is a stride through **t.** into eternity,
T-17 II.4:4 you will barely have **t.** to thank God for it.
T-17 III.4:1 **T.** is indeed unkind to the unholy
T-17 III.4:2 For **t.** *is* cruel in the ego's hands, as it is
T-17 IV.11:5 picture of timelessness, set in a frame of **t.**
T-17 IV.11:8 borrowed from eternity and set in **t.** for
T-17 IV.14:1 framed, for **t.** cannot contain eternity.
T-17 V.3:1 Holy Spirit wastes no **t.** in introducing the
T-17 V.5:1 ego given **t.** to reinterpret each slow step
T-17 V.6:1 This is the **t.** for *faith.* You let this goal be
T-17 V.6:6 brother in what but seems to be a trying **t.**
T-17 V.12:1 forgotten if you allow **t.** to close over it. It
T-17 V.12:2 and gracious in your awareness of **t.**, but
T-17 V.13:4 You reinforce this every **t.** you attack your
T-18 I.4:4 brought truth to illusion, infinity to **t.**,
T-18 II.3:7 a **t.** it seems as if the world were given you
T-18 II.5:12 All your **t.** is spent in dreaming. Your
T-18 III.7:5 Let not **t.** worry you, for all the fear that
T-18 III.7:6 past. **T.** has been readjusted to help us do,
T-18 V.7:1 Whoever is saner at the **t.** the threat is
T-18 VI.12:2 **T.** is not relevant; it can occur with
T-18 VI.13:6 the lifting of the barriers of **t.** and space,
T-18 VII.3:4 real. **T.** controls it entirely, for sin is never
T-18 VII.4:5 to teach more than they learned in **t.**, but
T-18 VII.4:5 in time, but it does aim at saving **t.**. You
T-18 VII.4:11 means are tedious and very **t.** consuming,
T-18 VII.5:2 A holy relationship is a means of saving **t.**
T-18 VII.6:1 one day find in his own way, at his own **t.**.
T-18 VII.6:2 You do not need this **t.**. Time has been
T-18 VII.6:3 **T.** has been saved for you because you
T-18 VII.6:4 means this course is using to save you **t.**.
T-18 VII.6:6 for *you.* Save **t.** for me by only this one
T-18 VII.7:3 centuries of effort, and escape from **t.**.
T-18 VII.7:5 For here is **t.** denied, and past and future
T-18 VII.7:6 Who needs do nothing has no need for **t.**.
T-18 IX.12:5 never was a **t.** in which you knew it not.
T-19 I.16:1 to interfere with it and make it slave to **t.**.
T-19 III.5:1 In **t.**, the Holy Spirit clearly sees the Son
T-19 III.5:3 of the difference between **t.** and eternity.
T-19 III.5:4 when correction is completed, **t.** *is* eternity
T-19 III.5:5 to look on **t.** differently and see beyond it,
T19 IV.C.10:6 born in **t.** but nourished in eternity.
T19 IV.D.17:4 It is almost Easter, the **t.** of resurrection.
T-20 I.4:6 The **t.** of Easter is a time of joy, and not of
T-20 I.4:6 The time of Easter is a **t.** of joy, and not of
T-20 I.4:8 For Easter is the **t.** of your salvation, along
T-20 II.6:6 toy you would pick up from **t.** to time and
T-20 II.6:6 toy you would pick up from time to **t.** and
T-20 II.8:5 home has called to you since **t.** began, nor
T-20 IV.8:1 can be at peace when, while you are in **t.**,
T-20 V.1:4 Only in **t.** can anything be lost, and never
T-20 V.1:5 the parts of God's Son gradually join in **t.**,
T-20 V.1:5 with each joining is the end of **t.** brought
T-20 V.2:2 Each speaks in **t.** of what is far beyond it.
T-20 V.5:8 through **t.** like golden light is all the same;
T-20 V.6:1 each holy instant as a different point in **t.**.
T-20 VI.8:7 In that unholy instant **t.** was born, and

T-20...... VI.8:8 that held together for a little while in t.,
T-20.... VI.11:2 it prisoner in a tiny spot of space and t.,
T-20.... VI.12:3 but one. This is no t. for sadness. Perhaps
T-20..... VII.5:2 The unholy instant *is* the t. of bodies. But
T-21...... IV.5:1 recognized him perfectly since t. began.
T-21....... V.5:3 of God wait upon t. to be accomplished.
T-21... VII.10:3 same as are the other three, except in t..
T-21... VII.13:1 form that shifts with t. and place, is an
T-21.... VIII.5:6 t. is powerless because of your desire for
T-22....... in.1:3 could never see it in the same place and t..
T-22....... I.10:3 For what is t. to what was always so?
T-22....... II.3:7 to joy, for t. gives way to the eternal. Only
T-22....... II.3:8 but everything in t. can change with time.
T-22....... II.3:8 but everything in time can change with t..
T-22....... II.8:7 choice. For t. you made, and time you can
T-22....... II.8:7 time you made, and t. you can command.
T-22....... II.8:8 are no more a slave to t. than to the world
T-22..... II.12:2 How still it rests, in t. and yet beyond,
T-22..... II.12:4 T. waits upon its will, and earth will be as
T-22...... VI.6:8 No trace of anything in t. can long remain
T-23....... in.5:3 not let t. intrude upon your sight of him.
T-24...... VI.4:3 by the world, by t. and all appearances,
T-24...... VI.6:3 no sight nor place nor t. where He is not.
T-24...... VI.7:2 and through t. that seems to have no end,
T-24.... VI.12:1 with little effort and with little t., and
T-24..... VII.4:2 The body, yes, a little; not from t., but
T-24..... VII.6:7 state of true creation, found not within t.,
T-24..... VII.7:3 from; not born of size nor place nor t.,
T-25......... I.7:1 of t. and place as if they were discrete, for
T-25....... II.2:2 respect, at any t. or place, has anything
T-25...... III.6:3 him out of darkness into light at any t..
T-25...... III.6:4 The t. he chooses can be any time, for
T-25...... III.6:4 The time he chooses can be any t., for
T-25...... III.9:8 instant when all t. becomes a means to
T-25...... IV.5:7 other place; no other state nor t.. Nothing
T-25....... V.2:9 you, each t. you look upon your brother.
T-25...... VI.5:3 is the only function meaningful in t.. It is
T-25...... VI.5:7 it. Then is t. no more. Yet while in time,
T-25...... VI.5:8 Yet while in t., there is still much to do.
T-25.... VI.5:10 He *has* a special part in t. for so he chose,
T-25...... VI.7:7 and will remain in t. and in eternity alike.
T-25..... VII.7:3 the special t. and place in which you think
T-25..... VII.7:3 and where you can be free of place and t.,
T-25..... VII.7:4 Son of God cannot be bound by t. nor
T-26......... I.6:6 die each t. you see in him a sin deserving
T-26......... I.7:7 Born again each instant, untouched by t.,
T-26....... II.1:7 all t. and will not rise again in any form.
T-26....... II.3:4 regard to size, complexity, or place and t.,
T-26....... II.5:7 Each t. you keep a problem for yourself to
T-26...... III.2:2 and when you reach it is apart from t..
T-26...... III.3:6 place and t. and choice have meaning still
T-26....... V.1:9 while t. remains and choice is meaningful
T-26....... V.2:1 Nothing is ever lost but t., which in the
T-26....... V.3:3 T. lasted but an instant in your mind,
T-26....... V.3:4 so is all t. past, and everything exactly as
T-26....... V.3:5 of t. in which the first mistake was made,
T-26....... V.3:6 And in that tiny instant t. was gone, for
T-26....... V.4:1 you live in t. and know not it is gone, the
T-26....... V.4:1 and senseless maze you still perceive in t.,
T-26....... V.5:4 very long ago, for such a tiny interval of t.
T-26....... V.5:5 back, as if it could be made again in t..
T-26....... V.6:1 Forgiveness is the great release from t.. It
T-26....... V.6:6 a place and t. that have long since gone by
T-26....... V.6:9 imagine he is elsewhere, and in another t.
T-26....... V.7:3 much can his own illusions about t. and
T-26....... V.9:1 Forget the t. of terror that has been so
T-26..... V.10:1 a road long since a memory of t. gone by?
T-26..... V.12:1 not change the laws of t. nor of eternity.
T-26..... V.12:3 of the hallucination t. and death are real,
T-26..... V.12:4 terrible illusion was denied in but the t. it
T-26..... V.12:4 illusion for all t. and every circumstance.
T-26..... V.13:1 when the t. of terror took the place of love
T-26..... V.13:4 all of t. is but the mad belief that what is
T-26..... VII.4:3 answer is eternal, though it works in t.,
T-26..... VII.4:4 the laws of t. do not affect its workings. It
T-26..... VII.8:8 They limit you to t. and place, and give a
T-26.... VIII.1:1 interval between the t. when you forgive,
T-26.... VIII.1:3 For t. and space are one illusion, which
T-26.... VIII.1:4 beyond your mind you think of it as t..
T-26 ... VIII.2:1 and this space you perceive as t. because
T-26 ... VIII.3:2 the risk of loss is great between the t. its
T-26 ... VIII.3:6 Do not project this fear to t., for time is
T-26 ... VIII.3:6 for t. is not the enemy that you perceive.
T-26 ... VIII.3:7 T. is as neutral as the body is, except in
T-26 ... VIII.3:8 you then would want a little t. in which
T-26 ... VIII.3:9 but makes the interval between the t. in
T-26 ... VIII.4:1 *now,* and cannot be perceived in future t..
T-26 ... VIII.5:9 only interval of t. that sin and fear have
T-26 ... VIII.5:9 overlooked, but which is all there is to t..
T-26 ... VIII.6:1 out of all correction takes no t. at all. Yet
T-26 ... VIII.6:5 unfold in t. and fear they may not come,
T-26 ... VIII.7:8 until the t. of liberation is at hand. Given
T-26 ... VIII.8:3 This interval in t., when retribution is
T-26 ... VIII.9:6 cause must be delayed until a future t., is
T-26 ... VIII.9:7 one. Look not to t., but to the little space
T-26 ... VIII.9:8 And do not let it be disguised as t., and so
T-27 ..... III.3:8 the t. devoted to its seeing be perceived as
T-27 ..... III.3:8 be perceived as idly spent, a t. unoccupied
T-27 ..... III.4:1 unused interval of t. not seen as spent and
T-27 ..... III.5:6 until the t. when aids are meaningless and
T-27 ..... IV.2:1 Thus it must be that t. is not involved
T-27 .... V.2:14 is sufficient. Miracles wait not on t..
T-27 .... VII.8:5 as is the weather or the t. of day. It loves
T-27 .... VII.9:3 you the one decider of your destiny in t..
T-27 .. VII.12:4 of fear, the t. of terror and of ancient hate,
T-27 ... VIII.1:4 In the brief t. allotted it to live, it seeks for
T-27 ... VIII.3:1 from the t. of birth to dying are the theme
T-27 ... VIII.5:5 was a t. when he knew nothing of a body,
T-27 ... VIII.6:4 that t. cannot intrude upon eternity. It is
T-27 ... VIII.6:5 that t. can come to circumvent eternity,
T-27 ... VIII.6:5 eternity, which *means* there is no t..
T-27 ... VIII.7:1 A timelessness in which is t. made real; a
T-28 ........ I.4:7 part of t. where guilt appears to linger still
T-28 ........ I.5:1 use of memory is quite apart from t.. He
T-28 ........ I.5:9 their effects appear to be increased by t.,
T-28 ........ I.6:1 Yet t. is but another phase of what does
T-28 ........ I.6:3 T. neither takes away nor can restore.
T-28 ........ I.8:3 because there never was a t. in which He
T-28 ........ I.9:4 untouched by t. and interference. Never
T-28 ....... I.10:3 There was no t. in which His Son could be
T-28 ....... I.11:2 It reaches gently from that quiet t., and
T-28 ....... I.11:4 there can be no pause in t. to cause the
T-28 ....... I.12:1 He to Whom t. is given offers thanks for
T-28 ..... III.9:7 enter not, for t. waits not upon this feast,
T-28 ..... V.6:5 left no room for them in any place or t..
T-28 ..... V.6:6 For it fills every place and every t., and
T-28 ..... VI.6:7 God reminds him of it every t. he does
T-29 ........ I.1:1 There is no t., no place, no state where
T-29 ........ I.4:6 you and he agree to meet from t. to time,
T-29 ........ I.4:6 you and he agree to meet from time to t.,
T-29 ........ I.4:7 to you the t. in which to build again your
T-29 ....... II.7:7 The body can appear to change with t.,
T-29 ...... V.1:2 There is a place in you which t. has left,
T-29 ......... VI.h Forgiveness and the End of T.
T-29 ..... VI.2:9 all things that change with t. and bloom
T-29 ... VI.2:10 Where t. has set an end is not where the
T-29 ... VI.2:12 as he is, for t. appointed not his destiny,
T-29 ... VI.2:14 t. waits upon forgiveness that the things
T-29 ... VI.2:14 things of t. may disappear because they
T-29 ..... VI.4:4 All other goals are set in t. and change
T-29 ..... VI.4:4 and change that t. might be preserved,
T-29 ..... VI.4:5 Forgiveness does not aim at keeping t.,
T-29 ..... VI.4:8 T. can set no end to its fulfillment nor its
T-29 ..... VI.6:4 comes quietly to take the place of t..
T-29 .... VII.1:2 fail, and you will weep each t. an idol falls.
T-29 .... VII.9:3 Save t., my brother; learn what time is for
T-29 .... VII.9:3 Save time, my brother; learn what t. is for
T-29 ... VIII.6:2 the infinite, a t. transcending the eternal.
T-29 ... VIII.6:3 power and place and t. are given form,
T-29 ... VIII.6:4 the timeless to be made the slaves of t..
T-29 ... VIII.7:3 a place where t. can interrupt eternity? A
T-29 ..... IX.6:1 a t. when childhood should be passed and
T-29 ..... IX.7:7 can enter here, for t. is almost over. And
T-29 ..... IX.8:4 has not heard it since before all t. began.
T-29 ..... IX.8:7 it not. And where is t., when dreams of
T-30 ...... in.1:4 will help a little, every t. it is attempted.
T-30 ........ I.1:5 set, adopted consciously each t. you wake,
T-30 ........ I.4:1 at any t. you think of it and have a quiet
T-30 ..... III.6:4 a t. in which His Thoughts were absent or
T-30 ..... III.7:7 as it was before the t. when you forgot,
T-30 ..... III.8:7 was no t. it was not there; no instant
T-30 ..... III.9:4 the t. that keeps this star invisible to earth
T-30 ..... V.10:3 *never was a t. an idol brought you anything*
T-30 .... VII.1:6 which is different every t. you think of it.
T-31 ........ I.6:6 day, since t. began and learning had been
T-31 ....... II.1:3 must be prepared; no t. to be expended,
T-31 ....... II.2:6 each t. you think you must decide on
T-31 ..... III.1:4 by a span of t. you cannot realize. You
T-31 ..... IV.1:5 a little t. is given you to use for you alone;
T-31 ..... IV.1:5 a t. when everyone conflicts with you, but
T-31 ..... IV.3:3 t. must come when everyone begins to see
T-31 ..... IV.3:6 And yet this was the t. they could have
T-31 ..... IV.4:7 understand you but waste t. unless you go
T-31 ....... V.1:7 And by the t. you reach "maturity" you
T-31 ..... V.16:3 be some confusion every t. there is a shift,
T-31 ..... V.17:2 come a t. when images have all gone by,
T-31 . VIII.12:2 in the abode You set for Him before t. was
W-in.......... 2:2 They do not require a great deal of t., and
W-pI ...... 4.3:1 and will be repeated from t. to time in
W-pI ...... 4.3:1 time to t. in somewhat different form.
W-pI ...... 7.2:1 ideas about t. are very difficult to change,
W-pI ...... 7.2:1 everything you believe is rooted in t., and
W-pI ...... 7.2:2 precisely why you need new ideas about t.
W-pI ...... 7.2:3 This first t. idea is not really so strange as
W-pI ...... 8.1:4 about t. from which your seeing suffers.
W-pI ...... 8.1:5 the present, which is the only t. there is. It
W-pI ...... 8.1:6 is. It therefore cannot understand t., and
W-pI .... 10.2:1 second t. we have used this kind of idea.
W-pI .... 10.2:3 This t. the idea is introduced with "My
W-pI .... 10.5:1 any thought that distresses you at any t..
W-pI .... 10.5:3 is not recommended that this t. period be
W-pI .... 12.2:2 Look around you, this t. quite slowly. Try
W-pI .... 12.2:3 involves a fairly constant t. interval. Do
W-pI .... 12.2:4 Do not allow the t. of the shift to become
W-pI .... 12.2:6 rests on equal attention and equal t.. This
W-pI .... 12.4:1 sure that you do not alter the t. intervals
W-pI .... 13.4:1 more than a minute or so at most each t.,
W-pI .... 15.4:6 should be repeated quite slowly each t..
W-pI .... 19.3:2 for the thoughts it contains at that t.. As
W-pI .... 19.5:1 shortening the length of t. involved, if
W-pI .... 20.1:2 virtually no attempt to direct the t. for
W-pI .... 21.1:2 This t., however, specific mind-searching
W-pI .... 22.3:1 times today, for at least a minute each t..
W-pI .... 23.7:3 and you are asked at this t. only to treat
W-pI .... 26.5:2 the t. may be reduced to a minute if the
W-pI .... 26.6:4 because a longer t. than usual should be
W-pI .... 27.1:5 the t. when the idea will be wholly true a
W-pI .... 27.3:4 you set a definite t. interval for using the
W-pI .... 27.3:5 or otherwise occupied at the t.. You can
W-pI .... 31.2:3 During that t., look about you slowly
W-pI .... 32.4:3 a t. when few distractions are anticipated,
W-pI .... 34.2:2 to be undertaken at any t. in between that
W-pI .... 35.9:1 t. and apply the idea for today to them,
W-pI .... 38.1:2 It is beyond every restriction of t., space,
W-pI .... 38.5:1 From t. to time you may want to vary this
W-pI .... 38.5:1 to t. you may want to vary this procedure,
W-pI .... 40.3:1 Today's exercises take little t. and no
W-pI .... 41.7:1 From t. to time, you may repeat the idea
W-pI .... 41.7:1 From time to t., you may repeat the idea
W-pI .... 41.8:5 results even the first t. it is attempted,
W-pI .... 42.2:2 you can receive it any t. and anywhere,
W-pI .... 42.2:3 through t. and space is not at random.
W-pI .... 42.2:4 but be in the right place at the right t..
W-pI .... 42.3:1 close as possible to the t. you go to sleep.
W-pI .... 42.3:2 by yourself, at a t. when you feel ready,
W-pI .... 42.3:2 it is to be concerned with the t. as such.
W-pI .... 43.4:2 the most convenient and suitable t. that
W-pI .... 43.4:4 Then glance around you for a short t.,
W-pI .... 43.9:1 presents itself to your awareness at the t.,
W-pI .... 43.9:2 to allow any long periods of t. to slip by
W-pI .... 44.4:2 A longer t. is highly recommended, but
W-pI .... 44.4:2 but only if you find the t. slipping by with
W-pI .... 44.6:2 helpful to remind yourself, from t. to time
W-pI .... 44.6:2 helpful to remind yourself, from time to t.
W-pI .. 44.11:1 or closed as seems better to you at the t..
W-pI .... 46.7:3 They will be needed at any t. during the
W-pI .... 48.2:3 eyes open at any t. and in any situation. It

W-pI.....50.1:1 today and tomorrow and throughout **t.**.
W-pI.....52.3:5 that I am trying to use **t.** against God. Let
W-pI.....62.3:1 while each **t.** you forgive you call upon the
W-pI.....62.4:3 who seem to be far away in space and **t.**,
W-pI.....64.4:4 every **t.** you choose whether or not to
W-pI.....65.3:4 searching you have done since **t.** began.
W-pI.....65.4:1 at approximately the same **t.** each day.
W-pI.....65.4:2 Try, also, to determine this **t.** in advance,
W-pI.....65.4:3 so that you have set apart the **t.** for God,
W-pI.....67.4:1 **t.** to time to replace distracting thoughts.
W-pI.....67.4:1 time to **t.** to replace distracting thoughts.
W-pI.....70.6:3 be a good **t.** to lay aside for each of them,
W-pI.....73.9:4 the **t.** appointed for the release of the Son
W-pI.....75.2:4 the **t.** of light begins for you and everyone
W-pI.....75.8:3 From this **t.** forth you will see differently.
W-pI.....75.8:5 that has been promised you since **t.** began
W-pI.....75.8:5 and in which is the end of **t.** ensured.
W-pI.....75.9:2 so that today is a **t.** for special celebration.
W-pI.....79.3:5 no **t.** in which you feel completely free of
W-pI.....79.5:5 and rise to haunt you from **t.** to time, only
W-pI.....79.5:5 and rise to haunt you from time to **t.**, only
W-pI.....79.9:1 periods for today will not be set by **t.**, but
WpI. rII.in.3:1 of the **t.** listening quietly but attentively.
W-pI.....90.3:2 problems only because I am misusing **t.**.
W-pI.....90.3:3 **t.** must elapse before it can be worked out
W-pI.....90.3:5 so that they cannot be separated by **t.**.
W-pI.....90.4:4 *it. T. cannot separate this problem from its*
W-pI.....91.5:1 for a quiet **t.** in which you try to leave
W-pI...92.11:2 will use the day in preparation for the **t.** at
W-pI.....95.5:1 have other advantages for you at this **t.**. In
W-pI.....95.5:2 to forget about it for long periods of **t.**.
W-pI.....95.6:1 is necessary for you at this **t.**, planned to
W-pI.....95.6:2 it. Regularity in terms of **t.** is not the ideal
W-pI...95.14:8 understand each **t.** you do so, someone
W-pI.....96.2:2 series of expenditures of **t.** and effort,
W-pI.....96.6:1 Waste no more **t.** on this. Who can
W-pI...96.11:5 Every **t.** you spend five minutes of the
W-pI...96.12:1 Each **t.** today you tell your frantic mind
W-pI.....97.3:2 Each **t.** you practice, awareness is brought
W-pI.....97.3:3 and over, for the miracle makes use of **t.**,
W-pI.....97.4:1 the miracle in which all **t.** stands still; the
W-pI.....97.4:1 a **t.** that has no limit and that has no end.
W-pI.....97.5:3 increase in healing power each **t.**
W-pI.....97.8:3 Self. Listen for His assurance every **t.** you
W-pI.....98.3:4 completely in the perfect **t.** and place.
W-pI.....98.5:1 worth five minutes of your **t.** each hour to
W-pI.....98.6:2 can exchange a little of your **t.** for peace of
W-pI.....98.6:3 And since **t.** has no meaning, you are
W-pI.....98.9:6 exchanging every instant of the **t.** you
W-pI...98.10:1 let your **t.** be spent in happy preparation
W-pI...98.10:2 wait for the glad **t.** to come to you again.
W-pI...98.10:3 often, and do not forget each **t.** you do so,
W-pI...98.10:3 mind be readied for the happy **t.** to come:
W-pI...98.11:1 once more to spend a little **t.** with you, be
W-pI...98.11:1 and spend a happy **t.** again with Him. Tell
W-pI.....99.5:2 apart from **t.** in that its Source is timeless.
W-pI.....99.5:3 Yet it operates in **t.**, because of your belief
W-pI.....99.5:3 time, because of your belief that **t.** is real.
W-pI.100.10:7 every **t.** you tell yourself you are essential
W-pI...104.2:3 the gifts that we inherited before **t.** was,
W-pI...104.2:3 be ours when **t.** has passed into eternity.
W-pI...105.9:1 thus with Him each **t.** you can today, but
W-pI...107.2:3 Try to remember when there was a **t.**, –
W-pI...107.2:4 extended to the end of **t.** and to eternity.
W-pI.107.11:2 Each **t.** you tell yourself with confidence,
W-pI.108.10:2 be far better understood from this **t.** on,
W-pI.108.10:3 still faster and more sure each **t.** you say,
W-pI...109.5:2 while **t.** goes by without its touch upon
W-pI...109.5:8 Take **t.** today to slip away from dreams
W-pI...109.6:2 The world is born again each **t.** you rest,
W-pI...109.7:2 And the **t.** when rest will be the only thing
W-pI...109.9:4 T. is not the guardian of what we give
W-pI...109.9:6 their resting place each **t.** we tell ourselves
W-pI...110.1:1 will repeat today's idea from **t.** to time.
W-pI...110.1:1 will repeat today's idea from time to **t.**.
W-pI...110.2:1 that any mind has made at any **t.** or place.
W-pI...110.2:4 is enough to let **t.** be the means for all the
W-pI...110.2:4 for all the world to learn escape from **t.**,
W-pI...110.2:4 every change that **t.** appears to bring in
WpI. rIII.in2:2 it is impossible at the appointed **t.**. Nor is
WpI. rIII.in3:1 the **t.** to it that you are asked to give. Do
WpIrIII.in10:5 your mind to rest a little **t.** in silence and
W-pI.122.12:2 been held in store for us since **t.** began,
W-pI...124.6:3 and apart from distance as apart from **t.**.
W-pI.124.10:3 thankfully aware no **t.** was ever better
W-pI...125.1:5 must hear to usher in the quiet **t.** of peace.
W-pI...125.4:2 of salvation and the holy **t.** of peace. We
W-pI...127.7:1 and in **t.** beyond the count of years to
W-pI...127.7:2 then, be glad to give some **t.** to God today
W-pI...127.7:2 there is no better use for **t.** than this.
W-pI...128.7:3 little, every **t.** you let your mind escape its
W-pI...129.2:1 It might be worth a little **t.** to think once
W-pI...129.2:6 This is the world of **t.**, where all things
W-pI...129.3:2 exactly as you want them throughout **t.**?
W-pI...131.6:3 T. is the great illusion it is past or in the
W-pI...131.6:7 as far removed from **t.** as is a tiny candle
W-pI...131.8:6 is present now, beyond the reach of **t.**.
W-pI...131.9:2 God make **t.** to take away the Will of God
W-pI.131.14:5 for we come to the appointed **t.** and place
W-pI.131.15:1 today should be a **t.** of special gladness,
W-pI.131.15:2 Salvation's **t.** has come. Today is set by
W-pI.131.15:3 be a **t.** of grace for you and for the world.
W-pI...132.3:1 The present now remains the only **t.**.
W-pI...132.9:3 and no **t.** that can bring change to your
W-pI...132.9:4 How can a world of **t.** and place exist, if
W-pI...133.4:3 until you had considered all of them in **t.**;
W-pI...133.6:3 T. can never take away a value that is real.
W-pI.134.14:1 that the **t.** of joining be no more delayed.
W-pI.134.15:3 thought of him, and each **t.** ask yourself,
W-pI.134.16:4 relief. The **t.** remaining should be given to
W-pI...135.5:4 say your home is open to the thief of **t.**,
W-pI.135.15:3 T. becomes a future emphasis, to be
W-pI.135.19:1 as this life becomes a holy instant, set in **t.**
W-pI.135.20:2 the ancient plan, begun when **t.** was born.
W-pI.135.21:1 that **t.** today with present confidence, for
W-pI.136.13:1 that demonstrates that **t.** is an illusion.
W-pI.136.13:2 For **t.** lets you think what God has given
W-pI.136.13:3 Thoughts of God are quite apart from **t.**.
W-pI.136.13:4 For **t.** is but another meaningless defense
W-pI.136.14:3 It is found at any **t.**; today, if you will
W-pI.136.18:3 guaranteed, because it is not limited by **t.**,
W-pI.137.11:2 Nor does **t.** elapse between the instant
W-pI.137.13:3 Is not a little **t.** a small expense to offer for
W-pI...138.3:2 the aim of effort and expenditure of **t.**.
W-pI...138.3:3 **t.** is but a waste and effort dissipated. It is
W-pI...138.3:4 in return, and **t.** goes by without results.
W-pI...138.7:1 choice that **t.** was made to help us make.
W-pI...138.9:3 judged again, this **t.** with Heaven's help.
W-pI.138.12:3 in a brief quiet **t.** devoted to maintaining
W-pI...139.7:3 again until the **t.** Atonement is accepted,
W-pI.140.11:4 and thus delay the **t.** when we can hear
WpI. rIV.in1:1 **t.** aware we are preparing for the second
WpI. rIV.in5:1 Begin each day with **t.** devoted to the
WpI. rIV.in7:3 you are using **t.** for its intended purpose.
WpI. rIV.in8:2 **t.** enough to see the gifts that they contain
WpI. rIV.in9:3 **t.** of blessing and of happiness for us; and
W-pI.151.13:1 the beginning of the **t.** we spend with God
W-pI.153.13:3 Now a quiet **t.** has come, in which we put
W-pI.153.15:5 hour is too short a **t.** to spend with God.
W-pI.153.18:1 In **t.**, with practice, you will never cease
W-pI.153.18:3 even though your **t.** is spent in offering
W-pI.153.19:5 We call upon His strength each **t.** we feel
W-pI.155.11:1 **t.** has closed the door on all the things
W-pI...157.1:2 a special **t.** of promise in your calendar of
W-pI...157.1:3 is a **t.** Heaven has set apart to shine upon,
W-pI...157.3:2 to alter **t.** sufficiently to rise above its laws
W-pI...157.7:1 becomes a little closer to the end of **t.**; a
W-pI...157.7:3 The **t.** will come when you will not return
W-pI...158.2:8 Son are one will come in **t.** to every mind.
W-pI...158.2:9 is that **t.** determined by the mind itself,
W-pI...158.3:1 The **t.** is set already. It appears to be
W-pI...158.3:5 it. For **t.** but seems to go in one direction.
W-pI...158.4:1 T. is a trick, a sleight of hand, a vast
W-pI...158.5:2 It revealed itself to him at its appointed **t.**.
W-pI.158.11:1 revelation comes, for that is not of **t.**. Yet
W-pI.158.11:2 Yet **t.** has still one gift to give, in which
W-pI...162.1:2 From **t.** to time we will repeat it, as we
W-pI...162.1:2 From time to **t.** we will repeat it, as we
W-pI...162.3:3 each **t.** he practices the words of truth.
W-pI...163.3:3 when the **t.** has come for its arrival. It will
W-pI...164.1:1 What **t.** but now can truth be recognized
W-pI...164.1:2 The present is the only **t.** there is. And so
W-pI...164.1:4 He looks past **t.**, and sees eternity as
W-pI...164.3:2 quiet is the **t.** you give to spend with Him,
W-pI.166.11:4 points to all the gifts you have each **t.** the
W-pI...167.4:3 it in kind as well as distance, **t.** and form.
W-pI...167.9:3 It dreams of **t.**; an interval in which what
W-pI...169.4:2 the mind determines when that **t.** will be,
W-pI...169.6:4 beyond salvation; past all thought of **t.**,
W-pI...169.7:2 which bear witness that the **t.** the mind
W-pI...169.8:2 He recognized all that **t.** holds, and gave it
W-pI...169.8:2 from a point where **t.** was ended, when it
W-pI...169.9:2 be here. Whatever **t.** the mind has set for
W-pI.169.10:3 for those in **t.** can speak of things beyond,
W-pI.169.12:3 that grace provides will end in **t.**, for
W-pI.169.12:3 the thought of **t.** but for a little while.
W-pI...170.8:2 the **t.** of your release from abject slavery.
W-pI.170.11:2 look for the last **t.** upon this bit of carven
W-pI.170.11:5 This **t.** you leave it there. And you return
WpI...rV.in1:2 This **t.** we are ready to give more effort
WpI...rV.in1:2 effort and more **t.** to what we undertake.
WpI...rV.in5:3 This review will shorten **t.** immeasurably,
WpI...rV.in7:1 My resurrection comes again each **t.**
WpI...rV.in7:2 I am renewed each **t.** a brother learns
WpI...rV.in7:3 pain. I am reborn each **t.** a brother's mind
WpI...rV.in8:3 we devote our **t.** and effort to them. And
WpI...rV.in8:8 before **t.** was and kept unchanged by time
WpI...rV.in8:8 before time was and kept unchanged by **t.**
WpI...rV.in8:8 safe, as it will be at last when **t.** is done.
WpI.rV.in10:1 Let this review become a **t.** in which we
WpI.rV.in10:1 for you, yet one as old as **t.** and older still.
WpI.rV.in10:7 that it is free of all illusions every **t.** we say
WpI.rV.in11:2 we start and end each period of practice **t.**
Wi181-200 1:2 asked for total dedication all the **t.** as yet.
W-pI...181.3:4 for us within this interval of **t.** wherein we
W-pI...181.5:7 in the **t.** of practicing with one intent; to
W-pI...182.2:2 in games they play to occupy their **t.**, and
W-pI...182.5:7 But give Him just a little **t.** to be Himself,
W-pI.182.10:1 each **t.** a wanderer would leave his home.
W-pI.182.10:3 Go home with Him from **t.** to time today.
W-pI.182.10:3 Go home with Him from time to **t.** today.
W-pI.182.11:1 Take **t.** today to lay aside your shield
W-pI...184.1:6 all happenings in terms of place and **t.**; all
W-pI...185.1:3 for you in any form; in any place or **t.**.
W-pI...187.4:4 will change and grow unrecognizable in **t.**
W-pI...190.4:2 **t.** has come to laugh at such insane ideas.
W-pI...190.8:4 love, and **t.** replace eternity and Heaven.
W-pI...191.8:1 the rites of death echoed since **t.** began.
W-pI...191.8:2 For **t.** has lost its hold upon the world.
W-pI...192.8:4 he spends his **t.** in keeping watch on him.
W-pI...192.9:4 Every **t.** you feel a stab of anger, realize
W-pI...193.9:4 none but waiting their appointed **t.** to fall
W-pI.193.10:4 T. was made for this. Use it today for
W-pI.193.10:6 devote what **t.** you can to serve its proper
W-pI.193.10:6 let the **t.** be less than meets your deepest
W-pI.193.12:1 Each hour, spend a little **t.** today, and in
W-pI.193.12:3 of **t.** are easily unloosened in this way. Let
W-pI.193.12:5 in peace eternal in the world of **t.**.
W-pI...194.3:4 is a **t.** of your release from sadness, pain
W-pI...194.4:4 the lack of sequence really found in **t.**.
W-pI...194.5:2 becomes the instant in which **t.** escapes
W-pI...194.5:3 slave to **t.** transformed into a holy instant,
W-pI.195.10:1 shorten our learning **t.** by more than you
W-pI...196.4:3 one. It is not **t.** we need for this. It is but
W-pI.196.11:1 for you until the **t.** when it can kill at last.
W-pI.196.11:2 is the **t.** as well in which salvation comes.
W-pI.198.13:4 Now is the **t.** for your deliverance. The
W-pI.198.13:5 The **t.** has come. The time has come today
W-pI.198.13:6 time has come. The **t.** has come today.
W-pI...199.2:1 all ways, beyond the laws of **t.** and space,
W-pI...199.8:6 His Love and happiness each **t.** you say: *I*
W-pI...200.9:3 and needless wasted **t.** on thorny byways.
W-pI.200.11:8 and draw still nearer every **t.** we say:
WpI rVI.in.1:2 the **t.** you give morning and evening,
WpI rVI.in.3:7 And we repeat it every **t.** the hour strikes,
WpI rVI.in.4:2 we attempt, this **t.**, to reach a quickened
WpI rVI.in.7:2 say and think, each **t.** you turn to Him. He

Wpl rVI.in.7:3 to you, each **t.** you call to Him to help you
W-pI...204.1:2 *reminds me that I am His Son, not slave to* **t.***,*
W-pII ....in.2:6 spending **t.** with Him each morning and
W-pII ....in.2:7 not consider **t.** a matter of duration now.
W-pII ....in.5:1 Now is the **t.** of prophecy fulfilled. Now
W-pII ....in.5:3 No step remains for **t.** to separate from its
W-pII ....in.8:5 has called to us unceasingly since **t.** began
W-pII ..in.11:2 From **t.** to time, instructions on a theme
W-pII ..in.11:2 From time to **t.**, instructions on a theme
W-pII .230.2:2 *here now, for my creation was apart from* **t.***,*
W-pII .....2.1:3 It guarantees that **t.** will have an end, and
W-pII .....2.1:3 that have been born in **t.** will end as well.
W-pII .....2.5:2 freedom is returned, that **t.** is almost over
W-pII .232.1:2 *every minute be a* **t.** *in which I dwell with You*
W-pII .233.1:4 *obtained, and wasting* **t.** *in vain imaginings.*
W-pII .234.1:1 Today we will anticipate the **t.** when
W-pII .241.1:2 It is a **t.** of special celebration. For today
W-pII .241.1:6 is the **t.** of hope for countless millions.
W-pII .264.1:3 *In You* **t.** *disappears, and place becomes a*
W-pII .270.1:4 *instant more of* **t.** *which ends forever, as*
W-pII .....6.5:1 symbol that the **t.** for learning now is over
W-pII .....6.5:3 no need of learning or perception or of **t.**,
W-pII .275.1:2 day been chosen as the **t.** when we will
W-pII .277.1:5 *He is not slave to any laws of* **t.***. He is as You*
W-pII .279.1:2 there a **t.** when he appears to be in prison,
W-pII .286.1:3 *that has been chosen as the* **t.** *in which I come*
W-pII .....8.4:3 The real world signifies the end of **t.**, for
W-pII .....8.4:3 for its perception makes **t.** purposeless.
W-pII .....8.5:1 need of **t.** when it has served His purpose.
W-pII .....8.5:2 take His final step, and **t.** has disappeared
W-pII .....9.3:2 The Second Coming is the **t.** in which all
W-pII .....9.4:1 event in **t.** which time itself can not affect.
W-pII .....9.4:1 event in time which **t.** itself can not affect.
W-pII ....308.h This instant is the only **t.** there is.
W-pII .308.1:1 of **t.** in such a way that I defeat my aim. If
W-pII .308.1:2 If I elect to reach past **t.** to timelessness, I
W-pII .308.1:2 change my perception of what **t.** is for.
W-pII .308.1:4 in which I can be saved from **t.** is now. For
W-pII .308.2:3 *instant is the* **t.** *You have appointed for Your*
W-pII .310.1:2 *And what I will experience is not of* **t.** *at all.*
W-pII .316.1:3 a brother has received throughout all **t.**,
W-pII .316.1:3 throughout all time, and past all **t.** as well
W-pII .317.1:3 I am the slave of **t.** and human destiny.
W-pII ...11.1:3 no **t.** when all that it created was not there
W-pII ...11.1:4 Nor will there be a **t.** when anything that
W-pII ...11.1:5 unchanged through **t.** and after time is
W-pII ...11.1:5 unchanged through time and after **t.** is
W-pII ...11.2:4 One will still be One when **t.** is over; and
W-pII ...11.2:4 be changed throughout the course of **t.**,
W-pII ...11.2:4 as it was before the thought of **t.** began.
W-pII .346.1:2 *share eternity, for* **t.** *has stepped aside today*
W-pII .346.1:3 *I do not seek the things of* **t.***, and so I will not*
W-pII .346.1:4 *all laws of* **t.** *and things perceived in time.*
W-pII .346.1:4 *all laws of time and things perceived in* **t.***. I*
W-pII .354.1:1 *me as Your Son, beyond the reach of* **t.***, and*
Wfl ........in.2:3 In the dream of **t.** it seems to be far off.
Wfl ........in.6:5 all that there will be throughout all **t.** and
W-ep .........5:3 for you each **t.** there is a choice to make.
W-ep .........5:5 And so we walk with Him from this **t.** on,
M-in ..........1:4 a relatively small proportion of one's **t.**.
M-in ..........2:2 believe one or the other is true all the **t.**.
M-1 ...........2:5 It goes on all the **t.** everywhere. It calls for
M-1 ...........2:8 Yet it is all a matter of **t.**. Everyone will
M-1 .........2:11 Their function is to save **t.**. Each one
M-1 .........2:13 thousand years of **t.** as the world judges it
M-1 .........2:14 it. To the Call Itself **t.** has no meaning.
M-1 ...........3:6 no language; in any place or **t.** or manner.
M-1 ...........4:3 They merely save **t.**. Yet it is time alone
M-1 ...........4:4 Yet it is **t.** alone that winds on wearily,
M-1 ...........4:7 But **t.**, with its illusions of change and
M-1 ...........4:8 Yet **t.** has an ending, and it is this that the
M-1 ...........4:9 For **t.** is in their hands. Such was their
M-2 ...........1:4 Again, it is only a matter of **t.**. Once he
M-2 ...........1:6 **T.** waits on his choice, but not on whom
M-2 ...........2:1 the concept of **t.** that the course sets forth
M-2 ...........2:4 the Will of God is entirely apart from **t.**.
M-2 ...........2:7 In **t.** this happened very long ago. In
M-2 ...........3:1 The world of **t.** is the world of illusion.
M-2 ...........3:5 already happened at any **t.** you choose,
M-2 ...........4:1 **T.** really, then, goes backward to an
M-2 ...........4:4 The pupil comes at the right **t.** to the right
M-2 ...........4:7 but seems to take **t.** in the working-out.
M-3 ...........3:1 a concept as meaningless in reality as is **t.**.
M-3 ...........3:3 In **t.**, the teacher of God seems to begin to
M-3 ...........3:4 We have covered the illusion of **t.** already,
M-3 ...........4:1 he can from the other person at that **t.**. In
M-3 ...........4:3 sustained relationship, in which, for a **t.**,
M-3 ...........4:5 each has learned the most he can at the **t.**.
M-3 ...........5:5 be quite hostile to each other for some **t.**,
M-4 ...........1:5 set in **t.** as a means of leading out of time.
M-4 ...........1:5 set in time as a means of leading out of **t.**.
M-4 ...........2:2 in **t.** it can be said that the advanced
M-4 ..... I.A.6:2 This is a quiet **t.**, in which the teacher of
M-4 ..... I.A.7:7 impossible to reach for a long, long **t.**. He
M-4 ....VIII.1:3 at a **t.** perhaps unknown to him as yet,
M-4 ....VIII.1:4 The **t.** will be as right as is the answer.
M-4 ....VIII.1:7 Perhaps it was not understood at the **t.**.
M-4 ..VIII.1:10 ultimate interpretation of all things in **t.**,
M-4 ...... IX.1:5 remaining carefully limited for a **t.**. To
M-6 ...........2:4 And what is **t.** before the gifts of God? We
M-8 ...........6:7 from size and shape and **t.** and place–for
M-10 .........1:6 **t.** and "bad" judgment at another time.
M-10 .........1:6 time and "bad" judgment at another **t.**.
M-10 .........1:8 **t.** the student may disagree with what his
M-10 .........6:6 of passing **t.** and growing hopelessness; of
M-11 .........2:2 **t.** ask yourself whether your judgment or
M-13 .........5:7 places, each **t.** believing it is there, and
M-13 .........5:7 there, and each **t.** disappointed in the end
M-14 .........3:3 But **t.** stands still, and waits on the goal of
M-15 .......1:10 **T.** pauses as eternity comes near, and
M-15 .........2:7 One instant out of **t.** can bring time's end.
M-16 .........2:8 obvious advantages in terms of saving **t.**.
M-16 .........3:1 beginning, it is wise to think in terms of **t.**
M-16 .........3:3 of **t.** is an essential early emphasis which,
M-16 .........3:4 safely say that **t.** devoted to starting the
M-16 .........3:4 starting the day right does indeed save **t.**.
M-16 .........3:5 How much **t.** should be so spent? This
M-16 .........4:3 to spend **t.** with God as soon as possible,
M-16 .........4:7 as possible after waking take your quiet **t.**,
M-16 .........4:9 and drop away. If not, that is the **t.** to stop
M-16 .........5:2 your quiet **t.** should be fairly early in the
M-16 .........5:6 to sleep is a desirable **t.** to devote to God.
M-16 .........5:8 If it is expedient to spend this **t.** earlier, at
M-16 .........7:1 How simply and how easily does **t.** slip
M-16 .........8:2 particularly during the **t.** when his mind
M-16 .........8:4 not of him, but will be given him at any **t.**,
M-19 .........2:7 the pathway ceases and **t.** ends with it.
M-22 .........2:1 a **t.** excludes some problem areas from it.
M-23 .........7:4 a very present help in **t.** of trouble; a
M-24 .........4:5 teach that theoretical issues but waste **t.**,
M-24 .........6:7 There is no other **t.**. No teaching that
M-26 .........2:8 The **t.** will come when this is understood.
M-26 .........3:3 be maintained for much of the **t.** on earth.
M-28 .........4:1 the **t.** of everlasting things is now at hand.
M-29 .........1:4 must be remembered that only **t.** divides
M-29 .........7:8 for waiting implies **t.** and He is timeless.
M-29 .........8:4 *around the world, To close all things of* **t.***; to*
C-1 ...........5:4 Here **t.** and illusions end together.
C-3 ...........6:5 shift from place to place; from **t.** to time.
C-3 ...........6:5 shift from place to place; from time to **t.**.
C-4 ...........1:4 last in **t.** a little while longer than others.
C-4 ...........1:5 **t.** will come when all things visible will
C-4 ...........3:4 But for the **t.** it lasts it comes to heal. For
C-4 ...........4:5 with **t.** forever ended as the world spins
C-4 ...........5:8 For place has gone as well, along with **t.**.
C-5 ...........1:5 But they have names which differ for a **t.**,
C-5 ...........1:5 differ for a time, for **t.** needs symbols,
C-6 ...........5:6 And you will be with him when **t.** is over
C-ep...........2:5 within eternity and through all **t.** as well.
P-1............5:4 Psychotherapy can only save him **t.**. The
P-1............5:5 The Holy Spirit uses **t.** as He thinks best,
P-1............5:6 is one of the means He uses to save **t.**, and
P-2.........II.1:5 made perfect in **t.** and restored to eternity
P-2........IV.6:4 at the same **t.** making a new self-concept
P-2......... V.7:2 In **t.** no effort can be made in vain. It is
P-3..........II.6:5 But only little **t.** is saved. The new dreams
P-3..........II.7:5 remain on earth until the closing of **t.**.
P-3..........II.8:2 he reaches this in **t.** he can go towards it.
P-3..........II.9:1 can save enormous **t.** if it is properly used.
P-3........II.10:8 Except in **t.**. In time there can be a great
P-3........II.10:9 In **t.** there can be a great lag between the
P-3......II.10:11 because **t.** does not exist and the Will of
S-1.........in.1:7 be throughout eternity, when **t.** is done.
S-1.........in.1:8 For such it was before **t.** seemed to be.
S-1.........in.2:1 To you who are in **t.** a little while, prayer
S-1...........I.5:1 go, a quiet **t.** of listening and loving. It
S-1........ III.4:2 **t.** be followed by a deep retreat into fear.
S-1........ IV.4:1 a newborn chance each **t.** you pray. And
S-1..........V.4:3 the place appointed for the **t.** when you
S-1..........V.4:4 you. Here will **t.** end forever. At this gate
S-3..........II.3:3 form in which death comes when it is **t.** to
S-3..........II.6:4 before **t.** was and still but waits for him.
S-3........ IV.2:5 **T.** remains only to let the last embrace of
S-3........ IV.8:2 where **t.** and distance have no meaning.
S-3........ IV.9:1 Creation leans across the bars of **t.** to lift

## time's 8

T-2 .........II.6:9 but the whole Atonement stands at **t.** end
T-13 ..... IV.7:3 The Holy Spirit interprets **t.** purpose as
T-13 ..... VI.4:6 destroy **t.** continuity by breaking it into
T-26 ..... IX.4:2 When They come, **t.** purpose is fulfilled.
W-pII . 308.1:3 **T.** purpose cannot be to keep the past and
W-pII ... 13.1:5 Thus it stays within **t.** limits. Yet it paves
M-15 ......... 2:7 One instant out of time can bring **t.** end.
C-4 ............ 7:6 of Christ has shone away **t.** final instant,

## time-bound 1

S-1........ IV.4:5 What **t.** thing can give you more than this

## time-control 1

T-1 .........V.2:3 therefore, accepts the **t.** factor gladly. He

## time-dependent 1

T-2 .........V.9:5 of which you are capable now are **t.**.

## timeless 25

T-1 ........I.47:3 the usual laws of time. In this sense it is **t.**.
T-3 ..... III.2:10 Knowledge is **t.**, because certainty is not
T-3 ..... III.5:12 altar within and is **t.** because it is certain.
T-4 .........II.4:6 real creations, which are as **t.** as you are.
T-5 ..... III.11:2 time, and reinterpret it into the **t.**. He
T-7 ..........I.6:5 meaningful, and the temporary into the **t.**
T-7 ..........I.7:9 What is **t.** is always there, because its
T-10 .....V.14:9 If you will accept only what is **t.** as real,
T-13 ..... VI.6:7 continuity is **t.** and their communication
T-13 ..... VI.8:3 In **t.** union with them is your continuity,
T-15 .......II.6:3 single second, and to experience it as **t.**, is
T-16 .... VII.7:5 not prevent the **t.** from being what it is,
T-22 .......II.3:8 Only the **t.** must remain unchanged, but
T-22 ..... VI.6:8 long remain in a mind that serves the **t.**.
T-23 ......in.5:2 beyond it, measureless and **t.** as eternity.
T-24 .......V.9:4 you, and that this Oneness is endless, **t.**,
T-29 ... VIII.6:4 loss, the **t.** to be made the slaves of time.
W-pI .... 99.5:2 It is apart from time in that its Source is **t.**
W-pI .. 104.2:4 gifts that are within us now, for they are **t.**
W-pI .. 110.4:1 saved to quietly extend into a **t.** future. If
W-pI .. 124.6:3 Their thoughts are **t.**, and apart from
W-pI .. 131.5:1 affect His perfect, **t.** and unchanging Love
W-pI .. 157.1:3 upon, and cast a **t.** light upon this day,
M-29 ......... 7:8 wait, for waiting implies time and He is **t.**.
S-2.........in.1:7 Unlike the **t.** nature of its sister, prayer,

## timelessness 28

T-2 ... V.A.17:5 under my direction, but **t.** belongs to God
T-2 ... V.A.17:7 each other. In **t.** we coexist with God.
T-13 ... VIII.4:4 His message speaks of **t.** in time, and that
T-14 ..... IX.1:7 making of time to take the place of **t.** lay
T-15 ........V.9:6 The Holy Spirit's **t.** lies only here. For in
T-16 ... IV.13:6 the bridge to **t.** you understand nothing.
T-16 ... IV.13:7 as you step lightly across it, upheld *by* **t.**,
T-17 ... IV.11:5 It is a picture of **t.**, set in a frame of time.

| | |
|---|---|
| T-25... VIII.3:7 | and triumph over eternity and **t.** and life? |
| T-27... VIII.7:1 | A **t.** in which is time made real; a part of |
| T-29...... VI.6:4 | *is* a little while till **t.** comes quietly to take |
| T-29...... IX.8:5 | brings **t.** so close the song of Heaven can |
| W-pI..... 97.4:2 | Him Who promised to lay **t.** beside them. |
| W-pI..... 98.9:6 | of the time you offer Him for **t.** and peace. |
| W-pI... 105.4:3 | limitless to the unlimited, eternity to **t.**, |
| W-pI... 109.5:2 | In **t.** you rest, while time goes by without |
| W-pI. 127.10:1 | disappears before the **t.** of what you learn. |
| W-pI... 129.5:1 | you stand an instant's space away from **t.**. |
| W-pI. 132.11:1 | make what does not share His **t.** and Love |
| W-pI. 169.13:3 | Christ but his who went a moment into **t.**, |
| W-pI. 198.12:6 | between this single sight and **t.** itself, you |
| W-pII.. 234.1:2 | has elapsed between eternity and **t.**. So |
| W-pII...... 4.3:3 | God's Son is evil; **t.** must have an end; |
| W-pII.. 308.1:2 | If I elect to reach past time to **t.**, I must |
| W-pII.. 308.1:7 | to the world, restoring it to **t.** and love. |
| W-pII.... 13.1:6 | for the return of **t.** and love's awakening, |
| S-1......... II.8:1 | of every prayer, giving it **t.** instead of end. |
| S-2........... I.8:6 | to formlessness, beyond all limits into **t.**, |

## times 99

| | |
|---|---|
| T-3......... II.2:3 | innocent are apt to be quite foolish at **t.**. |
| T-4........ IV.2:1 | but I have also said, and many **t.**, that you |
| T-5....... VII.2:3 | Some of them have healed the sick at **t.**, |
| T-7....... VII.1:3 | Nor is it possible to love it totally at **t.**. |
| T-9........... I.5:1 | I have emphasized many **t.** that the Holy |
| T-9....... VII.4:4 | because at such **t.** its confusion increases. |
| T-17....... V.8:2 | for it will seem at **t.** to have no purpose. A |
| T-18..... VII.2:2 | It has perhaps faded at **t.** from your sight, |
| T-21...... IV.6:4 | At **t.** it still deceives you. Yet in your saner |
| T-22.......... I.6:4 | different things to him at different **t.**. |
| T-22....... II.9:5 | illusion we have seen many **t.** before. |
| T-23..... II.16:3 | how it appears to function many **t.** before |
| T-30.......... I.5:1 | still be **t.** when you have judged already. |
| T-31....... II.4:3 | hate as well his not assuming it at **t.** you |
| T-31....... V.2:8 | companions and it looks, at **t.** with pity, |
| T-31....... V.9:1 | some lack of ease at **t.** and some distress, |
| W-pI....... 4.6:2 | more than three or four **t.** during the day. |
| W-pI....... 5.7:6 | Three or four **t.** during the day is enough. |
| W-pI....... 8.6:1 | can be done four or five **t.** during the day, |
| W-pI....... 8.6:2 | find it trying, three or four **t.** is sufficient. |
| W-pI..... 12.6:1 | Three or four **t.** is enough for practicing |
| W-pI..... 13.4:1 | about three or four **t.** for not more than a |
| W-pI..... 19.1:2 | You will notice that at **t.** the ideas related |
| W-pI..... 19.1:2 | while at other **t.** the order is reversed. The |
| W-pI..... 22.3:1 | the world about you at least five **t.** today, |
| W-pI..... 31.2:3 | while repeating the idea two or three **t.**. |
| W-pI..... 32.3:1 | for today two or three **t.** while looking |
| W-pI..... 33.4:2 | and repeat the idea to yourself several **t.**. |
| W-pI..... 36.3:1 | and repeat the idea for today several **t.**, |
| W-pI... 36.3:10 | Several **t.** during these practice periods, |
| W-pI..... 39.9:1 | today's idea to yourself slowly a few **t.**. |
| W-pI... 39.11:1 | made some three or four **t.** an hour and |
| W-pI..... 44.7:1 | slowly, repeating the idea several **t.** more. |
| W-pI..... 48.2:4 | the idea slowly to yourself several **t.**. It is |
| W-pI..... 64.8:2 | At **t.**, do the exercises with your eyes |
| W-pI..... 64.8:3 | At other **t.**, keep your eyes open after |
| W-pI..... 67.5:3 | Four or five **t.** an hour, and perhaps even |
| W-pI..... 68.7:4 | the idea several **t.** an hour in this form: |
| W-pI... 71.10:5 | today's idea some six or seven **t.** an hour. |
| W-pI... 73.11:5 | This should be repeated several **t.** an hour |
| W-pI..... 74.3:1 | by repeating these thoughts several **t.**, |
| W-pI..... 75.6:7 | While you wait, repeat several **t.**, slowly |
| W-pI... 76.12:1 | today; at least four or five **t.** an hour, as |
| W-pI..... 78.4:5 | you see as difficult at **t.** or hard to please, |
| W-pI..... 78.9:1 | God thanks you for these quiet **t.** today |
| WpI. rII.in.2:2 | them over slowly, several **t.** if you wish, |
| W-pI..... 91.5:1 | Three **t.** today, set aside about ten |
| W-pI... 91.11:1 | Five or six **t.** an hour, at reasonably |
| W-pI..... 94.3:2 | you. Begin these **t.** of searching with these |
| W-pI... 95.11:5 | Repeat this several **t.**, and then attempt to |
| W-pI... 99.12:2 | this between the **t.** you give five minutes |
| W-pI... 104.5:2 | sight of them between the **t.** we come to |
| W-pI... 106.4:4 | He comes with miracles a thousand **t.** as |
| W-pI... 107.2:5 | that you felt be multiplied a hundred **t.**, |
| WpI. rIII.in9:2 | inclined to practice only at appointed **t.**, |
| WpIrIII.in11:5 | to serve you in all ways, all **t.** and places, |
| W-pI... 124.6:2 | in **t.** gone by and times as yet to come, as |
| W-pI... 124.6:2 | in times gone by and **t.** as yet to come, as |
| W-pI... 125.7:1 | Three **t.** today, at times most suitable for |
| W-pI... 125.7:1 | times today, at **t.** most suitable for silence |
| W-pI... 126.4:1 | yet undeserved, a gift bestowed at **t.**, at |
| W-pI... 126.4:1 | bestowed at times, at other **t.** withheld. |
| W-pI... 127.2:3 | And thus he thinks that he can love at **t.**, |
| W-pI... 127.2:3 | he can love at times, and hate at other **t.**. |
| W-pI. 127.12:2 | At least three **t.** an hour think of one who |
| W-pI... 128.7:1 | Give it ten minutes rest three **t.** today. |
| W-pI... 130.7:1 | Six **t.** today, in thanks and gratitude, we |
| W-pI. 131.10:3 | ten minutes to this goal three **t.** today, |
| W-pI. 134.17:1 | for there will still be many **t.** when you |
| W-pI. 135.24:5 | give up nothing in these **t.** today when, |
| W-pI. 151.13:2 | We introduce these **t.** with but a single, |
| W-pI. 153.16:2 | At **t.**, perhaps, a minute, even less, will be |
| W-pI. 153.16:4 | At other **t.** the business of the world will |
| W-pI. 154.12:2 | this said a hundred ways, a hundred **t.**, |
| W-pI... 156.8:2 | should be asked a thousand **t.** a day, till |
| W-pI... 159.5:3 | transparent, faintly seen, at **t.** forgot, and |
| W-pI... 161.6:4 | many **t.** been urged to look beyond the |
| W-pI... 169.8:3 | We have repeated several **t.** before that |
| W-pI... 182.1:6 | tiny throb, at other **t.** hardly remembered |
| W-pI. 185.10:5 | You have been weak at **t.**, uncertain in |
| W-pI. 186.10:4 | change ten **t.** an hour at their most secure |
| WpI rVI.in.6:6 | give these **t.** of quiet to the Teacher Who |
| W-pII..... in.1:4 | the **t.** in which we leave the world of pain, |
| W-pII..... in.3:1 | that thought to introduce our **t.** of rest, |
| W-pII..... in.4:5 | So our **t.** with Him will now be spent. We |
| W-pII..... in.6:2 | Father, we give these holy **t.** to You, in |
| W-pII.. 236.1:2 | At **t.**, it does not seem I am its king at all. |
| W-pII.. 284.1:5 | to be but said and then repeated many **t.**; |
| M-4 ..... I.A.8:3 | in all "emergencies" as well as tranquil **t.**. |
| M-6 ........... 2:5 | We have referred many **t.** in the text to |
| M-10 ......... 4:1 | Remember how many **t.** you thought you |
| M-10 ......... 4:3 | know how many **t.** you merely thought |
| M-16 ......... 7:7 | state at different **t.** and different places, |
| M-16 ......... 8:5 | There are **t.** his certainty will waver, and |
| M-17 ......... 2:6 | How many **t.** has it been emphasized that |
| M-24 ......... 1:2 | has no meaning either once or many **t.**. |
| P-1............. 1:5 | Yet there are **t.** and situations in which an |
| P-2....... VII.7:4 | He tries to heal, and thus at **t.** he may. But |
| P-3........ III.8:5 | is in every circumstance and at all **t.**. |

## timid 2

| | |
|---|---|
| T-20...... III.4:2 | you thread your **t.** way through constant |
| W-pI. 153.20:2 | Be not afraid nor **t.**. There can be no |

## tiniest 4

| | |
|---|---|
| T-22.... VI.8:10 | overlook the **t.** mistake be lost to anyone. |
| T-24..... VII.1:6 | from the least slight, the **t.** attack, the |
| W-pI. 154.12:3 | has denied the **t.** of blessings to His Son. |
| P-2......... V.6:5 | advance, the **t.** of whispers of His Name. |

## tininess 1

| | |
|---|---|
| T-16..... V.13:1 | them to obscure their **t.** and His greatness |

## tiny 79

| | |
|---|---|
| T-15....... I.11:4 | **t.** instant to offer you the whole of Heaven |
| T-17.. IV.12:10 | them. One is a **t.** picture, hard to see at all |
| T-18.......... I.7:9 | Their **t.** differences in form are no real |
| T-18... VIII.2:2 | you limit your awareness to its **t.** senses, |
| T-18... VIII.2:5 | The body is a **t.** fence around a little part |
| T-18... VIII.3:3 | fragment of your mind is such a **t.** part of |
| T-18... VIII.3:4 | this **t.** sunbeam has decided it is the sun; |
| T-18... VIII.4:2 | and hated by a **t.** segment of themselves. |
| T-18... VIII.5:3 | created. Each **t.** fragment seems to be self- |
| T-18... VIII.6:1 | that this **t.** part regards itself as you. It is |
| T-18... VIII.7:5 | you remain within your **t.** kingdom, a |
| T-18... VIII.8:4 | In your **t.** kingdom you have so little! |
| T-18. VIII.11:6 | And your shining Self will lift the **t.** aspect |
| T-18...... IX.1:3 | Therefore, it is the **t.** part of yourself, the |
| T-18.... IX.1:10 | its barricades is still a **t.** segment of the |
| T19... IV.A.2:9 | sand, a wall of dust, a **t.** seeming barrier, |
| T19... IV.A.7:4 | causing no more than **t.** interruptions in |
| T19.... IV.A.8:1 | This feather of a wish, this **t.** illusion, this |
| T19. IV.A.14:4 | of charity, no **t.** expression of forgiveness, |
| T19.... IV.C.5:6 | nothing. It is the result of a **t.**, mad idea of |
| T19.. IV.C.10:5 | In its **t.** hands it holds, in perfect safety, |
| T-20...... III.7:8 | so **t.** and so meaningless it slips unnoticed |
| T-20...... VI.5:2 | secret room, a **t.** spot of senseless mystery |
| T-20.... VI.11:2 | it prisoner in a **t.** spot of space and time, |
| T-20.... VI.11:3 | instant of despair, a **t.** island of dry sand, |
| T-21........ II.1:2 | rests; the **t.** change of mind by which the |
| T-21....... V.2:3 | it is sure that you will see yourself as **t.**, |
| T-22......... I.8:7 | new and yet as old as He, a **t.** newcomer, |
| T-22....... V.4:7 | **t.** mouse or everything that God created? |
| T-22...... VI.9:5 | Him the **t.** gifts He can extend forever. He |
| T-23....... in.4:4 | nor for a **t.** stirring of guilt's attraction. |
| T-24........ II.1:5 | not chosen to make of him a **t.** measure of |
| T-24........ II.4:4 | Its **t.** answer, soundless in the melody |
| T-24...... II.13:2 | where none is welcome but your **t.** self. |
| T-24....... V.4:2 | unlit but by the shifting **t.** gleams that |
| T-24.... VI.12:4 | a **t.** willingness, a nod to God, a greeting |
| T-25......... I.5:5 | Holy Spirit links the other part–the **t.**, |
| T-26......... I.5:4 | and **t.** crumb of happiness that you allot |
| T-26........ II.7:4 | than just a **t.** sigh before they disappear, |
| T-26...... IV.5:4 | **t.** spot that sin proclaimed to be its own. |
| T-26...... IV.5:5 | And what was **t.** then has soared into a |
| T-26...... IV.6:1 | **t.** spot of sin that stands between you and |
| T-26....... V.3:5 | **t.** tick of time in which the first mistake |
| T-26....... V.3:6 | And in that **t.** instant time was gone, for |
| T-26....... V.5:1 | The **t.** instant you would keep and make |
| T-26....... V.5:4 | very long ago, for such a **t.** interval of time |
| T-26... VII.14:6 | A **t.** sacrifice is just the same in its effects |
| T-27..... VI.6:6 | to bless the world, a **t.** stab of pain, a little |
| T-27... VII.11:3 | between a **t.** you and an enormous world, |
| T-27.... VIII.6:2 | eternity, where all is one, there crept a **t.**, |
| T-28...... VI.5:4 | **t.** oath to be forever faithful unto death. |
| T-29...... III.3:1 | no more, perhaps, than just a **t.** spark, a |
| T-29....... V.7:6 | each with his **t.** spear and rusted sword, |
| T-30......... I.9:4 | This **t.** opening will be enough to let you |
| T-30....... I.11:1 | (6) This **t.** grain of wisdom will suffice to |
| T-31.... VIII.1:3 | has; his grasp cannot exceed its **t.** reach. |
| T-31.. VIII.11:5 | to Heaven grows from **t.** scattered threads |
| W-pI..... 28.3:4 | its meaning to your **t.** experience of tables |
| W-pI..... 67.6:1 | practice periods that this is not your **t.**, |
| W-pI..... 93.9:5 | by hiding Its majesty behind the **t.** idols |
| W-pI..... 97.6:2 | radiance of the sun outshine the **t.** gleam |
| W-pI..... 98.7:1 | give Him your **t.** gift of but five minutes. |
| W-pI... 126.8:5 | And if you only catch a **t.** glimpse of the |
| W-pI... 131.6:7 | time as is a **t.** candle from a distant star, |
| W-pI. 131.13:3 | A **t.** moment of surprise, perhaps, will |
| W-pI... 153.8:3 | the Son of God; its **t.** instant for eternity. |
| W-pI... 182.1:6 | sometimes not more than a **t.** throb, at |
| W-pI... 182.6:3 | shut out, His **t.** voice so readily obscured, |
| W-pI... 183.5:2 | Repeat His Name, and all the **t.**, nameless |
| W-pI... 191.3:2 | a **t.** particle of dust against the legions of |
| W-pII. 234.1:2 | Merely a **t.** instant has elapsed between |
| W-pII. 300.2:5 | *would go beyond that* **t.** *instant to eternity.* |
| M-4......... I.2:2 | would attempt to fly with the **t.** wings of a |
| M-14......... 4:3 | leave the world and go beyond its **t.** reach |
| M-18......... 3:4 | Its little space and **t.** breath become the |
| M-20......... 6:8 | your **t.** frail imaginings apart from Him? |
| P-2....... VII.5:6 | nor is the **t.** self of one alone against the |
| S-2........... I.6:5 | Mistakes are **t.** shadows, quickly gone, |
| S-3........... I.2:3 | linked to its unstable, **t.** breath. Death |

## tire 2

| | |
|---|---|
| T-11...... VI.3:8 | the distortions you introduce that **t.** you. |
| T-29......... I.5:6 | and what will **t.** it and make it sick. And |

## tired 19

| | |
|---|---|
| T-3........ VI.5:1 | When you feel **t.**, it is because you have |
| T-3........ VI.5:1 | have judged yourself as capable of being **t.** |
| T-3........ VI.5:4 | makes you feel **t.** because it is essentially |
| T-3........ VI.5:5 | You are not really capable of being **t.**, but |
| T-5....... II.10:6 | The world is very **t.**, because it is the idea |
| T-13..... VII.3:5 | for it is old and **t.** and ready to return to |
| T-14...... IV.6:7 | **t.** will find this is more restful than sleep. |
| T-18.. VIII.13:2 | You are still worn and **t.**, and the desert's |
| T19.... IV.B.5:5 | to let peace through to bless the **t.** world! |

T-22......IV.4:6 which you will bring to light the **t.** eyes of
T-25......IV.3:2 you to all the weary eyes and **t.** hearts that
T-31....VIII.8:4 **t.** eyes I bring a vision of a different world
W-pI...109.6:1 today, a **t.** mind is suddenly made glad, a
W-pI...109.7:2 is comes closer to all worn and **t.** minds,
W-pI...153.6:4 folly, or a silly game a **t.** child might play,
W-pI...188.3:5 It brings renewal to all **t.** hearts, and
W-pI...195.7:1 let our brothers lean their **t.** heads against
W-pII .345.2:2 to offer miracles to bless the **t.** world. It
M-1 ...........4:4 on wearily, and the world is very **t.** now. It

### title 1

M-16 .........3:7 He cannot claim that **t.** until he has gone

### to 14958

### today 801

T-16....... II.8:5 **T.**, let us resolve together to accept the
T-30.........I.2:2 *T. I will make no decisions by myself.* This
T-30.......I.16:8 Whose kingdom is the world for you **t.**?
W-pI.......4.4:1 thoughts for application of the idea for **t.**,
W-pI.......5.2:1 When using the idea for **t.** for a specific
W-pI.......5.7:2 Apply the idea for **t.** to each of them,
W-pI.......7.4:3 idea for **t.** indiscriminately to whatever
W-pI.......8.3:1 purpose of the exercises for **t.** is to begin
W-pI.......8.4:1 exercises for **t.** should be done with eyes
W-pI.......8.6:3 emotion that the idea for **t.** may induce,
W-pI.....10.4:1 the idea for **t.** quite slowly to yourself.
W-pI.....11.4:1 Three practice periods **t.** will probably be
W-pI.....12.6:1 is enough for practicing the idea for **t.**.
W-pI.....13.4:1 The exercises for **t.**, which should be
W-pI.....14.1:1 The idea for **t.** is, of course, the reason
W-pI.....14.2:1 The exercises for **t.** are to be practiced
W-pI.....14.3:1 The idea for **t.** is another step in learning
W-pI.....14.7:1 The idea for **t.** can, of course, be applied
W-pI.....15.4:1 In practicing the idea for **t.**, repeat it first
W-pI.....16.1:1 idea for **t.** is a beginning step in dispelling
W-pI.....16.4:1 In applying the idea for **t.**, search your
W-pI.....18.1:1 The idea for **t.** is another step in learning
W-pI.....18.2:2 the exercises for **t.** emphasize this aspect
W-pI.....18.3:1 of the idea for **t.** as randomly as possible,
W-pI.....19.1:1 The idea for **t.** is obviously the reason
W-pI.....19.2:1 **T.** we are again emphasizing the fact that
W-pI.....19.3:2 The idea for **t.** is to be repeated first, and
W-pI.....20.4:1 The exercises for **t.** consist in reminding
W-pI.....20.5:1 and positively at least twice an hour **t.**,
W-pI.....21.1:1 idea for **t.** is obviously a continuation and
W-pI.....22.3:1 the world about you at least five times **t.**,
W-pI.....23.1:1 The idea for **t.** contains the only way out
W-pI.....23.5:1 idea for **t.** introduces the thought that you
W-pI.....24.2:3 The idea for **t.** is a step toward opening
W-pI.....24.3:1 The exercises for **t.** require much more
W-pI.....24.3:2 periods which should be undertaken **t.**,
W-pI.....24.5:1 In applying the idea for **t.**, name each
W-pI.....25.4:1 make any sense out of the exercises for **t.**,
W-pI.....25.5:3 The idea for **t.** is a step in this direction.
W-pI.....25.6:2 with a slow repetition of the idea for **t.**,
W-pI.....26.3:1 idea for **t.** introduces the thought that you
W-pI.....26.6:1 should begin with repeating the idea for **t.**
W-pI.....27.3:1 The idea for **t.** needs many repetitions for
W-pI.....28.1:1 **T.** we are really giving specific
W-pI.....28.6:1 as a subject for applying the idea for **t.**,
W-pI.....28.7:1 have six two-minute practice periods **t.**, in
W-pI.....29.1:1 The idea for **t.** explains why you can see
W-pI.....29.3:1 Try then, **t.**, to begin to learn how to look
W-pI.....29.4:1 for **t.** should follow a now familiar pattern
W-pI...29.5:10 repeat the idea for **t.** at least once an hour,
W-pI.....30.1:1 idea for **t.** is the springboard for vision.
W-pI.....30.2:1 **T.** we are trying to use a new kind of
W-pI.....31.2:1 of practice with the idea for **t.** are needed,
W-pI.....31.4:1 for **t.** as often as possible during the day.
W-pI.....31.5:1 The idea for **t.** is also a particularly useful
W-pI.....32.1:1 **T.** we are continuing to develop the
W-pI.....32.2:1 The idea for **t.**, like the preceding ones,
W-pI.....32.2:2 for **t.** will again include two phases, one
W-pI.....32.3:1 the idea for **t.** two or three times while
W-pI.....32.3:4 Repeat the idea for **t.** unhurriedly as often
W-pI.....32.6:1 The idea for **t.** should also be applied
W-pI.....34.1:1 The idea for **t.** begins to describe the
W-pI.....34.3:3 repeating the idea for **t.** slowly as you
W-pI.....35.3:1 idea for **t.** presents a very different view of
W-pI.....35.3:3 the emphasis for **t.** is on the perceiver,
W-pI.....35.4:1 the three five-minute practice periods **t.**,
W-pI.....35.6:1 the idea for **t.** might be as follows: *I see*
W-pI.....35.9:1 the time and apply the idea for **t.** to them,
W-pI.....36.2:1 practice periods are required for **t.**. Try to
W-pI.....36.3:1 your eyes and repeat the idea for **t.** several
W-pI.....37.4:1 begin with the repetition of the idea for **t.**,
W-pI.....37.5:1 for **t.** to your outer world if you so desire;
W-pI.....38.4:1 a full five minutes, repeat the idea for **t.**,
W-pI.....38.4:4 Use this form in applying the idea for **t.**:
W-pI.....39.5:1 for the four longer practice periods for **t.**,
W-pI.....39.8:2 the idea for **t.** to each of them in this way:
W-pI.....40.1:1 **T.** we will begin to assert some of the
W-pI.....40.1:2 No long practice periods are required **t.**,
W-pI.....40.3:2 effort. Repeat the idea for **t.**, and then add
W-pI.....41.2:4 The idea for **t.** has the power to end all
W-pI.....41.5:3 **T.** we will make our first real attempt to
W-pI.....41.6:1 will be only one long practice period **t.**. In
W-pI.....42.1:1 idea for **t.** combines two very powerful
W-pI.....42.3:1 three-to-five-minute practice periods **t.**,
W-pI.....42.4:1 periods by repeating the idea for **t.** slowly,
W-pI.....42.5:1 clearly related to the idea for **t.** is suitable.
W-pI.....42.7:1 periods that would be beneficial **t.**. The
W-pI.....43.4:1 practice periods are required **t.**, one as
W-pI.....43.4:3 the idea for **t.** to yourself with eyes open.
W-pI.....43.9:2 Try **t.** not to allow any long periods of
W-pI.....44.1:1 **T.** we are continuing the idea for
W-pI.....44.3:1 **T.** we are going to attempt to reach that
W-pI.....44.4:1 Have at least three practice periods **t.**,
W-pI.....44.4:3 The form of practice we will use **t.** is the
W-pI.....44.5:2 to learn the form of exercise we will use **t.**,
W-pI...44.11:3 Above all, be determined not to forget **t.**.
W-pI.....45.3:2 **T.** we will attempt to reach them. We will
W-pI.....45.4:1 for **t.** will take the same general form that
W-pI.....45.5:3 to feel confident that we will succeed **t.**. It
W-pI.....45.6:1 the exercises for **t.** by repeating the idea
W-pI.....45.8:1 which the exercises for **t.** are directed.
W-pI.....45.9:1 In the shorter exercise periods for **t.**, try
W-pI.....46.7:1 for **t.** in the original or in a related form,
W-pI.....47.4:1 **T.** we will try to reach past your own
W-pI.....47.4:2 practice periods are necessary **t.**, and
W-pI.....48.1:1 The idea for **t.** simply states a fact. It is
W-pI.....49.2:4 Try **t.** not to listen to it. Try to identify
W-pI.....49.3:1 least four five-minute practice periods **t.**,
W-pI.....49.5:3 repeat the idea for **t.** whenever you can,
W-pI.....50.1:1 **t.** and tomorrow and throughout time. In
W-pI.....50.4:4 is the answer to whatever confronts you **t.**
W-pI.....50.4:6 Tell yourself this often **t.**. It is a
W-pI.....50.5:1 For ten minutes, twice **t.**, morning and
W-pI.....50.5:1 for **t.** sink deep into your consciousness.
WpI... rI.in.1:1 Beginning with **t.** we will have a series of
W-pI........51.h review for **t.** covers the following ideas:
W-pI........53.h **T.** we will review the following:
W-pI........54.h These are the review ideas for **t.**:
W-pI........56.h Our review for **t.** covers the following:
W-pI........57.h **T.** let us review these ideas:
W-pI........58.h These ideas are for review **t.**:
W-pI........59.h The following ideas are for review **t.**:
W-pI.....59.2:3 Let me not look to my own eyes to see **t.**.
W-pI.....59.2:6 Let me call upon this gift **t.**, so that this
W-pI.....61.4:1 about this idea as often as possible **t.**. It is
W-pI.....61.5:1 as possible should be undertaken **t.**,
W-pI.....61.7:4 Try **t.** to begin to build a firm foundation
W-pI.....62.5:1 your eyes if possible, say to yourself **t.**:
W-pI.....63.3:1 will be happy to remember it very often **t.**
W-pI.....64.5:1 Let us remember this **t.**. Let us remind
W-pI.....64.5:3 you will make **t.** by remembering they are
W-pI.....64.6:1 **T.**, then, let us practice with these
W-pI.....64.6:5 or fifteen minutes **t.** to reflecting on this
W-pI.....65.1:1 idea for **t.** reaffirms your commitment to
W-pI.....65.3:1 **T.**, and for a number of days to follow,
W-pI.....65.7:1 Finally, repeat the idea for **t.** once more,
W-pI.....66.3:1 **T.** we will try to go past this wholly
W-pI.....66.4:1 Our longer practice period **t.** has as its
W-pI ....66.9:1 this during the longer practice period **t.**.
W-pI ...66.9:6 We need great honesty **t.**. Remember the
W-pI ..66.10:8 try **t.** to realize that only the truth is true.
W-pI ..66.11:1 be most helpful **t.** if undertaken twice an
W-pI ....67.1:6 effort **t.** to reach this truth about you, and
W-pI ....67.2:8 We are trying **t.** to undo your definition
W-pI ....67.4:1 to repeat the idea for **t.** from time to time
W-pI ....67.4:4 do much **t.** to bring that awareness nearer
W-pI ....67.5:1 will be particularly helpful **t.** to practice
W-pI ....68.4:4 **T.** we will try to find out how you would
W-pI ....69.2:1 **T.** let us make another real attempt to
W-pI ....69.3:1 our longer practice period **t.** with the full
W-pI ....69.3:5 ancient search **t.** by finding the light in us,
W-pI ....69.5:5 of substance. We will make this attempt **t.**
W-pI ....69.6:1 much you want to reach the light in you **t.**
W-pI ....69.8:1 Have confidence in your Father **t.**, and be
W-pI ....69.9:8 to hold anything against anyone **t.**.
W-pI ....70.1:1 temptation not to believe the idea for **t.**.
W-pI ....70.5:1 **T.** we practice realizing that God's Will
W-pI ....70.5:3 Therefore, in accepting the idea for **t.**, we
W-pI ....70.6:1 ready for two longer practice periods **t.**,
W-pI ....70.7:1 periods by repeating the idea for **t.**,
W-pI ..70.10:1 the short and frequent practice periods **t.**,
W-pI ....71.6:3 The idea for **t.** is the answer. Only God's
W-pI ....71.7:1 us practice recognizing this certainty **t.**.
W-pI ....71.8:1 for **t.** by thinking about today's idea, and
W-pI ..71.10:2 to all temptation to hold grievances **t.**,
W-pI ....72.8:1 will try **t.** to stop these senseless attacks
W-pI ..72.10:1 the longer practice periods **t.** is to become
W-pI ..72.13:1 periods an hour will be enough for **t.**,
W-pI ....73.1:1 **T.** we are considering the will you share
W-pI ....73.4:1 **T.** we will try once more to reach the
W-pI ....73.6:8 to succeed in what we are trying to do **t.**.
W-pI ....73.7:1 We will succeed **t.** if you remember that
W-pI ....73.7:6 are. **T.** it is the ego that stands powerless
W-pI ....73.8:1 we undertake the exercises for **t.** in happy
W-pI ....73.8:3 **T.** let your will be done, and end forever
W-pI ....73.9:4 You will succeed **t.**, the time appointed
W-pI ....74.1:1 idea for **t.** can be regarded as the central
W-pI ....74.2:1 for **t.** are directed towards finding it. The
W-pI ....74.2:5 Let us try to recognize this **t.**, and
W-pI ....74.6:3 quickly repeat the idea for **t.** and try again
W-pI ....74.7:1 at regular and predetermined intervals **t.**,
W-pI ....74.7:3 *I seek His peace* **t.**. Then try to find what
W-pI ....74.7:5 if possible, would be well spent on this **t.**.
W-pI ....75.2:1 **T.** we celebrate the happy ending to your
W-pI ....75.2:4 **T.** the time of light begins for you and
W-pI ....75.2:7 **T.** we see a different world, because the
W-pI ....75.3:1 Our exercises for **t.** will be happy ones, in
W-pI ....75.3:3 **T.** we will accept the new world as what
W-pI ....75.4:4 inevitable. **T.** the real world rises before
W-pI ....75.5:1 to see the ego's shadow on the world **t.**.
W-pI ....75.6:1 Dwell not upon the past **t.**. Keep a
W-pI ....75.6:3 You have forgiven the world **t.**. You can
W-pI ....75.8:4 **T.** the light has come. And you will see
W-pI ....75.9:2 so that **t.** is a time for special celebration.
W-pI ....75.9:6 upon your eyes, you cannot fail to see **t.**.
W-pI ....75.9:7 that you will gladly extend **t.** forever.
W-pI ..75.11:2 of yourself and see it everywhere **t.**, as we
W-pI ....76.2:1 **T.** we will be glad you cannot prove it.
W-pI ....76.2:3 idea for **t.** tells you once again how simple
W-pI ....76.7:2 will devote **t.** to rejoicing that this is so. It
W-pI ....76.8:1 the longer practice periods **t.** with a short
W-pI ....76.9:2 Dismiss all foolish magical beliefs **t.**, and
W-pI ..76.11:1 Let us **t.** open God's channels to Him,
W-pI ..76.12:1 this dedication as often as possible **t.**; at
W-pI ....77.1:6 Identity. It is this that we will celebrate **t.**.
W-pI ....77.3:1 **T.** we will claim the miracles which are
W-pI ....77.3:5 **T.**, however, we will also make sure that
W-pI ....77.6:5 is no room for doubt and uncertainty **t.**.
W-pI ....77.7:2 fact. Tell yourself often **t.**: *I am entitled to*
W-pI ....78.2:1 **T.** we go beyond the grievances, to look
W-pI ....78.4:1 **T.** we will attempt to see God's Son. We
W-pI ....78.5:5 Let him be savior unto you **t.**. Such is his
W-pI ....78.6:1 practice periods **t.** will see him in this role
W-pI ....78.9:1 these quiet times **t.** in which you laid your
W-pI ....79.7:1 periods **t.** we will ask what the problem is,
W-pI ....79.8:1 The exercises for **t.** will be successful to
W-pI ....79.9:1 shorter practice periods for **t.** will not be

W-pI.....79.9:2 You will see many problems **t.**, each one
W-pI...79.10:1 not deceived by the form of problems **t.**.
W-pI.....80.2:2 Repeat this over and over to yourself **t.**,
W-pI.....80.3:1 You are entitled to peace **t.**. A problem
W-pI.....80.4:1 In our longer practice periods **t.**, we will
W-pI.....80.6:1 yourself often **t.** that your problems have
W-pI.....80.6:3 sure to apply the idea for **t.** to any specific
W-pI.....80.7:1 be determined not to collect grievances **t.**.
W-pI........81.h Our ideas for review **t.** are:
W-pI........82.h We will review these ideas **t.**:
W-pI........83.h T. let us review these ideas:
W-pI.....84.1:5 I would recognize my reality **t.**. I will
W-pI.....84.3:6 I am determined not to attack my Self **t.**,
W-pI.....85.3:2 T. I will recognize where my salvation is.
W-pI........86.h These ideas are for review **t.**:
W-pI........87.h Our review **t.** will cover these ideas:
W-pI.....87.1:2 I will use the power of my will **t.**. It is not
W-pI.....87.1:4 Light shall be my guide **t.**. I will follow it
W-pI.....87.3:2 safe **t.** because there is no will but God's.
W-pI.....87.3:5 T. I will recognize that all this has not
W-pI........88.h T. we will review these ideas:
W-pI........89.h These are our review ideas for **t.**:
W-pI.....90.1:2 solved. Let me realize **t.** that the problem
W-pI.....90.1:4 T. I would remember the simplicity of
W-pI.....91.4:3 T. we will devote ourselves to the attempt
W-pI.....91.5:1 Three times **t.**, set aside about ten
W-pI.....91.6:6 ends is needed for our exercises **t.**. What
W-pI.....92.1:1 for **t.** is an extension of the previous one.
W-pI.....92.9:3 meeting place we try **t.** to find and rest in,
W-pI...92.10:1 Let us give twenty minutes twice **t.** to join
W-pI...92.10:4 Leave, then, the dark a little while **t.**, and
W-pI...92.11:3 us repeat as often as we can the idea for **t.**,
W-pI.....93.3:1 T. we question this, not from the point of
W-pI.....93.8:1 In our longer exercise periods **t.**, which
W-pI...93.11:5 can do much for the world's salvation **t.**.
W-pI...93.11:6 You can do much **t.** to bring you closer to
W-pI...93.11:7 do much **t.** to bring the conviction to your
W-pI.....94.1:1 T. we continue with the one idea which
W-pI.....94.3:1 T. we will again devote the first five
W-pI.....94.5:4 Tell yourself frequently **t.** that you are as
W-pI.....94.5:8 every effort to do the hourly exercises **t.**.
W-pI.....95.3:1 We will attempt **t.** to be aware only of
W-pI.....95.3:3 In patience and in hope we try again **t.**.
W-pI...95.10:4 T. we will affirm this truth again, and try
W-pI...95.11:1 the practice periods **t.** with this assurance
W-pI...95.14:1 Do not forget **t.**. We need your help; your
W-pI...95.14:3 to you in confidence that you will try **t.**.
W-pI...95.14:6 Do not forget **t.**. Throughout the day do
W-pI...95.15:2 To everyone you meet **t.**, be sure to give
W-pI.....96.8:1 We will attempt **t.** to find this thought,
W-pI...96.11:1 Your Self knows that you cannot fail **t.**.
W-pI...96.12:1 Each time **t.** you tell your frantic mind
W-pI.....97.1:4 Practice this truth **t.** as often as you can,
W-pI.....97.3:1 T. we try to bring reality still closer to
W-pI.....97.4:4 Give Him the minutes which He needs **t.**,
W-pI.....97.8:1 each practice period **t.** gladly to Him. And
W-pI.....97.8:3 time you speak the words He offers you **t.**,
W-pI.....97.8:5 else. The Holy Spirit gives you peace **t.**.
W-pI.....98.1:1 T. is a day of special dedication. We take
W-pI.....98.1:2 We take a stand on but one side **t.**. We
W-pI.....98.1:5 We dedicate ourselves to truth **t.**, and to
W-pI.....98.2:2 All our doubts we lay aside **t.**, and take
W-pI.....98.3:5 They took the stand which we will take **t.**,
W-pI.....98.4:1 us; all who took the stand we take **t.** will
W-pI.....98.4:4 We do not choose but for ourselves **t.**.
W-pI.....98.7:1 Each hour **t.** give Him your tiny gift of
W-pI.....98.7:5 T. you practice with Him, as you say: *I will*
W-pI.....98.8:2 that you may give them to the world **t.**.
W-pI.....99.7:1 be sure you practice well the idea for **t.**.
W-pI.....99.9:1 Practice His Thought **t.**, and let His light
W-pI.....99.9:5 Think of these things in practicing **t.**, and
W-pI.....99.9:5 start the lesson that we learn **t.** with this
W-pI...99.11:1 There is a special message for **t.** which
W-pI...100.5:1 We will not let ourselves be sad **t.**. For if
W-pI...100.6:1 T. we will attempt to understand joy is
W-pI...100.6:4 You are God's messenger **t.**. You bring
W-pI...100.7:1 We will prepare ourselves for this **t.**, in
W-pI.100.10:3 You are His messenger **t.**. And you must
W-pI.100.10:5 forget the idea for **t.** between your hourly
W-pI.100.10:6 It is your Self Who calls to you **t.**. And it is
W-pI...101.1:1 T. we will continue with the theme of
W-pI...101.5:1 You need the practice periods **t.**. The
W-pI...101.5:5 with this thought as often as we can **t.**,
W-pI...101.7:2 T. escape from madness. You are set on
W-pI...101.7:5 sin. Remember this **t.**, and tell yourself as
W-pI...102.2:1 T. we try to loose its weakened hold still
W-pI...102.2:6 you free **t.** to join the happy Will of God.
W-pI...102.4:1 Begin your practice periods **t.** with this
W-pI...102.5:3 five-minute rests, pause frequently **t.**, to
W-pI...103.2:3 error we will try again to bring to truth **t.**,
W-pI...103.2:6 Begin your periods of practicing **t.** with
W-pI...103.3:1 within your mind each waking hour **t.**.
W-pI...103.3:6 *And it is happiness I seek* **t.**. *I cannot fail,*
W-pI...104.2:1 T. we would remove all meaningless and
W-pI...104.2:6 wait to have them. They belong to us **t.**.
W-pI...104.3:2 Our longer practice periods **t.**, the hourly
W-pI...104.4:3 We come in confidence **t.**, aware that
W-pI...104.5:1 do we clear the way for Him **t.** by simply
W-pI...105.1:2 T. we will accept them, knowing they
W-pI...105.5:1 T. accept God's peace and joy as yours.
W-pI...105.5:6 Receive His gift of joy and peace **t.**, and
W-pI...105.6:1 T. our practice periods will start a little
W-pI...105.6:2 Begin **t.** by thinking of those brothers
W-pI...105.7:3 be free of all that would prevent success **t.**
W-pI...105.8:1 You must succeed **t.**, if you prepare your
W-pI...105.9:1 thus with Him each time you can **t.**, but
W-pI...105.9:3 not to interfere **t.** with what He wills. And
W-pI...106.2:2 Be still **t.** and listen to the truth. Be not
W-pI...106.3:1 afraid **t.** to circumvent the voices of the
W-pI...106.3:4 Be still **t.** and listen to the truth. Go past
W-pI...106.3:6 love. Hear only Him **t.**, and do not wait to
W-pI...106.3:7 to reach Him longer. Hear one Voice **t.**.
W-pI...106.4:1 T. the promise of God's Word is kept.
W-pI...106.4:8 Prepare yourself for miracles **t.**. Today
W-pI...106.4:9 T. allow your Father's ancient pledge to
W-pI...106.5:1 Hear Him **t.**, and listen to the Word
W-pI...106.5:4 Hear Him **t.**, and offer Him your voice to
W-pI...106.5:4 to hear the Word that He will speak **t.**.
W-pI...106.6:2 It is here, and will **t.** be given unto you.
W-pI...106.6:4 Listen **t.**, and you will hear a Voice which
W-pI...106.7:3 T. we practice giving, not the way you
W-pI...106.9:1 Be still and listen to the truth **t.**. For each
W-pI.106.10:1 T. the holy Word of God is kept through
W-pI.106.10:2 Do not forget **t.** to reinforce your choice
W-pI.106.10:2 given to yourself as often as is possible **t.**:
W-pI.106.10:4 *I am the messenger of God* **t.**, *My voice is His,*
W-pI...107.6:5 T. belongs to truth. Give truth its due,
W-pI...107.7:3 own. T. we practice on the happy note of
W-pI...107.7:4 of illusion are not our approach **t.**. We are
W-pI...107.7:6 We do not doubt we walk with truth **t.**,
W-pI...107.9:2 Him. You speak to Him **t.**, and make your
W-pI.107.11:1 Do not forget your function for **t.**. Each
W-pI...108.7:1 T. we practice with the special case of
W-pI...108.7:4 receive. T. we will attempt to offer peace
W-pI...108.8:1 practice periods with the instruction for **t.**
W-pI.108.10:1 simple lesson for **t.** will teach you much.
W-pI.108.10:3 now. Think of the exercises for **t.** as quick
W-pI...109.1:1 ask for rest **t.**, and quietness unshaken by
W-pI...109.5:3 You rest **t.**. And as you close your eyes,
W-pI...109.5:8 Take time **t.** to slip away from dreams
W-pI...109.6:1 Each hour that you take your rest **t.**, a
W-pI...109.7:1 With each five minutes that you rest **t.**,
W-pI...109.8:1 You rest within the peace of God **t.**, and
W-pI...109.8:2 you. You will be faithful to your trust **t.**,
W-pI...109.9:1 You rest within the peace of God **t.**, quiet
W-pI...109.9:3 what we give **t.** we have received already.
W-pI...109.9:4 is not the guardian of what we give **t.**. We
W-pI...110.9:2 T. honor your Self. Let graven images you
W-pI...110.9:3 instead of what he is be worshipped not **t.**
W-pI.110.10:1 Seek Him **t.**, and find Him. He will be
W-pI.110.10:4 T. we make a great advance to truth by
W-pI.110.10:4 our hands and hearts and minds to God **t.**
W-pI.110.11:1 thoughts for all who meet with us **t.**. For
WpI. rIII.in1:1 Our next review begins **t.**. We will review
W-pI...118.1:2 *T. I will accept God's peace and joy, in glad*
W-pI...119.2:2 *I will forgive all things* **t.**, *that I may learn*
W-pI...120.1:2 *I rest in God* **t.**, *and let Him work in me and*
W-pI...120.2:3 *T. I lay aside all sick illusions of myself, and*
W-pI...121.8:1 T. we practice learning to forgive. If you
W-pI...121.8:2 can learn **t.** to take the key to happiness,
W-pI...121.9:2 Yet we will try to learn **t.** that they are one
W-pI...122.6:6 Let us **t.** rejoice that this is so, for here we
W-pI...122.7:6 God wills salvation be received **t.**, and
W-pI...122.8:1 Open your eyes **t.** and look upon a happy
W-pI...122.9:1 we undertake our practicing **t.** with hope
W-pI...122.9:2 Earnestly and gladly will we seek for it **t.**,
W-pI.122.11:2 T. it will be given you to feel the peace
W-pI.122.12:1 Before the light you will receive **t.** the
W-pI.122.12:2 for us since time began, kept waiting for **t.**
W-pI.122.13:2 T. all things you want are given you. Let
W-pI.122.14:4 *T. I have accepted this as true. Today I have*
W-pI.122.14:5 *as true. T. I have received the gifts of God.*
W-pI...123.1:1 T. let us be thankful. We have come to
W-pI...123.2:2 Be glad **t.**, in loving thankfulness, your
W-pI...123.2:4 Him and His creation. Give Him thanks **t.**
W-pI...123.4:1 T. in gratitude we lift our hearts above
W-pI...123.4:2 We sing the song of thankfulness **t.**, in
W-pI...123.4:3 T. we smile on everyone we see, and walk
W-pI...123.6:2 Receive the thanks of God **t.**, as you give
W-pI...123.7:1 yours to Him for fifteen minutes twice **t.**.
W-pI...124.1:1 T. we will again give thanks for our
W-pI...124.4:1 T. we will not doubt His Love for us, nor
W-pI...124.4:3 Him **t.** in recognition and remembrance.
W-pI...124.4:6 T. we see only the loving and the lovable.
W-pI...124.7:5 T. we would experience ourselves at one
W-pI...124.8:1 Peace be to you **t.**. Secure your peace by
W-pI...124.8:3 you. Sometime **t.**, whenever it seems best,
W-pI...124.8:5 trust God's Voice to speak as He sees fit **t.**,
W-pI...124.9:2 You may not be ready to accept the gain **t.**
W-pI.124.10:1 Perhaps **t.**, perhaps tomorrow, you will
W-pI.124.11:1 Perhaps **t.**, perhaps tomorrow, you will
W-pI.124.11:3 yet you can be sure someday, perhaps **t.**,
W-pI.124.12:1 frame that holds the mirror offered you **t.**
W-pI......125.h In quiet I receive God's Word **t.**.
W-pI...125.1:2 Your Father wills you hear His Word **t.**.
W-pI...125.1:4 Hear Him **t.**. No peace is possible until
W-pI...125.3:1 In stillness we will hear God's Voice **t.**
W-pI...125.3:2 We will not judge ourselves **t.**, for what
W-pI...125.3:5 T. we will not listen to the world, but wait
W-pI...125.4:3 We gather at the throne of God **t.**, the
W-pI...125.6:1 T. He speaks to you. His Voice awaits
W-pI...125.6:4 is peace within you to be called upon **t.**, to
W-pI...125.7:1 Three times **t.**, at times most suitable for
W-pI...125.8:4 In quiet listen to your Self **t.**, and let Him
W-pI...125.9:2 practicing **t.** lift you above the thinking of
W-pI...125.9:5 true. As every hour passes by **t.**, be still a
W-pI...126.8:1 T. we try to understand the truth that
W-pI...126.8:4 Give Him your faith **t.**, and ask Him that
W-pI...126.8:4 that He share your practicing in truth **t.**.
W-pI...126.8:5 that lies in the idea we practice for **t.**, this
W-pI...126.9:1 Give fifteen minutes twice **t.** to the
W-pI.126.11:1 can, remind yourself you have a goal **t.**;
W-pI...127.6:4 T. we practice making free your mind of
W-pI...127.6:5 T. we take the largest single step this
W-pI...127.7:1 faintest glimmering of what love means **t.**
W-pI...127.7:2 then, be glad to give some time to God **t.**,
W-pI...127.8:1 fifteen minutes twice **t.** escape from every
W-pI...127.9:4 will shine through your idle thoughts **t.**,
W-pI.127.10:1 T. the legion of the future years of
W-pI.127.10:2 Let us give thanks **t.** that we are spared a
W-pI.127.10:3 T. we leave the past behind us, nevermore
W-pI...128.3:1 Escape **t.** the chains you place upon your
W-pI...128.5:1 T. we practice letting go all thought of
W-pI...128.7:1 Give it ten minutes rest three times **t.**.
W-pI...129.6:4 Let it be given you **t.**. It waits but for your
W-pI...129.8:1 T. the lights of Heaven bend to you, to
W-pI...129.8:4 A day of grace is given you **t.**, and we give
W-pI...130.4:8 T. we will not seek for them, nor waste
W-pI...130.6:1 T. we will attempt no compromise where
W-pI...130.6:3 What we would learn **t.** is more than just
W-pI...130.7:1 Six times **t.**, in thanks and gratitude, we
W-pI.130.10:1 Dismiss temptation easily **t.** whenever it
W-pI...131.6:2 It is here **t.**. Time is the great illusion it is
W-pI...131.9:1 T. we will not choose a paradox in place
W-pI.131.10:1 foolish thoughts like these behind **t.**, and
W-pI.131.10:2 truth, and it is truth we seek to reach **t.**.
W-pI.131.10:3 ten minutes to this goal three times **t.**,

W-pII..275.2:1 *Your healing Voice protects all things t.,*
W-pII..278.2:3 *T., I would not dream. I choose the way to*
W-pII..279.2:1 *I will accept Your promises t., and give my*
W-pII..280.2:1 *T. let me give honor to Your Son, for thus*
W-pII..281.2:1 I will not hurt myself t.. For I am far
W-pII.....282.h I will not be afraid of love t..
W-pII..282.1:1 If I could realize but this t., salvation
W-pII..282.2:5 *a mistake. Let me not be afraid of truth t..*
W-pII..284.1:8 And I would go beyond these words t.,
W-pII..284.2:2 *Let me not fail to trust in You t., accepting*
W-pII.....285.h My holiness shines bright and clear t..
W-pII..285.1:1 T. I wake with joy, expecting but the
W-pII..285.1:4 avail me if insanity departs from me t.,
W-pII.....286.h The hush of Heaven holds my heart t..
W-pII..286.1:1 *Father, how still t.! How quietly do all*
W-pII..286.2:1 The stillness of t. will give us hope that
W-pII..286.2:2 T. we will not doubt the end which God
W-pII.....288.h Let me forget my brother's past t..
W-pII..288.2:1 Forgive me, then, t.. And you will know
W-pII..290.2:1 *You, and ask Your strength to hold me up t.,*
W-pII..290.2:4 *And I am sure that I will see my happiness t..*
W-pII..291.1:1 Christ's vision looks through me t.. His
W-pII..291.1:4 What loveliness we look upon t.! What
W-pII..293.2:1 *let not Your holy world escape my sight t..*
W-pII..293.2:4 *I would see only this world before my eyes t..*
W-pII294.1:10 off. Let me not see it more than this t.; of
W-pII.....295.h The Holy Spirit looks through me t..
W-pII..295.1:1 Christ asks that He may use my eyes t.,
W-pII..295.2:2 *Help me to use the eyes of Christ t., and thus*
W-pII.....296.h The Holy Spirit speaks through me t..
W-pII..296.1:1 *The Holy Spirit needs my voice t., that all*
W-pII..296.1:4 *Word Your holy Voice will speak to me t..*
W-pII..296.2:1 We teach t. what we would learn, and
W-pII..298.2:1 *Father, I come to You t., because I would not*
W-pII..300.1:3 we seek, unclouded, obvious and sure, t..
W-pII..300.2:1 *We seek Your holy world t.. For we, Your*
W-pII..300.2:4 *give thanks t. the world endures but for an*
W-pII..301.1:4 *Let me t. behold it uncondemned, through*
W-pII..301.1:7 *gone. Father, I will not judge Your world t..*
W-pII..301.2:4 and we will look upon God's world t..
W-pII..302.1:7 *Let me forgive Your holy world t., that I may*
W-pII.....303.h The holy Christ is born in me t..
W-pII..303.1:1 Watch with me, angels, watch with me t..
W-pII..303.1:6 here, for He is born again in me t..
W-pII..305.2:2 *Help us t. but to accept Your gift, and judge it*
W-pII.....306.h The gift of Christ is all I seek t..
W-pII..306.1:1 What but Christ's vision would I use t.,
W-pII..306.1:2 T. I can forget the world I made. Today I
W-pII..306.1:3 T. I can go past all fear, and be restored to
W-pII..306.1:4 T. I am redeemed, and born anew into a
W-pII.....309.h I will not fear to look within t..
W-pII..309.2:1 *The step I take t., my Father, is my sure*
W-pII.....310.h In fearlessness and love I spend t..
W-pII..310.1:4 *to me, and that it is Your Will I be set free t..*
W-pII..310.2:4 There is no room in us for fear t., for we
W-pII..311.1:5 Let us not use it t., but make a gift of it to
W-pII..311.2:1 *Father, we wait with open mind t., to hear*
W-pII..312.2:1 *for t. except to look upon a liberated world,*
W-pII..312.2:2 *this is Your Will for me t., and therefore it*
W-pII..313.2:1 Let us t. behold each other in the sight of
W-pII..313.2:4 Brother, come and join with me t.. We
W-pII..315.2:1 *to me t. and every day from every Son of God*
W-pII..316.2:1 *Father, I would accept Your gifts t.. I do not*
W-pII..317.2:1 *Father, Your way is what I choose t.. Where*
W-pII..318.2:1 *Let me t., my Father, take the role You offer*
W-pII..321.2:1 T. we answer for the world, which will be
W-pII..326.2:1 Let us t. behold earth disappear, at first
W-pII..329.2:1 T. we will accept our union with each
W-pII.....330.h I will not hurt myself again t..
W-pII..330.1:6 Let us choose t. that He be our Identity,
W-pII..330.2:3 *You. We would return to It t., to be made free*
W-pII..331.2:2 upon the holy sights forgiveness shows t.,
W-pII..332.2:1 *We would not bind the world again t.. Fear*
W-pII.....334.h T. I claim the gifts forgiveness gives.
W-pII..334.1:3 me not accept such meager gifts again t..
W-pII..334.1:5 This is my choice t.. And so I go to find
W-pII..334.2:4 *T. I would behold my brother sinless. This*
W-pII..339.1:9 resolve t. to ask for what we really want,
W-pII.....340.h I can be free of suffering t..
W-pII..340.1:1 *Father, I thank You for t., and for the*
W-pII..340.1:2 *day is holy, for t. Your Son will be redeemed.*
W-pII..340.1:5 *Thanks for t., my Father. I was born into this*
W-pII..340.1:6 *he made, which is released along with him t..*
W-pII..340.2:1 Be glad t.! Be glad! There is no room for
W-pII..340.2:3 room for anything but joy and thanks t..
W-pII..340.2:5 Not one of us but will be saved t.. Not one
W-pII..342.1:6 *Let me not wait again t.. Let me forgive all*
W-pII..343.2:4 And it is this that we would learn t..
W-pII.....344.h T. I learn the law of love; that what I give
W-pII.....345.h I offer only miracles t.. For I would have
W-pII..345.1:7 *Then let me give this gift alone t., which,*
W-pII..345.2:1 Peace to all seeking hearts t.. The light
W-pII..345.2:3 It will find rest t., for we will offer what
W-pII.....346.h T. the peace of God envelops me, And I
W-pII..346.1:1 *Father, I wake t. with miracles correcting*
W-pII..346.1:2 *share eternity, for time has stepped aside t.. I*
W-pII..346.1:4 *What I seek t. transcends all laws of time and*
W-pII..346.2:1 And when the evening comes t., we will
W-pII..346.2:2 For we will learn t. what peace is ours,
W-pII..347.1:4 *freedom, and I choose to claim Your gift t..*
W-pII..347.1:9 *Let Him judge t.. I do not know my will, but*
W-pII..347.2:1 Listen t.. Be very still, and hear the gentle
W-pII.....349.h T. I let Christ's vision look upon All
W-pII..352.1:8 *hear Your Voice and find Your peace t.. For I*
W-pII.....353.h hands, my feet t. Have but one purpose;
W-pII..353.1:1 *Father, I give all that is mine t. to Christ, to*
W-pII.....355.h When I accept God's Word. Why not t.?
W-pII..357.1:4 *And as I look upon Your Son t., I hear Your*
W-pII..359.1:1 *Father, t. we will forgive Your world, and let*
M-27 .........2:3 it off without regret or care, perhaps t..

## today's 154

W-pI.......4.2:1 the subjects for the application of t. idea,
W-pI.......5.6:1 to apply t. idea to some perceived sources
W-pI.......6.2:1 T. idea is useful for application to
W-pI.....10.5:1 T. thought can obviously serve for any
W-pI.....11.1:3 T. idea introduces the concept that your
W-pI.....11.2:1 The practice periods for t. idea are to be
W-pI.....12.3:7 mind are suitable subjects for t. exercises.
W-pI.....12.4:1 the time intervals between applying t.
W-pI.....13.1:1 T. idea is really another form of the
W-pI.....13.4:2 eyes closed, repeat t. idea to yourself.
W-pI.....14.2:3 more than three practice periods with t.
W-pI.....14.5:1 subjects for the application of t. idea also
W-pI.....14.6:7 the practice periods by repeating t. idea:
W-pI.....15.4:4 subjects for the application of t. idea. It is
W-pI.....15.5:3 than three application periods for t. idea
W-pI.....16.4:4 it, is a suitable subject for applying t. idea.
W-pI.....16.5:4 use t. idea whenever you are aware of a
W-pI.....17.2:1 In applying t. idea, say to yourself, with
W-pI.....18.2:1 T. idea does not refer to what you see as
W-pI.....19.3:1 or so of mind searching which t. exercises
W-pI.....19.5:1 the "as needed" application of t. idea, at
W-pI.....20.4:2 T. idea also tacitly implies the recognition
W-pI.....20.5:1 Repeat t. idea slowly and positively at
W-pI.....22.1:1 T. idea accurately describes the way
W-pI.....23.6:1 periods are required in applying t. idea.
W-pI.....23.7:3 them as the same in t. practice periods.
W-pI.....24.4:1 periods should begin with repeating t.
W-pI.....25.1:2 T. idea explains why nothing you see
W-pI.....25.6:8 next subject, and apply t. idea as before.
W-pI.....26.4:1 Practice with t. idea will help you to
W-pI.....26.5:1 periods are required in applying t. idea. A
W-pI.....26.6:5 one. T. idea should be applied as follows:
W-pI.....26.9:3 by repeating t. idea to yourself once more
W-pI.....27.1:1 T. idea expresses something stronger
W-pI.....27.1:5 The purpose of t. exercises is to bring the
W-pI.....27.4:2 How much do you want t. idea to be true?
W-pI.....27.4:6 sincere while you were repeating t. idea,
W-pI.....28.7:2 equal sincerity as t. idea is applied to it, in
W-pI.....29.1:5 well. T. idea is the whole basis for vision.
W-pI.....29.3:6 you will understand t. idea perfectly. And
W-pI.....29.4:2 t. idea because of its wholly alien nature.
W-pI.....30.3:1 T. idea should be applied as often as
W-pI.....30.4:2 you can actually see, as you apply t. idea.
W-pI.....30.5:3 to applying t. idea with your eyes closed,
W-pI.....30.5:4 without. T. idea applies equally to both.
W-pI.....31.1:1 T. idea is the introduction to your
W-pI.....31.3:5 repeat t. idea to yourself as often as you
W-pI.....32.2:3 mind. In t. exercises, try to introduce the
W-pI.....33.1:1 T. idea is an attempt to recognize that
W-pI.....33.3:2 Specific applications of t. idea should also
W-pI.....33.4:1 Remember to apply t. idea the instant
W-pI.....34.2:1 periods are required for t. exercises. One
W-pI.....34.2:4 the applications of t. idea should be made
W-pI.....34.6:2 than one application of t. idea to help you
W-pI.....35.1:1 T. idea does not describe the way you see
W-pI.....35.3:3 kind of application for t. idea because the
W-pI.....35.4:1 begin by repeating t. idea to yourself, and
W-pI.....35.7:3 and use them in applying t. idea. After
W-pI.....35.8:2 but merely relax and repeat t. idea slowly
W-pI.....36.1:1 T. idea extends the idea for yesterday
W-pI.....37.4:1 T. four longer exercise periods, each to
W-pI.....38.3:4 In t. exercises, we will apply the power of
W-pI.....38.5:5 purpose of t. exercises is to begin to instill
W-pI.....39.3:6 T. exercises will apply to you, recognizing
W-pI.....39.6:1 as usual, by repeating t. idea to yourself.
W-pI.....39.7:1 kind are suitable subjects for t. exercises.
W-pI.....39.9:1 t. idea to yourself slowly a few times. You
W-pI...39.11:1 ask yourself this question, repeat t. idea,
W-pI.....40.3:1 T. exercises take little time and no effort.
W-pI.....41.1:1 T. idea will eventually overcome
W-pI.....41.6:3 practice period, repeat t. idea very slowly.
W-pI.....41.9:1 Throughout the day use t. idea often,
W-pI.....42.6:1 is not appropriate for t. exercises. Try
W-pI.....43.5:2 phase, close your eyes, repeat t. idea again
W-pI.....43.5:8 more or less directly to t. idea is suitable.
W-pI.....43.6:1 are clearly out of accord with t. idea, or if
W-pI.....43.7:1 In applying t. idea in the shorter practice
W-pI.....43.8:1 T. idea should also be applied
W-pI.....43.9:2 to slip by without remembering t. idea,
W-pI.....44.7:1 by repeating t. idea with your eyes open,
W-pI.....44.9:1 form, pause long enough to repeat t. idea,
W-pI.....45.1:1 T. idea holds the key to what your real
W-pI.....46.3:1 T. exercises require at least three full five-
W-pI.....46.3:2 periods by repeating t. idea to yourself, as
W-pI.....46.5:1 purpose of the first phase of t. practice
W-pI.....46.6:7 a repetition of t. idea as originally stated.
W-pI.....48.2:1 T. practice periods will be very short,
W-pI.....49.5:1 not forget to repeat t. idea very frequently
W-pI........52.h T. review covers these ideas:
W-pI........55.h T. review includes the following:
W-pI........60.h These ideas are for t. review:
W-pI.....61.2:1 t. idea is the epitome of self-glorification.
W-pI.....61.3:1 that you accept t. idea because it is God's
W-pI.....61.7:1 T. idea goes far beyond the ego's petty
W-pI.....62.4:1 and end this day by practicing t. idea, and
W-pI.....63.4:3 should be lost for reinforcing t. idea.
W-pI.....64.1:1 T. idea is merely another way of saying
W-pI.....64.7:1 applications of t. idea throughout the day
W-pI.....65.3:2 T. idea offers you escape from all your
W-pI.....65.8:1 an hour, use this form in applying t. idea:
W-pI.....65.8:5 totally changed when you accept t. idea
W-pI.....66.4:4 T. exercises are an attempt to go beyond
W-pI...66.10:5 us. T. idea is another giant stride in the
W-pI.....67.1:1 T. idea is a complete and accurate
W-pI.....68.5:1 Begin t. extended practice period by
W-pI.....68.7:1 a quick application of t. idea in this form,
W-pI.....69.9:1 of t. idea to you and your happiness,
W-pI.....70.2:1 seeming cost of accepting t. idea is this: It
W-pI.....70.2:3 way. T. idea places you in charge of the
W-pI.....71.8:1 for today by thinking about t. idea, and
W-pI...71.10:2 respond to them with this form of t. idea:
W-pI...71.10:5 remember t. idea some six or seven times
W-pI...73.11:6 apply t. idea in this form immediately you
W-pI.....74.2:1 There is great peace in t. idea, and the
W-pI...76.11:4 will repeat t. idea until we have listened
W-pI........84.h These are the ideas for t. review:
W-pI........85.h T. review will cover these ideas:
W-pI...91.11:2 be sure to meet temptation with t. idea.
W-pI.....95.1:1 T. idea accurately describes you as God
W-pI...95.14:8 Repeat t. idea as frequently as possible,
W-pI...95.15:2 sure to give the promise of t. idea and tell
W-pI.....97.1:1 T. idea identifies you with your one Self.
W-pI.....98.7:2 the words you use in practicing t. idea the
W-pI.....98.7:3 and make each repetition of t. idea a total

Wpl .. rV.in6:3 overcome. We walk t.. I must understand
Wpl .. rV.in8:2 T. we review these thoughts. Together we
Wpl .. rV.in8:3 T. we devote our time and effort to them.
Wpl .. rV.in8:4 And t. we will teach them to our brothers.
Wpl .. rV.in8:8 made whole we go t. to our ancient home,
Wpl .. rV.in9:5 To Him we go t.. Take your brother's
W-pI.187.10:2 Thought, we stand t. as one Son of God.
W-pI ...192.8:3 free, for he is bound t. with his prisoner.
W-pII.....in.8:1 spent t. in the search for truth and God,
W-pII..221.2:2 God is here, because we wait t.. I am sure
W-pII..225.2:3 Now we follow it in peace t.. You have
W-pII......2.4:1 to this holy place, and spend a while t..
W-pII......2.4:6 has gone, and we have come t. in the light
W-pII..233.2:2 And as we walk t., we will give this day to
W-pII..263.2:2 walk t. to our Father's house as brothers
W-pII..271.1:3 as they come t. all perception disappears.
W-pII..295.1:6 For all of us must be redeemed t.. Fear
W-pII..299.1:3 Will, t., understands it. And Our Will,
W-pII..299.1:4 it. And Our Will, t., knows that it is so.
W-pII......9.5:5 do God's Will, and join t. in its holy light.
W-pII..310.2:1 We spend this day t., you and I. And all
W-pII..324.2:3 We walk t., for we follow Him. And it is
W-pII....14.2:2 days of this one year we gave to God t.,
W-pII....14.4:3 minds that join t. as we bless the world.
W-pII.....354.h We stand t., Christ and I, in peace And
Wfl ........in.2:5 to go. Let us t. follow in the way that truth
M-2............4:3 teacher seem to come t. in the present,
M-2............5:1 pupil and teacher come t., a teaching-
M-2............5:3 any two who join t. for learning purposes.
M-3............1:7 because t. they have the potential for a
M-3............2:2 students "happening" to walk home t..
M-16..........1:6 so they can learn the lessons for the day t.
C-1.............5:4 Himself. Here time and illusions end t..
C-2...........10:4 is? Problem and answer lie t. here, and
C-4.............6:7 guilt and forgiveness for an instant lie t.,
P-2...........I.1:2 in psychotherapy those have come t. who
P-2...........I.1:5 need. Perhaps they will come t. again and
P-2.........II.5:7 T. they can find a pathway out, for no one
P-2........IV.3:2 sometimes t. and sometimes in grim
S-1.........II.8:6 And then all things will be transformed t.,
S-1........IV.1:8 this change of mind: *We go t., you and I.*
S-1........IV.2:5 Even t. you may ask for things, and thus
S-1........IV.2:6 You may ask t. for specifics, and not
S-1........IV.3:1 enough, if those who pray t. do not ask,

## token 1

T-15... VIII.1:3 He must side with every sign or t. of your

## told 44

T-1...........I.4:3 You will be t. all you need to know.
T-4.........V.4:6 Being t. by the ego that it is really part of
T-4.........V.4:6 is also t. that the body cannot protect it.
T-5.........in.1:2 happy. I have t. you to think how many
T-5.......VII.4:2 yourself because, as I t. you before, the
T-6...........I.2:5 I have already t. you that you can always
T-6...........I.2:6 I have also t. you that the crucifixion was
T-6.......... I.16:1 remember that I t. them myself that there
T-6.........V.3:3 a child would experience if he were t.,
T-6......V.C.4:2 it. I have already t. you that you can be as
T-7...........I.1:5 I have already t. you that only in this
T-8...........I.1:9 I have t. you what knowledge offers you,
T-9..... VIII.3:2 I t. you that the ego is aware of threat to
T-11.... VIII.5:4 to be t. that if you ask you will receive.
T-12.........I.1:1 You have been t. not to make error real,
T-13.......II.7:3 t. again and again that it will set you free,
T-13.......IV.1:3 been t. that your function in this world is
T-15.....V.10:7 have been t. to offer miracles as I direct,
T-16.......II.1:2 t. that it must include everyone to *be* holy.
T-16.......II.3:2 And when you are t. what is natural, you
T-18.......IX.1:1 been t. to bring the darkness to the light,
T-18.......IX.1:2 And you have also been t. that error must
T-19.......III.5:7 must accept as true what it is t. through it
T-22.......IV.2:5 There will be nothing you will not be t., if
T-25.... VIII.6:6 they are t. that they have never sinned.
T-26.... VIII.6:6 t. that everything brings good that comes
T-27.... VIII.1:8 and joys are different and can be t. apart.
T-28.... VI.1:10 It accepts no role, but does what it is t.,
T-29....... II.8:6 For He is t. that part of Him belongs to
T-29... VII.1:10 that you are t. where happiness abides,
T-31.........I.1:9 t. exactly how to tell one from the other,
W-pI.....79.7:6 We will be t.. Then we will ask for the
W-pI.....79.7:8 ask for the solution to it. And we will be t.
W-pI.....91.3:1 To be t. that what you do not see is there
W-pI...106.1:1 mind, that has not t. you what salvation is
W-pI.135.23:2 are plans to make, you will be t. of them.
W-pII.....in.4:1 to take the step to us that He has t. us,
W-ep .........5:3 You will be t. exactly what God wills for
M-7 ...........4:4 to be t. that continued concern is attack.
M-16 ..........1:5 He will be t. all that his role should be,
M-24 .........4:6 that will be helpful, he will be t. about it.
M-24 .........4:7 it. He will also be t. how to use it. What
S-1 ...........I.2:1 t. to ask the Holy Spirit for the answer to
S-1 ...........I.2:2 You have also been t. that there is only

## tolerance 4

T-2........ III.3:5 T. for pain may be high, but it is not
W-pI.....95.8:4 t. for weakness will enable us to overlook
W-pI...126.3:3 He has not earned your charitable t.,
M-4 ......... III.h Tolerance

## tolerant 2

T-2........ VI.4:6 You are much too t. of mind wandering,
M-4 ...... IX.2:6 And being confident, it is t.. Faithfulness,

## tolerate 10

T-2........ III.4:6 makes it increasingly unable to t. delay,
T-3........ VI.5:3 if only because you cannot t. the idea of
T-9...... VIII.2:9 not to t. self-abasement and seek relief.
T-9..... VIII.6:1 depends solely on your willingness to t. it.
T-12...... III.7:2 conflict of this magnitude he cannot t.. A
T-13...... IV.5:3 The ego cannot t. release from the past,
T-15.........I.3:2 life, and what it wants for you it cannot t..
T-18....... II.2:5 both of the ego's inability to t. reality, and
T-29.........I.5:6 It dictates what its health can t., and what
T-31....... V.4:1 proudly wears can t. attack in self-defense

## tombs 1

T-28....... V.7:5 and no darkened t. where terror rises

## tomorrow 4

W-pI.....50.1:1 you, today and t. and throughout time. In
W-pI.124.10:1 Perhaps today, perhaps t., you will see
W-pI.124.11:1 Perhaps today, perhaps t., you will look
W-pI.124.11:3 sure someday, perhaps today, perhaps t.,

## tongue 6

T-14...... VI.6:3 how can this t. mean anything? Yet even
T-18...... IX.3:6 of it; its t. cannot relay its messages. Yet
T-22.........I.6:6 does not understand will be his native t.,
T-22.........I.8:3 For his will be no alien t.. He will need no
T-31.........I.8:3 the selfsame t. in which the call was made
W-pII.....353.h My eyes, my t., my hands, my feet today

## tongues 5

T-9...........I.6:1 It is impossible to communicate in alien t.
T-27.........I.6:7 your brother and yourself in different t..
T-27....... II.5:8 with power greater than a thousand t..
W-pII..268.2:1 today, nor let our ears attend to lying t..
M-23 .........7:2 in different t. and appeal to different

## tonight 1

W-pI.138.12:1 Before we close our eyes in sleep t., we

## too 141

T-1......... II.4:4 would be t. great for you to encompass.
T-1.......VII.4:3 parts of the course rest t. heavily on these
T-1.......VII.4:5 you may become much t. fearful of what
T-2......... V.6:4 and the body in itself is t. dense. The
T-2........ VI.4:6 are much t. tolerant of mind wandering,
T-4....... II.11:1 It cannot be emphasized t. often that
T-4........ III.1:7 You, t., have a Kingdom that your spirit
T-4...... IV.11:3 t. confused to recognize your own hope.
T-5..... III.10:6 You are at home there, t., because it is a
T-5........ IV.2:8 ideas that are t. weak to increase, but
T-5....... IV.3:10 the light of the Kingdom, making them, t.
T-6.......V.A.4:4 We have t. much to accomplish on behalf
T-7..........II.1:3 If you, t., see him this way, you are seeing
T-7......... V.3:6 This situation, t., can be used either for
T-7...... VII.1:12 is t. powerful to be subject to exclusion.
T-7........ X.5:10 However, this, t., is merely a matter of his
T-8........ VI.1:3 so they t. can lay aside their weakness and
T-8........ IX.3:8 Yet the Holy Spirit, t., has use for sleep,
T-9........ IV.4:1 The ego, t., has a plan of forgiveness
T-10...... III.4:3 taught by sick minds t. divided to know
T-11.......in.1:5 Remember, t., that their results are as
T-11.........I.8:8 t. often repeated that you do not know it.
T-11..VIII.14:3 you t. will laugh at your fears and replace
T-12...... III.7:2 His insane thoughts, t., must be in his
T-12..... VII.8:5 Love, t., is recognized by its messengers.
T-13...... IV.9:1 You, t., will interpret the function of time
T-13...... IX.8:5 are t. afraid to look upon the light within.
T-14...... IX.1:9 the past, t., was changed and interposed
T-14........X.7:2 much t. confused either to recognize love,
T-14........X.7:3 love. You are t. bound to form, and not to
T-15.......I.4:12 ego tries, and all t. frequently succeeds, in
T-15...... III.2:3 is much t. poor a gift to satisfy you. It is
T-15...... III.8:5 it t. little to understand its magnitude.
T-16........II.6:9 come t. near to truth to renounce it now,
T-16...... IV.2:5 Be not unwilling now; you are t. near, and
T-16.... VI.10:2 for you have come t. far to yield to the
T-17..... IV.11:2 It is a picture, t., set in a frame. Yet if you
T-17..... V.14:6 Yet because it is within, the gladness, t., is
T-17..... VII.6:7 Nothing t. small or too enormous, too
T-17..... VII.6:7 Nothing too small or t. enormous, too
T-17..... VII.6:7 too enormous, t. weak or too compelling,
T-17..... VII.6:7 too enormous, too weak or t. compelling,
T-18..... VII.1:1 You still have t. much faith in the body as
T-18.... VIII.9:8 but has grown t. weary to go on alone.
T-18.... IX.11:6 There is t. much to learn. The readiness
T19. IV.A.16:1 Love, t., would set a feast before you, on
T19....IV.B.2:4 "sacrifice" you feel to be t. great to make,
T19....IV.B.2:4 too great to make, t. much to ask of you.
T19..IV.B.17:3 the Holy Spirit, t., is a communication
T19....IV.C.1:6 Guilt, t., is feared and fearful. Yet it could
T19. IV.D.10:1 Nor is it possible to look on this t. soon.
T-20....... V.3:2 for itself, and therefore values him t. little
T-21........II.1:5 judgment, to be t. much to pay for peace.
T-21...... IV.2:6 the ego claims it is; t. loudly and too often
T-21...... IV.2:6 the ego claims it is; too loudly and t. often
T-21...... IV.3:3 whole defensive system t. seriously for it
T-24........II.9:1 along the way of truth; t. far to falter now.
T-24....... V.1:4 Specialness, t., takes joy in what it sees,
T-24....... V.5:3 They are illusions, t., as much as yours.
T-24..... VI.12:3 nor do you deem this cost t. heavy. But a
T-24..... VI.12:4 and tedious, t. heavy to be borne. Yet to
T-24..... VII.1:6 No effort is t. great, no cost too much, no
T-24..... VII.1:6 No effort is too great, no cost t. much, no
T-24..... VII.1:6 no price t. dear to save his specialness
T-25.........I.5:1 presents itself to you as separate, t.. Not
T-25...... III.8:8 The Holy Spirit, t., sees what He sees as
T-25...... IV.4:6 twisted forms t. far away for recognition,
T-25....VIII.8:5 and is t. weak to save from punishment.
T-25..VIII.13:3 not because you are a miserable sinner t..
T-26....... V.5:1 eternal, passed away in Heaven t. soon for
T-26....... V.5:2 What disappeared t. quickly to affect the
T-26....... V.5:3 t. short to make a world in answer to
T-26... VII.11:7 Here does the Son of God ask not t. much
T-26... VII.11:7 of God ask not too much, but far t. little.
T-26...... IX.2:1 it t. much to ask a little trust for him who
T-27...... VI.2:3 You can have pleasure, t., but only at the
T-27...... VI.6:1 Love, t., has symbols in a world of sin.
T-27....VIII.5:6 illusion, t. ridiculous for anything but to
T-29.........I.1:9 Be wary, then; let Him not come t. close,
T-29........II.1:3 rough and far t. difficult for you to follow
T-30...... VI.5:3 you learn that you must be forgiven t..
T-31.........I.2:8 it hard to learn or t. complex to grasp.

T-31 I.5:4 Its lessons are not true; t. hard to learn,
T-31 I.5:4 true; too hard to learn, t. difficult to see,
T-31 I.5:4 see, and t. opposed to what is really true.
T-31 IV.7:3 find this course to be t. difficult to learn,
T-31 VII.1:2 yet t. alien to your thinking to be helpful,
T-31 VII.2:4 for you are t. confused about yourself. But
W-pI 4.5:4 You are t. inexperienced as yet to avoid a
W-pI 7.3:3 not your aesthetic reactions to the cup, t.,
W-pI 12.6:3 You may find even this t. long. Terminate
W-pI 26.5:2 to a minute if the discomfort is t. great.
W-pI 53.4:4 It is in my mind t., because He created it
W-pI 70.1:3 So, t., does the source of guilt. You see
W-pI 75.9:1 The shorter practice periods, t., will be
W-pI 77.8:1 Remember, t., not to be satisfied with
W-pI 98.4:2 Those still uncertain, t., will join with us,
W-pI 108.9:4 It might be helpful, t., to think of one to
W-pI 109.7:2 minds, t. weary now to go their way alone
W-pI 121.8:3 forgiveness and receive forgiveness, t..
W-pI 124.11:2 a joy t. deep for you to comprehend, a
W-pI 124.11:2 a sight t. holy for the body's eyes to see.
W-pI 133.2:1 You do not ask t. much of life, but far too
W-pI 133.2:1 do not ask too much of life, but far t. little
W-pI 133.11:3 and t. dangerous to be the nothingness it
W-pI 135.7:2 This cannot be t. often emphasized. It will
W-pI 152.2:1 is extreme, and t. inclusive to be true. Yet
W-pI 152.3:6 can not be t. often said and thought about
W-pI 153.6:4 becomes t. sleepy to remember what he
W-pI 153.15:5 hour is t. short a time to spend with God.
W-pI 158.5:6 because the Mind of Christ beholds it t..
W-pI 163.3:1 t. quickly lost however hard to gain,
W-pI 166.4:4 here he is afraid indeed, and homeless, t.;
Wi181-200 2:1 and t. limited to let you see the value of
W-pI 193.11:3 We have been gone t. long, and we would
W-pI 196.12:6 Yet your redemption, t., will come from
W-pII 268.1:4 *For thus will I be able, t., to recognize my Self*
W-pII 343.1:6 *I, t., must give. And so all things are given*
W-pII 14.2:5 words can speak of this and teach it, t., if
M-2 4:6 So has the teacher, t., made an inevitable
M-8 6:7 it–so t. are illusions without distinctions
M-15 3:2 t. small and meaningless to occupy your
M-17 4:3 t., of the intensity of the anger that is
M-17 4:4 t. mild to be even clearly recognized. Or it
M-17 6:11 Him, it seems to you He has forgotten, t..
M-21 3:12 Word stands for. And this, t., is enough.
M-24 4:1 be t. strongly emphasized that this course
M-26 1:6 They, t., have not attained the necessary
M-26 4:9 be t. concerned with goals for which you
C-2 7:6 And look an instant, t., on what you left
C-3 5:1 Forgiveness is a symbol, t., but as the
P-2 II.6:7 His eyes is t. fragmented to be meaningful
P-2 III.4:4 t. advanced to believe in sickness and too
P-2 III.4:4 to believe in sickness and t. near to God
P-2 IV.10:5 It cannot be t. strongly emphasized that
P-2 VI.7:3 statement cannot be t. often remembered
P-3 II.9:9 Many patients, t., consider this strange
S-1 in.1:3 Endless the harmony, and endless, t., the
S-1 II.4:4 have need of prayer, and great need, t..
S-3 in.1:3 should not be t. strongly emphasized, for
S-3 II.2:3 But we are thankful, t., the need is done

**took** 17

T-16 III.5:6 the place of what you t. in to replace them
T-16 VI.8:5 it t. to fix your mind so firmly on illusions
T-18 IX.13:2 it calls to you to follow the course it t.,
T-20 I.4:3 it. I was a stranger and you t. me in, not
T-26 V.12:4 the time it t. for God to give His Answer
T-26 V.13:1 when the time of terror t. the place of love
T-26 VII.15:3 justify a miracle whatever form they t.. In
T-28 I.5:9 by time, which t. away their cause.
T-28 IV.6:4 But if you t. your own away would he be
T-30 V.7:4 their hands it was Christ's hand they t.,
W-pI 98.3:5 They t. the stand which we will take today
W-pI 98.4:1 us; all who t. the stand we take today will
W-pI 105.2:2 than was received by him who t. the gift.
W-pI 135.18:3 blessing shine in every step you ever t..
W-pI 158.9:4 It matters not what form they t., nor how
W-pI 160.6:7 in, and t. no alien thought to be Itself.
S-3 IV.9:7 healed My Son and t. him from the cross.

**tool** 1

T-27 IV.5:6 An honest question is a learning t. that

**top** 1

S-1 II.7:2 At the t. there is a transformation much

**topple** 1

T-28 VII.5:11 The wind will t. it, and rain will come and

**tops** 1

T-18 IX.6:3 softly to the mountain t. that rise above it

**torment** 2

T-12 VII.13:5 It will t. you while you live, but its hatred
T-31 VII.10:2 be miserable, and remain in hell and t.?

**torn** 10

T-5 V.3:10 a part of Him has been t. away by you.
T-6 I.9:2 I was betrayed, abandoned, beaten, t.,
T-13 XI.1:5 No one finds himself ravaged and t. in
T-19 III.6:4 be split, and t. between good and evil;
T-23 II.12:8 secret gift, t. from your brother's body,
T-23 III.6:10 the body, t. between the natural desire to
T-25 VIII.6:4 to strike them dead with lightning bolts t.
W-pI 74.1:5 idea that you are t. by conflicting goals.
W-pI 109.4:2 and while the world is t. by winds of hate
W-pI 121.3:1 The unforgiving mind is t. with doubt,

**torture** 1

T-27 VIII.2:7 slave of bodies that would hurt and t. it.

**tortured** 3

T-14 V.8:6 and attract all t. minds to join with you in
T19. IV.D.16:4 of guilt from his disturbed and t. mind.
W-pI 192.6:1 pain was lifted from a sick and t. mind. Is

**toss** 1

T19. IV.D.16:5 and t. it lightly and with happy laughter

**tossed** 1

T-20 II.6:5 no plaything to be t. about a while and

**tosses** 1

T-27 VIII.2:3 and t. them away for senseless things it

**total** 71

T-1 V.3:3 All His children have His t. Love, and all
T-2 II.7:1 The Atonement is a t. commitment. You
T-3 II.2:2 is not real *until* it is t.. The partly innocent
T-3 V.9:7 God's miracles are as t. as His Thoughts
T-4 VII.4:5 which becomes t. only by recognizing all
T-5 V.5:9 it recognizes that only t. allegiance can be
T-6 II.6:5 It is t. inclusion. You cannot change it
T-6 V.C.10:10 inclusion is t. and creation is without
T-7 VI.1:5 and they will affect his t. perception. That
T-7 VI.4:2 Knowledge is t., and the ego does not
T-7 VI.5:2 It perceives their threat as t., because it
T-7 VI.5:2 all commitments the mind makes are t..
T-7 VI.8:7 true. If truth is t., the untrue cannot exist.
T-7 VI.8:8 Commitment to either must be t.; they
T-7 VI.9:8 perceiving in t. contradiction to the Holy
T-7 VII.1:1 deprived, because denial is as t. as love. It
T-7 IX.7:4 The miracle is a lesson in t. perception.
T-7 X.1:2 which is t. confusion about everything. If
T-8 I.6:1 The t. senselessness of such a curriculum
T-8 I.6:2 are in t. disagreement about everything.
T-8 II.2:2 t. disregard of anything it teaches make
T-8 III.2:3 you, being an experience of t. willingness.
T-8 IX.2:2 because t. harmlessness is the condition
T-9 VII.7:2 and this produces a t. lack of knowledge
T-9 VII.7:2 simply because knowledge is t.. Not to
T-9 VIII.9:8 without you because His grandeur is t.,
T-11 II.3:1 And denial is as t. as love. You cannot
T-12 VIII.8:3 invisible, for beholding it is t. perception.
T-13 III.9:3 not offering t. love you will not be healed
T-15 VI.1:3 relationships are seen as t. commitments,
T-15 X.7:2 For t. love would demand total sacrifice.
T-15 X.7:2 For total love would demand t. sacrifice.
T-15 X.7:6 t. Love would completely destroy you.
T-15 X.8:4 if God would demand t. sacrifice of you, it
T-15 X.8:6 you, and does demand t. sacrifice of you.
T-15 X.9:3 must choose between t. freedom and total
T-15 X.9:3 between total freedom and t. bondage,
T-15 XI.2:8 Love must be t. to give Him welcome, for
T-15 XI.3:3 nothing behind, for release is t., and
T-16 V.10:3 t. context in which it is thought to occur.
T-16 VI.4:5 Great Rays would establish the t. lack of
T-16 VII.2:2 with the past and its t. commitment to it.
T-18 I.5:3 it a world of t. unreality *had* to emerge.
T-18 VIII.4:4 its t. dependence on them for its being.
T-18 VIII.8:2 itself. Its t. lack of limit *is* its meaning. It is
T-25 VII.11:6 destruction be the t. cost of any gain at all
T-25 VIII.4:6 for the cost of sin, but not the t. cost. The
T-25 VIII.4:9 And in the t. cost, the greater his the less
T-26 I.2:2 of complete disunity and t. lack of joining
T-26 II.5:1 to yourself, remember this: Justice is t..
T-26 IV.1:2 the gate behind which t. lack of limits lies.
T-26 X.1:6 occurs at all it will be t.. And its presence,
T-27 I.1:8 For sacrifice is t.. If it could occur at all it
T-27 I.4:8 death; a form of vengeance not yet t.. Yet
T-27 V.8:10 t. transfer of your learning is not made by
T-27 V.11:3 Its t. value need not be appraised by you
T-29 I.4:7 for it gets away from t. sacrifice and gives
T-31 V.8:5 of what you now believe for t. loss of self,
W-in 5:2 t. transfer to everyone and everything is
W-pI 65.1:3 obviously necessary for a t. commitment.
W-pI 98.7:3 repetition of today's idea a t. dedication,
W-pI 163.6:2 For death is t.. Either all things die, or else
W-pI 169.6:2 comes to every mind when t. recognition
Wi181-200 1:2 asked for t. dedication all the time as yet.
Wi181-200 1:4 that you will give your t. willingness to
W-pI 195.8:6 is complete you will have t. gratitude, for
W-pII 319.2:1 *Father, Your Will is t.. And the goal which*
M-13 7:1 Do not forget that sacrifice is t.. There
M-24 6:3 Atonement might be equated with t.
M-24 6:3 past and t. lack of interest in the future.
S-1 II.1:3 fuses into t. communication with God. In

**totality** 13

T-4 III.1:6 a message which in its t. transcends the
T-7 VI.4:2 is total, and the ego does not believe in t..
T-7 VII.h The T. of the Kingdom
T-7 VII.10:10 it. Understand totally by understanding t.
T-7 IX.2:3 prevail against a t. that includes God, and
T-7 IX.2:3 includes God, and any t. *must* include God
T-7 IX.7:5 By including any part of t. in the lesson,
T-11 V.13:3 The attempt to understand t. by breaking
T-15 V.2:3 certain aspects of the t. and look to them
T-27 III.5:1 be pictured, so there is no symbol for t..
W-pII 311.1:4 cannot see t. and therefore judges falsely.
W-pII 319.1:5 thinks that what one gains, t. must lose.
W-pII 319.2:2 *And the goal which stems from it shares its t.*

**totally** 75

T-1 I.38:3 to perceive t. rather than selectively.
T-1 VII.3:11 Fantasies become t. unnecessary as the
T-2 II.1:10 This peace is t. incapable of being shaken
T-2 VII.3:12 and Effect relationships t. different from
T-2 VIII.3:4 a concept t. opposed to right-mindedness
T-3 I.4:1 Sacrifice is a notion t. unknown to God.
T-3 II.1:8 No one, therefore, is able to deny truth t.,
T-3 V.5:6 Ingenuity is t. divorced from knowledge,
T-3 V.10:2 those who perceive have not t. accepted
T-3 VI.3:1 and your brothers t. without judgment.

T-4........ I.2:14 make the t. lifeless out of the life-given.
T-4........ I.10:1 and become t. without investment in fear.
T-4........ VI.1:7 and always will be t. unaffected by your
T-4..... VII.3:12 cannot t. lose the ability to communicate,
T-5........... I.1:9 While this kind of thinking is t. alien to
T-5....... V.2:11 a t. meaningless concept except to the ego
T-6........ III.3:1 own mind perceives itself as t. harmless.
T-7......... II.7:8 It is t. free, because nothing discordant
T-7........ III.5:2 This is t. beyond question, and when you
T-7......... V.3:7 This belief is its t. insane premise, and so
T-7......... V.9:6 The ego is t. unable to understand this,
T-7........ VI.3:5 ego draws upon the one source that is t.
T-7...... VI.8:11 that two t. contradictory thought systems
T-7........ VI.9:1 and you are t. committed to neither. Your
T-7........ VI.9:2 is t. beyond question except by you, when
T-7........ VI.9:6 decide. The ego believes this t., being fully
T-7........ VI.9:8 ego therefore is t. committed to untruth,
T-7....... VII.1:3 Nor is it possible to love it t. at times. You
T-7....... VII.1:4 You cannot be t. committed sometimes.
T-7... VII.10:10 Understand t. by understanding totality.
T-7..... VIII.6:2 time, because it is a t. incredible belief,
T-8......... II.1:8 ego is t. confused and totally confusing.
T-8......... II.1:8 ego is totally confused and t. confusing.
T-8........ IX.2:2 The reality of everything is t. harmless,
T-9........... I.3:4 something of which you are t. unaware.
T-9........... I.9:4 security of reality, fear is t. meaningless.
T-9........ I.11:3 the impossible in order to be happy is t.
T-9........ IV.8:4 Anyone who elects a t. insane guide must
T-9........ IV.8:4 insane guide must be t. insane himself.
T-9........ VI.7:6 Everything else would be t. meaningless.
T-9..... VIII.4:3 in it. Grandeur is t. without illusions, and
T-11....... V.7:3 The ego is t. confused about reality, but it
T-12...... III.9:6 world you made is therefore t. chaotic,
T-12...... IV.3:2 would be t. inadequate in love's presence,
T-12....... V.9:3 it. The curriculum is t. unambiguous,
T-13....... X.6:3 must learn that guilt is always t. insane,
T-13...... XI.2:1 His Son's imagined "enemy" is t. unreal.
T-14......... I.3:8 the world is t. insane and leads to nothing
T-14.... IV.10:1 guiltless and the guilty are t. incapable of
T-14....... X.8:1 content, and is t. unconcerned with it. To
T-16..... V.16:4 choosing possible, and they are t. unreal.
T-16...... VI.4:1 The special relationship is t. meaningless
T-17...... III.2:2 relationships into which they enter are t.
T-17...... IV.5:2 It does not realize that it is t. insane. And
T-18......... I.7:7 shifting and t. meaningless patterns that
T-18... VIII.5:3 but by no means t. dependent on its one
T-19......... I.6:7 and seen as t. unreconcilable with truth,
T-19......... I.7:4 system, but t. disconnected to each other.
T-19...... III.6:2 what is part of Him is t. unlike the rest. If
T-20...... III.8:1 judgment of what is t. bereft of judgment
T-21....... V.7:9 Only the t. insane can disregard them,
T-26...... IV.2:3 parting here, for everything is t. forgiven.
T-31......... I.2:6 that what is t. confused is easier to learn
W-pI........ 1.3:4 idea for the day, use it t. indiscriminately.
W-pI...... 20.2:6 because your mind is t. undisciplined,
W-pI...... 38.1:3 Your holiness is t. unlimited in its power
W-pI...... 39.1:2 simple, very clear and t. unambiguous.
W-pI...... 53.2:7 what is t. insane and has no meaning.
W-pI...... 53.3:2 The t. insane engenders fear because it is
W-pI...... 65.8:5 see now that will be t. changed when you
W-pI.170.10:1 Where does the t. insane belief in gods of
W-pII.... 10.2:2 it sees the world as t. forgiven, without
M-in .......... 3:2 questions may be t. unrelated to what you
M-10.......... 1:1 is t. misunderstood by the world. It is
M-20.......... 2:2 way it is t. unlike all previous experiences.

## totter 1

W-pI... 136.7:3 all your world appears to t. and prepare

## touch 50

T-1........ I.45:2 It may t. many people you have not even
T-7...... XI.3:11 everything you see and t. and remember,
T-13......... I.4:3 he fears and that he sees will never t. him,
T-13...... VI.8:2 and t. them with the touch of Christ. In
T-13...... VI.8:2 and touch them with the t. of Christ. In
T-13..... VII.3:6 not the power to t. the living world at all.
T-13..... VII.4:1 world has the power to t. you even here,
T-13..... VII.7:1 God's Will that nothing t. His Son except
T-14....... X.1:4 Reach out of time and t. it, with the help
T-15....... III.6:9 T. no one, then, with littleness in the
T-15....... V.8:1 how to bring a t. of Heaven to them here.
T-15...... XI.2:9 No fear can t. the Host Who cradles God
T-18...... IX.6:6 Try but to t. it and it disappears; attempt
T19.... IV.C.2:5 T. any one of them with the gentle hands
T-20...... IV.4:3 Nothing but this can t. them, for they see
T-22...... IV.7:6 brother's, and t. this heavy-seeming block
T-23...... IV.8:8 no t. of doubt can ever mar your certainty
T-24...... VII.5:2 cannot t. it with the false ideas you made,
T-26...... IV.3:4 the universe to t. the Heart of all creation?
T-27......... I.5:1 Now in the hands made gentle by His t.,
T-27......... I.5:8 and no attack can ever t. him with the
T-29......... I.4:4 And then your bodies seem to get in t.,
T-29....... V.6:1 light the t. of evil on it may appear to be.
T-30.... IV.4:11 See none in them and they will t. you not.
T-30.... VIII.3:4 a prayer the miracle t. not some dreams,
T-31...... VI.1:8 all Heaven bends to t. your eyes and bless
W-pI...... 26.8:2 thoroughly than to t. on a larger number.
W-pI...... 69.2:3 to get in t. with the salvation of the world.
W-pI...... 69.6:3 Reach out and t. them in your mind.
W-pI...... 93.6:5 Nothing can t. it, or change what God
W-pI...... 99.4:2 without attack and with no t. of pain?
W-pI... 109.5:2 while time goes by without its t. upon you
W-pI... 124.1:4 Everything we t. takes on a shining light
W-pI.137.10:1 t. or those who seem to have no contact
W-pI... 151.3:6 You think your fingers t. reality, and close
W-pI... 151.7:2 nor what your fingers' t. reports of him.
W-pI.151.11:2 and every happening that seems to t. on
W-pI... 157.3:1 it will be given you to feel a t. of Heaven,
W-pI... 157.5:1 from your fingertips to those you t., and
W-pI... 166.8:1 should feel Christ's t. upon your shoulder
W-pI.166.12:2 His t. on you has made you like Himself.
W-pI.166.13:5 comes to those who feel the t. of Christ,
W-pI.166.14:5 Your hand becomes the giver of Christ's t.
W-pI.166.15:2 of what Christ's t. can offer everyone. God
W-pI.166.15:4 to accept His gifts, and feel the t. of Christ
W-pII...... 4.1:5 need have they of sights or sounds or t.?
W-pII..... 289.h The past is over. It can t. me not.
W-pII.. 355.1:4 *it. Even now my fingers t. it. It is very close.*
P-2......... V.5:6 a hand to reach His Son and t. his heart.
P-3......... II.3:6 rise and grow; a patient will t. his heart,

## touched 16

T-13....... in.3:6 Adam's "sin" could have t. no one, had he
T-13....... X.2:3 For all relationships that guilt has t. are
T-13... X.11:11 *unto his Father that no guilt has ever t. him.*
T-13.... X.12:1 him has t. his innocence in any way. His
T-14......... I.2:7 area of your perception that it has not t.,
T-14.... III.17:5 who will be t. in any way by the decision.
T-16....... V.1:5 attempted that have not been t. upon.
T-18......... I.7:6 t. with insanity and swirling lightly off on
T-23...... III.6:6 on it in safety from above and not be t..
T-25...... II.8:3 The darkness t. him not, nor you who
T-29....... II.4:7 t. the holy ground whereon you stand,
W-pI... 158.7:3 the body; an idea beyond what can be t., a
W-pI... 161.7:3 a form he can be t. and seen and heard,
W-pI... 164.4:3 in you the thought of sin has never t.. All
W-pI... 166.9:2 Christ's hand has t. your shoulder, and
M-14 ....... 2:11 not be destroyed nor attacked nor even t..

## touches 4

T-17....... II.2:5 strongest thing that t. on this world at all.
T-17....... II.5:4 spot His reason t. grows alive with beauty
T-17..... VII.8:9 and t. everyone to whom the situation's
W-pI... 110.8:1 saved, with power to save whoever t. Him

## touching 2

T-4......... V.6:3 just as it does with all issues t. on the real
T-30....... V.3:5 a little longer, with his feet still t. earth.

## touchstone 1

W-pI... 157.5:3 it becomes the t. for the holy Thoughts of

## toward 66

T-2......... V.6:6 has learned to look beyond it t. the light.
T-2......... V.7:5 also looks immediately t. the Atonement.
T-2......... V.7:7 is merely channelized t. correction.
T-2...... VIII.4:1 first step t. freedom involves a sorting out
T-2...... VIII.5:5 judgment cannot be directed t. yourself,
T-4........... I.2:3 perceive it as a move t. further separation,
T-4.......... II.5:6 Your attitudes even t. this are necessarily
T-4........ III.8:3 you have taken the first step t. preparing
T-5........... I.7:5 own integration t. the paths of creation. It
T-6......... I.16:2 thought system t. which I am guiding you
T-6.......... II.9:7 can inspire perception and lead it t. God.
T-6...... V.B.9:1 a giant step t. the unified perception that
T-6...... V.B.9:2 be pushing t. the center of your thought
T-6...... V.C.3:1 is a major step t. fundamental change.
T-7........ IV.2:2 intermediary step t. the knowledge that
T-8...... VIII.1:1 Attitudes t. the body are attitudes toward
T-8...... VIII.1:1 toward the body are attitudes t. attack.
T-9.......... II.8:6 not going beyond yourself but t. yourself.
T-11......... II.1:1 step t. recognizing what you truly want.
T-11...... III.5:6 Turn t. the light, for the little spark in you
T-12... VII.13:6 your destruction is the one end t. which it
T-16...... III.2:6 all your learning has been directed t.
T-17...... III.3:4 t. further fragmentation and unreality.
T-17....... V.2:1 step t. the perception of the real world, is
T-18...... III.3:5 You go t. love still hating it, and terribly
T-21...... III.1:2 t. which the seeming union is adjusted.
T-21...... III.7:1 served sin are redirected now t. holiness.
T-21....... V.8:3 perception t. what the mind has valued.
T-21... VI.7:10 leads steadily away from madness t. the
T-22... VI.9:10 look away from it and t. your brother.
T-25....... V.5:3 And so you walk t. Heaven or toward hell,
T-25....... V.5:3 And so you walk toward Heaven or t. hell,
T-25....... V.6:1 the Son of God may cherish t. himself, is
T-26... III.1:11 a necessary step in the advance t. oneness
T-26...... V.1:11 You but choose whether to go t. Heaven,
T-30....... V.7:3 been surely set away from idols t. reality.
T-31.. VIII.11:1 looks with fixed determination t. the light
W-pI....... 4.3:2 the first steps t. the goal of separating the
W-pI..... 14.3:6 direction is t. perfect safety and perfect
W-pI..... 24.2:3 The idea for today is a step t. opening
W-pI..... 26.8:3 those that occur to you t. the end, less
W-pI..... 29.4:2 Try to avoid the tendency t. self-directed
W-pI..... 35.5:2 T. the latter part of the exercise period,
W-pI..... 45.8:1 this Foundation t. which the exercises for
W-pI..... 60.3:4 everything I see will lean t. me to bless me
W-pI..... 60.4:4 I am walking steadily on t. truth. There is
W-pI..... 61.3:3 giant stride t. taking your rightful place in
W-pI..... 74.1:1 t. which all our exercises are directed.
W-pI..... 78.4:3 the world reversed, as we look out t. truth
W-pI..... 79.9:3 Our efforts will be directed t. recognizing
W-pI..... 94.5:9 you do will be a giant stride t. your release
W-pI... 121.9:2 t. one whom you think of as an enemy,
W-pI. 155.11:3 And we step forth t. this, as we progress
W-pI. 186.10:3 and concentrated drive t. goals like these?
W-pI... 194.1:1 idea takes another step t. quick salvation,
W-pI... 200.8:4 is easy, sloping gently t. the bridge where
W-pI. 200.10:5 And you look up and on t. Heaven, with
WpI rVI.in.7:4 by day, advancing t. the goal He set for us
W-pII .... in.1:5 end t. which our practicing was always
M-4 ........... 1:6 born in the holy relationship t. which the
M-4 .... IX.2:10 T. Them it looks, seeking until it finds.
M-9 ........... 2:5 world's training is directed t. achieving a
M-25 ......... 1:6 be directed t. this one great final surprise,
C-in ........... 2:6 experience t. which the course is directed.
C-3............. 1:1 is for God and t. God but not of Him. It is
P-2........... I.1:9 direction is one of progress t. the truth.

## towards 15

T-1........ III.9:1 t. those who can use them for themselves.
T-4........... I.2:2 of it as a move t. healing the separation.
T-4....... II.11:2 perception is a steppingstone t. it. The
T-4........ VI.2:3 Whenever you act egotistically t. another,
T-5...... VI.11:7 speaking for patience t. the Sonship in
T-6...... V.A.6:7 than take the next step t. its resolution.
T-6.... V.C.4:10 direct it t. creation within the Kingdom.
T-6...... V.C.5:3 and goes beyond them t. real integration.
T-12......... I.8:4 taken a step away from reality, not t. it.

W-pI.....74.2:1 exercises for today are directed t. finding
W-pI.....95.3:2 again direct our exercises t. reaching your
W-pI...127.6:5 in your advance t. its established goal.
C-in ...........3:2 it is planned only to set the direction t. it.
C-3.............1:4 it leads away from error and not t. it.
P-3.........II.8:2 he reaches this in time he can go t. it.

**tower** 1

T-26......IV.3:4 altar to rise and t. far above the world,

**toy** 4

T-20....... II.6:6 a t. you would pick up from time to time
T-20....VIII.7:1 Judgment is but a t., a whim, the
T-29...... IX.5:4 Or can a t. grow large and dangerous and
T-29...... IX.5:9 And so he makes of anything a t., to make

**toys** 27

T-29.........I.9:4 What t. or trinkets in the gap could serve
T-29...... IX.4:4 idols are the t. you dream you play with.
T-29...... IX.4:5 Who has need of t. but children? They
T-29...... IX.4:6 and give their t. the power to move about,
T-29...... IX.4:7 Yet everything their t. appear to do is in
T-29...... IX.4:8 up the dream in which their t. are real,
T-29...... IX.5:2 The t. have turned against the child who
T-29...... IX.5:5 thoughts and gives them to the t. instead.
T-29...... IX.6:2 Seek not to retain the t. of children. Put
T-30...... IV.2:1 gods you made are blown-up children's t..
T-30...... IV.3:1 there is filled with t. in countless forms.
T-30...... IV.3:6 laugh at popping heads and squeaking t.,
T-30...... IV.3:9 Yet *is* he at the mercy of his t.? And *can*
T-30...... IV.4:6 They are but t., my child, so do not grieve
T-30...... IV.4:9 but merely looked upon as children's t.
T-30...... IV.5:9 Look calmly at its t., and understand that
T-30...... IV.8:2 without the t. of terror that you made. No
T-30...... IV.8:8 The gap is emptied of the t. of fear, and
W-pI.....39.1:3 with intellectual feats nor logical t.. We
W-pI...151.8:4 guilt, unwilling now to play with t. of sin;
W-pI.153.12:2 replace their fearful t. with joyous games,
W-pI.153.13:3 come, in which we put away the t. of guilt,
W-pI.182.12:7 for all the t. of battle you have made. And
W-pII .....4.5:2 put away these sharp-edged children's t.?
W-pII .258.1:3 while the t. and trinkets of the world are
W-pII .346.1:7 *forgetting all the foolish t. I made as I behold*
M-13 .........4:3 adult resent the giving up of children's t.?

**trace** 17

T-13...... XI.5:1 and every t. of guilt that His dear Son has
T19. IV.D.16:4 remove all t. of guilt from his disturbed
T-20...... VI.9:1 and leave no t. behind their going. The
T-22...... VI.6:8 No t. of anything in time can long remain
T-23.......I.10:3 and let forgiveness sweep away all t. of
T-24...... VI.1:1 so complete that not one t. of conflict still
T-26...... X.6:2 a t. of all the happy sparkle that salvation
T-27..... II.3:11 and retains no t. of condemnation that he
T-31..VIII.12:4 No t. of it remains. Not one illusion is
W-pI.....75.2:6 old one has left no t. upon it in its passing
W-pI...107.1:4 not a t. by which to be remembered. They
W-pI.135.19:1 future undisturbed, without a t. of sorrow
W-pII .239.1:3 He shares His glory any t. of sin and guilt?
M-26 .........2:1 directly, retaining no t. of worldly limits
C-2.............6:8 come: Its opposite has gone without a t..
C-6.............5:6 and no t. remains of dreams of spite in
S-2...........I.9:6 There can be no t. of it remaining, if the

**trade** 4

T-16....... V.7:3 tries to "t." itself for the self of another.
T-26...... IX.2:3 would you t. Them for an ancient hate?
W-pI.....77.8:3 *I will not t. miracles for grievances. I want*
C-ep...........1:9 you wait for this and t. it for illusions,

**traded** 2

W-pI.....73.3:1 in which guilt is t. back and forth, and
S-1...........I.4:6 this be t. for a bit of trifling advice about a

**traffic** 1

W-pI.....73.2:3 the ego employs to t. in grievances. They

**tragedy** 2

W-pI...166.8:5 And what becomes of all the t. you sought
M-25 .........4:8 turned to weakness are t. indeed. Yet

**tragic** 6

T-3 ..........I.2:3 applications and genuinely t. on a wider
T-5 ....... VI.1:3 not matter in eternity, but it is t. in time.
W-pI.....41.2:5 is, despite the serious and t. forms it may
W-pI...131.7:1 goals, its painful pleasures and its t. joys.
W-pI...166.6:3 Yet is he really t., when you see that he is
S-2..........II.8:3 them by as worthless in their t. offerings.

**train** 7

T-6 ........ V.2:4 you t. them to recognize the difference
W-in..........1:4 purpose of this workbook to t. your mind
W-in..........4:1 The purpose of the workbook is to t. your
W-pI.......4.1:6 if you t. yourself to look at your thoughts,
W-pI.......4.3:2 The aim here is to t. you in the first steps
W-pI.......8.3:1 for today is to begin to t. your mind to
W-pII .258.1:1 All that is needful is to t. our minds to

**trained** 9

T-2 ......VII.1:9 but you can be t. to think that way. All
T-7 ....... XI.5:9 You have t. yourself not to recognize it,
T19..IV.A.12:3 Fear's messengers are t. through terror,
T19..IV.A.14:1 send instead of those you t. through fear.
T-21 .......II.5:3 You t. it in its testimony, and as it gave it
W-pI.....44.4:3 and easy one in the world for the t. mind,
C-1 ............7:5 world, and can be t. to do so increasingly.
C-1 ............7:6 and can be t. demonstrates that it cannot
S-3........ III.2:4 Someone knows better, has been better t.,

**training** 20

T-1 ......VII.4:1 This is a course in mind t.. All learning
T-2 ....VII.1:10 All miracle workers need that kind of t..
T-12 ..... VI.6:5 the transfer of t. under the Holy Spirit's
W-in..........2:4 The t. period is one year. The exercises
W-in..........5:1 Transfer of t. in true perception does not
W-in..........5:1 as does transfer of the t. of the world. If
W-in..........6:4 This will interfere with transfer of t.. The
W-pI.......4.3:4 It is also the beginning of t. your mind to
W-pI.....44.3:3 and represents a major goal of mind t.. It
W-pI.....44.3:5 t. must be accomplished if you are to see.
W-pI.....65.4:4 part of the long-range disciplinary t. your
W-pI.....95.4:4 discipline, and of your need for mind t.. It
M-4 ...... IV.1:8 but must learn,–and fairly early in his t.,
M-9 ...........1:4 step in the newly made teacher of God's t.
M-9 ...........1:5 since t. is always highly individualized.
M-9 ...........1:7 are given a slowly evolving t. program, in
M-9 ...........2:1 As the teacher of God advances in his t.,
M-9 ...........2:5 world's t. is directed toward achieving a
M-16 .......11:9 All through their t., every day and every
P-3..........II.2:2 For this, however, he needs special t.,

**trains** 2

M-9 ...........2:6 world t. for reliance on one's judgment as
M-9 ...........2:7 Our curriculum t. for the relinquishment

**traitor** 4

T-12 .. VII.14:1 The ego is not a t. to God, to Whom
T-12 .. VII.14:2 a t. to you who believe that you have been
W-pI...190.3:2 as mad, and seen as t. to Himself. If God
S-1..........II.4:7 Be t. to no one, or you will be treacherous

**traits** 2

M-4 ...........1:1 surface t. of God's teachers are not at all
M-4 ........II.1:1 All other t. of God's teachers rest on trust

**tranquil** 11

T19 ...IV.A.1:4 its t. dwelling place from which it gently
T-29 .......V.2:4 and quiet, t. in the might of its Creator,
W-pI .. 107.9:6 give you peace so deep and t. that you will
W-pI 198.11:3 is there t. light across the face of earth,
W-pII ..... 7.1:5 has made possible perception's t. end.
W-pII . 326.1:8 *Your effects into the t. Heaven of Your Love,*
WpII361-5.1:3 And if I need but stillness and a t., open
M-4 ..... I.A.8:3 on in all "emergencies" as well as t. times.
M-20 ......... 4:8 A t. mind is not a little gift. Would you
M-28 ......... 4:1 are t. with a stir of deep anticipation, for
S-2........... I.6:6 remains in t. silence and in perfect peace.

**tranquility** 7

W-pI .. 108.7:5 us. Light is t., and in that peace is vision
W-pI .. 122.8:3 your heart with deep t. as ancient truths,
W-pI .. 124.5:2 are restored to the t. and peace of mind in
W-pII . 273.1:1 are now ready for a day of undisturbed t..
W-pII ... 12.3:4 and undisturbed, in deepest silence and t.
M-4 ..... I.A.8:4 Indeed, the t. is their result; the outcome
M-4 ..... I.A.8:9 to change t. for something more desirable

**transcend** 14

T-1 ........I.17:1 Miracles t. the body. They are sudden
T-8 .........V.6:8 my hand because you want to t. the ego.
T-11 ..... VI.2:3 t. your prison and ascend to the Father?
T-12 .......V.5:2 provided by a Teacher Who can t. your
T-15 ......I.14:5 Long enough to t. all of the ego's making,
T-18 ... IX.12:6 and yours of Him so far t. all learning that
T-20 ..... VI.9:5 Then lay aside the body and quietly t. it,
T-30 ... VIII.1:8 It must t. all form to be itself. It cannot
W-pI .. 181.1:1 in your ability to t. doubt and lack of sure
W-pI .. 181.2:8 And you will not t. their sight and see the
W-pI .. 181.6:3 should such blocks arise we will t. them
C-1 ............ 7:4 but it cannot t. the perceptual realm. At
P-2..........II.8:5 Only by doing this is it possible to t. the
P-2........ III.2:2 the process, therefore, is to t. these limits.

**transcended** 4

T-12 .... VII.3:3 and space, of magnitude and mass is t.,
T-20 ..... VI.9:7 can attract the mind that has t. them, and
T-27 .......V.3:2 to a state of mind that has t. conflict, and
M-23 ....... 3:10 transcends the body has t. limitation.

**transcendence** 1

T-11 ..... VI.1:6 over the ego, not by attack but by t.. For

**transcendent** 1

P-1............. 2:3 more t. aim can there be than to recall the

**transcending** 3

T-8 .........V.4:4 success in t. the ego is guaranteed by God
T-29 ... VIII.6:2 beyond the infinite, a time t. the eternal.
P-2........ III.2:3 for t. all limitations has been given them.

**transcends** 19

T-1 ........I.48:2 Only revelation t. it, having nothing to do
T-2 .......V.10:5 I said before that only revelation t. time.
T-2 ...... VII.6:3 Sonship in its Oneness t. the sum of its
T-3 .........V.8:6 t. the laws governing perception, because
T-4 ....... III.1:6 which in its totality t. the sum of its parts.
T-11 ......V.16:4 and no thought system t. its source. Yet
T-14 ........X.2:7 is the one thing you can do that t. order,
T-15 .......I.15:3 He Who t. time for you understands what
T-15 ..... VI.3:5 t. the concept of loss of power completely.
W-pI .. 122.1:4 of worth and beauty that t. the world? Do
W-pI .. 123.3:5 Be thankful that your value far t. your
W-pI .. 157.9:2 there will be an instant which t. all vision,
W-pI .. 158.6:5 for it t. what needs to be accomplished.
W-pI 183.11:6 in which communication far t. all words,
WpI.rVI.in.3:7 have a function that t. the world we see.

W-pII..269.1:4 *I ask for the illusion which t. all those I made.*
W-pII..346.1:4 *What I seek today t. all laws of time and*
M-23........3:10 t. the body has transcended limitation.
M-25..........2:7 Who t. these limits in any way is merely

**transfer** 23

T-5...........I.6:4 that t. to it is at last possible. Perception
T-5........III.1:2 for the t. of perception to knowledge, so
T-7.........II.1:1 the elements they share, can t. easily to it.
T-7.....VIII.3:5 their t. value is limited by his confusion.
T-11...VIII.1:9 is the t. of all perception to knowledge.
T-12.......V.6:4 You cannot t. what you have not learned,
T-12......VI.6:3 so holy that its t. to holiness is merely its
T-12......VI.6:5 the t. of training under the Holy Spirit's
T-13...VIII.3:1 with knowledge, making t. to it possible.
T-25.........I.7:5 use all learning to t. illusions to the truth,
T-27.......V.8:8 All learning aims at t., which becomes
T-27.....V.8:10 total t. of your learning is not made by
T-27.....V.10:1 t. of your learning to the One Who really
W-in..........5:1 T. of training in true perception does not
W-in..........5:1 as does t. of the training of the world. If
W-in..........5:2 total t. to everyone and everything is
W-in..........6:4 This will interfere with t. of training. The
W-in..........7:3 the conditions necessary for this kind of t.
W-pI.121.12:2 a friend. Try to t. the light you learned to
M-4......I.A.4:3 ability to t. what he has learned to new
M-4......I.A.6:4 to see the t. value of what he has learned.
M-4......I.A.8:4 consistency of thought and full t.. This is
M-5........II.4:5 The t. value of one true idea has no end or

**transferred** 3

T-5...........I.6:5 knowledge, but it can be t. to knowledge,
T-5...........I.6:6 the literal meaning of t. or "carried over,"
T-18.......II.9:6 dream of waking is easily t. to its reality.

**transfers** 1

T-12......VI.6:4 Love t. to love without any interference,

**transfiguration** 2

W-pI.124.10:1 you will see your own t. in the glass this
W-pI.151.16:3 Through your t. is the world redeemed,

**transform** 7

T-9.....VIII.9:5 t. to the Will of God does not exist at all.
T-17......III.6:9 will let this spark t. the relationship so
T-17.......IV.2:3 special relationships, but would t. them.
T-18. VIII.11:1 t. it into a garden of peace and welcome.
W-pI.....23.4:5 and so t. them that you will love them,
W-pI...157.5:3 For your experience today will so t. your
M-5........II.4:4 learning will generalize and t. the world.

**transformation** 3

T-17....IV.14:4 a t. of both pictures can at last occur. And
W-pI...164.5:6 eyes of Christ. Now is its t. clear to you.
S-1.........II.7:2 At the top there is a t. much like your own

**transformed** 25

T-13.....X.14:3 t. into kindness will never more be what it
T-14........V.1:2 it t. into a radiant message of God's Love,
T-15......I.15:9 of God's creation, it is t. into forever. Give
T-17......III.5:4 And the t. past is made like the present.
T-17....IV.15:1 is t. into what lies beyond the picture. As
T-17........V.2:2 old, unholy relationship, t. and seen anew
T-17.....VII.9:3 lead you to illusions t. to means for truth.
T-18. VIII.10:4 see your little garden gently t. into the
T-18....IX.10:6 of light; nothing perceived, forgiven nor t.
T19. IV.A.15:2 The world will be t. before your sight,
T-21........II.1:2 to have your whole relationship t. to joy;
T-22.........in.4:4 And here is sight of differences t. to vision
T-23.........I.4:4 as an intruder on your peace is here t.,
T-26........II.7:5 cure, has been t. into a universal blessing.
T-26.....V.14:5 your hate has been t. into a world of love.
W-pI...138.7:2 now t. from the intent you gave it; that it
W-pI.151.14:2 And as each thought is thus t., it takes on
W-pI.161.12:6 see him suddenly t. from enemy to savior;
W-pI.166.15:4 Be witness in your happiness to how t. the
W-pI...194.5:3 was slave to time t. into a holy instant,
W-pII..249.1:6 it quickly is t. into the light that it reflects.
W-pII..326.2:1 us today behold earth disappear, at first t.
M-28.........4:6 light their purpose is t. and understood.
S-1.........II.8:6 And then all things will be t. together,
S-2.......in.1:11 Accomplish this and you have been t..

**Transformer** 1

T-17.......II.5:2 The great T. of perception will undertake

**transforming** 2

T-7........XI.5:2 of other minds, t. them into majesty. The
W-pI...156.5:5 you, t. in Its gentle light all things unto Its

**transforms** 2

T-17.......II.6:2 For forgiveness literally t. vision, and lets
T-17... VIII.3:4 This power instantly t. all situations into

**transgressions** 1

T-27.....II.1:10 And if you forgive him his t., you but add

**transient** 2

T-20......III.7:5 Ask not this t. stranger, "What am I?" He
W-pI...122.3:5 fancied value, trivial effect or t. promise,

**transition** 8

T-13......IV.4:5 the present only as a brief t. to the future,
T-16......VI.7:1 more than a t. in the perspective of reality
T-16......VI.7:4 In the t. there is a period of confusion, in
T-16......VI.8:2 it will keep gentle pace with you in your t.
T-16......VI.8:5 which precedes the actual t., is far shorter
T-22......VI.3:5 the soft t. from means to end as easy as is
T-26..............h THE T.
W-pI.159.10:5 a sweet t. can be made from death to life;

**transitory** 3

W-pI...107.3:3 no room for t. thoughts and dead ideas to
W-pI...152.5:1 with t. states by definition false. And that
W-pI.184.10:1 learning of the world becomes a t. phase;

**translate** 12

T-7.......VII.7:4 His patience can t. attack into blessing.
T-11. VIII.13:3 is helped to t. his "ghost" into a curtain,
T-12.........I.8:3 Holy Spirit must still t. the fear into truth.
T-12.......I.10:4 fear with love and t. error into truth. And
T-14.....X.11:1 Spirit t. His communications through you
T-15.......II.2:3 He has appointed to t. time into eternity.
T-15.......V.5:3 He can t. them into holiness by removing
T-16.......II.5:5 For His task is to t. the miracle into the
T-25......VI.5:4 to t. specialness from sin into salvation.
W-pI...192.3:5 power to t. in form the wholly formless.
W-pII..270.1:1 *and it has power to t. all that the body's eyes*
M-29.........6:5 the power to t. your prayers of the heart

**translated** 13

T-1.........II.2:1 personal and cannot be meaningfully t..
T-7.........II.4:2 must be t. for those who speak different
T-7........IV.4:4 must be t. into a way of remembering.
T-9.........V.7:7 perception ultimately is t. into knowledge
T-11... VIII.1:5 and only real perception will be t. into
T-12.......V.7:2 T. into curricular terms this means, "Try
T-12... VIII.8:6 perception is easily t. into knowledge, for
T-14.....VII.5:8 t. by the Holy Spirit from means of self-
T-15.....IX.1:5 is t. into knowledge by the part that God
T-16......IV.2:5 perfect safety, t. quietly from war to peace
W-pII......6.4:1 them come to Him, to be t. into truth. He
W-pII .....7.2:2 For sights and sounds must be t. from the
P-2........VI.5:3 So closely is one t. into the other, that a

**translates** 11

T-6......V.A.2:4 have made and t. it into a learning device.
T-6......V.A.5:1 to God, t. communication into being, just
T-6......V.A.5:1 ultimately t. perception into knowledge.
T-7..........II.4:3 he must alter the form of what he t., never
T-7..........II.5:2 t. only to preserve the original meaning in
T-9........IV.3:3 He t. what you have made into what God
T-9.........V.7:8 and t. his perception into sureness by
T-15.........II.2:7 altar, where He gently t. hell into Heaven.
T-20..VIII.10:4 t. your nightmares into happy dreams;
T-26......IV.1:2 It t. the world of sin into a simple world,
P-2........VI.3:1 t.; it does not hear. The eye reproduces; it

**translating** 3

T-7...........I.6:5 the task of t. the useless into the useful,
T-7..........II.5:1 purpose in t. is exactly the opposite. He
P-2........VI.3:4 reproducing its desires and t. them into

**translation** 6

*See also* re-translation

T-3........IV.6:2 why perception involves an exchange or t.
T-6......V.C.5:8 He is getting you ready for the t. of *having*
T-7..........II.7:6 no t. because it is perfectly understood,
T-8.......VII.7:2 the t. of one order of reality into another.
T-11....VIII.1:8 not its destruction, but its t. into Heaven.
T-12........II.1:1 are merely the t. of denial into truth. If to

**translations** 1

T-7..........II.6:6 You will not understand His t. while you

**Translator** 2

*translator*

T-7..........II.4:5 Holy Spirit is the T. of the laws of God to
W-pI...157.8:2 dreams of life, T. of perception into truth,

**translator** 1

*Translator*

T-7..........II.4:3 Nevertheless, a good t., although he must

**transmits** 2

T-18......IX.2:5 and the messages it t. to you who made it
T19..IV.B.14:4 It t. to you the feelings that you want.

**transmitting** 1

T-5..........II.1:6 God Himself keeps your will alive by t. it

**transparency** 1

T-18......IX.5:3 Its thinness and t. are not apparent until

**transparent** 2

W-pI.138.11:3 to what is real, is flimsy and t. in the light.
W-pI...159.5:3 solid here are merely shadows there; t.,

**transport** 2

T-28.......I.15:7 and it is He Who will t. His Son across it.
W-pI.....50.3:3 It will t. you into a state of mind that

**transportation** 1

T-18....VI.11:4 will consider what this "t." really entails,

**transported** 2

T-16......III.8:5 who would cross over is literally t. there.

**trembling** 2
T-17....... II.8:2 world, **t.** with readiness to be given you.
T-23.......in.5:7 Who can walk **t.** in a fearful world, and

**tremendous** 2
T-3........ VI.3:1 no idea of the **t.** release and deep peace
P-2...... IV.10:1 then, has a **t.** responsibility. He must

**trespasses** 3
T-31...... VI.6:4 forgiving, for you have forgiven it its **t.**,
W-pI.198.10:4 forgive the **t.** you thought Them guilty of,
P-2......... V.7:6 to forgive himself for all the **t.** with which

**trial** 4
T-14....... V.6:6 is no pain, no **t.**, no fear that teaching this
T-14...... XI.9:4 or pain or **t.** you have has been undone.
W-pI..... 50.3:2 It will lift you out of every **t.**, and raise you
W-pII..292.2:2 *for every* **t.** *we think we still must meet.*

**trials** 2
T-31... VIII.3:1 **T.** are but lessons that you failed to learn
W-pII..292.1:4 of all problems we perceive, all **t.** we see,

**tribulation** 1
T-4...... I.13:10 *have* **t.** *because I have overcome the world.*

**tribulations** 1
W-pI...193.5:2 words the Holy Spirit speaks in all your **t.**,

**tribute** 6
T-15...... III.3:2 that it is true and is but a **t.** to your power
T-15...... III.4:6 you, in **t.** to your magnitude and not your
T-18........ II.1:5 you, and change it into a **t.** to your ego,
T-20.... VI.11:7 to spend this instant paying **t.** to the body
T-24..... VII.2:6 All of the **t.** you have given specialness
W-pI.184.12:6 you made as fitting **t.** to the Son He loves.

**trick** 2
T-4........ IV.1:7 the **t.** of its existence except with mirrors?
W-pI...158.4:1 Time is a **t.**, a sleight of hand, a vast

**tricks** 2
T-13...... III.6:6 all the **t.** and games you offer it can heal it
M-25.......... 3:8 Only by **t.** of magic are special powers

**tried** 34
T-4......... V.6:2 the one function the ego has **t.** to develop,
T-8....... VII.9:5 the mind you **t.** to separate *from* spirit can
T-9......... II.1:1 Everyone who ever **t.** to use prayer to ask
T-9........ IV.4:8 Many have **t.** to do this in my name,
T-11......... I.4:3 you have **t.** to limit what He created, and
T-11..... VII.3:7 autonomy you **t.** to create unlike your
T-12....... II.9:1 have **t.** to banish love have not succeeded,
T-12....... V.4:4 You **t.** to make the separation eternal,
T-12....... V.8:1 You who have **t.** to learn what you do not
T-12... VIII.7:1 matter how much distance you have **t.** to
T-14...... IV.8:3 **t.** to throw yourself away and valued God
T-14...... XI.1:3 **t.** to keep power for yourself have "lost" it
T-15....... X.9:4 You have **t.** many compromises in the
T-16....... II.9:2 never **t.** to solve anything yourself and
T-16...... III.5:4 more to you than you **t.** to take away. He
T-17.... IV.13:1 You who have **t.** so hard, and are still
T-18....... V.2:1 you have **t.** to remove all fear and hatred
T-18. VIII.11:6 **t.** to hide from Heaven straight to Heaven
T-21.......in.2:3 and catastrophe, you **t.** to crucify him. If
T-22...... I.2:12 hard you **t.** to understand its messages.
T-22..... II.11:9 for you, not what you **t.** to give yourself.
T-22...... III.8:6 **t.** to see your sins in him to save yourself.
T-28..... VII.5:5 Yet all it means is that you **t.** to keep a
W-pI..... 56.1:6 I have **t.** to give my inheritance away in
W-pI..... 59.4:5 I have **t.** to define what seeing is, and I
W-pI..... 66.9:2 and the many ways in which you **t.** to find
W-pI..... 70.4:1 have **t.** to do just the opposite, making
W-pI... 108.6:1 it can be **t.** so easily and seen as true. And
W-pI... 108.6:2 works, in every circumstance where it is **t.**
W-pI.136.16:4 that it **t.** to authorize the body to obey.
W-pI... 138.6:2 all the choices you have **t.** to make this is
W-pI.184.15:3 *we have* **t.** *to cast across Your Own reality.*
W-pII..322.1:2 go I find the gifts illusions **t.** to hide,
M-7 .......... 2:1 Whenever a teacher of God has **t.** to be a

**tries** 34
T-4.......... I.8:1 ego **t.** to exploit all situations into forms
T-4......... II.7:8 and **t.** to satisfy itself through the body.
T-4......... V.2:5 **t.** to conceal not only "unacceptable"
T-5......... V.5:9 It **t.** to usurp all the functions of God as it
T-6...... V.B.6:3 The ego **t.** to persuade you that it is up to
T-7......... V.2:3 The ego thus **t.** to teach you that the body
T-7......... V.4:2 Magic always **t.** to weaken. Healing
T-7........ VI.8:1 **t.** to persuade you that you have done this
T-7..... VIII.2:2 The ego always **t.** to preserve conflict. It is
T-7..... VIII.2:4 The ego therefore **t.** to persuade you that
T-8......... II.3:7 undoing of everything the ego **t.** to teach.
T-8......... II.4:1 ego **t.** to teach that you want to oppose
T-8........ III.5:6 The ego **t.** to find them in yourself alone,
T-8........ IX.6:1 mind, **t.** to separate it from the body in an
T-12...... III.6:5 and he always **t.** to handle it by making
T-13...... IV.5:3 ego **t.** to preserve its image by responding
T-15....... I.4:12 Again the ego **t.**, and all too frequently
T-15......... I.5:2 that it **t.** to take the life of someone who
T-15...... IX.3:3 to utilize the means by which it **t.** to turn
T-16....... V.7:3 **t.** to "trade" itself for the self of another.
T-16....... V.7:5 Each partner **t.** to sacrifice the self he does
T-20..... VII.5:1 the means by which the ego **t.** to make the
T-21.... III.10:5 which **t.** to use the body to carry out the
T-22...... VI.1:8 one but yearns for freedom and **t.** to find
T-27... VIII.1:7 It **t.** to look for pleasure, and avoid the
T-27... VIII.1:8 it **t.** to teach itself its pains and joys are
W-pI..... 97.1:2 **t.** to weave opposing factors into unity. It
W-pI.133.10:1 though he **t.** to keep its halo clear within
W-pI... 140.1:3 When it **t.** to heal the mind, it sees no
W-pI... 190.4:5 and **t.** to demonstrate must still be true.
M-18 ......... 1:2 **t.** to establish its error or demonstrate its
P-2........ III.3:4 hears and **t.** to answer in the form of help.
P-2........ IV.9:2 he will attack the one who **t.** to save him
P-2....... VII.7:4 He **t.** to heal, and thus at times he may.

**trifling** 3
T-27... VIII.8:4 consequences, but without their **t.** cause.
W-pI... 164.8:2 Your **t.** treasures put away, and leave a
S-1........... I.4:6 this be traded for a bit of **t.** advice about a

**Trinity** 11
T-3......... II.5:4 The Son of God is part of the Holy **T.**, but
T-3......... II.5:4 of the Holy Trinity, but the **T.** Itself is One
T-3........ IV.1:7 the Levels of the **T.** are capable of unity.
T-5.......... I.4:1 the Holy **T.** that has a symbolic function.
T-5........ III.1:4 He is part of the Holy **T.**, because His
T-7.......... I.7:5 that He is the First in the Holy **T.** Itself.
T-8........ IV.8:9 The Holy **T.** is holy *because* It is One. If
T-8...... IV.8:10 are perceiving the Holy **T.** as separated.
T-8...... IV.8:12 of It, the Holy **T.** is as bereft as you are.
T-8........ VI.5:3 Your creations are your gift to the Holy **T.**
T-8........ VI.8:9 and thus increase the joy of the Holy **T.**.

**trinkets** 4
T-20....... II.1:1 all the **t.** made to hang upon the body, or
T-21...... IV.6:7 remaining **t.** still seem to shine and catch
T-29......... I.9:4 What toys or **t.** in the gap could serve to
W-pII..258.1:3 toys and **t.** of the world are sought instead

**trip** 1
T-20...... IV.8:5 and leaving in your way no stones to **t.** on

**triumph** 27
T-9...... VIII.7:8 You cannot **t.**, but you *are* exalted. And in
T-11...... VI.1:6 is the complete **t.** of Christ over the ego,
T-16......... I.5:1 The **t.** of weakness is not what you would
T-16......... I.5:2 And yet you recognize no **t.** but this. This
T-16...... IV.5:2 hate is at all concerned with the "**t.** of love
T-16...... IV.5:3 of love can **t.** over the illusion of hate, but
T-16....... V.5:5 To the ego completion lies in **t.**, and in
T-16....... V.5:5 the "victory" even to the final **t.** over God.
T-16....... V.6:3 relationship is the **t.** of this confusion. It
T-16..... V.10:1 the special relationship as a **t.** over God,
T-18........ II.3:8 trying to **t.** over it and make it serve you.
T19.... IV.C.7:7 the **t.** of the ego's making over creation,
T-23......... I.2:6 it thinks that **t.** over you is possible. And
T-23......... I.4:5 **t.** and attack of any kind are all unknown.
T-23......... I.5:5 of yourself, a wish to **t.** over what you are,
T-23......... I.6:8 it. Illusions cannot **t.** over truth, nor can
T-24......... I.5:8 For specialness is **t.**, and its victory is his
T-24......... I.6:7 love have meaning where the goal is **t.**?
T-25... VII.11:6 suffering. For otherwise would evil **t.**, and
T-25.... VIII.3:7 and death is seen as victory and **t.** over
W-pI... 136.9:3 and chaos sits in **t.** on His throne.
W-pI. 136.12:2 It does not make appeal to might nor **t.**. It
W-pI... 152.7:1 to truth, and suffers death to **t.** over life;
W-pI... 163.7:3 Their stronger will could **t.** over His, and
W-pI... 190.8:4 In pain does fear appear to **t.** over love,
W-pII .236.1:3 It seems to **t.** over me, and tell me what to
M-5 ......... I.2:2 Son and the **t.** of his Father over him. It

**triumphant** 1
T-16......... I.4:7 yield not to the ego's **t.** use of empathy for

**triumphed** 1
T-16..... V.12:4 as the sign that form has **t.** over content,

**triumphing** 1
T-16..... V.11:3 truth, **t.** over it and leaving it helpless. See

**triumphs** 4
T-16.... IV.4:10 it are broken, fear rushes in and hatred **t.**.
T-16...... IV.5:1 There are no **t.** of love. Only hate is at all
T-16....... V.4:1 love from God, that the ego's hatred **t.**.
P-2....... VII.8:2 and all its little **t.** and its dreams of death.

**trivial** 9
T19... IV.D.7:6 mad desire, no **t.** impulse to forget again,
W-pI..... 16.3:3 **t.** and not worth bothering about that it is
W-pI..... 20.3:4 the salvation of the world be a **t.** purpose?
W-pI..... 47.7:3 Let go all the **t.** things that churn and
W-pI..... 50.1:3 placed in the most **t.** and insane symbols;
W-pI..... 63.2:4 you. Accept no **t.** purpose or meaningless
W-pI..... 65.4:3 the **t.** purposes and goals you will pursue.
W-pI... 122.3:5 value, **t.** effect or transient promise, never
W-pI. 138.11:5 it is recognized as but a foolish, **t.** mistake

**trouble** 3
W-pI..... 80.3:2 that has been resolved cannot **t.** you.
W-ep ......... 1:6 you need for anything that seems to **t.** you
M-23 ......... 7:4 without a very present help in time of **t.**; a

**troubled** 1
T-10....... V.5:3 yourself that you need be **t.** over nothing.

**troubles** 2
T-3........ VI.8:5 frightening to them, but hardly **t.** God.
W-ep ......... 1:5 Whatever **t.** you, be certain that He has

## truce 1

T-23......III.6:1 Mistake not **t.** for peace, nor compromise

## true 641

*See also* Appendix C

T-1...........I.9:2 are always miraculous in the **t.** sense, the
T-1.........I.23:1 and place all levels in **t.** perspective. This
T-1.........I.38:3 He separates the **t.** from the false by His
T-1.........I.49:3 the error. This is its **t.** indiscriminateness.
T-1.........I.50:1 accepting what is in accord with it as **t.**,
T-1.........II.1:4 result in **t.** closeness to others. Revelation
T-1.........V.3:4 Son in his **t.** relationship with the Father.
T-1.........V.5:1 Whatever is **t.** is eternal, and cannot
T-1.........V.5:7 to place it at the disposal of *t.* Authority.
T-1........VI.4:5 can believe what no one else thinks is **t.**. It
T-1........VI.4:6 It is **t.** for you because it was made by you.
T-1........VI.5:3 In sorting out the false from the **t.**, the
T-1.......VII.2:5 to do this is the body's only **t.** usefulness.
T-2...........I.2:6 This is as **t.** of the Son as of the Father. In
T-2...........I.3:3 what is not **t.** unless you choose to do so.
T-2.........II.2:1 **T.** denial is a powerful protective device.
T-2........III.1:8 **t.** holiness lies at the inner altar around
T-2........III.5:2 waste themselves and their **t.** creative
T-2.........V.5:6 the mind to its **t.** position as the learner.
T-2........VI.8:9 the fear. This is how **t.** healing occurs.
T-2.......VII.1:8 enable you to do this, which is perfectly **t.**
T-2.......VII.2:4 genuine respect for **t.** cause and effect as a
T-2.......VII.4:4 The **t.** resolution rests entirely on mastery
T-2.......VII.5:5 What you believe is **t.** for you. In this
T-2.......VII.6:6 wholeness in the **t.** sense be understood.
T-2.......VIII.4:1 a sorting out of the false from the **t.**. This
T-2.......VIII.4:2 reflects the **t.** meaning of the Apocalypse.
T-3...........I.7:5 perfectly aware of everything that is **t.**.
T-3...........I.7:9 that all the other lessons I taught are **t.**. If
T-3...........I.8:1 The innocence of God is the **t.** state of the
T-3...........II.h Miracles as **T.** Perception
T-3.........II.1:4 They are all **t.** or all false. It is essential
T-3.........II.2:5 Innocent or **t.** perception means that you
T-3.........II.5:8 the innocent defend **t.** perception instead
T-3.........II.6:1 in them and invest it only in what is **t.**.
T-3.........II.6:2 You cannot make untruth **t.**. If you are
T-3.........II.6:3 what is **t.** in everything you perceive, you
T-3.........II.6:3 you perceive, you let it be **t.** for you. Truth
T-3........III.1:8 fear and **t.** perceptions foster love, but
T-3......III.1:10 **T.** perception is the basis for knowledge,
T-3........III.4:1 **T.** vision is the natural perception of
T-3......IV.3:10 can never make your misperceptions **t.**,
T-3.........V.2:3 specific purpose has no **t.** generalizability.
T-3.........V.8:4 All of it is equally **t.**, and knowing any
T-3........VI.2:8 be **t.** unless you also believe that what you
T-3........VI.8:7 creations are given their **t.** Authorship,
T-3........VI.8:8 Being uncertain of your **t.** Authorship,
T-3.......VII.4:7 it. You cannot make it **t.**. And, as I said
T-3.......VII.6:3 will shine from the **t.** Foundation of life,
T-4...........I.3:6 When I remind you of your **t.** creation,
T-4...........I.5:2 This is the one **t.** goal of the teacher. It is
T-4.........II.5:1 even though this is anything but **t.**. Babies
T-4.........II.7:6 This is as **t.** of body appetites as it is of the
T-4.....II.11:10 It is as **t.** now as it ever was or ever will be,
T-4........III.2:5 My role is to separate the **t.** from the false
T-4........III.7:7 but I will not uphold it unless it is **t.**. I will
T-4......III.10:4 would undertake to believe what is not **t.**,
T-4........IV.9:2 because I know these images are not **t.**."
T-4.......VII.3:1 the same way to everything it knows is **t.**,
T-4.......VII.3:2 it make any attempt to establish what is **t.**
T-4.......VII.3:3 It knows that what is **t.** is everything that
T-5...........I.4:9 before of the higher or "**t.**" perception,
T-5.........II.9:5 the one choice that resembles **t.** creation.
T-5........III.5:4 **t.** and false perceptions are themselves
T-5........IV.1:3 and teach you that only what is loving is **t.**
T-5......VI.11:3 still **t.** that where you look to find yourself
T-6...........I.7:3 it there Himself, and so it is **t.** forever.
T-6...........I.7:4 in it, and therefore accepted it as **t.** for me
T-6...........I.7:5 of God, but first believe that it is **t.** for you
T-6.........I.11:6 to show this was **t.** in an extreme case,
T-6.........II.6:7 It is forever **t.**. It is not a belief, but a Fact.
T-6.........II.6:9 Anything that God created is as **t.** as He is
T-6.........II.9:2 is as **t.** of God's Thinking as it is of yours.
T-6.......II.10:2 but He does not believe in what is not **t.**.
T-6.......II.10:3 your mind can also believe only what is **t.**.
T-6.......II.11:9 He perceives only what is **t.** in your mind,
T-6.......II.11:9 outward only to what is **t.** in other minds.
T-6.......III.1:7 hear and teach and learn what is not **t.**.
T-6.......III.2:8 If that is **t.**, and it is true indeed, do not
T-6.......III.2:8 If that is true, and it is **t.** indeed, do not
T-6.......IV.6:8 for you, because they are beautiful and **t.**.
T-6.......IV.7:6 as God because you are as **t.** as He is, but
T-6.......IV.9:2 This is not **t.** of anything that God created
T-6......IV.11:4 however, not because the laws are **t.**, but
T-6.........V.1:2 wrongly, having believed what was not **t.**.
T-6...V.B.1:10 If the center of the thought system is **t.**,
T-6...V.B.3:10 to both as if what you do believe is not **t.**.
T-6.....V.B.6:2 Only one is **t.**, and therefore only one is
T-6.....V.B.6:3 it is up to you to decide which voice is **t.**,
T-6.....V.C.1:2 out the **t.** from the false in your mind, and
T-6.....V.C.5:2 You create by your **t.** being, but what you
T-6...V.C.10:5 what you made because it was not **t.**.
T-6...V.C.10:8 it is already **t.** and needs no protection. It
T-7..........I.6:4 God. This is **t.**, but it is hard to explain in
T-7..........I.6:4 and nothing that is **t.** need be explained.
T-7..........I.7:8 will take was therefore **t.** in the beginning,
T-7..........I.7:8 therefore true in the beginning, is **t.** now,
T-7..........I.7:8 is true now, and will be **t.** forever. What is
T-7.......III.3:6 you have accepted the impossible as **t.**. Is
T-7.......III.4:2 believe you can attend to what is not **t.**,
T-7........V.7:5 **T.** learning is constant, and so vital in its
T-7....V.10:12 this, because you perceive only what is **t.**.
T-7......V.11:6 This is **t.** communion with the Holy Spirit
T-7.......VI.7:6 is necessary against beliefs that are not **t.**,
T-7.......VI.7:7 something, you have made it **t.** for you.
T-7.......VI.8:6 of truth, because the ego itself is not **t.**. If
T-7.....VI.8:10 as long as you do not recognize what is **t.**.
T-7.......VI.9:7 it. It is not **t.**. The ego therefore is totally
T-7.....VIII.1:1 also **t.** that without extension there can be
T-7.....VIII.6:1 is beyond belief and His perception is **t.**.
T-7.....VIII.7:3 and affirming your **t.** identification with
T-7.........X.3:3 not whether what the Holy Spirit says is **t.**
T-8.......III.7:9 have no power, because they are not **t.**.
T-8.....III.7:10 to produce is no more **t.** than they are.
T-8.......IV.8:5 sight of your **t.** identification with me and
T-8........V.6:5 the journey is the way to what is **t.**. Leave
T-8.......VI.2:3 Only one is **t.**. I am come to tell you that
T-8.......VI.2:4 choice of which is **t.** is not yours to make.
T-8.......VI.5:8 therefore there is no other gift that is **t.**.
T-8......VII.8:6 it is because the **t.** goal of the curriculum
T-8....VII.11:4 but foster illness, because it is not **t.**. A
T-8....VII.15:5 Therefore it is not **t.**. No more are any of
T-8....VII.16:1 from imagined results of what is not **t.**.
T-8.....VIII.1:3 it is incapable of **t.** generalizations, and
T-8.....VIII.5:1 is still **t.** that the body has no function of
T-8.....VIII.5:2 as such, its **t.** function is obscured. This is
T-8.....VIII.5:7 interpretation of the body rests are **t.**;
T-8.....VIII.6:7 of truth is to collect information that is **t.**.
T-8.....VIII.7:6 one thing about the ego that is wholly **t.**.
T-8.......IX.5:4 only between the false and the **t.**,
T-8.......IX.5:4 the true, replacing the false with the **t.**.
T-9..........I.4:2 sort out the **t.** from the false in your mind
T-9.........II.1:2 only **t.** in connection with specific things
T-9.........II.3:1 prayer is answered, and this is indeed **t.**.
T-9.........II.4:5 are **t.** because of the truth that is in him.
T-9.........II.4:6 the truth in him, and his words will *be* **t.**.
T-9.......III.3:2 his errors. This *must* be **t.**, since there is no
T-9.......IV.1:4 Accept as **t.** only what your brother is, if
T-9.......IV.8:5 is it **t.** that you do not realize the guide is
T-9.....IV.11:6 fearful, but no one calls them **t.**. Children
T-9.....IV.11:7 so, for a while, the tales are **t.** for them.
T-9.........V.9:4 will convince you that the words are **t.**. By
T-9......VII.4:1 in your mind, and they cannot both be **t.**.
T-9......VII.7:6 because He knows its foundation is not **t.**.
T-9......VII.7:9 If it comes from God, He knows it to be **t.**.
T-9.....VIII.6:3 is God's answer to the ego, because it is **t.**.
T-9.....VIII.7:2 Truth does not vacillate; it is always **t.**.
T-9.....VIII.7:5 Yet it must be insane because it is not **t.**.
T-9.....VIII.8:2 you of the **t.** witnesses to your reality.
T-9...VIII.11:7 but the Source is **t.** and so is Its answer.
T-10.....III.7:7 I have only one message, and it is **t.**. Your
T-10......V.5:2 were, what you have made would be **t.**,
T-10.....V.14:3 this is not **t.** in eternity it *is* true in time, so
T-10.....V.14:3 this is not true in eternity it *is* **t.** in time, so
T-11......in.1:2 sides fairly, you will realize this must be **t.**
T-11......in.4:7 I will lead you to your **t.** Father, Who hath
T-11......III.2:5 if your will is His it cannot be **t.** of you,
T-11......III.2:5 be true of you, because it is not **t.** of Him.
T-11......III.3:2 He wills has happened, for it was always **t.**
T-11........V.5:2 being out of accord with your **t.** nature.
T-11......V.11:2 the impossible and the false from the **t.**.
T-11......V.14:5 is meaningless, inconsistency must be **t.**.
T-11......V.17:3 for nothing can prove that a lie is **t.**. What
T-11......V.18:3 to the thought system you want to be **t.**.
T-11......VI.4:7 This is as **t.** now as it will ever be, for the
T-11.....VII.1:4 a new earth, yet this cannot be literally **t.**,
T-11.....VII.2:8 false and the **t.** and making no distinction
T-11.....VII.3:5 For perceptions cannot be partly **t.**. If you
T-11.....VII.3:6 and illusion, you cannot tell which is **t.**.
T-11.....VII.3:8 Yet everything **t.** *is* like Him. Perceiving
T-11.....VII.4:9 recognition that reality is only what is **t.**.
T-11....VIII.1:2 in the end, teaches that only reality is **t.**.
T-11....VIII.1:5 an instant to realize that this alone is **t.**.
T-11....VIII.1:6 the good and the bad, the false and the **t.**.
T-11....VIII.3:2 Not one thought you hold is wholly **t.**.
T-12.........I.1:2 have to make it real because it is not **t.**.
T-12.........I.3:3 Every loving thought is **t.**. Everything else
T-12.........I.6:8 divided state, His remain consistently **t.**.
T-12........I.10:6 to your eternal knowledge that union is **t.**.
T-12......IV.6:2 and whatever is **t.** is the Will of the Father
T-12.....VII.8:4 that the witnesses for opposition are **t.**,
T-12..VII.15:2 this is **t.** when you look within and *see* me.
T-12....VIII.3:1 When you made visible what is not **t.**,
T-12....VIII.3:1 not true, what *is* **t.** became invisible to you.
T-13.........I.4:3 in it the Holy Spirit knows it is not **t.**. The
T-13.......I.11:5 Son of God, He knows that this is **t.**. And
T-13.......I.11:6 And being **t.** for you, you cannot attack
T-13........V.7:5 what you have offered yourself is not **t.**,
T-13......VI.6:2 it holds the only things that are forever **t.**.
T-13.....VII.2:4 Both are not **t.**, yet either one will seem as
T-13.....VII.5:3 who judges what is **t.** and what is false.
T-13.....VII.8:4 thing that is wholly **t.** and wholly yours.
T-13.....VII.9:3 In these lie your **t.** perceptions, for the
T-13....VIII.5:2 **t.** perception of one aspect of the whole.
T-13......IX.4:1 Spirit can separate the false and the **t.**,
T-13......IX.4:2 has become as **t.** for you as innocence.
T-13......IX.6:4 you learn that it is **t.** for you. Remember
T-13........X.1:3 which attention is diverted, must be **t.**;
T-13........X.9:3 Yet it is forever **t.**. In shining peace within
T-13......X.11:6 Until you recognize that this is **t.**, you will
T-13......XI.4:4 Him to demonstrate which must be **t.**. He
T-13....XI.11:1 is not **t.** must be reconciled with truth.
T-13....XI.11:7 how can you remember what was never **t.**
T-14.........I.4:2 knows to be **t.** you have denied yourself,
T-14......II.1:11 you *can* learn how to make the untrue **t.**.
T-14........II.2:1 the fundamental teaching that *truth* is **t.**.
T-14........II.2:6 is **t.** and what is not is perfectly apparent,
T-14........II.3:1 and teaches, simply, that all this is not **t.**.
T-14........II.3:3 *truth is* **t.**. *Nothing else matters, nothing*
T-14........II.4:2 Like God, He knows it to be **t.**. He brings
T-14........II.5:1 When you teach anyone that truth is **t.**,
T-14........II.6:2 on the firm foundation that truth is **t.**. For
T-14........II.6:3 For what is builded there *is* **t.**, and built on
T-14........II.7:3 For truth *is* **t.**. What else could ever be, or
T-14........II.8:8 he sing the dirge of sorrow when this is **t.**?
T-14......III.4:5 be reconciled and cannot both be **t.**. You
T-14......III.9:3 It is not **t.** that you can make decisions by
T-14....III.12:3 against it, for being of Him it must be **t.**.
T-14......IV.9:3 you the **t.** condition of the Son of God. It
T-14........V.2:3 his **t.** function remains unfulfilled in him.
T-14......VI.4:1 to life simply because destruction is not **t.**
T-14......VI.7:4 and offering your **t.** communication to
T-14.....VII.3:2 From their point of view it is not **t.**. Yet it
T-14.....VII.3:3 Yet it is **t.** because God knows it. These
T-14......IX.2:5 It merely vanishes because it is not **t.**.
T-14........X.2:5 it is not **t.** that anything without order of
T-14........X.4:4 is **t.** of the thoughts that cross the mind of
T-14........X.9:7 The fact of union tells them it is not **t.**.
T-14......X.12:1 miracle is the recognition that this is **t.**.
T-14......XI.1:9 false, and of your attempts to undo the **t.**.
T-14......XI.5:1 to recognize if what you learned is **t.**. If

T-14......XI.5:3 Unless all this is **t.**, there are dark lessons
T-15......III.3:2 it is **t.** and is but a tribute to your power.
T-16........... I.h **T.** Empathy
T-16.........I.4:1 **T.** empathy is of Him Who knows what it
T-16....... II.6:6 has come. It is **t.**, just as you fear, that to
T-16....... II.6:7 But what you think you know was never **t.**
T-16......III.6:6 For what you taught is **t.**. Alone, you
T-16......IV.6:2 it. It is not necessary to seek for what is **t.**,
T-16......IV.7:1 Recognize this, for it is **t.**, and truth must
T-16....... V.3:6 a direction exactly opposite of what is **t.**.
T-16..... V.14:1 are not fearful because they are not **t.**.
T-16..... V.14:2 the extent to which you *want* them to be **t.**.
T-16.....VII.9:7 to bring you the **t.** condition of Heaven.
T-16...VII.12:1 *us to accept our* **t.** *relationship with You, in*
T-17.........I.5:7 in reality, because everything there is **t.**.
T-17......III.7:6 sees, because He knows that only this is **t.**.
T-17......III.9:6 Thought systems are but **t.** or false, and
T-17......III.9:7 Only the Thoughts of God are **t.**. And all
T-17......III.9:8 as **t.** as is the holy Source from which they
T-17.....IV.16:1 of relationship and know it to be **t.**. Let us
T-17....... V.9:6 which your **t.** intent was never absent.
T-17......VI.4:4 The **t.** becomes what can be used to meet
T-17... VIII.4:4 was never **t.**. For what the "something
T-18....... II.2:1 they have no concern with what is **t.**.
T-18..... II.5:17 try to make your sleeping dreams come **t.**.
T-18....... V.4:1 Happy dreams come **t.**, not because they
T-18......IX.3:2 witness to this world, pronouncing it as **t.**
T-19.........I.7:2 This will remain forever **t.**, however much
T-19....... II.5:3 system; lovely and powerful, wholly **t.**,
T-19......III.2:5 What must be punished, must be **t.**. And
T-19......III.2:6 And what is **t.** must be eternal, and will
T-19......III.5:7 must accept as **t.** what it is told through it
T19..IV.B.16:1 believe not the impossible is **t.**. Forget not
T19... IV.C.6:5 Death, were it **t.**, would be the final and
T-20......III.1:6 adjustments necessary, because it is not **t.**
T-20......III.8:3 to adjust the world to make its answer **t.**.
T-20......IV.1:8 already given and received all that is **t.**.
T-20....VI.10:1 the **t.** relationship the Son of God has
T-20....VI.10:5 way to **t.** relationships held gently open,
T-20....VI.12:9 given one **t.** relationship beyond the body
T-20.....VII.4:3 lifted, so what was always **t.** is recognized.
T-20... VIII.9:7 It still is **t.** that nothing is without. Yet
T-21....... II.1:3 And being **t.**, it is so simple that it cannot
T-21....... II.5:3 convinced yourself that what it saw was **t.**
T-21....... V.7:3 as much a **t.** Effect of this same Source as
T-22.........I.3:8 to suspect that what it tells you is not **t.**.
T-22.........I.3:9 be **t.** *because* you do not understand it.
T-22....... II.5:4 idea as what will make it either **t.** or false.
T-22....... II.7:5 all. For it is wholly **t.** or wholly false, and
T-22....... II.9:4 If this were **t.**, thoughts would not be the
T-22..... II.10:6 Are you not glad to learn it is not **t.**? Is it
T-22..... II.12:6 has no exceptions, and what it wills is **t.**.
T-22......III.5:7 between you and the truth, is wholly **t.**.
T-22......III.7:2 You can change form *because* it is not **t.**. It
T-22....... V.1:4 They go against what must be **t.**. The
T-22....VI.13:7 to decide which must be **t.** is whether you
T-22..VI.13:10 truth, to teach you what *is* natural and **t.**.
T-22....VI.15:7 or the same, and teach you which is **t.**.
T-23.........I.4:8 possibly establish this, and make it **t.**?
T-23.........I.6:1 the belief the one that conquers will be **t.**.
T-23.........I.6:4 Both are not **t.**. And so it matters not
T-23...... I.10:1 illusion, being as **t.** and holy as Himself.
T-23...... I.10:6 you from everything that is not **t.**. You
T-23...... I.11:6 do battle only to establish which form is **t.**
T-23....... II.2:3 some are more valuable and therefore **t.**.
T-23....... II.2:4 it **t.** by his attack on what another values.
T-23....... II.9:2 if the others are accepted, must be **t.**. This
T-23..... II.14:2 protects madness is the belief that it is **t.**.
T-23..... II.14:6 around, with madness sanity, illusions **t.**,
T-23..... II.16:6 one of these laws is **t.** sees what it says.
T-23..... II.18:1 You would maintain, and think it **t.**, that
T-23..... II.19:9 are but forms. Their content is never **t.**.
T-23..... II.20:4 a certain witness that these laws are **t.**.
T-23......III.1:1 **t.** you do not recognize some of the forms
T-23......III.1:2 If it is **t.** attack in any form will hurt you,
T-23......IV.1:5 Heaven is wholly **t.**. No difference enters,
T-23......IV.2:3 Yet if they both are **t.**, then must they be
T-24....... V.1:4 joy in what it sees, although it is not **t.**.
T-24....... V.1:6 it. What you wish is **t.** for you. Nor is it
T-24.....VII.3:5 what is **t.** in him must be as true in you.
T-24.....VII.3:5 what is true in him must be as **t.** in you.
T-24.....VII.5:5 you see in it has meaning, and if that is **t.**,
T-24.....VII.6:7 This is the state of **t.** creation, found not
T-24.....VII.7:5 All this is **t.**, and yet it has no meaning to
T-24...VII.8:10 a wish; an image that you wanted to be **t.**.
T-24.....VII.9:6 It is the means to make your wish come **t.**.
T-25....... II.3:1 Is it not also **t.** that you have found some
T-25....... V.1:6 truth, for each attests the other must be **t.**
T-25.....VII.3:4 as **t.** has any meaning in His Mind at all.
T-25.....VII.3:7 If one belief so deeply valued here were **t.**,
T-25.....VII.3:8 And if but one Thought of His is **t.**, then
T-25.....VII.4:7 any form of reason, believes this to be **t.**.
T-25...VII.11:3 If this were **t.**, then God is mad indeed!
T-25...VII.12:6 And sin must be impossible, if this is **t.**.
T-25. VIII.5:10 it aside, unaided, and perceive it is not **t.**?
T-25... VIII.9:1 ask of you who think that all of this is **t.**?
T-25. VIII.12:2 in every circumstance, that this is **t.**. Nor
T-25......IX.3:2 And this must be **t.**, because He asks no
T-26....... II.2:6 If this were **t.**, then God would be unfair;
T-26....... II.4:3 to the Son of God, and therefore is not **t.**.
T-26......III.3:3 truth, a segment of the universe made **t.**.
T-26......III.7:7 been withdrawn from what was never **t.**,
T-26......III.7:7 to give it up, and choose what *must* be **t.**?
T-26..... V.6:10 he can delude himself that this is **t.**, and
T-26..... V.12:2 hinder not the **t.** existence of the here and
T-26.....VII.4:1 and what is **t.** of knowledge is not true of
T-26.....VII.4:1 is not **t.** of anything that is apart from it.
T-26.....VII.5:3 The laws of truth forever will be **t.**, and
T-26.....VII.6:4 it appears some are more **t.** than others,
T-26.....VII.6:9 Not one is **t.** in any way, and all must
T-26.....VII.7:6 not establish that the picture must be **t.**.
T-26.....VII.8:2 And truth needs no defense to make it **t.**.
T-26...VII.10:1 asks but a little wish that what is **t.** be true
T-26...VII.10:1 asks but a little wish that what is true be **t.**
T-26...VII.10:3 but a willingness that truth be **t.**? What
T-26...VII.13:2 **t.**: that He created you as part of Him,
T-26...VII.13:2 be **t.** because ideas leave not their source.
T-26...VII.13:4 This is as **t.** of what is idly wished as what
T-26...VII.13:5 their source is to invite illusions to be **t.**,
T-26...VII.20:5 it can make what always has been **t.** be
T-27.........I.6:2 because it proves illusions are not **t.**. It is
T-27.........I.8:2 If this were **t.**, there would be reason to
T-27....... II.3:6 in whom **t.** forgiveness rests can suffer.
T-27......III.4:7 Yet **t.** undoing must be kind. And so the
T-27......IV.4:5 this: "Of these illusions, which of them *is* **t.**
T-27....IV.4:12 The others are not **t.**. What can the body
T-27......VI.3:7 make a witness **t.** because you called him
T-27......VI.6:2 for what is past forgiveness and is **t.**. How
T-27... VIII.4:3 That this is all the body does is **t.**, for it is
T-27. VIII.10:2 what the form of the attack, this still is **t.**.
T-27. VIII.10:4 pain and suffering you feel, this is still **t.**.
T-27. VIII.13:7 be unlike each other; that they both be **t.**.
T-28....... II.7:1 a dream, and that its content is not **t.**.
T-28.....VII.5:5 to keep a promise to be **t.** to faithlessness.
T-29......IV.1:2 They are dreams *because* they are not **t.**.
T-29......IX.2:9 dreams, where idols are your "**t.**" identity
T-30......IV.1:8 arose between yourself and what is **t.**.
T-30......VI.7:1 must be **t.** the miracle can heal all forms
T-30......VI.7:2 are real, and which appearances are **t.**. If
T-30.....VII.1:3 meaning changes constantly, and yet is **t.**.
T-31.........I.1:2 it says is what was never **t.** is not true now
T-31.........I.1:2 it says is what was never true is not **t.** now
T-31.........I.1:5 to learn by anyone who wants it to be **t.**?
T-31.........I.1:7 is it to see that what is false can not be **t.**,
T-31.........I.1:7 not be true, and what is **t.** can not be false
T-31.........I.1:8 you perceive no differences in false and **t.**.
T-31.........I.5:4 and teach you that Its lessons are not **t.**;
T-31.........I.5:4 to see, and too opposed to what is really **t.**
T-31....... II.2:7 Neither is **t.**. Nor are they different. Yet
T-31....... II.8:8 you did not want, and that were never **t.**.
T-31......IV.3:8 is **t.** indeed there is no choice at all within
T-31....... V.7:5 Not one of them is **t.**, and many come
T-31..... V.11:1 the one who would not think it **t.** is you.
T-31......VI.1:5 all you see and think is real and hold as **t.**.
T-31......VI.4:4 In Heaven as on earth this is forever **t.**. It
T-31.....VII.8:2 To every part of **t.** creation has the Lord
W-in..........3:1 with the acquisition of **t.** perception.
W-in..........5:1 Transfer of training in **t.** perception does
W-in..........5:2 If **t.** perception has been achieved in
W-in..........5:3 exception held apart from **t.** perception
W-in..........6:5 of **t.** perception is that it has no limits. It
W-in..........8:6 to you, and will show you that they are **t.**.
W-pI.......5.1:4 This is not **t.**. However, until you learn
W-pI.......7.4:2 This is equally **t.** of whatever you look at.
W-pI.......8.2:1 one wholly **t.** thought one can hold about
W-pI.....15.3:5 they merely symbolize **t.** perception, and
W-pI.....16.1:5 They are merely **t.** or false. Those that are
W-pI.....16.1:6 Those that are **t.** create their own likeness
W-pI.....17.3:3 as yet of any thought that is really **t.**, and
W-pI.....19.2:4 it must be **t.** if salvation is possible at all.
W-pI.....27.1:5 the idea will be wholly **t.** a little nearer.
W-pI.....27.4:2 much do you want today's idea to be **t.**?
W-pI.....35.5:5 direction in reality. They are merely not **t.**
W-pI.....37.1:1 of your **t.** function in the world, or why
W-pI.....48.1:5 it for those who want illusions to be **t.**.
W-pI.....51.5:3 I am constantly trying to make them **t.**.
W-pI.....54.1:6 thoughts cannot be neither **t.** nor false.
W-pI.....61.3:1 **T.** humility requires that you accept
W-pI.....61.3:1 it is God's Voice which tells you it is **t.**.
W-pI.....62.5:5 in your mind is the awareness they are **t.**.
W-pI.....65.6:4 *slate let my* **t.** *function be written for me.* You
W-pI.....66.8:2 Him. Which is **t.**? Unless God gave your
W-pI...66.10:8 try today to realize that only the truth is **t.**
W-pI...72.11:7 answer will be **t.** because of Whom you
W-pI.....74.2:2 it. The idea itself is wholly **t.**. Therefore it
W-pI.....75.7:6 He will show you what **t.** vision sees. It is
W-pI.....77.1:5 It is merely a statement of your **t.** Identity
W-pI.....78.7:1 savior shining in the light of **t.** forgiveness
W-pI.....87.1:6 I will experience the peace of **t.** perception
W-pI.....91.6:1 with this statement of **t.** cause and effect
W-pI.....93.1:3 think if what is **t.** about you were revealed
W-pI.....93.2:3 all this is **t.** by what you now believe.
W-pI.....93.6:3 It is **t.**. Your sinlessness is guaranteed by
W-pI.....93.9:2 One Self is **t.**; the other is not there. Try to
W-pI...93.11:7 mind that the idea for the day is **t.** indeed.
W-pI.....94.2:1 **T.** light is strength, and strength is
W-pI...95.10:3 This is the truth, and nothing else is **t.**.
W-pI...95.10:4 which there is no doubt that only this is **t.**
W-pI...95.12:2 **t.** creation may extend the allness and the
W-pI.....97.8:3 and let Him tell your mind that they are **t.**
W-pI.....98.9:4 joy and certainty that what you say is **t.**.
W-pI.....99.5:5 does He know one thing must still be **t.**;
W-pI...99.11:2 If you are tempted to believe them **t.**,
W-pI...101.2:3 be illusion, for they cannot both be **t.**.
W-pI...103.3:4 with this assurance, kind and wholly **t.**:
W-pI...105.4:2 yours. **T.** giving is creation. It extends the
W-pI...105.8:3 assure you that the words you speak are **t.**
W-pI...106.4:5 His miracles are **t.**. They will not fade
W-pI...108.1:3 into one concept which is wholly **t.**? Even
W-pI...108.2:1 **T.** light that makes true vision possible is
W-pI...108.2:1 True light that makes **t.** vision possible is
W-pI...108.6:1 it can be tried so easily and seen as **t.**. And
W-pI...110.1:2 and the world, if you believed that it is **t.**.
W-pI.122.14:4 *Today I have accepted this as* **t.**. *Today I have*
W-pI...123.4:2 has willed to be our **t.** Identity in Him.
W-pI...125.9:4 between the wholly indivisible and **t.**. As
W-pI...126.3:3 him beneath a **t.** equality with you. He
W-pI...126.5:1 If this be **t.**, forgiveness has no grounds
W-pI...126.7:5 And **t.** forgiveness, as the means by which
W-pI.126.11:4 *I need to learn that this is* **t.** *is with me now.*
W-pI...128.1:3 No one but must accept this thought as **t.**,
W-pI...128.3:3 that leads to **t.** awareness of your Self.
W-pI.130.10:2 or **t.** is what you see and only what you
W-pI.131.10:1 and turn your mind to **t.** ideas instead.
W-pI.131.10:3 **t.** ideas arising in the place of thoughts
W-pI.131.11:6 such a world, and which you think are **t.**.
W-pI...132.8:2 idea is **t.** because the world does not exist.
W-pI...134.2:1 fact that pardon is not asked for what is **t.**
W-pI...134.3:2 deceive yourself by making an illusion **t.**.
W-pI...134.4:2 sin as **t.** and not believe forgiveness is a lie
W-pI...134.8:4 way your **t.** forgiveness opens up to you.
W-pI...134.9:1 way to find the door to **t.** forgiveness, and
W-pI.134.14:1 Today we practice **t.** forgiveness, that the
W-pI.135.12:3 But when it has accepted this as **t.**, then is
W-pI...136.6:1 without regard to all their **t.** relationships
W-pI...136.8:4 Thus is your "**t.**" identity preserved, and
W-pI...137.4:2 But healing demonstrates that truth is **t.**.

W-pI...138.2:5 Yet what is **t.** in God's creation cannot
W-pI...138.4:6 all. For truth is **t.**, and nothing else is true.
W-pI...138.4:6 truth is true, and nothing else is **t.**. There
W-pI...139.6:5 sad belief that what is universal here is **t.**?
W-pI...139.7:1 Nothing the world believes is **t.**. It is a
W-pI...140.9:5 and can be cured because they are not **t.**.
WpI. rIV.in2:8 from his awareness. Yet it is forever **t.**.
WpI. rIV.in3:1 **t.** forgiveness may be carefully concealed.
W-pI...152.2:1 is extreme, and too inclusive to be **t.**. Yet
W-pI...152.3:1 is the recognition that the truth is **t.**, and
W-pI...152.3:1 the truth is true, and nothing else is **t.**.
W-pI...152.3:4 the second, is the first no longer **t.**. Truth
W-pI...152.3:7 what is not **t.** is true as well as what is true
W-pI...152.3:7 what is not true is **t.** as well as what is true
W-pI...152.3:7 what is not true is true as well as what is **t.**
W-pI...152.3:9 Nothing but the truth is **t.**, and what is
W-pI...152.9:1 Today we practice **t.** humility,
W-pI...152.9:4 and lift our hearts in **t.** humility instead to
W-pI.152.11:1 that lies are false, and only truth is **t.**. We
W-pI...153.8:2 For our **t.** purpose is to save the world,
W-pI.153.14:6 smile at last, on learning that it is not **t.**.
W-pI.153.18:1 where you will walk in **t.** defenselessness.
W-pI.154.11:5 we may be the **t.** receivers of the gifts He
W-pI.154.14:1 minds, and realize these holy words are **t.**
W-pI...156.1:4 If this be **t.**, how can you be apart from
W-pI...156.2:2 Truth must be **t.** throughout, if it be true.
W-pI...156.2:2 Truth must be true throughout, if it be **t.**.
W-pI.158.11:2 in which **t.** knowledge is reflected in a way
W-pI...161.5:4 Love needs no symbols, being **t.**. But fear
W-pI...163.6:5 one thought entirely can not be **t.**, unless
W-pI...164.5:3 of judgment left to Him Who judges **t.**.
W-pI...166.2:4 and **t.** believes in two creators; or in one,
W-pI...169.1:3 the mind prepares itself for **t.** acceptance.
WpI...rV.in4:2 more meaningful, more personal and **t.**,
WpI.rV.in11:5 have recognized the words we speak are **t.**
W-pI...181.8:4 we seek for in the name of **t.** perception,
W-pI...182.1:2 in your mind you know that this is **t.**. A
W-pI...184.3:4 be seen as meaningful; a cause of **t.** effect,
W-pI...184.6:6 What denies that it is **t.** is but illusion, for
W-pI...184.8:3 is **t.** in earth and Heaven is beyond your
W-pI...184.8:5 His **t.** Identity is hidden from you by what
W-pI...184.9:5 where **t.** communication can be found.
W-pI.184.10:2 the one acknowledgment of what is **t.**.
W-pI...186.1:2 Here is the thought of **t.** humility, which
W-pI...186.5:1 to prove the false is **t.** has brought to you.
W-pI...187.1:6 which the world and **t.** perception differ.
W-pI...189.6:1 as we seek to reach to what is **t.** in us, and
W-pI...189.7:2 of everything it thinks is either **t.** or false,
W-pI...189.9:5 there, if it be **t.** and can be surely reached.
W-pI...190.4:5 and tries to demonstrate must still be **t.**.
W-pI...191.5:3 can accept his **t.** Identity is truly saved.
W-pI...193.2:5 which perception is made **t.** and beautiful
W-pI...196.6:4 to anyone who thinks this thought is **t.**.
W-pI...200.3:4 To ask that what is false be **t.** can only fail.
W-pI...200.6:5 that he imagines, yet believes are **t.**, a
W-pI...211.1:2 *silence and in **t.** humility I seek God's glory,*
W-pII ....in.9:4 and we no longer think illusions **t.**. The
W-pII ......1.2:1 not raise to doubt, although it is not **t.**.
W-pII .224.1:1 My **t.** Identity is so secure, so lofty,
W-pII .228.1:3 I accept as **t.** what He proclaims as false?
W-pII .228.1:4 Who knows the **t.** condition of His Son?
W-pII .230.1:6 this be denied me, when it is forever **t.**?
W-pII .234.1:5 Son. This we accept as wholly **t.** today.
W-pII .237.2:2 *Him Who is Your Son, and my **t.** Self as well.*
W-pII .240.1:3 Not one thing in this world is **t.**. It does
W-pII .....3.1:4 has been changed to one of **t.** forgiveness,
W-pII .....4.2:7 will seek instead for witnesses to what is **t.**
W-pII .252.2:1 *Father, You know my **t.** Identity. Reveal It*
W-pII .260.2:1 and Therein we find our **t.** Identity at last.
W-pII .271.1:2 witnesses to what is **t.** in God's creation.
W-pII .275.1:1 no more **t.** today than any other day. Yet
W-pII .281.1:7 *The Thoughts I think with You alone are **t.**.*
W-pII ....283.h My **t.** Identity abides in You.
W-pII .283.1:8 *Is not Your Son my **t.** Identity, when You*
W-pII .284.1:5 and next to be accepted as but partly **t.**,
W-pII .296.1:2 *are apart from Yours, for only Yours are **t.**.*
W-pII .300.2:3 *to be restored to Heaven and our **t.** Identity.*
W-pII .....9.1:2 what is forever and forever **t.**. It is the
W-pII .....9.3:2 name of **t.** creation and the Will of God.
W-pII .309.1:5 I think I made another will that is not **t.**,
W-pII .309.2:3 *to my Self, and there I find my **t.** Identity.*
W-pII ...10.1:1 is false, and what is **t.** has never changed.
W-pII ...10.1:3 see a world that has accepted this as **t.**,
W-pII .313.1:6 *Now let His **t.** perception come to me, that I*
W-pII .327.1:3 learn from my experience that this is **t.**,
W-pII ...12.1:3 death, and what opposes God alone is **t.**.
W-pII .345.1:7 *alone today, which, born of **t.** forgiveness,*
M-in ..........2:2 believe one or the other is **t.** all the time.
M-4 .....VII.1:3 no one can be generous in the **t.** sense. To
M-4 ...VII.2:12 These he can give away in **t.** generosity,
M-4 ....VIII.1:5 And this is **t.** for everything that happens
M-4 ......IX.2:1 **T.** faithfulness, however, does not deviate
M-4 ......IX.2:9 in the **t.** sense is always directed. Toward
M-4 ........X.3:6 teachers to bring **t.** learning to the world.
M-4 ........X.3:7 bring, for that is "**t.** learning" in the world
M-5 ........II.4:4 their **t.** sequence in one respect, and the
M-5 ........II.4:5 transfer value of one **t.** idea has no end or
M-5 ......III.2:3 what the patient has accepted as **t.**. As
M-6 ...........4:2 it is trust that makes **t.** giving possible.
M-8 ...........2:4 The mind therefore seeks to make it **t.** out
M-8 ...........4:6 it concludes that the categories must be **t.**
M-10 .........6:8 be. Not one is **t.**. For he has given up their
M-11 .........1:8 But it is **t.** that the world must be looked
M-11 .........2:2 or the Word of God is more likely to be **t.**.
M-13 .........6:2 In one sense this is **t.**, for you hold dear
M-14 .......5:10 And now sit down in **t.** humility, and
M-15 .........2:2 Do you believe that this is wholly **t.**? No;
M-15 .........2:5 this Judgment and to recognize that it is **t.**
M-16 .........1:4 Seeing this and understanding that it is **t.**,
M-16 .........8:6 is a sorry substitute for **t.** assistance. It is
M-16 .......10:8 to accept magic as **t.** must be abandoned
M-17 .......9:13 fear, and thus forever real and always **t.**.
M-18 .........1:1 nature,–and only this is **t.** correction,–
M-18 .........4:2 has made an interpretation that is not **t.**.
M-19 .........2:3 possible because, while it is not **t.** in itself,
M-19 .........3:5 for not one "sin" but seems forever **t.**.
M-20 .........2:7 it is not a contrast of **t.** differences. The
M-20 .........6:3 that contradicts His Will, yet can be **t.**.
M-22 .........4:8 It is **t.** of all things that God created. In it
M-23 .........4:7 the **t.** conditions for your homecoming.
M-23 .........6:6 on us. No one who has become a **t.** and
M-24 .........1:3 cannot, then, be **t.** in any real sense. Our
M-29 .........5:4 you is simply to accept your **t.** inheritance
C-2 ............3:1 definition for a lie that serves to make it **t.**
C-4 ...............h **T.** PERCEPTION – KNOWLEDGE
C-4 ............3:2 for false perception must be ***t.** perception.*
C-4 ............3:5 For **t.** perception is a remedy with many
C-4 ............3:6 salvation, Atonement, **t.** perception, all
C-4 ............3:8 **T.** perception is the means by which the
C-4 ............3:9 exist. And it is this that **t.** perception sees.
C-4 ............4:2 **t.** perception looks on it as nothing more
C-4 ............6:1 This is the shift that **t.** perception brings:
C-4 ............7:2 Gone is perception, false and **t.** alike.
C-5 ............1:8 Son while he believes his fantasies are **t.**.
C-5 ............2:5 he saw the false without accepting it as **t.**.
C-5 ............3:4 obscure to you, between the false and **t.**.
C-6 ............3:4 principle; the bringer of **t.** perception, the
P-1.............5:2 as false and to accept the truth as **t.**. His
P-2.........in.2:6 but only at the cost of making illusions **t.**.
P-2...........I.2:2 ego fosters; that it is capable of **t.** change,
P-2...........I.2:2 true change, and therefore of **t.** creativity.
P-2..........II.2:7 the seeming obstacles to **t.** awareness?
P-2..........II.4:5 but knowledge of God has no **t.** opposite.
P-2..........II.7:1 As **t.** religion heals, so must true
P-2..........II.7:1 so must **t.** psychotherapy be religious. But
P-2........IV.7:4 make illusions **t.** through false perception
P-2.......VII.4:3 his life to the function of **t.** healing. Before
P-2.......VII.5:1 passing of guilt is the **t.** aim of therapy
P-3...........I.1:8 come. This could hardly be **t.**. To demand
P-3...........I.2:7 What you hear is **t.**. Would God send His
S-1..............I.h **T.** Prayer
S-1...........I.1:6 **T.** prayer must avoid the pitfall of asking
S-1...........I.3:4 In **t.** prayer you hear only the song. All
S-1...........I.4:1 secret of **t.** prayer is to forget the things
S-1...........I.7:1 Praying to Christ in anyone is **t.** prayer
S-1...........I.7:7 who knows that this is **t.** is to be answered
S-1..........II.2:3 also **t.** that no one who is uncertain of his
S-1........III.6:8 he lose the only **t.** goal that is given him.
S-1..........V.1:1 Prayer is a way to **t.** humility. And here
S-1..........V.1:3 and **t.** humility will come at last to grace
S-2...........I.2:1 of the world far better than its **t.** objective
S-2........III.6:8 made free to save as **t.** forgiveness is
S-3...........I.3:1 can be healed as an effect of **t.** forgiveness
S-3...........I.5:1 **t.** healing and its faulty counterpart. The
S-3...........I.5:3 to kill, so healing can be false as well as **t.**;
S-3.............II.h False versus **T.** Healing
S-3..........II.3:3 If there has been **t.** healing, this can be the
S-3..........II.4:2 first **t.** healing must have come to bless
S-3..........II.5:9 What is false cannot be partly **t.**. If you
S-3........III.1:5 For it is this that makes **t.** healing possible
S-3........III.1:8 the meaning of **t.** healing has been lost,
S-3........III.3:4 **T.** healing cannot come from inequality
S-3........IV.2:6 This instant is the goal of all **t.** healers,

**truer** 6

T-4 ........I.12:4 humble, and this gives them **t.** perception
T-9 ...VIII.10:9 evaluation of yourself is **t.** than God's.
T-23 ........I.9:2 truths; the conqueror to be the **t.**, the
W-pI .. 140.9:4 not exist is **t.** in some forms than others.
W-pI .. 166.9:4 Perhaps God's Word is **t.** than your own.
W-pI .. 188.2:6 sight, be it of dreams or from a **t.** Source,

**truest** 2

W-pI .. 154.6:4 become their first receivers in the **t.** sense,
M-17 ....... 8:11 and thus forgotten in the **t.** sense.

**truly** 120

T-1 ....... III.7:4 As an expression of what you **t.** are, the
T-2 ....... IV.5:2 In fact, if it is used **t.**, it will inevitably be
T-2 .......V.1:11 of creative ability that is **t.** meaningful.
T-2 ...V.A.18:2 *I am here only to be **t.** helpful. I am here to*
T-2 .....VIII.2:7 number become **t.** miracle-minded, this
T-3 .........I.6:3 of the **t.** loved to others who are like them
T-3 ..........I.8:5 That is why their altars are **t.** radiant.
T-3 .........II.2:5 you never misperceive and always see **t.**.
T-3 .........II.5:7 can be perceived only by the **t.** innocent.
T-3 .........II.5:9 wish to attack, and therefore they see **t.**.
T-3 .........II.6:5 If you perceive **t.** you are cancelling out
T-4 ........in.1:8 **t.** inspired are enlightened and cannot
T-4 .........II.6:1 sense of abundance can be **t.** charitable.
T-4 ....... III.4:7 into any mind that **t.** wants it, but it must
T-4 ....... III.4:7 that truly wants it, but it must want it **t.**.
T-4 ....... III.6:5 Those who call **t.** are always answered.
T-4 ....... III.7:9 in impatience, you will surely ask me **t.**.
T-4 ..... IV.8:10 Let it be judged **t.** and you must withdraw
T-4 ....... VI.4:3 done this, it denies all **t.** natural impulses,
T-4 ...... VII.3:8 beings of a like order can **t.** communicate,
T-4 ...... VII.8:3 The **t.** helpful are invulnerable, because
T-4 ...... VII.8:7 The **t.** helpful are God's miracle workers,
T-4 ...... VII.8:8 you to wherever you can be **t.** helpful, and
T-5 ..........I.7:3 of attack and is therefore **t.** open. This
T-5 .........V.2:3 What is **t.** blessed is incapable of giving
T-5 ..... VI.10:4 it speaks for Him and therefore speaks **t.**.
T-5 ..... VI.10:7 not hear it, because He can only witness **t.**
T-5 ..... VI.12:7 He is the only blessing you can **t.** give,
T-5 ..... VI.12:7 can truly give, because He is **t.** blessed.
T-6 ....... IV.3:4 the Holy Spirit answers **t.** He answers for
T-7 ....... IV.7:1 that is where the laws of God operate **t.**,
T-7 ....... IV.7:1 only **t.** because they are the laws of truth.
T-7 .......V.11:2 and as we see them **t.** they will be healed.
T-7 ..... VI.10:3 creation **t.** you cannot know the Creator,
T-7 ....... XI.1:1 The Holy Spirit will always guide you **t.**,
T-8 ...... VII.4:6 it is. Use it for truth and you will see it **t.**.
T-8 .....VIII.6:9 give rise in order to judge them **t.**.
T-9 .........II.4:4 Can you ask of the Holy Spirit **t.**, and
T-9 .........II.7:8 to anything else or you will not hear **t.**.
T-9 ....... III.6:3 you can see him **t.**, because it is possible
T-9 ....... III.6:3 it is possible for you to see yourself **t.**. It is
T-9 ...... VII.3:2 what you are, and so He evaluates you **t.**.
T-10 ...... IV.2:4 because of your ability to evaluate it **t.**, to
T-11 .......I.10:1 be happy unless you do what you will **t.**,
T-11 .......II.1:1 step toward recognizing what you **t.** want.
T-11 ..... IV.4:2 it is **t.** the beginning of the dawn of light.
T-11 .....V.16:6 the ego teach **t.** when it overlooks truth?

T-11. VIII.14:5 learn to perceive t. they are not afraid.
T-12.........I.6:2 your awareness if you perceive them t..
T-12.........I.7:3 if you want It in truth, It will be t. yours.
T-12....... II.9:7 Holy Spirit will judge, and He will judge t.
T-12.... III.10:7 changed, and there you will learn to see t..
T-12.... III.10:8 look out in peace and behold the world t..
T-12... VIII.8:5 invisible, for you will at last have seen t..
T-13.... III.10:3 ask this of a Father Who t. loved His Son.
T-13...... VI.1:1 To perceive t. is to be aware of all reality
T-14...... VI.7:4 who would communicate as t. with you.
T-14....... X.9:5 For no one alone can judge the ego t.. Yet
T-15..... VII.5:3 and let the Holy Spirit judge them t.. For
T-15....... X.2:1 The holy instant is t. the time of Christ.
T-16..... VII.8:1 What God has given you is t. given, and
T-16..... VII.8:1 you is truly given, and will be t. received.
T-17...... VI.5:6 to you and you will see the outcome t., for
T-18..... VII.6:7 allegiance, a t. undivided loyalty. Believe
T-19...... IV.3:4 Spirit, but you can see your brothers t..
T19..IV.B.17:2 must also be received, to be t. given. For
T19.IV.D.15:4 it. And he will give it t., for it will be both
T-20....... II.2:1 bodies, if they be t. given and received.
T-22...... III.5:8 as if it were a solid wall, see t.? It is held
T-24...... VI.8:2 from himself, nor you who see him t.. His
T-24.... VI.10:7 The Christ in you can see your brother t..
T-25. VIII.11:2 For just *one* witness is enough, if he sees t..
T-26... VII.13:4 of what is idly wished as what is t. willed,
T-27..... II.3:11 lies the proof that he has t. pardoned, and
T-27...... IV.6:6 because it answers questions t. asked. The
T-27. VIII.12:3 undone by but a single lesson t. learned.
T-28.........I.1:8 gone, and what has t. gone has no effects.
T-29.........I.4:7 you t. believe diminishes as you and your
T-31.... VI.6:10 And what could hurt the t. innocent?
W-pI..... 14.3:2 exchange, which can t. be called salvation
W-pI..... 42.2:1 strength, and what He gives is t. given.
W-pI..... 42.4:6 *God gives t., or: God's gifts to me must be*
W-pI..... 46.2:4 forgiveness can t. be called salvation. It is
W-pI..... 49.4:7 reach the place where you are t. welcome.
W-pI..... 52.4:2 is now, it can t. be said that I see nothing.
W-pI..... 89.2:4 *you instead. Seen t., this offers me a miracle.*
W-pI... 104.4:1 and seek instead that which is t. ours, as
W-pI... 105.1:6 guilt. The t. given gift entails no loss. It is
W-pI... 107.6:4 is impossible that anyone could seek it t.,
W-pI. 133.13:2 to value but the t. valuable and the real.
W-pI. 135.22:3 And we are given t., as we say: *If I defend*
W-pI. 136.18:2 be enough to serve all t. useful purposes.
W-pI... 140.7:6 no core, and nothing that is t. different?
W-pI... 152.8:1 Let us today be t. humble, and accept
W-pI... 185.6:4 meet with acceptance and be t. learned.
W-pI. 185.11:1 No one who t. seeks the peace of God can
W-pI. 186.11:1 your t. given function stands out clear
W-pI... 191.5:3 can accept his true Identity is t. saved.
WpI rVI.in.1:3 for salvation, if it were learned t.. Each
W-pII..250.2:4 *Today I would see t., that this day I may at*
W-pII....... 7.3:3 to restore your mind to where it t. is at
W-pII..316.1:5 and enter in where I am t. welcome and at
M-4........ II.1:7 Such are the t. honest. At no level are they
M-6........... 4:1 about the gift that makes it t. given. And
M-7.......... 1:10 lacked the trust that makes for giving t.,
M-17.......... 3:2 A lesson t. taught can lead to nothing but
M-29.......... 8:5 *in A world unseen, unheard, yet t. there.*
P-2.........in.1:6 is an error, to that extent is he t. saved.
P-2......... V.1:6 of self that holds in darkness what is t. felt
P-2........ VI.2:5 make this ugly sound seem t. beautiful.
S-1......... II.6:7 Pray t. for your enemies, for herein lies
S-1........ IV.2:4 is not the goal that prayer should t. seek.
S-1......... V.2:3 t. humble have no goal but God because
S-1....... V.3:11 pray only for what you t. share with him.
S-2...........I.1:4 is not understood, *nor t. sought for.* What
S-2...........I.6:1 Forgiveness, t. given, is the way in which
S-2......... II.2:1 to save a "baser" one from what he t. is.
S-3........ III.4:8 is, for never thus can it be t. healed.
S-3........ III.6:6 is no fear in one who has been t. healed,
S-3........ IV.2:1 prayer, and the effect of mercy t. taught,

## trumpet 2

T-27........ II.6:7 be the last t. that the world will ever hear.
W-pI... 162.2:4 They are the t. of awakening that sounds

## trumpets 1

T-28.......I.13:4 The t. of eternity resound throughout the

## trust 130

T-2........ III.5:1 perfect comfort that comes from perfect t.
T-2......... V.4:2 but maintain a consistent t. in mine. If
T-4...........I.8:3 You who made it cannot t. it, because in
T-4........ VI.3:1 You have very little t. in me as yet, but it
T-4........ VI.6:1 My t. in you is greater than yours in me
T-4........ VI.6:4 The Holy One shares my t., and accepts
T-7....... VII.9:1 God, the ego is incapable of t.. Projecting
T-7......... X.5:7 this confusion, t. becomes impossible. No
T-7......... X.5:8 No one gladly obeys a guide he does not t.
T-9......... II.6:7 will not know the t. I have in you unless
T-9......... II.6:8 will not t. the guidance of the Holy Spirit,
T-9....... V.8:11 T. Him, for help is His function, and He is
T-11.......I.11:1 You are asked to t. the Holy Spirit only
T-11....... II.5:8 You can safely t. His patience, for He
T-11. VIII.13:2 ask someone they t. for the meaning of
T-12....... II.7:5 T. in my help, for I did not walk alone,
T-12....... II.8:5 Give me but a little t. in the name of the
T-12....... II.8:5 the name of the complete t. I have in you,
T-12....... V.4:2 t. your own love when you attack it. You
T-13....... X.13:5 My t. in you is without limit, and without
T-14.... III.17:5 T. Him to answer quickly, surely, and
T-14.... III.19:4 *so I t. Him to communicate to me all that He*
T-14....... V.2:7 you share with God He holds in t. for you.
T-14.... XI.12:2 But whenever they t. themselves, they will
T-17....... II.8:5 and walk with Him in t. out of this world,
T-18...... IV.2:1 T. not your good intentions. They are not
T-18...... IV.2:3 enough. But t. implicitly your willingness,
T-21....... II.6:9 your belief and t. in this is strong indeed.
T-24...... IV.1:1 is a lack of t. in anyone except yourself.
T-25... VIII.6:4 they t. Him not to strike them dead with
T-25... VIII.9:3 You are not asked to t. Him far. No more
T-26... VIII.2:2 This makes t. impossible. And you cannot
T-26... VIII.2:3 believe that t. would settle every problem
T-26...... IX.2:1 a little t. for him who carries Christ to you
T-27....... II.1:4 stand firmly in the way of t. and peace,
T-27....... II.1:4 that the frail can have no t. and that the
T-27....... II.1:5 his brother, and could love and t. him still
T-29.........I.1:7 How could you t. Him, then? For He must
T-31...... VI.2:5 have t. where so much change is seen, for
T-31...... VI.6:8 is seen as stable, fully worthy of your t.; a
T-31..... VII.1:7 Nor does he t. the "good" in anyone,
T-31..... VII.1:8 treachery, and t. becomes impossible.
T-31..... VII.2:8 as you give your t. to what is good in him,
W-pI........ 47.h God is the strength in which I t..
W-pI..... 47.2:2 to put your t. where trust is unwarranted,
W-pI..... 47.2:2 to put your trust where t. is unwarranted,
W-pI..... 47.4:5 yourself: *God is the strength in which I t..*
W-pI..... 47.8:3 are giving your t. to the strength of God.
W-pI..... 53.3:2 and offers no grounds for t.. Nothing in
W-pI..... 53.3:7 this belief, and place my t. in reality. In
W-pI..... 60.2:1 (47) God is the strength in which I t.. It is
W-pI..... 75.8:1 you cannot fail because you t. in Him.
WpI..rII.in.4:5 T. it to see you through, and carry you
W-pI..... 81.3:5 Yet I will t. that, in the light, I will see it as
W-pI... 92.11:2 at night when we will meet again in t.. Let
W-pI..... 98.9:3 and peace and t. will be His gifts; His
W-pI... 107.4:3 trusted with a perfect t. in all the seeming
W-pI... 109.8:2 you. You will be faithful to your t. today,
WpI. rIII.in6:3 What can you t. but what is in your mind
WpI. rIII.in7:1 You have been given them in perfect t.; in
WpI. rIII.in7:2 in that same t. and confidence and faith.
WpI. rIII.in7:5 Since it has His t., His means must surely
W-pI... 122.4:2 less than halfway diligence and partial t..
W-pI... 124.8:5 We will t. God's Voice to speak as He sees
W-pI. 126.11:5 *And I will t. in Him.* Then spend a quiet
W-pI. 135.19:1 Your present t. in Him is the defense that
W-pI. 135.19:2 Let no defenses but your present t. direct
W-pI. 135.24:2 And in the light and joy of simple t., you
W-pI... 151.2:5 Why would you t. them so implicitly?
W-pI. 153.17:1 we will observe our t. as ministers of God,
W-pI. 155.13:4 given you your brothers in His t. that you
W-pI. 155.13:4 trust that you are worthy of His t. in you.
W-pI. 155.13:6 His t. has made your pathway certain and
W-pI. 155.14:1 His Love, reminding you how great His t.;
W-pI... 157.1:1 This is a day of silence and of t.. It is a
W-pI... 159.5:2 And in its power can you safely t. to carry
W-pI... 163.1:2 as anger, faithlessness and lack of t.;
W-pI... 163.2:3 alone is real, inevitable, worthy of their t..
W-pI... 166.1:2 God's t. in you is limitless. He knows His
W-pI. 166.13:6 not tempt you to be unfaithful to your t..
W-pI...... 181.h I t. my brothers, who are one with me.
W-pI... 181.6:5 *upon. I t. my brothers, who are one with me.*
W-pI... 181.9:6 we give our t. to the experience we ask for
W-pI... 186.3:2 perfect t. He holds in you who are His Son
W-pI... 201.1:1 (181) I t. my brothers, who are one with
W-pII ....in.4:2 his madness, nor betrayed his t. in Him.
W-pII . 232.2:4 T. all things to Him. Let Him reveal all
W-pII . 238.1:1 *Father, Your t. in me has been so great, I*
W-pII . 284.2:2 *Let me not fail to t. in You today, accepting*
W-pII . 286.2:3 We t. in Him, and in our Self, Who still is
W-pII . 316.2:3 *Yet I t. that You Who gave them will provide*
W-pII . 321.1:5 *But I t. in You. You Who endowed me with*
W-pII . 349.2:3 And so we t. in Him to send us miracles
Wfl........in.1:5 treacherous beyond the hope of t. and the
W-ep......... 4:4 He has earned your t. by speaking daily to
W-ep......... 6:1 We t. our ways to Him and say "Amen."
W-ep......... 6:2 in His way, and t. all things to Him. In
M-4.............I.h Trust
M-4.........I.1:4 The teachers of God have t. in the world,
M-4.........I.2:1 to t. one's own petty strength again. Who
M-4........I.A.h Development of T.
M-4........II.1:1 All other traits of God's teachers rest on t.
M-4........II.2:6 the t. on which God's teachers rest secure
M-4...... III.1:6 Judgment implies a lack of t., and trust
M-4...... III.1:6 and t. remains the bedrock of the teacher
M-4.... III.1:10 destroys honesty and shatters t.. No
M-4....... V.1:9 God's teachers t. in Him. And they are
M-4.... VI.1:10 But he learns faster as his t. increases. It is
M-4..... VII.1:3 teachers this one rests ultimately on t., for
M-4..... VII.1:3 for without t. no one can be generous in
M-4.... VIII.1:9 Patience is natural to those who t.. Sure of
M-4...... IX.1:3 and his t. not yet firmly established.
M-4...... IX.1:4 Faithfulness is the teacher of God's t. in
M-4...... IX.2:3 Being unswerving, it is full of t.. Being
M-6........... 2:9 and t. that it will be accepted when it is
M-6........... 3:6 T. is an essential part of giving; in fact, it
M-6........... 4:2 And it is t. that makes true giving possible
M-7......... 1:10 lacked the t. that makes for giving truly,
M-7........... 3:1 It is in this that the teacher of God must t.
M-7........... 4:1 is a mistake in the form of lack of t.. As
M-7........... 4:6 Yet love without t. is impossible, and
M-7........... 4:6 and doubt and t. cannot coexist. And
M-7........... 4:9 workers, for they have put their t. in Him.
M-7........... 5:2 necessarily implies that t. has been placed
M-10.......... 5:9 Whose judgment he has chosen now to t.,
M-13......... 6:9 hope in all the world that they can t..
M-14......... 4:6 He need merely t. that, if God's Voice tells
M-16....... 11:5 the day except to put your t. in magic, for
M-27......... 4:1 God nor re-establish any grounds for t.. If
S-2........ III.1:6 asks for t. and willingness to learn how to

## trusted 2

T-5......... V.5:9 that only total allegiance can be t..
W-pI... 107.4:3 t. with a perfect trust in all the seeming

## trusting 9

T-14... VII.5:14 you do, t. Him only to the small extent of
T-18...... IX.3:7 t. Him not to abandon you and leave you
T-26.... VIII.1:1 receive the benefits of t. in your brother.
W-pI..... 47.1:1 If you are t. in your own strength, you
W-pI..... 47.5:3 t. yourself that you will gain confidence.
W-pI..... 48.3:1 sign that you are t. in your own strength.
W-pI... 181.1:1 T. your brothers is essential to
WpI rVI.in.7:4 and t. Him completely for the way each
M-4........II.1:3 Only the t. can afford honesty, for only

## trusts 3

T-7......... X.6:2 God Himself t. you, and therefore your
W-pI... 182.7:2 He t. in you. He came because He knew
M-14......... 4:8 he t. that He will show him how to learn it

**trustworthiness** 1
T-7......... X.6:2 and therefore your t. is beyond question.

**trustworthy** 3
T-7......... X.6:1 The Holy Spirit is perfectly t., as you are.
T-8......VIII.4:2 appears to be innocent and t. because you
W-pI...166.2:4 solid, t. and true believes in two creators;

**Truth** 1
*truth*
W-pI...118.2:2 *and let me hear the mighty Voice for T. Itself*

**truth** 1235
*Truth*
T-1.........I.14:1 Miracles bear witness to t.. They are
T-1.........I.20:1 the spirit, not the body, is the altar of t..
T-1.........I.36:1 your perceptions with t. as God created it.
T-1........ III.5:1 Error cannot really threaten t., which can
T-1........IV.2:4 and the miracle acknowledges only t.. It
T-1........IV.3:4 T. is always abundant. Those who
T-1........VI.2:2 had not distorted your perception of t.,
T-2...........I.1:7 can fill it with your own ideas instead of t.
T-2...........I.5:3 to distinguish between t. on the one hand,
T-2......... II.2:5 it. Denial of error is a strong defense of t.,
T-2......... II.2:5 but denial of t. results in miscreation, the
T-2......... II.2:7 miscreate, because it recognizes only t..
T-2......... II.3:1 You can defend t. as well as error. The
T-2........ III.4:4 over all others, looking past error to t..
T-2......... V.5:5 then give to them is the t. that their minds
T-2....V.A.14:1 of this error and an affirmation of the t..
T-2........ VI.2:6 The t. is that you are responsible for what
T-2........ VI.2:8 the t. by "giving" autonomy to behavior.
T-3...........I.2:1 position, but rather to protect the t.. It is
T-3...........I.5:5 mind knows the t. and this is its strength.
T-3...........I.7:1 Atonement itself radiates nothing but t..
T-3...........I.7:6 demonstrated that nothing can destroy t..
T-3...........I.8:4 The understanding of the innocent is t..
T-3......... II.1:8 No one, therefore, is able to deny t. totally
T-3......... II.3:5 If nothing but the t. exists, right-minded
T-3......... II.6:4 T. overcomes all error, and those who live
T-3......... II.6:6 your acceptance of their t. so they can
T-3...... III.1:10 is the affirmation of t. and beyond all
T-3...... III.5:13 perceive the t. is not the same as to know
T-3........IV.6:7 T. will always overcome error in this way.
T-3........IV.7:2 T. cannot deal with errors that you want.
T-3......... V.5:7 thinking is *not* the t. that shall set you free,
T-3......... V.8:3 T. can only be known. All of it is equally
T-3....... V.10:2 and given themselves over to t..
T-3.......VII.5:4 will surely dissolve in the light of t.,
T-3.......VII.5:6 it. Your starting point is t., and you must
T-3.....VII.6:11 The world is not left by death but by t.,
T-3.....VII.6:11 t. can be known by all those for whom the
T-4........ III.2:5 so t. can break through the barriers the
T-4...... III.10:4 then protect this belief at the cost of t.?
T-4........ IV.9:1 are a mirror of t., in which God Himself
T-5...........I.4:9 is so near to t. that God Himself can flow
T-5...... III.11:5 You have not made t., but truth can still
T-5...... III.11:5 not made truth, but t. can still set you free
T-5........ IV.1:4 T. is beyond your ability to destroy, but
T-6...........I.6:4 perfect immunity, which is the t. in you,
T-6.........I.10:3 be perceived as the way, the t. and the life.
T-6....... II.6:10 t. lies only in its perfect inclusion in Him
T-6........ III.4:2 you will learn the t. that will set you free,
T-6........ IV.6:7 you will see the t. around you and in you,
T-6.......IV.11:9 you made with the t. He created for you,
T-6....V.B.1:10 system is true, only t. extends from it. But
T-6......V.B.6:3 Holy Spirit teaches you that t. was created
T-6......V.C.8:9 Vigilance is not necessary for t., but it is
T-6......V.C.9:1 T. is without illusions and therefore
T-6......V.C.9:3 When you threw t. away you saw yourself
T-7......... II.5:5 the use of t. to convince His Sons of truth.
T-7......... II.5:5 the use of truth to convince His Sons of t..
T-7......... II.5:6 The extension of t., which *is* the law of the
T-7......... II.5:6 rests only on the knowledge of what t. is.
T-7........ III.1:9 you, *you* are the way, the t. and the life.
T-7...........IV.h Healing as the Recognition of T.
T-7 ....... IV.1:1 T. can only *be* recognized and *need* only be
T-7 ....... IV.7:1 only truly because they are the laws of t..
T-7 ........ V.9:3 The other shows you only t., which you
T-7 ...... V.11:1 unto me, and learn of the t. in you. The
T-7 ....... VI.8:6 it. It wants no part of t., because the ego
T-7 ....... VI.8:7 true. If t. is total, the untrue cannot exist.
T-7 ..... VI.8:11 contradictory thought systems share t.,
T-7 .....VIII.6:1 t. is beyond belief and His perception is
T-7 ....... IX.1:7 To spirit this is t., because it knows its
T-7 ....... IX.6:6 In t. it is impossible. Your Self-fullness is
T-7 .........X.2:4 t. has nothing to do with your willingness.
T-7 .........X.2:5 T. is God's Will. Share His Will and you
T-7 .........X.8:6 Every miracle is thus a lesson in t., and by
T-7 .........X.8:6 offering t. you are learning the difference
T-7 ....... XI.5:7 Nothing is so easy to recognize as t.. This
T-7 ....... XI.6:1 is t.?" since truth is the environment by
T-7 ....... XI.6:1 is truth?" since t. is the environment by
T-7 ....... XI.7:1 You cannot deny part of t.. You do not
T-8 ..... IV.8:13 can be imprisoned if Its t. is to be known.
T-8 ........ V.1:3 delusional believe that t. will assail them,
T-8 ........ V.1:4 Judging t. as something they do not want,
T-8 ........ V.3:3 of His power in you, but in that lies all t..
T-8 ........ V.4:3 The t. in both of us is beyond the ego. Our
T-8 ....... VI.9:8 T. can only be experienced. It cannot be
T-8 ..... VI.9:10 can make you aware of the conditions of t.
T-8 ..... VI.9:11 but t. will dawn upon you of itself.
T-8 ...... VII.4:6 it is. Use it for t. and you will see it truly.
T-8 .....VIII.6:7 function of t. is to collect information that
T-8 .....VIII.8:5 choose not to accept anything except t..
T-9 ..........I.1:3 illusions, since reality can only uphold t..
T-9 ..........I.3:2 The association of t. and fear, which
T-9 ..........I.3:2 of those who do not know what t. is. All
T-9 ..........I.7:6 Yet you cannot be safe *from* t., but only *in*
T-9 ..........I.7:6 you cannot be safe *from* truth, but only *in* t.
T-9 ..........I.9:3 are one. In the presence of t., there are no
T-9 ........I.11:1 waste of energy you expend in denying t..
T-9 ........I.14:5 do not try to look beyond yourself for t.,
T-9 ........I.14:5 for truth, for t. can only be within you.
T-9 .........II.4:5 are true because of the t. that is in him.
T-9 .........II.4:6 You will unite with the t. in him, and his
T-9 .........II.4:8 me. Listening to t. is the only way you can
T-9 .........II.5:6 can so holy a brother tell you except t.?
T-9 .........II.5:9 giving t. to his words and making you
T-9 .........II.7:1 I love you for the t. in you, as God does.
T-9 .........II.8:3 you if you learn to ask only t. of them. Do
T-9 .........II.8:5 this way you are seeking the t. in you. This
T-9 ....... III.6:5 do not come from the t. that is in him,
T-9 ....... III.6:5 that is in him, and only this t. is yours.
T-9 ....... III.6:6 can have no effect at all on the t. in you.
T-9 ....... III.7:3 keep it, see only t. beside you for you walk
T-9 ..... IV.12:3 heals, because it is the awareness of t..
T-9 ........ V.2:3 searches fantasies for t. must be unhealed,
T-9 ........ V.2:3 he does not know where to look for t., and
T-9 ...... VII.8:4 it. The t. about you is so lofty that nothing
T-9 .....VIII.7:1 T. and littleness are denials of each other
T-9 .....VIII.7:1 of each other because grandeur is t..
T-9 .....VIII.7:2 T. does not vacillate; it is always true.
T-9 .....VIII.8:3 T. is not obscure nor hidden, but its
T-9 ...VIII.11:1 Yet if t. is indivisible, your evaluation of
T-10 ........I.4:3 impossible because you will want only t.,
T-10 .......II.1:3 because the dissociation is an attack on t..
T-10 .......II.3:3 The ability to accept t. in this world is the
T-10 .......II.4:4 that this is always an attack on t., and
T-10 .......II.4:4 is always an attack on truth, and t. is God,
T-10 ..... III.3:5 God reminds him of the t. about himself,
T-10 ..... IV.2:5 because t. and illusions are irreconcilable.
T-10 ..... IV.2:6 T. is whole, and cannot be known by part
T-10 ..... IV.6:6 yourself and your reality affect t. at all.
T-11 .......II.2:2 become. If you have denied t., what better
T-11 ...... V.1:4 for we are merely looking honestly for t..
T-11 ...... V.1:6 together, and then look beyond it to t..
T-11 ...... V.3:5 Yet the t. is very simple: *All power is of God*
T-11 .... V.10:6 that you have successfully attacked t., you
T-11 .... V.12:2 fulfilling your function as it exists in t..
T-11 .... V.13:4 understanding and t. lie in separation,
T-11 .... V.14:2 The ego focuses on error and overlooks t..
T-11 .... V.14:3 mistake consistent t. must be meaningless
T-11 .... V.14:5 is obvious. If consistent t. is meaningless,
T-11 .... V.14:6 system: Error is real and t. is error.
T-11 .....V.16:6 the ego teach truly when it overlooks t.?
T-11 .....V.17:5 not deny, and it will demonstrate its t..
T-11 .... VII.3:6 true. If you believe in t. and illusion, you
T-11 .... VII.4:5 it. T. is not absent here, but it is obscure.
T-11 ... VIII.4:1 one can withhold t. except from himself.
T-11 ... VIII.4:3 and do not defend yourself against t.. You
T-11 ... VIII.7:7 willing to ask the t. of God without fear,
T-11 ... VIII.8:4 Believe that the t. is in me, for I know that
T-11 ... VIII.8:6 Ask for t. of any Son of God, and you have
T-11 . VIII.14:6 ask for t. again when they are frightened.
T-11 . VIII.15:1 Would you not exchange your fears for t.,
T-11 . VIII.15:3 the t. about yourself from the Holy Spirit,
T-12 .........I.1:3 true. But t. is real in its own right, and to
T-12 .........I.1:3 believe in t. *you do not have to do anything.*
T-12 .........I.1:8 and having done this you will overlook t..
T-12 .........I.5:2 for t. to him has become what he wants it
T-12 .........I.7:3 you want It to be, and if you want It in t.,
T-12 .........I.8:3 Spirit must still translate the fear into t.. If
T-12 .......I.10:3 for the awareness of t. cannot be denied.
T-12 .......I.10:4 fear with love and translate error into t..
T-12 ........II.1:1 are merely the translation of denial into t.
T-12 ........II.1:4 the t. about themselves they could not be
T-12 ........II.1:5 thus becomes *to deny the denial of t..* The
T-12 ........II.1:6 must heal themselves, for the t. is in them
T-12 ........II.8:7 perfection is not so difficult as to deny t.,
T-12 ... III.10:6 world to this altar, for it is the altar to t..
T-12 .. VII.12:1 because you have decided to manifest t..
T-12 ... VIII.4:4 you have made invisible is the only t., and
T-12 ... VIII.6:7 invisible the only t. that this world holds.
T-12 ... VIII.7:1 interpose between your awareness and t..
T-13 .........I.9:3 you of His Son, and what he is in t.. For
T-13 ........II.4:5 for the ego cannot protect you against t.,
T-13 ........II.5:1 In the calm light of t., let us recognize
T-13 ........II.8:6 For you believe that, in the presence of t.,
T-13 ..... III.8:4 place of t. as you see it in your brothers,
T-13 .....V.11:7 this vision of the t. in them came all the
T-13 ..... VI.5:4 from you, for t. lies only in the present,
T-13 ..... VI.7:6 *forth.* And they will not deny the t. in you,
T-13 ... VI.12:1 out of quiet recognition of the t. in them.
T-13 ..... IX.6:1 affirm the t. of guiltlessness unto yourself.
T-13 ..... IX.8:9 knows Himself, and knows the t. in you.
T-13 ........X.9:5 Fear not to look upon the lovely t. in you.
T-13 ..... XI.6:5 T. comes of its own will unto its own.
T-13 ..... XI.6:6 you have learned that you belong to t., it
T-13 ... XI.11:1 what is not true must be reconciled with t.
T-13 ... XI.11:8 It is this reconciliation with t., and only
T-13 ... XI.11:8 this reconciliation with truth, and only t.,
T-14 ............ h TEACHING FOR T.
T-14 ...... in.1:8 the simple conclusions that speak for t.,
T-14 ...... in.1:8 that speak for truth, and only t..
T-14 .........I.2:1 Indirect proof of t. is needed in a world
T-14 .........I.2:5 off and wholly separated from the t.. This
T-14 .........I.3:5 And it is these, and not the t., that he has
T-14 .........I.5:2 but He must introduce the simple t. into a
T-14 ........II.2:1 the fundamental teaching that *t.* is true.
T-14 ........II.2:5 Nothing is so alien to you as the simple t.,
T-14 ........II.3:3 *The t. is true. Nothing else matters, nothing*
T-14 ........II.3:8 *no deception there, but only the simple t..*
T-14 ........II.4:1 Like you, the Holy Spirit did not make t..
T-14 ........II.4:3 He brings the light of t. into the darkness,
T-14 ........II.5:1 When you teach anyone that t. is true,
T-14 ........II.6:2 on the firm foundation that t. is true. For
T-14 ........II.6:3 is builded there *is* true, and built on t.. The
T-14 ........II.6:5 With t. before you, you will not look back.
T-14 ........II.7:3 For t. *is* true. What else could ever be, or
T-14 ........II.8:5 it is impossible to deny the simple t.. For
T-14 ..... III.4:6 are no alternatives except t. and illusion.
T-14 ... III.12:1 Would you deny the t. of God's decision,
T-14 ..... IV.1:5 see the t. of what you have acknowledged.
T-14 ..... IV.1:6 Yet t. is offered first to be received, even
T-14 ..... IV.3:1 all that obscured the t. in your most holy
T-14 ..... IV.5:6 Holiness that join together as the t. in you
T-14 ..... VI.4:2 the t. of one must make the falsity of its
T-14 .... VII.1:5 is not real must disappear, for t. *is* union.
T-14 .... VII.1:8 rather than a helper in the search for t..
T-14 .... VII.2:1 search for t. is but the honest searching
T-14 .... VII.2:1 out of everything that interferes with t..
T-14 .... VII.2:2 T. *is.* It can neither be lost nor sought nor
T-14 .... VII.2:7 insane system of belief, the t. lies hidden.

T-14.....VII.2:8 cannot know this, for by hiding t. in fear,
T-14.....VII.5:2 T. does not struggle against ignorance,
T-14.....VII.5:6 Holy Spirit uses defenses on behalf of t.
T-14... VIII.3:7 glory and His Son's belong to you in t..
T-14... VIII.4:1 There is no substitute for t.. And truth
T-14... VIII.4:2 And t. will make this plain to you as you
T-14... VIII.4:2 the place where you must meet with t..
T-14... VIII.4:5 Such is the t.. Nothing can change the
T-14......IX.1:4 Bringing illusion to t., or the ego to God,
T-14......IX.1:8 Thus t. was made past, and the present
T-14......IX.2:1 the ego to God is but to bring error to t.,
T-14......IX.3:1 does t. release you from everything that it
T-14......IX.8:6 as part of Him, hold Him in them in t..
T-14......IX.8:7 They do not merely reflect t., for they *are*
T-14......IX.8:7 do not merely reflect truth, for they *are* t..
T-14....... X.1:7 the reflection of t. draws everyone to truth
T-14....... X.1:7 the reflection of truth draws everyone to t.
T-14....... X.2:2 its t. becomes the only perception the Son
T-14....... X.9:6 or more join together in searching for t.,
T-14.........XI.h The Test of T.
T-14......XI.1:8 and t. is beyond semblance of any kind.
T-14......XI.4:1 judge the t. and value of this course. Yet
T-14......XI.4:6 lessons must be brought willingly to t.,
T-15....... II.1:9 removed? T. is so far beyond time that all
T-15......IV.6:1 this course is simple is that t. is simple.
T-15....... V.4:5 as learning experiences that point to t..
T-15......VI.8:2 is remembered together, as is t.. There is
T-15... VIII.1:3 to learn of Him what the t. must be. He is
T-15......IX.7:5 the only t. that you could ever want. All
T-15......IX.7:6 that you could ever want. All t. *is* here.
T-16.........I.7:3 is not the way, for it leads not to life and t.
T-16....... II.2:1 the t. of just a little part of the whole. And
T-16....... II.5:2 be in joyously accepting t. for what it is,
T-16....... II.5:3 Honor the t. that has been given you, and
T-16....... II.6:1 you of the t. of what you do not want. Yet
T-16....... II.6:8 to it, and denying the evidence for t.? For
T-16....... II.6:9 come too near to t. to renounce it now,
T-16....... II.9:7 This year invest in t., and let it work in
T-16......III.2:8 spoke for the cause of t. and its effects.
T-16......III.4:6 not by your own projection, but in t.. And
T-16....III.4:10 And the seeming conflict between t. and
T-16....III.4:10 yourself from the illusion and not from t..
T-16......IV.5:6 in the choice between t. and illusion. Seen
T-16......IV.7:1 and t. must be recognized if it is to be
T-16......IV.7:6 You have come close to t., and only this
T-16......IV.8:4 substitute for what makes you whole in t.,
T-16....IV.10:3 are the veil behind which t. is hidden. To
T-16....IV.10:4 only needful to value t. beyond all fantasy,
T-16....IV.10:4 unwilling to settle for illusion in place of t.
T-16....IV.11:5 your completion lies in t., and nowhere
T-16....IV.12:1 Father can no more forget the t. in you
T-16....IV.12:5 now, and let nothing stand in the way of t.
T-16....IV.12:6 last useless journey away from t. together,
T-16..IV.13:10 The way to t. is open. Follow it with me.
T-16..... V.11:2 So fearful has the t. become to you that
T-16..... V.11:3 you made with power you wrested from t.
T-16..... V.14:3 And to the same extent you are denying t.
T-16..... V.14:3 the simple choice between t. and illusion;
T-16..... V.15:4 to lead away from t. and into fantasy. Yet
T-16..... V.16:1 it is but the choice between t. and illusion.
T-16..... V.16:2 For here is t., separated from illusion and
T-16....VI.10:5 See no illusion of t. and beauty there. And
T-16....VI.10:6 *is* a place where t. and beauty wait for you.
T-16.....VII.6:2 and uses opposites to point to t.. The holy
T-16.....VII.6:6 Everything is gone except the t..
T-16.....VII.7:1 between your experience of t. and illusion
T-16...VII.10:1 you always choose between t. and illusion
T-16...VII.11:6 The t. lies there and nowhere else. You
T-17........... I.h Bringing Fantasy to T.
T-17.........I.2:5 What you use in fantasy you deny to t..
T-17.........I.2:6 to t. to use for you is safe from fantasy.
T-17.........I.3:1 some things you would withhold from t..
T-17.........I.3:2 You believe t. cannot deal with them only
T-17.........I.3:2 because you would keep them from t..
T-17.........I.4:3 learn to deal with part of the t. in one way
T-17.........I.4:4 fragment t. is to destroy it by rendering it
T-17.........I.5:1 Think you that you can bring t. to fantasy
T-17.........I.5:1 learn what t. means from the perspective
T-17.........I.5:2 T. *has* no meaning in illusion. The frame of
T-17.........I.5:4 When you try to bring t. to illusions, you
T-17.........I.5:5 But to give illusions to t. is to enable truth
T-17.........I.5:5 to enable t. to teach that the illusions are
T-17.........I.5:6 Reserve not one idea aside from t., or you
T-17.........I.6:1 the t. to Him Who knows the truth, and
T-17.........I.6:1 the truth to Him Who knows the t., and
T-17.........I.6:1 truth, and in Whom all is brought to t..
T-17.........I.6:6 of you away from t. and from salvation.
T-17.........I.6:7 to t. what was denied by both of you. And
T-17....... II.2:3 and there are no fantasies to hide the t..
T-17....... III.2:3 the exclusion of the t. about the other,
T-17....... III.8:5 And what is thus let go is all the t. the past
T-17....... III.9:1 to choose to join with t. or with illusion.
T-17....... III.9:4 or the world of guilt and fear, t. or illusion
T-17.... III.10:5 t. that I would interpose between you and
T-17......IV.3:2 predominance that, when t. calls to you,
T-17......IV.3:3 that you will not hear the call of t..
T-17......IV.4:4 holds within itself the t. about everything.
T-17......IV.4:5 And the t. is that the Holy Spirit is in close
T-17....IV.10:1 instant is so important in the defense of t.
T-17....IV.10:2 The t. itself needs no defense, but you do
T-17....IV.10:3 are t. accept an idea so dangerous to truth
T-17....IV.10:3 are truth accept an idea so dangerous to t.
T-17....IV.10:3 to truth, you threaten t. with destruction.
T-17....IV.10:4 must now be undertaken, to keep t. whole
T-17..... V.14:1 together in the holy presence of t. itself.
T-17......VI.4:3 Holy Spirit's sorting out of t. and falsity.
T-17......VI.5:1 goal of t. has further practical advantages.
T-17......VI.5:2 If the situation is used for t. and sanity, its
T-17......VI.5:4 *is*. If peace is the condition of t. and sanity,
T-17......VI.5:5 T. comes of itself. If you experience peace,
T-17......VI.5:6 the t. has come to you and you will see the
T-17......VI.6:1 goal of t. requires faith. Faith is implicit in
T-17......VI.6:3 Where the goal of t. is set, there faith
T-17......VI.7:2 unity, and must obscure the goal of t..
T-17......VI.7:4 T. has not come because faith has been
T-17......VI.7:5 of the situation the goal of t. would bring.
T-17......VI.7:6 is not the condition in which t. can enter.
T-17.....VII.3:3 But if the goal is t., this is impossible.
T-17.....VII.3:9 to faith will never interfere with t.. But
T-17...VII.3:10 used *against* t. will always destroy faith. If
T-17.....VII.6:1 as closely tied to faithlessness as faith to t.
T-17.....VII.6:2 in any situation dedicated in advance to t.
T-17.....VII.8:6 and is not there to interfere with t.. There
T-17.....VII.8:9 light of t. shines from the center of the
T-17.....VII.9:3 to illusions transformed to means for t..
T-17.....VII.9:4 T. calls for faith, and faith makes room
T-17.....VII.9:4 calls for faith, and faith makes room for t..
T-17...VII.10:4 from loneliness because the t. has come.
T-17... VIII.1:3 that faith might answer to the call of t..
T-17... VIII.2:2 Let t. be what it is. Do not intrude upon it
T-17... VIII.2:5 faith is asked of you, for t. asks nothing.
T-17... VIII.3:7 strain of refusing faith to t. is enormous,
T-17... VIII.3:8 answer t. with faith entails no strain at all.
T-17... VIII.4:6 strain of refusing to give faith to t., and
T-17... VIII.6:1 When you accepted t. as the goal for your
T-18.........I.4:2 it was the substitution of illusion for t.; of
T-18.........I.4:4 one error, which brought t. to illusion,
T-18.........I.6:2 and drawn between you and the t.. For
T-18.........I.6:3 For t. extends inward, where the idea of
T-18.........I.6:6 For t. brought to this could only remain
T-18.........I.7:2 The t. will save you. It has not left you, to
T-18.........I.7:5 it is the other way; that t. is outside, and
T-18.........I.8:3 you gently back to the t. and safety within
T-18.........I.8:4 that you have placed outside you to the t..
T-18.........I.9:1 set the course inward to the t. you share.
T-18.........I.9:4 only the t. in your brother can abide. Here
T-18.........I.9:7 Here is the radiant t., to which the Holy
T-18.......I.10:3 firmly joined in t. that only God is there.
T-18.......I.11:2 been gently brought unto the t. in you,
T-18.......I.11:2 you, blessing your relationship with t..
T-18.......I.11:4 relationship, with the t. shining upon it!
T-18....... II.2:2 can be utilized to substitute illusions for t.
T-18....... II.8:4 changed from one of dreams to one of t..
T-18....... II.8:6 the choice between the t. and *all* illusions.
T-18....... II.9:3 Its coming means that you have chosen t.,
T-18....... II.9:5 the t. of Heaven join in the Will of God.
T-18...... III.1:1 spent your life in bringing t. to illusion,
T-18...... III.1:5 that you could hide from t. forever, in
T-18...... III.2:1 rush to darkness, shrinking from the t.,
T-18...... III.2:2 your goal is the advance from fear to t..
T-18...... III.3:1 T. has rushed to meet you since you
T-18...... III.5:6 and walk with you in your advance to t..
T-18...... IV.7:5 is a powerful contribution to the t., and
T-18....... V.1:2 the difference between t. and illusion, the
T-19.........I.1:1 a situation has been dedicated wholly to t.
T-19.........I.1:3 for what is dedicated to t. as its only goal
T-19.........I.1:3 as its only goal is brought to t. *by* faith.
T-19.........I.3:6 there, hearing what t. has never said and
T-19.........I.4:6 "enemy" of healing and the opposite of t..
T-19.........I.5:6 dedicated to illusions; faith wholly to t..
T-19.........I.5:8 T. is the absence of illusion; illusion the
T-19.........I.5:8 of illusion; illusion the absence of t.. Both
T-19.........I.6:7 all attempts to keep both t. and illusion in
T-19.........I.6:7 illusion; and given up when brought to t.,
T-19.........I.6:7 and seen as totally unreconcilable with t.,
T-19.........I.7:1 T. and illusion have no connection. This
T-19.........I.7:3 But illusions are always connected, as is t..
T-19.........I.7:8 identification safe from the "attack" of t..
T-19.......I.15:2 it calls on t. to enter and make lovely what
T-19.......I.15:3 T. follows faith and peace, completing the
T-19.......I.15:5 has been learned. Yet t. will stay forever.
T-19........II.4:1 religion is that sin is not error but t., and
T-19........II.4:5 an attempt to wrest creation away from t.,
T-19........II.6:6 is a mistake, it can be undone easily by t..
T-19........II.6:7 can be corrected, if t. be left to judge it.
T-19........II.6:8 But if the mistake is given the status of t.,
T-19......II.6:10 As t. it is inviolate, and everything is
T-19......II.6:11 As a mistake, *it* must be brought to t.. It is
T-19........II.7:3 the "t." from which escape will always be
T19. IV.A.6:10 And in the goal of t. which you accepted
T19....IV.A.9:1 feather be before the great wings of t.?
T19. IV.A.10:2 the nature of love to look upon only the t.,
T19....IV.B.7:1 holy relationship t. proclaims the truth,
T19....IV.B.7:1 holy relationship truth proclaims the t.,
T19....IV.C.7:2 the great dark savior from the light of t.,
T19..IV.C.11:4 to the t. or falsity of the idea which they
T19... IV.D.8:5 it has no power to keep you from the t..
T-20.........I.1:1 of victory and the acceptance of the t.. Let
T-20.........I.2:2 the acceptance of the t. and its expression.
T-20...... III.1:7 Who need adjust to t., which calls on only
T-20...... III.3:1 The holy do not interfere with t.. They
T-20...... III.3:2 within the t. they recognize their holiness,
T-20...... III.7:2 the home of t. and who will wander off.
T-20...... III.7:8 slips unnoticed through the universe of t.,
T-20.... III.7:10 in all the seeing universe of t. you ask,
T-20...... III.8:2 answer, and adjust to it as if it were the t.?
T-20.... VI.10:3 firm foundation is eternally upheld by t.,
T-20..... VII.4:8 both must be undone for purposes of t..
T-20..... VII.6:6 Here are illusions never brought to t., and
T-20....VIII.1:2 T. is restored to you through your desire,
T-20....VIII.4:7 would you rather look on it than on the t.
T-21.........II.5:8 it taken from him and be replaced with t..
T-21.........II.7:6 that is asked of you is to make room for t..
T-21.......II.13:1 Yet the t. is you and your brother were
T-21...... III.2:1 accepted the idea of making room for t..
T-21...... IV.3:5 you join with what is part of you in t..
T-21....... V.8:1 the great deceiver's needs as well as t.. But
T-21...... VI.6:7 with what you hold more dear than t.?
T-21.... VI.7:10 away from madness toward the goal of t..
T-21.... VI.7:11 will lay down the burden of denying t..
T-21.... VI.7:12 the burden that is terrible, and not the t..
T-21... VII.5:14 *want to see what I denied because it is the t.?*
T-21..... VII.6:6 that t. may be the enemy you yet may find
T-21..... VII.7:1 Forget not that the choice of sin or t.,
T-21... VII.10:5 But t. is constant, and implies a state
T-21.... VIII.1:7 Yet he did not desire it *because* it was the t.
T-22.......in.3:6 not his own reality *because* it is the t.. Just
T-22.........I.5:3 you, you will understand *because* it is the t.
T-22.........I.9:9 him; such he believed *because* it was the t..
T-22.......I.10:5 And t. came instantly, to show you where
T-22.......I.10:6 It is denial of illusions that calls on t., for
T-22........II.1:1 of illusions is not disillusionment but t..
T-22........II.1:2 Only to the ego, to which t. is meaningless
T-22........II.1:3 In t. they are the same. Both bring the
T-22........II.1:6 covered, and hidden from the joy of t..
T-22........II.2:1 T. is the opposite of illusions because it
T-22........II.3:9 not imagined, illusions must give way to t.

| | |
|---|---|
| T-22 II.4:2 | T. is the same and misery the same, but |
| T-22 II.4:4 | against the t. makes all truth meaningless, |
| T-22 II.4:4 | against the truth makes all t. meaningless, |
| T-22 II.10:7 | the illusions that you made replaced the t. |
| T-22 II.11:8 | you gave him for the one he has in t.? |
| T-22 III.5:7 | wall that stands between you and the t., is |
| T-22 III.7:6 | and must perceive illusions as the t.. |
| T-22 III.7:7 | the truth. Could it, then, recognize the t.? |
| T-22 IV.6:4 | opens the way to t. to more than you. |
| T-22 V.1:9 | way of t. when only weakness interferes? |
| T-22 V.2:2 | Always to justify what goes against the t., |
| T-22 V.2:4 | to insanity, to save you from the t.? And |
| T-22 V.3:4 | In t. you and your brother stand together, |
| T-22 V.5:5 | immovable; this Force is irresistible in t.. |
| T-22 V.6:6 | not one that t. cannot pass over lightly, |
| T-22 VI.13:10 | other experiences, more in line with t., to |
| T-22 VI.15:7 | Let t. decide if you and your brother be |
| T-23 in.3:3 | awareness of the t. releases everything |
| T-23 in.4:3 | happy world you walk, with t. beside you! |
| T-23 I.5:4 | Yet t. can never be forgotten by itself, and |
| T-23 I.6:2 | *is* no conflict between them and the t.. Nor |
| T-23 I.6:8 | Illusions cannot triumph over t., nor can |
| T-23 I.7:3 | T. does not fight against illusions, nor do |
| T-23 I.7:3 | do illusions fight against the t.. Illusions |
| T-23 I.7:6 | But t. is indivisible, and far beyond their |
| T-23 I.7:10 | And t. stands radiant, apart from conflict, |
| T-23 I.9:1 | disappears when it is brought to t.! For it |
| T-23 I.12:1 | Illusion meets illusion; t., itself. The |
| T-23 II.1:3 | to be an obstacle to reason and to t.. Let |
| T-23 II.1:5 | to make meaningless, and to attack the t.. |
| T-23 II.2:1 | law is that the t. is different for everyone. |
| T-23 II.3:2 | establishes degrees of t. among illusions, |
| T-23 II.3:5 | brought to t. instead of to each other, they |
| T-23 II.3:6 | more resistant to the t. than can another. |
| T-23 II.6:3 | that He be asked about the t. of what has |
| T-23 II.14:3 | function of insanity to take the place of t.. |
| T-23 II.14:4 | It must be seen as t. to be believed. And if |
| T-23 II.14:5 | And if it is the t., then must its opposite, |
| T-23 II.14:5 | must its opposite, which was the t. before, |
| T-23 II.16:4 | In t. it does not function, yet in dreams, |
| T-23 II.21:4 | still deeper into terror and away from t.. |
| T-23 IV.1:12 | Every illusion is an assault on t., and every |
| T-23 IV.1:12 | of love because it seems to be of equal t.. |
| T-23 IV.2:1 | What can be equal to the t., yet different? |
| T-23 IV.5:11 | How can the t. of miracles be recognized |
| T-24 in.2:9 | The t. arises from what He knows. And |
| T-24 I.9:1 | must defend illusions against the t.. For |
| T-24 II.2:9 | illusions of yourself are dearer than the t.. |
| T-24 II.3:7 | it carefully in sin, to keep it "safe" from t. |
| T-24 II.4:2 | your specialness against the t. of what you |
| T-24 II.4:2 | you really are, how can you know the t.? |
| T-24 II.5:3 | and one with different meaning, is the t.. |
| T-24 II.5:4 | Yet how can t. be different to each one? |
| T-24 II.6:4 | as his mind accepts the t. about himself, |
| T-24 II.6:5 | only "cost" of t.: You will no longer see |
| T-24 II.7:2 | can change the t. in him and in yourself. |
| T-24 II.7:3 | certain that the t. is just the same in both. |
| T-24 II.7:8 | between you. What is one is joined in t.. |
| T-24 II.9:1 | You have come far along the way of t.; |
| T-24 II.9:5 | holy place does t. stand waiting to receive |
| T-24 II.11:6 | And only specialness could make the t. of |
| T-24 II.13:4 | God, away from t. and from salvation. |
| T-24 III.3:2 | T. is not frail. Illusions leave it perfectly |
| T-24 III.3:4 | But specialness is not the t. in you. *It* can |
| T-24 IV.3:10 | that all illusions are "threatened" by the t. |
| T-24 IV.4:5 | and give it meaning that the t. denies. All |
| T-24 V.3:2 | The Christ in you looks only on the t., and |
| T-24 VI.5:3 | not his specialness obscure the t. in him, |
| T-24 VI.7:2 | have no end, until the t. be your decision. |
| T-24 VI.7:6 | that you might see the t. about yourself, |
| T-24 VI.11:5 | this; you wanted specialness to be the t.. |
| T-24 VI.12:5 | dedication to the t. as God established it |
| T-24 VI.12:5 | of t. itself is given to provide the means, |
| T-24 VII.1:1 | the specialness he wants to be the t.! His |
| T-24 VII.3:3 | Seek not to make your specialness the t., |
| T-24 VII.3:4 | you to see his holiness *because* it is the t.. |
| T-24 VII.4:8 | around him, that the t. may shine on him, |
| T-24 VII.5:7 | as means for t. shares in its holiness, and |
| T-24 VII.10:10 | made it, and speak for its reality and t.. |
| T-24 VII.11:9 | his wish by giving it appearances of t.. Yet |
| T-25 I.h | The Link to T. |
| T-25 I.5:2 | Not that it is in t., but that the link that |
| T-25 I.5:2 | given you to join the t. may reach to you |
| T-25 I.5:3 | One, as all your brothers join as one in t.. |
| T-25 I.7:5 | all learning to transfer illusions to the t., |
| T-25 I.7:5 | beyond them to the t. that *is* beyond them. |
| T-25 III.8:13 | it is to change its state from error into t.. |
| T-25 IV.5:12 | your own mistakes be brought to t. than |
| T-25 V.1:6 | believe in one unless the other were the t., |
| T-25 V.4:8 | proper function, the only one he has in t., |
| T-25 VII.3:6 | And what is madness cannot be the t.. If |
| T-25 VII.4:4 | to believe one thought opposed to t., he |
| T-25 VII.4:10 | the changeless if it does not rest on t.? |
| T-25 VII.6:5 | the madness and rest peacefully on t.. |
| T-25 VII.6:6 | changeless and eternal t. of what you are. |
| T-25 VII.12:4 | single rock of t. can faith in God's eternal |
| T-25 VII.13:7 | And this is sane because it is the t.. |
| T-25 VIII.8:1 | knows that they are wholly innocent in t.. |
| T-25 IX.1:8 | mean that t. has greater value now than |
| T-25 IX.1:9 | recognize that t. must be revealed to you, |
| T-26 I.4:7 | bodies, however much he witnesses to t.? |
| T-26 I.5:1 | to t. instead of to illusion merely ask that |
| T-26 II.2:4 | for Him to bring to t. than is another. For |
| T-26 III.1:3 | one reality, one t. and but one Son. |
| T-26 III.1:8 | The t. is simple; it is one, without an |
| T-26 III.1:10 | is? The t. makes no decisions, for there is |
| T-26 III.2:3 | all illusions are laid down beside the t., |
| T-26 III.3:3 | words imply a limited reality, a partial t., |
| T-26 III.4:2 | But what is t. to him must be brought to |
| T-26 III.4:3 | It is the judgment of the t. upon illusion, |
| T-26 IV.5:1 | a world that will become an altar to the t., |
| T-26 V.4:3 | ago, before its unreality gave way to t.. |
| T-26 V.8:3 | this a hindrance to the t. the past is gone, |
| T-26 VI.1:8 | find the safety that the t. alone can give? |
| T-26 VI.2:8 | for what illusion can replace the t.? |
| T-26 VI.3:4 | And it is He Who is your only Friend in t.. |
| T-26 VII.3:2 | Not in t., but in the world of shadows and |
| T-26 VII.3:5 | is t. unchanged. It cannot be perceived, |
| T-26 VII.3:8 | Brought to t., its senselessness is quite |
| T-26 VII.3:9 | Kept apart from t., it seems to have a |
| T-26 VII.4:1 | Perception's laws are opposite to t., and |
| T-26 VII.5:2 | because they *are* reversals of the laws of t.. |
| T-26 VII.5:3 | The laws of t. forever will be true, and |
| T-26 VII.6:1 | be less amenable to t. than are the rest. |
| T-26 VII.6:2 | less willingly offered to t. for healing and |
| T-26 VII.6:3 | No illusion has any t. in it. Yet it appears |
| T-26 VII.6:6 | What relevance has preference to the t.? |
| T-26 VII.6:11 | His Will has no foundation in the t.. |
| T-26 VII.8:2 | And t. needs no defense to make it true. |
| T-26 VII.10:3 | but a willingness that t. be true? What |
| T-26 VII.16:1 | because the t. is in your memory. And to |
| T-26 VII.20:5 | by this little gift of t. but let to be itself, |
| T-27 I.5:4 | witnesses to the eternal t. that you cannot |
| T-27 I.10:5 | the t. and value that it represents. Let it |
| T-27 II.2:6 | seeks to pardon what it thinks to be the t.. |
| T-27 III.1:8 | a silent invitation to the t. to enter, and to |
| T-27 III.4:3 | and where He is there must the t. abide. |
| T-27 III.4:6 | Nothing points beyond the t., for what |
| T-27 III.5:5 | by which the t. is represented temporarily |
| T-27 VI.3:8 | The t. is found in him if it is truth he |
| T-27 VI.3:8 | is found in him if it is t. he represents. |
| T-27 VI.8:6 | And t. will be revealed to you who chose |
| T-27 VII.6:8 | What conceals the t. is not where you |
| T-27 VII.6:8 | is not where you should look to *find* the t.. |
| T-27 VII.11:3 | with different dreams about the t. in you. |
| T-27 VIII.8:1 | The world but demonstrates an ancient t. |
| T-27 VIII.10:3 | of enemy and of attacker, still is this the t. |
| T-27 VIII.11:3 | will make answer with this very simple t.. |
| T-28 I.3:3 | that is not used to interfere with t.. All |
| T-28 I.6:2 | to keep concealed the t. about yourself. |
| T-28 IV.6:5 | to his, and his attest the t. of yours. Yet if |
| T-28 IV.6:6 | Yet if you see there is no t. in yours, his |
| T-28 V.3:10 | What can be between illusion and the t.? |
| T-28 V.3:11 | you, must be a dream and cannot be the t. |
| T-28 V.4:1 | t. to be the place where all your safety lies, |
| T-28 V.6:2 | perhaps, all put together to attest its t.. |
| T-28 V.6:4 | gap that separates the t. from dreams and |
| T-28 V.6:5 | T. has left no room for them in any place |
| T-28 VII.3:5 | this, because it lacks foundation in the t.. |
| T-29 II.1:2 | Why would you not acclaim the t. instead |
| T-29 III.3:1 | bodies and of death is yet one theme of t.; |
| T-29 IV.1:1 | believe that t. can be but some illusions? |
| T-29 IV.1:3 | equal lack of t. becomes the basis for the |
| T-29 VII.1:12 | But it is given you to know the t., and not |
| T-29 VII.2:3 | his coming, he denies the t. about himself, |
| T-29 VII.6:1 | the t. within from being known to you, |
| T-29 VII.9:8 | you must protect against the light of t.. |
| T-29 VIII.5:5 | The miracle does not restore the t., the |
| T-29 VIII.5:6 | veil, and lets the t. shine unencumbered, |
| T-29 IX.1:4 | and ask yourself if it be not the t. that you |
| T-30 III.1:10 | loss. Decide for t. and everything is yours. |
| T-30 IV.h | The T. behind Illusions |
| T-30 IV.1:3 | For the t. behind them is so lovely and so |
| T-30 IV.1:4 | The t. could never be attacked. And this |
| T-30 IV.5:3 | and they bring fear *because* they hide the t. |
| T-30 VI.4:9 | t. that you can merit neither more nor less |
| T-30 VI.7:3 | healing, one illusion must be part of t.. |
| T-30 VI.7:8 | that have replaced the t. about God's Son. |
| T-30 VI.9:3 | if you would know the t. about yourself. |
| T-30 VI.9:6 | is this except a simple statement of the t.? |
| T-30 VI.10:1 | an error that could change the t. in him. It |
| T-31 I.5:4 | stand implacable before the Voice of t., |
| T-31 I.13:5 | away, and left a place for t. to be reborn. |
| T-31 II.1:2 | It is not vanquished that the t. be known, |
| T-31 II.1:4 | ancient battle being waged against the t., |
| T-31 II.1:4 | against the truth, but t. does not respond. |
| T-31 II.1:6 | He has no enemy in t.. And can he be |
| T-31 II.2:1 | between you and the t. of what you are. |
| T-31 II.2:4 | But afterwards, the t. is given you. You |
| T-31 II.2:5 | You would establish t.. And by your wish |
| T-31 II.8:6 | and learn the t. of what you really want. |
| T-31 II.10:6 | same as yours, as he is like yourself in t.. |
| T-31 IV.6:4 | is but the search for different forms of t.. |
| T-31 IV.6:5 | this would *keep* the t. from being reached. |
| T-31 IV.8:5 | How utterly opposed to t. is this, when all |
| T-31 V.7:10 | make a single picture representing t.. |
| T-31 V.17:3 | unsealed and open mind that t. returns, |
| T-31 V.17:4 | been laid by is t. revealed exactly as it is. |
| T-31 V.17:5 | is the t. left free to enter in its sanctuary, |
| T-31 VI.4:5 | think the t. about yourself must really be. |
| T-31 VI.5:1 | will stand against the t. of what you are. |
| T-31 VI.5:2 | are. Undoing t. would be impossible. But |
| T-31 VI.7:4 | The t. in you remains as radiant as a star, |
| T-31 VII.1:4 | For it must deal in contrasts, not in t., |
| T-31 VII.7:1 | a shield, a silent barricade before the t., |
| T-31 VIII.3:3 | unhealed, nor any image left to veil the t.. |
| T-31 VIII.5:7 | by, and nothing left to interfere with t.. |
| W-pI 8.3:2 | preoccupy your mind, the t. is blocked. |
| W-pI 12.5:3 | and let the t. be written upon it for you, it |
| W-pI 12.5:6 | It is this that is meaningless in t.. Beneath |
| W-pI 12.5:8 | The t. upsets you now, but when your |
| W-pI 16.2:3 | you have contributes to t. or to illusion; |
| W-pI 16.2:3 | it extends the t. or it multiplies illusions. |
| W-pI 35.3:2 | it describes you as you must really be in t.. |
| W-pI 41.5:2 | you, when the t. is hidden deep within, |
| W-pI 43.1:7 | sees it. Therefore, that is its function in t.. |
| W-pI 45.4:3 | We will deny the world in favor of t.. We |
| W-pI 45.6:6 | thoughts that cover the t. in your mind, |
| W-pI 48.1:3 | In t. there is nothing to fear. It is very easy |
| W-pI 49.1:2 | The part of your mind in which t. abides |
| W-pI 50.4:8 | acknowledgment of the t. about yourself. |
| W-pI 50.5:2 | thoughts come to help you recognize its t. |
| W-pI 55.1:7 | to see the witnesses to the t. in me, rather |
| W-pI 55.5:7 | I have given it, and learning the t. about it |
| W-pI 56.2:5 | As it is replaced by t., vision will surely be |
| W-pI 56.3:3 | I see it now, t. cannot enter my awareness. |
| W-pI 56.4:2 | I have made, the t. remains unchanged. |
| W-pI 56.4:6 | and recognize the t. beyond them all. |
| W-pI 57.3:3 | and my thoughts are the opposite of t.. |
| W-pI 58.1:4 | the innocence that is the t. about me. |
| W-pI 58.3:5 | them all by asserting the t. about me. In |
| W-pI 60.4:4 | I am walking steadily on toward t.. There |
| W-pI 61.1:2 | a statement of the t. about yourself. It is |
| W-pI 61.1:7 | created by God. It simply states the t.. |
| W-pI 61.4:3 | you have made about yourself to the t., |
| W-pI 61.6:2 | acknowledgment of the t. about yourself, |
| W-pI 62.1:4 | does the t. about yourself return to your |

| | |
|---|---|
| W-pI.....62.2:4 | you are learning how to remember the t.. |
| W-pI.....65.6:5 | your illusions of purpose be replaced by t. |
| W-pI.....66.3:1 | and arrive at the t. about your function. |
| W-pI.....66.3:4 | the ego by listening to its attacks on t.. |
| W-pI.....66.3:5 | be glad that we can find out what t. is. |
| W-pI.....66.4:4 | a common content where it exists in t.. |
| W-pI.....66.7:4 | home of the Holy Spirit, where t. abides. |
| W-pI...66.10:1 | You will listen to madness or hear the t.. |
| W-pI...66.10:7 | All t. stands on the other. Let us try today |
| W-pI...66.10:8 | try today to realize that only the t. is true. |
| W-pI.....67.1:6 | effort today to reach this t. about you, and |
| W-pI.....67.1:6 | fully, if only for a moment, that it is the t.. |
| W-pI.....67.2:2 | will begin by repeating this t. about you, |
| W-pI.....67.3:1 | about yourself to the t. in you. If love |
| W-pI.....67.4:2 | thoughts related to the t. about yourself. |
| W-pI.....67.5:2 | You need to hear the t. about yourself as |
| W-pI.....67.5:4 | itself. Hear the t. about yourself in this. |
| W-pI.....67.6:3 | your Self. This is the Voice of t., replacing |
| W-pI.....67.6:3 | with the simple t. about the Son of God. |
| W-pI.....72.5:3 | and offering illusions in place of t.. The |
| W-pI.....72.7:4 | may not hear the Voice of t. and welcome |
| W-pI.....72.8:4 | yourself in a body and the t. outside you, |
| W-pI.....72.9:1 | The light of t. is in us, where it was placed |
| W-pI.....72.9:4 | state. To recognize the light of t. in us is to |
| W-pI...72.11:6 | it. We are asking it of t.. Be certain, then, |
| W-pI.....73.6:6 | Such is your will in t.. And so salvation is |
| W-pI.....76.7:3 | It is no longer a t. that we would hide. We |
| W-pI.....76.7:4 | instead it is a t. that keeps us free forever. |
| W-pI.....76.9:2 | to hear the Voice that speaks the t. to you. |
| W-pI.....77.2:3 | It is inherent in the t. of what you are. It is |
| W-pI.....77.3:4 | ask no more than what belongs to us in t.. |
| W-pI.....78.4:3 | world reversed, as we look out toward t., |
| W-pI.....78.7:1 | knows this Son of God in his reality and t. |
| W-pI.....80.2:4 | deception aside, and seen the light of t.. |
| WpI. rII.in.5:1 | dedications to the way, the t. and the life. |
| W-pI.....88.1:5 | I always choose between t. and illusion; |
| W-pI.....89.3:4 | to have all my illusions be replaced with t. |
| W-pI...91.6:10 | t. of what you are calls on the strength in |
| W-pI.....92.4:7 | Strength is the t. about you; weakness is |
| W-pI.....92.5:1 | Strength comes from t., and shines with |
| W-pI.....92.5:3 | itself. T. is a savior and can only will for |
| W-pI...92.10:4 | closing the body's eyes and asking t. to |
| W-pI.....93.1:2 | see the t. about you he would be repelled, |
| W-pI.....93.7:3 | you made, the t. about you is unchanged. |
| W-pI.....93.8:1 | begin by stating the t. about your creation |
| W-pI...93.10:6 | that this is a statement of the t. about you. |
| W-pI.....94.3:1 | hour to the attempt to feel the t. in you. |
| W-pI.....94.4:1 | and wait in silent expectancy for the t.. |
| W-pI.....95.9:4 | you would defend illusions against the t.. |
| W-pI...95.10:3 | This is the t., and nothing else is true. |
| W-pI...95.10:4 | Today we will affirm this t. again, and try |
| W-pI...95.12:3 | to teach the world the t. about yourself. |
| W-pI...95.13:5 | Mind that is this Self, the holy t. in you. |
| W-pI...95.14:8 | hope, the stirring of the t. within his mind |
| W-pI.....96.2:1 | that t. and illusion cannot be reconciled, |
| W-pI.....96.6:3 | What could the resolution mean in t.? |
| W-pI.....97.1:3 | It simply states the t.. Practice this truth |
| W-pI.....97.1:4 | Practice this t. today as often as you can, |
| W-pI.....97.2:1 | We state again the t. about your Self, the |
| W-pI.....97.4:4 | who asks; replaces error with the simple t. |
| W-pI.....98.1:3 | We side with t. and let illusions go. We |
| W-pI.....98.1:5 | We dedicate ourselves to t. today, and to |
| W-pI.....99.2:1 | T. and illusions both are equal now, for |
| W-pI.....99.2:3 | borderland between the t. and the illusion |
| W-pI.....99.2:4 | It reflects the t. because it is the means by |
| W-pI.....99.2:5 | t. because it undoes what was never done. |
| W-pI.....99.4:2 | What plan could hold the t. inviolate, yet |
| W-pI.....99.6:1 | the Thought that brings illusions to the t., |
| W-pI.....99.9:5 | today with this instruction in the way of t. |
| W-pI...99.10:1 | would oppose the t. of your completion, |
| W-pI...99.11:2 | not withstand the t. these mighty words |
| W-pI...101.7:7 | *This is the t., because there is no sin.* |
| W-pI...103.2:2 | These images, with no reality in t., bear |
| W-pI...103.2:3 | error we will try again to bring to t. today, |
| W-pI...103.3:2 | the happiness it brings as t. replaces fear, |
| W-pI...103.3:7 | *today. I cannot fail, because I seek the t..* |
| W-pI......104.h | I seek but what belongs to me in t.. |
| W-pI...104.2:2 | His are the gifts that are our own in t.. His |
| W-pI...104.3:2 | five minutes given t. for your salvation, |
| W-pI...104.3:3 | *I seek but what belongs to me in t., And joy* |
| W-pI...104.4:3 | aware that what belongs to us in t. is what |
| W-pI...104.4:4 | else, for nothing else belongs to us in t.. |
| W-pI...104.5:4 | *I seek but what belongs to me in t.. God's* |
| W-pI......106.h | Let me be still and listen to the t.. |
| W-pI...106.1:1 | then you will hear the mighty Voice of t., |
| W-pI...106.2:2 | Be still today and listen to the t.. Be not |
| W-pI...106.2:4 | Attend them not, but listen to the t.. |
| W-pI...106.3:4 | Be still today and listen to the t.. Go past |
| W-pI...106.7:5 | *I will be still and listen to the t.. What does it* |
| W-pI...106.9:1 | Be still and listen to the t. today. For each |
| W-pI...106.9:2 | thousand minds are opened to the t. and |
| W-pI...106.9:3 | who pause to ask that t. be given them, |
| W-pI.106.10:3 | *Let me be still and listen to the t.. I am the* |
| W-pI......107.h | T. will correct all errors in my mind. |
| W-pI...107.1:1 | What can correct illusions but the t.? |
| W-pI...107.1:3 | Where t. has entered errors disappear. |
| W-pI...107.1:7 | dust they come and go, for only t. remains |
| W-pI...107.3:1 | mind will rest in when the t. has come. |
| W-pI...107.3:3 | When t. has come all pain is over, for |
| W-pI...107.3:4 | mind. T. occupies your mind completely, |
| W-pI...107.3:5 | have no place because the t. has come, |
| W-pI...107.3:6 | not be found, for t. is everywhere forever, |
| W-pI...107.4:1 | When t. has come it does not stay a while |
| W-pI...107.4:4 | when t. corrects the errors in your mind. |
| W-pI...107.5:1 | When t. has come it harbors in its wings |
| W-pI...107.5:2 | gift of healing, for the t. needs no defense, |
| W-pI...107.5:3 | can be brought to t. to be corrected. But |
| W-pI...107.5:4 | But the t. stands far beyond illusions, and |
| W-pI...107.5:4 | be brought to them to turn them into t.. |
| W-pI...107.6:1 | T. does not come and go nor shift nor |
| W-pI...107.6:5 | Today belongs to t.. Give truth its due, |
| W-pI...107.6:6 | Give t. its due, and it will give you yours. |
| W-pI...107.6:9 | dreams be gone. Let t. correct them all. |
| W-pI...107.7:3 | note of certainty that has been born of t.. |
| W-pI...107.7:6 | We do not doubt we walk with t. today, |
| W-pI...107.9:1 | T. will correct all errors in your mind |
| W-pI...107.9:5 | *T. will correct all errors in my mind, And I* |
| W-pI...107.9:6 | *Self.* Then let Him lead you gently to the t., |
| W-pI.107.10:2 | which the t. that goes with you will carry |
| W-pI.107.11:2 | "T. will correct all errors in my mind," |
| W-pI......108.h | To give and to receive are one in t.. |
| W-pI...108.4:1 | of one Thought whose t. does not depend |
| W-pI...108.5:3 | be directed by the One Who knows the t.. |
| W-pI...108.8:2 | say: *To give and to receive are one in t.. I will* |
| W-pI.108.10:3 | say, "To give and to receive are one in t.." |
| W-pI...109.2:4 | has power to wake the sleeping t. in you, |
| W-pI...109.2:4 | t. in everyone and everything there is. |
| W-pI...109.3:5 | no appearance but will turn to t. before |
| W-pI...109.4:3 | Yours is the rest of t.. Appearances cannot |
| W-pI...110.1:3 | Its t. would mean that you have made no |
| W-pI...110.3:1 | you, appearances cannot replace the t., |
| W-pI...110.5:2 | great restorer of the t. to the awareness of |
| W-pI...110.5:4 | This is the t. that comes to set you free. |
| W-pI...110.5:5 | This is the t. that God has promised you. |
| W-pI.110.10:4 | a great advance to t. by letting idols go, |
| W-pI.110.11:5 | *me.* Let us declare this t. as often as we can. |
| W-pI...111.1:3 | *the light of holiness and t. light up my mind,* |
| W-pI...117.2:1 | (104) I seek but what belongs to me in t.. |
| W-pI...117.2:4 | *to me. I would accept all that is mine in t..* |
| W-pI...117.3:4 | hour: I seek but what belongs to me in t.. |
| W-pI...118.2:1 | (106) Let me be still and listen to the t.. |
| W-pI...118.3:4 | hour: Let me be still and listen to the t.. |
| W-pI...119.1:1 | (107) T. will correct all errors in my mind |
| W-pI...119.2:1 | (108) To give and to receive are one in t.. |
| W-pI...119.2:2 | *that I may learn how to accept the t. in me,* |
| W-pI...119.3:2 | T. will correct all errors in my mind. On |
| W-pI...119.3:4 | hour: To give and to receive are one in t.. |
| W-pI...122.6:7 | this extremely simple statement of the t.. |
| W-pI.122.13:4 | change; the light of t. behind appearances |
| W-pI...123.1:3 | and no implacable resistance to the t.. A |
| W-pI...124.2:4 | Our shining footprints point the way to t., |
| W-pI...126.8:1 | the t. that giver and receiver are the same. |
| W-pI...126.8:4 | that He share your practicing in t. today. |
| W-pI.126.10:4 | the Voice of t. and healing speak to you, |
| W-pI...127.5:3 | upholds but violates the t. of what love is, |
| W-pI...127.9:3 | of t. within your mind wherever you give |
| W-pI...127.9:4 | and help you understand the t. of love. In |
| W-pI...130.3:3 | T. is eclipsed by fear, and what remains is |
| W-pI...130.9:3 | expressed in tangible perception and in t.. |
| W-pI......131.h | No one can fail who seeks to reach the t.. |
| W-pI...131.9:1 | we will not choose a paradox in place of t.. |
| W-pI.131.10:2 | No one can fail who seeks to reach the t., |
| W-pI.131.10:2 | truth, and it is t. we seek to reach today. |
| W-pI.131.10:3 | and neither source nor substance in the t.. |
| W-pI.131.12:2 | no one can fail who seeks to reach the t.. |
| W-pI.131.13:3 | you in the light reflects the t. you knew, |
| W-pI.131.15:7 | *me. No one can fail who seeks to reach the t..* |
| W-pI...132.1:4 | are as strong in their effects as is the t.. A |
| W-pI...132.4:5 | t. you found exactly what you looked for |
| W-pI...132.6:4 | can let himself be led along the road to t.. |
| W-pI...132.7:4 | because what they behold must be the t., |
| W-pI.132.12:2 | not of illusions, but as God in t.. God |
| W-pI.132.13:4 | Deny illusions, but accept the t.. Deny |
| W-pI...133.8:7 | It does not even tell the t. as it perceives it, |
| W-pI...134.1:1 | and a complete denial of the t.. In such a |
| W-pI...134.2:4 | T. is God's creation, and to pardon that is |
| W-pI...134.2:5 | All t. belongs to Him, reflects His laws |
| W-pI...134.3:1 | you still believe you must forgive the t., |
| W-pI...134.3:2 | look past what is there; to overlook the t., |
| W-pI...134.4:4 | It says the t. is false, and smiles on the |
| W-pI...134.5:2 | name, for pardon is a treachery to t.. Guilt |
| W-pI...134.6:2 | and gently lays them at the feet of t.. And |
| W-pI...134.7:1 | stands for t. in the illusions of the world. |
| W-pI...134.7:5 | "My brother, what you think is not the t.. |
| W-pI...134.8:1 | that it sees illusions as illusions, not as t.. |
| W-pI...134.8:2 | of lies; the great restorer of the simple t.. |
| W-pI...134.8:3 | what is not there, it opens up the way to t. |
| W-pI.134.10:1 | Himself intended it to be, and as it is in t.. |
| W-pI.134.10:3 | In t. is innocence the only thing there is. |
| W-pI.134.10:4 | stands between illusions and the t.; |
| W-pI.134.11:1 | of hatred and attack brought silently to t.. |
| W-pI.135.10:1 | have been corrected and replaced with t.. |
| W-pI.135.14:2 | its own protection, at the cost of t.. This is |
| W-pI.135.17:1 | you undertake to make against the t.. |
| W-pI.135.19:2 | t. that only your defenses would conceal. |
| W-pI.135.21:3 | t. to dawn upon our minds with certainty. |
| W-pI.135.22:1 | from every thought that blocks the t. from |
| W-pI.135.26:8 | *Son of God needs no defense against the t. of* |
| W-pI......136.h | Sickness is a defense against the t.. |
| W-pI...136.1:5 | approach that carries all of them to t., and |
| W-pI...136.2:4 | aim of all defenses is to keep the t. from |
| W-pI...136.3:2 | magic wands you wave when t. appears to |
| W-pI...136.7:3 | an instant t. arises in your own deluded |
| W-pI...136.7:4 | that t. may go away and threaten your |
| W-pI...136.8:1 | can succeed in shielding you from t.? |
| W-pI...136.8:2 | and so you must be separate from the t.. |
| W-pI...136.9:1 | Thus is the body stronger than the t., |
| W-pI.136.10:2 | blind by your illusions, t. turned into lies, |
| W-pI.136.10:4 | and react to them as if they were the t.? |
| W-pI.136.11:4 | suffer sickness or distort the t. in any way. |
| W-pI.136.12:1 | Such is the simple t.. It does not make |
| W-pI.136.12:4 | T. merely wants to give you happiness, for |
| W-pI.136.13:2 | God has given you is not the t. right now, |
| W-pI.136.13:4 | defense you made against the t.. Yet what |
| W-pI.136.14:1 | T. has a power far beyond defense, for no |
| W-pI.136.14:1 | remain where t. has been allowed to enter |
| W-pI.136.14:3 | to practice giving welcome to the t.. |
| W-pI.136.15:2 | to ask the t. to come to us and set us free. |
| W-pI.136.15:3 | And t. will come, for it has never been |
| W-pI.136.15:5 | and let t. be as it has always been: *Sickness* |
| W-pI.136.15:6 | *Sickness is a defense against the t.. I will* |
| W-pI.136.15:7 | *I will accept the t. of what I am, and let my* |
| W-pI.136.16:1 | peace and t. arise to take the place of war |
| W-pI.136.16:2 | and keep defended from the light of t.. |
| W-pI.136.20:4 | *Sickness is a defense against the t.. But I am* |
| W-pI...137.4:1 | would prove that lies must be the t.. But |
| W-pI...137.4:2 | But healing demonstrates that t. is true. |
| W-pI...137.4:4 | to accept what always was the simple t., |
| W-pI...137.4:6 | So healing, never needed by the t., must |
| W-pI...137.5:1 | the dream of sickness in the name of t., |
| W-pI...137.5:1 | in the name of truth, but not in t. itself. |
| W-pI...137.5:3 | dreams embroider into pictures of the t.. |
| W-pI...137.7:1 | which you hold before the simple t.. |
| W-pI...137.8:2 | that dreams will not prevail against the t.. |
| W-pI.137.11:4 | For here is t. bestowed, and here are all |
| W-pI.137.11:4 | and here are all illusions brought to t.. |
| W-pI.137.12:6 | we ask that only t. will occupy our minds; |

W-pI...138.2:3 It is this strange perception of the **t.** that
W-pI...138.2:6 **T.** cannot come where it could only be
W-pI...138.2:7 be the error **t.** can be brought to illusions.
W-pI...138.2:8 Opposition makes the **t.** unwelcome, and
W-pI...138.4:6 all. For **t.** is true, and nothing else is true.
W-pI...138.4:8 instead. There is no contradiction to the **t.**
W-pI...138.5:2 And the **t.** cannot be learned, but only
W-pI...138.5:6 have accepted as the **t.** of what you are,
W-pI...138.6:5 choice in which is **t.** accepted or denied.
W-pI...138.8:2 be safe, and magically armored against **t.**.
W-pI...138.9:4 as the **t.** dismisses them as causeless. Now
W-pI.138.11:2 has nothing but an appearance of the **t.**.
W-pI...139.5:4 into what knows and does not know the **t.**
W-pI.139.10:2 but merely to accept the **t.** about yourself,
W-pI.139.11:6 recall how dear our brothers are to us in **t.**
W-pI...140.3:3 heralds of the dawn of **t.** upon the mind.
W-pI...140.6:5 It is merely an appeal to **t.**, which cannot
W-pI...140.7:4 brings illusions to the **t.** is really changed.
W-pI.140.10:4 a single Voice which speaks to us of **t.**,
WpI. rIV.in1:1 part of learning how the **t.** can be applied.
WpI. rIV.in2:3 and represents the **t.** of What you are and
WpI. rIV.in4:2 self-deceptions cannot take the place of **t.**.
W-pI...146.1:1 No one can fail who seeks to reach the **t.**.
W-pI...148.2:1 (136) Sickness is a defense against the **t.**.
W-pI...151.3:6 fingers touch reality, and close upon the **t.**
W-pI...151.9:7 the gap between illusions and the **t.**.
W-pI.151.11:1 elements in them which represent the **t.**,
W-pI.151.13:3 Him Who sees the elements of **t.** in them.
W-pI.151.14:2 from the Mind which saw the **t.** in it, and
W-pI.151.17:3 the joyous news that **t.** has no illusions,
W-pI...152.2:2 Yet can **t.** have exceptions? If you have the
W-pI...152.2:6 **T.** must be all-inclusive, if it be the truth
W-pI...152.2:6 must be all-inclusive, if it be the **t.** at all.
W-pI...152.2:7 for to do so is to contradict the **t.** entirely.
W-pI...152.3:1 is the recognition that the **t.** is true, and
W-pI...152.3:5 **T.** cannot have an opposite. This can not
W-pI...152.3:7 well as what is true, then part of **t.** is false.
W-pI...152.3:8 And **t.** has lost its meaning. Nothing but
W-pI...152.3:9 Nothing but the **t.** is true, and what is
W-pI...152.4:4 thus the **t.** appears to have some aspects
W-pI...152.5:3 which sets the **t.** apart from falsehood,
W-pI...152.5:3 and the false kept separate from the **t.**, as
W-pI...152.7:1 His Will, invented opposites to **t.**, and
W-pI...152.9:3 But **t.** is humble in acknowledging its
W-pI.152.11:1 that lies are false, and only **t.** is true. We
W-pI.152.11:2 true. We think of **t.** alone as we arise, and
W-pI.152.12:3 thoughts, the **t.** of God for self-deceptions
W-pI.153.10:2 ministers have chosen that the **t.** be with
W-pI.153.14:2 we go to take our rightful place where **t.**
W-pI...155.2:5 let illusions walk ahead of **t.** is madness.
W-pI...155.2:6 let illusion sink behind the **t.** and let the
W-pI...155.2:6 truth and let the **t.** stand forth as what it is
W-pI...155.3:3 They cannot learn directly from the **t.**,
W-pI...155.3:4 beyond illusion to the simple **t.** in them.
W-pI...155.4:1 If **t.** demanded they give up the world, it
W-pI...155.6:4 Nor can the **t.**, which walks ahead of you,
W-pI...155.7:3 All this steps back as **t.** comes forth in you
W-pI...155.7:5 of it, for they mistake illusion for the **t.**.
W-pI...155.8:2 It asks that you accept the **t.**, and let it go
W-pI...155.9:2 you are tempted still to walk ahead of **t.**,
W-pI...155.9:3 walk with certainty of purpose to the **t.**. It
W-pI.155.10:1 be no gap, no distance between **t.** and you
W-pI.155.10:2 keep the **t.** apart from God's completion,
W-pI.155.10:3 Step back in faith and let **t.** lead the way.
W-pI.155.11:2 be no wish to be illusion rather than the **t.**
W-pI.155.11:3 along the way that **t.** points out to us. This
W-pI.155.11:6 For as **t.** goes before us, so it goes before
W-pI.155.12:6 The **t.** that walks before us now is one
W-pI...156.1:1 Today's idea but states the simple **t.** that
W-pI...156.2:2 **T.** must be true throughout, if it be true. It
W-pI...157.8:2 of life, Translator of perception into **t.**,
W-pI.159.10:7 His dream awakens us to **t.**. His vision
W-pI...160.2:1 to the **t.** he speaks a different language,
W-pI...160.2:1 looks upon a world **t.** does not know, and
W-pI...160.2:1 understands what **t.** regards as senseless.
W-pI...161.4:3 Such is the **t.**. Yet do these thoughts make
W-pI...162.3:2 and wakens with the **t.** before him always.
W-pI...162.3:3 each time he practices the words of **t.**.
W-pI...164.1:1 What time but now can **t.** be recognized?
W-pI...165.1:1 your own denial of the **t.** that lies beyond?
W-pI...166.3:3 deny their presence, contradict the **t.**, and
W-pI...166.7:4 down lest you might catch a glimpse of **t.**,
W-pI...167.1:1 different kinds of life, for life is like the **t.**.
W-pI.167.3:11 die. Its **t.** established you as one with God.
W-pI...167.7:2 created it, because it is not opposite in **t.**.
W-pI.167.10:1 Let us today be children of the **t.**, and not
W-pI...169.1:1 like the state prevailing in the unity of **t.**.
W-pI...169.4:3 of God to hasten the experience of **t.**, and
W-pI.169.13:4 and in need of you as witness to the **t.**?
WpI.rV.in10:6 practice but an ancient **t.** we knew before
W-pI...184.4:1 purposefully set against the given **t.**. Its
W-pI.184.13:3 see, but have not interfered with **t.** at all.
W-pI.184.15:6 *And we accept the **t.** You give, in place of*
W-pI...185.3:2 For minds can only join in **t.**. In dreams,
W-pI.185.12:5 that ever seemed to take the place of **t.**.
W-pI...186.6:5 Sin can not tarnish the **t.** in you, and
W-pI...187.1:8 The **t.** maintains that giving will increase
W-pI...188.5:4 because he recognized the **t.** in him. The
W-pI...190.3:1 Pain is a sign illusions reign in place of **t.**.
W-pI.190.10:6 Pain is deception; joy alone is **t.**.
W-pI.190.11:1 we choose between illusions and the **t.**, or
W-pI...191.4:5 In this one **t.** are all illusions gone. In this
W-pI...193.4:4 No one can hide forever from a **t.** so very
W-pI.193.11:6 **T.** is His message; truth His teaching is.
W-pI.193.11:6 Truth is His message; **t.** His teaching is.
W-pI...194.8:2 thoughts of sin and evil with the **t.** of love.
W-pI...196.2:2 threat, is quick to cite the **t.** to save its lies.
W-pI...196.2:3 it fail to understand the **t.** it uses thus. But
W-pI...196.3:2 distort the **t.** will not deceive you longer.
W-pI...198.2:5 To condemn is thus impossible in **t.**.
W-pI...198.3:5 It is not itself the **t.**. Yet does it point to
W-pI...198.3:6 Yet does it point to where the **t.** must be,
W-pI...198.8:2 of any kind are strange and alien to the **t.**.
W-pI...198.8:3 And what but **t.** could have a Thought
W-pI...198.9:2 **t.** bestows these words upon your mind,
W-pI...199.1:5 this were the **t.**, the mind were vulnerable
W-pI...200.6:2 In **t.** it has no function, and does nothing.
WpI rVI.in.3:8 it deaf to reason, sanity and simple **t.**.
W-pII ....in.1:3 now we seek direct experience of **t.** alone.
W-pII ....in.8:1 together in the search for **t.** and God,
W-pII ....in.9:3 that our insane desires were the **t.**. Now
W-pII ..... 1.4:5 must learn to welcome **t.** exactly as it is.
W-pII . 222.1:5 who knows the **t.** of what He speaks today
W-pII . 224.1:7 only this. This is illusion's end. It is the **t.**.
W-pII . 226.1:5 not sought for illusions to replace the **t.**.
W-pII . 227.1:5 *up, and lay them down before the feet of **t.**, to*
W-pII . 229.1:5 the **t.** of the Identity I sought to lose, but
W-pII . 231.1:6 *else could I desire but the **t.** about myself?*
W-pII . 237.1:1 Today I will accept the **t.** about myself.
W-pII . 239.1:1 Let not the **t.** about ourselves today be
W-pII ..... 3.1:4 another light; and one which leads to **t.**,
W-pII ..... 3.3:4 its illusions but a solid base where **t.** exists
W-pII ..... 3.3:5 is but illusion which is kept apart from **t.**.
W-pII ..... 3.4:1 As sight was made to lead away from **t.**, it
W-pII . 243.2:3 *memory, and **t.** must shine in all of us as one.*
W-pII . 244.2:1 And there we are in **t.**. No storms can
W-pII . 247.1:4 what His sight shows me as the simple **t.**,
W-pII . 248.1:1 I have disowned the **t.**. Now let me be as
W-pII . 248.1:6 and did but mock the **t.** about myself.
W-pII ..... 4.1:2 seeks to let illusions take the place of **t.**.
W-pII ..... 4.1:3 it sees illusions where the **t.** should be,
W-pII ..... 4.1:9 And **t.** can be but filled with knowledge,
W-pII ..... 4.2:6 **T.** can be its aim as well as lies. The senses
W-pII .....251.h I am in need of nothing but the **t.**.
W-pII . 251.1:5 But now I see that I need only **t.**. In that
W-pII . 252.2:2 *Your Son, that I may waken to the **t.** in You,*
W-pII . 254.1:3 *but this: I come to You to ask You for the **t.**.*
W-pII . 254.1:4 *And **t.** is but Your Will, which I would share*
W-pII . 255.1:4 bear witness to the **t.** of what He says.
W-pII ..... 5.3:3 For only love creates in **t.**, and truth can
W-pII ..... 5.3:3 love creates in truth, and **t.** can never fear.
W-pII ..... 5.5:3 Your safety lies in **t.**, and not in lies. Love
W-pII . 262.2:1 recognize this day the **t.** about ourselves.
W-pII . 269.1:3 *to surpass perception and return to **t.**. I ask*
W-pII . 270.1:4 *his Father, lets his dreams be brought to **t.**,*
W-pII ..... 6.3:2 is the only part of you that has reality in **t.**
W-pII ..... 6.4:1 come to Him, to be translated into **t.**. He
W-pII . 271.1:1 to what I want to be the **t.** for me. Today I
W-pII . 272.1:1 *Father, the **t.** belongs to me. My home is set*
W-pII . 274.1:3 *as well the **t.** will enter where illusions were,*
W-pII . 277.2:5 he cannot be bound unless God's **t.** can lie
W-pII . 278.1:5 For **t.** is free, and what is bound is not a
W-pII . 278.1:5 free, and what is bound is not a part of **t.**.
W-pII . 278.2:1 *Father, I ask for nothing but the **t.**. I have*
W-pII . 278.2:5 *of fear. For **t.** is safe, and only love is sure.*
W-pII . 279.1:3 are gone, with **t.** established in their place.
W-pII . 280.1:2 for him, but only in illusions, not in **t.**. No
W-pII ..... 7.1:1 mediates between illusions and the **t.**.
W-pII ..... 7.1:2 gift to everyone who turns to Him for **t.**.
W-pII ..... 7.1:3 provides are dreams all carried to the **t.**,
W-pII ..... 7.2:3 has achieved the only goal it has in **t.**. For
W-pII ..... 7.2:4 itself, to be replaced by the eternal **t.**.
W-pII . 282.1:3 while **t.** remains forever living in the joy of
W-pII . 282.2:2 *Such is the **t.**. And can the truth be changed*
W-pII . 282.2:3 *And can the **t.** be changed by merely giving it*
W-pII . 282.2:5 *a mistake. Let me not be afraid of **t.** today.*
W-pII . 284.1:5 This is the **t.**, at first to be but said and
W-pII . 284.1:6 and more, and finally accepted as the **t.**.
W-pII . 284.1:8 arrive at full acceptance of the **t.** in them.
W-pII . 284.2:2 *Your gifts; accepting but the joyous as the **t.**.*
W-pII . 287.2:4 *of dreams and futile substitutions for the **t.**?*
W-pII ..... 8.5:2 it goes, and leaving but the **t.** to be itself.
W-pII . 303.2:4 *He is but what I really am in **t.**. He is the Son*
W-pII . 305.1:3 envelops it, and gently carries it to **t.**, no
W-pII . 307.1:5 *nothing contradicts the holy **t.** that I remain*
W-pII ... 10.3:1 accept this holy **t.**: God's Judgment is the
W-pII . 311.1:1 made to be a weapon used against the **t.**.
W-pII . 319.1:1 has been removed, and only **t.** remains.
W-pII . 319.1:2 For arrogance opposes **t.**. But when there
W-pII . 319.1:3 no arrogance the **t.** will come immediately
W-pII ... 11.3:1 all illusions, for creation is the **t.**. Creation
W-pII . 323.2:1 And as we pay the debt we owe to **t.**, –a
W-pII . 323.2:1 **t.** returns to us in wholeness and in joy.
W-pII . 325.2:1 *Our Father, Your ideas reflect the **t.**, and*
W-pII . 325.2:2 *for Yours and Yours alone establish **t.**.*
W-pII . 329.1:2 *Yet what I am in **t.** is but Your Will, extended*
W-pII . 331.1:9 *Death is illusion; life, eternal **t.**. There is no*
W-pII . 332.1:2 **T.** undoes its evil dreams by shining them
W-pII . 332.1:3 **T.** never makes attack. It merely is. And
W-pII . 333.1:4 the **t.** can shine upon it as it disappears.
W-pII . 335.1:3 it stands for what I want to be the **t.**. It is
W-pII . 336.1:4 and opens the hidden altar to the **t.**. Its
W-pII ... 13.2:2 law of **t.** the world does not obey, because
W-pII ... 13.2:4 Now is perception open to the **t.**. Now is
W-pII . 342.1:8 *last, forget illusions in the blazing light of **t.**,*
W-pII . 347.1:6 *sees what I behold, and yet He knows the **t.**.*
W-pII ... 14.2:4 **t.** of what we are is not for words to speak
W-pII ... 14.3:7 only with giving welcome to the **t.**.
W-pII .... 357.h **T.** answers every call we make to God,
Wfl........ in.2:4 And yet, in **t.**, it is already here; already
Wfl........ in.2:5 follow in the way that **t.** points out to us.
Wfl........ in.4:4 the **t.** and life that shows the way to us. In
Wfl........ in.5:7 son because he failed to understand the **t.**
W-ep......... 2:6 And thus He speaks of freedom and of **t.**.
M-in.......... 5:7 remain a source of strength and **t.** forever.
M-2........... 2:2 Atonement corrects illusions, not **t.**.
M-4..... I.A.5:5 his own best interests on behalf of **t.**. He
M-4...... VI.1:2 no dreams that need defense against the **t.**
M-4........X.2:3 They have in **t.** abandoned the world, and
M-4........X.3:2 knowledge and eternal **t.** do not appear in
M-5...... III.3:6 The **t.** in their minds reaches out to the
M-5...... III.3:6 out to the **t.** in the minds of their brothers
M-5...... III.3:7 They are thus brought to **t.**; truth is not
M-5...... III.3:7 to truth; **t.** is not brought to them. So are
M-6........... 1:2 be brought to **t.** and keep the illusions.
M-6........... 1:3 **T.** demonstrates illusions have no value.
M-8........... 2:5 of creation; attempts to bring **t.** to lies.
M-8........... 2:6 Finding **t.** unacceptable, the mind revolts
M-8........... 2:6 mind revolts against **t.** and gives itself an
M-8........... 6:9 The one answer to all illusions is **t.**.
M-10......... 1:2 with wisdom, and substitutes for **t.**. As
M-12......... 3:6 the fear that **t.** would encounter in them.
M-12......... 3:7 Do not forget that **t.** can come only where
M-13......... 1:1 Although in **t.** the term sacrifice is
M-13......... 5:3 price that must be paid for the denial of **t.**.
M-13....... 6:11 If you would sacrifice the **t.**, they stay in
M-13....... 7:15 It seems to happen at the "sacrifice" of **t.**.

M-14........1:10 They have been brought to t., and truth
M-14........1:10 brought to truth, and t. saw them not. It
M-15..........1:3 Who could flee forever from the t.? But
M-17..........4:8 They obscure the t., and this can never be
M-17..........4:9 Either t. is apparent, or it is not. It cannot
M-17........4:11 is unaware of t. must look upon illusions.
M-17..........9:2 In t. it has no power to make anything.
M-18..........1:1 interpretation with fact, or illusion with t.
M-18..........2:2 can they proclaim the t. about themselves
M-18..........2:6 to teach all minds the t. of what they are,
M-18..........3:5 t. becomes diminutive and meaningless.
M-18..........3:7 *You but mistake interpretation for the t..*
M-19..........2:2 the one interpretation that leads to t..
M-19..........2:3 justice includes nothing that opposes t..
M-19..........2:4 no inherent conflict between justice and t.
M-20..........6:5 In t. there was no conflict, for His Will is
M-22..........6:8 he believes about himself is not the t.. It is
M-24........6:10 be said that their t. lies in their usefulness.
M-26..........1:3 where all barriers to t. have been removed
M-27..........7:2 nor let attack conceal the t. from you.
M-27..........7:4 task to let the illusion be carried to the t..
M-27..........7:6 T. neither moves nor wavers nor sinks
M-28........3:11 There is no opposition to the t.. And now
M-28........3:12 And now the t. can come at last. How
M-28..........4:8 world, as it is lifted up and brought to t..
M-28..........6:6 the t. about the holy Son of God. He is
M-28..........6:8 because he let God's Voice proclaim the t.
M-29..........4:6 The Holy Spirit knows the t. about you.
M-29........4:10 Who knows the t. has not forgotten it. His
C-in............2:3 that it is a defense against t. in the form of
C-2.............3:2 there be a t. that lies conceal effectively.
C-3.............2:1 gap between their perception and the t..
C-3.............6:4 No, not in t., for truth goes nowhere. But
C-3.............6:4 No, not in truth, for t. goes nowhere. But
C-3.............8:1 see the t. about yourself reflected there.
C-4.............6:3 all illusions brought to t. and laid upon
P-1.............1:1 is to remove the blocks to t.. Its aim is to
P-1.............2:3 than to recall the way, the t. and the life,
P-1.............5:1 The patient need not think of t. as God in
P-1.............5:2 he must begin to separate t. from illusion,
P-1.............5:2 as false and to accept the t. as true. His
P-2...........I.1:9 direction is one of progress toward the t..
P-2...........I.2:9 different. Illusions are illusions; t. is truth.
P-2...........I.2:9 different. Illusions are illusions; truth is t..
P-2.........II.2:6 Neither is t. itself, but both can lead to
P-2.........II.2:6 is truth itself, but both can lead to t..
P-2.........II.2:7 What can be necessary to find t., which
P-2.........II.4:2 where there is forgiveness t. must come. It
P-2........III.1:6 is all there is to light the way to t..
P-2........IV.1:5 a decision that t. can lie and must be lies.
P-2........IV.6:6 T. being brought to illusions, reality now
P-2........IV.7:3 illness is real it cannot be overlooked in t.,
P-2........IV.7:5 cannot heal, for it opposes t.. Perhaps an
P-2....IV.11:10 The t. is simple, being one for all.
P-2.........V.1:1 While t. is simple, it must still be taught
P-2.........V.2:4 The t. is simple. Yet it must be taught to
P-2.........V.4:5 that He will hear and answer them in t..
P-2.........V.7:5 And the t. will come to us only through
P-2........VI.2:4 first the willingness to question the "t." of
P-2.......VII.7:7 alien to the t. and poor in wisdom,
S-1.........in.2:4 to the t. of union in his Father and himself
S-1........I.7:11 Christ is in both of you. That is its only t..
S-1.......V.3:10 And so he is in t.. Now can you pray only
S-2.......III.4:8 God's Will is t., and you are one with Him
S-3...........I.4:5 home, but it will never be his home in t..
S-3........III.3:4 assumed and then accepted as the t., and
S-3........IV.6:5 hard against the love that is the t. in you.

## truth's 6

T-23.....II.21:4 form in the progression of t. reversal,
T-27......VI.3:7 true because you called him by t. name.
T-31.......II.1:2 nor fought against to lose to t. appeal.
W-pI...169.4:3 mind that recognizes t. effects on you.
W-pI.184.12:3 unified; all space is filled with t. reflection
W-pII..357.1:1 *Forgiveness, t. reflection, tells me how to*

## truthful 1

T-30......IV.1:7 attack but false ideas, and never t. ones.

## truths 3

T-23.........I.9:2 as it is seen as war between conflicting t.;
W-pI.....91.9:1 try to experience these t. about yourself.
W-pI...122.8:3 heart with deep tranquility as ancient t.,

## try 224

T-3.........V.5:2 You may t. to "interpret" meaning, but
T-4...........I.5:5 is natural for the ego to t. to protect itself
T-4...........I.8:4 sane solution is not to t. to change reality,
T-4.........I.11:2 t. to make this impoverished house stand.
T-4.........II.8:2 can only turn to other egos and t. to unite
T-4........III.8:3 If you will really t. to do this, you have
T-6...........I.6:5 Do not t. to protect it yourself, or you are
T-6.........II.2:4 you t. to keep the fact that you attacked
T-6......V.A.6:7 point they may t. to accept the conflict,
T-7.......V.10:8 I t. to share an illusion with the most holy
T-7......VI.11:8 Do not t. to understand it because, if you
T-8.........V.5:9 or you will t. to go in different directions
T-9.........I.14:5 do not t. to look beyond yourself for truth
T-11......IV.2:1 Could you t. to make God homeless and
T-11......VI.3:9 t. to limit what you see by narrow little
T-12.......V.6:2 and do not t. to set up curriculum goals
T-12.......V.7:2 means, "T. to learn but do not succeed."
T-13.......II.3:5 it will t. to destroy it because it is afraid.
T-14......III.7:3 him that, whatever he may t. to do to you,
T-14....III.11:7 Do not t. to escape the gift of God He so
T-14.......V.4:2 Do not t. to steal it from him, or you will
T-14......XI.3:8 in which you t. to see can only obscure.
T-15......III.2:5 You are free to t. as many as you wish, but
T-15......IV.4:5 practice, t. to give over every plan you
T-15......IV.9:8 t. only to be vigilant against deception,
T-15.......X.9:7 Do not t. to project it from you and see it
T-15......XI.1:5 t. longer to keep apart your thoughts and
T-15......XI.4:6 you endow it with fear and t. to cast it out
T-15......XI.4:8 And who can t. to resolve the "conflict" of
T-16.........I.6:3 not t. to substitute your "miracle" for this
T-16.........II.2:3 still t. to keep understanding to yourself.
T-17.........I.5:4 When you t. to bring truth to illusions,
T-17......VI.3:2 and t. to piece together what it must have
T-18.....II.5:17 is the means by which you t. to make your
T-18......IV.5:8 prepare yourself for Him, t. to think thus:
T-18......IX.6:6 T. but to touch it and it disappears;
T-18....IX.11:2 Nor is there any need for us to t. to speak
T-19......IV.1:2 Some of them you will t. to impose.
T-21.........I.5:3 They t. to reach each other, and they fail,
T-21.........I.5:5 and t. to think if you remember what we
T-21.......III.7:2 and whom you t. to limit to the body you
T-21.....VII.5:8 it. Nor should he t.. For if he focuses on
T-22......III.3:3 the help of reason would t. to pass it. The
T-23.......in.2:3 it, and t. to weaken it because of this; and
T-25. VIII.13:9 and t. to take away from whom he judges.
T-27... VIII.3:4 This single lesson does it t. to teach again,
T-29......IV.6:4 And do not t. to hurt him when he fails to
T-29.....VII.4:1 you t. to bring about your death. For you
T-29.....VII.8:3 t. to see in it a place of idols found outside
T-29....IX.10:2 another t. to worship idols and to keep
T-30.........I.1:9 Then t. again to have the day you want.
T-30.........I.7:1 T. to observe this rule without delay,
T-31......IV.3:2 Perhaps you would prefer to t. them all,
T-31......IV.4:1 Why would you seek to t. another road,
W-pI.......2.2:3 T. to apply the exercise with equal ease to
W-pI.......3.1:7 T. to lay such feelings aside, and merely
W-pI.......5.7:1 t. to identify a number of different forms
W-pI.....10.4:5 T. to avoid classification of any kind. In
W-pI.....12.2:3 slowly. T. to pace yourself so that the slow
W-pI.....12.2:4 become markedly longer or shorter, but t.
W-pI.....13.6:2 t. not even to think of it except during the
W-pI.....15.5:1 t. to make the selection as random as
W-pI.....21.3:1 T., therefore, not to let the "little"
W-pI.....21.5:1 T. to be as specific as possible. You may,
W-pI.....24.5:4 on. T. to cover as many different kinds of
W-pI.....25.2:5 you will t. to withdraw the goals you have
W-pI.....26.8:4 you. T., however, to treat them all alike to
W-pI.....27.3:3 You might t. for every fifteen or twenty
W-pI.....27.4:5 t. to keep on your schedule from then on.
W-pI.....29.3:1 T. then, today, to begin to learn how to
W-pI.....29.4:2 T. to avoid the tendency toward self-
W-pI.....30.4:2 t. to think of things beyond your present
W-pI.....31.3:2 T. not to establish any kind of hierarchy
W-pI.....31.3:4 but t. to let the stream move on evenly
W-pI.....32.2:3 t. to introduce the thought that both are
W-pI.....32.3:3 world. T. to treat them both as equally as
W-pI.....33.2:2 T. to remain equally uninvolved in both,
W-pI.....34.6:2 t. to take several minutes and devote
W-pI.....35.5:3 T. to recognize that the direction of your
W-pI.....36.2:2 T. to distribute them fairly evenly, and
W-pI.....38.4:2 T. to make as little distinction as possible
W-pI.....40.1:4 If you forget, t. again. If there are long
W-pI.....40.1:5 If there are long interruptions, t. again.
W-pI.....40.1:6 again. Whenever you remember, t. again.
W-pI.....41.6:5 T., instead, to get a sense of turning
W-pI.....41.6:6 T. to enter very deeply into your own
W-pI.....41.7:2 most of all, t. to sink down and inward,
W-pI.....42.4:3 t. to think of nothing except thoughts
W-pI.....42.6:2 exercises. T. merely to step back and let
W-pI.....43.7:2 t. to remember to tell him silently: *God is*
W-pI.....43.7:6 t. not to make distinctions of this kind at
W-pI.....43.9:2 T. today not to allow any long periods of
W-pI.....44.7:2 Then t. to sink into your mind, letting go
W-pI.....44.7:5 T. to observe your passing thoughts
W-pI.....44.9:3 T., however, to return to the exercises
W-pI...44.10:2 T. to think of light, formless and without
W-pI.....45.4:6 we will t. to recognize that only what God
W-pI.....45.5:1 We will also t. to understand that only
W-pI.....45.5:2 And we will also t. to remember that we
W-pI.....45.6:6 Then t. to go past all the unreal thoughts
W-pI.....45.9:1 t. to remember how important it is to you
W-pI.....47.4:1 Today we will t. to reach past your own
W-pI.....47.5:1 Now t. to slip past all concerns related to
W-pI.....47.7:1 t. to reach down into your mind to a place
W-pI.....49.2:4 T. today not to listen to it. Try to identify
W-pI.....49.2:5 T. to identify with the part of your mind
W-pI.....49.2:6 T. to hear God's Voice call to you lovingly
W-pI.....49.3:2 We will t. actually to hear God's Voice
WpI...rI.in.3:2 T., rather, to emphasize the central point,
W-pI.....59.3:7 these I choose when I t. to see through the
W-pI.....61.7:4 weeks. T. today to begin to build a firm
W-pI.....64.6:3 *Let me not t. to substitute mine for God's.*
W-pI.....65.3:1 in which you t. to understand and accept
W-pI.....65.4:1 T., if possible, to undertake the daily
W-pI.....65.4:2 T., also, to determine this time in advance
W-pI.....65.5:4 t. to uncover each thought that arises to
W-pI.....65.6:2 T., however, to continue a minute or so
W-pI.....65.6:5 but t. to get the sense of being willing to
W-pI.....66.3:1 Today we will t. to go past this wholly
W-pI.....66.5:5 T. to see the logic in this sequence, even if
W-pI...66.10:2 T. to make this choice as you think about
W-pI...66.10:8 Let us t. today to realize that only the
W-pI.....67.3:1 t. to let all thoughts drop away for a brief
W-pI.....67.3:1 and then t. to reach past all your images
W-pI.....67.6:1 T. to realize in the shorter practice
W-pI.....68.4:4 Today we will t. to find out how you
W-pI.....68.6:5 return. T. to feel safety surrounding you,
W-pI.....68.6:6 up. T. to believe, however briefly, that
W-pI.....69.4:1 t. to let go of all the content that generally
W-pI.....69.6:1 world, t. to settle down in perfect stillness
W-pI.....69.8:3 it. T., as you attempt to go through the
W-pI.....69.8:4 mind. T. to remember that you are at last
W-pI.....69.8:5 T. to keep the thought clearly in mind
W-pI.....70.8:1 we will t. again to reach the light in you,
W-pI.....70.9:2 T. to pass the clouds by whatever means
W-pI...71.10:5 T. to remember today's idea some six or
W-pI.....72.7:2 the body, and t. to hurt and humiliate it.
W-pI.....72.7:3 love the body, and t. to glorify and exalt it
W-pI.....72.8:1 We will t. today to stop these senseless
W-pI.....72.8:2 We will t. to welcome it instead. Your
W-pI.....72.8:5 we are going to t. to see this differently.
W-pI...72.10:5 we are going to t. to lay judgment aside,
W-pI.....73.4:1 Today we will t. once more to reach the
W-pI.....74.2:5 Let us t. to recognize this today, and
W-pI.....74.5:1 close your eyes and t. to experience the
W-pI.....74.6:3 repeat the idea for today and t. again. Do
W-pI.....74.7:4 Then t. to find what you are seeking.

W-pI.....79.7:3 will t. to free our minds of all the many
W-pI.....79.7:4 We will t. to realize that we have only one
W-pI...79.10:4 t. to suspend all judgment about what the
WpI..rII.in.3:1 but t. to spend the major part of the time
W-pI.....87.3:4 I t. to attack only when I am afraid, and
W-pI.....87.3:4 and only when I t. to attack can I believe
W-pI.....91.5:1 you t. to leave your weakness behind.
W-pI.....91.9:1 period, t. to experience these truths about
W-pI.....91.9:4 T. to remove your faith from it, if only for
W-pI.....92.9:3 meeting place we t. today to find and rest
W-pI.....93.9:3 T. to experience the unity of your one Self
W-pI.....93.9:4 T. to appreciate Its Holiness and the love
W-pI.....93.9:5 T. not to interfere with the Self which
W-pI...93.10:2 T., however, to do so when you can. At
W-pI...93.10:6 Then t. to devote at least a minute or so to
W-pI.....94.3:5 Now t. to reach the Son of God in you.
W-pI.....95.3:3 In patience and in hope we t. again today.
W-pI.....95.7:5 and an unwillingness to t. again.
W-pI...95.10:4 and t. to reach the place in you in which
W-pI...95.14:3 to you in confidence that you will t. today
W-pI.....96.2:1 be reconciled, no matter how you t., what
W-pI.....97.3:1 Today we t. to bring reality still closer to
W-pI.....99.7:2 T. to perceive the strength in what you
W-pI...100.8:1 Now let us t. to find that joy that proves
W-pI...101.4:3 he t. to listen and accept Its offering? If
W-pI...102.2:1 Today we t. to loose its weakened hold
W-pI...103.2:3 we will t. again to bring to truth today,
W-pI...105.1:3 And we will t. to understand these gifts
W-pI...107.2:3 T. to remember when there was a time,
W-pI...107.2:4 Then t. to picture what it would be like to
W-pI...110.7:1 t. to discover in your mind the Self Who
WpI. rIII.in8:2 at least t. to divide them so you undertake
WpIrIII.in10:6 but t. to keep the thought with you, and
WpIrIII.in11:6 kind. T., then, to take it with you in the
W-pI...121.9:2 Yet we will t. to learn today that they are
W-pI.121.10:1 actively despise, or merely t. to overlook.
W-pI.121.11:2 a while. T. to perceive some light in him
W-pI.121.11:3 T. to find some little spark of brightness
W-pI.121.11:4 and then t. to let this light extend until it
W-pI.121.12:2 T. to transfer the light you learned to see
W-pI...126.8:1 Today we t. to understand the truth that
W-pI...131.4:4 seek vainly, though he t. to force delay,
W-pI...131.8:5 Let us not t. longer to impose an alien will
W-pI.131.12:2 it. But before you t. to open it, remind
W-pI...133.2:4 It does not t. to substitute utopian ideas
W-pI.135.26:1 T. not to shape this day as you believe
W-pI...140.7:1 Let us not t. today to seek to cure what
W-pI...140.8:2 will t. today to find the source of healing,
W-pI...168.1:5 We t. to hide from Him, and suffer from
W-pI...169.7:1 This is beyond experience we t. to hasten.
WpI.rV.in12:4 and t. and try again to go beyond them to
WpI.rV.in12:4 and try and t. again to go beyond them to
W-pI...182.2:2 some t. to put by their suffering in games
W-pI...185.7:5 nor t. to make another bargain in the
W-pI...187.4:4 time, however much you t. to keep it safe.
W-pI.193.10:3 not t. to hold it off another day, another
W-pI.193.12:2 t. to give it application to the happenings
W-pI...195.1:3 And they t. to be content because another
W-pI...195.3:3 Now can you but t. to bring him down to
W-pI.196.12:5 but you your mind can t. to crucify. Yet
W-pII .242.1:2 and so to t. to lead my life alone must be
W-pII .246.1:2 Let me not t. to hurt God's Son, and think
W-pII .250.1:2 me not t. to obscure the holy light in him,
W-pII .277.1:3 *by which I t. to make the body more secure.*
W-pII .307.1:3 *Let me not t. to make another will, for it is*
W-pII .327.2:2 *Let me attempt therefore to t. them, and to*
M-4 ...... VI.1:3 They do not t. to make themselves. Their
M-6 ........... 1:7 patient might even t. to destroy himself.
M-10 ......... 6:2 But it is difficult indeed to t. to keep it.
M-11 ......... 2:3 that it is pointless to t. to reconcile them.
M-16 ......... 8:3 He can but t., and his success depends on
C-ep........... 3:4 And now we t. again. Our new beginning
P-2......... V.4:7 to guide us, as we t. to help our brothers.
P-3........ III.2:1 healer would t. to heal for money, and he
S-2.........in.1:2 to t. to rise above prayer's bottom step, or
S-2....... II.6:10 t. to strike a bargain with the Son of God,
S-2......... II.7:2 t. to reinforce his guilt and thus your own

**trying** 66

T-1 ...... VII.5:5 it. I am also t. to do the same with yours.
T-4 .......... I.3:5 but I am t. to teach you how its thought
T-4 ....... IV.2:6 it is much easier than t. to think against it
T-4 ..... IV.10:8 ego is t. to convince you that it is real and
T-4 ........ V.5:6 what you are t. to learn is of value to you.
T-6 ..... V.B.6:4 that you are t. to undo a decision that was
T-7 ...VIII.3:11 their projections are t. to creep back in.
T-7 ....... XI.2:5 There is no point in t.. A Son of God is
T-8 .........II.1:4 ego does not know what it is t. to teach. It
T-8 .........II.1:5 It is t. to teach you what you are without
T-8 ....... IX.3:4 pathetic way of t. not to see by rendering
T-9 ........I.14:4 because you are t. to make yourself unreal
T-9 ........ V.1:4 he is t. to give what he has not received. If
T-12 ........I.1:7 If you decide that someone is really t. to
T-12 ...... V.3:2 and if you are t. to attack them you will be
T-12 ...... V.7:5 If you are t. to learn how not to learn, and
T-12 ..... VI.1:1 The ego is t. to teach you how to gain the
T-13 .......II.7:3 sometimes react as if it is t. to imprison
T-13 ..... XI.2:2 You are but t. to escape a bitter war from
T-14 ..... IV.5:5 and t. to teach him guilt instead of love.
T-16 ..... IV.4:5 are t. to live with guilt rather than die of it
T-16 ..... VI.5:3 they are t. to decrease their magnitude.
T-17 ........I.5:4 illusions, you are t. to make illusions real,
T-17 ... IV.13:1 who have tried so hard, and are still t., to
T-17 ...... V.6:6 brother in what but seems to be a t. time.
T-18 .......II.3:8 it, t. to triumph over it and make it serve
T-20 .......II.1:5 and t. to justify your own interpretation
T-22 .......II.6:8 is no point in t. to avoid this one decision.
T-26 .. VII.13:6 be possible in t. to deceive the Son of God
W-pI....... 2.2:1 around you, t. to avoid selection by size,
W-pI....... 8.6:2 you. If you find it t., three or four times is
W-pI..... 11.3:4 from worry that we are t. to achieve. On
W-pI..... 23.2:3 There is no point in t. to change the world
W-pI..... 30.2:1 we are t. to use a new kind of "projection.
W-pI..... 30.2:3 t. to see in the world what is in our minds,
W-pI..... 30.2:4 Thus, we are t. to join with what we see,
W-pI..... 30.3:2 and t. to realize that the idea applies to
W-pI..... 41.7:3 You are t. to reach past all these things.
W-pI..... 41.7:4 are t. to leave appearances and approach
W-pI..... 45.8:5 For such is the place you are t. to reach.
W-pI..... 45.8:6 as yet to realize how high you are t. to go.
W-pI..... 49.4:6 We are t. to reach your real home. We are
W-pI..... 49.4:7 We are t. to reach the place where you are
W-pI..... 49.4:8 truly welcome. We are t. to reach God.
W-pI..... 51.3:5 There is no sense in t. to understand it.
W-pI..... 51.4:2 because I am t. to think without God.
W-pI..... 51.5:2 I am constantly t. to justify my thoughts.
W-pI..... 51.5:3 I am constantly t. to make them true.
W-pI..... 52.3:5 Let me understand that I am t. to use time
W-pI..... 64.8:2 t. to concentrate on the thoughts you are
W-pI..... 65.7:1 to t. to focus on its importance to you, the
W-pI..... 67.2:8 We are t. today to undo your definition of
W-pI..... 67.2:9 We are also t. to emphasize that you are
W-pI..... 68.6:4 the practice period t. to think of yourself
W-pI..... 69.2:2 to thinking about what we are t. to do.
W-pI..... 69.2:4 We are t. to see past the veil of darkness
W-pI..... 69.2:5 We are t. to let the veil be lifted, and to
W-pI..... 69.6:1 you are t. to do for yourself and the world
W-pI..... 72.4:4 actively t. to hold him to it by confusing it
W-pI..... 72.5:3 In t. to present Himself as the Author of
W-pI..... 73.6:8 to succeed in what we are t. to do today.
W-pI..... 79.8:4 You are t. to recognize that you have been
W-pI..... 93.8:4 of the practice period in t. to experience
W-pI... 198.5:3 teach, instead of t. to dismiss His words,
M-in .......... 3:9 that the self you are t. to protect is real.
M-25 ......... 2:3 be little point in t. to teach salvation. It

**tune** 2

W-pI. 169.11:5 that does not beat as yet in t. with God.
P-2........ VI.2:2 given us literally "to change our t.." The

**turmoil** 8

T-5 .........II.7:6 even in the midst of the t. you may make.
T-12 .......II.5:5 Learn to be quiet in the midst of t., for
T19..IV.B.10:4 body can bring you neither peace nor t.;
T-30 ... III.10:2 by the t. and the terror of the world, the
WpI... rI.in.4:4 quiet with you, and to heal distress and t..
W-pI .... 75.1:6 and t. and death have disappeared. The
W-pI .. 109.1:2 midst of all the t. born of clashing dreams
W-pI .. 121.2:1 peace and soar above the t. of the world.

**turn** 87

T-1 ..... VI.1:10 This, in t., depends on your perception of
T-2 .........II.4:7 not, however, t. it into a weapon of attack
T-2 .........V.1:3 This misperception arises in t. from the
T-4 .........II.8:2 a fearful state that it can only t. to other
T-4 .........V.4:7 to which the ego replies, "T. to me." The
T-4 ....... VI.3:1 it will increase as you t. more and more
T-5 .........V.8:6 and it will t. it back to full creation at any
T-6 ..... V.A.6:2 it is necessary that you t. in that direction.
T-6 ... V.C.10:6 you must now t. your effort against it.
T-8 .........II.2:3 a Son of God should t. to find himself?
T-9 .......II.11:9 this, in t., is the measure of how much
T-11 ..... III.5:6 T. toward the light, for the little spark in
T-11 .....V.15:4 it is this universe which, in t., becomes its
T-12 .......V.5:6 You would hardly t. to them to establish
T-13 .......II.8:6 might t. on yourself and destroy yourself.
T-13 .... VII.3:7 and so although you t. in sadness from it,
T-14 ......in.1:8 Let us now t. away from them, and follow
T-14 .......X.1:5 And you will t. from time to holiness, as
T-14 ..... XI.7:3 not meet, if he but t. to Him ever so little.
T-14 ..... XI.7:4 His Son to t. to Him and remain Himself.
T-15 ... VIII.2:9 T., then, in peace from guilt to God and
T-15 ..... IX.3:3 to t. its purpose into accomplishment.
T-15 ..... IX.6:3 as great as His, you can t. away from love.
T-16 .......II.5:6 and do not t. away from all the witnesses
T-16 ... IV.12:5 T. with me firmly away from all illusions
T-18 ........I.8:2 you. And t. you to the stately calm within,
T-19 .......II.3:1 t. the power of his mind against himself.
T-20 ..... III.7:9 you t. to ask the meaning of the universe.
T-20 ... VIII.5:3 t. in your distress and need for help unto
T-21 .... VII.2:8 to attack his brother or t. upon himself as
T-22 .......II.3:6 Joy does not t. to sorrow, for the eternal
T-23 ........I.8:9 t. in peace to the rememberance of God,
T-23 ......I.11:1 can the resting place of God t. on itself,
T-23 .......II.7:2 impossible to t. to Him for help in misery.
T-24 ..... III.3:7 and t. and whirl about with every breeze.
T-24 ..... VI.1:3 will scatter with the wind and t. to dust.
T-25 ..... VI.2:2 And they t. away from sunlight and the
T-28 ..... IV.1:2 and let him t. illusions on himself. Nor do
T-29 ........I.1:5 His gentleness t. sometimes to attack, and
T-29 ........I.3:6 and him, lest he t. again into an enemy.
T-29 ..... IX.5:7 t. against him for his treachery to them.
W-pI ...... 2.1:4 T. your head so that you include whatever
W-pI ...... 2.1:5 t. around and apply the idea to what was
W-pI .... 61.6:2 t. to sleep as you reaffirm your function
W-pI .... 68.6:2 all, thinking of each one in t. as you do so:
W-pI .... 99.9:8 t. to Him Who shares your function here,
W-pI .. 101.6:4 But t. to it in confidence that it will set
W-pI .. 107.5:4 be brought to them to t. them into truth.
W-pI .. 109.3:5 no appearance but will t. to truth before
W-pI .. 110.3:1 the truth, health cannot t. to sickness, nor
WpIrIII.in10:6 Then t. to other things, but try to keep
W-pI .. 121.1:3 that appear to threaten you at every t.,
W-pI 121.12:1 and t. your mind to one you call a friend.
W-pI .. 122.7:2 not t. away in aimless wandering again.
W-pI .. 128.1:2 hopes that t. to bitter ashes of despair. No
W-pI 131.10:1 and t. your mind to true ideas instead. No
W-pI .. 153.2:6 knows not where to t. to find escape from
W-pI 153.15:5 ceases to arise to t. us from our purpose,
W-pI 153.16:4 a little while, and t. our thoughts to God.
W-pI .. 159.9:4 and t. the world into a garden like the one
W-pI .. 161.7:5 compelled to t. upon itself and to destroy.
W-pI .. 170.5:2 to which you t. for solace and escape from
W-pI .. 181.6:2 and t. our eyes upon our own mistakes,
W-pI .. 181.9:3 as we t. our minds to practicing today.
W-pI .. 183.1:4 a bond to which they t. for their identity.
W-pI 183.10:1 T. to the Name of God for your release,
W-pI 185.10:5 it, and where to t. for help in the attempt.
W-pI .. 197.1:3 Yet you t. them to attack again, unless
WpI.rVI.in.7:2 say and think, each time you t. to Him.
W-pI .. 207.1:3 *I need but t. to Him, and every sorrow melts*
W-pII . 229.1:4 that I will t. away no longer from the holy
W-pII . 272.2:2 dream, we t. aside and ask ourselves if we,

W-pII 7.3:1 nor t. away from His replacement for the
W-pII 350.1:6 *Therefore, my Father, I would t. to You.*
Wfl in.1:3 Let us t. to Him Who leads the way and
W-ep 1:5 if you simply t. to Him and ask it of Him.
W-ep 5:5 and t. to Him for guidance and for peace
M-5 III.2:11 brothers to t. away from death: "Behold,
M-13 6:8 heard it as yet, and they can but t. to you.
M-14 5:9 To t. hell into Heaven is the function of
M-18 4:3 let him t. within to his eternal Guide, and
M-22 5:10 lost it. T. quickly to your Teacher, and let
M-23 6:8 Then t. to one who laid all limits by, and
M-28 3:6 Thoughts t. to Heaven and away from hell
P-3 II.1:5 that a large number of others t. for help.
P-3 II.6:6 temporary appeal and t. to dreams of fear
S-2 III.6:10 to God you t. to hear what you should do.

## turned 22

T-2 I.4:6 If a light is suddenly t. on while someone
T-2 II.7:6 can be t. against you very unexpectedly.
T-2 V.4:3 and has t. it upside down. All forms of
T-4 II.8:10 creative effort can be t. to mythology. It
T-8 VII.10:7 to attack, because it has t. against itself.
T-14 VII.5:8 made, must be gently t. to your own good
T-17 VII.6:7 but will be gently t. to its use and purpose
T-20 VIII.6:4 sin is t. to blessing under His gentle gaze.
T-21 VII.3:12 And love is t. to hate as easily. This is no
T-22 I.11:9 home prepared for Them as earth is t. to
T-22 II.3:7 But sorrow can be t. to joy, for time gives
T-23 II.14:6 Such a reversal, completely t. around,
T-25 III.6:5 t. to an event which justifies his love. He
T-28 II.8:3 But what he made has t. against him,
T-28 IV.1:3 Nor do you wish that they be t., instead,
T-29 IV.5:7 And dreams of sadness thus are t. to joy.
T-29 IX.5:2 toys have t. against the child who thought
T-31 IV.5:1 to be t. away from all the roadways of the
W-pI 136.10:2 blind by your illusions, truth t. into lies,
W-pI 159.7:4 one will be t. away from this new home,
M-25 4:8 itself. Strengths t. to weakness are tragedy
P-3 III.6:1 should be t. away because he cannot pay.

## turning 17

T-2 III.3:7 firmly established, it becomes a t. point.
T-2 V.7:1 t. away from the belief in physical sight.
T-4 V.4:8 so there is no point in t. to *it* for protection
T-5 IV.4:6 This is the meaning of "t. the other cheek.
T-6 V.A.6:4 your perception and t. it right-side up.
T-18 I.8:1 and t. till they disappear from sight, far,
T-18 VI.6:8 place of God's Son, and t. it against him.
T-21 VII.4:6 attack by t. into something else. How
T-23 II.17:7 find safety from attack by t. on himself?
T-30 I.10:1 Now you have reached the t. point,
W-pI 41.6:5 Try, instead, to get a sense of t. inward,
W-pI 122.10:2 for we have reached the t. point at which
W-pI 123.1:3 There is no thought of t. back, and no
W-pI 157.2:1 another crucial t. point in the curriculum.
W-pI 185.9:7 be gone with every twist and t. of the road
M-14 2:7 t. to Him in silence to receive His Word.
S-3 I.1:5 so its healing but delays its t. back to dust

## turns 17

T-2 II.7:8 The miracle t. the defense of Atonement
T-6 IV.4:5 mind, the ego t. to the body as its ally,
T-9 IV.10:1 and who t. to fantasy unless he despairs
T-21 VII.3:11 A flower t. into a poisoned spear, a child
T-21 VII.4:6 And as it runs it t. against itself, thinking
T-26 IV.2:1 Forgiveness t. the world of sin into a
T-30 II.5:1 God t. to you to ask the world be saved,
W-pI 24.6:2 of your goals, however the situation t. out
W-pI 121.7:2 and t. to you imploringly for Heaven here
WpI rV.in7:3 I am reborn each time a brother's mind t.
W-pII 7.1:2 gift to everyone who t. to Him for truth.
M-11 4:9 What else but a Thought of God t. hell to
M-16 7:5 t. with all of them recognizes no order of
M-17 3:5 single aim of the teacher t. the divided
M-29 8:2 *God t. to you for help to save the world.*
P-3 III.5:11 Where God's Son t. against himself, he
S-1 in.2:4 t. in holy gladness to the truth of union in

## twenty 3

W-pI 27.3:3 might try for every fifteen or t. minutes. It
W-pI 92.10:1 Let us give t. minutes twice today to join
WpI rVI.in.2:1 has bestowed on us in our last t. lessons.

## twice 19

T-4 in.1:1 go with a brother t. as far as he asks. It
W-pI 1.4:1 not be done more than t. a day each,
W-pI 20.5:1 and positively at least t. an hour today,
W-pI 29.5:11 At least once or t., you should experience
W-pI 50.5:1 For ten minutes, t. today, morning and
W-pI 66.11:1 helpful today if undertaken t. an hour,
W-pI 92.10:1 minutes t. today to join this meeting. Let
WpI. rIII.in5:1 is this: Devote five minutes t. a day, or
W-pI 123.7:1 yours to Him for fifteen minutes t. today.
W-pI 126.9:1 Give fifteen minutes t. today to the
W-pI 127.8:1 fifteen minutes t. today escape from every
W-pI 132.15:1 in which we practice t. today with this: *I*
W-pI 134.5:5 are pitifully mocked and t. condemned;
W-pI 134.14:4 let us give a quarter of an hour t. today,
W-pI 135.22:1 minutes t. today we rest from senseless
W-pI 136.15:2 And we will give a quarter of an hour t. to
W-pI 159.9:5 Now are they t. blessed. The messages
W-pI 184.8:7 And thus his unity is t. denied, for you
M-21 1:10 They are thus t. removed from reality.

## twilight 1

T-25 VI.2:1 to the dim effects perceived at t.. And

## twinge 3

T-23 IV.6:3 There is a stab of pain, a t. of guilt, and
T-24 I.8:4 Every t. of malice, or stab of hate or wish
W-pI 21.2:5 that a slight t. of annoyance is nothing

## twinkling 1

T-2 I.3:4 All that can literally disappear in the t. of

## twist 8

T-1 VII.3:5 needs. T. reality in any way and you are
T-3 I.3:11 possible to t. symbols around if you wish.
T-25 VII.3:10 nor t. it into something it is not. For only
T-30 V.1:4 to t. and fit into the dream of fear. Instead
W-pI 136.2:3 it, change it, render it inept, distort it, t. it
W-pI 136.8:5 suffer, t. your limbs and stop your heart,
W-pI 185.9:7 gone with every t. and turning of the road
W-pII 1.4:2 nor seeks to t. it to appearances it likes. It

## twisted 19

T-11 V.6:8 and has t. even your longing for God into
T-13 VII.5:2 From such a t. reference point, what
T-14 I.5:2 so t. and so complex you cannot see that
T-14 II.2:3 Simplicity is very difficult for t. minds.
T-14 VI.6:4 this strange and t. effort to communicate
T-17 II.6:2 removing all illusions that had t. your
T-18 I.7:1 When you seem to see some t. form of
T-18 IX.4:2 are all the illusions, all the t. thoughts, all
T19 IV.C.8:3 no grim commandments nor t. rituals of
T-23 II.22:4 the t. stairway that leads from Heaven.
T-25 IV.4:6 in t. forms too far away for recognition,
W-pI 76.3:1 and t. laws you have set up to save you.
W-pI 134.2:1 This t. view of what forgiveness means is
W-pI 134.3:3 t. viewpoint but reflects the hold that the
W-pI 159.3:4 can show but t. images in broken parts.
P-2 V.2:3 reverse his t. way of looking at the world;
P-2 V.2:3 the world; his t. way of looking at himself.
S-2 I.2:6 God's mercy has become a t. knife that
S-3 IV.6:1 such t. thoughts upon your hearts. You

## twisting 3

T-1 VII.3:2 they always involve t. perception into
W-pI 191.6:5 world t. in agony because your fears have
W-pII 1.3:2 its goal, t. and overturning what it sees as

## twists 1

W-pI 153.1:1 world, its t. of fortune and its bitter jests,

## two 201

*See also* two-edged, two-minute, two-minutes, two-way

T-1 II.4:7 but there are t. parts to the statement in
T-1 IV.1:1 from darkness involves t. stages: First, the
T-1 V.5:3 its choice is that it cannot serve t. masters
T-2 II.7:6 weak precisely because it has t. edges, and
T-2 III.3:9 The alternating investment in the t. levels
T-2 IV.1:3 healing" is to combine t. orders of reality
T-2 IV.2:9 This error can take t. forms; it can be
T-2 V.A.17:3 t. statements are not in the same order of
T-2 VI.5:2 This situation arises in t. ways: First, you
T-2 VII.7:3 The t. should not be confused. As soon as
T-4 I.2:5 the same thought system can stand on t.
T-4 VII.8:2 because the t. beliefs must coexist. The
T-5 I.1:1 Healing is a thought by which t. minds
T-5 II.3:4 choose to hear one of t. voices within you.
T-5 II.8:9 devotion has given you the t. voices, and
T-5 III.1:3 the separation between the t. ways of
T-5 III.3:1 There are t. diametrically opposed ways
T-5 VI.3:5 you? The t. voices speak for different
T-6 V.B.5:1 way out of conflict between t. opposing
T-6 V.B.5:2 accept t. thought systems which are in
T-7 II.2:9 you can respond to t. conflicting voices.
T-7 II.6:6 you listen to t. ways of interpreting them.
T-7 V.9:1 As you can hear t. voices, so you can see
T-7 V.9:1 hear two voices, so you can see in t. ways.
T-7 VI.8:11 is true. While you believe that t. totally
T-7 VI.9:1 its allegiance between t. kingdoms, and
T-7 VIII.3:1 t. major errors involved in this attempt.
T-7 X.3:4 and are, in fact, very apt to confuse the t..
T-8 I.5:5 it is planned by t. teachers, each believing
T-8 I.5:6 out by these t. teachers simultaneously,
T-8 I.6:2 You cannot learn simultaneously from t.
T-8 III.4:6 Whenever t. Sons of God meet, they are
T-8 VIII.2:1 t. voices fighting for its possession. In this
T-8 VIII.5:7 Sickness is meaningful only if the t. basic
T-9 VII.h The T. Evaluations
T-9 VII.4:1 have t. conflicting evaluations of yourself
T-9 VIII.3:2 these t. very different kinds of threat. Its
T-12 VI.6:4 any interference, for the t. are one. As you
T-12 VII.5:6 in. T. ways of looking at the world are in
T-12 VII.6:6 if you seek for t. goals you will find them,
T-12 VII.7:7 for it represents the acceptance of t. goals,
T-13 V.h The T. Emotions
T-13 V.1:1 I have said you have but t. emotions, love
T-13 V.5:1 You have but t. emotions, yet in your
T-13 V.10:1 You have but t. emotions, and one you
T-13 VII.10:9 *yes!* As Mediator between the t. worlds, He
T-14 VI.7:5 You speak t. languages at once, and this
T-14 VII.4:3 of thinking whereby t. systems of belief
T-14 X.7:1 Spirit's one division into t. categories; one
T-14 X.9:6 t. or more join together in searching for
T-14 X.11:6 more than these t. orders of thought.
T-15 I.h The T. Uses of Time
T-15 X.7:3 of the t. is judged as the lesser of two evils
T-15 X.7:3 of the two is judged as the lesser of t. evils
T-16 II.4:3 When t. minds join as one and share one
T-16 III.6:1 You are not t. selves in conflict. What is
T-16 V.11:5 is erected in between t. separate people,
T-16 VI.5:3 When t. individuals seek to become one,
T-17 I.2:4 You cannot be faithful to t. masters who
T-17 IV.h The T. Pictures
T-17 IV.12:1 T. gifts are offered you. Each is complete,
T-17 V.5:5 undertaken by t. individuals for their
T-17 V.5:6 As these t. contemplate their relationship
T-18 III.7:7 for no t. minds can join in the desire for
T-18 IV.1:6 will add the ego to Him and confuse the t.
T-18 IX.h The T. Worlds

T19. IV.A.11:3 Perception cannot obey t. masters, each
T-20...... IV.6:5 The ark of peace is entered t. by two, yet
T-20...... IV.6:5 The ark of peace is entered two by t., yet
T-20...... IV.7:2 of your brother serves but you t. alone.
T-20...... IV.7:3 hands of every t. who enter here to rest.
T-20....... V.2:3 T. voices raised together call to the hearts
T-20.... VIII.9:1 Only t. purposes are possible. And one is
T-21.......in.2:5 choice that lies between these t. decisions.
T-21...... II.10:8 and to confuse the t. is merely to fail to
T-22.......in.1:3 No t. can look on sin together, for they
T-22.........I.7:6 no t. brothers can unite except through
T-23.........I.3:8 nothingness; t. are as meaningless as one
T-23.........I.6:1 yourself is but the battle of t. illusions,
T-23.........I.7:8 yet the war of t. illusions is a state where
T-23.........I.8:1 Conflict must be between t. forces. It
T-23.........I.8:4 And *by* attacking it you make t. illusions of
T-24...... III.4:7 is it possible the t. can ever be the same,
T-24.... VI.12:2 Yet of the t., it is this one you find more
T-24... VII.11:1 And thus are t. sons made, and both
T-25...... III.3:3 But this world has t. who made it, and
T-25...... III.7:5 For these t. questions are the same. And
T-25...... III.7:7 from the belief there are t. ways to see.
T-26...... III.7:4 choice between t. things so clearly unalike
T-26....... V.1:7 There are t. teachers only, who point in
T-26....... V.1:9 There are but t. directions you can take,
T-26..... VII.7:4 Then would God's Will be split in t., and
T-26..... VII.7:4 to the laws of t. opposing powers, until
T-27....... II.2:8 and yet, because I am the better of the t., I
T-27...... II.12:7 And these t. halves appear to represent a
T-27...... II.12:7 a split within a self perceived as t..
T-27...... II.13:2 is. From an idea of self as t., there comes a
T-27...... II.13:2 view of function split between the t.. And
T-27....... V.8:8 within t. situations that are seen as one,
T-27... VII.11:1 choices can be made between t. states,
T-28....... V.6:2 of glass, a piece of wood, a thread or t.,
T-28..... VII.3:2 no allegiance to be split between the t..
T-29.........I.4:1 one of space between t. separate bodies.
T-29..... VII.8:3 by splitting what you are between the t..
T-30.........I.4:3 These t. procedures, practiced well, will
T-30.......I.17:1 It needs but t. who would have happiness
T-30.......I.17:2 It needs but t. to understand that they
T-30.......I.17:4 have. It needs but t.. These two are joined
T-30.......I.17:5 These t. are joined before there can be a
T-30...... III.2:4 What idol can make t. of what is one?
T-30.... III.11:5 You have not t. realities, but one. Nor can
T-31.........I.7:1 The lessons to be learned are only t..
T-31....... II.2:6 by your wish you set t. choices to be made
T-31....... II.3:5 these roles, forever split between the t..
T-31....... II.5:5 T. calls you make to him, as he to you.
T-31....... II.5:6 Between these t. *is* choice, because from
T-31....... V.2:5 be. For it is made to serve t. purposes, but
T-31..... V.10:6 t. parts to what you think yourself to be.
T-31..... VI.1:2 There is no compromise between the t.. If
T-31... VII.14:7 There are but t.. Be not deceived by what
W-in.......... 3:1 workbook is divided into t. main sections,
W-pI....... 6.3:1 remind yourself of the t. cautions stated
W-pI....... 9.1:1 follows from the t. preceding ones. But
W-pI..... 23.5:3 The first t. steps in this process require
W-pI..... 23.5:6 By taking the first t. steps, you will see
W-pI..... 24.3:3 T. minutes are suggested for each of the
W-pI..... 26.5:2 A full t. minutes should be attempted for
W-pI..... 31.1:4 speaking, the form includes t. aspects,
W-pI..... 31.2:1 T. longer periods of practice with the
W-pI..... 31.2:3 while repeating the idea t. or three times.
W-pI..... 32.2:2 for today will again include t. phases, one
W-pI..... 32.3:1 the idea for today t. or three times while
W-pI..... 32.4:1 For the t. longer practice periods three to
W-pI..... 37.5:1 use any combination of these t. phases of
W-pI..... 42.1:1 today combines t. very powerful thoughts
W-pI..... 42.3:1 will have t. three-to-five-minute practice
W-pI..... 45.9:2 Take a minute or t., as you repeat the idea
W-pI..... 46.3:3 spend a minute or t. in searching your
W-pI..... 47.4:4 Then spend a minute or t. in searching
WpI... rI.in.2:3 once. Devote t. minutes or more to each
W-pI..... 61.5:1 each one need not exceed a minute or t..
W-pI..... 61.6:3 t. practice periods may be longer than the
W-pI..... 62.5:4 Then devote a minute or t. to considering
W-pI..... 63.4:1 in the minute or t. that you should devote
W-pI..... 64.8:1 T. forms of shorter practice periods are
W-pI..... 65.1:5 only function necessarily entails t. phases;
W-pI..... 66.5:6 It is only if the first t. thoughts are wrong
W-pI..... 66.7:2 that there are only t. parts of your mind.
W-pI..... 70.6:1 ready for t. longer practice periods today,
W-pI..... 71.5:3 and you will attempt to follow t. plans for
W-pI..... 71.8:1 Begin the t. longer practice periods for
W-pI..... 71.8:1 idea, and realizing that it contains t. parts
W-pI... 72.13:1 One or perhaps t. shorter practice
W-pI..... 74.7:5 A minute or t. every half an hour, with
WpI..rII.in.1:2 review left off, and cover t. ideas each day.
W-pI..... 96.1:1 are one Self, you experience yourself as t.;
W-pI..... 96.3:2 T. selves in conflict could not be resolved,
W-pI..... 96.3:3 your Self, nor can your Self be split in t.,
W-pI..... 96.3:5 Make no attempt to reconcile the t., for
W-pI..... 98.1:4 We will not vacillate between the t., but
WpI..rIII.in1:2 We will review t. recent lessons every day
WpIrIII.in10:2 Attempt to give your daily t. ideas a brief
W-pI...... 130.h It is impossible to see t. worlds.
W-pI... 130.5:1 impossible to see t. worlds which have no
W-pI... 130.6:3 the lesson that you cannot see t. worlds. It
W-pI... 130.8:5 say: *It is impossible to see t. worlds. Let me*
W-pI. 130.11:4 *It is impossible to see t. worlds. I seek my*
W-pI... 131.7:4 He did not make t. minds, with Heaven as
W-pI... 131.8:2 Nor is His creation split in t.. How could
W-pI... 133.4:1 We have already stressed there are but t.,
W-pI. 133.11:3 thus you do not realize there are but t.,
W-pI. 133.13:3 Our t. extended practice periods of fifteen
WpI. rIV.in7:1 merely read each of the t. ideas assigned
WpI. rIV.in8:2 repeat the t. ideas you practice for the day
W-pI... 145.2:1 (130) It is impossible to see t. worlds.
W-pI... 166.2:4 and true believes in t. creators; or in one,
W-pI... 170.3:2 splitting your mind into t. camps which
W-pI... 185.2:9 should any t. agree these words express
W-pI... 185.3:1 T. minds with one intent become so
W-pI... 185.3:3 In dreams, no t. can share the same intent
M-in.......... 2:2 There are only t. thought systems, and
M-2........... 5:3 God's Teacher speaks to any t. who join
M-3........... 2:2 "chance" meeting of t. apparent strangers
M-3........... 2:2 t. students "happening" to walk home
M-3........... 2:6 it is possible for t. people to lose sight of
M-3........... 4:3 a time, t. people enter into a fairly intense
M-8........... 6:5 the understanding that only t. categories
M-8........... 6:6 And of these t., but one is real. Just as
M-16......... 4:7 continuing a minute or t. after you begin
M-16....... 10:9 t. aspects of one error and no more, he
M-23......... 4:4 that the little space between the t. is lost,
C-1............ 2:4 described in the course *as if* it has t. parts;
C-1............ 7:1 always between t. choices or two voices.
C-1............ 7:1 always between two choices or t. voices.
P-2..........II.6:5 If any t. are joined, He must be there. It
P-2........ III.2:6 or go no further than a step or t. from hell
P-2......... V.4:3 t. come very close to God in this attempt,
P-2......... V.4:4 Where t. have joined for healing, God is
P-2......... V.6:1 t. have joined. And now God's promises
P-2....... VII.8:1 the joining of t. brothers really means.
P-3........II.4:11 only message that any t. should ever give

## two-edged 2

T-2.........II.4:8 the only defense that is not a t. sword. It
T-2....... IV.3:6 of the Atonement to t. application. This is

## two-minute 2

W-pI .... 28.7:1 We will have six t. practice periods today
W-pI .... 29.4:1 six t. practice periods for today should

## two-minutes 1

W-pI .... 25.6:1 Six practice periods, each of t. duration,

## two-way 2

T-2.........II.7:6 A t. defense is inherently weak precisely
W-pI .... 66.2:3 is. It is not a t. battle. The ego attacks and

## twofold 1

T-12 ..... III.2:6 The question is always t.; first, *what* is to

## type 5

T-1........I.46:2 do not involve this t. of communication,
T-2....... IV.1:5 a remedy and any t. of healing is a result.
T-2..... IV.2:10 itself, neither t. of confusion need occur.
T-2..... VI.5:10 the error from the first to the second t.,
T-3..... VI.2:12 cannot be avoided in any t. of judgment,

## types 1

T-16........I.2:1 t. of problems and in certain people.

## typewriter 1

W-pI...... 9.3:3 *I do not see this t. as it is now. I do not see this*

## typical 3

T-4.........V.4:9 is none, but it does have a t. solution. It
T-9....... IV.7:1 The confusion of functions is so t. of the
T-31..... III.1:3 a habit of response so t. of everything you

## tyrannical 1

T19 .. IV.D.4:3 makes life seem to be ugly, cruel and t..

## tyrannize 1

T-18..... IX.1:5 sole ruler of the kingdom it set apart to t.

## tyrannous 1

T-1.........V.5:5 under t. rather than Authoritative control

## tyranny 3

T-1.... VII.3:12 through usurpation, which produces t..
T-8....... IV.6:7 cannot be learned by t. of any kind, and
W-pI .. 76.12:2 of freedom from all danger and all t.. It is

## tyrants 1

T-1.........V.5:6 because such are the dictates of t.. To

# U

**ugliness** 5

T-15.....VII.3:6 for **u.** such as this belongs not in your
T-17....... II.2:6 all **u.** into beauty that will enchant you,
T-17...... III.5:7 the spark of beauty hidden in the **u.** of the
T-17...... III.9:4 The spark of beauty or the veil of **u.**, the
M-10..........6:4 of the **u.** he sees about him is its outcome.

**ugly** 9

T-8.......VII.4:3 it. The body is beautiful or **u.**, peaceful or
T-16....VI.10:4 What guilt has wrought is **u.**, fearful and
T-17....... II.5:4 seemed **u.** in the darkness of your lack of
T19...IV.D.4:3 of death that makes life seem to be **u.**,
W-pI.....95.2:1 creation; weak, vicious, **u.** and sinful,
W-pI.121.11:3 the **u.** picture that you hold of him. Look
Wfl........in.1:5 that made the world seem **u.** and unsafe,
P-2........IV.2:6 shadow, grotesque and **u.** since it mimics
P-2........VI.2:5 make this **u.** sound seem truly beautiful.

**ultimate** 21

T-1......... V.2:4 closer to the **u.** release from time, in
T-6......V.B.8:6 this step is essential for the **u.** decision, it
T-6......V.C.3:5 It therefore makes the **u.** choice inevitable
T-7.......VII.8:5 is the **u.** basis for all the ego's projection.
T-12...... I.8:10 That is the **u.** value in learning to perceive
T-12...VII.13:2 The death penalty is the ego's **u.** goal, for
T-13...........I.1:1 **u.** aim is to make themselves unnecessary
T-13........II.1:1 The **u.** purpose of projection is always to
T-16....... V.5:6 In this it sees the **u.** freedom of the self,
T-18.....VII.6:1 Here is the **u.** release which everyone will
W-pI.....12.5:9 That is the **u.** purpose of these exercises.
W-pI...132.5:1 you wish, and herein lies your **u.** release.
W-pI...184.6:6 is true is but illusion, for it is the **u.** reality
W-pII......1.5:1 in hope, and certain of your **u.** success. He
M-3............1:2 although the **u.** goal is always the same; to
M-4.. VIII.1:10 the **u.** interpretation of all things in time,
M-5..........I.2:3 represents the **u.** defiance in a direct form
M-16..........3:2 This is by no means the **u.** criterion, but
M-24..........1:1 the **u.** sense, reincarnation is impossible.
P-2.........in.1:4 for reality, it has achieved its **u.** success.
S-3.........in.1:2 of assurance of success in **u.** attainment of

**ultimately** 37

T-1......... V.4:1 **U.**, every member of the family of God
T-1........VI.3:5 **U.**, space is as meaningless as time. Both
T-2...........I.4:1 All fear is **u.** reducible to the basic
T-2......... II.5:1 itself, and **u.** to make learning complete.
T-2........ III.3:8 point. This **u.** reawakens spiritual vision,
T-2......III.5:13 is the guarantee that they will **u.** succeed.
T-2.....VII.5:10 **u.** no compromise is possible between
T-2.......VII.6:5 is why the conflict cannot **u.** be resolved
T-2..... VIII.4:3 Apocalypse. Everyone will **u.** look upon
T-3........III.6:4 and time, and will **u.** replace them. That
T-3......VI.10:4 All fear comes **u.**, and sometimes by way
T-4...........I.3:2 be. Learning is **u.** perceived as frightening
T-6.........in.1:2 which must **u.** be accepted as one's own
T-6...........I.4:1 Assault can **u.** be made only on the body.
T-6......... II.7:3 knowledge, you will **u.** remember it. The
T-6......V.A.5:1 just as He **u.** translates perception into
T-6......V.C.4:9 Holy Spirit will **u.** teach you that you need
T-7........III.4:7 is how *having* and *being* are **u.** reconciled,
T-7........IV.3:8 **U.**, then, they all contribute to one result,
T-8.......VII.8:4 it is **u.** why the world itself is depressing.
T-9...........I.9:1 **U.** everyone must remember the Will of
T-9...........I.9:1 **u.** everyone must recognize himself. This
T-9........ I.14:4 anxiety, depression and **u.** panic, because
T-9......... V.7:7 is how perception **u.** is translated into
T-13....... II.3:3 crucifixion of God's Son can **u.** satisfy it.
T-13....... II.6:4 course stems **u.** from this interpretation,
T-18...... VI.1:2 That is what you must **u.** learn, for it is
T-18...VII.4:10 All such attempts will **u.** succeed because
T-27...... III.5:2 Reality is **u.** known without a form,
T-27...... III.6:9 will **u.** take the place of every learning aid
W-pI.......5.1:6 in **u.** recognizing they are all the same.
W-pI.....19.4:3 of order in this connection will **u.** make
W-pI.....26.1:5 It is this law that will **u.** save you, but you
W-pI...161.7:3 touched and seen and heard, and **u.** killed
M-4 .....VII.1:3 of God's teachers this one rests **u.** on trust
M-4 ..... X.2:12 aim, at which all learning **u.** converges. It
M-13 .........1:2 its meaning is temporary and will **u.** fade

**un-understandable** 1

M-11 .........3:6 is the **u.** made understandable. How is

**unabated** 1

C-1.............4:3 Creation continues **u.** because that is the

**unable** 34

T-2........ III.4:6 makes it increasingly **u.** to tolerate delay,
T-2......... V.2:4 may be **u.** to accept the real Source of the
T-2......... V.3:5 will be **u.** to re-establish right-mindedness
T-3........ VI.1:4 you will be **u.** to avoid judging your own.
T-3.......VII.1:8 because otherwise you will be **u.** to escape
T-4........ III.7:5 of fear, or you will be **u.** to ask me to do so
T-5........ III.5:6 would be **u.** to understand the change.
T-6......V.C.8:2 of its wholeness and will be **u.** to teach it.
T-7......... V.9:6 The ego is totally **u.** to understand this,
T-7....... X.5:13 **U.** to follow this guidance without fear, he
T-12......IV.3:2 Being **u.** to love, the ego would be totally
T-12....... V.3:2 are trying to attack them you will be **u.** to
T-13......VI.1:7 be **u.** to perceive the reality that is now.
T-13.....VII.4:3 answers, being **u.** to deny a call for help,
T-14....IV.10:2 himself, making both **u.** to communicate,
T-14...... XI.8:6 are **u.** to depend on miracles to answer all
T-15.... III.10:7 and **u.** to accept anything for yourself. But
T-16......VI.2:5 or Love will be **u.** to find you and comfort
T-17... V.11:10 yourself **u.** to express the holy instant,
T19....IV.C.8:1 ego's might, **u.** to protect the life that He
T-20... VIII.6:6 **u.** to overlook it in any form and seeing it
T-22...... III.2:2 and reason will be **u.** to see your errors
T-22...... III.5:6 **u.** to look beyond the granite block of sin,
T-22...... III.6:6 **u.** to go beyond the form to meaning.
T-31....... V.3:1 for the world is wicked and **u.** to provide
T-31... VIII.1:2 in what must die, **u.** to escape its frailty,
W-pI.....43.6:1 if you seem to be **u.** to think of anything,
W-pI.....45.8:6 You will probably be **u.** as yet to realize
W-pI.....72.2:3 **u.** to reach other minds except through
W-pI...135.4:3 prey, **u.** to protect itself and needing your
W-pI. 153.16:4 we will be **u.** to withdraw a little while,
W-pI...160.7:3 You are **u.** now to recognize this stranger
M-21 .........4:3 words, being as yet **u.** to hear in silence.
M-22 .........5:5 fact, be **u.** to recognize his brother at all,

**unacceptable** 4

T-4......... V.2:2 God. Thoughts of God are **u.** to the ego,
T-4......... V.2:5 to conceal not only "**u.**" body impulses,
T-13...... IV.2:1 oblivion nor hell is as **u.** to you as Heaven.
M-8 ...........2:6 Finding truth **u.**, the mind revolts against

**unaccepted** 1

W-pI...154.9:3 offer what you need, nor has it been left **u.**

**unaccomplished** 1

T-31.....VII.6:1 here remain forever **u.** and undone. And

**unacknowledged** 1

W-pI...110.9:5 yourself while He is **u.** and unknown.

**unadjusted** 1

T-20....VIII.6:3 in **u.** form and suited perfectly to meet it.

**unaffected** 8

T-2...........I.5:6 you are perfectly **u.** by all expressions of
T-4........ VI.1:7 totally **u.** by your attempts to dissociate it
T-8...........I.6:5 Your reality is **u.** by both, but if you listen
T-21...VII.13:8 leave the thinker's mind, or leave him **u.**.
T-29...... IX.6:8 real world **u.** by the world he thinks is real
T-30.... III.10:2 you. Completely **u.** by the turmoil and the
W-pI.....83.4:3 *and my function remains wholly* **u.** *by this.*
W-pII .350.1:4 *What he is, is* **u.** *by his thoughts. But what he*

**unafraid** 6

T-21...... IV.8:2 met and joined, and looks upon the ego **u.**
T-25...... IV.4:7 stand in quiet, in innocence and wholly **u.**
W-pI.....58.4:5 And because I am **u.**, everyone must share
W-pI...109.9:1 the peace of God today, quiet and **u.**.
W-pI...158.1:2 purely mind, sinless forever, wholly **u.**,
W-pII ....in.7:1 in silence, **u.** and certain of Your coming.

**unaided** 1

T-25..VIII.5:10 of punishment that they lay it aside, **u.**,

**unalike** 1

T-26...... III.7:4 choice between two things so clearly **u.**.

**Unalterable** 1

*unalterable*

T-4..........II.2:3 they were not made by or with the **U.**. It is

**unalterable** 6

*Unalterable*

T-1......... V.5:2 is therefore **u.** because it is already perfect
T-5......... V.6:5 that the alternatives themselves are **u.**.
T-6..........II.6:4 It is completely **u.**. It is total inclusion.
T-17..... V.14:8 Yet the goal is fixed, firm and **u.**, and the
W-pI.....93.7:4 Creation is eternal and **u.**. Your
W-pI. 136.11:7 What is **u.** cannot change. And what is

**unambiguous** 9

T-3...........I.6:5 Atonement is entirely **u.**. It is perfectly
T-12....... V.9:3 The curriculum is totally **u.**, because the
T-13...... XI.3:8 Heaven is perfectly **u.**. Everything is clear
T-25...... VI.2:4 the eyes than what is wholly clear and **u.**.
W-pI.....39.1:2 are very simple, very clear and totally **u.**.
W-pI.....81.3:3 clear and perfectly **u.** before my sight. My
W-pI... 129.4:1 Communication, **u.** and plain as day,
W-pI. 186.11:1 function stands out clear and wholly **u.**.
W-pI... 199.6:3 The body's purpose now is **u.**. And it

**unamenable** 1
T-2......... V.6:5 the learner, and is therefore **u.** to learning

**unanswered** 14
T-13...... VI.9:4 His Son called upon Him and remained **u.**
T-19...... III.4:9 that you would keep unheard and thus **u.**
T-21........VII.h The Last **U.** Question
T-21......VII.8:1 to the last question you have left **u.** still.
T-23..... II.11:1 And now there is a vague **u.** question, not
T-26....... V.4:4 one illusion still remains **u.** in your mind.
T-27...... IV.7:4 question, though they leave the first **u.**. In
T-31.........I.8:3 nor left **u.** in the selfsame tongue in which
W-pI.135.23:4 which remains **u.** yet in need of answering
W-pI.185.11:4 Who could be **u.** who requests an answer
W-pII ....in.3:4 not remain **u.** when he calls His Name.
W-pII ....358.h No call to God can be unheard nor left **U.**
M-21 .........3:3 **u.** in the perception of the one who asks.
M-28 .........3:7 for what remains **u.** or incomplete? The

**unapproachable** 1
T-19....... II.5:2 quite **u.** except with reverence and awe. It

**unaskable** 1
W-pI.169.14:7 We do not ask for the **u.**. We do not look

**unasked** 2
T-21....... V.4:6 is obvious, simple and remains **u.**. But
T-27..... VII.7:3 to thrust upon you, uninvited and **u.**,

**unassailable** 3
T-5......... V.2:4 to the ego because its peace is **u.**. It is
W-pI... 153.9:1 need no defense because we are created **u.**
W-pI... 190.2:4 for attack on what is wholly **u.**. It is a

**unassailed** 2
W-pI... 137.3:4 his Self with all Its parts intact and **u.**. In
W-pI.139.10:1 is **u.** by his belief he knows not what he is.

**unassembled** 1
W-pI... 136.2:3 it, or reduce it to a little pile of **u.** parts.

**unattached** 1
W-pII .223.1:1 separate entity that moved in isolation, **u.**

**unattacked** 1
T-27.......I.10:6 to represent an endless life, forever **u.**.

**unattainable** 3
T-15...... IX.3:5 that the ego, whose goals are altogether **u.**
W-pII .259.1:1 that makes the goal of God seem **u.**. What
W-pII .....7.3:2 which you would attain what is forever **u.**.

**unattained** 1
S-1......... II.8:4 forgiveness, itself an illusion, remains **u.**.

**unattested** 1
T-27....... V.2:2 As long as it is **u.**, it remains without

**unavailable** 1
M-23 .......3:11 greatest teacher be **u.** to those who follow

**unawakened** 1
W-pI.169.13:4 of you remains outside, unknowing, **u.**,

**unaware** 32
T-1 ....... IV.2:9 empty shell and is **u.** of the spirit within.
T-3 ..........I.7:4 is wisdom because it is **u.** of evil, and evil
T-4 .........II.8:6 Spirit in its knowledge is **u.** of the ego. It
T-4 .........II.8:8 all. While the ego is equally **u.** of spirit, it
T-7 ....... IV.1:7 does not exist, but those who sleep are **u.**.
T-7 ....... IV.1:8 Because they are **u.**, they do not know.
T-7 ...... VII.5:2 **u.** of your gift because you do not give it.
T-9 ..........I.3:4 something of which you are totally **u.**.
T-9 ....... III.2:2 **u.** of what errors are and what correction
T-9 ...... VII.3:6 you. It is **u.** of what you are, and wholly
T-11 .... V.13:5 **U.** that the belief cannot be established,
T-18 ... VIII.4:2 **u.** that they are feared and hated by a tiny
T-18 .VIII.12:5 together you could no more be **u.** of love
T-18 ... IX.1:10 and holy, serene and **u.** of what you think
T-18 ..... IX.3:6 it not; its senses remain quite **u.** of it; its
T19 IV.B.14:10 ego hides it, for it would keep you **u.** of it.
T-21 ...... V.6:5 meaningful to ask why you are **u.** of what
T-26 ...... V.5:7 lives in memories alone is **u.** of where he
T-27 .... VII.7:3 Once you were **u.** of what the cause of
T-30 .... III.7:5 It was always there, but you were **u.** of it.
T-30 ... III.10:4 safe, completely **u.** of all the world that
T-30 . III.11:10 Son of God Himself, are **u.** of your reality.
T-31 ......I.13:1 **u.** of any thoughts of evil or of good that
W-pI..... 17.3:3 **u.** as yet of any thought that is really true,
W-pI... 95.10:2 attempts to keep you **u.** you are one Self,
W-pI... 138.8:3 And these decisions are made **u.**, to keep
W-pI... 157.9:1 now, serenely **u.** of everything except His
W-pI... 198.8:1 and **u.** of any condemnation which could
W-pII ... 11.4:2 and **u.** of our eternal unity with Him. Yet
M-17 ....... 4:11 is **u.** of truth must look upon illusions.
M-25 ......... 1:3 has many abilities of which he is **u.**. As his
M-26 ......... 2:6 Nor is there anyone of whom they are **u.**.

**unawareness** 4
T-7 ....... IX.3:7 their reality than your **u.** of your spirit
T-18 ... VI.11:4 realize that it is a sudden **u.** of the body,
W-pI. 138.10:1 it is raised from its protective shield of **u.**,
W-pII . 258.1:3 to allow God's grace to shine in **u.**, while

**unbelief** 3
T-1 ....... VI.4:1 of this world is to use it to correct your **u.**.
T-7 ....... VI.4:3 This **u.** is its origin, and while the ego
P-2..........II.4:5 Belief implies that **u.** is possible, but

**unbelievable** 7
T-7 ........VIII.h The **U.** Belief
T-7 ..... VIII.6:2 can keep a belief he has judged to be **u.**.
T-7 ..... VIII.6:4 cannot be understood because it is **u.**.
T-7 ..... VIII.6:5 of perception based on the **u.** is apparent,
T-7 ..... VIII.7:1 ego is **u.** and will forever be unbelievable.
T-7 ..... VIII.7:1 ego is unbelievable and will forever be **u.**.
T-7 ..... VIII.7:2 the **u.** cannot make this judgment alone.

**unbelievers** 1
T-9 ..........I.9:3 of truth, there are no **u.** and no sacrifices.

**unbelieving** 1
T-11 ...... V.9:1 you to regard yourself as supercilious, **u.**,

**unbidden** 1
W-pII . 253.1:1 anything should come to me **u.** by myself.

**unbind** 1
W-pI... 129.5:3 as you **u.** your mind from little things the

**unblemished** 1
S-1..........II.8:6 and returned **u.** into the Mind of God.

**unborn** 3
T-24 .... VII.2:2 created and creating, born and **u.** as yet,
W-pI .... 98.4:3 those as yet **u.** will hear the call we heard,
W-pI .. 109.9:5 We give to those **u.** and those passed by,

**unbound** 4
T-31 .....V.17:3 that truth returns, unhindered and **u.**.
W-pI 193.12:5 Thus will you remain **u.**, in peace eternal
W-pI .. 199.2:1 time and space, **u.** by any preconceptions,
W-pI .. 204.1:2 *time,* **u.** *by laws which rule the world of sick*

**unbroken** 5
T-13 ..... VI.6:7 is timeless and their communication is **u.**,
T-13 ..... VI.8:3 continuity, **u.** because it is wholly shared.
T-14 . VIII.2:15 here. **U.** and uninterrupted love flows
T-15 ..... XI.7:2 remains **u.** even if the body is destroyed,
T-20 ..... VI.1:5 is one of perfect union and **u.** continuity.

**unburdened** 3
W-pI .... 61.4:3 in peace, **u.** and certain of your purpose.
W-pI 170.11:6 return to a new world, **u.** by its weight;
M-10 ......... 5:5 Now can the teacher of God rise up **u.**,

**unceasingly** 5
T-14 .......X.5:2 It shifts **u.** across the mirror of your mind,
W-pI .. 182.5:3 He desires to go home so deeply, so **u.**,
W-pI .. 182.7:4 He whispers of His home **u.** to you. For
W-pI 182.11:5 yet He asks **u.** that you return with Him,
W-pII .... in.8:5 Love has called to us **u.** since time began.

**uncertain** 34
T-3 ....... IV.3:5 It is necessarily **u.** about what it is. It has
T-3 ....... VI.8:8 Being **u.** of your true Authorship, you
T-10 ...... in.3:1 about you, for He is not **u.** of Himself.
T-12 .......II.4:4 them. It is easy to help an **u.** child, for he
T-15 .......II.4:9 If you remain **u.**, it is only because you
T-17 ..... VI.2:1 In any situation in which you are **u.**, the
T-18 ... VI.11:9 And while this lasts you are not **u.** of your
T-20 ........I.2:6 and lilies in the other, **u.** which to give.
T-20 ..... III.9:3 **u.** whether to let it go or to take hold on
T-21 ........I.3:7 yet because you still remain **u.** that vision
T-21 ... VIII.3:8 Yet what he is **u.** of, God cannot give. For
T-21 ... VIII.3:9 he does not desire it while he remains **u.**,
T-24 .... VII.7:5 one thought with purpose still **u.**, or one
T-28 ..... III.1:2 first, **u.** steps to be directed up the ladder
T-28 ..... III.7:5 concealed within a separate and **u.** bit of
T-28 .......V.7:3 with vague **u.** forms and changing shapes,
T-30 .... VII.7:2 you will believe the world is an **u.** place,
T-31 ... VIII.7:1 to everyone who wanders in the world **u.**,
W-pI .... 49.1:4 distracted, disorganized and highly **u.**.
W-pI .... 79.3:2 you are still **u.** about what the problem is.
W-pI .. 96.11:2 your mind remains **u.** yet a little while. Be
W-pI .... 97.6:2 firefly makes an **u.** moment and goes out.
W-pI .... 98.4:2 Those still **u.**, too, will join with us, and,
W-pI .. 131.7:1 its ways; its shifting patterns and **u.** goals,
W-pI .. 139.5:1 Thus he becomes **u.** of his life, for what it
W-pI .. 156.2:3 itself, nor be in parts **u.** and in others sure
W-pI .. 160.5:4 who he is, **u.** of all things but this; that he
W-pI .. 163.3:1 however hard to gain, **u.** in their outcome
W-pI 169.11:5 salvation comes a little nearer each **u.**
W-pI 185.10:5 been weak at times, **u.** in your purpose,
W-pI 186.10:2 and vague, **u.** and ambiguous. Who could
W-pI 186.10:4 so **u.** that they change ten times an hour
W-pII . 256.1:4 are? Who would still be **u.**? Who could be
S-1..........II.2:3 Yet it is also true that no one who is **u.** of

**uncertainly** 7
T-20 ... VI.11:3 bereft of water and set **u.** upon oblivion.
T-22 .......II.7:7 no middle ground where you can pause **u.**
T-28 .... VII.3:3 grasp **u.** at any straw that seems to hold
T-29 ........I.7:4 because it seems to come and go **u.**, and
W-pI .... 94.3:7 left Its home in God to walk the world **u.**.
WpI...rV.in1:5 doubts have made us walk **u.** and slowly

W-pI...182.3:2 home. He goes **u.** about in endless search,

**uncertainties** 3

T-24.....VII.7:3 time, nor held to limits or **u.** of any kind.
W-pI.136.19:2 or make plans against **u.** to come, you
M-25..........5:7 "power's" **u.** with increasing deception.

**uncertainty** 28

T-3........III.1:4 certain. **U.** means that you do not know.
T-3........IV.5:1 because it brings the mind into areas of **u.**
T-3........VI.3:4 All **u.** comes from the belief that you are
T-3......VI.8:10 dispute over authorship has left such **u.** in
T-6........IV.8:1 into being was the beginning of **u.**,
T-9.......VII.3:9 It cannot exceed it because of its **u.**. And
T-9.......VII.4:7 to viciousness, since its **u.** is increased.
T-14...VII.3:10 **U.** brought to certainty does not retain
T19. IV.C.11:5 with such seeming **u.** of meaning, judge it
T-22.....V.3:11 Only **u.** can be defensive. And all
T-22.....V.3:12 And all **u.** is doubt about yourself.
T-26.......V.4:5 **U.** was brought to certainty so long ago
T-26.VII.11:13 **u.** be what you want? Or is it a mistake
T-29.......IX.9:2 the guilt and pain of self-betrayal and **u.**,
T-30.........I.2:6 but produce confusion and **u.** and fear.
T-30.......VII.7:2 place, in which you walk in danger and **u.**.
T-30... VIII.6:2 to prefer a dream allow **u.** to enter here.
W-pI.....77.6:5 There is no room for doubt and **u.** today.
W-pI...121.1:3 bring **u.** to all your hopes of ever finding
W-pI...121.1:4 here the end of all **u.** ensured at last.
W-pI...128.4:3 and pain; one moment of **u.** and doubt.
W-pI...139.1:3 what is choice except **u.** of what we are?
W-pI...139.3:1 **U.** about what you must be is self-
W-pI...151.1:4 is but a cloak for the **u.** it would conceal.
W-pI...165.4:6 Till you welcome it as yours, **u.** remains.
WpI.. rV.in6:4 I must understand **u.** and pain, although I
M-7...........2:5 must recognize that his own **u.** is not love
C-in...........2:7 possible because here alone **u.** ends.

**unchain** 2

T-5........VI.2:8 role is only to **u.** your will and set it free.
T-15.......II.3:6 holy instant you will **u.** all your brothers,

**unchallenged** 1

WpI rVI.in.5:2 Permit no idle thought to go **u.**. If you

**unchangeable** 16

T-5.......V.6:11 what God creates is irreversible and **u.**.
T-7......VI.13:4 Yet because God's Will is **u.**, no conflict of
T-19......III.5:7 sin is the belief that your perception is **u.**,
T19...IV.A.7:3 and **u.** dedication to sin and its results.
T-30......III.8:4 of you is like a star, **u.** in an eternal sky.
T-30......VI.5:6 a special form of error that remains **u.**,
W-pI.....67.2:1 and its wholly unchanged and **u.** nature.
W-pI...152.5:1 As God created you, you must remain **u.**,
W-pI...187.4:6 behind the form of things that lives **u.**.
W-pI...190.6:5 holy joy, unchanged, unchanging and **u.**,
W-pII..283.1:2 *as it always was, for Your creation is* ***u.***. *Let*
M-4......II.2:10 unchanging and **u.** beyond appearances;
M-18..........2:4 **u.** condition of all that God created. Now
M-27..........1:4 **u.** belief of the world that all things in it
C-ep...........2:6 it still; unchanged, unchanging and **u.**.
S-2.........in.1:4 feet secure; your purpose steadfast and **u.**.

**unchanged** 29

T-4...........I.8:5 which stands **u.** beyond the reach of your
T-13....XI.10:4 will remain **u.** throughout eternity. You
T-17.......V.9:5 remember a goal **u.** throughout eternity?
T-22.......II.3:8 Only the timeless must remain **u.**, but
T-25.......II.6:8 all corruption, **u.** and perfect in eternity.
T-25......III.5:4 to obscure the sinlessness that shines **u.**,
T-25.......V.3:4 **u.** in content in whatever form the call is
T-26.....VII.3:5 Yet is truth **u.**. It cannot be perceived, but
T-26.....VII.9:6 Facts are **u.**. Yet facts can be denied and
T-29.......II.7:8 means the mind remains **u.** in its belief of
T-30......III.7:6 of you is perfectly **u.** by your forgetting. It
T-30.....VII.4:4 it everywhere, **u.** by circumstance. And so
W-pI.....45.7:2 are there in your mind now, completely **u.**
W-pI.....56.4:2 image I have made, the truth remains **u.**.
W-pI.....67.2:1 its wholly **u.** and unchangeable nature.
W-pI.....93.7:3 made, the truth about you is **u.**. Creation
W-pI...127.1:5 It is like itself, **u.** throughout. It never
WpI...rV.in8:8 for us before time was and kept **u.** by time
W-pI...190.6:5 Your Self is radiant in this holy joy, **u.**,
W-pII..230.2:3 *was born into Your Mind is shining there* ***u.***.
W-pII......4.5:6 Creation is **u.**. Would you still hold return
W-pII......6.1:5 He abides **u.** forever in the Mind of God.
W-pII....11.1:5 **u.** through time and after time is done.
W-pII..336.2:2 *Your Word remains* ***u.*** *within my mind,*
M-18 .........2:4 of sinlessness, the one **u.**, unchangeable
C-ep...........2:6 And holds it still; **u.**, unchanging and
P-2........IV.2:5 decision, and how can its shadow be **u.**?
S-2...........I.6:5 which still remains **u.** behind them all.
S-3 ......... II.6:1 cure, leaving the cause of illness still **u.**,

**unchanging** 5

W-pI...131.5:1 affect His perfect, timeless and **u.** Love.
W-pI...190.6:5 joy, unchanged, **u.** and unchangeable,
M-4 .... II.2:10 **u.** and unchangeable beyond appearances
C-3.............3:5 adapts itself to need; the content is **u.**, as
C-ep...........2:6 it still; unchanged, **u.** and unchangeable.

**unclear** 1

T-26......III.4:6 the same and what is different remain **u.**.

**unclosed** 1

W-ep .........5:7 which God has held **u.** to welcome us.

**unclouded** 5

T-10......IV.2:1 Reality can dawn only on an **u.** mind. It is
T-14......III.13:7 obscure your innocence from your **u.**
T-31...VII.13:3 a wholly open mind, **u.** by old concepts,
W-pI.186.10:1 go, and leave your mind **u.** and serene,
W-pII...300.1:3 And it is this serenity we seek, **u.**, obvious

**unconcerned** 4

T-2.........V.4:2 are completely **u.** about your readiness,
T-14.......X.8:1 content, and is totally **u.** with it. To the
W-pI...129.2:3 indeed, unstable, cruel, **u.** with you, quick
P-3.........II.3:2 healer may be arrogant, selfish, **u.**, and

**uncondemned** 2

W-pII..301.1:4 *Let me today behold it* ***u.***, *through happy*
C-2.............9:5 what it is, is wholly **u.** and wholly pure.

**unconflicted** 2

T-8.........II.3:8 of the curriculum that must be **u.**, but
W-pII..296.2:2 so our learning goal becomes an **u.** one,

**unconscious** 4

T-12.......I.8:13 in **u.** recognition of what has been denied.
T-27.....VII.1:3 the dreamer is **u.** of what brought on the
W-pI...136.3:3 seem to be **u.** but because of the rapidity
W-pI...138.8:1 beliefs can gain **u.** hold of great intensity,

**unconsciously** 3

T-6.........II.2:4 By doing this **u.**, you try to keep the fact
T-15.....VII.9:5 him, perhaps in little ways, perhaps "**u.**,"
W-pI...136.4:2 All this cannot be done **u.**. But afterwards

**unconsciousness** 2

T-8........IX.4:7 a form of death than death is a form of **u.**.
T-8........IX.4:8 Complete **u.** is impossible. You can rest in

**uncontained** 1

T-28........II.2:4 the nature of the innocent to be forever **u.**

**uncorrectable** 3

T-19...... III.3:6 that it was an error, but keeping it **u.**.
T-22...... III.2:5 what you thought was **u.** can be corrected
T-25...... IX.1:2 they are sins and not mistakes, forever **u.**,

**uncorrected** 4

T-17.........I.3:6 perspective on reality be warped and **u.**.
T-21...... VI.1:6 **u.** error of any kind deceives you about
W-pI...181.7:3 upon sin will bring, and **u.** will remain.
P-2........ VI.2:1 only an instant, and then dismiss it **u.**.

**uncorrupted** 1

W-pI...134.8:1 is so **u.** that it sees illusions as illusions,

**uncover** 4

T-13...... III.7:5 for any thoughts you may fear to **u.**. For
T-17........II.5:2 and **u.** to you the seeming reasons for
T-17...... III.6:7 Let Him **u.** the hidden spark of beauty in
W-pI.....65.5:4 Rather, try to **u.** each thought that arises

**uncovered** 4

T-13........II.5:5 but you have not **u.** its source. For the ego
T-13...... III.6:5 in this mind is so apparent, when it is **u.**,
T-21......II.13:4 are gone, because its source has been **u.**.
W-pI.......6.2:2 to each upsetting thought **u.** in the search

**uncovering** 2

T-9......... V.2:2 How, then, can "**u.**" them make them real
W-pI.....24.4:2 should be on **u.** the outcome you want.

**uncreative** 2

T-1.........I.14:3 destructive; or rather, the **u.** use of mind.
T-5........ VI.9:4 because it is **u.** and therefore unsharing, it

**undeceived** 1

M-4 ...... VI.1:9 Slowly at first he lets himself be **u.**. But he

**undeceiver** 1

W-pI...134.8:2 that it becomes the **u.** in the face of lies;

**undefended** 2

T-22....... V.3:8 you in quiet, **u.** and wholly undefending,
W-pI.135.24:5 up nothing in these times today when, **u.**,

**undefending** 1

T-22....... V.3:8 you in quiet, undefended and wholly **u.**,

**undefiled** 4

T-26........II.8:4 of His Love kept perfectly intact and **u.**.
WpI.rV.in10:3 Name. Your glory **u.** forever. And your
W-pII .309.2:2 *Your altar stands serene and* ***u.***. *It is the holy*
W-pII .313.1:6 *completely* ***u.*** *upon the altar to Your holy*

**undefinable** 1

C-2.............3:4 Who can define the **u.**? And yet there is

**undependability** 1

T-14...... XI.8:5 and use this fancied **u.** as an excuse for

### undependable 3

T-14 XI.8:5 Thus would you make Him **u.**, and use
W-pI 53.3:2 engenders fear because it is completely **u.**,
M-27 1:6 and unsure; the **u.** and the unsteady,

### under 72

T-1 I.5:2 They should not be **u.** conscious control.
T-1 I.37:3 places you **u.** the Atonement principle,
T-1 I.47:2 time interval not **u.** the usual laws of time
T-1 III.4:4 will be acting **u.** direct communication.
T-1 III.4:5 and **u.** my guidance miracles lead to the
T-1 V.5:5 but places itself **u.** tyrannous rather than
T-2 V.2:5 **U.** these conditions, it is safer for you to
T-2 V.A.17:5 Time is **u.** my direction, but timelessness
T-2 VI.2:9 you place what you think **u.** my guidance.
T-2 VI.6:1 **u.** my guidance without conscious effort,
T-2 VII.7:9 you that time and space are **u.** my control
T-3 IV.7:7 mind if you will bring it **u.** my guidance.
T-3 VI.3:4 that you are **u.** the coercion of judgment.
T-4 II.8:11 can do so, however, only **u.** one condition
T-8 VII.13:5 is brought **u.** the purpose of the mind, it
T-8 VIII.9:10 of the proper perspective on life **u.** the
T-8 IX.4:3 give it? **U.** which teacher did you place it?
T-9 II.6:2 directed by the Holy Spirit **u.** the laws of
T-10 IV.4:7 that is not **u.** them does not exist. "Laws
T-12 II.4:6 hiding your head **u.** the cover of the heavy
T-12 IV.4:5 **u.** His guidance you cannot be defeated.
T-12 V.5:2 that you can progress only **u.** constant,
T-12 V.8:6 **U.** the proper learning conditions, which
T-12 VI.6:5 the transfer of training **u.** the Holy Spirit's
T-12 VII.1:1 has occurred **u.** the right guidance, for
T-13 III.2:1 **U.** the ego's dark foundation is the
T-13 IV.3:1 **U.** the circumstances, would it not be
T-13 IV.8:2 of past and future, **u.** its direction, is the
T-13 VII.13:4 **U.** His guidance you will travel light and
T-13 VIII.2:7 can reach everywhere **u.** His guidance, for
T-13 VIII.4:6 that spring to light **u.** His loving gaze are
T-13 VIII.8:2 me **u.** the holy banner of His teaching,
T-14 VII.2:7 **U.** each cornerstone of fear on which you
T-15 V.4:6 truth. **U.** His teaching, every relationship
T-15 V.5:4 You can place any relationship **u.** His care
T-15 VI.1:3 within it. **U.** the Holy Spirit's teaching all
T-15 VI.5:7 for this alone is natural **u.** the laws of God
T-17 II.2:2 with everything sparkling **u.** the open sun
T-17 V.6:5 purify what He has taken **u.** His guidance
T-18 II.1:6 as **u.** attack and highly vulnerable to it.
T-18 VIII.9:8 And **u.** its beneficence your little garden
T19 IV.B.13:2 **U.** fear's orders the body will pursue guilt,
T19 IV.C.8:1 **U.** the dusty edge of its distorted world
T-20 VIII.6:4 sin is turned to blessing **u.** His gentle gaze
T-20 VIII.11:1 to quiet views of gardens **u.** open skies,
T-22 in.2:8 living with their bodies perhaps **u.** a
T-22 in.3:7 Just **u.** Heaven does he stand, but close
T-24 VI.10:4 yourself **u.** the laws you see as ruling him.
W-pI 28.5:3 Hidden **u.** all your ideas about it is its real
W-pI 40.2:4 practice quite well **u.** any circumstances,
W-pI 41.5:2 **u.** a heavy cloud of insane thoughts,
W-pI 45.7:1 **U.** all the senseless thoughts and mad
W-pI 56.1:2 who I am when I see myself as **u.** constant
W-pI 66.9:2 to find salvation **u.** the ego's guidance.
W-pI 73.10:5 of the practice period **u.** Their guidance.
W-pI 76.h I am **u.** no laws but God's.
W-pI 76.4:2 and put them **u.** different names in a long
W-pI 76.9:3 says there is no loss **u.** the laws of God.
W-pI 76.11:6 period concludes: *I am* **u.** *no laws but God's.*
W-pI 79.5:5 remain unsolved **u.** a cloud of denial, and
W-pI 88.3:1 (76) I am **u.** no laws but God's. Here is
W-pI 88.3:3 freedom. I am **u.** no laws but God's. I am
W-pI 89.1:2 because I am **u.** no laws but God's. His
W-pI 105.6:2 are their right **u.** the equal laws of God.
W-pI 127.6:4 obey; of all the limits **u.** which you live,
W-pI 196.2:2 because the ego, **u.** what it sees as threat,
W-pII 13.1:6 fear must slip away **u.** the gentle remedy
M-24 2:1 would not, **u.** any circumstances, be the
M-25 3:2 the Holy Spirit, and used **u.** His direction,
M-25 5:3 may still be strong enough to rally **u.** this
M-29 2:6 and all aspects are **u.** the Holy Spirit's
P-1 5:6 Psychotherapy **u.** His direction is one of

### underestimate 6

T-5 V.2:11 do not **u.** the power of the ego's belief in it
T-7 III.3:5 **u.** your need to be vigilant *against* this idea
T-11 V.16:1 **u.** the appeal of the ego's demonstrations
T-11 VI.5:1 **u.** the power of the devotion of God's Son
T-14 I.2:6 and do not **u.** the extent of its insanity.
T-16 VII.3:1 Do not **u.** the intensity of the ego's drive

### underfoot 1

W-pI. 200.10:4 Now are they **u.**. And you look up and on

### underground 2

T-15 X.5:1 which it burrows **u.** and hides in darkness
T-16 IV.1:6 but will merely drive it **u.** and out of sight.

### underlie 1

S-1 II.3:4 guilt that inevitably **u.** any prayer of need.

### underlies 6

T-7 VIII.4:4 makes, **u.** its whole use of projection. It
T-8 VIII.3:4 the obvious attack that **u.** the sickness. If
T19 IV.B.13:5 It is this idea that **u.** all of the ego's heavy
W-pI 108.6:3 at the one Thought which **u.** them all.
W-pI 166.2:1 paradox that **u.** the making of the world.
W-pI 167.2:4 It is the one idea which **u.** all feelings that

### underlying 12

T-1 II.6:8 It does so by the **u.** recognition of perfect
T-2 V.1:4 of the **u.** fear that the mind can hurt itself.
T-3 III.3:3 to counteract an **u.** fear that the future
T-12 I.9:7 affirmation of the **u.** belief it masks, you
T-12 I.10:1 every defense against it, the **u.** appeal *for* it
T-14 X.9:3 the **u.** lack of content makes a cohesive
T-17 IV.7:2 The **u.** basis for their effectiveness is that
T-19 II.2:6 grand illusion **u.** all the ego's grandiosity.
T-25 VII.11:1 reflects the **u.** tenet God must be insane.
W-pI 79.6:3 Perceiving the **u.** constancy in all the
W-pI 151.2:6 Why but because of **u.** doubt, which you
M-in 3:6 teaching **u.** what you say that teaches you.

### undermine 2

T-8 VIII.8:8 Holy Spirit seeks to restore, never to **u.**.
W-pI. 153.19:5 our defenses **u.** our certainty of purpose.

### undermined 1

W-pI 153.2:5 Now are the weak still further **u.**, for there

### undermining 2

T-4 II.5:1 **U.** the ego's thought system must be
T-12 I.9:7 **u.** its perceived usefulness by rendering it

### underneath 9

T-15 I.6:3 For **u.** its fanatical insistence that the past
T-18 IX.3:5 are no messages that speak of what lies **u.**,
T-21 IV.2:7 For **u.** this constant shout and frantic
T-27 VII.12:2 Yet **u.** this dream is yet another, in which
W-pI 151.1:6 a doubt because of all the doubting **u.**.
W-pI 151.5:3 **u.** remains the hidden doubt that what it
W-pI 193.4:2 Yet that is the content **u.** the form. It is
W-pII 293.2:2 *the world is singing* **u.** *the sounds of fear.*
S-3 IV.7:5 **U.** the sounds of harsh and bitter striving

### underpinnings 2

T-1 V.6:5 rests. As these false **u.** are given up, the
T-31 V.11:2 world you see, if all its **u.** were removed?

### understand 421

T-1 IV.1:5 communion but will also **u.** peace and joy
T-2 II.3:2 The means are easier to **u.** after the value
T-2 IV.1:9 not **u.** healing because of your own fear.
T-2 IV.5:3 that the recipient can **u.** without fear.
T-2 V.1:1 it is essential that they fully **u.** the fear of
T-2 VIII.2:2 This is because you do not **u.** it. Judgment
T-2 VIII.3:6 come to **u.** what is worthy and what is not
T-3 I.5:1 do not **u.** the meaning of the symbol.
T-3 VII.2:2 you really **u.** the strength of the mind.
T-4 I.9:7 you awaken you will not be able to **u.** this,
T-4 I.13:5 I could not **u.** their importance to you if I
T-4 II.11:7 be careful, however, that you really **u.** it.
T-4 III.1:1 hard to **u.** what "The Kingdom of Heaven
T-4 III.2:3 will find it very helpful if you **u.** it fully.
T-4 IV.11:11 I **u.** that miracles are natural, because
T-4 VI.1:1 the ego, you do not **u.** the situation as it is
T-5 I.4:5 makes the Holy Spirit difficult to **u.**,
T-5 III.5:6 mind would be unable to **u.** the change.
T-5 III.7:3 enables Him to **u.** the laws of God, for
T-5 III.8:1 You cannot **u.** yourself alone. This is
T-5 III.10:2 to teach you that you do not **u.** it. The
T-5 III.11:6 Spirit looks, and **u.** as He understands.
T-5 IV.6:7 are, and **u.** they belong to God as you do.
T-5 VI.9:2 be undone, a word the ego cannot even **u.**
T-6 I.2:8 will help you **u.** your own role as a teacher
T-6 I.16:1 that there was much they would **u.** later,
T-6 IV.3:1 You cannot **u.** the conflict until you fully
T-6 IV.3:1 the conflict until you fully **u.** the basic fact
T-6 V.2:4 will **u.** they need not be afraid of dreams.
T-6 V.A.4:3 you do not **u.** it and cannot use it. We
T-7 I.4:2 but it cannot **u.** that to be like another
T-7 II.4:5 laws of God to those who do not **u.** them.
T-7 II.6:6 You will not **u.** His translations while you
T-7 II.6:7 forget or relinquish one to **u.** the other.
T-7 V.1:4 unhealed healer obviously does not **u.** his
T-7 V.4:5 quite evident that he does not **u.** God if he
T-7 V.9:3 which you will love because you will **u.** it.
T-7 V.9:4 because what you **u.** you can identify with
T-7 V.9:6 love. The ego is totally unable to **u.** this,
T-7 V.9:6 this, because it does not **u.** what it makes,
T-7 VI.2:2 and therefore does not **u.** what love is. If it
T-7 VI.2:3 is. If it does not **u.** what love is, it cannot
T-7 VI.6:5 Spirit does not want you to **u.** conflict; He
T-7 VI.11:8 Do not try to **u.** it because, if you do, you
T-7 VII.10:10 it. **U.** totally by understanding totality.
T-7 VIII.4:5 It does not **u.** what mind is, and therefore
T-7 VIII.4:5 is, and therefore does not **u.** what *you* are.
T-8 I.3:8 cannot **u.** the state that prevails within it.
T-8 II.1:7 It does not **u.** anything else. As a teacher,
T-8 III.6:7 you will **u.** why you once believed that,
T-8 V.2:2 if you are to **u.** what it is and what you are
T-8 V.2:9 will realize this when you **u.** that there is
T-8 VI.6:6 You do not **u.** this because you do not
T-8 VI.6:6 this because you do not **u.** Him. No one
T-8 VI.6:7 not accept his function can **u.** what it is,
T-8 VI.8:10 You do not **u.** this, because you who are
T-8 VI.8:11 Given this belief, you cannot **u.** anything.
T-8 VII.3:2 will **u.** the power of the mind that is in
T-9 III.1:3 They **u.** this kind of sense, because it is
T-9 III.3:3 attempt to **u.** anything that arises from it.
T-9 III.3:4 Since He does not **u.** it, He does not judge
T-9 III.5:4 you cannot **u.** how all errors are undone.
T-9 III.8:9 You do not **u.** how to use it. He will teach
T-9 IV.2:2 You do not **u.** how to overlook errors, or
T-9 IV.6:3 recognizing that you do not **u.** what it is.
T-9 V.8:12 you will **u.** that you are not obeying the
T-9 VII.4:2 because you do not **u.** how lofty the Holy
T-9 VIII.1:4 this occurs, even though it does not **u.** it,
T-9 VIII.3:1 ego does not **u.** the difference between
T-10 II.4:4 **u.** that this is always an attack on truth,
T-10 II.4:5 you will **u.** why it is that you always attack
T-10 V.1:4 but they do not **u.** what it means. They do
T-10 V.14:9 will begin to **u.** eternity and make it yours
T-11 II.3:3 without meaning to you, you will not **u.** it
T-11 II.3:4 To deny meaning is to fail to **u.**. You can
T-11 II.3:6 need it because you do not **u.** yourself,
T-11 III.7:10 cannot **u.** wholeness unless you are whole
T-11 V.13:3 attempt to **u.** totality by breaking it down

| | |
|---|---|
| T-11.....V.15:1 | The ego makes no attempt to **u.** this, and |
| T-11... VIII.2:2 | that they do not **u.** what they perceive, |
| T-11... VIII.2:3 | of believing that you **u.** what you perceive |
| T-11... VIII.3:5 | is your great need, for you **u.** nothing. |
| T-11... VIII.5:1 | sufficiently specific for you to **u.** and use. |
| T-11... VIII.7:1 | child of God, you do not **u.** your Father. |
| T-11. VIII.14:4 | minds of children who do not **u.** reality. It |
| T-11VIII.14:10 | For you do not **u.** them, and because you |
| T-12.........I.1:4 | **U.** that you do not respond to anything |
| T-12.........I.2:2 | your own ability to **u.** what you perceive. |
| T-12.........I.5:1 | to tell you not to judge what you do not **u.** |
| T-12....... II.4:1 | terrify them because they do not **u.** them. |
| T-12....... II.4:4 | he recognizes that he does not **u.** what his |
| T-12....... II.4:5 | Yet you believe that you do **u.** yours. |
| T-12..... II.10:3 | You do not **u.** how to use what He knows. |
| T-12...... III.5:5 | **u.** that they dwell in abundance and that |
| T-12....... V.6:2 | to teach yourself what you do not **u.**, and |
| T-12....... V.8:6 | which you can neither provide nor **u.**, you |
| T-12.....VII.3:4 | His results, you will **u.** where He must be, |
| T-13.......in.3:7 | those who do not **u.** Him could believe it. |
| T-13.........I.6:2 | him as guiltless can you **u.** his oneness. |
| T-13.........I.8:4 | believes this can **u.** what "always" means, |
| T-13....... II.6:4 | yet **u.** that any fear you may experience in |
| T-13......V.11:5 | And all this will they **u.**, because they |
| T-13.....VII.8:2 | Yet here it *is*, and you can **u.** it *now*. God |
| T-13....... X.3:6 | they love, and cannot **u.** what loving is. |
| T-14....... II.3:9 | *And you will love it because you will* ***u.*** *it.* |
| T-14.... III.10:4 | And they will fail to **u.** the simple fact that |
| T-14.... III.10:8 | Yet because they do not **u.** their will, the |
| T-14.... III.12:5 | know not of salvation, for you do not **u.** it |
| T-14......IV.4:1 | You need not **u.** creation to do what must |
| T-14......IV.7:7 | Do not endow Him with attributes you **u.**. |
| T-14......IV.7:8 | not, and anything you **u.** is not of Him. |
| T-14......IV.8:4 | **u.** how much your Father loves you, for |
| T-14......IV.8:4 | experience of the world to help you **u.** it. |
| T-14....... V.3:6 | To accuse is *not to* ***u.***. The happy learners |
| T-14......VI.1:2 | Nothing you **u.** is fearful. It is only in |
| T-14......VI.1:5 | because you do not **u.** its meaning. If you |
| T-14......VI.6:1 | do not **u.** the language you have made. It |
| T-14......IX.6:5 | for everyone to see, no one can fail to **u.**. |
| T-14....... X.3:3 | legion. This is not difficult to **u.**, once you |
| T-14....... X.8:4 | you **u.** something of the "dynamics" of |
| T-14....... X.8:4 | let me assure you that you **u.** nothing of it |
| T-14....... X.8:5 | it. For of yourself you could not **u.** it. The |
| T-14......X.11:1 | through you, so you can **u.** them. God has |
| T-14......XI.3:5 | ever learned can help you **u.** the present, |
| T-14......XI.3:8 | attempt to **u.** any event or anything or |
| T-14....XI.12:4 | Think not you **u.** anything until you pass |
| T-15......II.4:12 | so clearly of Him that you will hear and **u.** |
| T-15......III.1:2 | But be sure you **u.** what littleness is, and |
| T-15......III.8:5 | valuing it too little to **u.** its magnitude. |
| T-15....... V.1:4 | past, for without it you do not **u.** anything |
| T-15....... V.1:5 | that you do not **u.** what anything means. |
| T-15....... V.3:1 | parts of reality and **u.** what love means. If |
| T-15....... V.3:2 | knows no special love, how can you **u.** it? |
| T-15......V.10:4 | from His, and it is impossible to **u.** it. God |
| T-15......VI.7:3 | His Self, you will learn to **u.** Selfhood. |
| T-15......VI.8:7 | you will begin to **u.** what your Creator is, |
| T-15...VII.14:8 | And you **u.** that your completion is God's, |
| T-15... VIII.5:1 | to free you of what He does not **u.**. And |
| T-15... VIII.5:3 | He would teach you what you do not **u.**. |
| T-15... VIII.5:6 | not **u.** your problem in communication, |
| T-15... VIII.6:1 | cannot know, and what you do not **u.**. It |
| T-15....... X.9:6 | of God, and therefore very easy to **u.**. Do |
| T-15......XI.7:3 | And if you **u.** this lesson, you will realize |
| T-16.........I.1:1 | for that is what you must *refuse* to **u.**. That |
| T-16.........I.1:5 | He does not **u.** suffering, and would have |
| T-16.........I.4:6 | how to respond to what you do not **u.**. Be |
| T-16....... II.1:1 | still think that holiness is impossible to **u.** |
| T-16....... II.1:3 | for the nature of miracles you do not **u.**. |
| T-16....... II.1:6 | when you do not **u.** the miracle itself? |
| T-16....... II.1:7 | is no more difficult to **u.** than is the whole |
| T-16....... II.2:2 | you think you might be better able to **u.**. |
| T-16....... II.2:4 | of miracles is this: You do not **u.** them, |
| T-16....... II.2:7 | to accomplish what you do not **u.**. And so |
| T-16....... II.2:8 | must be Something in you that *does* **u.**. |
| T-16....... II.3:2 | are told what is natural, you cannot **u.** it. |
| T-16....... II.3:5 | And if you could **u.** their meaning, their |
| T-16....... II.4:4 | of your gift enables Him to **u.** it, and you |
| T-16....... II.4:5 | that you must **u.** it or else it is not real. |
| T-16....... II.5:3 | given you, and be glad you do not **u.** it. |
| T-16.....IV.13:6 | the bridge to timelessness you **u.** nothing. |
| T-16....... VI.1:7 | impossible to define it otherwise and **u.** it. |
| T-16....... VI.9:2 | **u.** the Thought that *knows* what you are. |
| T-17...... III.1:8 | do not **u.** how they came into your mind, |
| T-17......IV.4:2 | the ego did not **u.** what had been created, |
| T-17....... V.8:1 | Accept with gladness what you do not **u.**, |
| T-18.... III.4:11 | You do not **u.** what you accepted, but |
| T-18.... III.4:12 | was necessary was merely the *wish* to **u.**. |
| T-18......IV.1:9 | holy instant far greater than you can **u.**. It |
| T-18......IV.7:6 | emphasized that you need **u.** nothing. |
| T-18....... V.4:4 | is an undertaking impossible for you to **u.** |
| T-20...... III.1:7 | truth, which calls on only what he is, to **u.** |
| T-20...... III.9:2 | takes a while for them to **u.** what freedom |
| T-20...... VI.3:4 | They do not **u.** what they are offered, and |
| T-21.........I.4:5 | They do not **u.** the lessons *keep* them blind |
| T-21..... II.10:8 | the two is merely to fail to **u.** them both. |
| T-21....... V.3:6 | ego because it does not **u.** how separate |
| T-21....... V.4:4 | mind devoid of reason **u.** what reason is, |
| T-21...... VI.4:5 | you will not **u.** the body or yourself. |
| T-21...... VI.7:9 | Reason is given you to **u.** that this is so. |
| T-21.... VI.10:4 | tell you that you can **u.** what you must be. |
| T-21.....VII.5:7 | not necessary that he **u.** how he can see it. |
| T-21.....VII.5:9 | For if he focuses on what he cannot **u.**, he |
| T-21... VIII.2:2 | you would desire it although you **u.** it not. |
| T-22.......in.1:5 | error, and one the other cannot **u.**. |
| T-22.........I.2:8 | This *you* would **u.**. The brain interprets to |
| T-22.........I.2:10 | But what it says you cannot **u.**. Yet you |
| T-22.........I.2:12 | long and hard you tried to **u.** its messages |
| T-22.........I.3:1 | to **u.** what fails entirely to reach you. You |
| T-22.........I.3:2 | have received no messages at all you **u.**. |
| T-22.........I.3:9 | it cannot be true *because* you do not **u.** it. |
| T-22.........I.5:1 | you, along with everything that you can **u.** |
| T-22.........I.5:3 | show you, you will **u.** *because* it is the truth |
| T-22.........I.5:7 | by an interpreter you cannot **u.**. |
| T-22.........I.6:1 | you have received and failed to **u.**, this |
| T-22.........I.6:3 | do not **u.** it yet only because your whole |
| T-22.........I.6:6 | and does not **u.** will be his native tongue, |
| T-22.........I.7:3 | and he will speak the language you can **u.**. |
| T-22.........I.8:2 | child will teach you what you do not **u.**, |
| T-22.... VI.13:8 | position of what you **u.** you seem to be, |
| T-23.......in.6:3 | So will you come to **u.** all that is given you |
| T-23....... II.3:3 | to **u.** that miracles apply to all of them. |
| T-23..... II.11:4 | you "**u.**" the reason why you found it not. |
| T-23...... III.4:6 | this and love for that and **u.** forgiveness. |
| T-23......IV.4:4 | Holy Spirit **u.** how to increase your little |
| T-24....... II.1:7 | **u.** it is yourself that you diminish thus. |
| T-24....... II.7:5 | it is one you and your brother both can **u.** |
| T-24.... VI.12:3 | The "sacrifice" of self you **u.**, nor do you |
| T-24.... VI.13:1 | be sure you **u.** what made this judgment. |
| T-25.........I.5:2 | may reach to you through what you **u.**. |
| T-25.........I.7:4 | It use the language that this mind can **u.**, |
| T-25....... II.7:2 | and **u.** the Mind that thought it, not in |
| T-25....... II.8:1 | and **u.** your brother as his Father's Mind |
| T-25..... II.10:5 | giving it, you learn to **u.** His gift to you. |
| T-25....... V.6:4 | forgiveness will you **u.** His Love for you; |
| T-25...... VI.7:7 | all attack, and let him **u.** that he is safe, as |
| T-25.....VII.6:1 | and **u.** that everything that meets this one |
| T-25.....VII.9:4 | Until he comes to **u.** it cost him his sanity, |
| T-25...VII.11:7 | and **u.** that it must be either God or this |
| T-25... VIII.6:1 | meaningful to **u.** the Holy Spirit's justice. |
| T-25... VIII.6:8 | than vengeance, which they **u.** and love. |
| T-25... VIII.8:2 | fair, and cannot **u.** that they are innocent. |
| T-25. VIII.12:1 | if you **u.** it is impossible the Son of God |
| T-25. VIII.13:4 | special really **u.** that justice is the same for |
| T-26....... II.1:1 | difficult to **u.** the reasons why you do not |
| T-26....... V.1:1 | do not **u.** that miracles are all the same. |
| T-26... VIII.7:6 | with "reasoning" you do not **u.** it now, |
| T-27...... III.1:9 | Who can **u.** a double concept, such as |
| T-27...... V.11:3 | let you **u.** that you have benefited from it. |
| T-27... VIII.6:4 | **u.** that time cannot intrude upon eternity. |
| T-27. VIII.11:6 | you will **u.** that miracles reflect the simple |
| T-28.........I.7:4 | And so you cannot **u.** what they are for. |
| T-28.......I.10:1 | your own Creator cannot **u.** it is not He |
| T-28.......I.14:2 | does he **u.** what he has made is causeless, |
| T-28......IV.6:6 | go, and he will **u.** what made the dream. |
| T-28....... V.4:7 | to perceive as it can judge or **u.** or know. |
| T-28...... VI.1:5 | its purpose is and cannot **u.** what it is for. |
| T-29........II.1:5 | up nothing, until you **u.** there is no loss, |
| T-29...... III.1:9 | strength could fail to **u.** this must be so. |
| T-29.... III.3:10 | and **u.** what really fills the gap so long |
| T-29....... V.6:2 | **u.** how great the cost of holding anything |
| T-29.....VII.3:2 | **u.** the idol that he seeks *is* but his death. Its |
| T-29...... IX.6:9 | laws been changed because he does not **u.** |
| T-30.......I.17:2 | two to **u.** that they cannot decide alone, |
| T-30........II.1:1 | not **u.** that to oppose the Holy Spirit is to |
| T-30......IV.5:9 | and **u.** that they are idols which but dance |
| T-30......IV.6:3 | this will be done, for this you cannot **u.**. |
| T-30......IV.6:4 | But you will **u.** that mighty changes have |
| T-30....... V.1:5 | to **u.** all things created as they really are. |
| T-30... VI.10:1 | will **u.** he could not make an error that |
| T-30.....VII.6:4 | you both can **u.** the sacrifice of meaning is |
| T-30.....VII.7:8 | and to **u.** with them forgiveness has been |
| T-31.........I.2:6 | is totally confused is easier to learn and **u.** |
| T-31.........I.8:4 | will **u.** it was this call that everyone and |
| T-31.......I.10:4 | You do not **u.** Who calls to you beyond |
| T-31........II.8:8 | will **u.** you need but come away without |
| T-31.... IV.3:10 | and in this you come to **u.** what it is for. |
| T-31......IV.4:7 | and **u.** you but waste time unless you go |
| T-31......IV.7:5 | If this be difficult to **u.**, then is this course |
| T-31...... VI.3:3 | **u.** how to behold a world apart from it. It |
| T-31...... VI.3:6 | You do not **u.** how what you see arose to |
| W-in..........4:2 | so that you will **u.** that each of them is |
| W-pI..........3.h | I do not **u.** anything I see in this room |
| W-pI.......3.2:1 | realize how little you really **u.** about them |
| W-pI.......7.1:5 | why you do not **u.** anything you see. It is |
| W-pI.......8.1:6 | It therefore cannot **u.** time, and cannot, in |
| W-pI.......8.1:6 | time, and cannot, in fact, **u.** anything. |
| W-pI.......9.1:4 | the recognition that you do not **u.** is a |
| W-pI.......9.1:6 | not need to practice what you already **u.**. |
| W-pI.....12.3:6 | may not yet **u.** why these "nice" adjectives |
| W-pI.....14.2:4 | be because you really **u.** what they are for. |
| W-pI.....15.2:2 | You will begin to **u.** it when you have seen |
| W-pI.....16.3:4 | idea in many forms before you really **u.** it. |
| W-pI.....19.2:4 | will yet **u.** that it must be true if salvation |
| W-pI.....25.4:4 | **u.** that a telephone is for the purpose of |
| W-pI.....25.4:5 | not **u.** is what you want to reach him for. |
| W-pI.....26.4:1 | to **u.** that vulnerability or invulnerability |
| W-pI.....29.3:6 | world, you will **u.** today's idea perfectly. |
| W-pI.....29.3:7 | will not **u.** how you could ever have found |
| W-pI.....41.5:1 | We **u.** that you do not believe all this. |
| W-pI.....45.5:1 | We will also try to **u.** that only what God |
| W-pI.....45.9:1 | it is to you to **u.** the holiness of the mind |
| W-pI.....51.3:1 | (3) I do not **u.** anything I see. How could I |
| W-pI.....51.3:2 | I **u.** what I see when I have judged it amiss |
| W-pI.....51.3:4 | I do not **u.** what I see because it is not |
| W-pI.....51.3:5 | There is no sense in trying to **u.** it. But |
| W-pI.....52.3:5 | Let me **u.** that I am trying to use time |
| W-pI.....55.1:4 | such things is proof that I do not **u.** God. |
| W-pI.....55.1:5 | Therefore I also do not **u.** His Son. What I |
| W-pI.....57.4:3 | I will **u.** that peace, not war, abides in it. |
| W-pI.....57.5:3 | I begin to **u.** that this peace comes from |
| W-pI.....57.5:6 | begin to **u.** the holiness of all living things |
| W-pI.....59.2:6 | so that this day may help me to **u.** eternity |
| W-pI.....59.4:6 | to **u.** that God is the light in which I see. |
| W-pI.....61.2:2 | the ego does not **u.** humility, mistaking it |
| W-pI.....62.3:2 | to **u.** what forgiveness will do for you? It |
| W-pI.....65.3:1 | in which you try to **u.** and accept what the |
| W-pI...72.10:3 | it, we cannot **u.** what God's plan for us is. |
| W-pI...72.10:8 | *Tell me, that I may* ***u.***. Then we will wait in |
| W-pI...72.12:4 | *Tell me, that I may* ***u.***. He will answer. Be |
| W-pI.....74.3:1 | firm determination to **u.** what they mean, |
| W-pI.....75.7:2 | **U.** that the Holy Spirit never fails to give |
| W-pI.....76.1:4 | Yet to **u.** that this is so, you must first |
| W-pI.....76.5:5 | It would not **u.** it is its own enemy; that it |
| W-pI.....79.6:3 | you would **u.** that you have the means to |
| W-pI.....81.3:4 | function is, for I do not yet **u.** forgiveness. |
| W-pI.....90.1:3 | Let me also **u.** that the solution is always a |
| W-pI.....90.3:7 | I will **u.** it is impossible that I could have a |
| W-pI.....95.2:5 | It does not **u.** you are the Son of God, for |
| W-pI...95.14:8 | as possible, and **u.** each time you do so, |
| W-pI.....97.4:4 | to help you **u.** with Him you are the spirit |
| W-pI.....98.9:2 | will enable you to **u.** your special function |
| W-pI... 100.6:1 | will attempt to **u.** joy is our function here. |
| W-pI... 105.1:3 | try to **u.** these gifts increase as we receive |
| W-pI... 105.5:3 | You will **u.** that what completes Him |
| W-pI... 106.7:3 | practice giving, not the way you **u.** it now, |

W-pI...106.8:4 world becomes ready to **u.** and to receive.
W-pI.110.10:3 you will **u.** how worthless are your idols,
WpI. rIII.in2:1 **u.**, of course, that it may be impossible for
W-pI...123.8:1 will **u.** how lovingly He holds you in His
W-pI.124.11:1 **u.** the sinless light you see belongs to you;
W-pI.124.11:2 will be a sense of love you cannot **u.**, a joy
W-pI.124.11:3 you will **u.** and comprehend and see.
W-pI...126.1:3 **u.** the means by which salvation comes to
W-pI...126.6:1 You do not **u.** forgiveness. As you see it,
W-pI...126.8:1 Today we try to **u.** the truth that giver
W-pI...126.9:1 today to the attempt to **u.** today's idea. It
W-pI.126.10:1 the world that does not **u.** forgiveness,
W-pI.126.10:4 you, and you will **u.** the words He speaks,
W-pI...127.2:5 believe these things of love is not to **u.** it.
W-pI...127.7:2 **u.** there is no better use for time than this.
W-pI...127.9:4 today, and help you **u.** the truth of love.
W-pI...129.8:3 your mind can see it plainly, and can **u.**.
W-pI...129.9:1 Now do we **u.** there is no loss. For we
W-pI.131.13:2 clear that you can **u.** all things you see.
W-pI...132.5:4 mind if you would **u.** the lesson for today.
W-pI...132.7:2 form which they can **u.** and recognize.
W-pI.132.16:2 although you may not fully **u.** as yet that
W-pI...138.2:5 is reflected in some form the world can **u.**.
WpI. rIV.in4:4 our minds to **u.** the lessons that we read,
W-pI...151.3:7 This is awareness that you **u.**, and think
W-pI...153.5:3 You do not **u.** how much you have been
W-pI...154.3:2 it to you, giving you the strength to **u.** it,
W-pI...154.7:2 they **u.** the messages by giving them away
W-pI...154.8:6 No one can receive and **u.** he has received
W-pI...155.4:4 of loss still deeper, which they did not **u.**.
W-pI...155.9:4 something they **u.** to lead the way.
W-pI...159.2:1 You **u.** that you are healed when you give
W-pI.166.10:5 There was a need He did not **u.**, to which
W-pI.166.13:2 do not **u.** they but pursue their wishes. It
W-pI.167.11:3 have no opposite, we **u.** there is one life,
W-pI.169.10:1 clarify what no one in the world can **u.**.
WpI...rV.in2:5 *lead a little child along a way he does not* **u.**.
WpI...rV.in6:4 I must **u.** uncertainty and pain, although I
W-pI...182.3:4 He does not **u.** he builds in vain. The
W-pI...184.9:5 communicate in ways the world can **u.**,
W-pI.184.10:2 Here you **u.** the Word, the Name which
W-pI.184.14:1 Son, we **u.** that they have but one Name,
W-pI...185.6:2 mind that seeks for it in honesty can **u.**.
W-pI.190.10:1 Here will you **u.** there is no pain. Here
W-pI...192.2:2 **u.** a language far beyond his simple grasp
W-pI...192.7:3 think we **u.** is but confusion born of error.
W-pI...193.1:2 His Will extends to what He does not **u.**,
W-pI...194.4:4 And so you are not asked to **u.** the lack of
W-pI...196.1:4 And you will **u.** his safety is your own,
W-pI...196.2:1 Perhaps at first you will not **u.** how
W-pI...196.2:3 Yet must it fail to **u.** the truth it uses thus.
W-pI...196.8:3 For once you **u.** it is impossible that you
WpI rVI.in.4:4 from all we did not know and failed to **u.**.
W-pII ..in.10:2 come to **u.** that we need only call to God,
W-pII .240.2:4 *in Your Name, that we may* **u.** *his holiness,*
W-pII .242.1:2 I do not **u.** the world, and so to try to lead
W-pII .243.1:3 I **u.** the whole from bits of my perception,
W-pII .248.2:4 *and my own. Now do I* **u.** *that they are one.*
W-pII .275.1:2 we will seek and hear and learn and **u.**.
W-pII .275.1:4 God tells us of things we cannot **u.** alone,
W-pII .286.1:3 *to* **u.** *the lesson that there is no need that I do*
W-pII .299.1:1 far beyond my own ability to **u.** or know.
W-pII .301.2:3 We wept because we did not **u.**. But we
W-pII .302.1:7 *its holiness and* **u.** *it but reflects my own.*
W-pII .311.1:4 be. It judges what it cannot **u.**, because it
W-pII .321.1:1 *I did not* **u.** *what made me free, nor what my*
W-pII .337.1:6 from harm, to **u.** my Father loves His Son;
W-pII ...13.2:2 because it fails entirely to **u.** its ways.
W-pII ...13.4:1 of what it cannot see and does not **u.**. Yet
Wfl ........in.5:4 sanity, in which we **u.** that anger is insane
Wfl ........in.5:7 at his son because he failed to **u.** the truth
Wfl ........in.6:1 in honesty to God and say we did not **u.**,
M-2 ........... 2:1 order to **u.** the teaching-learning plan of
M-3 ........... 3:1 is difficult to **u.** that levels of teaching the
M-4 ..... I.A.4:5 It takes great learning to **u.** that all things,
M-4 ..... I.A.7:2 Now must the teacher of God **u.** that he
M-5 ...... III.1:5 for those who do not **u.** what healing is.
M-12 ......... 3:6 A voice they **u.** and listen to, without the
M-12 ......... 4:3 the mind will **u.** because of their Source.
M-13 ......... 3:1 for the mind to **u.** that all the "pleasures"
M-14 ......... 3:8 Can you **u.** this? No; it is meaningless to
M-20 ......... 5:7 and you will **u.** that everything that God
M-21 ......... 1:7 God does not **u.** words, for they were
M-23 ......... 7:1 you in a language you can love and **u.**. Are
M-26 ......... 4:4 you must **u.** what needs to be escaped.
M-29 ....... 2:11 for decisions about which you **u.** so little?
C-2 .......... 1:10 name it but to help us **u.** that it is nothing
C-2 .......... 10:6 **u.** the way is short and Heaven is his goal?
P-1 ............. 4:2 and to **u.** that what he thought projected
P-2 ..........II.7:5 does not **u.** that healing comes from God.
P-2 ........ IV.5:5 who can **u.** this without the Word of God,
P-2 ......... V.7:8 of Christ, and **u.** that it is but our own.
P-2 ........ VI.1:6 **u.** that it is he who sings it to himself. To
P-2 ....... VII.9:1 as this, if you but **u.** your proper role. But
P-3 ...........I.4:9 be able to hear the call and **u.** that it is his
P-3 ..........II.8:6 Even those who have begun to **u.** what
P-3 ..........II.9:4 **u.** there is no order of difficulty in healing
P-3 ........ III.2:9 for he could never **u.** what healing is. He
S-1 ........ III.6:9 Think of the cost, and **u.** it well. All other
S-1 ......... V.3:2 you how to **u.** your glory as God's Son,
S-2 ........ III.1:7 asks, and seeks to **u.** the Will of God. His
S-2 ........ III.2:3 then, seek to **u.** what is beyond you yet,
S-2 ........ III.4:4 His is a justice He can **u.**, but you cannot
S-2 ........ III.5:7 that you can **u.** and you can also use. Do
S-3 ........ III.5:1 and **u.** that all their Source creates is one
S-3 ........ IV.7:3 I love, who does not **u.** that he is healed,

## understandable 16

*See also* un-understandable

T-4 ....... III.1:2 This is because it is not **u.** to the ego,
T-5 ....... III.6:1 one level of the mind is not **u.** to another.
T-7 ....... VI.6:5 conflict is meaningless, it is not **u.**. As I
T-9 ........ V.3:7 is **u.** that there have been revolts against
T-11 .... V.15:1 to understand this, and it is clearly not **u.**,
T-15 ...VIII.5:7 It is only you who believe that it is **u.**. The
T-15 ...VIII.5:8 The Holy Spirit knows that it is not **u.**,
T-16 ..........I.1:5 and would have you teach it is not **u.**.
T-22 ..........I.5:7 will it ever be made **u.** by an interpreter
T-25 ...VIII.8:3 Love is not **u.** to sinners because they
W-pI..... 51.3:4 understand what I see because it is not **u.**.
W-pI... 161.4:6 yet fundamentally not understood nor **u.**.
M-11 ......... 3:6 is the un-understandable made **u.**. How is
M-12 ......... 3:2 because reality is not **u.** to the deluded.
C-4 .......... 5:11 then will overlook will not be **u.** to you,
C-4 ............ 7:1 changeless, certain, pure and wholly **u.**,

## understanding 124

T-2 ..........II.1:8 Your **u.** will then inevitably value wrongly
T-2 ..........II.1:9 of "the peace of God which passeth **u.**."
T-2 ......... V.4:1 his own readiness is endangering his **u.**.
T-3 ...........I.8:4 The **u.** of the innocent is truth. That is
T-3 ..........II.5:9 U. the lesson of the Atonement they are
T-4 ..........II.1:4 and examples are irrelevant to its **u.**.
T-4 ........ III.4:6 ambivalence the concept is beyond its **u.**.
T-5 ........ III.7:4 ego makes, not by destruction but by **u.**
T-5 ........ III.7:5 U. is light, and light leads to knowledge.
T-5 ...... III.11:7 His **u.** looks back to God in remembrance
T-7 ....... V.6:11 U. means consistency because God means
T-7 ......... V.9:4 it. U. is appreciation, because what you
T-7 ......... V.9:5 is how God Himself created you; in **u.**, in
T-7 ........ VI.6:6 **u.** brings appreciation and appreciation
T-7 ........ VI.8:5 the light of your **u.** would dispel it. It
T-7 ........ VI.9:5 fact. They are problems of **u.**, since their
T-7 .... VII.10:7 as lonely without **u.** this as God Himself is
T-7 .... VII.10:8 The peace of God is **u.** this. There is only
T-7 .. VII.10:10 into it. Understand totally by **u.** totality.
T-8 ........ III.1:4 want **u.** and enlightenment you will learn
T-8 ........ III.1:7 U. His function perfectly He fulfills it
T-8 .... VII.12:5 confusion that blocks the **u.** of both.
T-9 ........ V.6:5 unless it is understood, since light *is* **u.**. A
T-9 ....... VI.7:4 perfect communication born of perfect **u.**.
T-11 ..........II.1:5 to Him because, in your perfect **u.** of Him,
T-11 ..........II.1:6 and His Kingdom your **u.** is not perfect,
T-11 ..........II.2:1 Healing thus becomes a lesson in **u.**, and
T-11 ...... IV.1:6 hate part of your Self all your **u.** is lost,
T-11 ....... V.3:1 this lesson in "ego dynamics" by **u.** that
T-11 ..... V.13:4 that power, **u.** and truth lie in separation,
T-11 .... VII.3:9 because it will make you capable of **u.** it.
T-11 ... VIII.3:6 do not accept it, for **u.** is your inheritance.
T-11 . VIII.14:5 is only their lack of **u.** that frightens them,
T-13 ..........II.9:5 In this **u.** lies your remembering, for it is
T-13 ...... IV.6:6 you from awakening and **u.** they are past.
T-13 ..... VII.8:1 of God passeth your **u.** only in the past.
T-14 ... IV.10:1 are totally incapable of **u.** one another.
T-14 ...... VI.1:1 of dark for light, of ignorance for **u.**.
T-14 ... VIII.4:3 gentle **u.** which can lead you nowhere else
T-14 .........X.8:1 The ego is incapable of **u.** content, and is
T-14 ...... XI.3:9 at all in darkness to illuminate your **u.**,
T-14 .... XI.12:4 peace and **u.** go together and never can be
T-14 .... XI.13:1 unless the effects of **u.** are with them, can
T-14 .... XI.14:3 reciprocate, for His faith in you is His **u.**.
T-14 .... XI.14:8 For **u.** is in you, and from it peace must
T-15 ...........I.7:3 is what prevents you from **u.** the present,
T-15 ...... VI.7:5 But remember that **u.** is of the mind, and
T-16 ...........I.1:7 **u.** that healing pain is not accomplished
T-16 ..........II.2:3 you would still try to keep **u.** to yourself.
T-16 ..........II.2:6 Therefore your **u.** cannot be necessary.
T-16 ..........II.4:4 it, and you to use His **u.** on your behalf. It
T-16 ..........II.5:6 His **u.** of the miracle be enough for you,
T-16 ... VI.11:1 over will be the **u.** of where Heaven *is.*
T-17 ...........I.4:5 of reality is a perspective without **u.**; a
T-17 ...... VI.1:7 in an **u.** far broader than you now possess
T-17 ...... VI.3:7 **u.** doubtful and evaluation impossible.
T-17 ...... VI.7:5 Thus do you lose the **u.** of the situation
T-17 ..... VII.1:6 in the way of **u.** would have been removed
T-18 ... III.4:11 remember that your **u.** is not necessary.
T-18 ...... IV.7:5 still convinced that your **u.** is a powerful
T-18 ..........V.2:6 On your little faith, joined with His **u.**, He
T-20 ..... V.7:10 His **u.** recognize it and love it as your own
T-20 ...... VI.9:4 instant, which offers you peace and **u.**?
T-21 ..........II.7:7 to make or do what lies beyond your **u.**.
T-21 ...... III.8:4 faith had limited their **u.** of the world,
T-21 ... VIII.2:1 of joy is a condition quite alien to your **u.**.
T-22 ...........I.5:2 will perceive no difficulty in **u.** what this
T-22 ...........I.6:1 is open to your **u.** and can be understood.
T-22 ..........II.8:6 *How* He will do it is beyond your **u.**, but
T-22 ...... III.6:8 sight of form means **u.** has been obscured
T-23 ..........II.1:4 may look beyond them, **u.** what they are,
T-25 ...........I.5:4 separate, and Christ abides within your **u.**
T-25 ..........V.6:5 the **u.** that he is the way to Heaven or to
T-25 . VIII.12:4 The **u.** that you need comes not of you,
T-25 . VIII.12:6 His **u.** will be yours. And so the Holy
T-26 .. VII.12:6 still feel guilty, though without **u.** why.
T-30 ...... III.2:9 you want, you lose the **u.** of its purpose.
T-30 ..........V.2:1 it is thought that **u.** is acquired by attack.
T-30 ..........V.2:2 There, it is clear that by attack is **u.** lost.
T-30 ..........V.4:2 how this can be, for **u.** this is Heaven itself
T-30 ..........V.8:6 His gratitude to you is past your **u.**, for
T-30 ...... VI.3:1 This **u.** is the only change that lets the
T-31 ..... V.12:4 is some **u.** that you chose for both of you,
W-pI ....... 9.1:3 However, **u.** is not necessary at this point.
W-pI ....... 9.1:5 are concerned with practice, not with **u.**.
W-pI ....... 9.1:7 It would indeed be circular to aim at **u.**,
W-pI ....... 9.2:5 **u.** will finally come to lighten every corner
W-pI ..... 25.2:3 you incapable of **u.** what anything is for.
W-pI ..... 42.5:2 **u.** some of your thoughts contain. Let
W-pI ..... 45.8:7 with the little **u.** you have already gained,
W-pI ..... 58.1:5 Seen through **u.** eyes, the holiness of the
W-pI ..... 58.4:5 unafraid, everyone must share in my **u.**,
W-pI ..... 70.1:6 in the same place. In **u.** this you are saved.
W-pI ..... 80.1:4 problem, and **u.** that it has been solved.
W-pI .. 101.1:2 is a key idea in **u.** what salvation means.
W-pI .. 108.4:3 **u.** is the base on which all opposites are
W-pI 126.10:2 and ask for help in **u.** what it really means
W-pI 134.11:3 his dream by **u.** what he thought he saw
W-pI 134.13:2 that leads to any **u.** of the laws it follows,
W-pI .. 138.9:3 is veiled in shadows must be raised to **u.**,
WpI..rIV.in3:1 our preparation with some **u.** of the many
WpI...rV.in1:3 we are preparing for another phase of **u.**.
W-pI .. 188.5:3 And the means for giving it are in his **u.**.
W-pI .. 192.7:3 Our **u.** is so limited that what we think we
W-pII . 347.1:7 *it is not real, and in His* **u.** *it is healed. He*
M-2 ........... 1:2 is best for them in view of their level of **u.**.
M-4 ...... VI.1:4 comes from their **u.** Who created them.
M-5 ........... 1:1 an **u.** of what the illusion of sickness is for

M-8 1:7 Look not to them for peace and **u.**.
M-8 6:5 Teacher; the **u.** that only two categories
M-12 4:4 From this **u.** will come the recognition, in
M-16 1:4 Seeing this and **u.** that it is true, he rests
M-20 6:2 simple **u.** that His Will is wholly without
M-26 1:6 have not attained the necessary **u.** as yet,
C-1 3:3 an equivalent of "spirit," with the **u.** that,
P-3 I.4:8 Who calls on him is far beyond his **u.**. Yet
P-3 II.5:8 His **u.** begins with recognizing this, and
P-3 II.7:2 This is a necessary **u.** for the healed healer
P-3 II.7:4 can hold this **u.** consistently in his mind,
P-3 II.7:5 and let their **u.** remain on earth until the
P-3 III.5:8 will lose this **u.** unless they remember
S-1 II.3:2 in honest belief, though not yet with **u.**. A
S-2 III.1:8 far beyond your **u.** and your simple grasp.
S-3 IV.4:4 And in this **u.** you are healed. In prayer

## understands 52

T-5 III.6:3 of God, so the Holy Spirit **u.** it perfectly.
T-5 III.10:2 only what your mind already **u.** to teach
T-5 III.11:6 Spirit looks, and understand as He **u.**. His
T-6 I.2:6 release from fear to anyone who **u.** it.
T-7 IV.4:1 Spirit, Who **u.** how to use them properly.
T-7 IV.4:4 but the Holy Spirit **u.** that your forgetting
T-8 III.2:4 The Holy Spirit **u.** how to teach this, but
T-12 I.6:6 one Teacher of reality, Who **u.** what it is.
T-12 V.9:2 Him and **u.** His curriculum for learning it.
T-14 III.10:8 will, the Holy Spirit quietly **u.** it for them,
T-15 I.15:3 time for you **u.** what time is for. Holiness
T-15 VIII.5:8 and yet He **u.** it because you made it.
T-15 IX.1:5 for it is the only step in it He **u.**. Therefore
T-16 I.2:4 Having identified with what it thinks it **u.**,
T-16 VII.10:4 Messenger **u.** how to restore the Kingdom
T-23 IV.4:5 Also He **u.** how your relationship is raised
T-25 VIII.9:5 but **u.** as well that you cannot accept it for
T-26 III.6:2 For no one **u.** what is the same, and seems
T-26 IV.4:6 so that he **u.** that love cannot be feared?
T-27 V.8:2 And no one **u.** the nature of his problem.
T-27 V.10:1 learning to the One Who really **u.** its laws,
T-27 VIII.4:5 he **u.** he gave them their effects by causing
T-28 I.14:4 **u.** he never had a need for doing anything
T-30 V.4:5 of God knows everything his Father **u.**,
T-30 V.4:5 understands, and **u.** it perfectly with Him.
T-31 I.3:1 No one who **u.** what you have learned,
T-31 VII.6:4 mind. Give it instead to Him Who **u.** the
T-31 VII.8:6 and **u.** he looks on everyone as he beholds
W-pI 95.2:5 of God, for it is senseless and **u.** nothing.
W-pI.134.14:4 Guide Who **u.** the meaning of forgiveness
W-pI 136.1:1 one can heal unless he **u.** what purpose
W-pI 136.1:2 he **u.** as well its purpose has no meaning.
W-pI 140.4:2 For the mind which **u.** that sickness can
W-pI 160.2:1 and **u.** what truth regards as senseless.
WpI.. rV.in4:5 Its Thoughts; knows Its Creator, **u.** Itself,
W-pI 182.2:5 would deny he **u.** the words we speak?
W-pI 187.6:2 Who **u.** what giving means must laugh at
W-pI 198.2:4 It is not a law that knowledge **u.**, for
W-pII 7.3:2 The Holy Spirit **u.** the means you made,
W-pII..299.1:3 Our Will, together, **u.** it. And Our Will,
W-pII..303.1:5 And let Him hear the sounds He **u.**, and
W-pII..347.1:7 *He looks on pain, and yet He* **u.** *it is not real,*
M-4 VI.1:6 God until he fully **u.** that defenses are but
M-21 3:11 Spirit alone **u.** what this Word stands for.
M-29 6:2 He **u.** the requests of your heart, and
M-29 6:6 He **u.** that an attack is a call for help. And
P-2 IV.4:2 can cure, and not one of them **u.** healing.
P-2 VII.6:4 **u.** all power in earth and Heaven belongs
P-3 I.4:2 **u.** that his part is necessary to the whole,
S-1 III.2:3 come from one who **u.** that they are calls
S-3 I.3:3 by a mind which **u.** that it must overlook
S-3 III.1:4 it made by one who **u.** the other is exactly

## understating 1

T-1 VII.5:4 Atonement without either over- or **u.** it. I

## understood 122

T-1 IV.4:4 itself, if properly **u.**, offers only protection
T-2 IV.2:10 When it is **u.** that the mind, the only level
T-2 IV.3:6 if properly **u.**, shares the invulnerability
T-2 V.10:7 It must be **u.**, however, that whenever you
T-2 V.A.15:2 this has occurred healing cannot be **u.**.
T-2 VII.6:6 of wholeness in the true sense be **u.**. Any
T-3 I.5:2 Correctly **u.**, it is a very simple symbol
T-3 II.1:2 cannot be **u.** in terms of opposites. It is
T-3 V.7:2 "Image" can be **u.** as "thought," and
T-3 VII.3:1 before, but its meaning must be clearly **u.**.
T-4 in.1:5 properly **u.** is the opposite of fatigue. To
T-4 II.11:11 is it **u.** by being compared to an opposite.
T-5 II.2:4 not have **u.** the Call to right thinking. The
T-5 IV.2:11 must be **u.** as a pure act of sharing. That is
T-5 IV.4:1 because I **u.** that I could not atone for
T-5 VI.9:1 if the word "perish" is **u.** as "be undone."
T-6 I.1:5 in what it teaches, if it is properly **u.**.
T-6 I.3:5 must be fully **u.** *as* impossible. Otherwise,
T-6 I.15:4 Judas as they did, if they had really **u.** me.
T-6 V.3:5 easily **u.** and very easily remembered.
T-7 I.7:4 It must be **u.** that the word "first" as
T-7 II.7:6 no translation because it is perfectly **u.**,
T-7 V.6:10 is consistent it cannot be inconsistently **u.**
T-7 VI.6:7 Nothing else can be **u.**, because nothing
T-7 VI.11:8 believing that it can be **u.** and is therefore
T-7 VIII.2:1 of projection must be fully **u.** before the
T-7 VIII.6:4 cannot be **u.** because it is unbelievable.
T-8 VI.4:1 he had not **u.** its worthlessness at the time
T-8 VII.12:4 the One Light in which it can be really **u.**.
T-9 V.6:5 Nothing will change unless it is **u.**, since
T-10 IV.4:3 their laws cannot be **u.** together. The laws
T-12 V.5:7 If they **u.** what is beyond them, they
T-12 V.9:1 Your learning potential, properly **u.**, is
T-13 II.8:1 from guilt, and this is correct if it is **u.**.
T-13 III.10:5 shattered, for he no longer **u.** his Father.
T-14 XI.15:6 by which you recognize that you have **u.**.
T-15 V.11:6 has meaning, and only there can it be **u.**.
T-15 VI.7:4 And therein is love's meaning **u.**. But
T-16 V.1:3 All these must be **u.** for what they are.
T-16 VII.6:4 holy instant it is **u.** that the past is gone,
T-17 VI.1:3 The simple is merely what is easily **u.**, and
T-18 V.1:2 If you already **u.** the difference between
T-19 I.8:1 **u.** how much this strange concealment
T19..IV.B.12:2 It is essential that this relationship be **u.**,
T19 IV.B.14:11 if he but **u.** he sends them to himself?
T-20 VI.2:5 to be known, completely **u.** and shared. It
T-20 VIII.7:4 What if you really **u.** you made it up?
T-21 II.1:3 that it cannot fail to be completely **u.**.
T-22 I.6:1 open to your understanding and can be **u.**
T-22 III.1:7 If it is not the body's sight, it *must* be **u.**.
T-22 III.1:9 It can be **u.**. And here do reason and the
T-23 II.1:1 can be brought to light, though never **u.**.
T-23 II.1:5 It is essential it be **u.** what they are for,
T-23 III.3:10 as one. Does this make sense? Can it be **u.**
T-24 VI.7:6 at last in terms you recognized and **u.**?
T-24 VII.6:10 a holy home for your creations is it **u.**.
T-24 VII.8:5 upside down until its purpose has been **u.**
T-25 I.5:6 In this world this is not **u.**, but can be
T-25 I.6:3 But this is **u.** by mind perceived as one,
T-25 VI.6:4 is seen and **u.** as each one takes his part in
T-25 VII.8:4 which he lives, and thought he **u.** before.
T-26 VII.1:2 the laws of healing must be **u.** before the
T-26 VII.11:6 It is not **u.** apart from Him, and therefore
T-27 II.16:2 With half a mind this is not **u.**. Leave,
T-27 V.11:8 Infinity cannot be **u.** by merely counting
T-28 II.6:2 design exists that could be found and **u.**.
T-28 V.5:5 sights that *can* be seen and heard and **u.**.
T-29 IV.1:3 that you have **u.** that dreams are dreams;
T-30 I.15:4 Let this be **u.**, and you can see there
T-30 I.17:3 For they have **u.** the basic law that makes
T-30 V.1:6 things must be first forgiven, and *then* **u.**.
T-30 V.2:4 is **u.** as the sole cause of pain in any form.
T-30 V.2:6 by which it can be gained can now be **u.**.
T-30 V.5:3 has **u.** that idols are nothing and nowhere
T-30 VII.6:7 no light by which they can be seen and **u.**.
T-31 I.9:2 call to life, and **u.** that it is but your own.
T-31 IV.5:1 of the world, unless he **u.** their real futility
W-pI 25.4:3 Yet purpose cannot be **u.** at these levels.
W-pI 51.3:6 for what can be seen and **u.** and loved. I
W-pI 76.11:4 and **u.** there are no laws but God's. Then
W-pI 92.2:2 If you but **u.** the nature of thought, you
W-pI 100.2:5 be **u.** by those to whom He sends you.
W-pI 108.4:2 Here it is **u.** that both occur together, that
W-pI.108.10:2 will be far better **u.** from this time on, and
W-pI 129.3:3 language is unspoken and yet surely **u.**.
W-pI 137.6:4 that can be seen and justified and fully **u.**.
W-pI 138.9:2 alternatives are accurately seen and **u.**. All
W-pI 161.4:6 fundamentally not **u.** nor understandable
W-pI.169.10:2 comes, it will be known and fully **u.**. Now
W-pI 193.6:2 these words when we have **u.** their power
W-pI 196.1:1 this is firmly **u.** and kept in full awareness
WpI rVI.in.2:2 Each contains the whole curriculum if **u.**,
WpI rVI.in.4:3 forget all that we thought we knew and **u.**.
W-pII .321.1:4 *made nor* **u.** *the way to find my freedom. But*
W-pII .344.1:2 *own. I have not* **u.** *what giving means, and*
W-pII 359.h And all sin Is **u.** as merely a mistake.
M-2 3:4 What has been learned and **u.** and long
M-4 I.A.3:3 and it is rarely **u.** initially that their lack of
M-4 IV.2:8 for they have **u.** their evil thoughts came
M-4 VIII.1:7 Perhaps it was not **u.** at the time. Even so,
M-4 X.1:1 is easily **u.** when its relation to forgiveness
M-22 3:1 That forgiveness is healing needs to be **u.**
M-22 7:7 Yet this will not be **u.** until God's teacher
M-26 2:8 The time will come when this is **u.**. And
M-28 4:6 light their purpose is transformed and **u.**.
M-28 6:7 has heard God's Word and **u.** its meaning
C-3 3:3 the content it is His Will that it be **u.**. And
C-3 8:5 God is not seen but only **u.**. His Son is not
P-1 2:6 For psychotherapy, correctly **u.**, teaches
P-2 IV.5:4 overcome until the meaning of love is **u.**.
P-2 IV.11:5 Seen rightly, its purpose can be **u.**. What
P-3 II.7:1 because only then it can be **u.** that there is
P-3 III.5:6 they have heard His Word and **u.** it. All
S-1 II.8:8 to its attainment, however, need to be **u.**,
S-1 III.1:4 Praying for others, if rightly **u.**, becomes a
S-1 V.3:12 For you have **u.** he never left, and you,
S-2 I.1:4 at first, because salvation is not **u.**, *nor*
S-2 II.3:1 form, still very like the first if it is **u.**, does
S-3 II.1:2 kindly meant but not completely **u.** as yet
S-3 III.6:5 any more be feared because it has been **u.**.
S-3 IV.4:3 You have **u.** that you forgive and pray but
S-3 IV.4:5 Source, and **u.** that you have never left.

## undertake 39

T-2 IV.1:8 To **u.** this you cannot be fearful yourself.
T-2 V.1:1 are ready to **u.** their function in this world
T-4 in.3:11 We have another journey to **u.**, and if you
T-4 in.3:11 carefully they will help prepare you to **u.**
T-4 I.13:6 Let us **u.** to learn this lesson together so
T-4 III.10:4 would **u.** to believe what is not true, and
T-9 III.8:2 Do not **u.** His function, or you will forget
T-11 II.4:3 to go far beyond the healing you would **u.**
T-11 III.5:4 you but **u.** a journey that is not real. The
T-12 IV.5:1 You *will* **u.** a journey because you are not
T-13 VII.14:1 Whenever you are tempted to **u.** a useless
T-13 VII.15:3 you **u.** a quiet journey to the peace of God
T-14 III.13:3 Every decision you **u.** alone but signifies
T-14 VI.1:1 The journey that we **u.** together is the
T-14 X.10:6 it. If you **u.** the search together, you bring
T-15 III.4:5 of littleness is a task the little cannot **u.**.
T-17 II.5:2 of perception will **u.** with you the careful
T-26 V.2:5 Nothing you **u.** with certain purpose and
T-29 I.5:5 to go there, what is feasible for you to **u.**,
T-31 IV.4:2 that all must **u.** who still believe there is
W-in 2:6 **u.** to do more than one set of exercises a
W-pI 65.4:1 to **u.** the daily extended practice periods
W-pI 69.2:2 Before we **u.** this in our more extended
W-pI 69.8:5 that what you **u.** with God must succeed.
W-pI 70.6:2 still let you decide when to **u.** them. We
W-pI 73.6:9 We **u.** it with your blessing and your glad
W-pI 73.8:1 we **u.** the exercises for today in happy
W-pI 86.1:6 I will **u.** no more idle seeking. Only God's
WpI. rIII.in2:1 it may be impossible for you to **u.** what is
WpI. rIII.in8:2 divide them so you **u.** one in the morning,
W-pI 122.9:1 we **u.** our practicing today with hope and
W-pI.135.14:2 mind would **u.** its own protection, at the
W-pI.135.17:1 the plans you **u.** to make against the truth
W-pI 137.9:2 how little practice you need **u.** to let His

WpI. rIV.in2:1 that unifies each step in the review we **u.**,
W-pI. 154.10:1 this joining that we **u.** to recognize today.
W-pI... 158.3:6 We but **u.** a journey that is over. Yet it
WpI...rV.in1:2 more effort and more time to what we **u.**.
W-pII ....in.7:8 certainty, we **u.** these last few steps to You

## undertaken 25

T-2...........I.2:4 Extension, as **u.** by God, is similar to the
T-2......VIII.3:1 thought of as a procedure **u.** by God.
T-2......VIII.3:2 it will be **u.** by my brothers with my help.
T-4......... V.5:3 Meaningful seeking is consciously **u.**,
T-4........ VI.8:3 It cannot be **u.** successfully by those who
T-9......... V.1:2 This is because it is **u.** by unhealed healers
T-14....... II.1:4 confused you that you have **u.** to learn to
T-16...... IV.1:3 is hidden, is **u.** solely to offset the hate,
T-17.... IV.10:4 And your defense must now be **u.**, to keep
T-17....... V.5:5 **u.** by two individuals for their unholy
T-19...... IV.2:3 nothing **u.** with the Holy Spirit remains
T19... IV.A.5:5 fail to be accomplished, wherever it is **u.**?
T-20.........I.3:1 the whole journey the Son of God has **u.**.
T-20...... III.1:4 in fact, is lost if any shift or change is **u.**.
T-23.........I.5:1 The war against yourself was **u.** to teach
W-pI..... 11.2:1 for today's idea are to be **u.** somewhat
W-pI..... 11.4:2 to do more, as many as five may be **u.**.
W-pI..... 19.3:1 require is to be **u.** with eyes closed. The
W-pI..... 24.3:2 practice periods which should be **u.** today
W-pI..... 34.2:2 an additional one to be **u.** at any time in
W-pI..... 43.4:2 third may be **u.** at the most convenient
W-pI..... 61.5:1 periods as possible should be **u.** today,
W-pI..... 65.8:1 which should be **u.** at least once an hour,
W-pI... 66.11:1 be most helpful today if **u.** twice an hour,
W-pI..... 74.7:1 **u.** at regular and predetermined intervals

## undertakes 4

T-12...... IV.2:1 ego **u.** is therefore bound to be defeated.
T19. IV.D.21:2 And no one **u.** to do what he believes is
T-22....... II.6:4 and no one **u.** to do what holds no hope
W-pI..... 95.4:2 mind to wander, if it **u.** extended practice.

## undertaking 5

T-4....... VII.4:2 communication is judged to be worth **u.**.
T-5........ III.4:6 are **u.** an ego-alien journey with the ego as
T-18....... V.4:4 is an **u.** impossible for you to understand.
W-pI..... 20.1:2 no attempt to direct the time for **u.** them,
W-pI... 107.8:1 with you upon this **u.** that He be in your

## undertakings 2

T-14....... X.8:7 the **u.** of students who would "analyze" it,
W-pI... 124.1:2 and strength available to us in all our **u.**.

## undertook 4

T-1........ III.1:1 process of Atonement, which I **u.** to begin
T-6.........I.11:6 I **u.** to show this was true in an extreme
T-17..... V.11:1 You **u.**, together, to invite the Holy Spirit
T-18...... III.8:5 meaningless journey that you **u.** apart,

## undeserved 3

W-pI... 126.4:1 a charitable whim, benevolent yet **u.**, a
W-pI... 126.5:2 choose to give indulgently an **u.** reprieve.
W-pI... 134.1:1 righteous wrath, a gift unjustified and **u.**,

## undesirable 5

T-6...... V.C.3:4 between the desirable and the **u.**. It
T-7..... VII.11:1 insane, wholly delusional and wholly **u.**,
T-14..... VII.4:1 on bringing what is **u.** to the desirable;
W-pI..... 35.4:2 positive or negative, desirable or **u.**,
M-8 ......... 3:11 is seen is real or illusory, desirable or **u.**,

## undesired 1

M-17 ......... 2:4 little value, and must lead to **u.** outcomes.

## undimmed 3

T-13 .... V.10:5 perfect radiance that is **u.** by your dreams
W-pI..... 56.4:3 across the face of love, its light remains **u.**
W-pI... 158.7:3 what can be touched, a purity **u.** by errors

## undisciplined 2

W-pI..... 20.2:6 them now, because your mind is totally **u.**
W-pI..... 44.3:3 particularly difficult form for the **u.** mind,

## undisguised 1

P-2........ VI.4:2 it is. Seen **u.** it is intolerable. Without

## undismayed 4

T-22 ..... VI.7:3 through which you walk completely **u.**?
W-pI... 100.8:5 **u.** by all the little thoughts and foolish
W-pI... 109.3:2 Completely **u.**, this thought will carry you
W-pII . 232.2:5 and be you **u.** because you are His Son.

## undisturbable 1

W-pII . 305.1:1 deep and quiet, **u.** and wholly changeless,

## undisturbed 10

T-20 ..... VI.2:2 on love, and rests on it serene and **u.**. The
T-24 ..... III.3:3 leave it perfectly unmoved and **u.**. But
T-30 ... III.10:2 of forms that fear can take; quite **u.**, the
W-pI... 109.4:2 of hate your rest remains completely **u.**.
W-pI. 135.19:1 is the defense that promises a future **u.**.
W-pI... 138.8:3 are made unaware, to keep them safely **u.**;
W-pI... 193.1:2 happiness His Son inherited of Him be **u.**;
W-pII . 273.1:1 are now ready for a day of **u.** tranquility.
W-pII ... 12.3:4 peace, forever conflict-free and **u.**, in
W-pII . 360.1:2 *Rays remain forever still and* **u.** *within me. I*

## undivided 12

T-2 ....... VI.6:3 to do comes from your **u.** decision. There
T-2 ..... VII.7:4 but it is by no means necessarily **u.**. The
T-5 ....... IV.2:6 the higher part, returning it **u.** to creation
T-8 ........... V.h The U. Will of the Sonship
T-8 ........ V.1:8 This Mind is invincible because it is **u.**.
T-8 ........ V.2:1 The **u.** will of the Sonship is the perfect
T-12 ....... V.1:1 Only love is strong because it is **u.**. The
T-12 ....... V.9:4 accord. You need offer only **u.** attention.
T-15 ..... IX.7:4 Accepting it as **u.** you join Him wholly, in
T-18 .... VII.6:7 a statement of allegiance, a truly **u.** loyalty
W-pI... 199.6:4 perfect in the ability to serve an **u.** goal. In
P-2...........I.3:5 His goal is wholly **u.** always. Whatever

## undo 41

T-1 ........I.13:3 They **u.** the past in the present, and thus
T-1 ....... III.1:6 learn to **u.** error and act to correct it. The
T-2 ....... IV.2:1 Atonement plan is to **u.** error at all levels.
T-2 ........ V.5:4 place yourself in a position to **u.** the level
T-3 ....... VI.8:6 is, however, eager to **u.** it, not to punish
T-4 ..........I.4:6 **u.** it by not changing your mind about it.
T-5 ....... IV.2:8 them you did not realize how to **u.** them.
T-5 ....... VI.7:3 will **u.** it in you because it does not belong
T-5 ... VII.6:10 *Holy Spirit will* **u.** *all the consequences of my*
T-6 ........in.1:6 The way to **u.** an insane conclusion is to
T-6 .... V.B.6:4 that you are trying to **u.** a decision that
T-7 ....... III.5:5 His sole function is to **u.** the questionable
T-7 ....... IV.5:5 is the way to **u.** the belief in differences,
T-7 ........ V.8:8 you help him **u.** the change his ego thinks
T-7 .......X.6:10 That is His Will, and you cannot **u.** it.
T-9 ....... IV.1:1 to **u.** the belief that anything is for you
T-9 ....... IV.2:7 The way to **u.** them, therefore, is not *of* you
T-9 ....... IV.5:1 learned of me does not use fear to **u.** fear.
T-9 ....... IV.5:4 you must **u.** what you have made in order
T-9 ..... VIII.2:6 delusional attempt to outdo, but not to **u.**
T-11 ...... V.1:6 We will **u.** this error quietly together, and
T-11 ...... V.5:2 way to **u.** its results is merely to recognize
T-13 ... XI.11:1 The Holy Spirit will **u.** for you everything
T-14 ........I.5:4 you who cannot **u.** what you have made,
T-14 ... III.13:7 His decision to **u.** everything that would
T-14 ..... XI.1:9 false, and of your attempts to **u.** the true.
T-14 ..... XI.3:5 present, or teach you how to **u.** the past.
T-15 ........I.7:5 uses it to **u.** the fear by which the ego
T-15 ........I.8:1 The Holy Spirit would **u.** all of this *now.*
T-15 ..... IX.6:7 the Holy Spirit must **u.** to set him free.
T-20 .... VII.8:4 from Him Who would **u.** your teaching.
T-27 .......II.6:4 Thus does the miracle **u.** all things the
T-27 ..... VI.6:3 is bound by laws that it came solely to **u.**!
T-27 . VIII.11:6 done this thing, and it is this I would **u.**."
T-28 ........I.1:2 All it does is to **u.**. And thus it cancels out
T-30 ..... VI.5:7 mistake that had the power to **u.** creation,
T-31 ..... VI.3:4 It is your world salvation will **u.**, and let
W-pI .... 67.2:8 We are trying today to **u.** your definition
W-pI .. 197.3:4 you would **u.** by taking back your gifts,
M-29 ......... 8:4 *visible; and to* **u.** *All things that change.*
S-3...........I.4:1 What he has done now must God's Son **u.**

## undoes 14

T-1 ....... III.5:7 Atonement **u.** all errors in this respect,
T-1 ..... III.5:11 **u.** their distortions and frees them from
T-2 .........II.6:5 It **u.** your past errors, thus making it
T-2 ....... III.2:1 where it **u.** the separation and restores
T-5 ....... III.5:6 He **u.** it at the same level on which the ego
T-7 ....... III.5:3 The Answer merely **u.** the question by
T-7 ....... VI.6:1 Spirit **u.** illusions without attacking them,
T-11 .......V.2:9 Clarity **u.** confusion by definition, and to
T-17 ..... III.6:3 of problems where it is, and there **u.** it.
W-pI .... 46.2:3 thus **u.** what fear has produced, returning
W-pI .... 58.3:5 My holiness **u.** them all by asserting the
W-pI .... 99.2:5 truth because it **u.** what was never done.
W-pII . 332.1:2 Truth **u.** its evil dreams by shining them
W-pII ... 13.1:4 It **u.** error, but does not attempt to go

## undoing 51

T-1 ........I.26:2 "Atoning" means "**u.**." The undoing of
T-1 ........I.26:3 The **u.** of fear is an essential part of the
T-2 ....... VI.7:1 The first corrective step in **u.** the error is
T-3 ....... III.2:6 illusions is the first step in **u.** them. The
T-5 ....... III.5:5 Holy Spirit has the task of **u.** what the ego
T-5 ....... IV.6:1 The Holy Spirit atones in all of us by **u.**,
T-5 .........V.7:9 except by accepting the solution of **u.**.
T-5 ...... VII.6:3 the first step in the **u.** is to recognize that
T-5 ...... VII.6:4 yourself fully aware that the **u.** process,
T-6 ..... V.B.3:1 The first step in the reversal or **u.** process
T-6 ..... V.B.3:1 process is the **u.** of the getting concept.
T-6 ..... V.C.2:5 The **u.** is necessary only in your mind, so
T-8 .........II.3:7 the **u.** of everything the ego tries to teach.
T-8 ....... III.7:7 why He has given you the means for **u.** it.
T-10 .......V.6:6 if you accept denial, you can accept its **u.**.
T-10 .....V.11:6 you the means for **u.** what you have made
T-11 .......V.9:2 Minimizing fear, but not its **u.**, is the
T-11 ..... VI.7:5 For the **u.** of the crucifixion of God's Son
T-12 ........I.8:5 disguise as a crucial step in the **u.** of the
T-12 .. VII.14:3 is why the **u.** of guilt is an essential part of
T-13 ..... IX.2:1 Release from guilt is the ego's whole **u.**.
T-14 ........I.3:7 *by* him, for the Source of their **u.** is in him.
T-14 ........I.4:3 U. *is* indirect, as doing is. You were created
T-14 ... IX.2:10 U. is for unreality. And this reality will do
T-16 ..... IV.2:3 go through this last **u.** quite unharmed,
T-17 ..... III.6:4 each step in His **u.** is the separation more
T-18 .......II.7:1 for **u.** guilt in everyone blessed through
T-18 ..... IV.8:7 which thought it did, is its **u.** needful.
T-18 .......V.1:1 Prepare you *now* for the **u.** of what never
T-20 .......II.7:5 **u.** of illusion that God Himself could give.
T-20 ... VIII.1:6 Desire now its whole **u.**, and it is done for
T-21 .......II.8:5 U. is not your task, but it *is* up to you to
T-21 .......V.9:1 with your Father's, to the **u.** of insanity.
T-22 ...... in.1:7 **u.** the effects of what you both believed
T-22 ..... III.1:1 thought system is the beginning of its **u.**,
T-25 ..... VI.6:4 as each one takes his part in its **u.**, as he
T-26 ..... III.6:5 within this one lies the **u.** of every illusion
T-27 .......II.4:6 their **u.** lies the proof that they are merely
T-27 ..... III.4:7 Yet true **u.** must be kind. And so the first
T-27 .... VII.6:6 mighty legions of its witnesses for its **u.**.
T-28 ............ h THE U. OF FEAR

T-30...... I.13:4 need for practicing the rules for its **u.**. Let
T-31......VI.2:1 Salvation is **u.**. If you choose to see the
T-31......VI.2:6 Salvation is **u.** of all this. For constancy
T-31......VI.5:2 are. **U.** truth would be impossible. But
W-in..........3:1 dealing with the **u.** of the way you see now
W-pI........9.1:4 is a prerequisite for **u.** your false ideas.
W-pI.....43.2:3 is the **u.** of what never was, perception
W-pII......2.3:1 is **u.** in the sense that it does nothing,
M-4......I.A.3:1 what might be called "a period of **u.**."
M-18..........4:6 means correction, or the **u.** of errors.

**undone** 76

T-2........III.2:3 be **u.** for the restoration of the temple,
T-4........IV.2:5 you have done and left **u.** accordingly,
T-5......IV.1:11 to be as one, the ego fades away and is **u.**.
T-5......... V.2:2 you have made is **u.** by the Holy Spirit,
T-5.......V.7:10 your wrong thinking if it could not be **u.**.
T-5........VI.9:1 the word "perish" is understood as "be **u.**.
T-5........VI.9:2 Every loveless thought must be **u.**, a word
T-5........VI.9:3 the ego, to be **u.** means to be destroyed.
T-5.......VII.5:3 this way is yours, and can therefore be **u.**.
T-5.......VII.5:4 be **u.** by repentance in the usual sense,
T-5.......VII.5:5 error rather than allow it to be **u.** for you.
T-7......III.2:11 ego, then, is always being **u.**, and does
T-7..... VIII.2:1 projection and anger can be finally **u.**.
T-7..... VIII.5:6 to the Holy Spirit to be **u.** completely, so
T-8........III.7:8 your wrong decisions are **u.** completely,
T-9.........III.5:4 cannot understand how all errors are **u.**.
T-11......IV.5:3 That is why blame must be **u.**, not seen
T-13.........I.4:5 has already **u.** everything unworthy of the
T-13.......IX.6:6 will see it there, for it *is* there until it is **u.**.
T-13.......IX.6:8 it not, for while you do, it cannot be **u.**.
T-14....... II.5:6 Be glad it is **u.**, for when you look at it in
T-14....... II.5:6 you look at it in simple honesty, it *is* **u.**. I
T-14......IV.3:1 in your most holy mind be **u.** for you, and
T-14.....IV.4:10 deceit, for thus are darkness and deceit **u.**
T-14... VIII.1:5 judgment of the Holy Spirit, and there **u.**.
T-14......IX.2:2 It is **u.** because the contradiction can no
T-14......IX.2:9 it real. This cannot be **u.**. Undoing is for
T-14......XI.2:1 Be willing, then, for all of it to be **u.**, and
T-14......XI.9:4 fear or pain or trial you have has been **u.**.
T-17....... II.3:5 reach. Fantasies are all **u.**, and no one and
T-17......III.5:8 of separation, and where it must be **u.**.
T-17......III.6:4 is the separation more and more **u.**, and
T-17......III.6:6 in separation is that it must be **u.**. Let
T-18....IX.12:4 interference; that is what needs to be **u.**.
T-19....... II.6:6 is a mistake, it can be **u.** easily by truth.
T19.IV.D.19:2 has established for salvation will be left **u.**
T-20.....VII.4:8 And both must be **u.** for purposes of truth
T-22.......in.4:2 Here is belief in differences **u.**. Here is the
T-22......IV.2:3 of Heaven to uphold it cannot be **u.**. Your
T-23.........I.8:9 Let all this madness be **u.** for you, and
T-23..... II.22:5 any instant it is possible to have all this **u.**
T-25......IX.1:1 errors cannot be **u.** by Heaven's justice?
T-26....... II.7:4 to be forever **u.** and unremembered.
T-26......III.7:1 where the separation is **u.** by change of
T-26....... V.6:5 For what has been **u.** no longer is. And
T-26....... V.9:1 that has been so long ago corrected and **u.**
T-26.....VII.5:1 its effects be utterly **u.** and without cause.
T-26......IX.3:6 What hate has wrought have They **u.**.
T-26....... X.1:1 to be **u.** for you to realize Their Presence?
T-27....... II.4:5 that cannot be **u.** and overlooked entirely.
T-27....... II.6:4 all things the world attests can never be **u.**
T-27...VII.12:6 unreality. And it is here that it will be **u.**.
T-27. VIII.12:3 all of them are easily **u.** by but a single
T-28...... I.13:5 made to render unremembered and **u.**.
T-28..... II.10:3 dreams are the effects of yours **u.**, and
T-28..... II.12:7 gone, and all the dreaming of the world **u.**
T-30.........I.7:6 Yet this decision still can be **u.**, by simple
T-30...... I.13:3 dream of judgment has forever been **u.**.
T-30.....VII.6:4 understand the sacrifice of meaning is **u.**.
T-31....... V.8:3 you see this concept of the self must be **u.**,
T-31..... V.16:7 you. Yet have no fear it will not be **u.**.
T-31.....VII.6:1 remain forever unaccomplished and **u.**.
W-pI.....57.1:2 that can be completely **u.** if I so choose?
W-pI.....91.6:7 What you think you are is a belief to be **u.**
W-pI.....94.1:1 renders the ego silent and entirely **u.**. You
W-pI.....99.4:2 offer means by which they are **u.** without
W-pI...110.4:1 In this one thought is all the past **u.**; the
W-pI...158.9:6 gone with them, **u.** and never to be done.
W-pI...168.4:5 is still **u.** when your forgiveness rests on
W-pI...191.7:1 Be glad today how very easily is hell **u.**.
W-pI...192.2:4 it is the means by which untruth can be **u.**
W-pI...195.8:4 The fear of God is now **u.** at last, and we
W-pI...198.1:5 and those it seemed to have will be **u.**.
W-pII.....in.9:4 Now we are glad that this is all **u.**, and we
M-28 .........3:3 is wholly corrected and all mistakes **u.**.
S-2 ........ III.4:3 What you have chosen still can be **u.**, for

**undreamed** 1

T-1.........I.45:2 and produce **u.** of changes in situations of

**undue** 2

W-pI.....39.8:1 **u.** emphasis on any one in particular,
W-pI.....65.6:2 not strain or make **u.** effort in doing this.

**unduly** 1

T-2......... II.3:8 time if you do not protract this step **u.**.

**uneasiness** 5

T-4....... V.4:11 the question can and does produce **u.**, but
T-22.........I.1:6 where, you wonder, does your strange **u.**,
W-pI.....11.4:2 or no **u.** and an inclination to do more, as
W-pI.....16.5:4 of a particular thought that arouses **u.**.
W-pI.....39.6:2 form they appear; **u.**, depression, anger,

**uneasy** 2

W-pI.....15.5:2 the practice periods, if you begin to feel **u.**
W-pI.....27.2:2 become **u.** about the lack of reservation

**unencumbered** 3

T-19......IV.1:4 cover them, extending past completely **u.**.
T-29... VIII.5:6 lifts the veil, and lets the truth shine **u.**,
W-pI.133.14:1 what waits for everyone who reaches, **u.**,

**unequal** 4

T-8.......IV.5:10 were not so the Sons of God would be **u.**.
T-13.....VII.2:5 because their real attraction to you is **u.**.
M-8 ...........1:2 **u.** heights and diverse sizes, on varying
S-3........IV.1:9 can bestow **u.** gifts on those less fortunate

**unequivocal** 9

T-4......III.7:10 I will come in response to a single **u.** call.
T-5....... II.10:2 This Mind is **u.**, because it hears only one
T-6......V.C.4:5 This lesson is **u.** in that it teaches there
T-8........IV.5:6 The decision to unite must be **u.**, or the
T-12.........I.9:9 conceals to clear-cut **u.** predominance,
T-17......VI.1:1 purpose is extremely simple, but it is **u.**.
T-17......VI.1:2 In fact, in order to be simple it *must* be **u.**.
T-17... VIII.1:4 the clear and **u.** demonstration of the
W-pI...199.6:5 conflict-free and **u.** response to mind with

**unequivocally** 2

T-2......... V.8:1 to accept **u.** that healing is necessary.
T-13... VIII.1:5 the mind that knows this **u.** knows also it

**uneven** 1

M-8 ...........1:2 **u.** background and shifting foreground,

**unexpected** 2

W-pI.....15.3:2 different forms, some of them quite **u.**.
M-25 .........6:3 And the more unusual and **u.** the power,

**unexpectedly** 2

T-2..........II.7:6 and can be turned against you very **u.**.
W-pI.....79.5:4 Some spring up **u.**, just as you think you

**unfailing** 4

W-pI.....41.9:3 on the **u.** companionship that is yours; on
W-pI.....50.4:3 you; eternal, changeless and forever **u.**.
W-pI...130.9:2 called upon the great **u.** power which will
M-4 ...... IV.2:7 must come from harm in place of the **u.**,

**unfailingly** 1

M-17 .........3:6 answer will enter the teacher's mind **u.**.

**unfair** 20

T-25..VIII.10:2 **u.** indeed to all the holiness that is in him,
T-25...... IX.3:3 it greater, harder to resolve and more **u.**.
T-25...... IX.3:5 is **u.** must be corrected *because* it is unfair.
T-25...... IX.3:5 is unfair must be corrected *because* it is **u.**.
T-25...... IX.7:1 Son be more **u.** than he has sought to be.
T-26........II.2:6 If this were true, then God would be **u.**;
T-26........II.4:9 hurt God's Son must be **u.** and therefore
T-26........X.1:2 you think it is **u.** and not to be allowed.
T-26........X.1:3 When you perceive it as **u.**, you think that
T-26........X.2:1 attack in certain forms to be **u.** to you? It
T-26........X.2:3 how could some be evaluated as **u.**? Some
T-26........X.3:4 to be **u.** and not your just deserts. Yet it is
T-26........X.5:1 think your brother is **u.** to you because
T-26........X.5:1 must be **u.** to make the other innocent.
T-27.........I.2:4 been **u.** will come to him in righteousness
T-27........II.2:2 they are the witnesses that pardon is **u.**.
W-pI... 134.1:1 entails an **u.** sacrifice of righteous wrath,
M-17 .........6:1 How can this **u.** battle be resolved? Its
M-22 .........6:4 Not to believe this is to be **u.** to God, and
P-2..........II.4:3 It would be **u.** indeed if belief in God were

**unfairly** 9

T-25...... IX.3:6 in which one, at least, is seen **u.**. Thus is
T-25...... IX.4:6 loser; no one left **u.** treated and deprived,
T-26........X.3:2 You cannot be **u.** treated. The belief you
T-26........X.4:1 temptation to perceive yourself **u.** treated
T-26........X.6:1 this injustice does to you who judge **u.**,
T-26........X.6:3 **u.** left without a purpose in a futile world.
T-27.........I.1:1 wish to be **u.** treated is a compromise
T-27.........I.1:6 And if you are **u.** treated, he must suffer
T-27.........I.3:1 **u.** treated or in need of anything, you but

**unfairness** 8

T-25..VIII.10:8 protect from all **u.** you might seek to offer
T-25..VIII.14:7 decide, and never fear that you, in your **u.**
T-25...... IX.3:4 the Holy Spirit could see **u.** as a resolution
T-26....... V.9:7 own **u.** to yourself has He protected you.
T-26........X.3:1 **U.** and attack are one mistake, so firmly
T-26........X.5:7 each **u.** that the world appears to lay upon
T-26........X.6:4 has all **u.** been resolved and been replaced
T-27.........I.1:6 treated, he must suffer the **u.** that you see.

**unfaithful** 2

W-pI. 166.13:6 Let sorrow not tempt you to be **u.** to your
M-22 .........6:4 is to be unfair to God, and thus **u.** to Him.

**unfamiliar** 3

T-4..........II.3:5 Surprise is a reasonable response to the **u.**
T-21.........I.6:1 dim, perhaps, and yet not altogether **u.**,
T-23......II.16:3 Nor is it **u.**; we have seen how it appears

**unfavorably** 1

T-12... VII.13:1 look without and react **u.** to what you see,

**unfinished** 1

T-19......IV.2:3 with the Holy Spirit remains **u.**. You can

**unfold** 2

T-26....VIII.6:5 Why wait till they **u.** in time and fear they
W-pI...164.5:4 in His judgment will a world **u.** in perfect

**unforgivable** 5

T-24......III.1:5 And so he calls it "**u.**," and makes it sin.
T-25......III.8:5 and damned forever, being forever **u.**. If,
T-25......IX.6:9 is salvation's justice if some errors are **u.**,
T-30......VI.2:3 You do not forgive the **u.**, nor overlook a
W-pI...134.5:2 It merely is a further sign that sin is **u.**, at

**unforgiven** 6

T-24......III.2:7 birthright to it, leaving him alone and **u.**,
T-25......IX.9:5 **u.** have no mercy to bestow upon another
T-26.......V.8:1 The **u.** is a voice that calls from out a past
T-26....VIII.8:3 little space that lies between you, **u.** still.
W-pI...75.11:2 replace the **u.** world you thought was real.
P-2........VI.1:2 unforgiving are sick, believing they are **u.**.

**unforgiveness** 12

W-pI...193.4:1 all distress does not appear to be but **u.**.
W-pI...193.7:4 And there remains an **u.** hiding in the
M-9...........1:8 and all dark cornerstones of **u.** removed.
P-2.........II.3:3 the remembrance of God are forms of **u.**,
P-2.........II.4:6 and it is to this that all **u.** leads. And
P-2........VI.4:1 thus keep **u.** unrecognized for what it is.
P-2........VI.4:5 so. For when an **u.** is not recognized, the
P-2........VI.5:1 takes many forms, and so does **u.**. The
P-2........VI.5:3 clearly to the form of **u.** that it represents.
P-2........VI.5:5 that only forgiveness heals an **u.**, and only
P-2........VI.5:5 and only an **u.** can possibly give rise to
S-3...........I.2:1 The body's cause is **u.** of the Son of God.

**unforgiving** 23

T-14......IV.3:5 restore what always was to your **u.** mind.
T19.IV.D.11:4 complete forgiveness you still stand **u.**.
T-24......III.4:6 It will forevermore be **u.**, for that is what
T-26.......V.5:5 Yet in each **u.** act or thought, in every
W-pI...121.2:1 The **u.** mind is full of fear, and offers love
W-pI...121.2:2 The **u.** mind is sad, without the hope of
W-pI...121.3:1 The **u.** mind is torn with doubt, confused
W-pI...121.3:2 the **u.** mind perceive but its damnation?
W-pI...121.4:1 The **u.** mind sees no mistakes, but only
W-pI...121.5:1 The **u.** mind is in despair, without the
W-pI...121.7:1 Each **u.** mind presents you with an
W-pI...121.7:5 The **u.** mind must learn through your
W-pI...121.9:1 The **u.** mind does not believe that giving
W-pI.121.13:4 in bringing happiness to every **u.** mind,
W-pI...122.3:1 who look with **u.** eyes upon the world. It
WpI. rIV.in3:2 defenses that protect your **u.** thoughts
W-pI...193.9:2 leave an **u.** thought without correction,
W-pI...194.9:4 If we accept an **u.** thought, it will be soon
W-pI...198.9:5 suffering that fails to hide an **u.** thought.
W-pII .....1.2:1 An **u.** thought is one which makes a
W-pII .....1.3:1 **u.** thought does many things. In frantic
P-2........VI.1:2 else. The **u.** are sick, believing they are
S-3...........I.1:3 and witnesses to **u.** thoughts that injure

**unfortunate** 3

T-2......IV.3:13 denies this **u.** aspect of the mind's power,
T-3...........I.1:6 This particularly **u.** interpretation, which
T-9........IV.8:3 qualifications as a guide are singularly **u.**,

**unfounded** 1

W-pI...134.3:2 **u.** effort to deceive yourself by making an

**unfulfilled** 8

T-7 ....... IX.3:5 joy, so that you perceive yourself as **u.**.
T-7 ....... IX.3:6 Unless you create you *are* **u.**, but God does
T-14 ...... V.2:3 that his true function remains **u.** in him.
T-15 . XI.10:10 born, and take your place, so long left **u.**,
T-29 ..... IV.3:1 to function **u.** as you perceive the function
WpI..rII.in.5:4 each day not to leave your function **u.**.
W-pI...100.6:2 If you are sad, your part is **u.**, and all the
S-3........ IV.8:4 Without you is creation **u.**. Return to Me

**unfulfillment** 1

T-7 ....... IX.3:6 God does not know **u.** and therefore you

**ungenerous** 1

W-pI...133.4:3 be most **u.** to you to let alternatives be

**unguarded** 1

T-2 ......VII.2:1 I cannot let you leave your mind **u.**, or

**unhampered** 1

W-pI....... 3.2:2 a perfectly open mind, **u.** by judgment, in

**unhappiness** 4

T-30 ......I.13:1 day if you prevent **u.** from entering at all.
W-pI..... 38.4:1 sense of loss or **u.** of any kind as you see it
W-pI..... 64.5:4 Each one will lead to happiness or **u.**. Can
W-pII . 244.1:3 *suffer, be endangered, or experience* ***u.***,

**unhappy** 8

T-3 ....... VI.8:6 because He knows that it makes them **u.**.
T-6 .........II.5:7 are not in this world, for the world *is* **u.**.
T-8 ..........I.5:2 If the outcome of yours has made you **u.**,
T-14 ........II.3:2 **u.** learners who would teach themselves
T-14 ..... III.4:6 or guiltless, bound or free, **u.** or happy.
W-pI....... 4.1:4 If you are already aware of **u.** thoughts,
W-pI..... 70.5:2 want to be sick, because it makes us **u.**.
W-pII ..... 8.2:1 each **u.** thought reflected in your world; a

**unharmed** 4

T-16 ..... IV.2:3 will go through this last undoing quite **u.**,
T-18 ..... VI.7:7 you would not escape from it, leaving it **u.**
T19. IV.D.12:3 still, to keep what seems to be yourself **u.**.
T-21 ........I.1:2 walk **u.** through open doorways that they

**unhealed** 27

T-5 ....... IV.2:6 **u.** part of your mind to the higher part,
T-7 ........ V.1:4 **u.** healer obviously does not understand
T-7 ........ V.7:1 The **u.** healer wants gratitude from his
T-9 ........... V.h The U. Healer
T-9 ........ V.1:2 is because it is undertaken by **u.** healers,
T-9 ........ V.1:3 consider the **u.** healer more carefully now.
T-9 ........ V.1:5 If an **u.** healer is a theologian, for example
T-9 ........ V.2:3 searches fantasies for truth must be **u.**,
T-9 ........ V.3:2 The **u.** healer cannot do this because he
T-9 ........ V.3:3 it. All **u.** healers follow the ego's plan for
T-9 ........ V.5:4 real has happened to the **u.** healer, and he
T-9 ........ V.5:6 **u.** healer therefore does not know how to
T-9 ........ V.7:3 The **u.** healer cannot do this for him,
T-16 ... IV.1:10 remain unrecognized, and therefore **u.**.
T-26 .. VII.10:4 remain **u.** and broken from a unity which
T-27 .......II.2:1 The **u.** cannot pardon. For they are the
T-27 .......II.8:5 as he consents to suffer, you will be **u.**.
T-27 .....II.15:3 mistakes in one **u.** and set the other free.
T-28 ..... III.3:5 in sickness, to preserve the little gap **u.**,
T-31 ...VIII.3:3 He would not leave one source of pain **u.**,
W-pI. 135.13:1 the plans the **u.** mind sets up to save itself
P-2....... VII.4:2 All "**u.** healers" make this fundamental
P-2....... VII.4:3 or the **u.** healer would instantly become a
P-2....... VII.5:8 obvious. No **u.** healer can be wholly sane.
P-2....... VII.7:3 The **u.** healer cannot but be fearful of his
P-3..........II.3:2 The **u.** healer may be arrogant, selfish,
P-3........ III.2:1 an **u.** healer would try to heal for money,

**unheard** 10

T-19 ..... III.4:9 you would keep **u.** and thus unanswered?
T-24 .......II.4:5 seems silent and **u.** before its "mightiness.
T-27 ..... IV.6:8 whom," it will remain unrecognized, **u.**,
T-28 ..... VI.4:6 Unstated and **u.** in consciousness is every
T-31 ........I.8:3 with you. And never does a call remain **u.**,
T-31 ........I.9:1 whole, and that you do not leave its call **u.**
W-pI .. 123.5:6 An **u.** message will not save the world,
W-pI .. 182.6:3 call for help almost **u.** amid the grating
W-pII .... 358.h call to God can be **u.** nor left Unanswered.
M-29 ......... 8:5 *you is ushered in A world unseen,* ***u.***, *yet*

**unheeding** 2

W-pI 136.11:2 universe remains **u.** of the laws by which
W-pI .. 151.8:4 sin; **u.** of the body's witnesses before the

**unhelpful** 1

T-9 .........V.4:1 the ego's plan are as **u.** as the older ones,

**unhindered** 2

T-18 ... IX.10:4 God Himself can take the final step **u.**, for
T-31 .....V.17:3 mind that truth returns, **u.** and unbound.

**unholiness** 6

T-14 ..... IX.1:3 It merely brings **u.** to holiness; or what
T-17 ... III.2:10 For **u.** seeks to reinforce itself, as holiness
T-18 .......II.6:9 As its **u.** kept it a thing apart, its holiness
T-20 .... VII.5:4 is quite in keeping with the purpose of **u.**.
W-pI .... 39.4:5 God does not know **u.**. Can it be He does
W-pI 151.12:2 and the world, past every witness for **u.**,

**unholy** 49

*See also* Appendix C

T-14 ........I.4:5 blocked by the capricious and **u.** whim of
T-15 .......V.5:3 **u.** the reason you made them may be, He
T-17 ... III.1:12 into **u.** alliances to support the ego's goals
T-17 ..... III.2:7 bodies are central to all **u.** relationships is
T-17 ..... III.2:9 that go to make the relationship **u.**. For
T-17 ..... III.3:1 In the **u.** relationship, it is not the body
T-17 ..... III.3:4 and the breaking off of the **u.** relationship
T-17 ..... III.4:1 is indeed unkind to the **u.** relationship.
T-17 ..... III.4:3 attraction of the **u.** relationship begins to
T-17 ..... III.4:5 The "ideal" of the **u.** relationship thus
T-17 ..... III.5:7 the ugliness of the **u.** relationship where
T-17 ..... III.7:7 the relationship unreal, and therefore **u.**,
T-17 ..... III.8:1 into a continuing, **u.** alliance with the ego
T-17 ..... III.8:3 the relationships the **u.** alliance dictates
T-17 ..... III.8:4 the purpose of the **u.** alliance are retained,
T-17 .......V.1:7 And as the **u.** relationship is a continuing
T-17 .......V.2:2 It is the old, **u.** relationship, transformed
T-17 .......V.2:4 the reversal of the **u.** relationship. Be
T-17 .......V.3:6 it. In its **u.** condition, *your* goal was all that
T-17 .......V.3:9 For once the **u.** relationship has accepted
T-17 .......V.4:5 Set firmly in the **u.** relationship, there is
T-17 .......V.5:5 by two individuals for their **u.** purposes,
T-18 .......V.4:5 bring **u.** means to its accomplishment.
T-18 ... IX.13:1 its **u.** purpose has been safely brought
T-20 ..... III.6:1 in a holy relationship can long remain **u.**?
T-20 ..... III.8:4 for the meaning of your **u.** relationship,
T-20 ... III.8:10 the one thing that still would have it be **u.**
T-20 ..... VI.1:4 Son of God invented an **u.** relationship
T-20 ..... VI.2:1 of both a holy and an **u.** relationship. The
T-20 ..... VI.4:4 And its relationships must be **u.**, for what
T-20 ..... VI.5:3 Here the **u.** relationship escapes reality,
T-20 ..... VI.8:3 An **u.** relationship is no relationship. It is
T-20 ..... VI.8:6 with God **u.** seemed to be possible, all
T-20 ..... VI.8:7 In that **u.** instant time was born, and
T-20 ..... VI.9:2 The **u.** instant of their seeming power is
T-20 ..... VI.9:4 Is the malevolence of the **u.** relationship,
T-20 ... VI.10:4 **u.** instant is exchanged in gladness for the

T-20....VI.11:3 And this **u.** instant seems to be life; an
T-20....VI.11:8 him to replace the **u.** one he chose before.
T-20....VI.12:2 to you than its **u.** seeming counterpart,
T-20.....VII.5:1 tries to make the **u.** relationship seem real
T-20.....VII.5:2 The **u.** instant *is* the time of bodies. But the
T-20.....VII.6:7 in **u.** relationships with other bodies,
T-22.......in.2:5 an **u.** relationship is based on differences,
T-22.........I.7:2 reborn itself from an **u.** relationship, and
T-22......III.9:2 **U.** values will produce confusion, and in
T-22......III.9:3 In an **u.** relationship, each one is valued
W-pI.....43.2:4 Made by the Son of God for an **u.** purpose
W-pI...163.5:1 **U.** in defeat, he has become what death

### unhurried 3
W-pI.....11.3:2 words, however, should be used in an **u.**,
W-pI.....33.1:3 though **u.** applications are essential.
W-pI.....34.4:1 the idea to yourself in an **u.** manner,

### unhurriedly 4
W-pI...29.5:10 you as you say the words **u.** to yourself. At
W-pI.....32.3:4 the idea for today **u.** as often as you wish,
W-pI.....36.4:2 slowly, as effortlessly and **u.** as possible.
WpI. rIV.in8:2 the two ideas you practice for the day **u.**,

### unification 2
T-8........IX.9:1 **u.** of purpose, then, is the Holy Spirit's
T-12......VI.6:7 that they share the **u.** of the laws of God.

### unified 39
T-1........VI.2:5 **U.** needs lead to unified action, because
T-1........VI.2:5 Unified needs lead to **u.** action, because
T-2........VI.6:9 be corrected only by accepting a **u.** goal.
T-6........III.2:5 This is the one lesson that is perfectly **u.**,
T-6......V.B.9:1 a giant step toward the **u.** perception that
T-6......V.C.1:6 perfectly consistent and perfectly **u.**.
T-7......III.2:12 mind cannot be **u.** in allegiance to the ego
T-7........IV.3:5 the Holy Spirit has a **u.** goal for the effort.
T-7........IV.3:6 goal, the abilities themselves become **u.**.
T-7........IV.5:1 The ego's goal is as **u.** as the Holy Spirit's,
T-8.........V.1:5 them your **u.** mind on their behalf, as I
T-8.....VII.12:3 of the body can be **u.** only by one purpose
T-8.....VII.14:6 to the **u.** purpose of the curriculum, and
T-8.....VII.15:1 Joy is **u.** purpose, and unified purpose is
T-8.....VII.15:1 purpose, and **u.** purpose is only God's.
T-8.....VII.15:2 When yours is **u.** it is His. Believe you can
T-8........IX.8:7 is split, and does not accept a **u.** purpose.
T-11.........I.3:1 not part of God, His Will would not be **u.**.
T-14.......V.6:1 taking their part in the **u.** curriculum of
T-20.......V.1:7 one who has a single purpose, **u.** and sure
T-27.....II.11:2 anyone perceive a function **u.** which has
T-27.....II.16:5 lies the means whereby your mind is **u.**.
T-28.......VI.6:7 be sick, but lets his mind be healed and **u.**
W-pI.....24.6:2 that you have no **u.** outcome in mind, and
W-pI.....25.1:7 this that your goals become **u.**. It is in
W-pI.....42.7:2 that you are studying a **u.** thought system
W-pI...108.2:2 a state of mind that has become so **u.** that
W-pI...108.5:1 One thought, completely **u.**, will serve to
W-pI.151.11:2 one frame of reference, wholly **u.** and sure
W-pI.151.14:4 remains is **u.** into a perfect Thought that
Wi181-200 1:3 of peace such **u.** commitment will bestow,
W-pI.184.12:3 All names are **u.**; all space is filled with
W-pII..234.1:3 in thoughts which are forever **u.** as one.
W-pII..271.1:4 and the Son; Creator and creation **u.**.
M-22..........1:3 it is the source of a wholly **u.** perception.
C-1.............1:4 The **u.** spirit is God's one Son, or Christ.
C-1.............4:2 to be imprisoned while the mind is not **u.**.
C-1.............4:4 This Will is always **u.** and therefore has
S-1........IV.3:2 satisfied; all separate wishes **u.** in one.

### unifies 8
T-7.........II.2:3 because it **u.** by increasing and integrates
T-7.....VIII.1:4 It is the law that **u.** the Kingdom, and
T-11.....V.15:2 perceptions which it **u.** on behalf of itself.
T-23......IV.7:4 Only a purpose **u.**, and those who share a
T-27.....II.16:6 His single purpose **u.** the halves of you
W-pI...108.4:3 frame of reference which **u.** this Thought.
WpI. rIV.in2:1 theme that **u.** each step in the review we
W-pI.184.11:3 a single Source which **u.** all things within

### uniformly 1
T-4.......II.10:2 right perception is **u.** without attack, and

### unify 6
T-6......V.C.2:3 but only in order to **u.** the mind so it can
T-7........IV.5:3 Holy Spirit always seeks to **u.** and heal. As
W-pI...108.5:1 unified, will serve to **u.** all thought. This is
WpI...rV.in3:6 *the Word You offer us to* **u.** *our practicing, as*
W-pI.184.13:5 One Name we use to **u.** our sight.
W-pII..257.1:4 that we may **u.** our thoughts and actions

### unifying 1
T-14.......V.8:4 Son. Joy is its **u.** attribute, with no one left

### unimpeded 1
M-28.........2:5 of God shines **u.** across the world. Christ's

### unimportance 1
T-4.........I.13:4 with them, and lets me teach you their **u.**.

### unimportant 5
T-9.........V.6:6 an "**u.** mind" esteem itself without magic.
T-15.....VII.8:3 goes or what it thinks, for this seems **u.**.
W-pI.....16.3:3 temptation to dismiss fear thoughts as **u.**,
W-pI.....18.1:1 to what you see are never neutral or **u.**. It
W-pI.....25.6:2 your eye, near or far, "important" or "**u.**,"

### unintelligibility 1
T-14......VI.7:5 at once, and this must lead to **u.**. Yet if

### unintelligible 2
T-27......III.1:8 idea a something it is not, and make it **u.**.
T-30...VII.6:13 meaning. It must be forever **u.**. This is not

### unintentional 1
W-pI...136.3:1 Defenses are not **u.**, nor are they made

### uninterested 1
P-3.........II.3:3 He may be **u.** in healing as his major goal.

### uninterrupted 2
T-14. VIII.2:15 Unbroken and **u.** love flows constantly
T-17......III.4:8 of it, and join with fantasies in **u.** "bliss."

### uninvited 1
T-27.....VII.7:3 to thrust upon you, **u.** and unasked, must

### uninvolved 2
T-11.......V.9:1 shallow, callous, **u.** and even desperate,
W-pI.....33.2:2 Try to remain equally **u.** in both, and to

### union 90
T-3........V.1:3 by the **u.** of my will with the Father's. We
T-5.........II.1:7 of this **u.** of Will between Father and Son.
T-5........IV.1:9 and the **u.** of the Sonship is its protection.
T-8........III.3:3 created, in **u.** with the perfect Creator.
T-8......IV.3:11 you, so we can teach them peace and **u.**.
T-8........IV.5:4 Separation is overcome by **u.**. It cannot be
T-8......IV.8:10 If you exclude yourself from this **u.**, you
T-8.........V.3:5 be to the **u.** of God and His holy Sons! All
T-8.........V.4:2 Our **u.** is therefore the way to renounce
T-8.......VII.4:5 Spirit to use on behalf of **u.** of the Sonship
T-12........I.10:6 For the separation is only the denial of **u.**,
T-12........I.10:6 to your eternal knowledge that **u.** is true.
T-13......VI.8:3 timeless **u.** with them is your continuity,
T-13........X.3:1 **u.** with a brother in which you seek to lay
T-13........X.3:2 him, because your **u.** with him is not real.
T-13........X.7:5 He has seen separation, but knows of **u.**.
T-14.......V.8:5 to its safe embrace of love and **u.**. Stand
T-14.....VII.1:4 your mind, and they are reconciled by **u.**,
T-14.....VII.1:5 are. In **u.**, everything that is not real must
T-14.....VII.1:5 is not real must disappear, for truth *is* **u.**.
T-14....VIII.5:2 Heaven itself is **u.** with all of creation, and
T-14........X.9:7 The fact of **u.** tells them it is not true.
T-15.....VII.9:2 suffering and sacrifice as the price of **u.**.
T-15...VII.11:6 The **u.** of bodies thus becomes the way in
T-15......IX.4:7 and their **u.** need only be accepted and
T-15......IX.7:4 place no limits on your **u.** with Him. The
T-15........X.1:1 the perfect **u.** of the Father and the Son.
T-15........X.3:3 our **u.** you will accept all of our brothers.
T-15........X.3:4 of **u.** is the only gift that I was born to give
T-16......IV.8:5 creations were created in **u.** with them.
T-16....IV.10:1 to **u.** in yourself *must* lead to knowledge,
T-16....IV.12:2 Him and created by His joy in **u.** with you
T-16.......V.3:7 of love is known, love is the same as **u.**.
T-16.......V.5:4 knows that completion lies first in **u.**, and
T-16.......V.5:4 in union, and then in the extension of **u.**.
T-16.......V.5:8 And therefore **u.**, which is a condition in
T-16.......V.6:4 a kind of **u.** from which union is excluded,
T-16.......V.6:4 a kind of union from which **u.** is excluded,
T-16.......V.6:4 for the attempt at **u.** rests on exclusion.
T-16.......V.7:4 This is not **u.**, for there is no increase and
T-16.......V.8:3 other, the ego sees "a **u.** made in Heaven."
T-16......VI.2:3 God, no longer seek for **u.** in separation,
T-16......VI.5:4 for the separate **u.** excludes the universe.
T-16......VI.5:6 If one such **u.** were made in perfect faith,
T-17......III.2:6 become attempts at **u.** through the body,
T-17......III.3:1 of the other with which **u.** is attempted,
T-17......III.4:7 attempt at **u.** becomes a way of excluding
T-17......III.4:7 the one with whom the **u.** was sought. For
T-17......III.6:4 and more undone, and **u.** brought closer.
T-18....VI.11:7 limited awareness, and lost your fear of **u.**
T-18......IX.2:1 does surround it has brought **u.** to you,
T-19.........I.4:2 body cannot be used for purposes of **u.**. If
T-19........I.10:2 Faith is the acknowledgment of **u.**. It is
T-19.....III.10:3 against a **u.** Heaven has smiled upon.
T19. IV.A.10:2 it would unite in holy **u.** and completion.
T19....IV.B.5:3 obstacle that you can place before our **u.**,
T19....IV.B.7:4 holy **u.** of the Father and the Son in you!
T19....IV.C.7:7 Here is the final end of **u.**, the triumph of
T19....IV.C.9:2 protected by your **u.** with your brother,
T19... IV.D.3:4 to allow **u.** to call you out of separation;
T-20......III.2:4 keep them separate and prevent their **u.**.
T-20.....III.10:3 For what is Heaven but **u.**, direct and
T-20.....III.11:1 given me the certainty our **u.** will be soon.
T-20......VI.1:5 one of perfect **u.** and unbroken continuity
T-21......II.12:3 His **u.** with It is the source of his creating.
T-21.......III.1:2 toward which the seeming **u.** is adjusted.
T-21.......V.9:1 by your will in **u.** with your Father's, to
T-22.......in.4:5 to the logical conclusion of your **u.**. It
T-22.......V.5:1 awareness of your **u.** with your brother!
T-22....VI.14:5 of the **u.** of the Creator and His Son. From
T-25..VIII.11:6 strengthened by their **u.** with each other.
T-26.........I.4:9 his song of **u.** and of love be heard at all.
T-26......III.7:1 what once was specialness, and now is **u.**?
T-28......IV.7:3 if someone else accepts his **u.** with him.
T-30.......I.16:4 can be caused without some form of **u.**,
W-pI...154.4:3 created it, and of His lasting **u.** with itself.
WpI...rV.in4:5 Its constant state of **u.** with Its Father and
W-pI...185.4:2 Sometimes it takes the form of **u.**, but
W-pI.200.11:6 For peace is **u.**, if it be of God. We seek no
W-pII .253.2:2 *is but Your Will in perfect* **u.** *with my own,*
W-pII ...10.3:2 happiness, and **u.** with your own Identity.
W-pII .329.2:1 our **u.** with each other and our Source.
M-5 ......III.3:8 but by the **u.** of the one Will with itself.
M-26 .........3:1 a brief experience of direct **u.** with God.
P-2..........II.5:4 way, a **u.** of purpose between patient and
S-1.........in.2:4 to the truth of **u.** in his Father and himself

S-2......... II.2:6 There is no **u.** here, but only grief. This is
S-3........... III.h Separation versus **U.**
S-3......... III.5:7 separation must be healed by love and **u.**.
S-3...... IV.1:10 sing of their **u.** and their thanks to God.

## unions 2

T-15..... VII.9:1 with which the ego would "bless" all **u.**.
T-16...... VI.5:2 separate **u.** and to become one by losing.

## unique 5

T-1......... II.6:5 The miracle thus has the **u.** property of
T-1........ IV.3:2 It has no **u.** properties of its own. It is an
T-2......... II.6:8 plan has a **u.** relationship to time. Until
T-14....... X.2:6 The miracle, therefore, has a **u.** function,
T-14....... X.2:6 is motivated by a **u.** Teacher Who brings

## unison 1

S-3........ IV.7:3 his joyful thanks in **u.** with all creation, in

## unite 52

T-1......... II.1:6 Miracles **u.** you directly with your brother
T-1........ III.3:4 that serve the Holy Spirit **u.** with me for
T-3........ IV.7:7 I cannot **u.** your will with God's for you,
T-4......... II.8:2 to other egos and try to **u.** with them in a
T-4........ IV.8:3 and mine can **u.** in shining your ego away,
T-8........ IV.3:4 My mission was simply to **u.** the will of
T-8........ IV.5:6 The decision to **u.** must be unequivocal,
T-8......... V.2:5 to heal is to **u.** with those who are like you
T-8......... V.3:4 As we **u.**, we unite with Him. Glory be to
T-8......... V.3:4 As we unite, we **u.** with Him. Glory be to
T-8......... V.4:1 When you **u.** with me you are uniting
T-8......... V.4:1 myself and therefore cannot **u.** with yours
T-9......... II.4:6 You will **u.** with the truth in him, and his
T-11....... II.1:4 To **u.** *having* and *being* is to unite your will
T-11....... II.1:4 *having* and *being* is to **u.** your will with His,
T-12..VIII.7:11 function of love to **u.** all things unto itself,
T-13...... III.8:3 hidden, you will only to **u.** with the Father
T-13..... V.7:10 we are united so would we **u.** with them.
T-13...... VI.7:1 in the light that would **u.** you with them,
T-13....VIII.8:2 **U.** with me under the holy banner of His
T-13....VIII.8:3 will all **u.** in the eternity of God the Father
T-13....... X.2:9 No one who would **u.** in any way with
T-14....... V.5:1 and nothing else can **u.** us in this world.
T-14....VIII.3:5 **U.** with what you are. You cannot join
T-15..... V.10:8 the holy instant you **u.** directly with God,
T-15...... VI.5:3 **u.** this idea with the Mind that thought it,
T-16.... IV.12:2 made from your willingness to **u.** with
T-18.........I.2:6 One would **u.**; the other separate.
T-18.... VI.11:5 It becomes part of you, as you **u.** with it.
T-19.........I.5:4 and separate; faith would **u.** and heal.
T-19...... III.7:2 While you believe that bodies can **u.**, you
T19. IV.A.10:2 it would **u.** in holy union and completion.
T19..IV.B.10:3 Yet it can **u.** only with what already is at
T-20.... III.10:7 And here would I **u.** with you, my friend,
T-22.........I.7:6 two brothers can **u.** except through Christ
T-24..... VII.7:4 Here do the means and end **u.** as one, nor
T-25.........I.7:3 this mind, and does **u.** all things together,
T-25....... V.3:4 the call is made, that you **u.** with him, and
T-26...VII.19:3 Let us **u.** in bringing blessing to the world
T-28...... IV.2:7 And with the mind you would **u.**, but
W-pI.....89.3:2 idea do I **u.** my will with the Holy Spirit's,
W-pI.....92.5:7 **u.** in purpose and forgiveness and in love.
W-pI.....92.9:2 Strength and light **u.** in you, and where
W-pI...104.3:1 we but **u.** our will with what God wills,
W-pI.121.13:1 let your "enemy" and friend **u.** in blessing
WpI. rIV.in6:4 you who are complete as you **u.** with Him,
W-pI...161.8:2 attack, and howling to **u.** with him again.
W-pI...162.6:2 eager to **u.** with one like him in holiness?
W-pI...185.4:4 Minds cannot **u.** in dreams. They merely
W-pI.185.13:2 God gives but to **u.**. To take away is
W-pII .326.1:8 *all separate thoughts* **u.** *in glory as the Son of*
S-1......... II.6:2 If you **u.** with anyone in prayer, you make

## united 64

T-1....... III.7:2 being **u.** this mind goes out to everyone,
T-4...... III.1:12 *is perfectly* **u.** *and perfectly protected, and*
T-4....... III.2:6 our **u.** strength the ego cannot prevail.
T-4...... VII.8:7 we are all **u.** in the joy of the Kingdom. I
T-5..... IV.1:10 the Kingdom because the Sonship is **u.**. In
T-6.........II.8:2 All His Thoughts are thus perfectly **u.**
T-6.......II.12:5 is **u.** He offers the whole Kingdom always.
T-7.........II.7:7 is perfectly direct and perfectly **u.**. It is
T-8........ V.3:6 All glory lies in Them *because* They are **u.**.
T-8........ V.4:6 Nothing can prevail against our **u.** wills
T-8.... VII.13:4 is therefore nothing more than **u.** purpose
T-9...... VII.2:1 then, that in this joint will you are all **u.**,
T-11 .......I.11:8 be One, and **u.** with Him in His Oneness.
T-13.... V.7:10 as we are **u.** so would we unite with them.
T-13 .....X.14:6 **U.** in this praise we stand before the gates
T-13..... XI.3:1 When we are all **u.** in Heaven, you will
T-14.... V.11:9 of us, **u.** as one within the Cause of peace.
T-14 .VIII.2:11 meeting place where God, **u.** with His Son
T-15.... V.10:2 **u.** in your blessing it becomes one to you.
T-15.... VII.9:2 **u.** at its altar accept suffering and sacrifice
T-16..... III.8:4 **u.** will of all who make Heaven what it is,
T-18........I.2:4 Being **u.**, they are one because they are
T-18... IX.13:3 were **u.** is but the messenger of love, sent
T-19........I.2:5 It is this joining Him in a **u.** purpose that
T-19........I.7:4 Each is **u.**, a complete thought system,
T-19......I.10:5 **u.** in your purpose to be released from
T-19......I.12:7 Who joined you, and in Whom you are **u.**
T-20........I.2:9 cannot be **u.** in crucifixion and in death.
T-21..... VI.9:5 Love plans is like Itself in this: Being **u.**, It
T-26..VII.15:8 His Kingdom is **u.**; thus it was created,
T-27.....II.16:3 then, correction to the Mind that is **u.**,
T-27...VIII.1:3 **u.** in the dust with other bodies dying like
T-28..... IV.7:5 gone if someone wills to be **u.** with him.
T-30..... III.6:9 It is forever One, eternally **u.** and at peace
T-30...... V.2:8 world has been **u.** in belief the purpose of
T-30...... V.3:4 he is **u.** in his purpose with himself. There
T-30.... VII.5:6 one **u.** goal does this become impossible,
W-pI.....56.4:4 is my will, **u.** with the Will of my Father.
W-pI...73.10:4 joined with the power of God and **u.** with
W-pI...91.10:4 are **u.** with you in this practice period, in
W-pI........95.h I am one Self, **u.** with my Creator.
W-pI.....95.3:2 your one Self, which is **u.** with Its Creator.
W-pI...95.10:2 you are one Self, **u.** with your Creator, at
W-pI...95.11:2 *I am one Self,* **u.** *with my Creator, at one with*
W-pI...95.12:1 **u.** and secure in light and joy and peace.
W-pI...95.13:2 of God, **u.** with your brothers in that Self;
W-pI...95.13:2 that Self; **u.** with your Father in His Will.
W-pI...95.15:1 you are one Self, **u.** with your Father, is a
W-pI...95.15:3 *Self with me,* **u.** *with our Creator in this Self. I*
W-pI...113.1:1 (95) I am one Self, **u.** with my Creator.
W-pI...113.3:2 I am one Self, **u.** with my Creator. On the
W-pI.154.11:5 And He needs our will **u.** with His Own,
W-pI...159.4:3 receiver are **u.** in extension here on earth,
W-pI...167.5:2 Ideas remain **u.** to their source. They can
W-pI...169.5:6 itself. It has **u.** with its Source. And like its
W-pI...183.1:4 and thus are they **u.** in a bond to which
W-pI.184.15:2 *In It we are* **u.** *with all living things, and You*
W-pI...199.3:3 lives **u.** with the home that it has made. It
W-pII .239.2:3 *We are one,* **u.** *in this light and one with You,*
W-pII .241.1:7 They will be **u.** now, as you forgive them
W-pII .262.1:8 *are our Source, eternally* **u.** *in Your Love;*
W-pII .266.2:1 in each of us; **u.** in the holy Love of God.
W-pII .330.1:4 joy, as is the Will of God **u.** with its own.
S-3........ IV.4:5 In prayer you have **u.** with your Source,

## unites 14

T-1.........II.1:5 Revelation **u.** you directly with God.
T-18... VI.11:8 to what has freed you, and **u.** with it. And
T-19......I.12:7 Yet faith **u.** you in the holiness you see,
T-23..... III.5:5 No one **u.** with enemies, nor is at one
T-25........I.7:2 a Oneness which **u.** all things within Itself
T-27...... VI.1:6 **u.** all those who share in it within itself.
T-27 ..VII.15:1 who **u.** with you in holy innocence. And
W-pI.....92.4:3 It **u.** with light, of which it is a part. It sees
W-pI...100.1:3 separate minds **u.** them in one purpose,
W-pI.151.17:2 the world **u.** with us and happily accepts
W-pI...160.9:2 His Own and joyously **u.** with them. They
W-pI 184.15:8 *Your Name* **u.** *us in the oneness which is our*
W-pI .. 186.1:6 It **u.** all wills on earth in Heaven's plan to
W-pI .. 188.3:6 everyone **u.** in giving thanks to you who

## unities 1

C-3........... 8:4 Unity of **u.** that stands behind all joining

## uniting 13

T-1....... III.7:3 is one, **u.** all creations with their Creator.
T-3....... IV.7:6 By **u.** my will with that of my Creator, I
T-8....... III.2:6 God's, **u.** it with His power and glory and
T-8.........V.3:7 and to our joy in **u.** with His Will for us.
T-8.........V.4:1 unite with me you are **u.** without the ego,
T-8...... VII.2:5 minds and **u.** them with yours and mine.
T-8...... VII.3:4 In the service of **u.** it becomes a beautiful
T-18......I.13:2 the Sonship with healing and **u.** comfort.
T-19........I.4:3 in which **u.** with him becomes impossible
T-28..... III.2:5 **U.** with a brother's mind prevents the
W-pI 185.14:1 **u.** our desires with the need of every heart
W-pII..... 6.1:2 the Self we share, **u.** us with one another,
W-pII .283.2:2 to all things, **u.** lovingly with all the world

## Unity 1

*unity*

C-3........... 8:4 **U.** of unities that stands behind all joining

## unity 46

*Unity*

T-3....... IV.1:7 the Levels of the Trinity are capable of **u.**.
T-8....... III.3:2 Their **u.** together by extending Their joint
T-12......I.10:5 dream of separation with the fact of **u.**.
T-13........I.6:3 projecting separation in place of **u.**. You
T-14.......V.6:2 is no **u.** of learning goals apart from this.
T-17..... VI.7:2 except that this attempt conflicts with **u.**,
T-20.......V.2:4 in that single heartbeat is the **u.** of love
T-20.......V.2:5 to hold the **u.** of the Son of God together.
T-21.... VII.1:8 protect his **u.** or see him shattered and
T-26 .. VII.10:4 and broken from a **u.** which holds all
T-26 .. VII.19:6 The **u.** that specialness denies will save
T-27........I.1:2 and make a **u.** of what can never join?
T-31... IV.10:3 out. In **u.** with Him do they abide, and in
W-pI.... 93.9:3 Try to experience the **u.** of your one Self.
W-pI.... 95.1:3 Yours is the **u.** of all creation. Your perfect
W-pI.... 95.1:4 Your perfect **u.** makes change in you
W-pI .. 95.12:2 may extend the allness and the **u.** of God.
W-pI.... 97.1:2 nor tries to weave opposing factors into **u.**
W-pI .. 99.10:1 truth of your completion, **u.** and peace.
W-pI .. 110.4:2 other minds, and only **u.** within your own
W-pI .. 125.8:3 and of peace, of **u.** of will and purpose,
W-pI .. 126.6:5 your **u.** with him to your awareness. It is
W-pI .. 137.3:5 and without the **u.** that gives It life. But
W-pI .. 154.3:3 becomes His messenger of **u.** with Him.
W-pI 167.11:3 created in a **u.** of life that cannot separate
W-pI .. 169.1:1 like the state prevailing in the **u.** of truth.
W-pI 169.13:3 and brought a clear reflection of the **u.** he
W-pI .. 184.1:4 By this you carve it out of **u.**. By this you
W-pI .. 184.2:2 and see as well nothing where there is **u.**;
W-pI .. 184.2:4 split you think you are established as a **u.**
W-pI .. 184.4:4 a sense of **u.** or vision that sees differently,
W-pI .. 184.8:7 And thus his **u.** is twice denied, for you
W-pI .. 184.9:5 the **u.** where true communication can be
W-pI .. 195.5:4 awareness of the **u.** we share with them,
W-pII . 262.2:2 We would come home, and rest in **u.**. For
W-pII . 268.1:3 *be willing to withdraw my wishes from its* **u.**,
W-pII ... 11.4:2 and unaware of our eternal **u.** with Him.
W-pII ... 11.4:5 know their oneness and their **u.** with their
M-12......... 3:8 their **u.** could not be recognized directly.
M-12......... 4:5 is enough to let the thought of **u.** come in,
M-12....... 6:10 **U.** alone is not a thing of dreams. And it is
M-14....... 3:10 it is the final lesson in which **u.** is restored
M-28......... 5:9 are lost, for **u.** of purpose has been found.
C-3........... 5:2 so the **u.** that it reflects becomes His Will.
S-1..........II.5:5 has become a statement of the **u.** of Christ
S-3......... III.1:8 to obscure the **u.** that is the Son of God.

**Universal** 3
*universal*
T-5...........I.4:6 from the Holy Spirit or the **U.** Inspiration,
T-9...........I.8:8 ask the **U.** Giver for what you do not want
T-19.........I.3:4 see itself as separated from the **U.** Purpose

**universal** 27
*Universal*
T-1........ I.27:1 miracle is a **u.** blessing from God through
T-1........ I.40:2 is a way of perceiving the **u.** mark of God.
T-2.......... II.1:2 are natural, corrective, healing and **u.**.
T-3.......... II.2:4 **u.** application that it becomes wisdom.
T-4.......VII.3:9 since its quality is **u.** in application and
T-6.......... II.5:5 is the one need in this world that is **u.**. To
T-12......VI.6:6 and everything, for its applicability is **u.**.
T-17......VI.1:6 you do not yet realize their **u.** application.
T-18......VI.8:3 the **u.** communication that is an eternal
T-22......VI.9:1 What can it be but **u.** blessing to look on
T-25....IX.10:9 Its offering is **u.**, and it teaches but one
T-26....... II.7:5 has been transformed into a **u.** blessing.
T-30......III.1:2 But your will is **u.**, being limitless. And so
T-31.........I.9:1 does not share the **u.** Will that it be whole
W-pI.....72.7:1 This is the **u.** belief of the world you see.
W-pI...137.3:6 to attack the **u.** Oneness of God's Son.
W-pI...139.6:3 Yet it is the **u.** question of the world.
W-pI...139.6:5 in the sad belief that what is **u.** here is true
W-pII....13.3:5 upon the **u.** altar to Creator and creation
W-pII..345.1:2 *to me, reminding me the law of love is* **u.**.
M-1............2:4 is **u.**. It goes on all the time everywhere. It
M-1............4:1 teachers of a special form of the **u.** course.
M-2............1:2 because the form of the **u.** curriculum that
M-3............3:1 the **u.** course is a concept as meaningless
M-22..........6:1 The offer of Atonement is **u.**. It is equally
C-in............2:5 **u.** theology is impossible, but a universal
C-in............2:5 but a **u.** experience is not only possible

**universality** 2
T-5...........I.7:2 First, its **u.** is perfectly clear, and no one
T-7........IV.6:9 the laws of God, and recognizing their **u.**.

**universally** 2
W-pI...188.5:6 In quietness is it acknowledged **u.**. For
W-pI...197.4:5 In your gratitude are they accepted **u.**,

**universe** 106
T-5........III.2:5 the laws of the **u.** of which it is a part. It is
T-7......VI.10:6 powerful force in the **u.** as if it were weak,
T-10......IV.6:5 by them He established the **u.** as what it is
T-11.........I.2:3 no endings in God, Whose **u.** is Himself.
T-11.........I.2:4 Can you exclude yourself from the **u.**, or
T-11.........I.2:4 the universe, or from God Who *is* the **u.**? I
T-11.........I.5:1 laws of the **u.** do not permit contradiction
T-11.........I.5:5 end to God and His Son, for we *are* the **u.**.
T-11....... I.5:10 The **u.** of love does not stop because you
T-11..... V.15:3 This, then, becomes the **u.** it perceives.
T-11..... V.15:4 And it is this **u.** which, in turn, becomes
T-12... VIII.5:4 should hardly aspire to control the **u.**. But
T-13....... V.6:4 reality as if you were alone in all the **u.**. In
T-14....... II.6:4 The **u.** of learning will open up before you
T-15....... II.6:8 deny the Presence of what the **u.** bows to,
T-15....... II.6:9 recognition of the **u.** that witnesses to It,
T-15... VIII.4:4 Your relationships are with the **u.**. And
T-15... VIII.4:5 And this **u.**, being of God, is far beyond
T-15.......XI.6:5 keep away holds all the meaning of the **u.**,
T-15.......XI.6:5 and holds the **u.** together in its meaning.
T-15.......XI.6:6 Unless the **u.** were joined in you it would
T-16......III.6:3 hold Him and whom He holds are the **u.**,
T-16......III.6:4 have taught this, and from far off in the **u.**
T-16......VI.5:4 for the separate union excludes the **u.**. Far
T-16......VI.5:6 in perfect faith, the **u.** would enter into it.
T-17.....VII.6:8 The **u.** will serve it gladly, as it serves the
T-17.....VII.6:8 will serve it gladly, as it serves the **u.**. But
T-17.....VII.7:3 stars and to the **u.** that lies beyond them,
T-18........ I.11:7 **u.** within you stands with you, together
T-18.....VII.5:3 brother restores the **u.** to both of you.
T-18... VIII.3:2 of dust it bids you fight against the **u.**.
T-18... VIII.3:5 illusion, holding itself apart against the **u.**
T19... IV.A.3:7 your brother seems mightier than the **u.**,
T19... IV.A.3:7 it would hold back the **u.** and its Creator.
T19... IV.D.1:4 of the **u.** and of the universe of universes,
T19... IV.D.1:4 of the universe and of the **u.** of universes,
T-20...... III.7:6 only thing in all the **u.** that does not know
T-20...... III.7:8 it slips unnoticed through the **u.** of truth,
T-20...... III.7:9 it you turn to ask the meaning of the **u.**.
T-20..... III.7:10 thing in all the seeing **u.** of truth you ask,
T-20....... V.8:2 shares his Father's certainty the **u.** rests in
T-20....... V.8:4 that the Creator of the **u.** should offer it to
T-20...... VI.5:7 place in all the **u.** where it can not be seen
T-21....... II.3:4 is possible within the **u.** as God created it,
T-22....... V.4:3 frightened mouse that would attack the **u.**
T-22....... V.4:5 throughout the **u.** forever sings as one?
T-22.... VI.11:7 than to attack the great Creator of the **u.**,
T-22.. VI.12:10 And this is so because the **u.** is one. You
T-22.... VI.15:1 your brother shines throughout the **u.**,
T-23...... IV.2:7 can a body be extended to hold the **u.**?
T-24.......in.1:8 back the Will that holds the **u.** secure?
T-24.........I.4:1 for there is nothing in the **u.** unlike itself.
T-24.........I.4:7 On its behalf they fight against the **u.**, for
T-24..... II.10:7 that both might share the **u.** with Him
T-24...... III.6:1 Forgive the great Creator of the **u.**, the
T-24.... IV.3:13 Given to Him, the **u.** is yours. Offered to
T-24...... VI.2:2 There could be no **u.** and no reality. For
T-24...... VI.3:1 Nothing is lost to you in all the **u.**.
T-24.... VI.11:3 In its eyes you are a separate **u.**, with all
T-25...... III.4:1 law itself upholds the **u.** as God created it,
T-25. VIII.14:1 You have the right to all the **u.**; to perfect
T-26...... III.3:3 truth, a segment of the **u.** made true. This
T-26...... IV.3:4 reach beyond the **u.** to touch the Heart of
T-26...... IV.5:5 the **u.** has joined with but a single voice.
T-27. VIII.12:5 The **u.** proclaims it so. Yet to its witnesses
T-28....... II.1:8 But in itself it holds the **u.** of all creation,
T-29...... VI.2:6 only thing in all the **u.** that must be one.
T-30....... II.4:4 you co-creator of the **u.** along with Him.
T-31.... VI.3:11 within the **u.** that God created that must
T-31.....VII.7:7 you love beside you, and the **u.** with them
T-31.....VII.8:1 Behold your role within the **u.**! To every
W-pI.....28.5:3 the purpose it shares with all the **u.**.
W-pI.....28.6:1 really asking to see the purpose of the **u.**.
W-pI.....29.2:4 that a table shares the purpose of the **u.**.
W-pI.....29.2:5 of the **u.** shares the purpose of its Creator.
W-pI.....52.5:7 the thinking of the **u.** than to obscure all
W-pI.....54.4:3 I think or say or do teaches all the **u.**. A
W-pI.....68.5:5 in all the **u.** in your perception of yourself.
W-pI.....69.7:2 call on the power of the **u.** to help you,
W-pI.....70.2:3 Today's idea places you in charge of the **u.**
W-pI...110.1:3 changed the **u.** so that what God created
W-pI...124.1:5 and with the **u.** we go our way rejoicing,
W-pI.136.10:2 and all the **u.** made slave to laws which
W-pI.136.11:2 The **u.** remains unheeding of the laws by
W-pI...152.8:3 your rightful place as co-creator of the **u.**,
W-pI...156.5:1 light in you is what the **u.** longs to behold.
W-pI.182.11:5 for love. He rules the **u.**, and yet He asks
W-pI.183.11:4 **u.** consists of nothing but the Son of God,
W-pI...188.5:7 looks upon is your perception of the **u.**.
W-pI...191.3:2 own Identity, and you assail the **u.** alone,
W-pI...196.5:5 destroy his life and blot him from the **u.**,
W-pI...201.1:3 *blessed with oneness with the* **u.** *and God,*
W-pII.....253.h My Self is ruler of the **u.**.
W-pII..253.2:2 *My Self, which rules the* **u.**, *is but Your Will*
W-pII..341.1:2 *and deep and still the* **u.** *smiles back on You,*
W-pII..341.1:3 *as His Son, a* **u.** *of Thought completing Him.*
M-20 .......6:11 The **u.** beyond the sun and stars, and all
M-27 .........2:1 this perception of the **u.** as God created it,
M-28 .........4:5 of fear and misperceptions of the **u.**. All
C-2.............8:1 and the self that seemed alone in all the **u.**
P-2........IV.1:4 the **u.** as you would have created it. It is a
P-2........VI.2:6 rhythm of the **u.**," "the herald angel's
P-2.......VII.5:6 tiny self of one alone against the **u.** able to
S-1......... V.1:4 it does not claim that you must rule the **u.**
S-3......... II.1:9 thoughts and raging anger at the **u.**. It
S-3......IV.10:3 The **u.** is waiting your release because it is

**universes** 1
T19... IV.D.1:4 of the universe and of the universe of **u.**,

**unjoined** 1
T-24.... VI.11:2 and **u.** with anything beyond the body. In

**unjust** 10
T-25VIII.11:12 For that would be **u.** to innocence.
T-25...... IX.6:2 what would be **u.** to him cannot occur.
T-25...... IX.7:7 No one can be **u.** to you, unless you have
T-25...... IX.7:7 you, unless you have decided first to *be* **u.**.
T-25...... IX.8:1 you were **u.** to one with equal rights. Seek
T-26........II.8:2 He cannot be **u.** to anyone or anything,
T-26....VIII.7:8 This is not reason, for it is **u.**, and clearly
T-26........X.3:7 more **u.** than that he be deprived of what
T-27.........I.2:5 **u.** vengeance that you suffer now belongs
M-19 ......... 1:5 on justice, since all attack can only be **u.**.

**unjustifiable** 2
T-6...........I.6:8 There can be no justification for the **u.**.
T-6.........I.11:4 are constantly engaged in justifying the **u.**

**unjustified** 5
T-13........X.8:6 wholly **u.** and wholly without reason, you
T-22... VI.12:3 It is **u.** in any form, because it has no
T-30...... VI.2:6 If pardon were **u.**, you would be asked to
T-30...... VI.3:5 **U.** forgiveness is attack. And this is all the
W-pI... 134.1:1 righteous wrath, a gift **u.** and undeserved,

**unjustly** 2
T-17... VII.3:11 as if you had been **u.** deprived of it.
T-27..... VII.1:3 attacked **u.** and by something not himself

**unkind** 1
T-17...... III.4:1 is indeed **u.** to the unholy relationship.

**unknowing** 8
T-14..... VII.3:1 possible to convince the **u.** that they know
T-14..... VII.3:4 opposite viewpoints on what the "**u.**" are.
T-14..... VII.3:5 To God, **u.** is impossible. It is therefore
T-14..... VII.3:7 It is only this belief that the **u.** have, and
T-31... VII.15:3 Their savior stands, **u.** and unknown,
W-pI. 169.13:4 while a part of you remains outside, **u.**,
W-pI. 186.13:1 Voice is calling from the known to the **u.**.
C-3.............2:1 a way in which the **u.** can bridge the gap

**unknowingly** 1
T-25.......in.2:4 And so he carries Him **u.**, and does not

**unknowingness** 1
T-14....VIII.4:6 the knowledge, given you by God, into **u.**.

**unknown** 30
T-3...........I.4:1 Sacrifice is a notion totally **u.** to God. It
T-7........ IV.1:7 is **u.** to Him and therefore does not exist,
T-8........ VI.7:7 does make the Son's function **u.** to him,
T-8........ VI.7:8 And because it is not **u.** to his Creator, it
T-11....... IV.3:2 you share, and your Self must be **u.** to you
T-12........II.8:3 You do not fear the **u.** but the known.
T-14.........I.1:8 what has been done for you, **u.** to you,
T-14...... VI.1:7 cannot be shared, and so its value is **u.**.
T-20...... VI.6:8 God seem fearful to you, and kept **u.**.
T-21.........I.1:1 for what it really looks like is **u.** to them.
T-21...... III.4:8 In Heaven they are **u.**. Yet Heaven is
T-21...... IV.2:2 Its rule is tempered, and its **u.** "enemy,"
T-23.........I.4:5 triumph and attack of any kind are all **u.**.
T-24.........I.2:2 are kept **u.** and never brought to reason,
T-26..... VII.9:7 facts can be denied and thus **u.**, though

T-26..... X.1:11 door to Theirs, and keeps Them there **u.**.
T-27...... III.6:6 other half of what it represents remains **u.**
T-31...VII.15:3 Their savior stands, unknowing and **u.**,
W-pI.....91.2:8 use it because its presence is **u.** to you.
W-pI...110.9:5 while He is unacknowledged and **u.**.
W-pI...158.3:7 Yet it seems to have a future still **u.** to us.
W-pI...160.1:3 And thus you are **u.** to you. What is your
W-pI...166.5:1 God's gifts go with him, all **u.** to him. He
W-pI...168.5:3 but He to Whom all error is **u.** is yet the
W-pI...182.1:4 feel an alien here, from somewhere all **u.**.
W-pI.185.10:4 seek above all things, perhaps **u.** to them,
W-pI...192.4:1 gently looks upon all things **u.** in Heaven,
W-pI...200.6:3 For it is **u.** in Heaven. It is only hell where
M-4 ....VIII.1:3 at a time perhaps **u.** to him as yet, but not
P-2......... V.1:3 that, to be safe, one must control the **u.**.

## unlearn 2

T-6...... III.3:10 and you can **u.** it by not teaching it.
T-14.... III.18:3 **U.** isolation through His loving guidance,

## unlearned 4

T-14....... II.6:1 learned to the Holy Spirit, to be **u.** for you
T-24......VII.7:5 still retains one **u.** lesson in his memory,
T-31....... V.8:4 Nor can it be **u.** except by lessons aimed
W-pI...158.6:4 Experience– **u.**, untaught, unseen–is

## unlearning 1

M-4 ....... X.3:7 Properly speaking it is **u.** that they bring,

## unless 186

T-1........ III.6:5 appropriately **u.** you perceive correctly.
T-1......... V.3:4 as little children" means that **u.** you fully
T-1.........VI.1:2 No learning is acquired by anyone **u.** he
T-2...........I.3:3 what is not true **u.** you choose to do so.
T-2......... V.8:5 state becomes doubly dangerous **u.** it *is*
T-2....V.A.15:3 is an empty gesture **u.** it entails correction
T-3........VI.2:8 be true **u.** you also believe that what you
T-4...........I.1:3 and **u.** they share their lessons conviction
T-4...........I.5:5 want to obey its laws **u.** *you* believe them.
T-4........ III.7:7 made, but I will not uphold it **u.** it is true.
T-4....... V.6:11 remain in effect **u.** you change your mind.
T-4.......VII.6:4 But **u.** you take your part in the creation,
T-5........ III.1:3 must be in His Mind because, **u.** it were,
T-5........VII.2:4 **U.** the healer heals himself, he cannot
T-6.........in.1:3 Anger cannot occur **u.** you believe that
T-6.........I.15:5 man with a kiss?" **u.** I believed in betrayal
T-6........ IV.4:4 **U.** you do believe it you will not side with
T-7......... V.3:5 but this cannot occur **u.** the body has
T-7......... V.5:2 **U.** the healer always heals by Him the
T-7........ VI.7:3 not require vigilance **u.** it is conflicted. If
T-7...... VI.10:3 **U.** you perceive His creation truly you
T-7.......VII.8:1 Attack could never promote attack **u.** you
T-7.......VII.8:2 lose anything **u.** you do not value it, and
T-7......... IX.3:6 **U.** you create you *are* unfulfilled, but God
T-8...........I.2:1 you **u.** you give it the power to do so. The
T-8........ IV.1:1 **u.** you experience only this you must be
T-8........ IV.4:3 it? For **u.** you do, you will not receive it. If
T-8...... IV.8:12 **U.** you take your place in It and fulfill
T-8........ VI.6:7 accept his function **u.** he knows what *he* is.
T-9...........I.1:2 have occurred **u.** the mind were already
T-9...........I.6:5 be communicated **u.** it makes sense. How
T-9......... II.6:7 the trust I have in you **u.** you extend it.
T-9......... II.6:8 that it is for you **u.** you hear it in others. It
T-9......... III.5:4 **U.** this becomes the one way in which you
T-9......... IV.6:4 and **u.** you accept this you cannot learn
T-9...... IV.10:1 and who turns to fantasy **u.** he despairs of
T-9......... V.6:5 Nothing will change **u.** it is understood,
T-9......... V.7:2 but the point is lost **u.** he is also helped to
T-9.......VII.2:5 in peace **u.** you accept the Atonement,
T-9.......VII.2:8 cannot overlook it **u.** you are not looking.
T-9......VIII.4:4 **u.** you do not allow the ego to attack it.
T-10....... II.1:1 **U.** you first know something you cannot
T-10....... V.3:4 **U.** you are sick you cannot keep the gods
T-11.......I.10:1 be happy **u.** you do what you will truly,
T-11...... III.1:4 **U.** you hurt yourself you could never
T-11 ... III.7:10 understand wholeness **u.** you are whole,
T-11 ....... V.1:1 escape from illusions **u.** he looks at them,
T-11 ..... V.18:5 of him **u.** you have evoked false witnesses
T-11 ..... VI.9:5 and **u.** you give all that you have received
T-12 .....VII.4:2 And **u.** you do, you will not realize He is
T-12 .. VII.15:4 the Father **u.** He had also given it to you?
T-12 ...VIII.3:8 **u.** He had given you a way to remember
T-13 ..... IV.6:2 hold over you **u.** you bring them with you
T-13 ..... IV.6:5 **U.** you learn that past pain is an illusion,
T-13 ..... VI.2:4 the present, ***u.** you are afraid of light.* And
T-13 ..... VI.4:2 **u.** you force continuity on them. You can
T-13 ..... VI.6:1 you, and **u.** you bring them with you, you
T-13 .....X.11:1 Sons **u.** you love them all and equally.
T-13 ..... XI.1:2 and ravaged by a cruel war **u.** he believes
T-14 .........I.1:8 **u.** you do what you would have to do if it
T-14 ........II.1:4 that **u.** you learn it you will not be happy.
T-14 ..... IV.7:1 **U.** you are guiltless you cannot know
T-14 ..... VI.2:3 **u.** it is concealed from love's beneficence.
T-14 .... VII.6:6 and **u.** you look with Him He cannot see.
T-14 .....X.10:5 it not **u.** he joins with you in seeking it. If
T-14 ..... XI.5:3 **U.** all this is true, there are dark lessons in
T-14 ... XI.13:1 those who recognize they cannot know **u.**
T-15 ........II.1:5 For **u.** God is bound, you cannot be. An
T-15 ..... IV.1:1 **u.** you believe that what God wills takes
T-15 ....... V.6:6 **U.** you had seen yourself as without love,
T-15 ..... XI.6:6 **U.** the universe were joined in you it
T-15 ... XI.10:6 ***u.** I want to use you to imprison myself. In*
T-16 ..... III.3:4 taught freedom **u.** you did believe in it.
T-16 .... V.11:2 become to you that **u.** it is weak and little,
T-16 .... V.15:2 And **u.** love's meaning is restored to you,
T-16 ..... VI.1:3 **u.** a relationship has special value it has
T-17 .........I.3:6 **U.** you give it back, it is inevitable that
T-17 ... VII.6:4 No relationship is holy **u.** its holiness goes
T-18 ........II.1:6 wish **u.** you saw yourself as one with the
T-18 ..... VI.3:7 **U.** the mind believes the body is actually
T-18 ... VII.4:1 the holy instant without reservation **u.**,
T-19 ........II.1:5 and will forever so remain **u.** a mind not
T-19 ..... III.3:5 stop and let it go, **u.** the guilt remains. For
T19....IV.A.1:2 it. For it cannot extend **u.** you keep it. You
T19....IV.C.1:4 No one can die **u.** he chooses death. What
T19... IV.D.9:1 **u.** he has accepted the Atonement and
T19... IV.D.9:2 this far **u.** his brother walked beside him.
T19. IV.D.10:6 that it is over **u.** you realize its purpose is
T-20 ........II.6:4 you use what I have given **u.** you share it.
T-20 ..... IV.1:1 hurt you **u.** you give it the power to do so.
T-20 .... VII.7:7 judgment has no value **u.** the goal is sin.
T-21 ..... VI.3:3 itself **u.** the body *were* the mind. For only
T-21 ..... VI.6:7 How can a fact be fearful **u.** it disagrees
T-21 ... VIII.3:9 giving must be incomplete **u.** it is received
T-22 .....II.10:2 you **u.** you still would be apart from your
T-22 ... VI.11:2 frail and easily destroyed **u.** his Father is?
T-23 ......in.1:5 and no one can attack **u.** he thinks he has.
T-23 .........I.1:4 impossible **u.** belief in victory is cherished
T-23 .....II.12:2 is justified **u.** you know what it is for? And
T-25 ..... IV.1:7 the hope of change **u.** the aim is changed.
T-25 ....... V.1:6 believe in one **u.** the other were the truth,
T-25 .... V.4:10 it be regained **u.** the way is shown to him
T-25 ..... IX.6:4 **u.** someone deserves to suffer more and
T-25 ..... IX.7:7 you, **u.** you have decided first to *be* unjust.
T-25 ..... IX.8:1 **U.** you think that all your brothers have
T-26 ..... III.5:3 **u.** he recognizes they are not the same?
T-26 ..... IV.1:5 No one forgives **u.** he has believed in sin,
T-26 ... VIII.3:2 **U.** you so perceive it, you will be afraid of
T-26 ... VIII.5:4 fear effects **u.** he thought they had been
T-27 ........II.4:1 Forgiveness is not real **u.** it brings a
T-27 ........II.4:4 innocence be justified **u.** his sins have no
T-27 ..... IV.6:8 And so, **u.** the answer tells "of whom," it
T-27 .. VII.13:4 **u.** a gentler dream preceded his awaking,
T-27 ... VIII.4:4 to figures in a dream **u.** he sees them as if
T-27 .VIII.10:6 no effect on you **u.** you failed to recognize
T-28 ..... IV.1:6 **U.** you help him, you will suffer pain with
T-28 ..... VI.5:3 **U.** you both agree that is your wish, it can
T-29 .........I.5:1 your brother's **u.** you wanted it to be a
T-29 ..... III.1:8 **U.** he gives he will not know he has, for
T-29 ... III.1:10 so. For who could give **u.** he has, and who
T-29 ...... V.7:4 Because **u.** the Holy Spirit gives the dream
T-29 ..... VI.3:2 die it must **u.** it does not take this purpose
T-29 ... VIII.8:5 No one comes **u.** he worshipped them,
T-29 ..... IX.3:3 for one **u.** he were in terror and despair?
T-30 .........I.5:2 **u.** you quickly straighten out your mind
T-30 ........II.2:4 **U.** you do your will you are not free. And
T-30 ...... VI.3:2 Fear cannot arise **u.** attack is justified, and
T-30 ... VIII.4:6 is no miracle that can be given you **u.** you
T-31 ........II.1:5 be hurt in such a war, **u.** he hurts himself?
T-31 ........II.4:5 is. **U.** he serves it, he has not fulfilled the
T-31 ........II.6:9 way **u.** you keep him safely by your side.
T-31 ..... III.4:9 could never change **u.** the mind preferred
T-31 ..... IV.4:7 understand you but waste time **u.** you go
T-31 ..... IV.5:1 world, **u.** he understood their real futility?
T-31 ..... IV.9:4 it must have **u.** it be but futile wandering?
T-31 ..... V.17:1 images of you **u.** you want to learn them.
T-31 .... VII.6:3 **u.** you choose to hold it past the hope of
W-pI ...... 1.4:2 or so, **u.** that entails a sense of hurry.
W-pI ...... 8.6:1 during the day, **u.** you find it irritates you.
W-pI ..... 14.2:3 today's idea **u.** you find them comfortable
W-pI ..... 15.5:3 **u.** you feel completely comfortable with it
W-pI ..... 38.6:1 apply the idea in its original form **u.** a
W-pI ..... 42.5:3 Let them come without censoring **u.** you
W-pI ..... 44.7:3 be stopped in this **u.** you choose to stop it
W-pI ..... 44.9:1 your eyes closed **u.** you are aware of fear.
W-pI .. 44.10:3 world **u.** you give them the power to do so
W-pI ..... 53.2:6 need not see it at all **u.** I choose to value it.
W-pI ..... 66.6:5 not. **U.** God gives you only happiness, He
W-pI ..... 66.8:3 **U.** God gave your function to you, it must
W-pI ..... 76.3:2 that you would starve **u.** you have stacks
W-pI ..... 76.3:4 you are alone **u.** another body is with you.
W-pI ..... 82.3:4 it. And **u.** I fulfill my function, I will not
W-pI ..... 95.5:2 that, **u.** you are reminded of your purpose
W-pI .. 126.7:2 He ask you for a gift **u.** it was for you?
W-pI .. 129.1:2 for **u.** you see that there is something else
W-pI .. 131.3:3 you search, **u.** you give it power to do so.
W-pI 132.11:4 **U.** it does, it is not real, and cannot be at
W-pI .. 133.3:2 **U.** they meet these sound requirements,
W-pI .. 135.1:1 himself **u.** he thought he were attacked,
W-pI 135.15:2 for, **u.** it makes its own provisions. Time
W-pI .. 136.1:1 No one can heal **u.** he understands what
W-pI .. 139.4:2 never be alive at all **u.** he knew the answer
W-pI .. 152.1:1 can suffer loss **u.** it be his own decision.
W-pI .. 152.1:3 **u.** these are the outcomes that he wants.
W-pI .. 160.3:3 **u.** he thought there were another home
W-pI .. 163.6:5 not be true, **u.** its opposite is proven false.
W-pI .. 166.1:5 And yet, **u.** your will is one with His, His
W-pI .. 187.1:1 No one can give **u.** he has. In fact, giving
W-pI .. 197.1:3 **u.** you find external gratitude and lavish
W-pI .. 200.1:5 of God, **u.** you seek for misery and pain.
W-pII .... in.5:7 could have never come this far **u.** you saw,
W-pII . 277.2:5 he cannot be bound **u.** God's truth can lie
W-pII . 289.1:1 **U.** the past is over in my mind, the real
W-pII . 290.1:1 **U.** I look upon what is not there, my
W-pII . 301.1:1 *Father,* ***u.*** *I judge I cannot weep. Nor can I*
W-pII . 304.1:2 looks upon, **u.** it is His vision that I use.
M-4 ..... I.A.3:4 How can lack of value be perceived **u.** the
M-4 ..... I.A.5:4 valueless **u.** the next obvious step is taken.
M-5 .........I.1:2 choose suffering **u.** he thought it brought
M-21 ......... 2:3 **U.** a specific referent does occur to the
M-22 ......... 3:8 to the Holy Spirit **u.** the body is killed?
M-24 ......... 5:3 belief **u.** his internal Teacher so advised.
M-25 ......... 5:7 **u.** the individual changes his mind about
C-5 ............ 2:4 Yet who can save **u.** he sees illusions and
P-3........ III.5:8 lose this understanding **u.** they remember
S-2...........I.5:5 You have no freedom **u.** he gives it to you.

## unlike 42

T-4 ..........I.9:3 You have chosen to create **u.** Him, and
T-10 .......V.5:5 make creators who are **u.** your Creator,
T-10 .......V.5:5 could have created a Son who was **u.** Him.
T-10 .......V.5:6 is sharing, it cannot create what is **u.** itself
T-11 ...... III.7:5 For what is **u.** God cannot enter His Mind
T-11 .......V.5:4 extension of His Will cannot be **u.** itself.
T-11 .... VII.3:7 autonomy you tried to create **u.** your
T-11 .... VII.3:7 what you made is capable of being **u.** Him
T-12 ..... III.9:5 it is governed by the desire to be **u.** God,
T-13 .....X.11:5 Seek not to love **u.** Him, for there is no
T-14 ... IV.10:2 sees the other **u.** the way he sees himself.
T-15 .......V.3:2 If you would love **u.** to God, Who knows
T-16 ..... VI.1:4 is **u.** the relationship of God and His Son,
T-16 ..... VI.1:4 that are **u.** this one *must* be unnatural. For

T-19......III.1:8 only an avenger, with a mind **u.** your own
T-19......III.6:2 what is part of Him is totally **u.** the rest. If
T-21.....VII.6:2 one still seems fearful, and **u.** the others.
T-22.......in.2:8 a world of strangers, **u.** themselves, living
T-23....... II.2:5 and those who hold them seem to be **u.**,
T-24.........I.4:1 there is nothing in the universe **u.** itself.
T-24....... II.3:4 the "creator" who creates **u.** the Father,
T-25.....IX.10:7 Because it does not make the same **u.**, it
T-27. VIII.13:7 is impossible is that you be **u.** each other;
T-28....... II.3:6 mind, creating with effects **u.** yourself.
T-28......III.9:1 a feast **u.** indeed to those the dreaming of
T-28......IV.6:2 because what is the same appears to be **u.**.
T-29....... II.7:3 To change is to attain a state **u.** the one in
T-29......VI.3:4 can set a goal **u.** God's purpose for you,
W-pI.......4.1:1 **U.** the preceding ones, these exercises do
W-pI.....68.1:6 from your Source and make you **u.** Him.
W-pI.....68.1:7 can conceive of his Creator as **u.** himself.
W-pI.....72.4:6 as well. A creator wholly **u.** his creation is
W-pI.....96.5:4 Now must it reconcile **u.** with like, for this
W-pI.127.10:4 future dawns **u.** the past in every attribute
W-pI.132.11:5 creation is **u.** the world in every way. And
W-pI.135.16:4 to guarantee a future quite **u.** the past,
W-pI...137.8:4 attribute it proves that laws **u.** the ones
M-10..........3:1 **u.** the goal of the world's learning, is the
M-20..........2:2 way it is totally **u.** all previous experiences
M-23..........3:9 can one who is one with God be **u.** Him?
C-3............1:4 **U.** all other illusions it leads away from
S-2.........in.1:7 **U.** the timeless nature of its sister, prayer,

### unlikely 4

T-31.....V.10:1 your brother made of you seems most **u.**.
W-pI.......9.1:2 **u.** that it will mean anything to you as yet.
M-9...........1:4 is most **u.** that changes in attitudes would
M-24..........5:4 And this is most **u.**. He might be advised

### unlimited 37

T-5......... II.6:4 that its creative power is **u.** and choice is
T-5....... II.12:5 the Call for God is the Call to the **u.**. Child
T-6....... II.13:4 This alignment with light is **u.**, because it
T-8......... II.7:3 no boundaries because its extension is **u.**,
T-8......... II.7:7 and glory, and are therefore as **u.** as He is.
T-8.......VII.3:5 way of making **u.** what you have limited.
T-8.....VII.16:6 there *is* **u.** communication and therefore
T-8.....VII.16:6 and therefore **u.** power and wholeness.
T-12....... V.9:7 of God's Son. His learning is as **u.** as he is.
T-13....VI.11:8 Light is **u.**, and spreads across this world
T-15......IX.1:1 from them, so **u.** that they reach to God.
T-15......IX.2:5 must be **u.** in order to have meaning, and
T-15......IX.6:3 His attraction for you remains **u.**, but
T-15....... X.2:2 and his **u.** power is thus restored to him.
T-16.......V.11:1 How can you grant **u.** power to what you
T-18......IV.4:2 combined with the **u.** power of God's Will
T-18... VIII.1:3 its origin, and it was made to limit the **u.**.
T-20......II.10:2 free, **u.** in his communion with all that is
T-20......VI.9:3 of the holy instant and its **u.** beneficence?
T-22....VI.14:8 Joy is **u.**, because each shining thought of
T-26....VII.14:5 everything is his, **u.** by loss of any kind.
T-27......III.7:5 to interfere with power **u.** and single
T-27.....V.10:1 that they remain unviolated and **u.**. Your
T-28......III.9:3 Guests have brought **u.** supply with Them
T-30......III.3:2 Wholeness has no form because it is **u.**.
W-pI.....30.5:1 vision is not only **u.** by space and distance
W-pI.....38.1:3 holiness is totally **u.** in its power because
W-pI.....58.3:2 do. My holiness is **u.** in its power to heal,
W-pI.....58.3:2 heal, because it is **u.** in its power to save.
W-pI.....91.8:6 *I am not limited, but* **u.**. *I am not doubtful,*
W-pI...105.4:3 It extends the limitless to the **u.**, eternity
W-pI...127.4:5 upon Himself, and so are you **u.** as well.
W-pI...129.4:1 plain as day, remains **u.** for all eternity.
W-pI...162.4:3 kept complete because its sharing is **u.**.
W-pI...199.2:1 that serves the Holy Spirit is **u.** forever, in
W-pII..315.2:2 *My brothers are* **u.** *in all their gifts to me.*
M-3............5:2 him with **u.** opportunities for learning.

### unlit 1

T-24....... V.4:2 **u.** but by the shifting tiny gleams that

### unloosened 1

W-pI.193.12:3 The chains of time are easily **u.** in this way

### unlost 1

W-pI.159.10:8 to our **u.** and everlasting sanctity in God.

### unlovable 1

M-11 .........2:6 the world; your judgment says it is **u.**.

### unloving 9

T-7.......VII.3:2 of you is deprived, **u.** and vulnerable. You
T-9.......VII.4:5 has evaluated you as **u.** and you are going
T-9.......VII.5:1 to see yourself as **u.** you will not be happy.
T-13.... III.10:4 Therefore you made of Him an **u.** father,
W-pI.....34.3:2 which you are harboring **u.** thoughts.
W-pI.....39.6:2 search out your **u.** thoughts in whatever
W-pI.....39.6:3 they take, they are **u.** and therefore fearful
W-pI.....39.7:1 you associate with **u.** thoughts of any kind
W-pI.....39.8:3 *My* **u.** *thoughts about_are keeping me in*

### unmade 2

T-10......III.9:6 and will be **u.** for you the instant you
T-21...VII.10:4 can be made, and then **u.** and made again

### unmarked 1

W-pI...192.4:1 and leaves the world a clean and **u.** slate

### unmerciful 1

T-13....... X.9:1 been **u.** to yourself do not remember your

### unmerited 2

T-30......VI.4:3 God the sure result of seeing pardon as **u.**.
W-pI...126.4:2 **U.**, withholding it is just, nor is it fair that

### unmet 2

T-16.........I.7:4 No needs will long be left **u.** if you leave
W-pI...159.6:5 no need **u.** within this golden treasury of

### unmindful 4

T-2......IV.3:12 to protect the mind by denying the **u.**. If
T-18... VIII.6:1 **u.** that this tiny part regards itself as you.
T-29....... II.9:5 **u.** that the failure does not lie in that it is
W-pI...140.6:3 not sick, **u.** where the need for healing is.

### unmistakable 1

T-17....IV.15:1 of light, in clear-cut and **u.** contrast, is

### unmoved 2

T-24......III.3:3 leave it perfectly **u.** and undisturbed. But
W-pI...198.8:1 The stillness of your Self remains **u.**,

### unnatural 17

T-5......... V.4:8 Guilt is a sure sign that your thinking is **u.**
T-5......... V.4:9 **U.** thinking will always be attended with
T-8......... II.4:2 This **u.** lesson cannot be learned, and the
T-13.....VI.2:2 Yet this is *u.* because it is delusional. When
T-14....III.18:1 You taught yourself the most **u.** habit of
T-16....... II.3:1 to hurt your mind has made it so **u.** that it
T-16....... V.3:5 is not natural at all seem to be the **u.** ones.
T-16....... V.6:1 special relationship is a strange and **u.**
T-16......VI.1:4 that are unlike this one *must* be **u.**. For
T-21....... V.3:6 Miracles seem **u.** to the ego because it
T-23....III.6:10 and the **u.** intent to murder and to die.
T-27.........I.7:2 one of their **u.** desires and strange needs.
T-30......VI.2:4 asked to make **u.** responses which are
W-pI.....44.4:3 just as it seems to be the most **u.** and
W-pI...161.2:2 But part of it is now **u.**. It does not look
W-pI...191.3:1 weird, **u.** and ghostly thought that mocks
M-25 .........1:2 There are, of course, no "**u.**" powers, and

### unnaturally 1

T-8.......VII.7:7 use the body **u.** is to lose sight of the Holy

### unnecessary 16

T-1..........II.6:5 it renders the interval of time it spans **u.**.
T-1......... V.1:1 a state in which they become **u.**. When
T-1.....VII.3:11 Fantasies become totally **u.** as the wholly
T-2..........II.6:5 errors, thus making it **u.** for you to keep
T-2........ III.4:6 delay, realizing that it only adds **u.** pain.
T-2......... V.9:1 the separation, before which it was **u.**.
T-4....... II.11:3 realization that *all* perception is **u.**. This
T-4........ III.1:3 The word "within" is **u.**. The Kingdom of
T-5........ VI.3:6 Alternate interpretations were **u.** until the
T-5...... VI.12:3 producing results *now* it renders time **u.**.
T-6.........I.11:2 Spirit, Whom we share, makes this **u.**. To
T-6....... II.11:2 Holy Spirit tells you that even return is **u.**,
T-6....V.C.10:4 only until you learn that effort itself is **u.**.
T-13.........I.1:1 ultimate aim is to make themselves **u.** by
T-13...... IV.7:3 purpose as rendering the need for time **u.**.
T-22.........I.3:7 would, of course, render this quite **u.**. Yet

### unneeded 4

W-pI.183.10:3 and all requests **u.** when God's Son calls
W-pII .294.1:9 It is but functionless, **u.** and cast off. Let
W-pII .301.1:2 *or feel I am abandoned or* **u.** *in the world.*
S-2.........in.1:8 it becomes **u.** when the rising up is done.

### unneedful 1

S-1..........II.7:8 or vain desires, **u.** now of anything at all.

### unnoticed 3

T-20...... III.7:8 and so meaningless it slips **u.** through the
T-29....... V.2:3 in this world but passes by, **u.** and unseen
W-pI...108.2:3 while what is not the same remains **u.**, for

### unnourishing 1

W-pI...159.8:3 can never grow in its **u.** and shallow soil.

### unoccupied 6

T-21........II.7:2 and **u.** the altar where the gifts belong.
T-26...... VI.3:2 its emptiness has left yours empty and **u.**?
T-27...... III.3:8 be perceived as idly spent, a time **u.**.
T-27...... III.6:1 the space so lately left **u.** and vacant will
T-31.....VII.9:2 that holds your brother off **u.** by love. Yet
W-pII .319.1:3 and fill up the space the ego left **u.** by lies.

### unopened 1

T-31...VII.15:3 unknown, beholding them with eyes **u.**.

### unopposed 2

T-27...... III.1:5 Power is **u.**, to be itself. No weakness can
W-pI...167.8:4 Forever **u.** by opposites of any kind, the

### unpictured 1

T-27...... III.5:2 known without a form, **u.** and unseen.

### unpleasant 2

W-pI.....12.4:1 think is pleasant and what you think is **u.**.
W-pI.....17.3:1 to be animate or inanimate; pleasant or **u.**

### unpredictability 1

T-9........IV.8:2 whether its **u.** places the ego in a sound

**unpredictable** 2
T-9 IV.7:6 It is **u.** in its responses, because it has no
T19 IV.A.8:3 to be more erratic and **u.** than before. Yet

**unproductive** 1
T-18 VIII.8:6 Look at the desert–dry and **u.,** scorched

**unprotected** 2
T-16 V.2:2 the Sonship open to attack and **u.** from it.
T-17 IV.13:6 itself, seeing at last that, **u.** by the frame,

**unquestioned** 1
T-20 VII.5:5 remain **u.** while the end is cherished.

**unquiet** 1
T-28 I.11:4 miracle delay in hastening to all **u.** minds,

**unreachable** 1
T-18 VI.7:5 in a separate prison, removed and **u.,**

**unready** 1
M-29 2:3 needs but a smile, being as yet **u.** for more

**unreal** 58
T-in 2:3 *Nothing **u.** exists.* Herein lies the peace of
T-1 I.39:1 Holy Spirit identifies error as false or **u..**
T-1 III.9:3 of size exists on a plane that is itself **u..**
T-3 VI.2:11 way you are placing your belief in the **u..**
T-6 II.9:6 Although perception of any kind is **u.,**
T-7 III.2:5 only by experiencing yourself as **u..** This
T-7 III.3:7 from saying you perceive yourself as **u.?**
T-8 VII.15:8 Yet if all condemnation is **u.,** and it must
T-8 VII.15:8 it must be **u.** since it is a form of attack,
T-9 I.13:4 make the **u.** because the absence of reality
T-9 I.14:4 because you are trying to make yourself **u.**
T-9 IV.5:2 it make real the **u.** and then destroy it.
T-9 IV.5:3 beginning, and thus keeping it **u.** for you.
T-9 V.2:1 be shared, and this is why they are **u..**
T-9 V.4:4 if the dreamer were also identified as **u..**
T-12 I.4:2 of the need for healing by making it **u..**
T-12 VIII.7:6 looked upon the **u.** and found despair.
T-12 VIII.7:7 Yet by seeking the **u.,** what else could you
T-12 VIII.7:8 The **u.** world *is* a thing of despair, for it can
T-13 X.11:3 all your relationships and making them **u.**
T-13 XI.1:4 the war is between real and **u.** powers, he
T-13 XI.2:1 His Son's imagined "enemy" is totally **u..**
T-14 VII.2:6 it becomes **u.** to you *because* you hid it and
T-15 V.2:2 relationships, and thus make them **u..** If
T-16 II.5:1 yours while you are bent on making it **u.?**
T-16 V.16:4 choosing possible, and they are totally **u..**
T-17 I.2:3 devoting it to "evil," it also makes it **u..**
T-17 I.5:5 truth to teach that the illusions are **u.,**
T-17 III.7:7 You have made the relationship **u.,** and
T-18 II.8:2 that dreams can make a world that is **u..**
T-20 VIII.7:5 and destroy themselves, are wholly **u.?**
T-21 II.7:5 you otherwise must therefore seem **u..** All
T-21 II.9:3 Faith in the **u.** leads to adjustments of
T-21 VI.3:4 bodies can be separate, and therefore **u..**
T-22 II.3:9 to other dreams that are but equally **u..**
T-23 in.1:4 it not, for how can the **u.** be hidden? No
T-26 V.9:5 whose accomplishment can only be **u..**
T-27 VI.1:7 Pleasure and pain are equally **u.,** because
T-30 IV.7:3 and not to look upon the **u.** as reality.
T-30 VIII.2:9 are shown to be **u.** *because* they change.
T-30 VIII.4:2 between reality and your awareness is **u.,**
W-pI 16.3:3 all as equally destructive, but equally **u..**
W-pI 35.4:3 All of them are equally **u.,** because you do
W-pI 45.4:2 will attempt to leave the **u.** and seek for
W-pI 45.6:6 Then try to go past all the **u.** thoughts
W-pI 87.1:3 and afraid of things unseen and **u..** Light
W-pI 93.5:5 It is **u.,** and nothing more than that. It
W-pI 130.4:6 They can be valued, but remain **u..** They
W-pI 130.5:5 the **u.** are all there are to choose between,
W-pI 130.10:2 The **u.** or the real, the false or true is what
W-pI 198.1:4 lay it down as valueless, unwanted and **u..**
M-8 6:4 put them all in one category; they are **u..**
M-20 3:12 that is perceived as nonexistent and **u..**
M-22 5:5 so he is seeing in his brother only the **u..**
C-3 6:7 As a perception it is part **u..** And yet this
C-5 1:5 for time needs symbols, being itself **u..**
P-2 IV.10:7 function to teach that guilt, being **u.,**
P-2 IV.10:9 it must remain unwanted as well as **u..**

**unrealistic** 1
P-2 in.4:4 and therapists alike accept **u.** goals not

**unrealities** 1
W-pI 140.6:2 It does not make distinctions among **u..**

**unreality** 24
T-1 VII.3:2 always involve twisting perception into **u.**
T-7 VI.2:4 of **u.** and results in utter confusion. Your
T-10 IV.2:3 the willingness to judge **u.** for what it is.
T-11 V.10:5 fear **u.** *because* you have denied yourself.
T-12 I.8:12 that it is, the **u.** of fear must dawn on you.
T-13 VIII.3:7 be seen, and they will replace aspects of **u.**
T-13 XI.2:8 as one into the **u.** from which they came.
T-14 IX.2:10 Undoing is for **u..** And this reality will do
T-17 III.3:4 toward further fragmentation and **u..** The
T-18 I.5:3 from it a world of total **u.** *had* to emerge.
T-18 II.5:19 determination to keep your hold on **u.,**
T-19 III.h The **U.** of Sin
T-21 V.2:4 and feelings of impermanence and **u..**
T-26 V.4:3 long ago, before its **u.** gave way to truth.
T-27 VII.12:5 Here is the cause of **u..** And it is here that
T-30 IV.8:8 of the toys of fear, and then its **u.** is plain.
T-30 VIII.3:4 keep their **u.** obscure and give to them
W-pI 13.2:3 to demonstrate its own impotence and **u..**
W-pI 130.7:2 attempt to bring with us a little part of **u.,**
W-pI 134.6:1 is sin's **u.** that makes forgiveness natural
W-pI 184.10:3 but only to proclaim its **u.** in terms which
W-pII 342.1:3 *have given me the means to prove its **u.** to me*
M-8 5:3 Will he agree more quickly to the **u.** of a
C-2 3:3 The ego's **u.** is not denied by words nor is

**unreasonable** 3
T-10 IV.3:6 and then the mind does become **u..** By
W-pI 170.6:4 It is their enemies who are **u.** and insane,
M-7 4:4 appear **u.** at first to be told that continued

**unreceived** 1
W-pI 126.7:6 What remains as **u.** has not been given,

**unrecognizable** 2
W-pI 136.5:5 Defenses must make facts **u..** They aim at
W-pI 187.4:4 For this will change and grow **u.** in time,

**unrecognized** 16
T-14 VII.2:5 Yet it can be recognized or **u.,** real or false
T-16 IV.1:10 And until you do, the split will remain **u.,**
T19 IV.C.4:5 all are part of your **u.** dedication to death.
T-24 I.2:2 an **u.** belief is a decision to war in secret,
T-24 I.2:6 **u.** and swift to challenge you to combat
T-24 I.3:1 a hidden belief, to be defended though **u.,**
T-24 I.8:1 comes from each **u.** belief in specialness.
T-25 VI.3:4 He does not will your savior be **u.** by you.
T-27 IV.6:8 answer tells "of whom," it will remain **u.,**
T-29 VIII.1:3 For idols are **u.** as such, and never seen
W-pI 107.1:2 illusions that remain **u.** for what they are?
W-pI 138.10:2 decide between the clearly seen and the **u.**
W-pI 163.1:1 that takes on many forms, often **u..** It may
W-pI 185.9:7 and turning of the road, to reappear, **u.,**
M-8 4:5 U. by itself, it has itself asked to be given
P-2 VI.4:1 thus keep unforgiveness **u.** for what it is.

**unreconcilable** 1
T-19 I.6:7 to truth, and seen as totally **u.** with truth,

**unredeemed** 2
T-16 I.5:4 The **u.** cannot redeem, yet they have a
T19 IV.D.16:6 brow, nor nail him to it, **u.** and hopeless.

**unrelated** 2
T-31 VI.2:2 behold a world of separation, **u.** things,
M-in 3:2 questions may be totally **u.** to what you

**unrelenting** 3
T19 IV.A.8:2 It is no longer an **u.** barrier to peace. Its
T19 IV.C.8:5 merciless and **u.** orders you laid upon it,
P-2 IV.3:2 misery now stalk the earth in **u.** waves,

**unreliable** 1
T-22 I.6:4 makes and what he hears are highly **u.,**

**unremembered** 12
T19 IV.D.3:3 beyond the veil forever blotted out and **u.**
T-21 I.6:1 in which you heard completely **u..** Not the
T-26 II.7:4 disappear, to be forever undone and **u..**
T-28 I.8:2 It is not past because He let It not be **u..** It
T-28 I.8:5 Father's Will that He be **u.** by His Son.
T-28 I.11:5 its place will not be wholly **u.** afterwards.
T-28 I.13:5 fear was made to render **u.** and undone.
T-30 III.7:3 An **u.** thought is born again to you when
T-30 V.7:6 For He must be **u.** till His Son has reached
T-31 VII.10:5 will yet meet; the **u.** and the not yet born.
W-pI 164.3:3 sins forgot, and all your sorrows **u..** On
S-1 II.7:3 The things of earth are left behind, all **u..**

**unresolved** 5
T-25 IX.7:6 is to decide it should remain unsettled, **u.,**
T-27 VII.2:3 which were made to keep the problem **u.?**
W-pI 24.4:1 eyes, for **u.** situations about which you are
W-pI 24.7:1 each **u.** situation that crosses your mind
W-pI 26.6:1 your eyes and reviewing the **u.** questions

**unrewarding** 2
T-15 VII.4:6 endless, **u.** chain of special relationships,
T-25 II.3:2 the hopeless and **u.** task you set yourself.

**unsafe** 6
T-6 V.3:3 because it will hurt you and make you **u.;**
T-14 VI.3:2 They are neither safe nor **u..** They do not
T-30 IV.2:5 mean his world is made chaotic and **u..**
T-30 VII.7:4 a state so seemingly **u.** that fear must rise.
W-pI 135.5:4 **u.** it must be guarded with your very life.
Wfl in.1:5 sin that made the world seem ugly and **u.,**

**unsatisfied** 3
T-15 I.4:6 death, which it craves for you, leaves it **u..**
W-pI 159.6:5 no sickness not already healed, no lack **u.,**
W-pI 185.11:3 can remain **u.** who asks for what he has

**unsatisfying** 3
T-16 IV.3:7 broken or becomes **u.** on the grounds of
W-pI 12.3:6 a "satisfying world" implies an "**u.**" one.
W-pI 164.8:5 to be sought above the world's **u.** goals?

**unsaved** 1
T-29 III.4:3 will not forget his savior, leaving him **u..**

**unscrupulous** 1
T-23..... II.10:3 attack by the **u.** behavior of the enemy,

**unsealed** 1
T-31..... V.17:3 this **u.** and open mind that truth returns,

**unseeing** 1
T-21.........I.1:5 but which stand open before **u.** eyes,

**unseen** 13
T-10...... IV.8:3 the greater light, for the Rays are there **u.**.
T-11.......in.3:3 Remember the Rays that are there **u.**. The
T-27...... III.5:2 known without a form, unpictured and **u.**
T-29....... V.2:3 world but passes by, unnoticed and **u.**.
W-pI.....87.1:3 and afraid of things **u.** and unreal. Light
W-pI.....91.2:2 in darkness, the miracle remains **u.**. Thus
W-pI...158.6:4 Experience–unlearned, untaught, **u.–is**
W-pI...158.9:3 **U.** by One they merely disappear, because
W-pI.158.11:2 so accurate its image shares its **u.** holiness
W-pI...189.4:1 Yet is the world of hatred equally **u.** and
M-25..........3:6 the past, unusual attunement with the "**u.**
M-29..........8:5 *you is ushered in A world* **u.**, *unheard, yet*
P-2......... II.6:7 **u.** through His eyes is too fragmented to

**unselected** 1
W-pI.....35.6:1 A suitable **u.** list for applying the idea for

**unselective** 1
T-28.........I.3:3 It is an **u.** memory, that is not used to

**unselectively** 1
W-pI.....64.8:3 and then look slowly and **u.** around you,

**unseparated** 4
T-3......... V.5:3 as separated and **u.** at the same time. It is
T-14. VIII.2:13 The holy meeting place of the **u.** Father
T19... IV.D.7:7 within you, **u.** from it and completely one
T-28..... VII.2:9 What is **u.** must be joined. And what is

**unsettled** 2
T-25...... IX.7:6 His help is to decide it should remain **u.**,
W-pI.....26.6:3 Any problem as yet **u.** that tends to recur

**unsettling** 1
M-4...... I.A.7:1 The next stage is indeed "a period of **u.**."

**unshakable** 2
T-4........ III.3:6 knowledge of permanence and **u.** being.
T-21... VIII.2:4 is **u.** as is the Love of God for His creation.

**unshaken** 3
T-2........ I.5:12 It enables you to remain **u.** by lack of love
W-pI.....99.5:4 **U.** does the Holy Spirit look on what you
W-pI...109.1:1 quietness **u.** by the world's appearances.

**unshared** 6
T-5........ IV.2:2 Its existence is **u.**. It does not die; it was
T-5........ IV.2:8 burden of **u.** ideas that are too weak to
T-28....... V.2:2 **U.**, they are perceived as meaningless.
W-pI.....73.1:4 The ego's idle wishes are **u.**, and therefore
W-pI...156.3:2 of His remains **u.** by everything that lives.
W-pI.185.12:4 alone? No gift of God can be **u.**. It is this

**unsharing** 1
T-5........ VI.9:4 because it is uncreative and therefore **u.**,

**unshed** 1
W-pI...193.9:4 wiped away, with none remaining yet **u.**,

**unsheltering** 1
T-4.........I.11:1 has built a shabby and **u.** home for you,

**unsolvable** 1
T-17..... VII.1:7 remove yourself from it and make it **u.**.

**unsolved** 5
T-25...... IX.4:6 Yet does the problem still remain **u.**, for
W-pI.....79.4:1 to keep the problem of separation **u.**. The
W-pI.....79.5:5 Others remain **u.** under a cloud of denial,
W-pI.....79.5:5 time, only to be hidden again but still **u.**.
W-pI...138.6:3 could decide the rest, this one remains **u.**.

**unsought** 1
W-pI...136.7:2 not a thing that happens to you, quite **u.**,

**unsound** 1
W-pI...126.4:1 Thus is forgiveness basically **u.**;

**unspeakable** 2
T-1......... II.2:7 Revelation is literally **u.** because it is an
T-1......... II.2:7 because it is an experience of **u.** love.

**unspoken** 1
W-pI...129.3:3 language is **u.** and yet surely understood.

**unstable** 8
T-1......... V.6:5 is temporarily experienced as **u.**. However
T-3......... V.3:5 In this sense, when your behavior is **u.**,
T-3...... VI.11:4 of reality by the **u.** scales of desire. Wishes
T-4...... IV.11:8 the dis-spirited or to stabilize the **u.**? I do
T19... IV.A.8:4 Yet what could be more **u.** than a tightly
W-pI...129.2:3 The world you see is merciless indeed, **u.**,
S-1......... II.3:3 and usually **u.** sense of identification has
S-3...........I.2:3 is tied to its command and linked to its **u.**

**unstated** 1
T-28...... VI.4:6 **U.** and unheard in consciousness is every

**unsteady** 2
W-pI...107.7:4 The shaky and **u.** footsteps of illusion are
M-27.........1:6 and unsure; the undependable and the **u.**,

**unsubstantial** 4
T-18...... IX.8:3 their **u.** nature as He leads you past them,
T-28...... III.5:2 and as **u.** as the empty place between the
T-28....... V.7:3 changing shapes, forever **u.** and unsure.
W-pI.186.10:1 These **u.** images will go, and leave your

**unsuited** 2
T-17....... V.3:5 and clearly **u.** to the purpose that has
W-pI...160.4:2 fear or you who are **u.** to the home which

**unsullied** 1
T-24....... II.1:6 and stately, clean and honest, pure and **u.**

**unsung** 1
C-ep...........4:6 instant, though it seems to be **u.** forever.

**unsupported** 2
W-pI.153.19:4 leaves our weakness **u.** by His strength.
W-pII.327.1:1 to take salvation on the basis of an **u.** faith

**unsure** 11
T-21... VII.12:1 you are **u.** the others have been answered
T-28....... V.7:3 shapes, forever unsubstantial and **u.**. Yet
W-pI..... 59.1:3 How can I be doubtful and **u.** of myself
W-pI...139.6:1 yourself, and be **u.** of what you really are.
W-pI...163.3:1 All things but death are seen to be **u.**, too
W-pI.185.10:5 your purpose, and **u.** of what you wanted,
W-pI.186.12:4 inconsistent and **u.** of everything? Let not
W-pII.256.1:5 Who could be **u.** of who he is? And who
W-pII.257.1:1 I can be but confused, **u.** of what I am,
W-pII.276.1:6 we deny our Self, to be **u.** of Who we are,
M-27.........1:6 the changing and **u.**; the undependable

**unswerving** 3
T-14.... III.12:1 place of His calm and **u.** value of His Son?
T-25.... VIII.2:2 that your faith in it be strong, **u.**, and
M-4...... IX.2:3 Being **u.**, it is full of trust. Being based on

**untainted** 1
W-pI...188.6:6 **u.** by the dream of worldly things outside

**untarnished** 1
T-15.........I.8:4 Each instant is a clean, **u.** birth, in which

**untaught** 1
W-pI...158.6:4 Experience–unlearned, **u.**, unseen–is

**untenable** 2
T-3........ VI.7:5 **u.** position is the result of the authority
M-7...........2:6 His position has thus become **u.**, for he is

**unterrified** 1
T19... IV.D.9:1 No one can look upon the fear of God **u.**,

**unthinkable** 2
T-14...... XI.2:2 of God, a lesson so **u.** that only the insane
W-pI...168.2:2 be forever satisfied; despair of any kind **u.**

**until** 218

**unto** 163
T-1..........II.4:1 "No man cometh **u.** the Father but by me
T-1........ III.6:2 The Golden Rule asks you to do **u.** others
T-1........ III.6:2 others as you would have them do **u.** you.
T-3...... IV.7:15 now, and they will find rest **u.** their souls.
T-5........ IV.6:8 by rendering **u.** God the things that are
T-5........ VI.8:1 fathers **u.** the third and fourth generation,
T-7........ V.11:1 Come therefore **u.** me, and learn of the
T-8........ IV.2:4 you always, even **u.** the end of the world.
T-8........ IX.3:2 All forms of sickness, even **u.** death, are
T-10...... III.6:6 When I said, "My peace I give **u.** you,"
T-11...... IV.6:6 Come **u.** me who hold it open for you, for
T-11...... IV.8:4 Peace be **u.** you who rest in God, and in
T-11....... V.4:5 sufficient **u.** itself and independent of any
T-11...... VI.4:9 For we ascend **u.** the Father together, as it
T-11...... VI.9:3 not perceive that I have done them **u.** you.
T-11.... VIII.9:3 Father accepts him and heal him **u.** Christ
T-11..VIII.15:5 last step for you, by raising you **u.** Himself
T-12........II.3:4 he really wants is to offer it **u.** yourself, for
T-12...... VI.3:6 Make the world real **u.** yourself, for the
T-12..VIII.7:11 function of love to unite all things **u.** itself
T-13....... V.5:4 Everyone draws nigh **u.** what he loves,
T-13....... V.7:9 drawing nigh **u.** them you will draw them
T-13....... V.9:7 And He will not return **u.** the Father until

T-13....... V.9:7 extended your perception even **u.** Him.
T-13.... VI.12:1 Awaking **u.** Christ is following the laws of
T-13.... VI.13:9 And so it is that he can call **u.** himself the
T-13..... VII.7:1 and nothing else comes nigh **u.** him. He is
T-13..... VII.8:6 yours, being the gift of God **u.** His Son.
T-13..... VII.9:5 Yet the dreams of love lead **u.** knowledge.
T-13... VII.14:2 say: *The Holy Spirit leads me **u.** Christ, and*
T-13... VII.16:5 teach you to awaken **u.** us and to yourself.
T-13... VII.17:9 give thanks **u.** his Father for his purity.
T-13.... VIII.6:2 will offer them **u.** His Father as they were
T-13.... VIII.6:2 His Father as they were offered **u.** Him.
T-13.. VIII.10:3 Nor do you witness **u.** Him, for reality is
T-13...... IX.3:2 faithful **u.** darkness and you will not see,
T-13...... IX.4:5 you have denied the witness **u.** yours. You
T-13...... IX.5:1 thought that he has done this **u.** you.
T-13...... IX.6:1 the truth of guiltlessness **u.** yourself. In
T-13... X.11:11 *and offer thanks **u.** his Father that no guilt*
T-13..... X.13:2 even **u.** the worth that God has placed
T-13..... X.13:3 and all my faith and my belief I offer **u.** it.
T-13..... X.14:4 fitting as a hymn of praise **u.** your Father.
T-13...... XI.2:4 the hymn of freedom rising **u.** Heaven.
T-13...... XI.6:5 Truth comes of its own will **u.** its own.
T-14......... I.2:4 you must direct your thoughts **u.** oblivion
T-14.... III.17:7 take **u.** yourself the sole responsibility for
T-14...... IV.2:1 created by Him like **u.** Himself and part of
T-14....... V.8:1 be **u.** everyone who becomes a teacher of
T-14..... VII.7:9 through Him, and through Him **u.** God.
T-14.... VIII.2:2 the one promise given **u.** Him to lay upon
T-15....... I.14:5 ego's making, and ascend **u.** your Father.
T-15...... III.6:9 of Christ, eternal Host **u.** His Father.
T-15...... VI.6:8 through me the Holy Spirit gives it **u.** you,
T-17....... II.1:4 And nothing will you value like **u.** this,
T-18....... I.11:2 been gently brought **u.** the truth in you,
T-18...... III.8:7 back into darkness and forward **u.** God,
T-19....... I.11:6 forth to gather witnesses **u.** its coming,
T-19....... I.12:5 offers you faith to give **u.** your brother.
T-19....... I.14:1 has raised **u.** Himself and both of you. Lay
T-19...... IV.1:7 everyone who draws nigh **u.** your temple,
T19..IV.B.17:3 and offering His messages **u.** the Son.
T19. IV.D.18:5 So will we prepare together the way **u.** the
T-20....... II.2:5 to those who come **u.** its chosen home, or
T-20....... II.7:7 Son of God looks **u.** you for his release.
T-20...... III.9:4 raise your eyes **u.** your strong companion,
T-20.... III.11:1 Your gift **u.** your brother has given me
T-20.... III.11:5 look **u.** the Son to lead them to the Father
T-20.... VI.11:2 spot of space and time, beholden **u.** death
T-20.... VI.12:6 God as equal things are like **u.** each other.
T-20.... VIII.5:3 distress and need for help **u.** the helpless?
T-20.... VIII.8:5 take **u.** yourself the power you gave them,
T-21....... II.3:8 savior, that he may give salvation **u.** you.
T-21.... VIII.2:8 comes as surely **u.** those who see the final
T-22....... I.11:2 For He is always drawn **u.** Himself. What
T-22...... IV.3:9 His messenger, returning Him **u.** Himself.
T-23..... II.15:8 Give thanks **u.** the hero on love's throne,
T-23...... IV.3:2 to create **u.** His Son because it is His Own.
T-24....... II.3:4 His Son like to itself and not like **u.** Him.
T-24....... II.8:6 only that he may return it **u.** you. It is not
T-24..... II.10:4 not keep one part of what He is **u.** Himself
T-24..... II.13:3 Nothing is sacred here but **u.** you, and
T-24...... III.8:4 you will that this be done **u.** your savior?
T-24....... V.8:4 a brother **u.** you except he be as perfect as
T-24...... VI.8:1 is sacrament and benediction **u.** you. His
T-25......... I.1:6 you are manifest **u.** your holy brother, as
T-25......... I.1:7 the meeting of the holy Christ **u.** Himself;
T-25......... I.3:4 nor gives the slightest witness **u.** anything
T-25......... I.4:3 may release all that it looks upon **u.** itself.
T-25..... II.10:6 He offers **u.** the Father and the Son alike.
T-25....... V.3:5 answer by returning **u.** God what is His
T-25.. VIII.10:8 justice would be done **u.** the Son He loves,
T-25.. VIII.12:8 witness **u.** his sinlessness and not his sins.
T-26..... V.10:7 restored **u.** his Father's perfect Love. And
T-26..... VII.7:4 apart, and relegates attack **u.** Himself.
T-26...... IX.1:1 for God calls lovingly **u.** your brother,
T-26....... X.5:3 you seek to add **u.** the purpose given it.
T-27......... I.5:5 Show this **u.** your brother, who will see
T-27......... I.8:1 but witnesses **u.** the strange belief that sin
T-27....... II.6:1 less to him than it has given **u.** you. So
T-27....... II.6:7 to His Son, and of the Son **u.** His Own,
T-27....... II.8:4 knows your healing is the witness **u.** his,
T-27...... V.2:1 Health is the witness **u.** health. As long as
T-27.... V.11:9 for He knows it is a gift of love **u.** His Son,
T-27.... V.11:9 His Son, and therefore is it given **u.** Him.
T-27..... VI.5:7 fear. As fear is witness **u.** death, so is the
T-27..... VI.5:7 death, so is the miracle the witness **u.** life.
T-27... VIII.6:1 the dream he gave away **u.** the dreamer,
T-27 .VIII.10:1 this: that you are doing this **u.** yourself.
T-28...... I.12:3 How gladly does He offer them **u.** the one
T-28..... VI.5:4 tiny oath to be forever faithful **u.** death.
T-28.... VII.7:7 be used to liberate God's Son **u.** his home.
T-29..... II.10:4 dwell in what was built as temple **u.** death
T-29..... II.10:5 and it is this that makes him savior **u.** you
T-29... III.3:13 By your gift of freedom is it given **u.** you.
T-29...... V.6:2 and lead God's Son **u.** his Father's house.
T-29...... V.8:6 all dreams, **u.** the peace of everlasting life.
T-29.... VII.9:5 there. Your holy mind is altar **u.** God, and
T-29..... IX.2:2 to hell, and God made enemy **u.** His Son.
T-30.... V.10:5 Be merciful **u.** your brother, then. And do
T-31.... VII.4:5 For your forgiveness, offered **u.** him, has
T-31.. VII.15:1 Let not the world's light, given **u.** you, be
T-31... VIII.2:7 you have brought your weakness **u.** Him,
T-31... VIII.3:4 from you whom God created altar **u.** joy.
W-pI..... 78.5:5 Let him be savior **u.** you today. Such is his
W-pI..... 78.7:1 in the light of true forgiveness, given **u.** us
W-pI... 92.10:2 Let yourself be brought **u.** your Self. Its
W-pI... 96.12:3 how much is given **u.** you to give this day,
W-pI... 105.4:3 eternity to timelessness, and love **u.** itself.
W-pI... 106.6:2 It is here, and will today be given **u.** you.
W-pI... 110.8:1 Word that tells him he is brother **u.** Him.
W-pI... 126.4:5 are gracious **u.** him by giving him what he
W-pI... 156.5:5 all things **u.** Its likeness and Its purity.
W-pI... 159.9:7 And they return them gladly **u.** Him.
W-pI... 160.6:8 will call Its Own **u.** Itself in recognition of
WpI...rV.in3:5 *may walk more certainly and quickly **u.** You.*
W-pI... 182.5:3 voice cries **u.** you to let Him rest a while.
W-pI... 189.7:5 with wholly empty hands **u.** your God.
W-pI. 189.10:5 *And it is **u.** You we look for them. Our hands*
W-pI. 190.11:2 gratitude **u.** our Teacher fill our hearts, as
W-pI... 191.9:1 power is given **u.** you in earth and Heaven
W-pI. 193.11:2 arise in haste and go **u.** our Father's house
W-pI... 194.3:4 so each instant given **u.** God in passing,
W-pI... 197.7:2 Self for this, for He is grateful only **u.** God
W-pI... 197.7:2 and He gives thanks for you **u.** Himself.
W-pI... 197.9:5 All that you do is given **u.** Him. All that
W-pI... 216.1:2 *All that I do I do **u.** myself. If I attack, I suffer.*
W-pII . 221.2:6 we are, and to reveal Himself **u.** His Son.
W-pII . 233.2:4 a day of countless gifts and mercies **u.** us.
W-pII . 245.2:3 we share the Word that He has given **u.** us
W-pII ..... 6.3:4 Yet will these dreams be given **u.** Christ,
W-pII . 274.2:2 today, because the day is given **u.** love.
W-pII . 319.1:6 I learn that what one gains is given **u.** all.
W-pII .... 320.h My Father gives all power **u.** me.
W-pII . 343.1:7 *all things are given **u.** me forever and forever*
W-pII .... 357.h and then Returning **u.** us to be itself.
Wfl........ in.3:2 U. us the aim is given to forgive the world
Wfl........ in.4:5 us through our forgiveness, given **u.** him.
C-5............ 5:9 at last and carry it with you **u.** your God.
S-1......... in.1:2 returns the thanks it offers Him **u.** the
S-2........... I.8:6 song that all creation sings **u.** its God.
S-2........ III.3:2 haste to go at last **u.** your Father's house.
S-3........ IV.6:1 Come **u.** Me, My children, once again,

## untouchable 1

W-pI. 153.10:1 how secure you rest, **u.** within its light.

## untouched 19

T-7....... XI.3:4 him? Does it keep his heart **u.** by fear, and
T-13........ I.5:6 his purity shines **u.** forever in God's Mind
T-13... VIII.8:2 will leave no one **u.** and no one left alone.
T-13..... X.12:2 wholly **u.** by guilt and wholly loving, is
T-14...... V.7:2 No one can be **u.** by teaching such as this.
T-15..... III.6:1 **u.** by every little gift the world of littleness
T-20..... II.10:3 are the lilies of his innocence **u.** by guilt,
T-20..... III.9:6 yet his holiness remained **u.** and perfect,
T-23...... I.7:10 conflict, **u.** and quiet in the peace of God.
T-26........ I.7:7 Born again each instant, **u.** by time, and
T-28........ I.9:4 perfectly **u.** by time and interference.
T-29..... IV.1:6 dreams to leave **u.** by its beneficence. You
W-pI .. 182.8:3 beyond all words, **u.** by fear and doubt,
W-pI .. 198.8:1 unmoved, **u.** by thoughts like these, and
W-pII . 229.2:1 *I am; for keeping my Identity **u.** and sinless,*
W-pII ..... 5.2:4 For if his oneness still remained **u.**, who
W-pII ..... 6.2:4 remains **u.** by anything the body's eyes
W-pII . 289.2:2 *world the past has left **u.** and free of sin. Here*
W-pII . 299.2:5 *It stands forever perfect and **u.**. In it are all*

## untrained 5

W-in.......... 1:3 An **u.** mind can accomplish nothing. It is
W-pI ...... 9.2:1 is difficult for the **u.** mind to believe that
W-pI .... 44.3:4 requires precisely what the **u.** mind lacks.
W-pI .... 44.4:3 unnatural and difficult for the **u.** mind.
W-pI .... 44.5:1 Your mind is no longer wholly **u.**. You

## untroubled 4

W-pI .. 193.9:3 ensure his holy rest remain **u.** and serene,
W-pI .. 194.9:2 For in God's Hands we rest **u.**, sure that
W-pII . 329.1:9 *And I am safe, **u.** and serene, in endless joy,*
M-16..... 11:11 its light can shine again on an **u.** mind.

## untrue 19

T-1....... VI.5:1 All aspects of fear are **u.** because they do
T-7....... VI.7:6 Holy Spirit if you had not believed the **u.**.
T-7....... VI.8:7 is total, the **u.** cannot exist. Commitment
T-9..... VIII.6:5 are **u.** and are therefore on the same level.
T-14..... II.1:11 that you *can* learn how to make the **u.** true.
T-16..... III.1:4 look upon it fairly, and perceive it was **u.**.
T-18... IX.14:3 Forgiveness removes only the **u.**, lifting
T-20..... IV.1:9 The **u.** He has neither received nor given.
T-23....... II.3:3 that they are all the same and equally **u.**,
T-23....... II.3:4 kind can be corrected *because* they are **u.**.
T-26..... III.2:3 the truth, where they are judged to be **u.**.
T-26... VIII.8:1 this illusion has a cause which, though **u.**,
T-28.... VII.1:6 is no one who could be **u.** to what He wills
W-pI .... 78.4:5 or **u.** to the ideal he should accept as his,
W-pI .. 140.9:3 between what is **u.** and equally untrue.
W-pI .. 140.9:3 between what is untrue and equally **u.**.
W-pII ..... 4.3:1 issuing from thoughts that are **u.**. They
M-8........... 2:3 importance, but is recognized as being **u.**.
S-2........ III.4:7 Illusions are **u.**. God's Will is truth, and

## untrustworthy 1

T-7......... X.5:8 but this does not mean that the guide is **u.**

## untruth 4

T-2.......... I.3:2 "lies of the serpent," all he heard was **u.**.
T-3......... II.6:2 true. You cannot make **u.** true. If you are
T-7....... VI.9:8 ego therefore is totally committed to **u.**,
W-pI .. 192.2:4 it is the means by which **u.** can be undone

## ununified 1

W-pI .. 184.3:1 a series of discrete events, of things **u.**, of

## unused 3

T-17... VIII.1:3 of faithlessness, withheld and left **u.**, that
T-17... VIII.3:2 wherever faithlessness is laid aside, **u.**.
T-27..... III.4:1 an **u.** interval of time not seen as spent

## unusual 3

M-25......... 3:6 the past, **u.** attunement with the "unseen,
M-25......... 4:5 appeal in **u.** abilities that can be curiously
M-25......... 6:3 the more **u.** and unexpected the power,

## unveil 1

T-31... VIII.7:2 and through the Christ in you **u.** his eyes,

**unveiled** 4

T-20.......II.8:8 lies, ready to be **u.** and freed from all the
T-23.....II.12:8 Behold, **u.**, the ego's secret gift, torn from
W-pI.198.10:1 Christ appears **u.** at last in this one dream
S-2..........I.9:5 must be **u.** in all its treachery, and then let

**unviolated** 1

T-27.....V.10:1 that they remain **u.** and unlimited. Your

**unwanted** 4

T-31......I.11:2 it is a state of mind **u.** that becomes the
W-pI...183.4:2 nameless and **u.** thing before God's Name
W-pI...198.1:4 you lay it down as valueless, **u.** and unreal
P-2......IV.10:9 thus it must remain **u.** as well as unreal.

**unwarranted** 2

T-30......VI.3:4 While you regard it as a gift **u.**, it must
W-pI.....47.2:2 can is to put your trust where trust is **u.**,

**unwavering** 2

T-31.......V.6:4 points to him, **u.** and deadly in its aim. It
WpI..rV.in1:5 footsteps have not been **u.**, and doubts

**unweakened** 1

T-27......III.4:4 **U.** power, with no opposite, is what

**unwelcome** 4

T-31......VI.6:9 Who is **u.** to the kind in heart? And what
W-pI...138.2:8 Opposition makes the truth **u.**, and it
W-pI...192.6:2 Is this **u.**? Is it to be feared? Or is it to be
C-3............7:2 Even the wished-for can become **u.**. That

**unwelcoming** 1

T-11.......II.5:1 Holy Spirit cannot speak to an **u.** host,

**unwilling** 31

T-3..........I.2:6 many have been **u.** to give it up in view of
T-4.........in.2:6 forever **u.** to depart from its Foundation.
T-4........III.7:3 forever **u.** to destroy what you have made.
T-8........VI.7:1 An "**u.** will" does not mean anything,
T-8........VI.7:2 you think you are **u.** to will with God, you
T-12.........I.5:3 If you are **u.** to perceive an appeal for help
T-12.........I.5:3 you are **u.** to give help and to receive it.
T-12......III.1:5 if you were **u.** to share their poverty. For
T-13.........I.7:4 time, being forever **u.** to be without him.
T-13...VII.11:6 and render you **u.** to question the value
T-15......I.12:1 while you are **u.** to give it to your brothers
T-15......I.13:6 **u.** to give what you would receive of Him,
T-15....III.11:1 **u.** to attempt to grasp for peace yourself,
T-15......VI.2:1 because you are **u.** to accept the fact that
T-15.......X.6:4 you. You are **u.** to recognize that the ego,
T-16......IV.2:5 Be not **u.** now; you are too near, and you
T-16....IV.10:4 entirely **u.** to settle for illusion in place of
T-16.......V.3:1 most appeal to those **u.** to relinquish guilt
T-17......III.6:8 will be **u.** ever to lose the sight of it again.
T-17....III.6:10 become increasingly **u.** to let it be hidden
T-18......IV.8:2 and remain **u.** to give place to One Who
T19...IV.A.2:3 seems to be the cost you are so **u.** to pay?
T19...IV.A.3:2 Yet you are still **u.** to let it join you wholly
T-21......IV.3:6 entirely **u.** to look within and see it not.
T-30.........I.5:3 this has happened if you feel yourself **u.** to
T-30.........I.8:1 (4) If you are so **u.** to receive you cannot
WpI.rIII.in3:1 because you are **u.** to devote the time to it
WpI.rIII.in4:2 are **u.** to cooperate in practicing salvation
W-pI...151.8:4 at guilt, **u.** now to play with toys of sin;
C-3............2:4 that makes them **u.** merely to rise up and
S-3.........II.3:2 to be thrust down in pain upon **u.** flesh,

**unwillingly** 2

W-pI.....73.9:2 of an alien power, thrust upon you **u.**. It is
W-pI...132.4:4 but came **u.** to what was made already,

**unwillingness** 17

T-1........III.1:6 share my **u.** to accept error in yourself
T-2........III.1:9 and an **u.** to reach the altar itself. The real
T-2.........V.8:1 of healing arises in the end from an **u.** to
T-5........III.4:5 Itself, but It is limited by your **u.** to hear It
T-9.......VII.7:2 kind is always associated with **u.** to know,
T-11.........I.5:8 for your **u.** to accept His Fatherhood has
T-12.........I.4:3 except for your **u.** to accept reality as it is,
T-15.........I.3:5 its **u.** for you to find peace even in death,
T-16....VI.12:4 to atone for your **u.** by His perfect faith,
T-16....VI.12:5 recognition of your **u.** for your release,
T-16...VII.12:4 *The sleep of forgetfulness is only the* **u.** *to*
T-22.......V.6:8 For it is your **u.** to overlook what seems to
T-31.........I.1:6 Only **u.** to learn it could make such an
W-pI.....95.7:5 be corrected, and an **u.** to try again.
W-pI.....95.8:2 held back only by your **u.** to let them go.
WpI.rIII.in3:3 in this. **U.** can be most carefully concealed
WpI.rIII.in3:4 to uphold a camouflage for your **u.**.

**unwise** 3

T-1.......VII.5:8 **u.** to start on these steps without careful
T-3..........I.2:2 It is **u.** to accept any concept if you have
T-6..........I.8:7 all respects, they are **u.** not to follow him.

**unwitnessed** 1

T-13. VIII.10:1 Yet in this world your perfection is **u.**.

**unwittingly** 1

T-2.........V.1:2 Otherwise they may **u.** foster the belief

**unworthiness** 4

T-7......VI.11:3 as unworthy and attack them for their **u.**.
T-11......VI.4:4 perceive **u.** in a brother and not perceive
T-18...VII.4:11 from a state of present **u.** and inadequacy.
W-pI.133.10:2 the rust a sign of deep **u.** within himself.

**unworthy** 36

T-2......IV.3:11 in a particularly **u.** form of denial. The
T-2......IV.3:12 The term "**u.**" here implies only that it is
T-3..........I.1:9 words have clearly stated is **u.** of His Son?
T-3........VI.5:2 it is because you have judged him as **u.**.
T-3........VI.5:3 the idea of being more **u.** than they are.
T-4.........I.10:7 a false and **u.** picture of yourself to others,
T-7......VI.11:3 perceive them as **u.** and attack them for
T-8......VI.5:12 made only the decision to be **u.** of both.
T-8......VI.5:13 yourself **u.** because you are the treasure of
T-9.......VII.8:4 that nothing **u.** of God is worthy of you.
T-10......IV.5:7 made is so **u.** of you that you could hardly
T-11.....V.17:3 can demonstrate that His Son is **u.**, for
T-11.....VI.3:9 little beliefs that are **u.** of God's Son. For
T-12...VII.13:1 yourself **u.** and have condemned yourself
T-13.......in.1:2 as **u.** of love and deserving of punishment
T-13.........I.4:5 undone everything **u.** of the Son of God,
T-13........V.7:3 is **u.** of you because it is unworthy of Him.
T-13........V.7:3 is unworthy of you because it is **u.** of Him.
T-14......IV.4:9 nor anyone **u.** of His perfect Love. Fail not
T-15......III.2:2 for you will have judged yourself **u.** of it.
T-16.....V.10:8 hating it you have made it little and **u.**,
T-16.....V.11:2 unless it is weak and little, and **u.** of value,
T-18......IV.3:5 not create His dwelling place **u.** of Him.
T-18......IV.4:8 If you maintain you are **u.** of learning this,
T-19.........I.8:3 withholding faith you see what is **u.** of it,
T-19.........I.11:2 of God, and judges him **u.** of forgiveness.
T-22.........I.9:1 God did not entrust His Son to the **u.**.
T-25......IX.9:4 lost, condemns you as **u.** of forgiveness.
T-27......II.14:4 hate, **u.** to be part of you and thus outside
W-pI.....45.9:3 that are **u.** of Him Whose host you are.
W-pI.....64.3:2 you to regard yourself as **u.** of the task
W-pI...126.3:2 You give charity to one **u.**, merely to
W-pI...126.3:3 which you bestow on one **u.** of the gift,
W-pI...137.6:1 not healing is **u.** of your function here.
W-pI...197.4:1 not matter if another thinks your gifts **u.**.
S-2..........II.3:3 since both have been **u.** and deserve the

**up** 344

*See also* blown-up

T-in..........2:1 be summed **u.** very simply in this way:
T-1.........I.37:2 breaking **u.** erroneous perception and
T-1..........II.4:4 In the process of "rising **u.**," I am higher
T-1........III.4:6 does direct, leaving it **u.** to you to follow.
T-1.........V.6:5 As these false underpinnings are given **u.**,
T-1........VI.3:3 introduced vertically from the bottom **u.**.
T-1........VI.3:4 such as "**u.**" and "down" are meaningful.
T-2.........I.1:12 direction of your own creation is **u.** to you
T-2..........I.3:6 is there reference to his waking **u.**. The
T-2.......V.1:11 then, that inducing the mind to give **u.** its
T-2........VI.5:8 because you have not made **u.** your mind.
T-2.....VII.5:11 in this respect can be given **u.**. It only
T-3..........I.2:6 many have been unwilling to give it **u.** in
T-3........IV.7:4 but to correct error from the bottom **u.**.
T-3.........V.4:3 but is also one that is **u.** to you to supply.
T-4.........in.3:6 endless until they are voluntarily given **u.**.
T-4..........I.5:4 remember that laws are set **u.** to protect
T-4........III.2:5 has set **u.** and can shine into your mind.
T-4........III.7:1 your mind to give **u.** every idea you ever
T-4........IV.1:8 you look to find yourself is **u.** to you.
T-4........IV.6:3 have given **u.** this voluntary dis-spiriting,
T-4.........V.6:6 Preoccupations with problems set **u.** to be
T-5..........I.3:2 that I can reach **u.** and bring the Holy
T-5..........II.5:3 By choosing one you give **u.** the other.
T-5.........V.8:8 Having given **u.** its disordered thought,
T-5......VI.10:5 you, however carefully you have built it **u.**
T-5......VI.11:3 you look to find yourself is **u.** to you. Your
T-6......V.A.6:4 perception and turning it right-side **u.**.
T-6......V.B.6:3 it is **u.** to you to decide which voice is true
T-6......V.B.7:2 be insane to believe that it is **u.** to you to
T-7........VI.5:5 The mind can, however, make **u.** illusions
T-7........VI.8:9 must give **u.** the idea of conflict entirely
T-7........VI.9:5 that what you are is **u.** to you to decide.
T-7......VI.11:3 Therefore they make **u.** images, perceive
T-7....VIII.1:10 This choice is **u.** to you, but it is not up to
T-7....VIII.1:10 but it is not **u.** to you to decide whether or
T-7......VIII.2:3 that you will insist on giving it **u.**. The ego
T-7......VIII.2:4 lest you give the ego **u.** and free yourself.
T-7.........X.3:8 Spirit, and you will be giving **u.** the ego.
T-8..........I.3:4 which you are giving **u.** by attacking them
T-8..........I.3:5 How can you have what you give **u.**? You
T-8..........I.3:6 to have, but you do not give it **u.** yourself.
T-8..........I.3:7 yourself. When you give **u.** peace, you are
T-8....VIII.1:12 In perception the whole is built **u.** of parts
T-8......VIII.8:4 the ego's skill in building **u.** false cases.
T-8........IX.2:7 And this part only is **u.** to you. The rest is
T-9..........I.3:5 You have set **u.** this strange situation so
T-9..........II.5:1 your brother gives you is **u.** to you. What
T-9........III.4:6 It is the giving **u.** of correction in yourself.
T-9........III.6:4 It is not **u.** to you to change your brother,
T-9.........V.5:8 He believes that it is **u.** to him to teach the
T-9......VIII.4:2 will give **u.** all investment in it. Grandeur
T-10.......in.2:7 to everything you perceive is **u.** to you,
T-10.......in.3:8 and you will realize how much is **u.** to you
T-10........II.2:1 to give **u.** the dissociation of reality brings
T-10........II.2:4 Give **u.** gladly everything that would
T-10..III.10:11 fear you have been willing to give **u.** your
T-10....III.11:4 can give **u.** the god of sickness for your
T-10....III.11:4 to do so if you give him **u.** for yourself.
T-10......IV.5:1 You are not free to give **u.** freedom, but
T-11.......in.3:7 and bravely hold it **u.** to the foundation of
T-11......VI.1:2 are built **u.** on the basis of experience,
T-12......IV.1:4 be summed **u.** simply as: "Seek and do *not*
T-12.......V.6:2 and do not try to set **u.** curriculum goals
T-12.......V.8:7 situation as you have set it **u.** is reversed.
T-12.....VII.7:1 what you project or extend is **u.** to you,
T-12....VIII.3:4 Yet it is no more **u.** to you to decide what
T-12....VIII.3:4 than it is **u.** to you to decide what reality
T-13.........I.3:5 end it will roll **u.** like a long carpet spread
T-13....III.12:8 hears His answer but will give **u.** insanity.
T-13......IV.2:3 and oblivion are ideas that you made **u.**,

T-13....... V.1:7 make **u.** a private world that cannot be
T-13....... V.2:2 are made **u.** only of his reactions to his
T-13...VII.11:6 to tighten **u.** your world against the light,
T-13..VIII.10:5 earth are lifted **u.** to Heaven and to Him.
T-14.........I.3:7 But they can be given **u.** *by* him, for the
T-14....... II.6:4 universe of learning will open **u.** before
T-14....... II.7:2 and open **u.** the way to freedom for you.
T-14...... IV.5:6 Give **u.** this frantic and insane attempt
T-15...... III.6:5 that littleness can be blown **u.** into a sense
T-15...... IX.3:2 give **u.** every use the ego has for the body,
T-16... V.12:10 No rituals that you have set **u.** in which
T-16..... VI.8:1 abruptly lifted **u.** and hurled into reality.
T-16.... VI.10:7 to give **u.** nothing *because* it is nothing.
T-16.... VI.11:4 that for all this you gave **u.** *nothing!* The
T-17....... II.4:1 opened **u.** the world to beauty will vanish.
T-17...... III.9:1 It is still **u.** to you to choose to join with
T-17...VII.3:11 not to have it made **u.** to you elsewhere,
T-18...... IV.4:4 believe that it is **u.** to you to establish the
T-18...... VI.8:6 It is *not* made **u.** of different parts, which
T-18.... VI.11:7 really happens is that you have given **u.**
T-18....VIII.8:6 –that makes **u.** your little kingdom. And
T-18....VIII.9:2 See how life springs **u.** everywhere! The
T-19.......I.5:10 set **u.** a goal forever impossible to attain,
T-19.........I.6:7 and given **u.** when brought to truth, and
T-19....... II.6:5 wants; a world it rules, made **u.** of bodies,
T19... IV.A.9:4 little wisp is lifted **u.** and carried away,
T19... IV.D.5:4 exaltation of the body is given **u.** in favor
T19... IV.D.8:4 It does not open **u.** its secrets, and bid
T19... IV.D.8:7 lift **u.** your eyes and look on your brother
T-20....... II.6:6 pick **u.** from time to time and then put by
T-20..... II.8:11 Let us lift **u.** our eyes together, not in fear
T-20...... III.4:3 *You made this* **u.**. It is a picture of what you
T-20...... III.9:1 leap **u.** in joy the instant they are made
T-20...... IV.1:3 lose. It is not **u.** to you to give power at all.
T-20...... IV.2:6 what you would receive of him is **u.** to you
T-20..... VII.6:4 about him are not held **u.** to his reality.
T-20....VIII.7:4 if you really understood you made it **u.**?
T-21....... II.7:3 have set **u.** your idols to something else.
T-21....... II.8:5 task, but it *is* **u.** to you to welcome it or not
T-21..... VII.2:5 raising **u.** their helplessness against him.
T-21...VII.13:2 it is attained by giving **u.** the wish for the
T-22...... VI.8:7 them, and where and when, is **u.** to Him.
T-22...... VI.9:9 offer to your brother lights **u.** the world.
T-23.......in.4:4 Do not give **u.** this world of freedom for a
T-23.........I.4:9 **u.** to you to say what shall be part of you
T-23...... III.3:2 want; to take a little and give **u.** the rest.
T-23...... III.3:3 Salvation gives **u.** nothing. It is complete
T-23...... IV.5:1 Be lifted **u.**, and from a higher place look
T-23...... IV.6:6 will gently lean to you, and hold you **u.**.
T-24....... II.6:6 Is it a sacrifice to give **u.** nothing, and to
T-25....... II.3:2 you still from giving **u.** the hopeless and
T-25....... II.4:4 is but a means to hold the picture **u.**, so
T-25....... II.7:3 Its holiness lights **u.** the sinlessness the
T-25...... III.1:5 this, to hold it **u.** and offer it support.
T-25...... III.5:4 be, and light the body **u.** instead of it. The
T-25... VII.3:12 The rest is **u.** to God, and not to you.
T-25....VIII.4:7 all that you would keep, and not give **u.**.
T-25...... IX.4:6 can set **u.** a state in which there is no loser
T-26.........I.1:5 a giving **u.** of power in the name of saving
T-26...... III.7:3 **u.** all attempts to choose between them,
T-26...... III.7:7 was never true, can it be hard to give it **u.**,
T-26....... V.9:3 Can it be **u.** to you to see the past and put
T-26...... IX.3:5 of Them have miracles sprung **u.** as grass
T-26...... IX.4:4 What hatred claimed is given **u.** to love,
T-26...... IX.4:4 and freedom lights **u.** every living thing
T-26...... IX.5:3 what was held apart from light is given **u.**,
T-26...... IX.6:2 where a home for Them has been set **u.**.
T-26...... IX.7:2 Your footprints lighten **u.** the world, for
T-26........ X.6:2 can you perceive to lighten **u.** your way.
T-27....... V.3:4 dead, are gently lifted **u.** and comforted.
T-27....... V.8:1 these specific shapes make **u.** the world.
T-27..... V.11:8 by merely counting **u.** its separate parts.
T-27..... VII.2:2 is, and not the way that you have set it **u.**.
T-27..... VII.2:6 No one has difficulty making **u.** his mind
T-27..... VII.8:7 shadow, leaping **u.** and down according
T-27...VII.11:2 effects, when only one is seen as **u.** to him
T-27...VII.14:7 has come to lighten **u.** your sleeping face.
T-27...VII.15:4 instead of counting **u.** the hurts he gave.
T-28.........I.2:7 is a skill made **u.** by you to take the place

T-28 ......I.15:6 that he be lifted **u.** and gently carried over
T-28 .......II.7:3 them when he perceives he made them **u.**.
T-28 .....II.12:3 the active role in making **u.** the dream.
T-28 ..... III.1:2 to be directed **u.** the ladder separation led
T-28 ..... III.1:5 **u.** to waking and the ending of the dream.
T-28 ..... III.5:4 and covered **u.** the space which seemed to
T-28 ... IV.10:6 and its giving **u.** would be a sacrifice. But
T-29 .........I.5:7 And its "inherent" weaknesses set **u.** the
T-29 .......II.1:5 Until you realize you give **u.** nothing,
T-29 ...... V.1:3 **u.** to gladden God the Father and the Son.
T-29 .... VII.4:3 To sacrifice is to give **u.**, and thus to be
T-29 .... VII.4:4 And by this giving **u.** is life renounced.
T-29 .... VII.8:1 and open **u.** a road of hope and of release
T-29 ... VIII.4:5 hand could be held **u.** to block God's way
T-29 ..... IX.1:3 and look to idols that they raise him **u.**?
T-29 ..... IX.4:8 are eager to forget that they made **u.** the
T-30 ........I.3:2 You still make **u.** your mind, and *then*
T-30 .......II.1:7 He did not set His Kingdom **u.** alone. And
T-30 ..... III.9:1 it safe, forever lifted **u.** and anchored sure
T-30 ..... IV.1:1 and thus you will not see you made it **u.**.
T-30 ..... IV.2:2 **u.** as a closed box is opened suddenly, or
T-30 ...... V.9:4 Give **u.** the world! But not to sacrifice.
T-31 ........I.4:4 And every lesson that makes **u.** the world
W-pI....... 4.2:3 which are being covered **u.** by them. The
W-pI....... 7.3:2 your past experiences of picking **u.** a cup,
W-pI..... 11.2:3 look about, near and far, **u.** and down,–
W-pI........23.h world I see by giving **u.** attack thoughts.
W-pI..... 23.1:4 Every thought you have makes **u.** some
W-pI..... 23.6:4 *I see by giving* **u.** *attack thoughts about–.*
W-pI..... 25.5:1 to be willing to give **u.** the goals you have
W-pI..... 29.3:6 you the holiness that lights **u.** the world,
W-pI..... 30.1:2 this idea will the world open **u.** before you
W-pI..... 32.1:3 can give it **u.** as easily as you made it up.
W-pI..... 32.1:3 can give it up as easily as you made it **u.**.
W-pI..... 35.7:3 Pick **u.** any specific situation that occurs
W-pI..... 35.8:2 think **u.** specific things to fill the interval,
W-pI..... 35.9:1 pick **u.** a specific attribute or attributes
W-pI..... 41.6:2 morning, as soon as you get **u.** if possible,
W-pI..... 44.5:4 all the thoughts that you have made **u.**.
W-pI..... 45.7:1 which you have cluttered **u.** your mind
W-pI..... 52.1:5 replaced reality with illusions I made **u.**.
W-pI..... 52.3:6 that in so doing I am giving **u.** nothing.
W-pI..... 55.3:1 this world by giving **u.** attack thoughts.
W-pI..... 57.1:9 I would give **u.** my insane wishes and
W-pI..... 57.2:2 I made **u.** the prison in which I see myself.
W-pI..... 57.4:2 of the rules I made **u.** for it to obey. I will
W-pI..... 60.1:6 reach down to me and raise me **u.** to Him.
W-pI..... 60.5:3 His Love lights **u.** the world for me to see.
W-pI..... 66.7:3 by the ego, and is made **u.** of illusions.
W-pI..... 68.6:5 hovering over you and holding you **u.**.
W-pI..... 69.3:5 holding it **u.** for everyone who searches
W-pI..... 69.7:1 sense of being lifted **u.** and carried ahead.
W-pI..... 71.1:1 may not realize that the ego has set **u.** a
W-pI..... 76.3:1 twisted laws you have set **u.** to save you.
W-pI..... 76.5:4 mind holds **u.** to hide what really suffers.
W-pI..... 78.1:3 And as you raise it **u.** before your eyes,
W-pI..... 79.5:4 Some spring **u.** unexpectedly, just as you
W-pI..... 81.1:2 given the function of lighting **u.** the world
W-pI..... 88.3:4 I am constantly tempted to make **u.** other
W-pI..... 92.1:3 idea of what seeing means is tied **u.** with
W-pI..... 98.9:3 He will open **u.** the way to happiness, and
W-pI..... 99.9:1 seek out and lighten **u.** all darkened spots
W-pI... 105.8:2 let all bars to peace and joy be lifted **u.**,
W-pI. 110.11:7 is the key that opens **u.** the gate of Heaven
WpI..rIII.in2:3 that you catch **u.** in terms of numbers.
W-pI... 111.1:3 *light of holiness and truth light* **u.** *my mind,*
W-pI... 122.3:1 Forgiveness lets the veil be lifted **u.** that
W-pI... 122.8:3 it rises **u.** to greet your open eyes, and fill
W-pI... 127.9:3 mind wherever you give **u.** a false belief,
W-pI... 129.1:3 emphasis is not on giving **u.** the world,
W-pI... 130.4:2 differences you believe make **u.** the world.
W-pI... 130.4:4 Love's enemy has made them **u.**. Yet love
W-pI... 134.8:3 is not there, it opens **u.** the way to truth,
W-pI... 134.8:4 way your true forgiveness opens **u.** to you.
W-pI. 134.14:3 lighting **u.** the way for all our brothers,
W-pI. 134.16:3 will begin to sense a lifting **u.**, a lightening
W-pI. 135.13:1 **u.** to save itself must make the body sick.
W-pI. 135.15:1 in setting **u.** control of future happenings.
W-pI. 135.20:3 until the world is lighted **u.** with joy. And

W-pI 135.24:5 give **u.** nothing in these times today when
W-pI .. 136.4:1 and sets **u.** a series of defenses to reduce
W-pI 136.10:3 illusions but the one who made them **u.**?
W-pI 152.11:5 in silence, giving **u.** all self-deceptions, as
W-pI .. 153.2:4 sets **u.** a system of defense that cannot
W-pI 153.19:3 We rise **u.** strong in Christ, and let our
W-pI 154.14:1 world recedes as we light **u.** our minds,
W-pI .. 155.4:1 If truth demanded they give **u.** the world,
W-pI .. 155.5:4 on the way that God has opened **u.** to you
W-pI .. 155.8:2 you, lighting **u.** the path of ransom from
W-pI .. 158.8:2 nor set **u.** a goal that does not merely
W-pI .. 166.6:3 him and open **u.** his treasures to be free?
W-pI .. 166.9:1 and justice has caught **u.** with you at last.
W-pI .. 168.3:2 by which God leans to us and lifts us **u.**,
W-pI .. 168.4:3 hearts rise **u.** and claim the light as theirs.
W-pI .. 170.3:2 Yet your defense sets **u.** an enemy within;
WpI...rV.in3:2 *And if we stumble, You will raise us* **u.**. *If we*
WpI...rV.in5:4 was sent to open **u.** the path of light to us,
WpI.rV.in11:4 thoughts to hold it **u.** before our minds,
Wi181-200 1:1 of firming **u.** your willingness to make
Wi181-200 2:4 peace that comes as you give **u.** your tight
W-pI .. 181.1:1 to establishing and holding **u.** your faith
W-pI .. 182.4:6 It is His Holiness that lights **u.** Heaven,
W-pI .. 184.1:2 made **u.** names for everything you see.
W-pI .. 189.9:8 and lightens **u.** the world in innocence.
W-pI .. 191.8:1 has lighted **u.** all dark and ancient caverns
W-pI .. 192.6:5 We are one, and therefore give **u.** nothing
W-pI 193.13:5 to earth at last, to raise it **u.** to Heaven.
W-pI 200.10:5 And you look **u.** and on toward Heaven,
WpI.rVI.in.3:8 of everything that clutters **u.** the mind,
WpI.rVI.in.5:4 the thought which you denied be given **u.**,
W-pII .... in.8:3 go. His Hand has held us **u.**. His Thoughts
W-pII . 227.1:5 *Now I give them* **u.**, *and lay them down*
W-pII . 229.2:1 *the thoughts of sin my foolish mind made* **u.**.
W-pII . 290.2:1 *and ask Your strength to hold me* **u.** *today,*
W-pII . 292.1:3 Yet it is **u.** to us when this is reached; how
W-pII ..... 9.3:1 beyond itself, and reaches **u.** to God. The
W-pII . 319.1:3 fill **u.** the space the ego left unoccupied by
W-pII .... 322.h I can give **u.** but what was never real.
W-pII . 322.2:3 *me, I can give* **u.** *nothing You gave me. What*
W-pII . 323.1:1 *Son; You ask him to give* **u.** *all suffering, all*
W-pII . 325.1:2 makes **u.** an image of the thing the mind
W-pII . 325.2:1 *mine apart from Yours but make* **u.** *dreams.*
W-pII ... 13.5:4 And everywhere the signs of life spring **u.**,
M-in .......... 3:1 The curriculum you set **u.** is therefore
M-4 ......... I.1:4 governed by the laws the world made **u.**.
M-4 ..... I.A.5:2 is interpreted as giving **u.** the desirable, it
M-4 ..... I.A.5:7 as he actually does give **u.** the valueless.
M-4 ..... I.A.6:6 "Give **u.** what you do not want, and keep
M-4 ..... VII.1:4 "giving away" in the sense of "giving **u.**."
M-4 ...... IX.1:6 To give **u.** all problems to one Answer is
M-5 ...... II.2:12 merely rise **u.** without their aid and say, "I
M-6 ........... 2:5 storehouse of treasures laid **u.** equally for
M-6 ........... 2:8 **u.** to him to judge when his gift should be
M-9 ........... 2:3 of God learns to give **u.** his own judgment
M-9 ........... 2:4 The giving **u.** of judgment, the obvious
M-10 ......... 2:2 In giving **u.** judgment, he is merely giving
M-10 ......... 2:2 is merely giving **u.** what he did not have.
M-10 ......... 2:3 He gives **u.** an illusion; or better, he has
M-10 ......... 2:3 or better, he has an illusion of giving **u.**.
M-10 ......... 5:5 the teacher of God rise **u.** unburdened,
M-10 ......... 6:9 For he has given **u.** their cause, and they,
M-11 ....... 4:10 leans down in answer, to raise it **u.** again.
M-13 ......... 1:6 sacrifice to give **u.** the things of this world
M-13 ......... 4:1 on giving **u.** the pleasures of the world. Is
M-13 ......... 4:2 Is it a sacrifice to give **u.** pain? Does an
M-13 ......... 4:3 an adult resent the giving **u.** of children's
M-13 ......... 6:4 It always means the giving **u.** of what you
M-13 ......... 7:3 You cannot give **u.** Heaven partially. You
M-13 ....... 7:13 have set **u.** a situation that is impossible.
M-15 ......... 3:1 contempt; give **u.** these foolish thoughts!
M-16 ......... 2:5 the very goals for which they were set **u.**.
M-16 ......... 5:4 It is better to sit **u.**, in whatever position
M-16 ......... 6:7 What you give **u.** is merely the illusion of
M-16 ....... 10:9 merely chooses to give **u.** all that he never
M-19 ......... 3:3 of the world built **u.** in just this way. "Sins
M-20 ......... 4:4 recognize that you have picked it **u.** again.
M-22 ......... 7:4 not **u.** to God's teachers to set limits upon
M-22 ......... 7:4 it is not **u.** to them to judge His Son. And

M-24..........1:7 about it really useful in lighting **u.** the way
M-25..........1:2 to make **u.** a power that does not exist. It
M-27..........3:2 like a shield held **u.** to obscure the sun.
M-28..........4:7 rise **u.** from the dust and look upon our
M-28..........4:8 as it is lifted **u.** and brought to truth.
C-2............9:2 cover **u.** the world the ego made. No
C-3............2:4 to rise **u.** and to return to Him in peace.
C-4............8:3 Here He leans down to lift you **u.** to Him,
C-ep.........1:11 the Holy of the Holies opens **u.** an ancient
C-ep...........3:6 Look **u.** and see His Word among the
C-ep...........3:7 Look **u.** and find your certain destiny the
P-1............3:3 attacked as well, is a concept he made **u.**.
P-1............5:9 end. But that is **u.** to Him. We are all His
P-2.........in.4:3 will learn to give **u.** their original goals,
P-2.........in.4:5 are finally given **u.** in the minds of both.
P-3...........I.1:6 This is not **u.** to you to decide. There is a
S-1.........in.3:1 of God, and rising **u.** as God created you,
S-1.........in.3:3 and hold you **u.** as you ascend the shining
S-1...........I.5:5 a giving **u.** of yourself to be at one with
S-1...........I.6:4 you and helps to raise you **u.** to Him. One
S-1......... II.7:1 Prayer is a ladder reaching **u.** to Heaven.
S-1......... II.8:5 Prayer is tied **u.** with learning until the
S-1........ III.1:6 goals, until it reaches even **u.** to God.
S-1........ III.4:1 Guilt must be given **u.**, and not
S-1........ III.6:1 always made to set **u.** jailers and to hide
S-1........ IV.2:1 to help in prayer, and so reach **u.** yourself.
S-1........ IV.2:5 set **u.** but an illusion of a goal you share.
S-1......... V.1:2 And here again it rises slowly **u.**, and
S-2.........in.1:4 Both must come to hold you **u.** and keep
S-2.........in.1:8 unneeded when the rising **u.** is done. Yet
S-2......... II.8:8 prayer will lift you **u.** and bring you home
S-2........ III.2:3 but let it be a way to draw you **u.** to where
S-2........ III.2:4 Give **u.** all else, for there *is* nothing else.
S-3........ IV.1:9 and given **u.** all separate dreams of special
S-3........ IV.4:2 prayer has risen **u.** and called to God,
S-3........ IV.9:2 Lift **u.** your hearts to greet its advent. See

### upheld 13

T-11..... V.12:6 U. by fear, this is what the ego would have
T-16.... IV.13:7 step lightly across it, **u.** *by* timelessness,
T19... IV.D.3:1 **u.** by the belief in death and protected by
T-20...... IV.4:5 It is **u.** through all temptation to imprison
T-20.... VI.10:3 Its firm foundation is eternally **u.** by truth
T-21...... V.10:4 Faith and belief, **u.** by reason, cannot fail
T-27..... II.15:7 is. If He **u.** divided function, you were lost
T-28...... III.3:5 protected, cherished, and **u.** by firm belief
W-pI... 76.10:1 thought **u.** the world you thought you saw
W-pI... 130.9:5 strength **u.** you as you made this choice.
WpI.. rV.in1:4 more sincere, with faith **u.** more surely.
W-pII.....in.5:2 are all ancient promises **u.** and fully kept.
W-pII......3.3:4 base where truth exists, **u.** apart from lies.

### uphold 14

T-4....... III.7:7 made, but I will not **u.** it unless it is true.
T-5........ VI.4:2 based on the error they were made to **u.**.
T-9...........I.1:3 illusions, since reality can only **u.** truth.
T-10....... IV.4:1 Will, and His laws are established to **u.** it.
T-15....... II.3:5 attempt to support it and **u.** its weakness,
T-20...... III.1:3 calls upon defenses to **u.** it against reality.
T-21....... II.9:6 false, you will **u.** it by not realizing all the
T-22...... IV.2:3 of Heaven to **u.** it cannot be undone. Your
T-23...... III.4:4 salvation is impossible cannot **u.** a quiet,
T-25....... II.3:3 to **u.** pursuit of what has always failed, on
T-30...... VI.3:4 it must **u.** the guilt you would "forgive."
T-31.........I.5:2 but to **u.** a wish that it could be opposed,
WpI . rIII.in3:4 to **u.** a camouflage for your unwillingness.
M-29..........4:9 of the world that was made to **u.** it. But

### upholdeth 1

T-25.........I.3:4 anything the purpose in your mind **u.** not

### upholding 3

T-11....... V.9:3 separation without **u.** it through fear, and
T-23...... IV.9:8 Who with the Love of God **u.** him could
W-pI..... 77.4:3 rights, you are **u.** the rights of everyone.

### upholds 7

T-23..... II.20:4 others. Each one **u.** these laws completely,
T-24....... V.1:9 power of a wish **u.** illusions as strongly as
T-25...... III.3:6 Not one but it **u.** in its perception; not
T-25...... III.4:1 law itself **u.** the universe as God created it
T-25..... VII.4:1 To justify one value that the world **u.** is to
T-31...... III.7:2 And what they see **u.** their freedom from
W-pI... 127.5:3 the world **u.** but violates the truth of what

### upon 800

### uprooted 5

T-1........ V.6:3 All shallow roots must be **u.**, because they
T-16..... VII.6:4 has been **u.** and has disappeared. The
T-18.... IX.13:1 has been **u.** from the world of shadows,
T-19...... III.8:5 belief in sin has been **u.** in its smile of love
T19... IV.A.7:2 this little wish, **u.** and floating aimlessly,

### uproots 1

T-1........ III.5:7 this respect, and thus **u.** the source of fear

### upset 30

T-10.......in.2:5 What can **u.** you except the ephemeral,
W-pI..........5.h I am never **u.** for the reason I think.
W-pI.......5.1:2 you believe is the cause of your **u.**, using
W-pI.......5.1:3 to you. The **u.** may seem to be fear, worry,
W-pI.......5.2:1 perceived cause of an **u.** in any form, use
W-pI.......5.2:1 name of the form in which you see the **u.**,
W-pI.......5.3:1 for "sources" of **u.** in which you believe,
W-pI.......5.3:1 and forms of **u.** which you think result.
W-pI.......5.6:1 perceived sources of **u.** than to others. If
W-pI.......5.6:3 *keep this form of* **u.** *and let the others go. For*
W-pI.......5.7:1 of different forms of **u.** that are disturbing
W-pI.......5.7:2 both the source of the **u.** as you perceive it
W-pI..........6.h I am **u.** because I see something that is
W-pI.......6.1:2 to name both the form of **u.** (anger, fear,
W-pI.......6.2:1 to anything that seems to **u.** you, and can
W-pI.......6.3:5 And: *I cannot keep this form of* **u.** *and let the*
W-pI.......7.1:7 you are never **u.** for the reason you think.
W-pI.......7.1:8 the reason why you are **u.** because you see
W-pI........12.h I am **u.** because I see a meaningless world
W-pI.....12.4:4 *I am* **u.** *because I see a meaningless world.*
W-pI.....12.5:2 then, should a meaningless world **u.** you?
W-pI.....51.5:1 (5) I am never **u.** for the reason I think.
W-pI.....51.5:2 think. I am never **u.** for the reason I think
W-pI.....52.1:1 (6) I am **u.** because I see what is not there
W-pI.....52.1:3 is impossible that it could **u.** me. Reality
W-pI.....52.1:5 When I am **u.**, it is always because I have
W-pI.....52.1:8 of mine. I am always **u.** by nothing.
W-pI.....53.2:1 I am **u.** because I see a meaningless world.
W-pI.....70.2:2 or disturb your peace or **u.** you in any way
W-pI... 122.1:6 and a rest so perfect it can never be **u.**?

### upsets 7

T-24...... III.3:1 that you did not anticipate **u.** your world,
W-pI.......5.4:3 *There are no small* **u.**. *They are all equally*
W-pI.......6.3:2 *There are no small* **u.**. *They are all equally*
W-pI.....12.1:2 that what **u.** you is a frightening world, or
W-pI.....12.5:8 The truth **u.** you now, but when your
W-pI.....20.5:3 any situation, person or event that **u.** you.
M-8 ...........1:5 completely **u.** the mental balance. What

### upsetting 5

W-pI.......6.2:2 application of the idea to each **u.** thought
W-pI.......6.3:1 to some **u.** thoughts more than to others,
WpI...rI.in.4:3 most in situations that appear to be **u.**,
W-pI.....52.1:6 are **u.** because I have given them reality,
W-pI.....53.2:2 Insane thoughts are **u.**. They produce a

### upside 10

*See also* upside-down

T-1........ V.6:7 Nor can anything that holds it **u.** down be
T-2........ V.4:3 and has turned it **u.** down. All forms of
T-6...... V.B.4:1 U. down as always, the ego perceives the
T-18.........I.6:4 and **u.** down arose from this projection of
T-19........II.6:2 such a world could everything be **u.** down
T-24..... VII.8:5 that all perception still is **u.** down until its
T-26..... VII.5:3 be reversed; yet can be seen as **u.** down.
W-pI..... 57.3:3 at it. I see everything **u.** down, and my
W-pII . 328.1:1 all things we perceive are **u.** down until
W-pII ... 13.2:3 perception which was **u.** down before,

### upside-down 7

T-1........ V.6:6 is less stable than an **u.** orientation. Nor
T-2...... IV.4:10 This is likely to occur when **u.** perception
T-2......VIII.5:2 an outstanding example of **u.** perception.
T-3...........I.1:5 the crucifixion is seen from an **u.** point of
T-6.........I.15:1 some of the examples of **u.** thinking in the
T-6...... V.A.6:5 This conflicts with the **u.** perception you
W-pI..... 72.8:3 Your **u.** perception has been ruinous to

### urge 6

T-4........ IV.2:9 and **u.** you to follow my example as you
T-13........II.3:3 for the ego's destructive **u.** is so intense
W-pI..... 95.7:1 and **u.** you to omit as few as possible.
W-pI... 169.4:3 **u.** you to bear witness to the Word of God
W-pI... 188.8:2 **u.** you gently to accept His Word for what
C-2............8:1 of pain, the fear of dying and the **u.** to kill,

### urged 8

W-pI..... 21.1:3 Five practice periods are **u.**, allowing a
W-pI..... 39.5:1 full five minutes are **u.** for the four longer
W-pI..... 40.1:3 **u.** to attempt this schedule and to adhere
W-pI..... 47.4:2 and longer and more frequent ones are **u.**.
WpI. rIII.in1:3 are **u.** to follow just as closely as you can.
W-pI... 151.4:2 have often been **u.** to refrain from judging
W-pI... 161.6:4 times been **u.** to look beyond the body,
WpI rVI.in.3:8 for the day, no form of exercise is **u.**,

### urgency 3

T-16...... VI.8:3 The **u.** is only in dislodging your mind
T-31....... V.6:8 are but silently, and yet with ceaseless **u.**,
W-pI..... 11.2:4 haste, and with no sense of **u.** or effort.

### urgent 2

T-5....... VII.4:4 your part in it, and how **u.** it is to fulfill it.
W-pI... 159.6:4 his least request or his most **u.** need.

### urgently 1

W-pI... 166.3:2 **u.** he may be called to claim them as his

### urges 4

T-13... VII.11:2 the ego **u.** you again and again to get, it
T19..IV.B.15:3 it **u.** you to send out all your messages of
W-pI... 137.9:1 means by which the Holy Spirit **u.** you to
W-pI. 186.12:6 you, and **u.** that you now remember Him.

### urging 1

T-2........ VI.6:6 I will therefore repeat it, **u.** you to listen.

### Us 4

- God and Jesus

*us*

T-2....... VII.3:6 You have misperceived or miscreated **U.**,
T-9...... IV.12:2 God, and is perfectly satisfying to all of **U.**
T-11.........I.2:5 are one with you, for you are part of **U.**.
T-12...... VI.5:1 you will surely do, you will remember **U.**.

**us** 583
• Jesus
*noise word*
*Us*

T-1....... II.3:12 between **u.** now is that I have nothing else
T-4.........I.13:6 myself. Let **u.** undertake to learn this
T-4........ III.6:3 Let **u.** ask the Father in my name to keep
T-4........ III.7:6 can help you only as our Father created **u.**
T-5...........I.2:1 Let **u.** start our process of reawakening
T-5....... II.11:4 Let **u.** restate "My yoke is easy and my
T-5....... II.11:4 light" in this way; "Let **u.** join together,
T-5........ IV.6:1 Holy Spirit atones in all of **u.** by undoing,
T-6...........I.1:1 let **u.** consider the crucifixion again. I did
T-6........ II.13:5 Each of **u.** is the light of the world, and by
T-8......... V.3:7 to our joy in uniting with His Will for **u.**.
T-8......... V.4:3 The truth in both of **u.** is beyond the ego.
T-8......... V.4:4 this confidence for both of **u.** and all of us.
T-8......... V.4:4 this confidence for both of us and all of **u.**.
T-8......... V.4:5 because I received it of Him for **u.** all.
T-8......... V.5:5 join the journey with **u.** and cannot do so.
T-8......... V.6:3 me is yours. Let **u.** not lose sight of His
T-8......... V.6:3 for which God's Voice speaks in all of **u.**.
T-8........VI.1:3 weakness and add their strength to **u.**.
T-8........VI.1:4 us. God's welcome waits for **u.** all, and He
T-8........VI.1:4 He will welcome **u.** as I am welcoming you
T-8........VI.3:1 **u.** glorify Him Whom the world denies,
T-8........VI.8:5 whole power of God's Son lies in all of **u.**,
T-8........VI.8:5 lies in all of us, but not in any of **u.** alone.
T-8........VI.8:6 God would not have **u.** be alone because
T-9......... II.2:1 Let **u.** suppose, then, that what you ask of
T-9......... V.1:3 Let **u.** consider the unhealed healer more
T-11....... V.1:4 Let **u.** be very calm in doing this, for we
T-11....... V.3:1 Let **u.** begin this lesson in "ego dynamics
T-11....VIII.8:7 Not one of **u.** but has the answer in him,
T-12....... II.5:1 Let **u.** not save nightmares, for they are
T-12....... II.5:4 Let **u.** not delay this, for your dream of
T-12....... II.7:7 that peace goes with ***u.*** on the journey?
T-12...VII.10:5 safety of the Mind which created **u.**. For
T-13....... II.5:1 let **u.** recognize that you believe you have
T-13..... V.7:11 The Father welcomes all of **u.** in gladness,
T-13....VII.16:5 you to awaken unto **u.** and to yourself.
T-13....VIII.8:2 the power of God's Son will move in **u.**,
T-13..... X.12:3 Let **u.** look upon him together and love
T-13..... X.14:2 that none of **u.** alone can even think of it.
T-14.......in.1:8 Let **u.** now turn away from them, and
T-14....... V.5:1 and nothing else can unite **u.** in this world
T-14....... V.9:2 me. Our power comes not of **u.**, but of our
T-14....... V.9:3 we know Him, as He knows **u.** guiltless.
T-14..... V.11:9 let **u.** join him in the holy place of peace
T-14..... V.11:9 holy place of peace which is for all of **u.**,
T-15...... III.9:9 Let **u.** join in honoring you, who must
T-15...... VI.7:1 It is through ***u.*** that peace will come. Join
T-15..... VII.5:3 release him, let **u.** look more closely at the
T-15....VIII.2:4 Let **u.** join together in making the holy
T-15...... XI.3:2 and let **u.** celebrate our release together
T-15...... XI.3:2 together by releasing everyone with **u.**.
T-15...... XI.3:5 to **u.** and disappear in our presence, and
T-15...... XI.8:2 joy. Let **u.** join in celebrating peace by
T-15...... XI.8:5 He joins **u.** in the celebration of His Son's
T-16...... II.8:5 let **u.** resolve together to accept the joyful
T-16.... IV.13:9 the Love of God in **u.** together cannot lift.
T-16..... V.10:2 Let **u.** not think of its fearful nature, nor
T-16...VII.12:1 *Forgive* ***u.*** *our illusions, Father, and help us*
T-16...VII.12:1 *help* ***u.*** *to accept our true relationship with*
T-16...VII.12:3 *be in* ***u.*** *that needs forgiveness when Yours is*
T-16...VII.12:5 *Let* ***u.*** *not wander into temptation, for the*
T-16...VII.12:6 *And let* ***u.*** *receive only what You have given,*
T-17.... IV.16:2 Let **u.** ascend in peace together to the
T-17.... IV.16:4 They are in **u.**, through His ascendance.
T-18.......I.10:9 Let **u.** join in Him in peace and gratitude,
T-18...... III.2:5 Let **u.** then join quickly in an instant of
T-18...... III.3:9 **u.** who travel surely and very swiftly away
T-18...... III.5:7 And where we go we carry God with **u.**.
T-18...... III.7:6 Time has been readjusted to help **u.** do,
T-18.... IX.11:2 Nor is there any need for **u.** to try to speak
T-18.... IX.11:5 for **u.** to dwell on what cannot be attained
T19. IV.A.17:6 I teach that bodies cannot keep **u.** apart?
T19....IV.B.5:6 it be difficult for **u.** to walk past barriers
T19....IV.B.9:6 He Who is our home is homeless with **u.**.
T19... IV.D.9:6 Let **u.** join together in a holy instant, here
T19... IV.D.9:7 let **u.** join in faith that He Who brought us
T19... IV.D.9:7 Who brought **u.** here together will offer
T19. IV.D.17:5 Let **u.** give redemption to each other and
T-20 ........I.1:2 Let **u.** not spend this holy week brooding
T-20 .....II.8:11 Let **u.** lift up our eyes together, not in fear
T-20 .....II.8:12 And there will be no fear in **u.**, for in our
T-20 .......II.9:5 The holiness that leads **u.** is within us, as
T-20 .......II.9:5 The holiness that leads us is within **u.**, as
T-20 .......II.9:6 were meant to find by Him Who leads **u.**.
T-20 ... III.10:5 separation between **u.** become impossible
T-20 ...... V.8:3 Let **u.** consider now what he must learn,
T-20 ....VII.2:5 not, let **u.** admit that *you* are inconsistent.
T-22 .......II.9:1 Let **u.** look closer at the whole illusion
T-22 ... VI.10:7 Let **u.** look straight at how this error came
T-23 ......in.5:1 Let **u.** not let littleness lead God's Son
T-23 .......II.1:4 Let **u.**, then, look upon them calmly, that
T-25 .... VII.3:1 Let **u.** go back to what we said before,
T-26 .... VII.1:3 Let **u.** review the principles that we have
T-26 .. VII.12:1 Let **u.** consider what the error is, so it can
T-26 .. VII.19:3 Let **u.** unite in bringing blessing to the
T-26 .. VII.19:4 can save each one of **u.** can save us all.
T-26 .. VII.19:4 can save each one of us can save **u.** all.
T-27 ... VIII.5:3 Then let **u.** merely look upon the dream's
T-27 ... VIII.6:1 Let **u.** return the dream he gave away
T-29 ...... V.8:4 Let **u.** be glad indeed that this is so, and
T-29 .... VII.7:1 Let **u.** forget the purpose of the world the
T-30 ......I.13:5 Let **u.**, then, consider once again the very
T-30 .... VII.7:7 so that they mean the same to all of **u.**.
T-30 .... VII.7:8 language lets **u.** speak to all our brothers,
T-30 .... VII.7:8 them forgiveness has been given to **u.** all,
T-31 ......I.12:1 Let **u.** be still an instant, and forget all
T-31 ......I.12:2 is. Let **u.** remember not our own ideas of
T-31 .......II.2:1 Let **u.** review again what seems to stand
T-31 .......II.6:4 Then let **u.** wait an instant and be still,
T-31 .......II.6:5 This brother neither leads nor follows **u.**,
T-31 .......II.6:5 but walks beside **u.** on the selfsame road.
T-31 .......II.6:6 He is like **u.**, as near or far away from
T-31 .......II.6:7 make no gains he does not make with **u.**,
T-31 ..... III.6:1 Let **u.** be glad that you will see what you
T-31 ...... V.9:2 Let **u.** consider, then, what proof there is
T-31 .... V.10:6 so? Let **u.** forget the concept's foolishness,
T-31 ... VIII.9:1 Let **u.** be glad that we can walk the world,
T-31 ... VIII.9:3 to lift **u.** high above the thorny roads we
T-31 .VIII.12:8 we have reached where all of **u.** are one,
T-31 .VIII.12:8 we are home, where You would have **u.** be
W-pI..... 30.2:4 see, rather than keeping it apart from **u.**.
W-pI..... 45.4:4 let the thoughts of the world hold **u.** back.
W-pI..... 45.4:5 let the beliefs of the world tell **u.** that what
W-pI..... 45.4:5 what God would have **u.** do is impossible.
W-pI..... 45.4:6 what God would have **u.** do is possible.
W-pI..... 45.5:1 would have **u.** do is what we want to do.
W-pI..... 45.5:2 fail in doing what He would have **u.** do.
W-pI........57.h Today let **u.** review these ideas:
W-pI..... 62.4:1 Let **u.** be glad to begin and end this day
W-pI..... 64.5:1 Let **u.** remember this today. Let us
W-pI..... 64.5:2 today. Let **u.** remind ourselves of it in the
W-pI..... 64.6:1 then, let **u.** practice with these thoughts:
W-pI..... 66.5:7 Let **u.**, then, think about the premises for
W-pI... 66.10:4 For God Himself shares it with **u.**. Today's
W-pI... 66.10:8 Let **u.** try today to realize that only the
W-pI..... 69.2:1 Today let **u.** make another real attempt to
W-pI..... 69.2:2 let **u.** devote several minutes to thinking
W-pI..... 69.3:1 Let **u.** begin our longer practice period
W-pI..... 69.3:1 to reach what is dearer to **u.** than all else.
W-pI..... 69.3:5 Let **u.** end the ancient search today by
W-pI..... 69.3:5 search today by finding the light in **u.**,
W-pI..... 69.3:5 searches with **u.** to look upon and rejoice.
W-pI..... 70.5:2 God wants **u.** to be healed, and we do not
W-pI..... 70.5:2 to be sick, because it makes **u.** unhappy.
W-pI..... 70.5:4 He does not want **u.** to be sick. Neither do
W-pI..... 70.5:6 do we. He wants **u.** to be healed. So do we.
W-pI..... 71.7:1 Let **u.** practice recognizing this certainty
W-pI..... 71.7:2 And let **u.** rejoice that there is an answer
W-pI..... 71.9:1 this, let **u.** devote the remainder of the
W-pI..... 71.9:1 to asking God to reveal His plan to **u.**. Ask
W-pI..... 72.3:2 But let **u.** consider the kinds of things you
W-pI..... 72.6:4 Let **u.** accept this and be glad. As a body,
W-pI..... 72.9:1 The light of truth is in **u.**, where it was
W-pI .... 72.9:2 It is the body that is outside **u.**, and is not
W-pI .... 72.9:4 in **u.** is to recognize ourselves as we are.
W-pI .. 72.10:1 has already been accomplished in **u.**. To
W-pI .. 72.10:3 understand what God's plan for **u.** is. We
W-pI .. 72.10:5 aside, and ask what God's plan for **u.** is:
W-pI .... 73.8:2 No idle wishes can detain **u.**, nor deceive
W-pI .... 73.8:2 nor deceive **u.** with an illusion of strength.
W-pI .... 74.2:5 Let **u.** try to recognize this today, and
W-pI .... 75.3:2 and hide the world forgiveness offers **u.**.
W-pI .... 75.4:1 at the world that our forgiveness shows **u.**
W-pI .... 75.4:4 the real world rises before **u.** in gladness,
W-pI .... 75.4:5 Sight is given **u.**, now that the light has
W-pI .... 76.7:4 it is a truth that keeps **u.** free forever.
W-pI .. 76.11:1 Let **u.** today open God's channels to Him,
W-pI .. 76.11:1 and let His Will extend through **u.** to Him
W-pI .. 76.11:3 His Voice will speak of this to **u.**, as well as
W-pI .... 77.3:4 no more than what belongs to **u.** in truth.
W-pI .... 78.7:1 Then let **u.** ask of Him Who knows this
W-pI .... 78.7:1 the light of true forgiveness, given unto **u.**
W-pI .. 78.10:1 to **u.** as part of God's salvation plan, and
W-pI .. 78.10:2 we allow each one we meet to save **u.**, and
W-pI .... 80.7:1 Let **u.** be determined not to collect
W-pI .... 80.7:2 today. Let **u.** be determined to be free of
W-pI ....... 83.h Today let **u.** review these ideas:
W-pI .. 92.10:1 Let **u.** give twenty minutes twice today to
W-pI .. 92.10:4 to show **u.** how to find the meeting place
W-pI .. 92.11:3 Let **u.** repeat as often as we can the idea
W-pI .... 95.8:3 them go. Let **u.** therefore be determined,
W-pI .... 95.8:4 for weakness will enable **u.** to overlook it,
W-pI .... 98.1:8 is, and take the part assigned to **u.** by God
W-pI .... 98.4:1 They will be with **u.**; all who took the
W-pI .... 98.4:1 the stand we take today will gladly offer **u.**
W-pI .... 98.4:2 Those still uncertain, too, will join with **u.**
W-pI .. 100.7:1 feeling happiness arise in **u.** according to
W-pI .. 100.8:1 Now let **u.** try to find that joy that proves
W-pI .. 100.8:1 to **u.** and all the world God's Will for us. It
W-pI .. 100.8:1 to us and all the world God's Will for **u.**. It
W-pI .. 104.2:4 His are the gifts that are within **u.** now,
W-pI .. 104.2:6 to have them. They belong to **u.** today.
W-pI .. 104.4:1 we ask to recognize what God has given **u.**
W-pI .. 104.4:2 to find what has been given **u.** by Him.
W-pI .. 104.4:3 that what belongs to **u.** in truth is what
W-pI .. 104.4:4 else, for nothing else belongs to **u.** in truth
W-pI .. 104.5:1 and peace belong to **u.** as His eternal gifts.
W-pI .. 105.1:2 accept them, knowing they belong to **u.**.
W-pI .. 107.7:2 We merely ask for what belongs to **u.**,
W-pI .. 108.7:4 and see how quickly peace returns to **u.**.
W-pI .. 108.7:5 and in that peace is vision given **u.**, and
W-pI 110.11:1 thoughts for all who meet with **u.** today.
W-pI 110.11:3 Son, our holy Self, the Christ in each of **u.**:
W-pI 110.11:5 Let **u.** declare this truth as often as we can
W-pI .. 122.6:6 Let **u.** today rejoice that this is so, for here
W-pI 122.12:2 been held in store for **u.** since time began,
W-pI .. 123.1:1 Today let **u.** be thankful. We have come
W-pI .. 123.4:3 as we go to do what is appointed **u.** to do.
W-pI .. 123.5:2 to speak the saving Word of God to **u.**.
W-pI .. 124.1:2 available to **u.** in all our undertakings. We
W-pI .. 124.1:5 that God Himself goes everywhere with **u.**
W-pI .. 124.2:5 come to follow **u.** will recognize the way
W-pI .. 124.2:5 yet still remains with **u.** as we walk on.
W-pI .. 124.3:1 who went before or stayed with **u.** a while.
W-pI .. 124.3:2 Who loves **u.** with the equal love in which
W-pI .. 124.3:2 on **u.** and offers us the happiness we gave.
W-pI .. 124.3:2 on us and offers **u.** the happiness we gave.
W-pI .. 124.4:1 Today we will not doubt His Love for **u.**,
W-pI .. 124.7:7 from our Father, it is healed along with **u.**.
W-pI .. 126.2:1 Let **u.** consider what you do believe, in
W-pI .. 127.7:2 Let **u.** together, then, be glad to give some
W-pI 127.10:2 learn. Let **u.** give thanks today that we are
W-pI 127.10:3 past. Today we leave the past behind **u.**,
W-pI 127.11:3 Now are they all made free, along with **u.**.
W-pI 127.12:1 leave a part of **u.** outside our love if we
W-pI .. 130.7:2 nor attempt to bring with **u.** a little part of
W-pI .. 131.8:5 Let **u.** not try longer to impose an alien
W-pI 132.14:4 we are in the home our Father set for **u.**,
W-pI 132.14:5 created **u.** would loose the world this day
W-pI .. 134.1:1 Let **u.** review the meaning of "forgive,"
W-pI 134.14:3 follow **u.** to the reality we share with them
W-pI 134.14:4 let **u.** give a quarter of an hour twice today

W-pI.134.14:4 forgiveness, and was sent to **u.** to teach it.
W-pI.134.14:5 teach it. Let **u.** ask of Him: *Let me perceive*
W-pI...135.4:1 Let **u.** consider first what you defend. It
W-pI.135.21:1 for this is part of what was planned for **u.**.
W-pI.135.21:2 **u.** for our accomplishment of this today.
W-pI.136.15:2 ask the truth to come to **u.** and set us free.
W-pI.136.15:2 ask the truth to come to us and set **u.** free.
W-pI.136.15:3 come, for it has never been apart from **u.**.
W-pI.136.15:5 prayer, to help **u.** rise above defensiveness
W-pI...138.7:1 that time was made to help **u.** make. Such
W-pI...139.1:2 to accept ourselves as God created **u.**.
W-pI...139.8:5 Let **u.** not allow our holy minds to occupy
W-pI...139.9:3 Let **u.** not forget the goal that we accepted
W-pI...139.9:5 what everyone must be, along with **u.**. Fail
W-pI.139.11:4 gave to **u.** when He created us like Him.
W-pI.139.11:4 gave to us when He created **u.** like Him.
W-pI.139.11:6 how dear our brothers are to **u.** in truth,
W-pI.139.11:6 truth, how much a part of **u.** is every mind
W-pI.139.11:6 how faithful they have really been to **u.**,
W-pI.139.12:1 that would distract **u.** from our holy aim.
W-pI...140.7:1 Let **u.** not try today to seek to cure what
W-pI...140.8:2 because our Father placed it there for **u.**.
W-pI...140.8:3 It is not farther from **u.** than ourselves. It
W-pI...140.8:4 It is as near to **u.** as our own thoughts; so
W-pI...140.9:1 misled today by what appears to **u.** as sick
W-pI.140.10:4 a single Voice which speaks to **u.** of truth,
W-pI.140.11:1 speak to **u.** five minutes as the day begins,
W-pI.140.11:4 when we can hear our Father speak to **u.**.
W-pI.140.12:3 *Speak to* **u.***, Father, that we may be healed.*
W-pI.140.12:4 feel salvation cover **u.** with soft protection
W-pI.140.12:4 minds, nor offer proof to **u.** that it is real.
W-pI.140.12:6 given **u.** as we attend in silence and in joy.
W-pI.140.12:7 This is the day when healing comes to **u.**.
WpI.rIV.in3:1 Let **u.** begin our preparation with some
WpI.rIV.in4:4 and see the meaning that they offer **u.**.
WpI.rIV.in9:2 than this to give **u.** happiness and rest,
WpI.rIV.in9:3 time of blessing and of happiness for **u.**;
W-pI.151.16:4 to Him Who has restored our sanity to **u.**.
W-pI.151.17:2 world unites with **u.** and happily accepts
W-pI.151.17:3 and the peace of God, through **u.**, belongs
W-pI...152.8:1 Let **u.** today be truly humble, and accept
W-pI...152.9:4 to Him Who has created **u.** immaculate,
W-pI.152.11:5 ask our Self that He reveal Himself to **u.**.
W-pI...153.8:2 the endless joy our function offers **u.**. We
W-pI.153.15:5 to arise to turn **u.** from our purpose, we
W-pI.153.16:4 the business of the world will close on **u.**,
W-pI.153.17:2 what He would have **u.** do the hour that is
W-pI.153.17:2 all the gifts He gave **u.** in the one gone by.
W-pI.153.19:3 remember that His strength abides in **u.**.
W-pI.153.19:4 that He remains beside **u.** through the day
W-pI.153.19:6 We will pause a moment, as He tells **u.**, "I
W-pI...154.1:1 Let **u.** today be neither arrogant nor
W-pI...154.1:5 nor can we know what role is best for **u.**;
W-pI.154.10:2 minds apart from Him Who speaks for **u.**,
W-pI.154.10:3 Him. He alone can speak to **u.** and for us,
W-pI.154.10:3 Him. He alone can speak to us and for **u.**,
W-pI.154.11:1 have, that we may recognize His gifts to **u.**
W-pI.154.11:2 our voice that He may speak through **u.**.
W-pI.154.11:4 needs our feet to bring **u.** where He wills,
W-pI.154.12:1 Let **u.** but learn this lesson for today: We
W-pI.154.14:2 message sent to **u.** today from our Creator
W-pI.155.11:3 along the way that truth points out to **u.**.
W-pI.155.11:6 way. For as truth goes before **u.**, so it goes
W-pI.155.11:6 before our brothers who will follow **u.**.
W-pI.155.12:6 that walks before **u.** now is one with Him,
W-pI.155.12:6 and leads **u.** to where He has always been.
W-pI...157.2:2 prepares **u.** for what we have yet to learn.
W-pI...157.2:3 It brings **u.** to the door where learning
W-pI...157.2:4 It leaves **u.** here an instant, and we go
W-pI...158.3:7 seems to have a future still unknown to **u.**.
W-pI.159.10:6 Let **u.** an instant dream with Him. His
W-pI.159.10:7 His dream awakens **u.** to truth. His vision
W-pI...161.3:4 to teach **u.** from a different point of view,
W-pI...161.5:1 feel limits our freedom, makes **u.** suffer,
W-pI...163.8:9 And it is given **u.** to look past death, and
W-pI...163.9:6 *And we abide where You have placed* **u.***, in*
W-pI...164.7:2 We will receive but what is given **u.** from
W-pI...164.7:6 the light in which our Savior looks on **u.**,
W-pI...164.7:6 given **u.** through His forgiving vision, not
W-pI...165.8:1 not upon ourselves, to give **u.** certainty.
W-pI.167.10:1 Let **u.** today be children of the truth, and
W-pI.167.12:1 Source from which perfection comes to **u.**
W-pI...168.1:1 God speaks to **u.**. Shall we not speak to
W-pI...168.1:4 He makes no attempt to hide from **u.**. We
W-pI...168.3:2 by which God leans to **u.** and lifts us up,
W-pI...168.3:2 by which God leans to us and lifts **u.** up,
W-pI...168.3:4 and takes **u.** in His Arms and sweeps away
W-pI...168.5:1 for we receive what has been given **u.**. Our
W-pI...168.5:3 by giving **u.** the means to lay them down,
W-pI...168.6:1 And He descends to meet **u.**, as we come
W-pI...168.6:2 prepared for **u.** He gives and we receive.
W-pI...168.6:4 He gave to **u.** through His Own Voice, His
W-pI.169.14:9 give in the grace that has been given **u.**.
W-pI...170.9:2 fear. Let **u.** remember what the text has
W-pI.170.13:2 *No cruelty abides in* **u.***, for there is none in*
W-pI.170.13:5 *our brothers, knowing they are one with* **u.**.
W-pI.170.13:7 *thanks for them who render* **u.** *complete. In*
W-pI.170.13:9 *are we because Your Holiness has set* **u.** *free.*
WpI...rV.in1:5 doubts have made **u.** walk uncertainly
WpI...rV.in2:2 *and our holy minds be still, and speak to* **u.**.
WpI...rV.in3:2 *And if we stumble, You will raise* **u.** *up. If we*
WpI...rV.in3:4 *off, but You will not forget to call* **u.** *back.*
WpI...rV.in3:6 *the Word You offer* **u.** *to unify our practicing*
WpI...rV.in3:6 *review the thoughts that You have given* **u.**.
WpI...rV.in5:1 waits to meet **u.** at the journey's ending.
WpI...rV.in5:2 Every step we take brings **u.** a little nearer.
WpI...rV.in5:4 Let **u.** raise our hearts from dust to life, as
WpI...rV.in5:4 to life, as we remember this is promised **u.**
WpI...rV.in5:4 was sent to open up the path of light to **u.**,
WpI...rV.in5:4 up the path of light to us, and teach **u.**,
WpI...rV.in8:8 prepared for **u.** before time was and kept
W-pI...181.3:4 for **u.** within this interval of time wherein
W-pI...181.5:6 will believe will not intrude upon **u.** now.
W-pI...181.6:2 And if a brother's sins occur to **u.**, our
W-pI...181.7:1 to keep **u.** safe throughout the day. We do
W-pI...181.8:5 He feels for **u.** becomes our own as well.
W-pI.183.11:8 And in His Name, it shall be given **u.**.
W-pI.184.14:3 separations disappear which kept **u.** blind
W-pI.184.15:8 *Your Name unites* **u.** *in the oneness which is*
W-pI...185.7:1 Let **u.** today devote our practicing to
W-pI...185.7:4 do not request another dream be given **u.**.
W-pI.185.14:2 With Help like this beside **u.**, can we fail
W-pI.185.14:2 as we request the peace of God be given **u.**
W-pI...186.2:1 Let **u.** not fight our function. We did not
W-pI...186.2:4 The means are given **u.** by which it will be
W-pI...186.2:6 is given **u.** to do, we have the strength to
W-pI...186.2:7 assigned to **u.** by One Who knows us well.
W-pI...186.2:7 assigned to us by One Who knows **u.** well.
W-pI...186.4:1 reveal to **u.** what He would have us do.
W-pI...186.4:1 reveal to us what He would have **u.** do.
W-pI...186.4:2 adequacy for the function He will offer **u.**.
W-pI...186.4:4 And if He deems **u.** worthy, so we are. It is
W-pI...186.8:2 will accept the function God has given **u.**,
W-pI...186.8:5 and our emotions raise **u.** high indeed, or
W-pI...186.8:5 or dash **u.** to the ground in hopelessness.
W-pI.187.10:3 Whose innocence has joined **u.** all as one,
W-pI.187.11:6 it will be returned to **u.** in form of lilies we
W-pI.187.11:6 in **u.** and offers us His Holiness as ours.
W-pI.187.11:6 in us and offers **u.** His Holiness as ours.
W-pI...188.9:1 coming nearer to the light in **u.** today. We
W-pI...188.9:5 them, ordering that they depart from **u.**.
W-pI.188.10:1 that the peace of God still shines in **u.**,
W-pI.188.10:1 **u.** to all living things that share our life.
W-pI.188.10:2 world from what we thought it did to **u.**.
W-pI...189.6:1 as we seek to reach to what is true in **u.**,
W-pI...189.6:1 its Love which knows **u.** perfect as itself,
W-pI...189.6:1 which is the gift its Love bestows on **u.**.
W-pI...189.6:3 as sure as Love itself, to which it carries **u.**
W-pI.189.10:2 *we have called, and You have answered* **u.**.
W-pI.189.10:7 *no beliefs of what we are, or Who created* **u.**.
W-pI.189.10:9 *own as well, be done in* **u.** *and in the world,*
W-pI.193.11:4 let **u.** think about all things we saved to
W-pI.193.11:5 Let **u.** give them all to Him Who knows
W-pI.193.11:7 are the lessons God would have **u.** learn.
W-pI...194.9:2 sure that only good can come to **u.**. If we
W-pI...194.9:5 for **u.** that leaves temptation far behind.
W-pI...195.4:4 that in **u.** all things will find their freedom
W-pI...195.5:4 Let **u.** not compare ourselves with them,
W-pI...195.5:4 with them, as they must share with **u.**.
W-pI...195.6:3 we fail to recognize the gifts of God to **u.**.
W-pI...195.7:3 would find, the way is opening at last to **u.**
W-pI...195.9:3 self-perception which regards **u.** in a place
W-pI...195.9:3 a thought or care for **u.** or for our future.
W-pI...195.9:5 God has cared for **u.**, and calls us Son.
W-pI...195.9:5 God has cared for us, and calls **u.** Son.
W-pI...196.4:1 we take in leading **u.** from bondage to the
W-pI...196.4:2 Let **u.** take this step today, that we may
W-pI...196.4:2 may quickly go the way salvation shows **u.**
W-pI.198.13:2 brought **u.** here will not forsake us now.
W-pI.198.13:2 brought us here will not forsake **u.** now.
W-pI.198.13:3 For He would give to **u.** the gift that God
W-pI.198.13:3 that God has given **u.** through Him today.
W-pI...200.9:1 Let **u.** not lose our way again today. We
W-pI.200.11:4 Peace be to **u.** today. For we have found a
WpI rVI.in.2:1 bestowed on **u.** in our last twenty lessons.
WpI rVI.in.4:4 For thus is freedom given **u.** from all we
WpI rVI.in.7:4 Let **u.** offer Him the whole review we now
WpI rVI.in.7:4 and let **u.** also not forget to Whom it has
WpI rVI.in.7:4 advancing toward the goal He set for **u.**;
WpI rVI.in.7:4 for us; allowing Him to teach **u.** how to go
W-pII ....in.2:6 and at night, as long as makes **u.** happy.
W-pII ....in.4:1 the step to **u.** that He has told us, through
W-pII ....in.4:1 to take the step to us that He has told **u.**,
W-pII ....in.4:3 invitation that He seeks to make **u.** happy
W-pII ....in.4:6 and then we wait for Him to come to **u.**.
W-pII ....in.6:2 in gratitude to Him Who taught **u.** how to
W-pII ....in.6:2 for its replacement, given **u.** by You. We
W-pII ....in.6:5 Accept these little gifts of thanks from **u.**,
W-pII ....in.7:2 way by following the Guide You sent to **u.**
W-pII ....in.7:3 know the way, but You did not forget **u.**.
W-pII ....in.7:4 we know that You will not forget **u.** now.
W-pII ....in.8:2 We have found the way He chose for **u.**,
W-pII ....in.8:2 choice to follow it as He would have **u.** go.
W-pII ....in.8:3 His Hand has held **u.** up. His Thoughts
W-pII ....in.8:5 His Love has called to **u.** unceasingly since
W-pII ....in.9:7 safely home, where He would have **u.** be.
W-pII ..in.10:8 This year has brought **u.** to eternity.
W-pII .221.2:6 to hear Him speak to **u.** of what we are,
W-pII .....2.4:1 Let **u.** come daily to this holy place, and
W-pII .....2.4:3 a hint of all the glory given **u.** by God. The
W-pII .231.2:5 only this is what it will be given **u.** to find.
W-pII .233.2:1 Today we have one Guide to lead **u.** on.
W-pII .233.2:4 day of countless gifts and mercies unto **u.**.
W-pII .238.2:1 to think how much our Father loves **u.**.
W-pII .239.1:2 Let **u.** instead be thankful for the gifts our
W-pII .239.1:2 be thankful for the gifts our Father gave **u.**
W-pII .240.1:6 Let **u.** not be deceived today. We are the
W-pII .240.1:8 There is no fear in **u.**, for we are each a
W-pII .....3.5:1 Let **u.** not rest content until the world has
W-pII .....3.5:2 Let **u.** not be satisfied until forgiveness
W-pII .....3.5:3 let **u.** not attempt to change our function.
W-pII .245.2:3 Who speaks to **u.** as we relate His Word;
W-pII .245.2:3 share the Word that He has given unto **u.**.
W-pII .254.2:6 God speaks to **u.** and tells us of our will,
W-pII .254.2:6 God speaks to us and tells **u.** of our will,
W-pII .257.1:4 and great depression. Let **u.** therefore be
W-pII .257.1:4 only what God would have **u.** do this day.
W-pII .259.1:2 What else could blind **u.** to the obvious,
W-pII .263.2:1 let **u.** look on all we see through holy
W-pII .263.2:2 Let all appearances seem pure to **u.**, that
W-pII .264.2:3 in what will save the world, along with **u.**?
W-pII .266.2:1 own, acknowledging our Self in each of **u.**;
W-pII .266.2:2 How many saviors God has given **u.**! How
W-pII .266.2:3 and given **u.** the sight to look on them?
W-pII .....6.1:2 Self we share, uniting **u.** with one another,
W-pII .....6.5:2 let **u.** seek to find Christ's face and look on
W-pII .272.2:2 if we hear temptation call to **u.** to stay and
W-pII .273.1:3 let **u.** learn how to dismiss it and return to
W-pII .274.2:1 A special blessing comes to **u.** today,
W-pII .275.1:1 Let **u.** today attend the Voice for God,
W-pII .275.1:4 Voice for God tells **u.** of things we cannot
W-pII .276.1:5 Let **u.** accept His Fatherhood, and all is
W-pII .276.1:5 accept His Fatherhood, and all is given **u.**.
W-pII .276.1:7 Who gave His Word to **u.** in our creation,
W-pII .277.2:1 Let **u.** not worship idols, nor believe in
W-pII .283.2:1 Source, and everything created part of **u.**.
W-pII .283.2:2 our forgiveness has made one with **u.**.

T-15.....XI.10:6 *unless I want to* **u.** *you to imprison myself. In*
T-16.........I.1:3 provided you let Him **u.** it in His way. His
T-16.........I.3:6 Do not **u.** empathy to make the past real,
T-16.........I.4:2 you let Him **u.** your capacity for strength,
T-16.........I.4:7 triumphant **u.** of empathy for its glory.
T-16....... II.4:4 have offered it to Him to **u.** as He sees fit,
T-16....... II.4:4 to **u.** His understanding on your behalf. It
T-16......IV.4:5 and **u.** them for any purpose which they
T-16......VI.8:2 is kind, and if you **u.** it on behalf of reality
T-17.........I.2:5 What you **u.** in fantasy you deny to truth.
T-17.........I.2:6 to truth to **u.** for you is safe from fantasy.
T-17......V.2:7 to the Holy Spirit, to **u.** for His purposes.
T-17.....V.13:1 a condition in which you cannot **u.** it. As
T-17.....V.15:1 effects of the holy instant and **u.** them to
T-17......VI.1:7 is essential at this point to **u.** them in each
T-17.....VII.5:3 **U.** not your faithlessness. Let it enter and
T-17.....VII.5:4 and look upon it calmly, but do not **u.** it.
T-17.....VII.5:6 **U.** it, and it will carry you straight to
T-17.....VII.6:7 will be gently turned to its **u.** and purpose
T-17.....VII.7:2 And you can **u.** *this* in perfect safety. Yet
T-17.....VII.7:3 if you would **u.** the faithlessness instead.
T-17...VII.10:6 **U.** not your faithlessness against it, for it
T-17... VIII.3:3 Holy Spirit's purpose is free to **u.** instead.
T-17... VIII.5:3 let yourself **u.** faithlessness against him.
T-18....... II.6:6 But He does **u.** it differently, as a help to
T-18....... V.2:8 will you **u.** it to ascend to Heaven alone.
T-18....... V.4:6 is required to receive the means and **u.**
T-18......VI.4:8 does not condemn it and can **u.** it lovingly
T-18......VI.6:1 to **u.** the body as the scapegoat for guilt,
T-18.....VII.6:5 You are not making **u.** of the course if you
T-18.....VII.8:4 center will you be directed how to **u.** the
T-19.........I.3:3 the purpose that the mind would **u.** it for.
T-19.........I.9:4 You do not **u.** anything your brother has
T19....IV.B.9:3 and **u.** it for the Son of God's release. It is
T19..IV.B.10:8 for its accomplishment, and justify its **u.**.
T19..IV.B.11:7 **U.** not your error as the justification for
T19. IV.C.11:9 *of sin and death, nor* **u.** *it for destruction.*
T19IV.C.11:10 *it an obstacle to peace, but let You* **u.** *it for me*
T-20....... II.1:1 upon the body, or to cover it or for its **u.**.
T-20....... II.6:3 And yet I cannot **u.** your gift of lilies while
T-20....... II.6:4 **u.** what I have given unless you share it.
T-20....... V.5:1 brother's body is as little **u.** to you as it is
T-20....... V.5:4 sight that sees the body has no **u.** which
T-21......III.6:1 The Holy Spirit has a **u.** for all the means
T-21......III.6:3 He sees the means you **u.**, but not the
T-21.....III.10:5 which tries to **u.** the body to carry out the
T-21.....III.12:7 can **u.** them still to save itself from what it
T-21....... V.9:3 and those who **u.** it have gained a means
T-21...VII.10:8 let an "enemy" tempt you to **u.** the body's
T-22....... II.6:3 their **u.** will you gain faith in them. Yet to
T-22......VI.8:9 He will **u.** every one of them for peace.
T-22......VI.9:5 Save no dark secrets that He cannot **u.**,
T-23.......in.1:4 of strength attack would **u.** to cover frailty
T-23.......in.2:2 You will believe that everything you **u.** for
T-24....... II.2:4 who can **u.** him as the gauge of littleness,
T-24......VI.4:4 you will **u.** the world for what is not its
T-24.VII.11:12 and **u.** perception for a different purpose.
T-25.........I.7:4 Yet must It **u.** the language that this mind
T-25.........I.7:5 must **u.** all learning to transfer illusions to
T-25......VI.4:1 of specialness; His **u.** of what you made,
T-25... VIII.1:1 The Holy Spirit can **u.** all that you give to
T-25... VIII.1:2 But He cannot **u.** what you withhold, for
T-26...VII.18:1 To **u.** the power God has given you as He
T-26...VII.18:2 nor to make **u.** of what He gave to answer
T-27......III.5:7 No learning aid has **u.** that can extend
T-27......III.5:9 interval it has a **u.** that now you fear, but
T-27......VI.3:2 You **u.** its eyes to see, its ears to hear, and
T-27......VI.3:4 tells you but the names you gave to it to **u.**
T-28.........I.3:6 await their **u.**. They have no dedication
T-28.........I.4:1 Spirit can indeed make **u.** of memory, for
T-28.........I.5:1 Spirit's **u.** of memory is quite apart from
T-28.........I.5:2 seek to **u.** it as a means to keep the past,
T-28.........I.6:4 And yet you make strange **u.** of it, as if the
T-28.........I.6:7 is held in memory as you make **u.** of it,
T-29....... V.8:1 that has been kept apart from **u.** by Him
T-29....VI.2:14 may disappear because they have no **u.**.
T-29......VI.4:5 time, but at its ending, when it has no **u.**.
T-30.....VII.7:7 through His **u.** of symbols are we joined,
T-31......IV.1:5 little time is given you to **u.** for you alone;
T-31......IV.5:3 is none, what power of decision can he **u.**?
T-31......IV.5:4 with learning where it really has a **u.**. And
T-31.....VII.1:2 Salvation does not seek to **u.** a means as
T-31.....VII.6:5 Alternatives are in your mind to **u.**, and
W-in..........8:5 You are asked only to **u.** them. It is their
W-in..........8:6 **u.** that will give them meaning to you,
W-in..........9:4 reactions to the ideas may be, **u.** them.
W-pI.......1.3:4 for the day, **u.** it totally indiscriminately.
W-pI.......3.1:7 and merely **u.** these things exactly as you
W-pI.......4.1:4 thoughts, **u.** them as subjects for the idea.
W-pI.......4.2:2 be afraid to **u.** "good" thoughts as well as
W-pI.......4.5:1 You can also **u.** the idea for a particular
W-pI.......5.2:1 **u.** both the name of the form in which
W-pI.....12.3:5 occur to you, **u.** them along with the rest.
W-pI.....14.5:3 Do not **u.** general terms. For example, do
W-pI.....16.5:4 **u.** today's idea whenever you are aware of
W-pI.....26.6:4 will not be able to **u.** very many for any
W-pI.....26.8:1 available for each situation you **u.**, and
W-pI.....28.6:2 subject that you **u.** in the practice periods.
W-pI.....30.2:1 are trying to **u.** a new kind of "projection.
W-pI.....31.1:3 we will **u.** a form of practice which will be
W-pI.....31.5:1 is also a particularly useful one to **u.** as a
W-pI.....34.6:1 or worry, **u.** the idea in its original form.
W-pI.....35.3:3 We will **u.** a somewhat different kind of
W-pI.....35.7:3 and **u.** them in applying today's idea.
W-pI.....37.5:1 you may **u.** any combination of these two
W-pI.....37.6:3 essential to **u.** the idea if anyone seems to
W-pI.....38.4:4 **U.** this form in applying the idea for today
W-pI.....38.6:2 **u.** the more specific form in applying the
W-pI...39.10:3 However you elect to **u.** it, the idea should
W-pI.....41.9:1 Throughout the day **u.** today's idea often,
W-pI.....44.3:2 will **u.** a form of exercise which has been
W-pI.....44.4:3 The form of practice we will **u.** today is
W-pI.....44.5:2 learn the form of exercise we will **u.** today
W-pI.....44.8:3 only one that has any real **u.** to you at all.
W-pI.....47.8:2 **U.** it as your answer to any disturbance.
W-pI.....48.2:3 You can **u.** it with your eyes open at any
W-pI.....48.2:5 that you **u.** the idea immediately, should
WpI...rI.in.6:2 **U.** them as they are given here. It is not
W-pI.....52.3:5 that I am trying to **u.** time against God.
W-pI.....55.5:3 I attempt to **u.** everyone and everything.
W-pI.....62.4:1 **u.** it as frequently as possible throughout
W-pI.....64.2:2 **u.** for all the illusions you have made, and
W-pI.....65.4:4 Holy Spirit can **u.** it consistently for the
W-pI.....65.6:5 *me.* You need not **u.** these exact words, but
W-pI.....65.8:1 hour, **u.** this form in applying today's idea
W-pI.....67.2:7 He defines Himself is appropriate for **u.**.
W-pI.....76.4:2 that have no **u.** and serve no purpose.
W-pI.....79.6:4 And you would **u.** the means, because you
WpI..rII.in.6:4 the particular words you **u.** that matter.
W-pI.....81.4:4 *my will. I will not* **u.** *this for an alien purpose.*
W-pI.....82.4:2 *me not* **u.** *this to hide my function from me.*
W-pI.....82.4:3 *I would* **u.** *this as an opportunity to fulfill my*
W-pI.....83.2:4 *Let me not* **u.** *this to justify a function God*
W-pI.....84.4:3 *I will not* **u.** *this to attack love. Let this not*
W-pI.....85.2:2 *Let me not* **u.** *this as a block to sight. The*
W-pI.....87.1:2 I will **u.** the power of my will today. It is
W-pI.....89.1:5 that I may **u.** it on behalf of the function
W-pI.....89.2:1 might **u.** these suggestions for specific
W-pI.........90.h For this review we will **u.** these ideas:
W-pI.....91.2:8 You cannot **u.** it because its presence is
W-pI...92.11:2 will **u.** the day in preparation for the time
W-pI...93.10:1 or even able to **u.** the first five minutes of
W-pI.....95.4:1 **u.** of the first five minutes of every waking
W-pI.....95.7:3 **u.** your lapses from this schedule as an
W-pI.....96.2:1 what means you **u.** and where you see the
W-pI.....96.4:1 Spirit makes **u.** of mind as means to find
W-pI.....96.9:3 *Its Thoughts are mine to* **u.**. Then seek Its
W-pI.....97.3:3 and over, for the miracle makes **u.** of time
W-pI.....97.8:4 **U.** them against temptation, and escape
W-pI.....98.7:2 He will give the words you **u.** in practicing
W-pI...108.7:2 will **u.** this simple lesson in the obvious
WpI. rIII.in5:1 format you should **u.** for these reviews is
WpI. rIII.in6:1 your mind, and let it **u.** them as it chooses
WpI. rIII.in6:2 Give it faith that it will **u.** them wisely,
WpI. rIII.in6:6 gave as they were given you for it to **u.**.
WpI. rIII.in7:1 confidence that you would **u.** them well;
WpI. rIII.in7:1 their messages and **u.** them for yourself.
WpI. rIII.in9:4 you. Here is another chance to **u.** it well.
WpIrIII.in10:3 **U.** one on the hour, and the other one a
WpIrIII.in12:1 of the thought to **u.** each hour, and the
W-pI... 121.8:2 happiness, and **u.** it on your own behalf.
W-pI... 126.1:3 you, and would not hesitate to **u.** it now.
W-pI... 127.7:2 understand there is no better **u.** for time
W-pI... 128.1:1 you; nothing that you can **u.** in any way,
W-pI... 131.2:3 Who can **u.** such senseless means, and
W-pI... 136.3:3 with which you choose to **u.** them. In that
WpI. rIV.in7:6 will **u.** no format for our practicing but
W-pI... 161.3:2 now it is specifics we must **u.** in practicing
W-pI... 161.3:4 Yet He can **u.** but what we made, to teach
W-pI... 161.3:4 so we can see a different **u.** in everything.
W-pI. 161.12:5 Be sure you **u.** it instantly, should you be
W-pI... 162.4:2 For the words we **u.** are mighty, and they
WpI.rV.in11:4 **u.** the thoughts to hold it up before our
WpI.rV.in12:2 comes from practice, not the means we **u.**
WpI.rV.in12:4 We **u.** the words, and try and try again to
W-pI... 181.7:1 we will also **u.** this thought to keep us safe
W-pI... 183.6:5 other word we **u.** except at the beginning,
W-pI... 184.9:2 have need to **u.** the symbols of the world a
W-pI. 184.11:1 **U.** all the little names and symbols which
W-pI. 184.11:4 **U.** all the names the world bestows on
W-pI. 184.13:5 One Name we **u.** to unify our sight.
W-pI. 184.14:1 And though we **u.** a different name for
W-pI. 184.14:2 It is this Name we **u.** in practicing. And
W-pI. 184.14:3 And through Its **u.**, all foolish separations
W-pI... 185.8:3 the words you **u.** in making your requests.
W-pI... 191.6:3 You have no need to **u.** it cruelly, and
W-pI. 193.10:5 this. **U.** it today for what its purpose is.
W-pI... 199.7:3 can make **u.** of your escape from bondage
WpI rVI.in.1:2 **u.** the idea as often as you can between
WpI rVI.in.2:5 to **u.** them all and let them blend as one,
W-pII ....in.1:2 We **u.** them but as guides on which we do
W-pII ....in.2:8 **u.** as much as we will need for the result
W-pII ....in.3:1 and we will **u.** that thought to introduce
W-pII ..in.11:1 One further **u.** for words we still retain.
W-pII ....270.h I will not **u.** the body's eyes today.
W-pII ....271.h Christ's is the vision I will **u.** today.
W-pII . 285.1:4 For what would be the **u.** of pain to me,
W-pII . 294.1:4 What **u.** has God's beloved Son for what
W-pII . 294.1:6 Its neutrality protects it while it has a **u.**.
W-pII . 294.2:3 *then,* **u.** *this dream to help Your plan that we*
W-pII . 295.1:1 Christ asks that He may **u.** my eyes today
W-pII . 295.2:2 *Help me to* **u.** *the eyes of Christ today, and*
W-pII . 296.1:2 *me, for I would* **u.** *no words but Yours, and*
W-pII . 304.1:2 looks upon, unless it is His vision that I **u.**
W-pII . 306.1:1 What but Christ's vision would I **u.** today
W-pII . 311.1:5 Let us not **u.** it today, but make a gift of it
W-pII . 311.1:5 of it to Him Who has a different **u.** for it.
W-pII . 314.2:1 *past, and choose to* **u.** *the present to be free.*
W-pII ....347.h is The weapon I would **u.** against myself,
W-pII ... 14.2:1 Our **u.** for words is almost over now. Yet
W-pII ....353.h given Christ To **u.** to bless the world with
W-pII . 353.1:1 **u.** *in any way that best will serve the purpose*
WfI........in.1:2 We **u.** them but at the beginning of our
M-in..........3:3 Yet it is impossible not to **u.** the content
M-5 ........II.2:1 a purpose for which it would **u.** the body,
M-5 ..... II.2:12 their aid and say, "I have no **u.** for this."
M-7 ...........2:5 He must **u.** his reason to tell himself that
M-12 .........4:4 really is; the only **u.** there really is for it.
M-12 .........4:6 but because of what they **u.** the body for,
M-12 .........5:1 you **u.** the body for it will become to you.
M-12 .........5:2 you. **U.** it for sin or for attack, which is the
M-12 .........5:4 **U.** it to bring the Word of God to those
M-13 .........1:2 it came when there is no more **u.** for it.
M-16 .........2:4 each one must **u.** them as best he can in
M-21 .........1:4 heart, not to the words you **u.** in praying.
M-21 .........4:1 to avoid the **u.** of words in his teaching?
M-21 .........4:4 however, learn to **u.** words in a new way.
M-21 .........5:9 the words they **u.** the power of His Spirit,
M-24 .........4:7 it. He will also be told how to **u.** it. What
M-25 .........4:2 and He can **u.** only genuine abilities.
P-2........ III.2:4 of this potentiality they are willing to **u.**.
P-2....... VII.4:6 Guilt is inevitable in those who **u.** their
P-3..........II.1:9 but they may be called upon to **u.** special
P-3..........II.3:1 Even this the Holy Spirit can **u.**, and will
P-3..........II.3:1 this the Holy Spirit can use, and will **u.**,
P-3..........II.6:8 as much good as each can accept and **u.**.
S-2...........I.1:3 the steps of prayer cannot but **u.** it thus.

|  |  |
|---|---|
| S-2 ... I.6:4 | Christ's vision does not **u.** your eyes, but |
| S-2 ... I.9:2 | but who can **u.** a key when he has lost the |
| S-2 ... II.7:5 | a way to **u.** forgiveness for the goal of God |
| S-2 ... III.5:7 | you can understand and you can also **u.**. |
| S-2 ... III.7:7 | Give it to Him to **u.** instead of you, and |
| S-3 ... III.4:1 | one can **u.** to offer help for someone else? |

## used 113

|  |  |
|---|---|
| T-2 ... II.1:13 | It is not **u.** to hide anything, but to correct |
| T-2 ... II.4:1 | that cannot be **u.** destructively because it |
| T-2 ... III.1:2 | defenses have been **u.** almost entirely to |
| T-2 ... III.1:4 | be **u.** as a means for attaining "atonement |
| T-2 ... IV.5:2 | In fact, if it is **u.** truly, it will inevitably be |
| T-2 ... VII.1:9 | are not **u.** to miracle-minded thinking, |
| T-3 ... II.4:1 | Will because you have **u.** your own mind, |
| T-3 ... IV.4:3 | term "right-mindedness" is properly **u.** as |
| T-3 ... VI.5:9 | that it will someday be **u.** against you. |
| T-3 ... VII.4:9 | and all your defenses are **u.** to attack ideas |
| T-4 ... IV.8:7 | defense, can be **u.** to attack or protect; to |
| T-4 ... IV.10:4 | judgment, which is **u.** only for protection, |
| T-4 ... VI.2:4 | The term "holy" can be **u.** here because, |
| T-6 ... I.18:2 | and must be **u.** for their joint salvation. |
| T-7 ... IV.2:10 | it can be **u.** as a way out of conflict, as all |
| T-7 ... V.1:1 | is quite apart from what they are **u.** for. |
| T-7 ... V.3:6 | can be **u.** either for healing or for magic, |
| T-7 ... VII.1:9 | of being **u.** positively as well as negatively. |
| T-7 ... VII.1:10 | **U.** negatively it will be destructive, |
| T-7 ... VII.1:10 | destructive, because it will be **u.** for attack |
| T-8 ... VII.7:5 | for which the body can be **u.**. This is the |
| T-8 ... VII.11:5 | its usefulness if it is **u.** for anything else. |
| T-8 ... VIII.9:3 | you. Everything **u.** in accordance with its |
| T-8 ... VIII.9:4 | Everything **u.** otherwise is. Do not allow |
| T-8 ... IX.4:1 | wake is the sign of how you have **u.** sleep. |
| T-9 ... V.1:1 | is far more widely **u.** than God's. This is |
| T-9 ... VIII.9:6 | because it is **u.** to replace your grandeur. |
| T-11 ... VI.2:5 | because the word is **u.** both for awareness |
| T-13 ... III.4:4 | you have **u.** the world to cover your love, |
| T-13 ... X.2:3 | are **u.** but to avoid the person *and* the guilt |
| T-13 ... X.2:5 | are holy, and cannot be **u.** by you at all. |
| T-13 ... X.2:6 | They are **u.** only by the Holy Spirit, and it |
| T-14 ... X.4:2 | may indeed be so **u.** to this that it causes |
| T-14 ... X.4:3 | Yet you are also **u.** to classifying some of |
| T-16 ... I.1:2 | always **u.** to form a special relationship in |
| T-16 ... II.9:5 | forces, to be **u.** and not held idly by. They |
| T-17 ... II.4:2 | been **u.** for learning will have no function. |
| T-17 ... III.3:3 | What can be **u.** for fantasies of vengeance, |
| T-17 ... III.4:2 | hands, as it is kind when **u.** for gentleness |
| T-17 ... VI.4:4 | becomes what can be **u.** to meet the goal. |
| T-17 ... VI.5:2 | If the situation is **u.** for truth and sanity, |
| T-17 ... VII.3:10 | faithlessness **u.** *against* truth will always |
| T-17 ... VII.6:3 | and **u.** your faithlessness against him. No |
| T-18 ... I.3:7 | and **u.** as the standard for comparison of |
| T-18 ... II.6:2 | You would have **u.** them to remain asleep. |
| T-18 ... II.8:6 | You are so **u.** to choosing among dreams |
| T-18 ... VI.5:1 | for salvation, and **u.** for purposes of love? |
| T-19 ... I.3:5 | its weapon, **u.** against this Purpose, to |
| T-19 ... I.4:2 | body cannot be **u.** for purposes of union. |
| T-20 ... V.5:2 | it is **u.** only as the Holy Spirit teaches, it |
| T-22 ... II.6:2 | purpose be accomplished, they can be **u.**. |
| T-22 ... VI.2:1 | mind is **u.** as means whose value lies in its |
| T-22 ... VI.4:3 | and nothing given it but will be **u.**. This |
| T-22 ... VI.15:5 | gift. For it was given you to be **u.**, and not |
| T-25 ... VI.2:1 | Eyes become **u.** to darkness, and the light |
| T-26 ... V.2:3 | when it can be **u.** to reach a goal as high |
| T-26 ... VII.18:1 | given you as He would have it **u.** is natural |
| T-27 ... I.5:3 | one has not been **u.** for purpose of attack, |
| T-27 ... III.1:3 | power **u.** to weaken is employed to limit. |
| T-28 ... I.2:8 | it can be **u.** to serve another purpose, and |
| T-28 ... I.2:9 | It can be **u.** to heal and not to hurt, if you |
| T-28 ... I.3:3 | that is not **u.** to interfere with truth. All |
| T-28 ... VI.2:9 | hate. It can be **u.** for hate, but it cannot be |
| T-28 ... VII.4:2 | **u.** to witness to the dream of separation |
| T-28 ... VII.7:7 | be **u.** to liberate God's Son unto his home. |
| T-29 ... IX.7:4 | one is **u.** to substitute for something else, |
| T-29 ... IX.7:5 | No one is **u.** for something he is not, for |
| T-30 ... VII.6:1 | symbols that are **u.** mean different things |
| T-31 ... V.7:8 | not be **u.** to demonstrate the world is real. |
| W-pI ... 5.1:1 | preceding one, can be **u.** with any person, |
| W-pI ... 6.2:1 | be **u.** throughout the day for that purpose |
| W-pI ... 10.2:1 | second time we have **u.** this kind of idea. |
| W-pI ... 11.3:2 | however, should be **u.** in an unhurried, |
| W-pI ... 13.2:3 | otherwise be **u.** to demonstrate its own |
| W-pI ... 16.4:2 | This is quite difficult until you get **u.** to it. |
| W-pI ... 26.1:6 | it can be **u.** for your own best interests, |
| W-pI ... 27.3:2 | It should be **u.** at least every half hour, |
| W-pI ... 29.1:4 | it explains every idea we have **u.** thus far, |
| W-pI ... 30.4:2 | To help you begin to get **u.** to this idea, |
| W-pI ... 31.1:3 | practice which will be **u.** more and more, |
| W-pI ... 35.8:4 | force nor discrimination should be **u.**. |
| W-pI ... 39.1:2 | ideas **u.** for the exercises are very simple, |
| W-pI ... 45.4:1 | that we **u.** in applying yesterday's idea. |
| W-pI. 72.10:12 | We have **u.** our grievances to close our |
| W-pI ... 78.4:4 | you have **u.** as target for your grievances, |
| WpI.rV.in12:1 | Yet are the words but aids, and to be **u.**, |
| W-pI ... 198.1:4 | for yourself can be now **u.** against you, till |
| W-pII . 300.1:1 | thought which can be **u.** to say that death |
| W-pII . 311.1:1 | made to be a weapon **u.** against the truth. |
| W-pII . 311.1:2 | It separates what it is being **u.** against, |
| M-6 ... 3:7 | it is **u.** as the giver deems appropriate? |
| M-7 ... 2:3 | the Holy Spirit so accepted it and so **u.** it. |
| M-10 ... 5:13 | now he laughs, he **u.** to come to weep. |
| M-23 ... 4:3 | a symbol that is safely **u.** as a replacement |
| M-24 ... 1:5 | depends, of course, on what it is **u.** for. If |
| M-24 ... 1:6 | If it is **u.** to strengthen the recognition of |
| M-25 ... 3:2 | Holy Spirit, and **u.** under His direction, |
| M-25 ... 3:4 | consideration is how they are **u.**. Taking |
| M-25 ... 4:1 | Nothing that is genuine is **u.** to deceive. |
| M-25 ... 4:3 | What is **u.** for magic is useless to Him. |
| M-25 ... 4:4 | But what He uses cannot be **u.** for magic. |
| M-25 ... 5:6 | ability, and cannot be **u.** dependably. It is |
| M-25 ... 6:5 | have been **u.** to call upon the devil, which |
| C-in ... 5:3 | these are some of the terms that are **u.**. |
| C-1 ... 1:1 | term *mind* is **u.** to represent the activating |
| C-1 ... 3:2 | The term "soul" is not **u.** except in direct |
| P-3 ... II.9:1 | can save enormous time if it is properly **u.** |
| P-3 ... III.1:2 | this world be **u.** by the Holy Spirit to help |
| S-1 ... III.6:2 | are **u.** for goals that substitute for God, |
| S-2 ... I.1:5 | was meant to heal is **u.** to hurt because |
| S-3 ... II.2:1 | body has been kindly **u.** to help the Son of |
| S-3 ... III.3:4 | and **u.** to help restore the wounded and to |
| S-3 ... III.6:6 | has entered now where idols **u.** to stand, |

## useful 26

|  |  |
|---|---|
| T-1 ... I.15:4 | cease when it is no longer **u.** in facilitating |
| T-1 ... II.2:5 | They are more **u.** now because of their |
| T-1 ... III.9:4 | it would not be **u.** if it were bound by laws |
| T-4 ... III.2:1 | because it is **u.** in moments of temptation. |
| T-5 ... VI.12:4 | to be abolished when it is no longer **u.**. |
| T-7 ... I.6:5 | task of translating the useless into the **u.**, |
| T-14 ... III.1:4 | salvation, and serves no **u.** function at all. |
| T-15 ... V.1:1 | the Holy Spirit's most **u.** learning device |
| T-16 ... I.1:3 | to empathize is very **u.** to the Holy Spirit, |
| T-18 ... V.5:4 | Yet it is very **u.** to the Holy Spirit, Who |
| T19 ... IV.C.5:1 | as long as it is **u.** for your holy purpose. |
| T-21 ... III.1:6 | to make it **u.** to Him and harmless to you. |
| W-pI ... 3.2:3 | equally suitable and therefore equally **u.**. |
| W-pI ... 4.5:2 | This practice is **u.**, but is not a substitute |
| W-pI ... 6.2:1 | Today's idea is **u.** for application to |
| W-pI ... 31.5:1 | for today is also a particularly **u.** one to |
| W-pI ... 83.4:1 | Some **u.** forms for specific applications of |
| W-pI ... 87.4:1 | are some **u.** forms of this idea for specific |
| W-pI ... 88.2:1 | prove **u.** forms for specific applications of |
| W-pI ... 88.4:1 | in applying this idea, these would be **u.**: |
| W-pI ... 89.4:1 | **U.** specific forms for applying this idea |
| W-pI ... 90.4:1 | the idea will be **u.** for specific applications |
| W-pI. 136.18:2 | be enough to serve all truly **u.** purposes. |
| W-pI. 186.13:5 | on the form most **u.** in a world of form. |
| W-pI ... 199.4:4 | as **u.** form for what the mind must do. It |
| M-24 ... 1:7 | about it really **u.** in lighting up the way? |

## usefulness 15

|  |  |
|---|---|
| T-1 ... VII.2:5 | to do this is the body's only true **u.**. |
| T-8 ... VII.11:5 | loses its **u.** if it is used for anything else. |
| T-12 ... I.9:7 | its perceived **u.** by rendering it useless. |
| T-31 ... II.4:6 | he has no purpose and no **u.** to you. |
| W-pI .. 108.6:1 | and receiving are the same has special **u.**, |
| WpIrIII.in11:4 | Its **u.** is limitless to you. And it is meant to |
| W-pI .. 135.8:2 | the mind can operate until its **u.** is over. |
| W-pI .. 135.8:3 | would want to keep it when its **u.** is done? |
| W-pI 136.17:5 | does. Its **u.** remains and nothing more. |
| W-pII294.1:10 | fit to serve, to keep its **u.** while it can serve |
| M-12 ... 5:6 | When its **u.** is done it is laid by, and that |
| M-24 ... 3:3 | of him, it would merely limit his **u.**, as |
| M-24 ... 6:10 | can be said that their truth lies in their **u.**. |
| M-25 ... 6:3 | the power, the greater its potential **u.**. |
| S-3 ... II.1:10 | end has come for **u.** of body functioning. |

## useless 33

|  |  |
|---|---|
| T-2 ... III.5:2 | their true creative powers on **u.** attempts |
| T-2 ... VII.4:2 | attempting the mastery of fear is **u.**. In |
| T-4 ... in.2:5 | Do not embark on **u.** journeys, because |
| T-4 ... in.3:1 | to the cross should be the last "**u.** journey. |
| T-4 ... in.3:3 | can accept it as your own last **u.** journey, |
| T-4 ... II.8:5 | and thus establish its own existence are **u.** |
| T-4 ... IV.7:4 | are **u.** to themselves and to me, but only |
| T-6 ... I.2:6 | the last **u.** journey the Sonship need take, |
| T-6 ... IV.8:2 | Your abilities are **u.** in the presence of |
| T-7 ... I.6:5 | task of translating the **u.** into the useful, |
| T-12 ... I.9:7 | its perceived usefulness by rendering it **u.**. |
| T-12 ... II.10:5 | His knowledge remains **u.** to you. Surely |
| T-13 ... I.4:1 | Son of God has set himself is **u.** indeed, |
| T-13 .. VII.14:1 | to undertake a **u.** journey that would lead |
| T-15 ... I.7:5 | which the ego would make the present **u.**. |
| T-16 ... IV.12:6 | We will take the last **u.** journey away from |
| T-16 ... VII.3:9 | less obvious is that the present is **u.** to you |
| T-17 ... VI.4:5 | becomes the **u.** from this point of view. |
| T-17 ... VII.7:3 | your little faithlessness can make it **u.**, if |
| T-18 ... IX.12:6 | not. Learning is **u.** in the Presence of your |
| T-18 ... IX.14:1 | else, and memory will be as **u.** as learning, |
| T-20 ... II.1:2 | all the **u.** things made for its eyes to see. |
| T-23 ... II.7:3 | Who caused it, to Whom appeal is **u.**. |
| T-25 ... V.4:3 | So must it remain **u.** to both. Together, it |
| T-28 ... II.11:6 | The miracle is **u.** if you learn but that the |
| W-pI ... 91.2:7 | The light is **u.** to you then, even though it |
| W-pI 134.12:4 | can remove the ponderous and **u.** armor |
| W-pI .. 195.3:3 | to lie in death with you, as **u.** as yourself; |
| W-pII ... 10.2:6 | Bodies now are **u.**, and will therefore fade |
| M-25 ... 4:3 | What is used for magic is **u.** to Him. But |
| P-2 ... V.3:2 | And yet it would be **u.** in an ideal state. |
| P-3 ... III.3:1 | of this world are indeed **u.** to the world's |
| S-1 ... V.2:4 | Enemies are **u.** now, because humility |

## uselessness 2

|  |  |
|---|---|
| T-12 ... V.3:1 | will never realize the utter **u.** of attack |
| M-14 ... 1:8 | Their **u.** is recognized, and they are gone. |

## uses 46

|  |  |
|---|---|
| T-5 ... I.3:4 | in Christ Jesus," and **u.** this as a blessing. |
| T-5 ... III.10:2 | Teacher. He **u.** only what your mind |
| T-6 ... II.3:7 | The ego **u.** projection only to destroy your |
| T-6 ... II.10:1 | The Holy Spirit **u.** time, but does not |
| T-6 ... II.10:2 | from God He **u.** everything for good, but |
| T-6 ... IV.5:1 | ego **u.** the body to conspire against your |
| T-6 ... V.A.2:5 | He reinterprets what the ego **u.** as an |
| T-6 ... V.A.5:3 | ego **u.** the body for attack, for pleasure |
| T-7 ... IV.4:2 | He **u.** them only for healing, because He |
| T-8 ... VII.10:4 | if it **u.** the body to go beyond itself. By |
| T-8 ... VIII.6:3 | The ego **u.** this as its best argument for |
| T-14 ... in.1:4 | Holy Spirit **u.** logic as easily and as well as |
| T-14 ... VII.5:6 | The Holy Spirit **u.** defenses on behalf of |
| T-15 ... I.h | The Two **U.** of Time |
| T-15 ... I.2:3 | the Holy Spirit **u.** time in His Own way, |
| T-15 ... I.2:6 | **u.** time to support its belief in destruction |
| T-15 ... I.2:7 | Holy Spirit, **u.** time to convince you of the |
| T-15 ... I.7:5 | **u.** it to undo the fear by which the ego |
| T-15 ... V.4:5 | the Holy Spirit **u.** special relationships, |
| T-15 ... X.1:4 | them both, though not as the ego **u.** them |
| T-16 ... I.2:1 | the ego **u.** it is destructive lies in the fact |
| T-16 ... VII.6:2 | and **u.** opposites to point to truth. The |
| T-17 ... IV.8:1 | frame of all the defenses the ego **u.**. Its |
| T-18 ... I.2:1 | The Holy Spirit never **u.** substitutes. |

| | |
|---|---|
| T-18 ....... II.6:1 | dreams and **u.** them as means for waking. |
| T-18 ....... II.7:6 | **u.** everyone who calls on Him as means |
| T-18 ....... VI.4:2 | **u.** what it does to hurt the body to prove |
| T-21 ...... III.6:2 | But as He **u.** them they lead away from sin |
| T-21 ....... V.8:7 | The ego never **u.** it, because it does not |
| T-25 ...... VI.5:4 | the means the Holy Spirit **u.** to translate |
| T-28 ...... VI.3:3 | it is, but for the **u.** you have made of it. |
| W-pI ..... 91.7:2 | the Holy Spirit **u.** to replace the image of a |
| W-pI ..... 97.5:3 | them as his thoughts, and **u.** them to heal. |
| WpI . rIII.in6:4 | the means the Holy Spirit **u.** will not fail. |
| W-pI ... 133.8:7 | for it needs to keep the halo which it **u.** to |
| W-pI ... 162.4:2 | to change the mind of him who **u.** them. |
| W-pI.184.11:3 | The Holy Spirit **u.** all of them, but He |
| W-pI ... 196.2:3 | it fail to understand the truth it **u.** thus. |
| W-pII .. 305.1:1 | Who **u.** but Christ's vision finds a peace |
| M-6 ............ 1:6 | if the patient **u.** sickness as a way of life, |
| M-10 .......... 1:3 | As the world **u.** the term, an individual is |
| M-25 .......... 4:4 | But what He **u.** cannot be used for magic. |
| C-in ............ 3:3 | Therefore it **u.** words, which are symbolic |
| P-1 ............. 5:5 | The Holy Spirit **u.** time as He thinks best, |
| P-1 ............. 5:6 | is one of the means He **u.** to save time, |
| P-2 ......... II.7:2 | no good teacher **u.** one approach to every |

## usher 1

| | |
|---|---|
| W-pI ... 125.1:5 | must hear to **u.** in the quiet time of peace. |

## ushered 2

| | |
|---|---|
| M-29 .......... 8:5 | *you is* ***u.*** *in A world unseen, unheard, yet* |
| P-2 ......... V.1:5 | it is **u.** in by the belief that there are forces |

## ushers 1

| | |
|---|---|
| W-pI ... 157.1:4 | day is holy, for it **u.** in a new experience; a |

## using 39

| | |
|---|---|
| T-6 ........ I.14:1 | **u.** it as a weapon for assault rather than as |
| T-7 ..... VIII.2:5 | U. its own warped version of the laws of |
| T-8 ..... VII.10:1 | of **u.** the body solely for communication. |
| T-9 ....... VII.5:4 | escape from its evaluation of you by **u.** its |
| T-14 ...... III.2:1 | you are accustomed to **u.** guiltlessness |
| T-15 ....... I.4:12 | both, by **u.** dissociation for holding its |
| T-18 ...... VI.4:8 | made and **u.** it to save him from illusions. |
| T-18 ...... VII.6:4 | special means this course is **u.** to save you |
| T-18 ...... VII.6:5 | **u.** means which have served others well, |
| T-22 ...... VI.3:6 | **u.** your body only to serve the sinless. |
| T-31 ... VIII.2:5 | never **u.** weakness to direct your actions, |
| W-pI ....... 4.4:1 | In **u.** your thoughts for application of the |
| W-pI ....... 5.1:2 | upset, **u.** the description of the feeling in |
| W-pI ....... 5.2:1 | When **u.** the idea for today for a specific |
| W-pI ....... 5.7:2 | **u.** the name of both the source of the |
| W-pI ..... 11.2:4 | in **u.** the idea merely repeat it to yourself, |
| W-pI ..... 12.3:2 | **u.** whatever descriptive terms happen to |
| W-pI ..... 15.4:1 | **u.** its name and letting your eyes rest on it |
| W-pI ..... 23.6:1 | Besides **u.** it throughout the day as the |
| W-pI ..... 24.3:1 | honesty than you are accustomed to **u.**. A |
| W-pI ..... 27.1:3 | You may feel hesitant about **u.** the idea, |
| W-pI ..... 27.3:4 | you set a definite time interval for **u.** the |
| W-pI ..... 28.6:1 | In **u.** the table as a subject for applying |
| W-pI ..... 30.5:3 | **u.** whatever subjects come to mind, and |
| W-pI ..... 37.4:5 | occurs to you, **u.** his name and saying: *My* |
| W-pI ..... 37.6:2 | you meet, **u.** his name as you do so. It is |
| W-pI ..... 64.4:2 | function is to be happy by **u.** the means |
| W-pI ..... 64.8:2 | to concentrate on the thoughts you are **u.**. |
| WpI ..rII.in.6:1 | **u.** the original form of the idea for general |
| W-pI ..... 81.4:1 | forms for **u.** this idea might include: *Let* |
| W-pI ..... 95.5:3 | yet formed the habit of **u.** the idea as an |
| W-pI ..... 95.7:2 | U. the first five minutes of the hour will |
| W-pI ..... 97.4:1 | in which a minute spent in **u.** these ideas |
| W-pI.134.15:2 | but realize that you are **u.** his "offenses" |
| WpI. rIV.in7:3 | you are **u.** time for its intended purpose. |
| W-pI ... 164.2:5 | Self, **u.** your voice to give His glad consent |
| W-pI ... 190.3:6 | love and **u.** pain to prove that God is dead |
| W-pI ... 192.7:2 | **u.** reason but to justify our rage and our |
| M-3 ........... 4:3 | U. the term in this way, the second level |

## usual 15

| | |
|---|---|
| T-1 ......... I.47:2 | interval not under the **u.** laws of time. In |
| T-3 ......... V.6:4 | the **u.** sense becomes utterly meaningless. |
| T-5 ....... VII.5:4 | be undone by repentance in the **u.** sense, |
| W-pI ....... 4.2:1 | today's idea, the **u.** specificity is required. |
| W-pI ....... 8.4:3 | search your mind for the **u.** minute or so, |
| W-pI ..... 16.5:4 | As **u.**, use today's idea whenever you are |
| W-pI ..... 17.3:1 | **u.**, it is essential to make no distinctions |
| W-pI ..... 26.6:4 | longer time than **u.** should be spent with |
| W-pI ..... 28.8:1 | As **u.**, the applications should include the |
| W-pI ..... 39.6:1 | Begin the practice periods as **u.**, by |
| W-pI ..... 46.3:2 | by repeating today's idea to yourself, as **u.** |
| W-pI ..... 47.4:3 | Close your eyes and begin, as **u.**, by |
| W-pI ... 72.13:1 | they will be somewhat longer than **u.**. |
| M-4 ..... VII.1:2 | It is not the **u.** meaning of the word; in |
| M-10 ......... 3:1 | judgment in the **u.** sense is impossible. |

## usually 15

| | |
|---|---|
| T-1 ........ IV.1:2 | hide. This step **u.** entails fear. Second, the |
| T-2 ........ III.3:9 | of perception is **u.** experienced as conflict, |
| T-2 ......... V.2:4 | egocentricity and fear **u.** occur together, |
| T-2 ........ VI.5:7 | a sense of coercion that **u.** produces rage, |
| T-2 ....... VII.7:4 | is **u.** some degree of desire to accomplish, |
| T-3 ........ III.3:3 | that is **u.** an attempt to counteract an |
| T-4 ......... II.9:1 | since myths are **u.** related to ego origins, |
| T-4 ......... II.9:4 | beginning is **u.** associated with physical |
| T-9 ......... V.4:6 | one which it **u.** notes even in its confusion |
| T-16 ....... V.3:3 | Here they are **u.** judged to be acceptable |
| M-4 ..... I.A.3:2 | not be painful, but it **u.** is so experienced. |
| M-7 ........... 4:3 | U. it seems to be just the opposite. It does |
| M-9 ........... 2:4 | God's Voice, is **u.** a fairly slow process, |
| S-1 ......... II.3:3 | understanding. A vague and **u.** unstable |
| S-1 ......... II.4:2 | the way in which they are **u.** interpreted. |

## usurp 4

| | |
|---|---|
| T-2 ........... I.4:1 | have the ability to **u.** the power of God. Of |
| T-5 ......... V.5:9 | It tries to **u.** all the functions of God as it |
| T-26 ...... VI.3:2 | Would you allow one shadow to **u.** the |
| W-pI ... 152.8:5 | to **u.** the altar to the Father and the Son. |

## usurpation 1

| | |
|---|---|
| T-1 ..... VII.3:12 | Reality is "lost" through **u.**, which |

## usurped 4

| | |
|---|---|
| T-3 ........ VI.8:4 | believe they have **u.** the power of God. |
| T-3 ........ VI.9:2 | You have not **u.** the power of God, but |
| M-5 ......... I.2:8 | thus entirely **u.** the throne of his Creator. |
| M-17 ......... 7:3 | mind, "You have **u.** the place of God. |

## usurping 3

| | |
|---|---|
| T-3 ....... VII.4:1 | for **u.** the ability for self-creating. This is |
| T-5 ......... V.3:3 | as based on the concept of **u.** God's power |
| M-29 ......... 3:6 | imagined **u.** of functions not your own is |

## usurps 2

| | |
|---|---|
| T-10 ...... III.4:3 | that creation shares power and never **u.** it |
| M-17 ......... 5:8 | Who **u.** the place of God and takes it for |

## utilize 9

| | |
|---|---|
| T-2 ........ IV.4:6 | case it may be wise to **u.** a compromise |
| T-4 ..... VII.3:12 | it may refuse to **u.** it on behalf of being. |
| T-7 .... VIII.1:10 | decide whether or not you will **u.** the law. |
| T-15 .... VIII.1:4 | He is swift to **u.** whatever you offer Him |
| T-15 ...... IX.3:3 | you will choose to **u.** the means by which |
| T-29 ...... IV.6:5 | Who can **u.** all dreams as means to serve |
| W-pI ..... 44.3:2 | before, and which we will **u.** increasingly. |
| M-25 ......... 6:8 | they lay upon themselves if they **u.** their |
| P-3 .......... II.9:8 | Some **u.** the relationship merely to collect |

## utilized 5

| | |
|---|---|
| T-3 ......... V.5:5 | it is **u.** in a futile attempt to escape from |
| T-4 ....... VII.2:2 | as it is **u.** to establish separateness rather |
| T-8 ........ IX.4:5 | you **u.** sleep according to His purpose. |
| T-18 ........ II.2:2 | can be **u.** to substitute illusions for truth. |
| W-pI ..... 32.4:2 | More than five can be **u.**, if you find the |

## utilizes 2

| | |
|---|---|
| T-7 ...... VIII.2:5 | the ego **u.** the power of the mind only to |
| T-13 .... VIII.1:5 | in eternity, and **u.** no perception at all. It |

## utopian 1

| | |
|---|---|
| W-pI ... 133.2:4 | try to substitute **u.** ideas for satisfactions |

## utter 2

| | |
|---|---|
| T-7 ........ VI.2:4 | of unreality and results in **u.** confusion. |
| T-12 ....... V.3:1 | You will never realize the **u.** uselessness |

## utterly 8

| | |
|---|---|
| T-3 ........... I.3:8 | how **u.** impossible this assumption is, and |
| T-3 ......... V.6:4 | the usual sense becomes **u.** meaningless. |
| T-12 ...... IV.3:1 | wants to find what would **u.** defeat him. |
| T-14 ........ X.9:2 | joining them is incoherent and **u.** chaotic. |
| T-18 ..... VII.2:1 | done; you have not **u.** forgotten the body. |
| T19 ... IV.D.7:1 | It seems to you the world will **u.** abandon |
| T-26 ..... VII.5:1 | only there can its effects be **u.** undone and |
| T-31 ...... IV.8:5 | How **u.** opposed to truth is this, when all |

# V

T-14......III.2:2 that guilt and guiltlessness are both of v.,
T-14......III.2:6 appreciation of the v. of your guiltlessness
T-14....III.10:7 to provide that offers them anything of v..
T-14....III.12:1 of His calm and unswerving v. of His Son?
T-14.......V.1:9 Heaven. There is nothing of v. here, and
T-14.......V.1:9 of value here, and everything of v. there.
T-14......VI.1:7 Nothing has hidden v., for what is hidden
T-14......VI.1:7 be shared, and so its v. is unknown. The
T-14......VI.1:8 but v. always lies in joint appreciation.
T-14......XI.4:1 judge the truth and v. of this course. Yet
T-15.........I.5:5 even there, its only v. is that it is no more.
T-15......III.3:3 the v. that you put upon yourself. Believe
T-15......IV.3:2 And v. no plan of the ego before the plan
T-15......IV.3:6 v. of His Will for you in your own mind.
T-15......IV.8:2 breaking communication holds v. to you.
T-15.......V.6:3 less v. on one and more on the other. You
T-15.....VII.3:3 choose to let go what he believes has v..
T-15.....VII.3:4 Yet the attraction of guilt has v. to you
T-15...VII.14:6 sudden recognition of the v. of his part in
T-15... VIII.2:3 learn the v. of what you have cast aside,
T-15......IX.7:1 no v. on it as a means of getting anything,
T-16.........I.3:1 anything you v. to come of a relationship.
T-16......IV.3:4 is not perceived as a v. in itself, but as a
T-16....IV.10:4 only needful to v. truth beyond all fantasy
T-16....IV.13:1 completion, can they have any v. to you?
T-16.......V.2:4 but if you consider how you v. it and why,
T-16.......V.7:6 and of giving nothing of v. in return. How
T-16.......V.7:7 How much v. can he place upon a self that
T-16.......V.9:2 for only the deprived could v. specialness.
T-16.....V.11:2 it is weak and little, and unworthy of v.,
T-16......VI.1:2 special relationship has v. only to the ego.
T-16......VI.1:3 unless a relationship has special v. it has
T-16......VI.4:2 If you v. it, you must also value the body.
T-16......VI.4:2 If you value it, you must also v. the body.
T-16......VI.4:3 body. And what you v. you will keep. The
T-16......VI.4:5 total lack of v. of the special relationship,
T-16......VI.4:6 disappear, because its v. would be lost.
T-16......VI.5:1 You see the world you v.. On this side of
T-16......VI.6:4 the v. of the body is so diminished in your
T-16......VI.6:5 will realize that the only v. the body has is
T-17.......II.1:4 And nothing will you v. like unto this, nor
T-17......III.3:3 separated off as being the only parts of v..
T-17......III.5:6 reality and its v. in your perception of it.
T-17......III.9:3 the choice depends on which you v. more.
T-17......IV.7:6 Its purpose is to be of v. *in itself,* and to
T-17......IV.9:5 What you v. is the frame, for there you
T-17....IV.12:4 their v. by comparing a picture to a frame
T-17....IV.15:5 wholly without v. and entirely deprived of
T-17......VI.4:1 The v. of deciding in advance what you
T-17.....VII.5:8 the goal, but with the v. of the goal to you.
T-18.....II.5:20 while you see more v. in sleeping than in
T-18.....VII.7:2 withdrawn the body's v. from your mind.
T19. IV.A.17:7 Mine was of no greater v. than yours; no
T19....IV.B.2:1 v. that you think peace would rob you of.
T-20.......II.1:5 interpretation of its v. by his acceptance.
T-20.......II.1:6 acknowledges the lack of v. he places on
T-20.......II.2:3 Only the mind can v., and only the mind
T-20.......II.3:5 v. that you lay upon your brother and on
T-20.......V.3:1 to overestimate your brother's v.. Only
T-20....VI.12:2 The holy instant is of greater v. now to
T-20.....VII.7:7 judgment has no v. unless the goal is sin.
T-20... VIII.3:4 And place no v. on your brother's body,
T-20... VIII.4:5 What can you v. more than this? Why do
T-21......III.6:4 their v. as a means for what He wills for
T-21....III.10:6 an inescapable belief of those who v. sin.
T-21......VI.1:2 It does not v. *them,* but their correction.
T-22......III.9:1 born, must v. holiness above all else.
T-22......VI.1:3 Which do you v.? Which is your goal? For
T-22......VI.1:7 is reached the v. of the means decreases,
T-22......VI.2:1 the mind is used as means whose v. lies in
T-22......VI.8:1 see your v. through your brother's eyes,
T-22....VI.12:7 Yet wherein lies its v., except in the desire
T-23.......in.6:6 What can you v. more than this? For here
T-23.......II.8:7 which does not v. what the ego cherishes.
T-23.......II.9:6 they seek to share the things they v.. And
T-23.....II.20:2 quite possible to v. some above the others
T-23......IV.9:4 nor could he v. the body's offerings. The
T-24.......in.2:1 to question every v. that you hold. Not
T-24.........I.4:7 for nothing in the world they v. more.
T-24.......II.2:9 To v. specialness is to esteem an alien will
T-25......II.1:7 The only v. that the past can hold is that
T-25......III.1:1 To the extent to which you v. guilt, to
T-25.....VI.7:2 Think not you lack a special v. here. You
T-25.....VII.4:1 To justify one v. that the world upholds
T-25......IX.1:8 truth has greater v. now than all illusions.
T-26......V.10:3 corrected, is of no concern nor v.. Let the
T-26.....VII.6:2 is possible that some are given greater v.,
T-27.......I.10:5 the truth and v. that it represents. Let it
T-27.....V.11:3 Its total v. need not be appraised by you
T-29... VIII.1:6 that you would v. more than what he is.
T-29... VIII.2:4 lacks, and add the v. that you do not have
T-30........V.1:3 The v. of forgiveness is perceived and
T-31.....VII.2:1 thoughts as long as you see v. in attack.
W-pI......12.2:7 step in learning to give them all equal v..
W-pI......28.5:2 beautiful and clean and of infinite v., full
W-pI......28.7:2 to acknowledge the equal v. of them all in
W-pI......44.8:1 you are doing; its inestimable v. to you,
W-pI......53.2:6 not see it at all unless I choose to v. it.
W-pI......53.2:7 I do not choose to v. what is totally insane
WpI. rIII.in4:3 When you withdraw the v. given them,
WpI. rIII.in9:1 important, and perhaps of even greater v.
W-pI...122.3:5 What fancied v., trivial effect or transient
W-pI...122.7:5 The world can give no gifts of any v. to a
W-pI...123.3:5 thankful that your v. far transcends your
W-pI.126.11:1 special v. to yourself and all your brothers
W-pI...127.8:4 Withdraw all v. you have placed upon its
W-pI...128.2:1 Each thing you v. here is but a chain that
W-pI...128.3:2 For what you v. you make part of you as
W-pI...128.3:3 things you seek to make your v. greater in
W-pI...128.7:2 you will not v. anything you see as much
W-pI...128.8:2 think you see some v. in an aspect or an
W-pI...129.2:1 once more about the v. of this world.
W-pI...129.2:2 no loss in letting go all thought of v. here.
W-pI...129.5:4 V. them not, and they will disappear.
W-pI...129.6:2 for you in choosing not to v. nothingness?
W-pI...130.1:4 this, for what you v. you must want to see
W-pI...130.1:5 see a world his mind has not accorded v..
W-pI...130.8:6 *God offers me and see no v. in this world,*
W-pI......133.h I will not v. what is valueless.
W-pI...133.6:2 A temporary v. is without all value. Time
W-pI...133.6:2 A temporary value is without all v.. Time
W-pI...133.6:3 Time can never take away a v. that is real.
W-pI...133.8:2 Why is the choice you make of v. to you?
W-pI.133.13:2 an honest willingness to v. but the truly
W-pI.133.13:4 *I will not v. what is valueless, and only what*
W-pI.133.13:4 *is valueless, and only what has v. do I seek,*
W-pI.133.14:3 *I will not v. what is valueless, for what is*
W-pI...135.6:4 set its v. far beyond a little pile of dust
W-pI.135.25:6 plans or magical beliefs can still have v.,
W-pI...147.1:1 (133) I will not v. what is valueless.
W-pI...158.8:2 that faintly can compare with this in v.;
W-pI...164.9:3 see the v. your acceptance gives the world
Wi181-200 2:1 too limited to let you see the v. of our goal
W-pI...182.8:1 valueless ideas cease to have v. in your
W-pI...186.5:3 Judge not your v. to it. If God's Voice
W-pI...187.4:1 you v. by the act of giving them away, and
W-pI...187.4:3 Yet v. not its form. For this will change
W-pI...187.5:8 to lose is always something he will v. less
W-pI...187.8:2 is no place for sacrifice in what has any v..
W-pII..226.1:3 If I believe it has a v. as I see it now, so will
W-pII..226.1:4 But if I see no v. in the world as I behold it
W-pII..315.1:2 in v. far beyond all things of which I can
M-4 .....I.A.3:3 their lack of v. is merely being recognized.
M-4 .....I.A.3:4 How can lack of v. be perceived unless the
M-4 .....I.A.4:7 The word "v." can apply to nothing else.
M-4 .....I.A.6:4 see the transfer v. of what he has learned.
M-4 .......II.1:3 afford honesty, for only they can see its v..
M-5 .........I.1:1 the sufferer no longer sees any v. in pain.
M-5 .........I.1:2 something, and something of v. to him?
M-5 ........II.4:5 transfer v. of one true idea has no end or
M-6 ..........1:3 Truth demonstrates illusions have no v..
M-17 ..........2:4 wish that makes the help of little v., and
M-21 ..........5:4 All these are judgments that have no v..
M-24 ..........2:4 if it heartens them its v. is self-evident. It
M-25 ..........3:6 Nor does their v. lie in proving anything;
M-25 ..........5:1 Even those who no longer v. the material
S-1 ........III.3:7 who sees no v. or advantage to himself in

## valued 15

T-6......V.C.9:4 By making another kingdom that you v.,
T-14......IV.8:3 throw yourself away and v. God so little,
T-14....VIII.2:2 great or small, however much or little v.,
T-20.....VII.7:5 nor is it v. as a separate thing apart from
T-20.....VII.7:6 means seem real because the goal is v..
T-21.......V.8:3 perception toward what the mind has v..
T-21....VIII.1:5 he v. the inconstant more than constancy.
T-22......III.9:3 each one is v. because he seems to justify
T-25.....VII.3:7 If one belief so deeply v. here were true,
W-pI...130.4:6 They can be v., but remain unreal. They
W-pI.131.12:4 now; no other goal is v. now nor sought,
W-pI...133.2:2 you buy, to eminence as v. by the world,
W-pI...183.4:3 will forget the names of all the gods you v.
M-4 .....I.A.4:3 most of the things he v. before will merely
M-4 .....I.A.4:4 Because he has v. what is really valueless,

## valueless 22

T-20......VI.4:6 away, for all that it could offer is seen as v.
W-pI......133.h I will not value what is v..
W-pI...133.6:1 will not last forever, what you chose is v..
W-pI.133.12:1 All things are valuable or v., worthy or
W-pI.133.13:4 *I will not value what is v., and only what has*
W-pI.133.14:3 *I will not value what is v., for what is valuable*
W-pI...135.8:2 v. and hardly worth the least defense,
W-pI...147.1:1 (133) I will not value what is v..
W-pI...164.6:4 The valuable and v. are both perceived
W-pI...166.5:5 world contains is v. before its magnitude.
Wi181-200 2:6 be sure of what you want, and what is v..
W-pI...182.8:1 when v. ideas cease to have value in your
W-pI...183.4:5 They become anonymous and v. to you,
W-pI...188.3:4 all thoughts of the ephemeral and v.. It
W-pI...198.1:4 used against you, till you lay it down as v.,
M-4 .....I.A.4:4 Because he has valued what is really v., he
M-4 .....I.A.5:4 v. unless the next obvious step is taken.
M-4 .....I.A.5:7 this only as he actually does give up the v.
M-4 .....I.A.7:2 know what was valuable and what was v..
M-4 .....I.A.7:3 so far was that he did not want the v., and
M-4 .....VII.2:3 it would be v. to him by definition. What
P-3........III.6:8 and how v. is money in comparison.

## valuelessness 1

M-5 ........II.1:1 to which the v. of sickness is recognized.

## values 23

T-7.......VII.4:3 V. are relative, but they are powerful
T-8......VI.5:13 of God, and what He v. is valuable. There
T-13......XI.3:7 In Heaven is everything God v., and
T-15.......V.8:3 Without the v. from the past, you would
T-20.......V.3:2 for itself, and therefore v. him too little.
T-20.....VIII.8:8 each different and with different v.. Yet
T-20..VIII.8:10 is no order; only a seeming hierarchy of v.
T-22.......III.9:2 Unholy v. will produce confusion, and in
T-23........II.2:4 it true by his attack on what another v..
T-23........II.2:5 And this is justified because the v. differ,
T-23........II.9:1 The ego v. only what it takes. This leads
T-25......VI.6:2 not imposed on you, its v. are not yours.
T-25......IX.1:5 you will forego all v. of this world in favor
T-26.......III.2:3 where conflicting v. meet and all illusions
W-pI...128.5:1 thought of v. we have given to the world.
W-pI...128.5:4 beyond all little v. and diminished goals.
W-pI...130.1:4 Your v. are determiners of this, for what
W-pI...135.7:5 your needs, your v. and your dreams.
W-pII .298.1:4 journeys, mad careers and artificial v..
M-8 ..........3:7 Its hierarchy of v. is projected outward,
M-8 ..........4:3 to it according to its preconceived v.,
M-13 .........4:6 the sacrifice its v. would demand of him.
P-3........III.2:1 not succeed to the extent to which he v. it.

## valuing 7

T-2..........II.1:7 If you are afraid, you are v. wrongly. Your
T-9.......II.10:6 V. it little, you will not appreciate it and
T-12....VIII.6:8 V. nothing, you have sought nothing. By
T-13.......II.4:3 by not v. its interpretation of salvation,
T-13......IX.3:5 The power of your v. will make it so.

T-15 III.8:5 gifts, thus **v.** it too little to understand its
T-20 VIII.1:3 you closed off by **v.** the "something else,"

### vanish 21

T-7 VIII.5:6 so that all their effects will **v.** from your
T-11 III.3:5 bleak little world will **v.** into nothingness,
T-11 VIII.1:7 even the real world will **v.** from your sight
T-12 II.4:2 enlightenment and accept it, their fears **v.**
T-13 III.3:3 world you thought you made would **v.**.
T-14 VIII.5:7 Your little gifts will **v.** on the altar, where
T-15 X.5:10 this one idea, your fear of love would **v.**.
T-17 II.4:1 that opened up the world to beauty will **v.**
T-17 II.7:3 become a dream, and **v.** from his mind.
T19 IV.D.6:5 "protectors" and your "home" will **v.**.
T-24 II.6:4 will **v.** as his mind accepts the truth about
T-26 II.3:4 not think so if you saw them **v.** one by one
W-pI 58.3:6 I share with God Himself, all idols **v.**.
W-pI 81.2:4 *This shadow will **v.** before the light.*
W-pI 91.4:2 great this strength, your doubts would **v.**.
W-pI 107.1:4 They merely **v.**, leaving not a trace by
W-pI 151.7:4 you are **v.** before the splendor He beholds
W-pI 162.1:5 illusions **v.** as these words are spoken. For
W-pII 3.1:4 world must disappear and all its errors **v.**.
W-pII 326.1:8 *Heaven of Your Love, where earth will **v.**,*
C-3 6:8 And yet this part will **v.**. What remains is

### vanished 4

T-20 VI.8:8 together for a little while in time, and **v.**.
T-27 VI.5:9 dying live, the dead arise, and pain has **v.**.
W-pI 73.4:4 it. Darkness has **v.**. The ego's idle wishes
W-pI 198.11:6 you ever thought you made completely **v.**

### vanishes 7

T-14 VIII.3:4 of oneness, before which all separation **v.**.
T-14 IX.2:5 merely **v.** because it is not true. Different
T-15 VI.3:1 All separation **v.** as holiness is shared.
T-15 VI.8:4 Without its source exclusion **v.**. And this
T-19 III.8:7 be cherished but a little while before it **v.**.
T-27 III.7:1 Forgiveness **v.** and symbols fade, and
W-pI 131.13:2 light the way, so that all darkness **v.**, and

### vanity 1

T-27 I.6:11 and **v.** of real concern with anything at all

### vanquish 1

W-pI 151.6:3 doubts their lord can not completely **v.**.

### vanquished 2

T-23 I.9:3 crowned as real, the other **v.** and despised
T-31 II.1:2 It is not **v.** that the truth be known, nor

### vanquisher 1

T-23 I.9:2 and the **v.** of the illusion that was less real

### vantage 1

T-25 VII.12:7 **v.** point from which the Holy Spirit gives

### vaporous 1

W-pI 162.1:5 its misty clouds and **v.** illusions vanish as

### variability 2

T-15 I.15:6 forever beyond attack and without **v.**.
T19 IV.A.8:6 The **v.** the little remnant induces merely

### variable 6

T-4 II.2:2 else he perceives, which is equally **v.**.
T-11 VII.3:2 That is why its perceptions are so **v.**. It
T-11 VIII.11:1 not accept your brother's **v.** perception of
T-18 I.3:5 appears to introduce quite **v.** behavior, a
T-29 I.8:1 goals, is your excuse for **v.** goals you hold,
W-pI 17.1:6 In view of its highly **v.** nature, this is

### variance 5

T-9 I.11:3 totally at **v.** with the principle of creation.
T-18 I.1:2 perceive at once how much at **v.** this is
T-23 in.4:7 purpose is at **v.** with littleness of any kind.
T-23 in.4:8 of any kind. And so it is at **v.** with sin.
P-2 in.3:1 patient's goal and the therapist's are at **v.**.

### variation 3

T-3 VI.7:1 and at that level there is almost endless **v.**.
T-4 II.2:1 to enormous **v.** because of its instability.
T-13 XI.3:11 There is no **v.**. There is no interruption.

### variations 2

T-17 II.4:3 no **v.** that made perception possible will
W-pI 38.5:4 Introduce whatever **v.** appeal to you, but

### varied 1

W-pI 79.5:2 varying forms and with such **v.** content,

### varies 5

T-3 III.1:8 brings certainty because all perception **v.**.
T-6 V.C.1:10 The Holy Spirit never **v.** on this point,
T-25 IV.1:6 It is not the aim, as such, that **v.**. Yet it is
M-1 3:2 The form of the course **v.** greatly. So do
P-2 IV.8:2 real is the belief that illness **v.** in intensity;

### variety 2

T-27 VIII.3:3 and seems to show a great **v.** of places and
W-pI 39.10:1 you should feel free to introduce **v.** into

### various 7

T-2 II.6:9 its **v.** phases will proceed in time, but the
T-19 IV.1:3 and from **v.** aspects of the world outside.
W-pI 35.4:1 your mind for the **v.** kinds of descriptive
W-pI 35.7:2 They will occur to you as **v.** situations,
W-pI 43.8:1 to **v.** situations and events that may occur
W-pI 70.7:5 in possessions, in **v.** situations and events
S-1 II.3:4 to ask for things of this world in **v.** forms,

### vary 8

T-6 V.C.1:9 The ego's beliefs on this crucial issue **v.**,
T-7 V.5:2 always heals by Him the results will **v.**.
T-9 VIII.11:4 it. It does not **v.**. It merely *is*. Ask the Holy
W-pI 38.5:1 to time you may want to **v.** this procedure
W-pI 39.10:2 itself as you **v.** the method of applying it.
W-pI 43.7:1 periods, the form may **v.** according to the
W-pI 46.6:1 of the application may **v.** considerably,
M-4 1:2 their experiences of the world **v.** greatly,

### varying 2

W-pI 79.5:2 **v.** forms and with such varied content,
M-8 1:2 sizes, on **v.** degrees of darkness and light,

### vassals 1

W-pI 151.6:4 believe to doubt his **v.** is to doubt yourself

### vast 8

T-18 I.5:3 It was so **v.** and so completely incredible
T-24 II.4:5 And that **v.** song of honor and of love for
T-28 I.4:4 as **v.** as those you let the world impose on
W-pI 69.4:2 Think of your mind as a **v.** circle,
W-pI 79.4:2 present you with a **v.** number of problems
W-pI 139.3:1 must be is self-deception on a scale so **v.**,
W-pI 152.4:3 It is concealed behind a **v.** array of choices
W-pI 158.4:1 a **v.** illusion in which figures come and go

### vastly 1

M-4 1:2 they come from **v.** different backgrounds,

### vault 1

T-26 V.10:7 death, a **v.** God's Son entered an instant,

### vaults 2

T-28 I.5:7 Committed to its **v.**, the history of all the
T-31 V.6:6 And in these shrouded **v.** are all his sins

### vehicle 1

W-pI 199.4:5 thus becomes a **v.** which helps forgiveness

### veil 62

T-12 I.9:11 **v.** that you have drawn across the face of
T-13 VII.16:10 like a **v.** of light across the world's sad face
T-13 IX.7:3 You throw a dark **v.** over it, and cannot
T-15 VI.6:2 Only the **v.** that has been drawn across
T-15 VI.6:4 swiftly as the **v.** of time is pushed aside.
T-15 VI.6:5 not yet experienced the lifting of the **v.**,
T-16 IV.10:3 are the **v.** behind which truth is hidden.
T-16 IV.10:4 To lift the **v.** that seems so dark and heavy
T-16 IV.13:9 is no **v.** the Love of God in us together
T-17 III.9:4 The spark of beauty or the **v.** of ugliness,
T-18 IX.5:4 you see it as a fragile **v.** before the light.
T19 IV.D.2:1 like a heavy **v.** before the face of Christ.
T19 IV.D.2:2 brush the **v.** aside and run to meet Him,
T19 IV.D.2:3 For this dark **v.**, which seems to make the
T19 IV.D.3:1 is the darkest **v.**, upheld by the belief in
T19 IV.D.3:2 in secret to the ego never to lift this **v.**, not
T19 IV.D.3:3 **v.** forever blotted out and unremembered
T19 IV.D.6:4 if you look on this and let the **v.** be lifted,
T19 IV.D.7:7 beyond the **v.** is also deep within you,
T19 IV.D.i.h The Lifting of the **V.**
T19 IV.D.14:3 because you cast the **v.** of sin upon Him to
T19 IV.D.19:1 disappear into the Presence beyond the **v.**
T19 IV.D.21:3 that it would lift you far beyond the **v.**,
T-20 I.4:2 of the face of Christ behind the **v.**, looking
T-20 II.8:1 home is on the other side, beyond the **v.**.
T-20 II.9:4 We go beyond the **v.** of fear, lighting each
T-20 III.10:3 perfect, and without the **v.** of fear upon it
T-20 V.7:6 The **v.** that hides the gift hides him as well
T-22 IV.3:1 before the **v.** of sin that hangs between
T-22 IV.3:3 for it is but a **v.** that stands between you.
T-22 IV.3:5 has reached you even here, before the **v.**.
T-22 IV.4:6 beautiful the sight you saw beyond the **v.**,
T-22 IV.6:4 This **v.** you and your brother lift together
T-22 IV.7:5 Standing before the **v.**, it still seems
T-24 VI.6:5 Let not your eyes be blinded by the **v.** of
T-25 I.4:5 The **v.** is lifted through its gentleness, and
T-25 I.4:6 to let Him draw aside the **v.** that seems to
T-25 II.7:3 and casts a **v.** of light across the picture's
T-26 X.2:7 Their Presence is obscured by any **v.** that
T-29 VIII.3:6 before His face like a dark **v.** that seems to
T-29 VIII.3:9 a **v.** can banish what it seems to separate,
T-29 VIII.4:1 This world of idols *is* a **v.** across the face of
T-29 VIII.5:5 the light the **v.** between has not put out. It
T-29 VIII.5:6 It merely lifts the **v.**, and lets the truth
T-31 VI.3:8 The **v.** of ignorance is drawn across the
T-31 VII.8:7 and now the **v.** is lifted from his sight.
T-31 VII.9:1 The **v.** across the face of Christ, the fear
T-31 VII.13:7 see beyond the **v.** of old ideas and ancient
T-31 VIII.3:3 nor any image left to **v.** the truth. He
W-pI 21.2:5 nothing but a **v.** drawn over intense fury.
W-pI 56.4:3 every **v.** I have drawn across the face of
W-pI 69.1:3 But as the **v.** of your grievances is lifted,
W-pI 69.2:4 the **v.** of darkness that keeps it concealed.
W-pI 69.2:5 We are trying to let the **v.** be lifted, and to
W-pI 95.12:3 to lift the **v.** of darkness from the world,
W-pI 106.5:1 which lifts the **v.** that lies upon the earth,

W-pI...122.3:1 Forgiveness lets the v. be lifted up that
W-pI.122.11:2 joy the lifting of the v. holds out to you.
C-4............4:2 on it as nothing more than just a fragile v.
P-2.........V.7:8 the v. of guilt that shrouds the Son of God
P-3.....II.10:10 This is the v. across the face of Christ. Yet
S-3.........II.6:3 a world in which there is no v. of sin to

## veiled 4

T-18......IX.4:4 its intensity is v. by its heavy coverings,
W-pI...138.9:3 All that is v. in shadows must be raised to
W-pII......1.2:3 distortions are more v. and more obscure;
S-1.........V.3:3 A dream has v. the face of Christ from you

## veils 3

T-14.......V.4:5 but shine away the heavy v. of guilt within
T-24.....II.12:4 from eyes it v. but looks on sight of death.
T-29......IV.3:4 v. the heavy lump of fear that is their core

## veins 1

W-pI.....76.3:3 or some fluid pushed into your v. through

## veneer 1

W-pI...133.9:1 Yet is its camouflage a thin v., which

## venerates 1

T-22......III.4:5 is but error in a special form the ego v.. It

## vengeance 77

T-3...........I.3:1 The statement "V. is mine, sayeth the
T-5........VI.7:1 "V. is mine, sayeth the Lord" is easily
T-5........VI.7:2 emphasizes that v. cannot be shared. Give
T-15.........I.7:7 all-encompassing, demanding v. forever.
T-16.....VII.2:1 special relationship takes v. on the past.
T-16.....VII.3:1 of the ego's drive for v. on the past. It is
T-16.....VII.3:5 of the v. it believes you so justly merit. Yet
T-16.....VII.5:1 to be an acting out of v. that you seek.
T-16.....VII.5:3 is the acting out of v. on yourself. Yet
T-16.....VII.5:7 for it. And v. becomes your substitute for
T-16.....VII.5:7 and the escape from v. becomes your loss.
T-16.....VII.6:3 belief in salvation through v. for the past.
T-16.....VII.6:4 passing the drive for v. has been uprooted
T-17......III.2:2 The shadow figures always speak for v.,
T-17......III.2:4 there, and make of both the slaves of v..
T-17......III.2:6 only bodies can be seen as means for v..
T-17......III.3:3 What can be used for fantasies of v., and
T-17......III.3:3 with those on whom v. is really sought, is
T-17....III.10:6 Atonement be lost to you in dreams of v..
T-17......VI.3:6 it; is it acceptable, or does it call for v.?
T-18......VI.5:2 from fantasies of v. to release from them?
T-18......VI.6:7 instrument of v. and the perceived source
T-18......VI.7:2 and where you have sown the seeds of v.,
T-18......VI.8:2 The home of v. is not yours; the place you
T-18......IX.4:2 the v. and betrayal that were made to
T19...IV.D.6:3 and the fear of v. of the ego you swore in
T-21.....VII.2:6 of the powerless, to wage their war of v.,
T-23........II.8:2 Atonement thus becomes a myth, and v.,
T-23.....II.12:7 Here is what makes your v. justified.
T-23.....II.13:3 Nor will God end His v. upon both, for in
T-24.........I.8:3 God Himself must honor it or suffer v..
T-25.......VI.1:5 He is not an arbiter of v., nor a punisher
T-25...VIII.3:2 To the world, justice and v. are the same,
T-25...VIII.4:4 For that is v. in whatever form it takes.
T-25...VIII.5:5 fair to everyone. V. is alien to God's Mind
T-25...VIII.5:7 Fairness and v. are impossible, for each
T-25...VIII.6:2 avoid the v. that their own belief in justice
T-25...VIII.6:8 to themselves and to their world than v.,
T-25...VIII.7:2 to work God's v. on them in the guise of a
T-25...VIII.8:4 is love perceived as weak, and v. strong.
T-25...VIII.8:6 But v. without love has gained in strength
T-25...VIII.8:7 And what but v. now can help and save,
T-25.VIII.10:8 seek to offer, believing v. is his proper due
T-25VIII.11:11 does love correct mistakes, but not in v..
T-25.VIII.12:1 impossible the Son of God could merit v..
T-25.VIII.14:4 And you are safe from v. in all forms. The
T-25......IX.1:2 uncorrectable, and to be met with v., not
T-25......IX.4:6 deprived, and thus with grounds for v..
T-25......IX.4:7 Problem solving cannot be v., which at
T-25......IX.6:9 warrant v. in place of healing and return
T-25......IX.9:4 bitterness, with v. justified and mercy lost
T-26.......II.2:6 be possible, attack be justified and v. fair.
T-27.........I.2:5 unjust v. that you suffer now belongs to
T-27.........I.4:8 a "little" death; a form of v. not yet total.
T-27.....VII.4:6 V. must have a focus. Otherwise is the
T-27...VIII.7:5 It brings its v., not your own. It keeps you
T-28.......II.8:6 And hate it for the v. it would offer them.
T-28.......II.8:7 It is their v. on the body which appears to
W-pI.....13.5:2 thought because of the "v." of the "enemy
W-pI........22.h What I see is a form of v..
W-pI.....22.1:2 world, he sees v. about to strike at him.
W-pI.....22.3:6 *What I see is a form of v.*. At the end of each
W-pI.....23.3:1 and everything in it is a symbol of v.. Each
W-pI.....55.2:1 (22) What I see is a form of v.. The world
W-pI...129.3:1 hate cannot exist and v. has no meaning?
W-pI.153.14:4 defense against a v. he can not escape, is
W-pI.170.10:1 insane belief in gods of v. come from?
W-pI...190.3:5 God. For v. is not part of love. And fear,
W-pI...195.3:2 Now is v. all there is to wish for. Now can
W-pI...196.1:1 yourself, nor make your body slave to v..
W-pI...196.9:2 world, and need not fear its v. and pursuit
Wfl........in.5:4 is mad, and v. merely foolish fantasy. We
M-17.........5:9 abated, and v. that can never be satisfied.
C-2.............8:1 hate, the need for v. and the cries of pain,
S-1........III.2:2 They call for v., not for love. Nor do they
S-3.........II.6:2 brief respite as it waits to take its v. on the
S-3........IV.5:6 V. is His. His great destroyer, death. And

## vengeance's 1

T-26.....VII.7:5 and brought His Love at last to v. heels.

## vengeful 4

T-25...VIII.5:6 To be just is to be fair, and not be v..
W-pI.....23.3:1 you see is a v. world, and everything in it
W-pI.138.11:4 now, for what was made enormous, v.,
S-1........III.2:4 They call upon a v. god, and it is he who

## venture 2

T-4........VI.8:2 Salvation is a collaborative v.. It cannot
T-8........IV.4:8 That is why healing is a collaborative v..

## verbal 1

M-in..........3:4 To this the v. content of your teaching is

## verbally 1

T-9........III.2:7 is right. You do not tell him this v., if he is

## verdict 3

T-5......VI.10:8 v. will always be "thine is the Kingdom,"
M-4......IV.1:5 It is a v. of guilt upon a brother, and
M-19.........1:6 is the Holy Spirit's v. upon the world.

## version 8

T-7.....VIII.2:5 its own warped v. of the laws of God, the
T-15.......I.4:15 Such is the ego's v. of immortality. And it
T-15.......I.4:16 And it is this the ego's v. of time supports.
T-25.VIII.14:5 replace God's justice with a v. of its own.
T-27.....VII.1:2 demented v. of salvation clearly shown.
T-30.........I.7:3 what your v. of the question asks will gain
W-pI.....79.8:3 of your v. of what your problems are. You
W-pI.....95.2:2 Such is your v. of yourself; a self divided

## versus 10

T-3..........III.h Perception v. Knowledge
T-3.........VII.h Creating v. the Self-Image
T-9........VIII.h Grandeur v. Grandiosity
T-15.........III.h Littleness v. Magnitude
T-19..........II.h Sin v. Error
T-21.........VI.h Reason v. Madness
T-24.........IV.h Specialness v. Sinlessness
T-31..........V.h Self-Concept v. Self
S-3............II.h False v. True Healing
S-3...........III.h Separation v. Union

## vertical 2

T-1..........II.4:2 terms of a v. rather than a horizontal axis.
T-1..........II.6:3 shift from horizontal to v. perception.

## vertically 1

T-1........VI.3:3 correction must be introduced v. from

## very 258

## vestige 1

T-24........II.9:2 every v. of the fear of God will melt away

## vestiges 1

T-31....VIII.9:2 And thus will all the v. of hell, the secret

## vicinity 1

W-pI.....25.4:4 is not physically in your immediate v..

## vicious 9

T-3...........I.4:2 from fear, and frightened people can be v.
T-5........VI.8:1 as interpreted by the ego, is particularly v.
T-10......III.4:7 self-sufficient, very v. and very vulnerable
T19. IV.A.12:5 starving and made very v. by their master
T-27..VIII.10:6 them be as hateful and as v. as they may,
W-pI.....22.1:4 becomes an increasingly v. circle until he
W-pI.....95.2:1 parody on God's creation; weak, v., ugly
W-pI...101.4:4 match the v. wishes in which sin is born.
W-pI...191.1:4 What could it be but v. and afraid, fearful

## viciously 1

T-5........III.8:9 you believe there is strife you will react v.,

## viciousness 5

T-5........VI.2:7 exchange guilt for joy, v. for love, and
T-9.......VII.3:7 of suspiciousness at best and v. at worst.
T-9.......VII.4:7 shift abruptly from suspiciousness to v.,
T-9......VIII.2:7 vacillates between suspiciousness and v..
T-9......VIII.2:9 It shifts to v. when you decide not to

## victim 20

T-15......XI.5:2 also perceive yourself as a v. of sacrifice,
T-25....VIII.3:3 The laws of sin demand a v.. Who it may
T-25....VIII.4:8 up. So is the v. seen as partly you, with
T-27......II.11:4 And thus does he become your v., not
T-27.....VII.1:4 He is the v. of this "something else,"
T-27.....VII.4:8 would be a v. of attack he did not choose.
T-27.....VII.8:4 a v. to a dream conceived and cherished
T-27...VII.14:4 is the murderer and who shall be the v..
T-28........II.5:5 attack are you the v. in a dying body slain.
T-28........II.5:6 no one asked to be the v. and the sufferer.
T-28........II.7:8 As v., he is suffering from its effects, but
T-28......II.11:4 sickness, and employed the body to be v.,
T-28......VI.1:9 be victimized, but cannot feel itself as v..
W-pI.........31.h I am not the v. of the world I see.
W-pI.....32.1:2 You are not the v. of the world you see
W-pI.....57.1:1 (31) I am not the v. of the world I see.
W-pI.....57.1:2 How can I be the v. of a world that can be
W-pI.....76.5:3 the mind will fail to see it is the v. of itself.
W-pI...153.5:5 of God as but a v. to attack by fantasies,
W-pII.....5.2:7 Who could be v.? Who the murderer?

**victimize** 1

T-28......VI.1:6 It does not **v.**, because it has no will, no

**victimized** 2

T-26....... X.4:6 of this, and **v.** despite your innocence?
T-28......VI.1:9 It can be **v.**, but cannot feel itself as victim

**victims** 1

W-pI...101.3:3 welcome boon of death to **v.** who are little

**victor** 6

T-23.........I.7:9 There is no **v.** and there is no victory. And
T-29.....VII.3:4 within, and prove that he is **v.** over him.
W-pI....92.6:4 a **v.** over limitations that but grow in
W-pI...190.3:6 dead, has shown that death is **v.** over life.
W-pII .....5.2:5 Who could be **v.**? Who could be his prey?
W-pII ...12.2:3 it has become a **v.** over God Himself. And

**victorious** 2

T-23.........I.1:5 you believe the ego has the power to be **v.**.
W-pI.....35.6:7 *I see myself as* **v.**. *I see myself as losing out.*

**victory** 15

T-16....... V.5:5 of the "**v.**" even to the final triumph over
T19....IV.C.7:7 creation, the **v.** of lifelessness on Life Itself
T-20.........I.1:1 celebration of **v.** and the acceptance of the
T-20.........I.3:2 He started with the sign of **v.**, the promise
T-21.....VII.4:5 another, and never comes to rest in **v.**.
T-23.........I.1:4 impossible unless belief in **v.** is cherished.
T-23.........I.2:2 Is **v.** conceivable? And if it were, is this a
T-23.........I.2:3 if it were, is this a **v.** that you would want?
T-23.........I.2:5 Is this a **v.**? The ego always marches to
T-23........I.3:10 The **v.** it seeks is meaningless as is itself.
T-23.........I.7:9 There is no victor and there is no **v.**. And
T-24.........I.5:8 and its **v.** is his defeat and shame. How
T-25....VIII.3:7 and death is seen as **v.** and triumph over
M-8 ...........2:6 truth and gives itself an illusion of **v.**.
S-3......... II.6:1 until it brings a cruel death in seeming **v.**.

**view** 44

T-3...........I.1:5 is seen from an upside-down point of **v.**, it
T-3...........I.2:6 in **v.** of its prominent value as a defense.
T-3........IV.4:4 miracle in **v.** of how you perceive yourself.
T-8.....VIII.3:4 argument from the ego's point of **v.**,
T-14.....VII.3:2 From their point of **v.** it is not true. Yet it
T-14.....VII.3:6 It is therefore not a point of **v.** at all, but
T-14.....VII.3:9 Their creation was not a point of **v.**, but
T-17....... V.5:6 from the point of **v.** of this new purpose,
T-17......VI.4:5 becomes the useless from this point of **v.**.
T-18.....VII.2:5 you a different **v.** of it when you return.
T-21......III.8:4 should another point of **v.** be given them.
T-25.....VII.6:7 each reflects a **v.** of what the Father and
T-26....... X.1:2 a differential **v.** of when attack is justified,
T-26....... X.4:2 In this **v.**, you seek to find an innocence
T-27.......I.11:3 leaves no space in which a different **v.**,
T-27..... II.13:2 comes a necessary **v.** of function split
T-27......IV.1:4 of **v.** is not an answer in another light.
T-27......IV.3:8 but only to restate its point of **v.**.
T-28......III.2:4 your minds from separate points of **v.**.
T-28......VI.2:1 It is indeed a senseless point of **v.** to hold
T-31.......V.13:4 Nor can this be explained by either **v.**.
T-31......VII.5:2 because they do not cloud your **v.** of him.
T-31......VII.9:3 the mirror to another **v.** of what he is, and
W-pI.....17.1:6 In **v.** of its highly variable nature, this is
W-pI.....35.3:1 presents a very different **v.** of yourself. By
W-pI.....69.9:1 will want to do as often as possible in **v.** of
W-pI.....72.5:4 makes this **v.** of God quite convincing. In
W-pI.....93.3:1 not from the point of **v.** of what you think
W-pI...105.3:1 has set is to reverse your **v.** of giving, so
W-pI...130.6:4 from the point of **v.** from which you see it.
W-pI...134.1:2 In such a **v.**, forgiveness must be seen as
W-pI...134.2:1 This twisted **v.** of what forgiveness means
W-pI...134.5:1 Pardon is no escape in such a **v.**. It
W-pI...134.5:5 Those who are forgiven from the **v.** their
W-pI...161.3:4 to teach us from a different point of **v.**, so
W-pII .....1.1:4 And in that **v.** are all your sins forgiven.
W-pII .....1.3:4 to pose a contradiction to its point of **v.**.
M-2 ...........1:2 them in **v.** of their level of understanding.
M-3 ...........1:4 point of **v.** he cannot meet everyone, nor
P-2.........in.1:1 is a process that changes the **v.** of the self.
P-2........IV.6:1 as the result of a **v.** of the self as weak,
P-2.......VII.5:5 point of **v.** would such a role be possible.
P-3........III.7:1 **v.** of payment may well seem impractical,
S-3..........II.5:4 What healing has occurred in such a **v.** of

**viewpoint** 9

T-3 .........II.2:4 until their innocence becomes a **v.** with
T-4 .........II.4:8 belief you are regarding it from an ego **v.**.
T-5 ......III.4:6 you because, by adopting the ego's **v.**, you
T-13 .......II.1:2 attempts to get rid of guilt from its **v.** only
T-14 .......X.3:5 From the world's **v.**, this is impossible.
T-17 ..... VI.6:9 Yet this is so only from the **v.** of the ego,
T-25 .... VII.6:7 be, to make that **v.** meaningful and sane.
W-pI...134.3:3 This twisted **v.** but reflects the hold that
S-3..........II.5:6 **v.** must be fostered by the healing that the

**viewpoints** 1

T-14 .... VII.3:4 opposite **v.** on what the "unknowing" are.

**views** 5

T-8 .....VIII.4:3 a strong witness on behalf of the ego's **v.**.
T-20 .VIII.11:1 to quiet **v.** of gardens under open skies,
T-27 .....II.15:6 Your separate **v.** of what your function is.
T-30 ...VIII.2:4 by changing **v.** of him that you perceive as
W-pI..... 61.7:1 the ego's petty **v.** of what you are and

**vigilance** 26

T-4 ..... III.10:3 Consider how much **v.** you have been
T-4 ..... IV.11:3 I am your **v.** in this, because you are too
T-4 ......... V.1:3 The ego exerts maximal **v.** about what it
T-6 ..... V.C.4:1 this step calls for consistent **v.** against it.
T-6 ..... V.C.4:4 difficulty, but with clear-cut priority for **v.**
T-6 ..... V.C.8:6 This is why **v.** is essential. Doubts about
T-6 ..... V.C.8:9 you. **V.** is not necessary for truth, but it is
T-6 ..... V.C.9:6 Your **v.** against this sickness is the way to
T-6 ..... V.C.9:9 **V.** was required of me as much as of you,
T-6 ... V.C.10:3 Your **v.** is the sign that you *want* Him to
T-6 ... V.C.10:4 **V.** does require effort, but only until you
T-7 ....... III.1:6 Your **v.** does not establish it as yours, but
T-7 .......... VI.h From **V.** to Peace
T-7 ....... VI.7:3 does not require **v.** unless it is conflicted.
T-7 ....... VI.7:4 and **v.** has therefore become essential.
T-7 ....... VI.7:5 **V.** has no place in peace. It is necessary
T-7 ..... VI.8:10 This requires **v.** only as long as you do not
T-7 ..... VI.8:11 share truth, your need for **v.** is apparent.
T-9 ...... III.1:1 the kind of **v.** the Holy Spirit would have
T-10 .......II.6:6 this **v.** that makes you afraid to remember
T-11 .... V.18:2 the kingdom you have chosen for your **v.**.
T-15 ..... III.1:7 choices open to your striving and your **v.**.
T-15 ..... III.4:4 require **v.** to protect your magnitude in
T-24 ... VI.11:4 have pursued this goal with **v.** you never
T-24 ... VI.12:1 you pursue another goal with far less **v.**;
S-2........ III.6:8 to come from His eternal **v.** and Love.

**vigilant** 23

T-4 ....... IV.1:4 to keep, and what you are **v.** to save. Your
T-4 ....... IV.4:2 as **v.** against the ego's dictates as for them
T-4 ....... IV.6:4 Yet you are not sufficiently **v.** against the
T-5 ..... III.8:11 Holy Spirit is as **v.** as the ego to the call of
T-6 ........ V.C.h Be **V.** Only for God and His Kingdom
T-6 ..... V.C.2:8 is: *Be* **v.** *only for God and His Kingdom.*
T-6 ..... V.C.3:2 there is something you must be **v.** *against.*
T-6 ..... V.C.4:2 you can be as **v.** against the ego as for it.
T-6 ..... V.C.4:8 long as you must be **v.** against anything,
T-6 ..... V.C.7:5 is why you must be **v.** on God's behalf.
T-6 ..... V.C.8:2 Now you must be **v.** to hold its oneness in
T-7 ..........I.2:8 become **v.** only for God and His Kingdom
T-7 ....... III.3:5 underestimate your need to be **v.** *against*
T-7 ....... VI.7:1 **v.** for anything *but* God and His Kingdom.
T-7 ..... VI.12:3 and you must be **v.** against this divided
T-7 .....VIII.3:9 is why those who project are **v.** for their
T-10 .......II.6:5 yourself **v.** *against* God and His Kingdom.
T-10 ..... III.4:9 Is this the image you would be **v.** to save?
T-10 ... III.10:4 gods, and how **v.** you are on their behalf.
T-11 .......V.7:4 It is much more **v.** than you are, because
T-15 ..... IV.9:8 then, try only to be **v.** against deception,
T-31 .. VII.14:1 **v.** against temptation, then, remembering
W-pI .. 95.14:5 Be **v.**. Do not forget today. Throughout

**violate** 3

T-10 ......in.1:5 can **v.** God's laws in your imagination,
T-12 .... VII.3:2 for miracles **v.** every law of reality as this
T-19 .......II.2:2 lacks. To sin would be to **v.** reality, and to

**violated** 4

T-4 ....... IV.5:1 that the ego has indeed **v.** the laws of God
T-10 ........I.2:5 you awaken to were **v.** while you slept. Is
T-18 .......II.2:3 **v.** in them becomes apparent. Yet they
T-27 .......V.9:4 have been properly perceived but never **v.**

**violates** 1

W-pI .. 127.5:3 upholds but **v.** the truth of what love is,

**violating** 3

T-8 ..... IV.5:14 with it and thereby **v.** God's Will for you.
T-8 .....VIII.8:8 louder without **v.** your freedom of choice,
T-29 ......I.3:10 And **v.** this was thought to be a breach of

**violation** 3

T-3 ..........I.4:3 be vicious. Sacrificing in any way is a **v.** of
T-8 .........II.4:2 the attempt to learn it is a **v.** of your own
T-16 ..... IV.7:3 In fundamental **v.** of love's one condition,

**violence** 9

T-18 ..... VI.7:2 sown the seeds of vengeance, **v.** and death
T-18 ... VI.13:1 There is no **v.** at all in this escape. The
T-20 .VIII.11:1 you have looked on scenes of **v.** and death
T-23 ... IV.1:12 and every one does **v.** to the idea of love
T-24 ........I.2:6 to **v.** far more inclusive than you think,
T-24 ..... VI.4:4 will not escape its laws of **v.** and death.
T-25 ..... III.8:1 world of **v.** and hate that seems to stand
W-pII . 249.2:2 *them with thoughts of* **v.** *and death. Now*
M-17 ......... 4:5 rage, accompanied by thoughts of **v.**,

**violent** 1

W-pI .... 12.1:2 world, or a sad world, or a **v.** world, or an

**virtually** 4

T-2 .....VIII.1:2 where a belief in magic is **v.** inevitable.
T-2 .....VIII.2:7 process can be **v.** immeasurable. It is
T-3 ....... VI.5:6 of constant judgment is **v.** intolerable. It
W-pI .... 20.1:2 There has been **v.** no attempt to direct the

**virtuous** 1

W-pI .. 35.6:10 *I see myself as charitable. I see myself as* **v.**.

**vise** 1

W-pII . 249.2:2 *them, held them in a* **v.** *of bitterness, and*

**visible** 10

T-12 ...VIII.3:1 When you made **v.** what is not true, what
T-12 ...VIII.3:4 to decide what is **v.** and what is invisible,
T-12 .VIII.6:11 of what you have made **v.** to yourself.
T-14 ..... IV.3:6 becomes real and **v.** to those who use it.

T-16......VI.6:3 holds the Great Rays within it is also v.,
W-pI.....30.1:3 you saw before be even faintly v. to you.
W-pI...164.5:2 Now is what is really there made v., while
M-26..........2:2 because, although they are no longer v.,
M-29..........8:4 *of time; to end the sight Of all things v.; and*
C-4............1:5 come when all things v. will have an end.

## vision 313

T-1.......VII.2:3 body to another, because v. is still so dim.
T-1.......VII.2:4 your perception so you can achieve real v.
T-1.......VII.3:1 Fantasy is a distorted form of v..
T-2......III.1:11 the structure at all because it is perfect v..
T-2........III.3:8 This ultimately reawakens spiritual v.,
T-2........III.4:1 Spiritual v. literally cannot see error, and
T-2........III.4:3 Spiritual v. looks within and recognizes
T-2........III.4:5 Because of the strength of its v., it brings
T-2.........V.8:4 real v. is obscured, because you cannot
T-3.........II.5:7 Yet this v. can be perceived only by the
T-3........III.4:1 True v. is the natural perception of
T-3........III.4:4 A "v. of God" would be a miracle rather
T-5........III.8:6 v. frightens the ego because it is so calm.
T-10.......IV.5:9 your v. will automatically look beyond it,
T-12.......II.9:6 to real v. without looking upon them, for
T-12.....III.10:7 There you will see your v. changed, and
T-12.........VI.h The V. of Christ
T-12.......VI.4:2 He knows that they have not lost their v.,
T-12.......VI.4:4 see with love if you accept His v. as yours.
T-12.......VI.4:5 The Holy Spirit keeps the v. of Christ for
T-12.......VI.4:6 and He longs to share His v. with you. He
T-12... VIII.4:3 ask, and a v. will correct the perception of
T-12... VIII.6:6 through His v. your perception is healed.
T-12... VIII.7:2 Son can be seen because his v. is shared.
T-13.......III.7:2 for the Holy Spirit's v. is merciful and His
T-13.......V.6:7 And the v. of Christ is not in your sight,
T-13.......V.8:1 V. depends on light. You cannot see in
T-13.......V.8:5 for sight of it depends upon denying v..
T-13.......V.8:6 denying v. it does not follow you cannot
T-13.......V.9:1 Do not seek v. through your eyes, for you
T-13.......V.9:2 and yet still within you, is the v. of Christ,
T-13.......V.9:3 Your "v." comes from fear, as His from
T-13.....V.10:3 See through the v. that is given you, for
T-13.....V.10:3 through Christ's v. He beholds Himself.
T-13.....V.10:6 Him, for His v. is His gift of love to you,
T-13.....V.11:6 In the sanity of His v. they looked upon
T-13.....V.11:7 And with this v. of the truth in them came
T-13.......VI.7:4 the light of perfect v. is freely given as it is
T-13.....VI.13:8 he slept, Christ's v. did not leave him.
T-13.....VII.2:1 of it is costing you a different kind of v..
T-13.....VII.6:2 his own, he will deny the v. of the other,
T-13... VIII.2:7 v. of Christ beholds everything in light.
T-13... VIII.4:4 Christ's v. looks on everything with love.
T-13... VIII.4:5 Yet even Christ's v. is not His reality. The
T-13... VIII.5:5 to make Christ's v. possible even here.
T-13... VIII.6:6 Christ's v. is His gift to you. His Being is
T-13.......X.9:6 the cloud of guilt that dims your v., and
T-13...X.10:11 And in Christ's v. He would show you the
T-14.......II.8:3 v. of Christ is given the very instant that it
T-14.....VII.6:7 The v. of Christ is not for Him alone, but
T-14.....VII.7:5 yours, comes not from double v., but
T-14.....VII.7:7 The single v. which the Holy Spirit offers
T-15.......II.5:5 blind you to this world by its own v., you
T-15......IX.1:1 Holy Spirit release your v. and let you see
T-15......IX.1:2 shift to v. that is accomplished in the holy
T-15......IX.6:7 And limit not your v. of God's Son to
T-17.......II.6:2 For forgiveness literally transforms v.,
T-19.........I.2:3 and in this v. does the Holy Spirit share.
T-19......III.5:2 On this you share His v.. Yet you do not
T-19....III.10:6 you who were sightless have been given v.
T-20..............h THE V. OF HOLINESS
T-20.......II.5:3 purpose as their own share also His v..
T-20.......II.6:5 it. The Holy Spirit's v. is no idle gift, no
T-20.......II.7:1 have the v. now to look past all illusions.
T-20.......II.7:5 your v. has become the greatest power for
T-20.....II.8:12 fear in us, for in our v. will be no illusions;
T-20.......II.9:3 and look on him with the new v. that
T-20.....II.11:1 released from crucifixion through your v.,
T-20.......V.4:4 your grateful v. that you will merely love
T-20.......V.4:7 V. or judgment is your choice, but never
T-20.....V.7:10 And through His v. will you see it, and
T-20.....VII.5:7 you have chosen judgment and not v.. For
T-20.....VII.5:8 For v., like relationships, has no order.
T-20.....VII.7:1 between this vain imagining and v.. The
T-20.....VII.8:2 To see the body is the sign that you lack v.
T-20.....VII.8:4 v. is learned from Him Who would undo
T-20.....VII.8:5 v. cannot see the body because it cannot
T-20.....VII.9:5 The means is v.. For what the seeing look
T-20.....VII.9:8 was the v. that made his seeing possible.
T-20...... VIII.h The V. of Sinlessness
T-20... VIII.1:1 V. will come to you at first in glimpses,
T-20... VIII.1:5 V. would not be necessary had judgment
T-20. VIII.2:10 V. is freely given to those who ask to see.
T-20... VIII.3:1 the Holy Spirit's v. and to rejoice in along
T-20... VIII.3:3 may rise before your v. and give you joy.
T-20... VIII.4:2 v. that makes it yours is ready to be given.
T-20... VIII.4:3 the v. that enables you to see the body not
T-20... VIII.5:7 no perplexity that v. will not solve. All is
T-20... VIII.5:8 All is redeemed when looked upon with v.
T-20... VIII.6:1 looked upon with v. falls gently into place
T-20... VIII.7:2 But v. sets all things right, bringing them
T-20. VIII.10:4 V. is the means by which the Holy Spirit
T-20. VIII.11:1 need persuade you to accept the gift of v.?
T-20. VIII.11:2 And after v., who is there who could
T-21......in.1:10 Everything looked upon with v. is healed
T-21.........I.2:5 directions, but v. shows you where to go.
T-21.........I.3:7 v. gives you more than judgment does,
T-21.........I.9:1 This is the v. of the Son of God, whom
T-21.........I.9:4 Accept the v. that can show you this, and
T-21.......I.10:3 will look upon the v. of the Son of God,
T-21....... II.2:1 is the only thing that you need do for v.,
T-21....... II.7:1 in holiness and v. to see it easily enough.
T-21....... II.8:3 comes of v. and suspended judgment.
T-21..... II.10:1 When v. is denied, confusion of cause
T-21......... III.h Faith, Belief and V.
T-21...... III.4:1 Faith and belief and v. are the means by
T-21...... III.4:5 faith and His belief and v. are all for you.
T-21...... III.4:7 For faith and v. and belief are meaningful
T-21...... III.6:6 you that the v. of a holy relationship is all
T-21...... III.7:1 Faith and belief become attached to v., as
T-21...... III.8:3 sees far beyond the body, supporting v.,
T-21...... III.8:6 choose to look away from sin are given v.,
T-21.... III.12:2 of v. it is looked upon quite differently.
T-21....... V.3:1 There is another v. and another Voice in
T-21..... V.10:5 in this change is room made way for v..
T-21..... V.10:6 V. extends beyond itself, as does the
T-21.....VII.7:5 or let him be revealed to you through v.?
T-21...VII.13:3 be perceived except through constant v..
T-21...VII.13:4 And constant v. can be given only those
T-21... VIII.2:5 in its v. as its Creator is in what He knows
T-22.......in.4:4 is sight of differences transformed to v..
T-22.........I.2:6 If this is not your v., what can it show to
T-22.........I.2:7 brain cannot interpret what your v. sees.
T-22.........I.3:7 you. Your v. would, of course, render this
T-22.........I.5:2 in understanding what this v. tells you,
T-22.........I.5:4 your v. can convey to you what you can
T-22.........I.7:3 in this infant is your v. returned to you,
T-22.........I.7:6 through Christ, Whose v. sees them one.
T-22.........I.9:6 each other through a v. not of the body,
T-22....... II.8:4 And v. cannot damn, but only bless.
T-22..... II.12:8 His home with v. that overlooks the world
T-22..... II.13:1 in quiet here with Christ is share His v..
T-22..... II.13:2 Quickly and gladly is His v. given anyone
T-22...... III.1:5 is the beginning of a v. that has meaning.
T-22...... III.1:6 V. is sense, quite literally. If it is not the
T-22...... III.5:7 To this distorted form of v. the outside of
T-22...... III.8:2 Let not the v. of his holiness, the sight of
T-22...... VI.6:3 can deny himself the v. that he brings to
T-23...... III.4:8 it? It can be kept shining before your v.,
T-24....... II.5:6 Christ's v. is their "enemy," for it sees not
T-24....... V.7:3 He gives them v. for their sightless eyes,
T-24...... VI.6:6 the v. you were meant to see from you.
T-25....... II.8:8 this seeing is the v. shared that looks on
T-25...... III.8:9 But on His v. sin cannot encroach, for sin
T-25...... IV.3:5 there is a v. that extends to all of them,
T-31..............h THE FINAL V.
T-31...... VI.1:4 There is no choice in v. but this one.
T-31...... VI.5:4 One v., clearly seen, that does not fit the
T-31........VII.h The Savior's V.
T-31..... VII.7:2 that dims your sight and warps your v., so
T-31..... VII.7:7 the v. and the inner Guide all lead you out
T-31..... VII.8:6 this single v. does he see the face of Christ
T-31...VII.11:5 him. This is the savior's v.; that he see his
T-31...VII.13:1 The savior's v. is as innocent of what
T-31...VII.13:7 dear against the v. of the Christ in you.
T-31...VII.15:2 the savior's v. is withheld and what they
T-31....VIII.8:4 tired eyes I bring a v. of a different world,
T-31....VIII.8:5 Yet this a v. is which you must share with
W-pI.......8.3:3 is the first step to opening the way to v..
W-pI.....10.3:5 see it. As such, it is the prerequisite for v..
W-pI.....15.1:7 place of seeing, replacing v. with illusions.
W-pI.....15.2:3 That is the beginning of real v.. You can
W-pI.....15.2:4 You can be certain that real v. will come
W-pI.....20.3:1 Your decision to see is all that v. requires.
W-pI.....20.3:8 your determination to see is v. given you.
W-pI.....23.4:4 gone? V. already holds a replacement for
W-pI.....27.1:2 It gives v. priority among your desires.
W-pI.....27.2:3 *V. has no cost to anyone.* If fear of loss still
W-pI.....28.5:1 could, in fact, gain v. from just that table,
W-pI.....29.1:5 well. Today's idea is the whole basis for v.
W-pI.....29.3:6 When v. has shown you the holiness that
W-pI.....30.1:1 idea for today is the springboard for v..
W-pI.....30.2:5 difference between v. and the way you see
W-pI.....30.4:1 Real v. is not limited to concepts such as
W-pI.....30.5:1 Real v. is not only unlimited by space
W-pI.....35.1:2 however, describe what v. will show you.
W-pI.....35.2:6 image. This is not v.. Images cannot see.
W-pI.....37.1:4 everyone gains through your holy v.. It
W-pI.....37.2:5 restored to his awareness through your v..
W-pI.....39.7:3 on them that will save you and give you v.
W-pI.........42.h God is my strength. V. is His gift.
W-pI.....42.1:5 rather than your own, that offers v. to you
W-pI.....42.4:5 *V. must be possible. God gives truly,* or:
W-pI.....43.3:3 If v. is real, and it is real to the extent to
W-pI.....44.2:4 making v. possible in every circumstance.
W-pI.....45.1:2 think you see is related to v. in any way.
W-pI.....45.1:5 any resemblance to what v. will show you.
W-pI.....51.1:4 I think I see now is taking the place of v..
W-pI.....51.1:5 no meaning, so that v. may take its place.
W-pI.....51.2:3 This is not v.. It is merely an illusion of
W-pI.....52.4:5 What I have chosen to see has cost me v..
W-pI.....56.2:2 I am, I realize that v. is my greatest need.
W-pI.....56.2:5 by truth, v. will surely be given me. And
W-pI.....56.2:6 me. And with this v., I will look upon the
W-pI.....59.2:2 V. is His gift. Let me not look to my own
W-pI.....59.2:4 of seeing for the v. that is given by God.
W-pI.....59.2:5 Christ's v. is His gift, and He has given it
W-pI.....59.3:8 Yet the v. of Christ has been given me to
W-pI.....59.3:9 It is through this v. that I choose to see.
W-pI.....59.4:7 Let me welcome v. and the happy world it
W-pI.....60.5:5 I look upon the world with the v. He has
W-pI.....75.7:1 that your forgiveness entitles you to v..
W-pI.....75.7:6 He will show you what true v. sees. It is
W-pI...75.11:2 beginning of your v. and the sight of the
W-pI.....85.1:5 light and v. must be joined for me to see.
W-pI.....91.1:1 miracles and v. necessarily go together.
W-pI.....91.1:5 Its presence is not caused by your v.; its
W-pI...100.5:2 essential to God's plan, as well as to our v.
W-pI...108.1:1 V. depends upon today's idea. The light
W-pI...108.2:1 True light that makes true v. possible is
W-pI...108.3:1 the light that shows no opposites, and v.,
W-pI...108.6:2 to other areas of doubt and double v..
W-pI...108.7:5 and in that peace is v. given us, and we
W-pI...109.2:4 whose v. sees beyond appearances to that
W-pI...110.2:1 and give you perfect v. that will heal all
W-pI...125.9:2 and free your v. from the body's eyes.
W-pI. 133.10:1 he tries to keep its halo clear within his v.,
W-pI. 151.10:2 gives you v. which can look beyond these
W-pI...157.5:2 A v. reaches everyone you meet, and
W-pI...157.6:1 to bring the v. of what you experience this
W-pI...157.6:3 leaves a v. in our eyes which we can offer
W-pI...157.7:2 the light more sure; the v. more distinct.
W-pI...157.9:2 The v. of His face will stay with you, but
W-pI...157.9:2 will be an instant which transcends all v.,
W-pI...157.9:4 Yet the v. speaks of your remembrance
W-pI...158.2:7 be shared directly, in the way that v. can.
W-pI...158.5:3 But v. is his gift. This he can give directly,
W-pI...158.5:4 has a v. He can give to anyone who asks.

W-pI...158.5:6 Yet there is a v. which the Holy Spirit sees
W-pI...158.6:6 Our concern is with Christ's v.. This we
W-pI...158.7:1 Christ's v. has one law. It does not look
W-pI...158.9:1 has v. that has power to overlook them all
W-pI...158.9:3 a v. of the holiness that lies beyond them
W-pI.158.10:2 And thus Christ's v. looks on you as well.
W-pI.158.10:5 chance to let Christ's v. shine on you, and
W-pI.158.11:4 Christ's v. looks upon ourselves as well.
W-pI...159.3:1 Christ's v. is a miracle. It comes from far
W-pI...159.3:3 Christ's v. pictures Heaven, for it sees a
W-pI...159.4:1 Christ's v. is the miracle in which all
W-pI...159.5:1 v. is the bridge between the worlds. And
W-pI...159.5:4 Holiness has been restored to v., and the
W-pI...159.8:1 Christ's v. is the holy ground in which
W-pI.159.10:8 His v. gives the means for a return to our
W-pI...160.9:2 His v. sees no strangers, but beholds His
W-pI...161.6:4 of love's "enemy" Christ's v. does not see.
W-pI...161.9:3 in Christ's v. is his loveliness reflected in a
W-pI.161.10:2 and you will come today nearer Christ's v.
W-pI...162.4:5 God. Christ's v. has restored your sight by
W-pI...164.6:2 Your v., given you from far beyond all
W-pI...164.7:6 freedom given us through His forgiving v.
W-pI...164.8:5 Christ's v. worthy to be sought above the
W-pI...165.5:5 to let it fade away from your ecstatic v.?
W-pI.166.11:2 it now has been replaced by v. which
W-pI.167.12:6 No v. now is needed. For the wakened
W-pI...168.4:2 will disappear, and v. first will come, with
W-pI.170.11:6 in the v. that your choice restored to you.
WiI81-200 2:1 special blocks that keep your v. narrow,
W-pI...181.2:4 Your v. now will shift, to give support to
W-pI...181.7:3 seems to block the v. of our sinlessness,
W-pI...184.4:1 is the way reality is made by partial v.,
W-pI...184.4:4 a sense of unity or v. that sees differently,
W-pI...184.5:1 other v. still remain a natural direction
W-pI...188.2:5 to look within, for there all v. starts.
W-pI...188.2:6 the shadow of the seen through inward v..
W-pI...188.3:5 hearts, and lights all v. as it passes by. All
W-pI...188.5:7 inward v. looks upon is your perception
W-pI...192.6:1 that, for Christ's v. and the gift of sight,
W-pI...193.2:3 and give him v. that will lead him back to
W-pI.198.12:6 In this v. of the Son, so brief that not an
W-pI.198.12:6 itself, you see the v. of yourself, and then
W-pI.198.13:1 would stand between this v. and our sight
W-pI...218.1:2 *My condemnation keeps my v. dark, and*
W-pI...218.1:2 *sightless eyes I cannot see the v. of my glory.*
W-pII ....in.6:5 as through Christ's v. we behold a world
W-pII .247.1:3 means whereby Christ's v. comes to me.
W-pII .260.1:6 *my sinlessness arise again before Christ's v.,*
W-pII ....263.h My holy v. sees all things as pure.
W-pII .263.2:1 see through holy v. and the eyes of Christ.
W-pII .269.2:2 We share one v., as we look upon the face
W-pII .270.1:1 *Father, Christ's v. is Your gift to me, and it*
W-pII ....271.h Christ's is the v. I will use today.
W-pII .271.2:1 *Father, Christ's v. is the way to You. What*
W-pII .290.1:3 have Christ's v. come to me this very day.
W-pII .291.1:1 Christ's v. looks through me today. His
W-pII .291.1:2 peace, and offers this same v. to the world
W-pII .291.1:3 And I accept this v. in its name, both for
W-pII .302.1:6 *Christ's v. changes darkness into light, for*
W-pII .304.1:2 looks upon, unless it is His v. that I use.
W-pII .305.1:1 Christ's v. finds a peace so deep and quiet
W-pII .306.1:1 What but Christ's v. would I use today,
W-pII .313.1:1 *is a v. which beholds all things as sinless, so*
W-pII .313.1:3 *This v. is Your gift. The eyes of Christ look on*
W-pII .313.2:6 our v. it becomes as holy as the light in us.
W-pII .340.1:4 *him to find Christ's v. through forgiveness,*
W-pII ....349.h Today I let Christ's v. look upon All
W-pII ...14.4:1 the eyes through which Christ's v. sees a
M-13 .........4:4 Does one whose v. has already glimpsed
M-18 .........2:5 ears, and bring Christ's v. to eyes that see.
M-19 .......5:10 V. is now restored. What had been lost
M-23 .........5:8 Christ's v. shines in perfect constancy. He
M-28 .........3:3 V. is wholly corrected and all mistakes
M-28 .........5:4 What remains that v. could accomplish?
M-28 .........6:3 and seeing there the v. of Christ's face to
C-1.............5:2 Christ's v. sees the real world in its place.
C-1.............5:3 This is the final v., the last perception, the
C-5.............5:5 your will with his, your sight will be his v.
C-6.............3:4 the inherent power of the v. of Christ. He
P-2..........II.5:4 first through Christ's v. and then through
P-2..........II.9:2 who stands apart can receive Christ's v.. It
P-2.......VII.3:4 His v. heals perception and sickness
S-2...........I.6:4 Christ's v. does not use your eyes, but you
S-2...........I.7:1 to learn forgiveness as His v. lets it be.
S-3..........II.3:5 is clearer now; His v. more sustained in us

## visions 1

T-3 ....... III.4:6 That is why v., however holy, do not last.

## visit 1

T-5 ....... VI.8:1 "I will v. the sins of the fathers unto the

## vistas 1

M-19 ......... 2:6 the enormous opening v. that rise to meet

## vital 1

T-7 ........ V.7:5 so v. in its power for change that a Son of

## vitality 2

T-25 ...VIII.8:7 helpless hands, bereft of justice and v.,
M-27 ......... 1:2 think of life as being born, aging, losing v.

## vividly 1

W-pI....... 8.4:2 matter how v. you may picture a thought,

## vocation 3

T-5 .........II.2:3 This is the v. of the mind. The mind had
T-5 .......II.10:9 What better v. could there be for any part
T-7 ........ V.1:4 obviously does not understand his own v.

## Voice 255

*voice*

T-1 ..........I.4:2 life. His V. will direct you very specifically.
T-4 ....... IV.1:1 If you cannot hear the V. for God, it is
T-5 ..........I.5:4 The V. of the Holy Spirit is the Call to
T-5 ........... II.h The V. for God
T-5 .........II.3:8 His is the V. that calls you back to where
T-5 .........II.3:9 world to hear only that V. and no other. It
T-5 .........II.5:6 chose to leave Him He gave you a V. to
T-5 .........II.6:9 in their minds was not the V. for His Will,
T-5 .........II.7:1 V. of the Holy Spirit does not command,
T-5 .........II.7:7 The V. for God is always quiet, because It
T-5 .........II.8:6 V. for God comes from your own altars to
T-5 .......II.10:2 only one V. and answers in only one way.
T-5 ....... III.4:1 The V. of the Holy Spirit is weak in you.
T-5 ....... IV.1:7 from the Holy Spirit, the V. for creation.
T-5 ..... IV.2:12 even in this world to listen to one V.. If
T-5 ....... IV.4:1 I heard one V. because I understood that
T-5 ....... IV.4:2 Listening to one V. implies the decision to
T-5 ..... VI.11:7 His V. was in me as It is in you, speaking
T-5 ...... VII.1:6 His V. reminds you always that all hope is
T-5 ...... VII.3:1 you can know the V. for God is in you?
T-6 ..........I.8:1 not share my decision to hear only one V.,
T-6 ........I.10:4 one V. you are never called on to sacrifice.
T-6 ........I.19:2 If you will listen to His V. you will know
T-6 .........II.4:2 by the mind, which has a better V.. The
T-6 ........ V.2:1 by a gentle V. that will not frighten them,
T-6 ..... V.B.4:5 of the Holy Spirit's V. makes it impossible
T-6 ..... V.B.5:4 called upon the V. for peace to help you.
T-6 ..... V.B.6:4 the quiet power of the Holy Spirit's V.,
T-6 ..... V.C.7:3 V. for God speaks only for belief beyond
T-7 ....... IV.1:3 since inspiration comes from the V. for
T-7 ....... IV.1:5 it proceeds from His V. and from His laws
T-7 ....... IV.5:7 accord with His, because it serves His V.,
T-7 ........ V.6:9 on because it is inspired by His V., and is
T-7 ..... VI.10:2 from this will obscure God's V. in you,
T-7 .........X.7:3 His V. will teach you how to distinguish
T-8 .........II.3:5 His V. teaches only in accordance with
T-8 .........II.8:6 every Son of God to the V. for his Creator,
T-8 .........II.8:6 because It is the V. for his creations and
T-8 ....... IV.3:9 to hear His V. and abide in His Will. As
T-8 ........V.6:3 one for which God's V. speaks in all of us.
T-8 ...... VII.5:9 V. which He has established as part of you
T-8 ...... VII.9:7 His V. abides in it by directing the use to
T-8 .....VIII.8:7 Spirit's V. is as loud as your willingness to
T-8 ...VIII.9:10 what life is, being the V. for Life Itself.
T-9 .........II.5:5 and His V. speaks to you through him.
T-9 .........II.6:5 hear the V. for God in yourself alone,
T-9 .......II.6:10 God have created a V. for you alone?
T-9 .........II.7:5 my brothers in whom God's V. speaks.
T-9 ...VIII.10:3 God, through His V., reminds you of it,
T-10 .......II.2:5 His V. will tell you that you are part of
T-10 ...... III.8:2 all illusions because you heard His V.. But
T-10 ... III.11:3 His V. still calls you to return, and He will
T-10 ..... IV.7:4 the miracle worker has heard God's V., he
T-11 ......I.11:2 He is the V. for God, but never forget that
T-11 .......II.4:2 your ears to the V. of the Holy Spirit,
T-11 .......II.5:2 but His V. grows faint in alien company.
T-11 ..... IV.5:7 Creator, he will hear the V. for his Father.
T-12 ...VIII.4:3 A V. will answer every question you ask,
T-13 ..... XI.5:4 reactions to the Holy Spirit's V. may be,
T-13 ..... XI.7:7 would communicate. His V. *will* be heard.
T-15 .. VII.10:6 in His V. your own need to communicate.
T-16 .......II.8:4 His V. has spoken clearly, and yet you
T19 ... IV.C.7:2 the silencer of the V. that speaks for God.
T19 .. IV.D.5:9 you heard the V. of Love beyond them,
T-21 .......V.1:6 small V. for God is not drowned out by all
T-21 .......V.3:1 and another V. in which your freedom lies
T-23 ..... III.2:1 blessing and a sign the V. for God speaks
T-24 .......II.5:1 never will you hear the V. for God beside
T-24 ..... VI.5:6 but through the V. that speaks for God in
T-24 .... VII.1:5 while it calls to him he hears no other V..
T-26 ..... IX.1:1 you must be from whom the V. for God
T-26 ..... IX.1:1 may awake in him the V. that answers to
T-27 .....V.1:12 else. Yet by your listening His V. extends,
T-27 .. VII.13:4 the V. that calls with love to waken him;
T-29 .......V.4:2 Be very still and hear God's V. in him, and
T-29 .. VII.10:5 and do not seek to drown His V. in chants
T-30 ......I.16:4 a dream of judgment or the V. for God.
T-30 .......II.3:3 Him Who is His V. and yours as well,
T-31 ........I.4:4 so great the Holy Spirit's V. seems small
T-31 ........I.5:4 stand implacable before the V. of truth,
T-31 ........I.6:1 this a little V., so small and still It cannot
T-31 ........I.6:3 power of His Will is in the V. that speaks
T-31 .......II.7:6 Because He hears one V., He cannot hear
W-pI .... 47.3:2 His V. speaks for Him in all situations and
W-pI .... 47.3:4 And the V. which speaks for Him thinks
W-pI ....... 49.h God's V. speaks to me all through the day
W-pI .... 49.1:1 It is quite possible to listen to God's V. all
W-pI .... 49.2:1 that is listening to the V. for God is calm,
W-pI .... 49.2:6 Try to hear God's V. call to you lovingly,
W-pI .... 49.3:2 We will try actually to hear God's V.
W-pI .... 49.3:4 He wants you to hear His V.. He gave It to
W-pI .... 49.5:3 you are inviting God's V. to speak to you.
W-pI .... 60.4:1 God's V. speaks to me all through the day.
W-pI .... 60.4:2 in which God's V. ceases to call on my
W-pI .... 60.4:3 in which His V. fails to direct my thoughts
W-pI .... 60.4:5 because God's V. is the only Voice and the
W-pI .... 60.4:5 because God's Voice is the only V. and the
W-pI .... 60.5:2 As I listen to God's V., I am sustained by
W-pI .... 61.3:1 it is God's V. which tells you it is true.
W-pI .... 66.8:1 is established by God through His V., or is
W-pI .... 66.9:8 the only alternative to the Holy Spirit's V..
W-pI .... 67.6:2 This is the V. for God, reminding you of
W-pI .... 67.6:3 your Self. This is the V. of truth, replacing
W-pI .... 71.9:7 to your willingness to hear His V.. Refuse
W-pI .... 72.7:4 may not hear the V. of truth and welcome
W-pI 72.10:11 loudly that we have not listened to His V..
W-pI .... 76.9:2 to hear the V. that speaks the truth to you
W-pI .. 76.11:3 His V. will speak of this to us, as well as of
W-pI .... 96.7:3 His V. accepted it for you and answered in
W-pI .... 97.4:4 calls through His V. to every living thing;
W-pI .. 101.4:2 can to drown the V. which offers it to him
W-pI .. 105.8:3 and let His V. assure you that the words
W-pI .. 106.1:1 then you will hear the mighty V. of truth,
W-pI .. 106.2:1 speak to you through His appointed V.,
W-pI .. 106.3:7 to reach Him longer. Hear one V. today.
W-pI .. 106.6:4 and you will hear a V. which will resound
W-pI .. 118.2:2 *and let me hear the mighty V. for Truth Itself*

## voice 73
*Voice*



## voices 15



## void 1

**voids** 1

| | |
|---|---|
| T-11.........I.3:5 | cannot be blocked, and it has no v.. It |

**volatile** 1

| | |
|---|---|
| T-8...........I.5:8 | The v. have no direction. They cannot |

**volition** 2

| | |
|---|---|
| T-13...... III.5:5 | for it enters of its own v. and cares not for |
| T-14...... IV.6:3 | your own v. seems to make deciding hard. |

**voluntarily** 1

| | |
|---|---|
| T-4.........in.3:6 | are endless until they are v. given up. Do |

**voluntary** 2

| | |
|---|---|
| T-in ........... 1:3 | *Only the time you take it is v.. Free will does* |
| T-4........ IV.6:3 | you have given up this v. dis-spiriting, |

**vow** 3

| | |
|---|---|
| T19... IV.D.3:2 | and to its sovereignty is but the solemn v. |
| T-24 ..... III.4:6 | secret v. that what God wants for you will |
| T-28 ..... VI.4:3 | This is the secret v. that you have made |

**vows** 2

| | |
|---|---|
| T-28 ........ VI.h | The Secret V. |
| T-28 ..... VI.6:8 | secret v. are powerless before the Will of |

**vulnerability** 7

| | |
|---|---|
| T-2 ........ V.2:6 | As long as your sense of v. persists, you |
| T-4 ........ V.4:2 | safe, since the body's v. is its own best |
| T-8 ..... VIII.6:2 | It is a witness to your frailty, your v., and |
| T-9 ..... VIII.3:3 | profound sense of v. renders it incapable |
| T-20 ... VIII.5:1 | the sign of weakness, v. and loss of power. |
| W-pI..... 26.4:1 | to understand that v. or invulnerability is |
| M-7 ........... 5:4 | Perhaps there is a fear of weakness and v.. |

**vulnerable** 20

| | |
|---|---|
| T-1 ....... III.5:2 | Only the error is actually v.. You are free |
| T-1 ..... III.5:10 | makes them v. to the distortions of others |
| T-2 .........V.2:3 | afraid makes your mind v. to miscreation. |
| T-4 .........II.6:9 | This "self-esteem" is always v. to stress, |
| T-6 ........I.14:3 | imperfect love made them v. to projection |
| T-7 ...... VII.3:2 | of you is deprived, unloving and v.. You |
| T-8 .... VII.10:7 | been blocked has allowed itself to be v. to |
| T-10 ..... III.4:7 | self-sufficient, very vicious and very v.. Is |
| T-18 .......II.1:6 | on you, as under attack and highly v. to it. |
| T-18 ..... VI.6:5 | your "enemy"; weak, v. and treacherous, |
| T-21 .......V.2:3 | you will see yourself as tiny, v. and afraid. |
| T-22 ... VI.10:6 | You see yourself as v., frail and easily |
| T-24 ..... III.3:1 | so v. and open to attack that just a word, |
| T-27 ......I.6:10 | demonstrate how frail and v. is your life; |
| W-pI .... 26.2:3 | therefore make you v. in your own mind, |
| W-pI .... 26.3:2 | must entail the belief that you are v., their |
| W-pI ..... 26.4:3 | thoughts can make you think you are v.. |
| W-pI .. 199.1:5 | were the truth, the mind were v. indeed! |
| P-2.........in.3:5 | wants to make the v. invulnerable and the |
| P-2........ IV.6:1 | the result of a view of the self as weak, v., |

**wage** 3

| | |
|---|---|
| T-21..... VII.2:6 | powerless, to w. their war of vengeance, |
| T-24.........I.9:5 | of battle which you w. against him. Here |
| T-25...... III.3:5 | off; the perfect battleground to w. its wars |

**waged** 1

| | |
|---|---|
| T-31....... II.1:4 | ancient battle being w. against the truth, |

**wages** 2

| | |
|---|---|
| T-10....... V.1:5 | and in this sense the w. of sin *is* death. The |
| T-19....... II.3:6 | For the w. of sin *is* death, and how can the |

**wait** 93

| | |
|---|---|
| T-1......... V.1:5 | You can w., delay, paralyze yourself, or |
| T-1......... V.2:1 | to w. on time any longer than is necessary |
| T-4......... III.7:8 | I must w. as long as you choose to forsake |
| T-4......... III.7:9 | Because I w. in love and not in impatience |
| T-5......... VI.1:1 | but His Kingdom is bereft while *you* w.. |
| T-7......... III.2:2 | it. It does not w. in time. It merely rests in |
| T-8......... IV.6:4 | I will w. until you change your mind. |
| T-9......... IV.9:2 | Judgment, but welcome it and do not w., |
| T-9...... VIII.3:6 | immediately. If you do not, it will w.. |
| T-13..... VII.6:5 | You w. but for yourself. To give this sad |
| T-13... VII.12:8 | He wills no delay to w. upon your joyous |
| T-14...... IX.7:1 | w. to make the mirror of your mind clean |
| T-16...... III.9:2 | w. for you will not draw you safely across. |
| T-16.... VI.10:6 | a place where truth and beauty w. for you |
| T-16.... VI.11:6 | W. no longer, for the Love of God and *you* |
| T-17....... II.8:3 | you this is so intense He would not w., |
| T-18...... IV.4:6 | They do not w. upon your willingness for |
| T-19...... IV.1:8 | You will not w. to give him this, for you |
| T-20.... II.11:5 | altar where the strength and freedom w., |
| T-20..... III.4:2 | hoping at most that death will w. a little |
| T-20....... V.3:5 | see it, but w. in patience for its coming. It |
| T-21....... V.5:3 | of God w. upon time to be accomplished. |
| T-24.......in.1:9 | God does not w. upon illusions to let Him |
| T-24...... III.5:6 | as one Mind They w. for all illusions to be |
| T-26 ...VIII.6:5 | Why w. till they unfold in time and fear |
| T-27 .... V.2:14 | is sufficient. Miracles w. not on time. |
| T-29 ...... V.3:1 | gives to you who w. upon the Son of God, |
| T-30 ..... III.8:3 | They w. for welcome and remembering. |
| T-30 ...... V.3:5 | he can barely stay and w. a little longer, |
| T-30 ...... V.3:6 | is he glad to w. till every hand is joined, |
| T-31 .......II.6:4 | Then let us w. an instant and be still, |
| W-pI..... 42.3:2 | to w. until you can sit quietly by yourself, |
| W-pI..... 63.4:2 | not, however, w. for such an opportunity. |
| W-pI... 72.10:9 | Then we will w. in quiet for His answer. |
| W-pI... 72.13:6 | *Father?* Then w. a minute or so in silence, |
| W-pI..... 75.6:6 | You merely w. to have it shown to you. |
| W-pI..... 75.6:7 | While you w., repeat several times, slowly |
| W-pI..... 75.7:5 | He will be with you as you watch and w.. |
| W-pI..... 75.7:8 | W. patiently for Him. He will be there. |
| W-pI..... 75.8:2 | And tell yourself you w. in certainty to |
| W-pI..... 77.5:1 | w. quietly for the assurance that your |
| W-pI..... 78.2:3 | We will not w. before the shield of hate, |
| W-pI..... 79.7:5 | will ask what it is, and w. for the answer. |
| W-pI..... 90.4:2 | *I need not w. for this to be resolved. The* |
| W-pI..... 94.4:1 | and w. in silent expectancy for the truth. |
| W-pI..... 96.8:4 | It. W. patiently, and let Him speak to you |
| W-pI... 98.10:2 | Repeat today's idea while you w. for the |
| W-pI... 104.2:5 | And we need not w. to have them. They |
| W-pI... 106.3:6 | today, and do not w. to reach Him longer. |
| W-pI... 106.5:4 | to all the multitude who w. to hear the |
| W-pI... 125.3:5 | but w. in silence for the Word of God. |
| W-pI... 130.8:4 | You w. for God to help you, as you say: *It* |
| W-pI... 131.6:1 | Why w. for Heaven? It is here today. |
| W-pI. 132.12:2 | creations w. for this release to give you |
| W-pI. 152.11:5 | *be.* Then will we w. in silence, giving up all |
| W-pI. 152.12:1 | patience w. for Him throughout the day, |
| W-pI. 153.17:2 | by and w. on Him and listen to His Voice, |
| W-pI... 154.8:4 | w. to give the messages you have received. |
| W-pI. 154.11:4 | who w. in misery may be at last delivered. |
| WpI.rV.in12:3 | We w. for the experience, and recognize |
| W-pI... 182.7:7 | He will w. until you hear His gentle Voice |
| W-pI... 188.1:1 | Why w. for Heaven? Those who seek the |
| W-pI... 188.2:2 | Why w. to find it in the future, or believe |
| W-pII .... in.2:2 | w. in quiet expectation for our God and |
| W-pII .... in.2:5 | along the road, and now we w. for Him. |
| W-pII .... in.4:1 | and w. for Him to take the step to us that |
| W-pII .... in.4:6 | and then we w. for Him to come to us. |
| W-pII .... in.5:5 | Sit silently and w. upon your Father. He |
| W-pII .... in.7:1 | And now we w. in silence, unafraid and |
| W-pII . 221.1:3 | *of my mind, I w. and listen for Your Voice.* |
| W-pII . 221.2:1 | Now do we w. in quiet. God is here, |
| W-pII . 221.2:2 | God is here, because we w. together. I am |
| W-pII . 221.2:6 | joined. We w. with one intent; to hear our |
| W-pII ..... 2.5:2 | to w. until his Father is remembered, |
| W-pII . 279.1:5 | I w. in chains which have been severed for |
| W-pII . 289.2:5 | *Shall I demand that You w. longer for Your* |
| W-pII . 311.2:1 | *Father, we w. with open mind today, to hear* |
| W-pII . 334.1:1 | I will not w. another day to find the |
| W-pII . 342.1:6 | *Let me not w. again today. Let me forgive all* |
| W-pII . 355.1:1 | *Why should I w., my Father, for the joy You* |
| W-pII . 355.1:6 | *not w. an instant more to be at peace forever.* |
| W-ep ......... 6:3 | In confidence we w. His answers, as we |
| M-4 .... VIII.1:1 | certain of the outcome can afford to w., |
| M-4 .... VIII.1:1 | can afford to wait, and w. without anxiety |
| M-6 ........... 1:9 | Healing must w., for his protection. |
| M-15 ....... 2:13 | aside in quiet listening, and w. for Him. |
| M-19 ......... 2:7 | fall short indeed of all that w. when the |
| M-27 ......... 3:4 | where worms w. to greet him and to last a |
| M-29 ......... 7:8 | God does not w., for waiting implies time |
| C-ep .......... 1:9 | you w. for this and trade it for illusions, |
| C-ep .......... 4:1 | Let us w. here in silence, and kneel down |
| P-2...........I.3:4 | But He will w., and His patience is infinite |
| S-3........ IV.8:3 | While you w. in sorrow Heaven's melody |

**waited** 5

| | |
|---|---|
| T-18 . VIII.13:4 | He has w. long to give you this. Receive it |
| T-30 .....II.1:10 | had but w. for your blessing to be born. |
| W-pI .. 125.5:1 | He has not w. until you return your mind |
| W-pII . 229.1:4 | So still It w. for my coming home, that I |
| S-1..........V.4:3 | you should come has w. long for you. |

**waiting** 42

| | |
|---|---|
| T-5 ....... VI.1:1 | God in His knowledge is not w., but His |
| T-5 ....... VI.1:2 | All the Sons of God are w. for your return |

M-16 ......... 4:7 as possible after w. take your quiet time,

## walk 111

T-1..... VII.3:13 as a single "slave" remains to w. the earth,
T-9........ III.7:3 only truth beside you for you w. together.
T-11....... III.4:6 Son. W. in light and do not see the dark
T-12........ II.7:5 Trust in my help, for I did not w. alone,
T-12........ II.7:5 I will w. with you as our Father walked
T-13.........I.3:6 God is guilty you will w. along this carpet,
T-13..... VII.1:2 where people w. alone and separate.
T-13... VII.16:2 We w. together on the way to quietness
T-17........ II.8:5 and w. with Him in trust out of this world
T-17........ V.9:4 w. together along a road far more familiar
T-18...... III.5:6 and w. with you in your advance to truth.
T-18..VIII.13:8 And w. into the garden love has prepared
T19.... IV.B.5:6 difficult for us to w. past barriers together
T19.... IV.C.2:3 They but w. past and it is gone. But what
T-20..... II.10:5 W. with him now rejoicing, for the savior
T-20..... II.11:3 brother w. the way of innocence together,
T-20.... VI.10:5 which you and your brother w. together,
T-20.... VIII.7:5 that those who seem to w. about in it, to
T-21.........I.1:2 or w. unharmed through open doorways
T-22...... IV.4:1 that you will see, who w. with Him! And
T-22...... IV.5:4 So shall you w. the world with me, whose
T-22....... V.1:9 And how can it be difficult to w. the way
T-22....... VI.7:3 shadow through which you w. completely
T-23........in.3:1 W. you in glory, with your head held
T-23........in.4:3 Think what a happy world you w., with
T-23........in.5:7 Who can w. trembling in a fearful world,
T-23........in.6:5 beautiful it is to w., clean and redeemed
T-23..... II.13:4 you w. in sanity with feet on solid ground,
T-23... II.22:12 not, you w. alone. Ask, then, your Friend
T-24....... V.4:2 And both will w. in danger, each intent,
T-24..... V.7:10 There is no journey but to w. with Him.
T-24... VII.11:1 and both appear to w. this earth without
T-25.... IV.5:12 you w. beyond the world of darkness into
T-25....... V.5:3 so you w. toward Heaven or toward hell,
T-25....... V.6:6 and you will w. the way you pointed out
T-26...... IX.7:2 you w. forgiveness gladly goes with you.
T-27.........I.1:3 W. you the gentle way, and you will fear
T-28....... V.3:6 and w. upon an alien ground which your
T-28...... VI.4:3 with every brother who would w. apart.
T-29....... II.4:6 help in giving them to all who w. apart,
T-30....... V.8:2 to w. with perfect confidence away from
T-30....... V.8:4 you the way that He must w. with you?
T-30....... V.10:8 in confidence w. with a happy heart that
T-30..... VII.7:2 which you w. in danger and uncertainty.
T-31....... II.9:3 be. He is afraid to w. with you, and thinks
T-31....... II.9:5 which is but to decide to w. with him, so
T-31...... II.11:3 or on following, you think you w. alone,
T-31...... II.11:4 light cannot be given while you w. alone,
T-31...... IV.1:8 you whatever road you choose to w. along
T-31....... V.5:4 and those who w. on them will not escape
T-31.... VIII.9:1 Let us be glad that we can w. the world,
W-pI..... 57.1:9 wishes and w. into the sunlight at last.
W-pI..... 70.9:1 easily w. on into the light of real salvation
W-pI..... 94.3:7 home in God to w. the world uncertainly.
W-pI... 106.3:2 world. W. lightly past their meaningless
W-pI... 107.7:6 We do not doubt we w. with truth today,
W-pI... 109.7:3 and energy restored to w. with lightened
W-pI. 122.12:2 Now we w. directly into light, and we
W-pI... 123.4:3 and w. with lightened footsteps as we go
W-pI... 124.2:4 our Companion as we w. the world a little
W-pI... 124.2:5 yet still remains with us as we w. on.
W-pI... 124.6:2 as in the ones who w. beside them now.
W-pI. 153.18:1 where you will w. in true defenselessness.
W-pI... 155.1:4 And the ones who w. the world as you do
W-pI... 155.2:5 let illusions w. ahead of truth is madness.
W-pI... 155.5:3 You w. this path as others walk, nor do
W-pI... 155.5:3 You walk this path as others w., nor do
W-pI... 155.9:1 W. safely now, yet carefully, because this
W-pI... 155.9:2 you are tempted still to w. ahead of truth,
W-pI... 155.9:3 your footsteps as you w. with certainty of
W-pI. 155.12:1 We w. to God. Pause and reflect on this.
W-pI. 155.12:5 God? We w. to God. The truth that walks
W-pI. 155.14:3 *way, For I would w. along the road to Him.*
W-pI...... 156.h I w. with God in perfect holiness.
W-pI... 156.1:5 you w. the world alone and separate from
W-pI... 156.2:4 You cannot w. the world apart from God,
W-pI... 156.4:4 on the ground that you may w. in softness
W-pI... 156.8:5 *I w. with God in perfect holiness. I light the*
W-pI... 157.3:2 its laws, and w. into eternity a while. This
W-pI. 166.13:4 Christ there is another way for them to w.
WpI... rV.in1:5 and doubts have made us w. uncertainly
WpI... rV.in3:5 *may w. more certainly and quickly unto You*
WpI... rV.in6:3 We w. together. I must understand
WpI... rV.in6:6 until you w. along the road with me.
WpI... rV.in9:6 hand, for this is not a way we w. alone. In
WpI... rV.in9:7 In him I w. with you, and you with me.
W-pI... 173.2:1 (156) I w. with God in perfect holiness.
W-pI...... 195.h Love is the way I w. in gratitude.
W-pI... 195.5:2 or who w. the way of hatred and the path
W-pI... 195.8:1 W., then, in gratitude the way of love.
W-pI. 195.10:6 For love can w. no road except the way of
W-pI. 195.10:6 and thus we go who w. the way to God.
W-pI... 215.1:1 (195) Love is the way I w. in gratitude.
W-pII. 233.2:2 And as we w. together, we will give this
W-pII..... 5.4:3 to help him w. along the road with him.
W-pII. 263.2:2 and w. together to our Father's house as
W-pII. 287.2:3 *that which leads to You could I desire to w.?*
W-pII. 288.1:6 *my heart, or I will lose the way to w. to You.*
W-pII. 324.2:3 We w. together, for we follow Him. And it
W-pII. 325.1:6 and help his brothers w. ahead with him,
W-ep......... 4:6 Now you w. with Him, as certain as is He
W-ep......... 5:5 And so we w. with Him from this time on,
W-ep......... 6:6 You do not w. alone. God's angels hover
M-3........... 2:2 "happening" to w. home together. These
M-10......... 5:5 rise up unburdened, and w. lightly on.
M-29......... 8:7 *And for all those who w. to God with me.*
C-2........... 7:4 extend before you as you w. in gentleness.
C-ep........... 1:5 remember that you w. with Him and with
C-ep........... 4:3 Now we are sure we do not w. alone. For
P-2........ III.1:2 should w. ahead of him to give him light
S-3.......... II.2:3 the need is done to w. the world of limits,

## walked 5

T-12....... II.7:5 walk with you as our Father w. with me.
T-12....... II.7:6 you not know that I w. with Him in peace
T-18...... III.1:1 to fantasy, have w. the way of dreams. For
T19... IV.D.9:2 this far unless his brother w. beside him.
T-22...... IV.4:3 and lonely journey where you w. alone.

## walking 13

T-18...... I.12:4 w. together with your brother out of this
T-19....... II.8:1 is like w. through a mist into the sun? For
T-22...... IV.6:5 saviors, w. the world with their Redeemer
T-25.... V.4:10 you, that you may find it, w. by his side.
T-31......... II.h W. with Christ
T-31... IV.10:8 w. there without your own reality at one
W-pI..... 57.1:6 I can leave simply by w. out. Nothing
W-pI..... 60.4:4 I am w. steadily on toward truth. There is
W-pI. 155.10:2 all illusions w. in the way you travelled
W-pI... 191.6:5 image of yourself w. the world in terror,
C-5........... 2:3 to be a separate being, w. by himself,
C-5........... 5:6 W. with him is just as natural as walking
C-5........... 5:6 as natural as w. with a brother whom you

## walks 32

T-17.. VII.10:1 Him Who w. with you in every situation.
T-18...... III.3:2 knew Who w. beside you on the way that
T-20...... IV.5:3 To each who w. this earth in seeming
T-20...... VI.2:7 It w. in sunlight, open-eyed and calm, in
T-23...... in.2:5 He w. in peace who travels sinlessly along
T-23...... in.2:6 For love w. with him there, protecting
T-24...... III.4:4 by everything that w. and breathes, or
T-24...... V.3:7 how lovingly He w. beside him, showing
T-24...... V.9:5 you, yet He w. beside you and before,
T-25...... in.2:7 he is, and w. with him within his holiness,
T-28...... VI.2:6 is changed, it w. as easily another way. It
T-29...... III.4:4 he w. through darkness to the everlasting
T-30....... II.5:2 And no one w. upon the earth but must
T-31....... II.6:5 us, but w. beside us on the selfsame road.
T-31...... V.1:4 Here it w. at home, where what it sees is
T-31.... VII.5:1 Have faith in him who w. with you, so
W-pI 131.14:2 w. with you the Spirit Heaven sent you,
W-pI.. 135.2:5 no one w. the world in armature but must
W-pI.. 155.6:4 Nor can the truth, which w. ahead of you,
W-pI 155.12:6 that w. before us now is one with Him,
W-pI.. 156.5:2 you, for they recognize Who w. with you.
W-pI.. 156.5:5 due to Holiness Itself, which w. with you,
W-pI.. 156.8:1 "Who w. with me?" This question should
W-pI.. 158.2:2 one who w. the world but has received it.
W-pI.. 166.6:1 bleed a little from the rocky road he w..
W-pI.. 166.6:3 and need but realize Who w. with him
W-pI 166.11:3 One w. with you Who gently answers all
W-pI.. 182.3:1 today for everyone who w. this world, for
W-pI.. 215.1:3 *He w. with me in love. And I give thanks to*
W-pII. 302.2:1 and w. beside us showing us the way. He
M-16....... 1:10 and sees the road on which he w. stretch
P-2........ III.1:1 that he w. slightly ahead of the patient,

## wall 20

T-4....... III.7:4 No one can see through a w., but I can
T-18. VIII.13:6 Him. Only a little w. of dust still stands
T-18..... IX.6:1 that seem to be a solid w. before the sun.
T19... IV.A.2:9 you let a little bank of sand, a w. of dust,
T19. IV.A.2:11 This little w. of hatred would still oppose
T19... IV.A.3:8 This little w. would hide the purpose of
T19. IV.A.4:11 little w. will fall away so quietly beneath
T19... IV.A.5:1 difficult than to surmount your little w..
T19... IV.A.6:4 Look not upon the little w. of shadows.
T-20... VI.11:2 seems to be a w. of flesh around the mind,
T-22..... III.5:7 w. that stands between you and the truth,
T-22..... III.5:8 at nothingness, as if it were a solid w., see
T-22..... IV.7:7 It is no solid w.. And only an illusion
T-25....... II.5:1 frame upon a w. and stands before it,
T-26........ I.2:3 entity is built a w. so seeming solid that it
T-26........ I.2:3 with what is locked away within the w..
T-29..... III.2:7 one with him without the w. the world
W-pI.... 17.2:6 say: *I do not see a neutral w., because my*
W-pI.... 36.3:5 *My holiness envelops that w.. My holiness*
W-pI.. 137.2:3 in pieces by a solid w. of sickened flesh,

## walled 1

W-pI.. 137.8:6 and minds that were w. off within a body

## walls 6

T-4....... III.7:3 through the w. you make to block it, and
W-pI.... 17.2:6 *my thoughts about w. are not neutral. I do*
W-pI 134.12:3 Nor need he erect the heavy w. of stone
W-pI.. 135.5:4 to make it beautiful or w. to make it safe,
M-25......... 2:6 for without them the w. that surround all
C-4........... 7:7 there is no journey, no belief in sin, no w.,

## wander 24

T-11..... III.5:4 you. When you w., you but undertake a
T-13... VIII.5:6 to all who think they w. in the darkness,
T-13... XI.11:5 From Him you cannot w., and there is no
T-14... VIII.3:1 mind w. not through darkened corridors,
T-15..... III.8:1 leave littleness behind, and w. not in vain
T-16... VI.12:1 Whenever your thoughts w. to a special
T-16.. VII.12:5 *Love. Let us not w. into temptation, for the*
T-18... VIII.9:3 who lost their way and w. in the dust.
T19 IV.D.10:8 choose whether to look upon it or w. on,
T-20........ I.3:3 not w. into the temptation of crucifixion,
T-20..... III.7:2 into the home of truth and who will w. off
T-21..... III.4:4 And when you w., He reminds you there
T-22...... in.2:8 so they w. through a world of strangers,
T-22........ I.1:7 without a plan of any kind except to w. off
T-26....... V.2:6 But it is hard indeed to w. off, alone and
T-27... VIII.4:2 And so you w. idly in and out of places
W-pI.... 62.5:6 Should your attention w., repeat the idea
W-pI.... 64.1:1 of saying "Let me not w. into temptation.
W-pI.... 95.4:2 at this point not to allow your mind to w.,
W-pI.. 123.2:2 yourself, nor let you w. in the dark alone.
WpI... rV.in3:4 *We w. off, but You will not forget to call us*
W-pI.. 200.9:3 if we attempt to w. can there be delay,
W-pI.. 220.1:2 *Let me not w. from the way of peace, for I am*
W-pII. 324.1:4 *I can but choose to w. off a while, and then*

**wandered** 6

T-20......III.7:2 who w. carelessly into the home of truth
T-22..........I.1:7 It is as though you w. in without a plan of
W-pI...125.5:2 you have w. off a little while from Him.
W-pII..317.2:5 *who thought mistakenly that he had w. from*
W-pII..329.1:1 *Father, I thought I w. from Your Will, defied*
S-3........IV.6:5 w. in a savage world with feet that bleed,

**wanderer** 2

T19....IV.B.9:8 you forever be a w. in search of peace?
W-pI.182.10:1 each time a w. would leave his home. For

**wandering** 14

T-2........VI.4:6 it. You are much too tolerant of mind w.,
T19...IV.A.7:4 Now it is aimless, w. pointlessly, causing
T19...IV.A.8:3 pointless w. makes its results appear to be
T-24......VI.9:2 A senseless w., without a purpose and
T-31......IV.9:4 it must have unless it be but futile w.? All
W-pI.....42.5:3 unless you find your mind is merely w.,
W-pI.....43.6:1 If you find your mind w.; if you begin to
WpI. rII.in.3:1 exercise period if you find your mind w.,
W-pI.....96.9:5 let your mind go w. in a world of dreams,
W-pI...122.7:2 Do not turn away in aimless w. again.
W-pI.131.13:3 did not quite forget in w. away in dreams.
W-pI.153.20:1 help you keep your mind from w. from its
W-pI...166.4:4 too; an outcast w. so far from home, so
W-pI...188.9:2 We take our w. thoughts, and gently

**wanderings** 1

W-pI...166.5:1 Yet in his lonely, senseless w., God's gifts

**wanders** 7

T-11......III.2:2 Kingdom is his, and yet he w. homeless.
T-29.....VII.2:5 And thus he w. aimlessly about, in search
T-31... VIII.7:1 everyone who w. in the world uncertain,
W-pI.....61.5:7 mind w. away from the central thought.
W-pI...131.4:6 When he w. off, he is led back to his
W-pI...166.5:4 He w. on, aware of the futility he sees
W-pI...166.5:5 Still he w. on in misery and poverty, alone

**wands** 1

W-pI...136.3:2 magic w. you wave when truth appears to

**wane** 1

W-pI...72.12:1 feel your confidence w. and your hope of

**waning** 1

M-27..........1:6 and w. in a certain way upon a certain

**want** 547

T-in............1:5 *can elect what you w. to take at a given time.*
T-1........IV.1:3 nothing you w. to hide even if you could.
T-1........VI.1:1 who w. peace can find it only by complete
T-2........VI.5:1 what you w. conflicts with what you do.
T-2........VI.5:6 doing what you do not wholly w. to do.
T-3........IV.7:2 Truth cannot deal with errors that you w..
T-3.........V.3:6 hardly w. to do it if you were in your right
T-4...........I.2:1 over their ideas because they w. to protect
T-4...........I.5:5 not natural for you to w. to obey its laws
T-4........III.4:7 that truly wants it, but it must w. it truly.
T-4........III.5:1 you will never w. to cover or hide it again.
T-4........IV.1:3 Yet this is what you w.. This is what you
T-4........IV.3:2 of something you w. and do not have.
T-4.........V.5:7 you may w. to learn has lasting value.
T-4.........V.5:8 many of the things you w. to learn may be
T-4........VI.4:3 but because you w. to believe that *you* are.
T-4........VI.5:8 you really w. the rewards of the ego in the
T-4........VI.7:2 to your brother is the only gift I w.. I will
T-4.......VII.5:1 but who w. to share it to increase their joy
T-4.......VII.7:3 but He does w. it brought to others. This
T-5.........in.3:2 You should w. to bless them in return,
T-5.........II.8:9 choose at which altar you w. to serve. The
T-5........IV.4:4 w. to show your brother anything except
T-5.........V.6:2 "What do you w.?" must be answered.
T-5.........V.7:4 you can think apart from God, and w. to.
T-5.........V.8:4 you w. you expect. This is not delusional.
T-5.......VII.3:6 means that you do not w. to be healed.
T-5.......VII.6:9 *I w. to decide otherwise, because I want to be*
T-5.......VII.6:9 *decide otherwise, because I w. to be at peace.*
T-6...........I.5:5 and one which I w. to share with you. If
T-6...........I.6:3 a lesson a Son of God should w. to teach if
T-6.........I.16:2 I do not w. you to allow any fear to enter
T-6.........II.3:8 that exists in you but which you do not w.
T-6.........II.9:8 the idea, and therefore does not w. it now
T-6......V.A.4:5 system I teach and w. you to teach. You
T-6......V.B.5:4 it. Yet you do w. peace, or you would not
T-6......V.B.8:3 is a positive affirmation of what you w..
T-6......V.C.2:1 w. you to teach error and learn it yourself.
T-6......V.C.6:2 you teach, and that you w. to learn peace.
T-6....V.C.10:1 is a statement of what you w. to believe,
T-6....V.C.10:3 is the sign that you *w.* Him to guide you.
T-7........IV.3:1 not w. to teach everyone all it has learned,
T-7........IV.6:3 *You do not w. it.* It is not a gift. It is nothing
T-7.......V.9:11 lies in you to give. Do you not w. to give it
T-7.......V.10:7 yours. I do not w. to share my body in
T-7.......V.10:9 Yet I do w. to share my mind with you
T-7......VI.4:10 maker, then, does not w. it. Rejection is
T-7........VI.6:5 Holy Spirit does not w. you to understand
T-7........VI.8:9 coexist in peace, and if you w. peace, you
T-7......VI.12:2 If you w. something else you will make
T-7.......VII.2:7 you w. to be *is* what you think you are.
T-7.......VII.2:8 What you w. to be, then, must determine
T-7.......VII.3:8 that he is what you would not w. to be.
T-7.....VII.3:11 and it must last as long as you w. it.
T-7.......VII.8:1 of depriving you of something you w.. Yet
T-7.......VII.8:2 do not value it, and therefore do not w. it.
T-7..... VIII.1:5 of getting rid of something it does not w..
T-7..... VIII.2:3 because it does not w. you to find conflict
T-7..... VIII.3:6 you do not w. by giving it away. Giving it
T-7.........X.1:3 really saw this result you could not w. it.
T-7.........X.1:4 only reason you could possibly w. any
T-7.........X.3:3 whether you w. to listen to what He says.
T-7.........X.5:2 guidance in any way, you w. to be weak.
T-7.........X.5:4 mean except that you w. to be fearful?
T-8...........I.2:6 not w. them on the basis of loss of peace,
T-8...........I.5:2 unhappy, and if you w. a different one,
T-8.........II.4:1 to teach that you w. to oppose God's Will.
T-8........III.1:4 w. understanding and enlightenment you
T-8........IV.4:2 Do you not w. to give it to the world as
T-8........IV.4:2 the world as much as you w. to receive it?
T-8........IV.4:4 If you w. to have it of me, you must give it
T-8........IV.4:7 The guidance must be what you w., or it
T-8........IV.6:3 His. If you w. to be like me I will help you,
T-8........IV.6:4 If you w. to be different, I will wait until
T-8.........V.1:4 truth as something they do not w., they
T-8.........V.6:8 hand because you w. to transcend the ego
T-8........VI.5:2 You w. your creations as He wants His.
T-8.......VI.5:10 And what else but joy would you w.? You
T-8........VI.8:1 "Do I w. to know my Father's Will for me
T-8.......VII.1:4 that attack can get you something you w..
T-8.....VII.16:4 what other hope would you w.? Freedom
T-8..... VIII.4:1 entirely out of keeping with what you w..
T-8..... VIII.4:4 w. the ego are predisposed to defend it.
T-8..... VIII.8:2 the distorting power of something you w.,
T-8..... VIII.8:3 of how what you w. distorts perception.
T-9...........I.3:3 awareness with something you do not w..
T-9...........I.3:6 is merely to remind you of what you w..
T-9...........I.6:6 be, when you ask for what you do not w.?
T-9...........I.7:2 You do not ask only for what you w.. This
T-9...........I.7:4 could not possibly give you what you w..
T-9...........I.8:7 cannot give you something you do not w..
T-9...........I.8:8 Universal Giver for what you do not w.,
T-9...........I.9:7 God is Love and you do w. Him. This *is*
T-9.........I.12:2 goal even though you do not w. it. But
T-9.........I.12:4 your mind to what you do not w.. How
T-9.........I.12:6 If you do not w. it, it was never created. If
T-9.........II.2:1 ask of the Holy Spirit is what you really w.
T-9.........II.2:2 of it would no longer *be* what you w.. This
T-9.......II.6:12 for you would not w. me to be deceived.
T-9.......II.10:6 not appreciate it and you will not w. it.
T-9.......II.11:9 is the measure of how much you w. it.
T-9.......II.12:4 His answer is all you can ask for and w..
T-9........III.5:3 w. to give yours over to the Holy Spirit,
T-9........III.8:5 that, but you do need to learn to w. it. For
T-9........VI.7:5 not w. anything the world has to offer.
T-9.......VII.8:5 Choose, then, what you w. in these terms,
T-9.......VII.8:6 You do not w. anything else. Return your
T-9......VIII.2:4 and you could not possibly w. it. The
T-9......VIII.6:2 and therefore you cannot w. the ego.
T-10.........I.4:3 impossible because you will w. only truth,
T-10........II.6:2 believe it can get you something you w.. It
T-10........II.6:3 w. something other than peace of mind,
T-10......III.5:1 whether its offering is really what you w.,
T-10......IV.5:7 of you that you could hardly w. it, if you
T-10.......V.2:2 you give because it is the message you w..
T-10.......V.3:4 in sickness could you possibly w. them.
T-11.........I.9:3 demand of you what you do not w. to give
T-11.........I.9:3 give, and thus deprive you of what you w..
T-11.......I.10:5 is the belief that makes you *w.* not to know
T-11........II.1:1 toward recognizing what you truly w..
T-11........II.1:6 what you really w. is therefore lost to you.
T-11........II.3:7 will, you do not know what you really w..
T-11........II.4:1 is a sign that you w. to make whole. And
T-11........II.5:3 your care is a sign that you w. Him. Think
T-11.......V.1:3 it, and since you realize you do not w. it,
T-11.....V.18:2 convinces you of what you w. to perceive,
T-11.....V.18:3 to the thought system you w. to be true.
T-11......VI.6:2 fact that it represents what you w. to be.
T-11....VIII.4:6 *Do I w. the problem or do I want the answer?*
T-11....VIII.4:6 *Do I want the problem or do I w. the answer?*
T-11..VIII.10:3 for It, you will give It because you w. It.
T-12.........I.1:2 If you w. to believe in error, you would
T-12.........I.7:3 recognize God's Answer as you w. It to be
T-12.........I.7:3 you want It to be, and if you w. It in truth,
T-12........II.6:1 still w. what God wills, and no nightmare
T-12.......II.10:1 the Holy Spirit everything you do not w..
T-12.......III.2:1 something you think you do not w. to do.
T-12.......III.9:7 For it is made out of what you do not w.,
T-12.....V.7:10 and succeed, for that is what you w.. But
T-12.....V.7:11 that there is something you w. to learn,
T-12.......V.8:1 what you do not w. should take heart, for
T-12.......V.9:6 you. For you really w. to learn aright, and
T-12......VI.2:7 Father but you do not really w. to do so,
T-12......VI.3:1 You do not w. the world. The only thing
T-12.....VII.6:7 are the same because you w. both of them
T-12.....VII.7:5 you w. in yourself you will make manifest,
T-12.....VII.7:6 you are projecting what you do not w., it
T-12.....VII.7:6 do not want, it is still because you *do* w. it.
T-12...VII.7:11 have accepted only one and w. but one.
T-12.....VII.8:1 you w. only love you will see nothing else.
T-12...VII.11:4 That is because you do not yet w. *only* that
T-12...VII.11:5 you will learn that you do w. only that.
T-12...VII.14:5 the ego, you believe that you w. death.
T-12...VII.14:6 from what you w. God does not save you.
T-13.......I.10:4 could you hold dear what you do not w.?
T-13........II.5:6 For the ego does w. to kill you, and if you
T-13........II.8:3 offerings, but though you do not w. them,
T-13......III.2:5 you do not w. the separation healed. You
T-13......III.2:9 for you. This is what you really w. to hide.
T-13.....VII.3:1 You do not really w. the world you see,
T-13.....VII.4:3 strange world you made but do not w..
T-13.....VII.9:2 you made for what you w. is the exchange
T-13...VII.14:1 from light, remember what you really w.,
T-13......XI.6:7 to help you realize that this is what you w.
T-13......XI.8:2 You may believe you w. It broken, and
T-14......III.2:3 You do not w. either alone, for without
T-14......III.5:7 what you do not w. without this penalty.
T-14....III.10:4 that what they do not w. must hurt them.
T-14....III.10:5 do not believe that what they w. is good.
T-14....III.10:8 gives them what they w. without effort,
T-14....III.10:8 of deciding what they w. and need alone.
T-14......IV.3:7 you must learn that it is all you w. to learn
T-14......IV.5:1 whether you w. to make decisions here.
T-14......IV.5:2 to decide against deciding what you w., in
T-14.....VII.1:1 do you w.? Light or darkness, knowledge
T-14.....VII.4:1 what you do not w. to what you do. You
T-14......XI.4:7 accept from you, because you do not w. it.
T-14......XI.6:4 that everything you learned you do not w.

T-14.... XI.13:2 all. For this it must be peace they w., and
T-14.... XI.14:1 w. peace you must abandon the teacher of
T-15...... IV.1:4 The one you w. it to be it is. The one you
T-15...... IV.1:9 into glad awareness while you do not w. it
T-15...... IV.2:4 much as you w. it will you bring it nearer.
T-15...... IV.4:4 instant any time and anywhere you w. it.
T-15...... IV.8:3 I w. to have perfect communication, and
T-15..... VII.7:1 attraction of what you do not w. seems to
T-15..... VII.7:1 than the attraction of what you do w.. For
T-15...... IX.1:5 accepted it as the only perception you w.,
T-15...... IX.2:2 gratification what you think you w.. The
T-15...... IX.7:5 the only truth that you could ever w.. All
T-15....... X.5:3 of the same idea, and one you do not w.,
T-15....... X.6:1 give all your guilt away whenever you w.,
T-15..... XI.9:5 they ever had, and ever w. to have.
T-15.... XI.10:6 *unless I w. to use you to imprison myself. In*
T-16......... I.3:1 you do not w. anything you value to come
T-16....... II.6:1 you of the truth of what you do not w..
T-16....... V.7:5 not w. for one he thinks he would prefer.
T-16...... V.10:1 as a triumph over God, would you w. it?
T-16...... V.12:5 Would you w. this to be possible, even
T-16...... V.13:2 of your completion you do not w. this.
T-16...... V.14:2 the extent to which you *w.* them to be true.
T-16...... VI.9:4 for you would not w. to be apart from it.
T-16... VII.2:11 serves some purpose that you w. fulfilled.
T-17....... II.8:1 How much do you w. salvation? It will
T-17.... III.6:10 For you will w. it more and more, and
T-17...... VI.2:1 simply, is "What do I w. to come of this?
T-17...... VI.2:8 It is aware of what it does not w., but only
T-17...... VI.4:1 what you w. to happen is simply that you
T-17.... VIII.3:1 Would you not w. to make a holy instant
T-18....... II.4:1 in which you literally scream, "I w. it thus
T-18....... II.5:1 it be, and that because you w. it you see it.
T-18...... IV.1:4 of recognizing that you w. it above all else
T-18....... V.4:3 Will be done," and not, "I w. it otherwise.
T-18...... VI.6:3 For it is still the fantasies you w., and they
T-18..... VI.14:1 is possible because you w. it. The sudden
T-19..... III.1:7 ego thinks you are, you will always w. it.
T-19..... III.2:7 For what you think is real you w., and will
T-19..... III.3:2 see clearly as a mistake you w. corrected.
T19... IV.A.2:1 Why would you w. peace homeless?
T19IV.A.17:10 believe that it can get you what you w..
T19.... IV.B.4:4 w. neither to get rid of peace nor limit it.
T19.... IV.B.4:6 You w. communion, not the feast of fear.
T19.... IV.B.4:7 You w. salvation, not the pain of guilt.
T19.... IV.B.4:8 guilt. And you w. your Father, not a little
T19.. IV.B.14:4 transmits to you the feelings that you w..
T-20....... V.3:6 worth when all you w. for him is peace.
T-20....... V.3:7 And what you w. for him you will receive.
T-20....... V.4:2 What would you w. except his offering?
T-20...... VI.9:3 substitute you w. for the eternal blessing
T-20...... VI.9:5 it, rising to welcome what you really w..
T-20.... VI.12:2 you have learned you really w. but one.
T-20..... VII.2:3 You recognize you w. the goal. Are you
T-20..... VII.2:6 w. a purpose you must be willing to want
T-20..... VII.2:6 must be willing to w. the means as well.
T-20..... VII.2:7 be sincere and say, "I w. this above all else
T-20..... VII.2:7 yet I do not w. to learn the means to get it
T-20.... VIII.2:1 Do you not w. to know your own Identity
T-20.... VIII.8:7 question never is whether you w. them,
T-20.... VIII.8:7 do you w. the purpose that they serve?
T-21......... I.3:3 happiness you w. to learn and not forget.
T-21....... II.4:6 you do not w. brought to the one you do.
T-21....... II.4:7 one you do is given you because you w. it.
T-21...... III.2:3 not your purpose and you no longer w. it.
T-21...... III.6:6 of a holy relationship is all you *w.* to see.
T-21...... IV.6:6 wish to look within, you do not w.. A few
T-21....... V.1:6 senseless ravings to those who w. to hear
T-21...... VI.8:5 assures you Heaven is what you w., and
T-21...... VI.8:5 Heaven is what you want, and all you w..
T-21... VII.5:14 *And do I w. to see what I denied because it is*
T-21..... VII.7:3 Whom you attack you *cannot* w. to heal.
T-21..... VII.7:7 what you w. to see must be your choice.
T-21..... VII.8:5 *Is this what I would see? Do I w. this?*
T-21... VII.10:8 And you can w. to see a sinless world, and
T-21... VII.11:7 When it is this you do not w., the rest are
T-21... VII.13:6 Desire what you w., and you will look on
T-22...... V.1:12 that needs defense you do not w., for
T-22...... VI.1:1 w. freedom of the body or of the mind?
T-22 ... VI.12:6 And this belief you w.. Yet wherein lies its
T-23 ........ I.2:3 it were, is this a victory that you would w.
T-23 ..... II.11:3 It must be what you w. but never found.
T-23 ..... II.12:1 But what is it you w. that needs his death
T-23 ..... III.3:2 is to accept but part of what you w.; to
T-23 ..... III.4:7 Would you not w. to recognize assault
T-23 ..... IV.8:2 They w. for nothing. Sorrow of any kind
T-24 ..... VI.7:1 body or his holiness as what you w. to see,
T-24 .... VII.9:5 is an image that you w. to be yourself. It is
T-25 ........ I.3:1 is a choice of what you w. yourself to be;
T-25 ........ I.3:1 yourself to be; the world you w. to live in,
T-25 ....... II.1:7 no rewards which you would w. to keep.
T-25 ..... III.1:3 believe it there because you w. it there.
T-25 ..... III.7:4 What do you w.? For these two questions
T-25 ..... III.7:9 w. to see peace and forgiveness descend
T-25 .. VII.13:1 make you sane and give you what you w.;
T-25 ..... IX.7:5 to solve for you means that you *w.* it solved
T-26 ....... II.6:4 For there are those you w. to suffer loss,
T-26 ....... II.7:2 one, for pain in any form you will not w..
T-26 ...... V.8:4 And do you w. that fearful instant kept,
T-26 VII.11:13 Can uncertainty be what you w.? Or is it a
T-26 .. VIII.3:8 you then would w. a little time in which
T-27 ..... III.6:3 in deciding that it is the only one you w..
T-27 ... IV.4:13 body get that you would w. the most of all
T-27 ... IV.4:15 But tell it what you w., and it will serve
T-27 ... IV.4:16 you what you w. and where to go for it. It
T-27 ..... IV.5:8 for he does not *w.* an honest answer where
T-27 .. VIII.2:3 it does not need and does not even w.. It
T-27 .. VIII.8:2 because you *w.* the guilt to rest on them.
T-27 . VIII.12:7 attest the thing you do not w. to know.
T-28 ..... II.10:2 and shows you its effects are what you w..
T-28 ..... III.3:6 for it is His coming that you w. above all
T-28 ... IV.10:3 w. to have the "benefits" of sickness when
T-28 ...... V.3:5 you will not w. to know your own Identity
T-28 ...... V.5:7 and make a witness to the world you w..
T-28 ..... VI.2:3 It behaves in ways you w., but never
T-28 ..... VI.3:1 thing you hate and fear and loathe and w.
T-28 ... VI.3:10 w. your mind to have and see and keep.
T-28 .... VII.1:4 that he could w. for something he has not
T-29 ..... IV.1:5 but only if you w. to live in dreams or to
T-29 ...... V.6:3 Would you not w. to be a friend to him,
T-29 .... VII.1:7 from a futile search for what you w.,
T-29 .... VII.8:6 because you w. their power as your own.
T-30 ........ I.1:8 But think about the kind of day you w.,
T-30 ........ I.1:9 Then try again to have the day you w..
T-30 ........ I.4:1 tell yourself again the kind of day you w.;
T-30 ........ I.4:1 have, the things you w. to happen to you,
T-30 ........ I.5:2 your mind to w. an answer that will work.
T-30 ........ I.6:1 (3) Remember once again the day you w.,
T-30 ........ I.7:3 until you believe the day you w. is one in
T-30 ........ I.7:4 day by robbing you of what you really w..
T-30 ........ I.9:3 something that you w. and that you need,
T-30 ...... I.11:2 but merely hope to get a thing you w..
T-30 ...... I.11:4 *I w. another way to look at this.* Now you
T-30 ...... I.11:5 and have remembered what you really w..
T-30 ...... I.11:6 the insane belief you w. it for the goal of
T-30 ...... I.11:7 in conflict when you ask for what you w.,
T-30 ...... I.16:2 adviser must agree on what you w. before
T-30 ...... I.16:7 The day you w. you offer to the world, for
T-30 ...... I.17:6 in mind, and you will have the day you w.
T-30 ....... II.2:8 Son made prisoner to what he does not w.
T-30 ..... III.1:7 This little thing I w., and it will be as
T-30 ..... III.2:6 You do not w. an idol. It is not your will
T-30 ..... III.2:9 you decide upon the form of what you w.,
T-30 ..... III.4:1 It never is the idol that you w.. But what
T-30 ..... III.4:2 w. indeed and have the right to ask for.
T-30 ..... III.4:8 It is not this you w.. Creation gives no
T-30 ..... IV.6:4 not w. whatever you believe an idol gives.
T-30 ..... IV.7:4 no longer for the things you do not w..
T-30 ... IV.8:11 him no single thing that he could ever w..
T-30 ...... V.7:2 and think they see an idol that they w..
T-30 ... VIII.3:3 those you would not w. to have reality.
T-30 ... VIII.4:6 that can be given you unless you w. it.
T-31 ....... I.11:1 and have an outcome that you do not w.?
T-31 ....... I.11:3 if you believe you w. disaster and disunity
T-31 ....... II.3:3 advantages you would not w. to lose. So
T-31 ....... II.4:3 you w. to let the follower in you arise, and
T-31 ....... II.5:2 What does he w. of you? What could he
T-31 ....... II.5:3 What could he w., but what you want of
T-31 ....... II.5:3 could he want, but what you w. of him?
T-31 ...... II.5:14 hear your voice requesting what you w..
T-31 ....... II.6:6 from what we w. as we will let him be. We
T-31 ....... II.8:6 and learn the truth of what you really w..
T-31 ....... II.8:8 away without the thoughts you did not w.
T-31 ..... II.10:3 He asks for what you w., and needs the
T-31 ... III.2:10 could the outcome be that you would w.?
T-31 ..... III.6:6 will not w. to hold in guilt your chosen
T-31 ....... V.4:3 The other side he does not w. to see. Yet it
T-31 ..... V.17:1 images of you unless you w. to learn them
T-31 ..... VI.1:7 for you have chosen that you w. it so. But
W-pI ...... 4.2:6 seeing impossible. You do not w. either.
W-pI .... 20.2:3 You w. salvation. You want to be happy.
W-pI .... 20.2:4 You w. to be happy. You want peace. You
W-pI .... 20.2:5 You w. peace. You do not have them now,
W-pI .... 20.3:2 What you w. is yours. Do not mistake the
W-pI .... 20.4:1 throughout the day that you w. to see.
W-pI .... 20.4:3 for a better one, and one you really w..
W-pI .... 22.2:1 this savage fantasy that you w. to escape.
W-pI .... 22.3:8 *this the world I really w. to see?* The answer
W-pI .... 23.2:1 it is these thoughts which you do not w..
W-pI .... 24.4:2 be on uncovering the outcome you w..
W-pI .... 25.4:5 is what you w. to reach him for. And it is
W-pI ....... 27.h Above all else I w. to see.
W-pI .... 27.2:1 when you say you w. to see above all else.
W-pI .... 27.4:2 much do you w. today's idea to be true?
W-pI ....... 28.h all else I w. to see things differently.
W-pI .... 28.2:1 all else I w. to see this table differently."
W-pI .... 28.3:1 all else I w. to see this table differently,"
W-pI .... 28.4:3 all else I w. to see this table differently,"
W-pI .... 28.8:2 *Above all else I w. to see this_differently.*
W-pI .... 30.2:3 and what we w. to recognize is there.
W-pI .... 32.1:5 While you w. it you will see it; when you
W-pI .... 32.1:5 it you will see it; when you no longer w. it,
W-pI .... 35.2:2 yourself with the environment you w..
W-pI .... 35.2:3 w. it to protect the image of yourself that
W-pI .... 38.5:1 to time you may w. to vary this procedure
W-pI .... 39.5:2 w. to exceed the minimum requirements,
W-pI .... 40.2:4 any circumstances, if you really w. to.
W-pI .... 45.5:1 God would have us do is what we w. to do
W-pI .... 48.1:5 it for those who w. illusions to be true.
W-pI .... 51.2:5 in my judgments, because I w. to see. My
W-pI .... 51.2:6 and I do not w. to see according to them.
W-pI .... 51.5:6 that has hurt me, and that I no longer w..
W-pI .... 56.2:1 (27) Above all else I w. to see.
W-pI .... 56.3:1 (28) Above all else I w. to see differently.
W-pI .... 57.2:5 in this belief, which I no longer w.. The
W-pI .... 61.4:1 will w. to think about this idea as often as
W-pI .... 61.6:3 find them helpful and w. to extend them.
W-pI .... 62.5:7 *remember this because I w. to be happy.*
W-pI .... 65.7:1 extent to which you really w. salvation in
W-pI .... 65.8:3 *I w. no other and I have no other.* Sometimes
W-pI .... 69.6:1 you w. to reach the light in you today,–
W-pI .... 69.9:1 will w. to do as often as possible in view of
W-pI .... 69.9:6 *Yet I w. to let it be revealed to me, for my*
W-pI .... 70.5:2 healed, and we do not really w. to be sick,
W-pI .... 70.5:4 He does not w. us to be sick. Neither do
W-pI .... 70.9:1 you, surely you do not w. to remain in the
W-pI .... 73.5:7 Do you really w. to be in hell? Do you
W-pI .... 73.5:8 you really w. to weep and suffer and die?
W-pI .... 73.6:3 You cannot w. this for yourself. There is a
W-pI .... 73.6:5 and it is happiness you really w.. Such is
W-pI .... 73.6:8 You w. to succeed in what we are trying to
W-pI .... 73.7:1 that you w. salvation for yourself. You
W-pI .... 73.7:2 You w. to accept God's plan because you
W-pI .... 73.7:3 oppose it, and you do not w. to do so.
W-pI .... 73.7:5 you w. the freedom to remember Who
W-pI .. 73.11:1 make a declaration of what you really w..
W-pI .... 75.3:3 accept the new world as what we w. to see
W-pI .... 75.4:2 This is what we w. to see, and only this.
W-pI .... 75.5:1 We do not w. to see the ego's shadow on
W-pI .... 77.8:4 *I w. only what belongs to me. God has*
WpI.. rII.in.3:4 that it belongs to you, and that you w. it.
W-pI .... 85.1:3 this, what do I w. my grievances for? They
W-pI .... 85.1:7 I w. to see, and this will be the means by
W-pI .... 85.2:5 *this away. I have no need for this. I w. to see.*
W-pI .... 89.3:6 I w. all of Heaven and only Heaven, as
W-pI .... 91.5:3 body. Faith goes to what you w., and you
W-pI .. 98.11:2 He will make you sure you w. this choice,

W-pI...99.10:3 You do not w. to be another self. You
W-pI...102.1:1 You do not w. to suffer. You may think it
W-pI...102.1:2 a little that it buys you what you w.. Yet
W-pI...104.5:5 *God's gifts of joy and peace are all I w..*
W-pI...106.1:1 that give you nothing that you really w.; if
WpI. rIII.in4:1 lost because you did not w. to do them,
W-pI...116.2:3 *What He has given me is all I w.. What He*
W-pI......122.h Forgiveness offers everything I w..
W-pI...122.1:1 could you w. forgiveness cannot give? Do
W-pI...122.1:2 Do you w. peace? Forgiveness offers it.
W-pI...122.1:4 it. Do you w. happiness, a quiet mind,
W-pI...122.1:5 world? Do you w. care and safety, and the
W-pI...122.1:6 w. a quietness that cannot be disturbed,
W-pI...122.3:3 would you w. forgiveness cannot give?
W-pI.122.13:1 Forgiveness offers everything you w..
W-pI.122.13:2 Today all things you w. are given you. Let
W-pI.122.14:3 *Forgiveness offers everything I w.. Today I*
W-pI......128.h The world I see holds nothing that I w..
W-pI...128.2:5 world you see holds nothing that you w..
W-pI...128.4:1 holds anything you w. to hold you back.
W-pI...128.8:4 *The world I see holds nothing that I w..*
W-pI......129.h Beyond this world there is a world I w..
W-pI...129.3:2 Is it loss to find all things you really w.,
W-pI...129.3:2 exactly as you w. them throughout time?
W-pI...129.4:6 you exchange it for the world you w..
W-pI...129.5:2 back to see again the world you do not w..
W-pI...129.6:3 world holds nothing that you really w.,
W-pI...129.6:3 what you choose instead you w. indeed!
W-pI...129.6:5 of all the things you seek but do not w..
W-pI...129.7:3 *Beyond this world there is a world I w..*
W-pI...129.7:4 *of this, for here is nothing that I really w..*
W-pI...129.9:4 this: *The world I see holds nothing that I w..*
W-pI...129.9:5 *Beyond this world there is a world I w..*
W-pI...130.1:3 reflects your choice of what you w. to see.
W-pI...130.1:4 for what you value you must w. to see,
W-pI...130.2:2 desire what he does not w. to have reality
W-pI...130.3:5 would you w. that this is shown to you?
W-pI...130.8:2 You do not w. illusions. And you come to
W-pI.130.11:5 *and this is not a part of what I w..*
W-pI...131.3:4 yet holding everything you really w..
W-pI...131.4:2 and must find the goal you really w.. No
W-pI...131.4:3 fail to w. this goal and reach it in the end.
W-pI...131.5:5 It will go because you do not w. it. You
W-pI...131.5:6 it. You will reach the goal you really w. as
W-pI...131.6:7 what you chose from what you really w..
W-pI.131.11:4 *the thoughts I w. to think are not my own.*
W-pI.131.12:4 nothing before this door you really w.,
W-pI.131.15:5 *Today I seek and find all that I w.. My single*
W-pI...132.2:4 of seeking what you do not w. to find.
W-pI...132.5:2 but your mind on what you w. to see, and
W-pI...133.3:1 which to test all things you think you w..
W-pI...135.8:3 w. to keep it when its usefulness is done?
W-pI...138.1:2 an opposite, and what we w. we choose. If
W-pI.138.12:4 acknowledging we chose but what we w.:
W-pI.138.12:6 *my mind, because it is the only thing I w..*
W-pI...139.4:3 shows he does not w. to be the thing he is.
W-pI...141.2:1 (122) Forgiveness offers everything I w..
W-pI...144.2:1 The world I see holds nothing that I w..
W-pI...145.1:1 Beyond this world there is a world I w..
W-pI...163.7:2 by those who did not w. Him to survive.
W-pI...164.8:1 letting go all things you think you w..
W-pI...164.9:4 But this you surely w.; you can exchange
W-pI...165.5:2 that you request the only thing you w..
Wi181-200 2:6 You will be sure of what you w., and what
W-pI...181.8:4 When seeing this is all we w. to see, when
W-pI......185.h I w. the peace of God.
W-pI...185.2:9 words express the only thing they w..
W-pI...185.5:1 To mean you w. the peace of God is to
W-pI...185.7:2 We w. the peace of God. This is no idle
W-pI.185.10:1 You w. the peace of God. And so do all
W-pI.185.10:4 For thus you reach to what they really w.,
W-pI...190.6:4 the joy of God as what you really w.. Your
W-pI...196.7:2 at least consider if you w. to go along this
W-pI...196.9:5 You are strong, and it is strength you w..
W-pI.200.11:3 ours, and only this will we accept and w..
WpI rVI.in.6:2 *This thought I do not w.. I choose instead*
W-pI...205.1:1 (185) I w. the peace of God. *The peace of*
W-pI...205.1:2 *The peace of God is everything I w.. The*
W-pII..225.1:2 *return it, for I w. it mine in full awareness,*
W-pII..226.1:4 I w. to keep as mine or search for as a goal
W-pII..231.1:4 *nothing else that I could ever really w. to find*
W-pII..242.2:3 *not ask for anything that we may think we w.*
W-pII..251.1:3 before I needed not, and did not even w..
W-pII..251.1:8 Now have I everything that I could w..
W-pII..251.2:2 *restored, and only that is what we really w..*
W-pII..253.1:4 not occur is what I do not w. to happen.
W-pII..254.2:3 not w. what they would bring with them.
W-pII..257.1:4 to remember what we w. today, that we
W-pII..258.2:3 *What could we w. but to remember You?*
W-pII..271.1:1 I am choosing what I w. to look upon, the
W-pII..271.1:1 to look upon, the sounds I w. to hear, the
W-pII..271.1:1 to what I w. to be the truth for me. Today
W-pII..297.1:1 gift I give, because it is the only gift I w..
W-pII..316.2:3 *worth, and cherish only them as what I w..*
W-pII..325.1:1 which starts with my idea of what I w..
W-pII..335.1:3 it stands for what I w. to be the truth. It is
W-pII..339.1:7 request that he would w. when he receives
W-pII..339.1:9 resolve today to ask for what we really w.,
W-pII..347.1:1 *Father, I w. what goes against my will, and*
W-pII..347.1:1 *my will, and do not w. what is my will to have*
W-pII..349.1:3 *because I have chosen it as the gift I w. to give*
W-pII.....358.h be sure; His answer is the one I really w..
W-pII..358.1:1 *I really am alone remember what I really w..*
W-pII..358.1:4 *mine as well, and all I w. is what You offer me*
W-ep .........2:4 of what you really w. and really need. His
M-in ..........2:5 a means of choosing what you w. to teach
M-in ..........2:5 teach on the basis of what you w. to learn.
M-2 ...........3:7 to decide when you w. to learn it. And as
M-4 .....I.A.6:6 "Give up what you do not w., and keep
M-4 .....I.A.7:3 so far was that he did not w. the valueless,
M-4 .....I.A.7:3 valueless, and that he did w. the valuable.
M-4 .....VII.2:3 does not w. anything he cannot give away
M-4 .....VII.2:4 What would he w. it *for*? He could only
M-4 .....VII.2:8 He does not w. to suffer. Why should he
M-4 ...VII.2:10 w. to keep for himself all things that are
M-7 ...........6:6 If you really w. the problem solved, you
M-7 ...........6:9 wishes. Be sure of what you w., and doubt
M-10 .......6:11 peace. Can it be difficult to w. but this?
M-13 .........6:4 means the giving up of what you w.. And
M-13 .........6:5 what, O teacher of God, is it that you w.?
M-14 .........1:6 that they serve a need or gratify a w..
M-16 .......11:1 Is not this an exchange that you would w.
M-20 .........4:6 and think of this: Is conflict what you w.,
M-22 .........3:9 who would w. salvation at such a price?
M-29 .........2:11 w. to be responsible for decisions about
P-2.........in.4:1 be, he must w. to change the patient's self-
S-1 ...........I.5:6 to ask because there is nothing left to w..
S-1 ......... II.2:6 for you have established what it is you w..
S-2 ...........I.4:3 You w. to see them there, and not in you.
S-2 ......... II.8:4 You do not w. to stay in slavery. You do
S-2 ......... II.8:5 You do not w. to be afraid of God. You
S-2 ......... II.8:6 You w. to see the sunlight and the glow of

### wanted 30

T-8...........I.4:4 it means that you did not get what you w..
T-8........VI.4:4 his father's treasure. He w. nothing else.
T-12....... V.4:4 w. to retain the characteristics of creation
T-13....... X.4:7 You w. not salvation in the past. Would
T-15.....VII.3:5 question will be why it was you ever w. it.
T19....IV.B.1:2 of guilt holds sway, peace is not w.. The
T-21... VIII.1:6 Surely he thought he w. happiness. Yet he
T-23......IV.9:7 there that offers less, yet could be w. more
T-24....VI.11:5 for this; you w. specialness to be the truth
T-24...VII.8:10 of a wish; an image that you w. to be true.
T-25......VI.7:3 You w. it, and it is given you. All that you
T-28....... II.4:5 that it pictures what you w. shown to you.
T-29.........I.5:1 brother's unless you w. it to be a cause of
T-29......IV.4:4 not matter if they be fulfilled or merely w.
T-29......IV.4:6 Dreams are not w. more or less. They are
T-29... VIII.1:9 or a circumstance, an object owned or w.,
T-30....... V.2:4 And idols are not w. there, for guilt is
T-30....... V.2:5 as things not w. and not striven for. The
T-30....... V.5:2 when they are still perceived but w. not.
T-30....... V.9:3 lies ahead is all you ever w. in your heart.
T-30....... V.9:6 You never w. it. What happiness have you
T-31.........I.2:8 you accomplished it because you w. to,
T-31.........I.8:7 had lost a friend who always w. to be part
W-pI.....70.8:6 imagined that endured, or that you w..
W-pI.....99.7:5 yourself the thought He w. this for you.
W-pI...185.3:4 the outcome w. not the same for both.
W-pI.185.10:5 your purpose, and unsure of what you w.,
W-pII ....in.9:2 We w. God to change Himself, and be
W-pII ..... 1.2:4 the aim that it has chosen as its w. goal?
S-2...........I.1:5 used to hurt because forgiveness is not w..

### wanting 20

T-2........ VI.5:4 should, but without entirely w. to do so.
T-2........ VI.6:8 because w. and doing are discordant. This
T-3........ VI.2:6 and rejected, or judged and found w.,
T-4........ III.4:8 and this kind of w. is wholly without the
T-4........ IV.8:8 brought to judgment and found w. there.
T-4......... V.5:5 Learning and w. to learn are inseparable.
T-4........ VI.6:7 them my strength as long as theirs is w..
T-7..... VII.11:3 W. this only you will *have* this only, and
T-8......... V.6:9 My strength will never be w., and if you
T-12..... VII.7:5 the world because you put it there by w. it
T-12... VII.13:4 W. to kill you as the final expression of its
T-18....... V.5:6 and nothing will be w. that would make
T19. IV.A.15:1 gives you, w. no messages but theirs, you
T19... IV.D.5:8 Your w. fear seemed to be holding them
T-20..... VII.3:8 your w. of the purpose has been shaken.
T-21........II.4:8 power of your w. must first be recognized
T-21........II.9:2 better demonstration of the power of w.,
T-25....... V.2:7 to maintain the wish, while w. innocence?
W-pI... 185.5:3 has looked on them, and found them w..
S-1..........II.1:5 At these levels prayer is merely w., out of

### wants 100

T-1........ VI.1:2 he w. to learn it and believes in some way
T-2........ VI.5:3 that w. to do something else is outraged.
T-2........ VI.6:8 so whenever it is conflicted in what it w.,
T-4........ III.4:7 into any mind that truly w. it, but it must
T-4........ III.4:8 means that it w. it without ambivalence,
T-5......... V.6:1 interpret them according to what it w.,
T-6........ IV.4:3 defense is attack, and w. *you* to believe it.
T-6.... V.A.5:11 back, because He w. you to keep it.
T-7......... V.7:1 healer w. gratitude from his brothers, but
T-7........ VI.4:9 No one who has everything w. the ego. Its
T-7........ VI.6:5 conflict; He w. you to realize that, because
T-7........ VI.8:3 as you are, it can see itself as it w. to be.
T-7........ VI.8:4 of its weakness the ego w. your allegiance,
T-7........ VI.8:5 The ego therefore w. to engage your mind
T-7........ VI.8:6 it. It w. no part of truth, because the ego
T-8........ VI.5:1 God w. only His Son because His Son is
T-8........ VI.5:2 You want your creations as He w. His.
T-8........ IX.6:1 ego, which always w. to weaken the mind,
T-8........ IX.6:6 The ego w. only what it hates. To the ego
T-8........ IX.6:8 in the power of attack, the ego w. attack.
T-9...........I.8:5 no one really w. either abandonment or
T-9......VIII.8:5 God w. you to behold what He created
T-11.........I.9:4 Would God, Who w. only your will, be
T-11..... V.10:1 from how the ego w. you to experience it,
T-11....... V.10:8 no one w. to find what he believes would
T-12.........I.5:2 to him has become what he w. it to be. If
T-12........II.3:4 he really w. is to offer it unto yourself, for
T-12...... III.4:8 is valuable and w. to accept nothing else.
T-12...... IV.3:1 surely obvious that no one w. to find what
T-12..... VII.6:8 and if it is split and w. to keep the split, it
T-12....VIII.5:2 that has obliterated it and w. to keep it so.
T-13.........I.1:2 The Holy Spirit w. only this, for sharing
T-13........II.1:2 ego w. to retain guilt *you* find it intolerable
T-13. VII.10:11 The ego w. to have things for salvation,
T-13...... XI.9:2 from what the Holy Spirit w. to teach you.
T-15.........I.3:2 and what it w. for you it cannot tolerate.
T-15.........I.3:3 The ego w. *you* dead, but not itself. The
T-15..... VII.6:3 and avoid delaying what it really w.. Yet
T-15..... VII.7:3 Yet this is what he thinks he w.. He is not
T-15..... VII.9:7 what the ego really w. you do not realize.
T-16...... VI.5:8 The ego w. but part of him, and sees only
T-17...... III.6:3 The Holy Spirit w. only to make His
T-17...... VI.2:7 know what it w. to come of the situation.
T-18....VIII.3:6 terrifies the little ripple and w. to swallow
T-19........II.6:5 from an idea of God to an ideal the ego w.
T-20.........II.2:4 every gift it offers depends on what it w..

T-20....... II.2:5 to receive the gifts it w. by offering them
T-20....... V.3:2 all it means is that it w. the other for itself
T-20...... VI.4:5 w. them solely for the offerings on which
T-21....... II.8:6 hand, for everyone believes in what he w..
T-21....... II.9:1 is how the ego deals with what it w., to
T-21....VIII.3:7 God has already given all that he really w.
T-22...... III.2:4 sin and mistakes, because it w. correction
T-22....... V.2:1 Consider what the ego w. defenses for.
T-23....... II.8:6 enable you to find escape from what it w..
T-23..... II.14:1 No one w. madness, nor does anyone
T-23..... II.17:9 condemning what it says it w. to save. Be
T-24...... III.4:6 a secret vow that what God w. for you will
T-24..... VII.1:1 the specialness he w. to be the truth! His
T-24... VII.10:8 means to offer to the "father" what he w..
T-25...... VI.2:5 the darkness and maintain he w. to see?
T-25..... VII.9:2 to him that it is an alternative he really w.
T-30...... IV.6:1 deceive the mind that w. to be deceived.
T-31.........I.1:5 be hard to learn by anyone who w. it to be
W-pI..... 49.3:4 He w. you to hear His Voice. He gave It to
W-pI..... 59.3:3 I can see what God w. me to see. I cannot
W-pI..... 62.4:2 day as happy for you as God w. you to be.
W-pI..... 70.3:4 He w. you to be healed, so He has kept the
W-pI..... 70.5:2 God w. us to be healed, and we do not
W-pI..... 70.5:6 do we. He w. us to be healed. So do we.
W-pI..... 76.5:5 enemy; that it attacks itself and w. to die.
W-pI... 100.7:4 or anyone who w. to take his place among
W-pI... 121.4:3 It w. to live, yet wishes it were dead. It
W-pI... 121.4:4 It w. forgiveness, yet it sees no hope. It
W-pI... 121.4:5 It w. escape, yet can conceive of none
W-pI... 130.1:6 fail to look upon what he believes he w..
W-pI... 133.8:6 For what the ego w. it fails to recognize. It
W-pI. 136.12:4 it. Truth merely w. to give you happiness,
W-pI... 152.1:3 unless these are the outcomes that he w..
W-pI... 153.6:4 too sleepy to remember what he w..
W-pI... 161.2:6 to your mind the sounds it w. to hear.
W-pI... 185.2:4 He w. the peace of God, and it is given
W-pI... 185.2:5 For that is all he w., and that is all he will
W-pI... 185.5:2 one means these words who w. illusions,
W-pI... 185.6:1 it w. is peace must join with other minds,
W-pI... 193.4:4 one but w. to see the simple lesson there.
W-pII . 242.2:5 *us. You know all our desires and our w.. And*
W-pII . 339.1:6 confused indeed about the things he w.;
M-4 ..... I.A.7:8 what he really w. in every circumstance.
M-13 ......... 3:3 to know not what it really w. to find. Who
M-21 ......... 3:4 if he w. what does not exist or seeks for
M-22 ......... 2:7 has decided on the direction he w. to take
M-22 ......... 4:2 anyone actually believe he w. to be sick.
M-25 ......... 4:6 which the Holy Spirit w. and needs. Yet
P-2.........in.1:5 anger brings him something he really w.,
P-2.........in.2:8 this price. Now he w. a "better" illusion.
P-2.........in.3:3 to get the changes he w. without changing
P-2.........in.3:5 w. to make the vulnerable invulnerable
S-1........ III.6:7 one who w. an enemy will fail to find one.
S-2........ III.1:3 evaluate the errors that it w. to overlook.

## war 69

T-5......... II.7:8 Peace is stronger than w. because it heals.
T-5......... II.7:9 W. is division, not increase. No one gains
T-5........ III.8:7 reality, w. is the guarantee of its survival.
T-5...... III.8:13 are as closely related as are time and w..
T-7........ III.3:1 itself at w. and therefore in need of allies.
T-7........ III.3:2 w. must look for brothers and recognize
T-7........ VI.7:4 within it that have led to a state of w., and
T-8...........I.3:1 Every response to the ego is a call to w.,
T-8...........I.3:1 to war, and w. does deprive you of peace.
T-8...........I.3:2 Yet in this w. there is no opponent. This
T-10...... IV.1:6 God is not at w. with the god of sickness
T-13.... III.11:2 In w. he demanded everything and found
T-13...... XI.1:2 conflict and ravaged by a cruel w. unless
T-13...... XI.1:2 that both opponents in the w. are real.
T-13...... XI.1:3 a w. would surely end his peace of mind,
T-13...... XI.1:4 the w. is between real and unreal powers,
T-13...... XI.2:2 a bitter w. from which you *have* escaped.
T-13...... XI.2:3 The w. is gone. For you have heard the
T-13...... XI.2:6 so you made not a w. that could endanger
T-13...... XI.2:8 The w., the guilt, the past are gone as one
T-14..... II.1:10 of dust, a body or a w. are one to you. For
T-16...... IV.2:5 safety, translated quietly from w. to peace
T-19 ..... III.6:3 is real, God must be at w. with Himself.
T-21 .... VII.2:6 powerless, to wage their w. of vengeance,
T-23 ............ h THE W. AGAINST YOURSELF
T-23 ......in.2:1 indeed becomes this w. against yourself!
T-23 ........I.1:2 for a mind at w. against itself remembers
T-23 ........I.1:3 means of w. are not the means of peace,
T-23 ........I.1:4 W. is impossible unless belief in victory is
T-23 ........I.1:7 you realize the ego is at w. with God.
T-23 ........I.2:1 Do you not realize a w. against yourself
T-23 ........I.2:1 against yourself would be a w. on God? Is
T-23 ........I.2:8 This is no w.; only the mad belief the Will
T-23 ........I.4:1 the w. against yourself is almost over. The
T-23 ........I.4:7 The Son of God at w. with his Creator is a
T-23 ........I.5:1 The w. against yourself was undertaken
T-23 ........I.6:1 w. against yourself is but the battle of two
T-23 ........I.7:8 yet the w. of two illusions is a state where
T-23 ........I.9:2 it is seen as w. between conflicting truths;
T-23 ......I.12:2 The meeting of illusions leads to w.. Peace
T-23 ......I.12:4 W. is the condition in which fear is born,
T-23 ......I.12:9 Yet far beyond this senseless w. it shines,
T-23 .......II.7:4 every aspect seems to be at w. with Him,
T-23 ..... IV.1:1 conflict, for there *is* no w. without attack.
T-24 ........I.1:5 And now must w., the substitute for
T-24 ........I.2:2 belief is a decision to w. in secret, where
T-24 ...... V.8:1 seek salvation in a w. with love, consider
T-25 ..... III.6:6 He will hear plainly that the calls to w. he
T-27 ...... V.3:3 and demonstrates that w. has no effects.
T-27 ...... V.3:4 all the hurt that w. has sought to bring,
T-27 .. VII.10:1 or death, waking or sleeping, peace or w.,
T-27 .. VII.13:3 his Father, and made w. upon himself. So
T-28 ...... V.3:7 You will make w. upon your Self, which
T-31 ......I.10:4 beyond each form of hate; each call to w..
T-31 .......II.1:5 Who could be hurt in such a w., unless he
W-pI..... 14.4:5 *God did not create that w., and so it is not*
W-pI..... 16.3:1 you have brings either peace or w.; either
W-pI..... 57.4:3 will understand that peace, not w., abides
W-pI. 136.16:1 take the place of w. and vain imaginings.
W-pI... 170.3:2 within; an alien thought at w. with you,
W-pII ..... 2.2:1 instant that his mind had thought of w..
M-4 ........II.2:2 only the wish to deceive that makes for w.
M-11 ......... 4:1 is impossible to those who look on w..
M-14 ......... 5:3 end in peace, because it is a place of w..
M-20 ......... 3:8 For what except attack will lead to w.?
M-20 ......... 3:9 And what but peace is opposite to w.?
M-20 ......... 3:11 peace is found, the w. is meaningless.
M-20 ......... 4:3 W. is again accepted as the one reality.
M-27 ......... 2:7 reigns and opposites make endless w..

## ward 1

W-pI..... 76.3:3 needle will w. off disease and death. You

## wariness 1

T-29 ........I.8:6 is a w. that is aroused by learning that the

## warlike 1

T-23 ........I.1:3 what the w. would remember is not love.

## warm 1

W-pI... 189.2:3 offers you a w. and gentle home in which

## warming 1

WpI. rIV.in4:3 of the tides, the w. of the water by the sun

## warmth 4

W-pI..... 92.2:3 that lights the sun and gives it all its w.; or
W-pI... 122.1:5 and the w. of sure protection always? Do
W-pI... 122.5:3 with w. and welcome calling from beyond
W-pI... 159.8:4 They need the light and w. and kindly

## warning 1

T-1 ........ V.4:3 not mocked" is not a w. but a reassurance

## warped 3

T-7 ..... VIII.2:5 its own w. version of the laws of God, the
T-17 ........I.3:6 that your perspective on reality be w. and
M-19 ......... 4:7 of w. perception through which you look.

## warps 1

T-31 .... VII.7:2 that dims your sight and w. your vision,

## warrant 4

T-25VIII.11:10 can be to w. an attack upon the innocent?
T-25 ..... IX.6:9 and w. vengeance in place of healing and
T-27 .......II.4:4 unless his sins have no effect to w. guilt?
W-pI .. 101.2:4 The sinful w. only death and pain, and it

## warranted 2

T-25 .......II.3:1 is w. on grounds that are not in this world
W-pI .... 51.5:4 anger is justified and my attacks are w..

## warrants 1

T-25 ..... IX.2:3 you. God's justice w. gratitude, not fear.

## warring 1

W-pI .... 95.2:2 yourself; a self divided into many w. parts

## warrior 1

W-pI .. 170.7:6 and no mighty w. to fight for them.

## warriors 1

T-24 ........I.2:4 of these hidden w. to disrupt your peace.

## wars 1

T-25 ..... III.3:5 the perfect battleground to wage its w.,

## wary 1

T-29 ........I.1:9 Be w., then; let Him not come too close,

## was 817

## wash 2

T-28 .... VII.7:4 The world will w. away and yet this house
W-pI .. 188.9:6 and w. them clean of strange desires and

## washed 4

T-18 ..... IX.9:4 innocence, w. in the waters of forgiveness
T-18 ... IX.13:1 the barriers of guilt, w. with forgiveness,
W-pI .... 75.6:2 w. of all past ideas and clean of every
W-pI .... 98.2:6 All our sins are w. away by realizing they

## washes 1

T-30 .......V.6:2 what you are, forgiveness w. joyfully away

## waste 14

T-1 .........V.2:2 Time can w. as well as be wasted. The
T-2 ....... III.5:2 they w. themselves and their true creative
T-9 ........I.11:1 the enormous w. of energy you expend in
T-15 ........I.2:5 It does not w. Him, as it does you. And all
T-15 ........I.2:6 all the w. that time seems to bring with it
T-20 . VIII.11:1 in dancing brooks that never w. away;
T-26 .......V.2:3 in it, why should you w. it going nowhere,
T-31 ..... IV.4:7 understand you but w. time unless you go
W-pI .... 29.5:9 *God is in that w. basket.* In addition to the
W-pI .... 96.6:1 W. no more time on this. Who can
W-pI .. 130.4:8 nor w. this day in seeking what can not be
W-pI .. 138.3:3 time is but a w. and effort dissipated. It is

W-pI...156.6:5 but who would w. an instant in approach
M-24..........4:5 teach that theoretical issues but w. time,

**wasted** 6

T-1......... V.2:2 Time can waste as well as be w.. The
T-3......... V.2:7 Inventiveness is w. effort even in its most
T-4.........in.3:4 Until you do so your life is indeed w.. It
W-pI...156.7:1 Yet you have w. many, many years on
W-pI...200.9:3 and needless w. time on thorny byways.
M-6...........4:7 How can it be w.? God's treasure house

**wastes** 1

T-17....... V.3:1 Holy Spirit w. no time in introducing the

**wasting** 1

W-pII..233.1:4 *be obtained, and w. time in vain imaginings.*

**watch** 26

T-4........III.7:5 it. W. your mind for the scraps of fear, or
T-4........III.8:1 W. carefully and see what it is you are
T-4........IV.6:1 W. your mind for the temptations of the
T-4........IV.8:5 W. your mind carefully for any beliefs
T-14......VI.2:5 sentinels of darkness w. over it carefully,
T19... IV.C.2:5 of forgiveness, and w. the chains fall away
T-22......III.6:6 W. how they stop at nothingness, unable
W-pI.....31.3:3 W. them come and go as dispassionately
W-pI.....31.3:5 As you sit and quietly w. your thoughts,
W-pI.....32.3:4 w. the images your imagination presents
W-pI.....34.3:3 slowly as you w. them arise in your mind,
W-pI.....65.5:2 w. your mind carefully to catch whatever
W-pI.....75.7:5 He will be with you as you w. and wait.
W-pI.127.11:2 we will w. it grow in health and strength,
W-pI...129.7:5 silent darkness w. the lights that are not
W-pI.131.11:5 For several minutes w. your mind and see
W-pI.151.13:3 And then we w. our thoughts, appealing
W-pI.161.11:4 W. him smile, and see familiar gestures
W-pI...168.4:3 and w. fear disappear from every face as
W-pI...191.3:3 and w. despair snatch from your fingers
W-pI...192.8:4 he spends his time in keeping w. on him.
W-pII..235.1:1 from this," and merely w. them disappear
W-pII..303.1:1 W. with me, angels, watch with me today
W-pII..303.1:1 Watch with me, angels, w. with me today
W-pII..316.1:4 angels w. its open doors that not one gift
M-12..........6:7 They w. the dream figures come and go,

**watched** 1

T-20. VIII.11:1 w. them change to quiet views of gardens

**watches** 7

T-7........XI.3:9 it. God w. over His children and denies
T-13.....VII.7:2 Himself, Who w. over him in everything.
T-13......XI.9:7 God w. over him and light surrounds him
T19. IV.D.21:3 w. over you in faith so gentle yet so strong
T-20......III.6:6 He Who w. over all perception answered.
T-23....... I.10:8 Over His home the Holy Spirit w., sure
W-pI...189.2:4 w. through the night as silent guardian of

**watchful** 2

T-26... VIII.2:4 little w. of interests perceived as separate.
W-pI...135.4:4 has such frailty that constant care and w.,

**watching** 4

T-20....... V.8:1 and feel the Holy Spirit w. over you in
W-pI.....10.4:6 might imagine that you are w. an oddly
W-pI.136.19:1 needs to be preserved by careful w.. If you
W-pII..281.2:3 placed me safe in Heaven, w. over me.

**water** 9

T-18... VIII.9:8 out to everyone who thirsts for living w.,
T-20....VI.11:3 of w. and set uncertainly upon oblivion.
T-20. VIII.11:1 life-giving w. running happily beside
T-28...... III.5:3 as fast, as w. rushes in to close the gap,
W-pI...135.6:4 far beyond a little pile of dust and w..
WpI. rIV.in4:3 tides, the warming of the w. by the sun,
W-pI...156.3:3 be of ice; the sea elect to be apart from w.,
W-pII..222.1:2 the w. which renews and cleanses me. He
W-pII.... 13.5:2 Now they have w.. Now the world is green

**waters** 1

T-18...... IX.9:4 washed in the w. of forgiveness, and

**wave** 1

W-pI...136.3:2 magic wands you w. when truth appears

**waver** 2

WpI..rII.in.4:1 not allow your intent to w. in the face of
M-16 .........8:5 There are times his certainty will w., and

**wavering** 2

T-25....... II.3:1 this; some glimmering,–inconstant, w.,
W-pI...123.1:4 the truth. A bit of w. remains, some small

**wavers** 1

M-27 .........7:6 Truth neither moves nor w. nor sinks

**waves** 4

T-28...... III.5:3 the gap, and as the w. in joining cover it.
T-28...... III.5:4 is the gap between the w. when they have
W-pI...156.4:4 The w. bow down before you, and the
P-2......... IV.3:2 now stalk the earth in unrelenting w.,

**waxen** 1

T19... IV.D.6:3 of guilt, the "holy" w. image of death, and

**waxing** 1

M-27 .........1:6 w. and waning in a certain way upon a

**way** 773
*See also* two-way

T-in ...........2:1 be summed up very simply in this w.:
T-1.........I.18:3 is a w. of loving your neighbor as yourself.
T-1.........I.28:1 Miracles are a w. of earning release from
T-1.........I.40:2 It is a w. of perceiving the universal mark
T-1......... II.4:1 that I am in any w. separate or different
T-1......... III.3:4 Miracles are the w. in which minds that
T-1........ VI.1:2 it and believes in some w. that he needs it.
T-1.......VII.3:5 needs. Twist reality in any w. and you are
T-2.......... II.7:2 Sons of God make in one w. or another. It
T-2........ III.3:6 dimly, that there *must* be a better w.. As
T-2........ IV.5:2 w. is most helpful to the receiver. This
T-2......... V.9:4 charity is a w. of perceiving the perfection
T-2....... V.10:1 Charity is a w. of looking at another as if
T-2....V.A.14:2 can correct in a w. that has any real effect.
T-2....V.A.16:3 they do" in no w. evaluates *what* they do.
T-2....V.A.18:1 calling for help, you think of it this w.:
T-2......... VI.7:4 steps may be summarized in this w.:
T-2.......VII.1:9 but you can be trained to think that w..
T-3...........I.2:8 believe our Father really thinks this w.? It
T-3...........I.3:5 His Mind does not create that w.. He does
T-3...........I.4:3 Sacrificing in any w. is a violation of my
T-3...........I.5:4 is another w. of saying the same thing.
T-3......... II.6:1 w. to correct distortions is to withdraw
T-3........ III.2:4 The miracle, being a w. of perceiving, is
T-3........ IV.5:5 and the only w. out of ambiguity is clear
T-3........ IV.6:7 will always overcome error in this w..
T-3........ IV.7:8 your misperceptions stand in your w..
T-3......... V.6:1 Prayer is a w. of asking for something. It
T-3......VI.2:11 Either w. you are placing your belief in
T-3......... VI.3:2 them in any w. is without meaning. In
T-3......VI.10:4 sometimes by w. of very devious routes,
T-3...... VI.11:1 not feel that he is imprisoned in some w..
T-4..........II.3:6 that the mind need not work that w., even
T-4..........II.3:6 even though it does work that w. now.
T-4....... II.4:10 God. Belief that there is another w. of
T-4..........II.8:1 which is merely another w. of describing
T-4......... V.1:3 the w. a balanced mind holds together.
T-4......... V.6:3 touching on the real question in any w..
T-4....... VI.6:1 moment, but it will not always be that w..
T-4......VII.3:1 the same w. to everything it knows is true,
T-5...........I.6:2 He also blessed His children with a w. of
T-5...........I.7:4 it does not obstruct it in any w.. Finally, it
T-5...........I.7:5 the w. beyond the healing that it brings,
T-5..........II.5:2 there is a right w. and also a wrong way,
T-5..........II.5:2 there is a right way and also a wrong w.,
T-5..........II.6:7 The Holy Spirit is one w. of choosing.
T-5..........II.7:6 you *of.* It brings to your mind the other w.,
T-5..........II.8:4 The Holy Spirit is the w. in which God's
T-5....... II.10:2 one Voice and answers in only one w..
T-5....... II.11:4 is easy and my burden light" in this w.;
T-5........ III.1:1 The w. to recognize your brother is by
T-5........ IV.1:2 the Atonement is the w. out of fear. The
T-5........ IV.3:3 Sharing is God's w. of creating, and also
T-5........ IV.6:2 the w. except by taking your brother with
T-5........ VI.2:9 possible moment and in every possible w.
T-5...... VI.12:2 w. in which time is exchanged for eternity
T-5.......VII.5:3 The decision to react in this w. is yours,
T-6.........in.1:3 that you are in no w. responsible for it.
T-6.........in.1:6 The w. to undo an insane conclusion is to
T-6...........I.5:3 When you do choose to react that w.,
T-6.........I.10:3 only w. in which I can be perceived as the
T-6.........I.10:3 way in which I can be perceived as the w.,
T-6.........I.10:6 is inevitably led to demonstrate His w. for
T-6.........I.14:1 interpret the crucifixion in any other w.,
T-6..........II.5:6 perceive yourself this w. is the only way in
T-6..........II.5:6 perceive yourself this way is the only w. in
T-6..........II.7:3 perception in a w. that reflects knowledge
T-6....... II.11:5 This is the w. in which you must perceive
T-6........ III.4:3 only w. to have peace is to teach peace. By
T-6........ IV.3:3 time or another and in one w. or another,
T-6........ IV.7:5 has given w. to creation and to its eternity
T-6........ IV.9:6 and never detract from it in any w.. You
T-6......... V.2:1 wake children in a more kindly w. than by
T-6......V.A.6:3 Having chosen to go that w., you place
T-6...... V.B.5:1 w. out of conflict between two opposing
T-6...... V.C.5:3 The w. to remember it is inherent in the
T-6...... V.C.9:6 against this sickness is the w. to heal it.
T-7...........I.2:4 in this w. can all creative power extend
T-7...........I.4:6 God does not limit His gifts in any w..
T-7..........II.1:3 If you, too, see him this w., you are seeing
T-7..........II.6:8 is the only w. you can learn consistency,
T-7........ III.1:9 I am always with you, *you* are the w., the
T-7........ IV.2:7 is merely a w. of remembering better. It is
T-7...... IV.2:10 it can be used as a w. out of conflict, as all
T-7........ IV.3:7 channelized in one direction, or in one w.
T-7........ IV.4:4 be translated into a w. of remembering.
T-7........ IV.5:1 be reconciled in any w. or to any extent.
T-7........ IV.5:5 is the w. to undo the belief in differences,
T-7........ IV.5:5 only w. of perceiving the Sonship as one.
T-7........ IV.6:9 w. of approaching knowledge by thinking
T-7........ IV.7:7 Healing is a w. of forgetting the sense of
T-7......... V.7:7 in no w. contradicts the changelessness of
T-7......... V.9:2 One w. shows you an image, or an idol
T-7........ VI.3:8 insane dilemma in a completely insane w.
T-7........VII.2:4 no w. for you to have it except by giving it
T-7........VII.4:4 only w. to dispel illusions is to withdraw
T-7........VII.5:7 Keep His w. to remember yourself, and
T-7........VII.5:7 and teach His w. lest you forget yourself.
T-7.....VII.10:9 is only one w. out of the world's thinking,
T-7.....VII.10:9 just as there was only one w. into it.
T-7.......VIII.4:2 There is no w. out of this, because it is
T-7......... X.5:2 long as you avoid His guidance in any w.,
T-7......... X.6:8 The only w. out of the error is to decide
T-8........ IV.5:3 Healing is the w. in which the separation
T-8......... V.4:2 union is therefore the w. to renounce the
T-8......... V.5:9 in different directions and will lose the w.
T-8......... V.6:1 The ego's w. is not mine, but it is also not
T-8......... V.6:5 the journey is the w. to what is true. Leave
T-8........VII.1:7 himself in this w. he is belittling himself,
T-8........VII.3:5 is God's w. of making unlimited what you

| | |
|---|---|
| T-8.......VII.5:5 | not see him this **w.** for your own salvation |
| T-8.....VII.11:1 | the only **w.** to guarantee help and healing. |
| T-8......VIII.6:1 | is a **w.** of demonstrating that you can be |
| T-8......VIII.6:8 | *Any* **w.** you handle error results in nothing |
| T-8........ IX.3:4 | This is a pathetic **w.** of trying not to see by |
| T-8........ IX.9:1 | is the Holy Spirit's only **w.** of healing. |
| T-8........ IX.9:3 | a chaotic thought system *is* the **w.** to heal it |
| T-9......... II.4:8 | to truth is the only **w.** you can hear it now |
| T-9......... II.8:4 | this **w.** can you learn how blessed you are. |
| T-9......... II.8:5 | following this **w.** you are seeking the truth |
| T-9....... II.12:4 | This is the **w.**, and the only way to have |
| T-9....... II.12:4 | way, and the only **w.** to have His answer, |
| T-9........ III.5:4 | the one **w.** in which you handle all errors, |
| T-9........ III.6:8 | guide and will therefore lose your **w.**. |
| T-9........ III.7:3 | If you would find your **w.** and keep it, see |
| T-9........IV.1:1 | because it is the **w.** to undo the belief that |
| T-9........IV.2:7 | The **w.** to undo them, therefore, is not *of* |
| T-9......... V.5:1 | the **w.** to counteract fear is to reduce the |
| T-9........ VI.6:3 | a **w.** of giving acceptance and receiving it. |
| T-9.......VII.2:5 | because the Atonement *is* the **w.** to peace. |
| T-10....... II.2:4 | stand in the **w.** of your remembering, for |
| T-10....... II.5:4 | is thus the **w.** in which your identification |
| T-10......IV.3:1 | it that **w.** is not to perceive it at all. If the |
| T-11.......in.3:5 | darker and more obscure becomes the **w.**. |
| T-11...... III.1:4 | yourself you could never suffer in any **w.**, |
| T-11...... III.4:1 | The **w.** is not hard, but it *is* very different. |
| T-11...... III.4:2 | Yours is the **w.** of pain, of which God |
| T-11...... III.4:3 | That **w.** is hard indeed, and very lonely. |
| T-11...... III.4:4 | go with you and abide with you on the **w.**. |
| T-11...... III.4:5 | dark journey is not the **w.** of God's Son. |
| T-11.... III.4:10 | for the light is here and the **w.** is clear. |
| T-11...... III.5:3 | You will never lose your **w.**, for God leads |
| T-11...... III.5:5 | The dark companions, the dark **w.**, are all |
| T-11....... V.1:1 | not looking is the **w.** they are protected. |
| T-11....... V.2:1 | of all that stands in the **w.** of knowledge? |
| T-11....... V.5:2 | and the **w.** to undo its results is merely to |
| T-11....VIII.9:4 | Who is in no **w.** separate from His Father, |
| T-12.........I.1:1 | real, and the **w.** to do this is very simple. |
| T-12.......I.6:10 | attempt to "help" a brother in your **w.**, |
| T-12.......... II.h | The **W.** to Remember God |
| T-12....... II.2:9 | yourself is thus the **w.** to remember God. |
| T-12..... II.2:10 | your forgetting is but the **w.** to remember |
| T-12....... II.6:5 | not let your hatred stand in the **w.** of love, |
| T-12....... II.9:5 | not by denying its full import in any **w.** |
| T-12...... III.5:2 | can be saved and the only **w.** to save it. |
| T-12...... III.7:9 | you would have to perceive it this **w.**. |
| T-12.......IV.1:2 | It never puts it this **w.**; on the contrary, |
| T-12....... V.8:2 | the **w.** to achieve a goal is not to attain it? |
| T-12....... V.9:2 | You can teach the **w.** to Him and learn it, |
| T-12....... V.9:2 | follow the Teacher Who knows the **w.** to |
| T-12....VIII.3:8 | and unless He had given you a **w.** to |
| T-12....VIII.8:8 | is but the **w.** back to what was never lost. |
| T-13.........I.5:3 | the **w.** to find release is not denied him. |
| T-13.........I.8:6 | is a **w.** of holding past and future in your |
| T-13.........I.9:3 | God's **w.** of reminding you of His Son, |
| T-13.......I.11:3 | and if it is real there *is* no **w.** to overcome it |
| T-13....... II.1:2 | stands in the **w.** of your remembering |
| T-13....... V.9:1 | made your **w.** of seeing that you might see |
| T-13..... V.10:2 | you. Each is a **w.** of seeing, and different |
| T-13.....VII.8:4 | The real world is the **w.** that leads you to |
| T-13...VII.12:2 | all things that do not block the **w.** to light. |
| T-13...VII.16:2 | the **w.** to quietness that is the gift of God. |
| T-13....... X.2:9 | No one who would unite in any **w.** with |
| T-13....... X.6:1 | you believe that guilt is justified in any **w.**, |
| T-13..... X.10:2 | other **w.** to look within and see the light |
| T-13..... X.12:1 | him has touched his innocence in any **w.**. |
| T-14....... II.7:2 | and open up the **w.** to freedom for you. |
| T-14...... III.2:6 | To wish for guilt in any **w.**, in any form, |
| T-14...... III.7:1 | **w.** to teach this simple lesson is merely |
| T-14.... III.14:2 | He knows the **w.**, and leads you gladly on |
| T-14.... III.17:5 | will be touched in any **w.** by the decision. |
| T-14.... III.19:2 | *He leadeth me and knows the **w.**, which I* |
| T-14.... IV.10:2 | the other unlike the **w.** he sees himself. |
| T-14....... V.6:1 | Teachers of innocence, each in his own **w.** |
| T-14.....VII.4:2 | that salvation must come to you this **w.**, if |
| T-14.....VII.7:1 | Joining with Him in seeing is the **w.** in |
| T-14....... X.6:2 | you that your **w.** of ordering is wrong, but |
| T-14....... X.6:2 | wrong, but that a better **w.** is offered you. |
| T-14...... XI.6:6 | peace is threatened or disturbed in any **w.** |
| T-14 ... XI.14:7 | Make **w.** for peace, and it will come. For |
| T-15 .........I.2:3 | the Holy Spirit uses time in His Own **w.**, |
| T-15 .........I.6:6 | only **w.** in which the ego allows the fear of |
| T-15 ........II.5:3 | gift of God is recognized in any other **w.**. |
| T-15 ...... IV.2:5 | find salvation in your own **w.** and have it. |
| T-15 ...... IV.7:2 | The only **w.** you could do that would be |
| T-15 ...... IV.7:4 | you find a **w.** to keep what you would |
| T-15 ..... V.10:9 | are joined in Christ are in no **w.** separate. |
| T-15 ...... VI.1:3 | do not conflict with one another in any **w.** |
| T-15 ... VI.5:10 | that he be bound, or limited in any **w.**. In |
| T-15 .....VII.4:1 | but in such a **w.** that you do not recognize |
| T-15 .....VII.6:1 | In one **w.** or another, every relationship |
| T-15 .. VII.11:6 | union of bodies thus becomes the **w.** in |
| T-16 .........I.1:3 | provided you let Him use it in His **w.**. His |
| T-16 .........I.1:4 | way. His **w.** is very different. He does not |
| T-16 .........I.3:2 | to hurt it nor to heal it in your own **w.**. |
| T-16 .........I.7:3 | That is not the **w.**, for it leads not to life |
| T-16 ........II.2:2 | whole. And this is but a **w.** of avoiding, or |
| T-16 ........II.2:3 | another **w.** in which you would still try to |
| T-16 ........II.2:4 | A better and far more helpful **w.** to think |
| T-16 ........II.3:3 | natural, for it is the **w.** God thinks, and |
| T-16 ... IV.12:5 | and let nothing stand in the **w.** of truth. |
| T-16 . IV.13:10 | The **w.** to truth is open. Follow it with me. |
| T-16 ...... VI.3:1 | **w.** in which the Holy Spirit asks your help |
| T-16 ... VI.11:7 | may the holy instant speed you on the **w.**, |
| T-16 .....VII.1:3 | which becomes a **w.** in which you seek to |
| T-17 .........I.4:3 | to deal with part of the truth in one **w.**, |
| T-17 .........I.4:3 | one way, and in another **w.** the other part. |
| T-17 ...... III.4:7 | the attempt at union becomes a **w.** of |
| T-17 ...... III.7:1 | to light your **w.** and make it clear to you. |
| T-17 ....... V.4:6 | accepted as the only **w.** out of the conflict, |
| T-17 ....... V.9:1 | salvation, and think you have lost your **w.** |
| T-17 ....... V.9:2 | *Your* **w.** *is* lost, but think not this is loss. In |
| T-17 ...... VI.5:8 | see the opposite of the ego's **w.** of looking, |
| T-17 .....VII.1:6 | interference in the **w.** of understanding |
| T-18 .........I.7:5 | You but believe it is the other **w.**; that |
| T-18 ........II.2:4 | Yet they are a **w.** of looking at the world, |
| T-18 ...... III.1:1 | to fantasy, have walked the **w.** of dreams. |
| T-18 ...... III.3:2 | beside you on the **w.** that you have chosen |
| T-18 ...... III.8:6 | brother, and you will light each other's **w.** |
| T-18 ...... IV.5:6 | than simple willingness to make **w.** for it. |
| T-18 .....VII.1:2 | or protection or enjoyment in some **w.**? |
| T-18 .....VII.5:1 | Your **w.** will be different, not in purpose |
| T-18 .....VII.6:1 | everyone will one day find in his own **w.**, |
| T-18 .....VII.7:4 | **w.** in which sin loses all attraction *right* |
| T-18 ...VIII.4:4 | And what it thinks it is in no **w.** changes |
| T-18 ...VIII.5:2 | living alone and in no **w.** joined to the |
| T-18 ...VIII.9:3 | who lost their **w.** and wander in the dust. |
| T-18 ...... IX.6:3 | gives **w.** softly to the mountain tops that |
| T-18 ... IX.11:3 | go, will go beyond it, but in a different **w.**. |
| T-19 .........I.6:7 | with truth, in any respect or in any **w.**. |
| T-19 .......I.16:4 | any **w.** except by the mind that thought it. |
| T-19 ........II.3:3 | would really change his reality in any **w.**, |
| T-19 ...... IV.1:5 | **w.** in which He will bring means and goal |
| T19..IV.A.17:4 | Salvation is looked upon as a **w.** by which |
| T19....IV.B.8:3 | raise to freedom, and bar my **w.** to you. |
| T19..IV.B.17:5 | returns to Him, seeking itself along the **w.** |
| T19....IV.C.6:2 | What better **w.** to teach the first and |
| T19... IV.D.5:1 | across is surmounted in just the same **w.**; |
| T19. IV.D.12:6 | that would heal it gives **w.** to fear. Brother |
| T19. IV.D.18:5 | the **w.** unto the resurrection of God's Son, |
| T-20 .........I.3:4 | his **w.** to his redemption and release. |
| T-20 .........I.3:6 | lilies speed him on his **w.** to resurrection. |
| T-20 ........II.9:2 | His innocence will light your **w.**, offering |
| T-20 ........II.9:4 | the veil of fear, lighting each other's **w.**. |
| T-20 ......II.10:1 | **w.** to Heaven and to the peace of Easter, |
| T-20 ......II.11:3 | brother walk the **w.** of innocence together |
| T-20 ...... III.1:5 | a **w.** of looking in which certainty is lost |
| T-20 ...... III.4:2 | your timid **w.** through constant dangers, |
| T-20 ...... IV.8:1 | be done before the **w.** to peace is open. |
| T-20 ...... IV.8:5 | leaving in your **w.** no stones to trip on, |
| T-20 ...... IV.8:5 | to trip on, and no obstacles to bar your **w.** |
| T-20 ... VI.10:5 | **w.** to true relationships held gently open, |
| T-21 .........I.2:4 | safety lies; and which **w.** leads to darkness |
| T-21 .........I.4:2 | They think they know their **w.** about in it. |
| T-21 ... III.11:4 | and cannot meaningfully join in any **w.**. It |
| T-21 ...... IV.8:3 | sin, follow in gladness the **w.** to certainty. |
| T-21 ...... IV.8:8 | The quiet **w.** is open. Follow it happily, |
| T-21 ..... V.10:5 | in this change is room made **w.** for vision. |
| T-21 ... VI.1:10 | reason would not make **w.** for correction |
| T-21 .....VII.3:8 | Any **w.** at all. It could be seen attacking |
| T-22 .......in.1:6 | and forgiven for its maker in the same **w.**. |
| T-22 ........II.1:4 | the **w.** to lose the misery the other brings. |
| T-22 ........II.3:7 | to joy, for time gives **w.** to the eternal. |
| T-22 ........II.3:9 | imagined, illusions must give **w.** to truth, |
| T-22 ........II.4:1 | Reason will tell you that the only **w.** to |
| T-22 ........II.4:1 | misery is to recognize it *and go the other **w.***. |
| T-22 ........II.4:2 | are different from each other in every **w.**, |
| T-22 ........II.5:4 | Yet reason looks on this another **w.**, for |
| T-22 ...... III.2:2 | errors and make **w.** for their correction. |
| T-22 ...... III.3:1 | but it makes **w.** for peace and brings you |
| T-22 ...... IV.1:2 | You must go either one **w.** or the other. |
| T-22 ...... IV.1:3 | the **w.** you went before you reached the |
| T-22 ...... IV.1:5 | The **w.** you came no longer matters. It can |
| T-22 ...... IV.1:8 | and not deciding on which **w.** to go. |
| T-22 ...... IV.2:1 | the first few steps along the right **w.** that |
| T-22 ...... IV.2:4 | Your **w.** is decided. There will be nothing |
| T-22 ...... IV.6:3 | seemed to rise and block their **w.** before. |
| T-22 ...... IV.6:4 | opens the **w.** to truth to more than you. |
| T-22 ........V.1:2 | or anger, nor by opposing them in any **w.**. |
| T-22 ........V.1:9 | walk the **w.** of truth when only weakness |
| T-22 ...... VI.9:7 | no blessing from it, nor limit it in any **w.**. |
| T-22 ... VI.12:4 | The only **w.** it could be justified is if you |
| T-23 .......in.2:5 | sinlessly along the **w.** love shows him. For |
| T-23 .......in.5:5 | Your innocence will light the **w.** to his, |
| T-23 .........I.6:8 | truth, nor can they threaten it in any **w.**. |
| T-23 ......II.22:6 | the stairs to Heaven or the **w.** to hell? |
| T-23 ...II.22:10 | Are you certain which **w.** you go? And are |
| T-24 .........I.6:3 | help him reach it in every **w.** you could, if |
| T-24 ........II.9:1 | You have come far along the **w.** of truth; |
| T-24 ...... III.6:5 | The **w.** is barred to love and to salvation. |
| T-24 ........V.4:1 | Yet let your specialness direct his **w.**, and |
| T-24 ........V.6:2 | there in gentleness and blessing all the **w.**. |
| T-24 ........V.9:5 | leading the **w.** that He must go to find |
| T-24 ...... VI.4:5 | in every **w.** and every circumstance, in all |
| T-24 .....VII.6:9 | any **w.** to learn what this condition means |
| T-25 ........II.2:4 | For one thing is sure; the **w.** you see, and |
| T-25 ........II.5:4 | for a while, without obscuring it in any **w.** |
| T-25 ........II.6:7 | you not the picture is destroyed in any **w.**. |
| T-25 ...... IV.1:7 | **w.** in which the aim is seen that makes the |
| T-25 ...... IV.1:8 | another **w.** and sought for differently. |
| T-25 ......V.4:10 | be regained unless the **w.** is shown to him |
| T-25 ........V.6:5 | that he is the **w.** to Heaven or to hell, as |
| T-25 ........V.6:6 | and you will walk the **w.** you pointed out |
| T-25 .. VII.1:11 | creation, when it opposes it in every **w.**? |
| T-25 .....VII.4:7 | Who thinks the world is sane in any **w.**, is |
| T-25 .....VII.6:4 | who believe theirs is the **w.** to sanity. But |
| T-25 .....VII.8:4 | another **w.** of looking at what he has seen |
| T-25 ...VIII.4:2 | Justice looks on all in the same **w.**. It is |
| T-25 .VIII.14:1 | eternal, joyous and complete in every **w.**, |
| T-25 ...... IX.4:4 | The world solves problems in another **w.**. |
| T-25 ...... IX.5:1 | is the **w.** in which the problem ends. It |
| T-25 ...... IX.7:8 | then must problems rise to block your **w.**, |
| T-26 ........II.3:5 | on what you see can limit God in any **w.**. |
| T-26 ...... IV.1:4 | is charity within the world gives **w.** to |
| T-26 ........V.1:8 | go along the **w.** your chosen teacher leads. |
| T-26 ......V.1:10 | road be made except the **w.** to Heaven. |
| T-26 ........V.2:4 | the **w.** to Heaven's gate is difficult at all. |
| T-26 ........V.3:4 | before the **w.** to nothingness was made. |
| T-26 ........V.4:3 | ago, before its unreality gave **w.** to truth. |
| T-26 ........V.6:4 | There *is* no other teacher and no other **w.**. |
| T-26 ........V.9:5 | And everything that points the **w.** in the |
| T-26 ........V.9:8 | your **w.** because there is no way but His, |
| T-26 ........V.9:8 | your way because there is no **w.** but His, |
| T-26 ......V.10:1 | his **w.** along a road long since a memory |
| T-26 .....VII.1:3 | arrange them in a **w.** that summarizes all |
| T-26 .....VII.6:9 | Not one is true in any **w.**, and all must |
| T-26 ........X.4:7 | Whatever **w.** the game of guilt is played, |
| T-26 ........X.6:2 | can you perceive to lighten up your **w.**. |
| T-27 .........I.1:3 | Walk you the gentle **w.**, and you will fear |
| T-27 .........I.7:7 | must come, whatever **w.** that life be spent |
| T-27 .........I.9:6 | that it may be judged in any **w.** at all. It |
| T-27 .......I.11:1 | simple **w.** to let this be achieved is merely |
| T-27 ........II.1:4 | stand firmly in the **w.** of trust and peace, |
| T-27 ......II.11:3 | must be a **w.** to punish sins you think are |
| T-27 ...... IV.1:7 | if God gave an answer there must be a **w.** |
| T-27 ...... IV.2:3 | God must have given you a **w.** of reaching |
| T-27 ...... IV.4:1 | within this world are but a **w.** of looking, |

| | |
|---|---|
| T-27.......V.1:1 | The only w. to heal is to be healed. The |
| T-27.......V.9:5 | you not the w. that you perceive them. |
| T-27.....VII.2:2 | it is, and not the w. that you have set it up |
| T-27.....VII.2:3 | another w. to solve a problem that is very |
| T-27.....VII.7:5 | you in any w. request them for yourself. |
| T-28.........I.5:2 | the past, but rather as a w. to let it go. |
| T-28.........I.6:7 | it is a w. to hold the past against the now. |
| T-28........I.13:3 | the w. of glad awakening to present peace |
| T-28........I.15:3 | better w. to close the little gap between |
| T-28........II.9:1 | which proceeds to go the other w., begins. |
| T-28.......III.1:5 | will the w. be made serene and simple in |
| T-28.......IV.2:1 | w. of finding certainty right here and now |
| T-28.......VI.2:6 | is changed, it walks as easily another w.. |
| T-29.........I.1:3 | no w. in which a gap could be conceived |
| T-29.........I.3:3 | make the w. to light seem dark and fearful |
| T-29........II.1:3 | marked it is impossible to lose the w., |
| T-29........II.1:4 | hell instead of looking on it as a simple w. |
| T-29........II.1:5 | regrets about the w. that you have chosen |
| T-29.......III.3:7 | as heavy shadows must give w. to light. |
| T-29.....III.3:11 | the gentle w. of kindness to God's Son. |
| T-29.......III.4:1 | Make w. for love, which you did not |
| T-29.......IV.2:8 | for which the miracle prepares the w.. |
| T-29........V.7:5 | form it takes in some w. calls for death. |
| T-29....VIII.2:3 | reality. In some w., you believe they will |
| T-29....VIII.4:5 | hand could be held up to block God's w.? |
| T-29....VIII.6:5 | given to all living things, give w. to chaos. |
| T-29.....IX.10:6 | judgment seemed to be the w. to save him |
| T-30.........I.1:8 | and tell yourself there is a w. in which this |
| T-30.........I.7:3 | of being answered in a different w. from |
| T-30.........I.8:3 | and paves the w. for the next easy step. |
| T-30.........I.9:1 | that you do not like the w. you feel, what |
| T-30.........I.9:3 | because you do not like the w. you feel. |
| T-30........I.11:4 | *I want another w. to look at this.* Now you |
| T-30........I.12:3 | *Perhaps there is another w. to look at this.* |
| T-30........V.8:4 | delay in showing you the w. that He must |
| T-30......V.9:11 | Be speeded on your w. by honesty, and let |
| T-30.......VI.1:9 | responding in a w. which is not justified, |
| T-30.......VI.9:3 | There is no w. to think of him but this, if |
| T-31........II.3:1 | free, for it will have one outcome either w. |
| T-31........II.6:9 | we go separately along the w. unless you |
| T-31........II.9:6 | Thus it is a w. you go together, not alone. |
| T-31......II.11:4 | and so you cannot see which w. you go. |
| T-31......II.11:8 | but cannot make the w. itself grow dark. |
| T-31.......IV.3:4 | saw no w. except the pathways offered by |
| T-31.......IV.4:1 | you have learned the w. the lesson starts, |
| T-31.......IV.5:2 | with this, to seek another w. instead? For |
| T-31.......IV.7:2 | makes no sense, and cannot be the w.. To |
| T-31.......IV.7:4 | every road that leads the other w. will not |
| T-31........V.8:2 | roads nor realize the w. you see yourself. |
| T-31........V.8:3 | Now must the Holy Spirit find a w. to |
| T-31......V.12:3 | and at least makes w. for active choice, |
| T-31.......VI.4:1 | you must make the w. to Heaven plain. |
| T-31.....VII.6:5 | use, and you can see yourself another w.. |
| T-31....VIII.6:4 | the w. to his salvation and release. Choose |
| W-in..........3:1 | with the undoing of the w. you see now, |
| W-in..........4:1 | to train your mind in a systematic w. to a |
| W-in..........6:6 | It is the opposite of the w. you see now. |
| W-pI.......3.1:1 | idea in the same w. as the previous ones, |
| W-pI.......8.3:3 | is the first step to opening the w. to vision |
| W-pI.....10.3:3 | This is merely another w. of repeating our |
| W-pI.....13.4:1 | practiced in a somewhat different w. from |
| W-pI.....15.3:7 | to you. But they will prepare the w. to it. |
| W-pI.....17.1:3 | to believe that it is the other w. around. |
| W-pI.....17.1:4 | This is not the w. the world thinks, but |
| W-pI.....17.1:4 | you must learn that it is the w. you think. |
| W-pI.....22.1:1 | the w. anyone who holds attack thoughts |
| W-pI.....23.1:1 | only w. out of fear that will ever succeed. |
| W-pI.....23.1:3 | But this w. cannot fail. Every thought you |
| W-pI.....24.1:2 | action, and no w. of judging the result. |
| W-pI.....25.3:1 | Another w. of describing the goals you |
| W-pI.....25.5:2 | or "bad," is the only w. to accomplish this |
| W-pI.....28.1:4 | have started on the w. to keeping them. |
| W-pI.....30.2:5 | difference between vision and the w. you |
| W-pI........33.h | is another w. of looking at the world. |
| W-pI.....33.3:4 | say: *There is another w. of looking at this.* |
| W-pI.....34.1:1 | that prevail in the other w. of seeing. |
| W-pI.....34.5:1 | peace of mind is threatened in any w.. |
| W-pI.....35.1:1 | not describe the w. you see yourself now. |
| W-pI.....35.7:1 | not think of these terms in an abstract w.. |
| W-pI.....37.2:1 | There is no other w. in which the idea of |
| W-pI.....37.2:2 | other w. of seeing will inevitably demand |
| W-pI.....39.8:2 | idea for today to each of them in this w.: |
| W-pI.....41.8:4 | The w. will open, if you believe that it is |
| W-pI.....43.5:2 | add to the idea in your own personal w.. |
| W-pI.....43.8:1 | which seem to distress you in any w.. For |
| W-pI.....44.5:4 | While you practice in this w., you leave |
| W-pI.....45.1:2 | think you see is related to vision in any w. |
| W-pI.....47.1:4 | in such a w. that only good can come of it |
| W-pI.....49.1:1 | your regular activities in any w.. The part |
| W-pI.....52.1:7 | in any w. by this confusion of mine. I am |
| W-pI.....53.5:5 | Yet God's w. is sure. The images I have |
| W-pI.....57.3:1 | is another w. of looking at the world. |
| W-pI.....57.3:2 | there must be another w. of looking at it. |
| W-pI.....64.1:1 | Today's idea is merely another w. of |
| W-pI.....64.4:3 | There is no other w.. Therefore, every |
| W-pI.....65.2:1 | This is the only w. in which you can take |
| W-pI.....65.2:2 | only w. in which you can say and mean, |
| W-pI.....65.2:3 | the only w. in which you can find peace of |
| W-pI.....68.6:6 | that nothing can harm you in any w.. At |
| W-pI.....69.5:4 | which is the only w. in which you would |
| W-pI.....70.2:2 | disturb your peace or upset you in any w.. |
| W-pI.....70.3:3 | That is the w. your mind has worked, but |
| W-pI.....70.7:2 | You might put it this w.: *My salvation* |
| W-pI...71.10:6 | no better w. to spend a half minute or less |
| W-pI...73.10:6 | Join with Them as They lead the w.. |
| W-pI.....74.5:1 | you have cleared your mind in this w., |
| W-pI.....78.2:2 | will reverse the w. you see by not allowing |
| W-pI.....78.7:1 | that we may look on him a different w., |
| W-pI.....80.2:3 | opening the w. for the Holy Spirit to give |
| WpI..rII.in.5:1 | practice periods as dedications to the w., |
| W-pI.....82.4:4 | *but cannot change my function in any w..* |
| W-pI.....86.3:5 | my own best interests in this insane w.. |
| W-pI.....95.9:4 | another w. in which you would defend |
| W-pI.....96.7:2 | in your mind, and offers it the w. to peace |
| W-pI.....97.6:3 | nor will you be able to forget the w. again. |
| W-pI.....98.2:4 | Not one mistake stands in our w.. For we |
| W-pI.....98.9:3 | He will open up the w. to happiness, and |
| W-pI.....99.9:5 | with this instruction in the w. of truth: |
| W-pI...101.4:2 | and attempt in every w. he can to drown |
| W-pI...104.5:1 | So do we clear the w. for Him today by |
| W-pI...105.3:3 | will learn a different w. of looking at a gift |
| W-pI...106.2:1 | the w. to peace to those who cannot see. |
| W-pI...106.7:3 | giving, not the w. you understand it now, |
| W-pI...106.8:3 | world from thinking giving is a w. to lose. |
| W-pI...109.5:2 | your rest can never change in any w. at all |
| W-pI...109.7:2 | minds, too weary now to go their w. alone |
| WpI. rIII.in9:2 | and then go on your w. to other things, |
| W-pI...119.1:2 | *mistaken when I think I can be hurt in any w.* |
| W-pI...121.1:3 | the w. to safety in apparent dangers that |
| W-pI...121.7:7 | Who was given you to show the w. to you. |
| W-pI.122.10:3 | And now the w. is short that yet we travel. |
| W-pI...124.1:5 | with the universe we go our w. rejoicing, |
| W-pI...124.2:4 | shining footprints point the w. to truth, |
| W-pI...124.2:5 | come to follow us will recognize the w. |
| W-pI...124.5:1 | of pain, and pain gives w. to peace. We |
| W-pI...126.2:3 | help are not in any w. related to your own |
| W-pI...127.1:2 | for this, a kind for that; a w. of loving one, |
| W-pI...127.1:2 | one, another w. of loving still another. |
| W-pI...128.1:1 | you; nothing that you can use in any w., |
| W-pI...131.2:2 | There is no w. to reach them, for the |
| W-pI...131.7:4 | which is Heaven's opposite in every w.. |
| W-pI.131.13:2 | it. Angels light the w., so that all darkness |
| W-pI.132.10:1 | the lesson for today except another w. of |
| W-pI.132.11:5 | creation is unlike the world in every w.. |
| W-pI...134.8:3 | is not there, it opens up the w. to truth, |
| W-pI...134.8:4 | Now are you free to follow in the w. your |
| W-pI...134.9:1 | is a very simple w. to find the door to true |
| W-pI.134.12:5 | to point the w. to those who follow him. |
| W-pI.134.14:3 | lighting up the w. for all our brothers, |
| W-pI.135.16:5 | all, for present confidence directs the w.. |
| W-pI.136.11:4 | sickness or distort the truth in any w.. |
| W-pI...138.1:3 | is the w. we make what we perceive, and |
| W-pI.139.10:2 | go your w. rejoicing in the endless Love of |
| WpI. rIV.in1:4 | their central thoughts in such a w. as will |
| W-pI...151.7:1 | will clear the w. to recognize yourself, and |
| W-pI.151.11:2 | in any w. from His one frame of reference, |
| W-pI......155.h | I will step back and let Him lead the w.. |
| W-pI...155.1:1 | a w. of living in the world that is not here, |
| W-pI...155.1:5 | perceived the w. will recognize you also, |
| W-pI...155.2:3 | then they step back and let it lead the w.. |
| W-pI...155.5:2 | This is the w. appointed for you now. You |
| W-pI...155.5:4 | on the w. that God has opened up to you, |
| W-pI...155.6:4 | now, while on the w. you call to them, |
| W-pI...155.7:3 | and set them on the w. to happiness. |
| W-pI...155.9:4 | something they understand to lead the w. |
| W-pI.155.10:2 | And all illusions walking in the w. you |
| W-pI.155.10:3 | Step back in faith and let truth lead the w. |
| W-pI.155.11:3 | we progress along the w. that truth points |
| W-pI.155.11:5 | We must not lose our w.. For as truth |
| W-pI.155.12:3 | Could any w. be holier, or more deserving |
| W-pI.155.12:4 | w. could give you more than everything, |
| W-pI.155.12:7 | What w. but this could be a path that you |
| W-pI.155.14:3 | *I will step back and let Him lead the w., For I* |
| W-pI...156.6:1 | This is the w. salvation works. As you |
| W-pI...157.3:2 | come far enough along the w. to alter |
| W-pI...158.2:7 | shared directly, in the w. that vision can. |
| W-pI.158.11:2 | true knowledge is reflected in a w. so |
| W-pI.159.10:3 | but follow in the w. He has established. |
| W-pI...160.6:4 | His w. is lost, except a miracle will search |
| W-pI...163.7:3 | His, and so eternal life gave w. to death. |
| W-pI...165.2:6 | your resting place and smooth your w., |
| W-pI...166.6:3 | see that he is following the w. he chose, |
| W-pI...166.7:4 | You go on your appointed w., with eyes |
| W-pI...166.9:6 | and go the w. you chose without your Self |
| W-pI.166.13:4 | learned of Christ there is another w. for |
| W-pI...170.4:1 | self-defense proceeds on its imagined w., |
| W-pI.170.12:6 | Now has fear made w. for love, as God |
| WpI...rV.in2:5 | *little child along a w. he does not understand* |
| WpI...rV.in2:6 | *is safe because his father leads the w. for him.* |
| WpI...rV.in3:3 | *If we forget the w., we count upon Your sure* |
| WpI...rV.in6:5 | still retaining in his mind the w. that led |
| WpI...rV.in7:2 | learns there is a w. from misery and pain. |
| WpI...rV.in9:6 | hand, for this is not a w. we walk alone. In |
| W-pI...173.1:1 | I will step back and let Him lead the w.. |
| Wi181-200 1:4 | to following the w. the course sets forth. |
| W-pI...181.3:1 | we first let all such little focuses give w. to |
| W-pI...181.4:3 | you will inevitably lose your w. again. |
| W-pI...181.6:1 | goal if anger blocks our w. in any form. |
| W-pI.182.12:8 | And now the w. is open, and the journey |
| W-pI...184.4:1 | is the w. reality is made by partial vision, |
| W-pI...185.6:3 | in such a w. that he can not mistake it, if |
| W-pI...186.3:3 | be different in any w. from what you are. |
| W-pI...186.5:1 | is one w., and only one, to be released |
| W-pI...188.6:5 | They know the w.. For honest thoughts, |
| W-pI...189.6:2 | us. We learn the w. today. It is as sure as |
| W-pI...189.8:1 | Is it not He Who knows the w. to you? |
| W-pI...189.8:2 | You need not know the w. to Him. Your |
| W-pI...189.8:7 | w. to reach Him is merely to let Him be. |
| W-pI...189.8:8 | that w. is your reality proclaimed as well. |
| W-pI...189.9:1 | so today we do not choose the w. in which |
| W-pI...189.9:6 | knows His Son, and knows the w. to him. |
| W-pI...189.9:7 | His Son to show Him how to find His w.. |
| W-pI.189.10:1 | *Father, we do not know the w. to You. But* |
| W-pI.189.10:8 | *Yours is the w. that we would find and follow* |
| W-pI...190.5:2 | mind can hurt or injure you in any w.. |
| W-pI...190.8:5 | rules and little joys give w. before the |
| W-pI...191.5:4 | Who pointed out the w. to happiness that |
| W-pI...192.8:6 | freedom that the w. to liberty depends for |
| W-pI...192.9:3 | The w. is simple. Every time you feel a |
| W-pI.192.10:3 | that you accept the w. to freedom now. |
| W-pI...193.9:2 | or nail to hurt His holy Son in any w.. He |
| W-pI.193.11:5 | to Him Who knows the w. to look upon |
| W-pI.193.12:3 | of time are easily unloosened in this w.. |
| W-pI.193.13:1 | a w. to look on everything that lets it be to |
| W-pI...194.6:2 | a w. of quick reaction to temptation, you |
| W-pI...194.7:6 | pain has found his w. to present peace, |
| W-pI......195.h | Love is the w. I walk in gratitude. |
| W-pI...195.2:3 | and follow in the w. He sets before them, |
| W-pI...195.5:2 | the w. of hatred and the path of death. All |
| W-pI...195.7:3 | would find, the w. is opening at last to us. |
| W-pI...195.8:1 | Walk, then, in gratitude the w. of love. |
| W-pI.195.10:1 | Our gratitude will pave the w. to Him, |
| W-pI.195.10:6 | walk no road except the w. of gratitude, |
| W-pI.195.10:6 | and thus we go who walk the w. to God. |
| W-pI...196.4:2 | may quickly go the w. salvation shows us, |
| W-pI...198.4:2 | How could there be another w., when this |
| W-pI...200.7:6 | Yet can he learn to look on it another w., |

| | |
|---|---|
| W-pI...200.8:2 | to the gate of Heaven and the **w.** beyond. |
| W-pI...200.8:4 | Now the **w.** is easy, sloping gently toward |
| W-pI...200.9:1 | Let us not lose our **w.** again today. We go |
| W-pI.200.11:5 | happy **w.** to leave the world of ambiguity, |
| WpI rVI.in.7:4 | for the **w.** each practice period can best |
| W-pI...213.1:3 | *I learn of Him becomes the* **w.** *I am set free.* |
| W-pI...215.1:1 | (195) Love is the **w.** I walk in gratitude. |
| W-pI...215.1:4 | *thanks to Him for showing me the* **w.** *to go.* |
| W-pI...220.1:2 | *Let me not wander from the* **w.** *of peace, for I* |
| W-pII ....in.7:2 | sought to find our **w.** by following the |
| W-pII ....in.7:3 | We did not know the **w.**, but You did not |
| W-pII ....in.8:2 | We have found the **w.** He chose for us, |
| W-pII ..in.10:6 | We will accept the **w.** God's plan will end, |
| W-pII ..in.10:6 | will end, as we received the **w.** it started. |
| W-pII .225.1:3 | *the* **w.** *Your loving Son is led along to You!* |
| W-pII .225.2:2 | The **w.** is open. Now we follow it in peace |
| W-pII .....2.1:1 | that you would find your **w.** to Him at last |
| W-pII .242.1:5 | and it is He Who knows the **w.** to God. |
| W-pII .242.2:6 | *we need in helping us to find the* **w.** *to You.* |
| W-pII .246.1:1 | me not think that I can find the **w.** to God |
| W-pII .246.2:1 | *the* **w.** *You choose for me to come to You, my* |
| W-pII .256.1:1 | **w.** to God is through forgiveness here. |
| W-pII .256.1:2 | There is no other **w.**. If sin had not been |
| W-pII .256.1:3 | have been to find the **w.** to where you are? |
| W-pII .256.2:1 | *would we come to You in Your appointed* **w.** |
| W-pII .256.2:2 | *the* **w.** *Your sacred Word has pointed out to* |
| W-pII .258.2:1 | *is but to follow in the* **w.** *that leads to You.* |
| W-pII .266.2:3 | How can we lose the **w.** to Him, when He |
| W-pII .269.1:2 | *to become the* **w.** *to show me my mistakes,* |
| W-pII .271.2:1 | *Father, Christ's vision is the* **w.** *to You.* |
| W-pII .273.1:3 | If we give **w.** to a disturbance, let us learn |
| W-pII .278.1:3 | If I am bound in any **w.**, I do not know my |
| W-pII .278.2:4 | *I choose the* **w.** *to You instead of madness* |
| W-pII .280.2:1 | *Your Son, for thus alone I find the* **w.** *to You.* |
| W-pII .281.1:2 | *When I think that I am hurt in any* **w.**, *it is* |
| W-pII .286.2:1 | give us hope that we have found the **w.**, |
| W-pII .287.2:3 | *What* **w.** *but that which leads to You could I* |
| W-pII .287.2:7 | *What* **w.** *but this could I expect to recognize* |
| W-pII .288.1:1 | *This is the thought that leads the* **w.** *to You,* |
| W-pII .288.1:4 | *is the hand that leads me on the* **w.** *to You.* |
| W-pII .288.1:6 | *my heart, or I will lose the* **w.** *to walk to You.* |
| W-pII .291.2:3 | *I do not know the* **w.** *to You. But You are* |
| W-pII .297.1:4 | be the **w.** I live within a world that needs |
| W-pII .298.2:1 | *because I would not follow any* **w.** *but Yours.* |
| W-pII .298.2:3 | *me. Certain is Your* **w.**. *And I am grateful for* |
| W-pII .300.2:2 | *Your loving Sons, have lost our* **w.** *a while.* |
| W-pII .....9.2:3 | lights the Second Coming's **w.**, because it |
| W-pII .....9.3:1 | teaches, making **w.** for the Last Judgment, |
| W-pII .302.2:1 | and walks beside us showing us the **w.**. |
| W-pII .308.1:1 | I have conceived of time in such a **w.** that |
| W-pII .315.1:5 | finds the **w.** to God becomes my savior, |
| W-pII .315.1:5 | my savior, pointing out the **w.** to me, and |
| W-pII ....317.h | I follow in the **w.** appointed me. |
| W-pII .317.1:4 | when I willingly and gladly go the **w.** my |
| W-pII .317.2:1 | *Father, Your* **w.** *is what I choose today.* |
| W-pII .317.2:3 | *Your* **w.** *is certain, and the end secure. The* |
| W-pII .321.1:4 | *nor understood the* **w.** *to find my freedom.* |
| W-pII .321.1:7 | **w.** *to You is opening and clear to me at last.* |
| W-pII .321.2:2 | the certain **w.** our Father has established. |
| W-pII .324.1:2 | *You have set the* **w.** *I am to go, the role to take* |
| W-pII .324.1:3 | *path. I cannot lose the* **w.**. *I can but choose to* |
| W-pII .324.1:6 | *brothers all can follow in the* **w.** *I lead them.* |
| W-pII .324.1:7 | *Yet I merely follow in the* **w.** *to You, as You* |
| W-pII .324.2:1 | So let us follow One Who knows the **w.**. |
| W-pII .325.1:6 | and find the **w.** to Heaven and to God. |
| W-pII .328.1:2 | is the **w.** in which salvation is obtained. |
| W-pII .329.2:4 | Through it we find our **w.** at last to God. |
| W-pII .331.1:2 | *and be left without a certain* **w.** *to his release* |
| W-pII .333.2:1 | *doubt, and light the* **w.** *for our return to You.* |
| W-pII .336.1:2 | gives **w.** entirely to what remains forever |
| W-pII ...13.1:6 | paves the **w.** for the return of timelessness |
| W-pII .342.2:3 | the world goes with us on our **w.** to God. |
| W-pII .345.1:7 | *lights the* **w.** *that I must travel to remember* |
| W-pII .351.1:5 | *beside me, and my* **w.** *secure and clear.* |
| W-pII .352.1:4 | *have given me a* **w.** *to find Your peace again.* |
| W-pII .352.1:5 | *redeemed when I elect to follow in this* **w.**. |
| W-pII .353.1:1 | *use in any* **w.** *that best will serve the purpose* |
| W-pII .357.1:4 | *Voice instructing me to find the* **w.** *to You, as* |
| W-pII .357.1:4 | *to You, as You appointed that the* **w.** *shall be* |
| Wfl........in.1:3 | leads the **w.** and makes our footsteps sure |
| Wfl........in.2:1 | the only **w.** to find the peace that God has |
| Wfl........in.2:2 | **w.** that everyone must travel in the end, |
| Wfl........in.2:4 | us as gracious guidance in the **w.** to go. |
| Wfl........in.2:5 | follow in the **w.** that truth points out to us |
| Wfl........in.2:6 | many brothers who are seeking for the **w.**, |
| Wfl........in.4:2 | points the **w.** to Him and to the Heaven of |
| Wfl........in.4:4 | He is the **w.**, the truth and life that shows |
| Wfl........in.4:4 | the truth and life that shows the **w.** to us. |
| W-ep......... 1:7 | He knows the **w.** to solve all problems, |
| W-ep......... 5:6 | Joy attends our **w.**. For we go homeward |
| W-ep......... 6:2 | In peace we will continue in His **w.**, and |
| M-1........... 2:9 | end, but the end can be a long, long **w.** off |
| M-3........... 3:5 | Perhaps the best **w.** to demonstrate that |
| M-3........... 4:3 | Using the term in this **w.**, the second level |
| M-4..... I.A.6:5 | at which he sees in it his whole **w.** out. |
| M-4..... I.A.8:6 | here, the **w.** to Heaven is open and easy. |
| M-4...... IV.2:6 | hell when he perceives a **w.** to Heaven? |
| M-4...... V.1:11 | They hold His gifts and follow in His **w.**, |
| M-4..... VII.1:8 | In the clearest **w.** possible, and at the |
| M-4......X.2:10 | paves the **w.** for what goes far beyond all |
| M-6........... 1:6 | if the patient uses sickness as a **w.** of life, |
| M-6........... 1:6 | of life, believing healing is the **w.** to death |
| M-10......... 3:4 | everything involved in them in any **w.**. |
| M-10......... 4:9 | and everything involved in any **w.**. And |
| M-11......... 3:4 | yet out of which no **w.** seems possible, |
| M-13....... 8:12 | What other **w.** is there to save His Son? |
| M-14......... 1:9 | How but in this **w.** are all illusions ended? |
| M-16......... 2:4 | use them as best he can in his own **w.**. |
| M-16......... 8:1 | the **w.** the teacher of God has yet to travel, |
| M-17......... 2:1 | respond to magic in a **w.** that reinforces it |
| M-17......... 8:3 | There is a **w.** in which escape is possible. |
| M-17......... 8:7 | this is even dimly grasped, the **w.** is open. |
| M-18......... 2:2 | Only in this **w.** can they proclaim the |
| M-19......... 3:3 | of the world built up in just this **w.**. "Sins" |
| M-20......... 1:5 | each reflects a different step along the **w.**. |
| M-20......... 2:2 | in every **w.** it is totally unlike all previous |
| M-20......... 3:4 | Who sees anger as justified in any **w.** or |
| M-21......... 4:4 | however, learn to use words in a new **w.**. |
| M-21......... 4:6 | "I will step back and let Him lead the **w.**." |
| M-22......... 2:5 | Anywhere along the **w.**, the necessary |
| M-22......... 2:6 | If the **w.** seems long, let him be content. |
| M-22......... 5:9 | Lead not the **w.**, for you have lost it. Turn |
| M-23......... 1:2 | will give **w.** to temptation in this world. |
| M-23......... 4:6 | gratitude to God becomes the **w.** in which |
| M-23......... 5:1 | Jesus has led the **w.**. Why would you not |
| M-23......... 7:2 | possible, to lead the **w.** to those who |
| M-24......... 1:7 | about it really useful in lighting up the **w.** |
| M-24......... 2:5 | **w.** to salvation can be found by those who |
| M-24......... 5:5 | he is misusing the belief in some **w.** that is |
| M-25......... 1:6 | ones that may come to him on the **w.**. |
| M-25......... 2:7 | any **w.** is merely becoming more natural. |
| M-25......... 3:1 | be gathered on the **w.** can be very helpful. |
| M-27......... 1:5 | This is regarded as "the **w.** of nature," not |
| M-27......... 1:6 | waxing and waning in a certain **w.** upon a |
| M-29....... 3:11 | It is the **w.** out of hell for you. |
| C-in........... 5:2 | away to make **w.** for the central teaching. |
| C-2............ 5:1 | The ego's opposite in every **w.**, –in origin |
| C-2............ 7:5 | at the helpers all along the **w.** you travel, |
| C-2.......... 10:6 | the **w.** is short and Heaven is his goal? |
| C-3............ 2:1 | **w.** in which the unknowing can bridge the |
| C-5............ 3:2 | He led the **w.** for you to follow him. He |
| C-5............ 3:5 | life in any **w.** be changed by sin and evil, |
| C-ep........... 1:2 | Doubt along the **w.** will come and go and |
| C-ep........... 3:3 | on before and lost our **w.** a little while. |
| C-ep........... 4:2 | arise and go in faith along the **w.** to Him. |
| C-ep........... 4:5 | know that we will never lose the **w.** again. |
| C-ep........... 5:2 | had lost our **w.** but He has found it for us. |
| P-in........... 1:8 | Either **w.**, the task is the same; the patient |
| P-1............. 2:3 | aim can there be than to recall the **w.**, the |
| P-1............. 3:2 | often regards them in that **w.** himself. |
| P-2.........in.1:4 | it can make **w.** for reality, it has achieved |
| P-2.........in.4:1 | in some **w.** that he believes is real. The |
| P-2...........I.2:4 | "Resistance" is its **w.** of looking at things; |
| P-2...........I.3:2 | Either **w.**, it sets a limit on psychotherapy |
| P-2...........I.4:5 | are patients who need him just that **w.**. |
| P-2..........II.5:4 | in. In the same **w.**, a union of purpose |
| P-2..........II.6:4 | for they have found the **w.** to call to Him. |
| P-2........ III.1:6 | accepted is all there is to light the **w.** to |
| P-2..........V.1:1 | their **w.** in endless mazes of complexity. |
| P-2..........V.2:3 | his twisted **w.** of looking at the world; his |
| P-2..........V.2:3 | world; his twisted **w.** of looking at himself |
| P-2..........V.8:2 | There is one **w.** alone by which we come |
| P-2..........V.8:6 | There is no other **w.** to hear His Voice. |
| P-2..........V.8:7 | There is no other **w.** to seek His Son. |
| P-2..........V.8:8 | There is no other **w.** to find your Self. |
| P-2....... VII.4:1 | in no **w.** confuses himself with God. All |
| P-2....... VII.6:2 | The advanced therapist in no **w.** can ever |
| P-2....... VII.9:5 | You lost the **w.**. And can you now expect |
| P-3........... I.3:6 | whatever **w.** can be most helpful to both |
| P-3..........II.4:7 | **w.** God chose for the return of His Son. In |
| P-3..........II.8:3 | holy instants can be his along the **w.**. |
| P-3.........II.10:7 | does not limit the Holy Spirit in any **w.**. |
| S-1.........in.3:5 | is. This is the **w.**. It is God's gift to you. |
| S-1........... I.1:1 | is a **w.** offered by the Holy Spirit to reach |
| S-1........... I.4:3 | it. Also in the same **w.**, in prayer you |
| S-1........... I.5:2 | it is a **w.** of remembering your holiness. |
| S-1..........II.2:3 | of his Identity can avoid praying in this **w.** |
| S-1..........II.4:2 | **w.** in which they are usually interpreted. |
| S-1........ IV.2:3 | The **w.** is open, and hope is justified. Yet |
| S-1........ IV.3:3 | asks to have the past repeated in some **w.**. |
| S-1..........V.1:1 | Prayer is a **w.** to true humility. And here |
| S-2........... I.6:1 | **w.** in which your only hope of freedom |
| S-2..........II.7:5 | a **w.** to use forgiveness for the goal of God |
| S-2........ III.1:9 | Yet He has willed you learn the **w.** to Him, |
| S-2........ III.2:3 | but let it be a **w.** to draw you up to where |
| S-2........ III.3:2 | the **w.** to make of every call a help to you, |
| S-3..........II.1:3 | Only false healing can give **w.** to fear, so |
| S-3..........II.2:1 | Son of God along the **w.** he goes to God. |
| S-3........ III.6:6 | stand, and fear has given **w.** at last to God |

## ways 59

| | |
|---|---|
| T-2....... VI.5:2 | This situation arises in two **w.**: First, you |
| T-2.....VIII.1:1 | One of the **w.** in which you can correct |
| T-3....... III.2:3 | can see in many **w.** because perception |
| T-4.........II.4:6 | they resemble in many **w.** how you will |
| T-4...... VII.2:7 | **w.** to everything it perceives as related. |
| T-5....... III.1:3 | the separation between the two **w.** of |
| T-5....... III.3:1 | opposed **w.** of seeing your brother. They |
| T-5....... IV.5:1 | Teaching is done in many **w.**, above all |
| T-7.........II.6:6 | you listen to two **w.** of interpreting them. |
| T-7....... III.1:6 | enable you to use it always and in all **w.**. |
| T-7.........V.9:1 | hear two voices, so you can see in two **w.**. |
| T-7.....VIII.2:3 | very ingenious in devising **w.** that seem to |
| T-8.......... I.6:4 | different things in entirely different **w.**, |
| T-12..... VII.5:6 | Two **w.** of looking at the world are in your |
| T-15.... VII.9:5 | and wounding him, perhaps in little **w.**, |
| T-17.......V.8:3 | and to remind you of all the **w.** you once |
| T-17.......V.9:1 | You are very new in the **w.** of salvation, |
| T-22... III.1:10 | the ego separate, to go their separate **w.**. |
| T-22..... VI.2:1 | contrive **w.** to achieve the body's freedom |
| T-25..... III.7:7 | from the belief there are two **w.** to see. |
| T-26.......V.1:4 | And you can learn it in many different **w.**. |
| T-26.......V.1:7 | teachers only, who point in different **w.**. |
| T-27..... IV.1:3 | has no answer, for it is seen in different **w.** |
| T-27..... VI.4:2 | names that speak in other **w.** for its reality |
| T-27...VIII.2:1 | in many **w.** to prove it is autonomous and |
| T-27...VIII.3:3 | has but one purpose, taught in many **w.**. |
| T-28..... VI.2:3 | It behaves in **w.** you want, but never |
| T-29........ I.4:5 | for you and him to go your separate **w.**. |
| T-31.......V.7:9 | growing in its **w.** and finally "maturing" |
| W-pI .... 66.9:2 | and the many **w.** in which you tried to |
| W-pI .... 71.5:3 | that are diametrically opposed in all **w.**. |
| W-pI .... 76.8:2 | the body's protection in innumerable **w.**. |
| W-pI .... 93.2:3 | you have sought salvation in strange **w.**; |
| W-pI .. 100.1:2 | separate lives and go their separate **w.**. |
| WpIrIII.in11:5 | And it is meant to serve you in all **w.**, all |
| W-pI .. 126.2:2 | and able to behave in **w.** which have no |
| W-pI .. 128.1:3 | soar beyond its petty scope and little **w.**. |
| W-pI .. 131.7:1 | this strange world you made and all its **w.** |
| W-pI 135.20:2 | will lead you on in **w.** appointed for your |
| W-pI 152.11:2 | and spend five minutes practicing its **w.**, |
| W-pI 153.18:1 | Voice guiding your footsteps into quiet **w.** |
| W-pI 154.12:2 | You have heard this said a hundred **w.**, a |
| W-pI .. 155.7:3 | to lead your brothers from the **w.** of death |
| W-pI 155.13:2 | not to **w.** that seem to lead you elsewhere. |
| W-pI .. 157.7:1 | of time; a little more like Heaven in its **w.**; |

W-pI...160.1:1 Fear is a stranger to the w. of love.
W-pI...184.9:5 in w. the world can understand, but
W-pI.189.10:4 *Salvation's w. are not our own, for they*
W-pI...196.3:2 For the w. in which the ego would distort
W-pI...198.4:3 a thousand w. in which it must be wrong;
W-pI...199.2:1 Holy Spirit is unlimited forever, in all w.,
W-pII..297.2:1 *Father, how certain are Your w.; how sure*
W-pII....13.2:2 it fails entirely to understand its w..
Wfl ........in.1:5 and destroying, dangerous in all its w.,
W-ep .........6:1 We trust our w. to Him and say "Amen."
M-in ..........5:6 over and over, in many, many w., until
M-13..........5:7 in a thousand w. and in a thousand places
P-3 ......III.8:11 forget how very simple are the w. of God:
S-3 ......... II.4:1 a kind forgiveness of the w. of earth, can

## We 1

• Christ
*we*

W-pII.....354.h W. stand together, Christ and I, in peace

## we 1651

• Jesus
*noise word*
*We*

T-2........IV.2:3 W. have referred to miracles as the means
T-2... V.A.17:6 In time w. exist for and with each other.
T-2... V.A.17:7 In timelessness w. coexist with God.
T-2.......VII.7:7 W. have already attempted to correct the
T-3...........I.2:9 that w. must be sure that nothing of this
T-3........III.1:1 W. have been emphasizing perception,
T-3......... V.1:4 W. can now establish a distinction that
T-3......... V.3:1 Knowing, as w. have already observed,
T-3........VI.1:1 W. have already discussed the Last
T-3.......VII.1:2 a difference w. have already discussed.
T-3.......VII.3:1 W. have discussed the fall or separation
T-4...... in.3:11 W.ave another journey to undertake,
T-4........ I.13:6 so w. can be free of them together. I need
T-4........III.8:2 for w. must hide nothing from each other.
T-4........III.8:4 W. will prepare for this together, for once
T-4........III.9:7 is why w. make no distinction between
T-4......IV.11:5 with mine, and together w. are invincible.
T-4........VI.1:5 W. cannot safely let it go at that, however,
T-4.......VII.8:7 I direct until w. are all united in the joy of
T-5........ II.9:1 yours, because w. were created as equals.
T-5........ II.11:2 As w. share this goal, we increase its
T-5........ II.11:2 w. increase its power to attract the whole
T-5........ II.12:1 but w. must respond to the same Mind to
T-5........ II.12:5 w. can accomplish together has no limits,
T-5........III.1:2 so w. can use the terms as if they were
T-5........IV.8:6 and w. know what God creates is eternal.
T-5......IV.8:12 W. cannot lose. My judgment is as strong
T-5......IV.8:13 Heart and Hands w. have our being. His
T-5......... V.3:3 W. spoke before of the authority problem
T-5......... V.8:2 W. have said this before, but did not
T-5......VI.12:4 W. have repeatedly said that time is a
T-6......... I.6:11 me, and w. will become equal as teachers.
T-6......... I.10:1 W. are still equal as learners, although we
T-6......... I.10:1 w. do not need to have equal experiences.
T-6......... I.11:2 because the Holy Spirit, Whom w. share,
T-6......... II.1:5 W. have said before that the separation
T-6......... II.4:1 W. have learned, however, that there *is* an
T-6........ II.13:5 in this light w. proclaim the Kingdom of
T-6........III.1:1 As w. have already emphasized, every
T-6......V.A.1:5 life. If w. share the same mind, you can
T-6......V.A.4:4 it. W. have too much to accomplish on
T-6......V.B.3:3 and w. can clarify this still further now. At
T-6......V.C.1:1 W. said before that the Holy Spirit is
T-7......... V.2:4 Yet w. have learned that behavior is not
T-7........ V.10:9 with you because w. are of one Mind, and
T-7........ V.11:2 The mind w. share is shared by all our
T-7........ V.11:2 as w. see them truly they will be healed.
T-7..... VIII.1:1 W. have said that without projection
T-8......... II.5:1 W. have said that the Holy Spirit teaches
T-8......IV.3:11 so w. can teach them peace and union.
T-8........IV.6:3 I will help you, knowing that w. are alike.
T-8......... V.1:6 Alone w. can do nothing, but together our
T-8......... V.3:2 His power to you because w. are sharing it
T-8......... V.3:4 As w. unite, we unite with Him. Glory be
T-8......... V.3:4 As we unite, w. unite with Him. Glory be
T-8......... V.3:7 miracles w. do bear witness to the Will of
T-8........ VI.1:1 W. are the joint will of the Sonship,
T-8........ VI.1:2 W. begin the journey back by setting out
T-8........ VI.1:2 and gather in our brothers as w. continue
T-8........ VI.8:4 from each other w. cannot function at all.
T-8........ VI.8:8 Our creations are as holy as w. are, and
T-8........ VI.8:8 are, and w. are the Sons of God Himself,
T-8........ VI.8:9 Through our creations w. extend our love,
T-8........ VI.9:3 W. cannot be separated. Whom God has
T-8....... VI.9:11 Together w. can meet its conditions, but
T-8........ IX.7:3 of love because w. share this Oneness.
T-8........ IX.8:5 you limit yourself w. are not of one mind,
T-9........ VI.3:8 for yourself because w. are part of you,
T-9........ VI.3:8 everything w. do belongs to you as well.
T-9..... VIII.2:7 W. said before that the ego vacillates
T-11.........I.5:5 to God and His Son, for w. *are* the universe
T-11....... V.1:3 W. are ready to look more closely at the
T-11....... V.1:3 w. have the lamp that will dispel it, and
T-11....... V.1:4 w. are merely looking honestly for truth.
T-11....... V.1:5 w. must look first at this to see beyond it,
T-11....... V.1:6 W. will undo this error quietly together,
T-11....... V.4:1 When w. look at the ego, then, we are not
T-11....... V.4:1 then, w. are not considering dynamics but
T-11...... VI.4:9 For w. ascend unto the Father together, as
T-11. VIII.11:4 w. heal together as we live together and
T-11. VIII.11:4 as w. live together and love together. Be
T-12.........I.8:5 w. have repeatedly emphasized the need
T-12.......I.8:11 W. have already learned that fear and
T-12....... II.8:2 W. will but be making perfect to you what
T-12....... II.8:5 and w. will easily accomplish the goal of
T-12....... II.8:7 and what w. can accomplish together will
T-12....... II.9:5 When w. have overcome fear–not by
T-12..... II.10:1 W. are therefore embarking on an
T-12...VII.10:6 For w. are there in the peace of the Father,
T-12...VII.11:6 w. will look upon the real world together.
T-13....... II.4:5 So it is this secret that w. must look upon,
T-13...... III.1:4 Atonement. W. have said that no one will
T-13..... V.7:10 and w. will draw them from their private
T-13..... V.7:10 as w. are united so would we unite with
T-13..... V.7:10 are united so would w. unite with them.
T-13..... V.7:11 and gladness is what w. should offer Him.
T-13...VII.16:2 W. walk together on the way to quietness
T-13...VII.16:4 W. will restore to you the peace of mind
T-13...VII.16:4 peace of mind that w. must find together.
T-13.VII.16:10 w. will spread it like a veil of light across
T-13.VII.16:10 w. hide our brothers from the world, and
T-13...VII.17:1 W. cannot sing redemption's hymn alone
T-13... VIII.8:2 as w. grow in strength the power of God's
T-13... VIII.8:2 and w. will leave no one untouched and
T-13... VIII.8:3 and w. will all unite in the eternity of God
T-13...... X.14:2 Alone w. are all lowly, but together we
T-13...... X.14:2 but together w. shine with brightness so
T-13...... X.14:6 United in this praise w. stand before the
T-13...... X.14:6 w. will surely enter in our sinlessness.
T-13...... XI.3:1 When w. are all united in Heaven, you
T-14.......in.1:6 W. have followed much of the ego's logic,
T-14.......in.1:7 w. have realized that they cannot be seen
T-14....... V.5:1 W. are all joined in the Atonement here,
T-14....... V.9:3 guiltlessness w. know Him, as He knows
T-14...... VI.1:1 The journey that w. undertake together is
T-14...... VI.8:5 W. must open all doors and let the light
T-14...... X.12:5 W. have already learned that this Identity
T-14.... XI.11:2 As w. are held as one in God, so do we
T-14.... XI.11:2 one in God, so do w. learn as one in Him.
T-15.........I.4:9 W. have seen this strange paradox in the
T-15...... III.9:4 so that together w. can replace the shabby
T-15..... III.11:3 that w. may release all those who would
T-15..... III.11:4 Thus will w. let no one forget what you
T-15....... V.2:2 W. have said that to limit love to part of
T-15...... VI.2:5 In the holy instant w. share our faith in
T-15...... VI.2:5 faith in God's Son because w. recognize,
T-15...... VI.2:5 of his worth w. cannot doubt his holiness.
T-15...... VI.2:6 doubt his holiness. And so w. love him.
T-15......VII.3:5 As w. bring it to light, your only question
T-15......VII.4:1 W. said before that the ego attempts to
T-15..... X.1:10 The time of Christ w. celebrate together,
T-15..... X.1:10 for it has no meaning if w. are apart.
T-15........X.3:1 W. who are one cannot give separately.
T-15...... XI.8:3 to perceive w. are deprived of nothing?
T-15...... XI.9:3 And w. but celebrate His Wholeness as we
T-15...... XI.9:3 as w. welcome Him into ourselves. Those
T-15.... XI.10:9 to do, and w. have been long delayed.
T-16...... III.1:1 W. have already learned that everyone
T-16...... IV.7:5 It is essential that w. look very closely at
T-16.... IV.12:6 W. will take the last useless journey away
T-16.... IV.12:6 and then together w. go straight to God,
T-16..... VII.6:2 W. said before that the Holy Spirit must
T-17...... IV.6:4 Yet w. have looked at it far closer than we
T-17...... IV.6:4 at it far closer than w. have at many other
T-17.... IV.16:3 W. will gain everything by giving Him the
T-18.......I.10:9 and perfect reality, which w. share in Him
T-18......II.7:10 For w. are joined as in one purpose, being
T-18...... III.5:1 Each instant that w. spend together will
T-18...... III.5:7 And where w. go we carry God with us.
T-18...... III.5:7 And where we go w. carry God with us.
T-18...... III.7:4 W. are made whole in our desire to make
T-18...... IV.7:6 is. Yet w. have emphasized that you need
T-18.... IX.11:3 W. need remember only that whoever
T-19.........I.1:1 W. said before that when a situation has
T-19.........I.1:3 Yet w. also said that peace without faith
T19....IV.B.1:1 W. said that peace must first surmount
T19....IV.B.5:4 W. will surmount all obstacles together,
T19....IV.B.5:4 w. stand within the gates and not outside.
T19....IV.B.7:3 And w. are there together, in the quiet
T19....IV.B.8:5 communion, where w. are joined already,
T19..IV.C.2:14 W. know that an idea leaves not its source
T19..IV.C.2:15 is the result of the thought w. call the ego,
T19. IV.D.16:1 of resurrection, to which w. come again;
T19. IV.D.16:1 to which we come again; to which w. will
T19. IV.D.17:5 it, that w. may rise as one in resurrection,
T19. IV.D.17:9 that w. might meet here in this holy place,
T19. IV.D.18:5 So will w. prepare together the way unto
T19. IV.D.19:1 Together w. will disappear into the
T-20.........I.2:3 This week w. celebrate life, not death.
T-20.........I.2:4 w. honor the perfect purity of the Son of
T-20.........I.2:9 W. cannot be united in crucifixion and in
T-20.......II.8:12 the home w. share in quietness and where
T-20.......II.8:12 and where w. live in gentleness and peace,
T-20........II.9:4 joy. W. go beyond the veil of fear, lighting
T-20........II.9:6 will w. find what we were meant to find
T-20........II.9:6 will we find what w. were meant to find
T-20.......II.10:1 in which w. join in glad awareness that
T-20.... III.10:4 it? Here are w. one, looking with perfect
T-20..... VII.1:1 W. have said much about discrepancies
T-20..... VII.1:2 But w. have also said the means to meet
T-20..... VII.3:8 it. Before w. look at them a little closer,
T-21.........I.5:5 you remember what w. will speak of now.
T-21........II.1:1 W. have repeated how little is asked of
T-21........II.9:1 W. have already said that wishful
T-21.......II.10:4 w. spoke of your desire to create your own
T-21..... VII.6:4 W. said this year would emphasize the
T-22.........I.2:1 w. have heard a very similar description
T-22........II.9:5 And here w. see again another form of the
T-22........II.9:5 illusion w. have seen many times before.
T-23........II.1:4 calmly, that w. may look beyond them,
T-23.......II.16:3 w. have seen how it appears to function
T-24..... VII.8:4 do w. deal with them as if they were. It is
T-25..... VII.3:1 Let us go back to what w. said before, and
T-26.... III.1:14 Nor is it necessary w. dwell on anything
T-26...... III.3:2 W. have referred to it as the real world.
T-26..... VII.1:3 review the principles that w. have covered
T-26..... VII.9:3 W. call it "wish" because it still conceives
T-27....VIII.5:9 W. can remember this, if we but look
T-27....VIII.5:9 this, if w. but look directly at their cause.
T-27..VIII.5:10 And w. will see the grounds for laughter,
T-27....VIII.6:4 Together, w. can laugh them both away,
T-28...... III.1:4 Here is where w. must begin. And having
T-30.......in.1:7 So now w. need to practice them awhile,
T-30.......in.1:8 W. seek to make them habits now, so you
T-30.......I.14:1 W. said you can begin a happy day with
T-30..... VII.7:6 W. have one Interpreter. And through His
T-30..... VII.7:7 through His use of symbols are w. joined,
T-30..... VII.7:8 all, and thus w. can communicate again.
T-31.......I.12:1 and forget all things w. ever learned, all
T-31.......I.12:1 we ever learned, all thoughts w. had, and
T-31.......I.12:1 and every preconception that w. hold of

W-pI.....95.3:2 W. will again direct our exercises towards
W-pI.....95.3:3 In patience and in hope w. try again today
W-pI.....95.7:1 W. will, therefore, keep to the five-
W-pI.....95.8:5 If w. give it power to do this, we are
W-pI.....95.8:5 to do this, w. are regarding it as strength,
W-pI...95.10:4 Today w. will affirm this truth again, and
W-pI...95.14:2 W. need your help; your little part in
W-pI.....96.8:1 W. will attempt today to find this
W-pI.....97.2:1 W. state again the truth about your Self,
W-pI.....97.3:1 Today w. try to bring reality still closer to
W-pI.....98.1:2 W. take a stand on but one side today.
W-pI.....98.1:3 W. side with truth and let illusions go.
W-pI.....98.1:4 W. will not vacillate between the two, but
W-pI.....98.1:5 W. dedicate ourselves to truth today, and
W-pI.....98.1:6 W. will not argue it is something else. We
W-pI.....98.1:7 W. will not seek for it where it is not. In
W-pI.....98.1:8 In gladness w. accept it as it is, and take
W-pI.....98.2:2 All our doubts w. lay aside today, and
W-pI.....98.2:3 W. have a mighty purpose to fulfill, and
W-pI.....98.2:3 everything w. need with which to reach
W-pI.....98.2:5 For w. have been absolved from errors.
W-pI.....98.3:5 took the stand which w. will take today,
W-pI.....98.3:5 that w. may share their certainty and thus
W-pI.....98.4:1 all who took the stand w. take today will
W-pI.....98.4:3 as yet unborn will hear the call w. heard,
W-pI.....98.4:4 W. do not choose but for ourselves today.
W-pI.....99.9:5 and start the lesson that w. learn today
W-pI...100.5:1 W. will not let ourselves be sad today. For
W-pI...100.5:2 For if w. do, we fail to take the part that is
W-pI...100.5:2 w. fail to take the part that is essential to
W-pI...100.6:1 Today w. will attempt to understand joy
W-pI...100.7:1 W. will prepare ourselves for this today,
W-pI...101.1:1 Today w. will continue with the theme of
W-pI...101.5:5 W. practice with this thought as often as
W-pI...101.5:5 with this thought as often as w. can today,
W-pI...102.2:1 Today w. try to loose its weakened hold
W-pI...102.3:1 several days w. will continue to devote
W-pI...103.2:3 error w. will try again to bring to truth
W-pI...104.2:1 Today w. would remove all meaningless
W-pI...104.2:1 which w. have placed upon the holy altar
W-pI...104.2:3 the gifts that w. inherited before time was
W-pI...104.2:5 And w. need not wait to have them. They
W-pI...104.3:1 Therefore, w. choose to have them now,
W-pI...104.3:1 choosing them in place of what w. made,
W-pI...104.3:1 w. but unite our will with what God wills,
W-pI...104.4:1 All this w. lay aside, and seek instead that
W-pI...104.4:1 w. ask to recognize what God has given us
W-pI...104.4:2 us. W. clear a holy place within our minds
W-pI...104.4:2 w. come to find what has been given us by
W-pI...104.4:3 W. come in confidence today, aware that
W-pI...104.4:4 And w. would wish for nothing else, for
W-pI...104.5:1 So do w. clear the way for Him today by
W-pI...104.5:2 gifts. W. will not let ourselves lose sight of
W-pI...104.5:2 the times w. come to seek for them where
W-pI...104.5:3 will w. bring to mind as often as we can:
W-pI...104.5:3 will we bring to mind as often as w. can:
W-pI...105.1:2 Today w. will accept them, knowing they
W-pI...105.1:3 And w. will try to understand these gifts
W-pI...105.1:3 these gifts increase as w. receive them.
W-pI...105.8:1 if you prepare your mind as w. suggest.
W-pI...106.7:3 Today w. practice giving, not the way you
W-pI...107.7:1 W. do not ask for what we do not have.
W-pI...107.7:1 We do not ask for what w. do not have.
W-pI...107.7:2 W. merely ask for what belongs to us, that
W-pI...107.7:2 to us, that w. may recognize it as our own.
W-pI...107.7:3 Today w. practice on the happy note of
W-pI...107.7:5 W. are as certain of success as we are sure
W-pI...107.7:5 We are as certain of success as w. are sure
W-pI...107.7:5 as certain of success as we are sure w. live
W-pI...107.7:6 W. do not doubt we walk with truth today
W-pI...107.7:6 We do not doubt w. walk with truth today
W-pI...107.7:6 into all the exercises that w. do this day.
W-pI...108.7:1 Today w. practice with the special case of
W-pI...108.7:2 receiving. W. will use this simple lesson in
W-pI...108.7:2 because it has results w. cannot miss. To
W-pI...108.7:4 Today w. will attempt to offer peace to
W-pI...108.7:5 peace is vision given us, and w. can see.
W-pI...108.8:1 So w. begin the practice periods with the
W-pI.108.10:2 w. will make much faster progress now.
W-pI...109.1:1 W. ask for rest today, and quietness
W-pI...109.1:2 W. ask for peace and stillness, in the
W-pI...109.1:3 W. ask for safety and for happiness,
W-pI...109.1:3 w. seem to look on danger and on sorrow.
W-pI...109.1:4 And w. have the thought that will answer
W-pI...109.1:4 answer our asking with what w. request.
W-pI...109.9:3 W. rest together here, for thus our rest is
W-pI...109.9:3 w. give today we have received already.
W-pI...109.9:3 we give today w. have received already.
W-pI...109.9:4 is not the guardian of what w. give today.
W-pI...109.9:5 W. give to those unborn and those passed
W-pI...109.9:6 And w. remind them of their resting place
W-pI...109.9:6 resting place each time w. tell ourselves,
W-pI...110.1:1 W. will repeat today's idea from time to
W-pI.110.10:4 Today w. make a great advance to truth
W-pI.110.11:1 W. will remember Him throughout the
W-pI.110.11:2 For it is thus that w. remember Him. And
W-pI.110.11:3 And w. will say, that we may be reminded
W-pI.110.11:3 say, that w. may be reminded of His Son,
W-pI.110.11:5 Let us declare this truth as often as w. can.
WpI. rIII.in1:2 W. will review two recent lessons every
WpI. rIII.in1:3 W. will observe a special format for these
WpI. rIII.in2:1 W. understand, of course, that it may be
WpI. rIII.in8:1 W. emphasize the benefits to you if you
WpIrIII.in10:1 w. stress the need to let your learning not
WpIrIII.in12:3 that w. come from these reviews with
WpIrIII.in12:3 w. will continue on more solid ground,
W-pI...121.8:1 Today w. practice learning to forgive. If
W-pI...121.8:3 behalf. W. will devote ten minutes in the
W-pI...121.9:2 Yet w. will try to learn today that they are
W-pI...121.9:3 one, w. will extend the lesson to yourself,
W-pI...122.6:6 that this is so, for here w. have an answer,
W-pI...122.9:1 w. undertake our practicing today with
W-pI...122.9:2 and gladly will w. seek for it today, aware
W-pI...122.9:2 aware w. hold the key within our hands,
W-pI...122.9:2 Heaven's answer to the hell w. made, but
W-pI...122.9:2 but where w. would remain no more.
W-pI.122.10:1 Morning and evening do w. gladly give a
W-pI.122.10:2 for w. have reached the turning point at
W-pI.122.10:3 now the way is short that yet w. travel.
W-pI.122.10:4 W. are close indeed to the appointed
W-pI.122.12:2 Now w. walk directly into light, and we
W-pI.122.12:2 w. receive the gifts that have been held in
W-pI...123.1:2 W. have come to gentler pathways and to
W-pI...123.4:1 gratitude w. lift our hearts above despair,
W-pI...123.4:2 W. sing the song of thankfulness today, in
W-pI...123.4:3 Today w. smile on everyone we see, and
W-pI...123.4:3 Today we smile on everyone w. see, and
W-pI...123.4:3 as w. go to do what is appointed us to do.
W-pI...123.5:1 W. do not go alone. And we give thanks
W-pI...123.5:2 And w. give thanks that in our solitude a
W-pI...124.1:1 Today w. will again give thanks for our
W-pI...124.1:2 is safe, protection guaranteed in all w. do,
W-pI...124.1:3 W. can fail in nothing. Everything we
W-pI...124.1:4 Everything w. touch takes on a shining
W-pI...124.1:5 with the universe w. go our way rejoicing,
W-pI...124.2:2 everything w. see reflects the holiness
W-pI...124.2:4 is our Companion as w. walk the world a
W-pI...124.2:5 because the light w. carry stays behind,
W-pI...124.2:5 yet still remains with us as w. walk on.
W-pI...124.3:1 w. receive is our eternal gift to those who
W-pI...124.3:2 the equal love in which w. were created,
W-pI...124.3:2 on us and offers us the happiness w. gave.
W-pI...124.4:1 Today w. will not doubt His Love for us,
W-pI...124.4:3 W. are one with Him today in recognition
W-pI...124.4:4 W. feel Him in our hearts. Our minds
W-pI...124.4:5 behold His loveliness in all w. look upon.
W-pI...124.4:6 Today w. see only the loving and the
W-pI...124.5:1 W. see it in appearances of pain, and
W-pI...124.5:2 W. see it in the frantic, in the sad and the
W-pI...124.5:3 w. see it in the dying and the dead as well,
W-pI...124.5:4 life. All this w. see because we saw it first
W-pI...124.5:4 see because w. saw it first within ourselves
W-pI...124.7:1 W. join in this awareness as we say that
W-pI...124.7:1 as w. say that we are one with God. For in
W-pI...124.7:1 as we say that w. are one with God. For in
W-pI...124.7:2 words w. say as well that we are saved and
W-pI...124.7:2 words we say as well that w. are saved and
W-pI...124.7:2 that w. can save and heal accordingly. We
W-pI...124.7:3 W. have accepted, and we now would give
W-pI...124.7:3 We have accepted, and w. now would give
W-pI...124.7:4 w. would keep the gifts our Father gave.
W-pI...124.7:5 Today w. would experience ourselves at
W-pI...124.7:7 w. deny our separation from our Father, it
W-pI...124.8:4 which w. give no rules nor special words
W-pI...124.8:5 W. will trust God's Voice to speak as He
W-pI...125.3:1 In stillness w. will hear God's Voice today
W-pI...125.3:2 W. will not judge ourselves today, for
W-pI...125.3:2 today, for what w. are can not be judged.
W-pI...125.3:3 W. stand apart from all the judgments
W-pI...125.3:5 Today w. will not listen to the world, but
W-pI...125.4:3 W. gather at the throne of God today, the
W-pI...126.8:1 Today w. try to understand the truth that
W-pI...126.8:5 that lies in the idea w. practice for today,
W-pI...127.6:4 Today w. practice making free your mind
W-pI...127.6:5 Today w. take the largest single step this
W-pI.127.10:2 that w. are spared a future like the past.
W-pI.127.10:3 past. Today w. leave the past behind us,
W-pI.127.10:4 w. raise our eyes upon a different present,
W-pI.127.11:2 And w. will watch it grow in health and
W-pI.127.12:1 W. will remember them throughout the
W-pI.127.12:1 w. cannot leave a part of us outside our
W-pI.127.12:1 outside our love if w. would know our Self
W-pI...128.5:1 Today w. practice letting go all thought
W-pI...128.5:1 of values w. have given to the world. We
W-pI...128.5:2 W. leave it free of purposes we gave its
W-pI...128.5:2 leave it free of purposes w. gave its aspects
W-pI...128.5:3 W. hold it purposeless within our minds,
W-pI...128.5:3 and loosen it from all w. wish it were.
W-pI...128.5:4 Thus do w. lift the chains that bar the
W-pI...129.1:1 from the one w. practiced yesterday. You
W-pI...129.3:3 at last for what w. cannot speak of, for
W-pI...129.8:4 is given you today, and w. give thanks.
W-pI...129.8:5 This day w. realize that what you feared to
W-pI...129.9:1 Now do w. understand there is no loss.
W-pI...129.9:2 For w. have seen its opposite at last, and
W-pI...129.9:2 and w. are grateful that the choice is made
W-pI...130.4:8 Today w. will not seek for them, nor
W-pI...130.6:1 Today w. will attempt no compromise
W-pI...130.6:3 w. would learn today is more than just the
W-pI...130.7:1 w. gladly give five minutes to the thought
W-pI...130.7:2 W. will not make a thousand meaningless
W-pI...130.7:2 w. devote our minds to finding only what
W-pI...131.9:1 Today w. will not choose a paradox in
W-pI.131.10:2 and it is truth w. seek to reach today. We
W-pI.131.10:3 W. will devote ten minutes to this goal
W-pI.131.10:3 and w. will ask to see the rising of the real
W-pI.131.10:3 the foolish images that w. hold dear, with
W-pI.131.11:1 This w. acknowledge as we start upon our
W-pI.131.11:1 acknowledge as w. start upon our practice
W-pI.131.14:5 w. come to the appointed time and place
W-pI...132.8:1 and in the exercises that w. do today.
W-pI.132.14:1 all the idle thoughts w. ever held about it,
W-pI.132.14:1 and about all living things w. see upon it.
W-pI.132.14:3 No more can w.. For we are in the home
W-pI.132.14:4 w. are in the home our Father set for us,
W-pI.132.14:5 And w. who are as He created us would
W-pI.132.14:5 one of our illusions, that w. may be free.
W-pI.132.15:1 in which w. practice twice today with this:
W-pI...133.1:2 This w. will do today. We will not speak
W-pI...133.1:3 do today. W. will not speak of lofty, world-
W-pI...133.3:1 Today w. list the real criteria by which to
W-pI...133.4:1 W. have already stressed there are but
W-pI...133.4:2 range is set, and this w. cannot change. It
W-pI.133.11:1 w. come to the criterion for choice that is
W-pI.133.13:2 W. will attempt to reach this state today,
W-pI.134.14:1 Today w. practice true forgiveness, that
W-pI.134.14:2 w. would meet with our reality in freedom
W-pI.134.14:3 follow us to the reality w. share with them
W-pI.135.21:1 W. will anticipate that time today with
W-pI.135.21:2 W. will be sure that everything we need is
W-pI.135.21:2 We will be sure that everything w. need is
W-pI.135.21:3 W. make no plans for how it will be done,
W-pI.135.22:1 today w. rest from senseless planning,
W-pI.135.22:2 Today w. will receive instead of plan, that
W-pI.135.22:2 plan, that w. may give instead of organize.
W-pI.135.22:3 w. are given truly, as we say: *If I defend*
W-pI.135.22:3 we are given truly, as w. say: *If I defend*

W-pI.135.25:2 Today **w.** will remember Him. For this is
W-pI.136.15:2 **w.** will give a quarter of an hour twice to
W-pI.136.15:4 for just this invitation which **w.** give today
W-pI.136.15:5 **W.** introduce it with a healing prayer, to
W-pI.137.12:6 Today **w.** ask that only truth will occupy
W-pI.137.13:1 **W.** will remember, as the hour strikes,
W-pI.137.13:1 that **w.** may carry healing to the world,
W-pI.137.14:1 Yet must **w.** be prepared for such a gift.
W-pI.137.14:2 And so **w.** will begin the day with this,
W-pI.137.14:2 **w.** will conclude today at night as well:
W-pI.137.15:3 Now **w.** come together to make well all
W-pI.137.15:4 Nor will **w.** let this function be forgot as
W-pI...138.1:1 **w.** believe there are alternatives to choose
W-pI...138.1:2 **W.** think that all things have an opposite,
W-pI...138.1:2 an opposite, and what **w.** want we choose.
W-pI...138.1:2 an opposite, and what we want **w.** choose.
W-pI...138.1:3 is the way **w.** make what we perceive, and
W-pI...138.1:3 is the way we make what **w.** perceive, and
W-pI...138.1:3 we perceive, and what **w.** think is real.
W-pI...138.5:4 But knowledge is beyond the goals **w.** seek
W-pI...138.7:1 So **w.** begin today considering the choice
W-pI.138.10:5 And shall **w.** hesitate to choose today?
W-pI.138.11:1 **W.** make the choice for Heaven as we
W-pI.138.11:1 make the choice for Heaven as **w.** wake,
W-pI.138.11:1 spend five minutes making sure that **w.**
W-pI.138.11:2 **W.** recognize we make a conscious choice
W-pI.138.11:2 We recognize **w.** make a conscious choice
W-pI.138.12:1 Before **w.** close our eyes in sleep tonight,
W-pI.138.12:1 **w.** reaffirm the choice that we have made
W-pI.138.12:1 we reaffirm the choice that **w.** have made
W-pI.138.12:2 And now **w.** give the last five minutes of
W-pI.138.12:2 day to the decision with which **w.** awoke.
W-pI.138.12:3 passed, **w.** have declared our choice again,
W-pI.138.12:4 And finally, **w.** close the day with this,
W-pI.138.12:4 this, acknowledging **w.** chose but what we
W-pI.138.12:4 we chose but what **w.** want: *Heaven is the*
W-pI...139.1:2 For here **w.** come to a decision to accept
W-pI...139.1:3 is choice except uncertainty of what **w.** are
W-pI...139.9:1 **W.** have a mission here. We did not come
W-pI...139.9:2 **W.** did not come to reinforce the madness
W-pI...139.9:2 the madness that **w.** once believed in. Let
W-pI...139.9:3 Let us not forget the goal that **w.** accepted
W-pI...139.9:4 just our happiness alone **w.** came to gain.
W-pI...139.9:5 What **w.** accept as what we are proclaims
W-pI...139.9:5 as what **w.** are proclaims what everyone
W-pI.139.10:3 It is but this that **w.** are asked to do. It is
W-pI.139.10:4 to do. It is but this that **w.** will do today.
W-pI.139.11:1 the morning and at night **w.** will devote to
W-pI.139.11:2 **W.** start with this review of what our
W-pI.139.11:4 **W.** have not lost the knowledge that God
W-pI.139.11:5 **W.** can remember it for everyone, for in
W-pI.139.12:1 **w.** repeat our dedication to our cause
W-pI.139.12:1 as **w.** lay aside all thoughts that would
W-pI...140.8:1 Today **w.** seek to change our minds about
W-pI...140.8:1 sickness, for **w.** seek a cure for all illusions
W-pI...140.8:2 **W.** will try today to find the source of
W-pI...140.8:5 **W.** need but seek it and it must be found.
W-pI...140.9:1 **W.** will not be misled today by what
W-pI...140.9:2 **W.** go beyond appearances today and
W-pI...140.9:3 **W.** will succeed to the extent to which we
W-pI...140.9:3 to the extent to which **w.** realize that there
W-pI.140.10:1 do **w.** lay aside our amulets, our charms
W-pI.140.10:2 **W.** will be still and listen for the Voice of
W-pI.140.10:4 Today **w.** hear a single Voice which speaks
W-pI.140.11:1 **W.** waken hearing Him, and let Him
W-pI.140.11:1 five minutes more before **w.** go to sleep.
W-pI.140.11:4 **W.** have no need to make them different,
W-pI.140.11:4 thus delay the time when **w.** can hear our
W-pI.140.11:5 to us. **W.** hear Him now. We come to Him
W-pI.140.11:6 hear Him now. **W.** come to Him today.
W-pI.140.12:1 nothing in our hands to which **w.** cling,
W-pI.140.12:1 lifted hearts and listening minds **w.** pray:
W-pI.140.12:3 *Speak to us, Father, that* ***w.*** *may be healed.*
W-pI.140.12:4 And **w.** will feel salvation cover us with
W-pI.140.12:5 This will **w.** learn today. And we will say
W-pI.140.12:6 **w.** will say our prayer for healing hourly,
W-pI.140.12:6 given us as **w.** attend in silence and in joy.
W-pI.140.12:8 ends, and **w.** remember Who we really are
W-pI.140.12:8 ends, and we remember Who **w.** really are

WpI. rIV.in1:1 Now **w.** review again, this time aware we
WpI. rIV.in1:1 this time aware **w.** are preparing for the
WpI. rIV.in1:2 Today **w.** will begin to concentrate on
WpI. rIV.in1:4 **w.** review the recent lessons and their
WpI. rIV.in1:4 the readiness that **w.** would now achieve.
WpI. rIV.in2:1 each step in the review **w.** undertake,
WpI. rIV.in4:4 So do **w.** start each practice period in this
WpI. rIV.in4:4 to understand the lessons that **w.** read,
WpI. rIV.in7:6 **w.** will use no format for our practicing
WpI. rIV.in9:1 **W.** add no other thoughts, but let these
WpI. rIV.in9:2 are. **W.** need no more than this to give us
WpI. rIV.in9:2 and all our Father wills that **w.** receive as
WpI. rIV.in9:2 receive as the inheritance **w.** have of Him.
WpI. rIV.in9:3 Each day of practicing, as **w.** review, we
WpI. rIV.in9:3 we review, **w.** close as we began, repeating
WpI. rIV.in9:3 we review, we close as **w.** began, repeating
W-pI.151.13:1 **W.** practice wordlessly today, except at
W-pI.151.13:1 beginning of the time **w.** spend with God.
W-pI.151.13:2 **W.** introduce these times with but a single
W-pI.151.13:3 begins. And then **w.** watch our thoughts,
W-pI.151.16:4 Now do **w.** lift our resurrected minds in
W-pI.151.17:1 And **w.** will hourly remember Him Who
W-pI.151.17:2 As **w.** give thanks, the world unites with
W-pI...152.8:1 accept what **w.** have made as what it is.
W-pI...152.9:1 Today **w.** practice true humility,
W-pI...152.9:4 **W.** lay aside the arrogance which says
W-pI...152.9:4 arrogance which says that **w.** are sinners,
W-pI...152.9:4 guilty and afraid, ashamed of what **w.** are;
W-pI.152.10:2 And **w.** accept of Him that which we are,
W-pI.152.10:2 And we accept of Him that which **w.** are,
W-pI.152.11:1 Now do **w.** join in glad acknowledgment
W-pI.152.11:2 **W.** think of truth alone as we arise, and
W-pI.152.11:2 We think of truth alone as **w.** arise, and
W-pI.152.11:5 Then will **w.** wait in silence, giving up all
W-pI.152.11:5 as **w.** humbly ask our Self that He reveal
W-pI...153.8:1 **W.** will not play such childish games
W-pI...153.8:2 **w.** would not exchange for foolishness the
W-pI...153.8:3 us. **W.** would not let our happiness slip by
W-pI...153.8:3 **w.** mistook the figures in it for the Son of
W-pI...153.9:1 **W.** look past dreams today, and
W-pI...153.9:1 recognize that **w.** need no defense because
W-pI...153.9:1 we need no defense because **w.** are created
W-pI...153.9:2 Now **w.** cannot fear, for we have left all
W-pI...153.9:2 for **w.** have left all fearful thoughts behind
W-pI...153.9:3 And in defenselessness **w.** stand secure,
W-pI...153.9:3 sure **w.** will fulfill our chosen purpose, as
W-pI.153.13:3 in which **w.** put away the toys of guilt, and
W-pI.153.14:1 **W.** pause but for a moment more, to play
W-pI.153.14:2 And then **w.** go to take our rightful place
W-pI.153.15:1 Today **w.** practice in a form we will
W-pI.153.15:1 we practice in a form **w.** will maintain for
W-pI.153.15:2 **W.** will begin each day by giving our
W-pI.153.15:3 the least **w.** give to preparation for a day
W-pI.153.15:3 in which salvation is the only goal **w.** have
W-pI.153.15:5 **w.** will find that half an hour is too short a
W-pI.153.15:6 Nor will **w.** willingly give less at night, in
W-pI.153.16:1 as **w.** remember to be faithful to the Will
W-pI.153.16:1 be faithful to the Will **w.** share with God.
W-pI.153.16:2 most that **w.** can offer as the hour strikes.
W-pI.153.16:3 Sometimes **w.** will forget. At other times
W-pI.153.16:4 and **w.** will be unable to withdraw a little
W-pI.153.17:1 Yet when **w.** can, we will observe our
W-pI.153.17:1 **w.** will observe our trust as ministers of
W-pI.153.17:2 And **w.** will quietly sit by and wait on Him
W-pI.153.19:2 **W.** clothe ourselves in it, as we prepare to
W-pI.153.19:2 in it, as **w.** prepare to meet the day. We
W-pI.153.19:3 **W.** rise up strong in Christ, and let our
W-pI.153.19:3 as **w.** remember that His strength abides
W-pI.153.19:4 **W.** will remind ourselves that He remains
W-pI.153.19:5 **W.** call upon His strength each time we
W-pI.153.19:5 His strength each time **w.** feel the threat
W-pI.153.19:6 **W.** will pause a moment, as He tells us, "I
W-pI...154.1:2 **W.** have gone beyond such foolishness.
W-pI...154.1:3 **W.** cannot judge ourselves, nor need we
W-pI...154.1:3 cannot judge ourselves, nor need **w.** do so
W-pI...154.1:5 nor can **w.** know what role is best for us;
W-pI...154.1:5 **w.** can do within a larger plan we cannot
W-pI...154.1:5 a larger plan **w.** cannot see in its entirety.
W-pI...154.1:7 what **w.** think is weakness can be strength

W-pI .. 154.1:7 what **w.** believe to be our strength is often
W-pI 154.10:1 that **w.** undertake to recognize today. We
W-pI 154.10:2 **W.** will not seek to keep our minds apart
W-pI 154.10:2 is but our voice **w.** hear as we attend Him.
W-pI 154.10:2 is but our voice we hear as **w.** attend Him.
W-pI 154.11:1 **W.** practice giving Him what He would
W-pI 154.11:1 have, that **w.** may recognize His gifts to us
W-pI 154.11:5 that **w.** may be the true receivers of the
W-pI 154.12:1 **W.** will not recognize what we receive
W-pI 154.12:1 recognize what **w.** receive until we give it.
W-pI 154.12:1 recognize what we receive until **w.** give it.
W-pI 154.14:1 world recedes as **w.** light up our minds,
W-pI 154.14:3 Creator. Now **w.** demonstrate how they
W-pI 154.14:4 For as **w.** prove that we accept no will we
W-pI 154.14:4 that **w.** accept no will we do not share, our
W-pI 154.14:4 that we accept no will **w.** do not share, our
W-pI 154.14:4 and **w.** will recognize what we received.
W-pI 154.14:4 and we will recognize what **w.** received.
W-pI .. 155.3:1 This is the simple choice **w.** make today.
W-pI 155.11:3 And **w.** step forth toward this, as we
W-pI 155.11:3 as **w.** progress along the way that truth
W-pI 155.11:4 final journey, which **w.** make for everyone
W-pI 155.11:5 **W.** must not lose our way. For as truth
W-pI 155.12:1 **W.** walk to God. Pause and reflect on this
W-pI 155.12:5 **W.** walk to God. The truth that walks
W-pI 155.14:2 **w.** practice gladly with this thought today:
W-pI .. 156.2:1 **W.** are not inconsistent in the thoughts
W-pI .. 156.2:1 that **w.** present in our curriculum. Truth
W-pI .. 157.2:2 **W.** add a new dimension now; a fresh
W-pI .. 157.2:2 a light on all that **w.** have learned already,
W-pI .. 157.2:2 prepares us for what **w.** have yet to learn.
W-pI .. 157.2:3 and **w.** catch a glimpse of what lies past
W-pI .. 157.2:4 us here an instant, and **w.** go beyond it,
W-pI .. 157.6:2 world. **W.** cannot give experience like this
W-pI .. 157.6:3 it leaves a vision in our eyes which **w.** can
W-pI .. 157.8:1 Today **w.** will embark upon a course you
W-pI .. 157.9:1 Into Christ's Presence will **w.** enter now,
W-pI .. 158.3:6 **W.** but undertake a journey that is over.
W-pI .. 158.4:5 For **w.** but see the journey from the point
W-pI .. 158.4:5 on it, imagining **w.** make it once again;
W-pI .. 158.6:7 is with Christ's vision. This **w.** can attain.
W-pI 158.11:3 **W.** practice seeing with the eyes of Christ
W-pI 158.11:4 And by the holy gifts **w.** give, Christ's
W-pI .. 160.9:1 Today **w.** offer thanks that Christ has
W-pI .. 161.1:1 Today **w.** practice differently, and take a
W-pI .. 161.1:2 in which **w.** practice with today's idea.
W-pI .. 161.3:2 it is specifics **w.** must use in practicing.
W-pI .. 161.3:3 **W.** give them to the Holy Spirit, that He
W-pI .. 161.3:3 is different from the one **w.** gave to them.
W-pI .. 161.3:4 Yet He can use but what **w.** made, to
W-pI .. 161.3:4 so **w.** can see a different use in everything.
W-pI .. 161.4:8 **W.** need to see a little, that we learn a lot.
W-pI .. 161.4:8 We need to see a little, that **w.** learn a lot.
W-pI .. 161.5:1 It seems to be the body that **w.** feel limits
W-pI 161.10:1 Today **w.** practice in a form we have
W-pI 161.10:1 in a form **w.** have attempted earlier. Your
W-pI .. 162.1:2 From time to time **w.** will repeat it, as we
W-pI .. 162.1:2 it, as **w.** reach another stage in learning. It
W-pI .. 162.4:1 Today **w.** practice simply. For the words
W-pI .. 162.4:2 For the words **w.** use are mighty, and they
W-pI .. 162.5:1 **W.** honor you today. Yours is the right to
W-pI .. 163.6:5 For here again **w.** see an obvious position,
W-pI .. 163.6:5 which **w.** must accept if we be sane; what
W-pI .. 163.6:5 which we must accept if **w.** be sane; what
W-pI .. 163.8:5 and **w.** renounce it now in every form, for
W-pI .. 163.8:8 This the stand **w.** take today. And it is
W-pI .. 163.9:2 ***W.*** *are Your messengers, and we would look*
W-pI .. 163.9:2 ***w.*** *would look upon the glorious reflection*
W-pI .. 163.9:3 ***W.*** *live and move in You alone. We are not*
W-pI .. 163.9:4 ***W.*** *are not separate from Your eternal life.*
W-pI .. 163.9:6 *And* ***w.*** *abide where You have placed us, in*
W-pI .. 163.9:6 *the life* ***w.*** *share with You and with all living*
W-pI .. 163.9:7 ***W.*** *accept Your Thoughts as ours, and our*
W-pI ..... 164.h are **w.** one with Him Who is our Source.
W-pI .. 164.1:3 **w.** come to look upon what is forever
W-pI .. 164.7:1 **W.** will not judge today. We will receive
W-pI .. 164.7:2 **W.** will receive but what is given us from
W-pI .. 164.7:4 All that **w.** see will but increase our joy,
W-pI .. 164.7:5 **W.** stand forgiven in the sight of Christ,

W-pI...164.7:6 W. bless the world, as we behold it in the
W-pI...164.7:6 as w. behold it in the light in which our
W-pI...164.9:2 W. can change the world, if you
W-pI...165.8:1 W. count on God, and not upon
W-pI...165.8:2 Name w. practice as His Word directs we
W-pI...165.8:2 we practice as His Word directs w. do. His
W-pI.166.11:1 Now do w. live, for now we cannot die.
W-pI.166.11:1 Now do we live, for now w. cannot die.
W-pI...167.2:3 Yet w. have learned that the idea of death
W-pI.167.10:2 Our life is not as w. imagine it. Who
W-pI.167.10:4 is? W. will not ask for death in any form
W-pI.167.10:5 will w. let imagined opposites to life abide
W-pI.167.11:1 His holy home w. strive to keep today as
W-pI.167.11:2 He is Lord of what w. think today. And in
W-pI.167.11:3 opposite, w. understand there is one life,
W-pI.167.11:3 is one life, and that w. share with Him,
W-pI.167.12:1 W. share one life because we have one
W-pI.167.12:1 share one life because w. have one Source,
W-pI.167.12:2 As w. were, so are we now and will forever
W-pI.167.12:2 we were, so are w. now and will forever be
W-pI...168.1:2 to us. Shall w. not speak to Him? He is not
W-pI...168.1:5 W. try to hide from Him, and suffer from
W-pI...168.3:1 Today w. ask of God the gift He has most
W-pI...168.3:3 All steps but this w. learn, instructed by
W-pI...168.5:1 for w. receive what has been given us. Our
W-pI...168.5:3 W. acknowledge our mistakes, but He to
W-pI...168.6:1 descends to meet us, as w. come to Him.
W-pI...168.6:2 prepared for us He gives and w. receive.
W-pI...168.6:4 To Him w. pray today, returning but the
W-pI...169.3:4 w. prepare for grace in that an open mind
W-pI...169.4:1 W. have perhaps appeared to contradict
W-pI...169.4:2 But w. have also said the mind determines
W-pI...169.4:3 And yet w. urge you to bear witness to the
W-pI...169.5:4 W. say "God is," and then we cease to
W-pI...169.5:4 say "God is," and then w. cease to speak,
W-pI...169.6:1 W. cannot speak nor write nor even think
W-pI...169.7:1 is beyond experience w. try to hasten. Yet
W-pI...169.7:3 W. do not hasten it, in that what you will
W-pI...169.8:3 W. have repeated several times before
W-pI...169.9:3 W. merely take the part assigned long
W-pI.169.10:3 Now w. have work to do, for those in time
W-pI.169.12:2 And now w. ask for grace, the final gift
W-pI.169.14:5 W. ask for grace, and for experience that
W-pI.169.14:6 W. welcome the release it offers everyone.
W-pI.169.14:7 W. do not ask for the unaskable. We do
W-pI.169.14:8 W. do not look beyond what grace can
W-pI.169.14:9 For this w. can give in the grace that has
W-pI.169.15:2 what could be more than what w. ask this
W-pI.169.15:2 day of Him Who gives the grace w. ask, as
W-pI...170.2:4 Today w. learn a lesson which can save
W-pI...170.7:1 Today w. look upon this cruel god
W-pI...170.7:2 w. note that though his lips are smeared
W-pI...170.7:4 W. need not defy his power. He has none.
W-pI.170.13:1 *Father, w. are like You. No cruelty abides in*
W-pI.170.13:4 *And w. bless the world with what we have*
W-pI.170.13:4 *with what w. have received from You alone.*
W-pI.170.13:5 *W. choose again, and make our choice for all*
W-pI.170.13:6 *us. W. bring them Your salvation as we have*
W-pI.170.13:6 *us. We bring them Your salvation as w. have*
W-pI.170.13:7 *And w. give thanks for them who render us*
W-pI.170.13:8 *In them w. see Your glory, and in them we*
W-pI.170.13:8 *see Your glory, and in them w. find our peace*
W-pI.170.13:9 *are w. because Your Holiness has set us free.*
WpI 170.13:10 *has set us free. And w. give thanks. Amen.*
WpI.. rV.in1:1 W. now review again. This time we are
WpI.. rV.in1:2 This time w. are ready to give more effort
WpI.. rV.in1:2 and more time to what w. undertake. We
WpI.. rV.in1:3 undertake. W. recognize we are preparing
WpI.. rV.in1:3 recognize w. are preparing for another
WpI.. rV.in1:4 W. would take this step completely, that
WpI.. rV.in1:4 that w. may go on again more certain,
WpI.. rV.in1:6 But now w. hasten on, for we approach a
WpI.. rV.in1:6 on, for w. approach a greater certainty, a
WpI.. rV.in2:3 *W. have no words to give to You. We would*
WpI.. rV.in2:4 *You. W. would but listen to Your Word, and*
WpI.. rV.in3:1 *So do w. bring our practicing to You. And if*
WpI.. rV.in3:2 *And if w. stumble, You will raise us up. If we*
WpI.. rV.in3:3 *up. If w. forget the way, we count upon Your*
WpI.. rV.in3:3 *way, w. count upon Your sure remembering*
WpI...rV.in3:4 *W. wander off, but You will not forget to call*
WpI...rV.in3:5 *that w. may walk more certainly and quickly*
WpI...rV.in3:6 *w. accept the Word You offer us to unify our*
WpI...rV.in3:6 *w. review the thoughts that You have given*
WpI...rV.in4:1 precede the thoughts that w. review. Each
WpI...rV.in4:2 more descriptive of the holy Self w. share
WpI...rV.in5:2 Every step w. take brings us a little nearer.
WpI...rV.in5:3 if w. keep in mind that this remains our
WpI...rV.in5:3 and as w. practice it is this to which we
WpI...rV.in5:3 it is this to which w. are approaching. Let
WpI...rV.in5:4 to life, as w. remember this is promised us
WpI...rV.in5:4 to return to the eternal Self w. thought we
WpI...rV.in5:4 to the eternal Self we thought w. lost.
WpI...rV.in6:3 W. walk together. I must understand
WpI...rV.in8:2 Him. Together w. review these thoughts.
WpI...rV.in8:3 Together w. devote our time and effort to
WpI...rV.in8:4 And together w. will teach them to our
WpI...rV.in8:8 whole w. go together to our ancient home
WpI...rV.in9:5 own. To Him w. go together. Take your
WpI...rV.in9:6 hand, for this is not a way w. walk alone.
WpI rV.in10:1 which w. share a new experience for you,
WpI rV.in10:6 W. practice but an ancient truth we knew
WpI rV.in10:6 We practice but an ancient truth w. knew
WpI rV.in10:7 And w. remind the world that it is free of
WpI rV.in10:7 it is free of all illusions every time w. say:
WpI rV.in11:1 With this w. start each day of our review.
WpI rV.in11:2 With this w. start and end each period of
WpI rV.in11:3 And with this thought w. sleep, to waken
WpI rV.in11:4 that w. review but we surround with it,
WpI rV.in11:4 that we review but w. surround with it,
WpI rV.in11:5 thus, when w. have finished this review,
WpI rV.in11:5 w. will have recognized the words we
WpI rV.in11:5 will have recognized the words w. speak
WpI rV.in12:2 W. place faith in the experience that
WpI rV.in12:2 from practice, not the means w. use. We
WpI rV.in12:3 W. wait for the experience, and recognize
WpI rV.in12:4 W. use the words, and try and try again to
WpI rV.in12:5 as w. approach the Source of meaning. It
WpI rV.in12:6 of meaning. It is Here that w. find rest.
W-pI...177.2:1 are w. one with Him Who is our Source.
Wi181-200 2:2 W. are attempting now to lift these blocks
Wi181-200 3:1 so w. start our journey beyond words by
Wi181-200 3:4 So w. now attempt to go past all defenses
W-pI...181.3:1 w. first let all such little focuses give way
W-pI...181.3:2 W. instruct our minds that it is this we
W-pI...181.3:2 instruct our minds that it is this w. seek,
W-pI...181.3:3 W. do not care about our future goals.
W-pI...181.3:4 And what w. saw an instant previous has
W-pI...181.3:4 wherein w. practice changing our intent.
W-pI...181.3:5 W. seek for innocence and nothing else.
W-pI...181.3:6 W. seek for it with no concern but now.
W-pI...181.5:5 W. lay these pointless limitations by a
W-pI...181.5:6 W. do not look to past beliefs, and what
W-pI...181.5:6 and what w. will believe will not intrude
W-pI...181.5:7 W. enter in the time of practicing with
W-pI...181.6:1 W. recognize that we have lost this goal if
W-pI...181.6:1 We recognize that w. have lost this goal if
W-pI...181.6:2 which w. will magnify and call our "sins."
W-pI...181.6:3 should such blocks arise w. will transcend
W-pI...181.6:3 our minds to change their focus, as w. say:
W-pI...181.7:1 And w. will also use this thought to keep
W-pI...181.7:2 W. do not seek for long-range goals. As
W-pI...181.7:3 w. seek but for surcease an instant from
W-pI...181.8:1 Nor do w. ask for fantasies. For what we
W-pI...181.8:2 what w. seek to look upon is really there.
W-pI...181.8:3 w. will behold a wholly sinless world.
W-pI...181.8:4 When seeing this is all w. want to see,
W-pI...181.8:4 this is all w. seek for in the name of true
W-pI...181.8:6 will become the only thing w. see reflected
W-pI...181.9:1 sins becomes the proof that w. are sinless.
W-pI...181.9:2 And our love for everyone w. look upon
W-pI...181.9:3 W. seek for this remembrance as we turn
W-pI...181.9:3 seek for this remembrance as w. turn our
W-pI...181.9:4 W. look neither ahead nor backwards.
W-pI...181.9:5 W. look straight into the present. And we
W-pI...181.9:6 And w. give our trust to the experience we
W-pI...181.9:6 our trust to the experience w. ask for now.
W-pI...182.2:1 No one but knows whereof w. speak. Yet
W-pI...182.2:4 maintain that what w. speak of is illusion,
W-pI...182.2:5 deny he understands the words w. speak?
W-pI...182.3:1 W. speak today for everyone who walks
W-pI...183.6:5 other word w. use except at the beginning
W-pI...183.6:5 when w. say today's idea but once. And
W-pI...183.6:6 occupies our minds, the only wish w. have
W-pI...183.6:6 Name of everything that w. desire to see;
W-pI...183.6:6 of everything that w. would call our own.
W-pI...183.7:1 Thus do w. give an invitation which can
W-pI.183.11:7 w. would experience this peace today.
W-pI.184.13:4 One Name w. bring into our practicing.
W-pI.184.13:5 One Name w. use to unify our sight.
W-pI.184.14:1 And though w. use a different name for
W-pI.184.14:1 w. understand that they have but one
W-pI.184.14:2 It is this Name w. use in practicing. And
W-pI.184.14:4 w. are given strength to see beyond them.
W-pI.184.14:5 with blessings w. can give as we receive.
W-pI.184.14:5 with blessings we can give as w. receive.
W-pI.184.15:2 *In It w. are united with all living things, and*
W-pI.184.15:3 *w. made and call by many different names is*
W-pI.184.15:3 *w. have tried to cast across Your Own reality*
W-pI.184.15:4 *And w. are glad and thankful we were wrong*
W-pI.184.15:4 *And we are glad and thankful w. were wrong*
W-pI.184.15:5 *All our mistakes w. give to You, that we may*
W-pI.184.15:5 *that w. may be absolved from all effects our*
W-pI.184.15:6 *And w. accept the truth You give, in place of*
W-pI.184.15:7 *our salvation and escape from what w. made*
W-pI...185.7:1 that w. really mean the words we say. We
W-pI...185.7:1 that we really mean the words w. say. We
W-pI...185.7:2 W. want the peace of God. This is no idle
W-pI.185.14:1 It is this one intent w. seek today, uniting
W-pI.185.14:2 can w. fail today as we request the peace
W-pI.185.14:2 as w. request the peace of God be given us
W-pI...186.2:2 W. did not establish it. It is not our idea.
W-pI...186.2:5 All that w. are asked to do is to accept our
W-pI...186.2:5 arrogance that w. are worthy. What is
W-pI...186.2:6 given us to do, w. have the strength to do.
W-pI...186.3:6 this? Today w. will not shrink from our
W-pI...186.4:1 All false humility w. lay aside today, that
W-pI...186.4:1 that w. may listen to God's Voice reveal to
W-pI...186.4:2 do. W. do not doubt our adequacy for the
W-pI...186.4:3 W. will be certain only that He knows our
W-pI...186.4:4 And if He deems us worthy, so w. are. It is
W-pI...186.8:1 And so w. find our peace. We will accept
W-pI...186.8:2 W. will accept the function God has given
W-pI...186.8:2 that w. can make another for ourselves.
W-pI...186.8:4 W. can laugh or weep, and greet the day
W-pI...186.8:5 Our very being seems to change as w.
W-pI...187.1:3 W. have made this point before. What
W-pI...187.2:3 w. have learned that things but represent
W-pI.187.10:1 Now are w. one in thought, for fear has
W-pI.187.10:2 w. stand together as one Son of God. Not
W-pI.187.10:3 us all as one, w. stand in blessedness, and
W-pI.187.10:3 in blessedness, and give as w. receive. The
W-pI.187.10:5 And as w. look within, we see the purity
W-pI.187.10:5 w. see the purity of Heaven shine in our
W-pI.187.11:1 Now are w. blessed, and now we bless the
W-pI.187.11:1 we blessed, and now w. bless the world.
W-pI.187.11:2 w. have looked upon we would extend, for
W-pI.187.11:2 we have looked upon w. would extend, for
W-pI.187.11:2 extend, for w. would see it everywhere.
W-pI.187.11:3 W. would behold it shining with the grace
W-pI.187.11:4 W. would not have it be withheld from
W-pI.187.11:4 be withheld from anything w. look upon.
W-pI.187.11:5 is ours, w. offer it to everything we see.
W-pI.187.11:5 is ours, we offer it to everything w. see.
W-pI.187.11:6 For where w. see it, it will be returned to
W-pI.187.11:6 in form of lilies w. can lay upon our altar,
W-pI...188.9:1 W. practice coming nearer to the light in
W-pI...188.9:2 W. take our wandering thoughts, and
W-pI...188.9:2 with all the thoughts w. share with God.
W-pI...188.9:3 W. will not let them stray. We let the light
W-pI...188.9:4 W. let the light within our minds direct
W-pI...188.9:5 W. have betrayed them, ordering that
W-pI...188.9:6 us. But now w. call them back, and wash
W-pI...188.9:7 W. restore to them the holiness of their
W-pI.188.10:1 and w. acknowledge that the peace of God
W-pI.188.10:2 W. will forgive them all, absolving all the
W-pI.188.10:2 world from what w. thought it did to us.
W-pI.188.10:3 w. who make the world as we would have

W-pI.188.10:3 who make the world as **w.** would have it.
W-pI.188.10:4 Now **w.** choose that it be innocent, devoid
W-pI.188.10:5 And **w.** lay our saving blessing on it, as we
W-pI.188.10:5 we lay our saving blessing on it, as **w.** say:
W-pI...189.1:6 reflection of the thought **w.** practice now.
W-pI...189.6:1 Today **w.** pass illusions, as we seek to
W-pI...189.6:1 as **w.** seek to reach to what is true in us,
W-pI...189.6:2 us. **W.** learn the way today. It is as sure as
W-pI...189.9:1 And so today **w.** do not choose the way in
W-pI...189.9:1 not choose the way in which **w.** go to Him
W-pI...189.9:2 But **w.** do choose to let Him come. And
W-pI...189.9:3 And with this choice **w.** rest. And in our
W-pI.189.10:1 *Father,* ***w.*** *do not know the way to You. But*
W-pI.189.10:2 *But* ***w.*** *have called, and You have answered*
W-pI.189.10:3 ***W.*** *will not interfere. Salvation's ways are*
W-pI.189.10:5 *And it is unto You* ***w.*** *look for them. Our*
W-pI.189.10:7 ***W.*** *have no thoughts we think apart from*
W-pI.189.10:7 *have no thoughts* ***w.*** *think apart from You,*
W-pI.189.10:7 *You, and cherish no beliefs of what* ***w.*** *are, or*
W-pI.189.10:8 *is the way that* ***w.*** *would find and follow. And*
W-pI.189.10:9 *And* ***w.*** *ask but that Your Will, which is our*
W-pI.190.11:1 so again **w.** make the only choice that ever
W-pI.190.11:1 **w.** choose between illusions and the truth,
W-pI.190.11:2 as **w.** are free to choose our joy instead of
W-pI...192.6:5 **W.** are one, and therefore give up nothing
W-pI...192.6:6 But **w.** have indeed been given everything
W-pI...192.7:1 **w.** need forgiveness to perceive that this is
W-pI...192.7:2 is so. Without its kindly light **w.** grope in
W-pI...192.7:3 that what **w.** think we understand is but
W-pI...192.7:3 that what we think **w.** understand is but
W-pI...192.7:4 **W.** are lost in mists of shifting dreams
W-pI...193.6:1 **w.** not learn to say these words when we
W-pI...193.6:1 not learn to say these words when **w.** are
W-pI...193.6:2 **w.** not learn to say these words when we
W-pI...193.6:2 not learn to say these words when **w.** have
W-pI.193.10:1 **W.** will attempt today to overcome a
W-pI.193.11:2 For now **w.** would arise in haste and go
W-pI.193.11:3 **W.** have been gone too long, and we
W-pI.193.11:3 long, and **w.** would linger here no more.
W-pI.193.11:4 And as **w.** practice, let us think about all
W-pI.193.11:4 all things **w.** saved to settle by ourselves,
W-pI...194.1:4 far are **w.** progressing now from earth!
W-pI...194.1:5 How close are **w.** approaching to our goal!
W-pI...194.9:1 Now are **w.** saved indeed. For in God's
W-pI...194.9:2 For in God's Hands **w.** rest untroubled,
W-pI...194.9:3 If **w.** forget, we will be gently reassured. If
W-pI...194.9:3 If we forget, **w.** will be gently reassured. If
W-pI...194.9:4 If **w.** accept an unforgiving thought, it will
W-pI...194.9:5 And if **w.** are tempted to attack, we will
W-pI...194.9:5 **w.** will appeal to Him Who guards our
W-pI...194.9:6 for **w.** have chosen that we be its friend.
W-pI...194.9:6 for we have chosen that **w.** be its friend.
W-pI...195.4:4 **W.** offer thanks to God our Father that in
W-pI...195.5:4 thus **w.** split them off from our awareness
W-pI...195.5:4 awareness of the unity **w.** share with them
W-pI...195.6:1 **W.** thank our Father for one thing alone;
W-pI...195.6:1 that **w.** are separate from no living thing,
W-pI...195.6:2 And **w.** rejoice that no exceptions ever can
W-pI...195.6:3 **W.** give thanks for every living thing, for
W-pI...195.6:3 for otherwise **w.** offer thanks for nothing,
W-pI...195.6:3 **w.** fail to recognize the gifts of God to us.
W-pI...195.7:2 **W.** offer thanks for them. For if we can
W-pI...195.7:3 For if **w.** can direct them to the peace that
W-pI...195.7:3 them to the peace that **w.** would find, the
W-pI...195.7:4 clarity as **w.** are willing once again to hear
W-pI...195.8:2 forgotten when **w.** lay comparisons aside.
W-pI...195.8:4 at last, and **w.** forgive without comparing.
W-pI...195.8:5 Thus **w.** cannot choose to overlook some
W-pI...195.9:1 Today **w.** learn to think of gratitude in
W-pI...195.9:2 **W.** have been given everything. If we
W-pI...195.9:3 If **w.** refuse to recognize it, we are not
W-pI...195.9:3 it, **w.** are not entitled therefore to our
W-pI...195.9:3 pursuit, where **w.** are badgered ceaselessly
W-pI...195.9:4 Gratitude becomes the single thought **w.**
W-pI.195.10:6 and thus **w.** go who walk the way to God.
W-pI...196.2:1 be found in the idea **w.** practice for today.
W-pI...196.4:1 Today's idea is one step **w.** take in leading
W-pI...196.4:2 that **w.** may quickly go the way salvation
W-pI...196.4:3 It is not time **w.** need for this. It is but
W-pI...196.8:2 From there **w.** go ahead quite rapidly. For
W-pI...196.9:1 be heard in the idea **w.** practice for today.
W-pI.196.12:3 kind and merciful is the idea **w.** practice!
W-pI...197.1:1 the second step **w.** take to free your mind
W-pI...198.2:7 must **w.** deal with them a while as if they
W-pI...198.9:1 Today **w.** practice letting freedom come
W-pI.198.13:1 Today **w.** come still nearer to the end of
W-pI.198.13:2 **w.** are glad that we have come this far,
W-pI.198.13:2 we are glad that **w.** have come this far,
W-pI...199.5:4 **W.** sound the call of freedom round the
W-pI...200.9:2 **W.** go to Heaven, and the path is straight.
W-pI...200.9:3 if **w.** attempt to wander can there be delay
W-pI.200.11:1 Today **w.** seek no idols. Peace can not be
W-pI.200.11:3 and only this will **w.** accept and want.
W-pI.200.11:5 For **w.** have found a simple, happy way to
W-pI.200.11:7 **W.** seek no further. We are close to home,
W-pI.200.11:8 **W.** are close to home, and draw still
W-pI.200.11:8 and draw still nearer every time **w.** say:
WpI rVI.in.1:1 this review **w.** take but one idea each day,
WpI rVI.in.2:1 With this in mind **w.** start our practicing,
WpI rVI.in.2:1 in which **w.** carefully review the thoughts
WpI rVI.in.2:5 And so **w.** need to use them all and let
WpI rVI.in.2:5 as each contributes to the whole **w.** learn.
WpI rVI.in.3:1 with which **w.** start and end each lesson.
WpI rVI.in.3:7 **w.** repeat it every time the hour strikes, or
WpI rVI.in.3:7 time the hour strikes, or **w.** remember, in
WpI rVI.in.3:7 **w.** have a function that transcends the
WpI rVI.in.3:7 function that transcends the world **w.** see.
WpI rVI.in.3:8 the special thought **w.** practice for the day
WpI rVI.in.4:1 **W.** will attempt to get beyond all words
WpI rVI.in.4:2 For **w.** attempt, this time, to reach a
WpI rVI.in.4:3 **W.** merely close our eyes, and then forget
WpI rVI.in.4:3 that **w.** thought we knew and understood.
WpI rVI.in.4:3 that we thought **w.** knew and understood.
WpI rVI.in.4:4 thus is freedom given us from all **w.** did
WpI rVI.in.5:4 quick exchange for the idea **w.** practice for
WpI rVI.in.6:5 **w.** will add but a few formal expressions
WpI rVI.in.6:6 **w.** give these times of quiet to the Teacher
WpI rVI.in.7:4 offer Him the whole review **w.** now begin,
WpI rVI.in.7:4 has been given, as **w.** practice day by day,
W-pII ....in.1:2 **W.** use them but as guides on which we
W-pII ....in.1:2 as guides on which **w.** do not now depend
W-pII ....in.1:3 For now **w.** seek direct experience of truth
W-pII ....in.1:4 times in which **w.** leave the world of pain,
W-pII ....in.1:5 Now **w.** begin to reach the goal this course
W-pII ....in.2:1 Now **w.** attempt to let the exercise be
W-pII ....in.2:2 For **w.** wait in quiet expectation for our
W-pII ....in.2:4 And **w.** are sure His promises are kept.
W-pII ....in.2:5 **W.** have come far along the road, and
W-pII ....in.2:5 along the road, and now **w.** wait for Him.
W-pII ....in.2:6 **W.** will continue spending time with Him
W-pII ....in.2:7 **W.** will not consider time a matter of
W-pII ....in.2:8 **W.** use as much as we will need for the
W-pII ....in.2:8 use as much as **w.** will need for the result
W-pII ....in.2:8 we will need for the result that **w.** desire.
W-pII ....in.2:9 will **w.** forget our hourly remembrance in
W-pII ....in.2:9 calling to God when **w.** have need of Him
W-pII ....in.2:9 Him as **w.** are tempted to forget our goal.
W-pII ....in.3:1 **W.** will continue with a central thought
W-pII ....in.3:1 and **w.** will use that thought to introduce
W-pII ....in.3:2 **w.** will not content ourselves with simple
W-pII ....in.3:2 conclude the year that **w.** have given God.
W-pII ....in.3:3 **W.** say some simple words of welcome,
W-pII ....in.3:4 **W.** have called on Him, and He has
W-pII ....in.4:1 Now do **w.** come to Him with but His
W-pII ....in.4:1 not fail to take when **w.** invited Him. He
W-pII ....in.4:4 **W.** will offer it, and it will be accepted. So
W-pII ....in.4:6 **W.** say the words of invitation that His
W-pII ....in.4:6 and then **w.** wait for Him to come to us.
W-pII ....in.5:4 For now **w.** cannot fail. Sit silently and
W-pII ....in.6:1 I am so close to you **w.** cannot fail. Father
W-pII ....in.6:2 Father, **w.** give these holy times to You, in
W-pII ....in.6:3 You. **W.** look not backward now. We look
W-pII ....in.6:4 **W.** look ahead, and fix our eyes upon the
W-pII ....in.6:5 Christ's vision **w.** behold a world beyond
W-pII ....in.6:5 behold a world beyond the one **w.** made,
W-pII ....in.7:1 And now **w.** wait in silence, unafraid and
W-pII ....in.7:2 coming. **W.** have sought to find our way
W-pII ....in.7:3 **W.** did not know the way, but You did not
W-pII ....in.7:4 **w.** know that You will not forget us now.
W-pII ....in.7:5 **W.** ask but that Your ancient promises be
W-pII ....in.7:6 keep. **W.** will with You in asking this. The
W-pII ....in.7:8 **w.** undertake these last few steps to You,
W-pII ....in.8:1 And so **w.** start upon the final part of this
W-pII ....in.8:1 **w.** have spent together in the search for
W-pII ....in.8:2 **W.** have found the way He chose for us,
W-pII ....in.9:1 **W.** had a wish that God would fail to
W-pII ....in.9:2 **W.** wanted God to change Himself, and
W-pII ....in.9:2 and be what **w.** would make of Him. And
W-pII ....in.9:3 And **w.** believed that our insane desires
W-pII ....in.9:4 Now **w.** are glad that this is all undone,
W-pII ....in.9:4 and **w.** no longer think illusions true. The
W-pII ....in.9:7 **w.** who are God's Sons are safely home,
W-pII ..in.10:2 **w.** will come to understand that we need
W-pII ..in.10:2 to understand that **w.** need only call to
W-pII ..in.10:3 words, **w.** need but feel His Love. Instead
W-pII ..in.10:4 of prayers, **w.** need but call His Name.
W-pII ..in.10:5 **w.** need but be still and let all things be
W-pII ..in.10:6 **W.** will accept the way God's plan will
W-pII ..in.10:6 will end, as **w.** received the way it started.
W-pII ..in.11:1 One further use for words **w.** still retain.
W-pII ..in.11:5 **W.** give the first of these instructions now
W-pII .221.2:1 Now do **w.** wait in quiet. God is here,
W-pII .221.2:2 God is here, because **w.** wait together.
W-pII .221.2:6 **W.** wait with one intent; to hear our
W-pII .221.2:6 to hear Him speak to us of what **w.** are,
W-pII .225.2:1 Brother, **w.** find that stillness now. The
W-pII .225.2:3 Now **w.** follow it in peace together. You
W-pII .225.2:5 **W.** are one, and it is but this oneness that
W-pII .225.2:5 one, and it is but this oneness that **w.** seek
W-pII .225.2:5 **w.** accomplish these few final steps which
W-pII .227.2:1 today **w.** find our glad return to Heaven,
W-pII .227.2:1 to Heaven, which **w.** never really left. The
W-pII ..... 2.4:2 Here **w.** share our final dream. It is a
W-pII ..... 2.4:6 and **w.** have come together in the light.
W-pII ..... 2.5:1 From here **w.** give salvation to the world,
W-pII .231.2:4 This **w.** seek. And only this is what it will
W-pII .233.2:1 Today **w.** have one Guide to lead us on.
W-pII .233.2:2 And as **w.** walk together, we will give this
W-pII .233.2:2 together, **w.** will give this day to Him with
W-pII .234.1:1 Today **w.** will anticipate the time when
W-pII .234.1:1 **w.** have reached the holy peace we never
W-pII .234.1:1 have reached the holy peace **w.** never left.
W-pII .234.1:5 Son. This **w.** accept as wholly true today.
W-pII .238.2:1 **w.** pause to think how much our Father
W-pII .239.1:3 Can **w.** see in those with whom He shares
W-pII .239.1:4 And can it be that **w.** are not among them
W-pII .240.1:7 **W.** are the Sons of God. There is no fear
W-pII .240.1:8 in us, for **w.** are each a part of Love Itself.
W-pII ..... 3.5:4 **W.** must save the world. For we who
W-pII ..... 3.5:5 **w.** who made it must behold it through
W-pII .244.2:1 And there **w.** are in truth. No storms can
W-pII .244.2:3 In God **w.** are secure. For what can come
W-pII .245.2:1 And so **w.** go in peace. To all the world
W-pII .245.2:2 world **w.** give the message that we have
W-pII .245.2:2 we give the message that **w.** have received.
W-pII .245.2:3 thus **w.** come to hear the Voice for God,
W-pII .245.2:3 Who speaks to us as **w.** relate His Word;
W-pII .245.2:3 Love **w.** recognize because we share the
W-pII .245.2:3 Love we recognize because **w.** share the
W-pII ..... 4.5:2 Shall **w.** not put away these sharp-edged
W-pII .254.2:1 Today **w.** let no ego thoughts direct our
W-pII .254.2:2 **w.** quietly step back and look at them,
W-pII .254.2:2 and look at them, and then **w.** let them go
W-pII .254.2:3 **W.** do not want what they would bring
W-pII .254.2:4 And so **w.** do not choose to keep them.
W-pII .254.2:6 will, as **w.** have chosen to remember Him.
W-pII .256.1:7 Here **w.** can but dream. But we can dream
W-pII .256.1:8 But **w.** can dream we have forgiven him in
W-pII .256.1:8 But we can dream **w.** have forgiven him in
W-pII .256.1:8 and it is this **w.** choose to dream today.
W-pII .257.1:4 to remember what **w.** want today, that we
W-pII .257.1:4 **w.** may unify our thoughts and actions
W-pII .258.1:3 Shall **w.** continue to allow God's grace to
W-pII .258.1:5 **W.** have no aim but to remember Him.
W-pII .260.2:1 Therein **w.** find our true Identity at last.
W-pII .260.2:2 Holy indeed are **w.**, because our Source
W-pII .260.2:3 **w.** who are His Sons are like each other,

W-pII......5.3:5 w. can change the purpose that the body
W-pII......5.3:5 by changing what w. think that it is for.
W-pII..262.2:1 W. who are one would recognize this day
W-pII..262.2:2 W. would come home, and rest in unity.
W-pII..263.2:1 while w. still remain outside the gate of
W-pII..263.2:1 let us look on all w. see through holy
W-pII..263.2:2 us, that w. may pass them by in innocence
W-pII..264.2:3 Must w. not join in what will save the
W-pII..266.2:1 This day w. enter into Paradise, calling
W-pII..266.2:3 How can w. lose the way to Him, when He
W-pII..268.2:5 safe. And it is only this w. seek today.
W-pII..269.2:2 W. share one vision, as we look upon the
W-pII..269.2:2 w. look upon the face of Him Whose Self
W-pII..269.2:3 W. are one because of Him Who is the
W-pII..270.2:3 His sight w. offer healing to the world
W-pII......6.1:2 He is the Self w. share, uniting us with
W-pII......6.5:3 As w. behold His glory, will we know we
W-pII......6.5:3 will w. know we have no need of learning
W-pII......6.5:3 will we know w. have no need of learning
W-pII..272.2:1 Today w. pass illusions by. And if we
W-pII..272.2:2 if w. hear temptation call to us to stay and
W-pII..272.2:2 w. turn aside and ask ourselves if we, the
W-pII..272.2:2 we turn aside and ask ourselves if w., the
W-pII..273.1:1 Perhaps w. are now ready for a day of
W-pII..273.1:2 yet feasible, w. are content and even more
W-pII..273.1:3 If w. give way to a disturbance, let us learn
W-pII..273.1:4 W. need but tell our minds, with certainty
W-pII..275.1:2 day been chosen as the time when w. will
W-pII..275.1:4 Voice for God tells us of things w. cannot
W-pII..276.1:6 Deny w. were created in His Love and we
W-pII..276.1:6 created in His Love and w. deny our Self,
W-pII..276.1:6 deny our Self, to be unsure of who w. are,
W-pII..276.1:6 is, and for what purpose w. have come.
W-pII..276.1:7 w. need but to acknowledge Him Who
W-pII..283.2:1 Now are w. One in shared Identity, with
W-pII..283.2:2 us. And so w. offer blessing to all things,
W-pII..286.2:1 give us hope that w. have found the way,
W-pII..286.2:2 Today w. will not doubt the end which
W-pII..286.2:3 W. trust in Him, and in our Self, Who still
W-pII......8.5:4 And as w. look upon a world forgiven, it is
W-pII..291.1:4 well. What loveliness w. look upon today!
W-pII..291.1:5 What holiness w. see surrounding us!
W-pII..291.1:6 recognize it is a holiness in which w. share
W-pII..292.1:3 how long w. let an alien will appear to be
W-pII..292.1:4 And while w. think this will is real, we will
W-pII..292.1:4 w. will not find the end He has appointed
W-pII..292.1:4 the outcome of all problems w. perceive,
W-pII..292.1:4 all problems we perceive, all trials w. see,
W-pII..292.1:4 we see, and every situation that w. meet.
W-pII..292.1:7 W. will seek and we will find according to
W-pII..292.1:7 seek and w. will find according to His Will
W-pII..296.2:1 W. teach today what we would learn, and
W-pII..296.2:1 We teach today what w. would learn, and
W-pII..296.2:3 when w. allow His teaching to persuade
W-pII..300.1:3 And it is this serenity w. seek, unclouded,
W-pII......9.5:5 Let us rejoice that w. can do God's Will,
W-pII......9.5:6 w. can reach our Father's Love through
W-pII..301.2:3 W. wept because we did not understand.
W-pII..301.2:3 We wept because w. did not understand.
W-pII..301.2:4 But w. have learned the world we saw was
W-pII..301.2:4 have learned the world w. saw was false,
W-pII..301.2:4 and w. will look upon God's world today.
W-pII..302.2:1 Our Love awaits us as w. go to Him, and
W-pII..302.2:3 He the End w. seek, and He the Means by
W-pII..302.2:3 and He the Means by which w. go to Him.
W-pII..307.2:1 prayer w. enter silently into a state where
W-pII..307.2:1 because w. join our holy will with God's,
W-pII..310.2:1 W. spend this day together, you and I.
W-pII..310.2:3 W. are restored to peace and holiness.
W-pII..310.2:4 for w. have welcomed love into our hearts
W-pII..311.1:6 w. have made against ourselves, and re-
W-pII..312.1:2 w. therefore see what we would look upon
W-pII..312.1:2 we therefore see what w. would look upon
W-pII..312.1:3 serve to offer us what w. would have. It is
W-pII..312.1:4 impossible to overlook what w. would see
W-pII..312.1:4 fail to see what w. have chosen to behold.
W-pII..313.2:2 How beautiful w. are! How holy and how
W-pII..313.2:5 W. save the world when we have joined.
W-pII..313.2:5 We save the world when w. have joined.
W-pII....11.4:1 W. are creation; we the Sons of God. We
W-pII....11.4:1 We are creation; w. the Sons of God. We
W-pII....11.4:2 W. seem to be discrete, and unaware of
W-pII....11.5:2 to us. W. hear His Voice, and we forgive
W-pII....11.5:2 and w. forgive creation in the Name of its
W-pII..321.2:1 Today w. answer for the world, which
W-pII..321.2:2 glad are w. to find our freedom through
W-pII..321.2:3 when w. learn our freedom can be found
W-pII..323.2:1 And as w. pay the debt we owe to truth,
W-pII..323.2:1 And as we pay the debt w. owe to truth,
W-pII..323.2:1 and of images w. worshipped falsely
W-pII..323.2:2 W. are deceived no longer. Love has now
W-pII..323.2:4 And w. are at peace again, for fear has
W-pII..324.2:2 W. need not tarry, and we cannot stray
W-pII..324.2:2 and w. cannot stray except an instant
W-pII..324.2:3 W. walk together, for we follow Him. And
W-pII..324.2:3 We walk together, for w. follow Him. And
W-pII..328.1:1 for all things w. perceive are upside down
W-pII..328.1:1 down until w. listen to the Voice for God.
W-pII..328.1:2 It seems that w. will gain autonomy but
W-pII..328.1:3 Yet all w. find is sickness, suffering and
W-pII..328.1:6 Him that w. must go to recognize our will.
W-pII..329.2:1 Today w. will accept our union with each
W-pII..329.2:2 W. have no will apart from His, and all of
W-pII..329.2:3 Through it w. recognize that we are one.
W-pII..329.2:3 Through it we recognize that w. are one.
W-pII..329.2:4 Through it w. find our way at last to God.
W-pII..330.1:2 Why should w. attack our minds, and
W-pII..330.1:3 should w. teach them they are powerless,
W-pII..331.2:1 God's Will is One, and that w. share it.
W-pII..331.2:2 today, that w. may find the peace of God.
W-pII..339.1:9 today to ask for what w. really want, and
W-pII..339.1:9 that w. may spend this day in fearlessness
W-pII..341.2:2 us. And in its kind reflection w. are saved.
W-pII..342.2:3 And as w. go, the world goes with us on
W-pII..343.2:4 And it is this that w. would learn today.
W-pII..344.2:1 How near w. are to one another, as we go
W-pII..344.2:1 we are to one another, as w. go to God.
W-pII..345.2:3 for w. will offer what we have received.
W-pII..345.2:3 for we will offer what w. have received.
W-pII..346.2:1 w. will remember nothing but the peace
W-pII..346.2:2 For w. will learn today what peace is ours,
W-pII..346.2:2 w. forget all things except God's Love.
W-pII..348.2:2 that w. choose to be our will as well as His
W-pII..349.2:3 so w. trust in Him to send us miracles to
W-pII..349.2:3 and heal our minds as w. return to Him.
W-pII..350.2:1 And as w. gather miracles from Him, we
W-pII..350.2:1 from Him, w. will indeed be grateful. For
W-pII..350.2:2 For as w. remember Him, His Son will be
W-pII....14.2:2 of this one year w. gave to God together,
W-pII....14.2:2 w. found a single purpose that we shared.
W-pII....14.2:2 we found a single purpose that w. shared.
W-pII....14.2:4 The truth of what w. are is not for words
W-pII....14.2:5 Yet w. can realize our function here, and
W-pII....14.2:5 it, too, if w. exemplify the words in us.
W-pII....14.3:1 W. are the bringers of salvation. We
W-pII....14.3:2 W. accept our part as saviors of the world,
W-pII....14.3:4 us. W. look on everyone as brother, and
W-pII....14.3:5 W. do not seek a function that is past the
W-pII....14.3:6 Knowledge will return when w. have done
W-pII....14.3:7 part. W. are concerned only with giving
W-pII....14.4:3 that join together as w. bless the world.
W-pII....14.4:4 oneness that w. have attained we call to
W-pII....14.4:4 have attained w. call to all our brothers,
W-pII....14.5:1 W. are the holy messengers of God who
W-pII....14.5:1 us, w. learn that it is written on our hearts
W-pII....14.5:2 changed about the aim for which w. came
W-pII....14.5:2 we came, and which w. seek to serve. We
W-pII....14.5:3 W. bring glad tidings to the Son of God,
Wfl........in.1:2 W. use them but at the beginning of our
Wfl........in.1:2 remind us that w. seek to go beyond them
Wfl........in.1:4 To Him w. leave these lessons, as to Him
Wfl........in.1:4 as to Him w. give our lives henceforth. For
Wfl........in.1:5 w. would not return again to the belief in
Wfl........in.3:4 It is His ending to the dream w. seek, and
Wfl........in.3:5 For all that w. forgive we will not fail to
Wfl........in.3:5 For all that we forgive w. will not fail to
Wfl........in.4:3 And shall w. not forgive our brother, who
Wfl........in.5:1 W. will not end this year without the gift
Wfl........in.5:2 W. are forgiven now. And we are saved
Wfl........in.5:3 And w. are saved from all the wrath we
Wfl........in.5:3 all the wrath w. thought belonged to God,
Wfl........in.5:4 W. are restored to sanity, in which we
Wfl........in.5:4 which w. understand that anger is insane,
Wfl........in.5:5 W. have been saved from wrath because
Wfl........in.5:5 saved from wrath because w. learned we
Wfl........in.5:5 because we learned w. were mistaken.
Wfl........in.6:1 W. come in honesty to God and say we
Wfl........in.6:1 come in honesty to God and say w. did
W-ep.........5:2 To this w. say "Amen." You will be told
W-ep.........5:5 so w. walk with Him from this time on,
W-ep.........5:7 w. go homeward to an open door which
W-ep.........6:1 W. trust our ways to Him and say "Amen
W-ep.........6:2 In peace w. will continue in His way, and
W-ep.........6:3 In confidence w. wait His answers, as we
W-ep.........6:3 as w. ask His Will in everything we do. He
W-ep.........6:3 as we ask His Will in everything w. do. He
W-ep.........6:4 He loves God's Son as w. would love him.
M-3...........3:4 it. W. have covered the illusion of time
M-3...........4:2 only, w. can speak of levels of teaching.
M-6...........2:5 W. have referred many times in the text
M-7...........1:4 is certain, as w. have already said it is,
M-11.........2:1 w. come to the question of judgment. This
M-16.........3:4 w. can safely say that time devoted to
M-16.........3:7 workbook, since w. are learning within
M-17.........7:5 Here w. have the fear of God most starkly
M-19.......5:12 descends on all the world, and w. can see.
M-19.......5:13 the world, and we can see. And w. can see!
M-23.........2:1 W. have repeatedly said that one who has
M-23.........6:2 Yet w. have witnesses. It is to them that
M-23.........6:4 learning far exceeds what w. can learn.
M-23.........6:5 w. teach the limitations we have laid on us
M-23.........6:5 we teach the limitations w. have laid on us
M-23.........7:5 Yet do w. need a many-faceted curriculum
M-27.........1:3 W. have asked this question before, but
M-27.........1:3 now w. need to consider it more carefully.
M-28.........4:7 And w., God's children, rise up from the
M-28.........5:5 W. have seen the face of Christ, His
M-28.........5:6 Holy are w. because His Holiness has set
M-28.........5:7 And w. accept His Holiness as ours; as it is
M-28.........5:8 us so will w. be forever and forever, and
M-28.........5:8 and w. wish for nothing but His Will to be
M-28.........6:1 but w. are not prepared as yet to welcome
C-2..........1:10 W. name it but to help us understand that
C-2............4:1 W. cannot really make a definition for
C-2............4:1 the ego is, but w. *can* say what it is not.
C-2............4:3 from this that w. deduce all that the ego is
C-2............5:1 effect and consequence– w. call a miracle.
C-2............5:2 w. find all that is not the ego in this world.
C-2............5:3 and here alone w. look on what the ego
C-2............5:3 for here w. see all that it seemed to do,
C-2............6:1 there was darkness now w. see the light.
C-3..........4:12 is the final step. And this w. leave to God.
C-3............6:2 is. W. can but go from nothingness to
C-5............1:6 but w. will not go beyond the names the
C-ep...........2:4 W. *have* begun the journey. Long ago the
C-ep...........3:2 W. only start again an ancient journey
C-ep...........3:3 new. W. have begun again upon a road we
C-ep...........3:3 begun again upon a road w. travelled on
C-ep...........3:4 And now w. try again. Our new beginning
C-ep...........4:3 Now w. are sure we do not walk alone. For
C-ep...........4:3 Now we are sure w. do not walk alone. For
C-ep...........4:5 Now w. know that we will never lose the
C-ep...........4:5 know that w. will never lose the way again
C-ep...........5:2 W. had lost our way but He has found it
C-ep...........5:3 and the end of all w. thought we made.
C-ep...........5:3 and the end of all we thought w. made.
C-ep...........5:5 W. who complete Him offer thanks to
P-1...........5:10 W. are all His psychotherapists, for He
P-2...........I.2:3 When w. speak of "the saving illusion" or
P-2...........I.2:3 final dream," this is not what w. mean,
P-2........IV.3:6 w. have said already and will say again, all
P-2........IV.7:2 And as w. have already emphasized,
P-2.........V.3:3 W. speak of ideal teaching in a world in
P-2.........V.3:4 But still w. speak of what can yet be done
P-2.........V.4:7 W. have His Word to guide us, as we try
P-2.........V.4:7 to guide us, as w. try to help our brothers.
P-2.........V.4:8 not forget that w. are helpless of ourselves

| | |
|---|---|
| P-2......... V.5:4 | And what w. do for him becomes the gift |
| P-2......... V.5:4 | for him becomes the gift w. give to God. |
| P-2......... V.7:4 | W. are deceived already, if we think there |
| P-2......... V.7:4 | if w. think there is a need of healing. And |
| P-2......... V.7:8 | And as w. see the sinlessness in him come |
| P-2......... V.7:8 | w. will behold in him the face of Christ, |
| P-2......... V.8:1 | Will, and do what it has chosen that w. do |
| P-2......... V.8:2 | which w. come to where all dreams began |
| P-2......... V.8:3 | And it is there that w. will lay them down, |
| S-1........ III.1:1 | W. said that prayer is always for yourself, |
| S-2...........I.9:3 | Therefore w. make distinctions, so that |
| S-3......... II.2:2 | God. W. thank the body, then, for all the |
| S-3......... II.2:3 | But w. are thankful, too, the need is done |
| S-3......... II.2:4 | Now w. can behold Him without blinders, |
| S-3......... II.2:4 | that w. have learned to look upon again. |
| S-3......... II.3:1 | W. call it death, but it is liberty. It does |
| S-3......... II.3:4 | ended. Now w. go in peace to freer air and |
| S-3......... II.3:4 | to see the gifts w. gave were saved for us. |

## we 105

- noise word

  *Jesus*
  *We*

## weak 62

| | |
|---|---|
| T-2......... II.7:6 | two-way defense is inherently w. precisely |
| T-3....... VII.1:6 | that a thought system based on lies is w.. |
| T-5........ III.4:1 | The Voice of the Holy Spirit is w. in you. |
| T-5........ III.4:4 | in yourself while It is so w. in your mind. |
| T-5........ III.4:5 | It is not w. in Itself, but It is limited by |
| T-5........ IV.2:8 | unshared ideas that are too w. to increase, |
| T-7...... VI.10:6 | force in the universe as if it were w., |
| T-7...... VI.11:1 | part in it, God's creation is seen as w., |
| T-7......... X.5:2 | guidance in any way, you want to be w.. |
| T-12........ V.1:3 | you must have perceived yourself as w.. |
| T-15...... VI.3:4 | always lose if you perceive yourself as w.. |
| T-15..... VII.2:6 | an attraction so w. that it would have no |
| T-15...... IX.6:5 | your sight grows w. and dim and limited, |
| T-16..... V.11:2 | to you that unless it is w. and little, and |
| T-17..... VII.6:7 | too enormous, too w. or too compelling, |
| T-18...... VI.6:5 | have made your body your "enemy"; w., |
| T-18..VIII.12:1 | and entered fully at your w. request. You |
| T-20...... III.9:1 | starved and emaciated, w. and exhausted, |
| T-20....VIII.5:5 | will seem to make your savior w.. Yet it is |
| T-21..... VII.4:1 | The army of the powerless is w. indeed. It |
| T-22........ V.4:1 | w. is fear; how little and how meaningless |
| T-22........ V.6:2 | feel that you are w. because you are alone. |
| T-22.... VI.11:2 | How can God's Son be w. and frail and |
| T-23.......in.1:6 | and what is w. is not the Will of God. |
| T-23.......in.5:6 | perceive the little and the w. about him? |
| T-23........ II.5:6 | One becomes w., the other strong by his |
| T-24.........I.4:5 | feel w. and frail because of differences, for |
| T-25....VIII.8:4 | else. And thus is love perceived as w., and |
| T-25....VIII.8:5 | and is too w. to save from punishment. |
| T-25..VIII.11:7 | Without love is justice prejudiced and w.. |
| T-27........ II.6:6 | the w. and miserable cry of death and |
| T-27...... III.1:3 | W. strength is meaningless, and power |
| T-27...... III.1:4 | And therefore it must be limited and w., |
| T-27...... III.3:2 | or to endow with power or to see as w.. |
| T-29.........I.5:7 | do, and keep your purpose limited and w. |
| T-29.........I.7:5 | see how limited and w. is your allegiance, |
| T-29...... III.2:2 | He made w. because He shared His Love? |
| T-30.........I.1:6 | find resistance strong and dedication w., |
| T-31....VIII.5:1 | as w. and miserable with these words: |
| W-pI.....16.1:4 | are not big or little; powerful or w.. They |
| W-pI.....47.2:4 | can put his faith in strength and feel w.? |
| W-pI.....91.8:4 | *I am not w., but strong. I am not helpless, but* |
| W-pI.....92.3:3 | the likeness of itself; the small, the w., the |
| W-pI.....95.2:1 | a ridiculous parody on God's creation; w., |
| W-pI.....96.5:2 | and sees itself as helpless, limited and w.. |
| W-pI...121.3:1 | sees; afraid and angry, w. and blustering, |
| W-pI...135.4:2 | It must be something that is very w. and |
| W-pI...136.7:2 | makes you w. and brings you suffering. It |
| W-pI...151.4:5 | senses carefully, to prove how w. you are; |
| W-pI...153.2:5 | Now are the w. still further undermined, |
| Wi181-200 1:1 | to make your w. commitment strong; |
| W-pI.185.10:5 | You have been w. at times, uncertain in |
| W-pI... 186.6:3 | You are not w., as is the image of yourself. |
| W-pI... 190.5:5 | power to make you ill or sad, or w. or frail |
| W-pI... 191.9:1 | You who perceive yourself as w. and frail, |
| W-pI... 195.5:2 | who will escape with you; the sick, the w., |
| W-pI... 196.9:7 | You have sought to be both w. and bound |
| W-pII ... 12.1:3 | that strength is w. and love is fearful, life |
| M-5 .........I.2:6 | will be killed to prove to him how w. and |
| M-12 ......... 5:3 | Because it is sinful it is w., and being weak |
| M-12 ......... 5:3 | Because it is sinful it is weak, and being w. |
| P-2........ IV.6:1 | as the result of a view of the self as w., |

## weaken 17

| | |
|---|---|
| T-3 ...... VII.2:3 | You also realize that you cannot w. it, any |
| T-3 ...... VII.2:3 | weaken it, any more than you can w. God. |
| T-7 ........ V.2:5 | will w. you as a teacher and a learner |
| T-7 ........ V.4:2 | Magic always tries to w.. Healing |
| T-8 ....... IX.6:1 | ego, which always wants to w. the mind, |
| T-11 ...... V.8:2 | your independence and w. your power. |
| T-12 ...... V.2:7 | attacks on yourself have failed to w. you, |
| T-16 ........I.2:5 | the ego always empathizes to w., and to |
| T-16 ........I.2:5 | to weaken, and to w. is always to attack. |
| T-16 .... VII.7:4 | will w. the experience of Him for a while, |
| T-18 ......I.12:5 | still further w. and break apart what is |
| T-22 .... V.1:12 | anything that needs defense will w. you. |
| T-23 ......in.2:3 | against it, and try to w. it because of this; |
| T-27 ..... III.1:2 | For opposition would w. it, and weakened |
| T-27 ..... III.1:3 | and power used to w. is employed to limit |
| T-27 ..... III.1:7 | To w. is to limit, and impose an opposite |
| W-pI..... 26.3:2 | their effect is to w. you in your own eyes. |

## weakened 8

*See also* fear-weakened

| | |
|---|---|
| T-6 ........I.17:1 | to develop your w. ability to be grateful, |
| T-7 ..... VI.11:1 | those who see themselves as w. do attack. |
| T-12 ...... V.1:4 | was effective, you behold yourself as w.. |
| T-12 ...... V.7:7 | has so w. your mind that you cannot love, |
| T-27 ..... III.1:2 | and w. power is a contradiction in ideas. |
| T-27 ..... III.1:9 | such as "w. power" or "hateful love"? |
| T-27 ..... III.2:1 | a symbol for a "hateful love," a "w. power |
| W-pI... 102.2:1 | we try to loose its w. hold still further, |

## weakening 4

| | |
|---|---|
| T-2 ....... III.3:8 | simultaneously w. the investment in |
| T-6 ..... V.B.1:7 | not share a thought system, you are w. it. |
| T-10 ...... IV.7:4 | a sick brother by w. his belief in sickness, |
| T-12 ...... V.1:6 | that attack was successful in w. you. |

## weakens 1

| | |
|---|---|
| T-6 ..........I.8:1 | it w. them as teachers and as learners. Yet |

## weaker 3

| | |
|---|---|
| T-2 ........ V.9:6 | Charity is really a w. reflection of a much |
| T-12 ...... V.1:5 | as equal, and regarding yourself as w., |
| T-27 ...VIII.2:6 | it is a conqueror of bodies w. than itself. |

## weakness 81

| | |
|---|---|
| T-3 ..........I.5:6 | innocence with strength, not with w.. |
| T-4 ........I.11:3 | Its w. is your strength. Only God could |
| T-7 ....... VI.8:4 | to be. Aware of its w. the ego wants your |
| T-7 .......X.4:11 | This is the ego's w. and your strength. |
| T-7 .........X.5:3 | Yet w. is frightening. What else, then, can |
| T-8 ....... VI.1:3 | aside their w. and add their strength to us |
| T-8 ....... IX.6:5 | ego despises w., even though it makes |
| T-13 ..... III.3:2 | love with w. and hatred with strength, |
| T-13 ..... III.3:2 | real power seems to you as your real w.. |
| T-15 .......II.3:5 | an attempt to support it and uphold its w. |
| T-15 .......II.3:6 | to support either their w. or your own. |
| T-15 .......II.6:6 | only your w. that will depart from you in |
| T-15 ..... III.9:4 | to guilt and w. with the glad awareness of |
| T-16 ........I.2:7 | and will gain in strength and not in w.. |
| T-16 ........I.4:2 | your capacity for strength, and not for w.. |
| T-16 ........I.5:1 | The triumph of w. is not what you would |
| T-16 ........I.6:1 | is lost in any relationship that looks to w., |
| T-16 .......II.7:2 | power of holiness and the w. of attack are |
| T-16 .......II.7:3 | that holiness is w. and attack is power. |
| T19 ...IV.A.8:5 | Its seeming stability is its pervasive w., |
| T19 .. IV.D.8:5 | It would not have you see its w., and learn |
| T-20 ... VIII.5:1 | The body is the sign of w., vulnerability |
| T-21 .......II.4:9 | must accept its strength, and not its w.. |
| T-21 ..... IV.7:3 | The ego's w. is its strength. The song of |
| T-21 ..... IV.8:1 | the ego's w. is revealed in both your sight. |
| T-21 ... VI.11:7 | Such is his strength, and not his w.. He is |
| T-22 ..........V.h | W. and Defensiveness |
| T-22 .......V.1:8 | Only illusions need defense because of w.. |
| T-22 .......V.1:9 | the way of truth when only w. interferes? |
| T-22 .......V.3:9 | Here can no w. enter, for here is no attack |
| T-23 ......in.1:1 | opposite of frailty and w. is sinlessness? |
| T-23 ......in.1:3 | cannot fear, for sin of any kind is w.. The |
| T-23 ......in.1:6 | in enemies is therefore the belief in w., |
| T-27 .......II.9:3 | Their helplessness and w. represent the |
| T-27 ..... III.1:6 | No w. can intrude on it without changing |
| T-28 .... VII.6:2 | chains and heavy anchors, when its w. lies |
| T-29 ........I.8:2 | You do not fear its w., but its lack of |
| T-29 ........I.8:2 | its weakness, but its lack of strength *or* w.. |
| T-31 ... VIII.2:3 | your w. and the strength of Christ in you. |
| T-31 ... VIII.2:5 | by never using w. to direct your actions, |
| T-31 ... VIII.2:7 | For you have brought your w. unto Him, |
| T-31 ... VIII.4:4 | His strength instead of their own w., seen |
| T-31 ... VIII.5:5 | replacing all your w. with the strength |
| T-31 ... VIII.6:2 | as pain, as w. and as suffering and loss, is |
| T-31 ... VIII.6:4 | and close the door upon his dreams of w., |
| W-pI .... 47.2:3 | Who can put his faith in w. and feel safe? |
| W-pI .... 47.4:1 | your own w. to the Source of real strength |
| W-pI .... 48.3:2 | let His strength take the place of your w.. |
| W-pI .... 62.3:1 | in every attack you call upon your own w. |
| W-pI .... 62.3:3 | It will remove all sense of w., strain and |
| W-pI .... 91.4:5 | The miracles your sense of w. hides will |
| W-pI .... 91.5:1 | in which you try to leave your w. behind. |
| W-pI .... 91.9:3 | strength. Remember that all sense of w. is |
| W-pI .... 92.1:2 | of strength, and darkness in terms of w.. |
| W-pI .... 92.3:2 | His strength denies your w.. It is your |
| W-pI .... 92.3:3 | your w. that sees through the body's eyes, |
| W-pI .... 92.4:7 | you; w. is an idol falsely worshipped and |
| W-pI .... 92.5:1 | it; w. reflects the darkness of its maker. It |
| W-pI .... 92.6:1 | W., which looks in darkness, cannot see |
| W-pI .... 95.8:4 | for w. will enable us to overlook it, rather |
| W-pI .... 95.8:5 | and are confusing strength with w.. |
| W-pI .. 111.2:3 | *My w. is the dark His gift dispels, by giving* |
| W-pI .. 135.2:2 | is an acknowledgment of an inherent w.; |
| W-pI .. 137.8:6 | For by its gentle hand is w. overcome, and |
| W-pI .. 153.2:4 | For it attests to w., and sets up a system of |
| W-pI .. 153.6:3 | Christ's strength and your own w., seen |
| W-pI .. 153.7:1 | Defensiveness is w.. It proclaims you |
| W-pI 153.19:3 | strong in Christ, and let our w. disappear, |
| W-pI 153.19:4 | our w. unsupported by His strength. We |
| W-pI .. 154.1:7 | And what we think is w. can be strength; |
| W-pI .. 197.2:2 | and w. must become salvation to you. See |
| M-4 ...... IV.2:7 | And who would choose the w. that must |
| M-5 .........I.1:5 | It is the choice of w., in the mistaken |
| M-5 .........I.2:7 | death himself, his w. is his strength. Now |
| M-7 ........... 5:4 | there is a fear of w. and vulnerability. |
| M-25 ......... 4:8 | Strengths turned to w. are tragedy indeed |
| M-25 ......... 4:9 | to the Holy Spirit must be given to w., for |
| M-29 ......... 7:2 | Remember your w. is His strength. But do |
| M-29 ......... 7:4 | you perceive as your w. is but illusion. |
| P-2....... VII.7:1 | are not afraid to offer w. to God's Son. |
| S-1..........II.2:1 | involve feelings of w. and inadequacy, |

## weaknesses 2

| | |
|---|---|
| T-29 ........I.5:7 | its "inherent" w. set up the limitations on |
| W-pI .. 135.9:2 | For you have seen in it the faults, the w., |

## wealth 2

| | |
|---|---|
| T-26 ..... IV.6:2 | that withholds the w. of Heaven from you |
| T-29 ... VIII.8:8 | more beauty, more intelligence, more w., |

## weapon 14

| | |
|---|---|
| T-2 .........II.4:7 | not, however, turn it into a w. of attack, |
| T-3 ..... VI.5:10 | as a w. of defense for your own authority. |

W-pII .316.1:5 enter in where I am truly w. and at home,
W-pII .322.1:2 tried to hide, awaiting me in shining w.,
W-pII ...14.3:7 concerned only with giving w. to the truth
W-ep .........5:7 which God has held unclosed to w. us.
M-6 ...........2:2 The instant it is w. it is there. Where
M-11 .........4:6 redeemed it and made it fit to w. peace.
M-15 .........1:5 One day each one will w. it, and on that
M-28 .........6:1 not prepared as yet to w. them with joy.
C-ep...........5:3 Let us go and bid Him w. Who returns to
P-3........ III.8:7 Let the Christ in you bid him w., for that
S-1......... III.4:7 of escape makes it difficult to w. freedom,
S-3......... II.3:2 flesh, but as a gentle w. to release. If there
S-3......... II.5:3 how could it be w. when it must be feared
S-3......... II.6:4 in the home that stands ready to w. him,

## welcomed 13

T-8........ VI.4:3 he came home the father w. him with joy,
T-18..... VII.1:6 Atonement is not w. by those who prefer
T-18..VIII.13:3 Yet He Whom you w. has come to you,
T19. IV.A.16:2 which everyone is w. as an honored guest.
T-22....... VI.8:8 them where they are received and w.. He
T-30....... V.2:6 of freedom has been grasped and w., and
W-pI... 104.1:5 They are not w. gladly by a mind that has
W-pI... 196.8:5 be w. back within the holy mind He never
W-pII .303.1:4 Let Christ be w. where He is at home. And
W-pII .310.2:4 today, for we have w. love into our hearts.
M-12 .........3:7 can come only where it is w. without fear.
M-28 .........2:4 Love is no longer feared, but gladly w..
C-ep...........5:4 where God is w. and His Son with Him.

## welcomes 6

T-1........ III.7:5 mind then naturally w. the Host within
T-5...... III.8:11 it with His strength just as the ego w. it.
T-13..... V.7:11 The Father w. all of us in gladness, and
W-pI... 189.2:2 It w. you, rejoices that you came, and
M-26 .......4:10 God takes you where you are and w. you.
S-2........ III.7:4 it arise to Christ, Who w. it as gift to Him.

## welcoming 7

T-5...... III.8:12 Spirit counters this welcome by w. peace.
T-8........ VI.1:4 all, and He will welcome us as I am w. you
T-11....... II.7:7 Real freedom depends on w. reality, and
T-26...... VI.2:4 and forgiveness from your w. embrace.
W-pI... 159.7:6 except the gift of his acceptance of his w..
W-pII .293.1:3 seem bright and clear and safe and w.,
M-4 ....... X.2:6 And above all are all things w., for threat

## welded 1

T-1........ III.9:2 others, a strong chain of Atonement is w..

## welfare 1

T-22.... VI.10:1 your learning depends the w. of the world

## well 274

*See also* well-known, well-structured
T-1......... V.2:2 Time can waste as w. as be wasted. The
T-2......... II.3:1 You can defend truth as w. as error. The
T-2....... V.10:8 of you. This corrects retroactively as w. as
T-2........ VI.2:4 that you would do w. to look at clearly.
T-4...........I.8:6 beloved Son in whom He is w. pleased.
T-4........ II.5:2 may w. harm themselves if you do not. In
T-4........ IV.8:6 Judge how w. you have done this by your
T-4....... VII.4:1 as w. as being rest on communication.
T-5........ III.2:4 of yourself, as w. as of all His creations.
T-6.........I.16:8 lessons must be learned now as w. as then
T-6......... II.9:3 is split, you can perceive as w. as think.
T-6......... II.9:6 and the Holy Spirit can therefore use it w.
T-6........ IV.1:3 and does not mean its maker w.. It
T-6........ IV.1:5 If it meant you w. it would be glad, as the
T-6....... V.A.5:6 Perhaps you think that fear as w. as love
T-7......... II.2:5 in this world as w. as in the Kingdom.
T-7....... VII.1:9 being used positively as w. as negatively.
T-7....... VII.6:2 beloved Sons in whom He is w. pleased.
T-7 ....... XI.2:2 environment and does not function w..
T-7 ....... XI.6:1 your natural environment you may w. ask
T-8 ..... VIII.8:1 might w. ask how the voice of something
T-9 ....... VI.3:8 everything we do belongs to you as w..
T-12 .........I.8:6 the ego. Consider how w. the Holy Spirit's
T-13 ..... IV.4:1 that your questioning might w. begin.
T-13 ..... VI.4:1 Time can release as w. as imprison,
T-14 ...... in.1:4 logic as easily and as w. as does the ego,
T-15 .........I.5:3 For it tells him hell is here as w., and bids
T-15 .... VII.4:3 The ego wishes no one w.. Yet its survival
T-15 .... VII.7:6 accept the guilt and sacrifice himself as w.
T-16 .........I.6:7 recognizes foolish needs as w. as real ones
T-16 ...... III.1:2 You may have taught w., and yet you may
T-18 .... VII.6:5 using means which have served others w.,
T19.... IV.A.6:2 For Heaven knows you w., as you know
T-20 ....... II.5:4 from every altar now is yours as w. as His.
T-20 ...... V.7:6 The veil that hides the gift hides him as w.
T-20 .... VII.2:6 must be willing to want the means as w..
T-20 .... VII.3:2 He asks no more to give the means as w..
T-20 .... VII.3:9 the means to do so must be possible as w.
T-21 .........I.9:1 of the Son of God, whom you know w..
T-21 .........I.9:5 know the ancient song, and know it w..
T-21 .......I.10:1 of their Creator gives praise to them as w..
T-21 ...... V.8:1 the great deceiver's needs as w. as truth.
T-22 ..... II.12:9 not have this holy home be yours as w.?
T-23 ..... IV.3:5 and what is His must be His Son's as w..
T-23 ..... IV.6:4 This you know w.. When they occur leave
T-24 ... III.8:12 The print of nails is on your hands as w..
T-24 ..... IV.4:2 do consider, and consider w., whether it
T-24 ..... IV.5:6 specialness his "enemy," and yours as w..
T-24 ..... VI.6:5 the face of Christ from him, and you as w.
T-24 ..... VI.9:4 who condemned himself, and you as w.,
T-24 .... VII.6:5 God is a Means as w. as End. In Heaven,
T-24 .. VII.10:6 beloved son, in whom I am w. pleased."
T-24 VII.11:13 what you see will serve that purpose w.,
T-25 ..... VI.7:4 made can serve salvation easily and w..
T-25 ... VIII.5:3 But justice does He know, and knows it w.
T-25 ... VIII.9:5 understands as w. that you cannot accept
T-25 ... VIII.9:7 you accept brings joy to Him as w. as you.
T-26 .VIII.9:10 Should not His happiness be yours as w.?
T-26 ..... IX.1:4 as w. while you attack His chosen home,
T-26 ..... IX.6:4 to be Their resting place as w. as yours.
T-27 .........I.9:5 a purpose, it is seen as neither sick nor w.,
T-27 ....... II.3:5 their brothers and themselves as w.. For
T-27 ....... II.7:3 Your healing saves him pain as w. as you,
T-27 ....... II.7:3 are healed because you wished him w..
T-27 ... IV.4:15 want, and it will serve you lovingly and w.
T-27 ...... V.5:3 Consider w. its question. It is asked of you
T-28 ....... II.5:2 and can accept another dream as w.. But
T-28 ....... II.6:8 He sees illusions of himself as sick or w.,
T-28 ..... IV.5:2 believe that it is your reality as w. as his.
T-28 ..... IV.6:4 he be free of them, and of his own as w..
T-28 .... VII.4:9 And you are sick or w., accordingly.
T-29 ..... VI.5:3 in the world but must be changed as w..
T-29 ... VIII.9:8 give the same to every living thing as w..
T-30 .........I.1:5 each time you wake, will put you w. ahead
T-30 .........I.4:3 These two procedures, practiced w., will
T-30 .......I.12:5 and so the answer will make sense as w..
T-30 .......I.16:1 The second rule as w. is but a fact. For
T-30 .......I.16:6 for yourself and for the world as w.. The
T-30 ....... II.3:3 Him Who is His Voice and yours as w.,
T-30 .... V.10:6 that he will pay the cost as w. as you. For
T-31 ....... II.4:3 hate as w. his not assuming it at times you
T-31 ....... II.5:4 what you choose you choose as w. for him
T-31 ..... II.5:13 And listen w.! For he is asking what will
T-31 ..... III.1:4 Learn this, and learn it w., for it is here
T-31 ...... V.1:2 It fits it w.. For this an image is that suits
T-31 ...... V.6:5 It points to you as w., but this is kept still
T-31 ...... V.9:7 must have made the world as w. as you to
T-31 .... VII.3:2 "baser" part of you, and thus of him as w.
T-31 .. VII.14:2 think as w. upon the thing that you would
W-pI....... 4.2:2 to use "good" thoughts as w. as "bad."
W-pI..... 23.3:3 One can w. ask if this can be called seeing.
W-pI..... 29.1:4 thus far, and all subsequent ones as w..
W-pI..... 30.4:2 range as w. as those you can actually see,
W-pI..... 30.5:3 more accustomed to this idea as w.,
W-pI..... 35.5:2 descriptive terms may w. cross your mind
W-pI..... 36.1:3 are holy, your sight must be holy as w..
W-pI..... 40.2:4 quite w. under any circumstances, if you
W-pI .... 45.2:7 They are in your mind as w., where He is.
W-pI .... 46.4:1 exercises w. you should have no difficulty
W-pI .... 53.1:4 I have real thoughts as w. as insane ones.
W-pI .... 54.2:6 know the world I see can change as w..
W-pI .... 54.3:7 me will dawn on their sight as w. as mine.
W-pI .... 62.4:3 as w. as those who seem to be far away in
W-pI .... 64.5:2 at night, and all through the day as w..
W-pI .... 65.4:3 w. as for all the trivial purposes and goals
W-pI .... 70.3:1 the realization that salvation is there as w.
W-pI .... 70.6:3 again be w. to decide in advance when
W-pI .... 72.4:5 Son is only a body, so must He be as w..
W-pI .... 72.6:3 Very w.. Let us accept this and be glad. As
W-pI .... 73.6:7 And so salvation is your will as w.. You
W-pI .... 74.7:5 possible, would be w. spent on this today.
W-pI .. 76.11:3 w. as of the joys of Heaven which His laws
W-pI .. 76.12:1 as w. as in response to any temptation to
W-pI .... 78.6:4 body with its flaws and better points as w.
W-pI .. 78.10:4 you both, and all the sightless ones as w.,
WpI.. rII.in.6:1 in the shorter practice periods as w.,
W-pI .... 87.4:3 *you are His Son, [name], and mine as w..*
W-pI .... 94.2:3 the guarantee of strength and light as w..
W-pI .... 95.7:4 There may w. be a temptation to regard
W-pI .... 98.9:5 that you have on earth as w. as Heaven.
W-pI .... 99.7:1 be sure you practice w. the idea for today.
W-pI .. 100.5:2 to God's plan, as w. as to our vision.
W-pI .. 103.1:5 And therefore joy is everywhere as w.. Yet
W-pI .. 105.5:3 Him must complete His Son as w.. He
W-pI .. 107.8:2 which gave the gift of life to Him as w.. He
W-pI .. 109.8:3 from far across the world, and near as w.;
WpI..rIII.in7:1 confidence that you would use them w.;
WpI..rIII.in7:5 His means must surely merit yours as w..
WpI..rIII.in9:4 to you. Here is another chance to use it w.
WpIrIII.in10:6 keep your peace throughout the day as w.
WpIrIII.in12:1 one to be applied on each half hour as w..
W-pI .. 121.6:3 forgiveness must be learned by you as w.,
W-pI .. 123.1:4 but you can w. be grateful for your gains,
W-pI .. 123.3:2 Give thanks as w. that you are changeless,
W-pI .. 123.5:5 thanking Him the thanks are yours as w..
W-pI .. 124.5:3 we see it in the dying and the dead as w.,
W-pI .. 124.7:2 we say as w. that we are saved and healed;
W-pI .. 127.4:5 Himself, and so are you unlimited as w..
W-pI .. 127.5:3 of what love is, and what you are as w..
W-pI .. 128.8:1 your mind throughout the day as w.. And
W-pI .. 131.4:2 glad as w. to learn you search for Heaven,
W-pI 131.11:6 real. Review the thoughts as w. which are
W-pI 132.16:1 world, as w. as to the ones you see nearby,
W-pI .. 136.1:2 as w. its purpose has no meaning. Being
W-pI 136.17:2 will recognize you practiced w. by this:
W-pI 136.17:3 will be no sense of feeling ill or feeling w.,
W-pI 136.18:4 You need do nothing now to make it w.,
W-pI 137.14:2 we will conclude today at night as w.:
W-pI 137.15:3 Now we come together to make w. all that
W-pI .. 138.1:3 If Heaven exists there must be hell as w.,
W-pI .. 138.7:5 the conflict is to end your life as w..
W-pI .. 140.1:5 so the patient now perceives himself as w.
W-pI .. 140.2:2 he found a magic formula to make him w.
W-pI .. 151.9:6 Let Him be Judge as w. of everything that
W-pI .. 152.3:7 is not true is true as w. as what is true,
W-pI 152.10:3 To recognize God's Son implies as w. that
W-pI .. 153.1:1 to take away again; attend this lesson w..
W-pI 153.10:6 God, by His election and their own as w.?
W-pI .. 154.2:1 Whose function is to speak for you as w..
W-pI .. 154.9:5 would have them be received by you as w.
W-pI 155.10:2 you travelled will be gone from you as w.,
W-pI .. 156.3:1 He is, there must be holiness as w. as life.
W-pI .. 157.7:4 now it has a purpose, and will serve it w..
W-pI .. 158.1:5 It was given as w. to every living thing, for
W-pI 158.10:2 thus Christ's vision looks on you as w..
W-pI 158.11:4 Christ's vision looks upon ourselves as w..
W-pI .. 163.7:4 And with the Father died the Son as w..
W-pI .. 163.8:5 for their salvation and our own as w..
W-pI 166.12:7 He speaks as w. of what becomes your
W-pI .. 167.4:3 apart from it in kind as w. as distance,
W-pI 167.11:3 all creation, with their thoughts as w.,
W-pI .. 181.1:4 and past his seeming sins as w. as yours.
W-pI .. 181.8:5 He feels for us becomes our own as w..
W-pI .. 182.5:5 You are His home as w.. He will return.
W-pI .. 183.9:4 play in its salvation, and your own as w..
W-pI .. 184.2:2 and see as w. nothing where there is unity

W-pI...184.3:3 and thus reality was given them as **w.**. For
W-pI...184.9:3 But be you not deceived by them as **w.**.
W-pI.185.10:3 For them as **w.** as for yourself, you ask but
W-pI...186.1:5 of God is done on earth as **w.** as Heaven.
W-pI...186.2:7 assigned to us by One Who knows us **w.**.
W-pI...187.5:6 who retains; another who will give as **w.**.
W-pI...187.6:4 take. He laughs as **w.** at pain and loss, at
W-pI...187.8:5 first to you, it now is yours to give as **w.**.
W-pI...188.1:5 bear the light in you are alien here as **w.**.
W-pI...188.4:1 world restores the memory to you as **w.**.
W-pI...188.7:4 but they must remain with you as **w.**, for
W-pI...189.8:8 that way is your reality proclaimed as **w.**.
W-pI.189.10:9 *but that Your Will, which is our own as* **w.**,
W-pI...191.1:2 And here as **w.** is all the world released.
W-pI...191.6:2 as **w.** that you have freed the world. You
W-pI...194.4:6 the past and present in His Hands as **w.**,
W-pI.196.11:2 is the time as **w.** in which salvation comes
W-pI...197.3:2 Yet your thanks belong to you as **w.**, for
W-pI.198.10:3 on earth and in your holy home as **w.**. Be
W-pI...199.5:3 will not gain in added gifts to you as **w.**.
W-pI...199.6:5 the body serves, and serves its purpose **w.**
W-pI...199.8:4 Then practice **w.** the thought the Holy
W-pI...203.1:2 *and of sin, because it is my own as* **w.** *as His.*
W-pII......1.3:3 by which it would accomplish it as **w.**. It
W-pII..224.1:2 It lights the world as **w.**. It is the gift my
W-pII..224.1:3 gave to me; the one as **w.** I give the world.
W-pII......2.1:3 that have been born in time will end as **w.**
W-pII..231.2:2 and with the One as **w.** Who is our Father
W-pII..233.1:4 *I give You all my acts as* **w.**, *that I may do*
W-pII..237.2:2 *Him Who is Your Son, and my true Self as* **w.**
W-pII..238.1:5 *And I must be steadfast in holiness as* **w.**,
W-pII..240.2:4 *feel the love for him which is Your Own as* **w.**.
W-pII......3.1:5 has gone, and its effects are gone as **w.**.
W-pII..246.2:3 *that what You will is what I will as* **w.**, *and*
W-pII..247.2:3 *to me as part of You, and my own Self as* **w.**.
W-pII..248.2:1 *and lets me love Your Son again as* **w.**. *Father*
W-pII......4.2:6 Truth can be its aim as **w.** as lies. The
W-pII..257.1:2 contradicting goals and serve them **w.**.
W-pII..257.2:3 *And thus our purpose must be Yours as* **w.**, *if*
W-pII..265.2:1 *but reflects Your Thoughts, and mine as* **w.**.
W-pII......6.1:2 us with one another, and with God as **w.**.
W-pII..274.1:3 **w.** *the truth will enter where illusions were,*
W-pII..280.2:3 *and what is Yours belongs to me as* **w.**.
W-pII..291.1:3 both for myself and for the world as **w.**.
W-pII..294.1:2 And can I be another thing as **w.**? Did
W-pII....10.2:4 There it was born, and there it ends as **w.**.
W-pII..312.2:2 *and therefore it must be my goal as* **w.**.
W-pII..315.1:5 that what he learned is surely mine as **w.**.
W-pII..316.1:3 all time, and past all time as **w.**. My
W-pII..317.1:4 all my brothers and already mine as **w.**.
W-pII..318.1:8 I am salvation's means and end as **w.**.
W-pII..320.2:1 *extend to all the world as* **w.** *through me.*
W-pII..335.2:3 *in Your Son I find the memory of You as* **w.**.
W-pII..343.1:5 *becomes impossible for me as* **w.** *as You. I,*
W-pII..348.2:2 that we choose to be our will as **w.** as His.
W-pII....14.2:3 with me, so what I am are you as **w.**. The
W-pII..354.1:5 *Thus must I be one with You as* **w.** *as Him.*
W-pII..358.1:4 *Your Voice, my Father, then is mine as* **w.**,
W-ep .........5:1 The end is certain, and the means as **w.**.
M-in ..........1:6 continues into sleeping thoughts as **w.**.
M-4......I.A.8:3 all "emergencies" as **w.** as tranquil times.
M-4..... V.1:13 looks down on them in thanks as **w.**. His
M-4.... VIII.1:6 The past as **w.** held no mistakes; nothing
M-4.... VIII.1:6 **w.** as him to whom it seemed to happen.
M-10..........1:8 himself may **w.** be inconsistent in what he
M-11..........1:3 things that seem impossible, as **w.** as this.
M-16..........2:6 be said that it is **w.** to start the day right.
M-17..........1:7 He can be sure as **w.** that he has asked for
M-22..........4:3 of himself and of all others as **w.**. Nor is it
M-24..........3:3 as **w.** as his own decision making. Our
M-25..........1:4 may **w.** develop abilities that seem quite
M-26..........3:6 not happen, so be it as **w.**. All worldly
M-27..........3:5 worms as **w.** are doomed to be destroyed
M-29........5:10 confidence will be **w.** founded indeed.
M-29..........8:7 *of God, Knowing they are on my behalf as* **w.**
C-in............2:2 who seek clarification will find it as **w.**.
C-1.............3:1 in this part but sees the other part as **w.**.
C-2.............7:2 A dream as **w.**. But look at all the aspects
C-4.............5:8 For place has gone as **w.**, along with time.
C-6.............5:5 He offers thanks to you as **w.** as him for
C-ep...........2:5 within eternity and through all time as **w.**
P-1.............3:3 which can attack and be attacked as **w.**, is
P-2.........in.3:2 therapist as **w.** as the patient may cherish
P-2...........I.3:1 of a therapist as **w.** as of a patient. Either
P-2......IV.10:9 it must remain unwanted as **w.** as unreal.
P-2......... V.4:8 for what to teach as **w.** as what to learn.
P-2...... VI.4:10 cure what cannot be sick and make it **w.**?
P-3...........I.3:3 You can see others as **w.**, for seeing is not
P-3......... II.8:2 Yet **w.** before he reaches this in time he
P-3......... III.5:1 It has **w.** been said that to him who hath
P-3......... III.7:1 view of payment may **w.** seem impractical
P-3......... III.8:7 for that same Christ is in him as **w.**. Deny
S-1......... III.6:9 Think of the cost, and understand it **w.**.
S-2...........I.5:8 But you can free him and yourself as **w.**.
S-2...........I.8:5 As He would give, so must you give as **w.**.
S-2......... III.5:5 you look on him, and speak for Him as **w.**
S-3...........I.5:3 to kill, so healing can be false as **w.** as true
S-3......... IV.8:1 so soon it might as **w.** have never been.

## well-known 1

T-31....... V.4:1 not a **w.** fact the world deals harshly with

## well-structured 1

T-12..... II.10:1 **w.** and carefully planned program aimed

## wells 1

W-pI...189.4:2 look out from the endless **w.** of joy within

## went 10

T-22...... IV.1:3 you **w.** before you reached the branch,
T-25...... III.2:5 could be sure His sanity **w.** there with him
T-28.........I.2:3 In its passing **w.** its consequences, left
T-30..... VII.2:5 see another meaning in what **w.** before.
T-31.........I.3:1 and the pains to which you **w.** to practice
W-pI...124.3:1 who **w.** before or stayed with us a while.
W-pI.169.13:3 his who **w.** a moment into timelessness,
W-pII..306.2:1 *to You, remembering we never* **w.** *away;*
M-20 .........2:3 It calls to mind nothing that **w.** before. It
M-23 .........6:8 **w.** beyond the farthest reach of learning.

## wept 1

W-pII..301.2:3 We **w.** because we did not understand.

## were 365

## wet 1

T-31....... V.3:2 face is often **w.** with tears at the injustices

## What 6

*what*

T-25.........I.7:3 And so **W.** is within this mind, and does
T-31..... V.17:9 And **W.** you are will tell you of Itself.
W-pI...95.15:4 *I honor you because of* **W.** *I am, and What*
W-pI...95.15:4 *you because of What I am, and* **W.** *He is,*
WpI. rIV.in2:3 of **W.** you are and What your Father is. It
WpI. rIV.in2:3 of What you are and **W.** your Father is.

## what 4222

*What*

## whatever 159

## when 989

## whence 1

W-pI...107.1:6 to nothingness, returning **w.** they came.

## whenever 72

T-1........ III.5:8 **W.** you experience God's reassurances as
T-2..........II.3:7 The means are available **w.** you ask. You
T-2......... III.5:9 **W.** you are afraid you *are* deceived, and
T-2........ V.10:7 that **w.** you offer a miracle to another, you
T-2....... VI.2:10 **W.** you are afraid, it is a sure sign that you
T-2........ VI.5:1 arising **w.** what you want conflicts with
T-2........ VI.5:8 **W.** there is fear, it is because you have not
T-2........ VI.6:8 does so **w.** it is conflicted in what it wants,
T-2....... VII.5:4 **W.** light enters darkness, the darkness is
T-4........ IV.2:2 and this is so **w.** you are not joyous, then
T-4........ VI.2:3 **W.** you act egotistically towards another,
T-4....... VII.8:1 is praised **w.** any mind learns to be wholly
T-5......... V.3:6 **W.** you respond to your ego you will
T-5....... VII.5:1 **W.** you are not wholly joyous, it is
T-7....... VII.1:1 **W.** you deny a blessing to a brother *you*
T-7....... VII.9:3 **W.** a brother attacks another, that *is* what
T-7........ IX.5:1 into your awareness **w.** you will let Him.
T-7........ XI.6:5 **W.** you heal a brother by recognizing his
T-8........ III.4:6 **W.** two Sons of God meet, they are given
T-8........ III.5:4 lost. **W.** you are with anyone, you have
T-8........ III.5:8 are. **W.** you are with a brother, you are
T-8......... V.5:5 **W.** fear intrudes anywhere along the road
T-8....... VII.8:6 **W.** the reaction to learning is depression,
T-8..... VII.14:3 **W.** you see another as limited to or by the
T-8........ IX.4:4 **W.** you wake dispiritedly, it was not given
T-9........ VI.4:4 creation **w.** you recognize part of creation
T-9....... VII.8:1 **W.** you question your value, say: *God*
T-9......VIII.1:3 you. **W.** you become aware of it, however
T-10....... V.2:5 for **w.** you see your brothers without it,
T-11.........I.8:9 **W.** what the Holy Spirit tells you appears
T-11........II.5:5 **W.** you ask the ego to enter, you lessen
T-12........ III.3:1 **W.** you become angry with a brother, for
T-12... VII.13:1 then, that **w.** you look without and react
T-13..... VII.5:5 for **w.** judgment enters reality has slipped
T-13... VII.14:1 **W.** you are tempted to undertake a
T-14...... III.3:3 **W.** the pain of guilt seems to attract you,
T-14...... III.9:1 **W.** you choose to make decisions for
T-14.... III.19:1 **W.** you are in doubt what you should do,
T-14..... XI.12:2 But **w.** they trust themselves, they will not
T-14..... XI.13:3 **W.** you think you know, peace will depart
T-14..... XI.13:4 **W.** you fully realize that you know not,
T-15... VII.10:1 **W.** you are angry, you can be sure that
T-15........X.6:1 can give all your guilt away **w.** you want,
T-16........II.4:2 You have succeeded **w.** you have reached
T-16........II.7:5 But remember also that **w.** you listened to
T-16..... V.12:1 **W.** any form of special relationship
T-16.... VI.12:1 **W.** your thoughts wander to a special
T-23.........I.8:5 And this occurs **w.** you look on anything
T-27.........I.3:1 **W.** you consent to suffer pain, to be
T-28...... VI.4:4 again, **w.** you perceive yourself attacked.
T-29..... VII.4:1 **W.** you attempt to reach a goal in which
T-29...... IX.9:1 **W.** you feel fear in any form,–and you
T-31...... III.2:5 You answer "yes" **w.** you attack, for by
W-pI..... 12.6:4 the exercises **w.** you experience a sense of
W-pI..... 16.5:4 use today's idea **w.** you are aware of a
W-pI..... 30.3:2 **W.** you have a moment or so, repeat it to
W-pI..... 34.5:1 and made **w.** you feel your peace of mind
W-pI..... 40.1:3 schedule and to adhere to it **w.** possible. If
W-pI..... 40.1:6 try again. **W.** you remember, try again.
W-pI..... 48.2:4 that you take a minute or so **w.** possible
W-pI..... 49.5:3 and repeat the idea for today **w.** you can,
W-pI..... 68.7:1 **w.** any thought of grievance arises against
W-pI... 72.12:1 **W.** you feel your confidence wane and
W-pI..... 77.7:4 Ask for them **w.** a situation arises in
W-pI..... 77.7:6 are fully entitled to receive it **w.** you ask.
W-pI... 79.10:2 today. **W.** any difficulty seems to rise, tell
WpIrIII.in11:5 places, and **w.** you need help of any kind.
W-pI... 124.8:3 Sometime today, **w.** it seems best, devote
W-pI. 130.10:1 Dismiss temptation easily today **w.** it
W-pI. 132.17:1 say **w.** you are tempted to deny the power
W-pI. 185.13:1 lose and everyone must gain **w.** any gift of
M-7 ...........2:1 **W.** a teacher of God has tried to be a

### where 857

### whereby 12

| | |
|---|---|
| T-14.....VII.4:3 | of thinking w. two systems of belief which |
| T-26...VII.19:2 | And be the means w. your brother finds |
| T-27..... II.16:5 | lies the means w. your mind is unified. |
| T-30.....VII.4:1 | means w. perception can be stabilized, |
| T-31.......I.11:2 | the means w. the choice is reassessed; |
| W-pI.159.10:5 | w. a sweet transition can be made from |
| W-pI...168.2:6 | asks the means of Him w. its sleep is done |
| W-pI...195.2:2 | the certain means w. all pain is healed, |
| W-pI...200.4:5 | given you to find the means w. the world |
| W-pII .247.1:3 | means w. Christ's vision comes to me. Let |
| W-pII .327.2:4 | *You give the means w. conviction comes,* |
| P-3........ III.3:5 | only gift w. all healing is accomplished. |

### wherein 12

| | |
|---|---|
| T-14.... III.15:8 | from the loving Mind w. he was created, |
| T-15.........I.9:7 | From this holy instant w. holiness was |
| T-22.... VI.12:7 | Yet w. lies its value, except in the desire to |
| T-24...... VI.8:6 | w. you see the judgment you have laid on |
| T-25.........I.2:8 | your sinfulness, w. you stand condemned |
| T-27....VIII.3:3 | places and events w. its "hero" finds itself |
| WpIrIV.in10:2 | in the peace w. He wills you be forever, |
| W-pI...153.3:1 | w. another circle bound it and another |
| W-pI...157.4:3 | joy, w. you quickly leave the world behind |
| W-pI...181.3:4 | time w. we practice changing our intent. |
| W-pI...182.4:6 | w. are earth and Heaven joined as one. |
| W-pII .222.1:3 | He is my home, w. I live and move; the |

### whereof 1

| | |
|---|---|
| W-pI...182.2:1 | No one but knows w. we speak. Yet some |

### whereon 7

| | |
|---|---|
| T-18...... IX.8:3 | is a world of light w. they cast no shadows |
| T-26....... V.7:1 | this a hindrance to the place w. he stands |
| T-26...... IX.2:4 | The ground w. you stand is holy ground |
| T-26...... IX.4:6 | to join Them on the ground w. you stand. |
| T-28.....VII.6:2 | the little gap of nothingness w. it stands? |
| T-29....... II.4:7 | touched the holy ground w. you stand, |
| W-pII .....2.3:4 | holy Name of God w. His Word is written |

### wherever 29

| | |
|---|---|
| T-2....V.A.18:5 | *I am content to be w. He wishes, knowing He* |
| T-4.......VII.8:8 | direct you to w. you can be truly helpful, |
| T-6....... II.12:5 | same. W. He looks He sees Himself, and |
| T-8.....IV.2:12 | more than darkness can abide w. you go. |
| T-10...... IV.1:9 | to you, and w. you think you see him, he |
| T-11....... II.2:6 | thought you hold, w. you perceive it, lies |
| T-14.....VII.2:4 | It is there, w. you are, being within you. |
| T-14..... X.12:7 | your Identity w. It is not recognized, you |
| T-17.....VIII.3:2 | freely given w. faithlessness is laid aside, |
| T19... IV.A.5:5 | to be accomplished, w. it is undertaken? |
| T-29....... II.3:4 | gone, and love must come w. they are not. |
| T-31.....VIII.1:1 | would teach, in all its forms, w. it occurs. |
| T-31.....VIII.6:3 | see all pain, in every form, w. it occurs, |
| W-pI........41.h | God goes with me w. I go. |
| W-pI.....41.4:1 | its Source goes with you w. you go. You |
| W-pI.....41.4:2 | Source of all joy goes with you w. you go. |
| W-pI.....41.4:3 | Source of all life goes with you w. you go. |
| W-pI.....41.4:4 | because God goes with you w. you go. |
| W-pI...41.10:1 | remembering that God goes with you w. |
| W-pI.....42.2:2 | it any time and anywhere, w. you are, and |
| W-pI.....59.1:1 | (41) God goes with me w. I go. How can I |
| W-pI.....59.1:7 | perfect because God goes with me w. I go. |
| W-pI.....72.9:6 | instead. And w. His plan is accepted, it is |
| W-pI.....75.1:5 | and you bring peace with you w. you go. |
| W-pI...127.9:3 | your mind w. you give up a false belief, a |
| W-pI...160.6:3 | himself can find no home w. he may look, |
| W-pII .244.1:1 | *Your Son is safe w. he may be, for You are* |
| W-pII .313.1:2 | *And love will come w. it is asked. This vision* |
| S-1...........I.6:7 | w. he may be and whatever form he may |

### whether 54

| | |
|---|---|
| T-3 ....... VI.2:5 | of what is judged, w. in you or in others. |
| T-3 ..... VI.2:10 | it does not matter w. your judgment is |
| T-3 ..... VI.8:10 | it may even doubt w. you really exist at all |
| T-4 .........II.5:5 | Yet w. or not you recognize it now, you |
| T-4 ..... III.10:2 | odds, w. you are asleep or awake. |
| T-4 ..... IV.11:2 | Holy Spirit, w. you are asleep or awake, |
| T-7 ....... VI.1:5 | depending on w. the ego or the Holy |
| T-7 ...VIII.1:10 | to decide w. or not you will utilize the law |
| T-7 .........X.3:3 | is not w. what the Holy Spirit says is true, |
| T-7 .........X.3:3 | but w. you want to listen to what He says. |
| T-9 ....... IV.8:2 | w. its unpredictability places the ego in a |
| T-9 ....VIII.3:4 | its only decision is w. to attack now or to |
| T-10 ..... III.5:1 | w. its offering is really what you want, for |
| T-11 .......II.7:6 | ego is nothing, w. you invite it in or not. |
| T-11 ..... VI.5:2 | w. it be the god he made or the God Who |
| T-12 ..... IV.5:2 | home w. you realize where it is or not. If |
| T-14 ..... III.5:6 | W. he does this or does it not will make |
| T-14 ... III.11:9 | decide w. or not you are deserving of it. |
| T-14 ..... IV.5:1 | carefully w. you want to make decisions |
| T-15 .......II.4:5 | your choice w. they support the ego or the |
| T-16 .... V.16:1 | decision w. or not to listen to this course |
| T-17 ..... VI.3:6 | left to make is w. or not the ego likes it; is |
| T-18 ... VI.13:6 | questioning w. or not all this is possible. |
| T19. IV.D.10:8 | choose w. to look upon it or wander on, |
| T-20 ..... III.9:3 | uncertain w. to let it go or to take hold on |
| T-20 ...VIII.8:7 | the question never is w. you want them, |
| T-21 ........I.3:5 | Your question is w. the means by which |
| T-21 .... VII.7:1 | power, is the choice of w. to attack or heal |
| T-21 .... VII.7:5 | this decision but the choice w. to see him |
| T-22 ... VI.13:7 | is w. you and your brother are different. |
| T-23 .......II.6:4 | the choice w. to take his word for it or be |
| T-23 .....II.22:6 | know w. you chose the stairs to Heaven or |
| T-24 ..... IV.4:2 | w. it is your wish that you might see your |
| T-26 .......II.4:8 | to judge w. the hurt be large or little. He |
| T-26 ..... V.1:11 | You but choose w. to go toward Heaven, |
| T-29 ... IV.4:11 | But w. it succeeds or fails is not its core, |
| T-30 ..... III.9:2 | depend on w. it is seen on earth or not. |
| T-31 ..VII.12:6 | of w. you would join with what you see, or |
| W-pI....... 7.3:4 | How else would you know w. or not this |
| W-pI..... 28.1:3 | The question of w. you will keep them in |
| W-pI..... 49.1:2 | with God, w. you are aware of it or not. It |
| W-pI..... 52.4:4 | is not w. to see the past or the present; the |
| W-pI..... 52.4:4 | the choice is merely w. to see or not. |
| W-pI..... 64.4:4 | every time you choose w. or not to fulfill |
| W-pI..... 64.4:4 | are really choosing w. or not to be happy. |
| W-pI..... 66.9:7 | consider also w. it was ever reasonable to |
| W-pI..... 67.4:4 | w. you feel you have succeeded or not. |
| M-in .......... 2:4 | The question is not w. you will teach, for |
| M-4 ..... I.A.4:2 | things on the basis of w. they increase the |
| M-8 ......... 3:11 | decides w. what is seen is real or illusory, |
| M-11 ......... 2:2 | This time ask yourself w. your judgment |
| M-22 ......... 2:1 | rapid, depending on w. he recognizes the |
| M-23 ......... 3:7 | ask yourself honestly w. it is likely that he |
| S-1 ...........I.2:4 | must be made w. they be illusions or not. |

### which 2081

### while 104

- noun

*noise word*

| | |
|---|---|
| T-1 ...... VII.2:3 | The Love of God, for a little w., must still |
| T-4 .........II.5:8 | Be patient a w. and remember that the |
| T-9 .... IV.11:7 | may believe them, and so, for a w., the |
| T-11 ...... V.1:5 | of the ego will be our lesson for a w., for |
| T-12 .......II.7:1 | A little w. and you will see me, for I am |
| T-13 .......X.5:5 | within you all the w. you dreamed of guilt |
| T-16 .....II.6:10 | can delay this now, but only a little w.. |
| T-16 .... VII.7:4 | will weaken the experience of Him for a w. |
| T-19 ..... III.8:7 | cherished but a little w. before it vanishes. |
| T19.... IV.D.9:4 | Stand you here a w. and tremble not. You |
| T-20 .......II.6:5 | no plaything to be tossed about a w. and |
| T-20 ..... III.9:2 | It takes a w. for them to understand what |
| T-20 ..... IV.6:7 | enter without fear and where he rests a w. |
| T-20 ..... VI.8:8 | that held together for a little w. in time, |
| T-25 .......II.5:4 | to see. The body holds it for a w., without |
| T-25 ..... IV.4:6 | light. They linger for a w., a little while, in |
| T-25 ..... IV.4:6 | linger for a while, a little w., in twisted |
| T-25 ... IV.5:11 | entered it and were mistaken for a little w. |
| T-26 ... VIII.3:8 | in which forgiveness is withheld a little w. |
| T-27 ... VIII.1:3 | outside the body, lives a little w. and dies, |
| T-27 ... VIII.9:3 | its foolish cause and laugh with Him a w.. |
| T-28 ........ I.1:7 | of them and loved them for a little w.. The |
| T-28 ..... III.5:4 | to keep them separate for a little w.? |
| T-28 .... VII.7:8 | is it made a home of holiness a little w., |
| T-29 ........ I.3:5 | made your friendship possible a little w.. |
| T-29 ..... VI.6:3 | is to dwell a little w. in such a happy place |
| T-29 ..... VI.6:4 | *is* a little w. till timelessness comes quietly |
| T-29 ... VIII.6:6 | as his Father, come to hate a little w.; to |
| T-29 ... IX.10:6 | the w. he is remembering what he forgot, |
| T-30 ..... IV.4:4 | They seem to dance a little w., according |
| T-31 ... IV.2:12 | On some you travel gaily for a w., before |
| T-31 ..... VI.6:8 | your trust; a happy place to rest in for a w. |
| T-31 .. VII.10:5 | and those you knew a long w. since, and |
| W-pI .... 61.5:6 | about these statements for a short w., |
| W-pI .... 65.6:1 | After a w., interfering thoughts will |
| W-pI .... 66.5:7 | us, then, think about the premises for a w. |
| W-pI .. 66.11:3 | about them a little w. as you say them. |
| W-pI .... 78.1:4 | Yet all the w. it waits for you in light, but |
| W-pI .. 92.10:4 | Leave, then, the dark a little w. today, and |
| W-pI .... 95.7:1 | practice periods for a w., and urge you to |
| W-pI .. 96.11:2 | mind remains uncertain yet a little w.. Be |
| W-pI .. 105.7:1 | Think of your "enemies" a little w., and |
| W-pI .. 105.8:3 | joy are mine," and close your eyes a w., |
| W-pI .. 107.4:1 | When truth has come it does not stay a w. |
| W-pI .. 108.9:1 | Say each one slowly and then pause a w., |
| W-pI .. 109.2:5 | came and yet will come to linger for a w.. |
| W-pI 121.11:1 | him in your mind, and look at him a w.. |
| W-pI 121.12:1 | Look at this changed perception for a w., |
| W-pI .. 124.2:4 | as we walk the world a little w.. And those |
| W-pI .. 124.3:1 | who went before or stayed with us a w.. |
| W-pI .. 125.5:2 | have wandered off a little w. from Him. |
| W-pI .. 125.6:2 | be heard until your mind is quiet for a w., |
| W-pI .. 128.6:1 | Pause and be still a little w., and see how |
| W-pI .. 128.6:2 | It will be grateful to be free a w.. It knows |
| W-pI .. 129.2:4 | all things that you have cherished for a w.. |
| W-pI .. 132.6:5 | or perhaps step back a w. and then return |
| W-pI 135.13:2 | and which needs its service for a little w.. |
| W-pI .. 151.2:3 | though you learned a long w. since your |
| W-pI 153.15:1 | in a form we will maintain for quite a w.. |
| W-pI 153.16:4 | we will be unable to withdraw a little w., |
| W-pI 155.14:1 | but that you think of Him a w. each day, |
| W-pI .. 157.3:2 | above its laws, and walk into eternity a w.. |
| W-pI .. 157.6:3 | and Heaven is remembered for a w.. |
| W-pI .. 163.5:4 | while all the w. its worshippers agree, and |
| W-pI .. 167.9:2 | Source, it merely seems to go to sleep a w. |
| W-pI 169.12:3 | the thought of time but for a little w.. |
| WpI...rV.in6:2 | I share your doubts and fears a little w., |
| Wi181-200 3:4 | go past all defenses for a little w. each day. |
| W-pI .. 181.3:2 | we seek, and only this, for just a little w.. |
| W-pI .. 181.5:5 | these pointless limitations by a little w.. |
| W-pI .. 181.6:3 | So, for a little w., without regard to past |
| W-pI .. 182.5:3 | voice cries unto you to let Him rest a w.. |
| W-pI 182.12:9 | go home with Him, and be at peace a w.. |
| W-pI .. 184.9:2 | need to use the symbols of the world a w.. |
| W-pI .. 189.2:3 | and gentle home in which to stay a w.. It |
| W-pI .. 195.7:1 | against our shoulders as they rest a w.. |
| W-pI .. 197.6:2 | the gifts of God are lent but for a little w., |
| W-pI .. 198.2:7 | must we deal with them a w. as if they had |
| W-pII .. in.11:4 | slowly read and thought about a little w., |
| W-pII . 222.2:1 | *now, and ask to rest with You in peace a w..* |
| W-pII ..... 2.4:1 | to this holy place, and spend a w. together |
| W-pII ..... 4.4:4 | But all the w. his Father shines on him, |
| W-pII294.1:10 | today; of service for a w. and fit to serve, |
| W-pII . 300.2:2 | *we, Your loving Sons, have lost our way a w..* |
| W-pII . 324.1:4 | *I can but choose to wander off a w., and then* |
| W-pII . 325.1:6 | he can rest a w. before he journeys on, |
| W-pII . 353.1:4 | *A w. I work with Him to serve His purpose.* |
| M-4 ..... I.A.6:2 | the teacher of God rests a w. in reasonable |
| M-4 ... I.A.6:12 | him. Now he rests a w., and gathers them |
| M-12 ......... 6:2 | teachers choose to look on dreams a w.. It |
| M-13 ......... 2:5 | a w. about what the world calls sacrifice. |
| M-14 ......... 3:1 | this seems to be a long, long w. away. |
| M-27 ......... 3:4 | and to last a little w. by his destruction. |
| C-2 .......... 10:6 | And who would not go on a little w. when |
| C-4 ............ 1:4 | last in time a little w. longer than others. |

C-6 ............ 5:7 place the hymn to God is heard a little **w.**.
C-ep ........... 3:3 on before and lost our way a little **w.**. And
P-2 ........ IV.7:6 of health is substituted for a little **w.**, but
P-2 ....... VII.7:5 except to some extent and for a little **w.**.
P-3 ........ III.7:7 Then stop a **w.**, long enough to think of
S-1 ......... in.2:1 To you who are in time a little **w.**, prayer
S-2 ........ III.7:3 Rest a **w.** in this; do not attempt to judge
S-3 ......... II.3:3 it is time to rest a **w.** from labor gladly
S-3 ......... II.6:2 It can be held at bay a little **w.**, and there

## while 232

• noise word
*noun*

## whim 6

T-14 ......... I.4:5 the capricious and unholy **w.** of death and
T-20 ... VIII.7:1 Judgment is but a toy, a **w.**, the senseless
W-pI ... 126.4:1 basically unsound; a charitable **w.**,
W-pI ... 126.5:5 indeed, if your salvation rested on a **w.**?
W-pI ... 134.1:2 course appear to rest salvation on a **w.**.
W-pI ... 156.6:5 to God Himself for such a senseless **w.**?

## whirl 1

T-24 ...... III.3:7 and turn and **w.** about with every breeze.

## whisper 4

T-14 ...... IX.3:2 is so gentle you need but **w.** to it, and all
T-24 ...... III.3:1 just a word, a little **w.** that you do not like
W-pI ... 156.4:4 wind sinks to a **w.** round your holy head.
W-pI ... 163.5:4 the ground, they **w.** fearfully that it is so.

## whispered 3

T-20 ..... III.6:5 They gently questioned it and **w.**, "What
T-24 ..... VII.1:6 slight, the tiniest attack, the **w.** doubt, the
M-8 ............ 5:4 easily a **w.** demand to kill than a shout?

## whispering 1

T19.IV.A.16:1 and a softly joyous **w.** is ever heard. This

## whispers 6

T19..IV.B.13:8 happiness. Yet to itself it **w.**, "It is death."
T-24 ... VII.10:6 Yet your specialness **w.**, "Here is my own
T-27 ....... V.5:2 dying bring reproach, and suffering **w.**,
W-pI ... 151.9:4 What **w.** of the ego can He hear? What
W-pI ... 182.7:4 He **w.** of His home unceasingly to you.
P-2 ......... V.6:5 advance, the tiniest of **w.** of His Name. To

## whit 1

T-29 ... VIII.3:9 nor darken by one **w.** the light itself.

## white 5

*See also* snow-white

T-20 ......... I.2:1 the **w.** and holy sign the Son of God is
T-26 ....... IX.3:1 be all **w.** and sparkling in the summer sun
T-30 ...... III.8:6 Yet still and **w.** and lovely will it shine
W-pI ... 134.4:4 as blameless as the grass; as **w.** as snow. It
M-17 .......... 8:5 an intense **w.** light against a black horizon

## whiteness 1

T-20 ......... I.3:6 But let the **w.** of your shining gift of lilies

## Who 160

• God
*God and Christ/Self*
*Christ/Self*
*Holy Spirit*
*who*

T-1 ........ VI.4:3 your Creator, **W.** has perfect faith in His
T-2 ........ III.3:3 Creator, **W.** set the limits on your ability
T-2 ...... VIII.1:3 **W.** was expressing the same Will in His
T-4 ......... I.10:5 **W.** is as incapable of deception as is the
T-4 ....... VII.5:1 God, **W.** encompasses all being, created
T-5 ......... II.3:6 by God, **W.** asks you only to listen to it.
T-5 ........ IV.6:5 to forsake myself and God **W.** created me.
T-6 ....... II.6:10 inclusion in Him **W.** alone is perfect. To
T-6 ...... IV.10:5 **W.** knows that His creations are perfect,
T-7 ......... I.7:12 You also do not know **W.** created it. God
T-7 ........ IV.1:4 **W.** knows His creations as perfectly whole
T-7 ........ IV.7:5 All being is in Him **W.** is all Being. You
T-7 ....... V.6:15 **W.** created you by sharing His Being with
T-7 ....... V.10:2 to forget yourself and Him **W.** created you
T-7 ....... V.10:4 your remembrance of me and of Him **W.**
T-7 ......... X.7:2 of God, **W.** has not left you comfortless.
T-7 ........ XI.6:8 denying yours and that of God **W.** created
T-8 ........... I.1:5 made by God, **W.** makes no bargains. It is
T-8 ......... II.3:4 It is never God **W.** coerces you, because
T-8 ......... II.7:7 are part of Him **W.** is all power and glory,
T-8 ........ III.7:1 you are part of God, **W.** is everything. His
T-8 ...... IV.2:13 of yourself, and of Him **W.** sent me to you
T-8 ......... V.5:4 the journey back to God **W.** is our home.
T-9 ........ III.7:9 is of God, **W.** does not know of arrogance.
T-9 ..... VIII.4:8 is of God, **W.** created it out of His Love.
T-9 ... VIII.10:6 God, **W.** knows your value, would not
T-10 ...... III.4:5 you are part of God, **W.** is all power. A
T-10 ....... V.4:4 without the Father, **W.** alone is his Help.
T-11 ....... in.4:7 to your true Father, **W.** hath need of you,
T-11 ......... I.2:4 universe, or from God **W.** *is* the universe? I
T-11 ......... I.4:2 **W.** placed no limits on His creation or
T-11 ......... I.9:4 Would God, **W.** wants only your will, be
T-11 ....... V.6:4 the ego's arrogance to Him **W.** wills not to
T-11 ....... VI.5:2 god he made or the God **W.** created him.
T-12 ... VII.10:6 **W.** wills to extend His peace through you.
T-13 ........ in.3:6 the Father **W.** drove him out of Paradise.
T-13 .... III.10:3 ask this of a Father **W.** truly loved His Son
T-13 ..... VII.7:2 **W.** watches over him in everything. The
T-13 ... VIII.2:3 being in the Mind of God, **W.** knows you.
T-13 ....... X.9:7 is as pure as He **W.** raised it to Himself.
T-14 .... III.15:7 the Love of God, **W.** has remembered you
T-14 ...... IV.1:7 God the Father, **W.** is both First and One.
T-14 ...... IV.8:7 Would you know of One **W.** gives forever,
T-14 ...... IV.8:7 and **W.** knows of nothing except giving?
T-14 ...... X.12:8 **W.** wills to be with His Son forever, will
T-15 ...... III.6:8 magnitude is of Him **W.** dwells in you,
T-15 ...... IV.7:5 God **W.** surrounds all of you together.
T-15 ....... V.3:2 unlike to God, **W.** knows no special love,
T-15 ..... VII.5:3 in the Name of Him **W.** would release him
T-15 ... VIII.3:5 for He comes from One **W.** cannot fail.
T-15 ... VIII.4:7 His Father, **W.** is His one relationship, in
T-15 ..... XI.2:7 need but invite Him in **W.** is there already
T-15 ..... XI.8:4 return it to the Father, **W.** gave it to me.
T-15 ..... XI.9:4 Him, being host to Him **W.** created them.
T-16 ...... III.8:1 for what He is **W.** created you as you are.
T-16 .. IV.11:14 all the Love of God, **W.** forgot you not.
T-16 .... IV.13:5 fearlessly the Call of Him **W.** gave eternity
T-17 ....... II.3:3 No one but Him **W.** planned salvation
T-18 ......... I.8:2 God you never left, and **W.** never left you.
T-18 .... IV.5:10 *He W. established His dwelling place in me*
T-18 .... IX.11:4 Him **W.** is complete where He begins, and
T19 .... IV.B.9:6 He **W.** is our home is homeless with us. Is
T19 .... IV.C.3:3 God, **W.** created neither sin nor death,
T19.IV.D.18:5 of his Father, **W.** knows no sin, no death,
T-20 ...... IV.1:8 **W.** has already given and received all that
T-20 ....... V.2:7 you remember **W.** gave the gifts to Him to
T-21 .... II.13:1 **W.** created you together and as one. See
T-23 ...... I.10:2 of You, **W.** dwell as One and not apart.
T-23 ...... I.11:1 seek to overcome the One **W.** dwells there
T-23 ....... II.7:3 He has become the "enemy" **W.** caused it,
T-24 ....... II.8:7 It is not God **W.** has condemned His Son,
T-24 .... II.10:7 **W.** chose that love could never be divided
T-24 ..... III.5:8 **W.** knows that death is not your will,
T-24 ..... III.7:6 die, but not by Him **W.** made not death;
T-24 ....... V.8:3 **W.** willed not to be without His Son could
T-24 .... VI.10:6 **W.** loves each part of Him with equal love
T-26 ......... I.7:8 only one was given him by One **W.** knows
T-27 ...... VI.4:7 to your life in Him **W.** knows no death.
T-28 ...... I.10:1 it is not He **W.** laid a judgment on His Son
T-28 ...... I.15:7 it is He **W.** will transport His Son across it
T-28 ...... III.6:4 thus make room for Him **W.** wills to come
T-28 ..... VII.1:5 of Either, **W.** have promised to be One.
T-30 ........ II.3:6 Remember Him **W.** has created you, and
T-30 ........ II.4:4 you, **W.** has made you co-creator of the
T-30 ........ II.4:7 forgiven Him **W.** gave your will to you.
T-30 ....... V.4:1 because it is but God **W.** could create a
T-30 .... VIII.3:7 you, but not of God **W.** knows no limits.
W-pI ..... 56.5:4 of God, **W.** has not left His Thoughts.
W-pI ... 72.12:1 of infinity, **W.** created you like Himself:
W-pI ..... 94.2:3 He **W.** ensured your sinlessness must be
W-pI ... 95.15:4 *am, and What He is, W. loves us both as One.*
W-pI ..... 97.4:2 and count on Him **W.** promised to lay
W-pI ..... 98.9:5 then of Him **W.** knows the function that
W-pI ... 100.9:5 when He **W.** calls to you is God Himself?
W-pI ... 104.1:3 **W.** cannot fail to give you what He wills.
W-pI ... 106.3:5 **W.** holds your happiness within His Hand
W-pI ... 114.2:2 *W. has created me for what I am and will*
W-pI ... 124.3:2 **W.** loves us with the equal love in which
W-pI. 151.12:3 and your Creator, **W.** is One with Him. So
W-pI ... 152.9:4 to Him **W.** has created us immaculate,
W-pI. 153.12:2 designed by One **W.** loves His children,
W-pI. 153.12:2 and **W.** would replace their fearful toys
W-pI ... 154.4:3 becomes aware again of **W.** created it, and
W-pI. 155.10:5 go. But One **W.** knows goes with you. Let
W-pI ... 156.5:2 you, for they recognize **W.** walks with you
W-pI ...... 164.h are we one with Him **W.** is our Source.
W-pI ... 168.5:3 is yet the One **W.** answers our mistakes by
W-pI ... 177.2:1 are we one with Him **W.** is our Source.
W-pI. 184.15:2 *things, and You W. are their one Creator.*
W-pI ... 186.9:3 He **W.** is changeless shares His attributes
W-pI. 186.11:3 It comes from One **W.** knows no error,
W-pI. 186.12:2 impossible, remember **W.** it is that asks,
W-pI. 186.12:4 **W.** knows all things exactly as they are, or
W-pI. 186.12:6 you by your Creator **W.** remembers you,
W-pI. 187.10:3 Not separate from Him **W.** is our Source;
W-pI. 187.11:6 **W.** dwells in us and offers us His Holiness
W-pI ... 188.1:7 with you from Him **W.** is your Source. It
W-pI ... 189.8:1 Is it not He **W.** knows the way to you?
W-pI. 189.10:7 *no beliefs of what we are, or W. created us.*
W-pI ... 193.2:5 Yet it is He **W.** gives the means by which
W-pI ... 193.2:6 It is He **W.** answers what His Son would
W-pI ... 194.9:5 we will appeal to Him **W.** guards our rest
W-pI ... 195.1:7 gratitude is due to Him alone **W.** made all
W-pI ... 195.2:2 to fail in gratitude to One **W.** offers you
W-pI ... 195.6:2 the One **W.** is Himself completion. We
W-pII .... in.8:1 for truth and God, **W.** is its one Creator.
W-pII . 228.1:4 One **W.** knows the true condition of His
W-pII . 231.2:2 and with the One as well **W.** is our Father.
W-pII . 232.2:3 fear. Have faith in Him **W.** is your Father.
W-pII . 245.2:3 **W.** speaks to us as we relate His Word;
W-pII . 253.1:6 with them and Him **W.** has created me.
W-pII . 260.1:2 *my Source, remaining part of W. created me*
W-pII . 262.1:8 *and we are part of You W. are our Source,*
W-pII . 274.2:1 to us today, from Him **W.** is our Father.
W-pII . 276.1:6 unsure of Who we are, of **W.** our Father is,
W-pII . 276.1:7 to acknowledge Him **W.** gave His Word
W-pII ..... 8.5:4 **W.** calls to us and comes to take us home,
W-pII . 299.1:2 my Father, **W.** created it, acknowledges
W-pII . 310.2:2 and joy to Him **W.** gave salvation to us,
W-pII . 310.2:2 gave salvation to us, and **W.** set us free.
W-pII . 316.2:3 *I trust that You W. gave them will provide*
W-pII . 321.1:6 *You W. endowed me with my freedom as*
W-pII . 322.1:4 Holy One **W.** still abides in Him forever,
W-pII . 324.1:1 *One W. gave the plan for my salvation to me.*
W-pII . 324.2:1 So let us follow One **W.** knows the way.
W-pII . 324.2:4 And it is He **W.** makes the ending sure,
W-pII . 337.2:1 *You W. created me in sinlessness are not*
M-4 ...... IV.2:9 thoughts with Him **W.** is their Source.
M-4 ...... VI.1:4 their understanding **W.** created them.
M-7 ........... 3:7 him remember **W.** gave the gift and Who
M-7 ........... 3:7 Who gave the gift and **W.** received it.
M-17 ....... 6:10 of **W.** your great "opponent" really is.
C-ep ........... 2:2 to Him **W.** loves you as He loves Himself.
C-ep ........... 4:1 to Him **W.** called to us and helped us hear
P-2 ....... VII.6:5 Whose Love is in him and **W.** cannot fail.
P-3 ......... I.2:12 or hear the Voice of Him **W.** is God in you
S-1 ......... in.1:2 **W.** returns the thanks it offers Him unto
S-3 ........ IV.4:2 and called to God, **W.** hears and answers.
S-3 ........ IV.5:5 He **W.** is Love becomes the source of fear,

S-3 IV.8:5 Return to Me **W.** never left My Son.

## Who 2

- God and Christ/Self
  *God*
  *Christ/Self*
  *Holy Spirit*
  *who*

T-26 IX.2:4 stand is holy ground because of Them **W.**,
C-6 4:2 your Self and your Creator, **W.** are One.

## Who 59

- Christ/Self
  *God*
  *God and Christ/Self*
  *Holy Spirit*
  *who*

T-11 IV.7:4 **W.** lives in His Creator and shines with
T-11 VIII.9:4 Christ is the Son of God **W.** is in no way
T-13 V.9:2 vision of Christ, **W.** looks on all in light.
T-14 II.7:8 the hands of Christ **W.** gives it to you, that
T-15 XI.2:9 Host **W.** cradles God in the time of Christ,
T-16 III.7:5 to your Self, **W.** teaches you what He is,
T19.IV.D.14:1 Friend, the Christ **W.** stands beside you.
T-25 I.1:1 you to do, since it is He **W.** does it. And in
T-26 VI.3:4 it is He **W.** is your only Friend in truth. He
T-31 II.7:1 and answer to the Christ **W.** calls to you.
T-31 II.11:7 you is One **W.** holds the light before you,
T-31 II.11:9 And He **W.** travels with you *has* the light.
W-pI 52.2:5 forgiven myself and remembered **W.** I am
W-pI 56.5:3 of **W.** I am because I have forgotten it. It
W-pI 58.5:5 or deprivation or pain because of **W.** I am
W-pI 63.4:5 And **W.** but your Self must be His Son?
W-pI 73.7:5 freedom to remember **W.** you really are.
W-pI 81.1:5 In its peace let me remember **W.** I am.
W-pI 84.3:6 today, so that I can remember **W.** I am.
W-pI 97.2:1 Self, the holy Son of God **W.** rests in you,
W-pI 100.9:3 Him **W.** waits that you may look on Him?
W-pI.100.10:6 It is your Self **W.** calls to you today. And it
W-pI 107.8:1 Begin by asking Him **W.** goes with you
W-pI 107.9:5 *mind, And I will rest in Him* **W.** *is my Self.*
W-pI.107.11:2 and Him **W.** would release the world, as
W-pI 110.7:1 the Self **W.** is the holy Son of God Himself
W-pI 110.8:1 Seek Him within you **W.** is Christ in you,
W-pI 110.8:1 the Savior **W.** has been forever saved,
W-pI 120.2:3 *and let my Father tell me* **W.** *I really am.*
W-pI 121.6:5 your mind as one to Him **W.** is your Self,
W-pI 121.6:5 Who is your Self, and **W.** can never sin.
W-pI.137.14:4 *mind of God's one Son,* **W.** *is my only Self.*
W-pI.140.12:8 ends, and we remember **W.** we really are.
W-pI.152.11:6 And He **W.** never left will come again to
W-pI 164.5:3 of judgment left to Him **W.** judges true.
W-pI 166.6:3 and need but realize **W.** walks with him
W-pI.166.11:3 One walks with you **W.** gently answers all
W-pI 182.4:3 a Child in you **W.** seeks His Father's house
W-pI 182.5:2 It is this Child **W.** knows His Father. He
W-pI.182.10:2 Child, **W.** comes defenseless and Who is
W-pI.182.10:2 comes defenseless and **W.** is protected by
W-pII .237.2:2 *I come to You through Him* **W.** *is Your Son,*
W-pII .238.1:5 *certainty that he is safe* **W.** *still is part of You,*
W-pII .261.1:8 only there will I remember **W.** I really am.
W-pII .269.2:3 one because of Him **W.** is the Son of God;
W-pII .269.2:3 of God; of Him **W.** is our own Identity.
W-pII 6.2:5 salvation, yet does He remain the Self **W.**,
W-pII .276.1:6 unsure of **W.** we are, of Who our Father is,
W-pII .282.1:4 He loves, and **W.** remains my one Identity
W-pII .286.2:3 and in our Self, **W.** still is One with Him.
M-12 1:3 becomes the Self **W.** is the Son of God. He
M-22 5:1 it is because he has forgotten **W.** he is.
M-25 1:5 glorious surprise of remembering **W.** he is
C-6 1:5 Christ, His real Son, **W.** is part of Him.
C-ep 5:3 and bid Him welcome **W.** returns to us to
P-3 I.4:8 of God. **W.** calls on him is far beyond his
P-3 II.9:10 Yet at each meeting there is One **W.** says,
S-1 II.2:1 by a Son of God who knows **W.** he is. No
S-2 III.7:4 to Christ, **W.** welcomes it as gift to Him.

## Who 149

- Holy Spirit
  *God*
  *God and Christ/Self*
  *Christ/Self*
  *who*

T-2 V.A.18:3 *I am here to represent Him* **W.** *sent me. I do*
T-2 V.A.18:4 *to do, because He* **W.** *sent me will direct me. I*
T-5 VI.7:3 **W.** will undo it in you because it does not
T-5 VI.12:5 Holy Spirit, **W.** speaks for God in time,
T-6 V.A.5:1 Holy Spirit, **W.** leads to God, translates
T-7 IV.4:1 Spirit, **W.** understands how to use them
T-7 V.11:6 **W.** sees the altar of God in everyone, and
T-7 IX.5:1 Holy Spirit, **W.** is in your mind, knows of
T-8 III.1:4 to listen to the Teacher **W.** knows of light,
T-8 VIII.9:8 Spirit, **W.** perceives no attack on anything
T-8 VIII.9:10 of the one Teacher **W.** knows what life is,
T-9 I.3:5 a Guide **W.** *does* know what your reality is.
T-9 II.7:4 in you, **W.** speaks to me through you. If
T-9 V.9:1 the Guide **W.** tells you what to do. If you
T-11 II.7:8 **W.** abides with you merely by recognizing
T-11 VIII.6:4 the Holy Spirit, **W.** wills only to restore,
T-11 .VIII.14:9 their reality is from the One **W.** knows it,
T-11 .VIII.15:3 the Holy Spirit, **W.** will teach you that, as
T-12 I.6:6 of reality, **W.** understands what it is. He
T-12 V.5:2 provided by a Teacher **W.** can transcend
T-12 V.9:2 follow the Teacher **W.** knows the way to
T-13 VIII.8:1 through Him **W.** knows of freedom. Unite
T-14 I.3:9 there is One **W.** knows it leads to nothing,
T-14 III.11:3 **W.** gives you everything will simply offer
T-14 III.13:1 The One **W.** knows the plan of God that
T-14 III.15:5 Be quiet in your faith in Him **W.** loves you
T-14 IV.5:4 Leave all decisions to the One **W.** speaks
T-14 IV.9:5 Holy Spirit, **W.** remembers this for you,
T-14 V.2:6 you do, but He **W.** knows is with you. His
T-14 VII.5:12 Leave that to Him **W.** knows. You are not
T-14 X.2:6 motivated by a unique Teacher **W.** brings
T-14 XI.4:7 **W.** teaches light He will accept from you,
T-14 XI.10:1 He **W.** has freed you from the past would
T-15 I.7:5 Holy Spirit, **W.** knows only the present,
T-15 I.15:3 **W.** transcends time for you understands
T-15 VIII.6:4 **W.** knows it must be possible because it is
T-16 I.4:1 empathy is of Him **W.** knows what it is.
T-16 II.5:4 are natural to the One **W.** speaks for God.
T-16 II.9:8 Have faith in Him **W.** has faith in you.
T-17 I.3:5 away from Him **W.** would release you.
T-17 I.6:1 the truth to Him **W.** knows the truth, and
T-17 III.5:7 is given to Him **W.** gives it life and beauty.
T-17 III.7:8 Give the past to Him **W.** can change your
T-17 IV.4:1 **W.** was God's Answer to the separation.
T-17 V.7:6 Have faith in Him **W.** answered you. He
T-17 V.15:2 to Him **W.** gave you your release, and
T-17 V.15:2 and **W.** would extend it through you.
T-17 VII.10:1 Him **W.** walks with you in every situation.
T-18 III.3:2 you knew **W.** walks beside you on the way
T-18 IV.1:8 is He **W.** adds the greatness and the might
T-18 IV.6:5 holy instant belongs to Him **W.** gives it.
T-18 IV.8:2 unwilling to give place to One **W.** knows.
T-18 V.5:4 Holy Spirit, **W.** *has* a special function here.
T-18 IX.2:1 the One **W.** does surround it has brought
T-19 I.12:7 but in the sight of Him **W.** joined you,
T-19 III.5:9 its Teacher, **W.** is one with it, would bring
T-19 IV.2:7 He **W.** offered your relationship the gift of
T19 IV.A.5:8 He **W.** answered you would call. His
T19 IV.B.8:4 not possible to keep away One **W.** is there
T19 IV.D.8:6 Guide **W.** brought you here remains with
T19 IV.D.9:7 let us join in faith that He **W.** brought us
T-20 II.9:6 we were meant to find by Him **W.** leads us
T-20 III.6:6 **W.** watches over all perception answered.
T-20 IV.1:4 Spirit, **W.** knows that as you give you gain
T-20 IV.6:2 For He **W.** knows the rest will see to it
T-20 V.2:7 Forget not **W.** has given you the gifts you
T-20 V.7:9 have faith that He **W.** sees the gift in you
T-20 VI.5:7 **W.** sees the face of Christ choose as His
T-20 VII.2:2 means to Him **W.** changed the purpose.
T-20 VII.8:4 from Him **W.** would undo your teaching.
T-21 II.3:6 to Him **W.** must decide for God for you.
T-21 III.9:9 He **W.** loves the world is seeing it for you,
T-21 VI.8:6 Listen to Him **W.** speaks with reason, and
T-22 VI.9:11 be dispelled by Him **W.** knows the light,
T-25 III.5:1 another Maker **W.** can reconcile its goal
T-25 VII.10:3 One **W.** speaks for Him can show you this
T-25 VIII.8:1 but have a Judge **W.** knows that they are
T-27 II.10:2 It belongs to One **W.** knows of fairness,
T-27 II.16:1 Correction must be left to One **W.** knows
T-27 V.4:5 the One **W.** blesses you loves all the world
T-27 V.8:9 only be attained by One **W.** does not see
T-27 V.9:6 but there is One within you **W.** is right.
T-27 V.10:1 to the One **W.** really understands its laws,
T-27 V.10:1 and **W.** will guarantee that they remain
T-27 VI.5:6 The One **W.** brings the miracle perceives
T-27 VI.6:6 One **W.** sends forth miracles to bless the
T-27 .VIII.12:1 all forms of suffering to Him **W.** knows
T-29 II.5:2 Yet He **W.** entered in but waits for you to
T-29 II.5:5 where He is **W.** brought them with Him,
T-29 IV.6:5 **W.** can utilize all dreams as means to
T-29 V.8:1 **W.** sees a different function for a dream.
T-30 II.3:3 Him **W.** is His Voice and yours as well,
T-30 VIII.4:7 and He **W.** gives all miracles has not been
T-31 I.10:4 understand **W.** calls to you beyond each
T-31 VII.6:4 Give it instead to Him **W.** understands
W-pI 76.9:3 You will be listening to One **W.** says there
W-pI 76.10:1 Hear Him **W.** tells you this, and realize
W-pI 78.7:1 Then let us ask of Him **W.** knows this Son
W-pI 96.8:1 Him **W.** speaks to you from your one Self.
W-pI 96.8:3 from this one Self through Him **W.** is the
W-pI 96.11:5 seeking Him **W.** joins your mind and Self,
W-pI 99.9:8 turn to Him **W.** shares your function here
W-pI 99.12:2 with Him **W.** shares God's plan with you.
W-pI 106.6:3 will learn your function from the One **W.**
W-pI 108.5:3 directed by the One **W.** knows the truth.
WpI..rIII.in6:2 by the One **W.** gave the thoughts to you.
W-pI 121.6:3 **W.** represents the other Self in you.
W-pI 121.7:7 the Teacher **W.** was given you to show the
W-pI 134.14:4 spend it with the Guide **W.** understands
W-pI 151.9:3 body mean to Him **W.** knows the glory of
W-pI 151.13:3 appealing silently to Him **W.** sees the
W-pI 151.16:4 to Him **W.** has restored our sanity to us.
W-pI 151.17:1 Him **W.** is salvation and deliverance.
W-pI 154.9:5 He **W.** has received for you the messages
W-pI 154.10:2 minds apart from Him **W.** speaks for us,
W-pI 155.3:4 so they need a Teacher **W.** perceives their
W-pI 155.3:4 but **W.** still can look beyond illusion to
W-pI 169.7:3 Him **W.** teaches what forgiveness means.
W-pI 169.9:3 as perfectly fulfilled by Him **W.** wrote
W-pI 169.15:2 this day of Him **W.** gives the grace we ask,
WpI...rV.in8:1 to you from Him **W.** sees your bitter need,
W-pI 186.2:7 assigned to us by One **W.** knows us well.
W-pI 191.5:4 gratitude to Him **W.** pointed out the way
W-pI 192.3:5 Yet God created One **W.** has the power to
W-pI 193.2:3 for One **W.** can correct his erring sight,
W-pI 193.11:5 Let us give them all to Him **W.** knows the
W-pI 198.5:2 to thank the One **W.** gives salvation, and
W-pI 198.13:2 and recognize that He **W.** brought us here
W-pI 199.7:5 give your mind to Him **W.** calls to you to
WpI.rVI.in.6:6 quiet to the Teacher **W.** instructs in quiet,
W-pI 220.1:3 *But let me follow Him* **W.** *leads me home,*
W-pII in.6:2 in gratitude to Him **W.** taught us how to
W-pII 1.5:1 to do, through Him **W.** is your Guide,
W-pII .242.1:3 is One **W.** knows all that is best for me.
W-pII .242.1:5 and it is He **W.** knows the way to God.
W-pII .255.1:3 have faith in Him **W.** says I am God's Son.
W-pII .311.1:5 gift of it to Him **W.** has a different use for
W-pII .352.1:7 *memory of You, and One* **W.** *leads me to it.*
W-pII .358.1:1 *You* **W.** *remember what I really am alone*
Wfl in.1:3 Let us turn to Him **W.** leads the way and
M-6 4:4 mind of the giver **W.** gives the gift to him.
M-7 2:5 given the problem to One **W.** cannot fail,
M-16 7:4 He has a Guide **W.** will not fail. He need
M-29 2:12 have a Teacher **W.** cannot make a mistake
M-29 4:10 the Teacher **W.** knows the truth has not
C-1 3:1 **W.** abides in this part but sees the other
C-6 4:4 therefore it is He **W.** proves Them One.
S-2 III.2:7 task, and it is He **W.** will respond for you.
S-2 III.7:2 has a Teacher **W.** will fail in nothing. Rest

## who 27

- Jesus
  - *noise word*
  - *Who*

| | |
|---|---|
| T-1........III.4:1 | am the only one w. can perform miracles |
| T-3...........I.5:1 | God w. taketh away the sins of the world, |
| T-3........IV.7:3 | I was a man w. remembered spirit and its |
| T-6........IV.9:6 | follow w. will strengthen your command, |
| T-8.........V.5:2 | me w. know it for you and you will find it. |
| T-11......IV.6:6 | Come unto me w. hold it open for you, for |
| T-15......III.7:1 | with me w. decided for holiness for you. It |
| T-15....III.10:1 | with me, w. has decided to abide with you |
| T-15.......X.3:1 | We w. are one cannot give separately. |
| T-18......III.3:9 | Yet what is that to us w. travel surely and |
| T-20...........I.4:3 | and you took me in, not knowing w. I was |
| W-pI.132.14:5 | we w. are as He created us would loose the |
| WpI.. rV.in6:2 | that you may come to me w. recognize the |
| W-pI.188.10:3 | we w. make the world as we would have it |
| W-pI.195.10:6 | and thus we go w. walk the way to God. |
| W-pII.....in.9:7 | and we w. are God's Sons are safely home, |
| W-pII......3.5:5 | For we w. made it must behold it through |
| W-pII..260.2:3 | And we w. are His Sons are like each other |
| W-pII..262.2:1 | We w. are one would recognize this day |
| W-pII....14.5:1 | holy messengers of God w. speak for Him, |
| M-23..........3:9 | can one w. is one with God be unlike Him |
| M-23..........6:8 | Then turn to one w. laid all limits by, and |
| C-5.............2:1 | name of *Jesus* is the name of one w. was a |
| C-5.............4:3 | dreams. Arise with him w. showed you |
| C-5.............4:3 | you owe him this w. shared your dreams |
| C-5.............5:7 | w. would be only brother to the world. |
| C-ep...........5:5 | We w. complete Him offer thanks to Him, |

## who 1325

- noise word
  - *Jesus*
  - *Who*

## whoever 12

| | |
|---|---|
| T-4.......VII.8:8 | to w. can follow my guidance through you |
| T-16.......V.8:2 | w. seems to possess a special self is "loved |
| T-18.......V.7:1 | W. is saner at the time the threat is |
| T-18....IX.11:3 | remember only that w. attains the real |
| T-27. VIII.10:3 | is true. W. takes the role of enemy and of |
| T-28......VI.5:4 | W. says, "There is no gap between my |
| W-pI...110.8:1 | saved, with power to save w. touches Him |
| C-3.............4:8 | W. looks on this no longer sees the world. |
| P-3........III.6:5 | W. comes has been sent. Perhaps he was |
| P-3........III.7:8 | W. asks your help can show you where. |
| P-3........III.8:6 | W. He sends you will reach you, holding |
| S-2........III.1:7 | He gives His Teacher to w. asks, and seeks |

## whole 290

*See also* part-whole

| | |
|---|---|
| T-1........III.8:4 | of my complete awareness of the w. plan. |
| T-1.........V.3:8 | When this occurs the w. family of God, or |
| T-1.........V.4:5 | creation is w., and the mark of wholeness |
| T-2.........II.6:9 | the w. Atonement stands at time's end. At |
| T-2........IV.2:8 | The w. distortion that made magic rests |
| T-2........IV.5:6 | The w. aim of the miracle is to raise the |
| T-2........VI.7:3 | w. process of correction becomes nothing |
| T-2.......VII.6:2 | must be an integral part of the w. Sonship |
| T-3...........I.2:2 | w. frame of reference in order to justify it. |
| T-3........III.2:3 | this means that it is not w. or consistent. |
| T-3........IV.5:9 | spirit that it derives its w. power to make |
| T-4.........II.6:7 | w. perception of other egos as real is only |
| T-4........II.11:3 | The w. value of right perception lies in the |
| T-4........III.1:6 | This is the w. message of the Atonement; |
| T-4........VI.2:4 | much you are indebted to the w. Sonship, |
| T-4.......VII.2:1 | the ego perceives is a separate w., without |
| T-4.......VII.7:1 | you until you know it with your w. mind. |
| T-5.........in.2:2 | the only possible w. state is that of love. |
| T-5.........in.2:4 | only possible w. state is the wholly joyous |
| T-5........ I.1:14 | the w. belief in the false association the |
| T-5...........I.5:5 | and the w. Sonship is healed there will be |
| T-5.........II.2:5 | until the w. mind returns to creating. |
| T-5.......II.7:11 | gain the w. world and lose his own soul? |
| T-5.......II.10:9 | the perfect integration that can make it w. |
| T-5.......II.11:2 | its power to attract the w. Sonship, and to |
| T-5.........V.2:5 | invulnerable to disruption because it is w. |
| T-5........VI.9:5 | Kingdom, where your w. mind belongs. |
| T-5.......VII.2:2 | their faith because their faith was not w.. |
| T-5.......VII.2:5 | of being healed *because* God created it w.. |
| T-6.........I.15:6 | w. message of the crucifixion was simply |
| T-6.........II.1:2 | be appreciated except by a w. mind that |
| T-6.......II.10:5 | tells you to return your w. mind to God, |
| T-6.......II.12:5 | is united He offers the w. Kingdom always |
| T-6........IV.1:7 | the foundation of its w. thought system. |
| T-6.........V.1:4 | when He knows your mind only as w.? |
| T-6......V.C.5:6 | it is. Since it is w., you are teaching peace |
| T-6......V.C.8:1 | teach the w. Sonship without exception |
| T-7...........I.6:2 | because the Kingdom of God is w.. I have |
| T-7.........II.1:2 | as sick, he is perceiving himself as not w., |
| T-7.........II.4:4 | his w. purpose is to change the form so |
| T-7........IV.1:4 | Who knows His creations as perfectly w.. |
| T-7........IV.4:2 | healing, because He knows you only as w. |
| T-7.........V.5:3 | only the conflict-free are w.. By accepting |
| T-7.......V.6:13 | because your w. meaning and your only |
| T-7.......V.9:10 | The w. glory and perfect joy that *is* the |
| T-7.......V.11:4 | back upon you and on the w. Sonship, |
| T-7.....VII.3:10 | last until the Sonship knows itself as w.. |
| T-7.....VIII.4:4 | makes, underlies its w. use of projection. |
| T-7.....VIII.5:6 | your mind and from the Sonship as a w.. |
| T-7.....VIII.7:1 | The w. purpose of this course is to teach |
| T-7.....VIII.7:3 | the w. Kingdom as literally part of you. |
| T-7........IX.2:2 | The power of the w. Sonship and of its |
| T-7........IX.2:2 | equally w. and equal in perfection. The |
| T-7........IX.3:4 | ego's w. thought system blocks extension, |
| T-7........IX.4:3 | from yourself and you are not w.. A split |
| T-7........IX.5:3 | being created for the Sonship as a w.. |
| T-7........IX.6:9 | only the w. can be born of Its Wholeness. |
| T-7........IX.7:5 | in the lesson, you have included the w.. |
| T-7.........X.1:4 | of it is because you do not see the w. of it. |
| T-7.........X.3:7 | is the cause of the w. idea of sacrifice. |
| T-7.........X.6:7 | The w. separation lies in this error. The |
| T-7........XI.6:4 | that only the w. Sonship is worthy to be |
| T-7........XI.6:4 | only the w. Sonship can create like Him. |
| T-8........IV.5:6 | or the mind itself is divided and not w.. |
| T-8.........V.2:4 | Yet to heal is still to make w.. Therefore, |
| T-8........VI.8:5 | The w. power of God's Son lies in all of us |
| T-8.......VII.9:1 | not even the body is perceived as w.. Its |
| T-8.....VII.10:2 | Since this is natural it heals by making w., |
| T-8.....VII.10:3 | All mind is w., and the belief that part of |
| T-8.....VII.13:5 | it becomes w. because the mind's purpose |
| T-8.....VII.14:4 | when your w. purpose for learning should |
| T-8... VIII.1:10 | The w. does define the part, but the part |
| T-8... VIII.1:10 | part, but the part does not define the w.. |
| T-8... VIII.1:12 | perception the w. is built up of parts that |
| T-8... VIII.1:15 | is no difference between the part and w.. |
| T-8........IX.2:9 | so powerful that it will bring the w. to you |
| T-8.......IX.2:10 | your little part, and let the w. be yours. |
| T-8........IX.7:4 | Our minds are w. because they are one. If |
| T-9........VI.4:5 | to your wholeness because each part *is* w.. |
| T-9.......VII.6:8 | open the w. thought system to question. |
| T-9.......VII.7:3 | keep the ego's w. thought system intact. |
| T-10......III.7:5 | you, and it is this value that makes you w. |
| T-10......III.7:6 | A w. mind is not idolatrous, and does not |
| T-10......III.7:8 | make you w. when you have faith in me. |
| T-10......IV.2:6 | Truth is w., and cannot be known by part |
| T-11.......in.2:8 | or its w. thought system will not stand. |
| T-11.......I.10:4 | is your w. sickness and your whole fear. |
| T-11.......I.10:4 | is your whole sickness and your w. fear. |
| T-11.......II.4:1 | is a sign that you want to make w.. And |
| T-11.......II.4:3 | your small willingness to make w. He will |
| T-11.......II.4:3 | Own complete Will and make yours w.. |
| T-11....III.7:10 | understand wholeness unless you are w., |
| T-11.......III.8:1 | mind you can accept the w. Sonship and |
| T-11......IV.8:4 | in God, and in whom the w. Sonship rests |
| T-11.......V.3:3 | w. separation fallacy lies in the belief that |
| T-11.......V.6:2 | w. creative function lies in your complete |
| T-11......VI.6:2 | w. compelling power lies in the fact that it |
| T-11....VI.10:6 | w. power of God is in every part of Him, |
| T-12.........I.2:2 | w. process represents a clear-cut attempt |
| T-12.......II.3:3 | You will be made w. as you make whole, |
| T-12.......II.3:3 | You will be made whole as you make w., |
| T-12......IV.6:8 | is w. and all His extensions are like Him. |
| T-12.......V.8:7 | and will not be so until the w. learning |
| T-12......VI.1:1 | gain the w. world and lose your own soul. |
| T-12.....VII.1:5 | this holy perception you will be made w., |
| T-13......III.3:3 | and the w. world you thought you made |
| T-13......III.4:1 | built your w. insane belief system because |
| T-13.......V.2:3 | he made them, and that they are not w.. |
| T-13......VI.8:5 | no darkness in him anywhere, for he is w. |
| T-13....VIII.2:2 | Every aspect is w., and therefore no |
| T-13....VIII.5:2 | the true perception of one aspect of the w. |
| T-13....VIII.5:3 | Though every aspect *is* the w., you cannot |
| T-13......IX.2:1 | Release from guilt is the ego's w. undoing |
| T-14......III.2:3 | not see yourself as w. and therefore happy |
| T-14......III.2:4 | Yet you are w. only in your guiltlessness, |
| T-14......III.9:5 | Every decision is made for the w. Sonship, |
| T-15........I.11:4 | tiny instant to offer you the w. of Heaven. |
| T-15........I.15:2 | little to restore God's w. power to you. He |
| T-15.........II.1:7 | quickly offer you the w. lesson of peace. |
| T-15......IV.1:9 | for it holds the w. release from littleness. |
| T-15......VI.8:3 | and with it goes the w. basis for exclusion. |
| T-15......XI.1:1 | Fear not to recognize the w. idea of |
| T-15......XI.2:5 | the w. idea of sacrifice loses all meaning. |
| T-16.........I.7:8 | give through Him is for the w. Sonship, |
| T-16.........II.1:7 | difficult to understand than is the w.. If |
| T-16.........II.2:1 | the truth of just a little part of the w.. And |
| T-16.........II.2:2 | of avoiding, or looking away from the w., |
| T-16.........II.2:4 | understand them, either in part or in w.. |
| T-16.........II.3:3 | The recognition of the part as w., and of |
| T-16.........II.3:3 | of the w. in every part is perfectly natural, |
| T-16......IV.8:4 | substitute for what makes you w. in truth, |
| T-16.. IV.11:10 | Whom God remembers must be w.. And |
| T-16.. IV.11:11 | has never forgotten what makes Him w.. |
| T-16.....V.10:3 | attributes of the w. religion of separation, |
| T-16.....V.15:4 | w. thought system is a carefully contrived |
| T-16......VI.4:7 | your w. investment in seeing it would be |
| T-16......VI.5:7 | does not include even one w. individual. |
| T-17.........I.3:4 | must do to your appreciation of the w.! |
| T-17......IV.4:3 | The w. defense system the ego evolved to |
| T-17......IV.5:7 | part of it, as insane as the w.. The special |
| T-17......IV.6:7 | this one, and you have retained the w.. |
| T-17......IV.9:8 | system, for these aspects enclose the w., |
| T-17....IV.10:4 | now be undertaken, to keep truth w.. The |
| T-17....IV.11:8 | the w. thought system of the ego lies in its |
| T-17....IV.11:8 | so the w. of Heaven lies in this instant, |
| T-17....IV.15:5 | your remembrance, offering you the w. of |
| T-17....IV.16:6 | It shines in every part of Him, as in the w. |
| T-17....IV.16:7 | The w. reality of your relationship with |
| T-17.......V.5:2 | about what the w. relationship is for. As |
| T-17......VI.6:4 | The Holy Spirit sees the situation as a w.. |
| T-17......VI.6:9 | does not perceive the situation as a w.. |
| T-17...VII.8:11 | that does not involve your w. relationship |
| T-17...VII.8:13 | the purpose of your w. relationship, and |
| T-17....VIII.1:4 | and every situation, seen as a w.. Faith |
| T-18.........I.4:5 | Your w. world rests upon it. Everything |
| T-18.......I.11:1 | for in it lies the Sonship, w. and beautiful, |
| T-18.......I.11:3 | His w. creation have entered it together. |
| T-18.......I.12:7 | join in making w. what has been ravaged |
| T-18......III.7:4 | are made w. in our desire to make whole. |
| T-18......III.7:4 | are made whole in our desire to make w.. |
| T-18......IV.8:3 | w. belief in orders of difficulty in miracles |
| T-18....VI.11:6 | with it. And both become w., as neither is |
| T-18.....VII.3:7 | *now.* Its w. attraction is imaginary, and |
| T-18....VIII.2:6 | splintered from the w., proclaiming that |
| T-18....VIII.3:3 | of it that, could you but appreciate the w., |
| T-18....VIII.4:5 | Its w. existence still remains in them. |
| T-18....VIII.5:3 | needing the w. to give it any meaning, for |
| T-18....VIII.6:2 | nor would the W. be whole without it. It |
| T-18....VIII.6:2 | nor would the Whole be w. without it. It |
| T-18....VIII.6:5 | little aspect is no different from the w., |
| T-18....VIII.7:7 | surrounding it with love is the glorious w. |
| T-18..VIII.11:7 | No part of love calls on the w. in vain. No |
| T-18......IX.1:5 | it is the Son of God, w. and omnipotent, |
| T-18......IX.4:1 | seems to be the w. foundation on which |
| T-18......IX.7:1 | bank it is easy to see a w. world rising. A |
| T-19.........I.1:4 | is perceived as meaningful and as a w.. |
| T-19.........I.2:5 | this purpose real, because you make it w.. |
| T-19.........I.5:3 | would remove all limitations and make w. |
| T-19........II.3:5 | wild insanity inherent in the w. idea of sin |
| T-19........II.8:1 | easily escaped from that its w. correction |
| T19....IV.A.1:6 | If it would spread across the w. creation, |

| | |
|---|---|
| T19... IV.A.3:4 | is a limit you would place upon the w.. |
| T19... IV.B.9:1 | give the Holy Spirit the w. idea of sacrifice |
| T19..IV.B.13:2 | maintains the w. illusion of its existence. |
| T-20.........I.1:5 | he looks upon himself as healed and w.. |
| T-20.........I.3:1 | holy week is the symbol of the w. journey |
| T-20....... II.4:3 | me still, and who is w. without him? Be |
| T-20....... II.4:4 | you may look upon the Son of God as w.. |
| T-20...... IV.6:4 | nor is the w. completed without your part |
| T-20...... IV.7:3 | For the w. new world rests in the hands of |
| T-20... VIII.1:6 | Desire now its w. undoing, and it is done |
| T-21.........I.6:2 | Not the w. song has stayed with you, but |
| T-21....... II.1:2 | your w. relationship transformed to joy; |
| T-21....... II.6:3 | see in it the w. exchange of separation for |
| T-21..... II.13:2 | otherwise, and you deny your w. reality. |
| T-21...... IV.3:3 | ask it now are threatening the ego's w. |
| T-21....... V.1:9 | entirely your w. belief in what you are. |
| T-21....... V.4:1 | You do not realize the w. extent to which |
| T-21...... VI.7:6 | you it is given you to change his w. mind, |
| T-21...... VI.7:7 | correction of his errors and make him w.. |
| T-21...... VI.7:8 | is his w. salvation seen as complete with |
| T-22.......in.3:3 | it by joining with another, w. as himself. |
| T-22.........I.6:3 | your w. communication is like a baby's. |
| T-22....... II.9:1 | Let us look closer at the w. illusion that |
| T-22...... III.2:1 | ego's w. continuance depends on its belief |
| T-22...... III.4:3 | a distorted fragment of the w. without the |
| T-22...... III.4:3 | the meaning that the w. would give. And |
| T-22...... IV.1:4 | The w. purpose of coming this far was to |
| T-22....... V.3:2 | It is still w., and nothing has been taken |
| T-22... VI.12:5 | a part of the creation without the w., the |
| T-23.... II.21:6 | w. descent from Heaven lies in each one. |
| T-24....... II.8:5 | make you w. in mind and one with him. |
| T-24....... V.2:4 | the w. contributes nothing to the parts to |
| T-24...... VI.2:3 | For what God wills is w., and part of Him |
| T-24...... VI.5:1 | and behold in him the w. reversal of the |
| T-24..... VII.8:7 | makes it hard to grasp the w. extent to |
| T-25.........I.1:7 | w. and pure and worthy of His everlasting |
| T-25....... V.1:1 | this: The w. desire to attack is gone, and |
| T-25..... VII.5:1 | the power to change the w. foundation of |
| T-25... VII.11:1 | w. belief that someone loses but reflects |
| T-25... VII.12:8 | For here your special function is made w., |
| T-25... VII.12:8 | because it shares the function of the w.. |
| T-26....... II.2:5 | mistake; the w. idea that loss is possible, |
| T-26...... IV.3:8 | and all their radiance made w. again. |
| T-26... VII.14:6 | in its effects as is the w. idea of sacrifice. If |
| T-26....... X.5:2 | one purpose for your w. relationship. |
| T-27.........I.1:9 | all it would entail the w. of God's creation |
| T-28...... II.11:5 | Yet half the lesson will not teach the w.. |
| T-28...... IV.8:3 | Identity, which the w. picture represents, |
| T-28...... IV.9:6 | the w. is in each one. And every aspect of |
| T-29....... V.1:1 | place in you where this w. world has been |
| T-29....... V.4:3 | He was created that you might be w., for |
| T-29..... VII.4:6 | The search implies you are not w. within |
| T-29..... VII.5:4 | be life, and what is sacrificed cannot be w. |
| T-30...... III.3:7 | alone and separated off from what is w.. |
| T-30...... III.5:4 | For more than w. is meaningless. If there |
| T-30...... III.5:8 | What is not w. cannot make whole. But |
| T-30...... III.5:8 | What is not whole cannot make w.. But |
| T-30.... III.5:11 | but in the w. completely lovely Thought |
| T-30...... VI.7:6 | keep an image of yourself that is not w., |
| T-30...... VI.8:3 | To heal is to make w.. And what is whole |
| T-30...... VI.8:4 | And what is w. can have no missing parts |
| T-30.... VIII.5:4 | you would not have him healed and w.. |
| T-31.........I.8:8 | part of God's creation to the w. is heard |
| T-31.........I.9:1 | not share the universal Will that it be w., |
| W-pI..... 16.2:2 | of a w. world can hardly be called idle. |
| W-pI..... 29.1:5 | Today's idea is the w. basis for vision. |
| W-pI..... 37.2:7 | see themselves as w. make no demands. |
| W-pI..... 39.3:7 | your world, the w. world stands to benefit |
| W-pI..... 71.8:1 | each making equal contribution to the w.. |
| W-pI... 95.12:3 | are one Self, complete and healed and w., |
| W-pI..... 97.7:2 | *God, free of all limits, safe and healed and w.* |
| W-pI... 113.1:2 | *mine, because I am one Self, completely w.,* |
| W-pI. 121.12:3 | savior, saved and saving, healed and w.. |
| W-pI... 128.7:3 | w. perspective on the world will shift by |
| W-pI... 136.2:4 | is to keep the truth from being w.. The |
| W-pI... 136.2:5 | seen as if each one were w. within itself. |
| W-pI... 136.6:1 | Every defense takes fragments of the w., |
| W-pI... 136.6:1 | illusions of a w. that is not there. It is this |
| W-pI... 136.6:3 | When parts are wrested from the w. and |
| W-pI... 136.6:3 | symbols standing for attack upon the w.; |
| W-pI... 136.6:3 | in effect, and never to be seen as w. again. |
| W-pI... 152.1:7 | Here is its w. reality for you. And it is only |
| W-pI... 159.2:3 | and thus do you perceive that you are w.. |
| W-pI... 161.2:4 | It sees instead but fragments of the w., for |
| WpI...rV.in8:8 | am made w. we go together to our ancient |
| W-pI... 186.5:4 | your part, and that the w. depends on you |
| W-pI... 191.5:4 | changed his w. perspective of the world. |
| WpI rVI.in.2:2 | contains the w. curriculum if understood, |
| WpI rVI.in.2:5 | as each contributes to the w. we learn. |
| WpI rVI.in.7:4 | us offer Him the w. review we now begin, |
| W-pI... 201.1:3 | *Father, one Creator of the w. that is my Self,* |
| W-pII . 243.1:3 | the w. from bits of my perception, which |
| W-pII . 270.2:3 | Him, the holy Son whom God created w.; |
| W-pII ... 11.3:2 | making every part container of the w.. Its |
| W-pII ... 14.1:1 | *I am God's Son, complete and healed and w.* |
| M-4 ..... I.A.6:5 | at which he sees in it his w. way out. |
| M-4 ...... III.1:6 | of the teacher of God's w. thought system |
| M-5 ........II.3:4 | It costs the w. world you see, for the |
| M-15 ....... 1:11 | *Holy are you, eternal, free and w., at peace* |
| M-20 ....... 5:10 | the Holy Spirit's w. curriculum specified |
| M-23 ......... 3:3 | w. relationship of the Son to the Father |
| M-28 ......... 3:9 | The w. reversal is accomplished. Nothing |
| M-29 ......... 3:7 | The w. world you see reflects the illusion |
| P-2.........in.1:5 | Its w. function, in the end, is to help the |
| P-2.........in.2:4 | Their w. equilibrium rests on the insane |
| P-3...........I.4:2 | that his part is necessary to the w., and |
| P-3...........I.4:2 | it he will recognize the w. when his part is |
| S-3........ III.1:1 | heals the body in a part, but never as a w.. |
| S-3........ IV.3:5 | as dear to Him as is the w. of His creation, |

## wholehearted 1

| | |
|---|---|
| T-5 ........in.2:1 | To be w. you must be happy. If fear and |

## wholeheartedly 1

| | |
|---|---|
| T-5 ........in.1:7 | deprive others of the joy of responding w. |

## Wholeness 19

*wholeness*

| | |
|---|---|
| T-5 ....... IV.4:3 | God's W. is the Wholeness of His Son. |
| T-5 ....... IV.4:3 | God's Wholeness is the W. of His Son. |
| T-6 ........I.12:1 | to enable the Sonship to know its W.. |
| T-6 .........II.1:2 | W. of God, which is His peace, cannot be |
| T-6 .........II.1:2 | that recognizes the W. of God's creation. |
| T-7 ....... IX.6:9 | and only the whole can be born of Its W.. |
| T-8 ....... VI.1:1 | will of the Sonship, whose W. is for all. |
| T-8 ....... IX.9:6 | part of His health, since it is part of His W. |
| T-11 ... III.7:10 | if he would know the W. of his Father. |
| T-11 ..... IV.3:7 | for the protection of the W. of His Son. |
| T-11 ..... IV.7:3 | of Him as yourself, and of His W. as yours |
| T-15 ..... XI.9:3 | His W. as we welcome Him into ourselves |
| T-16 ... IV.10:2 | and thus denies the W. of your Father. |
| T-16 . IV.11:12 | completion lie the memory of His W. and |
| T-16 .. V.12:11 | for the W. of God have any influence at all |
| T-26 .........I.4:7 | What witness to the W. of God's Son is |
| T-28 .... VII.1:8 | and in Whose W. there can be no gap? |
| T-29 .........I.1:3 | could be conceived of in the W. that is His |
| W-pI. 132.13:1 | of God Himself and thus destroy His W.. |

## wholeness 60

*Wholeness*

| | |
|---|---|
| T-1 ........I.41:1 | W. is the perceptual content of miracles. |
| T-1 ........... V.h | W. and Spirit |
| T-1 ......... V.4:5 | is whole, and the mark of w. is holiness. |
| T-2 ........ III.2:1 | and restores the w. of the mind. Before |
| T-2 ...... VII.6:6 | of w. in the true sense be understood. Any |
| T-3 ...........I.6:1 | and strives only to protect its w.. It cannot |
| T-5 ................h | HEALING AND W. |
| T-5 ....... IV.4:4 | your brother anything except your w.. |
| T-5 ...... VII.2:8 | you. Sanity is w., and the sanity of your |
| T-6 .........II.8:3 | Spirit enables you to perceive this w. *now.* |
| T-6 .........II.8:5 | His Kingdom until you know of its w.. |
| T-6 ..... V.C.8:1 | demonstrates that you perceive its w., and |
| T-6 ..... V.C.8:2 | of its w. and will be unable to teach it. The |
| T-6 ..... V.C.8:3 | The w. of the Kingdom does not depend |
| T-6 ..... V.C.8:3 | but your awareness of its w. does. It is |
| T-7 ..........II.2:2 | and restores its w. in your mind. This |
| T-7 ....... IV.4:3 | whole. By healing you learn of w., and by |
| T-7 ....... IV.4:3 | learning of w. you learn to remember God |
| T-7 ..... VI.10:4 | of the Creator and the creation is your w., |
| T-7 ..... VIII.7:5 | w. has no limits because being is infinity. |
| T-7 ....... IX.4:4 | of its w. to dawn upon it and heal it. This |
| T-7 ....... IX.4:5 | This reawakens the w. in it, and restores it |
| T-7 ....... IX.4:5 | Kingdom because of its acceptance of w.. |
| T-7 ....... IX.7:1 | extensions which maintain It in w. and |
| T-8 ... VII.16:6 | and therefore unlimited power and w.. |
| T-8 .... VII.16:7 | The power of w. is extension. Do not |
| T-8 ....... IX.3:1 | W. heals because it is of the mind. All |
| T-9 ....... VI.4:5 | adds to your w. because each part *is* whole. |
| T-9 ....... VI.4:6 | W. is indivisible, but you cannot learn of |
| T-9 ....... VI.4:6 | of your w. until you see it everywhere. |
| T-10 ..... III.3:7 | remind him of his w. and remember your |
| T-11 ........II.4:2 | of the Holy Spirit, Whose message is w.. |
| T-11 ... III.7:10 | understand w. unless you are whole, and |
| T-11 ..... V.13:2 | of w. comes only through acceptance, for |
| T-12 ..... IV.7:1 | The Atonement is not the price of your w. |
| T-12 ..... IV.7:1 | it *is* the price of your awareness of your w.. |
| T-12 . VIII.7:11 | all things together by extending its w.. |
| T-13 ..... VI.8:6 | Call all your brothers to witness to his w., |
| T-13 ..... VI.9:2 | for in their w. you will see your own. And |
| T-13 .....X.13:6 | Kingdom in honor of its w. that is of God. |
| T-15 .. VII.14:7 | in it. In the protection of your w., all are |
| T-17 ... VI.6:10 | for it has faith in separation and not in w.. |
| T-18 .........I.4:2 | illusion for truth; of fragmentation for w.. |
| T-19 .........I.1:2 | by which the w. of the dedication can be |
| T-19 .........I.6:2 | and divided into little parts of seeming w., |
| T-28 .... VII.2:2 | you deny yourself your w. and your health |
| T-30 ..... III.3:2 | W. has no form because it is unlimited. |
| T-30 ..... III.3:8 | for the search for w. to be made beyond |
| W-pI .... 37.2:5 | w. restored to his awareness through your |
| W-pI .. 127.3:8 | w. is the power holding everything as one, |
| W-pI 151.14:1 | w. and the happiness God wills His Son, |
| W-pI .. 152.9:3 | its changelessness and its eternal w., all- |
| WpI.rV.in10:4 | your w. now complete, as God established |
| W-pI .. 184.4:2 | Its enemy is w.. It conceives of little things |
| W-pI .. 195.6:2 | can be made which would reduce our w., |
| W-pII . 323.2:1 | truth returns to us in w. and in joy. We |
| M-19 ......... 3:4 | in which all thought of w. must be lost. |
| M-19 ......... 4:2 | It restores to your awareness the w. of the |
| M-19 ......... 4:4 | must decay and die, but w. is immortal. It |
| S-3...... IV.1:10 | has restored their w. so they can forgive, |

## wholes 1

| | |
|---|---|
| W-pI .. 136.6:3 | seen as separate and w. within themselves |

## wholly 244

| | |
|---|---|
| T-1 ....... III.2:3 | His work is w. lovable and wholly loving. |
| T-1 ....... III.2:3 | His work is wholly lovable and w. loving. |
| T-1 ... VII.3:11 | the w. satisfying nature of reality becomes |
| T-2 ....... VI.5:6 | are doing what you do not w. want to do. |
| T-3 ........I.2:11 | w. benign lesson the Atonement teaches |
| T-4 ........I.11:6 | it. Of this you can be w. certain. God is as |
| T-4 ........I.12:5 | are w. worthy of Him and only of Him. |
| T-4 ....... III.4:8 | of wanting is w. without the ego's "drive |
| T-4 ...... VII.8:1 | any mind learns to be w. helpful. This is |
| T-4 ...... VII.8:2 | is impossible without being w. harmless, |
| T-5 ........in.1:7 | attempt to heal without being w. joyous |
| T-5 ........in.2:2 | to be w. fearful and remain alive, the only |
| T-5 ........in.2:4 | only possible whole state is the w. joyous. |
| T-5 ..........I.1:4 | If you do not choose to be w. joyous, your |
| T-5 ...... VII.5:1 | Whenever you are not w. joyous, it is |
| T-5 ...... VII.6:2 | not to be w. joyous if that is how you feel. |
| T-6 ........in.1:4 | Given these three w. irrational premises, |
| T-6 ..........I.1:5 | of the crucifixion that is w. devoid of fear, |
| T-6 ..........I.1:5 | and therefore w. benign in what it teaches |
| T-6 ........I.16:1 | were not w. ready to follow me at the time |
| T-6 ....... III.3:4 | The perfectly safe are w. benign. They |
| T-6 ....... III.3:6 | Without anxiety the mind is w. kind, and |
| T-6 ....... IV.7:3 | Having finally been w. answered, *it has* |
| T-6 .........V.1:5 | and know that His children are w. joyous. |
| T-6 ..... V.B.8:7 | nothing is difficult that is *w.* desired. To |

T-6......V.B.8:8 To desire w. is to create, and creating
T-6....V.C.1:11 and so He alone can keep you w. joyous.
T-6....V.C.10:8 This recognition is w. without effort since
T-7.........V.6:8 on, because everything of God is w. real.
T-7......VI.12:1 you have not judged sanity as w. desirable
T-7.....VII.11:1 of the ego's thought system as w. insane,
T-7.....VII.11:1 w. delusional and wholly undesirable,
T-7.....VII.11:1 wholly delusional and w. undesirable,
T-7.....VII.11:2 to perceive any part of creation as w. real,
T-7.....VII.11:2 real, w. perfect and wholly desirable.
T-7.....VII.11:2 real, wholly perfect and w. desirable.
T-7........XI.1:7 the ego perceives nothing as w. desirable.
T-8...........I.1:9 you do not yet regard this as w. desirable.
T-8.........V.2:1 creator, being w. in the likeness of God,
T-8......VI.10:4 who are beloved of God are w. blessed.
T-8..... VIII.7:6 the one thing about the ego that is w. true
T-9.......VII.3:6 w. mistrustful of everything it perceives
T-9.......VII.8:5 not offer to God as w. fitting for Him. You
T-10.........I.4:1 everything the instant you desire it w., for
T-10.........I.4:1 it wholly, for if to desire w. is to create,
T-10.......V.9:9 Your Father created you w. without sin,
T-10.......V.9:9 sin, w. without pain and wholly without
T-10.......V.9:9 pain and w. without suffering of any kind.
T-10......V.12:1 If God knows His children as w. sinless, it
T-10......V.12:2 knows His children as w. without pain, it
T-10......V.12:3 If God knows His children to be w. joyous
T-11.......II.6:1 your will and your Father's be w. joined.
T-11.......IV.6:2 But come w. without condemnation, for
T-11.......IV.7:2 knows His Son as w. blameless as Himself
T-11... VIII.3:2 Not one thought you hold is w. true. The
T-12.......IV.2:4 of its source the ego is not w. split off, or
T-13...... I.11:8 And being w. pure, you are invulnerable.
T-13......VI.8:3 unbroken because it is w. shared. God's
T-13.....VII.8:4 one thing that is w. true and wholly yours
T-13.....VII.8:4 one thing that is wholly true and w. yours
T-13.......X.8:6 w. unjustified and wholly without reason,
T-13.......X.8:6 wholly unjustified and w. without reason,
T-13.......X.8:6 look upon the Atonement and accept it w.
T-13......X.12:2 w. untouched by guilt and wholly loving,
T-13......X.12:2 wholly untouched by guilt and w. loving,
T-13......XI.1:5 perceives them as w. without meaning.
T-13......XI.3:2 that you value here do you value w., and
T-13......XI.3:4 w. of value. It can merely be appreciated
T-13......XI.4:1 for nothing in this world is w. shared.
T-13......XI.4:2 you what is capable of being w. shared. It
T-13......XI.8:3 be w. closed and separated from Him.
T-14.........I.2:5 closed off and w. separated from the truth
T-14.........I.3:2 your thoughts w. of you, the thought
T-14......III.7:7 His guilt is w. without cause, and being
T-14....III.12:2 everything that He created, for it *is* w. pure
T-14.......V.3:1 Blessed Son of a w. blessing Father, joy
T-14......VI.4:6 The other is w. without sense of any kind.
T-14... VIII.1:8 what He promised God He is w. faithful,
T-14... VIII.2:4 replaced by gifts w. acceptable to Father
T-14......XI.5:2 If you are w. free of fear of any kind, and
T-15.........I.9:6 free and w. without condemnation. From
T-15..... II.4:13 have w. released through the Holy Spirit.
T-15........II.5:6 complete, accomplished and given w..
T-15....III.11:1 If you are w. willing to leave salvation to
T-15......IV.8:3 and am I w. willing to let everything that
T-15......VI.2:5 together, that he is w. worthy of it, and in
T-15......VI.4:6 w. without loss and only with gain.
T-15.....VII.1:5 Being w. pure, everyone joined in it has
T-15.......IX.2:2 it is impossible to recognize as w. without
T-15.......IX.7:4 Accepting it as undivided you join Him w.
T-16........II.3:4 W. natural perception would show you
T-16.....II.6:12 again will you be w. willing not to listen.
T-16........II.8:6 and w. kind to everyone and everything.
T-16......III.3:3 teach successfully w. without conviction,
T-16......IV.9:1 completion, for you will be w. in God,
T-16......IV.9:1 special, but only to be w. like to Him,
T-16......IV.9:5 be w. willing to abandon all illusions. In
T-16......IV.9:6 relationship in which you are w. willing to
T-16....IV.10:1 completion rests, w. compatible with His.
T-16....IV.11:8 He loves you, w. without illusion, as you
T-16....IV.11:9 love. For love *is* w. without illusion, and
T-16....IV.11:9 illusion, and therefore w. without fear.
T-16.......VI.8:8 For you are no longer w. insane, and you
T-16....VI.10:3 Only the w. insane could look on death
T-17.......II.3:2 but this is given, complete and w. perfect.
T-17....IV.12:5 or the comparison is w. without meaning.
T-17....IV.15:5 w. without value and entirely deprived of
T-17.......V.7:9 You are not now w. insane. Can you deny
T-17.....VII.5:5 of illusion, and w. faithful to its master.
T-17...VII.10:2 are no longer w. insane, nor no longer
T-18.......V.7:5 *me. Yet it is w. possible for us to share it now.*
T-18.....VII.3:4 entirely, for sin is never w. in the present.
T-18......IX.6:2 impenetrable appearance is w. an illusion
T-19.........I.1:1 a situation has been dedicated w. to truth,
T-19.........I.5:6 Faithlessness is w. dedicated to illusions;
T-19.........I.5:6 dedicated to illusions; faith w. to truth.
T-19.......I.12:3 and w. acceptable to his Father as to Him.
T-19.......II.5:2 sin is w. sacrosanct to its thought system,
T-19.......II.5:3 ego's system; lovely and powerful, w. true
T19... IV.A.3:2 you are still unwilling to let it join you w..
T19. IV.A.10:7 Being w. without attack, it could not be
T19. IV.A.11:6 is w. absent from love's gentle perception.
T19..IV.B.10:1 kind, infinite in its patience and w. loving
T19..IV.B.10:2 It will accept you w., and give you peace.
T19..IV.C.10:1 What danger can assail the w. innocent?
T-20......VI.1:3 And this is w. loving and forever. Yet has
T-20......VI.1:7 The one created by his Father is w. Self-
T-20......VI.1:8 one he made is w. self-destructive and self-
T-20... VIII.7:5 and destroy themselves, are w. unreal?
T-21.......II.8:4 and w. independent of inference and
T-21......IV.4:2 you. Not w. mad, you have been willing to
T-21...VII.11:7 you do not want, the rest are w. answered
T-21... VIII.4:3 really asks if you are willing to be w. sane.
T-22.........I.2:5 whose sight is w. independent of the eyes
T-22.......II.7:5 at all. For it is w. true or wholly false, and
T-22.......II.7:5 at all. For it is wholly true or w. false, and
T-22......III.5:7 between you and the truth, is w. true. Yet
T-22.......V.3:8 in quiet, undefended and w. undefending
T-23......IV.1:5 Heaven is w. true. No difference enters,
T-23......IV.8:5 same, eternally complete and w. shared.
T-24......III.1:6 How can he then give his forgiveness w.,
T-24......III.1:7 it is sure he would receive it w. the instant
T-25.....II.10:2 for the w. pure have never sinned. Give,
T-25......IV.4:7 in quiet, in innocence and w. unafraid.
T-25.......V.2:6 whatever he perceives as w. innocent?
T-25......VI.2:4 than what is w. clear and unambiguous.
T-25.....VII.6:4 for a world perceived as w. mad to sinners
T-25... VIII.1:5 You need not give it to Him w. willingly,
T-25... VIII.5:4 For He is w. fair to everyone. Vengeance
T-25... VIII.8:1 knows that they are w. innocent in truth.
T-25......IX.6:5 And is this justice to the w. innocent? A
T-26......III.2:5 is every thought made pure and w. simple
T-26...VII.10:2 see with Heaven, w. perfect and complete.
T-27.........I.1:2 Who can combine the w. incompatible,
T-27.......II.8:6 is purposeless and w. without cause.
T-27......III.3:3 The picture has been w. cancelled out,
T-27......III.3:7 you see is w. absent and has never been.
T-27......III.5:3 not yet a power known as w. free of limits
T-27......III.7:2 A power w. limitless has come, not to
T-28.......I.11:5 will not be w. unremembered afterwards.
T-28.......V.6:6 every time, and makes them w. indivisible
T-28.....VII.2:8 You accept it w. or accept it not. What is
T-29......II.4:3 enter, for you did not w. welcome Him.
T-30.......I.17:2 the joy they asked for will be w. shared.
T-31.......V.12:3 concept of the self from what is w. passive
T-31......VII.2:5 your sight as w. worthy of forgiveness,
T-31......VII.2:5 your concept of yourself is w. changed.
T-31...VII.13:3 at all. And thus it serves a w. open mind,
W-pI.......8.2:1 one w. true thought one can hold about
W-pI.....19.2:2 This is rarely a w. welcome idea at first,
W-pI.....27.1:5 the idea will be w. true a little nearer.
W-pI.....29.4:2 today's idea because of its w. alien nature.
W-pI.....44.5:1 Your mind is no longer w. untrained.
W-pI.....45.7:4 but the Foundation on which it rests is w.
W-pI.....49.2:1 God is calm, always at rest and w. certain.
W-pI.....66.3:1 we will try to go past this w. meaningless
W-pI.....67.2:1 and its w. unchanged and unchangeable
W-pI.....72.4:6 as well. A creator w. unlike his creation is
W-pI.....73.9:1 only His, is w. in accord with your will. It
W-pI.....74.2:2 it. The idea itself is w. true. Therefore it
W-pI.....83.4:3 *my function remains w. unaffected by this.*
W-pI...101.3:4 wrath is boundless, merciless, but w. just.
W-pI...103.3:4 with this assurance, kind and w. true: *God*
W-pI...108.1:3 into one concept which is w. true? Even
W-pI...108.5:2 forgive one brother w. is enough to bring
W-pI...125.9:4 interposed between the w. indivisible and
W-pI...129.4:4 is direct and w. shared and wholly one.
W-pI...129.4:4 is direct and wholly shared and w. one.
W-pI...131.6:6 is now, without a past and w. futureless.
W-pI...134.6:1 makes forgiveness natural and w. sane, a
W-pI.136.11:8 change. And what is w. sinless cannot sin.
W-pI.136.15:7 *I am, and let my mind be w. healed today.*
W-pI.138.10:3 valuable; the other as a w. worthless thing
W-pI.151.11:2 frame of reference, w. unified and sure.
W-pI...158.1:2 purely mind, sinless forever, w. unafraid,
W-pI...162.4:3 w. is it changed that it is now the treasury
W-pI...166.9:6 Perhaps He has not w. been outwitted by
W-pI...170.3:2 two camps which seem w. irreconcilable.
W-pI...181.8:3 we will behold a w. sinless world. When
W-pI.186.11:1 stands out clear and w. unambiguous.
W-pI...189.3:4 The other one is w. meaningless. A world
W-pI...189.7:5 and come with w. empty hands unto your
W-pI...190.2:2 Can they be anything but w. false? Pain is
W-pI...190.2:4 for attack on what is w. unassailable. It is
W-pI...191.7:5 is everything you look on w. changed.
W-pI...192.3:5 power to translate in form the w. formless
W-pI...193.1:2 eternally open and w. limitless in Him.
W-pI.196.10:1 so w. that escape appears quite hopeless.
W-pII .224.1:1 great, w. beneficent and free from guilt,
W-pII .234.1:5 the Son. This we accept as w. true today.
W-pII .242.2:2 *We come with w. open minds. We do not ask*
W-pII .268.2:4 Only reality is w. safe. And it is only this
W-pII .286.2:1 travelled far along it to a w. certain goal.
W-pII .291.2:4 *But You are w. certain. Father, guide Your*
W-pII ....294.h My body is a w. neutral thing.
W-pII .305.1:1 quiet, undisturbable and w. changeless,
W-pII ... 10.2:2 forgiven, without sin and w. purposeless.
W-pII .328.2:3 *It is Your Will that I be w. safe, eternally at*
W-pII .354.1:1 *of time, and w. free of every law but Yours. I*
M-4 .....I.A.5:6 realized as yet how w. impossible such a
M-4 ......IV.2:1 Therefore, God's teachers are w. gentle.
M-4 ......IX.2:2 Being consistent, it is w. honest. Being
M-8 ...........6:7 Just as reality is w. real, apart from size
M-10 .........3:5 judgment would be w. fair to everyone on
M-10 .......4:10 And He is w. fair to everyone, for there is
M-12 .........1:2 One w. perfect teacher, whose learning is
M-12 .........1:4 was always w. spirit now no longer sees
M-15 .........2:2 Do you believe that this is w. true? No;
M-18 .........2:1 react to magic thoughts w. without anger.
M-19 .........4:7 a Judgment w. lacking in condemnation
M-20 .........6:2 understanding that His Will is w. without
M-22 .........1:3 it is the source of a w. unified perception.
M-28 .........3:3 is w. corrected and all mistakes undone.
M-29 .......4:11 benefit to all, being w. devoid of attack.
C-in .........3:10 Only in that does it remain w. consistent
C-2.............9:5 it is, is w. uncondemned and wholly pure.
C-2.............9:5 it is, is wholly uncondemned and w. pure.
C-4.............7:1 certain, pure and w. understandable,
P-2...........I.3:5 infinite. His goal is w. undivided always.
P-2..........II.6:6 is, but they must share it w. to succeed. It
P-2........ III.1:4 this One be w. absent if the goal is healing
P-2........ III.3:7 One w. egoless therapist could heal the
P-2.......VII.5:8 No unhealed healer can be w. sane.
S-3........ III.5:4 It heals no part, but w. and forever. Now

**Whom** 25

• God
*Christ/Self*
*Holy Spirit*
*whom*

T-5...... VI.11:6 from W. I learned of infinite patience. His
T-8........ VI.3:1 Let us glorify Him W. the world denies,
T-8.......VII.6:3 He of W. you are has willed your power
T-11....VIII.9:6 in your Father, in W. no deceit is possible.
T-12...VII.14:1 to God, to W. treachery is impossible. But
T-13..... V.7:13 And it is God W. you must offer them, to
T-14...... VI.6:7 for He knows with W. you are in perfect
T-15...... III.6:8 Who dwells in you, and in W. you dwell.
T-19........II.7:6 then, the death of God, W. sin has killed!
T-21.......IV.2:2 unknown "enemy," W. it cannot even see,
T-22........II.5:6 to W. nothing He wills can be impossible,

T-22....... V.3:6 your Father W. you would defend against.
T-23.........I.4:5 God Himself, to W. all conflict, triumph
T-23....... II.7:3 Who caused it, to W. appeal is useless.
T-24....... II.3:5 himself, and Him of W. they are a part.
T-24...... VI.6:4 memory of Him in W. your brother lives,
T-26...... IX.8:1 as host again to Him by W. it was created.
T-27... VII.15:7 W. you see as offering both life and death
T-30.... III.10:5 left the Mind of its Creator W. it knows,
W-pI... 72.11:7 answer will be true because of W. you ask.
W-pI... 123.7:2 you will realize to W. you offer thanks,
W-pI... 123.7:2 W. He thanks as you are thanking Him.
W-pI... 168.5:3 but He to W. all error is unknown is yet
W-pI... 196.8:5 And God, W. you had thought to banish,
P-2......... V.8:5 It will be God to W. you answer, for you

**Whom** 11
• Christ/Self
*God*
*Holy Spirit*
*whom*

T19. IV.D.14:6 of sin, know not W. they attack.
T-24.........I.3:4 whose Self is his, and W. he knows? Only
T-26...... VI.2:3 in W. all power in earth and Heaven rests.
T-26...... VI.3:3 take the place of Him W. God has called
T-26...... VI.3:5 and only He to W. they have been given
W-pI. 161.12:1 And He will answer W. you called upon.
W-pI... 217.1:3 *can I find the Self to W. my thanks are due?* I
W-pII . 253.2:1 *are the Self W. You created Son, creating like*
W-pII ..... 6.5:3 Self, the Christ W. God created as His Son
W-pII . 279.2:2 *My Father loves the Son W. He created as*
W-pII . 282.1:4 Self W. God created as the Son He loves,

**Whom** 19
• Holy Spirit
*God*
*Christ/Self*
*whom*

T-6.........I.11:2 because the Holy Spirit, W. we share,
T-11....... II.6:5 The Guest W. God sent you will teach you
T-14.... III.14:5 Salvation is of Him to W. God gave it for
T-14..... VII.7:3 Sharing perception with Him W. God has
T-14...... XI.4:3 child of light by Him to W. God gave it.
T-14.... XI.6:10 Guide W. God has given you will speak to
T-17.........I.6:1 the truth, and in W. all is brought to truth
T-18.. VIII.13:3 Yet He W. you welcomed has come to you
T-19.......I.11:1 God, through Him W. God has given you.
T-19.......I.12:7 Who joined you, and in W. you are united
T19... IV.A.7:1 get rid of Him W. you invited in and push
T-28.......I.12:1 to W. time is given offers thanks for every
W-pI..... 99.6:4 with the One to W. the plan was given.
WpI rVI.in.7:4 us also not forget to W. it has been given,
W-pII ..... 3.4:2 W. God appointed Savior to the world.
W-ep ......... 2:4 follow Him W. you accepted as your voice
M-16 ......... 7:5 to W. he turns with all of them recognizes
M-29 ......... 3:8 To return the function to the One to W. it
C-6............ 1:1 W. he called down upon the earth after he

**whom** 193
*Whom*

**whomever** 1

**Whose** 34
• God
*Christ/Self*
*Holy Spirit*
*whose*

T-5...... IV.8:13 in W. Heart and Hands we have our being
T-7......... X.8:1 W. Will you do not know because you are
T-11.........I.2:3 endings in God, W. universe is Himself.
T-11.......I.11:7 to be like Him, W. Will it is that it be so.
T-11....... V.6:2 on God, W. function He shares with you.
T-11.... VIII.9:4 Father, W. every thought is as loving as
T-13 .......II.1:2 W. pull is so strong that you cannot resist
T-13 ...... XI.8:4 peace still flows to you from Him W. Will
T-14 ..... IV.7:1 know God, W. Will is that you know Him
T-15 ..... III.8:4 born in you in honor of Him W. host you
T-15 .. VII.14:8 W. only need is to have you be complete.
T-15 .......X.7:6 W. total Love would completely destroy
T-15 ..... XI.2:9 He protects, and W. power protects Him.
T-18 ... IX.12:6 W. acknowledgment of you and yours of
T19.... IV.C.3:5 of their Creator, W. Will it is they live.
T-21 .......II.6:4 W. Will cannot be separate from his own.
T-22 ... VI.11:7 of the universe, W. power you know.
T-24 ..... III.6:6 forgiven Him W. Will it is you rest forever
T-25 .... VII.4:3 with the Mind W. Thought created him.
T-28 ..... VI.6:8 the Will of God, W. promises he shares.
T-28 .... VII.1:8 and in W. Wholeness there can be no gap
T-30 .......II.4:9 apart from Him W. holy Will you share.
W-pI..... 45.9:3 that are unworthy of Him W. host you are
W-pI... 102.5:2 W. Love created him as loving as Himself.
W-pI... 151.9:2 the Mind W. Thought created your reality
W-pI. 198.12:5 Itself, so like to Him W. Son he is, that to
W-pII .... in.7:7 the Son, W. holy Will created all that is,
W-pII . 238.2:2 to Him W. Love is made complete in him.
W-pII . 245.2:3 W. Love we recognize because we share
W-pII ... 11.5:2 W. Holiness His Own creation shares;
W-pII ... 11.5:2 shares; W. Holiness is still a part of us.
P-2....... VII.6:5 W. Love is in him and Who cannot fail.
S-3........ IV.1:3 whom He speaks for God, W. Voice He is,
S-3........ IV.3:4 W. Love has never changed and never will

**Whose** 11
• Christ/Self
*God*
*Holy Spirit*
*whose*

T-22 ........I.7:6 through Christ, W. vision sees them one.
T-30 ...... V.7:4 they will look on Him W. hand they hold.
T-30 ...... V.8:1 you have recognized W. hand you hold!
T-30 ...... V.8:3 For He W. hand you hold was waiting but
T-30 .... V.10:7 will not perceive W. loving hand you hold
W-pI... 113.2:2 *W. knowledge still remains within my mind*
W-pI... 183.5:1 and call upon your Self, W. Name is His.
W-pI. 187.10:3 Self W. innocence has joined us all as one,
W-pII . 269.2:2 look upon the face of Him W. Self is ours.
C-1 ............ 6:3 Christ Mind, W. Will is One with God's.
C-6 ............ 5:4 W. part in its redemption you have made

**Whose** 20
• Holy Spirit
*God*
*Christ/Self*
*whose*

T-5 .......II.12:2 the Holy Spirit, W. Will is for God always.
T-6 .......II.11:7 the Holy Spirit, W. Mind is fixed on God.
T-8 ........ V.2:1 wholly in the likeness of God, W. Will it is
T-11 .......II.4:2 the Holy Spirit, W. message is wholeness.
T-14 ... III.17:1 W. equal Love is given equally to all alike!
T-15 .......II.2:4 W. joy it is to teach God's holy Son his
T-15 ... VIII.6:5 And let Him W. teaching is only of God
T-16 ........I.7:4 all to Him W. function is to meet them.
T-17 ... VIII.6:7 separate from Him W. Call you answered.
T-18 ..... IV.6:6 yourself to Him W. function is release. Do
T-20 ... VIII.5:9 with it the laws beloved of Him W. sight it
T-22 .......II.8:5 W. function is to save, will save. *How* He
W-pI. 135.18:1 gently planned by One W. only purpose is
W-pI... 154.2:1 W. function is to speak for you as well.
M-10 ......... 4:7 Someone with you W. judgment is perfect
M-10 ......... 5:9 gave himself to Him W. judgment he has
M-25 ......... 2:5 W. Presence is always there and Whose
M-25 ......... 2:5 Presence is always there and W. Voice is
M-28 ......... 6:5 and given Him W. function judgment is.
P-1............ 1:4 God has given everyone a Teacher W.

**whose** 2
• Jesus
*noise word*
*Whose*

T-9 .........II.4:3 in me w. faith in you cannot be shaken.
T-22 ...... IV.5:4 me, w. message has not yet been given

**whose** 97
• noise word
*Jesus*
*Whose*

**whosoever** 1

T-2 .... VII.5:14 that w. believeth in him should not perish

**why** 238

T-1 ........I.17:3 from the bodily level. That is w. they heal.
T-1 .........II.2:2 is w. any attempt to describe it in words is
T-1 ....... IV.4:2 and w. I could demonstrate that death
T-1 ....... VI.4:5 That is w. you can believe what no one
T-2 .........II.1:9 is w. the Bible speaks of "the peace of God
T-2 ....... VI.2:3 W. should you condone insane thinking?
T-2 ....... VI.3:3 That is w. you feel responsible for it. You
T-2 ....... VI.9:2 right thinking to realize w. fear occurs.
T-2 ...... VII.6:5 That is w. the conflict cannot ultimately
T-3 ........I.3:10 It is also w. you may believe from time to
T-3 ..........I.8:5 That is w. their altars are truly radiant.
T-3 ....... III.1:9 is w. it is not knowledge. True perception
T-3 ....... III.4:6 That is w. visions, however holy, do not
T-3 ....... IV.3:9 w. you cannot escape from fear until you
T-3 ..... IV.3:11 That is w. you must eventually choose to
T-3 ....... IV.6:2 is w. perception involves an exchange or
T-3 ....... VI.4:3 This is w. you see it in nightmares, or in
T-3 .... VII.4:12 That is w. you cannot create and are filled
T-3 ...... VII.5:9 and that is w. you become so fearful. As
T-4 ......I.13:11 *That is w. you should be of good cheer.*
T-4 .........II.3:4 w. is it surprising that it occurred in the
T-4 .........II.7:4 That is w. the concept of "getting" arose
T-4 .........II.8:9 This is w. self-esteem in ego terms must
T-4 ....... III.3:1 It is surely apparent by now w. the ego
T-4 ....... III.5:2 and hiding is w. the light cannot enter.
T-4 ....... III.9:7 is w. we make no distinction between
T-4 ..... IV.11:8 W. do you believe it is harder for me to
T-4 .... VII.3:12 That is w. the mind cannot totally lose the
T-4 ...... VII.5:3 is w. God created you. Divine Abstraction
T-5 ........ in.2:6 That is w. it makes no difference to what
T-5 ........ in.3:7 That is w. the healer's prayer is: *Let me*
T-5 .........II.3:4 That is w. you must choose to hear one of
T-5 ....... III.4:2 That is w. you must share It. It must be
T-5 .........V.6:2 That is w. the question, "What do you
T-5 ...... VII.3:1 W. should you listen to the endless
T-6 ....... III.2:1 That is w. you must teach only one lesson
T-6 ....... IV.2:2 That is w. attack within the Kingdom is
T-6 ..... IV.11:1 is w. the Holy Spirit never commands. To
T-6 ..... V.B.3:9 is the real reason w., in many respects,
T-6 ..... V.B.6:5 is w. I suggested before that you remind
T-6 ..... V.C.1:9 that is w. it promotes different moods.
T-6 ..... V.C.7:5 is w. you must be vigilant on God's behalf
T-6 ..... V.C.8:6 This is w. vigilance is essential. Doubts
T-7 .........II.6:3 w. the Holy Spirit's teaching is a lesson in
T-7 .........II.7:9 That is w. it is the Kingdom of God. It
T-7 ....... III.2:6 This is w. the ego is insane; it teaches that
T-7 ....... III.5:4 That is w. the Holy Spirit never questions.
T-7 ....... V.10:4 That is w. they need your remembrance
T-7 ....... VI.1:3 it. That is w. attack is never discrete, and
T-7 ....... VI.1:3 and w. it must be relinquished entirely. If
T-7 ....... VI.3:3 That is w. the ego never recognizes what
T-7 ...... VII.1:8 w. denying any part of it means you have
T-7 ..... VIII.3:9 That is w. those who project are vigilant
T-7 ....... IX.4:7 w. there is perfect peace in the Kingdom.
T-7 .........X.4:1 That is w. you need to demonstrate the
T-8 .........II.3:3 That is w. the ego is the denial of free will.
T-8 ....... III.2:5 That is w. you need Him, and why God
T-8 ....... III.2:5 need Him, and w. God gave Him to you.
T-8 ....... III.6:7 will understand w. you once believed that

T-3 II.3:6 with the same **W.** has any real existence.
T-3 II.4:1 of God's **W.** because you have used your
T-3 II.4:6 **W.** of the Sonship and the Father are One,
T-3 II.5:5 because They are of one Mind and one **W.**
T-4 VII.3:5 This communication is the **W.** of God.
T-4 VII.3:7 for the reception of His Mind and **W.**.
T-5 II.1:7 this union of **W.** between Father and Son.
T-5 II.6:9 their minds was not the Voice for His **W.**,
T-5 II.8:4 which God's **W.** is done on earth as it is in
T-5 II.12:2 Holy Spirit, Whose **W.** is for God always.
T-5 VII.1:7 escape His care because that is not His **W.**
T-5 VII.4:3 that is not in accord with His holy **W.**. I
T-7 I.4:4 is to limit giving, and this is not God's **W.**.
T-7 I.7:14 obscured, because it is His **W.** to share it.
T-7 IV.2:4 This is God's **W.** and yours. The laws of
T-7 IV.6:1 think you can oppose the **W.** of God is a
T-7 VI.13:4 Yet because God's **W.** is unchangeable, no
T-7 VII.5:5 because that is not the **W.** of your Creator
T-7 VII.10:1 You *are* the **W.** of God. Do not accept
T-7 IX.6:2 it was the **W.** of God to give it to you, He
T-7 IX.6:3 it was His **W.** that you have it forever, He
T-7 IX.6:5 God's **W.** is meaningful only to the insane
T-7 X.2:5 Truth is God's **W.**. Share His Will and you
T-7 X.2:6 Will. Share His **W.** and you share what He
T-7 X.2:7 knows. Deny His **W.** as yours, and you are
T-7 X.4:3 of God's **W.** can be better for you. You
T-7 X.4:4 is possible to *do* the opposite of God's **W.**.
T-7 X.6:4 I said before that you are the **W.** of God.
T-7 X.6:5 God. His **W.** is not an idle wish, and your
T-7 X.6:5 identification with His **W.** is not optional,
T-7 X.6:6 Sharing His **W.** with me is not really open
T-7 X.6:10 That is His **W.**, and you cannot undo it.
T-7 X.7:2 accomplished for you by the **W.** of God,
T-7 X.7:4 whose will must be the **W.** of the Father,
T-7 X.7:4 Father, because the Father's **W.** *is* His Son.
T-7 X.8:1 are in accord with the **W.** of God, Whose
T-7 X.8:1 Whose **W.** you do not know because you
T-7 X.8:3 are God's **W.** and do not accept His Will,
T-7 X.8:3 are God's Will and do not accept His **W.**,
T-7 XI.1:2 **W.** for everyone because He speaks for the
T-8 I.1:7 Knowledge *is* His **W.**. If you are opposing
T-8 I.1:8 If you are opposing His **W.**, how can you
T-8 II.3:4 you, because He shares His **W.** with you.
T-8 II.3:5 teaches only in accordance with His **W.**,
T-8 II.4:1 teach that you want to oppose God's **W.**.
T-8 II.4:3 that the **W.** of the Son is the Father's. The
T-8 II.6:3 it is not God's **W.** to *be* without you. When
T-8 II.7:1 I meant: The **W.** of God is without limit,
T-8 II.7:5 **W.** of God because that is how you were
T-8 III.2:1 fulfill the **W.** of God perfectly is the only
T-8 III.2:3 God's **W.** cannot be forced upon you,
T-8 III.3:1 **W.** of the Father and of the Son are One,
T-8 III.3:2 together by extending Their joint **W.**.
T-8 IV.1:1 If God's **W.** for you is complete peace and
T-8 IV.1:1 must be refusing to acknowledge His **W.**.
T-8 IV.1:2 His Will. His **W.** does not vacillate, being
T-8 IV.3:1 You were in darkness until God's **W.** was
T-8 IV.3:4 the Sonship with the **W.** of the Father by
T-8 IV.3:4 by being aware of the Father's **W.** myself.
T-8 IV.3:9 to hear His Voice and abide in His **W.**. As
T-8 IV.5:14 it and thereby violating God's **W.** for you.
T-8 IV.6:1 nothing God created can oppose His **W.**.
T-8 IV.6:8 in will, all being the **W.** of their Father.
T-8 IV.7:10 freedom, which is His **W.** for all His Sons.
T-8 V.2:1 in the likeness of God, Whose **W.** it is.
T-8 V.2:3 from the **W.** of God which *is* yourself. Yet
T-8 V.2:12 your awareness that the **W.** of God is One
T-8 V.3:7 to the **W.** of the Father for His Son, and to
T-8 V.3:7 to our joy in uniting with His **W.** for us.
T-8 V.5:1 Would you know the **W.** of God for you?
T-8 VI.2:7 His **W.** has saved you, not from yourself
T-8 VI.6:2 His **W.** *to* you is His Will *for* you. He would
T-8 VI.6:2 His Will *to* you is His **W.** *for* you. He would
T-8 VI.6:8 *he* is. Creation is the **W.** of God. His Will
T-8 VI.6:9 His **W.** created you to create. Your will
T-8 VI.7:3 God's **W.** *is* Thought. It cannot be
T-8 VI.8:1 I want to know my Father's **W.** for me?"
T-8 VI.10:2 He has given His **W.** to His treasure,
T-8 VII.6:3 perfectly accomplish His holy **W.** for you
T-8 IX.9:8 Yet it is still His **W.** for you, and His Will
T-8 IX.9:8 **W.** must stand forever and in all things.
T-9 I.1:1 Fear of the **W.** of God is one of the
T-9 I.1:4 The very fact that the **W.** of God, which is
T-9 I.1:5 the **W.** of God of which you are afraid, but
T-9 I.4:2 hidden and recognize the **W.** of God there
T-9 I.4:3 His recognition of this **W.** can make it real
T-9 I.5:2 is not God's **W.** because it is not yours.
T-9 I.6:2 that, and only that is Your joint **W.**. A
T-9 I.8:2 there is no God or that God's **W.** is fearful
T-9 I.9:1 everyone must remember the **W.** of God,
T-9 I.10:7 the Holy Spirit deny the **W.** of God? And
T-9 I.14:1 then, that God's **W.** is already possible,
T-9 VII.1:1 God's **W.** is your salvation. Would He
T-9 VIII.9:5 transform to the **W.** of God does not exist
T-10 II.3:5 Nothing is beyond His **W.** for you. But
T-10 III.9:5 because he is not the **W.** of the Father. He
T-10 IV.1:7 he cannot be reconciled with God's **W.**. If
T-10 IV.3:4 part of your mind from God's **W.**. This
T-10 IV.4:1 mind at peace because peace is His **W.**,
T-10 IV.5:5 been, and nothing but His **W.** will ever be
T-10 IV.5:6 created through His laws and by His **W.**,
T-10 V.4:1 the mind of God's Son against His **W.**.
T-11 I.3:1 part of God, His **W.** would not be unified.
T-11 I.6:7 To give without limit is God's **W.** for you,
T-11 I.7:9 And being an extension of His **W.**, yours
T-11 I.8:3 God's **W.** is that you are His Son. By
T-11 I.8:5 must ask what God's **W.** is in everything,
T-11 I.8:7 Him, therefore, what God's **W.** is for you,
T-11 I.9:1 it appear as if God's **W.** is outside yourself
T-11 I.9:2 for God's **W.** and yours to conflict. God,
T-11 I.9:9 Immortality is His **W.** for His Son, and
T-11 I.10:2 It is immutable by God's **W.** and yours,
T-11 I.10:2 otherwise His **W.** would not be extended.
T-11 I.10:3 You are afraid to know God's **W.**, because
T-11 I.11:3 He shares His **W.** with you; He does not
T-11 I.11:6 **W.** of your Father is to know your own.
T-11 I.11:7 be like Him, Whose **W.** it is that it be so.
T-11 I.11:8 so. God's **W.** is that His Son be One, and
T-11 II.1:5 of Him, you know there is but one **W.**. Yet
T-11 II.4:3 Own complete **W.** and make yours whole.
T-11 III.1:4 way, for that is not God's **W.** for His Son.
T-11 III.3:3 and you have said, "God's **W.** is mine,"
T-11 III.6:3 Him, and accept His **W.** for you in peace.
T-11 IV.2:4 on your power is not the **W.** of God.
T-11 V.5:4 His **W.** is One *because* the extension of His
T-11 V.5:4 of His **W.** cannot be unlike itself. The real
T-11 V.5:5 the ego's idle wishes and the **W.** of God,
T-11 V.12:4 cannot be found apart from Your joint **W.**
T-11 VI.4:7 be, for the resurrection is the **W.** of God,
T-11 VI.8:2 God's Son, for the **W.** of God cannot die.
T-11 VI.10:6 nothing contradictory to His **W.** is either
T-11 VII.4:8 God because it is His **W.** to be known.
T-12 II.6:2 must accomplish it because it is His **W.**.
T-12 IV.6:2 death is not your Father's **W.** nor yours,
T-12 IV.6:2 whatever is true is the **W.** of the Father.
T-13 VII.6:7 Christ will always offer you the **W.** of God
T-13 VII.7:1 It is God's **W.** that nothing touch His Son
T-13 X.9:9 His **W.** is like His Father's, and He offers
T-13 XI.5:4 may occur to you, God's **W.** *is* done. You
T-13 XI.6:9 to do. The **W.** of God can fail in nothing.
T-13 XI.7:4 because insanity is not the **W.** of God. If
T-13 XI.8:4 flows to you from Him Whose **W.** is peace
T-13 XI.8:8 The Holy Spirit knows only of His **W.**.
T-13 XI.10:7 **W.** of God must be accepted as your will.
T-14 IV.7:1 God, Whose **W.** is that you know Him.
T-14 VIII.5:3 Heaven remains the **W.** of God for you.
T-14 XI.11:8 This is the **W.** of God for all creation, and
T-14 XI.14:5 abandon, for it is not His **W.** to do so.
T-15 III.10:2 knowing His **W.** is constant and at peace
T-15 III.10:3 will be content with nothing but His **W.**.
T-15 IV.1:2 delay the recognition that His **W.** is so.
T-15 IV.3:6 value of His **W.** for you in your own mind.
T-15 IV.8:6 being the acceptance of the single **W.** that
T-15 VIII.6:4 be possible because it is the **W.** of God.
T-16 VI.1:6 except as its Creator defined it by His **W.**.
T-16 VII.8:4 You will receive *because* it is His **W.** to give
T-16 VII.12:5 *temptation of the Son of God is not Your* **W.**.
T-17 IV.2:7 have made is a substitute for God's **W.**,
T-18 II.9:5 the truth of Heaven join in the **W.** of God.
T-18 II.9:7 your will joined with the **W.** of God. And
T-18 II.9:8 **W.** would have accomplished has never
T-18 III.4:14 The **W.** of God is granted you. For you
T-18 III.5:3 with all the power of the Holy Spirit's **W.**.
T-18 III.5:4 desire from His **W.** and from His strength
T-18 IV.3:6 to be, you must be interfering with His **W.**
T-18 IV.3:7 to come from you, but only from His **W.**.
T-18 IV.4:2 with the unlimited power of God's **W.**.
T-18 V.4:3 Their message is, "Thy **W.** be done," and
T-18 VI.5:5 what He would have it be, being His **W.**.
T-18 VI.5:6 You cannot make His **W.** destructive. You
T-19 II.2:5 **W.** of God open to opposition and defeat.
T-19 III.8:2 that could attack His **W.** and overcome it;
T19 IV.A.2:11 hatred would still oppose the **W.** of God,
T19 IV.A.3:3 You still oppose the **W.** of God, just by a
T19 IV.A.3:5 God's **W.** is One, not many. It has no
T19 IV.A.4:5 It cannot contain the **W.** of God. Peace
T19 IV.C.2:9 It is the **W.** of God. What is impossible to
T19 IV.C.2:10 to you who chose His **W.** as yours? What
T19 IV.C.3:1 innocence, and to the **W.** of God Himself.
T19 IV.C.3:5 of their Creator, Whose **W.** it is they live.
T19 IV.C.3:6 They are not following His **W.**; they are
T19 IV.C.4:4 are but honoring the **W.** of his Creator.
T19 IV.C.10:7 your brother, and see in it the **W.** of God.
T-20 IV.4:3 their power according to the **W.** of God.
T-21 in.2:4 you joined the **W.** of God to set him free.
T-21 II.6:4 and thus without the **W.** of his Creator,
T-21 II.6:4 **W.** cannot be separate from his own. This
T-21 V.5:3 nor does the **W.** of God wait upon time to
T-21 V.5:4 joined the **W.** of God must be in you now,
T-21 V.6:3 of you that knows His **W.** and shares it. It
T-21 VIII.4:1 complete God's **W.** and are His happiness
T-22 I.1:3 Yet if you *are* His **W.**, what you must then
T-22 I.4:1 What could be secret from God's **W.**? Yet
T-22 I.11:8 This is your Father's **W.** for you, and
T-22 II.9:6 himself different and oppose His **W.**,
T-22 V.4:8 by this mouse, but by the **W.** of God. And
T-22 VI.7:4 wills are His, *because* they serve His **W.**.
T-22 VI.10:3 Think you the **W.** of God is powerless? Is
T-23 in.1:6 and what is weak is not the **W.** of God.
T-23 I.2:8 only the mad belief the **W.** of God can be
T-23 II.8:2 not forgiveness, is the **W.** of God. From
T-24 in.1:7 Peace will be yours *because* it is His **W.**.
T-24 in.1:8 the **W.** that holds the universe secure?
T-24 in.1:12 has the power to defeat what is Their **W.**?
T-24 I.9:2 but an attack upon the **W.** of God? You
T-24 II.2:8 and thus run counter to the **W.** of God.
T-24 III.2:2 your puny might against the **W.** of God.
T-24 III.4:6 and that you will oppose His **W.** forever.
T-24 III.6:6 you have forgiven Him Whose **W.** it is you
T-24 III.8:2 Such is the **W.** of God and of His Son.
T-24 III.8:5 to join His **W.** to save you both from hell.
T-24 III.8:13 Forgive your Father it was not His **W.** that
T-24 VI.2:3 and part of Him because His **W.** is One.
T-24 VI.3:4 It is His **W.** you share His Love for you,
T-24 VI.10:6 will disappear before the **W.** of God, Who
T-24 VII.11:7 The Son of God retains his Father's **W.**.
T-25 I.5:4 the part of you that shares His Father's **W.**
T-25 I.6:2 knows the **W.** of God and what you really
T-25 II.9:12 It is not His **W.** to be alone. And neither is
T-25 II.10:7 power over you except His **W.** and yours,
T-25 II.10:7 Will and yours, which but extends His **W.**
T-25 II.11:1 Himself is One and not divided in His **W.**
T-25 II.11:3 **W.** is brought together as you join in will,
T-25 IV.5:5 supersede the **W.** of God and of His Son,
T-25 V.6:2 is God made free to let His **W.** be done. In
T-25 V.6:3 in what the **W.** of God must be for you. In
T-25 VII.2:1 is just as strong as is God's **W.** for life.
T-25 VII.2:5 What is immutable besides His **W.**? And
T-25 VII.2:7 What wish can rise against His **W.**, and be
T-25 VII.2:8 nothing is changeless but the **W.** of God,
T-25 VII.7:5 Yet if His **W.** is seen as madness, then the
T-25 VII.10:4 It is God's **W.** that you remember this,
T-25 VII.13:3 can suffer for the **W.** of God to be fulfilled
T-25 VII.13:4 Salvation is His **W.** *because* you share it.
T-26 I.8:2 and sacrifice his Father's **W.** for him?
T-26 II.8:6 your Father's **W.** that you should offer or
T-26 V.9:2 Can sin withstand the **W.** of God? Can it

T-26.....V.14:4 There is no hindrance to the **W.** of God,
T-26......VI.3:1 loneliness is not the **W.** of God. Would
T-26...VII.6:10 all. God's **W.** is One. And any wish that
T-26...VII.6:11 His **W.** has no foundation in the truth.
T-26.....VII.7:4 Then would God's **W.** be split in two, and
T-26.....VII.9:4 state, and not in opposition to God's **W.**.
T-26...VII.10:6 his wishes and the **W.** of God are one.
T-26...VII.11:1 What is the **W.** of God? He wills His Son
T-28.........I.8:5 Father's **W.** that He be unremembered by
T-28...... I.10:3 for what was causeless and against His **W.**
T-28...... I.15:9 be excluded from the **W.** that is for you.
T-28.....V.1:11 exist because God shared His **W.** with you
T-28......VI.6:8 vows are powerless before the **W.** of God,
T-28.....VII.1:5 Father and the Son is not the **W.** of Either,
T-28.....VII.7:8 it shares your Father's **W.** with you.
T-29... VIII.7:5 nô room for anything to be except His **W.**
T-29. VIII.8:13 And it is this that is against God's **W.**.
T-30....... II.4:9 apart from Him Whose holy **W.** you share
T-30......III.4:4 Your will to be complete is but God's **W.**,
T-30......IV.7:5 strength of idle wishes for the **W.** of God.
T-30......V.11:1 The **W.** of God forever lies in those whose
T-30......V.11:4 thus the **W.** of God must reach to their
T-30......VI.5:7 replace it and destroy the **W.** of God.
T-30......VI.9:5 of evil that can overcome the **W.** of God;
T-31.........I.5:2 It was not made to do the **W.** of God, but
T-31.........I.6:3 His **W.** is in the Voice that speaks for Him
T-31.........I.9:1 share the universal **W.** that it be whole,
T-31... VIII.4:5 joined in all the power of the **W.** of God.
T-31. VIII.10:5 And as I would but do Your holy **W.**, so
T-31. VIII.11:3 And can You fail in what is but Your **W.**?
T-31. VIII.12:6 Thy **W.** is done, complete and perfectly,
W-pI.....19.2:5 be possible because it is the **W.** of God.
W-pI.....42.1:3 You will see because it is the **W.** of God. It
W-pI.....45.5:4 we will succeed today. It is the **W.** of God.
W-pI.....49.3:3 we are joining our will with the **W.** of God
W-pI.....54.5:5 that my will and the **W.** of God are one.
W-pI.....56.4:4 my will, united with the **W.** of my Father.
W-pI.....59.3:5 else. Beyond His **W.** lie only illusions. It is
W-pI.....69.7:3 light. You are in accord with His **W.**. You
W-pI.....69.8:6 you, that His **W.** and yours be done.
W-pI.....70.5:1 we practice realizing that God's **W.** and
W-pI.....73.3:2 a world have been created by the **W.** the
W-pI.....73.3:4 Son? Creation is the **W.** of Both together.
W-pI.....73.4:2 because it does not oppose the **W.** of God.
W-pI...73.10:3 *the light that reflects God's **W.** and mine.*
W-pI.....74.1:2 God's is the only **W.**. When you have
W-pI.....74.1:6 As an expression of the **W.** of God, you
W-pI.....75.7:7 It is His **W.**, and you have joined with
W-pI.....76.6:2 you have made in opposition to God's **W.**.
W-pI...76.11:1 and let His **W.** extend through us to Him.
W-pI.....77.5:5 are but asking that the **W.** of God be done
W-pI.....87.4:2 *this in accordance with the **W.** of God. It is*
W-pI.....87.4:3 *It is God's **W.** you are His Son, [name], and*
W-pI.....87.4:4 *This is part of God's **W.** for me, however I*
W-pI.....93.3:2 thoughts are not according to God's **W.**.
W-pI.....93.4:2 yourself cannot withstand the **W.** of God.
W-pI.....93.5:9 when it would contradict the **W.** of God?
W-pI...95.13:2 Self; united with your Father in His **W.**.
W-pI.....96.8:4 do, restored to It and free to serve Its **W.**.
W-pI.....99.1:2 apart or different from the **W.** of God.
W-pI.....99.5:5 God is still Love, and this is not His **W.**.
W-pI.....99.6:8 *God still is Love, and this is not His **W.**.*
W-pI.....99.7:4 you. All the world of pain is not His **W.**.
W-pI.....99.7:6 the thoughts that never were His **W.**.
W-pI.....99.9:2 It is God's **W.** your mind be one with His.
W-pI.....99.9:3 It is God's **W.** that He has but one Son. It
W-pI.....99.9:4 It is God's **W.** that His one Son is you.
W-pI...99.11:4 *God still is Love, and this is not His **W.**.*
W-pI...100.2:1 God's **W.** for you is perfect happiness.
W-pI...100.2:2 should you choose to go against His **W.**?
W-pI...100.7:1 us according to our Father's **W.** and ours.
W-pI...100.8:1 to us and all the world God's **W.** for us. It
W-pI......101.h God's **W.** for me is perfect happiness.
W-pI...101.6:1 God's **W.** for you is perfect happiness
W-pI...101.6:3 Fear not the **W.** of God. But turn to it in
W-pI...101.6:6 *God's **W.** for me is perfect happiness. There*
W-pI...101.7:6 *God's **W.** for me is perfect happiness. This is*
W-pI......102.h I share God's **W.** for happiness for me.
W-pI...102.2:6 free today to join the happy **W.** of God.

W-pI...102.3:1 the happiness God's **W.** has placed in you
W-pI...102.4:1 with this acceptance of God's **W.** for you: *I*
W-pI...102.4:2 *share God's **W.** for happiness for me, and I*
W-pI...102.4:4 your choice, and that you share God's **W.**.
W-pI...102.5:4 are joining with God's **W.** in doing this.
W-pI...104.5:1 recognizing that His **W.** is done already,
W-pI...116.1:1 God's **W.** for me is perfect happiness.
W-pI...116.1:2 *God's **W.** is perfect happiness for me. And I*
W-pI...116.2:1 I share God's **W.** for happiness for me. *I*
W-pI...116.2:2 *share my Father's **W.** for me, His Son. What*
W-pI...116.3:2 God's **W.** for me is perfect happiness. On
W-pI...116.3:4 I share God's **W.** for happiness for me.
W-pI...125.9:4 of God the Son joins in his Father's **W.**, at
W-pI...125.9:4 the Word in which the **W.** of God the Son
W-pI...131.6:5 How could the **W.** of God be in the past,
W-pI...131.8:4 lose what the Eternal **W.** has given him to
W-pI...131.9:2 make time to take away the **W.** of God?
W-pI...136.9:2 by a decision stronger than His **W.**. His
W-pI.136.11:1 knows not of your plans to change His **W.**
W-pI.137.12:1 Would you not offer shelter to God's **W.**?
W-pI.151.13:4 that do not contradict the **W.** of God.
W-pI...152.7:1 that God made chaos, contradicts His **W.**,
W-pI.152.11:4 *as what my Father's **W.** created me to be.*
W-pI.153.11:2 but few have come to realize His **W.** is but
W-pI.153.16:1 to be faithful to the **W.** we share with God
W-pI.154.10:3 Word; the giving and receiving of His **W.**.
W-pI...158.5:5 The Father's **W.** and His are joined in
W-pI...163.4:3 creation, stronger than God's **W.** for life,
W-pI...163.4:4 **W.** of Father and of Son defeated finally,
W-pI...163.9:5 *There is no death, for death is not Your **W.**.*
W-pI...165.8:5 and in our minds, according to His **W.**.
W-pI...166.2:2 This world is not the **W.** of God, and so it
W-pI.166.10:1 God's **W.** does not oppose. It merely is. It
W-pI.166.10:4 not know about a plan so alien to His **W.**.
W-pI...168.2:4 the means by which His **W.** is recognized?
W-pI...168.6:3 Such is His **W.**, because He loves His Son.
W-pI...181.9:7 Our sinlessness is but the **W.** of God. This
W-pI...185.3:1 what they will becomes the **W.** of God.
W-pI.185.11:2 by denying to himself what is God's **W.**.
W-pI.185.13:4 can be sure you share one **W.** with Him,
W-pI.185.13:5 you share one **W.** with all your brothers,
W-pI...186.1:5 acknowledges the **W.** of God is done on
W-pI.189.10:9 *And we ask but that Your **W.**, which is our*
W-pI...192.1:1 holy **W.** that you complete Himself, and
W-pI...193.1:2 Yet His **W.** extends to what He does not
W-pI...193.1:3 in Him. That is His **W.**. And thus His Will
W-pI...193.1:4 And thus His **W.** provides the means to
W-pI...193.3:2 His **W.** reflects them all, and they reflect
W-pI...197.7:4 Father is secure, because Their **W.** is One.
W-pI...200.7:1 in opposition to God's **W.** and to his own,
W-pI...210.1:3 *I thought apart from Him and from His **W.**.*
W-pI...210.1:4 *His **W.** is joy, and only joy for His beloved*
W-pII.....in.7:5 be kept which are Your **W.** to keep. We
W-pII.....in.7:7 the Son, Whose holy **W.** created all that is
W-pII...... 1.1:7 free to take its place is now the **W.** of God.
W-pII..230.2:6 *gave. It is Your **W.** that gave it to Your Son.*
W-pII..233.1:4 *that I may do Your **W.** instead of seeking*
W-pII..235.1:2 my Father's **W.** for me is only happiness,
W-pII..236.1:8 And thus I set it free to do the **W.** of God.
W-pII..245.1:8 *For I would save Your Son, as is Your **W.**,*
W-pII..246.2:2 *in that will I succeed, because it is Your **W.**.*
W-pII......4.3:4 His **W.** forever overcome by death, love
W-pII..253.2:2 *is but Your **W.** in perfect union with my own*
W-pII..254.1:4 *And truth is but Your **W.**, which I would*
W-pII..272.1:2 *home is set in Heaven by Your **W.** and mine.*
W-pII..290.2:1 *me up today, while I but seek to do Your **W.**.*
W-pII..292.1:6 For God's **W.** is done in earth and Heaven
W-pII..292.1:7 seek and we will find according to His **W.**,
W-pII..299.1:3 Our **W.**, together, understands it. And
W-pII..299.1:4 And Our **W.**, together, knows that it is so.
W-pII..299.2:8 *because it is Your **W.** that You be known.*
W-pII......9.3:2 name of true creation and the **W.** of God.
W-pII......9.5:5 Let us rejoice that we can do God's **W.**,
W-pII..305.2:1 *us, because it is Your **W.** that we be saved.*
W-pII..307.1:1 *Father, Your **W.** is mine, and only that.*
W-pII..307.1:4 *Your **W.** alone can bring me happiness, and*
W-pII..307.1:5 *You can give, I must accept Your **W.** for me,*
W-pII..309.1:1 it is God's **W.** that it be there forever and
W-pII..309.1:3 to deny my Father's **W.** is to deny my own

W-pII .310.1:4 *me, and that it is Your **W.** I be set free today.*
W-pII .312.2:2 *Father, this is Your **W.** for me today, and*
W-pII .319.1:6 And yet it is the **W.** of God I learn that
W-pII .319.2:1 *Father, Your **W.** is total. And the goal which*
W-pII .319.2:4 *be the **W.** my Self has shared with You?*
W-pII .320.1:6 the power of my Father's **W.** abides.
W-pII .320.2:1 *Your **W.** can do all things in me, and then*
W-pII .320.2:2 *me. There is no limit on Your **W.**. And so all*
W-pII ... 11.3:2 for in creation is His **W.** complete in every
W-pII ... 11.3:3 inviolate; forever held within His holy **W.**,
W-pII ... 11.4:6 only to let God's **W.** be done on earth,
W-pII .326.1:5 *because it is Your **W.** to have a Son so like his*
W-pII .326.2:1 forgiven, fade entirely into God's holy **W.**.
W-pII .328.1:4 for us, nor is there any second to His **W.**.
W-pII .328.2:3 *It is Your **W.** that I be wholly safe, eternally*
W-pII .328.2:4 *And happily I share that **W.** which You, my*
W-pII .329.1:1 *Father, I thought I wandered from Your **W.**,*
W-pII .329.1:2 *Yours. Yet what I am in truth is but Your **W.**,*
W-pII .329.1:9 *joy, because it is Your **W.** that it be so.*
W-pII .329.2:2 all of us are one because His **W.** is shared
W-pII .330.1:4 as is the **W.** of God united with its own.
W-pII ... 12.1:2 "will" that sees the **W.** of God as enemy,
W-pII ... 12.2:4 "sees" the **W.** of God has been destroyed.
W-pII .331.1:6 *There is no will except the **W.** of Love. Fear is*
W-pII331.1:10 *There is no opposition to Your **W.**. There is*
W-pII .331.2:1 shows us that God's **W.** is One, and that
W-pII .334.2:5 *This Your **W.** for me, for so will I behold my*
W-ep ......... 6:3 as we ask His **W.** in everything we do. He
M-1 ........... 4:6 for what can change the **W.** of God? But
M-2 ........... 2:4 the **W.** of God is entirely apart from time.
M-2 ........... 4:7 God's **W.** in everything but seems to take
M-3 ........... 3:5 no levels, being a reflection of His **W.**.
M-5 ...... III.3:8 but by the union of the one **W.** with itself.
M-12 ......... 1:8 Thus does he share God's **W.**, and bring
M-14 ....... 5:13 His **W.** be done. It cannot be otherwise.
M-16 ....... 10:1 There is no substitute for the **W.** of God.
M-17 ......... 5:4 will that can oppose the **W.** of God, also
M-20 ......... 6:2 that His **W.** is wholly without opposite.
M-20 ......... 6:3 is no thought that contradicts His **W.**, yet
M-20 ......... 6:4 His **W.** and yours but seemed to be reality
M-20 ......... 6:5 there was no conflict, for His **W.** is yours.
M-20 ......... 6:6 mighty **W.** of God Himself His gift to you.
M-20 ......... 6:9 The **W.** of God is One and all there is.
M-20 ....... 6:12 God's peace is the condition for His **W.**.
M-27 ......... 1:6 path,–all this is taken as the **W.** of God.
M-28 ......... 5:8 we wish for nothing but His **W.** to be our
C-1............. 4:2 the potential for creating, but its **W.**,
C-1............. 4:3 unabated because that is the **W.** of God.
C-1............. 4:4 **W.** is always unified and therefore has no
C-1............. 6:3 Mind, Whose **W.** is One with God's.
C-3............. 3:3 content it is His **W.** that it be understood.
C-3............. 5:1 of His **W.** alone it cannot be divided. And
C-3............. 5:2 the unity that it reflects becomes His **W.**.
C-3............. 6:1 God's **W.** is all there is. We can but go
C-3............. 6:9 remains is peace eternal and the **W.** of
C-3............. 7:4 But **W.** is constant, as the gift of God. And
C-ep............ 2:3 away, and it is done according to His **W.**.
P-2......... V.4:6 directs, because it is according to His **W.**.
P-2......... V.8:1 Let us stand silently before God's **W.**,
P-3....... II.10:5 the **W.** of God that he take his place in the
P-3....... II.10:6 **W.** of God that his patient be helped to
P-3.... II.10:11 time does not exist and the **W.** of God has
S-1........ IV.3:1 ask, before all else, what is the **W.** of God.
S-1......... V.2:5 it is, knowing creation is the **W.** of God.
S-2........ III.1:7 and seeks to understand the **W.** of God.
S-2........ III.2:1 not by your plans but by His holy **W.**. His
S-2........ III.4:8 God's **W.** is truth, and you are one with
S-2........ III.4:8 you are one with Him in **W.** and purpose

**will** 323

- noun
  *verb*
  *noise word (auxiliary verb)*
  *Will*

T-in ........... 1:4 *Free **w.** does not mean that you can establish*
T-2........... I.2:8 God's endowment of the Son with free **w.**,
T-2......... I.3:10 your free **w.** was given you for your joy in
T-2.......... II.2:6 and re-establishes the freedom of the **w.**.

T-2 II.2:7 the w. is really free it cannot miscreate,
T-2 III.3:2 may appear to contradict free w. because
T-2 III.3:4 An imprisoned w. engenders a situation
T-2 VIII.1:3 Your w. to create was given you by your
T-2 VIII.1:4 you create is necessarily a matter of w.. It
T-2 VIII.3:8 and imprisoned w. cannot but continue.
T-3 II.4:4 and the w. is not free to assert itself. To be
T-3 II.4:5 To be one is to be of one mind or w..
T-3 IV.7:6 By uniting my w. with that of my Creator,
T-3 IV.7:7 I cannot unite your w. with God's for you,
T-3 V.1:3 by the union of my w. with the Father's.
T-3 VI.11:2 free w. he must regard his will as not free,
T-3 VI.11:2 free will he must regard his w. as not free,
T-3 VI.11:3 Free w. must lead to freedom. Judgment
T-4 III.6:1 No force except your own w. is strong
T-4 VI.6:4 my w. is never out of accord with His. I
T-5 II.1:5 Your w. is still in you because God placed
T-5 II.1:6 it. God Himself keeps your w. alive by
T-5 II.6:4 In the holy state the w. is free, so that its
T-5 IV.7:4 joint w. of the Sonship is the only creator
T-5 VI.2:8 My role is only to unchain your w. and set
T-5 VI.11:6 because my w. is that of our Father, from
T-6 V.C.9:5 What you made has imprisoned your w.,
T-7 IV.6:2 that it can offer you its own "w." as a gift.
T-7 VI.13:4 unchangeable, no conflict of w. is possible
T-7 VI.13:6 separation, is your w. *because* it is God's,
T-7 VII.10:2 Do not accept anything else as your w., or
T-7 IX.2:9 Created by sharing, its w. is to create. It
T-7 X.4:8 w. is as powerful as His because it *is* His.
T-7 X.7:4 whose w. must be the Will of the Father,
T-8 I.1:6 behalf of an imaginary w. that is not His.
T-8 II.2:9 Your w. is *in* your nature, and therefore
T-8 II.3:1 you anything as long as your w. is free,
T-8 II.3:2 It is not your w. to be imprisoned because
T-8 II.3:2 to be imprisoned because your w. is free.
T-8 II.3:3 That is why the ego is the denial of free w.
T-8 II.3:6 lesson is that your w. and God's cannot be
T-8 II.4:2 you afraid of your w. *because* it is free. The
T-8 II.4:3 any imprisoning of the w. of a Son of God
T-8 II.6:4 you have learned that your w. is God's,
T-8 III.2:6 His teaching will release your w. to God's,
T-8 IV.3:4 My mission was simply to unite the w. of
T-8 IV.3:9 My w. is His, and your decision to hear
T-8 IV.5:1 Healing reflects our joint w.. This is
T-8 IV.5:12 you. Your w. is as free as mine, and God
T-8 IV.6:2 God gave your w. its power, which I can
T-8 IV.6:8 God's Sons are equal in w., all being the
T-8 IV.7:1 your w. were not mine it would not be our
T-8 V.h The Undivided W. of the Sonship
T-8 V.2:1 undivided w. of the Sonship is the perfect
T-8 V.2:3 belief that your w. is separate from mine,
T-8 V.2:9 no separation between your w. and mine.
T-8 VI.1:1 We are the joint w. of the Sonship, whose
T-8 VI.6:10 w. was not created separate from His, and
T-8 VI.7:1 "unwilling w." does not mean anything,
T-8 VI.10:5 and free the holy w. of all those who are as
T-8 IX.5:2 to wake is the reflection of the w. to love,
T-9 I.2:1 Your w. is not the ego's, and that is why
T-9 I.3:7 attempting to force an alien w. upon you.
T-9 I.3:8 Him, to re-establish your own w. in your
T-9 I.4:1 your w. beyond your own awareness,
T-9 I.5:3 no difference between your w. and God's.
T-9 I.6:7 Yet as long as you are afraid of your w.,
T-9 I.7:8 Your w. is your salvation because it is the
T-9 I.8:1 believe that its w. is stronger than God's.
T-9 I.8:2 believes that its w. is different from His, it
T-9 I.8:9 because it was never your w. for *you.*
T-9 I.9:2 recognition that his w. and God's are one.
T-9 I.9:8 This *is* your w.. Ask for this and you will be
T-9 VII.1:9 Is it possible that this is not also your w.?
T-9 VII.1:10 possible that this is not also the w. of your
T-9 VII.2:1 that in this joint w. you are all united, and
T-10 in.3:6 anything, then, exceed your w.? Nothing
T-10 I.4:3 want only truth, and being at last your w.,
T-10 II.3:6 But signify your w. to remember Him,
T-11 I.7:7 God wills to create, and your w. is His. It
T-11 I.7:8 to create, since your w. follows from His.
T-11 I.8:4 By denying this you deny your own w.,
T-11 I.8:9 because you have not recognized your w..
T-11 I.9:4 Would God, Who wants only your w., be
T-11 I.9:5 Your w. is His life, which He has given to
T-11 I.9:9 for His Son, and His Son's w. for himself.
T-11 I.9:11 Him. Creation is your w. *because* it is His.
T-11 I.11:7 For it is your w. to be like Him, Whose
T-11 I.11:9 of the recognition that your w. is His.
T-11 II.1:4 and *being* is to unite your w. with His, for
T-11 II.3:7 do. Having forgotten your w., you do not
T-11 II.6:1 only in this can your w. and your Father's
T-11 III.2:1 he does, believing his w. is not his own.
T-11 III.2:5 if your w. is His it cannot be true of you,
T-11 III.8:2 Him, because it is your w. not to be alone.
T-11 IV.2:4 the power of your w. cannot be lessened
T-11 VI.5:8 only have you learn your w. and follow it,
T-12 II.6:3 your purpose, for it is your w. to do so.
T-12 III.9:5 a world of w. because it is governed by the
T-12 III.9:5 to be unlike God, and this desire is not w..
T-12 IV.7:4 For spirit is w., and will is the "price" of
T-12 IV.7:4 will, and w. is the "price" of the Kingdom.
T-13 VI.12:1 is following the laws of love of your free w.
T-13 VII.6:6 errors for the peace of God is but *your* w..
T-13 XI.6:5 Truth comes of its own w. unto its own.
T-13 XI.10:7 Will of God must be accepted as your w..
T-14 I.4:5 but indirect expressions of the w. to live,
T-14 III.10:6 Yet w. was given them because it is holy,
T-14 III.10:7 There is nothing their w. fails to provide
T-14 III.10:8 because they do not understand their w.,
T-14 III.14:3 learn that what God wills for you *is* your w.
T-14 VII.7:8 Behold your w., accepting it as His, with
T-15 VIII.2:8 The w. of your creations calls to you, to
T-15 VIII.2:8 calls to you, to share your w. with them.
T-15 IX.5:3 For it is your w. to be in Heaven, where
T-15 XI.10:13 made holy for you. This is our w.. Amen.
T-16 III.8:4 united w. of all who make Heaven what it
T-18 II.9:7 this dream reflects your w. joined with the
T-18 VI.5:7 make fantasies in which your w. conflicts
T-19 III.8:2 capable of making another w. that could
T-19 III.8:2 it; and give His Son a w. apart from His,
T-19 III.8:3 creation would have a different w.,
T19 IV.B.4:5 between your w. and its accomplishment?
T19 IV.D.7:3 This is the re-establishment of *your* w..
T19 IV.D.7:4 thoughts that come to you against your w.
T19 IV.D.7:5 It *is* your w. to look on this. No mad desire,
T19 IV.D.7:6 seeming death can stand against your w..
T-20 III.10:1 Such is my w. for you and your brother,
T-21 II.6:4 happen to the Son of God without his w.;
T-21 II.6:5 is the Son of God's replacement for his w.,
T-21 II.7:4 This other "w.," which seems to tell you
T-21 V.5:1 without your w. and your consent. It must
T-21 V.6:2 and in this your w. must be included.
T-21 V.9:1 by your w. in union with your Father's, to
T-21 VI.4:3 But the insane know not their w., for they
T-21 VIII.4:1 happiness, whose w. is powerful as His, a
T-22 I.1:2 you and your Creator have a different w..
T-22 I.4:3 secrets be except another "w." that is your
T-22 II.10:2 Creator, and with a w. opposed to His.
T-22 II.12:4 Time waits upon its w., and earth will be
T-22 II.12:5 Here is no separate w., nor the desire that
T-22 II.12:6 Its w. has no exceptions, and what it wills
T-22 III.9:4 what impels him to sin against his w..
T-22 VI.4:6 Only in your joint w. does healing lie. For
T-22 VI.4:8 your w. and your brother's are joined.
T-22 VI.10:2 that would deny the power of your w..
T-23 in.1:8 And God is feared as an opposing w..
T-23 IV.4:6 that murder in any form is not your w..
T-24 I.8:2 your brother bow to it against his w.. And
T-24 II.2:9 is to esteem an alien w. to which illusions
T-24 III.5:2 would have no separation, like an alien w.
T-24 III.5:8 Who knows that death is not your w.,
T-24 III.5:8 "Thy w. be done" because you think it is.
T-24 III.8:9 They ask of you but that your w. be done.
T-24 V.1:8 makes real, as surely as does w. create.
T-24 VII.11:8 perceives an alien w. and wishes it were so
T-25 II.11:3 Will is brought together as you join in w.,
T-25 VIII.1:3 He wrested it from you against your w..
T-25 VIII.1:4 not learn it *is* your w. to be without it. You
T-26 VII.11:14 Or is it a mistake about your w., and what
T-26 VII.14:8 will he know himself, nor recognize his w.
T-27 I.6:3 It is not w. for life but wish for death that
T-28 III.6:2 destroy the alien w. that He created not.
T-28 VI.1:6 It does not victimize, because it has no w.,
T-28 VI.6:9 And what he substitutes is not his w., who
T-28 VII.1:8 w. can come between what must be One,
T-30 II.h Freedom of W.
T-30 II.1:2 He tells you but your w.; He speaks for
T-30 II.1:4 for you that you may do your w. through
T-30 II.1:5 God *asks* you do your w.. He joins with *you*
T-30 II.1:8 And Heaven itself but represents your w.,
T-30 II.2:1 How wonderful it is to do your w.! For
T-30 II.2:4 Unless you do your w. you are not free.
T-30 II.2:6 w. when He gave you His perfect Answer.
T-30 II.2:7 reminded of His Love and learn your w..
T-30 II.3:3 your w. to hate and be a prisoner to fear, a
T-30 II.3:4 Your w. is boundless; it is not your will
T-30 II.3:4 it is not your w. that it be bound. What
T-30 II.3:6 and through your w. created everything.
T-30 II.3:7 for it is by your w. that it was born. No
T-30 II.3:8 you, for it was set in Heaven by your w..
T-30 II.4:5 keep your w. forever and forever limitless.
T-30 II.4:7 But you w. not forgive the world until you
T-30 II.4:7 forgiven Him Who gave your w. to you.
T-30 II.4:8 it is by your w. the world is given freedom
T-30 II.5:2 shares your freedom as he shares your w..
T-30 II.5:3 It *is* your w. to heal him, and because you
T-30 III.1:2 But your w. is universal, being limitless.
T-30 III.1:8 it is your w. that everything be yours.
T-30 III.2:7 It is not your w. to have one. It will not
T-30 III.2:10 So you see your w. within the idol, thus
T-30 III.2:11 Yet this could never be your w., because
T-30 III.4:4 Your w. to be complete is but God's Will,
T-30 III.4:7 your w. could not be satisfied with empty
T-30 III.5:3 stands his holy w. to be but what he is.
T-30 III.5:10 Your w. *is* granted. Not in any form that
T-30 IV.7:4 You are but asked to let your w. be done,
T-30 IV.8:12 He is delivered from illusions by his w.,
T-30 V.11:3 they were free to learn their w. is one. And
T-31 I.3:6 to teach you that your w. is not your own,
T-31 I.5:2 w. apart from it was yet more real than it.
T-31 VI.4:3 Your w. be done! In Heaven as on earth
T-31 VI.4:7 God Himself has said, "Your w. be done."
T-31 VI.7:1 Your w. be done, you holy child of God.
T-31 VI.7:5 And you *are* worthy that your w. be done!
W-pI 20.3:7 His w. is done because all power is given
W-pI 49.3:3 we are joining our w. with the Will of God
W-pI 53.5:6 because it is not my w. that they do so.
W-pI 53.5:7 so. My w. is His, and I will place no other
W-pI 54.5:5 let it teach me that my w. and the Will of
W-pI 56.4:4 Beyond all my insane wishes is my w.,
W-pI 69.7:4 You cannot fail because your w. is His.
W-pI 69.8:4 you are at last joining your w. to God's.
W-pI 73.1:1 are considering the w. you share with God
W-pI 73.1:3 w. you share with God has all the power
W-pI 73.3:1 w. is lost to you in this strange bartering,
W-pI 73.4:1 world that is in accordance with your w..
W-pI 73.4:6 shines upon this world reflects your w.,
W-pI 73.5:4 lifts the darkness, reasserts your w., and
W-pI 73.6:6 Such is your w. in truth. And so salvation
W-pI 73.6:7 And so salvation is your w. as well. You
W-pI 73.7:3 You have no w. that can really oppose it,
W-pI 73.7:6 ego that stands powerless before your w..
W-pI 73.7:7 Your w. is free, and nothing can prevail
W-pI 73.8:1 that we will find what it is your w. to find,
W-pI 73.8:1 remember what it is your w. to remember.
W-pI 73.8:3 Today let your w. be done, and end
W-pI 73.9:1 only His, is wholly in accord with your w..
W-pI 73.9:5 His w. is now restored to his awareness.
W-pI 73.10:1 determining to keep your w. clearly in
W-pI 73.10:4 Then let your w. assert itself, joined with
W-pI 73.11:4 *light. Darkness is not my w..* This should be
W-pI 74.h There is no w. but God's.
W-pI 74.1:3 you have recognized that your w. is His.
W-pI 74.3:2 *There is no w. but God's. I cannot be in*
W-pI 74.3:7 *My w. is God's. My will and God's are one.*
W-pI 74.3:8 *My w. and God's are one. God wills peace for*
W-pI 74.3:12 *There is no w. but God's. These conflict*
W-pI 74.4:3 *There is no w. but God's. I share it with Him.*
W-pI 74.7:2 *There is no w. but God's. I seek His peace*
WpI rII.in.4:4 Do not forget that your w. has power over

W-pI.....81.4:3 *Let me not separate my function from my* **w.**
W-pI.....87.1:2 I will use the power of my **w.** today. It is
W-pI.....87.1:3 It is not my **w.** to grope about in darkness,
W-pI.....87.3:1 (74) There is no **w.** but God's. I am safe
W-pI.....87.3:2 today because there is no **w.** but God's. I
W-pI.....87.3:3 only when I believe there is another **w.**. I
W-pI.....87.3:6 I am safe because there is no **w.** but God's.
W-pI.....89.3:2 do I unite my **w.** with the Holy Spirit's,
W-pI.....91.5:4 Your **w.** remains your teacher, and your
W-pI.....91.5:4 your **w.** has all the strength to do what it
W-pI...104.3:1 we but unite our **w.** with what God wills,
W-pI...116.1:3 *the belief there is another* **w.** *apart from His.*
W-pI...125.2:2 surely to his Father's house by his own **w.**,
W-pI...125.5:4 of his madness that his **w.** is not his own.
W-pI...125.8:3 and of peace, of unity of **w.** and purpose,
W-pI...131.8:5 an alien **w.** upon God's single purpose. He
W-pI...154.4:4 in which its **w.** and that of God are joined.
W-pI.154.11:5 He needs our **w.** united with His Own,
W-pI.154.14:4 that we accept no **w.** we do not share, our
W-pI...157.4:2 having joined your **w.** with His this day,
W-pI...163.7:3 Their stronger **w.** could triumph over His,
W-pI...163.9:7 *ours, and our* **w.** *is one with Yours eternally.*
W-pI...166.1:5 And yet, unless your **w.** is one with His,
W-pI...166.1:6 you think there is another **w.** than His?
W-pI...166.2:3 real must still believe there is another **w.**,
W-pI.166.12:7 your **w.** when you accept these gifts, and
W-pI...169.6:2 when total recognition that its **w.** is God's
W-pI...184.2:4 which functions with an independent **w.**.
W-pI...190.5:7 they will accept your holy **w.** as theirs.
W-pII.....in.5:6 you have recognized it is your **w.** He do so
W-pII.....in.5:7 you saw, however dimly, that it is your **w.**.
W-pII..227.1:1 *today that I am free, because my* **w.** *is Yours.*
W-pII..227.1:2 *I thought to make another* **w.**. *Yet nothing*
W-pII..227.1:7 *Father, I know my* **w.** *is one with Yours.*
W-pII..231.2:1 This is your **w.**, my brother. And you
W-pII..231.2:2 And you share this **w.** with me, and with
W-pII..253.1:6 world to my creations, children of my **w.**,
W-pII..254.2:6 God speaks to us and tells us of our **w.**, as
W-pII..257.2:2 *today that we can have no* **w.** *but Yours. And*
W-pII..270.1:5 *him. And now his* **w.** *is one with Yours. His*
W-pII..292.1:3 let an alien **w.** appear to be opposing His.
W-pII..292.1:4 And while we think this **w.** is real, we will
W-pII..292.1:7 which guarantees that our **w.** is done.
W-pII.....307.h Conflicting wishes cannot be my **w.**.
W-pII..307.1:2 *There is no other* **w.** *for me to have. Let me*
W-pII..307.1:3 *Let me not try to make another* **w.**, *for it is*
W-pII..307.1:5 *Your Son is one with You in being and in* **w.**,
W-pII..307.2:1 because we join our holy **w.** with God's, in
W-pII..309.1:2 Son, whose **w.** is limitless as is His Own,
W-pII..309.1:4 To look within is but to find my **w.** as God
W-pII..309.1:5 I think I made another **w.** that is not true,
W-pII..320.1:4 His holy **w.** can never be denied, because
W-pII..321.1:9 *in You alone. Father, it is my* **w.** *that I return.*
W-pII..328.1:6 And since our **w.** is His, it is to Him that
W-pII..328.1:6 Him that we must go to recognize our **w.**.
W-pII..328.2:1 *There is no* **w.** *but Yours. And I am glad that*
W-pII..329.1:1 *a second* **w.** *more powerful than Yours. Yet*
W-pII..329.1:5 *where my* **w.** *became forever one with Yours*
W-pII..329.1:8 *my* **w.** *is Yours. And I am safe, untroubled*
W-pII..329.2:2 We have no **w.** apart from His, and all of
W-pII....12.1:2 "**w.**" that sees the Will of God as enemy,
W-pII.....331.h There is no conflict, for my **w.** is Yours.
W-pII..331.1:6 *There is no* **w.** *except the Will of Love. Fear is*
W-pII..331.1:7 *and has no* **w.** *that can conflict with Yours.*
W-pII331.1:11 *Will. There is no conflict, for my* **w.** *is Yours.*
W-pII..347.1:1 *Father, I want what goes against my* **w.**, *and*
W-pII..347.1:1 *will, and do not want what is my* **w.** *to have.*
W-pII347.1:10 *I do not know my* **w.**, *but He is sure it is Your*
W-pII..348.2:2 that we choose to be our **w.** as well as His.
W-ep .........2:4 Therefore obey your **w.**, and follow Him
M-2.............3:5 **w.** is free you can accept what has already
M-4........ II.2:9 because they never do their **w.** alone.
M-4.....IV.2:10 And so their **w.**, which always was His
M-5....... III.3:8 they dispelled, not by the **w.** of another,
M-5....... III.3:9 to see no **w.** as separate from their own,
M-16..........9:2 to substitute another **w.** for God's. These
M-16........11:6 "There is no **w.** but God's." His teachers
M-17..........5:4 mind which believes it has a separate **w.**
M-28..........5:9 Illusions of another **w.** are lost, for unity
C-1............7:2 **W.** is not involved in perception at any
C-3............2:2 they do not think it is their **w.** to do so.
C-5............5:5 And when you join your **w.** with his, your

## will 68

• verb
*noun*
*noise word (auxiliary verb)*
*Will*

T-3...... VI.11:8 say, "*W.* ye first the Kingdom of Heaven,"
T-6.........I.11:7 so extreme. I **w.** with God that none of His
T-7...........I.4:5 To **w.** with God is to create like Him. God
T-7....... X.4:10 impossible, but you can **w.** only with God.
T-7....... X.8:1 you are confused about what *you* **w.**. This
T-8......... II.6:4 you could no more **w.** to be without Him
T-8......... II.6:4 Him than He could **w.** to be without you.
T-8........ III.7:6 **w.** anyone to suffer for a wrong decision,
T-8...... IV.5:13 I cannot **w.** what God does not will. I can
T-8...... IV.5:13 I cannot will what God does not **w.**. I can
T-8........ VI.2:6 did not **w.** the destruction of His creations
T-8...... VI.6:10 from His, and so you must **w.** as He wills.
T-8........ VI.7:2 think you are unwilling to **w.** with God,
T-8........ VI.8:6 alone because *He* does not **w.** to be alone.
T-9.........I.11:4 creation. God could not **w.** that happiness
T-9....... II.12:6 *Because I* **w.** *to know myself, I see you as*
T-10...... III.1:3 No one can **w.** to destroy himself. When
T-11.........I.1:6 for God Himself did not **w.** to be alone.
T-11.........I.5:7 Because He did not **w.** to be alone, He
T-11.........I.6:3 you because God did not **w.** to be alone?
T-11.........I.7:8 follows, then, that you **w.** to create, since
T-11.........I.8:1 Yet what you **w.** you do not know. This is
T-11.......I.9:10 God's Son cannot **w.** death for himself
T-11.......I.10:1 be happy unless you do what you **w.** truly,
T-11.......I.11:2 forget that God did not **w.** to be alone. He
T-11....... II.1:5 And you **w.** yourself to Him because, in
T-11...... III.2:4 when He did not **w.** to be alone Himself?
T-11....... V.5:3 I said before that to **w.** contrary to God is
T-11...... VI.5:6 nothing, for He does not **w.** to take away.
T-12...... III.9:4 You still cannot **w.** against Him, and that
T-13...... III.3:4 God, and He does not **w.** to be excluded.
T-13...... III.8:3 you **w.** only to unite with the Father, in
T-13...... XI.8:7 and will always **w.** you nothing else. The
T-14...... XI.5:4 You think you do not **w.** for God's Son
T-14...... XI.5:6 that you **w.** with the Father and His Son.
T-15.... III.10:2 I **w.** as my Father wills, knowing His Will
T-15... VIII.2:6 His Son share, and **w.** to meet together.
T-20.... III.11:6 else would they go but where they **w.** to be
T-22........I.11:7 here you **w.** with Him and with His Father
T-24...... III.5:2 what He wills for you and what you **w.**.
T-24...... III.5:4 How could They **w.** the death of love itself
T-24...... III.8:4 you **w.** that this be done unto your savior?
T-24....... V.8:3 could never **w.** that you be brotherless.
T-25.........I.6:2 the Will of God and what you really **w.**.
T-25..... II.9:10 by those who **w.** to make their Father's
T-25...... VI.3:5 He **w.** that he remain without the function
T-25..... VII.2:4 what He did not **w.** cannot be changed?
T-25..... VII.7:4 nor place nor anything God did not **w.**.
T-26....... II.6:7 because you could not **w.** he suffer loss.
T-31... VIII.4:6 And what they **w.** is only what He wills.
W-pI.........73.h I **w.** there be light.
W-pI...73.10:2 *I* **w.** *there be light. Let me behold the light*
W-pI...73.11:3 *I* **w.** *there be light. Darkness is not my will.*
W-pI......75.3:5 We **w.** to see the light; the light has come.
W-pI......87.1:1 (73) I **w.** there be light. I will use the
W-pI......87.2:2 *This cannot hide the light I* **w.** *to see. You*
W-pI......92.5:3 and can only **w.** for happiness and peace
W-pI...185.3:1 what they **w.** becomes the Will of God.
W-pII.....in.7:6 We **w.** with You in asking this. The Father
W-pII.....231.h Father, I **w.** but to remember You.
W-pII..246.2:3 *I would recognize that what You* **w.** *is what I*
W-pII..246.2:3 *that what You will is what I* **w.** *as well, and*
W-pII..257.2:3 *if we would reach the peace You* **w.** *for us.*
W-pII..277.2:5 and God can **w.** that He deceive Himself.
W-pII..301.1:3 *it not, and therefore is it only what You* **w.**.
W-pII..309.1:2 as is His Own, can **w.** no change in this.
W-pII.....329.h I have already chosen what You **w.**.
M-27 .........1:7 one asks if a benign Creator could **w.** this.

## will 3958

• noise word (auxiliary verb)
*noun*
*verb*
*Will*

## willed 26

T-3...... VI.11:7 that what is wished is as real as what is **w.**.
T-4........ III.6:4 it asks only for what He has already **w.**.
T-8........ III.1:1 and to you because He has so **w.** it. Ask
T-8...... VI.10:1 What God has **w.** for you *is* yours. He has
T-8....... VII.6:3 are has **w.** your power and glory for you,
T-10.........I.4:1 you will have **w.** away the separation,
T-13...... XI.8:7 God **w.** you Heaven, and will always will
T-16..... VII.8:6 When He **w.** that His Son be free, His Son
T-19........II.4:3 created him, and **w.** that he be forever. Is
T-20.....VIII.4:1 what God **w.** and gave you shall be yours.
T-21........II.6:6 himself without what God has **w.** for him.
T-24........II.10:5 special, then He **w.** His Son to be like Him
T-24....... V.8:3 **w.** not to be without His Son could never
T-26.........I.7:3 make of Them what God **w.** not They be.
T-26... VII.13:4 of what is idly wished as what is truly **w.**,
T-26... VII.17:5 of God because his Father **w.** that it be so.
T-27... VII.13:5 God **w.** he waken gently and with joy, and
T-31.........I.6:2 God **w.** not His Son forget Him. And the
W-pI... 123.4:2 God has **w.** to be our true Identity in Him.
WpI. rIV.in6:3 Hosts be yours, as He Himself has **w.** it be
W-pI... 152.7:4 you can perceive what God **w.** not to be.
W-pI... 193.9:5 has **w.** that laughter should replace each
W-pII ....in.5:6 He has **w.** to come to you when you have
W-pII . 280.1:6 God, whose Father **w.** that he be limitless,
W-pII ... 11.2:4 What God has **w.** to be forever One will
S-2........ III.1:9 Yet He has **w.** you learn the way to Him,

## willing 143

T-1........ III.1:8 to do them, but you must be ready and **w.**
T-1........ IV.1:5 you have become **w.** to hide nothing, you
T-1........ IV.1:5 nothing, you will not only be **w.** to enter
T-1........ VI.5:2 To whatever extent you are **w.** to submit
T-2........ VI.6:2 cannot ask more than you are **w.** to do.
T-3..........II.6:3 are **w.** to accept what is true in everything
T-3......... V.5:7 to engage in it when you are **w.** to let it go.
T-3...... VI.11:6 wish is to imply that **w.** is not sufficient.
T-3....... VII.2:7 and they are **w.** to "sell" him their souls in
T-4...........I.4:7 are **w.** to renounce the role of guardian of
T-4...........I.7:5 I am **w.** to do this, because I have no right
T-4...... III.10:3 have been **w.** to exert to protect your ego,
T-5....... IV.2:6 It will increase as you are **w.** to return the
T-7...........I.4:2 It is always **w.** to strike a bargain, but it
T-7........ VI.5:3 it is **w.** to attach itself to anything else.
T-7...... VI.13:3 God's, you would be **w.** without meaning.
T-7......VIII.5:4 are **w.** to accept sole responsibility for the
T-7......... X.1:5 You are **w.** to look at the ego's premises,
T-8........ III.6:4 and you will know it if you are **w.** to look
T-8..... VII.14:4 Are you **w.** to accept this, when your
T-9...........I.5:4 you would recognize that **w.** is salvation
T-9.........I.12:2 **W.** against reality, though impossible,
T-9.......VIII.6:2 If you are **w.** to look upon your grandeur
T-10.........II.2:5 you are part of Him when you are **w.** to
T-10...... III.5:2 To obtain this you are **w.** to attack the
T-10...... III.5:3 And you are **w.** to keep it hidden, to
T-10.. III.10:11 fear you have been **w.** to give up your own
T-10...... IV.5:7 want it, if you were **w.** to see it as it is. You
T-10....... V.3:6 It means that you are **w.** not to know
T-11.......in.3:8 Be **w.** to judge it with perfect honesty.
T-11.........II.6:5 the little spark and are **w.** to let it grow.
T-11....... V.5:3 to God is wishful thinking and not real **w.**
T-11...... VI.3:6 you will become less and less **w.** to deny.
T-11....VIII.7:7 Blessed are you who are **w.** to ask the
T-11..VIII.10:3 become **w.** to accept this Help by asking
T-11..VIII.13:2 and are **w.** to let their own interpretations
T-12.........I.4:2 It is only this that makes you **w.** to engage
T-12...... III.9:2 Perhaps you are **w.** to accept even death
T-13...... III.2:4 You would be **w.** to look even upon your
T-13.... VI.12:3 who accept love of you become your **w.**
T-13........X.1:4 **w.** to look upon all kinds of "sources,"
T-14..... X.10:2 are not alone, and are **w.** to remember it.

T-14 XI.2:1 Be w., then, for all of it to be undone, and
T-14 XI.8:3 w. to acknowledge that it *is* impossible.
T-14 XI.11:8 creation, and all creation joins in w. this.
T-14 XI.12:1 who have become w. to learn everything,
T-15 I.11:4 It takes far longer to teach you to be w. to
T-15 III.4:10 God is not w. that His Son be content
T-15 III.11:1 If you are wholly w. to leave salvation to
T-15 IV.4:3 clear because you have been w. to meet its
T-15 IV.8:3 and am I wholly w. to let everything that
T-15 VII.5:5 know, but you will become w. to find out,
T-15 VII.5:5 w. first to perceive what you have made of
T-15 IX.1:3 you will become w. to make it permanent.
T-15 IX.5:2 of this and long remain w. to linger here.
T-15 X.3:2 are w. to accept our relationship as real,
T-15 X.5:3 When you are w. to regard them, not as
T-16 II.6:12 again will you be wholly w. not to listen.
T-16 III.2:5 you are w. to judge yourself accordingly.
T-16 III.8:3 as he is w. to expend some little effort on
T-16 IV.9:1 be wholly in God, w. for nothing special,
T-16 IV.9:5 God, be wholly w. to abandon all illusions
T-16 IV.9:6 you are wholly w. to accept completion,
T-16 VI.7:5 for it means only that you have been w. to
T-17 I.6:1 Be w., then, to give all you have held
T-17 III.1:5 Be w. to forgive the Son of God for what
T-17 IV.6:4 that you have been more w. to let go.
T-18 II.4:6 fearful, but this you are not w. to accept.
T-18 II.9:3 because you have been w. to let your
T-18 III.6:2 been w. to bring the darkness to light,
T-18 IV.5:13 *be w. not to substitute my own in place of it.*
T-18 VI.14:7 simply because you have been w. to let go
T-18 VII.4:1 instant, you are w. to see no past or future
T-18 IX.3:7 are w. to follow the Holy Spirit through
T-18 IX.6:3 to hold back anyone w. to climb above it
T-19 III.1:5 itself a w. captive to its sick appeal. Sin is
T-20 VII.2:4 Are you not also w. to accept the means?
T-20 VII.2:6 you must be w. to want the means as well.
T-20 VIII.3:3 is. Be w., then, to see your brother sinless,
T-21 II.4:10 accept correction if it is w. to see that it
T-21 II.5:8 Be w., then, to have it taken from him and
T-21 II.8:1 Be w., for an instant, to leave your altars
T-21 IV.4:2 you have been w. to look on much of your
T-21 IV.4:9 w. to see the Holy Spirit's purpose as its
T-21 VI.8:7 Be w. to let reason be the means by which
T-21 VII.5:6 he must be w. to perceive a world where it
T-21 VII.11:2 each one asks if you are w. to exchange
T-21 VIII.4:3 really asks if you are w. to be wholly sane.
T-22 II.13:2 who is but w. to see his brother sinless.
T-22 IV.5:8 share it have become its w. guardian and
T-23 III.5:4 Would they be w. to accept the fact their
T-25 II.1:8 only thus will you be w. to relinquish it,
T-25 IX.1:3 w. to be released from all effects of sin?
T-25 IX.2:2 disappears, and you are w. it be given you
T-26 II.7:1 when you are w. to receive correction for
T-27 VIII.5:1 How w. are you to escape effects of all the
T-29 IV.2:8 You would not then be w. to awake, for
T-29 VI.1:1 How w. are you to forgive your brother?
T-29 IX.1:1 The slave of idols is a w. slave. For willing
T-29 IX.1:2 w. he must be to let himself bow down in
T-30 I.12:2 mind, not certain yet, but w. to be shown:
T-30 II.2:9 He joins with you in w. you be free. And
T-30 VIII.4:9 he becomes the w. slave of what he chose
T-31 III.4:5 but the w. mind that would abide in it. It
T-31 IV.5:1 Who would be w. to be turned away
T-31 VII.5:3 you be w. that this happy change occur.
W-pI 5.6:1 You may also find yourself less w. to
W-pI 22.1:4 circle until he is w. to change how he sees.
W-pI 25.5:1 is crucial to your learning to be w. to give
W-pI 28.1:4 If you are w. at least to make them now,
W-pI 48.3:3 The instant you are w. to do this there is
W-pI 51.2:5 I am w. to recognize the lack of validity in
W-pI 51.3:7 now for this merely by being w. to do so.
W-pI 51.4:6 I am w. to recognize that my thoughts do
W-pI 51.5:7 that I no longer want. I am w. to let it go.
W-pI 55.4:4 I am w. to follow the Guide God has given
W-pI 59.2:4 to see today. Let me be w. to exchange my
W-pI 65.6:5 but try to get the sense of being w. to have
W-pI 68.4:1 Would you not be w. to relinquish your
W-pI 71.5:2 will, you must be w. to seek there only.
W-pI 73.9:6 w. this very day to look upon the light in
W-pI 80.1:1 If you are w. to recognize your problems,
W-pI 93.10:1 You may not be w. or even able to use the
W-pI 95.8:3 to be w. to forgive ourselves for our lapses
W-pI 121.8:2 If you are w., you can learn today to take
W-pI 126.10:3 Be w. to be taught. Be glad to hear the
W-pI 161.10:4 you will not be w. to accept the witnesses
W-pI 181.9:8 God. This instant is our w. one with His.
W-pI 182.9:2 w. to become a little Child that you might
W-pI 191.10:8 heart w. to bring your weary brothers rest
W-pI 195.7:4 gathers clarity as we are w. once again to
W-pII 268.1:3 *be w. to withdraw my wishes from its unity,*
W-pII 330.1:4 The mind that is made w. to accept God's
M-4 VIII.1:8 is w. to reconsider all his past decisions, if
M-5 III.1:4 already w. to change their minds he has
M-7 1:9 must be w. to change his mind about it.
M-14 4:5 approach it; to be w. to go in its direction.
C-in 2:3 however, be w. to overlook controversy,
P-1 3:4 sometimes even w. to "sacrifice" his "life"
P-1 4:2 must become w. to reverse his thinking,
P-1 5:2 becoming increasingly w. to see illusions
P-2 III.2:4 of this potentiality they are w. to use. The
S-2 III.1:9 to Him, and in His w. there is certainty.

## willingly 15

T-8 V.6:10 I give it w. and gladly, because I need you
T-13 VI.12:2 The attraction of light must draw you w.,
T-14 XI.4:6 dark lessons must be brought w. to truth,
T-15 IV.4:2 w. and gladly give over every plan but His
T-20 VIII.2:3 Would you not w. be free of misery, and
T-22 VI.7:5 And serve it w.. And could remembrance
T-22 VI.8:7 Accept this one and serve it w., for what
T-23 II.9:6 For enemies do not give w. to one another
T-25 VIII.1:5 You need not give it to Him wholly w., for
T-26 VII.6:2 less w. offered to truth for healing and for
T-30 V.5:3 How w. the mind can let them go when it
W-pI 97.4:2 Give, then, these minutes w., and count
W-pI 153.15:6 God. Nor will we w. give less at night, in
W-pI 169.1:4 it can be gently laid and w. received; an
W-pII 317.1:4 But when I w. and gladly go the way my

## willingness 105

*See also* Appendix C

T-2 VI.3:4 your behavior, and this *is* a matter of w..
T-2 VI.4:4 always entail a w. to be separate. At that
T-2 VI.6:1 a w. that you have not developed as yet.
T-4 VII.8:6 this joy with its individual w. to share in it
T-5 in.1:6 Joy calls forth an integrated w. to share it,
T-5 II.3:10 It takes effort and great w. to learn. It is
T-5 VII.3:5 and your w. to side with its separateness.
T-5 VII.3:6 This w. means that you do not want to be
T-6 V.C.10:1 entails a w. to relinquish everything else.
T-7 X.2:4 outcome depends on the w. to see it, but
T-7 X.2:4 its truth has nothing to do with your w..
T-8 III.2:3 upon you, being an experience of total w..
T-8 VIII.8:5 Nor can anyone doubt your w. to listen
T-8 VIII.8:7 Voice is as loud as your w. to listen. It
T-9 II.11:7 recognition of having is the w. for giving,
T-9 II.11:7 this w. can you recognize what you have.
T-9 IV.6:3 Miracles are merely the sign of your w. to
T-9 VIII.6:1 depends solely on your w. to tolerate it. If
T-10 II.2:3 the Holy Spirit only your w. to remember,
T-10 III.9:6 signify your w. to accept only the eternal.
T-10 IV.2:2 acceptance depends on your w. to have it.
T-10 IV.2:3 the w. to judge unreality for what it is. To
T-11 I.7:5 depends on your w. to give as He gives.
T-11 II.2:3 for in your w. to join them is your healing
T-11 II.4:2 And this w. opens your ears to the Voice
T-11 II.4:3 for beside your small w. to make whole
T-11 II.6:6 Your w. need not be perfect, because His
T-11 V.6:3 you. By His w. to share it, He became as
T-11 VII.2:7 necessary is a w. to perceive nothing else.
T-11 VIII.3:8 Yet your w. to learn of Him depends on
T-11 VIII.3:8 on your w. to question everything you
T-12 I.3:6 appropriate except the w. to give it to him
T-12 II.10:5 you must look at it yourself in perfect w.,
T-13 VI.12:2 you willingly, and w. is signified by giving
T-13 VII.4:4 is w. to learn the one you made is false.
T-14 V.3:5 here is to devote yourself, with active w.,
T-15 I.12:5 They attest to your w. to *be* released, and
T-15 IV.2:1 must therefore rest upon your w. to let all
T-15 IV.5:3 mind of the host of God depends on w.,
T-15 IV.8:6 is given and received with equal w., being
T-15 V.5:4 offer Him your w. to have it serve no need
T-15 VII.14:5 thoughts. The w. to communicate attracts
T-15 VIII.1:3 w. to learn of Him what the truth must be
T-15 VIII.2:5 need of your w. to strive for this that you
T-15 IX.1:4 Given this w. it will not leave you, for it *is*
T-16 II.4:5 your w. while you believe that you must
T-16 III.7:2 have chosen this by your own w. to teach.
T-16 IV.11:14 your w. to love and all the Love of God,
T-16 IV.12:2 made from your w. to unite with Him and
T-16 VI.10:7 w. to give up nothing *because* it is nothing.
T-16 VI.12:2 you. He needs only your w. to share His
T-16 VI.12:3 w. need not be complete because His is
T-16 VI.12:5 your release, His perfect w. is given you.
T-17 I.6:3 your w. to have this be accomplished. He
T-17 IV.11:3 only be accepted through your w. to focus
T-18 II.2:5 of your w. to change reality on its behalf.
T-18 III.2:3 for which you signified your w.. Fear
T-18 III.6:2 and this w. has given strength to everyone
T-18 IV.h The Little W.
T-18 IV.1:3 desire and the w. to let it come precede its
T-18 IV.2:3 But trust implicitly your w., whatever else
T-18 IV.2:8 instant lies in your w. to let it be what it is
T-18 IV.2:9 w. for this lies also your acceptance of
T-18 IV.3:7 need the strength of w. to come from you,
T-18 IV.4:1 does not come from your little w. alone. It
T-18 IV.4:2 the result of your small w. combined with
T-18 IV.4:6 not wait upon your w. for what they are.
T-18 IV.4:7 Your w. is needed only to make it possible
T-18 IV.5:6 more than simple w. to make way for it.
T-18 V.2:5 part is only to offer Him a little w. to let
T-18 V.6:1 instantly and offer the Holy Spirit your w.
T-21 II.1:2 It is the same small w. you need to have
T-22 II.13:3 And no one can remain beyond this w., if
T-22 VI.8:10 Nor will one little smile or w. to overlook
T-24 in.2:1 learn this course requires w. to question
T-24 VI.12:4 But a tiny w., a nod to God, a greeting to
T-25 IV.5:12 w. to bring the light of Heaven with you,
T-25 VIII.1:2 cannot take it from you without your w..
T-25 IX.2:4 holds out his hand in w. they be received.
T-26 VII.10:1 a little w. to overlook what is not there; a
T-26 VII.10:3 is forgiveness but a w. that truth be true?
T-28 IV.10:8 Your w. to let illusions go is all the Healer
T-30 in.1:3 thing alone; your w. to practice every step
T-30 VI.8:1 brother with the w. to see him as he is.
T-30 VI.8:2 keep a part of him outside your w. that he
W-pI 71.9:7 in proportion to your w. to hear His Voice
W-pI 71.9:9 proves that you have some w. to listen.
W-pI 89.3:4 By this idea do I express my w. to have all
W-pI 122.4:2 requests, halfhearted w. to hear, and less
W-pI 129.7:1 Practice your w. to make this change ten
W-pI 133.13:2 honest w. to value but the truly valuable
W-pI 134.16:3 been practicing thus far in w. and honesty
W-pI 136.5:2 given w. to reconsider the decision which
WI181-200 1:1 point of firming up your w. to make your
WI181-200 1:4 you will give your total w. to following the
W-pI 196.4:4 It is but w.. For what would seem to need
W-pII 9.1:3 w. to let forgiveness rest upon all things
W-pII 9.5:4 And most of all it needs your w.. Let us
M-4 I.A.7:6 He thought he learned w., but now he
M-4 I.A.7:6 that he does not know what the w. is for.
M-17 8:4 but it requires patience and abundant w..
P-2 III.2:5 The w. may come from either one at the
P-2 V.6:5 asked for more than just the smallest w.,
P-2 VI.2:4 But first the w. to question the "truth" of
S-2 III.1:6 for trust and w. to learn how to be free.

## wills 124

T-3 IV.5:4 Until then it w. only to know. Afterwards
T-3 IV.5:6 proper function only when it w. to know.
T-5 VII.3:3 He w. to keep it in perfect peace, because
T-7 IX.1:1 creative power, but God w. to release it.
T-7 IX.1:2 He no more w. you to deprive yourself of
T-7 IX.1:2 than He w. to deprive Himself of His. Do
T-7 IX.2:10 contain God, but w. to extend His Being.

T-7......... X.4:6 Yet God w.. He does not wish. Your will is
T-8......... III.7:5 God w. no one suffer. He does not will
T-8......... V.4:6 our united w. because nothing can prevail
T-8...... VI.6:10 from His, and so you must will as He w..
T-9....... VII.1:3 it? If He w. you to have it, He must have
T-9....... VII.1:8 God w. you perfect happiness now. Is it
T-11......... I.1:4 He w. His Son to be and where he is. In
T-11......... I.6:7 is His and that He w. to share with you.
T-11......... I.7:7 God w. to create, and your will is His. It
T-11....... II.1:4 your will with His, for He w. you Himself.
T-11...... III.3:1 child, if you knew what God w. for you,
T-11...... III.3:2 And what He w. has happened, for it was
T-11...... III.3:7 what God w. for Himself He wills for you,
T-11...... III.3:7 what God wills for Himself He w. for you,
T-11...... III.3:7 for you, and what He w. for you is yours.
T-11...... III.5:2 his glory, for God w. him to be glorious,
T-11...... IV.8:1 glory he w. to share as his Father shares it
T-11....... V.6:4 Who w. not to be independent of you. He
T-11... VIII.6:4 the Holy Spirit, Who w. only to restore,
T-11. VIII.12:5 you, for He w. to heal the Son of God, in
T-12........ II.3:4 Father w. you to know your brother as
T-12........ II.6:1 still want what God w., and no nightmare
T-12...... VI.2:3 you what He loves, for He w. to share it.
T-12... VII.10:6 Who w. to extend His peace through you.
T-13... VII.12:8 He w. no delay to wait upon your joyous
T-13...... XI.7:1 be sufficient: God w. you be in Heaven,
T-13...... XI.7:3 prevail against the peace God w. for you.
T-13...... XI.8:9 is sure, and what He w. is as sure as He is.
T-14.... III.11:6 are worthy of everything God w. for you.
T-14.... III.14:3 learn that what God w. for you *is* your will.
T-14. VIII.2:14 w. with His Son is quite impossible here.
T-14..... X.12:8 Who w. to be with His Son forever, will
T-14...... XI.5:4 for God's Son what his Father w. for him.
T-15...... III.6:2 side against Him in what He w. for you.
T-15.... III.10:2 I will as my Father w., knowing His Will is
T-15...... IV.1:1 you believe that what God w. takes time.
T-15.... VI.5:10 the laws of God as what he gladly w., it is
T-15... VIII.3:7 and nothing that he w. can be denied.
T-16....... II.7:7 God w. you better. Could you not look
T-18...... IV.3:6 believe He cannot enter where He w. to be
T-18...... IV.8:4 Everything God w. is not only possible,
T-18....... V.3:4 Yet it is possible, because God w. it. Nor
T-19...... III.6:5 have created what w. to destroy Him, and
T19... IV.C.3:3 death, w. not that you be bound by them.
T-21..... II.11:5 made has power to make you what it w.,
T-21...... III.6:4 value as a means for what He w. for you.
T-21....... V.5:2 for what God w. for him he must receive.
T-21....... V.5:3 For God w. not apart from him, nor does
T-22....... II.5:6 Whom nothing He w. can be impossible,
T-22....... II.6:5 *You* know what your Creator w. is possible
T-22..... II.12:6 has no exceptions, and what it w. is true.
T-22...... VI.7:4 interfere with those whose w. are His, and
T-22...... VI.7:4 and they will recognize their w. are His,
T-24....... in.1:6 it be He cannot enter where He w. to be?
T-24...... III.5:2 rise between what He w. for you and what
T-24...... III.5:3 the same, for neither One w. specialness.
T-24...... VI.2:3 For what God w. is whole, and part of
T-24.... VI.13:5 all, for only what His Father w. is possible
T-25...... VI.1:8 And being in accord with what God w.,
T-26... VII.11:2 He w. His Son have everything. And this
T-26... VII.13:2 God w. you learn what always has been
T-26... VII.16:6 instead of what his Father w. for him. Yet
T-26... VII.16:7 because his Father w. that he should live.
T-26... VII.18:3 little senseless wish instead of what He w.
T-27....... IV.1:7 for what He w. already has been done.
T-28....... I.15:6 Father w. that he be lifted up and gently
T-28....... I.15:8 no fear that He will fail in what He w..
T-28...... III.6:4 thus make room for Him Who w. to come
T-28...... IV.7:5 gone if someone w. to be united with him.
T-28..... VII.1:6 untrue to what He w. as part of what He is
T-30...... II.4:4 Think not He w. to bind you, Who has
T-31...... VI.7:3 your Father w. of you can never change.
T-31... VIII.4:6 And what they will is only what He w..
W-pI..... 74.3:9 *one. God w. peace for His Son.* During this
W-pI..... 89.3:6 and only Heaven, as God w. me to have.
W-pI..... 99.8:3 upon no obstacle to what He w. for you.
W-pI... 100.2:3 that you might be restored to what He w..
W-pI... 100.4:4 They are the proof that God w. perfect
W-pI... 100.5:4 how great the happiness He w. for you.
W-pI... 100.6:3 and w. no sorrow rises to abate his joy; no
W-pI... 104.1:3 Who cannot fail to give you what He w..
W-pI... 104.3:1 we but unite our will with what God w.,
W-pI... 105.9:2 call to Him to give you what He w. to give,
W-pI... 105.9:2 He wills to give, and w. you to receive.
W-pI... 105.9:3 not to interfere today with what He w..
W-pI... 107.6:8 Your Father w. these dreams be gone. Let
W-pI... 122.7:6 God w. salvation be received today, and
W-pI... 125.1:2 Your Father w. you hear His Word today.
W-pI... 125.5:4 Son, and w. that he remain as part of Him
W-pI... 131.6:4 be, if it is where God w. His Son to be.
W-pI... 131.6:6 What He w. is now, without a past and
W-pI... 131.8:6 He is here because He w. to be, and what
W-pI... 131.8:6 wills to be, and what He w. is present now
W-pI. 136.12:5 what God w. for you must be received.
W-pI. 136.13:5 Yet what He w. is here, and you remain as
WpI. rIV.in9:2 and all our Father w. that we receive as
WpIrIV.in10:2 in the peace wherein He w. you be forever
W-pI. 151.14:1 and the happiness God w. His Son, as
W-pI. 154.11:4 He needs our feet to bring us where He w.
W-pI... 157.4:1 for what you ask for now is what He w..
W-pI... 165.1:2 and the eternal life your Father w. for you
W-pI... 166.2:3 leads to opposite effects from those He w.
W-pI. 167.11:1 it, and w. it be forever and forever. He is
WpI... rV.in9:8 Our Father w. His Son be one with Him.
W-pI. 185.12:2 when you but ask for what He w. for you?
W-pI... 186.1:6 It unites all w. on earth in Heaven's plan
W-pI... 193.1:2 He w. the happiness His Son inherited of
W-pII..... 235.h God in His mercy w. that I be saved.
W-pII.. 235.1:1 myself, "God w. that I be saved from this,
W-pII.. 235.1:5 saved because God in His mercy w. it so.
W-pII.. 255.1:6 to finding what my Father w. for me,
W-pII...... 7.5:4 when all He w. is that you be complete?
W-pII.. 320.1:3 w. with his Creator and Redeemer must
W-pII.. 328.1:4 This is not what our Father w. for us, nor
W-ep......... 5:3 You will be told exactly what God w. for
S-2........ III.2:2 is, and how to give it as He w. it be. Do
S-3........ IV.1:6 because they know that this is what He w.

## win 8

T-6........ III.4:5 Only thus can you w. back the knowledge
T-23......... I.8:7 nothing cannot w. reality through battle.
T-23...... IV.8:7 can offer something you can w.. Can it be
T-25...... IX.4:5 is decided who shall w. and who shall lose
W-pI. 153.12:4 Everyone who plays must w., and in his
W-pI... 200.2:2 Attempt no more to w. through losing,
W-pI... 200.3:2 Ask for this, and you can only w.. To ask
M-25......... 5:3 temptation to w. back strength by guile.

## wind 7

*See also* wind-swept

T-18......... I.7:6 like feathers dancing insanely in the w.,
T-18......... I.8:1 Let them all go, dancing in the w.,
T-23......... I.4:7 as ridiculous as nature roaring at the w. in
T-24...... VI.1:3 will scatter with the w. and turn to dust.
T-28.... VII.3:4 and count on it as shelter from the w.?
T-28.... VII.5:11 The w. will topple it, and rain will come
W-pI... 156.4:4 while the w. sinks to a whisper round

## wind-swept 1

W-pI... 186.9:5 They blow across his mind like w. leaves

## window 6

T-24... VI.11:3 and every w. barred against the light.
W-pI.......... 1.h in this room [on this street, from this w.,
W-pI.......... 2.h in this room [on this street, from this w.,
W-pI.......... 3.h in this room [on this street, from this w.,
W-pI.......... 4.h in this room [on this street, from this w.,
W-pI..... 37.4:3 *My holiness blesses that w.. My holiness*

## windows 1

T-28... VII.5:10 and lock the w. and make fast the bolts.

## winds 4

T-25...... IX.7:8 and peace be scattered by the w. of hate.
T-28..... VII.7:3 The w. will blow upon it and the rain will
W-pI... 109.4:2 and while the world is torn by w. of hate
M-1........... 4:4 Yet it is time alone that w. on wearily, and

## wing 1

S-3........ IV.2:3 w. and all the living things upon the earth

## wings 14

T-16......... I.6:2 it silently by enveloping it in healing w..
T19. IV.A.4:11 away so quietly beneath the w. of peace.
T19.... IV.A.9:1 feather be before the great w. of truth?
T-20...... IV.4:7 for those with little w. have not accepted
W-pI... 95.14:8 the gentle rustling of the w. of peace.
W-pI... 101.7:3 today's idea brings w. to speed you on,
W-pI... 107.5:1 come it harbors in its w. the gift of perfect
W-pI... 109.6:1 glad, a bird with broken w. begins to sing,
W-pI... 121.2:1 no place where it can spread its w. in
W-pI... 128.6:4 But free its w., and it will fly in sureness
W-pI... 183.2:2 they spread out their w. to keep you safe,
M-4......... I.2:2 would attempt to fly with the tiny w. of a
S-2......... in.1:1 Forgiveness offers w. to prayer, to make
S-2......... II.8:8 Your w. are free, and prayer will lift you

## winning 2

T19.... IV.A.5:4 Each is a gentle w. over from the appeal of
W-pI. 153.12:4 in his w. is the gain to everyone ensured.

## winter 1

T-26...... IX.7:3 him from bitter w. and the freezing cold.

## winter's 1

T19.... IV.A.9:6 and shiver in remembrance of the w. cold

## wipe 4

T-26.... VIII.3:4 *would* w. out the space you see between
W-pII.... 301.h And God Himself shall w. away all tears.
W-pII.... 10.4:3 can heal all sorrow, w. away all tears, and
W-pII. 336.2:1 *quiet may forgiveness w. away my dreams of*

## wiped 3

T-27......... I.5:5 tear is w. away in laughter and in love.
W-pI..... 94.1:3 held are w. away forever by this one idea.
W-pI... 193.9:4 And He would have all tears be w. away,

## wisdom 24

T-1.......... II.3:7 and obedience for his greater w.. He is
T-3........... I.7:4 is w. because it is unaware of evil, and evil
T-3.......... II.2:4 universal application that it becomes w..
T-5...... IV.8:13 My judgment is as strong as the w. of God
T-6......... V.4:1 and those who lack w. *are* children. Yet He
T-14.... III.13:2 His w. is capable of guiding you to follow
T-14.... III.16:4 Learn of His w. and His Love, and teach
T-18........ II.6:1 The Holy Spirit, ever practical in His w.,
T-25.... VIII.2:6 little faith that w. could be found in such
T-29...... IX.6:4 powerful, but with the little w. of a child.
T-30....... I.11:1 grain of w. will suffice to take you further.
WpI. rIII.in6:5 The w. of your mind will come to your
W-pI. 135.11:2 through listening to w. that is not its own.
W-pI... 186.4:3 our strengths, our w. and our holiness.
W-pI... 186.6:2 the w. and the holiness to go beyond all
W-pII. 233.1:7 *who questions not the w. of the Infinite, nor*
M-10......... 1:2 world. It is actually confused with w., and
M-10......... 4:5 making? W. is not judgment; it is the
M-23......... 6:3 It is to them that w. should appeal. There
M-24......... 3:5 part of w. to add sectarian controversies
M-29......... 5:8 that w. will be given you when you need it
P-1............ 1:4 given everyone a Teacher Whose w. and
P-2....... VII.5:6 assume he has such w. except in madness.

T-26...VII.19:2 the peace in which your w. are fulfilled.
T-26...VII.19:8 No w. lie between a brother and his own.
T-27......IV.6:3 to separate your w. from the answer, so it
T-28....... II.7:6 to show him that his w. have been done.
T-29......IX.4:8 real, nor recognize their w. are their own.
T-30......IV.7:5 the strength of idle w. for the Will of God.
T-31..... V.15:8 see a picture of your secret w.. Nothing
W-pI.....56.1:4 All my hopes and w. and plans appear to
W-pI.....56.4:4 Beyond all my insane w. is my will, united
W-pI.....57.1:9 I would give up my insane w. and walk
W-pI.....73.1:2 This is not the same as the ego's idle w.,
W-pI.....73.1:4 in it. The ego's idle w. are unshared, and
W-pI.....73.1:5 Its w. are not idle in the sense that they
W-pI.....73.2:1 Idle w. and grievances are partners or co-
W-pI.....73.2:2 The w. of the ego gave rise to it, and the
W-pI.....73.4:5 The ego's idle w. have been withdrawn.
W-pI.....73.8:2 No idle w. can detain us, nor deceive us
W-pI.....73.9:4 Son of God from hell and from all idle w..
W-pI...101.4:4 match the vicious w. in which sin is born.
W-pI...121.4:3 wants to live, yet w. it were dead. It wants
W-pI...132.4:3 And what you behold upon it are your w.,
W-pI.136.16:4 It will be healed of all the sickly w. that it
W-pI...163.2:2 all hopes and w. in its blighting grasp; all
W-pI.166.13:2 not understand they but pursue their w..
W-pI...188.9:6 clean of strange desires and disordered w.
W-pI...190.7:5 Your idle w. represent its pains. Your
W-pII..268.1:3 *be willing to withdraw my w. from its unity,*
W-pII.....307.h Conflicting w. cannot be my will.
W-pII..325.1:4 From insane w. comes an insane world.
M-7............6:8 Doubt is the result of conflicting w.. Be
M-28..........1:9 all other w. and all other concerns. It is
C-3.............7:1 There are no w. now for wishes change.
C-3.............7:1 There are no wishes now for w. change.
S-1........IV.1:6 Their separate w. are their arsenals; their
S-1........IV.3:2 satisfied; all separate w. unified in one.

### wishful 2

T-11....... V.5:3 to God is w. thinking and not real willing.
T-21....... II.9:1 We have already said that w. thinking is

### wishing 1

T-24....... V.1:8 is so. W. makes real, as surely as does will

### wisp 2

T19... IV.A.9:4 this little w. is lifted up and carried away,
T-21.........I.6:2 with you, but just a little w. of melody,

### with 3053

### withdraw 22

T-3......... II.6:1 to correct distortions is to w. your faith in
T-4......... I.10:1 it you will w. all protection from the ego,
T-4......IV.8:10 judged truly and you must w. allegiance,
T-4........VI.8:1 you w. from him I become distant to you.
T-6........IV.1:4 maker may w. his support from it at any
T-7.......VII.4:4 illusions is to w. all investment from them
T-8........IX.7:6 Yet you cannot w. from me alone. You
T-8........IX.7:7 You can only w. from yourself *and* me.
T-9...... VIII.3:4 to attack now or to w. to attack later. If
T-12....... II.2:4 to it. He must himself w. that power,
T-15......IX.6:4 What you invest in guilt you w. from God
T-21......IV.6:6 that all the gifts it would w. from you, in
T-29.........I.3:7 you approached, did he but instantly w..
W-pI.....25.2:5 will try to w. the goals you have assigned
W-pI.....28.3:1 you are making a commitment to w. your
W-pI.....28.5:1 if you would w. all your own ideas from it,
W-pI.....53.3:7 Now I choose to w. this belief, and place
WpI. rIII.in4:3 When you w. the value given them, allow
W-pI...127.8:4 W. all value you have placed upon its
W-pI.153.16:4 and we will be unable to w. a little while,
W-pI...197.6:1 W. the gifts you give, and you will think
W-pII..268.1:3 *me be willing to w. my wishes from its unity,*

### withdrawal 3

W-pI.....74.5:3 to mistake these attempts for w., but the
W-pI.....74.6:3 it. If you feel yourself slipping off into w.,
W-pI.....74.6:5 gain in refusing to allow retreat into w.,

### withdrawing 6

T-7..... VIII.5:2 it, so you can dispel it by w. belief from it.
T-8........ IX.3:6 Sleep is w.; waking is joining. Dreams are
T-8........ IX.7:5 If you are sick you are w. from me. Yet
T-15.....VII.3:2 it clearly, and by w. your investment in it,
T-21...... III.3:4 in them, w. faith that they can hold him,
W-pI.....55.5:7 real purpose by w. the one I have given it,

### withdrawn 16

T-8.......VII.6:4 He has not w. His gifts from you, but you
T-8.......VII.6:4 you believe you have w. them from Him.
T-11......IV.4:5 painful, for as blame is w. from without,
T-13....... V.6:1 to you that you have w. into insanity. You
T-14.....VII.4:6 acceptance must be w. from one of them.
T-16......VI.4:7 investment in seeing it would be w. from
T-18.....VII.7:2 have w. the body's value from your mind.
T-26......III.7:7 has been w. from what was never true,
T-29... VIII.6:1 by belief, and when it is w. the idol "dies."
W-pI.....73.4:5 The ego's idle wishes have been w.. Yet
W-pI...184.7:5 can be w. as they are raised to doubt.
W-pI...197.1:4 be received with honor, lest they be w..
W-pI...197.6:1 think that what is given you has been w..
M-7 ...........3:9 He thought the gifts of God could be w..
M-16 .....11:10 Fear is w. from them, and so they go. And
M-25 .........5:2 investment has been w. from the world's

### withdraws 2

T-28....... V.1:8 But who w. his mind from sharing them *is*
M-22 .........7:8 he w. his judgment from the Son of God,

### wither 2

T-3.......VII.6:1 no fruit will be cut off and will w. away.
T-13.....in.2:10 bodies w. and gasp and are laid in the

### withered 2

T-18......IX.1:9 the w. kingdom in which you set it off,
W-pI...163.2:2 to hold all living things within its w. hand

### withering 4

T-20..... II.10:3 cold chill of fear and w. blight of sin alike.
T-26......IX.3:8 all the blight and w. have passed forever
W-pI...190.9:4 and put aside the w. assaults with which
S-2 ..........I.7:4 God's mercy would remove this w. and

### withers 1

T-24...VII.10:3 It grows and w., flourishes and dies. And

### withheld 26

T-5........IV.7:3 of God's ideas is w. from the Kingdom.
T-7.........I.7:15 is fully shared be w. and then revealed?
T-15... VIII.4:2 gift, for as He w. Himself not from you,
T-15... VIII.4:2 not from you, He w. not His creation.
T-17...... VI.7:4 denied, being w. from where it rightfully
T-17... VIII.1:3 of faithlessness, w. and left unused, that
T-17... VIII.3:6 fact, from which faith can no longer be w.
T19... IV.A.4:7 Salvation cannot be w. from you. It is
T-23..... II.10:1 position and attack for what has been w.;
T-23...... III.4:5 Forgiveness cannot be w. a little. Nor is it
T-25...... IX.6:7 some, to be w. from others as less worthy,
T-26... VIII.3:8 in which forgiveness is w. a little while.
T-26... VIII.3:9 is w. from you and given seem dangerous,
T-26...... IX.5:1 for this gift of what has been w. so long.
T-27....... V.4:6 for you have w. its peace and comfort,
T-30... VIII.4:4 have asked it be w. from power to heal all
T-31...VII.15:2 vision is w. and what they see is death.
W-pI... 126.4:1 a gift bestowed at times, at other times w.
W-pI... 126.4:2 it fair that you should suffer when it is w..
W-pI... 127.2:4 remain itself although it is w. from others
W-pI... 151.4:2 not because it is a right to be w. from you.
W-pI. 187.11:4 have it be w. from anything we look upon
M-22 ....... 1:12 heal? What miracle can be w. from him?
M-22 ......... 7:9 should be given and where it should be w.
M-25 ......... 4:9 for what is w. from love is given to fear,
C-2............. 9:3 No miracle is now w. from anyone. The

### withhold 30

T-7........ IX.1:3 Do not w. your gifts to the Sonship, or
T-7........ IX.1:3 the Sonship, or you w. yourself from God!
T-8........ VI.6:3 w. creation from you because His joy is in
T-11....VIII.4:1 No one can w. truth except from himself.
T-12.........I.4:3 and which you therefore w. from yourself.
T-14....... V.3:8 for you will not w. it from them alone.
T-14....... V.5:4 Do not w. this glad acknowledgment, for
T-14...... XI.9:1 have you give He would w. from you? You
T-17.........I.3:1 are some things you would w. from truth.
T-17..... V.10:4 in His blessing, and w. not yours upon it.
T-17....VIII.6:4 forever changeless can you now w. from it
T19. IV.D.15:6 Let him w. it not, for by receiving it you
T-20.. VI.12:11 And can they long w. the memory of their
T-21........II.4:2 W. it, and you keep the world as now you
T-22...... VI.9:7 He will w. no blessing from it, nor limit it
T-23...... III.2:5 W. forgiveness from your brother and
T-24.........I.1:2 w. the smallest gift is not to know love's
T-24...... VI.8:2 His errors cannot w. God's blessing from
T-24..... VII.1:3 his specialness demands does he w..
T-25....VIII.1:2 But He cannot use what you w., for He
T-27....... V.7:4 No reinforcement will its thanks w. from
T-28...... III.2:3 you w. agreement and accept the part you
W-pI.....46.1:4 illusions, while those who w. forgiveness
W-pI... 164.9:8 Can you w. so little, when His Hand holds
W-pI. 166.14:3 If you are sick, you but w. their healing.
W-pI. 191.10:6 Do not w. salvation longer. Look about
W-pII .279.2:3 *Would You w. the gifts You gave to me?*
W-ep ......... 1:6 He will not w. all answers that you need
M-22 ......... 2:9 what was required, would God w. the rest
P-3........ III.2:8 To w. it from where it rightfully belongs

### withholding 2

T-19.........I.8:3 by w. faith you see what is unworthy of it,
W-pI... 126.4:2 Unmerited, w. it is just, nor is it fair that

### withholds 2

T-10..... V.14:1 because love shares and arrogance w.. As
T-26...... IV.6:2 that w. the wealth of Heaven from you.

### within 505

T-1..........II.6:9 it, thus eliminating certain intervals w. it.
T-1....... II.6:10 however, w. the larger temporal sequence
T-1........ III.7:5 the Host w. and the stranger without.
T-1........ IV.2:9 shell and is unaware of the spirit w.. But
T-2...........I.3:9 It still remains w. you, however, to extend
T-2........ III.1:1 Atonement can only be accepted w. you
T-2........ III.2:4 heals the separation by placing w. you the
T-2........ III.4:3 Spiritual vision looks w. and recognizes
T-2....... V.10:4 still lies w. the limitations of this world.
T-3..........II.5:5 One. There is no confusion w. Its Levels,
T-3....... III.5:12 the altar w. and is timeless because it is
T-4...........I.2:7 the ego nor reduce the conflict w. it. The
T-4...........I.8:5 of your ego but w. easy reach of spirit.
T-4........ III.1:1 of Heaven is w. you" really means. This is
T-4........ III.1:3 word "w." is unnecessary. The Kingdom
T-5..........II.3:4 choose to hear one of two voices w. you.
T-5..... II.10:10 only this through the Holy Spirit w. you,
T-5....... II.12:6 away as you answer the Holy Spirit w. you
T-5........ IV.1:4 but entirely w. your ability to accept. It
T-5........ IV.8:6 They came from the Holy Spirit w. you,
T-5....... VII.6:4 nevertheless w. you because God placed it
T-6..........II.8:2 united w. themselves and with each other
T-6........ IV.2:2 why attack w. the Kingdom is impossible.
T-6........ IV.2:4 not remain w. the Kingdom without love,

| | |
|---|---|
| T-6....V.C.4:10 | direct it towards creation **w.** the Kingdom |
| T-6......V.C.9:1 | illusions and therefore **w.** the Kingdom. |
| T-7......... II.2:2 | This places you both **w.** the Kingdom, |
| T-7..... V.10:11 | because it encompasses all things **w.** itself |
| T-7........ VI.7:4 | conflicting components **w.** it that have led |
| T-7......VIII.3:8 | outside you have excluded it from **w.** is a |
| T-8...........I.3:8 | understand the state that prevails **w.** it. |
| T-8......... II.7:1 | limit, and all power and glory lie **w.** it. It |
| T-8........ IV.4:6 | You must accept guidance from **w.**. The |
| T-9...........I.3:8 | effort, **w.** the limits you impose on Him, |
| T-9.........I.14:5 | for truth, for truth can only be **w.** you. |
| T-9....... VII.6:1 | an insane belief system from **w.** it. Its |
| T-9....... VII.6:6 | **W.** the system that dictated this choice |
| T-9....... VII.6:8 | meaningless **w.** the ego's thought system, |
| T-9....... VII.7:5 | it, because **w.** it its foundation does stand. |
| T-9....VIII.10:3 | Himself keeps your extensions safe **w.**. it. |
| T-11...... IV.4:5 | there is a strong tendency to harbor it **w.**. |
| T-11...... IV.4:6 | is no distinction between **w.** and without. |
| T-11...... VI.9:1 | own call, for the Call to awake is **w.** you. If |
| T-11....VIII.8:3 | The Kingdom of Heaven *is* **w.** you. Believe |
| T-12.........I.2:5 | pitting one level **w.** it against another. |
| T-12...... III.7:3 | opposed thoughts **w.** itself is intolerable. |
| T-12...... IV.5:4 | You do not remember how to look **w.** for |
| T-12........VII.h | Looking **W.** |
| T-12..... VII.7:8 | a divided world outside itself, but not **w.**. |
| T-12..... VII.9:5 | looked **w.** and thought you saw the power |
| T-12..... VII.9:5 | power to give something else **w.** yourself. |
| T-12... VII.10:1 | looked **w.** and are afraid of what you saw. |
| T-12... VII.11:6 | And you will see me as you look **w.**, and |
| T-12... VII.12:1 | When you look **w.** and see me, it will be |
| T-12... VII.12:2 | it you will see it both without and **w.**. You |
| T-12... VII.12:3 | see it without *because* you saw it first **w.**. |
| T-12... VII.12:4 | is a judgment of what you beheld **w.**. If it |
| T-12... VII.15:2 | this is true when you look **w.** and *see* me. |
| T-12....VIII.1:2 | has hidden His Son safely **w.** Himself, and |
| T-13...... III.1:9 | find **w.** yourself something you fear even |
| T-13....... V.4:3 | where what is **w.** appears to be without. |
| T-13....... V.4:4 | Yet what is **w.** they do not see, for the |
| T-13....... V.9:2 | Beyond this darkness, and yet still **w.** you, |
| T-13....... V.9:6 | He loves what He sees **w.** you, and He |
| T-13..... V.10:5 | dreams He sees God's guiltless Son **w.** you |
| T-13..... V.11:5 | because they looked **w.** and saw beyond |
| T-13..... VI.6:3 | All healing lies **w.** it because its continuity |
| T-13..... VII.5:9 | He lives **w.** you in the quiet present, and |
| T-13..... VII.7:5 | on love, for it is all about him and **w.** him. |
| T-13... VII.13:7 | **W.** himself he has no needs, for light |
| T-13....... IX.7:1 | for while you see one spot of guilt **w.** you, |
| T-13....... IX.7:3 | cannot see it because you cannot look **w.**. |
| T-13....... IX.7:6 | you would look **w.** you would see only the |
| T-13....... IX.8:1 | Do not be afraid to look **w.**. The ego tells |
| T-13....... IX.8:2 | ego tells you all is black with guilt **w.** you, |
| T-13....... IX.8:5 | are too afraid to look upon the light **w.**. |
| T-13....... IX.8:6 | **W.** you is not what you believe is there, |
| T-13....... IX.8:7 | in. **W.** you is the holy sign of perfect faith |
| T-13... IX.8:13 | then, upon the light He placed **w.** you, |
| T-13....... X.3:5 | suffer, they will not look **w.** and let it go. |
| T-13....... X.5:5 | shone **w.** you all the while you dreamed of |
| T-13....... X.5:5 | of guilt, and would not look **w.** and see it. |
| T-13....... X.6:1 | whatever he may do, you will not look **w.**, |
| T-13....... X.8:4 | has looked **w.** and seen the radiance there |
| T-13....... X.9:4 | shining peace **w.** you is the perfect purity |
| T-13...... X.10:2 | no other way to look **w.** and see the light |
| T-13...... X.10:5 | reason, to look **w.** and see your holiness. |
| T-13... X.10:11 | perfect purity that is forever **w.** God's Son |
| T-13...... X.12:2 | guilt and wholly loving, is bright **w.** you. |
| T-13...... XI.8:1 | Link that God Himself placed **w.** you, |
| T-13... XI.10:1 | God has placed **w.** him the glad Call to |
| T-14.... III.18:2 | Him, and with everything that is **w.** Him, |
| T-14.... III.18:2 | that is within Him, as it is **w.** yourself. |
| T-14...... IV.1:3 | of your brother's guiltlessness shining **w.** |
| T-14...... IV.4:6 | you out of Himself, but still **w.** Him. He |
| T-14.... IV.10:5 | have placed **w.** your mind cannot exist, |
| T-14....... V.4:5 | veils of guilt **w.** which the Son of God has |
| T-14....... V.7:7 | bring **w.** its safety and its perfect peace. |
| T-14....... V.8:3 | **W.** its holy circle is everyone whom God |
| T-14....... V.8:6 | Stand quietly **w.** this circle, and attract all |
| T-14....... V.8:7 | Abide with me **w.** it, as a teacher of |
| T-14....... V.9:4 | I stand **w.** the circle, calling you to peace. |
| T-14....... V.9:8 | Stand not outside, but join with me **w.**. |
| T-14 .... V.11:1 | Each one you see you place **w.** the holy |
| T-14 .... V.11:9 | of us, united as one **w.** the Cause of peace. |
| T-14 ..... VI.2:1 | dwells **w.** you is merely perfect openness, |
| T-14 .... VII.2:4 | It is there, wherever you are, being **w.** you |
| T-14 .VIII.2:10 | All this is safe **w.** you, where the Holy |
| T-14 ..... IX.3:9 | the Presence that dwells **w.** it *is* Holiness. |
| T-15 ..... IV.5:1 | I stand **w.** the holy instant, as clear as you |
| T-15 ..... VI.1:2 | part of a relationship and find peace **w.** it. |
| T-15 ..... VI.5:4 | By holding it **w.** itself, there *is* no loss. The |
| T-15 ..... XI.2:2 | yourself, but shining in the Heaven **w.**, |
| T-15 ..... XI.4:7 | as loathsome, and live **w.** himself in peace |
| T-16 ..... III.4:4 | Yet **w.** you is everything you taught. What |
| T-16 ..... III.8:4 | make Heaven what it is, being joined **w.** it |
| T-16 ..... IV.3:3 | barricades against it, and keep **w.** them. |
| T-16 ..... IV.6:1 | **w.** yourself that you have built against it. |
| T-16 ..... IV.6:5 | can be certain that you perceive hatred **w.** |
| T-16 ..... VI.6:3 | holds the Great Rays **w.** it is also visible, |
| T-16 ... VI.11:5 | that returns to take its rightful place **w.** it. |
| T-17 ..... IV.4:4 | holds **w.** itself the truth about everything. |
| T-17 .... V.12:2 | awareness of time, but not concealed **w.** it |
| T-17 .... V.14:6 | Yet because it is **w.**, the gladness, too, is |
| T-18 ........I.6:6 | to this could only remain **w.** in quiet, and |
| T-18 ........I.7:5 | truth is outside, and error and guilt **w.**. |
| T-18 ........I.8:2 | you. And turn you to the stately calm **w.**, |
| T-18 ........I.8:3 | you gently back to the truth and safety **w.**. |
| T-18 ........I.9:3 | **W.** yourself you love your brother with a |
| T-18 .......I.11:7 | The universe **w.** you stands with you, |
| T-18 .......I.12:4 | the loveliness and joy the other holds **w.** it |
| T-18 .......II.5:3 | Yet here is a world, clearly **w.** your mind, |
| T-18 .......II.7:2 | will share with all who come **w.** your sight |
| T-18 ...... V.5:3 | All that remains of dreams **w.** it is that it |
| T-18 ...... VI.1:6 | outside this Oneness, and nothing else **w.**. |
| T-18 ...... VI.8:8 | out. **W.** itself it has no limits, and there is |
| T-18 ... VI.8:10 | you entirely; you **w.** it and it within you. |
| T-18 ... VI.8:10 | you entirely; you within it and it **w.** you. |
| T-18 ... VI.14:3 | to you to be yourself, **w.** its safe embrace. |
| T-18 .... VII.7:7 | make a place **w.** you where the activity of |
| T-18 ... VIII.1:5 | see yourself **w.** a body know yourself as an |
| T-18 ... VIII.2:6 | proclaiming that **w.** it is your kingdom, |
| T-18 ... VIII.3:1 | **W.** this kingdom the ego rules, and |
| T-18 ... VIII.7:5 | Would you remain **w.** your tiny kingdom, |
| T-18 ... IX.1:10 | **W.** its barricades is still a tiny segment of |
| T-18 ... IX.12:2 | Its meaning lies **w.** itself. And learning |
| T-18 ... IX.14:3 | carrying it, safe and sure **w.** its gentleness, |
| T-19 ..... IV.1:6 | He lay, deep **w.** you and your brother, will |
| T-19 ..... IV.2:2 | the peace that already lies deeply **w.** must |
| T19....IV.A.1:5 | how can it abide **w.** the Son of God? If it |
| T19....IV.A.3:1 | Spirit's purpose rests in peace **w.** you. Yet |
| T19....IV.B.5:4 | for we stand **w.** the gates and not outside. |
| T19....IV.B.5:5 | How easily the gates are opened from **w.**, |
| T19....IV.B.6:6 | what I signify to you you see **w.** yourself? |
| T19....IV.B.7:2 | Salvation flows from deep **w.** the home |
| T19....IV.B.8:3 | I am **w.** your holy relationship, yet you |
| T19..IV.B.16:5 | **w.** which is his death equally inevitable. |
| T19....IV.C.9:6 | is deathless, and **w.** it lies the end of death |
| T19... IV.D.7:7 | from beyond the veil is also deep **w.** you, |
| T19. IV.D.18:3 | the sins he thinks he sees **w.** himself. |
| T19. IV.D.21:3 | safely **w.** the sure protection of his Father. |
| T-20 .......II.9:2 | shining from the holy altar **w.** him where |
| T-20 .......II.9:5 | The holiness that leads us is **w.** us, as is |
| T-20 .....II.10:2 | in his communion with all that is **w.** him. |
| T-20 ..... III.3:2 | **w.** the truth they recognize their holiness, |
| T-20 ..... III.4:7 | look out in sorrow from what is sad **w.**, |
| T-20 ... III.11:4 | Looking with charity **w.**, what can it fear |
| T-20 ... III.11:5 | and the pure in heart see God **w.** His Son, |
| T-20 ..... IV.3:3 | would see **w.** your savior from insanity? |
| T-20 ..... IV.5:2 | the power of sinlessness **w.** your brother, |
| T-20 ..... VI.6:8 | realize is what you fear **w.** your brother, |
| T-20 ... VI.10:2 | Holy Spirit rests **w.** it in the certainty it |
| T-20 ... VIII.7:2 | bringing them gently **w.** the kindly sway |
| T-20 ... VIII.9:6 | the outside world, projected from **w.**, |
| T-20 . VIII.10:2 | meaning always looks **w.** to find itself, |
| T-20 . VIII.10:3 | must thus reflect the sight you saw **w.**; or |
| T-21 ......in.2:8 | the power to give it joy must lie **w.** you. |
| T-21 ........I.8:5 | anywhere. **W.** it everything is joined in |
| T-21 ........I.9:3 | you are; a part of this, with all of it **w.**, |
| T-21 .......II.3:4 | possible **w.** the universe as God created it, |
| T-21 .......II.8:4 | it is possible to look **w.** and see what must |
| T-21 ........ IV.h | The Fear to Look **W.** |
| T-21 ..... IV.1:3 | look **w.** and see the sin you think is there. |
| T-21 ..... IV.2:8 | look **w.** because of sin is yet another fear, |
| T-21 ..... IV.3:1 | What if you looked **w.** and saw no sin? |
| T-21 ..... IV.3:6 | entirely unwilling to look **w.** and see it not |
| T-21 ..... IV.4:1 | limited and incomplete, yet born **w.** you. |
| T-21 ..... IV.6:6 | at your "presumptuous" wish to look **w.**, |
| T-22 ......in.1:4 | yet believed by each to be **w.** himself. And |
| T-22 ......in.3:2 | Each one has looked **w.** and seen no lack. |
| T-22 ..... III.9:4 | Each sees **w.** the other what impels him to |
| T-22 .......V.5:4 | Yet **w.** you is a Force that no illusions can |
| T-23 ........I.1:5 | Conflict **w.** you must imply that you |
| T-23 .......II.7:4 | Nor can salvation lie **w.** the Son, whose |
| T-23 ..... III.5:1 | its behalf, cannot perceive it lies **w.** them. |
| T-23 ..... III.6:7 | But from **w.** it you can find no safety. Not |
| T-24 .......II.8:1 | the loveliness that you will see **w.** yourself |
| T-24 ..... IV.5:2 | you have beheld some sin **w.** your brother |
| T-24 .......V.6:3 | the fear you thought you saw **w.** yourself. |
| T-24 .......V.9:4 | **w.** your grasp because your hands are His. |
| T-24 .......V.9:5 | He is **w.** you, yet He walks beside you and |
| T-24 ..... VI.3:3 | Thought **w.** His Mind is absent from your |
| T-24 ..... VI.6:4 | **W.** your brother's holiness, the perfect |
| T-24 ..... VI.6:8 | to you. He *is* set forth **w.** his holiness. |
| T-24 ... VI.11:3 | the power to hold itself complete **w.** itself, |
| T-24 .... VII.2:2 | What is **w.** your brother still contains all |
| T-24 .... VII.6:7 | state of true creation, found not **w.** time, |
| T-24 .. VII.10:1 | beyond itself, and no escape **w.** its sight. |
| T-24 .. VII.11:3 | son. The other rests **w.**, his Father's Son, |
| T-24 .. VII.11:3 | Son, **w.** your brother as he is in you. Their |
| T-25 ......in.1:3 | thus it must be that you are not **w.** a body |
| T-25 ......in.1:4 | What is **w.** you cannot be outside. And it |
| T-25 ......in.1:8 | Christ is **w.** a frame of Holiness whose |
| T-25 ......in.2:7 | he is, and walks with him **w.** his holiness, |
| T-25 ......in.2:7 | as is his specialness set forth **w.** his body. |
| T-25 ........I.5:4 | and Christ abides **w.** your understanding, |
| T-25 ........I.7:2 | a Oneness which unites all things **w.** Itself |
| T-25 ........I.7:3 | And so What is **w.** this mind, and does |
| T-25 .......II.4:2 | Be glad that it is gone **w.** your mind, to |
| T-25 .......II.5:3 | has set **w.** this frame is all there is to see. |
| T-25 .......II.5:5 | He supports and frames **w.** Himself. His |
| T-25 .......II.6:6 | God has set His masterpiece **w.** a frame |
| T-25 .......II.8:1 | **W.** the darkness see the savior *from* the |
| T-25 .......II.8:5 | strength, and both will gladly look **w.**, |
| T-25 ..... III.4:1 | link that kept it still **w.** the laws of God; |
| T-25 ..... III.6:3 | he has come with Heaven's Help **w.** him, |
| T-25 ... IV.4:10 | enough to hold the world **w.** its peace. |
| T-25 ..... VI.4:3 | complete **w.** a world where incompletion |
| T-25 .... VII.3:3 | of His makes any sense at all **w.** this world |
| T-25 .... VII.6:5 | sin is equally insane **w.** the sight of love, |
| T-25 .... VII.9:3 | and all the sin he sees **w.** the world, offer |
| T-25 ... VIII.7:3 | dressed to deceive **w.** an angel's cloak. |
| T-25 . VIII.12:3 | you look to your experience **w.** the world, |
| T-25 . VIII.12:3 | of all that is really happening **w.** yourself. |
| T-26 ........I.2:3 | join with what is locked away **w.** the wall. |
| T-26 ........I.4:7 | Son is seen **w.** a world of separate bodies, |
| T-26 ........I.8:3 | Condemn him not by seeing him **w.** the |
| T-26 ..... III.6:5 | Yet **w.** this one lies the undoing of every |
| T-26 ..... IV.1:4 | is charity **w.** the world gives way to simple |
| T-26 ..... IV.5:4 | the altar that was raised **w.** the tiny spot |
| T-26 .......V.3:5 | made, and all of them **w.** that one mistake |
| T-26 .......V.3:5 | one, and all of them that came **w.** the first |
| T-26 .. VII.10:2 | In joyous answer will creation rise **w.** you, |
| T-26 .. VII.10:4 | a unity which holds all things **w.** itself? |
| T-26 .. VII.18:5 | which is not resolved **w.** its gracious light. |
| T-26 ... VIII.4:2 | can it be overlooked except **w.** the present |
| T-26 ... VIII.5:1 | make for safety all are laid **w.** the future, |
| T-26 ... VIII.5:9 | **w.** the only interval of time that sin and |
| T-26 ..... IX.1:6 | eyes on him who carries Christ **w.** him, |
| T-26 ..... IX.6:4 | to dwell **w.** the temple offered Them, to |
| T-26 ..... IX.8:4 | and ancient scars are healed **w.** His sight. |
| T-26 .......X.6:4 | Spirit has brought injustice to the light **w.** |
| T-27 ........I.8:1 | end alike **w.** the termination of the grave. |
| T-27 .....II.12:7 | represent a split **w.** a self perceived as two |
| T-27 ..... III.6:5 | and is incomplete, **w.** itself it is the same. |
| T-27 ..... IV.3:1 | problems but **w.** the holy instant's surety. |
| T-27 ..... IV.4:1 | All questions asked **w.** this world are but |
| T-27 ..... IV.5:3 | Thus is all questioning **w.** the world a |
| T-27 ..... IV.5:4 | witnesses are but the senses from **w.** itself |
| T-27 ..... IV.5:4 | contained **w.** the questions that are asked. |
| T-27 ..... IV.6:1 | Only **w.** the holy instant can an honest |

T-27......IV.6:9 that is not entailed w. the question asked.
T-27......IV.7:4 *is.* W. the world the answers merely raise
T-27....... V.4:5 nothing w. the world that could be feared
T-27....... V.8:8 complete w. two situations that are seen
T-27....... V.9:6 but there is One w. you Who is right.
T-27..... V.11:4 occurred w. the instant that love entered
T-27...... VI.1:6 unites all those who share in it w. itself.
T-27...... VI.2:2 one message: "You are here, w. this body,
T-27...... VI.3:1 This body, purposeless w. itself, holds all
T-27...... VI.4:4 could contain what you believe it holds w.
T-27...... VI.6:6 plaintive cry for help w. a world of misery
T-27..... VII.4:2 those w. the world are joined in sharing.
T-27..... VII.7:1 to sin all stand w. one little space. And it
T-27..... VII.8:7 plot conceived w. the idle dreaming of the
T-27... VIII.7:1 mind w. a body all are forms of circularity
T-27... VIII.7:6 It keeps you narrowly confined w. a body,
T-27... VIII.7:6 sinful things the body does w. its dream.
T-28.........I.5:5 Like to the body, it is purposeless w. itself
T-28.........I.5:8 alive, the present dead, are stored w. it,
T-28....... II.2:8 the mind is recognized as not w. the body
T-28....... II.3:6 A mind w. a body and a world of other
T-28....... II.6:1 that anyone has dreamed w. the world.
T-28...... III.7:1 keep w. the storehouse of the world. The
T-28...... III.7:5 And what are you who live w. the world
T-28...... III.7:5 concealed w. a separate and uncertain bit
T-28...... IV.8:5 that the miracle will place w. the little gap
T-28.... IV.10:5 then, would you perceive w. the gap? The
T-28....... V.5:8 seen w. the gap that you imagined, and
T-28....... V.7:6 of sin that you will see w. yourself, when
T-28..... VII.7:4 for its strength lies not w. itself alone. It is
T-29.........I.5:2 it with a power that lies not w. itself. And
T-29...... III.3:1 W. the dream of bodies and of death is
T-29...... III.3:6 of light where God abides w. the darkness
T-29...... III.5:6 This is the spark that shines w. the dream
T-29...... IV.2:3 The fear is seen w., without, or both. Or it
T-29....... V.2:3 so deep w. that nothing in this world but
T-29....... V.2:4 intrude upon the sacred Son of God w..
T-29..... VII.3:4 Yet does he seek to kill God's Son w., and
T-29..... VII.4:6 search implies you are not whole w. and
T-29..... VII.6:1 the truth w. from being known to you,
T-29..... VII.6:3 God dwells w., and your completion lies
T-29..... VII.8:3 to make complete what is w. by splitting
T-29... VIII.2:7 This is the penalty for looking not w. for
T-29... VIII.4:3 its source abides w. your mind where God
T-29... VIII.9:6 If Heaven is w., why would you seek for
T-29...... IX.3:5 laid upon himself w. the dream he made.
T-29...... IX.4:2 you sinful and put out the light w. you.
T-29...... IX.8:5 abides forever deep w. the Son of God.
T-30..... III.2:10 So you see your will w. the idol, thus
T-30...... III.6:8 parts in what exists w. God's Mind. It is
T-30...... III.7:8 the same w. the interval when you forgot.
T-30....... V.8:2 W. your hand is everything you need to
T-30...... VI.7:6 and will remain afraid to look w. and find
T-31.........I.8:4 everything w. the world has always made,
T-31...... I.11:4 Hear not the call for this w. yourself. But
T-31.... III.3:10 you are sin you lock the mind w. the body
T-31...... III.4:7 dies, because that mind is sick w. itself.
T-31...... IV.1:5 w. the narrow band from birth to death,
T-31...... IV.3:8 there is no choice at all w. the world. But
T-31...... IV.4:8 clear, and perfectly w. your learning grasp
T-31...... IV.9:4 What road in all the world will lead w.,
T-31....... V.2:9 It believes that it is good w. an evil world.
T-31....... V.7:9 For all of them are made w. the world,
T-31.... VI.3:11 What could there be w. the universe that
T-31..... VII.6:3 keep it static and concealed w. your mind.
T-31..... VII.8:1 Behold your role w. the universe! To
T-31... VII.11:3 holy eyes that look upon the innocence w.
T-31.... VIII.8:3 own release. There is no place for hell w. a
W-pI.......4.3:3 as outside you, and the meaningful w.. It
W-pI.....10.3:1 are meaningless, outside rather than w.;
W-pI.....30.3:2 now if it were w. the range of your sight.
W-pI.....30.5:3 mind, and looking w. rather than without
W-pI.....31.1:2 you see without and the world you see w..
W-pI.....41.3:1 Deep w. you is everything that is perfect,
W-pI.....41.5:2 you, when the truth is hidden deep w.,
W-pI.....44.2:1 to see, you must recognize that light is w.,
W-pI.....50.4:3 all your faith in the Love of God w. you;
W-pI.....50.4:5 Through the Love of God w. you, you can
W-pI.....57.5:3 this peace comes from deep w. myself.
W-pI...70.10:8 *W. me is the world's salvation and my own.*
W-pI.....73.5:1 of the world can only mirror what is w..
W-pI.....77.3:3 that the Kingdom of God is w. you, and
W-pI.....85.3:7 But from w. me it will reach beyond, and
W-pI.....91.4:4 makes all miracles w. your easy reach,
W-pI.....92.2:3 or that you held the world w. your hand,
W-pI.....95.1:2 You are one w. yourself, and one with
W-pI...95.13:4 His strength w. you and His Love forever
W-pI...95.13:5 and it is given you to feel this Self w. you,
W-pI...95.14:8 hope, the stirring of the truth w. his mind
W-pI.....96.3:1 be resolved w. the framework they are set.
W-pI.....96.4:4 perceive itself w. a body it confuses with
W-pI.....96.7:1 remain w. your mind and in the Mind of
W-pI.....96.8:2 will be a search for Him w. your mind.
W-pI.....99.3:1 w. a mind where both of them exist? The
W-pI.....99.5:1 Him w. the Mind of God and in your own
W-pI...100.8:5 Look deep w. you, undismayed by all the
W-pI...102.4:3 seek this function deep w. your mind, for
W-pI...103.3:1 this one correction to be placed w. your
W-pI...104.2:4 His are the gifts that are w. us now, for
W-pI...104.4:2 a holy place w. our minds before His altar
W-pI...106.3:5 Who holds your happiness w. His Hand,
W-pI...109.8:1 You rest w. the peace of God today, and
W-pI...109.9:1 You rest w. the peace of God today, quiet
W-pI...110.4:2 other minds, and only unity w. your own.
W-pI...110.8:1 Seek Him w. you Who is Christ in you,
WpI. rIII.in6:1 Place the ideas w. your mind, and let it
W-pI...111.1:3 *my mind, and let me see the innocence w..*
W-pI...113.2:2 *Whose knowledge still remains w. my mind*
W-pI.121.11:4 picture till you see a light somewhere w. it
W-pI...122.6:2 while all of Heaven waits for you w.?
W-pI...122.9:2 aware we hold the key w. our hands,
W-pI...124.2:2 we see reflects the holiness w. the mind at
W-pI...124.5:4 we see because we saw it first w. ourselves
W-pI.124.10:2 w. your mind and waiting to be found.
W-pI...125.1:3 from deep w. your mind where He abides.
W-pI...125.4:3 quiet place w. the mind where He abides
W-pI...125.6:4 is peace w. you to be called upon today, to
W-pI...127.6:1 Seek not w. the world to find your Self.
W-pI...127.9:3 will place a spark of truth w. your mind
W-pI...128.5:3 We hold it purposeless w. our minds, and
W-pI.130.11:2 still remains w. your range of choice, to
W-pI...131.1:2 immortality w. the darkness of the dream
W-pI...132.3:5 the bitter thoughts of death w. your mind
W-pI.132.10:3 you maintain the world w. your mind in
W-pI.133.10:1 he tries to keep its halo clear w. his vision,
W-pI.133.10:2 a sign of deep unworthiness w. himself.
W-pI.135.25:5 learn the part for you w. the plan of God.
W-pI...136.2:5 are seen as if each one were whole w. itself
W-pI...136.6:3 as separate and wholes w. themselves,
W-pI...137.8:6 off w. a body free to join with other minds
W-pI.137.11:3 who accepts it not w. his mind becomes a
W-pI...138.5:4 to teach w. the framework of this course.
W-pI...151.5:5 It is w. itself it sees the guilt. It is its own
W-pI.151.12:2 every witness for unholiness, w. the Holy,
W-pI...152.6:4 mind that lives w. a body that must die?
W-pI...153.2:5 without and still a greater treachery w..
W-pI.153.10:1 secure you rest, untouchable w. its light.
W-pI...154.1:5 do w. a larger plan we cannot see in its
W-pI...158.6:2 is a quiet place w. the world made holy by
W-pI...159.6:5 unmet w. this golden treasury of Christ.
W-pI...162.1:5 and all things seen w. its misty clouds and
W-pI...163.2:2 hold all living things w. its withered hand
W-pI...163.4:2 Himself perceived w. an idol made of dust
W-pI...164.6:2 from far beyond all things w. the world,
W-pI...164.8:2 and leave a clean and open space w. your
W-pI...165.4:5 Conviction lies w. it. Till you welcome it
W-pI...165.7:5 Sureness must abide w. you who are host
W-pI...167.6:3 cannot make a body, nor abide w. a body.
W-pI...167.8:4 changelessly, but yet w. themselves, for
W-pI...167.9:2 or a false condition not w. its Source, it
W-pI...168.3:1 most carefully preserved w. our hearts,
W-pI...169.2:1 God w. a world of seeming hate and fear.
W-pI...170.3:2 Yet your defense sets up an enemy w.; an
W-pI...181.3:4 for us w. this interval of time wherein we
W-pI...181.5:7 intent; to look upon the sinlessness w..
W-pI...182.5:7 be Himself, w. the peace that is His home,
W-pI...182.7:7 until you hear His gentle Voice w. you,
W-pI...183.1:5 are, even w. a world that does not know;
W-pI...183.5:4 Name along with him w. your quiet mind,
W-pI.183.10:2 this is necessary, for it holds them all w. it
W-pI.184.11:3 Source which unifies all things w. Itself.
W-pI.187.10:5 And as we look w., we see the purity of
W-pI...188.2:5 It is not difficult to look w., for there all
W-pI...188.5:2 Who recognizes it w. himself must give it.
W-pI...188.6:2 The light w. you is sufficient. It alone has
W-pI...188.6:4 and let your thoughts fly to the peace w..
W-pI...188.7:4 as well, for they were born w. your mind,
W-pI...188.9:4 light w. our minds direct them to come
W-pI......189.h I feel the Love of God w. me now.
W-pI...189.1:7 feel the Love of God w. you is to see the
W-pI...189.4:2 look out from the endless wells of joy w..
W-pI...189.5:3 You will look upon that which you feel w..
W-pI...189.5:4 If hatred finds a place w. your heart, you
W-pI...189.5:5 If you feel the Love of God w. you, you
W-pI...189.9:8 Love shines outward from its home w.,
W-pI...191.2:6 not speak of frailty w. you and without;
W-pI...192.1:2 such a function mean w. a world of envy,
W-pI...194.8:4 has also placed the world w. the Hands to
W-pI...195.3:3 left w. his grasping fingers as in yours.
W-pI...196.3:4 you will see w. today's idea the light of
W-pI...196.8:5 be welcomed back w. the holy mind He
W-pI.196.10:3 outward, and returned from outside to w.
W-pI.196.11:1 an instant, is a murderer perceived w. you
W-pI...197.8:2 you contain all things w. your Self. And
W-pI...199.6:6 which the mind w. the Holy Spirit seeks.
W-pI...199.7:2 still believe they are enslaved w. a body.
W-pI...200.8:2 begins w. the world perceived as different
W-pI...200.8:4 where freedom lies w. the peace of God.
W-pI...207.1:2 *blessing shines upon me from w. my heart,*
W-pI...208.1:4 *It is w. my heart, which witnesses to God*
W-pI...209.1:1 (189) I feel the Love of God w. me now.
W-pI...209.1:5 *The Love of God w. me sets me free.* I am not
W-pII .222.1:2 He is my Source of life, the life w., the air I
W-pII .223.1:1 unattached, and housed w. a body. Now I
W-pII .225.1:2 *in my mind and keeping it w. its kindly light,*
W-pII ..... 2.4:4 birds have come to live w. their branches.
W-pII .252.1:3 an intensity that holds all things w. it, in
W-pII ..... 5.1:2 It is w. this fence he thinks he lives, to die
W-pII ..... 5.1:3 w. this fence he thinks that he is safe from
W-pII ..... 5.1:5 he be certain he remains w. the body,
W-pII .261.1:2 and think I live w. the citadel where I am
W-pII .264.1:5 *the Love which holds all things w. itself.*
W-pII .264.1:7 *to be at peace w. Your everlasting Love.*
W-pII .267.1:6 and held forever quiet and at peace w. His
W-pII ..... 6.1:3 still abides w. the Mind that is His Source
W-pII ..... 6.3:1 at peace w. the Heaven of your holy mind.
W-pII .278.1:1 If I accept that I am prisoner w. a body,
W-pII .288.1:6 *Let me not cherish it w. my heart, or I will*
W-pII ..... 8.3:4 sees arises from a mind at peace w. itself.
W-pII .297.1:4 way I live w. a world that needs salvation,
W-pII ..... 9.2:1 and hold you safe w. its gentle advent,
W-pII .... 309.h I will not fear to look w. today.
W-pII .309.1:1 W. me is eternal innocence, because it is
W-pII .309.1:4 To look w. is but to find my will as God
W-pII .309.1:5 is. I fear to look w. because I think I made
W-pII .309.1:7 W. me is the Holiness of God. Within me
W-pII .309.1:8 of God. W. me is the memory of Him.
W-pII .313.1:6 *of sin and look w. upon my sinlessness,*
W-pII ... 11.3:3 inviolate; forever held w. His holy Will,
W-pII .331.1:4 *to die w. a world of pain and cruelty. How*
W-pII .332.1:6 in, and take its rightful place w. the mind.
W-pII .336.1:5 the mind, and call it to return and look w.
W-pII .336.2:2 *Then let me, Father, look w., and find Your*
W-pII .336.2:2 *Your Word remains unchanged w. my mind*
W-pII ... 13.1:5 Thus it stays w. time's limits. Yet it paves
W-pII .350.1:2 *all things w. himself as You created him.*
W-pII .352.1:7 *I have w. me both the memory of You, and*
W-pII .360.1:2 *remain forever still and undisturbed w. me.*
M-8 ........... 6:7 place–for differences cannot exist w. it–
M-16 .......... 3:7 since we are learning w. the framework of
M-16 .......... 6:2 limitless because all things are freed w. it.
M-18 .......... 4:3 Then let him turn w. to his eternal Guide,
C-in ........... 3:1 course remains w. the ego framework,
C-4............. 6:1 brings: What was projected out is seen w.
C-4............. 6:7 expect? But seen w. your mind, guilt and
C-5............. 2:3 w. a body that appeared to hold his self
C-ep........... 2:5 w. eternity and through all time as well.

| | |
|---|---|
| T-14......III.8:7 | to look upon w. imposing on himself the |
| T-14....III.10:8 | and gives them what they want w. effort, |
| T-14....III.14:4 | W. His guidance you will think you know |
| T-14......IV.4:9 | therefore, be anyone w. His Holiness, nor |
| T-14......IV.7:4 | He cannot be known w. His Son, whose |
| T-14......IV.8:2 | It is here w. your making, but not without |
| T-14......IV.8:2 | here without your making, but not w. you |
| T-14....IV.10:7 | with God is life. Nothing w. it is at all. |
| T-14.....V.11:3 | If you leave him w., you join him there. |
| T-14.....V.11:5 | Refuse to accept anyone as w. the blessing |
| T-14......VI.3:7 | W. protection of obscurity only the light |
| T-14......VI.4:6 | The other is wholly w. sense of any kind. |
| T-14.....VII.1:8 | Yet the perception must be w. deceit, for |
| T-14...VIII.2:3 | No altar stands to God w. His Son. And |
| T-14......IX.3:4 | you. Yet w. Him you are nothing. The |
| T-14......IX.8:3 | w. regard for what is brought to it. Those |
| T-14.......X.2:5 | anything w. order of difficulty can occur. |
| T-15.........I.4:7 | the ego's teaching is w. the fear of death. |
| T-15.........I.8:3 | w. its shadow reaching out into the future |
| T-15.........I.9:2 | For what is time w. a past and future? It |
| T-15.........I.9:6 | free and wholly w. condemnation. From |
| T-15.........I.9:7 | again you will go forth in time w. fear, |
| T-15......I.10:1 | Time is inconceivable w. change, yet |
| T-15......I.15:6 | forever beyond attack and w. variability. |
| T-15.......II.2:2 | of peace is eternal *because* it is w. fear. It |
| T-15....III.4:11 | For He is not content w. His Son, and His |
| T-15......III.7:5 | to His Son's creations, but w. leaving you. |
| T-15.......V.1:4 | Judgment becomes impossible w. the past |
| T-15.......V.1:4 | for w. it you do not understand anything. |
| T-15.......V.1:6 | of this because you believe that w. the ego |
| T-15.......V.1:7 | Yet I assure you that w. the ego, all would |
| T-15.......V.6:6 | Unless you had seen yourself as w. love, |
| T-15.......V.8:3 | W. the values from the past, you would |
| T-15.......V.9:7 | have no need to look w. and snatch love |
| T-15......VI.2:2 | seek w. for what you cannot find without. |
| T-15......VI.2:2 | seek without for what you cannot find w.. |
| T-15......VI.4:6 | wholly w. loss and only with gain. Herein |
| T-15......VI.6:5 | behind it, can have faith in love w. fear. |
| T-15......VI.8:4 | W. its source exclusion vanishes. And this |
| T-15.....VII.2:3 | to enter into any relationship w. anger, |
| T-15.....VII.7:8 | It is only by attack w. forgiveness that the |
| T-15.....VII.9:5 | yet never w. demand of sacrifice. The fury |
| T-15...VII.13:3 | that it can overcome even this w. fear. |
| T-15......IX.2:2 | it is impossible to recognize as wholly w. |
| T-15......IX.3:1 | of relationships w. limits is given you. But |
| T-15......IX.5:5 | you would see w. the limits the ego would |
| T-15.......X.5:8 | you cannot conceive of love w. sacrifice. |
| T-15......XI.3:5 | and w. pain there can be no sacrifice. And |
| T-15......XI.3:6 | And w. sacrifice there love *must* be. |
| T-15......XI.4:8 | w. experiencing himself as incomplete |
| T-15......XI.5:3 | aside w. a sense of sacrifice and loss? And |
| T-15......XI.5:4 | and loss w. attempting to restore himself? |
| T-15......XI.6:6 | and to be w. Him *is* to be without meaning |
| T-15......XI.6:6 | and to be without Him *is* to be w. meaning |
| T-15......XI.7:1 | are joined w. the body's interference, and |
| T-16.........I.6:8 | you how to meet both w. losing either. |
| T-16......III.3:3 | to teach successfully wholly w. conviction |
| T-16......IV.2:2 | of love is w. meaning if love is everything. |
| T-16......IV.8:5 | Your relationship with them is w. guilt, |
| T-16......IV.8:6 | w. which you could never be complete. |
| T-16....IV.11:8 | He loves you, wholly w. illusion, as you |
| T-16....IV.11:9 | love. For love *is* wholly w. illusion, and |
| T-16....IV.11:9 | illusion, and therefore wholly w. fear. |
| T-16......VI.4:1 | is totally meaningless w. a body. If you |
| T-16......VI.5:5 | in, for God is left w. and *nothing* taken in. |
| T-16......VI.7:7 | relationship. W. this illusion there could |
| T-16......VI.8:4 | you homeless and w. a frame of reference. |
| T-16.....VII.1:1 | let the past go w. relinquishing the special |
| T-16.....VII.1:4 | for choosing a special partner w. the past? |
| T-16.....VII.3:6 | w. your alliance in your own destruction, |
| T-16...VII.10:2 | power of God and all His Love, w. limit, |
| T-17.........I.4:5 | reality is a perspective w. understanding; |
| T-17.......II.5:1 | the old, the world you see w. forgiveness. |
| T-17.......II.5:5 | of God made in insanity could be w. a |
| T-17......III.2:3 | W. exception, these relationships have as |
| T-17......III.7:5 | has left no part of it w. Himself. This is |
| T-17......IV.7:7 | the frame w. the picture you cannot have. |
| T-17......IV.9:4 | You cannot have the frame w. the picture. |
| T-17....IV.11:7 | W. the frame, the picture is seen as what |
| T-17....IV.12:5 | or the comparison is wholly w. meaning. |
| T-17....IV.15:5 | wholly w. value and entirely deprived of |
| T-17.......V.1:5 | Yet w. expression it is not remembered. |
| T-17.......V.4:2 | its former goal completely w. attraction, |
| T-17......VI.3:1 | W. a clear-cut, positive goal, set at the |
| T-17......VI.5:4 | truth and sanity, and cannot be w. them, |
| T-17.....VII.4:6 | What situation can you be in w. faith, and |
| T-18......III.7:7 | the desire for love w. love's joining them. |
| T-18......IV.2:6 | If you could come w. them you would not |
| T-18.......V.3:8 | A purpose such as this, w. the means, is |
| T-18.......V.6:6 | instant come to either of you w. the other. |
| T-18.......V.7:4 | *It is not possible that I can have it w. him, or* |
| T-18.......V.7:4 | *that I can have it without him, or he w. me.* |
| T-18......VI.7:7 | leaving it unharmed, w. your guilt upon it |
| T-18......VI.9:8 | forever, and forever w. alternative. And |
| T-18....VI.12:3 | even a general idea w. specific reference. |
| T-18....VI.12:4 | join it w. reservation because you love it, |
| T-18.....VII.2:5 | you spend w. awareness of it gives you a |
| T-18.....VII.4:1 | to accept the holy instant w. reservation |
| T-18.....VII.4:2 | prepare for it w. placing it in the future. |
| T-18...VIII.1:7 | You cannot even think of God w. a body, |
| T-18...VIII.4:6 | W. the sun the sunbeam would be gone; |
| T-18...VIII.4:6 | the ripple w. the ocean is inconceivable. |
| T-18...VIII.6:2 | nor would the Whole be whole w. it. It is |
| T-18. VIII.11:3 | will come because you came w. the body, |
| T-18. VIII.12:4 | alone than He knows you w. your brother |
| T-18......IX.9:2 | seen anew, w. the shadow of guilt upon it. |
| T-19.........I.1:3 | that peace w. faith will never be attained, |
| T-19.........I.2:7 | The body is healed because you came w. it |
| T-19.........I.6:2 | of seeming wholeness, but w. connection. |
| T-19......III.3:3 | results, but w. the loss of its appeal. And |
| T-19......IV.2:7 | w. which it would have been forever |
| T19...IV.A.4:6 | flow across it, and join you w. hindrance. |
| T19...IV.A.5:2 | of your holy relationship, w. this barrier, |
| T19. IV.A.10:7 | Being wholly w. attack, it could not be |
| T19....IV.B.9:2 | w. the limits that would hold its extension |
| T19..IV.B.16:5 | body as himself, w. which he would die, |
| T19...IV.D.1:1 | What would you see w. the fear of death? |
| T19...IV.D.9:3 | it w. complete forgiveness of his brother |
| T19.IV.D.10:5 | journey w. a purpose is still meaningless, |
| T19.IV.D.19:3 | w. which is the journey meaningless. Here |
| T19.IV.D.21:6 | still w. conviction they have a purpose. |
| T-20.......II.4:3 | against me still, and who is whole w. him? |
| T-20......III.3:3 | w. attempting to adjust themselves to it, |
| T-20......III.7:3 | off. He came w. a purpose, but he will not |
| T-20....III.10:2 | there is only holiness and joining w. limit. |
| T-20....III.10:3 | and perfect, and w. the veil of fear upon it |
| T-20....III.11:4 | with charity within, what can it fear w.? |
| T-20......IV.1:8 | Being w. illusion of what you are, the |
| T-20......IV.6:2 | knows the rest will see to it w. your help. |
| T-20......IV.6:4 | lies all of it, w. which is no part complete, |
| T-20......IV.6:4 | nor is the whole completed w. your part. |
| T-20......IV.6:7 | enter w. fear and where he rests a while, |
| T-20......IV.6:8 | he enter, to rest and to remember, w. you |
| T-20......IV.7:5 | been achieved that you will rest w. them? |
| T-20......IV.8:4 | will not arrange for you w. your effort. He |
| T-20......VI.9:2 | frail as is a snowflake, but w. its loveliness |
| T-20.....VII.7:5 | is meaningless w. the end for which it was |
| T-20.....VII.9:1 | "How can I see my brother w. the body?" |
| T-20...VIII.9:7 | It still is true that nothing is w.. Yet upon |
| T-21.....in.1:11 | Nothing perceived w. it means anything. |
| T-21.......II.6:4 | happen to the Son of God w. his will; and |
| T-21.......II.6:4 | will; and thus w. the Will of his Creator, |
| T-21.......II.6:6 | himself w. what God has willed for him. |
| T-21.....II.10:8 | Nothing can have effects w. a cause, and |
| T-21......III.9:9 | it for you, w. one spot of sin upon it, and |
| T-21.......V.5:1 | established w. your will and your consent. |
| T-21......VI.2:1 | or refused by you w. your brother. Sin |
| T-21......VI.3:1 | for himself, as God thinks not w. His Son. |
| T-21......VI.6:2 | Father forever, w. a hope of safe return. |
| T-21......VI.7:2 | instead w. the other being blessed by it, |
| T-21.....VII.5:2 | There can be no faith in sin w. an enemy. |
| T-21.....VII.9:4 | if you choose to see a world w. an enemy, |
| T-21...VII.12:4 | answered "yes" w. perceiving that "yes" |
| T-22.........I.1:7 | though you wandered in w. a plan of any |
| T-22.........I.5:5 | w. a need to be interpreted to you. What |
| T-22.......II.4:2 | way, in every instance and w. exception. |
| T-22......III.3:2 | set like a heavy gate, locked and w. a key, |
| T-22......III.3:3 | No one who looks on it w. the help of |
| T-22......III.4:3 | a distorted fragment of the whole w. the |
| T-22.....VI.12:5 | attack a part of the creation w. the whole, |
| T-22.....VI.12:5 | without the whole, the Son w. the Father; |
| T-22.....VI.12:5 | Father; and to attack another w. yourself, |
| T-22.....VI.12:5 | or hurt yourself w. the other feeling pain. |
| T-23.........III.h | Salvation w. Compromise |
| T-23......IV.1:1 | in conflict, for there *is* no war w. attack. |
| T-24........II.3:2 | is impossible even to imagine w. this base |
| T-24......III.4:1 | W. foundation nothing is secure. Would |
| T-24......III.6:6 | w. the heat and malice of one thought of |
| T-24.......V.8:3 | He Who willed not to be w. His Son could |
| T-24......VI.2:1 | W. you there would be a lack in God, a |
| T-24......VI.2:1 | a Heaven incomplete, a Son w. a Father. |
| T-24......VI.9:2 | wandering, w. a purpose and without |
| T-24......VI.9:2 | and w. accomplishment of any kind, is all |
| T-24......VII.9:3 | And w. a light it seems that it is gone. Yet |
| T-24...VII.11:1 | and both appear to walk this earth w. a |
| T-25........II.4:7 | W. the picture is the frame without its |
| T-25........II.4:7 | the picture is the frame w. its meaning. Its |
| T-25........II.5:4 | it for a while, w. obscuring it in any way. |
| T-25......III.4:1 | and maintained w. some link that kept it |
| T-25.......V.1:2 | and is meaningless w. the goal of sin. |
| T-25.......V.6:1 | is God believed to be w. the power to save |
| T-25.......V.6:5 | w. the understanding that he is the way to |
| T-25......VI.3:5 | will that he remain w. the function that |
| T-25......VII.9:5 | Nor is he left w. escape from madness, for |
| T-25......VII.9:6 | w. a special function in the hope of peace, |
| T-25...VII.10:6 | w. the differences which would have |
| T-25....VIII.1:2 | take it from you w. your willingness. For |
| T-25....VIII.1:4 | would not learn it *is* your will to be w. it. |
| T-25....VIII.2:2 | w. attack from all beliefs opposed to it. |
| T-25....VIII.3:7 | be defined w. insanity where love means |
| T-25....VIII.8:6 | vengeance w. love has gained in strength |
| T-25..VIII.11:7 | W. love is justice prejudiced and weak. |
| T-25..VIII.11:8 | And love w. justice is impossible. For love |
| T-25..VIII.11:9 | love is fair, and cannot chasten w. cause. |
| T-25..VIII.13:1 | W. impartiality there is no justice. How |
| T-25......IX.7:6 | To keep it for yourself to solve w. His help |
| T-26.........I.2:3 | as if what is inside can never reach w., |
| T-26.........I.4:3 | God's Son perceive himself w. his Father? |
| T-26.........I.4:4 | And his Father be w. His Son? Yet every |
| T-26.........I.4:5 | that they be separate and w. the other. |
| T-26.........I.5:2 | W. your special function has this world |
| T-26........II.3:4 | them vanish one by one, w. regard to size, |
| T-26........II.7:5 | a special problem, a mistake w. a remedy, |
| T-26........II.7:5 | a remedy, or an affliction w. a cure, has |
| T-26......III.1:8 | truth is simple; it is one, w. an opposite. |
| T-26......IV.5:3 | w. a voice that adds its power to the song, |
| T-26......VI.2:5 | W. Him you are friendless. Seek not |
| T-26.....VII.5:1 | its effects be utterly undone and w. cause. |
| T-26...VII.11:9 | this he cannot do w. a sense of isolation, |
| T-26...VII.12:6 | feel guilty, though w. understanding why. |
| T-26...VII.13:5 | is to invite illusions to be true, w. success. |
| T-26...VII.14:2 | healing of effect w. the cause can merely |
| T-26....VIII.5:3 | Who can predict effects w. a cause? And |
| T-26..VIII.7:10 | asks for what He gave w. a cost at all. |
| T-26......IX.2:1 | and left w. a single one you cherish still? |
| T-26........X.2:6 | equally w. a cause or consequence, and |
| T-26........X.5:7 | w. the function that the Holy Spirit sees. |
| T-26........X.6:3 | unfairly left w. a purpose in a futile world. |
| T-27.........I.8:3 | as neutral and w. a goal inherent in itself. |
| T-27.........I.9:5 | Pictured w. a purpose, it is seen as neither |
| T-27........I.11:6 | This thing w. a purpose cannot hide the |
| T-27........II.5:2 | healing proves that separation is w. effect. |
| T-27........II.8:6 | is purposeless and wholly w. cause. Show |
| T-27......II.14:5 | And only what is left w. his presence is |
| T-27......III.1:6 | it w. changing it into something it is not. |
| T-27......III.3:5 | Who can perceive effect w. a cause? What |
| T-27......III.5:2 | Reality is ultimately known w. a form, |
| T-27......III.7:5 | complete and happy, w. opposite. You do |
| T-27.......V.1:2 | The miracle extends w. your help, but you |
| T-27.......V.2:2 | it is unattested, it remains w. conviction. |
| T-27.....V.2:12 | if only for an instant, you love w. attack. |
| T-27.......V.4:2 | w. attack is necessary that all this occur. |
| T-27.....V.11:4 | in w. attack will stay with you forever. |
| T-27......VI.1:8 | for they have a goal w. a meaning. And |
| T-27.....VII.2:4 | W. the clouds the problem will emerge in |
| T-27...VII.13:4 | he could not waken to reality w. the sweat |
| T-27...VII.13:5 | joy, and gave him means to waken w. fear |

| | |
|---|---|
| T-27....VIII.1:2 | There is no dream w. it, nor does it exist |
| T-27....VIII.1:2 | nor does it exist w. the dream in which it |
| T-27....VIII.8:4 | consequences, but w. their trifling cause. |
| T-27....VIII.8:5 | W. the cause do its effects seem serious |
| T-28.........I.2:3 | went its consequences, left w. a cause. |
| T-28.........I.3:4 | Him, w. the content and the purposes for |
| T-28.........I.3:5 | They are but skills w. an application. |
| T-28....... II.1:1 | W. a cause there can be no effects, and |
| T-28....... II.1:1 | effects, and yet w. effects there is no cause |
| T-28....... II.1:8 | w. beginning and without an end. |
| T-28....... II.1:8 | without beginning and w. an end. |
| T-28....... II.2:4 | uncontained, w. a barrier or limitation. |
| T-28....... II.6:8 | w. a stable cause with guaranteed effects. |
| T-28...... II.7:11 | he fears is cause w. the consequences that |
| T-28....... III.1:7 | W. support, the dream will fade away |
| T-28....... III.1:7 | the dream will fade away w. effects. For it |
| T-28....... III.2:3 | its guilt w. your aid in letting it perceive |
| T-28....... III.8:3 | so sickness will now be seen w. a cause. |
| T-28....... IV.1:8 | both become illusions, and w. identity. |
| T-28....... IV.7:4 | can not remain w. a witness or a cause. |
| T-28....... V.5:6 | For eyes and ears are senses w. sense, and |
| T-28.... VI.1:10 | no role, but does what it is told, w. attack. |
| T-28....... VI.4:2 | yet you think it is your self, and that, w. it, |
| T-28..... VII.5:2 | think w. affecting those apart from you. |
| T-29.........I.3:6 | w. a gap perceived between you and him, |
| T-29.........I.9:3 | W. the fear of God, what could induce |
| T-29....... II.1:4 | as a simple way, w. a sacrifice or any loss, |
| T-29....... II.2:3 | happens suddenly, as an effect w. a cause. |
| T-29....... II.5:8 | now can do could not be done w. the love |
| T-29....... III.2:7 | one with him w. the wall the world has |
| T-29....... IV.2:3 | The fear is seen within, w., or both. Or it |
| T-29....... V.8:3 | w. the hope of change and betterment, for |
| T-29.... VI.4:11 | it be as one forever and forever, w. end. |
| T-29..... VII.4:3 | thus to be w. and to have suffered loss. |
| T-29....VIII.4:2 | yet a thought w. the power to change one |
| T-30.........I.4:3 | will serve to let you be directed w. fear, |
| T-30.........I.7:1 | Try to observe this rule w. delay, despite |
| T-30.......I.16:4 | can be caused w. some form of union, be |
| T-30....... II.2:5 | His Son w. what he has chosen for himself |
| T-30...... IV.4:9 | toys w. a single meaning of their own. See |
| T-30...... IV.8:2 | w. the toys of terror that you made. No |
| T-30....... V.5:4 | can guilt and sin be seen w. a purpose, |
| T-31.........I.4:3 | step, however difficult, w. complaint, |
| T-31.........I.9:2 | W. your answer is it left to die, as it is |
| T-31.......I.13:4 | him, w. the past that sentenced him to die |
| T-31....... II.8:2 | Come w. all thought of what you ever |
| T-31....... II.8:3 | the new w. your opposition or intent. |
| T-31....... II.8:8 | away w. the thoughts you did not want, |
| T-31..... II.10:1 | An instant spent w. your old ideas of who |
| T-31...... IV.4:3 | Learn now, w. despair, there is no hope of |
| T-31...... IV.5:5 | if it be applied in situations w. choice? |
| T-31...... IV.9:6 | die, w. their Source forever in themselves. |
| T-31.... IV.10:8 | there w. your own reality at one with you? |
| T-31....... V.1:6 | This is its purpose; that you come w. a self |
| T-31...... VI.3:3 | For you can see the body w. help, but do |
| T-31...... VI.6:7 | and w. the promise of corruption and the |
| T-31..... VII.3:5 | you see w. the Aid that God has given you |
| W-pI....... 3.1:1 | ones, w. making distinctions of any kind. |
| W-pI..... 10.4:4 | available to you, w. selection or judgment |
| W-pI..... 11.2:4 | it to yourself, being sure to do so w. haste, |
| W-pI..... 13.1:3 | Nothing w. meaning exists. However, it |
| W-pI..... 13.3:1 | the meaningless, and accept it w. fear. If |
| W-pI..... 25.6:7 | w. shifting your eyes from the subject |
| W-pI..... 27.3:6 | short sentence to yourself w. disturbing |
| W-pI..... 30.5:3 | mind, and looking within rather than w.. |
| W-pI..... 31.1:2 | you see w. and the world you see within. |
| W-pI..... 31.3:4 | w. any special investment on your part. |
| W-pI..... 33.1:4 | but w. an abrupt sense of shifting. |
| W-pI..... 34.4:1 | w. applying it to anything in particular. |
| W-pI..... 36.1:4 | "Sinless" means w. sin. You cannot be |
| W-pI..... 36.1:5 | sin. You cannot be w. sin a little. You are |
| W-pI..... 39.8:1 | w. conscious selection and without undue |
| W-pI..... 39.8:1 | without conscious selection and w. undue |
| W-pI..... 42.5:3 | Let them come w. censoring unless you |
| W-pI..... 43.1:4 | W. this link with God, perception would |
| W-pI..... 43.5:1 | w. self-directed inclusion or exclusion. |
| W-pI..... 43.9:2 | to slip by w. remembering today's idea, |
| W-pI..... 44.2:1 | must recognize that light is within, not w. |
| W-pI..... 44.7:5 | your passing thoughts w. involvement, |
| W-pI... 44.10:2 | Try to think of light, formless and w. limit |
| W-pI..... 49.1:1 | the day w. interrupting your regular |
| W-pI..... 49.2:3 | and distraught, but w. reality of any kind. |
| W-pI..... 50.4:5 | resolve all seeming difficulties w. effort |
| W-pI..... 51.4:2 | because I am trying to think w. God. |
| W-pI..... 54.1:4 | But thoughts cannot be w. effects. As the |
| W-pI..... 55.3:3 | else. W. attack thoughts I could not see a |
| W-pI..... 68.4:4 | to find out how you would feel w. them. If |
| W-pI..... 72.9:3 | be w. a body is to be in our natural state. |
| W-pI. 72.10:10 | for salvation w. waiting to hear what it is. |
| W-pI..... 73.5:2 | light nor darkness can be found w.. |
| W-pI..... 74.2:4 | W. illusions conflict is impossible. Let us |
| W-pI..... 75.9:6 | W. the darkness of the past upon your |
| W-pI..... 92.8:2 | can leave w. a miracle before his eyes, and |
| W-pI..... 96.4:5 | W. its function then it has no peace, and |
| W-pI..... 98.3:2 | escapes from fancied threats w. reality. |
| W-pI..... 99.4:2 | which they are undone w. attack and with |
| W-pI... 100.3:2 | plan. W. your joy, His joy is incomplete. |
| W-pI... 100.3:3 | W. your smile, the world cannot be saved |
| W-pI... 102.2:1 | is purposeless, w. a cause and with no |
| W-pI... 107.1:5 | They are gone because, w. belief, they |
| W-pI... 107.2:1 | what a state of mind w. illusions is? How |
| W-pI... 107.3:2 | W. illusions there could be no fear, no |
| W-pI... 109.5:2 | while time goes by w. its touch upon you, |
| WpI..rIII.in9:2 | w. applying what you learned to them. As |
| W-pI... 121.2:2 | w. the hope of respite and release from |
| W-pI... 121.5:1 | w. the prospect of a future which can |
| W-pI... 123.3:1 | remain shining on you, forever w. change. |
| W-pI... 125.3:1 | today w. intrusion of our petty thoughts, |
| W-pI... 125.3:1 | petty thoughts, w. our personal desires, |
| W-pI... 125.3:1 | and w. all judgment of His holy Word. |
| W-pI... 126.2:4 | You further think that they can sin w. |
| W-pI... 126.6:2 | w. requiring correction in your mind. It |
| W-pI... 127.3:7 | is not. Love is a law w. an opposite. Its |
| W-pI... 127.7:1 | advanced in distance w. measure and in |
| W-pI... 128.2:3 | w. delaying to perceive some hope where |
| W-pI... 131.6:6 | is now, w. a past and wholly futureless. It |
| W-pI... 133.6:2 | A temporary value is w. all value. Time |
| W-pI. 133.12:5 | you make choices easily and w. pain. |
| W-pI. 135.16:4 | w. a continuity of any old ideas and sick |
| W-pI. 135.19:1 | a future undisturbed, w. a trace of sorrow |
| W-pI. 135.20:1 | W. defenses, you become a light which |
| W-pI. 135.25:5 | in you, for now you come w. defense, to |
| W-pI. 135.26:2 | that comes to you w. your planning. |
| W-pI... 136.1:3 | and w. a meaningful intent of any kind, it |
| W-pI... 136.3:1 | nor are they made w. awareness. They are |
| W-pI... 136.6:1 | assembles them w. regard to all their true |
| W-pI... 137.3:5 | and w. the unity that gives It life. But |
| W-pI... 138.3:3 | W. decision, time is but a waste and effort |
| W-pI... 138.3:4 | in return, and time goes by w. results. |
| W-pI... 138.9:5 | Now are they w. effects. They cannot be |
| W-pI... 151.1:6 | w. a doubt because of all the doubting |
| W-pI... 152.1:4 | And no one dies w. his own consent. |
| W-pI... 152.3:3 | W. the first, the second has no meaning. |
| W-pI... 152.3:4 | But w. the second, is the first no longer |
| W-pI... 153.2:5 | treachery w. and still a greater treachery |
| W-pI... 153.9:1 | w. all thought or wish or dream in which |
| W-pI... 154.2:3 | He does not work w. your own consent. |
| W-pI... 156.2:4 | God, because you could not be w. Him. |
| W-pI... 158.7:5 | w. the slightest fading of the light it sees. |
| W-pI... 161.5:3 | Fear w. symbols calls for no response, for |
| W-pI... 164.9:1 | Let not today slip by w. the gifts it holds |
| W-pI... 166.1:4 | He gives w. exception, holding nothing |
| W-pI... 166.4:3 | W. the world he made is he an outcast; |
| W-pI... 166.9:6 | and go the way you chose w. your Self. |
| W-pI... 170.1:1 | No one attacks w. intent to hurt. This can |
| W-pI... 170.3:1 | seems to be the enemy w. that you attack. |
| WpI...rV.in8:7 | I am incomplete w. your part in me. And |
| W-pI... 181.6:3 | a little while, w. regard to past or future, |
| W-pI... 181.9:2 | conceive of anything w. Its sinlessness. |
| W-pI... 182.2:5 | w. defensiveness and self-deception, |
| W-pI... 182.9:2 | how strong is he who comes w. defenses, |
| W-pI. 182.11:1 | you raised against an enemy w. existence. |
| W-pI... 183.2:1 | Name can not be heard w. response, nor |
| W-pI... 183.2:1 | nor said w. an echo in the mind that calls |
| W-pI... 185.6:4 | But if he asks w. sincerity, there is no |
| W-pI... 186.1:3 | to you, w. insisting on another role. It |
| W-pI... 190.9:1 | and come w. defense into the quiet place |
| W-pI... 191.2:6 | not speak of frailty within you and w.; no |
| W-pI .. 191.3:2 | you assail the universe alone, w. a friend, |
| W-pI .. 192.5:1 | mind w. the body cannot make mistakes. |
| W-pI .. 192.7:2 | W. its kindly light we grope in darkness, |
| W-pI .. 193.9:2 | an unforgiving thought w. correction, nor |
| W-pI .. 193.9:3 | remain untroubled and serene, w. a care, |
| W-pI .. 195.8:4 | at last, and we forgive w. comparing. |
| W-pI .. 195.9:3 | and pushed about w. a thought or care for |
| W-pI .. 196.5:5 | universe, w. the fear of hell upon his heart |
| W-pI .. 196.8:4 | cannot then believe that fear is caused w.. |
| W-pI .. 199.6:6 | W. the power to enslave, it is a worthy |
| W-pI .. 219.1:5 | *w. confusion as to what my Father loves* |
| W-pII ..... 1.3:4 | reality, w. concern for anything that |
| W-pII ..... 2.2:2 | before, for peace was given w. opposite, |
| W-pII .... 247.h | W. forgiveness I will still be blind. |
| W-pII . 257.1:3 | can he function w. deep distress and great |
| W-pII ..... 5.4:2 | was made to fence him into hell w. escape |
| W-pII . 264.1:5 | *or w. the Love which holds all things within* |
| W-pII ..... 7.4:2 | W. forgiveness will your dreams remain |
| W-pII . 288.1:2 | *I cannot come to You w. my brother. And to* |
| W-pII . 290.1:4 | What I perceive w. God's Own Correction |
| W-pII . 294.1:7 | And afterwards, w. a purpose, it is laid |
| W-pII . 298.1:1 | permits my love to be accepted w. fear. |
| W-pII ..... 9.1:3 | things w. exception and without reserve. |
| W-pII ..... 9.1:3 | things without exception and w. reserve. |
| W-pII . 308.1:6 | birth of Christ is now, w. a past or future. |
| W-pII ... 10.2:2 | forgiven, w. sin and wholly purposeless. |
| W-pII ... 10.2:3 | W. a cause, and now without a function |
| W-pII ... 10.2:3 | and now w. a function in Christ's sight, it |
| W-pII ... 11.1:1 | infinite, and everywhere w. all limit. Only |
| W-pII . 331.1:2 | *and be left w. a certain way to his release?* |
| W-pII . 332.1:7 | W. forgiveness is the mind in chains, |
| W-pII . 336.1:5 | to find what it has vainly sought w.. For |
| W-pII . 339.1:9 | in fearlessness, w. confusing pain with joy |
| W-pII ... 14.1:3 | *impossible, and joy established w. opposite.* |
| Wfl........ in.5:1 | We will not end this year w. the gift our |
| M-1 ........... 4:5 | It is old and worn and w. hope. There was |
| M-4 ...... III.1:3 | Judgment w. self-deception is impossible. |
| M-4 ...... III.1:8 | goes. W. judgment are all things equally |
| M-4 ...... III.1:9 | W. judgment are all men brothers, for |
| M-4 ..... VII.1:3 | for w. trust no one can be generous in the |
| M-4 ....VIII.1:1 | can afford to wait, and wait w. anxiety. |
| M-5 ........... 1:2 | is for. Healing is impossible w. this. |
| M-5 ......II.2:12 | could merely rise up w. their aid and say, |
| M-5 ......II.4:11 | w. distortion and without fear, they |
| M-5 ......II.4:11 | and w. fear, they re-establish Heaven. |
| M-7 ........... 4:6 | Yet love w. trust is impossible, and doubt |
| M-8 ........... 6:7 | it–so too are illusions w. distinctions. |
| M-10 ......... 4:3 | right, w. ever realizing you were wrong? |
| M-11 ......... 3:4 | one w. meaning and devoid of sense, yet |
| M-12 ......... 3:6 | w. the fear that truth would encounter in |
| M-12 ......... 3:7 | come only where it is welcomed w. fear. |
| M-13 ......... 3:3 | mind condemned itself to seek w. finding; |
| M-16 ......... 1:7 | one is sent w. a learning goal already set, |
| M-17 ....... 7:12 | for what was done cannot be done w.. |
| M-18 ......... 2:1 | react to magic thoughts wholly w. anger. |
| M-20 ......... 4:5 | now what happiness was yours w. it, that |
| M-20 ......... 6:2 | that His Will is wholly w. opposite. There |
| M-23 ......... 7:4 | God leave anyone w. a very present help |
| M-25 ......... 2:6 | for w. them the walls that surround all |
| M-26 ......... 4:2 | escape from them, but not to be w. them. |
| M-27 ......... 2:3 | ready to break it off w. regret or care, |
| M-27 ......... 6:3 | W. the idea of death there is no world. All |
| M-29 ......... 2:5 | of God has come this far w. realizing that. |
| M-29 ......... 5:5 | cannot say anything w. consulting Him? |
| C-2 ............ 6:8 | has come: Its opposite has gone w. a trace |
| C-4 ............ 2:4 | that God created is forever w. sin and |
| C-4 ............ 2:4 | without sin and therefore is forever w. |
| C-4 ............ 7:6 | world w. a purpose and without a cause. |
| C-4 ............ 7:6 | world without a purpose and w. a cause. |
| C-5 ............ 2:5 | he saw the false w. accepting it as true. |
| C-5 ............ 6:6 | from them w. accepting him into your life |
| P-in ........... 1:6 | to start to open his mind w. formal help, |
| P-2......... in.2:3 | as it is, but w. the suffering that it entails. |
| P-2......... in.3:3 | the changes he wants w. changing his self- |
| P-2..........II.1:3 | within an instant and w. a word. Yet he |
| P-2..........II.2:2 | term w. perceiving the contradiction at all |
| P-2..........II.4:7 | w. knowledge one can have only belief. |
| P-2........ III.1:3 | W. this One, both will merely stumble |
| P-2........ III.3:7 | therapist could heal the world w. a word, |

P-2........III.4:3 therapist cannot progress w. the patient,
P-2........IV.5:5 can understand this w. the Word of God,
P-2......IV.10:2 must meet attack w. attack, and therefore
P-2......IV.10:2 without attack, and therefore w. defense.
P-2.........V.7:6 he would condemn himself w. a cause.
P-2........VI.4:3 W. protection it could not endure. Here is
P-2........VI.4:4 but w. the recognition that this is so. For
P-2.......VII.7:7 w. the god who must be given him?
P-3......III.6:11 everyone must gain a blessing w. cost.
P-3........III.7:7 for salvation w. recognizing where to look
S-1...........I.6:5 the goodness of God prays w. fear. And
S-1...........I.6:6 who prays w. fear cannot but reach Him.
S-1.........II.2:5 Everyone prays w. ceasing. Ask and you
S-1.........II.3:5 W. guilt there is no scarcity. The sinless
S-1.........II.7:7 w. needs of any kind, and clad forever in
S-1.........II.7:8 of thanks to your Creator, sung w. words,
S-1........III.4:2 Nor can this be done w. some pain, and a
S-1........III.4:8 be released w. an insane fear for yourself?
S-1........IV.2:6 that you are asking for effects w. the cause
S-1.........V.3:9 *I cannot go w. you, for you are a part of me.*
S-2.........in.1:2 W. its strong support it would be vain to
S-3.........II.2:4 Now we can behold Him w. blinders, in
S-3........III.5:9 W. Him there is no healing, for there is
S-3........III.6:4 And now w. a cause, it cannot come again
S-3........IV.6:1 w. such twisted thoughts upon your
S-3........IV.8:4 W. you is creation unfulfilled. Return to
S-3......IV.10:2 The song of prayer is silent w. you. The

### withstand 11

T-1........III.5:1 threaten truth, which can always w. it.
T-3...........I.7:7 Good can w. any form of evil, as light
T-12.......II.6:5 can w. the Love of Christ for His Father,
T-13.......II.4:4 ego can w. your raising all else to question
T-13....XI.10:3 His sleep will not w. the Call to wake. The
T-21......I.10:2 made will not w. the memory of this song.
T-26.......V.9:2 Can sin w. the Will of God? Can it be up
T-30......VI.5:8 appearances that could w. the miracle,
T-31.........I.6:6 and incredible in difficulty will w. the
W-pI.....93.4:2 of yourself cannot w. the Will of God.
W-pI...99.11:2 remember that appearances can not w.

### withstood 1

T-13.....VII.3:3 built has w. the crumbling assault of time.

### Witness 1

*witness*

T-27......VI.4:1 God's W. sees no witnesses against the

### witness 118

*Witness*

T-1........I.14:1 Miracles bear w. to truth. They are
T-1........IV.4:6 you that I will w. for anyone who lets me,
T-1........IV.4:8 it. Those who w. for me are expressing,
T-4........I.10:2 now because fear is a w. to the separation,
T-4........I.10:2 and your ego rejoices when you w. to it.
T-5........VI.4:4 even interprets Scripture as a w. for itself.
T-5......VI.10:3 and every w. to guilt in God's creations is
T-5......VI.10:3 is bearing false w. to God Himself. Appeal
T-5......VI.10:7 not hear it, because He can only w. truly.
T-8.........V.3:7 miracles we do bear w. to the Will of the
T-8.....VIII.3:5 not give this false w. to the ego's stand.
T-8.....VIII.4:1 It is hard to perceive sickness as a false w.
T-8.....VIII.4:2 This w., then, appears to be innocent and
T-8.....VIII.4:3 a strong w. on behalf of the ego's views.
T-8.....VIII.4:9 When the ego calls on a w., it has already
T-8.....VIII.4:9 witness, it has already made the w. an ally
T-8.....VIII.6:2 It is a w. to your frailty, your vulnerability
T-9........VI.5:5 who w. to its reality as the Son does to the
T-11.....V.18:1 becomes a w. for Christ or for the ego,
T-11.....V.18:3 Everything you perceive is a w. to the
T-11.....V.18:5 You cannot accept false w. of him unless
T-12.........I.5:2 with a personal investment is a reliable w.
T-13.........V.9:4 sees for you, as your w. to the real world.
T-13......VI.8:6 all your brothers to w. to his wholeness,
T-13......VI.8:8 Son is the w. that his light is of his Father.
T-13......VI.9:2 whom you heal bear w. to your healing,
T-13....VI.13:7 ceased to be his Father's w. and his own.
T-13....VIII.9:2 You are the w. to the Fatherhood of God,
T-13. VIII.10:2 not, and so you do not share His w. to it.
T-13. VIII.10:3 it. Nor do you w. unto Him, for reality is
T-13. VIII.10:4 waits your w. to His Son and to Himself.
T-13. VIII.10:6 They w. to what you do not know, and as
T-13......IX.4:5 doing you have denied the w. unto yours.
T-14.....X.6:10 miracle itself is but the w. that you have
T-15.......II.4:2 they w. to the ego in your perception, and
T-15.....II.4:12 You will be sure because the w. to Him
T-15.....II.4:13 will doubt until you hear one w. whom
T-15.......VI.4:3 his success as w. to the possibility of yours
T-17....III.1:10 hoping that their w. will enable you to
T-17....III.1:12 your relationships the w. to its power.
T-18.......IX.3:2 And these messages bear w. to this world,
T19....IV.B.7:7 as everyone offers you w. of the end of sin,
T-20.... VIII.9:6 adjusts to sin and seems to w. to its reality
T-21........in.1:5 It is the w. to your state of mind, the
T-21........in.2:6 you will see the w. to the choice you made
T-21........II.5:1 see is but the idle w. that you were right.
T-21........II.5:2 This w. is insane. You trained it in its
T-21.....V.1:10 Perception is a w. but to this, and never to
T-23.....II.20:4 a certain w. that these laws are true. The
T-24.VII.10:10 Son's creation gave Him joy and w. to His
T-25.........I.3:4 nor gives the slightest w. unto anything
T-25. VIII.11:2 For just *one* w. is enough, if he sees truly.
T-25. VIII.12:1 perfect w. to the power of love and justice,
T-25. VIII.12:8 Son has found a w. unto his sinlessness
T-25.......IX.7:3 He cannot perceive He bears no w. to.
T-26.........I.4:7 What w. to the Wholeness of God's Son is
T-26.........I.6:3 and take the rest his w. offers on behalf of
T-26.........I.6:4 nor see what it is given him to w. to, that
T-26.........I.7:3 and make your eyes and ears bear w. to
T-27.........I.3:6 becomes the perfect w. to his innocence.
T-27.........I.4:1 The power of w. is beyond belief because
T-27.........I.4:2 w. is believed because he points beyond
T-27.........I.4:3 w. that you send lest he forget the injuries
T-27.........I.4:7 For sickness is the w. to his guilt, and
T-27.........I.7:1 The strongest w. to futility, that bolsters
T-27.......II.3:1 To w. sin and yet forgive it is a paradox
T-27.......II.5:4 The power of w. comes from your belief.
T-27.......II.8:4 knows your healing is the w. unto his, and
T-27.......V.2:1 Health is the w. unto health. As long as it
T-27.......V.2:3 and must provide a w. that compels belief
T-27.......V.3:2 each one is born into this world as w. to a
T-27.......V.6:8 And what you see the world will w., and
T-27.......V.6:8 see the world will witness, and will w. to.
T-27......VI.2:2 For either w. is the same, and carries but
T-27......VI.3:7 make a w. true because you called him by
T-27......VI.4:7 for each w. to the body's death He sends a
T-27......VI.4:7 the body's death He sends a w. to your life
T-27......VI.4:8 Each miracle He brings is w. that the body
T-27......VI.5:7 As fear is w. unto death, so is the miracle
T-27......VI.5:7 death, so is the miracle the w. unto life. It
T-27......VI.5:8 life. It is a w. no one can deny, for it is the
T-27....VI.6:11 strength of miracles for what they w. to.
T-27......VI.7:1 Be you then w. to the miracle, and not the
T-27.....VII.5:5 effects, which then bear w. to the cause,
T-27.....VII.6:2 Forget not that the w. to the world of evil
T-27.....VII.6:5 And it is this the world bears w. to. Seek
T-28.......I.10:4 would w. to is but the fear of God. He has
T-28......III.8:5 of guilt to bring you w. to what never was.
T-28......IV.7:4 can not remain without a w. or a cause.
T-28.......V.5:3 a dream; your ears bear w. to illusion.
T-28.......V.5:7 and make a w. to the world you want. Let
T-28.....VII.4:2 used to w. to the dream of separation and
T-29......III.2:5 Deny Him not His w. in the dream His
T-29....III.3:11 God's w. has set forth the gentle way of
W-pI...103.2:2 reality in truth, bear w. to the fear of God,
W-pI...121.5:3 sees bears w. that its judgment is correct.
W-pI...151.3:2 upon the w. that your senses offer you.
W-pI...151.3:3 Yet w. never falser was than this. But how
W-pI...151.7:3 which merely bear false w. to God's Son.
W-pI...151.9:2 for He bears w. to your beautiful creation,
W-pI.151.12:2 the world, past every w. for unholiness,
W-pI...163.5:3 says but this: "Here lies a w. God is dead."
W-pI.166.15:4 w. in your happiness to how transformed
W-pI...169.4:3 urge you to bear w. to the Word of God to
W-pI...169.7:2 it the experiences which bear w. that the
W-pI.169.13:4 and in need of you as w. to the truth?
W-pI...190.2:3 Pain is but w. to the Son's mistakes in
W-pI...190.4:5 Their w., pain, is mad as they, and no
W-pI...191.2:5 is no sight that fails to w. this to you.
W-pII.....3.3:3 the world was made to w. and make real.
W-pII.250.1:1 the Son of God today, and w. to his glory.
W-pII.255.1:4 today bear w. to the truth of what He says
M-17.........9:7 certain w. that you do believe in it as fact.
M-19.........3:2 distorts perception and brings w. of the
S-2..........II.5:3 w. that it offers one who could be savior,
S-3.........in.1:2 Forgiveness' w. and an aid to prayer, a
S-3...........I.5:3 a w. to the power of the world or to the
S-3........IV.2:1 As w. to forgiveness, aid to prayer, and

### witnessed 6

T-13..VIII.10:3 unto Him, for reality is w. to as one. God
T-17.......V.1:2 is a practical device, w. to by its results.
T-27.......I.4:11 w. to the guilt in him which you perceived
T-27.......V.7:5 the sight to them, by which they w. it. The
W-pI...104.3:4 goals made of illusions, w. to by them,
W-pI...151.3:7 and think more real than what is w. to by

### witnesses 108

T-8......VIII.4:5 choice of w. should be suspect from the
T-8......VIII.4:6 upon w. who would disagree with its case,
T-9........VI.5:4 They will become the w. to your reality, as
T-9........VI.5:4 reality, as you were created w. to God's.
T-9........VI.6:2 miracles are the only w. to your reality
T-9......VIII.8:2 deprive you of the true w. to your reality.
T-9......VIII.8:3 to you lies in the joy you bring to its w.,
T-9......VIII.9:1 be arrogant when God Himself w. to it?
T-9......VIII.9:2 it? And what can be real that has no w.?
T-11........II.2:2 better w. to its reality could you have than
T-11.....V.16:2 perception chooses its w. carefully, and
T-11.....V.16:2 carefully, and its w. are consistent. The
T-11.....V.16:8 Its w. do attest to its denial, but hardly to
T-11.....V.17:6 w. for God stand in His light and behold
T-11.....V.18:5 you have evoked false w. against him. If
T-12.....VII.4:3 Miracles are His w., and speak for His
T-12.....VII.4:4 you only through the w. that speak for it.
T-12.....VII.6:2 you His w. if you will but look upon them.
T-12.....VII.7:3 And then you look out and behold his w..
T-12.....VII.8:2 The contradictory nature of the w. you
T-12.....VII.8:4 believe that the w. for opposition are true,
T-12...VII.11:2 Its holy w. will surround you because you
T-12...VII.11:9 all that you see but w. to your decision.
T-13.......V.2:4 whole. For these figures have no w., being
T-13.......V.7:9 as w. to the reality you share with God.
T-13.......V.9:5 forth its w. and drawing them to you. He
T-13......VI.7:5 you look at Christ and call His w. to shine
T-13......VI.9:1 as you call forth the w. to His creation.
T-13....VI.10:2 you. Yet you will find it through its w., for
T-13....VI.12:3 your willing w. to the love you gave them,
T-13....VI.13:9 the w. that teach him that he never slept.
T-13....VIII.9:2 you the power to create the w. to yours,
T-13....VIII.9:3 deny the w. to your fatherhood in Heaven
T-13......IX.6:6 see as guilty become the w. to guilt in you,
T-13......IX.6:9 where the w. to your fatherhood rejoice.
T-15........II.4:3 more compelling w. for the Holy Spirit.
T-15........II.6:9 recognition of the universe that w. to It,
T-16........II.5:6 the w. that He has given you to His reality
T-16........II.6:5 and honor the w. who bring you the glad
T-16........II.8:1 for you have many w. that speak of it so
T-16......II.9:10 it. Can you be alone with w. like these?
T-16......III.2:8 care you have exerted in choosing its w.,
T-16......III.6:4 the w. to your teaching have gathered to
T-16.......V.9:5 only illusions can be the w. to its "reality.
T-17......III.1:6 The shadow figures are the w. you bring
T-17......III.8:5 offer to the present as w. for its reality.
T-17......III.8:6 is kept but w. to the reality of dreams.
T-17.....VII.1:1 situation are the w. to your lack of faith.
T-19.......I.11:6 sent forth to gather w. unto its coming,
T-21......IV.1:9 that sin is there but w. to your desire that
T-21.......V.7:8 see, because the w. on its behalf are clear.
T-24.....VII.8:9 Yet it but w. to what you taught. It is the
T-25..VIII.10:5 What honest w. could they call forth to

| | |
|---|---|
| T-26.........I.4:7 | bodies, however much he w. to truth? He |
| T-26.........I.5:1 | see the w. to truth instead of to illusion |
| T-26.....VII.8:3 | Illusions have no w. and no effects. Who |
| T-27.........I.5:4 | It w. to the eternal truth that you cannot |
| T-27.........I.6:6 | the w. that are called forth to be believed, |
| T-27.........I.6:9 | to show how lovely are the w. for guilt. |
| T-27.........I.8:1 | but w. unto the strange belief that sin and |
| T-27.........I.9:9 | For now it w. to nothing yet, its purpose |
| T-27....... II.2:2 | For they are the w. that pardon is unfair. |
| T-27...... IV.5:4 | Just as the body's w. are but the senses |
| T-27....... V.7:5 | It will call forth its w. to show the face of |
| T-27..... V.10:3 | to you by all the many different w. it finds |
| T-27..... V.11:7 | Yet all the w. that you behold will be far |
| T-27.........VI.h | The W. to Sin |
| T-27...... VI.2:4 | These w. are joined by many more. Each |
| T-27...... VI.2:6 | Except for this, the w. of sin are all alike. |
| T-27...... VI.2:9 | Sin's w. but shift from name to name, as |
| T-27.... VI.2:11 | Sin's w. hear but the call of death. |
| T-27...... VI.3:4 | when you call forth the w. to its reality. |
| T-27...... VI.4:1 | Witness sees no w. against the body. |
| T-27...... VI.4:2 | Neither does He harken to the w. by other |
| T-27...... VI.4:9 | heal alike, for all sin's w. do His replace. |
| T-27...... VI.5:1 | in the names by which sin's w. are called. |
| T-27...... VI.6:4 | have different w. with different strengths. |
| T-27..... VII.6:6 | among the mighty legions of its w. for its |
| T-27..... VII.7:1 | w. to sin all stand within one little space. |
| T-27..VIII.12:6 | so. Yet to its w. you pay no heed at all. For |
| T-28...... IV.6:5 | Your dreams are w. to his, and his attest |
| T-29......... III.h | God's W. |
| W-pI..... 54.2:2 | What I see w. to what I think. If I did not |
| W-pI..... 54.5:3 | I would look upon the w. that show me |
| W-pI..... 55.1:7 | I am determined to see the w. to the truth |
| W-pI... 151.2:4 | they have been faulty w. indeed! Why |
| W-pI... 151.6:2 | The w. it sends to prove to you its evil is |
| W-pI... 151.7:3 | He passes by such idle w., which merely |
| W-pI... 151.8:4 | sin; unheeding of the body's w. before the |
| W-pI. 151.16:2 | the world, replacing w. to sin and death. |
| W-pI. 161.10:4 | accept the w. your body's eyes call forth. |
| W-pI... 166.7:2 | the w. with proof to show this is not you. |
| W-pI... 181.2:7 | if focused on, are w. to sins in you. And |
| W-pI... 190.1:7 | w. to God the Father's hatred of His Son, |
| W-pI... 208.1:4 | *is within my heart, which w. to God Himself.* |
| W-pII . 240.1:5 | It w. but to your own illusions of yourself. |
| W-pII ..... 4.2:7 | will seek instead for w. to what is true. |
| W-pII . 271.1:1 | w. to what I want to be the truth for me. |
| W-pII . 271.1:2 | the w. to what is true in God's creation. In |
| W-pII ..... 7.2:2 | from the w. of fear to those of love. And |
| W-pII ..... 8.1:3 | and brings the w. of terror to your mind. |
| W-pII ..... 8.1:4 | and w. to fear can not be found. |
| W-pII ... 13.4:2 | faith will bring its w. to show that what it |
| M-in .......... 2:7 | a call to w. to attest to what you believe. It |
| M-23 ......... 6:2 | Yet we have w.. It is to them that wisdom |
| S-2......... II.5:7 | except to keep the w. of guilt away from |
| S-3.........in.1:1 | Prayer has both aids and w. which make |
| S-3...........I.1:3 | w. to unforgiving thoughts that injure |

**witnessing** 3

| | |
|---|---|
| T-1........IV.4:7 | it. Your w. demonstrates your belief, and |
| T-23..... II.20:5 | of the attack are no less certain in their w. |
| M-18 ......... 1:2 | he is but w. to its reality. Depression is |

**won** 2

| | |
|---|---|
| M-17 ....... 6:10 | Believe that you have w. it, but do not |
| M-26 ......... 3:3 | be w. after much devotion and dedication |

**wonder** 10

| | |
|---|---|
| T-13.........I.3:1 | be tempted to w. how you can be guiltless |
| T-13...... III.1:1 | You may w. why it is so crucial that you |
| T-14....... X.6:7 | You may w. how you who are still bound |
| T-15...... IV.7:5 | And then you w. why it is that you are not |
| T-17....... II.6:3 | The smallest leaf becomes a thing of w., |
| T-20...... IV.8:1 | may w. how you can be at peace when, |
| T-22.........I.1:6 | And where, you w., does your strange |
| T-28...... VI.1:7 | It does not w. what it is. And so it has no |
| W-pI..... 28.2:1 | You may w. why it is important to say, |
| W-pI. 135.24:2 | you will but w. why you ever thought that |

**wondered** 1

| | |
|---|---|
| T-20 ...... III.5:1 | you not w. what the world is really like; |

**wonderful** 5

| | |
|---|---|
| T-4 ...... VII.6:2 | that you should tell Him how w. He is. He |
| T-21 ........I.6:3 | how w. the setting where you heard it, |
| T-26 ..... IV.2:1 | of sin into a world of glory, w. to see. Each |
| T-30 .......II.2:1 | How w. it is to do your will! For that is |
| W-pI... 106.4:4 | and as w. as those you ever dreamed or |

**wondering** 2

| | |
|---|---|
| T-14 .. VII.5:11 | delay in your return to peace by w. how |
| W-pII . 342.1:5 | *w. if I should enter in and be at home. Let me* |

**wonderment** 1

| | |
|---|---|
| T-17 .......II.2:6 | cease to cause you w. at its perfection. |

**wood** 1

| | |
|---|---|
| T-28 ...... V.6:2 | made of little bits of glass, a piece of w., a |

**wooden** 1

| | |
|---|---|
| T-30 ..... IV.2:2 | child is frightened when a w. head springs |

**woolly** 1

| | |
|---|---|
| T-30 ..... IV.2:2 | or when a soft and silent w. bear begins to |

**Word** 117
*word*

| | |
|---|---|
| T-8 ...... VII.7:1 | "The W. (or thought) was made flesh." |
| W-pI..... 12.5:7 | your words is written the W. of God. The |
| W-pI..... 14.3:1 | and see the W. of God in their place. The |
| W-pI... 106.4:1 | Today the promise of God's W. is kept. |
| W-pI... 106.5:1 | and listen to the W. which lifts the veil |
| W-pI... 106.5:4 | to hear the W. that He will speak today. |
| W-pI... 106.9:2 | and they will hear the holy W. you hear. |
| W-pI. 106.10:1 | Today the holy W. of God is kept |
| W-pI. 106.10:2 | and to receive the W. by this reminder, |
| W-pI... 110.5:6 | This is the W. in which all sorrow ends. |
| W-pI... 110.8:1 | asking for the W. that tells him he is |
| W-pI. 110.11:6 | This is the W. of God that sets you free. |
| W-pI... 114.2:2 | *my function be but to accept the W. of God,* |
| W-pI... 123.5:2 | come to speak the saving W. of God to us. |
| W-pI... 123.5:4 | His W. is soundless if it be not heard. In |
| W-pI....... 125.h | In quiet I receive God's W. today. |
| W-pI... 125.1:2 | Your Father wills you hear His W. today. |
| W-pI... 125.1:5 | until His W. is heard around the world; |
| W-pI... 125.2:2 | given the W. of God to be his Guide, |
| W-pI... 125.3:1 | and without all judgment of His holy W.. |
| W-pI... 125.3:5 | but wait in silence for the W. of God. |
| W-pI... 125.4:2 | His Voice would give to you His holy W., |
| W-pI... 125.5:1 | your mind to Him to give His W. to you. |
| W-pI... 125.6:2 | for His W. can not be heard until your |
| W-pI... 125.6:3 | Await His W. in quiet. There is peace |
| W-pI... 125.7:1 | instead a gentle listening to the W. of God |
| W-pI... 125.8:3 | It is the W. of freedom and of peace, of |
| W-pI... 125.9:4 | You will hear the W. in which the Will of |
| W-pI... 125.9:5 | this day; in quiet to receive the W. of God. |
| W-pI. 137.15:2 | and to receive the W. of God to take the |
| WpIrIV.in10:1 | who practice thus the keeping of His W.. |
| W-pI... 143.1:1 | (125) In quiet I receive God's W. today. |
| W-pI... 151.9:2 | Accept His W. for what you are, for He |
| W-pI... 154.5:4 | his proper part as bringer of the W.. |
| W-pI. 154.10:3 | the getting and the giving of God's W.; |
| W-pI... 162.2:1 | Here is the W. by which the Son became |
| W-pI... 165.8:2 | Name we practice as His W. directs we do |
| W-pI... 166.9:4 | Perhaps God's W. is truer than your own. |
| W-pI... 168.6:4 | gave to us through His Own Voice, His W. |
| W-pI... 169.4:3 | urge you to bear witness to the W. of God |
| WpI...rV.in2:4 | *We would but listen to Your W., and make it* |
| WpI...rV.in3:6 | *the W. You offer us to unify our practicing,* |
| W-pI. 184.10:2 | Here you understand the W., the Name |
| W-pI 184.13:2 | must come to supplement the W.. But |
| W-pI .. 188.8:2 | urge you gently to accept His W. for what |
| W-pI .. 192.4:1 | which the W. of God can now replace the |
| W-pI .. 195.7:4 | forgotten W. re-echoes in our memory, |
| W-pI .. 198.6:7 | the W. of God will come to take its place, |
| W-pI 198.11:4 | now the W. of God alone remains upon it. |
| W-pII .... in.4:1 | but His W. upon our minds and hearts, |
| W-pII . 228.1:4 | Or shall I take His W. for what I am, since |
| W-pII . 228.2:6 | *to receive Your W. alone for what I really am.* |
| W-pII ..... 2.1:4 | well. God's W. is given every mind which |
| W-pII ..... 2.3:4 | Name of God whereon His W. is written, |
| W-pII . 234.2:2 | *and the W. which You have given us that we* |
| W-pII . 245.2:3 | Who speaks to us as we relate His W.; |
| W-pII . 245.2:3 | we share the W. that He has given unto us |
| W-pII . 254.1:2 | *to hear Your Voice and to receive Your W..* |
| W-pII . 256.2:2 | *find the way Your sacred W. has pointed out* |
| W-pII .... 276.h | The W. of God is given me to speak. |
| W-pII . 276.1:1 | What is the W. of God? "My Son is pure |
| W-pII . 276.1:4 | the W. His Son did not create with Him, |
| W-pII . 276.1:7 | Who gave His W. to us in our creation, to |
| W-pII . 276.2:1 | *Father, Your W. is mine. And it is this that I* |
| W-pII . 296.1:1 | *Your Voice, and hear Your W. through me.* |
| W-pII . 296.1:4 | *hear the W. Your holy Voice will speak to me* |
| W-pII ..... 9.1:3 | to God's W. to take illusion's place; the |
| W-pII . 327.2:3 | *Your W. is one with You. You give the means* |
| W-pII . 336.2:2 | *W. remains unchanged within my mind,* |
| W-pII ... 13.3:5 | And each is laid before the W. of God, |
| W-pII . 341.2:1 | for it contains the W. of God to us. And in |
| W-pII ... 14.5:1 | carrying His W. to everyone whom He has |
| W-pII .... 355.h | that I will give, When I accept God's W.. |
| W-pII . 355.1:2 | *will keep Your W. You gave Your Son in exile* |
| W-pII . 357.1:3 | *instructs me patiently to hear Your W., and* |
| W-ep ......... 3:3 | for His sure direction and His certain W.. |
| W-ep ......... 3:4 | His is the W. that God has given you. His |
| W-ep ......... 3:5 | His is the W. you chose to be your own. |
| M-4...... IX.1:4 | in the W. of God to set all things right; |
| M-4...... IX.2:8 | implies acceptance of the W. of God and |
| M-5 ...... III.2:7 | With God's W. in their minds they come |
| M-5 ...... III.2:9 | not their voice that speaks the W. of God. |
| M-11 ......... 1:3 | Yet the W. of God promises other things |
| M-11 ......... 1:4 | His W. has promised peace. It has also |
| M-11 ......... 1:6 | His W. assures us that He loves the world. |
| M-11 ......... 1:7 | God's W. has promised that peace is |
| M-11 ......... 2:2 | or the W. of God is more likely to be true. |
| M-11 ......... 2:6 | God's W. assures you that He loves the |
| M-12 ......... 5:4 | the W. of God to those who have it not, |
| M-13 ......... 3:5 | through God's W. could this be possible. |
| M-13 ......... 7:5 | The W. of God has no exceptions. It is |
| M-13 ....... 8:11 | God holds out His W. to you, for He has |
| M-14 ......... 2:7 | to Him in silence to receive His W.. The |
| M-14 ....... 5:12 | His W. says otherwise. His Will be done. |
| M-18 ......... 2:5 | can speak the W. of God to listening ears, |
| M-18 ......... 2:7 | completely in His sight and in God's W.. |
| M-18 ......... 3:2 | is taken as replacement for God's W.. The |
| M-21 ....... 3:10 | Only the W. of God has any meaning, |
| M-21 ....... 3:11 | understands what this W. stands for. And |
| M-21 ......... 5:8 | have God's W. behind their symbols. And |
| M-22 ......... 1:6 | Atonement is the W. of God. Accept His |
| M-22 ......... 1:7 | Accept His W. and what remains to make |
| M-22 ......... 1:8 | Accept His W. and every miracle has been |
| M-23 ......... 4:4 | the shining symbol for the W. of God, so |
| M-26 ......... 1:2 | and His W. is written on everyone's heart. |
| M-28 ....... 3:10 | is left to contradict the W. of God. There |
| M-28 ......... 6:7 | he has heard God's W. and understood its |
| C-6 ............ 4:5 | in that form He speaks God's W. to you. |
| C-ep .......... 1:5 | Him and with His W. upon your heart. |
| C-ep .......... 3:6 | Look up and see His W. among the stars, |
| P-2........ IV.5:5 | understand this without the W. of God, |
| P-2..........V.4:7 | We have His W. to guide us, as we try to |
| P-2..........V.5:6 | voice through which to speak His holy W. |
| P-3......... III.5:6 | they have heard His W. and understood it |
| S-3..........II.3:5 | sustained in us; His Voice, the W. of God, |
| S-3........ III.5:6 | place is written now the holy W. of God. |
| S-3........ IV.7:1 | comes for Me and speaks My W. to you. |

**word** 37
*Word*

| | |
|---|---|
| T-1 ....... III.2:2 | My w., which is the resurrection and the |

T-3.........V.4:6 w. "image" is always perception-related,
T-4.........in.1:5 a w. which properly understood is the
T-4.........I.9:10 The w. "inevitable" is fearful to the ego,
T-4.........III.1:3 The w. "within" is unnecessary. The
T-5.........I.4:8 The w. "know" is proper in this context,
T-5.........V.2:2 w. "create" is appropriate here because,
T-5.........VI.9:1 w. "perish" is understood as "be undone."
T-5.........VI.9:2 a w. the ego cannot even understand. To
T-6.........III.1:3 The w. "knows" is correct here, because
T-7.........I.7:4 It must be understood that the w. "first"
T-11.......VI.2:5 because the w. is used both for awareness
T19.IV.A.12:2 it, and return with w. of what they saw.
T19.IV.A.13:2 bring you w. of bones and skin and flesh.
T-23.......II.6:4 to take his w. for it or be mistaken. This
T-24.......III.3:1 and open to attack that just a w., a little
W-pI.....23.3:4 not fantasy a better w. for such a process,
W-pI...125.8:2 It is your w. He speaks. It is the Word of
W-pI...140.1:1 "Cure" is a w. that cannot be applied to
WpI.rIV.in7:4 Let each w. shine with the meaning God
W-pI...168.6:4 but the w. He gave to us through His Own
W-pI...183.6:5 other w. we use except at the beginning,
W-pI...183.6:6 becomes our only thought, our only w.,
W-pII..315.1:4 speaks a w. of gratitude or mercy, and my
WpII361-5.1:1 And if I need a w. to help me, He will give
M-4......I.A.4:7 The w. "value" can apply to nothing else.
M-4........II.1:6 any other thought; no act belies your w.;
M-4........II.1:6 and no w. lacks agreement with another.
M-4.....VII.1:2 It is not the usual meaning of the w.; in
M-4.....VII.1:8 the w. means the exact opposite to the
M-21..........2:3 to the mind in conjunction with the w.,
M-21..........2:3 the w. has little or no practical meaning,
P-2........II.1:3 within an instant and without a w.. Yet he
P-2........III.3:7 could heal the world without a w., merely
P-2........IV.4:1 w. "cure" has come into disrepute among
P-2........IV.5:1 and the w. is perhaps questionable here,
P-2........IV.6:5 In a w., error is accepted as real and dealt

## wordless 1

W-pII.. in.11:2 our daily lessons and the periods of w.,

## wordlessly 1

W-pI.151.13:1 practice w. today, except at the beginning

## words 169

T-1.........II.2:2 attempt to describe it in w. is impossible.
T-3...........I.1:9 kind of thinking which His Own w. have
T-3...........I.2:5 The very w. are meaningless. It has been
T-3.........I.3:11 I have made every effort to use w. that are
T-3.........V.2:1 the w. "create" and "make" have become
T-3........VI.6:2 mercy. Your w. should reflect only mercy,
T-4.........in.2:3 These w. are inspired because they reflect
T-6.........V.3:4 better to use only three w.: "Do only that!
T-7...........I.6:4 explain in w. because words are symbols,
T-7...........I.6:4 explain in words because w. are symbols,
T-9.........II.4:5 Believe his w. are true because of the
T-9.........II.4:6 the truth in him, and his w. will *be* true. As
T-9.........II.5:9 his w. and making you able to hear them.
T-9.......II.5:10 His w. are the Holy Spirit's answer to you.
T-9........IV.4:8 forgetting that my w. make perfect sense
T-9.........V.9:3 Its results are more convincing than its w.
T-9.........V.9:4 will convince you that the w. are true. By
T-11.....V.17:8 to them, and it is His w. they speak.
T-14.......X.8:9 this fact behind impressive sounding w.,
T-18....IX.11:2 speak of what must forever lie beyond w..
T-22.......III.1:5 This is not a play on w., for here is the
T-26.......III.3:3 here, in that the w. imply a limited reality
T-27.......VI.1:2 and keep His w. from your awareness.
T-31...VIII.5:1 as weak and miserable with these w.: *I am*
T-31...VIII.8:1 fail to hear my voice and listen to my w..
W-pI.....11.3:2 The w., however, should be used in an
W-pI.....12.5:7 your w. is written the Word of God. The
W-pI.....12.5:8 now, but when your w. have been erased,
W-pI....29.5:10 as you say the w. unhurriedly to yourself.
W-pI.....41.9:2 of what you are saying; what the w. mean.
W-pI.....62.5:5 for your heart will recognize these w., and
W-pI.....65.6:5 You need not use these exact w., but try
W-pI.....66.11:3 to repeat these w. slowly and think about
WpI..rII.in.6:4 not the particular w. you use that matter.
W-pI.....94.3:2 these times of searching with these w.:
W-pI.....94.5:5 who seems to irritate you with these w.:
W-pI.....95.11:3 meaning of the w. to sink into your mind,
W-pI.....95.11:5 to feel the meaning that the w. convey.
W-pI.....97.7:1 with the w. the Holy Spirit speaks to you,
W-pI.....97.8:3 time you speak the w. He offers you today
W-pI.....97.8:6 Receive His w., and offer them to Him.
W-pI.....98.7:2 He will give the w. you use in practicing
W-pI.....98.7:3 His w. will join with yours, and make
W-pI.....98.7:4 will bring the light to all the w. you say,
W-pI.....98.8:1 He will accept your w. and give them back
W-pI.....98.9:1 Give Him the w., and He will do the rest.
W-pI.....98.9:3 will be His gifts; His answer to your w..
W-pI.....99.7:2 these are w. in which your freedom lies.
W-pI...99.11:2 not withstand the truth these mighty w.
W-pI...105.8:3 assure you that the w. you speak are true.
W-pI...105.9:2 to say the w. which call to Him to give you
W-pI.122.12:1 world arise you have no w. to picture.
W-pI...124.7:2 For in these w. we say as well that we are
W-pI...124.8:4 nor special w. to guide your meditation.
W-pI.126.10:4 and you will understand the w. He speaks
W-pI.126.10:4 and recognize He speaks your w. to you.
W-pI...129.3:3 you go from there to where w. fail entirely
W-pI...129.4:3 Their language has no w., for what They
WpI.rIV.in2:1 which can be simply stated in these w.:
W-pI.152.12:1 hourly invite Him with the w. with which
W-pI.154.14:1 minds, and realize these holy w. are true.
W-pI...156.8:4 in answering your question with these w.:
W-pI...161.1:2 in the simple w. in which we practice with
W-pI...161.4:5 w. bring perfect clarity with them to you?
W-pI...162.1:4 w. are sacred, for they are the words God
W-pI...162.1:4 for they are the w. God gave in answer to
W-pI...162.1:5 illusions vanish as these w. are spoken.
W-pI...162.2:3 There is no dream these w. will not dispel
W-pI...162.3:1 indeed is he who makes these w. his own;
W-pI...162.3:3 each time he practices the w. of truth.
W-pI...162.4:2 For the w. we use are mighty, and they
W-pI...162.6:4 These w. dispel the night, and darkness is
W-pI...169.5:4 for in that knowledge w. are meaningless.
W-pI.169.10:3 listen to w. which explain what is to come
W-pI.169.10:4 Yet what meaning can the w. convey to
WpI...rV.in2:3 *We have no w. to give to You. We would but*
WpI...rV.in9:2 I need; that you will hear the w. I speak,
WpI rV.in11:3 again with these same w. upon our lips, to
WpI rV.in11:5 have recognized the w. we speak are true.
WpI rV.in12:1 Yet are the w. but aids, and to be used,
WpI rV.in12:4 We use the w., and try and try again to go
Wi181-200 2:3 W. alone can not convey the sense of
Wi181-200 2:5 that w. become of little consequence. You
Wi181-200 3:1 our journey beyond w. by concentrating
W-pI...182.2:5 deny he understands the w. we speak?
W-pI...182.8:3 silent and at peace, beyond all w.,
W-pI.183.10:3 it. W. are insignificant, and all requests
W-pI.183.11:6 communication far transcends all w., and
W-pI.183.11:6 height whatever w. could possibly convey
W-pI...185.1:1 To say these w. is nothing. But to mean
W-pI...185.1:2 But to mean these w. is everything. If you
W-pI...185.2:1 one can mean these w. and not be healed.
W-pI...185.2:6 Many have said these w.. But few indeed
W-pI...185.2:9 these w. express the only thing they want.
W-pI...185.5:2 one means these w. who wants illusions,
W-pI...185.7:1 that we really mean the w. we say. We
W-pI...185.7:4 w. do not request another dream be given
W-pI...185.7:6 mean these w. acknowledges illusions are
W-pI...185.8:3 the w. you use in making your requests.
W-pI...186.5:5 The arrogant must cling to w., afraid to
W-pI...193.5:2 These are the w. the Holy Spirit speaks in
W-pI...193.5:3 are the w. with which temptation ends,
W-pI...193.5:4 are the w. which end the dream of sin,
W-pI...193.5:5 the w. by which salvation comes to all the
W-pI...193.6:1 learn to say these w. when we are tempted
W-pI...193.6:2 we not learn to say these w. when we have
W-pI...193.6:3 These are w. which give you power over
W-pI...193.6:4 when you hold these w. in full awareness,
W-pI...193.6:4 forget these w. apply to everything you
W-pI.193.13:4 of suffering, repeat these selfsame w..
W-pI...198.5:3 teach, instead of trying to dismiss His w.,
W-pI...198.6:1 His w. will work. His words will save. His
W-pI...198.6:2 His w. will save. His words contain all
W-pI...198.6:3 His w. contain all hope, all blessing and
W-pI...198.6:4 His w. are born in God, and come to you
W-pI...198.6:5 His w. have heard the song of Heaven. For
W-pI...198.6:6 are the w. in which all merge as one at last
W-pI...198.9:2 truth bestows these w. upon your mind,
WpI rVI.in.4:1 We will attempt to get beyond all w. and
W-pII ....in.1:1 W. will mean little now. We use them
W-pII ....in.3:3 We say some simple w. of welcome, and
W-pII ....in.4:6 We say the w. of invitation that His Voice
W-pII ..in.10:3 Instead of w., we need but feel His Love.
W-pII ..in.11:1 One further use for w. we still retain.
W-pII .222.2:1 *we have no w. except Your Name upon our*
W-pII .229.1:1 Identity, and find It in these w.: "Love,
W-pII .254.2:1 no ego thoughts direct our w. or actions.
W-pII .275.2:3 *thoughts to think, what w. to give the world.*
W-pII .284.1:8 And I would go beyond these w. today,
W-pII .296.1:2 *through me, for I would use no w. but Yours,*
W-pII ... 14.2:1 Our use for w. is almost over now. Yet in
W-pII ... 14.2:4 what we are is not for w. to speak of nor
W-pII ... 14.2:5 here, and w. can speak of this and teach it
W-pII ... 14.2:5 teach it, too, if we exemplify the w. in us.
Wfl........in.1:1 lessons will be left as free of w. as possible
Wfl........in.6:4 thus, for these are His Own w. to you.
Wfl........in.6:5 one ever have, for in these w. is all there is
M-in..........2:9 is not done by w. alone. Any situation
M-1...........3:6 actions or thoughts; in w. or soundlessly;
M-16.......10:7 Perhaps he prefers other w., or only one,
M-21............h IS THE ROLE OF W. IN HEALING?
M-21.........1:1 speaking, w. play no part at all in healing.
M-21.........1:4 the heart, not to the w. you use in praying
M-21.........1:5 the w. and the prayer are contradictory;
M-21.........1:7 God does not understand w., for they
M-21.........1:8 W. can be helpful, particularly for the
M-21.........1:9 that w. are but symbols of symbols. They
M-21.........2:1 symbols, w. have quite specific references
M-21.........2:6 The w., then, are symbols for the things
M-21.........3:9 His w. do not matter. Only the Word of
M-21.........4:1 then, to avoid the use of w. in his teaching
M-21.........4:3 many who must be reached through w.,
M-21.........4:4 however, learn to use w. in a new way.
M-21.........4:5 learns how to let his w. be chosen for him
M-21.........4:7 God accepts the w. which are offered him,
M-21.........5:6 Judge not the w. that come to you, but
M-21.........5:9 to the w. they use the power of His Spirit,
M-23.........7:1 him because his w. have reached you in a
M-29.........6:1 Holy Spirit does not depend on your w..
M-29.........6:8 be cruel if He let your w. replace His Own.
C-in...........3:3 Therefore it uses w., which are symbolic,
C-2.............2:5 behind the w. that seem to make it so.
C-2.............3:3 ego's unreality is not denied by w. nor is
C-5.............6:6 is possible to read his w. and benefit from
P-2..........II.2:2 to join contradictory w. into one term
S-1..........II.4:2 The contradiction lies not in the actual w.
S-1..........II.7:8 thanks to your Creator, sung without w.,
S-2........III.3:3 make your footsteps sure, your w. sincere;
S-2........III.5:7 in w. that you can understand and you

## work 66

T-1........III.1:7 The power to w. miracles belongs to you.
T-1........III.2:3 You are the w. of God, and His work is
T-1........III.2:3 His w. is wholly lovable and wholly loving
T-2........VI.3:7 at the symptom level, where it cannot w..
T-4..........II.3:6 forget that the mind need not w. that way
T-4..........II.3:6 way, even though it does w. that way now
T-4.......IV.11:2 I do w. with your higher mind, the home
T-4.........V.1:1 All things w. together for good. There are
T-5.........III.7:2 Him to w. with the ego's beliefs in its own
T-5......III.11:3 He must w. through opposites, because
T-5......III.11:3 because He must w. with and for a mind
T-5.......VII.4:2 been asked to w. out the plan of salvation
T-6......V.A.1:7 solution the ego attempts, *it will not w.*.
T-7........IV.2:1 Holy Spirit must w. *through* you to teach
T-7.........V.5:1 The Holy Spirit does not w. by chance,
T-8........VI.8:4 Our function is to w. together, because
T-9........IV.4:2 of course, makes no sense and will not w..
T-9........IV.6:4 is. His w. is not your function, and unless

T-9....... V.8:13 But the laws you are obeying w.. “The
T-9....... V.8:15 Only the good *can* w.. Nothing else works
T-10...... IV.4:4 The laws of God w. only for your good,
T-11...... VI.7:5 of God's Son is the w. of the redemption,
T-12......... I.9:8 useless. Defenses that do not w. at all are
T-12....... V.2:5 does not w. and cannot protect you. Yet
T-12..... VII.4:6 Do the Holy Spirit's w., for you share in
T-16....... II.9:7 year invest in truth, and let it w. in peace.
T-17....... V.8:1 its purpose w. in it to make it holy. You
T-17..... V.11:3 enormous efforts to help Him do His w..
T-17...... VI.1:5 He will w. with you to make it specific, for
T-20...... IV.8:3 a plan for your salvation that does not w..
T-25.... VIII.7:2 w. God's vengeance on them in the guise
T-27..... II.12:4 Yet must He w. with what is given Him,
T-30......... I.5:2 your mind to want an answer that will w..
W-pI..... 23.1:2 Nothing else will w.; everything else is
W-pI..... 23.1:5 with your thoughts, then, that we must w.
W-pI..... 69.8:6 power of God w. in you and through you,
W-pI......... 71.h Only God's plan for salvation will w..
W-pI..... 71.3:2 is acceptable provided that it will not w..
W-pI..... 71.6:4 Only God's plan for salvation will w..
W-pI..... 71.8:2 God's plan for your salvation will w., and
W-pI... 71.10:1 plan for salvation, and only His, will w..
W-pI... 71.10:4 *And only His plan will w..* Try to remember
W-pI..... 80.5:7 because of this that it is guaranteed to w..
W-pI..... 86.1:1 (71) Only God's plan for salvation will w.
W-pI..... 86.1:7 Only God's plan for salvation will w.. And
W-pI..... 86.3:2 that God's plan for salvation will not w..
W-pI..... 86.3:3 Yet only His plan will w.. By holding
W-pI..... 88.4:3 *I see only the laws of God at w. in this. Let me*
W-pI..... 88.4:4 *Let me allow God's laws to w. in this, and not*
W-pI..... 99.7:1 You who will yet w. miracles, be sure you
W-pI... 120.1:2 *today, and let Him w. in me and through me,*
W-pI... 153.2:4 sets up a system of defense that cannot w.
W-pI... 153.7:3 you see at w. in all the evils of the world?
W-pI... 154.2:3 He does not w. without your own consent
W-pI. 169.10:3 Now we have w. to do, for those in time
W-pI. 169.10:4 and rise and w. and go to sleep by them?
W-pI. 169.11:1 that you have w. to do to play your part.
W-pI... 198.6:1 His words will w.. His words will save.
W-pII ..... 5.2:3 impermanence is “proof” his fences w.,
W-pII . 345.1:3 *which can be recognized and seen to w.. The*
W-pII . 353.1:4 *A while I w. with Him to serve His purpose.*
M-in ........ 5:11 How can they w. out their own salvation
M-3 ........... 3:7 God's teachers w. at different levels, but
M-16 ....... 6:11 Your defenses will not w., but you are not
M-24 ......... 2:3 he can still w. out his salvation only now.
P-1 ............. 5:6 to prepare additional teachers for His w..

## workbook 15

W-in .......... 1:1 make the exercises in this w. meaningful.
W-in .......... 1:4 It is the purpose of this w. to train your
W-in .......... 3:1 The w. is divided into two main sections,
W-in .......... 4:1 purpose of the w. is to train your mind in
W-in .......... 8:1 Some of the ideas the w. presents you
W-in .......... 9:4 in applying the ideas the w. contains, and
W-pI..... 39.1:2 Like the text for which this w. was written
W-pI..... 39.2:5 text is, and you would not need a w. at all.
M-4 ..... VII.1:6 throughout the text and the w., but it is
M-16 ......... 3:7 that title until he has gone through the w.
M-16 ......... 3:8 practice periods, which the w. contains,
M-16 ......... 5:5 Having gone through the w., you must
M-21 ......... 4:6 case of the lesson in the w. that says, “I
M-29 ......... 1:2 of the major concepts in the text and w..
M-29 ......... 1:6 might do better to begin with the w.. Still

## worked 4

T-26....... II.2:3 And when the situation is w. out so no
W-pI..... 70.3:3 That is the way your mind has w., but
W-pI..... 90.3:3 time must elapse before it can be w. out.
W-pI..... 96.1:3 such solutions, and none of them has w..

## worker 15

*See also* Appendix C

T-1..... III.5:11 The miracle w. can only bless them, and
T-1........ III.7:2 the awareness of the miracle w. himself.
T-1 ........ V.2:3 The miracle w., therefore, accepts the
T-2 ........... V.h The Function of the Miracle W.
T-2 ........ V.3:2 of the miracle w. or the miracle receiver.
T-2 ........ V.3:5 that the miracle w. be in his right mind,
T-2 ........ V.5:1 *The sole responsibility of the miracle w. is to*
T-2 ...... VII.2:4 The miracle w. must have genuine respect
T-5 ........ V.7:8 sole responsibility of the miracle w. is to
T-9 ........ V.7:8 The miracle w. begins by perceiving light,
T-10 ..... IV.7:4 the miracle w. has heard God's Voice, he
T-12 ....... II.1:5 task of the miracle w. thus becomes *to*
M-7 ........... 3:2 w. is to accept the Atonement for himself.
M-7 ........... 3:3 teacher of God is a miracle w. because he
M-18 ......... 4:7 God becomes a miracle w. by definition.

## workers 6

T-2 ........ V.1:1 Before miracle w. are ready to undertake
T-2 ........ V.A.h Special Principles of Miracle W.
T-2 ... V.A.17:2 appeal for cooperation from miracle w..
T-2 .... VII.1:10 All miracle w. need that kind of training.
T-4 ...... VII.8:7 it. The truly helpful are God's miracle w.,
M-7 ........... 4:9 God's teachers the power to be miracle w.

## working 11

*See also* working-out

T-1 ......... II.2:6 w. miracles is important because freedom
T-2 ........ V.4:3 If your miracle w. inclinations are not
T-2 ...... VII.2:2 Miracle w. entails a full realization of the
T-8 .... VII.11:2 of a mind that is w. through the body, but
T-9 ........ V.5:7 correct because he is not w. correctively.
T-15 .. VII.12:1 but the w. of the ego's plan to establish its
T-26 ... VIII.6:1 w. out of all correction takes no time at all
T-26 ... VIII.6:2 acceptance of the w. out can seem to take
W-pI... 100.2:3 you to take in w. out His plan is given you
W-pI... 190.8:1 form, and w. havoc in your holy mind.
P-2........ III.4:6 w. through other patients to express his

## working-out 1

M-2 ........... 4:7 but seems to take time in the w.. What

## workings 2

T-25 ..... III.7:2 you to see the w. of the Helper given you
T-26 .... VII.4:4 God, the laws of time do not affect its w..

## works 24

T-1 ........ I.25:2 Atonement w. all the time and in all the
T-7 ........ V.5:1 healing that is of Him *always* w.. Unless
T-8 ....... IX.7:3 to do the w. of love because we share this
T-9 ...... V.8:14 “The good is what w.” is a sound though
T-9 ...... V.8:16 the good *can* work. Nothing else w. at all.
T-9 ........ V.9:2 you do it, you will see that it w.. Its results
T-11 ..... VI.1:7 does rise above the ego and all its w., and
T-11 ..... VI.9:3 Yet you must see the w. I do through you,
T-12 .. VII.13:6 is the one end toward which it w., and the
T-12 ... VIII.2:5 its w. were not created by the Father, and
T-14 ....... II.4:5 nothing and from all the w. of nothing.
T-14 ... XI.10:8 God that He is there and w. through you.
T-14 ... XI.10:9 And all His w. are yours. He offers you a
T-14 ... XI.15:3 the mighty w. that He will do through you
T-26 .... VII.4:3 answer is eternal, though it w. in time,
T-27 ... VIII.2:3 It w. to get them, doing senseless things,
T-28 ........ I.6:2 It w. hand in hand with all the other
T-30 ........ I.9:3 This w. against the sense of opposition,
W-pI..... 71.5:1 plan for salvation w. simply because, by
W-pI... 108.6:2 this special case has proved it always w.,
W-pI... 156.6:1 This is the way salvation w.. As you step
W-pII ... 12.4:1 not to see the ego and its thoughts, its w.,
M-12 ......... 2:9 And God w. through them now as one,
M-16 ....... 11:8 one simple-minded illusion;–that it w..

## world 2062

*See also* world-encompassing; Appendix C

T-1 ....... VI.4:1 this w. is to use it to correct your unbelief.
T-2 .......... I.3:7 up. The w. has not yet experienced any
T-2 ..... III.5:12 must learn to look upon the w. as a means
T-2 ....... IV.3:8 part of your experience in the physical w..
T-2 ..... IV.3:10 impossible to deny its existence in this w..
T-2 ......... V.1:1 to undertake their function in this w., it is
T-2 ....... V.10:4 still lies within the limitations of this w..
T-2 .... VII.3:13 The fundamental conflict in this w., then,
T-2 .... VII.5:14 the w. that he gave his only begotten Son,
T-3 .......... I.5:1 of God who taketh away the sins of the w.
T-3 .......... I.6:4 The lamb “taketh away the sins of the w.”
T-3 ......... V.9:6 w. believes that if anyone has everything,
T-3 ...... VII.6:9 Your Kingdom is not of this w. because it
T-3 ...... VII.6:9 it was given you from beyond this w..
T-3 .... VII.6:10 Only in this w. is the idea of an authority
T-3 .... VII.6:11 The w. is not left by death but by truth,
T-4 .......... I.4:4 ego and believe in a w. that rests upon it.
T-4 ...... I.13:10 *w. you need not have tribulation because I*
T-4 ...... I.13:10 *tribulation because I have overcome the w..*
T-4 ....... II.11:5 long as you appear to be living in this w..
T-4 ....... II.11:8 Who is the “you” who are living in this w.
T-4 ....... III.4:6 love in this w. is without this ambivalence
T-5 ........ I.1:14 the concept that the w. is one of ideas, the
T-5 ......... II.3:9 possible even in this w. to hear only that
T-5 ....... II.7:11 gain the whole w. and lose his own soul?
T-5 ....... II.10:3 You are the light of the w. with me. Rest
T-5 ....... II.10:6 The w. is very tired, because it is the idea
T-5 ..... III.11:1 The ego made the w. as it perceives it,
T-5 ..... III.11:1 made, sees the w. as a teaching device for
T-5 ..... IV.2:12 even in this w. to listen to one Voice. If
T-5 ....... VI.4:1 reverse a lower court's decisions in this w.
T-5 ..... VI.11:1 I said “I am come as a light into the w.,”
T-6 .......... I.5:3 that I was persecuted as the w. judges,
T-6 .......... I.9:2 As the w. judges these things, but not as
T-6 ......... II.5:5 is the one need in this w. that is universal.
T-6 ......... II.5:6 in which you can find happiness in the w..
T-6 ......... II.5:7 that you are not in this w., for the world *is*
T-6 ......... II.5:7 are not in this world, for the w. *is* unhappy
T-6 ....... II.13:4 it is in alignment with the light of the w..
T-6 ....... II.13:5 Each of us is the light of the w., and by
T-7 .......... I.1:6 Even in this w. there is a parallel. Parents
T-7 ......... II.1:1 kind of thinking in this w. that resembles
T-7 ......... II.2:5 mind in this w. as well as in the Kingdom.
T-7 ......... II.2:6 the content is different in this w., because
T-7 ......... II.2:8 operate in this w. is that by obeying them,
T-7 ......... II.2:9 adapted to the circumstances of this w.,
T-7 ......... V.3:2 Spirit's form of communication in this w.,
T-7 ......... V.7:5 one instant and change the w. in the next.
T-7 ..... VI.11:4 That is all the w. of the ego is. Nothing. It
T-7 ......... X.1:1 is the result of premises, just as this w. is.
T-7 ....... XI.1:3 is therefore the easiest thing in the w.,
T-7 ....... XI.1:3 that is easy, because it is not of the w.. It
T-7 ....... XI.1:5 The w. goes against your nature, being
T-7 ....... XI.1:6 The w. perceives orders of difficulty in
T-8 ....... IV.2:1 into a w. that does deny itself everything.
T-8 ....... IV.2:4 you always, even unto the end of the w..
T-8 ....... IV.2:5 That is why I am the light of the w.. If I
T-8 ....... IV.2:6 If I am with you in the loneliness of the w.
T-8 ....... IV.2:8 purpose, then, is still to overcome the w..
T-8 ....... IV.3:5 in accepting it is the problem of this w..
T-8 ....... IV.3:6 in this sense I *am* the salvation of the w..
T-8 ....... IV.3:7 w. must therefore despise and reject me,
T-8 ....... IV.3:7 the w. *is* the belief that love is impossible.
T-8 ....... IV.3:8 you are denying the w. and accepting God
T-8 ....... IV.4:1 the w. needs peace as much as you do? Do
T-8 ....... IV.4:2 to the w. as much as you want to receive it
T-8 ....... VI.1:5 of God for anything the w. has to offer.
T-8 ....... VI.2:1 The w. can add nothing to the power and
T-8 ....... VI.2:2 You cannot behold the w. and know God.
T-8 ....... VI.3:1 Let us glorify Him Whom the w. denies,
T-8 ....... VI.3:1 over His Kingdom the w. has no power.
T-8 ...... VII.8:3 is the most depressing thing in the w.. In
T-8 ...... VII.8:4 ultimately why the w. itself is depressing.
T-8 ...... VII.9:1 In this w., not even the body is perceived
T-8 .... VII.16:8 Do not arrest your thought in this w., and
T-8 ..... VIII.2:1 body exists in a w. that seems to contain
T-9 ....... V.8:12 you are not obeying the laws of this w..
T-9 ....... VI.7:5 not want anything the w. has to offer.
T-9 ....... VI.7:8 brother in this w. and accept nothing else
T-10 ...... in.1:4 in the w. can take this responsibility from
T-10 ....... II.2:6 in this w. delay your remembering of Him

T-10....... II.3:3 The ability to accept truth in this **w.** is the
T-10...... III.6:3 in this **w.** is the counterpart of value in
T-11...... III.3:5 little **w.** will vanish into nothingness, and
T-11..... VII.1:1 The **w.** as you perceive it cannot have
T-11..... VII.1:1 the Father, for the **w.** is not as you see it.
T-11..... VII.1:3 must be another **w.** that you do not see.
T-11..... VII.1:6 **w.** that awaits your perception when you
T-11..... VII.2:2 in this **w.** are the world's only reality.
T-11..... VII.2:6 The real **w.** can actually be perceived. All
T-11..... VII.3:9 Perceiving only the real **w.** will lead you to
T-11..... VII.4:4 these beliefs are the **w.** as you perceive it.
T-11..... VII.4:7 believe that you can perceive the real **w.** is
T-11..... VII.4:9 real **w.** is all that the Holy Spirit has saved
T-11... VIII.1:4 When you perceive the real **w.**, you will
T-11... VIII.1:7 the real **w.** will vanish from your sight.
T-11... VIII.1:8 The end of the **w.** is not its destruction,
T-11... VIII.1:9 reinterpretation of the **w.** is the transfer
T-11... VIII.7:2 You believe in a **w.** that takes, because
T-11... VIII.7:3 you have lost sight of the real **w.**. You are
T-11... VIII.7:4 You are afraid of the **w.** as you see it, but
T-11... VIII.7:4 but the real **w.** is still yours for the asking.
T-11. VIII.10:1 In the real **w.** there is no sickness, for
T-11. VIII.11:2 you share the real **w.** as you share Heaven,
T-11. VIII.15:4 will accept the real **w.** in place of the false
T-12..... II.10:7 reason for fearing the **w.** as you perceive it
T-12...... III.1:2 have no investment in anything in this **w.**,
T-12...... III.6:5 sort of insane "arrangement" with the **w.**.
T-12...... III.6:6 perceives this **w.** as outside himself, for
T-12...... III.6:7 He does not realize that he makes this **w.**,
T-12...... III.6:7 world, for there is no **w.** outside of him.
T-12...... III.7:1 reality, the real **w.** must be in his mind.
T-12...... III.7:5 as the outside **w.** is merely your attempt
T-12...... III.7:7 at odds with the **w.** as you perceive it,
T-12.... III.7:10 you can perceive the **w.** as it really is.
T-12...... III.8:1 that God so loved the **w.** that He gave it to
T-12...... III.8:2 God does love the real **w.**, and those who
T-12...... III.8:2 its reality cannot see the **w.** of death. For
T-12...... III.8:3 For death is not of the real **w.**, in which
T-12...... III.8:4 God gave you the real **w.** in exchange for
T-12...... III.9:1 **w.** you perceive is a world of separation.
T-12...... III.9:1 world you perceive is a **w.** of separation.
T-12...... III.9:4 you have no control over the **w.** you made
T-12...... III.9:5 It is not a **w.** of will because it is governed
T-12...... III.9:6 **w.** you made is therefore totally chaotic,
T-12...... III.9:8 this **w.** is only in the mind of its maker,
T-12.... III.10:4 You have defiled the altar, but not the **w.**.
T-12.... III.10:6 your perceptions of the **w.** to this altar,
T-12.... III.10:8 look out in peace and behold the **w.** truly.
T-12.... III.10:9 your investment in the **w.** as you project it
T-12.... III.10:9 the real **w.** to you from the altar of God.
T-12...... IV.5:1 because you are not at home in this **w.**.
T-12...... VI.1:1 gain the whole **w.** and lose your own soul.
T-12...... VI.1:2 your soul and there is no gain in the **w.**,
T-12...... VI.3:1 You do not want the **w.**. The only thing
T-12...... VI.3:6 Make the **w.** real unto yourself, for the
T-12...... VI.3:6 for the real **w.** is the gift of the Holy Spirit,
T-12...... VI.4:7 the real **w.** because God gave you Heaven.
T-12...... VI.4:9 begins with his investment in the real **w.**,
T-12.... VI.4:10 the Holy Spirit blesses the real **w.** in Their
T-12...... VI.5:1 When you have seen this real **w.**, as you
T-12...... VI.5:4 then the real **w.** will spring to your sight,
T-12...... VI.5:6 He looks quietly on the real **w.**, which He
T-12...... VI.7:4 The **w.** has no purpose as it blends into
T-12...... VI.7:5 real **w.** has slipped quietly into Heaven,
T-12..... VII.1:4 to all situations you will gain the real **w.**.
T-12..... VII.2:1 Everyone in the **w.** must play his part in
T-12..... VII.2:1 recognize that the **w.** has been redeemed.
T-12..... VII.3:2 enables you to do is clearly not of this **w.**,
T-12..... VII.3:2 every law of reality as this **w.** judges it.
T-12..... VII.5:6 ways of looking at the **w.** are in your mind
T-12..... VII.7:5 will accept it from the **w.** because you put
T-12..... VII.7:8 mind then sees a divided **w.** outside itself,
T-12... VII.7:10 Yet as long as you perceive the **w.** as split,
T-12..... VII.9:1 freedom as a prisoner of this **w.**. You can
T-12... VII.11:6 and we will look upon the real **w.** together
T-12... VII.11:7 only the real **w.** exists and only the real
T-12... VII.11:7 exists and only the real **w.** can be seen. As
T-12... VII.15:6 as you look out upon a **w.** that cannot die.
T-12... VIII.1:3 You attack the real **w.** every day and every
T-12... VIII.6:7 invisible the only truth that this **w.** holds.
T-12... VIII.7:8 The unreal **w.** *is* a thing of despair, for it
T-12... VIII.8:1 real **w.** was given you by God in loving
T-12... VIII.8:1 the **w.** you made and the world you see.
T-12... VIII.8:1 the world you made and the **w.** you see.
T-13............. h THE GUILTLESS **W.**
T-13....... in.2:2 The **w.** you see is the delusional system of
T-13....... in.2:3 Look carefully at this **w.**, and you will
T-13....... in.2:4 For this **w.** is the symbol of punishment,
T-13....... in.3:1 If this were the real **w.**, God *would* be
T-13....... in.3:5 Only the **w.** of guilt could demand this,
T-13....... in.4:1 This **w.** *is* a picture of the crucifixion of
T-13....... in.4:2 be crucified, this is the **w.** you will see. Yet
T-13......... I.2:1 In the strange **w.** that you have made the
T-13......... I.2:3 **w.** of retribution rose in the black cloud
T-13......... I.5:8 Deny your **w.** and judge him not, for his
T-13...... III.3:3 whole **w.** you thought you made would
T-13...... III.4:3 You think you have made a **w.** God would
T-13...... III.4:3 you do, you would throw this **w.** away,
T-13...... III.4:4 you have used the **w.** to cover your love,
T-13...... IV.1:3 that your function in this **w.** is healing,
T-13...... IV.7:5 of eternity that this **w.** offers. It is in the
T-13...... IV.9:2 accept your function in the **w.** of time as
T-13....... V.1:7 up a private **w.** that cannot be shared. For
T-13....... V.1:9 In this **w.** their maker moves alone, for
T-13....... V.2:1 Each one peoples his **w.** with figures from
T-13....... V.3:1 that the insane relate to their insane **w.**.
T-13....... V.3:6 in him a shadow figure in your private **w.**.
T-13....... V.5:1 yet in your private **w.** you react to each of
T-13....... V.5:2 For love cannot abide in a **w.** apart, where
T-13....... V.5:7 private **w.** is filled with figures of fear you
T-13....... V.6:1 As you look with open eyes upon your **w.**,
T-13....... V.7:7 come forth from your private **w.** in peace.
T-13....... V.8:3 Yet in darkness, in the private **w.** of sleep,
T-13....... V.8:7 a private **w.** and rule your own perception
T-13....... V.9:4 sees for you, as your witness to the real **w.**
T-13....... V.9:5 looking always on the real **w.**, and calling
T-13..... V.11:7 the beauty of the **w.** to shine upon them.
T-13.... VI.11:1 There is a light that this **w.** cannot give.
T-13.... VI.11:3 forth to call you from the **w.** and follow it.
T-13.... VI.11:4 attract you as nothing in this **w.** can do.
T-13.... VI.11:5 you will lay aside the **w.** and find another.
T-13.... VI.11:6 This other **w.** is bright with love which
T-13.... VI.11:8 and spreads across this **w.** in quiet joy. All
T-13.... VI.13:3 the real **w.** for you when you awake. In
T-13........ VII.h Attainment of the Real **W.**
T-13..... VII.1:1 Sit quietly and look upon the **w.** you see,
T-13..... VII.1:1 tell yourself: "The real **w.** is not like this.
T-13..... VII.2:1 The **w.** you see must be denied, for sight
T-13..... VII.3:1 You do not really want the **w.** you see, for
T-13..... VII.3:6 This aching **w.** has not the power to touch
T-13..... VII.3:6 not the power to touch the living **w.** at all.
T-13..... VII.3:7 that leads away from it into another **w.**.
T-13..... VII.4:1 real **w.** has the power to touch you even
T-13..... VII.4:3 this strange **w.** you made but do not want
T-13..... VII.4:4 All that you need to give this **w.** away in
T-13..... VII.5:1 about the **w.** because you have misjudged
T-13..... VII.5:9 into the **w.** He holds out to you in love.
T-13..... VII.6:1 No one in this distracted **w.** but has seen
T-13..... VII.6:1 some glimpses of the other **w.** about him.
T-13..... VII.6:6 give this sad **w.** over and exchange your
T-13..... VII.7:3 **w.** about him shines with love because
T-13..... VII.7:6 He must deny the **w.** of pain the instant
T-13..... VII.7:7 recognizes that the **w.** is one with him.
T-13..... VII.8:4 The real **w.** is the way that leads you to
T-13..... VII.9:3 the Holy Spirit corrects the **w.** of dreams,
T-13..... VII.9:7 and the real **w.** is but your welcome of
T-13... VII.10:4 In your **w.** you do need things. It is a
T-13... VII.10:5 a **w.** of scarcity in which you find yourself
T-13... VII.10:6 Yet can you find yourself in such a **w.**?
T-13... VII.11:6 to tighten up your **w.** against the light,
T-13... VII.11:6 value that this **w.** can really hold for you.
T-13... VII.13:6 become, no **w.** outside himself holds his
T-13... VII.15:1 peace of mind this **w.** may set before you.
T-13... VII.16:7 Salvation from the **w.** lies only here. My
T-13... VII.16:9 for all the **w.** has offered but to take away.
T-13. VII.16:10 which we hide our brothers from the **w.**,
T-13... VIII.1:3 therefore no one in the **w.** can know. It
T-13... VIII.1:4 indeed be impossible to be in the **w.** with
T-13.... VIII.5:4 the darkness, and enabling the **w.** to see.
T-13.... VIII.5:5 the darkened **w.** to make Christ's vision
T-13.... VIII.9:1 in this **w.** join you to your brothers, so do
T-13.. VIII.10:1 in this **w.** your perfection is unwitnessed.
T-13...... IX.3:1 The **w.** can give you only what you gave it
T-13...... IX.7:2 And by projecting it the **w.** seems dark,
T-13........ X.8:3 alone in a dark **w.** where pain is pressing
T-13.... XI.3:13 that no dream in this **w.** has ever brought
T-13...... XI.4:1 Nothing in this **w.** can give this peace, for
T-13...... XI.4:1 for nothing in this **w.** is wholly shared.
T-14....... in.1:2 Yet in this **w.** you do not know it. But you
T-14......... I.2:1 truth is needed in a **w.** made of denial and
T-14......... I.2:3 of the **w.** must therefore lead to nothing,
T-14......... I.2:6 the truth. This *is* an insane **w.**, and do not
T-14......... I.3:8 is nothing in the **w.** to teach him that the
T-14......... I.3:8 **w.** is totally insane and leads to nothing.
T-14.... III.15:2 this **w.** or Heaven could possibly commit.
T-14...... IV.8:4 of the **w.** to help you understand it. There
T-14....... V.1:8 Leave the **w.** of death behind, and return
T-14....... V.5:1 and nothing else can unite us in this **w.**.
T-14....... V.5:2 So will the **w.** of separation slip away, and
T-14..... VII.7:7 intense you could not wish, for all the **w.**,
T-14...... IX.5:1 this **w.** you can become a spotless mirror,
T-14...... IX.7:1 shining in you, can bring to all the **w.**, you
T-14...... IX.7:1 the image of the holiness that heals the **w.**
T-14........ X.1:6 Heaven here, and bring this **w.** to Heaven.
T-14........ X.2:4 **w.** you seem to live in is a world of limits.
T-14........ X.2:4 world you seem to live in is a **w.** of limits.
T-14........ X.2:5 In this **w.**, it is not true that anything
T-14........ X.2:6 brings the laws of another **w.** to this one.
T-15........ II.5:5 blind you to this **w.** by its own vision, you
T-15...... III.1:5 Everything in this **w.** is little because it is
T-15...... III.1:5 because it is a **w.** made out of littleness, in
T-15...... III.1:6 strive for anything in this **w.** in the belief
T-15...... III.4:4 to protect your magnitude in this **w.**. To
T-15...... III.4:5 awareness in a **w.** of littleness is a task the
T-15...... III.6:1 gift the **w.** of littleness would offer you.
T-15...... III.7:1 the birth of holiness into this **w.**, join with
T-15...... III.7:6 Far beyond your little **w.** but still in you,
T-15...... III.9:7 My Kingdom is not of this **w.** because it is
T-15...... IV.3:4 to the **w.** for its release from littleness.
T-15...... VI.5:1 In the **w.** of scarcity, love has no meaning
T-15...... VI.5:9 of this **w.** cease to hold any meaning at all
T-15.... VIII.1:2 use everything in this **w.** for your release.
T-15........ X.1:2 For in this **w.**, the attraction of guilt does
T-15........ X.1:5 you would celebrate my birth into the **w.**.
T-16...... IV.9:4 Seek not for this in the bleak **w.** of illusion
T-16....... V.3:6 For this **w.** *is* the opposite of Heaven,
T-16......... VI.h The Bridge to the Real **W.**
T-16...... VI.5:1 You see the **w.** you value. On this side of
T-16...... VI.5:2 bridge you see the **w.** of separate bodies,
T-16...... VI.7:5 that seemed to hold your **w.** together.
T-17.......... II.h The Forgiven **W.**
T-17........ II.2:2 It is the real **w.**, bright and clean and new,
T-17........ II.2:4 bridge between that **w.** and this is so little
T-17........ II.2:5 thing that touches on this **w.** at all. This
T-17........ II.3:4 The real **w.**, in its loveliness, you learn to
T-17........ II.4:1 opened up the **w.** to beauty will vanish.
T-17........ II.4:4 The perception of the real **w.** will be so
T-17........ II.4:5 the real **w.** and have been made ready for
T-17........ II.5:1 real **w.** is attained simply by the complete
T-17........ II.5:1 old, the **w.** you see without forgiveness.
T-17........ II.5:2 searching of the mind that made this **w.**,
T-17........ II.6:1 you look upon the **w.** with forgiving eyes.
T-17........ II.6:2 lets you see the real **w.** reaching quietly
T-17........ II.7:1 forgiven **w.** the Son of God is lifted easily
T-17........ II.8:2 It will give you the real **w.**, trembling with
T-17........ II.8:5 and walk with Him in trust out of this **w.**,
T-17........ II.8:5 into the real **w.** of beauty and forgiveness.
T-17...... III.9:4 the real **w.** or the world of guilt and fear,
T-17...... III.9:4 the real world or the **w.** of guilt and fear,
T-17...... IV.2:1 In this **w.** it is impossible to create. Yet it
T-17...... IV.3:1 very real relationships even in this **w.**. Yet
T-17....... V.1:1 of the holy instant in living in this **w.**. Like
T-17....... V.2:1 step toward the perception of the real **w.**,
T-18......... I.4:5 Your whole **w.** rests upon it. Everything
T-18......... I.5:3 it a **w.** of total unreality *had* to emerge.
T-18......... I.6:2 The **w.** arose to hide it, and became the
T-18......... I.6:4 Do you really think it strange that a **w.** in

T-18.........I.6:6 projection by which this w. was made.
T-18.........I.7:3 into the mad w. and so depart from you.
T-18.........I.9:2 In the mad w. outside you nothing can be
T-18.......I.12:4 out of this w. and through another, to the
T-18.......I.13:1 to the most holy function this w. contains
T-18....... II.1:1 a w. that seems quite real arise in dreams?
T-18....... II.1:2 Yet think what this w. is. It is clearly not
T-18....... II.1:3 It is clearly not the w. you saw before you
T-18....... II.1:4 Rather it is a distortion of the w., planned
T-18....... II.2:4 Yet they are a way of looking at the w.,
T-18....... II.3:7 a time it seems as if the w. were given you,
T-18....... II.4:5 a w. that you prefer *is* terrifying. Your
T-18....... II.5:1 to make a w. as you would have it be, and
T-18....... II.5:3 Yet here is a w., clearly within your mind,
T-18..... II.5:10 wish to make another w. that is not real
T-18..... II.5:11 form of this same w. you see in dreams.
T-18....... II.8:2 that dreams can make a w. that is unreal.
T-18....... II.9:4 the Holy Spirit has gently laid the real w.;
T-18....... II.9:4 the real world; the w. of happy dreams,
T-18....... II.9:5 so do the real w. and the truth of Heaven
T-18....VIII.5:1 in a w. inhabited by bodies seem to be.
T-18...... IX.3:1 From the w. of bodies, made by insanity,
T-18...... IX.3:2 these messages bear witness to this w.,
T-18...... IX.4:1 foundation on which the w. is based.
T-18...... IX.4:2 w. could rise from it and keep it hidden.
T-18...... IX.7:1 bank it is easy to see a whole w. rising. A
T-18...... IX.7:5 it, you do not confuse it with the w. below
T-18...... IX.8:3 them is a w. of light whereon they cast no
T-18...... IX.8:4 shadows lie upon the w. beyond them,
T-18...... IX.9:1 This w. of light, this circle of brightness is
T-18...... IX.9:1 this circle of brightness is the real w.,
T-18...... IX.9:2 Here the w. outside is seen anew, without
T-18.... IX.11:3 only that whoever attains the real w.,
T-18.... IX.13:1 been uprooted from the w. of shadows,
T-18.... IX.13:1 and firmly rooted in the w. of light. From
T-18.... IX.14:3 the shadows from the w. and carrying it,
T-18.... IX.14:3 the bright w. of new and clean perception
T-19.......I.12:1 exchanged for knowledge as is the real w..
T-19....... II.6:1 indeed be said the ego made its w. on sin.
T-19....... II.6:2 sin. Only in such a w. could everything be
T-19....... II.6:5 to an ideal the ego wants; a w. it rules,
T-19...... III.7:3 perception of the w. in which the proof of
T-19...... IV.1:3 from various aspects of the w. outside.
T19. IV.A.4:12 send its messengers from you to all the w.
T19... IV.A.5:1 overcome the w. is no more difficult than
T19... IV.A.7:2 As you look upon the w., this little wish,
T19... IV.A.8:1 remains of what once seemed to be the w.
T19. IV.A.12:1 Relationships in this w. are the result of
T19. IV.A.12:1 world are the result of how the w. is seen.
T19. IV.A.13:1 not these savage messengers into the w.,
T19. IV.A.14:8 of safety, for they see the w. as kind.
T19. IV.A.15:2 w. will be transformed before your sight,
T19. IV.A.15:3 The w. contains no fear that you laid not
T19....IV.B.5:5 to let peace through to bless the tired w.!
T19....IV.B.6:5 if I surmounted guilt and overcame the w.
T19....IV.B.7:6 forth to all the w. the joyous message of
T19....IV.B.7:6 the end of guilt, and all the w. will answer
T19....IV.B.8:5 that will bring light to all the w.,
T19....IV.C.8:1 Under the dusty edge of its distorted w.
T19... IV.D.1:6 to sanity. For here your w. *does* end.
T19... IV.D.7:1 seems to you the w. will utterly abandon
T19... IV.D.7:2 will occur is you will leave the w. forever.
T19. IV.D.21:4 Here is the only purpose that gives this w.
T19. IV.D.21:4 and the long journey through this w.,
T-20...... III.3:6 You make the w. and then adjust to it,
T-20...... III.4:2 have made?–a w. of murder and attack,
T-20...... III.4:6 to a w. made fearful by their adjustments.
T-20...... III.5:1 not wondered what the w. is really like;
T-20...... III.5:2 w. you see is but a judgment on yourself.
T-20...... III.5:5 Such is the w. you see; a judgment on
T-20...... III.5:6 it loves, and placed outside you in the w..
T-20...... III.5:7 And to this w. must you adjust as long as
T-20...... III.5:8 This w. *is* merciless, and were it outside
T-20...... III.6:2 The w. the holy see is one with them, just
T-20...... III.6:2 as the w. the ego looks upon is like itself.
T-20...... III.6:3 The w. the holy see is beautiful because
T-20...... III.6:7 of the w. as answer to the question,
T-20...... III.6:8 The w. believes in sin, but the belief that
T-20...... III.8:3 The w. you look on is the answer that it
T-20 ..... III.8:3 given it power to adjust the w. to make its
T-20 ..... IV.1:2 as the laws of this w. interpret giving; as
T-20 ..... IV.1:5 nor to its results as this w. sees them,–
T-20 ..... IV.5:4 In the w. of separation each is appointed
T-20 ..... IV.6:5 beginning of another w. goes with them.
T-20 ..... IV.6:7 a new w. rises in which sin can enter not,
T-20 ..... IV.7:3 For the whole new w. rests in the hands of
T-20 ...... V.1:1 In this w., God's Son comes closest to
T-20 ...VIII.7:3 you recognized this w. is an hallucination
T-20 ...VIII.8:8 This w. seems to hold out many purposes,
T-20 ...VIII.9:6 are the means by which the outside w.,
T-20 .VIII.10:3 All meaning that you give the w. outside
T-21 ......in.1:2 w. you see is what you gave it, nothing
T-21 ......in.1:7 Therefore, seek not to change the w., but
T-21 ......in.1:7 choose to change your mind about the w..
T-21 ......in.2:1 and this you will project upon the w.. See
T-21 ......in.2:7 The w. you see but shows you how much
T-21 ........I.1:1 forget the w. the sightless "see" must be
T-21 ........I.2:2 to imagine what the w. must look like. It
T-21 ........I.4:1 become accustomed to their w. by their
T-21 ........I.4:7 And so they keep the w. they learned to
T-21 ........I.4:8 hate the w. they learned through pain.
T-21 ........I.7:3 would lose the w. you learned since then.
T-21 ........I.7:4 in the w. you learned is half so dear as this
T-21 .......II.4:2 it, and you keep the w. as now you see it.
T-21 .......II.4:6 Here is the w. you do not want brought to
T-21 ......II.4:10 is strong enough to make a w. can let it go
T-21 .......II.5:1 The w. you see is but the idle witness that
T-21 .......II.9:4 of a fearful w. to justify its purpose. What
T-21 .....II.11:1 you recognize you made the w. you see, as
T-21 .....II.11:5 think the w. you made has power to make
T-21 .....II.12:6 brother thinks he made the w. with you.
T-21 .....II.12:8 With you, he thinks the w. he made,
T-21 ..... III.4:2 the Holy Spirit leads you to the real w.,
T-21 ..... III.8:4 had limited their understanding of the w.,
T-21 ..... III.9:9 He Who loves the w. is seeing it for you,
T-21 ..... IV.7:4 which sings the praises of another w.,
T-21 ...... V.1:1 selects, and makes the w. you see. It
T-21 ...... V.2:6 the w. you made directs your destiny. For
T-21 ..... VI.2:4 himself as guilty and sees a sinless w.?
T-21 ..... VI.2:5 can see a sinful w. and look upon himself
T-21 .... VII.4:3 it can overrun the w. and *seek* an enemy.
T-21 .... VII.5:6 be willing to perceive a w. where it is not.
T-21 .. VII.5:11 *I desire a w. I rule instead of one that rules me*
T-21 .. VII.5:12 *a w. where I am powerful instead of helpless*
T-21 .. VII.5:13 *a w. in which I have no enemies and cannot*
T-21 .... VII.9:4 you choose to see a w. without an enemy,
T-21 .. VII.10:6 can desire a w. you rule that rules you not
T-21 .. VII.10:8 And you can want to see a sinless w., and
T-21 .. VII.11:2 the w. of sin for what the Holy Spirit sees,
T-21 .. VII.11:2 sees, since it is this the w. of sin denies.
T-21 .. VII.11:3 on sin are seeing the denial of the real w..
T-21 .. VII.11:4 constancy in your desire to see the real w.,
T-22 ......in.2:8 so they wander through a w. of strangers,
T-22 ......in.2:8 in the same room and yet a w. apart.
T-22 ........I.2:3 Reason would tell you that the w. you see
T-22 ........I.2:5 of the eyes that look upon the w.. If this is
T-22 ........I.3:8 asking it to explain to you the w. it sees,
T-22 .......I.3:11 does not lead you through a w. of misery,
T-22 .......I.4:10 lead you through the w. it made for you.
T-22 .......II.2:6 in the dark w. of misery is to select some
T-22 .......II.8:8 a slave to time than to the w. you made.
T-22 .....II.12:8 home with vision that overlooks the w..
T-22 ..... III.4:7 its heavy anchor in the shifting w. it made
T-22 ..... IV.3:7 it into a darkened w. that needs the light.
T-22 ..... IV.5:4 So shall you walk the w. with me, whose
T-22 ..... IV.6:5 walking the w. with their Redeemer, and
T-22 ..... VI.8:2 Through this releasing is the w. released.
T-22 ..... VI.9:9 you offer to your brother lights up the w..
T-22 ... VI.10:1 learning depends the welfare of the w..
T-23 ......in.4:3 Think what a happy w. you walk, with
T-23 ......in.4:4 give up this w. of freedom for a little sigh
T-23 ......in.5:7 Who can walk trembling in a fearful w.,
T-23 ......in.6:4 forgiveness will the w. sparkle and shine,
T-23 ......in.6:5 a w. in bitter need of the redemption that
T-23 ........I.8:8 Why would you fill your w. with conflicts
T-23 .......II.1:6 are the laws that rule the w. you made.
T-23 .....II.10:4 But in a savage w. the kind cannot survive
T-23 .....II.13:4 w. where meaning can be found, consider
T-24 ........I.4:7 for nothing in the w. they value more.
T-24 .......II.6:4 Father. And all the w. he made, and all his
T-24 ..... III.3:1 that you did not anticipate upsets your w.
T-24 ..... III.7:1 surrounded by a w. of loveliness they do
T-24 ..... IV.1:7 can only mean destruction of the w.,
T-24 ..... IV.5:2 Only this is certain in this shifting w. that
T-24 ..... VI.1:1 your brother's holiness the w. is still, and
T-24 ..... VI.3:4 He conceived of you before the w. began,
T-24 ..... VI.3:7 saves you from a w. that He created not.
T-24 ..... VI.4:1 the healing of God's Son is all the w. is for
T-24 ..... VI.4:3 all you wish to be accomplished by the w.,
T-24 ..... VI.4:4 will use the w. for what is not its purpose,
T-24 ..... VI.5:1 of the laws that seem to rule this w.. See
T-24 .... VII.1:1 to this w. defend the specialness he wants
T-25 ........I.3:1 yourself to be; the w. you want to live in,
T-25 ........I.5:6 In this w. this is not understood, but can
T-25 .......II.1:3 satisfaction in the w. as you perceive it.
T-25 .......II.2:1 hope of satisfaction from the w. you see?
T-25 .......II.3:1 on grounds that are not in this w.? And
T-25 ..... III.1:1 that extent will you perceive a w. in which
T-25 ..... III.1:6 is perception's form, adapted to this w.,
T-25 ..... III.2:1 obtain directly to a w. perception rules,
T-25 ..... III.2:1 for such a w. could not have been created
T-25 ..... III.2:3 Not that the w. where this reflection is, is
T-25 ..... III.3:3 But this w. has two who made it, and they
T-25 ..... III.4:1 There is another Maker of the w., the
T-25 ..... III.5:1 is another purpose in the w. that error
T-25 ..... III.5:2 In His perception of the w., nothing is
T-25 ..... III.5:6 the Maker of the w. correct your error,
T-25 ..... III.7:2 to see the w. He made instead of yours.
T-25 ..... III.7:8 This w. has much to offer to your peace,
T-25 ..... III.8:1 Maker of the w. of gentleness has perfect
T-25 ..... III.8:1 to offset the w. of violence and hate that
T-25 ... III.9:10 the purpose of the w. you see is chosen,
T-25 ..... IV.3:1 You maker of a w. that is not so, take rest
T-25 ..... IV.3:1 take rest and comfort in another w. where
T-25 ..... IV.3:2 w. you bring with you to all the weary
T-25 ..... IV.3:4 can rise a w. they will rejoice to look upon
T-25 ..... IV.3:6 this widening w. of light the darkness that
T-25 ..... IV.4:9 a home in Heaven the w. cannot destroy.
T-25 ... IV.4:10 it is large enough to hold the w. within its
T-25 ... IV.5:11 This can you bring to all the w., and all
T-25 ... IV.5:12 walk beyond the w. of darkness into light
T-25 ..... VI.1:2 can see no evil; nothing in the w. to fear,
T-25 ..... VI.3:6 see no function in the w. for them to fill;
T-25 ..... VI.4:3 make himself complete within a w. where
T-25 ..... VI.5:6 every function of this w. completed with
T-25 ..... VI.6:1 than a reminder this w. is not your home.
T-25 .... VII.1:2 thing in all the w. that cannot change. It is
T-25 .... VII.1:4 And on its changelessness the w. depends
T-25 .... VII.1:5 The magic of the w. can seem to hide the
T-25 .... VII.1:9 The w. is safe from love to everyone who
T-25 .... VII.2:2 Nor can the basis of a w. He did not make
T-25 .... VII.3:2 is mad, or is this w. a place of madness.
T-25 .... VII.3:3 His makes any sense at all within this w..
T-25 .... VII.3:4 And nothing that the w. believes as true
T-25 .... VII.3:8 the w. gives any meaning to are false, and
T-25 .... VII.4:1 To justify one value that the w. upholds
T-25 .... VII.4:7 Who thinks the w. is sane in any way, is
T-25 .... VII.4:9 w. is meaningless *because* it rests on sin.
T-25 .... VII.5:1 of the w. you see to something else; a
T-25 .... VII.5:1 can be based, another w. perceived. And
T-25 .... VII.6:4 the basis for a w. perceived as wholly mad
T-25 .... VII.6:6 Each sees a w. immutable, as each defines
T-25 .... VII.8:2 He to raise a saner w. to meet the sight of
T-25 .... VII.8:3 one which will not attack the w. he sees,
T-25 .... VII.8:4 and recognizes as the w. in which he lives,
T-25 .... VII.9:3 and all the sin he sees within the w., offer
T-25 .. VII.11:2 For in this w. it seems that one must gain
T-25 .. VII.11:4 basic tenet, "Sin is real, and rules the w.?"
T-25 ... VIII.3:1 salvation of which the w. knows nothing.
T-25 ... VIII.3:2 To the w., justice and vengeance are the
T-25 ... VIII.6:7 Their w. depends on sin's stability. And
T-25 ... VIII.6:8 and to their w. than vengeance, which
T-25 .VIII.12:3 you look to your experience within the w.,
T-25 .VIII.14:5 The w. deceives, but it cannot replace
T-25 ..... IX.1:5 of this w. in favor of the peace of Heaven.
T-25 ..... IX.4:4 The w. solves problems in another way. It
T-26 ........I.1:7 Look at the w., and you will see nothing

T-26.........I.2:1 The **w.** you see is based on "sacrifice" of
T-26.........I.4:7 Son is seen within a **w.** of separate bodies,
T-26.........I.4:8 He is invisible in such a **w.**. Nor can his
T-26...... I.4:10 him to make the **w.** recede before his song
T-26.........I.5:1 they might see a purpose in the **w.** that
T-26.........I.5:2 function has this **w.** no meaning for you.
T-26.........I.6:3 brother sings to you, and let the **w.** recede
T-26.........I.8:1 all injustice the **w.** would lay upon him.
T-26...... III.2:1 that stands between this **w.** and Heaven.
T-26...... III.3:2 We have referred to it as the real **w.**. And
T-26...... III.4:2 possible, the final judgment upon this **w.**.
T-26...... III.4:6 But in this **w.** there are no simple facts,
T-26.... III.4:10 In the real **w.** is choosing simplified.
T-26...... III.6:1 in this complex and overcomplicated **w.**.
T-26...... III.6:3 The real **w.** is the area of choice made real
T-26...... IV.1:2 the **w.** of sin into a simple world, where
T-26...... IV.1:2 the world of sin into a simple **w.**, where
T-26...... IV.1:4 charity within the **w.** gives way to simple
T-26...... IV.2:1 turns the **w.** of sin into a world of glory,
T-26...... IV.2:1 turns the world of sin into a **w.** of glory,
T-26...... IV.3:4 altar to rise and tower far above the **w.**,
T-26...... IV.5:1 a **w.** that will become an altar to the truth,
T-26....... V.2:2 meaningless to the real Teacher of the **w.**.
T-26....... V.5:3 short to make a **w.** in answer to creation,
T-26....... V.5:3 to creation,–did this **w.** appear to rise.
T-26..... V.12:3 now. The real **w.** is the second part of the
T-26..... V.14:3 reached the **w.** that lies at Heaven's gate.
T-26..... V.14:5 and behold the **w.** in which perception of
T-26..... V.14:5 has been transformed into a **w.** of love.
T-26...... VI.1:1 Anything in this **w.** that you believe is
T-26...... VI.1:5 has entered all the **w.** of sick illusions. All
T-26...... VI.3:5 He brings you gifts that are not of this **w.**,
T-26..... VII.3:2 **w.** of shadows and illusions built on sin.
T-26..... VII.4:2 God given answer to the **w.** of sickness,
T-26..... VII.4:5 It is in this **w.**, but not a part of it. For it is
T-26..... VII.7:4 becomes impatient, splits the **w.** apart,
T-26..... VII.8:5 and serves to bring the joy this **w.** denies
T-26..... VII.9:3 reached beyond the **w.** of choice entirely.
T-26... VII.10:1 **w.** that death and desolation seem to rule.
T-26... VII.10:2 to replace the **w.** you see with Heaven,
T-26... VII.11:6 and therefore has no meaning in this **w.**.
T-26... VII.12:4 error does the **w.** of sin and sacrifice arise.
T-26... VII.12:5 **w.** is an attempt to prove your innocence,
T-26... VII.19:3 blessing to the **w.** of sin and death. For
T-26...... IX.3:2 become a living temple in a **w.** of light.
T-26...... IX.5:3 between the light of Heaven and the **w.**.
T-26...... IX.7:2 in. Your footprints lighten up the **w.**, for
T-26....... X.5:5 for the **w.** is purposeless except for this.
T-26....... X.5:6 all purpose from the **w.** and from yourself
T-26....... X.5:7 each unfairness that the **w.** appears to lay
T-26....... X.6:2 The **w.** grows dim and threatening, not a
T-26....... X.6:3 left without a purpose in a futile **w.**. The
T-26....... X.6:4 The **w.** is fair because the Holy Spirit has
T-27.........I.6:3 for death that is the motivation for this **w.**
T-27....... II.6:4 things the **w.** attests can never be undone.
T-27....... II.6:7 the last trumpet that the **w.** will ever hear.
T-27....... II.8:2 Spirit and the **w.** interpret differently.
T-27....... II.8:3 **w.** perceives it as a statement of the "fact"
T-27...... III.7:8 the **w.** of symbols and of limitations. He
T-27...... IV.3:5 The **w.** can only ask a double question.
T-27...... IV.4:1 this **w.** are but a way of looking, not a
T-27...... IV.4:4 The **w.** asks but one question. It is this:
T-27...... IV.4:7 from all the pain of which this **w.** is made
T-27...... IV.5:3 the **w.** a form of propaganda for itself.
T-27...... IV.5:4 questions of the **w.** contained within the
T-27...... IV.6:7 of the **w.** but ask of whom is sacrifice
T-27...... IV.7:1 attempt to solve no problems in a **w.** from
T-27...... IV.7:4 *is.* Within the **w.** the answers merely raise
T-27....... V.3:2 each one is born into this **w.** as witness to
T-27....... V.4:5 the One Who blesses you loves all the **w.**,
T-27....... V.4:5 leaves nothing within the **w.** that could be
T-27....... V.4:6 blessing, will the **w.** indeed seem fearful,
T-27....... V.5:1 a **w.** so bitterly bereft be looked on as a
T-27....... V.5:5 dying **w.** asks only that you rest an instant
T-27....... V.6:1 is left behind on your returning to the **w.**.
T-27....... V.6:3 Life is given you to give the dying **w.**. And
T-27....... V.6:8 And what you see the **w.** will witness, and
T-27....... V.7:1 is your healing everything the **w.** requires,
T-27....... V.7:3 will the **w.** remind you gently of what you
T-27....... V.7:6 The **w.** of accusation is replaced by one in
T-27....... V.8:1 and these specific shapes make up the **w.**.
T-27...... VI.6:1 Love, too, has symbols in a **w.** of sin. The
T-27...... VI.6:6 Who sends forth miracles to bless the **w.**,
T-27...... VI.6:6 cry for help within a **w.** of misery. It is
T-27...... VI.7:3 suffering and sorrow of the **w.** have made
T-27...... VI.8:1 resurrection of the **w.** awaits your healing
T-27...... VI.8:1 may demonstrate the healing of the **w.**.
T-27..... VII.1:1 all that the **w.** has done to injure you.
T-27..... VII.3:1 The "reasoning" by which the **w.** is made
T-27..... VII.3:6 it looks as if the **w.** were hurting you. And
T-27..... VII.4:2 those within the **w.** are joined in sharing.
T-27..... VII.4:4 condemnation of the **w.** will rest on him.
T-27..... VII.5:1 This is the purpose of the **w.** he sees. And
T-27..... VII.5:2 the **w.** provides the means by which this
T-27..... VII.6:1 part you play in salvaging the **w.** from
T-27..... VII.6:2 Forget not that the witness to the **w.** of
T-27..... VII.6:2 for what has seen a need for evil in the **w.**.
T-27..... VII.6:5 And it is this the **w.** bears witness to. Seek
T-27..... VII.7:2 the cause of your perspective on the **w.**.
T-27..... VII.7:3 the **w.** appeared to thrust upon you,
T-27..... VII.8:1 from a dream the **w.** is dreaming for him.
T-27..... VII.8:7 within the idle dreaming of the **w.**.
T-27... VII.10:2 because the **w.** equates the body with the
T-27... VII.11:3 between a tiny you and an enormous **w.**,
T-27... VII.11:4 of the **w.** and what you dream in secret.
T-27... VII.11:6 The dreaming of the **w.** is but a part of
T-27... VII.12:2 destroyer of your brother and the **w.** alike
T-27... VII.13:1 *You* are the dreamer of the **w.** of dreams.
T-27... VIII.1:1 central figure in the dreaming of the **w.**.
T-27... VIII.1:3 bodies, born into the **w.** outside the body,
T-27... VIII.2:1 dreaming of the **w.** takes many forms,
T-27... VIII.2:2 the **w.** proclaims as valuable and real. It
T-27... VIII.3:1 theme of every dream the **w.** has ever had.
T-27... VIII.5:1 of all the dreams the **w.** has ever had? Is it
T-27... VIII.5:4 the **w.** remembers his attack upon himself
T-27... VIII.5:5 could never have conceived this **w.** as real.
T-27... VIII.7:2 The **w.** you see depicts exactly what you
T-27... VIII.7:4 a guilty **w.** that dreams your dreams and
T-27... VIII.8:1 **w.** but demonstrates an ancient truth;
T-27. VIII.13:1 perceive the **w.** when this is recognized!
T-27. VIII.13:2 When you forgive the **w.** your guilt, you
T-27. VIII.13:5 has maintained you separate from the **w.**,
T-28.........I.1:6 This **w.** was over long ago. The thoughts
T-28.........I.4:4 the **w.** imposes on it are as vast as those
T-28.........I.4:4 vast as those you let the **w.** impose on you
T-28........I.14:7 fear, and past the **w.** of sin entirely.
T-28....... II.3:6 within a body and a **w.** of other bodies,
T-28....... II.6:1 This **w.** is causeless, as is every dream
T-28....... II.6:1 that anyone has dreamed within the **w.**.
T-28...... II.10:6 this much of the dream; the **w.** is neutral,
T-28...... II.12:1 This **w.** is full of miracles. They stand in
T-28...... II.12:7 and all the dreaming of the **w.** undone.
T-28...... III.4:1 and love was never in the **w.** of dreams.
T-28...... III.7:1 keep within the storehouse of the **w.**. The
T-28...... III.7:4 the **w.** except a little gap perceived to tear
T-28...... III.7:5 the **w.** except a picture of the Son of God
T-28...... III.8:1 but let your **w.** be gently lit by miracles.
T-28...... III.9:1 those the dreaming of the **w.** has shown.
T-28....... V.4:2 Here is a **w.** established that is sick, and
T-28....... V.4:2 and this the **w.** the body's eyes perceive.
T-28....... V.5:4 made to look upon a **w.** that is not there;
T-28....... V.5:7 and make a witness to the **w.** you want.
T-28....... V.7:1 in a **w.** perceived to be existing here. The
T-28....... V.7:2 The **w.** you see does not exist, because the
T-28..... VII.2:3 for healing, and the **w.** waits with him.
T-28..... VII.5:2 **w.** is but the dream that you can be alone,
T-28..... VII.7:4 The **w.** will wash away and yet this house
T-29....... II.6:3 for on confusion has this **w.** been based,
T-29...... III.2:7 one with him without the wall the **w.** has
T-29....... V.1:1 place in you where this whole **w.** has been
T-29....... V.2:3 so deep within that nothing in this **w.** but
T-29....... V.5:6 their hold on every vain illusion of the **w.**.
T-29....... V.7:6 have come to worship in a separated **w.**,
T-29....... V.8:3 Yet nothing in the **w.** of dreams remains
T-29....... V.8:4 is so, and seek not the eternal in this **w.**.
T-29....... V.8:5 from dreaming of a **w.** outside yourself.
T-29...... VI.5:1 **w.** will bind your feet and tie your hands
T-29...... VI.5:3 in the **w.** but must be changed as well. For
T-29...... VI.6:1 How lovely is the **w.** whose purpose is
T-29...... VI.6:4 Nor can it be forgot, in such a **w.**, it *is* a
T-29..... VII.6:1 All idols of this **w.** were made to keep the
T-29..... VII.7:1 the purpose of the **w.** the past has given it.
T-29..... VII.8:1 you do not know the purpose of the **w.**.
T-29..... VII.9:4 And speed the end of idols in a **w.** made
T-29..... VII.9:9 all the **w.** becomes the means by which
T-29.... VIII.2:3 for safety in a **w.** perceived as dangerous,
T-29.... VIII.2:6 apart from all the misery the **w.** reflects.
T-29.... VIII.2:7 quiet calm that liberates you from the **w.**,
T-29.... VIII.4:1 **w.** of idols *is* a veil across the face of Christ,
T-29.... VIII.6:3 Here the **w.** of idols has been set by the
T-29.... VIII.6:3 shape the **w.** where the impossible has
T-29.... VIII.8:4 The **w.** believes in idols. No one comes
T-29...... IX.4:6 They pretend they rule the **w.**, and give
T-29...... IX.5:9 to make his **w.** remain outside himself,
T-29...... IX.6:7 and he is afraid of all the chaos in a **w.** he
T-29...... IX.6:8 Yet is the real **w.** unaffected by the world
T-29...... IX.6:8 unaffected by the **w.** he thinks is real. Nor
T-29...... IX.7:1 The real **w.** still is but a dream. Except
T-30.......I.16:6 adviser, for yourself and for the **w.** as well
T-30.......I.16:7 The day you want you offer to the **w.**, for
T-30.......I.16:7 reinforce the rule of your adviser in the **w.**
T-30.......I.16:8 Whose kingdom is the **w.** for you today?
T-30.......I.17:1 this day to promise it to all the **w.**. It
T-30.......I.17:6 and give it to the **w.** by having it yourself.
T-30.......I.17:7 the **w.** by your decision for a happy day.
T-30........II.3:2 For thus was hatred born into the **w.**, and
T-30........II.4:1 you for anger in a **w.** that merely waits
T-30........II.4:6 This **w.** awaits the freedom you will give
T-30........II.4:7 But you will not forgive the **w.** until you
T-30........II.4:8 it is by your will the **w.** is given freedom.
T-30........II.5:1 God turns to you to ask the **w.** be saved,
T-30.... III.10:2 by the turmoil and the terror of the **w.**,
T-30.... III.10:4 unaware of all the **w.** that worships idols,
T-30.... III.11:2 a **w.** which your reality knows nothing of?
T-30..... IV.2:5 mean his **w.** is made chaotic and unsafe.
T-30....... V.1:1 The real **w.** is the state of mind in which
T-30....... V.1:1 purpose of the **w.** is seen to be forgiveness
T-30....... V.2:7 The **w.** becomes a place of hope, because
T-30....... V.2:8 because the **w.** has been united in belief
T-30....... V.2:8 of the **w.** is one which all must share, if
T-30....... V.4:3 the real **w.** has a purpose still beneath
T-30....... V.5:1 The real **w.** still falls short of this, for this
T-30....... V.5:2 The real **w.** is a state in which the mind
T-30....... V.7:1 brothers join in purpose in the **w.** of fear,
T-30....... V.7:1 stand already at the edge of the real **w.**.
T-30....... V.8:1 the narrow boundaries of the **w.** of fear
T-30....... V.9:1 An ancient hate is passing from the **w.**.
T-30....... V.9:4 Give up the **w.**! But not to sacrifice. You
T-30...... VI.1:4 real **w.** given in exchange for dreams of
T-30...... VI.3:1 the only change that lets the real **w.** rise to
T-30...... VI.3:3 The real **w.** is achieved when you perceive
T-30...... VI.3:6 And this is all the **w.** can ever give. It
T-30...... VI.4:1 false forgiveness which the **w.** employs to
T-30...... VI.5:7 and to make a **w.** that could replace it and
T-30..... VII.1:1 meaning of the **w.** to your interpretation?
T-30..... VII.1:4 Holy Spirit looks upon the **w.** as with one
T-30..... VII.4:1 given to the **w.** and all experiences here.
T-30..... VII.5:1 purpose, which you share with all the **w.**.
T-30..... VII.5:2 nothing in the **w.** can be opposed to it, for
T-30..... VII.7:2 will believe the **w.** is an uncertain place, in
T-31.........I.3:2 There is no greater power in the **w.**. The
T-31.........I.3:3 The **w.** was made by it, and even now
T-31.........I.4:3 until a **w.** was built that suited you. And
T-31.........I.4:4 that makes up the **w.** arises from the first
T-31.........I.4:5 The **w.** began with one strange lesson,
T-31.........I.5:5 skill the Holy Spirit sees in all the **w.**. His
T-31.........I.7:2 Each has its outcome in a different **w.**.
T-31.........I.7:3 each **w.** follows surely from its source.
T-31.........I.7:4 that God's Son is guilty is the **w.** you see.
T-31.........I.7:5 see. It is a **w.** of terror and despair. Nor is
T-31.......I.7:11 God's Son is innocent, and see another **w.**
T-31.........I.8:1 is guiltless is a **w.** in which there is no fear
T-31.........I.8:4 everything within the **w.** has always made
T-31.........I.8:8 throughout the **w.** this second lesson
T-31.......I.10:3 and pleads that love restore the dying **w.**.
T-31.......I.11:6 And all the **w.** will give you joy and peace.
T-31.....I.11:10 Its outcome is the **w.** you look upon.

T-31.......I.12:2 not our own ideas of what the w. is for.
T-31......III.5:2 rules, and orders that the w. be like itself;
T-31......IV.1:1 There is a tendency to think the w. can
T-31......IV.2:2 But the w. has none to offer. All its roads
T-31......IV.2:6 The w. was made that problems could not
T-31......IV.3:3 The roads this w. can offer seem to be
T-31......IV.3:4 way except the pathways offered by the w.
T-31......IV.3:8 there is no choice at all within the w.. But
T-31......IV.4:3 there is no hope of answer in the w.. But
T-31......IV.4:5 Seek not another signpost in the w. that
T-31......IV.5:1 away from all the roadways of the w.,
T-31......IV.6:1 The learning that the w. can offer but one
T-31......IV.6:3 come to learn to find a road the w. does
T-31......IV.6:4 search for different pathways in the w. is
T-31......IV.8:4 All choices in the w. depend on this; you
T-31......IV.9:3 No pathway in the w. can lead to Him,
T-31......IV.9:4 What road in all the w. will lead within,
T-31.......V.1:1 learning of the w. is built upon a concept
T-31.......V.1:3 is that suits a w. of shadows and illusions.
T-31.......V.1:5 the self is what the learning of the w. is for
T-31.......V.1:7 it, to meet the w. on equal terms, at one
T-31.......V.2:4 The concept of the self the w. would teach
T-31.......V.2:9 It believes that it is good within an evil w..
T-31.......V.3:1 for the w. is wicked and unable to provide
T-31.......V.3:2 the injustices the w. accords to those who
T-31.......V.4:1 for is it not a well-known fact the w. deals
T-31.......V.4:4 the learning of the w. has set its sights, for
T-31.......V.5:4 of the self the w. smiles with approval, for
T-31.......V.5:4 the pathways of the w. are safely kept,
T-31.......V.7:7 Concepts maintain the w.. But they can
T-31.......V.7:8 not be used to demonstrate the w. is real.
T-31.......V.7:9 For all of them are made within the w.,
T-31.....V.7:10 idols, painted with the brushes of the w.,
T-31.......V.8:2 all learning that the w. directs begun and
T-31.......V.9:7 He must have made the w. as well as you
T-31.....V.10:9 If the w. be evil, there is still no need to
T-31.....V.11:2 And what would happen to the w. you see
T-31.....V.11:3 Your concept of the w. depends upon this
T-31.....V.14:1 been the great preoccupation of the w..
T-31.....V.15:6 To see a guilty w. is but the sign your
T-31.....V.15:6 your learning has been guided by the w.,
T-31.....V.16:3 you thankful that the learning of the w. is
T-31.....V.17:1 The w. can teach no images of you unless
T-31.....V.17:6 the w. is more afraid to hear than this: *I do*
T-31.....V.17:7 *am, or how to look upon the w. or on myself.*
T-31......VI.1:6 this one choice does all your w. depend,
T-31......VI.1:8 that you may see the w. of flesh no more
T-31......VI.2:2 the body, you behold a w. of separation,
T-31......VI.3:3 how to behold a w. apart from it. It is
T-31......VI.3:4 it. It is your w. salvation will undo, and let
T-31......VI.3:4 and let you see another w. your eyes could
T-31......VI.4:2 the w. that will replace the one you made.
T-31......VI.5:4 change the w. for eyes that learn to see,
T-31......VI.6:2 Then the w. is harmless in your sight. Do
T-31......VI.6:4 Then is the w. forgiving, for you have
T-31......VI.6:6 So is all the w. perceived as treacherous,
T-31......VI.6:8 So the w. is seen as stable, fully worthy of
T-31.....VII.3:4 when you have reached the w. beyond the
T-31.....VII.3:6 you. And in His sight there *is* another w..
T-31.....VII.4:1 You live in that w. just as much as this.
T-31.....VII.6:6 yourself as needed for salvation of the w.,
T-31...VII.15:1 given unto you, be hidden from the w.. It
T-31....VIII.1:5 *take your place among the saviors of the w.,*
T-31....VIII.4:4 The saviors of the w., who see like Him,
T-31....VIII.4:5 They will redeem the w., for they are
T-31....VIII.7:1 who wanders in the w. uncertain, lonely,
T-31....VIII.8:3 for hell within a w. whose loveliness can
T-31....VIII.8:4 tired eyes I bring a vision of a different w.,
T-31....VIII.9:1 Let us be glad that we can walk the w.,
T-31..VIII.10:7 the w. with every choice they make. For
T-31..VIII.11:5 chorus from a w. redeemed from hell, and
W-in..........4:1 of everyone and everything in the w.. The
W-in..........5:1 as does transfer of the training of the w..
W-pI........11.h are showing me a meaningless w..
W-pI.....11.1:1 the reversal of the thinking of the w.. It
W-pI.....11.1:2 as if the w. determines what you perceive.
W-pI.....11.1:3 your thoughts determine the w. you see.
W-pI........12.h I am upset because I see a meaningless w.
W-pI.....12.1:2 that what upsets you is a frightening w.,
W-pI.....12.1:2 you is a frightening world, or a sad w., or
W-pI.....12.1:2 world, or a sad world, or a violent w., or
W-pI.....12.1:2 world, or a violent world, or an insane w..
W-pI.....12.1:4 it by you. The w. is meaningless in itself.
W-pI.....12.3:2 *I think I see a fearful w., a dangerous world, a*
W-pI.....12.3:2 *I think I see a fearful world, a dangerous w.,*
W-pI.....12.3:2 *world, a dangerous world, a hostile w., a sad*
W-pI.....12.3:2 *a dangerous world, a hostile world, a sad w.,*
W-pI.....12.3:2 *a hostile world, a sad world, a wicked w.,*
W-pI.....12.3:2 *a sad world, a wicked world, a crazy w.,* and
W-pI.....12.3:4 example, you might think of "a good w.,"
W-pI.....12.3:4 of "a good world," or "a satisfying w.." If
W-pI.....12.3:6 that a "good w." implies a "bad" one, and
W-pI.....12.3:6 "satisfying w." implies an "unsatisfying"
W-pI.....12.4:4 *I am upset because I see a meaningless w..*
W-pI.....12.5:2 then, should a meaningless w. upset you?
W-pI.....12.5:3 If you could accept the w. as meaningless
W-pI........13.h A meaningless w. engenders fear.
W-pI.....13.1:2 Actually, a meaningless w. is impossible.
W-pI.....13.3:2 is certain that you will endow the w. with
W-pI.....13.4:4 *I am looking at a meaningless w..* Repeat this
W-pI.....13.4:7 *A meaningless w. engenders fear because I*
W-pI........14.h God did not create a meaningless w..
W-pI.....14.1:1 why a meaningless w. is impossible.
W-pI.....14.1:4 w. you see has nothing to do with reality.
W-pI.....14.3:1 thoughts that you have written on the w.,
W-pI.....14.4:1 the horrors in the w. that cross your mind
W-pI.....14.6:2 These things are part of the w. you see.
W-pI.....14.6:8 idea: *God did not create a meaningless w..*
W-pI.....14.7:4 *God did not create a meaningless w.. He did*
W-pI.....16.2:2 of a whole w. can hardly be called idle.
W-pI.....17.1:1 and effect as it really operates in the w..
W-pI.....17.1:4 This is not the way the w. thinks, but you
W-pI.....20.1:5 The salvation of the w. depends on it. Yet
W-pI.....20.3:4 the salvation of the w. be a trivial purpose
W-pI.....20.3:5 And can the w. be saved if you are not?
W-pI.....20.5:6 of cause and effect as it operates in the w..
W-pI.....22.1:1 thoughts in his mind must see the w..
W-pI.....22.1:2 Having projected his anger onto the w.,
W-pI.....22.1:5 preoccupy him and people his entire w..
W-pI.....22.3:1 the w. about you at least five times today,
W-pI.....22.3:8 *Is this the w. I really want to see?* The answer
W-pI........23.h the w. I see by giving up attack thoughts.
W-pI.....23.1:4 makes up some segment of the w. you see.
W-pI.....23.1:5 your perception of the w. is to be changed
W-pI.....23.2:1 cause of the w. you see is attack thoughts,
W-pI.....23.2:2 There is no point in lamenting the w..
W-pI.....23.2:3 is no point in trying to change the w.. It is
W-pI.....23.2:5 in changing your thoughts about the w..
W-pI.....23.3:1 The w. you see is a vengeful world, and
W-pI.....23.3:1 The world you see is a vengeful w., and
W-pI.....23.4:1 You see the w. that you have made, but
W-pI.....23.4:2 You cannot be saved from the w., but you
W-pI.....23.4:3 is the w. you see when its cause is gone?
W-pI.....23.5:1 that you are not trapped in the w. you see,
W-pI.....23.6:4 *I can escape from the w. I see by giving up*
W-pI.....23.7:4 of identifying the cause of the w. you see.
W-pI.....25.2:1 You perceive the w. and everything in it
W-pI.....25.2:5 the goals you have assigned to the w.,
W-pI.....29.3:6 you the holiness that lights up the w., you
W-pI.....30.1:2 this idea will the w. open up before you,
W-pI.....30.2:3 to see in the w. what is in our minds, and
W-pI........31.h I am not the victim of the w. I see.
W-pI.....31.1:2 the w. you see without and the world you
W-pI.....31.1:2 you see without and the w. you see within
W-pI.....31.2:4 and apply the same idea to your inner w..
W-pI.....31.3:1 As you survey your inner w., merely let
W-pI.....31.4:3 in your freedom lies the freedom of the w.
W-pI........32.h I have invented the w. I see.
W-pI.....32.1:2 of the w. you see because you invented it.
W-pI.....32.2:2 one involving the w. you see outside you,
W-pI.....32.2:2 and the other the w. you see in your mind
W-pI.....32.3:1 at the w. you see as outside yourself. Then
W-pI.....32.3:2 your eyes and look around your inner w..
W-pI.....32.5:2 you survey either your inner or outer w..
W-pI........33.h There is another way of looking at the w..
W-pI.....33.1:1 the w. in both its outer and inner aspects.
W-pI.....33.2:1 the w. you perceive as outside yourself,
W-pI.....34.1:4 that a peaceful perception of the w. arises.
W-pI .... 34.2:4 your inner w. to which the applications of
W-pI .... 35.1:3 he is in this w. to believe this of himself.
W-pI .... 35.1:4 in this w. is because he does not believe it.
W-pI ....... 37.h My holiness blesses the w..
W-pI .... 37.1:1 of your true function in the w., or why
W-pI .... 37.1:2 is to see the w. through your own holiness
W-pI .... 37.1:3 Thus are you and the w. blessed together.
W-pI .... 37.3:1 Your holiness is the salvation of the w.. It
W-pI .... 37.3:2 you teach the w. that it is one with you,
W-pI .... 37.5:1 for today to your outer w. if you so desire;
W-pI .... 38.1:1 holiness reverses all the laws of the w.. It
W-pI .... 39.3:1 your holiness is the salvation of the w..
W-pI .... 39.3:6 is crucial to the salvation of the w.. As you
W-pI .... 39.3:7 As you apply the exercises to your w., the
W-pI .... 39.3:7 your world, the whole w. stands to benefit
W-pI .... 39.4:3 Your holiness is the salvation of the w.,
W-pI .... 41.2:1 what they believe to be "the ills of the w.."
W-pI .... 41.3:1 radiate through you and out into the w..
W-pI .... 41.6:5 past all the idle thoughts of the w.. Try to
W-pI .... 41.7:2 and inward, away from the w. and all the
W-pI .... 41.7:2 and all the foolish thoughts of the w.. You
W-pI .... 41.8:2 it is the most natural thing in the w.. You
W-pI .... 41.8:3 say it is the only natural thing in the w..
W-pI .... 43.5:5 *I see the w. as blessed. The world can show*
W-pI .... 43.5:6 *The w. can show me myself. I see my own*
W-pI .... 44.4:3 easy one in the w. for the trained mind,
W-pI .. 44.10:2 as you pass by the thoughts of this w..
W-pI .. 44.10:3 they cannot hold you to the w. unless you
W-pI .... 45.4:3 We will deny the w. in favor of truth. We
W-pI .... 45.4:4 not let the thoughts of the w. hold us back
W-pI .... 45.4:5 We will not let the beliefs of the w. tell us
W-pI .... 46.1:3 Forgiveness is the great need of this w.,
W-pI .... 46.1:3 but that is because it is a w. of illusions.
W-pI .... 49.1:3 in the w. and obeys the world's laws. It is
W-pI .... 49.4:4 and sights and sounds of this insane w..
W-pI .... 49.5:3 you can, closing your eyes on the w., and
W-pI .... 50.1:2 In this w., you believe you are sustained
W-pI .... 50.3:2 perceived dangers of this w. into a climate
W-pI .... 52.2:2 look about, I condemn the w. I look upon.
W-pI .... 53.1:1 are showing me a meaningless w.. Since
W-pI .... 53.1:2 the w. that pictures them can have no
W-pI .... 53.1:3 What is producing this w. is insane, and
W-pI .... 53.1:5 I can therefore see a real w., if I look to my
W-pI .... 53.2:1 I am upset because I see a meaningless w..
W-pI .... 53.2:3 a w. in which there is no order anywhere.
W-pI .... 53.2:4 rules a w. that represents chaotic thinking
W-pI .... 53.2:5 I cannot live in peace in such a w.. I am
W-pI .... 53.2:6 I am grateful that this w. is not real, and
W-pI .... 53.3:1 (13) A meaningless w. engenders fear.
W-pI .... 53.3:5 But such a w. is not real. I have given it
W-pI .... 53.3:8 I will escape all the effects of the w. of fear
W-pI .... 53.4:1 (14) God did not create a meaningless w..
W-pI .... 53.4:2 meaningless w. exist if God did not create
W-pI .... 53.5:4 The fact that I see a w. in which there is
W-pI .... 54.1:3 make a false w. or lead me to the real one.
W-pI .... 54.1:5 w. I see arises from my thinking errors, so
W-pI .... 54.1:5 so will the real w. rise before my eyes as I
W-pI .... 54.2:4 thought. Let me look on the w. I see as the
W-pI .... 54.2:6 I also know the w. I see can change as well
W-pI .... 54.3:2 private thoughts, I cannot see a private w.
W-pI .... 54.3:3 it could form the basis of the w. I see. Yet
W-pI .... 54.3:7 And the w. my real thoughts show me will
W-pI .... 54.5:3 the thinking of the w. has been changed.
W-pI .... 54.5:5 I would look upon the real w., and let it
W-pI .... 55.2:2 The w. I see is hardly the representation
W-pI .... 55.2:6 save me from this perception of the w.,
W-pI .... 55.3:1 from this w. by giving up attack thoughts.
W-pI .... 55.3:3 thoughts I could not see a w. of attack. As
W-pI .... 55.3:4 I will see a w. of peace and safety and joy.
W-pI .... 55.4:3 bind me closer to the w. of illusions. I am
W-pI .... 55.5:4 It is for this that I believe the w. is for.
W-pI .... 55.5:6 the w. has led to a frightening picture of it
W-pI .... 56.1:4 to be at the mercy of a w. I cannot control
W-pI .... 56.1:6 away in exchange for the w. I see. But God
W-pI .... 56.2:3 The w. I see attests to the fearful nature of
W-pI .... 56.2:6 I will look upon the w. and on myself with
W-pI .... 56.3:2 The w. I see holds my fearful self-image in
W-pI .... 56.3:3 While I see the w. as I see it now, truth
W-pI .... 56.3:4 the door behind this w. be opened for me,

| | |
|---|---|
| W-pI.....56.3:4 | it to the **w.** that reflects the Love of God. |
| W-pI.....57.1:1 | (31) I am not the victim of the **w.** I see. |
| W-pI.....57.1:2 | How can I be the victim of a **w.** that can |
| W-pI.....57.1:7 | Nothing holds me in this **w.**. Only my |
| W-pI.....57.2:1 | (32) I have invented the **w.** I see. I made |
| W-pI.....57.3:1 | There is another way of looking at the **w.**. |
| W-pI.....57.3:2 | purpose of the **w.** is not the one I ascribed |
| W-pI.....57.3:4 | I see the **w.** as a prison for God's Son. It |
| W-pI.....57.3:5 | the **w.** is really a place where he can be set |
| W-pI.....57.3:6 | I would look upon the **w.** as it is, and see |
| W-pI.....57.4:2 | When I see the **w.** as a place of freedom, I |
| W-pI.....57.5:3 | the peace of the **w.** with my brothers, I |
| W-pI.....57.5:4 | The **w.** I look upon has taken on the light |
| W-pI.....58.1:2 | does the perception of the real **w.** come. |
| W-pI.....58.1:5 | eyes, the holiness of the **w.** is all I see, for I |
| W-pI.....58.2:1 | (37) My holiness blesses the **w.**. The |
| W-pI.....58.2:5 | holiness of the **w.** shine forth for everyone |
| W-pI.....58.4:3 | is also recognizing the salvation of the **w.**. |
| W-pI.....58.4:5 | is the gift of God to me and to the **w.**. |
| W-pI.....59.4:7 | vision and the happy **w.** it will show me. |
| W-pI.....60.3:2 | the **w.** will look to me when I can see it! It |
| W-pI.....60.3:6 | be to fear in a **w.** that I have forgiven, and |
| W-pI.....60.5:3 | His Love lights up the **w.** for me to see. As |
| W-pI.....60.5:5 | I look upon the **w.** with the vision He has |
| W-pI........61.h | I am the light of the **w.**. |
| W-pI.....61.1:1 | is the light of the **w.** except God's Son? |
| W-pI.....61.2:4 | be the light of the **w.** if that is the function |
| W-pI.....61.5:3 | *I am the light of the* **w.**. *That is my only* |
| W-pI.....61.7:5 | You are the light of the **w.**. God has built |
| W-pI........62.h | is my function as the light of the **w.**. |
| W-pI.....62.1:1 | will bring the **w.** of darkness to the light. |
| W-pI.....62.1:3 | that you are the light of the **w.**. Through |
| W-pI.....62.2:1 | about yourself and the **w.** are one. That is |
| W-pI.....62.5:2 | *is my function as the light of the* **w.**. *I would* |
| W-pI........63.h | The light of the **w.** brings peace to every |
| W-pI.....63.2:1 | the light of the **w.** with such a function. |
| W-pI.....63.3:4 | *light of the* **w.** *brings peace to every mind* |
| W-pI.....63.3:5 | *has appointed for the salvation of the* **w.**. |
| W-pI.....64.1:2 | purpose of the **w.** you see is to obscure |
| W-pI.....64.2:3 | **w.** is a place where you learn to forgive |
| W-pI.....64.3:1 | function here is to be the light of the **w.**, |
| W-pI.....64.6:6 | of your function to you and to the **w.**. |
| W-pI.....64.8:4 | *This is the* **w.** *it is my function to save.* |
| W-pI.....65.2:1 | rightful place among the saviors of the **w.**. |
| W-pI.....67.1:2 | are. This is why you are the light of the **w.**. |
| W-pI.....68.6:4 | in a **w.** that protects you and loves you, |
| W-pI........69.h | grievances hide the light of the **w.** in me. |
| W-pI.....69.1:2 | grievances are hiding the light of the **w.** in |
| W-pI.....69.1:5 | in the light of the **w.** that saves you both. |
| W-pI.....69.2:3 | to get in touch with the salvation of the **w.** |
| W-pI.....69.6:1 | are trying to do for yourself and the **w.**, |
| W-pI.....69.9:1 | the light of the **w.** from your awareness. |
| W-pI.....69.9:4 | *My grievances hide the light of the* **w.** *in me.* |
| W-pI.....69.9:6 | *for my salvation and the salvation of the* **w.**. |
| W-pI.....69.9:8 | *I hold this grievance the light of the* **w.** *will be* |
| W-pI...70.10:4 | are in charge of the salvation of the **w.**. |
| W-pI.....72.7:1 | is the universal belief of the **w.** you see. |
| W-pI.....73.1:5 | they can make a **w.** of illusions in which |
| W-pI.....73.2:1 | or co-makers in picturing the **w.** you see. |
| W-pI.....73.3:2 | **w.** have been created by the Will the Son |
| W-pI.....73.3:5 | Would God create a **w.** that kills Himself? |
| W-pI.....73.4:1 | the **w.** that is in accordance with your will |
| W-pI.....73.4:6 | that shines upon this **w.** reflects your will, |
| W-pI.....73.5:1 | of the **w.** can only mirror what is within. |
| W-pI.....73.5:3 | mind, and you look out on a darkened **w.**. |
| W-pI.....73.5:4 | will, and lets you look upon a **w.** of light. |
| W-pI.....75.2:5 | It is a new era, in which a new **w.** is born. |
| W-pI.....75.2:7 | Today we see a different **w.**, because the |
| W-pI.....75.3:2 | sight and hide the **w.** forgiveness offers us |
| W-pI.....75.3:3 | accept the new **w.** as what we want to see. |
| W-pI.....75.4:1 | at the **w.** that our forgiveness shows us. |
| W-pI.....75.4:4 | the real **w.** rises before us in gladness, to |
| W-pI.....75.5:1 | to see the ego's shadow on the **w.** today. |
| W-pI.....75.5:2 | see Heaven's reflection lie across the **w.**. |
| W-pI.....75.5:5 | *The light has come. I have forgiven the* **w.**. |
| W-pI.....75.6:3 | You have forgiven the **w.** today. You can |
| W-pI.....75.6:9 | *The light has come. I have forgiven the* **w.**. |
| W-pI.....75.7:4 | You have forgiven the **w.**. He will be with |
| W-pI...75.7:11 | light has come. You have forgiven the **w.**. |
| W-pI.....75.8:2 | to look upon the **w.** He promised you. |
| W-pI.....75.8:5 | And you will see the **w.** that has been |
| W-pI...75.10:3 | *come. I have forgiven the* **w.**. Should you be |
| W-pI...75.11:2 | of your vision and the sight of the real **w.**, |
| W-pI...75.11:2 | has come to replace the unforgiven **w.** you |
| W-pI...76.10:1 | upheld the **w.** you thought you saw. Then |
| W-pI.....77.3:2 | full release from the **w.** you made. You |
| W-pI.....77.4:4 | Miracles do not obey the laws of this **w.**. |
| W-pI.....77.5:2 | You have asked for the salvation of the **w.** |
| W-pI.....78.4:3 | So is the seeing of the **w.** reversed, as we |
| W-pI.....78.9:2 | The **w.** and Heaven join in thanking you, |
| W-pI.....78.9:2 | as you are saved, and all the **w.** with you. |
| W-pI.....79.1:3 | solved. This is the situation of the **w.**. The |
| W-pI.....79.2:1 | Everyone in this **w.** seems to have his |
| W-pI.....79.4:2 | The **w.** seems to present you with a vast |
| W-pI.....79.5:1 | all the problems the **w.** appears to hold. |
| W-pI.....81.1:1 | (61) I am the light of the **w.**. How holy |
| W-pI.....81.1:2 | given the function of lighting up the **w.**! |
| W-pI.....81.2:2 | *Let me not obscure the light of the* **w.** *in me.* |
| W-pI.....81.2:3 | *me. Let the light of the* **w.** *shine through this* |
| W-pI.....81.3:1 | is my function as the light of the **w.**. It is |
| W-pI.....82.1:1 | light of the **w.** brings peace to every mind |
| W-pI.....82.1:2 | of the **w.** finds expression through me. |
| W-pI.....82.1:3 | become aware of the light of the **w.** in me. |
| W-pI.....82.1:4 | is the means by which the **w.** is healed, |
| W-pI.....82.1:5 | Let me, then, forgive the **w.**, that it may |
| W-pI.....82.2:3 | *I share the light of the* **w.** *with you, [name].* |
| W-pI.....85.1:1 | grievances hide the light of the **w.** in me. |
| W-pI.....85.2:3 | *The light of the* **w.** *will shine all this away.* |
| W-pI.....92.2:3 | or that you held the **w.** within your hand, |
| W-pI.....92.6:2 | and nothing in the **w.** that it would share. |
| W-pI.....94.1:3 | The sounds of this **w.** are still, the sights |
| W-pI.....94.1:3 | are still, the sights of this **w.** disappear, |
| W-pI.....94.1:3 | and all the thoughts that this **w.** ever held |
| W-pI.....94.3:7 | home in God to walk the **w.** uncertainly. |
| W-pI...95.12:3 | to lift the veil of darkness from the **w.**, |
| W-pI...95.12:3 | to teach the **w.** the truth about yourself. |
| W-pI...95.14:2 | part in bringing happiness to all the **w.**. |
| W-pI...95.15:1 | is a call to all the **w.** to be at one with you. |
| W-pI.....96.9:5 | mind go wandering in a **w.** of dreams, to |
| W-pI.....97.5:1 | carry them around this aching **w.** where |
| W-pI.....97.7:1 | let them echo round the **w.** through Him: |
| W-pI.....97.7:2 | *free to forgive, and free to save the* **w.**. |
| W-pI.....98.6:1 | kind, and joy the **w.** does not contain. |
| W-pI.....98.8:1 | will light the **w.** with hope and gladness. |
| W-pI.....98.8:2 | that you may give them to the **w.** today. |
| W-pI.....99.7:4 | All the **w.** of pain is not His Will. Forgive |
| W-pI...100.3:3 | your smile, the **w.** cannot be saved. While |
| W-pI...100.3:4 | means to save the **w.** is dim and lusterless |
| W-pI...100.5:4 | Thus do you fail to show the **w.** how great |
| W-pI...100.6:2 | and all the **w.** is thus deprived of joy, |
| W-pI...100.6:3 | **w.** can see how much He loves His Son, |
| W-pI...100.8:1 | to us and all the **w.** God's Will for us. It is |
| W-pI.100.10:7 | to God's plan for the salvation of the **w.**. |
| W-pI...104.3:4 | Then lay aside the conflicts of the **w.** that |
| W-pI...104.3:4 | and sought for only in a **w.** of dreams. |
| W-pI...105.1:4 | are not like to the gifts the **w.** can give, in |
| W-pI...105.2:3 | means pervades all levels of the **w.** you see |
| W-pI...106.3:1 | today to circumvent the voices of the **w.**. |
| W-pI...106.6:4 | resound throughout the **w.** through you. |
| W-pI...106.8:3 | will free the **w.** from thinking giving is a |
| W-pI...106.8:4 | **w.** becomes ready to understand and to |
| W-pI.106.10:1 | can teach the **w.** what giving means by |
| W-pI...107.4:3 | the appearances the **w.** presents engender |
| W-pI...107.9:6 | will return to the familiar **w.** reluctantly. |
| W-pI.107.10:1 | will be glad to look again upon this **w.**. |
| W-pI.107.10:2 | that goes with you will carry to the **w.**. |
| W-pI.107.10:3 | and the errors that surround the **w.** will |
| W-pI.107.11:2 | speak for all the **w.** and Him Who would |
| W-pI.107.11:2 | world and Him Who would release the **w.** |
| W-pI...109.2:5 | Here is the end of suffering for all the **w.**, |
| W-pI...109.4:2 | and while the **w.** is torn by winds of hate |
| W-pI...109.6:2 | The **w.** is born again each time you rest, |
| W-pI...109.6:2 | to bring the peace of God into the **w.**, that |
| W-pI...109.7:1 | you rest today, the **w.** is nearer waking. |
| W-pI...109.8:3 | and let them come from far across the **w.**, |
| W-pI...110.1:2 | would be enough to save you and the **w.**, |
| W-pI...110.2:4 | for all the **w.** to learn escape from time, |
| W-pI...110.3:3 | to light the **w.** and free it from the past. |
| W-pI...110.5:2 | of the truth to the awareness of the **w.**. |
| W-pI...110.8:1 | you, the Son of God and brother to the **w.** |
| W-pI...115.1:2 | *to forgive the* **w.** *for all the errors I have made* |
| W-pI...115.1:3 | *thus am I released from them with all the* **w.**. |
| W-pI...115.2:2 | *to the plan of God for the salvation of the* **w.**. |
| W-pI...115.2:3 | *He gave me His plan that I might save the* **w.**. |
| W-pI...121.1:2 | is the key to meaning in a **w.** that seems to |
| W-pI...121.2:1 | and soar above the turmoil of the **w.**. The |
| W-pI...121.4:2 | It looks upon the **w.** with sightless eyes, |
| W-pI...121.5:2 | its judgment of the **w.** as irreversible, and |
| W-pI...122.1:4 | worth and beauty that transcends the **w.**? |
| W-pI...122.3:1 | look with unforgiving eyes upon the **w.**. It |
| W-pI...122.6:7 | All the complexities the **w.** has spun of |
| W-pI...122.7:4 | It is the gift of God, and not the **w.**. The |
| W-pI...122.7:5 | The **w.** can give no gifts of any value to a |
| W-pI...122.8:1 | upon a happy **w.** of safety and of peace. |
| W-pI.122.12:1 | today the **w.** will fade until it disappears, |
| W-pI.122.12:1 | see another **w.** arise you have no words to |
| W-pI.122.13:3 | you return again to meet a **w.** of shifting |
| W-pI...123.5:6 | An unheard message will not save the **w.**, |
| W-pI...123.6:1 | and lets It echo round and round the **w.**. |
| W-pI...123.6:5 | the **w.** with gladness and with gratitude. |
| W-pI...123.7:3 | power to save the **w.** eons more quickly |
| W-pI...123.8:2 | His Son, that he might rise above the **w.**, |
| W-pI...124.2:4 | as we walk the **w.** a little while. And those |
| W-pI...124.7:5 | **w.** may share our recognition of reality. In |
| W-pI...124.7:6 | In our experience the **w.** is freed. As we |
| W-pI...125.1:5 | until His Word is heard around the **w.**; |
| W-pI...125.1:5 | accepts the message that the **w.** must hear |
| W-pI...125.2:1 | This **w.** will change through you. No |
| W-pI...125.3:3 | the **w.** has laid upon the Son of God. It |
| W-pI...125.3:5 | Today we will not listen to the **w.**, but |
| W-pI...125.4:2 | to spread across the **w.** the tidings of |
| W-pI...125.7:1 | minutes set apart from listening to the **w.**, |
| W-pI...125.9:2 | today lift you above the thinking of the **w.** |
| W-pI...126.1:1 | alien to the ego and the thinking of the **w.** |
| W-pI...126.8:5 | for today, this is a day of glory for the **w.**. |
| W-pI.126.10:1 | close your eyes upon the **w.** that does not |
| W-pI...127.5:1 | No law the **w.** obeys can help you grasp |
| W-pI...127.5:2 | What the **w.** believes was made to hide |
| W-pI...127.5:3 | There is not one principle the **w.** upholds |
| W-pI...127.6:1 | Seek not within the **w.** to find your Self. |
| W-pI...127.8:3 | **w.** that seems to hold you prisoner can be |
| W-pI.127.11:1 | The **w.** in infancy is newly born. And we |
| W-pI.127.11:2 | to learn to cast aside the **w.** they thought |
| W-pI......128.h | The **w.** I see holds nothing that I want. |
| W-pI...128.1:1 | **w.** you see holds nothing that you need to |
| W-pI...128.1:3 | if he would leave the **w.** behind and soar |
| W-pI...128.2:1 | is but a chain that binds you to the **w.**, |
| W-pI...128.2:3 | this **w.** contains is that you pass it by, |
| W-pI...128.2:5 | **w.** you see holds nothing that you want. |
| W-pI...128.4:1 | permit temptation to believe the **w.** holds |
| W-pI...128.5:1 | thought of values we have given to the **w.**. |
| W-pI...128.5:4 | that bar the door to freedom from the **w.**, |
| W-pI...128.6:1 | and see how far you rise above the **w.**, |
| W-pI...128.7:3 | whole perspective on the **w.** will shift by |
| W-pI...128.7:4 | The **w.** is not where it belongs. And you |
| W-pI...128.7:5 | to rest when you release it from the **w.**. |
| W-pI...128.8:2 | value in an aspect or an image of the **w.**, |
| W-pI...128.8:4 | *The* **w.** *I see holds nothing that I want.* |
| W-pI......129.h | Beyond this **w.** there is a world I want. |
| W-pI......129.h | Beyond this world there is a **w.** I want. |
| W-pI...129.1:2 | stop with the idea the **w.** is worthless, for |
| W-pI...129.1:3 | Our emphasis is not on giving up the **w.**, |
| W-pI...129.1:4 | Think you this **w.** can offer that to you? |
| W-pI...129.2:1 | once more about the value of this **w.**. |
| W-pI...129.2:3 | here. The **w.** you see is merciless indeed, |
| W-pI...129.2:6 | This is the **w.** of time, where all things |
| W-pI...129.3:1 | a **w.** instead where losing is impossible; |
| W-pI...129.4:5 | this are you who stay bound to this **w.**. |
| W-pI...129.4:6 | when you exchange it for the **w.** you want. |
| W-pI...129.5:2 | back to see again the **w.** you do not want. |
| W-pI...129.5:3 | Here is the **w.** that comes to take its place, |
| W-pI...129.5:3 | the **w.** sets forth to keep you prisoner. |
| W-pI...129.6:3 | **w.** holds nothing that you really want, but |
| W-pI...129.7:3 | this: *Beyond this* **w.** *there is a world I want.* |
| W-pI...129.7:3 | this: *Beyond this world there is a* **w.** *I want.* |
| W-pI...129.7:4 | *I choose to see that* **w.** *instead of this, for here* |
| W-pI...129.7:5 | Then close your eyes upon the **w.** you see, |

| | |
|---|---|
| W-pI...129.7:5 | that are not of this **w.** light one by one, |
| W-pI...129.8:1 | as you rest beyond the **w.** of darkness. |
| W-pI...129.9:4 | this: *The* **w.** *I see holds nothing that I want.* |
| W-pI...129.9:5 | *I want. Beyond this* **w.** *there is a world I want.* |
| W-pI...129.9:5 | *I want. Beyond this world there is a* **w.** *I want.* |
| W-pI...130.1:5 | see a **w.** his mind has not accorded value. |
| W-pI...130.2:3 | choose to see a **w.** of which he is afraid? |
| W-pI...130.3:1 | What, then, can fear project upon the **w.**? |
| W-pI...130.4:2 | of differences you believe make up the **w.**. |
| W-pI...130.6:2 | **w.** you see is proof you have already made |
| W-pI...130.8:1 | Begin your searching for the other **w.** by |
| W-pI...130.8:3 | hands of all the petty treasures of this **w.**. |
| W-pI...130.8:6 | *God offers me and see no value in this* **w.**, |
| W-pI...131.3:3 | **w.** can not dictate the goal for which you |
| W-pI...131.3:4 | beyond the **w.** and every worldly thought, |
| W-pI...131.7:1 | this strange **w.** you made and all its ways; |
| W-pI.131.10:3 | will ask to see the rising of the real **w.** to |
| W-pI.131.11:3 | this: *I ask to see a different* **w.**, *and think a* |
| W-pI.131.11:4 | *made. The* **w.** *I seek I did not make alone, the* |
| W-pI.131.11:5 | closed, the senseless **w.** you think is real. |
| W-pI.131.11:6 | well which are compatible with such a **w.**, |
| W-pI.131.13:3 | before you realize the **w.** you see before |
| W-pI.131.14:5 | here, and all the seeking of the **w.**, which |
| W-pI.131.15:3 | be a time of grace for you and for the **w.**. |
| W-pI......132.h | I loose the **w.** from all I thought it was. |
| W-pI...132.1:1 | keeps the **w.** in chains but your beliefs? |
| W-pI...132.1:2 | And what can save the **w.** except your Self |
| W-pI...132.1:5 | A madman thinks the **w.** he sees is real, |
| W-pI...132.3:2 | Here in the present is the **w.** set free. For |
| W-pI...132.3:3 | fears, you find escape and give it to the **w.** |
| W-pI...132.3:4 | have enslaved the **w.** with all your fears, |
| W-pI...132.3:4 | and keep the **w.** a prisoner to your beliefs. |
| W-pI...132.4:1 | The **w.** is nothing in itself. Your mind |
| W-pI...132.4:4 | you think you did not make the **w.**, but |
| W-pI...132.5:1 | There is no **w.** apart from what you wish, |
| W-pI...132.5:2 | and all the **w.** must change accordingly. |
| W-pI...132.5:5 | tells you that you made the **w.** you see, |
| W-pI...132.6:1 | into a **w.** quite separate from yourself, |
| W-pI...132.6:2 | There is no **w.**! This is the central thought |
| W-pI...132.7:1 | who are prepared to learn there is no **w.**, |
| W-pI...132.7:4 | find it in experience that is not of this **w.**, |
| W-pI...132.7:4 | which shows them that the **w.** does not |
| W-pI...132.7:4 | truth, and yet it clearly contradicts the **w.**. |
| W-pI...132.8:2 | idea is true because the **w.** does not exist. |
| W-pI...132.9:4 | How can a **w.** of time and place exist, if |
| W-pI.132.10:1 | know your Self is the salvation of the **w.**? |
| W-pI.132.10:2 | To free the **w.** from every kind of pain is |
| W-pI.132.10:3 | no **w.** apart from your ideas because ideas |
| W-pI.132.10:3 | you maintain the **w.** within your mind in |
| W-pI.132.11:2 | Are these inherent in the **w.** you see? |
| W-pI.132.11:5 | If you are real the **w.** you see is false, for |
| W-pI.132.11:5 | for God's creation is unlike the **w.** in every |
| W-pI.132.12:1 | Release the **w.**! Your real creations wait |
| W-pI.132.13:1 | is no **w.** because it is a thought apart from |
| W-pI.132.13:2 | a **w.** which comes from this idea be real? |
| W-pI.132.13:5 | are a shadow briefly laid upon a dying **w.**. |
| W-pI.132.13:6 | and you will look upon a **w.** released. |
| W-pI.132.14:1 | Today our purpose is to free the **w.** from |
| W-pI.132.14:5 | He created us would loose the **w.** this day |
| W-pI.132.15:2 | *would loose the* **w.** *from all I thought it was.* |
| W-pI.132.15:3 | *was. For I am real because the* **w.** *is not, and I* |
| W-pI.132.15:4 | be changed so that the **w.** is freed, along |
| W-pI.132.16:1 | comes to many brothers far across the **w.**, |
| W-pI.132.16:1 | send out these thoughts to bless the **w.**. |
| W-pI.132.17:1 | sent through your ideas to all the **w.**, and |
| W-pI.132.17:2 | *I loose the* **w.** *from all I thought it was, and* |
| W-pI...133.2:2 | you buy, to eminence as valued by the **w.**, |
| W-pI...133.2:4 | for satisfactions which the **w.** contains. |
| W-pI...133.2:5 | There are no satisfactions in the **w.**. |
| W-pI...134.7:1 | stands for truth in the illusions of the **w.**. |
| W-pI.134.10:4 | the **w.** you see and that which lies beyond; |
| W-pI.134.13:1 | for the **w.** cannot perceive its meaning, |
| W-pI.134.13:2 | no thought in all the **w.** that leads to any |
| W-pI.134.13:3 | is as alien to the **w.** as is your own reality. |
| W-pI.134.15:2 | his "offenses" but to save the **w.** from all |
| W-pI...135.2:3 | The **w.** is based on this insane belief. And |
| W-pI...135.2:5 | no one walks the **w.** in armature but must |
| W-pI.135.20:3 | will be increased until the **w.** is lighted up |
| W-pI.135.26:4 | And all the **w.** will take this giant stride, |
| W-pI...136.7:3 | your **w.** appears to totter and prepare to |
| W-pI...137.3:1 | **w.** obeys the laws that sickness serves, but |
| W-pI...137.5:3 | Just as the real **w.** will arise to take the |
| W-pI...137.6:2 | Christ to those who dream the **w.** is real. |
| W-pI...137.7:1 | **w.** will occupy the place of what you made |
| W-pI...137.9:1 | glad exchange of all the **w.** of sorrow for a |
| W-pI...137.9:1 | for a **w.** where sadness cannot enter, are |
| W-pI.137.10:2 | how great your offering to all the **w.**, |
| W-pI.137.13:1 | may carry healing to the **w.**, exchanging |
| W-pI.137.14:4 | *And I would share my healing with the* **w.**, |
| W-pI...138.1:1 | In this **w.** Heaven is a choice, because |
| W-pI...138.2:5 | in some form the **w.** can understand. |
| W-pI...138.6:1 | In this insanely complicated **w.**, Heaven |
| W-pI...139.6:3 | Yet it is the universal question of the **w.**. |
| W-pI...139.6:4 | What does this mean except the **w.** is mad |
| W-pI...139.7:1 | Nothing the **w.** believes is true. It is a |
| W-pI.139.12:2 | the **w.** would weave around the holy Son |
| W-pI...140.1:1 | to any remedy the **w.** accepts as beneficial |
| W-pI...140.1:2 | What the **w.** perceives as therapeutic is |
| W-pI...140.3:1 | are different from the dreaming of the **w.**, |
| W-pI...140.7:3 | There is no remedy the **w.** provides that |
| WpI. rIV.in9:3 | restored the **w.** from darkness to the light |
| W-pI...144.2:1 | The **w.** I see holds nothing that I want. |
| W-pI...145.1:1 | Beyond this **w.** there is a world I want. |
| W-pI...145.1:1 | Beyond this world there is a **w.** I want. |
| W-pI...146.2:1 | I loose the **w.** from all I thought it was. |
| W-pI...151.2:1 | You do not seem to doubt the **w.** you see. |
| W-pI...151.3:4 | But how else do you judge the **w.** you see? |
| W-pI...151.9:6 | that seems to happen to you in this **w.**. |
| W-pI.151.11:3 | sin, and only Heaven's blessing on the **w.**. |
| W-pI.151.12:2 | see. It stands beyond the body and the **w.**, |
| W-pI.151.16:2 | lay the gift of snow-white lilies on the **w.**, |
| W-pI.151.16:3 | your transfiguration is the **w.** redeemed, |
| W-pI.151.17:2 | the **w.** unites with us and happily accepts |
| W-pI.151.17:3 | carry round the **w.** the joyous news that |
| W-pI...152.1:6 | Here is your **w.**, complete in all details. |
| W-pI...152.6:1 | you made the **w.** you see is arrogance? |
| W-pI...152.6:5 | to think He made a **w.** where such things |
| W-pI...152.6:7 | Yet only madness makes a **w.** like this. |
| W-pI...153.1:1 | who feel threatened by this changing **w.**, |
| W-pI...153.1:2 | The **w.** provides no safety. It is rooted in |
| W-pI...153.2:1 | The **w.** gives rise but to defensiveness. |
| W-pI...153.4:3 | the **w.** encourages is so much deeper, and |
| W-pI...153.7:3 | you see at work in all the evils of the **w.**? |
| W-pI...153.8:2 | For our true purpose is to save the **w.**, and |
| W-pI...153.9:3 | extends its holy blessing through the **w.**. |
| W-pI.153.11:3 | holds the **w.** in grim imprisonment. Nor |
| W-pI.153.13:1 | in a fearful **w.** made mad by sin and guilt; |
| W-pI.153.14:4 | day bring the last chapter closer to the **w.**, |
| W-pI.153.16:4 | the business of the **w.** will close on us, and |
| W-pI.153.18:3 | is spent in offering salvation to the **w.**. |
| W-pI.153.18:4 | plan for the salvation of the **w.** and yours? |
| W-pI...154.4:1 | Son, that sets apart salvation from the **w.**. |
| W-pI...154.4:2 | which speaks of laws the **w.** does not obey |
| W-pI...154.6:1 | sets them off from those the **w.** appoints. |
| W-pI.154.14:1 | The **w.** recedes as we light up our minds, |
| W-pI...155.1:1 | is a way of living in the **w.** that is not here, |
| W-pI...155.1:4 | walk the **w.** as you do recognize their own |
| W-pI...155.2:1 | The **w.** is an illusion. Those who choose |
| W-pI...155.4:1 | If truth demanded they give up the **w.**, it |
| W-pI...155.4:2 | the **w.** while still believing its reality. And |
| W-pI...155.4:4 | Others have chosen nothing but the **w.**, |
| W-pI.155.13:1 | set upon the road that leads the **w.** to God |
| W-pI...156.1:5 | walk the **w.** alone and separate from your |
| W-pI...156.2:4 | You cannot walk the **w.** apart from God, |
| W-pI...156.4:1 | that the **w.** is sanctified because of you. |
| W-pI...156.6:2 | steps forward and encompasses the **w.**. It |
| W-pI...156.8:6 | *I light the* **w.**, *I light my mind and all the* |
| W-pI...157.4:3 | wherein you quickly leave the **w.** behind. |
| W-pI...157.6:1 | you experience this day to light the **w.**. |
| W-pI...157.6:3 | in which the **w.** is quietly forgot, and |
| W-pI...157.7:1 | the **w.** to which you will return becomes a |
| W-pI...158.2:2 | one who walks the **w.** but has received it. |
| W-pI...158.6:1 | Here is the joining of the **w.** of doubt and |
| W-pI...158.6:2 | a quiet place within the **w.** made holy by |
| W-pI...158.8:2 | the **w.** can not give anything that faintly |
| W-pI...159.1:3 | Here the laws of Heaven and the **w.** agree. |
| W-pI...159.1:5 | The **w.** believes that to possess a thing, it |
| W-pI...159.3:3 | for it sees a **w.** so like to Heaven that what |
| W-pI .. 159.3:4 | The darkened glass the **w.** presents can |
| W-pI .. 159.3:5 | The real **w.** pictures Heaven's innocence. |
| W-pI .. 159.5:2 | this **w.** into one made holy by forgiveness. |
| W-pI .. 159.7:1 | **w.** remember what was lost when it was |
| W-pI .. 159.8:3 | can be brought from here back to the **w.**, |
| W-pI .. 159.9:2 | when they are carried back into the **w.**. |
| W-pI .. 159.9:4 | and turn the **w.** into a garden like the one |
| W-pI 159.10:4 | has dreamed the dream of a forgiven **w.**. |
| W-pI .. 160.2:1 | looks upon a **w.** truth does not know, and |
| W-pI .. 160.9:1 | to search the **w.** for what belongs to Him. |
| W-pI .. 161.1:4 | the **w.** passed safely by and Heaven now |
| W-pI .. 161.2:4 | thus could it invent the partial **w.** you see. |
| W-pI .. 162.1:1 | firmly in the mind, would save the **w.**. |
| W-pI .. 162.1:4 | God gave in answer to the **w.** you made. |
| W-pI .. 162.2:4 | of awakening that sounds around the **w.**. |
| W-pI .. 162.3:3 | He will save the **w.**, because he gives the |
| W-pI .. 162.3:3 | gives the **w.** what he receives each time he |
| W-pI .. 162.4:3 | all His Love, to be distributed to all the **w.** |
| W-pI .. 162.5:3 | when holiness like this has blessed the **w.** |
| W-pI .. 162.6:5 | The light is come today to bless the **w.**. |
| W-pI .. 164.1:5 | sounds the senseless, busy **w.** engenders, |
| W-pI .. 164.2:1 | The **w.** fades easily away before His sight. |
| W-pI .. 164.2:3 | dim. A melody from far beyond the **w.** |
| W-pI .. 164.3:2 | give to spend with Him, beyond the **w.**. |
| W-pI .. 164.3:4 | that come from nearer than the **w.** are |
| W-pI .. 164.4:1 | silence into which the **w.** can not intrude. |
| W-pI .. 164.5:4 | And in His judgment will a **w.** unfold in |
| W-pI .. 164.6:1 | Brother, this day is sacred to the **w.**. Your |
| W-pI .. 164.6:2 | from far beyond all things within the **w.**, |
| W-pI .. 164.6:3 | the healing and salvation of the **w.**. The |
| W-pI .. 164.7:2 | us from judgment made beyond the **w.**. |
| W-pI .. 164.7:5 | Christ, with all the **w.** forgiven in our own |
| W-pI .. 164.7:6 | We bless the **w.**, as we behold it in the |
| W-pI .. 164.8:3 | of your most holy mind to save the **w.**. Is |
| W-pI .. 164.9:2 | acceptance. We can change the **w.**, if you |
| W-pI .. 164.9:3 | see the value your acceptance gives the **w.** |
| W-pI .. 165.1:1 | makes this **w.** seem real except your own |
| W-pI .. 165.6:3 | now you are among the saviors of the **w.**. |
| W-pI .. 166.2:1 | that underlies the making of the **w.**. This |
| W-pI .. 166.2:2 | This **w.** is not the Will of God, and so it is |
| W-pI .. 166.2:4 | looks upon the **w.** and judges it as certain, |
| W-pI .. 166.3:3 | and suffer to preserve the **w.** he made. |
| W-pI .. 166.4:3 | Without the **w.** he made is he an outcast; |
| W-pI .. 166.5:5 | so great that everything the **w.** contains is |
| W-pI 166.15:8 | And now you go to share it with the **w.**. |
| W-pI .. 167.2:1 | In this **w.**, there appears to be a state that |
| W-pI .. 168.4:2 | the means by which this **w.** will disappear |
| W-pI .. 168.4:3 | see a light that covers all the **w.** in love, |
| W-pI .. 169.1:2 | for it leads beyond the **w.** entirely. It is |
| W-pI .. 169.2:1 | God within a **w.** of seeming hate and fear. |
| W-pI .. 169.2:2 | so opposite to everything the **w.** contains, |
| W-pI .. 169.2:2 | grace can not believe the **w.** of fear is real. |
| W-pI .. 169.6:6 | him. The **w.** has never been at all. Eternity |
| W-pI 169.10:1 | what no one in the **w.** can understand. |
| W-pI 169.13:3 | he felt an instant back to bless the **w.**? |
| W-pI 169.15:2 | Yet in the **w.**, what could be more than |
| W-pI 170.11:6 | And you return to a new **w.**, unburdened |
| W-pI 170.13:4 | *bless the* **w.** *with what we have received from* |
| WpI...rV.in9:2 | the words I speak, and give them to the **w.** |
| WpI...rV.in9:3 | my hands through which I save the **w.**. |
| WpI.rV.in10:6 | before illusion seemed to claim the **w.**. |
| WpI.rV.in10:7 | And we remind the **w.** that it is free of all |
| W-pI .. 181.8:3 | we will behold a wholly sinless **w.**. When |
| W-pI .. 181.8:6 | we see reflected in the **w.** and in ourselves |
| W-pI .. 181.9:1 | The **w.** which once proclaimed our sins |
| W-pI .. 182.1:1 | **w.** you seem to live in is not home to you. |
| W-pI .. 182.3:1 | today for everyone who walks this **w.**, for |
| W-pI .. 182.6:3 | and harsh and rasping noises of the **w.**. |
| W-pI .. 182.7:5 | lives an outcast in a **w.** of alien thoughts. |
| W-pI .. 182.8:1 | an instant, when the **w.** recedes from you, |
| W-pI .. 183.1:5 | are, even within a **w.** that does not know; |
| W-pI .. 183.3:1 | the **w.** responds by laying down illusions. |
| W-pI .. 183.3:2 | the **w.** holds dear has suddenly gone by, |
| W-pI .. 183.3:5 | as happy laughter comes to bless the **w.**. |
| W-pI .. 183.7:3 | with names of idols cherished by the **w.**. |
| W-pI .. 183.9:2 | You can escape all bondage of the **w.**, and |
| W-pI .. 183.9:2 | give the **w.** the same release you found. |
| W-pI .. 183.9:3 | You can remember what the **w.** forgot, |
| W-pI .. 184.3:1 | the **w.** becomes a series of discrete events, |

W-pI...184.6:1 the sum of the inheritance the w. bestows
W-pI...184.6:2 and symbols that assert the w. is real. It is
W-pI...184.7:1 is the teaching of the w.. It is a phase of
W-pI...184.7:4 Learning that stops with what the w.
W-pI...184.7:5 all the arbitrary names the w. bestows can
W-pI...184.8:1 Think not you made the w.. Illusions, yes
W-pI...184.9:1 asked to go beyond all symbols of the w.,
W-pI...184.9:2 need to use the symbols of the w. a while.
W-pI...184.9:5 in ways the w. can understand, but which
W-pI.184.10:1 of the w. becomes a transitory phase; a
W-pI.184.10:3 meaning in the w. that darkness rules.
W-pI.184.11:1 which delineate the w. of darkness. Yet
W-pI.184.11:4 Use all the names the w. bestows on them
W-pI.184.12:5 of the w. to take the place of Heaven. In
W-pI...185.2:8 You have but to look upon the w. you see
W-pI...185.2:9 are. The w. would be completely changed,
W-pI......186.h Salvation of the w. depends on me.
W-pI...186.1:6 on earth in Heaven's plan to save the w.,
W-pI...186.7:4 Salvation of the w. depends on you, and
W-pI.186.10:4 The functions which the w. esteems are so
W-pI.186.13:5 on the form most useful in a w. of form.
W-pI.186.14:5 of the w. depends on you who can forgive.
W-pI......187.h I bless the w. because I bless myself.
W-pI...187.1:6 which the w. and true perception differ.
W-pI...187.1:7 the w. asserts that you have lost what you
W-pI...187.3:2 If you are to save the w., you first accept
W-pI...187.5:5 in the sense the w. conceives of them.
W-pI.187.11:1 are we blessed, and now we bless the w..
W-pI...188.1:5 Light is not of the w., yet you who bear
W-pI...188.3:1 from your heart extends around the w.. It
W-pI...188.4:1 reminds the w. of what it has forgotten,
W-pI...188.4:1 the w. restores the memory to you as well.
W-pI...188.4:4 to the gifts you have to offer to the w..
W-pI...188.6:4 to you. Exclude the outer w., and let your
W-pI.188.10:2 the w. from what we thought it did to us.
W-pI.188.10:3 we who make the w. as we would have it.
W-pI...189.1:1 is a light in you the w. can not perceive.
W-pI...189.1:2 this light, for you are blinded by the w..
W-pI...189.1:7 of God within you is to see the w. anew,
W-pI...189.2:1 Who could feel fear in such a w. as this?
W-pI...189.3:1 This is the w. the Love of God reveals. It
W-pI...189.3:2 so different from the w. you see through
W-pI...189.3:5 meaningless. A w. in which forgiveness
W-pI...189.3:5 who see a w. of hatred rising from attack,
W-pI...189.4:1 Yet is the w. of hatred equally unseen
W-pI...189.4:2 Their w. reflects the quietness and peace
W-pI...189.5:4 your heart, you will perceive a fearful w.,
W-pI...189.5:5 will look out on a w. of mercy and of love.
W-pI...189.7:1 concepts you have learned about the w.;
W-pI...189.7:5 Forget this w., forget this course, and
W-pI...189.9:8 and lightens up the w. in innocence.
W-pI.189.10:9 *is our own as well, be done in us and in the w.*
W-pI...190.5:5 is nothing in the w. that has the power to
W-pI...190.6:1 this awhile: The w. you see does nothing.
W-pI...190.7:1 The w. may seem to cause you pain. And
W-pI...190.7:2 And yet the w., as causeless, has no power
W-pI...190.8:5 the w. becomes a cruel and a bitter place,
W-pI.190.11:2 light of Heaven for the darkness of the w..
W-pI...191.1:1 of release from bondage of the w.. And
W-pI...191.1:2 And here as well is all the w. released.
W-pI...191.1:3 the w. the role of jailer to the Son of God.
W-pI...191.2:1 have you done that this should be your w.
W-pI...191.5:1 and you have risen far above the w., and
W-pI...191.5:4 changed his whole perspective of the w..
W-pI...191.6:2 learn as well that you have freed the w..
W-pI...191.6:5 image of yourself walking the w. in terror,
W-pI...191.6:5 w. twisting in agony because your fears
W-pI...191.8:2 For time has lost its hold upon the w..
W-pI...191.8:3 to give the w. the gift of his forgiveness.
W-pI...191.8:4 Who could see the w. as dark and sinful,
W-pI...191.9:3 in a w. which shows no mercy to you. Yet
W-pI.191.10:1 eyes, return again to bless the w. he made
W-pI.191.10:5 Your glory is the light that saves the w..
W-pI.191.10:7 Look about the w., and see the suffering
W-pI.191.11:3 of the w. until you find it in yourself. They
W-pI.191.11:7 Remember this, and all the w. is free.
W-pI...192.1:2 such a function mean within a w. of envy,
W-pI...192.2:1 have a function in the w. in its own terms.
W-pI...192.3:1 cannot even be conceived of in the w.. It
W-pI...192.4:1 and leaves the w. a clean and unmarked
W-pI...192.8:5 become the w. in which his jailer lives,
W-pI...193.5:5 by which salvation comes to all the w..
W-pI.193.12:5 in peace eternal in the w. of time.
W-pI.193.13:1 step to Him, and to salvation of the w.. To
W-pI...194.2:2 released the w. from all imprisonment by
W-pI...194.2:3 thus becomes the gift you give the w.,
W-pI...194.4:3 Yet in this w., the temporal progression
W-pI...194.5:3 in God's Son is freed to bless the w.. Now
W-pI...194.5:4 shines upon a w. made free with him, to
W-pI...194.6:2 you extend your learning to the w.. And
W-pI...194.6:3 so will the w. perceive that it is saved.
W-pI...194.7:6 certainty of care the w. can never threaten
W-pI...194.8:3 of love. Think you the w. could fail to gain
W-pI...194.8:4 to God has also placed the w. within the
W-pI...194.8:5 the sick illusions of the w. along with his,
W-pI...194.9:6 No longer is the w. our enemy, for we
W-pI...195.1:1 for those who look upon the w. amiss.
W-pI...195.1:7 of sorrow disappear throughout the w..
W-pI...196.9:2 you you crucify, you did not hurt the w.,
W-pI...197.3:1 The w. must thank you when you offer it
W-pI...198.7:1 w. has many seeming separate haunts
W-pI.198.10:1 is remembered instantly; the w. forgotten
W-pI.198.11:1 Now is there silence all around the w..
W-pI...199.5:3 not gain thereby in power to help the w.,
W-pI...199.5:4 the call of freedom round the w. with this
W-pI...199.8:5 you in it; the w. is blessed along with you,
W-pI...200.4:3 This w. is not where you belong. You are
W-pI...200.4:5 find the means whereby the w. no longer
W-pI...200.5:2 your mind about the purpose of the w., if
W-pI...200.5:3 will be bound till all the w. is seen by you
W-pI...200.7:1 He has one Son who cannot make a w. in
W-pI...200.7:2 What could he hope to find in such a w.?
W-pI...200.7:5 as he looks on it, the w. can but deceive?
W-pI...200.8:1 will cross, to leave this w. behind. But
W-pI...200.8:2 within the w. perceived as different, and
W-pI...200.9:7 what appears to be a w. apart from God,
W-pI.200.11:5 happy way to leave the w. of ambiguity,
WpI rVI.in.1:4 and to the w. from every form of bondage
WpI rVI.in.3:7 a function that transcends the w. we see.
WpI rVI.in.7:4 become a loving gift of freedom to the w..
W-pI...204.1:2 *by laws which rule the w. of sick illusions,*
W-pI...206.1:1 (186) Salvation of the w. depends on me.
W-pI...207.1:1 (187) I bless the w. because I bless myself
W-pI...212.1:2 *me free from all the vain illusions of the w..*
W-pII.....in.1:4 the times in which we leave the w. of pain,
W-pII.....in.6:2 how to leave the w. of sorrow in exchange
W-pII.....in.6:5 Christ's vision we behold a w. beyond the
W-pII.....in.6:5 that w. to be the full replacement of our
W-pII..224.1:2 It lights the w. as well. It is the gift my
W-pII..224.1:3 gave to me; the one as well I give the w..
W-pII..224.2:3 *me, Father, now, for I am weary of the w. I see*
W-pII..226.1:1 If I so choose, I can depart this w. entirely
W-pII..226.1:2 of mind about the purpose of the w.. If I
W-pII..226.1:4 But if I see no value in the w. as I behold it
W-pII......2.3:1 to support the w. of dreams and malice.
W-pII......2.5:1 From here we give salvation to the w., for
W-pII......2.5:2 call to all the w. that freedom is returned,
W-pII......2.5:2 are done, eternity has shined away the w.,
W-pII..237.1:2 to shine upon the w. throughout the day.
W-pII..237.1:3 day. I bring the w. the tidings of salvation
W-pII..237.1:4 I behold the w. that Christ would have me
W-pII..240.1:2 look upon a w. which is impossible. Not
W-pII..240.1:3 Not one thing in this w. is true. It does
W-pII.........3.h What Is the W.?
W-pII......3.1:1 The w. is false perception. It is born of
W-pII......3.1:4 will the w. be seen in quite another light;
W-pII......3.1:4 where all the w. must disappear and all its
W-pII......3.2:1 The w. was made as an attack on God. It
W-pII......3.2:4 Thus the w. was meant to be a place
W-pII......3.3:3 the w. was made to witness and make real
W-pII......3.4:2 Whom God appointed Savior to the w..
W-pII......3.4:3 His light, and see the w. as He beholds it.
W-pII......3.5:1 the w. has joined our changed perception.
W-pII......3.5:4 We must save the w.. For we who made it
W-pII..241.1:3 to the darkened w. where its release is set.
W-pII..241.1:5 salvation dawns today upon a w. set free.
W-pII..242.1:2 I do not understand the w., and so to try
W-pII.....244.h I am in danger nowhere in the w..
W-pII .245.2:2 To all the w. we give the message that we
W-pII .249.1:1 a picture of a w. where suffering is over,
W-pII .249.1:5 The w. becomes a place of joy, abundance
W-pII .252.1:4 burning impulses which move the w., but
W-pII .252.1:5 How far beyond this w. my Self must be,
W-pII .253.1:2 Even in this w., it is I who rule my destiny
W-pII .253.1:6 thus am I led past this w. to my creations,
W-pII .258.1:3 and trinkets of the w. are sought instead?
W-pII .264.2:3 Must we not join in what will save the w.,
W-pII .265.1:1 I have indeed misunderstood the w.,
W-pII .265.1:3 I to think that what I feared was in the w.,
W-pII .265.1:4 alone. Today I see the w. in the celestial
W-pII .265.1:6 the light of Heaven shining on the w..
W-pII .265.2:1 *In quiet would I look upon the w., which but*
W-pII .266.2:3 filled the w. with those who point to Him,
W-pII .267.1:4 and all I need to save the w. is given me.
W-pII .269.1:5 *Today I choose to see a w. forgiven, in which*
W-pII .270.1:1 *eyes behold into the sight of a forgiven w..*
W-pII .270.1:2 *How glorious and gracious is this w.! Yet*
W-pII .270.1:4 *can give. The w. forgiven signifies Your Son*
W-pII .270.2:3 we offer healing to the w. through Him,
W-pII ..... 6.4:3 the w. and peace has come to every Son of
W-pII .271.1:3 sight, the w. and God's creation meet,
W-pII .271.1:4 kindly sight redeems the w. from death,
W-pII .275.2:3 *thoughts to think, what words to give the w..*
W-pII .278.1:1 in a w. in which all things that seem to
W-pII .278.1:2 the laws the w. obeys must I obey; the
W-pII .282.1:1 salvation would be reached for all the w..
W-pII .283.2:2 all things, uniting lovingly with all the w.,
W-pII .289.1:1 mind, the real w. must escape my sight.
W-pII .289.1:3 I then perceive the w. forgiveness offers?
W-pII .289.1:4 the w. that can be looked on only now. It
W-pII .289.2:2 *a present w. the past has left untouched and*
W-pII ........8.h What Is the Real W.?
W-pII ..... 8.1:1 The real w. is a symbol, like the rest of
W-pII ..... 8.1:3 Your w. is seen through eyes of fear, and
W-pII ..... 8.1:4 The real w. cannot be perceived except
W-pII ..... 8.1:4 so they see a w. where terror is impossible
W-pII ..... 8.2:1 The real w. holds a counterpart for each
W-pII ..... 8.2:1 unhappy thought reflected in your w.; a
W-pII ..... 8.2:1 sounds of battle which your w. contains.
W-pII ..... 8.2:2 The real w. shows a world seen differently
W-pII ..... 8.2:2 The real world shows a w. seen differently
W-pII ..... 8.3:4 The w. it sees arises from a mind at peace
W-pII ..... 8.4:1 real w. is the symbol that the dream of sin
W-pII ..... 8.4:3 The real w. signifies the end of time, for
W-pII ..... 8.5:4 And as we look upon a w. forgiven, it is
W-pII .291.1:2 and offers this same vision to the w.. And
W-pII .291.1:3 both for myself and for the w. as well.
W-pII .293.1:3 Can the w. seem bright and clear and safe
W-pII .293.1:5 the w. shines in reflection of its holy light,
W-pII .293.1:5 light, and I perceive a w. forgiven at last.
W-pII .293.2:1 *let not Your holy w. escape my sight today.*
W-pII .293.2:2 *w. is singing underneath the sounds of fear.*
W-pII .293.2:3 *real w. which the present holds safe from all*
W-pII .293.2:4 *would see only this w. before my eyes today.*
W-pII .295.1:1 my eyes today, and thus redeem the w..
W-pII .295.1:3 that seemed to settle on the w. are gone.
W-pII .295.1:5 As I am saved, the w. is saved with me.
W-pII .296.1:1 *that all the w. may listen to Your Voice, and*
W-pII .296.1:3 *I would be savior to the w. I made. For having*
W-pII .296.2:3 we allow His teaching to persuade the w.,
W-pII .297.1:4 way I live within a w. that needs salvation,
W-pII ....300.h Only an instant does this w. endure.
W-pII .300.2:1 *We seek Your holy w. today. For we, Your*
W-pII .300.2:4 *today the w. endures but for an instant. We*
W-pII ..... 9.2:1 it to embrace the w. and hold you safe
W-pII .301.1:2 *feel I am abandoned or unneeded in the w..*
W-pII .301.1:5 *Let me see Your w. instead of mine. And all*
W-pII .301.1:7 *gone. Father, I will not judge Your w. today.*
W-pII .301.2:1 God's w. is happy. Those who look on it
W-pII .301.2:2 we have learned the w. we saw was false,
W-pII .301.2:4 and we will look upon God's w. today.
W-pII .302.1:2 *Your holy w. awaits us, as our sight is finally*
W-pII .302.1:7 *Let me forgive Your holy w. today, that I may*
W-pII ....304.h Let not my w. obscure the sight of Christ.
W-pII .304.1:1 my holy sight, if I intrude my w. upon it.
W-pII .304.1:5 I would bless the w. by looking on it
W-pII .304.2:2 *forgive, and thus receive salvation for the w..*

| | |
|---|---|
| C-4 4:1 | w. stands like a block before Christ's face. |
| C-4 4:5 | and in that instant is the w. forgot, with |
| C-4 4:5 | with time forever ended as the w. spins |
| C-4 5:1 | w. forgiven cannot last. It was the home |
| C-4 5:5 | The w. of bodies is the world of sin, for |
| C-4 5:5 | The world of bodies is the w. of sin, for |
| C-4 5:7 | remains to keep a separated w. in place? |
| C-4 5:9 | Only the body makes the w. seem real, for |
| C-4 7:6 | and now is the last perception of the w. |
| C-4 8:3 | into holiness; out of the w. and to eternity |
| C-5 5:7 | him who would be only brother to the w.. |
| C-6 3:5 | light in which the forgiven w. is perceived |
| C-6 5:1 | You are His manifestation in this w.. |
| C-6 5:4 | with you he is the shining Savior of the w. |
| C-6 5:5 | with him when he began to save the w.. |
| C-ep 1:11 | an ancient door that leads beyond the w.? |
| C-ep 3:7 | your certain destiny the w. would hide |
| C-ep 4:7 | until the w. is still an instant and forgets |
| C-ep 5:1 | Let us go out and meet the newborn w., |
| C-ep 5:4 | this new day looks on a different w. where |
| P-in 1:4 | manifestations of this w. seem real indeed |
| P-1 1:3 | it rests. No one in this w. escapes fear, but |
| P-1 3:6 | and helpless midst the power of the w.. |
| P-1 4:2 | were made by his projections on the w.. |
| P-1 4:3 | The w. he sees does therefore not exist. |
| P-2 II.2:2 | religion. In this w., there is an astonishing |
| P-2 II.3:5 | w. has marshalled all its forces against |
| P-2 II.3:5 | it lies the ending of the w. and all it stands |
| P-2 II.6:4 | comes to those who would restore His w., |
| P-2 III.3:7 | could heal the w. without a word, merely |
| P-2 IV.4:1 | more "respectable" therapists of the w., |
| P-2 IV.5:1 | the "healers" of the w. may recognize the |
| P-2 IV.5:3 | has some merit in a w. where "degrees of |
| P-2 V.2:3 | his twisted way of looking at the w.; his |
| P-2 V.3:1 | If this w. were ideal, there could perhaps |
| P-2 V.3:3 | speak of ideal teaching in a w. in which |
| P-2 V.3:7 | out his brother as his savior from the w.. |
| P-2 V.4:2 | Nothing in the w. is holier than helping |
| P-2 VII.8:2 | And then forget the w. and all its little |
| P-2 VII.8:3 | now can be remembered of the w. of guilt |
| P-3 I.4:6 | the door on the savior of the w. to let in a |
| P-3 II.5:6 | of this w. do not expect this outcome, and |
| P-3 II.6:8 | is a place for all relationships in this w., |
| P-3 II.7:5 | some in this w. who have come very close, |
| P-3 II.7:8 | God. They are the Saviors of the w.. Their |
| P-3 III.1:2 | His plan that everything in this w. be used |
| P-3 III.3:1 | therapists of this w. are indeed useless to |
| P-3 III.5:4 | This is the law of God, and not of the w.. |
| P-3 III.7:1 | and in the eyes of the w. it would be so. |
| P-3 III.8:9 | Remember the sorrowful story of the w., |
| P-3 III.8:12 | *lost in the darkness of the w. until you asked* |
| S-1 II.3:1 | for in this w. prayer is reparative, and so |
| S-1 II.3:4 | ask for things of this w. in various forms, |
| S-1 II.4:3 | have limited prayer to the laws of this w., |
| S-1 V.1:3 | it was alone and stood against the w.. |
| S-1 V.3:1 | Now prayer is lifted from the w. of things |
| S-2 in.1:12 | Accomplish this and you will save the w.. |
| S-2 I.2:1 | of the w. far better than its true objective, |
| S-2 I.4:5 | it is the only happy dream in all the w.; |
| S-2 I.5:1 | This is the great deception of the w., and |
| S-2 I.6:2 | illusion of a w. appears to be your home. |
| S-2 I.7:5 | sight the w. becomes as holy as Himself. |
| S-2 I.10:1 | This is the w. of opposites. And you must |
| S-2 I.10:2 | while this w. retains reality for you. Yet |
| S-2 I.10:5 | ascend above the w. of chaos into peace. |
| S-2 II.1:1 | forms, being a weapon of the w. of form. |
| S-2 II.7:5 | Within the w. of opposites there is a way |
| S-3 I.1:2 | to be just, according to the usage of the w. |
| S-3 I.5:2 | The w. of opposites is healing's place, for |
| S-3 I.5:3 | As prayer within the w. can ask amiss and |
| S-3 I.5:3 | of the w. or to the everlasting Love of God |
| S-3 II.2:3 | the need is done to walk the w. of limits, |
| S-3 II.4:2 | it dreamed about and laid upon the w.. |
| S-3 II.4:4 | the w. and it is ready to depart in peace, |
| S-3 II.5:1 | This is not death according to the w., for |
| S-3 II.5:6 | by the healing that the w. cannot conceive |
| S-3 II.6:3 | a w. in which there is no veil of sin to keep |
| S-3 III.3:1 | the aim of healing as the w. conceives of it |
| S-3 IV.2:2 | And the w. responds in quickened chorus |
| S-3 IV.2:5 | earth an instant, as the w. is shined away. |
| S-3 IV.3:6 | you for shifting dreams within a sorry w.? |
| S-3 IV.6:5 | nor wandered in a savage w. with feet that |
| S-3 IV.6:6 | prayer beyond the sorry reaches of the w.. |
| S-3 IV.9:1 | time to lift the heavy burden from the w.. |
| S-3 IV.10:7 | whatever you may think about the w., |

## world's 55

| | |
|---|---|
| T-3 V.9:5 | condition entirely alien to the w. thinking |
| T-7 VII.10:9 | is only one way out of the w. thinking, |
| T-11 VII.2:2 | in this world are the w. only reality. They |
| T-12 I.10:1 | look upon love, which *is* the w. reality, |
| T-12 III.7:1 | thoughts of God's Son are the w. reality, |
| T-12 VI.1:5 | costs you the w. reality by denying yours, |
| T-13.VII.16:10 | it like a veil of light across the w. sad face, |
| T-14 X.3:5 | From the w. viewpoint, this is impossible. |
| T-18 III.4:3 | In your relationship is this w. light. And |
| T-19 II.6:4 | solidness that this w. foundation seems to |
| T-22 IV.6:5 | lifted from their minds are this w. saviors, |
| T-24 VI.6:4 | frame for your salvation and the w., is set |
| T-25 VII.1:8 | a wish to make this w. foundation sure as |
| T-25 IX.5:6 | Not as it is seen through this w. eyes, but |
| T-26 IV.1:1 | is this w. equivalent of Heaven's justice. It |
| T-27 VII.1:2 | w. demented version of salvation clearly |
| T-27 VII.4:2 | The w. escape from condemnation is a |
| T-30 V.6:1 | is the real w. purpose gently brought into |
| T-31 V.1:1 | of the self adjusted to the w. reality. It fits |
| T-31 V.4:4 | sights, for it is here the w. "reality" is set, |
| T-31 V.8:2 | that you will choose to follow this w. laws, |
| T-31 VII.1:5 | In this w. concepts are the guilty "bad"; |
| T-31 VII.15:1 | Let not the w. light, given unto you, be |
| W-pI 37.2:1 | can be removed from the w. thinking. |
| W-pI 49.1:3 | in the world and obeys the w. laws. It is |
| W-pI 55.5:7 | of it. Let me open my mind to the w. real |
| W-pI 64.3:3 | The w. salvation awaits your forgiveness, |
| W-pI 67.1:3 | why God appointed you as the w. savior. |
| W-pI 70.10:8 | *Within me is the w. salvation and my own.* |
| W-pI 93.11:5 | can do much for the w. salvation today. |
| W-pI 109.1:1 | unshaken by the w. appearances. We ask |
| W-pI 126.5:4 | allow the w. salvation to depend on this? |
| W-pI 137.1:2 | healing is the opposite of all the w. ideas |
| W-pI 162.6:6 | of God, and in that recognition is the w.. |
| W-pI 164.8:5 | be sought above the w. unsatisfying goals |
| W-pI.166.14:6 | entrusted with the w. release from pain. |
| W-pI 169.1:2 | It is the w. most lofty aspiration, for it |
| W-pI 184.2:1 | by which the w. perception is achieved. |
| W-pI 189.6:4 | w. apparent reasoning but serve to hide. |
| W-pII 321.2:3 | And how sure is all the w. salvation, when |
| M-in 4:4 | Everyone who follows the w. curriculum, |
| M-4 VII.1:7 | of its reversal of the w. thinking. In the |
| M-8 1:1 | is the basis for the w. perception. It rests |
| M-8 1:5 | of as more desirable by the w. standards, |
| M-9 2:5 | w. training is directed toward achieving a |
| M-10 3:1 | unlike the goal of the w. learning, is the |
| M-12 2:5 | to be many, for that is what is the w. need |
| M-13 2:4 | in the w. terms that does not involve the |
| M-13 5:8 | do not find" remains this w. stern decree, |
| M-13 5:8 | pursues the w. goals can do otherwise. |
| M-17 5:2 | the w. thought system becomes apparent. |
| M-25 5:2 | withdrawn from the w. material gifts, the |
| M-28 1:3 | Spirit's interpretation of the w. purpose; |
| P-3 II.2:4 | Most of the w. teaching follows a |
| P-3 III.3:1 | are indeed useless to the w. salvation. |

## world-encompassing 1

| | |
|---|---|
| W-pI 133.1:3 | We will not speak of lofty, w. ideas, but |

## worldly 10

| | |
|---|---|
| T-27 I.6:5 | real. No w. thought or act or feeling has a |
| T-27 VI.6:6 | a tiny stab of pain, a little w. pleasure, |
| T-31 IV.9:3 | to Him, nor any w. goal be one with His. |
| W-pI 131.3:4 | beyond the world and every w. thought, |
| W-pI 183.2:2 | and shelter you from every w. thought |
| W-pI 188.6:6 | by the dream of w. things outside yourself |
| W-pI 191.5:1 | all the w. thoughts that hold it prisoner. |
| M-26 2:1 | directly, retaining no trace of w. limits |
| M-26 3:7 | All w. states must be illusory. If God were |
| P-3 III.7:2 | Yet not one w. thought is really practical. |

## worlds 22

| | |
|---|---|
| T-10 V.9:11 | Your mind is capable of creating w., but it |
| T-13 V.2:1 | is because of this that private w. do differ. |
| T-13 V.4:3 | And so they separate into their private w., |
| T-13 V.7:10 | we will draw them from their private w., |
| T-13 V.10:2 | and different w. arise from their different |
| T-13 VII.2:2 | *You cannot see both w.,* for each of them |
| T-13 VII.10:9 | *yes!* As Mediator between the two w., He |
| T-13 VII.13:5 | Son is not a traveller through outer w.. |
| T-16 V.6:2 | w. has merely led to fantasies of both, and |
| T-17 II.2:4 | it is the meeting place of w. so different. |
| T-18 IX.h | The Two W. |
| T-26 III.4:8 | herein lies the difference between the w.. |
| T-26 V.11:8 | This is the borderland between the w., |
| T-26 V.14:2 | on the ground that lies between the w.. |
| W-pI 32.2:1 | ones, applies to your inner and outer w., |
| W-pI 130.h | It is impossible to see two w.. |
| W-pI 130.5:1 | two w. which have no overlap of any kind. |
| W-pI 130.6:3 | just the lesson that you cannot see two w.. |
| W-pI 130.8:5 | *It is impossible to see two w.. Let me accept* |
| W-pI.130.11:4 | this: *It is impossible to see two w.. I seek my* |
| W-pI 145.2:1 | (130) It is impossible to see two w.. |
| W-pI 159.5:1 | vision is the bridge between the w.. And |

## worms 2

| | |
|---|---|
| M-27 3:4 | where w. wait to greet him and to last a |
| M-27 3:5 | w. as well are doomed to be destroyed as |

## worn 4

| | |
|---|---|
| T-18 VIII.13:2 | You are still w. and tired, and the desert's |
| W-pI 109.7:2 | is comes closer to all w. and tired minds, |
| W-pI 166.6:1 | He seems a sorry figure; weary, w., in |
| M-1 4:5 | It is old and w. and without hope. There |

## worried 2

| | |
|---|---|
| W-pI 5.7:4 | *I am not w. about_for the reason I think. I am* |
| W-pI 6.1:5 | *am w. about_because I see something that is* |

## worries 1

| | |
|---|---|
| T-15 I.1:1 | what it means to have no cares, no w., no |

## worry 12

| | |
|---|---|
| T-2 V.A.18:4 | *I do not have to w. about what to say or what* |
| T-16 II.1:6 | Why should you w. how the miracle |
| T-18 III.7:5 | Let not time w. you, for all the fear that |
| W-pI 5.1:3 | upset may seem to be fear, w., depression |
| W-pI 6.1:2 | both the form of upset (anger, fear, w., |
| W-pI 11.3:4 | from w. that we are trying to achieve. On |
| W-pI 26.6:2 | may take the form of depression, w., |
| W-pI 34.6:1 | such as depression, anxiety or w., use the |
| W-pI 34.6:4 | *or w. [or my thoughts about this situation,* |
| W-pI 39.6:2 | uneasiness, depression, anger, fear, w., |
| W-pI 41.1:3 | anxiety, w., a deep sense of helplessness, |
| W-pI 194.7:1 | What w. can beset the one who gives his |

## worse 2

| | |
|---|---|
| T-3 III.3:3 | that the future will be w. than the present |
| T-24 I.5:7 | He who is "w." than you must be attacked |

## worsening 1

| | |
|---|---|
| P-2 V.6:9 | may even seem to be a w. and not a help. |

## worship 23

| | |
|---|---|
| T-7 V.9:2 | or an idol that you may w. out of fear, but |
| T-10 III.1:7 | those who make idols do w. them. The |
| T-10 III.4:1 | God is sick is to w. the same idol he does. |
| T-10 III.4:8 | Is this the idol you would w.? Is this the |

T-10 III.11:6 him you will bow down and **w.** him,
T-10 IV.1:9 refuse to **w.** him in whatever form he may
T-20 VI.6:4 and kept apart from those who **w.** them.
T-21 II.6:7 upon your altars, and which you **w.**. And
T-29 V.7:6 have come to **w.** in a separated world,
T-29 VII.1:4 Each idol that you **w.** when God calls will
T-29 VII.6:2 It is vain to **w.** idols in the hope of peace.
T-29 IX.1:2 bow down in **w.** to what has no life, and
T-29 IX.3:4 its **w.** is the worship of despair and terror,
T-29 IX.3:4 its worship is the **w.** of despair and terror,
T-29 IX.10:2 another try to **w.** idols and to keep attack.
T-30 IV.5:10 Give them not your **w.**, for they are not
W-pI 84.1:6 I will **w.** no idols, nor raise my own self-
W-pI 163.6:1 It is impossible to **w.** death in any form,
W-pI 170.6:2 those who **w.** them obey their dictates,
W-pI 170.9:5 For fear is loved by those who **w.** it, and
W-pII 277.2:1 Let us not **w.** idols, nor believe in any law
W-pII 283.1:3 *Let me not w. idols. I am he my Father loves.*
P-3 II.9:8 to collect bodies to **w.** at their shrine, and

## worshipful 1

T-1 II.3:2 for miracles because a state of awe is **w.**,

## worshipfully 1

W-pI 183.4:5 little names, you stood before them **w.**,

## worshipped 7

T-20 VI.6:4 that are **w.** here are shrouded in mystery,
T-29 VIII.1:5 is obscure, and they are feared and **w.**,
T-29 VIII.8:5 No one comes unless he **w.** them, and still
W-pI 92.4:7 weakness is an idol falsely **w.** and adored
W-pI 110.9:3 God instead of what he is be **w.** not today.
W-pI 194.3:2 be set upon a throne, and **w.** faithfully. In
W-pII 323.2:1 go of self-deceptions and of images we **w.**

## worshipper 2

T-23 II.4:1 of chaos, dear indeed to every **w.** of sin, is
T-29 VIII.8:6 Each **w.** of idols harbors hope his special

## worshippers 10

T-10 III.1:8 their **w.** are the Sons of God in sickness.
T-11 VI.5:4 demands that he crucify, and his **w.** obey.
T-14 IX.3:8 though His **w.** placed other gods upon it.
T-15 I.6:4 for it would have its **w.** still believe that it
T19. IV.D.14:6 The "enemies" of Christ, the **w.** of sin,
T-20 II.3:3 to it the **w.** of what he placed upon it,
T-22 III.4:7 and where its **w.** are bound to bodies,
W-pI 163.5:4 still again, while all the while its **w.** agree,
W-pI 163.8:1 Death's **w.** may be afraid. And yet, can
W-pI 170.10:3 Yet must the **w.** of fear perceive their own

## worshipping 3

T-16 V.13:1 and by **w.** them to obscure their tininess
W-pI 163.1:3 but reflections of the **w.** of death as savior
W-pI 192.7:4 our minds engaged in **w.** what is not there

## worships 2

T-11 VI.5:1 nor the power the god he **w.** has over him.
T-30 III.10:4 unaware of all the world that **w.** idols,

## worst 6

T-2 IV.3:4 **w.** a faulty use of a learning device can do
T-9 VII.3:7 at best and viciousness at **w.**. That is its
T-23 II.19:4 At best it seems like life; at **w.**, like death.
W-pI 197.1:5 think God's gifts are loans at best; at **w.**,
M-24 1:10 At **w.**, it induces inertia in the present. In
P-2 IV.4:3 At **w.**, they but make the body real in

## worth 59

T-1 I.18:4 and your neighbor's **w.** simultaneously.
T-2 VI.8:2 this **w.** is re-established by the Atonement
T-3 V.10:7 Your **w.** is beyond perception because it is
T-3 VII.2:7 their souls in return for gifts of no real **w.**.
T-4 I.7:1 Your **w.** is not established by teaching or
T-4 I.7:2 Your **w.** is established by God. As long as
T-4 I.7:6 or make is necessary to establish your **w.**.
T-4 IV.7:2 including yourself, is **w.** consistent effort.
T-4 VI.5:5 as he changes his mind about its **w.**. I am
T-4 VII.4:2 is judged to be **w.** undertaking. Being is
T-5 II.8:12 made on the basis of which call is **w.** more
T-5 VI.6:1 to mean what you consider **w.** cultivating
T-5 VI.11:5 Is not a child of God **w.** patience? I have
T-7 VII.7:3 the inestimable **w.** of every Son of God,
T-7 XI.2:8 own **w.** is beyond anything he can make.
T-7 XI.3:1 you have made and judge its **w.** fairly. Is it
T-7 XI.6:5 you heal a brother by recognizing his **w.**,
T-8 VI.5:14 can be no question of its **w.**, because its
T-9 II.10:2 is in proportion to your judgment of **w.**. If
T-12 VI.2:4 always, He cannot let you forget your **w.**.
T-13 X.13:2 unto the **w.** that God has placed upon you
T-14 III.15:1 Seek not to appraise the **w.** of God's Son
T-15 VI.2:5 of his **w.** we cannot doubt his holiness.
T-20 V.3:6 you to see your brother's **w.** when all you
T-20 V.4:1 estimate the **w.** of him who offers peace to
T-20 V.4:3 His **w.** has been established by his Father,
T-20 VII.8:10 will be evaluated as **w.** the seeing, and so
T-23 II.9:7 would keep from you must be **w.** having,
T-24 I.5:3 make the body dear and **w.** preserving.
T-24 VII.3:1 know your **w.** while specialness claims
T-25 II.2:3 this respect is hardly **w.** delaying change
T-25 VIII.10:4 his death, and could not see his **w.** at all.
T-26 II.7:4 **w.** no more than just a tiny sigh before
T-26 VI.1:1 valuable and **w.** striving for can hurt you,
T-27 I.7:3 and not esteem the **w.** of passing joys?
T-27 VII.8:7 is his **w.** that he is but a dancing shadow,
T-28 VII.7:7 and neither less nor more in **w.** than the
W-pI 16.3:3 trivial and not **w.** bothering about that it
W-pI 20.3:3 an indication that our goal is of little **w.**.
W-pI 98.5:1 Is it not **w.** five minutes of your time each
W-pI 98.5:2 **w.** five minutes hourly to recognize your
W-pI 122.1:4 a sense of **w.** and beauty that transcends
W-pI 126.9:3 means, and let you realize its **w.** to you.
W-pI 128.3:3 limit you further, hide your **w.** from you,
W-pI 128.4:3 here is **w.** one instant of delay and pain;
W-pI 128.4:5 of **w.** can not be found in worthlessness.
W-pI 129.2:1 It might be **w.** a little time to think once
W-pI 133.3:2 they are not **w.** desiring at all, for they can
W-pI 133.12:1 entirely desirable or not **w.** the slightest
W-pI 135.8:2 valueless and hardly **w.** the least defense,
W-pI 137.13:2 not a minute of the hour **w.** the giving to
W-pI 139.4:4 has judged against it and denied its **w.**,
W-pI 154.1:5 It is not our part to judge our **w.**, nor can
W-pI 157.7:1 and all goals but this become of little **w.**,
W-pI 159.10:2 to give. Are you not **w.** the gift, when God
W-pII 316.2:3 *by which I can behold them, see their w., and*
W-pII 344.1:6 *me gifts beyond the w. of anything on earth.*
M-4 IX.1:9 degree, however small, is **w.** achieving.
M-5 I.1:3 price to pay for something of greater **w.**.

## worthiness 1

T-2 VIII.4:4 on its own creations because of their **w.**.

## worthless 8

W-pI 50.2:4 Do not put your faith in the **w.**. It will not
W-pI 105.9:1 less is **w.** when you cannot give Him more
W-pI 110.10:3 you will understand how **w.** are your idols
W-pI 128.4:4 The **w.** offer nothing. Certainty of worth
W-pI 129.1:2 cannot stop with the idea the world is **w.**,
W-pI 138.10:3 as valuable; the other as a wholly **w.** thing
W-pI 165.3:2 all else as **w.** in comparison with them?
S-2 II.8:3 lay them by as **w.** in their tragic offerings.

## worthlessness 5

T-8 VI.4:1 he had not understood its **w.** at the time.
T-20 II.1:6 Yet still the gift proclaims his **w.** to you,
T-21 V.2:4 will experience depression, a sense of **w.**,
W-pI 128.4:5 Certainty of worth can not be found in **w.**.
W-pI 183.10:6 of God becomes his judgment of their **w.**.

## worthy 69

T-2 III.5:4 is **w.** of being offered at the altar of God,
T-2 III.5:5 and is entirely **w.** of receiving perfection.
T-2 VI.8:1 a sign of respect *from* the **w.** *to* the worthy.
T-2 VI.8:1 a sign of respect *from* the worthy *to* the **w.**.
T-2 VIII.3:6 to understand what is **w.** and what is not.
T-3 V.2:8 of invention is not **w.** of the abstract
T-4 I.11:4 make a home that is **w.** of His creations,
T-4 I.12:5 are wholly **w.** of Him and only of Him.
T-4 I.12:6 Nothing else is sufficiently **w.** to be a gift
T-4 III.6:1 strong enough or **w.** enough to guide you.
T-5 in.3:5 Only God's holy children are **w.** channels
T-5 IV.3:10 making them, too, **w.** of being shared.
T-5 VI.6:2 judgment of what is **w.** makes it worthy
T-5 VI.6:2 of what is worthy makes it **w.** for you.
T-5 VII.2:5 that every mind God created is equally **w.**
T-6 in.1:4 that a brother is **w.** of attack rather than
T-7 VII.6:1 whom God Himself created **w.** of honor,
T-7 VII.7:1 teacher sufficiently **w.** to teach another.
T-7 XI.2:8 the only environment that is **w.** of him,
T-7 XI.3:2 Is it **w.** to be a home for a child of God?
T-7 XI.6:4 Sonship is **w.** to be co-creator with God,
T-8 VI.3:2 else, but because nothing else is **w.** of him
T-9 VII.8:4 nothing unworthy of God is **w.** of you.
T-11 III.8:2 will be **w.** to dwell in the temple with Him
T-14 III.11:4 done to make you **w.** of the gift of God.
T-14 III.11:6 you are **w.** of everything God wills for you
T-14 VIII.2:4 there that is not equally **w.** of Both, but
T-14 VIII.5:5 and only what is **w.** of the Father will be
T-15 III.8:4 that you must be **w.** of the Prince of Peace
T-15 VI.2:5 together, that he is wholly **w.** of it, and in
T-18 IV.3:3 fixed conviction that you are not **w.** of it.
T-18 IV.5:9 *I who am host to God am w. of Him. He Who*
T-18 VI.6:5 **w.** of the hate that you invest in it. How
T-20 II.2:6 what their minds judge to be **w.** of them.
T-20 II.3:3 upon it, making it **w.** of their devotion.
T-22 I.9:2 what is part of Him is **w.** of being joined.
T-24 IV.1:3 hated and **w.** only of destruction.
T-25 I.1:7 and pure and **w.** of His everlasting Love.
T-25 VII.6:1 meets this one demand is **w.** of your faith.
T-25 IX.6:7 to be withheld from others as less **w.**,
T-26 VI.2:2 This is no friendship **w.** of God's Son, nor
T-29 V.6:4 If God esteems him **w.** of Himself, would
T-29 VIII.5:4 **w.** of the gift of Heaven and eternal peace.
T-31 VI.2:5 is seen, for who is **w.** if he be but dust?
T-31 VI.6:8 is seen as stable, fully **w.** of your trust; a
T-31 VI.7:5 And you *are* **w.** that your will be done!
T-31 VII.2:5 your sight as wholly **w.** of forgiveness,
W-pI 91.7:4 solid and more sure; more **w.** of your faith
W-pI 91.9:5 with the more **w.** in you as we go along.
WpIrIII.in11:6 the day and make it holy, **w.** of God's Son,
W-pI 122.3:4 What gifts but these are **w.** to be sought?
W-pI 126.7:3 evaluate such petty gifts as **w.** of His Son?
W-pI 128.2:3 only purpose **w.** of your mind this world
W-pI 133.12:1 valueless, **w.** or not of being sought at all,
W-pI 135.4:5 fail to serve the Son of God as **w.** host?
W-pI 151.7:1 be Judge of what is **w.** of your own belief.
W-pI 155.13:3 not a **w.** guide for you who are God's Son.
W-pI 155.13:4 trust that you are **w.** of His trust in you.
W-pI 163.2:3 it alone is real, inevitable, **w.** of their trust
W-pI 164.6:5 what is **w.** of your love receives your love,
W-pI 164.8:4 Is not this purpose **w.** to be yours? Is not
W-pI 164.8:5 Christ's vision **w.** to be sought above the
W-pI 186.2:5 self-deceiving arrogance that we are **w.**.
W-pI 186.4:4 And if He deems us **w.**, so we are. It is but
W-pI 189.7:2 good or bad, of every thought it judges **w.**
W-pI 199.6:6 it is a **w.** servant of the freedom which the
W-pI 200.6:5 yet believes are true, a **w.** purpose? Who
W-pII 238.1:1 *trust in me has been so great, I must be w..*
P-2 V.3:6 all he has to give is **w.** of the therapist. For

**would** 1829

**would-be** 1
M-10..........1:8 with what his w. teacher says about them,

**wounded** 2
T-16.....VII.1:3 you seek to restore your w. self-esteem.
S-3........III.3:4 and used to help restore the w. and to

**wounding** 1
T-15.....VII.9:5 seems always to be attacking and w. him,

**wounds** 1
T-27.....VII.4:9 And thus he suffers from the w. a knife he

**wove** 1
T-24.......V.2:3 there, and w. a picture out of nothing. For

**woven** 5
T-9......IV.11:5 than the fantasies into which they are w..
T-14.......II.2:4 and reactions that you have w. out of it.
T-17......IV.8:3 Into the frame are w. all sorts of fanciful
W-pII..334.1:2 while they are w. out of thoughts that rest
P-2........VI.2:5 distortions w. inextricably into the self-

**wrapped** 2
T-24.......II.3:7 instead of peace, and w. it carefully in sin,
T-29......IV.3:4 in which they may be w. but slightly veils

**wrapping** 2
T-17......IV.9:6 frame is only the w. for the gift of conflict.
T-23......III.2:2 The w. does not make the gift you give.

**wrappings** 2
T-17....IV.13:4 as you search it out amid its w.. As each
T-29......IV.3:5 and not the w. in which it is bound.

**wrath** 10
T-6........I.14:3 the "w. of God" as His retaliatory weapon
T-23.....II.11:2 be wrested in righteous w. from this most
T-25...VIII.6:3 and perceive the "w." of God in Him. Nor
T-27.....VII.3:2 Your presence justifies my w., and you
W-pI...101.3:4 Its w. is boundless, merciless, but wholly
W-pI...134.1:1 entails an unfair sacrifice of righteous w.,
W-pI...161.8:4 shrieks in w., and claws the air in frantic
Wfl........in.5:3 we are saved from all the w. we thought
Wfl........in.5:5 from w. because we learned we were
S-2.........II.3:3 deserve the retribution of the w. of God.

**wrenched** 1
T-13...VII.11:3 it, it will be w. and hurled into the dust.

**wrest** 2
T-19.......II.4:5 attempt to w. creation away from truth,
W-pI...170.8:4 to love what you have sought to w. from it

**wrested** 4
T-16.....V.11:3 you made with power you w. from truth,
T-23.....II.11:2 be w. in righteous wrath from this most
T-25...VIII.1:3 believe He w. it from you against your will
W-pI...136.6:3 When parts are w. from the whole and

**wrestle** 1
T-18.....VII.5:7 who w. with temptation and fight against

**wretched** 1
W-pI...151.4:5 how black with sin, how w. in your guilt.

**writ** 2
T-27.........I.3:2 are w. in Heaven in your blood and death,
T-27.........I.3:3 Yet this is w. in hell and not in Heaven,

**write** 6
T-28.........I.5:4 It does not w. the message, nor appoint
T-30.....VII.1:7 script you w. for every minute in the day,
T-30...VII.6:15 senseless, isolated scripts you w. in sleep.
W-pI.....12.5:4 to w. upon it what you would have it be.
W-pI...154.6:4 they did not w. the messages they bear,
W-pI...169.6:1 speak nor w. nor even think of this at all.

**writes** 3
W-pI...154.5:1 the one who w. the message he delivers.
W-pI...163.5:4 And this it w. again and still again, while
P-2.........II.6:3 Or is it he who w. that gives the invitation

**written** 18
T-4........III.2:1 This is w. in the form of a prayer because
T19IV.A.10:10 which return to it with messages w. in the
W-pI.....12.5:3 and let the truth be w. upon it for you, it
W-pI.....12.5:7 your words is w. the Word of God. The
W-pI.....13.2:2 to whose meaning is to be w. in the empty
W-pI.....14.3:1 thoughts that you have w. on the world,
W-pI.....39.1:2 the text for which this workbook was w.,
W-pI.....65.6:4 *clean slate let my true function be w. for me.*
WpI. rIII.in5:2 that are w. down for each day's exercise.
W-pI...158.4:3 The script is w.. When experience will
W-pI...163.5:2 epitaph, which death itself has w., gives
W-pI...192.4:1 the senseless symbols w. there before.
W-pII.......2.3:4 Name of God whereon His Word is w.,
W-pII....14.5:1 to us, we learn that it is w. on our hearts.
M-26.........1:2 and His Word is w. on everyone's heart.
C-ep...........2:5 Long ago the end was w. in the stars and
P-2.........II.6:1 does it make how the invitation is w.?
S-3........III.5:6 place is w. now the holy Word of God.

**wrong** 77
*See also* wrong-minded, wrong-mindedness
T-1...........I.6:2 they do not occur something has gone w..
T-3.....VI.2:10 whether your judgment is right or w..
T-4.....IV.10:4 cannot be w. because it never attacks.
T-5.........II.5:2 there is a right way and also a w. way, one
T-5.......II.7:12 to the w. voice you *have* lost sight of your
T-5.......II.11:1 When you are tempted by the w. voice,
T-5.......V.6:14 But you are w.. The function of thought
T-5.......V.7:10 your w. thinking if it could not be undone
T-5........VI.4:2 The ego's decisions are always w., because
T-5.....VII.6:10 *of my w. decision if I will let Him. I choose to*
T-6......IV.10:2 and proved to you that you were w.. This
T-6.....V.B.1:4 and can therefore teach yourself w.. Many
T-8...........I.4:1 past learning must have taught you the w.
T-8........III.7:6 not will anyone to suffer for a w. decision,
T-8........III.7:8 your w. decisions are undone completely,
T-8........III.7:9 W. decisions have no power, because they
T-8........IX.1:7 be sick, because only perception can be w.
T-8........IX.2:1 W. perception is the wish that things be
T-9........III.2:4 a brother, you are telling him that he is w.
T-9.....III.2:10 His ego is always w., no matter what it
T-9........III.5:6 if you think he is w. you are condemning
T-9........III.6:8 the w. guide and will therefore lose your
T-9........IV.6:2 they do not occur something has gone w..
T-9......IV.10:3 reality is fearful is w. can God be right.
T-9......IV.10:5 Be glad, then, that you have been w., but
T-9......IV.10:6 no more have been w. than God can.
T-9..........V.8:9 helping, and the w. choice will not help.
T-12...VII.12:5 If it is your judgment it will be w., for
T-13......IV.3:1 it not be more desirable to have been w.,
T-13......IV.3:1 even apart from the fact that you were w.?
T-13.....VII.5:1 w. about the world because you have
T-14......III.9:1 destructively, and the decision will be w..
T-14......IV.4:5 God is right and you are w. about yourself
T-14.....VII.3:7 and by it they are w. about themselves.
T-14........X.6:2 show you that your way of ordering is w.,
T-17....IV.13:1 to fit the better picture into the w. frame
T-17.....VI.3:3 And you will be w.. Not only is your
T-18......IV.4:3 w. in thinking that it is needful to prepare
T-18......VI.9:5 it is. Yet this could only be if God were w..
T-19........II.1:2 can be corrected, and the w. made right.
T-21.........I.1:5 Your cues for inference are w., and so you
T-21......II.4:10 if it is willing to see that it was w..
T-21......VI.2:7 But reason tells you that this must be w..
T-21...VII.13:5 that he is w. who sees himself as helpless.
T-21....VIII.3:5 He may be w. in what he asks, where, and
T-22......IV.1:7 reaches this far can make the w. decision,
T-24.........I.5:1 is the great dictator of the w. decisions.
T-25......III.8:6 sin's perception must have been w.. And
T-27.......V.9:6 You are w., but there is One within you
T-30.........I.9:2 *And so I hope I have been w..* This works
T-30.......I.10:3 you would be better off if you were w..
T-30.......I.11:6 the goal of being right when you are w..
T-30.......I.15:6 And if you think there is, you must be w..
T-30......IV.3:4 rules for safety, since the rules were w..
T-30....VI.10:6 Is his Father w. about His Son? Or have
T-31.......I.10:3 How w. are you who fail to hear the call
T-31.......I.11:1 the w. decision on what you would learn,
W-pI.....24.1:3 of the situation, and that perception is w..
W-pI.....59.4:5 define what seeing is, and I have been w..
W-pI.....66.5:6 are w. that the conclusion could be false.
W-pI.....93.3:4 This is enough to prove that they are w.,
W-pI.....99.1:2 both imply that something has gone w.;
W-pI...100.7:6 have indeed been w. in your belief that
W-pI...131.4:5 When he is w., he finds correction. When
W-pI...134.4:6 It would see as right the plainly w.; the
W-pI.184.15:4 *And we are glad and thankful we were w.. All*
W-pI...190.1:1 Pain is a w. perspective. When it is
W-pI...193.7:1 How can you tell when you are seeing w.,
W-pI...198.4:3 a thousand ways in which it must be w.; a
M-10.........4:1 for judgment, and how w. you were! Is
M-10.........4:3 right, without ever realizing you were w.?
M-11.........2:8 right? For one of you is w.. It must be so.
M-18.........3:8 *And you are w.. But a mistake is not a sin, nor*
M-22.........5:8 You have been w.. Lead not the way, for
C-1............5:1 The mind can be right or w., depending
P-1............5:5 time as He thinks best, and He is never w.
P-2...........I.2:5 interpretations will be w. of necessity,

**wrong-minded** 2
T-3........IV.2:3 ego is a w. attempt to perceive yourself as
T-3........IV.4:2 You can be right-minded or w., and even

**wrong-mindedness** 4
T-2....V.A.13:1 (3) Never confuse right- and w..
T-3........IV.4:3 is properly used as the correction for "w.,
T-4.......II.10:2 attack, and therefore w. is obliterated.
C-1............6:1 *W.* listens to the ego and makes illusions;

**wrongly** 15
T-2..........II.1:7 If you are afraid, you are valuing w.. Your
T-2..........II.1:8 will then inevitably value w., and by
T-2........IV.2:5 error. The body can act w. only when it is
T-2........VI.3:2 When you are fearful, you have chosen w.
T-4........IV.2:2 mood tells you that you have chosen w.,
T-4........IV.2:3 In every case you have thought w. about
T-4........VI.6:3 and I do not choose God's channels w..
T-5.......VII.6:3 to recognize that you actively decided w.,
T-5.......VII.6:7 *I must have decided w., because I am not at*
T-6.........V.1:2 Him. You had already taught yourself w.,
T-6.......V.B.1:4 it is quite apparent that you can teach w.,
T-10......IV.3:7 By defining the mind w., you perceive it
T-10......IV.3:7 wrongly, you perceive it as functioning w.
T-12......III.1:3 are merely those who have invested w.,
M-29.........7:3 But do not read this hastily or w.. If His

**wrongs** 1
M-29.........7:9 your dreams of danger and selected "w.."

**wrote** 2

T-30.....VII.3:9 but to show you **w.** a fearful script, and
W-pI...169.9:3 Who **w.** salvation's script in His Creator's

**wrought** 6

T-16 ... VI.10:4 What guilt has **w.** is ugly, fearful and very
T-19 ........I.8:2 the devastation **w.** by your faithlessness,
T-26 ..... IX.3:6 What hate has **w.** have They undone. And
W-pI .. 101.6:4 sin has **w.** in feverish imagination. Say:
W-pI .. 153.4:3 no idea of all the devastation it has **w.**.
W-pI .. 167.9:3 the changes **w.** are substanceless, and all

# y

**ye** 12

T-1......... V.3:4 "Except **y.** become as little children"
T-3........ VI.1:4 says "Judge not that **y.** be not judged," it
T-3.......VI.11:8 "Seek **y.** first the Kingdom of Heaven" say
T-3.......VI.11:8 say, "*Will* **y.** first the Kingdom of Heaven,"
T-4......... V.5:2 "Seek and **y.** shall find" does not mean
T-5........ VI.6:1 **y.** sow, so shall ye reap" He interprets to
T-5........ VI.6:1 **y.** reap" He interprets to mean what you
T-7........IV.7:1 Seek **y.** first the Kingdom of Heaven,
T-9......... V.9:6 *By their fruits* **y.** *shall know them, and they*
T-11...... VI.1:5 are **y.** who have not seen and still believe,
T-16...... III.2:2 earlier, "By their fruits **y.** shall know them
T19....IV.B.7:4 O come **y.** faithful to the holy union of the

**year** 17

T-15.... XI.10:1 time in which a new **y.** will soon be born
T-15.... XI.10:8 So will the **y.** begin in joy and freedom.
T-15.. XI.10:10 Accept the holy instant as this **y.** is born,
T-15.. XI.10:11 this **y.** different by making it all the same.
T-16....... II.7:1 This is a **y.** of joy, in which your listening
T-16....... II.8:2 This **y.** determine not to deny what has
T-16....... II.9:4 the **y.** for the application of the ideas that
T-16....... II.9:7 This **y.** invest in truth, and let it work in
T-16...... III.7:1 This **y.** you will begin to learn, and make
T-16..... V.17:1 **y.** is thus the time to make the easiest
T-21..... VII.6:4 We said this **y.** would emphasize the
W-in.......... 2:4 training period is one **y.**. The exercises are
W-pII ....in.3:2 conclude the **y.** that we have given God.
W-pII ....in.8:1 upon the final part of this one holy **y.**,
W-pII ..in.10:8 This **y.** has brought us to eternity.
W-pII ... 14.2:2 of this one **y.** we gave to God together,
Wfl ........in.5:1 We will not end this **y.** without the gift

**yearn** 2

T-14....... V.1:5 You **y.** for Him, as He for you. This is
W-pI. 182.12:2 It is for this you **y.**. This is your heart's

**yearning** 4

T-14....... V.1:4 Would you deny His **y.** to be known? You
T-20...... IV.7:4 forgetting all the rest and **y.** only to have
T-30...... III.3:1 for every idol lies the **y.** for completion.
W-pI...76.10:6 About His **y.** for His only Son, created as

**yearns** 4

T-7........ IX.2:8 Spirit **y.** to share its being as its Creator
T-19...... III.1:5 to it, and the mind hears it and **y.** for it,
T-22....... VI.1:8 one but **y.** for freedom and tries to find it.
W-pII ..... 7.3:1 knew how much your Father **y.** to have

**years** 17

T-1......... II.6:7 that might have taken thousands of **y.**. It
T-2......VIII.2:5 separation occurred over millions of **y.**,
T-6...........I.3:1 for **y.** as if you were being crucified. This
T-15 .......II.3:5 days, hours and even **y.** in chaining your
T-20 ..... III.9:1 Prisoners bound with heavy chains for **y.**,
T-26 ..... IX.4:1 is a hundred or a thousand **y.** to Them, or
T-28 ..... III.7:4 and break it into days and months and **y.**
T-28 ..... III.9:7 Here can the lean **y.** enter not, for time
W-pI..... 27.4:6 you have saved yourself many **y.** of effort.
W-pI..... 97.3:2 a thousand **y.** or more are saved. The
W-pI... 123.7:3 to you in terms of **y.** for every second;
W-pI... 127.7:1 beyond the count of **y.** to your release. Let
W-pI. 127.10:1 Today the legion of the future **y.** of
W-pI... 128.1:2 and you are saved from **y.** of misery, from
W-pI... 156.7:1 many **y.** on just this foolish thought. The
W-pI... 196.4:5 seem to need a thousand **y.** can easily be
M-1 ......... 2:13 thousand **y.** of time as the world judges it.

**yes** 23

T-13 .. VII.10:8 because of Him the answer is a joyous *y.!*
T-14 ......in.1:1 **Y.**, you are blessed indeed. Yet in this
T-19 ..... III.5:6 In error, **y.**, for this can be corrected by
T-21 ........II.1:4 Rejected **y.**, but not ambiguous. And if
T-21 ...... V.7:4 O **y.**, you know this, and more than this
T-21 ..... VI.8:3 In madness, **y.**. And yet what madness
T-21 .... VII.4:3 **Y.**, it can overrun the world and *seek* an
T-21 .... VII.4:5 **Y.**, it can *dream* it found an enemy, but
T-21 .. VII.11:5 By answering the final question "**y.**," you
T-21 .. VII.12:3 made, the answer is both "**y.**" and "no."
T-21 .. VII.12:4 answered "**y.**" without perceiving that
T-21 .. VII.12:4 perceiving that "**y.**" must mean "not no."
T-21 ... VIII.1:2 To bodies, **y.**! The thoughts that seem to
T-22 ...... V.5:3 **Y.**, to the body's eyes it looks like an
T-24 .... VII.4:2 The body, **y.**, a little; not from time, but
T-25 ..... IX.1:5 For if you answer "**y.**" it means you will
T-27 ........II.1:2 To many, **y.**. For accusation is a bar to
T-31 ..... III.2:5 You answer "**y.**" whenever you attack, for
W-pI..... 68.2:3 Oh, **y.**! For he who holds grievances
W-pI... 184.8:2 Illusions, **y.**! But what is true in earth and
M-15 ......... 1:1 Indeed, **y.**! No one can escape God's Final
M-20 ......... 2:6 There is a contrast, **y.**, between this thing
C-5 ............ 5:2 O **y.**, along with you. His little life on

**yesterday** 6

W-pI..... 28.1:1 specific application to the idea for **y.**. In
W-pI..... 29.2:4 Yet we emphasized **y.** that a table shares
W-pI..... 36.1:1 for **y.** from the perceiver to the perceived.
W-pI..... 44.1:1 Today we are continuing the idea for **y.**,
W-pI... 129.1:1 that follows from the one we practiced **y.**.
W-pI... 158.2:6 lesson **y.** evoked a theme found early in

**yesterday's** 1

W-pI..... 45.4:1 form that we used in applying **y.** idea. We

**yet** 1467

**yield** 12

T-12 .. VII.15:1 are tempted to **y.** to the desire for death,
T-14 ..... III.3:3 attract you, remember that if you **y.** to it,
T-14 ..... VI.2:2 fearful. Attack will always **y.** to love if it is
T-16 ........I.4:7 and **y.** not to the ego's triumphant use of
T-16 .......II.6:9 and you *will* **y.** to its compelling attraction.
T-16 ... VI.10:2 for you have come too far to **y.** to the
T-24 ... VI.11:4 with vigilance you never thought to **y.**,
T-26 .... VII.6:9 and all must **y.** with equal ease to what
T-31 ... VIII.6:3 **Y.** not to this, and you will see all pain, in
W-pI .... 31.5:2 It is a declaration that you will not **y.** to it,
W-pI .... 97.8:4 escape its sorry consequences if you **y.** to
W-pI 136.19:2 **y.** to judgment or make plans against

**yielded** 1

T19 ... IV.C.9:1 as its appeal is **y.** to love's real attraction.

**yielding** 1

T19 . IV.B.16:4 Not one but must believe that **y.** to the

**yields** 2

T-14 ..... VI.4:1 **y.** to life simply because destruction is not
T19 .. IV.D.5:1 fear that raised it **y.** to the love beyond,

**yoke** 2

T-5 .......II.11:3 Remember that "**y.**" means "join together
T-5 .......II.11:4 "message." Let us restate "My **y.** is easy

**You** 355

- God
  *Christ/Self*
  *Holy Spirit*
  *you*

T-13 .....X.12:6 I thank **Y.**, Father, for the purity of Your
T-13 .....X.12:6 whom **Y.** have created guiltless forever.
T-16 .. VII.12:1 *us to accept our true relationship with* **Y.**, *in*
T-16 .. VII.12:6 *And let us receive only what* **Y.** *have given,*
T-16 .. VII.12:6 *minds which* **Y.** *created and which You love.*
T-16 .. VII.12:6 *minds which You created and which* **Y.** *love.*
T-23 ......I.10:2 Him and of yourself is home to Both of **Y.**,
T-28 ..... IV.9:1 I thank **Y.**, Father, knowing You will
T-28 ..... IV.9:1 knowing **Y.** will come to close each little
T-30 ..... VI.9:4 *I thank* **Y.**, *Father, for Your perfect Son, and*
T-31 . VIII.10:1 I thank **Y.**, Father, for these holy ones
T-31 . VIII.10:3 come to me as **Y.** are sure of what they are
T-31 . VIII.10:4 because **Y.** gave it me on their behalf. And
T-31 . VIII.11:2 Give me my own, for they belong to **Y.**.
T-31 . VIII.11:3 And can **Y.** fail in what is but Your Will?
T-31 . VIII.11:4 I give **Y.** thanks for what my brothers are.
T-31 . VIII.11:5 from hell, and giving thanks to **Y.**.

T-31. VIII.12:2 the abode Y. set for Him before time was,
T-31. VIII.12:6 perfectly, and all creation recognizes Y.,
T-31. VIII.12:6 and knows Y. as the only Source it has.
T-31. VIII.12:7 everything that lives and moves in Y.. For
T-31. VIII.12:8 we are home, where Y. would have us be.
W-pI.....71.9:3 What would Y. have me do? Where would
W-pI.....71.9:4 Where would Y. have me go? What would
W-pI.....71.9:5 What would Y. have me say, and to whom?
W-pI...163.9:3 We live and move in Y. alone. We are not
W-pI...163.9:6 And we abide where Y. have placed us, in the
W-pI...163.9:6 life we share with Y. and with all living things
W-pI...163.9:6 things, to be like Y. and part of You forever.
W-pI...163.9:6 things, to be like You and part of Y. forever.
W-pI...168.6:7 Father, I come to Y.. And You will come to
W-pI...168.6:8 And Y. will come to me who ask. I am the Son
W-pI...168.6:9 come to me who ask. I am the Son Y. love.
W-pI.170.13:1 Father, we are like Y.. No cruelty abides in
W-pI.170.13:2 cruelty abides in us, for there is none in Y..
W-pI.170.13:4 with what we have received from Y. alone.
WpI.. rV.in2:3 We have no words to give to Y.. We would
WpI.. rV.in3:1 So do we bring our practicing to Y.. And if
WpI.. rV.in3:2 And if we stumble, Y. will raise us up. If we
WpI.. rV.in3:4 off, but Y. will not forget to call us back.
WpI.. rV.in3:5 walk more certainly and quickly unto Y..
WpI.. rV.in3:6 the Word Y. offer us to unify our practicing,
WpI.. rV.in3:6 we review the thoughts that Y. have given us.
W-pI.184.15:2 things, and Y. Who are their one Creator.
W-pI.184.15:5 All our mistakes we give to Y., that we may be
W-pI.184.15:6 And we accept the truth Y. give, in place of
W-pI.189.10:1 Father, we do not know the way to Y.. But we
W-pI.189.10:2 But we have called, and Y. have answered us.
W-pI.189.10:4 ways are not our own, for they belong to Y..
W-pI.189.10:5 And it is unto Y. we look for them. Our hands
W-pI.189.10:7 We have no thoughts we think apart from Y.
W-pII.....in.6:2 Father, we give these holy times to Y., in
W-pII.....in.6:2 for its replacement, given us by Y.. We
W-pII.....in.7:2 way by following the Guide Y. sent to us.
W-pII.....in.7:3 not know the way, but Y. did not forget us
W-pII.....in.7:4 we know that Y. will not forget us now.
W-pII.....in.7:6 We will with Y. in asking this. The Father
W-pII.....in.7:8 we undertake these last few steps to Y.,
W-pII.....in.7:8 which will not fail the Son who calls to Y..
W-pII..221.1:1 I come to Y. today to seek the peace that You
W-pII..221.1:1 today to seek the peace that Y. alone can give
W-pII..221.1:5 love, sure Y. will hear my call and answer me.
W-pII..222.2:1 now, and ask to rest with Y. in peace a while.
W-pII..223.2:4 And we would not forget Y. longer. We are
W-pII..224.2:1 My Name, O Father, still is known to Y..
W-pII..224.2:4 Reveal what Y. would have me see instead.
W-pII..225.1:1 same, and Y. have given all Your Love to me.
W-pII..225.1:3 the way Your loving Son is led along to Y.!
W-pII..227.1:3 nothing that I thought apart from Y. exists.
W-pII..228.2:3 remains a part of me, as I am part of Y.. And
W-pII..229.2:1 Father, my thanks to Y. for what I am; for
W-pII..229.2:2 And thanks to Y. for saving me from them.
W-pII..230.2:1 seek the peace Y. gave as mine in my creation
W-pII..230.2:4 I am as Y. created me. I need but call on You
W-pII..230.2:5 need but call on Y. to find the peace You gave
W-pII..230.2:5 need but call on You to find the peace Y. gave
W-pII.....231.h Father, I will but to remember Y..
W-pII..231.1:5 find. Let me remember Y.. What else could I
W-pII..232.1:2 minute be a time in which I dwell with Y..
W-pII..232.1:3 thanksgiving that Y. have remained with me
W-pII..232.1:3 be there to hear my call to Y. and answer me.
W-pII..232.1:4 all my thoughts be still of Y. and of Your Love
W-pII..233.1:1 Father, I give Y. all my thoughts today.
W-pII..233.1:4 give Y. all my acts as well, that I may do Your
W-pII..233.1:5 Today I come to Y.. I will step back and
W-pII..233.1:6 I will step back and merely follow Y.. Be You
W-pII..233.1:7 You. Be Y. the Guide, and I the follower who
W-pII..234.2:1 We thank Y., Father, that we cannot lose the
W-pII..234.2:1 lose the memory of Y. and of Your Love. We
W-pII..234.2:2 for all the gifts Y. have bestowed on us, for all
W-pII..234.2:2 the Word which Y. have given us that we are
W-pII..235.2:2 and made my sinlessness forever part of Y..
W-pII..235.2:3 no guilt nor sin in me, for there is none in Y..
W-pII..236.2:2 I rule my mind, and offer it to Y.. Accept my
W-pII..237.2:2 I come to Y. through Him Who is Your Son,
W-pII..238.1:2 Y. created me, and know me as I am. And yet
W-pII..238.1:3 Y. placed Your Son's salvation in my hands,
W-pII..238.1:4 I must be beloved of Y. indeed. And I must be
W-pII..238.1:5 Y. would give Your Son to me in certainty
W-pII..238.1:5 certainty that he is safe Who still is part of Y.
W-pII..239.2:1 thank Y., Father, for the light that shines
W-pII..239.2:2 And we honor it, because Y. share it with us.
W-pII..239.2:3 are one, united in this light and one with Y.,
W-pII..240.2:2 Would Y. allow Your Son to suffer? Give us
W-pII..241.2:1 now, and so we come at last to Y. again.
W-pII..242.2:1 And so we give today to Y.. We come with
W-pII..242.2:4 Give us what Y. would have received by us.
W-pII..242.2:5 Y. know all our desires and our wants. And
W-pII..242.2:6 Y. will give us everything we need in helping
W-pII..242.2:6 we need in helping us to find the way to Y..
W-pII..244.1:1 he may be, for Y. are there with him. He need
W-pII..244.1:3 unhappiness, when he belongs to Y.,
W-pII..246.2:1 the way Y. choose for me to come to You, my
W-pII..246.2:1 the way You choose for me to come to Y., my
W-pII..246.2:3 I would recognize that what Y. will is what I
W-pII..247.2:3 them, and gave them all to me as part of Y.,
W-pII..247.2:4 Today I honor Y. through them, and thus I
W-pII..248.2:1 Father, my ancient love for Y. returns, and
W-pII..248.2:2 Father, I am as Y. created me. Now is Your
W-pII..249.2:1 Father, we would return our minds to Y..
W-pII..249.2:3 death. Now would we rest again in Y., as You
W-pII..249.2:3 would we rest again in You, as Y. created us.
W-pII..251.2:2 What we denied ourselves Y. have restored,
W-pII..252.2:1 Father, Y. know my true Identity. Reveal It
W-pII..252.2:2 Your Son, that I may waken to the truth in Y.,
W-pII..253.2:1 Y. are the Self Whom You created Son,
W-pII..253.2:1 You are the Self Whom Y. created Son,
W-pII..253.2:1 Son, creating like Yourself and One with Y..
W-pII..254.1:2 In deepest silence I would come to Y., to hear
W-pII..254.1:3 but this: I come to Y. to ask You for the truth.
W-pII..254.1:3 but this: I come to You to ask Y. for the truth.
W-pII..254.1:4 Will, which I would share with Y. today.
W-pII..255.2:1 so, my Father, would I pass this day with Y..
W-pII..255.2:2 Your Son has not forgotten Y.. The peace
W-pII..255.2:3 The peace Y. gave him still is in his mind, and
W-pII..256.2:1 would we come to Y. in Your appointed way.
W-pII..257.2:3 if we would reach the peace Y. will for us.
W-pII..258.2:1 is but to follow in the way that leads to Y.. We
W-pII..258.2:3 What could we want but to remember Y.?
W-pII..259.2:4 Y. are the Source of everything there is. And
W-pII..259.2:5 And everything that is remains with Y., and
W-pII..259.2:5 that is remains with You, and Y. with it.
W-pII..260.1:3 Your Son, my Father, calls on Y. today. Let
W-pII..260.1:4 Let me remember Y. created me. Let me
W-pII..261.2:2 I would come, my Father, home to Y. today.
W-pII..261.2:3 I choose to be as Y. created me, and find the
W-pII..261.2:3 and find the Son whom Y. created as my Self.
W-pII..262.1:1 Father, Y. have one Son. And it is he that I
W-pII..262.1:6 must bear Your Name, for Y. created him.
W-pII..262.1:8 and we are part of Y. Who are our Source,
W-pII..263.1:2 what Y. created as if it could be made sinful?
W-pII..263.1:4 loveliness with which Y. blessed creation; all
W-pII..263.1:4 its joy, and its eternal, quiet home in Y..
W-pII..264.1:1 Father, Y. stand before me and behind,
W-pII..264.1:2 I go. Y. are in all the things I look upon, the
W-pII..264.1:3 In Y. time disappears, and place becomes a
W-pII..264.1:7 We come to Y. in Your Own Name today, to
W-pII..266.1:1 Father, Y. gave me all Your Sons, to be my
W-pII..266.1:2 In them are Y. reflected, and in them does
W-pII..268.1:1 critic, Lord, today, and judge against Y.. Let
W-pII..268.1:3 its unity, and thus to let it be as Y. created it.
W-pII..268.1:4 too, to recognize my Self as Y. created me. In
W-pII..269.1:2 means which Y. have chosen to become the
W-pII..269.1:3 perception through the Guide Y. gave to me,
W-pII..271.2:1 Father, Christ's vision is the way to Y.. What
W-pII..272.1:6 I will accept no less than Y. have given me.
W-pII..272.1:8 safe. God's Son must be as Y. created him.
W-pII..273.2:2 can rob me of what Y. would have me keep?
W-pII..273.2:4 so the peace Y. gave Your Son is with me still,
W-pII..273.2:4 quietness and in my own eternal love for Y..
W-pII..274.1:1 I would let all things be as Y. created them,
W-pII..274.1:3 Your Son will know he is as Y. created him.
W-pII..275.2:1 all things today, and so I leave all things to Y.
W-pII..276.2:2 as I am loved and blessed and saved by Y..
W-pII..277.1:6 He is as Y. created him, because he knows no
W-pII .278.2:4 to Y. instead of madness and instead of fear.
W-pII .279.2:3 Would Y. withhold the gifts You gave to me?
W-pII .279.2:3 Would You withhold the gifts Y. gave to me?
W-pII .280.2:1 Your Son, for thus alone I find the way to Y..
W-pII .280.2:2 on the Son Y. love and You created limitless.
W-pII .280.2:2 on the Son You love and Y. created limitless.
W-pII .281.1:2 who I am, and that I am as Y. created me.
W-pII .281.1:4 or hurt or ill, I have forgotten what Y. think,
W-pII .281.1:6 The Thoughts I think with Y. can only bless.
W-pII .281.1:7 The Thoughts I think with Y. alone are true.
W-pII ....283.h My true Identity abides in Y..
W-pII .283.1:6 Is not what is beloved of Y. secure? Is not the
W-pII .283.1:8 Identity, when Y. created everything that is?
W-pII .284.2:1 Father, what Y. have given cannot hurt, so
W-pII .284.2:2 Let me not fail to trust in Y. today, accepting
W-pII .285.2:3 sanity. Your Son is still as Y. created him. My
W-pII .285.2:4 My holiness is part of me, and also part of Y..
W-pII .286.1:4 In Y. is every choice already made. In You
W-pII .286.1:5 In Y. has every conflict been resolved. In You
W-pII .286.1:6 Y. is everything I hope to find already given
W-pII ....287.h Y. are my goal, my Father. Only You.
W-pII ....287.h You are my goal, my Father. Only Y..
W-pII .287.2:1 Y. are my goal, my Father. What but You
W-pII .287.2:2 What but Y. could I desire to have? What
W-pII .287.2:3 that which leads to Y. could I desire to walk?
W-pII .287.2:4 except the memory of Y. could signify to me
W-pII .287.2:5 Y. are my only goal. Your Son would be as
W-pII .287.2:6 Your Son would be as Y. created him. What
W-pII .288.1:1 This is the thought that leads the way to Y.,
W-pII .288.1:2 I cannot come to Y. without my brother.
W-pII .288.1:3 must recognize what Y. created one with me
W-pII .288.1:4 is the hand that leads me on the way to Y..
W-pII .288.1:6 my heart, or I will lose the way to walk to Y..
W-pII .288.1:8 Let me not attack the savior Y. have given me
W-pII .289.2:2 Y. have offered me Your Own replacement,
W-pII .289.2:5 Shall I demand that Y. wait longer for Your
W-pII .289.2:5 Your Son to find the loveliness Y. planned to
W-pII .290.2:1 With this resolve I come to Y., and ask Your
W-pII .290.2:2 Y. cannot fail to hear me, Father. What I ask
W-pII .290.2:3 What I ask have Y. already given me. And I
W-pII .291.2:1 is quiet, to receive the Thoughts Y. offer me.
W-pII .291.2:2 And I accept what comes from Y., instead of
W-pII .291.2:3 I do not know the way to Y.. But You are
W-pII .291.2:4 But Y. are wholly certain. Father, guide Your
W-pII .291.2:5 Son along the quiet path that leads to Y.. Let
W-pII .291.2:6 and let the memory of Y. return to me.
W-pII .292.2:1 We thank Y., Father, for Your guarantee of
W-pII .292.2:2 delay the happy endings Y. have promised
W-pII .296.1:2 I am resolved to let Y. speak through me, for I
W-pII .297.2:2 Thanks be to Y. for Your eternal gifts, and
W-pII .297.2:2 gifts, and thanks to Y. for my Identity.
W-pII ....298.h I love Y., Father, and I love Your Son.
W-pII .298.2:1 Father, I come to Y. today, because I would
W-pII .298.2:2 Y. are beside me. Certain is Your way. And I
W-pII .299.2:6 healed, for they remain as Y. created them.
W-pII .299.2:8 because it is Your Will that Y. be known.
W-pII .301.1:3 it not, and therefore is it only what Y. will.
W-pII .302.1:4 But we had forgot the Son whom Y. created.
W-pII .303.2:3 He is the Self that Y. have given me. He is but
W-pII .303.2:5 He is the Son Y. love above all things. He is
W-pII .303.2:6 He is my Self as Y. created me. It is not Christ
W-pII .304.2:1 Y. lead me from the darkness to the light;
W-pII .304.2:3 that he may find again the memory of Y., and
W-pII .304.2:3 of You, and of Your Son as Y. created him.
W-pII .306.2:1 our Father, we return to Y., remembering
W-pII .306.2:2 hearts and minds, asking but what Y. give.
W-pII .307.1:5 If I would have what only Y. can give, I must
W-pII .307.1:5 Your Son is one with Y. in being and in will,
W-pII .307.1:5 the holy truth that I remain as Y. created me.
W-pII .308.2:3 is the time Y. have appointed for Your Son's
W-pII .310.1:1 This day, my Father, would I spend with Y.,
W-pII .310.1:1 You, as Y. have chosen all my days should be.
W-pII .310.1:4 be Your sweet reminder to remember Y.,
W-pII .311.2:1 to hear Your Judgment of the Son Y. love.
W-pII .311.2:3 he whom Y. created as Your Son must be.
W-pII .313.1:6 Y. have kept completely undefiled upon the
W-pII .314.2:2 sure that Y. will keep Your present promises
W-pII .315.2:1 I thank Y., Father, for the many gifts that
W-pII .316.2:3 I trust that Y. Who gave them will provide

W-pII .317.2:4 *The memory of Y. awaits me there. And all*
W-pII .317.2:5 *which Y. have promised to Your Son, who*
W-pII .318.2:1 *take the role Y. offer me in Your request that*
W-pII .318.2:2 *in me become as surely reconciled to Y..*
W-pII .319.2:3 *of the world could Y. have given me? And*
W-pII .319.2:4 *could be the Will my Self has shared with Y.?*
W-pII ....321.h Father, my freedom is in Y. alone.
W-pII .321.1:5 *But I trust in Y.. You Who endowed me with*
W-pII .321.1:6 *Y. Who endowed me with my freedom as*
W-pII .321.1:7 *way to Y. is opening and clear to me at last.*
W-pII .321.1:8 *Father, my freedom is in Y. alone. Father, it*
W-pII .322.2:1 *Father, to Y. all sacrifice remains forever*
W-pII .322.2:3 *As Y. created me, I can give up nothing You*
W-pII .322.2:3 *created me, I can give up nothing Y. gave me.*
W-pII .322.2:4 *What Y. did not give has no reality. What*
W-pII .323.1:1 *only "sacrifice" Y. ask of Your beloved Son;*
W-pII .323.1:1 *Son; Y. ask him to give up all suffering, all*
W-pII .323.1:2 *Such is the "sacrifice" Y. ask of me, and one I*
W-pII .324.1:1 *Y. are the One Who gave the plan for my*
W-pII .324.1:2 *Y. have set the way I am to go, the role to take,*
W-pII .324.1:7 *Yet I merely follow in the way to Y., as You*
W-pII .324.1:7 *You, as Y. direct me and would have me go.*
W-pII .326.1:2 *and Y. forever and forever are my Cause. As*
W-pII .326.1:3 *As Y. created me I have remained. Where*
W-pII .326.1:4 *Where Y. established me I still abide. And all*
W-pII .326.1:6 *God, and so I have the power to create like Y.*
W-pII .326.1:8 *and at the end I know that Y. will gather Your*
W-pII ....327.h I need but call and Y. will answer me.
W-pII .327.2:1 *thank Y. that Your promises will never fail in*
W-pII .327.2:3 *not. Your Word is one with Y.. You give the*
W-pII .327.2:4 *You. Y. give the means whereby conviction*
W-pII .328.2:2 *contradicts what Y. would have me be. It is*
W-pII .328.2:4 *And happily I share that Will which Y., my*
W-pII ....329.h I have already chosen what Y. will.
W-pII .329.1:4 *As Y. are One, so am I one with You. And this*
W-pII .329.1:4 *As You are One, so am I one with Y.. And this*
W-pII .330.2:2 *to know our one Identity we share with Y..*
W-pII .331.1:3 *Y. love me, Father. You could never leave me*
W-pII .331.1:4 *Y. could never leave me desolate, to die*
W-pII .332.2:6 *while Y. are holding freedom out to us.*
W-pII .333.2:1 *forgiveness is the light Y. chose to shine*
W-pII .333.2:1 *doubt, and light the way for our return to Y..*
W-pII .334.2:3 *can be his solace but what Y. are offering to*
W-pII .335.2:3 *in Your Son I find the memory of Y. as well.*
W-pII .337.2:1 *Y. Who created me in sinlessness are not*
W-pII .338.2:3 *until I learn that Y. have given me the only*
W-pII .338.2:5 *the Thought Y. gave me promises to lead me*
W-pII .339.2:2 *I do; requesting only what Y. offer me,*
W-pII .339.2:2 *accepting only Thoughts Y. share with me.*
W-pII .340.1:1 *Father, I thank Y. for today, and for the*
W-pII .341.1:2 *is holy. I am he on whom Y. smile in love and*
W-pII .341.1:2 *deep and still the universe smiles back on Y.,*
W-pII .341.1:3 *Love bestowed upon us, living one with Y.,*
W-pII .342.1:1 *I thank Y., Father, for Your plan to save me*
W-pII .342.1:3 *And Y. have given me the means to prove its*
W-pII .342.1:7 *creation be as Y. would have it be and as it is.*
W-pII .342.1:8 *light of truth, as memory of Y. returns to me.*
W-pII .343.1:3 *Y. only give. You never take away. And You*
W-pII .343.1:4 *Y. never take away. And You created me to*
W-pII .343.1:5 *And Y. created me to be like You, so sacrifice*
W-pII .343.1:5 *And You created me to be like Y., so sacrifice*
W-pII .343.1:5 *becomes impossible for me as well as Y.. I,*
W-pII .343.1:9 *having the function of completing Y.. I am*
W-pII .344.1:9 *And thus Your Son arises and returns to Y..*
W-pII .345.1:7 *the way that I must travel to remember Y..*
W-pII .346.1:2 *the day I share with Y. as I will share eternity,*
W-pII .346.1:6 *I would abide in Y., and know no laws except*
W-pII .346.1:7 *find the peace which Y. created for Your Son*
W-pII .347.1:4 *But Y. have offered freedom, and I choose to*
W-pII .347.1:5 *to the One Y. gave to me to judge for me. He*
W-pII ....348.h for anger or for fear, For Y. surround me.
W-pII .348.1:1 *Father, let me remember Y. are here, and I*
W-pII .348.1:3 *the perfect peace and joy I share with Y..*
W-pII .348.1:8 *when Y. created me in holiness as perfect as*
W-pII .350.1:2 *all things within himself as Y. created him.*
W-pII .350.1:6 *Therefore, my Father, I would turn to Y..*
W-pII .352.1:2 *Through this I come to Y.. Judgment will*
W-pII .352.1:4 *reminds me Y. have given me a way to find*
W-pII .352.1:6 *way. Y. have not left me comfortless. I have*
W-pII .352.1:7 *I have within me both the memory of Y., and*
W-pII .352.1:9 *Identity, and find in It the memory of Y..*
W-pII .354.1:5 *Thus must I be one with Y. as well as Him.*
W-pII .354.1:6 *is Christ except Your Son as Y. created Him?*
W-pII .355.1:1 *I wait, my Father, for the joy Y. promised me*
W-pII .355.1:2 *For Y. will keep Your Word You gave Your*
W-pII .355.1:2 *keep Your Word Y. gave Your Son in exile.*
W-pII .355.1:7 *It is Y. I choose, and my Identity along with*
W-pII .355.1:7 *You I choose, and my Identity along with Y..*
W-pII .355.1:8 *and know Y. as his Father and Creator, and*
W-pII .356.1:1 *Y. promised You would never fail to answer*
W-pII .356.1:1 *You promised Y. would never fail to answer*
W-pII .356.1:1 *answer any call Your Son might make to Y..*
W-pII .356.1:3 *He is Your Son, and Y. will answer him. The*
W-pII .357.1:4 *Voice instructing me to find the way to Y., as*
W-pII .357.1:4 *to You, as Y. appointed that the way shall be:*
W-pII .358.1:4 *as well, and all I want is what Y. offer me, in*
W-pII .358.1:4 *me, in just the form Y. choose that it be mine.*
W-pII .359.1:4 *What Y. created sinless so abides forever*
W-pII .360.1:1 *peace that I would give, receiving it of Y..*
W-pII .360.1:2 *I am Your Son, forever just as Y. created me,*
W-pII .360.1:6 *Your Son is like to Y. in perfect sinlessness.*

**You** 2
• Christ/Self
*God*
*Holy Spirit*
*you*

W-pI..... 93.9:7 Here you are; This is Y.. And light and joy
W-pI... 107.8:3 Father knows that Y. are Both the same. It

**You** 10
• Holy Spirit
*God*
*Christ/Self*
*you*

T-14 .. VII.6:10 when Both of Y. together look on them.
T19IV.C.11:10 *it an obstacle to peace, but let Y. use it for me,*
W-pI..... 78.7:3 *Let me behold my savior in this one Y. have*
W-pII .358.1:1 *Y. Who remember what I really am alone*
W-pII .358.1:2 *Y. speak for God, and so You speak for me.*
W-pII .358.1:2 *You speak for God, and so Y. speak for me.*
W-pII .358.1:3 *what Y. give me comes from God Himself.*
WpII ..361-5.h This holy instant would I give to Y.. Be
WpII ..361-5.h Be Y. in charge. For I would follow You,
WpII ..361-5.h For I would follow Y., Certain that Your

**you** 17701
*You*

**Your** 342
• God
*Holy Spirit*
*your*

T-11 .... V.12:4 cannot be found apart from Y. joint Will.
T-13 .....X.12:6 Father, for the purity of Y. most holy Son,
T-16 .. VII.12:4 *to remember Y. forgiveness and Your Love.*
T-16 .. VII.12:4 *to remember Your forgiveness and Y. Love.*
T-16 .. VII.12:5 *temptation of the Son of God is not Y. Will.*
T-28 ..... IV.9:1 between the broken pieces of Y. holy Son.
T-28 ..... IV.9:2 Y. Holiness, complete and perfect, lies in
T-30 ..... VI.9:4 *I thank You, Father, for Y. perfect Son, and*
T-31 .VIII.10:1 who are my brothers as they are Y. Sons.
T-31 .VIII.10:5 And as I would but do Y. holy Will, so will
T-31 .VIII.11:3 And can You fail in what is but Y. Will?
T-31 .VIII.12:7 Clear in Y. likeness does the light shine
W-pI... 163.9:2 *We are Y. messengers, and we would look*
W-pI... 163.9:2 *of Y. Love which shines in everything. We*
W-pI... 163.9:4 *We are not separate from Y. eternal life.*
W-pI... 163.9:5 *There is no death, for death is not Y. Will.*
W-pI... 163.9:7 *We accept Y. Thoughts as ours, and our will*
W-pI...... 168.h Y. grace is given me. I claim it now.
W-pI... 168.6:5 *Y. grace is given me. I claim it now. Father,*
W-pI. 170.13:3 *Y. peace is ours. And we bless the world with*
W-pI. 170.13:6 *them Y. salvation as we have received it now.*
W-pI 170.13:8 *In them we see Y. glory, and in them we find*
W-pI 170.13:9 *are we because Y. Holiness has set us free.*
WpI... rV.in2:4 *We would but listen to Y. Word, and make it*
WpI... rV.in3:3 *way, we count upon Y. sure remembering.*
W-pI .. 179.2:1 (168) Y. grace is given me. I claim it now.
W-pI 184.15:3 *we have tried to cast across Y. Own reality.*
W-pI 184.15:7 *Y. Name is our salvation and escape from*
W-pI 184.15:8 *Y. Name unites us in the oneness which is*
W-pI 189.10:6 *Our hands are open to receive Y. gifts. We*
W-pI 189.10:9 *And we ask but that Y. Will, which is our*
W-pII .... in.7:1 silence, unafraid and certain of Y. coming
W-pII .... in.7:5 We ask but that Y. ancient promises be
W-pII .... in.7:5 be kept which are Y. Will to keep. We will
W-pII .... in.7:8 You, and rest in confidence upon Y. Love,
W-pII . 221.1:3 *of my mind, I wait and listen for Y. Voice. My*
W-pII . 221.1:5 *I come to hear Y. Voice in silence and in*
W-pII . 222.2:1 *no words except Y. Name upon our lips and*
W-pII . 222.2:1 *as we come quietly into Y. Presence now,*
W-pII . 223.2:2 *For we who are Y. holy Son are sinless. We*
W-pII . 223.2:3 *for guilt proclaims that we are not Y. Son.*
W-pII . 223.2:7 *and we acknowledge that we are Y. Son.*
W-pII . 225.1:1 *Father, I must return Y. Love for me, for*
W-pII . 225.1:1 *same, and You have given all Y. Love to me.*
W-pII . 225.1:3 *still the way Y. loving Son is led along to You!*
W-pII . 226.2:2 *Y. Arms are open and I hear Your Voice.*
W-pII . 226.2:2 *Your Arms are open and I hear Y. Voice.*
W-pII . 228.2:6 *to receive Y. Word alone for what I really am.*
W-pII . 230.2:3 *The peace in which Y. Son was born into*
W-pII . 230.2:3 *into Y. Mind is shining there unchanged.*
W-pII . 230.2:6 *gave. It is Y. Will that gave it to Your Son.*
W-pII . 230.2:6 *gave. It is Your Will that gave it to Y. Son.*
W-pII . 231.1:1 *What can I seek for, Father, but Y. Love?*
W-pII . 231.1:3 *Yet is Y. Love the only thing I seek, or ever*
W-pII . 232.1:4 *all my thoughts be still of You and of Y. Love.*
W-pII . 232.1:5 *me sleep sure of my safety, certain of Y. care,*
W-pII . 232.1:5 *of Your care, and happily aware I am Y. Son.*
W-pII . 233.1:3 *In place of them, give me Y. Own. I give You*
W-pII . 233.1:4 *that I may do Y. Will instead of seeking goals*
W-pII . 233.1:7 *but which is yet Y. perfect gift to me.*
W-pII .... 234.h Father, today I am Y. Son again.
W-pII . 234.2:1 *lose the memory of You and of Y. Love. We*
W-pII . 234.2:2 *we have received, for Y. eternal patience,*
W-pII . 235.2:1 *Father, Y. Holiness is mine. Your Love*
W-pII . 235.2:2 *is mine. Y. Love created me, and made my*
W-pII . 236.2:1 *Father, my mind is open to Y. Thoughts,*
W-pII . 237.2:2 *I come to You through Him Who is Y. Son,*
W-pII . 238.1:1 *Father, Y. trust in me has been so great, I*
W-pII . 238.1:3 *You placed Y. Son's salvation in my hands,*
W-pII . 238.1:5 *that You would give Y. Son to me in certainty*
W-pII . 240.2:2 *Would You allow Y. Son to suffer? Give us*
W-pII . 240.2:3 *Give us faith today to recognize Y. Son, and*
W-pII . 240.2:4 *Let us forgive him in Y. Name, that we may*
W-pII . 240.2:4 *feel the love for him which is Y. Own as well.*
W-pII . 241.2:2 *Father, Y. Son, who never left, returns to*
W-pII . 243.2:3 *one because each part contains Y. memory,*
W-pII . 244.1:1 *Y. Son is safe wherever he may be, for You*
W-pII . 244.1:2 *He need but call upon Y. Name, and he will*
W-pII . 244.1:2 *and he will recollect his safety and Y. Love,*
W-pII . 244.1:3 *loving, in the safety of Y. Fatherly embrace?*
W-pII .... 245.h Y. peace is with me, Father. I am safe.
W-pII . 245.1:1 *Y. peace surrounds me, Father. Where I go,*
W-pII . 245.1:2 *Where I go, Y. peace goes there with me. It*
W-pII . 245.1:5 *I give Y. peace to those who suffer pain, or*
W-pII . 245.1:7 *Let me bring Y. peace with me. For I would*
W-pII . 245.1:8 *For I would save Y. Son, as is Your Will, that I*
W-pII . 245.1:8 *For I would save Your Son, as is Y. Will, that I*
W-pII . 246.2:2 *For in that will I succeed, because it is Y. Will*
W-pII . 246.2:4 *that. And so I choose to love Y. Son. Amen.*
W-pII . 247.2:2 *My brothers are Y. Sons. Your Fatherhood*
W-pII . 247.2:3 *Y. Fatherhood created them, and gave them*
W-pII . 248.2:1 *returns, and lets me love Y. Son again as well*
W-pII . 248.2:3 *Now is Y. Love remembered, and my own.*
W-pII . 250.2:1 *He is Y. Son, my Father. And today I would*
W-pII . 252.2:2 *Reveal It now to me who am Y. Son, that I*
W-pII . 253.2:2 *is but Y. Will in perfect union with my own,*
W-pII . 254.1:1 *Father, today I would but hear Y. Voice. In*
W-pII . 254.1:2 *to hear Y. Voice and to receive Your Word.*
W-pII . 254.1:2 *to hear Your Voice and to receive Y. Word.*
W-pII . 254.1:4 *And truth is but Y. Will, which I would share*

W-pII..255.2:2 Y. Son has not forgotten You. The peace You
W-pII..256.2:1 would we come to You in Y. appointed way.
W-pII..256.2:2 We have no goal except to hear Y. Voice, and
W-pII..256.2:2 find the way Y. sacred Word has pointed out
W-pII..257.2:1 is Y. chosen means for our salvation. Let us
W-pII..260.1:2 Yet, as Y. Thought, I have not left my Source,
W-pII..260.1:3 Y. Son, my Father, calls on You today. Let me
W-pII..262.1:3 He is Y. one creation. Why should I perceive
W-pII..262.1:6 For Y. Son must bear Your Name, for You
W-pII..262.1:6 For Your Son must bear Y. Name, for You
W-pII..262.1:8 are our Source, eternally united in Y. Love;
W-pII..263.1:1 Father, Y. Mind created all that is, Your
W-pII..263.1:1 created all that is, Y. Spirit entered into it,
W-pII..263.1:1 Spirit entered into it, Y. Love gave life to it.
W-pII..264.1:4 surrounds Y. Son and keeps him safe is Love
W-pII..264.1:5 holiness; that stands beyond Y. one creation,
W-pII..264.1:6 Father, Y. Son is like Yourself. We come to
W-pII..264.1:7 We come to You in Y. Own Name today, to
W-pII..264.1:7 to be at peace within Y. everlasting Love.
W-pII..265.2:1 the world, which but reflects Y. Thoughts,
W-pII..266.1:1 Father, You gave me all Y. Sons, to be my
W-pII..266.1:1 in sight; the bearers of Y. holy Voice to me. In
W-pII..266.1:3 Let not Y. Son forget Your holy Name. Let
W-pII..266.1:3 Let not Your Son forget Y. holy Name. Let
W-pII..266.1:4 Let not Y. Son forget his holy Source. Let not
W-pII..266.1:5 Let not Y. Son forget his Name is Yours.
W-pII..267.2:1 Let me attend Y. Answer, not my own.
W-pII..268.1:1 Let me not be Y. critic, Lord, today, and
W-pII..268.1:2 me not attempt to interfere with Y. creation,
W-pII..269.1:1 I ask Y. blessing on my sight today. It is the
W-pII..269.1:5 to me; that nothing is, except Y. holy Son.
W-pII..270.1:1 Father, Christ's vision is Y. gift to me, and it
W-pII..270.1:4 can give. The world forgiven signifies Y. Son
W-pII..270.1:4 ends forever, as Y. memory returns to him.
W-pII..270.1:6 His function now is but Y. Own, and every
W-pII..270.1:6 and every thought except Y. Own is gone.
W-pII..271.2:2 invites Y. memory to be restored to me. And
W-pII..272.1:2 me. My home is set in Heaven by Y. Will and
W-pII..272.1:5 What but Y. memory can satisfy Your Son?
W-pII..272.1:5 What but Your memory can satisfy Y. Son?
W-pII..272.1:7 I am surrounded by Y. Love, forever still,
W-pII..273.2:1 Father, Y. peace is mine. What need have I
W-pII..273.2:3 I cannot lose Y. gifts to me. And so the peace
W-pII..273.2:4 so the peace You gave Y. Son is with me still,
W-pII..274.1:1 and give Y. Son the honor due his sinlessness
W-pII..274.1:3 Y. Son will know he is as You created him.
W-pII..275.2:1 Y. healing Voice protects all things today,
W-pII..275.2:3 Y. Voice will tell me what to do and where to
W-pII..275.2:5 Y. Voice protects all things through me.
W-pII..276.2:1 Father, Y. Word is mine. And it is this that I
W-pII.....277.h Let me not bind Y. Son with laws I made.
W-pII..277.1:1 Y. Son is free, my Father. Let me not imagine
W-pII..279.2:1 I will accept Y. promises today, and give my
W-pII..280.2:1 Today let me give honor to Y. Son, for thus
W-pII..281.1:1 Father, Y. Son is perfect. When I think that I
W-pII..281.1:3 Y. Thoughts can only bring me happiness. If
W-pII..281.1:4 ideas in place of where Y. Thoughts belong,
W-pII..282.2:1 Father, Y. Name is Love and so is mine. Such
W-pII..283.1:2 always was, for Y. creation is unchangeable.
W-pII..283.1:8 Is not Y. Son my true Identity, when You
W-pII..284.2:2 today, accepting but the joyous as Y. gifts;
W-pII..285.2:3 sanity. Y. Son is still as You created him. My
W-pII..286.1:7 Y. peace is mine. My heart is quiet, and my
W-pII..286.1:9 Y. Love is Heaven, and Your Love is mine.
W-pII..286.1:9 Your Love is Heaven, and Y. Love is mine.
W-pII..287.2:6 Y. Son would be as You created him. What
W-pII..288.1:9 But let me honor him who bears Y. Name,
W-pII..289.2:2 You have offered me Y. Own replacement,
W-pII..289.2:4 And here am I made ready for Y. final step.
W-pII..289.2:5 for Y. Son to find the loveliness You planned
W-pII..290.2:1 You, and ask Y. strength to hold me up today
W-pII..290.2:1 me up today, while I but seek to do Y. Will.
W-pII..291.2:5 guide Y. Son along the quiet path that leads
W-pII..292.2:1 for Y. guarantee of only happy outcomes in
W-pII..293.2:1 let not Y. holy world escape my sight today.
W-pII..294.2:1 My body, Father, cannot be Y. Son. And
W-pII..294.2:3 then, use this dream to help Y. plan that we
W-pII..296.1:1 that all the world may listen to Y. Voice, and
W-pII..296.1:1 Your Voice, and hear Y. Word through me.
W-pII..296.1:4 hear the Word Y. holy Voice will speak to me
W-pII..297.2:1 Father, how certain are Y. ways; how sure
W-pII..297.2:1 set already, and accomplished by Y. grace.
W-pII..297.2:2 Thanks be to You for Y. eternal gifts, and
W-pII.....298.h I love You, Father, and I love Y. Son.
W-pII..298.2:3 Certain is Y. way. And I am grateful for Your
W-pII..298.2:4 grateful for Y. holy gifts of certain sanctuary,
W-pII..299.2:8 because it is Y. Will that You be known.
W-pII..300.2:1 We seek Y. holy world today. For we, Your
W-pII..300.2:2 For we, Y. loving Sons, have lost our way a
W-pII..300.2:3 But we have listened to Y. Voice, and learned
W-pII..301.1:5 Let me see Y. world instead of mine. And all
W-pII..301.1:7 gone. Father, I will not judge Y. world today.
W-pII..302.1:2 Y. holy world awaits us, as our sight is finally
W-pII..302.1:7 Let me forgive Y. holy world today, that I
W-pII..303.2:1 Y. Son is welcome, Father. He has come to
W-pII..303.2:8 Safe in Y. Arms let me receive Your Son.
W-pII..303.2:8 Safe in Your Arms let me receive Y. Son.
W-pII..304.2:3 It is Y. gift, my Father, given me to offer to
W-pII..304.2:3 my Father, given me to offer to Y. holy Son,
W-pII..304.2:3 of You, and of Y. Son as You created him.
W-pII..305.2:1 us, because it is Y. Will that we be saved.
W-pII..305.2:2 Help us today but to accept Y. gift, and judge
W-pII..306.2:1 went away; remembering Y. holy gifts to us.
W-pII..306.2:3 cannot make an offering sufficient for Y. Son
W-pII..306.2:4 Son. But in Y. Love the gift of Christ is his.
W-pII..307.1:1 Father, Y. Will is mine, and only that. There
W-pII..307.1:4 Y. Will alone can bring me happiness, and
W-pII..307.1:5 You can give, I must accept Y. Will for me,
W-pII..307.1:5 Y. Son is one with You in being and in will,
W-pII..308.2:3 time You have appointed for Y. Son's release
W-pII..309.2:2 Y. altar stands serene and undefiled. It is the
W-pII..310.1:3 hours, for it comes from Heaven to Y. Son.
W-pII..310.1:4 will be Y. sweet reminder to remember You,
W-pII..310.1:4 You, Y. gracious calling to Your holy Son,
W-pII..310.1:4 You, Your gracious calling to Y. holy Son,
W-pII..310.1:4 holy Son, the sign Y. grace has come to me,
W-pII..310.1:4 to me, and that it is Y. Will I be set free today.
W-pII..311.2:1 to hear Y. Judgment of the Son You love. We
W-pII..311.2:3 And so we let Y. Love decide what he whom
W-pII..311.2:3 he whom You created as Y. Son must be.
W-pII..312.2:2 Father, this is Y. Will for me today, and
W-pII..313.1:3 This vision is Y. gift. The eyes of Christ look
W-pII..313.1:6 undefiled upon the altar to Y. holy Son, the
W-pII..314.2:2 free. Now do we leave the future in Y. Hands,
W-pII..314.2:2 sure that You will keep Y. present promises,
W-pII..316.2:1 Father, I would accept Y. gifts today. I do
W-pII..317.2:1 Father, Y. way is what I choose today.
W-pII..317.2:3 do. Y. way is certain, and the end secure. The
W-pII..317.2:5 And all my sorrows end in Y. embrace,
W-pII..317.2:5 which You have promised to Y. Son, who
W-pII..317.2:5 from the sure protection of Y. loving Arms.
W-pII..318.2:1 take the role You offer me in Y. request that I
W-pII..319.2:1 Father, Y. Will is total. And the goal which
W-pII..320.2:1 Y. Will can do all things in me, and then
W-pII..320.2:2 There is no limit on Y. Will. And so all power
W-pII..320.2:3 And so all power has been given to Y. Son.
W-pII..321.1:2 in vain until I heard Y. Voice directing me.
W-pII..321.1:6 as Y. holy Son will not be lost to me. Your
W-pII..321.1:7 Y. Voice directs me, and the way to You is
W-pII..323.1:1 only "sacrifice" You ask of Y. beloved Son;
W-pII..323.1:1 freely let Y. Love come streaming in to his
W-pII..323.1:1 of pain, and giving him Y. Own eternal joy.
W-pII..323.1:2 "cost" of restoration of Y. memory to me, for
W-pII..324.1:5 Y. loving Voice will always call me back, and
W-pII..325.2:1 Our Father, Y. ideas reflect the truth, and
W-pII..326.1:1 Father, I was created in Y. Mind, a holy
W-pII..326.1:2 I am forever Y. Effect, and You forever and
W-pII..326.1:5 And all Y. attributes abide in me, because it
W-pII..326.1:5 because it is Y. Will to have a Son so like his
W-pII..326.1:8 Y. plan I follow here, and at the end I know
W-pII..326.1:8 You will gather Y. effects into the tranquil
W-pII..326.1:8 effects into the tranquil Heaven of Y. Love,
W-pII..327.2:1 I thank You that Y. promises will never fail in
W-pII..327.2:3 Y. Word is one with You. You give the means
W-pII..327.2:4 surety of Y. abiding Love is gained at last.
W-pII..328.2:3 It is Y. Will that I be wholly safe, eternally at
W-pII..329.1:1 Father, I thought I wandered from Y. Will,
W-pII..329.1:2 Yours. Yet what I am in truth is but Y. Will,
W-pII .329.1:9 endless joy, because it is Y. Will that it be so.
W-pII .330.2:1 Father, Y. Son can not be hurt. And if we
W-pII .331.1:1 believe Y. Son could cause himself to suffer!
W-pII331.1:10 There is no opposition to Y. Will. There is no
W-pII .332.2:3 Y. Love has given us the means to set it free.
W-pII .333.2:4 anything, being Y. gift to Your beloved Son.
W-pII .333.2:4 anything, being Your gift to Y. beloved Son.
W-pII .334.2:2 For Y. Son can be content with nothing less
W-pII .334.2:5 This Y. Will for me, for so will I behold my
W-pII .335.2:1 could restore Y. memory to me, except to see
W-pII .335.2:3 in Y. Son I find the memory of You as well.
W-pII .336.2:2 and find Y. promise of my sinlessness is kept
W-pII .336.2:2 Y. Word remains unchanged within my
W-pII .336.2:2 my mind, Y. Love is still abiding in my heart.
W-pII .338.2:1 Y. plan is sure, my Father,–only Yours. All
W-pII .338.2:5 because it holds Y. promise to Your Son.
W-pII .338.2:5 because it holds Your promise to Y. Son.
W-pII .339.2:1 Father, this is Y. day. It is a day in which I
W-pII .339.2:2 myself, but hear Y. Voice in everything I do;
W-pII .340.1:2 is holy, for today Y. Son will be redeemed.
W-pII .340.1:4 For he will hear Y. Voice directing him to
W-pII .340.1:6 joy and freedom for Y. holy Son and for the
W-pII .341.1:1 Father, Y. Son is holy. I am he on whom You
W-pII .341.1:2 smiles back on You, and shares Y. Holiness.
W-pII .341.1:3 how holy, then, are we, abiding in Y. Smile,
W-pII .341.1:3 Smile, with all Y. Love bestowed upon us,
W-pII .342.1:1 for Y. plan to save me from the hell I made. It
W-pII .342.1:8 it is. Let me remember that I am Y. Son, and
W-pII .343.1:9 Y. Son can make no sacrifice, for he must be
W-pII343.1:10 I am complete because I am Y. Son. I cannot
W-pII .344.1:1 This is Y. law, my Father, not my own. I have
W-pII .344.1:9 And thus Y. Son arises and returns to You.
W-pII .345.1:1 Father, a miracle reflects Y. gifts to me, Your
W-pII .345.1:1 a miracle reflects Your gifts to me, Y. Son.
W-pII .345.1:6 to Y. gifts than any other gift that I can give.
W-pII .346.1:5 I would forget all things except Y. Love.
W-pII .346.1:6 You, and know no laws except Y. law of love.
W-pII .346.1:7 find the peace which You created for Y. Son,
W-pII .346.1:7 toys I made as I behold Y. glory and my own.
W-pII .347.1:4 freedom, and I choose to claim Y. gift today.
W-pII347.1:10 not know my will, but He is sure it is Y. Own.
W-pII347.1:11 for me, and call Y. miracles to come to me.
W-pII ....348.h need That I perceive, Y. grace suffices me.
W-pII .348.1:6 when Y. eternal promise goes with me?
W-pII .348.1:8 created me in holiness as perfect as Y. Own?
W-pII .349.1:4 Y. gifts are mine. Each one that I accept gives
W-pII .349.1:6 I learn Y. healing miracles belong to me.
W-pII .350.1:3 him. Y. memory depends on his forgiveness.
W-pII .350.1:7 Only Y. memory will set me free. And only
W-pII .350.1:8 my forgiveness teaches me to let Y. memory
W-pII .351.1:1 Who is my brother but Y. holy Son? And if I
W-pII .351.1:4 also see my brother sinless, as Y. holy Son.
W-pII .351.1:6 then, for me, my Father, through Y. Voice.
W-pII .351.1:7 For He alone gives judgment in Y. Name.
W-pII .352.1:4 have given me a way to find Y. peace again.
W-pII .352.1:8 hear Y. Voice and find Your peace today. For
W-pII .352.1:8 hear Your Voice and find Y. peace today. For
W-pII .354.1:1 with the Christ establishes me as Y. Son,
W-pII .354.1:6 is Christ except Y. Son as You created Him?
W-pII .355.1:2 will keep Y. Word You gave Your Son in exile
W-pII .355.1:2 will keep Your Word You gave Y. Son in exile
W-pII .355.1:8 Y. Son would be Himself, and know You as
W-pII .356.1:1 to answer any call Y. Son might make to You.
W-pII .356.1:3 He is Y. Son, and You will answer him. The
W-pII .356.1:4 him. The miracle reflects Y. Love, and thus it
W-pII .356.1:5 Y. Name replaces every thought of sin, and
W-pII .356.1:6 Y. Name gives answer to Your Son, because
W-pII .356.1:6 Your Name gives answer to Y. Son, because
W-pII .356.1:6 because to call Y. Name is but to call his own.
W-pII .357.1:2 Y. holy Son is pointed out to me, first in my
W-pII .357.1:3 Y. Voice instructs me patiently to hear Your
W-pII .357.1:3 instructs me patiently to hear Y. Word, and
W-pII .357.1:4 And as I look upon Y. Son today, I hear Your
W-pII .357.1:4 I hear Y. Voice instructing me to find the way
W-pII .358.1:4 Y. Voice, my Father, then is mine as well, and
W-pII .358.1:6 let me not forget Y. Love and care, keeping
W-pII .358.1:6 care, keeping Y. promise to Your Son in my
W-pII .358.1:6 care, keeping Your promise to Y. Son in my
W-pII .359.1:1 Father, today we will forgive Y. world, and

W-pII .359.1:1 *Your world, and let creation be* **Y.** *Own. We*
W-pII .360.1:1 *Father, it is* **Y.** *peace that I would give,*
W-pII .360.1:2 *I am* **Y.** *Son, forever just as You created me,*
W-pII .360.1:6 **Y.** *Son is like to You in perfect sinlessness.*
S-2 ........ III.5:1 **Y.** holy Son?" should be the only thing

## Your 1
• Holy Spirit
*God*
*your*

WpII...361-5.h Certain that **Y.** direction gives me peace.

## your 5849
*Your*

## Yours 37
• God
*yours*

T-16...VII.12:2 *Our holiness is* **Y.**. *What can there be in us*
T-16...VII.12:3 *us that needs forgiveness when* **Y.** *is perfect?*
T-31..VIII.10:2 My faith in them is **Y.**. I am as sure that
W-pI...163.9:7 *as ours, and our will is one with* **Y.** *eternally.*
W-pI. 184.15:1 *Father, our Name is* **Y.**. *In It we are united*
W-pI. 189.10:8 **Y.** *is the way that we would find and follow.*
W-pII .223.2:7 *Our Name is* **Y.**, *and we acknowledge that*
W-pII .227.1:1 *it is today that I am free, because my will is* **Y.**
W-pII .227.1:7 *Father, I know my will is one with* **Y.**.
W-pII .236.2:1 *and closed today to every thought but* **Y.**.
W-pII .236.2:3 *it to You. Accept my gift, for it is* **Y.** *to me.*
W-pII .253.2:2 *own, which can but offer glad assent to* **Y.**,
W-pII .257.2:2 *forget today that we can have no will but* **Y.**.
W-pII .257.2:3 *And thus our purpose must be* **Y.** *as well, if*
W-pII .266.1:5 *Let not Your Son forget his Name is* **Y.**.
W-pII .270.1:5 *And now his will is one with* **Y.**. *His function*
W-pII .280.2:3 *The honor that I give to him is* **Y.**, *and what is*
W-pII .280.2:3 *Yours, and what is* **Y.** *belongs to me as well.*
W-pII .285.2:1 *Father, my holiness is* **Y.**. *Let me rejoice in it,*
W-pII .296.1:2 *through me, for I would use no words but* **Y.**,
W-pII .296.1:2 *have no thoughts which are apart from* **Y.**,
W-pII .296.1:2 *are apart from Yours, for only* **Y.** *are true.*
W-pII .298.2:1 *because I would not follow any way but* **Y.**.
W-pII .307.1:4 *can bring me happiness, and only* **Y.** *exists.*
W-pII .325.2:1 *and mine apart from* **Y.** *but make up dreams*
W-pII .325.2:2 *Let me behold what only* **Y.** *reflect, for Yours*
W-pII .325.2:2 *for* **Y.** *and Yours alone establish truth.*
W-pII .325.2:2 *for Yours and* **Y.** *alone establish truth.*
W-pII .328.2:1 *There is no will but* **Y.**. *And I am glad that*
W-pII .329.1:1 *a second will more powerful than* **Y.**. *Yet*
W-pII .329.1:5 *where my will became forever one with* **Y.**.
W-pII .329.1:8 *my will is* **Y.**. *And I am safe, untroubled and*
W-pII .... 331.h There is no conflict, for my will is **Y.**.
W-pII .331.1:7 *and has no will that can conflict with* **Y.**.
W-pII331.1:11 *Will. There is no conflict, for my will is* **Y.**.
W-pII .338.2:1 *Your plan is sure, my Father,–only* **Y.**. *All*
W-pII .354.1:1 *of time, and wholly free of every law but* **Y.**.

## yours 443
*Yours*

## Yourself 2
• God
*yourself*

W-pII .253.2:1 *Son, creating like* **Y.** *and One with You. My*
W-pII .264.1:6 *Father, Your Son is like* **Y.**. *We come to You*

## yourself 1295
*Yourself*

## yourselves 1

# APPENDIX A

Complete list of words and number of occurrences

# Complete list of words and number of occurrences

## A

a 4997
abandon 21
abandoned 18
abandoning 4
abandonment 5
abate 2
abated 1
abide 65
abides 57
abideth 3
abiding 6
abilities 23
ability 68
abject 1
able 36
abode 5
abolish 4
abolished 6
abolishes 3
abolishing 2
about 403
above 68
Abraham 1
abrupt 1
abruptly 3
absence 11
absent 25
absolute 1
absolutely 2
absolution 1
absolve 1
absolved 6
absolving 1
abstract 8
Abstraction 1
abstraction 3
absurd 1
absurdity 1
abundance 15
abundant 2
abuse 3
accept 499
acceptable 24
acceptance 88
accepted 163
accepting 64
accepts 40
access 1
accessibility 1
accessible 3
accident 5
accidental 1
accidents 1
acclaim 1
accommodate 1
accompanied 1
accomplish 38
accomplished 101
accomplishment 34
accomplishments 9
accord 45
accordance 7
accorded 8
according 47
accordingly 23
accords 2
account 5
accounts 1
accurate 6
accurately 4
accusation 3
accuse 9
accused 1
accuser 2
accusers 2
accusing 2
accustomed 12
achieve 30
achieved 30
achievement 3
achievements 1
achieving 4
aching 2
acknowledge 34
acknowledged 11
acknowledges 17
acknowledging 12
acknowledgment 34
acquired 7
acquires 1
acquisition 1
across 58
act 36
acted 6
acting 11
action 10
actions 16
activate 1
activating 1
active 11
actively 10
activities 5
activity 6
acts 12
actual 8
actually 41
acute 5
Adam 4
Adam's 1
adapt 2
adapted 6
adapts 2
add 44
added 11
adding 11
addition 6
additional 5
addressed 1
adds 14
adequacy 3
adhere 3
adheres 1
adhering 1
adjectives 1
adjust 14
adjusted 4
adjusting 1
adjustment 5
adjustments 10
adjusts 1
admit 3
admitted 1
adopted 2
adopting 1
adored 1
adorn 1
adornment 1
adult 3
advance 27
advanced 18
advancement 2
advances 5
advancing 4
advantage 9
advantageous 1
advantages 5
advent 3
adventures 1
adverse 2
adversely 1
advertise 1
advice 5
advised 3
adviser 3
advocate 2
advocated 1
advocates 2
advocating 1
aesthetic 1
affect 15
affected 3
affecting 2
affects 2
affirm 3
affirmation 4
affirmations 2
affirming 5
affliction 2
afford 4
affront 2
affronted 1
afraid 187
after 51
afterwards 11
again 301
against 311
age 2
age-old 1
ageless 1
agent 1
agents 3
aging 2
ago 14
agony 7
agree 10
agreeable 1
agreed 8
agreeing 2
agreement 11
agrees 2
ahead 23
Aid 1
aid 19
aids 11
aim 74
aimed 5
aiming 1
aimless 2
aimlessly 3
aimlessness 1
aims 17
air 5
airplane 1
alarm 1
alcove 1
alert 5
alertness 2
alien 60
aligning 2
alignment 6
alike 25
alive 26
All 3
all 3027
all-embracing 3
all-encompassed 1
all-encompassing 8
all-inclusive 4
all-inclusiveness 1
All-Loving 1
allay 2
allays 1
allegiance 31
allegorical 1
alliance 8
alliances 3
allied 1
allies 2
allness 1
allot 1
allots 2
allotted 4
allow 70
allowance 2
allowed 18
allowing 17
allows 8
ally 8
almost 32
alone 362
along 117
Alpha 1
already 207
also 262
altar 99
altars 11
alter 10
alterable 1
alteration 3
alterations 1
Alternate 2
alternate 1
• adjective
alternate 5
• verb
alternating 3
Alternative 1
alternative 25
alternatives 26
alters 4
although 103
altogether 5
always 438
am 589
amazing 1
ambiguity 3
ambiguous 4
ambiguously 1
ambivalence 3
Amen 17
amenable 1
amid 3
amiss 9
amnesia 1
among 51
amount 8
amounts 1
amplified 1
amplify 1
amulets 1
an 980
analyses 1
analysis 1
analyze 3
analyzes 1
analyzing 4
anchor 2
anchored 2
anchors 1
ancient 70
and 15958
anew 6
angel's 2
angels 9
anger 89
angered 2
angry 24
anguish 1
animals 2
animate 1
annoyance 1
anonymous 3
Another 1
another 375
another's 14
Answer 42
answer 364
answered 76
answering 9
answers 49

## B

## C

## E

## G



## H

## I

limit . . . . . 95
limitation . . . . . 14
limitations . . . . . 22
limited . . . . . 88
limiting . . . . . 9
limitless . . . . . 53
limitlessness . . . . . 3
limits . . . . . 80
line . . . . . 20
lines . . . . . 3
linger . . . . . 10
lingered . . . . . 1
lingering . . . . . 7
lingers . . . . . 2
link . . . . . 20
linked . . . . . 1
linking . . . . . 1
links . . . . . 2
lion . . . . . 2
Lips . . . . . 1
lips . . . . . 9
list . . . . . 11
listen . . . . . 108
listened . . . . . 10
listening . . . . . 28
listens . . . . . 7
lit . . . . . 9
litanies . . . . . 1
litany . . . . . 1
literal . . . . . 6
literally . . . . . 35
little . . . . . 475
littleness . . . . . 68
littlest . . . . . 1
live . . . . . 104
lived . . . . . 3
lives . . . . . 44
liveth . . . . . 2
living . . . . . 76
load . . . . . 1
loan . . . . . 1
loans . . . . . 1
loathe . . . . . 1
loathsome . . . . . 2
lock . . . . . 4
locked . . . . . 12
locks . . . . . 2
loftier . . . . . 1
loftiest . . . . . 2
lofty . . . . . 6
logic . . . . . 8
logical . . . . . 15
logically . . . . . 1
loneliness . . . . . 24
lonely . . . . . 26
long . . . . . 225
long-held . . . . . 1
long-range . . . . . 4
longed . . . . . 1
longer . . . . . 198
longing . . . . . 3
longings . . . . . 1
longitudinal . . . . . 1
longs . . . . . 2
look . . . . . 666
looked . . . . . 61
looking . . . . . 81
looks . . . . . 149
loom . . . . . 1
loose . . . . . 7
loosed . . . . . 1
loosen . . . . . 2
loosened . . . . . 3
loosening . . . . . 2
Lord . . . . . 14
lord . . . . . 8
lordliness . . . . . 1
lose . . . . . 131
loser . . . . . 4
loses . . . . . 19
losing . . . . . 20
loss . . . . . 150
lost . . . . . 166
lot . . . . . 5
loud . . . . . 4
louder . . . . . 3
loudly . . . . . 7
lovable . . . . . 4
Love . . . . . 383
love . . . . . 1069
Love's . . . . . 3
love's . . . . . 40
love-encompassment . . 1
loved . . . . . 30
loveless . . . . . 4
lovelessly . . . . . 2
loveliest . . . . . 1
loveliness . . . . . 38
lovely . . . . . 29
loves . . . . . 103
loving . . . . . 104
lovingly . . . . . 19
low . . . . . 3
lower . . . . . 9
lower-order . . . . . 1
lowered . . . . . 1
lowest . . . . . 1
lowly . . . . . 1
loyalty . . . . . 2
lump . . . . . 1
lure . . . . . 1
lurk . . . . . 1
lurking . . . . . 1
lurks . . . . . 1
lusterless . . . . . 1
lying . . . . . 2


## M


mad . . . . . 51
made . . . . . 1023
madhouse . . . . . 1
madman . . . . . 5
madman's . . . . . 2
madness . . . . . 99
magazine . . . . . 1
magic . . . . . 62
magic's . . . . . 1
magic-miracle . . . . . 1
magical . . . . . 9
magically . . . . . 1
magnificence . . . . . 1
magnified . . . . . 2
magnify . . . . . 2
Magnitude . . . . . 1
magnitude . . . . . 31
main . . . . . 7
maintain . . . . . 41
maintained . . . . . 20
maintaining . . . . . 10
maintains . . . . . 8
Majesty . . . . . 3
majesty . . . . . 5
major . . . . . 30
majority . . . . . 1
make . . . . . 889
make-believe . . . . . 1
Maker . . . . . 4
maker . . . . . 33
maker's . . . . . 1
makes . . . . . 319
making . . . . . 147
malady . . . . . 1
malevolence . . . . . 1
malice . . . . . 11
man . . . . . 18
man's . . . . . 1
managed . . . . . 1
maneuver . . . . . 2
manger . . . . . 1
manifest . . . . . 26
manifestation . . . . . 4
manifestations . . . . . 6
manifested . . . . . 1
manifestly . . . . . 1
mankind . . . . . 1
manner . . . . . 5
manual . . . . . 6
many . . . . . 210
many-faceted . . . . . 1
mar . . . . . 5
march . . . . . 1
marches . . . . . 1
marching . . . . . 1
margins . . . . . 1
mark . . . . . 6
marked . . . . . 2
markedly . . . . . 1
marks . . . . . 1
marshalled . . . . . 2
martyr . . . . . 3
martyred . . . . . 1
martyrs . . . . . 1
mask . . . . . 1
masks . . . . . 1
mass . . . . . 1
massed . . . . . 2
massive . . . . . 1
master . . . . . 11
mastered . . . . . 2
masterpiece . . . . . 8
masters . . . . . 3
mastery . . . . . 6
match . . . . . 2
material . . . . . 6
matter . . . . . 82
matters . . . . . 19
maturing . . . . . 1
maturity . . . . . 2
maxim . . . . . 1
maximal . . . . . 7
maximizes . . . . . 1
maximum . . . . . 3
may . . . . . 579
maybe . . . . . 1
maze . . . . . 1
mazes . . . . . 1
Me . . . . . 14
• God
Me . . . . . 3
• Holy Spirit
me . . . . . 264
• Jesus
me . . . . . 844
• noise word
meager . . . . . 7
mean . . . . . 137
meaning . . . . . 359
meaningful . . . . . 70
meaningfully . . . . . 7
meaningfulness . . . . . 1
meaningless . . . . . 198
meaninglessly . . . . . 1
meaninglessness . . . 6
meanings . . . . . 1
Means . . . . . 2
means . . . . . 340
• noun
means . . . . . 194
• verb
meant . . . . . 38
meanwhile . . . . . 7
measure . . . . . 10
measured . . . . . 1
measureless . . . . . 1
mechanics . . . . . 1
mechanism . . . . . 4
mechanisms . . . . . 3
mediates . . . . . 3
mediating . . . . . 1
Mediator . . . . . 3
mediator . . . . . 1
medication . . . . . 1
medications . . . . . 1
medicine . . . . . 2
medicines . . . . . 1
meditation . . . . . 2
medium . . . . . 12
meek . . . . . 2
meekness . . . . . 1
meet . . . . . 112
meeting . . . . . 30
meetings . . . . . 1
meets . . . . . 10
melodies . . . . . 1
melody . . . . . 8
melt . . . . . 5
melting . . . . . 1
melts . . . . . 2
member . . . . . 1
members . . . . . 2
memories . . . . . 5
memory . . . . . 116
men . . . . . 8
menace . . . . . 1
mental . . . . . 6
mentally . . . . . 1
mention . . . . . 1
mentioned . . . . . 1
mercies . . . . . 1
merciful . . . . . 17
merciless . . . . . 10
mercilessness . . . . . 1
mercy . . . . . 51
mere . . . . . 8
merely . . . . . 385
merest . . . . . 1
merge . . . . . 2
merit . . . . . 11
merited . . . . . 1
meriting . . . . . 1
merits . . . . . 3
message . . . . . 73
messages . . . . . 55
Messenger . . . . . 1
messenger . . . . . 19
messengers . . . . . 29
met . . . . . 18
metal . . . . . 2
meted . . . . . 2
method . . . . . 4
methods . . . . . 4
meting . . . . . 1
microscopic . . . . . 1
middle . . . . . 3
middlemen . . . . . 1
midst . . . . . 11
might . . . . . 124
mightier . . . . . 3
mightily . . . . . 1
mightiness . . . . . 2
mighty . . . . . 30
mild . . . . . 2
milder . . . . . 1
milestone . . . . . 1
millions . . . . . 2
mimics . . . . . 1
Mind . . . . . 143
mind . . . . . 1607
mind's . . . . . 14
mind-searching . . . 5
mindful . . . . . 2
mindless . . . . . 7
minds . . . . . 206
Mine . . . . . 3
• God
mine . . . . . 31
• Jesus
mine . . . . . 64
• noise word
miniature . . . . . 3
minimal . . . . . 1
minimize . . . . . 1
minimizes . . . . . 1
minimizing . . . . . 3
minimum . . . . . 1
ministering . . . . . 1
ministers . . . . . 8
ministry . . . . . 5
minor . . . . . 3
minute . . . . . 58
minutes . . . . . 82
miracle . . . . . 310
miracle's . . . . . 1
miracle-based . . . . . 1
miracle-minded . . . 6
miracle-mindedness 5
miracle-readiness . 1
miracles . . . . . 246
miraculous . . . . . 5
miraculously . . . . . 1
mirages . . . . . 1
mirror . . . . . 22

mirrored . . . . . . . . . . 1
mirroring . . . . . . . . . 1
mirrors . . . . . . . . . . . 1
misapplication. . . . . 1
misconception . . . . . 1
misconstrue . . . . . . . 1
miscreate . . . . . . . . 10
miscreated . . . . . . . . 1
miscreation . . . . . . . 8
miscreations. . . . . . . 7
miscreative . . . . . . . . 1
misdirected . . . . . . . 3
misdirecting. . . . . . . 1
miserable . . . . . . . . 12
miseries. . . . . . . . . . . 1
misery . . . . . . . . . . . 69
misguide . . . . . . . . . . 1
misguided. . . . . . . . . 4
mishandled. . . . . . . . 1
misinterpretation . . 1
misinterpreted. . . . . 1
misinterpreting. . . . 1
misjudged. . . . . . . . . 1
misleading . . . . . . . . 1
misled . . . . . . . . . . . . 1
misperceive . . . . . . . 6
misperceived . . . . . . 2
misperceiving . . . . . 1
misperception . . . . 11
misperceptions . . . . 9
misplaced . . . . . . . . . 5
miss . . . . . . . . . . . . . . 4
missed . . . . . . . . . . . . 2
missing . . . . . . . . . . . 8
mission . . . . . . . . . . 25
misstep . . . . . . . . . . . 1
missteps . . . . . . . . . . 1
mist . . . . . . . . . . . . . . 1
mistake . . . . . . . . . . 95
mistaken . . . . . . . . . 34
mistakenly . . . . . . . . 1
mistakes . . . . . . . . . 82
mistaking . . . . . . . . . 1
misthought. . . . . . . . 2
mistook . . . . . . . . . . . 4
mistrust. . . . . . . . . . . 1
mistrustful . . . . . . . . 2
mists . . . . . . . . . . . . . 4
misty . . . . . . . . . . . . . 2
misunderstand . . . . 2
misunderstanding. . 2
misunderstands. . . . 1
misunderstood . . . 15
misuse . . . . . . . . . . . . 8
misused . . . . . . . . . . . 6
misusing . . . . . . . . . . 5
mitigate. . . . . . . . . . . 1
mixture . . . . . . . . . . . 1
mobilize . . . . . . . . . . 1
mock . . . . . . . . . . . . . 1
mocked . . . . . . . . . . . 4
mockery . . . . . . . . . . 5
mocks . . . . . . . . . . . . 1
model . . . . . . . . . . . . 9
modesty . . . . . . . . . . 1
moment . . . . . . . . . 49
moments . . . . . . . . . 2
momentum . . . . . . . 1
money . . . . . . . . . . . . 9
monster . . . . . . . . . . 1
monsters. . . . . . . . . . 2
months . . . . . . . . . . . 1
mood. . . . . . . . . . . . . 4
moods . . . . . . . . . . . . 1
moon. . . . . . . . . . . . . 2
more . . . . . . . . . . . 752
more-than-everything . . . . . . . 1
morning . . . . . . . . . 33
mortal. . . . . . . . . . . . 5
most. . . . . . . . . . . 117
mother . . . . . . . . . . . 1
motion . . . . . . . . . . . 2
motivate . . . . . . . . . . 2
motivated. . . . . . . . . 2
motivating . . . . . . . . 1
motivation . . . . . . . 23
motivators . . . . . . . . 1
motives . . . . . . . . . . . 5
mound . . . . . . . . . . . 1
mountain . . . . . . . . . 3
mountains . . . . . . . . 3
mourn . . . . . . . . . . . . 3
mourner . . . . . . . . . . 2
mournful . . . . . . . . . 1
mourning . . . . . . . . . 3
mouse . . . . . . . . . . . . 5
mouth . . . . . . . . . . . . 1
move . . . . . . . . . . . . 22
moved . . . . . . . . . . . . 2
moves . . . . . . . . . . . . 3
moving . . . . . . . . . . . 1
much . . . . . . . . . . . 183
multiplied . . . . . . . . 5
multiplies . . . . . . . . . 1
multiply . . . . . . . . . . 2
multitude . . . . . . . . . 2
murder . . . . . . . . . . 39
murderer . . . . . . . . . 8
murderers . . . . . . . . 1
murderous . . . . . . . . 6
music. . . . . . . . . . . . . 1
musings . . . . . . . . . . 1
must . . . . . . . . . . 1561
mute . . . . . . . . . . . . . 1
mutual . . . . . . . . . . . 2
mutually. . . . . . . . . . 1
My. . . . . . . . . . . . . . 18
• God
My. . . . . . . . . . . . . . . 1
• Christ
My. . . . . . . . . . . . . . . 2
• Holy Spirit
my . . . . . . . . . . . . . 185
• Jesus
my . . . . . . . . . . . . . 847
• noise word
myriad . . . . . . . . . . . 2
Myself. . . . . . . . . . . . 2
• God
myself. . . . . . . . . . . 17
• Jesus
myself. . . . . . . . . . 113
• noise word
mysteries . . . . . . . . . 2
mysterious. . . . . . . . 1
mystery . . . . . . . . . . 3
myth . . . . . . . . . . . . . 1
mythological . . . . . . 1
mythology . . . . . . . . 1
myths . . . . . . . . . . . . 4


## N


nail . . . . . . . . . . . . . . 2
nailed . . . . . . . . . . . . 2
nails . . . . . . . . . . . . . 8
Name . . . . . . . . . . 114
name. . . . . . . . . . . 110
Name's . . . . . . . . . . . 1
named. . . . . . . . . . . . 5
nameless . . . . . . . . . 6
namelessness . . . . . 1
names . . . . . . . . . . . 30
naming. . . . . . . . . . . 3
narrow . . . . . . . . . . . 6
narrowed . . . . . . . . . 2
narrowly . . . . . . . . . 1
native . . . . . . . . . . . . 2
natural . . . . . . . . . . 85
naturally . . . . . . . . . 9
nature. . . . . . . . . . . 46
nature's . . . . . . . . . . 1
natures . . . . . . . . . . . 1
near. . . . . . . . . . . . . 30
nearby . . . . . . . . . . . 1
nearer. . . . . . . . . . . 29
nearest . . . . . . . . . . . 1
neatly . . . . . . . . . . . . 1
necessarily. . . . . . . 16
necessary . . . . . . . 134
necessity . . . . . . . . . 5
need . . . . . . . . . . . 657
needed . . . . . . . . . . 56
needful. . . . . . . . . . . 12
needing . . . . . . . . . . . 6
needle . . . . . . . . . . . . 1
needless. . . . . . . . . . . 7
needlessly . . . . . . . . . 2
needs . . . . . . . . . . . 187
needy . . . . . . . . . . . . . 1
negative. . . . . . . . . . . 7
negatively . . . . . . . . . 2
neglect . . . . . . . . . . . . 1
neglecting . . . . . . . . . 1
neighbor . . . . . . . . . . 3
neighbor's. . . . . . . . . 1
neither. . . . . . . . . . 108
nemesis . . . . . . . . . . . 1
nestles . . . . . . . . . . . . 1
neutral. . . . . . . . . . . 29
neutrality . . . . . . . . . 1
never . . . . . . . . . . . 652
never-changing . . . . 1
never-ending . . . . . . 1
nevermore . . . . . . . . 2
nevertheless . . . . . . . 9
new. . . . . . . . . . . . . . 79
newborn . . . . . . . . . . 3
newcomer . . . . . . . . . 1
newer . . . . . . . . . . . . . 2
newly . . . . . . . . . . . . . 4
newness. . . . . . . . . . . 2
news . . . . . . . . . . . . . 3
next . . . . . . . . . . . . . 46
nice. . . . . . . . . . . . . . . 1
nicer. . . . . . . . . . . . . . 1
nigh . . . . . . . . . . . . . . 4
night. . . . . . . . . . . . . 27
nightmare . . . . . . . . . 6
nightmares . . . . . . . 19
nights. . . . . . . . . . . . . 1
no . . . . . . . . . . . . 2735
nod . . . . . . . . . . . . . . . 1
noise. . . . . . . . . . . . . . 1
noises . . . . . . . . . . . . . 1
non-creative . . . . . . . 1
non-mental . . . . . . . . 1
non-right-minded . . 1
non-threat. . . . . . . . . 1
none . . . . . . . . . . . . . 68
nonessentials . . . . . . 1
nonexistence . . . . . . 1
nonexistent. . . . . . . . 3
nonhuman . . . . . . . . 1
nor . . . . . . . . . . . . . 603
normal. . . . . . . . . . . . 1
not . . . . . . . . . . . 6735
not-right-mindedness. . . . . . . 2
note . . . . . . . . . . . . . 10
noted. . . . . . . . . . . . . 1
notes . . . . . . . . . . . . . 3
nothing. . . . . . . . 1003
nothingness . . . . . . 52
notice. . . . . . . . . . . . . 7
noticeable. . . . . . . . . 1
noticed . . . . . . . . . . . 5
noting . . . . . . . . . . . . 2
notion . . . . . . . . . . . 10
notions . . . . . . . . . . . 3
nourished. . . . . . . . . 2
nourishment . . . . . . 1
now . . . . . . . . . . . . 945
nowhere . . . . . . . . . 47
number. . . . . . . . . . 23
numbered. . . . . . . . . 2
numbers . . . . . . . . . . 2
nursed. . . . . . . . . . . . 1
nurtured. . . . . . . . . . 1
nutrition. . . . . . . . . . 1


## O


O. . . . . . . . . . . . . . . . 10
oath . . . . . . . . . . . . . . 2
obedience . . . . . . . . . 7
obey . . . . . . . . . . . . . 26
obeyed. . . . . . . . . . . . 3
obeying . . . . . . . . . . . 7
obeys . . . . . . . . . . . . 12
object. . . . . . . . . . . . . 7
objectionable. . . . . . 1
objections. . . . . . . . . 1
objective . . . . . . . . . . 2
objectively . . . . . . . . 1
objects. . . . . . . . . . . . 1
obliterate . . . . . . . . . 4
obliterated . . . . . . . . 6
obliterates . . . . . . . . 2
oblivion. . . . . . . . . . 11
oblivious. . . . . . . . . . 1
obscure . . . . . . . . . . 69
obscured. . . . . . . . . 25
obscures . . . . . . . . . 10
obscuring . . . . . . . . . 8
obscurity. . . . . . . . . . 3
observable . . . . . . . . 1
observe . . . . . . . . . . . 5
observed. . . . . . . . . . 4
observes . . . . . . . . . . 1
observing . . . . . . . . . 1
obsessed . . . . . . . . . . 3
obstacle. . . . . . . . . . 28
obstacles. . . . . . . . . 24
obstruct . . . . . . . . . . 2
obstructing . . . . . . . 1
obstruction . . . . . . . 2
obstructions . . . . . . 1
obtain . . . . . . . . . . . . 8
obtained. . . . . . . . . . 6
obvious. . . . . . . . . . 78
obviously . . . . . . . . 19
obviousness. . . . . . . 4
occasion . . . . . . . . . . 1
occasionally. . . . . . . 2
occupied. . . . . . . . . . 4
occupies . . . . . . . . . . 4
occupy . . . . . . . . . . . 7
occupying . . . . . . . . 1
occur . . . . . . . . . . . 75
occurred. . . . . . . . . 31
occurrence. . . . . . . . 1
occurrences . . . . . . . 1
occurring . . . . . . . . . 1
occurs . . . . . . . . . . . 42
ocean. . . . . . . . . . . . 11
oddly. . . . . . . . . . . . . 1
odds . . . . . . . . . . . . . 3
of. . . . . . . . . . . . 12735
off . . . . . . . . . . . . . . 83
off-balanced . . . . . . 1
offended. . . . . . . . . . 4
offending . . . . . . . . . 1
offends . . . . . . . . . . . 2
offense . . . . . . . . . . . 4
offenses . . . . . . . . . . 2
offer . . . . . . . . . . . 320
offered . . . . . . . . . . 88
offering. . . . . . . . . . 72
offerings. . . . . . . . . 11
offers. . . . . . . . . . . 163
official. . . . . . . . . . . 1
officially . . . . . . . . . 1
offset. . . . . . . . . . . . . 4
offspring . . . . . . . . . 1
oft . . . . . . . . . . . . . . . 1
often . . . . . . . . . . . . 77
oh. . . . . . . . . . . . . . . 1
old . . . . . . . . . . . . . . 23
older . . . . . . . . . . . . . 3
Omega . . . . . . . . . . . 1
omit. . . . . . . . . . . . . . 2
omits. . . . . . . . . . . . . 1
omitted. . . . . . . . . . . 2
omitting . . . . . . . . . . 1
omnipotence. . . . . . 3
omnipotent . . . . . . . 1
omniscient. . . . . . . . 2
on. . . . . . . . . . . . . 1454
once. . . . . . . . . . . . 153
One . . . . . . . . . . . . . 28
• God
One . . . . . . . . . . . . . . 2
• God and Christ

# P

## S

silencer . . . 1
silences . . . 1
silent . . . 22
silently . . . 17
silly . . . 3
silver . . . 3
similar . . . 6
similarity . . . 1
similarly . . . 4
simple . . . 158
simple-minded . . . 1
simplest . . . 8
simplicity . . . 12
simplified . . . 1
simply . . . 87
simultaneous . . . 5
simultaneously . . . 14
sin . . . 544
sin's . . . 8
since . . . 179
sincere . . . 9
sincerely . . . 2
sincerity . . . 9
sinful . . . 31
sinfulness . . . 9
sing . . . 14
singing . . . 4
single . . . 74
sings . . . 15
singularly . . . 1
sink . . . 11
sinking . . . 1
sinks . . . 2
sinless . . . 61
sinlessly . . . 2
Sinlessness . . . 3
sinlessness . . . 97
sinned . . . 16
sinner . . . 7
sinner's . . . 1
sinners . . . 10
sins . . . 100
sister . . . 2
sit . . . 16
sits . . . 1
situation . . . 155
situation's . . . 1
situations . . . 38
six . . . 8
size . . . 13
sizes . . . 1
skeleton . . . 1
skies . . . 1
skill . . . 7
skills . . . 2
skin . . . 1
skip . . . 1
sky . . . 7
slain . . . 6
slate . . . 2
slaughter . . . 1
slave . . . 26
slavery . . . 10
slaves . . . 4
sleep . . . 66
sleepeth . . . 1
sleeping . . . 27
sleeps . . . 10
sleepy . . . 1
sleight . . . 1
slept . . . 6
slight . . . 7
slightest . . . 8
slightly . . . 4
slights . . . 1
slip . . . 17
slipped . . . 2
slipping . . . 2
slips . . . 5
sloping . . . 1
slow . . . 9
slower . . . 1
slowly . . . 47
small . . . 37
smaller . . . 4
smallest . . . 6
smash . . . 1
smeared . . . 1
smile . . . 20
smiled . . . 2
smiles . . . 11
smiling . . . 1
smoke . . . 1
smooth . . . 1
smoother . . . 1
smoothly . . . 1
snake . . . 1
snares . . . 1
snarling . . . 1
snatch . . . 6
snatches . . . 1
snow . . . 4
snow-white . . . 2
snowflake . . . 2
snuffed . . . 1
so . . . 1456
so-called . . . 3
soar . . . 2
soared . . . 1
soars . . . 1
sobering . . . 1
soft . . . 10
softer . . . 1
softly . . . 6
softness . . . 1
soil . . . 2
solace . . . 4
sold . . . 2
sole . . . 15
solely . . . 19
solemn . . . 2
solid . . . 26
solidity . . . 1
solidness . . . 1
solitary . . . 5
solitude . . . 6
solution . . . 32
solutions . . . 3
solve . . . 27
solved . . . 28
solves . . . 3
solving . . . 5
some . . . 243
somebody . . . 1
someday . . . 4
somehow . . . 11
Someone . . . 1
someone . . . 81
someone's . . . 1
Something . . . 2
something . . . 221
sometime . . . 3
sometimes . . . 46
somewhat . . . 7
somewhere . . . 14
Son . . . 1320
son . . . 20
Son's . . . 24
song . . . 57
songs . . . 1
Sons . . . 79
sons . . . 3
Sonship . . . 104
soon . . . 29
sooner . . . 7
soothes . . . 1
sorrow . . . 44
sorrowful . . . 3
sorrows . . . 6
sorry . . . 13
sort . . . 6
sorting . . . 8
sorts . . . 3
sought . . . 69
soul . . . 9
souls . . . 2
sound . . . 31
sounding . . . 1
soundless . . . 5
soundlessly . . . 1
sounds . . . 42
Source . . . 102
source . . . 129
sources . . . 6
sovereignty . . . 2
sow . . . 1
sown . . . 1
space . . . 65
space-time . . . 1
span . . . 2
spans . . . 1
spare . . . 2
spared . . . 1
spares . . . 1
spark . . . 28
sparkle . . . 2
sparkles . . . 4
sparkling . . . 3
sparrow . . . 2
spawn . . . 1
speak . . . 122
speaking . . . 16
speaks . . . 115
spear . . . 3
special . . . 241
specialized . . . 1
specially . . . 1
specialness . . . 116
specific . . . 87
specifically . . . 23
specificity . . . 4
specifics . . . 6
specified . . . 1
specify . . . 4
specious . . . 1
speck . . . 3
spectacles . . . 1
speculation . . . 1
speed . . . 6
speeded . . . 1
spells . . . 1
spend . . . 41
spending . . . 1
spends . . . 1
spent . . . 23
sphere . . . 4
spinning . . . 1
spins . . . 1
Spirit . . . 11
spirit . . . 128
Spirit's . . . 139
spirit's . . . 7
spirit-identification 1
spiritual . . . 12
spiritualized . . . 1
spite . . . 8
splendid . . . 1
splendor . . . 2
splintered . . . 2
split . . . 81
splits . . . 3
splitting . . . 4
spoil . . . 1
spoke . . . 6
spoken . . . 8
sponsors . . . 2
spot . . . 14
spotless . . . 2
spots . . . 3
spread . . . 7
spreads . . . 2
spring . . . 5
springboard . . . 1
springs . . . 3
sprung . . . 1
spun . . . 1
spurious . . . 2
squandered . . . 1
squeak . . . 1
squeaking . . . 1
squeaks . . . 1
stab . . . 5
stability . . . 11
stabilize . . . 4
stabilized . . . 2
stable . . . 13
stacks . . . 1
stage . . . 11
stages . . . 3
stagger . . . 2
staggering . . . 1
stain . . . 4
stairs . . . 1
stairway . . . 2
stake . . . 2
stalk . . . 1
stalks . . . 2
stamp . . . 3
stamps . . . 1
stance . . . 1
stand . . . 165
standard . . . 2
standards . . . 1
standing . . . 9
standpoint . . . 1
stands . . . 132
star . . . 11
stares . . . 1
stark . . . 2
starkly . . . 1
stars . . . 9
start . . . 31
started . . . 9
starting . . . 7
startling . . . 4
starts . . . 9
starvation . . . 1
starve . . . 2
starved . . . 3
starves . . . 1
starving . . . 3
state . . . 149
stated . . . 15
stately . . . 2
statement . . . 66
statements . . . 5
states . . . 17
static . . . 1
stating . . . 3
status . . . 4
stay . . . 31
stayed . . . 3
stays . . . 5
steadfast . . . 4
steadfastly . . . 2
steadily . . . 7
steady . . . 4
steal . . . 4
steel . . . 1
steep . . . 1
steeped . . . 1
stem . . . 6
stemming . . . 1
stems . . . 13
step . . . 193
stepped . . . 4
stepping . . . 2
steppingstone . . . 1
steps . . . 35
stern . . . 2
stick . . . 1
stifle . . . 1
still . . . 84
• quiet, peaceful
still . . . 535
• other
stilled . . . 3
stillness . . . 28
sting . . . 2
stir . . . 1
stirring . . . 3
stirs . . . 1
stole . . . 2
stolen . . . 1
stone . . . 10
stones . . . 3
stood . . . 9
stoop . . . 1
stop . . . 21
stopped . . . 2
stopping . . . 1
stops . . . 5

## T

## U

urging 1
Us 4
• God and Jesus
us 583
• Jesus
us 44
• noise word
usage 1
usages 1
use 350
used 113
useful 26
usefulness 15
useless 33
uselessness 2
uses 46
usher 1
ushered 2
ushers 1
using 39
usual 15
usually 15
usurp 4
usurpation 1
usurped 4
usurping 3
usurps 2
utilize 9
utilized 5
utilizes 2
utopian 1
utter 2
utterly 8

# V

vacant 6
vacillate 3
vacillates 1
vacillations 3
vacuum 1
vague 6
vaguely 1
vain 34
vainly 4
valid 1
validity 5
valuable 26
value 234
valued 15
valueless 22
valuelessness 1
values 23
valuing 7
vanish 21
vanished 4
vanishes 7
vanity 1
vanquish 1
vanquished 2
vanquisher 1
vantage 1
vaporous 1
variability 2
variable 6
variance 5
variation 3
variations 2
varied 1
varies 5
variety 2
various 7
vary 8
varying 2
vassals 1
vast 8
vastly 1
vault 1
vaults 2
vehicle 1
veil 62
veiled 4
veils 3
veins 1
veneer 1
venerates 1
vengeance 77
vengeance's 1
vengeful 4
venture 2
verbal 1
verbally 1
verdict 3
version 8
versus 10
vertical 2
vertically 1
very 258
vestige 1
vestiges 1
vicinity 1
vicious 9
viciously 1
viciousness 5
victim 20
victimize 1
victimized 2
victims 1
victor 6
victorious 2
victory 15
view 44
viewpoint 9
viewpoints 1
views 5
vigilance 26
vigilant 23
violate 3
violated 4
violates 1
violating 3
violation 3
violence 9
violent 1
virtually 4
virtuous 1
vise 1
visible 10
vision 313
visions 1
visit 1
vistas 1
vital 1
vitality 2
vividly 1
vocation 3
Voice 255
voice 73
voices 15
void 1
voids 1
volatile 1
volition 2
voluntarily 1
voluntary 2
vow 3
vows 2
vulnerability 7
vulnerable 20

# W

wage 3
waged 1
wages 2
wait 93
waited 5
waiting 42
waits 61
wake 30
waken 30
wakened 4
wakening 6
wakens 2
wakes 1
waking 40
walk 111
walked 5
walking 13
walks 32
wall 20
walled 1
walls 6
wander 24
wandered 6
wanderer 2
wandering 14
wanderings 1
wanders 7
wands 1
wane 1
waning 1
want 547
wanted 30
wanting 20
wants 100
war 69
ward 1
wariness 1
warlike 1
warm 1
warming 1
warmth 4
warning 1
warped 3
warps 1
warrant 4
warranted 2
warrants 1
warring 1
warrior 1
warriors 1
wars 1
wary 1
was 817
wash 2
washed 4
washes 1
waste 14
wasted 6
wastes 1
wasting 1
watch 26
watched 1
watches 7
watchful 2
watching 4
water 9
waters 1
wave 1
waver 2
wavering 2
wavers 1
waves 4
waxen 1
waxing 1
way 773
ways 59
We 1
• Christ
we 1651
• Jesus
we 105
• noise word
weak 62
weaken 17
weakened 8
weakening 4
weakens 1
weaker 3
weakness 81
weaknesses 2
wealth 2
weapon 14
weapons 1
wearily 2
weariness 2
wearing 1
wearisome 1
wears 2
weary 13
wearying 3
weather 2
weave 6
weaves 1
weaving 2
week 7
weeks 1
weep 11
weeps 1
weight 5
weighty 1
weird 8
welcome 106
welcomed 13
welcomes 6
welcoming 7
welded 1
welfare 1
well 274
well-known 1
well-structured 1
wells 1
went 10
wept 1
were 365
wet 1
What 6
what 4222
• noise word
whatever 159
when 989
whence 1
whenever 72
where 857
whereby 12
wherein 12
whereof 1
whereon 7
wherever 29
whether 54
which 2081
while 104
• noun
while 232
• noise word
whim 6
whirl 1
whisper 4
whispered 3
whispering 1
whispers 6
whit 1
white 5
whiteness 1
Who 160
• God
Who 2
• God and Christ/Self
Who 59
• Christ/Self
Who 149
• Holy Spirit
who 27
• Jesus
who 1325
• noise word
whoever 12
whole 290
wholehearted 1
wholeheartedly 1
Wholeness 19
wholeness 60
wholes 1
wholly 244
Whom 25
• God
Whom 11
• Christ/Self
Whom 19
• Holy Spirit
whom 193
• noise word
whomever 1
Whose 34
• God
Whose 11
• Christ/Self
Whose 20
• Holy Spirit
whose 2
• Jesus
whose 97
• noise word
whosoever 1
why 238
wicked 4
wide 5

widely 1
widening 2
wider 2
wild 8
wildest 1
wildly 1
Will 467
will 323
• noun
will 68
• verb
will 3958
• noise word (auxiliary verb)
willed 26
willing 143
willingly 15
willingness 105
wills 124
win 8
wind 7
wind-swept 1
window 6
windows 1
winds 4
wing 1
wings 14
winning 2
winter 1
winter's 1
wipe 4
wiped 3
wisdom 24
wise 8
wisely 1
wiser 6
wish 175
wished 6
wished-for 1
wishes 52
wishful 2
wishing 1
wisp 2
with 3053
withdraw 22
withdrawal 3
withdrawing 6
withdrawn 16
withdraws 2
wither 2
withered 2
withering 4
withers 1
withheld 26
withhold 30
withholding 2
withholds 2
within 505
without 728
withstand 11
withstood 1
Witness 1
witness 118
witnessed 6
witnesses 108
witnessing 3
won 2
wonder 10
wondered 1
wonderful 5
wondering 2
wonderment 1
wood 1
wooden 1
woolly 1
Word 117
word 37
wordless 1
wordlessly 1
words 169
work 66
workbook 15
worked 4
worker 15
workers 6
working 11
working-out 1
workings 2
works 24
world 2062
world's 55
world-encompassing 1
worldly 10
worlds 22
worms 2
worn 4
worried 2
worries 1
worry 12
worse 2
worsening 1
worship 23
worshipful 1
worshipfully 1
worshipped 7
worshipper 2
worshippers 10
worshipping 3
worships 2
worst 6
worth 59
worthiness 1
worthless 8
worthlessness 5
worthy 69
would 1829
would-be 1
wounded 2
wounding 1
wounds 1
wove 1
woven 5
wrapped 2
wrapping 2
wrappings 2
wrath 10
wrenched 1
wrest 2
wrested 4
wrestle 1
wretched 1
writ 2
write 6
writes 3
written 18
wrong 77
wrong-minded 2
wrong-mindedness 4
wrongly 15
wrongs 1
wrote 2
wrought 6

Y

ye 12
year 17
yearn 2
yearning 4
yearns 4
years 17
yes 23
yesterday 6
yesterday's 1
yet 1467
yield 12
yielded 1
yielding 1
yields 2
yoke 2
You 355
• God
You 2
• Christ/Self
You 10
• Holy Spirit
you 17701
• noise word
Your 342
• God
Your 1
• Holy Spirit
your 5849
• noise word
Yours 37
• God
yours 443
• noise word
Yourself 2
• God
yourself 1295
• noise word
yourselves 1

# Total word counts by book

*A Course in Miracles*:

text ........ 288,532
workbook for students ........ 146,252
manual for teachers ........ 24,990
clarification of terms ........ 4,922

Supplements:

*Psychotherapy* ........ 9,608
*The Song of Prayer* ........ 9,317

Combined:

Total words ........ 483,621
Total unique words ........ 8,277

# APPENDIX B

## Noise words and split words

# Noise words

a
about
also
am
an
and
are
as
at
be
because
been
but
by
can
cannot
could

did
do
does
done
else
else's
for
from
had
has
have
he
him
himself
his
how
however

I
if
in
into
is
it
its
itself
may
me
mine
my
myself
nor
not
of
on

only
or
our
ourselves
should
since
so
some
than
that
the
their
theirs
them
themselves
then
there

therefore
these
they
this
those
through
thus
to
until
upon
us
very
was
we
were
what
whatever

when
where
which
who
whom
whomever
whose
with
would
yet
you
your
yours
yourself
yourselves

# Split words

## Pronouns

**He**
God
Christ/Self
Holy Spirit

**he**
Jesus
noise word

**Him**
God
Christ/Self
Holy Spirit

**him**
Jesus
noise word

**Himself**
God
Christ/Self
Holy Spirit

**himself**
Jesus
noise word

**His**
God
Christ/Self
Holy Spirit

**his**
Jesus
noise word

**I**
God
Christ
Holy Spirit
Jesus
noise word

**It**

**it**
noise word

**Its**

**its**
noise word

**Itself**

**itself**
noise word

**Me**
God
Holy Spirit

**me**
Jesus
noise word

**Mine**
God

**mine**
Jesus
noise word

**My**
God
Christ
Holy Spirit

**my**
Jesus
noise word

**Myself**
God

**myself**
Jesus
noise word

**One**
God
God and Christ
Christ
Holy Spirit
Unity

**one**
Jesus
other

**Our**
God and Jesus

**our**
Jesus
noise word

**ours**
Jesus

**ourselves**
Jesus
noise word

**Their**

**their**
noise word

**Theirs**

**theirs**
noise word

**Them**

**them**
noise word

**Themselves**

**themselves**
noise word

**They**

**they**
noise word

**Thy**

**thy**
noise word

**Us**
God and Jesus

**us**
Jesus
noise word

**We**
Christ

**we**
Jesus
noise word

**Who**
God
God and Christ/Self
Christ/Self
Holy Spirit

**who**
Jesus
noise word

**Whom**
God
Christ/Self
Holy Spirit

**whom**
noise word

**Whose**
God
Christ/Self
Holy Spirit

**whose**
Jesus
noise word

**You**
God
Christ/Self
Holy Spirit

**you**
noise word

**Your**
God
Holy Spirit

**your**
noise word

**Yours**
God

**yours**
noise word

**Yourself**
God

**yourself**
noise word

## Words split by meaning or part of speech

**Alternate**

**alternate**
adjective
verb

**Arms**

**arms**
body
weapons

**Being**

**being**
existence
verb, adverb

**content**
happiness
meaning

**course**
*A Course in Miracles*
curriculum
direction
of course

**cross**
noun
verb

**having**
noun
verb

**just**
fair, deserved
other

**Means**
God

**means**
noun
verb

**One**
God
God and Christ
Christ
Holy Spirit
Unity

**one**
Jesus
other

**past**
noun
other

**present**
verb
noun
other

**rest**
peace, repose
remainder
other

**rested**
peace, repose
other

**resting**
peace, repose
other

**rests**
peace, repose
other

**still**
quiet, peaceful
other

**subject**
noun
other

**while**
noun
noise word

**Will**

**will**
noun
verb
noise word
(auxiliary verb)

# Split words

## Uppercase words that refer to Heaven, God, Christ or the Holy Spirit

These words also appear in lowercase. The listings in the Concordance are divided into uppercase and lowercase.

Abstraction
Aid
All
Alternate
Alternative
Another
Answer
Arms
Atonement
Author
Authority
Authorship
Autonomy
Awakening
Beginning
Being
Both
Bridge
Brother
Call
Cause
Certainty
Changeless
Child
Coming
Communication
Companion
Companionship
Correction
Court
Creator
Divine
Each
Effect
Effects
Either
End
Eternal
Everlasting
Everywhere
Fact
Father
Father's
Fatherhood
Fatherless
Final
First
Force
Formlessness
Foundation
Friend
Gift
Given
Giver
God
Guest
Guests
Guide
Hand
Hands
He
Healer
Heart
Heaven
Help
Helper
Helpers
Here
Higher
Him
Himself
His
Holiness
Holy
Host
I
Identity
Infinite
Innocence
Inspiration
Interpreter
It
Its
Itself
Judge
Judgment
Kingdom
Last
Levels
Life
Light
Lips
Lord
Love
Love's
Magnitude
Majesty
Maker
Means
Mediator
Messenger
Me
Mind
Mine
My
Myself
Name
One
Oneness
Order
Other
Our
Ourselves
Own
Perfection
Presence
Protector
Purpose
Ray
Rays
Redeemer
Relationship
Saints
Savior
Saviors
Second
Self
Self-centered
Sinlessness
Someone
Something
Son
Song
Sons
Source
Spirit
Spirit's
Teacher
Teachers
Their
Theirs
Them
Themselves
Therapist
Therein
They
Thought
Thoughts
Thy
Translator
Truth
Unalterable
Unity
Universal
Us
Voice
We
What
Who
Wholeness
Whom
Whose
Will
Witness
Word
You
Your
Yours
Yourself

**The following words appear in uppercase only.**

All-Loving
Alpha
Atonement's
Authoritative
Christ
Christ's
Comforter
Coming's
Corrector
Creator's
Divinity
Fatherly
God's
God-created
God-destructive
God-proof
Godlike
Heaven's
Heaven-born
Heavens
Holies
Hosts
Jesus
Name's
Omega
One-mindedness
Paradise
Prime
Prince
Redeemer's
Resource
Self-encompassing
Self-extending
Self-fullness
Self-love
Selfhood
Son's
Sonship
Transformer
Trinity

# APPENDIX C

## Terms and Phrases

# Terms and Phrases

Only the most important terms and phrases—the ones almost all students would be most likely to recognize—have been included here. The emphasis in these listings is on meaning rather than the strict adherence to the form or actual word that is found in the Concordance. Thus, for example, *small willingness* is included under the term *a little willingness*, and *innocent perception* is included under the term *true perception*. The various listings are complete regarding the occurrences of the *exact* wording of the term or phrase, but limits were placed on the variations allowed.

## accept the Atonement 57

| | |
|---|---|
| T-1 I.44:1 | an inner awareness of Christ and the acceptance of His Atonement. |
| T-2 I.4:4 | The escape is brought about by your acceptance of the Atonement, |
| T-2 III.1:1 | The Atonement can only be accepted within you by releasing the |
| T-2 III.3:1 | acceptance of the Atonement by everyone is only a matter of time. |
| T-2 V.4:4 | not-right-mindedness are the result of refusal to accept the Atonement |
| T-2 V.4:4 | are the result of refusal to accept the Atonement for yourself. |
| T-2 V.4:5 | If you do accept it, you are in a position to recognize that those who |
| T-2 V.5:1 | sole *responsibility of the miracle worker is to accept the Atonement for* |
| T-2 VI.7:3 | in the larger process of accepting the Atonement as the remedy. |
| T-2 VII.5:9 | establishes a state of mind in which the Atonement can be accepted |
| T-3 V.10:2 | totally accepted the Atonement and given themselves over to truth. |
| T-5 V.7:8 | sole responsibility of the miracle worker is to accept the Atonement |
| T-5 V.8:6 | it back to full creation at any minute if it accept the Atonement first. |
| T-7 VIII.7:3 | By accepting the Atonement for yourself, you are deciding against |
| T-8 III.6:5 | have really looked at it you *will* accept the Atonement for yourself. |
| T-9 h | THE ACCEPTANCE OF THE ATONEMENT |
| T-9 VII.2:5 | Yet you cannot abide in peace unless you accept the Atonement, |
| T-12 VII.1:5 | Atonement will radiate from your acceptance of it for yourself to |
| T-13 in.2:1 | of the separation, as the acceptance of the Atonement is its end. |
| T-13 I.6:1 | When you have accepted the Atonement for yourself, you will |
| T-13 I.9:1 | Accepting the Atonement teaches you what immortality is, |
| T-13 IX.6:3 | you free of it, accept His offer of Atonement for all your brothers. |
| T-13 X.5:5 | For you will have accepted the Atonement, which shone within you |
| T-13 X.8:6 | you will not fear to look upon the Atonement and accept it wholly. |
| T-14 I.1:7 | accepting the Atonement for yourself and learning you are guiltless. |
| T-14 III.3:7 | *I choose to testify to my acceptance of the Atonement, not to its rejection* |
| T-14 III.7:4 | teach him that the Atonement, which you have accepted for yourself, |
| T-14 III.10:1 | Those who accept the Atonement *are* invulnerable. But those who |
| T-14 III.12:4 | in every mind that quietly accepts the plan God set for its Atonement |
| T-18 VII.1:4 | one accept Atonement for himself who still accepts sin as his goal. |
| T-19 I.9:2 | It is the sign that you have accepted the Atonement for yourself, |
| T19 IV.D.9:1 | unless he has accepted the Atonement and learned illusions are not |
| T-22 VI.4:7 | For here your healing is, and here will you accept Atonement. |
| T-22 VI.5:3 | the same Atonement you accepted in your relationship corrects the |
| T-28 IV.1:1 | Accepting the Atonement for yourself means not to give support to |
| W-pI 101.5:3 | Accept Atonement with an open mind, which cherishes no |
| W-pI 139.h | I will accept Atonement for myself. |
| W-pI 139.7:3 | And they will come again until the time Atonement is accepted, |
| W-pI. 139.10:2 | Today accept Atonement, not to change reality, but merely to |
| W-pI. 139.11:3 | *I will accept Atonement for myself, For I remain as God created me.* |
| W-pI. 139.12:4 | *I will accept Atonement for myself, For I remain as God created me.* |
| W-pI 150.1:1 | (139) I will accept Atonement for myself. |
| W-pII .297.1:4 | salvation, and that will be saved as I accept Atonement for myself. |
| W-pII .318.2:1 | the *role You offer me in Your request that I accept Atonement for myself* |
| W-pII .337.1:4 | I must accept Atonement for myself, and nothing more. |
| W-pII .337.2:2 | mistaken *when I thought I sinned, but I accept Atonement for myself.* |
| M-6 1:5 | Having accepted the Atonement for himself, he has also accepted it |
| M-7 3:2 | of the miracle worker is to accept the Atonement for himself. |
| M-14 3:4 | remain the instant any one of them accepts Atonement for himself. |
| M-18 4:5 | responsibility of God's teacher is to accept the Atonement for himself. |
| M-22 1:5 | Accept Atonement and you are healed. Atonement is the Word of |
| M-22 1:10 | teacher of God has taken accepting the Atonement for himself as his |
| M-22 5:4 | In so doing, he has refused to accept the Atonement for himself, |
| M-23 2:1 | has perfectly accepted the Atonement for himself can heal the world |
| M-28 1:3 | of the world's purpose; the acceptance of the Atonement for oneself. |
| P-2 II.8:6 | you and I, accept Atonement and learn to give it as it was received. |
| P-3 II.3:9 | and heal it. He has accepted the Atonement for himself. |

## face of Christ 74

| | |
|---|---|
| T-4 IV.1:5 | to save the face of your ego, and you do not seek the face of Christ. |
| T19 IV.D.2:1 | to be surmounted hangs like a heavy veil before the face of Christ. |
| T19 IV.D.2:2 | Yet as His face rises beyond it, shining with joy because He is in His |
| T19 IV.D.2:3 | Love that light His face with glory appear as streams of blood, |
| T19 IV.D.2:3 | which seems to make the face of Christ Himself like to a leper's, |
| T19 IV.D.4:6 | so you could look upon the face of Christ and join Him in His Father |
| T-20 I.4:2 | If you see glimpses of the face of Christ behind the veil, looking |
| T-20 IV.5:6 | one finds his savior when he is ready to look upon the face of Christ, |
| T-20 IV.7:4 | face of Christ shines on them and they remember the laws of God, |
| T-20 V.4:5 | see the face of Christ and yet insist that judgment still has meaning? |
| T-20 V.6:7 | already given, the face of Christ you yet will look upon already seen. |
| T-20 VI.5:7 | Would He Who sees the face of Christ choose as His home the only |
| T-20 VI.12:10 | Can they be long held back from looking on the face of Christ? |
| T-22 IV.3:1 | before the veil of sin that hangs between you and the face of Christ. |
| T-24 VI.6:5 | by the veil of specialness that hides the face of Christ from him, |
| T-25 I.4:5 | gentleness, and nothing hides the face of Christ from its beholders. |
| T-26 IV.3:2 | And here you see the face of Christ, arising in its place. |
| T-26 IV.3:3 | behold the face of Christ and not recall His Father as He really is? |
| T-26 IX.2:2 | brother and yourself obscures the face of Christ and memory of God |
| T-27 V.6:5 | them sight to see beyond all suffering and see Christ's face instead. |
| T-27 V.7:5 | to show the face of Christ to you who brought the sight to them, |
| T-29 VIII.3:6 | before His face like a dark veil that seems to shut you off from Him, |
| T-29 VIII.4:1 | This world of idols *is* a veil across the face of Christ, because its |
| T-30 V.7:5 | The face of Christ is looked upon before the Father is remembered. |
| T-31 VII.8:6 | And in this single vision does he see the face of Christ, |
| T-31 VII.9:1 | The veil across the face of Christ, the fear of God and of salvation, |
| T-31 VII.13:7 | door held open for the face of Christ to shine upon the one who asks |
| T-31 VIII.3:5 | release your mind from everything that hides His face from you. |
| T-31 VIII.4:3 | appears to hide the face of Christ is powerless before His majesty, |
| T-31 VIII.12:5 | spot of darkness still remains to hide the face of Christ from anyone. |
| W-pI 122.3:1 | Forgiveness lets the veil be lifted up that hides the face of Christ |
| W-pI 124.9:5 | And you will see Christ's face upon it, in reflection of your own. |
| W-pI 151.8:4 | of the body's witnesses before the rapture of Christ's holy face. |
| W-pI. 151.10:2 | appearances, and can behold the gentle face of Christ in all of them. |
| W-pI. 151.12:4 | So will you see the holy face of Christ in everything, and hear in |
| W-pI 157.9:1 | serenely unaware of everything except His shining face and perfect |
| W-pI 157.9:2 | The vision of His face will stay with you, but there will be an instant |
| W-pI 169.6:4 | past all thought of time, forgiveness and the holy face of Christ. |
| W-pI. 169.13:3 | is the face of Christ but his who went a moment into timelessness, |
| W-pI. 198.10:1 | as the face of Christ appears unveiled at last in this one dream. |
| W-pI. 198.10:4 | and see your innocence shining upon you from the face of Christ. |
| W-pII .223.2:1 | *Our Father, let us see the face of Christ instead of our mistakes.* |
| W-pII .229.1:4 | that I will turn away no longer from the holy face of Christ. |
| W-pII 269.h | My sight goes forth to look upon Christ's face. |
| W-pII .269.1:5 | *to see a world forgiven, in which everyone shows me the face of Christ,* |
| W-pII 6.4:3 | to keep things separate, for what remains to see except Christ's face |
| W-pII 6.5:2 | therefore let us seek to find Christ's face and look on nothing else. |
| M-4 X.2:7 | No clouds remain to hide the face of Christ. Now is the goal |
| M-13 4:4 | the face of Christ look back with longing on a slaughter house? |
| M-22 4:5 | mind *and* body, seeing only the face of Christ shining in front of him, |
| M-28 2:6 | Christ's face is seen in every living thing, and nothing is held in |
| M-28 5:5 | We have seen the face of Christ, His sinlessness, His Love behind all |
| M-28 6:3 | there the vision of Christ's face to take the place of what they dream |
| C-3 h | FORGIVENESS – THE FACE OF CHRIST |

## happy dream 21



## holy encounter 6



## holy instant 156

T-16.....VII.8:7 holy instant is His reminder that His Son will always be exactly as
T-16.....VII.9:7 In the holy instant this is done for you in time, to bring you the true
T-16...VII.11:1 Seek and *find* His message in the holy instant, where all illusions are
T-17....IV.10:1 That is why the holy instant is so important in the defense of truth.
T-17....IV.11:1 The holy instant is a miniature of Heaven, sent you *from* Heaven.
T-17....IV.11:4 The holy instant is a miniature of eternity. It is a picture of
T-17....IV.16:8 The holy instant shines alike on all relationships, for in it they *are*
T-17....... V.1:1 holy relationship is the expression of the holy instant in living in
T-17....... V.1:2 everything about salvation, the holy instant is a practical device,
T-17....... V.1:3 The holy instant never fails. The experience of it is always felt.
T-17..... V.10:2 You have joined with many in the holy instant, and they have
T-17... V.11:10 and gratitude you make yourself unable to express the holy instant,
T-17..... V.12:5 To give thanks to your brother is to appreciate the holy instant,
T-17..... V.13:1 You *have* received the holy instant, but you may have established a
T-17..... V.15:1 you will also accept the effects of the holy instant and use them to
T-17... VIII.1:1 The holy instant is nothing more than a special case, or an extreme
T-17... VIII.1:4 The holy instant is the shining example, the clear and unequivocal
T-17... VIII.3:1 Would you not want to make a holy instant of every situation?
T-18...... III.7:3 it back to darkness, from the holy instant to which you brought it.
T-18......IV.1:1 The holy instant is the result of your determination to be holy.
T-18......IV.1:9 you to make the holy instant far greater than you can understand.
T-18......IV.2:6 you could come without them you would not need the holy instant.
T-18......IV.2:8 of the holy instant lies in your willingness to let it be what it is.
T-18......IV.3:3 difficulty with the holy instant arises from your fixed conviction
T-18......IV.4:1 The holy instant does not come from your little willingness alone.
T-18......IV.5:4 In preparing for the holy instant, do not attempt to make yourself
T-18......IV.6:5 The preparation for the holy instant belongs to Him Who gives it.
T-18......IV.7:1 It is this that makes the holy instant so easy and so natural.
T-18......IV.8:2 If you believe the holy instant is difficult for you, it is because you
T-18....... V.1:3 The holy instant, the holy relationship, the Holy Spirit's teaching,
T-18....... V.2:1 Never approach the holy instant after you have tried to remove all
T-18....... V.3:1 reborn and blessed in every holy instant you do not arrange,
T-18....... V.6:1 let Him exchange this instant for the holy one that you would rather
T-18....... V.6:6 that the holy instant come to either of you without the other. And it
T-18....... V.7:3 *I desire this holy instant for myself, that I may share it with my brother,*
T-18....... V.7:6 *And so I choose this instant as the one to offer to the Holy Spirit, that*
T-18....VI.13:6 you experience much of what happens in the holy instant;
T-18....VI.14:2 with your desire for it is the irresistible appeal the holy instant holds.
T-18.....VII.4:1 is impossible to accept the holy instant without reservation unless,
T-18. VIII.11:1 holy instant is your invitation to love to enter into your bleak and

T-18..VIII.11:4 In the holy instant, you ask of love only what it offers everyone,
T-18.... IX.13:3 holy instant in which you and your brother were united is but the
T-19.......I.10:5 Each one appears just as he is perceived in the holy instant, united
T-19.......I.14:1 In the holy instant, you and your brother stand before the altar
T-19.... III.10:1 In the holy instant, you will see the smile of Heaven shining on
T-19.... III.10:4 Your perception was healed in the holy instant Heaven gave you.
T19. IV.A.16:3 And in a holy instant grace is said by everyone together, as they join
T19... IV.D.9:6 Let us join together in a holy instant, here in this place where the
T19... IV.D.9:6 here in this place where the purpose, given in a holy instant
T-20....... V.5:6 should it take so many holy instants to let this be accomplished,
T-20....... V.6:1 You look upon each holy instant as a different point in time.
T-20...... VI.9:3 the holy instant and its unlimited beneficence? Is the malevolence
T-20...... VI.9:4 so invested in a false attraction your preference to the holy instant,
T-20.... VI.10:4 the unholy instant is exchanged in gladness for the holy one of safe
T-20.... VI.11:8 Here he can accept the holy instant, offered him to replace the
T-20.... VI.12:2 holy instant is of greater value now to you than its unholy seeming
T-21........II.4:5 In the holy instant is this exchange effected and maintained.
T-21........II.8:2 The holy instant is not an instant of creation, but of recognition.
T-21....VIII.5:1 What is the holy instant but God's appeal to you to recognize what
T-27...... IV.2:4 Such is the holy instant. It is here that all your problems should be
T-27...... IV.3:1 Attempt to solve no problems but within the holy instant's surety.
T-27...... IV.6:1 within the holy instant can an honest question honestly be asked.
T-27...... IV.6:9 The holy instant is the interval in which the mind is still enough to
T-27...... IV.7:5 In the holy instant, you can bring the question to the answer,
T-27....... V.3:1 The holy instant is the miracle's abiding place. From there, each
T-27....... V.4:4 from you, when you accept the blessing that the holy instant brings
T-27....... V.6:1 Come to the holy instant and be healed, for nothing that is there
T-27....... V.6:5 The holy instant's radiance will light your eyes, and give them sight
T-27...... VI.8:2 holy instant will replace all sin if you but carry its effects with you.
T-27....VIII.9:8 will leave the holy instant with your laughter and your brother's
W-pI. 135.19:1 joy that constantly increases, as this life becomes a holy instant, set
W-pI. 169.13:2 are laid; to be returned by you from holy instants you receive,
W-pI... 194.5:3 instant which was slave to time transformed into a holy instant,
W-pII ....in.3:2 content ourselves with simple practicing in the remaining holy instants
W-pII ..in.11:4 while, preceding one of the holy and blessed instants in the day.
W-pII ....227.h This is my holy instant of release.
W-pII . 227.1:6 *This is my holy instant of release. Father, I know my will is one with*
W-pII ....241.h This holy instant is salvation come.
WpII ..361-5.h This holy instant would I give to You. Be You in charge.
P-3..........II.8:3 Many holy instants can be his along the way. A goal marks the end

## Holy One 9

T-4........ III.7:2 retain thousands of little scraps of fear that prevent the Holy One
T-4........ III.8:3 the first step toward preparing your mind for the Holy One to enter
T-4........IV.9:3 Then let the Holy One shine on you in peace, knowing that this and
T-4........VI.6:4 The Holy One shares my trust, and accepts my Atonement
T-4........VI.7:1 I will go with you to the Holy One, and through my perception He

T-23.......I.11:3 light grows dim, the temple of the Holy One becomes a house of sin
T-24...... III.6:7 Forgive the Holy One the specialness He could not give, and that
W-pI... 157.8:2 But the Holy One, the Giver of the happy dreams of life, Translator
W-pII . 322.1:4 likeness of Himself, the Holy One Who still abides in Him forever,

## I am as God created me 144

T-3......... V.3:4 Nevertheless, you are perfectly stable as God created you.
T-5.......VII.2:6 You are merely asked to return to God the mind as He created it.
T-6......V.C.5:4 God put there, you are acknowledging your mind as God created it.
T-7......... V.7:7 in no way contradicts the changelessness of mind as God created it,
T-9... VIII.10:8 To accept yourself as God created you cannot be arrogance,
T-10....... V.9:5 If you will accept yourself as God created you, you will be incapable
T-14...... V.9:10 Restore to God His Son as He created him, by teaching him his
T-16...... III.8:1 due for what you are, and for what He is Who created you as you are
T-23.........I.7:2 For you must be as God created you. Truth does not fight against
T-24..... II.14:5 of what you are to the acceptance of yourself as God created you.
T-24...... VI.3:6 Your brother *is* as He created him. And it is this that saves you from
T-26........ II.8:2 that is belongs to Him, and will forever be as He created it.
T-26...VII.18:2 It is not arrogant to also be a Father, who creates as God created him.
T-28....... II.1:5 Son that he must also be a father, who creates as God created him.
T-30...... III.5:5 limited to what is not in him, he would not be as God created him.
T-31... VIII.5:2 *I am as God created me. His Son can suffer nothing. And I am His Son*
T-31... VIII.6:1 You *are* as God created you, and so is every living thing you look
W-pI.....57.2:7 He is as God created him, and not what I would make of him.
W-pI.....93.4:1 sins are nothing, that you are as pure and holy as you were created,
W-pI.....93.7:1 the acceptance of but one thought;–you are as God created you,
W-pI.....93.7:2 Whatever evil you may think you did, you are as God created you.
W-pI.....93.7:6 You are and will forever be exactly as you were created.
W-pI........94.h I am as God created me.

W-pI..... 94.1:2 You are as God created you. The sounds of this world are still,
W-pI..... 94.2:2 If you remain as God created you, you must be strong and light
W-pI..... 94.2:4 You are as God created you. Darkness cannot obscure the glory of
W-pI..... 94.3:3 *I am as God created me. I am His Son eternally.*
W-pI..... 94.5:2 *I am as God created me. I am His Son eternally.*
W-pI..... 94.5:4 Tell yourself frequently today that you are as God created you.
W-pI..... 94.5:6 *You are as God created you. You are His Son eternally.*
W-pI..... 95.1:1 Today's idea accurately describes you as God created you.
W-pI...... 110.h I am as God created me.
W-pI... 110.1:4 If you remain as God created you fear has no meaning, evil is not
W-pI... 110.3:1 If you remain as God created you, appearances cannot replace the
W-pI... 110.3:2 All this has not occurred, if you remain as God created you.
W-pI... 110.4:2 If you are as God created you, then there has been no separation of
W-pI... 110.6:2 *I am as God created me. His Son can suffer nothing. And I am His Son*
W-pI... 110.9:1 You are as God created you. Today honor your Self.
W-pI. 110.11:4 *I am as God created me.* Let us declare this truth as often as we can.
W-pI... 112.2:1 (94) I am as God created me. *I will remain forever as I was, created by*
W-pI... 112.3:4 and peace abide in me. On the half hour: I am as God created me.
W-pI... 120.2:1 (110) I am as God created me. *I am God's Son. Today I lay aside all*
W-pI... 120.3:4 the hour: I rest in God. On the half hour: I am as God created me.
W-pI... 132.9:2 You are as God created you. There is no place where you can suffer,
W-pI... 132.9:4 a world of time and place exist, if you remain as God created you?
W-pI. 132.11:1 Yet if you are as God created you, you cannot think apart from

W-pI.132.14:5 we who are as He created us would loose the world this day from every
W-pI.132.15:2 *who remain as God created me would loose the world from all I thought*
W-pI.136.13:5 Yet what He wills is here, and you remain as He created you.
W-pI...139.1:2 here we come to a decision to accept ourselves as God created us.
W-pI.139.11:3 *I will accept Atonement for myself, For I remain as God created me.*
W-pI.139.12:4 *I will accept Atonement for myself, For I remain as God created me.*
W-pI...152.5:1 As God created you, you must remain unchangeable,
W-pI.152.11:4 *This day I will accept myself as what my Father's Will created me to be.*
W-pI...158.1:3 Nor have you left your Source, remaining as you were created.
W-pI......162.h I am as God created me.
W-pI...162.6:3 You are as God created you. These words dispel the night,
W-pI...176.2:1 (162) I am as God created me. God is but Love, and therefore so
W-pI.185.14:1 hate has sought to sever, but which still remains as God created it.
W-pI...191.4:2 You are as God created you. All else but this one thing is folly to
W-pI.192.10:7 He is as God created him. And you are what he is. Forgive him now
W-pI...197.8:2 For as you were created, you contain all things within your Self.
W-pI...197.8:3 And you are still as God created you. Nor can you dim the light of
WpI rVI.in.3:5 *For I am still as God created me.* The day begins and ends with this.
W-pI......201.h I am not a body. I am free. For I am still as God created me.
W-pI...201.1:6 I am not a body. I am free. For I am still as God created me.
W-pI......202.h I am not a body. I am free. For I am still as God created me.
W-pI...202.1:5 I am not a body. I am free. For I am still as God created me.
W-pI......203.h I am not a body. I am free. For I am still as God created me.
W-pI...203.1:5 I am not a body. I am free. For I am still as God created me.
W-pI......204.h I am not a body. I am free. For I am still as God created me.
W-pI...204.1:5 I am not a body. I am free. For I am still as God created me.
W-pI......205.h I am not a body. I am free. For I am still as God created me.
W-pI...205.1:6 I am not a body. I am free. For I am still as God created me.
W-pI......206.h I am not a body. I am free. For I am still as God created me.
W-pI...206.1:6 I am not a body. I am free. For I am still as God created me.
W-pI......207.h I am not a body. I am free. For I am still as God created me.
W-pI...207.1:6 I am not a body. I am free. For I am still as God created me.
W-pI......208.h I am not a body. I am free. For I am still as God created me.
W-pI...208.1:7 I am not a body. I am free. For I am still as God created me.
W-pI......209.h I am not a body. I am free. For I am still as God created me.
W-pI...209.1:8 I am not a body. I am free. For I am still as God created me.
W-pI......210.h I am not a body. I am free. For I am still as God created me.
W-pI...210.1:8 I am not a body. I am free. For I am still as God created me.
W-pI......211.h I am not a body. I am free. For I am still as God created me.
W-pI...211.1:5 I am not a body. I am free. For I am still as God created me.
W-pI......212.h I am not a body. I am free. For I am still as God created me.
W-pI...212.1:7 I am not a body. I am free. For I am still as God created me.
W-pI......213.h I am not a body. I am free. For I am still as God created me.
W-pI...213.1:7 I am not a body. I am free. For I am still as God created me.
W-pI......214.h I am not a body. I am free. For I am still as God created me.
W-pI...214.1:8 I am not a body. I am free. For I am still as God created me.
W-pI......215.h I am not a body. I am free. For I am still as God created me.
W-pI...215.1:7 I am not a body. I am free. For I am still as God created me.
W-pI......216.h I am not a body. I am free. For I am still as God created me.
W-pI...216.1:7 I am not a body. I am free. For I am still as God created me.
W-pI......217.h I am not a body. I am free. For I am still as God created me.
W-pI...217.1:6 I am not a body. I am free. For I am still as God created me.
W-pI......218.h I am not a body. I am free. For I am still as God created me.
W-pI...218.1:6 I am not a body. I am free. For I am still as God created me.
W-pI......219.h I am not a body. I am free. For I am still as God created me.
W-pI...219.1:8 I am not a body. I am free. For I am still as God created me.
W-pI......220.h I am not a body. I am free. For I am still as God created me.
W-pI...220.1:6 I am not a body. I am free. For I am still as God created me.
W-pII .230.2:4 *I am as You created me. I need but call on You to find the peace*
W-pII ....237.h Now would I be as God created me.
W-pII .239.1:4 and with perfect constancy, knowing he is as He created him?
W-pII .243.1:6 I free myself and what I look upon, to be in peace as God created us
W-pII .248.1:8 Now am I ready to accept him back as God created him, and as he
W-pII .248.2:2 *Father, I am as You created me. Now is Your Love remembered, and my*
W-pII .249.2:3 *Now would we rest again in You, as You created us.*
W-pII .261.2:3 *I choose to be as You created me, and find the Son whom You created as*
W-pII .268.1:3 *my wishes from its unity, and thus to let it be as You created it.*
W-pII .268.1:4 *For thus will I be able, too, to recognize my Self as You created me.*
W-pII ..... 6.1:1 Christ is God's Son as He created Him. He is the Self we share,
W-pII .272.1:8 *forever gentle and forever safe. God's Son must be as You created him.*
W-pII .274.1:1 *Father, today I would let all things be as You created them, and give*
W-pII .274.1:3 *replace all darkness, and Your Son will know he is as You created him.*
W-pII .277.1:6 *He is as You created him, because he knows no law except the law of*
W-pII .281.1:2 *is because I have forgotten who I am, and that I am as You created me.*
W-pII .282.1:2 accept myself as God Himself, my Father and my Source, created me.
W-pII .285.2:3 *Your Son is still as You created him. My holiness is part of me, and also*
W-pII .287.2:6 *Your Son would be as You created him. What way but this could I expect*
W-pII .299.2:6 *In it are all things healed, for they remain as You created them. And I can*
W-pII .303.2:6 *He is my Self as You created me. It is not Christ that can be crucified.*
W-pII .304.2:3 *find again the memory of You, and of Your Son as You created him.*
W-pII .307.1:5 *nothing contradicts the holy truth that I remain as You created me.*
W-pII .309.1:4 To look within is but to find my will as God created it, and as it is.
W-pII ... 11.4:6 earth, only to be restored to sanity, and to be but as God created us.
W-pII .322.2:3 *As You created me, I can give up nothing You gave me. What You did*
W-pII .326.1:3 *As You created me I have remained. Where You established me I still*
W-pII .354.1:6 *For who is Christ except Your Son as You created Him? And what am I*
W-pII .360.1:2 *I am Your Son, forever just as You created me, for the Great Rays remain*
M-5 ..... III.3:4 that he did not make himself, and must remain as God created him
M-12 ......... 1:9 is forever one, because he is as God created him. He has accepted
M-23 ......... 2:6 He has recognized himself as God created him, and in so doing he
M-28 ......... 5:8 As God created us so will we be forever and forever, and we wish for
M-29 ......... 4:4 As God created you, you *have* all power. The image you made of
M-29 ....... 7:10 God knows but His Son, and as was created so he is. In confidence I
C-2 ............ 2:4 God's Son as He created him abide in form or in a world of form?
C-6 ............ 1:1 identified with the Christ, the Son of God as He created Him.
S-1.........in.3:1 dreams, you holy Son of God, and rising up as God created you,
S-1..........II.5:6 has become holy, for it acknowledges the Son of God as he was created
S-2........ III.7:8 brother there beyond the door; the Son of God as He created him.

## ideas leave not their source 14

T-26.....VII.4:7 Ideas leave not their source, and their effects but seem to be apart
T-26...VII.12:3 the firm conviction that ideas can leave their source made real and
T-26...VII.13:2 Him, and this must still be true because ideas leave not their source.
T-26...VII.13:5 to believe ideas can leave their source is to invite illusions to be true,
T-29... VIII.3:3 Yet it is still a thought, and cannot leave the mind that is its source.
W-pI.....45.2:5 of God leave your mind, because thoughts do not leave their source.
W-pI...132.5:3 Ideas leave not their source. This central theme is often stated in
W-pI. 132.10:3 no world apart from your ideas because ideas leave not their source,
W-pI... 156.1:3 thought so often mentioned in the text; ideas leave not their source.
W-pI... 159.9:4 They do not leave their source, but carry its beneficence with them,
W-pI... 167.3:6 Ideas leave not their source. The emphasis this course has placed on
W-pI... 167.4:3 It is the fixed belief ideas can leave their source, and take on
W-pI... 167.5:2 Ideas remain united to their source. They can extend all that their
W-pI... 170.4:2 First, it is obvious ideas must leave their source, for it is you who

## last step 31

T-5...........I.6:6 of transferred or "carried over," since the last step is taken by God.
T-6......V.C.5:7 The final step will still be taken for you by God, but by the third
T-7............. I.h The Last Step
T-7...........I.6:3 that the last step in the reawakening of knowledge is taken by God.
T-7...........I.6:6 timeless. He can therefore tell you something about this last step.
T-7...........I.7:8 "last step" that God will take was therefore true in the beginning,
T-11. VIII.15:5 your Father will lean down to you and take the last step for you,
T-13... VIII.3:2 Yet the last step must be taken by God, because the last step in your
T-17....... II.4:5 For God will take the last step swiftly, when you have reached the
T-18.... IX.10:4 you are led, that God Himself can take the final step unhindered,
T-18.... IX.10:5 A step beyond this holy place of forgiveness,
T-18.... IX.10:5 a step still further inward but the one *you* cannot take,
T-19 ..... IV.3:8 When God has taken the last step Himself, the Holy Spirit will
T-27 ...... III.6:7 And thus is God left free to take the final step Himself.
T-30 ...... V.3:7 is he made ready for the step in which is all forgiveness left behind.
T-30 ...... V.4:1 The final step is God's, because it is but God Who could create a
W-pI... 129.5:1 Now is the last step certain; now you stand an instant's space away
W-pI... 168.3:2 God leans to us and lifts us up, taking salvation's final step Himself.
W-pI... 169.3:2 The final step must go beyond all learning.
W-pI. 193.13:6 God will take this final step Himself. Do not deny the little steps He
W-pI... 194.1:3 place of peace, where you await with certainty the final step of God.
W-pII ....in.2:3 He has promised He will take the final step Himself.
W-pII ....in.4:1 and wait for Him to take the step to us that He has told us,
W-pII .289.2:4 *And here am I made ready for Your final step.*

## little willingness 12



## miracle worker 21



## order of difficulty 34



## real world 101

## relationships

### special relationships 75

## special love 16

| | |
|---|---|
| T-15....... V.3:2 | If you would love unlike to God, Who knows no special love, how |
| T-15....... V.3:3 | To believe that *special* relationships, with *special* love, can offer you |
| T-15.....VII.1:1 | Beyond the poor attraction of the special love relationship, |
| T-16......IV.1:3 | For the special love relationship, in which the meaning of love is |
| T-16......IV.1:6 | The special love relationship will not offset it, but will merely drive |
| T-16......IV.3:1 | special love relationship is an attempt to limit the destructive effects |
| T-16......IV.3:4 | The special love relationship is not perceived as a value in itself, but |
| T-16......IV.3:5 | The special love partner is acceptable only as long as he serves this |
| T-16...... IV.7:1 | special love relationship is an attempt to bring love into separation. |
| T-16...... IV.7:3 | the special love relationship would accomplish the impossible. |
| T-16...... IV.8:4 | special love relationship is but a shabby substitute for what makes |
| T-16....... V.2:3 | special love relationship is the ego's chief weapon for keeping you |
| T-16....... V.3:1 | The special love relationship is the ego's most boasted gift, and one |
| T-16....... V.4:1 | is in the special relationship, born of the hidden wish for special love |
| T-16...... VI.1:3 | has special value it has no meaning, for it perceives all love as special |
| T-25...... VI.6:8 | was made his special grace. His special hate became his special love. |

## special hate (unholy) 23

| | |
|---|---|
| T-16......IV.1:1 | Be not afraid to look upon the special hate relationship, |
| T-17......III.3:1 | In the unholy relationship, it is not the body of the other with |
| T-17......III.3:4 | the maintaining and the breaking off of the unholy relationship is a |
| T-17......III.4:1 | Time is indeed unkind to the unholy relationship. |
| T-17......III.4:3 | The attraction of the unholy relationship begins to fade and to be |
| T-17......III.4:5 | The "ideal" of the unholy relationship thus becomes one in which |
| T-17......III.5:7 | the ugliness of the unholy relationship where hatred is remembered |
| T-17....... V.1:7 | the unholy relationship is a continuing hymn of hate in praise of its |
| T-17....... V.2:2 | It is the old, unholy relationship, transformed and seen anew. |
| T-17....... V.2:4 | accomplished, it represents the reversal of the unholy relationship. |
| T-17....... V.3:9 | For once the unholy relationship has accepted the goal of holiness, |
| T-17....... V.4:5 | Set firmly in the unholy relationship, there is no course except to |
| T-20...... III.8:4 | this puff of madness for the meaning of your unholy relationship, |
| T-20...... VI.1:4 | of God invented an unholy relationship between him and his Father |
| T-20...... VI.2:1 | than the experience of both a holy and an unholy relationship. |
| T-20...... VI.5:3 | Here the unholy relationship escapes reality, and seeks for crumbs |
| T-20...... VI.8:3 | An unholy relationship is no relationship. It is a state of isolation, |
| T-20...... VI.9:4 | Is the malevolence of the unholy relationship, so seeming powerful |
| T-20..... VII.5:1 | by which the ego tries to make the unholy relationship seem real. |
| T-22.......in.2:5 | For an unholy relationship is based on differences, where each one |
| T-22.........I.7:2 | relationship, so recently reborn itself from an unholy relationship, |
| T-22...... III.9:3 | In an unholy relationship, each one is valued because he seems to |
| T-25...... VI.6:8 | made his special grace. His special hate became his special love. |

## holy relationships 88

| | |
|---|---|
| T-13....... X.2:2 | No real relationship can rest on guilt, or even hold one spot of it to |
| T-13....... X.2:5 | And you forgot that real relationships are holy, and cannot be used |
| T-13....... X.4:4 | you and your brothers, with whom you find no real relationships |
| T-13..... X.11:1 | cannot enter into real relationships with any of God's Sons unless you |
| T-15...VII.13:3 | in Him and you is joined in a real relationship so holy and so strong, |
| T-15...... VIII.h | The Only Real Relationship |
| T-15... VIII.3:8 | You are forever in a relationship so holy that it calls to everyone to |
| T-15......IX.2:6 | by which you can establish real relationships, which have no limits |
| T-16...VII.11:4 | To join in close relationship with Him is to accept relationships as real, |
| T-17.............h | FORGIVENESS AND THE HOLY RELATIONSHIP |
| T-17......IV.2:6 | But the holy relationship shares God's purpose, rather than aiming |
| T-17......IV.3:1 | You have made very real relationships even in this world. |
| T-17......IV.4:7 | Him have all your holy relationships been carefully preserved, to |
| T-17....... V.1:1 | The holy relationship is the expression of the holy instant in living |
| T-17....... V.1:6 | holy relationship is a constant reminder of the experience in which |
| T-17....... V.1:7 | so is the holy relationship a happy song of praise to the Redeemer |
| T-17....... V.2:1 | The holy relationship, a major step toward the perception of the |
| T-17....... V.2:3 | The holy relationship is a phenomenal teaching accomplishment. |
| T-17..... V.7:14 | now, nor your brother. This relationship has been reborn as holy. |
| T-17..... V.10:3 | you comfortless, for God Himself has blessed your holy relationship |
| T-17.....VII.6:4 | No relationship is holy unless its holiness goes with it everywhere. |
| T-18...... I.11:4 | How lovely and how holy is your relationship, with the truth |
| T-18...... I.13:3 | This is offered you, in your holy relationship. Accept it here, |
| T-18....... II.7:1 | undoing guilt in everyone blessed through your holy relationship. |
| T-18....III.4:10 | The holiness of your relationship is established in Heaven. You do |
| T-18....... V.1:3 | The holy instant, the holy relationship, the Holy Spirit's teaching, |
| T-18....... V.3:1 | Through your holy relationship, reborn and blessed in every holy |
| T-18....... V.5:2 | Nor is your holy relationship a dream. All that remains of dreams |
| T-18....... V.6:1 | you feel the holiness of your relationship is threatened by anything, |
| T-18.....VII.5:2 | A holy relationship is a means of saving time. One instant spent |
| T-19...... I.12:5 | Your holy relationship, with its new purpose, offers you faith to |
| T-19......III.8:4 | Your holy relationship has, as its purpose now, the goal of proving |
| T19... IV.A.5:2 | For in the miracle of your holy relationship, without this barrier, is |
| T19... IV.A.5:9 | His home is in your holy relationship. Do not attempt to stand |
| T19. IV.A.16:2 | This is a feast that honors your holy relationship, and at which |
| T19....IV.B.4:9 | In your holy relationship is your Father's Son. He has not lost |
| T19....IV.B.5:3 | before our union, for in your holy relationship I am there already. |
| T19....IV.B.7:1 | From your holy relationship truth proclaims the truth, and love |
| T19....IV.B.8:3 | I am within your holy relationship, yet you would imprison me |
| T-20......III.2:5 | it difficult for you to recognize your holy relationship for what it is. |
| T-20......III.6:1 | Who in a holy relationship can long remain unholy? |
| T-20......III.8:9 | That is the purpose of your holy relationship. Ask not the means of |
| T-20......IV.6:6 | Each holy relationship must enter here, to learn its special function |
| T-20....... V.1:1 | God's Son comes closest to himself in a holy relationship. |
| T-20....... V.2:5 | Peace to your holy relationship, which has the power to hold the |
| T-20....... V.5:4 | the body has no use which serves the purpose of a holy relationship. |
| T-20...... VI.1:5 | real relationship is one of perfect union and unbroken continuity. |
| T-20...... VI.2:1 | than the experience of both a holy and an unholy relationship. |
| T-20.... VI.10:1 | The holy relationship reflects the true relationship the Son of God |
| T-20.... VI.12:5 | You have a *real* relationship, and it has meaning. |
| T-20.... VI.12:6 | as like your real relationship with God as equal things are like unto |
| T-20..... VII.1:1 | must be brought in line before your holy relationship can bring you |
| T-20..... VII.8:3 | can a holy relationship achieve its purpose through the means of sin |
| T-20....VIII.2:4 | Your holy relationship offers all this to you. As it was given you, so |
| T-20....VIII.6:9 | Your holy relationship, the source of your salvation, will be |
| T-21...... III.6:6 | teach you that the vision of a holy relationship is all you *want* to see. |
| T-21...... IV.3:5 | holy relationship is one in which you join with what is part of you in |
| T-21....VIII.5:7 | the holiness of your relationship and your *awareness* of its holiness. |
| T-22.............h | SALVATION AND THE HOLY RELATIONSHIP |
| T-22.......in.1:7 | The holiness of your relationship forgives you and your brother, |
| T-22.......in.3:1 | A holy relationship starts from a different premise. Each one has |
| T-22.......in.4:1 | Think what a holy relationship can teach! Here is belief in |
| T-22.....in.4:10 | For what is born into a holy relationship can never end. |
| T-22...........I.h | The Message of the Holy Relationship |
| T-22.........I.7:1 | So in each holy relationship is the ability to communicate instead |
| T-22.........I.7:2 | Yet a holy relationship, so recently reborn itself from an unholy |
| T-22.........I.8:7 | dependent on the holiness of your relationship to let Him live. |
| T-22.......I.11:3 | What is as like Him as a holy relationship? And what draws you and |
| T-22.......I.11:9 | drawn to God as surely as Both are drawn to every holy relationship |
| T-22......II.11:5 | What God has given to your holy relationship is there. For what He |
| T-22......II.12:1 | bright, endless circle that extends forever, is your holy relationship, |
| T-22...... III.9:1 | A holy relationship, however newly born, must value holiness |
| T-22...... III.9:7 | Yet reason sees a holy relationship as what it is; a common state of |
| T-22...... IV.7:4 | Such is the function of a holy relationship; to receive together and |
| T-22.........VI.h | The Light of the Holy Relationship |
| T-22...... VI.4:1 | This holy relationship, lovely in its innocence, mighty in strength, |
| T-22...... VI.4:4 | This holy relationship has the power to heal all pain, regardless of |
| T-22...... VI.5:1 | Before a holy relationship there is no sin. The form of error is no |
| T-22.... VI.14:1 | This is the function of your holy relationship. For what one thinks, |
| M-2 ........... 5:4 | The relationship is holy because of that purpose, and God has |
| M-2 ........... 5:4 | and God has promised to send His Spirit into any holy relationship. |
| M-3 ........... 1:2 | is always the same; to make of the relationship a holy relationship, |
| M-3 ........... 1:7 | because together they have the potential for a holy relationship. |
| M-3 ........... 4:6 | meet again, for it is the destiny of all relationships to become holy. |
| M-4 ........... 1:6 | born in the holy relationship toward which the teaching-learning |
| P-2....... VII.3:6 | capable of joining with the patient in a holy relationship in which |
| P-3........ III.4:4 | If their relationship is to be holy, whatever one needs is given by the |
| P-3........ III.4:5 | Herein is the relationship made holy, for herein both are healed. |

## true perception 82

| | |
|---|---|
| T-1 I.36:1 | thinking, aligning your perceptions with truth as God created it. |
| T-2 V.A.15:1 | power of the miracle induces the right perception for healing. |
| T-3 h | THE INNOCENT PERCEPTION |
| T-3 II.h | Miracles as True Perception |
| T-3 II.2:5 | Innocent or true perception means that you never misperceive and |
| T-3 II.5:8 | defend true perception instead of defending themselves against it. |
| T-3 III.1:8 | Misperceptions produce fear and true perceptions foster love, but |
| T-3 III.1:10 | True perception is the basis for knowledge, but knowing is the |
| T-3 III.4:1 | True vision is the natural perception of spiritual sight, but it is still |
| T-3 III.4:3 | It is, however, a means of right perception, which brings it into the |
| T-3 III.5:11 | Even in its most spiritualized form perception involves the body. |
| T-3 III.6:1 | Right perception is necessary before God can communicate |
| T-3 IV.4:1 | the knowing mind, because it is applicable only to right perception. |
| T-3 IV.4:3 | and applies to the state of mind that induces accurate perception. |
| T-3 IV.5:5 | ambiguously, and the only way out of ambiguity is clear perception. |
| T-3 IV.7:10 | Sane perception induces sane choosing. I cannot choose for you, |
| T-3 V.9:2 | Correct perception of your brother is necessary, because minds have |
| T-4 I.12:4 | because their egos are humble, and this gives them truer perception. |
| T-4 II.10:2 | automatically, because right perception is uniformly without attack, |
| T-4 II.11:2 | knowledge, while accurate perception is a steppingstone towards it. |
| T-4 II.11:3 | whole value of right perception lies in the inevitable realization that |
| T-4 VI.2:3 | of your indebtedness and the holy perception it would produce. |
| T-5 III.5:4 | notions, because true and false perceptions are themselves opposed. |
| T-6 III.1:3 | holds knowledge safe in your mind through His impartial perception. |
| T-6 V.B.9:1 | step toward the unified perception that reflects God's knowing. |
| T-7 IV.2:10 | it can be used as a way out of conflict, as all proper perception can. |
| T-7 IV.5:7 | The strength of right perception is so great that it brings the mind |
| T-7 VI.5:1 | appreciation, all recognition, all sane perception and all knowledge. |
| T-7 IX.7:4 | The miracle is a lesson in total perception. By including any part of |
| T-8 IX.h | Healing as Corrected Perception |
| T-8 IX.1:6 | rather, that the Holy Spirit teach you the right *perception* of the body |
| T-11 VIII.1:5 | Yet the swiftness with which your new and only real perception will |
| T-12 VI.7:2 | the holy perception of God's Son becomes so enlightened that light |
| T-12 VII.1:5 | world. For in this holy perception you will be made whole, and the |
| T-12 VIII.8:3 | make everything else invisible, for beholding it is total perception. |
| T-12 VIII.8:6 | Redeemed perception is easily translated into knowledge, for only |
| T-13 VII.9:3 | In these lie your true perceptions, for the Holy Spirit corrects the |
| T-13 VIII.3:1 | Perfect perception, then, has many elements in common with |
| T-13 VIII.5:2 | the Son of God is but the true perception of one aspect of the whole. |
| T-13 X.1:2 | and keep from your awareness the full perception that it is insane. |
| T-13 XI.4:2 | Perfect perception can merely show you what is capable of being wholly |
| T-16 II.3:4 | Wholly natural perception would show you instantly that order of |
| T-16 II.4:4 | fit, His natural perception of your gift enables Him to understand it |
| T-17 II.3:7 | this final blessing of God's Son upon himself, the real perception, |
| T-18 IX.9:4 | Here is the new perception, where everything is bright and shining |
| T-18 IX.14:3 | its gentleness, to the bright world of new and clean perception. |
| T-19 I.11:6 | It is the messenger of the new perception, sent forth to gather |
| T-19 III.9:3 | in the new perception the mind corrects it when it seems to be seen, |
| T19 IV.B.8:5 | the focus of the new perception that will bring light to all the world, |
| T-25 VII.5:1 | else; a basis not insane, on which a sane perception can be based, |
| W in.3:1 | you see now, and the second with the acquisition of true perception. |
| W in.5:1 | Transfer of training in true perception does not proceed as does |
| W in.5:2 | If true perception has been achieved in connection with any person, |
| W in.5:3 | hand, one exception held apart from true perception makes its |
| W in.6:5 | The very nature of true perception is that it has no limits. It is the |
| W-pI 15.3:5 | will not persist, because they merely symbolize true perception, |
| W-pI 34.1:4 | your peace of mind that a peaceful perception of the world arises. |
| W-pI 43.2:7 | Healed perception becomes the means by which the Son of God |
| W-pI 87.1:6 | This day I will experience the peace of true perception. |
| W-pI 108.3:3 | This is the light that heals because it brings single perception, based |
| W-pI 181.8:4 | to see, when this is all we seek for in the name of true perception, |
| W-pI 184.7:5 | another kind of learning can begin, a new perception can be gained, |
| W-pI 187.1:6 | It is the second phase on which the world and true perception differ |
| W-pI 193.2:5 | Who gives the means by which perception is made true and beautiful |
| W-pI 194.8:3 | and every living creature not respond with healed perception? |
| W-pI 200.8:2 | from this fresh perception to the gate of Heaven and the way beyond |
| W-pII 3.5:1 | not rest content until the world has joined our changed perception. |
| W-pII 269.1:3 | *It is given me to find a new perception through the Guide You gave to me,* |
| W-pII 313.h | Now let a new perception come to me. |
| W-pII 313.1:6 | *Now let His true perception come to me, that I may waken from the* |
| W-pII 314.1:1 | new perception of the world there comes a future very different |
| M-22 1:3 | in this world, because it is the source of a wholly unified perception. |
| C-4 h | TRUE PERCEPTION – KNOWLEDGE |
| C-4 3:2 | one correction possible for false perception must be *true perception.* |
| C-4 3:5 | For true perception is a remedy with many names. |
| C-4 3:6 | Forgiveness, salvation, Atonement, true perception, all are one. |
| C-4 3:8 | True perception is the means by which the world is saved from sin, |
| C-4 3:9 | sin, for sin does not exist. And it is this that true perception sees. |
| C-4 4:2 | true perception looks on it as nothing more than just a fragile veil, |
| C-4 6:1 | that true perception brings: What was projected out is seen within, |
| C-4 7:2 | Gone is perception, false and true alike. Gone is forgiveness, for its |
| C-6 3:4 | He is the great correction principle; the bringer of true perception, |